W9-AAW-508

World Index Maps / Welt Indexkarten / Indice de Mapas del Mundo
Index des Cartes du Monde / Índice de Mapas do Mundo

RAND McNALLY

The New International Atlas
Der Neue Internationale Atlas
El Nuevo Atlas Internacional
Le Nouvel Atlas International
O Nôvo Atlas Internacional

Twenty-Fifth Anniversary Edition

Rand McNally International Atlas Staff

Publisher
Andrew McNally III
Andrew McNally IV

Corporate Advisory Group
John S. Bakalar
Henry J. Feinberg
Jayne L. Fenton
Michael W. Dobson, Ph. D.

Editorial and Cartographic Direction
Russell L. Voisin
Jon M. Leverenz
V. Patrick Healy

Art and Design Direction
Chris Arvetis
Gordon Hartshorne

Coordination
David C. Zapenski

Geographic Research and Index
Susan Hudson
Keith Jennerjohn
Felix A. Lopez
Raymond T. Tobiaski
Richard L. Forstall
(Consultant)

Cartographic Editorial
Robert K. Argersinger
Winifred V. Farbman

Cartographic Compilation
Jill M. Stift
Nina Lusterman
Lynn N. Jasmer
Larry K. Tyler

Cartographic Production
James A. Purvis
L. Charlene Smith
Patty A. Porter
Barbara Smith
Wanda McDonald

Composition and Typesetting
Rajani Veeramachaneni

Terrain Illustrators
Ivan Barcaba
Evelyn Mitchell
Mary Jo Schrader

Advisory Board

Dr. Manlio Castiglioni
Italy

Dr. Arch C. Gerlach
United States

Dr. Ir. Cornelis Koeman
Netherlands

Dr. André Libault
Brazil

Brig. D. E. O. Thackwell
United Kingdom

Robert J. Voskuil
United States

Dr. Akira Watanabe
Japan

International Map Advisors

Europe
Prof. Dr. Emil Meynen
Germany
Dr. Sandor Rado
Hungary

Asia
Dr. Hisashi Sato
Japan

Australia
R. O. Buchanan
United Kingdom

Anglo-America
Dr. Arch C. Gerlach
United States

Latin America
Dr. André Libault
Brazil
Dra. Consuelo Soto Mora
Mexico
Dr. Jorge A. Vivó Escoto
Mexico

Metropolitan Area Maps
Prof. Harold M. Mayer
United States

The Real World

Developed by Rand McNally with Dr. Marvin W. Mikesell, University of Chicago. Artimus Keiffer, Kent State University, contributed the section on communication.

Editors
Jon M. Leverenz, Brett R. Gover.

Design Direction
John C. Nelson, Donna M. McGrath; designer: Vito M. DePinto.

Maps by the Cartographic Department of Rand McNally.

Satellite image on pages xvi-A·1: Mendoza, Argentina. Processed by Earth Information Systems Corporation, Austin, TX.; Laser film by Cirrus Technology, Inc., Nashua, NH. Data for communication section from TeleGeography, Inc., Washington, D.C.

The New International Atlas
25th Anniversary Edition
Revised 1998 Edition.

Copyright © 1994 by Rand McNally & Company. Copyright © 1969 by Rand McNally & Company as The International Atlas.

Printed in the United States of America.

Library of Congress Cataloging-in-Publication Data
Rand McNally and Company.
   The new international atlas. -- 25th anniversary ed.
      p.   cm..
   Includes index.
   ISBN 0-528-83808-3
   1. Atlases.   I. Title.
G1021.R23 1994 <G&M>
912--dc20
                           94-15784
                              CIP
                              MAP

Twenty-five years ago Rand McNally first published *The New International Atlas*. It was created through the cooperative efforts of an international cadre of cartographers, geographers, designers, and editors, under the leadership and direction of Rand McNally. The goal was to bring to a worldwide audience the most comprehensive, authoritative, and handsome atlas possible.

In the quarter of a century since the first printing, the *Atlas* has continued to portray with unsurpassed accuracy the Earth's surface and patterns of human settlement, and to chronicle the geographic changes affecting our lives. During this period it has been redesigned several times, and new maps have been added to the original selection. Today *The New International Atlas* is used throughout the world and is considered the standard of excellence for world reference atlases.

The editorial policies for the *Atlas* have been established with international use in mind. This approach has been carried into the maps through the utilization of the metric system of measurement, and through strong emphasis on the use of local geographic names. Essentially all names are in the local language; however, English is used for names of geographic features which cross international borders, and as an alternate form for major cities. The names of countries appear on most of the maps both in English and in the locally official forms.

Generic terms for physical features (mountain, island, cape, etc.) also appear in their local forms, not in English. Short glossaries translating the most common of these terms appear in the margins of most maps. A complete glossary of all the generic terms can be found toward the back of the *Atlas*. In the index to the *Atlas*, the

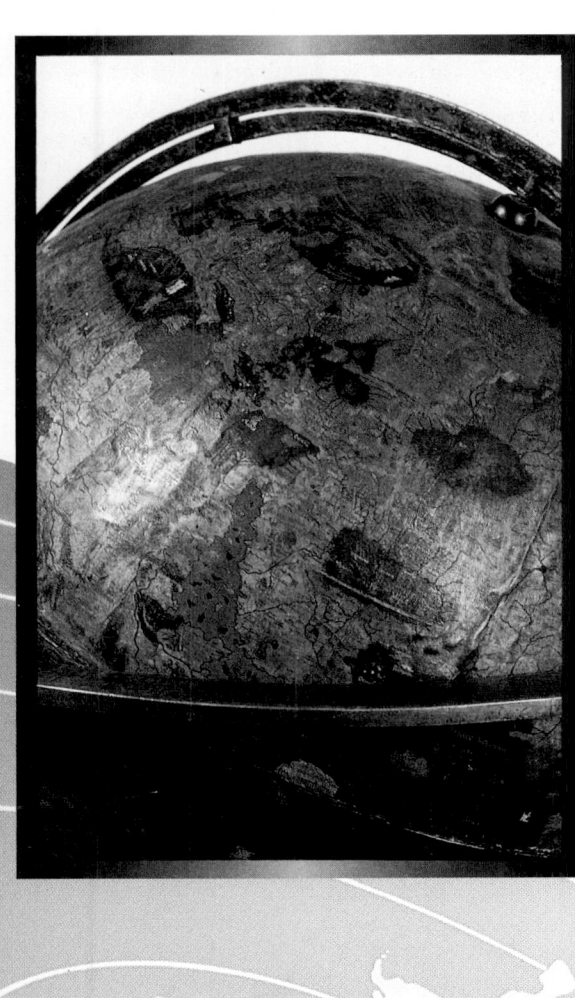

translation of generic terms is aided by the use of symbols.

The coverage of the world's regions has also been planned with international use in mind. There is an approximate balance between North America, Europe, and Asia, each with more than one-fifth of the total map pages. Africa, Australia/Oceania, and South America together account for the remaining one-third.

Another significant feature of the *Atlas* is the classification of the maps into five separate series, while using a limited number of map scales. This allows ready comparison of the nature and size of the Earth's regions. Each series has its own distinctive style and content. In the first of these series, the continents are portrayed at 1:24,000,000 in natural colors, as they might appear from about 4,000 miles in space. The series also includes maps of the oceans at 1:48,000,000 and the world at 1:75,000,000.

In the next series, the major world regions are uniformly portrayed at 1:12,000,000. These maps are primarily political in style and content. The third series covers virtually the entire inhabited area of the Earth at either 1:6,000,000 for the less dense regions, or 1:3,000,000 for Europe, most of North America, and the densest portions of South and East Asia. Physical and cultural detail are given approximately equal emphasis in this series.

In the fourth series, the scale of 1:1,000,000 has been used to portray key regions in each continent, selected for their exceptional importance, high population density, or complexity of development. The emphasis is on cultural detail, though relief is also shown. In the fifth and final series, the world's major metropolitan areas are mapped at 1:300,000. This series emphasizes the complex patterns characteristic of large urban areas.

The sequence of maps in the *Atlas* begins with the series of world, continent, and ocean maps. Next are the three series of regional maps, arranged within major regions from smallest scale (1:12,000,000) to largest scale (1:1,000,000). The metropolitan maps

(1:300,000) have been kept together in one section following the regional maps.

The map symbols used for specific features, shown on the Legend to Maps, are generally alike on all of the map scales, though reduced in size for smaller scales. The art form called shaded relief is used to symbolize the Earth's terrain on the maps in the *Atlas*. It uses variations from light through dark tones to give the maps their three-dimensional appearance. The expert craftsmanship used to depict the surface features in this manner adds beauty, drama, and important information to the maps, as well as a unique quality to the *Atlas*. On the 1:6,000,000 and 1:3,000,000 maps, the shaded relief appears in combination with altitude tints which represent variations in elevation.

In the concluding part of the *Atlas* are various tables and summaries for general reference, beginning with the comprehensive glossary of geographic terms. Following this is the World Information Table which lists the area, population, and political status for each major political unit. The world's largest metropolitan areas are then listed, followed by a list of the world's major cities and their populations. Finally, the Index provides map location references—map page, latitude and longitude—for more than 160,000 places.

Vorwort

Vor fünfundzwanzig Jahren veröffentlichte Rand McNally zum ersten Mal *Den Neuen Internationalen Atlas*. Dieses Werk wurde durch die Zusammenarbeit einer internationalen Gruppe von Kartographen, Geographen, Designern und Herausgebern unter der Leitung und Aufsicht von Rand McNally geschaffen. Das Ziel war, einem weltweiten Publikum den umfassendsten, autoritativsten und attraktivsten Atlas bereitzustellen.

Im Vierteljahrhundert seit der ersten Ausgabe zeigt der Atlas weiterhin die Erdoberfläche und die menschliche Besiedlung mit großer Genauigkeit und stellt die geographischen Veränderungen dar, die unser Leben beeinflussen. In diesem Zeitraum wurde der Atlas mehrmals revidiert und die ursprüngliche Auswahl durch neue Landkarten erweitert. Heute wird *Der Neue*

Internationale Atlas überall in der Welt benutzt und als Norm für ausgezeichnete Weltatlanten betrachtet.

Die redaktionellen Richtlinien für den *Atlas* wurden im Hinblick auf internationale Benutzung aufgestellt. Daher werden metrische Maßeinheiten und sowie örtliche geographische Namen benutzt. Im Prinzip erscheinen alle Namen in der jeweiligen Landessprache, jedoch wird Englisch für die Bezeichnung geographischer Merkmale, die Staatsgrenzen überschreiten, sowie als Alternativform für Großstädte eingesetzt. Die Ländernamen erscheinen auf den meisten Landkarten sowohl auf Englisch als auch in den örtlich geltenden Formen.

Gatungsbegriffe für geographische Eigenschaften (Gebirge, Inseln, Buchten usw.) werden ebenfalls in der jeweiligen Landessprache und nicht auf Englisch angegeben. Kurze Glossare mit Übersetzungen der üblichsten Begriffe erscheinen am Rande der meisten Landkarten. Ein vollständiges Glossar aller Gattungsnamen ist nahe dem Ende des *Atlasses* zu finden. Im Index für den gesamten *Atlas* wird die Übersetzung generischer Ausdrücke durch Symbole vereinfacht.

Auch die Behandlung der Weltregionen wurde nach internationalen Gesichtspunkten gestaltet. Die Behandlung von Nordamerika, Europa und Asien nimmt jeweils den gleichen Raum ein, und jeder dieser Kontinente umfaßt mehr als ein Fünftel der gesamten Landkartenseiten. Afrika, Australien/Ozeanien und Südamerika nehmen das restliche Drittel ein.

Ein weiteres wesentliches Merkmal des *Atlasses* ist die Klassifizierung der Landkarten in fünf getrennte Serien, wobei eine begrenzte Anzahl von Maßstäben eingesetzt wird. Dies ermöglicht mühelose Vergleiche der Bodenbeschaffenheit und der Größe der jeweiligen Erdregionen. Jede dieser Serien hat ihren eigenen distinktiven Stil und Inhalt. Die erste Serie zeigt die Kontinente im Maßstab 1:24 000 000 in Naturfarben, wie sie in einer Entfernung von 6600 Kilometern über der Erde sichtbar sind. Diese Serie enthält auch die Karten der Meere im Maßstab 1:48 000 000 und der Welt im Maßstab 1: 75 000 000.

In der folgenden Serie werden die größten Weltregionen gleichartig im Maßstab 1:12 000 000 dargestellt. Diese Landkarten sind in Stil und Inhalt hauptsächlich politisch gegliedert. Die dritte Serie deckt

die gesamten Besiedlungsgebiete der Erde entweder im Maßstab 1:6 000 000 bei den weniger dicht besiedelten Bereichen oder 1:3 000 000 bei Europa, einem Großteil von Nordamerika und sowie bei den am dichtesten besiedelten Gebiete in Süd- und Ostasien. Physische und kulturelle Details werden ungefähr gleichartig in dieser Serie betont.

Bei der vierten Serie wird der Maßstab 1:1 000 000 eingesetzt, um Schlüsselgebiete jedes Kontinents nach Wichtigkeit, Bevölkerungsdichte oder Komplexität der Entwicklung darzustellen. Die Betonung liegt auf kulturellem Detail, aber auch Relief wird gezeigt. Die fünfte und letzte Serie stellt die Bevölkerungszentren im Maßstab von 1:300 000 dar. Diese Serie hebt die komplexen Muster, die für große Stadtgebiete charakteristsich sind, hervor.

Die Abfolge der Karten im *Atlas* beginnt mit einer Anzahl von Welt-, Kontinent- und Meereskarten. Danach folgen drei Serien von regionalen Landkarten, die innerhalb größerer Gebiete von kleinerem Maßstab (1:12 000 000) bis größerem Maßstab (1:1 000 000) angeordnet sind. Die Großstadtkarten (1:300 000) sind in einem Teil nach den regionalen Landkarten zusammengefaßt.

Die Landkartensymbole für bestimmte Merkmale, die in der Legende der Landkarten auftreten, sind bei allen Maßstäben allgemein gleichartig, obwohl sie bei kleineren Maßstäben ebenfalls verkleinert sind. Schattierte Reliefkarten symbolisieren die Erdoberfläche auf den Landkarten im *Atlas*. Variationen von hellen und dunklen Farbtönen geben den Landkarten ein dreidimensionales Aussehen. Diese kartographische Kunstform, die zur Darstellung der Oberflächeneigenschaften eingesetzt wird, gibt den Landkarten Schönheit, Eindrucksstärke, bietet wichtige Informationen und verleiht

dem *Atlas* eine einzigartige Qualität. Auf den Landkarten im Maßstab 1:6 000 000 und 1:3 000 000 wird schattierte Reliefdarstellung zusammen mit Höhenfarbtönen eingesetzt und zeigt Höhenunterschiede.

Am Ende des *Atlasses* sind zahlreiche Tabellen und Zusammenfassungen als allgemeine Referenz zu finden, die mit einem umfassenden Glossar geographischer Begriffe beginnen. Danach folgt eine Weltinformationstabelle mit Bereichen, Bevölkerung und politischem Status der wesentlichsten Staaten. Dann werden die größten Bevölkerungsgebiete sowie eine Liste der Großstädte und deren Bevölkerungszahlen aufgeführt. Schließlich gibt der Index Hinweise auf die Landkarten mit Seitenzahlen sowie Breiten- und Längengraden für mehr als 160 000 Orte.

Prefacio

Vinte-cinco anos atrás a Rand McNally publicou *O Novo Atlas Internacional* pela primeira vez. Ele foi criado através dos esforços cooperativos de um quadro internacional de cartógrafos, geógrafos, desenhistas e editores, sob a liderança e direção da Rand McNally. A meta era trazer à uma audiência mundial o atlas mais compreensivo, autoritário e simpático possível.

Neste quarto de século desde a primeira impressão, o *Atlas* continuou a retratar a superfície da Terra e os padrões de colonização humana com grande exatidão, e o registro das mudanças geográficas que afetam as nossas vidas. Durante este período, ele foi redesenhado diversas vezes, e novos mapas foram somados à seleção original. Hoje, *O Novo Atlas Internacional* é utilizado ao redor do mundo e é considerado como sendo o padrão de excelência para os atlases mundiais de referência.

As políticas editoriais para o *Atlas* foram estabelecidas tendo em mente o uso internacional. Esta aproximação foi levada

aos mapas através da utilização do sistema métrico de medições, e pela forte ênfase ao uso dos nomes geográficos locais. Essencialmente todos os nomes estão na lingua local; porém, o Inglês é utilizado para os nomes das características geográficas que cruzam fronteiras internacionais, e como uma forma alternativa para cidades principais. Os nomes dos países aparecem na maioria dos mapas tanto em Inglês como na forma oficial local.

Têrmos genéricos para características físicas (montanha, ilha, cabo, etc.) também aparecem em sua forma local, não em Inglês. Glossários curtos traduzindo os mais comuns destes têrmos aparecem nas margens da maioria dos mapas. Um glossário completo de todos os têrmos genéricos pode ser encontrado ao final do *Atlas*. No índice do *Atlas*, uma tradução dos têrmos genéricos é auxiliada pelo uso de símbolos.

A cobertura das regiões mundiais também foram planejadas com o uso internacional em mente. Existe um balanço aproximado entre a América do Norte, Europa e Asia, cada um com mais de um quinto do total de páginas de mapas. África, Austrália/ Oceania, e América do Sul juntos compõem o um-terço restante.

Outra característica significante do *Atlas* é a classificação dos mapas em cinco séries separadas, enquanto usando um número limitado de escalas de mapas. Isto permite uma rápida comparação da natureza e do tamanho da regiões da Terra. Cada série possui seu próprio estilo e conteúdo distintos. Na primeira destas séries, os continentes estão retratados na escala de 1:24.000.000 em cores naturais, como eles poderiam parecer de aproximadamente 4.000 milhas no espaço. A série também inclui mapas dos oceanos em 1:48.000.000 e o mundo em 1:75.000.000.

Na próxima série, as principais regiões mundiais são retratadas uniformemente em 1:12.000.000. Estes mapas são primáriamente políticos quanto ao estilo e conteúdo. A terceira série cobre virtualmente todas as áreas habitadas da Terra em 1:6.000.000 para as regiões menos densas, ou 1:3.000.000 para a Europa, a maior parte da América do Norte, e as porções mais densas do Sul e do Leste da Asia. Uma ênfase aproximadamente igual aos detalhes físicos e culturais é dada nesta série.

Na quarta série, a escala de 1:1.000.000 foi utilizada para retratar as regiões chave de cada continente, selecionados pela sua excepcional importância, alta densidade populacional, ou complexidade do desenvolvimento. A ênfase é sobre o detalhe cultural, embora relevo também seja mostrado. Na quinta e última série, as principais áreas metropolitanas mundiais são mapeadas em 1:300.000. Esta série enfatiza os padrões complexos característicos de grandes áreas urbanas.

A sequência de mapas no *Atlas* inicia com a série de mapas do mundo, continente e oceano. A seguir vem três séries de mapas regionais, arranjados dentro de regiões principais desde a menor escala (1:12.000.000) até a maior escala (1:1.000.000). Os mapas metropolitanos (1:300.000) foram mantidos juntos numa seção seguinte aos mapas regionais.

Os símbolos de mapa utilizados para características específicas, mostrados na Inscrição dos Mapas, são geralmente os mesmos em todas as escalas dos mapas, embora reduzidos em tamanho para as escalas menores. A forma de arte chamada relevo sombreado é utilizado para simbolizar o terreno da Terra nos mapas do *Atlas*. A forma utiliza variações dos tons claros aos escuros para dar aos mapas sua aparência tri-dimensional. O artesanato especializado utilizado para retratar as caracteríticas da superfície desta forma soma beleza, drama e informações importantes aos mapas, também uma qualidade sem igual ao *Atlas*. Nos mapas de 1:6.000.000 e 1:3.000.000, o relevo sombreado aparece em combinação com matizes de altitude que representam variações na elevação.

Na parte que conclui o *Atlas* existem várias tabelas e sumários para referência geral, começando com o glossário compreensivo de têrmos geográficos. Em seguida a isso, está a Tabela de Informação do Mundo, que lista a área, população e status político para cada unidade política. As maiores áreas metropolitanas estão então listadas, seguidas por uma lista das maiores cidades do mundo e suas populações. Finalmente, o Índice proporciona referências de localização de mapas - página do mapa, latitude e longitude - para mais de 160.000 lugares.

Préface

Le *Nouvel Atlas International* fut publié pour la première fois par Rand McNally il y a vingt-cinq ans. Cet atlas fut le produit de la collaboration d'une équipe internationale de cartographes, de géographes, de concepteurs et de rédacteurs travaillant sous la direction de Rand McNally. Le but était de mettre un atlas faisant autorité, aussi complet et bien présenté que possible, à la disposition de lecteurs dans le monde entier.

Tout au long du quart de siècle qui s'est écoulé depuis sa première impression, l'*Atlas* a continué à illustrer avec une grande précision la surface de la Terre et son peuplement humain, et à faire la chronique des changements géographiques qui affectent notre vie. Pendant cette période, de nouvelles cartes ont été ajoutées à la sélection initiale, et sa conception même a été refondue à plusieurs reprises. Aujourd'hui, *Le Nouvel Atlas International* est utilisé dans le monde entier et est considéré comme la norme d'excellence pour les atlas mondiaux de référence.

Sur le plan rédactionnel, l'*Atlas* a véritablement été conçu pour un public international. Cette approche a été appliquée aux cartes en utilisant le système métrique et en employant autant que possible les noms géographiques locaux. En règle générale, tous les noms sont imprimés dans la langue du pays concerné ; cependant, la langue anglaise est utilisée pour les noms de structures géographiques qui dépassent les frontières internationales, et les grandes villes sont indiquées à la fois en anglais et dans la langue locale. Sur la plupart des cartes, les noms des pays sont indiqués en anglais et selon la forme officielle locale.

Les termes génériques pour les traits physiques (montagne, île, cap, etc.) apparaissent également dans leur forme locale plutôt que systématiquement en anglais. De brefs glossaires traduisant les termes génériques les plus usuels figurent en marge de la plupart des cartes. Un glossaire complet de tous les termes génériques est inclus vers la fin de l'*Atlas*. Dans l'index de l'*Atlas*, la compréhension des termes génériques est facilitée par l'emploi de symboles.

Le nombre de pages consacrées aux différents continents a également été décidé en pensant au public international. Il existe un équilibre approximatif entre l'Amérique du Nord, l'Europe et l'Asie - chacun de ces continents occupant plus de 20 pour cent du nombre total des pages de cartes. L'Afrique, l'Australie/Océanie et l'Amérique du Sud occupent ensemble le tiers restant des pages de cartes.

Une autre particularité intéressante de l'*Atlas* est la classification des cartes en cinq séries distinctes avec un nombre limité d'échelles. Ceci permet de comparer facilement la nature et la superficie des régions de la Terre. Chaque série a un style et un contenu distinctifs. Dans la première de ces séries, les continents sont représentés à l'échelle de 1:24 000 000 en couleurs naturelles, exactement comme ils apparaîtraient si vous les regardiez depuis plus de 6 000 km dans l'espace. Cette série comprend également des cartes des océans à 1:48 000 000 et du monde à 1:75 000 000.

Dans la série suivante, les principales régions du monde sont représentées de façon uniforme à l'échelle de 1:12 000 000. Ces cartes sont principalement politiques par leur style et par leurs détails. La troisième série couvre virtuellement toute la surface habitée de la Terre à l'échelle de 1:6 000 000 pour les régions faiblement peuplées ou de 1:3 000 000 pour l'Europe, la plus grande partie de l'Amérique du Nord et les régions à forte densité de population de l'Asie du Sud et de l'Est. Les cartes de cette série donnent une attention identique aux détails physiques et aux détails culturels.

Dans la quatrième série, l'échelle de 1:1 000 000 a été utilisée pour présenter les régions clés de chaque continent en raison de leur importance exceptionnelle, de leur forte densité de population ou de la complexité de leur développement. Les détails culturels sont mis en valeur, mais le relief y apparaît également. Dans la cinquième et dernière série, les principales agglomérations métropolitaines du monde sont présentées à l'échelle de 1:300 000. Cette série de cartes montre les caractéristiques complexes des grandes zones urbanisées.

La séquence de cartes de l'*Atlas* commence par les cartes du monde, des continents et des océans. Puis on trouve les trois séries de cartes régionales arrangées pour chaque grande région depuis la plus petite échelle (1:12 000 000) jusqu'à la plus grande (1:1 000 000). Toutes les cartes des zones métropolitaines (1:300 000) ont été regroupées dans la même section, à la suite des cartes régionales.

Les symboles des cartes utilisés pour des caractéristiques spécifiques, qui apparaissent sur la Légende des cartes, sont généralement les mêmes pour toutes les échelles de cartes, mais en dimensions réduites pour les échelles les plus petites. La méthode graphique dite du relief ombré est utilisée pour symboliser les traits physiques de la Terre sur les cartes de l'*Atlas*. Elle utilise des variations allant du plus clair au plus sombre pour donner aux cartes leur aspect tridimensionnel. Cette technique complexe qui est utilisée pour représenter les particularités de la surface terrestre de cette manière ajoute de la beauté, un aspect spectaculaire et des renseignements importants aux cartes, ainsi qu'une qualité unique à l'*Atlas*. Sur les cartes à une échelle de 1:6 000 000 et de 1:3 000 000, le relief ombré apparaît combiné avec des nuances de hauteurs qui représentent des variations diverses de l'altitude.

Enfin, dans la dernière partie de l'*Atlas*, on trouvera divers tableaux et résumés pour référence générale, en commençant par un glossaire complet des termes géographiques. Ce glossaire est suivi du Tableau des informations mondiales, qui indique la superficie, la population et le statut politique de chacune des principales unités politiques. La section suivante énumère les grandes zones métropolitaines du monde, puis les plus grandes villes du monde, ainsi que leur population. Enfin, l'*Index* donne les références nécessaires pour permettre de localiser plus de 160 000 points dans l'Atlas - page de la carte, latitude et longitude.

Prefácio

Hace veinticinco años Rand McNally publicó por primera vez *El Nuevo Atlas Internacional*. El mismo fue creado gracias a los esfuerzos de colaboración de un plantel internacional de cartógrafos, geógrafos, diseñadores y revisores, bajo el liderazgo y dirección de Rand McNally. El objetivo consistía en poner a la disposición de un público mundial el atlas más completo, más fidedigno y más hermoso posible.

Durante el cuarto de siglo desde su primera impresión, el *Atlas* ha seguido ilustrando con gran exactitud la superficie de la Tierra y las tendencias de las poblaciones, además de registrar los cambios geográficos que afectan nuestras vidas. Durante este período el diseño ha sido modificado varias veces, habiéndose añadido nuevos mapas a la selección original. Hoy día *El Nuevo Atlas Internacional* se utiliza en el mundo entero y es considerado como la norma por excelencia entre los atlas de referencia mundial.

Los principios editoriales que han guiado la elaboración del *Atlas* han sido establecidos teniendo presente el uso a nivel internacional. Este enfoque ha sido incorporado en los mapas mediante la utilización del sistema métrico de medidas y mediante un énfasis acentuado en el uso de los nombres geográficos locales. Esencialmente, todos los nombres aparecen en el idioma local; sin embargo, se ha utilizado el inglés para los nombres de rasgos geográficos que cruzan los confines internacionales y como forma alternativa para ciudades importantes. Los nombres de países aparecen tanto en inglés como en el idioma oficial de la localidad.

También los términos genéricos de accidentes físicos (como montañas, islas, cabos, etc.) figuran en los idiomas locales y no en inglés. En el margen de la mayoría de los mapas aparecen breves glosarios con la traducción de los términos más comunes. Un glosario completo de todos los términos genéricos se encuentra hacia el final del *Atlas*. En el índice alfabético del *Atlas*, la traducción de los términos genéricos es facilitada mediante el uso de símbolos.

También la cobertura de las regiones del mundo ha sido planificada teniendo presente el uso internacional. Existe un equilibrio aproximado entre Norteamérica, Europa y Asia, dedicando a cada continente más de un quinto del total de páginas con mapas. Africa, Australia/Oceanía y América del Sur comprenden, juntas, el tercio restante.

Otra característica significativa del *Atlas* está representada por la clasificación de los mapas en cinco series independientes, aun utilizando un número limitado de escalas. Esto permite una comparacón rápida de la naturaleza y dimensiones de las regiones terrestres. Cada serie está dotada de un estilo y contenido bien distinto. En la primera de estas series, los continentes están representados con una escala de 1:24.000.000 a colores naturales, tal como podrían aparecer desde una distancia de 4.000 millas en el espacio. La serie comprende también mapas de los océanos a una escala de 1:48.000.000 y del mundo a 1:75.000.000.

En la serie subsiguiente, se ilustran las principales regiones del mundo a una escala uniforme de 1:12.000.000. El estilo y el contenido de estos mapas es principalmente político. La tercera serie abarca prácticamente la totalidad de la superficie poblada de la Tierra a una escala de 1:6.000.000 para las regiones menos densamente pobladas o a 1:3.000.000 para Europa, la mayor parte de Norteamérica y las partes de mayor densidad de Asia del Sur y Asia Oriental. En esta serie se ha dedicado aproximadamente el mismo grado de énfasis a los detalles físicos y culturales.

En la cuarta serie, se ha utilizado una escala de 1:1.000.000 para ilustrar las regiones clave de cada continente, seleccionadas en base a su importancia excepcional, alta densidad de población o complejidad de desarrollo. Se ha prestado énfasis al detalle cultural, aun cuando se muestren también los relieves. En la quinta y última serie se han cartografiado las áreas metropolitanas de gran envergadura a una escala de 1:300.000. Esta serie pone énfasis en los patrones característicos de las grandes áreas urbanas.

La secuencia de mapas en el *Atlas* comienza con la serie de mapas del mundo, de los continentes y de los océanos. Seguidamente, aparecen las tres series de mapas regionales, dispuestas dentro de las regiones principales con escalas a partir desde la más pequeña (1:12.000.000) a la más grande (1:1.000.000). Los mapas metropolitanos (1:300.000) se han reunido juntos en una sola sección, a continuación de los mapas regionales.

Los símbolos utilizados en los mapas con respecto a accidentes específicos, indicados en la Leyenda de Mapas, son por lo general similares en todas las escalas, pero de dimensiones reducidas en el caso de escalas más pequeñas. La forma gráfica conocida como relieve sombreado se utiliza para simbolizar el terreno de la Tierra en los mapas del *Atlas*. Se hace uso de variaciones de tonos claros y oscuros para dar el aspecto tridimensional a los mapas. La pericia artística empleada para ilustrar de esta manera las características de superficie añade belleza, drama e información importante a los mapas, así como una calidad exclusiva al *Atlas*. En los mapas con escalas de 1:6.000.000 y 1:3.000.000, el relieve sombreado aparece en combinación con los matices de altitudes que representan las diferencias de altura.

En la parte final del *Atlas* figuran varias tablas y resúmenes como referencia general, comenzando con el glosario completo de los términos geográficos. A continuación de ello, aparece la Tabla de Información del Mundo que indica datos de superficie, población y estado político de cada unidad política importante. Luego se enumeran las áreas metropolitanas más grandes del mundo, seguidas por una lista de las principales ciudades del mundo y su población. Por último, el Indice alfabético proporciona referencias para la ubicación de los mapas como, por ejemplo, la página del mapa, latitud y longitud, correspondientes a más de 160.000 localidades.

Summary of Contents

Sumario del Contenido

Inhaltsverzeichnis

Table des Matières

Sumário

Lista de Mapas

Liste des Cartes

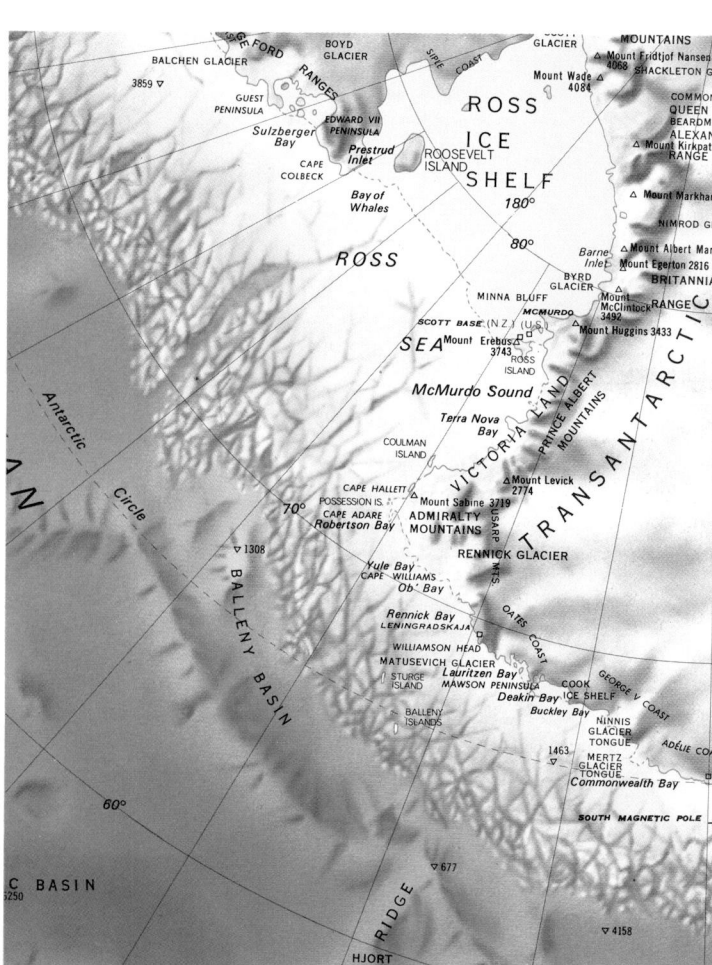

The design and color of the map symbols are consistent throughout the Regional and Metropolitan Area maps, although the size of the symbol varies with scale. An asterisk marks those symbols which appear only on the 1:300,000 scale maps.

The symbol 80-81 in the margin of a map directs the reader to a map of the adjoining area.

A separate legend on page 1 identifies the land and submarine features which appear on the World, Ocean, and Continent maps.

Der Entwurf und die Farbe der Kartensymbole sind einheitlich für alle Regionalkarten und Karten von Stadtregionen, während die Grösse des Symbols sich mit dem Massstab ändert. Ein Stern kennzeichnet diejenigen Symbole, welche nur auf den Karten im Masstab 1:300 000 erscheinen.

Kennzeichen 80-81 am rande einer Karte ist ein Hinweis für den Leser, die Karte eines angrenzenden Gebietes nachzuschlagen.

Eine andere Legende auf Seite 1 identifiziert die Land- und untermeerischen Phänomene, die auf den Weltkarten, Karten der Ozeane und Erdteile erscheinen.

El diseño y el color de los símbolos cartográficos son uniformes para todas los mapas regionales y de las áreas metropolitanas, aunque el tamaño del símbolo varía según la escala. Un asterisco distingue los símbolos que aparecen sólo en los mapas a 1:300 000.

El símbolo 80-81 al margen de un mapa dirige al lector a un mapa del área adyacente.

Otra leyenda, en la página 1, identifica la topografía terrestre y submarina que se encuentra en los mapas del Mundo, Océanos y Continentes.

La couleur et la forme des symboles cartographiques des cartes régionales et des cartes des zones métropolitaines sont identiques, bien que la grandeur des signes carie selon l'échelle. Un astérisque accompagne les symboles qui n'apparaissent que sur les cartes au 1:300 000.

Le symbole 80-81 en marge d'une carte renvoie le lecteur à une carte de la région voisine.

Pour les cartes du monde, des océans et des continents une légende séparée, à la page 1, donne le sens des symboles représentant les paysages continentaux et les formes de relief sous-marin.

A cor e a forma dos símbolos cartográficos dos mapas regionais e das áreas metropolitanas são idênticos, ainda que a dimensão do símbolo varie segundo a escala. Um asterisco distingue os símbolos que só aparecem nos mapas da escala de 1:300 000.

O símbolo 80-81 à margem de um mapa, remete o leitos a um mapa da região vizinha.

Nos mapas do mundo, dos oceanos e dos continentes uma legenda separada, na pág. 1, indica o sentido dos símbolos representativos das paisagens continentais e das formas do relevo submarino.

	Hydrographic Features	Hydrographische Objekte	Elementos Hidrográficos	Données Hydrographiques	Acidentes Hidrográficos
	Shoreline	Uferlinie	Línea costanera	Trait de côte	Linha costeira
	Undefined or Fluctuating Shoreline	Unbestimmte oder Veränderliche Uferlinie	Línea costanera indefinida o fluctuante	Trait de côte indéfini ou fluctuant	Linha costeira indefinida ou flutuante
Amur	River, Stream	Fluss, Strom	Río, Corriente	Rivière, Cours d'eau	Rio, curso d'água
	Intermittent Stream	Periodischer Fluss	Corriente intermitente	Cours d'eau périodique	Rio, curso d'água intermitente
SALTO ÁNGEL	Rapids, Falls	Stromschnellen, Wasserfälle	Rápidos, Cascadas	Rapides, Chutes d'eau	Corredeiras, quedas d'água
764 ▽	Depth of Water	Wassertiefe	Profundidad del aqua	Profondeur bathymétrique	Profundidade da água
8428 ▼	Greatest Depth (Atlantic, Indian, Pacific oceans)	Grösste Tiefe (Atlantischer, Indischer, Pazifischer Ozean)	Profundidad más grande (Océanos Atlántico, Índico, Pacífico)	Profondeur maximum (océans Atlantique, Indien, Pacifique)	Profundidade máxima (oceanos Atlântico, Índico, Pacífico)
Canal du Midi	Navigable Canal	Schiffbarer Kanal	Canal navegable	Canal navigable	Canal navegável
	Irrigation or Drainage Canal	Be- oder Entwässerungskanal	Canal de irrigación o desagüe	Canal d'irrigation ou de drainage	Canal de irrigação ou drenagem
Los Angeles Aqueduct	Aqueduct	Aquädukt	Acueducto	Aqueduc	Aqueduto
	Pier, Breakwater	Landungsbrücke, Wellenbrecher	Embarcadero, Rompeolas	Jetée, Brise-lames	Cais, Quebra-mar
GREAT BARRIER REEF	Reef	Riff	Arrecife	Récif	Recife
Kumdah ○	Uninhabited Oasis	Unbewohnte Oase	Oasis deshabitado	Oasis inhabitée	Oásis desabitado
L. Victoria	Lake, Reservoir	See, Stausee	Lago, Embalse	Lac, Réservoir	Lago, reservatório (represa)
	Intermittent Lake, Reservoir	Periodischer See, Stausee	Lago o Embalse intermitente	Lac ou Réservoir périodique	Lago, reservatório (represa) intermitente
Tuz Golu	Salt Lake	Salzsee	Lago salado	Lac salé	Lago salgado
	Dry Lake Bed	Trockener Seeboden	Lecho de lago seco	Fond de lac asséché	Leito de lago seco
The Everglades	Swamp	Sumpf	Pantano	Marais	Pântano
RIMO GLACIER	Glacier	Gletscher	Glaciar	Glacier	Geleira
(395)	Lake Surface Elevation	Seehöhe	Elevación del lago	Cote du niveau du lac	Altitude do nível do lago

	Topographic Features	Topographische Objekte	Elementos Topográficos	Données Topographiques	Acidentes Topográficos
Matterhorn 4478 △	Elevation Above Sea Level	Höhe über dem Meeresspiegel	Elevación sobre del nivel del mar	Cote au-dessus du niveau de la mer	Altitude acima do nível do mar
76 ▽	Elevation Below Sea Level	Höhe unter dem Meeresspiegel	Elevación bajo del nivel del mar	Cote au-dessous du niveau de la mer	Altitude abaixo do nível do mar
Mount Cook 3764 ▲	Highest Elevation in Country	Höchster Punkt des Landes	Elevación más alta en el país	Cote la plus élevée d'un pays	Altitude mais elevada de um país
133 ▼	Lowest Elevation in Country	Tiefster Punkt des Landes	Elevación más baja en el país	Cote la plus basse d'un pays	Altitude mais baixa de um país
(106)	Elevation of City	Höhenangabe einer Stadt	Elevación de ciudad	Altitude d'une ville	Altitude de uma cidade
Khyber Pass 1067 ≍	Mountain Pass	Pass	Paso	Col de montagne	Passo (de montanha)
*	Rock	Fels	Roca	Rocher	Rocha
	Lava	Lava	Lava	Lave	Lava
	Sand Area	Sandgebiet	Area de arena	Région sableuse, Erg	Região arenosa, Erg
	Salt Flat	Salzebene	Salar	Dépression salée	Depressão salgada
ANDES KUNLUN SHAN	Mountain Range, Plateau, Valley, etc.	Gebirge, Hochebene, Tal, usw.	Sierra, Meseta, Valle, etc.	Chaîne de montagnes, Plateau, Vallée, etc.	Cadeia de montanhas, Planalto, Vale, etc.
BAFFIN ISLAND NUNIVAK ISLAND	Island	Insel	Isla	Île	Ilha
POLUOSTROV KAMČATKA CABO DE HORNOS	Peninsula, Cape, Point, etc.	Halbinsel, Kap, Landspitze, usw.	Península, Cabo, Punta, etc.	Péninsule, Cap, Pointe, etc.	Península, Cabo, Ponta, etc.
	Elevations and depths are given in meters	Höhen und Tiefen sind in Metern angegeben	Elevaciones y profundidades se dan en metros	Cotes et profondeurs sont indiquées en mètres	Altitudes e profundidades são apresentadas em metros
	Highest Elevation and Lowest Elevation of a continent are underlined	Höchster und tiefster Punkt innerhalb eines Erdteils sind unterstrichen	Elevación más alta y más baja de un continente se subrayan	La cote la plus haute et la cote la plus basse d'un continent sont soulignées	As altitudes mais e menos elevadas de um continente são sublinhadas

Inhabited Localities / Bewohnte Orte / Lugares Poblados / Lieux Habités / Lugares Habitados

English	German	Spanish	French	Portuguese
Inhabited Localities	**Bewohnte Orte**	**Lugares Poblados**	**Lieux Habités**	**Lugares Habitados**
The symbol represents the number of inhabitants within the locality	Die Signatur entspricht der Einwohnerzahl des Ortes	El símbolo representa el número de habitantes dentro del lugar	Le symbole représente le nombre d'habitants de la localité	O símbolo representa o número de habitantes do lugar

1:300,000 1:1,000,000
1:3,000,000 1:6,000,000

- · 0–10,000
- ○ 10,000–25,000
- ⊙ 25,000–100,000
- ⊡ 100,000–250,000
- ▣ 250,000–1,000,000
- ■ >1,000,000

1:12,000,000

- · 0–50,000
- ⊙ 50,000–100,000
- ⊡ 100,000–250,000
- ▣ 250,000–1,000,000
- ■ >1,000,000

1:24,000,000
1:48,000,000

- · 0–100,000
- ⊙ 100,000–1,500,000x
- ■ >1,500,000

Écommoy Lisieux **Rouen**
Trouville Orléans **PARIS**

English	German	Spanish	French	Portuguese
The size of type indicates the relative economic and political importance of the locality	Die Schriftgrösse entspricht der relativen wirtschaftlichen und politischen Bedeutung des Ortes	El tamaño del tipo de imprenta indica la relativa importancia económica y política del lugar	La dimension des caractères indique l'importance économique et politique relative d'une localité	A dimensão dos caracteres tipográficos indica a importância econômica e política relativa do lugar
Hollywood □ *Westminster* — Section of a City, Neighborhood	Stadtteil, Nachbarschaft	Sección de una ciudad, Barrio	Arrondissement, Quartier	Seção de uma cidade, Bairro
Northland ■ *Center* — *Major Shopping Center	Haupteinkaufszentrum	Mercado principal	Centre commercial important	Centro comercial importante
BYRD □ — Scientific Station	Wissenschaftliche Station	Estación científica	Station scientifique	Estação científica
Bir Safâjah ○ — Inhabited Oasis	Bewohnte Oase	Oasis habitado	Oasis habitée	Oásis habitado
Kumdah ○ — Uninhabited Oasis	Unbewohnte Oase	Oasis deshabitado	Oasis inhabitée	Oásis desabitado
Urban Area (area of continuous industrial, commercial, and residential development)	Stadtgebiet (ausgedehntes Industrie-, Geschäfts- und Wohngebiet)	Zona urbanizada (área de desarrollo industrial, comercial y residencial)	Zone urbanisée (zone d'occupation continue par des industries, des commerces, des habitations)	Zona urbanizada (área de ocupação contínua por indústrias, estabelecimentos comerciais e habitações)
*Major Industrial Area	Hauptindustriegebiet	Zona principal industrial	Région industrielle importante	Zona industrial importante
*Wooded Area	Wald	Área de bosque	Région boisée	Área verde
*Local Park or Recreational Area	Park oder Erholungsgebiet	Parque municipal o área de recreo	Parc municipal ou zone de loisirs	Parque municipal ou área de lazer

Political Boundaries / Politische Grenzen / Límites Políticos / Frontières Politiques / Fronteiras e Limites

Scale	English	German	Spanish	French	Portuguese
	International (First-order political unit)	**Staatsgrenze** (Politische Einheit erster Ordnung)	**Internacionales** (Unidad política de primer orden)	**Internationales** (Entités politiques de premier ordre)	**Internacionais** (Unidade política de primeiro nível)
1:1** / 1:3, 1:3, 1:6 / 1:24, 1:48 / 1:12	Demarcated, Undemarcated, and Administrative (HUNGARY)	Markiert, unmarkiert, verwaltungstechnisch	Demarcado, No demarcado, y Administrativo	Délimitées, Non-délimitées, Administratives	Delimitados, Não delimitados, Administrativos
1:1 / 1:3, 1:3, 1:6 / 1:24, 1:48 / 1:12	Disputed de facto	Umstritten de facto	Disputado de hecho	Contestées de facto	Contestados de fato
1:1 / 1:3, 1:3, 1:6 / 1:24, 1:48 / 1:12	Disputed de jure	Umstritten de jure	Disputado de derecho	Contestées de jure	Contestados de direito
1:1 / 1:3, 1:3, 1:6 / 1:24, 1:48 / 1:12	Indefinite or Undefined	Unklar oder Unbestimmt	Indefinido o No determinado	Imprécises ou Non définies	Imprecisos ou Não definidos
1:1 / 1:3, 1:3, 1:6 / 1:24, 1:48 / 1:12	Demarcation Line	Demarkationslinie	Línea de demarcación	Ligne de démarcation	Linha de demarcação

Scale	English	German	Spanish	French	Portuguese
	Internal	**Verwaltungsgrenze**	**Internos**	**Intérieures**	**Limites Internos**
1:1 / 1:3, 1:6 / 1:12	State, Province, etc. (Second-order political unit) (PERNAMBUCO)	Land, Provinz, usw. (Politische Einheit zweiter Ordnung)	Estado, Provincia, etc. (Unidad política de segundo orden)	État, Province, etc. (Subdivision administrative de deuxième ordre)	Estado, Província, etc. (Unidade política de segundo nível)
1:1 / 1:3, 1:1	County, Oblast, etc. (Third-order political unit) (SIENA / WESTCHESTER)	Grafschaft, Oblast, usw. (Politische Einheit dritter Ordnung)	Condado, Oblast, etc. (Unidad política de tercer orden)	Comté, Oblast, etc. (Subdivision administrative de troisième ordre)	Condado, Oblast, etc. (Unidade política de terceiro nível)
1:3, 1:1	Okrug, Kreis, etc. (Fourth-order political unit) (ISERLOHN)	Okrug, Kreis, usw. (Politische Einheit vierter Ordnung)	Okrug, Kreis, etc. (Unidad política de cuarto orden)	Okrug, Kreis, etc. (Subdivision administrative de quatrième ordre)	Okrug, Kreis, etc. (Unidade política de quarto nível)
1:3, 1:1	City or Municipality (may appear in combination with another boundary symbol)	Stadt oder Gemeinde (kann zusammen mit einem anderen Begrenzungssymbol erscheinen)	Ciudad o Municipio (puede aparecer en combinación con otro símbolo de límite)	Ville ou Municipalité (peut paraître en combinaison avec un autre symbole de limites politiques)	Cidade ou Municipalidade (Pode aparecer em combinação com outro símbolo de limite político)
	Historical Region (No boundaries indicated) (NORMANDIE)	Historische Landschaft (Grenzen werden nicht gezeigt)	Región Histórica (Sin indicación de límites)	Région Historique (Sans indication de frontières)	Região Histórica (Sem indicação de fronteiras)

Capitals of Political Units / Hauptstädte politischer Einheiten / Capitales de Unidades Políticas / Capitales d'Entités Politiques / Capitais de Unidades Políticas

Sample	English	German	Spanish	French	Portuguese
BUDAPEST	Independent Nation	Unabhängiger Staat	Nación independiente	État indépendant	Estado independente
Cayenne	Dependency (Colony, protectorate, etc.)	Abhängiges Gebiet (Kolonie, Protektorat, usw.)	Dependencia (Colonia, protectorado, etc.)	Territoire dépendant (Colonie, protectorat, etc.)	Dependência (Colônia, protetorado, etc.)
GALAPAGOS (Ecuador)	Administering Country	Verwaltender Staat	País administrador	Pays administrateur	País administrador
Recife	State, Province, etc.	Land, Provinz, usw.	Estado, Provincia, etc.	État, Province, etc.	Estado, Província, etc.
Ambala / **Johnstown**	County, Oblast, etc.	Grafschaft, Oblast, usw.	Condado, Oblast, etc.	Comté, Oblast, etc.	Condado, Oblast, etc.
Iserlohn	Okrug, Kreis, etc.	Okrug, Kreis, usw.	Okrug, Kreis, etc.	Okrug, Kreis, etc.	Okrug, Kreis, etc.

**Scale in millions

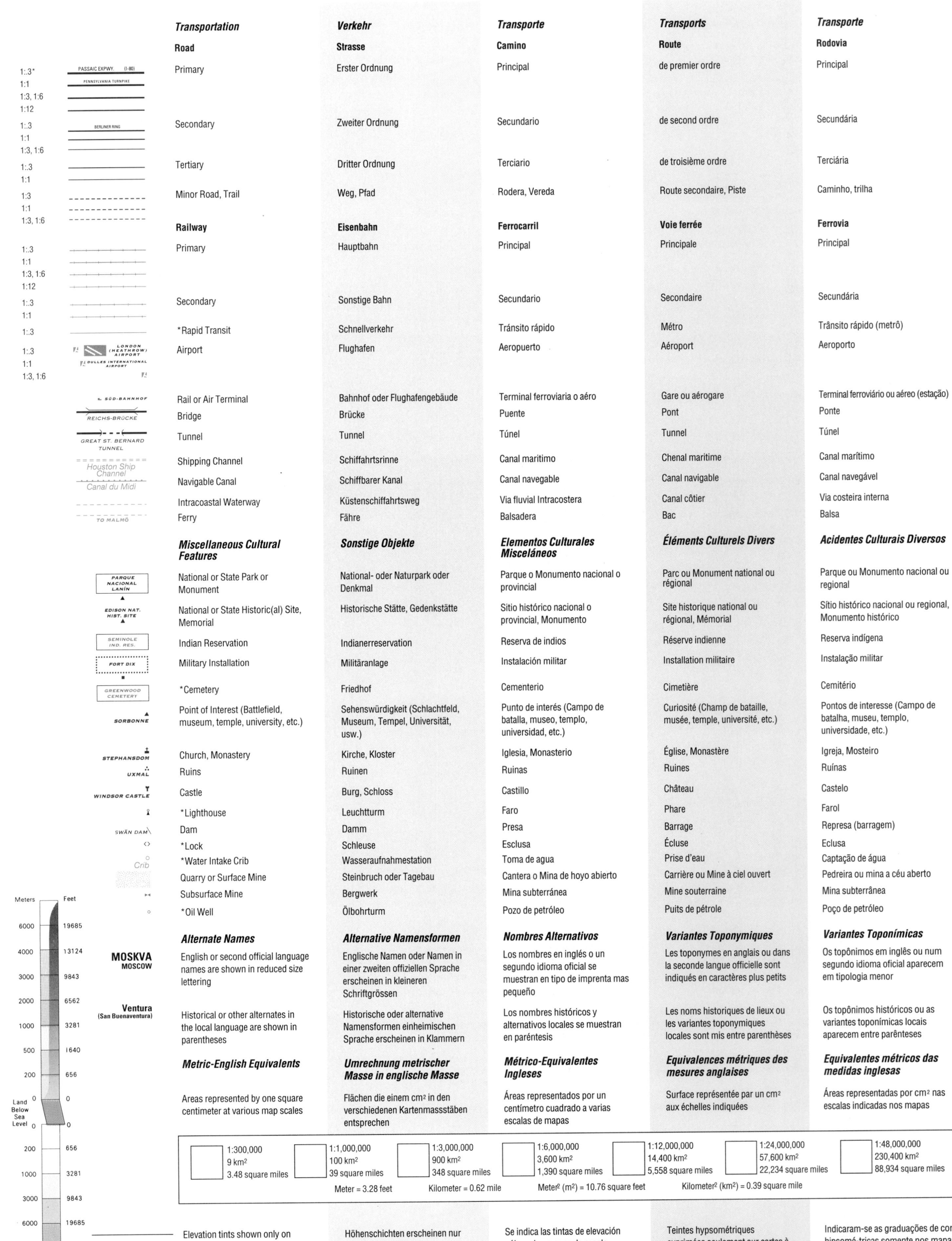

English	Deutsch	Español	Français	Português
Transportation	**Verkehr**	**Transporte**	**Transports**	**Transporte**
Road	**Strasse**	**Camino**	**Route**	**Rodovia**
Primary	Erster Ordnung	Principal	de premier ordre	Principal
Secondary	Zweiter Ordnung	Secundario	de second ordre	Secundária
Tertiary	Dritter Ordnung	Terciario	de troisième ordre	Terciária
Minor Road, Trail	Weg, Pfad	Rodera, Vereda	Route secondaire, Piste	Caminho, trilha
Railway	**Eisenbahn**	**Ferrocarril**	**Voie ferrée**	**Ferrovia**
Primary	Hauptbahn	Principal	Principale	Principal
Secondary	Sonstige Bahn	Secundario	Secondaire	Secundária
*Rapid Transit	Schnellverkehr	Tránsito rápido	Métro	Trânsito rápido (metrô)
Airport	Flughafen	Aeropuerto	Aéroport	Aeroporto
Rail or Air Terminal	Bahnhof oder Flughafengebäude	Terminal ferroviaria o aéro	Gare ou aérogare	Terminal ferroviário ou aéreo (estação)
Bridge	Brücke	Puente	Pont	Ponte
Tunnel	Tunnel	Túnel	Tunnel	Túnel
Shipping Channel	Schiffahrtsrinne	Canal maritimo	Chenal maritime	Canal marítimo
Navigable Canal	Schiffbarer Kanal	Canal navegable	Canal navigable	Canal navegável
Intracoastal Waterway	Küstenschiffahrtsweg	Via fluvial Intracostera	Canal côtier	Via costeira interna
Ferry	Fähre	Balsadera	Bac	Balsa
Miscellaneous Cultural Features	**Sonstige Objekte**	**Elementos Culturales Misceláneos**	**Éléments Culturels Divers**	**Acidentes Culturais Diversos**
National or State Park or Monument	National- oder Naturpark oder Denkmal	Parque o Monumento nacional o provincial	Parc ou Monument national ou régional	Parque ou Monumento nacional ou regional
National or State Historic(al) Site, Memorial	Historische Stätte, Gedenkstätte	Sitio histórico nacional o provincial, Monumento	Site historique national ou régional, Mémorial	Sítio histórico nacional ou regional, Monumento histórico
Indian Reservation	Indianerreservation	Reserva de indios	Réserve indienne	Reserva indígena
Military Installation	Militäranlage	Instalación militar	Installation militaire	Instalação militar
*Cemetery	Friedhof	Cementerio	Cimetière	Cemitério
Point of Interest (Battlefield, museum, temple, university, etc.)	Sehenswürdigkeit (Schlachtfeld, Museum, Tempel, Universität, usw.)	Punto de interés (Campo de batalla, museo, templo, universidad, etc.)	Curiosité (Champ de bataille, musée, temple, université, etc.)	Pontos de interesse (Campo de batalha, museu, templo, universidade, etc.)
Church, Monastery	Kirche, Kloster	Iglesia, Monasterio	Église, Monastère	Igreja, Mosteiro
Ruins	Ruinen	Ruinas	Ruines	Ruínas
Castle	Burg, Schloss	Castillo	Château	Castelo
*Lighthouse	Leuchtturm	Faro	Phare	Farol
Dam	Damm	Presa	Barrage	Represa (barragem)
*Lock	Schleuse	Esclusa	Écluse	Eclusa
*Water Intake Crib	Wasseraufnahmestation	Toma de agua	Prise d'eau	Captação de água
Quarry or Surface Mine	Steinbruch oder Tagebau	Cantera o Mine de hoyo abierto	Carrière ou Mine à ciel ouvert	Pedreira ou mina a céu aberto
Subsurface Mine	Bergwerk	Mina subterránea	Mine souterraine	Mina subterrânea
*Oil Well	Ölbohrturm	Pozo de petróleo	Puits de pétrole	Poço de petróleo
Alternate Names	**Alternative Namensformen**	**Nombres Alternativos**	**Variantes Toponymiques**	**Variantes Toponímicas**
English or second official language names are shown in reduced size lettering	Englische Namen oder Namen in einer zweiten offiziellen Sprache erscheinen in kleineren Schriftgrössen	Los nombres en inglés o un segundo idioma oficial se muestran en tipo de imprenta mas pequeño	Les toponymes en anglais ou dans la seconde langue officielle sont indiqués en caractères plus petits	Os topônimos em inglês ou num segundo idioma oficial aparecem em tipologia menor
Historical or other alternates in the local language are shown in parentheses	Historische oder alternative Namensformen einheimischen Sprache erscheinen in Klammern	Los nombres históricos y alternativos locales se muestran en paréntesis	Les noms historiques de lieux ou les variantes toponymiques locales sont mis entre parenthèses	Os topônimos históricos ou as variantes toponímicas locais aparecem entre parênteses
Metric-English Equivalents	**Umrechnung metrischer Masse in englische Masse**	**Métrico-Equivalentes Ingleses**	**Equivalences métriques des mesures anglaises**	**Equivalentes métricos das medidas inglesas**
Areas represented by one square centimeter at various map scales	Flächen die einem cm² in den verschiedenen Kartenmassstäben entsprechen	Áreas representados por un centímetro cuadrado a varias escalas de mapas	Surface représentée par un cm² aux échelles indiquées	Áreas representadas por cm² nas escalas indicadas nos mapas

PASSAIC EXPWY. (I-80)
PENNSYLVANIA TURNPIKE
BERLINER RING

1::3*
1:1
1:3, 1:6
1:12

1::3
1:1
1:3, 1:6

1::3
1:1

1:3
1:1
1:3, 1:6

1::3
1:1
1:3, 1:6
1:12

1::3
1:1

1::3

1::3
1:1
1:3, 1:6

L. SÜD-BAHNHOF
REICHS-BRÜCKE
GREAT ST. BERNARD TUNNEL
Houston Ship Channel
Canal du Midi
TO MALMÖ

LONDON (HEATHROW) AIRPORT
DULLES INTERNATIONAL AIRPORT

PARQUE NACIONAL LANÍN
EDISON NAT. HIST. SITE
SEMINOLE IND. RES.
FORT DIX
GREENWOOD CEMETERY
SORBONNE
STEPHANSDOM
UXMAL
WINDSOR CASTLE
SWAN DAM
Crib

MOSKVA
MOSCOW

Ventura
(San Buenaventura)

Meters	Feet
6000	19685
4000	13124
3000	9843
2000	6562
1000	3281
500	1640
200	656
0	0
Land Below Sea Level 0	0
200	656
1000	3281
3000	9843
6000	19685
9000	29520

1:300,000 9 km² 3.48 square miles	1:1,000,000 100 km² 39 square miles	1:3,000,000 900 km² 348 square miles	1:6,000,000 3,600 km² 1,390 square miles	1:12,000,000 14,400 km² 5,558 square miles	1:24,000,000 57,600 km² 22,234 square miles	1:48,000,000 230,400 km² 88,934 square miles

Meter = 3.28 feet   Kilometer = 0.62 mile   Meter² (m²) = 10.76 square feet   Kilometer² (km²) = 0.39 square mile

Elevation tints shown only on 1:3,000,000 and 1:6,000,000 scale maps	Höhenschichten erscheinen nur auf Karten im Massstab 1:3 000 000 und 1:6 000 000	Se indica las tintas de elevación sólo en los mapas de escala 1:3 000 000 y 1:6 000 000	Teintes hypsométriques exprimées seulement sur cartes à 1:3 000 000 et 1:6 000 000	Indicaram-se as graduações de cor hipsomé-tricas somente nos mapas de escalas 1:3 000 000 e 1:6 000 000

*Scale in millions

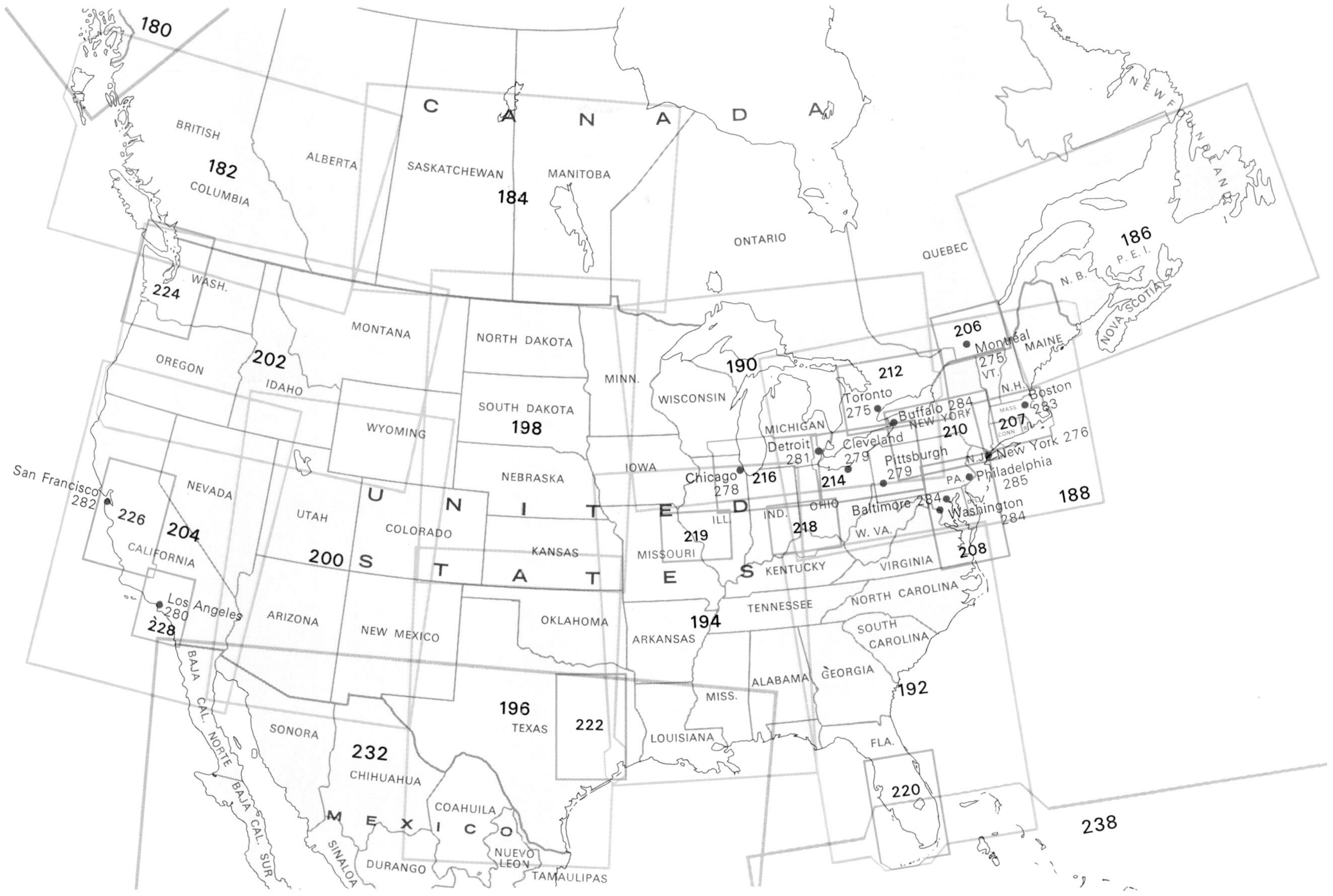
C A N A D A
BRITISH COLUMBIA
ALBERTA
SASKATCHEWAN
MANITOBA
ONTARIO
QUEBEC
NEWFOUNDLAND
N. B.
P. E. I.
NOVA SCOTIA
U N I T E D S T A T E S
WASH.
OREGON
IDAHO
MONTANA
WYOMING
NORTH DAKOTA
SOUTH DAKOTA
NEBRASKA
MINN.
WISCONSIN
MICHIGAN
IOWA
ILL.
IND.
OHIO
NEW YORK
PA.
N.J.
VT.
N.H.
MAINE
MASS.
CONN.
NEVADA
CALIFORNIA
UTAH
COLORADO
KANSAS
MISSOURI
KENTUCKY
W. VA.
VIRGINIA
ARIZONA
NEW MEXICO
OKLAHOMA
ARKANSAS
TENNESSEE
NORTH CAROLINA
SOUTH CAROLINA
ALABAMA
GEORGIA
MISS.
LOUISIANA
TEXAS
FLA.
M E X I C O
BAJA CAL. NORTE
BAJA CAL. SUR
SONORA
CHIHUAHUA
COAHUILA
NUEVO LEON
SINALOA
DURANGO
TAMAULIPAS
180
182
184
186
188
190
192
194
196
198
200
202
204
206
207
208
210
212
214
216
218
219
220
222
224
226
228
232
238
San Francisco 282
Los Angeles 280
Chicago 278
Detroit 281
Toronto 275
Montréal 275
Buffalo 284
Cleveland 279
Pittsburgh 279
Boston 283
New York 276
Philadelphia 285
Baltimore 284
Washington 284

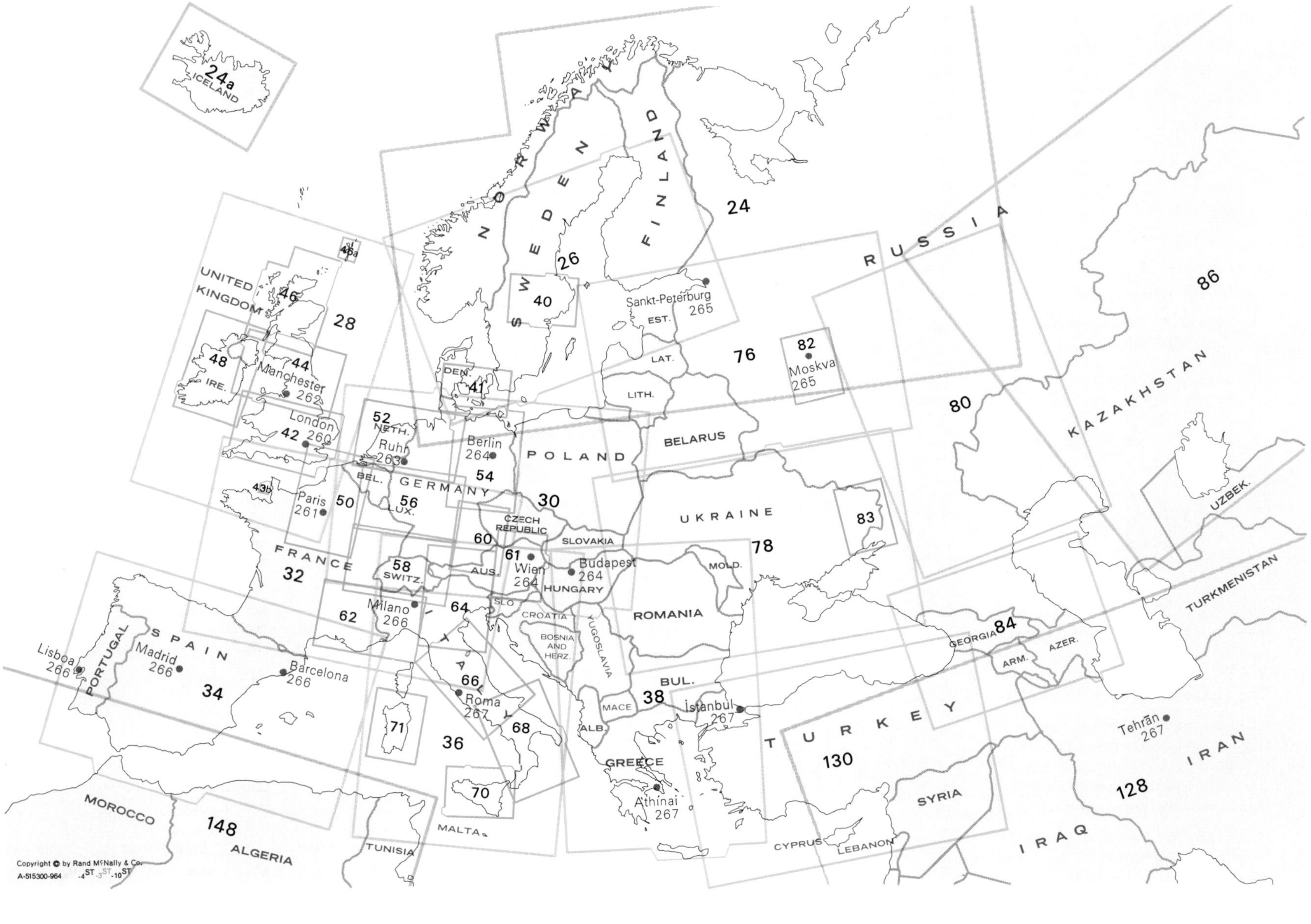
24a ICELAND
UNITED KINGDOM
IRE.
NORWAY
SWEDEN
FINLAND
RUSSIA
DEN.
NETH.
BEL.
LUX.
GERMANY
POLAND
BELARUS
EST.
LAT.
LITH.
UKRAINE
MOLD.
CZECH REPUBLIC
SLOVAKIA
AUS.
SWITZ.
HUNGARY
ROMANIA
SLO.
CROATIA
BOSNIA AND HERZ.
YUGOSLAVIA
MACE.
ALB.
BUL.
GREECE
FRANCE
SPAIN
PORTUGAL
ITALY
MALTA
MOROCCO
ALGERIA
TUNISIA
TURKEY
CYPRUS
LEBANON
SYRIA
IRAQ
IRAN
GEORGIA
ARM.
AZER.
KAZAKHSTAN
UZBEK.
TURKMENISTAN
24
26
28
30
32
34
36
38
40
41
42
43a
43b
44
46
48
50
52
54
56
58
60
61
62
64
66
68
70
71
76
78
80
82
83
84
86
128
130
148
Sankt-Peterburg 265
Moskva 265
Manchester 262
London 260
Berlin 264
Ruhr 263
Paris 261
Wien 264
Budapest 264
Milano 266
Lisboa 266
Madrid 266
Barcelona 266
Roma 267
İstanbul 267
Athínai 267
Tehrān 267

MAP COVERAGE / KARTENAUSSCHNITTE
CONTENIDO DEL ATLAS / TABLEAU D'ASSEMBLAGE/ABRANGÊNCIA DO MAPA

148 Page Reference / Seitenangabe
      Página de Referencia / Page de Référence / Página de Referência

Map Scale

Manila 269 ● 1:300,000

▨ 1:1,000,000   ☐ 1:6,000,000

☐ 1:3,000,000   ☐ 1:12,000,000

Enlarged maps of Anglo-America and Europe on page XIII.
Vergrösserte Karten von Anglo-Amerika und Europa auf Seite XIII.
Mapas aumentados de América Anglosajona y Europa, página XIII.
Cartes à grande échelle de l'Ámerique anglo-saxonne et de l'Europe à la page XIII.
Mapas ampliados da América Anglo-saxônica e da Europa, página XIII.

World, Ocean, and Continent maps on page 2-19.
Weltkarten, Karten der Ozeane und Erdteile auf Seiten 2-19.
Mapas del Mundo, Océanos y Continentes, páginas 2-19.
Cartes du Monde, des Océans et des Continents aux pages 2-19.
Mapas do Mundo, dos Oceanos e dos Continentes, páginas 2-19.

Additional Pacific Ocean Island maps on pages 174-175.
Zusätzliche Karten der Inseln des Pazifischen Ozeans auf Seite 174-175.
Mapas adicionales de las Islas del Océano Pacifico, páginas 174-175.
Cartes supplémentaires des Îles de l'Océan Pacifique aux pages 174-175.
Mapas suplementares das ilhas do Oceano Pacifico, páginas 174-175.

RUSSIA
Pacific Ocean
Indian Ocean
24
76
80
86
88
89
KAZAKHSTAN
MONGOLIA
CHINA
UKRAINE
78
Black Sea
Caspian Sea
84
85
TURKEY
130
TURKMENISTAN
UZBEKISTAN
KYRG.
TAJIKISTAN
AFGHANISTAN
IRAN
Tehrān 267
IRAQ
128
SYRIA
132
Al-Qahirah (Cairo) 273
142
EGYPT
Red Sea
SAUDI ARABIA
OMAN
YEMEN
140
SUDAN
ERITREA
DJIBOUTI
144
ETHIOPIA
SOMALIA
KENYA
UGANDA
RWANDA
BURUNDI
TANZANIA
154
COMOROS
157a
ZAMBIA
MALAWI
MOZAMBIQUE
ZIMBABWE
MADAGASCAR
157b
157c
MAURITIUS
REUNION
123
PAKISTAN
120
Delhi 272
NEPAL
124
INDIA
Calcutta 272
126
BHU.
BNGL.
Mumbai (Bombay) 272
122
SRI LANKA
102
107
104
105
Beijing (Peking) 271
98
KOREA
Soul 271
92
94
96
Tōkyō 268
Ōsaka 270
JAPAN
93b
RYUKYU ISLANDS
OKINAWA
174m
175d
106
Shanghai 269
100
T'aipei 269
TAIWAN
Xianggang (Hong Kong) 271
MYANMAR
LAOS
VIETNAM
THAILAND
Krung Thep (Bangkok) 269
CAMBODIA
Thanh-pho Ho Chi Minh (Saigon) 269
110
Manila 269
116
PHILIPPINES
175c
TRUK ISLANDS
175b
PALAU ISLANDS
BRUNEI
MALAYSIA
114
Singapore 271
SUMATRA
BORNEO
112
CELEBES
INDONESIA
Jakarta 269
115a
LESSER SUNDA ISLANDS
115b
JAVA
PAPUA NEW GUINEA
NEW GUINEA
164
SOLOMON ISLANDS
175e
VANUATU
175f
NEW CALEDONIA
175g
FIJI
AUSTRALIA
162
168a
168b
166
171a
170
171b
Sydney 274
169
Melbourne 274
TASMANIA
NEW ZEALAND
172

176
178
230
242
244
22
74
72
90
134
136
118
108
138
160

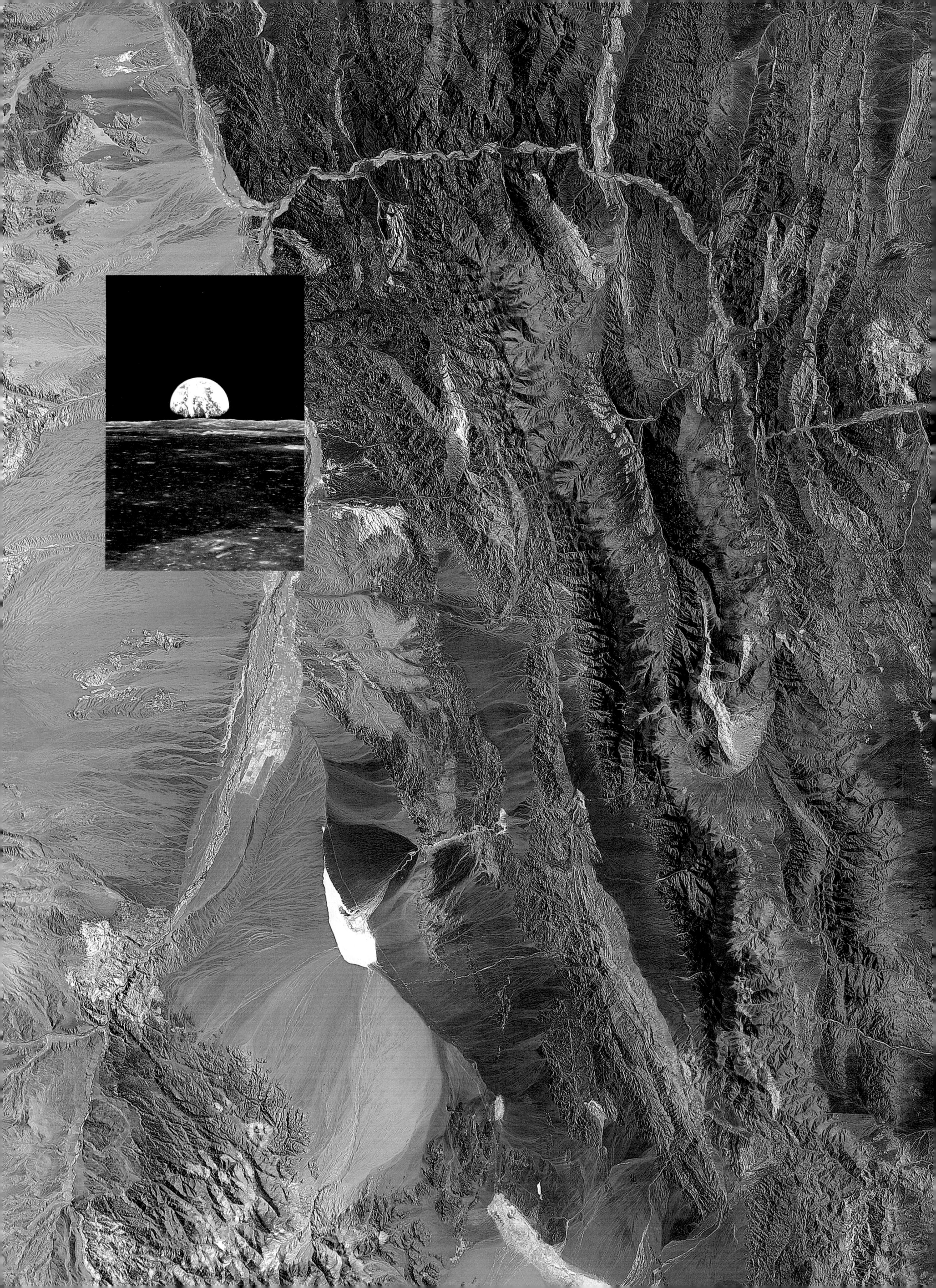

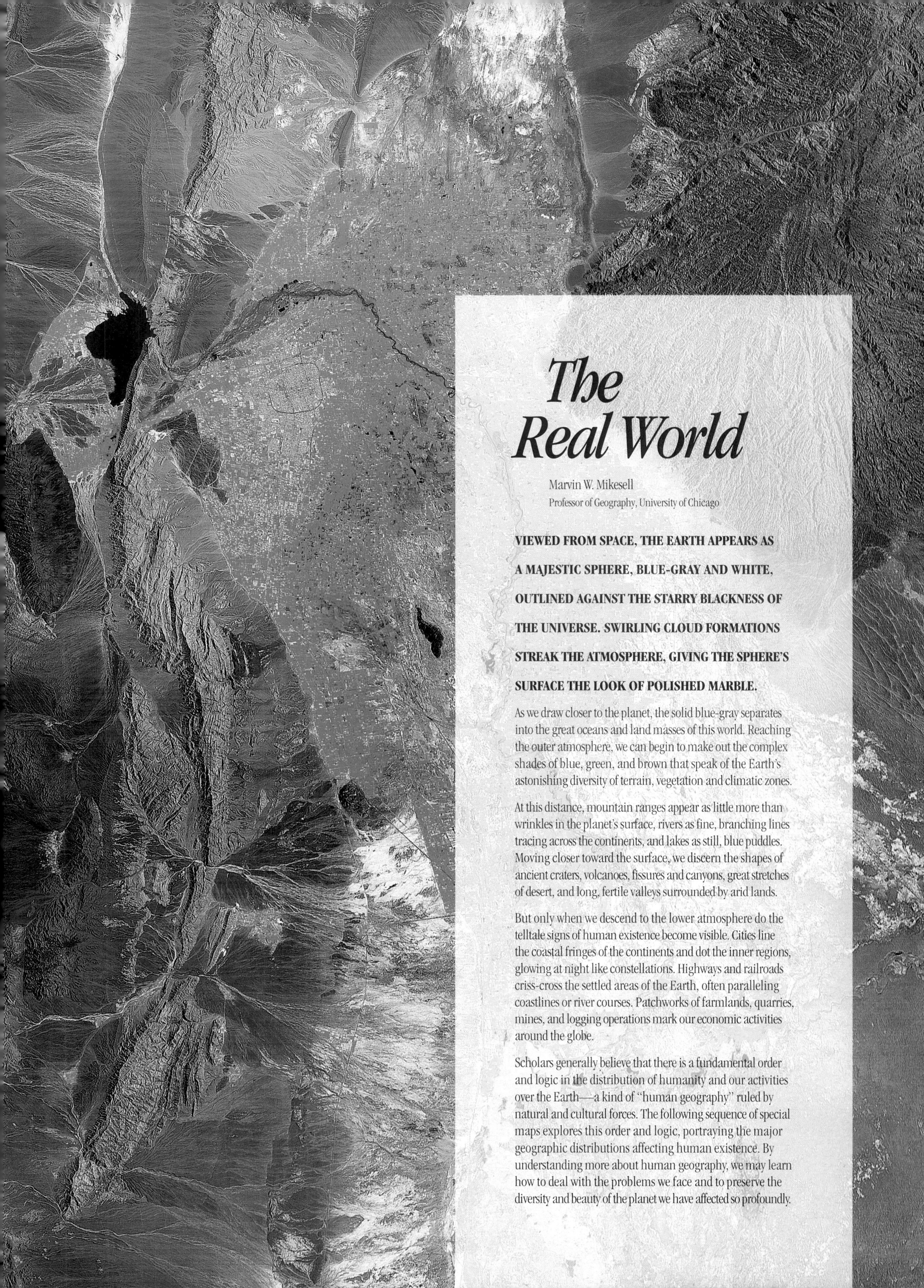

The Real World

Marvin W. Mikesell
Professor of Geography, University of Chicago

VIEWED FROM SPACE, THE EARTH APPEARS AS A MAJESTIC SPHERE, BLUE-GRAY AND WHITE, OUTLINED AGAINST THE STARRY BLACKNESS OF THE UNIVERSE. SWIRLING CLOUD FORMATIONS STREAK THE ATMOSPHERE, GIVING THE SPHERE'S SURFACE THE LOOK OF POLISHED MARBLE.

As we draw closer to the planet, the solid blue-gray separates into the great oceans and land masses of this world. Reaching the outer atmosphere, we can begin to make out the complex shades of blue, green, and brown that speak of the Earth's astonishing diversity of terrain, vegetation and climatic zones.

At this distance, mountain ranges appear as little more than wrinkles in the planet's surface, rivers as fine, branching lines tracing across the continents, and lakes as still, blue puddles. Moving closer toward the surface, we discern the shapes of ancient craters, volcanoes, fissures and canyons, great stretches of desert, and long, fertile valleys surrounded by arid lands.

But only when we descend to the lower atmosphere do the telltale signs of human existence become visible. Cities line the coastal fringes of the continents and dot the inner regions, glowing at night like constellations. Highways and railroads criss-cross the settled areas of the Earth, often paralleling coastlines or river courses. Patchworks of farmlands, quarries, mines, and logging operations mark our economic activities around the globe.

Scholars generally believe that there is a fundamental order and logic in the distribution of humanity and our activities over the Earth—a kind of "human geography" ruled by natural and cultural forces. The following sequence of special maps explores this order and logic, portraying the major geographic distributions affecting human existence. By understanding more about human geography, we may learn how to deal with the problems we face and to preserve the diversity and beauty of the planet we have affected so profoundly.

THE SURFACE OF OUR PLANET EXISTS IN A CONSTANT STATE OF CHANGE: CONTINENTS DRIFT TO NEW POSITIONS; OCEANS SHRINK AND DISAPPEAR WHILE NEW ONES ARE BEING

born; mountain ranges rise and gradually vanish. But on a human time scale, geologic processes are so gradual as to be almost unnoticeable. Only in the sudden, violent moments of an earthquake, a volcanic eruption, or a major storm do we glimpse the powerful forces that shape the face of our planet.

The greatest shaping force is the movement of the brittle crustal pieces that make up the Earth's surface. These pieces, called "tectonic plates," float on a dense fluid portion of the upper mantle. Convection currents rising from the lower mantle keep them in constant motion—colliding, moving apart, sliding over or under one another. The result is the tremendously varied terrain depicted on the relief map on these pages.

Asia's massive Himalayan mountains were born when the Indo-Australian Plate collided with the Eurasian Plate, crumpling the crustal material at the plate edges and slowly thrusting it upward to heights of five and a half miles above sea level. The Red Sea and Africa's great Rift Valley were created through a different kind of tectonic process: the African plate is literally splitting apart. Eventually, the land east of the rift will be torn from the continent to form an enormous offshore island.

In the vast Pacific Ocean, volcanic activity is creating a long chain of islands as the Pacific Plate slides over a "hot spot" in the mantle. The Hawaiian Islands are the newest additions to this chain, which stretches northwest all the way to Russia's Kamchatka Peninsula.

Besides plate movement, wind and water are the most powerful forces shaping the Earth's surface. Wind and rain carry away soil and sediment, while rivers sculpt valleys and gorges, such as the Grand Canyon, and create fertile flood plains and deltas. The advance and retreat of glaciers during the great ice ages vastly altered terrain in the northern latitudes. Norway's fjords and North America's Great Lakes are among the glaciers' legacies.

Over the last few centuries, humans have had an increasingly significant impact on the face of the Earth. We have turned arid regions into farmlands, and have made forests and grasslands into deserts. We have reclaimed land from the sea and dammed rivers to create new lakes. Our mining and quarrying operations have left huge scars on the landscape.

Today, as population soars and technology leaps forward, our potential for changing the face of the earth, and our responsibility to change it for the better, is greater than ever.

0   1000   2000   3000 Km.
0   1000   2000   3000 Mi.
Equatorial Scale
© Rand McNally
X-510000-792-1E-1E-1E-3B

CONTINENTAL DRIFT

Geologic evidence indicates that the Earth's landmasses have migrated to their present positions over millions of years. These maps illustrate the positions of the continents in the past and where they are at present.

225 million years ago.
All of the world's land masses were joined together, forming a single supercontinent which we call Pangaea. Panthalassa is the name given to the single ancestral ocean. The Tethys Sea, predecessor of the Mediterranean Sea, separated Eurasia and Africa.

180 million years ago.
Pangaea split up. The northern block of continents, Laurasia, drifted northward, and the southern block, Gondwanaland, broke up into South America/Africa, India, and Australia/Antarctica.

65 million years ago.
Madagascar moved away from Africa, and the Tethys Sea all but disappeared as the Mediterranean Sea began to form. The ocean basins took shape as South America moved from Africa and India headed toward a collision with Asia. Australia was still joined with Antarctica.

The present day.
India has completed its northward migration and collided with Asia to form the Himalayas. Australia and Antarctica have separated, and North America has split from Eurasia, leaving Greenland as an island between them. During the past 65 million years, nearly one-half of the world's ocean floor has been created.

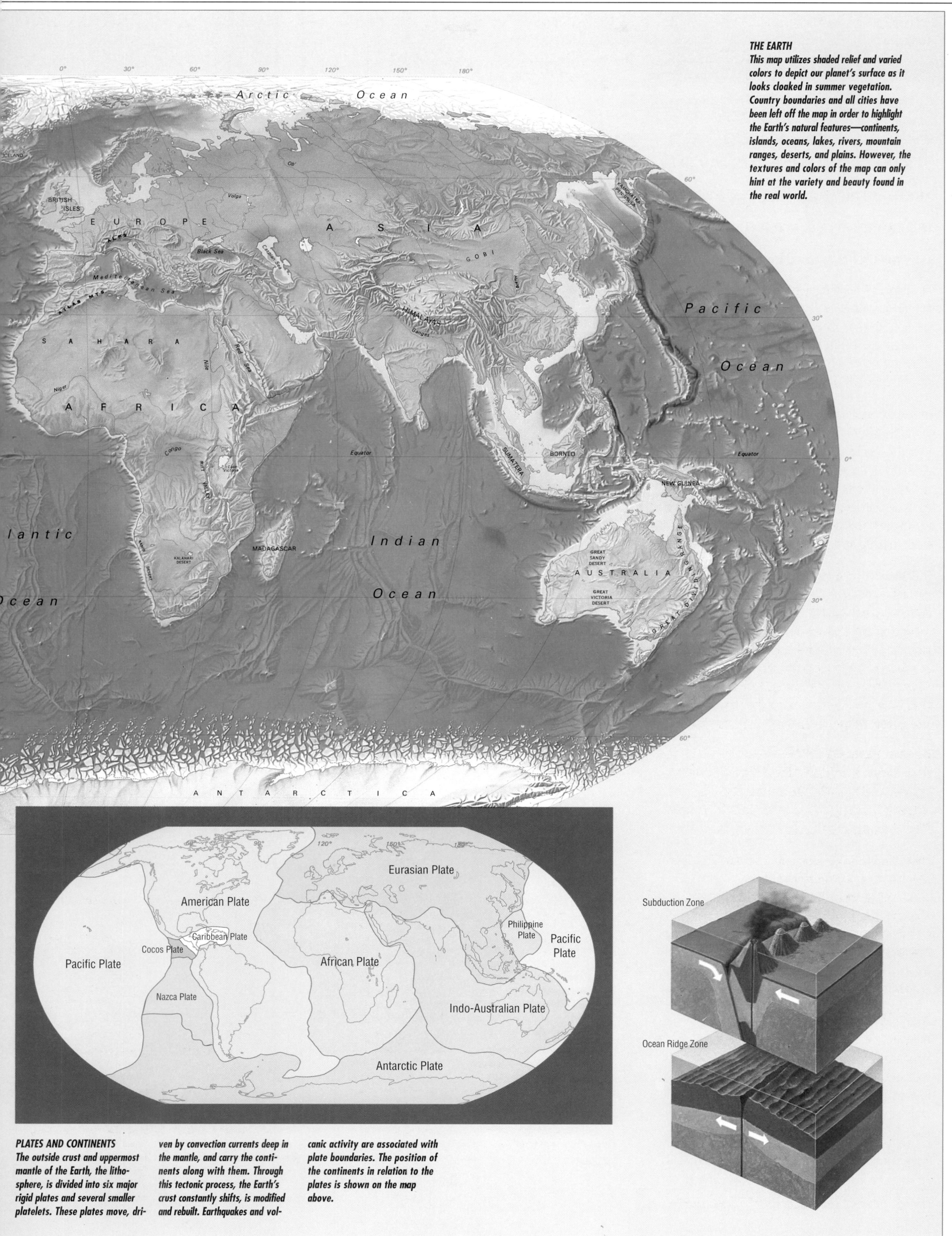

THE EARTH
This map utilizes shaded relief and varied colors to depict our planet's surface as it looks cloaked in summer vegetation. Country boundaries and all cities have been left off the map in order to highlight the Earth's natural features—continents, islands, oceans, lakes, rivers, mountain ranges, deserts, and plains. However, the textures and colors of the map can only hint at the variety and beauty found in the real world.

Subduction Zone

Ocean Ridge Zone

PLATES AND CONTINENTS
The outside crust and uppermost mantle of the Earth, the lithosphere, is divided into six major rigid plates and several smaller platelets. These plates move, driven by convection currents deep in the mantle, and carry the continents along with them. Through this tectonic process, the Earth's crust constantly shifts, is modified and rebuilt. Earthquakes and volcanic activity are associated with plate boundaries. The position of the continents in relation to the plates is shown on the map above.

WHILE CALM, CLEAR SKIES PREVAIL OVER NORTH AMERICA'S GREAT PLAINS, A VIOLENT HURRICANE BATTERS A CHAIN OF CARIBBEAN ISLANDS. IN EASTERN AFRICA, RAINSTORMS

break a two-year drought, but northern European farmers watch their crops dry up in a heat wave. Mild spring winds arrive over Argentina, and in southeast Asia monsoon winds bring lightning and torrential rains.

The infinite variety of our planet's weather is created by the complex relationship of air, water, and land. Air masses ebb and flow around the globe, as moist tropical air moves toward the poles and drier polar air descends toward the equator. The spinning of the Earth helps to direct the air masses. Ocean currents circulate "rivers" of warmer and cooler waters around the globe. Great mountain ranges trap air masses and disrupt the world-wide flow. The 23½° inclination of our planet as it revolves around the sun creates the yearly cycle of seasons.

Over time, this constant interaction of natural forces establishes consistent weather patterns which, in turn, define the major climatic regions of the world, which are depicted on the adjacent map. Within each region, char-acteristic soils and related plant and animal life evolve.

Generally predictable patterns of weather within these regions have permitted humanity to develop an array of economic and cultural systems, each closely related to the area's normal climatic conditions.

It is the abnormal climatic occurrence—sometimes called a "climatic anomaly"—that causes the most human turmoil, as well as shock to the natural order. For example, a combination of cold Pacific currents and dry air masses makes the northern coast of Chile one of the driest places on Earth. The lifestyle of the region is based upon this prevailing climate. When the phenomenon known as *El Niño* occurs, the usual northerly flow of cold air and water reverses itself, and warm equatorial air and water flow south onto the coast of Chile. These unexpected conditions dramatically increase rainfall, leading to disastrous flooding, and completely disrupting the cultural and natural order.

Today there is growing awareness and concern about humanity's increasing impact on climate. In many large urban areas, the heat-absorbing artificial terrain, combined with air pollution from automobiles and industry, has created "micro-climates" characterized by higher temperatures and excessive smog. A far greater potential problem is global warming resulting from the so-called "greenhouse effect." The burning of fossil fuels adds carbon dioxide to the atmosphere, which causes the atmosphere to trap heat that would normally radiate out into space. If global temperatures rise even a few degrees, the consequences could be disastrous.

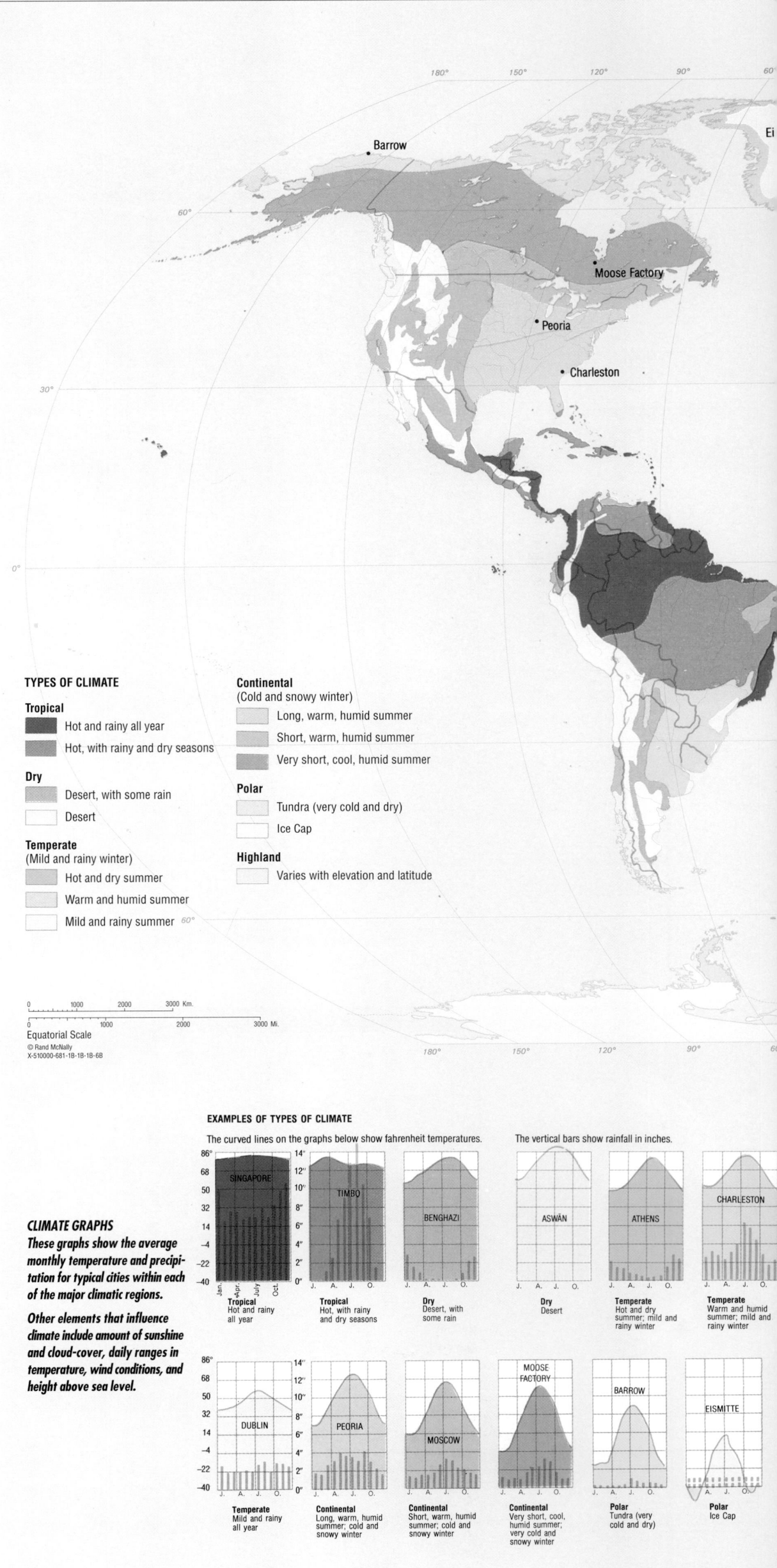

TYPES OF CLIMATE

Tropical
- Hot and rainy all year
- Hot, with rainy and dry seasons

Dry
- Desert, with some rain
- Desert

Temperate
(Mild and rainy winter)
- Hot and dry summer
- Warm and humid summer
- Mild and rainy summer

Continental
(Cold and snowy winter)
- Long, warm, humid summer
- Short, warm, humid summer
- Very short, cool, humid summer

Polar
- Tundra (very cold and dry)
- Ice Cap

Highland
- Varies with elevation and latitude

0   1000   2000   3000 Km.
0   1000   2000   3000 Mi.
Equatorial Scale
© Rand McNally
X-510000-681-1B-1B-1B-6B

EXAMPLES OF TYPES OF CLIMATE

The curved lines on the graphs below show fahrenheit temperatures. The vertical bars show rainfall in inches.

CLIMATE GRAPHS
These graphs show the average monthly temperature and precipitation for typical cities within each of the major climatic regions.

Other elements that influence climate include amount of sunshine and cloud-cover, daily ranges in temperature, wind conditions, and height above sea level.

SINGAPORE
Tropical
Hot and rainy all year

TIMBO
Tropical
Hot, with rainy and dry seasons

BENGHAZI
Dry
Desert, with some rain

ASWAN
Dry
Desert

ATHENS
Temperate
Hot and dry summer; mild and rainy winter

CHARLESTON
Temperate
Warm and humid summer; mild and rainy winter

DUBLIN
Temperate
Mild and rainy all year

PEORIA
Continental
Long, warm, humid summer; cold and snowy winter

MOSCOW
Continental
Short, warm, humid summer; cold and snowy winter

MOOSE FACTORY
Continental
Very short, cool, humid summer; very cold and snowy winter

BARROW
Polar
Tundra (very cold and dry)

EISMITTE
Polar
Ice Cap

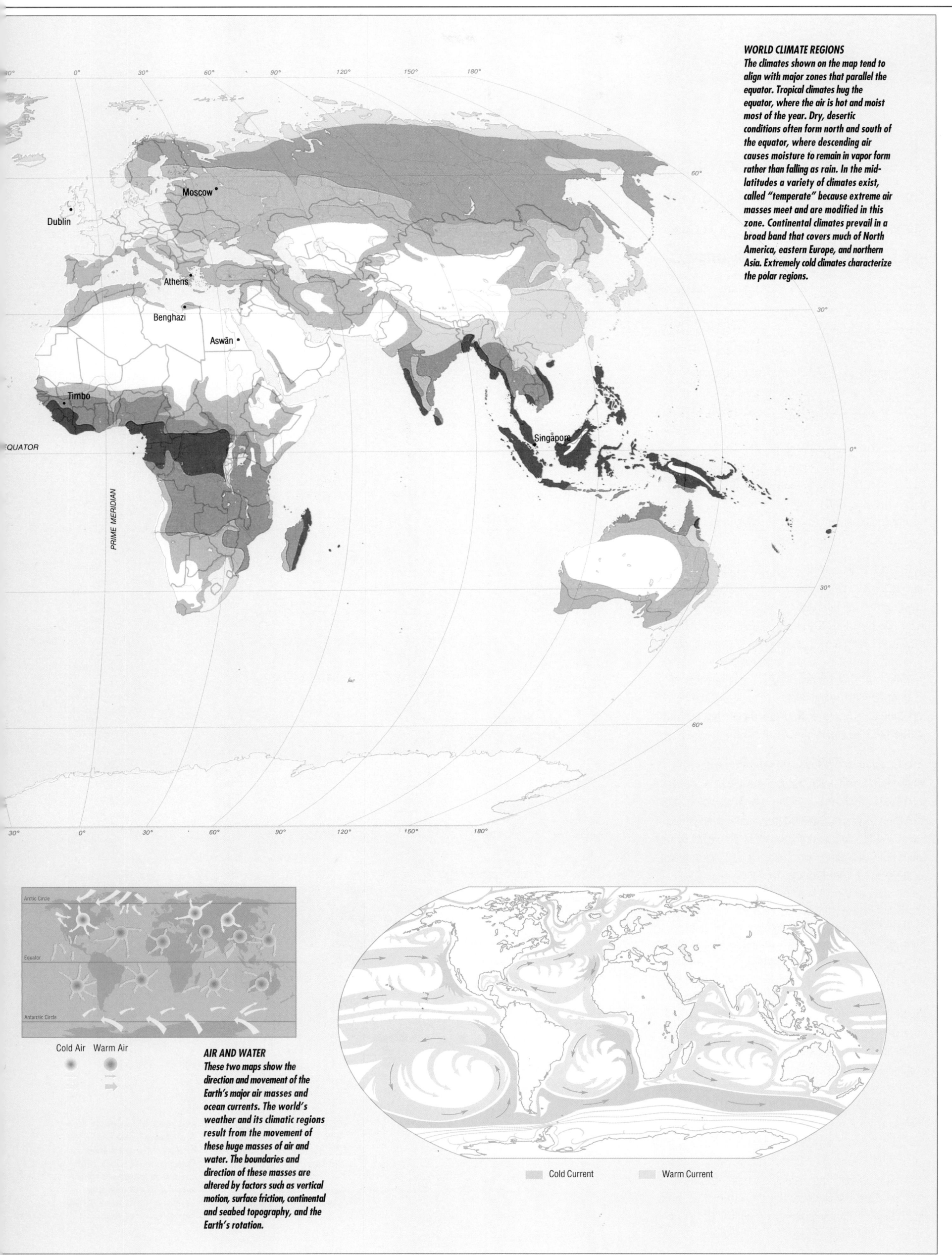

WORLD CLIMATE REGIONS
The climates shown on the map tend to align with major zones that parallel the equator. Tropical climates hug the equator, where the air is hot and moist most of the year. Dry, desertic conditions often form north and south of the equator, where descending air causes moisture to remain in vapor form rather than falling as rain. In the mid-latitudes a variety of climates exist, called "temperate" because extreme air masses meet and are modified in this zone. Continental climates prevail in a broad band that covers much of North America, eastern Europe, and northern Asia. Extremely cold climates characterize the polar regions.

Moscow

Dublin

Athens

Benghazi

Aswān

Timbo

EQUATOR

PRIME MERIDIAN

Singapore

Arctic Circle

Equator

Antarctic Circle

Cold Air   Warm Air

AIR AND WATER
These two maps show the direction and movement of the Earth's major air masses and ocean currents. The world's weather and its climatic regions result from the movement of these huge masses of air and water. The boundaries and direction of these masses are altered by factors such as vertical motion, surface friction, continental and seabed topography, and the Earth's rotation.

Cold Current   Warm Current

SETTLEMENT

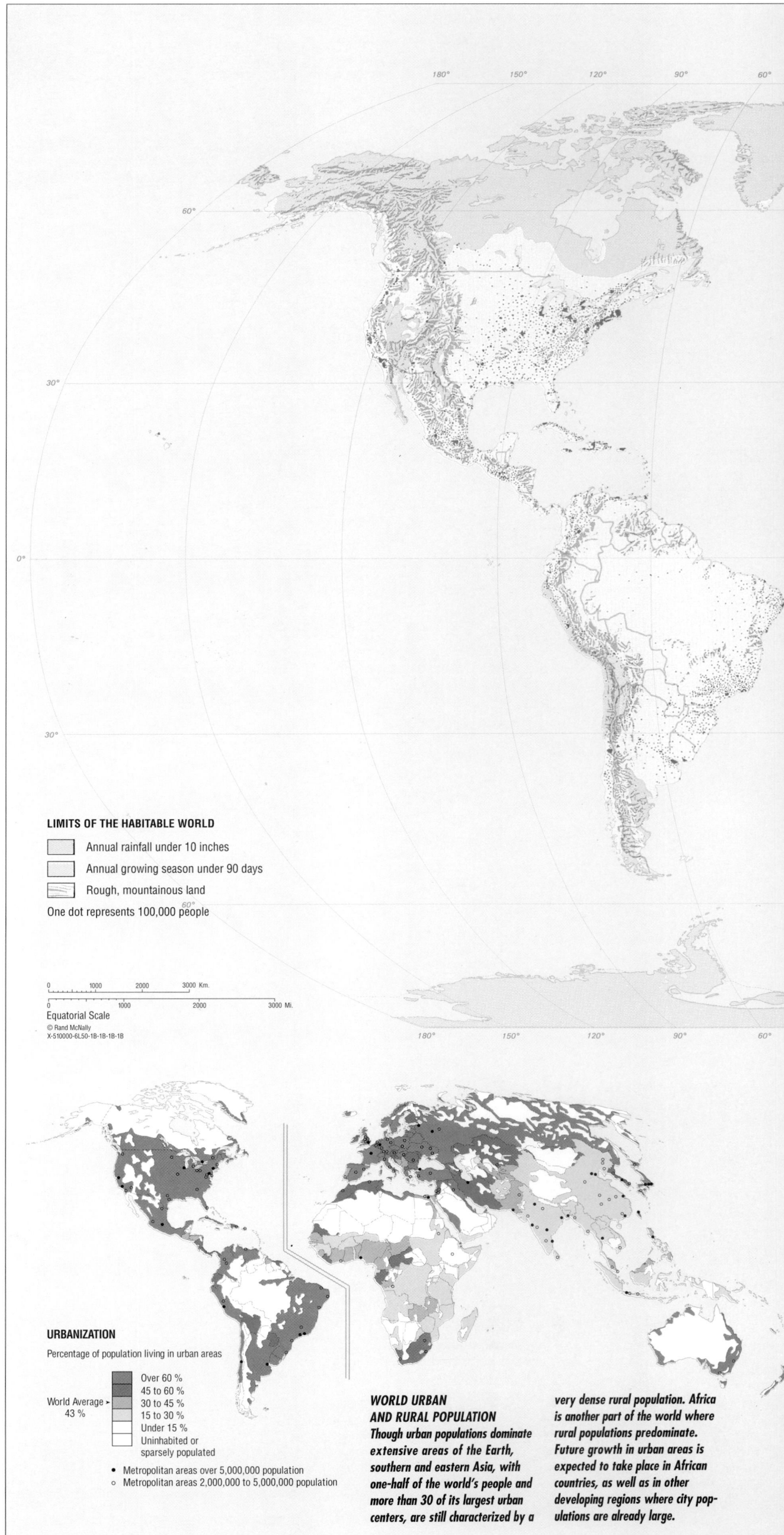

THE HISTORY OF HUMAN SETTLEMENT IS THE STORY OF A SEARCH FOR FERTILE LAND, ABUNDANT SOURCES OF WATER, SUITABLE TERRAIN, AND CLIMATES WITH ADEQUATE

growing seasons. Wherever nature supplies all of these elements, human settlements flourish. When they are scarce or disappear, communities are few and may eventually be abandoned.

Since humans began practicing agriculture about 10,000 years ago, the greatest limitation on settlement has been the length of the growing season. Areas with fewer than 90 days free of frost per year are not suitable for most forms of agriculture. Without an abundant food supply, settlements cannot grow beyond a limited size. Outside the regions where agriculture is viable, people must depend on imported food or live by hunting, fishing, and trapping—activities that can support only small communities.

Human settlement is also restricted by the amount of precipitation an area receives. Farming is not practical where annual rainfall is less than 10 inches (24.5 cm) in temperate areas and less than 20 inches (51 cm) in hotter regions. At various times, people have developed large-scale irrigation systems to pipe water into once-arid lands. In this way, human patterns of settlement have appeared in desert areas of the American Southwest, the Middle East, and parts of Africa. However, the process is costly and usually draws heavily on underground reservoirs.

Finally, terrain and soil also limit human settlement. Much of the world is simply too mountainous or the soil too poor for people to settle. At high elevations, the growing season is often too short for cultivation. Taiga forests and equatorial rainforests generally create a thin, acidic soil that is often too infertile to sustain permanent agricultural communities.

Human settlement patterns have shifted dramatically from rural to urban in the last two centuries. Advances in agricultural technology and methods have produced growing food supplies able to support larger and larger urban populations. The industrial and technological revolution has created job opportunities that are nearly always in urban areas. In 1925, approximately 20% of the world's population was urban. Today the figure is approaching 50%. It is estimated that by 2025, five out of eight people will live in cities.

Until the early part of this century, this trend was largely confined to the developed countries, but it has since spread to much of the rest of the world. Today the strongest urbanization trends are in the developing countries of South America and Africa, where the problems indigenous to urban living—overcrowding, pollution, inadequate sanitation, disease—are often magnified by inadequate economic resources.

LIMITS OF THE HABITABLE WORLD

Annual rainfall under 10 inches

Annual growing season under 90 days

Rough, mountainous land

One dot represents 100,000 people

| 0 | 1000 | 2000 | 3000 Km. |

| 0 | 1000 | 2000 | 3000 Mi. |

Equatorial Scale

© Rand McNally
X-510000-6L50-1B-1B-1B-1B

URBANIZATION

Percentage of population living in urban areas

Over 60 %

45 to 60 %

World Average ▶ 30 to 45 %

43 % 15 to 30 %

Under 15 %

Uninhabited or sparsely populated

• Metropolitan areas over 5,000,000 population

○ Metropolitan areas 2,000,000 to 5,000,000 population

WORLD URBAN AND RURAL POPULATION
Though urban populations dominate extensive areas of the Earth, southern and eastern Asia, with one-half of the world's people and more than 30 of its largest urban centers, are still characterized by a very dense rural population. Africa is another part of the world where rural populations predominate. Future growth in urban areas is expected to take place in African countries, as well as in other developing regions where city populations are already large.

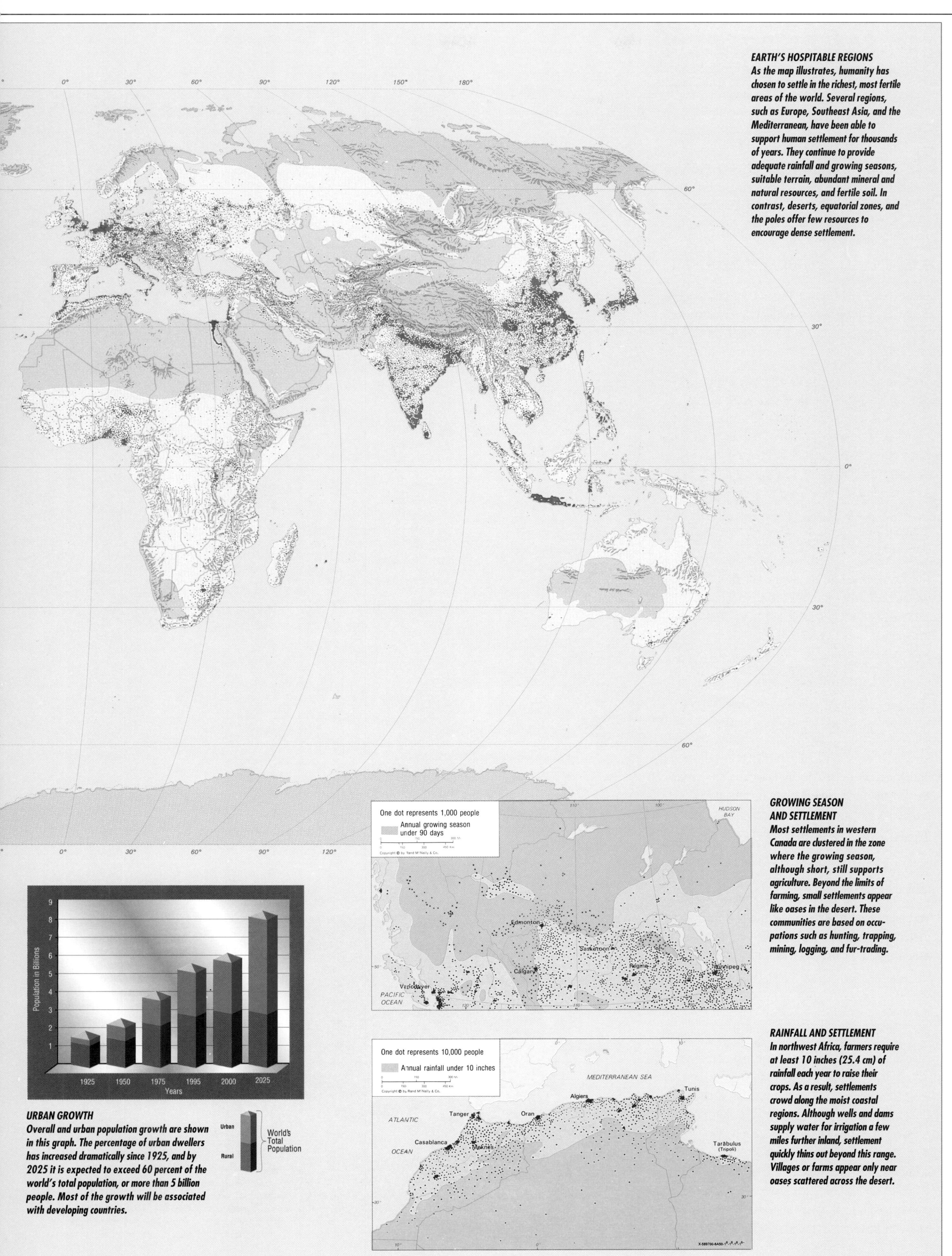

EARTH'S HOSPITABLE REGIONS
As the map illustrates, humanity has chosen to settle in the richest, most fertile areas of the world. Several regions, such as Europe, Southeast Asia, and the Mediterranean, have been able to support human settlement for thousands of years. They continue to provide adequate rainfall and growing seasons, suitable terrain, abundant mineral and natural resources, and fertile soil. In contrast, deserts, equatorial zones, and the poles offer few resources to encourage dense settlement.

GROWING SEASON AND SETTLEMENT
Most settlements in western Canada are clustered in the zone where the growing season, although short, still supports agriculture. Beyond the limits of farming, small settlements appear like oases in the desert. These communities are based on occupations such as hunting, trapping, mining, logging, and fur-trading.

One dot represents 1,000 people
Annual growing season under 90 days
Copyright © by Rand McNally & Co.

HUDSON BAY

Edmonton
Saskatoon
Calgary
Regina
Vancouver
Winnipeg
PACIFIC OCEAN

RAINFALL AND SETTLEMENT
In northwest Africa, farmers require at least 10 inches (25.4 cm) of rainfall each year to raise their crops. As a result, settlements crowd along the moist coastal regions. Although wells and dams supply water for irrigation a few miles further inland, settlement quickly thins out beyond this range. Villages or farms appear only near oases scattered across the desert.

One dot represents 10,000 people
Annual rainfall under 10 inches
Copyright © by Rand McNally & Co.

MEDITERRANEAN SEA
ATLANTIC OCEAN
Algiers
Tunis
Tanger
Oran
Casablanca
Meknes
Tarābulus (Tripoli)

URBAN GROWTH
Overall and urban population growth are shown in this graph. The percentage of urban dwellers has increased dramatically since 1925, and by 2025 it is expected to exceed 60 percent of the world's total population, or more than 5 billion people. Most of the growth will be associated with developing countries.

Population in Billions

1925 1950 1975 1995 2000 2025
Years

Urban
Rural
World's Total Population

X-589700-8A50-

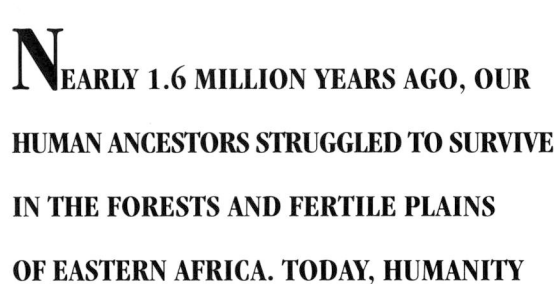

POPULATION

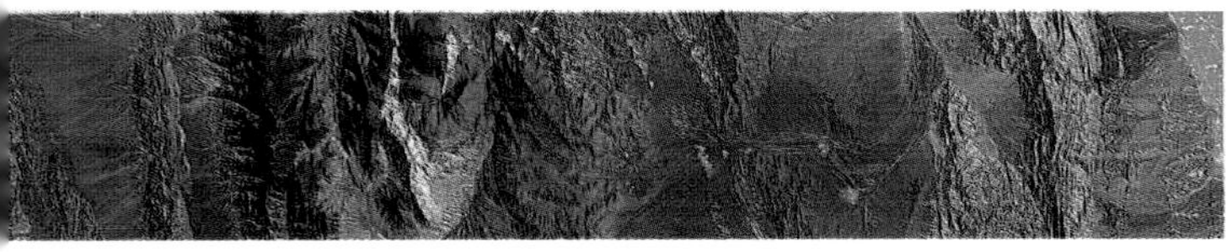

NEARLY 1.6 MILLION YEARS AGO, OUR HUMAN ANCESTORS STRUGGLED TO SURVIVE IN THE FORESTS AND FERTILE PLAINS OF EASTERN AFRICA. TODAY, HUMANITY

inhabits every continent on earth. World population is approaching 6 billion, with 80 million new lives added every year. More people are alive now than have existed since the dawn of human history.

This explosive growth is fueled not only by a rising birth rate but by longer average life spans and by a sharp reduction in the number of children who die young. With births far outstripping deaths, predictions are that world population will not stablize until the year 2010, when over 10 billion people will share the planet.

The most densely settled parts of the Earth appear in the industrial areas of Europe, North America, and Japan, and the predominantly rural areas of India, China, and Southeast Asia. In developed areas, modern technology has encouraged the growth of large urban districts. The heavily populated rural areas of Asian countries reflect nearly 4,000 years of agricultural civilization.

Even with the surge in population, however, substantial areas of the Earth remain underpopulated or virtually empty. Some regions offer striking contrasts between crowded and open spaces. In Russia, a narrow band of population stretches along the Trans-Siberian Railway. The eastern shore of the Mediterranean Sea, with its crowded coastal fringe of Israel, Lebanon, and Syria, stands out sharply against the barren, uninhabited land beyond.

Several natural and cultural factors help explain the uneven distribution of humanity. Nature imposes limits on agricultural development: many areas are too dry or mountainous or have growing seasons too short to support a large population. The harsher climate and terrain of the polar regions and great deserts of the world show only widely scattered human settlements.

Cultural factors also influence where populations are likely to concentrate. Nearly 2.5 billion people now live in urban centers, half of them in cities that number 500,000 or more. By the year 2000, the urban population in less-developed countries will double, as the rural poor seek greater opportunities in the already-crowded cities. Religion and cultural values also influence a nation's ability to control its birth rate. Until curbing population becomes a worldwide goal, our growing numbers will continue to exert increasing pressure on the Earth's resources.

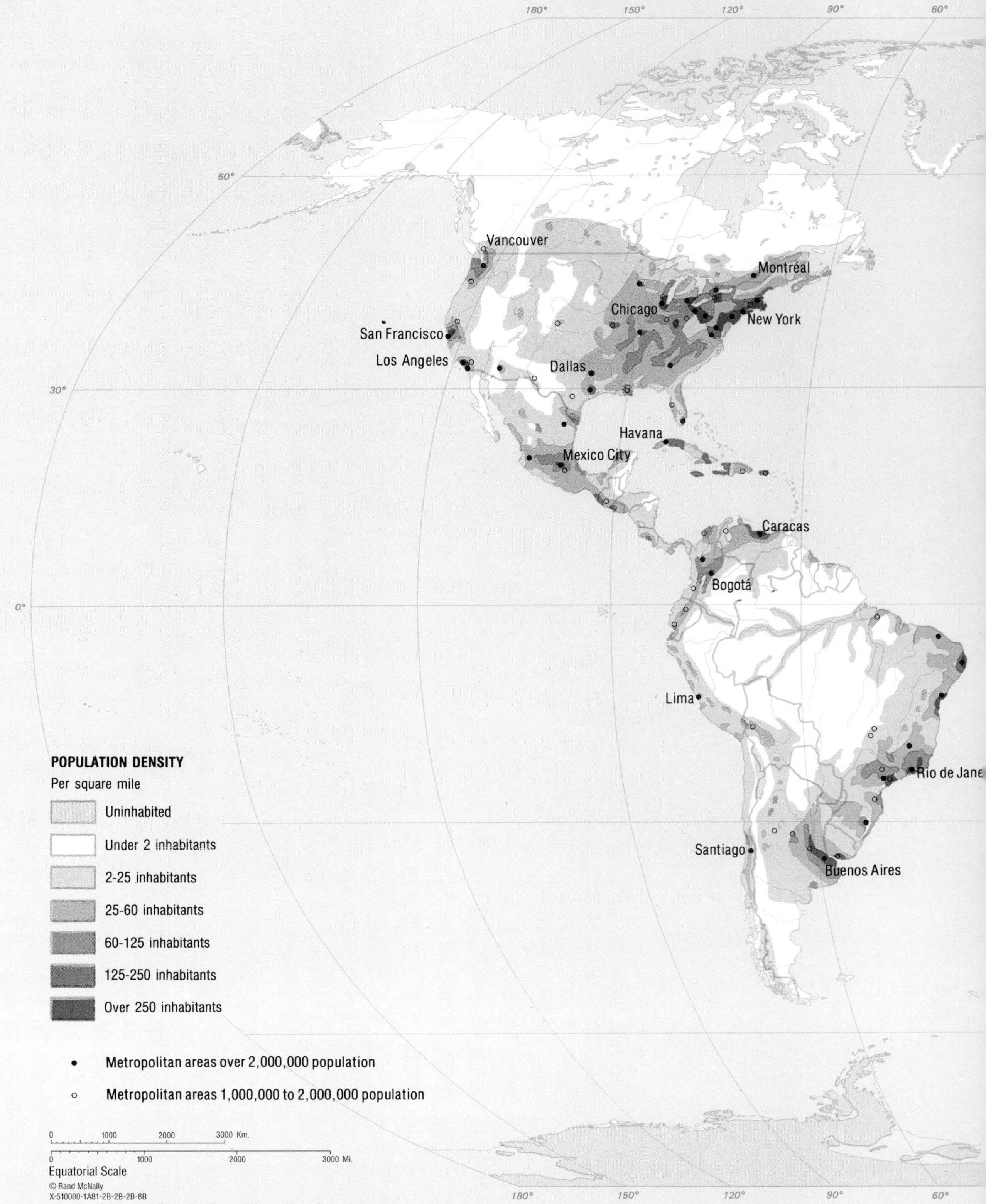

POPULATION DENSITY
Per square mile

- Uninhabited
- Under 2 inhabitants
- 2-25 inhabitants
- 25-60 inhabitants
- 60-125 inhabitants
- 125-250 inhabitants
- Over 250 inhabitants

- ● Metropolitan areas over 2,000,000 population
- ○ Metropolitan areas 1,000,000 to 2,000,000 population

0 1000 2000 3000 Km.
0 1000 2000 3000 Mi.
Equatorial Scale
© Rand McNally
X-510000-1A81-2B-2B-2B-8B

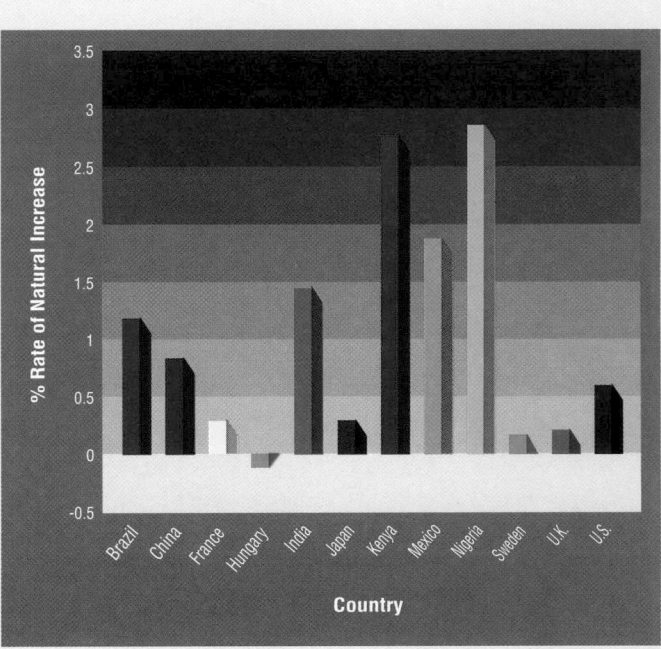

POPULATION GROWTH
In densely populated countries, extremely high growth rates can cripple efforts to develop viable economies. Through state-encouraged family planning, China has managed to decrease its growth rate and thus improve the economic well-being of its people. Low rates of growth in industrialized countries have resulted in economies which are able to support relatively high standards of living.

(Rate of natural growth per year = birth rate minus death rate. Immigration and emigration are not included in this formulation.)

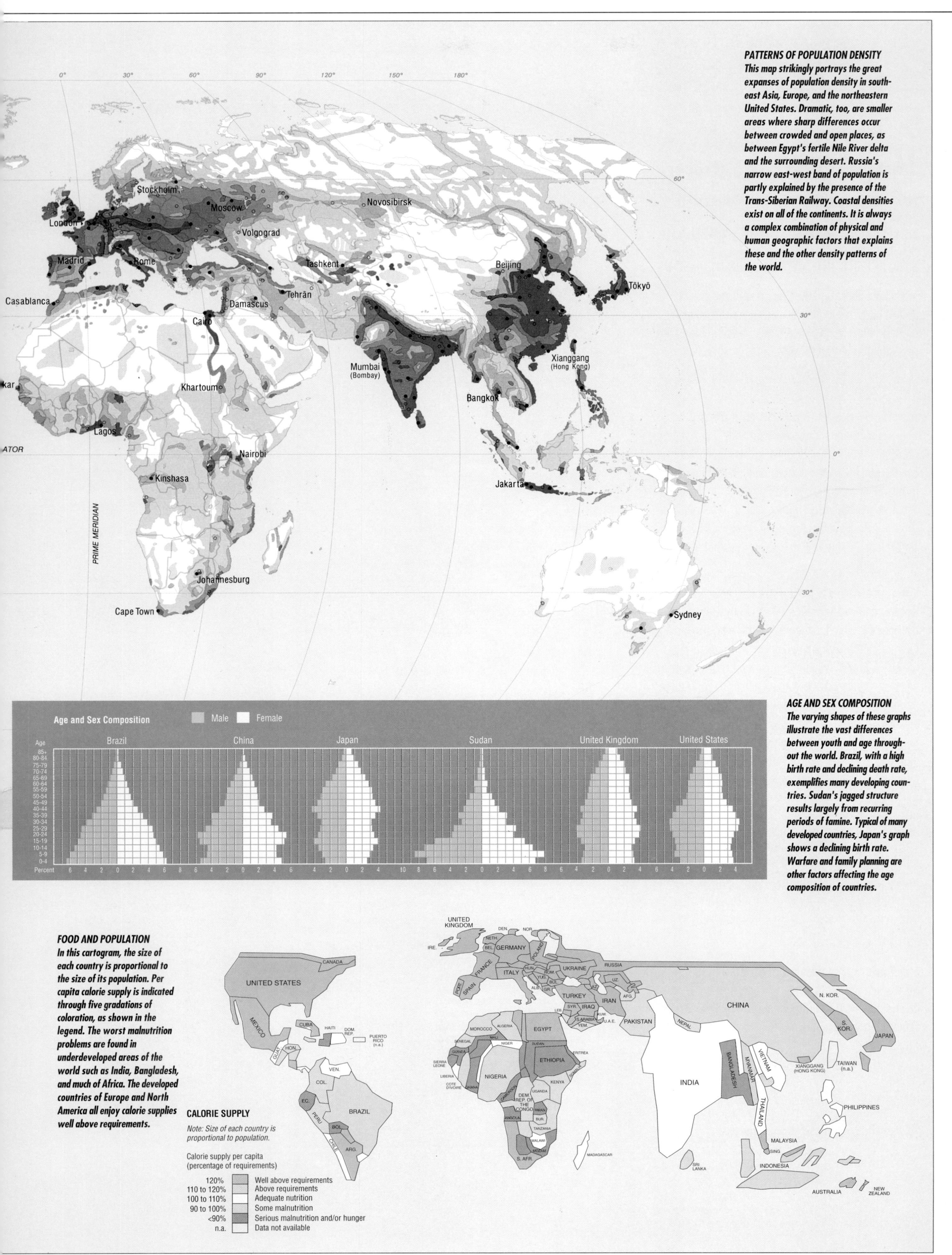

PATTERNS OF POPULATION DENSITY
This map strikingly portrays the great expanses of population density in southeast Asia, Europe, and the northeastern United States. Dramatic, too, are smaller areas where sharp differences occur between crowded and open places, as between Egypt's fertile Nile River delta and the surrounding desert. Russia's narrow east-west band of population is partly explained by the presence of the Trans-Siberian Railway. Coastal densities exist on all of the continents. It is always a complex combination of physical and human geographic factors that explains these and the other density patterns of the world.

Age and Sex Composition

Male   Female

Brazil   China   Japan   Sudan   United Kingdom   United States

Age: 85+, 80-84, 75-79, 70-74, 65-69, 60-64, 55-59, 50-54, 45-49, 40-44, 35-39, 30-34, 25-29, 20-24, 15-19, 10-14, 5-9, 0-4

AGE AND SEX COMPOSITION
The varying shapes of these graphs illustrate the vast differences between youth and age throughout the world. Brazil, with a high birth rate and declining death rate, exemplifies many developing countries. Sudan's jagged structure results largely from recurring periods of famine. Typical of many developed countries, Japan's graph shows a declining birth rate. Warfare and family planning are other factors affecting the age composition of countries.

FOOD AND POPULATION
In this cartogram, the size of each country is proportional to the size of its population. Per capita calorie supply is indicated through five gradations of coloration, as shown in the legend. The worst malnutrition problems are found in underdeveloped areas of the world such as India, Bangladesh, and much of Africa. The developed countries of Europe and North America all enjoy calorie supplies well above requirements.

CALORIE SUPPLY
Note: Size of each country is proportional to population.

Calorie supply per capita
(percentage of requirements)

120%	Well above requirements
110 to 120%	Above requirements
100 to 110%	Adequate nutrition
90 to 100%	Some malnutrition
<90%	Serious malnutrition and/or hunger
n.a.	Data not available

RESOURCES ALONE DO NOT ACCOUNT FOR THE DISTRIBUTION OF INDUSTRIAL DEVELOPMENT AROUND THE WORLD. THE LARGEST OIL AND NATURAL GAS DEPOSITS

are in the Sahara and the Persian Gulf region, yet most Middle Eastern countries have little industry beyond refineries. The location and development of industries depend upon several factors—energy, skilled labor, capital and technology, transportation, markets, government planning, and trade alliances.

In North America, industrial sites, large urban markets, and concentrations of resources coincide. These regions are also blessed with abundant skilled labor and large capital markets to fund development. In South America, industrial districts are confined primarily to the main urban centers. Some countries, such as Venezuela and Chile, have adequate natural resources but lack the skilled labor or national markets to sustain industrial development.

Europe, the former Soviet Union, and Japan have developed in widely different ways. In the industrial districts of England, Belgium, northern France, and Germany, large deposits of coal and iron ore have fueled the growth of heavy industries. But in countries where raw materials are scarce, such as Italy, development is due mainly to individual initiative. The pattern of development in the former Soviet Union is tied directly to this region's enormous stores of coal, oil, iron ore, and other natural resources. In contrast, nearly all of Japan's raw materials are imported. Ample capital and skilled labor have made this country a leader in such areas as electronics and automobiles.

Industrial development in other regions of the world reflects a mixture of natural resources and cultural influences. India has only one major industrial district, the product of government initiatives and local supplies of coal and oil. China is taking advantage of rich deposits of coal and iron ore and an abundant labor supply to move rapidly toward modernization. Africa, from an industrial point of view, remains the least developed continent. It has significant hydro-electric potential and mineral resources, but lacks skilled labor and capital.

The trend in industrial development is toward light industries such as electronics and food processing. Concentrations of this type of industry can be found near large urban centers in many countries, including Taiwan, the Philippines, Mexico, and Korea.

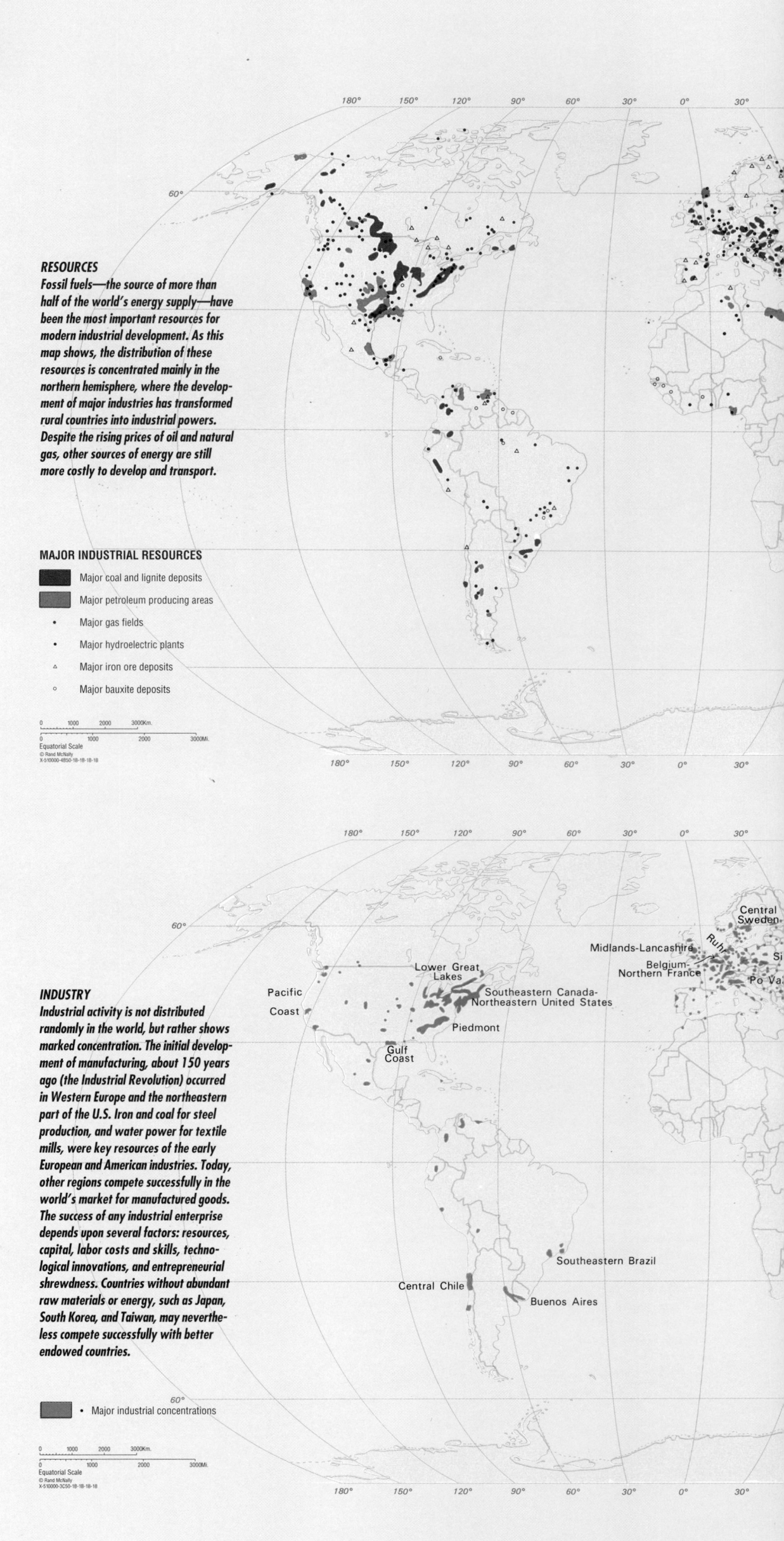

RESOURCES
Fossil fuels—the source of more than half of the world's energy supply—have been the most important resources for modern industrial development. As this map shows, the distribution of these resources is concentrated mainly in the northern hemisphere, where the development of major industries has transformed rural countries into industrial powers. Despite the rising prices of oil and natural gas, other sources of energy are still more costly to develop and transport.

MAJOR INDUSTRIAL RESOURCES

- Major coal and lignite deposits
- Major petroleum producing areas
- Major gas fields
- Major hydroelectric plants
- Major iron ore deposits
- Major bauxite deposits

0 1000 2000 3000 Km.
0 1000 2000 3000 Mi.
Equatorial Scale
© Rand McNally
X-510000-4850-18-18-18

INDUSTRY
Industrial activity is not distributed randomly in the world, but rather shows marked concentration. The initial development of manufacturing, about 150 years ago (the Industrial Revolution) occurred in Western Europe and the northeastern part of the U.S. Iron and coal for steel production, and water power for textile mills, were key resources of the early European and American industries. Today, other regions compete successfully in the world's market for manufactured goods. The success of any industrial enterprise depends upon several factors: resources, capital, labor costs and skills, technological innovations, and entrepreneurial shrewdness. Countries without abundant raw materials or energy, such as Japan, South Korea, and Taiwan, may nevertheless compete successfully with better endowed countries.

- Major industrial concentrations

0 1000 2000 3000 Km.
0 1000 2000 3000 Mi.
Equatorial Scale
© Rand McNally
X-510000-3C50-18-18-18-18

Pacific Coast
Lower Great Lakes
Southeastern Canada-Northeastern United States
Piedmont
Gulf Coast
Central Chile
Southeastern Brazil
Buenos Aires
Midlands-Lancashire
Belgium-Northern France
Central Sweden
Ruhr
Po Va
Si

ENERGY PRODUCTION AND CONSUMPTION

A large percentage of the world's energy is used for manufacturing. This fact helps explain the enormous variance—by country and by continent—in the production and consumption of energy. The United States, with only 5% of the world's population, consumes 25% of the world's energy, and nearly five times as much as Africa and South America combined.

However, the United States produces 80% of the energy it consumes, and is therefore less dependent on foreign sources than several other industrialized countries. Germany, for example, produces only 54% of the energy it consumes, and Japan only 7%.

Major energy exporting countries include oil-rich Saudi Arabia, Iran, and Venezuela.

Total World Production: 11,411,215,000 metric tons of coal equivalent
Total World Consumption: 11,037,655,000 metric tons of coal equivalent

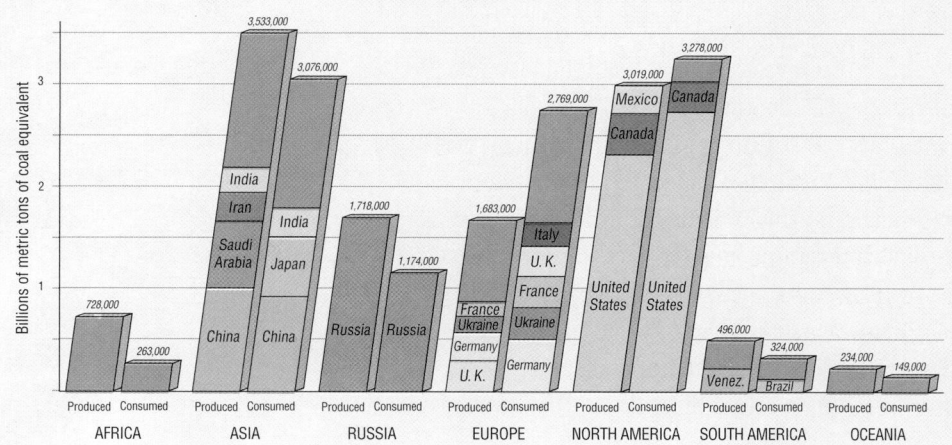

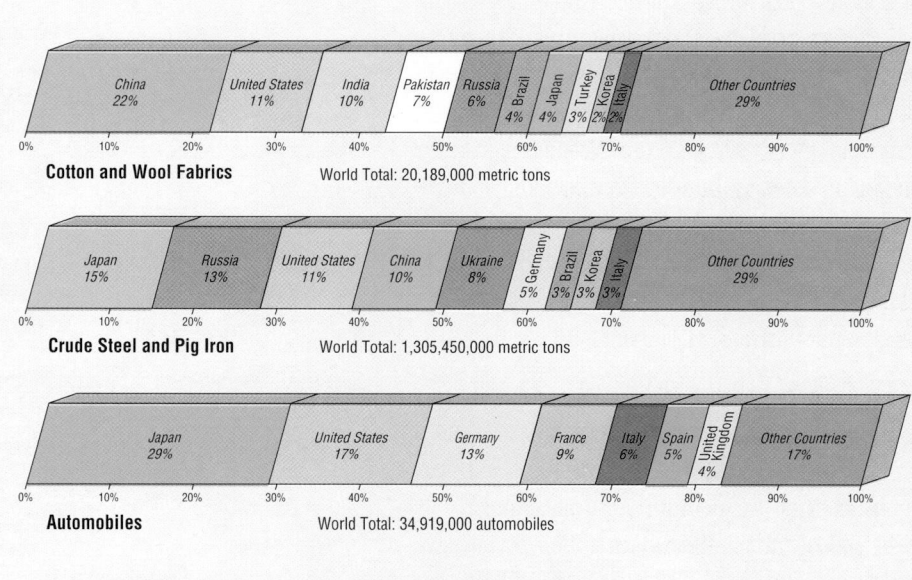

Cotton and Wool Fabrics   World Total: 20,189,000 metric tons

Crude Steel and Pig Iron   World Total: 1,305,450,000 metric tons

Automobiles   World Total: 34,919,000 automobiles

MANUFACTURING

These graphs deal with three very different types of manufacturing activities.

Textile manufacturing is a relatively basic industry—it does not require a great deal of technology, capital, or energy. Textiles are basic goods that are needed in every country, regardless of economic status. (It is not surprising that China, with 1.1 billion people, should lead this category.)

Crude steel and pig iron manufacturing provide a raw material that is used in many products, including automobiles, machinery, and building materials.

Automobile production is a rather sophisticated manufacturing activity, requiring significant amounts of energy and capital, and involving sophisticated technology and the complex logistics of assembling many different parts and materials.

More than anything else, the graphs show the industrial dominance of Japan, the U.S., China, and Europe (including Russia), which together produce 48% of the world's cotton and wool fabrics, 65% of the crude steel and pig iron, and 83% of the automobiles.

SINCE HUMANS FIRST BEGAN USING TOOLS, CULTIVATING THE SOIL, AND FASHIONING ARTICLES TO TRADE, THEY HAVE MADE USE OF THE EARTH'S RESOURCES TO EARN A living. Economic activities generally fall into two basic categories: herding and farming, and industrial production and commerce.

Nomadic herding and farming are perhaps the oldest economic activities practiced by humans. Today, only a smattering of people in Asia and Africa still follow the nomadic way of life. Farming, however, thrives in nearly every country, ranging from small family or tribal plots to the commercial farms of industrialized countries. Particularly in the United States, small, family-owned farms have given way to huge commercial agribusiness firms. With advanced methods of fertilization and mechanized harvesting, these agricultural businesses can raise enough food to feed the population of the country and still export surpluses around the world.

In contrast, subsistence farming, which produces little or no surplus for sale, is the mainstay of rural populations in Asia, Africa, and parts of South America. The large areas devoted to this type of farming represent essentially closed economic systems. It is in these areas that the challenge of economic development is greatest, for this type of farming is often the struggle on an impoverished people to wrest a living from tiny plots of land. Per capita income may be only a few hundred dollars per year. Release from such grinding poverty and toil is possible only where industries provide an alternative to rural life, and where systems of transportation and storage permit farming on a large scale.

Although subsistence agriculture still occupies large tracts of land in the world, developing countries are seeking to change this state of affairs in the near future. They wish to improve their agricultural output, increase industrialization, and raise their countries' standards of living.

Only a small portion of the Earth's surface is devoted to manufacturing and commerce—the foundations of national wealth and power. These areas generally coincide with the major urban centers of the world. In the United States alone, slightly over one percent of the land provides employment and residence for nearly 70 percent of the population. Urban centers in Europe are somewhat smaller but also account for a disproportionate amount of economic activity. As a result, per capita income in industrialized countries is high.

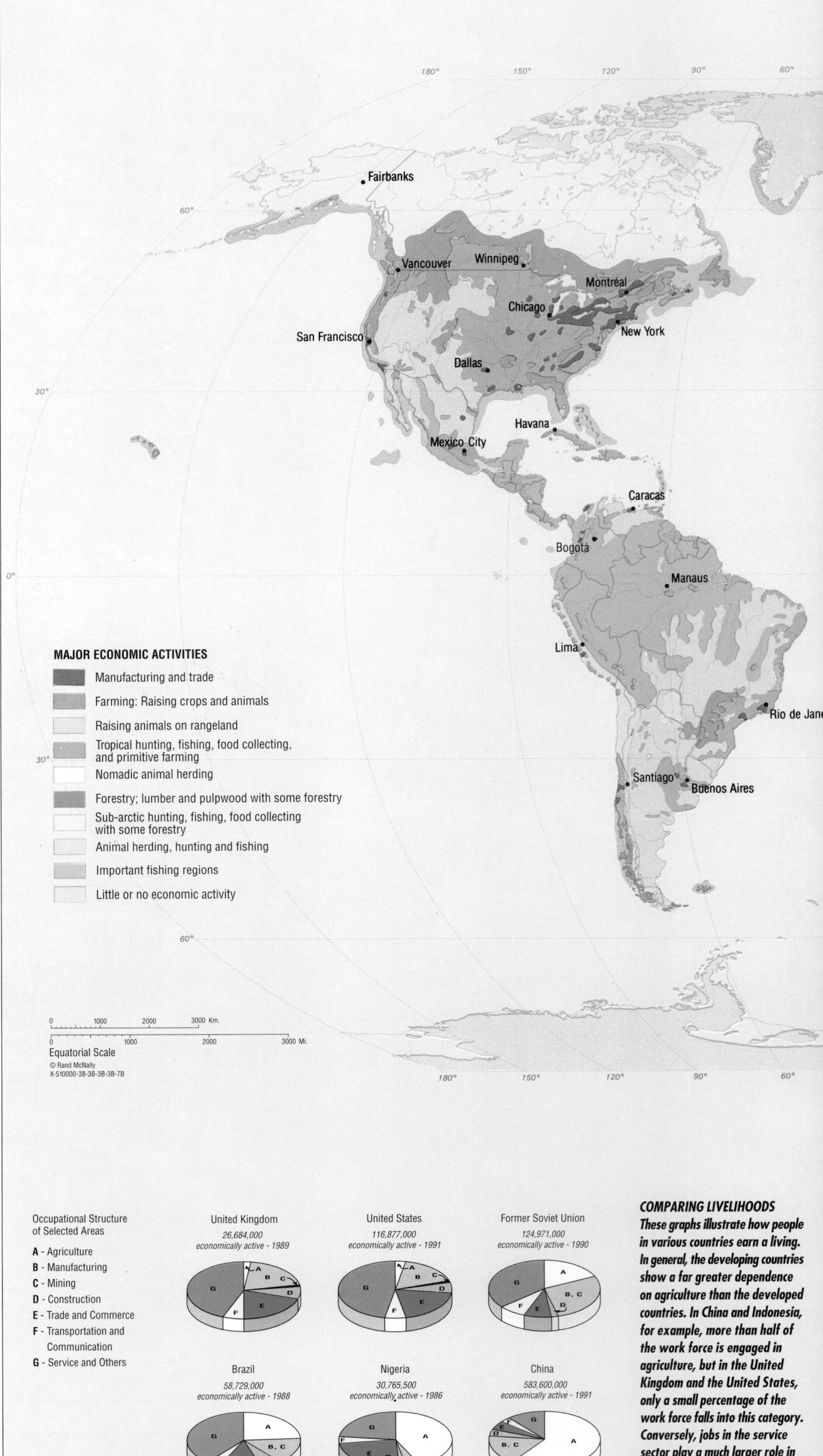

MAJOR ECONOMIC ACTIVITIES

- Manufacturing and trade
- Farming: Raising crops and animals
- Raising animals on rangeland
- Tropical hunting, fishing, food collecting, and primitive farming
- Nomadic animal herding
- Forestry; lumber and pulpwood with some forestry
- Sub-arctic hunting, fishing, food collecting with some forestry
- Animal herding, hunting and fishing
- Important fishing regions
- Little or no economic activity

Equatorial Scale
© Rand McNally
X-510000-38-38-38-38-38-78

Occupational Structure of Selected Areas

A - Agriculture
B - Manufacturing
C - Mining
D - Construction
E - Trade and Commerce
F - Transportation and Communication
G - Service and Others

United Kingdom
26,684,000
economically active - 1989

United States
116,877,000
economically active - 1991

Former Soviet Union
124,971,000
economically active - 1990

Brazil
58,729,000
economically active - 1988

Nigeria
30,765,500
economically active - 1986

China
583,600,000
economically active - 1991

COMPARING LIVELIHOODS
These graphs illustrate how people in various countries earn a living. In general, the developing countries show a far greater dependence on agriculture than the developed countries. In China and Indonesia, for example, more than half of the work force is engaged in agriculture, but in the United Kingdom and the United States, only a small percentage of the work force falls into this category. Conversely, jobs in the service sector play a much larger role in the developed countries than in the developing countries.

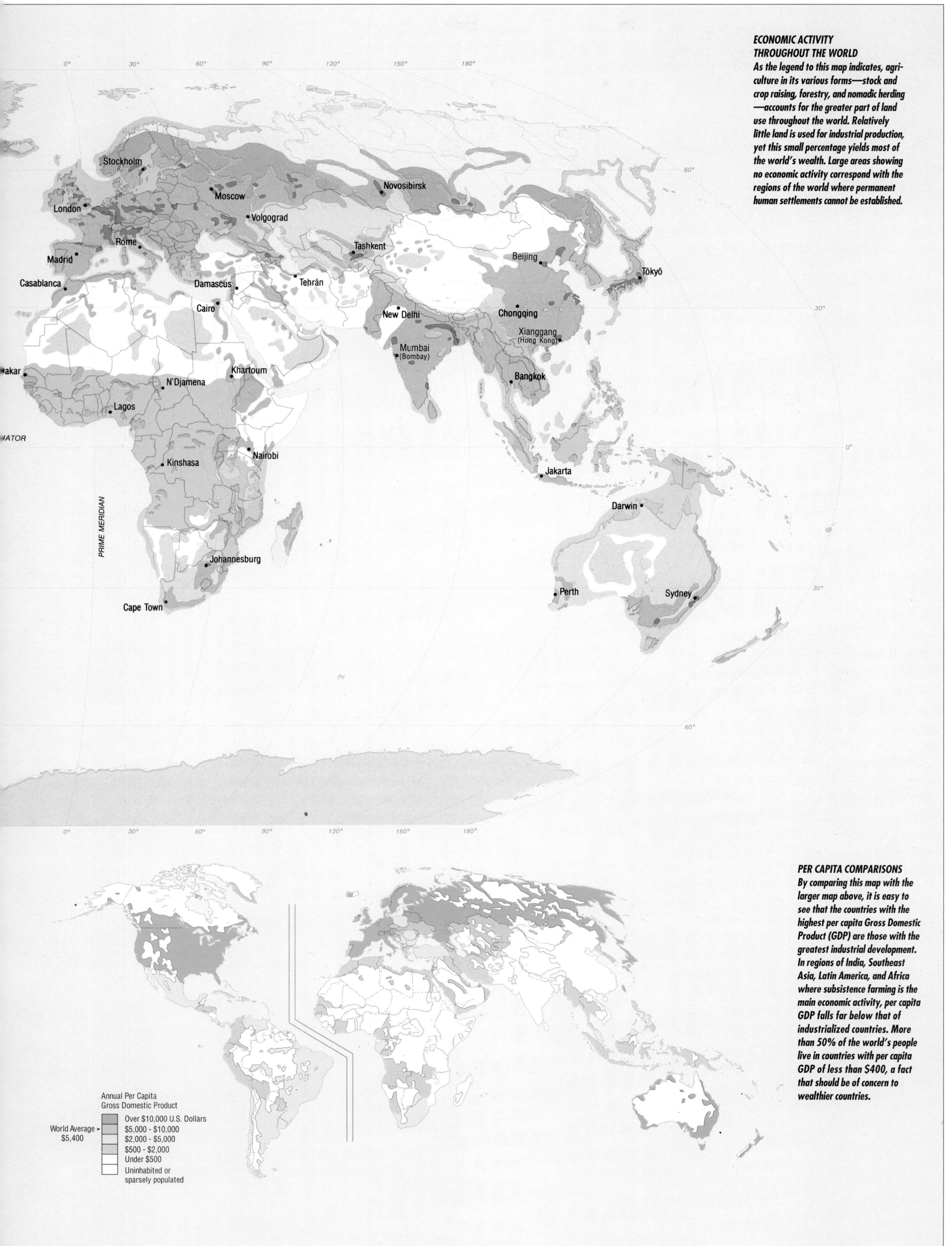

ECONOMIC ACTIVITY THROUGHOUT THE WORLD
As the legend to this map indicates, agriculture in its various forms—stock and crop raising, forestry, and nomadic herding—accounts for the greater part of land use throughout the world. Relatively little land is used for industrial production, yet this small percentage yields most of the world's wealth. Large areas showing no economic activity correspond with the regions of the world where permanent human settlements cannot be established.

Stockholm
London
Moscow
Novosibirsk
Volgograd
Rome
Madrid
Tashkent
Casablanca
Damascus
Beijing
Tōkyō
Cairo
Tehrān
New Delhi
Chongqing
Xianggang (Hong Kong)
Mumbai (Bombay)
Khartoum
Bangkok
N'Djamena
Lagos
Jakarta
Kinshasa
Nairobi
Darwin
Johannesburg
Perth
Sydney
Cape Town

PRIME MERIDIAN

PER CAPITA COMPARISONS
By comparing this map with the larger map above, it is easy to see that the countries with the highest per capita Gross Domestic Product (GDP) are those with the greatest industrial development. In regions of India, Southeast Asia, Latin America, and Africa where subsistence farming is the main economic activity, per capita GDP falls far below that of industrialized countries. More than 50% of the world's people live in countries with per capita GDP of less than $400, a fact that should be of concern to wealthier countries.

Annual Per Capita
Gross Domestic Product

World Average ▶
$5,400

- Over $10,000 U.S. Dollars
- $5,000 - $10,000
- $2,000 - $5,000
- $500 - $2,000
- Under $500
- Uninhabited or sparsely populated

WE HUMANS, UNLIKE ANY OTHER SPECIES ON EARTH, HAVE RADICALLY RESHAPED THE ENVIRONMENT TO SUIT OUR OWN NEEDS. OVER COUNTLESS CENTURIES, WE HAVE

cleared vast tracts of forest, dotted the landscape with cities—some covering hundreds of square miles—and altered the natural landscape to such a degree that we can almost speak of a "human-engineered" environment. But this reshaping carries a high price: mass extinctions of plant and animal life, damage to the atmosphere, and pollution on a worldwide scale. In the future, we must learn how to live in the world without destroying it.

The most obvious sign of our efforts to modify the environment has been the clearing of much of the world's forestland. At one time, the mid-latitude zones of both the Old and New Worlds were virtually covered with deciduous and evergreen trees. Over several hundred years, human settlers cleared the forests so vigorously that by the 17th century, wood was in short supply. These latitudes are now the most heavily populated on Earth, with new "forests" of glass, steel, and concrete.

The destruction of the world's forests and the overcultivation and overgrazing of exposed land has damaged the soil and accelerated the erosion process in many areas. The loss of productive land is especially serious today when a rapid increase in population raises the spectre of widespread famine.

Modern technology has enabled us to create artificial environments to live more comfortably in different climates. Central heating and cooling systems keep our buildings at a uniform temperature year-round. Some future planners envision entire dome-covered cities, with climate and temperature controlled by computer.

Pollution of air, water, and soil is perhaps the most pressing problem brought on by human activity. The Earth's atmosphere and hydrosphere are closed circulating systems. Industrial and household wastes are being dumped into these systems at a rate that far exceeds nature's ability to absorb them. Conservation and recycling programs seek to restore the environment and prevent further degradation. But much remains to be done, particularly in developing countries. The future quality of our environment will rest on our ability to cooperate as a world community.

THE NATURAL WORLD

This map shows the world's "natural" vegetation—that is, the vegetation patterns that are thought to have existed before humans began to have a significant impact on the world environment. Tropical and subtropical forests, which harbor a majority of the world's plant species, are clustered near the equator. Savanna and desert regions are found to the north and south of these forests, where hot and dry climates prevail. Mediterranean vegetation, temperate grasslands, and temperate forests appear mainly in the temperate zones of the northern hemisphere, where rainfall is abundant and growing seasons are long. North of these zones are great stretches of the northern coniferous forests called "taiga." The extreme northern and southern latitudes are characterized by tundra and polar ice cap. The world's mountainous regions, though shown here in a uniform color, actually support an incredible diversity of vegetation.

TODAY'S WORLD

The extent to which humans have impacted and reshaped the natural world is evident on this map. The Mediterranean area and most of Europe, once heavily forested, are now cropland, grassland, or near-desert environments. The same is true of south and east Asia. In North America, only pockets remain of the temperate forests and grasslands that once covered much of the central part of the continent. Vast urban areas have sprung up throughout the world, replacing the original environments.

Today, the eyes of the world are on South America, where the vast rain forest of the Amazon basin is being destroyed at a rapid pace to create new cropland and grazing land. This rain forest is thought to play an important role in the Earth's weather systems as well as in the purification of air through the absorption of carbon dioxide and the production of oxygen. Its destruction could be disastrous to the entire world ecosystem.

VEGETATION
This legend applies to both maps

 Tropical and subtropical forests

 Savanna

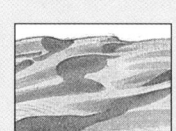 Desert

 Mediterranean

 Temperate grassland

 Temperate forest

 Taiga (northern forests)

 Tundra (lichen and moss)

 Mountain

Polar and high mountain

HUMAN ENVIRONMENTS
This legend applies to the bottom map only

 Cropland

 Cropland and woodland

 Cropland and grazing land

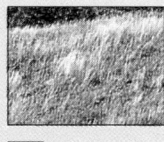 Grassland, grazing land

 Urban

TRANSPORTATION

EVERY GREAT CIVILIZATION IN HUMAN
HISTORY HAS CREATED A COMPLEX, OFTEN
FAR-FLUNG TRANSPORTATION NETWORK
LINKING IT TO THE OUTSIDE WORLD. CITIES
and industry in any era depend on supply lines and
trade routes to survive. As the adjacent map shows,
these land and sea routes underscore the world's uneven
distribution of human settlement.

The greatest systems of surface transportation are
found in North America and Europe, where nearly every
inhabited locale can be reached by car, train, bus, or
airline. This dense network thins out only in the western
United States and in western and northern Canada.
The more open network of the former Soviet Union
traces the well-populated area west of the Ural
Mountains and a narrow corridor between central Asia
and Siberia. South America's transportation network is
a study in contrasts between densely settled metropolitan
areas and the more inaccessible interior regions. Until
recently, much of the vast Amazon basin was accessible
only via waterways, but development of the rain forest
has spurred the construction of new highways and roads.
The Pan American Highway, stretching from Mexico to
Chile, is a major link among South American countries.

Africa, the Middle East, and Asia are more complex.
In Africa, only South Africa, northern Morocco, Algeria,
and Tunisia have well-developed transportation
systems. The Middle East boasts some of humanity's
oldest routes along the sea coast, but further inland the
desert has few roads. Only in the oil-producing regions
are transportation lines in abundant supply. Vast areas
of the Asian continent are sparsely populated, and
transportation facilities here are poor or nonexistent.
India and Pakistan have roads and rail systems built
on a European model, but only Japan's transportation
network rivals those of the United States and Europe. In
Australia, the transportation lines clearly mark where
human settlements end and the "outback" regions
begin. A single rail line cuts through the desert,
connecting rural settlements with the major cities
along the coast.

Transportation patterns also reveal something about
the culture and economic development of a country or
region. The complex network in Europe, for example,
means that every factory, farm, and home is connected
into a national and continental system of communication. In contrast, people in more remote areas may
not be exposed to new ideas and methods as easily.
Whether a country is connected into a vital network of
communication or is relatively isolated has a significant
impact on its rate of development and progress.

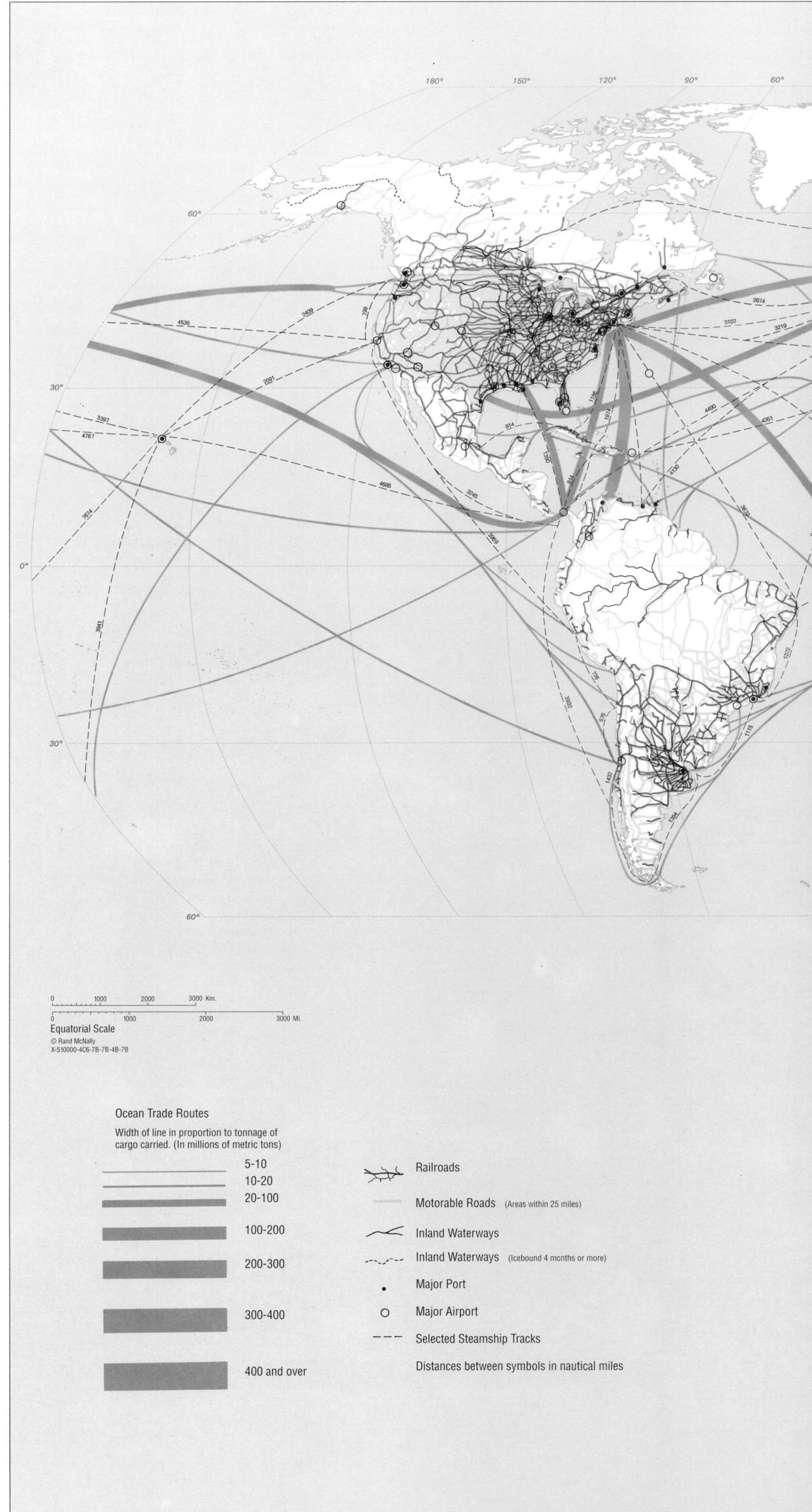

0   1000   2000   3000 Km.
0   1000   2000   3000 Mi.
Equatorial Scale
© Rand McNally
X-510000-4C6-7B-7B-4B-7B

Ocean Trade Routes
Width of line in proportion to tonnage of
cargo carried. (In millions of metric tons)

5-10
10-20
20-100

100-200

200-300

300-400

400 and over

Railroads

Motorable Roads (Areas within 25 miles)

Inland Waterways

Inland Waterways (Icebound 4 months or more)

• Major Port

○ Major Airport

--- Selected Steamship Tracks

Distances between symbols in nautical miles

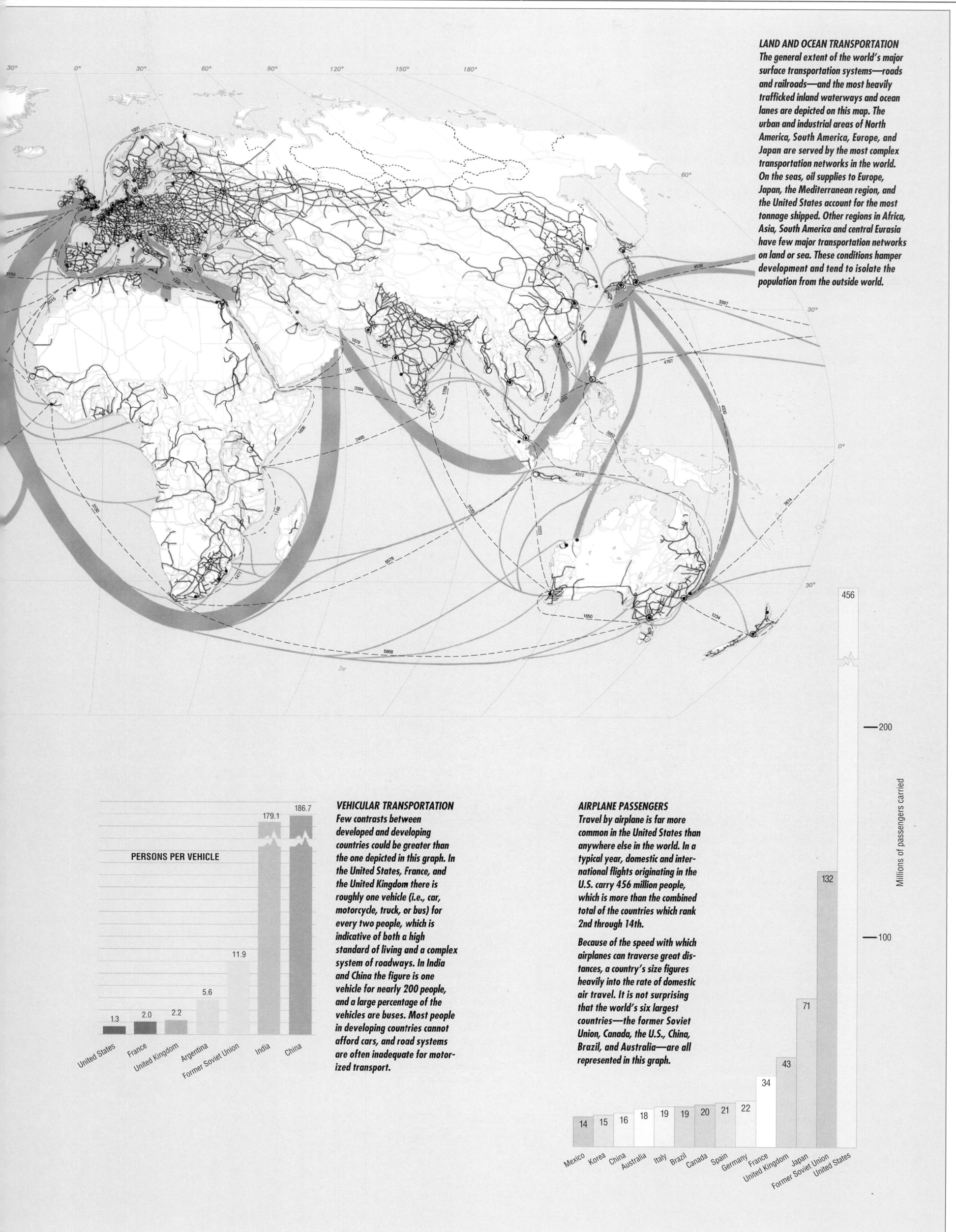

LAND AND OCEAN TRANSPORTATION
The general extent of the world's major surface transportation systems—roads and railroads—and the most heavily trafficked inland waterways and ocean lanes are depicted on this map. The urban and industrial areas of North America, South America, Europe, and Japan are served by the most complex transportation networks in the world. On the seas, oil supplies to Europe, Japan, the Mediterranean region, and the United States account for the most tonnage shipped. Other regions in Africa, Asia, South America and central Eurasia have few major transportation networks on land or sea. These conditions hamper development and tend to isolate the population from the outside world.

PERSONS PER VEHICLE

United States — 1.3
France — 2.0
United Kingdom — 2.2
Argentina — 5.6
Former Soviet Union — 11.9
India — 179.1
China — 186.7

VEHICULAR TRANSPORTATION
Few contrasts between developed and developing countries could be greater than the one depicted in this graph. In the United States, France, and the United Kingdom there is roughly one vehicle (i.e., car, motorcycle, truck, or bus) for every two people, which is indicative of both a high standard of living and a complex system of roadways. In India and China the figure is one vehicle for nearly 200 people, and a large percentage of the vehicles are buses. Most people in developing countries cannot afford cars, and road systems are often inadequate for motorized transport.

AIRPLANE PASSENGERS
Travel by airplane is far more common in the United States than anywhere else in the world. In a typical year, domestic and international flights originating in the U.S. carry 456 million people, which is more than the combined total of the countries which rank 2nd through 14th.

Because of the speed with which airplanes can traverse great distances, a country's size figures heavily into the rate of domestic air travel. It is not surprising that the world's six largest countries—the former Soviet Union, Canada, the U.S., China, Brazil, and Australia—are all represented in this graph.

Millions of passengers carried

456
— 200
— 100

Mexico — 14
Korea — 15
China — 16
Australia — 18
Italy — 19
Brazil — 19
Canada — 20
Spain — 21
Germany — 22
France — 34
United Kingdom — 43
Japan — 71
Former Soviet Union — 132
United States — 456

FEW ACTIVITIES HAVE HAD AS PROFOUND

AN IMPACT ON HUMAN DEVELOPMENT AS

COMMUNICATION. YET UNLIKE AGRICULTURE

OR TRANSPORTATION, COMMUNICATION

networks leave little imprint on the landscape. In modern times, this dynamic, invisible network has linked countries around the world, effectively conquering the barriers of time and distance. Today's telecommunications equipment can transmit and receive messages in milliseconds over distances that once took days, even months, to cross.

Throughout history, however, whether a country or region was included in a communications network or relatively isolated greatly affected its rate of cultural evolution. The invention of moveable type and printing in Europe in the 1400s, for example, had a tremendous cultural impact on the Western world. Information could now be disseminated to a wide audience, aiding in the exchange of ideas and new discoveries among the countries of Europe, North Africa, and the Far East. From that time on, the cultural development of these countries began to accelerate. Regions outside this network, such as sub-Saharan Africa and parts of Asia, slowly began to fall behind in technology and economic growth.

In the 1800s, advances in the understanding of electricity led to the invention of the telegraph, telephone, and radio. By 1866, the first transatlantic telegraph cable linked North America and Europe, laying the foundation for the modern era of electronic information exchange. Since the turn of the twentieth century, the explosive growth in communication devices and networks has ushered in the so-called "Information Age," the hallmark of which is the virtual elimination of geographic barriers to communication. Satellites, television and video, computer and data networks, modems, fax machines, electronic and voice mail, and cellular telephones have created a type of global information highway, along which information and communications flow with astonishing speed.

Although its full potential has not yet been realized, this new and vital highway is already beginning to transform the way we live, work, and view the world. For example, computer networking and fax machines allow many people in the service sector to work out of their homes instead of commuting to an office. Global positioning systems make it possible to track ocean-going vessels, trucks and individual parcels. Satellite geographic information systems aid in resource management by revealing global rates of deforestation, flood damage, and suburban sprawl.

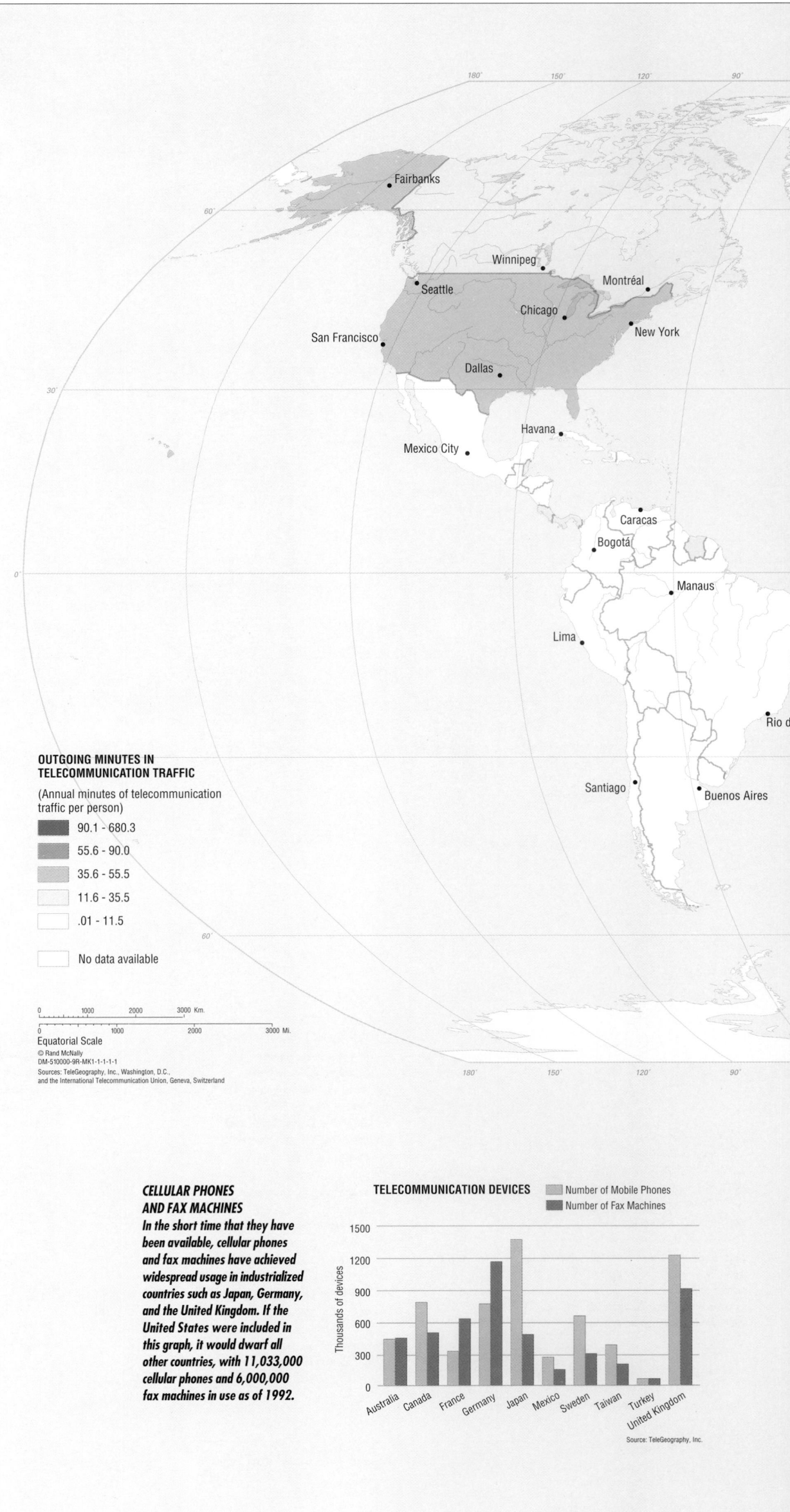

**OUTGOING MINUTES IN
TELECOMMUNICATION TRAFFIC**

(Annual minutes of telecommunication traffic per person)

- 90.1 - 680.3
- 55.6 - 90.0
- 35.6 - 55.5
- 11.6 - 35.5
- .01 - 11.5

- No data available

0   1000   2000   3000 Km.
0   1000   2000   3000 Mi.
Equatorial Scale
© Rand McNally
DM-510000-9R-MK1-1-1-1-1
Sources: TeleGeography, Inc., Washington, D.C.,
and the International Telecommunication Union, Geneva, Switzerland

***CELLULAR PHONES
AND FAX MACHINES***
In the short time that they have been available, cellular phones and fax machines have achieved widespread usage in industrialized countries such as Japan, Germany, and the United Kingdom. If the United States were included in this graph, it would dwarf all other countries, with 11,033,000 cellular phones and 6,000,000 fax machines in use as of 1992.

TELECOMMUNICATION DEVICES   ■ Number of Mobile Phones
■ Number of Fax Machines

Source: TeleGeography, Inc.

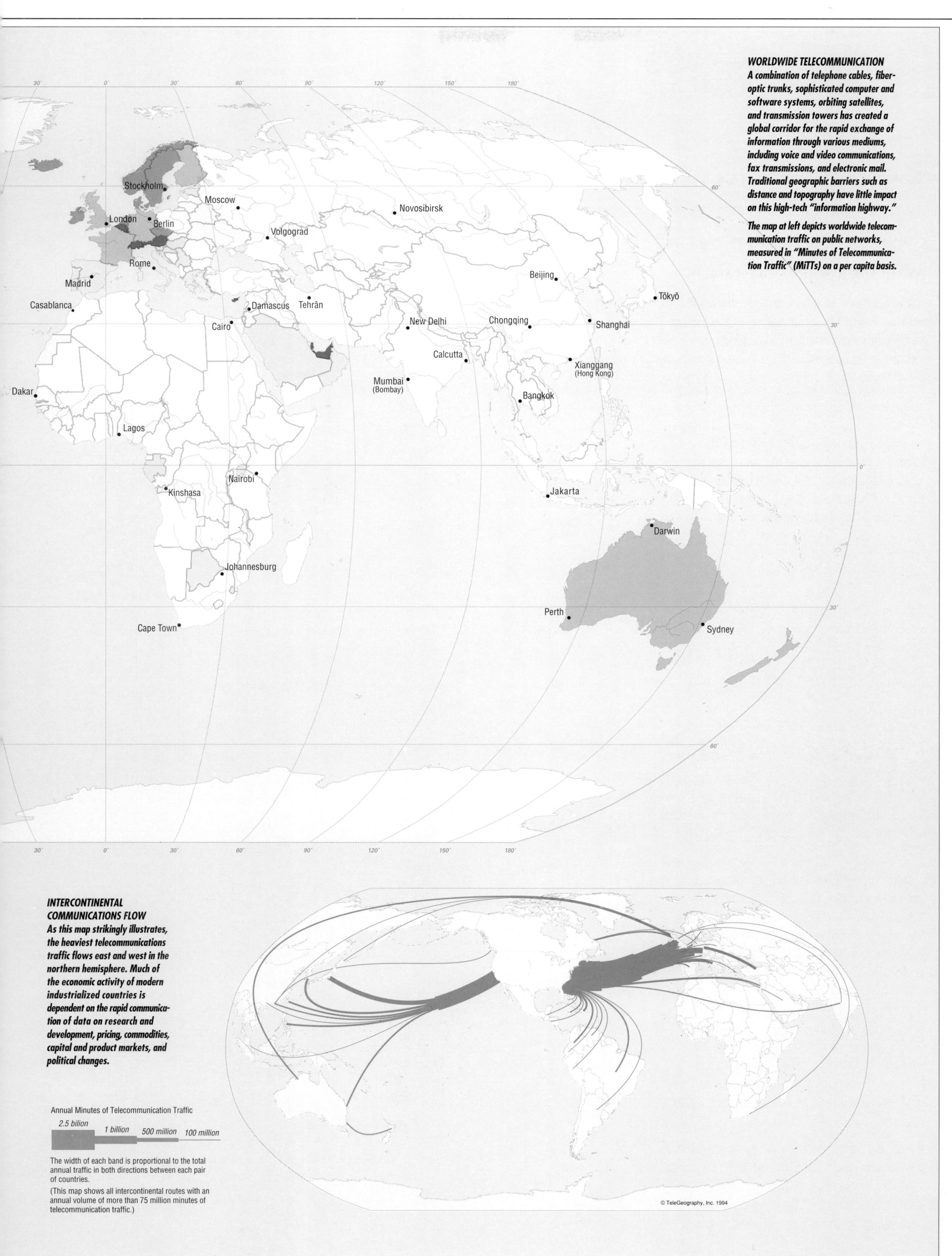

WORLDWIDE TELECOMMUNICATION
A combination of telephone cables, fiber-optic trunks, sophisticated computer and software systems, orbiting satellites, and transmission towers has created a global corridor for the rapid exchange of information through various mediums, including voice and video communications, fax transmissions, and electronic mail. Traditional geographic barriers such as distance and topography have little impact on this high-tech "information highway."

The map at left depicts worldwide telecommunication traffic on public networks, measured in "Minutes of Telecommunication Traffic" (MiTTs) on a per capita basis.

INTERCONTINENTAL COMMUNICATIONS FLOW
As this map strikingly illustrates, the heaviest telecommunications traffic flows east and west in the northern hemisphere. Much of the economic activity of modern industrialized countries is dependent on the rapid communication of data on research and development, pricing, commodities, capital and product markets, and political changes.

Annual Minutes of Telecommunication Traffic

2.5 bilion   1 billion   500 million   100 million

The width of each band is proportional to the total annual traffic in both directions between each pair of countries.

(This map shows all intercontinental routes with an annual volume of more than 75 million minutes of telecommunication traffic.)

© TeleGeography, Inc. 1994

LANGUAGE, RELIGION, AND ETHNIC IDENTITY—THESE HELP TO DEFINE HUMAN COMMUNITIES IN A WAY THAT TRANSCENDS POLITICAL BOUNDARIES. LANGUAGE, OF course, is the most effective means of communication among members of a group. It serves as a cohesive force for the members and helps to distinguish one community from another.

The map to the right shows only the major language groups, such as the Germanic branch of the Indo-European family. A map that displayed all known languages would require thousands of colors and labels. The Chinese branch of the Sino-Tibetan family ranks first in the number of speakers. English ranks second, but is the world's most important medium for scientific and commercial communication.

English enjoys absolute predominance in only four countries: the United Kingdom, the U.S., Australia, and New Zealand. However, it is spoken by a majority of people in Ireland and Canada and is the preferred second language in many other countries. French, Spanish, and Russian are also widely used as second languages. The importance of two other languages is suggested by the number of countries in which they have official status: Arabic (18 countries) and Spanish (20 countries).

Religion, like language, is a means of communication and a mechanism that promotes social cohesion. The map here shows the most important universalizing religions (Christianity, Islam, and Buddhism) that are held to be appropriate for all of humankind and so are propagated by missionary activities. Religions associated with particular peoples, such as Judaism and Hinduism, seldom entail missionary activity.

Countries cannot always be neatly divided into religious groups, however. In China, for example, Buddhism, Confucianism, and Taoism are so entwined that one has to speak of a Chinese religious system rather than a Chinese religion. Elsewhere in thé world, and especially in Africa, a wide array of tribal religions can be identified, and many of these have incorporated some of the practices and beliefs of one of the universalizing religions. Over time, most religions tend to split into factions or denominations. The division of Christianity into Catholic, Orthodox, and Protestant branches is striking evidence of this tendency, as is the split of the Islamic religion into Sunni and Shi'ite factions after the death of Muhammad in A.D. 632.

The country boundaries that appear as lines under the patterns of religions and languages remind us of an important fact about our world: very few of the 184 member states of the United Nations are nations in the strict or singular sense of the word. Most are a collection

Continued on page A·22

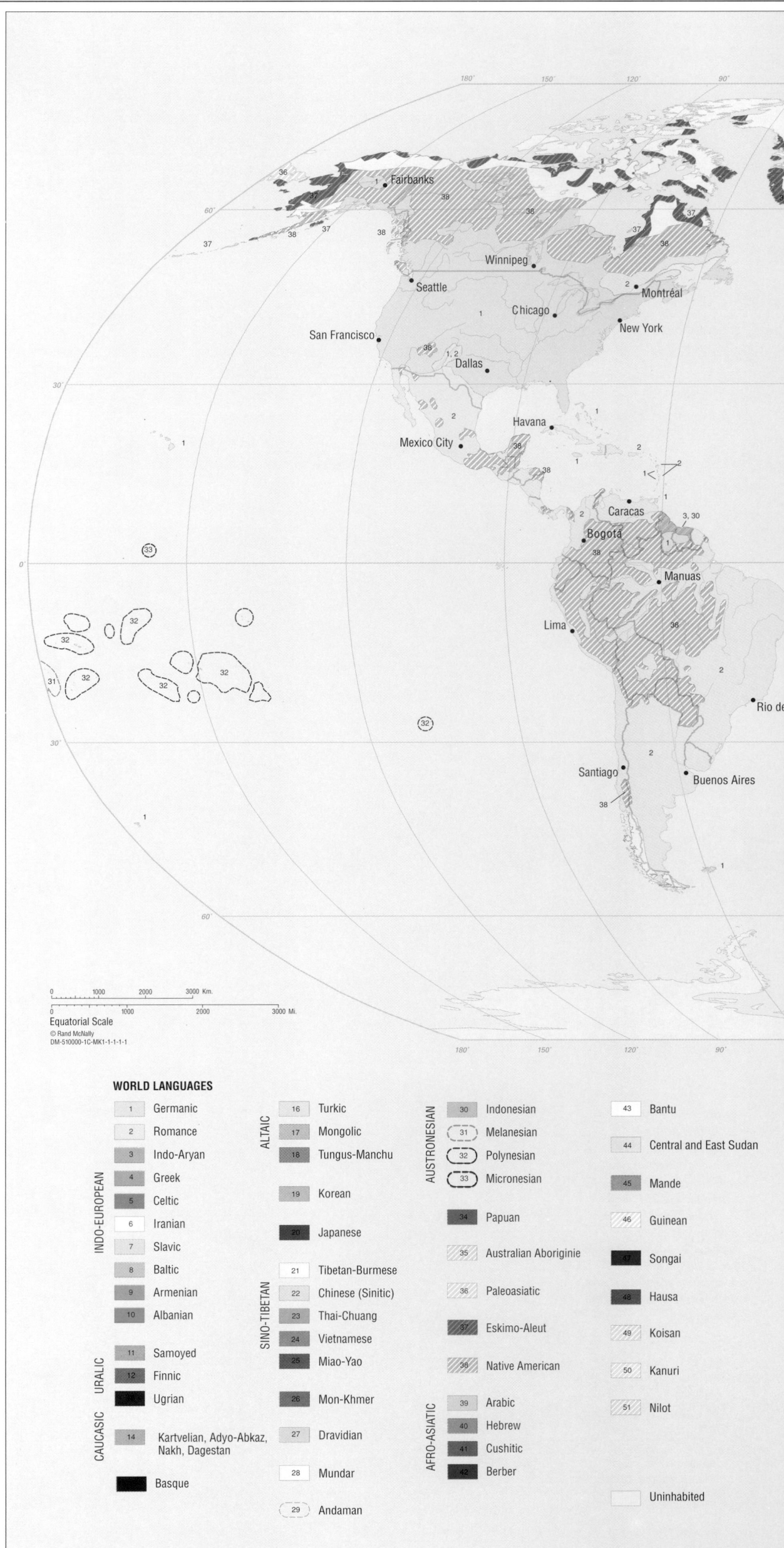

WORLD LANGUAGES

INDO-EUROPEAN
1 Germanic
2 Romance
3 Indo-Aryan
4 Greek
5 Celtic
6 Iranian
7 Slavic
8 Baltic
9 Armenian
10 Albanian

URALIC
11 Samoyed
12 Finnic
13 Ugrian

CAUCASIC
14 Kartvelian, Adyo-Abkaz, Nakh, Dagestan
15 Basque

ALTAIC
16 Turkic
17 Mongolic
18 Tungus-Manchu
19 Korean
20 Japanese

SINO-TIBETAN
21 Tibetan-Burmese
22 Chinese (Sinitic)
23 Thai-Chuang
24 Vietnamese
25 Miao-Yao
26 Mon-Khmer
27 Dravidian
28 Mundar
29 Andaman

AUSTRONESIAN
30 Indonesian
31 Melanesian
32 Polynesian
33 Micronesian
34 Papuan
35 Australian Aboriginie
36 Paleoasiatic
37 Eskimo-Aleut
38 Native American

AFRO-ASIATIC
39 Arabic
40 Hebrew
41 Cushitic
42 Berber

43 Bantu
44 Central and East Sudan
45 Mande
46 Guinean
47 Songai
48 Hausa
49 Koisan
50 Kanuri
51 Nilot

Uninhabited

0 1000 2000 3000 Km.
0 1000 2000 3000 Mi.
Equatorial Scale
© Rand McNally
DM-S10000-1C-MK1-1-1-1-1

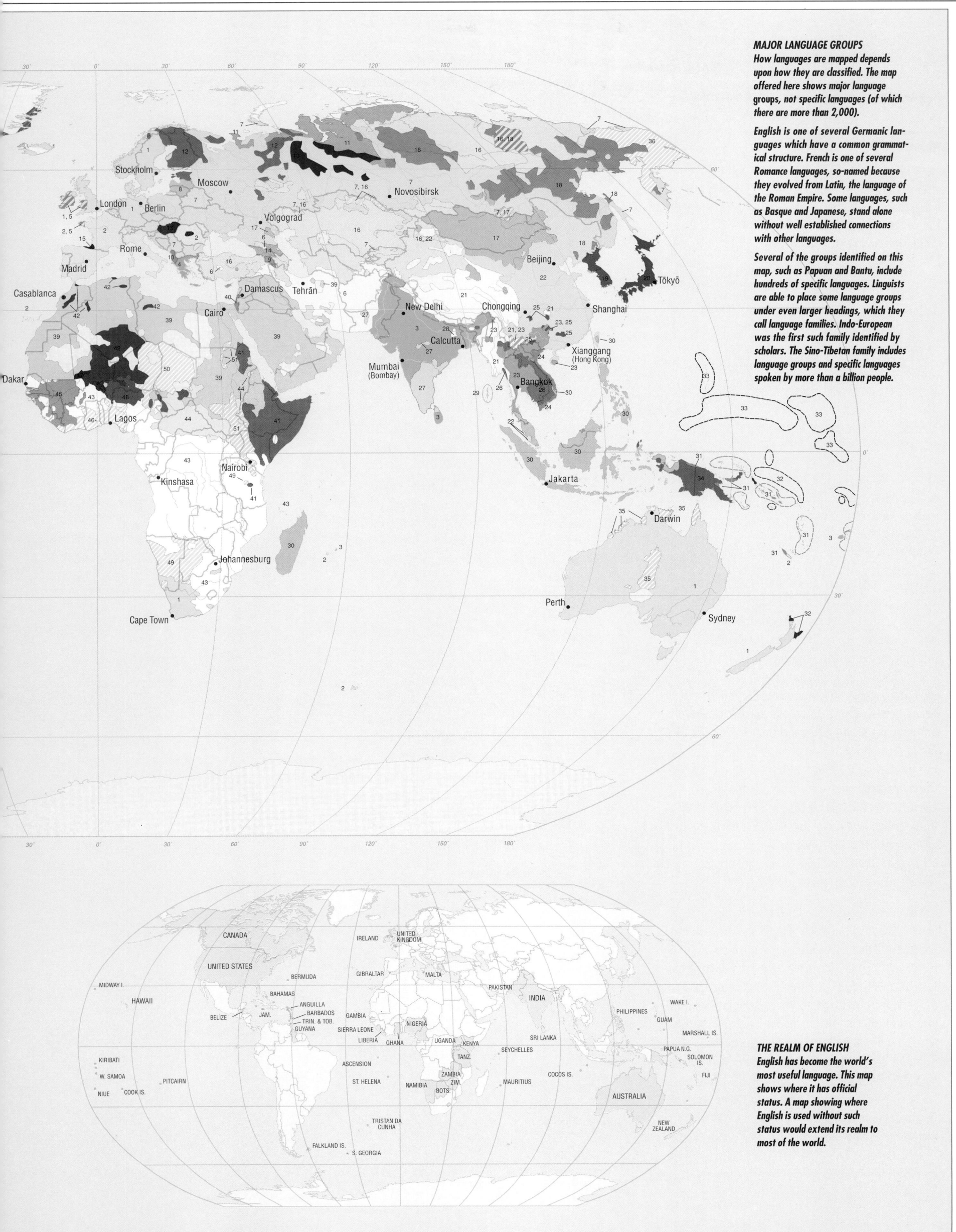

MAJOR LANGUAGE GROUPS
How languages are mapped depends upon how they are classified. The map offered here shows major language groups, not specific languages (of which there are more than 2,000).

English is one of several Germanic languages which have a common grammatical structure. French is one of several Romance languages, so-named because they evolved from Latin, the language of the Roman Empire. Some languages, such as Basque and Japanese, stand alone without well established connections with other languages.

Several of the groups identified on this map, such as Papuan and Bantu, include hundreds of specific languages. Linguists are able to place some language groups under even larger headings, which they call language families. Indo-European was the first such family identified by scholars. The Sino-Tibetan family includes language groups and specific languages spoken by more than a billion people.

THE REALM OF ENGLISH
English has become the world's most useful language. This map shows where it has official status. A map showing where English is used without such status would extend its realm to most of the world.

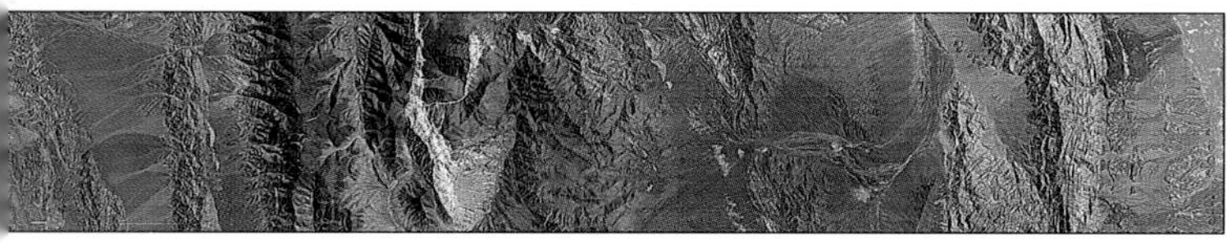

Continued from page A·20

of different groups speaking a variety of languages and maintaining diverse religious and cultural beliefs. In Western Europe, only Denmark and Portugal are homogeneous countries where everyone speaks the same language and belongs to the same church. In Africa, only Tunisia shares this distinction.

It is hard to find a comparable example in the Middle East, even among countries predominantly Islamic in faith and Arabic in speech. Saudi Arabia, if its large foreign labor population is ignored, is the only example of a true nation state in this region. Elsewhere in Asia, Japan and the two Korean states are rare exceptions to the more common pattern of cultural complexity. In Latin America, Spanish or Portuguese speech and Roman Catholicism are cultural common denominators, but Native American languages are still spoken in most countries. In contrast, Argentina and Brazil are cultural melting pots like the United States. Costa Rica and Uruguay may be the only New World states without significant minorities.

The fact that cultural uniformity is so rare, and only one perfect example can be cited (Iceland), means that the familiar political map not only differs from the less familiar maps of language and religion, but may actually conflict with them. Some countries have laws and institutions that permit citizens of different faiths and languages to live in peace and prosperity. For example, the Swiss live in harmony in spite of speaking four languages (German, French, Italian, and Romansch) and having Catholic and Protestant affiliations. Unfortunately, such happy examples of cultural accommodation are offset by numerous instances of tension and conflict. The ethnic warfare within recent decades in Sri Lanka, Bosnia, Sudan, Lebanon, and Rwanda are conspicuous examples of the potential for violence that often exists in states that are not true nation states or have borders that do not coincide with ethnic realities. The collapse of the Soviet Union exposed many problems of this nature.

Since the world is never likely to have only one language or one religion, comparison of maps showing cultural patterns with those indicating political jurisdiction reveals an important truth about our troubled world. In order to understand why ethnic conflict occurs so frequently we need an appropriate vocabulary. We need to be able to distinguish among the following cultural-political categories: *nation states* (homogeneous countries, such as Iceland and Denmark); *multinational states* (countries made up of diverse ethnic and linguistic groups, such as India); *multi-state nations* (multiple countries that share language and religion, such as the Arabic-Islamic realm); *non-nation states* (Vatican City is the only example); and, finally, *non-state nations* (regions where people share language and religion but have no political state, such as Kurdistan and Palestine).

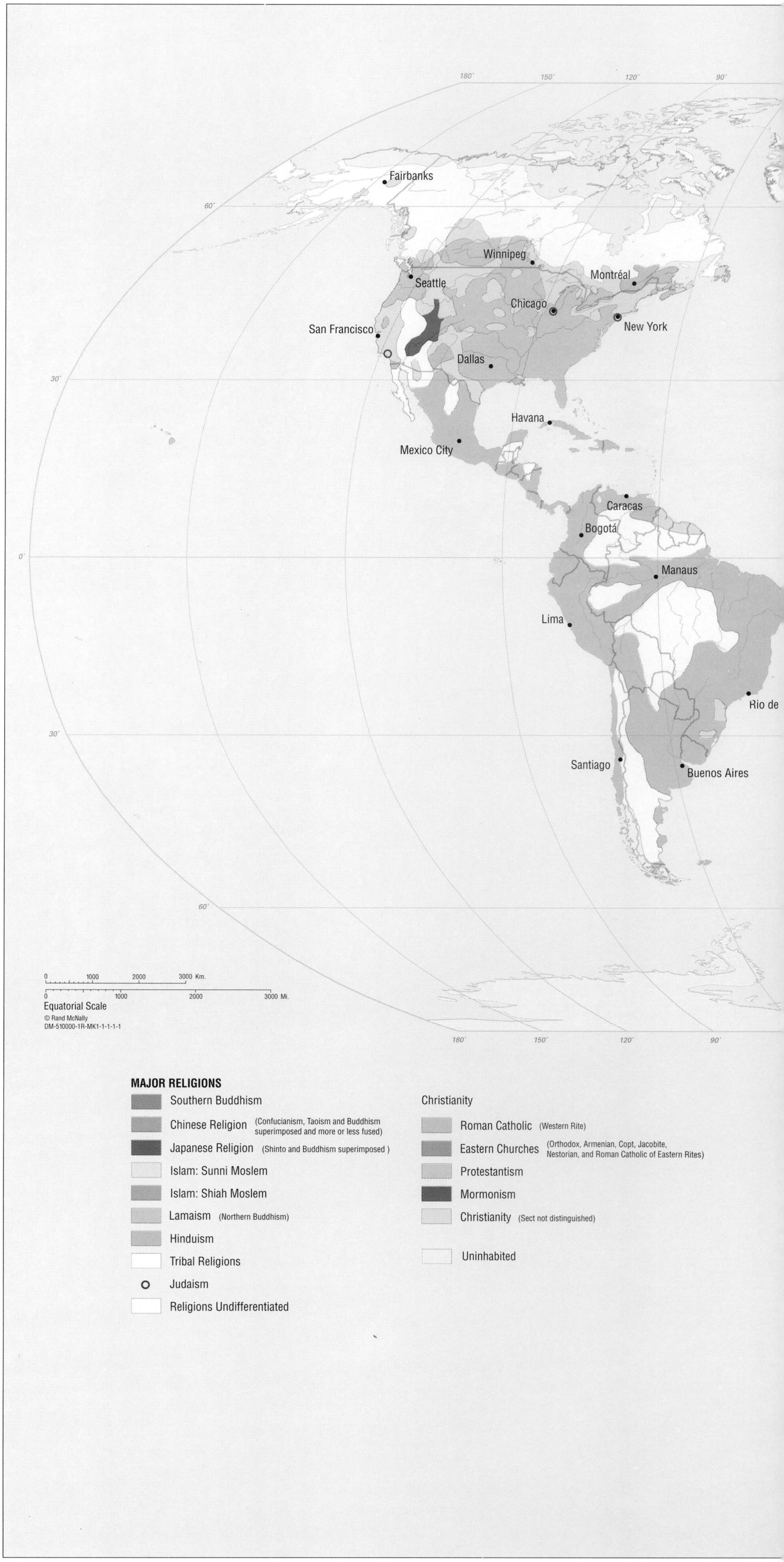

MAJOR RELIGIONS

- Southern Buddhism
- Chinese Religion (Confucianism, Taoism and Buddhism superimposed and more or less fused)
- Japanese Religion (Shinto and Buddhism superimposed)
- Islam: Sunni Moslem
- Islam: Shiah Moslem
- Lamaism (Northern Buddhism)
- Hinduism
- Tribal Religions
- Judaism
- Religions Undifferentiated

Christianity
- Roman Catholic (Western Rite)
- Eastern Churches (Orthodox, Armenian, Copt, Jacobite, Nestorian, and Roman Catholic of Eastern Rites)
- Protestantism
- Mormonism
- Christianity (Sect not distinguished)

- Uninhabited

Equatorial Scale
© Rand McNally
DM-510000-1R-MK1-1-1-1-1

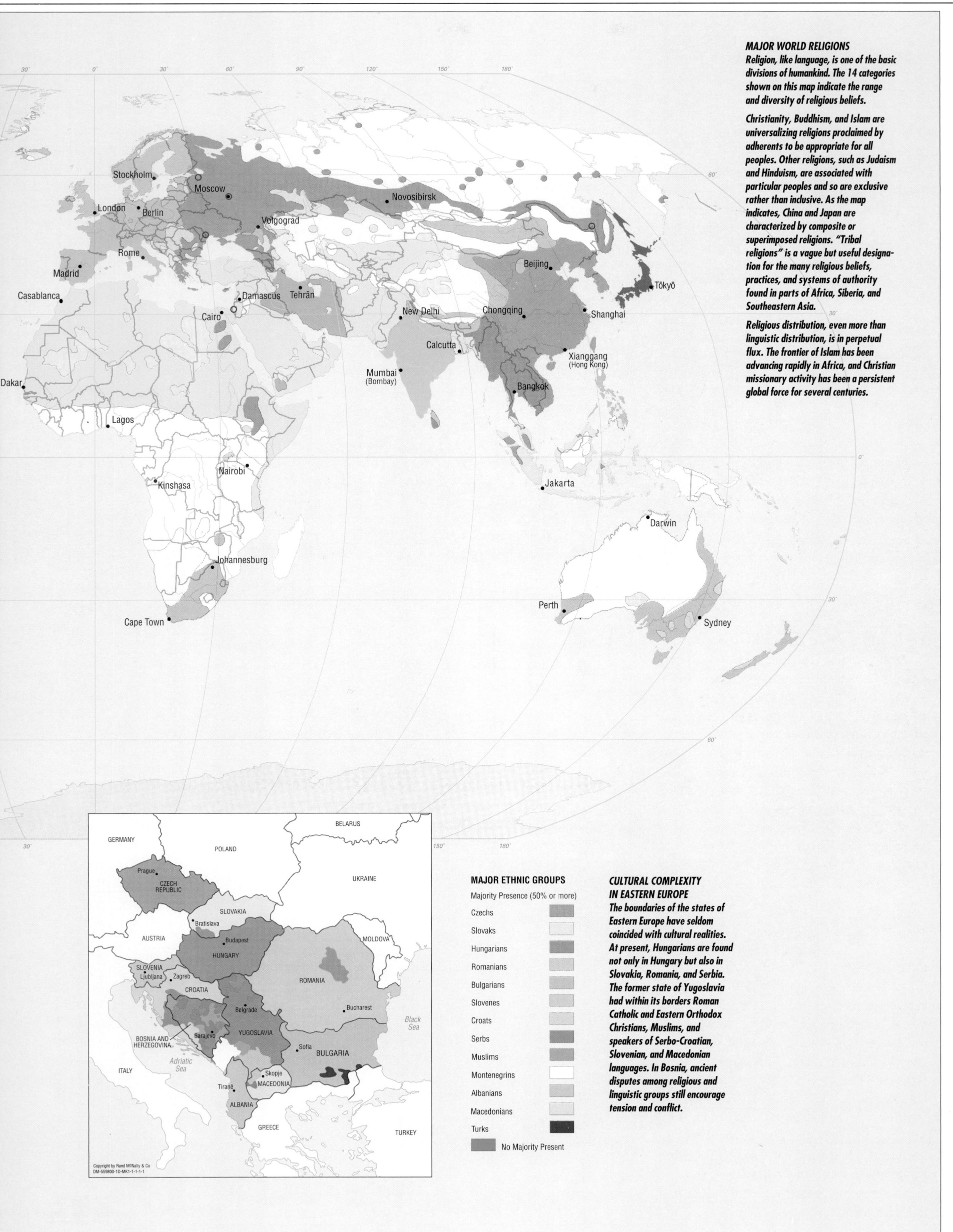

MAJOR WORLD RELIGIONS

Religion, like language, is one of the basic divisions of humankind. The 14 categories shown on this map indicate the range and diversity of religious beliefs.

Christianity, Buddhism, and Islam are universalizing religions proclaimed by adherents to be appropriate for all peoples. Other religions, such as Judaism and Hinduism, are associated with particular peoples and so are exclusive rather than inclusive. As the map indicates, China and Japan are characterized by composite or superimposed religions. "Tribal religions" is a vague but useful designation for the many religious beliefs, practices, and systems of authority found in parts of Africa, Siberia, and Southeastern Asia.

Religious distribution, even more than linguistic distribution, is in perpetual flux. The frontier of Islam has been advancing rapidly in Africa, and Christian missionary activity has been a persistent global force for several centuries.

MAJOR ETHNIC GROUPS

Majority Presence (50% or more)

- Czechs
- Slovaks
- Hungarians
- Romanians
- Bulgarians
- Slovenes
- Croats
- Serbs
- Muslims
- Montenegrins
- Albanians
- Macedonians
- Turks

No Majority Present

CULTURAL COMPLEXITY IN EASTERN EUROPE

The boundaries of the states of Eastern Europe have seldom coincided with cultural realities. At present, Hungarians are found not only in Hungary but also in Slovakia, Romania, and Serbia. The former state of Yugoslavia had within its borders Roman Catholic and Eastern Orthodox Christians, Muslims, and speakers of Serbo-Croatian, Slovenian, and Macedonian languages. In Bosnia, ancient disputes among religious and linguistic groups still encourage tension and conflict.

Copyright by Rand McNally & Co
DM-559800-1D-MK1-1-1-1-1

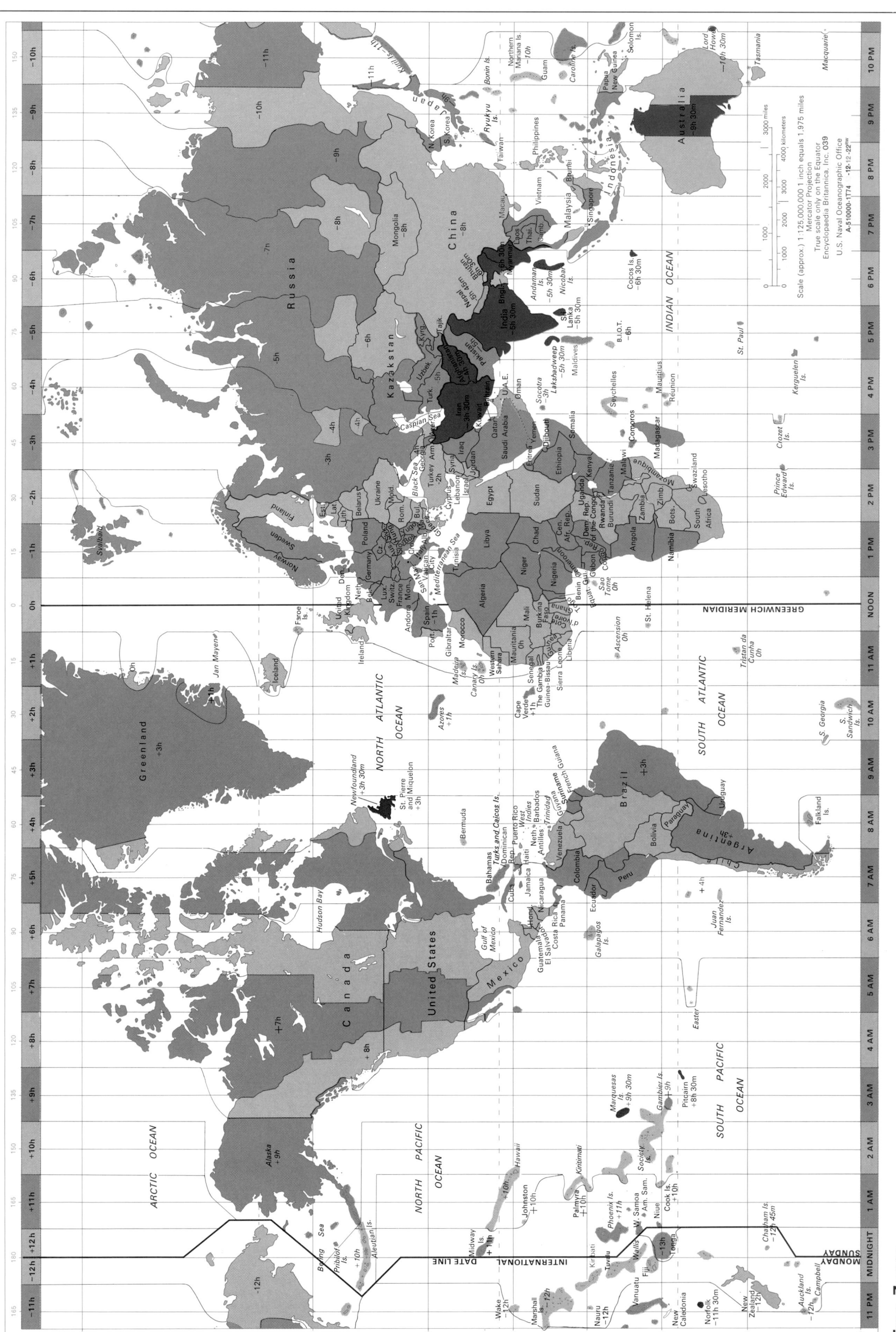

The standard time zone system, fixed by international agreement and by law in each country, is based on a theoretical division of the globe into 24 zones of 15° longitude each. The mid-meridian of each zone fixes the hour for the entire zone. The zero time zone extends 7½° east and 7½° west of the Greenwich meridian, 0° longitude. Since the earth rotates toward the east, time zones to the west of Greenwich are earlier, to the east, later.

Plus and minus hours at the top of the map are added to or subtracted from local time to find Greenwich time. Local standard time can be determined for any area in the world by adding one hour for each time zone counted in an easterly direction from

one's own, or by subtracting one hour for each zone counted in a westerly direction. To separate one day from the next, the 180th meridian has been designated as the international date line. On both sides of the line the time of day is the same, but west of the line it is one day later than it is to the east. Countries that adhere to the international zone system adopt the zone applicable to their location. Some countries, however, establish time zones based on political boundaries, or adopt the time zone of a neighboring unit. For all or part of the year some countries also advance their time by one hour, thereby utilizing more daylight hours each day.

Scale (approx.) 1:125,000,000 1 inch equals 1,975 miles
Mercator Projection
True scale only on the Equator
Encyclopædia Britannica, Inc. O39
U.S. Naval Oceanographic Office
A-510000-1T4 -12-12-22ᴺᵂ

Time Zones

Standard time zone of even-numbered hours from Greenwich time

Standard time zone of odd-numbered hours from Greenwich time

Time varies from the standard time zone by half an hour

Time varies from the standard time zone by other than half an hour

h m hours, minutes

World, Ocean, and Continent Maps / Weltkarten, Karten der Ozeane und Erdteile
Mapas del Mundo, Océanos y Continentes / Cartes du Monde, des Océans et des Continents
Mapas do Mundo, dos Oceanos e dos Continentes

1

THIS SECTION OPENS with World Political and World Physical maps at the scale of 1:75,000,000. There follow maps of the Pacific, Indian, and Atlantic oceans at the scale 1:48,000,000, the largest scale at which the total expanse of these bodies of water could be portrayed. Finally, a series of continent relief maps at the scale of 1:24,000,000 show a global view of the earth as it would appear from about 4,000 miles in space. The Azimuthal Equal-Area projection is used for the 1:24,000,000 maps, the scale being approximately that of a globe 20 inches in diameter.

The colors of the continent maps portray the land areas as if viewed from space during the growing season, without regard to the fact that the growing seasons are not concurrent in all areas. Underwater features and varying water depths are represented by shaded relief and different color tones. The result is a strong physical portrait of the earth's major land and submarine forms. The legend below shows how these different kinds of terrain and vegetation have been represented. The names of physical features—plateaus, basins, mountain ranges, seas, rivers, lakes, gulfs, trenches, bays, islands—predominate on these maps.

DIESER KARTENTEIL BEGINNT mit politischen und physischen Weltkarten im Massstab 1:75 Millionen. Dann folgen Karten des Pazifischen, Indischen und Atlantischen Ozeans in 1:48 Millionen, dem grössten Massstab, in dem diese Wasserflächen in ihrer ganzen Ausdehnung abgebildet werden konnten. Schliesslich folgt eine Reihe von Reliefkarten der Erdteile in 1:24 Millionen. Sie geben eine Übersicht der Erde, wie sie aus einer Entfernung von ungefähr 6 400 Kilometer aus dem Weltraum gewonnen würde. Den Karten im Massstab 1:24 Millionen liegt ein flächentreuer azimutaler Entwurf zugrunde, dieser Massstab entspricht ungefähr dem eines Globus von 50 cm Durchmesser.

Die Farben der Erdteilkarten bilden jedes Landgebiet so ab, wie es in der Vegetationsperiode aus der Vogelperspektive erschiene, ohne zu berücksichtigen, dass die Vegetationsperioden nicht in allen Gebieten gleichzeitig eintreten. Die Gliederung des Meeresbodens und die unterschiedlichen Meerestiefen werden durch Schummerung und verschiedene Farbstufen dargestellt. Das Ergebnis ist eine anschauliche physische Darstellung der wichtigsten terrestrischen und untermeerischen Formen der Erde. Die untenstehende Zeichenerklärung zeigt, wie diese verschiedenen Geländeformen und Vegetationsgebiete veranschaulicht werden. Namen physischer Objekte—Hochebenen, Becken, Gebirgszüge, Meere, Flüsse, Seen, Buchten, Gräben, Inseln—herrschen in diesen Karten vor.

ESTA SECCIÓN DA PRINCIPIO con los Mapas Políticos y Físicos del Mundo, a una escala de 1:75 000 000. A continuación están los mapas de los océanos Pacífico, Indico y Atlántico a una escala de 1:48 000 000, que es la mayor escala utilizable para la representación de esas masas de agua en toda su extensión. Por último, una serie de mapas del relieve de los continentes, a una escala de 1:24 000 000, proporcionan una vista global de la tierra tal como se apreciaría desde el espacio a una distancia aproximada de 6 400 kilómetros. La proyección azimutal equiárea se usa, para los mapas de 1:24 000 000, a una escala según la cual la tierra se reduciría a un globo de unos 50 cm de diámetro.

Los colores utilizados en los mapas de los continentes representan las diversas regiones de la tierra tal como se verían desde el espacio durante la estación en que la vegetación se desarrolla, sin tomar en cuenta que este fenómeno no se produce simultáneamente en todas las áreas. Las estructuras características del fondo marino y las variaciones de profundidad de los océanos se representan mediante relieve sombreado y distintos matices de color. El resultado es una imagen elocuente de las formas terrestres y submarinas más notables del planeta. La leyenda abajo explica cómo se representan estos diferentes tipos de terreno y vegetación. En estos mapas predomina la nomenclatura de elementos físicos: mesetas, cuencas, sierras, mares, ríos, lagos, golfos, bahías, trincheras, islas.

CETTE PARTIE comprend d'abord des cartes du monde politique et du monde physique à l'échelle de 1:75 000 000. Viennent ensuite les cartes des océans Pacifique, Indien et Atlantique à l'échelle de 1:48 000 000, la plus grande échelle qui a permis la reproduction complète de ces étendues d'eau. Pour terminer, une série de cartes en relief des continents à l'échelle de 1:24 000 000 donne une vue globale de la terre, telle qu'elle apparaîtrait vue de l'espace à une distance d'environ 6 400 kilomètres. La projection azimutale équivalente a été utilisée pour les cartes au 1:24 000 000ᵉ, dont l'échelle équivaut à celle d'un globe de 50 cm de diamètre environ.

Les couleurs des cartes font apparaître les continents tels qu'on les verrait de l'espace, pendant la saison de croissance végétale, mais sans tenir compte du fait que cette saison n'apparaît pas partout simultanément. Le relief sous-marin est représenté par un estompage et la profondeur des océans par une variation de la couleur. Il en résulte une reproduction vigoureuse des principaux paysages continentaux et des principales formes sous-marines. La légende ci-dessous indique de quelle façon ils sont cartographiés. Les noms d'éléments topographiques tels que plateaux, bassins, chaînes de montagnes, mers, cours d'eau, lacs, golfes, baies, crêtes, îles et fosses océaniques, prédominent dans ces cartes.

ESTA SEÇÃO PRINCIPIA com os mapas políticos e físicos do Mundo, em escala de 1:75 000 000. Seguem-se os mapas dos oceanos Pacífico, Índico e Atlântico na escala de 1:48 000 000, a maior escala que se pode utilizar para a representação dessas massas de água em toda a sua extensão. Finalmente, uma série de mapas de relevo dos continentes, na escala de 1:24 000 000, proporciona uma visão global da Terra tal como apareceria do espaço a uma distância aproximada de cerca de 6 400 km. A projeção azimutal equiárea foi usada para os mapas da escala de 1:24 000 000, segundo a qual a Terra se apresentaria como um globo de cerca de 50 cm de diâmetro.

As cores utilizadas nos mapas dos continentes representam as massas terrestres tal como apareceriam vistas do espaço durante a estação do crescimento vegetal, sem levar em conta que este fenômeno não se produz simultaneamente em todas as regiões. As características do fundo do mar e as variações de profundidade das águas são representadas por um relevo sombreado e por diferentes matizes de cor. O resultado proporciona uma imagem física eloqüente das principais formas terrestres e submarinas da Terra. As legendas abaixo explicam como foram representados os diversos tipos de terreno e de vegetação. Nestes mapas predomina a nomenclatura dos elementos físicos: planaltos, bacias, cadeias de montanhas, mares, rios, lagos, golfos, baías, fossas, ilhas.

Land Features / Land Phänomene / Elementos de la Tierra
Paysages Continentaux / Acidentes Continentais

Submarine Features / Untermeerische Phänomene
Elementos Submarinos / Formes de Relief Sous-marin / Acidentes do Revelo Submarino

Ice and Snow
Eis und Schnee
Hielo y nieve
Glace et neige
Gelo e neve

High Barren Area
Hochgebirgswüste
Alta zona árida
Région haute et aride
Alta zona árida

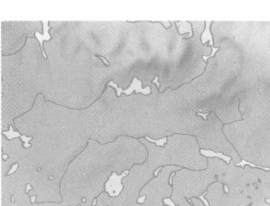

Tundra and Alpine
Tundra und Alpine Vegetation
Tundra y alpina
Toundra et végétation alpine
Tundra e vegetação alpina

Needleleaf Trees
Nadelwälder
Coníferas
Forêt de conifères
Coníferas

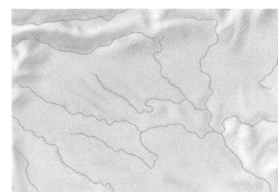

Broadleaf Trees
Laubwälder
Árboles de hojas anchas
Forêt à feuilles caduques
Árvores de folhas caducas

Tropical Rainforest
Tropischer Regenwald
Bosque tropical lluvioso
Forêt tropicale humide
Floresta tropical úmida

Grassland
Grasland
Pradera
Formations herbacées
Pradaria

Dry Scrub
Trockenes Buschland
Matorral
Brousse sèche
Caatinga

Desert
Wüste
Desierto
Désert
Deserto

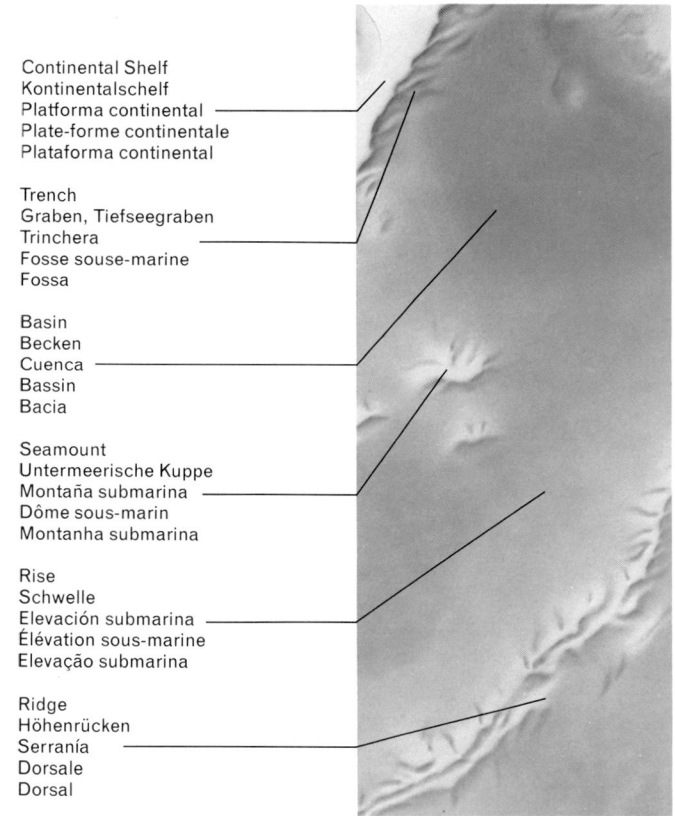

Continental Shelf
Kontinentalschelf
Platforma continental
Plate-forme continentale
Plataforma continental

Trench
Graben, Tiefseegraben
Trinchera
Fosse souse-marine
Fossa

Basin
Becken
Cuenca
Bassin
Bacia

Seamount
Untermeerische Kuppe
Montaña submarina
Dôme sous-marin
Montanha submarina

Rise
Schwelle
Elevación submarina
Élévation sous-marine
Elevação submarina

Ridge
Höhenrücken
Serranía
Dorsale
Dorsal

ARCTIC OCEAN
Beaufort Sea
GREENLAND
(Den.)
Greenland Sea
Baffin Bay
BAFFIN ISLAND
VICTORIA ISLAND
UNITED STATES
RUSSIA
Arctic Circle
Nome
Fairbanks
Mount McKinley 6194
Anchorage
Inuvik
Yellowknife
Bering Sea
Gulf of Alaska
Juneau
Hudson Bay
Churchill
Thule
Godhavn
Godthåb
Angmagssalik
Reykjavík
ICELAND
FAEROE ISLANDS (Den.)
ALEUTIAN ISLANDS
C A N A D A
ROCKY MOUNTAINS
Edmonton
Calgary
Vancouver
Seattle
Winnipeg
Lake Superior
Lake Huron
Portland
Minneapolis
Ottawa
Québec
Montréal
NEWFOUNDLAND
St. John's
Halifax
Toronto
Boston
DETROIT
CHICAGO
NORTH AMERICA
NEW YORK
PHILADELPHIA
WASHINGTON
APPALACHIAN MOUNTAINS
Salt Lake City
Denver
St. Louis
SAN FRANCISCO
UNITED STATES
LOS ANGELES
San Diego
Phoenix
El Paso
Dallas
Atlanta
Houston
New Orleans
BERMUDA (U.K.)
ATLANTIC OCEAN
AÇORES AZORES (Port.)
Glasgow
DUBLIN
IRELAND
Porto
PORTUGAL
LISBOA
GIBRALTAR (U.K.)
RABAT
Casablanca
MOROCCO
ARQUIPÉLAGO DA MADEIRA (Port.)
ISLAS CANARIAS CANARY ISLANDS (Sp.)
WESTERN SAHARA
MAURI-TANIA
Nouakchott
Tombouctou
CAPE VERDE
SENEGAL
DAKAR
GAMBIA
Banjul
Bamako
GUINEA-BISSAU
GUINEA
Conakry
SIERRA LEONE
Freetown
Monrovia
LIBERIA
Yamoussoukro
ABIDJAN
P A C I F I C
O C E A N
MIDWAY ISLANDS (U.S.)
HAWAIIAN ISLANDS (U.S.)
Honolulu
Tropic of Cancer
Gulf of Mexico
Monterrey
Miami
BAHAMAS
LA HABANA
CUBA
CABO SAN LUCAS
MEXICO
CIUDAD DE MÉXICO
MEXICO CITY
Guadalajara
DOMINICAN REPUBLIC
HAITI
Port-au-Prince
SANTO DOMINGO
SAN JUAN
PUERTO RICO (U.S.)
JAMAICA
Kingston
GUADELOUPE (Fr.)
MARTINIQUE (Fr.)
BARBADOS
TRINIDAD AND TOBAGO
Port of Spain
GUATEMALA
BELIZE
HONDURAS
Tegucigalpa
San Salvador
EL SALVADOR
NICARAGUA
Managua
SAN JOSÉ
COSTA RICA
Panamá
PANAMA
Caribbean Sea
JOHNSTON ATOLL (U.S.)
ÎLE CLIPPERTON (Fr.)
CARACAS
VENEZUELA
GUYANA
Georgetown
Paramaribo
SURINAME
FRENCH GUIANA
Medellín
SANTA FE DE BOGOTÁ
Cali
COLOMBIA
Equator
QUITO
ECUADOR
Guayaquil
ARCHIPIÉLAGO DE COLÓN GALAPAGOS ISLANDS (Ec.)
Manaus
Amazon
Belém
Fortaleza
CABO DE SÃO ROQUE
Natal
Recife
Iquitos
Trujillo
LIMA
PERU
ANDES
B R A Z I L
SOUTH AMERICA
Salvador
ATLANTIC OCEAN
KIRIBATI
PHOENIX ISLANDS
TOKELAU (N.Z.)
ÎLES MARQUISES
WALLIS AND FUTUNA (Fr.)
W. SAMOA
Apia
AM. SAMOA
FIJI
TONGA
NIUE (N.Z.)
COOK ISLANDS (N.Z.)
ÎLES TUAMOTU
FRENCH POLYNESIA
P O L Y N E S I A
Arequipa
LA PAZ
BOLIVIA
Sucre
Goiânia
BRASÍLIA
Belo Horizonte
SAINT HELENA (U.K.)
PARAGUAY
SÃO PAULO
RIO DE JANEIRO
Santos
Curitiba
Asunción
Antofagasta
Tropic of Capricorn
PITCAIRN (U.K.)
ISLA DE PASCUA EASTER ISLAND (Chile)
ISLA SAN AMBROSIO (Chile)
CHILE
Co. Aconcagua 6959
Córdoba
Porto Alegre
International Date Line
Valparaíso
SANTIAGO
Rosario
URUGUAY
BUENOS AIRES
MONTEVIDEO
ARCHIPIÉLAGO JUAN FERNÁNDEZ (Chile)
ARGENTINA
Concepción
Mar del Plata
Bahía Blanca
P A C I F I C
O C E A N
CHATHAM ISLANDS (N.Z.)
FALKLAND ISLANDS (U.K.)
Punta Arenas
CABO DE HORNOS CAPE HORN
SOUTH GEORGIA (U.K.)
Drake Passage
SOUTH ORKNEY ISLANDS (U.K.)
Antarctic Circle
ANTARCTIC PENINSULA
Bellingshausen Sea
Weddell Sea
Ross Sea
ROSS ICE SHELF
MARIE BYRD LAND
Vinson Massif 4897
A N T A R
180° 165° 150° 135° 120° 105° 90° 75° 60° 45° 30° 15° 0°
90° 75° 60° 45° 30° 15° 0° 15° 30° 45° 60° 75° 90°

ARCTIC OCEAN

NOVOSIBIRSKIJE
OSTROVA

Barents
Sea

VALBARD
(Nor.)

Hammerfest

NOVAJA
ZEML'A

ZEML'A FRANCA-IOSIFA

Karskoje
more

Dikson

Chatanga

Tiksi

more Laptevych

Murmansk

NORWAY

Narvik

SWEDEN

FINLAND

Vorkuta

Salechard

Noril'sk

Igarka

Verchojansk

Arctic Circle

Anadyr'

Bergen

Oslo

HELSINKI

Lapland

Archangel'sk

Ob'

Jenisej

Lena

Jakutsk

Magadan

Bering Sea

KØBENHAVN

STOCKHOLM

EST.

SANKT-PETERBURG
ST. PETERSBURG

LAT.

Niżnij Novgorod

Perm'

Jekaterinburg

Čel'abinsk

Omsk

Novosibirsk

Krasnojarsk

Irkutsk

Čita

Nikolajevsk

Ochotsk

Sea of
Okhotsk

Petropavlovsk-
Kamcatskij

ALEUTIAN IS.
(U.S.)

BERLIN

GERMANY

POLAND

BELARUS

MOSKVA

RUSSIA

Bonn

WARSZAWA

KYYIV

Volgograd

Samara

Karaganda

Ulaanbaatar

Chabarovsk

OSTROV
SACHALIN

KURIL'SKIJE
OSTROVA

CZECH
REP.

WIEN

UKRAINE

KAZAKHSTAN

ALTAI

MONGOLIA

Harbin

Vladivostok

Sapporo

JAPAN

SWITZ.

ALPS

HUNG.

BUDAPEST

MOLD.

Astracan'

gora El'brus

ALMATY

URÜMQI

TIEN
SHAN

GOBI

Hohhot

BEIJING
PEKING

Shenyang

N. KOREA

Dalian

PYONGYANG

Sendai

HONSHŪ

TOKYO

ÖSAKA

Milano

ROMA

ITALY

ROM.

BEOGRAD

BUL.

SOFIJA

Black Sea

AZER.

BAKI

UZBEKISTAN

TASKENT

KYRG.

TAJIK.

Shache

CHINA

Lanzhou

Tianjin

Qingdao

Xi'an

SOUL

S. KOREA

Pusan

Fukuoka

Napoli

ALB.

GREECE

ATHINAI

ISTANBUL

ANKARA

TURKEY

TURKMENISTAN

KABUL

Islāmābād

Rāwalpindi

Lhasa

Chengdu

Nanjing

Wuhan

SHANGHAI

NANSEI-
SHOTO

OGASAWARA-GUNTO
(Japan)

PACIFIC

TARĀBULUS

TRIPOLI

SYRIA

LEB.

TEHRĀN

BAGHDĀD

IRAN

Eşfahān

AFGHANISTAN

Lahore

Chongqing

Changsha

Fuzhou

T'AIPEI

TAIWAN

OCEAN

LIBYA

EGYPT

JORDAN

IRAQ

KUWAIT

QATAR

UNITED
ARAB
EMIRATES

Karāchi

PAKISTAN

DELHI

New Delhi

NEPAL

Mount
Everest
8848

BNGL.

DHAKA

Kunming

Guangzhou

Xianggang
(Hong Kong)

Philippine
Sea

NORTHERN
MARIANA
ISLANDS
(U.S.)

WAKE
ISLAND
(U.S.)

AR-RIYĀD

SAUDI

ARABIA

Aswan

AL-QĀHIRAH
CAIRO

AL-ISKANDARĪYAH
Alexandria

Masqat

OMAN

Ahmadābād

MUMBAI
(BOMBAY)

INDIA

Hyderābād

CALCUTTA

MYANMAR

Bay of
Bengal

YANGON

Tropic of Cancer

South
China
Sea

MANILA

PHILIPPINES

GUAM (U.S.)

MICRONESIA

MARSHALL
ISLANDS

SAHARA

AFRICA

NIGER

CHAD

SUDAN

AL-KHARTŪM

ERITREA

Şan'ā'

YEMEN

SUQUTRÁ
(Yem.)

Arabian
Sea

Bangalore

Chennai

ANDAMAN
ISLANDS
(India)

KRUNG THEP
BANGKOK

THAILAND

VIETNAM

GAMB.

Phnom Penh

FEDERATED STATES
OF MICRONESIA

PALAU

NIGERIA

ABUJA

CEN.
AFR. REP.

DJIBOUTI

Adan

Djibouti

GEES GWARDAFUY

Kochi

SRI LANKA

COLOMBO

NICOBAR
ISLANDS
(India)

Thanh Pho
Ho Chi Minh

Davao

BRUNEI

MALAYSIA

KUALA LUMPUR

SINGAPORE

NAURU

KIRIBATI

LAGOS

rto-Novo

CAMEROON

Douala

Yaoundé

Bangui

UATORIAL
GUINEA

Libreville

GABON

Brazzaville

KINSHASA

DEM. REP.
OF THE
CONGO

UGANDA

KAMPALA

Lake
Victoria

KENYA

NAIROBI

RWANDA

BURUNDI

Bujumbura

Lake
Tanganyika

MALDIVES

BRITISH
INDIAN OCEAN
TERRITORY

SEYCHELLES

Equator

Medan

SUMATERA

JAKARTA

JAWA

Palembang

Banjarmasin

BORNEO

SULAWESI

Ujungpandang

Surabaya

INDONESIA

TIMOR

Mount Wilhelm
4509

NEW
GUINEA

PAPUA
NEW GUINEA

Pt. Moresby

SOLOMON
ISLANDS

MELANESIA

TUVALU

Lubumbashi

ANGOLA

LUANDA

Lobito

ZAMBIA

Lusaka

TANZANIA

DODOMA

Mombasa

Zanzibar

DAR ES SALAAM

Muqdisho

SOMALIA

ETHIOPIA

ADIS ABEBA

Redsea

INDIAN

OCEAN

COCOS
ISLANDS
(Aust.)

CHRISTMAS ISLAND
(Aust.)

Darwin

Gulf of
Carpentaria

CAPE YORK

Cairns

Coral
Sea

VANUATU

NEW
CALEDONIA
(Fr.)

Nouméa

FIJI

Suva

Windhoek

NAMIBIA

Walvis Bay

BOTSWANA

Gaborone

ZIMBABWE

HARARE

Lilongwe

Mozambique Channel

ANTANANARIVO

MADAGASCAR

MAURITIUS

RÉUNION
(Fr.)

Tropic of Capricorn

Alice Springs

AUSTRALIA

Rockhampton

Brisbane

NORFOLK
ISLAND
(Aust.)

PRETORIA

MAPUTO

SWAZILAND

Johannesburg

LESOTHO

SOUTH
AFRICA

CAPE TOWN

CAPE AGULHAS

Port Elizabeth

Durban

MOZAMBIQUE

ÍLES KERGUÉLEN
(Fr.)

Perth

Adelaide

Melbourne

Mount Kosciusko
2228

Canberra

Sydney

Tasman Sea

NORTH ISLAND

Auckland

NEW
ZEALAND

Wellington

TASMANIA

Hobart

SOUTH
ISLAND

Christchurch

SOUTHERN

OCEAN

Antarctic Circle

ENDERBY LAND

WILKES LAND

Kilometers

Statute Miles

One centimeter represents 750 kilometers.
One inch represents approximately 1200 miles.

Robinson Projection

Scale 1:75,000,000

ARCTIC OCEAN
Beaufort Sea
Chukchi Sea
RUSSIA
Bering Sea
ALEUTIAN BASIN
ALEUTIAN TRENCH
UNITED STATES
ALASKA RANGE
Mount McKinley 6194
Mount Logan 5959
Gulf of Alaska
Arctic Circle
BROOKS RANGE
MACKENZIE MOUNTAINS
Great Bear Lake
Great Slave Lake
Lake Athabasca
Hudson Bay
Baffin Bay
BAFFIN ISLAND
GRØNLAND
Gunnbjørn Fjeld 3700
Greenland Sea
ICELAND
LABRADOR BASIN
Labrador Sea
CANADA
NORTH AMERICA
ROCKY MOUNTAINS
Mount Waddington 3994
Lake Winnipeg
Lake Superior
Lake Michigan
Lake Huron
Lake Erie
Lake Ontario
Montréal
CHICAGO
NEW YORK
UNITED STATES
GREAT PLAINS
Pikes Peak 4301
GREAT BASIN
SIERRA NEVADA
Mount Whitney 4418
LOS ANGELES
APPALACHIAN MOUNTAINS
OZARK PLATEAU
Mississippi
Houston
Gulf of Mexico
MEXICO
SIERRA MADRE OCCIDENTAL
SIERRA MADRE ORIENTAL
Pico de Orizaba 5610
CIUDAD DE MÉXICO
CUBA
GREATER ANTILLES
WEST INDIES
Caribbean Sea
VENEZUELAN BASIN
NORTH AMERICAN BASIN
Sargasso Sea
BERMUDA RISE
NEWFOUNDLAND BASIN
AZORES PLATEAU
ATLANTIC OCEAN
MID-ATLANTIC RIDGE
CAPE VERDE BASIN
GUIANA BASIN
SIERRA LEONE BASIN
PACIFIC OCEAN
MENDOCINO FRACTURE ZONE
MURRAY FRACTURE ZONE
HAWAIIAN RIDGE
HAWAIIAN ISLANDS
Tropic of Cancer
CLARION FRACTURE ZONE
CLIPPERTON FRACTURE ZONE
MIDDLE AMERICA TRENCH
CENTRAL PACIFIC BASIN
CHRISTMAS RIDGE
POLYNESIA
Equator
VENEZUELA
COLOMBIA
COCOS RIDGE
ARCHIPIÉLAGO DE COLÓN GALAPAGOS ISLANDS
Chimborazo 6310
Amazon
SOUTH AMERICA
BRAZIL
SELVAS
Recife
Nevado Huascarán 6746
LIMA
BOLIVIA
Lago Titicaca
ANDES
PERU-CHILE TRENCH
SÃO PAULO
RIO DE JANEIRO
PARAGUAY
GRAN CHACO
Nevado Ojos del Salado 6893
Cerro Aconcagua 6959
SANTIAGO
BUENOS AIRES
URUGUAY
PAMPA
ARGENTINA
PATAGONIA
ARGENTINE BASIN
BRAZIL BASIN
Tropic of Capricorn
EAST PACIFIC RISE
CHILE RISE
SOUTHWEST PACIFIC BASIN
SOUTHEAST PACIFIC BASIN
TONGA TRENCH
KERMADEC TRENCH
International Date Line
FALKLAND ISLANDS
FALKLAND PLATEAU
TIERRA DEL FUEGO
Drake Passage
Scotia Sea
SOUTH SHETLAND ISLANDS
SOUTH ORKNEY ISLANDS
SOUTH SANDWICH TRENCH
Antarctic Circle
Bellingshausen Sea
Amundsen Sea
Weddell Sea
Ross Sea
ROSS ICE SHELF
MARIE BYRD LAND
Mount Sidley 4181
Vinson Massif 4897
RONNE ICE SHELF
FILCHNER ICE SHELF
COATS LAND
NEW SCHWABENLAND
180° 165° 150° 135° 120° 105° 90° 75° 60° 45° 30° 15° 0°

One centimeter represents 750 kilometers.
One inch represents approximately 1200 miles.
Robinson Projection
Scale 1:75,000,000

GREENLAND
Greenland Sea
ICELAND
Norwegian Sea
Barents Sea
Arctic Circle
NORWAY
SWEDEN
FINLAND
IRELAND
UNITED KINGDOM
North Sea
Baltic Sea
DENMARK
FRANCE
SPAIN
POLAND
GERMANY
UKRAINE
ROMANIA
BULGARIA
HUNGARY
Black Sea
Caspian Sea
URAL'SKIJE GORY
URAL MOUNTAINS
ZAPADNO-SIBIRSKAJA RAVNINA
SREDNESIBIRSKOJE PLOSKOGORJE
RUSSIA
SIBERIA
KAZAKHSTAN
MONGOLIA
GOBI
ALTAI
ASIA
CHINA
TIEN SHAN
KUNLUN SHAN
HIMALAYAS
Mount Everest
TURKEY
SYRIA
IRAQ
IRAN
AFGHANISTAN
PAKISTAN
INDIA
NEPAL
BHUTAN
SAUDI ARABIA
YEMEN
OMAN
MEDITERRANEAN SEA
LIBYA
EGYPT
SAHARA
Tropic of Cancer
SUDAN
ETHIOPIA
SOMALIA
KENYA
AFRICA
TANZANIA
ZAMBIA
ZIMBABWE
MOZAMBIQUE
BOTSWANA
SOUTH AFRICA
MADAGASCAR
Mozambique Channel
Red Sea
Gulf of Aden
ARABIAN SEA
Bay of Bengal
SRI LANKA
MALDIVES
MYANMAR
THAILAND
VIETNAM
MALAYSIA
INDONESIA
PHILIPPINES
South China Sea
East China Sea
Yellow Sea
Sea of Japan
JAPAN
Sea of Okhotsk
Philippine Sea
PAPUA NEW GUINEA
AUSTRALIA
GREAT SANDY DESERT
GREAT VICTORIA DESERT
Great Australian Bight
Arafura Sea
Timor Sea
Coral Sea
GREAT DIVIDING RANGE
INDIAN OCEAN
Tropic of Capricorn
MID-INDIAN RIDGE
SOUTHWEST INDIAN RIDGE
NINETY-EAST RIDGE
SOUTHEAST INDIAN RIDGE
SOUTH INDIAN BASIN
ATLANTIC-INDIAN RIDGE
ATLANTIC-INDIAN BASIN
CROZET BASIN
AGULHAS BASIN
MADAGASCAR BASIN
WHARTON BASIN
PERTH BASIN
SOUTH AUSTRALIAN BASIN
SOUTHERN OCEAN
Antarctic Circle
ANTARCTICA
ENDERBY LAND
AMERY ICE SHELF
WILKES LAND
AMERICAN HIGHLAND
PRINCESS MARTHA COAST

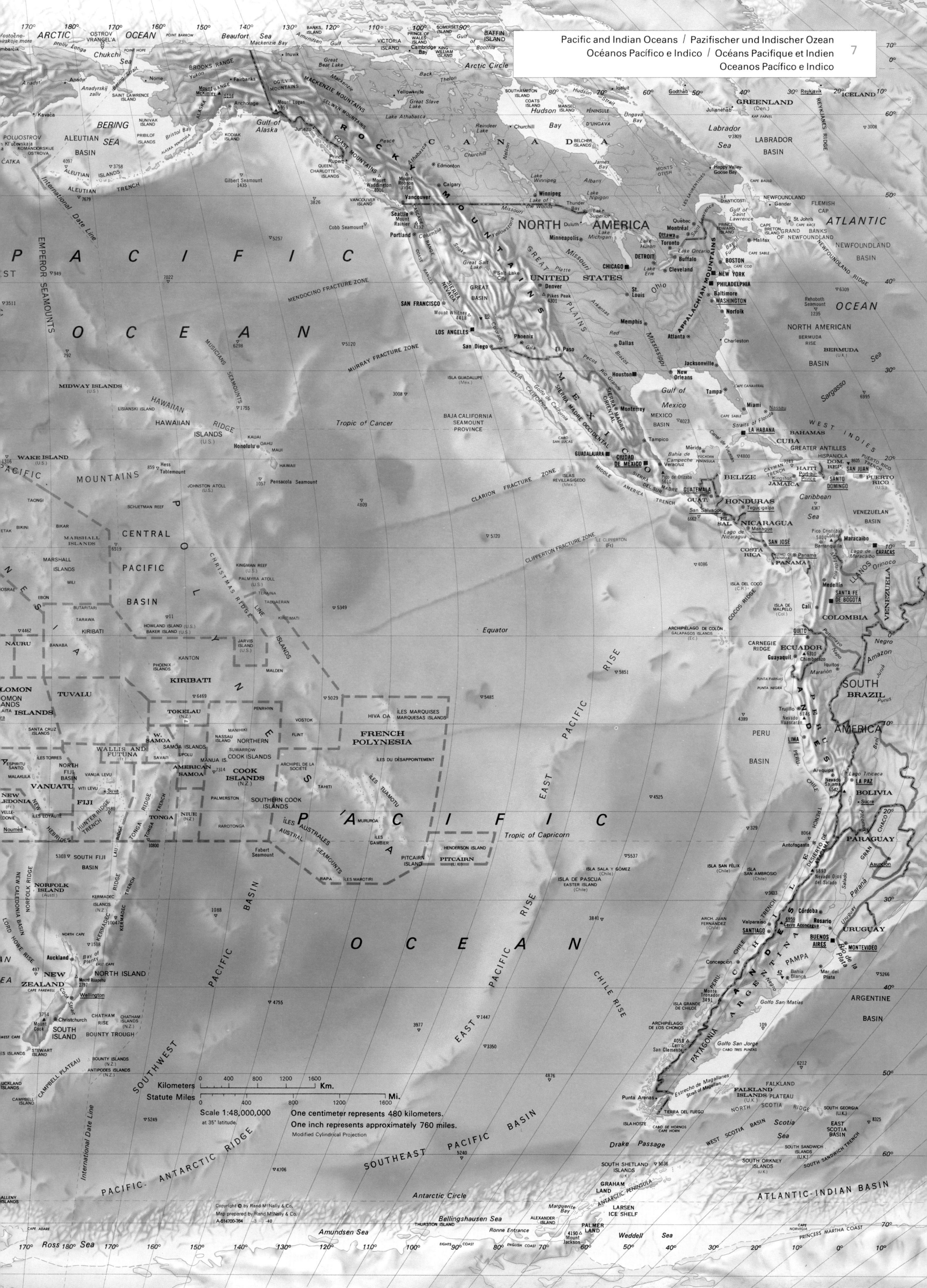

Pacific and Indian Oceans / Pazifischer und Indischer Ozean
Océanos Pacífico e Indico / Océans Pacifique et Indien
Oceanos Pacífico e Indico

7

Scale 1:48,000,000
One centimeter represents 480 kilometers.
at 35° latitude.
One inch represents approximately 760 miles.
Modified Cylindrical Projection

Atlantic Ocean / Atlantischer Ozean
Océano Atlántico / Océan Atlantique
Oceano Atlântico
NORTH AMERICA
CANADA
UNITED STATES
GREENLAND
ICELAND
EUROPE
AFRICA
SOUTH AMERICA
BRAZIL
ATLANTIC OCEAN
ATLANTIC OCEAN
PACIFIC OCEAN
INDIAN OCEAN
Caribbean Sea
Gulf of Mexico
Sargasso Sea
Mediterranean Sea
North Sea
Norwegian Sea
Barents Sea
Labrador Sea
Scotia Sea
Weddell Sea
Bellingshausen Sea
ANTARCTICA
MID-ATLANTIC RIDGE
NORTH AMERICAN BASIN
BRAZIL BASIN
ANGOLA BASIN
ARGENTINE BASIN
CAPE BASIN
AGULHAS BASIN
WEST EUROPEAN BASIN
LABRADOR BASIN
CAPE VERDE BASIN
GUIANA BASIN
SIERRA LEONE BASIN
GUINEA BASIN
Tropic of Cancer
Equator
Tropic of Capricorn
Arctic Circle
Antarctic Circle
Kilometers
Statute Miles
Scale 1:48,000,000
at 35° latitude
One centimeter represents 480 kilometers.
One inch represents approximately 760 miles.
Modified Cylindrical Projection
Copyright © by Rand McNally & Co.
Map prepared by Rand McNally & Co.
A-513700-764

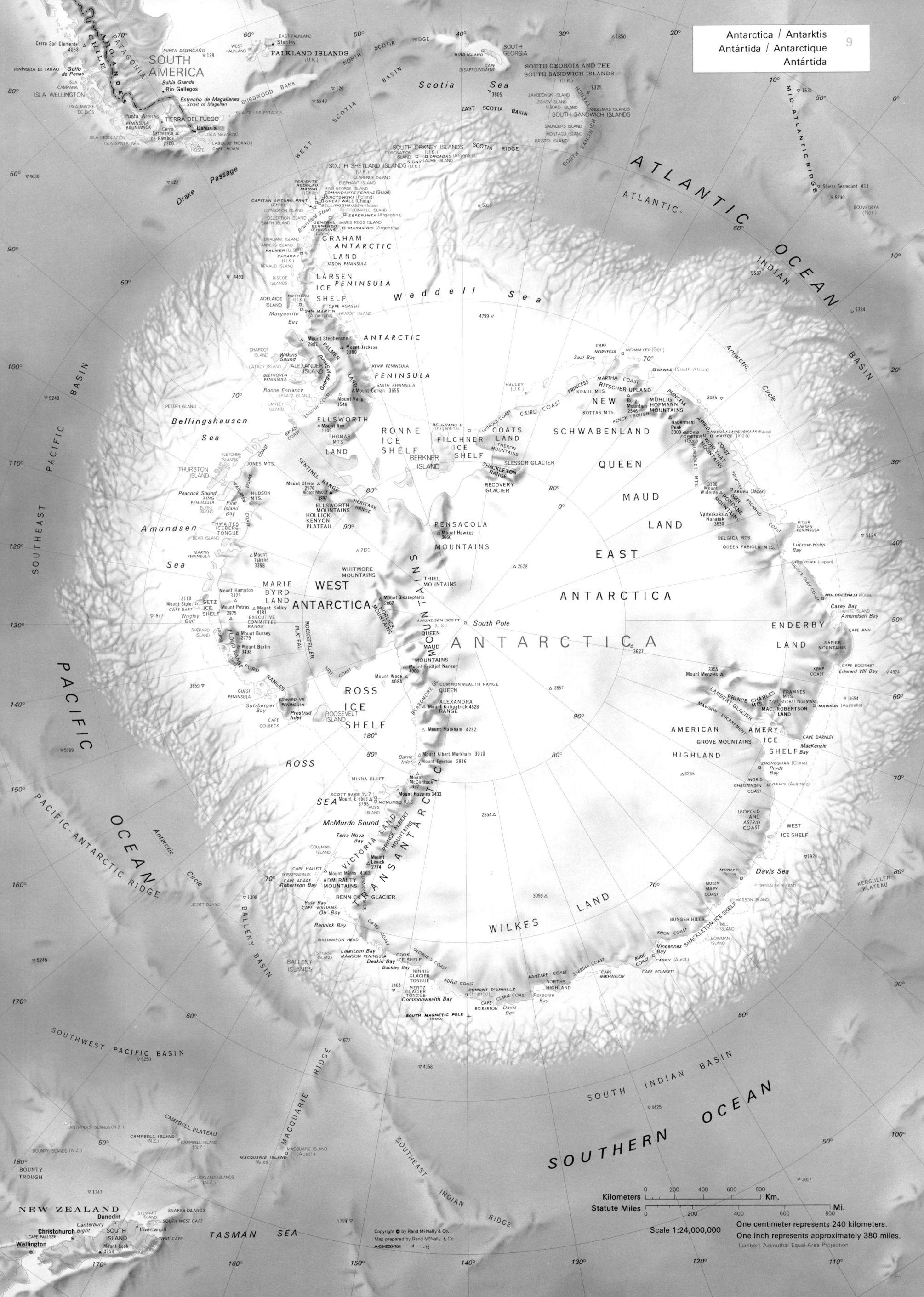

ATLANTIC OCEAN

ATLANTIC-

INDIAN

PACIFIC OCEAN

SOUTHEAST PACIFIC BASIN

PACIFIC-ANTARCTIC RIDGE

MID-ATLANTIC RIDGE

SOUTH AMERICA

Scotia Sea

FALKLAND ISLANDS

SOUTH GEORGIA AND THE SOUTH SANDWICH ISLANDS

SOUTH SANDWICH ISLANDS

SOUTH ORKNEY ISLANDS

SOUTH SHETLAND ISLANDS

Weddell Sea

GRAHAM ANTARCTIC LAND

LARSEN ICE SHELF

ANTARCTIC PENINSULA

ALEXANDER ISLAND

ELLSWORTH LAND

RONNE ICE SHELF

FILCHNER ICE SHELF

BERKNER ISLAND

COATS LAND

SCHWABENLAND

NEW

QUEEN MAUD LAND

EAST ANTARCTICA

ENDERBY LAND

AMERICAN HIGHLAND

AMERY ICE SHELF

MAC. ROBERTSON LAND

Bellingshausen Sea

Amundsen Sea

THURSTON ISLAND

PENSACOLA MOUNTAINS

WHITMORE MOUNTAINS

THIEL MOUNTAINS

South Pole

ANTARCTICA

MARIE BYRD LAND

WEST ANTARCTICA

QUEEN MAUD MOUNTAINS

ROSS ICE SHELF

ROSS SEA

ROOSEVELT ISLAND

TRANSANTARCTIC MOUNTAINS

VICTORIA LAND

ADMIRALTY MOUNTAINS

McMurdo Sound

WILKES LAND

Davis Sea

ENDERBY LAND

BALLENY ISLANDS

KERGUELEN PLATEAU

SOUTH INDIAN BASIN

SOUTHEAST INDIAN RIDGE

SOUTHERN OCEAN

NEW ZEALAND

TASMAN SEA

Christchurch

Wellington

Dunedin

Kilometers

Statute Miles

Scale 1:24,000,000

One centimeter represents 240 kilometers.
One inch represents approximately 380 miles.

Lambert Azimuthal Equal-Area Projection

Copyright © by Rand M\u0096Nally & Co.
Map prepared by Rand M\u0096Nally & Co.

ATLANTIC OCEAN
MID-ATLANTIC RIDGE
WEST EUROPEAN BASIN
AZORES-GIBRALTAR RIDGE
CANARY BASIN
ICELAND BASIN
IRMINGER BASIN
LABRADOR BASIN
Labrador Sea
REYKJANES RIDGE
ROCKALL RISE
NORWEGIAN BASIN
Norwegian Sea
LOFOTEN BASIN
GREENLAND BASIN
Greenland Sea
Barents Sea
Kara Sea
CANADA
GREENLAND (Den.)
Davis Strait
Denmark Strait
Arctic Circle
ICELAND
Reykjavík
FAEROE ISLANDS (Den.)
SPITSBERGEN SVALBARD (Nor.)
NOVAJA ZEMLJA
EUROPE
ASIA
RUSSIA
URAL'SKIJE GORY URAL MOUNTAINS
ZAPADNO-SIBIRSKAJA RAVNINA
KAZAKHSTAN
UZBEKISTAN
TURKMENISTAN
NORWAY
SWEDEN
FINLAND
DENMARK
UNITED KINGDOM
IRELAND
NETH.
BEL.
LUX.
GERMANY
POLAND
BELARUS
UKRAINE
EST.
LAT.
LITH.
CZECH REP.
SLOVAKIA
AUSTRIA
HUNGARY
SWITZ.
FRANCE
SPAIN
PORTUGAL
ANDORRA
ITALY
SLO.
CROATIA
BOSNIA AND HERZ.
YUGO.
MACE.
ALBANIA
GREECE
ROMANIA
MOLD.
BULGARIA
TURKEY
ASIA MINOR
GEORGIA
ARM.
AZER.
CAUCASUS
CYPRUS
NORTH CYPRUS
SYRIA
LEBANON
ISRAEL
JORDAN
IRAQ
IRAN
KUWAIT
BAHRAIN
QATAR
UNITED ARAB EMIRATES
OMAN
SAUDI ARABIA
ARABIAN PENINSULA
EGYPT
LIBYA
TUNISIA
ALGERIA
MOROCCO
WESTERN SAHARA
MAURITANIA
MALI
NIGER
SAHARA
CAPE VERDE
Mediterranean Sea
Black Sea
Caspian Sea
Aral Sea
Baltic Sea
North Sea
Adriatic Sea
Tyrrhenian Sea
Ionian Sea
Aegean Sea
Bay of Biscay
English Channel
Persian Gulf
Red Sea
Tropic of Cancer
ATLAS MOUNTAINS
ALPS
CARPATHIAN MOUNTAINS
PYRENEES
APPENNINO
MOSKVA
SANKT-PETERBURG
HELSINKI
STOCKHOLM
Oslo
KØBENHAVN
BERLIN
WARSZAWA
PRAHA
WIEN
BUDAPEST
BUCURESTI
SOFIJA
BEOGRAD
Tirane
ATHINAI
ISTANBUL
ANKARA
KYYIV
MINSK
Vilnius
RIGA
Tallinn
LONDON
DUBLIN
PARIS
BRUXELLES
AMSTERDAM
MADRID
LISBOA
BARCELONA
ROMA
MILANO
RABAT
CASABLANCA
EL DJAZAÏR ALGIERS
TUNIS
TARÂBULUS TRIPOLI
AL-QÂHIRAH CAIRO
AL-ISKANDARIYAH ALEXANDRIA
BAYRUT
DIMASHQ
'AMMAN
Yerushalayim Jerusalem
BAGHDÂD
TEHRÂN
BAKI BAKU
TBILISI
JEREVAN
AR-RIYÂD
AL-KUWAYT
Nouakchott

Europe and Africa / Europa und Afrika
Europa y África / Europe et Afrique
Europa e África

11

One centimeter represents 240 kilometers.
One inch represents approximately 380 miles.

Scale 1:24,000,000
Lambert Azimuthal Equal-Area Projection

ARCTIC
OCEAN
North Pole
ATLANTIC
OCEAN
GREENLAND
Greenland Sea
Norwegian Sea
Barents Sea
Kara Sea
Laptev Sea
Chukchi Sea
Bering Sea
Sea of Okhotsk
Sea of Japan
Yellow Sea
EAST CHINA SEA
Caspian Sea
Black Sea
Aral Sea
Baltic Sea
North Sea
ICELAND
SVALBARD
ZEML'A FRANCA-IOSIFA
FRANZ JOSEF LAND
NOVAJA ZEML'A
SEVERNAJA ZEML'A
NOVOSIBIRSKIJE OSTROVA
OSTROV VRANGEL'A
UNITED STATES
ALEUTIAN ISLANDS
KURIL'SKIJE OSTROVA
KURIL ISLANDS
OSTROV SACHALIN
SAKHALIN
HOKKAIDO
HONSHU
KYUSHU
UNITED KINGDOM
IRELAND
NORWAY
SWEDEN
FINLAND
DENMARK
NETHERLANDS
BELGIUM
GERMANY
POLAND
BELARUS
UKRAINE
ROMANIA
BULGARIA
HUNGARY
EUROPE
RUSSIA
SIBERIA
KAZAKHSTAN
UZBEKISTAN
TURKMENISTAN
KYRGYZSTAN
TAJIKISTAN
AFGHANISTAN
IRAN
IRAQ
SYRIA
TURKEY
ASIA MINOR
CAUCASUS
MONGOLIA
GOBI
ASIA
CHINA
NORTH KOREA
SOUTH KOREA
TIEN SHAN
ALTAI
KUNLUN SHAN
TARIM PENDI
PAMIR
HINDU KUSH
URAL'SKIJE GORY
URAL MOUNTAINS
ZAPADNO-SIBIRSKAJA RAVNINA
SREDNESIBIRSKOJE PLOSKOGORJE
CHREBET ČERSKOGO
DA HINGGAN LING
MOSKVA
SANKT-PETERBURG
LONDON
BERLIN
WARSZAWA
KYYIV
STOCKHOLM
HELSINKI
OSLO
KØBENHAVN
BUCUREŞTI
ISTANBUL
ANKARA
TEHRĀN
BAGHDĀD
BEIJING
SHANGHAI
SŎUL
P'YŎNGYANG
ULAANBAATAR
ALMATY
TAŠKENT
Novosibirsk
Omsk
Irkutsk
Jakutsk
Magadan
Vladivostok
Murmansk
Arctic Circle

AUSTRALIA

GIBSON DESERT

DARLING RANGE

Perth
PERTH BASIN

NORTH AUSTRALIAN BASIN

WHARTON BASIN

BROKEN RIDGE

CHRISTMAS ISLAND (Austl.)

COCOS ISLANDS (Austl.)

NINETYEAST RIDGE

I N D I A N   O C E A N

MID-INDIAN BASIN

INDIAN BASIN

MID-INDIAN RIDGE

CHAGOS LACCADIVE PLATEAU

CARLSBERG RIDGE

CHAGOS ARCHIPELAGO (Br.Ind.Oc.Terr.)

SOUTHWEST INDIAN RIDGE

RODRIGUES (Maur.)

MAURITIUS

REUNION (Fr.)

MASCARENE PLATEAU

MASCARENE BASIN

SEYCHELLES

SEYCHELLES BANK

NAZARETH BANK

CARGADOS CARAJOS SHOALS (Maur.)

SAYA DE MALHA BANK

MADAGASCAR

ANTANANARIVO

Betsiboka

Tropic of Capricorn

PHILIPPINES

MANILA
Quezon City

LUZON

SIERRA MADRE

Philippine Sea

Luzon Strait

TAIWAN Strait

GUANGZHOU (CANTON)
XIANGGANG (HONG KONG)
Macau

HAINAN DAO

SOUTH CHINA SEA

Hai Phong
Gulf of Tonkin
HA NOI

VIETNAM
LAOS
Vientiane
THAILAND
Mekong
CAMBODIA
KRUNG THEP (BANGKOK)
Phnum Penh
THANH PHO HO CHI MINH (SAIGON)

Gulf of Thailand

INDOCHINA

MYANMAR (BURMA)
Mandalay
YANGON (RANGOON)
Mawlamyine

Gulf of Martaban

Andaman Sea

ANDAMAN ISLANDS (India)

NICOBAR ISLANDS (India)

COCO ISLANDS

MALAYSIA
BRUNEI
KALIMANTAN
BORNEO
Banjarmasin
Kuching

MALAY PENINSULA
MALAYSIA
KUALA LUMPUR
SINGAPORE
George Town
Medan
Padang
SUMATERA

SUNDA SHELF

GREATER SUNDA ISLANDS

JAKARTA
Bandung
Palembang
SURABAYA
JAWA (JAVA)

JAVA TRENCH

Selat Sunda

Celebes Sea

SULAWESI (CELEBES)
Ujungpandang

NUSA TENGGARA

Sulu Sea

PHILIPPINE TRENCH

China
Guiyang
Kunming
Nanning
Liuzhou

NEPAL
Kathmandu
BHUTAN
Lhasa

HIMALAYAS

BANGLADESH
DHAKA
Chittagong

CALCUTTA
Patna
Ganges
Varanasi
Kanpur
DELHI
New Delhi

I N D I A

Nagpur
AHMADABAD
Pune
MUMBAI (BOMBAY)
Hyderabad
BANGALORE
Kochi
CHENNAI (MADRAS)
Hyderabad

SRI LANKA
COLOMBO
CAPE COMORIN

Gulf of Mannar
Palk Strait

Bay of Bengal

WESTERN GHATS
EASTERN GHATS

MALABAR COAST
COROMANDEL COAST

LACCADIVE SEA
Lakshadweep

LAKSHADWEEP (India)

MALDIVES
Male

Eight Degree Channel

Ten Degree Channel

PAKISTAN
KARACHI
Hyderabad
KIRTHAR RANGE

Gulf of Kutch
Gulf of Khambhat

ARABIAN SEA

ARABIAN BASIN

OMAN
Gulf of Oman

UNITED ARAB EMIRATES
QATAR
Gulf Persian

AR-RUB-AL-KHALI

ARABIAN PENINSULA

YEMEN
San'a
Gulf of Aden

ASIR

Red Sea
Bab el Mandeb

SOMALIA
Mogadishu

ETHIOPIA

DJIBOUTI

SOMALI BASIN

OWEN FRACTURE ZONE

Equator

Tropic of Cancer

Scale 1:24,000,000
One centimeter represents 240 kilometers.
One inch represents approximately 380 miles.
Lambert Azimuthal Equal-Area Projection

Statute Miles
Kilometers
Km.
Mi.

Copyright © by Rand McNally & Co.
Map prepared by Rand McNally & Co.
A-551200-784

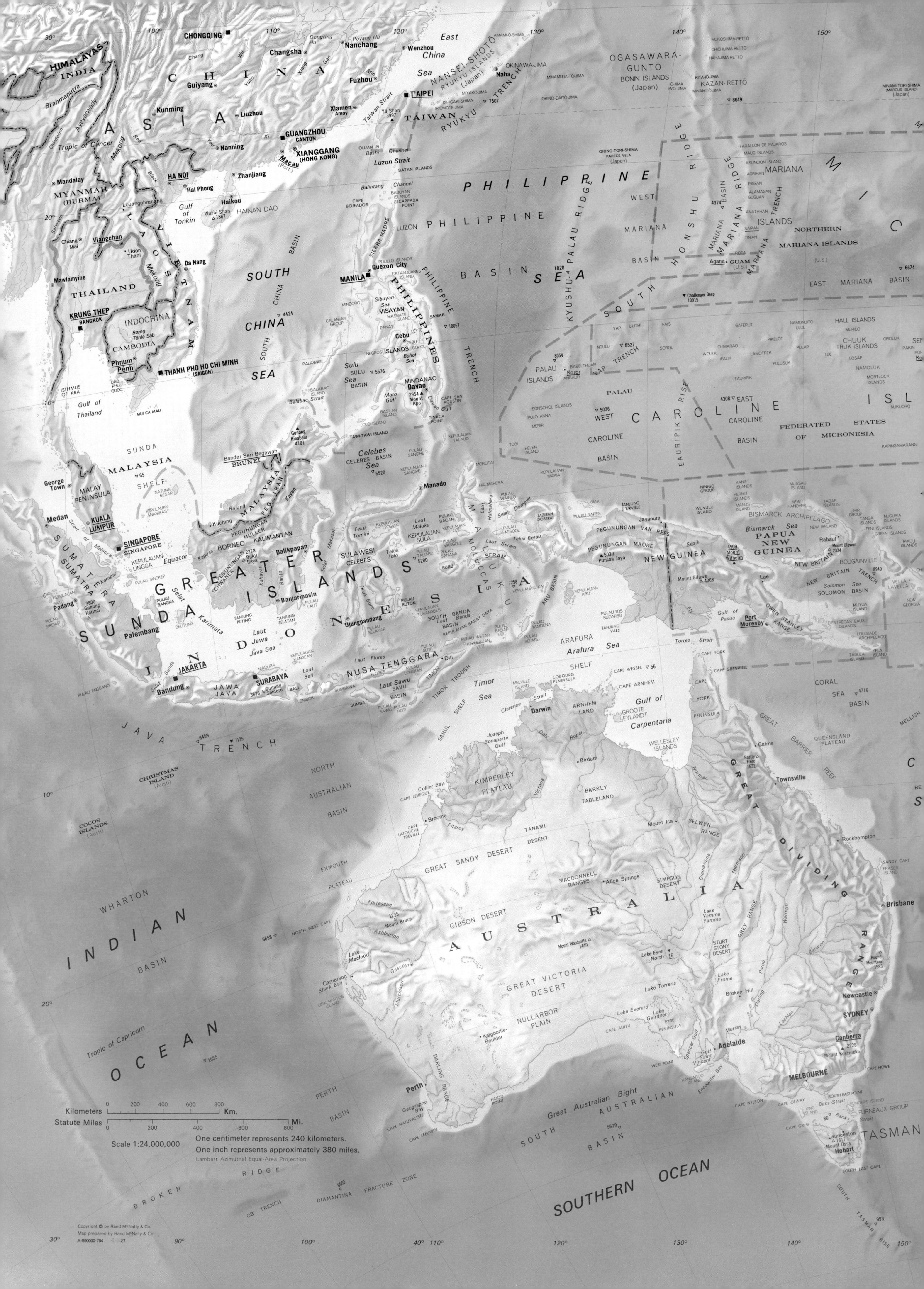
A S I A
C H I N A
CHONGQING
Changsha
Nanchang
Wenzhou
East China Sea
Guiyang
Fuzhou
Kunming
Liuzhou
Xiamen Amoy
T'AIPEI
TAIWAN
GUANGZHOU CANTON
XIANGGANG (HONG KONG)
Macau (Port.)
Nanning
Zhanjiang
HA NOI
Hai Phong
Haikou
HAINAN DAO
Gulf of Tonkin
HIMALAYAS
INDIA
Brahmaputra
Tropic of Cancer
Mekong
Mandalay
MYANMAR (BURMA)
LAOS
Viangchan
VIETNAM
Da Nang
Mawlamyine
THAILAND
KRUNG THEP BANGKOK
INDOCHINA
CAMBODIA
Phnum Pénh
THANH PHO HO CHI MINH (SAIGON)
Gulf of Thailand
SOUTH CHINA SEA
Luzon Strait
PHILIPPINE SEA
MANILA
Quezon City
PHILIPPINES
Cebu
MINDANAO
Davao
Sulu Sea
Celebes Sea
NANSEI-SHOTŌ RYUKYU ISLANDS (Japan)
Naha
OGASAWARA-GUNTŌ BONIN ISLANDS (Japan)
MARIANA ISLANDS
NORTHERN MARIANA ISLANDS
Agana
GUAM (U.S.)
Challenger Deep 10915
CAROLINE ISLANDS
FEDERATED STATES OF MICRONESIA
PALAU ISLANDS
Koror
MALAYSIA
Bandar Seri Begawan
BRUNEI
George Town
MALAY PENINSULA
KUALA LUMPUR
Medan
SINGAPORE
SUMATRA
BORNEO
KALIMANTAN
SULAWESI CELEBES
Balikpapan
Banjarmasin
Ujungpandang
Manado
MOLUCCAS
SERAM
GREATER SUNDA ISLANDS
INDONESIA
Padang
Palembang
JAKARTA
Bandung
JAWA JAVA
SURABAYA
Java Sea
NUSA TENGGARA
Dili
Timor Sea
NEW GUINEA
Jayapura
PAPUA NEW GUINEA
Port Moresby
BISMARCK ARCHIPELAGO
Rabaul
Solomon Sea
Arafura Sea
Torres Strait
Gulf of Carpentaria
Darwin
ARNHEM LAND
KIMBERLEY PLATEAU
Broome
GREAT SANDY DESERT
TANAMI DESERT
BARKLY TABLELAND
Mount Isa
Alice Springs
MACDONNELL RANGES
SIMPSON DESERT
GIBSON DESERT
A U S T R A L I A
GREAT VICTORIA DESERT
NULLARBOR PLAIN
Lake Eyre North
Lake Torrens
Kalgoorlie-Boulder
Perth
Adelaide
MELBOURNE
Canberra
SYDNEY
Newcastle
Brisbane
Rockhampton
Townsville
Cairns
GREAT DIVIDING RANGE
GREAT BARRIER REEF
CORAL SEA BASIN
Hobart
TASMAN
Great Australian Bight
SOUTHERN OCEAN
INDIAN OCEAN
JAVA TRENCH
CHRISTMAS ISLAND (Austl.)
COCOS ISLANDS (Austl.)
WHARTON BASIN
Tropic of Capricorn
Kilometers 0 200 400 600 800 Km.
Statute Miles 0 200 400 600 800 Mi.
Scale 1:24,000,000
One centimeter represents 240 kilometers.
One inch represents approximately 380 miles.
Lambert Azimuthal Equal-Area Projection
Copyright © by Rand McNally & Co.
Map prepared by Rand McNally & Co.

Australia and Oceania / Australien und Ozeanien
Australia y Oceanía / Australie et Océanie
Austrália e Oceania
15

170°   180°   170°   160°   150°
KURE   MIDWAY   PEARL AND   H A W A I I A N   ZONE
ATOLL   ISLANDS HERMES ATOLL   Tropic of Cancer
Guadalupe   (U.S.)   LISIANSKI
Seamount   ISLAND   GARDNER
                   LAYSAN   PINNACLES
                   ISLAND   (U.S.)
             Paul   FRENCH   NIHOA
             Seamount   FRIGATE   KAUAI   ISLANDS   FRACTURE
                         SHOALS   NECKER   RIDGE OAHU   MOLOKAI
   ▽ 6890   ▽ 1477   NECKER RIDGE   Honolulu LANAI MOLOKAI
                         ISLAND   UNITED   KA LAE MAUI
                Horizon   STATES   Swordfish HAWAII
▽ 1316   Tablemount   Seamount Mauna Kea Hilo
WAKE ISLAND   M O U N T A I N S   Hess   4205 HAWAII
   (U.S)   Tablemount Karin Seamount KA LAE Loihi
P A C I F I C   ▽ 859   Pensacola Seamount
                JOHNSTON ATOLL   Seamount 969
MARSHALL   Cape   (U.S.)   1057
ISLANDS   TAONG Johnson
         Tablemount   SCHJETMAN
MARSHALL   REEF
ISLANDS   4809
   BIKINI
ENEWETAK RONGELAP UTIRIK
  WOTHO UJAE AILUK   ▽ 6519 C E N T R A L   P A C I F I C
UAE LAE LIB KWAJALEIN WOTJE
RALIK NAMU MALOELAP
RONGELAPALAP ARNO   P A C I F I C
PINGELAP JALUIT MILI
KOSRAE EBON   KINGMAN REEF
      BUTARITARI   B A S I N   (U.S.)
MELANESIAN   PALMYRA   TERAINA
                TARAWA   ATOLL
   ▽ 4462 ABEMAMA KIRIBATI   (U.S.) TABUAERAN
NAURU KURIA NONOUTI   HOWLAND ISLAND (U.S.) KIRITIMATI
      BANABA BERU NIKUNAU BAKER ISLAND (U.S.)   ▽ 5349
BASIN   TABITEUEA ONOTOA WINSLOW
            TAMANA   REEF   JARVIS   Equator
   ▽ 1737 ARORAE   ISLAND   0°
                    KIRIBATI PHOENIX KANTON (U.S.)
SOLOMON   NANUMEA   ISLANDS ENDERBURY
ISLANDS TUVALU NUTAO NIKUMARORO BIRNIE RAWAKI
         NANUMANGA ISLANDS ORONA MANRA
ISLANDS   NIU   VAITUPU   MALDEN
      NUKUFETAL FUNAFUTI   STARBUCK
SANTA CRUZ NUKULAELAE   ▽ 6469   ▽ 5029
ISLANDS   NIULAKITA TOKELAU NUKUNONU   PENRHYN Merlin
VANIKOLO   (N.Z.) FAKAOFO   Seamount
SANTA CRUZ ROTUMA Combe Bank   ATAFU   NASSAU NORTHERN VOSTOK CAROLINE
BASIN 9175   ÎLES WALLIS SWAINS ISLAND COOK ISLANDS
ÎLES   Home Seamount ISLAND AMERICAN   MANIHIKI
TORRES NORTH Seamount WALLIS AND SAMOA SAMOA FLINT
VANUA LAVA FIJI   FUTUNA FUTUNA ISLANDS SUWARROW
ÎLES ▽ 1188 BANKS SANTA MARIA (Fr.) WESTERN Apia MANU'A ISLANDS 4846
ESPIRITU BASIN   ÎLE ALOFI SAMOA Pago ROSE MOTU-ONE BORA BORA
SANTO MAEWO   VANUA UPOLU Pago ISLAND MANUAE TAHAA MATAIVA ÎLES DU DÉSAPPOINTEMENT
VANUATU PENTECÔTE LEVU   TUTUILA SAMOA MAUPIHAA RAIATEA KAUKURA ÎLE TIKEI
MALAKULA AMBRYM FIJI ISLANDS TAVEUNI TAFAHI BASIN ▽ 7314 AITUTAKI SOCIETY RAIATEA FAKARAVA TUAMOTU
NEW   ÉFATÉ   VITI LAU   COOK ISLANDS MANUAE RIDGE TAHITI ANAA
Port Vila LEVU Koro GROUP TOKU ISLANDS (N.Z.) MITIARO ARCHIPEL DE LA SOCIÉTÉ HIKUERU RAVAHERE
HEBRIDES Sea   VAVA'U TONGA   TAKUTEA ATIU SOCIETY ISLANDS HAO
ERROMANGO KANDAVU ISLAND GROUP ISLANDS NIUE PALMERSTON AITUTAKI MAUKE MEHETIA NENGONENGO MANUHANGI
NEW TANNA FIJI ▽ 3580 ONO-LAU (N.Z.) SOUTHERN RAROTONGA MURUROA
CALEDONIA ÎLES LOYAUTÉ NEW LAU TONGATAPU COOK FRENCH HIKUERU VAHITAHI
(Fr.) NOUVELLE OUVÉA HEBRIDES RIDGE TONGATAPU TONGA ISLANDS MANGAIA ÎLES MARIA POLYNESIA
CALÉDONIE LIFOU Nuku'alofa ELA   ÎLES
Nouméa MARÉ ÎLE HUNTER HUNTER TONGA AUSTRALES
      TRENCH TONGA 10800   RIMATARA
   ▽ 5303 SOUTH LAU TRENCH   RURUTU ÎLES
NORFOLK FIJI RIDGE Osbourn   TUBUAI Tropic of AUSTRALES Capricorn
CALEDONIA BASIN   Seamount Fabert   RAIVAVAE
RIDGE NORFOLK RAOUL ISLAND RIDGE Seamount   A U S T R A L S E A M O U N T S RAPA
ISLAND   TRENCH   TEMATANGI
(Aust.) KERMADEC Currituck Seamount S O U T H W E S T ÎLES MAROTIRI
NORFOLK THREE KINGS IS. ISLANDS 10047 Seafox Seamount
CALEDONIA NORTH CAPE LOUISVILLE Louisville Seamount RAPA
LORD HOWE TAUROA KERMADEC RIDGE Burton Seamount P A C I F I C
ISLAND POINT ▽ 1518 Burton Seamount ▽ 1088
(Austl.) GREAT BARRIER ISLAND TRENCH
LORD HOWE RISE ▽ 8009 Auckland Bay of
T a s m a n NEW Plenty B A S I N
      New EAST CAPE
▽ 497 Plymouth NORTH ISLAND
CAPE EGMONT △ 2797 Napier Hawke Bay
S e a CAPE Ruapehu
▽ 5267 FAREWELL Wellington
ZEALAND Cook Strait CAPE PALLISER
M A N Mount Cook CHATHAM
   △ 3754 Christchurch RISE CHATHAM
SOUTH ISLAND Canterbury CHATHAM ISLANDS
S I N Bight ISLAND (N.Z.)
▽ 5267 WEST CAPE BOUNTY TROUGH
Invercargill ● Dunedin ▽ 4755
SOUTH WEST CAPE STEWART ISLAND BOUNTY
SNARES ISLANDS ISLANDS (N.Z.)
160° 170° CAMPBELL ANTIPODES 180° 170° 160° 150° 140° 130° 40°
PLATEAU ISLANDS (N.Z.)

ARCTIC
OCEAN
North Pole
ASIA
RUSSIA
SIBERIA
EUROPE
Sea of Okhotsk
OKHOTSK BASIN
POLUOSTROV KAMČATKA
BERING SEA
ALEUTIAN BASIN
ALEUTIAN TRENCH
ALEUTIAN ISLANDS
UNITED STATES
ALASKA
BROOKS RANGE
Beaufort Sea
Chukchi Sea
Vostočno-Sibirskoje more
East Siberian Sea
more Laptevych
Laptev Sea
Karskoje more
Kara Sea
Barents Sea
NOVOSIBIRSKIJE OSTROVA
SEVERNAJA ZEML'A
ZEML'A FRANCA-IOSIFA
FRANZ JOSEF LAND
NOVAJA ZEML'A
SVALBARD
SPITSBERGEN
Greenland Sea
GREENLAND BASIN
Norwegian Sea
NORWEGIAN BASIN
LOFOTEN BASIN
GREENLAND
(KALAALLIT NUNAAT)
ICELAND
Reykjavík
Denmark Strait
IRMINGER BASIN
REYKJANES RIDGE
ICELAND BASIN
ATLANTIC OCEAN
LABRADOR BASIN
Labrador Sea
Davis Strait
Baffin Bay
BAFFIN ISLAND
QUEEN ELIZABETH ISLANDS
ELLESMERE
VICTORIA ISLAND
BANKS ISLAND
Hudson Bay
CANADA
MACKENZIE MOUNTAINS
Arctic Circle
FINLAND
SWEDEN
NORWAY
Stockholm
Oslo
Helsinki
SANKT-PETERBURG
MOSKVA
Murmansk
Archangel'sk
Noril'sk
Jakutsk
Magadan
Anchorage
Chabarovsk
Petropavlovsk-Kamčatskij
North Sea
UNITED KINGDOM
Edinburgh
Glasgow
København
DENMARK

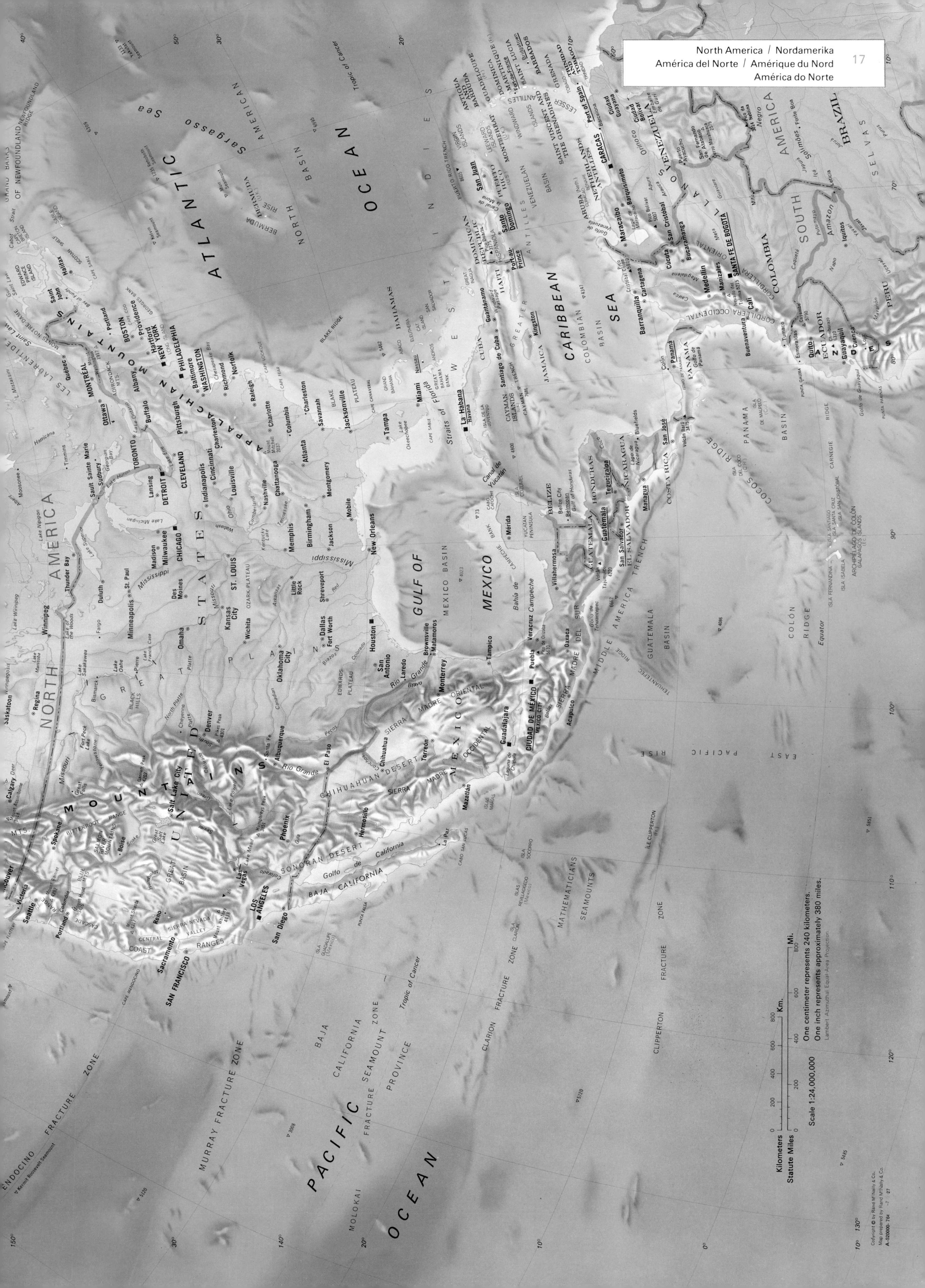
NORTH AMERICA
UNITED STATES
ATLANTIC OCEAN
PACIFIC OCEAN
GULF OF MEXICO
CARIBBEAN SEA
Sargasso Sea
APPALACHIAN MOUNTAINS
GREAT PLAINS
SIERRA MADRE ORIENTAL
SIERRA MADRE OCCIDENTAL
SIERRA MADRE DEL SUR
MEXICO
CUBA
JAMAICA
HAITI
BAHAMAS
HONDURAS
NICARAGUA
GUATEMALA
EL SALVADOR
COSTA RICA
PANAMA
BELIZE
COLOMBIA
VENEZUELA
ECUADOR
PERU
BRAZIL
SOUTH AMERICA
WASHINGTON
NEW YORK
PHILADELPHIA
BOSTON
CHICAGO
DETROIT
CLEVELAND
TORONTO
MONTRÉAL
Ottawa
ST. LOUIS
LOS ANGELES
SAN FRANCISCO
CIUDAD DE MÉXICO
La Habana
CARACAS
SANTA FE DE BOGOTÁ
Tropic of Cancer
Equator
Scale 1:24,000,000
One centimeter represents 240 kilometers.
One inch represents approximately 380 miles.
Lambert Azimuthal Equal-Area Projection
Kilometers
Statute Miles
Copyright © by Rand McNally & Co.
Map prepared by Rand McNally & Co.

NORTH AMERICA
UNITED STATES
ROCKY MTS.
APPALACHIAN MOUNTAINS
GREAT PLAINS
MEXICO
SIERRA MADRE ORIENTAL
SIERRA MADRE DEL SUR
GULF OF MEXICO
CARIBBEAN SEA
NORTH AMERICAN BASIN
ATLANTIC OCEAN
Sargasso Sea
MID-ATLANTIC RIDGE
CAPE VERDE BASIN
GUIANA BASIN
Tropic of Cancer
Equator
AZORES PLATEAU
BAHAMAS
CUBA
HAITI
DOMINICAN REPUBLIC
PUERTO RICO
JAMAICA
WEST INDIES
GREATER ANTILLES
LESSER ANTILLES
BELIZE
GUATEMALA
HONDURAS
EL SALVADOR
NICARAGUA
COSTA RICA
PANAMA
VENEZUELA
GUYANA
SURINAME
FRENCH GUIANA
COLOMBIA
ECUADOR
PERU
SOUTH AMERICA
BRAZIL
SELVAS
ANDES
LLANOS
MIDDLE AMERICA TRENCH
PERU-CHILE TRENCH
COCOS RIDGE
CARNEGIE RIDGE
COLÓN RIDGE
GUATEMALA BASIN
PANAMA BASIN
COLOMBIAN BASIN
VENEZUELAN BASIN
CHICAGO
NEW YORK
PHILADELPHIA
WASHINGTON
ST. LOUIS
Houston
New Orleans
Miami
CIUDAD DE MÉXICO
LA HABANA
SANTO DOMINGO
SAN JUAN
CARACAS
SANTA FE DE BOGOTÁ
QUITO
LIMA
Manaus
Belém
Amazon
Orinoco

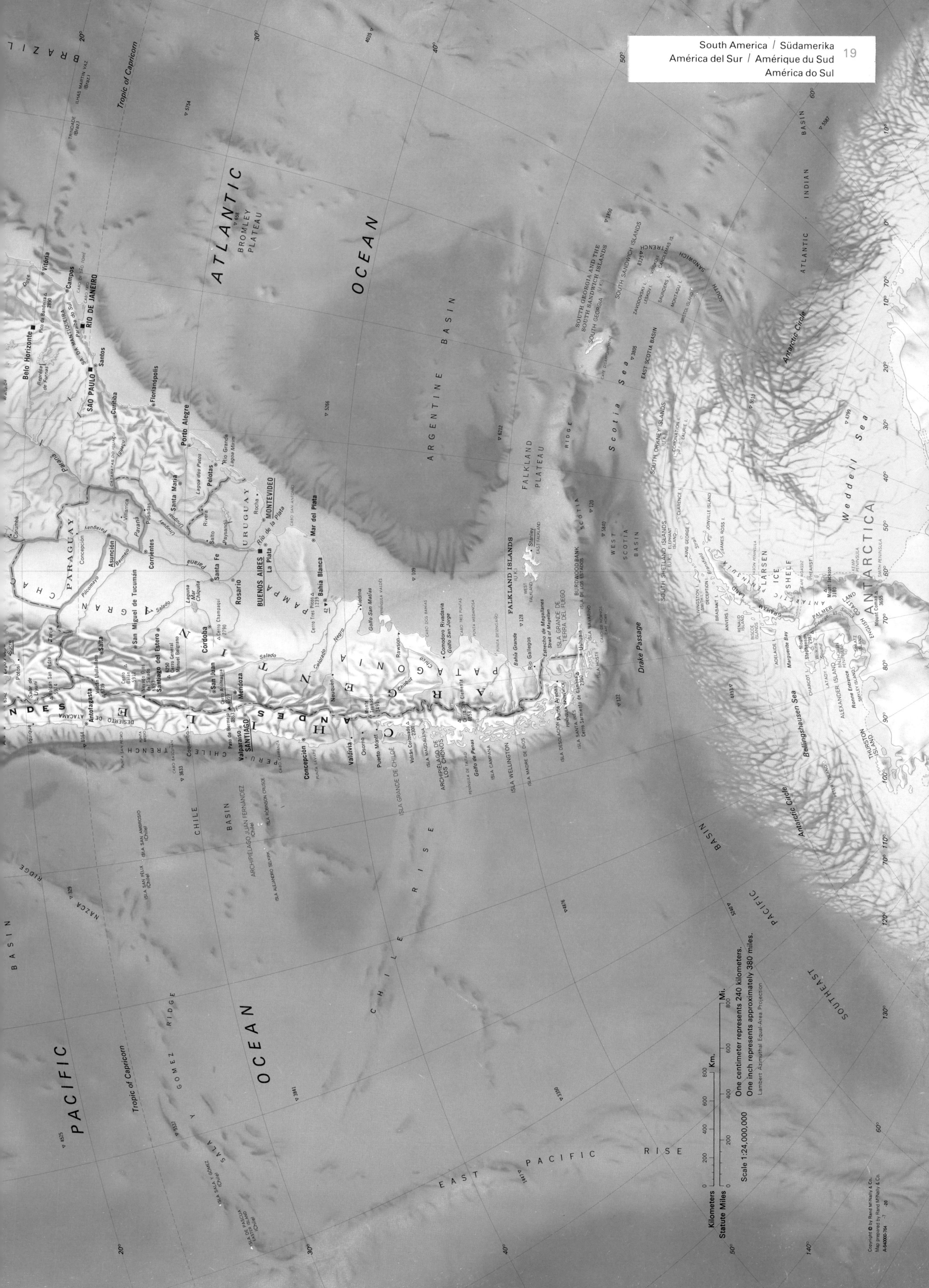

Kilometers

Statute Miles

Mi.

Km.

One centimeter represents 240 kilometers.
One inch represents approximately 380 miles.
Lambert Azimuthal Equal-Area Projection

Scale 1:24,000,000

Copyright © by Rand McNally & Co.
Map produced by Rand McNally & Co.
A-540000-764 -7 -26

THE REGIONAL MAPS consist of three basic series, each distinctive in style, but using common symbols to ensure ease of understanding (see Legend to Maps, pages x-xii). Every major land region, continent or subcontinent, is introduced by one or more maps at the scale of 1:12,000,000. There follow maps at 1:6,000,000 and 1:3,000,000 which cover the region in sections, in greater detail. Except for scale, the 1:6,000,000 and 1:3,000,000 maps are alike. Finally, selected areas of special importance in the region are shown at 1:1,000,000. Each scale is identified by a color bar, and a locater map with the same color may be found in the margin of the map page. A sample area at each of the scales, including centimeter-kilometer and inch-mile equivalents, appears on page 21.

The three basic series differ in content and emphasis. The 1:12,000,000 maps, which are primarily political, present an overview of each region. They show national boundaries and, in some cases, subordinate administrative subdivisions as well. These introductory maps make it possible to compare location, areal extent, and shape among the nations of the world. The distribution of cities, towns and metropolitan areas is shown in the context of broad physical configurations. A selection of the most important railways and highways also appears.

The 1:6,000,000 and 1:3,000,000 maps together constitute about half of the map pages and provide the basic reference coverage of the Atlas. They show sections of regions in great detail—in some cases individual countries (Japan and New Zealand), in others, parts of countries (central Mexico), in still others, larger regions (the Middle East). The more densely settled areas appear at the larger 1:3,000,000 scale, the remaining areas at 1:6,000,000. Maps at these two scales present political and cultural information against the background of a detailed physical portrait of the terrain, which is depicted by both shaded relief and a spectrum of altitude tints. Bathymetric tints are used to show offshore water depths. The transportation pattern shown includes major railways, two classes of roads, and airports that offer either international or jet service. The names and boundaries of political subdivisions are given for selected countries.

In the 1:1,000,000 series, strategic areas that are of special interest because of economic importance, dense settlement, or both, appear in even greater detail. This series is designed to show the pattern of cities, towns, roads, railways, bridges, airports, dams, reservoirs, and other interrelated features reflecting man's dense occupancy in these areas. The most important parks, places of historical interest, and recreational facilities are indicated. Three classes of highways and two classes of railways are shown, and major roads are named. All features are portrayed against a topographic background of shaded relief.

Inhabited places on the regional maps are classified in two distinct ways. Cities and towns of different *population size* are distinguished by the *size and shape of the symbol* that locates the place. The symbol reflects the population within the municipal or corporate limits, exclusive of any suburbs. In countries where the limits of a municipality include rural areas, the symbol represents only the urban or agglomerated population. The *relative political and economic importance* of a place which may be independent of the number of its inhabitants, is indicated by the *size of type* in which its name appears.

DIE REGIONALKARTEN bestehen aus drei Serien, die im Stil verschieden sind, der besseren Lesbarkeit halber aber gemeinsame Kartensignaturen verwenden (siehe "Zeichenerklärung" S. x-xii). Jede Grossregion, jeder Kontinent oder Subkontinent werden durch eine oder mehrere Karten im Massstab 1:12 Millionen eingeleitet. Es folgen sodann Karten in den Massstäben 1:6 und 1:3 Millionen, welche die Region in Teilen und grösseren Einzelheiten darstellen. Die Karten in 1:6 Millionen und 1:3 Millionen unterscheiden sich nur im Massstab. Schliesslich werden ausgewählte Gebiete von besonderer Bedeutung innerhalb der Region in 1:1 Million dargestellt. Jede Massstabsangabe ist durch ein Farbfeld gekennzeichnet, und ein Lagekärtchen in derselben Farbe erscheint am Rand der Kartenseite. Kartenausschnitte als Beispiele für jeden dieser Massstäbe mit Angabe des Verhältnisses Zentimeter zu Kilometer und Zoll ·zu Meilen sind auf Seite 21 aufgeführt.

Die drei Kartenreihen unterscheiden sich in Inhalt und Betonung. Die Karten im Massstab 1:12 Millionen, die vor allem politische Karten sind, geben einen Überblick über jede Region. Sie zeigen die Staatsgrenzen und in manchen Fällen auch die Grenzen von nachgeordneten Verwaltungseinheiten. Diese einführenden Karten ermöglichen einen Vergleich der Lage, Ausdehnung und Gestalt der Staaten der Erde. Die Verteilung der städtischen Ballungsgebiete, Grossstädte und Städte wird in ihrem Zusammenhang mit dem grossräumigen Formenschatz des Reliefs dargestellt. Gezeigt wird auch eine Auswahl der wichtigsten Eisenbahnlinien und Fernverkehrsstrassen.

Die Karten 1:6 Millionen und 1:3 Millionen machen zusammen mehr als die Hälfte der Kartenseiten aus und bilden den grundlegenden Teil des Atlas. Sie zeigen sehr inhaltsreiche Ausschnitte von Regionen—in einigen Fällen einzeln Länder (Japan und Neuseeland), in anderen Landesteile (Zentralmexiko) und wieder anderen Grossräume (Mittlerer Osten).

Die dichter besiedelten Gebiete sind im Massstab 1:3 Millionen dargestellt, die übrigen Gebiete im Massstab 1:6 Millionen. Die Karten in diesen beiden Massstäben liefern politische und kulturgeographische Informationen vor dem Hintergrund einer detaillierten Geländedarstellung, gekennzeichnet durch Reliefschummerung und eine Skala von Höhenschichten. Tiefenstufen werden verwendet, um die Meerestiefen jenseits der Küsten zu gliedern. Das abgebildete Verkehrsnetz umfasst wichtige Eisenbahnlinien, zwei Klassen von Strassen und Flughäfen, die entweder im internationalen Verkehr oder von Düsenflugzeugen angeflogen werden. Die Verwaltungsgliederung wird für eine grosse Zahl von Staaten gezeigt.

In der Kartenserie 1:1 Million sind mit noch zahlreicheren Einzelheiten zentrale Räume dargestellt, denen infolge ihrer wirtschaftlichen Bedeutung, dichten Besiedlung oder durch beide Faktoren bedingt besonderes Interesse zukommt. Diese Kartenserie wurde entwikelt, um die Verteilung der Grossstädte, Städte, Strassen, Eisenbahnen, Brücken, Flughäfen, Dämme, Stauseen und anderer Objekte zu zeigen, die Ausdruck sind für die dichte Besiedlung. Verzeichnet sind auch die wichtigsten Parks, Örtlichkeiten von historischem Interesse und Erholungsstätten. Drei Strassenklassen und zwei Klassen von Eisenbahnlinien werden unterschieden. Die Darstellung ist mit einer Reliefschummerung unterlegt.

Die Siedlungen auf den Regionalkarten sind auf zwei bestimmte Arten klassifiziert. Grossstädte und Städte unterschiedlicher *Einwohnerzahl* sind durch *Grösse und Form der Signatur* unterschieden, die den Ort lokalisiert. Die Signatur entspricht der Zahl der Einwohner innerhalb der Stadtgrenzen, schliesst also nicht eingemeindete Vororte aus. In Staaten, in denen ländliche Gebiete in die Stadtgemeinden einbezogen werden, entsprechen die Signaturen nur der in den zentralen Siedlungen ansässigen Bevölkerung. Die *relative politische und wirtschaftliche Bedeutung* eines Ortes, die von der Zahl seiner Einwohner unabhängig sein kann, ist ausgedrückt durch die *Schriftgrösse*, in welcher der Ortsname erscheint.

LOS MAPAS REGIONALES integran tres series básicas, cada una con su estilo propio; pero los símbolos usados son en todas los mismos para facilitar su comprensión (véanse las Leyendas para Mapas, páginas x-xii). Cada una de las grandes regiones, continentes o subcontinentes, se presenta a través de uno o varios mapas a la escala de 1:12 000 000. A continuación hay mapas a escalas de 1:6 000 000 y 1:3 000 000 que presentan la región correspondiente en secciones, con mayores detalles. Con excepción de su escala, los mapas de 1:6 000 000 y 1:3 000 000 tienen las mismas características. Por ultimo, aparecen a la escala de 1:1 000 000 áreas de cada región seleccionadas por su importancia. Cada escala se identifica por una barra de color, y un mapa-guía con el mismo color se presenta en el margen de la página de cada mapa. La página 21 ofrece como ejemplo un área-muestra a cada una de las escalas, incluyendo equivalentes en centímetros-kilómetros y pulgadas-millas.

Las tres series básicas son diferentes en contenido y en énfasis. Los mapas a escala de 1:12 000 000, fundamentalmente políticos, ofrecen una vista general de cada región. Indican las fronteras nacionales y, en algunos casos, las subdivisiones administrativas secundarias. Son mapas introductivos que permiten comparar la ubicación, extensión territorial y forma de las distintas naciones. La distribución de ciudades, poblados y áreas metropolitanas se aprecia en un contexto físico esbozado a grandes rasgos. Los detalles incluyen una selección de las vías férras y las carreteras más importantes.

Las series de mapas a 1:6 000 000 y a 1:3 000 000 ocupan entre ambas cerca de la mitad de los mapas del atlas y en ellas se concentra el material de consulta básico de la obra. Los mapas muestran secciones de regiones en gran detalle: en algunos casos países enteros, como Japón y Nueva Zelandia; en otros, partes de países, como el centro de México; y en otros, regiones mas extensas, como el Medio Oriente. Las áreas con mayor densidad de establecimientos humanos se presentan a una escala mayor, la de 1:3 000 000, y las demás a la escala de 1:6 000 000. En estas dos escalas los mapas contienen información política y cultural, sobre un fondo que ilustra en detalle la configuración física del terreno, utilizando sombreado para el relieve y toda una gama de tintes para indicar las altitudes. Un colorido batimétrico señala las variaciones de profundidad en el suelo marino. El esquema de las vías de comunicación incluye las principales vías férreas, dos clases de caminos, y los aeropuertos que ofrecen servicio nacional o internacional de jets. Las subdivisiones políticas secundarias se dan para una selección de varios países.

En la serie de mapas de 1:1 000 000, las áreas estratégicas de especial interés por su importancia económica, su densidad de población, o ambos factores combinados, aparecen aún con mayor detalle. Esta serie se diseñó para mostrar la distribución de ciudades, poblados, caminos, vías férreas, puentes, aeropuertos, presas, embalses y otros elementos similares, que reflejan la densidad de la ocupación humana. También se consignan los parques más importantes, los sitios de interés histórico, los campos de recreo, tres clases de carreteras, y dos de ferrocarriles, se da los nombres de los caminos más importantes. Todos estos elementos aparecen sobre un fondo topográfico de relieve sombreado.

En los mapas regionales se hacen dos clasificaciones distintas de los lugares habitados. Las ciudades y las poblaciones *de diferente densidad de habitantes* se distinguen por la *forma y tamaño del símbolo* que las localiza en el mapa. Este símbolo refleja el tamaño de la poblacióin dentro de sus límites municipales, sin tomar en cuenta los suburbios. En los países donde los límites de una municipalidad incluyen áreas rurales, el símbolo se limita a representar el conglomerado urbano de habitantes. La *importancia económica y política de un lugar*, la cual puede ser independiente del número de sus habitantes, se indica mediante el *tamaño del tipo de imprenta* en que aparece su nombre.

LES CARTES RÉGIONALES sont de trois types principaux, chacun d'un style différent mais avec des symboles communs pour faciliter la compréhension (voir la légende des cartes pages x-xii). Chaque grande région, continent ou subcontinent, est représentée par une ou plusieurs cartes à l'échelle de 1:12 000 000ᵉ. Viennent ensuite des cartes au 1:6 000 000ᵉ et au 1:3 000 000ᵉ qui couvrent la région par sections plus détaillées; hormis la différence d'échelle, ces cartes sont semblables. Enfin, des secteurs particulièrement importants sont représentés au 1:1 000 000ᵉ. À chaque échelle correspond une bande colorée et une carte repère de même couleur, dans la marge de chaque page. Un échantillon de cartes aux diverses échelles est représenté à droite. Chaque carte est accompagnée d'une double échelle graphique donnant les rapports centimètre/kilomètre et inch/mille correspondants.

Les trois catégories de cartes diffèrent par le contenu et par ce qu'elles mettent en relief. Les cartes au 1:12 000 000ᵉ, qui sont essentiellement politiques, donnent un aperçu général de chaque région. Elles indiquent les frontières nationales et, dans certains cas, les subdivisions administratives intérieures. Ces cartes d'introduction permettent de comparer la localisation, la superficie et la forme des pays du monde. La répartition des villes et des zones métropolitaines y apparaît dans le cadre des grandes régions naturelles. Les routes et les voies ferrées les plus importantes y figurent également.

Les cartes au 1:6 000 000ᵉ et au 1:3 000 000ᵉ forment la moitié de l'Atlas et en constituent la série cartographique essentielle. Elles représentent de façon plus détaillée une partie de pays (centre du Mexique), ou encore des régions plus vastes (Moyen-Orient) ou, parfois, des pays entiers (Japon, Nouvelle-Zélande). Les régions les plus peuplées sont représentées à plus grande échelle (1:3 000 000ᵉ) que les autres (1:6 000 000ᵉ). Ces cartes offrent des informations d'ordre politique et culturel sur un fond topographique précis où le relief est indiqué à la fois par un estompage et par des variations de couleur. Différentes teintes de bleu sont utilisées pour symboliser les profondeurs marines. Les réseaux de transport représentés comprennent les principales voies ferrées, deux catégories de routes et les aéroports internationaux ou desservis par les avions à réaction. Les subdivisions politiques d'un certain nombre de pays sont aussi tracées.

Dans la série de cartes au 1:1 000 000ᵉ, des régions très importantes, soit du fait de leur densité de population, soit du fait de leur rôle économique, sont représentées d'une manière encore plus détaillée. L'objectif de cette série de cartes est de montrer la répartition des villes, routes, voies ferrées, ponts, aéroports, barrages, lacs de barrages et autres données associées qui traduisent la densité de l'occupation humaine dans ces régions. Les parcs les plus importants, les sites historiques essentiels et les centres de loisirs sont indiqués. Toutes les informations se détachent sur un fond topographique où le relief apparaît en estompage.

Les centres urbains des cartes régionales sont classés de deux manières différentes. L'importance de la population des villes est indiquée par la dimension et la forme du symbole qui les situe sur la carte. Seule la population comprise dans les limites municipales est prise en considération; dans les pays où des espaces ruraux sont inclus dans les limites d'une municipalité, seule la population urbaine entre en ligne de compte. L'importance politique et économique relative d'une ville, qui n'est pas nécessairement liée au nombre d'habitants, est indiquée par la dimension des caractères qui composent son nom.

OS MAPAS REGIONAIS compreendem três séries básicas, cada uma em estilo diferente, mas que empregam os mesmos símbolos para facilitar sua compreensão (Ver as Legendas dos mapas, pág. x-xii). Os mapas de cada uma das principais regiões terrestres, continentes ou subcontinentes, são introduzidos por um ou mais mapas na escala de 1:12 000 000. Em seguida, vêm mapas, nas escalas de 1:6 000 000 e 1:3 000 000, que apresentam, com maiores detalhes, seções da região considerada. Exceto quanto à escala, os mapas de 1:6 000 000 e 1:3 000 000 têm as mesmas características. Finalmente, aparecem, na escala de 1:1 000 000, os mapas das áreas mais importantes da região considerada. A cada escala corresponde uma barra colorida e um indicador da mesma cor, que se encontra à margem da página de cada mapa. À página 21, acha-se um exemplo de cada escala, bem como a equivalência das relações centímetro/quilômetro e polegada/milha.

As três séries básicas de mapas são diferentes quanto ao conteúdo e à apresentação. Os mapas em escala de 1:12 000 000, que são essencialmente políticos, oferecem uma visão geral de cada região. Indicam as fronteiras nacionais e, em alguns casos, as subdivisões administrativas internas. Esses mapas servem de introdução e permitem avaliar e comparar a posição, superfície e forma dos países do Mundo. Neles está claramente indicada a distribuição das cidades e outros centros urbanos, bem como as principais características da configuração do solo. Encontra-se neles também uma seleção das ferrovias e rodovias mais importantes.

A série de mapas das escalas de 1:6 000 000 e de 1:3 000 000 constituem o principal material de referência do Atlas e representa cerca de metade do conjunto de mapas. Entre eles há mapas detalhados de parte de um país (centro do México), de um país inteiro (Japão e a Nova Zelândia) ou de uma região mais extensa (Oriente Médio). As áreas de maior densidade demográfica são apresentadas em escala maior, a de 1:3 000 000, e as demais, na escala de 1:6 000 000. Nessas duas escalas, os mapas fornecem informações de ordem política e cultural sobre um fundo que indica a configuração detalhada das particularidades físicas do solo, cujo relevo se destaca por contrastes de sombras e cores. Diversos matizes do azul traduzem o mapa batimétrico da profundidade ao largo das costas. Indicam também os aeroportos internacionais, as principais ferrovias, duas categorias de rodovias. As subdivisões políticas internas de numerosos países estão igualmente assinalados.

Na série de mapas da escala de 1:1 000 000, certas áreas, de interesse estratégico conjugado à importância econômica, densidade demográfica, ou ambos os elementos combinados, aparecem em forma ainda mais detalhada. O objetivo dessa série é representar a distribuição dos grandes centros urbanos, cidades, rodovias, ferrovias, pontes, aeroportos, represas, reservatórios e outras características associadas às grandes densidades demográficas. Indicam-se, também, os parques mais importantes, os lugares de interesse histórico, as áreas de lazer, três categorias de rodovias, e duas de ferrovias; e a nomenclatura dos grandes itinerários rodoviários. Todos esses elementos destacam-se sobre um fundo topográfico do relevo, executado em matizes das diversas cores.

Nos mapas regionais, assinalam-se os centros urbanos de dois modos. A grandeza da população das grandes cidades e dos centros urbanos secundários é representada pela dimensão e forma do símbolo que os localiza no mapa. O símbolo só reflete a população situada dentro de limites administrativos, sem levar em conta os subúrbios. Nos países onde os limites de uma municipalidade incluem zonas rurais, o símbolo representa apenas a população. A importância política e econômica de uma cidade, que não se relaciona necessariamente com o número de seus habitantes, é indicada pela dimensão dos caracteres tipográficos com que se compõe o seu nome.

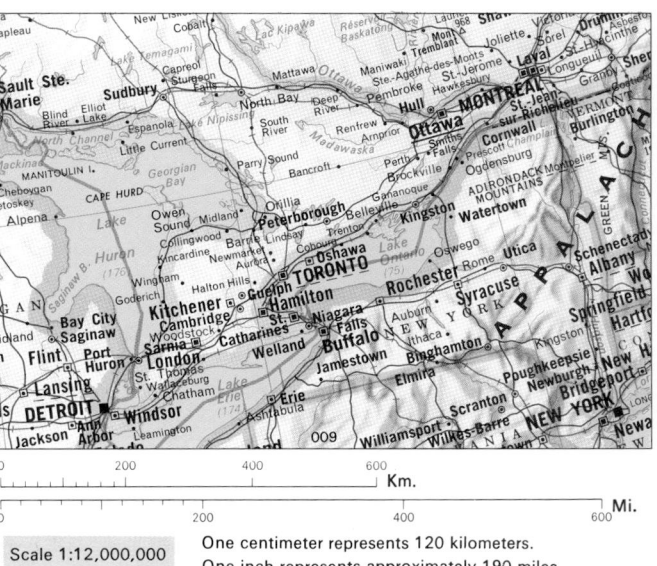

Scale 1:12,000,000   One centimeter represents 120 kilometers.
One inch represents approximately 190 miles.

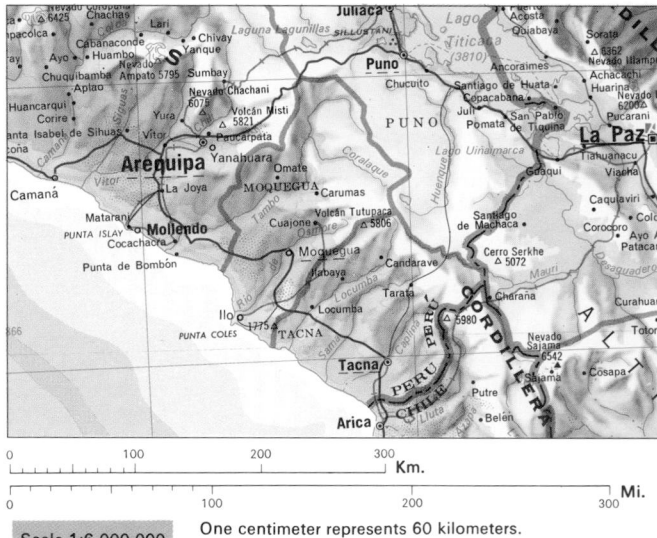

Scale 1:6,000,000   One centimeter represents 60 kilometers.
One inch represents approximately 95 miles.

Scale 1:3,000,000   One centimeter represents 30 kilometers.
One inch represents approximately 47 miles.

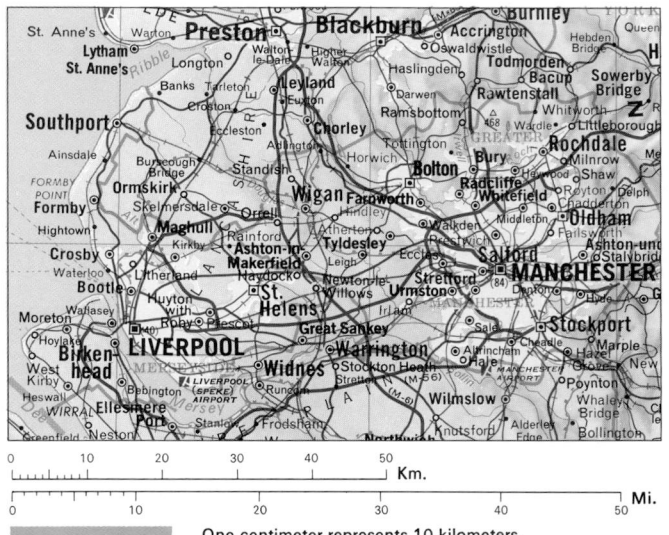

Scale 1:1,000,000   One centimeter represents 10 kilometers.
One inch represents approximately 16 miles.

MAP FORM	-älven	gora	île	islands	-øya	ozero	sea	vodochranilišče
ENGLISH	river	mountain	island	islands	island	lake	sea	reservoir
DEUTSCH	Fluss	Berg	Insel	Inseln	Insel	See	Meer	Stausee
ESPAÑOL	rio	montaña	isla	islas	isla	lago	mar	embalse
FRANÇAIS	rivière	montagne	île	îles	île	lac	mer	réservoir
PORTUGUÊS	rio	montanha	ilha	ilhas	ilha	lago	mar	reservatório

Copyright © by Rand McNally & Co.
Map prepared by Esselte Map Service AB, Stockholm
A-550000-264   -16.00 -31

BARENTS SEA

FINLAND

Murmansk
Severodvinsk
Archangel'sk
Syktyvkar
KOMI KRAJ

ZAPADNO SIBIRSKAJA RAVNINA

URAL'SKIJE GORY

HELSINKI
Tallinn
ESTONIA
SANKT-PETERBURG
ST. PETERSBURG (LENINGRAD)
Novgorod
Vologda
RUSSIA
Kirov
Perm'
Nižnij Tagil
Jekaterinburg (Sverdlovsk)
Čel'abinsk
URAL MOUNTAINS

RIGA
LATVIA
LITHUANIA
Pskov
Jaroslavl'
Ivanovo
Nižnij Novgorod (Gor'kij)
Kazan
TATARIJA
Ufa
BAŠKIRIJA
Magnitogorsk

VILNIUS
MINSK
BELARUS
Smolensk
Moscow MOSKVA
Vladimir
Tula
Penza
Uljanovsk
Toljatti
Samara
Orenburg

WARSAW
Br'ansk
Orel
Lipeck
Tambov
Saratov
Engel's
KAZAKHSTAN

KYYIV KIEV
Kharkiv
UKRAINE
Voronež
Kursk
Belgorod
Volgograd (Stalingrad)

L'viv
Dnipropetrovs'k
DONETS'K
Rostov-na-Donu
Astrachan'
KALMYKIJA
CASPIAN SEA
UZBEK

MOLDOVA
Chişinău
Odesa
Sea of Azov
Krasnodar
Novorossijsk
Stavropol'
Groznyj
TURKMENISTAN

BUCUREŞTI BUCHAREST
ROMANIA
BLACK SEA
Soči
CAUCASUS
GEORGIA
TBILISI
BAKI BAKU
AZERBAIJAN

SOFIJA SOFIA
BULGARIA
İstanbul
ANKARA
TURKEY
ARMENIA
YEREVAN
TEHRAN
IRAN

ATHINAI ATHENS
İzmir
Konya
Adana
SYRIA
IRAQ
BAGHDAD
Eşfahãn

CYPRUS
Nicosia

Kilometers | 0 | 200 | 400 | 600 | Km.
Statute Miles | 0 | 200 | 400 | 600 | Mi.

Scale 1:12,000,000
One centimeter represents 120 kilometers.
One inch represents approximately 190 miles.
Miller Oblated Stereographic Projection

Map continues pages 72-73

Map continues pages 118-119

a

MAP FORM	-älven	-fjorden	guba	-joki	-jökull	laäni	-øya	ozero
ENGLISH	river	fjord, lake	bay	river	glacier	province	island	lake
DEUTSCH	Fluss	Fjord, See	Bucht	Fluss	Gletscher	Provinz	Insel	See
ESPAÑOL	río	fiordo, lago	bahía	río	glaciar	provincia	isla	lago
FRANÇAIS	rivière	fjord, lac	baie	rivière	glacier	province	île	lac
PORTUGUÊS	rio	fiorde, lago	baia	rio	geleira	provincia	ilha	lago

Meters	Feet
6000	19685
4000	13124
3000	9843
2000	6562
1000	3281
500	1640
200	656
Land Below Sea Level	0
	0
200	656
1000	3281
3000	9843
6000	19685
9000	29520

Map continues
pages 76-77

Map continues
pages 86-87

Kilometers

Statute Miles

Km.

Mi.

Scale 1:6,000,000

One centimeter represents 60 kilometers.
One inch represents approximately 95 miles.

Lambert Conformal Conic Projection

Southern Scandinavia / Südskandinavien / Escandinavia Meridional
Scandinavie Méridionale / Escandinávia Meridional

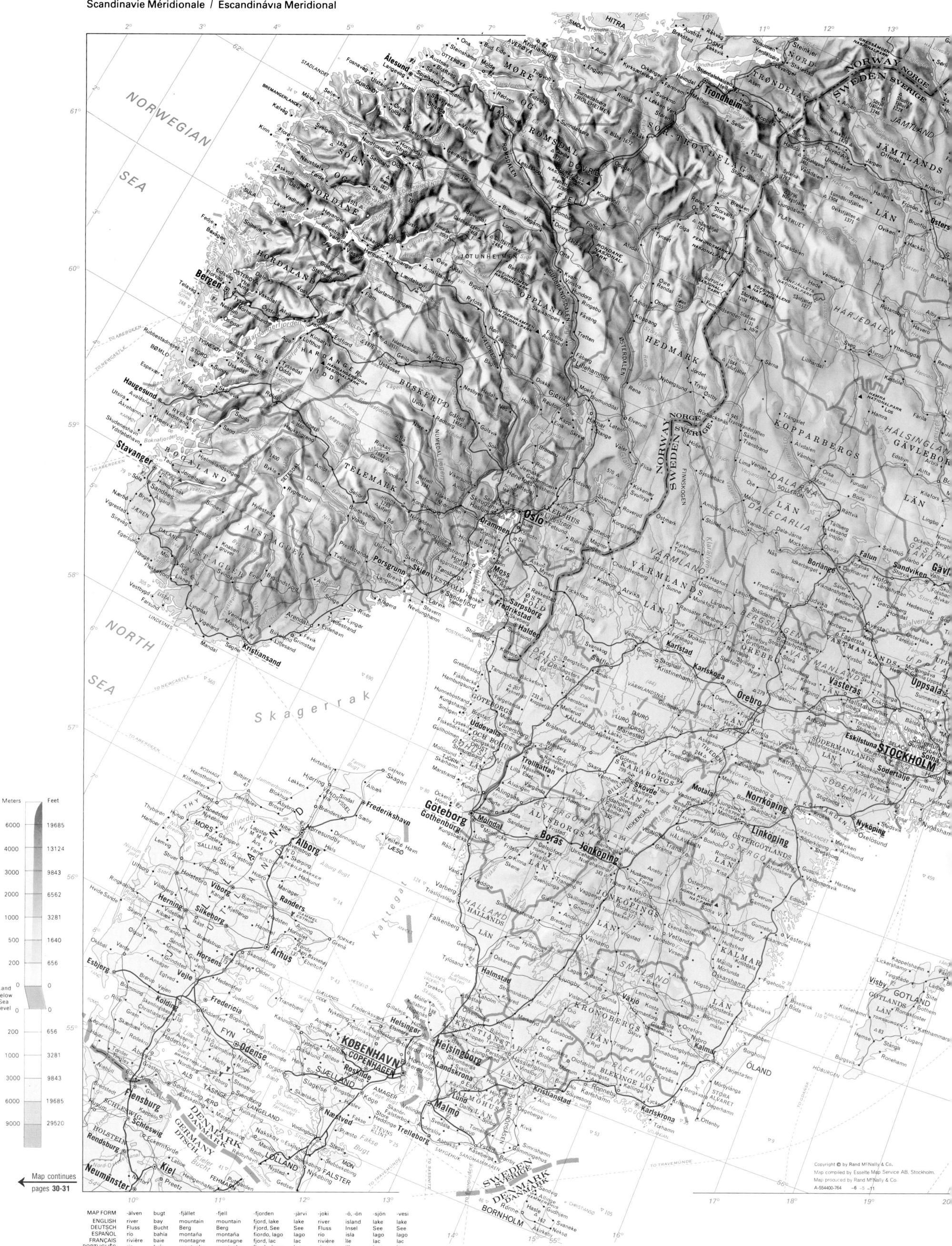

Meters	Feet
6000	19685
4000	13124
3000	9843
2000	6562
1000	3281
500	1640
200	656
0	0
Land Below Sea Level 0	0
200	656
1000	3281
3000	9843
6000	19685
9000	29520

Map continues
pages 30-31

MAP FORM	-älven	bugt	-fjället	-fjell	-fjorden	-järvi	-joki	-ö, -ön	-sjön	-vesi
ENGLISH	river	bay	mountain	mountain	fjord, lake	lake	river	island	lake	lake
DEUTSCH	Fluss	Bucht	Berg	Berg	Fjord, See	See	Fluss	Insel	See	See
ESPAÑOL	río	bahía	montaña	montaña	fiordo, lago	lago	río	isla	lago	lago
FRANÇAIS	rivière	baie	montagne	montagne	fjord, lac	lac	rivière	île	lac	lac
PORTUGUÊS	rio	baía	montanha	montanha	fiorde, lago	lago	rio	ilha	lago	lago

Copyright © by Rand McNally & Co.
Map compiled by Esselte Map Service AB, Stockholm.
Map produced by Rand McNally & Co.
A-554400-764   -6 -5 -11

Map continues
pages 24-25

Map continues
pages 76-77

Map continues
pages 76-77

Kilometers
Km.
Statute Miles
Mi.

Scale 1:3,000,000

One centimeter represents 30 kilometers.
One inch represents approximately 47 miles.
Conic Projection, Two Standard Parallels

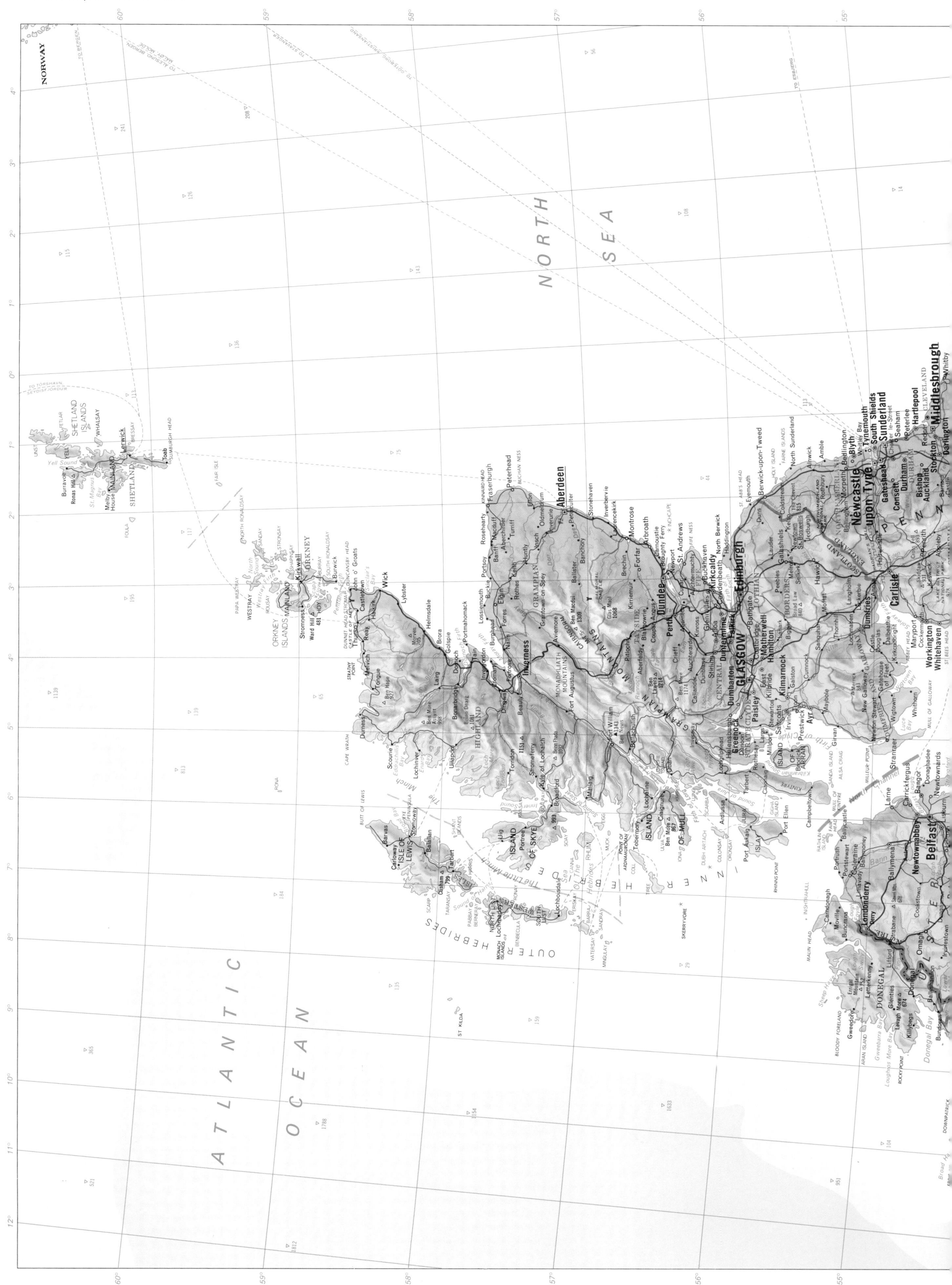
NORWAY
NORTH SEA
ATLANTIC OCEAN
SHETLAND ISLANDS
ORKNEY ISLANDS
OUTER HEBRIDES
Aberdeen
Dundee
Edinburgh
GLASGOW
Inverness
Newcastle upon Tyne
Sunderland
Middlesbrough
Carlisle
Belfast

Map continues
pages 30-31

Map continues
pages 32-33

Scale 1:3,000,000

One centimeter represents 30 kilometers.
One inch represents approximately 47 miles.

Conic Projection. Two Standard Parallels

Kilometers
Statute Miles

Mi.

Km.

MAP FORM	bay	ben	head	hills	island	loch	mountains	point	sound
ENGLISH	bay	mountain	headland	hills	island	lake; inlet	mountains	point	sound
DEUTSCH	Bucht	Berg	Landspitze	Hügel	Insel	See; Einfahrt	Berge	Landspitze	Sund
ESPAÑOL	bahía	montaña	promontorio	colinas	isla	lago; abra	montañas	punta	canal
FRANÇAIS	baie	montagne	promontoire	colinas	île	lac; bras de mer	montagnes	pointe	détroit
PORTUGUÊS	baía	montanha	promontório	colinas	ilha	lago; enseada	montanhas	pontes	canal

Copyright © by Rand McNally & Co.
Map prepared by George Philip & Son Ltd, London.

Meters	Feet
6000	19685
4000	13124
3000	9843
2000	6562
1000	3281
500	1640
200	656
0 Land Below Sea Level 0	0
200	656
1000	3281
3000	9843
6000	19685
9000	29520

ATLANTIC OCEAN

IRISH SEA

CELTIC SEA

English Channel
La Manche

St. George's Channel

IRELAND

UNITED KINGDOM
FRANCE

LONDON
DUBLIN
PARIS

Manchester
Liverpool
Birmingham
Leeds
Sheffield
Bristol
Cardiff
Kingston upon Hull

Map continues
pages 26-27

Map continues
pages 28-29

NORTH SEA

FRISIAN ISLANDS

Meters	Feet
6000	19685
4000	13124
3000	9843
2000	6562
1000	3281
500	1640
200	656
0 Land Below Sea Level	0
200	656
1000	3281
3000	9843
6000	19685
9000	29520

MAP FORM	Bucht	Gebirge	jezioro	Kanal	park narodowy	See	Wald
ENGLISH	bay	range	lake, lagoon	canal	national park	lake	forest, mountains
DEUTSCH	Bucht	Gebirge	See, Haff	Kanal	Nationalpark	See	Wald
ESPAÑOL	bahía	sierra	lago, laguna	canal	parque nacional	lago	bosque, montañas
FRANÇAIS	baie	chaîne	lac, lagune	canal	parc national	lac	forêt, montagnes
PORTUGUÊS	bala	serra	lago, laguna	canal	parque nacional	lago	floresta, montanhas

Kilometers 0   50   100   150 Km.

Statute Miles 0   50   100   150 Mi.

Scale 1:3,000,000

One centimeter represents 30 kilometers.
One inch represents approximately 47 miles.
Conic Projection, Two Standard Parallels.

Map continues
pages 76-77

Map continues
pages 78-79

Map continues
pages 36-37

Map continues
pages 28-29

Map continues
pages 34-35

MAP FORM	canal	cap	île	lago	mont (e)	monts	pointe	See
ENGLISH	canal	cape	island	lake	mount	mountains	point	lake
DEUTSCH	Kanal	Kap	Insel	See	Berg	Berge	Landspitze	See
ESPAÑOL	canal	cabo	isla	lago	monte	montes	punta	lago
FRANÇAIS	canal	cap	île	lac	mont	monts	pointe	lac
PORTUGUÉS	canal	cabo	ilha	lago	monte	montes	ponta	lago

Map continues
pages 30-31

Map continues
pages 36-37

Copyright © by Rand McNally & Co.
Map prepared by Rand McNally GmbH, Stuttgart.
A-559495-764   -10 -6 -17

Kilometers
Statute Miles

Scale 1:3,000,000

One centimeter represents 30 kilometers.
One inch represents approximately 47 miles.
Lambert Conformal Conic Projection

Spain and Portugal / Spanien und Portugal / España y Portugal
Espagne et Portugal / Espanha e Portugal

Meters	Feet
6000	19685
4000	13124
3000	9843
2000	6562
1000	3281
500	1640
200	656
0	0
Land Below Sea Level	
0	0
200	656
1000	3281
3000	9843
6000	19685
9000	29520

Copyright © by Rand McNally & Co.
Map prepared by Rand McNally GmbH, Stuttgart.
A-559900-764 -8 -7 -15

ESPAÑOL	bahía	cabo	isla	embalse	puerto	punta	ría	sierra
ENGLISH	bay	cape	island	reservoir	port	point	estuary	mountains
DEUTSCH	Bucht	Kap	Insel	Stausee	Hafen	Landspitze	Trichtermündung	Berge
FRANÇAIS	baie	cap	île	réservoir	port	pointe	estuaire	montagnes
PORTUGUÊS	baía	cabo	ilha	reservatório	porto	ponta	estuário	serra

Map continues
pages 32-33

MEDITERRANEAN SEA

ILLES BALEARS
BALEARIC ISLANDS

Map continues
pages 148-149

Kilometers
Statute Miles

Scale 1:3,000,000

One centimeter represents 30 kilometers.
One inch represents approximately 47 miles.

Conic Projection, Two Standard Parallels

Map continues
pages 38-39

Map continues
pages 30-31

Map continues
pages 32-33

BUDAPEST

BRATISLAVA

WIEN
VIENNA

Sankt
Pölten

Graz

MÜNCHEN
MUNICH

Salzburg

Linz

Innsbruck

Klagenfurt

Ljubljana

Zagreb

Trieste

Udine

Venezia
Venice

Padova

Verona

Brescia

Bergamo

Como

MILANO
MILAN

Pavia

Trento

Bolzano

Augsburg

Ulm

Zürich

Basel

Bern Berne

Lausanne

Genève

Torino
Turin

Asti

Genova
Genoa

Savona

San Remo

Nice

Cannes

MONACO

Bologna

Modena

Parma

Reggio
Emilia

Ferrara

Ravenna

Rimini

Pesaro
Fano

Ancona

Senigallia

Pescara

Chieti

L'Aquila

Terni

Perugia

Arezzo

Firenze
Florence

Prato

Pistoia

Lucca

Livorno
Leghorn

La
Spezia

Carrara
Massa

Viareggio

Pisa

Siena

Grosseto

Civitavecchia

Viterbo

Bastia

San Benedetto
del Tronto

Teramo

Macerata

Fabriano

Fermo

Ascoli
Piceno

Split

Sibenik

Zadar

Dubrovnik

Sarajevo

Mostar

Zenica

Banja Luka

Osijek

Pécs

Szombathely

Zalaegerszeg

Veszprém

Maribor

Varaždin

Sisak

Karlovac

Rijeka

Pula

Székesfehérvár

Dunaújváros

Győr

Komárno

Nitra

Nové Zámky

Wiener
Neustadt

Sopron

CORSE
CORSICA

Copyright © by Rand McNally & Co.
Map prepared by Rand McNally, GmbH, Stuttgart.
A-984996-764 -12 -7 -19

Seas and major labels

IONIAN SEA

ADRIATIC (coast)

TYRRHENIAN SEA — MARE TIRRENO

MEDITERRANEAN — MEDITERRANEO

Strait of Otranto

Golfo di Taranto

Golfo di Squillace

Strait of Sicily — of Sicily

Malta Channel

ITALY ITALIA / TUNISIA TUNISIE

ITALY ITALIA / TUNIS TUNISIE

Regions / Islands

SICILIA SICILY

SARDEGNA SARDINIA

PUGLIA — BASILICATA — CALABRIA — CAMPANIA — LUCANIA

MALTA

ISOLE EOLE — ISOLE EGADI — ISOLE PONZIANE — ISOLE PELAGIE

Major cities

Bari, Taranto, Brindisi, Lecce, Foggia, Barletta, Andria, Bisceglie, Trani, Molfetta, Manfredonia, Matera, Potenza, Cosenza, Catanzaro, Crotone, Reggio di Calabria, Messina, Catania, Siracusa, Ragusa, Gela, Agrigento, Caltanissetta, Enna, Marsala, Mazara del Vallo, Trapani, Palermo, Bagheria, Napoli Naples, Salerno, Avellino, Benevento, Caserta, Pozzuoli, Castellammare, Torre del Greco, Latina, Anzio, Gaeta

Cagliari, Sassari, Nuoro, Oristano, Iglesias, Carbonia, Alghero

Tunis, Bizerte, Sousse, Kairouan, Béja, Annaba (Bône), Guelma, Menzel Bourguiba

Valletta, Rabat (Victoria)

Map continuation

Map continues
pages 148-149

Glossary (MAP FORM)

ENGLISH	DEUTSCH	ESPAÑOL	FRANÇAIS	PORTUGUÊS
cape	Kap	cabo	cap	cabo
gulf	Golf	golfo	golfe	golfo
island	Insel	isla	île	ilha
lake	See	lago	lac	lago
mountain	Berg	monte	mont	monte
mountains	Gebirge	montes	monts	montes
point	Landspitze	punta	pointe	ponta
island	Insel	isla	île	ilha

capo ... golfo ... isola ... lago ... monte ... monti ... punta ... otok

Scale

Scale 1:3,000,000

Conic Projection, Two Standard Parallels

One centimeter represents 30 kilometers.
One inch represents approximately 47 miles.

Kilometers — Km.
Statute Miles — Mi.

0 50 100 150

Elevation legend

Meters	Feet
6000	19685
4000	13124
3000	9843
2000	6562
1000	3281
500	1640
200	656
0 Land Below Sea Level 0	0
200	656
1000	3281
3000	9843
6000	19685
9000	29520

TO MARSEILLE

FRANCE / ITALY

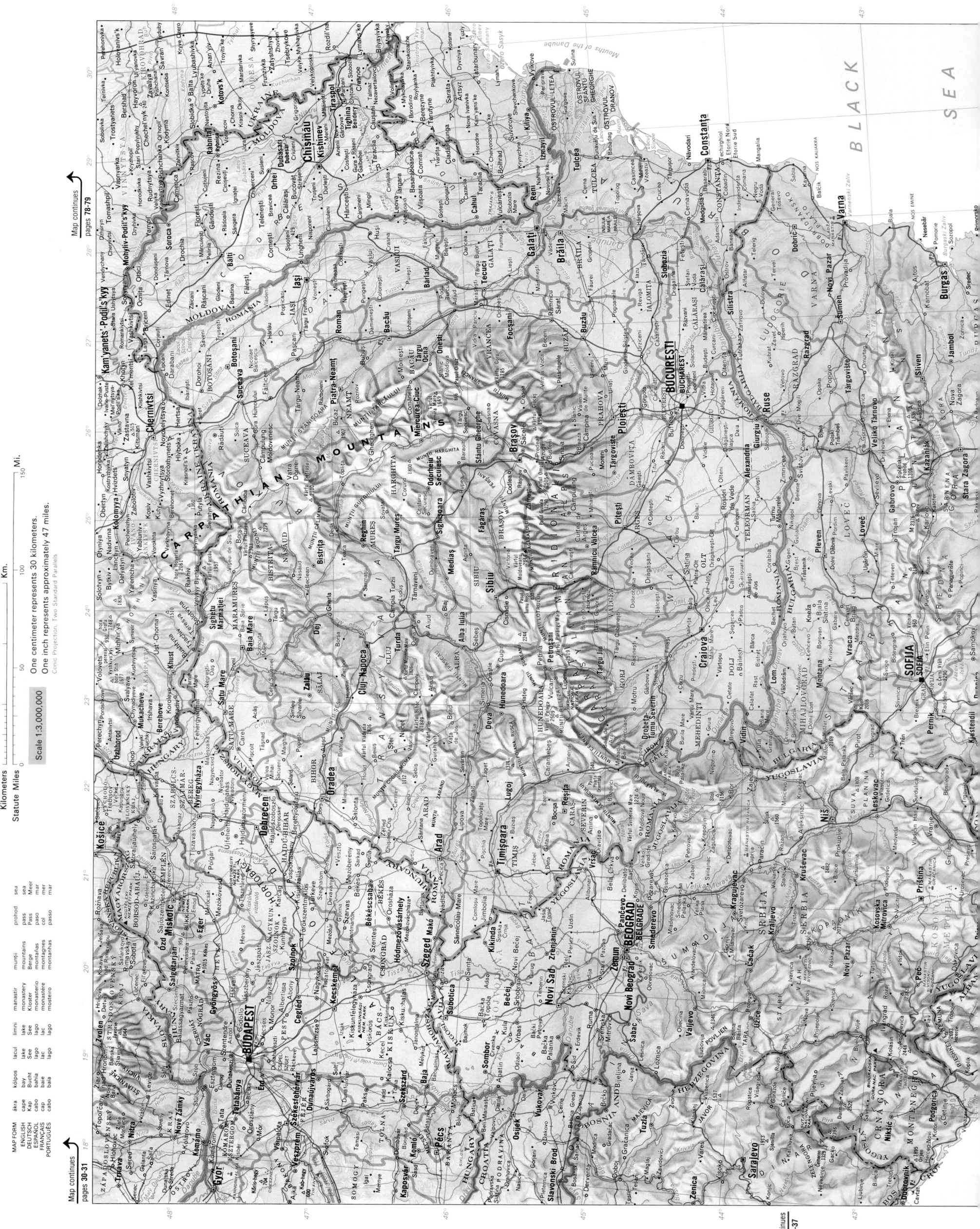

Map continues
pages 78-79

Map continues
pages 30-31

Map continues
pages 36-37

Scale 1:3,000,000

One centimeter represents 30 kilometers.
One inch represents approximately 47 miles.

Conic Projection, Two Standard Parallels

MAP FORM						
ENGLISH	åkra	kраj	kölpos	lacul	limni	manastir	munţii	prohod	sea
DEUTSCH	cape	See	bay	lake	lake	monastery	mountains	pass	sea
ESPAÑOL	Kap		Kap	Bucht	See	Kloster	Berge	Pass	Meer
FRANÇAIS	cap		cap	baie	lago	monasterio	montañas	paso	mar
PORTUGUÊS	cabo		cabo	baía	lago	monastère	montagnes	col	mer
	cabo		cabo	bahia	lago	mosteiro	montanhas	passo	mar

Map continues
pages 130-131

ISTANBUL

BULGARIA

TURKEY / TÜRKİYE

GREECE / ELLAS

ATHÍNAI/ATHENS

Thessaloníki / Salonika

KRÍTI / CRETE

RÓDHOS / RHODES

D'HODHEKÁNISOS / DODECANESE

KIKLÁDHES / CYCLADES

VÓREION AIYAÍON

NÓTION AIYAÍON

LÉSVOS / LESBOS

ÍKARÍA

SÁMOS

KHÍOS

LÍMNOS

ÁYION ÓROS

EÚVOIA

PELOPÓNNISOS

STEREÁ ELLÁS

ÍÓNIOI NÍSOI / IONIAN ISLANDS

KÉRKIRA / CORFU

AEGEAN SEA

ADRIATIC SEA

IONIAN SEA

MEDITERRANEAN SEA

Marmara Denizi / Sea of Marmara

ITALY

ALBANIA / SHQIPËRI

Tiranë

Durrës

Skopje

Titov Veles

Bitola

PLOVDIV

Haskovo

Kǔrdžali

Edirne

Kírklareli

Tekirdağ

Çorlu

Bursa

Bandırma

Çanakkale

Balıkesir

Edremit

Soma

Bergama

Manisa

İZMİR / Smyrna

Söke

Aydın

Nazilli

Denizli

Uşak

Kütahya

Ödemiş

Tire

Muğla

Xánthi

Komotiní

Alexandroúpolis

Kaválla

Dráma

Sérrai

Kilkís

Véroia

Katerini

Lárisa

Tríkala

Vólos

Lamía

Agrínion

Ioánnina

Préveza

Pátrai

Kalámai

Spárti

Pírgos

Khalkís

Piraiévs / Piraeus

Iráklion

Khaniá

Réthimnon

Feet: 19685 13124 9843 6562 3281 1640 656 0 | 0 656 3281 9843 19685 29520

Meters: 6000 4000 3000 2000 1000 500 200 0 | Land Below Sea Level | 0 200 1000 3000 6000 9000

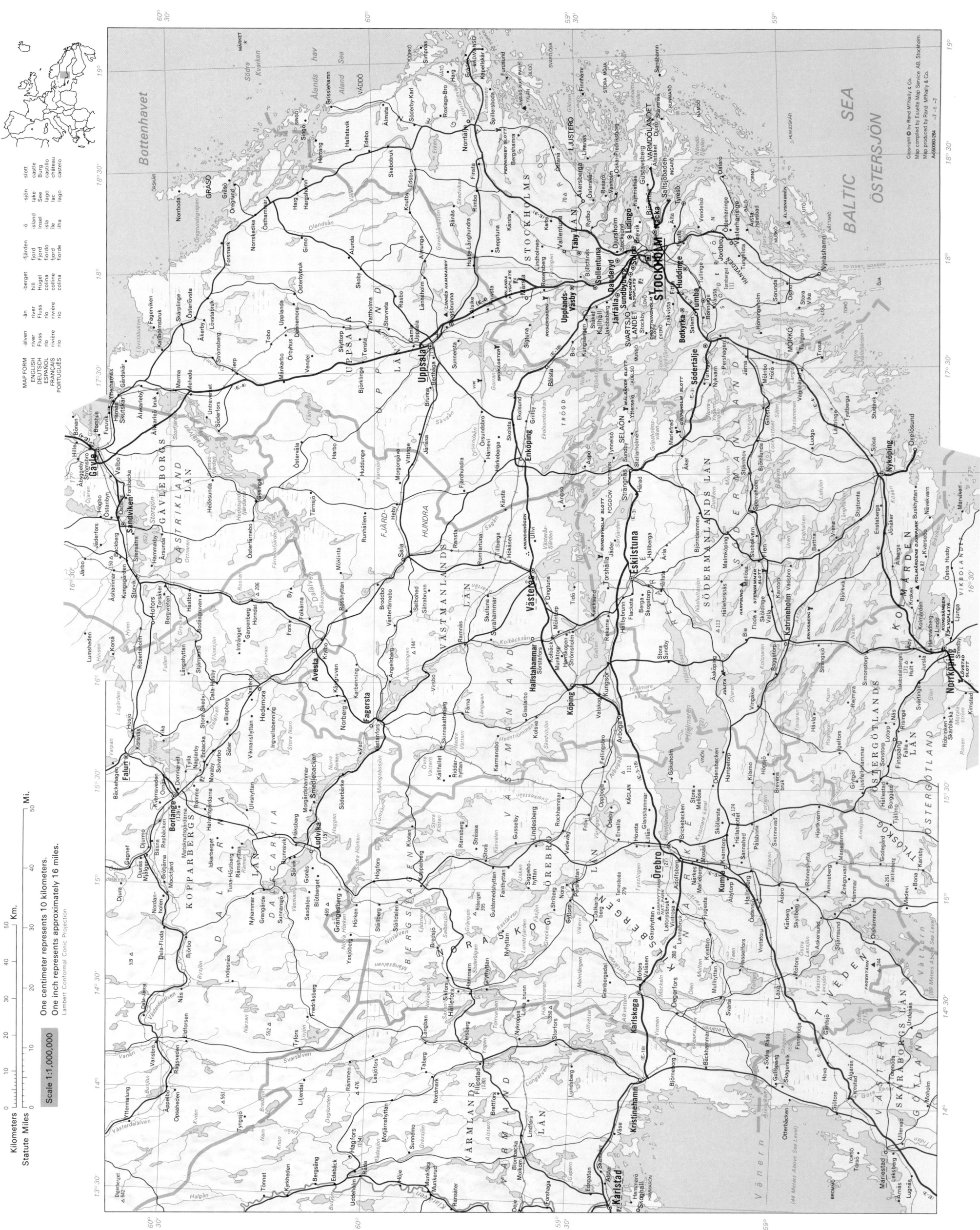
MAP FORM / ENGLISH / DEUTSCH / ESPAÑOL / FRANÇAIS / PORTUGUÊS
-älven: river, Fluss, río, rivière, rio
-ån: river, Fluss, río, rivière, rio
-berget: hill, Hügel, colina, colline, colina
-fjärden: fjord, Fjord, fiordo, fjord, fiorde
-ö: island, Insel, isla, île, ilha
-sjön: lake, See, lago, lac, lago
slott: castle, Burg, castillo, château, castelo
Kilometers
Statute Miles
Scale 1:1,000,000
One centimeter represents 10 kilometers.
One inch represents approximately 16 miles.
Lambert Conformal Conic Projection
Copyright © by Rand McNally & Co.
Map compiled by Esselte Map Service AB, Stockholm.
Map produced by Rand McNally & Co.
Bottenhavet
BALTIC SEA
ÖSTERSJÖN
Vänern
STOCKHOLM
Uppsala
Västerås
Örebro
Karlstad
Gävle
Falun
Borlänge
Nyköping
Norrköping
Eskilstuna
Södertälje
Norrtälje
Karlskoga
Kristinehamn

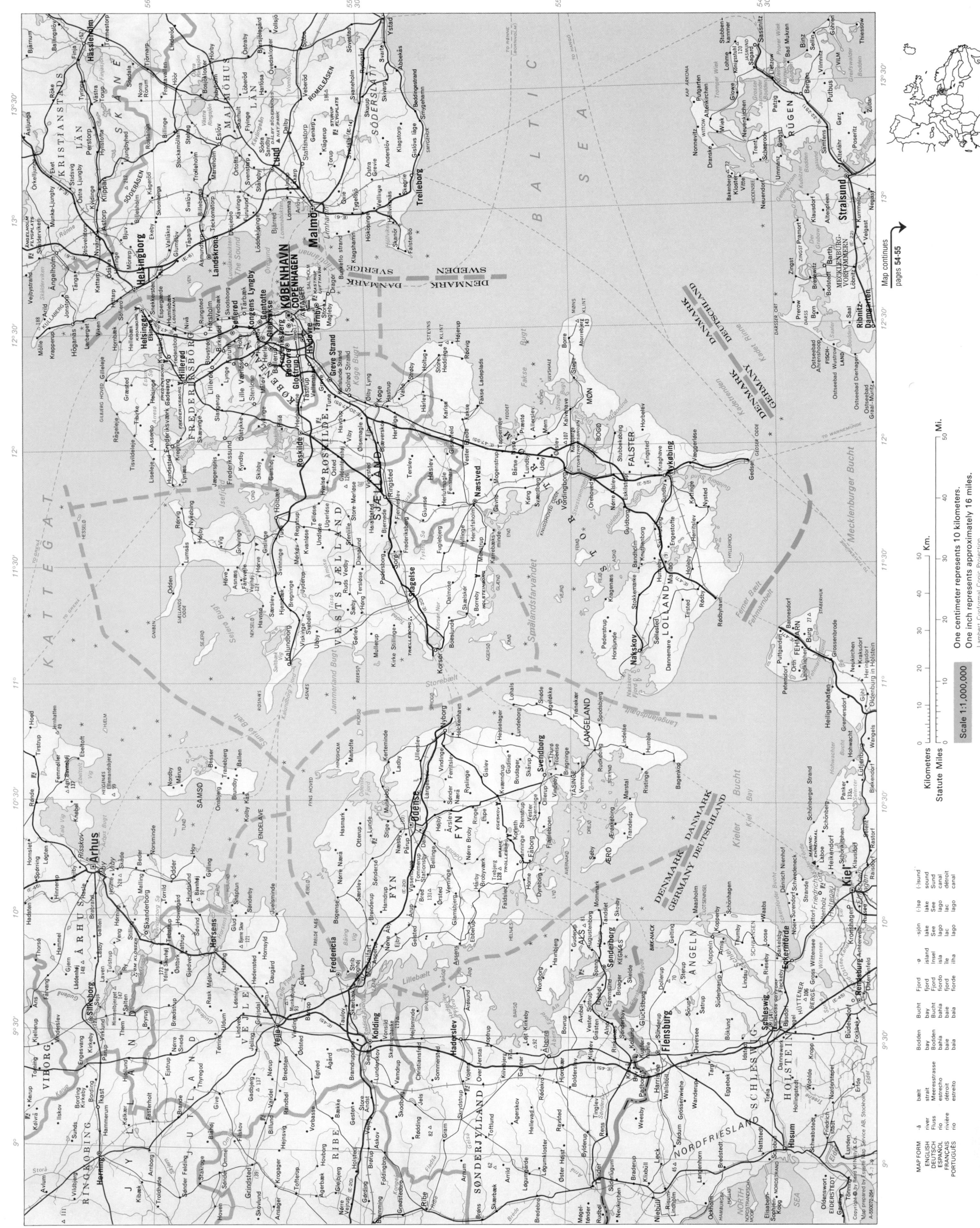

Map continues
pages 54-55

Scale 1:1,000,000

Kilometers
Statute Miles

One centimeter represents 10 kilometers.
One inch represents approximately 16 miles.

Lambert Conformal Conic Projection

MAPFORM						
ENGLISH	river	strait	bay	bay	island	lake	sound
DEUTSCH	Fluss	Meeresstrasse	Bodden	Bucht	Insel	See	Sund
ESPAÑOL	rio	estrecho	bahia	bahia	isla	lago	canal
FRANÇAIS	rivière	détroit	baie	baie	île	lac	canal
PORTUGUÊS	rio	estreito	baia	baia	ilha	lago	canal

Copyright © by Rand McNally & Co.
Map prepared by J.uppl. Geo Service AB, Stockholm
A-500075384

← Map continues
pages 48-49

ENGLISH	bay	drain	forest	head	hill	isle	marsh	point	vale
DEUTSCH	Bucht	Abzugsgraben	Wald	Landspitze	Hügel	Insel	Marsch	Landspitze	Tal
ESPAÑOL	bahía	acquia	bosque	promontorio	colina	isla	pantano	punta	valle
FRANÇAIS	baie	drainage	forêt	promontoire	colline	île	marais	pointe	dépression
PORTUGUÊS	baía	drenagem	floresta	promontório	colina	ilha	pântano	ponta	vale

Copyright © by Rand McNally & Co.
Map prepared by Rand McNally & Co.
A-656900-264   -9 -512

Map continues pages 44-45

Map continues pages 50-51

Kilometers | 0 10 20 30 40 50 Km.
Statute Miles | 0 10 20 30 40 50 Mi.

Scale 1:1,000,000
One centimeter represents 10 kilometers.
One inch represents approximately 16 miles.
Lambert Conformal Conic Projection

Map continues pages 46-47

Map continues pages 48-49

Londonderry / Derry
DONEGAL
Coleraine
Portrush
Portstewart
Ballymoney
Ballymena
Larne
Antrim
BELFAST
Newtownabbey
Bangor
Newtownards
Lisburn
Lurgan
Portadown
Armagh
Newry
Dundalk / Dún Dealgan
MONAGHAN
CAVAN
LOUTH
MEATH
Drogheda / Droichead Átha
Navan
Balbriggan
Skerries
Swords
Malahide
Portmarnock
Howth
DUBLIN — BAILE ÁTHA CLIATH
Dún Laoghaire
Bray
KILDARE
Naas
Droichead Nua
WICKLOW
Wicklow
Arklow
CARLOW
WEXFORD

NORTHERN IRELAND
NORTH CHANNEL
North Channel
IRISH SEA
ISLE OF MAN (U.K.)
Douglas
Ramsey
Peel
Castletown
Port Erin

IRELAND ÉIRE / UNITED KINGDOM

ANGLESEY
Holyhead
Llandudno
Colwyn Bay
Rhyl
Bangor
Caernarfon
SNOWDONIA
LLEYN PENINSULA

Kilmarnock
Ayr
Irvine
Troon
Prestwick
ISLAND OF ARRAN
Campbeltown
Girvan
Stranraer
Dumfries
STRATHCLYDE
GALLOWAY
MULL OF GALLOWAY
Workington
Whitehaven
Maryport
Barrow-in-Furness
LAKE DISTRICT

Copyright © by Rand McNally & Co.
Map prepared by Rand McNally & Co.
A-556800-264   -12 -9 -15

MAP FORM	bay	dale	firth	forest	head	loch	moor	water
ENGLISH	bay	dale	estuary	forest	head	lake; inlet	moor	water (lake, river)
DEUTSCH	Bucht	Weites Tal	Trichtermündung	Wald	Landspitze	See; Einfahrt	Moor	See, Fluss
ESPAÑOL	bahía	valle	estuario	bosque	promontorio	lago; abra	páramo	lago, río
FRANÇAIS	baie	vallée	estuaire	forêt	promontoire	lac; bras de mer	lande	lac, rivière
PORTUGUÊS	baía	vale	estuário	floresta	promontorio	lago; enseada	pântano	lago, rio

Kilometers 0 10 20 30 40 50 Km.

Statute Miles 0 10 20 30 40 50 Mi.

Scale 1:1,000,000
One centimeter represents 10 kilometers.
One inch represents approximately 16 miles.

Lambert Conformal Conic Projection

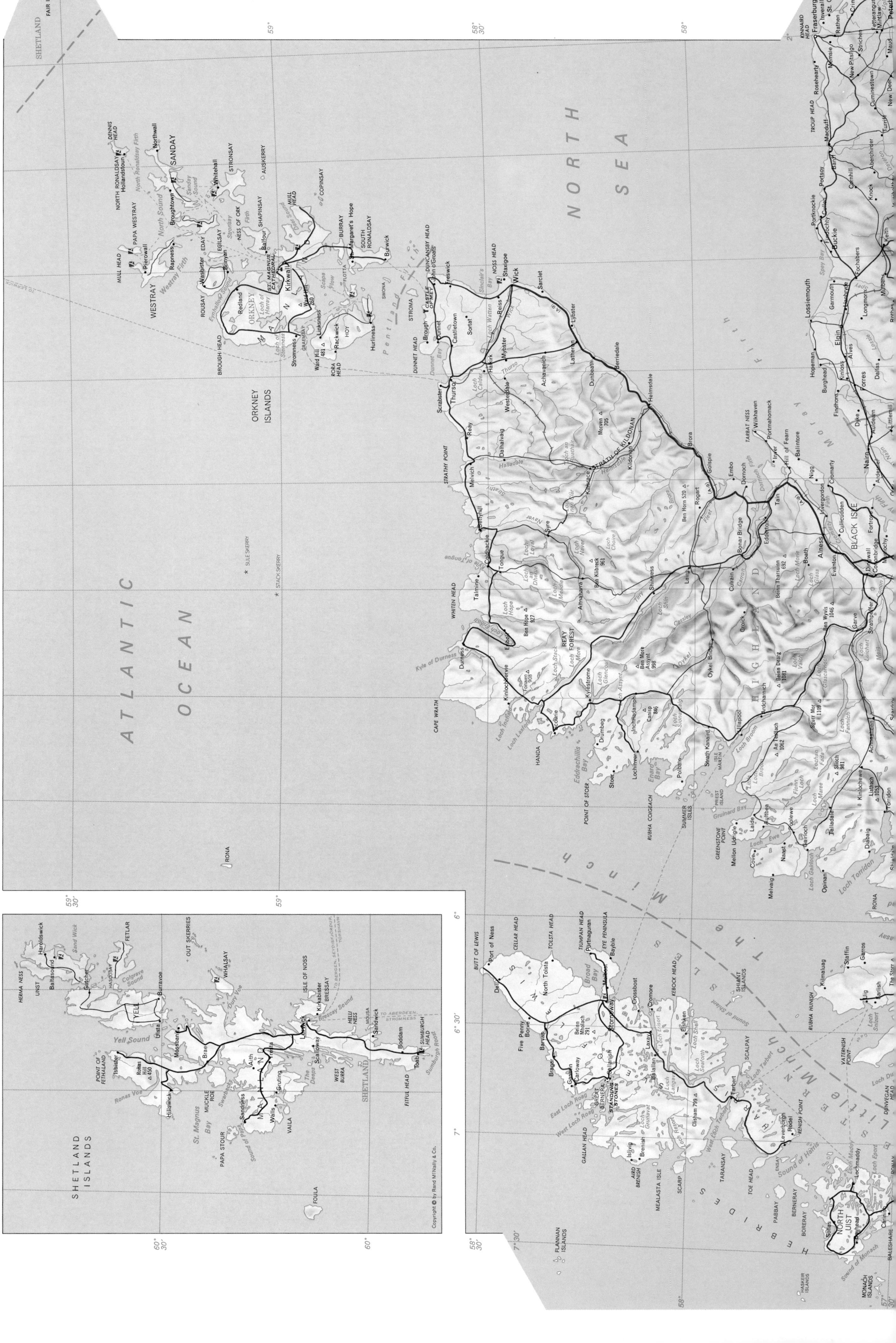
ATLANTIC
OCEAN
NORTH
SEA
ORKNEY ISLANDS
SHETLAND ISLANDS
The Minch
Little Minch
Moray Firth
Pentland Firth
Dornoch Firth
HIGHLAND
REAY FOREST
BLACK ISLE
NORTH UIST
HEBRIDES
FAIR ISLE
SHETLAND
WESTRAY
SANDAY
STRONSAY
ROUSAY
MAINLAND
HOY
SOUTH RONALDSAY
Kirkwall
Stromness
Thurso
Wick
John o'Groats
Dunnet
Castletown
Helmsdale
Brora
Golspie
Dornoch
Tain
Invergordon
Cromarty
Nairn
Forres
Elgin
Lossiemouth
Buckie
Banff
Macduff
Fraserburgh
Peterhead
Ullapool
Lochinver
Scourie
Durness
Tongue
Bettyhill
Lairg
Bonar Bridge
Stornoway
Tarbert
Lerwick
Scalloway
Sumburgh Head
Yell
Unst
Fetlar
Whalsay
Bressay
Foula
Papa Stour
BUTT OF LEWIS
CAPE WRATH
DUNNET HEAD
DUNCANSBY HEAD
STRATHY POINT
WHITEN HEAD
SULE SKERRY
STACK SKERRY
RONA
FLANNAN ISLANDS
SHIANT ISLANDS
SUMMER ISLES
MONACH ISLANDS
Copyright © by Rand McNally & Co.

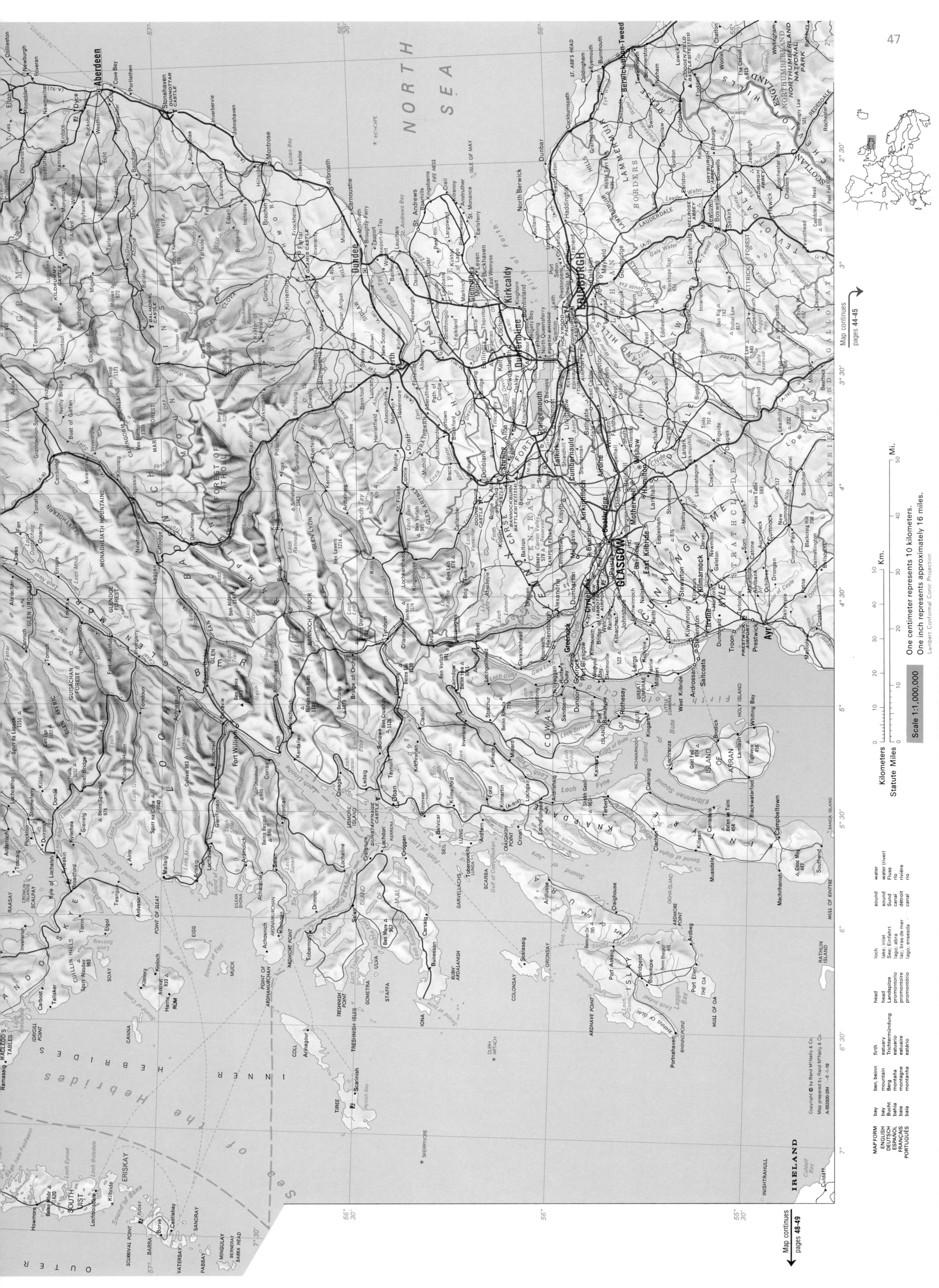

Map continues
pages 44-45

Map continues
pages 48-49

Scale 1:1,000,000

One centimeter represents 10 kilometers.
One inch represents approximately 16 miles.

Lambert Conformal Conic Projection

Kilometers
Statute Miles

Km.
Mi.

MAPFORM	bay	ben, beinn	firth	head	loch	sound	water
ENGLISH	bay	mountain	estuary	head	lake; inlet	sound	water (river)
DEUTSCH	Bucht	Berg	Trichtermündung	Landspitze	See; Einfahrt	Sund	Fluss
ESPAÑOL	bahía	montaña	estuario	promontorio	lago; abra	canal	río
FRANÇAIS	baie	montagne	estuaire	promontoire	lac; bras de mer	détroit	rivière
PORTUGUÊS	baía	montanha	estério	promontorio	lago; enseada	canal	río

Copyright © by Rand McNally & Co.
Map prepared by Rand McNally & Co.
A-550300-264   -8 -4-10

Map continues
pages 46-47

Map continues
pages 44-45

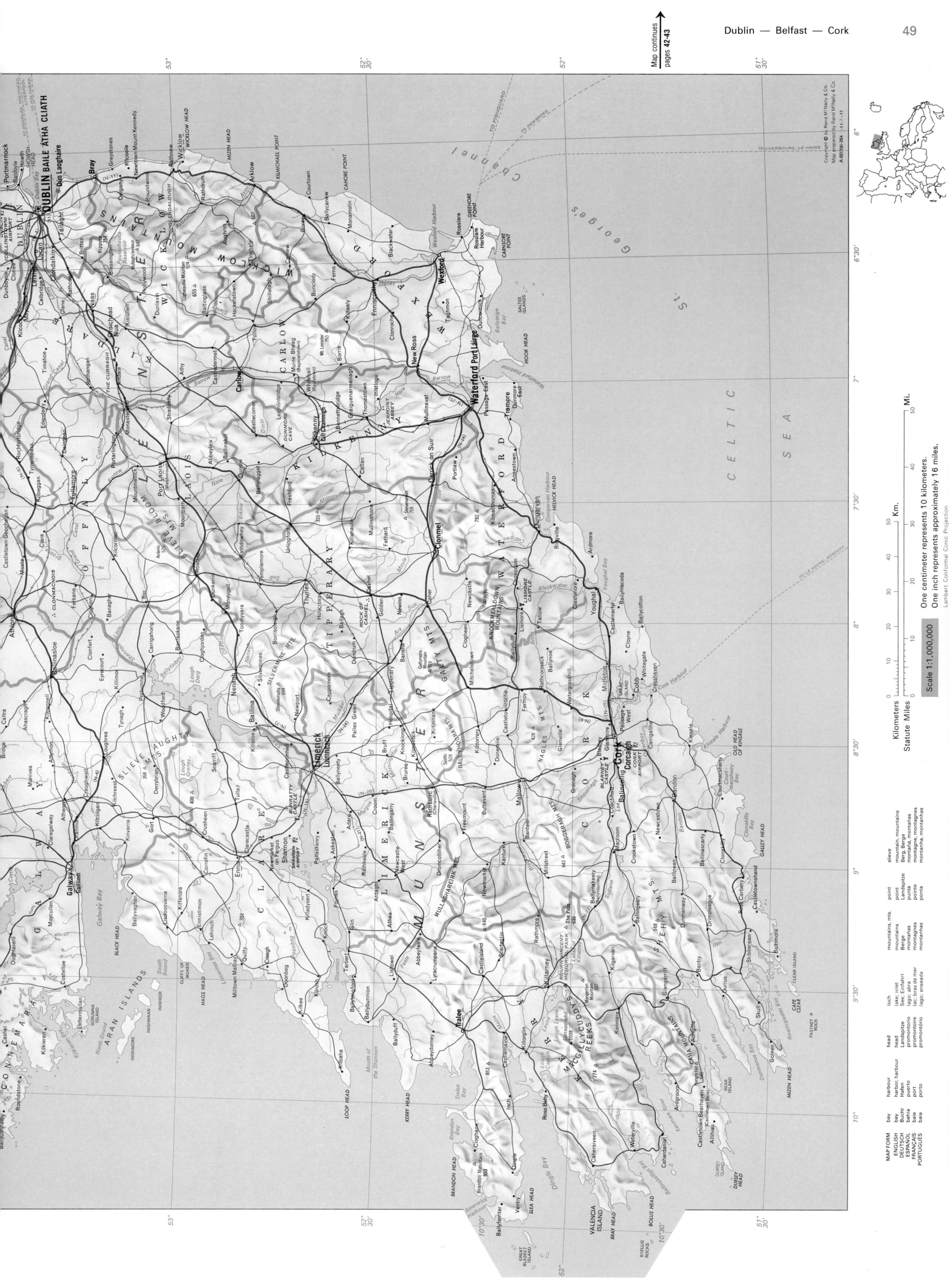

Map continues pages 42-43

Copyright © by Rand McNally & Co.
Map prepared by Rand McNally & Co.
A-557000-264   (-1)-7 -11

Scale 1:1,000,000

Kilometers
Statute Miles

One centimeter represents 10 kilometers.
One inch represents approximately 16 miles.

Lambert Conformal Conic Projection

MAP FORM	bay	harbour	head	loch	mountains, mts.	point	slieve
ENGLISH	bay	harbour, harbour	head	lake; inlet	mountains	point	mountain, mountains
DEUTSCH	Bucht	Hafen	Landspitze	See; Einfahrt	Berge	Landspitze	Berg, Berge
ESPAÑOL	bahía	puerto	promontorio	lago; abra	montañas	punta	montaña, montañas
FRANÇAIS	baie	port	promontoire	lac; bras de mer	montagnes	pointe	montagne, montagnes
PORTUGUÊS	baía	porto	promontório	lago; enseada	montanhas	ponta	montanha, montanhas

Map continues pages 56-57

Map continues pages 52-53

Map continues pages 42-43

Map continues
pages 58-59

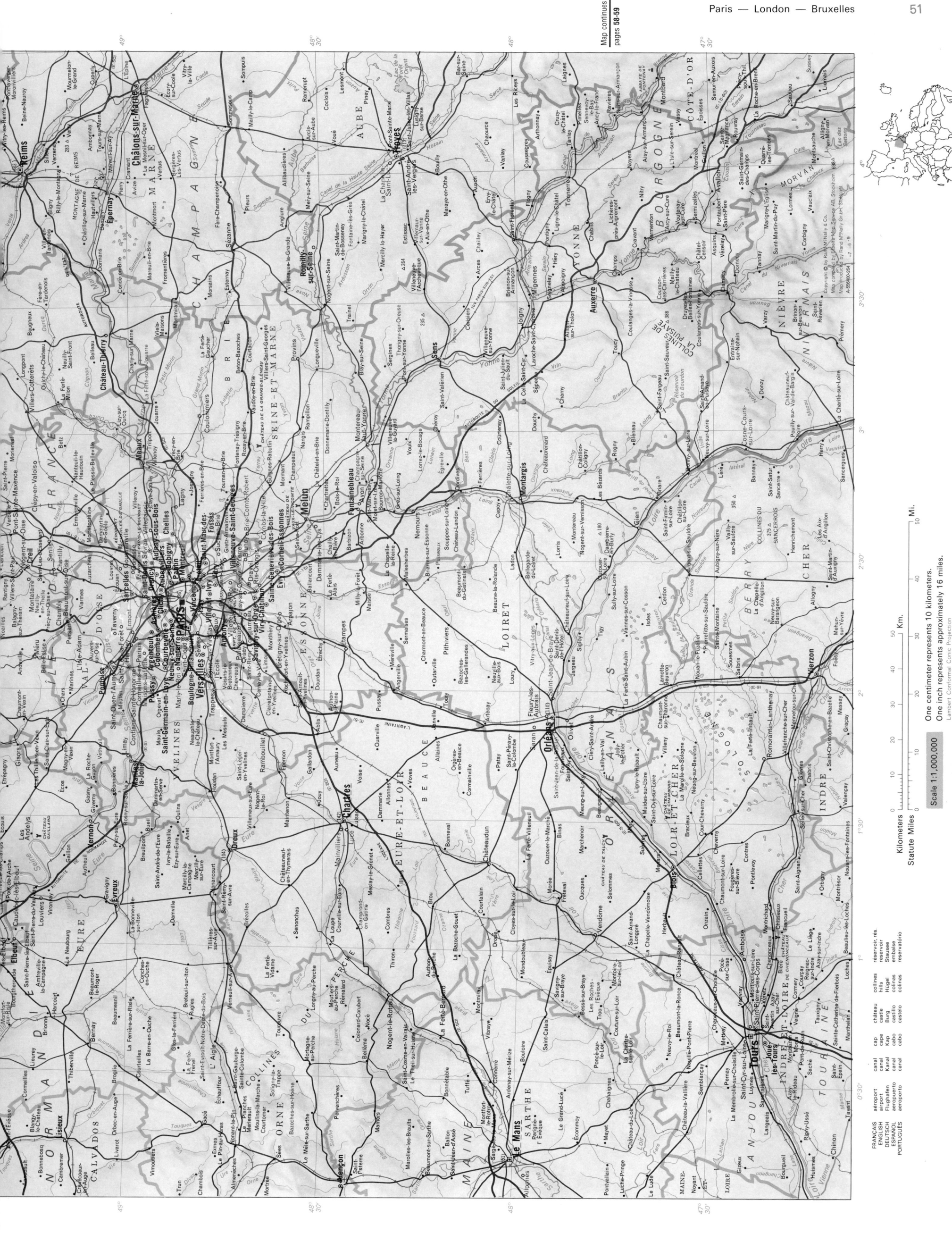

Scale 1:1,000,000

Kilometers

Statute Miles

One centimeter represents 10 kilometers.
One inch represents approximately 16 miles.
Lambert Conformal Conic Projection

FRANÇAIS	canal	cap	château	collines	reservoir/rés.
ENGLISH	canal	cape	castle	hills	reservoir
DEUTSCH	Kanal	Kap	Burg	Hügel	Stausee
ESPAÑOL	canal	cabo	castillo	colinas	embalse
PORTUGUÊS	canal	cabo	castelo	colinas	reservatorio

FRANÇAIS	aéroport
ENGLISH	airport
DEUTSCH	Flughafen
ESPAÑOL	aeropuerto
PORTUGUÊS	aeroporto

Map continues
pages 50-51

Map continues
pages 56-57

DEUTSCH	Gebirge	Kanal	Moor	Naturpark	Stausee	Talsperre	Wald
ENGLISH	range	canal	moor	reserve	reservoir	dam	forest, mountains
ESPAÑOL	sierra	canal	paramo	reserva	embalse	presa	bosque, montanas
FRANÇAIS	chaîne	canal	lande	réserve	réservoir	barrage	forêt, montagnes
PORTUGUÊS	serra	canal	pântano	reserva natural	reservatório	represa	floresta, montanhas

Kilometers

Statute Miles

Scale 1:1,000,000

One centimeter represents 10 kilometers.
One inch represents approximately 16 miles.

Lambert Conformal Conic Projection

BALTIC SEA
Pomeranian Bay
Mecklenburger Bucht
Rostock
Stralsund
Greifswald
Wismar
Schwerin
Lübeck
Kiel
HAMBURG
Szczecin (Stettin)
BERLIN
Potsdam
Brandenburg
Neubrandenburg
Stendal
Wittenberge
Salzwedel
Uelzen
Lüneburg
Wolfsburg
MECKLENBURG
UCKERMARK
ALTMARK
PRIGNITZ
HAVELLAND
BARNIM

Map continues page 41

Map continues pages 52-53

Map continues
page 60

Map continues
pages 56-57

Scale 1:1,000,000

One centimeter represents 10 kilometers.
One inch represents approximately 16 miles.
Lambert Conformal Conic Projection

Kilometers

Statute Miles

Mi.

Km.

DEUTSCH	Berg, Bg.	Bodden	Bucht	Gebirge	Heide	Kanal	See	Talsperre
ENGLISH	mountain	bay	bay	range	heath	canal	lake	dam
ESPAÑOL	montaña	bahía	bahía	sierra	matorral	canal	lago	presa
FRANÇAIS	montagne	baie	baie	chaîne	lande	canal	lac	barrage
PORTUGUÊS	montanha	baía	baía	serra	charneca	canal	lago	represa

Map continues
pages 52-53

Map continues
pages 50-51

Map continues
pages 58-59

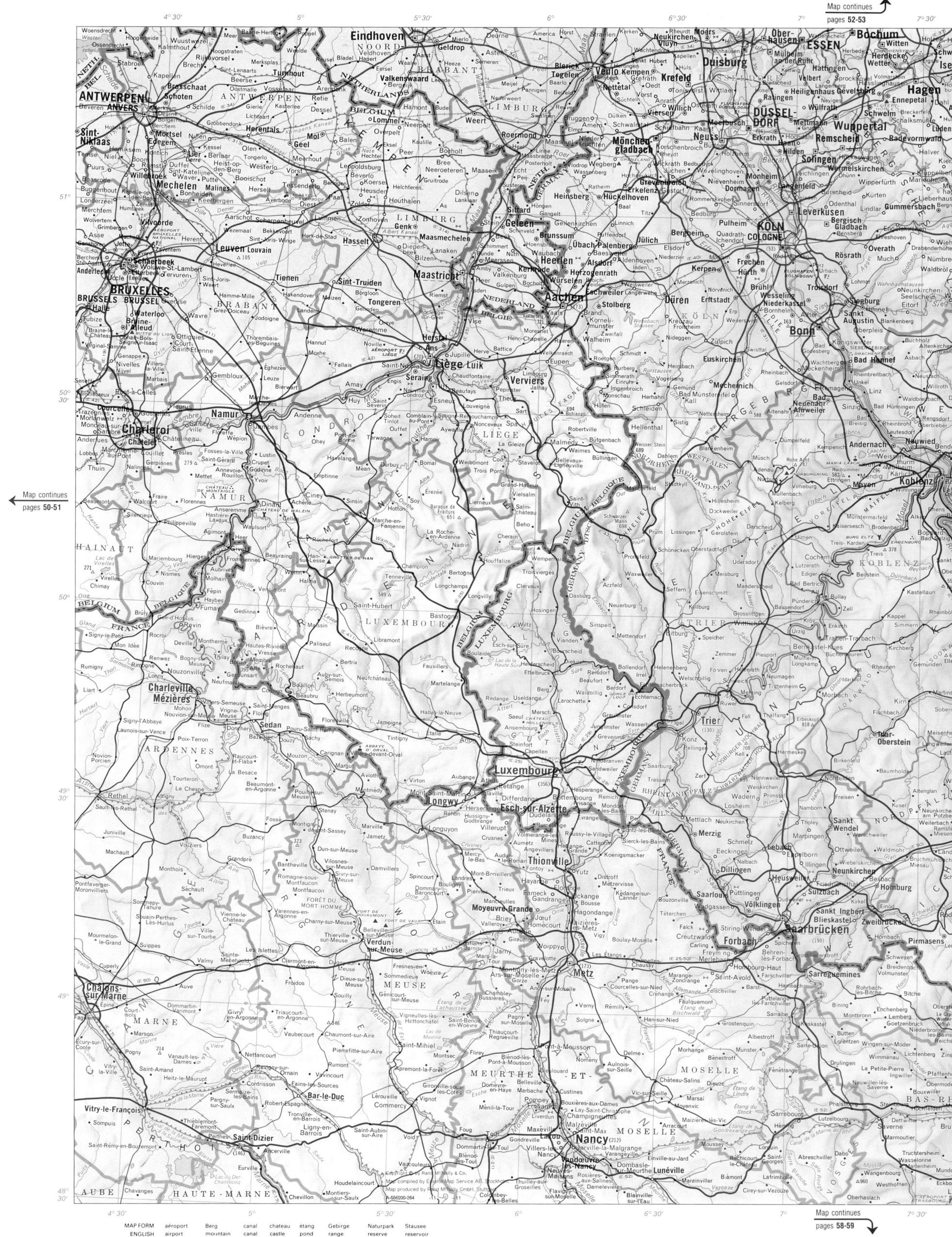

MAP FORM	aéroport	Berg	canal	chateau	étang	Gebirge	Naturpark	Stausee
ENGLISH	airport	mountain	canal	castle	pond	range	reserve	reservoir
DEUTSCH	Flughafen	Berg	Kanal	Burg	Teich	Gebirge	Naturpark	Stausee
ESPAÑOL	aeropuerto	montaña	canal	castillo	charca	cadena	reserva	embalse
FRANCAIS	aéroport	montagne	canal	château	étang	chaîne	réserve	réservoir
PORTUGUÊS	aeroporto	montanha	canal	castelo	lagoa	cordilheira	reserva	reservatório

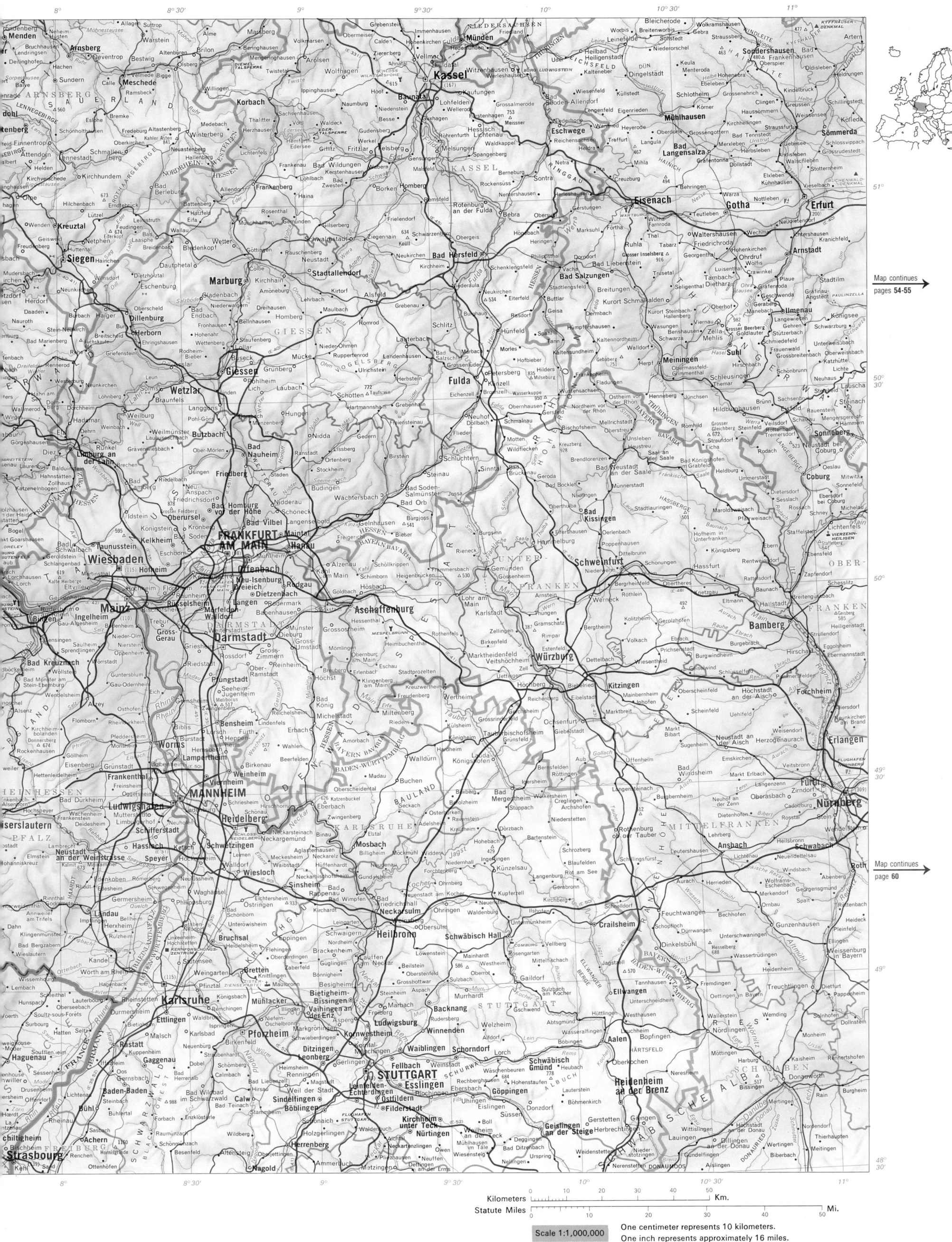

Map continues
pages 54-55 →

Map continues
page 60 →

Kilometers
Statute Miles

Scale 1:1,000,000
One centimeter represents 10 kilometers.
One inch represents approximately 16 miles.
Lambert Conformal Conic Projection

Map continues pages 50-51

MAP FORM	col	Horn	lago	mont	passo	piz, -zo	See	Spitze	val
ENGLISH	pass	peak	lake	mount	pass	peak	See	peak	valley
DEUTSCH	Pass	Horn	See	Berg	Pass	Gipfel	See	Spitze	Tal
ESPAÑOL	paso	pico	lago	monte	paso	pico	lago	pico	valle
FRANÇAIS	col	cime	lac	mont	col	cime	lac	cime	val
PORTUGUÊS	passo	pico	lago	monte	passo	pico	lago	pico	vale

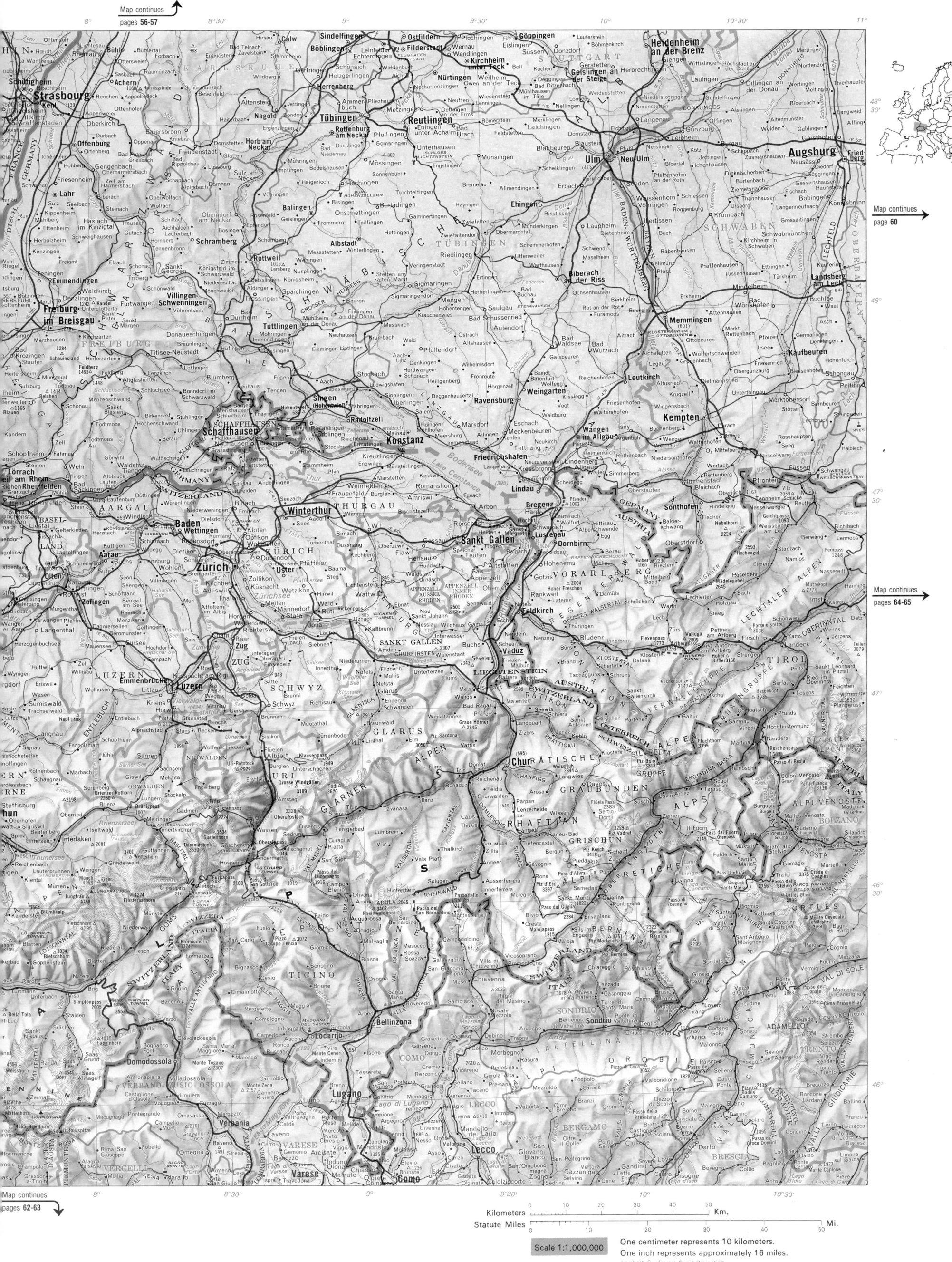

Map continues pages 56-57

Map continues page 60

Map continues pages 64-65

Map continues pages 62-63

Kilometers

Statute Miles

Scale 1:1,000,000   One centimeter represents 10 kilometers.
One inch represents approximately 16 miles.

Lambert Conformal Conic Projection

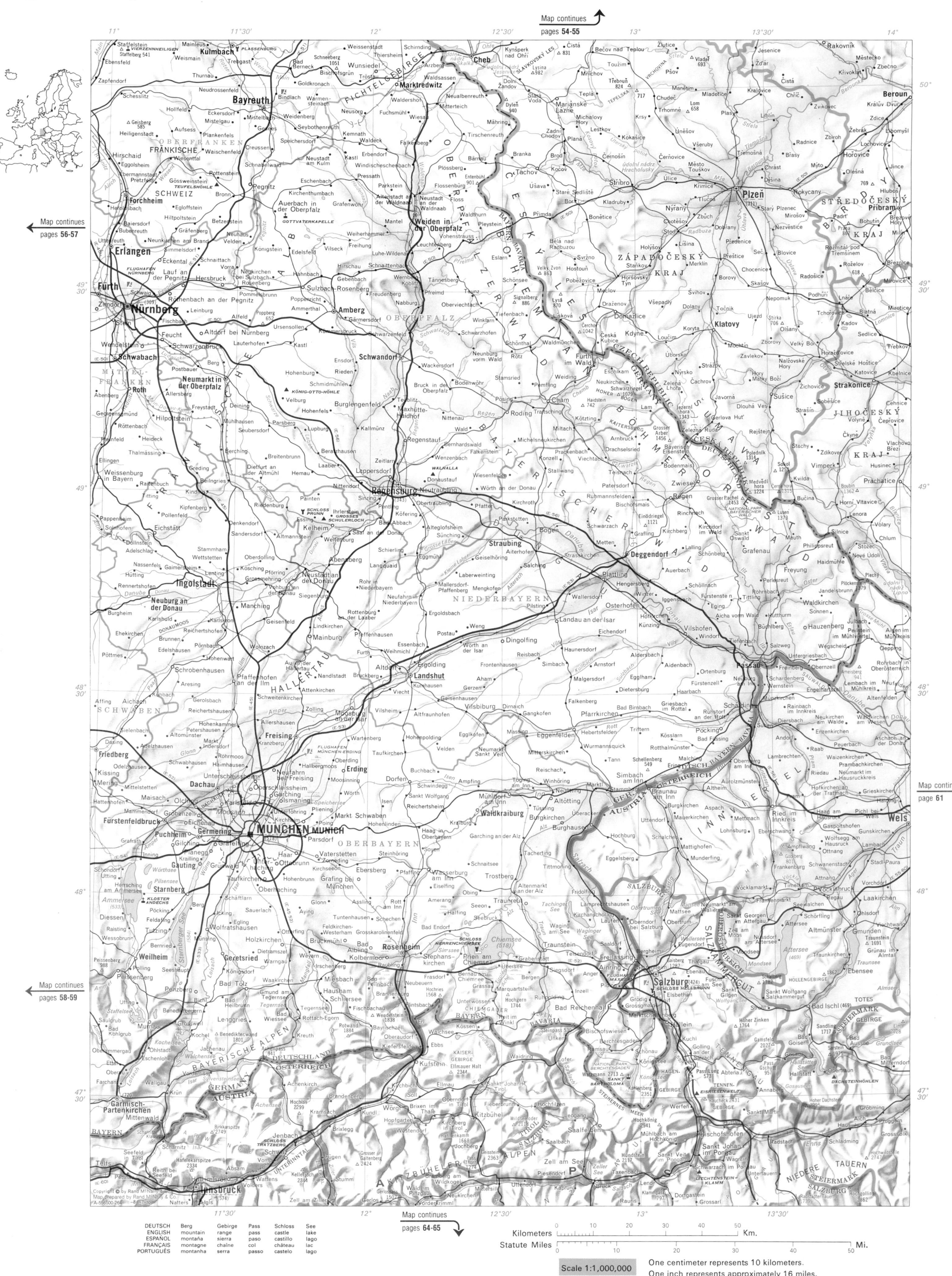

Map continues
pages 54-55

Map continues
pages 56-57

Map continues
pages 58-59

Map continues
page 61

Map continues
pages 64-65

DEUTSCH	Berg	Gebirge	Pass	Schloss	See
ENGLISH	mountain	range	pass	castle	lake
ESPAÑOL	montaña	sierra	paso	castillo	lago
FRANÇAIS	montagne	chaîne	col	château	lac
PORTUGUÊS	montanha	serra	passo	castelo	lago

Kilometers 0 10 20 30 40 50 Km.

Statute Miles 0 10 20 30 40 50 Mi.

Scale 1:1,000,000

One centimeter represents 10 kilometers.
One inch represents approximately 16 miles.
Modified Polyconic Projection

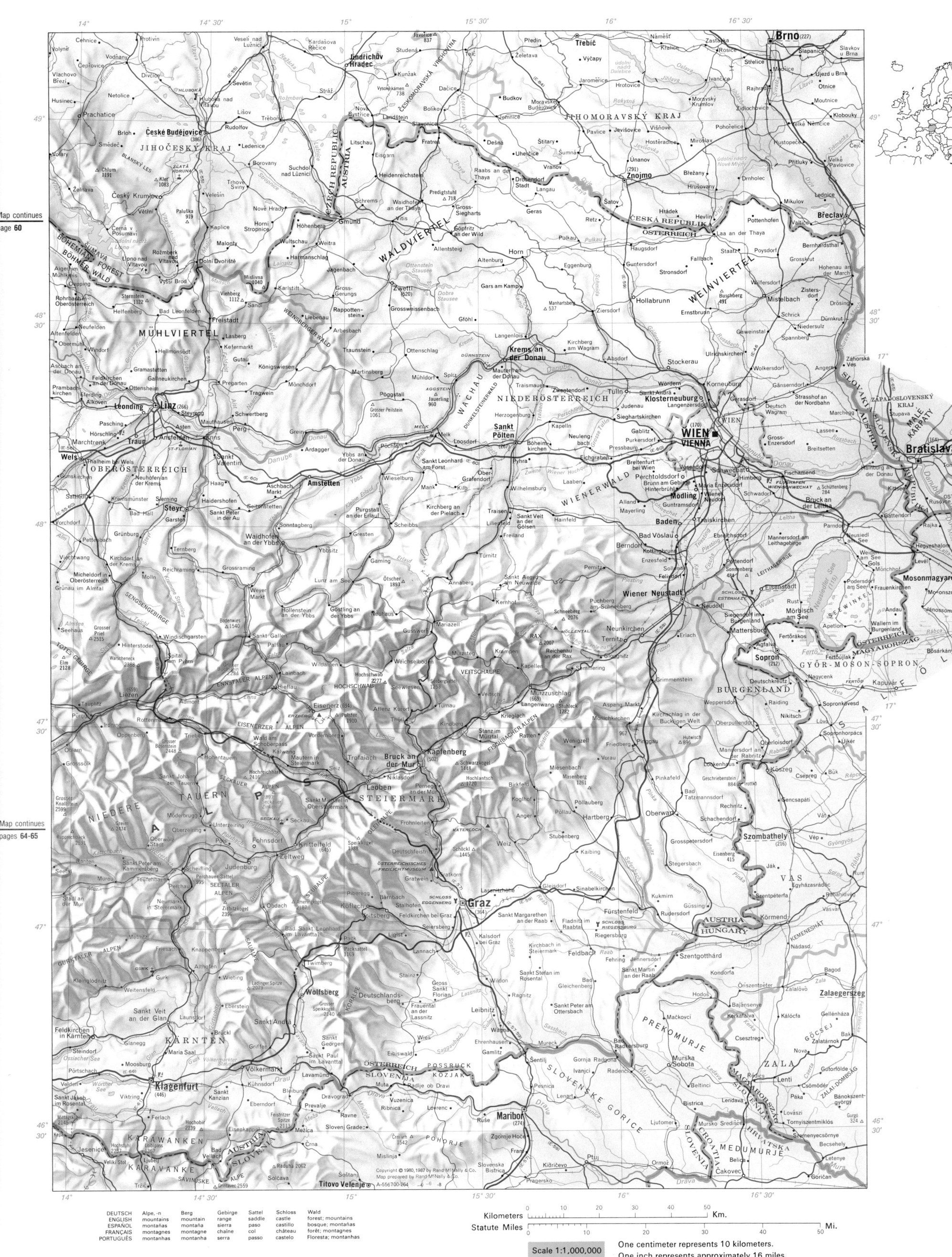

Map continues page 60

Map continues pages 64-65

	DEUTSCH	ENGLISH	ESPAÑOL	FRANÇAIS	PORTUGUÊS
Alpe, -n	mountains	montañas	montagnes	montanhas	
Berg	mountain	montaña	montagne	montanha	
Gebirge	range	sierra	chaîne	serra	
Sattel	saddle	paso	col	passo	
Schloss	castle	castillo	château	castelo	
Wald	forest; mountains	bosque; montañas	forêt; montagnes	Floresta; montanhas	

Kilometers

Statute Miles

Scale 1:1,000,000

One centimeter represents 10 kilometers.
One inch represents approximately 16 miles.

Lambert Conformal Conic Projection

Copyright © 1980, 1987 by Rand McNally & Co.
Map prepared by Rand McNally & Co.
A-556700-264

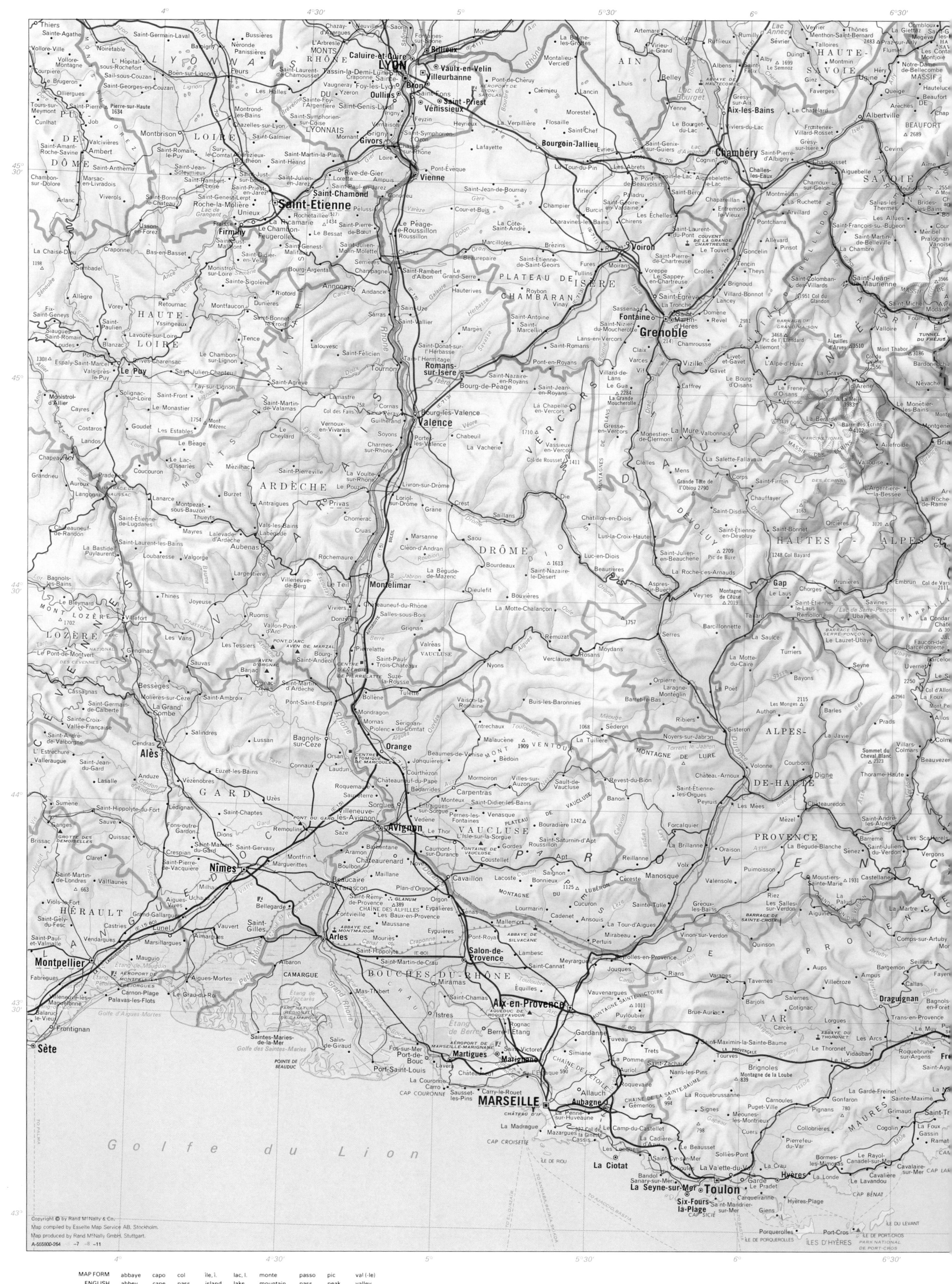

MAP FORM	abbaye	capo	col	île, i.	lac, l.	monte	passo	pic	val (-le)
ENGLISH	abbey	cape	pass	island	lake	mountain	pass	peak	valley
DEUTSCH	Abtei	Kap	Pass	Insel	See	Berg	Pass	Gipfel	Tal
ESPAÑOL	abadía	cabo	paso	isla	lago	montaña	paso	pico	valle
FRANÇAIS	abbaye	cap	col	île	lac	montagne	col	cime	val
PORTUGUÊS	abadia	cabo	passo	ilha	lago	montanha	passo	pico	vale

Map continues
pages 58-59

Map continues
pages 64-65

Golfo di Genova

Ligurian Sea
Mar Ligure

M E D I T E R R A N E A N   S E A

Kilometers
Statute Miles

Scale 1:1,000,000

One centimeter represents 10 kilometers.
One inch represents approximately 16 miles.

Lambert Conformal Conic Projection

Map continues page 61

Map continues page 60

Map continues pages 58-59

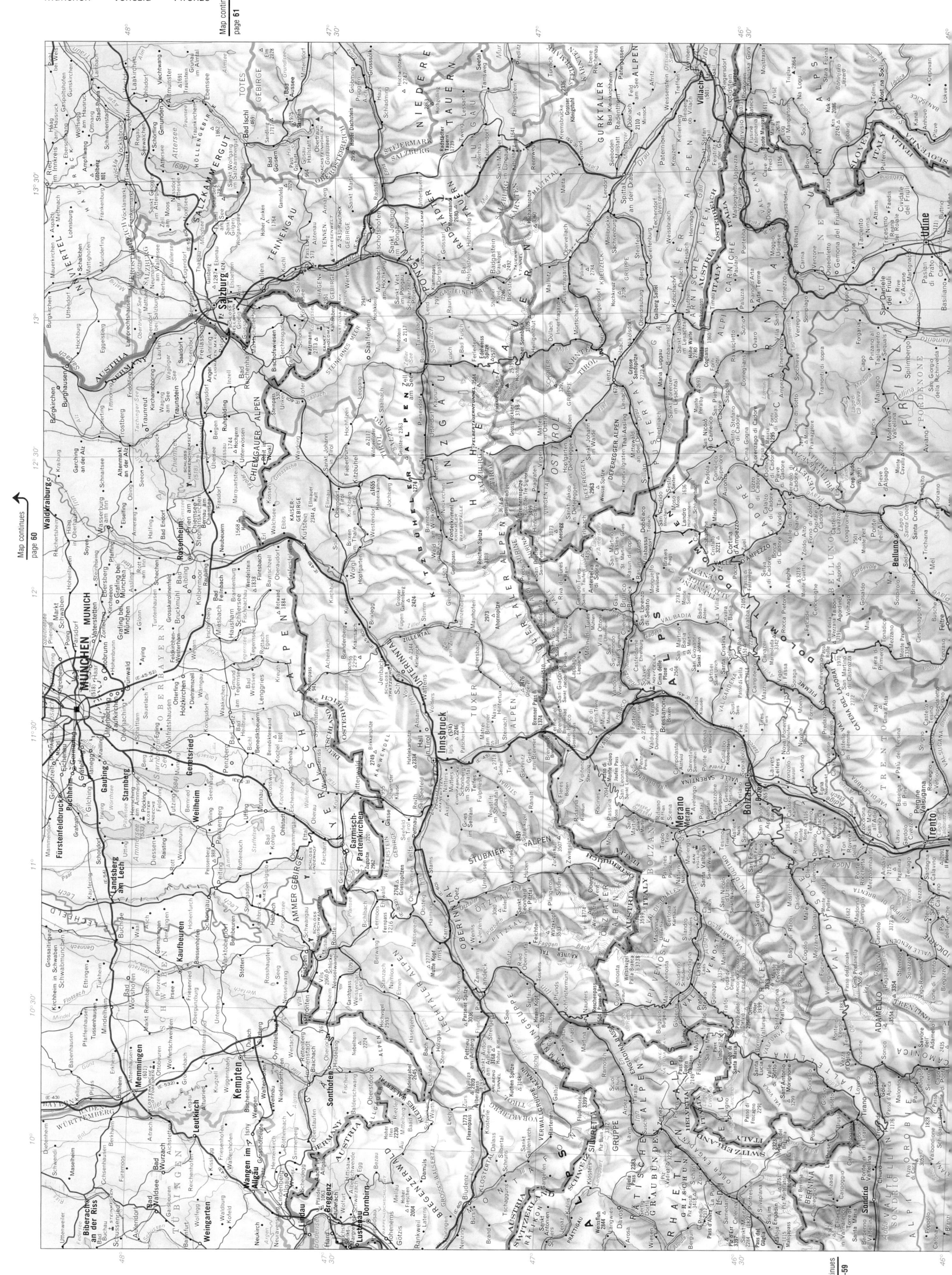

ADRIATIC SEA

MARE ADRIATICO

Gulf of Venice

Gulf of Trieste

LIGURIAN SEA

MAR LIGURE

Map continues pages 66-67

Map continues pages 62-63

Scale 1:1,000,000

Kilometers

Statute Miles

Km.

Mi.

One centimeter represents 10 kilometers.

One inch represents approximately 16 miles.

Lambert Conformal Conic Projection

Copyright © by Rand McNally & Co.
Map compiled by Esselte Map Service AB, Stockholm
Map produced by Rand McNally GmbH Stuttgart
A-660100-264 -7-a-12

MAP FORM								
ENGLISH	Alpen	Berg	Gebirge	cima	monte	piz	Schloss	See	Spitze
DEUTSCH	Alpen	Berg	Gebirge	peak	mountain	peak	castle	lake	peak
ESPAÑOL	Alps	mountain	range	Gipfel	Berg	Gipfel	Schloss	See	Spitze
FRANÇAIS	alpes	montaña	montaña	sierra	montaña	cime	castillo	lago	pico
PORTUGUÊS	montanhas	montagne	montagne	pico	montagne	cime	château	lac	pico
	montanhas	montanha	serra	pico	montanha	pico	castelo	lago	pico

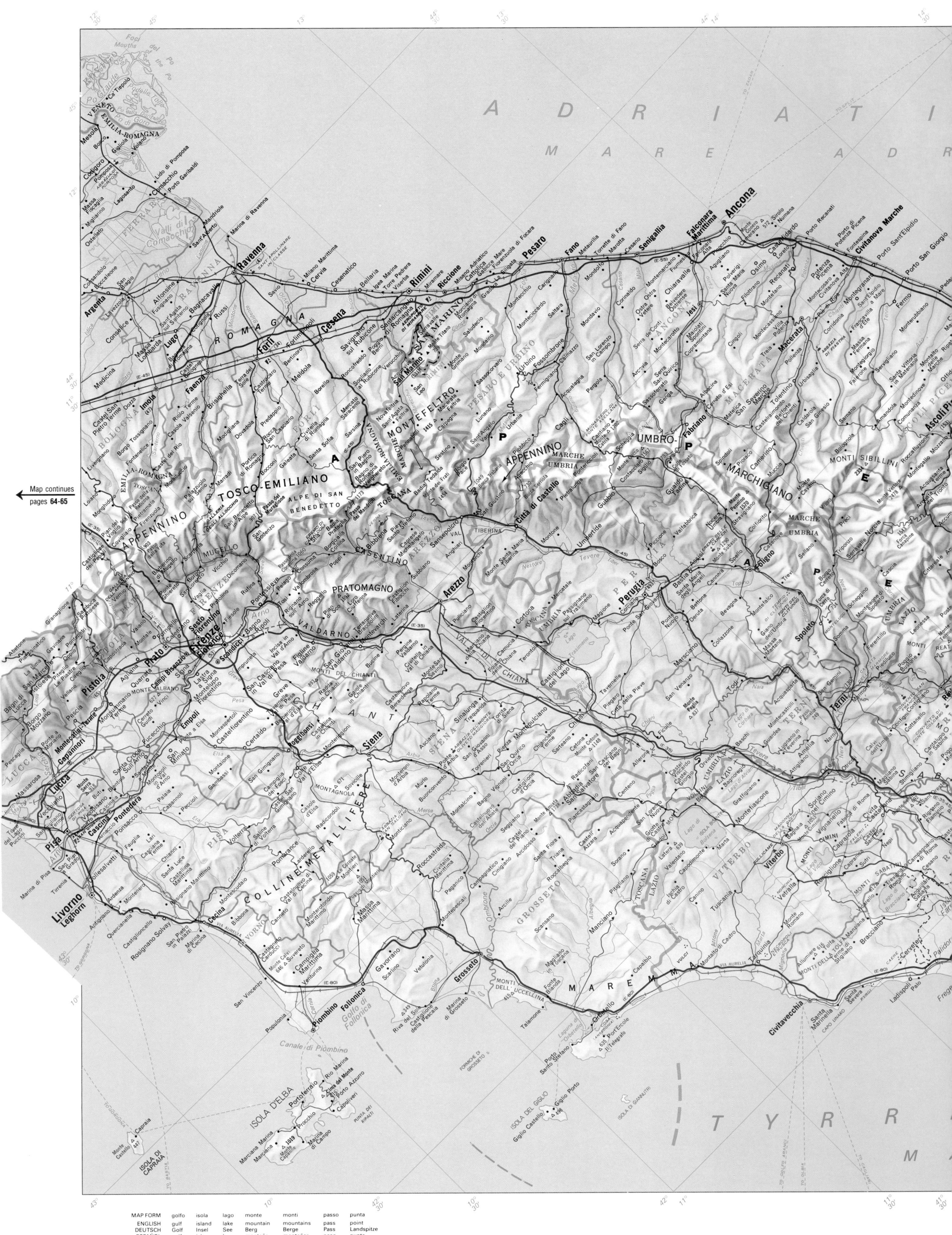

← Map continues
pages 64-65

MAP FORM	golfo	isola	lago	monte	monti	passo	punta
ENGLISH	gulf	island	lake	mountain	mountains	pass	point
DEUTSCH	Golf	Insel	See	Berg	Berge	Pass	Landspitze
ESPAÑOL	golfo	isla	lago	montaña	montañas	paso	punta
FRANÇAIS	golfe	île	lac	montagne	montagnes	col	pointe
PORTUGUÊS	golfo	ilha	lago	montanha	montanhas	passo	ponta

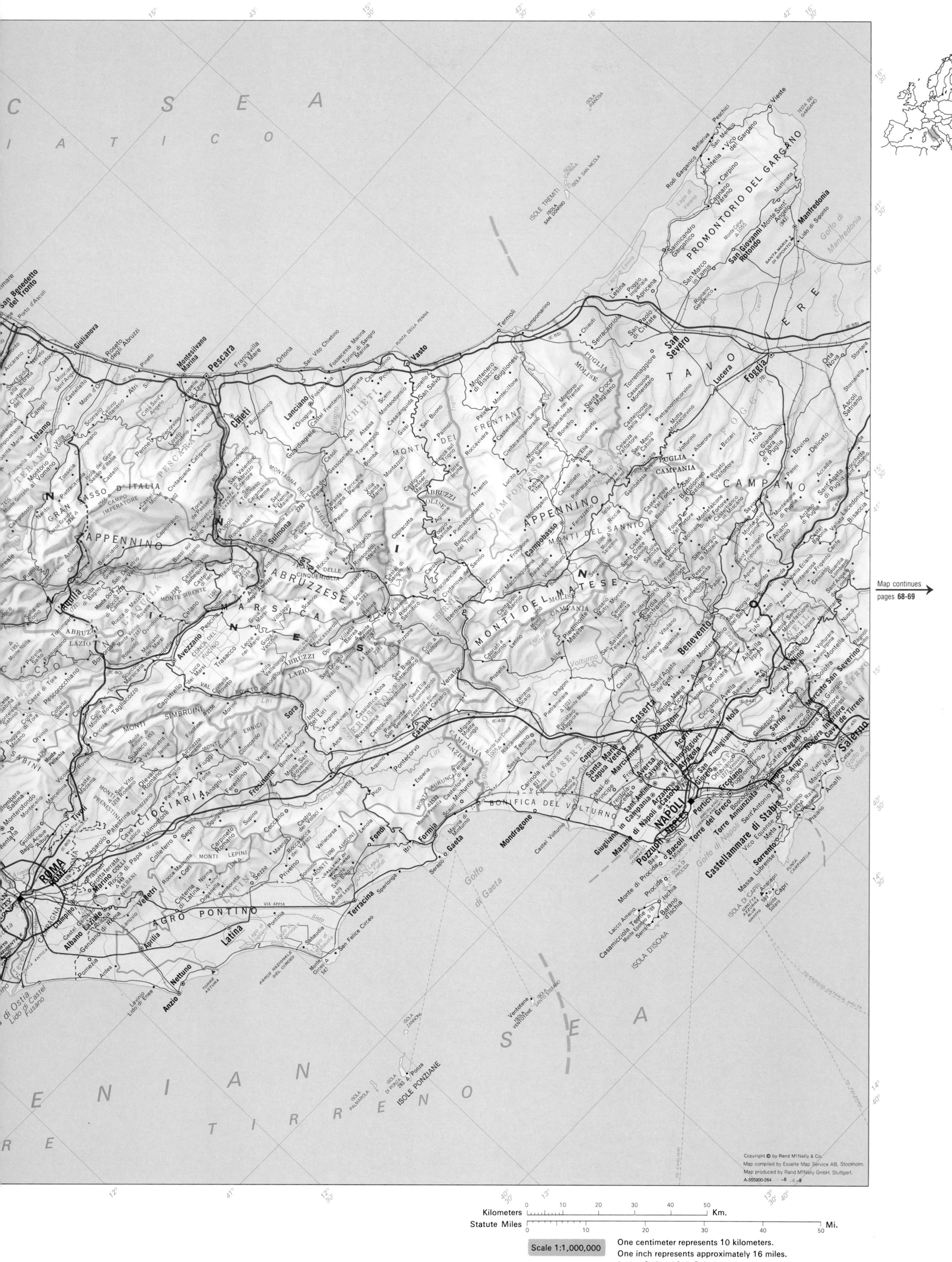

Map continues pages 68-69 →

Kilometers
Statute Miles

Scale 1:1,000,000

One centimeter represents 10 kilometers.
One inch represents approximately 16 miles.
Lambert Conformal Conic Projection

← Map continues pages 66-67

MAP FORM	capo	golfo	isola	lago	monte	monti	punta
ENGLISH	cape	gulf	island	lake	mountain	mountains	point
DEUTSCH	Kap	Golf	Insel	See	Berg	Berge	Landspitze
ESPAÑOL	cabo	golfo	isla	lago	montaña	montañas	punta
FRANÇAIS	cap	golfe	île	lac	montagne	montagnes	pointe
PORTUGUÊS	cabo	golfo	ilha	lago	montanha	montanhas	ponta

Strait of Otranto

San Cataldo

Lecce
LECCE
Galatina
Copertino
Nardò
MURGE
SALENTINE
PENISOLA SALENTINA
CAPO SANTA MARIA DI LEUCA
Gallipoli

Manduria
TARANTINE

Golfo di Taranto

MARE TIRRENO

IONIAN SEA
MARE IONIO

Capo Spulico

Crotone

Cirò Marina

SILA GRANDE
COSENZA
CATENA COSTIERA
SILA PICCOLA
Catanzaro
Golfo di Squillace

Nicastro
Golfo di Sant'Eufemia

Golfo di Gioia

Tropea

CALABRIA
SICILIA

SICILIA
SICILY

Reggio di Calabria

Messina

ISOLA STROMBOLI

Map continues
page 70

Kilometers 0 10 20 30 40 50 Km.
Statute Miles 0 10 20 30 40 50 Mi.

Scale 1:1,000,000
One centimeter represents 10 kilometers.
One inch represents approximately 16 miles.
Lambert Conformal Conic Projection

Map continues pages 68-69

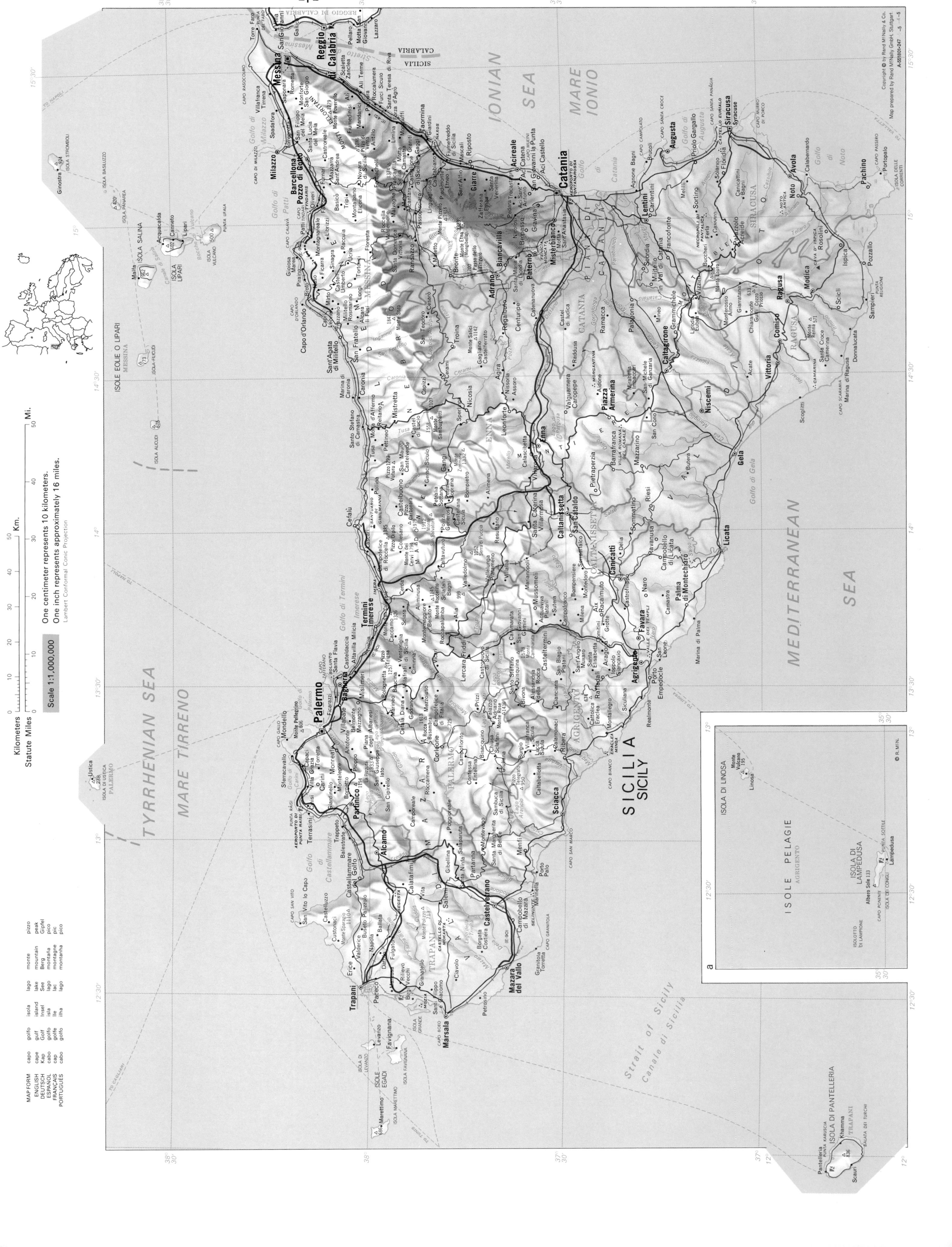

Kilometers

Statute Miles

Scale 1:1,000,000

One centimeter represents 10 kilometers.
One inch represents approximately 16 miles.
Lambert Conformal Conic Projection

MAP FORM			
ENGLISH	cape	island	gulf
DEUTSCH	Kap	Insel	Golf
ESPAÑOL	cabo	isla	golfo
FRANÇAIS	cap	île	golfe
PORTUGUÊS	cabo	ilha	golfo

monte	mountain	pizzo
	Berg	peak
	montaña	Gipfel
	montagne	pico
	montanha	pico

lago	lake
	See
	lago
	lac
	lago

TYRRHENIAN SEA

MARE TIRRENO

IONIAN SEA

MARE IONIO

MEDITERRANEAN SEA

Strait of Sicily

Canale di Sicilia

SICILIA

SICILY

ISOLE EOLIE O LIPARI

ISOLE PELAGIE

ISOLA DI PANTELLERIA

Palermo

Catania

Messina

Reggio di Calabria

Siracusa

Syracuse

Trapani

Marsala

Agrigento

Ragusa

Copyright © by Rand McNally & Co.

Map prepared by Rand McNally GmbH, Stuttgart

A-585801-247

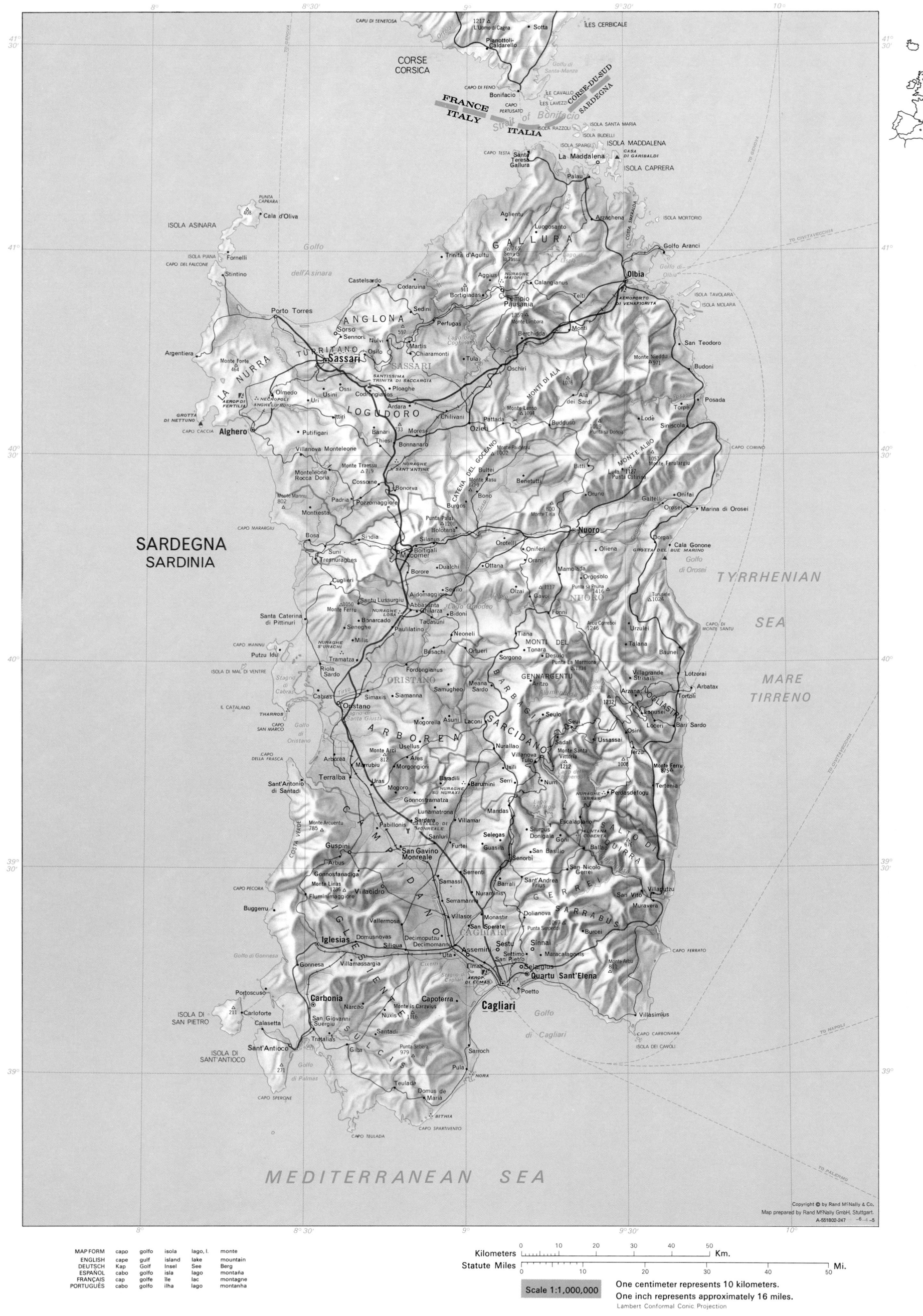

SARDEGNA
SARDINIA

TYRRHENIAN
SEA

MARE
TIRRENO

MEDITERRANEAN SEA

CORSE
CORSICA

FRANCE
ITALY

ITALIA

Copyright © by Rand McNally & Co.
Map prepared by Rand McNally GmbH, Stuttgart.
A-551802-247   -6-4-5

MAP FORM	capo	golfo	isola	lago, l.	monte
ENGLISH	cape	gulf	island	lake	mountain
DEUTSCH	Kap	Golf	Insel	See	Berg
ESPAÑOL	cabo	golfo	isla	lago	montaña
FRANÇAIS	cap	golfe	île	lac	montagne
PORTUGUÊS	cabo	golfo	ilha	lago	montanha

Kilometers
Statute Miles

0 10 20 30 40 50 Km.
0 10 20 30 40 50 Mi.

Scale 1:1,000,000

One centimeter represents 10 kilometers.
One inch represents approximately 16 miles.
Lambert Conformal Conic Projection

← Map continues pages 22-23

← Map continues pages 118-119

MAP FORM	chrebet	gora	guba	mys	ostrov	ozero	poluostrov	proliv	vodochranilišče
ENGLISH	range	mountain	bay	cape	island	lake	peninsula	strait	reservoir
DEUTSCH	Gebirge	Berg	Bucht	Kap	Insel	See	Halbinsel	Meeresstrasse	Stausee
ESPAÑOL	sierra	montaña	bahía	cabo	isla	lago	península	estrecho	embalse
FRANÇAIS	chaîne	montagne	baie	cap	île	lac	péninsule	détroit	réservoir
PORTUGUÊS	serra	montanha	bala	cabo	ilha	lago	peninsula	estreito	reservatório

Map continues
pages 74-75 →

Map continues
pages 90-91

Kilometers

Statute Miles

Scale 1:12,000,000   One centimeter represents 120 kilometers.
One inch represents approximately 190 miles.
Lambert Conformal Conic Projection

Copyright © by Rand McNally & Co.
Map prepared by Esselte Map Service AB, Stockholm
A-579594-264 -12 -37 -26

← Map continues
pages 72-73

Map continues
pages 90-91 →

MAP FORM	chrebet	gora	guba	mys	ostrov	ozero	poluostrov	proliv	vodochranilišče
ENGLISH	range	mountain	bay	cape	island	lake	peninsula	strait	reservoir
DEUTSCH	Gebirge	Berg	Bucht	Kap	Insel	See	Halbinsel	Meeresstrasse	Stausee
ESPAÑOL	sierra	montaña	bahía	cabo	isla	lago	península	estrecho	embalse
FRANÇAIS	chaîne	montagne	baie	cap	île	lac	péninsule	détroit	réservoir
PORTUGUÊS	serra	montanha	baía	cabo	ilha	lago	península	estreito	reservatório

Kilometers

Statute Miles

Scale 1:12,000,000

One centimeter represents 120 kilometers.
One inch represents approximately 190 miles.
Lambert Conformal Conic Projection

Copyright © by Rand McNally & Co.
Map prepared by Esselte Map Service AB, Stockholm.
A-579395-264   -8   -6   12

ALASKA
UNITED STATES

OSTROVA
Vostočno-Sibirskoje More
EAST SIBERIAN SEA

Chukchi Sea

OSTROVA ANŽU

Arctic Circle

Bering Sea

OSTROV KOTEL'NYJ

L'ACHOVSKIJE OSTROVA

SAINT LAWRENCE ISLAND

NUNIVAK ISLAND

KOLYMSKAJA NIZMENNOST'

JUKAGIRSKOJE PLOSKOGORJE

ANUJSKIJ CHREBET

PENŽINSKIJ CHREBET

KORJAKSKOJE NAGORJE

MOMSKIJ CHREBET

CHREBET ČERSKOGO

JAKUTIJA

SIBERIA

CHREBET

CHREBET SETTE-DABAN

CHREBET SUNTAR-CHAJATA

Jakutsk
Pokrovsk

Verchojansk

Magadan

Ochotsk

POLUOSTROV KAMČATKA
KAMCHATKA

SREDINNYJ CHREBET

Petropavlovsk-Kamčatskij

KOMANDORSKOJE OSTROVA

ALDANSKOJE NAGORJE

CHREBET DŽUGDŽUR

SEA OF OKHOTSK
OCHOTSKOJE MORE

STANOVOJ CHREBET

Ajan

SANTARSKIJE OSTROVA

OSTROV SACHALIN
SACHALIN

Komsomol'sk na-Amure

Svobodnyj

Blagoveščensk

Chabarovsk

BUREINSKIJ CHREBET

SICHOTE-ALIN

KURIL'SKIJE OSTROVA
KURIL ISLANDS

OSTROV URUP

Južno-Sachalinsk

Le Perouse Strait

Habomai, Shikotan, Kunashir, and Etorofu, occupied since 1945, are claimed by Japan pending a final peace treaty.

DAHINGAN LING

NEI MONGGOL
ZIZHIQU

MANCHURIA

CHINA

HEILONGJIANG

Qiqihar Tsitsihar

Harbin

JILIN

Mudanjiang

Ussurijsk

Art'om

Nachodka

Vladivostok

HOKKAIDŌ

Asahikawa

Kushiro

Obihiro

Sapporo

Otaru

Muroran

Hakodate

SEA OF JAPAN

JAPAN

HONSHŪ

Aomori

Hachinohe

Hirosaki

Akita

Morioka

PACIFIC OCEAN

Map continues
pages 26-27

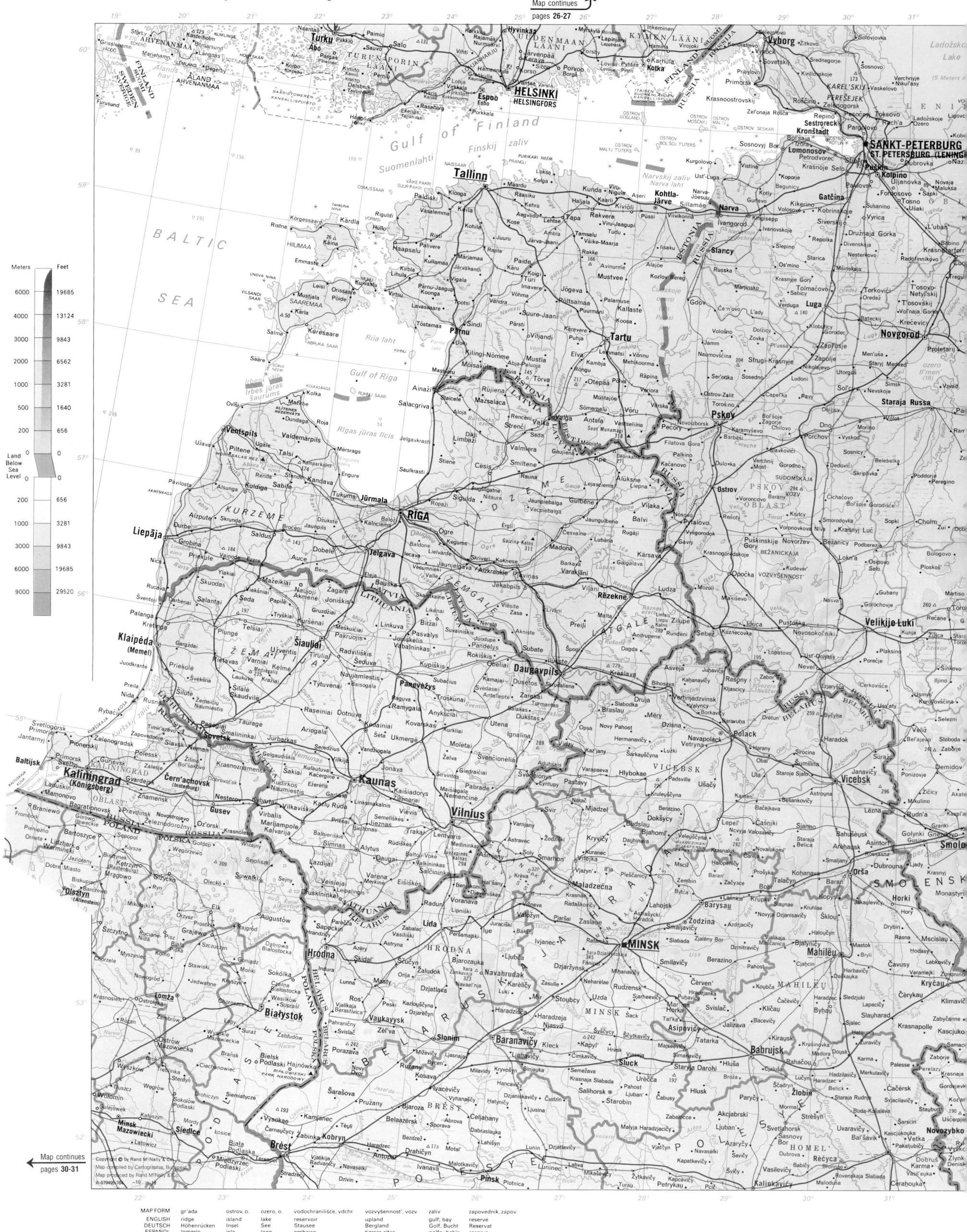

Map continues
pages 30-31

MAP FORM	gr'ada	ostrov, o.	ozero, o.	vodochranilišče, vdchr.	vozvyšennost', vozv.	zaliv	zapovednik, zapov.
ENGLISH	ridge	island	lake	reservoir	upland	gulf; bay	reserve
DEUTSCH	Höhenrücken	Insel	See	Stausee	Bergland	Golf; Bucht	Reservat
ESPAÑOL	lomerío	isla	lago	embalse	tierras altas	golfo; bahía	reserva
FRANÇAIS	crête	île	lac	réservoir	hautes terres	golfe; baie	réserve
PORTUGUÊS	cordilheira	ilha	lago	reservatório	terras altas	golfo; baía	reserva

Baltic and Moscow Regions / Baltenland und Mittelrussland / Regiones de Báltico y de Moscú
Républiques Baltes et la Région de Moscou / Regiões do Báltico e de Moscou

77

Map continues
pages 24-25

Map continues
pages 80-81

Map continues
pages 78-79

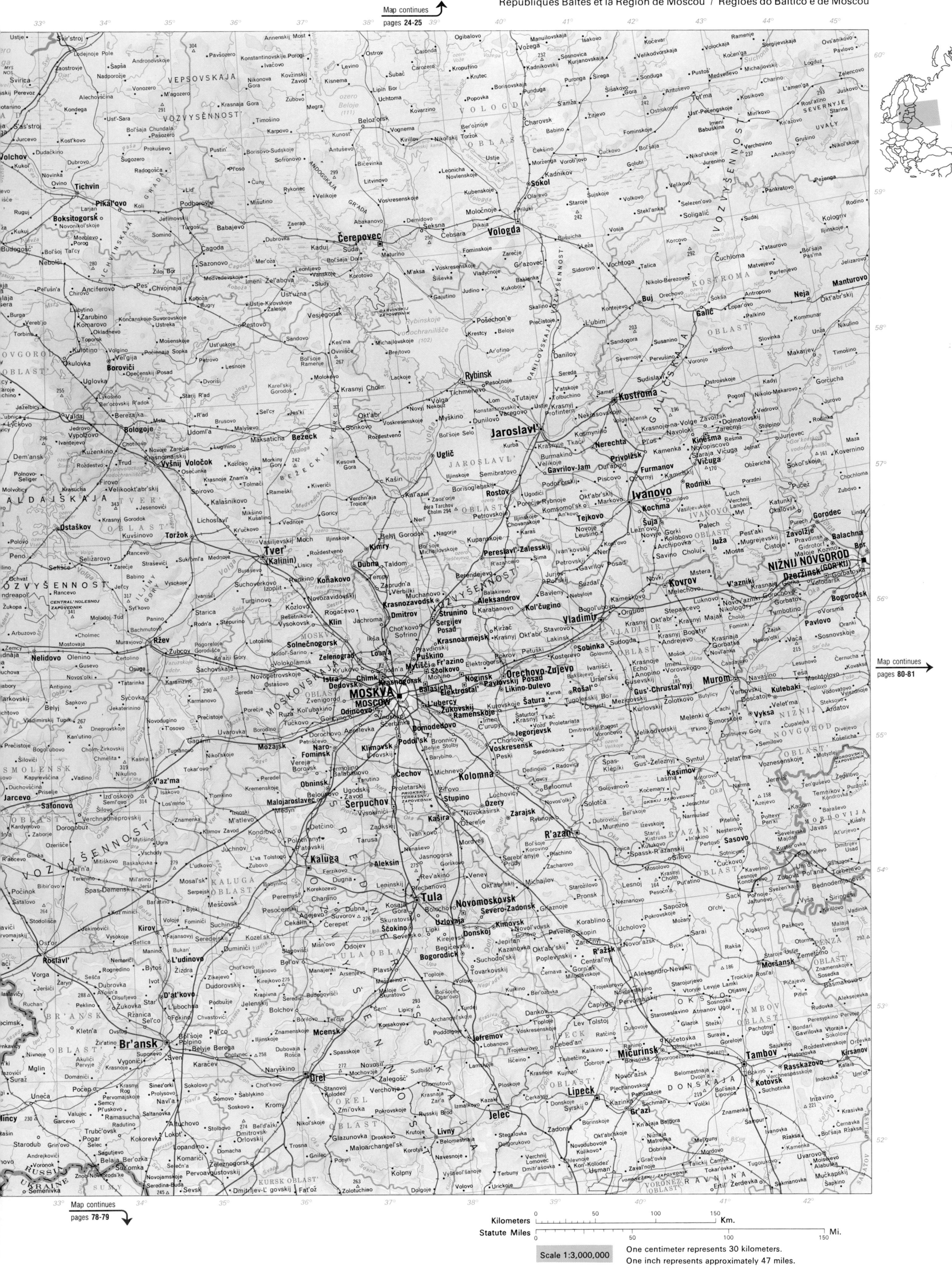

Kilometers

Km.

Statute Miles

Mi.

Scale 1:3,000,000   One centimeter represents 30 kilometers.
One inch represents approximately 47 miles.
Lambert Conformal Conic Projection

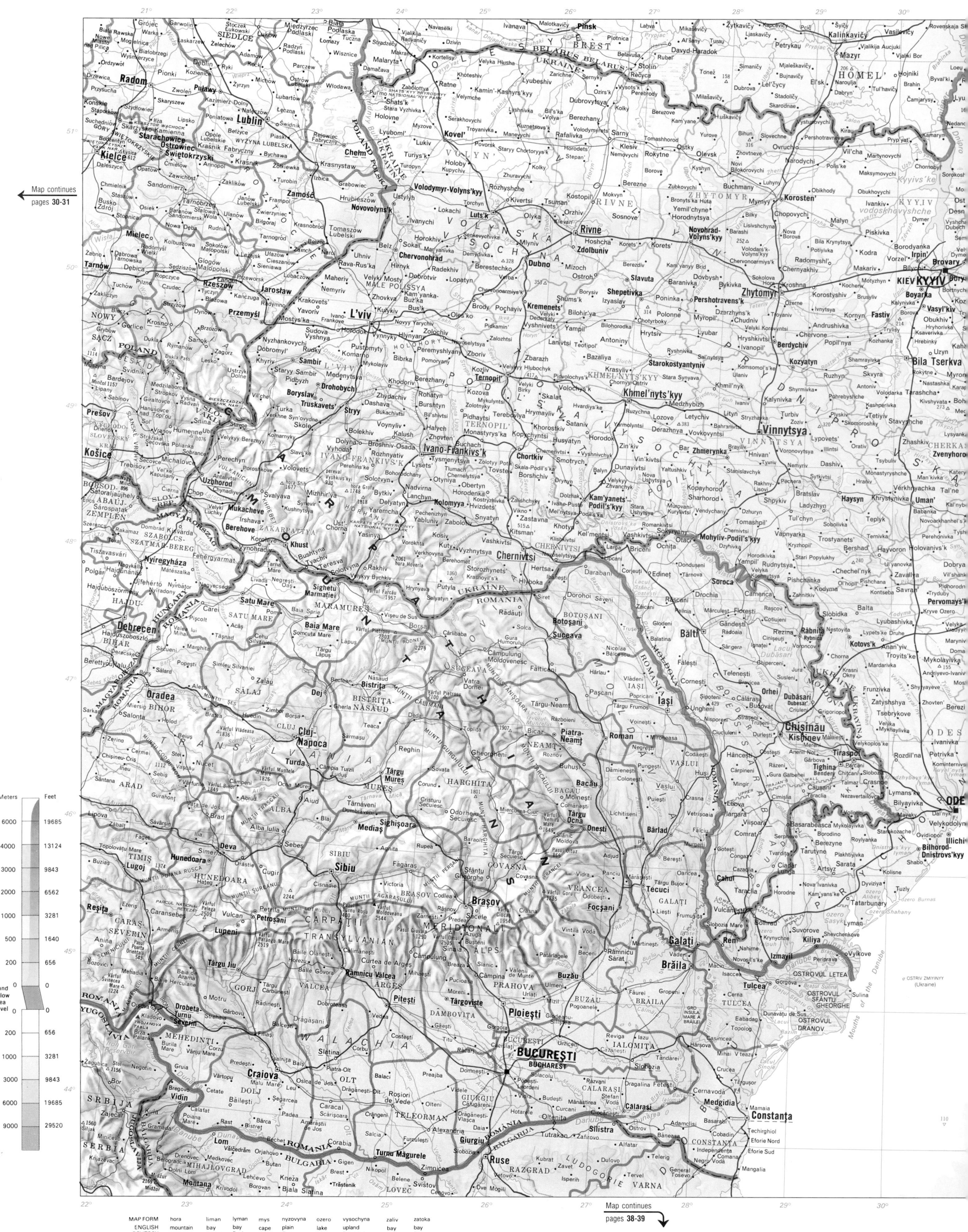

Map continues
pages 30-31

Map continues
pages 38-39

MAP FORM	hora	liman	lyman	mys	nyzovyna	ozero	vysochyna	zaliv	zatoka
ENGLISH	mountain	bay	bay	cape	plain	lake	upland	bay	bay
DEUTSCH	Berg	Bucht	Bucht	Kap	Ebene	See	Bergland	Bucht	Bucht
ESPAÑOL	montaña	bahía	bahía	cabo	llanura	lago	tierras altas	bahía	bahía
FRANÇAIS	montagne	baie	baie	cap	plaine	lac	hautes terres	baie	baie
PORTUGUÊS	montanha	baía	baía	cabo	planície	lago	terras altas	baía	baía

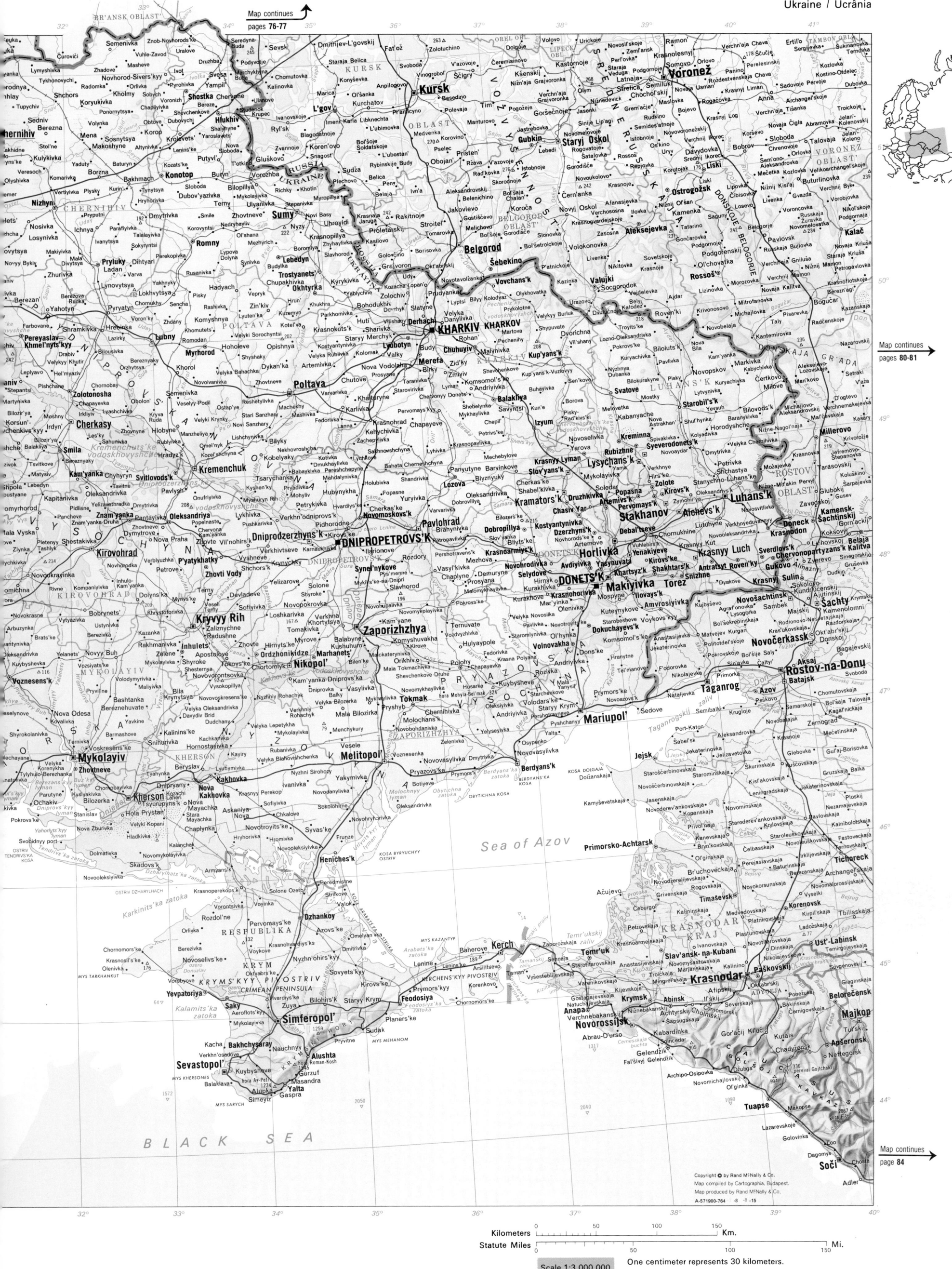

Map continues
pages 76-77

Map continues
pages 80-81

Map continues
pages 84

Sea of Azov

BLACK SEA

Kilometers   0   50   100   150   Km.

Statute Miles   0   50   150   Mi.

Scale 1:3,000,000

One centimeter represents 30 kilometers.
One inch represents approximately 47 miles.

Lambert Conformal Conic Projection

Map continues
pages 24-25

Map continues
pages 76-77

Map continues
pages 86-87

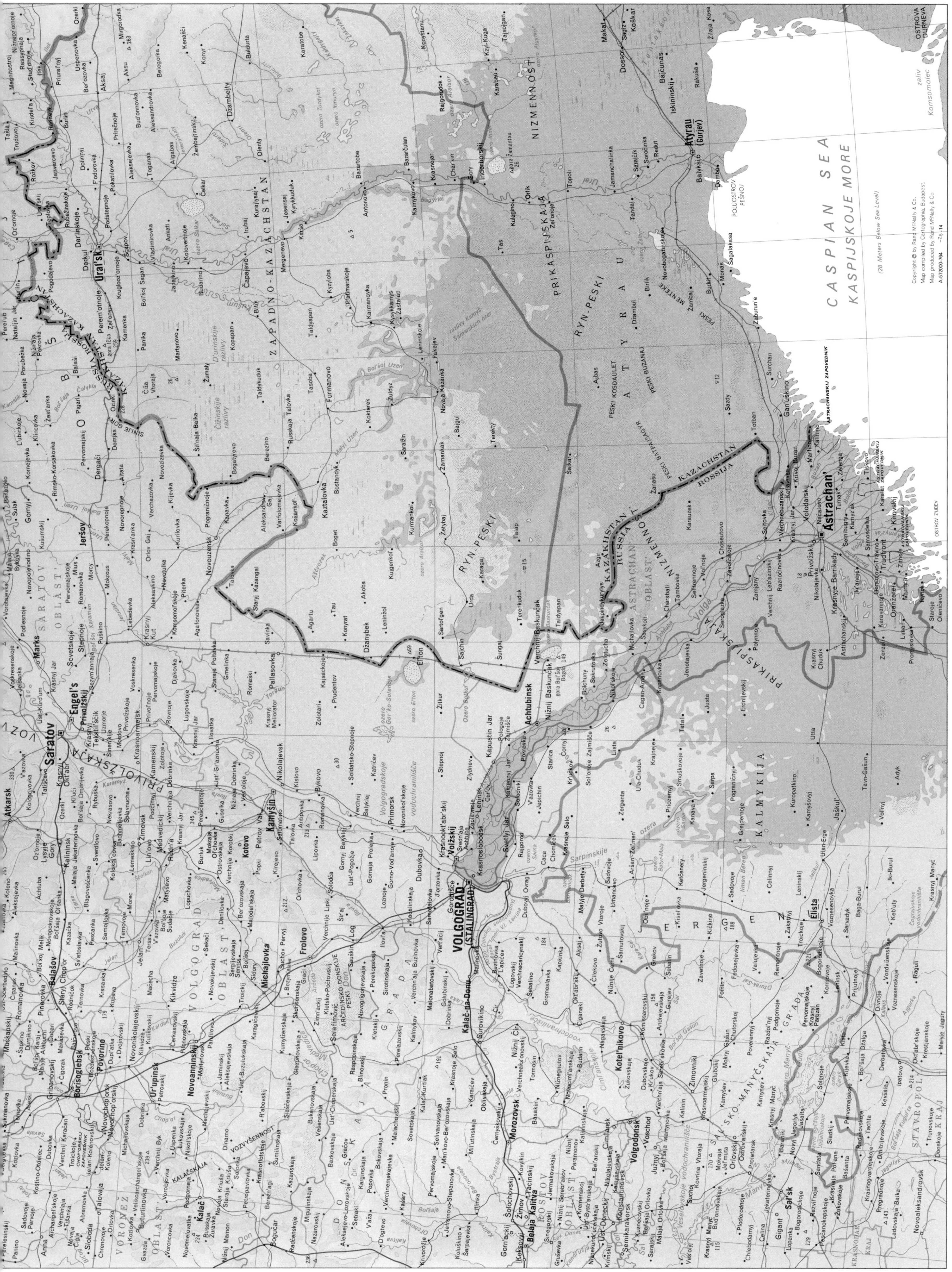

Map continues
pages 78-79

Map continues
page 84

CASPIAN SEA
KASPIJSKOJE MORE

zaliv Komsomolec

Copyright © by Rand McNally & Co.
Map compiled by Cartographia, Budapest.
Map produced by Rand McNally & Co.
A-572000.784   -74.-14

Scale 1:3,000,000

One centimeter represents 30 kilometers.
One inch represents approximately 47 miles.
Lambert Conformal Conic Projection

Kilometers
Statute Miles

MAP FORM							
ENGLISH	gory	ostrov	ozero	peski	vodochranilišče	vozvyšennost	vozvyšennost
DEUTSCH	Berge	Insel	See	Wüste	Stausee	Bergland	Reservoir
ESPAÑOL	montañas	isla	lago	desierto	embalse	tierras altas	reserva
FRANÇAIS	montagnes	île	lac	désert	réservoir	hautes terres	réserve
PORTUGUÊS	montanhas	ilha	lago	deserto	reservatório	terras altas	reserva
ENGLISH	mountains	island	lake	desert	reservoir	upland	reserve

Feet
19685
13124
9843
6562
3281
1640
656
0
Land Below Sea Level
0
656
3281
9843
19685
29520

Meters
6000
4000
3000
2000
1000
500
200
0
Land Below Sea Level
0
200
1000
3000
6000
9000

Mi.
150

Km.
150

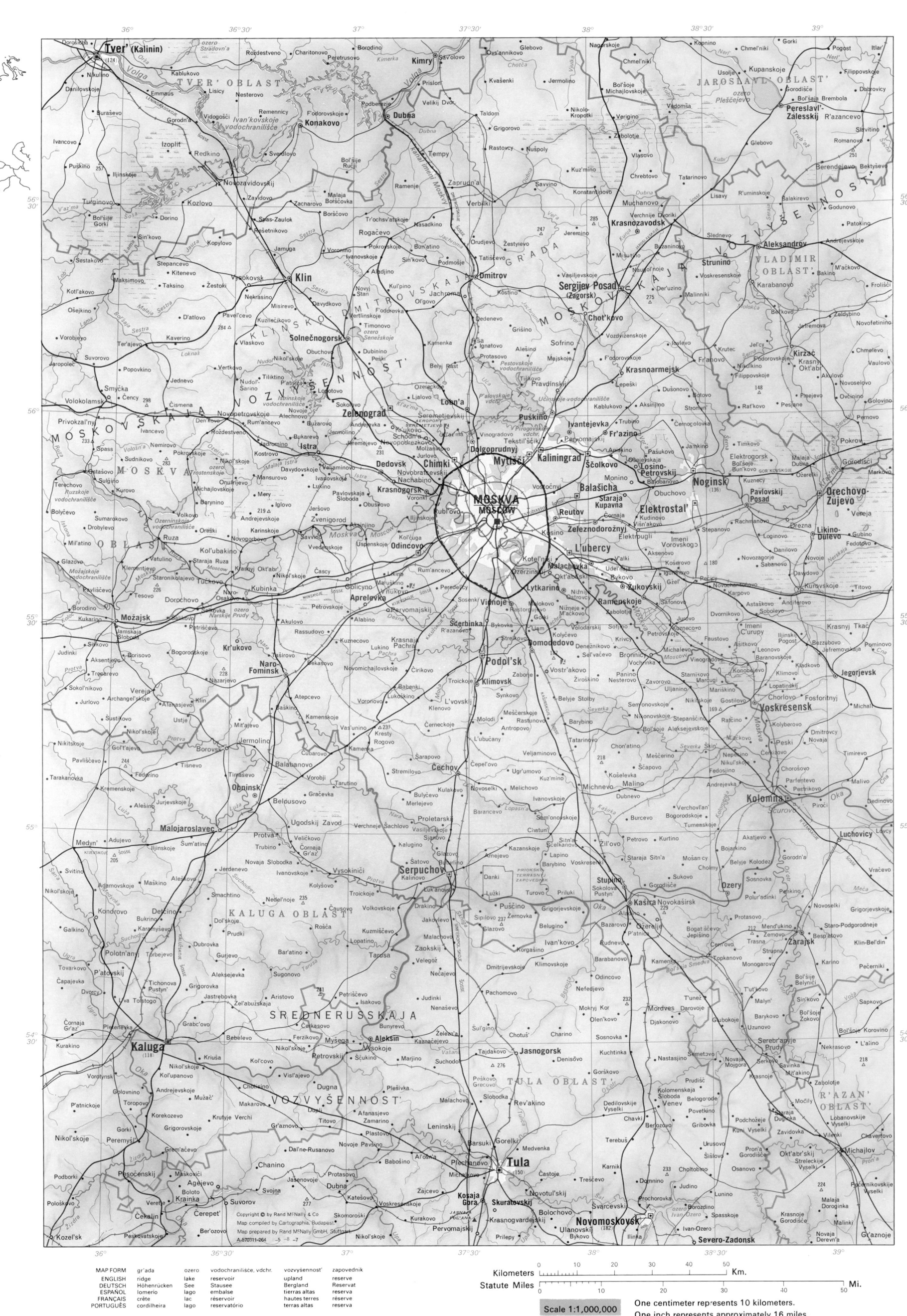

MAP FORM	gr′ada	ozero	vodochranilišče, vdchr.	vozvyšennost′	zapovednik
ENGLISH	ridge	lake	reservoir	upland	reserve
DEUTSCH	Höhenrücken	See	Stausee	Bergland	Reservat
ESPAÑOL	lomerío	lago	embalse	tierras altas	reserva
FRANÇAIS	crête	lac	réservoir	hautes terres	réserve
PORTUGUÊS	cordilheira	lago	reservatório	terras altas	reserva

Kilometers

Statute Miles

Scale 1:1,000,000

One centimeter represents 10 kilometers.
One inch represents approximately 16 miles.
Lambert Conformal Conic Projection

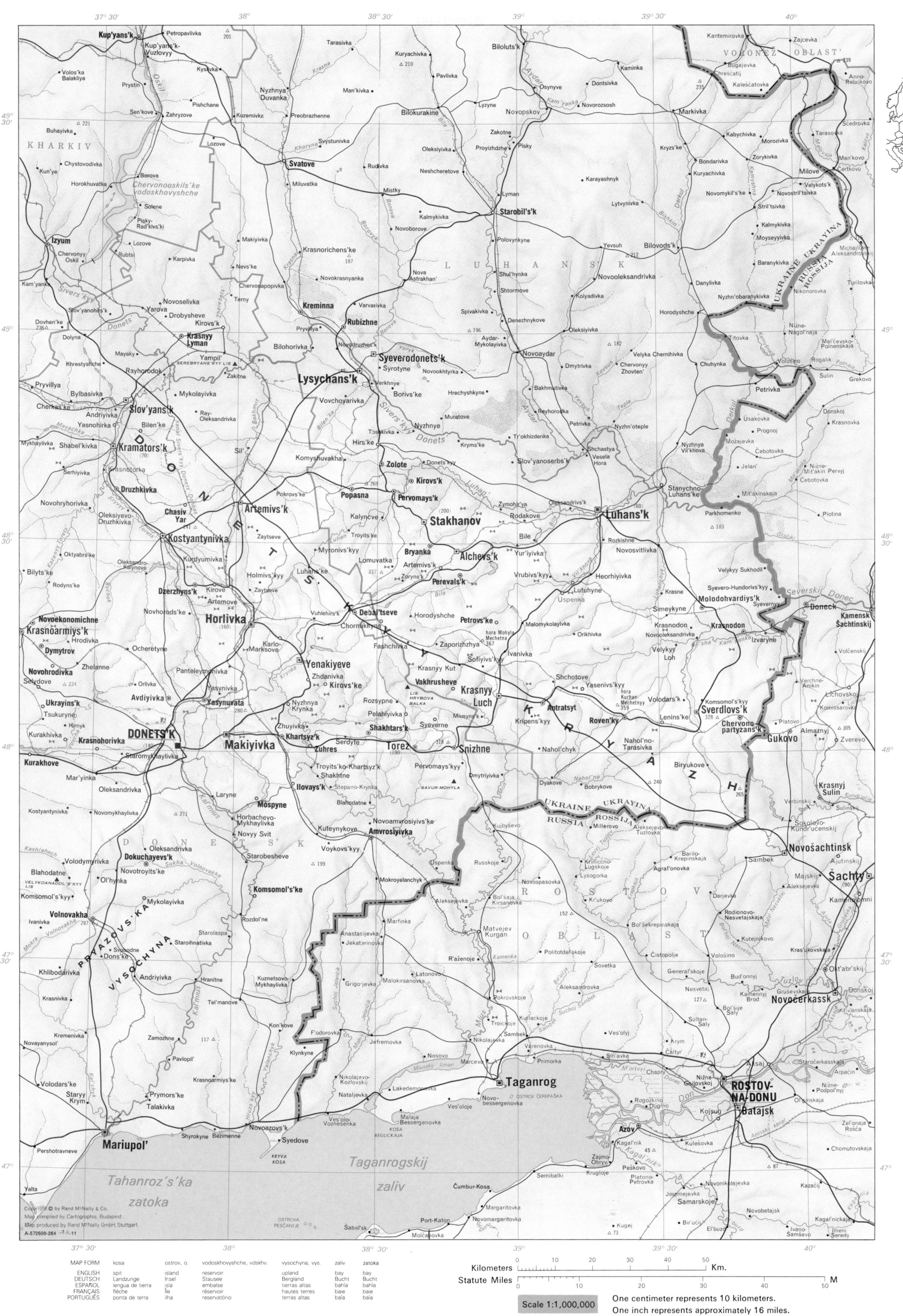

MAP FORM	kosa	ostrov, o.	vodoskhovyshche, vdskhv.	vysochyna, vys.	zaliv	zatoka
ENGLISH	spit	island	reservoir	upland	bay	bay
DEUTSCH	Landzunge	Insel	Stausee	Bergland	Bucht	Bucht
ESPAÑOL	lengua de tierra	isla	embalse	terras altas	bahía	bahía
FRANÇAIS	flèche	île	réservoir	hautes terres	baie	baie
PORTUGUÊS	ponta de terra	ilha	reservatório	terras altas	baía	baía

Kilometers

Statute Miles

One centimeter represents 10 kilometers.
One inch represents approximately 16 miles.

Scale 1:1,000,000

Lambert Conformal Conic Projection

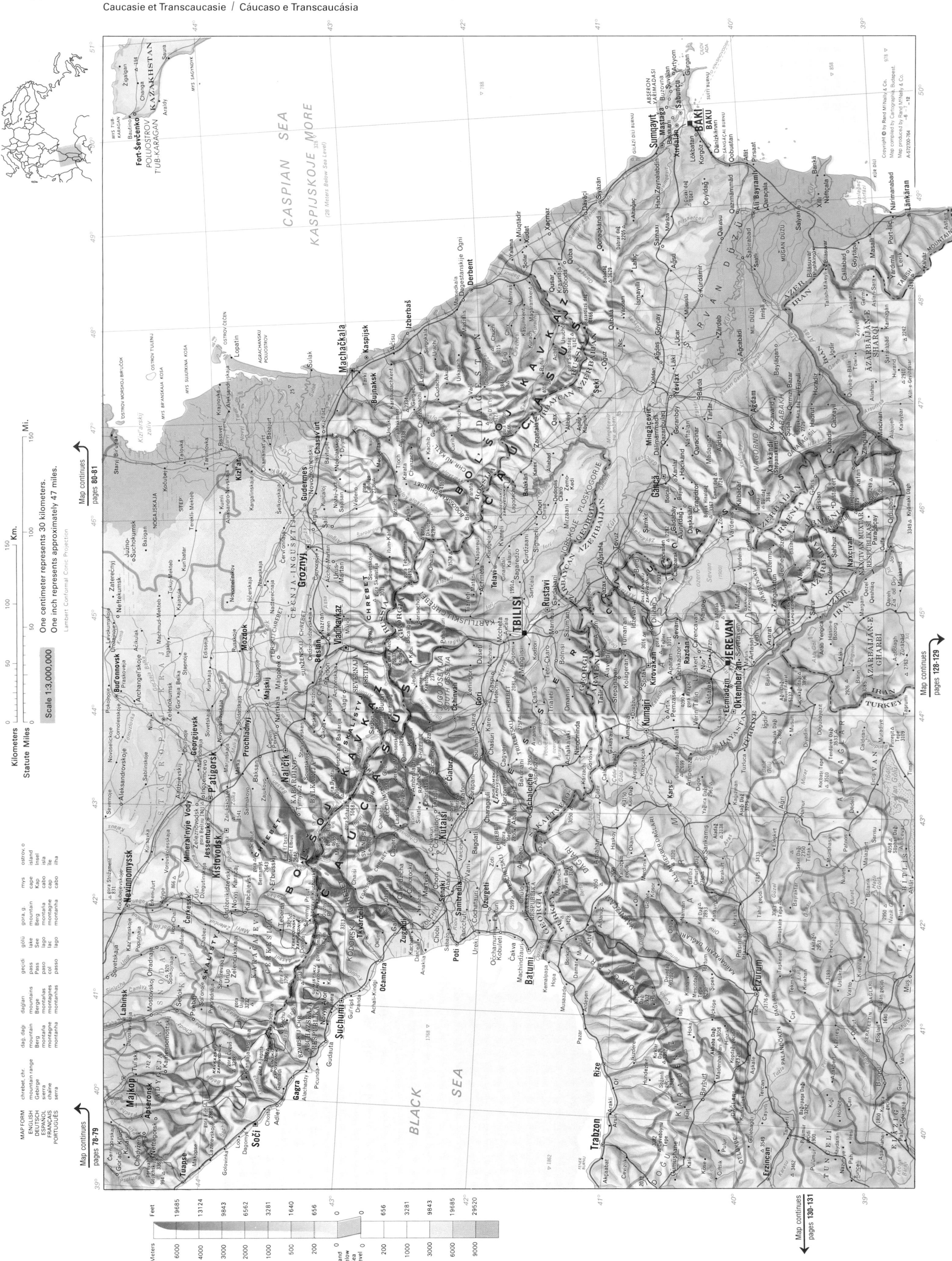

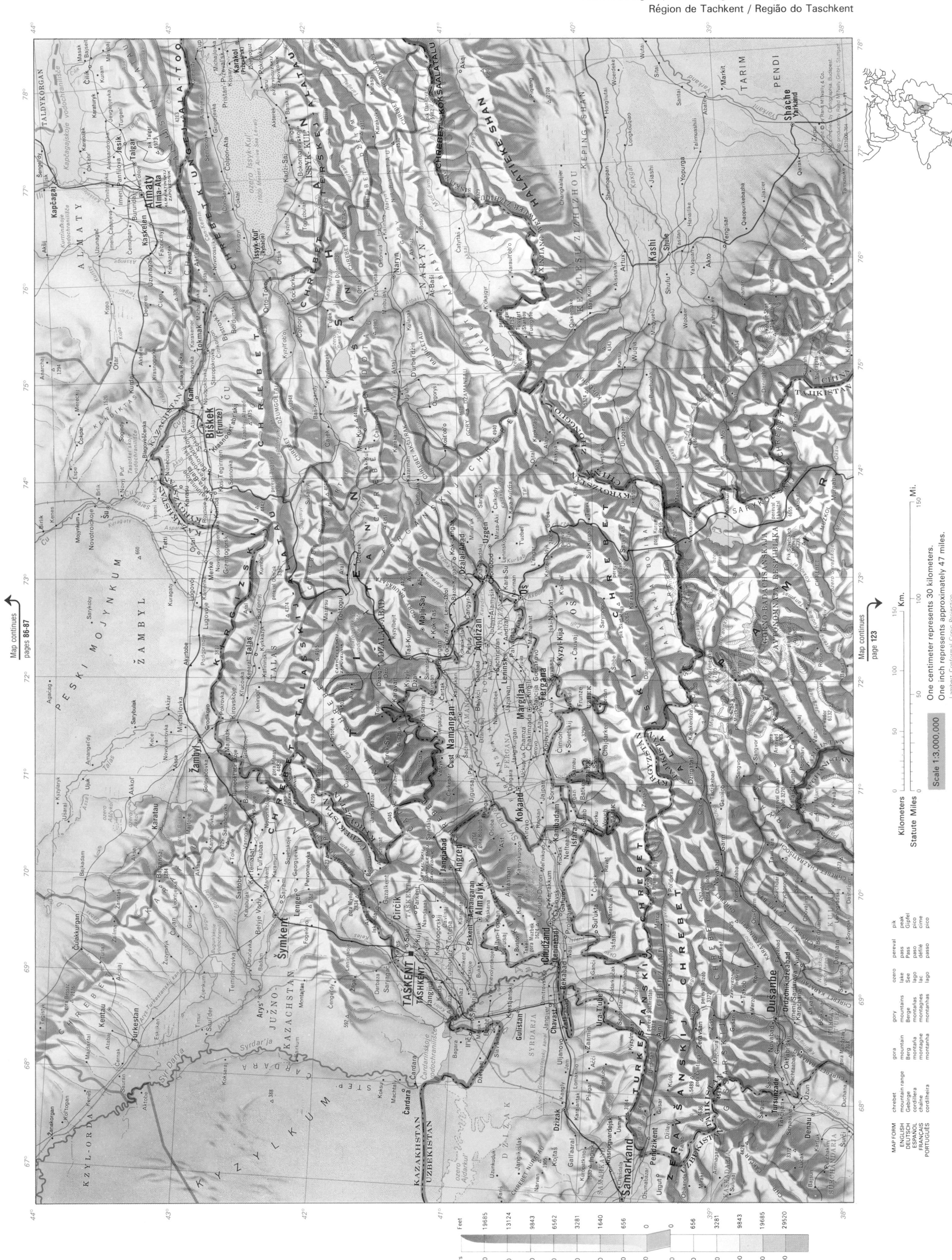

Map continues
pages 86-87

Map continues
page 123

Scale 1:3.000.000

One centimeter represents 30 kilometers.
One inch represents approximately 47 miles.

Lambert Conformal Conic Projection

Kilometers
Km.

Statute Miles
Mi.

MAP FORM					
ENGLISH	chrebet	gora	gory	gora	ozero	pereval	pik
DEUTSCH	mountain range	mountain	mountains	mountain	lake	pass	peak
ESPAÑOL	Gebirge	Berg	Berge	Berg	See	Pass	Gipfel
FRANÇAIS	cordillera	montaña	montañas	montaña	lago	paso	pico
PORTUGUÊS	chaîne	montagne	montagnes	montagne	lac	défilé	cime
	cordilheira	montanha	montanhas	montanha	lago	passo	pico

feet	Meters
19685	6000
13124	4000
9843	3000
6562	2000
3281	1000
1640	500
656	200
0	0
	Land Below Sea Level
656	200
3281	1000
9843	3000
19685	6000
29520	9000

86

Central Russia and Kazakhstan / Mittelrussland und Kasachstan / Rusia Central e Kazajstan
Russie Centrale et Kazakhstan / Rússia Central e Casaquistão

Map continues
pages 72-73

Map continues
pages 24-25

Map continues
pages 80-81

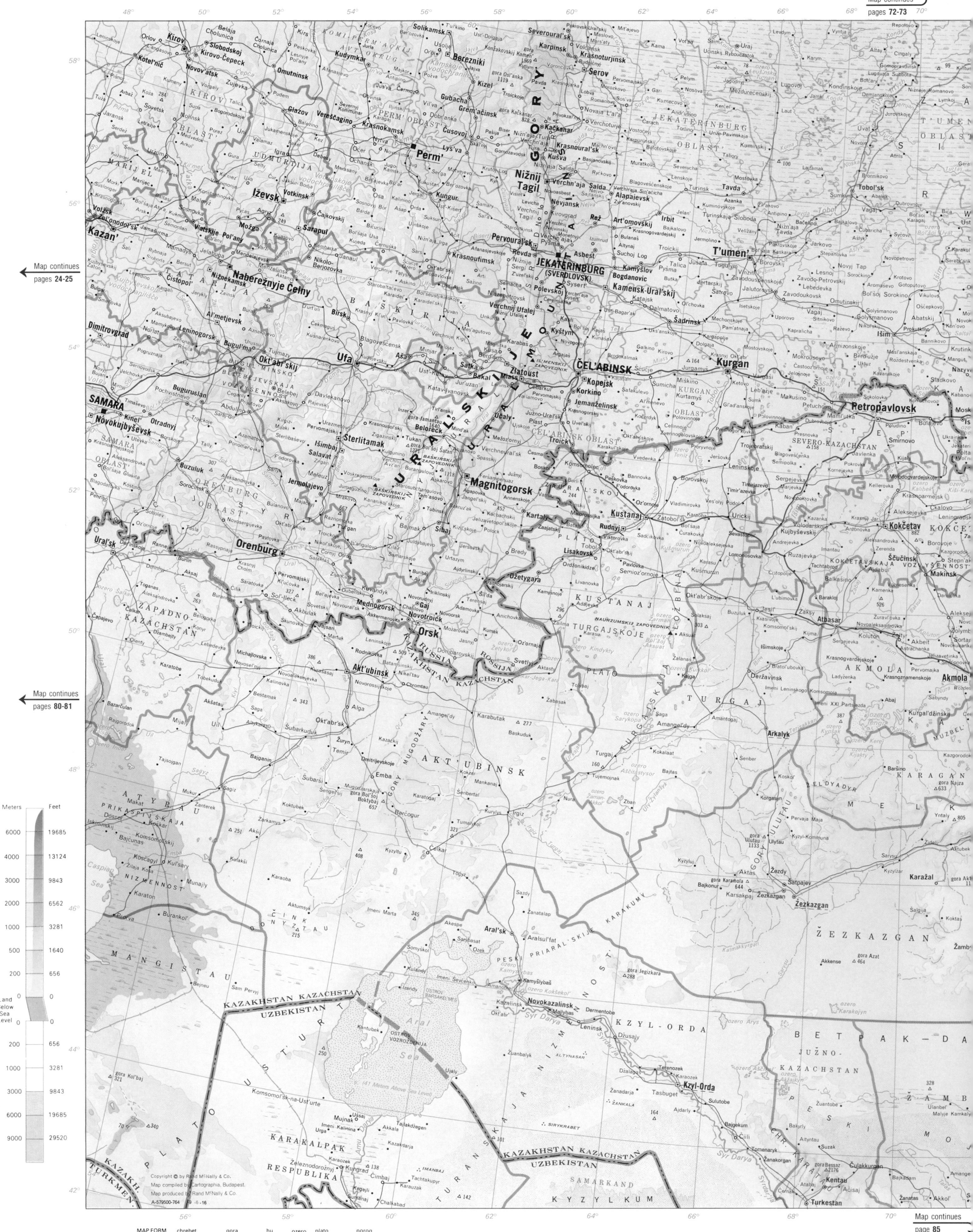

Map continues
page 85

MAP FORM	chrebet	gora	hu	ozero	plato	porog
ENGLISH	mountain range	mountain	lake	lake	plateau	waterfall
DEUTSCH	Gebirge	Berg	See	See	Hochebene	Wasserfall
ESPAÑOL	cordillera	montaña	lago	lago	meseta	cascada
FRANÇAIS	chaîne	montagne	lac	lac	plateau	chute d'eau
PORTUGUÊS	cordilheira	montanha	lago	lago	planalto	queda d'agua

Meters Feet
6000 19685
4000 13124
3000 9843
2000 6562
1000 3281
500 1640
200 656
Land Below Sea Level 0
0
200 656
1000 3281
3000 9843
6000 19685
9000 29520

Central Russia and Kazakhstan / Mittelrussland und Kasachstan / Rusia Central e Kazajstan
Russie Centrale et Kazakhstan / Rússia Central e Casaquistão

87

Map continues
page 88

Kilometers

Statute Miles

Scale 1:6,000,000

One centimeter represents 60 kilometers.
One inch represents approximately 95 miles.

Lambert Conformal Conic Projection

Lake Baikal Region / Baikalseegebiet / Región del Lago Baikal
Région du Lac Baïkal / Região do Lago Baikal

Map continues page 89

Map continues pages 74-75

Map continues pages 102-103

Map continues pages 86-87

Scale 1:6,000,000

One centimeter represents 60 kilometers.
One inch represents approximately 95 miles.

Lambert Conformal Conic Projection

Kilometers
Statute Miles

Km.
Mi.

MAP FORM						
ENGLISH	mountain range	mountain	mountain range	lake	lake	waterfall	mountains
DEUTSCH	Gebirge	Berg	Gebirge	See	See	Wasserfall	Berge
ESPAÑOL	cordillera	montaña	cordillera	lago	lago	cascada	montañas
FRANÇAIS	cordillère	montagne	cordillère	lac	lac	chute	montagnes
PORTUGUÊS	cordilheira	montanha	cordilheira	lago	lago	queda d'água	montanhas

chrebet — gora — nuruu — nuur — ozero. o. — porog — uul

Feet — Meters

Land Below Sea Level

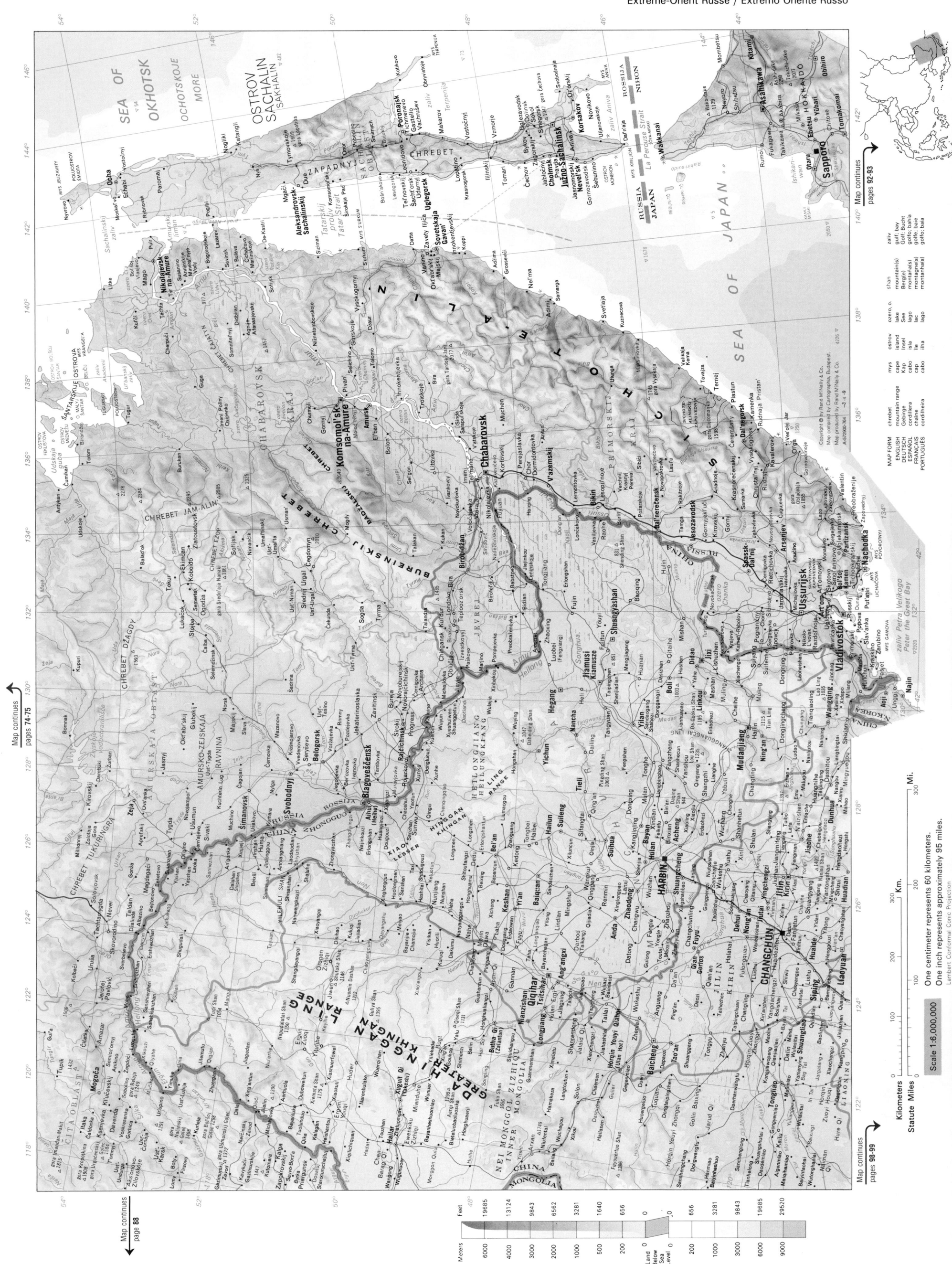

Map continues
pages 92-93

Map continues
pages 74-75

Map continues
pages 98-99

Map continues
page 88

MAP FORM		
ENGLISH		
DEUTSCH		
ESPAÑOL		
FRANÇAIS		
PORTUGUÊS		

chrebet	mountain range
Gebirge	
cordillera	
chaîne	
cordilheira	

mys	cape
Kap	
cabo	
cap	
cabo	

ostrov	island
Insel	
isla	
île	
ilha	

ozero, o.	lake
See	
lago	
lac	
lago	

shan	
Bergl.	
montaña(s)	
montagne(s)	
montanha(s)	

zaliv	
gulf, bay	
Golf, Bucht	
golfo, bahía	
golfe, baie	
golfo, baía	

Copyright © by Rand McNally & Co.
Map compiled by Cartographia, Budapest.
Map compiled by Rand McNally & Co.
A-82000-364 _ -2 _ 4 -9

Scale 1:6,000,000

One centimeter represents 60 kilometers.
One inch represents approximately 95 miles.

Lambert Conformal Conic Projection

Kilometers
Km. 0 100 200 300
Statute Miles
Mi. 0 100 200 300

Feet	Meters
19685	6000
13124	4000
9843	3000
6562	2000
3281	1000
1640	500
656	200
0	0
Land Below Sea Level	
0	0
656	200
3281	1000
9843	3000
19685	6000
29520	9000

Map continues
pages 74-75

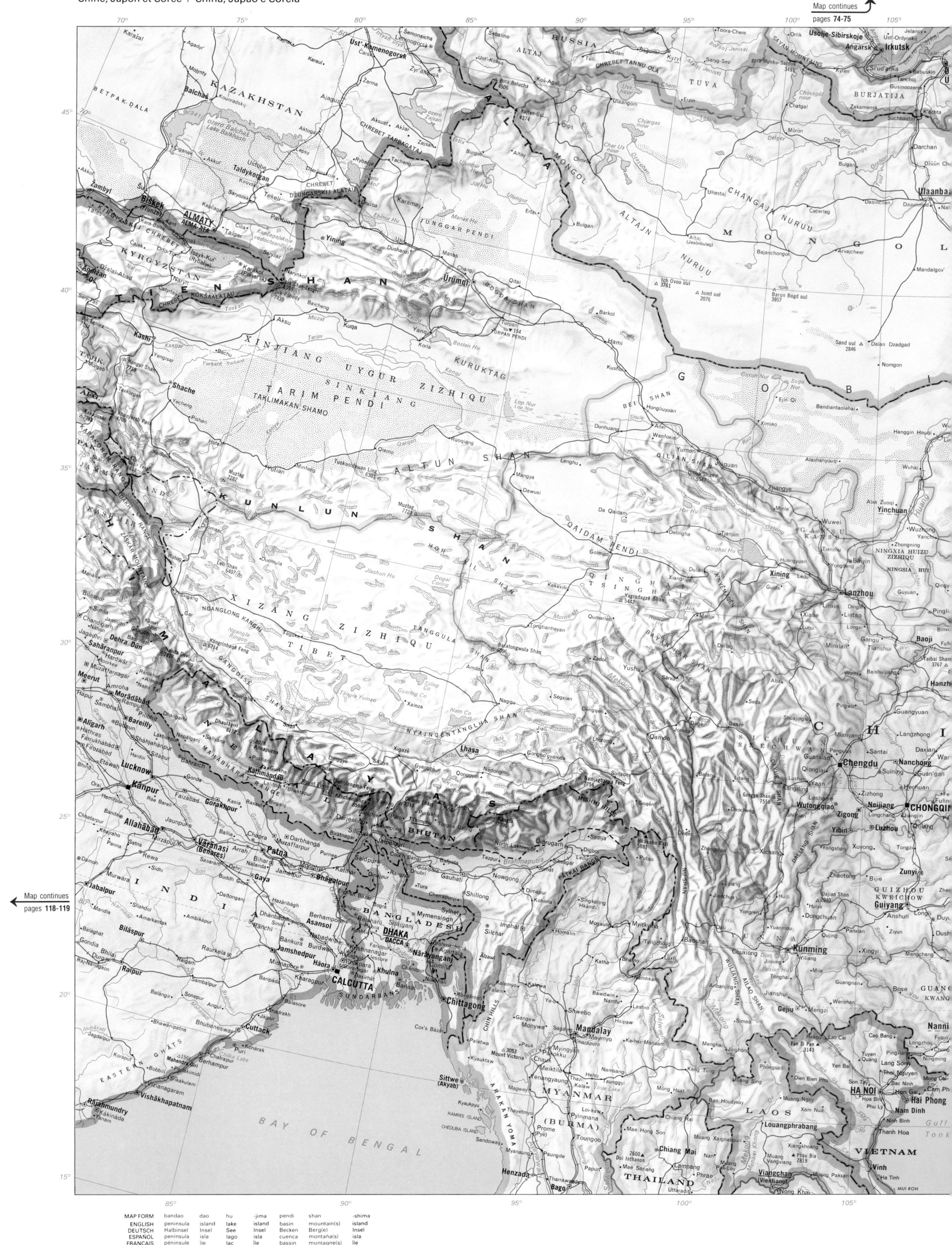

Map continues
pages 118-119

MAP FORM	bandao	dao	hu	-jima	pendi	shan	-shima
ENGLISH	peninsula	island	lake	island	basin	mountain(s)	island
DEUTSCH	Halbinsel	Insel	See	Insel	Becken	Berg(e)	Insel
ESPAÑOL	península	isla	lago	isla	cuenca	montaña(s)	isla
FRANÇAIS	péninsule	île	lac	île	bassin	montagne(s)	île
PORTUGUÊS	península	ilha	lago	ilha	bacia	montanha(s)	ilha

Map continues
pages **108-109**

Kilometers
Statute Miles

Scale 1:12,000,000

One centimeter represents 120 kilometers.
One inch represents approximately 190 miles.
Lambert Conformal Conic Projection

Copyright © by Rand McNally & Co.
Map prepared by Esselte Map Service AB, Stockholm
A-569700-264

RUSSIA
ROSSIJA
NIHON

JAPAN
NIHON

PACIFIC OCEAN

SEA OF OKHOTSK

KURIL'SKIJE OSTROVA
CHISHIMA-RETTŌ
KURIL ISLANDS

Habomai, Shikotan, Kunashir, and Etorofu, occupied by Japan and Etorofu claimed by Japan since 1945, are final peace treaty pending a final peace treaty

RUSSIA
ROSSIJA
NIHON

JAPAN

OSTROV
SACHALIN
SAKHALIN

Wakkanai

SEA OF JAPAN
NIHON-KAI

HOKKAIDŌ

TESHIO-SANCHI

KITAMI-SANCHI

Asahikawa
ISHIKARI

YŪBARI-SANCHI

Sapporo
Otaru

Tomakomai

Muroran

HIDAKA-SAMMYAKU

TOKACHI-HEIYA

Obihiro

KONSEN-DAICHI

Kushiro

Nemuro

HONSHŪ

Aomori

Hakodate

HONSHŪ

Hachinohe

PACIFIC OCEAN

HOKKAIDŌ

IWATE

KITAKAMI

Morioka

KŌCHI

Hachinohe

Aomori

TSUGARU-HEIYA

Hirosaki

Akita

DEWA-SANCHI

Sakata

Tsuruoka

Yamagata

Sendai

MIYAGI

ABUKUMA

KŌCHI

FUKUSHIMA

Koriyama

Niigata
ECHIGO

Sado-kaikyō

SADO

Nagaoka

Sanjo

Joetsu

Nagano

Matsumoto

Ueda

GUMMA

Maebashi

TOCHIGI

Mito

IBARAKI

Hitachi

Chōshi

Chiba

BŌSŌ-HANTŌ

TŌKYŌ

Yokohama
Kawasaki

Toyama

Kanazawa

HONSHŪ

PACIFIC OCEAN

WakfTaira)

Tsugaru-kaikyō

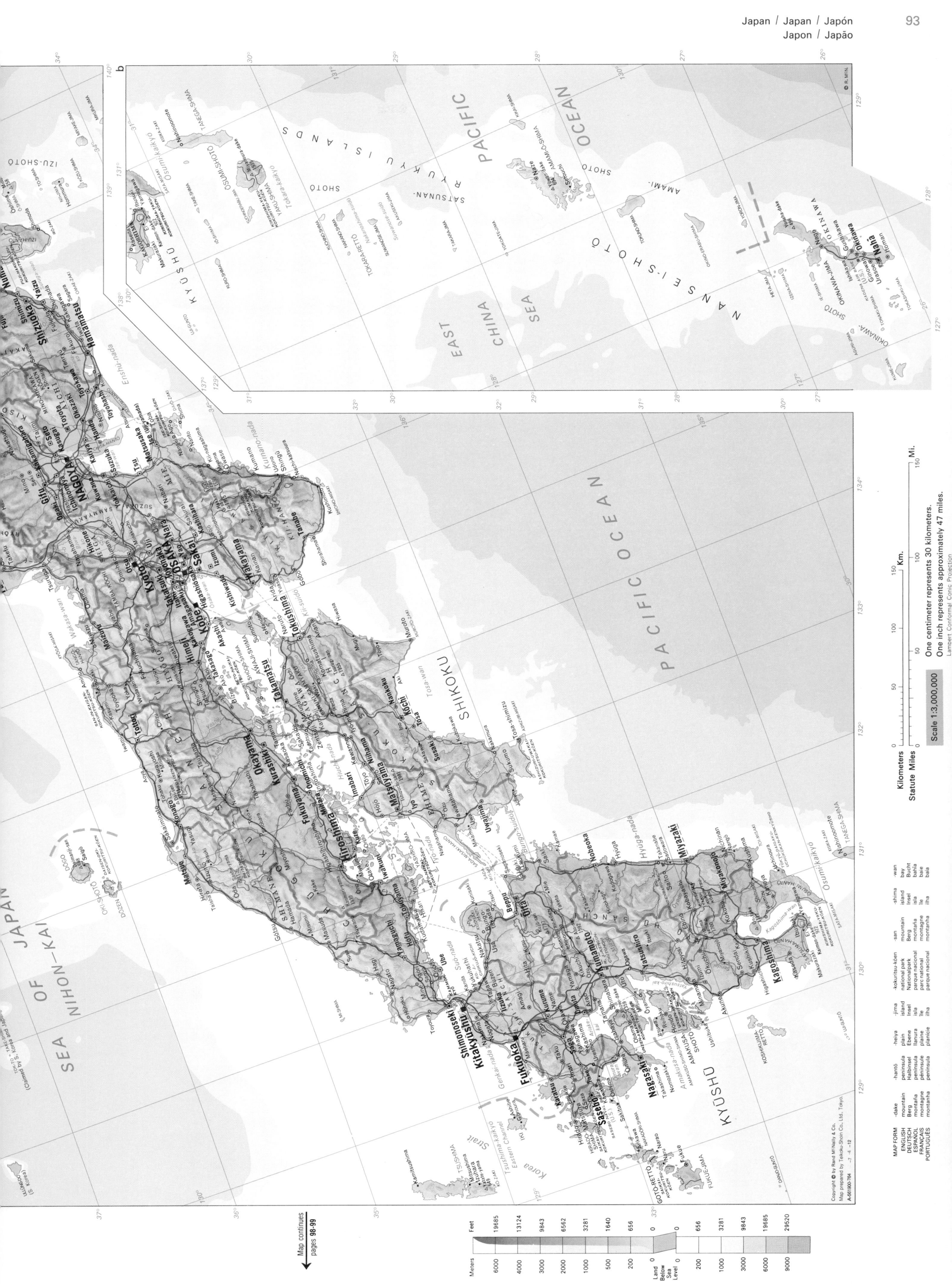

PACIFIC OCEAN

EAST CHINA SEA

RYUKYU ISLANDS

NANSEI-SHOTO

OKINAWA

Okinawa
Naha
Naman

SEA OF JAPAN
NIHON-KAI

(Claimed by S. Korea and Japan)

JAPAN

KYŪSHŪ

IZU-SHOTO

NAGOYA
Shizuoka Yaizu
Hamamatsu
Gifu

Kyoto
OSAKA Nara
KOBE Higashiosaka Sakai
Himeji

Wakayama

SHIKOKU

Tottori

Okayama
Kurashiki
Fukuyama

Hiroshima

Iwakuni

Tokushima

Takamatsu

Matsuyama

Kochi

Yamaguchi
Ube
Shimonoseki
Kitakyushu
Fukuoka

Beppu
Oita

Nobeoka

Miyazaki
Miyakonojo

Kumamoto
Yatsushiro

Kagoshima

Nagasaki
Sasebo

KYŪSHŪ

Map continues
pages 98-99

Scale 1:3,000,000

Kilometers
Statute Miles

One centimeter represents 30 kilometers.
One inch represents approximately 47 miles.
Lambert Conformal Conic Projection

MAP FORM	-dake	-hantō	-heiya	-jima	-kokuritsu-kōen	-san	-shima	-wan
ENGLISH	mountain	peninsula	plain	island	national park	mountain	island	bay
DEUTSCH	Berg	Halbinsel	Ebene	Insel	Nationalpark	Berg	Insel	Bucht
ESPAÑOL	montaña	península	llanura	isla	parque nacional	montaña	isla	bahía
FRANÇAIS	montagne	péninsule	plaine	île	parc national	montagne	île	baie
PORTUGUÊS	montanha	península	planície	ilha	parque nacional	montanha	ilha	baía

Feet
19685
13124
9843
6562
3281
1640
656
0

Meters
6000
4000
3000
2000
1000
500
200
0
Land
Below
Sea
Level
0
200
1000
3000
6000
9000

656
3281
9843
19685
29520

← Map continues pages 96-97

MAP FORM	-dake	-hantō	-kokutei-kōen	-misaki	-san	-tōge	-wan	-yama	-zaki
ENGLISH	mountain	peninsula	national park	cape	mountain	pass	bay	mountain	point
DEUTSCH	Berg	Halbinsel	Nationalpark	Kap	Berg	Pass	Bucht	Berg	Landspitze
ESPAÑOL	montaña	península	parque nacional	cabo	montaña	paso	bahía	montaña	punta
FRANÇAIS	montagne	péninsule	parc national	cap	montagne	col	baie	montagne	pointe
PORTUGUÊS	montanha	península	parque nacional	cabo	montanha	passo	baía	montanha	ponta

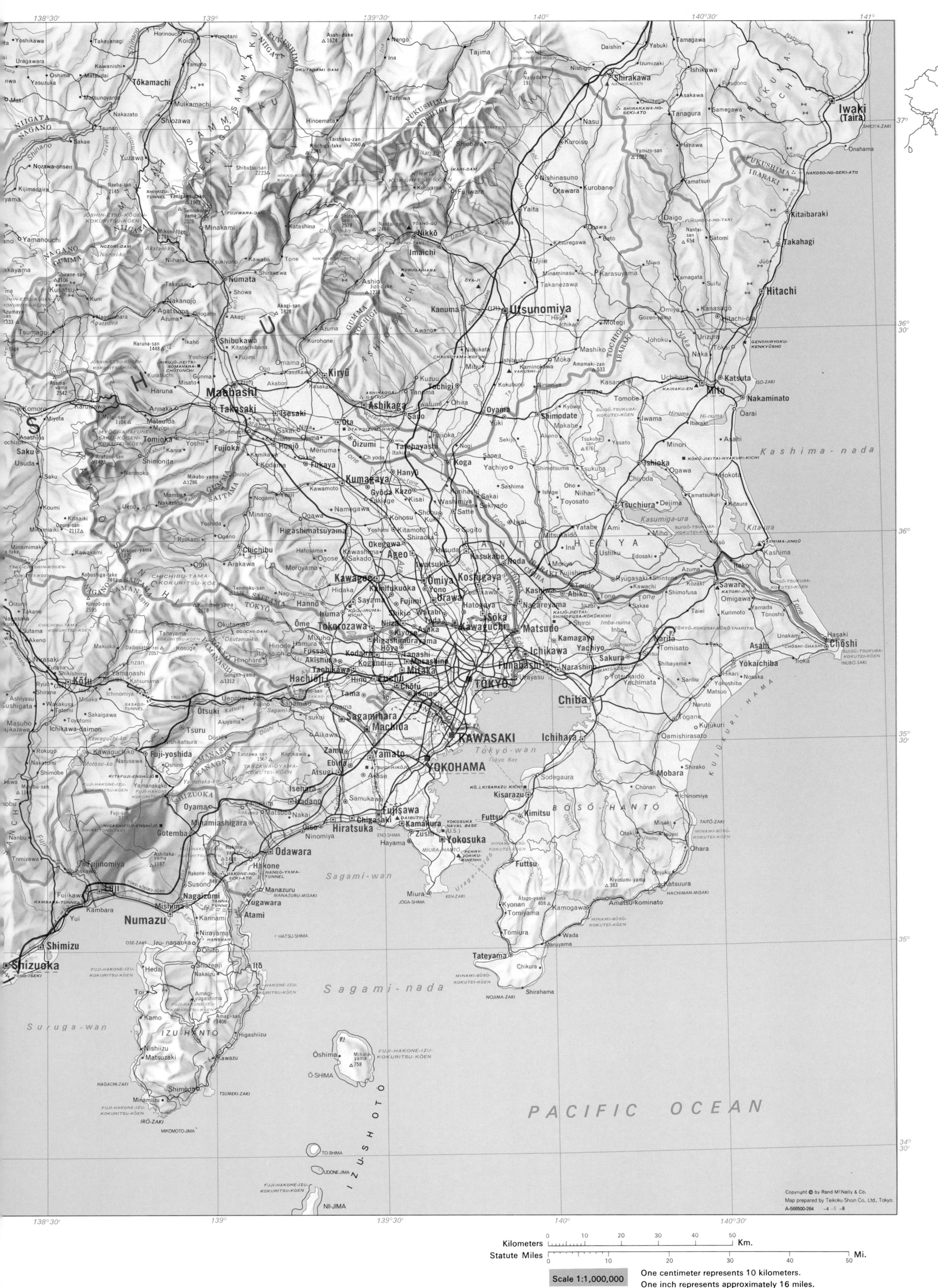

Kilometers
Statute Miles

Scale 1:1,000,000   One centimeter represents 10 kilometers.
One inch represents approximately 16 miles.
Lambert Conformal Conic Projection

SEA OF JAPAN
NIHON-KAI

KYŪSHŪ

MAP FORM	-jima	-misaki	-san	-sen	-shima	-tōge	-yama	-zen
ENGLISH	island	cape	mountain	mountain	island	pass	mountain	mountain
DEUTSCH	Insel	Kap	Berg	Berg	Insel	Pass	Berg	Berg
ESPAÑOL	isla	cabo	montaña	montaña	isla	paso	montaña	montaña
FRANÇAIS	île	cap	montagne	montagne	île	col	montagne	montagne
PORTUGUÊS	ilha	cabo	montanha	montanha	ilha	passo	montanha	montanha

Scale 1:1,000,000

One centimeter represents 10 kilometers.
One inch represents approximately 16 miles.
Lambert Conformal Conic Projection

98

Northeast China and Korea / Nordostchina und Korea / China Nor-oriental y Corea
Nord-Est de la Chine et Corée / Nordeste da China e Coréia

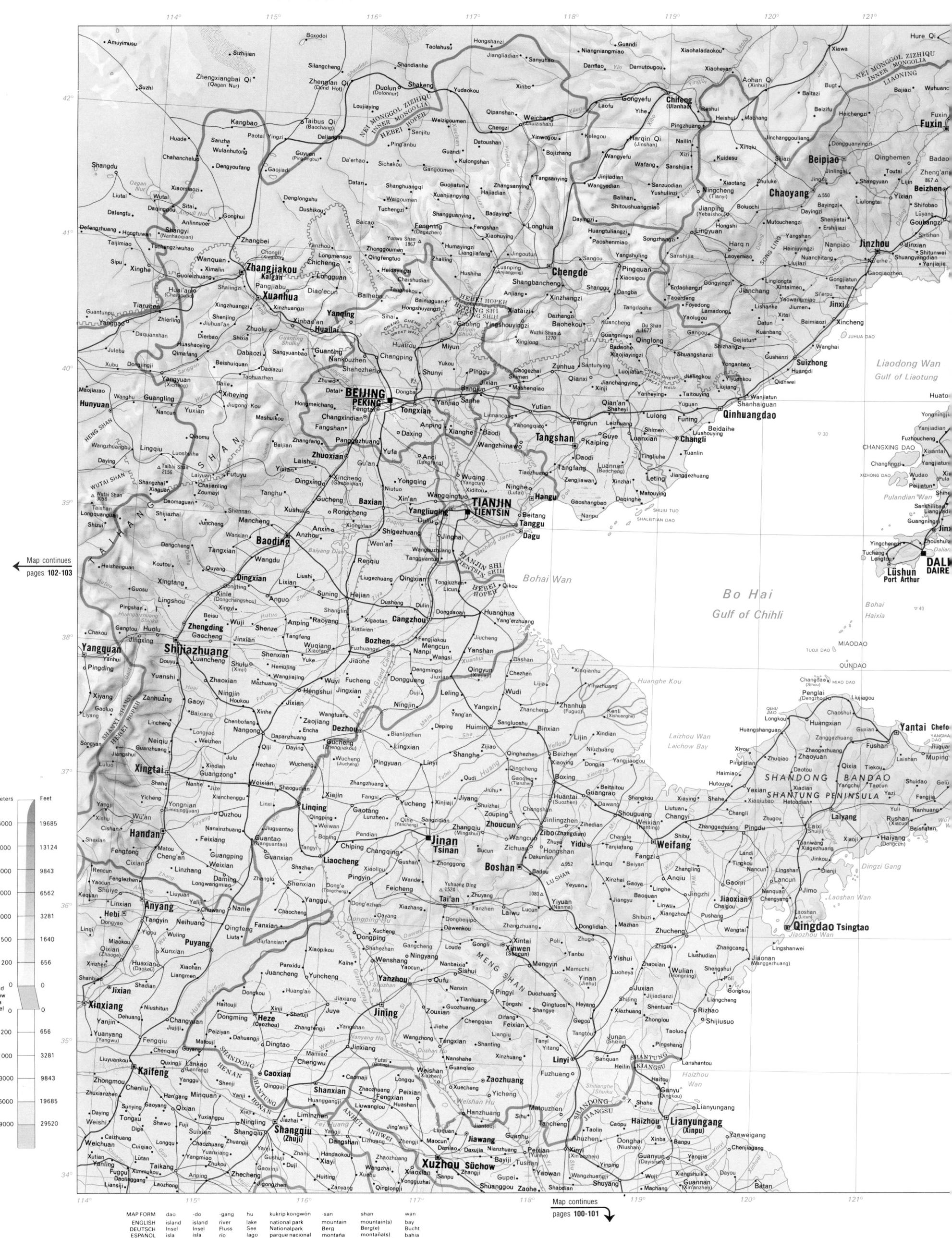

Map continues
pages 102-103

Map continues
pages 100-101

MAP FORM	dao	-do	-gang	hu	kukrip kongwŏn	-san	shan	wan
ENGLISH	island	island	river	lake	national park	mountain	mountain(s)	bay
DEUTSCH	Insel	Insel	Fluss	See	Nationalpark	Berg	Berg(e)	Bucht
ESPAÑOL	isla	isla	río	lago	parque nacional	montaña	montaña(s)	bahía
FRANÇAIS	île	île	rivière	lac	parc national	montagne	montagne(s)	baie
PORTUGUÊS	ilha	ilha	rio	lago	parque nacional	montanha	montanha(s)	baía

Map continues
page 89

Map continues
pages 92-93

MANCHURIA

CHINA

RUSSIA

Yanji Tumen Onsong Hunchun
Chaoyangchuan Longjing Namyang Kyŏng-wŏn
Yanji (Longjing) Ch'ŏngsong Krasking
Toudaogou Kaishantun Aoji Posjet
Unggi
Helong Sanhecun Hoeryŏng
Naping Musan Komusan Najin
HAMGYŎNG PUKDO Ch'ŏngjin
Nanam
Kyŏngsŏng

Kangping Gaojiadian Xifeng Yangdalinzi Dongfeng
Faku Damingcheng Kaiyuan Zhenxing Huinan (Chaoyang)
Tieling Hailong (Meihekou) Liangjiangkou

FUSHUN Tonghua Linjiang
SHENYANG MUKDEN

Hyesan YANGGANG-DO

Liaoyang Benxi Penhsi
Anshan Gongchangling

CHAGANG-DO
Kanggye

Dandong Sinŭiju
P'YŎNGAN PUKDO

Kimch'aek (Sŏngjin)

Tanch'ŏn

Pukch'ŏng
Sinch'ang
Sinp'o

Hamhŭng
Hŭngnam

HAMGYŎNG NAMDO

Anju
Sunch'ŏn

Wŏnsan

PYŎNGYANG

Namp'o Songnim

KANGWŎN DO

HWANGHAE PUKDO
Sariwŏn Chaeryŏng Sinch'ŏn

HWANGHAE NAMDO
Haeju Kaesŏng

NORTH KOREA
SOUTH KOREA

Sokch'o
Yangyang

SŎUL SEOUL
Inch'ŏn Sŏngnam-si
Suwŏn
Anyang

KANGWŎN DO
Wŏnju
Kangnŭng
Samch'ŏk

KYŎNGGI DO

Ch'ŏnan

CH'UNGCH'ŎNG PUKDO
Ch'ŏngju Chech'ŏn

Ch'ungju

CH'UNGCH'ŎNG NAMDO
Kongju Taejŏn

Andong

KYŎNGSANG PUKDO
Kimch'ŏn P'ohang
Taegu Kyŏngju

Kunsan Chŏnju
CHŎLLA PUKDO

Masan Chinhae
Pusan
Ulsan
Tongnae

KYŎNGSANG NAMDO
Chinju

CHŎLLA NAMDO
Kwangju Sunch'ŏn Yŏsu
Mokp'o

SEA OF JAPAN

KOREA STRAIT
JAPAN NIHON
TSUSHIMA

Korea Bay

YELLOW SEA

Weihai

KILOMETERS 0 50 100 150 Km.
Statute Miles 0 50 100 150 Mi.

Scale 1:3,000,000
One centimeter represents 30 kilometers.
One inch represents approximately 47 miles.
Lambert Conformal Conic Projection

Copyright © by Rand McNally & Co.
Map compiled by Cartographia, Budapest.
Map produced by Rand McNally & Co.
A-564400-764

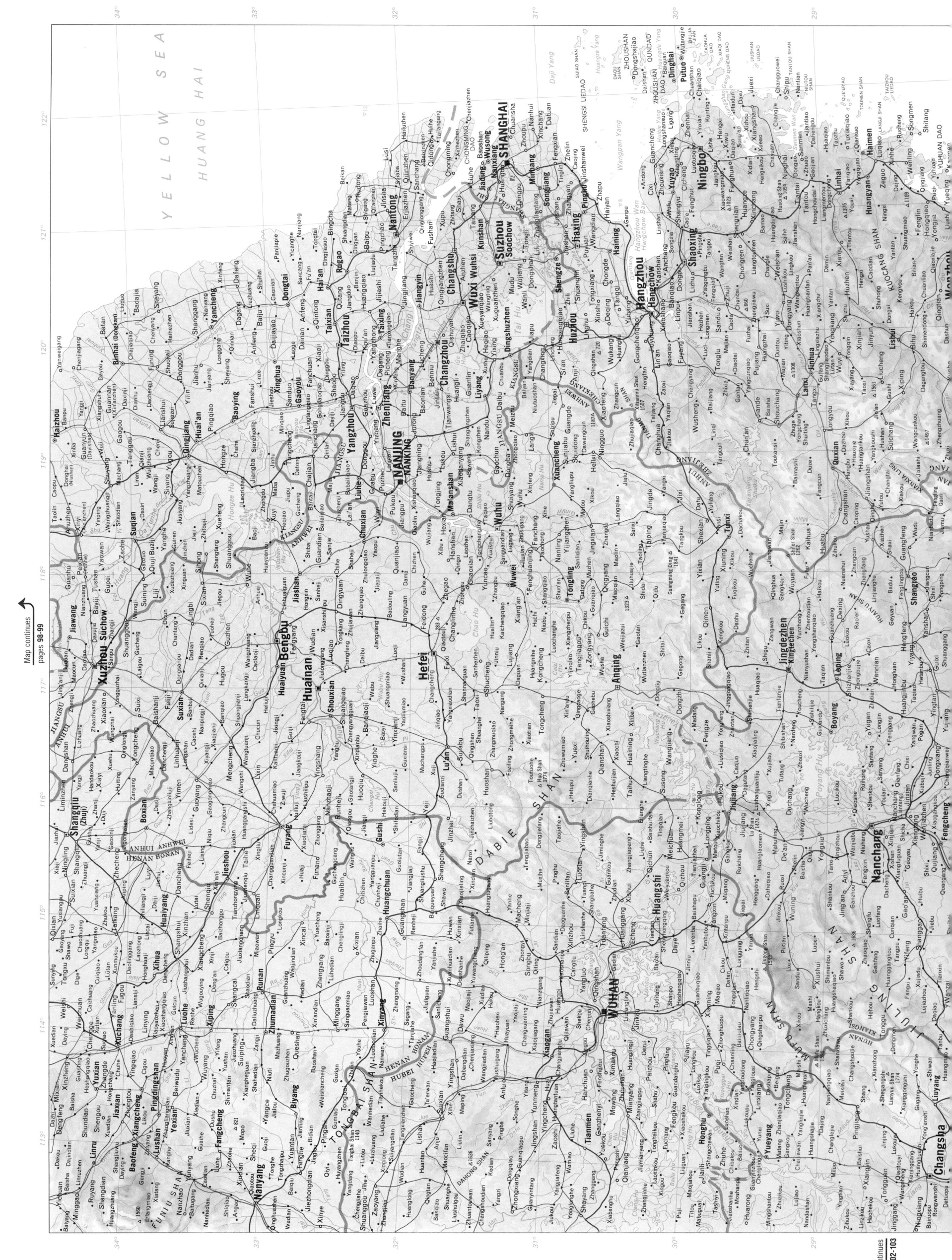

Map continues
pages 98-99

Map continues
pages 102-103

East and Southeast China / Ost- und Südostchina / Este y Sudeste de la China
Chine de l'Est et du Sud-Est / Leste e Sudeste da China

101

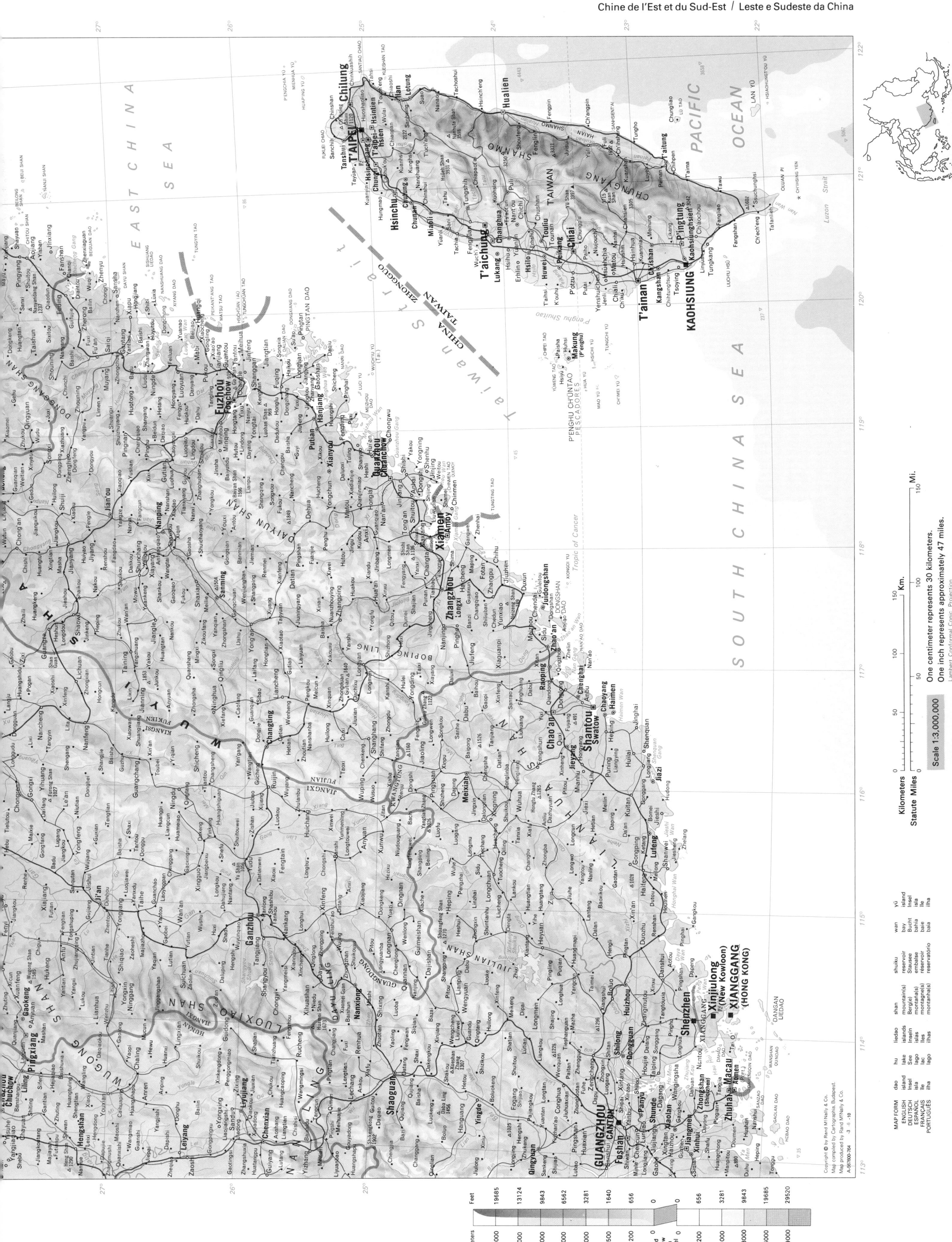

Copyright © by Rand McNally & Co.
Map compiled by Cartographia, Budapest.
Map produced by Rand McNally & Co.
A-597000-784   -3 -4 -10

Scale 1:3,000,000

One centimeter represents 30 kilometers.
One inch represents approximately 47 miles.
Lambert Conformal Conic Projection

MAP FORM					
ENGLISH	dao	hu	liedao	shan	shuiku
DEUTSCH	island	lake	islands	mountain(s)	reservoir
ESPAÑOL	Insel	See	Inseln	Berg(e)	Stausee
FRANÇAIS	isla	lago	islas	montaña(s)	embalse
PORTUGUÊS	île	lac	îles	montagne(s)	reservoir
	ilha	lago	ilhas	montanhas	reservatório

wan	yu	
bay	island	
Bucht	Insel	
bahía	isla	
baie	île	
baía	ilha	

Map continues pages 98-99

Map continues page 88

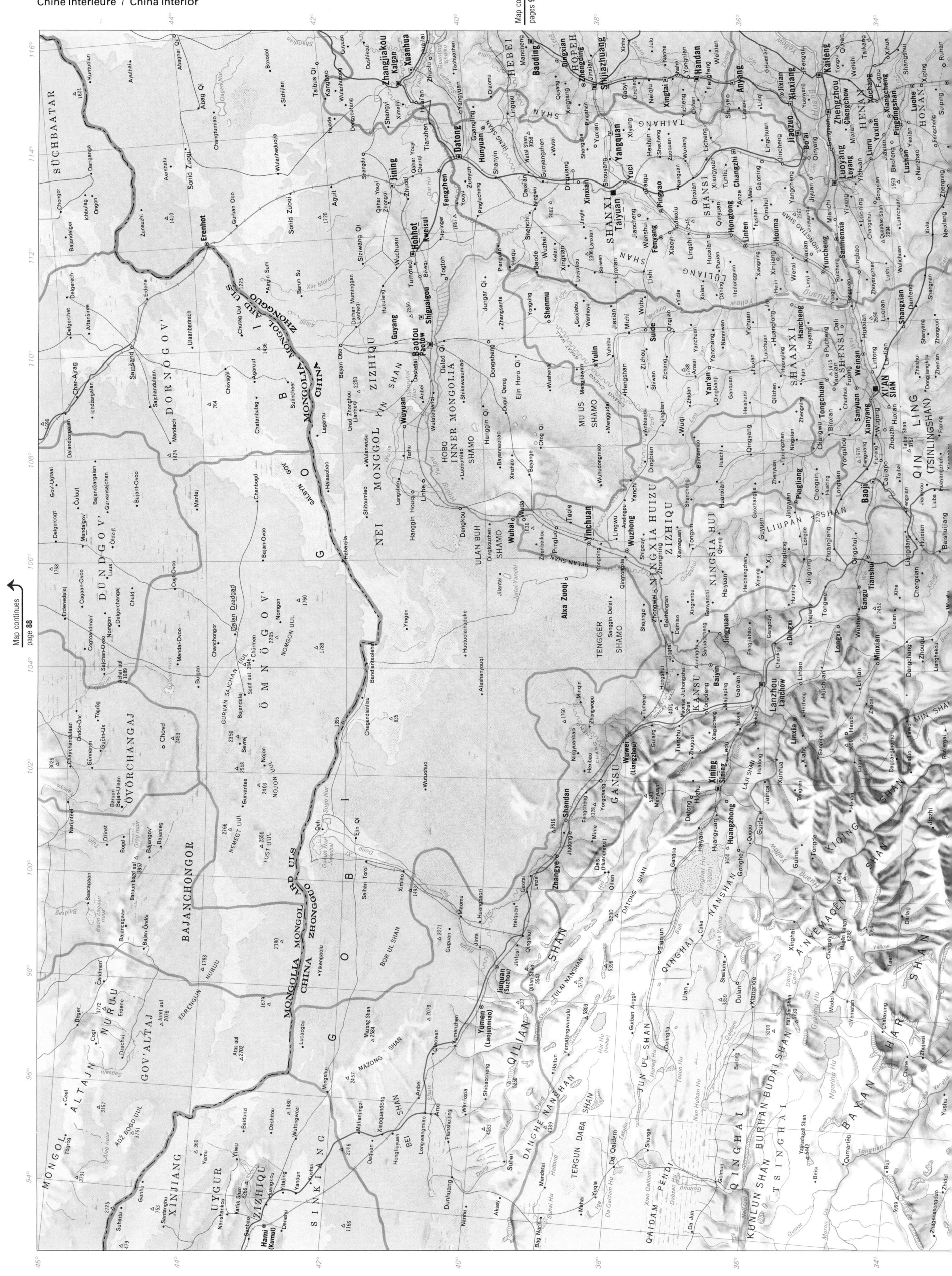
SÜCHBAATAR
DORNOGOV'
DUNDGOV'
ÖMNÖGOV'
ÖVÖRCHANGAJ
BAJANCHONGOR
GOV'ALTAJ
MONGOLIA
CHINA
NEI MONGGOL ZIZHIQU
INNER MONGOLIA
NINGXIA HUIZU ZIZHIQU
NINGSIA HUI
GANSU
KANSU
QINGHAI
TSINGHAI
SHAANXI
SHENSI
SHANXI
SHANSI
HEBEI
HOPEH
HENAN
HONAN
XINJIANG UYGUR ZIZHIQU
SINKIANG
G O B I
QILIAN SHAN
QIN LING (TSINLINGSHAN)
KUNLUN SHAN
BAYAN HAR SHAN
A'NYÊMAQÊN SHAN
TENGGER SHAMO
MU US SHAMO
HOBQ SHAMO
ULAN BUH SHAMO
Erenhot
Hohhot
Kweisui
Baotou
Paotow
Datong
Zhangjiakou
Kalgan
Shijiazhuang
Taiyuan
Yinchuan
Lanzhou
Lanchow
Xining
Sining
Xi'an
Sian
Zhengzhou
Chengchow
Luoyang
Yumen
Jiuquan
Zhangye
Wuwei
Hami
(Kumul)
Dunhuang
Golmud

Map continues pages 100-101

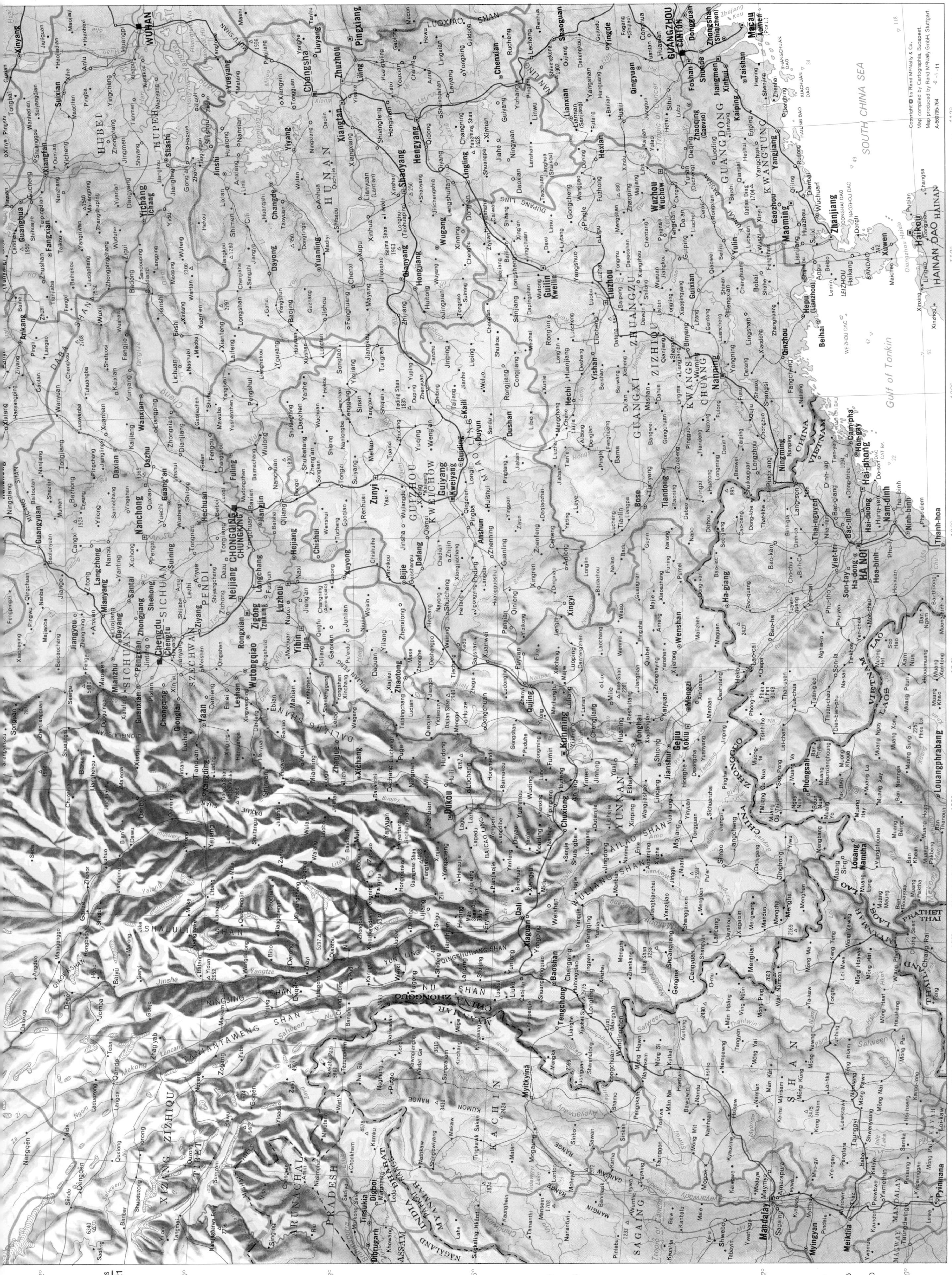

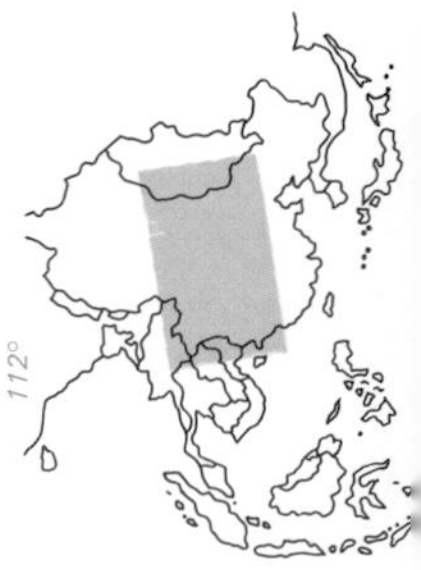

Map continues pages 110-111

Map continues pages 120-121

SOUTH CHINA SEA

Gulf of Tonkin

HUBEI / HUPEH

HUNAN

GUIZHOU / KWEICHOW

SICHUAN / SZECHWAN

YUNNAN

GUANGDONG / KWANGTUNG

GUANGXI ZIZHIQU / KWANGSI CHUANG

XIZANG ZIZHIQU / TIBET

VIETNAM

LAOS

PRATHET THAI / THAILAND

CHINA / ZHONGGUO

ZHONGGUO / CHINA

MYANMAR

INDIA

ARUNACHAL PRADESH

ASSAM

NAGALAND

SAGAING

MANDALAY

MAGWAY

KACHIN

SHAN

HAINAN DAO / HAINAN

Scale 1:6,000,000
One centimeter represents 60 kilometers.
One inch represents approximately 95 miles.
Lambert Conformal Conic Projection

Kilometers
Km.
Statute Miles
Mi.

MAP FORM	dao	hu	ling	shamo	shan	shuiku
ENGLISH	island	lake	mountains	desert	mountain(s)	reservoir
DEUTSCH	Insel	See	Berge	Wüste	Berge(l)	Stausee
ESPAÑOL	isla	lago	montañas	desierto	montaña(s)	embalse
FRANÇAIS	île	lac	montagnes	désert	montagne(s)	réservoir
PORTUGUÊS	ilha	lago	montanhas	deserto	montanha(s)	reservatório

Feet
19685
13124
9843
6562
3281
1640
656
0
Land Below Sea Level
0
656
3281
9843
19685
29520

Meters
6000
4000
3000
2000
1000
500
200
0
0
200
1000
3000
6000
9000

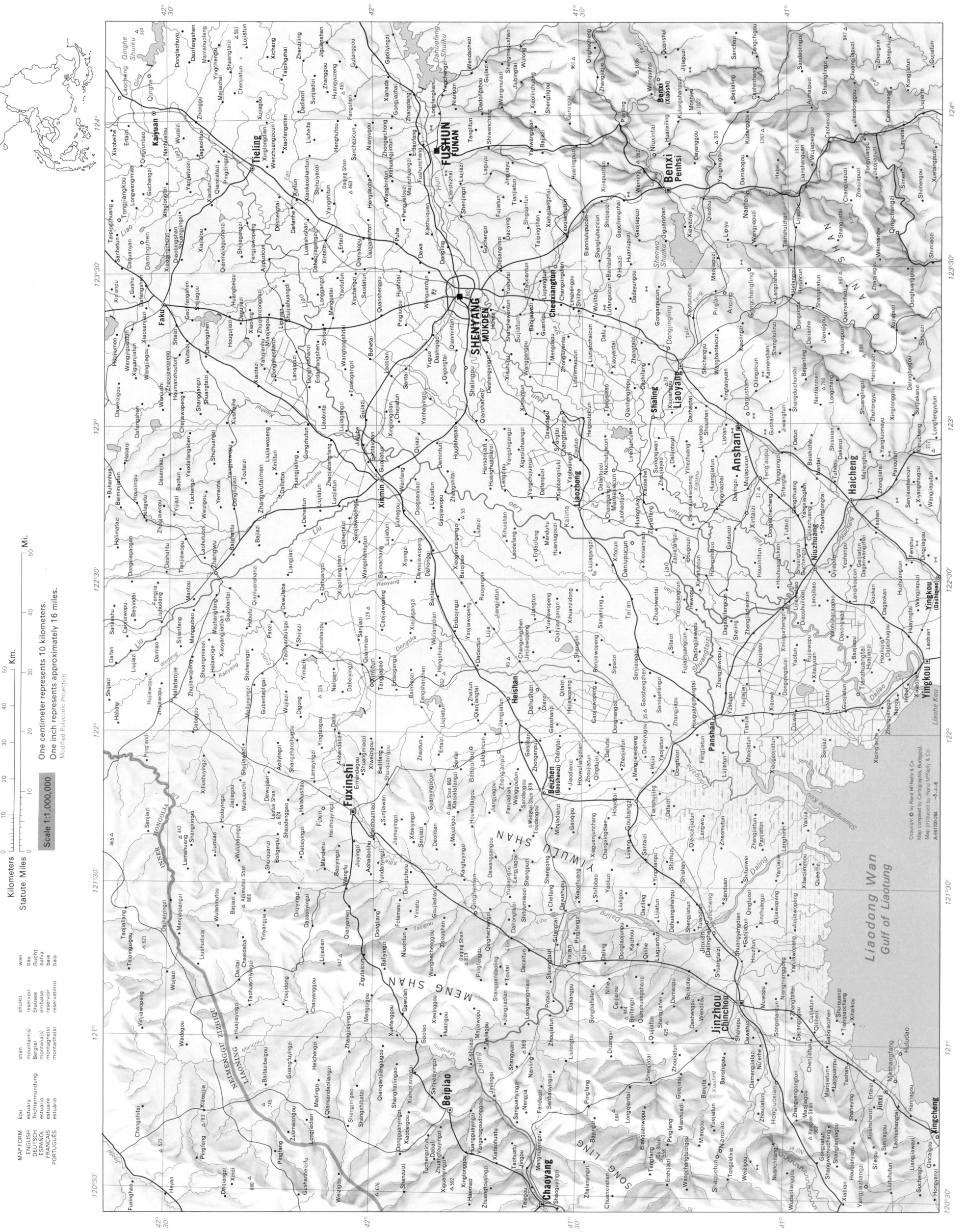

MAP FORM
ENGLISH
DEUTSCH
ESPAÑOL
FRANÇAIS
PORTUGUÊS

kou   estuary
             estuary
             Trichtermündung
             estuario
             estuaire
             estuário

shan   mountain(s)
             mountain(s)
             Berg(e)
             montaña(s)
             montagne(s)
             montanha(s)

shuiku   reservoir
             reservoir
             Stausee
             embalse
             reservoir
             reservatório

wan   bay
             bay
             Bucht
             bahía
             baie
             baía

Scale 1:1,000,000

One centimeter represents 10 kilometers.
One inch represents approximately 16 miles.

Modified Polyconic Projection

Kilometers

Statute Miles

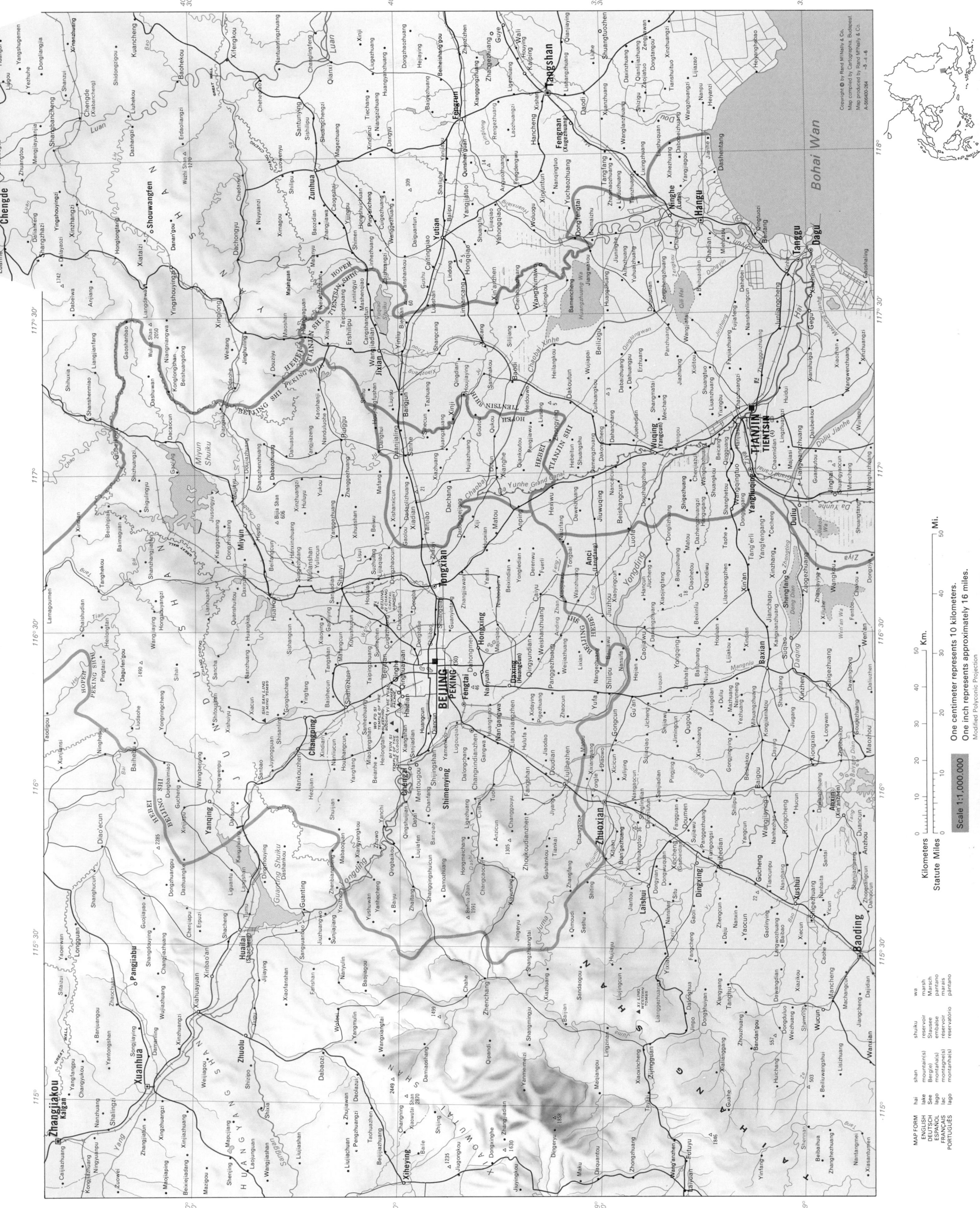

Bohai Wan

Scale 1:1,000,000

One centimeter represents 10 kilometers.
One inch represents approximately 16 miles.
Modified Polyconic Projection

Kilometers
Statute Miles

MAP FORM				
ENGLISH	hai	lake	shan	mountain(s)	shuiku	reservoir	wa	marsh
DEUTSCH		See		Berg(e)		Stausee		Marsch
ESPAÑOL		lago		montaña(s)		embalse		pantano
FRANÇAIS		lac		montagne(s)		reservoir		marais
PORTUGUÊS		lago		montanha(s)		reservatório		pântano

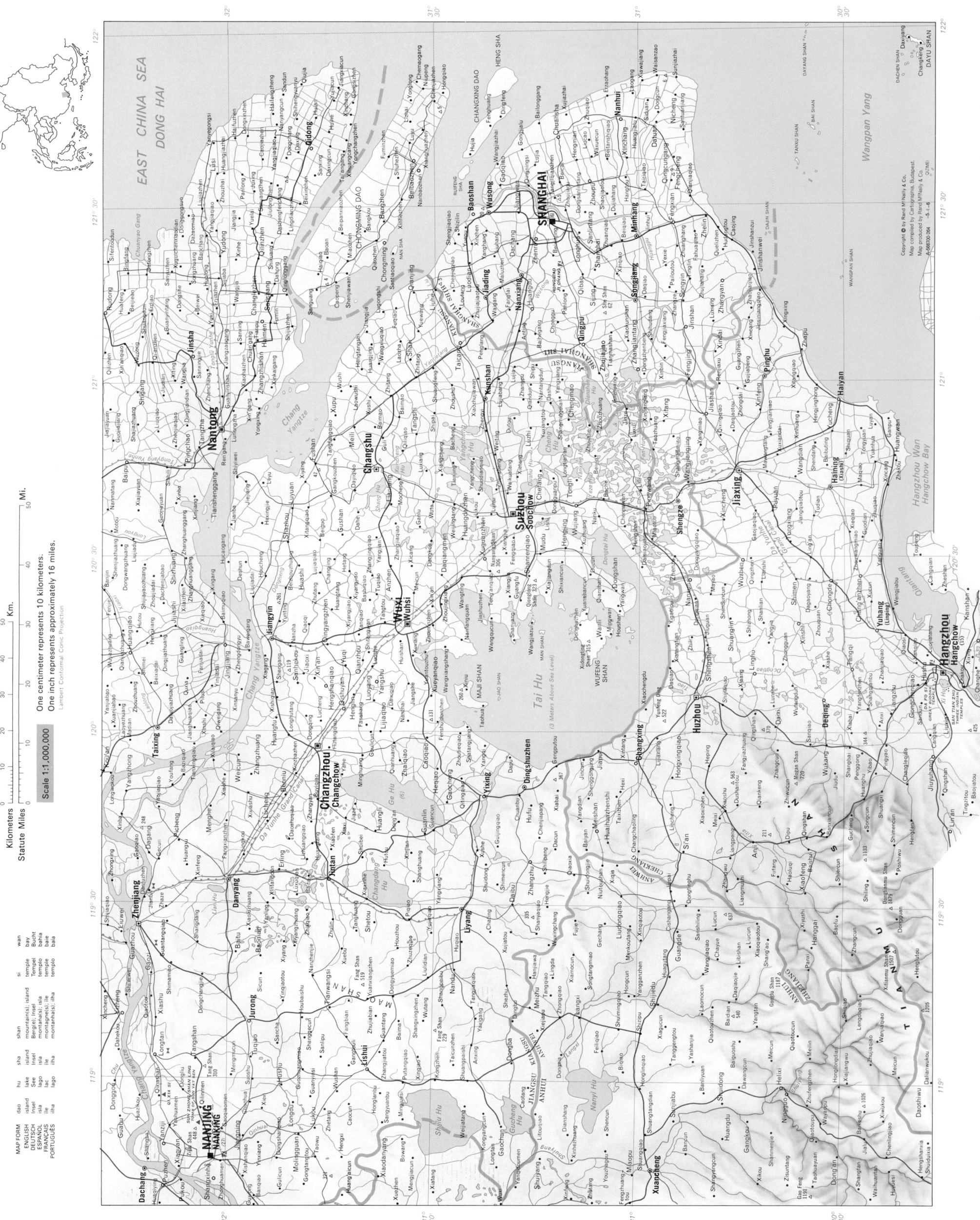

Scale 1:1,000,000

One centimeter represents 10 kilometers.
One inch represents approximately 16 miles.

Lambert Conformal Conic Projection

Kilometers
Statute Miles

Mi.
Km.

MAP FORM					
ENGLISH	island	lake	island	mountain(s); island	bay
DEUTSCH	Insel	See	Insel	Berg(e); Insel	Bucht
ESPAÑOL	isla	lago	isla	montaña(s); isla	bahía
FRANÇAIS	île	lac	île	montagne(s); île	baie
PORTUGUÊS	ilha	lago	ilha	montanha(s); ilha	baía
	sha	hu	dao	shan	wan
					temple
					Tempel
					templo
					temple
					templo
					si

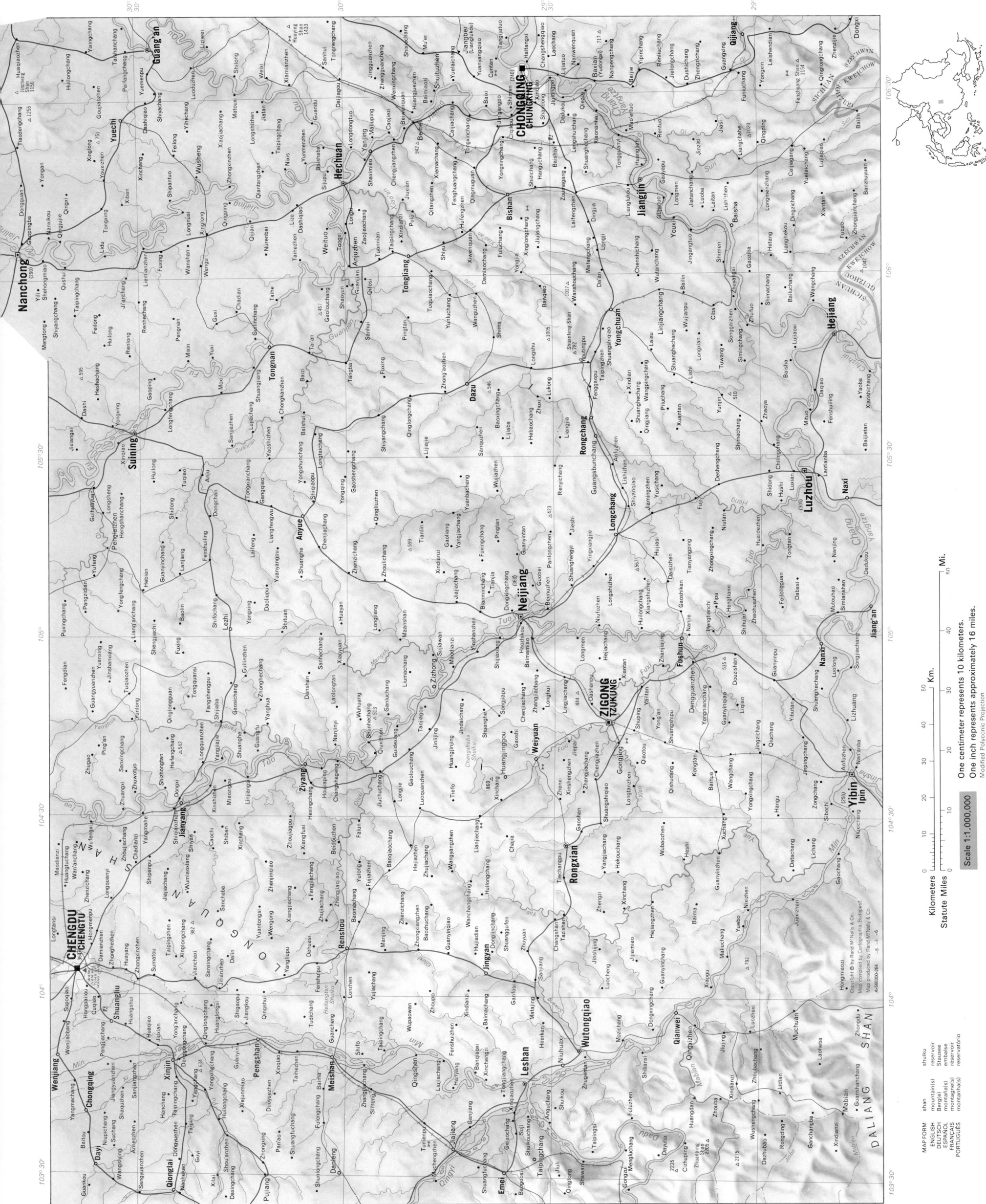

Scale 1:1,000,000

Kilometers

Statute Miles

One centimeter represents 10 kilometers.
One inch represents approximately 16 miles.
Modified Polycyclic Projection

MAP FORM	shan	shuiku
ENGLISH	mountain(s)	reservoir
DEUTSCH	Berg(e)	Stausee
ESPAÑOL	montaña(s)	embalse
FRANÇAIS	montagne(s)	réservoir
PORTUGUÊS	montanha(s)	reservatório

Map continues
pages 90-91

Map continues
pages 118-119

MAP FORM	gulf	gunung	island	kepulauan	pulau	sea	selat	strait
ENGLISH	gulf	mountain	island	islands	island	sea	strait	strait
DEUTSCH	Golf	Berg	Insel	Inseln	Insel	Meer	Meeresstrasse	Meeresstrasse
ESPAÑOL	golfo	montaña	isla	islas	isla	mar	estrecho	estrecho
FRANÇAIS	golfe	montagne	île	îles	île	mer	détroit	détroit
PORTUGUÊS	golfo	montanha	ilha	ilhas	ilha	mar	estreito	estreito

Copyright © by Rand McNally & Co.
Map prepared by Esselte Map Service AB, Stockholm.
A-569600-264   -12 -18

Tropic of Cancer

TAIWAN

T'AIWAN

PHILIPPINE

SEA

PACIFIC OCEAN

LUZON

PHILIPPINES

SAMAR

PANAY

LEYTE

NEGROS

CEBU

BOHOL

Cagayan
de Oro

MINDANAO

ZAMBOANGA
PENINSULA

Zamboanga

Davao

NORTHERN
MARIANA
ISLANDS
(U.S.)

MARIANA

ISLANDS

GUAM
(U.S.)

Agana

FEDERATED STATES OF MICRONESIA

PALAU ISLANDS

PALAU BELAU

CAROLINE   ISLANDS

CELEBES

SEA

KEPULAUAN TALAUD

SANGIHE

HALMAHERA

Manado

MINAHASA

Gorontalo

LAUT MALUKU
MOLUCCA SEA

Equator

PULAU
WAIGEO

JAZIRAH DOBERAI

PAPUA
NEW GUINEA

Jayapura (Sukarnapura)

PEGUNUNGAN VAN REES

SERAM CERAM SEA

KEPULAUAN
OBI

BURU

Ambon

SERAM CERAM

PEGUNUNGAN MAOKE

Puncak Jaya

N E W

G U I N E A

LAUT BANDA

BANDA SEA

KEPULAUAN
KAI

KEPULAUAN
ARU

KEPULAUAN
YAMDENA
KEPULAUAN TANIMBAR

Dili

TIMOR

ARAFURA   SEA

KEPULAUAN
BABAR

AUSTRALIA

Kupang

TIMOR SEA

CAPE YORK
PENINSULA

Map continues
pages 160-161

Kilometers   0   200   400   600   Km.
Statute Miles   0   200   400   600   Mi.

Scale 1:12,000,000

One centimeter represents 120 kilometers.
One inch represents approximately 190 miles.
Lambert Conformal Conic Projection

MAP FORM	dao	gunung	island	kepulauan	khao	kyun	pulau	shan
ENGLISH	island	mountain	island	islands	mountain	island	island	mountain(s)
DEUTSCH	Insel	Berg	Insel	Inseln	Berg	Insel	Insel	Berg(e)
ESPAÑOL	isla	montaña	isla	islas	montaña	isla	isla	montaña(s)
FRANÇAIS	île	montagne	île	îles	montagne	île	île	montagne(s)
PORTUGUÊS	ilha	montanha	ilha	ilhas	montanha	ilha	ilha	montanha(s)

Kilometers 0 100 200 300 Km.
Statute Miles 0 100 200 300 Mi.

Scale 1:6,000,000

One centimeter represents 60 kilometers.
One inch represents approximately 95 miles.
Lambert Conformal Conic Projection

Map continues pages 102-103

Map continues pages 120-121

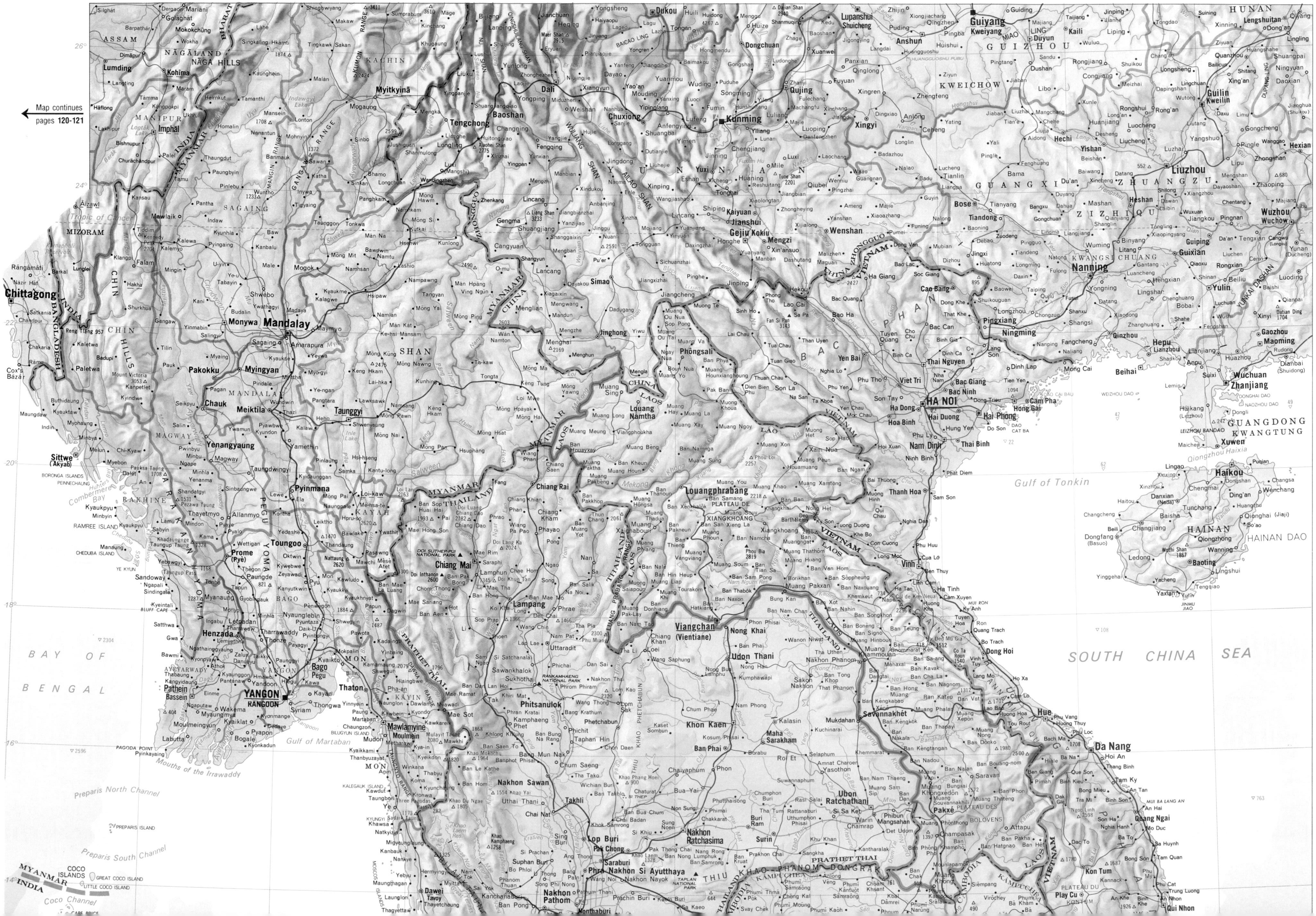

Myanmar, Thailand and Indochina/Myanmar, Thailand und Indochina/Myanmar, Siam e Indochina
Myanmar, Thaïlande et Indochine/Myanmar, Tailândia e Indochina

111

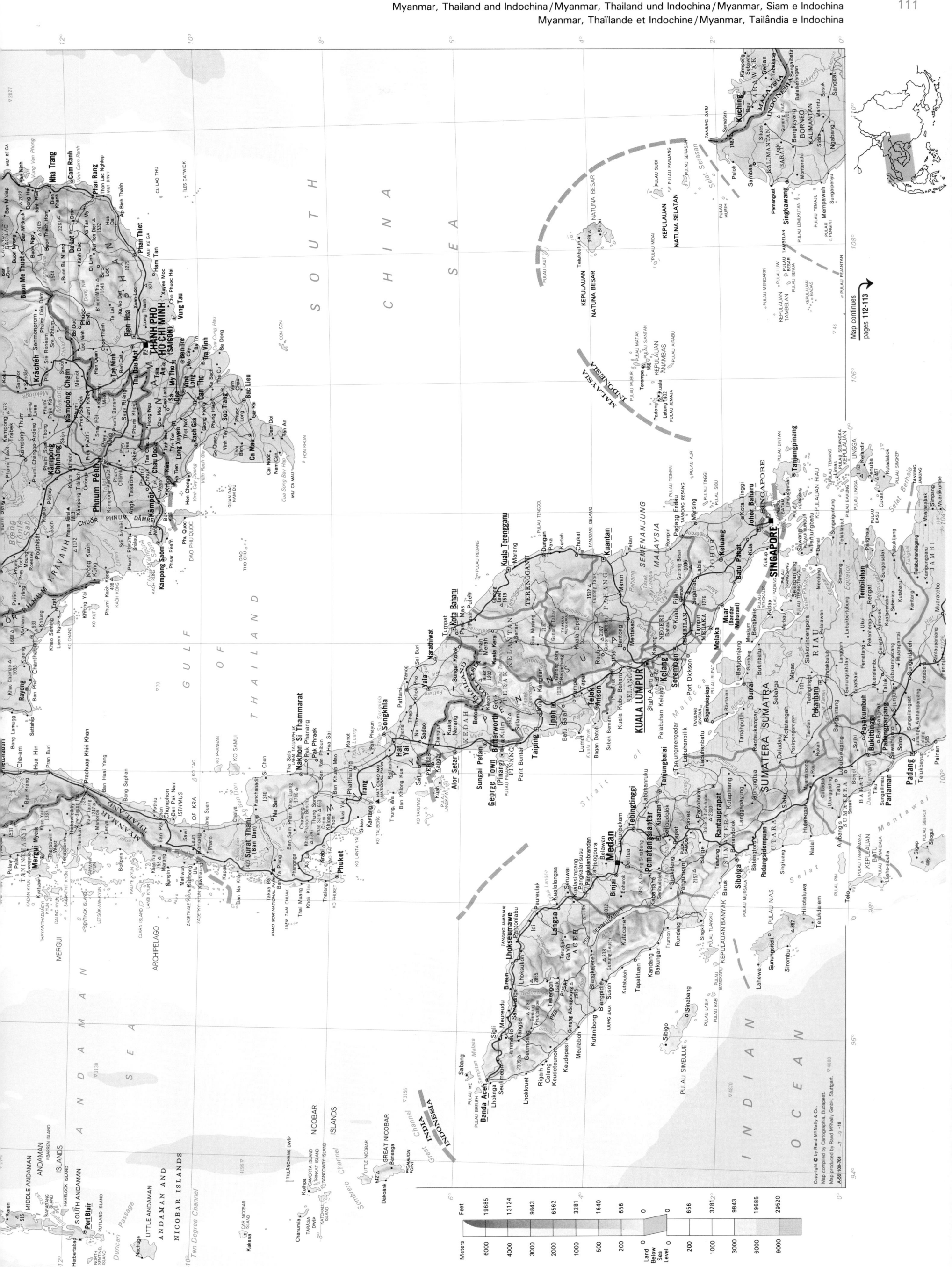

Map continues
pages 112-113

Feet
19685
13124
9843
6562
3281
1640
656
0
656
3282
9843
19685
29520

Meters
6000
4000
3000
2000
1000
500
200
0
Land
Below
Sea
Level
200
1000
3000
6000
9000

Copyright © by Rand McNally & Co.
Map compiled by Cartographia, Budapest.
Map produced by Rand McNally GmbH, Stuttgart.
A-06100-784

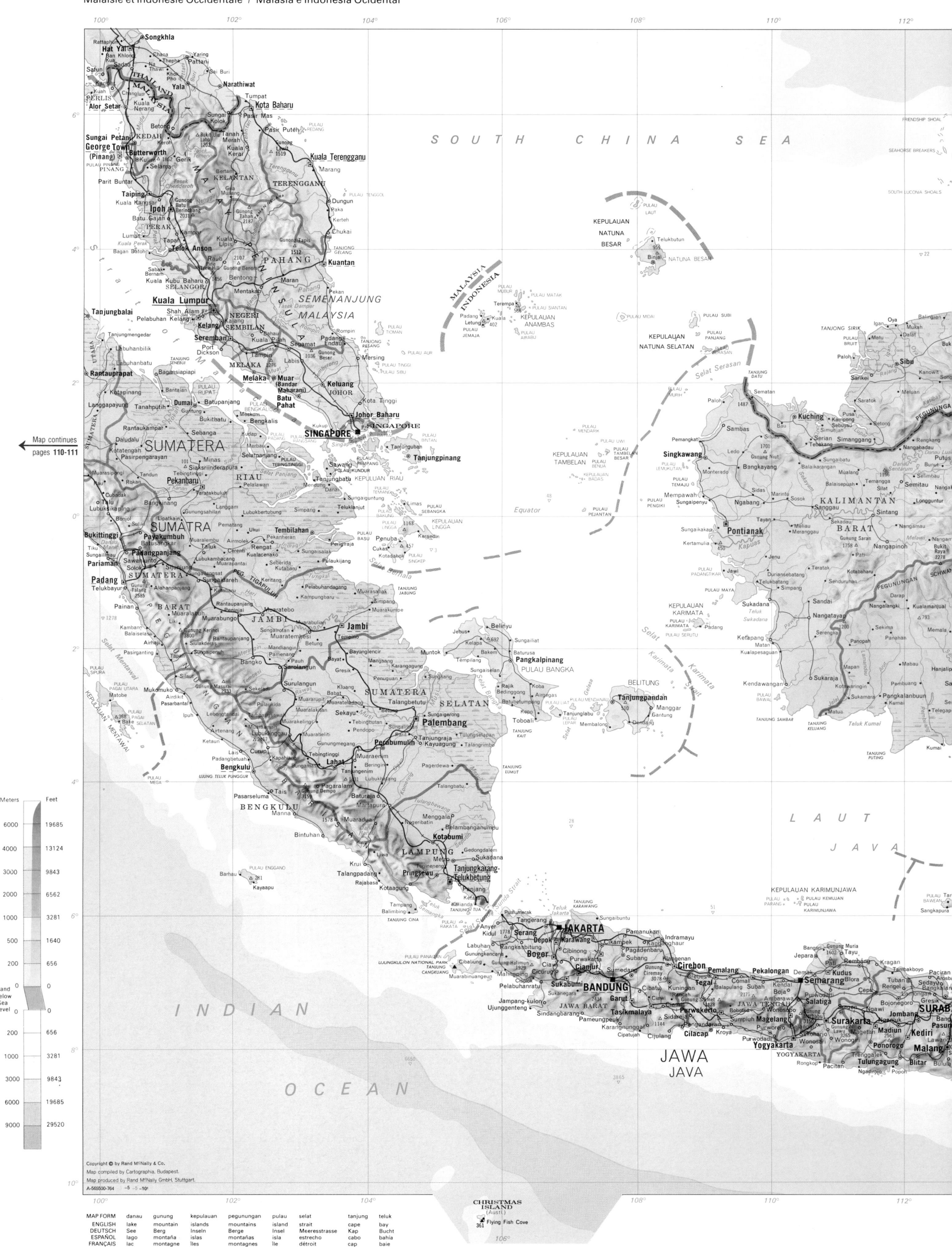

SOUTH CHINA SEA

MALAYSIA
INDONESIA

KEPULAUAN
NATUNA
BESAR

Map continues
pages **110-111**

SUMATERA

SUMATRA

KALIMANTAN
BARAT

Pontianak

Kuching

Singkawang

Kuala Lumpur

PENINSULAR
MALAYSIA

SINGAPORE

PEG. TIGAPULUH

Jambi

JAMBI

SUMATERA
SELATAN

Palembang

BELITUNG

Tanjungpandan

KEPULAUAN
KARIMATA

BENGKULU

Bengkulu

LAMPUNG

LAUT
JAWA

KEPULAUAN KARIMUNJAWA

INDIAN

OCEAN

JAKARTA

BANDUNG

JAWA BARAT

JAWA
JAVA

Semarang

SURAB

JAWA TENGAH

Surakarta

Yogyakarta

Meters	Feet
6000	19685
4000	13124
3000	9843
2000	6562
1000	3281
500	1640
200	656
0	0
Land Below Sea Level	
0	0
200	656
1000	3281
3000	9843
6000	19685
9000	29520

Copyright © by Rand McNally & Co.
Map compiled by Cartographia, Budapest.
Map produced by Rand McNally GmbH, Stuttgart.
A-565500-764

CHRISTMAS
ISLAND
(Austl.)
361 Flying Fish Cove

MAP FORM							
	danau	gunung	kepulauan	pegunungan	pulau	selat	tanjung	teluk
ENGLISH	lake	mountain	islands	mountains	island	strait	cape	bay
DEUTSCH	See	Berg	Inseln	Berge	Insel	Meeresstrasse	Kap	Bucht
ESPAÑOL	lago	montaña	islas	montañas	isla	estrecho	cabo	bahía
FRANÇAIS	lac	montagne	îles	montagnes	île	détroit	cap	baie
PORTUGUÊS	lago	montanha	ilhas	montanha	ilha	estreito	cabo	baía

Malaysia and Western Indonesia / Malaysia und westliches Indonesien
Malasia e Indonesia Occidental / Malaisie et Indonésie Occidentale
Malásia e Indonésia Ocidental

113

Map continues
pages **116-117**

Map continues
pages **164-165**

MALAYSIA
PHILIPPINES
SULU SEA
CELEBES SEA
LAUT MALUKU
MOLUCCA SEA
MINAHASA
MINDANAO
Davao
Zamboanga
Moro Gulf
JOLO ARCHIPELAGO
BORNEO
KALIMANTAN
KALIMANTAN TIMUR
SARAWAK
SABAH
BRUNEI
Bandar Seri Begawan
Kota Kinabalu (Jesselton)
Sandakan
Tawau
Tarakan
Samarinda
Balikpapan
Banjarmasin
Palangkaraya
KALIMANTAN TENGAH
KALIMANTAN SELATAN
SULAWESI
CELEBES
SULAWESI UTARA
SULAWESI TENGAH
SULAWESI SELATAN
SULAWESI TENGGARA
Manado
Gorontalo
Palu
Poso
Kendari
Palopo
Parepare
Singkang
Watampone (Bone)
Ujungpandang (Makasar)
Majene
Mamuju
Baubau
PULAU BUTON
PULAU MUNA
PULAU KABAENA
KEPULAUAN TUKANGBESI
MALUKU
BURU
BANDA SEA
LAUT BANDA
PULAU WETAR
KEPULAUAN ALOR
TIMOR
TIMOR TIMUR
Kupang
Dili
NUSA TENGGARA TIMUR
NUSA TENGGARA BARAT
FLORES
Ende
SUMBAWA
SUMBA
LOMBOK
BALI
Mataram
Denpasar
Singaraja
JAWA TIMUR
MADURA
Pamekasan
Situbondo
Banyuwangi
Jember
Laut Flores / Flores Sea
Laut Bali / Bali Sea
JAWA SEA
TIMOR SEA

Kilometers 0 100 200 300 Km.
Statute Miles 0 100 200 300 Mi.

Scale 1:6,000,000
One centimeter represents 60 kilometers.
One inch represents approximately 95 miles.
Mercator Projection

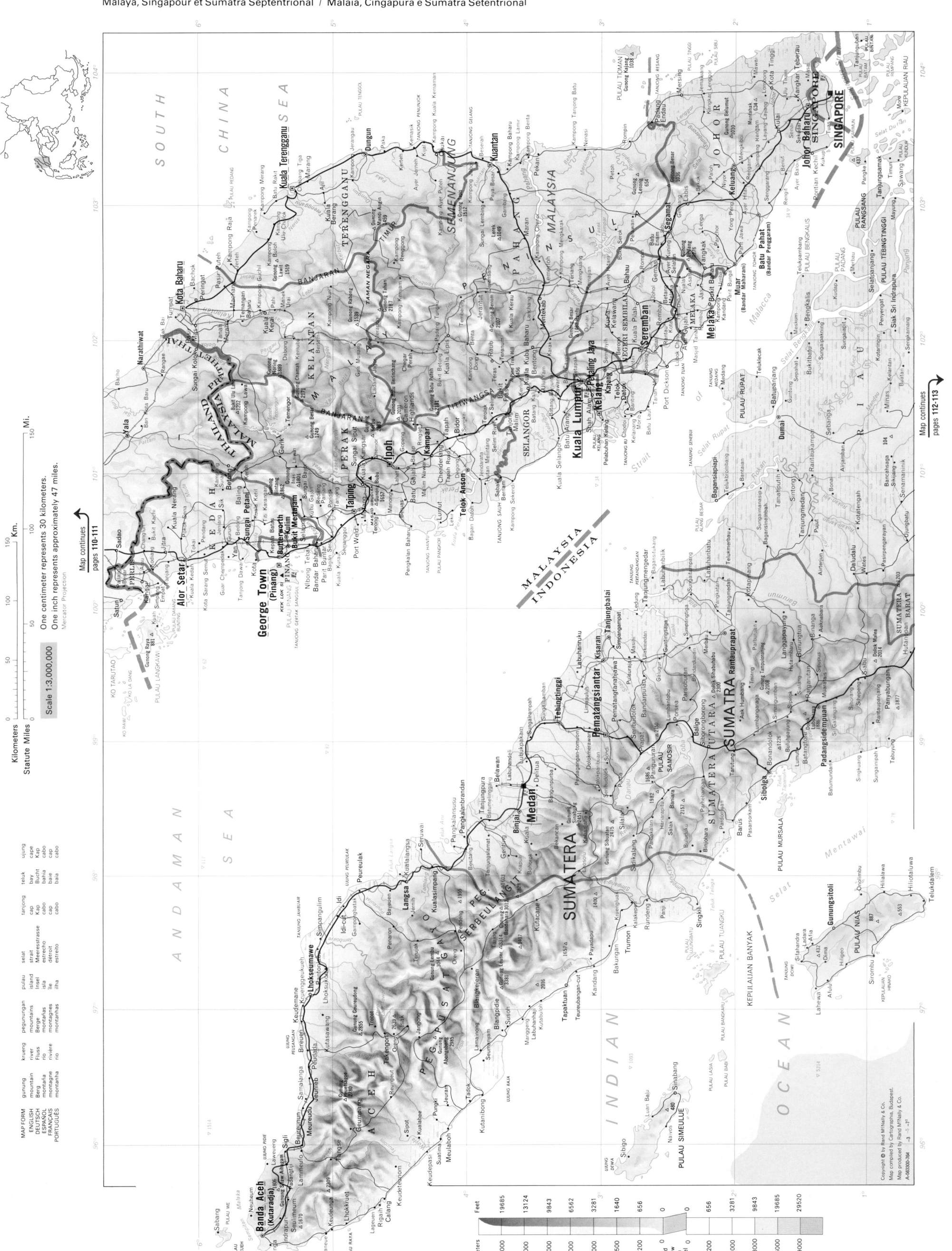

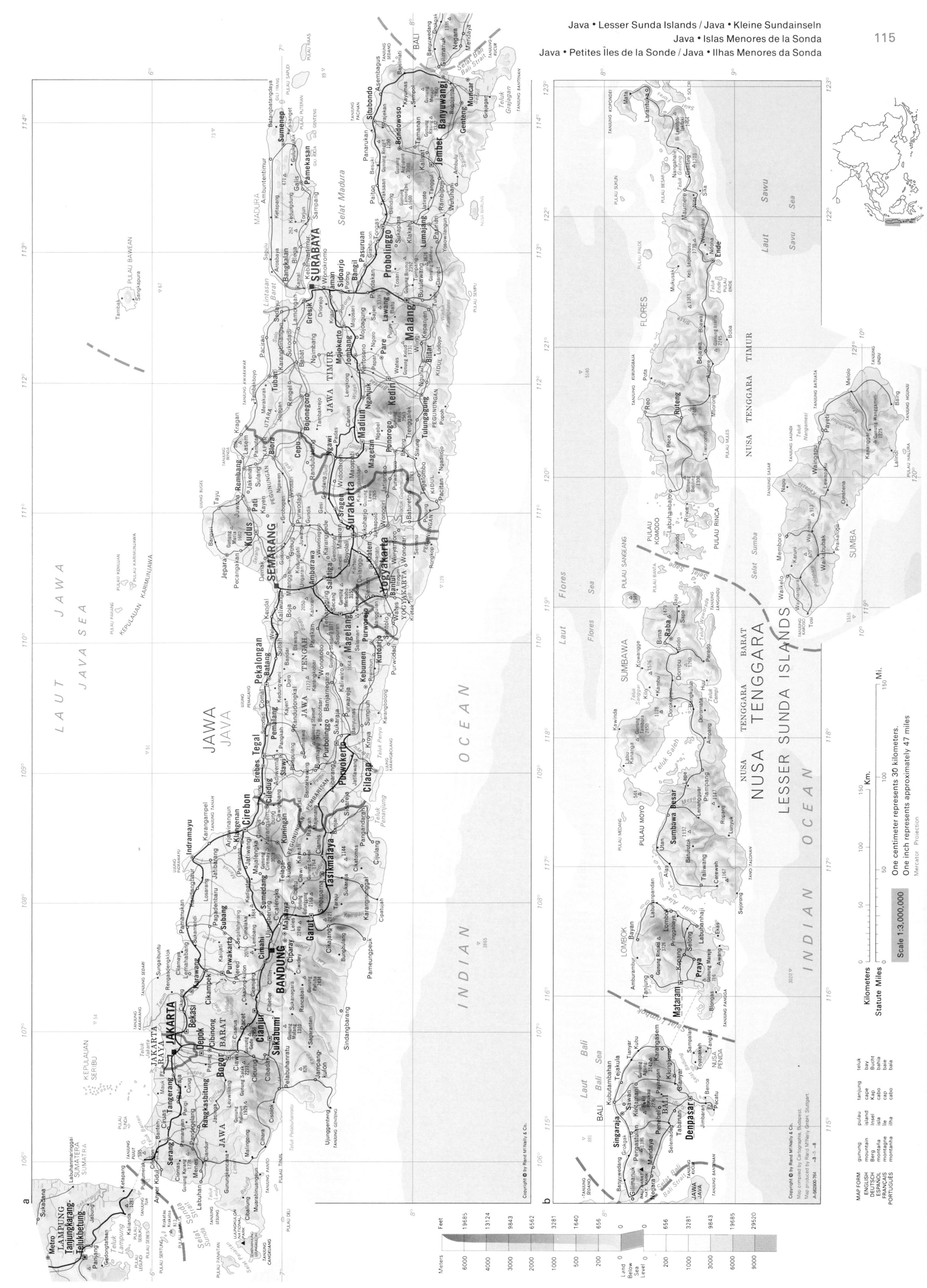

Java • Lesser Sunda Islands / Java • Kleine Sundainseln
Java • Islas Menores de la Sonda
Java • Petites Îles de la Sonde / Java • Ilhas Menores da Sonda

115

Scale 1:3,000,000

One centimeter represents 30 kilometers.
One inch represents approximately 47 miles.
Mercator Projection

MAP FORM
ENGLISH
DEUTSCH
ESPAÑOL
FRANÇAIS
PORTUGUÊS

gunung	mountain
	Berg
	montaña
	montagne
	montanha
pulau	island
	Insel
	isla
	île
	ilha
tanjung	cape
	Kap
	cabo
	cap
	cabo
teluk	bay
	Bucht
	bahía
	baie
	baía

Copyright © by Rand McNally & Co.

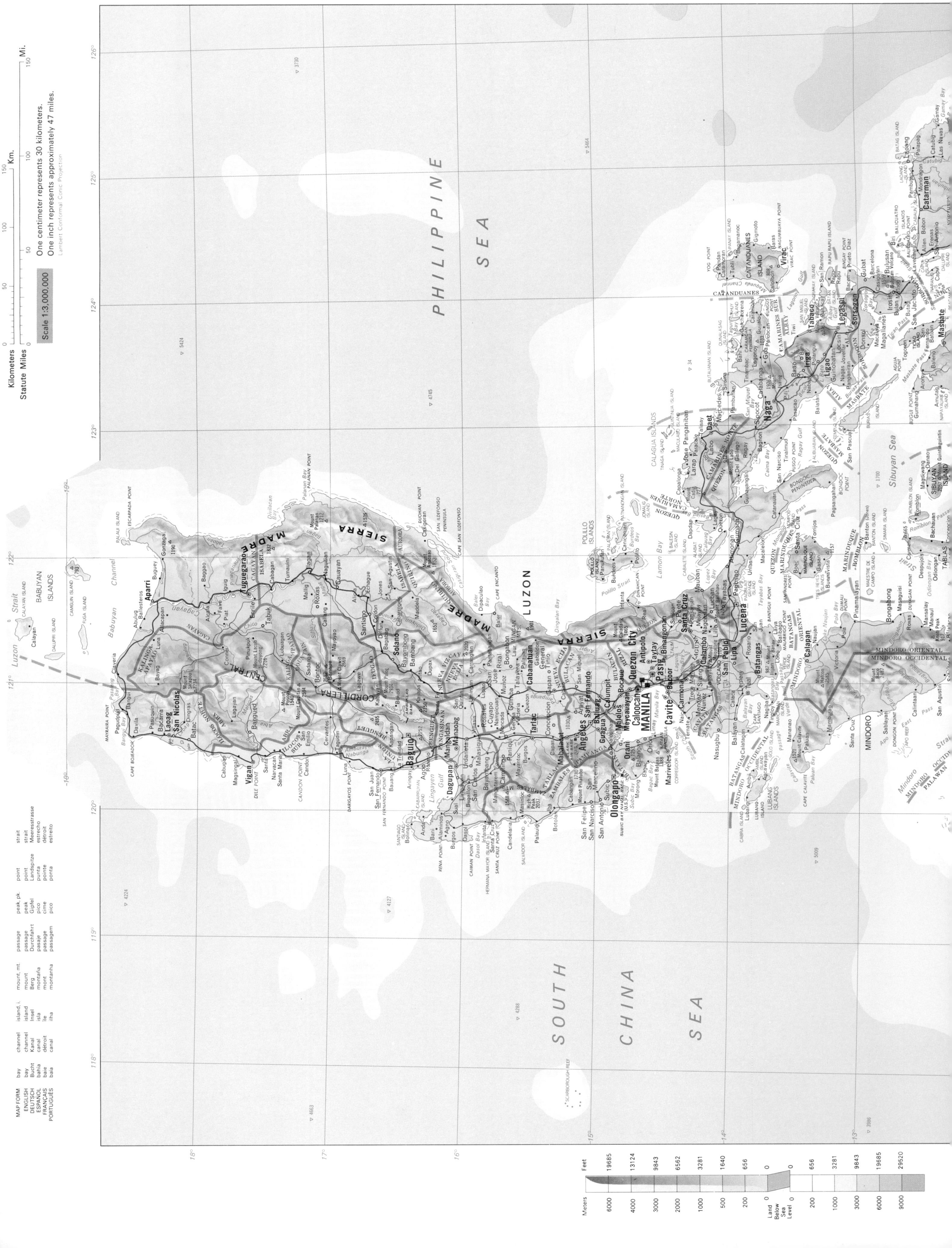

Mi.
150

Km.
150

100

50

One centimeter represents 30 kilometers.
One inch represents approximately 47 miles.

Scale 1:3,000,000

Lambert Conformal Conic Projection

Kilometers
Statute Miles

MAP FORM	bay	channel	island, i.	mount. mt.	passage	peak, pk.	point	strait
ENGLISH	bay	channel	island	mount	passage	peak	point	strait
DEUTSCH	Bucht	Kanal	Insel	Berg	Durchfahrt	Gipfel	Landspitze	Meeresstrasse
ESPAÑOL	bahia	canal	isla	montaña	pasaje	pico	punta	estrecho
FRANÇAIS	baie	canal	île	mont	passage	cime	pointe	détroit
PORTUGUÊS	baia	canal	ilha	montanha	passagem	pico	ponta	estreito

PHILIPPINE

SEA

SOUTH

CHINA

SEA

Sibuyan Sea

Mindoro Strait

LUZON

SIERRA MADRE

CENTRAL CORDILLERA

MANILA
Quezon City
Caloocan
Cavite
Angeles
San Fernando
Baguio
Dagupan
Vigan
Laoag
San Nicolas
Aparri
Tuguegarao
Olongapo
Batangas
Lucena
San Pablo
Calamba
Naga
Legaspi
Tabaco
Iriga
Daet
Virac
Masbate
Catarman
Calapan
Bongabong
Tarlac
Cabanatuan
Solano

BABUYAN ISLANDS

Luzon Strait

Babuyan Channel

MINDORO ORIENTAL
MINDORO OCCIDENTAL
MINDORO

PALAWAN

MARINDUQUE
ROMBLON

CATANDUANES
ISLAND

CAMARINES NORTE
CAMARINES SUR
ALBAY
SORSOGON
QUEZON
MASBATE

Feet		Meters
19685		6000
13124		4000
9843		3000
6562		2000
3281		1000
1640		500
656		200
0	Land Below Sea Level	0
0	Sea	0
656		200
3281		1000
9843		3000
19685		6000
29520		9000

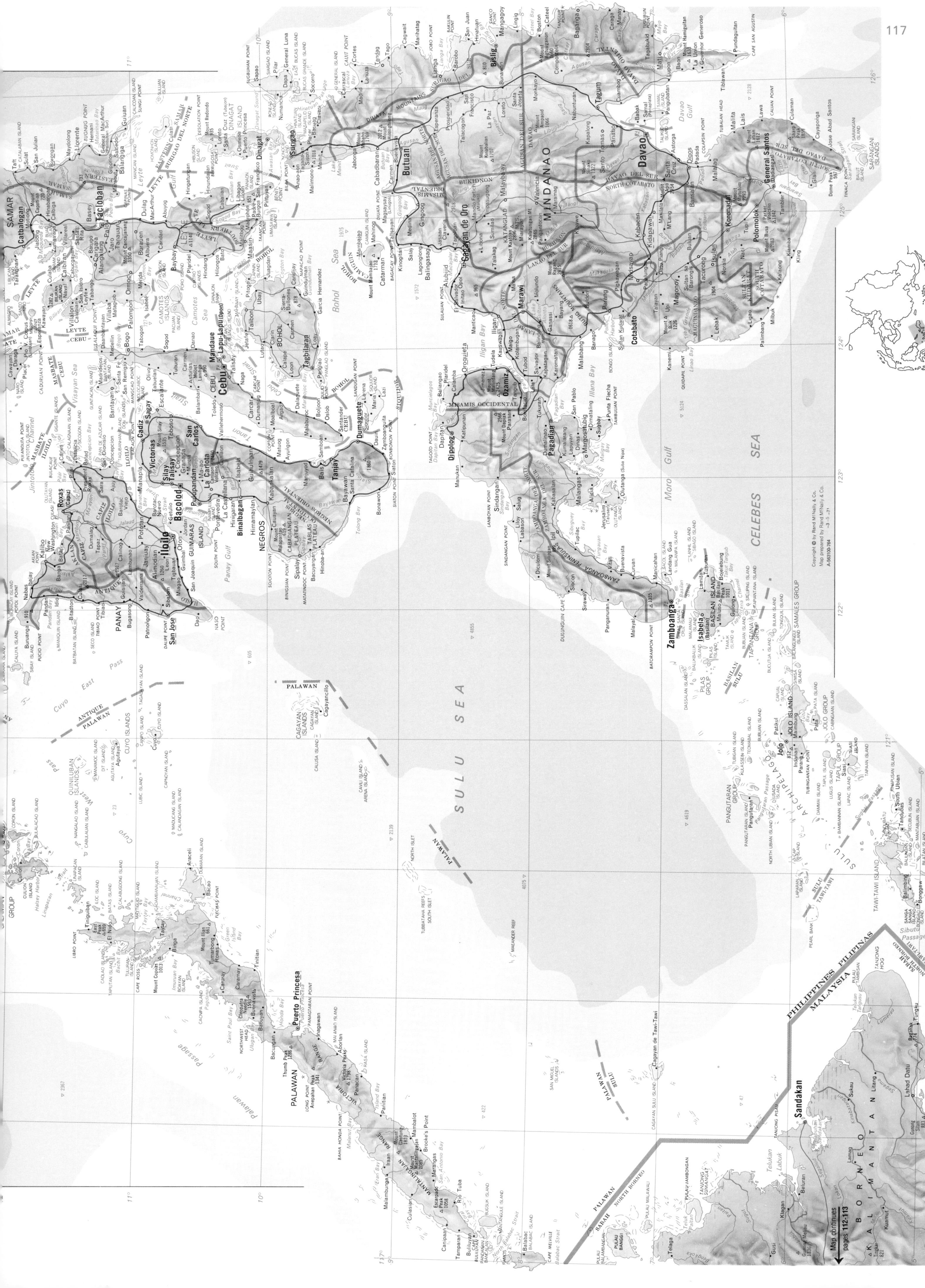

SAMAR

LEYTE

CEBU

BOHOL

NEGROS

PANAY

MASBATE

PALAWAN

MINDANAO

Tacloban

Catbalogan

Roxas

Iloilo

Bacolod

Cadiz

Victorias

Silay

Talisay

La Carlota

San Carlos

Binalbagan

Dumaguete

Cebu

Mandaue

Lapu-Lapu

Tagbilaran

Tanjay

Surigao

Butuan

Cagayan de Oro

Marawi

Ozamiz

Dipolog

Pagadian

Cotabato

Davao

Tagum

General Santos

Koronadal

Polomolok

Zamboanga

Isabela

Jolo

Sandakan

Puerto Princesa

San Jose

MISAMIS OCCIDENTAL

BUKIDNON

KATANGLAD

LANAO DEL NORTE

LANAO DEL SUR

NORTH COTABATO

DAVAO

DAVAO DEL SUR

SOUTH COTABATO

ZAMBOANGA DEL SUR

ZAMBOANGA DEL NORTE

SURIGAO DEL NORTE

AGUSAN

DIUATA MOUNTAINS

NEGROS OCCIDENTAL

NEGROS ORIENTAL

ANTIQUE

CAPIZ

ILOILO

AKLAN

GUIMARAS

MASBATE

CAMOTES ISLANDS

SULU SEA

CELEBES SEA

BOHOL SEA

Moro Gulf

Visayan Sea

Panay Gulf

Davao Gulf

Iligan Bay

Illana Bay

SULU ARCHIPELAGO

JOLO GROUP

TAPUL GROUP

SAMALES GROUP

TAWI-TAWI

BASILAN ISLAND

BASILAN

CUYO ISLANDS

CAGAYAN ISLANDS

PHILIPPINES PILIPINAS

MALAYSIA

BORNEO

KALIMANTAN

SABAH

NORTH BORNEO

Map continues pages 112-113

Map continues pages 22-23

Map continues pages 134-135

MAP FORM	gulf	jabal	jazirat	range	ra's	shan
ENGLISH	gulf	mountain	island	range	cape	mountain(s)
DEUTSCH	Golf	Berg	Insel	Gebirge	Kap	Berge(e)
ESPAÑOL	golfo	montaña	isla	sierra	cabo	montaña(s)
FRANCAIS	golfe	montagne	ile	chaine	cap	montagne(s)
PORTUGUÉS	golfo	montanha	ilha	serra	cabo	montanha(s)

Kilometers 0 — 200 — 400 — 600 Km.

Statute Miles 0 — 200 — 600 Mi.

Scale 1:12,000,000

One centimeter represents 120 kilometers.
One inch represents approximately 190 miles.
Lambert Conformal Conic Projection

India, Pakistan and Southwest Asia / Indien, Pakistan und Südwestasien / India, Pakistán y Asia Sud-occidental
Inde, Pakistan et Asie du Sud-Ouest / Índia, Paquistão e Ásia do Sudoeste

119

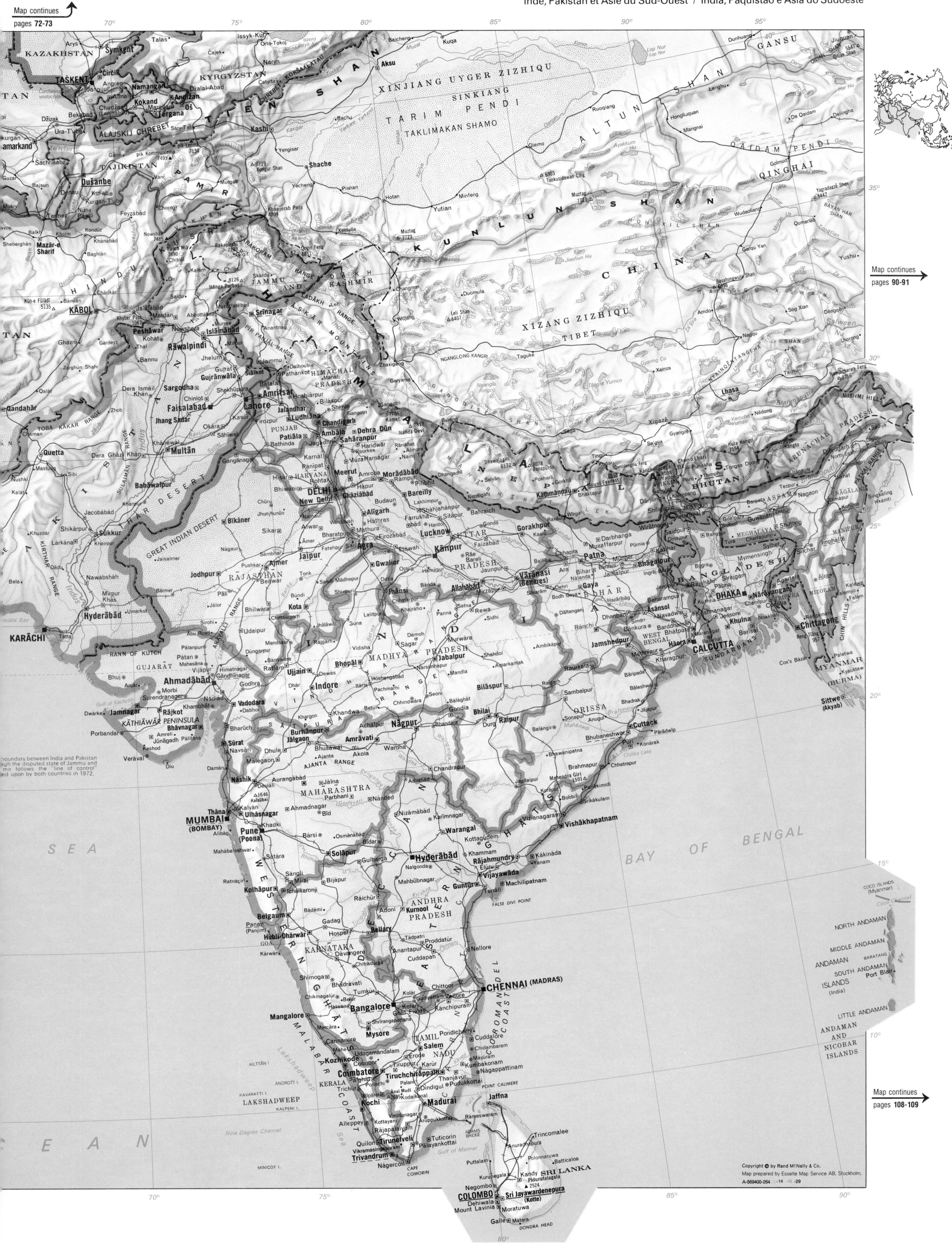

Map continues
pages 72-73

Map continues
pages 90-91

Map continues
pages 108-109

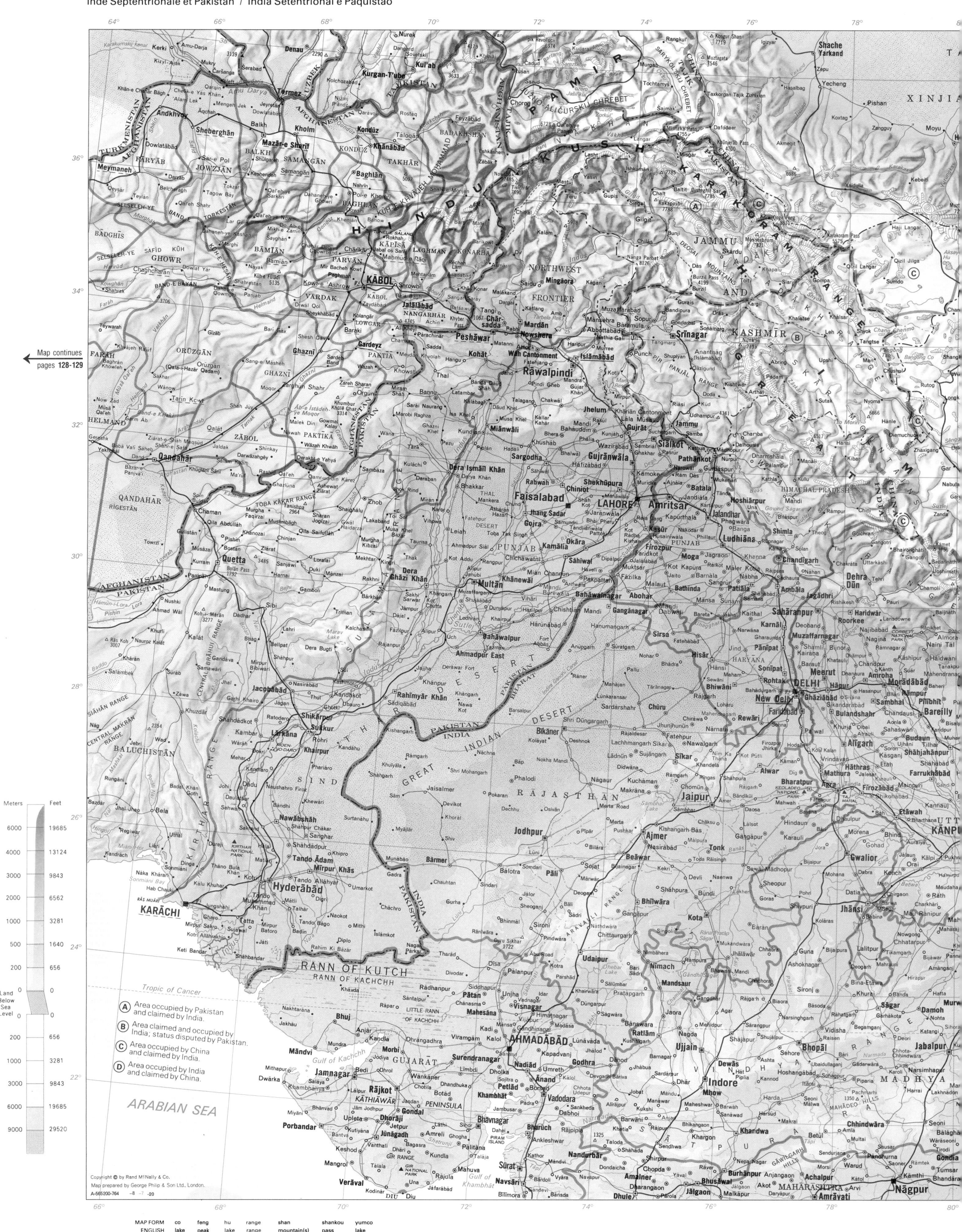

Map continues
pages 128-129

Meters   Feet
6000   19685
4000   13124
3000   9843
2000   6562
1000   3281
500   1640
200   656
Land   0
Below
Sea
Level   0
200   656
1000   3281
3000   9843
6000   19685
9000   29520

(A) Area occupied by Pakistan
and claimed by India.

(B) Area claimed and occupied by
India; status disputed by Pakistan.

(C) Area occupied by China
and claimed by India.

(D) Area occupied by India
and claimed by China.

Copyright © by Rand McNally & Co.
Map prepared by George Philip & Son Ltd., London.
A-565200-764   -8 -7 -20

MAP FORM	co	feng	hu	range	shan	shankou	yumco
ENGLISH	lake	peak	lake	range	mountain(s)	pass	lake
DEUTSCH	See	Gipfel	See	Gebirge	Berg(e)	Pass	See
ESPAÑOL	lago	pico	lago	sierra	montaña(s)	paso	lago
FRANÇAIS	lac	cime	lac	chaîne	montagne(s)	col	lac
PORTUGUÊS	lago	pico	lago	serra	montanha(s)	passo	lago

Northern India and Pakistan / Nordindien und Pakistan / India Septentrional y Pakistán
Inde Septentrionale et Pakistan / Índia Setentrional e Paquistão

121

Map continues
pages 102-103

Map continues
pages 110-111

Map continues
page 122

Kilometers

Statute Miles

Scale 1:6,000,000   One centimeter represents 60 kilometers.
One inch represents approximately 95 miles.
Lambert Conformal Conic Projection

BAY OF BENGAL

Southern India and Sri Lanka / Südindien und Sri Lanka / India Meridional y Sri Lanka
Inde Méridionale et Sri Lanka / Índia Meridional e Sri Lanka

Map continues
pages 120-121

ENGLISH   atoll   hills   island   lagoon   lake   range   reservoir
DEUTSCH   Atoll   Hügel   Insel   Haff   See   Gebirge   Stausee
ESPAÑOL   atolón   colinas   isla   laguna   lago   sierra   embalse
FRANÇAIS   atoll   collines   île   lagune   lac   chaîne   réservoir
PORTUGUÊS   atol   colinas   ilha   laguna   lago   serra   reservatório

Kilometers 0   100   200   300 Km.

Statute Miles 0   100   200   300 Mi.

Scale 1:6,000,000
One centimeter represents 60 kilometers.
One inch represents approximately 95 miles.
Lambert Conformal Conic Projection

Copyright © by Rand McNally & Co.
Map prepared by George Philip & Son Ltd., London.
A-565300-764   -3 □ -12

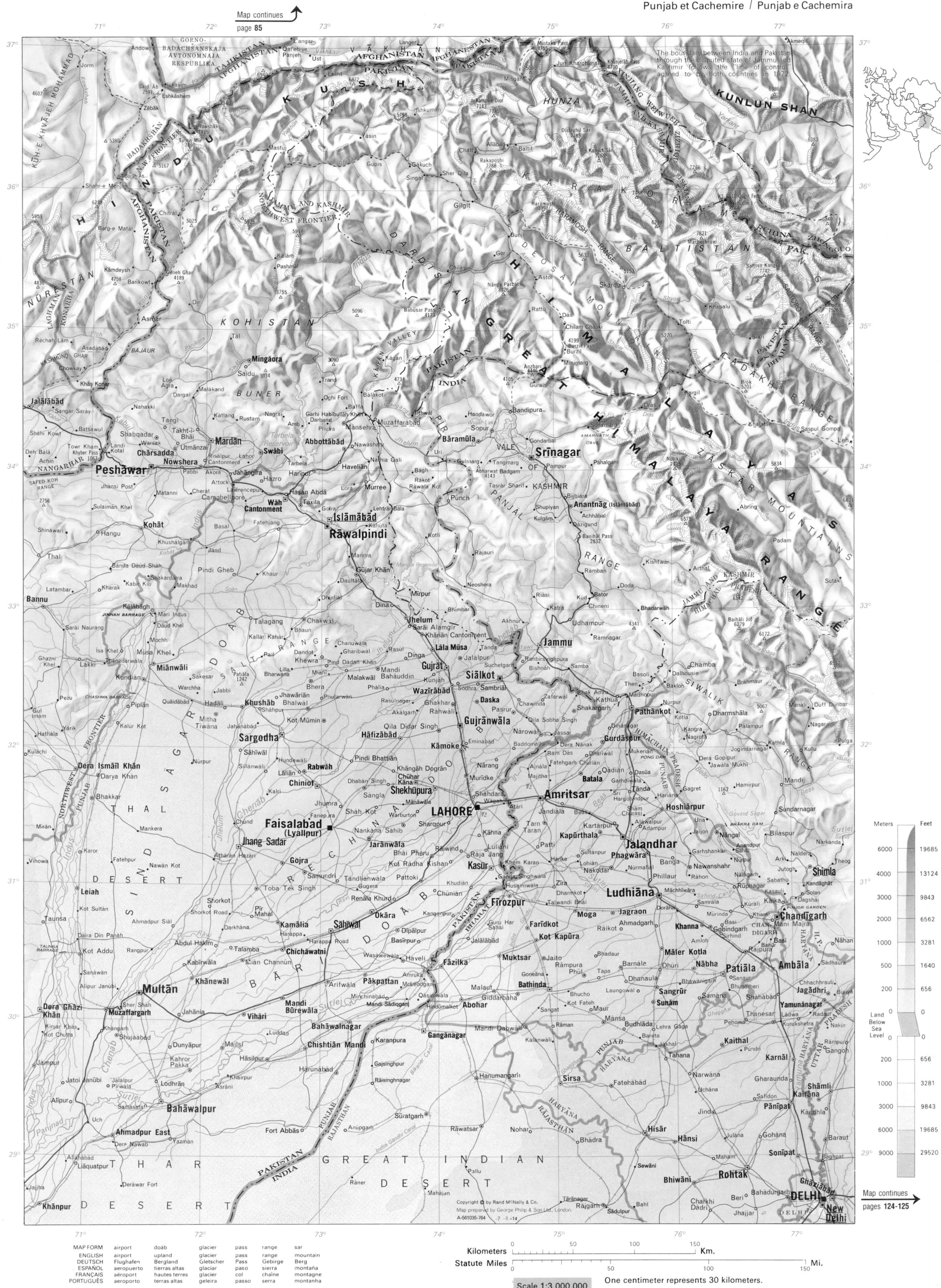

Map continues
page 85

The boundary between India and Pakistan
through the disputed state of Jammu and
Kashmir follows the "line of control"
agreed to by both countries in 1972.

Map continues
pages 124-125

Meters	Feet
6000	19685
4000	13124
3000	9843
2000	6562
1000	3281
500	1640
200	656
Land Below Sea Level	0
0	
200	656
1000	3281
3000	9843
6000	19685
9000	29520

MAP FORM	airport	doāb	glacier	pass	range	sar
ENGLISH	airport	upland	glacier	pass	range	mountain
DEUTSCH	Flughafen	Bergland	Gletscher	Pass	Gebirge	Berg
ESPAÑOL	aeropuerto	tierras altas	glaciar	paso	sierra	montaña
FRANÇAIS	aéroport	hautes terres	glacier	col	chaîne	montagne
PORTUGUÊS	aeroporto	terras altas	geleira	passo	serra	montanha

Kilometers
Statute Miles

Scale 1:3,000,000   One centimeter represents 30 kilometers.
One inch represents approximately 47 miles.
Lambert Conformal Conic Projection

Copyright © by Rand McNally & Co.
Map prepared by George Philip & Son Ltd., London.
A-561035-764

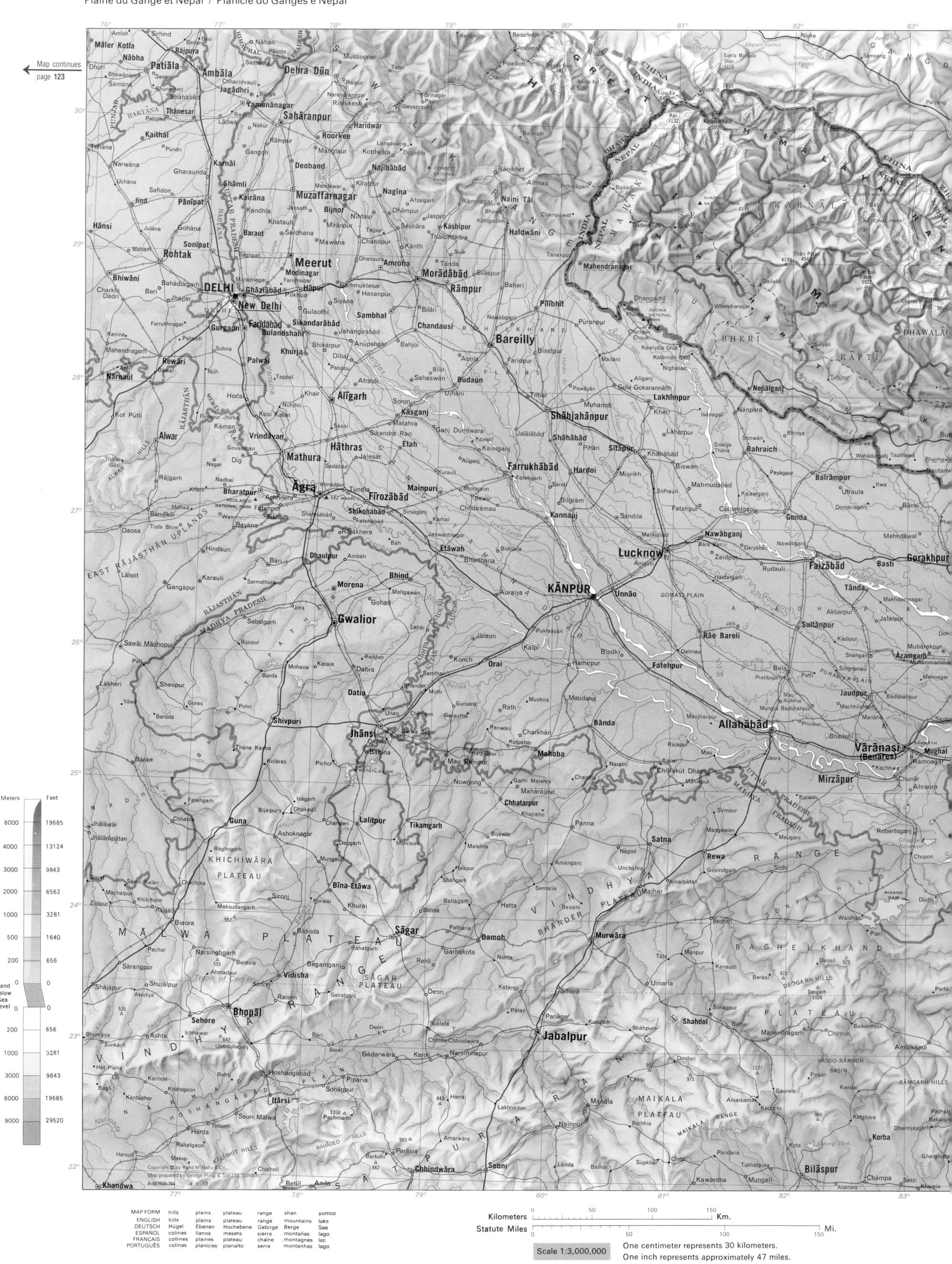

← Map continues page 123

MAP FORM	hills	plains	plateau	range	shan	yumco
ENGLISH	hills	plains	plateau	range	mountains	laks
DEUTSCH	Hügel	Ebenen	Hochebene	Gebirge	Berge	See
ESPAÑOL	colinas	llanos	meseta	sierra	montañas	lago
FRANÇAIS	collines	plaines	plateau	chaîne	montagnes	lac
PORTUGUÊS	colinas	planicies	planalto	serra	montanhas	lago

Kilometers   0   50   100   150   Km.

Statute Miles   0   50   100   150   Mi.

Scale 1:3,000,000

One centimeter represents 30 kilometers.
One inch represents approximately 47 miles.
Lambert Conformal Conic Projection

Meters / Feet

6000 — 19685
4000 — 13124
3000 — 9843
2000 — 6562
1000 — 3281
500 — 1640
200 — 656
0 — 0
Land Below Sea Level
0 — 0
200 — 656
1000 — 3281
3000 — 9843
6000 — 19685
9000 — 29520

Ganges Lowland and Nepal / Gangestiefland und Nepal / Llanuras del Ganges y Nepal
Plaine du Gange et Népal / Planície do Ganges e Nepal

125

Kilometers 0 10 20 30 40 50 Km.

Statute Miles 0 10 20 30 40 50 Mi.

Scale 1:1,000,000   One centimeter represents 10 kilometers.
One inch represents approximately 16 miles.
Lambert Conformal Conic Projection

Map continues page **84**

Map continues pages **130-131**

Map continues pages **140-141**

Map continues pages **144-145**

The Turkish Republic of Northern Cyprus unilaterally declared its independence on November 15, 1983.

Area occupied by Israel since June 1967

MEDITERRANEAN SEA

RED SEA

Area administered by Sudan

MAP FORM	harrat	jabal	jazireh	küh	mountain	ra's	sabkhat	wädi
ENGLISH	lava flow	mountain	island	mountain	cape	salt marsh	wadi
DEUTSCH	Lavastrom	Berg	Insel	Berg	Kap	Salzmarsch	Wadi
ESPAÑOL	corriente de lava	montaña	isla	montaña	cabo	pantano salado	uadi
FRANÇAIS	coulée de lave	montagne	île	montagne	cap	marais salé	wadi
PORTUGUÊS	corrente de lava	montanha	ilha	montanha	cabo	pântano salgado	uádi

Meters	Feet
6000	19685
4000	13124
3000	9843
2000	6562
1000	3281
500	1640
200	656
Land Below Sea Level 0	0
200	656
1000	3281
3000	9843
6000	19685
9000	29520

Administrative Boundary

CASPIAN SEA
(28 Meters Below Sea Level)

DAŠCHOVUZE

BALKAN

ACHAL

KARA

KUMY

LEBAN

UZBEKISTAN

BUCHARA

SAMARKAND

Kagan

Čardžou

Karši

KAŠKADARJA

TURKMENISTAN

MARYJ

AFGHANISTAN

FARYAB

BALKH

Mazar-e Sharif

Andkvoy

Sheberghan

Meymaneh

BADGHIS

BAMIAN

GHOWR

HERAT

OROZGAN

Herat

SELSELEH-YE SAFID KUH

FARAH

Farah

NIMRUZ

DASHT-E MARGOW

HELMAND

RIGESTAN

QANDAHAR

Qandahar

PAKISTAN

CHAGAI HILLS

SANDY DESERT

BALUCHISTAN

CENTRAL MAKRAN RANGE

SIAHAN RANGE

Bandar-e Anzali
(Bandar-e Pahlavi)
Rasht
Lahijan
Qazvin
RESHTEH-YE KUHHA-YE ALBORZ
ELBURZ MOUNTAINS
Karaj
TEHRAN
Eslamshahr
Qom
MARKAZI
Arak
Kashan
ESFAHAN
Najafabad
Esfahan
CHAHAR MAHAL VA BAKHTIARI
Masjed-e Soleyman
Shahr-e Kord
Qomsheh
YAZD
Yazd
SEMNAN
DASHT-E KAVIR
KAVIR-E NAMAK
KHORASAN
Mashhad
Sabzevar
Neyshabur
Torbat-e Heydariyeh
Torbat-e Jam
Birjand
DASHT-E LUT
KERMAN
Rafsanjan
Kerman
Sirjan
FARS
Shiraz
Kazerun
Marv Dasht
Fasa
Firuzabad
Jahrom
BUSHEHR
Bandar-e Bushehr
HORMOZGAN
Bandar-e 'Abbas
Zahedan
Zabol
SISTAN VA BALUCHESTAN
Iranshahr
BALUCHISTAN
MAKRAN COAST

Persian Gulf
Arabian Gulf

Al-Jubayl
BAHRAIN
AL-BAHRAYN
Ad-Dammam
Az-Zahran Dhahran
Al-Khubar
Al-Muharraq
Al-Manamah
QATAR
Al-Mubarraz
Al-Hufuf
Ad-Dawhah
Doha
Ar-Rayyan

UNITED ARAB EMIRATES
AL-IMARAT AL-'ARABIYAH
AL-MUTTAHIDAH

Abu Zaby
Abu Dhabi
Al-'Ayn
Dubayy
Ash-Shariqah

OMAN
'UMAN
Matrah
Masqat
Muscat

Gulf of Oman

Tropic of Cancer

Strait of Hormuz

Map continues
pages 120-121

Kilometers   0   100   200   300   Km.
Statute Miles 0   100   200   300   Mi.

Scale 1:6,000,000

One centimeter represents 60 kilometers.
One inch represents approximately 95 miles.
Lambert Conformal Conic Projection

Copyright © by Rand McNally & Co.
Map prepared by George Philip & Son Ltd., London.
A-569495-764   -15 -18 -28

Turkey and Cyprus / Türkei und Zypern / Turquía y Chipre
Turquie et Chypre / Turquia e Chipre

← Map continues
pages 38-39

The Turkish Republic of
Northern Cyprus unilaterally
declared its independence
on November 15, 1983.

	Meters	Feet
	6000	19685
	4000	13124
	3000	9843
	2000	6562
	1000	3281
	500	1640
	200	656
	0	0
Land Below Sea Level	0	0
	200	656
	1000	3281
	3000	9843
	6000	19685
	9000	29520

Copyright © by Rand McNally & Co.
Map prepared by George Philip & Son Ltd., London.
A-563900-764   -7 -8 -14

MAP FORM	burnu	dag, dağı	dağları	gölü	jabal	körfezi	sabkhat
ENGLISH	cape	mountain	mountains	lake	mountains	bay, gulf	salt marsh
DEUTSCH	Kap	Berg	Berge	See	Berge	Bucht, Golf	Salzmarsch
ESPAÑOL	cabo	montaña	montañas	lago	montañas	bahía, golfo	pantano salado
FRANÇAIS	cap	montagne	montagnes	lac	montagnes	baie, golfe	marais salé
PORTUGUÊS	cabo	montanha	montanhas	lago	montanhas	baia, golfo	pântano salgado

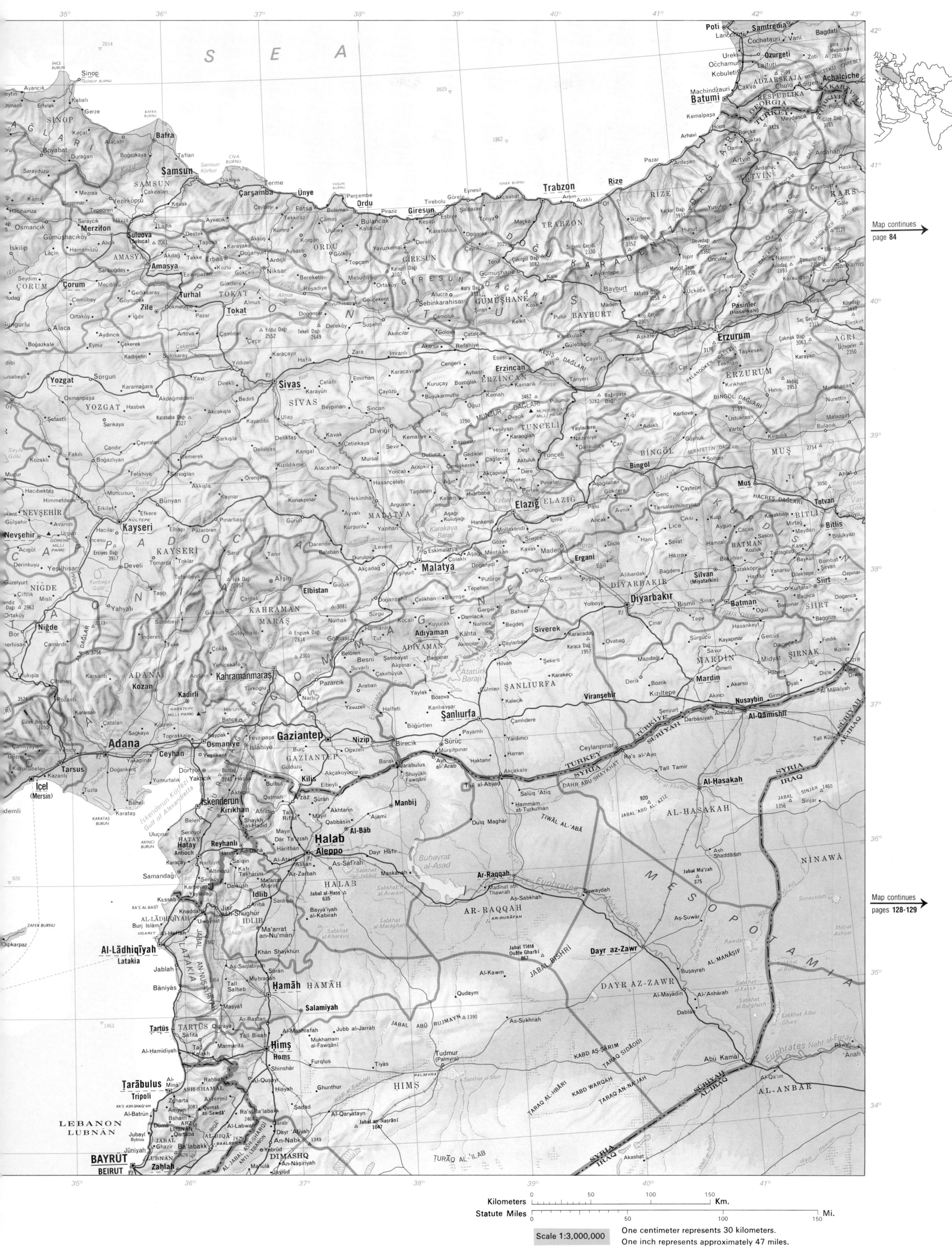

Map continues
page 84

Map continues
pages 128-129

Kilometers 0 50 100 150 Km.
Statute Miles 0 50 100 150 Mi.

Scale 1:3,000,000

One centimeter represents 30 kilometers.
One inch represents approximately 47 miles.
Conic Projection, Two Standard Parallels

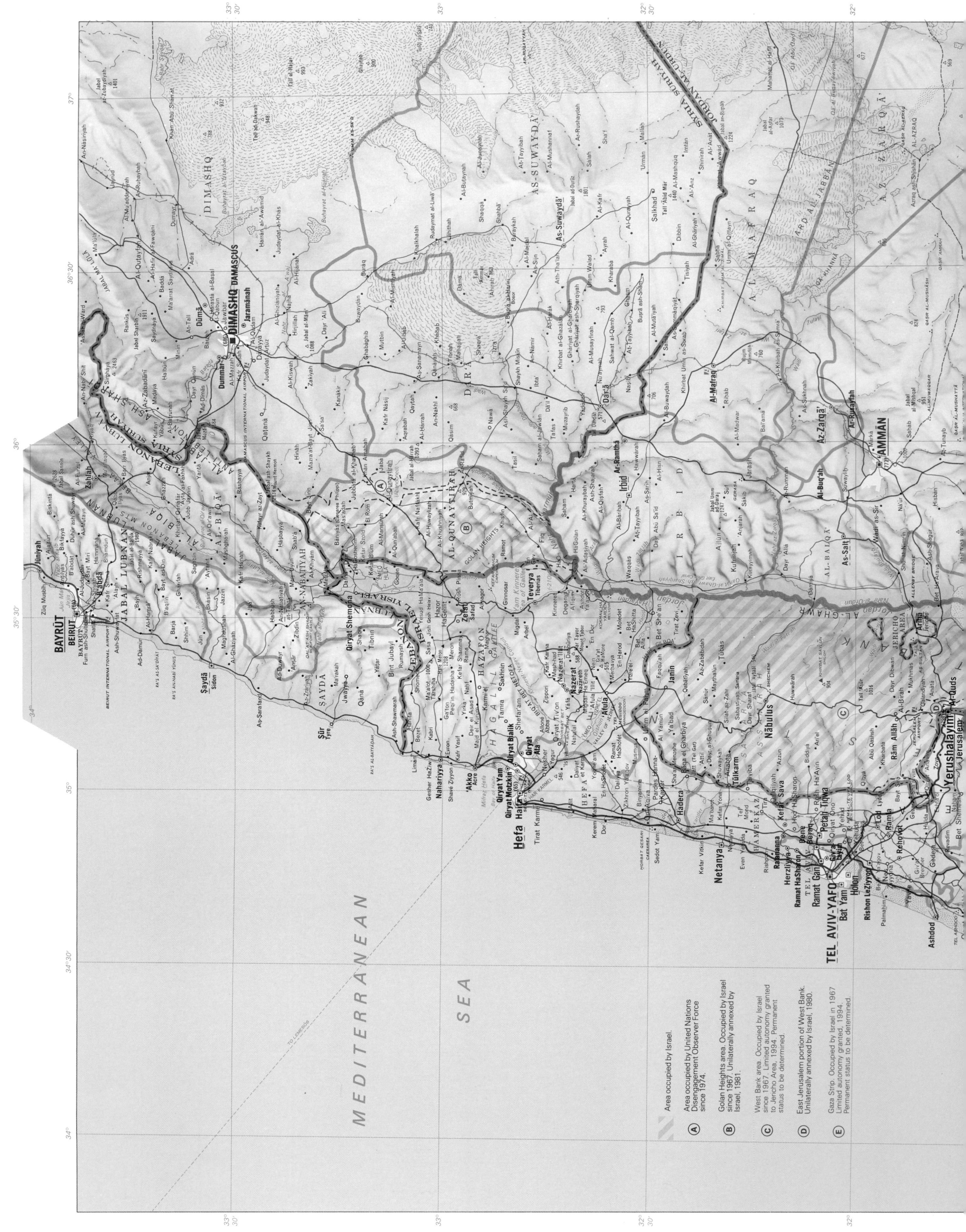

Area occupied by Israel.

(A) Area occupied by United Nations
Disengagement Observer Force
since 1974.

(B) Golan Heights area. Occupied by Israel
since 1967. Unilaterally annexed by
Israel, 1981.

(C) West Bank area. Occupied by Israel
since 1967. Limited autonomy granted
to Jericho Area, 1994. Permanent
status to be determined.

(D) East Jerusalem portion of West Bank.
Unilaterally annexed by Israel, 1980.

(E) Gaza Strip. Occupied by Israel in 1967.
Limited autonomy granted, 1994.
Permanent status to be determined.

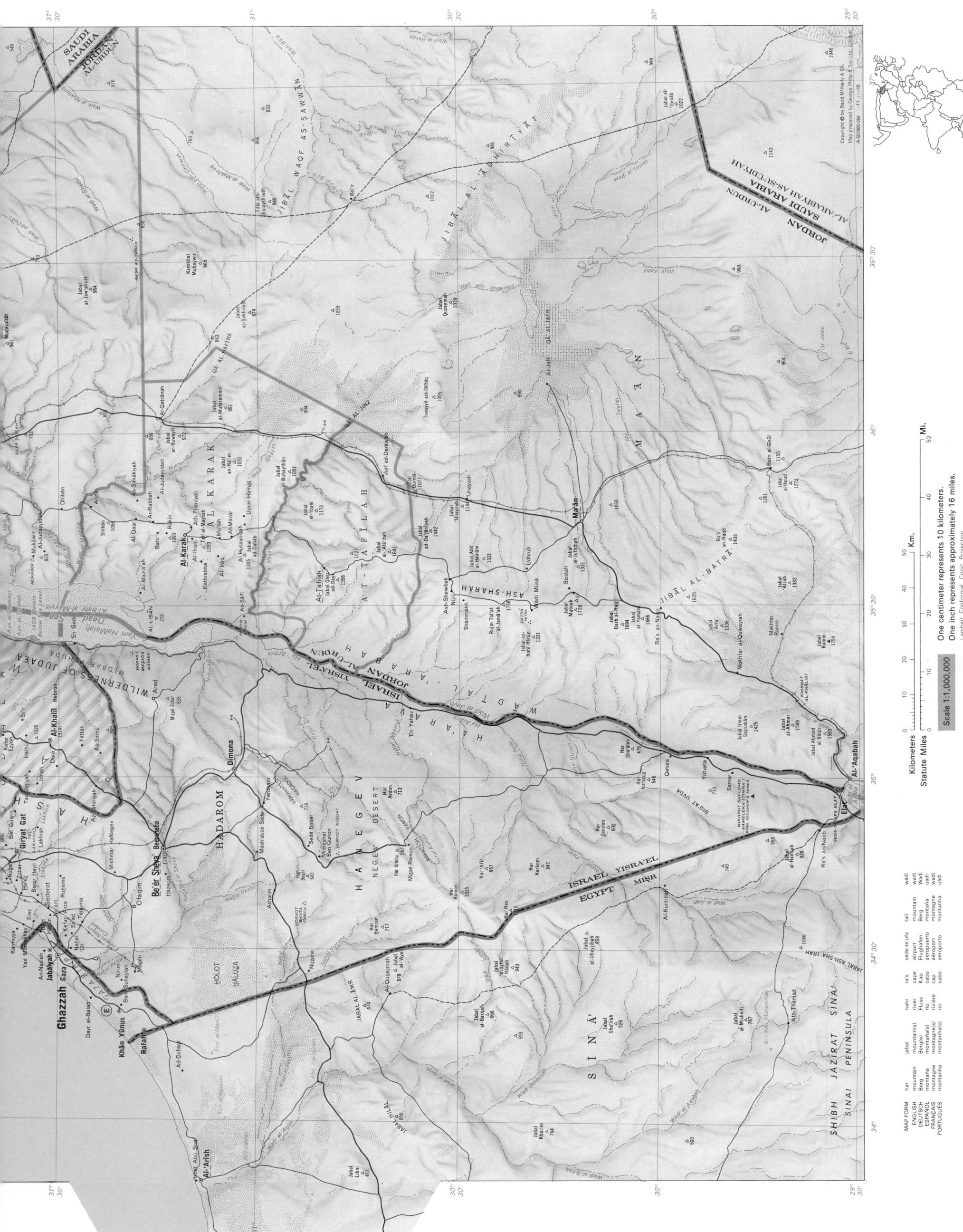

Scale 1:1,000,000

Kilometers
Statute Miles

Km.
Mi.

One centimeter represents 10 kilometers.
One inch represents approximately 16 miles.
Lambert Conformal Conic Projection

MAP FORM	har	jabal	sede-te'ufa	ra's	nahr	tall	wadi
ENGLISH	mountain	mountain(s)	airport	cape	river	mountain	wadi
DEUTSCH	Berg	Berg(e)	Flughafen	Kap	Fluss	Berg	Wadi
ESPAÑOL	montaña	montaña(s)	aeropuerto	cabo	río	montaña	wadi
FRANÇAIS	montagne	montagne(s)	aéroport	cap	rivière	montagne	uadi
PORTUGUÊS	montanha	montanha(s)	aeroporto	cabo	rio	montanha	

MAP FORM	bahr, bahr	chott	jabal	lake	mountains	oued	wahāt
ENGLISH	river, sea	salt marsh	mountain(s)	lake	mountains	wadi	oasis
DEUTSCH	Fluss, Meer	Salzmarsch	Berg(e)	See	Berge	Wadi	Oase
ESPAÑOL	río, mar	pantano salado	montaña(s)	lago	montañas	uadi	oasis
FRANÇAIS	rivière, mer	marais salé	montagne(s)	lac	montagnes	wadi	oasis
PORTUGUÊS	rio, mar	pântano salgado	montanha(s)	lago	montanhas	uádi	oásis

Western North Africa / West Nordafrika / Región Occidental de Africa Septentrional
Afrique du Nord Occidentale / África do Norte Ocidental

135

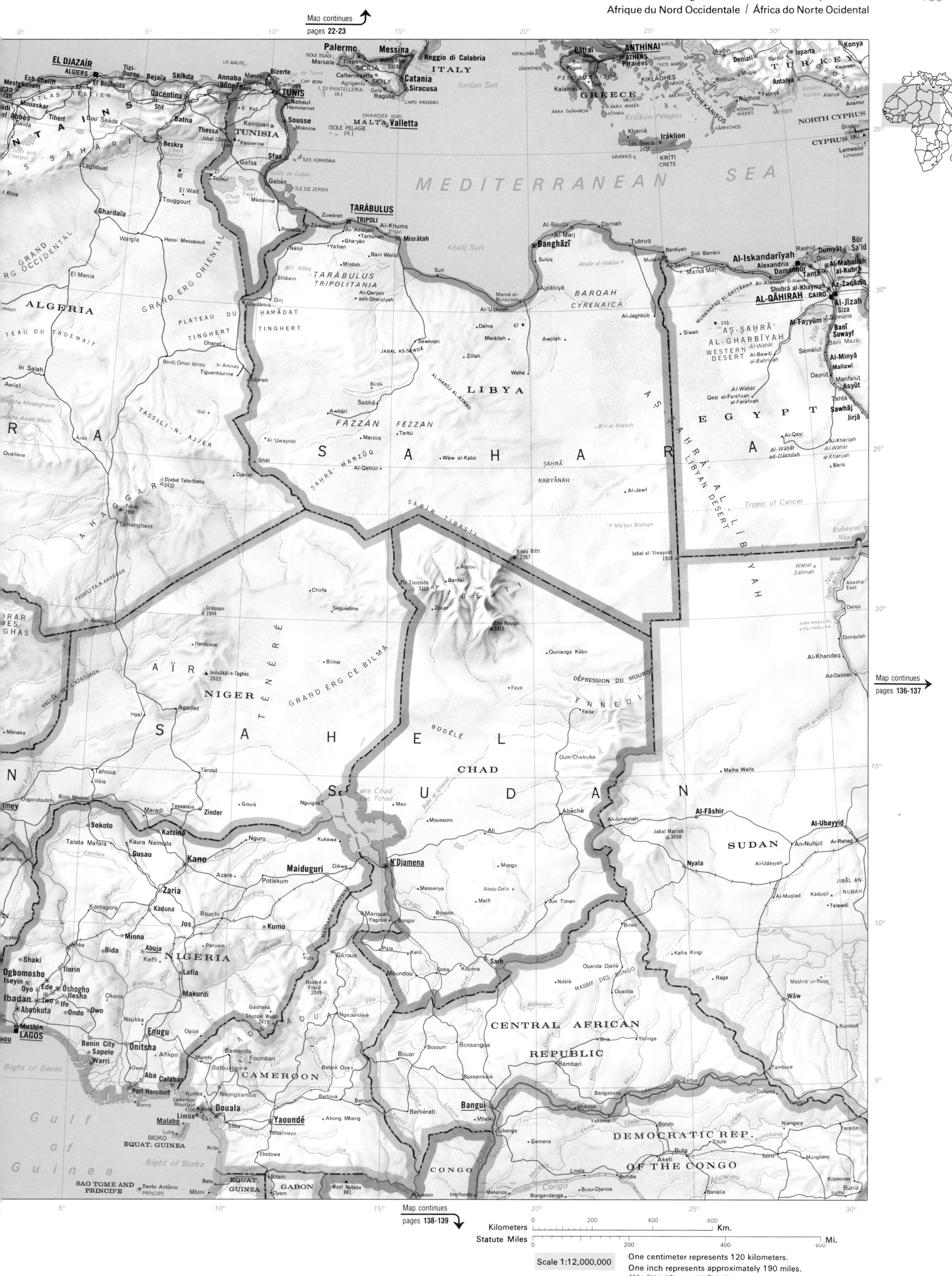

Map continues
pages 22-23

Map continues
pages 136-137

Map continues
pages 138-139

Kilometers 0   200   400   600   Km.
Statute Miles 0   200   400   600   Mi.

Scale 1:12,000,000
One centimeter represents 120 kilometers.
One inch represents approximately 190 miles.
Miller Oblated Stereographic Projection

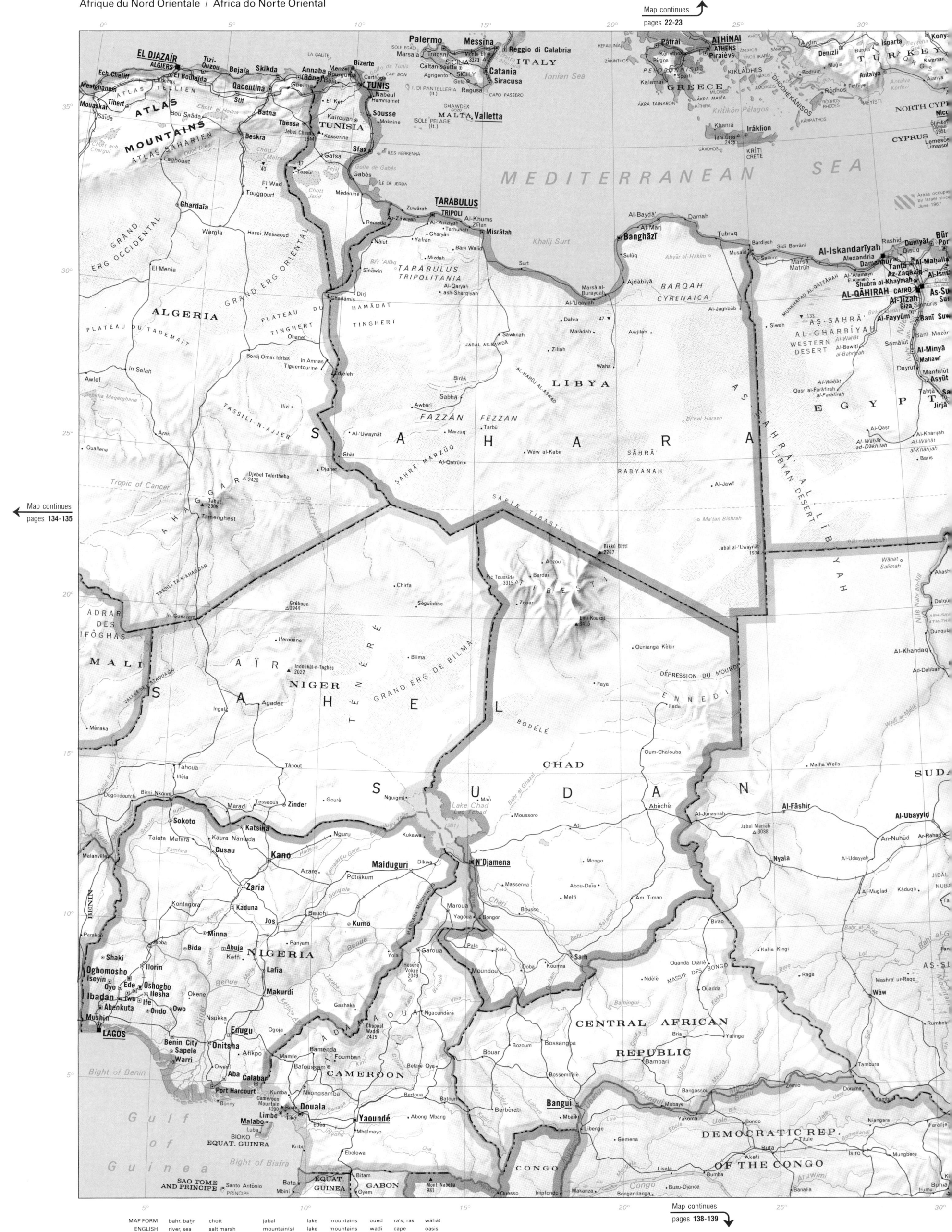

Map continues
pages 22-23

Map continues
pages 134-135

Map continues
pages 138-139

MAP FORM	bahr, bahr	chott	jabal	lake	mountains	oued	ra's; ras	wāhāt
ENGLISH	river, sea	salt marsh	mountain(s)	lake	mountains	wadi	cape	oasis
DEUTSCH	Fluss, Meer	Salzmarsch	Berg(e)	See	Berge	Wadi	Kap	Oase
ESPAÑOL	rio, mar	pantano salado	montaña(s)	lago	montañas	uadi	cabo	oasis
FRANÇAIS	rivière, mer	marais salé	montagne(s)	lac	montagnes	wadi	cap	oasis
PORTUGUÊS	rio, mar	pântano salgado	montanha(s)	lago	montanhas	uádi	cabo	oásis

Eastern North Africa / Ost Nordafrika / Región Oriental de Africa Septentrional
Afrique du Nord Orientale / África do Norte Oriental

137

Map continues
pages 118-119

Kilometers 0   200   400   600 Km.

Statute Miles 0   200   400   600 Mi.

Scale 1:12,000,000

One centimeter represents 120 kilometers.
One inch represents approximately 190 miles.
Miller Oblated Stereographic Projection

Copyright © by Rand McNally & Co.
Map prepared by Esselte Map Service AB, Stockholm.
A-589391 -264   -12 -12-26

Map continues
pages 136-137

MAP FORM	cape	ile	island	lake	mountains	plateau
ENGLISH	cape	island	island	lake	mountains	plateau
DEUTSCH	Kap	Insel	Insel	See	Berge	Hochebene
ESPAÑOL	cabo	isla	isla	lago	montañas	meseta
FRANÇAIS	cap	île	île	lac	montagnes	plateau
PORTUGUÊS	cabo	ilha	ilha	lago	montanhas	planalto

INDIAN OCEAN

SOMALIA

KENYA

NAIROBI

Mombasa

TANZANIA

SERENGETI PLAIN

MASAI STEPPE

Zanzibar

DAR ES SALAAM

MAFIA ISLAND

MALAWI

Lilongwe

Zomba
Blantyre
Tete

MOZAMBIQUE

Quelimane

Beira

CABO DELGADO

Nacala

Nampula

Moçambique

SEYCHELLES

AMIRANTE ISLANDS (Sey.)
ÎLE DESROCHES (Sey.)
PLATTE ISLAND (Sey.)

Victoria
SILHOUETTE
MAHÉ ISLAND
LA DIGUE
PRASLIN ISLAND

ALPHONSE ISLAND (Sey.)

COETIVY ISLAND (Sey.)

ALDABRA ISLAND (Sey.)

COSMOLEDO I. (Sey.)
SAINT PIERRE ISLAND (Sey.)
PROVIDENCE ISLAND (Sey.)
CERF ISLAND (Sey.)

ASSUMPTION ISLAND (Sey.)
ASTOVE ISLAND (Sey.)
FARQUHAR GROUP (Sey.)

AGALEGA ISLANDS (Mauritius)

COMOROS
Moroni
NJAZIDJA
Mutsamudu
NZWANI
MWALI
Fomboni
MAYOTTE (Fr.)
Dzaoudzi

ÎLES GLORIEUSES (Fr.)

CAP D'AMBRE
SAINT-SÉBASTIEN
CAP
Antsiranana

NOSY MITSIO
NOSY BE
Hell-Ville

MASSIF DU TSARATANANA
Maromokotro 2876

Sambava

Andapa
Antalaha

MADAGASCAR

Mahajanga

ANTANANARIVO

Antsirabe

Fianarantsoa

Toamasina

Toliara

CAP SAINTE-MARIE

Faradofay

ÎLE TROMELIN (Fr.)

Port Louis
Curepipe
Mahébourg
MAURITIUS

Le Port
Saint-Paul
Saint-Denis
Saint-Pierre
RÉUNION

MASCARENE ISLANDS

Tropic of Capricorn

INDIAN OCEAN

Kilometers
Statute Miles

Scale 1:12,000,000

One centimeter represents 120 kilometers.
One inch represents approximately 190 miles.
Miller Oblated Stereographic Projection

Map continues pages 128-129

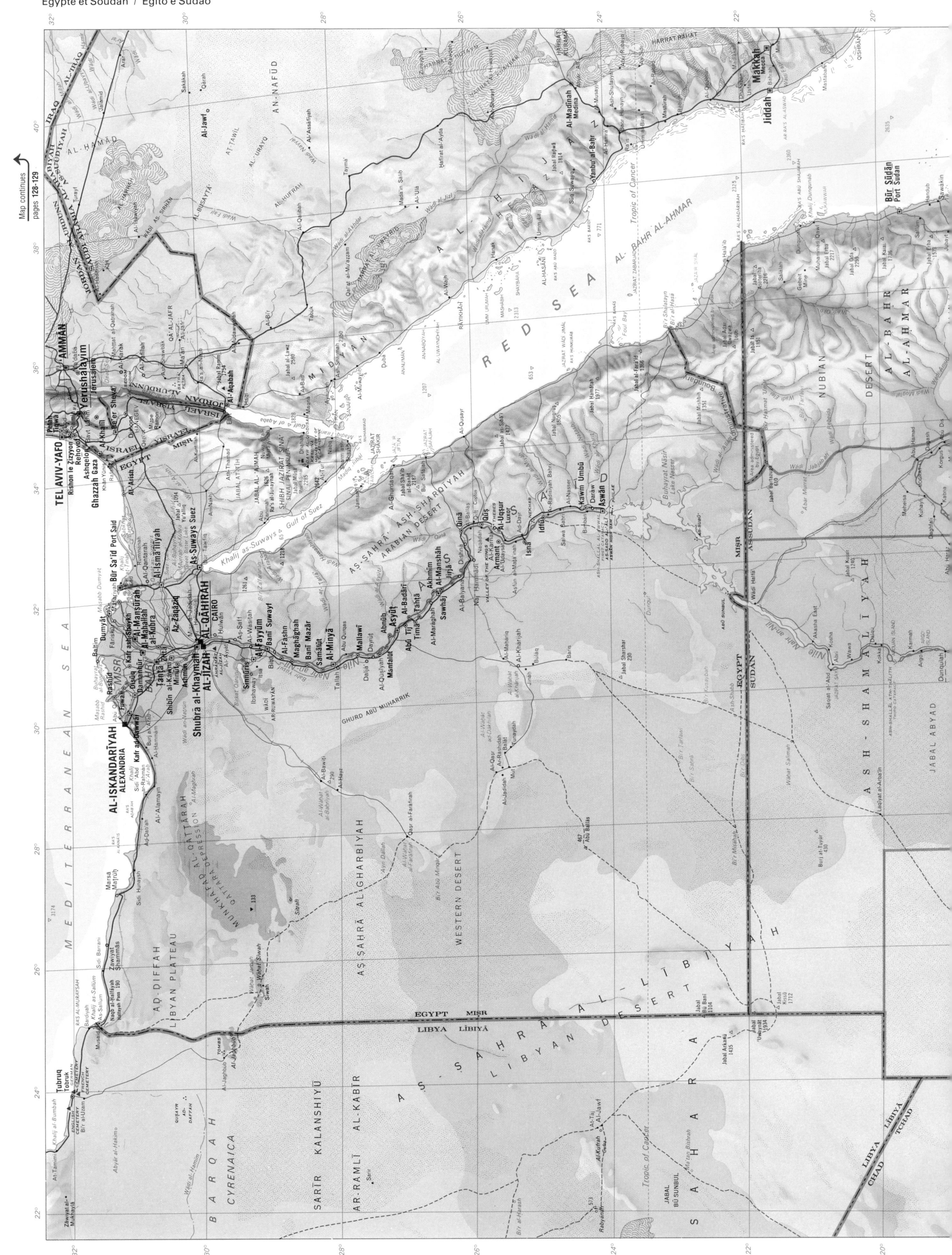
MEDITERRANEAN SEA
RED SEA
AL-BAHR AL-AHMAR
AL-ISKANDARĪYAH
ALEXANDRIA
AL-QĀHIRAH
CAIRO
AL-JĪZAH
TEL AVIV-YAFO
AMMĀN
Yerushalayim
Jerusalem
Būr Sa'īd Port Said
As-Suways Suez
Al-Ismā'īlīyah
Aswān
Al-Uqşur
Luxor
Asyūt
Al-Minyā
Makkah
Mecca
Jiddah
Al-Madīnah
Medina
Būr Sūdān
Port Sudan
Tubruq
Tobruk
Marsa Maţrūḥ
Sīwah
Al-Jawf
Al-Kufrah
WESTERN DESERT
ARABIAN DESERT
NUBIAN DESERT
LIBYAN DESERT
LIBYAN PLATEAU
CYRENAICA
AL-HIJAZ
MIDYAN
AN-NAFŪD
AL-HAMAD
Gulf of Suez
Gulf of Aqaba
Tropic of Cancer
Buhayrat Nāsir
Lake Nasser
EGYPT
MIŞR
LIBYA
LĪBIYĀ
SUDAN
AS-SŪDĀN
CHAD
TCHAD
ISRAEL
YISRA'EL
JORDAN
AL-URDUNN
SAUDI ARABIA
IRAQ
AL-'IRĀQ
MUNKHAFAD AL-QAŢŢĀRAH
QATTARA DEPRESSION
AŞ-ŞAḤRĀ' AL-GHARBĪYAH
AŞ-ŞAḤRĀ' ASH-SHARQĪYAH
AŞ-ŞAḤRĀ' AL-LĪBĪYAH
AŞ-ŞAḤRĀ' ASH-SHAMĀLĪYAH
SARĪR KALANSHIYŪ
AR-RAMLĪ AL-KABĪR
BARQAH
AD-DIFFAH
JABAL ABYAD
Nile
Nahr an-Nīl
32°
30°
28°
26°
24°
22°
20°
36°
38°
40°
34°

Map continues
pages 144-145

Map continues
pages 154-155

Map continues
pages 146-147

Scale 1:6,000,000

Kilometers
Statute Miles

One centimeter represents 60 kilometers.
One inch represents approximately 95 miles.
Lambert Azimuthal Equal-Area Projection

MAP FORM				
ENGLISH	bahr	river, sea	ra's	cape
DEUTSCH		Fluss, Meer		Kap
ESPAÑOL		río, mar		cabo
FRANÇAIS		rivière, mer		cap
PORTUGUÊS		rio, mar		cabo
	bi'r	well	khawr	wadi
		Brunnen		Wadi
		pozo		uadi
		puits		oued
		poço		uádi
	jazā'ir	islands	jazīrat	island
		Inseln		Insel
		islas		isla
		îles		île
		ilhas		ilha
	wādī	wadi	wāḥāt	oasis
		Wadi		Oase
		uadi		oasis
		oued		oasis
		uádi		oásis

Feet	Meters
19685	6000
13124	4000
9843	3000
6562	2000
3281	1000
1640	500
656	200
0	0 Land Below Sea Level
656	200
3281	1000
9843	3000
19685	6000
29520	9000

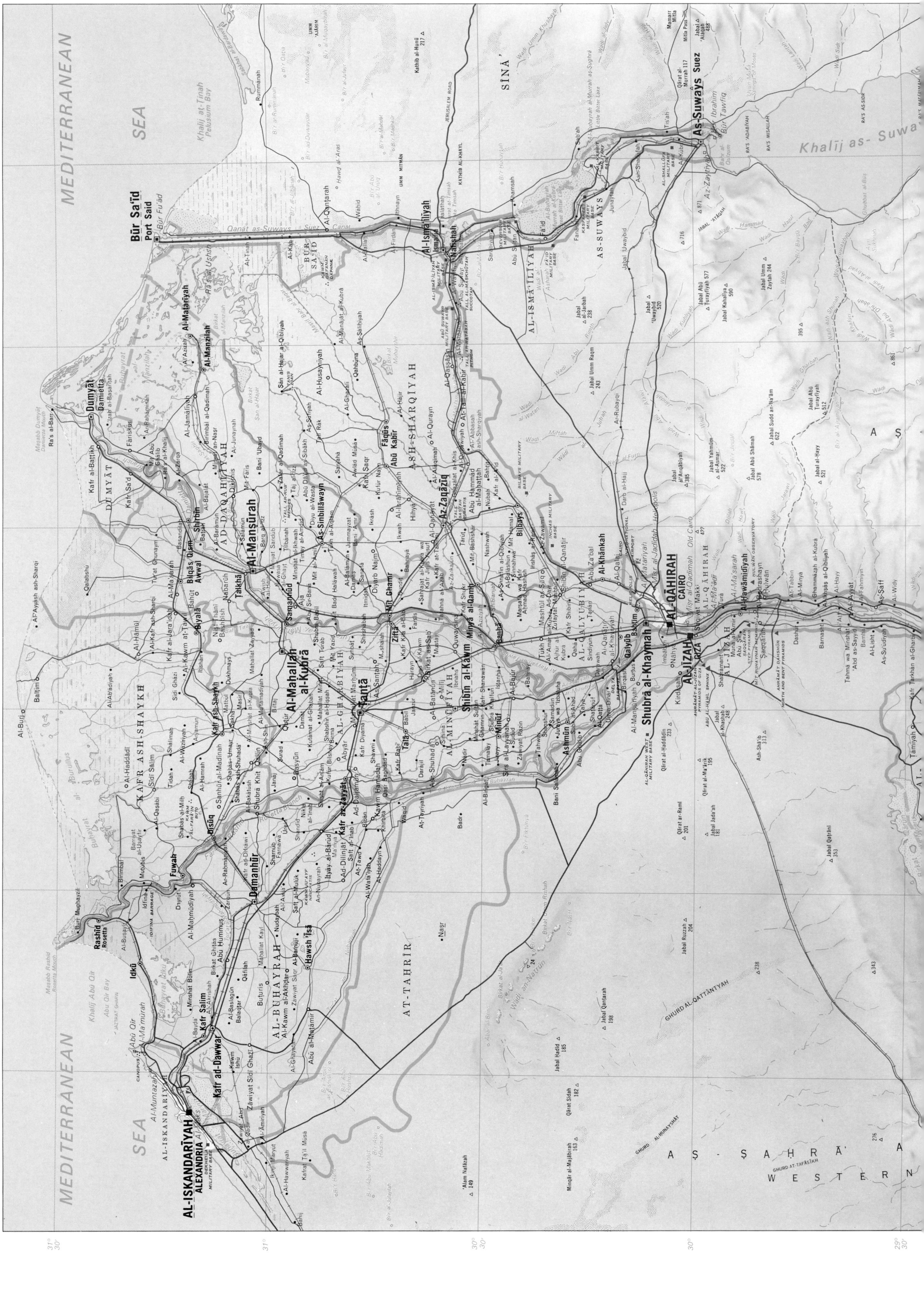
MEDITERRANEAN SEA
Khalīj as-Suways
AL-QĀHIRAH
CAIRO
AL-JĪZAH
AL-ISKANDARĪYAH
ALEXANDRIA
Būr Saʻīd
Port Said
As-Suways
Suez
Al-Ismāʻīlīyah
Ṭanṭā
Az-Zaqāzīq
Al-Manṣūrah
Dumyāṭ
Damietta
Rashīd
Rosetta
Damanhūr
Shubrā al-Khaymah
Al-Maḥallah al-Kubrā
Kafr ash-Shaykh
Banhā
Shibīn al-Kawm
Bilbays
Al-Buḥayrah
Ash-Sharqīyah
Ad-Daqahlīyah
Al-Minūfīyah
Al-Gharbīyah
Al-Qalyūbīyah
Kafr ash-Shaykh
Al-Ismāʻīlīyah
As-Suways
At-Taḥrīr
Sīnāʼ
Aṣ-Ṣaḥrāʼ
Western

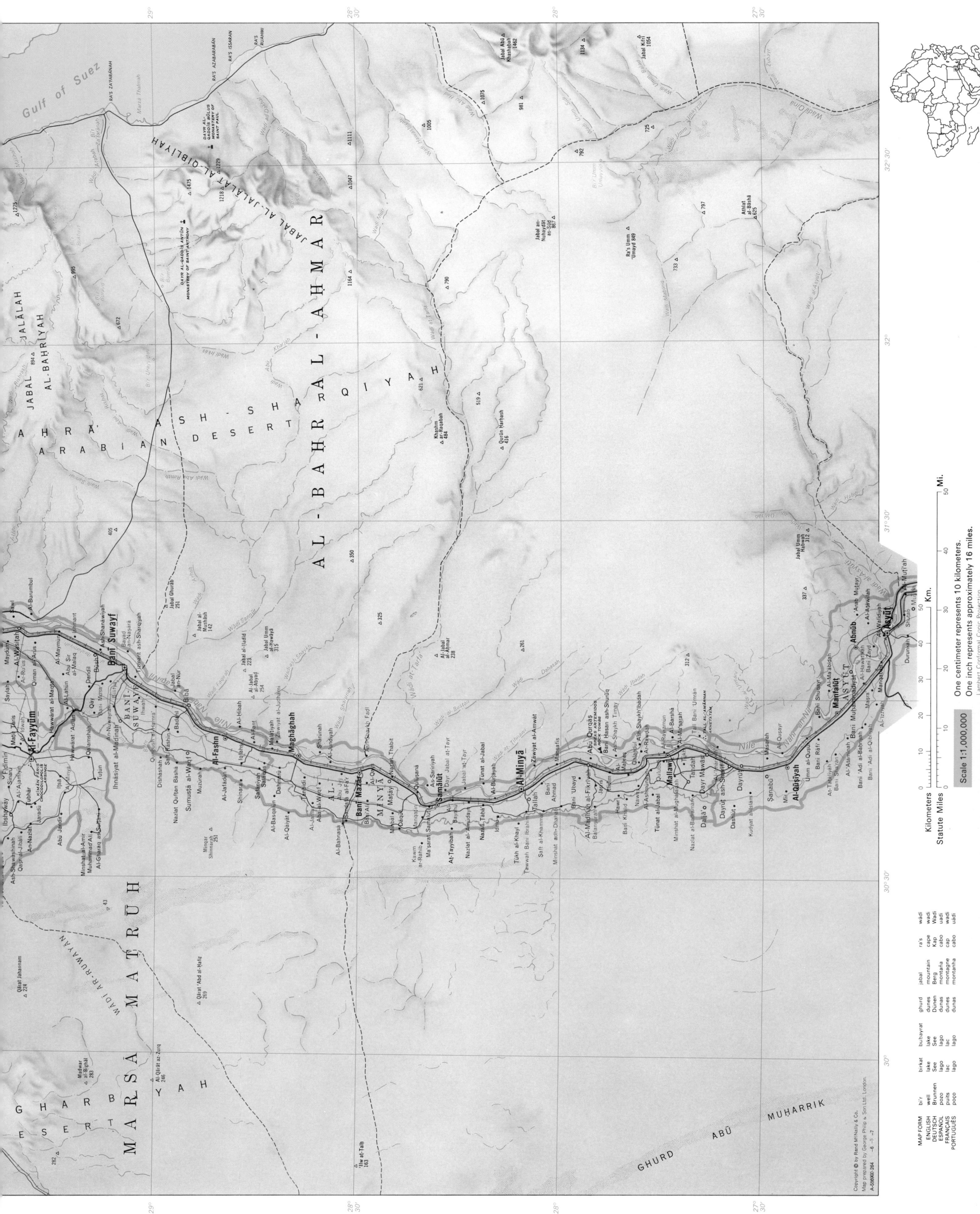

Scale 1:1,000,000

One centimeter represents 10 kilometers.
One inch represents approximately 16 miles.
Lambert Conformal Conic Projection

Copyright © by Rand McNally & Co.
Map prepared by George Philip & Son Ltd., London.
A-588600 264   -8, -3, -7

Kilometers

Statute Miles

Km.

Mi.

MAPFORM				
ENGLISH	bi'r	birkat	buḥayrat	ghurd
DEUTSCH	well	lake	lake	dunes
ESPAÑOL	Brunnen	See	See	Dünen
FRANÇAIS	puits	lago	lago	dunes
PORTUGUÊS	poço	lac	lac	dunes
	poço	lago	lago	dunes

jabal	ra's	wadi
mountain	cape	wadi
Berg	Kap	Wadi
montaña	cabo	uadi
montagne	cap	uadi
montanha	cabo	uadi

Map continues
pages 128–129

Map continues
pages 140–141

Ethiopia, Somalia and Yemen / Äthiopien, Somalia und Jemen / Etiopía, Somalía y Yemen
Ethiopie, Somalie et Yemen / Etiópia, Somália e Iêmen

145

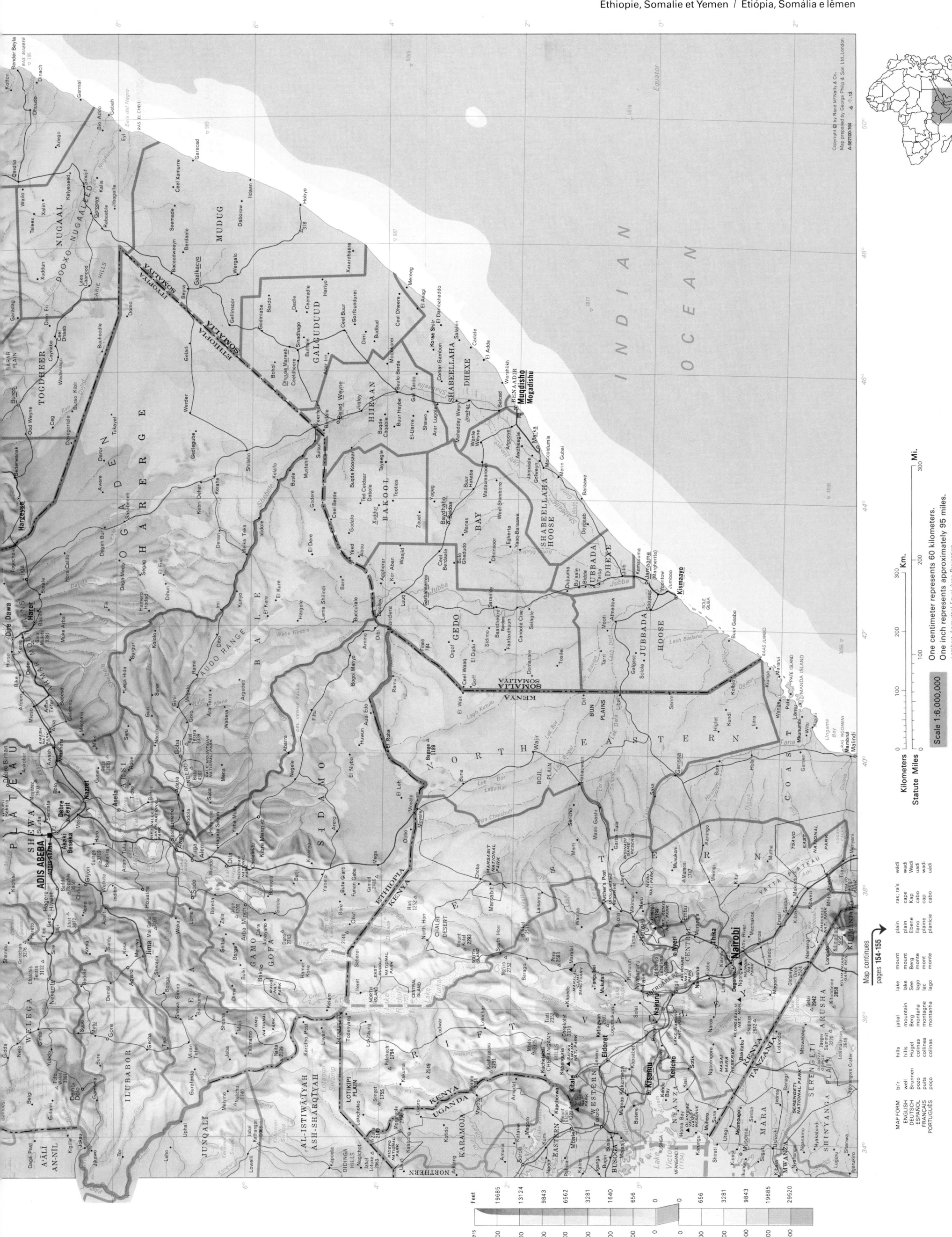

Map continues
pages 154-155

Copyright © by Rand McNally & Co.
Map prepared by George Philip & Son Ltd, London.

One centimeter represents 60 kilometers.
One inch represents approximately 95 miles.

Scale 1:16,000,000

MAP FORM							
ENGLISH	bir	hills	jabal	lake	mount	plain	ras, ra's	wadi
DEUTSCH	well	Hügel	Berg	See	Berg	Ebene	Kap	Wadi
ESPAÑOL	pozo	colinas	montaña	lago	mont	llano	cabo	uadi
FRANÇAIS	puits	colinas	montagne	lac	monte	plaine	cabo	wadi
PORTUGUÊS	poço	colinas	montanha	lago	monte	planície	cabo	wadi

Kilometers

Statute Miles

Mi.

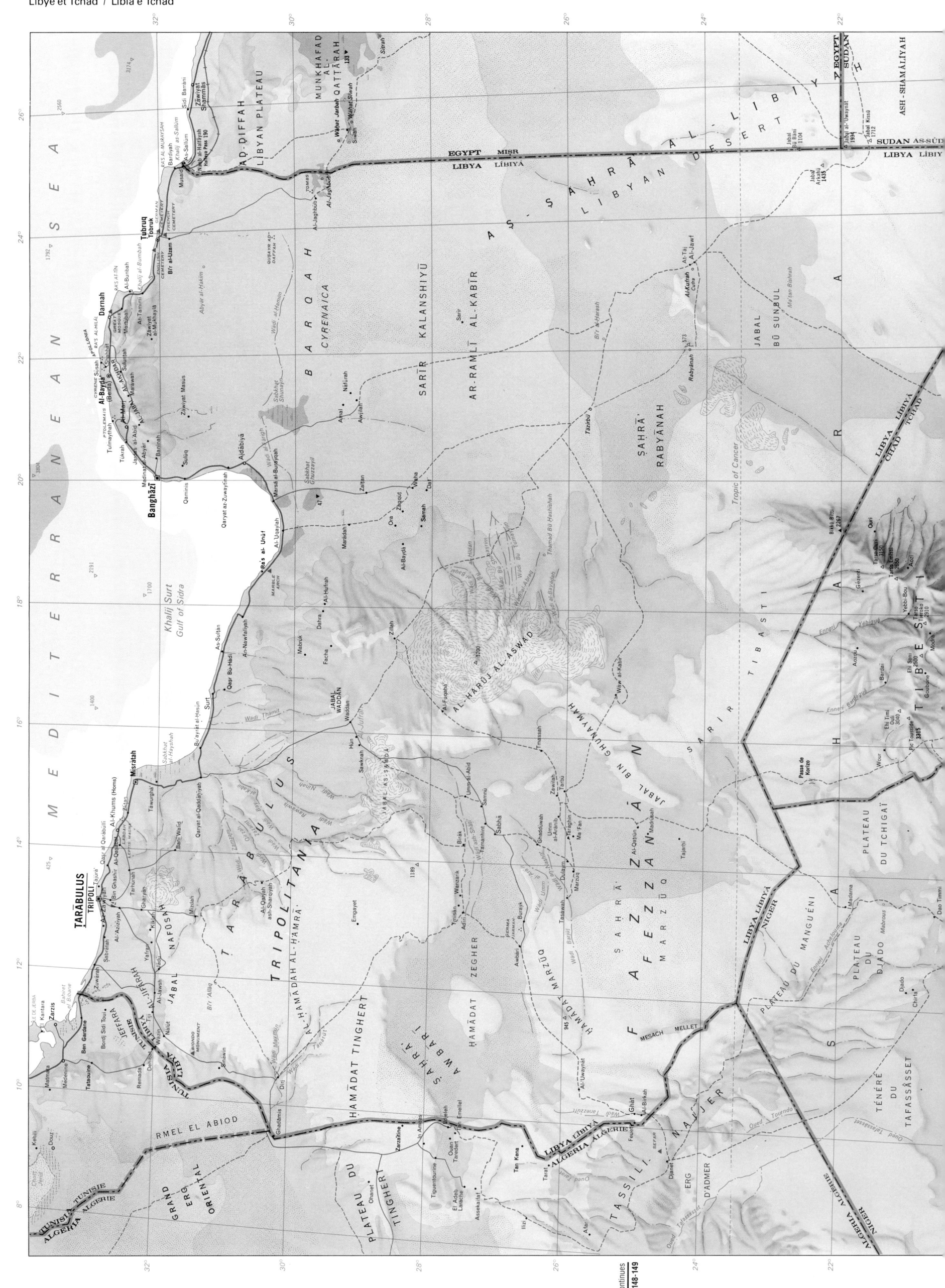
MEDITERRANEAN SEA
Khalij Surt
Gulf of Sidra
TARĀBULUS
TRIPOLI
Banghāzī
Ṭubruq
Tobruk
Darnah
Al-Bayḍā' (Beida)
Misrātah
Ajdābiyā
Surt
Zuwārah
Zarzis
Al-Khums (Homs)
BARQAH
CYRENAICA
AD-DIFFAH
LIBYAN PLATEAU
MUNKHAFAD AL-QAṬṬĀRAH
TARĀBULUS
TRIPOLITANIA
JABAL NAFŪSAH
AL-ḤAMĀDAH AL-ḤAMRĀ'
ḤAMĀDAT TINGHERT
FAZZĀN
FEZZAN
AṢ-ṢAḤRĀ' AL-LĪBĪYAH
LIBYAN DESERT
SARĪR KALANSHIYŪ
AR-RAMLĪ AL-KABĪR
ṢAḤRĀ' RABYĀNAH
JABAL BŪ SUNBUL
SARĪR TIBASTĪ
AL-HARŪJ AL-ASWAD
TIBESTI
Tropic of Cancer
Sabhā
Ghāt
Ghadāmis
Murzuq
Al-Kufrah
Al-Jaghbūb
EGYPT MIṢR
LIBYA LĪBIYĀ
SUDAN AS-SŪDĀN
LIBYA LĪBIYĀ CHAD TCHAD
LIBYA LĪBIYĀ NIGER
LIBYA LĪBIYĀ ALGERIA ALGÉRIE
TUNISIA TUNISIE
ALGERIA ALGÉRIE
GRAND ERG ORIENTAL
RMEL EL ABIOD
PLATEAU DU TINGHERT
TASSILI N'AJJER
ERG D'ADMER
PLATEAU DU DJADO
PLATEAU DU MANGUÉNI
PLATEAU DU TCHIGAÏ
TÉNÉRÉ DU TAFASSÂSSET
MESACH MELLET

Map continues pages 148-149

Map continues
pages 140-141

Map continues
pages 150-151

Map continues
pages 152-153

Scale 1:6,000,000

Kilometers
Statute Miles

One centimeter represents 60 kilometers.
One inch represents approximately 95 miles.
Lambert Azimuthal Equal-Area Projection

MAP FORM					
ENGLISH	bahi	hadjer	jabal	massif	ouadi	sarir	ra's
DEUTSCH	river	mountain	mountain	massif	wadi	desert	cape
ESPAÑOL	Fluss	Berg	Berg	Gebirgsmassiv	Wadi	Wüste	Kap
FRANÇAIS	rio	montaña	montaña	macizo	uadi	desierto	cabo
PORTUGUÊS	rivière	montagne	montagne	massif	wadi	desert	cap
	rio	montanha	montanha	maciço	uadi	deserto	cabo

Feet: 19685 13124 9843 6562 3281 1640 656 0 656 3281 9843 19685 29520

Meters: 6000 4000 3000 2000 1000 500 200 0 Land Below Sea Level 0 200 1000 3000 6000 9000

Major labels:

SUDAN AS-SŪDĀN

CHAD TCHAD

DĀRFŪR ASH-SHAMĀLĪYAH

DĀRFŪR AL-JANŪBĪYAH

DÉPRESSION DU MOURDI

ENNEDI

BORKOU-ENNEDI-TIBESTI

BORKOU

BODÉLÉ

ERG DU DJOURAB

BILTINE

OUADDAÏ

BATHA

GUÉRA

KANEM

LAC

Lake Chad / Lac Tchad

CHARI-BAGUIRMI

N'Djamena

SALAMAT

MOYEN-CHARI

BANGORAN

BAMINGUI

GRIBINGUI

CENTRAL AFRICAN REPUBLIC

RÉPUBLIQUE CENTRAFRICAINE

HAUTE-KOTTO

BAMINGUI

VAKAGA

BAHR AL-GHAZAL

MBOMOU

HAUT-MBOMOU

NIGER NIGERIA

ZINDER

DIFFA

KAOUAR

AGADEZ

AÏR

GRAND ERG DE BILMA

ERG DU TÉNÉRÉ

TANDJILÉ

MAYO-KEBBI

LOGONE-OCCIDENTAL

LOGONE-ORIENTAL

OUHAM

OUHAM-PENDE

NORD

CAMEROON CAMEROUN

NIGERIA

Maiduguri

Garoua

Ngaoundéré

Nyala

Al-Fāshir

Abéché

Sarh

Potiskum

Bauchi

Jos

Map continues
pages 34-35

a

Meters	Feet	
6000	19685	
4000	13124	
3000	9843	
2000	6562	
1000	3281	
500	1640	
200	656	
0	0	
Land Below Sea Level		
0	0	
200	656	
1000	3281	
3000	9843	
6000	19685	
9000	29520	

Azores inset

A T L A N T I C
O C E A N

CORVO
FLORES
Santa Cruz
das Flores
GRACIOSA
Santa Cruz
da Graciosa
TERCEIRA
Praia da Vitória
SÃO JORGE
FAIAL   Velas
Horta 235
São Mateus   PICO
Ponta do Pico
Angra do Heroísmo

SÃO MIGUEL   Ribeira Grande
Ponta
Delgada   Povoação
(Port.)

A Z O R E S

Vila do Porto
SANTA MARIA

© R. MIN.

ATLANTIC OCEAN

ARQUIPÉLAGO
DA MADEIRA
MADEIRA ISLANDS
(Port.)   PORTO SANTO
Pico Ruivo
1862   MADEIRA
Funchal   Machico
ILHAS DESERTAS

ILHAS SELVAGENS
(Mad. Is.)

ISLAS CANARIAS
CANARY ISLANDS
(Sp.)

ALEGRANZA
GRACIOSA
LA PALMA   670   LANZAROTE
Los
Llanos   PARQ. NAC. DE LA
CALDERA DE TABURIENTE   Arrecife
Roque de los   Santa Cruz   LOBOS
Muchachos   de la Palma
La Orotava   724   Puerto del Rosario
TENERIFE   San Cristóbal
de la Laguna   FUERTEVENTURA
Santa Cruz de Tenerife
LA GOMERA   San Miguel   CAP JUBY
San Sebastián   San Nicolás   Arucas   Tarfaya
de la Gomera   3715   Las Palmas
Valverde   Teide   de Gran Canaria
EL HIERRO   GRAN CANARIA

A T L A N T I C

O C E A N

Western Sahara has been
occupied by Morocco.

CAP BOUJDOUR

Tropic of Cancer

CAP BARBAS

CAP AGADIR

WESTERN SAHARA
MAURITANIA MAURITANIE

Nouâdhibou
La Gouêra
RÅS
NOUÂDHIBOU   DAKHLET
NOUADHIBOU   INCHIRI

Spain / Morocco region

BEJA
Córdoba
Odemira   Écija
CABO DE   Huelva   Sevilla
SÃO VICENTE   Lagos   Faro   Jerez   Antequera
CABO DE   Golfo de   de la Frontera   Mál
SANTA MARIA   Cádiz   Arcos de   Ronda
la Frontera
Cádiz   Estepona   Marbella
CABO TRAFALGAR   Algeciras   La Línea
Strait of Gibraltar   Gibraltar (U.K.)
CAP SPARTEL   Ceuta   Sp.
Tanger   Tétouan
Tangier   Bou Ahmed
Asilah   Chaouen   Al-Hoceima
Larache   R I F
Ksar-el-   Souk Larbat Gharb
Kebir   Ouezzane
Sidi Kacem   Fès
Salé   Kenitra   Meknès
RABAT   Sefrou
Mohammedia   Khemisset
(Fedala)   Ben-Slimane
CASABLANCA   Midelt
DAR-EL-BEIDA   Berrechid
Azemmour   Rommani
El-Jadida   Settat   Benahmed
(Mazagan)   Khouribga   Oued-Zem
Oualidia   Sidi Smaïl   Kasba-Tadla
RAS BEDDOUZA   Sidi Bennour   Fkir-ben-Salah   Beni-Mellal
Safi   Youssoufia   Bine-el-Ouidane
El-Kelâa   Dar-Ould-Zidouh
Benguerir   des-Srarhna
Chemaïa   Demnate   Er-Rachidia
Essaouira   Tamelelt   Azilal   Goulmima
(Mogador)   Ait-Ourir   Erfoud
CAP SIM   Marrakech   Ouarzazate   Rissani
Ounara   Boumalne
Imi-n'Tanout   Amizmiz   Asni   Tazenakht   Zagora
Tamanar   Jebel Toubkal   Tahouaite
Jebel Aoulime   3384
Agadir   3555   Tata
Ait-Melloul   Taroudant   Foum-Zguid
CAP RHIR   Tamri
Tiznit   Tata   Tagounit
HAUT ATLAS
ANTI ATLAS

Sidi Ifni   Bou Temeguida
Mirleft   Bou-Izakarn
Goulimine   Akka
Tan-Tan   Foum-el-Hisn   Assa
Tah   Tighmert   Assa
MOROCCO AL-MAGREB
WESTERN SAHARA

MOROCCO AL-MAGREB   ALGERIA ALGÉRIE
WESTERN SAHARA   Tindouf

La'youn   Hawza
LA'YOUN   Al Mahbas
El Aaiún   Al Mahbas
La'youn.   Smara
Lemsid

MAURITANIA MAURITANIE
ALGERIA ALGÉRIE

IGUIDI

EL EGLAB

Galtat Zemmour
Bir-Mogreïn
(Fort-Trinquet)
Aïn Ben Tili
ZEMMOUR
Dakhla
Bir Enzaran

TIRIS ZEMMOUR
Fdêrik
Zouérat
Kediet ej Jill
EL KHATT
MAQTEÎR
ADRAR
Atâr
Chinguetti
Ouâdane
Passe de
Ouarzata
Techlé
Ch, Chargui
HODH ECH
CHARGUI
MALI

TOMBOU

Copyright © by Rand McNally & Co.
Map prepared by George Philip & Son Ltd. London.
A-589791-764   -8   -12

Map continues
pages 150-151

MAP FORM	cap	chott	djebel	erg	hamada	jbel	oued	sebkha
ENGLISH	cape	intermittent lake	mountain	sand desert	desert	mountain	wadi	salt flat
DEUTSCH	Kap	periodischer See	Berg	Sandwüste	Wüste	Berg	Wadi	Salzebene
ESPAÑOL	cabo	lago intermitente	montaña	desierto arenoso	desierto	montaña	uadi	salar
FRANÇAIS	cap	lac périodique	montagne	désert de sable	désert	montagne	wadi	saline
PORTUGUÊS	cabo	lago intermitente	montanha	deserto arenoso	deserto	montanha	uádi	salina

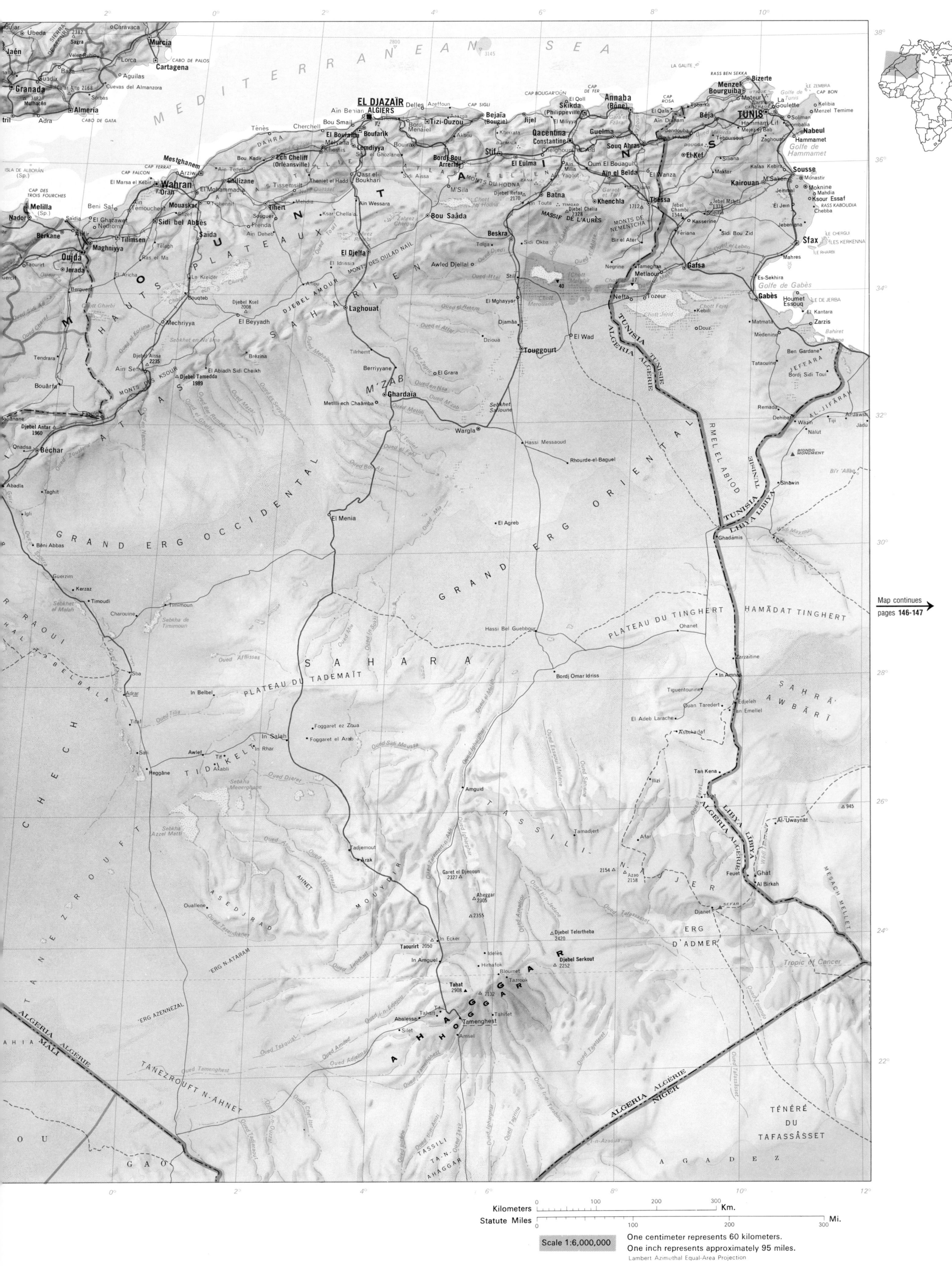

Map continues
pages 146-147

Kilometers

Km.

Statute Miles

Mi.

Scale 1:6,000,000

One centimeter represents 60 kilometers.
One inch represents approximately 95 miles.
Lambert Azimuthal Equal-Area Projection

Meters · Feet

Meters	Feet
6000	19685
4000	13124
3000	9843
2000	6562
1000	3281
500	1640
200	656
0	0
Land Below Sea Level	
0	0
200	656
1000	3281
3000	9843
6000	19685
9000	29520

	MAP FORM	coast	dhar	game reserve	ilha	lac	monts	mountains	vallée
	ENGLISH	coast	escarpment	game reserve	island	lake	mountains	mountains	valley
	DEUTSCH	Küste	Landstufe	Wildpark	Insel	See	Berge	Berge	Tal
	ESPAÑOL	costa	escarpa	vedado de caza	isla	lago	montes	montañas	valle
	FRANÇAIS	côte	escarpement	réserve à gibier	île	lac	monts	montagnes	vallée
	PORTUGUÊS	costa	escarpa	reserva de caça	ilha	lago	montes	montanhas	vale

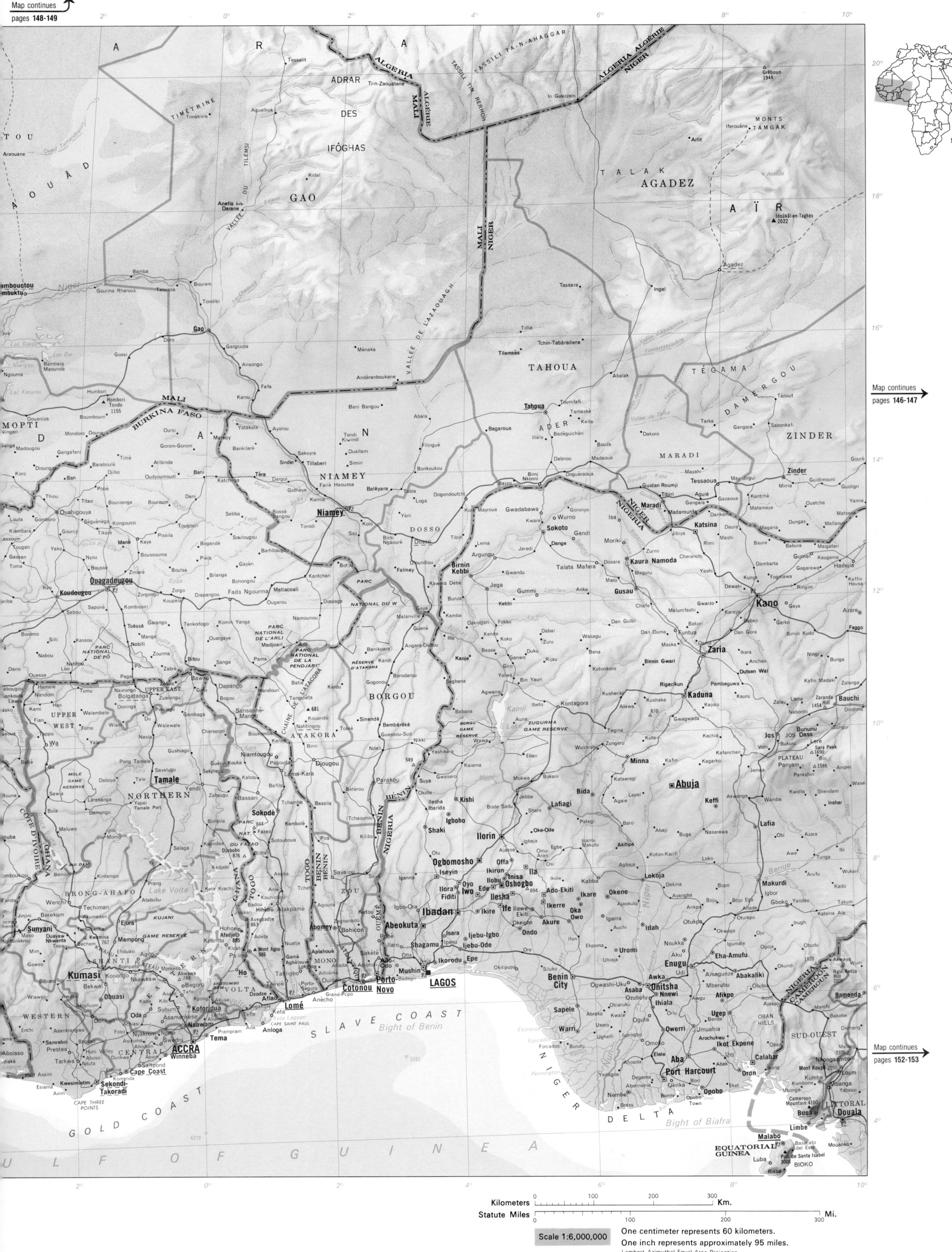

Map continues
pages 148-149

Map continues
pages 146-147

Map continues
pages 152-153

Kilometers 0 100 200 300 Km.
Statute Miles 0 100 200 300 Mi.

Scale 1:6,000,000
One centimeter represents 60 kilometers.
One inch represents approximately 95 miles.
Lambert Azimuthal Equal-Area Projection

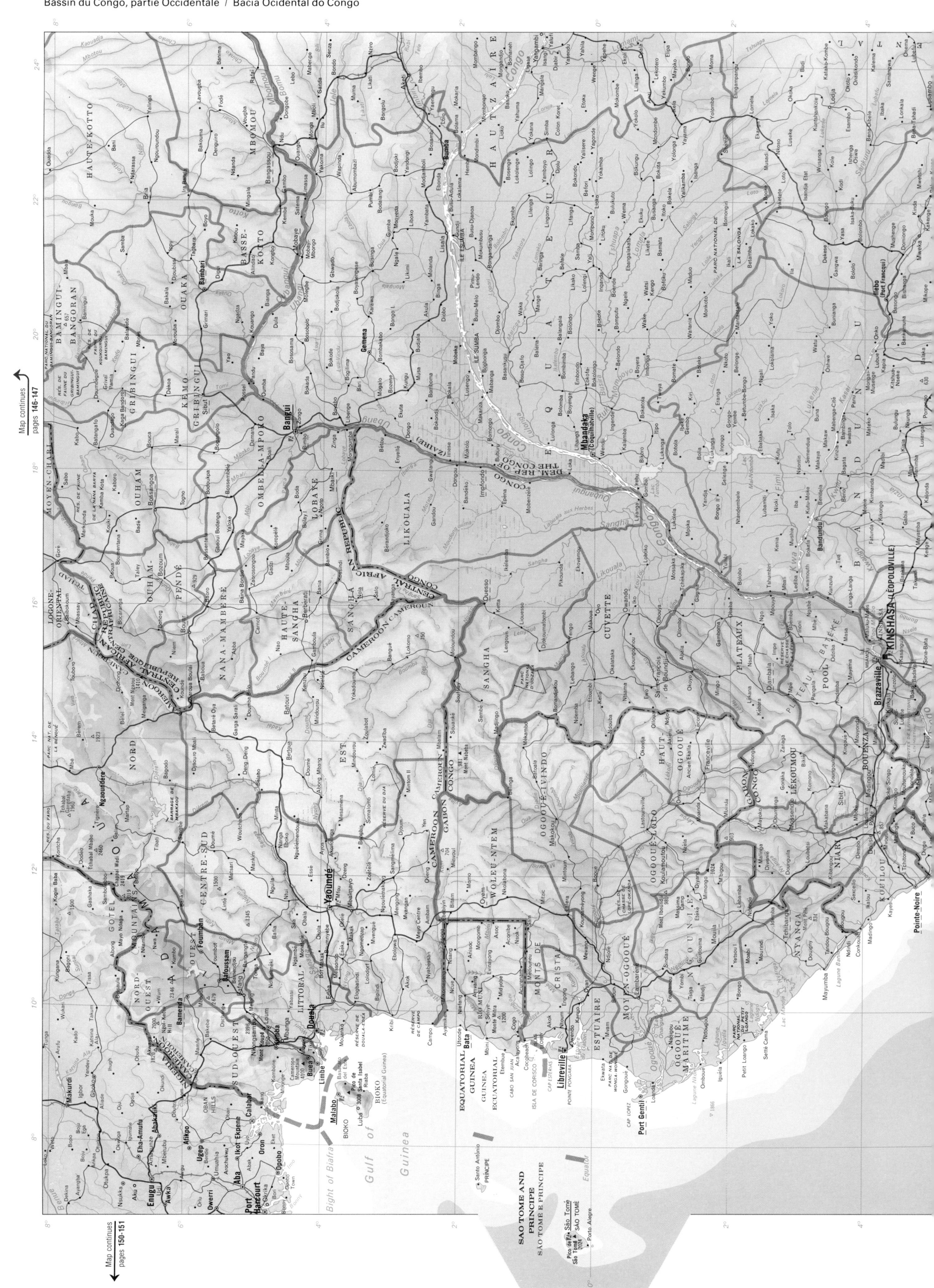

Map continues
pages 146-147

Map continues
pages 150-151

Western Congo Basin / Westliches Kongobecken / Cuenca Occidental del Congo
Bassin du Congo, partie Occidentale / Bacia Ocidental do Congo

153

ATLANTIC OCEAN

DEM. REP. OF THE CONGO (ZAIRE)

ANGOLA

ZAMBIA

NAMIBIA

BOTSWANA

Kananga (Luluabourg)
Mbuji-Mayi (Bakwanga)
Tshikapa
Mwene-Ditu
Kabinda
Gandajika

LUANDA
Lobito
Benguela
Malanje
Huambo (Nova Lisboa)
Lubango
Namibe

Provinces: KASAI OCCIDENTAL, KATANGA (SHABA), LUNDA NORTE, LUNDA SUL, MALANJE, CUANZA NORTE, CUANZA SUL, BENGUELA, HUAMBO, BIÉ, MOXICO, HUILA, CUANDO CUBANGO, CUNENE, NAMIBE, ZAIRE, UIGE

ZAMBIA NORTH-WESTERN, WESTERN

KASHJI PLAIN, LIUWA PLAIN, SILOWANA PLAINS, CAPRIVI ZIPFEL, NGAMILAND, OVAMBOLAND, OHANGWENA, OSHIKOTO, OMUSATI, OSHANA, KUNENE

NAMIB DESERT, SKELETON COAST

Map continues pages 154-155

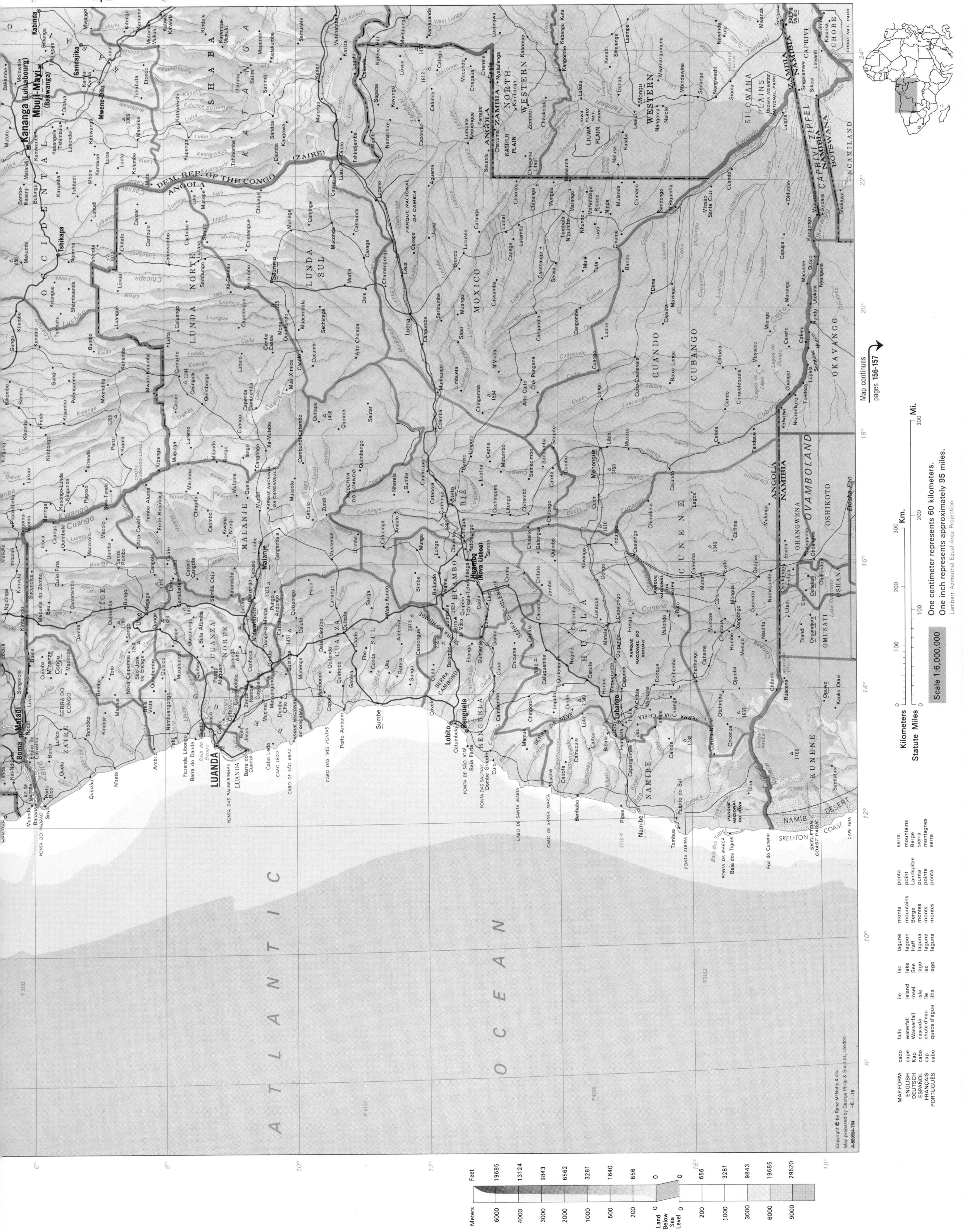

Map continues pages 156-157

Scale 1:6,000,000
One centimeter represents 60 kilometers.
One inch represents approximately 95 miles.
Lambert Azimuthal Equal-Area Projection

Kilometers
0   100   200   300   Km.

Statute Miles
0   100   200   300   Mi.

MAP FORM				
ENGLISH	serra	ponta	monts	laguna
DEUTSCH	mountains	point	mountains	lagoon
ESPAÑOL	Berge	Landspitze	Berge	Haff
FRANÇAIS	sierra	punta	montes	laguna
PORTUGUÊS	montagnes	pointe	montagnes	lagune
	serra	ponta	montes	laguna

lac	lie	falls	cabo
lake	island	waterfall	cape
See	Insel	Wasserfall	Kap
lago	isla	cascada	cabo
lac	île	chute d'eau	cap
lago	ilha	queda d'água	cabo

Feet / Meters elevation legend:
6000 / 19685
4000 / 13124
3000 / 9843
2000 / 6562
1000 / 3281
500 / 1640
200 / 656
0 / Land Below Sea Level / 0
200 / 656
1000 / 3281
3000 / 9843
6000 / 19685
9000 / 29520

154

East Africa and Eastern Congo Basin / Ostafrika und Östliches Kongobecken / África Oriental y Cuenca Oriental del Congo
Afrique Orientale et Bassin du Congo, partie Orientale / África Oriental e Bacia Oriental do Congo

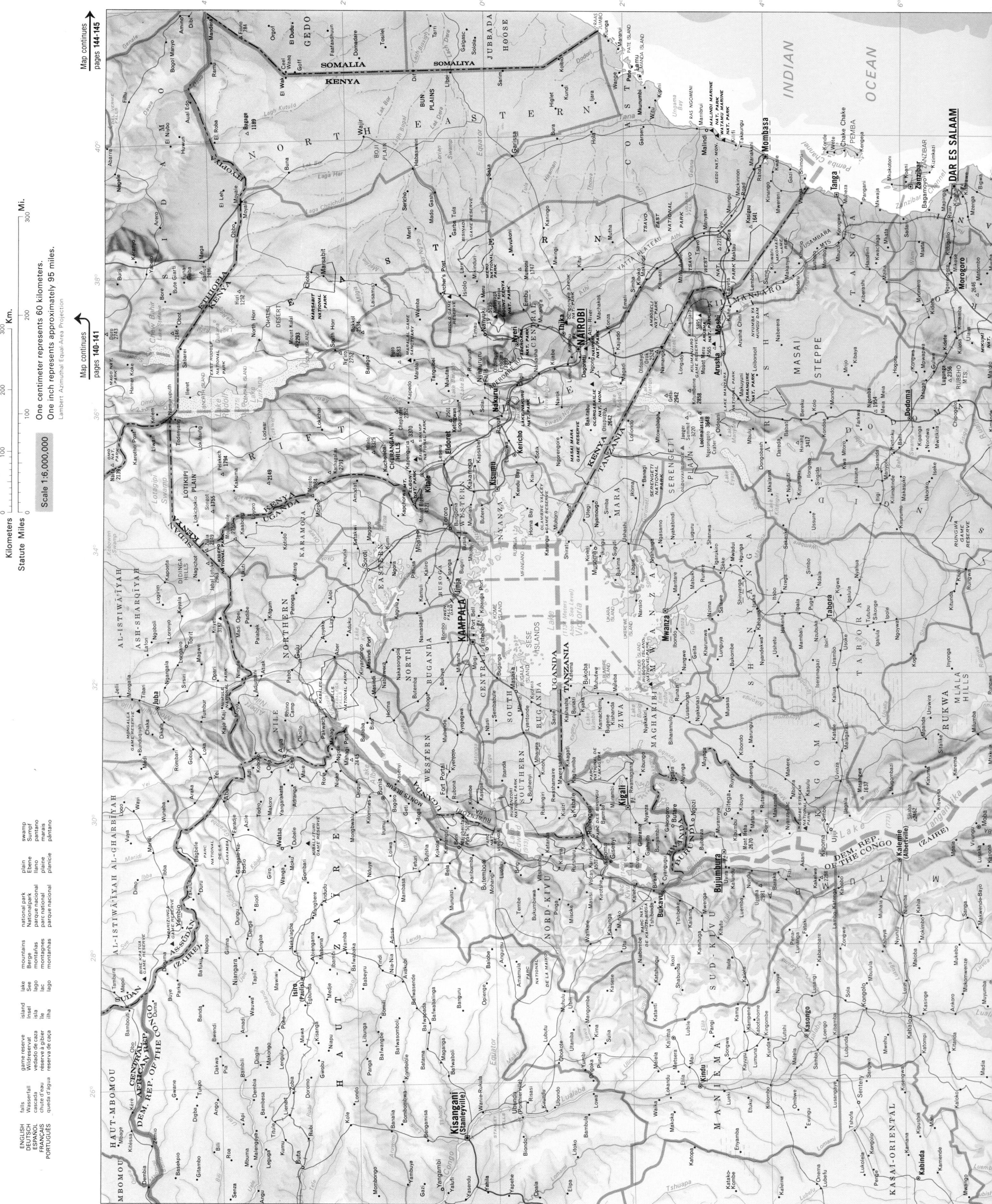

Map continues
pages 144-145

Map continues
pages 140-141

Map continues
pages 152-153

Scale 1:6,000,000

One centimeter represents 60 kilometers.
One inch represents approximately 95 miles.

Lambert Azimuthal Equal-Area Projection

ENGLISH	falls	game reserve	island	lake	mountains	national park	plain	swamp
DEUTSCH	Wasserfall	Wildreservat	Insel	See	Berge	Nationalpark	Ebene	Sumpf
ESPAÑOL	cascada	vedado de caza	isla	lago	montanas	parque nacional	llano	pantano
FRANÇAIS	chute d'eau	réserve d'animaux	île	lac	montagnes	parc national	plaine	marais
PORTUGUÊS	queda de água	reserva de caça	ilha	lago	montanhas	parque nacional	planície	pântano

INDIAN OCEAN

East Africa and Eastern Congo Basin / Ostafrika und Östliches Kongobecken / África Oriental y Cuenca Oriental del Congo
Afrique Orientale et Bassin du Congo, partie Orientale / África Oriental e Bacia Oriental do Congo

155

Map continues
pages 156-157

156

Southern Africa and Madagascar / Südafrika und Madagaskar / África Meridional y Madagascar
Afrique Méridionale et Madagascar / África Meridional e Madagascar

Map continues
pages 152-153

ATLANTIC

OCEAN

Meters / Feet (elevation scale)

Meters	Feet
6000	19685
4000	13124
3000	9843
2000	6562
1000	3281
500	1640
200	656
0	0
Land Below Sea Level	
0	0
200	656
1000	3281
3000	9843
6000	19685
9000	29520

Copyright © by Rand McNally & Co.
Map prepared by George Philip & Son Ltd., London.
A-589292-764   —8-10-22

MAP FORM	bay	berg, berge	cape	game reserve	ilha	lake	national park
ENGLISH	bay	mountain, mountains	cape	game reserve	island	lake	national park
DEUTSCH	Bucht	Berg, Berge	Kap	Wildpark	Insel	See	Nationalpark
ESPAÑOL	bahía	montaña, montañas	cabo	vedado de caza	isla	lago	parque nacional
FRANÇAIS	baie	montagne, montagnes	cap	réserve à gibier	île	lac	parc national
PORTUGUÊS	baía	montanha, montanhas	cabo	reserva de caça	ilha	lago	parque nacional

Kilometers   0   100   200   300   Km.
Statute Miles   0   100   200   300   Mi.

Scale 1:6,000,000
One centimeter represents 60 kilometers.
One inch represents approximately 95 miles.
Lambert Azimuthal Equal-Area Projection

Southern Africa and Madagascar / Südafrika und Madagaskar / África Meridional y Madagascar
Afrique Méridionale et Madagascar / África Meridional e Madagascar

157

Map continues
pages 154-155

Meters	Feet
6000	19685
4000	13124
3000	9843
2000	6562
1000	3281
500	1640
200	656
0	0

Land Below Sea Level

0	0
200	656
1000	3281
3000	9843
6000	19685
9000	29520

MAP FORM	bay	berge	cape	dam	game reserve	nationa park	pass	point
ENGLISH	bay	mountains	cape	dam	game reserve	nationa park	pass	point
DEUTSCH	Bucht	Berge	Kap	Damm	Wildpark	Nationalpark	Pass	Landspitze
ESPAÑOL	bahia	montañas	cabo	presa	vedado de caza	parque nacional	paso	punta
FRANÇAIS	baie	montagnes	cap	barrage	réserve à gibier	parc national	col	pointe
PORTUGUÊS	baía	montanhas	cabo	represa	reserva de caça	parque nacional	passo	ponta

South Africa

Major cities and places:

Pretoria, **Johannesburg**, **Soweto**, **Krugersdorp**, Kempton Park, **Germiston**, **Benoni**, Brakpan, **Springs**, Boksburg, Randfontein, Roodepoort-Maraisburg, **Witbank**, Middelburg, Nigel, Bethal, Ermelo, **Vereeniging**, Vanderbijlpark, **Potchefstroom**, Sasolburg, **Klerksdorp**, Stilfontein, Orkney, Parys, **Rustenburg**, Brits, Carletonville, Welkom, Virginia, **Kroonstad**, Odendaalsrus, Allanridge, **Bloemfontein**, Standerton, Bethlehem, Harrismith, **Ladysmith**, **Dundee**, **Newcastle**, Vryheid, **Maseru**, Ladybrand, **LESOTHO**, **Pietermaritzburg**, Edendale, **DURBAN**, Pinetown, Mariannhill, Stanger, **Richard's Bay**, **SWAZILAND**, Mbabane, Manzini, **Maputo (Lourenço Marques)**, **MOZAMBIQUE**, **MOÇAMBIQUE**

Queenstown, Umtata, **TRANSKEI**, **CISKEI**, King William's Town, Mdantsane, **East London / Oos-Londen**, Grahamstown, Fort Beaufort, **Port Elizabeth**, Port Alfred, Port Shepstone, Margate, Port Edward, Kokstad, Matatiele, Mount Fletcher

INDIAN OCEAN

DRAKENSBERG, **WITBERGE**, **STORMBERGE**, **WINTERBERGE**, **KAFFRARIA**, **TEMBULAND**, **GRIQUALAND**, **PONDOLAND**, **WILD COAST**, **EASTERN CAPE**, **KWAZULU-NATAL**, **GAUTENG**, **MPUMALANGA**, **NORTH-WEST**

Copyright © by Rand McNally & Co.
Map prepared by George Philip & Son Ltd., London.
A-584600-764   -7 -1 -15

Kilometers 0 50 100 150 Km.
Statute Miles 0 50 100 150 Mi.

Scale 1:3,000,000
One centimeter represents 30 kilometers.
One inch represents approximately 47 miles.
Lambert Conformal Conic Projection

Map continues
pages **108-109**

ENGLISH	bay	cape	island	lake	mount	point	range	reef
DEUTSCH	Bucht	Kap	Insel	See	Berg	Landspitze	Gebirge	Riff
ESPAÑOL	bahía	cabo	isla	lago	montaña	punta	cordillera	arrecife
FRANÇAIS	baie	cap	île	lac	mont	pointe	chaîne	récif
PORTUGUÊS	baía	cabo	ilha	lago	monte	ponta	cordilheira	recife

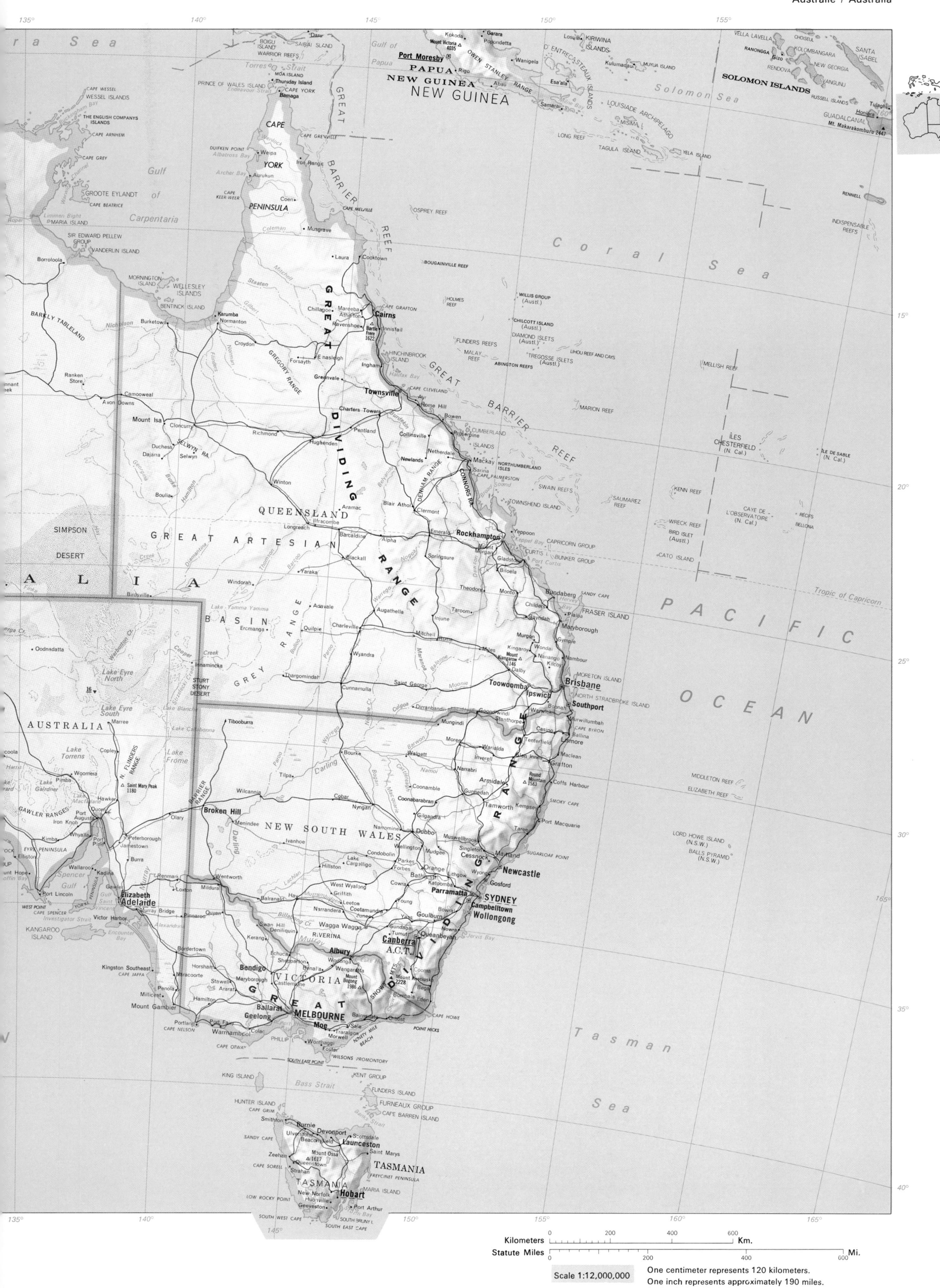

Kilometers

Statute Miles

One centimeter represents 120 kilometers.

One inch represents approximately 190 miles.

Lambert Conformal Conic Projection

162

Western and Central Australia / West- und Mittelaustralien / Australia Centro-occidental
Australie Occidentale et Centrale / Austrália Ocidental e Central

INDIAN   OCEAN

GREAT   SANDY   DESERT

WESTERN   AUSTRALIA

GIBSON   DESERT

LITTLE   SANDY
DESERT

Tropic of Capricorn

Meters	Feet
6000	19685
4000	13124
3000	9843
2000	6562
1000	3281
500	1640
200	656
0	0
Land Below Sea Level	
0	0
200	656
1000	3281
3000	9843
6000	19685
9000	29520

ENGLISH	bay	cape	creek, cr.	island, i.	lake, l.	mount	point	range
DEUTSCH	Bucht	Kap	Bach	Insel	See	Berg	Landspitze	Gebirge
ESPAÑOL	bahía	cabo	riachuelo	isla	lago	montaña	punta	cordillera
FRANÇAIS	baie	cap	crique	île	lac	mont	pointe	chaîne
PORTUGUÊS	baía	cabo	riacho	ilha	lago	monte	ponta	cordilheira

Western and Central Australia / West-und Mittelaustralien / Australia Centro-occidental
Australie Occidentale et Centrale / Austrália Ocidental e Central

163

Map continues
pages 164-165

Map continues
pages 166-167

Kilometers
Statute Miles
Km.
Mi.
0   100   200   300

Scale 1:6,000,000
One centimeter represents 60 kilometers.
One inch represents approximately 95 miles.
Lambert Conformal Conic Projection

← Map continues
pages 112-113

Map continues
pages 162-163 ↓

MAP FORM	bay	cape	island	kepulauan	mount	pulau	range	tanjung
ENGLISH	bay	cape	island	islands	mount	island	range	cape
DEUTSCH	Bucht	Kap	Insel	Inseln	Berg	Insel	Gebirge	Kap
ESPAÑOL	bahía	cabo	isla	islas	montaña	isla	cordillera	cabo
FRANÇAIS	baie	cap	île	îles	mont	île	chaîne	cap
PORTUGUÊS	baía	cabo	ilha	ilhas	monte	ilha	cordilheira	cabo

Northern Australia and New Guinea / Nordaustralien und Neuguinea / Australia Septentrional y Nueva Guinea
Australie Septentrionale et Nouvelle Guinée / Austrália Setentrional e Nova Guiné

165

Map continues
pages 166-167

Kilometers
Statute Miles

Scale 1:6,000,000

One centimeter represents 60 kilometers.
One inch represents approximately 95 miles.
Lambert Conformal Conic Projection

Copyright © by Rand McNally & Co.
Map prepared by George Philip & Son Ltd., London.
A-593000-764   -7 -8 -14

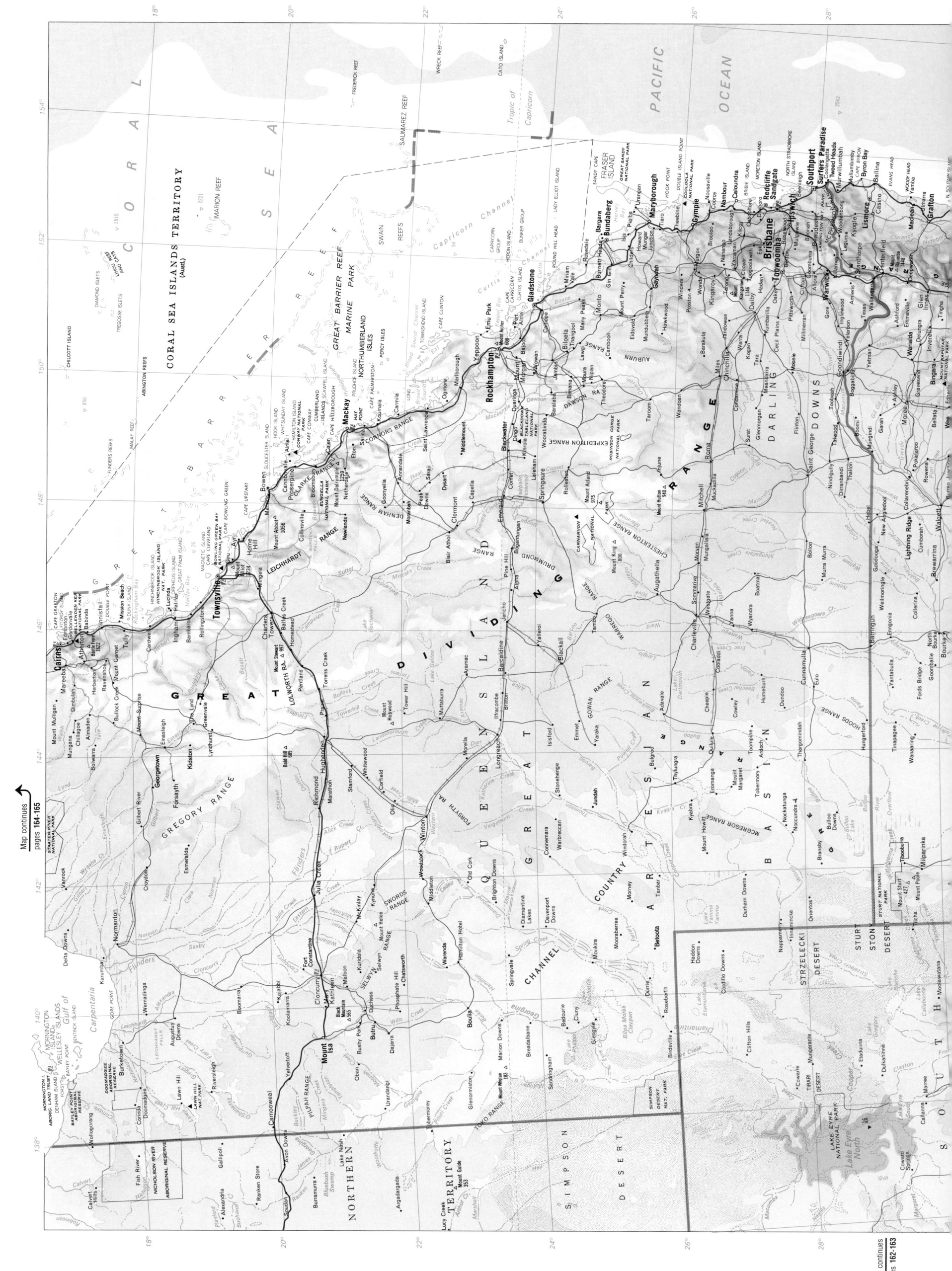

Map continues
pages 164-165

Map continues
pages 162-163

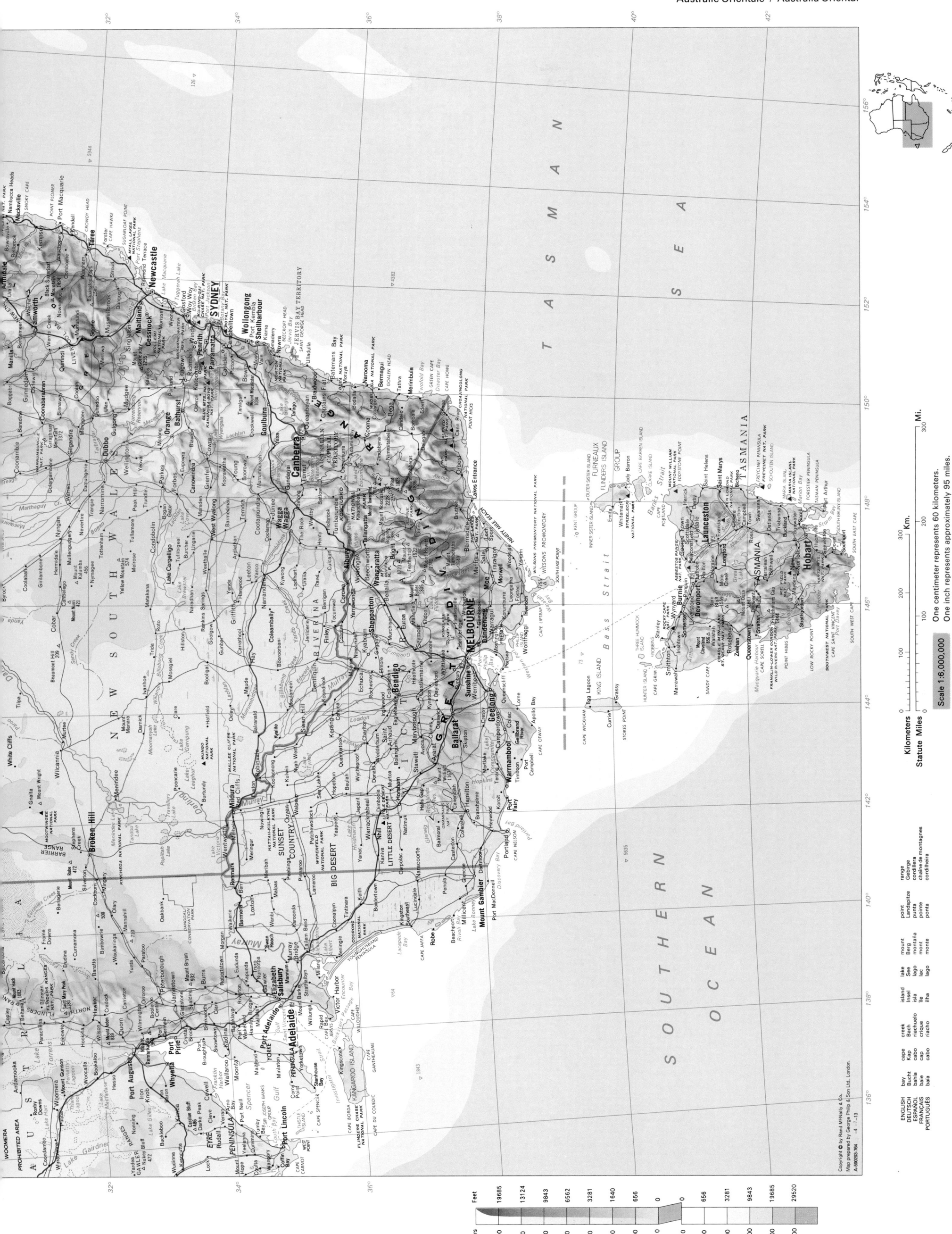

Scale 1:6,000,000

One centimeter represents 60 kilometers.
One inch represents approximately 95 miles.

Lambert Conformal Conic Projection

Kilometers
0   100   200   300   Km.

Statute Miles
0   100   200   300   Mi.

ENGLISH	bay	cape	creek	island	lake	mount	point	range
DEUTSCH	Bucht	Kap	Bach	Insel	See	Berg	Landspitze	Gebirge
ESPAÑOL	bahía	cabo	riachuelo	isla	lago	montaña	punta	cordillera
FRANÇAIS	baie	cap	crique	île	lac	mont	pointe	chaîne de montagnes
PORTUGUÊS	baía	cabo	riacho	ilha	lago	monte	ponta	cordilheira

Feet	Meters
19685	6000
13124	4000
9843	3000
6562	2000
3281	1000
1640	500
656	200
0	0 Land
0	Below 0 Sea Level
656	200
3281	1000
9843	3000
19685	6000
29520	9000

Copyright © by Rand McNally & Co.
Map prepared by George Philip & Son, Ltd., London.
A-590235-764   -4 -7- -13

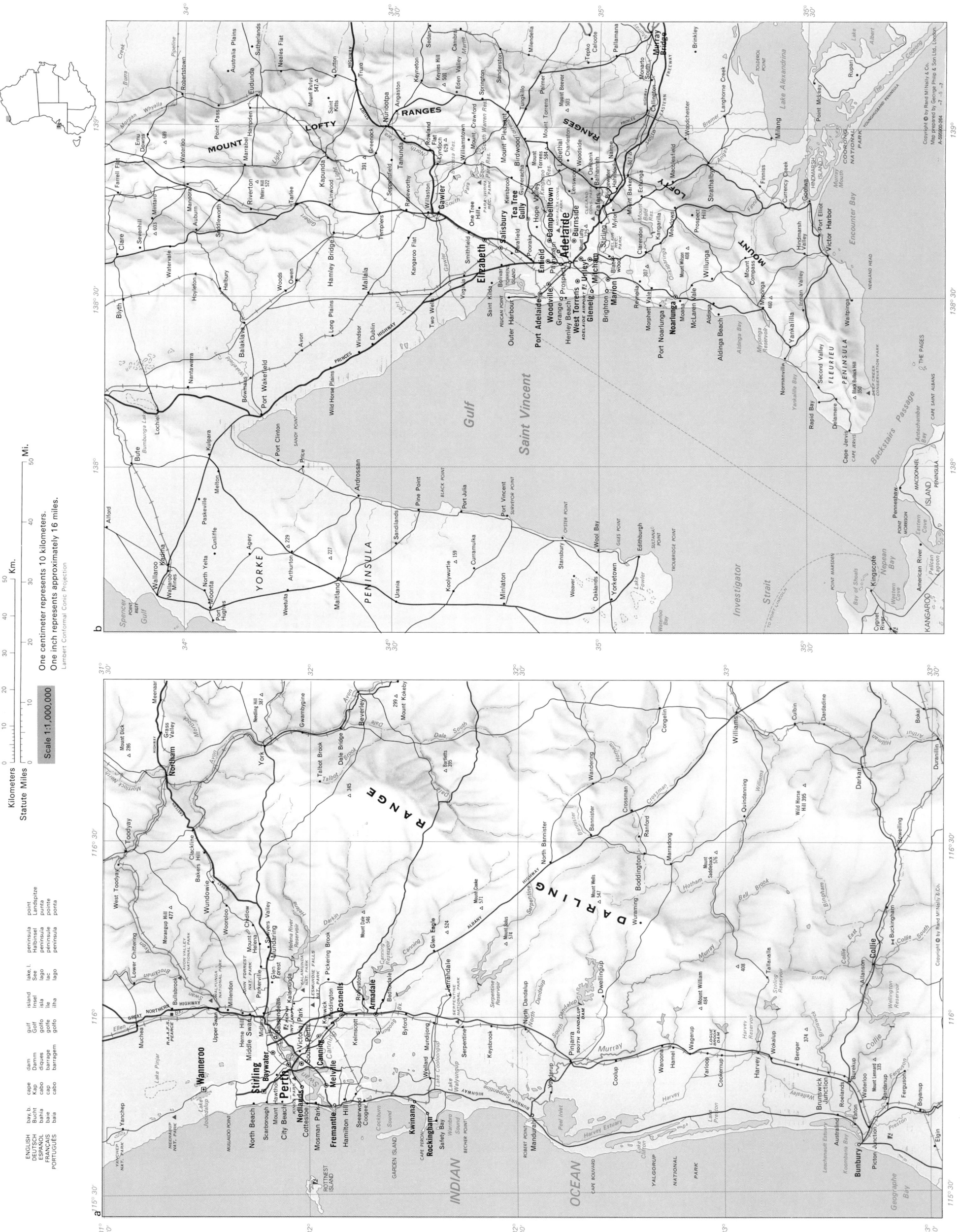

Scale 1:1,000,000

One centimeter represents 10 kilometers.
One inch represents approximately 16 miles.
Lambert Conformal Conic Projection

Kilometers
Statute Miles

ENGLISH	bay b.	cape	dam	gulf	island	lake, l.	peninsula	point
DEUTSCH	Bucht	Kap	Damm	Golf	Insel	See	Halbinsel	Landspitze
ESPAÑOL	bahía	cabo	diques	golfo	isla	lago	península	punta
FRANÇAIS	baie	cap	barrage	golfe	île	lac	péninsule	pointe
PORTUGUÊS	baía	cabo	barragem	golfo	ilha	lago	península	ponta

Mi.

Km.

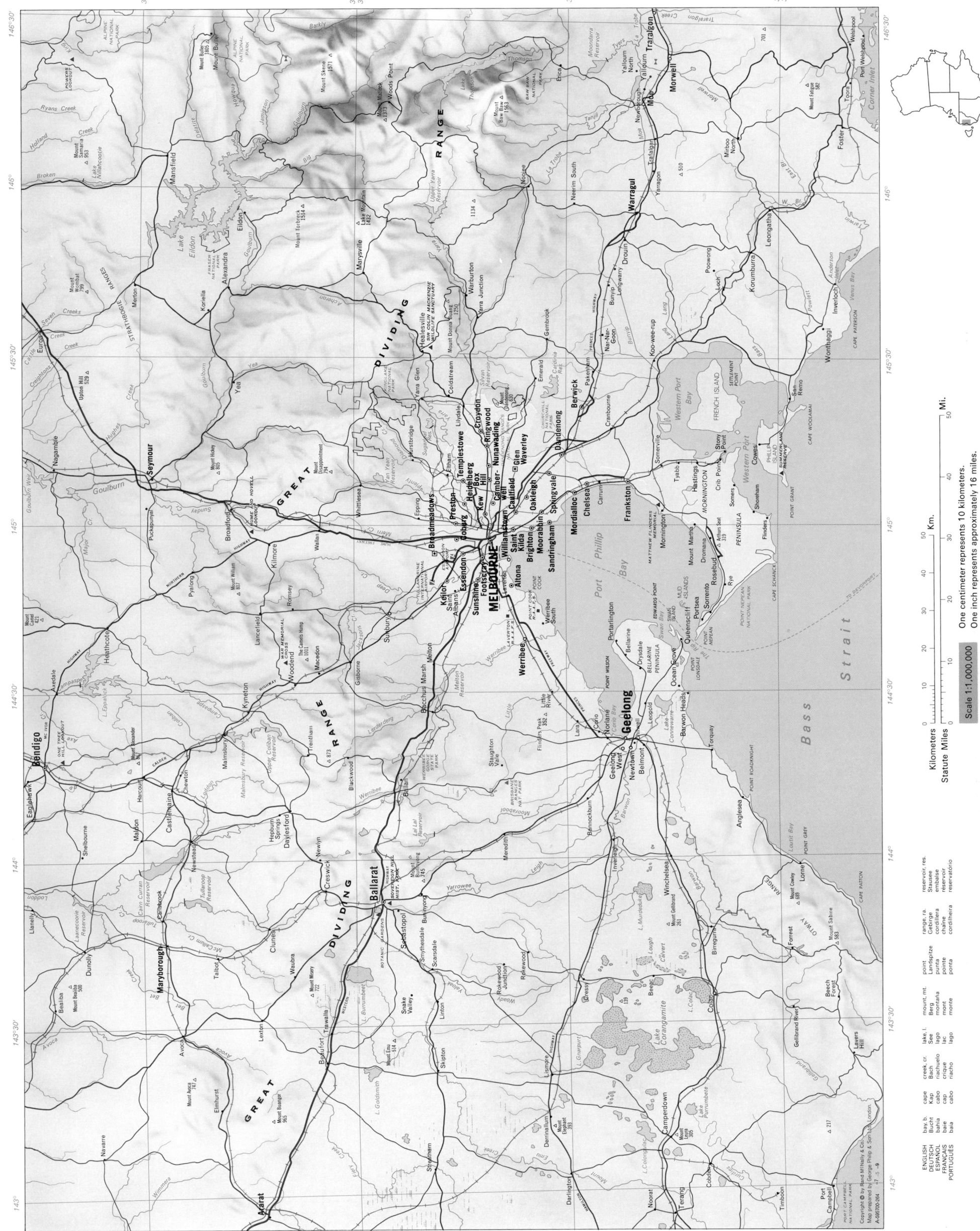

Scale 1:1,000,000

One centimeter represents 10 kilometers.
One inch represents approximately 16 miles.
Lambert Conformal Conic Projection

Kilometers

Statute Miles

ENGLISH	bay, b.	cape	creek, cr.	lake, l.	mount, mt.	point	range, ra.	reservoir, res.
DEUTSCH	Bucht	Kap	Bach	See	Berg	Landspitze	Gebirge	Stausee
ESPAÑOL	bahía	cabo	riachuelo	lago	montaña	punta	cordillera	embalse
FRANÇAIS	baie	cap	crique	lac	mont	pointe	chaîne	reservoir
PORTUGUÊS	baía	cabo	riacho	lago	monte	ponta	cordilheira	reservatório

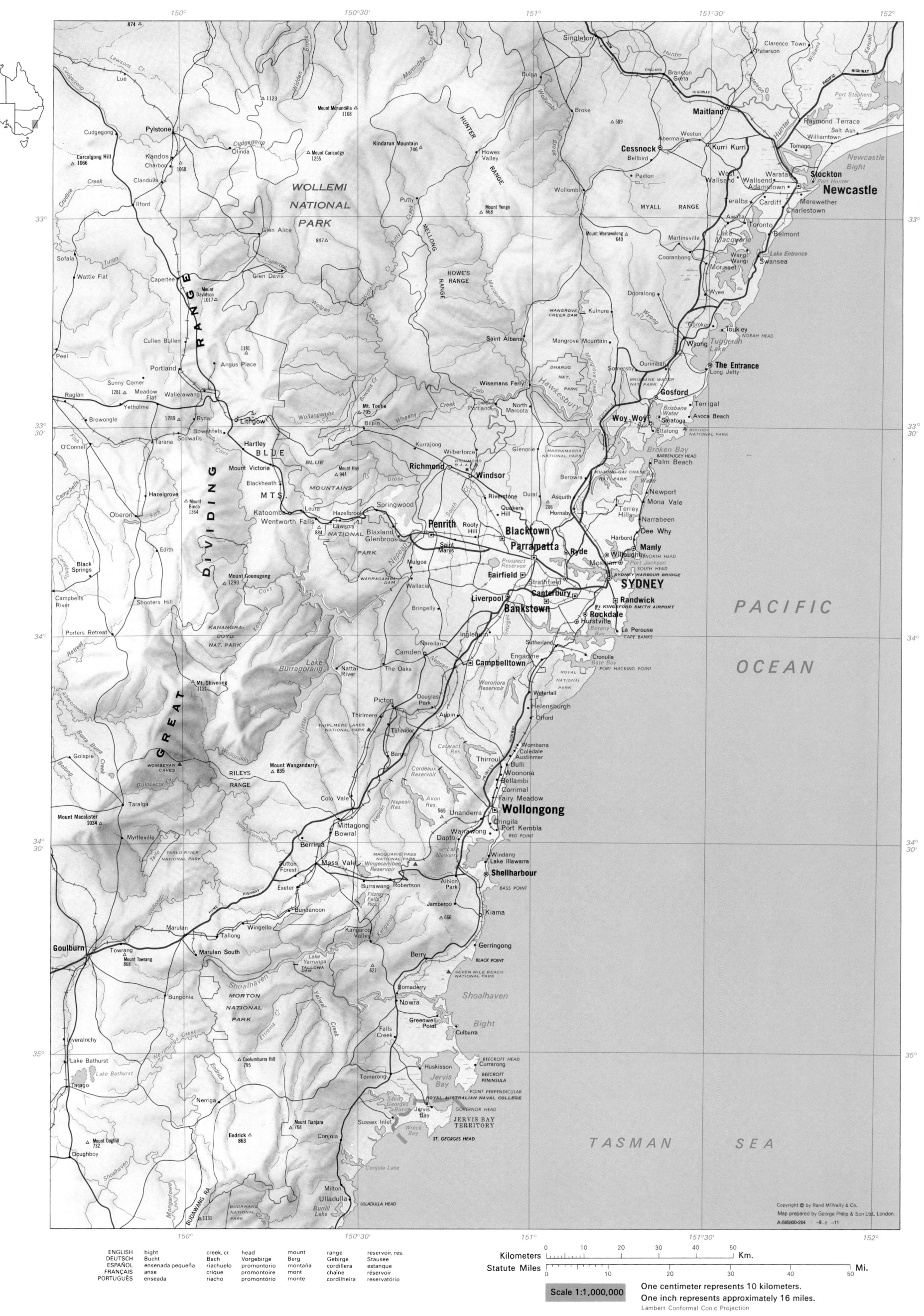

ENGLISH	bight	creek, cr.	head	mount	range	reservoir, res.
DEUTSCH	Bucht	Bach	Vorgebirge	Berg	Gebirge	Stausee
ESPAÑOL	ensenada pequeña	riachuelo	promontorio	montaña	cordillera	estanque
FRANÇAIS	anse	crique	promontoire	mont	chaîne	réservoir
PORTUGUÊS	enseada	riacho	promontório	monte	cordilheira	reservatório

Kilometers 0 10 20 30 40 50 Km.

Statute Miles 0 10 20 30 40 50 Mi.

Scale 1:1,000,000

One centimeter represents 10 kilometers.
One inch represents approximately 16 miles.
Lambert Conformal Conic Projection

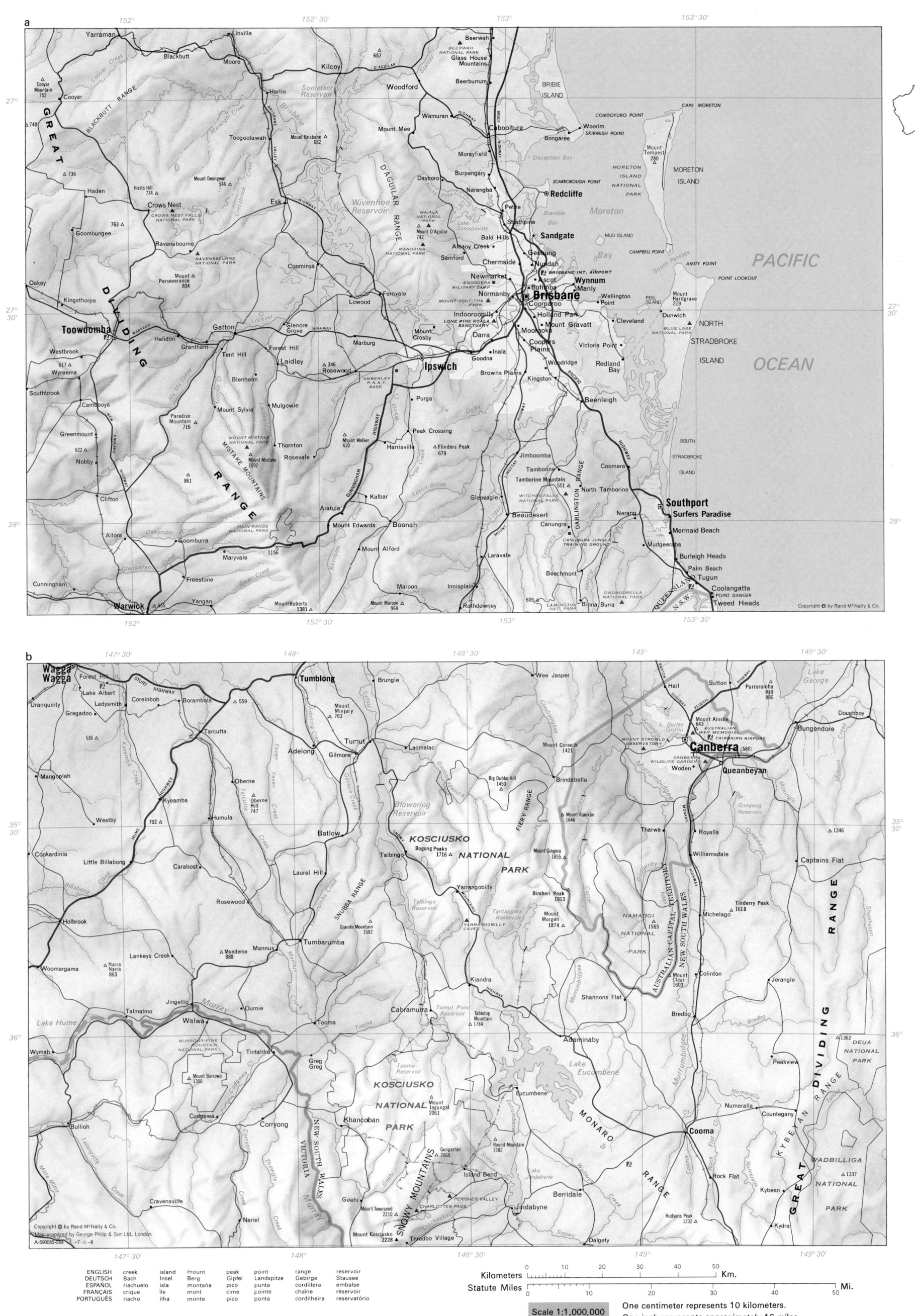

a

Yarraman
Linville
Blackbutt
Moore
Kilcoy
Cooyar
Mountain
752
Cooyar
Woodford
Harlin
Toogoolawah
Beerwah
BEERWAH
NATIONAL
PARK
Beerwah
Glass House
Mountains
657
O'Aguilar
Somerset
Reservoir
Beerburrum
BRIBIE
ISLAND
748
GREAT
Haden
Hirsts Hill
734
736
Mount Deongwar
546
Mount Brisbane
682
Wamuran
Caboolture
Morayfield
COMBOYURO POINT
CAPE MORETON
Bongaree
Woorim
SKIRMISH POINT
Crows Nest
BLACKBUTT RANGE
Mount Mee
Deception Bay
Mount
Tempest
280
Ravensbourne
Burpengary
Narangba
SCARBOROUGH POINT
MORETON
ISLAND
MORETON
ISLAND
763
Oakey
Kingsthorpe
DIVIDING
Coominya
D'AGUILAR
Dayboro
Petrie
Redcliffe
Bramble
Bay
Moreton
AMITY POINT
POINT LOOKOUT
PACIFIC
Toowoomba
Helidon
Fernvale
Samford
Albany Creek
Geebung
Bald Hills
Sandgate
Nudgah
Chermside
CAMPBELL POINT
MUD ISLAND
South Passage
OCEAN

Copyright © by Rand McNally & Co.

b

ENGLISH   creek   island   mount   peak   point   range   reservoir
DEUTSCH   Bach   Insel   Berg   Gipfel Landspitze Gebirge Stausee
ESPAÑOL   riachuelo isla   montaña pico   punta   cordillera embalse
FRANÇAIS   crique   île   mont   cime   pointe   chaîne   réservoir
PORTUGUÊS riacho   ilha   monte   pico   ponta   cordilheira reservatório

Kilometers   0   10   20   30   40   50   Km.
Statute Miles   0   10   20   30   40   50   Mi.

Scale 1:1,000,000   One centimeter represents 10 kilometers.
One inch represents approximately 16 miles.
Lambert Conformal Conic Projection

Copyright © by Rand McNally & Co.
Map prepared by George Philip & Son Ltd. London.
A-590055-201   -7-6 -8

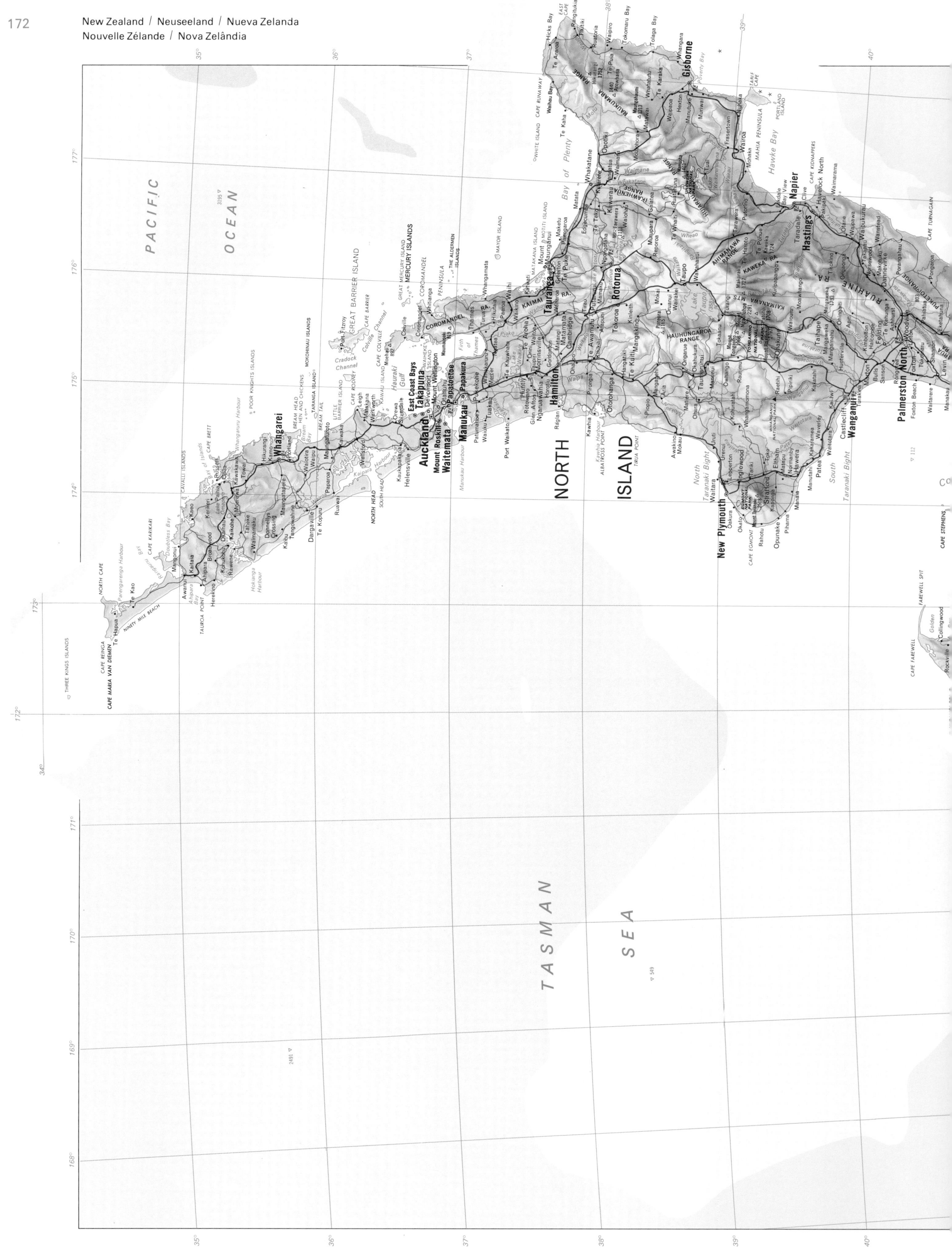

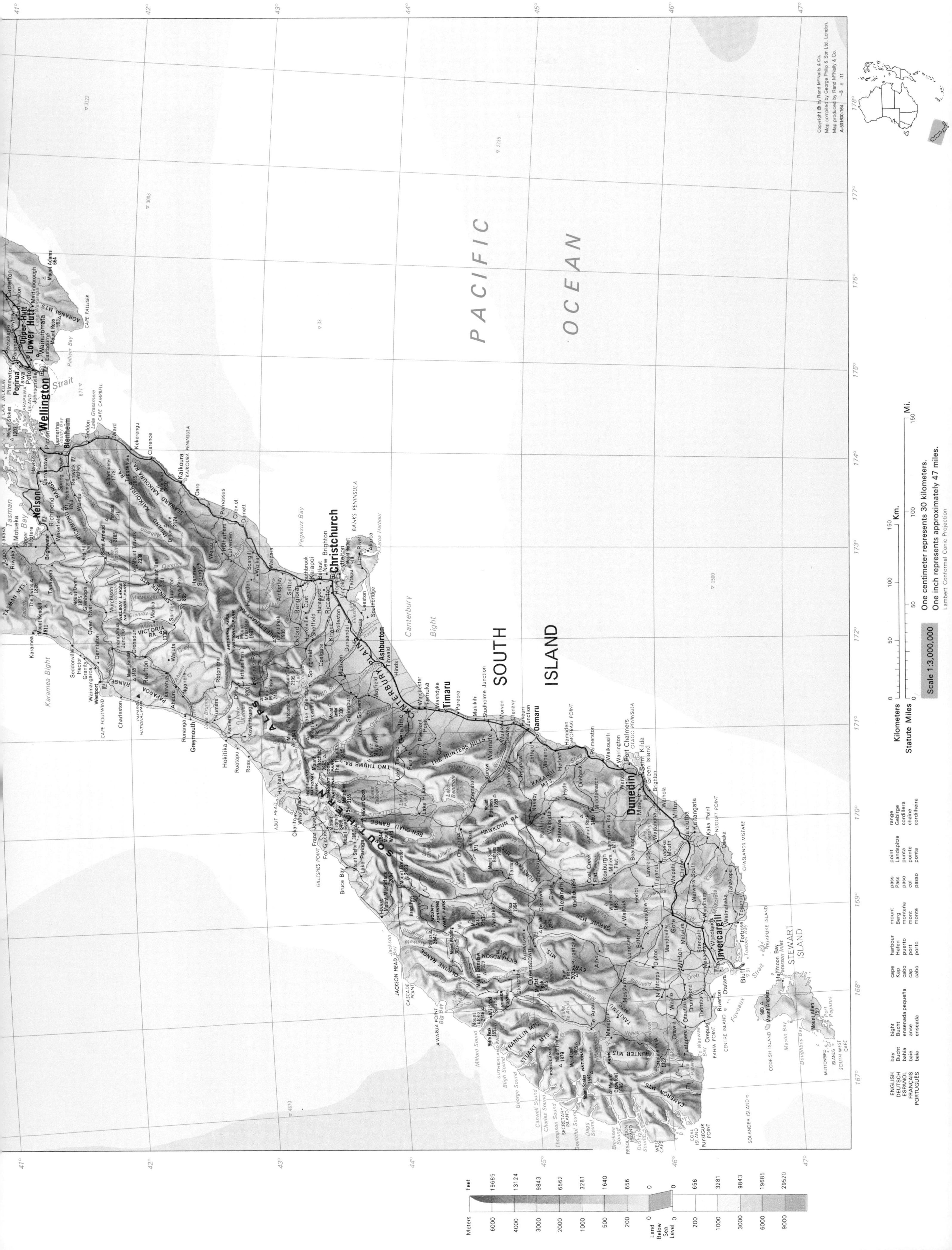
PACIFIC OCEAN
SOUTH ISLAND
STEWART ISLAND
Canterbury Bight
Pegasus Bay
Foveaux Strait
Wellington
Christchurch
Dunedin
Invercargill
Nelson
Blenheim
Timaru
Oamaru
Ashburton
Greymouth
SOUTHERN ALPS
CANTERBURY PLAINS
Kilometers
Statute Miles
Scale 1:3,000,000
One centimeter represents 30 kilometers.
One inch represents approximately 47 miles.
Lambert Conformal Conic Projection
Copyright © by Rand McNally & Co.
Map compiled by George Philip & Son Ltd, London.
Map produced by Rand McNally & Co.
Meters
Feet
Land Below Sea Level
ENGLISH bay bight cape harbour mount pass point range
DEUTSCH Bucht Bucht Kap Hafen Berg Pass Landspitze Gebirge
ESPAÑOL bahía ensenada pequeña cabo puerto montaña paso punta cordillera
FRANÇAIS baie anse cap port mont col pointe chaîne
PORTUGUÊS baía enseada cabo porto monte passo ponta cordilheira

Islands of the Pacific / Pazifische Inseln / Islas del Pacífico
Îles du Pacifique / Ilhas do Pacífico

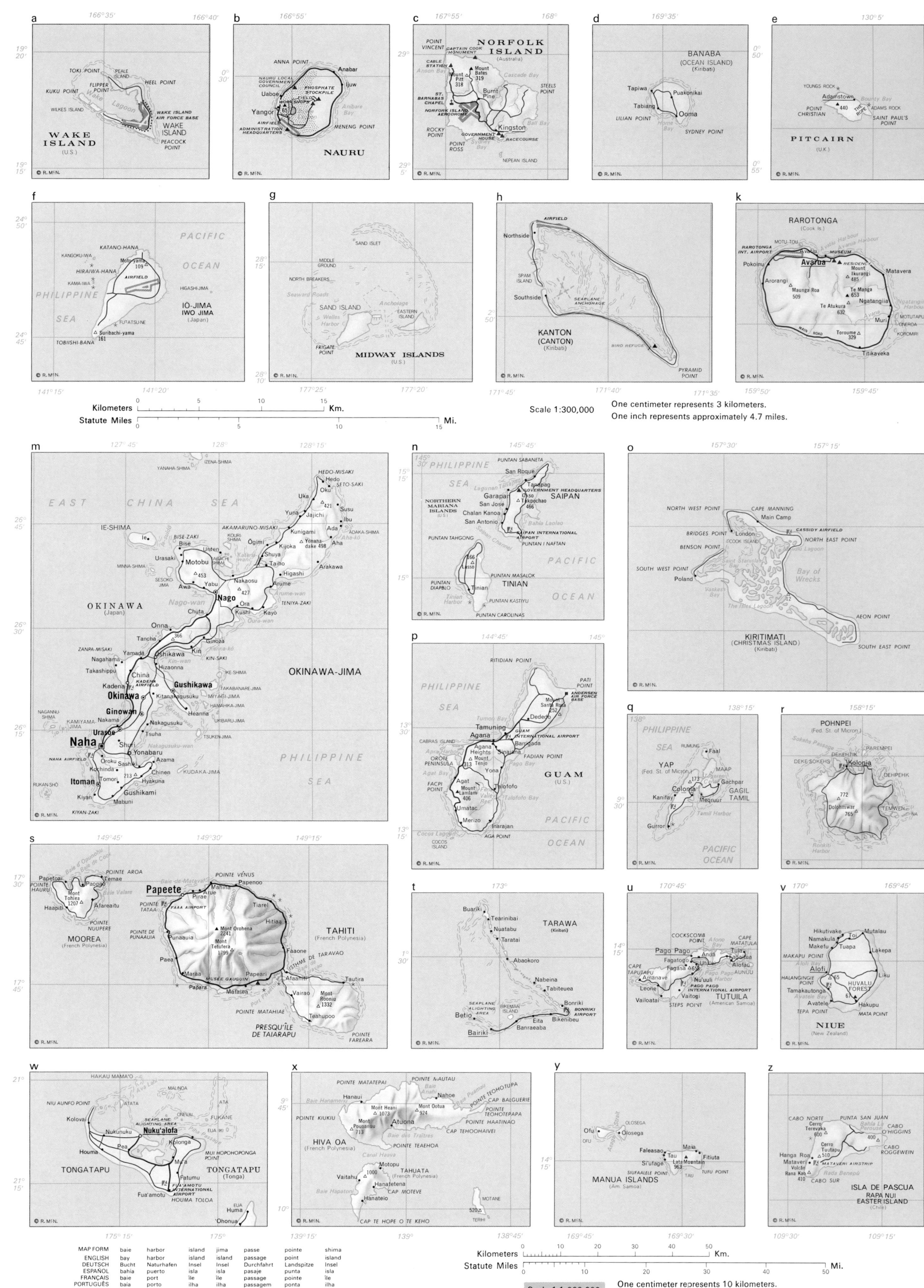

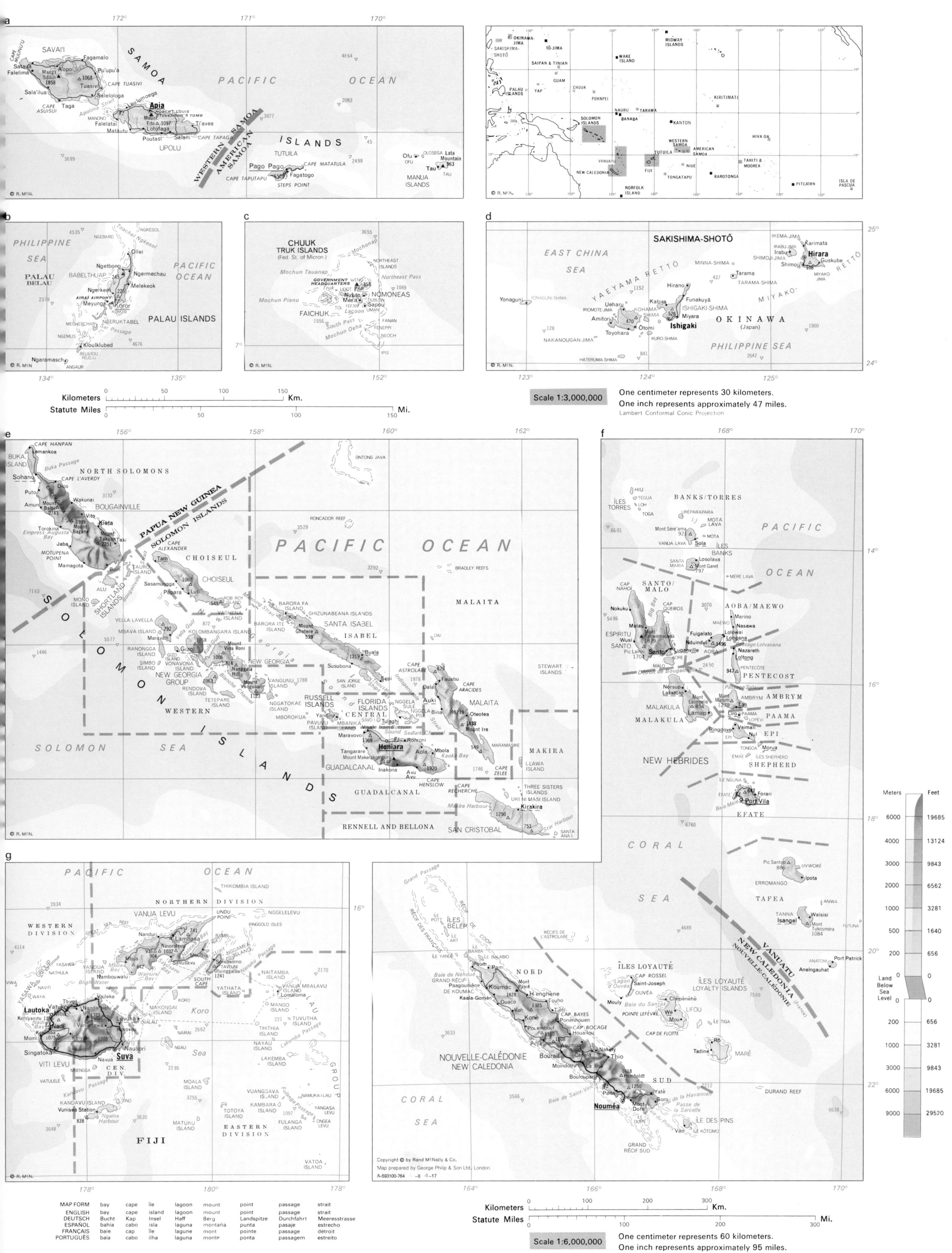

Scale 1:3,000,000

One centimeter represents 30 kilometers.

One inch represents approximately 47 miles.

Lambert Conformal Conic Projection

Scale 1:6,000,000

One centimeter represents 60 kilometers.

One inch represents approximately 95 miles.

Lambert Conformal Conic Projection

MAP FORM	bay	cape	île	lagoon	mount	point	passage	strait
ENGLISH	bay	cape	island	lagoon	mount	point	passage	strait
DEUTSCH	Bucht	Kap	Insel	Haff	Berg	Landspitze	Durchfahrt	Meeresstrasse
ESPAÑOL	bahía	cabo	isla	laguna	montaña	punta	pasaje	estrecho
FRANÇAIS	baie	cap	île	lagune	mont	pointe	passage	détroit
PORTUGUÊS	baía	cabo	ilha	laguna	monte	ponta	passagem	estreito

Map continues
pages 178-179 ➔

ENGLISH	bay	cape	island	lake, l	mountains, mts.	point	range	strait
DEUTSCH	Bucht	Kap	Insel	See	Berge	Landspitze	Gebirge	Meeresstrasse
ESPAÑOL	bahia	cabo	isla	lago	montañas	punta	sierra	estrecho
FRANÇAIS	baie	cap	île	lac	montagnes	pointe	chaîne	détroit
PORTUGUÊS	baia	cabo	ilha	lago	montanhas	ponta	serra	estreito

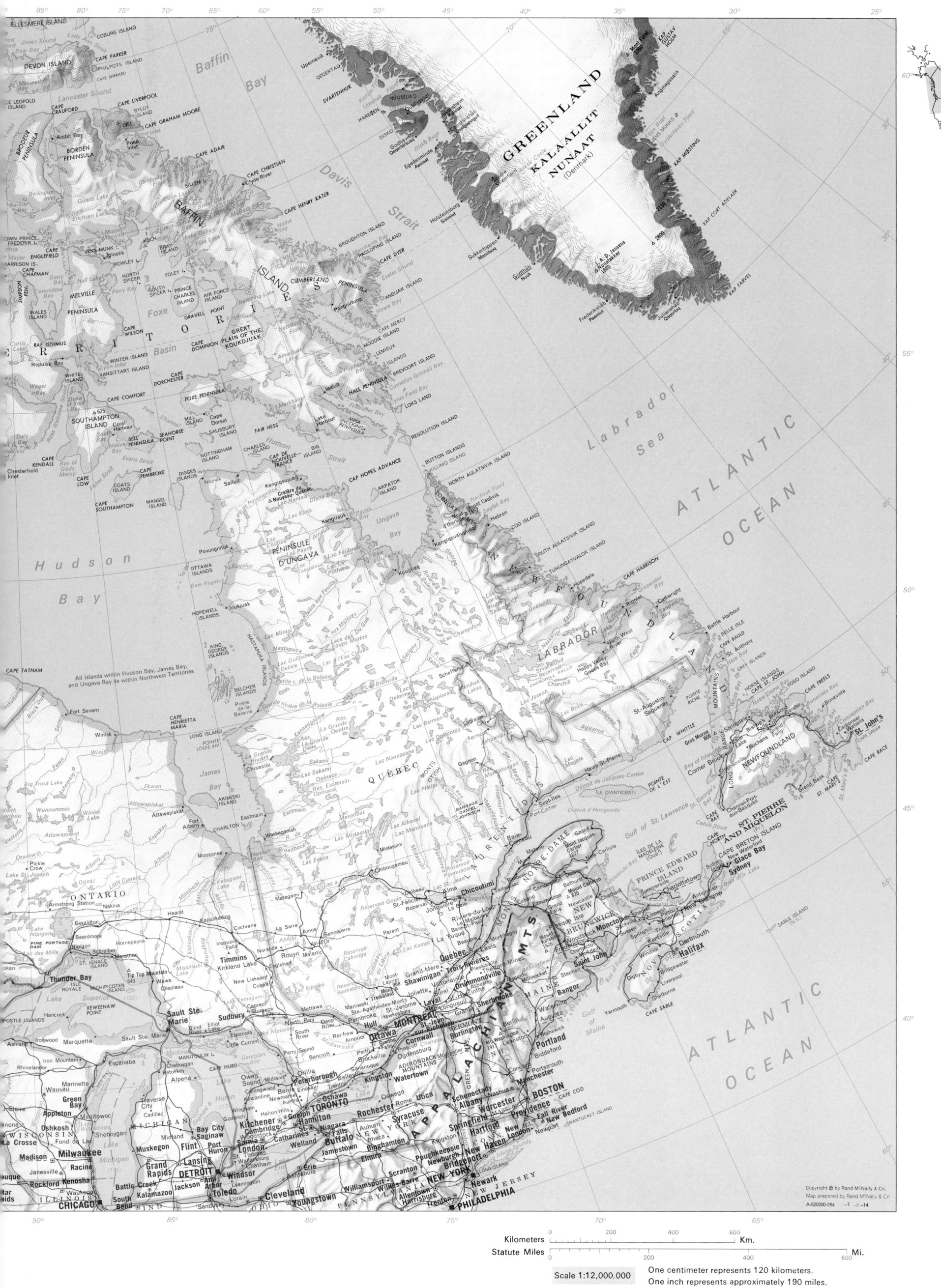

Kilometers
Statute Miles

Scale 1:12,000,000

One centimeter represents 120 kilometers.
One inch represents approximately 190 miles.
Lambert Conformal Conic Projection

	ENGLISH	bay	cape	desert	island	lake	mountains	peak	range
	DEUTSCH	Bucht	Kap	Wüste	Insel	See	Berge	Gipfel	Gebirge
	ESPAÑOL	bahía	cabo	desierto	isla	lago	montañas	pico	sierra
	FRANÇAIS	baie	cap	désert	ile	lac	montagnes	cime	chaine
	PORTUGUÊS	baia	cabo	deserto	ilha	lago	montanhas	pico	serra

Map continues
pages 230-231

Map continues
pages 176-177

Scale 1:12,000,000

One centimeter represents 120 kilometers.
One inch represents approximately 190 miles.

Albers Conical Equal-Area Projection

Meters	Feet
6000	19685
4000	13124
3000	9843
2000	6562
1000	3281
500	1640
200	656
	0
Land Below Sea Level	0
	0
200	656
1000	3281
3000	9843
6000	19685
9000	29520

	bay	cape	island, i.	lake, l.	mount, mt.	peak, pk.	point	volcano
ENGLISH	bay	cape	island, i.	lake, l.	mount, mt.	peak, pk.	point	volcano
DEUTSCH	Bucht	Kap	Insel	See	Berg	Gipfel	Landspitze	Vulkan
ESPAÑOL	bahía	cabo	isla	lago	monte	pico	punta	volcán
FRANÇAIS	baie	cap	île	lac	mont	cime	pointe	volcan
PORTUGUÊS	baía	cabo	ilha	lago	monte	pico	ponta	vulcão

Kilometers 0 100 200 300
Statute Miles 0 100 200 300 Mi.

Scale 1:6,000,000
One centimeter represents 60 kilometers.
One inch represents approximately 95 miles.
Lambert Conformal Conic Projection

Map continues
pages 176-177

Map continues
pages 182-183

Southwestern Canada / Südwestkanada / Canadá Sud-occidental
Sud-Ouest du Canada / Canadá: Sudoeste

Map continues
pages 180-181

Meters	Feet
6000	19685
4000	13124
3000	9843
2000	6562
1000	3281
500	1640
200	656
	0
Land Below Sea Level 0	0
200	656
1000	3281
3000	9843
6000	19685
9000	29520

Copyright © by Rand McNally & Co.
Map prepared by Rand McNally & Co.
A-520220-764   -5 -7 -9

ENGLISH	creek	Indian reserve	inlet	island	lake, l.	mountain	peak	provincial park	sound
DEUTSCH	Bach	Indianerreservation	Einfahrt	Insel	See	Berg	Gipfel	Provinz-Park	Sund
ESPAÑOL	riachuelo	reserva de Indios	abra	isla	lago	montaña	pico	parque de provincia	sonda
FRANÇAIS	crique	réserve indienne	bras de mer	île	lac	montagne	cime	parc provincial	détroit
PORTUGUÊS	riacho	reserva indigena	enseada	ilha	lago	montanha	pico	parque provincial	estreito

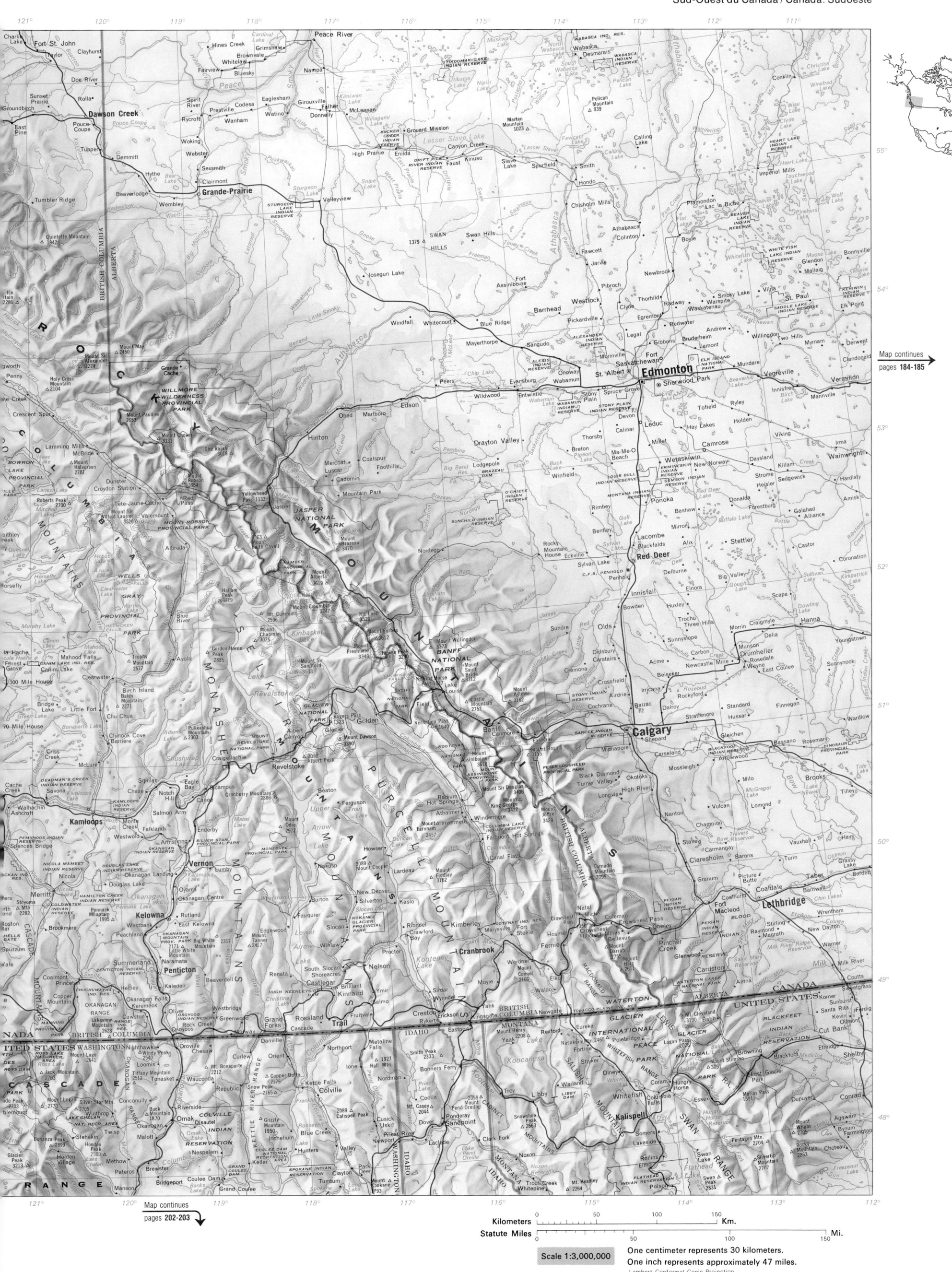

Map continues
pages 184-185

Map continues
pages 202-203

Kilometers
0   50   100   150
Km.

Statute Miles
0   50   100   150
Mi.

Scale 1:3,000,000
One centimeter represents 30 kilometers.
One inch represents approximately 47 miles.
Lambert Conformal Conic Projection

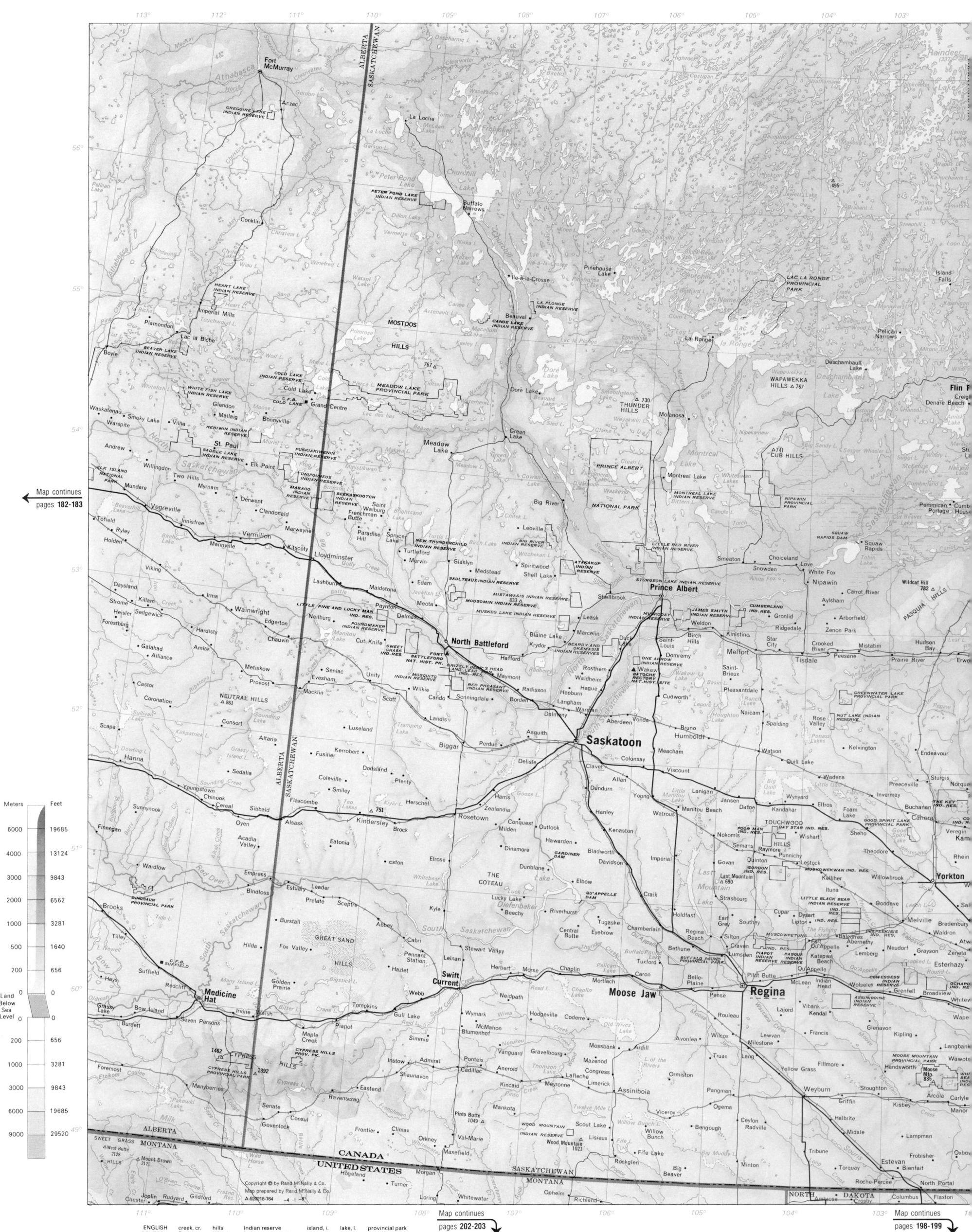

Map continues pages 182-183

Map continues pages 202-203

Map continues pages 198-199

		ENGLISH	creek, cr.	hills	Indian reserve	island, i.	lake, l.	provincial park
		DEUTSCH	Bach	Hügel	Indianerreservation	Insel	See	Provinz-Park
		ESPAÑOL	riachuelo	colinas	reserva de Indios	isla	lago	parque de provincia
		FRANÇAIS	crique	collines	réserve indienne	île	lac	parc provincial
		PORTUGUÊS	riacho	colinas	reserva indígena	ilha	lago	parque provincial

Copyright © by Rand McNally & Co.
Map prepared by Rand McNally & Co.
A-520018-764   -4   -8

South-Central Canada / Südliches Mittelkanada / Centro Meridional del Canadá
Canada Central, partie Méridionale / Canadá Central, parte meridional

185

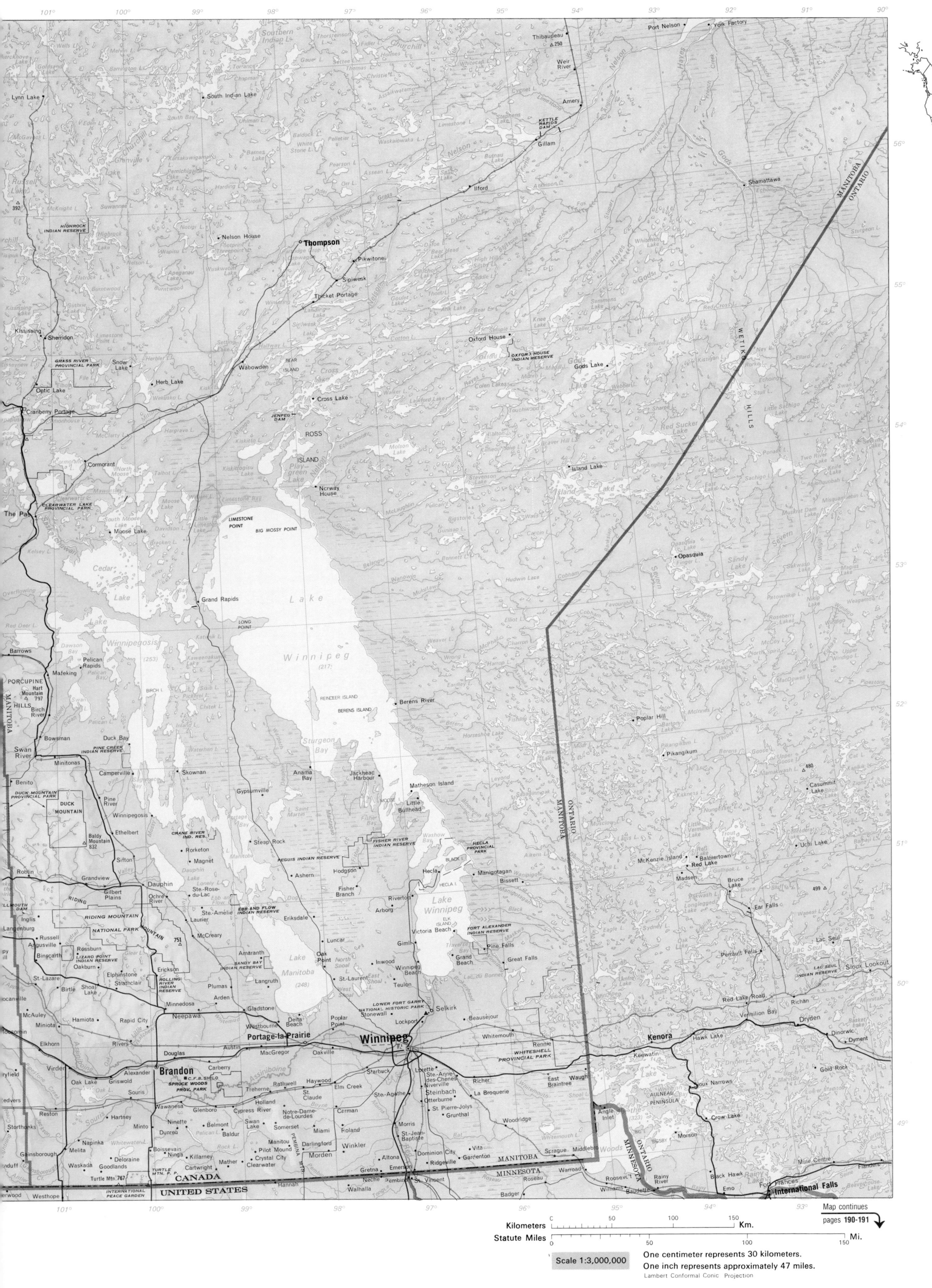

Kilometers

Statute Miles

Scale 1:3,000,000

One centimeter represents 30 kilometers.
One inch represents approximately 47 miles.
Lambert Conformal Conic Projection

Map continues
pages 190-191

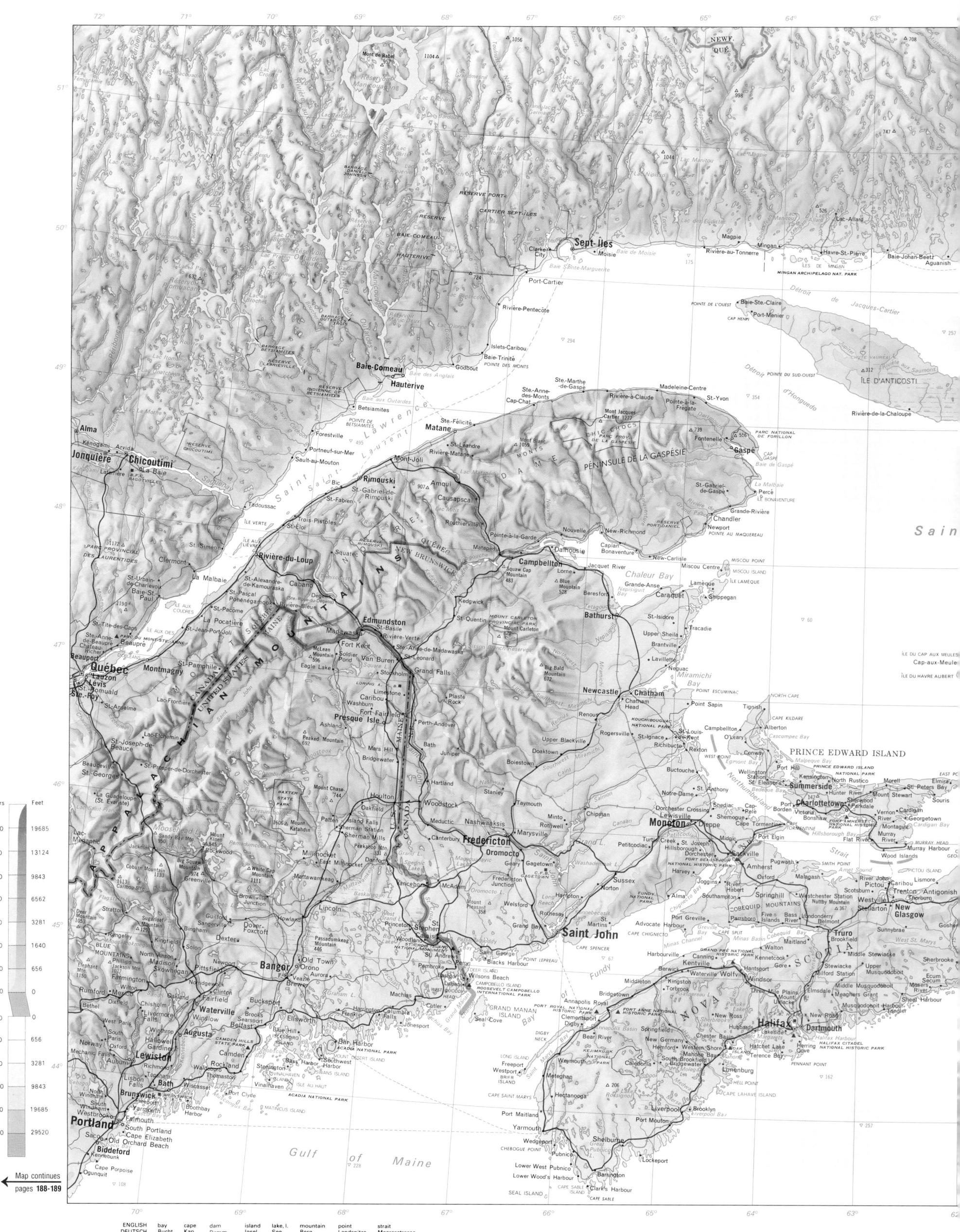

Map continues
pages **188-189**

Meters	Feet
6000	19685
4000	13124
3000	9843
2000	6562
1000	3281
500	1640
200	656
0	0
Land Below Sea Level	
0	0
200	656
1000	3281
3000	9843
6000	19685
9000	29520

ENGLISH	bay	cape	dam	island	lake, l.	mountain	point	strait
DEUTSCH	Bucht	Kap	Damm	Insel	See	Berg	Landspitze	Meeresstrasse
ESPAÑOL	bahía	cabo	presa	isla	lago	montaña	punta	estrecho
FRANÇAIS	baie	cap	barrage	île	lac	montagne	pointe	détroit
PORTUGUÊS	baía	cabo	represa	ilha	lago	montanha	ponta	estreito

LABRADOR
SEA

Gulf
of
Lawrence

NEWFOUNDLAND

Corner Brook

St. John's

Glace Bay
Sydney

SAINT PIERRE
AND MIQUELON
(France)
SAINT-PIERRE-
ET-MIQUELON

CANADA

ATLANTIC
OCEAN

SABLE ISLAND
(N.S.)

Kilometers   0   50   100   150   Km.
Statute Miles 0   50   100   150   Mi.

Scale 1:3,000,000

One centimeter represents 30 kilometers.
One inch represents approximately 47 miles.
Lambert Conformal Conic Projection

Copyright © by Rand McNally & Co.
Map prepared by Rand McNally & Co.
A-520219-764   3 5 -8'

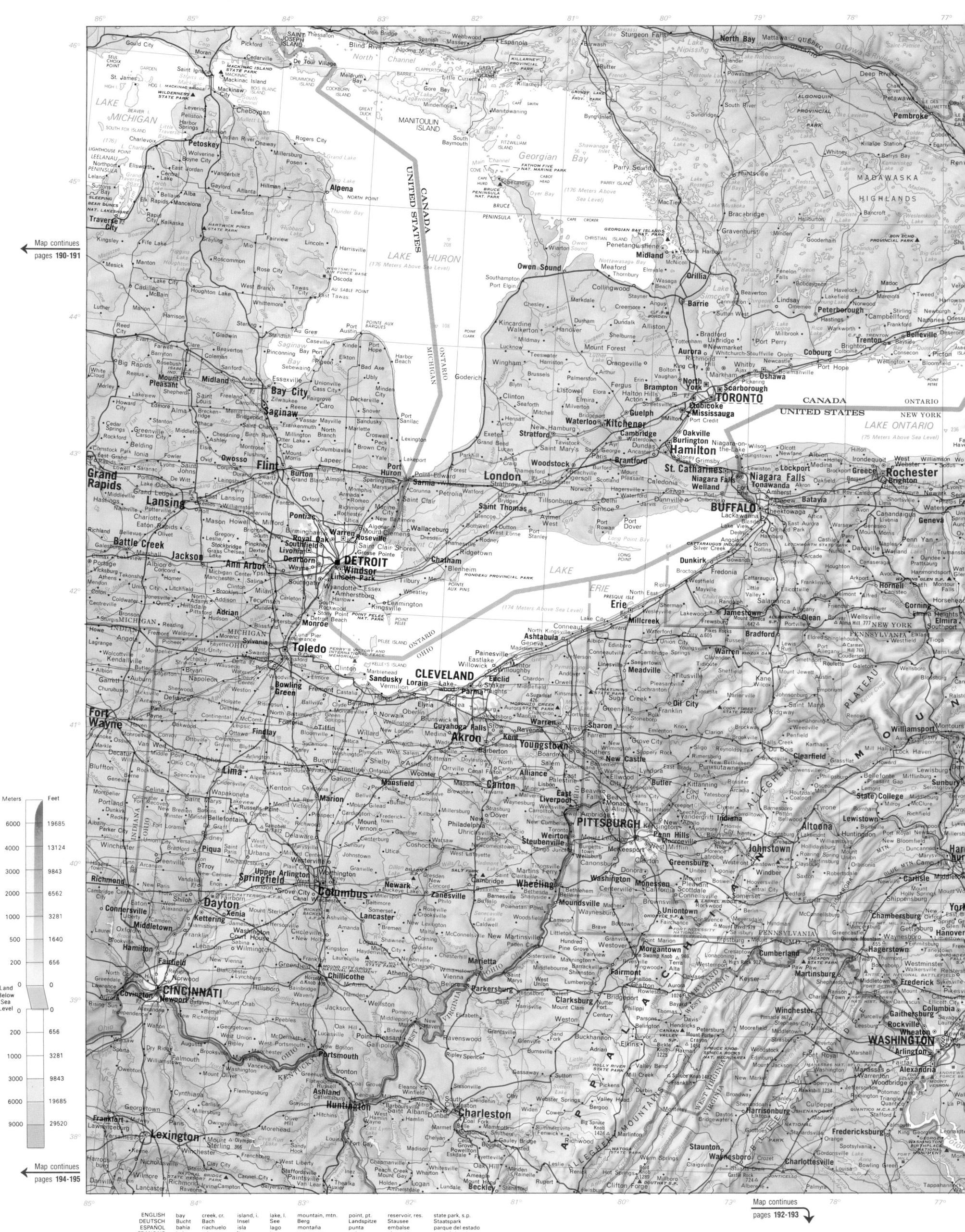

← Map continues pages 190-191

← Map continues pages 194-195

Map continues pages 192-193 →

	Meters	Feet
	6000	19685
	4000	13124
	3000	9843
	2000	6562
	1000	3281
	500	1640
	200	656
Land Below Sea Level	0	0
	0	0
	200	656
	1000	3281
	3000	9843
	6000	19685
	9000	29520

	bay	creek, cr.	island, i.	lake, l.	mountain, mtn.	point, pt.	reservoir, res.	state park, s.p.
ENGLISH	bay	creek, cr.	island, i.	lake, l.	mountain, mtn.	point, pt.	reservoir, res.	state park, s.p.
DEUTSCH	Bucht	Bach	Insel	See	Berg	Landspitze	Stausee	Staatspark
ESPAÑOL	bahía	riachuelo	isla	lago	montaña	punta	embalse	parque del estado
FRANÇAIS	baie	crique	île	lac	montagne	pointe	réservoir	parc régional
PORTUGUÊS	baía	riacho	ilha	lago	montanha	ponta	reservatório	parque estadual

Northeastern United States / Nordöstliche Vereinigte Staaten / Nor-este de los Estados Unidos
Nord-Est des États-Unis / Estados Unidos: Nordeste

189

Map continues
pages **186-187**

Kilometers

Statute Miles

Scale 1:3,000,000

One centimeter represents 30 kilometers.
One inch represents approximately 47 miles.
Albers Conical Equal-Area Projection

Copyright © by Rand McNally & Co.
Map prepared by Rand McNally & Co.
A-020596-764

Map continues
pages 184-185

← Map continues
pages 198-199

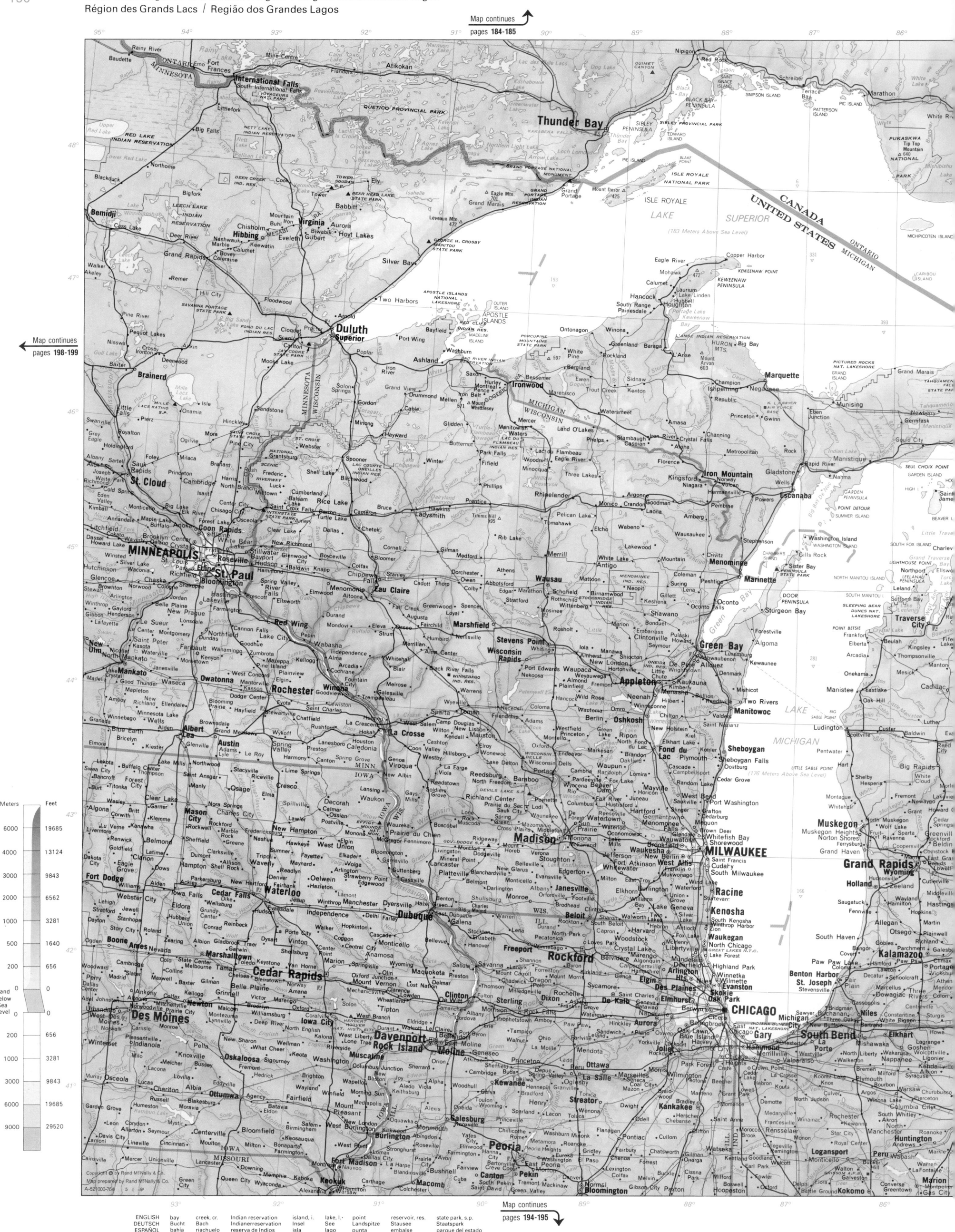

Map continues
pages 194-195 ↓

ENGLISH	bay	creek, cr.	Indian reservation	island, i.	lake, l.	point	reservoir, res.	state park, s.p.
DEUTSCH	Bucht	Bach	Indianerreservation	Insel	See	Landspitze	Stausee	Staatspark
ESPAÑOL	bahía	riachuelo	reserva de Indios	isla	lago	punta	embalse	parque del estado
FRANÇAIS	baie	crique	réserve indienne	île	lac	pointe	réservoir	parc régional
PORTUGUÊS	baía	riacho	reserva indígena	ilha	lago	ponta	reservatório	parque estadual

Meters / Feet

6000	19685
4000	13124
3000	9843
2000	6562
1000	3281
500	1640
200	656
0	0

Land Below Sea Level

0	0
200	656
1000	3281
3000	9843
6000	19685
9000	29520

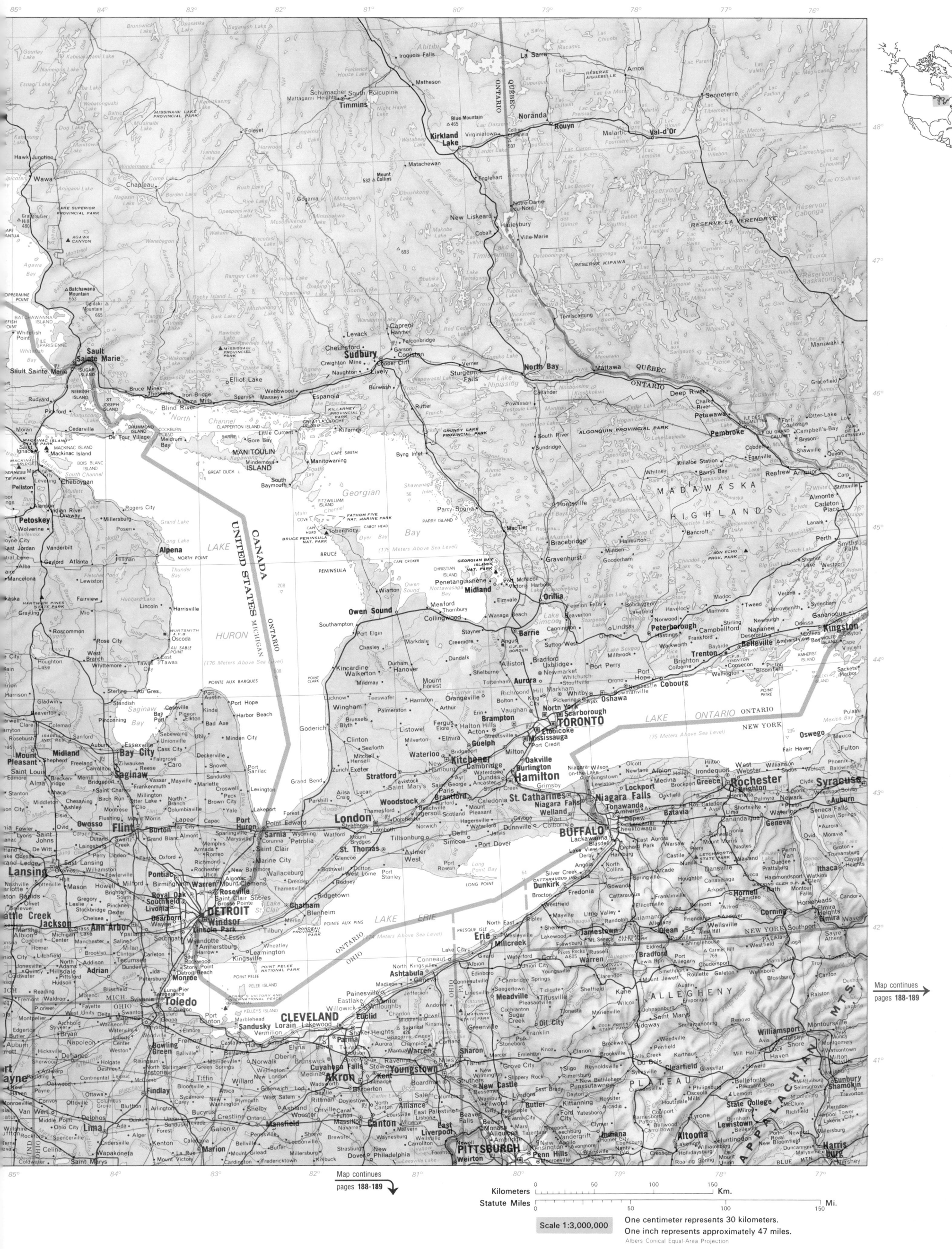

Map continues
pages **188-189**

Map continues
pages **188-189**

Kilometers

Statute Miles

Scale 1:3,000,000

One centimeter represents 30 kilometers.
One inch represents approximately 47 miles.
Albers Conical Equal-Area Projection

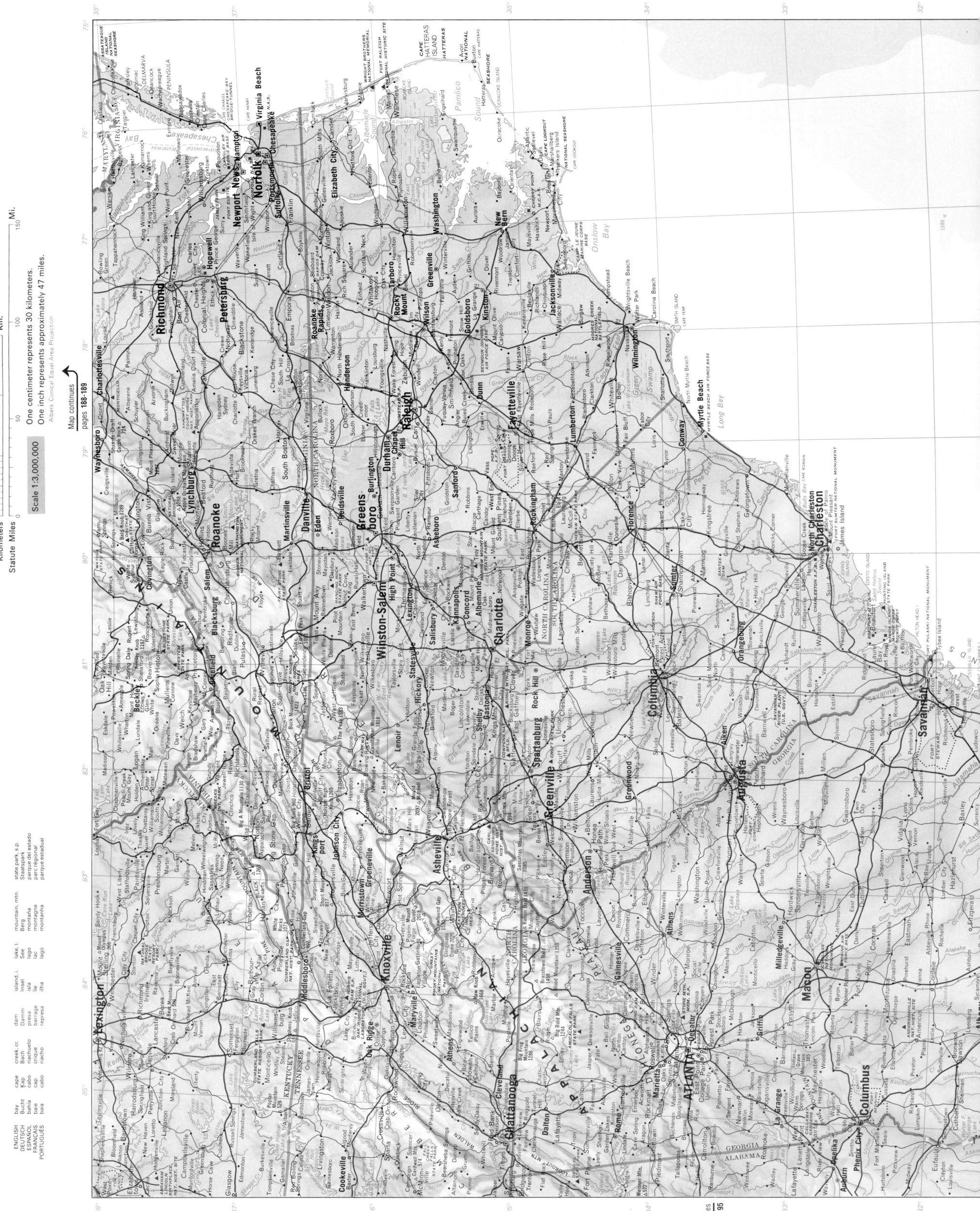

Map continues
pages 188-189

Map continues
pages 194-195

Scale 1:3,000,000

One centimeter represents 30 kilometers.
One inch represents approximately 47 miles.

Albers Conical Equal Area Projection

ENGLISH	DEUTSCH	ESPAÑOL	FRANÇAIS	PORTUGUÊS
bay	Bai	bahía	baie	baía
cape	Kap	cabo	cap	cabo
creek, cr.	Bach	riachuelo	crique	riacho
dam	Damm	presa	barrage	represa
island, i.	Insel	isla	île	ilha
lake, l.	See	lago	lac	lago
mountain, mtn.	Berg	montaña	montagne	montanha
state park, s.p.	Staatspark	parque del estado	parc régional	parque estadual

Southeastern United States / Südöstliche Vereinigte Staaten / Sud-este de los Estados Unidos
Sud-Est des États-Unis / Estados Unidos: Sudeste

193

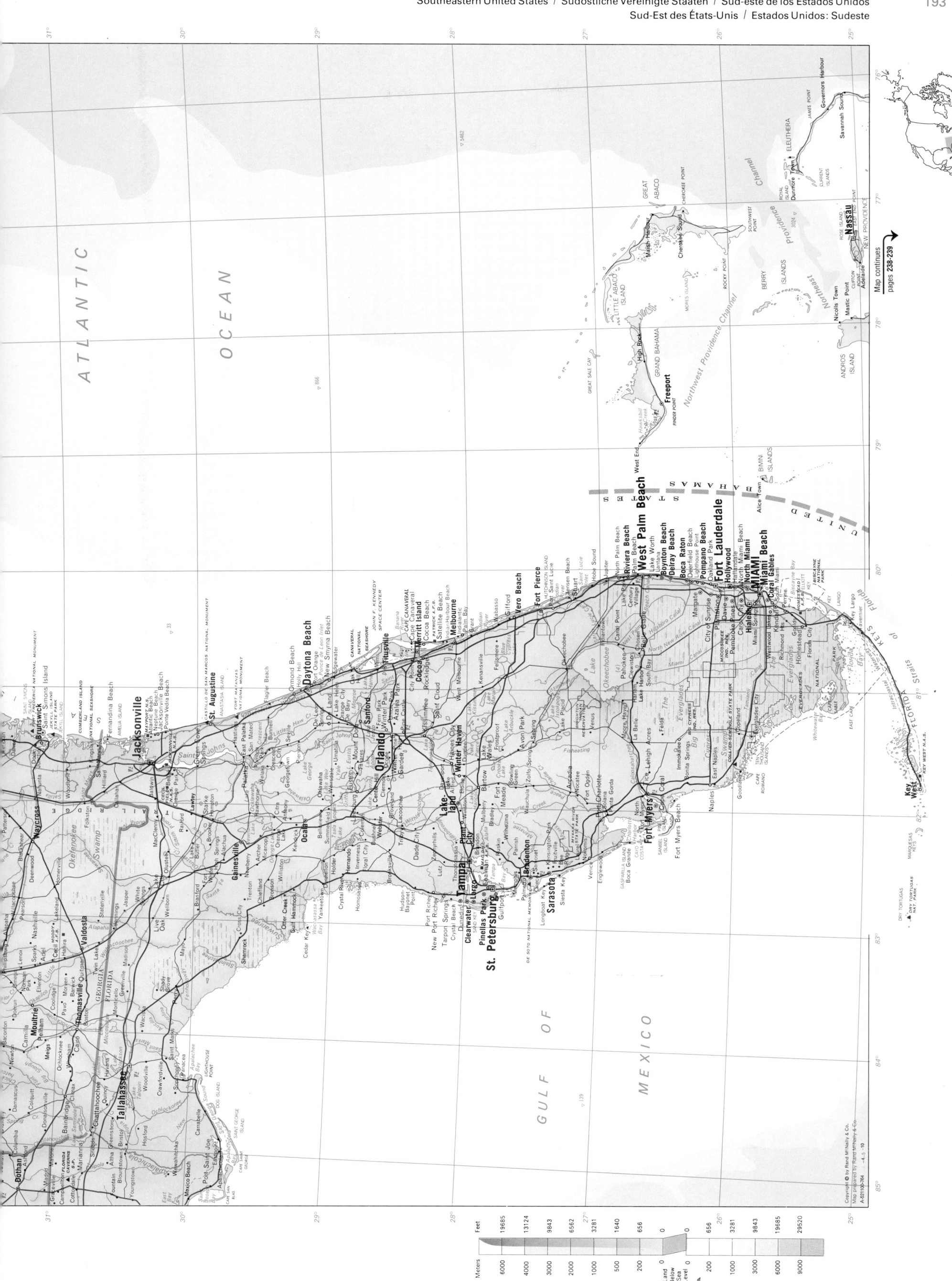

Map continues
pages 238-239

Feet	
19685	6000
13124	4000
9843	3000
6562	2000
3281	1000
1640	500
656	200
0	0
656	200
3281	1000
9843	3000
19685	6000
29520	9000

Meters

Land Below Sea Level

Map continues
pages 188–189

Map continues
pages 190–191

Map continues
pages 198–199

Map continues pages 192-193

Map continues pages 196-197

GULF OF MEXICO

Scale 1:3,000,000

Albers Conical Equal-Area Projection

One centimeter represents 30 kilometers.
One inch represents approximately 47 miles.

Kilometers
Km.
Statute Miles
Mi.

ENGLISH	DEUTSCH	ESPAÑOL	FRANÇAIS	PORTUGUÊS
bay	Bucht	bahía	baie	baía
bayou, bay.	Altwasser	ensenada	bayou	enseada
creek, cr.	Bach	riachuelo	crique	riacho
dam	Damm	presa	barrage	represa
lake	See	lago	lac	lago
mountain, mtn.	Berg	montaña	montagne	montanha
reservoir, res.	Stausee	embalse	réservoir	reservatório
state park, s.p.	Staatspark	parque del estado	parc régional	parque estadual

Land Below Sea Level

Meters	Feet
6000	19685
4000	13124
3000	9843
2000	6562
1000	3281
500	1640
200	656
0	0
200	656
1000	3281
3000	9843
6000	19685
9000	29520

196

Southern Great Plains / Südliche Grosse Ebenen / Grandes Llanos: zona meridional
Grandes Plaines, partie Méridionale / Grandes Planícies: zona meridional

Map continues
pages 194-195

Map continues
pages 198-199

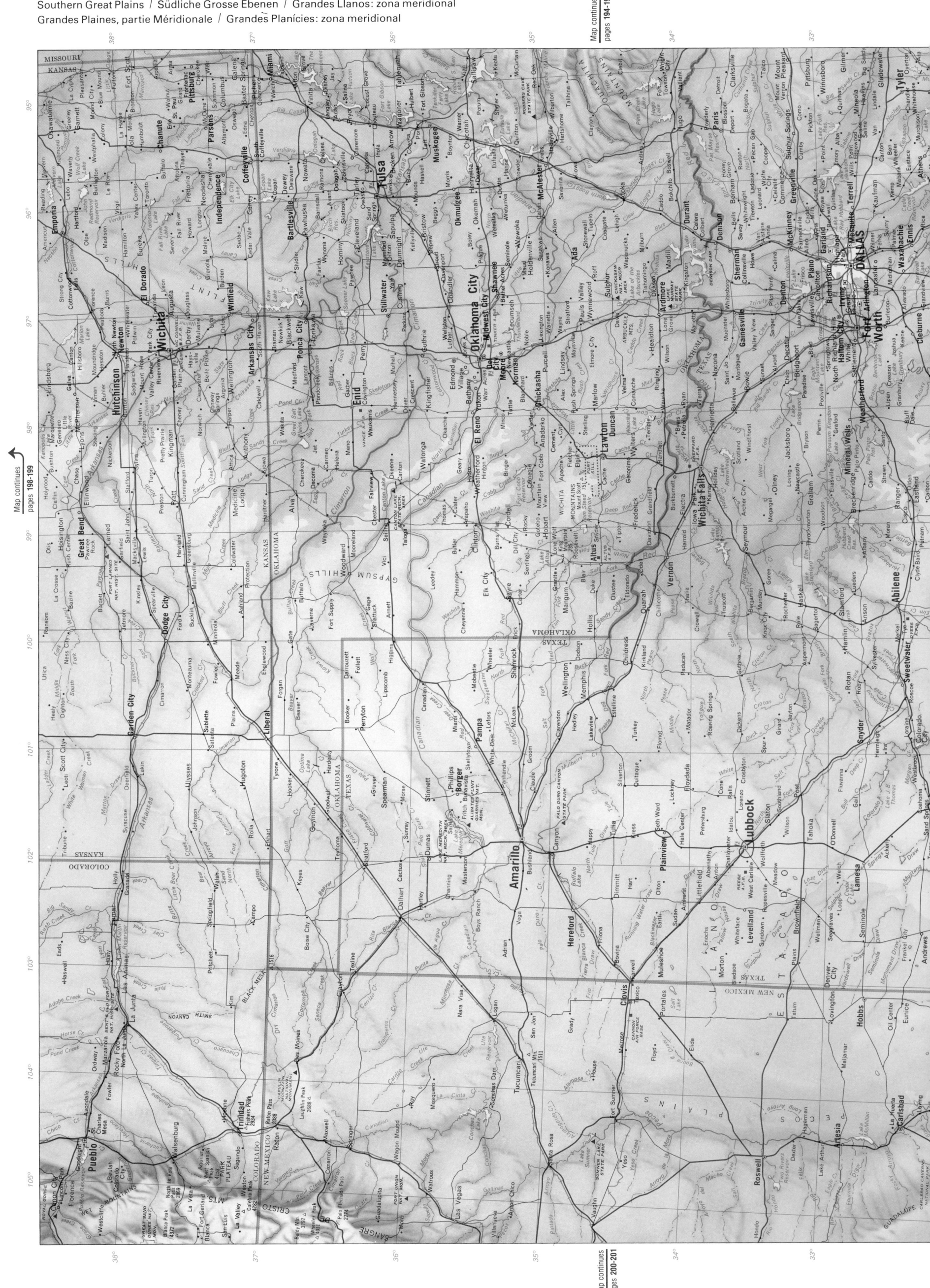

Map continues
pages 200-201

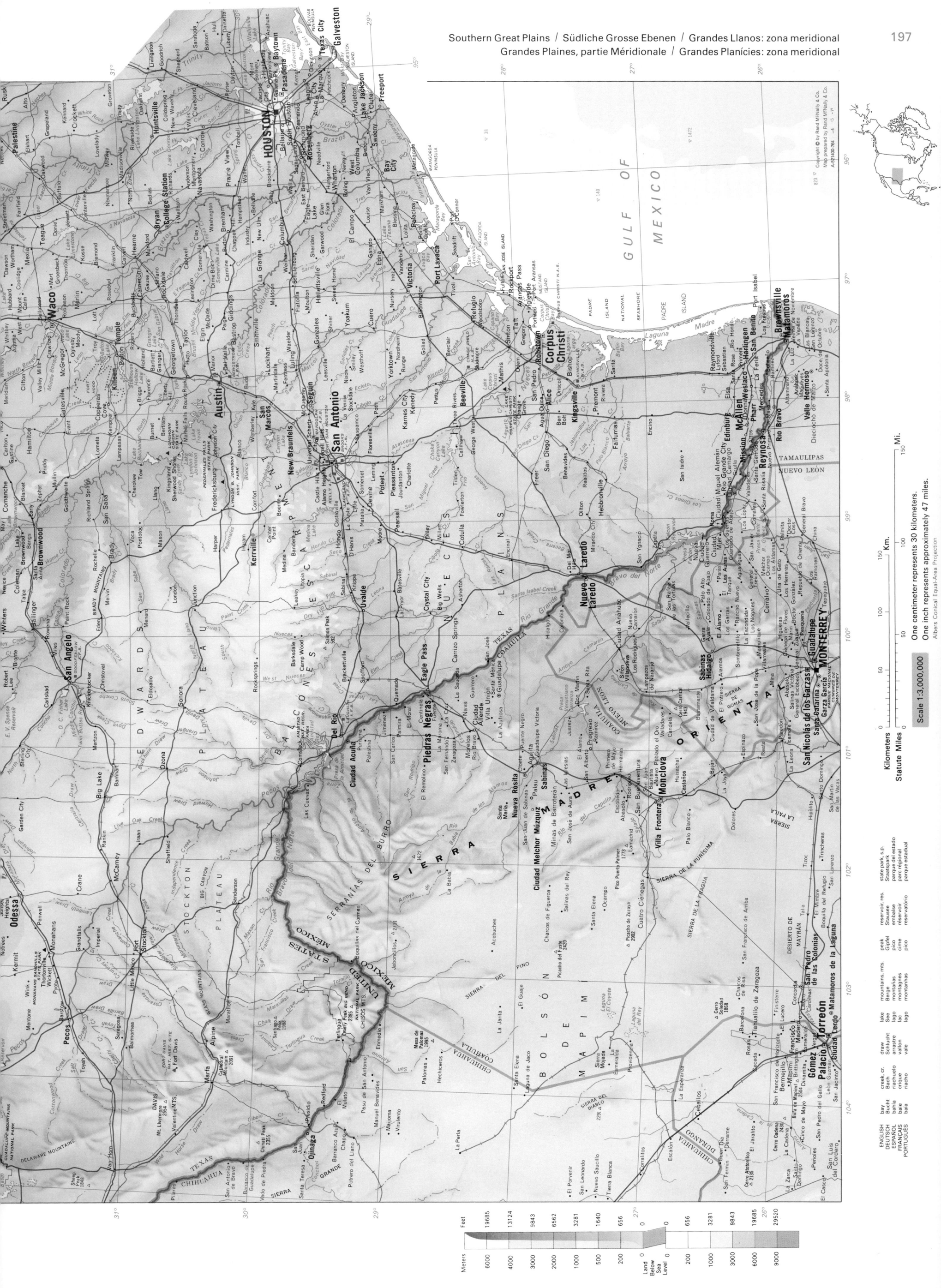

Southern Great Plains / Südliche Grosse Ebenen / Grandes Llanos: zona meridional
Grandes Plaines, partie Méridionale / Grandes Planícies: zona meridional

197

GULF OF MEXICO

Scale 1:3,000,000

One centimeter represents 30 kilometers.
One inch represents approximately 47 miles.

Albers Conical Equal-Area Projection

Kilometers
Statute Miles

ENGLISH	DEUTSCH	ESPAÑOL	FRANÇAIS	PORTUGUÊS
bay	Bucht	bahía	baie	baía
creek, cr.	Bach	riachuelo	crique	riacho
draw	Schlucht	arrastre	vallon	vale
lake	See	lago	lac	lago
mountains, mts.	Berge	montañas	montagnes	montanhas
peak	Gipfel	pico	cime	pico
reservoir, res.	Stausee	embalse	réservoir	reservatório
state park, s.p.	Staatspark	parque del estado	parc régional	parque estadual

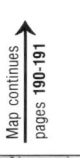

Map continues pages 190-191

Map continues pages 184-185

Map continues pages 202-203

Northern Great Plains / Nördliche Grosse Ebenen / Grandes Llanos: zona septentrional
Grandes Plaines, partie Septentrionale / Grandes Planícies: zona setentrional

199

Map continues pages 194-195

Map continues pages 196-197

Map continues pages 200-201

Scale 1:3,000,000

One centimeter represents 30 kilometers.
One inch represents approximately 47 miles.
Albers Conical Equal Area Projection

ENGLISH	DEUTSCH	FRANÇAIS	ESPAÑOL	PORTUGUÊS
state park	Staatspark	parc régional	parque del estado	parque estadual
reservoir, res.	Stausee	reservoir	embalse	reservatório
peak	Gipfel	cime	pico	pico
mountain, mtn.	Berg	montagne	montaña	montanha
lake, l.	See	lac	lago	lago
Indian reservation, Ind. res.	Indianerreservation	réserve indienne	reserva de Indios	reserva indígena
dam	Damm	barrage	presa	barragem
creek, cr.	Bach	ruisseau	riachuelo	riacho

Copyright © by Rand McNally & Co.
Map prepared by Rand McNally & Co.
A-621250-84

Kilometers
Statute Miles
Km.
Mi.

Southern Rocky Mountains / Südliches Felsengebirge / Montañas Rocosas: zona meridional
Montagnes Rocheuses, partie Méridionale / Montanhas Rochosas: zona meridional

Map continues pages 198-199
Map continues pages 202-203 
Map continues pages 204-205

Southern Rocky Mountains / Südliches Felsengebirge / Montañas Rocosas: zona meridional
Montagnes Rocheuses, partie Méridionale / Montanhas Rochosas: zona meridional

201

Scale 1:3,000,000

Kilometers

Statute Miles

One centimeter represents 30 kilometers.
One inch represents approximately 47 miles.

Albers Conical Equal-Area Projection

ENGLISH	creek, cr.	lake	Indian reservation	national monument, nat. mon.	mountains	peak	reservoir, res.	wash
DEUTSCH	Bach	See	Indianerreservation	Nationaldenkmal	Berge	Gipfel	Stausee	Trockenfluss
ESPAÑOL	riachuelo	lago	reserva de Indios	monumento nacional	montañas	pico	embalse	uadi
FRANÇAIS	crique	lac	réserve indienne	monument national	montagnes	cime	réservoir	wadi
PORTUGUÊS	riacho	lago	reserva indígena	monumento nacional	montanhas	pico	reservatório	uadi

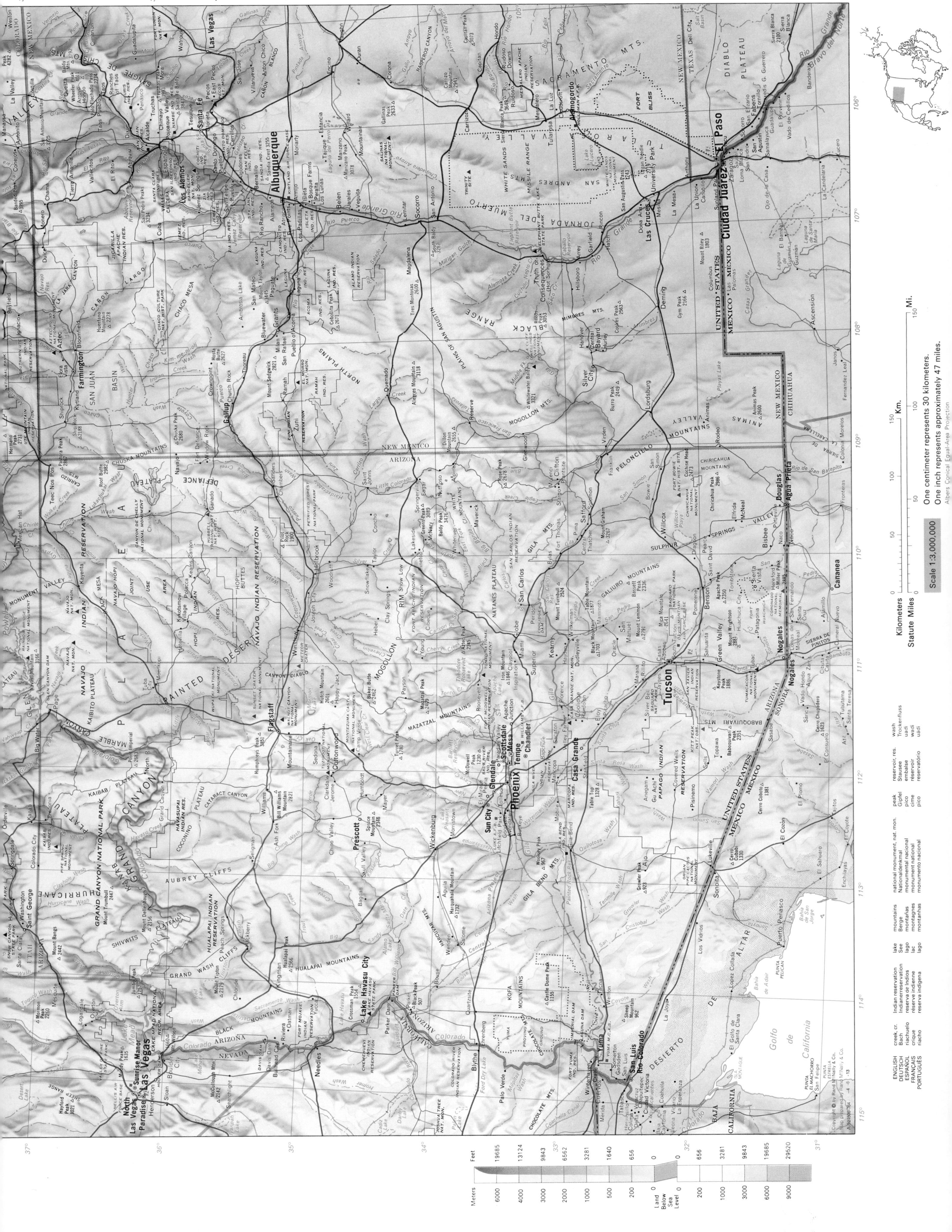

Feet
19685
13124
9843
6562
3281
1640
656
0
Land Below Sea Level
0
656
3281
9843
19685
29520

Meters
6000
4000
3000
2000
1000
500
200
0
Land Below Sea Level
0
200
1000
3000
6000
9000

Map continues
pages 182-183

Map continues
pages 204-205

	ENGLISH	creek, cr.	Indian reservation	lake, l.	mountain, mtn.	pass	peak	range	reservoir, res.
	DEUTSCH	Bach	Indianerreservation	See	Berg	Pass	Gipfel	Gebirge	Stausee
	ESPAÑOL	riachuelo	reserva de Indios	lago	montaña	paso	pico	sierra	embalse
	FRANÇAIS	crique	réserve indienne	lac	montagne	col	cime	chaîne	réservoir
	PORTUGUÊS	riacho	reserva indígena	lago	montanha	passo	pico	serra	reservatório

Northwestern United States / Nordwestliche Vereinigte Staaten / Nor-oeste de los Estados Unidos
Nord-Ouest des États-Unis / Noroeste dos Estados Unidos

203

Map continues
pages 184-185 ↑

Map continues
pages 198-199 →

Map continues
pages 200-201 ↓

Copyright © by Rand McNally & Co.
Map prepared by Rand McNally & Co.

A-800697-764   -4 -8 -9

Kilometers   0   50   100   150   Km.
Statute Miles   0   50   100   150   Mi.

Scale 1:3,000,000
One centimeter represents 30 kilometers.
One inch represents approximately 47 miles.
Albers Conical Equal-Area Projection

Map continues pages 200-201

Map continues pages 202-203

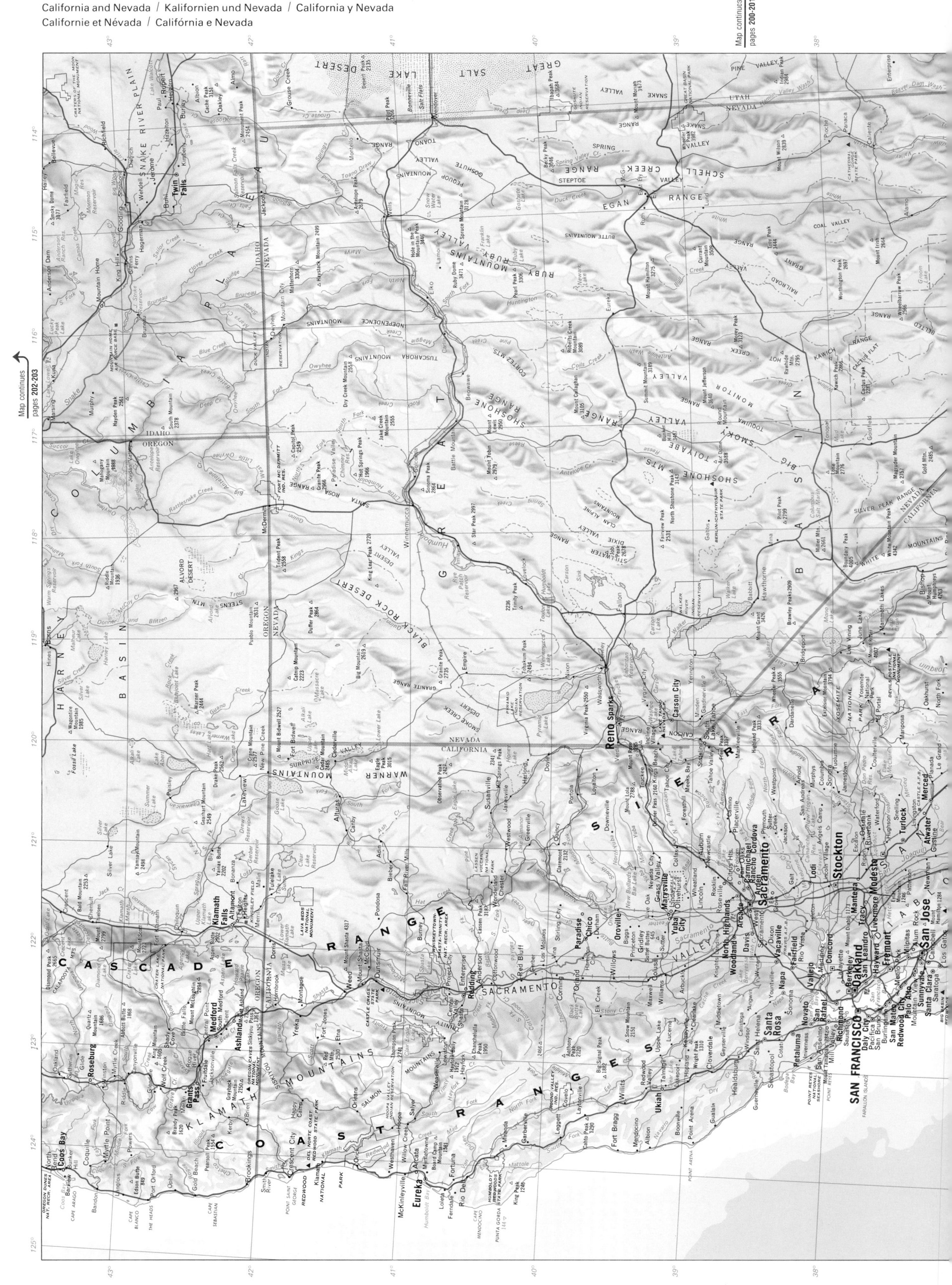

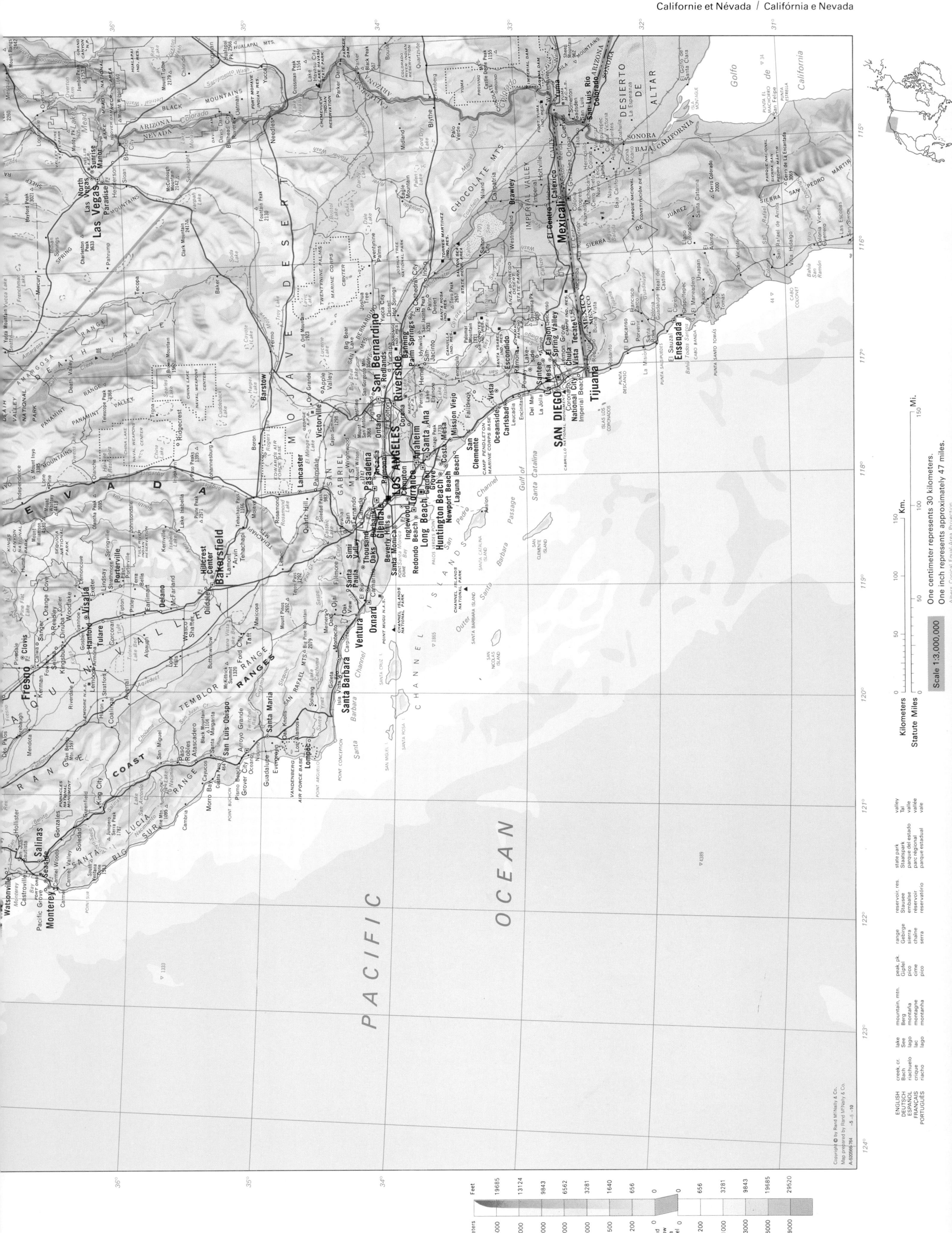

Scale 1:3,000,000

One centimeter represents 30 kilometers.
One inch represents approximately 47 miles.

Albers Conical Equal-Area Projection

Kilometers

Km.

Statute Miles

Mi.

ENGLISH	creek, cr.	lake	mountain, mtn.	peak, pk.	range	reservoir, res.	state park	valley
DEUTSCH	Bach	See	Berg	Gipfel	Gebirge	Stausee	Staatspark	Tal
ESPAÑOL	riachuelo	lago	montaña	pico	sierra	embalse	parque del estado	valle
FRANÇAIS	crique	lac	montagne	cime	chaîne	réservoir	parc régional	vallée
PORTUGUÊS	riacho	lago	montanha	pico	sierra	reservatório	parque estadual	vale

Feet	Meters
19685	6000
13124	4000
9843	3000
6562	2000
3281	1000
1640	500
656	200
0	0
	Land Below Sea Level
0	0
656	200
3281	1000
9843	3000
19685	6000
29520	9000

Copyright © by Rand McNally & Co.
Map prepared by Rand McNally & Co.
A-500066-784   -5.-5.-10

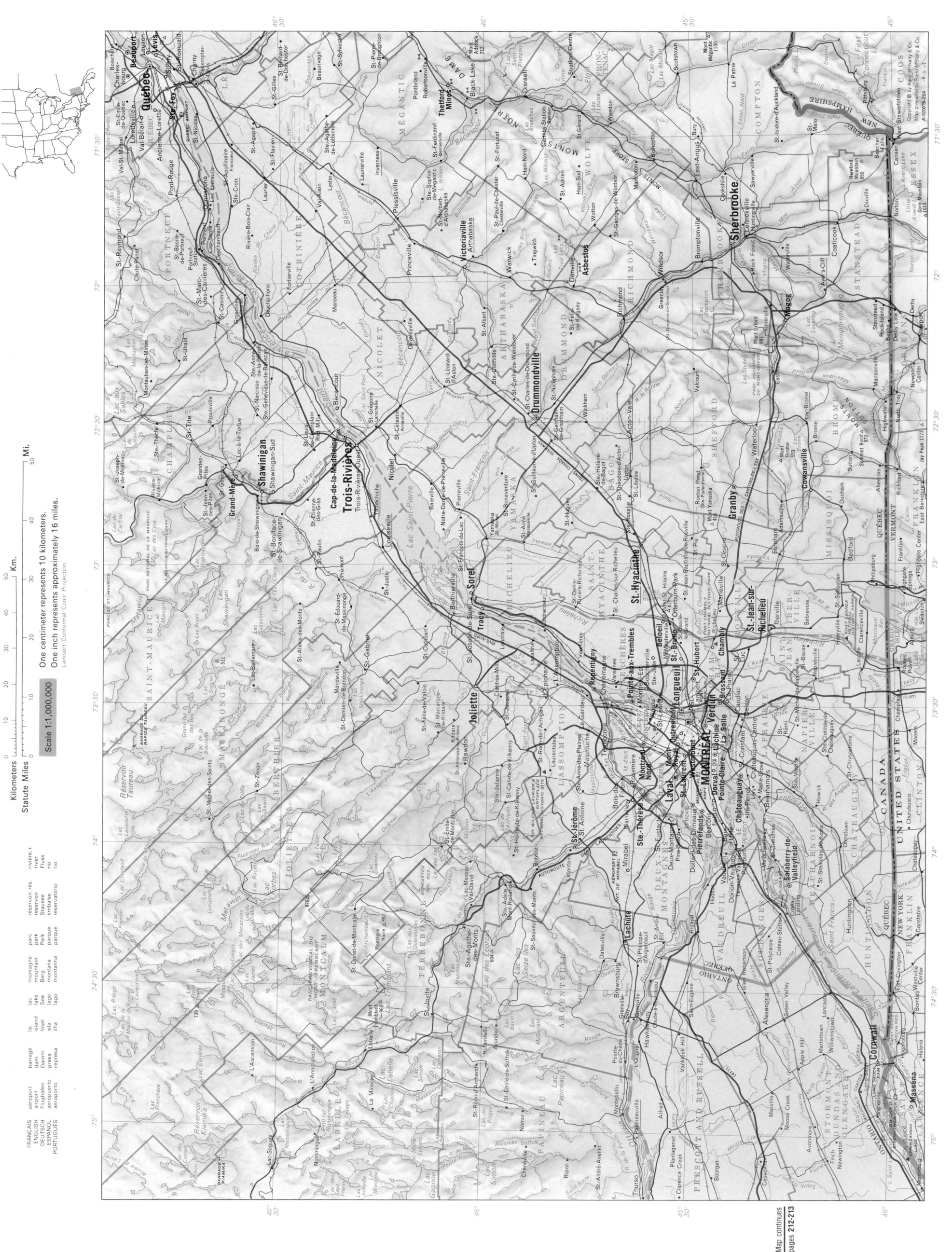
FRANÇAIS ENGLISH DEUTSCH ESPAÑOL PORTUGUÊS
aéroport airport Flughafen aeropuerto aeroporto
barrage dam Damm presa represa
île island Insel isla ilha
lac lake See lago lago
montagne mountain Berg montaña montanha
parc park Park parque parque
réservoir, rés. reservoir Stausee embalse reservatório
rivière, r. river Fluss río rio
Kilometers 0 10 20 30 40 50 Km.
Statute Miles 0 10 20 30 40 50 Mi.
Scale 1:1,000,000
One centimeter represents 10 kilometers.
One inch represents approximately 16 miles.
Lambert Conformal Conic Projection
Québec
Lévis
Ste-Foy
Thetford Mines
Victoriaville
Drummondville
Sherbrooke
Magog
Granby
Trois-Rivières
Cap-de-la-Madeleine
Shawinigan
Grand-Mère
Sorel
Joliette
St-Jérôme
Laval
MONTRÉAL
Longueuil
St-Hyacinthe
St-Jean-sur-Richelieu
Salaberry-de-Valleyfield
Cornwall
Massena
CANADA
UNITED STATES
QUÉBEC
VERMONT
NEW YORK
NEW HAMPSHIRE
ONTARIO
Copyright © by Rand McNally & Co.

Map continues pages 212-213

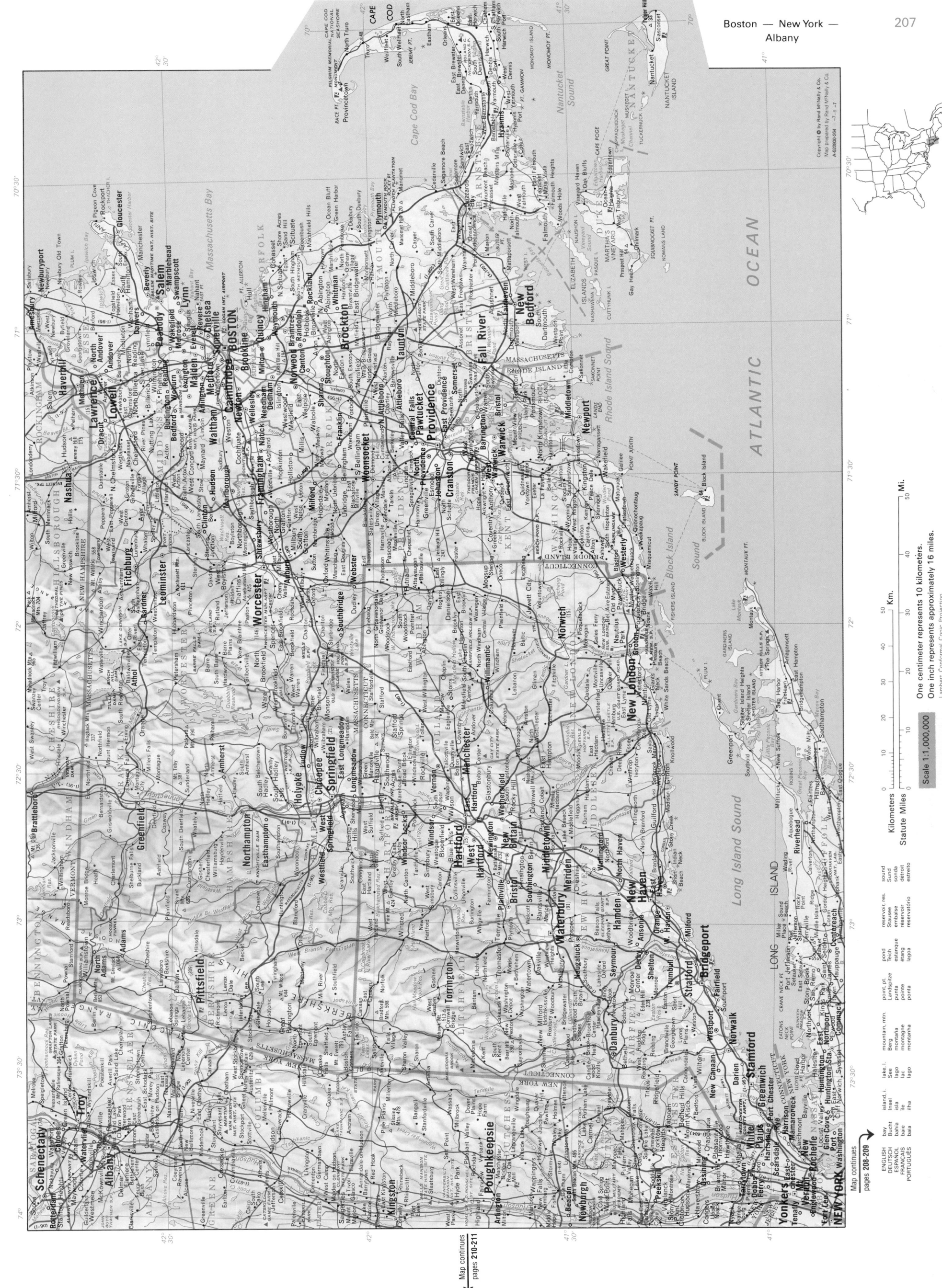

Scale 1:1,000,000

One centimeter represents 10 kilometers.
One inch represents approximately 16 miles.

Lambert Conformal Conic Projection

Map continues
pages 208-209

Map continues
pages 210-211

ENGLISH	bay	island, i.	lake, l.	mountain, mtn.	point, pt.	pond	reservoir, res.	sound
DEUTSCH	Bucht	Insel	See	Berg	Landspitze	Teich	Stausee	Sund
ESPAÑOL	bahía	isla	lago	montaña	punta	estanque	embalse	sonda
FRANÇAIS	baie	île	lac	montagne	pointe	étang	réservoir	détroit
PORTUGUÊS	baía	ilha	lago	montanha	ponta	lagoa	reservatório	estreito
Kilometers 0 10 20 30 40 50 Km.
Statute Miles 0 10 20 30 40 50 Mi.

Map continues pages 210-211

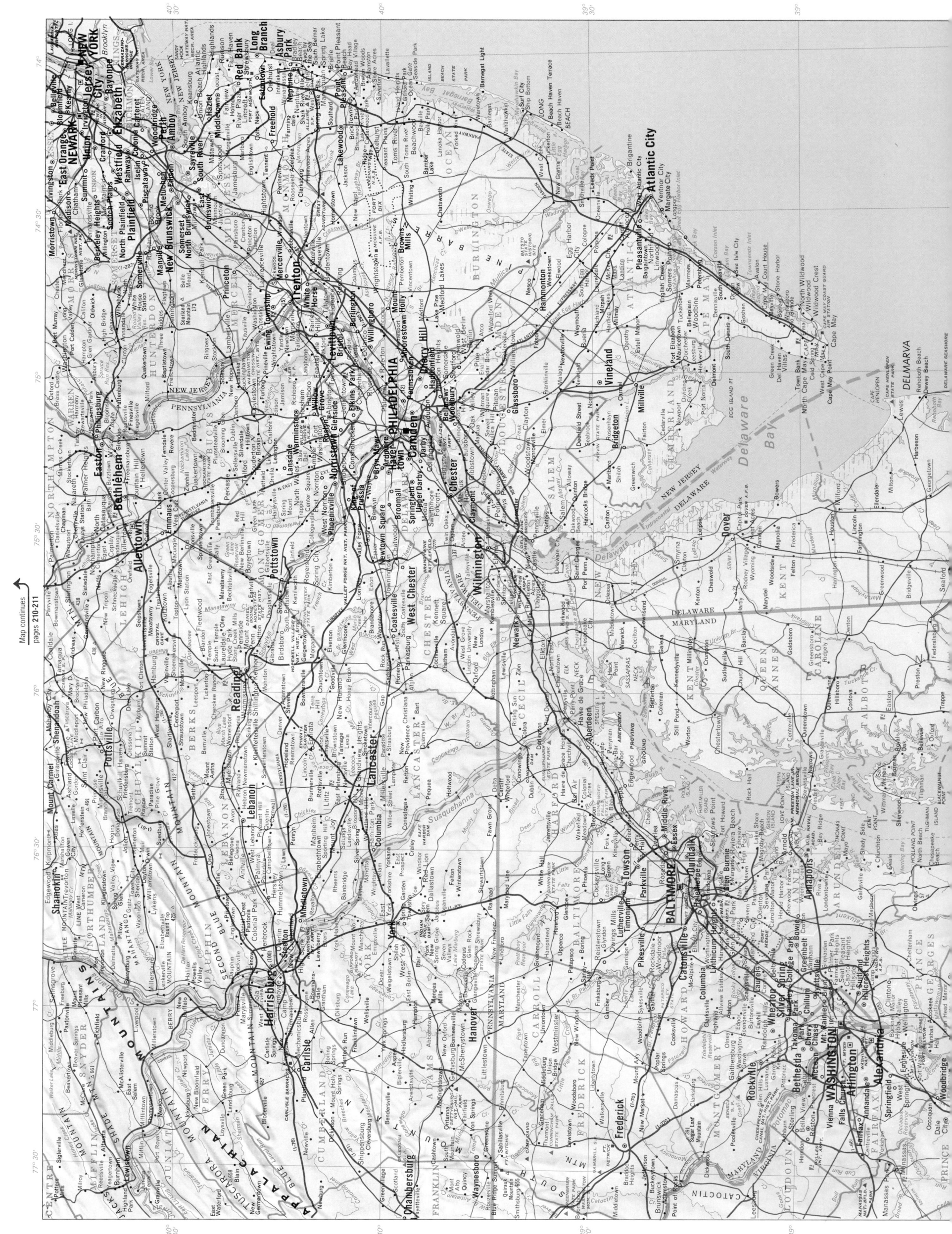
NEW YORK
NEWARK
Elizabeth
Jersey City
Trenton
Atlantic City
PHILADELPHIA
Camden
Wilmington
Allentown
Bethlehem
Reading
Lancaster
Harrisburg
York
BALTIMORE
WASHINGTON
Alexandria
Arlington
Annapolis
Dover
Vineland
Frederick
Hagerstown
Chambersburg
Delaware Bay
DELMARVA
NEW JERSEY
PENNSYLVANIA
DELAWARE
MARYLAND
VIRGINIA
APPALACHIAN
BLUE
MOUNTAIN

Scale 1:1,000,000

Kilometers
0   10   20   30   40   50   Km.

Statute Miles
0   10   20   30   40   50   Mi.

One centimeter represents 10 kilometers.
One inch represents approximately 16 miles.
Lambert Conformal Conic Projection

ENGLISH	airport, arpt.	bay	creek, cr.	inlet	island, Insel	mountain	point, pt.	reservoir, res.	state park
DEUTSCH	Flughafen	Bucht	Bach	Einfahrt	Insel	Berg	Landspitze	Stausee	Naturpark
ESPAÑOL	aeropuerto	bahía	riachuelo	abra	isla	montaña	punta	embalse	parque provincial
FRANÇAIS	aéroport	baie	ruisseau	bras de mer	île	montagne	pointe	par. régional	parc régional
PORTUGUÊS	aeroporto	baía	riacho	enseada	ilha	montanha	ponta	reservatório	parque estadual

ATLANTIC   OCEAN

PENINSULA

Chesapeake

Bay

Map continues
pages 212-213

Map continues
pages 214-215

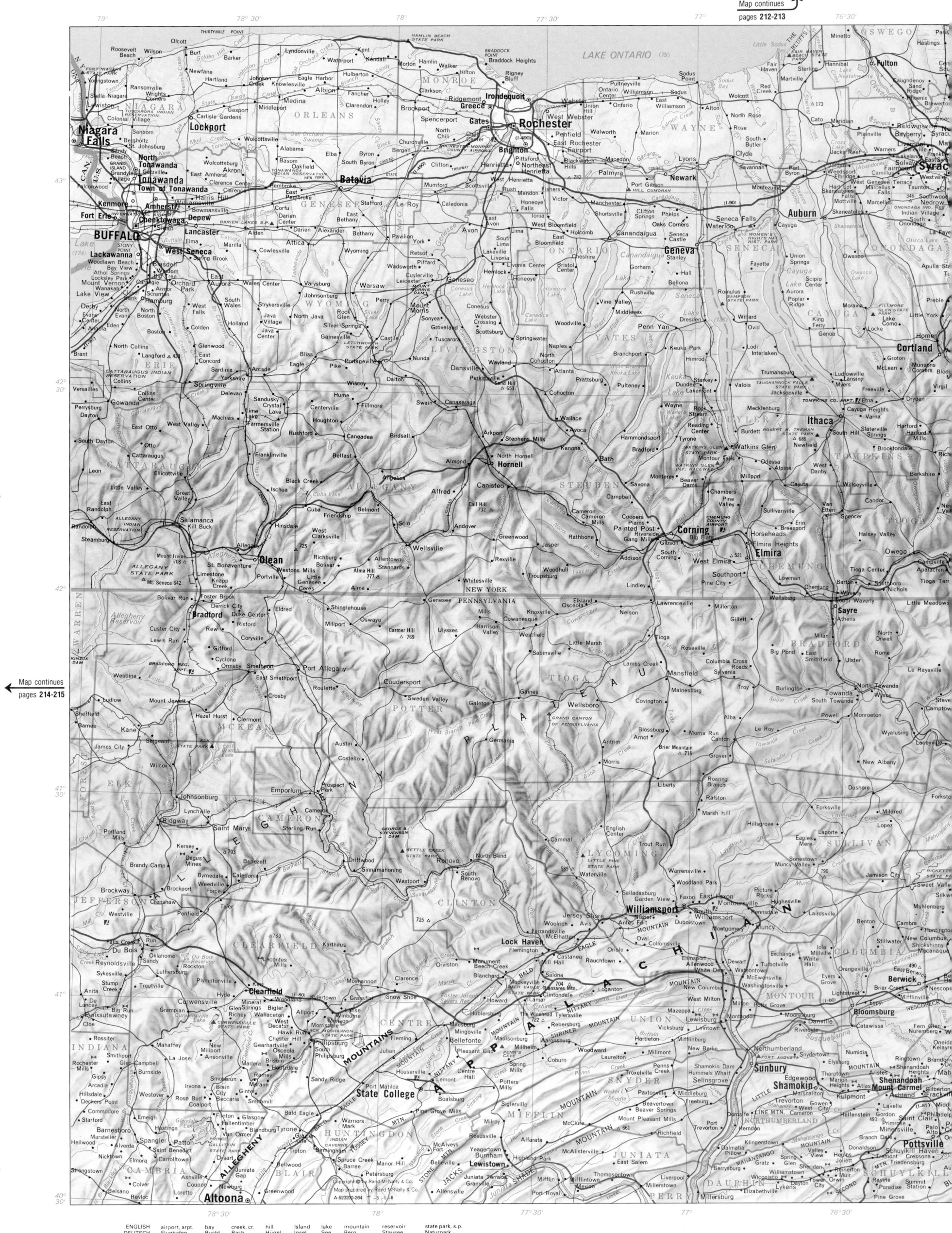

ENGLISH	airport, arpt.	bay	creek, cr.	hill	Island	lake	mountain	reservoir	state park, s.p.
DEUTSCH	Flughafen	Bucht	Bach	Hügel	Insel	See	Berg	reservoir	Naturpark
ESPAÑOL	aeropuerto	bahía	riachuelo	colina	isla	lago	montaña	embalse	parque provincial
FRANÇAIS	aéroport	baie	crique	colline	île	lac	montagne	réservoir	parc régional
PORTUGUÊS	aeroporto	baía	riacho	colina	ilha	lago	montanha	reservatório	parque estadual

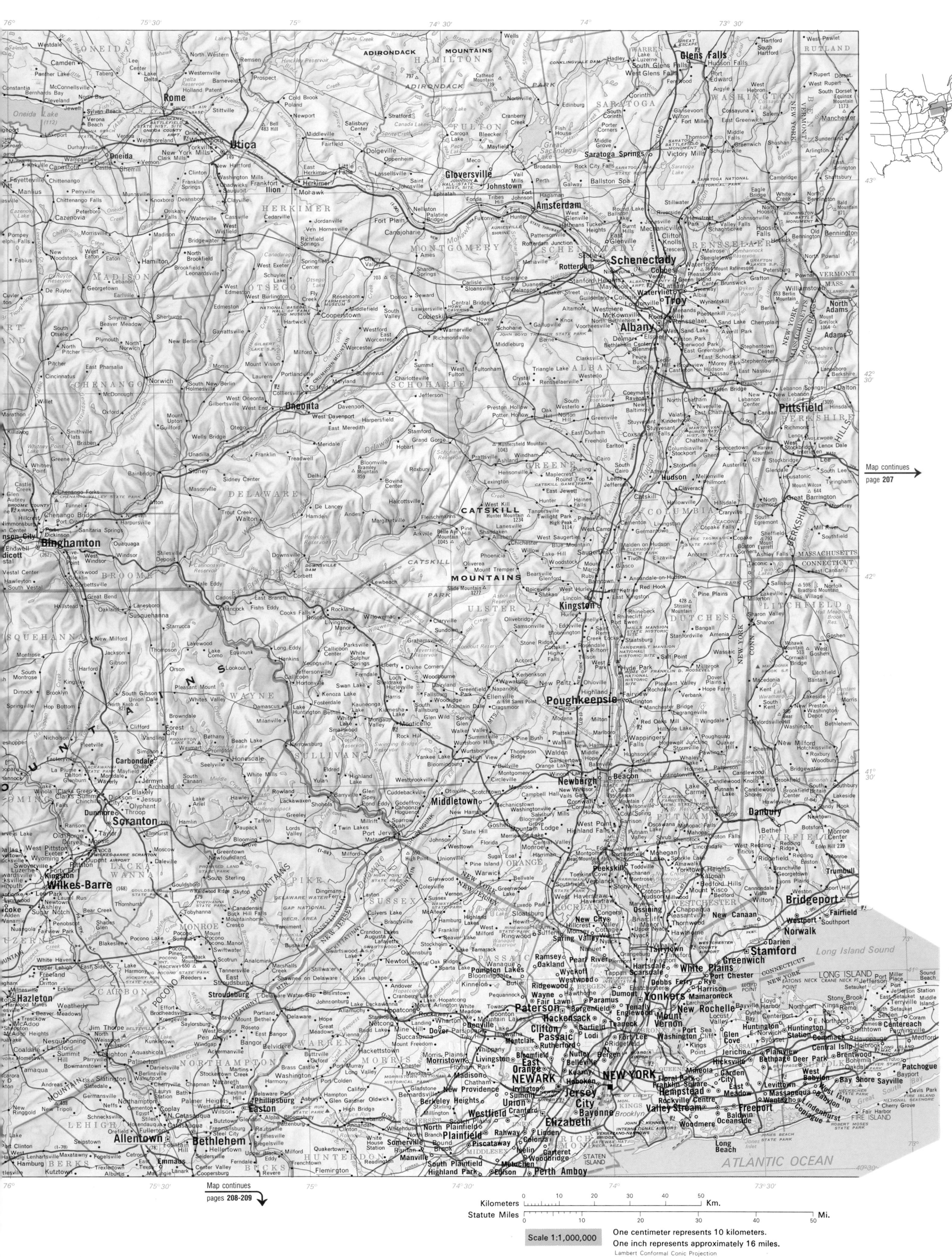

Map continues page 207 →

Map continues pages 208-209 →

Kilometers

Statute Miles

Scale 1:1,000,000

One centimeter represents 10 kilometers.
One inch represents approximately 16 miles.

Lambert Conformal Conic Projection

Map continues
pages 214-215

	ENGLISH	airport	bay	canal	channel	creek, cr.	Indian reservation	island	lake, l.	point
	DEUTSCH	Flughafen	Bucht	Kana	Kanal	Bach	Indianerreservation	Insel	See	Landspitze
	ESPAÑOL	aeropuerto	bahia	canal	canal	riachuelo	reserva de Indios	isla	lago	punta
	FRANÇAIS	aéroport	baie	canal	canal	crique	réserve indienne	île	lac	pointe
	PORTUGUÊS	aeroporto	baía	canal	canal	riacho	reserva indígena	ilha	lago	ponta

Map continues
page 206

Map continues
pages 210-211

Kilometers 0   10   20   30   40   50 Km.
Statute Miles 0   10   20   30   40   50 Mi.

Scale 1:1,000,000

One centimeter represents 10 kilometers.
One inch represents approximately 16 miles.

Lambert Conformal Conic Projection

214

Map continues
pages 216-217

Map continues
page 218

	ENGLISH	airport	creek, cr.	hill	lake, l.	mountain, mtn.	point, pt.	reservoir, res.	state park
	DEUTSCH	Flughafen	Bach	Hügel	See	Berg	Landspitze	Stausee	Naturpark
	ESPAÑOL	aeropuerto	riachuelo	colina	lago	montaña	punta	embalse	parque provincial
	FRANÇAIS	aéroport	crique	colline	lac	montagne	pointe	réservoir	parc régional
	PORTUGUÊS	aeroporto	riacho	colina	lago	montanha	ponta	reservatório	parque estadual

Copyright © by Rand McNally & Co.
Map prepared by Rand McNally & Co.
A-523500-264

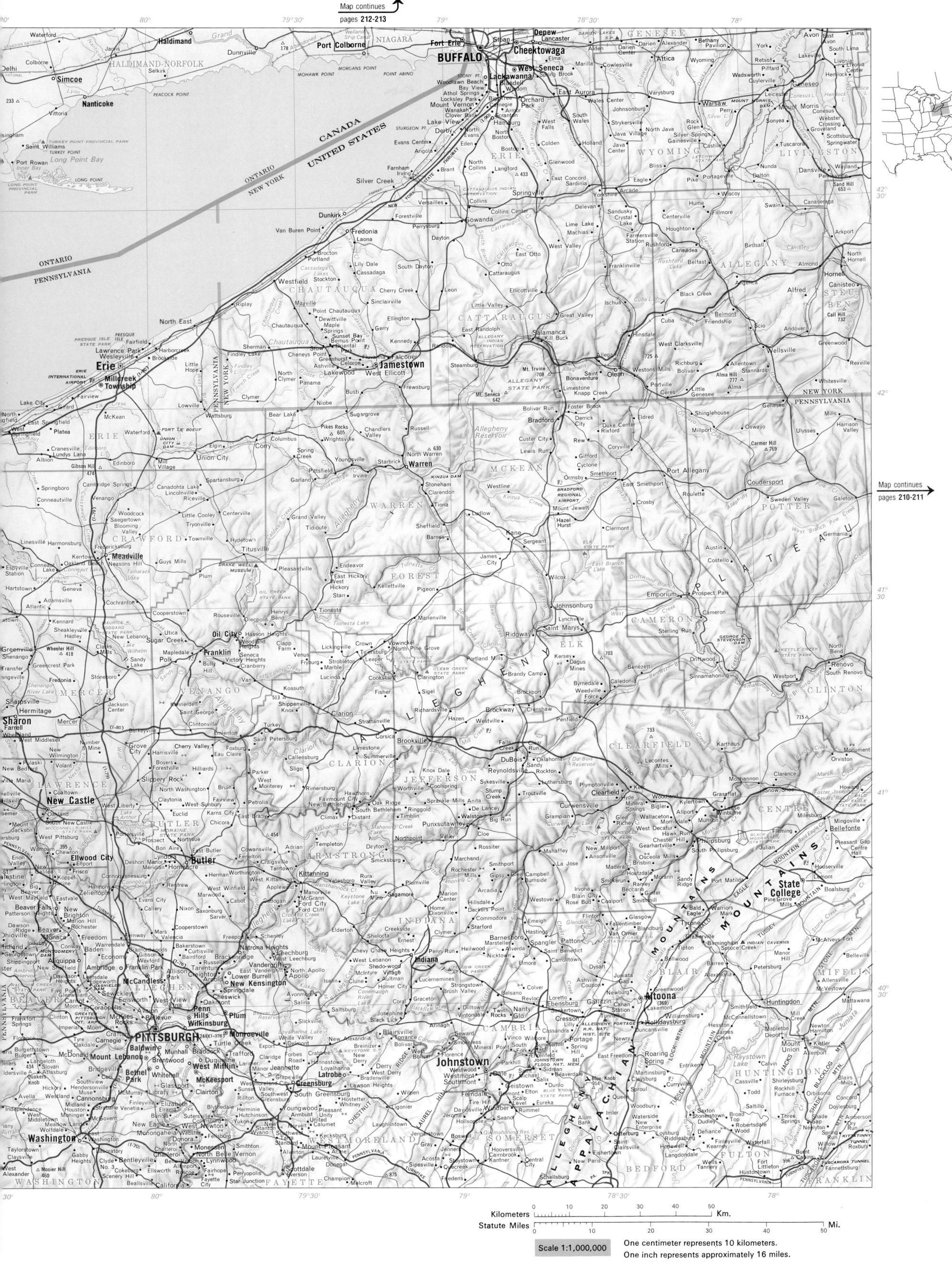

Map continues
pages 212-213

Map continues
pages 210-211

Kilometers

Statute Miles

Scale 1:1,000,000   One centimeter represents 10 kilometers.
One inch represents approximately 16 miles.
Lambert Conformal Conic Projection

ENGLISH	airport	creek, cr.	ditch	lake, l.	reservoir	state park, s.p.
DEUTSCH	Flughafen	Bach	Graben	See	Stausee	Naturpark
ESPAÑOL	aeropuerto	riachuelo	acequia	lago	embalse	parque provincial
FRANÇAIS	aéroport	crique	fossé	lac	réservoir	parc régional
PORTUGUÊS	aeroporto	riacho	fosso	lago	reservatório	parque estadual

Map continues pages 214-215

Map continues page 218

Kilometers 0 10 20 30 40 50 Km.

Statute Miles 0 10 20 30 40 50 Mi.

Scale 1:1,000,000

One centimeter represents 10 kilometers.
One inch represents approximately 16 miles.

Lambert Conformal Conic Projection

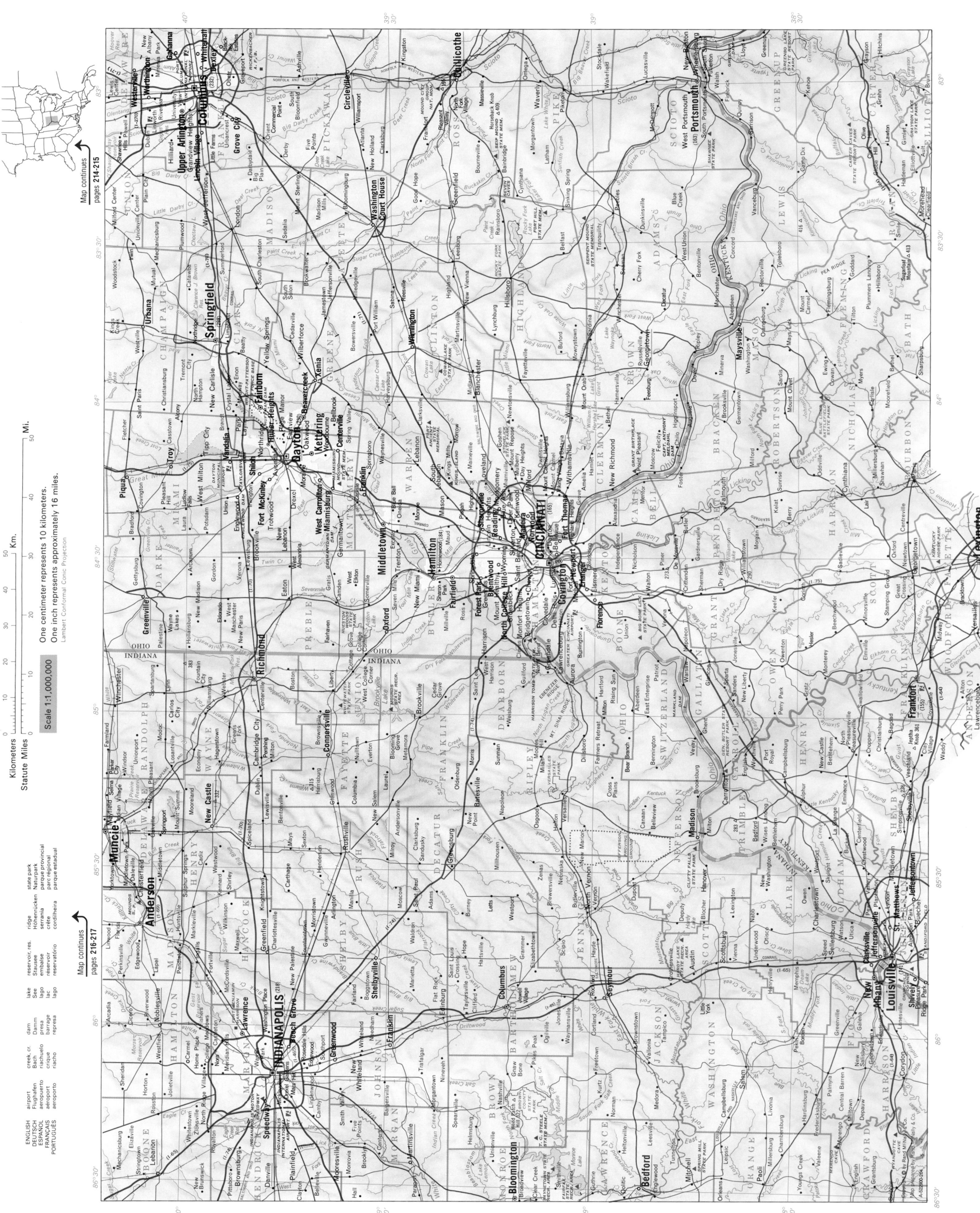

Scale 1:1,000,000

One centimeter represents 10 kilometers.
One inch represents approximately 16 miles.

Lambert Conformal Conic Projection

Map continues pages 214–215

Map continues pages 216–217

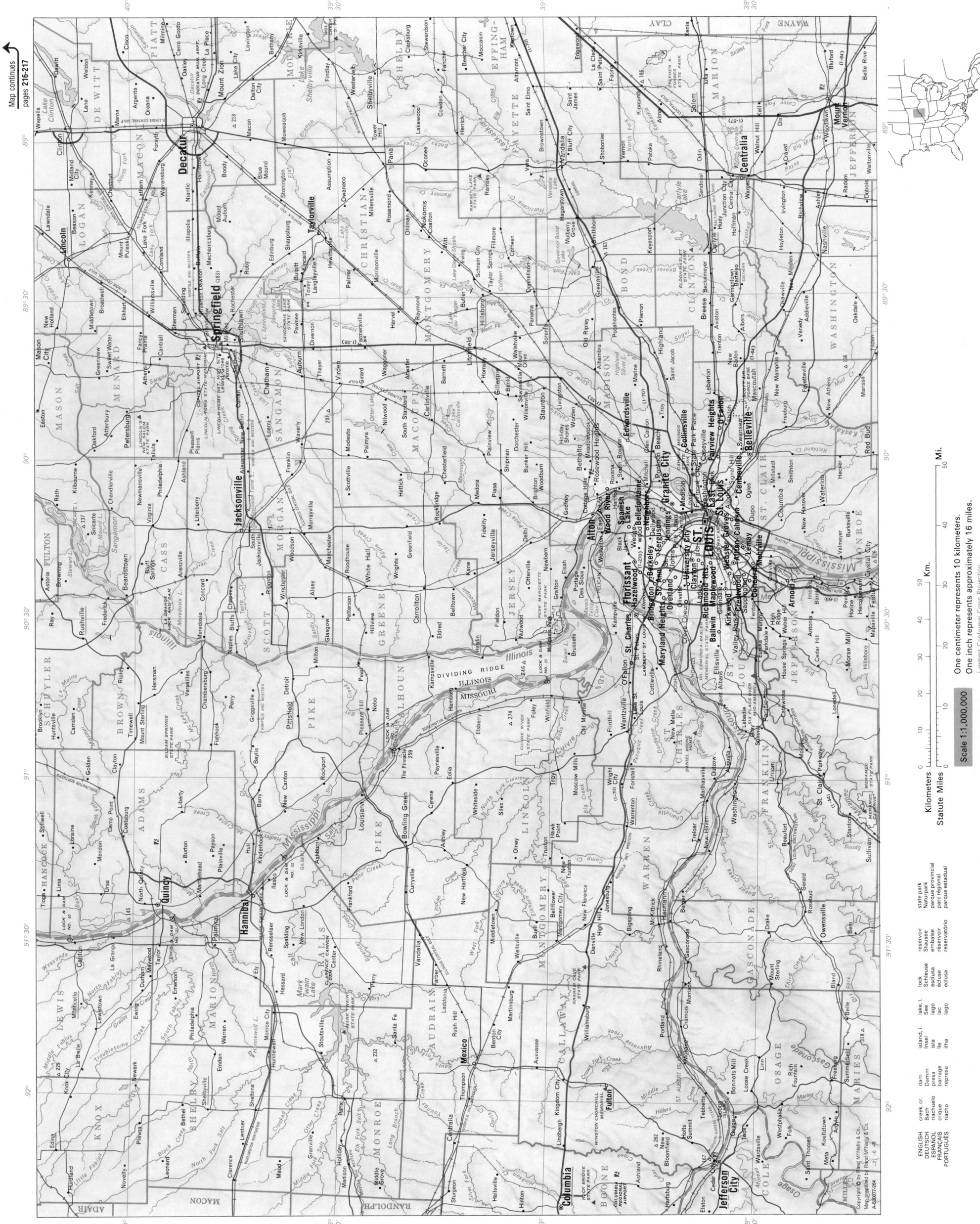

Map continues
pages 216-217

Scale 1:1,000,000

Kilometers

Statute Miles

One centimeter represents 10 kilometers.
One inch represents approximately 16 miles.

Lambert Conformal Conic Projection

ENGLISH	creek, cr.	dam	island, i.	lake, l.	lock	reservoir	state park
DEUTSCH	Bach	Damm	Insel	See			Natur-
ESPAÑOL	riachuelo	presa	isla	lago	esclusa	embalse	parque provincial
FRANÇAIS	crique	barrage	île	lac	écluse	reservoir	parc régional
PORTUGUÊS	riacho	represa	ilha	lago	eclusa	reservatório	parque estadual

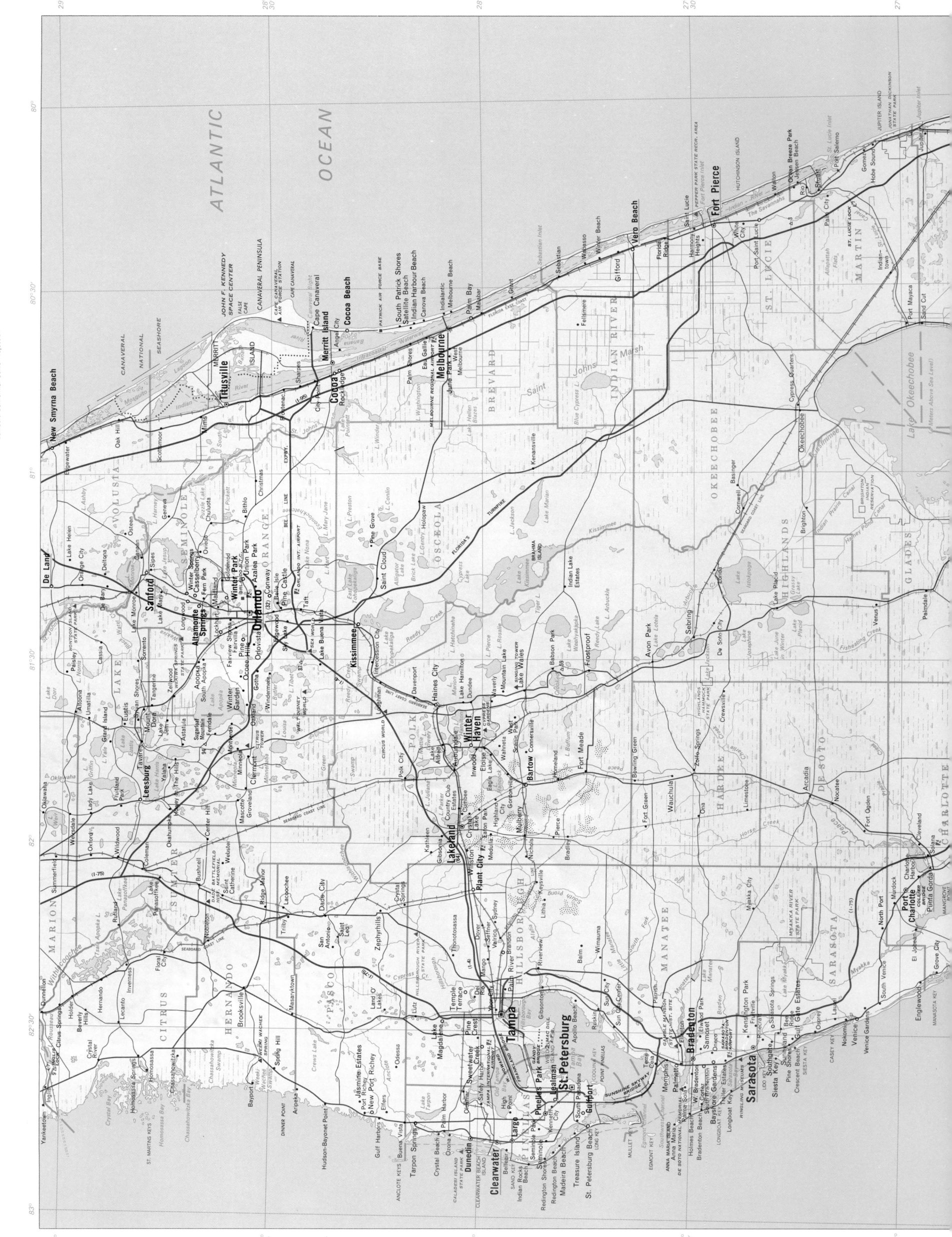

Scale 1:1,000,000
One centimeter represents 10 kilometers.
One inch represents approximately 16 miles.
Lambert Conformal Conic Projection

Riviera Beach
Palm Beach
West Palm Beach
Lake Worth
Lantana
Boynton Beach
Delray Beach
Highland Beach
Boca Raton
Deerfield Beach
Hillsboro Beach
Lighthouse Point
Pompano Beach
Lauderdale-by-the-Sea
Oakland Park
Wilton Manors
Fort Lauderdale
Hollywood
Hallandale
Golden Beach
North Miami Beach
North Miami
Bay Harbor Islands
Surfside
North Bay Village
MIAMI
Miami Beach
Key Biscayne
Coral Gables
South Miami
Kendall
Hialeah
Miami Springs
Opa-Locka
Carol City
Pembroke Pines
Miramar
Davie
Plantation
City of Sunrise
Lauderdale Lakes
North Andrews Gardens
Margate
Coral Springs
Pompano Beach Highlands
Westwood Lakes
Olympia Heights
Sweetwater
Richmond Heights
South Miami Heights
Perrine
Cutler Ridge
Goulds
Naranja
Leisure City
Homestead
Florida City
Key Largo
Tavernier
Plantation
Islamorada
Marathon
Big Pine Key
Stock Island
Key West
Flamingo
Belle Glade
South Bay
Lake Harbor
Clewiston
Harlem
La Belle
Immokalee
Felda
Corkscrew
Alva
Fort Myers Shores
Lehigh Acres
Fort Myers
Tice
Tanglewood
North Fort Myers
Fort Myers Villas
Cape Coral
Estero
Bonita Springs
Fort Myers Beach
Sanibel
Captiva
Saint James City
Bokeelia
Pineland
Matlacha
Boca Grande
Naples Park
North Naples
Naples
East Naples
Golden Gate
Marco
Goodland
Everglades City
Chokoloskee
Copeland
Ochopee
Monroe
PALM BEACH
BROWARD
DADE
HENDRY
COLLIER
MONROE
LEE
The Everglades
Big Cypress Swamp
Corkscrew Swamp
BIG CYPRESS NATIONAL PRESERVE
EVERGLADES NATIONAL PARK
BISCAYNE NATIONAL PARK
TAMIAMI TRAIL
Florida Bay
Biscayne Bay
CAPE SABLE
FLORIDA KEYS
TEN THOUSAND ISLANDS
GULF OF MEXICO
MARQUESAS KEYS
DRY TORTUGAS NATIONAL PARK
SEVENMILE BRIDGE
81°
80°30'
82°30'
26°
26° 30'
25° 30'
25°

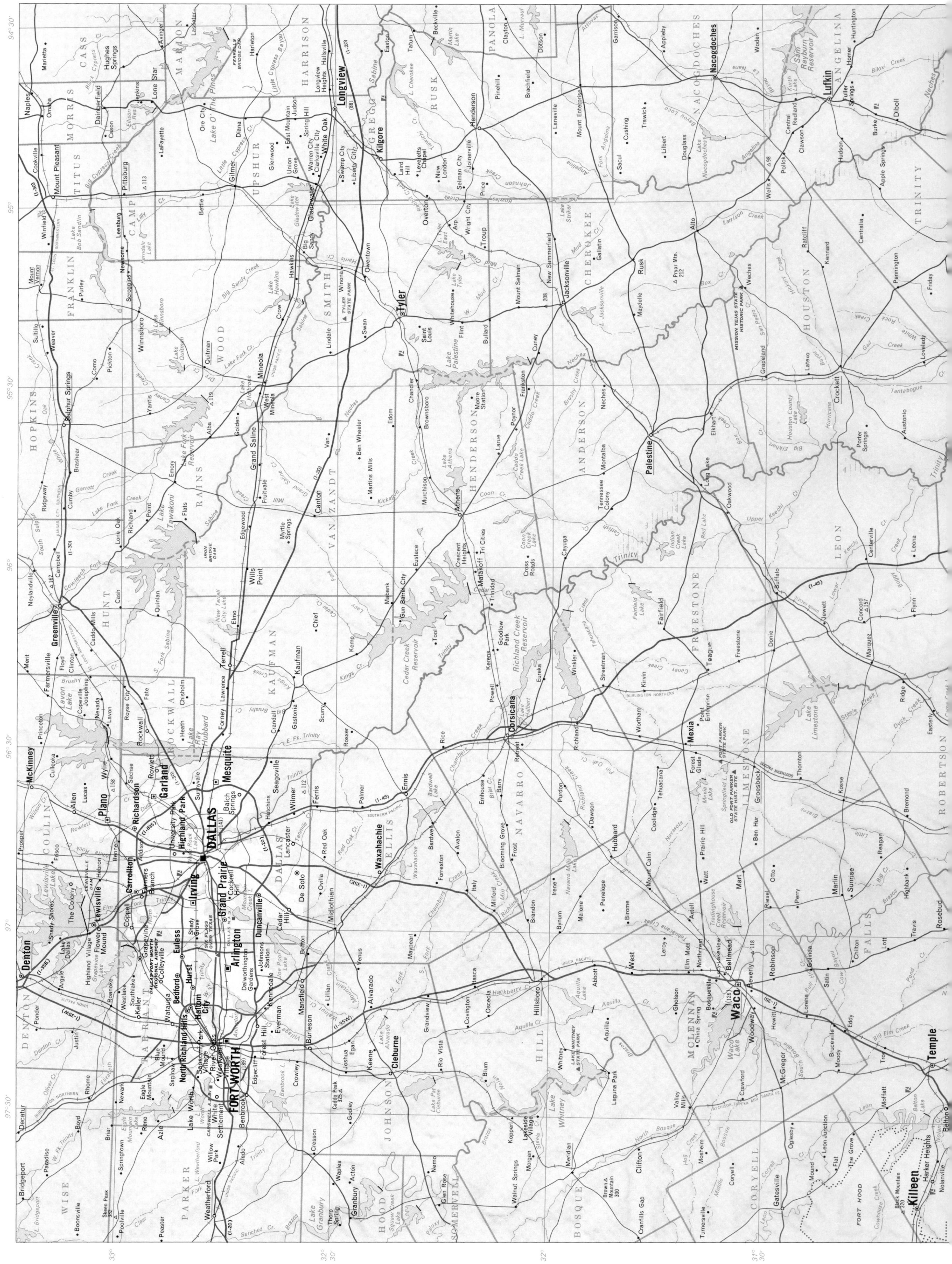
DALLAS
FORT WORTH
Waco
Tyler
Longview
Temple
Killeen
Denton
McKinney
Plano
Garland
Mesquite
Irving
Grand Prairie
Arlington
Richardson
Carrollton
Lewisville
Greenville
Sulphur Springs
Mount Pleasant
Palestine
Corsicana
Athens
Jacksonville
Nacogdoches
Lufkin
Kilgore
Henderson
Waxahachie
Ennis
Cleburne
Hillsboro
Mexia
Terrell
Kaufman
Canton
Crockett
Fairfield
Weatherford
Granbury
Mineola
Gilmer
Pittsburg
Daingerfield
Rusk
Marlin
Belton
Gatesville
Lake Whitney
Richland Creek Reservoir
Cedar Creek Reservoir
Lake Palestine
Lake Tawakoni
Lake Fork Reservoir
Lake Limestone
Lake O' The Pines
Sam Rayburn Reservoir
Trinity
Brazos
Neches
Sabine
DENTON
COLLIN
HUNT
HOPKINS
FRANKLIN
TITUS
MORRIS
CASS
MARION
HARRISON
UPSHUR
CAMP
WOOD
RAINS
ROCKWALL
KAUFMAN
VAN ZANDT
SMITH
GREGG
RUSK
PANOLA
NACOGDOCHES
CHEROKEE
HENDERSON
ANDERSON
HOUSTON
ANGELINA
TRINITY
LEON
FREESTONE
NAVARRO
ELLIS
DALLAS
TARRANT
PARKER
WISE
JOHNSON
HILL
LIMESTONE
ROBERTSON
FALLS
MCLENNAN
BOSQUE
CORYELL
HOOD
SOMERVELL
BELL

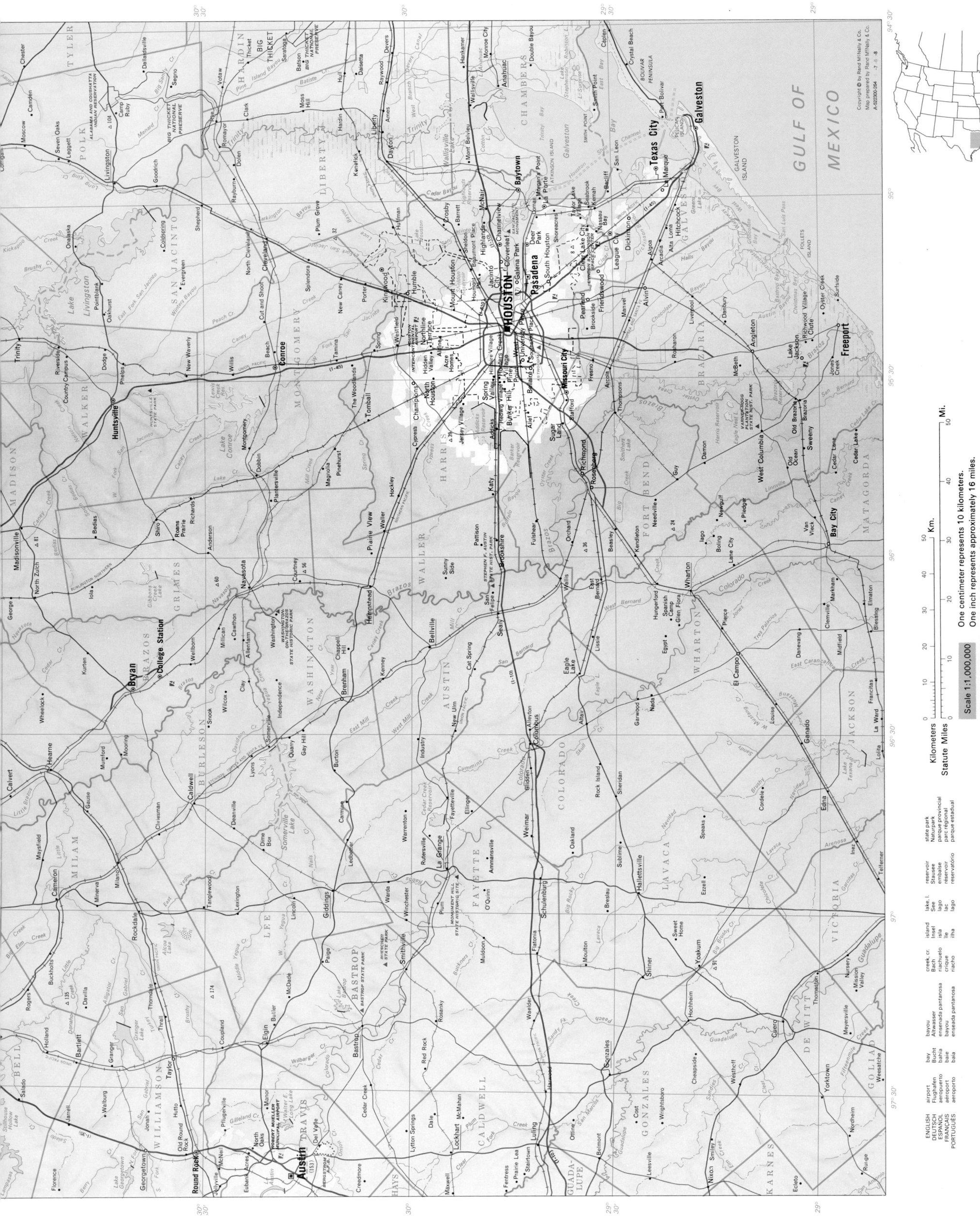

GULF OF MEXICO

Scale 1:1,000,000

One centimeter represents 10 kilometers.
One inch represents approximately 16 miles.
Lambert Conformal Conic Projection

ENGLISH	airport	bay	bayou	creek, cr.	island
DEUTSCH	Flughafen	Bucht	Bucht	Bach	Insel
ESPAÑOL	aeropuerto	bahía	ensenada pantanosa	riachuelo	isla
FRANÇAIS	aéroport	baie	bayou	crique	île
PORTUGUÊS	aeroporto	baía	enseada pantanosa	riacho	ilha

lake, l.	reservoir	state park
See	Stausee	Naturpark
lago	embalse	parque provincial
lac	réservoir	parc régional
lago	reservatório	parque estadual

VANCOUVER
Burnaby
North Vancouver
New Westminster
Richmond
Surrey
Delta
Coquitlam
Port Coquitlam
Maple Ridge
Mission
Matsqui
Abbotsford
Chilliwack
White Rock
Blaine
Bellingham
Mount Vernon
Anacortes
Everett
Lynnwood
Edmonds
SEATTLE
Bellevue
Kirkland
Redmond
Renton
Mercer Island
Federal Way
Auburn
Kent
Tacoma
Puyallup
Lakes District
University Place
Bremerton
Port Angeles
Port Townsend
Victoria
Esquimalt
Oak Bay
Sidney
Nanaimo
Ladysmith
Duncan
Port Alberni
CANADA
UNITED STATES
BRITISH COLUMBIA
WASHINGTON
Strait of Georgia
Strait of Juan de Fuca
Haro Strait
Puget Sound
VANCOUVER ISLAND
VANCOUVER ISLAND RANGES
OLYMPIC MOUNTAINS
OLYMPIC NATIONAL PARK
CASCADE MOUNTAINS
NORTH CASCADES NATIONAL PARK
WHATCOM
SKAGIT
SNOHOMISH
KING
CHELAN
MASON
JEFFERSON
CLALLAM
GRAYS HARBOR
SAN JUAN ISLANDS
WHIDBEY ISLAND
SEYMOUR RANGE
WENATCHEE MOUNTAINS
MANNING PROVINCIAL PARK

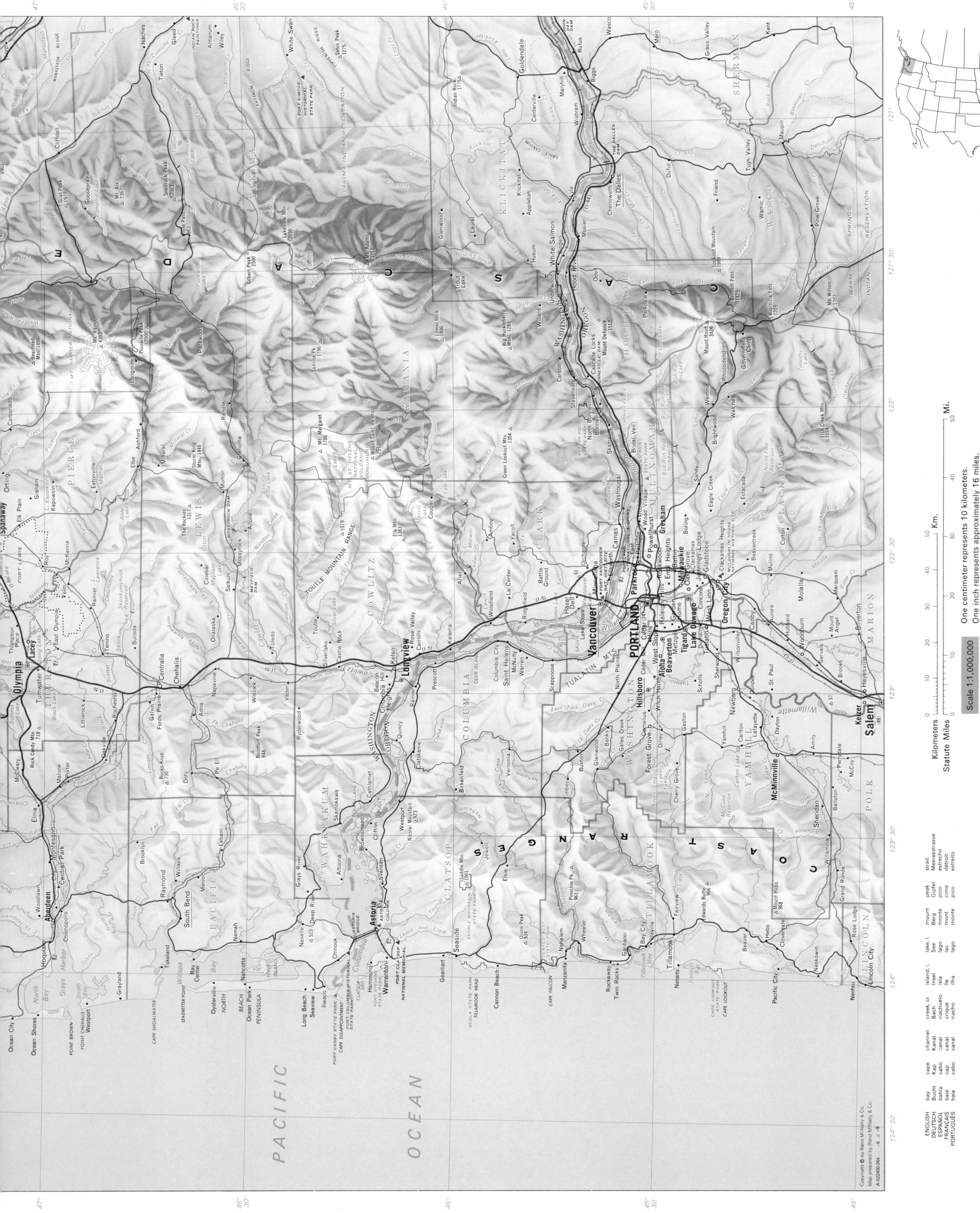

Scale 1:1,000,000

Kilometers

Statute Miles

One centimeter represents 10 kilometers.
One inch represents approximately 16 miles.
Lambert Conformal Conic Projection

Km.

Mi.

ENGLISH	bay	cape	channel	creek, cr.	island, i.	lake, l.	mount	peak	strait
DEUTSCH	Bucht	Kap	Kanal	Bach	Insel	See	Berg	Gipfel	Meeresstrasse
ESPAÑOL	bahía	cabo	canal	riachuelo	isla	lago	monte	pico	estrecho
FRANÇAIS	baie	cap	canal	crique	île	lac	monte	cime	détroit
PORTUGUÊS	baía	cabo	canal	riacho	ilha	lago	monte	pico	estreito

SIERRA NEVADA
SACRAMENTO VALLEY
CARSON RANGE
PINE NUT MOUNTAINS
SWEETWATER MTS.
CATHEDRAL RANGE
DESERT MTS.
Reno
Sparks
Carson City
Sacramento
Stockton
Modesto
Oakland
San Francisco
Berkeley
Richmond
Vallejo
Santa Rosa
Napa
Fairfield
Vacaville
Davis
Woodland
Yuba City
Marysville
Oroville
Roseville
Lodi
Tracy
Manteca
Livermore
Hayward
Fremont
Concord
Antioch
Pittsburg
Placerville
Auburn
Truckee
South Lake Tahoe
Lake Tahoe
Yosemite National Park
Turlock
Daly City
San Mateo
Palo Alto
Milpitas
39°30'
39°
38°30'
38°
37°30'
119°30'
120°
120°30'
121°
121°30'
122°
122°30'

Map continues page 228

Scale 1:1,000,000

Kilometers

Statute Miles

One centimeter represents 10 kilometers.
One inch represents approximately 16 miles.
Lambert Conformal Conic Projection

Km.

Mi.

ENGLISH
DEUTSCH
ESPAÑOL
FRANÇAIS
PORTUGUÊS

bay
Bucht
bahía
baie
baía

creek, cr.
Bach
riachuelo
crique
riacho

canal
Kanal
canal
canal
canal

lake, l.
See
lago
lac
lago

mountain, mtn.
Berg
montaña
montagne
montanha

pass
Pass
paso
col
passo

range
Gebirge
sierra
chaîne
serra

reservoir
Stausee
embalse
réservoir
reservatório

slough
verlandete Wasserfläche
pantano
fondrière
pântano

PACIFIC OCEAN

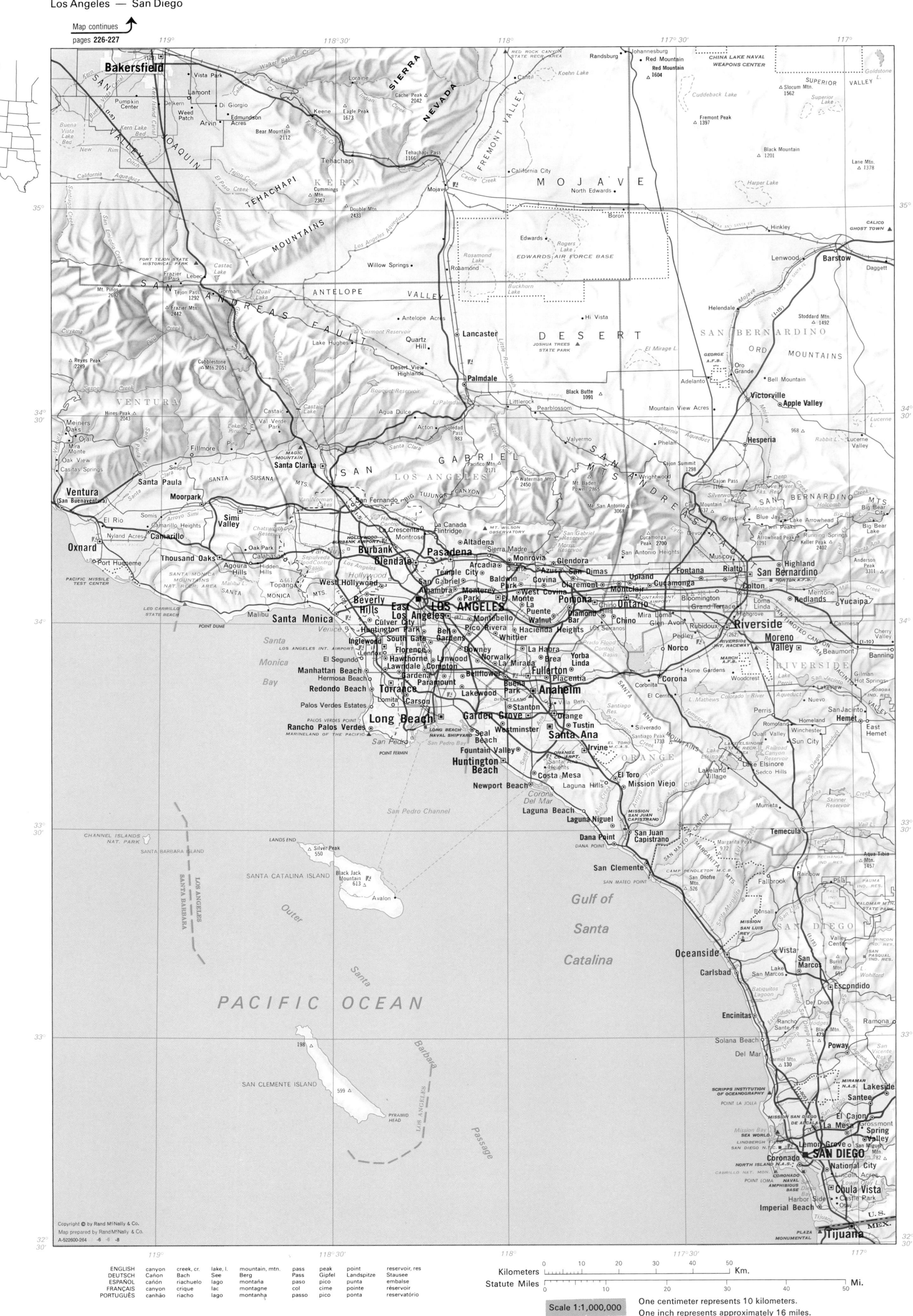

Map continues
pages 226-227

ENGLISH	canyon	creek, cr.	lake, l.	mountain, mtn.	pass	peak	point	reservoir, res
DEUTSCH	Cañon	Bach	See	Berg	Pass	Gipfel	Landspitze	Stausee
ESPAÑOL	cañón	riachuelo	lago	montaña	paso	pico	punta	embalse
FRANÇAIS	canyon	crique	lac	montagne	col	cime	pointe	réservoir
PORTUGUÊS	canhão	riacho	lago	montanha	passo	pico	ponta	reservatório

Copyright © by Rand McNally & Co.
Map prepared by Rand McNally & Co.
A-522600-264   -6   -8

Kilometers 0 10 20 30 40 50 Km.
Statute Miles 0 10 20 30 40 50 Mi.

Scale 1:1,000,000
One centimeter represents 10 kilometers.
One inch represents approximately 16 miles.
Lambert Conformal Conic Projection

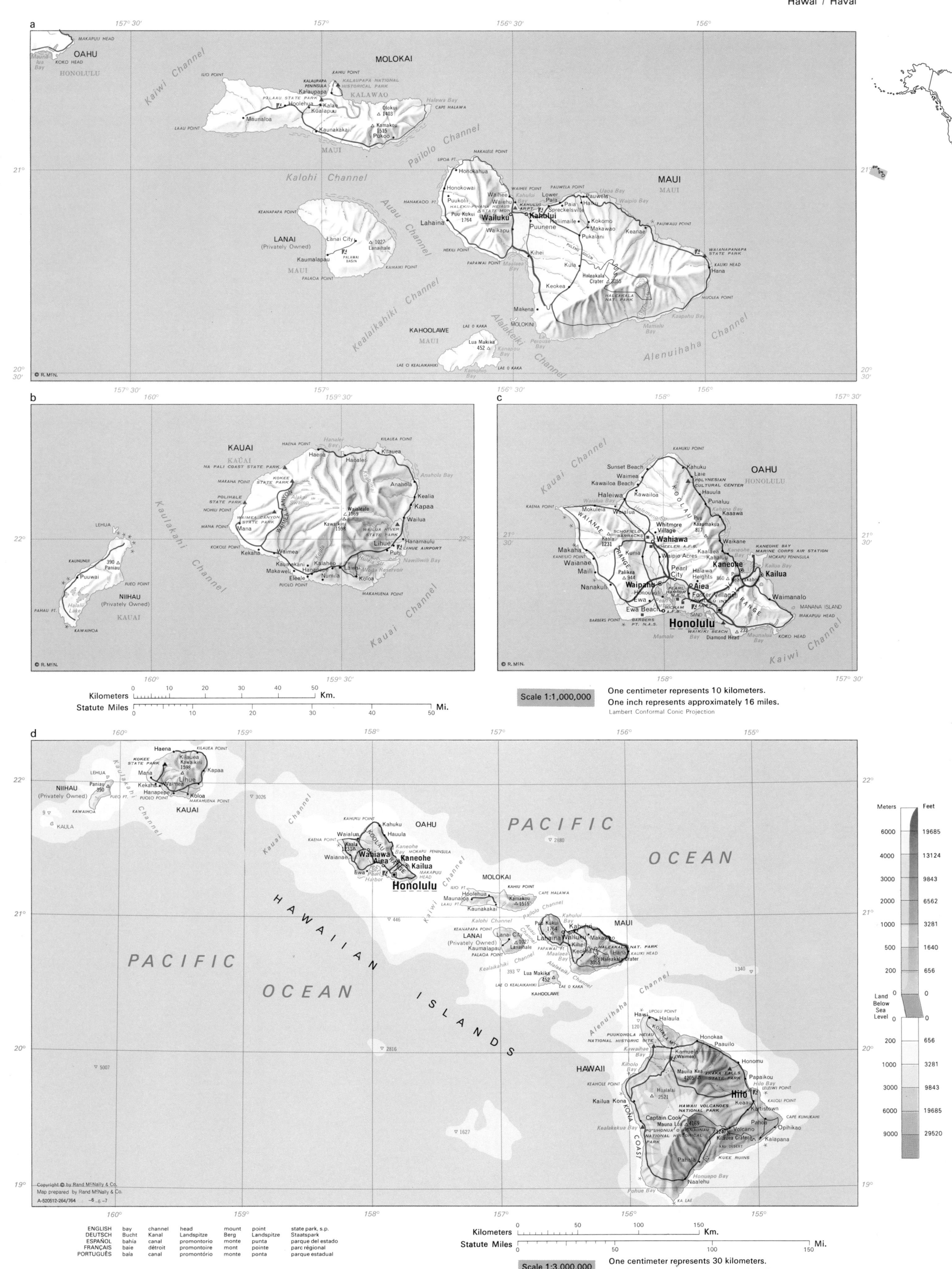

a

OAHU
MAKAPUU HEAD
KOKO HEAD
HONOLULU
Mamala Bay

MOLOKAI
KAHIU POINT
KALAUPAPA PENINSULA
KALAUPAPA NATIONAL HISTORICAL PARK
KALAWAO
PALAAU STATE PARK
Kalaupapa
Kalae
Hoolehua
Kualapuu
Olokui △1403
Kamakou △1515
Pukoo
Maunaloa
Kaunakakai
Halawa Bay
CAPE HALAWA
LAAU POINT
MAUI
Kalohi Channel
Pailolo Channel

LANAI
(Privately Owned)
KEANAPAPA POINT
Lanai City
△1027 Lanaihale
Kaumalapau
PALAWAI BASIN
KAMAIKI POINT
PALAOA POINT

LIPOA PT.
NAKALELE POINT
Honokohua
Honokowai
Puukolii
Kaanapali
Lahaina
HANAKAOO PT.
Waihee
Puukoli
Waihee
Waiehu
WAIHEE POINT
Kahului
KAHULUI ARPT.
Wailuku
Kahului
Waikapu
Puunene
Kihei
Spreckelsville
Haliimaile
Makawao
Keanae
Kula
Keokea
Haleakala Crater △3055
HALEAKALA NAT. PARK
Makena
MOLOKINI
PAUWELA POINT
Ulua Bay
Waipio Bay
Paia
Haiku
Kokomo
Pukalani
PAUWALU POINT
MAUI
WAIANAPANAPA STATE PARK
KAUIKI HEAD
Hana
MUOLEA POINT
Kaapohu Bay
Manalo Bay

Maalaea Bay
HEKILI POINT
PAPAWAI POINT
PUU OLAI

KAHOOLAWE
MAUI
LAE O KAKA
Lua Makika 452 △
KANAPOU Bay
LAE O KEALAIKAHIKI
Kamohio Bay
LAE O KAKA

Alalakeiki Channel
Kealaikahiki Channel
Auau Channel
Kaiwi Channel
Alenuihaha Channel

b

KAUAI
KAUAI
HAENA POINT
KILAUEA POINT
Hanalei Bay
NA PALI COAST STATE PARK
Haena
Hanalei
Kilauea
MAKAHA POINT
KOKEE STATE PARK
Anahola
Kealia
Kapaa
Wailua
POLIHALE STATE PARK
NOHILI POINT
WAIMEA CANYON STATE PARK
Waialeale △1569
Kawaikini △1598
WAILUA RIVER STATE PARK
Lihue
Hanamaulu
Mana
LIHUE AIRPORT
Nawiliwili Bay
MANA POINT
Kekaha
Waimea
Kaumakani
Kalaheo
Kalapaki
Lawai
Koloa
Hanapepe
Eleele
Numila
Waita Reservoir
KOKOLE POINT
PUOLO POINT
MAKAHUENA POINT

LEHUA
KAUNUUI
390 △ Paniau
Puuwai
NIIHAU
(Privately Owned)
Halalii Lake
PAHAU PT.
KAWAIHOA
FUTO POINT
KAUAI

Kaulakahi Channel
Kauai Channel

c

OAHU
HONOLULU
KAHUKU POINT
Sunset Beach
Waimea
Kawailoa Beach
Haleiwa
Kawailoa
Kahuku
Laie
POLYNESIAN CULTURAL CENTER
Haula
KAENA POINT
Mokuleia
Waialua
Punaluu
KOOLAU RANGE
Whitmore Village
Wahiawa
WHEELER A.F.B.
SCHOFIELD BARRACKS
△1231
Waikane
Kaaawa
Kahana Bay
WAIANAE RANGE
Makaha
KAENA POINT
Waianae
Maili
Nanakuli
Kumia
Waipio Acres
Kaalaea
Kaneohe Bay
MARINE CORPS AIR STATION
MOKAPU PENINSULA
Kaneohe
KANEOHE POINT
△944
Waipahu
Pearl City
Halawa Heights
860 △
Kailua
Kalihi
Aiea
Foster Village
Pearl Harbor
HICKAM A.F.B.
Ewa
Waimanalo
Waipio
Palikea △1231
Waikiki Beach
△33
MANANA ISLAND
MAKAPUU HEAD
Ewa Beach
BARBERS POINT N.A.S.
Honolulu
SAND I.
Diamond Head
KOKO HEAD
Mamala Bay
Maunalua Bay

Kaiwi Channel
Kauai Channel

Scale 1:1,000,000
One centimeter represents 10 kilometers.
One inch represents approximately 16 miles.
Lambert Conformal Conic Projection

Kilometers 0 10 20 30 40 50 Km.
Statute Miles 0 10 20 30 40 50 Mi.

© R. MEN.

d

NIIHAU
(Privately Owned)
LEHUA
Paniau 390
KAWAIHOA
KAULA
Haena
KOKEE STATE PARK
Kilauea
Kawaikini △1598
KILAUEA POINT
Kapaa
Mana
Kekaha Waimea Lihue
Hanapepe Koloa
PUOLO POINT
KAUAI
MAKAHUENA POINT
▽3026

PACIFIC
OCEAN

PACIFIC
OCEAN

HAWAIIAN ISLANDS

OAHU
KAHUKU POINT
Waialua
Kahuku
Hauula
KAENA POINT
KOOLAU RANGE
Kaneohe Bay
Wahiawa
Aiea
Kaneohe
Kailua
Waianae
Ewa
Pearl Harbor
Honolulu
MOKAPU PENINSULA
MAKAPUU HEAD
▽2880
▽446

MOLOKAI
ILIO PT.
KAHIU POINT
CAPE HALAWA
Hoolehua
Kamakou △1515
Maunaloa
Kaunakakai
Kalohi Channel
Pailolo Channel

LANAI
(Privately Owned)
Lanai City
△1027 Lanaihale
Kaumalapau
Puu Kukui △1764
Kahului
Wailuku
Makawao
MAUI
HALEAKALA NAT. PARK
Lahaina
Haleakala Crater △3055
Kula
Keokea
PAPAWAI POINT
Maalaea Bay
Lua Makika 452 △
KAHOOLAWE
LAE O KEALAIKAHIKI
LAE O KAKA
▽393
KEANAPAPA POINT

Kaulakahi Channel
Kauai Channel
Alenuihaha Channel

▽5007
▽2816
▽1627

UPOLU POINT
Hawi
Halaula
PUUKOHOLA HEIAU NATIONAL HISTORIC SITE
KOHALA MTS.
▽120
Honokaa
Paauilo
Kawaihae Bay
Kamuela (Waimea)
Honomu
Mauna Kea △4205
AKAKA FALLS STATE PARK
Papaikou
KEAHOLE POINT
Hilo
Hualalai △2521
Kiholo Bay
Hilo Bay
LELEIWI POINT
Kailua Kona
HAWAII VOLCANOES NATIONAL PARK
Keaau
Mauna Loa △4169
KEALAKEKUA BAY
Captain Cook
PUUHONUA O HONAUNAU NATIONAL HISTORICAL
Kurtistown
Volcano
Pahoa
Kilauea Crater
KAPOHO
CAPE KUMUKAHI
Opihikao
KUEE RUINS
KONA COAST
Pahala
Naalehu
KA LAE
HAWAII
Honuapo Bay
Pohue Bay
▽1340

Copyright © by Rand McNally & Co.
Map prepared by Rand McNally & Co.
A-520512-264/764 —6—.6—7

ENGLISH	bay	channel	head	mount	point	state park, s.p.
DEUTSCH	Bucht	Kanal	Landspitze	Berg	Landspitze	Staatspark
ESPAÑOL	bahía	canal	promontorio	monte	punta	parque del estado
FRANÇAIS	baie	détroit	promontoire	mont	pointe	parc régional
PORTUGUÊS	baía	canal	promontório	monte	ponta	parque estadual

Kilometers 0 50 100 150 Km.
Statute Miles 0 50 100 150 Mi.

Scale 1:3,000,000
One centimeter represents 30 kilometers.
One inch represents approximately 47 miles.
Lambert Conformal Conic Projection

Meters	Feet
6000	19685
4000	13124
3000	9843
2000	6562
1000	3281
500	1640
200	656
0	0
Land Below Sea Level	
0	0
200	656
1000	3281
3000	9843
6000	19685
9000	29520

Middle America / Mittelamerika / México, Centroamérica y Las Antillas
Mexique, Amérique Centrale et Région des Caraïbes / México, América Central e Antilhas

Map continues
pages **178-179**

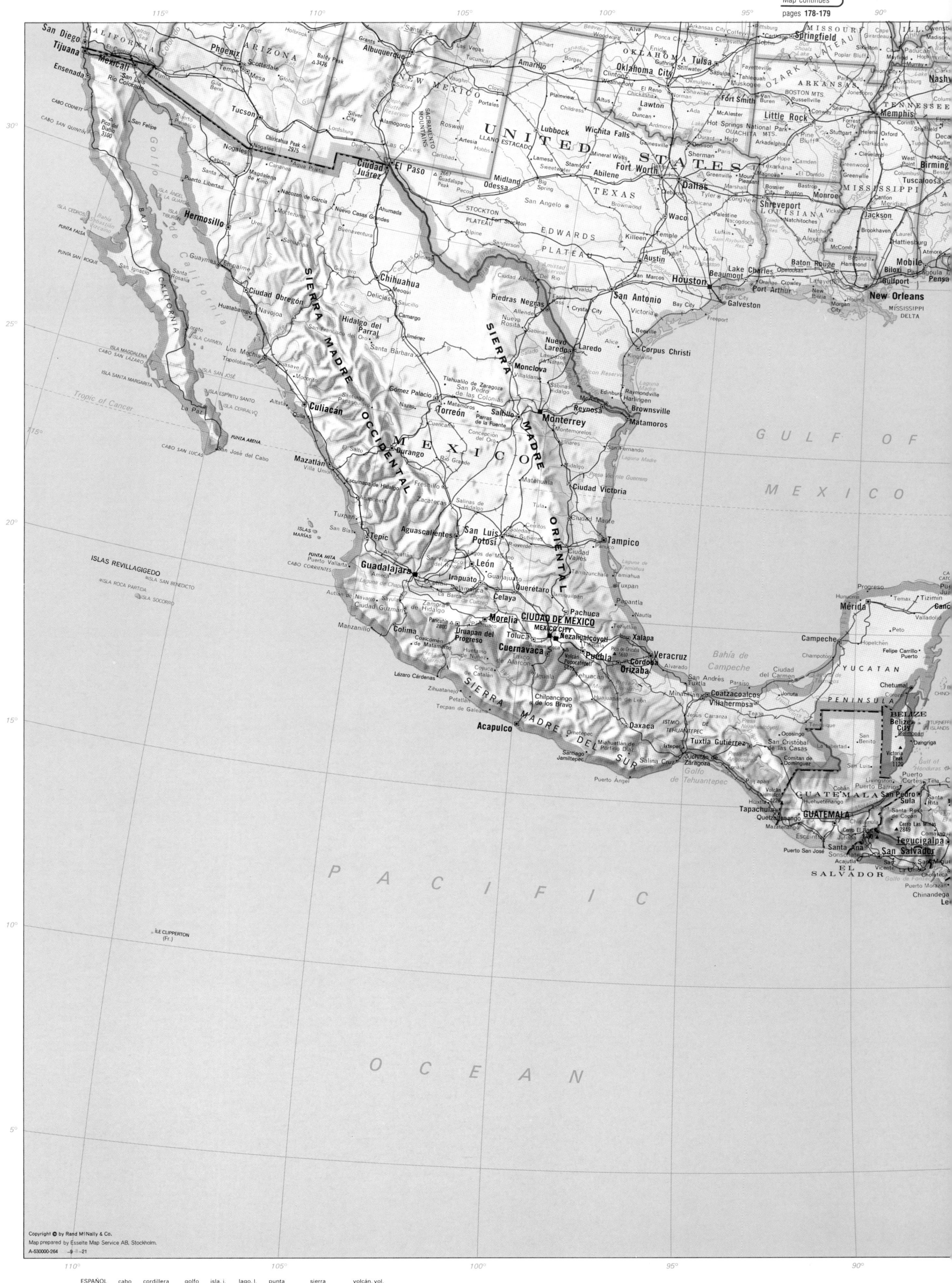

Copyright © by Rand McNally & Co.
Map prepared by Esselte Map Service AB, Stockholm.
A-530000-264

ESPAÑOL	cabo	cordillera	golfo	isla, i.	lago, l.	punta	sierra	volcán, vol.
ENGLISH	cape	mountains	gulf	island	lake	point	mountains	volcano
DEUTSCH	Kap	Berge	Golf	Insel	See	Landspitze	Berge	Vulkan
FRANÇAIS	cap	montagnes	golfe	île	lac	pointe	montagnes	volcan
PORTUGUÊS	cabo	cordilheira	golfo	ilha	lago	ponta	serra	vulcão

Middle America / Mittelamerika / México, Centroamérica y Las Antillas
Mexique, Amérique Centrale et Région des Caraïbes / México, América Central e Antilhas

231

Map continues
pages 242-243

Kilometers

Statute Miles

Scale 1:12,000,000

One centimeter represents 120 kilometers.
One inch represents approximately 190 miles.
Oblique Conic Conformal Projection

ESPAÑOL   bahía   cerro   isla   laguna   presa   punta   río   sierra
ENGLISH   bay   mountain island   lagoon   reservoir   point   river   mountains
DEUTSCH   Bucht   Berg   Insel   Haff   Stausee   Landspitze Fluss   Berge
FRANÇAIS   baie   montagne île   lagune   réservoir   pointe   rivière montagnes
PORTUGUÊS baía   montanha ilha   laguna   reservatório ponta   rio   serra

Kilometers 0 100 200 300 Km.

Statute Miles 0 100 200 300 Mi.

Scale 1:6,000,000

One centimeter represents 60 kilometers.
One inch represents approximately 95 miles.
Lambert Conformal Conic Projection

Meters Feet
6000   19685
4000   13124
3000   9843
2000   6562
1000   3281
500   1640
200   656
0   0

Land
Below   0   0
Sea
Level
200   656
1000   3281
3000   9843
6000   19685
9000   29520

Copyright © by Rand McNally & Co.
Map prepared by Rand McNally & Co.
A-531600-764

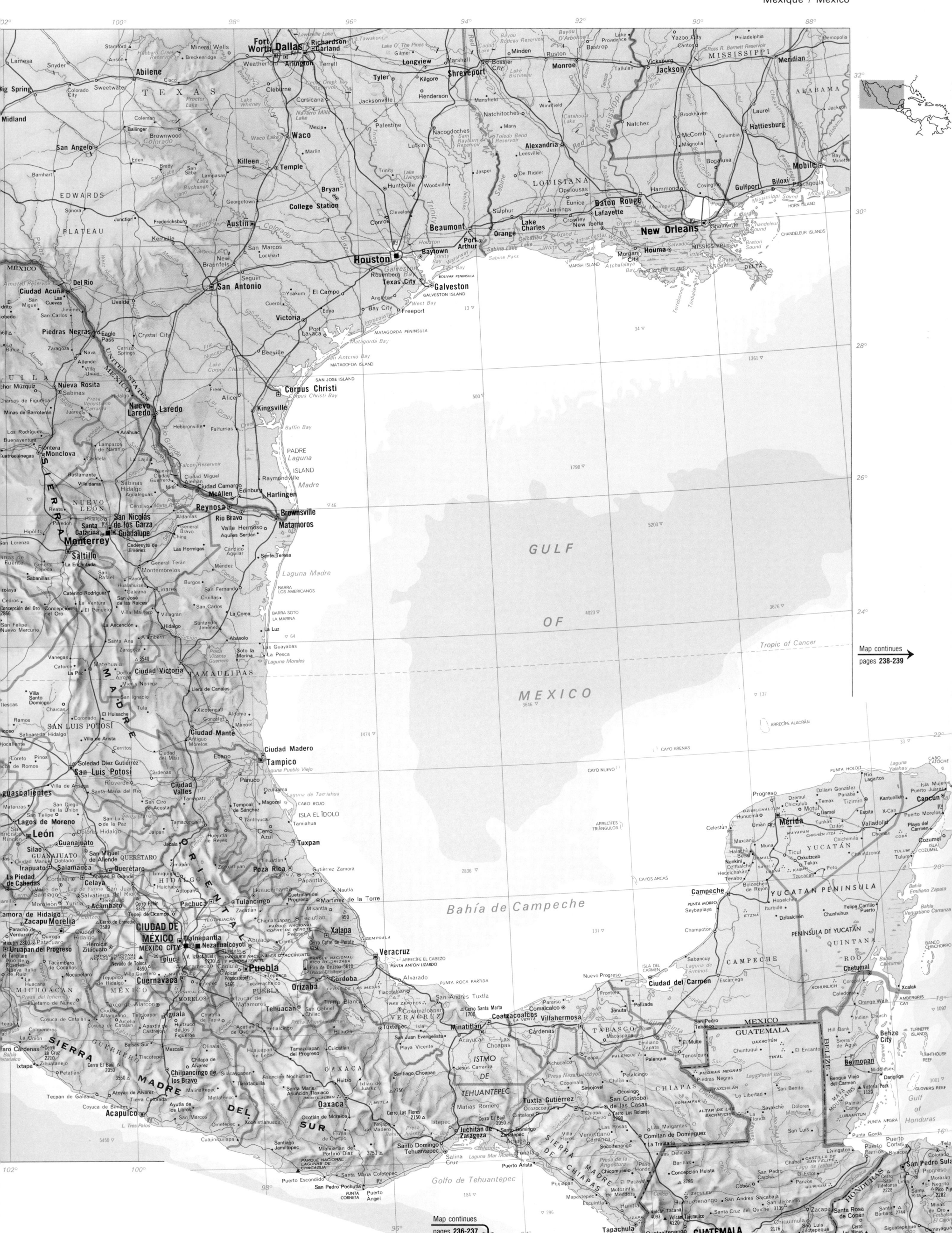

Map continues
pages 238-239

Map continues
pages 236-237

Map continues
pages 232-233

PACIFIC OCEAN

Meters	Feet
6000	19685
4000	13124
3000	9843
2000	6562
1000	3281
500	1640
200	656
0	0
Land Below Sea Level	
0	0
200	656
1000	3281
3000	9843
6000	19685
9000	29520

ESPAÑOL	arroyo	boca	cerro	lago	laguna	punta	rio	sierra	volcán
ENGLISH	brook	entrance	butte	lake	lagoon	point	river	ranges	volcano
DEUTSCH	Bach	Einfahrt	Restberg	See	Haff	Landspitze	Fluss	Bergketten	Vulkan
FRANÇAIS	ruisseau	entrée	butte	lac	lagune	pointe	rivière	chaîne	volcan
PORTUGUÊS	riacho	entrada	cerro	lago	laguna	ponta	rio	serra	vulcão

GULF OF MEXICO

Bahía de Campeche

Golfo de Tehuantepec

Map continues pages 232-233

Map continues pages 236-237

Kilometers | 0 | 50 | 100 | 150 | Km.
Statute Miles | 0 | 50 | 100 | 150 | Mi.

Scale 1:3,000,000

One centimeter represents 30 kilometers.
One inch represents approximately 47 miles.

Lambert Conformal Conic Projection

Map continues
pages 232-233

Map continues
pages 234-235

PETÉN

MEXICO
GUATEMALA
MÉXICO

BELIZE

Gulf of Honduras

ISLAS DE LA BAHÍA
ISLA DE ROATÁN

ISLAS DE LA BAHÍA

ALTA VERAPAZ

IZABAL

CHIAPAS

SIERRA MADRE DE CHIAPAS

HUEHUETENANGO

QUICHÉ

BAJA VERAPAZ

Puerto Cortés

Puerto Barrios

HONDURAS

La Ceiba

ATLÁNTIDA

CORDILLERA

YORO

San Pedro Sula

El Progreso

TOTONI-
CAPÁN

SANTA BÁRBARA

SIERRA DE LAS MINAS

ZACAPA

COPÁN

SAN MARCOS

Quetzaltenango

QUEZAL-
TENANGO

SOLOLÁ

CHIMAL-
TENANGO

GUATEMALA

JALAPA

CHIQUIMULA

COMAYAGUA

Comayagua

Tapachula

RETALHULEU

Mazatenango

SUCHITEPÉQUEZ

ESCUINTLA

Escuintla

SANTA ROSA

JUTIAPA

EL SALVADOR

OCOTEPEQUE

INTIBUCÁ

LEMPIRA

LA PAZ

FRANCISCO
MORAZÁN

Tegucigalpa

EL PARAÍSO

Puerto
San Jose

Santa Ana

San Salvador

Nueva San Salvador

Sonsonate

Mejicanos

Cojutepeque

San
Vicente

Zacatecoluca

Usulután

San Miguel

La Unión

CHOLUTECA

Choluteca

ESTELÍ

Estelí

MADRIZ

NUEVA SEGOVIA

Golfe de
Fonseca

CHINANDEGA

LEÓN

Chinandega

León

MANAGUA

Managua

PACIFIC

OCEAN

Masaya

Masaya

CARAZO

Meters		Feet
6000		19685
4000		13124
3000		9843
2000		6562
1000		3281
500		1640
200		656
0		0
Land Below Sea Level		
0		0
200		656
1000		3281
3000		9843
6000		19685
9000		29520

Copyright © by Rand McNally & Co.
Map prepared by Rand McNally & Co.
A-533600-764

ESPAÑOL	bahía	cerro	cordillera	isla	lago	laguna	punta	sierra	volcán
ENGLISH	bay	mountain	mountains	island	lake	lagoon	point	mountains	volcano
DEUTSCH	Bucht	Berg	Berge	Insel	See	Haff	Landspitze	Berge	Vulkan
FRANÇAIS	baie	montagne	montagnes	île	lac	lagune	pointe	montagnes	volcan
PORTUGUÊS	baía	montanha	cordilheira	ilha	lago	laguna	ponta	serra	vulcão

Map continues
pages 246-247

Kilometers   0   50   100   150   Km.

Statute Miles   0   50   100   150   Mi.

Scale 1:3,000,000

One centimeter represents 30 kilometers.

One inch represents approximately 47 miles.

Lambert Conformal Conic Projection

Caribbean Region / Mittelamerikanische Inselwelt / Región del Caribe
Région des Caraïbes / Região do Caribe

GULF OF MEXICO

UNITED STATES
FLORIDA

West Palm Beach
Palm Beach
Lake Worth
Delray Beach
Boca Raton
Pompano Beach
Fort Lauderdale
Hollywood
MIAMI
Miami Beach
Coral Gables
Homestead
Everglades National Park
Naples
Fort Myers
Belle Glade
Charlotte Harbor
Lake Okeechobee

West End
Freeport
GRAND BAHAMA
ABACO
Marsh Harbour
Dunmore Town
Nassau
NEW PROVIDENCE
ELEUTHERA
Governor's Harbour
Rock Sound
ANDROS
Andros Town
EXUMA
New Bight
Mount Alvernia
Port Howe
COLUMBUS POINT
CAT ISLAND
LONG ISLAND
Clarence Town
RAGGED ISLAND
Deadman's Cay
CROOKED ISLAND
RUM CAY
CAPE SANTA MARIA

BAHAMA

Key West
Key Largo
Florida Keys
Florida Bay
Straits of Florida

W E S T

LA HABANA
HAVANA
San Antonio de los Baños
San José de las Lajas
Matanzas
Cárdenas
Jovellanos
Artemisa
Guanajay
Güira de Melena
Güines
Colón
Unión de Reyes
Jagüey Grande
Pinar del Río
Mantua
Los Palacios
Consolación del Sur
Candelaria
Santa Clara
Placetas
Camajuaní
Caibarién
Sagua la Grande
Cienfuegos
Palmira
Cruces
Lajas
Sancti Spíritus
Trinidad
Ciego de Ávila
Florida
Camagüey
Las Tunas
Holguín
Bayamo
Manzanillo
Palma Soriano
Santiago de Cuba
Guantánamo
Banes
Baracoa

C U B A

CAYMAN ISLANDS (U.K.)
George Town
GRAND CAYMAN
LITTLE CAYMAN
CAYMAN BRAC

G R E A T E R

JAMAICA
Montego Bay
Falmouth
Saint Ann's Bay
Ocho Rios
Port Maria
Port Antonio
Mandeville
Kingston
Spanish Town
May Pen
Blue Mountain Peak
Morant Bay
MORANT POINT

C A R I B B E A N

ISLA DE LA JUVENTUD (ISLA DE PINOS)
Nueva Gerona

YUCATÁN
MÉXICO
Cancún
PUNTA CANCÚN
Playa del Carmen
Cozumel
ISLA COZUMEL
QUINTANA ROO
Tulum
COBÁ
YUCATAN PENINSULA
PENÍNSULA DE YUCATÁN

ISLAS DE LA BAHÍA
Roatán
Utila
Guanaja
CABO DE HONDURAS

Gulf of Honduras

GLOVERS REEF (Belize)
LIGHTHOUSE REEF (Belize)

HONDURAS
La Ceiba
Tela
Trujillo
Limón
Catacamas
Juticalpa
Tegucigalpa

LA MOSQUITIA

NICARAGUA
Puerto Cabezas
Waspam
Siuna
Bonanza
Bluefields
El Bluff
Bilwaskarma
Prinzapolka

COSTA RICA
SAN JOSÉ
Puerto Limón
Cartago
Puntarenas
Heredia

MANAGUA
Granada
Masaya
León
Chinandega
Lago de Nicaragua
Lago de Managua

SAN ANDRÉS Y PROVIDENCIA (Col.)
San Andrés
ISLA DE PROVIDENCIA

PACIFIC OCEAN

PANAMÁ
Colón
Bocas del Toro
ISTMO DE PANAMÁ

Santa Marta
Barranquilla
Soledad
Cartagena
Ciénaga
Sincelejo

Scale

Meters	Feet
6000	19685
4000	13124
3000	9843
2000	6562
1000	3281
500	1640
200	656
0	0
Land Below Sea Level 0	0
200	656
1000	3281
3000	9843
6000	19685
9000	29520

Map continues pages 232-233
Map continues pages 236-237

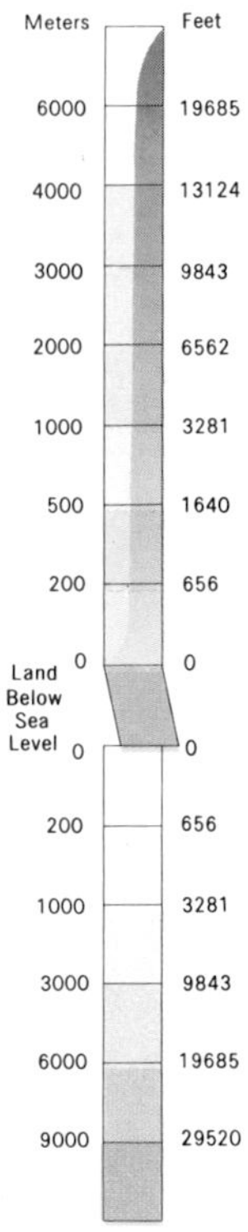

MAP FORM	bahía	cabo	cerro	channel	golfo	isla	passage	pico	punta
ENGLISH	bay	cape	mountain	channel	gulf	isle	passage	peak	point
DEUTSCH	Bucht	Kap	Berg	Kanal	Golf	Insel	Durchfahrt	Gipfel	Landspitze
ESPAÑOL	bahía	cabo	cerro	canal	golfo	isla	pasaje	pico	punta
FRANÇAIS	baie	cap	montagne	détroit	golfe	île	passage	cime	pointe
PORTUGUÊS	baía	cabo	montanha	canal	golfo	ilha	passagem	pico	ponta

Copyright © by Rand McNally & Co.
Map prepared by Rand McNally & Co.
A-530100-764

a

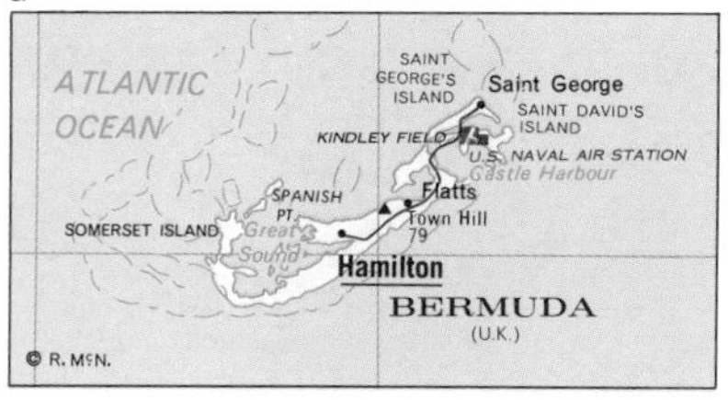

ATLANTIC OCEAN

SAINT GEORGE'S ISLAND
Saint George
SAINT DAVID'S ISLAND
KINDLEY FIELD
U.S. NAVAL AIR STATION
SPANISH POINT
Flatts
Castle Harbour
SOMERSET ISLAND
Town Hill
Hamilton
BERMUDA (U.K.)
R. MCN.

b

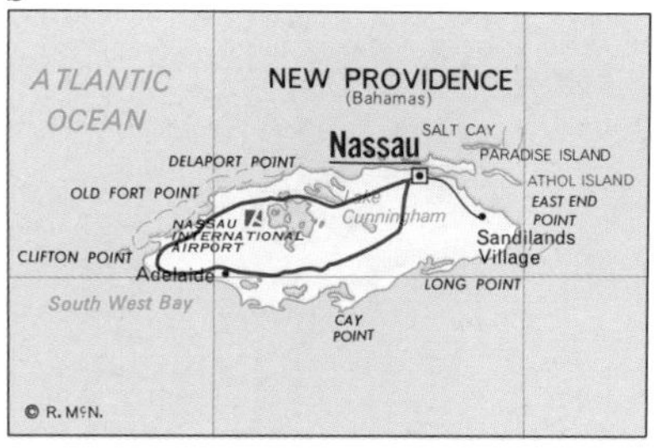

ATLANTIC OCEAN

NEW PROVIDENCE (Bahamas)
PARADISE ISLAND
DELAPORT POINT
SALT CAY
Nassau
OLD FORT POINT
NASSAU INTERNATIONAL AIRPORT
EAST END POINT
ATHOL ISLAND
CLIFTON POINT
Gunnrigham
Sandilands
Village
Adelaide
LONG POINT
South West Bay
CAY POINT
R. MCN.

c

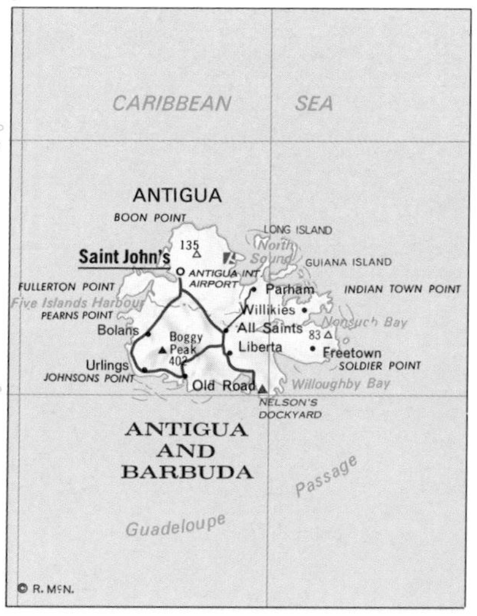

CARIBBEAN SEA

ANTIGUA
BOON POINT
LONG ISLAND
GUIANA ISLAND
Saint John's
Parham
INDIAN TOWN POINT
ANTIGUA INT. AIRPORT
FULLERTON POINT
Willikies
Five Islands Harbour
All Saints
PEARNS POINT
Bolans
Liberta
Nonsuch Bay
Urlings
Boggy Peak
JOHNSONS POINT
Old Road
Freetown
SOLDIER POINT
NELSON'S DOCKYARD
Willoughby Bay
ANTIGUA AND BARBUDA
Guadeloupe
Passage
R. MCN.

d

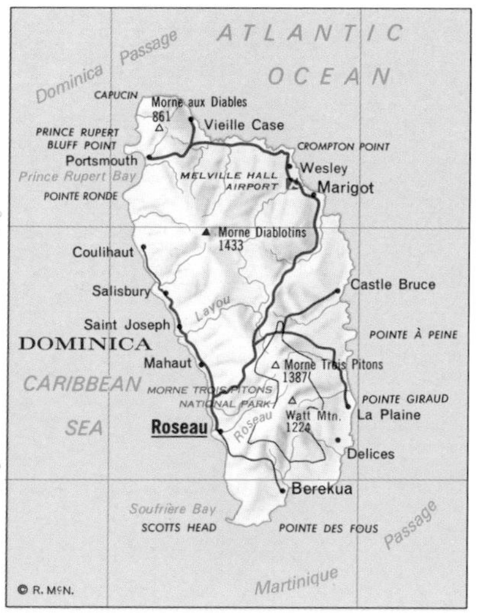

ATLANTIC OCEAN

Dominica
CAPUCIN
Morne aux Diables 861
PRINCE RUPERT BLUFF POINT
Vieille Case
CROMPTON POINT
Portsmouth
Prince Rupert Bay
Wesley
MELVILLE HALL AIRPORT
POINTE RONDE
Marigot
Coulihaut
Morne Diablotins 1433
Salisbury
Castle Bruce
Saint Joseph
POINTE À PEINE
DOMINICA
Mahaut
Morne Trois Pitons 1387
MORNE TROIS PITONS NATIONAL PARK
CARIBBEAN SEA
Roseau
POINTE GIRAUD
Watt Mtn. 1224
La Plaine
Delices
Souffrière Bay
Berekua
SCOTTS HEAD
POINTE DES FOUS
Martinique
Passage
R. MCN.

e

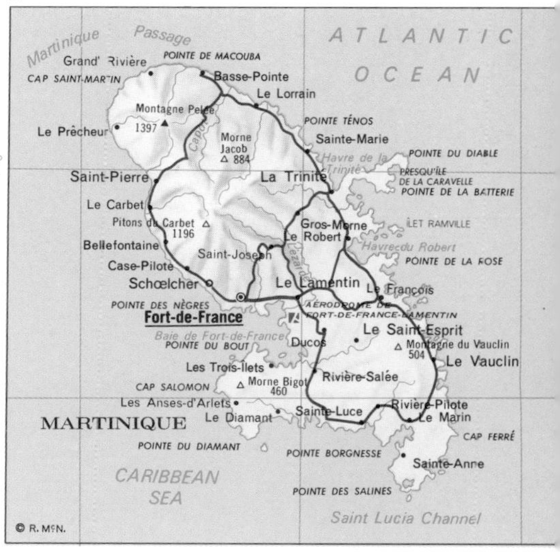

ATLANTIC OCEAN

Grand' Rivière
POINTE DE MACOUBA
CAP SAINT-MARTIN
Basse-Pointe
Le Lorrain
Le Prêcheur
Montagne Pelée 1397
POINTE TÉNOS
Morne Jacob 884
SAINTE-MARIE
Saint-Pierre
POINTE DU DIABLE
Le Carbet
Gros-Morne
PRESQU'ÎLE DE LA CARAVELLE
La Trinité
POINTE DE LA BATTERIE
Pitons du Carbet 1196
Le Robert
Bellefontaine
Saint-Joseph
HAVRE DU FORT DE LA ROSE
Case-Pilote
POINTE DES NÈGRES
Schœlcher
Le Lamentin
François
POINTE DU BOUT
AÉROPORT INT. FORT-DE-FRANCE LAMENTIN
Baie du Fort-de-France
Fort-de-France
Ducos
Le Saint-Esprit
Les Trois-Îlets
Daguai
Montagne du Vauclin 460
CAP SALOMON
Saint-Luce
Rivière-Salée
Le Vauclin
Le Diamant
Rivière-Pilote
Le Marin
POINTE DU DIAMANT
Sainte-Luce
CAP FERRÉ
MARTINIQUE
POINTE BORGNESSE
Sainte-Anne
POINTE DES SALINES
CARIBBEAN SEA
Saint Lucia Channel
R. MCN.

m

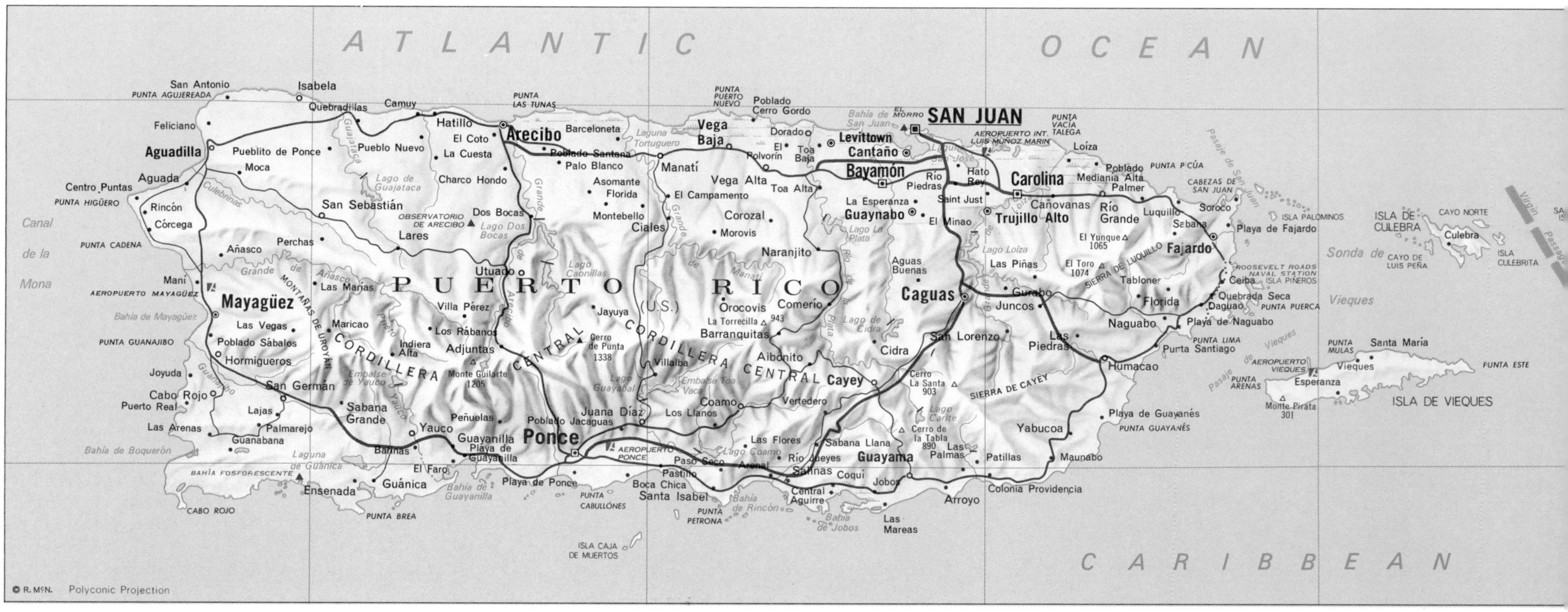

ATLANTIC OCEAN

San Antonio
PUNTA AGUEREADA
Isabela
Feliciano
Quebradillas
Camuy
PUNTA LAS TUNAS
Poblado Cerro Gordo
PUNTA PUERTO NUEVO
Bahía de San Juan
SAN JUAN
PUNTA VACIA TALEGA
Aguadilla
Hatillo
Barceloneta
Laguna Tortuguero
Vega Baja
Dorado
AEROPUERTO INT. LUIS MUÑOZ MARÍN
Loíza
Pueblo de Ponce
El Coto
Arecibo
Manatí
Levittown
PUNTA P. CÚA
Pueblo Nuevo
Rolando Santana
Palo Blanco
Cantaño
Poblado Medianía Alta Palmer
Aguada
Moca
Charco Hondo
Asomante
Florida
Vega Alta
Toa Baja
Bayamón
Río Piedras
Carolina
CABEZAS DE SAN JUAN
Centro Puntas
San Sebastián
Toa Alta
La Esperanza
Saint Just
Cañóvanas
Río Grande
Soroco
PUNTA HIGÜERO
Rincón
Lares
El Campamento
Guaynabo
El Minao
Trujillo Alto
Luquillo
Playa de Fajardo
ISLA DE CULEBRA
Córcega
Observatorio de Arecibo
Dos Bocas
Corozal
Aguas Buenas
El Yunque 1065
Fajardo
Culebra
Canal de la Mona
Anasco
Perchas
Lago Dos Bocas
Morovis
Naranjito
El Toro 1074
Tablonec
ISLA CULEBRITA
Mani
Las Marías
Utuado
PUERTO RICO (U.S.)
Comerío
Las Piñas
Ceiba
Quebrada Seca
Sonda de Vieques
Aeropuerto Mayagüez
Villa Alba
Jayuya
Lago Caonillas
La Torrecilla 943
Caguas
Juncos
ROOSEVELT ROADS NAVAL STATION
ISLA PIÑEROS
Mayagüez
Las Vegas
Los Rábanos
Barranquitas
Lago de Patillas
Naguabo
Playa de Naguabo
Vieques
Maricao
Cerro Alta
Indiera Alta
Adjuntas
Cerro de Punta 1338
CORDILLERA CENTRAL
Albonito
Cidra
San Lorenzo
Las Piedras
PUNTA MULAS
Esperanza
Santa María
Joyuda
Poblado Sábales
Hormigueros
Villalba
Cayey
Humacao
AEROPUERTO VIEQUES
PUNTA ESTE
San Germán
Monte Guilarte 1205
Coamo
SIERRA DE CAYEY
PUNTA ARENAS
Morne Pirata 301
ISLA DE VIEQUES
Cabo Rojo
Lajas
Sabana Grande
Peñuelas
Juana Díaz
Los Llanos
Cerro de la Santa 903
Yabucoa
Playa de Guayanés
Puerto Real
Yauco
Guayanilla
Playa de Guayanilla
Vertedero
Playa de Ponce
Las Flores
Sabana Llana
Las Palmas
PUNTA GUAYANÉS
Las Arenas
Guanabana
Laguna de Guánica
Ponce
Guayama
Patillas
Maunabo
BAHÍA FOSFORESCENTE
El Faro
Guánica
Boca Chica
Santa Isabel
Río Jueyes
Salinas
Arroyo
Colonia Providencia
CABO ROJO
Ensenada
Bahía de Guayanilla
Paso Seco
Coquí
Central Aguirre
Las Mareas
PUNTA BREA
AEROPUERTO PONCE
PUNTA CABULLONES
PUNTA PETRONA
PUNTA RINCÓN
Bahía de Jobos
CARIBBEAN
ISLA CAJA DE MUERTOS
R. MCN. Polyconic Projection

p

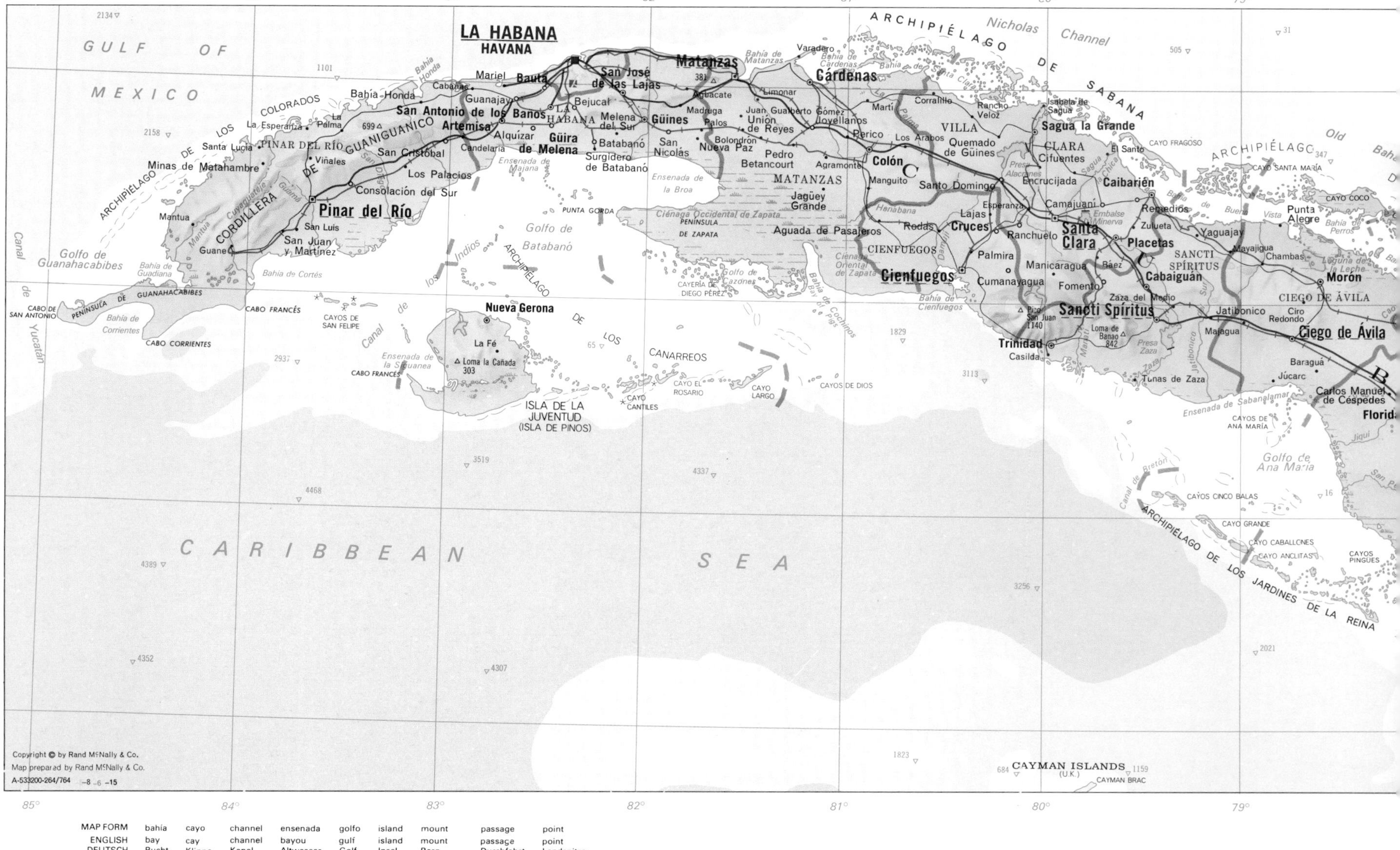

GULF OF MEXICO

2134
LA HABANA HAVANA
ARCHIPIÉLAGO DE SABANA
Nicholas Channel
Varadero
505
31
Mariel
Bauta
San José de las Lajas
Matanzas
Bahía de Matanzas
Cárdenas
Isabela de Sagua
1101
Bahía Honda
Cabañas
Guanajay
Bejucal
Güines
Limonar
Corralillo
Rancho Veloz
Sagua la Grande
CAYO FRAGOSO
COLORADOS
La Esperanza
San Antonio de los Baños
HABANA
Madruga
Jovellanos
VILLA
Caibarién
CAYO SANTA MARÍA
2158
La Palma
699
Artemisa
Alquízar
Unión de Reyes
Juan Gualberto Gómez
Perico
Los Arabos
CLARA
Cifuentes
El Santo
ARCHIPIÉLAGO
347
Minas de Matahambre
Santa Lucía
San Cristóbal
Candelaria
Güira de Melena
Palos
Nueva Paz
Pedro Betancourt
Agramonte
Santo Domingo
Encrucijada
Camajuaní
Remedios
Punta Alegre
Viñales
Los Palacios
Consolación del Sur
Surgidero de Batabanó
San Nicolás
Bolondrón
MATANZAS
Jagüey Grande
Manguito
Esperanza
Santa Clara
Placetas
Yaguajay
CORDILLERA DE
Pinar del Río
Guane
PINAR DEL RÍO
Ensenada de Majana
Ciénaga Occidental de Zapata
Aguada de Pasajeros
Lajas
Ranchuelo
Cruces
Manicaragua
Cabaiguán
SANCTI SPÍRITUS
Chambas
Morón
San Juan y Martínez
PUNTA GORDA
Golfo de Batabanó
PENÍNSULA DE ZAPATA
CIENFUEGOS
Palmira
Cumanayagua
Fomento
CIEGO DE ÁVILA
Mantua
Golfo de Guanahacabibes
Bahía de Cortés
ARCHIPIÉLAGO
Cienfuegos
Bahía de Cienfuegos
Zaza del Medio
Jatibonico
Ciro Redondo
CABO FRANCÉS
CAYOS DE SAN FELIPE
Nueva Gerona
Cienfuegos
Sancti Spíritus
Loma de Banao 842
Manga
Ciego de Ávila
PENÍNSULA DE GUANAHACABIBES
CABO CORRIENTES
La Fé
DE
Trinidad
Casilda
Zaza
Tunas de Zaza
Carlos Manuel de Céspedes
CABO SAN ANTONIO
Bahía de Corrientes
Loma la Cañada 303
LOS
CANARREOS
CAYOS DE DIOS
Baragua
Júcaro
Florida
ISLA DE LA JUVENTUD (ISLA DE PINOS)
CAYO LARGO
CAYOS DE SABANALAMAR
Golfo de Ana María
3519
CAYO CANTILES
CAYO EL ROSARIO
Ensenada de Sabanalamar
4468
4337
3113
CARIBBEAN SEA
4383
4352
4307
3256
2021
ARCHIPIÉLAGO DE LOS JARDINES DE LA REINA
1823
1159
CAYO CABALLONES
CAYMAN ISLANDS (U.K.)
CAYMAN BRAC
CAYOS CINCO BALAS
CAYOS PINGUES

Copyright © by Rand McNally & Co.
Map prepared by Rand McNally & Co.
A-533200-264/764 -8- -6 -15

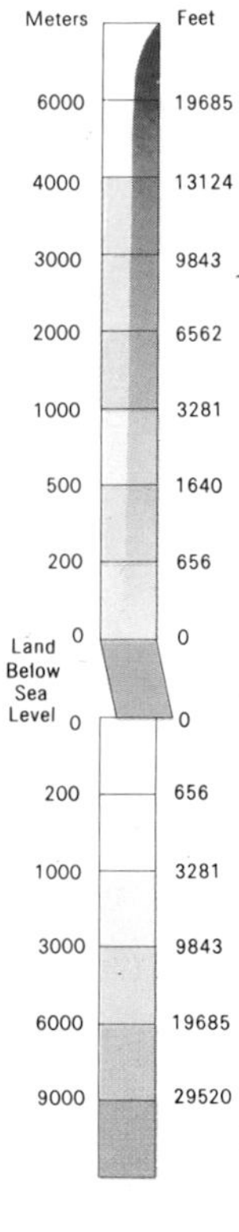

Meters Feet
6000 19685
4000 13124
3000 9843
2000 6562
1000 3281
500 1640
200 656
0 0
Land Below Sea Level 0 0
200 656
1000 3281
3000 9843
6000 19685
9000 29520

MAP FORM	bahía	cayo	channel	ensenada	golfo	island	mount	passage	point
ENGLISH	bay	cay	channel	bayou	gulf	island	mount	passage	point
DEUTSCH	Bucht	Klippe	Kanal	Altwasser	Golf	Insel	Berg	Durchfahrt	Landspitze
ESPAÑOL	bahía	cayo	canal	pasaje	golfo	isla	monte	pasaje	punta
FRANÇAIS	baie	caye	détroit	bayou	golfe	île	mont	passage	pointe
PORTUGUÊS	baía	baixio	canal	enseada	golfo	ilha	montanha	passagem	ponta

Islands of the West Indies / Westindische Inseln / Islas de ias Antillas
Îles des Antilles / Ilhas do Caribe (Índias Ocidentais)
241

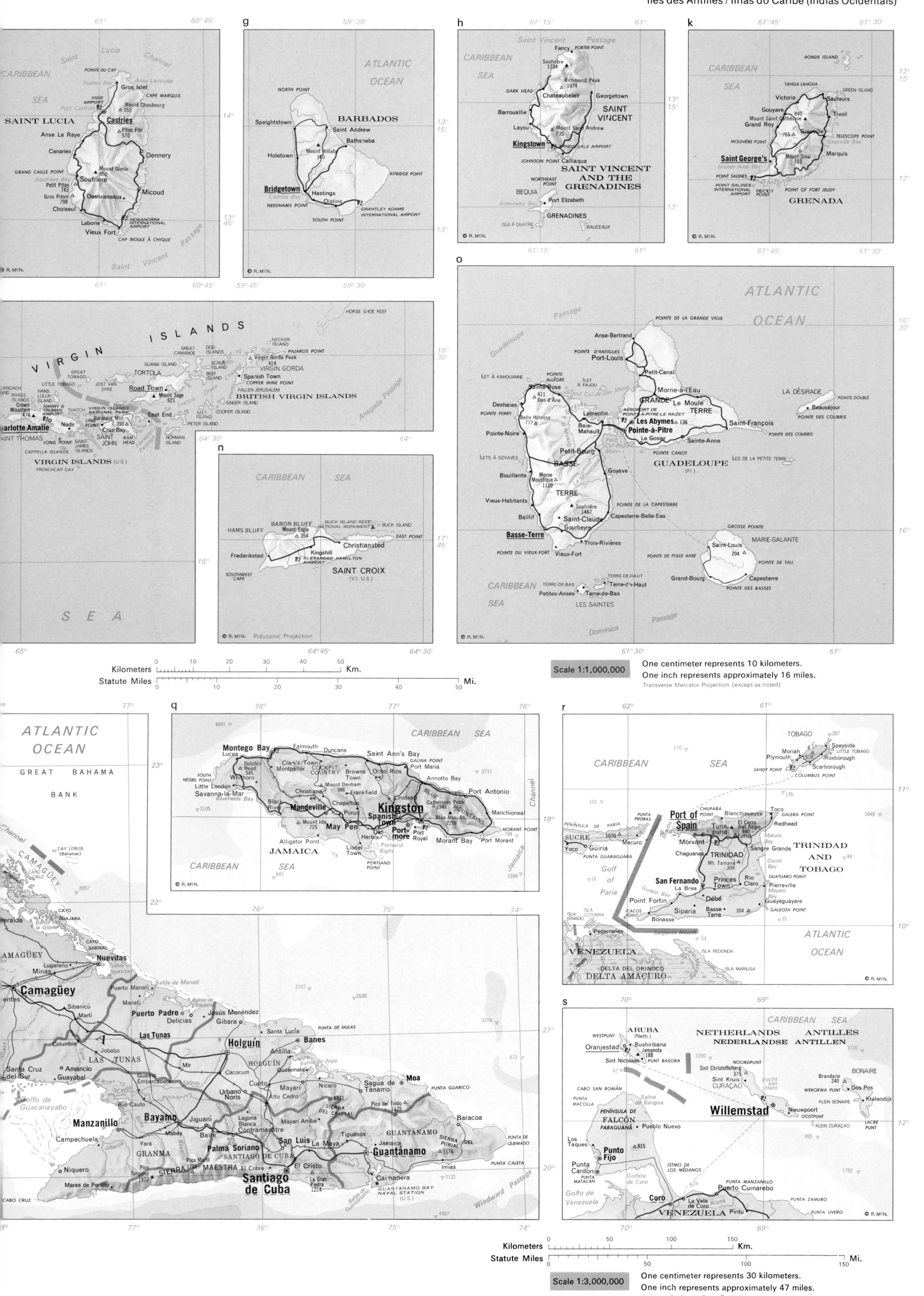

Map continues
pages 230-231

Kilometers
0   200   400   600
0   Km.

Statute Miles
0   200   400   600
0   Mi.

Scale 1:12,000,000

One centimeter represents 120 kilometers.
One inch represents approximately 190 miles.
Oblique Conic Conformal Projection

Northern South America / Südamerika, nördlicher Teil / América del Sur: zona septentrional
Amérique du Sud Septentrionale / América do Sul: zona setentrional

243

ATLANTIC OCEAN

BARBADOS
Bridgetown

TOBAGO

Georgetown
Paramaribo
Cayenne

SURINAME
FRENCH
GUIANA

GUYANA

▲ Juliana Top
1230

TUMUC-HUMAC MTS.

AMAPÁ

Macapá

ILHA DE MARAJÓ

Belém
Santarém
São Luís
Parnaíba
Fortaleza

Equator

PARÁ

MARANHÃO

Represa
de
Tucuruí

Marabá
Imperatriz
Teresina

CEARÁ

Mossoró
Natal

RIO GRANDE DO NORTE

PIAUÍ

SERRA DOS CARAJÁS

SERRA DO CACHIMBO

Juazeiro
do Norte
Campina Grande
João Pessoa
PARAÍBA
Olinda
Recife
Caruaru

PERNAMBUCO

Garanhuns

Represa
Boa
Esperança

Petrolina
Juazeiro
Paulo
Afonso

ALAGOAS

TOCANTINS

Maceió
Aracaju

SERRA DOS APIACÁS

SERRA DO RONCADOR

ILHA
DO
BANANAL

SERGIPE

BRAZIL

BAHIA

Feira de Santana
Alagoinhas
Salvador

MATO GROSSO

PLANALTO DO

MATO GROSSO

Cuiabá

Rondonópolis

GOIÁS

Vitória
da Conquista
Ilhéus
Itabuna

BRASÍLIA
Anápolis
Goiânia

CENTRAL

SERRA DO CAIAPÓ

Montes
Claros

MINAS GERAIS

MATO GROSSO
DO SUL

Corumbá

Campo Grande

Uberlândia
Uberaba

Governador
Valadares
ESPÍRITO
SANTO

Sete
Lagoas
Belo
Horizonte

Vitória
Vila Velha

Araçatuba
Presidente Prudente

SÃO PAULO

Ribeirão
Preto

Divinópolis

Juiz de Fora

Campinas
SÃO PAULO
Santos

Volta
Redonda
Nova
Iguaçu
Niterói
RIO DE JANEIRO

Tropic of Capricorn

Map continues
pages 244-245

MAP FORM	cerro	cordillera	ilha	lago	nevado	península	serra
ENGLISH	mountain	range	island	lake	mountain	peninsula	mountains
DEUTSCH	Berg	Gebirge	Insel	See	Berg	Halbinsel	Berge
ESPAÑOL	montaña	cordillera	isla	lago	montaña	península	montañas
FRANÇAIS	montagne	chaîne	île	lac	montagne	péninsule	montagnes
PORTUGUÊS	montanha	cordilheira	ilha	lago	montanha	península	montanhas

244

Southern South America / Südamerika, südlicher Teil / América del Sur: zona meridional
Amérique du Sud Méridionale / América do Sul: zona meridional

Map continues
pages 242-243

MAP FORM	cerro, co.	golfo	ilha	isla	lago	lagoa	monte	salar
ENGLISH	butte	gulf	island	isle	lake	lake	mountain	saltflat
DEUTSCH	Restberg	Golf	Insel	Insel	See	See	Berg	Salzebene
ESPAÑOL	cerro	golfo	isla	isla	lago	lago	montaña	salobral
FRANÇAIS	butte	golfe	île	île	lac	lac	montagne	salina
PORTUGUÊS	colina	golfo	ilha	ilha	lago	lago	montanha	salina

Southern South America / Südamerika, südlicher Teil / América del Sur: zona meridional
Amérique du Sud Méridionale / América do Sul: zona meridional

245

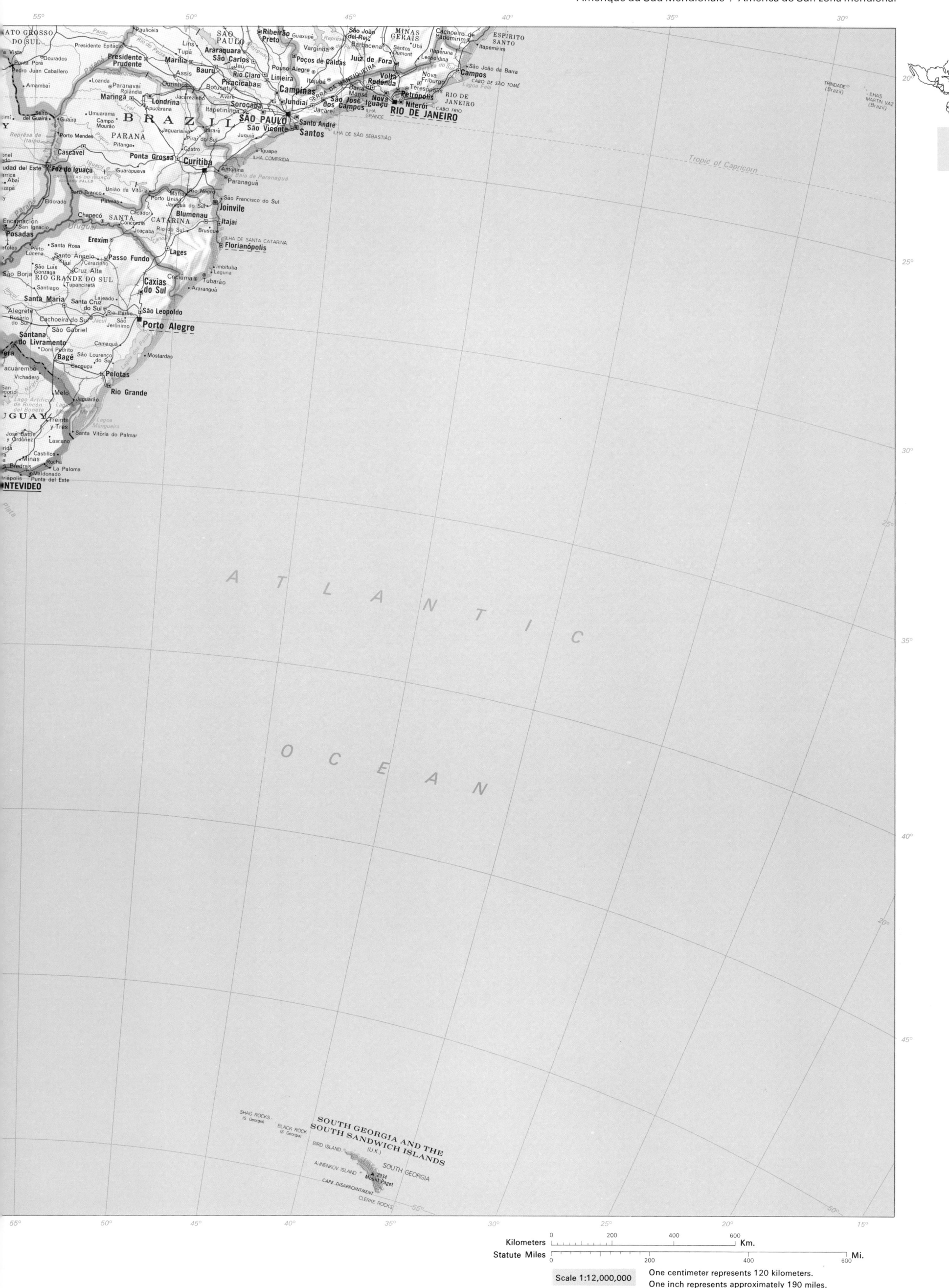

ATLANTIC

OCEAN

SOUTH GEORGIA AND THE
SOUTH SANDWICH ISLANDS
(U.K.)

| Kilometers | 0 | 200 | 400 | 600 | Km. |
| Statute Miles | 0 | 200 | 400 | 600 | Mi. |

Scale 1:12,000,000

One centimeter represents 120 kilometers.
One inch represents approximately 190 miles.
Oblique Conic Conformal Projection

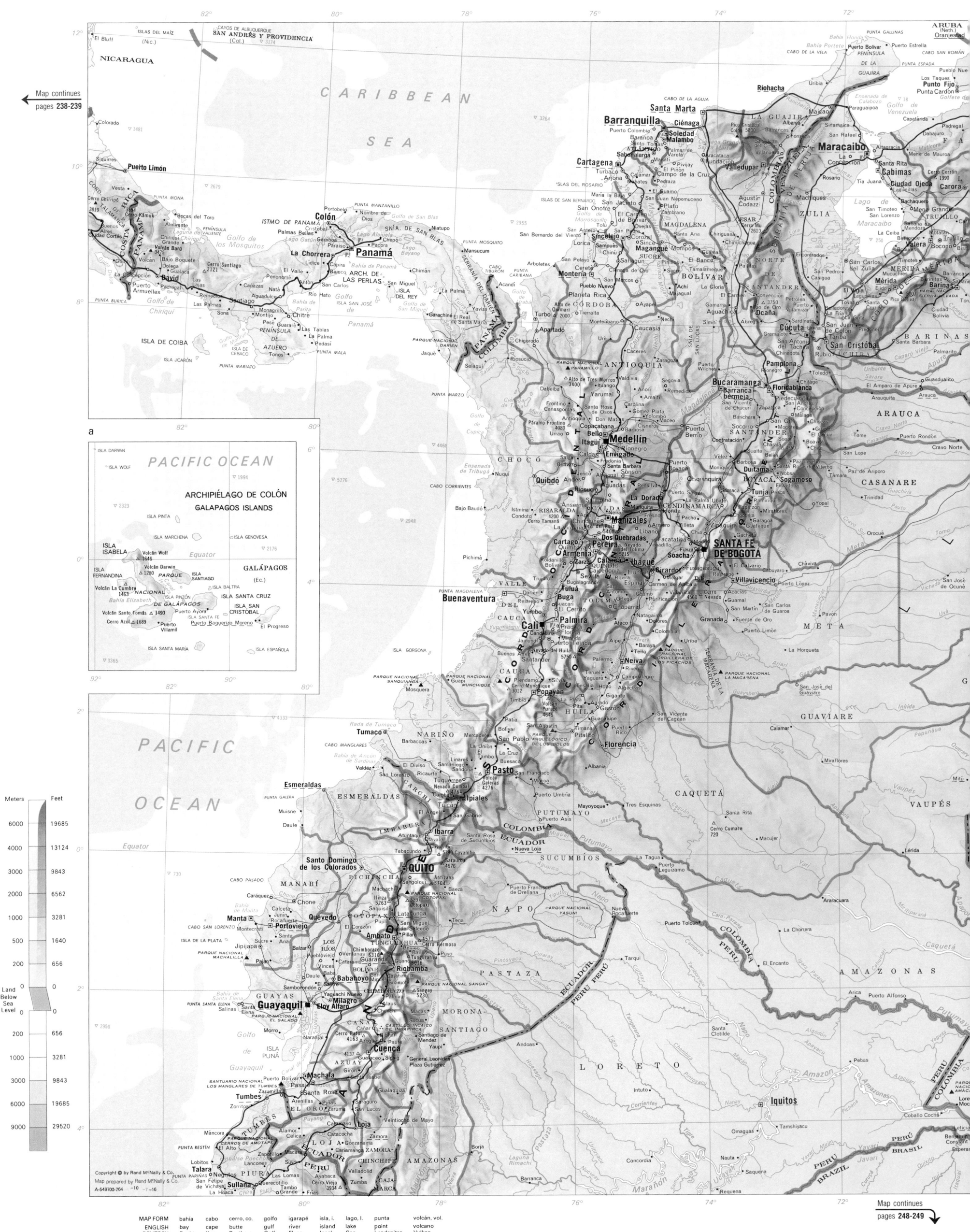

Map continues
pages 238-239

Map continues
pages 248-249

	MAP FORM	bahia	cabo	cerro, co.	golfo	igarapé	isla, i.	lago, l.	punta	volcán, vol.
	ENGLISH	bay	cape	butte	gulf	river	island	lake	point	volcano
	DEUTSCH	Bucht	Kap	Restberg	Golf	Fluss	Insel	See	Landspitze	Vulkan
	ESPAÑOL	bahía	cabo	cerro	golfo	río	isla	lago	punta	volcán
	FRANÇAIS	baie	cap	butte	golfe	rivière	île	lac	pointe	volcan
	PORTUGUÊS	baía	cabo	colina	golfo	rio	ilha	lago	ponta	vulcão

Colombia, Ecuador, Venezuela and Guyana / Kolumbien, Ecuador, Venezuela und Guayana / Colombia, Ecuador, Venezuela y Guyana
Colombie, Équateur, Venezuela et Guyane / Colômbia, Equador, Venezuela e Guiana

247

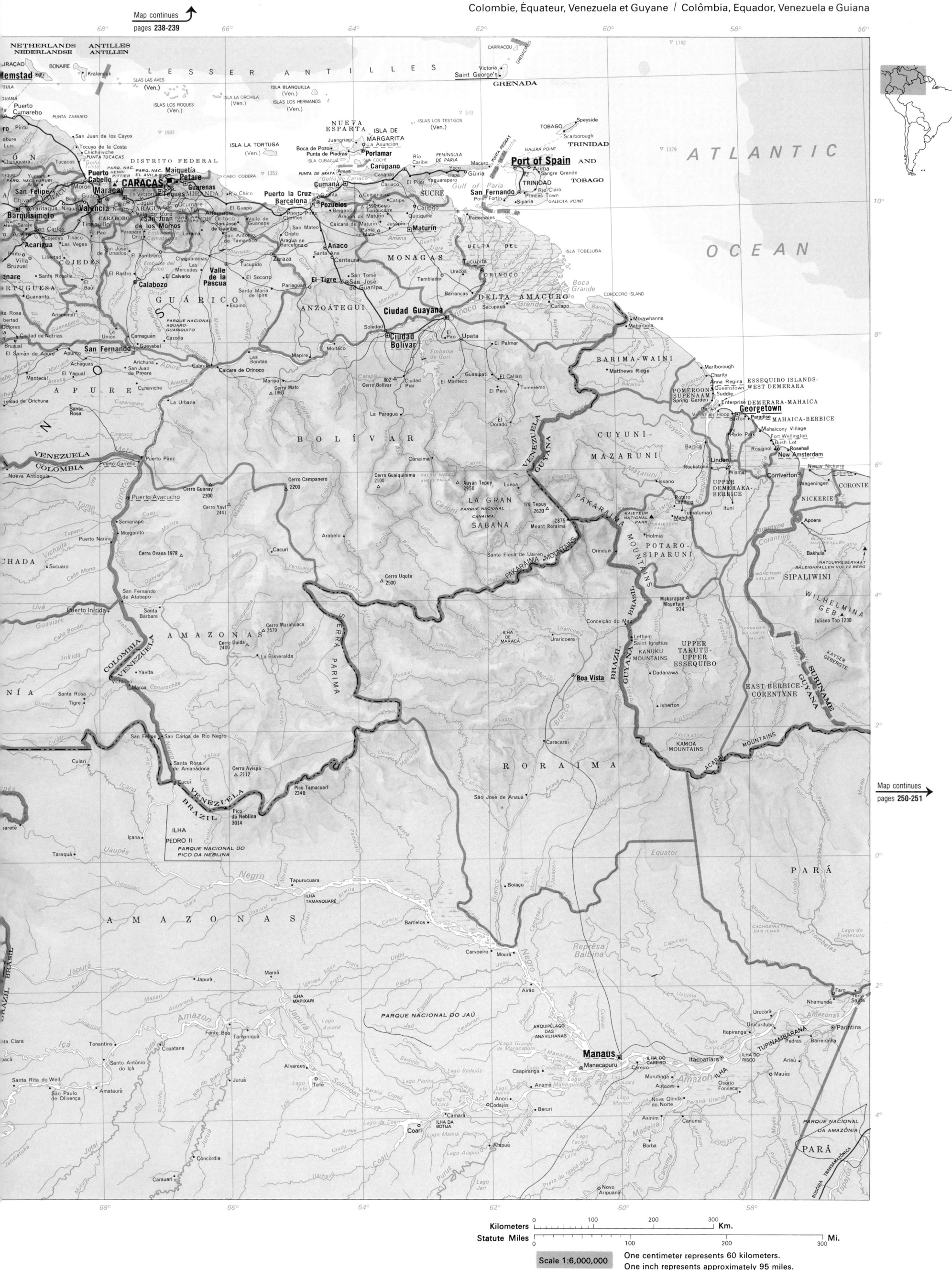

Map continues
pages 238-239

Map continues
pages 250-251

Kilometers 0 100 200 300 Km.
Statute Miles 0 100 200 300 Mi.

Scale 1:6,000,000
One centimeter represents 60 kilometers.
One inch represents approximately 95 miles.
Oblique Conic Conformal Projection

Meters   Feet

6000   19685

4000   13124

3000   9843

2000   6562

1000   3281

500   1640

200   656

0   0

Land
Below
Sea
Level   0

200   656

1000   3281

3000   9843

6000   19685

9000   29520

Copyright © by Rand McNally & Co.
Map prepared by Rand McNally & Co.
A-549792-764   -6   7-9

MAP FORM	cerro	cordillera	isla, i.	lago, l.	nevado	punta	rio	serra
ENGLISH	mountain	mountains	island	lake	mountain	point	river	mountains
DEUTSCH	Berg	Berge	Insel	See	Berg	Landspitze	Fluss	Berge
ESPAÑOL	montaña	montañas	isla	lago	nevado	punta	rio	sierra
FRANÇAIS	montagne	montagnes	ile	lac	montagne	pointe	rivière	montagnes
PORTUGUÊS	montanha	montanhas	ilha	lago	pico nevado	ponta	rio	serra

Peru, Bolivia and Western Brazil / Peru, Bolivien und westliches Brasilien / Perú, Bolivia y Brasil Occidental
Pérou, Bolivie et Brésil Occidental / Peru, Bolívia e Brasil Ocidental

249

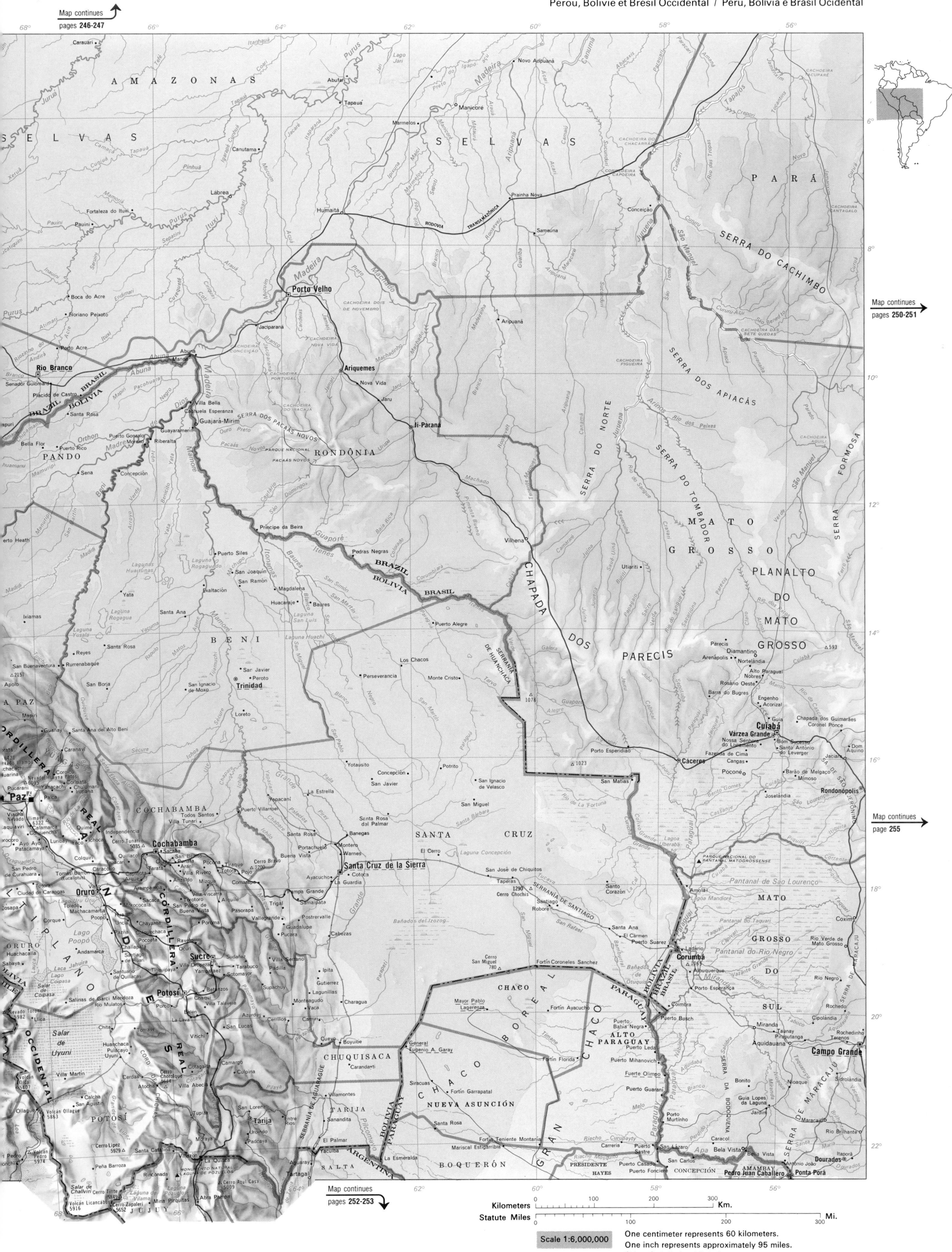

Map continues
pages 246-247

Map continues
pages 250-251

Map continues
page 255

Map continues
pages 252-253

Kilometers 0   100   200   300   Km.
Statute Miles 0   100   200   300   Mi.

Scale 1:6,000,000

One centimeter represents 60 kilometers.
One inch represents approximately 95 miles.

Oblique Conic Conformal Projection

Mahaicony
Village
Fort Wellington
Bush Lot
Rosehall
New Amsterdam
Rosignol
Corriverton

WANICA
COMME-
WIJNE

Nieuw Nickerie Totness
Nieuw Amsterdam
Paramaribo
Groningen
Lelydorp
MAROWIJNE
Onverwacht
Paranam
Moengo
Mana
Albina
Saint-Laurent-
du-Maroni
Iracoubo
Sinnamary
Kourou
Cayenne

CORONIE
NICKERIE
Wageningen

Apoera
Nickerie

SARAMACCA
PARA
Kwakoegron
Berg en Dal
Brokopondo
Apatou
Saint-
Élie
Tonate Remire
Matoury
Roura
ÎLE DU DIABLE
DEVILS ISLAND

NATUURPARK
BROWNSBERG
NATUURRESERVAAT
RALEIGHVALLEN
VOLTZ BERG
Stuwmeer

Kaw
Regina

Guisanbourg
POINTE BEHAGUE

BROKO-
PONDO
Grand-Santi
Mariapasoula

SAINT-
LAURENT-
DU-MARONI

Oiapoque
Saint-Georges
Clevelândia do Norte
CABO CACIPORÉ

Duanary

BAKHUIS
EAST
BERBICE-
CORENTYNE

SIPALIWINI
KAYSER
GEBERGTE

Tafelberg
1026
Juliana Top
1230
WILHELMINA GEB.
FREDERIK WILLEM
VALLEN

CAYENNE

Saül

Monte Tipoca
436
PARQUE NACIONAL
DO CABO ORANGE

830

Vila Velha

GUYANA
SURINAME GUYANA
SURINAME
BRAZIL
FRENCH GUIANA
GUYANE FRANÇAISE
BRAZIL

TUMUC- HUMAC MOUNTAINS

GUYANA
ACARAÍ MOUNTAINS
BRAZIL

Cunani
Calçoene

AMAPÁ

Serra do Navio
Amapá
Aporema

Lourenço

Ferreira Gomes
Porto Grande

ILHA DE MARACÁ
ILHA JIPIOCA
CABO NORTE
Sucuriju

ILHA BAILIQUE
Bailique
ILHA DO CURUÁ
ILHA JANAUCU
ILHA DE JURUPARI

Macapá
Pôrto Santana
Mazagão
Mazagão Velho
ILHA DO PARÁ

ILHA DO
CARÁ
ILHA
QUEIMADA
Afuá
Chaves
ILHA CHARAPUCU

ILHA CAVIANA
DE FORA
ARQUIPÉLAGO JURUPARI
ILHA MEXIANA

CABO MAGUARI
Baía de
Marajó

Salinópolis
Soure
Salvaterra
ILHA DE MARAJÓ

São Caetano
de Odivelas
Primavera
Maracanã
Curuçá
Marapanim
Vigia
Capanema
Piabas
Bragança

Boca
do Jari
ILHA URUBICAIA
ILHA DA
TARTARUGA
ILHA GRANDE
DO GURUPÁ

Almeirim
ILHA
URUTAÍ
Carrazedo
Vilarinho do
Monte
São Miguel dos Macacos
Anajás
ILHA DOS
MACACOS
Cachoeira do
Arari
Joanes
Colares
Condeixa

Castanhal
Ananindeua
Belém
Americano
Val-de-Cães
Abaetetuba
Moju

Candido Mendes

Oriximiná
Óbidos
Alenquer
Monte Alegre
Prainha
Porto de Moz
Breves
Muaná
Ponta de Pedras
Portel
Bagre
Curralinho
Melgaço
Pirá
Igarapé-Miri
Cametá

Terra Santa
Faro
Juruti
ILHA GRANDE
DO TAPARÁ
Santarém
Belterra
Veiros
Vitória
Curuçambaba
Baião
Tomé-Açu

Nhamundá
Urucará
Parintins
Boim
Aveiro
Senador José
Porfírio

AMAZONAS
Amazon

ILHA DO
VISCO
Itacoatiara
ILHA
TUPINAMBARANA
Maués

Osório Fonseca

Altamira

Tucuruí

PARQUE NACIONAL
DA AMAZÔNIA

Itaituba

RODOVIA
228
TRANSAMAZÔNICA

PARÁ

SERRA DOS CARAJÁS

Represa
de
Tucuruí

Itupiranga
Jacundá

Agailândia
MARANHÃO

Marabá
São João
do Araguaia
Imperatriz
Amarante do
Maranhão
Barra do Corda

Araguatins
Itaguatins
Montes
Altos
Sítio Novo
Grajaú

Carajás
898
Santa Isabel do Araguaia
Xambioá
Tocantinópolis
Nazaré
Porto Franco
Paranaidji
640
Fortaleza
dos Nogueiras
São Raimundo
das Mangabeiras
Resplandes

CACHOEIRA
DO CHIAVAPÁU

Conceição
Gradaús

SERRA
DO
CACHIMBO

Babaçulândia
Araguaína
Carolina
Riachão
Balsas
Ribeiro
Gonçalves

Itaporã
de Goiás
Couto do Magalhães
Pequizeiro
Conceição do
Araguaia

Itacajá

SERRA DO ESTRONDO

SERRA DO PENITENTE

CHAPADA DAS MANGABEIRAS

Cachimbo
Alta Floresta

Araguacema
Pedro Afonso
Dois Irmãos
de Goiás
Miracema do Tocantins
Tocantínia
Monte
Alegre do Piauí
Santa Filomena

SERRA DOS APIACÁS

SERRA DO TOMBADOR

Jauru
Porto dos Gaúchos

MATO GROSSO

SERRA FORMOSA

ILHA DO
BANANAL

PARQUE
NACIONAL
DO ARAGUAIA

Santa Terezinha
Cristalândia
Luciara
São Félix do
Araguaia
Duéré

Gurupi

Peixe

Pium
Monte
do Carmo
Ponte Alta
do Norte
Pindorama de Goiás
Brejinho
de Nazaré

TOCANTINS

Porto
Nacional
Palmas
Natividade
Dianópolis
Almas

Ponte Alta do Bom Jesus
Conceição do Norte
Barreiras

Sinop

Map continues
pages 246-247

Map continues
pages 248-249

Map continues
page 255

Meters | Feet
6000 | 19685
4000 | 13124
3000 | 9843
2000 | 6562
1000 | 3281
500 | 1640
200 | 656
0 | 0
Land
Below
Sea
Level
0 | 0
200 | 656
1000 | 3281
3000 | 9843
6000 | 19685
9000 | 29520

MAP FORM	cabo	cachoeira, cach.	ilha, i.	lago, l.	riacho	ribeirão, rão.	rio, r.	serra, sa.
ENGLISH	cape	waterfall	island	lake	creek	creek	river	mountains
DEUTSCH	Kap	Wasserfall	Insel	See	Bach	Bach	Fluss	Berge
ESPAÑOL	cabo	cascada	isla	lago	riachuelo	riachuelo	río	montañas
FRANÇAIS	cap	chute d'eau	île	lac	crique	crique	rivière	montagnes
PORTUGUÊS	cabo	queda d'água	ilha	lago	riacho	riacho	rio	montanhas

ATLANTIC

OCEAN

Equator

FORTALEZA

Natal

RECIFE

João Pessoa

Maceió

Aracaju

Teresina

Petrolina

Juazeiro

BAHIA

PIAUÍ

CEARÁ

RIO GRANDE DO NORTE

PARAÍBA

PERNAMBUCO

ALAGOAS

SERGIPE

Kilometers 0 100 200 300 Km.

Statute Miles 0 100 200 300 Mi.

Scale 1:6,000,000

One centimeter represents 60 kilometers.
One inch represents approximately 95 miles.

Oblique Conic Conformal Projection

Copyright © by Rand McNally & Co.
Map prepared by Rand McNally & Co.
A-540396-764

Map continues
pages 248-249

Map continues
page 254

MAP FORM	cabo	cerro	cuchilla	ilha	laguna	punta	salar	sierra	volcán
ENGLISH	cape	mountain	hills	island	lagoon; lake	point	saltflat	mountains	volcano
DEUTSCH	Kap	Berg	Hügel	Insel	Haff; See	Landspitze	Salzebene	Berge	Vulkan
ESPAÑOL	cabo	cerro	cuchilla	isla	laguna	punta	salobral	sierra	volcán
FRANÇAIS	cap	montagne	collines	île	lagune; lac	pointe	salina	montagnes	volcan
PORTUGUÊS	cabo	montanha	colina	ilha	laguna	ponta	salina	sierra	vulcão

Meters | Feet
6000 | 19685
4000 | 13124
3000 | 9843
2000 | 6562
1000 | 3281
500 | 1640
200 | 656
0 | 0
Land Below Sea Level
0 | 0
200 | 656
1000 | 3281
3000 | 9843
6000 | 19685
9000 | 29520

Copyright © by Rand McNally & Co.
Map prepared by Rand McNally & Co.
A-540191-764   —4-↓8

Central Argentina and Chile / Mittelargentinien und Mittelchile / Argentina y Chile: zonas centrales
Argentine et Chili, parties Centrales / Argentina e Chile: zonas centrais

253

Map continues
page 255

Kilometers
Statute Miles

Scale 1:6,000,000

One centimeter represents 60 kilometers.
One inch represents approximately 95 miles.
Oblique Conic Conformal Projection

Southern Argentina and Chile / Südliches Argentinien und südliches Chile / Argentina y Chile: zonas meridionales
Argentine et Chili, parties Méridionales / Argentina e Chile: zonas meridionais

Map continues
pages 252-253

MAP FORM
ENGLISH · bay · cape · mountain, hill · isle · lake · mountain · point
DEUTSCH · Bucht · Kap · Berg, Hügel · Insel · See · Berg · Landspitze
ESPAÑOL · bahia · cabo · cerro · isla · lago · monte · punta
FRANÇAIS · baie · cap · montagne, colline · île · lac · montagne · pointe
PORTUGUÊS · baia · cabo · montanha, colina · ilha · lago · monte · ponta

Kilometers   0   100   200   300   Km.
Statute Miles   0   100   200   300   Mi.

Scale 1:6,000,000
One centimeter represents 60 kilometers.
One inch represents approximately 95 miles.
Oblique Conic Conformal Projection

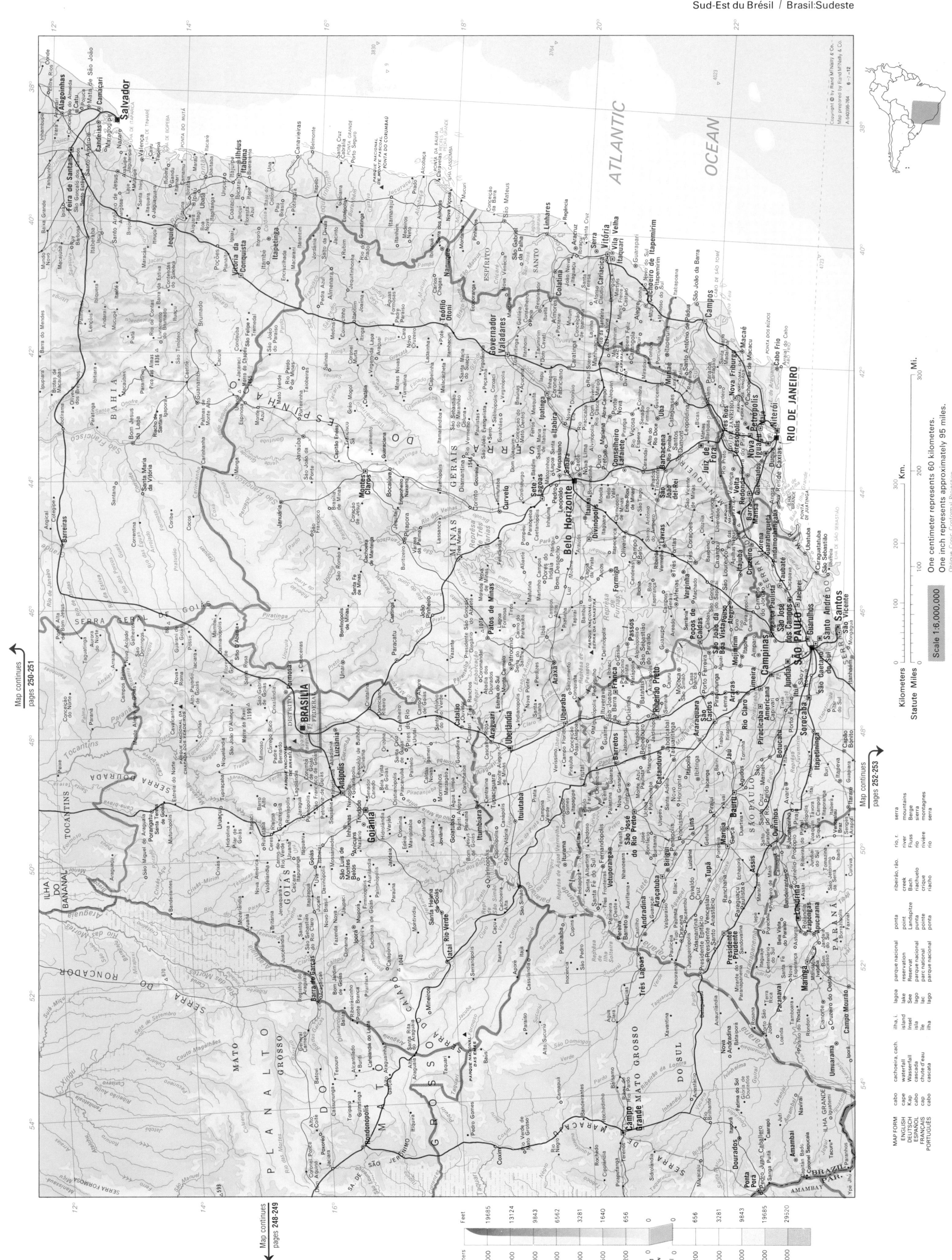

Map continues
pages 250-251

Map continues
pages 248-249

Map continues
pages 252-253

ATLANTIC

OCEAN

RIO DE JANEIRO

Scale 1:6,000,000

One centimeter represents 60 kilometers.
One inch represents approximately 95 miles.
Oblique Conic Conformal Projection

MAP FORM						
ENGLISH	cape	waterfall	point	lake	island	creek	river	mountains
DEUTSCH	Kap	Wasserfall	Landspitze	See	Insel	Bach	Fluss	Berge
ESPAÑOL	cabo	cascada	punta	lago	isla	riachuelo	rio	sierra
FRANÇAIS	cap	cascade	pointe	lac	île	ruisseau	rivière	chaîne
PORTUGUÊS	cabo	cascata	ponta	lago	ilha	riacho	rio	serra

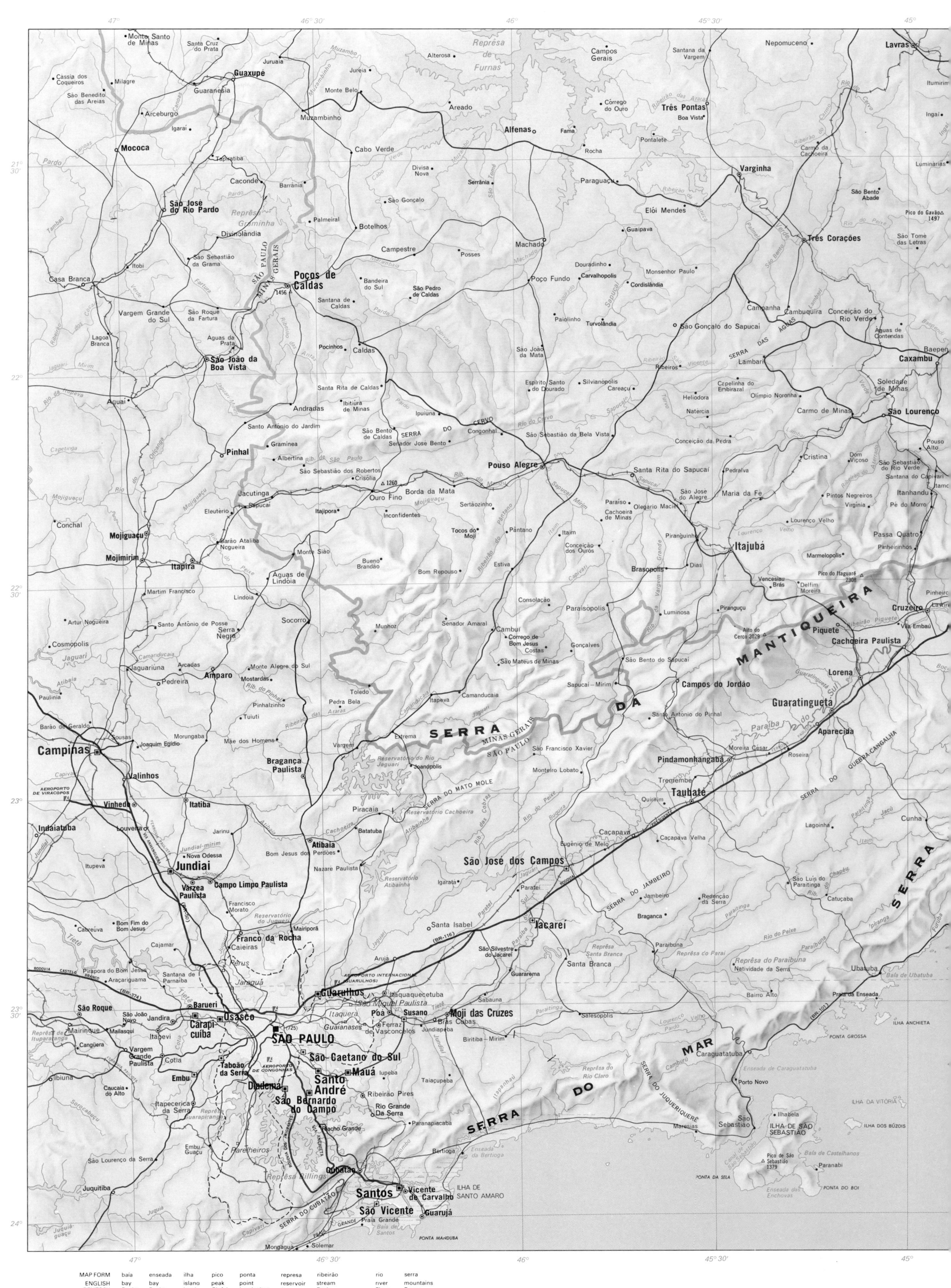

MAP FORM	baía	enseada	ilha	pico	ponta	represa	ribeirão	rio	serra
ENGLISH	bay	bay	island	peak	point	reservoir	stream	river	mountains
DEUTSCH	Bucht	Bucht	Insel	Gipfel	Landspitze	Stausee	Bach	Fluss	Berge
ESPAÑOL	bahia	bahia	isla	pico	punta	estanque	corriente de agua	rio	sierra
FRANÇAIS	baie	baie	île	cime	pointe	réservoir	cours d'eau	rivière	montagnes
PORTUGUÊS	baía	enseada	ilha	pico	ponta	represa	ribeirão	rio	serra

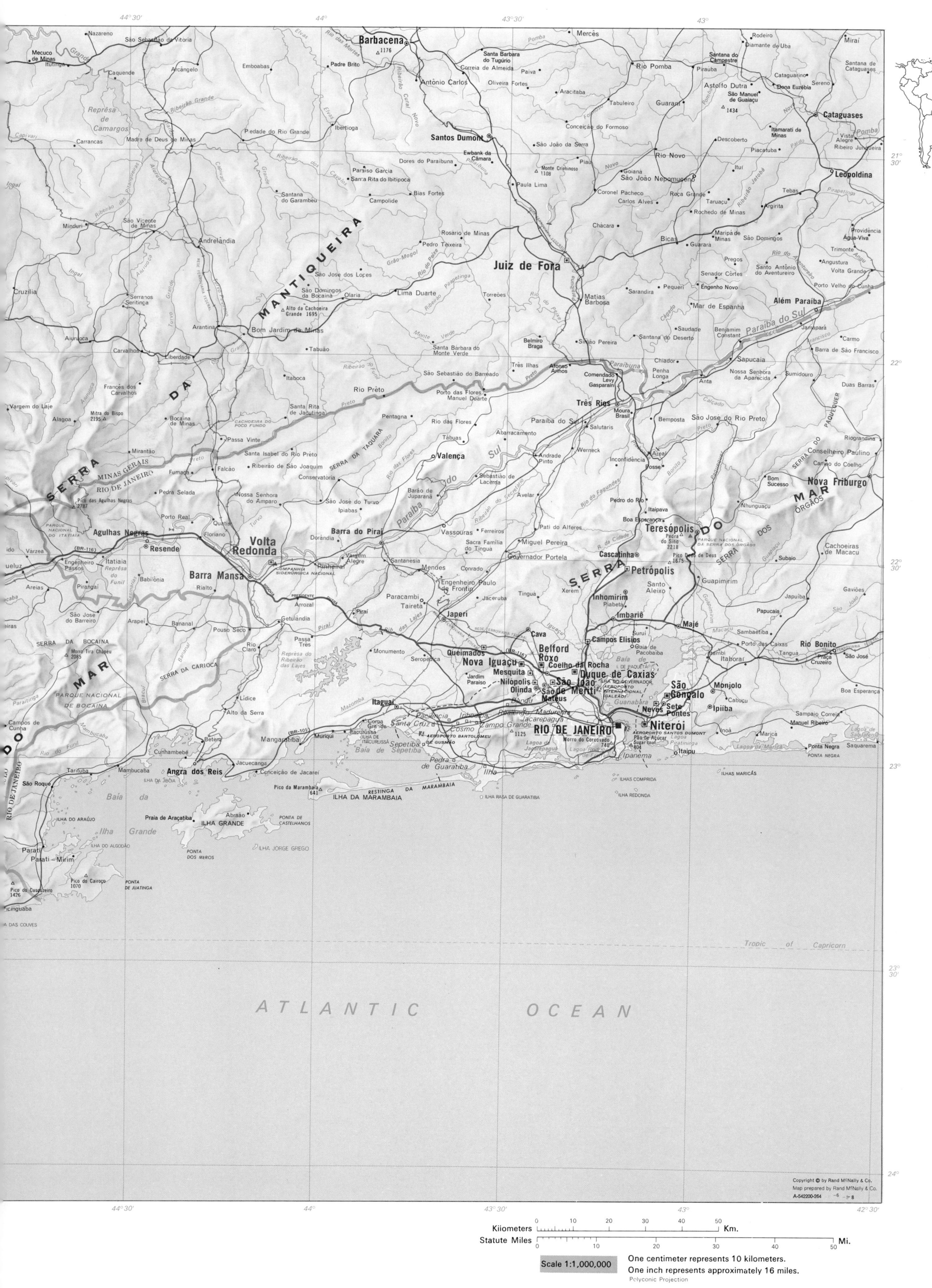

Kilometers | 0   10   20   30   40   50   Km.
Statute Miles | 0   10   20   30   40   50   Mi.

Scale 1:1,000,000

One centimeter represents 10 kilometers.
One inch represents approximately 16 miles.

Polyconic Projection

Copyright © by Rand McNally & Co.
Map prepared by Rand McNally & Co.
A-542200-264   -6 - -8

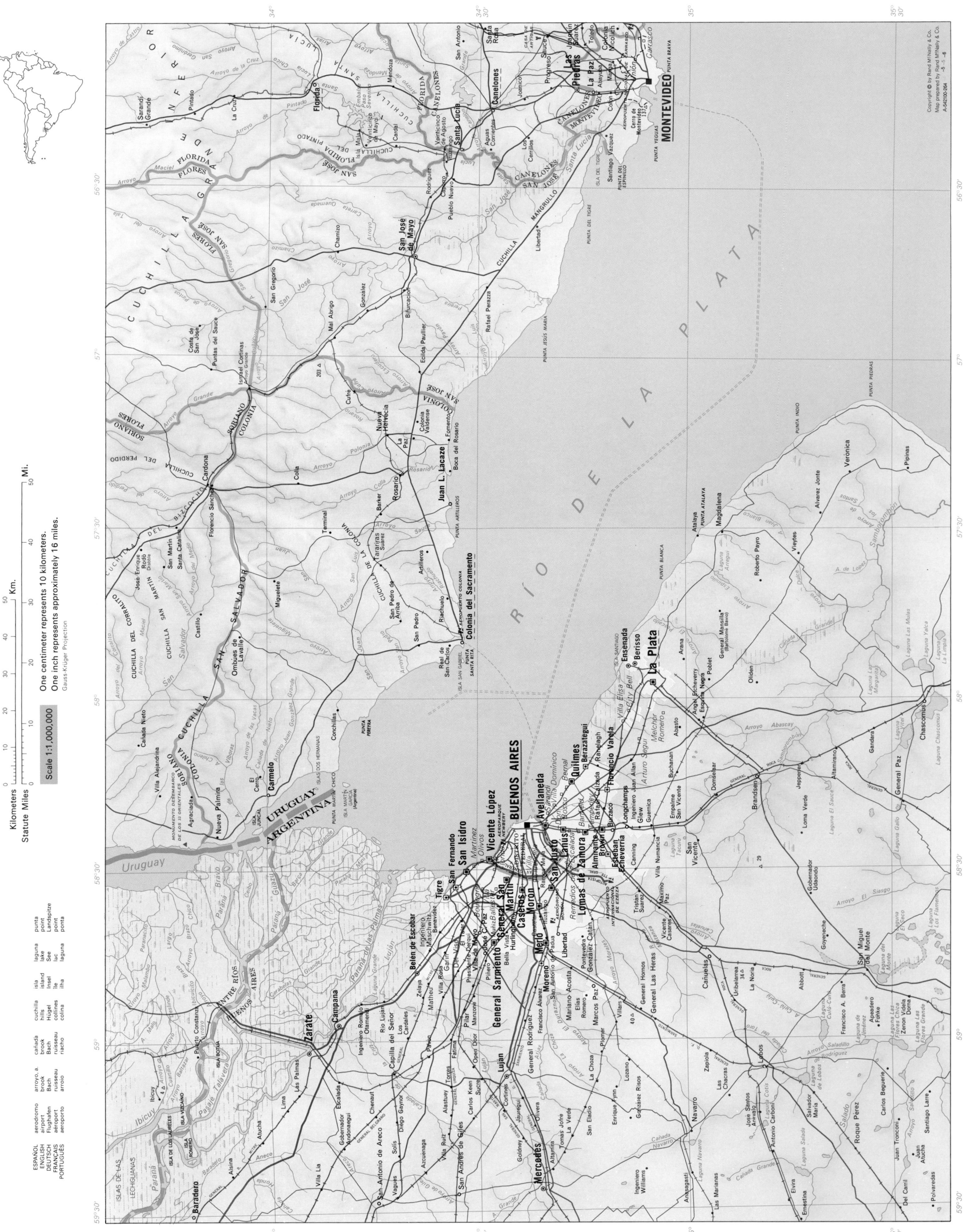

Copyright © by Rand McNally & Co.
Map prepared by Rand McNally & Co.
A-542100-264   -5-1 -6

Kilometers
Statute Miles

Scale 1:1,000,000

One centimeter represents 10 kilometers.
One inch represents approximately 16 miles.
Gauss-Krüger Projection

ESPAÑOL	ENGLISH	DEUTSCH	FRANÇAIS	PORTUGUÊS
aeródromo	airport	Flughafen	aéroport	aeroporto
arroyo, a.	brook	Bach	ruisseau	arroio
cañada	brook	Bach	ruisseau	riacho
cuchilla	hills	Hügel	collines	colina
isla	island	Insel	île	ilha
laguna	lake	See	lac	laguna
punta	point	Landspitze	point	ponta

MONTEVIDEO

BUENOS AIRES

RIO DE LA PLATA

URUGUAY
ARGENTINA

Metropolitan Area Maps/Karten von Stradtregionen
Mapas de las Areas Metropolitanas/Cartes des Zones Métropolitaines
Mapas das Áreas Metropolitanas

259

THIS SECTION CONSISTS of 60 maps of the world's major metropolitan areas, at the scale of 1:300,000. The maps show the generalized land-use patterns in and around each city—the total urban extent, major industrial areas, parks and preserves, and wooded areas. Airports are shown, as are many details of the highway and rail transportation networks. Selected points of interest appear, such as Fisherman's Wharf and Chinatown in San Francisco, the Welcome monument in Jakarta, the Temple of the Jade Buddha in Shanghai, and the Cristo Redentor statue in Rio de Janeiro.

The maps name and locate a great number of towns, villages, and suburbs, and also sections or neighborhoods within limits of the larger cities. Prominent physical features, including elevations, named and unnamed, have been indicated to give a general impression of the local topography. Shaded relief has been omitted, however, to permit display of such details as streams, parks, airport runways, important public buildings and monuments, and the names of major streets. The corporate limits of major cities are also outlined. For the symbols used on these maps see the Legend to Maps.

Maps of major world cities usually vary widely in scale, and heretofore have not been consistent in design and coverage. For this section, a special effort has been made to portray these varied metropolitan areas in as standard and comparable a fashion as possible. However, for a few cities (notably several in Asia) there has not been adequate source material to include certain information, such as major industrial areas and corporate limits.

The order of presentation is generally regional, with some exceptions where for ease of comparison major capitals or industrial centers or cities located in similar physical surroundings have been juxtaposed. Many American cities and some European cities, with their lower densities and more extensive areas, require larger maps than do Asiatic cities of comparable population. The total land area and population within the confines of each map are stated in the margin as a further aid to comparison.

DIESER KARTENTEIL UMFASST 60 Karten der bedeutendsten Stadtregionen der Erde im Massstab 1:300 000. Die Karten zeigen in generalisierter Form die Landnutzung in und um jede Stadt: die gesamte Ausdehnung des verstädterten Gebietes, wichtige Industriegebiete, Parks, Landflächen in Gemeinbesitz und Wald. Flughäfen werden ebenso dargestellt wie viele Einzelheiten des Strassen- und Eisenbahnnetzes. Bekannte Sehenswürdigkeiten sind eingetragen wie die "Fisherman's Wharf" und "Chinatown" in San Francisco, das Willkomm-Denkmal in Jakarta, der Tempel des Jade-Buddhas in Shanghai und die "Cristo Redentor"-Statue in Rio de Janeiro.

Die Karten verzeichnen Name and Lage einer grossen Zahl von Städten, Dörfern, Vororten ebenso wie eingemeindete Ortsteile bei grösseren Städten. Hervortretende physische Formen wie benannte und unbenannte Erhebungen sind aufgenommen, um eine allgemeine Vorstellung des lokalen Reliefs zu geben. Auf die Schummerung wurde jedoch verzichtet, um klar solche Einzelheiten wie Flüsse, Parks, Start- und Landebahnen der Flughäfen, bedeutende öffentliche Gebäude und Denkmäler sowie die Namen der wichtigsten Strassen herausstellen zu können. Eingetragen sind ferner die Gemeindegrenzen der wichtigsten Städte. Zu den auf diesen Karten verwendeten Signaturen siehe "Zeichenerklärung".

Karten der bedeutendsten Weltstädte differieren normalerweise sehr stark in ihren Massstäben und sind daher uneinheitlich in ihrer Gestaltung und Begrenzung. Deshalb wurde in diesem Kartenteil besonderer Wert darauf gelegt, die verschiedenen städtischen Ballungsgebiete in möglichst einheitlicher und vergleichbarer Form darzustellen. Für einige Städte, vor allem mehrere asiatische, war das Quellenmaterial jedoch nicht ausreichend genug, um gewisse Informationen wie Hauptindustriegebiete oder Stadtgrenzen einzutragen.

Im allgemeinen sind diese Karten nach regionalen Gesichtspunkten geordnet. Um Vergleiche zu erleichtern wurden einige Ausnahmen gemacht, indem wichtige Hauptstädte, Industriezentren oder Städte in vergleichbarer landschaftlicher Lage einander gegenübergestellt wurden. Viele amerikanische und einige europäische Städte mit ihrer geringen Bevölkerungsdichte, aber ausgedehnteren Fläche erfordern eine grössere Kartenfläche als asiatische Städte von vergleichbarer Bevölkerungszahl. Die gesamte Landfläche und die Bevölkerung innerhalb des dargestellten Gebietes ist am Kartenrand verzeichnet als ein weiteres Hilfsmittel für Vergleiche.

INTEGRAN ESTA SECCION 60 mapas de las áreas metropolitanas más importantes del mundo, a la escala de 1:300 000. Los mapas muestran los patrones de uso del suelo dentro de cada ciudad y en sus alrededores—la extensión total del conglomerado urbano, las principales áreas industriales, parques y reservas, y zonas boscosas. Aparecen los aeropuertos, así como muchos otros detalles de las redes de carreteras y ferrocarriles. Se seleccionaron también puntos de interés, como el Muelle de los Pescadores y el Barrio Chino de San Francisco, el monumento de Bienvenida de Jakarta, el Templo del Buda de Jade de Shanghai y la estatua del Cristo Redentor de Rio de Janeiro.

Los mapas incluyen los nombres y la ubicación de gran número de ciudades, poblaciones menores, suburbios, e inclusive barrios y distritos de algunas de las ciudades más importantes. Las características físicas sobresalientes, e incluso algunas elevaciones con o sin nombre, están indicados para dar una impresión general de la topografía local. Se omitió sin embargo el relieve sombreado, lo cual permite mostrar detalles como ríos y arroyos, parques, pistas de aterrizaje, edificios y monumentos públicos notables y los nombres de las calles principales. También están marcados los límites territoriales de las ciudades más grandes. Para la interpretación de los símbolos usados en estos mapas, véanse Leyendas para Mapas.

Los mapas de las ciudades más importantes del mundo varían generalmente en escala, y hasta ahora no han sido consistentes ni en diseño ni en contenido. En esta sección hemos hecho un esfuerzo de presentar las distintas áreas metropolitanas en la forma más uniforme posible, para facilitar sus comparaciones. Para algunas ciudades (la mayoría de ellas en Asia), no fué posible obtener de las propias fuentes material adecuado para la inclusión de ciertos datos, tales como las mayores áreas industriales y los límites municipales.

Los mapas de áreas metropolitanas se presentan por regiones, a excepción de unos cuantos que aparecen yuxtapuestos para facilitar la comparación entre grandes capitales, o centros comerciales, o ciudades ubicadas en contextos físicos similares. Muchas ciudades de América y algunas ciudades de Europa, por su baja densidad de población y su área extensa, requieren mapas más grandes que los ocupados por ciudades asiáticas con poblaciones comparables. Al margen de cada mapa se anotaron el área total y la población de territorio representado, lo cual facilita también las comparaciones.

CETTE PARTIE COMPREND 60 cartes des principales zones métropolitaines à l'échelle du 1:300 000ᵉ. Les cartes représentent les principaux types d'occupation du sol des villes et de leurs environs, c'est-à-dire de toute la zone urbanisée, les principales zones industrielles, les parcs et réserves naturelles, et les régions boisées. Les aéroports sont aussi représentés ainsi que de nombreux éléments des réseaux routier et ferroviaire. Certains lieux particulièrement intéressants sont indiqués, tels que le quai des pêcheurs et la ville chinoise à San Francisco, le monument de la Bienvenue à Jakarta, le temple du Bouddha de Jade à Shanghai et la statue du Christ Rédempteur à Rio de Janeiro.

Les cartes permettent de localiser un grand nombre de villes, villages et banlieues, ainsi que des quartiers de grandes villes. Les caractéristiques topographiques notables, comme les hauteurs sont indiquées même si elles ne portent pas de nom, pour donner une idée du site de l'aire métropolitaine. L'estompage du relief est cependant omis pour permettre de représenter cours d'eau, parks, pistes d'envol des aéroports, monuments et bâtiments publics importants, noms des principales rues, ainsi que les limites municipales des grandes villes. (Pour la signification des symboles voir légende.)

En général, les échelles des cartes des grandes villes du monde varient considérablement, et jusqu'ici la présentation et le contenu de ces cartes n'étaient pas comparables. Dans cette partie de l'Atlas, un effort spécial a été fait pour représenter les diverses zones métropolitaines de manière aussi homogène que possible. Cependant, dans certains cas (en Asie notamment), les documents de base n'étaient pas assez complets pour qu'il fût possible d'inclure avec précision des données comme les zones industrielles et les limites municipales.

L'ordre de présentation est régional, avec des exceptions quand, pour faciliter les comparaisons, de grandes capitales de grands centres industriels ou encore des villes possédant un même environnement naturel, sont juxtaposés. Beaucoup de villes américaines et quelques villes européennes ont une faible densité de population et une étendue considérable; elles requièrent, par conséquent, des cartes plus grandes que des villes asiatiques de population similaire. La superficie et la population de chaque carte sont indiquées dans la marge.

INTEGRAM ESTA SEÇÃO 60 mapas das áreas metropolitanas mais importantes do mundo, em escala de 1:300 000. Os mapas mostram os principais tipos de uso do solo em cada cidade e seus arredores, seja, a extensão total da zona urbanizada, as principais áreas industriais, os parques e reservas, e as áreas florestais. Mostram os aeroportos, e muitos detalhes das redes rodo e ferroviária. Indicam também pontos de interesse, selecionados, tais como o Cais dos Pescadores e o Bairro Chinês de San Francisco, o monumento de Boasvindas, em Jakarta, o templo do Buda de Jade, em Shanghai, e a Estátua do Cristo Redentor, no Rio de Janeiro.

Os mapas apresentam o nome e a localização de grande número de cidades, vilas e subúrbios, e incluem bairros das cidades mais importantes. Foram indicadas as características físicas principais, inclusive elevações, com ou sem nome, com o objetivo de proporcionar uma idéia geral da topografia local. No entanto, omitiu-se o sombreado do relevo, para permitir a indicação de detalhes tais como cursos d'água, parques, pistas de aeroportos, edifícios públicos e monumentos notáveis, e os nomes das principais ruas, bem como os limites municipais das grandes cidades. Para a interpretação dos símbolos usados nesses mapas, ver as *Legendas dos mapas.*

Os mapas das cidades mais importantes do mundo variam consideravelmente, de modo geral, quanto à escala, e até o presente não são comparáveis nem na forma de apresentação nem no conteúdo. Nesta seção, fez-se um esforço especial para representar as diversas áreas metropolitanas do modo mais uniforme e comparável possível. No entanto, para algumas cidades, a maioria das quais da Ásia, não foi possível obter fontes fidedignas de informações, tais como áreas industriais principais e limites municipais.

A ordem de apresentação dos mapas das áreas metropolitanas é geralmente regional, exceto em certos casos em que, para facilidade de comparação, capitais ou centros industriais e cidades importantes localizadas em meio físico semelhante foram justapostos. Muitas cidades da América e algumas da Europa, por sua baixa densidade demográfica e áreas mais extensas, exigem mapas maiores que as cidades asiáticas de população comparável. À margem de cada mapa indicam-se a área terrestre e a população total do território representado, também para maior facilidade de comparação.

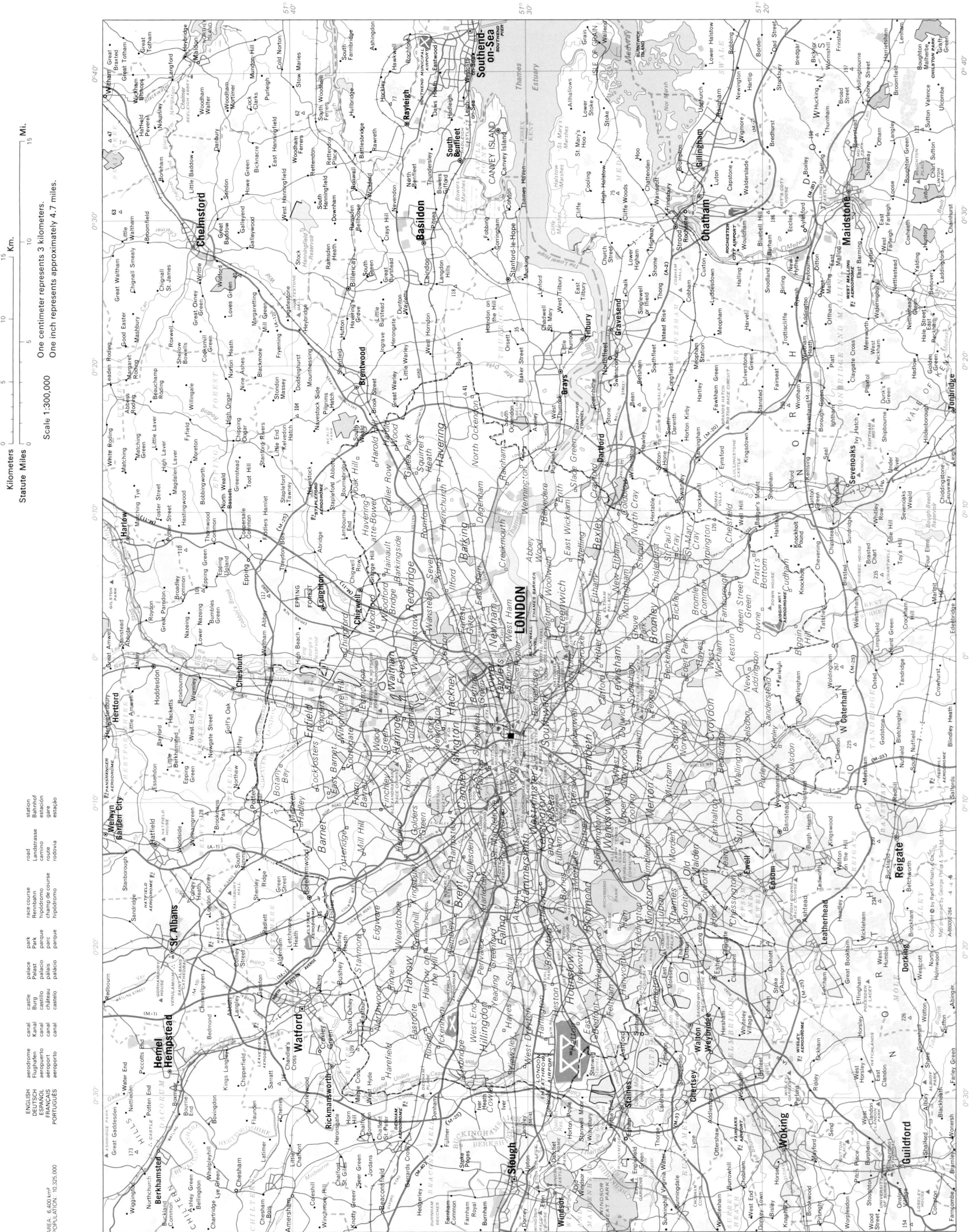

Scale 1:300,000

One centimeter represents 3 kilometers.
One inch represents approximately 4.7 miles.

ENGLISH	aerodrome	canal	castle	palace	park	race course	road	station
DEUTSCH	Flughafen	Kanal	Burg	Palast	Park	Rennbahn	Landstrasse	Bahnhof
ESPAÑOL	aeropuerto	canal	castillo	palacio	parque	hipódromo	camino	estación
FRANÇAIS	aéroport	canal	château	palais	parc	champ de course	route	gare
PORTUGUÊS	aeroporto	canal	castelo	palácio	parque	hipódromo	rodovia	estação

Kilometers
Statute Miles
Km.
Mi.

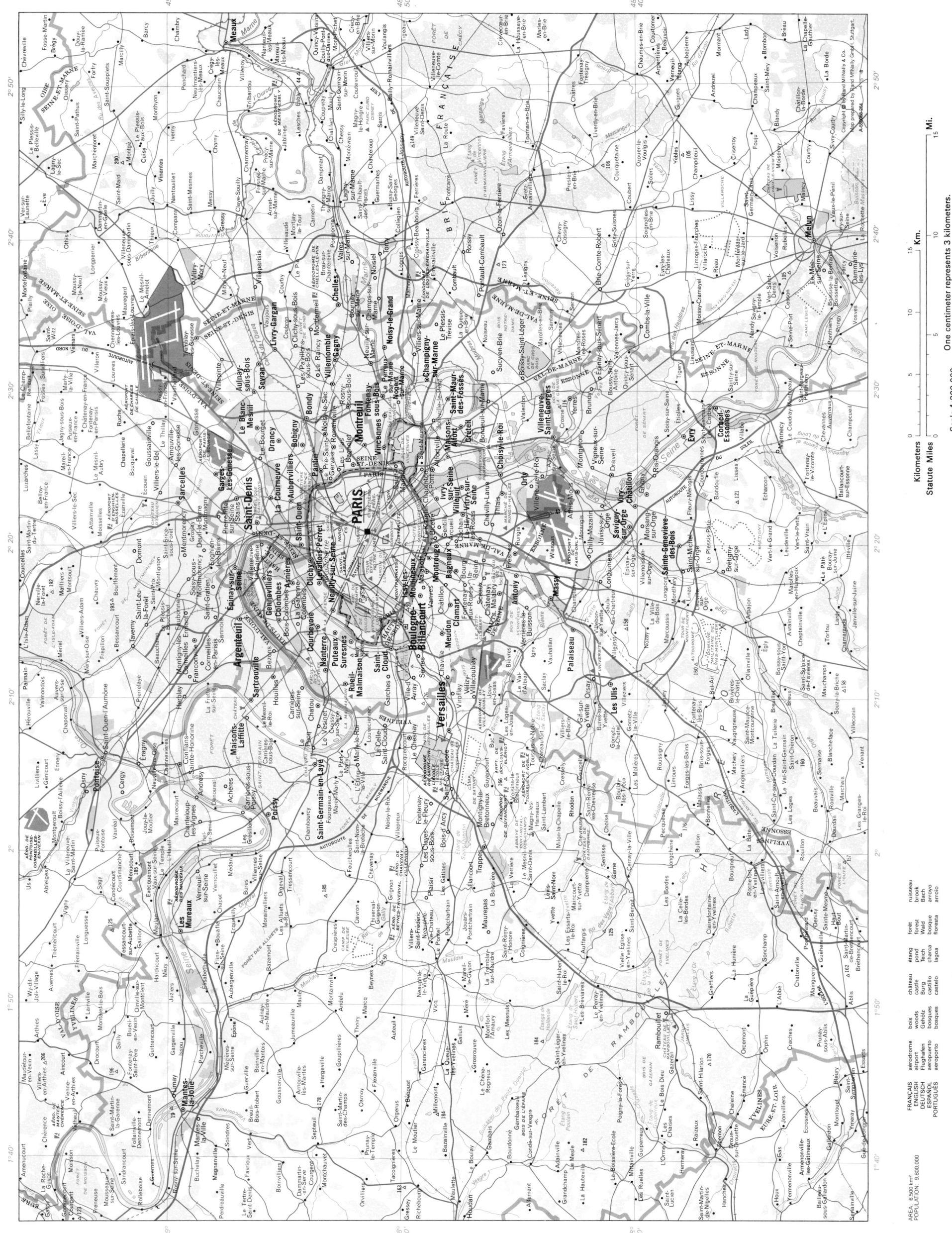

AREA 6,500 km²
POPULATION 9,800,000

FRANCAIS	aérodrome	bois	château	étang	forêt	ruisseau
ENGLISH	airport	woods	castle	pond	forest	brook
DEUTSCH	Flugplatz	Wald	Burg	Teich	Wald	Bach
ESPAÑOL	aeropuerto	bosques	castillo	charca	bosque	arroyo
PORTUGUÊS	aeroporto	bosques	castelo	lagoa	floresta	arroio

Kilometers 0 5 10 15 Km.

Statute Miles 0 5 10 15 Mi.

Scale 1:300,000

One centimeter represents 3 kilometers.
One inch represents approximately 4.7 miles.

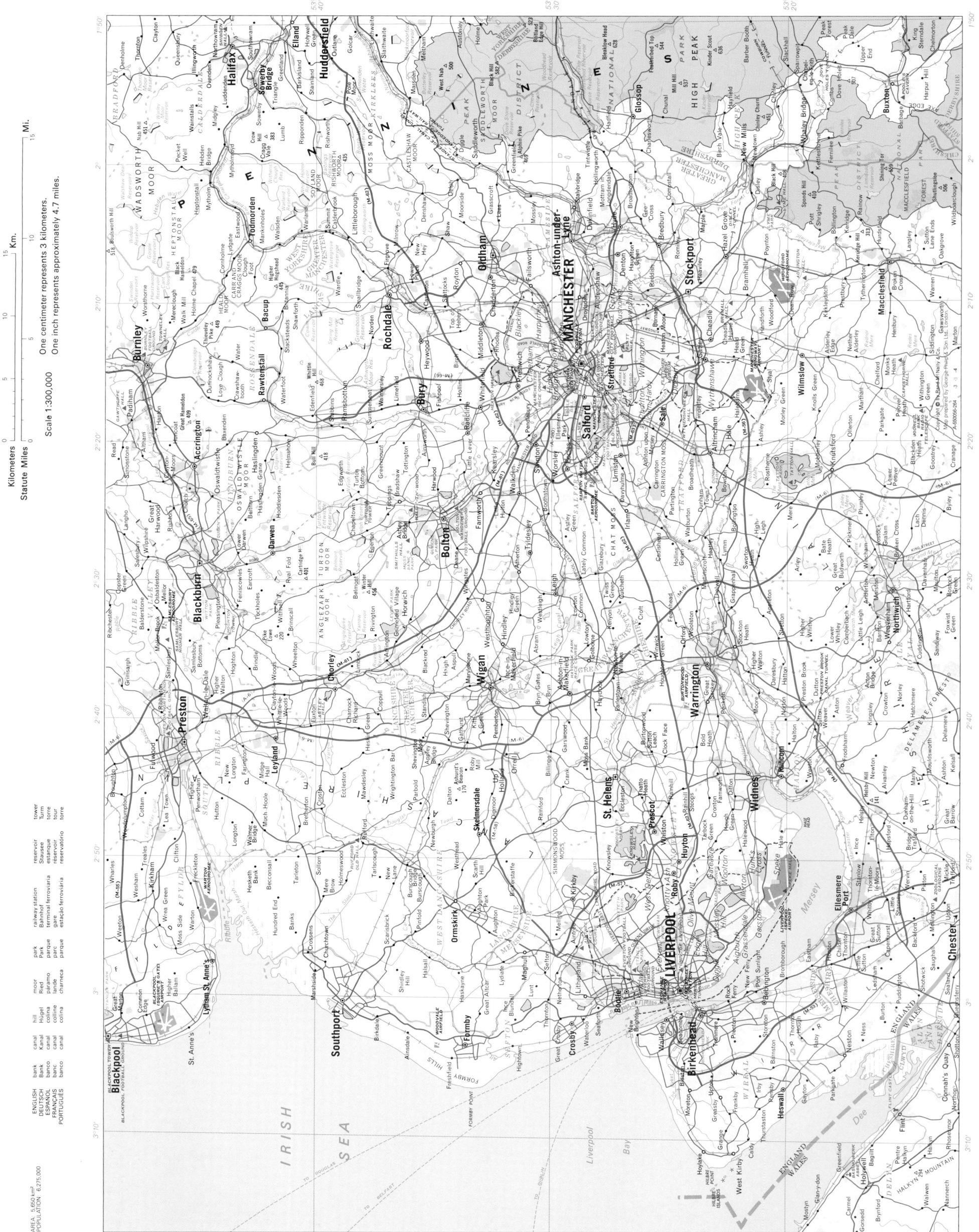

Scale 1:300,000

One centimeter represents 3 kilometers.
One inch represents approximately 4.7 miles.

Kilometers

Statute Miles

ENGLISH	bank	canal	hill	moor	park	railway station	reservoir	tower
DEUTSCH	Bank	Kanal	Hügel	Moor	Park	Bahnhof	Stausee	Turm
ESPAÑOL	banco	canal	colina	páramo	parque	terminal ferroviaria	estanque	torre
FRANCAIS	banc	canal	colline	lande	parc	gare	reservoir	tour
PORTUGUÊS	banco	canal	colina	charneca	parque	estação ferroviaria	reservoiro	torre

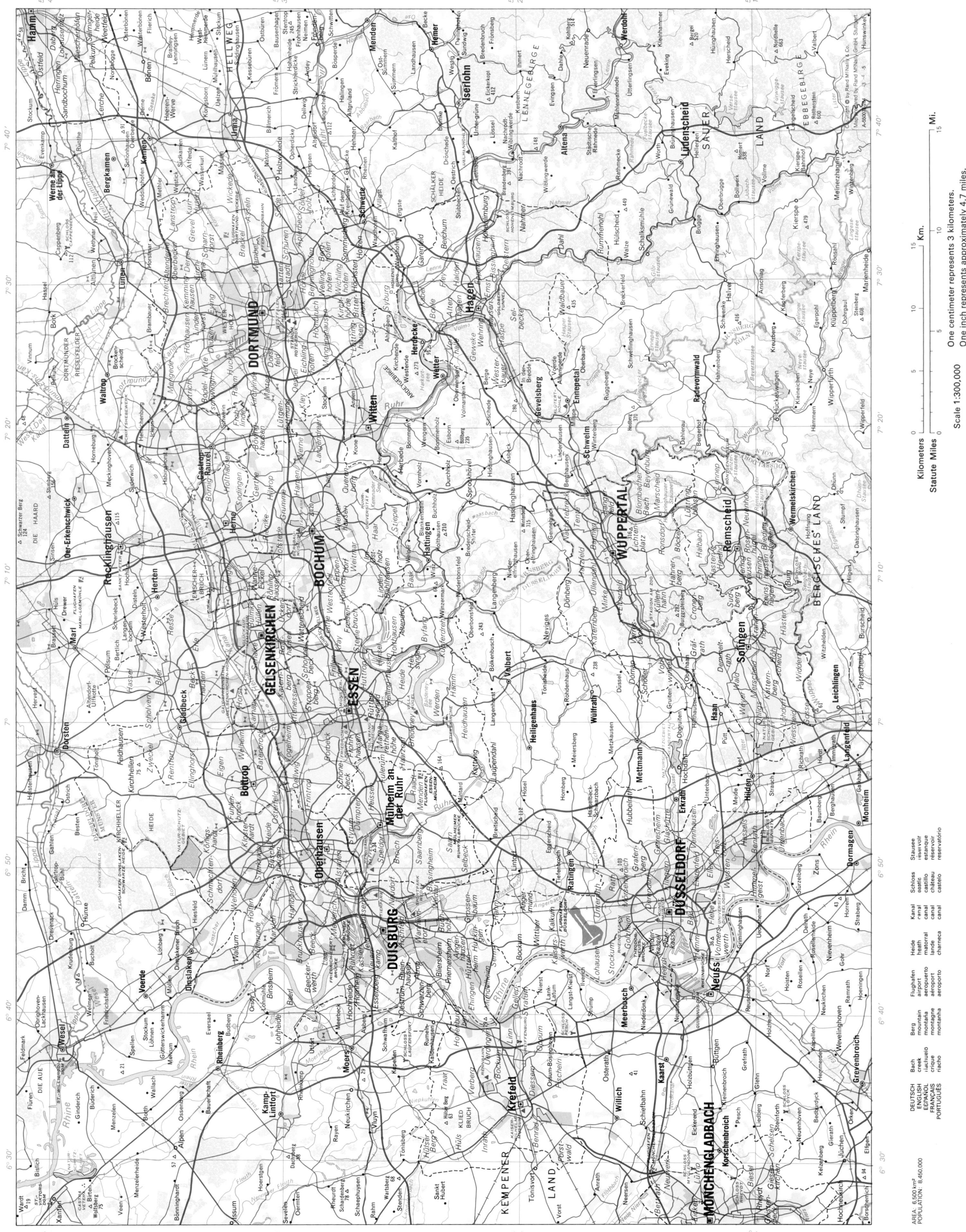

AREA 6,500 km²
POPULATION 8,450,000

DEUTSCH	Bach	Berg	Flughafen	Heide	Kanal	Schloss	Stausee
ENGLISH	creek	mountain	airport	heath	canal	castle	reservoir
ESPAÑOL	riachuelo	montaña	aeropuerto	matorral	canal	castillo	visaculf
FRANÇAIS	crique	montagne	aéroport	lande	canal	château	estanque
PORTUGUÊS	riacho	montanha	aeroporto	charneca	canal	castelo	reservatório

Scale 1:300,000

One centimeter represents 3 kilometers.

One inch represents approximately 4.7 miles.

Kilometers 0 ___ 5 ___ 10 ___ 15 Km.

Statute Miles 0 ___ 5 ___ 10 ___ 15 Mi.

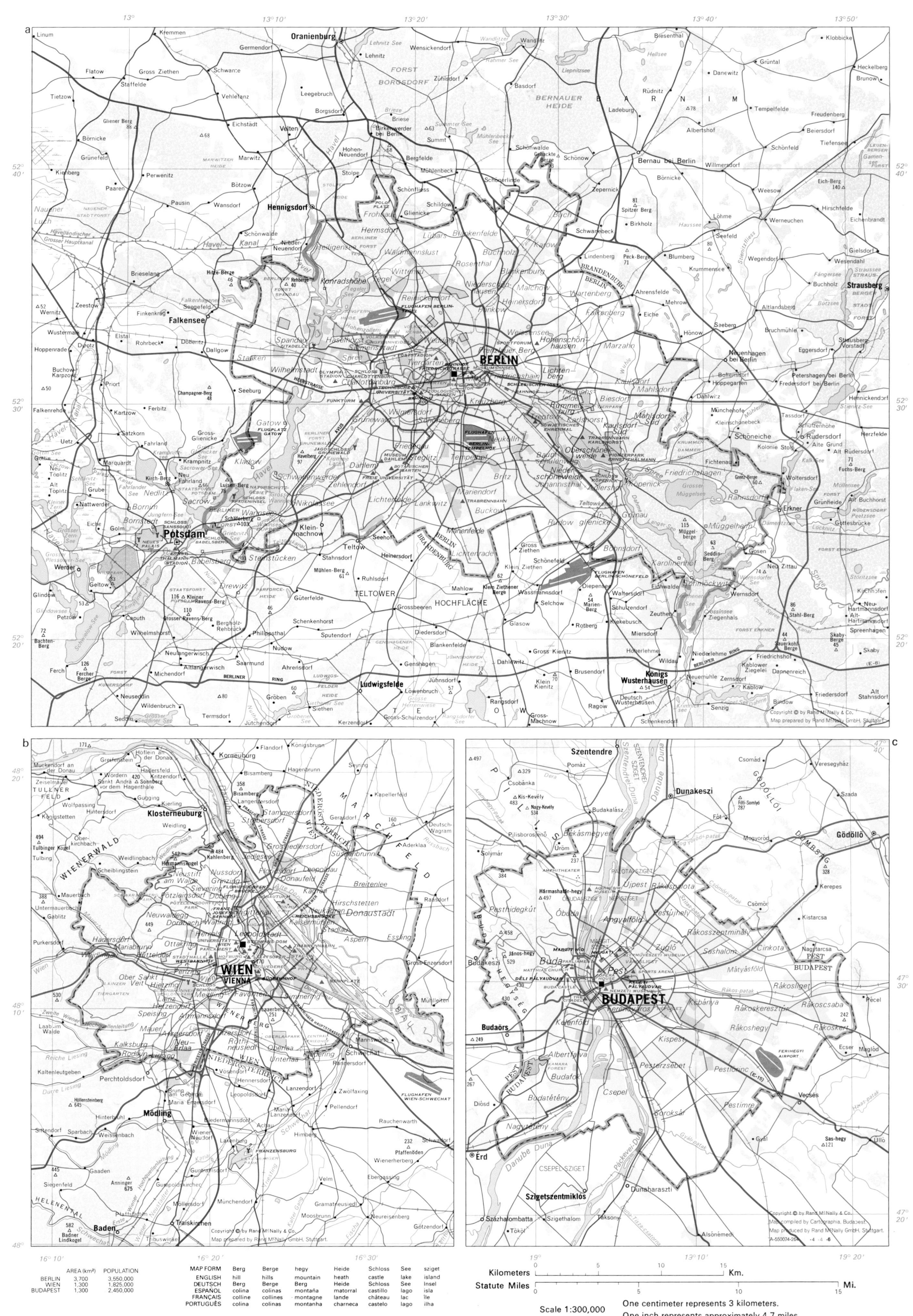

	AREA (km²)	POPULATION
BERLIN	3,700	3,550,000
WIEN	1,300	1,825,000
BUDAPEST	1,300	2,450,000

MAP FORM	Berg	Berge	hegy	Heide	Schloss	See	sziget
ENGLISH	hill	hills	mountain	heath	castle	lake	island
DEUTSCH	Berg	Berge	Berg	Heide	Schloss	See	Insel
ESPAÑOL	colina	colinas	montaña	matorral	castillo	lago	isla
FRANÇAIS	colline	collines	montagne	lande	château	lac	île
PORTUGUÊS	colina	colinas	montanha	charneca	castelo	lago	ilha

Kilometers

Statute Miles

Scale 1:300,000

One centimeter represents 3 kilometers.
One inch represents approximately 4.7 miles.

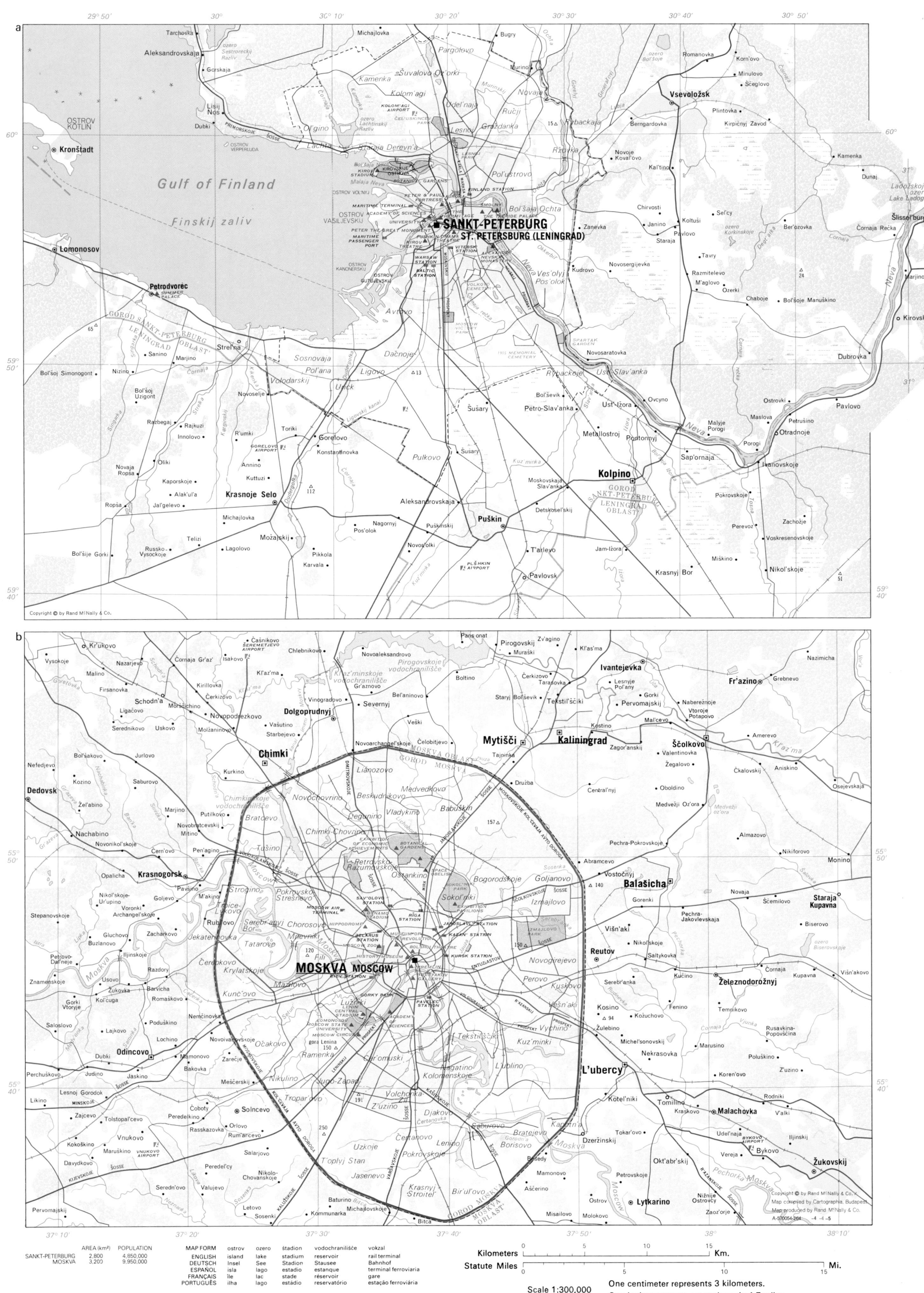

a

29° 50'   30°   30° 10'   30° 20'   30° 30'   30° 40'   30° 50'

Tarchovka
Aleksandrovskaja
Michajlovka
Bugry
Pargolovo
Romanovka
Korn'ovo
Minulovo
Ščeglovo
ozero
Gorskaja
Šuvalovo   Ožorki
Kamenka   Kolom'agi
Murino
Novoje   Vsevoložsk
Plintovka
Kirpičnyj Zavod

OSTROV
KOTLIN
Lisij
Nos
Ol'gino
ozero
Lachtinskij
Razliv
KOLOM'AGI
AIRPORT
ČEL'INCOV
Lesnoj   Gražd anka
15△   Rybackaja
Berngardovka
Ščeglovo
37°

Kronštadt
Dubki
PRIMORSKOJE
ŠOSSE
Staraja Derevn'a
Pol'ustrovo   Bol'šaja Ochta
Novoje
Koval'ovo
Kal'tino
Dunaj
Ladožskoje
ozero
Lake Ladoga

Gulf of Finland
Finskij zaliv
OSTROV VOLNYJ
MARITIME
TERMINAL
KIROV
STADIUM
KIROV
GARDENS
BOTANICAL GARDENS
PETER & PAUL
FORTRESS
FINLAND STATION
SMOLNY
Chirvosti
Sel'cy
Koltuši
Ber'ozovka
Čornaja Rečka
Šlissel'burg

ACADEMY OF SCIENCES
THE HERMITAGE THE PRIDE PALACE
Zanevka
Janino
Pavlovo
Staraja

OSTROV
VASIL'JEVSKIJ
UNIVERSITY
PETER THE GREAT MONUMENT
PUSHKIN MONUMENT
KIROV
THEATRE
SANKT-PETERBURG
ST. PETERSBURG (LENINGRAD)
Novosergijevka
Tavry
Razmitelevo

Lomonosov
MARITIME
PASSENGER
PORT
WARSAW
STATION
BALTIC
STATION
NEVSKIJ
VITEBSK
STATION
Ves'oly
Pos'olok
Kudrovo
M'aglovo
Ozerki
Chaboje
Bol'šoje Manuškino
Kirovsk

Petrodvorec
SUMMER
PALACE
OSTROV
KANONERSKIJ
OSTROV
GUTUJEVSKIJ
VOLKOV
CEMETERY
MOSCOW
VICTORY
PARK
1905 MEMORIAL
CEMETERY
SPARTAK
GARDEN
Novosaratovka
59°
50'

GOROD SANKT-PETERBURG
LENINGRAD   OBLAST'
65△
Strel'na
Avtovo
Dačnoje
Ligovo
Rybackoje   Ust'-Slav'anka
Ovcyno
Ostrovki
Maslova
Petrušino
Pavlovo
59°
50'

Bol'šoj Simonogont
Nizino
Sanino
Marjino
Sosnovaja
Pol'ana
△13
Bol'ševik
Petro-Slav'anka
Ust'-Ižora
Malyje
Porogi
Otradnoje

Bol'šoj
Uzigont
Razbegaj
Rajkuzi
R'umki
Toriki
Urick
Volodarskij
Novoselje
Ligovskij kanal
Šušary
Metallostroj
Pontonnyj
Sap'ornaja
Porogi
Ivanovskoje

Novaja
Ropsa
Oliki
Innolovo
Kaporskoje
GORELOVO
AIRPORT
Gorelovo
Konstantinovka
Pulkovo
Susary
Moskovskaja
Slav'anka
Kolpino
GOROD
SANKT-PETERBURG
LENINGRAD
OBLAST'
Pokrovskoje
Zachoje
Perevoz

Ropsa
Jal'gelevo
Kuttuzi
△112
Krasnoje Selo
Michajlovka
Alak'ul'a
Aleksandrovskaja
Detskobel'skij
Puškin
Nagornyj
Pos'olok
Puškinskij
Voskresenovskoje

Bol'šije Gorki
Russko-
Vysockoje
Telizi
Možajskij
Lagolovo
Pikkola
Novos'olki
T'arlevo
Jam-Ižora
Miškino
Nikol'skoje

Karvala
PŠKIN
AIRPORT
Pavlovsk
Krasnyj Bor
△51
59°
40'

Copyright © by Rand McNally & Co.

b

37° 10'   37° 20'   37° 30'   37° 40'   37° 50'   38°   38° 10'

Kr'ukovo
Čašnikovo
ŠEREMET'EVO
AIRPORT
Chlebnikovo
Pans onat
Pirogovskij
Zv'agino
Nazarjevo
Pirogovskoje
vodochranilišče
Muraški
Kl'as'ma
Nazimicha

Vysokoje
Malino
Nazarjevo
Čornaja Gr'az'
Isakovo
Novoaleksandrovo
Boltino
Čerkizovo
Lesnyje
Pol'any
Grebnevo
Ivantejevka
Fr'azino

Schodn'a
Kirillovka
Čerkizovo
Vinogradovo
Kl'az'ma
Gr'aznovo
Staryj Bol'ševik
Gorki
Tekstil'ščiki
Pervomajskij
Vtoroje
Potapovo

Ligačovo
Mörsčichino
Novopodrezkovo
Bel'aninovo
Veški
55°
50'

Serednikovo
Uskovo
Vašutino
Starbejevo
Dolgoprudnyj
GOROD MOSKVA
MOSKVA OBLAST'
Mytišči
Kaliningrad
Ščolkovo
Kl'az'ma
55°
50'

Bol'šakovo
Kozino
Jurlovo
Saburovo
Molžaninovo
Novoarchangel'skoje
Čelobitjevo
Tajninka
Valentinovka
Žegalovo
Aniskino

Dedovsk
Žel'abino
Marjino
Putilkovo
Chimki
Kurkino
Li'anozovo
Beskudnikovo
Druž ba
Central'nyj
Oboldino
Medvežji Oz'ora
Amerevo
Osejevskaja

Nachabino
Novonikol'skoje
Novobratcevskij
Mitino
Pen'agino
Chimkinskoje
vodochranilišče
Novočovrino
Degunino
Medvedkovo
Babuškino
Vladykino
157△
Pechra-Pokrovskoje
Almazovo

Cern'ovo
Tušino
Chimki-Chovanovo
Retrovsko-
Razumovskoje
BOTANICAL
GARDENS
Abramcevo
Nikiforovo
Monino

Opalicha
Krasnogorsk
Strogino
VDNH
EXHIBITION
SPACE
OBELISK
Sokol'niki
Bogorodskoje
Goljanovo
△140
Balašicha

Nikol'skoje-
Ur'upino
Voronki
Archangel'skoje
Pokrovskoje-
Strešnevo
Ostankino
Gorenki
Staraja
Kupavna

Stepanovskoje
Pavšino
M'akino
Ščukino
DINAMO
STADIUM
RIGA
STATION
Izmajlovo
Višn'aki
Novaja
Ščemilovo
Biserovo

Gluchovo
Zacharkovo
Rubl'ovo
Serebr'anyj
Bor
Chorošovo
HIPPODROME
MOSCOW AIR
TERMINAL
BELARUS
STATION
KAZAN' STATION
150△
Reutov
Saltykovka
ozero
Biserovskoje

Petrovo-
Dal'neje
Buzlanovo
Iljinskoje
Jekaterovka
Tatarovo
△120
Fili
HISTORY MUSEUM
BOL'ŠOJ THEATRE
KREMLIN
KURSK STATION
ENTUZIASTOV
Novogirejevo
Perovo
Serebr'anka
Čornaja
Kupavna
Višn'akovo
Železnodorožnyj

Znamenskoje
Usovo
Žukovka
Razdory
Krylatskoje
MOSKVA MOSCOW
Perovo
Kuskovo
Kučino

Gorki
Vtoryje
Barvicha
Korčuga
Romaškovo
Kunc'ovo
Mazilovo
GORKY PARK
PAVELEC
STATION
Novogrejevo
Kosino
Fenino
Temnikovo
Rusavkina-
Popovščina

Saloslovo
Poduškino
Lochino
Nemčinovka
LUŽNIKI
CENTRAL
STADIUM
KOMOMOSOL
MOSCOW STATE
UNIVERSITY
MOSCOW CIRCUS
ACADEMY OF
SCIENCES
△94
Kožuchovo
Žulebino
Michel'sonovskij
Marusino

Lajkovo
Novoivanovskoje
Očakovo
Zareče
gora Lenina
Ramenka
Čeromuški
Nagatino
Kolomenskoje
Kuz'minki
Ljublino
Nekrasovka
Poluškino

Odincovo
Dubki
Mamonovo
Bakovka
Meščerskoje
Nikulino
Sugo-Zapad
Volchonka
Z'uzino
Djakovo
△19
Saburovo
Brateevo
Borisovo
Moskva
Dzeržinskij
Koren'ovo
Z'uzino

Perchuškovo
Judino
Jaskino
△250
Solncevo
Uzkoje
Čertanovo
Lenino
L'ubercy
Kotel'niki
Tomilino
Kraskovo
Malachovka

Lesnoj Gorodok
MINSKOJE
ŠOSSE
Zajcevo
Peredelkino
Rasskazovka
Orlovo
Rum'ancevo
T'oplyj Stan
Jasenevo
Krasnyj
Stroitel'
Birul'ovo
Mamonovo
Okt'abr'skij
Udel'naja
BYKOVO
AIRPORT
Iljinskij

Likino
Tolstopal'cevo
Vnukovo
VNUKOVO
AIRPORT
Kokoškino
Maruškino
Nikolo-
Chovanskoje
Seredn'ovo
Valujevo
Čoboty
Baturino
Letovo
Sosenki
Mamonovo
Ostrov
Moskva
AšČerino
Misajlovo
Molokovo
Petrovskoje
Lytkarino
Nižnije
Ostrovcy
Zaoz'orje
Vereja
Bykovo
Žukovskij

Pervomajskij
Davydkovo
KIJEVSKOJE
ŠOSSE
Kommunarka
Michajlovka
Bitca
GOROD
MOSKVA
OBLAST'
Besedy
Tokar'ovo
Pechorka
Moskva

Copyright © by Rand McNally & Co.
Map compiled by Cartographia, Budapest
Map produced by Rand McNally & Co.
A-570054-264   -4 -4 -5

55°
40'

55°
40'

37° 20'   37° 30'   37° 40'   37° 50'   38° 10'

	AREA (km²)	POPULATION
SANKT-PETERBURG	2,800	4,950,000
MOSKVA	3,200	9,950,000

MAP FORM				
ENGLISH	ostrov	ozero	stadion	vodochranilišče	vokzal
	island	lake	stadium	reservoir	rail terminal
DEUTSCH	Insel	See	Stadion	Stausee	Bahnhof
ESPAÑOL	isla	lago	estadio	estanque	terminal ferroviaria
FRANÇAIS	île	lac	stade	réservoir	gare
PORTUGUÊS	ilha	lago	estádio	reservatório	estação ferroviária

Kilometers   0   5   10   15   Km.
Statute Miles   0   5   10   15   Mi.

Scale 1:300,000

One centimeter represents 3 kilometers.
One inch represents approximately 4.7 miles.

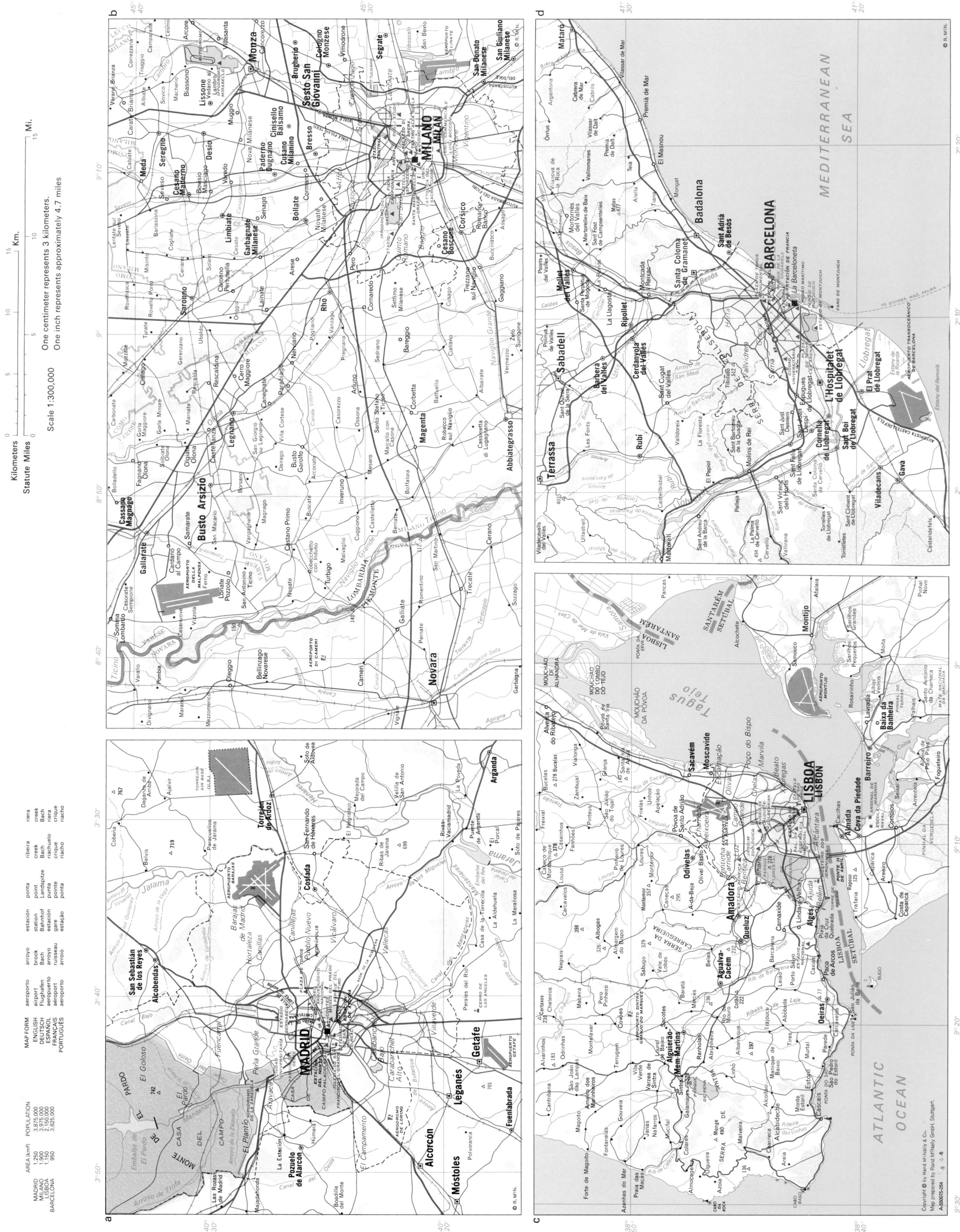

MADRID	AREA (km²)	POPULATION
MADRID	1,250	3,875,000
MILANO	1,900	3,975,000
LISBOA	1,150	2,150,000
BARCELONA	950	3,825,000

Kilometers / Statute Miles

Scale 1:300,000

One centimeter represents 3 kilometers.
One inch represents approximately 4.7 miles.

MAP FORM				
ENGLISH	aeropuerto	estación	ponta	ribera	riera
DEUTSCH	airport	station	point	creek	creek
ESPAÑOL	Flughafen	Bahnhof	Landspitze	riachuelo	riera
FRANCAIS	aeropuerto	estación	punta	ruisseau	riera
PORTUGUÊS	aeroporto	estação	ponta	riacho	riacho

Copyright © by Rand McNally & Co.
Map prepared by Rand McNally GmbH Stuttgart.

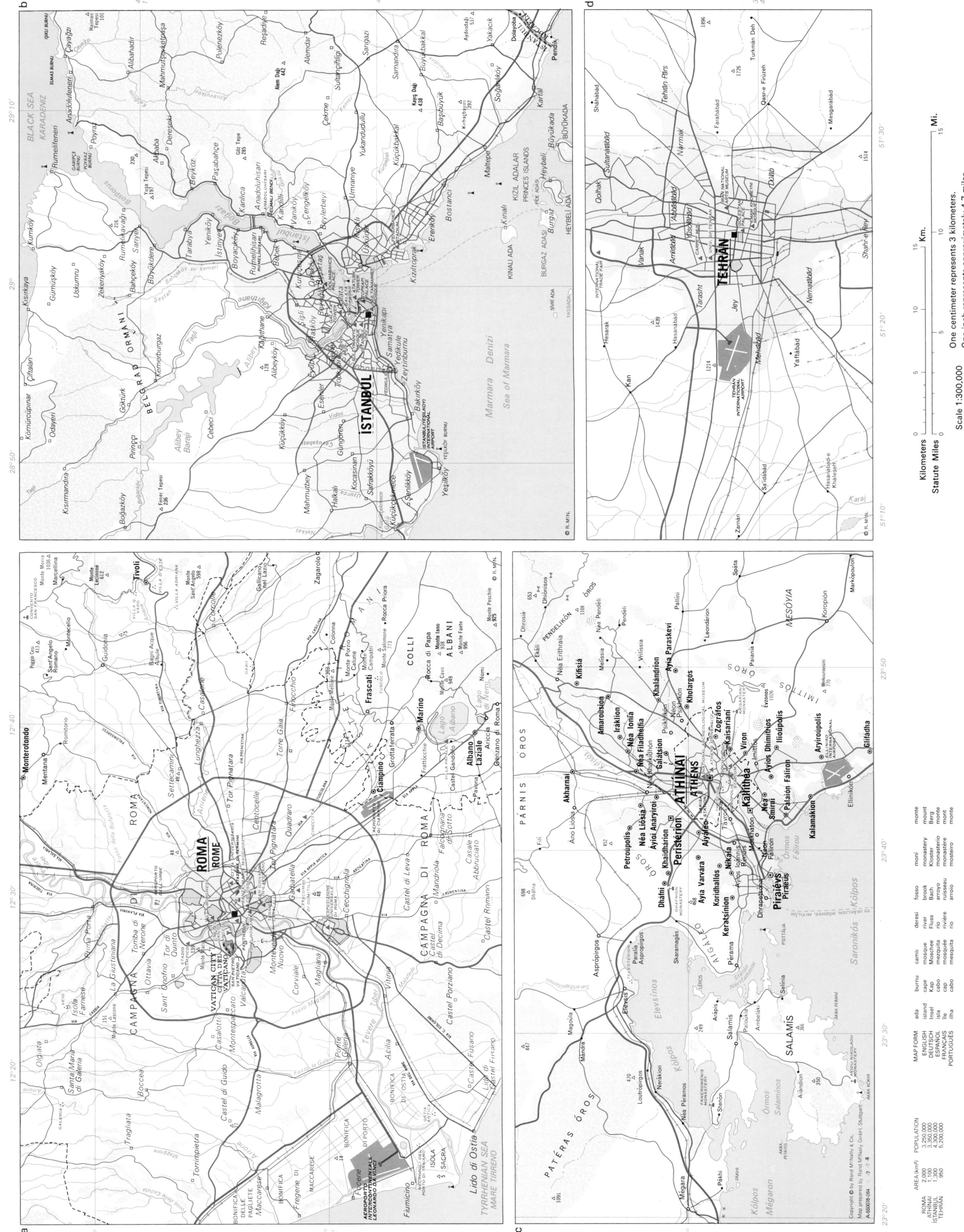

MAP FORM	ada	burnu	cami	deresi	fosso	moni		monte
ENGLISH	island	cape	mosque	river	brook	monastery		mount
DEUTSCH	Insel	Kap	Moschee	Fluss	Bach	Kloster		Berg
ESPAÑOL	isla	cabo	mezquita	rio	arroyo	monasterio		monte
FRANÇAIS	île	cap	mosquée	rivière	ruisseau	monastère		mont
PORTUGUÊS	ilha	cabo	mesquita	rio	arroio	mosteiro		monte

	AREA (km²)	POPULATION
ROMA	2,000	3,250,000
ATHÍNAI	1,100	3,350,000
İSTANBUL	1,300	4,300,000
TEHRĀN	950	5,200,000

Kilometers

Statute Miles

Km.

Mi.

Scale 1:300,000

One centimeter represents 3 kilometers.
One inch represents approximately 4.7 miles.

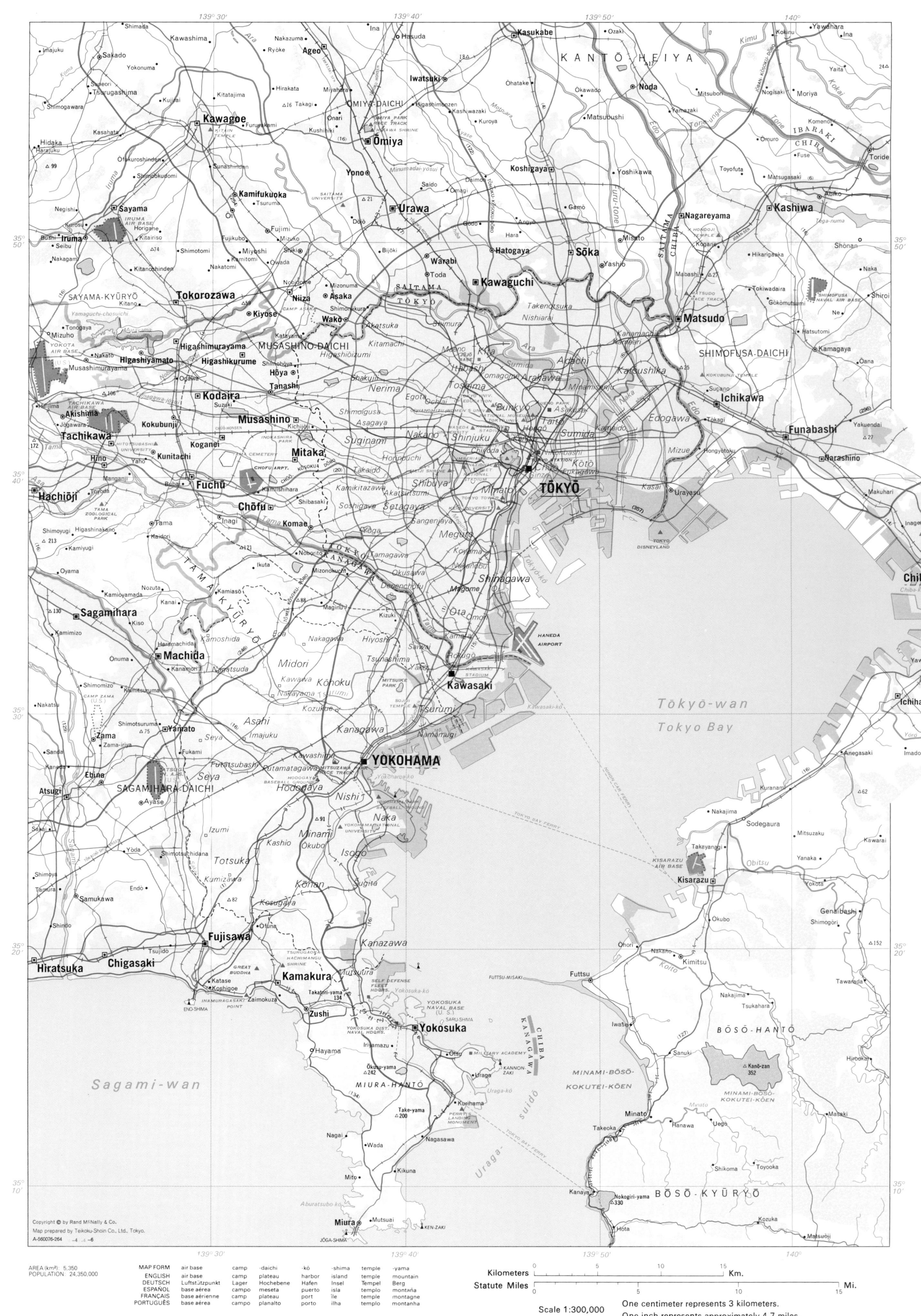

AREA (km²): 5,350
POPULATION: 24,350,000

MAP FORM					
ENGLISH	air base	camp	-daichi	-kō	-shima	temple	-yama
DEUTSCH	Luftstützpunkt	Lager	Hochebene	Hafen	Insel	Tempel	Berg
ESPAÑOL	base aérea	campo	meseta	puerto	isla	templo	montaña
FRANÇAIS	base aérienne	camp	plateau	port	île	temple	montagne
PORTUGUÊS	base aérea	campo	planalto	porto	ilha	templo	montanha

Kilometers

Statute Miles

Scale 1:300,000

One centimeter represents 3 kilometers.
One inch represents approximately 4.7 miles.

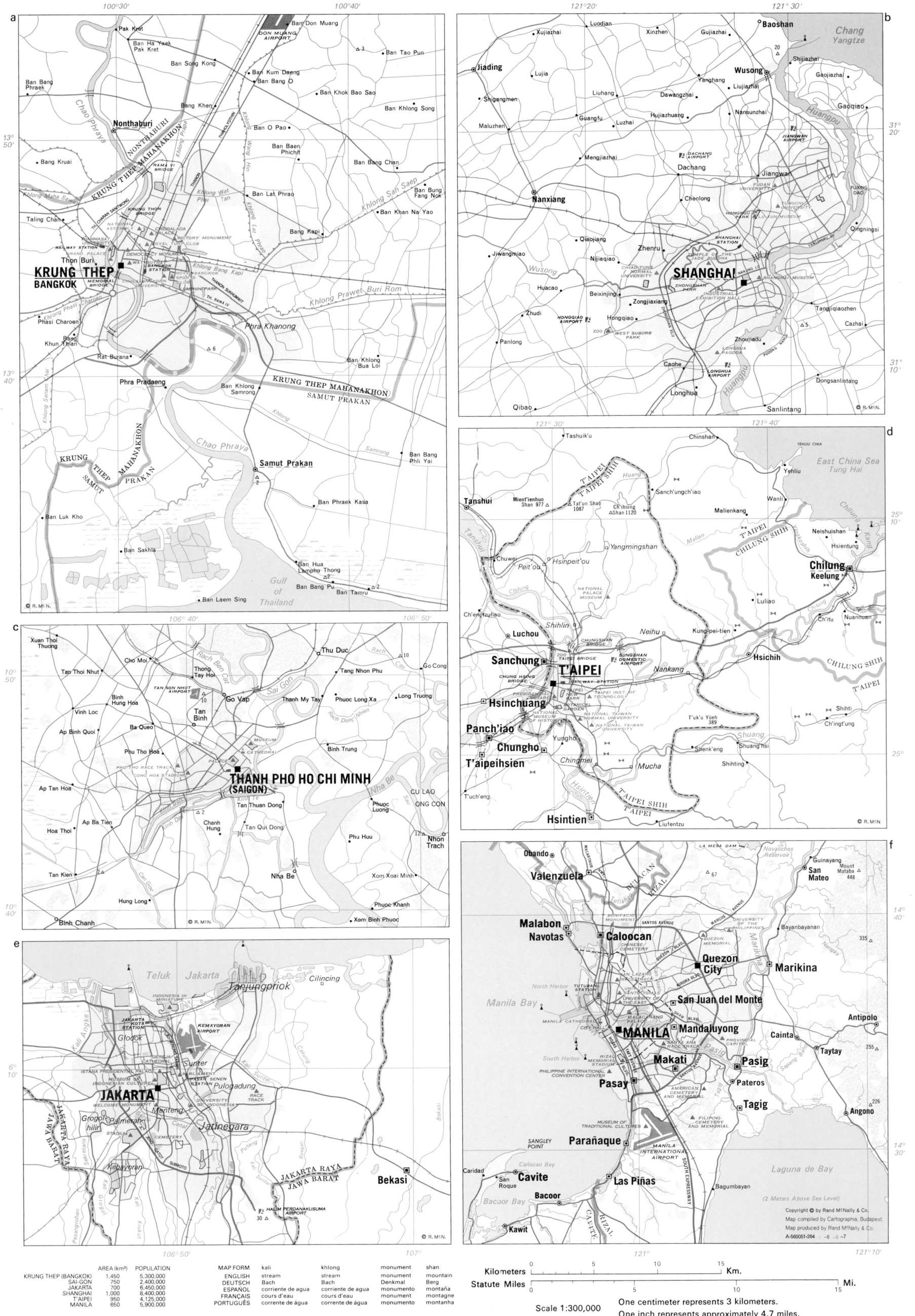

a (Krung Thep / Bangkok map)

Pak Kret
Ban Ha Yaek Pak Kret
Ban Song Kong
Ban Bang
Phraek
Bang Khen
Bang Kruai
Taling Chan
Thon Buri
KRUNG THEP
BANGKOK
Phasi Charoen
Bang Khun Thian
Rat Burana
Phra Pradaeng
Ban Luk Kho
Ban Sakhla
Samut Prakan
Nonthaburi
NONTHABURI
Chao Phraya
Khlong Maha Sawat
Khlong Bang Kapi
Khlong Phasi Charoen
Phra Khanong
KRUNG THEP MAHANAKHON
SAMUT PRAKAN
Gulf of Thailand
DON MUANG AIRPORT
Ban Don Muang
Ban Tao Pun
Ban Kum Daeng
Ban Bang O
Ban Khok Bao Sao
Ban Khlong Song
Ban Baen Phicht
Ban Bang Chan
Ban Bung Fang Nok
Ban Lat Phrao
Ban Khan Na Yao
Bang Kapi
Khlong San Saep
Khlong Prawet Buri Rom
Ban Khlong Bua Loi
Ban Khlong Samrong
Ban Bang Phli Yai
Ban Phraek Kasa
Ban Hua Lamphu Thong
Ban Bang Pu
Ban Tamru
Ban Laem Sing

c (Thanh Pho Ho Chi Minh / Saigon map)

Xuan Thoi Thuong
Tan Thoi Nhut
Cho Moi
Binh Hung Hoa
Vinh Loc
Ap Binh Quoi
Phu Tho Hoa
Ba Queo
Go Vap
Tan Binh
Thong Tay Hoi
Thanh My Tay
Phuoc Long Xa
Go Cong
Long Truong
Thu Duc
Tang Nhon Phu
THANH PHO HO CHI MINH (SAIGON)
Binh Trung
Phuoc Luong
Ap Tan Hoa
Hoa Thoi
Ap Ba Tien
Chanh Hung
Tan Thuan Dong
Tan Qui Dong
Phu Huu
CU LAO ONG CON
Tan Kien
Hung Long
Binh Chanh
Nha Be
Phuoc Khanh
Xom Xoai Minh
Xom Binh Phuoc
Nhon Trach
Rach Ben Cat
Sai Gon
TAN SON NHUT AIRPORT

e (Jakarta map)

Teluk Jakarta
Tanjungpriok
Cilincing
Jakarta Kota Station
Glodok
Kemayoran Airport
Sunter
Pulogadung
JAKARTA
Menteng
Jatinegara
Grogol
Palmerah
Kebayoran
JAKARTA RAYA
JAWA BARAT
Bekasi
Halim Perdanakusuma Airport

b (Shanghai map)

Jiading
Xujiazhai
Xinzhen
Luodian
Gujiazhai
Baoshan
Chang Yangtze
Lujia
Yanghang
Liujiazhai
Gaojiazhai
Wusong
Shijiazhai
Gaoqiao
Shigangmen
Liuhang
Dawangzhai
Guangfu
Luzhai
Hujiazhuang
Nansunzhai
Maluzhen
Mengjiazhai
Dachang
DACHANG AIRPORT
Jiangwan
JIANGWAN AIRPORT
FUXING DAO
Nanxiang
Cheolong
Qingningsi
Jiwangmiao
Qiaojiang
Zhenru
SHANGHAI STATION
Nijiaqiao
FUDAN UNIVERSITY
CHIAO-TUNG UNIVERSITY
Huacao
Beixinjing
SHANGHAI
Zhudi
Zongjiaxiang
HONGQIAO AIRPORT
Hongqiao
ZOO
WEST SUBURB PARK
Panlong
Caohe
LONGHUA PAGODA
Longhua
LONGHUA AIRPORT
Zhoujiadu
Tangjiaqiaozhen
Cazhai
Dongsanlintang
Qibao
Sanlintang
Wusong
Huangpu

d (T'aipei map)

Tashuik'u
Chinshan
YEHLIU CHIA
East China Sea Tung Hai
Mient'ienhuo Shan 977
T'at'un Shan 1087
Ch'ihsing Shan 1120
Yangmingshan
Sanch'ungch'iao
Wanli
Yehliu
Malienkang
Tanshui
T'AIPEI SHIH
Huang
Hsinpeit'ou
Peit'ou
Chuwei
Neishuishan
Hsientung
CHILUNG SHIH
Chilung Keelung
Ch'engtzuliao
Chilung
Shihlin
NATIONAL PALACE MUSEUM
Neihu
Kung-pei-tien
Ch'itu
Nuannuan
Luchou
CHUNGSHAN PARK
T'AIPEI BRIDGE
SUNGSHAN DOMESTIC AIRPORT
Sanchung
T'AIPEI
Nankang
Hsichih
CHILUNG SHIH
CHUNG HSING BRIDGE
RAILWAY STATION
PRESIDENTIAL PALACE
TAIPEI INST. OF TECHNOLOGY
T'AIPEI
Hsinchuang
NATIONAL MUSEUM OF HISTORY
NATIONAL TAIWAN NORMAL UNIVERSITY
T'u'k'u Yüeh 389
Shiti
Panch'iao
NATIONAL TAIWAN UNIVERSITY
Yungho
Ch'ingt'ung
Chungho
Shenk'eng
Shuang
T'aipeihsien
Chingmei
Mucha
Shuanghsi
Shihting
T'uch'eng
Hsintien
Hsintien
T'AIPEI SHIH
Liufentzu

f (Manila map)

Obando
LA MESA DAM
Novaliches Reservoir
Guinayan
San Mateo
Mount Mataba 448
Valenzuela
BULACAN RIZAL
67
Malabon
Navotas
BONIFACIO MONUMENT
SANTOS AVENUE
UNIVERSITY OF THE PHILIPPINES
Bayanbayanan
335
Caloocan
CHINESE CEMETERY
QUEZON MEMORIAL
Quezon City
Marikina
North Harbor
TUTUBAN STATION
UNIVERSITY OF THE EAST
San Juan del Monte
Antipolo
Manila Bay
MANILA CATHEDRAL
CITY HALL
BALARA FILTERS
Mandaluyong
Cainta
255
MANILA
SANTA ANA RACE TRACK
PROVINCIAL CAPITOL
Taytay
South Harbor
RIZAL MEMORIAL STADIUM
Makati
Pasig
Pateros
Pasay
AMERICAN CEMETERY AND MEMORIAL
Tagig
226
MUSEUM OF TRADITIONAL CULTURES
FILIPINO CEMETERY AND MEMORIAL
SANGLEY POINT
Parañaque
MANILA INTERNATIONAL AIRPORT
Cañacao Bay
Laguna de Bay
Caridad
San Roque
Cavite
Las Piñas
Bagumbayan
Bacoor
Bacoor Bay
CAVITE
RIZAL
SOUTH EXPRESSWAY
Kawit
Pasig

	AREA (km²)	POPULATION
KRUNG THEP (BANGKOK)	1,450	5,300,000
SAI-GON	750	2,400,000
JAKARTA	700	6,450,000
SHANGHAI	1,000	8,400,000
T'AIPEI	950	4,125,000
MANILA	650	5,900,000

MAP FORM				
	kali	khlong	monument	shan
ENGLISH	stream	stream	monument	mountain
DEUTSCH	Bach	Bach	Denkmal	Berg
ESPAÑOL	corriente de agua	corriente de agua	monumento	montaña
FRANÇAIS	cours d'eau	cours d'eau	monument	montagne
PORTUGUÊS	corrente de água	corrente de água	monumento	montanha

Kilometers
Statute Miles
0   5   10   15 Km.
0   5   10   15 Mi.

Scale 1:300,000

One centimeter represents 3 kilometers.
One inch represents approximately 4.7 miles.

Copyright © by Rand McNally & Co.
Map compiled by Cartographia, Budapest.
Map produced by Rand McNally & Co.
A-560051-264   -6 -6 -7

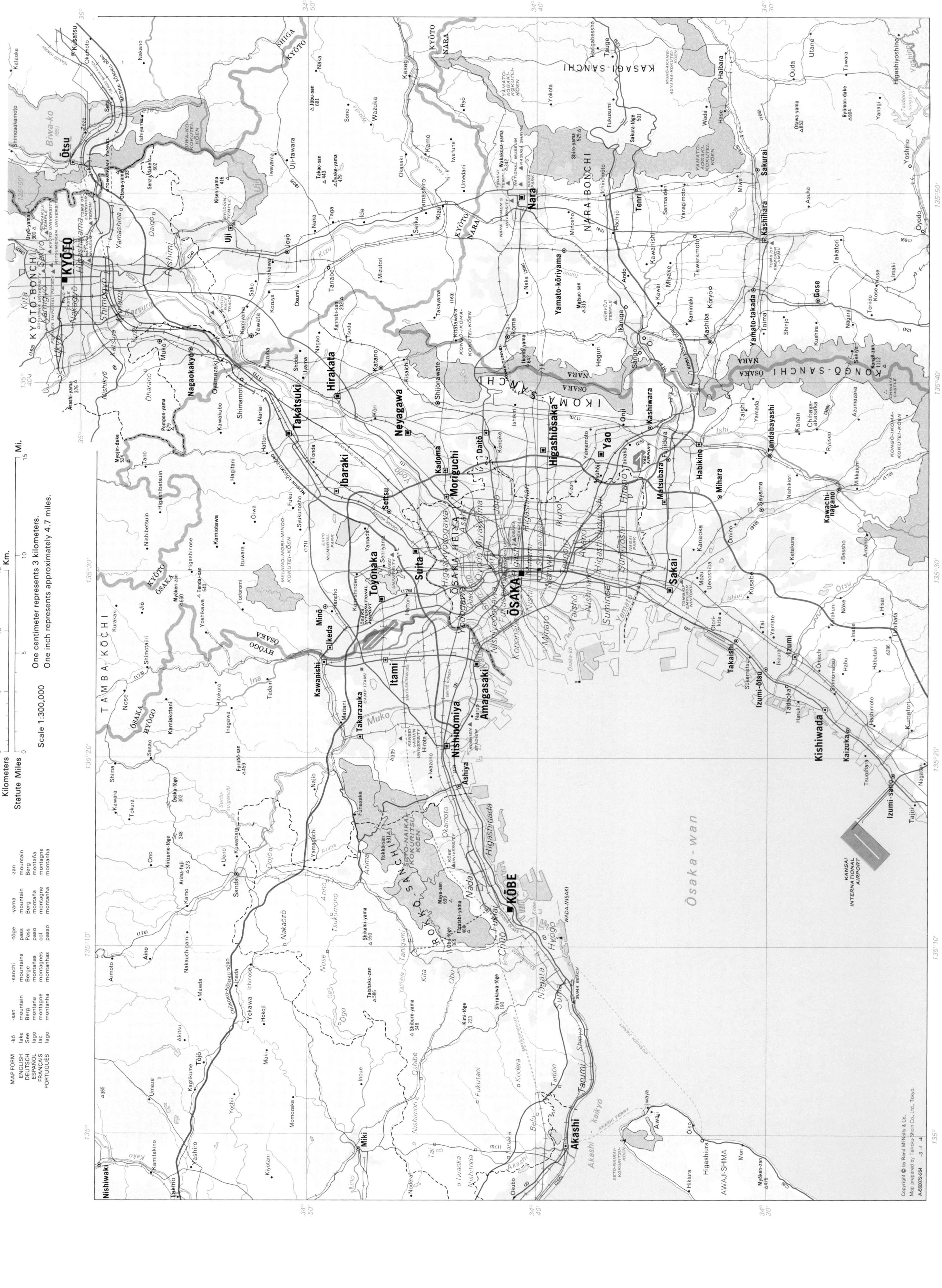
MAP FORM -kō -san -sanchi -tōge -yama -zan
ENGLISH lake mountain mountains pass mountain mountain
DEUTSCH See Berg Berge Pass Berg Berg
ESPAÑOL lago montaña montañas paso montaña montaña
FRANÇAIS lac montagne montagnes col montagne montagne
PORTUGUÊS lago montanha montanhas passo montanha montanha
Kilometers 0 5 10 15 Km.
Statute Miles 0 5 10 15 Mi.
Scale 1:300,000
One centimeter represents 3 kilometers.
One inch represents approximately 4.7 miles.
Copyright © by Rand McNally & Co.
Map prepared by Teikoku-Shoin Co., Ltd., Tokyo.
A-560072-264 -3 -4 -4
KYŌTO
ŌSAKA
KŌBE
Ōtsu
Nara
Sakai
Amagasaki
Nishinomiya
Akashi
Kishiwada
Takatsuki
Hirakata
Toyonaka
Suita
Ibaraki
Yao
Higashiōsaka
Uji
Ōsaka-wan
KANSAI INTERNATIONAL AIRPORT
AWAJI-SHIMA
Biwa-ko
KASAGI-SANCHI
NARA BONCHI
KYŌTO BONCHI
IKOMA-SANCHI
KONGŌ-SANCHI
RŌKKŌ-SANCHI
TAMBA-KŌCHI
ŌSAKA-HEIYA

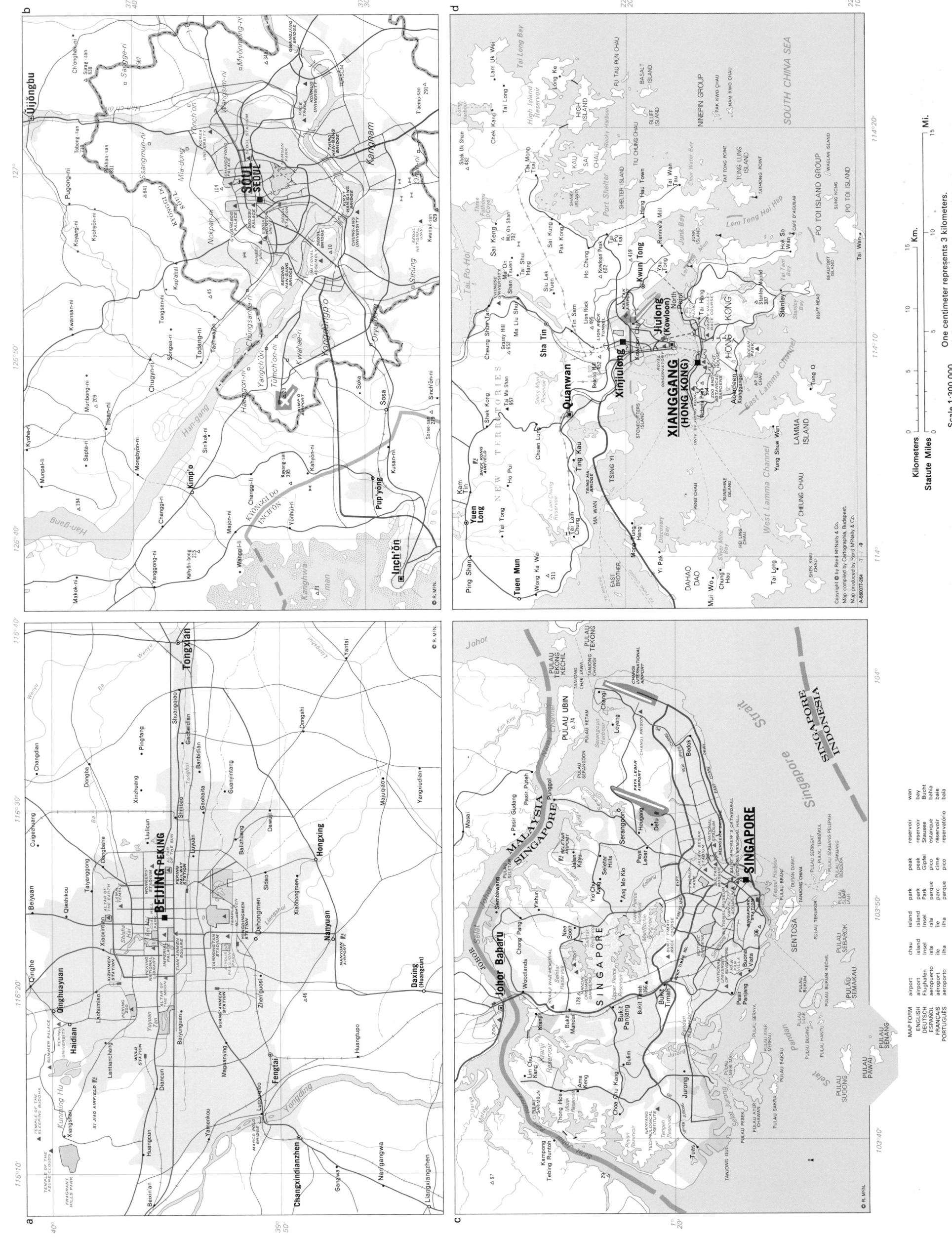

Scale 1:300,000

Kilometers

Statute Miles

One centimeter represents 3 kilometers.
One inch represents approximately 4.7 miles.

Copyright © by Rand McNally & Co.
Map compiled by Cartographia, Budapest.
Map produced by Rand McNally & Co.
A-560077-264

MAP FORM					
ENGLISH	airport	chau	island	park	peak	reservoir	bay
DEUTSCH	Flughafen	Insel	Insel	Park	Gipfel	Stausee	Bucht
ESPAÑOL	aeropuerto	isla	isla	parque	pico	estanque	bahía
FRANÇAIS	aéroport	île	île	parc	pic	réservoir	baie
PORTUGUÊS	aeroporto	ilha	ilha	parque	pico	reservatório	baía

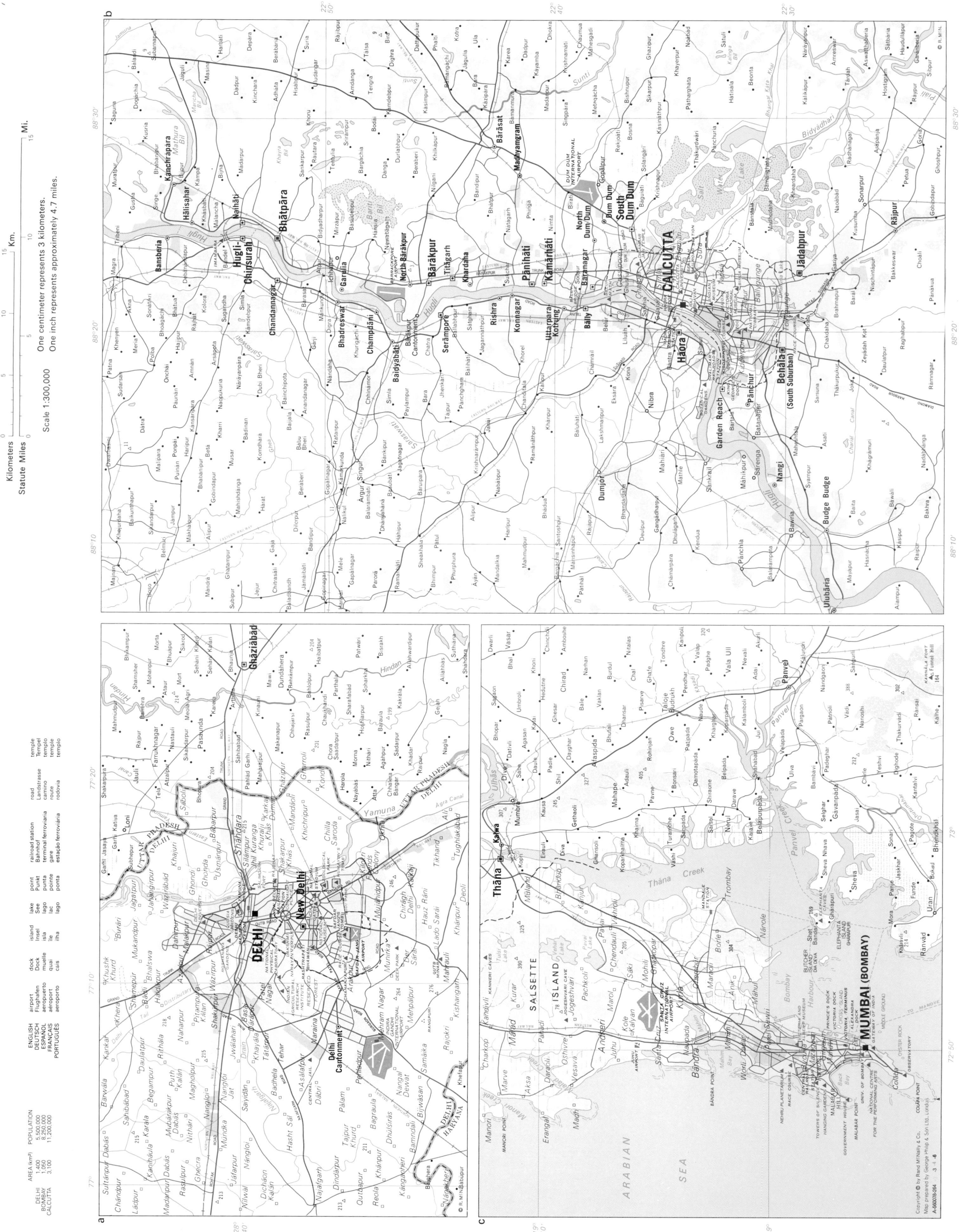

Kilometers

Statute Miles

Mi.

Km.

One centimeter represents 3 kilometers.
One inch represents approximately 4.7 miles.

Scale 1:300,000

	AREA (km²)	POPULATION
DELHI	1,400	6,500,000
BOMBAY	1,050	8,250,000
CALCUTTA	3,100	11,000,000

ENGLISH	DEUTSCH	ESPAÑOL	FRANÇAIS	PORTUGUÊS
airport	Flughafen	aeropuerto	aéroport	aeroporto
dock	Dock	muelle	dock	cais
island	Insel	isla	île	ilha
lake	See	lago	lac	lago
point	Punkt	punta	pointe	ponta
railroad station	Bahnhof	terminal ferroviaria	gare	estação ferroviária
road	Landstrasse	camino	route	rodovia
temple	Tempel	templo	temple	templo

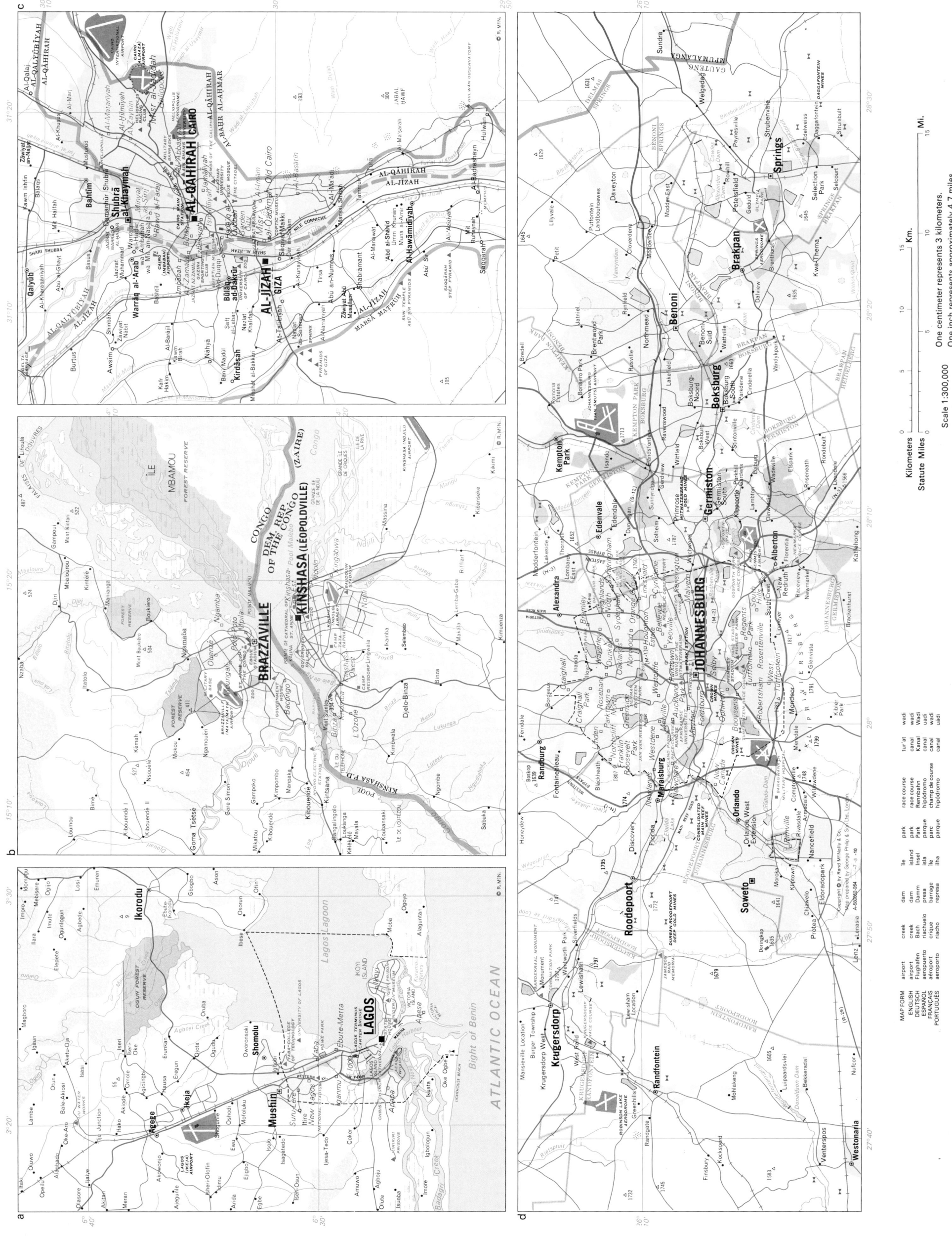

Scale 1:300,000

One centimeter represents 3 kilometers.
One inch represents approximately 4.7 miles.

MAP FORM					
ENGLISH	airport	creek	dam	lie	park	race course	tur'āt	wadi
DEUTSCH	airport	creek	dam	island	park	race course	canal	wadi
ESPAÑOL	Flughafen	Bach	Damm	Insel	Park	Rennbahn	Kanal	Wadi
FRANÇAIS	aeropuerto	riachuelo	presa	isla	parque	hipódromo	canal	uadi
PORTUGUÊS	aéroport	ruisseau	barrage	île	parc	champ de course	canal	uadi
	aeroporto	riacho	represa	ilha	parque	hipódromo	canal	uádi

Copyright © by Rand McNally & Co.
Map prepared by George Philip & Son Ltd., London.
A-662ar2-264   2·3·10

a

b

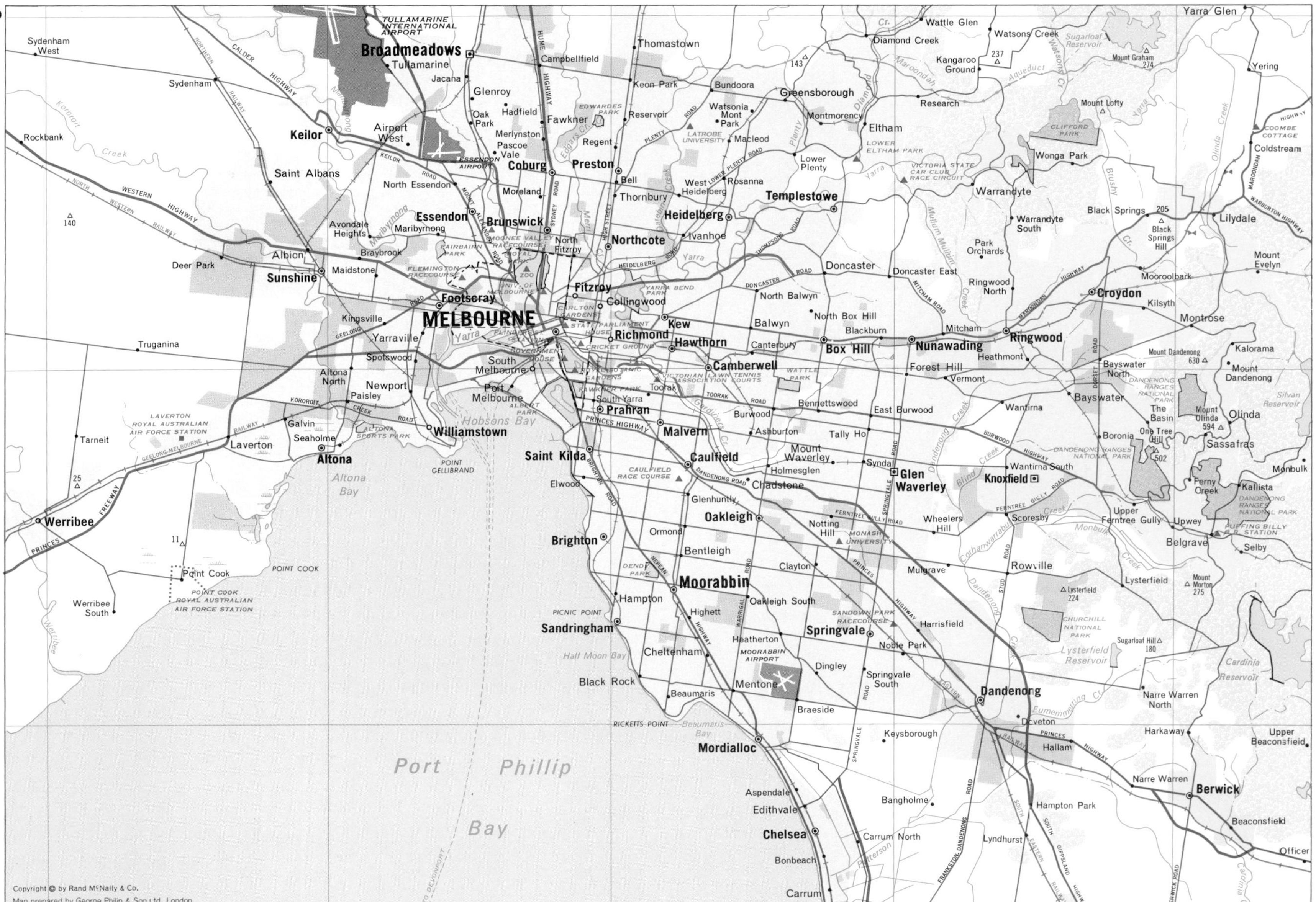

	AREA (km²)	POPULATION
MELBOURNE	2,600	2,425,000
SYDNEY	2,800	2,850,000

ENGLISH	bay, b.	bridge	creek, cr.	highway	point	road
DEUTSCH	Bucht	Brücke	Bach	Landstrasse	Landspitze	Landstrasse
ESPAÑOL	bahia	puente	riachuelo	camino	punta	camino
FRANÇAIS	baie	pont	crique	route	pointe	route
PORTUGUÊS	baia	ponte	riacho	rodovia	ponta	rodovia

Kilometers 0 5 10 15 Km.

Statute Miles 0 5 10 15 Mi.

Scale 1:300,000

One centimeter represents 3 kilometers.
One inch represents approximately 4.7 miles.

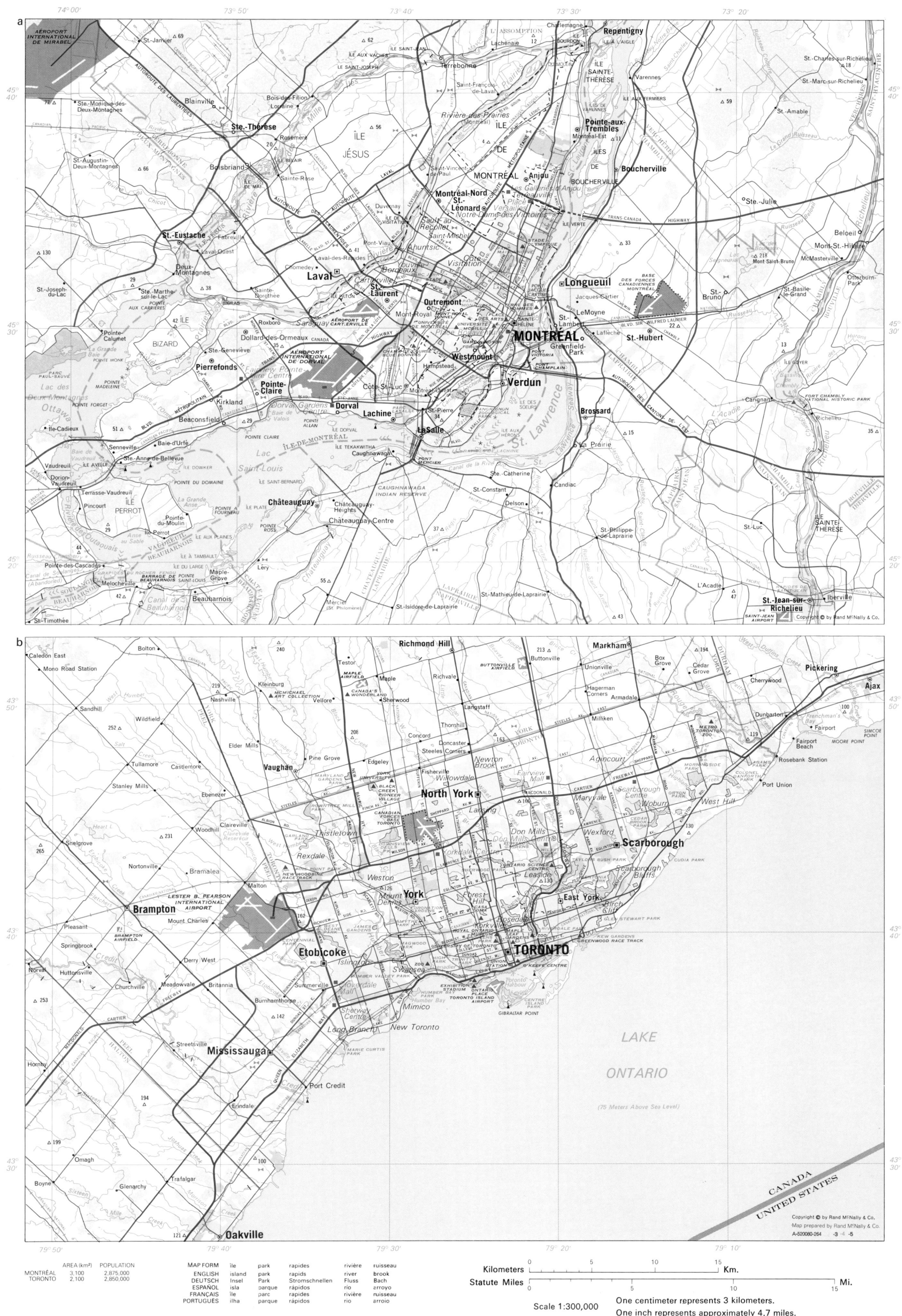

	AREA (km²)	POPULATION
MONTRÉAL	3,100	2,875,000
TORONTO	2,100	2,850,000

MAP FORM			
	île	park	rapides	rivière	ruisseau
ENGLISH	island	park	rapids	river	brook
DEUTSCH	Insel	Park	Stromschnellen	Fluss	Bach
ESPAÑOL	isla	parque	rápidos	rio	arroyo
FRANÇAIS	île	parc	rapides	rivière	ruisseau
PORTUGUÊS	ilha	parque	rápidos	rio	arroio

Kilometers

Statute Miles

Scale 1:300,000

One centimeter represents 3 kilometers.

One inch represents approximately 4.7 miles.

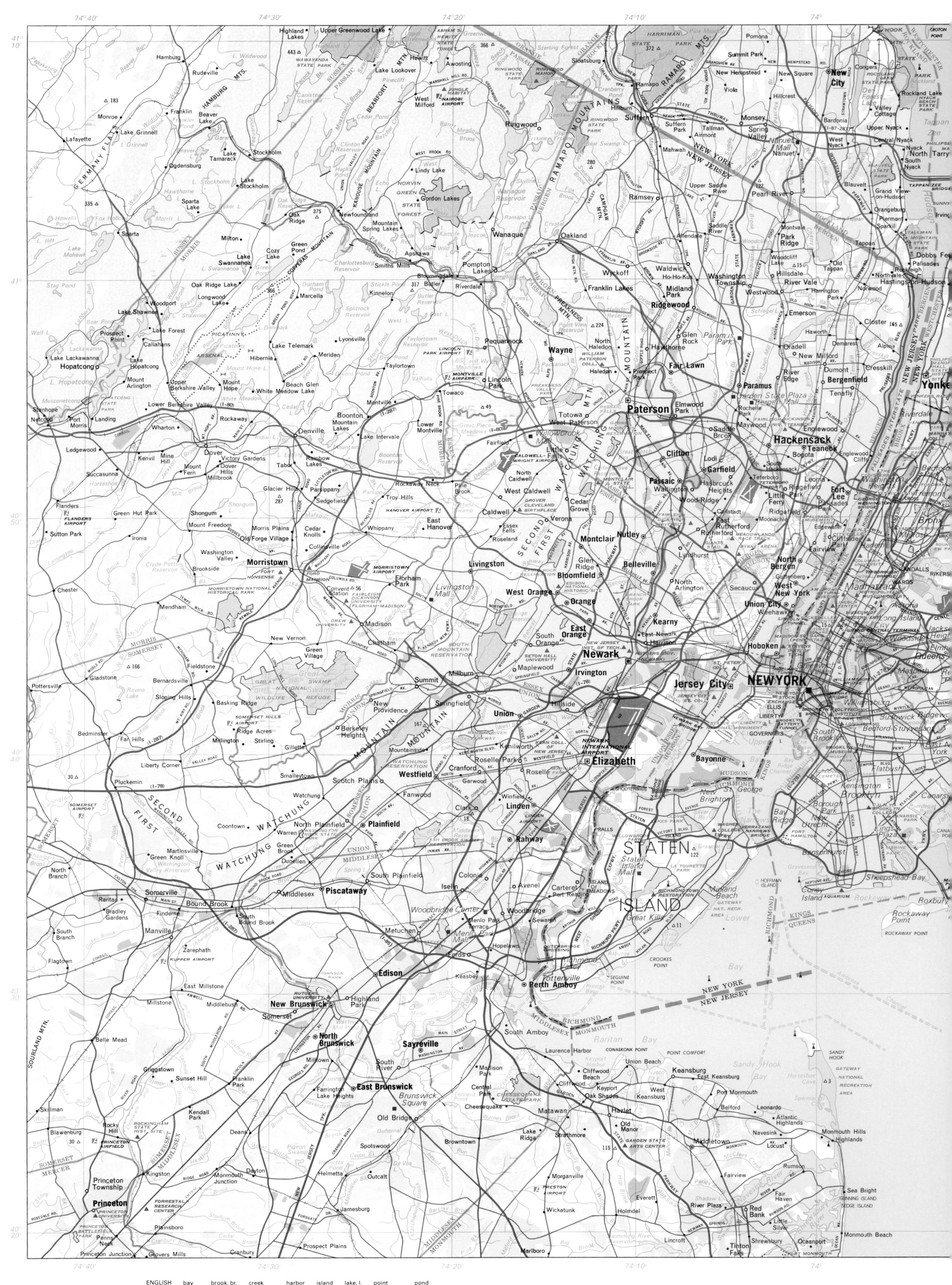

ENGLISH   bay   brook, br.   creek   harbor   island   lake, l.   point   pond
DEUTSCH   Bucht   Bach   Bach   Hafen   Insel   See   Landspitze   Teich
ESPAÑOL   bahía   arroyo   riachuelo puerto   isla   lago   punta   charca
FRANÇAIS   baie   ruisseau   crique   port   île   lac   pointe   étang
PORTUGUÊS   baía   arroio   riacho   porto   ilha   lago   ponta   lagoa

For complete glossary see page I·I.

Scale 1:300,000

One centimeter represents 3 kilometers.
One inch represents approximately 4.7 miles.

ENGLISH	airport	creek, cr.	harbor	lake, l.	park	woods
DEUTSCH	Flughafen	Bach	Hafen	See	Park	Gehölz
ESPAÑOL	aeropuerto	riachuelo	puerto	lago	parque	bosques
FRANÇAIS	aéroport	crique	port	lac	parc	bois
PORTUGUÊS	aeroporto	riacho	porto	lago	parque	bosques

Kilometers
Statute Miles

Scale 1:300,000

One centimeter represents 3 kilometers.
One inch represents approximately 4.7 miles.

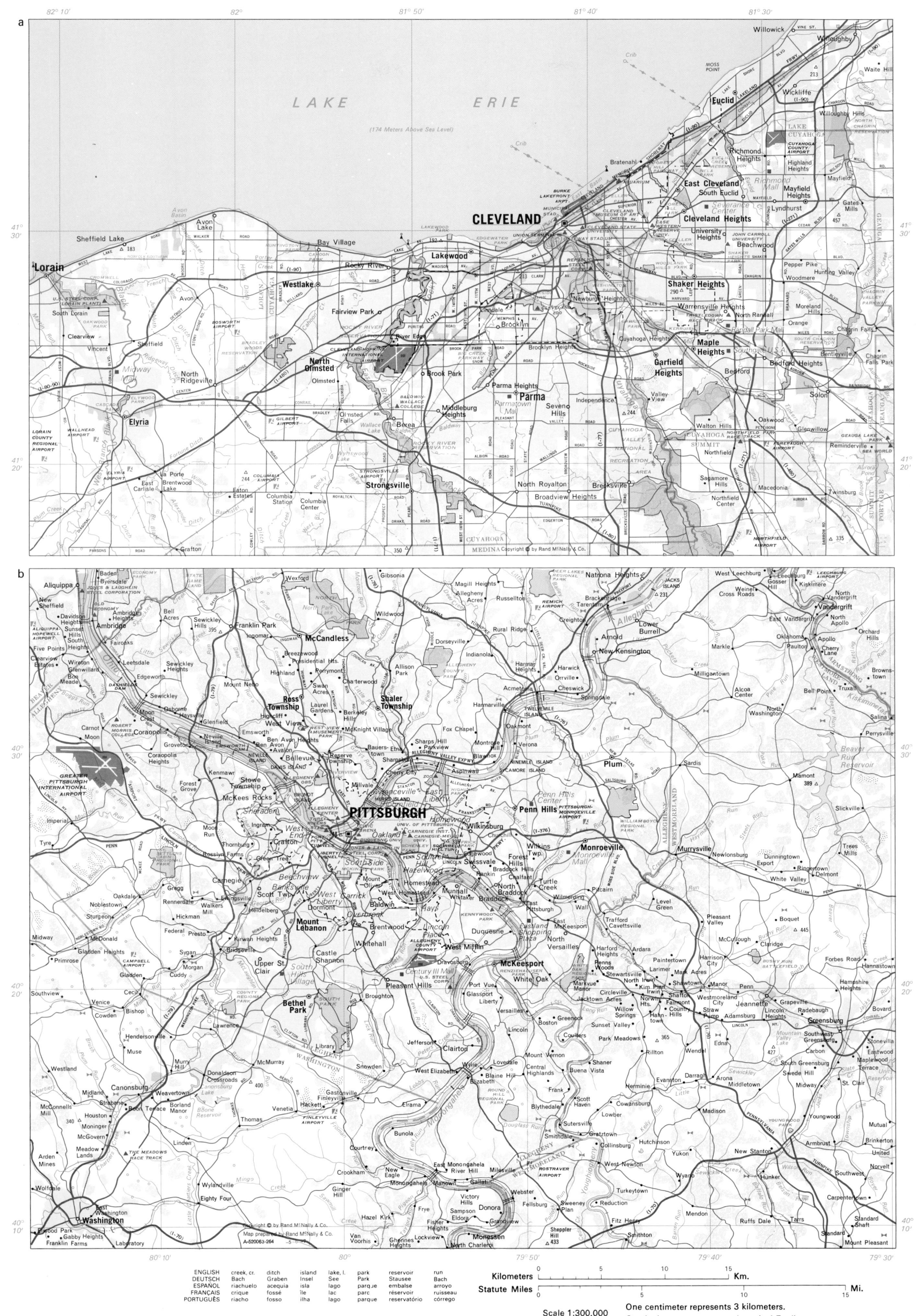

ENGLISH	creek, cr.	ditch	island	lake, l.	park	reservoir	run
DEUTSCH	Bach	Graben	Insel	See	Park	Stausee	Bach
ESPAÑOL	riachuelo	acequia	isla	lago	parque	embalse	arroyo
FRANÇAIS	crique	fossé	île	lac	parc	réservoir	ruisseau
PORTUGUÊS	riacho	fosso	ilha	lago	parque	reservatório	córrego

Kilometers

Statute Miles

Scale 1:300,000

One centimeter represents 3 kilometers.
One inch represents approximately 4.7 miles.

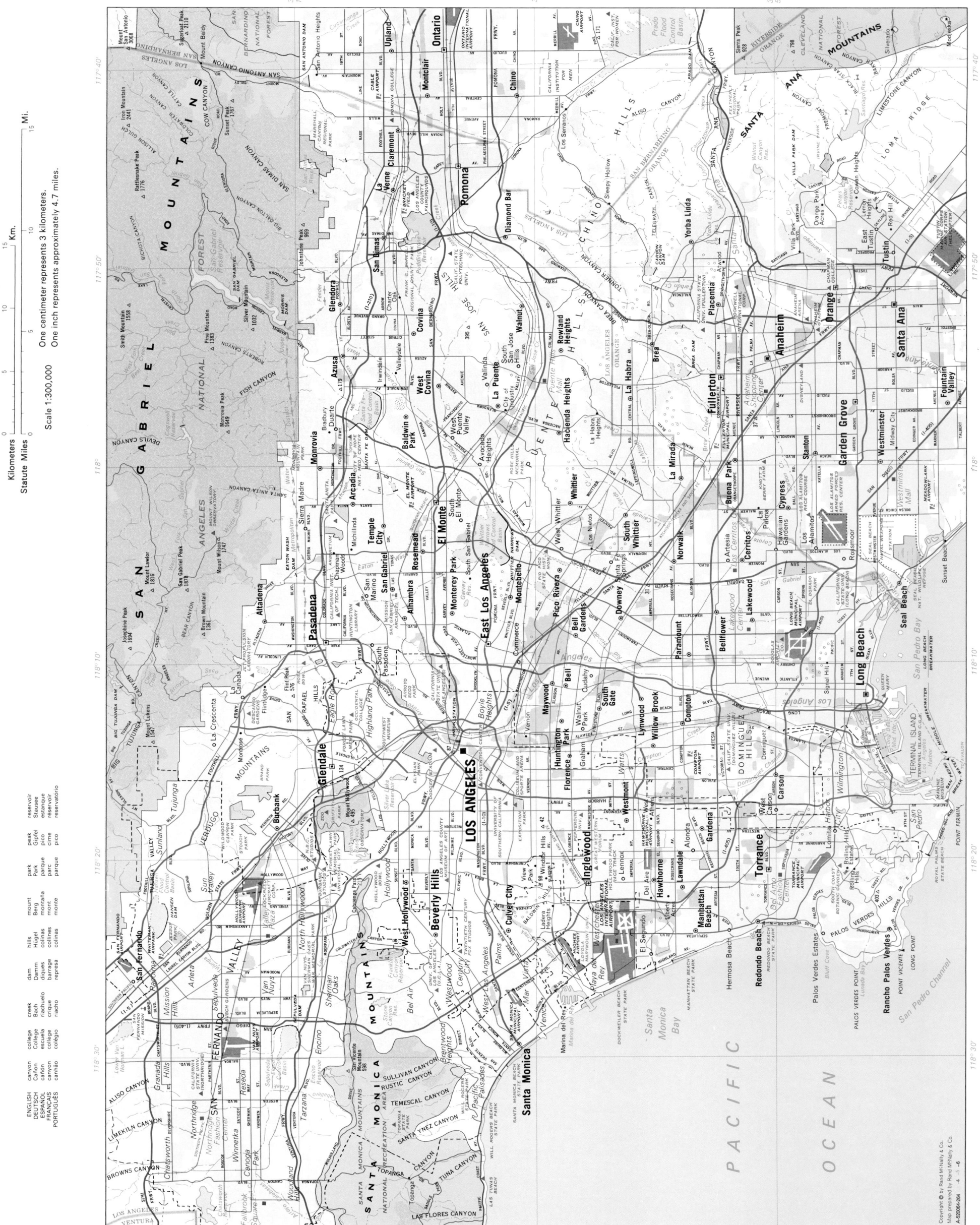

Kilometers
Statute Miles

Mi.

Km.

Scale 1:300,000

One centimeter represents 3 kilometers.
One inch represents approximately 4.7 miles.

ENGLISH	reservoir	peak	park	mount	hills	dam	creek	college	canyon
DEUTSCH	Stausee	Gipfel	Park	Berg	Hügel	Damm	Bach	College	Cañon
ESPAÑOL	reservorio	pico	parque	montaña	colinas	diques	riachuelo	escuela	cañon
FRANÇAIS	réservoir	pic	parc	mont	collines	barrage	cruque	collège	cañon
PORTUGUÉS	reservatório	pico	parque	monte	colinas	represa	riacho	colégio	canhão

Copyright © by Rand McNally & Co.
Map prepared by Rand McNally & Co.
A-582064-394   4 · 4 · 6 · -6

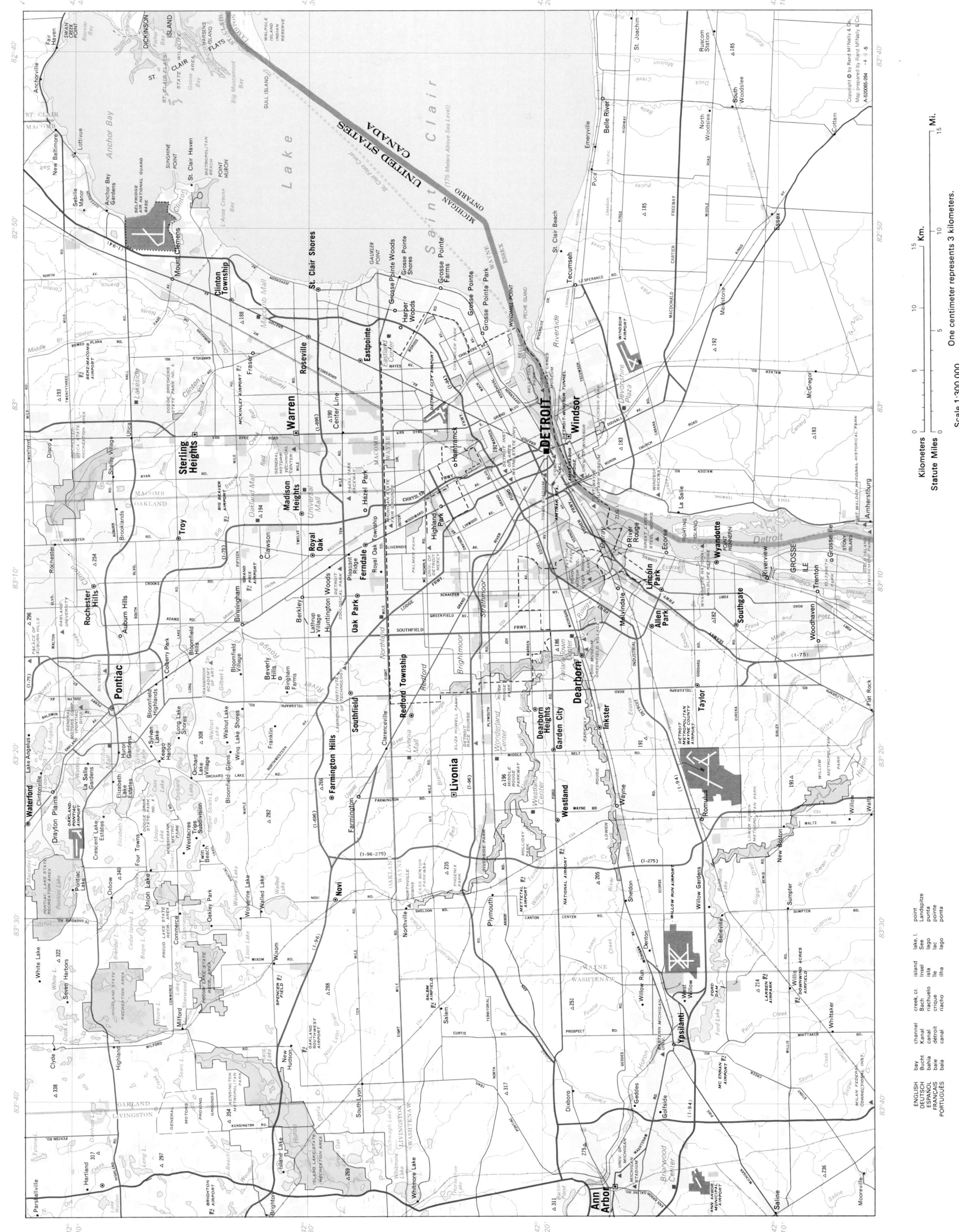

Scale 1:300,000

One centimeter represents 3 kilometers.
One inch represents approximately 4.7 miles.

Kilometers

Statute Miles

Mi.

Km.

ENGLISH	bay	creek, cr.	channel	island	lake, l.	point
DEUTSCH	Bucht	Bach	Kanal	Insel	See	Landspitze
ESPAÑOL	bahía	riachuelo	canal	isla	lago	punta
FRANÇAIS	baie	crique	détroit	île	lac	pointe
PORTUGUÊS	baía	riacho	canal	ilha	lago	ponta

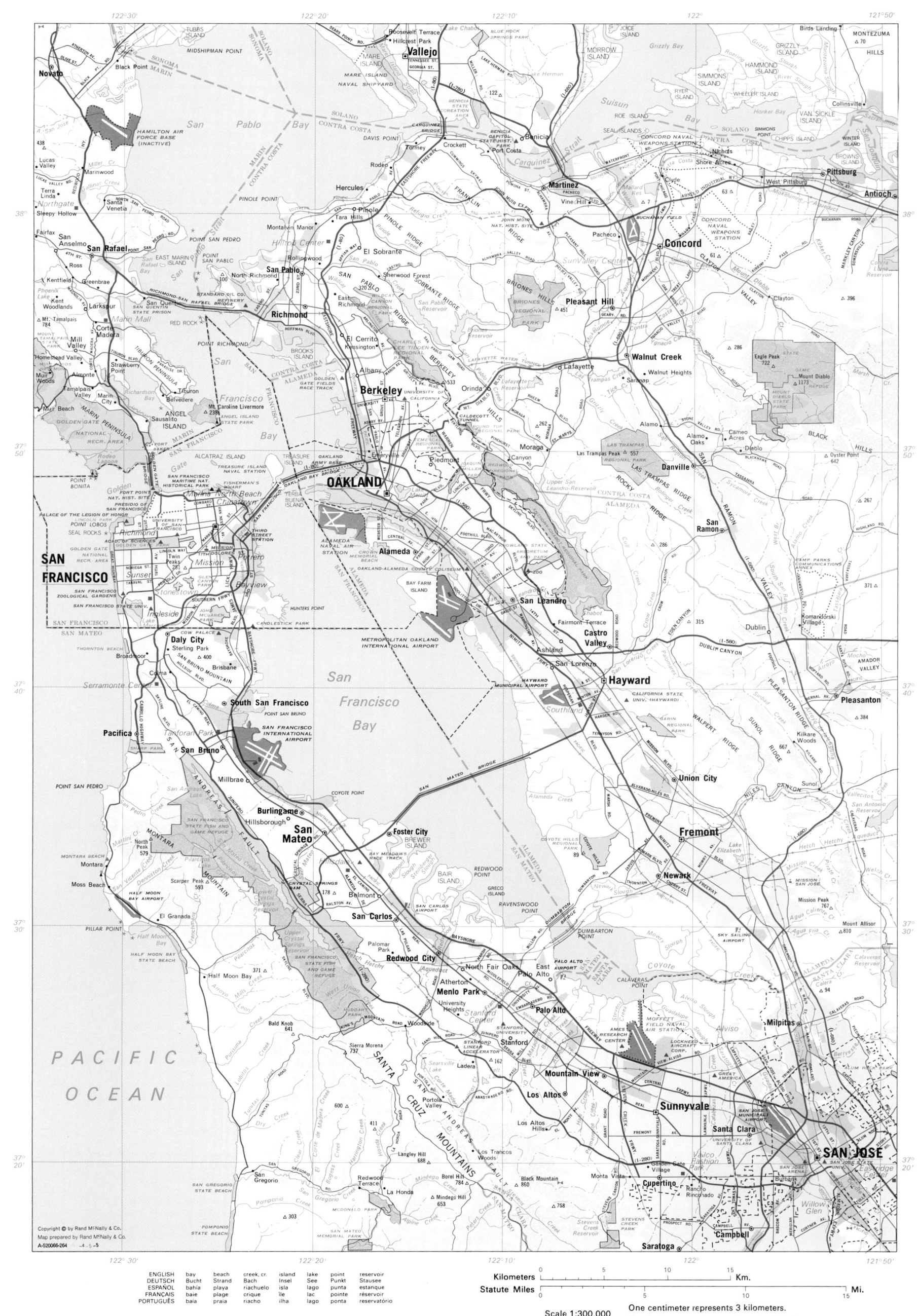

ENGLISH	bay	beach	creek, cr.	island	lake	point	reservoir
DEUTSCH	Bucht	Strand	Bach	Insel	See	Punkt	Stausee
ESPAÑOL	bahía	playa	riachuelo	isla	lago	punta	estanque
FRANÇAIS	baie	plage	crique	île	lac	pointe	réservoir
PORTUGUÊS	baía	praia	riacho	ilha	lago	ponta	reservatório

Kilometers

Statute Miles

Scale 1:300,000

One centimeter represents 3 kilometers.
One inch represents approximately 4.7 miles.

ATLANTIC OCEAN

Massachusetts Bay

Boston Bay

NEW HAMPSHIRE
MASSACHUSETTS

MASSACHUSETTS
RHODE ISLAND

Nashua **Lawrence** **Methuen** **Haverhill** **Newburyport** **Lowell** **Dracut** **Chelmsford** **Gloucester** **Salem** **Beverly** **Peabody** **Lynn** **Wakefield** **Woburn** **Lexington** **Concord** **Melrose** **Saugus** **Medford** **Arlington** **Malden** **Everett** **Revere** **Somerville** **Cambridge** **BOSTON** **Waltham** **Watertown** **Newton** **Brookline** **Wellesley** **Natick** **Framingham** **Needham** **Dedham** **Milton** **Quincy** **Weymouth** **Braintree** **Hull** **Norwood** **Westwood** **Randolph** **Walpole** **Stoughton** **Brockton** **Plymouth**

ENGLISH	bay	brook	island, i.	lake, l.	point	pond	reservation
DEUTSCH	Bucht	Bach	Insel	See	Landspitze	Teich	Reservat
ESPAÑOL	bahia	arroyo	isla	lago	punta	charca	parque nacional
FRANÇAIS	baie	ruisseau	île	lac	pointe	étang	reservation
PORTUGUÊS	baia	arroio	ilha	lago	ponta	lagoa	parque nacional

Kilometers   0   5   10   15   Km.

Statute Miles   0   5   10   15   Mi.

Scale 1:300,000

One centimeter represents 3 kilometers.
One inch represents approximately 4.7 miles.

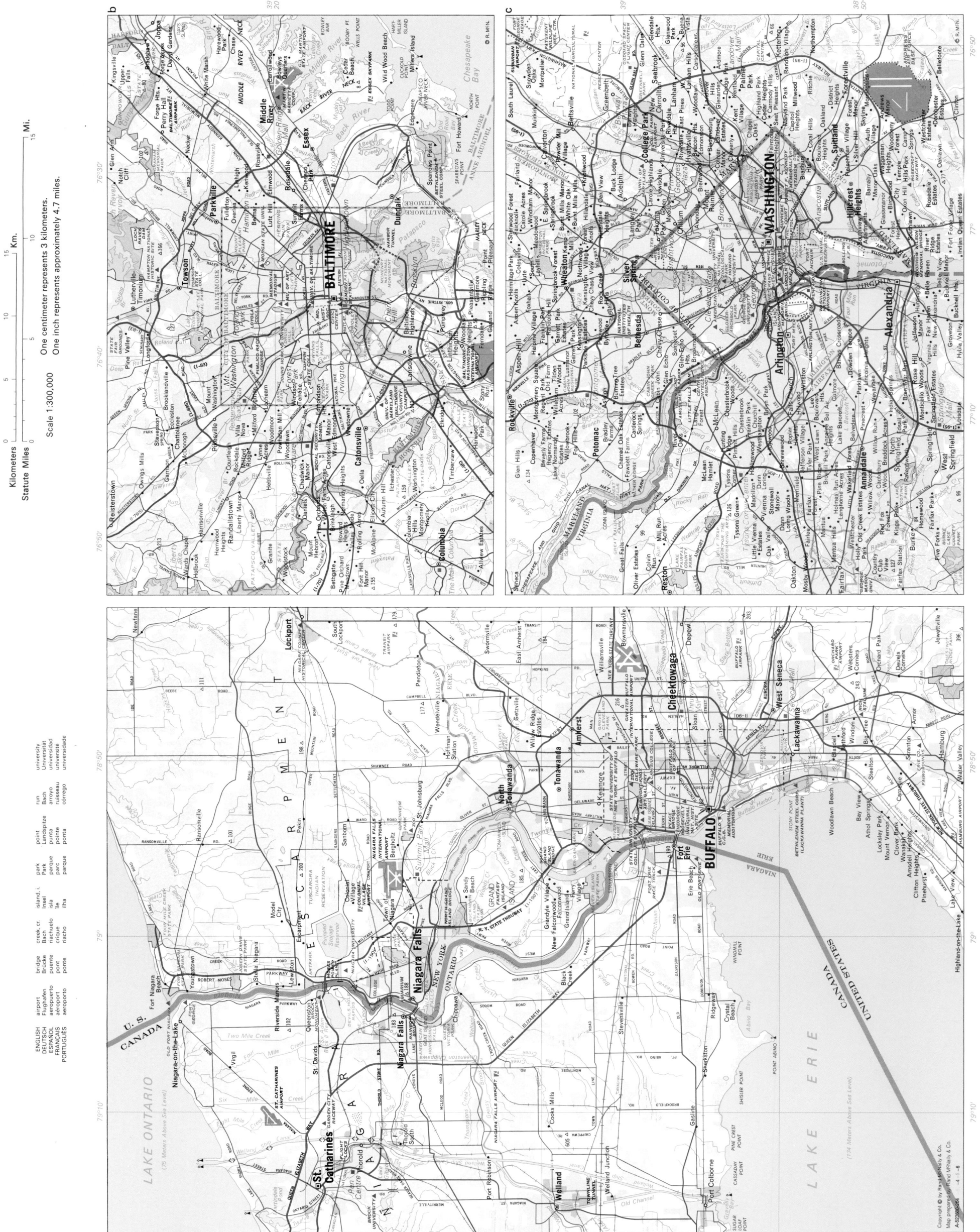

Kilometers
Statute Miles

Scale 1:300,000

One centimeter represents 3 kilometers.
One inch represents approximately 4.7 miles.

ENGLISH	airport	bridge	creek, cr.	island, i.	park	point	run	university
DEUTSCH	Flughafen	Brücke	Bach	Insel	Park	Landspitze	Bach	Universität
ESPAÑOL	aeropuerto	puente	riachuelo	isla	parque	punta	arroyo	universidad
FRANÇAIS	aéroport	pont	crique	île	parc	pointe	ruisseau	université
PORTUGUÊS	aeroporto	ponte	riacho	ilha	parque	ponta	córrego	universidade

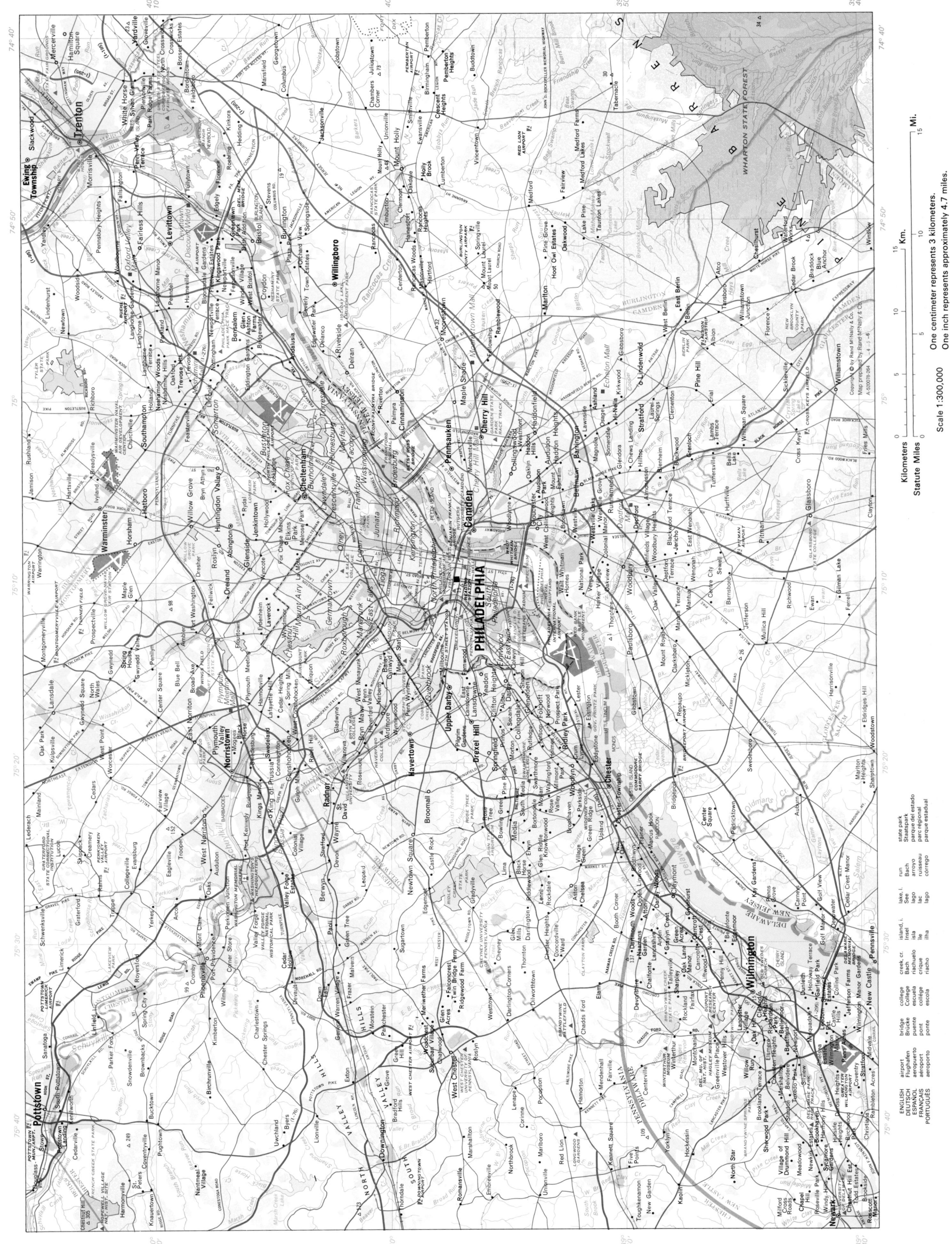

Kilometers

Statute Miles

Scale 1:300,000

One centimeter represents 3 kilometers.
One inch represents approximately 4.7 miles.

Mi.

Km.

ENGLISH	DEUTSCH	ESPAÑOL	FRANÇAIS	PORTUGUÊS
airport	Flughafen	aeropuerto	aeroport	aeroporto
bridge	Brücke	puente	pont	ponte
college	College	escuela	college	escola
creek, cr. Bach	riachuelo	crique	riacho
island, i. Insel	isla	île	ilha
lake, l. See	lago	lac	lago
run Bach	arroyo	ruisseau	córrego
state park Staatspark	parque del estado	parc régional	parque estadual

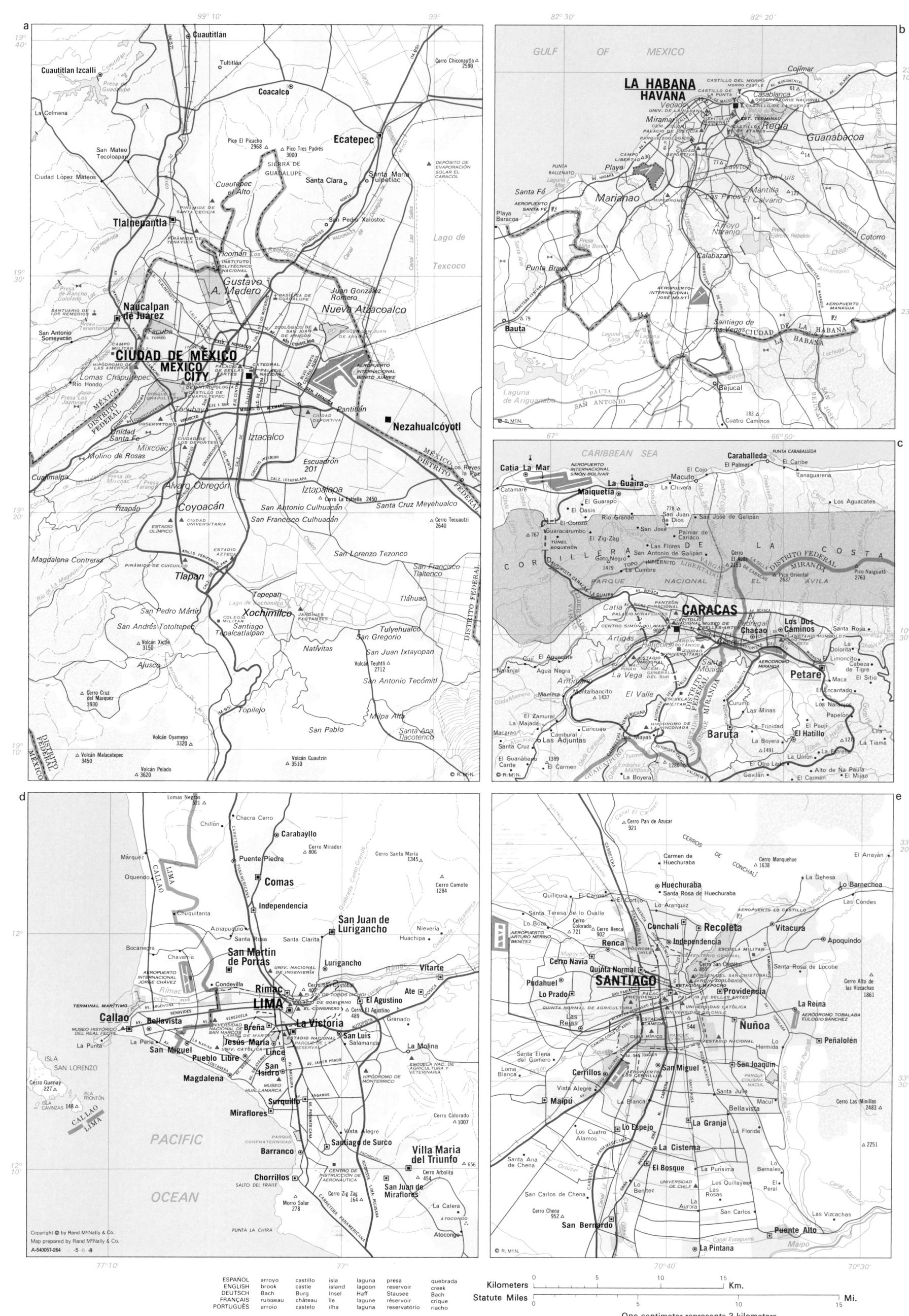

ESPAÑOL	arroyo	castillo	isla	laguna	presa	quebrada
ENGLISH	brook	castle	island	lagoon	reservoir	creek
DEUTSCH	Bach	Burg	Insel	Haff	Stausee	Bach
FRANÇAIS	ruisseau	château	île	lagune	réservoir	crique
PORTUGUÊS	arroio	castelo	ilha	laguna	reservatório	riacho

Kilometers   0   5   10   15   Km.

Statute Miles   0   5   10   15   Mi.

Scale 1:300,000

One centimeter represents 3 kilometers.
One inch represents approximately 4.7 miles.

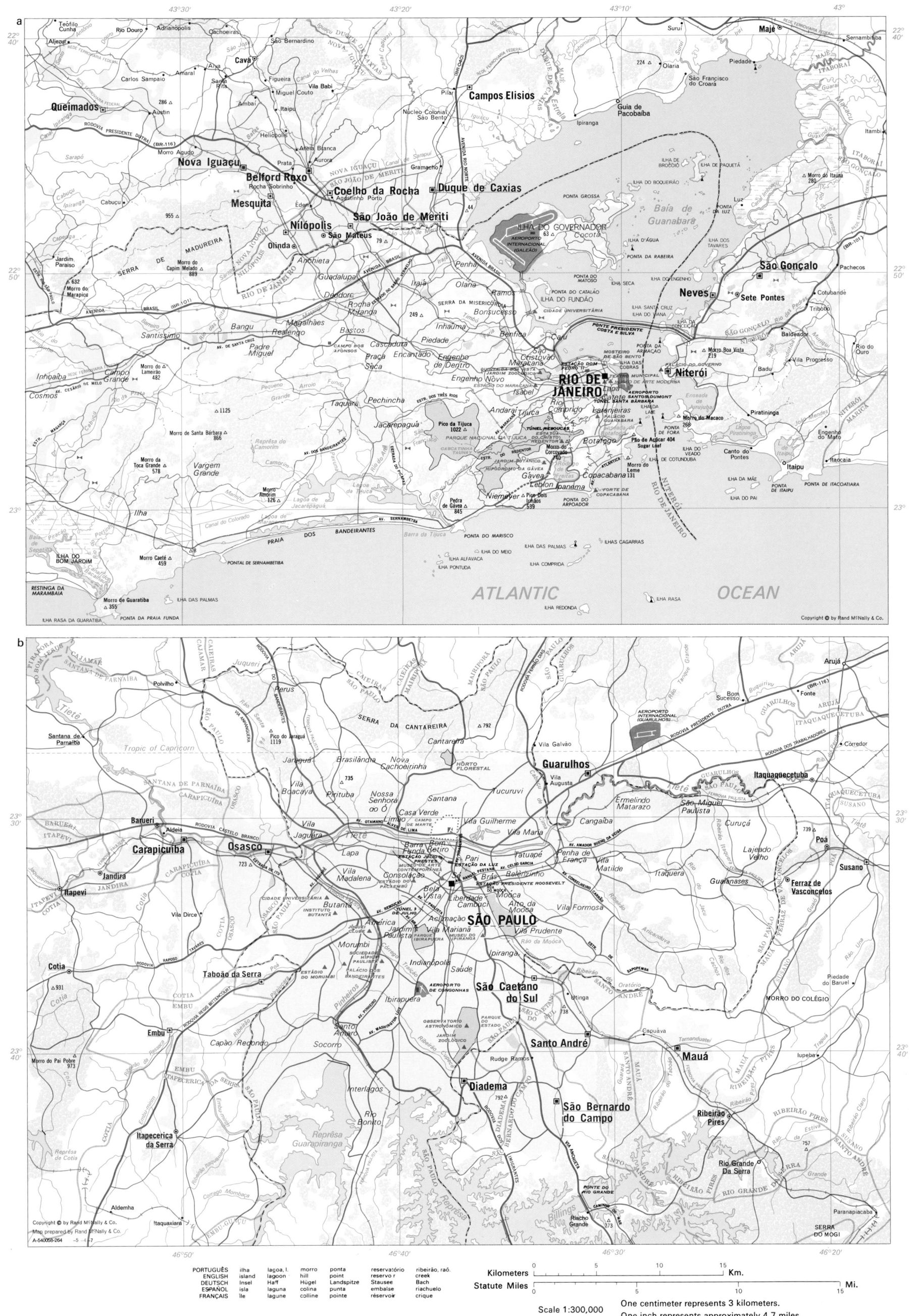

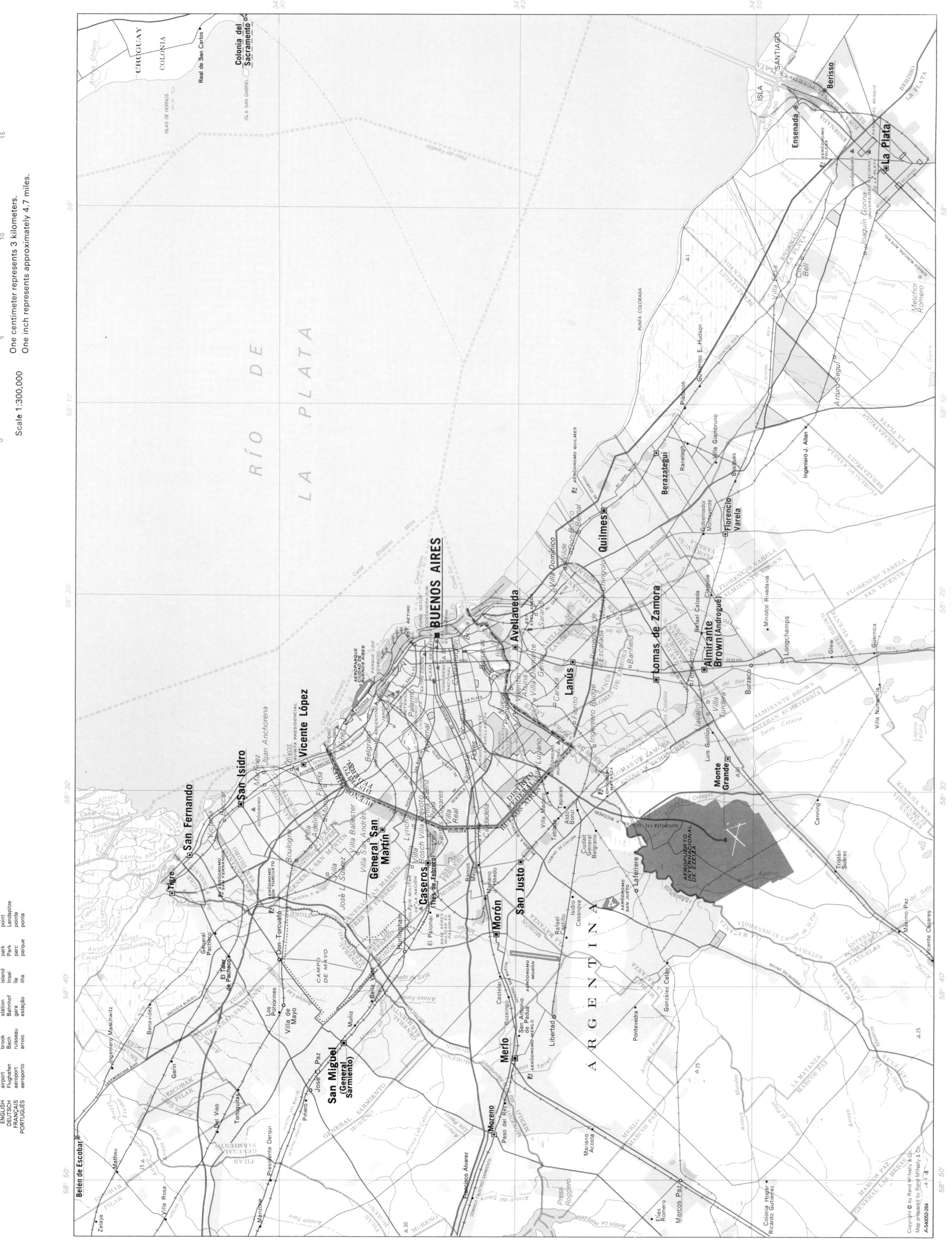

THE MAP FORM column of the glossary lists in alphabetical order the geographical terms, including any abbreviations, that appear on the maps. Terms preceded by a hyphen are those which commonly appear as endings in map names (for example, -san in Fuji-san, -älven in Dalälven). The languages of the terms are identified by abbreviations in *italics* (see Abbreviations of Language Names below). The glossary provides the English, German, Spanish, French, and Portuguese equivalent for each term.

As a rule, the translations were made from the map form to English, then from English into the other four languages. Since the glossary terms and translations refer to specific map features, some may vary from the customary dictionary definitions of the terms.

IN DER SPALTE "Geographische Begriffe" werden alle Begriffe und Abkürzungen in alphabetischer Ordnung aufgeführt, die in den Karten erscheinen. Begriffe mit vorgesetztem Bindestrich erscheinen normalerweise als Wortendungen in Kartennamen (z.B. -san in Fuji-san, -älven in Dalälven). In *Kursivschrift* sind die jeweiligen Abkürzungen angegeben für die Sprachen, in denen der Begriff wiedergegeben ist (siehe unten: Abkürzungen der Sprachen). Das Verzeichnis gibt für jeden Begriff den entsprechenden Ausdruck in englisch, deutsch, spanisch, französisch, und portugiesisch.

In der Regel wurde der Begriff in der Karte ins Englische übersetzt und dann vom Englischen in die vier anderen Sprachen. Da die Begriffe und Übersetzungen sich auf bestimmte Objekte in der Karte beziehen, können einige von ihnen von den in den üblichen Wörterbüchern aufgeführten Begriffsbestimmungen abweichen.

LOS TÉRMINOS GEOGRÁFICOS que aparecen en los mapas, incluyendo abreviaciones, son presentados en la columna de Términos Geográficas del Glosario, en orden alfabético. Los términos que están precedidos por un guión aparecen frecuentemente como terminaciones de los nombres en los mapas (por ejemplo, -san en Fuji-san, -älvan en Dalälven). Los idiomas que representan los términos están identificados por medio de abreviaciones en *cursiva* (véase abajo, Abreviaciones de los Idiomas Extranjeros). El Glosario provee el equivalente para cada término en inglés, alemán, español, francés y portugués.

Generalmente las traducciones están hechas de las formas originales de la terminología de los mapas que aparecen primero en inglés, y luego se traducen a las otras cuatro lenguas. Algunos términos y traducciones pueden aparecer distintas a las usadas en los diccionarios generales porque se refieren a los rasgos particulares de los mapas.

LE GLOSSAIRE cite par ordre alphabétique les termes géographiques et les abréviations utilisées. Les mots précédés d'un tiret sont des suffixes (par exemple, -san dans Fuji-san, -älven dans Dalälven). La langue d'origine du nom cité est indiquée par une abréviation en *italique* (voir Abréviations des noms de langues, ci-dessous). Le Glossaire donne chaque nom en anglais, allemand, espagnol, français, et portugais.

En général, les termes géographiques des cartes ont d'abord été traduits en anglais, puis de l'anglais dans les quatre autres langues. Les définitions de certains termes sont adaptées aux particularités de l'Atlas. Il peut arriver qu'elles diffèrent des définitions habituelles données par les dictionnaires.

A COLUNA 'TERMINOLOGIA', do *Glossário*, contém todos os termos geográficos que figuram nos mapas, em ordem alfabética e com as respectivas abreviações. Os termos precedidos por um hifen são os que freqüentemente aparecem nos mapas como sufixos de nomes tais como *-san* (em Fuji-san), *-älven* (em Dalälven). As línguas em que os termos são expressos estão identificadas por abreviações em *grifo* (ver abaixo, 'Abreviações das línguas estrangeiras'). O Glossário fornece o equivalente de cada termo em inglês, alemão, espanhol, português e francês.

De modo geral, as traduções foram feitas das formas originais da terminologia usada nos mapas para o inglês, e, em seguida, do inglês para as outras quatro línguas. Uma vez que os termos geográficos e traduções do *Glossário* referem-se a acidentes específicos de cada mapa, é possível que algumas definições sejam diferentes das consignadas nos dicionários gerais das línguas.

Abbreviations of Language Names / Abkürzungen der Nationalsprachen / Abreviaciones de los Idiomas Extranjeros
Abréviations des Noms de Langues / Abreviações dos Idiomas Estrangeiros

	ENGLISH	DEUTSCH	ESPAÑOL	FRANCAIS	PORTUGUÊS
Afk.	Afrikaans	Afrikaans	Africano	Afrikaans	Afrikaans
Alb.	Albanian	Albanisch	Albanesa	Albanais	Albanês
Ara.	Arabic	Arabisch	Árabe	Arabe	Árabe
Ber.	Berber	Berberisch	Bereber	Berbère	Berbere
Ben.	Bengali	Bengali	Bengali	Bengali	Bengali
Blg.	Bulgarian	Bulgarisch	Búlgaro	Bulgare	Búlgaro
Bur.	Burmese	Burmanisch	Birmano	Birman	Birmanês
Cat.	Catalan	Katalanisch	Catalán	Catalan	Catalão
Cbd.	Cambodian	Kambodschanisch	Camboyano	Cambodgien	Cambojano
Ch.	Chinese	Chinesisch	Chino	Chinois	Chinês
Czech	Czech	Tschechisch	Checo	Tchèque	Tcheco
Dan.	Danish	Dänisch	Danés	Danois	Dinamarquês
Du.	Dutch	Niederländisch	Holandés	Néerlandais	Holandês
Eng.	English	Englisch	Inglés	Anglais	Inglês
Est.	Estonian	Estnisch	Estonio	Esthonien	Estoniano
Finn.	Finnish	Finnisch	Finés	Finnois	Finlandês
Flm.	Flemish	Flämisch	Flamenco	Flamand	Flamengo
Fr.	French	Französisch	Francés	Français	Francês
Gae.	Gaelic	Gälisch	Gaélico	Gaélique	Gaélico
Ger.	German	Deutsch	Alemán	Allemand	Alemão
Gr.	Greek	Griechisch	Griego	Grec	Grego
Hau.	Hausa	Haussa	Hausa	Haoussa	Haussa
Heb.	Hebrew	Hebräisch	Hebreo	Hébreu	Hebraico
Hung.	Hungarian	Ungarisch	Húngaro	Hongrois	Húngaro
Ice.	Icelandic	Isländisch	Islandés	Islandais	Islandês
Indon.	Indonesian	Indonesisch	Indonesio	Indonésien	Indonésio
It.	Italian	Italienisch	Italiano	Italien	Italiano

	ENGLISH	DEUTSCH	ESPAÑOL	FRANCAIS	PORTUGUÊS
Jap.	Japanese	Japanisch	Japonés	Japonais	Japonês
Kor.	Korean	Koreanisch	Coreano	Coréen	Coreano
Lao.	Laotian	Laotisch	Laosiano	Laotien	Laosiano
Lapp.	Lappish	Lappisch	Lapón	Lapon	Lapão
Latv.	Latvian	Lettisch	Letón	Letton	Letão
Lith.	Lithuanian	Litauisch	Lituano	Lithuanien	Lituano
Mal.	Malay	Malaiisch	Malayo	Malais	Malaio
Mong.	Mongolian	Mongolisch	Mogol	Mongol	Mongol
Nor.	Norwegian	Norwegisch	Norvego	Norvégien	Norueguês
Pas.	Pashto	Paschtu	Pushtu	Pachtou	Pachtu
Per.	Persian	Persisch	Persa	Persan	Persa
Pol.	Polish	Polnisch	Polaco	Polonais	Polonês
Poly.	Polynesian	Polynesisch	Polinesio	Polynésien	Polinésio
Port.	Portuguese	Portugiesisch	Portugués	Portugais	Português
Rom.	Romanian	Rumänisch	Rumano	Roumain	Romeno
Rus.	Russian	Russisch	Ruso	Russe	Russo
S./C.	Serbo-Croatian	Serbokroatisch	Servio-croata	Serbo-croate	Servo-croata
Sin.	Sinhalese	Singhalesisch	Cingalés	Cinghalais	Cingalês
Slo.	Slovak	Slowakisch	Eslovaco	Slovaque	Eslovaco
Sp.	Spanish	Spanisch	Español	Espagnol	Espanhol
Swe.	Swedish	Schwedisch	Sueco	Suédois	Sueco
Thai	Thai	Thai	Tai	Thaï	Tailandês
Tib.	Tibetan	Tibetisch	Tibetano	Tibétain	Tibetano
Tur.	Turkish	Türkisch	Turco	Turc	Turco
Ukr.	Ukrainian	Ukrainisch	Ucranio	Ukrainien	Ucraniano
Viet.	Vietnamese	Vietnamesisch	Vietnamita	Vietnamien	Vietnamita
Welsh	Welsh	Walisisch	Galés	Gallois	Galês

A

ENGLISH	DEUTSCH	Map Form Geographische Begriffe Términos Geográficos Termes Géographiques Termos Geográficos	ESPAÑOL	FRANCAIS	PORTUGUÊS
river	Fluss	**-å** *Dan., Nor., Swe.*	río	rivière	rio
brook	Bach	**a., arroyo** *Sp.*	arroyo	ruisseau	córrego
river	Fluss	**āb** *Per.*	río	rivière	rio
army base	Heeres-stützpunkt	**a.b., army base** *Eng.*	base del ejército	base d'armée	base militar
well	Brunnen	**ābār** *Ara.*	pozo	puits	poço
abbey	Abtei	**abb., abbazia** *It.*	abadía	abbaye	abadia
abbey	Abtei	**abbaye** *Fr.*	abadía	abbaye	abadia
abbey	Abtei	**abbazia** *It.*	abadía	abbaye	abadia
abbey	Abtei	**abbey** *Eng.*	abadía	abbaye	abadia
aboriginal reserve	Eingeborenen-schutzgebiet	**aboriginal reserve** *Eng.*	zona de aborígenes	réserve d'indigènes	reserva indígena
abbey	Abtei	**Abtei** *Ger.*	abadía	abbaye	abadia
ditch	Graben	**acequia** *Sp.*	acequia	fossé	fosso
reservoir	Stausee	**ačude** *Port.*	embalse	réservoir	açude
island(s)	Insel(n)	**ada(lar)** *Tur.*	isla(s)	île(s)	ilha(s)
island	Insel	**adası** *Tur.*	isla	île	ilha
mountains	Berge	**adrar** *Ber.*	montañas	montagnes	montanhas
Atomic Energy Commission	Atomenergie-kommission	**A.E.C., Atomic Energy Commission** *Eng.*	Comisión de Energía Atomica	Commission de l'Énergie Atomique	Comissão de Energia Atômica
airport	Flughafen	**aérd., aérodrome** *Fr.*	aeródromo	aérodrome	aeródromo
airport	Flughafen	**aeródromo** *Port., Sp.*	aeródromo	aérodrome	aeródromo
airport	Flughafen	**aeroparque** *Sp.*	aeroparque	aéroport	aeroporto
airport	Flughafen	**aéroport** *Fr.*	aeropuerto	aéroport	aeroporto
airport	Flughafen	**aeroporto** *It., Port.*	aeropuerto	aéroport	aeroporto
airport	Flughafen	**aeropuerto** *Sp.*	aeropuerto	aéroport	aeroporto
air force base	Luftwaffen-stützpunkt	**a.f.b., air force base** *Eng.*	base aeronáutica	base aérienne	base aérea
wadi	Wadi	**ahzar** *Ara.*	uadi	wadi	uádi
peak	Gipfel	**aiguille** *Fr.*	pico	aiguille	pico
air base	Luftstützpunkt	**air base** *Eng.*	base aérea	base aérienne	base aérea
airfield	Flugplatz	**airfield** *Eng.*	camp de aviación	aérodrome	campo de pouso
air force base	Luftwaffen-stützpunkt	**air force base** *Eng.*	base aeronáutica	base aérienne	base aérea
airport	Flughafen	**airport** *Eng.*	aeropuerto	aéroport	aeroporto
cape	Kap	**ákra, akrotírion** *Gr.*	cabo	cap	cabo
hill	Hügel	**ʿalam, ʿalāmat** *Ara.*	colina	colline	colina

ENGLISH	DEUTSCH	Map Form Geographische Begriffe Términos Geográficos Termes Géographiques Termos Geográficos	ESPAÑOL	FRANCAIS	PORTUGUÊS
avenue	Allee	**alameda** *Sp.*	alameda	avenue	avenida
alps	Alpen	**alpes** *Fr.*	alpes	alpes	alpes
alps	Alpen	**alpi** *It.*	alpes	alpes	alpes
mountains, hills	Berge, Hügel	**altos** *Sp.*	altos	montagnes, collines	montanhas, colinas
river	Fluss	**-älv,-älven** *Swe.*	río	rivière	rio
amusement park	Vergnügungs-park	**amusement park** *Eng.*	parque de diversiones	parc récréatif	parque de diversões
river	Fluss	**-ån** *Swe.*	río	rivière	rio
anchorage	Ankerplatz	**anchorage** *Eng.*	ancladero	ancrage	ancoradouro
bay	Bucht	**angra** *Sp.*	angra	baie	baía
cove	kleine Bucht	**anse** *Fr.*	ensenada	anse	enseada
bay	Bucht	**ao** *Ch.*	bahía	baie	baía
bay	Bucht	**ao** *Thai*	bahía	baie	baía
aqueduct	Aquädukt	**aqueduc** *Fr.*	acueducto	aqueduc	aqueduto
aqueduct	Aquädukt	**aqueduct** *Eng.*	acueducto	aqueduc	aqueduto
archipelago	Archipel	**archipel** *Fr.*	archipiélago	archipel	arquipélago
archipelago	Archipel	**archipelag** *Rus.*	archipiélago	archipel	arquipélago
archipelago	Archipel	**archipelago** *Eng.*	archipiélago	archipel	arquipélago
archipelago	Archipel	**archipiélago** *Sp.*	archipiélago	archipel	arquipélago
arm	Arm	**arm** *Eng.*	brazo	bras	braço de rio
army base	Heeres-stützpunkt	**army base** *Eng.*	base del ejército	base d'armée	base militar
airport	Flughafen	**arpt., aéroport** *Fr.* **aeroporto** **aeropuerto** **airport**	aeropuerto	aéroport	aeroporto
archipelago	Archipel	**arquipélago** *Port.*	archipiélago	archipel	arquipélago
reef	Riff	**arrecife** *Sp.*	arrecife	récif	recife
brook	Bach	**arroyo** *Sp.*	arroyo	ruisseau	córrego, arroio
hills	Hügel	**-ås,-åsen** *Swe.*	colinas	collines	colinas
ridge	Höhenrücken	**ʿassâbet** *Ara.*	sierra	crête	serra
atoll	Atoll	**atol** *Port.*	atolón	atoll	atol
atoll	Atoll	**atoll** *Eng., Fr.*	atolón	atoll	atol
auditorium	Auditorium	**aud., auditorium** *Eng.*	auditorio	auditorium	auditório
race course	Rennbahn	**autodrome** *Fr.*	autódromo	autodrome	autódromo
race course	Rennbahn	**autodromo** *It.*	autódromo	autodrome	autódromo
expressway	Autobahn	**autopista** *Sp.*	autopista	autoroute	via expressa

290 Glossary and Abbreviations of Geographical Terms / Verzeichnis und Abkürzungen Geographischer Begriffe
Glosario y Abreviaciones de Términos Geográficos / Glossaire et Abréviations de Termes Géographiques
Glossário e Abreviações de Termos Geográficos

ENGLISH	DEUTSCH	Map Form / Geographische Begriffe / Términos Geográficos / Termes Géographiques / Termos Geográficos	ESPAÑOL	FRANCAIS	PORTUGUÊS
avenue	Allee	**av., avenida** *Port., Sp.* **avenue**	avenida	avenue	avenida
channel	Kanal	**ava** *Poly.*	canal, estrecho	canal, détroit	canal, estreito
avenue	Allee	**avenida** *Port., Sp.*	avenida	avenue	avenida
spring	Quelle	**'ayn** *Ara.*	manantial	source	manancial, fonte

B

ENGLISH	DEUTSCH	Map Form	ESPAÑOL	FRANCAIS	PORTUGUÊS
bay	Bucht	**baai** *Du.*	bahía	baie	baía
strait	Meeresstrasse	**bab** *Ara.*	estrecho	détroit	estreito
brook, creek	Bach	**Bach** *Ger.*	arroyo, riachuelo	ruisseau, crique	córrego, arroio
hill	Hügel	**-backen** *Swe.*	colina	colline	colina
bay	Bucht	**badia** *Cat.*	bahía	baie	baía
desert	Wüste	**bādiyat** *Ara.*	desierto	désert	deserto
strait	Meeresstrasse	**bælt** *Dan.*	estrecho	détroit	estreito
bay	Bucht	**bahía** *Sp.*	bahía	baie	baía
inlet	Einfahrt	**bahiret** *Ara.*	abra	bras de mer	enseada, estuário
railroad station	Bahnhof	**Bahnhof** *Ger.*	estacion de ferrocarril	gare	estação ferroviária
river, sea	Fluss, Meer	**bahr, bahr** *Ara.*	río, mar	rivière, mer	rio, mar
reservoir	Stausee	**baḩrat** *Ara.*	embalse	réservoir	reservatório
bay	Bucht	**baía** *Port.*	bahía	baie	baía
bay	Bucht	**baie** *Fr.*	bahía	baie	baía
reef, sand bar	Riff, Sandbarre	**bajo** *Sp.*	bajo	récif, banc de sable	recife, banco de areia
gorge	Schlucht	**balka** *Rus.*	garganta	gorge	garganta
dome	Kuppe	**ballon** *Fr.*	domo	ballon	domo
marsh	Marsch	**balta** *Rom.*	pantano	marais	pântano
cape	Kap	**-bana** *Jpn.*	cabo	cap	cabo
marsh	Marsch	**bañados** *Sp.*	bañados	marais	pântano
island	Insel	**-banare** *Jpn.*	isla	île	ilha
bank	Bank	**banco** *Sp.*	banco	banc	banco
peninsula	Halbinsel	**bandao** *Ch.*	península	péninsule	península
bank	Bank	**bank** *Eng.*	banco	banc	banco
shoal	Untiefe	**-banken** *Swe.*	bajo	haut-fond	escolho
sand bar	Sandbarre	**barra** *Sp.*	barra	banc de sable	banco de areia
dam	Damm	**barrage** *Fr.*	presa	barrage	represa
ravine	Tobel	**barranca** *Sp.*	barranca	ravin	ravina
air base	Luftstützpunkt	**base aérea** *Sp.*	base aérea	base aérienne	base aérea
basilica	Basilika	**basílica** *Sp.*	basílica	basilique	basílica
basilica	Basilika	**basilique** *Fr.*	basílica	basilique	basílica
basin	Becken	**basin** *Eng.*	cuenca	bassin	bacia
basin	Becken	**bassin** *Fr.*	cuenca	bassin	bacia
marsh	Marsch	**batakliği** *Tur.*	pantano	marais	pântano
river	Fluss	**batang** *Indon.*	río	rivière	rio
river	Fluss	**batha** *Ara.*	río	rivière	rio
marsh	Marsch	**bāţlāq** *Per.*	pantano	marais	pântano
battlefield	Schlachtfeld	**battlefield** *Eng.*	campo de batalla	champ de bataille	campo de batalha
mountain	Berg	**batu** *Mal.*	montaña	montagne	montanha
bay	Bucht	**bay** *Eng.*	bahía	baie	baía
bayou	Altwasser	**bayou** *Fr., Eng.*	ensenada pantanosa	bayou	enseada pantanosa
beach	Strand	**beach** *Eng.*	playa	plage	praia
mountain	Berg	**bein, beinn** *Gae.*	montaña	montagne	montanha
snowcapped mountains	Schneegipfel	**belogorje** *Rus.*	nevados	montagnes neigeuses	picos nevados
mountain	Berg	**ben** *Gae.*	montaña	montagne	montanha
mountain, hill	Berg	**Berg** *Ger.*	montaña, colina	montagne, colline	montanha, colina
mountains	Gebirge	**-berg** *Afk.*	montañas	montagnes	montanhas
hill(s), mountain(s)	Hügel, Berg(e)	**-berg** *Swe.*	colina(s), montaña(s)	colline(s), montagne(s)	colina(s), montanha(s)
mountains	Berge	**Berge** *Ger.*	montañas	montagnes	montanhas
mountains	Berge	**-berge** *Afk.*	montañas	montagnes	montanhas
hills, mountains	Hügel, Berge	**-bergen** *Swe.*	colinas, montañas	collines, montagnes	colinas, montanhas
hill, mountain	Hügel, Berg	**-berget** *Swe.*	colina, montaña	colline, montagne	colina, montanha
upland	Bergland	**Bergland** *Ger.*	tierras altas	hautes terres	terras altas
battlefield	Schlachtfeld	**bfld., battlefield** *Eng.*	campo de batalla	champ de bataille	campo de batalha
mountain, hill	Berg	**Bg., Berg** *Ger.*	montaña, colina	montagne, colline	montanha, colina
bridge	Brücke	**bge., bridge** *Eng.*	puente	pont	ponte
bight (bay)	Bucht	**bight** *Eng.*	bahía	baie	baía, enseada
bill (point)	Landspitze	**bill** *Eng.*	punta	pointe	ponta
valley	Tal	**biq'at** *Heb.*	valle	vallée	vale
well	Brunnen	**bi'r** *Ara.*	pozo	puits	poço
lake	See	**birkat** *Ara.*	lago	lac	lago
mountains	Berge	**bjeshkët** *Alb.*	montañas	montagnes	montanhas
brook	Bach	**bk., brook** *Eng.*	arroyo	ruisseau	córrego, arroio
upland	Bergland	**blaenau** *Welsh*	tierras altas	hautes terres	terras altas
bluff(s)	Steilufer	**bluff(s)** *Eng.*	acantilado(s)	falaise(s)	falésia(s)
boulevard	Boulevard	**blvd., boulevard** *Fr., Eng.*	boulevar	boulevard	bulevar
mountain	Berg	**b'nom** *Viet.*	montaña	montagne	montanha
river mouth	Flussmündung	**boca** *Sp.*	boca	embouchure	foz
river mouth, pass	Flussmündung, Pass	**bocca** *It.*	boca, paso	embouchure, col	foz, passo
bay	Bucht	**bocht** *Du.*	bahía	baie	baía
bay	Bodden	**Bodden** *Ger.*	bahía	baie	baía
lake	See	**bœng** *Cbd.*	lago	lac	lago
bog	Moor	**bog** *Eng.*	pantano	fondrière	pântano
strait	Meeresstrasse	**boğazı** *Tur.*	estrecho	détroit	estreito
range	Gebirge	**bogd** *Mong.*	sierra	chaîne	cordilheira
woods	Gehölz	**bois** *Fr.*	bosque	bois	bosque
enclosed basin	Becken	**bolsón** *Sp.*	bolsón	bassin fermée	bacia fechada
forest	Wald	**bory** *Pol.*	bosque	forêt	floresta
forest	Wald	**bosque** *Sp.*	bosque	forêt	floresta
boulevard	Boulevard	**boulevard** *Fr., Eng.*	boulevar	boulevard	bulevar
branch	Arm	**br., branch** *Eng.*	brazo	bras	braço
stream distributary	Flussarm	**braţul** *Rom.*	brazo de río	bras	braço de rio
breakwater	Wellenbrecher	**breakwater** *Eng.*	rompeolas	brise-lames	quebra-mar
glacier	Gletscher	**-breen** *Nor.*	glaciar	glacier	geleira
bridge	Brücke	**bridge** *Eng.*	puente	pont	ponte
marsh	Bruch	**Bruch** *Ger.*	pantano	marais	pântano
bridge	Brücke	**Brücke** *Ger.*	puente	pont	ponte
bridge	Brücke	**brug** *Du.*	puente	pont	ponte
bay	Bucht	**Bucht** *Ger.*	bahía	baie	baía
bay	Bucht	**buchta** *Rus.*	bahía	baie	baía
mountain	Berg	**bufa** *Sp.*	bufa	montagne	montanha
bay	Bucht	**bugt** *Dan.*	bahía	baie	baía
lake	See	**buhayrah** *Ara.*	lago	lac	lago
lake, lagoon	See, Lagune, Haff	**buhayrat** *Ara.*	lago, laguna	lac, lagune	lago, laguna
mountain, hill	Berg, Hügel	**bukit** *Indon., Mal.*	montaña, colina	montagne, colline	montanha, colina
bay	Bucht	**-bukten** *Swe.*	bahía	baie	baía
mountain	Berg	**bulu** *Indon.*	montaña	montagne	montanha
castle	Burg	**Burg** *Ger.*	castillo	château	castelo
hill	Hügel	**burj** *Ara.*	colina	colline	colina
brook	Bach	**burn** *Gae.*	riachuelo	crique	riacho
cape	Kap	**burnu, burun** *Tur.*	cabo	cap	cabo
bay	Busen	**Busen** *Ger.*	bahía	baie	baía
butte(s)	Restberg(e)	**butte(s)** *Eng., Fr.*	butte(s)	butte(s)	colina, outeiro

C

ENGLISH	DEUTSCH	Map Form	ESPAÑOL	FRANCAIS	PORTUGUÊS
cape	Kap	**c., cabo** *Sp.* **cap** **cape**	cabo	cap	cabo
street	Strasse	**c., calle** *Sp.*	calle	rue	rua
peaks	Gipfel	**cabezas** *Sp.*	cabezas	cimes	picos
cape	Kap	**cabo** *Port., Sp.*	cabo	cap	cabo
waterfall	Wasserfall	**cachoeira** *Port.*	cascada	chute d'eau	cachoeira
street	Strasse	**calle** *Sp.*	calle	rue	rua
parkway	Ferienstrasse	**calzada** *Sp.*	calzada	allée de parc	alameda de parque
mosque	Moschee	**camii** *Tur.*	mezquita	mosqée	mesquita
road	Landstrasse	**camino** *Sp.*	camino	route	rodovia
camp	Lager	**camp** *Eng., Fr.*	campo	camp	campo
plain	Ebene	**campo** *It.*	llanura	plaine	planície
brook, ravine	Bach, Tobel	**cañada** *Sp.*	cañada	ruisseau, ravin	ravina
canal	Kanal	**canal** *Eng.*	canal	canal	canal
canal, channel	Kanal	**canal** *Fr., Port., Sp.*	canal	canal	canal
canal, channel	Kanal	**canale** *It.*	canal	canal	canal
stream distributary	Flussarm	**caño** *Sp.*	caño	bras	braço de rio, igarapé
canyon	Cañon	**cañón** *Sp.*	cañón	canyon	canhão
canyon	Cañon	**canyon** *Eng.*	cañón	canyon	canhão
plateau	Hochebene	**cao nguyen** *Viet.*	meseta	plateau	planalto
cape	Kap	**cap** *Fr., Cat.*	cabo	cap	cabo
cape	Kap	**cape** *Eng.*	cabo	cap	cabo
capitol	Kapitol	**capitolio** *Sp.*	capitolio	capitole	capitólio
cape	Kap	**capo** *It.*	cabo	cap	cabo
captain	Kapitän	**capt., captain** *Eng.*	capitán	capitaine	capitão
highway	Strasse	**carretera** *Sp.*	carretera	route	rodovia
valley	Tal	**carse** *Gae.*	valle	vallée	vale
waterfall	Wasserfall	**cascada** *Sp.*	cascada	chute d'eau	queda d'água
waterfall	Wasserfall	**cascata** *It.*	cascada	chute d'eau	queda d'água
castle	Burg, Schloss	**castel, castello** *It.*	castillo	château	castelo
castle	Burg, Schloss	**castelo** *Port.*	castillo	château	castelo
castle	Burg, Schloss	**castillo** *Sp.*	castillo	château	castelo
castle	Burg, Schloss	**castle** *Eng.*	castillo	château	castelo
cataracts	Katarakten	**cataratas** *Port., Sp.*	cataratas	cataractes	cataratas
cathedral	Kathedrale	**catedral** *Sp.*	catedral	cathédrale	catedral
range	Gebirge	**catena** *Sp.*	catena	chaîne	cordilheira
cathedral	Kathedrale	**cathedral** *Eng.*	catedral	cathédrale	catedral
causeway	Dammweg	**causeway** *Eng.*	calzada	chaussée	calçada
upland	Bergland	**causse** *Fr.*	tierras altas	causse	terras altas
cave(s)	Höhle(n)	**cave(s)** *Eng.*	cueva(s)	caverne(s)	caverna(s)
cay (islet)	Klippe	**cay** *Eng.*	cayo	caye	baixio
cay(s), islet(s)	Klippe(n)	**cayo(s)** *Sp.*	cayo(s)	caye(s)	baixio(s)
cemetery	Friedhof	**cementerio** *Sp.*	cementerio	cimetière	cemitério
cemetery	Friedhof	**cemetery** *Eng.*	cementerio	cimetière	cemitério
mountain(s), hill(s)	Berg(e), Hügel	**cerro(s)** *Sp.*	cerro(s)	montagne(s), colline(s)	montanha(s), colina(s)
range	Gebirge	**chaîne** *Fr.*	sierra	chaîne	cordilheira
channel	Kanal	**channel** *Eng.*	canal, estrecho	canal, détroit	canal, estreito
hills	Hügel	**chapada** *Port.*	colinas	collines	chapada
island	Insel	**char** *Ben.*	isla	île	ilha
castle	Burg, Schloss	**château** *Fr.*	castillo	château	castelo
road	Landstrasse	**chemin** *Fr.*	camino	chemin	rodovia
bay	Bucht	**chhâk** *Cbd.*	bahía	baie	baía
lake	See	**chi** *Ch.*	lago	lac	lago
harbor, harbour	Hafen	**chiang** *Ch.*	puerto	port	porto
cape	Kap	**chiao** *Ch.*	cabo	cap	cabo
road	Landstrasse	**chin., chemin** *Fr.*	camino	chemin	rodovia
river	Fluss	**-ch'ŏn** *Kor.*	río	rivière	rio
reservoir	Stausee	**-chŏsuji** *Kor.*	embalse	réservoir	reservatório
intermittent lake, salt marsh	periodischer See, Salzmarsch	**chott** *Ara.*	lago intermitente, pantano salado	lac périodique, marais salé	lago intermitente, pântano salgado
range	Gebirge	**chr., chrebet** *Rus.*	sierra	chaîne	cordilheira
mountains	Berge	**chuŏr phnum** *Cbd.*	montañas	montagnes	montanhas
church	Kirche	**church** *Eng.*	iglesia	église	igreja
waterfalls	Wasserfälle	**chutes** *Fr.*	cascadas	chutes d'eau	quedas d'água
marsh	Marsch	**ciénaga** *Sp.*	ciénaga	marais	pântano
peak	Gipfel	**cima** *It., Sp.*	cima	cime	pico
peak	Gipfel	**cime** *Fr.*	cima	cime	pico
cemetery	Friedhof	**cimetière** *Fr.*	cementerio	cimetière	cemitério
city	Stadt	**città** *It.*	ciudad	ville	cidade
city	Stadt	**city** *Eng.*	ciudad	ville	cidade
city	Stadt	**ciudad** *Sp.*	ciudad	ville	cidade
claypan	Tonpfanne	**claypan** *Eng.*	capa de arcilla	couche argilleuse	camada de argila
cliff(s)	Kliff(e)	**cliff(s)** *Eng.*	risco(s)	falaise(s)	falésia(s)
lake	See	**co** *Tib.*	lago	lac	lago
mountain	Berg	**co** *Viet.*	montaña	montagne	montanha
mountain, hill	Berg, Hügel	**co., cerro** *Sp.*	cerro	montagne, colline	montanha, colina
coast	Küste	**coast** *Eng.*	costa	côte	costa
coast guard station	Küstenwacht-station	**coast guard station** *Eng.*	estación de los guardacostas	station des gardescôte	estação de guarda costeira
pass	Pass	**col** *Fr.*	paso	col	passo
college	Hochschule	**colegio** *Sp.*	colegio	collège	colégio
hill(s)	Hügel	**colina(s)** *Sp.*	colina(s)	colline(s)	colina(s)
college	Hochschule	**coll., college** *Eng.*	colegio	collège	colégio
hills	Hügel	**colli** *It.*	colinas	collines	colinas
hills	Hügel	**colline** *It.*	colinas	collines	colinas
hills	Hügel	**collines** *Fr.*	colinas	collines	colinas
common	Gemeindeland	**common** *Eng.*	campo común	commune	terra comum
islands	Inseln	**con** *Viet.*	islas	îles	ilhas
plain	Ebene	**conca** *It.*	llanura	plaine	planície
convent	Nonnenkloster	**convent** *Eng.*	convento	couvent	convento
convent	Nonnenkloster	**convento** *It., Port., Sp.*	convento	couvent	convento
range	Gebirge	**cord., cordillera** *Sp.*	cordillera	chaîne	cordilheira
mountain	Berg	**corno** *It.*	montaña	montagne	montanha
brook	Bach	**córrego** *Port.*	arroyo	ruisseau	córrego
coast	Küste	**costa** *Sp.*	costa	côte	costa
coast, hills	Küste, Hügel	**côte** *Fr.*	costa, colinas	côte	costa, colinas
hills	Hügel	**coteau** *Fr.*	colinas	coteau	colinas
coulee	breite Schlucht	**coulee** *Eng.*	rambla	coulée	barranco
coulee	breite Schlucht	**coulée** *Fr.*	rambla	coulée	barranco
county park	Park	**county park** *Eng.*	parque del condado	parc de comté	parque de condado
convent	Nonnenkloster	**couvent** *Fr.*	convento	couvent	convento
cove	kleine Bucht	**cove** *Eng.*	ensenada	anse	enseada
brook	Bach	**cr., creek** *Eng.*	riachuelo	crique	riacho
crag	Felsspitze	**crag** *Eng.*	despeñadero	pointe de rocher	despenhadeiro
crater	Krater	**crater** *Eng.*	cráter	cratère	cratera
crater	Krater	**cratère** *Fr.*	cráter	cratère	cratera
creek	Bach	**creek** *Eng.*	riachuelo	crique	riacho
peak	Gipfel	**croda** *It.*	pico	cime	pico
canal	Kanal	**csatorna** *Hung.*	canal	canal	canal
bay	Bucht	**cua** *Viet.*	bahía	baie	baía
hills, ridge	Hügel, Höhenrücken	**cuchilla** *Sp.*	cuchilla	collines, crête	coxilha
caves	Höhen	**cuevas** *Sp.*	cuevas	cavernes	cavernas
cove	kleine Bucht	**cul-de-sac** *Fr.*	ensenada	cul-de-sac	enseada
mountains	Berge	**culmea** *Rom.*	montañas	montagnes	montanhas
summit	Gipfel	**cumbre** *Sp.*	cumbre	sommet	cume

D

ENGLISH	DEUTSCH	Map Form	ESPAÑOL	FRANCAIS	PORTUGUÊS
mountain	Berg	**dağ, dağı** *Tur.*	montaña	montagne	montanha
mountains	Berge	**dāgh** *Per.*	montañas	montagnes	montanhas
mountains	Berge	**dağlar, dağları** *Tur.*	montañas	montagnes	montanhas
hill	Hügel	**dahr** *Ara.*	colina	colline	colina
plateau	Hochebene	**-dai, -daichi** *Jpn.*	meseta	plateau	planalto
mountain	Berg	**-dake** *Jpn.*	montaña	montagne	montanha
valley	Tal	**-dal, -dalen** *Nor., Swe.*	valle	vallée	vale
dale	weites Tal	**dale** *Eng.*	valle ancho	vallée large	vale aberto
dam	Damm	**dam** *Eng.*	presa	barrage	represa
lake	See	**danau** *Indon.*	lago	lac	lago
island	Insel	**dao** *Ch., Viet.*	isla	île	ilha
marsh	Marsch	**daqq** *Per.*	pantano	marais	pântano
lake	See	**daryācheh** *Per.*	lago	lac	lago
desert	Wüste	**dasht** *Per.*	desierto	désert	deserto
monastery	Kloster	**dayr** *Ara.*	monasterio	monastère	mosteiro
deep	Tiefe	**deep** *Eng.*	fosa marina	fossé marin	fossa submarina
delta	Delta	**delta** *Eng., Fr., Sp.*	delta	delta	delta

Glossary and Abbreviations of Geographical Terms / Verzeichnis und Abkürzungen Geographischer Begriffe 291
Glosario y Abreviaciones de Términos Geográficos / Glossaire et Abréviations de Termes Géographiques
Glossário e Abreviações de Termos Geográficos

ENGLISH	DEUTSCH	Map Form Geographische Begriffe Términos Geográficos Termes Géographiques Termos Geográficos	ESPAÑOL	FRANCAIS	PORTUGUÊS
sea	Meer	**deniz, denizi** *Tur.*	mar	mer	mar
monument	Denkmal	**Denkmal** *Ger.*	monumento	monument	monumento
pass	Pass	**deo** *Viet.*	paso	col	passo
depression	Senke	**depression** *Eng.*	depresión	dépression	depressão
river	Fluss	**deresi** *Tur.*	río	rivière	rio
desert	Wüste	**desert** *Eng.*	desierto	désert	deserto
desert	Wüste	**desierto** *Sp.*	desierto	désert	deserto
strait	Meeresstrasse	**détroit** *Fr.*	estrecho	détroit	estreito
escarpment	Landstufe	**dhar** *Ara.*	escarpa	escarpement	escarpa
canal	Kanal	**dhiórix** *Gr.*	canal	canal	canal
lake, marsh	See, Marsch	**dian** *Ch.*	lago, pantano	lac, marais	lago, pântano
channel	Kanal	**diep** *Du.*	canal, estrecho	canal, détroit	canal, estreito
dike	Deich	**dijk** *Du.*	dique	digue	dique
district	Distrikt	**district** *Eng.*	distrito	district	distrito
district	Distrikt	**distrito** *Sp.*	distrito	district	distrito
ditch	Graben	**ditch** *Eng.*	acequia	fossé	fosso
mountain(s)	Berg(e)	**djebel** *Ara.*	montaga(s)	montagne(s)	montanha(s)
fjord	Fjord	**-djúp** *Ice.*	fiordo	fjord	fiorde
channel, sound	Kanal, Sund	**-djupet** *Swe.*	canal, sonda	canal, détroit	canal, estreito
zoo	Zoo	**djurpark** *Swe.*	parque zoológico	zoo	jardim zoológico
island	Insel	**-do** *Kor.*	isla	île	ilha
interfluve	Erhebung	**doāb** *Per.*	interfluvio	interfluve	interflúvio
dock	Dock	**dock** *Eng.*	muelle	quai	doca
mountain	Berg	**doi** *Thai*	montaña	montagne	montanha
valley	Tal	**dolina** *Rus.*	valle	vallée	vale
mountain	Berg	**dolok** *Indon.*	montaña	montagne	montanha
hills	Hügel	**dombrovidék** *Hung.*	colinas	collines	colinas
hills	Hügel	**dombvidék** *Hung.*	colinas	collines	colinas
peak	Gipfel	**dos** *Fr.*	pico	dos	pico
downs (hills)	Hügelland	**downs** *Eng.*	colinas	collines	terras baixas (colinas)
drive	Fahrweg	**dr., drive** *Eng.*	calzada	avenue	avenida
drain (water-course)	Abzugsgraben	**drain** *Eng.*	desaguadero	drainage	escoadouro
draw (ravine)	kleines Tal	**draw** *Eng.*	valle pequeño	ravine	bacia, vale
drive	Fahrweg	**drive** *Eng.*	calzada	avenue	avenida
dry lake	Trockensee	**dry lake** *Eng.*	lago seco	lac asséché	lago seco
dunes	Dünen	**dunes** *Eng., Fr.*	dunas	dunes	dunas

E

ENGLISH	DEUTSCH	Map Form	ESPAÑOL	FRANCAIS	PORTUGUÊS
east	Ost	**e., east** *Eng.*	este	est	leste
school	Schule	**école** *Fr.*	escuela	école	escola
mountain	Berg	**-egga** *Nor.*	montaña	montagne	montanha
memorial	Ehrenmal	**Ehrenmal** *Ger.*	monumento	memorial	monumento
river	Fluss	**-elv,-elva** *Nor.*	río	rivière	rio
reservoir	Stausee	**embalse** *Sp.*	embalse	réservoir	reservatório
pier	Landungsbrücke	**embarcadero** *Sp.*	embarcadero	jetée	cais
valley	Tal	**'emeq** *Heb.*	valle	vallée	vale
monument	Denkmal	**emlékmü** *Hung.*	monumento	monument	monumento
spring	Quelle	**'en** *Heb.*	manantial	source	fonte, manancial
cove	kleine Bucht	**enseada** *Port.*	ensenada	anse	enseada
cove	kleine Bucht	**ensenada** *Sp.*	ensenada	anse	enseada
entrance	Einfahrt	**entrance** *Eng.*	entrada	entrée	entrada
forest	Wald	**erdö** *Hung.*	bosque	forêt	floresta
sand desert	Sandwüste	**erg** *Ara.*	desierto arenoso	désert de sable	deserto arenoso
escarpment	Landstufe	**escarpment** *Eng.*	escarpa	escarpement	escarpa
school	Schule	**escuela** *Sp.*	escuela	école	escola
highland	Hochland	**espigão** *Port.*	región montañosa	pays montagneux	espigão
station	Bahnhof, Stützpunkt	**est., estação** *Port.*	estación	station	estação
		estación			
stadium	Stadion	**estadio** *Sp.*	estadio	stade	estádio
reservoir	Stausee	**estanque** *Sp.*	estanque	réservoir	reservatório
estuary	Trichtermündung	**estero** *Sp.*	estero	estuaire	estuário
road	Landstrasse	**estr., estrada** *Port.*	camino	route	estrada
strait	Meeresstrasse	**estrecho** *Sp.*	estrecho	détroit	estreito
estuary	Trichtermündung	**estuary** *Eng.*	estuario	estuaire	estuário
pond	Teich	**étang** *Fr.*	charca	étang	lagoa, açude
expressway	Autobahn	**expy., expressway** *Eng.*	autopista	autoroute	via expressa
island	Insel	**-ey** *Ice.*	isla	île	ilha
lake	See	**ežeras** *Lith.*	lago	lac	lago
lake	See	**ezers** *Latv.*	lago	lac	lago

F

ENGLISH	DEUTSCH	Map Form	ESPAÑOL	FRANCAIS	PORTUGUÊS
faculty (school)	Fakultät	**faculté** *Fr.*	facultad	faculté	faculdade
fairground	Ausstellungsgelände	**fairground** *Eng.*	campo para ferias	champ de foire	terreno para feiras
cliff	Kliff	**falaise** *Fr.*	risco	falaise	falésia
fall(s) (waterfall)	Wasserfall	**falls(s)** *Eng.*	cascada	chute d'eau	queda d'água
waterfall	Fall	**Fall** *Ger.*	cascada	chute d'eau	queda d'água
waterfall	Wasserfall	**-fallet** *Swe.*	cascada	chute d'eau	queda d'água
river	Fluss	**far'** *Ara.*	río	rivière	rio
lighthouse	Leuchtturm	**faro** *Sp.*	faro	phare	farol
upland	Bergland	**farsh** *Ara.*	tierras altas	hautes terres	terras altas
fell (mountain, hill)	ödes Hügelland	**fell** *Eng.*	colina rocosa	colline rocheuse	colina rochosa
mountain	Berg	**-fell** *Ice.*	montaña	montagne	montanha
mountain	Berg	**feng** *Ch.*	montaña	montagne	montanha
upland	Bergland	**fennsík** *Hung.*	tierras altas	hautes terres	terras altas
ferry	Fähre	**ferry** *Eng.*	balsadera	bac	balsa
lake	See	**fertö** *Hung.*	lago	lac	lago
fortress	Feste	**Feste** *Ger.*	fortaleza	fort	fortaleza
estuary, strait	Trichtermündung, Meeresstrasse	**firth** *Eng.*	estuario, estrecho	estuaire, détroit	estuário, estreito
mountain(s)	Berg(e)	**fjäll(en)** *Swe.*	montaga(s)	montagne(s)	montanha(s)
mountain	Berg	**fjället** *Swe.*	montaña	montagne	montanha
fjord	Fjord	**fjärden** *Swe.*	fiordo	fjord	fiorde
mountain	Berg	**-fjell, -fjellet** *Nor.*	montaña	montagne	montanha
mountain	Berg	**-fjöll** *Ice.*	montaña	montagne	montanha
fjord	Fjord	**-fjord** *Nor.*	fiordo	fjord	fiorde
fjord, lake	Fjord, See	**-fjorden** *Nor., Swe.*	fiordo, lago	fjord, lac	fiorde, lago
fjord, bay	Fjord, Bucht	**-fjörur** *Ice.*	fiordo, bahía	fjord, baie	fiorde, baía
fork	Arm	**fk., fork** *Eng.*	brazo	bras	braço de rio
flat	Flachland	**flat** *Eng.*	llano	plat	planície
river	Fluss	**-fljót** *Ice.*	río	rivière	rio
bay	Bucht	**-flói** *Ice.*	bahía	baie	baía
flood control basin	Hochwasserrückhaltebecken	**flood control basin** *Eng.*	cuenca para controlar la inundación	bassin de contrôle d'inondation	bacia de controle de inundações
airport	Flugplatz	**Flughafen** *Ger.*	aeropuerto	aéroport	aeroporto
airport	Flugplatz	**Flugplatz** *Ger.*	aeropuerto	aérodrome	aeroporto
airport	Flughafen	**flygplats** *Swe.*	aeródromo	aérodrome	aeródromo
river mouth, pass	Flussmündung, Pass	**foce** *It.*	desembocadura, paso	embouchure, col	desembocadura, foz, passo
canal	Kanal	**föcsatorna** *Hung.*	canal	canal	canal
glacier	Gletscher	**-fonn** *Nor.*	glaciar	glacier	geleira
spring	Quelle	**fontaine** *Fr.*	manantial	fontaine	fonte, manancial
pass	Pass	**forca** *It.*	paso	col	passo
inlet	Förde	**Förde** *Ger.*	abra	bras de mer	enseada, estuário
foreland	Vorland	**foreland** *Eng.*	promontorio	promontoire	promontório
forest	Wald	**forest** *Eng.*	bosque	forêt	floresta
forest reserve	Waldreservat	**forest reserve** *Eng.*	reserva de bosque	réserve forestière	reserva florestal

ENGLISH	DEUTSCH	Map Form Geographische Begriffe Términos Geográficos Termes Géographiques Termos Geográficos	ESPAÑOL	FRANCAIS	PORTUGUÊS
forest	Wald	**forêt** *Fr.*	bosque	forêt	floresta
waterfall	Wasserfall	**-forsen** *Swe.*	cascada	chute d'eau	queda d'água
forest	Forst	**Forst** *Ger.*	bosque	forêt	floresta
fort	Fort	**fort** *Eng., Fr.*	fuerte	fort	forte
waterfall	Wasserfall	**-foss** *Ice.*	cascada	chute d'eau	queda d'água
waterfall	Wasserfall	**-fossen** *Nor.*	cascada	chute d'eau	queda d'água
brook	Bach	**fosso** *It.*	arroyo	ruisseau	córrego
pass	Pass	**foum** *Ara.*	paso	col	passo
fracture zone	Bruchzone	**fracture zone** *Eng.*	zona de fractura	zone de faille	zona de fratura
freeway	Autobahn	**frwy., freeway** *Eng.*	autopista	autoroute	via expressa
fort	Fort	**ft., fort** *Eng., Fr.*	fuerte	fort	forte
stream distributary	Flussarm	**furo** *Port.*	brazo de río	bras	furo

G

ENGLISH	DEUTSCH	Map Form	ESPAÑOL	FRANCAIS	PORTUGUÊS
mountain, hill	Berg, Hügel	**g., gora** *Rus.*	montaña, colina	montagne, colline	montanha, colina
mountain	Berg	**g., gunong** *Mal.* **gunung**	montaña	montagne	montanha
mountain	Berg	**-gai'sa** *Lapp.*	montga	montagne	montanha
tunnel	Tunnel	**galleria** *It.*	túnel	tunnel	túnel
gallery	Galerie	**gallery** *Eng.*	galería	galerie	galeria
game farm	Wildfarm	**game farm** *Eng.*	criadero de caza	ferme de gibier	fazenda de caça
game park	Wildpark	**game park** *Eng.*	vedado de caza	parc à gibier	parque de caça
game refuge	Wildgehege	**game refuge** *Eng.*	refugio de caza	refuge de gibier	refúgio de caça
game reserve	Wildreservat	**game reserve** *Eng.*	vedado de caza	réserve à gibier	reserva de caça
game sanctuary	Wildschutzgebiet	**game sanctuary** *Eng.*	vedado de caza	réserve à gibier	santuário de caça
bay	Bucht	**gang** *Ch.*	bahía	baie	baía
river	Fluss	**-gang** *Kor.*	río	rivière	rio
gap	Pass	**gap** *Eng.*	paso	col	passo
intermittent lake	periodischer See	**garaet** *Ara.*	lago intermitente	lac périodique	lago intermitente
garden	Garten	**gard., garden** *Eng.*	jardín	jardin	jardim
gardens	Gärten	**gardens** *Eng.*	jardines	jardins	jardins
mountain	Berg	**garet** *Ara.*	montaña	montagne	montanha
lake	See	**-gata** *Jpn.*	lago	lac	lago
gate	Tor	**gate** *Eng.*	puerta	porte	portão
mountain torrent	Wildbach	**gave** *Fr.*	torrente	gave	torrente
range	Gebirge	**gebergte** *Du.*	sierra	chaîne	cordilheira
range	Gebirge	**Gebirge** *Ger.*	sierra	chaîne	cordilheira
pass	Pass	**gečidi** *Tur.*	paso	col	passo
oasis, well	Oase, Brunnen	**ghadīr** *Ara.*	oasis, pozo	oasis, puits	oásis, poço
mountains	Gebirge	**ghar** *Pas.*	montañas	montagnes	montanhas
spring	Quelle	**ghayl** *Ara.*	manantial	source	manancial
bay	Bucht	**ghubbat** *Ara.*	bahía	baie	baía
dunes	Dünen	**ghurd** *Ara.*	dunas	dunes	dunas
island	Insel	**gili** *Indon.*	isla	île	ilha
peak	Gipfel	**Gipfel** *Ger.*	pico	cime	pico
hill	Hügel	**giva't** *Heb.*	colina	colline	colina
bay	Bucht	**gji** *Alb.*	bahía	baie	baía
glacier	Gletscher	**glacier** *Eng., Fr.*	glaciar	glacier	geleira
lake	See	**göl** *Tur.*	lago	lac	lago
bald mountains	kahle Berge	**gol'cy** *Rus.*	montañas calvas	monts chauves	montanhas calvas
gulf	Golf	**golf** *Cat.*	golfo	golfe	golfo
golf course	Golfplatz	**golf course** *Eng.*	campo de golf	champ de golf	campo de golfe
gulf	Golf	**golfe** *Fr.*	golfo	golfe	golfo
bay	Bucht	**golfete** *Sp.*	golfete	baie	baía
gulf	Golf	**golfo** *It., Sp.*	golfo	golfe	golfo
lake	See	**gölü** *Tur.*	lago	lac	lago
mountain, hill	Berg, Hügel	**gora** *Rus.*	montaña, colina	montagne, colline	montanha, colina
mountains	Berge	**gora** *S./C.*	montañas	montagnes	montanhas
mountain	Berg	**góra** *Pol.*	montaña	montagne	montanha
gorge	Schlucht	**gorge** *Eng., Fr.*	garganta	gorge	garganta
mountains, hills	Berge, Hügel	**gorje** *S./C.*	montañas, colinas	montagnes, collines	montanhas, colinas
ruins	Ruinen	**gorodišče** *Rus.*	ruinas	ruines	ruínas
mountains, hills	Berge, Hügel	**gory** *Rus.*	montañas, colinas	montagnes, collines	montanhas, colinas
mountains	Berge	**góry** *Pol.*	montañas	montagnes	montanhas
sinkhole	Schluckloch	**gouffre** *Fr.*	sumidero	gouffre	sumidouro
wadi	Wadi	**goulbin** *Hau.*	uadi	wadi	uádi
ditch	Graben	**Graben** *Ger.*	acequia	fossé	fosso
ridge	Höhenrücken	**gr'ada** *Rus.*	sierra	crête	cordilheira
mountain	Berg	**gradište** *Blg.*	montaña	montagne	montanha
ridges	Höhenrücken	**gr'ady** *Rus.*	sierras	crêtes	cordilheira
general	General	**gral., general** *Eng., Sp.*	general	général	geral
ridge	Grat	**Grat** *Ger.*	sierra	crête	cordilheira
grotto	Grotte	**grotta** *It.*	gruta	grotte	gruta
grotto	Grotte	**grotte** *Fr.*	gruta	grotte	gruta
group	Gruppe	**group** *Eng.*	grupo	groupe	grupo
island	Insel	**-grund** *Swe.*	isla	île	ilha
group	Gruppe	**grupo** *Sp.*	grupo	groupe	grupo
group	Gruppe	**groppo** *It.*	grupo	groupe	grupo
pass	Pass	**guan** *Ch.*	paso	col	passo
bay	Bucht	**guba** *Rus.*	bahía	baie	baía
mountain	Berg	**guelb** *Ara.*	montaña	montagne	montanha
gulch	Wildbachschlucht	**gulch** *Eng.*	quebrada	ravin	quebrada
gulf	Golf	**gulf** *Eng.*	golfo	golfe	golfo
mountain	Berg	**gunong** *Mal.*	montaña	montagne	montanha
mountain	Berg	**gunung** *Indon.*	montaña	montagne	montanha
islands	Inseln	**-guntō** *Jpn.*	islas	îles	ilhas

H

ENGLISH	DEUTSCH	Map Form	ESPAÑOL	FRANCAIS	PORTUGUÊS
upland	Bergland	**hadabat** *Ara.*	tierras altas	hautes terres	terras altas
mountain	Berg	**hadjer** *Ara.*	montaña	montagne	montanha
lagoon	Haff	**Haff** *Ger.*	laguna	lagune	laguna
sea, lake	Meer, See	**hai** *Ch.*	mar, lago	mer, lac	mar, lago
strait	Meeresstrasse	**haixia** *Ch.*	estrecho	détroit	estreito
reef	Riff	**hakau** *Poly.*	arrecife	récif	recife
peninsula	Halbinsel	**Halbinsel** *Ger.*	península	péninsule	península
hall	Halle	**hall** *Eng., Fr.*	salón	hall	hall
peninsula	Halbinsel	**-halvøya** *Nor.*	península	péninsule	península
beach	Strand	**-hama** *Jpn.*	playa	plage	praia
desert	Wüste	**hamada** *Ara.*	desierto	désert	deserto
plateau	Hochebene	**hammādat** *Ara.*	meseta	plateau	planalto
lake, marsh	See, Marsch	**hāmūn** *Per.*	lago, pantano	lac, marais	lago, pântano
point	Landspitze	**-hana** *Jpn.*	punta	pointe	ponta
peninsula	Halbinsel	**-hantō** *Jpn.*	península	péninsule	península
mountain, hill	Berg, Hügel	**har** *Heb.*	montaña, colina	montagne, colline	montanha, colina
harbor, harbour	Hafen	**harbor, harbour** *Eng.*	puerto	port	porto
mountains, hills	Berge, Hügel	**hare** *Heb.*	montañas, colinas	montagnes, collines	montanhas, colinas
ridge	Höhenrücken	**-harju** *Finn.*	sierra	crête	cordilheira
lava flow	Lavastrom	**harrat** *Ara.*	corriente de lava	coulée de lave	corrente de lava
hills	Hügel	**hauteurs** *Fr.*	colinas	hauteurs	colinas
sea, bay	Meer, Bucht	**-hav** *Swe.*	mar, bahía	mer, baie	mar, baía
harbor, harbour	Hafen	**havre** *Fr.*	puerto	havre	porto
oasis	Oase	**hawd** *Ara.*	oasis	oasis	oásis
lake	See	**hawr** *Ara.*	lago	lac	lago
harbor, harbour	Hafen	**hbr., harbor, harbour** *Eng.*	puerto	port	porto
headquarters	Hauptquartier	**hdqrs., headquarters** *Eng.*	cuartel general	guartier général	quartel-general
river	Fluss	**he** *Ch.*	río	rivière	rio
head (headland)	Landspitze	**head** *Eng.*	promontorio	promontoire	promontório

292 Glossary and Abbreviations of Geographical Terms / Verzeichnis und Abkürzungen Geographischer Begriffe
Glosario y Abreviaciones de Términos Geográficos / Glossaire et Abréviations de Termes Géographiques
Glossário e Abreviações de Termos Geográficos

ENGLISH	DEUTSCH	Map Form Geographische Begriffe Términos Geográficos Termes Géographiques Termos Geográficos	ESPAÑOL	FRANCAIS	PORTUGUÊS
heath	Heide	**heath** *Eng.*	matorral	lande	charneca
mountain(s)	Berg(e)	**hegy(ség)** *Hung.*	montaña(s)	montagne(s)	montanha(s)
heath	Heide	**Heide** *Ger.*	matorral	lande	charneca
plain	Ebene	**-heiya** *Jpn.*	llanura	plaine	planície
hills	Hügel	**-heuwells** *Afk.*	colinas	collines	colinas
highland	Hochland	**highland** *Eng.*	región montañosa	pays montagneux	terras altas
highway	Strasse	**highway** *Eng.*	carretera	route	rodovia
hill(s)	Hügel	**hill(s)** *Eng.*	colina(s)	colline(s)	colina(s)
race course	Rennbahn	**hipódromo** *Sp.*	hipódromo	hippodrome	hipódromo
race course	Rennbahn	**hippodrome** *Fr.*	hipódromo	hippodrome	hipódromo
historical	historisch	**hist., historical** *Eng.*	histórico	historique	histórico
historical park	historischer Park	**historical park** *Eng.*	parque histórico	parc historique	parque histórico
historic(al) site	historische Stätte	**historic(al) site** *Eng.*	sitio histórico	site historique	sítio histórico
Her Majesty's Air Station (U.K.)	Luftwaffen-stützpunkt (V.K.)	**H.M.A.S., Her Majesty's Air Station** *Eng.*	Real Estación Aeronáutica (R.U.)	Station Aérienne Royale (R.U.)	Estação Aérea Real (R.U.)
river	Fluss	**ho** *Ch.*	río	rivière	rio
reservoir	Stausee	**-ho** *Kor.*	embalse	réservoir	reservatório
mountain	Berg	**-hø** *Nor.*	montaña	montagne	montanha
plateau	Hochebene	**Hochebene** *Ger.*	meseta	plateau	planalto
forest	Hochwald	**Hochwald** *Ger.*	bosque	forêt	floresta
mountain	Berg	**-högarna** *Swe.*	montaña	montagne	montanha
height	Höhe	**Höhe** *Ger.*	altura	hauteur	elevação
cave(s)	Höhle(n)	**Höhle(n)** *Ger.*	cueva(s)	caverne(s)	caverna(s)
island	Insel	**-holm** *Dan.*	isla	île	ilha
hook	Haken	**hook** *Eng.*	gancho	crochet	cabo, promontório
mountain	Berg	**hora** *Czech, Slo.*	montaña	montagne	montanha
mountain, hill	Berg, Hügel	**hora** *Ukr.*	montaña, colina	montagne, colline	montanha, colina
point, peak	Horn	**Horn** *Ger.*	punta, pico	pointe, cime	ponta, pico
ruin	Ruine	**horva** *Heb.*	ruina	ruine	ruína
mountains	Berge	**hory** *Czech, Slo.*	montañas	montagnes	montanhas
mountains, hills	Berge, Hügel	**hory** *Ukr.*	montañas, colinas	montagnes, collines	montanhas, colinas
hospital	Krankenhaus	**hospital** *Eng., Sp.*	hospital	hôpital	hospital
point	Landspitze	**houma** *Poly.*	punta	pointe	ponta
house	Haus	**house** *Eng.*	casa	maison	casa
island	Insel	**hsü** *Ch.*	isla	île	ilha
lake, reservoir	See, Stausee	**hu** *Ch.*	lago, embalse	lac, réservoir	lago, reservatório
hill	Hügel	**Hügel** *Ger.*	colina	colline	colina
cape	Huk	**Huk** *Ger.*	cabo	cap	cabo
cape	Huk	**-huk** *Swe.*	cabo	cap	cabo
highway	Strasse	**hy., highway** *Eng.*	carretera	route	rodovia

I

island	Insel	**i., isla** *Sp.* **island**	isla	île	ilha
icefield	Eisdecke	**icefield** *Eng.*	helero	champ de glace	geleira
ice shelf	Schelfeis	**ice shelf** *Eng.*	corniza glacial	barrière de glace	banco de gelo
ice tongue	Eiszunge	**ice tongue** *Eng.*	lengua de glaciar	langue glaciaire	língua de geleira
dunes	Dünen	**idehan** *Ber.*	dunas	dunes	dunas
river	Fluss	**ig., igarapé** *Port.*	río	rivière	igarapé
church	Kirche	**iglesia** *Sp.*	iglesia	église	igreja
lake	See	**-ike** *Jpn.*	lago	lac	lago
island(s)	Insel(n)	**île(s)** *Fr.*	isla(s)	île(s)	ilha(s)
islet(s)	kleine Insel(n)	**îlet(s)** *Fr.*	isleta(s)	îlet(s)	ilhota(s)
island(s)	Insel(n)	**ilha(s)** *Port.*	isla(s)	île(s)	ilha(s)
islet(s)	kleine Insel(n)	**ilhéu(s)** *Port.*	isleta(s)	îlot(s)	ilhéu(s)
island	Insel	**illa** *Cat.*	isla	île	ilha
islands	Inseln	**illes** *Cat.*	islas	îles	ilhas
hill, upland	Hügel, Bergland	**'ilw** *Ara.*	colina, tierras altas	colline, hautes terres	colina, terras altas
hill	Hügel	**'ilwat** *Ara.*	colina	colline	colina
Indian reservation	Indianer-reservation	**Ind. res., Indian reservation** *Eng.*	reserva de Indios	réserve indienne	reserva indígena
inlet	Einfahrt	**inlet** *Eng.*	abra	bras de mer	enseada
island(s)	Insel(n)	**Insel(n)** *Ger.*	isla(s)	île(s)	ilha(s)
institute	Institut	**inst., institute** *Eng.*	instituto	institut	instituto
international	international	**int., international** *Eng.*	internacional	international	internacional
race course	Rennbahn	**ippodromo** *It.*	hipódromo	hippodrome	hipódromo
wadi	Wadi	**irhazer** *Ber.*	uadi	wadi	uádi
dunes	Dünen	**'irq** *Ara.*	dunas	dunes	dunas
islands	Inseln	**is., islands** *Eng.* **islas**	islas	îles	ilhas
island	Insel	**isla** *Sp.*	isla	île	ilha
island(s)	Insel(n)	**island(s)** *Eng.*	isla(s)	île(s)	ilha(s)
islands	Inseln	**islas** *Sp.*	islas	îles	ilhas
isle(s)	Insel(n)	**isle(s)** *Eng.*	isla(s)	île(s)	ilha(s)
islet(s)	kleine Insel(n)	**islet(s)** *Eng.*	isleta(s)	îlot(s)	ilhota(s)
islet	kleine Insel	**islote** *Sp.*	islote	îlot	ilhota
island	Insel	**isola** *It.*	isla	île	ilha
islands	Inseln	**isole** *It.*	islas	îles	ilhas
islet	kleine Insel	**isolotto** *It.*	isleta	îlot	ilhota
isthmus	Landenge	**isthme** *Fr.*	istmo	isthme	istmo
isthmus	Landenge	**isthmus** *Eng.*	istmo	isthme	istmo
isthmus	Landenge	**istmo** *Sp.*	istmo	isthme	istmo
island	Insel	**-iwa** *Jpn.*	isla	île	ilha

J

mountain(s)	Berg(e)	**jabal** *Ara.*	montaña(s)	montagne(s)	montanha(s)
cave	Höhle	**jama** *S./C.*	cueva	caverne	caverna
caves	Höhlen	**jame** *S./C.*	cuevas	cavernes	cavernas
garden	Garten	**jardin** *Fr.*	jardín	jardin	jardim
garden	Garten	**jardín** *Sp.*	jardín	jardin	jardim
gardens	Gärten	**jardines** *Sp.*	jardines	jardins	jardins
lake	See	**järv** *Est.*	lago	lac	lago
lake	See	**-järvi** *Finn.*	lago	lac	lago
mountains	Berge	**jary** *Rus.*	montañas	montagnes	montanhas
lake	See	**-jaur** *Lapp.*	lago	lac	lago
islands	Inseln	**jazā'ir** *Ara.*	islas	îles	ilhas
peninsula	Halbinsel	**jazirah** *Indon.*	península	péninsule	península
island	Insel	**jazīrat** *Ara.*	isla	île	ilha
island	Insel	**jazīreh** *Per.*	isla	île	ilha
reservoir	Stausee	**jazovir** *Blg.*	embalse	réservoir	reservatório
mountain(s)	Berg(e)	**jbel** *Ara.*	montaña(s)	montagne(s)	montanha(s)
lake	See	**jezero** *S./C.*	lago	lac	lago
lake, lagoon	See, Lagune, Haff	**jezioro** *Pol.*	lago, laguna	lac, lagune	lago, laguna
river	Fluss	**jiang** *Ch.*	río	rivière	rio
cape	Kap	**jiao** *Ch.*	cabo	cap	cabo
mountains	Berge	**jibāl** *Ara.*	montañas	montagnes	montanhas
island	Insel	**-jima** *Jpn.*	isla	île	ilha
saddle (pass)	Joch	**Joch** *Ger.*	paso	col	passo
river	Fluss	**-joki** *Finn.*	río	rivière	rio
glacier	Gletscher	**-jøkulen** *Nor.*	glaciar	glacier	geleria
glacier	Gletscher	**-jökull** *Ice.*	glaciar	glacier	geleria
gulf	Golf	**jūras līcis** *Latv.*	golfo	golfe	golfo
islands	Inseln	**juzur** *Ara.*	islas	îles	ilhas

K

mountains	Berge	**kabīr** *Per.*	montañas	montagnes	montanhas
dunes	Dünen	**kahal** *Ara.*	dunas	dunes	dunas
sea	Meer	**-kai** *Jpn.*	mar	mer	mar
strait	Meeresstrasse	**-kaikyō** *Jpn.*	estrecho	détroit	estreito
mountain	Berg	**-kaise** *Lapp.*	montaña	montagne	montanha
navy installation	Anlage de Marine	**ka.j., kaijō-jieitai** *Jpn.*	estación de la marina	installation navale	instalação naval
brook	Bach	**kali** *Indon.*	riachuelo	crique	riacho
mountain	Berg	**kalns** *Latv.*	montaña	montagne	montanha
ridge	Kamm	**Kamm** *Ger.*	sierra	crête	serra

ENGLISH	DEUTSCH	Map Form Geographische Begriffe Términos Geográficos Termes Géographiques Termos Geográficos	ESPAÑOL	FRANCAIS	PORTUGUÊS
canal	Kanal	**kanaal** *Du.*	canal	canal	canal
canal, channel	Kanal	**Kanal** *Ger.*	canal	canal	canal
canal, channel	Kanal	**kanal** *Rus., S./C., Swe., Ukr.*	canal	canal	canal
canal, channel	Kanal	**kana** *Pol.*	canal	canal	canal
canal, channel	Kanal	**kanalen** *Swe.*	canal	canal	canal
canal, channel	Kanal	**kanava** *Finn.*	canal	canal	canal
pass	Pass	**kandao** *Pas.*	paso	col	passo
river	Fluss	**-kang** *Kor.*	río	rivière	rio
moor	Moor	**-kangas** *Finn.*	páramo	lande	charneca
national park	Nationalpark	**kansallis-puisto** *Finn.*	parque nacional	parc national	parque nacional
island	Insel	**kaōh** *Cbd.*	isla	île	ilha
cape	Kap	**Kap** *Ger.*	cabo	cap	cabo
gorge	Schlucht	**kapija** *S./C.*	garganta	gorge	garganta
cape	Kap	**-kapp** *Nor.*	cabo	cap	cabo
dunes	Dünen	**kathīb** *Ara.*	dunas	dunes	dunas
desert	Wüste	**kavīr** *Per.*	desierto	désert	deserto
mountain	Berg	**kawlat** *Ara.*	montaña	montagne	montanha
hill	Hügel	**kawm** *Ara.*	colina	colline	colina
mountain	Berg	**kedīet** *Ara.*	montaña	montagne	montanha
lake	See	**kenohan** *Indon.*	lago	lac	lago
cape	Kap	**kep** *Alb.*	cabo	cap	cabo
islands	Inseln	**kepulauan** *Indon.*	islas	îles	ilhas
key(s), cay(s)	Klippe(n)	**key(s)** *Eng.*	cayo(s)	caye(s)	baixio(s)
intermittent lake	periodischer See	**khabrat** *Ara.*	lago intermitente	lac périodique	lago intermitente
gulf	Golf	**khalīj** *Ara.*	golfo	golfe	golfo
mountain	Berg	**khao** *Bur., Thai*	montaña	montagne	montanha
mountain	Berg	**khashm** *Ara.*	montaña	montagne	montanha
wadi	Wadi	**khatt** *Ara.*	uadi	wadi	uádi
wadi, river	Wadi, Fluss	**khawr** *Ara.*	uadi, río	wadi, rivière	uádi, rio
dam	Damm	**khazzān** *Ara.*	presa	barrage	represa
river, canal	Fluss, Kanal	**khlong** *Thai*	río, canal	rivière, canal	rio, canal
range	Gebirge	**khrebet** *Ukr.*	sierra	chaîne	cordilheira
dunes	Dünen	**khubb** *Ara.*	dunas	dunes	dunas
kill (river, channel)	Fluss, Kanal	**kill** *Eng.*	río, canal	rivière, canal	rio, canal
cemetery	Friedhof	**kladb., kladbišče** *Rus.*	cementerio	cimetière	cemitério
cloister	Kloster	**klasztory** *Pol.*	claustro	cloître	claustro, convento
cloister, monastery	Kloster	**Kloster** *Ger.*	claustro, monasterio	cloître, monastère	claustro, mosteiro
knob	Kuppe	**knob** *Eng.*	protuberancia	bosse	cerro, colina
island	Insel	**ko** *Thai*	isla	île	ilha
lake, lagoon	See, Lagune, Haff	**-ko** *Jpn.*	lago, laguna	lac, lagune	lago, laguna
harbor, harbour	Hafen	**-kō** *Jpn.*	puerto	port	porto
highland	Hochland	**-kōchi** *Jpn.*	región montañosa	pays montagneux	terras altas
mountain	Kogel	**Kogel** *Ger.*	montaña	montagne	montanha
plateau	Hochebene	**-kogen** *Jpn.*	meseta	plateau	planalto
mountains	Berge	**koh** *Per.*	montañas	montagnes	montanhas
air force installation	Anlage der Luftwaffe	**ko.j., kōkū-jieitai** *Jpn.*	estación aeronáutica	installation aérienne	instalação da força aérea
national park	Nationalpark	**-kokuritsu-kōen** *Jpn.*	parque nacional	parc national	parque nacional
national park	Nationalpark	**-kokutei-kōen** *Jpn.*	parque nacional	parc national	parque nacional
bay	Bucht	**kólpos** *Gr.*	bahía	baie	baía
mountain	Berg	**kong** *Indon.*	montaña	montagne	montanha
peak	Kopf	**Kopf** *Ger.*	pico	cime	pico
bridge	Brücke	**köprüsü** *Tur.*	puente	pont	ponte
gulf, bay	Golf, Bucht	**körfezi** *Tur.*	golfo, bahía	golfe, baie	golfo, baía
spit	Landzunge	**kosa** *Rus., Ukr.*	lengua de tierra	flèche	ponta de terra
rapids	Stromschnellen	**-koski** *Finn.*	rápidos	rapides	rápidos
pass	Pass	**kotal** *Per.*	paso	col	passo
basin	Becken	**kotlina** *Pol.*	cuenca	bassin	bacia
bay, pass	Bucht, Pass	**kou** *Ch.*	bahía, paso	baie, col	baía, passo
ridge	Höhenrücken	**kr'až** *Rus.*	sierra	crête	serra
escarpment	Landstufe	**kreb** *Ara.*	escarpa	escarpement	escarpa
fort	Fort	**krepost'** *Rus.*	fuerte	fort	forte
national park	Nationalpark	**krk., kokuritsu-kōen** *Jpn.*	parque nacional	parc national	parque nacional
ridge	Höhenrücken	**kryazh** *Ukr.*	sierra	crête	serra
national park	Nationalpark	**ktk., kokutei-kōen** *Jpn.*	parque nacional	parc national	parque nacional
bay	Bucht	**kuala** *Mal.*	bahía	baie	baía
mountain(s)	Berg(e)	**kūh(ha)** *Per.*	montaña(s)	montagne(s)	montanha(s)
hill	Hügel	**-kulle** *Swe.*	colina	colline	colina
dome	Kuppe	**Kuppe** *Ger.*	domo	dôme	domo
strait	Meeresstrasse	**-kurkku** *Finn.*	estrecho	détroit	estreito
channel	Kanal	**kyle** *Gae.*	canal, estrecho	canal, détroit	canal, estreito
island	Insel	**kyun** *Bur.*	isla	île	ilha
hills	Hügel	**-kyūryū** *Jpn.*	colinas	collines	colinas

L

lake	See	**l., lac** *Fr.* **lago lagoa lake**	lago	lac	lago, lagoa
pass	Pass	**la** *Tib.*	paso	col	passo
province	Provinz	**lääni** *Finn.*	provincia	province	província
lake(s)	See(n)	**lac(s)** *Fr.*	lago(s)	lac(s)	lago(s)
lake	See	**lacul** *Rom.*	lago	lac	lago
cape	Kap	**laem** *Thai*	cabo	cap	cabo
lagoon, lake	Lagune, Haff, See	**lag., laguna** *Sp.*	laguna	lagune, lac	laguna
lake	See	**lago** *It., Port., Sp.*	lago	lac	lago
lake, lagoon	See, Lagune, Haff	**lagoa** *Port.*	lago, laguna	lac, lagune	lagoa
lagoon	Lagune, Haff	**lagoon** *Eng.*	laguna	lagune	laguna
lakes	Seen	**lagos** *Port., Sp.*	lagos	lacs	lagos
lagoon, lake	Lagune, Haff, See	**laguna** *Sp.*	laguna	lagune, lac	laguna, lago
lagoon	Lagune, Haff	**lagune** *Fr.*	laguna	lagune	laguna
bay	Bucht	**laht** *Est.*	bahía	baie	baía
gulf	Golf	**-lahti** *Finn.*	golfo	golfe	golfo
lake(s)	See(n)	**lake(s)** *Eng.*	lago(s)	lac(s)	lago(s)
county	Grafschaft	**län** *Swe.*	condado	comté	condado
lake	Lanke (See)	**Lanke** *Ger.*	lago	lac	lago
sea	Meer	**laut** *Indon.*	mar	mer	mar
lava flow	Lavastrom	**lava flow** *Eng.*	corriente de lava	coulée de lave	corrente de lava
hill, mountain	Hügel, Berg	**law** *Eng.*	colina, montaña	colline, montagne	colina, montanha
mountains, forest	Berge, Wald	**les** *Czech*	montañas, bosque	montagnes, forêt	montanhas, floresta
forest	Wald	**les** *Rus.*	bosque	forêt	floresta
level (plain)	Niveau (Ebene)	**level** *Eng.*	nivel (llano)	niveau (plaine)	planície
islands	Inseln	**liedao** *Ch.*	islas	îles	ilhas
lighthouse	Leuchtturm	**lighthouse** *Eng.*	faro	phare	farol
estuary	Trichter-mündung	**liman** *Rus.*	estuario	estuaire	estuário
bay	Bucht	**limanı** *Tur.*	bahía	baie	baía
lake	See	**límni** *Gr.*	lago	lac	lago
mountain(s), peak	Berg(e), Gipfel	**ling** *Ch.*	montaña(s), pico	montagne(s), pic	montanha(s), pico
forest	Wald	**lis** *Ukr.*	bosque	forêt	floresta
plain(s)	Ebene(n)	**llano(s)** *Sp.*	llano(s)	plaine(s)	planície(s)
lake, reservoir	See, Stausee	**llyn** *Welsh*	lago, embalse	lac, réservoir	lago, reservatório
lake, inlet	See, Einfahrt	**loch** *Gae.*	lago, abra	lac, bras de mer	lago, angra
lock	Schleuse	**lock** *Eng.*	esclusa	écluse	eclusa
lock and dam	Damm mit Schleuse	**lock and dam** *Eng.*	presa y esclusa	écluse et barrage	represa e eclusa

Glossary and Abbreviations of Geographical Terms / Verzeichnis und Abkürzungen Geographischer Begriffe
Glosario y Abreviaciones de Términos Geográficos / Glossaire et Abréviations de Termes Géographiques
Glossário e Abreviações de Termos Geográficos
293

ENGLISH	DEUTSCH	Map Form Geographische Begriffe Términos Geográficos Termes Géographiques Termos Geográficos	ESPAÑOL	FRANCAIS	PORTUGUÊS
gorge	Schlucht	**log** *Rus.*	garganta	gorge	garganta
mountain	Berg	**loi** *Bur.*	montaña	montagne	montanha
hills	Hügel	**lomas** *Sp.*	lomas	collines	colinas
lake	See	**lough** *Gae.*	lago	lac	lago
lowland	Tiefland	**lowland** *Eng.*	tierra baja	terrain bas	terras baixas
marsh	Luch (Bruch)	**Luch** *Ger.*	pantano	marais	pântano
island	Insel	**-luoto** *Finn.*	isla	île	ilha
estuary	Trichtermündung	**lyman** *Ukr.*	estuario	estuaire	estuário

M

ENGLISH	DEUTSCH	Map Form	ESPAÑOL	FRANCAIS	PORTUGUÊS
mountains	Berge	**m., munţii** *Rom.*	montañas	montagnes	montanhas
island	Insel	**-maa** *Est.*	isla	île	ilha
strait	Meeresstrasse	**maḑīq** *Ara.*	estrecho	détroit	estreito
river	Fluss	**mae** *Thai*	río	rivière	rio
depression	Senke	**makhtesh** *Heb.*	depresión	dépression	depressão
bay	Bucht	**-man** *Kor.*	bahía	baie	baía
monastery	Kloster	**manastir** *S./C.*	monasterio	monastère	mosteiro
sea	Meer	**mar** *Sp., It.*	mar	mer	mar
marsh	Marsch	**marais** *Fr.*	pantano	marais	pântano
sea	Meer	**mare** *It.*	mar	mer	mar
marine corps air station	Flugstützpunkt des Marine-Corps	**marine corps air station** *Eng.*	estación aeronáutica de la infantería de marina	station aérienne de fusiliers marins	estação aérea de fuzileiros navais
marine corps base	Marine-Corps-Stützpunkt	**marine corps base** *Eng.*	base de la infantería de marina	base de fusiliers marins	base de fuzileiros navais
bay	Bucht	**marsā** *Ara.*	bahía	baie	baía
marsh	Marsch	**Marsch** *Ger.*	pantano	marais	pântano
marsh(es)	Marsch(en)	**marsh(es)** *Eng.*	pantano(s)	marais	pântano(s)
river mouth	Flussmündung	**maṣabb** *Ara.*	desembocadura	embouchure	desembocadura
canal	Kanal	**maṣrif** *Ara.*	canal	canal	canal
massif	Gebirgsmassiv	**massif** *Eng., Fr.*	macizo	massif	maciço
marine corps air station	Flugstützpunkt des Marine-Corps	**m.c.a.s., marine corps air station** *Eng.*	estación aeronáutica de la infantería de marina	station aérienne de fusiliers marins	estação aérea de fuzileiros navais
marine corps base	Marine-Corps-Stützpunkt	**m.c.b., marine corps base** *Eng.*	base de la infantería de marina	base de fusiliers marins	base de fuzileiros navais
meadow	Wiese	**meadow** *Eng.*	prado	prairie	pradaria
dunes	Dünen	**médanos** *Sp.*	médanos	dunes	dunas
sea, lake	Meer	**Meer** *Ger.*	mar, lago	mer, lac	mar, lago
sea, lake	Meer	**-meer** *Afk., Du.*	mar, lago	mer, lac	mar, lago
hills	Hügel	**melkosopočnik** *Rus.*	colinas	collines	colinas
memorial	Gedenkstätte	**mem., memorial** *Eng.*	monumento	mémorial	monumento
peninsula	Halbinsel	**menanjung** *Indon.*	península	péninsule	península
sea	Meer	**mer** *Fr.*	mar	mer	mar
mesa	Tafelberg	**mesa** *Sp.*	mesa	mesa	mesa
plateau	Hochebene	**meseta** *Sp.*	meseta	plateau	planalto
middle	Mittel-	**mid., middle** *Eng.*	medio	moyen	médio, central
spit	Landzunge	**mierzeja** *Pol.*	lengua de tierra	flèche	ponta de terra
bay	Bucht	**mifraz** *Heb.*	bahía	baie	baía
mines	Bergwerke	**mikhrot** *Heb.*	minas	mines	minas
military	militärisch	**mil., military** *Eng.*	militar	militaire	militar
harbor, harbour	Hafen	**-minato** *Jpn.*	puerto	port	porto
mine	Bergwerk	**mine** *Eng., Fr.*	mina	mine	mina
mountain	Berg	**-mine** *Jpn.*	montaña	montagne	montanha
cliff	Kliff	**minqār** *Ara.*	risco	falaise	falésia
cape	Kap	**-misaki** *Jpn.*	cabo	cap	cabo
mission	Mission	**mission** *Eng., Fr.*	misión	mission	missão
monument	Denkmal	**mon., monument** *Eng., Fr.*	monumento	monument	monumento
monastery	Kloster	**monasterio** *Sp.*	monasterio	monastère	mosteiro
monastery	Kloster	**monastero** *It.*	monasterio	monastère	mosteiro
monastery	Kloster	**monastery** *Eng.*	monasterio	monastère	mosteiro
monastery	Kloster	**moni** *Gr.*	monasterio	monastère	mosteiro
mount	Berg	**mont** *Fr.*	monte	mont	monte
mountain	Berg	**montagna** *It.*	montaña	montagne	montanha
mountain(s)	Berg(e)	**montagne(s)** *Fr.*	montaņa(s)	montagne(s)	montanha(s)
mountain(s)	Berg(e)	**montaña(s)** *Sp.*	montaña(s)	montagne(s)	montanha(s)
mount	Berg	**monte** *It., Port., Sp.*	monte	mont	monte
mountains	Berge	**montes** *Port., Sp.*	montes	monts	montes
mountains	Berge	**monti** *It.*	montes	monts	montes
mountains	Berge	**monts** *Fr.*	montes	monts	montes
monument	Denkmal	**monument** *Eng., Fr.*	monumento	monument	monumento
moor	Moor	**moor** *Eng.*	páramo	lande	pântano
moor	Moor	**Moor** *Ger.*	páramo	lande	pântano
sea	Meer	**more** *Rus., Ukr.*	mar	mer	mar
mountain	Berg	**-mori** *Jpn.*	montaña	montagne	montanha
mountain	Berg	**morne** *Fr.*	montaña	morne	montanha
hill, mountain	Hügel, Berg	**morro** *Port., Sp.*	morro	colline, montagne	morro
mosque	Moschee	**mosque** *Eng.*	mezquita	mosquée	mesquita
island, rock	Insel, Fels	**motu** *Poly.*	isla, roca	île, rocher	ilha, rochedo
island	Insel	**mouchão** *Port.*	isla	île	mouchão
mound	Erdhügel	**mound** *Eng.*	montículo	tertre	montículo
mount	Berg	**mount** *Eng.*	monte	mont	monte
mountain(s)	Berg(e)	**mountain(s)** *Eng.*	montaņa(s)	montagne(s)	montanha(s)
mouth (river mouth)	Mündung	**mouth** *Eng.*	desembocadura	embouchure	desembocadura
mount	Berg	**mt., mount** *Eng.*	monte	mont	monte
mountain	Berg	**mtn., mountain** *Eng.*	montaña	montagne	montanha
mountains	Berge	**mts., mountains** *Eng.*	montañas	montagnes	montanhas
point	Landspitze	**mui** *Viet.*	punta	pointe	ponta
headland	Landspitze	**mull** *Gae.*	promontorio	promontoire	promontório
depression	Senke	**munkhafaḑ** *Ara.*	depresión	dépression	depressão
mountain	Berg	**muntele** *Rom.*	montaña	montagne	montanha
mountains	Berge	**munţii** *Rom.*	montañas	montagnes	montanhas
museum	Museum	**museo** *It., Sp.*	museo	musée	museu
museum	Museum	**Museum** *Ger.*	museo	musée	museu
museum	Museum	**museum** *Eng.*	museo	musée	museu
museum	Museum	**múzeum** *Hung.*	museo	musée	museu
museum	Museum	**muzej** *Rus.*	museo	musée	museu
cape	Kap	**mys** *Rus., Ukr.*	cabo	cap	cabo

N

ENGLISH	DEUTSCH	Map Form	ESPAÑOL	FRANCAIS	PORTUGUÊS
north	Nord	**n., north** *Eng.*	norte	nord	norte
sea, gulf	Meer, Golf	**-nada** *Jpn.*	mar, golfo	mer, golfe	mar, golfo
desert	Wüste	**nafūd** *Ara.*	desierto	désert	deserto
plateau, mountains	Hochebene, Berge	**nagorje** *Rus.*	meseta, montañas	plateau, montagnes	planalto, montanhas
river	Fluss	**nahr** *Ara.*	río	rivière	rio
sea	Meer	**-naikai** *Jpn.*	mar	mer	mar
salt flat	Salzebene	**namakzār** *Per.*	salar	saline	salina
narrows	Meeresenge	**narrows** *Eng.*	angostura	goulet	estreito
peninsula	Halbinsel	**-näs** *Swe.*	península	péninsule	península
naval air station	Flugstützpunkt der Marine	**n.a.s., naval air station** *Eng.*	estación aeronáutica de la marina	station de forces aériennes navales	estação aérea da marinha
National Aeronautics and Space Administration	Nationale Aeronautik-und Weltraum-Behörde	**N.A.S.A., National Aeronautics and Space Administration** *Eng.*	Administración Nacional Aeronáutica y Espacial	Administration Nationale de l'Espace et Aéronautique	Administração Nacional do Espaço e Aeronâutica
national park	Nationalpark	**nasjonal park** *Nor.*	parque nacional	parc national	parque nacional
national	national	**nat., national** *Eng., Fr.*	nacional	national	nacional
national battlefield site	Schlachtfeld	**national battlefield site** *Eng.*	campo de batalla nacional	champ de bataille national	campo de batalha nacional
national cemetery	Nationalfriedhof	**national cemetery** *Eng.*	cementerio nacional	cimetière national	cemitério nacional
national forest	Wald in Gemeinbesitz	**national forest** *Eng.*	bosque nacional	forêt nationale	floresta nacional
national historical park	Park an historischer Stätte	**national historical park** *Eng.*	parque histórico nacional	parc historique national	parque histórico nacional
national historical site	historische Stätte	**national historical site** *Eng.*	lugar histórico nacional	site historique national	sítio histórico nacional
national laboratory	staatliche Forschungsanstalt	**national laboratory** *Eng.*	laboratorio nacional	laboratoire national	laboratório nacional
national memorial	nationale Gedenkstätte	**national memorial** *Eng.*	monumento nacional	memorial national	monumento nacional
national military park	Park bei einem Schlachtfeld	**national military park** *Eng.*	parque militar nacional	parc militaire national	parque militar nacional
national monument	National-denkmal	**national monument** *Eng.*	monumento nacional	monument national	monumento nacional
national park	Nationalpark	**national park** *Eng.*	parque nacional	parc nationale	parque nacional
national recreation area	Ausflugsgebiet	**national recreation area** *Eng.*	campo nacional de recreo	région de récréation national	área de lazer nacional
national seashore	öffentlicher Badestrand	**national seashore** *Eng.*	playa nacional	plage nationale	praia nacional
national park	Nationalpark	**natsional'nyy park** *Ukr.*	parque nacional	parc nationale	parque nacional
reserve	Naturpark	**Naturpark** *Ger.*	reserva natural	réserve naturelle	reserva natural
nature reserve	Naturschutzgebiet	**Naturschutzgebiet** *Ger.*	reserva natural	réserve naturelle	reserva natural
naval air station	Flugstützpunkt der Marine	**naval air station** *Eng.*	estación aeronáutica de la marina	station de forces aériennes navales	estação aérea da marinha
naval base	Flottenstützpunkt	**naval base** *Eng.*	base naval	base navale	base naval
naval station	Marinestation	**naval station** *Eng.*	estación naval	station navale	estação naval
naval base	Flottenstützpunkt	**n.b., naval base** *Eng.*	base naval	base navale	base naval
rock	Fels	**-ne** *Jpn.*	roca	rocher	rochedo
neck	Landenge	**neck** *Eng.*	istmo	isthme	istmo
necropolis (cemetery)	Friedhof	**necrópolis** *Sp.*	necrópolis	nécropole	necrópole
cape	Kap	**neem** *Est.*	cabo	cap	cabo
peninsula, point	Halbinsel, Landspitze	**-nes** *Ice., Nor.*	península, punta	péninsule, pointe	península, ponta
promontory	Vorgebirge	**ness** *Gae.*	promontorio	promontoire	promontório
snowcapped mountain(s)	Schneegipfel	**nev.(s)., nevado(s)** *Sp.*	nevado(s)	montagne(s) neigeuse(s)	pico(s) nevado(s)
mountain	Berg	**ngoc** *Viet.*	montaña	montagne	montanha
cape	Kap	**nina** *Est.*	cabo	cap	cabo
islands	Inseln	**nísoi** *Gr.*	islas	îles	ilhas
island	Insel	**nísos** *Gr.*	isla	île	ilha
lowland	Tiefland	**nizina** *Rus.*	tierra baja	terrain bas	terras baixas
lowland	Tiefland	**nižina** *Slo.*	tierra baja	terrain bas	terras baixas
lowland	Tiefland	**nizmennost'** *Rus.*	tierra baja	terrain bas	terras baixas
cape	Kap	**nos** *Blg.*	cabo	cap	cabo
naval station	Marinestation	**n.s., naval station** *Eng.*	estación naval	station navale	estação naval
nature reserve	Naturschutzgebiet	**Nsg., Naturschutzgebiet** *Ger.*	reserva natural	réserve naturelle	reserva natural
mountain	Berg	**nui** *Viet.*	montaña	montagne	montanha
lake	See	**-numa** *Jpn.*	lago	lac	lago
mountains	Berge	**nuruu** *Mong.*	montañas	montagnes	montanhas
island	Insel	**nusa** *Indon.*	isla	île	ilha
lake	See	**nuur** *Mong.*	lago	lac	lago
lowland	Tiefland	**nyzovyna** *Ukr.*	tierra baja	terrain bas	terras baixas

O

ENGLISH	DEUTSCH	Map Form	ESPAÑOL	FRANCAIS	PORTUGUÊS
island	Insel	**-ø** *Dan., Nor.*	isla	île	ilha
island	Insel	**-ö** *Swe.*	isla	île	ilha
island	Insel	**o., ostrov** *Rus.*	isla	île	ilha
islands	Inseln	**-öarna** *Swe.*	islas	îles	ilhas
oasis	Oase	**oasis** *Eng., Fr., Sp.*	oasis	oasis	oásis
observatory	Observatorium	**observatorio** *Sp.*	observatorio	observatoire	observatório
observatory	Observatorium	**observatory** *Eng.*	observatorio	observatoire	observatório
ocean	Ozean	**ocean** *Eng.*	océano	océan	oceano
island	Insel	**-ön** *Swe.*	isla	île	ilha
mountains	Berge	**óri** *Gr.*	montañas	montagnes	montanhas
bay	Bucht	**órmos** *Gr.*	bahía	baie	baía
mountain(s)	Berg(e)	**óros** *Gr.*	montaņa(s)	montagne(s)	montanha(s)
island	Insel	**ostriv** *Ukr.*	isla	île	ilha
island(s)	Insel(n)	**ostrov(a)** *Rus.*	isla(s)	île(s)	ilha(s)
island	Insel	**ostrovul** *Rom.*	isla	île	ilha
islands	Inseln	**otoci** *S./C.*	islas	îles	ilhas
island	Insel	**otok** *S./C.*	isla	île	ilha
wadi	Wadi	**ouadi** *Ara.*	uadi	wadi	uádi
wadi	Wadi	**oued** *Ara.*	uadi	wadi	uádi
outlet	Abfluss	**outlet** *Eng.*	desagüe	débouché	escoadouro
island	Insel	**-øy, -øya** *Nor.*	isla	île	ilha
lake	See	**oz., ozero** *Rus., Ukr.*	lago	lac	lago
lakes	Seen	**ozera** *Rus.*	lagos	lacs	lagos

P

ENGLISH	DEUTSCH	Map Form	ESPAÑOL	FRANCAIS	PORTUGUÊS
hills	Hügel	**pahorkatina** *Czech*	colinas	collines	colinas
palace	Palast	**pal., palace** *Eng.*	palacio	palais	palácio
palace	Palast	**palacio** *Sp.*	palacio	palais	palácio
palace	Palast	**palais** *Fr.*	palacio	palais	palácio
palace	Palast	**palazzo** *It.*	palacio	palais	palácio
palace	Palast	**paleis** *Du.*	palacio	palais	palácio
railroad station	Bahnhof	**pályaudvar** *Hung.*	estacion ferrocarril	gare	estação ferroviária
monument	Denkmal	**pam'atnik** *Rus.*	monumento	monument	monumento
plain	Ebene	**pampa** *Sp.*	pampa	plaine	pampa
basin	Becken	**pánev** *Czech*	cuenca	bassin	bacia
swamp	Sumpf	**pantanal** *Port., Sp.*	pantanal	marais	pantanal
marsh, swamp, reservoir	Marsch, Sumpf, Stausee	**pantano** *Sp.*	pantano	marais, réservoir	Pântano
moor	Moor	**páramo** *Sp.*	páramo	lande	pântano
park	Park	**parc** *Fr.*	parque	parc	parque
national park	Nationalpark	**parc national** *Fr.*	parque nacional	parc national	parque nacional
park	Park	**parco** *It.*	parque	parc	parque
national park	Nationalpark	**parco nazionale** *It.*	parque nacional	parc national	parque nacional
provincial park	Naturpark	**parc provincial** *Fr.*	parque de la provincia	parc provincial	parque provincial
park	Park	**Park** *Ger.*	parque	parc	parque
park	Park	**park** *Eng.*	parque	parc	parque
national park	Nationalpark	**park narodowy** *Pol.*	parque nacional	parc national	parque nacional
parkway	Ferienstrasse	**parkway** *Eng.*	calzada	allée de parc	alameda de parque
park	Park	**parque** *Port., Sp.*	parque	parc	parque
national park	Nationalpark	**parq. nac., parque nacional** *Port., Sp.*	parque nacional	parc national	parque nacional
beach	Strand	**part** *Hung.*	playa	plage	praia
strait	Meeresstrasse	**pas** *Fr.*	estrecho	détroit	estreito
passage	Durchfahrt	**pasaje** *Sp.*	pasaje	passage	passagem
pass	Pass	**paso** *Sp.*	paso	col	passo
pass	Pass	**Pass** *Ger.*	paso	col	passo
pass	Pass	**pass** *Eng.*	paso	col	passo
passage	Durchfahrt	**passage** *Eng., Fr.*	pasaje	passage	passagem
passage	Durchfahrt	**passe** *Fr.*	pasaje	passe	passagem
pass	Pass	**passo** *It.*	paso	col	passo
pass	Pass	**pasul** *Rom.*	paso	col	passo
brook	Bach	**patak** *Hung.*	riachuelo	crique	riacho
peak(s)	Gipfel	**peak(s)** *Eng.*	pico(s)	pic(s)	pico(s)
cave	Höhle	**pećina** *S./C.*	cueva	caverne	caverna
mountain	Berg	**pedra** *Port.*	montaña	montagne	montanha
mountains	Berge	**peg., pegunungan** *Indon.*	montañas	montagnes	montanhas
sea	Meer	**pélagos** *Gr.*	mar	mer	mar

294 Glossary and Abbreviations of Geographical Terms / Verzeichnis und Abkürzungen Geographischer Begriffe
Glosario y Abreviaciones de Términos Geográficos / Glossaire et Abréviations de Termes Géographiques
Glossário e Abreviações de Termos Geográficos

ENGLISH	DEUTSCH	Map Form Geographische Begriffe Términos Geográficos Termes Géographiques Termos Geográficos	ESPAÑOL	FRANCAIS	PORTUGUÊS
peninsula	Halbinsel	**pen., peninsula** *Eng.*	península	péninsule	península
peak, rock	Gipfel, Fels	**peña** *Sp.*	peña	pic, rocher	penha
peak, large rock	Gipfel, grosser Fels	**peñasco** *Sp.*	peñasco	pic, rocher	penhasco
basin	Becken	**pendi** *Ch.*	cuenca	bassin	bacia
peninsula	Halbinsel	**peninsula** *Eng.*	península	péninsule	península
peninsula	Halbinsel	**península** *Sp.*	península	péninsule	península
peninsula	Halbinsel	**péninsule** *Fr.*	península	péninsule	península
rock	Fels	**peñón** *Sp.*	peñón	rocher	rochedo
pass	Pass	**pereval** *Rus., Ukr.*	paso	col	passo
strait	Meeresstrasse	**pertuis** *Fr.*	estrecho	pertuis	estreito
sand desert	Sandwüste	**peski** *Rus.*	desierto arenoso	désert de sable	deserto arenoso
mountain	Berg	**phnum** *Cbd.*	montaña	montagne	montanha
mountain	Berg	**phou** *Lao.*	montaña	montagne	montanha
mountain	Berg	**phu** *Thai*	montaña	montagne	montanha
cape	Kap	**pi** *Ch.*	cabo	cap	cabo
plain	Ebene	**piano** *It.*	llanura	plaine	planície
peak	Gipfel	**pic** *Fr.*	pico	pic	pico
peak	Gipfel	**picacho** *Sp.*	picacho	pic	pico
peak	Gipfel	**picco** *It.*	pico	pic	pico
peak(s)	Gipfel	**pico(s)** *Port., Sp.*	pico(s)	pic(s)	pico(s)
pier	Landungsbrücke	**pier** *Eng.*	embarcadero	jetée	cais
mountain	Berg	**-piggen** *Nor.*	montaña	montagne	montanha
peak	Gipfel	**pik** *Rus.*	pico	pic	pico
forest	Wald	**pinhal** *Port.*	bosque	forêt	pinhal
peak	Gipfel	**pique** *Fr.*	pico	pique	pico
pyramid	Pyramide	**pirámide** *Sp.*	pirámide	pyramide	pirâmide
peak(s)	Gipfel	**piton(s)** *Fr.*	pico(s)	piton(s)	pico(s)
peninsula	Halbinsel	**pivostriv** *Ukr.*	península	péninsule	península
peak	Gipfel	**piz, pizzo** *It.*	pico	pic	pico
peak	Gipfel	**pk., peak** *Eng.*	pico	pic	pico
parkway	Ferienstrasse	**pkwy., parkway** *Eng.*	calzada	allée de parc	avenida
plain	Ebene	**plain** *Eng.*	llanura	plaine	planície
plain	Ebene	**plaine** *Fr.*	llanura	plaine	planície
plains	Ebenen	**plains** *Eng.*	llanura	plaines	planícies
plateau	Hochebene	**planalto** *Port.*	meseta	plateau	planalto
planetarium	Planetarium	**planetario** *Sp.*	planetario	planétarium	planetário
planetarium	Planetarium	**planetarium** *Eng.*	planetario	planétarium	planetário
mountain, range	Berg, Gebirge	**planina** *S./C.*	montaña, sierra	montagne, chaîne	montanha, cordilheira
plateau	Hochebene	**plateau** *Eng., Fr.*	meseta	plateau	planalto
plateau	Hochebene	**plato** *Afk., Blg., Rus.*	meseta	plateau	planalto
beach	Strand	**playa** *Sp.*	playa	plage	praia
square	Platz	**plaza** *Sp.*	plaza	place	praça
plateau	Hochebene	**plošina** *Czech*	meseta	plateau	planalto
plateau	Hochebene	**ploskogorje** *Rus.*	meseta	plateau	planalto
pass	Pass	**poarta** *Rom.*	paso	col	passo
hill	Hügel	**poggio** *It.*	colina	colline	colina
point	Landspitze	**point** *Eng.*	punta	pointe	ponta
point	Landspitze	**pointe** *Fr.*	punta	pointe	ponta
island	Insel	**pol** *Du.*	isla	île	ilha
plain, basin	Ebene, Becken	**polje** *S./C.*	llanura, cuenca	plaine, bassin	planície, bacia
peninsula	Halbinsel	**poluostrov** *Rus.*	península	péninsule	península
peninsula	Halbinsel	**poluotok** *S./C.*	península	péninsule	península
pond	Teich	**pond** *Eng.*	charca	étang	lago
peak	Gipfel	**-pong** *Kor.*	pico	cime	pico
bridge	Brücke	**pont** *Fr.*	puente	pont	ponte
point	Landspitze	**ponta, pontal** *Port.*	punta	pointe	ponta, pontal
bridge	Brücke	**ponte** *Port.*	puente	pont	ponte
pool	Tümpel	**pool** *Eng.*	charco	étang	charco
rapids	Stromschnellen	**porog** *Rus.*	rápidos	rapides	rápidos
port	Hafen	**port** *Eng., Fr.*	puerto	port	porto
port	Hafen	**porto** *It.*	puerto	port	porto
strait	Meeresstrasse	**porthmós** *Gr.*	estrecho	détroit	estreito
provincial park	Naturpark	**p.p., provincial park** *Eng.*	parque de la provincia	parc provincial	parque provincial
beach	Strand	**praia** *Port.*	playa	plage	praia
reservoir	Stausee	**přehr., přehradová nádrž** *Czech*	embalse	réservoir	reservatório
reservoir, dam	Stausee, Damm	**presa** *Sp.*	presa	réservoir, barrage	represa
peninsula	Halbinsel	**presqu'île** *Fr.*	península	presqu'île	península
reservoir	Stausee	**priehradová nádrž** *Slo.*	embalse	réservoir	reservatório
pass	Pass	**priesmyk** *Slo.*	paso	col	passo
prison	Gefängnis	**prison** *Eng.*	prisión	prison	prisão
pass	Pass	**prohod** *Blg.*	paso	col	passo
strait	Meeresstrasse	**proliv** *Rus.*	estrecho	détroit	estreito
promontory	Vorgebirge	**promontorio** *It., Sp.*	promontorio	promontoire	promontório
promontory	Vorgebirge	**promontory** *Eng.*	promontorio	promontoire	promontório
strait	Meeresstrasse	**protoka** *Ukr.*	estrecho	détroit	estreito
provincial park	Naturpark	**prov. park, provincial park** *Eng.*	parque de la provincia	parc provincial	parque provincial
reservoir	Stausee	**prudy** *Rus.*	embalse	réservoir	reservatório
pass	Pass	**průsmyk** *Czech*	paso	col	passo
pass	Pass	**przeęcz** *Pol.*	paso	col	passo
cape	Kap	**przylądek** *Pol.*	cabo	cap	cabo
point	Landspitze	**pt., point** *Eng.*	punta	pointe	ponta
railroad station	Bahnhof	**pu., pályaudvar** *Hung.*	estación de ferrocarril	gare	estação ferroviária
port	Hafen	**puerto** *Sp.*	puerto	port	porto
peak	Gipfel	**puig** *Cat.*	pico	cime	pico
island	Insel	**pulau** *Indon., Mal.*	isla	île	ilha
upland	Bergland	**puna** *Sp.*	puna	hautes terres	terras altas
peak	Gipfel	**puncak** *Indon.*	pico	cime	pico
point	Landspitze	**punt** *Du.*	punta	pointe	ponta
point, peak	Landspitze, Gipfel	**punta** *It., Sp.*	punta	pointe, cime	ponta
point	Landspitze	**puntilla** *Sp.*	puntilla	pointe	ponta pequena
forest	Wald	**puszcza** *Pol.*	bosque	forêt	floresta
pyramid	Pyramide	**pyramid** *Eng.*	pirámide	pyramide	pirâmide
			Q		
salt flat	Salzebene	**qā'** *Ara.*	salar	saline	salina
canal	Kanal	**qanāt** *Ara.*	canal	canal	canal
hill	Hügel	**qārat** *Ara.*	colina	colline	colina
hills	Hügel	**qārāt** *Ara.*	colinas	collines	colinas
dunes	Dünen	**qawz** *Ara.*	dunas	dunes	dunas
brook	Bach	**qbda., quebrada** *Sp.*	quebrada	crique	arroio
mountain	Berg	**qolleh** *Per.*	montaña	montagne	montanha
canal	Kanal	**-qu** *Ch.*	canal	canal	canal
quarry	Steinbruch	**quarry** *Eng.*	cantera	carrière	pedreira
brook	Bach	**quebrada** *Sp.*	quebrada	crique	arroio
rapids	Stromschnellen	**quedas** *Port.*	rápidos	rapides	quedas
islands	Inseln	**qundao** *Ch.*	islas	îles	ilhas
hill	Hügel	**qūr** *Ara.*	colina	colline	colina
mountain	Berg	**qurnat** *Ara.*	montaña	montagne	montanha
			R		
river	Fluss	**r., rio** *Port.* **rio** **river** **rivière**	río	rivière	rio
range	Gebirge	**ra., range** *Eng.*	sierra	chaîne	cordilheira
Royal Australian Air Force Station	Luftwaffenstützpunkt (Austl.)	**R.A.A.F.S., Royal Australian Air Force Station** *Eng.*	Real Estación Aeronáutica (Austl.)	Station Aérienne Royale (Austl.)	Real Estação da Força Aérea Australiana
race course	Rennbahn	**race course** *Eng.*	hipódromo	champ de course	hipódromo
race track	Rennbahn	**race track** *Eng.*	hipódromo	champ de course	hipódromo
raceway	Rennbahn	**raceway** *Eng.*	hipódromo	champ de course	hipódromo
river	Fluss	**rach** *Viet.*	río	rivière	rio

ENGLISH	DEUTSCH	Map Form Geographische Begriffe Términos Geográficos Termes Géographiques Termos Geográficos	ESPAÑOL	FRANCAIS	PORTUGUÊS
anchorage	Ankerplatz	**rada** *Sp.*	rada	ancrage	ancoradouro
cape	Kap	**rags** *Latv.*	cabo	cap	cabo
railroad	Eisenbahn	**railroad** *Eng.*	ferrocarril	chemin de fer	ferrovia
railway	Eisenbahn	**railway** *Eng.*	ferrocarril	chemin de fer	ferrovia
railway station	Bahnhof	**railway station** *Eng.*	estacíon de ferrocarril	gare	estação ferroviária
dunes	Dünen	**ramlat** *Ara.*	dunas	dunes	dunas
range(s)	Gebirge	**range(s)** *Eng.*	sierra(s)	chaîne(s)	cordilheira(s)
river	Fluss	**rão., ribeirão** *Port.*	río	rivière	rio, ribeirão
rapids	Stromschnellen	**rapides** *Fr.*	rápidos	rapides	rápidos
rapids	Stromschnellen	**rapids** *Eng.*	rápidos	rapides	rápidos
wadi	Wadi	**raqabat** *Ara.*	uadi	wadi	uádi
cape	Kap	**ras, ra's** *Ara.*	cabo	cap	cabo
cape	Kap	**rās** *Per.*	cabo	cap	cabo
ravine	Tobel	**ravine** *Eng.*	barranca	ravin	ravina
plain	Ebene	**ravnina** *Rus.*	llanura	plaine	planície
canal	Kanal	**rayyāh** *Ara.*	canal	canal	canal
flood plain	Überschwemmungsebene	**razlivy** *Rus.*	llanura de inundación	lit d'incndation	planície de inundação
road	Landstrasse	**rd., road** *Eng.*	camino	route	rodovia
reef	Riff	**récif** *Fr.*	arrecife	récif	recife
reefs	Riffe	**recifes** *Port.*	arrecifes	récifs	recifes
reefs	Riffe	**récifs** *Fr.*	arrecifes	récifs	recifes
reef(s)	Riff(e)	**reef(s)** *Eng.*	arrecife(s)	récif(s)	recife(s)
regional park	Regionalpark	**regional park** *Eng.*	parque regional	parc régional	parque regional
mountain	Berg	**-rei** *Jpn.*	montaña	montagne	montanha
race course	Rennbahn	**Rennbahn** *Ger.*	hipódromo	champ de course	hipódromo
dam, reservoir	Damm, Stausee	**represa** *Port.*	presa, embalse	barrage, réservoir	represa
airport	Flughafen	**repülötér** *Hung.*	aeropuerto	aéroport	aeroporto
reservoir	Stausee	**res., reservoir** *Eng.*	embalse	réservoir	reservatório
reservation	Reservat	**reservation** *Eng.*	reservación	réservation	reserva
reservoir	Stausee	**reservatório** *Port.*	embalse	réservoir	reservatório
reserve	Reservat	**reserve** *Eng.*	reserva	réserve	reserva
reserve	Reservat	**réserve** *Fr.*	reserva	réserve	reserva
game reserve	Wildreservat	**réserve de chasse** *Fr.*	vedado de caza	réserve de chasse	reserva de caça
reservoir	Stausee	**reservoir** *Eng.*	embalse	réservoir	reservatório
reservoir	Stausee	**réservoir** *Fr.*	embalse	réservoir	reservatório
beach	Strand	**restinga** *Port.*	playa	plage	praia
islands	Inseln	**-retto** *Jpn.*	islas	îles	ilhas
ria (inlet)	Ria	**ría** *Sp.*	ría	ria	ria
brook	Bach	**riacho** *Port., Sp.*	riacho	crique	riacho
brook	Bach	**riachuelo** *Sp.*	riachuelo	crique	riacho
brook	Bach	**rib., ribeira** *Port.*	riachuelo	crique	ribeira
river	Fluss	**ribeirão** *Port.*	río	rivière	ribeirão
ridge	Höhenrücken	**ridge** *Eng.*	sierra	crête	serra
moor	Ried	**Ried** *Ger.*	páramo	lande	pântano
brook	Bach	**riera** *Sp., Cat.*	riera	crique	riacho
national museum	Reichsmuseum	**rijksmuseum** *Du.*	museo nacional	musée national	museu nacional
army installation	Anlage des Heeres	**rikujō-jieitai** *Jpn.*	estación del ejército	installation militaire	instalação militar
river	Fluss	**rio** *Port.*	río	rivière	rio
river	Fluss	**río** *Sp.*	río	rivière	rio
river	Fluss	**riozinho** *Port.*	río	rivière	riozinho
rise (submarine)	Schwelle (untermeerische)	**rise** *Eng.*	elevación (submarina)	élévation (sous-marine)	elevação (submarina)
river	Fluss	**river** *Eng.*	río	rivière	rio
brook	Bach	**rivera** *Sp.*	rivera	ruisseau	córrego
coast	Küste	**riviera** *It.*	costa	côte	costa
river	Fluss	**rivière** *Fr.*	río	rivière	rio
army installation	Anlage des Heeres	**r.j., rikujō-jieitai** *Jpn.*	estación del ejército	installation militaire	instalação do exército
road	Landstrasse	**road** *Eng.*	camino	route	rodovia
roads (anchorage)	Ankerplatz	**roads** *Eng.*	ancladero	ancrage	ancoradouro
rock	Fels	**roca** *Sp.*	roca	rocher	rochedo
rock, mountain	Fels, Berg	**rocca** *It.*	roca, montaña	rocher, montagne	rochedo, montanha
rock(s)	Fels(en)	**rock(s)** *Eng.*	roca(s)	rocher(s)	rochedo(s)
cape	Kap	**rt** *S./C.*	cabo	cap	cabo
brook	Bach	**rû** *Fr.*	arroyo	rû	córrego
mountains	Berge	**rudohorie** *Slo.*	montañas	montagnes	montanhas
brook	Bach	**ruisseau** *Fr.*	arroyo	ruisseau	córrego
mountain	Berg	**rujm** *Ara.*	montaña	montagne	montanha
run (stream)	Bach	**run** *Eng.*	arroyo	ruisseau	córrego
			S		
south	Süd	**s., south** *Eng.*	sur	sud	sul
range	Gebirge	**sa., serra** *Port.*	sierra	chaîne	cordilheira
island	Insel	**saar** *Est.*	isla	île	ilha
savanna	Savanne	**sabana** *Sp.*	sabana	savane	savana
salt marsh, lagoon	Salzmarsch, Lagune, Haff	**sabkhat** *Ara.*	pantano salado, laguna	marais salé, lagune	pântano salgado, laguna
dam	Damm	**sadd** *Ara.*	presa	barrage	represa
wadi	Wadi	**saguia** *Ara.*	uadi	wadi	uádi
desert	Wüste	**ṣaḥrā'** *Ara.*	desierto	désert	deserto
cape	Kap	**-saki** *Jpn.*	cabo	cap	cabo
salt flat	Salzebene	**salar** *Sp.*	salar	saline	salina
salt marsh, salt flat	Salzmarsch, Salzebene	**salina(s)** *Sp.*	salina(s)	marais salé, saline	salina(s)
salt marsh, salt flat	Salzmarsch, Salzebene	**salines** *Fr.*	pantano salado, salinas, salar	salines	pântano salgado, salinas
salt flat	Salzebene	**salt flat** *Eng.*	salar	saline	salina
salt lake	Salzsee	**salt lake** *Eng.*	lago salado	lac salé	lago salgado
salt marsh	Salzmarsch	**salt marsh** *Eng.*	pantano salado	marais salé	pântano salgado
waterfall	Wasserfall	**salto(s)** *Port., Sp.*	salto(s)	chute d'eau	salto(s)
reservoir	Stausee	**samudra** *Sin.*	embalse	réservoir	reservatório
range	Gebirge	**-sammyaku** *Jpn.*	sierra	chaîne	cordilheira
mountain	Berg	**-san** *Jpn., Kor.*	montaña	montagne	montanha
mountains	Berge	**-sanchi** *Jpn.*	montañas	montagnes	montanhas
mountains	Berge	**-sanmaek** *Kor.*	montañas	montagnes	montanhas
shrine	Schrein	**santuario** *It., Sp.*	santuario	châsse	santuário
mountain	Berg	**sar** *Pas.*	montaña	montagne	montanha
island	Insel	**sari** *Est.*	isla	île	ilha
desert	Wüste	**sarīr** *Ara.*	desierto	désert	deserto
saddle (pass)	Sattel	**Sattel** *Ger.*	paso	col	passo
strait	Meeresstrasse	**šaurums** *Latv.*	estrecho	détroit	estreito
waterfall	Wasserfall	**saut** *Fr.*	cascada	saut	queda d'água
castle	Schloss	**Schloss** *Ger.*	castillo	château	castelo
gorge	Schlucht	**Schlucht** *Ger.*	garganta	gorge	garganta
school	Schule	**school** *Eng.*	escuela	école	escola
sea	Meer	**sea** *Eng.*	mar	mer	mar
seamount	untermeerische Kuppe	**seamount** *Eng.*	montaña submarina	montagne sous-marine	montanha submarina
sea scarp	Abbruch	**sea scarp** *Eng.*	cantil	escarpement sous-marine	escarpa submarina
dry lake	Trockensee	**sebjet** *Ara.*	lago seco	lac asséché	lago seco
salt flat	Salzebene	**sebkha** *Ara.*	salar	saline	salina
intermittent lake	periodischer See	**sebkra** *Ara.*	lago intermitente	lac périodique	lago intermitente
salt marsh	Salzmarsch	**sebkret** *Ara.*	pantano salado	marais salé	pântano salgado
airport	Flughafen	**sede-te'ufa** *Heb.*	aeropuerto	aéroport	aeroporto
saddle (pass)	Sattel	**sedlo** *Czech*	paso	col	passo
lake(s)	See(n)	**See(n)** *Ger.*	lago(s)	lac(s)	lago(s)
strait	Meeresstrasse	**selat** *Indon.*	estrecho	détroit	estreito
peninsula	Halbinsel	**semenanjung** *Indon.*	península	péninsule	península
seminary	Seminar	**seminary** *Eng.*	seminario	séminaire	seminário
mountain	Berg	**-sen** *Jpn.*	montaña	montagne	montanha
sound	Sund	**seno** *Sp.*	seno	détroit	estreito
mountains	Gebirge	**serra** *Cat.*	montañas	montagnes	montanhas
range, mountain	Gebirge, Berg	**serra** *Port.*	sierra	chaîne, montagne	serra

Glossary and Abbreviations of Geographical Terms / Verzeichnis und Abkürzungen Geographischer Begriffe
Glosario y Abreviaciones de Términos Geográficos / Glossaire et Abréviations de Termes Géographiques
Glossário e Abreviações de Termos Geográficos
295

ENGLISH	DEUTSCH	Map Form / Geographische Begriffe / Términos Geográficos / Termes Géographiques / Termos Geográficos	ESPAÑOL	FRANCAIS	PORTUGUÊS
ridge(s)	Höhenrücken	**serranía(s)** *Sp.*	serranía(s)	crête(s)	serrania(s)
island	Insel	**sha** *Ch.*	isla	île	ilha
rapids	Stromschnellen	**shallāl** *Ara.*	rápidos	rapides	rápidos
desert	Wüste	**shamo** *Ch.*	desierto	désert	deserto
mountain(s), island	Berg(e), Insel	**shan** *Ch.*	montaña(s), isla	montagne(s), île	montanha(s), ilha
pass	Pass	**shankou** *Ch.*	paso	col	passo
mountains	Berge	**shanmo** *Ch.*	montañas	montagnes	montanhas
bay	Bucht	**sharm** *Ara.*	bahía	baie	baía
peninsula	Halbinsel	**shibh jazīrat** *Ara.*	península	péninsule	península
island	Insel	**-shima** *Jpn.*	isla	île	ilha
reef	Riff	**-shō** *Jpn.*	arrecife	récif	recife
shoal(s)	Untiefe(n)	**shoal(s)** *Eng.*	bajo(s)	haut-fond(s)	baixio(s)
islands	Inseln	**-shotō** *Jpn.*	islas	îles	ilhas
shrine	Schrein	**shrine** *Eng.*	santuario	châsse	santuário
river	Fluss	**shui** *Ch.*	río	rivière	rio
reservoir	Stausee	**shuiku** *Ch.*	embalse	réservoir	reservatório
strait	Meeresstrasse	**shuitao** *Ch.*	estrecho	détroit	estreito
temple	Tempel	**si** *Ch.*	templo	temple	templo
range, ridge	Gebirge, Höhenrücken	**sierra** *Sp.*	sierra	chaîne, crête	serra
rapids	Stromschnellen	**šivera** *Rus.*	rápidos	rapides	rápidos
lake	See	**-sjø** *Nor.*	lago	lac	lago
lakes	Seen	**-sjöarna** *Swe.*	lagos	lacs	lagos
lake	See	**-sjøen** *Nor.*	lago	lac	lago
lake, bay	See, Bucht	**-sjön** *Swe.*	lago, bahía	lac, baie	lago, baía
island	Insel	**skär** *Swe.*	isla	île	ilha
forest	Wald	**-skog, -skogen** *Swe.*	bosque	forêt	floresta
mountain	Berg	**slieve** *Gae.*	montaña	montagne	montanha
castle	Schloss	**slot** *Du.*	castillo	château	castelo
castle	Schloss	**slott** *Swe.*	castillo	château	castelo
slough (swamp)	verlandende Wasserfläche	**slough** *Eng.*	pantano	fondrière	pântano, brejo
ridge	Höhenrücken	**snía., serranía** *Sp.*	serranía	crête	serrania
snowfield	Schneefeld	**snowfield** *Eng.*	ventisquero	champ de neige	campo de neve
lake	See	**-sø** *Dan.*	lago	lac	lago
sound	Sund	**sonda** *Sp.*	sonda	détroit	estreito
sound	Sund	**sound** *Eng.*	sonda	détroit	estreito
cave, tunnel	Höhle, Tunnel	**souterrain** *Fr.*	cueva, túnel	souterrain	caverna, túnel
state park	Naturpark	**s.p., state park** *Eng.*	parque provincial	parc régional	parque estadual
cave	Höhle	**špilja** *S./C.*	cueva	caverne	caverna
spit	Landzunge	**spit** *Eng.*	lengua de tierra	flèche	ponta de terra
peak	Spitze	**Spitze** *Ger.*	pico	cime	pico
spring	Quelle	**spr., spring** *Eng.*	manantial	source	fonte, manancial
square	Platz	**sq., square** *Eng.*	plaza	place	praça
range, ridge	Gebirge, Höhenrücken	**srra., sierra** *Sp.*	sierra	chaîne, crête	serra
saint	Sankt	**st., saint** *Eng., Fr.*	san, santa, santo	saint	são, santa, santo
street	Strasse	**st., street** *Eng.*	calle	rue	rua
saint	Sankt	**sta., santa** *Port., Sp.*	santa	sainte	santa
station	Bahnhof, Stützpunkt	**sta., station** *Eng., Fr.*	estación	station	estação
stadium	Stadion	**stad., stadium** *Eng.*	estadio	stade	estádio
stadium	Stadion	**stadio** *It.*	estadio	stade	estádio
stadium	Stadion	**Stadion** *Ger.*	estadio	stade	estádio
stadium	Stadion	**stadion** *Rus.*	estadio	stade	estádio
stadium	Stadion	**stadium** *Eng.*	estadio	stade	estádio
state beach	öffentlicher Badestrand	**state beach** *Eng.*	playa provincial	plage régionale	praia estadual
state forest	Wald in Gemeinbesitz	**state forest** *Eng.*	bosque provincial	forêt régionale	floresta estadual
state historical park	Park an historischer Stätte	**state historical park** *Eng.*	parque histórico provincial	parc historique régional	parque histórico estadual
state park	Naturpark	**state park** *Eng.*	parque provincial	parc régional	parque estadual
state recreation area	Ausflugsgebiet	**state recreation area** *Eng.*	zona de recreo provincial	zone récréative regionale	área de lazer estadual
station	Bahnhof, Stützpunkt	**station** *Eng., Fr.*	estación	station	estação
reservoir	Stausee	**Stausee** *Ger.*	embalse	réservoir	reservatório
station	Bahnhof, Stützpunkt	**stazione** *It.*	estación	station	estação
saint	Sankt	**ste., sainte** *Fr.*	santa	sainte	santa
mountains	Berge	**stěny** *Czech*	montañas	montagnes	montanhas
steppe	Steppe	**step'** *Rus.*	estepa	steppe	estepe
peak	Gipfel	**štít** *Slo.*	pico	cime	pico
saint	Sankt	**sto., santo** *Port., Sp.*	santo	saint	santo
strait(s)	Meeresstrasse	**strait(s)** *Eng.*	estrecho	détroit	estreito
stream	Strom	**stream** *Eng.*	corriente de agua	cours d'eau	curso d'água
street	Strasse	**street** *Eng.*	calle	rue	rua
strait	Meeresstrasse	**stretto** *It.*	estrecho	détroit	estreito
spit	Landzunge	**strilka** *Ukr.*	lengua de tierra	flèche	ponta de terra
stream	Strom	**Strom** *Ger.*	corriente de agua	cours d'eau	curso d'água
stream	Strom	**-ström, -strömmen** *Swe.*	corriente de agua	cours d'eau	curso d'água
river	Fluss	**-su** *Kor.*	río	rivière	rio
channel	Kanal	**-suidō** *Jpn.*	canal, estrecho	canal, détroit	canal, estreito
sound	Sund	**Sund** *Ger.*	sonda	détroit	estreito
sound	Sund	**-sund** *Swe.*	sonda	détroit	estreito
swamp	Sumpf	**swamp** *Eng.*	pantano	marais	pântano
ridge	Höhenrücken	**syrt** *Tur.*	sierra	crête	serra
island	Insel	**sziget** *Hung.*	isla	île	ilha

T

ENGLISH	DEUTSCH	Map Form	ESPAÑOL	FRANCAIS	PORTUGUÊS
tableland	Tafelland	**tableland** *Eng.*	mesa, altiplano	plateau	planalto
woods	Gehölz	**taillis** *Fr.*	bosque	taillis	bosque
reef	Riff	**taka** *Indon.*	arrecife	récif	recife
mountain	Berg	**-take** *Jpn.*	montaña	montagne	montanha
waterfall	Wasserfall	**-taki** *Jpn.*	cascada	chute d'eau	queda d'água
valley	Tal	**Tal** *Ger.*	valle	vallée	vale
mountain	Berg	**tall** *Ara.*	montaña	montagne	montanha
mountain, hill	Berg, Hügel	**tallat** *Ara.*	montaña, colina	montagne, colline	montanha, colina
hills	Hügel	**tallāt** *Ara.*	colinas	collines	colinas
dam	Talsperre	**Talsperre** *Ger.*	presa	barrage	represa
point	Landspitze	**-tangar, -tangi** *Ice.*	punta	pointe	ponta
cape	Kap	**tanjong** *Mal.*	cabo	cap	cabo
cape	Kap	**tanjung** *Indon.*	cabo	cap	cabo
island	Insel	**tao** *Ch.*	isla	île	ilha
hills	Hügel	**taraq** *Ara.*	colinas	collines	colinas
lake	See	**tasek** *Mal.*	lago	lac	lago
lake	See	**tasik** *Indon.*	lago	lac	lago
plateau	Hochebene	**tassili** *Ber.*	meseta	plateau	planalto
mountain	Berg	**taung** *Bur.*	montaña	montagne	montanha
range	Gebirge	**taungdan** *Bur.*	sierra	chaîne	cordilheira
theatre	Theater	**teatro** *It., Sp.*	teatro	théâtre	teatro
bay	Bucht	**teluk** *Indon.*	bahía	baie	baía
temple	Tempel	**temple** *Eng., Fr.*	templo	temple	templo
church	Kirche	**templom** *Hung.*	iglesia	église	igreja
desert	Wüste	**ténéré** *Ber.*	desierto	désert	deserto
peak, hill	Gipfel, Hügel	**tepe, tepesi** *Tur.*	pico, colina	cime, colline	pico, colina
territory	Territorium	**territory** *Eng.*	territorio	territoire	território
lagoon	Lagune, Haff	**thale** *Thai*	laguna	lagune	laguna
mountains	Berge	**thiu khao** *Thai*	montañas	montagnes	montanhas
mountain	Berg	**-tind,-tinderne** *Nor.*	montaña	montagne	montanha
ridge	Höhenrücken	**tiwāl** *Ara.*	sierra	crête	serra
mountain	Berg	**-tjåkko, tjöure** *Lapp.*	montaña	montagne	montanha
island	Insel	**-to** *Kor.*	isla	île	ilha
island	Insel	**-tō** *Jpn.*	isla	île	ilha
lake	See	**tó** *Hung.*	lago	lac	lago
pass	Pass	**-tōge** *Jpn.*	paso	col	passo
island	Insel	**tokong** *Mal.*	isla	île	ilha
lake	See	**tônlé** *Cbd.*	lago	lac	lago
mountain torrent	Wildbach	**torrente** *It., Sp.*	torrente	torrent	torrente
tower	Turm	**tower** *Eng.*	torre	tour	torre
turnpike	gebührenpflichtige Autobahn	**tpk., turnpike** *Eng.*	camino con peaje	grande route à péage	rodovia com pedágio
lake	See	**-träsk** *Swe.*	lago	lac	lago
trench	Tiefseegraben	**trench** *Eng.*	trinchera	tranchée	fossa submarina
trough	Tiefseegraben	**trough** *Eng.*	trinchera	tranchée	fossa submarina
volcano	Vulkan	**tulūl** *Ara.*	volcán	volcan	vulcão
tunnel	Tunnel	**túnel** *Sp.*	túnel	tunnel	túnel
tunnel	Tunnel	**tunnel** *Eng., Fr.*	túnel	tunnel	túnel
hill, mountain	Hügel, Berg	**-tunturi** *Finn.*	colina, montaña	colline, montagne	colina, montanha
island	Insel	**tuo** *Ch.*	isla	île	ilha
canal	Kanal	**tur'at** *Ara.*	canal	canal	canal
turnpike	gebührenpflichtige Autobahn	**turnpike** *Eng.*	camino con peaje	grande route à péage	rodovia com pedágio

U-V

ENGLISH	DEUTSCH	Map Form	ESPAÑOL	FRANCAIS	PORTUGUÊS
cape	Kap	**ujung** *Indon.*	cabo	cap	cabo
lagoon	Lagune, Haff	**-umi** *Jpn.*	laguna	lagune	laguna
United Nations	Vereinte Nationen	**U.N., United Nations** *Eng.*	Naciones Unidas	Nations Unies	Nações Unidas
canal	Kanal	**-unga** *Jpn.*	canal	canal	canal
university	Universität	**univ., universidad** *Sp.* **universidade università university**	universidad	université	universidade
university	Universität	**Universität** *Ger.*	universidad	université	universidade
university	Universität	**université** *Fr.*	universidad	université	universidade
university	Universität	**universitet** *Rus.*	universidad	université	universidade
upland	Bergland	**upland** *Eng.*	tierras altas	hautes terres	terras altas
lake	See	**-ura** *Jpn.*	lago	lac	lago
mountain(s)	Berg(e)	**uul** *Mong.*	montaña(s)	montagne(s)	montanha(s)
elevation(s)	Höhe(n)	**uval(y)** *Rus.*	altura(s)	élévation(s)	elevação(ões)
spring	Quelle	**'uyūn** *Ara.*	manantial	source	fonte, manancial
hill	Hügel	**-vaara** *Finn.*	colina	colline	colina
strait	Meeresstrasse	**väin** *Est.*	estrecho	détroit	estreito
valley	Tal	**val** *Fr., It.*	valle	val	vale
valley	Tal	**valle** *It., Sp.*	valle	vallée	vale
valley	Tal	**vallée** *Fr.*	valle	vallée	vale
waterfall	Wasserfall	**vallen** *Du.*	cascada	chute d'eau	queda d'água
valley	Tal	**valley** *Eng.*	valle	vallée	vale
valley	Tal	**vallon** *Fr.*	valle	vallon	vale
mountain	Berg	**vârful** *Rom.*	montaña	montagne	montanha
lake	See	**-vatn** *Ice., Nor.*	lago	lac	lago
lake	See	**-vatnet** *Nor.*	lago	lac	lago
lake	See	**-vattnett** *Swe.*	lago	lac	lago
reservoir	Stausee	**vdchr., vodochranilišče** *Rus.*	embalse	réservoir	reservatório
hills	Hügel	**-veden** *Swe.*	colinas	collines	colinas
upland	Bergland	**verch** *Rus.*	tierras altas	hautes terres	terras altas
lake	See	**-vesi** *Finn.*	lago	lac	lago
viaduct	Viadukt	**viaducto** *Sp.*	viaducto	viaduc	viaduto
plateau	Hochebene	**-vidda** *Nor.*	meseta	plateau	planalto
gulf	Golf	**-viken** *Swe.*	golfo	golfe	golfo
bay	Bucht	**vinh** *Viet.*	bahía	baie	baía
airport	Flughafen	**vliegveld** *Du.*	aeropuerto	aéroport	aeroporto
channel	Kanal	**vliet** *Du.*	canal, estrecho	canal, détroit	canal, estreito
canal	Kanal	**vodnyj put'** *Rus.*	canal	canal	canal
reservoir	Stausee	**vodochranilišče** *Rus.*	embalse	réservoir	reservatório
reservoir	Stausee	**vodoskhovyshche** *Ukr.*	embalse	réservoir	reservatório
railroad station	Bahnhof	**vokzal** *Rus.*	estación de ferrocarril	gare	estação ferroviária
volcano	Vulkan	**vol., volcán** *Sp.* **volcano**	volcán	volcan	vulcão
pass	Pass	**vorota** *Rus.*	paso	col	passo
upland	Bergland	**vozvyšennost'** *Rus.*	tierras altas	hautes terres	terras altas
mountain	Berg	**vrâh** *Blg.*	montaña	montagne	montanha
mountains	Berge	**vrchovina** *Czech, Slo.*	montañas	montagnes	montanhas
mountains	Berge	**vrchy** *Slo.*	montañas	montagnes	montanhas
peak	Gipfel	**vrh** *S./C.*	pico	cime	pico
volcano	Vulkan	**vulkan** *Rus.*	volcán	volcan	vulcão
bay	Bucht	**vung** *Viet.*	bahía	baie	baía
mountain, hill	Berg, Hügel	**-vuori** *Finn.*	montaña, colina	montagne, colline	montanha, colina
upland	Bergland	**vysochyna** *Ukr.*	tierras altas	hautes terres	terras altas

W-Z

ENGLISH	DEUTSCH	Map Form	ESPAÑOL	FRANCAIS	PORTUGUÊS
west	West	**w., west** *Eng.*	oeste	ouest	oeste
marsh	Marsch	**wa** *Ch.*	pantano	marais	pântano
wadi	Wadi	**wādī** *Ara.*	uadi	wadi	uádi
oasis	Oase	**wāhat, wāhāt** *Ara.*	oasis	oasis	oásis
forest, mountains	Wald	**Wald** *Ger.*	bosque, montañas	forêt, montagnes	floresta, montanhas
bay	Bucht	**wan** *Ch., Jap.*	bahía	baie	baía
wash	Wadi	**wash** *Eng.*	uadi	wadi	uádi
waterfalls	Wasserfälle	**Wasserfälle** *Ger.*	cascadas	chutes d'eau	quedas d'água
water (lake, river)	Wasser (See, Fluss)	**water** *Eng.*	agua (lago, río)	eau (lac, rivière)	água (lago, rio)
waterway	Wasserstrasse	**waterway** *Eng.*	canal	canal	canal
pond	Weiher	**Weiher** *Ger.*	charca	étang	charco
well	Brunnen	**well** *Eng.*	pozo	puits	poço
bay	Wiek	**Wiek** *Ger.*	bahía	baie	baía
woods	Gehölz	**woods** *Eng.*	bosque	bois	bosque
water (lake, river)	Wasser (See, Fluss)	**wr., water** *Eng.*	agua (lago, río)	eau (lac, rivière)	água (lago, rio)
strait	Meeresstrasse	**xia** *Ch.*	estrecho	détroit	estreito
lake, sea	See, Meer	**yam** *Heb.*	lago, mar	lac, mer	lago, mar
mountain	Berg	**-yama** *Jpn.*	montaña	montagne	montanha
bay	Bucht	**yang** *Ch.*	bahía	baie	baía
peninsula	Halbinsel	**yarımadası** *Tur.*	península	péninsule	península
mountain	Berg	**yebel** *Ara.*	montaña	montagne	montanha
rock, island	Fels, Insel	**yen** *Ch.*	roca, isla	rocher, île	rochedo, ilha
mountains	Berge	**yoma** *Bur.*	montañas	montagnes	montanhas
island	Insel	**yu** *Ch.*	isla	île	ilha
lake	See	**yumco** *Tib.*	lago	lac	lago
canal	Kanal	**yunhe** *Ch.*	canal	canal	canal
intermittent lake	periodischer See	**zahrez** *Ara.*	lago intermitente	lac périodique	lago intermitente
point	Landspitze	**-zaki** *Jpn.*	punta	pointe	ponta
lagoon	Lagune, Haff	**zalew** *Pol.*	laguna	lagune	laguna
gulf, bay	Golf, Bucht	**zaliv** *Rus.*	golfo, bahía	golfe, baie	golfo, baía
reserve	Reservat	**zapov., zapovednik** *Rus.*	reserva	réserve	reserva
gulf, bay	Golf, Bucht	**zatoka** *Ukr.*	golfo, bahía	golfe, baie	golfo, baía
sea, lake	Meer, See	**zee** *Du.*	mar, lago	mer, lac	mar, lago
autonomous province	autonome Provinz	**zizhiqu** *Ch.*	provincia autónoma	province autonome	província autônoma
zoo	Zoo	**zoo** *Eng.*	parque zoológico	zoo	jardim zoológico

THIS TABLE gives the area, population, population density, capital, and political status for every country in the world. The political units listed are categorized by political status in the last column of the table, as follows: A—independent countries; B—internally independent political entities which are under the protection of another country in matters of defense and foreign affairs; C—colonies and other dependent political units; and D—the major administrative subdivisions of Australia, Canada, China, the United Kingdom, and the United States. For comparison, the table also includes the continents and the world. For units categorized B, the names of protecting countries are specified in the political-status column. For units categorized C, the names of administering countries are given in parentheses in the first column.

The populations are estimates for January 1, 1995, made by Rand McNally on the basis of official data, United Nations estimates, and other available information.

IN DIESER ÜBERSICHT sind Fläche, Bevölkerung, Bevölkerungsdichte, Hauptstadt und politischer Status für jedes Land der Erde aufgeführt. Die politischen Einheiten sind in der letzten Spalte der Tabelle nach ihrem politischen Status wie folgt gegliedert: A—souveräne Staaten; B—innenpolitisch unabhängige Länder unter der Protektion eines anderen Landes in Angelegenheiten der Aussenpolitik und Verteidigung; C—Kolonien oder anderweitig abhängige Gebiete; D—die wichtigsten Verwaltungseinheiten von Australien, Kanada, China, dem Vereinigten Königreich und den Vereinigten Staaten. Für Vergleiche enthält die Übersicht auch Angaben über die Kontinente und die Welt. Für die unter B eingestuften Einheiten ist der Name des Schutzstaates in der Spalte Politischer Status aufgeführt. Für die unter C eingestuften Gebiete steht der Name des die Verwaltung ausübenden Landes in Klammern in der ersten Spalte.

Die Bevölkerungsangaben sind Schätzungen zum 1. Januar 1995, die Rand McNally auf der Grundlage amtlicher Zahlen, Schätzungen der Vereinten Nationen und anderer zugänglicher Informationen berechnet hat.

EL CUADRO ABAJO incluye la extensión, población y densidad de población, la capital y el estado político de todos los países del mundo. Las entidades políticas nombradas están clasificadas de acuerdo a su estado político en la última columna de la tabla, de esta manera: A—países independientes; B—entidades políticas internamente independientes las cuales se encuentran bajo la protección de otro país en cuanto a asuntos de defensa nacional y relaciones con el extranjero; C—colonias y otras entidades políticas dependientes; y D—las mayores subdivisiones administrativas de Australia, Canadá, China, el Reino Unido, y los Estados Unidos. Para servir de medida comparativa, el cuadro también incluye los continentes y el mundo. Para las entidades de la clasificación B, los nombres de los países protectores están especificados en la columna de estado político. Para las unidades bajo la categoría C, los nombres de los países administradores se encuentran entre paréntesis en la primera columna.

Las poblaciones son los estimados de Rand McNally, tomados el 1o. de Enero de 1995, en base a datos oficiales, estimados de las Naciones Unidas y varias otras informaciones disponibles.

CETTE TABLE donne, pour chaque pays du monde, les renseignements suivants: superficie, population, densité de population, capitale, statut politique. Les entités politiques sont classées, selon leur statut, dans la dernière colonne du tableau: A—pays indépendants; B—entités politiques indépendants intérieurement, mais qui se trouvent sous la protection d'un autre pays pour leur défense et leurs relations extérieures; C—colonies et autres entités politiques dépendantes; D—principales subdivisions administratives de l'Australie, du Canada, de la Chine, du Royaume-Uni, des États-Unis. Pour permettre les comparaisons, la table comprend aussi les continents et le monde. Pour les entités politiques de la catégorie B, les noms des pays protecteurs sont spécifiés dans la colonne "statut politique". Pour celles de la catégorie C, les noms des pays administrateurs sont mis entre parenthèses dans la première colonne.

Les chiffres concernant la population sont des estimations au 1er janvier 1995, établies par Rand McNally, d'après les sources officielles, les estimations des Nations Unies et autres informations disponibles.

A TABELA que se segue apresenta a área, a população, a densidade demográfica, a capital e o estatuto político de todos os países do mundo. As unidades políticas relacionadas na tabela estão classificadas de acordo com o respectivo estatuto político na última coluna, do seguinte modo: A—países independentes; B—unidades políticas internamente independentes mas que se encontram sob a proteção de outro país no tocante a assuntos de defesa nacional e negócios extrenos; C—colônias e outras unidades políticas dependentes; e D—subdivisões administrativas principais da Austrália, Canadá, China, Reino Unido e Estados Unidos. Para fins de comparabilidade, a tabela também inclui os continentes e o mundo. No tocante ás unidades classificadas em B, os nomes dos países protetores estão especificados na coluna relativa ao estatuto político. Para as unidades da categoria C, os nomes dos países administradores figuram entre parênteses na primeira coluna.

Os dados relativos à população são estimativas de Rand McNally para 1 de janeiro de 1995, com base em dados oficiais, estimativas das Nações Unidas e outras informações disponíveis.

NAME / NAME / NOMBRE / NOM / NOME English / Englisch Inglés / Anglais / Inglês	Local / Einheimisch Local / Local / Local	AREA / FLÄCHE AREA / SUPERFICIE / ÁREA sq. km.	sq. mi.	POPULATION BEVÖLKERUNG POBLACIÓN POPULATION POPULAÇÃO	DENSITY PER BEVÖLKERUNGSDICHTE PRO / DENSIDAD POR DENSITÉ / DENSIDADE POR sq. km.	sq. mi.	CAPITAL HAUPSTADT CAPITAL CAPITALE CAPITAL	POLITICAL STATUS POLITISCHER STATUS ESTADO POLITICO STATUS POLITIQUE ESTATUTO POLITICO
†Afghanistan	Afghānestān	652,225	251,826	19,715,000	30	78	Kābol (Kabul)	A
Africa	. . .	30,300,000	11,700,000	697,600,000	23	60	. . .	. . .
Alabama, U.S.	Alabama	135,775	52,423	4,254,000	31	81	Montgomery	D
Alaska, U.S.	Alaska	1,700,139	656,424	614,000	0.4	0.9	Juneau	D
†Albania	Shqipëri	28,748	11,100	3,394,000	118	306	Tiranë	A
Alberta, Can.	Alberta	661,190	255,287	2,632,000	4.0	10	Edmonton	D
†Algeria	Algérie (French) / Djazaïr (Arabic)	2,381,741	919,595	27,965,000	12	30	El Djazaïr (Algiers)	A
American Samoa (U.S.)	American Samoa (English) / Amerika Samoa (Samoan)	199	77	56,000	281	727	Pago Pago	C
†Andorra	Andorra	453	175	59,000	130	337	Andorra	B(Sp., Fr.)
†Angola	Angola	1,246,700	481,354	10,690,000	8.6	22	Luanda	A
Anguilla	Anguilla	91	35	7,100	78	203	The Valley	B(U.K.)
Anhwei, China	Anhui	139,000	53,668	59,490,000	428	1,108	Hefei	D
Antarctica	. . .	14,000,000	5,400,000	(1)	. . .	. . .	. . .	. . .
†Antigua and Barbuda	Antigua and Barbuda	442	171	67,000	152	392	St. John's	A
†Argentina	Argentina	2,780,400	1,073,519	34,083,000	12	32	Buenos Aires and Viedma (3)	A
Arizona, U.S.	Arizona	295,276	114,006	4,070,000	14	36	Phoenix	D
Arkansas, U.S.	Arkansas	137,742	53,182	2,468,000	18	46	Little Rock	D
†Armenia	Hayastan	29,800	11,506	3,794,000	127	330	Jerevan	A
Aruba	Aruba	193	75	67,000	347	893	Oranjestad	B(Neth.)
Asia	. . .	44,900,000	17,300,000	3,422,700,000	76	198	. . .	. . .
†Australia	Australia	7,682,300	2,966,155	18,205,000	2.4	6.1	Canberra	A
Australian Capital Territory, Austl.	Australian Capital Territory	2,400	927	309,000	129	333	Canberra	D
†Austria	Österreich	83,856	32,377	7,932,000	95	245	Wien (Vienna)	A
†Azerbaijan	Azärbaycan	86,600	33,436	7,491,000	87	224	Bakı (Baku)	A
†Bahamas	Bahamas	13,939	5,382	275,000	20	51	Nassau	A
†Bahrain	Al-Baḥrayn	691	267	563,000	815	2,109	Al-Manāmah	A
†Bangladesh	Bangladesh	143,998	55,598	119,370,000	829	2,147	Dhaka (Dacca)	A
†Barbados	Barbados	430	166	261,000	607	1,572	Bridgetown	A
†Belarus	Byelarus'	207,600	80,155	10,425,000	50	130	Minsk	A
†Belgium	Belgique (French) / België (Flemish)	30,518	11,783	10,075,000	330	855	Bruxelles (Brussels)	A
†Belize	Belize	22,963	8,866	212,000	9.2	24	Belmopan	A
†Benin	Bénin	112,600	43,475	5,433,000	48	125	Porto-Novo and Cotonou	A
Bermuda (U.K.)	Bermuda	54	21	61,000	1,130	2,905	Hamilton	C
†Bhutan	Druk-Yul	46,500	17,954	1,758,000	38	98	Thimphu	B(India)
†Bolivia	Bolivia	1,098,581	424,165	6,790,000	6.2	16	La Paz and Sucre	A
†Bosnia and Herzegovina	Bosna i Hercegovina	51,129	19,741	4,481,000	88	227	Sarajevo	A
†Botswana	Botswana	582,000	224,711	1,438,000	2.5	6.4	Gaborone	A
†Brazil	Brasil	8,511,996	3,286,500	159,690,000	19	49	Brasília	A
British Columbia, Can.	British Columbia (English) / Colombie-Britannique (French)	947,800	365,948	3,395,000	3.6	9.3	Victoria	D
British Indian Ocean Territory (U.K.)	British Indian Ocean Territory	60	23	(1)	. . .	. . .	. . .	C
British Virgin Islands (U.K.)	British Virgin Islands	153	59	13,000	85	220	Road Town	C
†Brunei	Brunei	5,765	2,226	289,000	50	130	Bandar Seri Begawan	A
†Bulgaria	Bălgarija	110,994	42,855	8,787,000	79	205	Sofija (Sofia)	A
†Burkina Faso	Burkina Faso	274,000	105,792	10,275,000	38	97	Ouagadougou	A
†Burundi	Burundi	27,830	10,745	6,192,000	222	576	Bujumbura	A
California, U.S.	California	424,002	163,707	32,090,000	76	196	Sacramento	D
†Cambodia	Kâmpŭchéa	181,035	69,898	9,713,000	54	139	Phnum Pénh (Phnom Penh)	A
†Cameroon	Cameroun (French) / Cameroon (English)	475,440	183,568	13,330,000	28	73	Yaoundé	A
†Canada	Canada	9,970,610	3,849,674	28,285,000	2.8	7.3	Ottawa	A
†Cape Verde	Cabo Verde	4,033	1,557	429,000	106	276	Praia	A
Cayman Islands (U.K.)	Cayman Islands	259	100	33,000	127	330	George Town	C
†Central African Republic	République centrafricaine	622,984	240,535	3,177,000	5.1	13	Bangui	A
†Chad	Tchad	1,284,000	495,755	6,396,000	5.0	13	N'Djamena	A
Chekiang, China	Zhejiang	101,800	39,305	43,930,000	432	1,118	Hangzhou	D
†Chile	Chile	756,626	292,135	14,050,000	19	48	Santiago	A
†China (excl. Taiwan)	Zhongguo	9,556,100	3,689,631	1,196,980,000	125	324	Beijing (Peking)	A
Christmas Island (Austl.)	Christmas Island	135	52	1,000	7.4	19	Settlement	C
Cocos (Keeling) Islands (Austl.)	Cocos (Keeling) Islands	14	5.4	600	43	111	. . .	C
†Colombia	Colombia	1,141,748	440,831	34,870,000	31	79	Santa Fe de Bogotá	A
Colorado, U.S.	Colorado	269,620	104,100	3,649,000	14	35	Denver	D
†Comoros (excl. Mayotte)	Comores (French) / Al-Qumur (Arabic)	2,235	863	540,000	242	626	Moroni	A
†Congo	Congo	342,000	132,047	2,474,000	7.2	19	Brazzaville	A
†Congo, Democratic Republic of the	Congo, République démocratique du Congo	2,344,858	905,355	43,365,000	18	48	Kinshasa	A
Connecticut, U.S.	Connecticut	14,358	5,544	3,266,000	227	589	Hartford	D
Cook Islands	Cook Islands	236	91	19,000	81	209	Avarua	B(N.Z.)
†Costa Rica	Costa Rica	51,100	19,730	3,379,000	66	171	San José	A
†Cote d'Ivoire	Côte d'Ivoire	322,500	124,518	14,540,000	45	117	Abidjan and Yamoussoukro	A
†Croatia	Hrvatska	56,538	21,829	4,801,000	85	220	Zagreb	A
†Cuba	Cuba	110,861	42,804	11,560,000	104	270	La Habana (Havana)	A
†Cyprus (excl. North Cyprus)	Kípros (Greek) / Kıbrıs (Turkish)	5,896	2,276	551,000	93	242	Nicosia (Levkosía)	A
Cyprus, North	Kuzey Kıbrıs	3,355	1,295	182,000	54	141	Nicosia (Lefkoşa)	A
†Czech Republic	Česká Republika	78,864	30,450	10,430,000	132	343	Praha (Prague)	A

World Information Table / Welt-Informationstabelle / Table de Información Mundial
Table d'Informations Mondiales / Tabela de Informação Mundial

297

NAME / NAME / NOMBRE / NOM / NOME		AREA / FLÄCHE AREA / SUPERFICIE / ÁREA		POPULATION BEVÖLKERUNG POBLACIÓN POPULATION POPULAÇÃO	DENSITY PER BEVÖLKERUNGSDICHTE PRO / DENSIDAD POR DENSITÉ / DENSIDADE POR		CAPITAL HAUPSTADT CAPITAL CAPITALE CAPITAL	POLITICAL STATUS POLITISCHER STATUS ESTADO POLÍTICO STATUS POLITIQUE ESTATUTO POLÍTICO
English / Englisch Inglés / Anglais / Inglês	Local / Einheimisch Local / Local / Local	sq. km.	sq. mi.		sq. km.	sq. mi.		
Delaware, U.S.	Delaware	6,447	2,489	709,000	110	285	Dover	D
†Denmark	Danmark	43,094	16,639	5,207,000	121	313	København (Copenhagen)	A
District of Columbia, U.S.	District of Columbia	177	68	575,000	3,249	8,456	Washington	D
†Djibouti	Djibouti	23,200	8,958	557,000	24	62	Djibouti	A
†Dominica	Dominica	790	305	89,000	113	292	Roseau	A
†Dominican Republic	República Dominicana	48,442	18,704	7,896,000	163	422	Santo Domingo	A
†Ecuador	Ecuador	272,045	105,037	11,015,000	40	105	Quito	A
†Egypt	Misr	1,001,449	386,662	58,100,000	58	150	Al-Qāhirah (Cairo)	A
†El Salvador	El Salvador	21,041	8,124	5,280,000	251	650	San Salvador	A
England, U.K.	England	130,410	50,352	48,730,000	374	968	London	D
†Equatorial Guinea	Guinea Ecuatorial	28,051	10,831	394,000	14	36	Malabo	A
†Eritrea	Ertra	93,679	36,170	3,458,000	37	96	Asmera	A
†Estonia	Eesti	45,100	17,413	1,515,000	34	87	Tallinn	A
†Ethiopia	Ītyop'iya	1,157,603	446,953	55,070,000	48	123	Adis Abeba	A
Europe	. . .	9,900,000	3,800,000	712,100,000	72	187	. . .	. . .
Faeroe Islands	Føroyar	1,399	540	49,000	35	91	Tórshavn	B(Den.)
Falkland Islands (U.K.) (2)	Falkland Islands	12,173	4,700	2,100	0.2	0.4	Stanley	C
†Fiji	Fiji (French) / Viti (Fijian)	18,274	7,056	775,000	42	110	Suva	A
†Finland	Suomi (Finnish) / Finland (Swedish)	338,145	130,559	5,098,000	15	39	Helsinki (Helsingfors)	A
Florida, U.S.	Florida	170,313	65,758	13,995,000	82	213	Tallahassee	D
†France (excl. Overseas Departments)	France	547,026	211,208	58,010,000	106	275	Paris	A
French Guiana (Fr.)	Guyane française	91,000	35,135	138,000	1.5	3.9	Cayenne	C
French Polynesia (Fr.)	Polynésie française	3,521	1,359	217,000	62	160	Papeete	C
Fukien, China	Fujian	120,000	46,332	31,720,000	264	685	Fuzhou	D
†Gabon	Gabon	267,667	103,347	1,035,000	3.9	10	Libreville	A
†Gambia	Gambia	10,689	4,127	1,082,000	101	262	Banjul	A
Gaza Strip	. . .	378	146	774,000	2,048	5,301	. . .	. . .
Georgia, U.S.	Georgia	153,953	59,441	7,065,000	46	119	Atlanta	D
†Georgia	Sakartvelo	69,700	26,911	5,704,000	82	212	Tbilisi	A
†Germany	Deutschland	356,955	137,822	81,710,000	229	593	Berlin and Bonn	A
†Ghana	Ghana	238,533	92,098	17,210,000	72	187	Accra	A
Gibraltar (U.K.)	Gibraltar	6.0	2.3	32,000	5,333	13,913	Gibraltar	C
Golan Heights	. . .	1,176	454	29,000	25	64	. . .	. . .
†Greece	Ellás	131,957	50,949	10,475,000	79	206	Athínai (Athens)	A
Greenland	Kalaallit Nunaat (Inuit) / Grønland (Danish)	2,175,600	840,004	57,000	. . .	0.1	Godthåb (Nuuk)	B(Den.)
†Grenada	Grenada	344	133	92,000	267	692	St. George's	A
Guadeloupe (incl. Dependencies) (Fr.)	Guadeloupe	1,780	687	432,000	243	629	Basse-Terre	C
Guam (U.S.)	Guam	541	209	152,000	281	727	Agana	C
†Guatemala	Guatemala	108,889	42,042	10,420,000	96	248	Guatemala	A
Guernsey (incl. Dependencies)	Guernsey	78	30	64,000	821	2,133	St. Peter Port	B(U.K.)
†Guinea	Guinée	245,857	94,926	6,469,000	26	68	Conakry	A
†Guinea-Bissau	Guiné-Bissau	36,125	13,948	1,111,000	31	80	Bissau	A
†Guyana	Guyana	214,969	83,000	726,000	3.4	8.7	Georgetown	A
Hainan, China	Hainan	34,000	13,127	6,945,000	204	529	Haikou	D
†Haiti	Haïti	27,750	10,714	7,069,000	255	660	Port-au-Prince	A
Hawaii, U.S.	Hawaii	28,313	10,932	1,181,000	42	108	Honolulu	D
Heilungkiang, China	Heilongjiang	469,000	181,082	37,345,000	80	206	Harbin	D
Honan, China	Henan	167,000	64,479	90,495,000	542	1,403	Zhengzhou	D
†Honduras	Honduras	112,088	43,277	5,822,000	52	135	Tegucigalpa	A
Hong Kong (Xianggang), China	Xianggang	1,072	414	5,927,000	5,529	14,316	Xianggang (Hong Kong)	D
Hopeh, China	Hebei	190,000	73,359	64,640,000	340	881	Shijiazhuang	D
Hunan, China	Hunan	210,000	81,081	64,280,000	306	793	Changsha	D
†Hungary	Magyarország	93,030	35,919	10,270,000	110	286	Budapest	A
Hupeh, China	Hubei	187,400	72,356	57,100,000	305	789	Wuhan	D
†Iceland	Ísland	103,000	39,769	265,000	2.6	6.7	Reykjavík	A
Idaho, U.S.	Idaho	216,456	83,574	1,129,000	5.2	14	Boise	D
Illinois, U.S.	Illinois	150,007	57,918	11,870,000	79	205	Springfield	D
†India (incl. part of Jammu and Kashmir)	India (English) / Bharat (Hindi)	3,203,975	1,237,062	909,150,000	284	735	New Delhi	A
Indiana, U.S.	Indiana	94,328	36,420	5,805,000	62	159	Indianapolis	D
†Indonesia	Indonesia	1,948,732	752,410	193,680,000	99	257	Jakarta	A
Inner Mongolia, China	Nei Monggol	1,183,000	456,759	22,745,000	19	50	Hohhot	D
Iowa, U.S.	Iowa	145,754	56,276	2,862,000	20	51	Des Moines	D
†Iran	Īrān	1,638,057	632,457	63,810,000	39	101	Tehrān	A
†Iraq	Al-'Irāq	438,317	169,235	20,250,000	46	120	Baghdād	A
†Ireland	Ireland (English) / Éire (Gaelic)	70,285	27,137	3,546,000	50	131	Dublin (Baile Átha Cliath)	A
Isle of Man	Isle of Man	572	221	72,000	126	326	Douglas	B(U.K.)
†Israel	Yisra'el (Hebrew) / Isrā'īl (Arabic)	20,770	8,019	5,059,000	244	631	Yerushalayim (Jerusalem)	A
†Italy	Italia	301,277	116,324	57,330,000	190	493	Roma (Rome)	A
†Jamaica	Jamaica	10,991	4,244	2,568,000	234	605	Kingston	A
†Japan	Nihon	377,801	145,870	125,360,000	332	859	Tōkyō	A
Jersey	Jersey	116	45	86,000	741	1,911	St. Helier	B(U.K.)
†Jordan	Al-Urdun	91,000	35,135	4,028,000	44	115	'Ammān	A
Kansas, U.S.	Kansas	213,110	82,282	2,575,000	12	31	Topeka	D
Kansu, China	Gansu	450,000	173,746	23,700,000	53	136	Lanzhou	D
†Kazakhstan	Kazakhstan	2,717,300	1,049,156	17,025,000	6.3	16	Alma-Ata (Almaty) and Akmola (3)	A
Kentucky, U.S.	Kentucky	104,665	40,411	3,835,000	37	95	Frankfort	D
†Kenya	Kenya	582,646	224,961	28,380,000	49	126	Nairobi	A
Kiangsi, China	Jiangxi	166,600	64,325	39,980,000	240	622	Nanchang	D
Kiangsu, China	Jiangsu	102,600	39,614	70,980,000	692	1,792	Nanjing (Nanking)	D
†Kiribati	Kiribati	811	313	79,000	97	252	Bairiki	A
Kirin, China	Jilin	187,000	72,201	26,095,000	140	361	Changchun	D
†Korea, North	Chosŏn-minjujuŭi-inmīn-konghwaguk	120,538	46,540	23,265,000	193	500	P'yŏngyang	A
†Korea, South	Taehan-min'guk	99,016	38,230	44,655,000	451	1,168	Sŏul (Seoul)	A
†Kuwait	Al-Kuwayt	17,818	6,880	1,866,000	105	271	Al-Kuwayt (Kuwait)	A
Kwangsi Chuang, China	Guangxi Zhuangzu	236,300	91,236	44,765,000	189	491	Nanning	D
Kwangtung, China	Guangdong	178,000	68,726	66,550,000	374	968	Guangzhou (Canton)	D
Kweichow, China	Guizhou	170,000	65,637	34,355,000	202	523	Guiyang	D
†Kyrgyzstan	Kyrgyzstan	198,500	76,641	4,541,000	23	59	Biškek (Frunze)	A
†Laos	Lao	236,800	91,429	4,768,000	20	52	Viangchan (Vientiane)	A
†Latvia	Latvija	63,700	24,595	2,532,000	40	103	Rīga	A
†Lebanon	Lubnān	10,400	4,015	3,660,000	352	912	Bayrūt (Beirut)	A
†Lesotho	Lesotho	30,355	11,720	1,967,000	65	168	Maseru	A
Liaoning, China	Liaoning	145,700	56,255	41,775,000	287	743	Shenyang (Mukden)	D
†Liberia	Liberia	99,067	38,250	2,771,000	28	72	Monrovia	A
†Libya	Lībiyā	1,759,540	679,362	5,148,000	2.9	7.6	Tarābulus (Tripoli)	A
†Liechtenstein	Liechtenstein	160	62	30,000	188	484	Vaduz	A
†Lithuania	Lietuva	65,300	25,212	3,757,000	58	149	Vilnius	A
Louisiana, U.S.	Louisiana	134,275	51,843	4,360,000	32	84	Baton Rouge	D
†Luxembourg	Luxembourg (French) / Lezebuurg (Luxembourgish)	2,586	998	396,000	153	397	Luxembourg	A
Macau (Port.)	Macau	18	7.0	396,000	22,000	56,571	Macau	C
†Macedonia	Makedonija	25,713	9,928	2,102,000	82	212	Skopje	A
†Madagascar	Madagasikara (Malagasy) / Madagascar (French)	587,041	226,658	13,645,000	23	60	Antananarivo	A
Maine, U.S.	Maine	91,653	35,387	1,260,000	14	36	Augusta	D
†Malawi	Malaŵi	118,484	45,747	8,984,000	76	196	Lilongwe	A
†Malaysia	Malaysia	329,758	127,320	19,505,000	59	153	Kuala Lumpur	A
†Maldives	Maldives	298	115	251,000	842	2,183	Male'	A
†Mali	Mali	1,248,574	482,077	9,585,000	7.7	20	Bamako	A
†Malta	Malta	316	122	368,000	1,165	3,016	Valletta	A
Manitoba, Can.	Manitoba	649,950	250,947	1,131,000	1.7	4.5	Winnipeg	D
†Marshall Islands	Marshall Islands	181	70	55,000	304	786	Majuro (island)	A
Martinique (Fr.)	Martinique	1,100	425	384,000	349	904	Fort-de-France	C
Maryland, U.S.	Maryland	32,135	12,407	5,045,000	157	407	Annapolis	D

World Information Table / Welt-Informationstabelle / Table de Información Mundial
Table d'Informations Mondiales / Tabela de Informação Mundial

NAME / NAME / NOMBRE / NOM / NOME		AREA / FLÄCHE AREA / SUPERFICIE / ÁREA		POPULATION BEVÖLKERUNG POBLACION POPULATION POPULAÇÃO	DENSITY PER BEVÖLKERUNGSDICHTE PRO / DENSIDAD POR DENSITÉ / DENSIDADE POR		CAPITAL HAUPSTADT CAPITAL CAPITALE CAPITAL	POLITICAL STATUS POLITISCHER STATUS ESTADO POLITICO STATUS POLITIQUE ESTATUTO POLITICO
English / Englisch Inglés / Anglais / Inglês	Local / Einheimisch Local / Local / Local	sq. km.	sq. mi.	POPULAÇÃO	sq. km.	sq. mi.		
Massachusetts, U.S.	Massachusetts	27,337	10,555	6,117,000	224	580	Boston	D
†Mauritania	Mauritanie (French) / Mūrītāniyā (Arabic)	1,025,520	395,956	2,228,000	2.2	5.6	Nouakchott	A
†Mauritius (incl. Dependencies)	Mauritius	2,040	788	1,121,000	550	1,423	Port Louis	A
Mayotte (Fr.) [4]	Mayotte	374	144	95,000	254	660	Dzaoudzi and Mamoudzou [3]	C
†Mexico	México	1,967,183	759,534	93,860,000	48	124	Ciudad de México (Mexico City)	A
Michigan, U.S.	Michigan	250,738	96,810	9,615,000	38	99	Lansing	D
†Micronesia, Federated States of	Federated States of Micronesia	702	271	122,000	174	450	Kolonia and Paliker [3]	A
Midway Islands (U.S.)	Midway Islands	5.2	2.0	500	96	250	. . .	C
Minnesota, U.S.	Minnesota	225,182	86,943	4,595,000	20	53	St. Paul	D
Mississippi, U.S.	Mississippi	125,443	48,434	2,678,000	21	55	Jackson	D
Missouri, U.S.	Missouri	180,546	69,709	5,330,000	30	76	Jefferson City	D
†Moldova	Moldova	33,700	13,012	4,377,000	130	336	Chişinău (Kishinev)	A
†Monaco	Monaco	1.9	0.7	31,000	16,316	44,286	Monaco	A
†Mongolia	Mongol Ard Uls	1,566,500	604,829	2,462,000	1.6	4.1	Ulaanbaatar (Ulan Bator)	A
Montana, U.S.	Montana	380,850	147,046	840,000	2.2	5.7	Helena	D
Montserrat (U.K.)	Montserrat	102	39	13,000	127	333	Plymouth	C
†Morocco (excl. Western Sahara)	Al-Magrib	446,550	172,414	26,890,000	60	156	Rabat	A
†Mozambique	Moçambique	799,380	308,642	17,860,000	22	58	Maputo	A
†Myanmar	Myanmar	676,577	261,228	44,675,000	66	171	Yangon (Rangoon)	A
†Namibia	Namibia	824,272	318,253	1,623,000	2.0	5.1	Windhoek	A
Nauru	Nauru (English) / Naoero (Nauruan)	21	8.1	10,000	476	1,235	Yaren District	A
Nebraska, U.S.	Nebraska	200,358	77,358	1,628,000	8.1	21	Lincoln	D
†Nepal	Nepāl	147,181	56,827	21,295,000	145	375	Kāthmāndū	A
†Netherlands	Nederland	41,864	16,164	15,425,000	368	954	Amsterdam and 's-Gravenhage (The Hague)	A
Netherlands Antilles	Nederlandse Antillen	800	309	187,000	234	605	Willemstad	B(Neth.)
Nevada, U.S.	Nevada	286,368	110,567	1,444,000	5.0	13	Carson City	D
New Brunswick, Can.	New Brunswick (English) / Nouveau-Brunswick (French)	73,440	28,355	764,000	10	27	Fredericton	D
New Caledonia (Fr.)	Nouvelle-Calédonie	19,058	7,358	183,000	9.6	25	Nouméa	C
Newfoundland, Can.	Newfoundland (English) / Terre-Neuve (French)	405,720	156,649	594,000	1.5	3.8	St. John's	D
New Hampshire, U.S.	New Hampshire	24,219	9,351	1,100,000	45	118	Concord	D
New Jersey, U.S.	New Jersey	22,590	8,722	7,985,000	353	916	Trenton	D
New Mexico, U.S.	New Mexico	314,939	121,598	1,655,000	5.3	14	Santa Fe	D
New South Wales, Austl.	New South Wales	801,600	309,500	6,171,000	7.7	20	Sydney	D
New York, U.S.	New York	141,089	54,475	18,460,000	131	339	Albany	D
†New Zealand	New Zealand	270,534	104,454	3,558,000	13	34	Wellington	A
†Nicaragua	Nicaragua	129,640	50,054	4,438,000	34	89	Managua	A
†Niger	Niger	1,267,000	489,191	9,125,000	7.2	19	Niamey	A
†Nigeria	Nigeria	923,768	356,669	97,300,000	105	273	Lagos and Abuja	A
Ningsia Hui, China	Ningxia Huizu	66,400	25,637	4,908,000	74	191	Yinchuan	D
Niue	Niue	259	100	1,900	7.3	19	Alofi	B(N.Z.)
Norfolk Island (Austl.)	Norfolk Island	36	14	2,700	75	193	Kingston	C
North America	. . .	24,700,000	9,500,000	453,300,000	18	48	. . .	. . .
North Carolina, U.S.	North Carolina	139,397	53,821	7,065,000	51	131	Raleigh	D
North Dakota, U.S.	North Dakota	183,123	70,704	656,000	3.6	9.3	Bismarck	D
Northern Ireland, U.K.	Northern Ireland	14,144	5,461	1,636,000	116	300	Belfast	D
Northern Mariana Islands	Northern Mariana Islands	477	184	51,000	107	277	Saipan (island)	B(U.S.)
Northern Territory, Austl.	Northern Territory	1,346,200	519,771	182,000	0.1	0.4	Darwin	D
Northwest Territories, Can.	Northwest Territories (English) / Territoires du Nord-Ouest (French)	3,426,320	1,322,910	57,000	. . .	. . .	Yellowknife	D
†Norway (incl. Svalbard and Jan Mayen)	Norge	386,975	149,412	4,339,000	11	29	Oslo	A
Nova Scotia, Can.	Nova Scotia (English) / Nouvelle-Écosse (French)	55,490	21,425	933,000	17	44	Halifax	D
Oceania (incl. Australia)	. . .	8,500,000	3,300,000	28,400,000	3.3	8.6	. . .	
Ohio, U.S.	Ohio	116,103	44,828	11,270,000	97	251	Columbus	D
Oklahoma, U.S.	Oklahoma	181,049	69,903	3,282,000	18	47	Oklahoma City	D
†Oman	'Umān	212,457	82,030	2,089,000	9.8	25	Masqat (Muscat)	A
Ontario, Can.	Ontario	1,068,580	412,581	10,435,000	9.8	25	Toronto	D
Oregon, U.S.	Oregon	254,819	98,386	3,098,000	12	31	Salem	D
†Pakistan (incl. part of Jammu and Kashmir)	Pākistān	879,902	339,732	129,630,000	147	382	Islāmābād	A
†Palau	Palau (English) / Belau (Palauan)	508	196	17,000	33	87	Koror and Melekeok [3]	A
†Panama	Panamá	75,517	29,157	2,654,000	35	91	Panamá	A
†Papua New Guinea	Papua New Guinea	462,840	178,704	4,057,000	8.8	23	Port Moresby	A
†Paraguay	Paraguay	406,752	157,048	4,400,000	11	28	Asunción	A
Peking, China	Beijing	16,800	6,487	11,490,000	684	1,771	Beijing (Peking)	D
Pennsylvania, U.S.	Pennsylvania	119,291	46,058	12,215,000	102	265	Harrisburg	D
†Peru	Perú	1,285,216	496,225	23,095,000	18	47	Lima	A
†Philippines	Philippines (English) / Pilipinas (Pilipino)	300,000	115,831	67,910,000	226	586	Manila	A
Pitcairn (incl. Dependencies) (U.K.)	Pitcairn	49	19	100	2.0	5.3	Adamstown	C
†Poland	Polska	313,895	121,196	38,730,000	123	320	Warszawa (Warsaw)	A
†Portugal	Portugal	91,985	35,516	9,907,000	108	279	Lisboa (Lisbon)	A
Prince Edward Island, Can.	Prince Edward Island (English) / Île-du Prince-Édouard (French)	5,660	2,185	141,000	25	65	Charlottetown	D
Puerto Rico	Puerto Rico	9,104	3,515	3,625,000	398	1,031	San Juan	B(U.S.)
†Qatar	Qatar	11,427	4,412	519,000	45	118	Ad-Dawhah (Doha)	A
Quebec, Can.	Québec	1,540,680	594,860	7,157,000	4.6	12	Québec	D
Queensland, Austl.	Queensland	1,727,200	666,876	3,259,000	1.9	4.9	Brisbane	D
Reunion (Fr.)	Réunion	2,510	969	660,000	263	681	Saint-Denis	C
Rhode Island, U.S.	Rhode Island	4,002	1,545	1,024,000	256	663	Providence	D
†Romania	România	237,500	91,699	22,745,000	96	248	Bucureşti (Bucharest)	A
†Russia	Rossija	17,075,400	6,592,849	150,500,000	8.8	23	Moskva (Moscow)	A
†Rwanda	Rwanda	26,338	10,169	7,343,000	279	722	Kigali	A
St. Helena (incl. Dependencies) (U.K.)	St. Helena	314	121	7,000	22	58	Jamestown	C
†St. Kitts and Nevis	St. Kitts and Nevis	269	104	42,000	156	404	Basseterre	A
†St. Lucia	St. Lucia	616	238	138,000	224	580	Castries	A
St. Pierre and Miquelon (Fr.)	Saint-Pierre-et-Miquelon	242	93	6,700	28	72	Saint-Pierre	C
†St. Vincent and the Grenadines	St. Vincent and the Grenadines	388	150	110,000	284	733	Kingstown	A
†San Marino	San Marino	61	24	24,000	393	1,000	San Marino	A
†Sao Tome and Principe	São Tomé e Príncipe	964	372	127,000	132	341	São Tomé	A
Saskatchewan, Can.	Saskatchewan	652,330	251,866	1,018,000	1.6	4.0	Regina	D
†Saudi Arabia	Al-'Arabīyah as-Su'ūdīyah	2,149,690	830,000	18,190,000	8.5	22	Ar-Riyāḍ (Riyadh)	A
Scotland, U.K.	Scotland	78,789	30,421	5,142,000	65	169	Edinburgh	D
†Senegal	Sénégal	196,712	75,951	8,862,000	45	117	Dakar	A
†Seychelles	Seychelles	453	175	75,000	166	429	Victoria	A
Shanghai, China	Shanghai	6,200	2,394	14,125,000	2,278	5,900	Shanghai	D
Shansi, China	Shanxi	156,000	60,232	30,405,000	195	505	Taiyuan	D
Shantung, China	Shandong	153,000	59,074	89,400,000	584	1,513	Jinan	D
Shensi, China	Shaanxi	205,000	79,151	34,830,000	170	440	Xi'an (Sian)	D
†Sierra Leone	Sierra Leone	72,325	27,925	4,690,000	65	168	Freetown	A
†Singapore	Singapore	636	246	2,921,000	4,593	11,874	Singapore	A
Sinkiang Uighur, China	Xinjiang Uygur	1,600,000	617,764	16,040,000	10	26	Ürümqi	D
†Slovakia	Slovenská Republika	49,035	18,933	5,353,000	109	283	Bratislava	A
†Slovenia	Slovenija	20,253	7,820	1,993,000	98	255	Ljubljana	A
†Solomon Islands	Solomon Islands	28,370	10,954	393,000	14	36	Honiara	A
†Somalia	Somaliya	637,657	246,201	7,187,000	11	29	Muqdisho (Mogadishu)	A

World Information Table / Welt-Informationstabelle / Table de Información Mundial
Table d'Informations Mondiales / Tabela de Informação Mundial

299

NAME / NAME / NOMBRE / NOM / NOME		AREA / FLÄCHE AREA / SUPERFICIE / ÁREA		POPULATION BEVÖLKERUNG POBLACIÓN POPULATION POPULAÇÃO	DENSITY PER BEVÖLKERUNGSDICHTE PRO / DENSIDAD POR DENSITÉ / DENSIDADE POR		CAPITAL HAUPTSTADT CAPITAL CAPITALE CAPITAL	POLITICAL STATUS POLITISCHER STATUS ESTADO POLÍTICO STATUS POLITIQUE ESTATUTO POLÍTICO
English / Englisch Inglés / Anglais / Inglês	Local / Einheimisch Local / Local / Local	sq. km.	sq. mi.		sq. km.	sq. mi.		
†South Africa	South Africa (English) / Suid-Afrika (Afrikaans)	1,219,909	471,010	44,500,000	36	94	Pretoria, Cape Town, and Bloemfontein	A
South America	. . .	17,800,000	6,900,000	313,900,000	18	45	. . .	. . .
South Australia, Austl.	South Australia	984,000	379,925	1,493,000	1.5	3.9	Adelaide	D
South Carolina, U.S.	South Carolina	82,898	32,007	3,702,000	45	116	Columbia	D
South Dakota, U.S.	South Dakota	199,745	77,121	735,000	3.7	9.5	Pierre	D
South Georgia and the South Sandwich Islands (U.K.)	South Georgia and the South Sandwich Islands	3,755	1,450	(1)	. . .	. . .	. . .	C
†Spain	España	504,750	194,885	39,260,000	78	201	Madrid	A
Spanish North Africa (Sp.) (5)	Plazas de Soberanía en el Norte de África	32	12	146,000	4,563	12,167	. . .	C
†Sri Lanka	Sri Lanka	64,652	24,962	18,240,000	282	731	Colombo and Sri Jayawardenapura	A
†Sudan	As-Sūdān	2,505,813	967,500	25,840,000	10	27	Al-Khartūm (Khartoum)	A
†Suriname	Suriname	163,820	63,251	426,000	2.6	6.7	Paramaribo	A
†Swaziland	Swaziland	17,364	6,704	889,000	51	133	Mbabane and Lobamba	A
†Sweden	Sverige	449,964	173,732	8,981,000	20	52	Stockholm	A
Switzerland	Schweiz (German) / Suisse (French) / Svizzera (Italian)	41,293	15,943	7,244,000	175	454	Bern (Berne)	A
†Syria	Sūrīyah	185,180	71,498	14,100,000	76	197	Dimashq (Damascus)	A
Szechwan, China	Sichuan	570,000	220,078	113,470,000	199	516	Chengdu	D
Taiwan	T'aiwan	36,002	13,900	21,150,000	587	1,522	T'aipei	A
†Tajikistan	Tojikiston	143,100	55,251	6,073,000	42	110	Dušanbe	A
†Tanzania	Tanzania	883,749	341,217	28,350,000	32	83	Dar es Salaam and Dodoma	A
Tasmania, Austl.	Tasmania	67,800	26,178	492,000	7.3	19	Hobart	D
Tennessee, U.S.	Tennessee	109,158	42,146	5,175,000	47	123	Nashville	D
Texas, U.S.	Texas	695,676	268,601	18,330,000	26	68	Austin	D
†Thailand	Prathet Thai	513,115	198,115	59,870,000	117	302	Krung Thep (Bangkok)	A
Tibet, China	Xizang	1,220,000	471,045	2,275,000	1.9	4.8	Lhasa	D
Tientsin, China	Tianjin	11,300	4,363	9,337,000	826	2,140	Tianjin (Tientsin)	D
†Togo	Togo	56,785	21,925	4,332,000	76	198	Lomé	A
Tokelau (N.Z.)	Tokelau	12	4.6	1,500	125	326	. . .	C
Tonga	Tonga	747	288	110,000	147	382	Nuku'alofa	A
†Trinidad and Tobago	Trinidad and Tobago	5,128	1,980	1,281,000	250	647	Port of Spain	A
Tsinghai, China	Qinghai	720,000	277,994	4,670,000	6.5	17	Xining	D
†Tunisia	Tunisie (French) / Tunis (Arabic)	163,610	63,170	8,806,000	54	139	Tunis	A
†Turkey	Türkiye	779,452	300,948	62,030,000	80	206	Ankara	A
†Turkmenistan	Türkmenistan	488,100	188,456	4,035,000	8.3	21	Aščhabad (Ashgabat)	A
Turks and Caicos Islands (U.K.)	Turks and Caicos Islands	500	193	14,000	28	73	Grand Turk	C
Tuvalu	Tuvalu	26	10	10,000	385	1,000	Funafuti	A
†Uganda	Uganda	241,139	93,104	18,270,000	76	196	Kampala	A
†Ukraine	Ukrayina	603,700	233,090	52,140,000	86	224	Kyyiv (Kiev)	A
†United Arab Emirates	Al-Imārāt al-'Arabīyah al-Muttahidah	83,600	32,278	2,855,000	34	88	Abū Ẓaby (Abu Dhabi)	A
†United Kingdom	United Kingdom	244,101	94,249	58,430,000	239	620	London	A
†United States	United States	9,809,431	3,787,425	262,530,000	27	69	Washington	A
†Uruguay	Uruguay	177,414	68,500	3,317,000	19	48	Montevideo	A
Utah, U.S.	Utah	219,902	84,904	1,890,000	8.6	22	Salt Lake City	D
†Uzbekistan	Ŭzbekiston	447,400	172,742	22,860,000	51	132	Taškent (Toshkent)	A
†Vanuatu	Vanuatu	12,190	4,707	161,000	13	34	Port Vila	A
Vatican City	Città del Vaticano	0.4	0.2	1,000	2,500	5,000	Città del Vaticano (Vatican City)	A
†Venezuela	Venezuela	912,050	352,145	21,395,000	23	61	Caracas	A
Vermont, U.S.	Vermont	24,903	9,615	578,000	23	60	Montpelier	D
Victoria, Austl.	Victoria	227,600	87,877	4,570,000	20	52	Melbourne	D
†Vietnam	Viet Nam	330,036	127,428	73,760,000	223	579	Ha Noi	A
Virginia, U.S.	Virginia	110,771	42,769	6,595,000	60	154	Richmond	D
Virgin Islands (U.S.)	Virgin Islands	344	133	97,000	282	729	Charlotte Amalie	C
Wake Island (U.S.)	Wake Island	7.8	3.0	300	38	100	. . .	C
Wales, U.K.	Wales	20,758	8,015	2,922,000	141	365	Cardiff	D
Wallis and Futuna (Fr.)	Wallis et Futuna	255	98	14,000	55	143	Mata-Utu	C
Washington, U.S.	Washington	184,674	71,303	5,360,000	29	75	Olympia	D
West Bank (incl. Jericho)		6,078	2,347	1,717,000	282	732	. . .	. . .
Western Australia, Austl.	Western Australia	2,525,500	975,101	1,729,000	0.7	1.8	Perth	D
Western Sahara		266,000	102,703	215,000	0.8	2.1	El Aaiún (Laayone)	. . .
†Western Samoa	Western Samoa (English) / Samoa i Sisifo (Samoan)	2,831	1,093	172,000	61	157	Apia	A
West Virginia, U.S.	West Virginia	62,759	24,231	1,838,000	29	76	Charleston	D
Wisconsin, U.S.	Wisconsin	169,653	65,503	5,120,000	30	78	Madison	D
Wyoming, U.S.	Wyoming	253,349	97,818	473,000	1.9	4.8	Cheyenne	D
†Yemen	Al-Yaman	527,968	203,850	12,910,000	24	63	San'ā'	A
Yugoslavia	Jugoslavija	102,173	39,449	10,765,000	105	273	Beograd (Belgrade)	A
Yukon Territory, Can.	Yukon Territory	483,450	186,661	28,000	0.1	0.2	Whitehorse	D
Yunnan, China	Yunnan	394,000	152,124	39,140,000	99	257	Kunming	D
†Zambia	Zambia	752,618	290,587	8,809,000	12	30	Lusaka	A
†Zimbabwe	Zimbabwe	390,757	150,872	11,075,000	28	73	Harare (Salisbury)	A
WORLD	. . .	150,100,000	57,900,000	5,628,000,000	37	97	. . .	. . .

† Member of the United Nations.
. . . None, or not applicable.
(1) No permanent population.
(2) Claimed by Argentina.
(3) Future capital.
(4) Claimed by Comoros.
(5) Comprises Ceuta, Melilla, and several small islands.

† Mitglied der Vereinten Nationen.
. . . Kein(e), oder nicht anwendbar.
(1) Bevölkerungszahl schwankend.
(2) Von Argentinien beansprucht.
(3) Zukünftige Hauptstadt.
(4) Von Komoren beansprucht.
(5) Umfasst Ceuta, Melilla und mehrere kleine Inseln.

† Miembro de las Naciones Unidas.
. . . Ninguno, o no se aplica.
(1) Sin población permanente.
(2) Reclamado por la Argentina.

(3) Capital futura.
(4) Reclamado por las Comores.
(5) Comprende Ceuta, Melilla y various islas pequeñas.

† Membre des Nations Unies.
. . . Pas d'information, ou pas applicable.
(1) Pas de population permanente.
(2) Revendiqué par l'Argentine.
(3) Capitale future.
(4) Revendiqué par les Comores.
(5) Inclus Ceuta, Melilla et plusieurs petites îles.

† Membro das Nações Unidas.
. . . Inexistente ou não aplicável.
(1) Sem população permanente.
(2) Reivindicado pela Argentina.
(3) Capital futuro.
(4) Reivindicado pelas Comores.
(5) Compreende Ceuta, Melilla e várias ilhas pequenas.

THIS TABLE lists the major metropolitan areas of the world according to their estimated population on January 1, 1994. For convenience in reference, the areas are grouped by major region with the total for each region given. The number of areas by population classification is given in parentheses with each size group.

For ease of comparison, each metropolitan area has been defined by Rand McNally according to consistent rules. A metropolitan area includes a central city, neighboring communities linked to it by continuous built-up areas, and more distant communities if the bulk of their population is supported by commuters to the central city. Some metropolitan areas have more than one central city; in such cases each central city is listed.

IN DIESER TABELLE sind die Hauptmetropolen der Welt verzeichnet, gemessen nach ihrer Bevölkerung, die nach dem Stand vom 1. Januar 1994 geschätzt wurde. Zur besseren Übersicht sind die Zonen nach grösseren Regionen gruppiert, wobei die Gesamtzahl für jede Region angegeben ist. Die Anzahl der Zonen ist nach Bevölkerung klassifiziert und in Klammern hinter denen nach Grössen sortierten Gruppen angegeben.

Zum einfacheren Vergleich ist jede Metropole von Rand McNally nach übereinstimmenden Massstäben definiert worden. Eine Metropole schliesst eine zentrale Stadt mit benachbarten Gemeinden, die mit ihr durch ununterbrochen bebaute Gebiete verbunden sind ein, sowie weiter entfernte Gemeinden, wenn der grösste Teil ihrer Bevölkerung von den Pendlern unterhalten wird. Einige Metropolen haben mehr als eine zentrale Stadt; in solchen Fällen ist jede dieser zentralen Städte angeführt.

ESTA TABLA indica las principales áreas metropolitanas del mundo, de acuerdo con su población calculada al 1 de enero de 1994. Para facilitar las referencias, las áreas se han agrupado por regiones principales, indicándose el total para cada región. El número de áreas, clasificadas por población, se indica entre paréntesis en los grupos de cada tamaño.

Para facilitar las comparaciones, Rand McNally ha definido cada área metropolitana de acuerdo con reglas consistentes. Un área metropolitana incluye una ciudad central, localidades vecinas vinculadas con ella mediante sectores construídos y contínuos, y localidades más distantes, si el grueso de su población lo constituye un núcleo que diariamente viaja a la ciudad central. Algunas áreas metropolitanas incluyen más de una ciudad central; en tales casos se indica cada una dichas ciudades.

CETTE TABLE contient la liste des aires métropolitaines les plus considérables dans le monde pour ce qui est du peuplement a la date du 1 er janvier 1994. Afin de faciliter la consultation, on a groupé les aires par grandes régions en indiquant la population totale pour chaque région, et, entre parenthéses, le nombre d'aires comprises dans celle-ci.

Afin de rendre plus faciles les comparaisons, Rand McNally a défini chaque aire métropolitaine selorègles cohérentes: une aire métropolitaine englobe une cité centrale ou métropole et l'environnement urbain continu qui s'y rattache; elle inclut également des agglomérations éloignées de la métropole lorsque la population de ces dernières est pour sa májorité constituée d'habitants se rendant quotidiennement dans la cité ou est situé le lieu de travail de ceux-ci. On trouvera quelques aires métropolitaines pourvues de plus d'une métropole. Dans ce cas, chaque métropole est mentionnée.

A TABELA que se segúe relaciona as principais áreas metropolitanas do mundo, de acordo com as respectivas populações, estimadas para 1 de janeiro de 1994. Para facilidade de referência, as áreas metropolitanas foram agrupadas dentro das regiões maiores, indicando-se, entre parênteses, os totais de cada região maior e o número de áreas metropolitanas, classificadas segundo a população, compreendidas em cada uma.

Para fins de comparabilidade, Rand McNally definiu cada área metropolitana de acordo com regras uniformes. Uma área metropolitana inclui uma cidade central, as localidades vizinhas ligadas a ela por áreas construídas contínuas, e as localidades mais distantes, desde que a maior parte de suas respectivas populações dependa economicamente da cidade central e que para ela viaje diariamente. Algumas áreas metropolitanas incluem mais de uma cidade central; em tais casos, indicam-se ambas as cidades.

CLASSIFICATION KLASSIFIZIERT CLASIFICADAS CLASSIFICATION CLASSIFICAÇÃO	ANGLO-AMERICA ANGLO-AMERIKA AMÉRICA ANGLOSAJONA AMÉRIQUE ANGLO-SAXONNE AMÉRICA ANGLO-SAXÔNICA	LATIN AMERICA LATEIN-AMERIKA AMÉRICA LATINA AMÉRIQUE LATINE AMÉRICA LATINA	EUROPE-RUSSIA EUROPA-RUSSLAND EUROPA-RUSIA EUROPE RUSSIE EUROPA RÚSSIA	ASIA ASIEN ASIA ASIE ÁSIA	AFRICA-OCEANIA AFRIKA-OZEANIEN AFRICA-OCEANÍA AFRIQUE-OCÉANIE ÁFRICA-OCEANIA
Over 25,000,000 (1)				Tōkyō-Yokohama	
15,000,000-25,000,000 (5)	New York	Ciudad de México (Mexico City) São Paulo		Ōsaka-Kōbe-Kyōto Sŏul (Seoul)	
10,000,000-15,000,000 (13)	Los Angeles	Buenos Aires Rio de Janeiro	London Moskva (Moscow) Paris	Calcutta Delhi-New Delhi Jakarta Manila Mumbai (Bombay) Shanghai	Al-Qāhirah (Cairo)
5,000,000-10,000,000 (22)	Chicago Philadelphia-Trenton- Wilmington San Francisco- Oakland-San Jose Toronto	Lima Santa Fe de Bogotá Santiago	Essen-Dortmund- Duisburg (Ruhr Area) Sankt-Peterburg (St. Petersburg)	Beijing (Peking) Chennai (Madras) Dhaka (Dacca) Hyderābād İstanbul Karāchi Krung Thep (Bangkok) Nagoya T'aipei Tehrān Tianjin (Tientsin) Xianggang (Hong Kong)	Lagos
3,000,000- 5,000,000 (40)	Boston Dallas-Fort Worth Detroit-Windsor Houston Miami-Fort Lauderdale Montréal San Diego-Tijuana Washington	Belo Horizonte Caracas Guadalajara Porto Alegre	Athínai (Athens) Barcelona Berlin Kyyiv (Kiev) Madrid Milano (Milan) Roma (Rome)	Ahmadābād Baghdād Bangalore Guangzhou (Canton) Harbin Kuala Lumpur Lahore Pusan Shenyang (Mukden) Singapore Surabaya Thanh Pho Ho Chi Minh (Saigon) Wuhan Yangon (Rangoon)	Al-Iskandarīyah (Alexandria) Casablanca El Djazaïr (Algiers) Johannesburg Kinshasa Melbourne Sydney
2,000,000- 3,000,000 (64)	Atlanta Baltimore Cleveland Minneapolis-St. Paul Phoenix Pittsburgh St. Louis Seattle-Tacoma	Curitiba Fortaleza La Habana (Havana) Medellín Monterrey Recife Salvador San Juan Santo Domingo	Amsterdam Birmingham Bruxelles (Brussels) Bucureşti (Bucharest) Budapest Donets'k-Makiyivka Frankfurt am Main Hamburg Katowice-Bytom- Gliwice Kharkiv Leeds-Bradford Lisboa (Lisbon) Liverpool Manchester München (Munich) Napoli (Naples) Nižnij Novgorod (Gorky) Stuttgart Warszawa (Warsaw) Wien (Vienna)	'Amman Ankara Bakı (Baku) Bandung Changchun Chengdu (Chengtu) Chittagong Chongqing (Chungking) Colombo Dalian (Dairen) Dimashq (Damascus) Fukuoka İzmir Kānpur Nanjing (Nanking) Pune (Poona) P'yongyang Sapporo-Otaru Taegu Taškent Tel Aviv-Yafo Xi'an (Sian)	Abidjan Adis Abeba Al-Khartūm-Umm Durmān (Khartoum- Omdurman) Cape Town Durban
Total/Gesamtzahl Total/Total/Total (145)	22	20	32	57	14

ALL URBAN CENTERS of 50,000 or more population and many other important or well-known cities and towns are listed in the following table. The populations are from recent censuses (designated C) or official estimates (designated E) for the dates specified. For a few cities, only unofficial estimates are available (designated U). For comparison, the total population of each country is also given. For each country, the date stated for the total population also applies to the cities, except those for which another date is specified.

Population estimates for 1995 for countries may be found in the World Information Table.

A population figure in parentheses and preceded by a star (★) is the population of a city's entire metropolitan area. To permit meaningful comparisons of metropolitan areas, these have been defined by Rand McNally according to consistent rules (see introduction to Metropolitan Areas Table), and in some cases may differ somewhat from the officially recognized metropolitan areas. Where a town is located within the metropolitan area of another city, that city's name is given in parentheses preceded by a star (★). The capital of a country is denoted by CAPITAL letters.

ALLE STÄDTISCHEN ZENTREN mit 50 000 oder mehr Einwohnern und zahlreiche andere bedeutende oder bekannte Städte sind in der folgenden Tabelle zusammengestellt. Die Bevölkerungszahlen stammen von neuesten Zählungen (mit C gekennzeichnet) oder amtlichen Schätzungen (E) zu den angegebenen Zeitpunkten. Für einige wenige Städte waren lediglich inoffizielle Schätzungen erhältlich (U). Zu Vergleichszwecken ist ferner die Gesamtbevölkerung jedes Landes angegeben. Das Bezugsjahr für die Einwohnerzahl eines Landes betrifft auch die Städte mit Ausnahme jener, bei denen ein anderes Datum angegeben ist.

Schätzungen der Bevölkerungszahlen der Länder für 1995 finden sich in der Welt-Informationstabelle.

Bevölkerungszahlen in Klammern mit vorangestelltem Stern (★) beziehen sich auf die gesamte Stadtregion einer Stadt. Um sinnvolle Vergleiche von Stadtregionen zu ermöglichen, wurden diese von Rand McNally nach einheitlichen Regeln festgelegt (siehe Einleitung: Tabelle der Stadtregionen), weshalb sie in einigen Fällen etwas von der offiziellen Abgrenzung von Stadtregionen abweichen können. Ist eine Stadt in die Stadtregion einer anderen Grossstadt einbezogen, so wird der Name der Stadtregion mit vorangestelltem Stern (★) in Klammern aufgeführt. Die Hauptstadt eines Landes wird durch GROSSBUCHSTABEN hervorgehoben.

TODAS LOS CENTROS URBANOS de 50 000 habitantes o más y muchos otros de importancia así como bien conocidas ciudades y pueblos están incluídos en la tabla que se presenta a continuación. El número de habitantes indicados está tomado del censo más reciente (cifras identificadas con la letra C) o estimados oficiales (E) para las fechas especificadas. Para algunas ciudades, sólo existen informes no oficiales (U). Para medida de comparación, la población total de cada país se encuentra incluída también.

Para permitir una comparación, se da la población total de cada país, referente al mismo año que se usa para las ciudades principles, excepto para aquellas en las que se especifica otra fecha. El número de habitantes para 1995 para los países, se encuentra en la Tabla de Información Mundial.

La segunda cifra para la población que aparece en paréntesis y está precedida por una estrella (★) constituye la población de un área metropolitana entera. Para permitir comparaciones validas de áreas metropolitanas, éstas fueron definidas por Rand McNally siguiendo las reglas establecidas para estos propósitos (véase la Introducción a la Tabla de las Areas Metropolitanas), y en algunas ocasiones pueden ser un poco distintas de las áreas metropolitanas oficialmente reconocidas. Cuando una población se encuentra dentro de los límites de un área metropolitana de otra ciudad, el nombre de ésta se da entre paréntesis precedido por una (★). La capital de un país se indica con letras MAYÚSCULAS.

TOUTES LES VILLES de plus de 50 000 habitants et des villes moins peuplées, mais cèlèbres ou importantes, sont mentionnées dans la table ci-dessous. Les chiffres donnant la population proviennent de recensements récents (référence C), ou d'estimations officielles (référence E), aux dates indiquées. Pour quelques villes, on dispose seulement d'estimations non officielles (référence U). La population totale de chaque pays est également donnée, ce qui permet des comparaisons. Dans chaque pays, la date des renseignements est identique pour les villes et le pays, sauf indication contraire.

On trouvera dans la table d'informations mondiales les estimations de la population en 1995 pour chaque pays.

Les chiffres entre parenthèses, précédés d'une étoile (★), indiquent la population de l'ensemble de la zone métropolitaine. Pour permettre d'établir des comparaisons significatives entre les zones métropolitaines, ces dernières ont été définies selon des critères uniformes par Rand McNally & Company (voir l'introduction à la table des zones métropolitaines). Parfois, les limites des zones métropolitaines ainsi définies diffèrent des limites officielles. Quand une ville fait partie de la zone métropolitaine d'une autre ville, le nom de celle-ci, précédé d'une étoile (★), est mis entre parenthèses. Le nom des capitales de pays est écrit en lettres MAJUSCULES.

TODOS OS CENTROS URBANOS de 50 000 habitantes e mais, bem como muitas outras cidades e vilas importantes ou muito conhecidas figuram na tabela que se apresenta em sequida. Os dados relativos à população referem-se a censos recentes (identificadas com a letra C), ou a estimativas oficiais (E) nas datas indicadas. Para algumas cidades só existem estimativas não oficiais (U). Para fins de comparabilidade, apresenta-se também a população total de cada país.

Para cada país, a data de referência da população total aplica-se também às cidades exceto quando especificado em contrário. As estimativas da população dos países para 1995 encontra-se na *Tabela de informaçoes mundiais.*

Um dado de população apresentado entre parênteses e precedido por uma estrela (★), refere-se à população de toda a área metropolitana. Para fins de comparabilidade, as áreas metropolitanas foram definidas por Rand McNally segundo regras coerentes (ver a 'Introdução' à *Tabela das áreas metropolitanas),* e em certos casos podem ser um pouco diferentes das áreas metropolitanas oficialmente reconhecidas. Quando um centro urbano esta localizado dentro dos limites da área metropolitana de outro, seu nome figura entre parênteses precedido por uma estrela (★). A capital de um país é indicada por letras MAIÚSCULAS.

AFGHANISTAN / Afghānestān	
1988 E	17,672,000
Herāt	177,300
Jalālābād (1982E)	58,000
• KĀBOL	1,424,400
Kondūz (1982E)	57,000
Mazār-e Sharīf	130,600
Qandahār	225,500
ALBANIA / Shqipëri	
1989 C	3,182,400
Durrës	82,700
Elbasan	80,700
Korçë	63,600
Shkodër	79,900
• TIRANË	238,100
Vlorë	71,700
ALGERIA / Algérie / Djazaïr	
1987 C	23,038,942
Aïn el Beïda	61,997
Aïn Oussera	44,270
Aïn Témouchent	47,479
Annaba (Bône)	305,526
Bab Ezzouar (★El Djazaïr)	55,211
Barika	56,488
Batna	181,601
Béchar	107,311
Bejaïa (Bougie)	114,534
Beskra	128,281
Bordj Bou Arreridj	84,264
Bordj el Kiffan (★El Djazaïr)	61,035
Boufarik	41,305
Bou Saâda	66,688
Ech Cheliff (Orléansville)	129,976
El Boulaïda	170,935
• EL DJAZAÏR (ALGIERS) (★2,547,983)	1,507,241
El Djelfa	84,207
El Eulma	67,933
El Wad	70,073
Ghardaïa	89,415
Ghilizane	80,091
Guelma	77,821
Jijel	62,793
Khemis	55,335
Khenchla	69,743
Laghouat	67,214
Lemdiyya	85,195
Maghniyya	52,275
Messaad	47,460
Mestghanem	114,037
Mouaskar	64,691
M'Sila	65,805
Qacentina	440,842
Saïda	80,825
Sidi bel Abbès	152,778
Skikda	128,747
Souq Ahras	83,015
Stif	170,182
Tbessa	107,559
Tihert	95,821
Tilimsen	126,882
Tizi-Ouzou	61,163
Touggourt	70,645
Wahran	628,558
Wargla	81,721
AMERICAN SAMOA / Amerika Samoa	
1990 C	46,773
• PAGO PAGO (▲14,295)	3,518
ANDORRA	
1991 E	54,507
• ANDORRA	20,437
ANGOLA	
1989 E	9,739,100
Benguela (1983E)	155,000
Huambo (Nova Lisboa) (1983E)	203,000
Lobito (1983E)	150,000
• LUANDA	1,459,900
Lubango (1984E)	95,915
Namibe (1981E)	100,000
ANGUILLA	
1984 C	6,680
South Hill	961
• THE VALLEY	1,042
ANTIGUA AND BARBUDA	
1977 E	72,000
• SAINT JOHN'S	24,359
ARGENTINA	
1991 C	32,608,560
Almirante Brown (★Buenos Aires)	448,762
Avellaneda (★Buenos Aires)	346,620
Bahía Blanca	255,145
Banda del Río Salí (★San Miguel de Tucumán)	50,282
Belén de Escobar (★Buenos Aires)	116,675
Berazategui (★Buenos Aires)	244,881
Berisso (★Buenos Aires)	72,703
• BUENOS AIRES (★11,000,000)	2,960,976
Campana (★Buenos Aires)	67,267
Caseros (Tres de Febrero) (★Buenos Aires)	349,221
Chimbas (★San Juan)	50,514
Comodoro Rivadavia	124,151
Concordia	116,491
Córdoba (★1,260,000)	1,148,305
Corrientes	257,766
Ensenada (★Buenos Aires)	47,192
Esteban Echeverría (★Buenos Aires)	274,303
Florencio Varela (★Buenos Aires)	249,006
Formosa	153,855
General San Martín (★Buenos Aires)	407,506
General Sarmiento (San Miguel) (★Buenos Aires)	646,891
Godoy Cruz (★Mendoza)	179,468
Gualeguaychú	64,620
Junín	70,138
Lanús (★Buenos Aires)	466,755
La Plata (★Buenos Aires)	520,449
La Rioja	104,494
Las Heras (★Mendoza)	145,823
Lomas de Zamora (★Buenos Aires)	572,769
Luján (★Mendoza)	54,241
Luján (★Buenos Aires)	66,226
Maipú (★Mendoza)	71,693
Mar del Plata	519,707
Mendoza (★770,000)	121,739
Mercedes	77,137
Merlo (★Buenos Aires)	386,304
Moreno (★Buenos Aires)	285,964
Morón (★Buenos Aires)	641,541
Necochea	59,775
Neuquén	167,076
Olavarría	72,821
Paraná	206,848
Pergamino	78,200
Pilar (★Buenos Aires)	113,428
Posadas	201,943
Presidencia Roque Sáenz Peña	64,476
Punta Alta	56,165
Quilmes (★Buenos Aires)	509,445
Rafaela	67,086
Resistencia (★291,083)	228,199
Río Cuarto	134,677
Río Gallegos	64,628
Rivadavia (★San Juan)	56,426
Rosario (★1,190,000)	894,645
Salta	367,099
San Carlos de Bariloche	77,750
San Fernando (★Buenos Aires)	141,496
San Fernando del Valle de Catamarca (★133,050)	110,269
San Francisco (★58,536)	55,828
San Isidro (★Buenos Aires)	299,022
San Juan (★353,476)	119,492
San Justo (★Buenos Aires)	1,111,811
San Lorenzo (▲130,242) (★Rosario)	38,509
San Luis	110,353
San Martín	64,821
San Miguel de Tucumán (★622,348)	470,604
San Nicolás de los Arroyos	114,752
San Rafael	94,776
San Salvador de Jujuy	181,318
Santa Fe (★394,888)	342,798
Santa Rosa	75,103
Santiago del Estero (★255,000)	189,490
San Vicente (★Buenos Aires)	74,890
Tandil	90,427
Tigre (★Buenos Aires)	253,748
Trelew	78,089
Venado Tuerto	58,678
Vicente López (★Buenos Aires)	289,142
Villa Krause (★San Juan)	83,266
Villa María	64,763
Villa Nueva (★Mendoza)	200,595
Zárate (▲91,820)	77,877
ARMENIA / Hayastan	
1989 C	3,283,000
Abovjan (1987E)	53,000
Ečmiadzin (★Jerevan) (1987E)	53,000
• JEREVAN (★1,315,000)	1,199,000
Kirovakan (1987E)	169,000
Kumajri	120,000
Razdan (1987E)	56,000
ARUBA	
1991 C	66,687
• ORANJESTAD	20,045
AUSTRALIA	
1991 C	16,850,330
Adelaide (★1,023,597)	14,843
Albury (★75,905)	40,154
Auburn (★Sydney)	48,566
Ballarat (★79,461)	34,501
Bankstown (★Sydney)	153,904
Bayswater (★Perth)	44,010
Bendigo (★67,315)	30,134
Berwick (★Melbourne)	69,144
Blacktown (★Sydney)	211,710
Blue Mountains (★Sydney)	69,420
Box Hill (★Melbourne)	45,139
Brisbane (★1,334,017)	751,115
Broadmeadows (★Melbourne)	102,996
Brunswick (★Melbourne)	39,886
Camberwell (★Melbourne)	83,799
Campbelltown (★Sydney)	137,879
CANBERRA (★303,846)	276,162
Canning (★Perth)	65,967
Canterbury (★Sydney)	129,232
Caulfield (★Melbourne)	67,776
Coburg (★Melbourne)	50,625
Cockburn (★Perth)	50,380
Coffs Harbour	51,520
Dandenong (★Melbourne)	57,275
Darwin (★78,400)	70,071
Doncaster (★Melbourne)	102,898
Enfield (★Adelaide)	61,502
Essendon (★Melbourne)	52,721

▲ Population of an entire municipality, commune, or district, including rural area.

• Largest city in country.
★ Population or designation of the metropolitan area, including suburbs.
C Census. E Official estimate.
U Unofficial estimate.

▲ Bevölkerung eines ganzen städtischen Verwaltungsgebietes, eines Kommunalbezirkes oder eines Distrikts, einschliesslich ländlicher Gebiete.
• Grösste Stadt des Landes.
★ Bevölkerung oder Bezeichnung der Stadtregion einschliesslich Vororte.
C Volkszählung. E Offizielle Schätzung.
U Inoffizielle Schätzung.

▲ Población de un municipio, comuna o distrito entero, incluyendo sus áreas rurales.

• Ciudad más grande de un país.
★ Población o designación de un área metropolitana, incluyendo los suburbios.
C Censo. E Estimado oficial.
U Estimado no oficial.

▲ Population d'une municipalité, d'une commune ou d'un district, zone rurale incluse.

• Ville la plus peuplée du pays.
★ Population de l'agglomération (ou nom de la zone métropolitaine englobante).
C Recensement. E Estimation officielle.
U Estimation non officielle.

▲ População de um municipio, comuna ou distrito, inclusive as respectivas áreas rurais.

• Maior cidade de um país.
★ População ou indicação de uma área metropolitana.
C Censo. E Estimativa oficial.
U Estimativa não oficial.

Fairfield (★Sydney)	175,099
Footscray (★Melbourne)	46,844
Frankston (★Melbourne)	84,986
Geelong (★145,325)	13,036
Gosford	128,956
Gosnells (★Perth)	69,560
Heidelberg (★Melbourne)	60,468
Hobart (★181,832)	47,106
Holroyd (★Sydney)	79,132
Hurstville (★Sydney)	63,757
Ipswich (★Brisbane)	73,299
Keilor (★Melbourne)	106,076
Knox (★Melbourne)	121,982
Kogarah (★Sydney)	46,518
Lake Macquarie (★Newcastle)	162,026
Launceston (★111,438)	66,747
Leichhardt (★Sydney)	58,484
Liverpool (★Sydney)	98,203
Logan (★Brisbane)	143,107
Mackay (★52,934)	23,052
Maitland	46,909
Malvern (★Melbourne)	41,340
Marion (★Adelaide)	73,942
Marrickville (★Sydney)	78,023
Melbourne (★3,022,439)	60,476
Melville (★Perth)	84,838
Mitcham (★Adelaide)	60,939
Moorabbin (★Melbourne)	94,161
Newcastle (★427,824)	131,305
Noarlunga (★Adelaide)	80,882
Northcote (★Melbourne)	46,547
North Sydney (★Sydney)	50,446
Nunawading (★Melbourne)	91,468
Oakleigh (★Melbourne)	55,151
Parramatta (★Sydney)	132,798
Penrith (★Sydney)	149,630
Perth (★1,143,249)	80,517
Prahran (★Melbourne)	42,193
Preston (★Melbourne)	76,996
Randwick (★Sydney)	115,349
Redcliffe (★Brisbane)	47,799
Rockdale (★Sydney)	84,074
Rockhampton (★62,787)	59,394
Ryde (★Sydney)	90,197
Saint Kilda (★Melbourne)	45,481
Salisbury (★Adelaide)	106,007
Shoalhaven	68,287
Southport (★268,662)	157,857
South Sydney (★Sydney)	77,818
Springvale (★Melbourne)	89,478
Stirling (★Perth)	172,731
Sunshine (★Melbourne)	94,020
• Sydney (★3,538,749)	13,501
Tea Tree Gully (★Adelaide)	83,969
Toowoomba	81,043
Townsville (★116,572)	87,288
Wagga Wagga	53,447
Wanneroo (★Perth)	167,873
Waverley (★Melbourne)	118,265
Waverley (★Sydney)	59,095
West Torrens (★Adelaide)	42,863
Willoughby (★Sydney)	51,503
Wollongong (★235,966)	211,417
Woodville (★Adelaide)	78,824
Woollahra (★Sydney)	49,904

AUSTRIA / Österreich

1991 C	7,795,786
Bruck an der Mur (★50,000)	14,046
Graz (★265,000)	237,810
Innsbruck (★200,000)	118,112
Klagenfurt (★118,000)	89,415
Leoben (★47,600)	28,897
Linz (★352,000)	203,044
Neunkirchen (★45,000)	10,216
Salzburg (★185,000)	143,978
Sankt Pölten (★69,500)	50,026
Steyr (★58,000)	39,337
Villach (★66,500)	54,640
Wels (★68,000)	52,594
• WIEN (VIENNA) (★1,900,000)	1,539,848

AZERBAIJAN / Azạrbaycan

1991 E	7,136,600
Äli Bayramlı	61,500
• BAKI (★2,020,000)	1,080,500
Gäncä	282,200
Mingäçevir	90,900
Naxçıvan	61,700
Şeki	63,200
Şumqayıt (★Bakı)	236,200
Xankändi (Stepanakert)	55,200

BAHAMAS

1990 C	254,685
Freeport (▲171,542)	28,200
• NASSAU	141,000

BAHRAIN / Al-Baḩrayn

1988 E	473,000
• AL-MANĀMAH (★273,000) (1986E)	82,700
Al-Muḩarraq (★Al-Manāmah)	78,000
Jidd Ḩafş (★Al-Manāmah)	48,000

BANGLADESH

1991 C	104,766,143
Barisāl	180,014
Begamganj (1981C)	69,623
Bhairab Bāzār	75,747
Bogra	93,114
Brāhmanbāria	84,067
Chāndpur	84,067
Chittagong (★2,342,662)	1,566,070
Chuādanga	65,222
Comilla (1981C)	184,132
• DHAKA (DACCA) (★6,537,308)	3,637,892
Dinājpur	136,657
Farīdpur	72,927
Gopālpur	45,174
Gulshan (★Dhaka) (1981C)	215,444
Jamālpur	108,416
Jessore	176,398
Jhenida	69,501
Khulna (★966,096)	601,051
Kishorganj	64,676
Kurīgrām	62,075
Kushtia	71,706
Mādārīpur	46,842
Mīrpur (★Dhaka) (1981C)	349,031
Mymensingh	138,662
Naogaon	109,156
Nārāyanganj (★Dhaka)	288,008
Narsinghdi	100,120
Nawābganj	131,260
Noākhāli	73,766
Pābna	113,146
Patuākhāli	50,344
Rājshāhi (★560,013)	324,532
Rangpur	220,849
Saidpur	110,494
Sātkhira	81,199
Sherpur	63,030
Sirājganj	100,003
Sītākunda (★Chittagong) (1981C)	237,520
Sylhet	114,284
Tangail	111,783
Tongi (★Dhaka)	165,099

BARBADOS

1990 C	260,491
• BRIDGETOWN (★125,000)	5,928

BELARUS / Belarus'

1991 E	10,260,400
Babrujsk	223,000
Baranavičy	166,700
Barysau̯	150,200
Brèst	277,000
Homel'	503,300
Hrodna	284,800
Kobryn	48,300
Lida	95,000
Mahilëu̯	363,000
Maladzečna	93,500
Mazyr	103,000
• MINSK (★1,694,000)	1,633,600
Navapolack	96,600
Orša	125,300
Pinsk	123,800
Polack	78,700
Rèčyca	69,400
Salihorsk	96,000
Sluck	60,100
Vicebsk	361,500
Žlobin	60,800
Žodzina	56,000

BELGIUM / België / Belgique

1991 C	9,978,681
Aalst (Alost) (★Bruxelles)	76,382
Anderlecht (★Bruxelles)	87,884
Antwerpen (★1,140,000)	467,518
Bastogne (▲12,187)	7,200
Brugge (Bruges) (★223,000)	117,063
• BRUXELLES (★2,385,000)	136,424
Charleroi (★480,000)	206,214
Etterbeek (★Bruxelles)	38,894
Forest (★Bruxelles)	46,437
Genk (★Hasselt)	61,339
Gent (Gand) (★467,000)	230,246
Hasselt (★295,000)	66,611
Ixelles (★Bruxelles)	72,610
Kortrijk (Courtrai) (★204,000)	76,141
La Louvière (★150,000)	76,432
Leuven (Louvain) (★178,000)	85,018
Liège (Luik) (★747,000)	194,596
Mechelen (Malines) (★122,000)	75,313
Molenbeek-St.-Jean (★Bruxelles)	68,759
Mons (Bergen) (★247,000)	91,726
Mouscron (★Lille, France)	53,513
Namur (★149,000)	130,443
Oostende (Ostende) (★124,000)	68,500
Roeselare (Roulers)	52,872
Saint-Gilles (★Bruxelles)	42,684
Schaerbeek (★Bruxelles)	102,702
Seraing (★Liège)	60,838
Sint-Niklaas (Saint-Nicolas)	68,203
Spa	10,140
Tournai (Doornik) (▲67,762)	45,400
Uccle (★Bruxelles)	73,721
Verviers (★104,000)	53,482
Waterloo (★Bruxelles)	27,860
Woluwe-Saint-Lambert (Sint-Lambrechts-Woluwe) (★Bruxelles)	47,963

BELIZE

1990 C	184,340
• Belize City	43,621
BELMOPAN	5,256

BENIN / Bénin

1984 E	3,825,000
Abomey	53,000
• COTONOU (1992C)	533,212
Parakou	92,000
PORTO-NOVO	164,000

BERMUDA

1991 C	58,460
• HAMILTON (★16,000)	1,100

BHUTAN / Druk-Yul

1982 E	1,333,000
• THIMPHU	12,000

BOLIVIA

1992 C	6,420,792
Cochabamba	407,825
El Alto (★La Paz)	405,492
• LA PAZ (★1,120,000)	713,378
Montero	52,021
Oruro	183,422
Potosí	112,078
Quillacollo	70,965
Riberalta	43,454
Santa Cruz de la Sierra	697,278
SUCRE	131,769
Tarija	90,113
Trinidad	57,328

BOSNIA AND HERZEGOVINA / Bosna i Hercegovina

1987 E	4,400,464
Banja Luka (▲193,890)	130,900
• SARAJEVO (▲479,688)	341,200
Tuzla (▲129,967)	67,300
Zenica (▲144,869)	67,500

BOTSWANA

1991 C	1,326,796
Francistown	65,244
• GABORONE	133,468
Selebi Phikwe	39,772

BRAZIL / Brasil

1991 C	146,917,459
Abaetetuba (▲100,016)	55,442
Abreu e Lima (▲76,568)	70,099
Alagoinhas (▲116,740)	97,819
Alegrete (▲78,879)	67,505
Almirante Tamandaré (▲66,090)	51,240
Altamira (▲120,441)	48,452
Alvorada (▲142,020) (★Porto Alegre)	132,582
Americana	153,592
Ananindeua (▲88,035)	73,941
Anápolis (▲239,047)	222,400
Anil (▲695,199)	81,879
Antônio Bezerra (▲1,765,794) (★Fortaleza)	193,682
Aparecida de Goiânia (▲178,326)	48,804
Apucarana (▲94,914)	80,048
Aracaju	401,676
Araçatuba (▲159,499)	146,977
Araguaína (▲103,396)	81,729
Araguari (▲91,202)	80,568
Arapiraca (▲165,379)	131,449
Arapongas (▲64,531)	59,996
Araraquara (▲166,732)	101,302
Araras (▲87,355)	79,002
Araucária (▲61,767)	53,522
Araxá	67,919
Assis (▲85,265)	72,004
Atibaia (▲86,193)	74,658
Avaré (▲61,063)	56,232
Bacabal (▲98,875)	64,844
Bagé (▲118,736)	89,372
Barbacena (▲99,895)	80,882
Barra Alegre (▲179,710)	58,445
Barra do Piraí (▲78,426)	59,202
Barra Mansa (▲171,671) (★Volta Redonda)	145,112
Barreiras (▲92,439)	70,701
Barreiros (▲139,318) (★Florianópolis)	58,694
Barretos (▲95,538)	88,935
Barueri (▲130,383)	66,722
Bauru	254,690
Bayeux (★João Pessoa)	77,047
Bebedouro (▲67,752)	60,792
Belém (★1,355,000)	765,476
Belford Roxo (▲1,293,611) (★Rio de Janeiro)	337,698
Belo Horizonte (★3,340,000)	1,529,566
Betim (★Belo Horizonte)	162,462
Birigui (▲75,054)	70,547
Blumenau (▲211,862)	185,200
Boa Vista (▲142,902)	118,958
Botucatu (▲90,620)	81,528
Bragança Paulista (▲108,602)	88,336
Brás Cubas (▲273,255)	65,538
BRASÍLIA	1,513,470
Brusque	53,438
Cabo (▲126,756)	68,594
Cabo Frio (▲84,635)	70,251
Caçapava (▲65,889)	58,145
Cáceres (▲77,475)	51,891
Cachoeira do Sul (▲89,148)	69,780
Cachoeirinha (★Porto Alegre)	87,976
Cachoeiro de Itapemirim (▲143,763)	112,099
Camaçari (▲113,615)	88,302
Camarajibe	99,431
Cambé (▲73,803)	66,767
Campina Grande	298,331
Campinas (★1,290,000)	759,032
Campo Comprido (▲1,313,094) (★Curitiba)	105,631
Campo Grande	516,403
Campo Mourão (▲82,280)	69,966
Campos (▲388,747)	277,482
Campos Elisios (▲665,343) (★Rio de Janeiro)	197,833
Candeias (▲67,936)	61,432
Canoas (★Porto Alegre)	269,234
Capuáva (▲615,112)	92,950
Carapicuíba (▲283,653) (★São Paulo)	207,264
Carapina (▲221,510) (★Vit2oria)	141,234
Carazinho (▲58,770)	49,010
Cariacica (▲274,455) (★Vitória)	91,888
Carpina (▲65,949)	50,962
Caruaru (▲213,573)	180,654
Cascatinha (▲255,261)	56,890
Cascavel (▲192,884)	175,332
Castanhal (▲101,963)	90,364
Catanduva	88,024
Caucaia (▲165,015) (★Fortaleza)	66,379
Cava (▲1,293,611)	59,506
Cavaleiro (▲486,774) (★Recife)	120,065
Caxias (▲146,730)	85,332
Caxias do Sul (▲290,969)	262,983
Chapecó (▲122,889)	93,697
Codó (▲111,679)	58,163
Coelho da Rocha (▲424,689) (★Rio de Janeiro)	152,045
Colatina (▲106,712)	71,094
Colombo (▲117,658) (★Curitiba)	110,161
Conselheiro Lafaiete (▲88,843)	82,619
Contagem (▲448,991) (★Belo Horizonte)	195,705
Corumbá (▲88,290)	75,235
Cotia (▲106,822)	90,469
Coxipó da Ponte (▲401,303)	140,130
Crato (▲91,413)	56,374
Criciúma (▲146,162)	99,375
Cruz Alta (▲68,784)	61,860
Cruzeiro	65,935
Cubatão (★Santos)	90,572
Cuiabá (▲401,303)	252,784
Curitiba (★1,815,000)	841,882
Diadema (★São Paulo)	305,068
Divinópolis (▲151,382)	141,984
Dourados (▲135,786)	116,817
Duque de Caxias (▲665,343) (★Rio de Janeiro)	325,903
Embu (★São Paulo)	155,851
Erechim (▲72,292)	61,509
Esteio (★Porto Alegre)	70,449
Eunápolis (▲70,561)	63,553
Feira de Santana (▲405,848)	340,034
Fernandópolis (▲56,125)	51,216
Ferraz de Vasconcelos (▲95,973) (★São Paulo)	65,319
Florianópolis (★420,000)	191,664
Formosa (▲62,974)	49,135
Fortaleza (★2,040,000)	743,335
Foz do Iguaçu	186,362
Franca	227,613
Francisco Morato	83,361
Franco da Rocha	79,534
Garanhuns (▲103,365)	86,593
Goiabeiras (▲258,243) (★Vitória)	74,086
Goiânia (★1,130,000)	912,136
Governador Valadares (▲230,403)	210,396
Gravatai (▲181,019) (★Porto Alegre)	166,954
Guaíba (▲83,119)	72,739
Guarapari (▲61,594)	54,994
Guarapuava (▲159,692)	107,046
Guaratinguetá (▲102,005)	84,660
Guarujá (▲209,814) (★Santos)	98,918
Guarulhos (▲786,355) (★São Paulo)	546,417
Gurupi (▲56,741)	51,005
Hortolândia (▲226,225)	78,011
Ibes (▲265,251) (★Vitória)	91,071
Icoraci (▲1,244,688) (★Belém)	67,458
Igapó (▲606,681)	117,251
Igarassu (▲79,713) (★Recife)	48,598
Ijuí (▲75,169)	58,627
Ilhéus (▲223,482)	135,117
Imbariê (▲665,343)	100,687
Imperatriz (▲276,440)	209,970
Indaiatuba (▲100,816)	91,752
Inhomirim (▲191,249)	76,031
Ipatinga (★179,710)	120,025
Ipiíba (▲778,831) (★Rio de Janeiro)	121,785
Itabira (▲85,284)	71,287
Itaboraí (▲161,398)	72,410
Itabuna (▲185,165)	170,434
Itaituba (▲116,541)	62,278
Itajaí	114,558
Itajubá (▲74,618)	68,469
Itambi (▲161,398)	48,891
Itapecerica da Serra (▲92,854) (★São Paulo)	84,479
Itaperuna (▲78,017)	55,484
Itapetininga (▲105,071)	84,703
Itapeva (▲81,858)	55,658
Itapevi (★São Paulo)	107,983
Itaquaquecetuba (★São Paulo)	164,665
Itaquari (▲274,455) (★Vitória)	169,145
Itatiba (▲61,587)	54,044
Itaúna	61,891
Itú (▲107,176)	88,838
Ituiutaba (▲84,581)	78,211
Itumbiara (▲79,457)	68,673
Jaboatão (▲486,774) (★Recife)	81,178
Jaboticabal (▲59,130)	53,027
Jacareí (▲163,843)	144,141
Jandira	62,573
Japeri (▲1,293,611)	65,576
Jaraguá do Sul (▲76,994)	62,578
Jardim Presidente Dutra (▲786,355) (★São Paulo)	229,987
Jataí (▲65,921)	53,431
Jaú (▲94,138)	80,331
Jequié (▲144,572)	114,542
Ji-Paraná (▲97,719)	75,384
João Monlevade	57,413
João Pessoa (★670,000)	497,308
Joinvile	326,208
Juàzeiro (▲128,691) (★Petrolina)	95,676
Juazeiro do Norte	163,527
Juiz de Fora	377,538
Jundiaí (▲288,644)	265,599
Jurema (▲165,015) (★Fortaleza)	75,463
Justinópolis (▲143,696) (★Belo Horizonte)	85,452
Lages (▲151,100)	137,169
Lavras (▲65,857)	60,690
Leme	64,525
Limeira (▲207,416)	177,591
Linhares (▲119,501)	73,082
Lins (▲59,218)	54,868
Londrina (▲389,959)	355,062
Lorena (▲73,167)	67,766
Luziânia (▲207,425)	194,128
Macaé (▲100,642)	57,581
Macapá (▲179,252)	146,523
Maceió (▲628,241)	554,727
Manaus	1,005,634
Marabá (▲122,231)	102,364
Marília (▲160,872)	144,906
Maringá	225,516
Matão	59,694
Mauá (★São Paulo)	294,631
Mesquita (▲1,293,611) (★Rio de Janeiro)	141,326
Messejana (▲1,765,794) (★Fortaleza)	229,507
Moji das Cruzes (▲273,255) (★São Paulo)	138,995
Mojiguaçu (▲107,440)	92,440
Mojimirim (▲64,750)	57,395
Mondubim (▲1,765,794) (★Fortaleza)	331,591
Monjolo (▲778,831) (★Rio de Janeiro)	137,974
Montes Claros (▲249,565)	223,046
Mossoró (▲191,959)	177,020
Muriaé (▲84,507)	65,406
Muribeca dos Guararapes (▲486,774) (★Recife)	217,905
Natal (▲606,681)	459,827
Neves (▲778,831) (★Rio de Janeiro)	151,087
Nilópolis (▲157,936) (★Rio de Janeiro)	104,671
Niterói (▲435,658) (★Rio de Janeiro)	400,586
Nossa Senhora do Socorro	67,443
Nova Brasilia (▲178,326) (★Goiânia)	126,701
Nova Friburgo (▲166,975)	111,020
Nova Iguaçu (▲1,293,611) (★Rio de Janeiro)	562,062
Nova Veneza (▲226,225)	82,203
Novo Hamburgo (★Porto Alegre)	201,334
Novo Mundo (▲1,313,094) (★Curitiba)	71,508
Olinda (▲157,936)	53,265
Olinda (★Recife)	341,059
Osasco (★São Paulo)	566,949
Ourinhos (▲76,912)	70,690
Palhoça (▲68,298) (★Florianópolis)	58,097
Paracatu (▲62,709)	49,656
Pará de Minas (▲61,066)	51,679
Paranaguá (▲107,601)	88,110
Paranavaí (▲71,173)	61,043
Parangaba (▲1,765,794) (★Fortaleza)	267,679
Parnaíba (▲127,992)	105,131
Parnamirim (▲63,253)	48,534
Parque Industrial (▲448,991) (★Belo Horizonte)	223,660
Passo do Sabão (▲169,079) (★Porto Alegre)	63,140
Passo Fundo (▲147,239)	135,158
Passos (▲84,618)	74,218
Patos (▲81,292)	76,378
Patos de Minas (▲102,766)	83,670

▲ Population of an entire municipality, commune, or district, including rural area.
• Largest city in country.
★ Population or designation of the metropolitan area, including suburbs.
C Census. **E** Official estimate. **U** Unofficial estimate.

▲ Bevölkerung eines ganzen städtischen Verwaltungsgebietes, eines Kommunalbezirkes oder eines Distrikts, einschliesslich ländlicher Gebiete.
• Grösste Stadt des Landes.
★ Bevölkerung oder Bezeichnung der Stadtregion einschliess-lich Vororte.
C Volkszählung. **E** Offizielle Schätzung. **U** Inoffizielle Schätzung.

Population of Cities and Towns / Einwohnerzahlen von Grossstädten / Habitantes en las Ciudades y Poblaciones
Population des Grands Centres et des Villes / População dos Centros Urbanos 303

Paulista (▲211,017) (★Recife)	53,566
Paulo Afonso (▲86,594)	74,326
Pelotas (▲290,660)	260,510
Petrolina (★300,000)	123,857
Petrópolis (▲255,261) (★Rio de Janeiro)	164,849
Pindamonhangaba (▲101,849)	71,449
Pinhais (▲106,764) (★Curitiba)	71,973
Pinheirinho (▲1,313,094) (★Curitiba)	117,518
Piracicaba (▲283,634)	223,170
Poá (★São Paulo)	72,151
Poços de Caldas	105,223
Ponta Grossa	219,955
Porto Alegre (★2,850,000)	1,247,352
Porto Velho (▲161,611)	56,973
Porto Velho (▲286,471)	226,196
Pouso Alegre (▲81,776)	73,875
Praia da Conceição (▲211,017) (★Recife)	97,635
Praia Grande (▲123,494)	97,173
Presidente Prudente	157,618
Queimados (▲1,293,611) (★Rio de Janeiro)	124,121
Recife (★2,880,000)	1,296,995
Resende (▲91,605)	52,261
Ribeirão Pires	62,240
Ribeirão Preto	416,486
Rio Branco (▲196,871)	136,457
Rio Claro	130,364
Rio de Janeiro (★11,050,000)	5,473,909
Rio Grande (▲172,408)	157,608
Rio Verde (▲95,894)	76,818
Rondonópolis (▲126,082)	87,307
Salto	72,076
Salvador (★2,340,000)	2,070,296
Santa Bárbara d'Oeste	141,230
Santa Cruz do Sul (▲117,779)	74,295
Santa Felicidade (▲1,313,094) (★Curitiba)	53,560
Santa Inês (▲64,655)	54,006
Santa Maria (▲217,604)	193,294
Santana do Livramento (▲80,145)	72,950
Santarém (▲264,779)	168,153
Santa Rita (▲94,412) (★João Pessoa)	74,396
Santa Rosa (▲58,262)	48,211
Santo André (▲615,112) (★São Paulo)	518,272
Santo Ângelo (▲76,461)	59,688
Santos (★1,165,000)	415,554
São Benedito (▲137,686) (★Belo Horizonte)	91,733
São Bernardo do Campo (★São Paulo)	550,030
São Borja (▲63,766)	52,493
São Caetano do Sul (★São Paulo)	149,203
São Carlos (▲158,186)	100,502
São Cristóvão	46,172
São Gabriel (▲59,024)	47,668
São Gonçalo (▲778,831) (★Rio de Janeiro)	296,021
São João da Boa Vista (▲69,090)	60,845
São João del-Rei (▲72,741)	63,680
São João de Meriti (▲424,689) (★Rio de Janeiro)	220,742
São José do Rio Preto	263,454
São José dos Campos (▲442,009)	385,879
São José dos Pinhais (▲128,170) (★Curitiba)	99,154
São Leopoldo (★Porto Alegre)	160,228
São Lourenco da Mata (▲85,889) (★Recife)	68,479
São Luís (★710,000)	164,334
São Mateus (▲424,689)	51,902
• São Paulo (★16,925,000)	9,393,753
São Vicente (★Santos)	268,467
Sapiranga (▲58,522)	51,387
Sapucaia do Sul (★Porto Alegre)	104,626
Serra (▲221,510)	62,398
Sertãozinho (▲78,753)	68,874
Sete Lagoas	139,910
Sete Pontes (▲778,831) (★Rio de Janeiro)	71,984
Sobral (▲127,459)	92,805
Sorocaba	348,952
Sumaré (▲226,225)	64,673
Susano (▲159,142) (★São Paulo)	110,414
Taboão da Serra (★São Paulo)	159,894
Tatuí (▲76,662)	68,808
Taubaté (▲206,416)	185,790
Teixeira de Freitas (▲85,227)	73,107
Telêmaco Borba (▲64,854)	50,774
Teófilo Otoni (▲140,676)	96,382
Teresina (★665,000)	556,073
Teresópolis (▲120,712)	96,516
Timon (▲107,394) (★Teresina)	90,577
Timóteo (▲58,393)	48,340
Toledo (▲94,857)	67,343
Três Corações (▲57,053)	49,138
Três Lagoas (▲68,067)	60,716
Três Rios (▲81,163)	60,201
Tubarão (▲95,058)	83,262
Tupã (▲61,290)	53,282
Ubá (▲66,422)	52,673
Uberaba (▲211,358)	198,565
Uberlândia	255,191
Umbará (▲1,313,094) (★Curitiba)	64,523
Umuarama (▲100,185)	66,995
Uruguaiana (▲117,437)	103,160
Valinhos (▲67,867)	59,896
Varginha (▲88,045)	82,263
Várzea Grande (▲161,611)	96,379
Várzea Paulista	67,911
Venda Nova (▲2,017,127) (★Belo Horizonte)	481,470
Viamão (▲169,079)	75,782
Vicente de Carvalho (▲209,814) (★Santos)	110,881
Vila Dirce (▲283,653)	59,144
Vila Velha (▲265,251) (★Vitória)	113,664
Vila Xavier (▲166,732)	50,922
Vitória (★810,000)	184,157
Vitória da Conquista (▲224,896)	179,868
Vitória de Santo Antão (▲106,661)	84,116
Volta Redonda (★430,000)	219,988
Votorantim	79,150
Votuporanga (▲66,037)	59,604

BRITISH VIRGIN ISLANDS

1980 C	12,034
• ROAD TOWN	2,479

BRUNEI

1981 C	192,832
• BANDAR SERI BEGAWAN (★64,000)	22,777
Seria	23,415

BULGARIA / Bâlgarija

1992 C	8,487,317
Asenovgrad	52,360
Blagoevgrad	71,476
Burgas	195,686
Dimitrovgrad	50,677
Dobrič	104,494
Gabrovo	76,522
Haskovo	80,700
Jambol	91,497
Kărdžali	45,793
Kazanlăk	60,095
Kjustendil	54,431
Loveč	48,242
Montana	52,476
Pazardžik	82,578
Pernik	90,549
Pleven	130,812
Plovdiv	341,058
Razgrad	40,933
Ruse	170,038
Silistra	48,360
Sliven	106,212
• SOFIJA (★1,280,000)	1,190,126
Ştara Zagora	150,518
Šumen	93,390
Varna	308,432
Veliko Tărnovo	67,540
Vidin	62,691
Vraca	75,518

BURKINA FASO

1985 C	7,964,705
Bobo Dioulasso	228,668
Koudougou	51,926
• OUAGADOUGOU	441,514
Ouahigouya	38,902

BURUNDI

1990 C	5,356,266
• BUJUMBURA	226,628

CAMBODIA / Kâmpŭchéa

1990 E	8,567,582
Bătdâmbâng	94,412
Kâmpóng Şaôm	67,452
• PHNUM PÉNH	620,000
Prey Vêng	41,456
Siĕmréab	76,434
Ta Khmau	34,947

CAMEROON / Cameroun

1987 C	9,312,429
Bafoussam	92,331
Bamenda	95,445
• Douala	712,251
Edéa	45,555
Fort-Foureau	48,620
Foumban	46,920
Garoua	122,584
Kumba	63,911
Maroua	111,630
Ngaoundéré	69,682
Nkongsamba	76,887
YAOUNDÉ	560,785

CANADA

1991 C	27,296,859

CANADA: ALBERTA

1991 C	2,545,553
Calgary (★754,033)	710,677
Edmonton (★839,924)	616,741
Lethbridge	60,974
Medicine Hat (★52,681)	43,625
Red Deer	58,134

CANADA: BRITISH COLUMBIA

1991 C	3,282,061
Burnaby (★Vancouver)	158,858
Chilliwack (★60,251)	49,531
Coquitlam (★Vancouver)	84,021
Delta (★Vancouver)	88,978
Kamloops (★67,856)	67,057
Kelowna (★111,846)	75,950
Nanaimo (★73,547)	60,129
Prince George	69,653
Richmond (★Vancouver)	126,624
Saanich (★Victoria)	95,577
Surrey (★Vancouver)	245,173
Vancouver (★1,602,502)	471,844
Victoria (★287,897)	71,228

CANADA: MANITOBA

1991 C	1,091,942
Winnipeg (★652,354)	616,790

CANADA: NEW BRUNSWICK

1991 C	723,900
Fredericton (★71,869)	46,466
Moncton (★106,503)	57,010
Saint John (★124,981)	74,969

CANADA: NEWFOUNDLAND

1991 C	568,474
Saint John's (★171,859)	95,770

CANADA: NORTHWEST TERRITORIES

1991 C	57,649
Yellowknife	15,179

CANADA: NOVA SCOTIA

1991 C	899,942
Dartmouth (★Halifax)	67,798
Halifax (★320,501)	114,455
Sydney (★116,100)	26,063

CANADA: ONTARIO

1991 C	10,084,885
Ajax (★Toronto)	57,350
Barrie (★92,165)	62,728
Brampton (★Toronto)	234,445
Brantford (★97,106)	81,997
Burlington (★Hamilton)	129,575
Cambridge (Galt) (★Kitchener)	92,772
Cornwall (★53,545)	47,137
East York (★Toronto)	102,696
Etobicoke (★Toronto)	309,993
Gloucester (★Ottawa)	101,677
Guelph (★97,213)	87,976
Hamilton (★599,760)	318,499
Kingston (★136,401)	56,597
Kitchener (★356,421)	168,282
Leamington (★35,792)	14,182
London (★381,522)	303,165
Markham (★Toronto)	153,811
Mississauga (★Toronto)	463,388
Nepean (★Ottawa)	107,627
Newcastle	49,479
Niagara Falls (★Saint Catharines)	75,399
North Bay (★63,285)	55,405
North York (★Toronto)	562,564
Oakville (★Toronto)	114,670
Oshawa (★240,104)	129,344
OTTAWA (★920,857)	313,987
Peterborough (★98,060)	68,371
Pickering (★Toronto)	68,631
Richmond Hill (★Toronto)	80,142
Saint Catharines (★364,552)	129,300
Sarnia (★87,870)	74,376
Sault Sainte Marie (★101,800)	81,476
Scarborough (★Toronto)	524,598
Stoney Creek (★Hamilton)	49,968
Sudbury (★157,613)	92,884
Thunder Bay (★124,427)	113,946
• Toronto (★3,893,046)	635,395
Vaughan (★Toronto)	111,359
Waterloo (★Kitchener)	71,181
Whitby (★Oshawa)	61,281
Windsor (★262,075)	191,435
York (★Toronto)	140,525

CANADA: PRINCE EDWARD ISLAND

1991 C	129,765
Charlottetown (★57,472)	15,396

CANADA: QUÉBEC

1991 C	6,895,963
Beauport (★Québec)	69,158
Brossard (★Montréal)	64,793
Charlesbourg (★Québec)	70,788
Chicoutimi (★160,928)	62,670
Drummondville (★60,092)	35,462
Gatineau (★Ottawa)	92,284
Hull (★Ottawa)	60,707
Jonquière (★Chicoutimi)	57,933
La Salle (★Montréal)	73,804
Laval (★Montréal)	314,398
Lévis (★Québec)	39,452
Longueuil (★Montréal)	129,874
Montréal (★3,127,242)	1,017,666
Montréal-Nord (★Montréal)	85,516
Pierrefonds (★Montréal)	48,735
Québec (★645,550)	167,517
Repentigny (★Montréal)	49,630
Sainte-Foy (★Québec)	71,133
Saint-Hubert (★Montréal)	74,027
Saint-Jean-sur-Richelieu (★68,378)	37,607
Saint-Laurent (★Montréal)	72,402
Saint-Léonard (★Montréal)	73,120
Shawinigan (★61,672)	19,931
Sherbrooke (★139,194)	76,429
Trois-Rivières (★136,303)	49,426
Verdun (★Montréal)	61,307

CANADA: SASKATCHEWAN

1991 C	988,928
Regina (★191,692)	179,178
Saskatoon (★210,023)	186,058

CANADA: YUKON

1991 C	27,797
Whitehorse	17,925

CAPE VERDE / Cabo Verde

1990 C	341,491
Mindelo	47,109
• PRAIA	61,644

CAYMAN ISLANDS

1989 C	25,355
• GEORGE TOWN	12,921

CENTRAL AFRICAN REPUBLIC / République centrafricaine

1989 E	2,841,000
Bambari	52,100
• BANGUI	596,800
Berbérati	45,400
Bouar	49,200

CHAD / Tchad

1993 C	6,288,261
Abéché	55,715
Moundou	99,607
• N'DJAMENA	546,572
Sarh	77,605

CHILE

1992 C	13,348,401
Antofagasta	225,316
Arica	161,333
Calama	103,970
Chillán	145,759
Concepción (★735,000)	326,784
Copiapó	98,188
Coquimbo	110,879
Coronel (★Concepción)	79,677
Curicó	77,733
Iquique	145,139
La Serena	109,293
Linares	59,658
Los Ángeles	94,716
Lota (★Concepción)	50,123
Osorno	114,239
Ovalle	53,515
Puente Alto (★Santiago)	254,127
Puerto Montt	110,139
Punta Arenas	109,110
Quilpué (★Valparaíso)	102,233
Rancagua	179,638
San Antonio	74,742
San Bernardo (★Santiago)	179,398
• SANTIAGO (★4,740,000)	4,295,593
Talca	15,971
Talcahuano (★Concepción)	244,034
Temuco	210,587
Valdivia	112,712
Vallenar	42,725
Valparaíso (★690,000)	274,228
Villa Alemana (★Valparaíso)	70,663
Viña del Mar (★Valparaíso)	303,589

CHINA / Zhongguo

1994 E	1,185,170,000
Abagnar Qi (▲100,700) (1986E)	71,700
Acheng (1985E)	100,304
Aihui (▲135,000) (1986E)	76,700
Aksu (▲345,900) (1986E)	143,100
Altay (▲141,700) (1986E)	62,800
Anci (Langfang) (▲522,800) (1986E)	122,100
Anda (▲425,500) (1986E)	130,200
Ankang (1985E)	89,188
Anqing (▲433,900) (1986E)	213,200
Anshan (1988E)	1,330,000
Anshun (▲214,700) (1986E)	128,800
Anyang (▲541,900) (1986E)	361,200
Baicheng (▲282,000) (1986E)	198,600
Baiquan (1985E)	50,996
Baiyin (▲301,900) (1986E)	157,100
Baoding (▲535,100) (1986E)	423,200
Baoji (▲359,500) (1986E)	286,200
Baoshan (▲688,400) (1986E)	52,300
Baotou (Paotow) (1988E)	1,130,000
Baoying (1985E)	50,479
Bei'an (▲440,500) (1986E)	199,500
Beihai (▲175,900) (1986E)	119,000
BEIJING (PEKING) (★7,320,000)	6,690,000
Beipiao (▲603,700) (1986E)	180,900
Bengbu (▲612,600) (1986E)	403,900
Benxi (Penhsi) (1988E)	860,000
Bijie (1985E)	54,871
Binxian (▲177,900) (1986E)	86,700
Binxian (1982C)	127,326
Boli (1985E)	61,990
Bose (▲271,400) (1986E)	82,000
Boshan (1975U)	100,000
Boxian (1985E)	63,222
Boxing (1982C)	57,554
Boyang (1985E)	60,688
Butha Qi (Zalantun) (▲389,500) (1986E)	111,300
Cangshan (Bianzhuang) (1982C)	79,334
Cangzhou (▲293,600) (1986E)	196,700
Changchun	2,470,000
Changde (▲220,800) (1986E)	178,200
Changge (1982C)	67,002
Changji (▲233,400) (1986E)	110,500
Changqing (1982C)	65,094
Changsha	1,510,000
Changshou (1985E)	51,923
Changshu (▲998,000) (1986E)	281,300
Changtu (1985E)	49,937
Changyi (1982C)	64,513
Changzhi (▲463,400) (1986E)	273,000
Changzhou (Changchow) (1986E)	522,700
Chao'an (▲1,214,500) (1986E)	265,400
Chaoxian (▲739,500) (1986E)	116,800
Chaoyang, Guangdong prov. (1985E)	85,968
Chaoyang, Liaoning prov. (▲318,900) (1986E)	180,300
Chengde (▲330,400) (1986E)	226,600
Chengdu (Chengtu)	2,760,000
Chenghai (1985E)	50,631
Chenxian (▲191,900) (1986E)	143,500
Chifeng (Ulanhad) (▲882,900) (1986E)	299,000
Chongqing (Chungking)	3,870,000
Chuxian (▲365,000) (1986E)	113,300
Chuxiong (▲379,400) (1986E)	67,700
Da'an (1985E)	70,552
Dachangzhen (1975U)	50,000
Dalian (Dairen)	2,400,000
Dandong (1986E)	579,800
Daqing (▲880,000) (1988E)	640,000
Dashiqiao (1985E)	68,898
Datong (1985E)	55,529
Datong (▲1,040,000) (1988E)	810,000
Dawa (1985E)	142,581
Daxian (▲209,400) (1986E)	142,000
Dehui (1985E)	60,247
Dengfeng (1982C)	49,746
Deqing (1982C)	48,726
Deyang (▲753,400) (1986E)	184,800
Dezhou (▲276,200) (1986E)	161,300
Didao (1975U)	50,000
Dinghai (1985E)	50,161
Dongchuan (Xincun) (▲275,100) (1986E)	67,400
Dongguan (▲1,208,500) (1986E)	254,900
Dongsheng (▲121,300) (1986E)	57,500
Dongtai (1985E)	65,788
Dongying (▲514,400) (1986E)	178,100
Dukou (▲551,200) (1986E)	380,200
Dunhua (▲448,000) (1986E)	217,100
Duyun (▲386,600) (1986E)	123,800
Echeng (▲938,000) (1986E)	217,400
Enshi (▲679,000) (1986E)	84,300
Erenhot (1986E)	7,200
Ergun Zuoqi (1985E)	55,970
Feixian (1982C)	73,246
Fengcheng (1985E)	66,745
Foshan (▲312,700) (1986E)	243,500
Fujin (1985E)	60,948
Fuling (▲973,500) (1986E)	166,300
Fushun (Funan) (1988E)	1,290,000
Fuxian (Wafangdian) (▲960,700) (1986E)	246,200
Fuxin (1988E)	700,000
Fuyang (▲195,200) (1986E)	143,400
Fuyu, Heilongjiang prov. (1985E)	48,670
Fuyu, Jilin prov. (1985E)	98,373
Fuzhou, Fujian prov.	1,380,000
Fuzhou, Jiangxi prov. (▲171,800) (1986E)	106,700
Gaixian (1985E)	67,587
Ganhe (1985E)	48,128
Ganzhou (▲346,000) (1986E)	191,600
Gaoqing (Tianzhen) (1982C)	70,411
Gaoyou (1985E)	57,844
Gejiu (Kokiu) (▲341,700) (1986E)	193,600
Golmud (1986E)	60,300
Gongchangling (1982C)	49,281
Guanghua (▲420,000) (1986E)	104,400
Guangyuan (▲805,500) (1986E)	162,200
Guangzhou (Canton)	3,750,000
Guanxian, Shandong prov. (1982C)	49,782
Guanxian, Sichuan prov. (1985E)	65,039
Guilin (Kweilin) (▲457,500) (1986E)	324,200

▲ Población de un municipio, comuna o distrito entero, incluyendo sus áreas rurales.
• Ciudad más grande de un país.
★ Población o designación de un área metropolitana, incluyendo los suburbios.
C Censo. **E** Estimado oficial. **U** Estimado no oficial.

▲ Population d'une municipalité, d'une commune ou d'un district, zone rurale incluse.
• Ville la plus peuplée du pays.
★ Population de l'agglomération (ou nom de la zone métropolitaine englobante).
C Recensement. **E** Estimation officielle. **U** Estimation non officielle.

▲ População de um municipio, comuna ou distrito, inclusive as respectivas áreas rurais.
• Maior cidade de um país.
★ População ou indicação de uma área metropolitana.
C Censo. **E** Estimativa oficial. **U** Estimativa não oficial.

Guixian (1985E)	61,970
Guiyang (Kweiyang)	1,080,000
Haicheng (▲984,800) (1986E)	210,700
Haifeng (1985E)	50,401
Haikou	340,000
Hailar (▲163,549) (1986E)	180,000
Hailin (1985E)	58,909
Hailong (Meihekou) (▲534,200) (1986E)	117,500
Hailun (1985E)	83,448
Haiyang (Dongcun) (1982C)	77,098
Hami (Kumul) (▲270,300) (1986E)	146,400
Hancheng (▲304,200) (1986E)	66,600
Handan (▲1,030,000) (1988E)	870,000
Hangu (1975U)	100,000
Hangzhou (Hangchow)	1,790,000
Hanzhong (▲415,000) (1986E)	151,700
Harbin	3,120,000
Hebi (▲321,600) (1986E)	158,500
Hechi (▲266,800) (1986E)	74,400
Hechuan (1985E)	65,237
Hefei	1,110,000
Hegang (1986E)	588,300
Helong (1985E)	62,665
Hengshui (▲286,500) (1986E)	83,100
Hengyang (▲601,300) (1986E)	419,200
Heshan (▲109,600) (1986E)	42,000
Heze (Caozhou) (▲1,001,500) (1986E)	115,400
Hohhot	730,000
Hongjiang (▲67,000) (1986E)	54,300
Horqin Youyi Qianqi (Ulan Hot) (▲192,100) (1986E)	129,100
Hotan (▲122,800) (1986E)	71,700
Houma (▲158,500) (1986E)	67,000
Huadian (1985E)	75,183
Huai'an (1985E)	65,673
Huaibei (▲447,200) (1986E)	252,100
Huaide (▲899,400) (1986E)	187,600
Huaihua (▲427,100) (1986E)	102,000
Huainan (▲1,110,000) (1988E)	700,000
Huaiyin (Wangying) (▲382,500) (1986E)	201,700
Huanan (1985E)	66,596
Huanggang (1982C)	65,961
Huangshi (1986E)	451,900
Huayun (Huarong) (▲313,500) (1986E)	81,000
Huinan (Chaoyang) (1985E)	52,429
Huizhou (▲182,100) (1986E)	117,000
Hulan (1985E)	74,989
Hunjiang (Badaojiang) (▲687,700) (1986E)	442,600
Huzhou (▲964,400) (1986E)	208,500
Jiading (1985E)	60,718
Jiamusi (Kiamusze) (▲557,700) (1986E)	429,800
Ji'an (▲184,300) (1986E)	132,200
Jiangling (1985E)	77,887
Jiangmen (▲231,700) (1986E)	168,800
Jiangyin (1985E)	66,476
Jiangyou (1985E)	72,663
Jian'ou (1985E)	55,180
Jiaohe (1985E)	51,504
Jiaojiang (▲385,200) (1986E)	82,300
Jiaoxian (1985E)	51,869
Jiaozuo (▲509,900) (1986E)	335,400
Jiawang (1975U)	50,000
Jiaxing (▲686,500) (1986E)	210,200
Jiayuguan (▲102,100) (1986E)	73,800
Jiexiu (1985E)	51,300
Jieyang (1985E)	98,531
Jilin (Kirin) (1988E)	1,200,000
Jinan (Tsinan)	2,150,000
Jinchang (Baijiazui) (▲136,000) (1986E)	90,500
Jincheng (▲612,700) (1986E)	99,900
Jingdezhen (Kingtechen) (▲569,700) (1986E)	304,000
Jingmen (▲946,500) (1986E)	227,000
Jinhua (▲799,900) (1986E)	147,800
Jining, Nei Monggol prov. (1986E)	163,300
Jining, Shandong prov. (▲765,700) (1986E)	222,600
Jinshi (▲219,700) (1986E)	73,700
Jinxi (▲634,300) (1986E)	223,100
Jinxian (1985E)	95,761
Jinzhou (Chinchou) (▲810,000) (1988E)	710,000
Jishou (▲194,500) (1986E)	59,500
Jishu (1985E)	75,587
Jiujiang (▲382,300) (1986E)	248,500
Jiulong (Kowloon) (★Xianggang) (1986C)	774,781
Jiuquan (Suzhou) (▲269,900) (1986E)	56,300
Jiutai (1985E)	63,021
Jixi (▲820,000) (1988E)	700,000
Jixian (1985E)	59,725
Juancheng (1982C)	54,110
Junan (Shizilu) (1982C)	90,222
Junxian (▲423,400) (1986E)	97,000
Juxian (1982C)	51,666
Kaifeng (▲629,100) (1986E)	458,800
Kaili (▲342,100) (1986E)	96,600
Kaiping (1985E)	54,145
Kaiyuan (▲342,100) (1986E)	96,600
Kaiyuan (1985E)	85,762
Karamay (▲168,868) (1986E)	185,300
Kashi (▲194,500) (1986E)	146,300
Keshan (1985E)	65,088
Korla (▲219,000) (1986E)	129,400
Kunming	1,500,000
Kunshan (1985E)	44,645
Kuytun (1986E)	60,200
Kwai Chung (★Xianggang) (1986C)	131,362
Laiwu (▲1,041,800) (1986E)	143,500
Langxiang (1985E)	64,658
Lanxi (1985E)	53,236
Lanxi (▲606,800) (1986E)	70,500
Lanzhou (Lanchow)	1,340,000
Lechang (1986E)	56,913
Lengshuijiang (▲277,600) (1986E)	101,700
Lengshuitan (▲362,000) (1986E)	60,900
Leshan (▲972,300) (1986E)	307,300
Lhasa (▲107,700) (1986E)	84,400
Lianyungang (Xinpu) (▲459,400) (1986E)	288,000
Liaocheng (▲724,300) (1986E)	119,000
Liaoyang (▲576,900) (1986E)	442,600
Liaoyuan (1986E)	370,400
Liling (▲856,300) (1986E)	107,100
Linfen (▲530,100) (1986E)	157,600
Lingling (▲515,300) (1986E)	72,700
Lingyuan (1985E)	66,825
Linhai (1985E)	52,653
Linhe (▲365,900) (1986E)	99,800
Linkou (1985E)	52,936
Linqing (▲603,000) (1986E)	87,000
Linqu (1982C)	84,196
Linxia (▲150,200) (1986E)	72,900
Linyi (▲1,365,000) (1986E)	190,000
Liuzhou (1988E)	680,000
Longjiang (1985E)	51,156
Longyan (▲378,500) (1986E)	114,500
Loudi (▲254,300) (1986E)	84,200
Lu'an (▲163,400) (1986E)	122,600
Lufeng (1985E)	53,015
Luohe (▲159,100) (1986E)	102,300
Luoyang (Loyang) (▲1,090,000) (1988E)	760,000
Luzhou (▲360,300) (1986E)	237,800
Ma'anshan (▲367,000) (1986E)	258,900
Manzhouli (1986E)	116,600
Maoming (▲434,900) (1986E)	118,600
Meixian (▲740,600) (1986E)	169,000
Mengyin (1982C)	70,602
Mianyang (▲848,500) (1986E)	233,900
Minhang (1975U)	60,000
Mishan (1985E)	54,919
Mixian (1982C)	64,776
Mudanjiang (1988E)	650,000
Nahe (1985E)	49,725
N'aizishen (1985E)	51,982
Nancha (1975U)	50,000
Nanchang	1,440,000
Nanchong (▲238,100) (1986E)	158,000
Nanjing (Nanking)	2,490,000
Nanning	960,000
Nanpiao (1982C)	67,274
Nanping (▲420,800) (1986E)	157,100
Nantong (▲411,000) (1986E)	308,800
Nanyang (▲294,800) (1986E)	199,400
Neihuang (1982C)	56,039
Neijiang (▲298,500) (1986E)	191,100
Ning'an (1985E)	49,334
Ningbo	1,100,000
Ningyang (1982C)	55,424
Nong'an (1985E)	55,966
Nunjiang (1985E)	59,276
Orogen Zizhiqi (1985E)	48,042
Panshan (▲343,100) (1986E)	248,100
Panshi (1985E)	59,270
Pingdingshan (▲819,900) (1986E)	363,200
Pingliang (▲362,500) (1986E)	85,400
Pingxiang, Jiangxi prov. (▲1,286,700) (1986E)	368,700
Pingyi (1982C)	89,373
Pingyin (1982C)	62,827
Potou (▲456,100) (1986E)	59,000
Puqi (1985E)	65,239
Putian (▲265,400) (1986E)	64,600
Putuo (1985E)	50,962
Puyang (▲1,086,100) (1986E)	131,000
Qian Gorlos (1985E)	79,494
Qingdao (Tsingtao)	2,300,000
Qinggang (1985E)	43,075
Qingjiang, Jiangsu prov. (▲246,617) (1982C)	150,000
Qingjiang, Jiangxi prov. (1985E)	42,698
Qingyuan (1985E)	51,756
Qinhuangdao (Chinwangtao) (▲436,000) (1986E)	307,500
Qinzhou (▲923,400) (1986E)	97,100
Qiqihar (Tsitsihar) (▲1,330,000) (1988E)	1,180,000
Qitaihe (▲309,900) (1986E)	166,400
Qixia (1982C)	54,158
Qixian (1982C)	53,041
Quanwan (★Xianggang)	514,241
Quanzhou (Chuanchou) (▲436,000) (1986E)	157,000
Qujing (▲758,000) (1986E)	135,000
Quxian (▲704,800) (1986E)	124,000
Raoping (1985E)	54,831
Rizhao (▲970,300) (1986E)	93,300
Rongcheng (1982C)	52,878
Rugao (1985E)	50,643
Rui'an (1985E)	57,993
Sanmenxia (Shanxian) (▲150,000) (1986E)	79,000
Sanming (▲214,300) (1986E)	144,900
• Shanghai (★11,010,000)	8,930,000
Shangqiu (Zhuji) (▲199,400) (1986E)	135,400
Shangrao (▲142,500) (1986E)	113,000
Shangshui (1982C)	50,191
Shantou (Swatow) (▲790,000) (1988E)	560,000
Shanwei (1985E)	61,234
Shaoguan (1986E)	363,100
Shaowu (▲266,700) (1986E)	81,400
Shaoxing (▲250,900) (1986E)	167,100
Shaoyang (▲465,900) (1986E)	218,600
Shashi (1986E)	253,700
Sha Tin (★Xianggang) (1986C)	355,810
Shenxian (1982C)	50,208
Shenyang (Mukden)	4,050,000
Shenzhen	640,000
Sheung Shui (1986C)	87,206
Shiguaigou (1975U)	50,000
Shihezi (▲549,300) (1987E)	304,700
Shijiazhuang	1,610,000
Shiyan (▲332,600) (1986E)	227,300
Shizuishan (▲317,400) (1986E)	225,500
Shouguang (1982C)	83,400
Shuangcheng (1985E)	91,163
Shuangliao (1985E)	67,326
Shuangyashan (1986E)	427,300
Shuicheng (▲2,216,500) (1986E)	363,500
Shulan (1986E)	50,582
Shunde (1985E)	50,262
Siping (▲357,800) (1986E)	280,100
Sishui (1982C)	82,990
Songjiang (1985E)	71,864
Songjianghe (1985E)	53,023
Suifenhe (▲21,700) (1986E)	13,900
Suihua (▲732,100) (1986E)	200,400
Suileng (1985E)	68,399
Suining (▲1,174,900) (1986E)	118,500
Suixian (▲1,281,600) (1986E)	187,700
Suqian (1985E)	50,742
Suxian (▲218,600) (1986E)	123,300
Suzhou (Soochow) (1988E)	740,000
Tai'an (▲1,325,400) (1986E)	215,900
Taiyuan	1,720,000
Taizhou (▲210,800) (1987E)	143,200
Tancheng (1982C)	61,857
Tangshan (▲1,440,000) (1988E)	1,080,000
Tao'an (1985E)	76,269
Tengxian (1985E)	53,254
Tianjin (Tientsin)	5,000,000
Tianshui (▲953,200) (1986E)	209,500
Tai Po (1986C)	119,679
Tiefa (▲146,367) (1982C)	60,000
Tieli (1985E)	102,527
Tieling (▲454,100) (1986E)	326,100
Tongchuan (▲393,200) (1986E)	268,900
Tonghua (▲367,400) (1986E)	290,200
Tongliao (▲253,100) (1986E)	190,100
Tongling (▲216,400) (1986E)	182,900
Tongren (1985E)	50,307
Tongxian (1985E)	97,168
Tuen Mun (★Xianggang) (1986C)	262,458
Tumen (▲99,700) (1986E)	77,600
Tunxi (▲104,500) (1986E)	61,800
Turpan (▲196,800) (1986E)	52,300
Ürümqi	1,130,000
Wangkui (1985E)	52,021
Wangqing (1985E)	61,237
Wanxian (▲280,800) (1986E)	138,700
Weifang (▲1,042,200) (1986E)	312,500
Weihai (▲220,800) (1986E)	83,000
Weinan (▲699,400) (1986E)	111,300
Weishan (Xiazhen) (1982C)	57,932
Weixian (Hanting) (1982C)	50,180
Wenzhou (▲530,600) (1986E)	372,200
Wuchang (1985E)	64,403
Wuhai (1986E)	266,000
Wuhan	3,870,000
Wuhu (▲502,200) (1986E)	396,000
Wulian (Hongning) (1982C)	51,718
Wusong (1982C)	64,017
Wuwei (Liangzhou) (▲804,000) (1986E)	115,500
Wuxi (Wuhsi) (1988E)	880,000
Wuzhong (▲402,400) (1986E)	48,600
Wuzhou (Wuchow) (▲261,500) (1986E)	194,800
Xiaguan (▲395,800) (1986E)	112,100
Xiamen (Amoy)	470,000
Xi'an (Sian)	2,410,000
Xiangfan (▲421,200) (1986E)	314,900
Xianggang (Hong Kong) (★4,770,000) (1991C)	1,250,993
Xiangtan (▲511,100) (1986E)	389,500
Xianning (▲402,200) (1986E)	122,200
Xianyang (▲641,800) (1986E)	285,900
Xiaogan (▲1,204,400) (1986E)	125,500
Xiaoshan (1985E)	63,074
Xichang (▲161,000) (1986E)	105,000
Xinghua (1985E)	75,573
Xinglongzhen (1982C)	52,961
Xingtai (▲350,800) (1986E)	265,600
Xinhui (1985E)	77,381
Xining (Sining) (1988E)	620,000
Xinjiulong (New Kowloon) (★Xianggang) (1986C)	1,526,910
Xinmin (1985E)	47,900
Xintai (▲1,157,300) (1986E)	171,400
Xinwen (Suncun) (1975U)	50,000
Xinxian (▲398,600) (1986E)	74,200
Xinxiang (▲540,500) (1986E)	411,000
Xinyang (▲234,200) (1986E)	169,100
Xinyu (▲610,600) (1986E)	140,200
Xuancheng (1985E)	52,387
Xuanhua (1975U)	140,000
Xuanwei (1982C)	70,081
Xuchang (▲247,200) (1986E)	167,800
Xuguit Qi (Yakeshi) (1986E)	390,000
Xuzhou (Süchow) (1988E)	860,000
Yaan (▲277,600) (1986E)	89,200
Yan'an (▲259,800) (1986E)	86,700
Yancheng (▲1,251,400) (1986E)	258,400
Yangcheng (1982C)	57,255
Yangjiang (1986E)	91,433
Yangquan (▲478,900) (1986E)	295,100
Yangzhou (▲417,300) (1986E)	321,500
Yanji (▲216,900) (1986E)	175,000
Yanji (Longjing) (1985E)	55,035
Yanling (1982C)	52,679
Yantai (Chefoo) (▲717,300) (1986E)	327,000
Yanzhou (1985E)	48,972
Yaxian (Sanya) (▲321,700) (1986E)	70,500
Yi'an (1986E)	54,253
Yibin (Ipin) (▲636,500) (1986E)	218,800
Yichang (Ichang) (1986E)	410,500
Yichuan (1982C)	58,914
Yichun, Heilongjiang prov. (1988E)	840,000
Yichun, Jiangxi prov. (▲770,200) (1986E)	132,600
Yidu (1985E)	54,838
Yilan (1985E)	50,436
Yima (▲84,800) (1986E)	53,700
Yinan (Jiehu) (1982C)	67,803
Yinchuan	430,000
Yingchengzi (1985E)	59,072
Yingkou (▲480,000) (1986E)	366,900
Yingtan (▲116,200) (1986E)	64,500
Yining (Kuldja) (▲232,000) (1986E)	153,200
Yiyang (▲365,000) (1986E)	155,300
Yiyuan (Nanma) (1982C)	53,800
Yong'an (▲269,000) (1986E)	105,100
Yongchuan (1985E)	70,444
Yuci (▲420,700) (1986E)	171,000
Yuen Long (1986C)	75,740
Yueyang (▲411,300) (1986E)	239,500
Yulin, Guangxi Zhuangzu prov. (▲1,228,800) (1986E)	115,600
Yulin, Shaanxi prov. (1985E)	51,610
Yumen (Laojunmiao) (▲160,100) (1986E)	84,300
Yuncheng, Shandong prov. (1982C)	54,262
Yuncheng, Shansi prov. (▲434,900) (1986E)	87,000
Yunyang (1982C)	54,903
Yushu (1985E)	57,222
Yuyao (▲772,700) (1986E)	169,700
Zaozhuang (▲1,592,000) (1986E)	292,200
Zhangjiakou (Kalgan) (▲640,000) (1988E)	500,000
Zhangye (▲394,200) (1986E)	73,000
Zhangzhou (Longxi) (▲310,400) (1986E)	159,400
Zhanjiang (▲920,900) (1986E)	335,500
Zhaodong (1985E)	99,836
Zhaoqing (Gaoyao) (▲187,600) (1986E)	145,700
Zhaotong (▲546,600) (1986E)	77,500
Zhaoyuan (1985E)	42,426
Zhaoyuan (1982C)	56,389
Zhengzhou (Chengchow)	1,690,000
Zhenjiang (1986E)	412,400
Zhongshan (Shiqizhen) (▲1,059,700) (1986E)	238,700
Zhoucun (1975U)	50,000
Zhoukouzhen (▲220,400) (1986E)	110,500
Zhuhai (▲155,000) (1986E)	88,800
Zhumadian (▲149,500) (1986E)	99,400
Zhuoxian (1985E)	54,523
Zhuzhou (Chuchow) (▲499,600) (1986E)	344,800
Zibo (Zhangdian) (▲2,370,000) (1988E)	840,000
Zigong (Tzukung) (▲909,300) (1986E)	361,700
Zixing (▲334,300) (1986E)	97,100
Ziyang (1985E)	57,349
Zouping (1982C)	49,274
Zouxian (1985E)	61,578
Zunyi (▲347,600) (1986E)	236,600

COLOMBIA

1985 C	27,867,326
Armenia	187,130
Barrancabermeja	137,406
Barranquilla (★1,140,000)	899,781
Bello (★Medellín)	212,861
Bucaramanga (★550,000)	352,326
Buenaventura	160,342
Buga	82,992
Cali (★1,400,000)	1,350,565
Cartagena	531,426
Cartago	97,791
Ciénaga	56,860
Cúcuta (★445,000)	379,478
Dos Quebradas (★Pereira)	101,480
Duitama	56,390
Envigado (★Medellín)	91,391
Florencia	66,430
Floridablanca (★Bucaramanga)	143,824
Girardot	70,078
Ibagué	292,965
Itagüí (★Medellín)	137,623
Magangué	49,160
Maicao	46,033
Malambo (★Barranquilla)	52,584
Manizales (★330,000)	299,352
Medellín (★2,095,000)	1,468,089
Montería	157,466
Neiva	194,556
Ocaña	51,443
Palmira	175,186
Pasto	197,407
Pereira (★390,000)	233,271
Popayán	141,964
• SANTA FE DE BOGOTÁ (★4,260,000)	3,982,941
Santa Marta	177,922
Sincelejo	120,537
Soacha (★Santa Fe de Bogotá)	109,051
Sogamoso	64,437
Soledad (★Barranquilla)	165,791
Tuluá	99,721
Tunja	93,792
Valledupar	142,771
Villa Rosario (★Cúcuta)	63,615
Villavicencio	178,685
Zipaquirá	45,676

COMOROS / Al-Qumur / Comores

1990 E	452,742
• MORONI	23,432

CONGO

1989 C	2,188,367
• BRAZZAVILLE	693,712
Dolisie	57,991
Pointe-Noire	350,139

CONGO, DEMOCRATIC REPUBLIC OF THE / République démocratique du Congo

1984 C	30,729,443
Bandundu	63,642
Beni	44,141
Boma	197,617
Bukavu	167,950
Bumba	51,197
Bunia	59,598
Butembo	73,312
Gandajika	64,878
Gbadolite	27,063
Gemena	63,052
Goma	77,908
Ilebo (Port-Francqui)	53,877
Isiro	78,268
Kalemie (Albertville)	73,528
Kamina	62,789
Kananga (Luluabourg)	298,693
Kikwit	149,296
Kindu	66,812
• KINSHASA (LÉOPOLDVILLE) (1986E)	3,000,000
Kipushi	53,207
Kisangani (Stanleyville)	317,581
Kolwezi	416,122
Likasi (Jadotville)	213,862
Lubumbashi (Élisabethville)	564,830
Matadi	138,798
Mbandaka (Coquilhatville)	137,291
Mbuji-Mayi (Bakwanga)	486,235
Mwene-Ditu	94,560
Tshikapa	116,016
Uvira	74,432

COOK ISLANDS

1991 C	18,617
• AVARUA	10,886

COSTA RICA

1988 E	2,851,000
Alajuela (▲147,400) (★San José)	33,800
Desamparados (★San José) (1984C)	43,352
Puerto Limón (▲62,600)	40,400
Puntarenas (▲86,400)	34,100
• SAN JOSÉ (★1,355,000)	278,600

CÔTE D'IVOIRE (IVORY COAST)

1988 C	10,815,694
Abengourou	59,114
• ABIDJAN	1,929,079
Agboville	46,045
Anyama	56,690
Bouaké	329,850
Daloa	121,842
Divo	72,350
Gagnoa	85,563
Korhogo	109,445
Man	89,575
San Pédro	70,611
YAMOUSSOUKRO	106,786

▲ Population of an entire municipality, commune, or district, including rural area.
• Largest city in country.
★ Population or designation of the metropolitan area, including suburbs.
C Census. **E** Official estimate. **U** Unofficial estimate.

▲ Bevölkerung eines ganzen städtischen Verwaltungsgebietes, eines Kommunalbezirkes oder eines Distrikts, einschliesslich ländlicher Gebiete.
• Grösste Stadt des Landes.
★ Bevölkerung oder Bezeichnung der Stadtregion einschliesslich Vororte.
C Volkszählung. **E** Offizielle Schätzung. **U** Inoffizielle Schätzung.

Population of Cities and Towns / Einwohnerzahlen von Grossstädten / Habitantes en las Ciudades y Poblaciones
Population des Grands Centres et des Villes / População dos Centros Urbanos 305

CROATIA / Hrvatska

1991 C	4,784,265
Bjelovar	42,066
Dubrovnik	55,638
Karlovac	70,729
Osijek	129,792
Pula	69,690
Rijeka	167,964
Šibenik	55,842
Sisak	60,564
Slavonski Brod	58,531
Split	200,459
Varaždin	48,834
Vukovar	45,963
Zadar	80,355
• ZAGREB	867,865

CUBA

1991 E	10,694,465
Bayamo	139,061
Camagüey	286,404
Cárdenas (▲84,590)	69,800
Ciego de Ávila	101,620
Cienfuegos	136,233
Florida	51,442
Guantánamo	215,864
Holguín	236,967
• LA HABANA (HAVANA) (★2,210,000)	2,119,059
Las Tunas	126,678
Manzanillo	108,668
Matanzas	119,510
Morón	49,793
Palma Soriano (▲124,543)	66,600
Pinar del Río	136,303
Sancti Spíritus	97,522
Santa Clara	203,753
Santiago de Cuba	434,541

CYPRUS / Kıbrıs / Kípros

1982 C	512,097
Lárnax (Larnaca) (★48,330)	35,823
Lemesós (Limassol) (★107,161)	74,782
• NICOSIA (LEVKOSÍA) (★185,000)	48,221

CYPRUS, NORTH / Kuzey Kıbrıs

1985 E	160,287
Gazimağusa (Famagusta)	19,428
• NICOSIA (LEFKOŞA)	37,400

CZECH REPUBLIC / Česká Republika

1991 C	10,298,731
Brno (★450,000)	387,986
Česká Lípa	39,667
České Budějovice (★114,000)	97,283
Český Těšín (★Třinec)	28,737
Cheb	31,847
Chomutov (★80,000)	53,191
Děčín (★72,000)	55,112
Frýdek-Místek (★Ostrava)	65,067
Havířov (★Ostrava)	86,267
Hodonín	30,736
Hradec Králové (★113,000)	99,889
Jablonec nad Nisou (★Liberec)	45,918
Jihlava	52,271
Karlovy Vary (Carlsbad)	56,291
Karviná (★Ostrava)	68,368
Kladno (★88,500)	71,735
Kolín	31,582
Kroměříž (★38,500)	28,962
Liberec (★175,000)	101,934
Litvínov (★Most)	29,085
Mladá Boleslav	44,471
Most (★135,000)	70,675
Nový Jičín	29,028
Olomouc (★126,000)	105,690
Opava (★78,000)	63,601
Orlová (★Ostrava)	36,307
Ostrava (★760,000)	327,553
Pardubice	94,857
Písek	29,542
Plzeň (★210,000)	173,129
• PRAHA (★1,328,000)	1,212,010
Přerov	51,341
Příbram	36,869
Prostějov	50,102
Šumperk	30,446
Tábor (★55,500)	36,329
Teplice (★94,000)	53,039
Třebíč	39,348
Třinec (★87,500)	45,189
Trutnov	31,957
Ústí nad Labem (★115,000)	99,739
Valašské Meziříčí	28,153
Vsetín	31,584
Zlín (★124,000)	84,634
Znojmo	39,910

DENMARK / Danmark

1992 E	5,162,126
Ålborg (▲156,614)	115,200
Århus (▲267,873)	207,300
Ballerup (★København)	45,476
Esbjerg (▲81,843)	72,200
Fredericia (▲46,617)	28,700
Frederiksberg (★København)	86,372
Gentofte (★København)	66,077
Gladsakse (★København)	60,604
Helsingør (Elsinore) (★København)	56,794
Horsens (▲55,123)	47,200
Hvidovre (★København)	48,754
• KØBENHAVN (★1,670,000)	464,566
Kolding (▲57,982)	42,700
Kongens Lyngby (★København)	49,612
Odense (▲179,487)	142,800
Randers	61,440
Rønne	15,236
Roskilde (▲50,158) (★København)	40,700
Vejle (▲51,845)	45,700

DJIBOUTI

1991 E	508,541
• DJIBOUTI	329,337

DOMINICA

1984 E	77,000
• ROSEAU	9,348

DOMINICAN REPUBLIC / República Dominicana

1990 E	7,169,800
Barahona	80,400
La Romana	147,800
La Vega	192,300
Mao	58,400
Puerto Plata	94,900
San Cristóbal	137,500
San Francisco de Macorís	165,300
San Juan de la Maguana	129,700
San Pedro de Macorís	144,300
Santiago de los Caballeros	489,500
• SANTO DOMINGO	2,411,900

ECUADOR

1990 C	9,648,189
Ambato	124,166
Babahoyo	50,285
Cuenca	194,981
Eloy Alfaro (★Guayaquil)	82,359
Esmeraldas	98,558
• Guayaquil	1,508,444
Ibarra	80,991
La Libertad	50,108
Loja	94,305
Machala	144,197
Manta	125,505
Milagro	93,637
Portoviejo	132,937
Quevedo	86,910
QUITO (★1,300,000)	1,100,847
Riobamba	94,505
Santo Domingo de los Colorados	114,422

EGYPT / Miṣr

1986 C	48,205,049
Abnūb	48,302
Abū Kabīr	68,394
Abū Tij	48,518
Akhmīm	70,494
Al-'Arīsh	67,337
Al-Fayyūm	213,070
Al-Hawāmidīyah (★Al-Qāhirah)	73,298
Al-Iskandarīyah (Alexandria) (★3,350,000)	2,926,859
Al-Ismā'īlīyah (★235,000)	158,045
Al-Jīzah (Giza) (★Al-Qāhirah)	1,883,189
Al-Maḥallah al-Kubrā	306,509
Al-Manṣūrah (★375,000)	317,508
Al-Manzilah	54,918
Al-Maṭarīyah	73,315
Al-Minyā	179,060
• AL-QĀHIRAH (CAIRO) (★9,300,000)	6,068,695
Al-Qanāṭir al-Khayrīyah	49,361
Al-Uqṣur (Luxor)	126,160
Armant	54,616
Ashmūn	54,450
As-Sinbillāwayn	60,159
As-Suways (Suez)	327,717
Aswān	190,579
Asyūṭ	272,986
Az-Zaqāzīq	244,354
Bahtīm (★Al-Qāhirah)	275,807
Banhā	115,701
Banī Mazār	47,982
Banī Suwayf	152,476
Bilbays	96,511
Bilqās Qism Awwal	73,040
Biyalā	47,702
Būlāq ad-Dakrūr (★Al-Qāhirah)	148,787
Būr Sa'īd (Port Said)	401,172
Būsh	54,655
Damanhūr	188,939
Dikirnis	48,616
Disūq	78,316
Dumyāṭ (Damietta)	89,069
Fāqūs	48,365
Hawsh 'Īsā	53,619
Idkū	70,724
Jirjā	71,564
Kafr ad-Dawwār (★Al-Iskandarīyah)	196,244
Kafr ash-Shaykh	103,301
Kafr az-Zayyāt	58,276
Kawm Umbū	52,506
Maghāghah	50,916
Mallawī	98,632
Manfalūṭ	52,281
Marsā Maṭrūḥ	43,157
Minūf	69,673
Mīt Ghamr (★100,000)	91,927
Qalyūb	84,413
Qinā	119,917
Rashīd (Rosetta)	51,789
Samālūṭ	62,404
Sāqiyat Makkī	51,062
Sawhāj	132,649
Shibīn al-Kawm	132,209
Shubrā al-Khaymah (★Al-Qāhirah)	714,594
Sinnūris	55,187
Tahtā	58,457
Ṭalkhā (★Al-Manṣūrah)	54,923
Ṭanṭā	336,517
Ṭimā	46,824
Warrāq al-'Arab (★Al-Qāhirah)	127,108
Ziftā (★Mīt Ghamr)	69,253

EL SALVADOR

1985 E	5,337,896
Delgado (★San Salvador)	67,684
Mejicanos (★San Salvador)	91,465
Nueva San Salvador (★San Salvador)	53,688
San Miguel	88,520
• SAN SALVADOR (★920,000)	462,652
Santa Ana	137,879
Soyapango (★San Salvador)	60,000

EQUATORIAL GUINEA / Guinea Ecuatorial

1983 C	300,000
• MALABO	31,630

ERITREA

1991 E	2,951,000
• ASMERA (1990E)	358,100
Mitsiwa (1986E)	16,576

ESTONIA / Eesti

1991 E	1,581,800
Kohtla-Järve	74,700
Narva	83,000
Pärnu	54,200
• TALLINN	481,500
Tartu	115,300

ETHIOPIA / Ityopiya

1986 E	44,927,000
• ADIS ABEBA (★1,990,000) (1990E)	1,912,500
Akaki Beseka (★Adis Abeba)	58,977
Awasa	39,693
Bahir Dar	59,951
Debre Zeyit	55,706
Dese	77,459
Dire Dawa (1990E)	127,400
Gonder	88,000
Harer	68,000
Jima	67,470
Mekele	66,640
Nazret	83,091

FAEROE ISLANDS / Føroyar

1990 E	47,946
• TÓRSHAVN	14,767

FALKLAND ISLANDS

1991 C	2,050
• STANLEY	1,557

FIJI

1986 C	715,375
Lautoka (★39,057)	28,728
• SUVA (★141,273)	69,665

FINLAND / Suomi

1993 E	5,054,982
Espoo (Esbo) (★Helsinki)	179,054
• HELSINKI (HELSINGFORS) (★1,045,000)	501,514
Joensuu	48,911
Jyväskylä (★93,000)	67,609
Kotka	56,462
Kouvola (★55,300)	32,151
Kuopio	82,340
Lahti (★108,300)	93,784
Lappeenranta	55,563
Oulu (★122,500)	103,538
Pori	76,331
Tampere (★241,200)	174,859
Turku (Åbo) (★228,500)	159,916
Vaasa (Vasa)	54,179
Vantaa (Vanda) (★Helsinki)	159,213

FRANCE

1990 C	56,614,493
Aix-en-Provence (★Marseille)	123,842
Ajaccio	58,315
Albi (★54,359)	46,579
Alès (★76,856)	41,037
Amiens (★156,120)	131,872
Angers (★208,282)	141,404
Angoulême (★102,908)	42,876
Annecy (★126,729)	49,644
Antibes (★Cannes)	63,248
Antony (★Paris)	57,771
Argenteuil (★Paris)	93,096
Arles (★54,309)	39,000
Armentières (★57,738)	25,219
Arras (★79,607)	38,983
Asnières [-sur-Seine] (★Paris)	71,850
Aubervilliers (★Paris)	67,557
Aulnay-sous-Bois (★Paris)	82,314
Avignon (★181,136)	86,939
Bastia (★52,446)	37,845
Bayonne (★164,378)	40,051
Beauvais (★57,704)	54,190
Belfort (★77,844)	50,125
Besançon (★122,623)	113,828
Béthune (★261,535)	24,556
Béziers (★76,304)	70,996
Blois (★65,132)	49,318
Bondy (★Paris)	46,676
Bordeaux (★760,000)	210,336
Boulogne-Billancourt (★Paris)	101,743
Boulogne-sur-Mer (★91,249)	43,678
Bourg-en-Bresse (★55,784)	40,972
Bourges (★94,731)	75,609
Brest (★201,480)	147,956
Brive-la-Gaillarde (★64,379)	49,765
Bruay-en-Artois (★Béthune)	24,927
Caen (★191,490)	112,846
Calais (★101,768)	75,309
Cambrai (★48,133)	33,092
Cannes (★335,647)	68,676
Carcassonne	43,470
Castres (★46,482)	44,812
Châlons-sur-Marne (★61,452)	48,423
Chalon-sur-Saône (★77,764)	54,575
Chambéry (★103,283)	54,120
Champigny-sur-Marne (★Paris)	79,486
Charleville-Mézières (★67,213)	57,008
Chartres (★85,933)	39,595
Châteauroux (★67,090)	50,969
Châtellerault (★36,298)	34,678
Cherbourg (★92,045)	27,121
Cholet	55,132
Clamart (★Paris)	47,227
Clermont-Ferrand (★254,416)	136,181
Clichy (★Paris)	48,030
Cognac (★27,468)	19,528
Colmar (★83,816)	63,498
Colombes (★Paris)	78,513
Compiègne (★67,057)	41,896
Courbevoie (★Paris)	65,389
Creil (★97,119)	31,956
Créteil (★Paris)	82,088
Denain (★Valenciennes)	19,544
Dieppe (★43,348)	35,894
Dijon (★230,451)	146,703
Douai (★199,562)	42,175
Drancy (★Paris)	60,707
Dunkerque (★190,879)	70,331
Elbeuf (★53,886)	16,604
Épinal (★62,140)	36,732
Épinay-sur-Seine (★Paris)	48,762
Évreux (★57,968)	49,103
Évry (★Paris)	45,531
Fontainebleau (★35,706)	15,714
Fontenay-sous-Bois (★Paris)	51,868
Forbach (★98,758)	27,076
Fréjus (★73,967)	41,486
Gennevilliers (★Paris)	44,818
Grenoble (★404,733)	150,758
Hagondange (★112,061)	8,222
Hayange (★Thionville)	15,638
Issy-les-Moulineaux (★Paris)	46,127
Ivry-sur-Seine (★Paris)	53,619
La Rochelle (★100,264)	71,094
La Seyne-sur-Mer (★Toulon)	59,968
Laval (★56,855)	50,473
Le Blanc-Mesnil (★Paris)	46,956
Le Havre (★253,627)	195,854
Le Mans (★189,107)	145,502
Lens (★323,174)	35,017
Le Puy (★43,499)	21,743
Levallois-Perret (★Paris)	47,548
Lille (★1,050,000)	172,142
Limoges (★170,065)	133,464
Longwy (★41,300)	15,439
Lorient (★115,488)	59,271
Lourdes	16,300
Lyon (★1,335,000)	415,487
Mâcon (★46,714)	37,275
Maisons-Alfort (★Paris)	53,375
Mantes-la-Jolie (★Paris)	45,087
Marseille (★1,225,000)	800,550
Martigues (★Marseille)	31,300
Maubeuge (★102,772)	34,989
Meaux (★63,006)	48,305
Melun (★107,705)	35,319
Menton (★Monaco, Monaco)	29,141
Mérignac (★Bordeaux)	57,273
Metz (★193,117)	119,594
Meudon (★Paris)	45,339
Montargis (★52,804)	15,020
Montbéliard (★117,510)	29,005
Montceau-les-Mines (★47,283)	22,999
Montluçon (★63,018)	44,248
Montpellier (★248,303)	207,996
Montreuil-sous-Bois (★Paris)	94,754
Moulins (★41,715)	22,799
Moyeuvre-Grande (★Hagondange)	9,203
Mulhouse (Mülhausen) (★223,856)	108,357
Nancy (★329,447)	99,351
Nanterre (★Paris)	84,565
Nantes (★496,078)	244,995
Neuilly-sur-Seine (★Paris)	61,768
Nevers (★58,915)	41,968
Nice (★516,740)	342,439
Nîmes (★138,527)	128,471
Niort (★65,792)	57,012
Noisy-le-Grand (★Paris)	54,032
Noisy-le-Sec (★Paris)	36,309
Orléans (★243,153)	105,111
Orly (★Paris)	21,646
Pantin (★Paris)	47,303
• PARIS (★10,275,000)	2,152,423
Pau (★144,674)	82,157
Périgueux (★63,322)	30,280
Perpignan (★157,873)	105,983
Pessac (★Bordeaux)	51,055
Poissy (★Paris)	36,745
Poitiers (★107,625)	78,894
Quimper (★65,954)	59,437
Reims (★206,437)	180,620
Rennes (★245,065)	197,536
Roanne (★77,160)	41,756
Rodez (★39,017)	24,701
Romans-sur-Isère (★49,212)	32,734
Roubaix (★Lille)	97,746
Rouen (★380,161)	102,723
Rueil-Malmaison (★Paris)	66,401
Saint-Brieuc (★83,861)	44,752
Saint-Chamond (★81,795)	38,878
Saint-Denis (★Paris)	89,988
Saint-Dizier (★40,097)	33,552
Saint-Étienne (★313,338)	199,396
Saint-Lô (★2,760)	21,546
Saint-Malo	48,057
Saint-Maur-des-Fossés (★Paris)	77,206
Saint-Nazaire (★131,511)	64,812
Saint-Ouen (★Paris)	42,343
Saint-Quentin (★71,113)	60,644
Sarcelles (★Paris)	56,833
Sartrouville (★Paris)	50,329
Sevran	48,478
Soissons (★46,168)	29,829
Strasbourg (★415,000)	252,338
Suresnes (★Paris)	35,998
Tarbes (★77,787)	47,566
Thionville (★132,413)	39,712
Toulon (★437,553)	167,619
Toulouse (★650,000)	358,688
Tourcoing (★Lille)	93,765
Tours (★282,152)	129,509
Troyes (★122,763)	59,255
Valence (★107,965)	63,437
Valenciennes (★338,392)	38,441
Vénissieux (★Lyon)	60,444
Verdun-sur-Meuse (★26,711)	20,753
Versailles (★Paris)	87,789
Vichy (★61,566)	27,714
Villefranche (★55,249)	29,542
Villejuif (★Paris)	48,405
Villeneuve-d'Ascq (★Lille)	65,320
Villeurbanne (★Lyon)	116,872
Vitry-sur-Seine (★Paris)	82,400
Wattrelos (★Lille)	43,675

FRENCH GUIANA / Guyane française

1982 C	73,022
• CAYENNE	38,091

FRENCH POLYNESIA / Polynésie française

1988 C	188,814
• PAPEETE (★80,000)	23,555

GABON

1985 E	1,312,000
Franceville	58,800
Lambaréné	49,500
• LIBREVILLE	235,700
Port Gentil	124,400

GAMBIA

1993 C	1,025,867
• BANJUL (★228,945)	42,407
Brikama	42,480

GAZA STRIP AND JERICHO AREA

1992 E	667,000
ARĪḤĀ (JERICHO) (1967C)	6,829
• Ghazzah (1986E)	235,000
Khān Yūnis (1986E)	98,370
Rafaḥ (1967C)	49,812

GEORGIA / Sakartvelo

1991 E	5,464,200
Batumi	137,500
Gori	70,100
Kutaisi	238,200
Poti	51,100
Rustavi (★Tbilisi)	161,900

▲ Población de un municipio, comuna o distrito entero, incluyendo sus áreas rurales.
• Ciudad más grande de un país.
★ Población o designación de un área metropolitana, incluyendo los suburbios.
C Censo. **E** Estimado oficial. **U** Estimado no oficial.

▲ Population d'une municipalité, d'une commune ou d'un district, zone rurale incluse.
• Ville la plus peuplée du pays.
★ Population de l'agglomération (ou nom de la zone métropolitaine englobante).
C Recensement. **E** Estimation officielle. **U** Estimation non officielle.

▲ População de um municipio, comuna ou distrito, inclusive as respectivas áreas rurais.
• Maior cidade de um país.
★ População ou indicação de uma área metropolitana.
C Censo. **E** Estimativa oficial. **U** Estimativa não oficial.

Suchumi	120,000
• TBILISI (★1,460,000)	1,279,000
Zugdidi	50,600

GERMANY / Deutschland

1994 E	81,338,093
Aachen (★550,000)	246,671
Aalen (★79,000)	66,333
Ahlen	55,657
Albstadt	50,057
Alsdorf (★Aachen)	46,747
Altenburg	46,647
Amberg	44,213
Arnsberg	77,847
Aschaffenburg (★152,000)	65,650
Augsburg (★430,000)	264,764
Baden-Baden	52,712
Bad Homburg (★Frankfurt am Main)	51,455
Bad Oeynhausen	48,365
Bad Salzuflen (★Herford)	54,979
Bamberg (★122,000)	70,770
Bautzen	45,351
Bayreuth (★88,000)	73,393
Bergheim (★Köln)	60,121
Bergisch Gladbach (★Köln)	104,991
Bergkamen (★Essen)	51,054
BERLIN (★4,200,000)	3,475,392
Bielefeld (★540,000)	324,674
Bitterfeld (★105,000)	17,027
Bocholt	70,272
Bochum (★Essen)	401,058
BONN (★580,000)	296,859
Bottrop (★Essen)	119,676
Brandenburg	89,208
Braunschweig (★320,000)	256,267
Bremen (★790,000)	551,604
Bremerhaven (★180,000)	131,492
Castrop-Rauxel (★Essen)	79,101
Celle	73,671
Chemnitz (★500,000)	279,520
Coburg	44,384
Cottbus	128,121
Cuxhaven	56,003
Dachau (★München)	36,294
Darmstadt (★315,000)	139,754
Delmenhorst (★Bremen)	77,127
Dessau (★138,000)	93,287
Detmold	72,109
Dinslaken (★Essen)	67,619
Dormagen (★Köln)	59,915
Dorsten (★Essen)	79,941
Dortmund (★Essen)	601,966
Dresden (★870,000)	479,273
Duisburg (★Essen)	536,797
Düren (★110,000)	89,852
Düsseldorf (★1,225,000)	574,936
Eberswalde-Finow	50,730
Eisenach	42,579
Eisenhüttenstadt	47,545
Emden	52,216
Erftstadt (★Köln)	47,228
Erfurt	200,799
Erkrath (★Düsseldorf)	49,299
Erlangen (★Nürnberg)	102,383
Eschweiler (★Aachen)	55,791
• Essen (★5,050,000)	622,380
Esslingen (★Stuttgart)	91,388
Euskirchen	51,247
Flensburg (★98,000)	87,994
Frankenthal (★Mannheim)	48,099
Frankfurt	83,850
Frankfurt am Main (★1,950,000)	659,803
Freiberg	46,537
Freiburg (★235,400)	197,384
Friedrichshafen	56,047
Fulda (★76,000)	58,711
Fürth (★Nürnberg)	108,097
Garbsen (★Hannover)	62,196
Garmisch-Partenkirchen	26,996
Gelsenkirchen (★Essen)	295,037
Gera	122,974
Giessen (★155,000)	73,705
Gladbeck (★Essen)	79,931
Göppingen (★155,000)	56,771
Görlitz	67,647
Goslar (★72,000)	46,191
Gotha	52,265
Göttingen	128,419
Greifswald	63,941
Grevenbroich (★Düsseldorf)	62,737
Gummersbach	52,374
Gütersloh (★Bielefeld)	91,634
Hagen (★Essen)	214,877
Halberstadt	43,033
Halle (★455,000)	295,372
Hamburg (★2,440,000)	1,702,887
Hameln (★65,000)	59,209
Hamm	182,390
Hanau (★Frankfurt am Main)	89,156
Hannover (★1,015,000)	524,823
Hattingen (★Essen)	58,481
Heidelberg (★Mannheim)	139,429
Heidenheim (★83,000)	52,670
Heilbronn (★250,000)	122,396
Herford (★123,000)	65,682
Herne (★Essen)	180,539
Herten (★Essen)	69,592
Hilden (★Düsseldorf)	55,296
Hildesheim (★126,000)	106,303
Hof	52,724
Hoyerswerda	60,894
Hürth (★Köln)	51,974
Ingolstadt (★150,000)	109,666
Iserlohn	98,478
Jena	100,093
Kaiserslautern (★133,000)	102,370
Kamen (★Essen)	46,519
Karlsruhe (★508,000)	277,998
Kassel (★385,000)	202,158
Kempten (Allgäu)	61,669
Kerpen (★Köln)	60,395
Kiel (★330,000)	248,931
Kleve	47,869
Koblenz (★170,000)	109,807
Köln (★1,820,000)	962,517
Konstanz	75,891
Krefeld (★Essen)	249,565
Landshut	59,637
Langenfeld (★Düsseldorf)	56,153
Langenhagen (★Hannover)	47,609
Leipzig (★720,000)	490,851
Leverkusen (★Köln)	161,761
Lingen	51,338
Lippstadt	65,822
Lübeck (★255,000)	217,269
Lüdenscheid	80,277
Ludwigsburg (★Stuttgart)	86,216
Ludwigshafen (★Mannheim)	168,130
Lüneburg	63,299
Lünen (★Essen)	89,741
Magdeburg (★400,000)	270,546
Mainz (★Wiesbaden)	185,487
Mannheim (★1,530,000)	318,025
Marburg	76,582
Marl (★Essen)	92,590
Meerbusch (★Düsseldorf)	53,249
Menden	57,538
Merseburg (★Halle)	41,528
Minden (★124,000)	80,423
Moers (★Essen)	106,631
Mönchengladbach (★420,000)	265,312
Mülheim an der Ruhr (★Essen)	177,175
München (Munich) (★1,930,000)	1,255,623
Münster	267,367
Neubrandenburg	85,540
Neumünster	82,014
Neunkirchen/Saar (★125,000)	51,997
Neuss (★Düsseldorf)	148,560
Neustadt an der Weinstrasse	53,782
Neu-Ulm (★Ulm)	51,068
Neuwied (★160,000)	65,740
Norderstedt (★Hamburg)	69,916
Nordhausen	44,744
Nordhorn	50,835
Nürnberg (★1,070,000)	498,945
Oberhausen (★Essen)	226,254
Offenbach (★Frankfurt am Main)	116,870
Offenburg	54,963
Oldenburg	147,701
Osnabrück (★275,000)	168,078
Paderborn	130,130
Passau	51,041
Peine	48,105
Pforzheim (★235,000)	117,450
Pirmasens	48,619
Pirna (★Dresden)	39,958
Plauen	69,387
Potsdam (★Berlin)	139,262
Pulheim (★Köln)	50,474
Rastatt	48,574
Ratingen (★Düsseldorf)	90,443
Ravensburg (★75,000)	47,099
Recklinghausen (★Essen)	127,150
Regensburg (★185,000)	125,337
Remscheid (★Wuppertal)	123,610
Reutlingen (★175,000)	107,607
Rheine	73,543
Riesa	42,656
Rosenheim	58,553
Rostock	237,307
Rüsselsheim (★Wiesbaden)	60,361
Saarbrücken (★365,000)	190,902
Saarlouis (★115,000)	38,347
Salzgitter	117,684
Sankt Augustin (★Bonn)	53,969
Schwäbisch Gmünd	63,701
Schwedt	49,594
Schweinfurt (★105,000)	55,284
Schwerin	122,189
Schwerte (★Essen)	50,955
Siegburg (★175,000)	36,628
Siegen (★195,000)	111,845
Sindelfingen (★Stuttgart)	59,930
Solingen (★Wuppertal)	166,064
Speyer	49,310
Stendal	47,252
Stolberg (★Aachen)	58,028
Stralsund	69,230
Stuttgart (★2,020,000)	594,406
Suhl	52,386
Trier (★122,000)	99,183
Troisdorf (★Siegburg)	67,584
Tübingen	83,553
Ulm (★220,000)	114,839
Unna (★Essen)	64,327
Velbert (★Essen)	89,643
Viersen (★Mönchengladbach)	77,204
Villingen-Schwenningen	81,315
Waiblingen (★Stuttgart)	50,259
Weimar	58,807
Wesel	61,111
Wetzlar (★100,000)	54,188
Wiesbaden (★800,000)	270,873
Wilhelmshaven (★122,000)	91,680
Wismar	53,149
Witten (★Essen)	105,807
Wittenberg	53,374
Wolfenbüttel (★Braunschweig)	53,812
Wolfsburg	128,032
Worms (★Mannheim)	79,155
Wuppertal (★850,000)	386,625
Würzburg (★195,000)	128,875
Zweibrücken (★105,000)	35,704
Zwickau (★180,000)	107,988

GHANA

1987 E	13,577,538
• ACCRA (★1,390,000)	949,113
Ashiaman (★Accra) (1984C)	49,427
Cape Coast (1984C)	86,620
Koforidua (1984C)	54,400
Kumasi (★540,000)	385,192
Obuasi (1984C)	60,146
Sekondi (★175,352) (1984C)	32,355
Tafo (★Kumasi) (1984C)	50,432
Takoradi (★Sekondi) (1984C)	61,527
Tamale (★171,661)	151,069
Tema (★179,076) (★Accra)	109,975
Teshie (★Accra) (1984C)	62,954

GIBRALTAR

1991 C	28,074
• GIBRALTAR	28,074

GREECE / Ellás

1991 C	10,259,900
Aiyáleo (★Athínai)	78,563
Akharnaí	59,698
Amaroúsion (★Athínai)	64,092
Ampelókipoi (★Thessaloníki)	40,093
• ATHÍNAI (ATHENS) (★3,150,000)	772,072
Áyios Dhimítrios (★Athínai)	57,574
Dráma	37,604
Ermoúpolis (★16,100)	13,030
Galátsion (★Athínai)	57,230
Glifádha (★Athínai)	63,306
Ilioúpolis (★Athínai)	75,037
Ioánnina	56,699
Iráklion (★127,600)	115,124
Kalámai (★45,100)	43,625
Kalamariá (★Thessaloníki)	80,698
Kallithéa (★Athínai)	114,233
Kardhítsa	30,289
Kateríni (★48,000)	43,613
Kavála	56,571
Keratsínion (★Athínai)	71,982
Khalándrion (★Athínai)	66,285
Khalkís	51,646
Khaniá (★65,500)	50,077
Khíos (★27,600)	22,894
Koridhallós (★Athínai)	63,184
Kórinthos (Corinth)	27,412
Lárisa (★125,600)	112,777
Návplion	11,897
Néa Ionía (★Athínai)	60,635
Néa Liósia (★Athínai)	78,326
Neápolis (★Thessaloníki)	30,568
Néa Smírni (★Athínai)	69,479
Níkaia (★Athínai)	87,597
Palaión Fáliron (★Athínai)	61,371
Pátrai (★172,800)	152,570
Peristérion (★Athínai)	137,288
Piraiévs (Piraeus) (★Athínai)	182,671
Ródhos (Rhodes)	42,400
Sérrai	49,380
Spárti (Sparta) (★15,500)	13,011
Thessaloníki (Salonika) (★755,000)	383,967
Thívai (Thebes)	19,505
Tríkala	44,232
Trípolis	22,429
Véroia	37,858
Víron (★Athínai)	58,523
Vólos (★106,200)	77,192
Zográfos (★Athínai)	80,492

GREENLAND / Grønland / Kalaallit Nunaat

1990 E	55,558
Egedesminde (Aasiaat)	3,308
• GODTHÅB (NUUK)	12,217
Holsteinsborg (Sisimiut)	4,871

GRENADA

1991 C	90,691
• SAINT GEORGE'S (★25,000)	4,439

GUADELOUPE

1990 C	387,034
BASSE-TERRE (★27,500)	14,082
Les Abymes (★Pointe-à-Pitre)	62,645
• Pointe-à-Pitre (★84,000)	26,031

GUAM

1990 C	133,152
• AGANA (★50,000)	1,139

GUATEMALA

1989 E	8,935,395
Escuintla	60,673
• GUATEMALA (★1,400,000)	1,057,210
Quetzaltenango	88,769

GUERNSEY

1991 C	58,867
• SAINT PETER PORT (★36,000)	16,648

GUINEA / Guinée

1986 E	6,225,000
• CONAKRY	800,000
Kankan	100,000
Kindia	80,000
Labé	110,000
Nzérékoré (1983C)	55,356

GUINEA-BISSAU / Guiné-Bissau

1988 E	945,000
• BISSAU	125,000

GUYANA

1983 E	918,000
• GEORGETOWN (★188,000)	78,500

HAITI / Haïti

1987 E	5,531,802
Cap-Haïtien	72,161
Gonaïves	37,034
• PORT-AU-PRINCE (★880,000)	797,000

HONDURAS

1988 C	4,443,721
Choluteca	54,481
El Progreso	60,058
La Ceiba	68,764
San Pedro Sula (★375,000)	287,350
• TEGUCIGALPA	576,661

HUNGARY / Magyarország

1994 E	10,277,000
Békéscsaba	67,475
• BUDAPEST (★2,515,000)	1,995,696
Debrecen	217,706
Dunaújváros	58,294
Eger	63,794
Győr	130,941
Hódmezővásárhely	50,745
Kaposvár	70,728
Kecskemét	105,559
Miskolc	189,655
Nagykanizsa	53,060
Nyíregyháza	115,643
Ózd	41,868
Pécs	172,177
Salgótarján	46,414
Sopron	56,324
Szeged	178,878
Székesfehérvár	109,666
Szolnok	80,859
Szombathely	85,932
Tatabánya	73,505
Vác	34,283
Veszprém	65,789
Zalaegerszeg	62,908

ICELAND / Ísland

1992 E	262,193
Akureyri	14,665
• REYKJAVÍK (★151,779)	100,850

INDIA / Bharat

1991 C	846,302,688
Abohar	107,163
Achalpur	96,229
Ādilābād	84,255
Ādityapur (★Jamshedpur)	77,803
Ādoni	136,182
Agartala	157,358
Āgra (★948,063)	891,790
Āgra Cantonment (★Āgra)	49,755
Ahmadābād (★3,312,216)	2,876,710
Ahmadnagar (★222,088)	181,339
Āīzawl	155,240
Ajmer	402,700
Akola	328,034
Akot	65,681
Alandur (★Madras)	125,244
Alīgarh	480,520
Alīpur Duār (★102,815)	65,241
Allahābād (★844,546)	792,858
Alleppey (★264,969)	174,666
Alwal (★Hyderābād)	66,471
Alwar (★210,146)	205,086
Amalner	76,442
Ambājogāi	57,159
Ambāla (★259,227)	119,338
Ambāla Cantonment (★Ambāla Sadar)	49,017
Ambāla Sadar	90,872
Ambāsamudram (★59,661)	33,893
Ambattur (★Madras)	215,424
Ambikāpur (★53,227)	50,277
Āmbūr	75,911
Amrāvati	421,576
Amreli (★69,366)	67,827
Amritsar	708,835
Amroha	137,061
Anakāpalle	84,356
Ānand (★174,480)	110,266
Anantapur	174,924
Anjār	51,209
Ankleshwar (★78,100)	51,739
Ara	157,082
Arakkonam	71,923
Arcot (★114,760)	45,205
Arni	54,898
Aruppukkottai	78,976
Asansol (★763,939)	262,188
Ashoknagar-Kalyangarh (★Hābra)	96,747
Āttūr	55,667
Auraiya	50,772
Aurangābād (★592,709)	573,272
Avadi (★Madras)	183,215
Āzamgarh	78,567
Badagara (★102,430)	72,434
Bagaha	64,627
Bāgalkot	76,903
Bahādurgarh	56,524
Baharampur (★126,400)	115,144
Bahraich	135,400
Baidyabāti (★Calcutta)	90,081
Bālāghāt (★67,151)	62,178
Balāngīr	69,920
Bāleshwar (★101,829)	85,442
Ballarpur (★92,438)	83,511
Ballia	84,063
Bally (★Calcutta)	184,474
Bally (★Calcutta)	73,322
Balrāmpur	59,619
Bālurghāt (★126,225)	119,796
Bānda	96,795
Bangalore (★4,130,288)	2,660,088
Bangaon	79,571
Bānkura	114,876
Bansberia (★Calcutta)	93,520
Bānswāra (★67,908)	66,632
Bāpatla	62,536
Bārākpur (★Calcutta)	133,265
Bārān	57,719
Baranagar (★Calcutta)	224,821
Bārāsat (★Calcutta)	102,660
Baraut	67,705
Barddhamān	245,079
Bareilly (★617,350)	587,211
Bargarh	51,205
Bāripada (★69,240)	49,619
Bārmer	68,625
Barnāla	75,430
Bārsi	88,810
Basīrhāt	101,409
Basti	67,371
Batala (★103,367)	86,006
Bathinda	159,114
Beāwar (★106,721)	105,363
Begusarai (★84,018)	71,424
Bela	65,945
Belampalli	66,780
Belgaum (★402,412)	326,399
Bellary	245,391
Bettiah	92,653
Betūl	63,534
Beypore	56,505
Bhadohi	64,010
Bhadrak	76,435
Bhadrāvati (★149,257)	55,475
Bhadrāvati New Town (★Bhadrāvati)	74,928
Bhadreswar (★Calcutta)	72,474
Bhāgalpur (★260,119)	253,225
Bhandāra	71,813
Bharatpur (★156,880)	148,519
Bharūch (★139,029)	133,102
Bhātpāra (★Calcutta)	304,952
Bhavāni (★97,160)	35,196
Bhāvnagar (★405,225)	402,338
Bhawānipatna	51,062
Bhilai (★685,474)	386,159
Bhīlwāra	183,965
Bhīmavaram	121,314
Bhind	109,755
Bhiwandi (★392,214)	379,070
Bhiwāni	121,629
Bhopāl	1,062,771
Bhubaneshwar	411,542
Bhuj (★121,009)	102,176
Bhusāwal (★159,799)	145,143
Bīd	112,434
Bīdar (★132,408)	108,016
Bihār	201,323
Bijāpur (★193,131)	186,939
Bijnor (★73,900)	66,486
Bīkāner	416,289
Bilāspur (★229,615)	179,633
Bilimora (★51,039)	42,052
Birlapur (★65,482)	20,320
Birnagar (★92,208)	20,015
Bishnupur	56,128
Bodhan	64,406
Bodināyakkanūr	66,500
Bokāro Steel City (★398,890)	333,683
Bolpur	52,760
Botād	64,603
Brahmapur	210,418
Brajrajnagar	69,667
Budaun	116,695
Budge Budge (★Calcutta)	72,951
Bulandshahr	127,201
Buldāna	52,767

▲ Population of an entire municipality, commune, or district, including rural area.
• Largest city in country.
★ Population or designation of the metropolitan area, including suburbs.
C Census. **E** Official estimate. **U** Unofficial estimate.

▲ Bevölkerung eines ganzen städtischen Verwaltungsgebietes, eines Kommunalbezirkes oder eines Distrikts, einschliesslich ländlicher Gebiete.
• Grösste Stadt des Landes.
★ Bevölkerung oder Bezeichnung der Stadtregion einschliesslich Vororte.
C Volkszählung. **E** Offizielle Schätzung. **U** Inoffizielle Schätzung.

Population of Cities and Towns / Einwohnerzahlen von Grossstädten / Habitantes en las Ciudades y Poblaciones
Population des Grands Centres et des Villes / População dos Centros Urbanos
307

Bulsār (★111,775)	57,909
Būndi	65,047
Burhānpur	172,710
Burnpur (★Āsānsol)	174,933
Calcutta (★11,021,918)	4,399,819
Cannanore (★Tellicherry)	65,238
Chāībāsa	56,729
Chākdaha	74,769
Chakradharpur (★47,666)	32,737
Chālisgaon	77,420
Champdāni (★Calcutta)	101,067
Chandannagar (★Calcutta)	120,378
Chandausi	82,748
Chandīgarh (★575,829)	504,094
Chāndpur	55,825
Chandrapur	226,105
Changanācheri	52,445
Channapatna	55,209
Chāpra	136,877
Chās	65,207
Chennai (Madras) (★5,421,985)	3,841,396
Chhatarpur (★75,594)	72,824
Chhindwāra (★96,858)	93,650
Chidambaram (★67,949)	58,740
Chikmagalūr	60,816
Chilakalūrupet	79,142
Chingleput	54,127
Chintāmani	50,394
Chīrāla (★142,778)	80,861
Chitradurga (★103,435)	87,069
Chittaranjan (★65,689)	47,186
Chittaurgarh	71,569
Chittoor	133,462
Chopda	49,234
Chūru	82,464
Coimbatore (★1,100,746)	816,321
Contai	53,484
Coonoor (★100,687)	48,003
Cuddalore	144,561
Cuddapah (★215,866)	121,463
Cuttack (★440,295)	403,418
Dabgram	147,217
Dabhoi	50,641
Dāhod (★96,632)	66,500
Dāltenganj	56,323
Damoh (★105,043)	95,661
Dānāpur (★Patna)	84,616
Dandeli	52,701
Darbhanga	218,391
Darjiling	73,062
Datia	64,477
Dāvangere (★287,233)	266,082
Dehra Dūn (★368,053)	270,159
Dehri	93,694
Delhi (★8,419,084)	7,206,704
Delhi Cantonment (★Delhi)	94,393
Deoband	66,208
Deoghar (★85,902)	76,380
Deolāli (★Nāsik)	44,331
Deoria	82,168
Dewās	164,364
Dhamtari	69,357
Dhanbad (★815,005)	151,789
Dhār	59,246
Dhārāpuram	48,393
Dharmapuri	59,318
Dharmavaram	78,961
Dhaulpur	68,533
Dholka (★54,352)	49,860
Dhorāji (★79,479)	77,748
Dhrāngadhra	57,961
Dhuburi	66,216
Dhule	278,317
Dibrugarh (★125,667)	120,127
Dimāpur	57,182
Dindigul	182,477
Dīsa	62,435
Dishergarh (★Āsānsol)	86,832
Dod Ballāpur	54,609
Dum Dum (★Calcutta)	40,961
Durg (★Bhilai)	150,645
Durgāpur	425,836
Elūru	212,866
Erode (★361,755)	159,323
Etah	78,458
Etāwah	124,072
Faizābād (★176,922)	124,437
Farīdābad (★Delhi)	617,717
Farīdkot	58,244
Farrukhābād (★208,727)	194,657
Fatehpur	117,675
Fathpur	66,387
Fāzilka	58,028
Fīrozābād (★270,536)	215,128
Fīrozpur	78,738
Fīrozpur Cantonment	53,094
Gadag	134,051
Gāndhidham	104,585
Gāndhinagar	123,359
Ganga Ghat	50,260
Gangānagar	161,482
Gangāpur (★68,886)	53,689
Gangāwati (★85,515)	64,843
Gangtok	25,024
Gārulia (★Calcutta)	80,918
Gaya (★294,427)	219,675
Ghāziābād (★511,759)	454,156
Ghāzīpur	76,547
Girīdīh	78,097
Godhra (★100,662)	96,813
Gokāk	52,080
Gonda	95,553
Gondal (★81,611)	80,584
Gondia	109,470
Gopichettipālaiyam	48,364
Gorakhpur	505,566
Gudivāda	101,656
Gudiyāttam (★90,557)	83,232
Gūdūr	55,984
Gulbarga (★310,920)	304,099
Guna	100,490
Guntakal	107,592
Guntūr	471,051
Gurdāspur	54,733
Gurgaon (★135,884)	121,486
Guruvayur (★118,632)	20,216
Guwāhāti	584,342
Gwalior (★717,780)	690,765
Hābra (★196,970)	100,223
Hājīpur	87,687
Haldwāni	104,195
Hālisahar (★Calcutta)	114,028
Hānsi	59,653
Hanumāngarh (★82,733)	78,525
Hāora (★Calcutta)	950,435
Hāpur	146,262
Hardoi	88,651
Haridwār (★187,392)	147,305
Harihar	66,647
Hassan (★108,706)	90,803
Hāthras	113,285
Hazārībāg	97,824
Himatnagar	51,461
Hindaun	60,780
Hindupur	104,651
Hinganghāt	78,715
Hingoli	54,457
Hisār (★181,255)	172,677
Hoshangābād	70,914
Hoshiārpur	122,705
Hospet (★134,799)	96,322
Hubli-Dhārwār	648,298
Hugli-Chinsurah (★Calcutta)	151,806
Hyderābād (★4,344,437)	3,043,896
Ichalkaranji (★235,979)	214,950
Imphāl (★202,839)	198,535
Indore (★1,109,056)	1,091,674
Ingrāj Bāzār (★177,164)	139,204
Itānagar	16,545
Itārsi (★84,626)	77,334
Jabalpur (★888,916)	741,927
Jabalpur Cantonment (★Jabalpur)	56,124
Jagādhri (★Yamunānagar)	67,386
Jagdalpur (★84,578)	66,154
Jagtiāl	67,591
Jahānābād	52,332
Jaipur (★1,518,235)	1,458,483
Jalandhar	509,510
Jālgaon	242,193
Jālna	174,985
Jalpāiguri	68,732
Jamālpur	86,112
Jamkhandi	48,143
Jammu (★223,361) (1981C)	206,135
Jamnagar (★381,646)	341,637
Jamshedpur (★829,171)	460,577
Jaora (★56,023)	54,997
Jaunpur	136,062
Jaypur	65,246
Jetpur (★95,397)	73,560
Jhānsi (★368,154)	300,850
Jharia (★Dhanbād)	69,641
Jhārsuguda	65,054
Jhunjhunūn	72,187
Jīnd	85,315
Jodhpur	666,279
Jorhāt (★112,030)	58,358
Jūnāgadh (★167,110)	130,484
Kadaiyanallūr	68,819
Kadiri	63,378
Kagaznagar	57,535
Kairāna	56,079
Kaithal	71,142
Kākināda (★327,541)	279,980
Kalamassery (★Cochin)	54,342
Kālol (★92,550)	82,137
Kalyān (★Bombay)	1,014,557
Kāmāreddi	48,666
Kāmārhāti (★Calcutta)	266,889
Kambam	52,435
Kāmthi (★127,151)	78,612
Kānchipuram (★171,129)	144,955
Kānchrāpāra (★Calcutta)	100,194
Kānnangād (★118,214)	57,165
Kannauj	58,932
Kānpur (★2,029,889)	1,874,409
Kānpur Cantonment (★Kānpur)	95,021
Kapra (★Hyderābād)	87,747
Kapūrthala	64,567
Karād	56,819
Kāraikāl	61,804
Kāraikkudi (★110,926)	71,965
Kāranja	48,866
Karauli	49,008
Karīmnagar	148,583
Karnāl (★176,131)	173,751
Karūr (★113,669)	73,418
Kārwār	51,022
Kāsaragod	50,126
Kāsganj	75,634
Kāshīpur	69,870
Katihār (★154,367)	135,436
Kātwa	55,541
Kāvali	65,910
Kāyankulam	67,151
Keshod	50,172
Khadki Cantonment (★Pune)	78,323
Khambhāt (★89,834)	76,746
Khāmgaon	73,692
Khammam (★149,077)	127,992
Khandwa	145,133
Khanna	71,990
Kharagpur (★264,842)	177,989
Kharagpur Railway Settlement (★Kharagpur)	84,252
Khardaha	88,358
Khargone	66,786
Khurja	80,305
Kishanganj	64,568
Kishangarh Bās	81,948
Koch Bihār (★92,820)	71,215
Kochi (Cochin) (★1,140,605)	564,589
Kodarma	53,577
Kohīma	51,418
Kolār	83,287
Kolār Gold Fields (★156,746)	72,485
Kolhāpur (★418,538)	406,370
Konnagar (★Calcutta)	62,200
Korba	124,501
Kota	537,371
Kot Kapūra	62,430
Kottagūdem (★102,137)	80,440
Kottayam (★166,552)	63,155
Kovilpatti	78,834
Kozhikode (★801,190)	419,831
Krishnagiri	60,315
Krishnanagar	121,110
Kukatpalle (★Hyderābād)	186,963
Kulti (★Asansol)	108,518
Kumārapālaiyam (★Bhavāni)	57,672
Kumbakonam (★150,540)	139,483
Kundla (★65,785)	64,815
Kurasia (★71,708)	15,898
Kurichi (★Coimbatore)	64,796
Kurnool (★275,360)	236,800
Lādnūn	48,205
Lakhīmpur	79,951
Lalbahadur Nagar (★Hyderābād)	155,514
Lalitpur	79,870
Lātūr	197,408
Luckeesarai	53,360
Lucknow (★1,669,204)	1,619,115
Lucknow Cantonment (★Lucknow)	50,089
Ludhiāna	1,042,740
Machilīpatnam (Bandar)	159,110
Madanapalle	73,820
Madgaon (Margao) (★72,400)	58,951
Mādhavaram (★Madras)	49,258
Madhubani	53,747
Madhyamgrām (★Calcutta)	69,252
Madurai (★1,085,914)	940,989
Mahbūbnagar	116,833
Mahesāna (★109,950)	88,201
Mahoba	56,247
Mahuva (★64,144)	59,912
Mainpuri	76,735
Makrāna (★66,720)	59,714
Malappuram (★142,204)	49,692
Malaut	56,868
Mālegaon	342,595
Māler Kotla	88,600
Malkajgiri (★Hyderābād)	127,178
Malkāpur	51,311
Mancheriyal	52,657
Mandsaur	95,907
Mandya	120,265
Mangalagiri	59,152
Mangalore (★426,341)	273,304
Mango (★Jamshedpur)	108,100
Manjeri	69,334
Manmād	61,312
Mannārgudi	56,552
Mānsa	55,089
Mathura (★235,922)	226,691
Maunath Bhanjan	136,697
Mawāna	51,701
Māyūram	76,837
Medinīpur	125,498
Meerut (★849,799)	753,778
Meerut Cantonment (★Meerut)	96,021
Melappālaiyam (★Tirunelveli)	68,347
Mettuppālaiyam	63,479
Mhow (★83,796)	74,987
Mira Bhayandar (★Bombay)	175,605
Miraj (★Sāngli)	121,593
Miryalaguda	65,879
Mirzāpur	169,336
Modinagar (★123,279)	101,660
Moga (★110,958)	108,304
Mokāma	59,528
Morādābād (★443,701)	429,214
Morbi (★120,117)	90,357
Morena	147,124
Mormugao (★90,429)	83,367
Motihāri (★83,255)	77,432
Mubārakpur (★62,733)	45,376
Mughal Sarāi (★91,505)	66,529
Muktsar	66,383
• Mumbai (Bombay) (★12,596,243)	9,925,891
Munger	150,112
Murwāra	163,431
Muzaffarnagar (★247,624)	240,609
Muzaffarpur	241,107
Mysore (★653,345)	480,692
Nābha	54,421
Nadiād (★170,217)	167,051
Nagaon	93,350
Nāgappattinam (★99,745)	86,489
Nāgaur	68,194
Nagda	79,622
Nāgercoil	190,084
Nagīna	58,513
Nāgpur (★1,664,006)	1,624,752
Naihāti (★Calcutta)	132,701
Najībābād	66,860
Nalasopara (★Bombay)	67,732
Nalgonda	84,910
Nānded (★309,316)	275,083
Nandurbār	78,378
Nandyāl	119,813
Nangi (★Calcutta)	52,958
Narasapur	56,362
Narasaraopet	88,726
Nārnaul	51,976
Nāshik (★725,341)	656,925
Navadwip (★155,905)	125,037
Navsāri (★190,946)	126,089
Nawābganj (★77,234)	64,582
Nawāda	53,174
Nawalgarh	51,190
Nedumangād	49,875
Neemuch (★90,474)	86,439
Nellore	316,606
New Bārākpur (★Calcutta)	63,795
New Bombay (★Bombay)	304,724
NEW DELHI (★Delhi)	301,297
Neyveli (★126,889)	118,080
Nipāni	51,624
Nirmal	57,761
Nizāmābād	241,034
North Bārākpur (★Calcutta)	100,606
North Dum Dum (★Calcutta)	149,965
Ongole (★128,648)	100,836
Orai	98,716
Osmānābād	68,019
Pālakodu	56,969
Palani (★76,209)	68,907
Pālanpur (★90,269)	80,657
Pālayankottai (★Tirunelveli)	98,399
Pālghāt (★180,033)	123,289
Pāli	136,842
Pallavaram (★Madras)	111,866
Palwal	59,168
Palwancha	53,102
Panaji (Panjim) (★85,515)	43,349
Pandharpur	79,902
Pānihāti (★Calcutta)	275,990
Pānīpat	191,212
Panruti	51,394
Panvel	58,986
Paramakkudi	72,321
Parbhani	190,255
Parli	72,670
Pātan (★97,025)	96,112
Pathānkot (★128,198)	123,930
Patiāla (★253,706)	238,368
Patna (★1,099,647)	917,243
Pattukkottai	58,062
Payyannūr	64,032
Periyakulam	46,744
Petlād	48,552
Phagwāra (★88,316)	83,163
Pīlibhīt	106,605
Pilkhua	51,162
Pimpri-Chinchwad (★Pune)	517,083
Pollāchi (★127,132)	86,897
Pondicherry (★401,437)	203,065
Ponmalai (★Tiruchchirāppalli)	69,639
Ponnāni	51,770
Ponnūru Nidubrolu	54,363
Porbandar (★160,671)	116,671
Port Blair	74,955
Proddatūr	133,914
Pudukkottai	99,058
Puliyangudi	53,287
Pune (Poona) (★2,493,987)	1,566,651
Pune Cantonment (★Pune)	82,139
Puri	125,199
Pūrnia (★136,918)	114,912
Puruliya	92,386
Pusad	55,931
Quilon (★362,572)	139,852
Qutubullapur (★Hyderābād)	106,591
Rabkavi Banhatti	60,609
Rāe Bareli	129,904
Rāichūr (★170,577)	157,551
Raiganj (★159,266)	151,045
Raigarh (★90,265)	86,767
Raipur (★462,694)	438,639
Rājahmundry (★401,397)	324,851
Rājapālaiyam	114,202
Rajendranagar (★Hyderābād)	84,520
Rajhara-Jharandalli	55,996
Rājkot (★654,490)	559,407
Rāj Nāndgaon	125,371
Rājpur (★86,451)	60,175
Rājpura	70,983
Rāmanagaram	50,437
Rāmanāthapuram	52,879
Rāmgarh (★82,328)	51,264
Rāmpur	243,742
Rānāghāt (★127,035)	62,532
Rānchi (★614,795)	599,306
Rānībennur	67,442
Rānīganj (★155,823)	61,997
Ratangarh	55,079
Ratlām (★195,776)	195,776
Ratnāgiri	56,529
Raurkela (★398,864)	215,509
Raurkela Civil Township (★Raurkela)	142,408
Rāyachoti	51,931
Rāyagāda	48,247
Rewa	128,981
Rewāri	75,342
Rishīkesh (★71,704)	44,487
Rishra (★Calcutta)	102,815
Robertson Pet (★Kolār Gold Fields)	68,230
Rohtak	216,096
Roorkee (★91,139)	80,262
Rudrapur	61,280
Sāgar (★257,119)	195,346
Sahāranpur	374,945
Saharsa	80,149
Sahaswān	51,080
Sāhibganj	49,257
Salem (★578,291)	366,712
Sāmalkot	48,760
Sambalpur (★193,297)	131,138
Sambhal	150,869
Sangamner	49,061
Sangareddi	50,123
Sāngli (★363,751)	193,197
Sangrūr	56,419
Sankarankovil	48,846
Sardārshahr	67,954
Sarni	84,379
Sāsarām	98,122
Sātāra	95,180
Satna (★160,500)	156,630
Sawāi Mādhopur (★77,690)	72,165
Secunderābād Cantonment (★Hyderābād)	171,148
Sehore	71,456
Seoni	64,532
Serampore (★Calcutta)	137,026
Serilungampalle (★Hyderābād)	72,320
Shahdol (★60,529)	55,508
Shāhjahānpur (★260,403)	237,713
Shāmli	70,853
Shāntipur	109,956
Shikohābād	62,829
Shiliguri	216,950
Shillong (★223,366)	131,719
Shimoga (★193,028)	179,258
Shivpuri	108,277
Shrirampur (★79,052)	71,368
Siddhapur (★51,794)	50,770
Siddipet	54,091
Sikandarābād	60,992
Sīkar	148,272
Silchar	115,483
Silvassa	11,725
Simla (★110,360)	82,054
Sindri (★Dhānbād)	72,333
Sircilla	50,048
Sirsa	112,841
Sītāmarhi (★67,336)	44,935
Sītāpur	121,842
Siuri	54,298
Sivakāsi (★102,175)	65,593
Siwān	63,125
Solāpur (★620,846)	604,215
Sonīpat	143,922
South Dum Dum (★Calcutta)	232,811
Srīkākulam	88,883
Srikalahasti	61,578
Srīnagar (★606,002) (1981C)	594,775
Srīrangam (★Tiruchchirāppali)	70,109
Srīvilliputtūr	68,644
Sujāngarh	70,843
Sultānpur	76,533
Sūrat (★1,518,950)	1,498,817
Surendranagar (★166,466)	106,110
Suriāpet	60,630
Tādepallegūdem	88,878
Tādpatri	71,068
Talipparamba	60,226
Tāmbaram (★Madras)	107,187
Tānda	70,605
Tanuku	62,913
Tellicherry (★463,962)	103,579
Tenāli	143,726
Tenkāsi	55,189
Tezpur	55,064
Thāna (★Bombay)	803,369
Thānesar	61,255
Thanjāvūr	202,013
Theni-Allinagaram	60,050
Thiruvārūr	49,195
Thrippunithura (★Cochin)	51,078
Tīkamgarh	54,173
Tindivanam	61,579
Tinsukia	73,918
Tiruchchirāppalli (★711,862)	387,223
Tiruchengodu	63,027
Tirunelveli (★366,869)	135,825
Tirupati (★188,904)	174,369
Tiruppattūr	55,282
Tiruppur (★306,237)	235,661
Tirūr	49,453
Tiruvalla	54,780

▲ Población de un municipio, comuna o distrito entero, incluyendo sus áreas rurales.
• Ciudad más grande de un país.
★ Población o designación de un área metropolitana, incluyendo los suburbios.
C Censo. E Estimado oficial. U Estimado no oficial.

▲ Population d'une municipalité, d'une commune ou d'un district, zone rurale incluse.
• Ville la plus peuplée du pays.
★ Population de l'agglomération (ou nom de la zone métropolitaine englobante).
C Recensement. E Estimation officielle.
U Estimation non officielle.

▲ População de um município, comuna ou distrito, inclusive as respectivas áreas rurais.
• Maior cidade de um país.
★ População ou indicação de uma área metropolitana.
C Censo. E Estimativa oficial. U Estimativa não oficial.

Tiruvannāmalai	109,196
Tiruvottiyūr (★Madras)	168,642
Titāgarh (★Calcutta)	114,085
Tonk	100,079
Trichūr (★275,053)	74,604
Trivandrum (★826,225)	524,006
Ttruchchendūr (★75,301)	27,420
Tumkūr (★179,877)	138,903
Tuticorin (★280,091)	199,854
Udagamandalam	81,763
Udaipur	308,571
Udamalpet	58,678
Udgīr	70,453
Ujjain	362,266
Ulhāsnagar (★Bombay)	369,077
Ulubāria	155,172
Unjha	51,003
Unnāo	107,425
Upleta	51,801
Uppal Kalan (★Hyderābād)	75,644
Uttarpara-Kotrung (★Calcutta)	101,268
Vadodara (★1,126,824)	1,031,346
Välpārai	106,523
Vāniyambādi (★92,307)	72,426
Vārānasi (Benares) (★1,030,863)	929,270
Vasai (Bassein) (★83,734)	39,781
Veerappanchattiram (★Erode)	61,649
Vejalpur (★Ahmadābād)	92,116
Vellore (★310,776)	175,061
Verāval (★120,178)	93,976
Vidisha	92,922
Vijayawāda (★845,756)	701,827
Vikramasingapuram	49,834
Viluppuram	88,788
Viramgām	50,788
Virār (★Bombay)	57,600
Virudunagar	70,971
Vishākhapatnam (★1,057,118)	752,037
Visnagar (★59,647)	57,869
Vizianagaram (★177,022)	160,359
Vriddhāchalam	52,819
Wadhwan (★Surendranager)	49,791
Warangal (★467,757)	447,657
Wardha	102,985
Wāshīm	49,140
Yamunānagar (★219,754)	144,346
Yavatmāl (★121,816)	108,578
Yemmiganur	65,089

INDONESIA

1990 C	179,378,946
Ambon (▲275,888)	205,193
Balikpapan	344,147
Banda Aceh (Kuturaja) (▲184,650)	143,360
Bandung (★2,220,000)	2,058,122
Banjarmasin	480,737
Bantul (▲696,944)	13,700
Banyuwangi (▲1,455,010)	92,800
Batang (▲591,647)	55,200
Bekasi (▲951,509) (★Jakarta)	146,400
Bengkulu	170,183
Binjai (▲181,866)	127,184
Blitar (★150,000)	118,933
Bogor (★620,000)	271,341
Bojonegoro (▲1,104,031)	63,700
Brebes (▲1,521,835)	49,500
Bukittinggi	83,753
Cianjur (▲1,420,228)	108,700
Cibinong (▲1,812,734)	264,100
Cikampek (▲1,152,405)	91,200
Cilacap (▲1,487,308)	141,900
Ciledug (▲1,244,151)	293,000
Cimahi (▲1,909,459) (★Bandung)	196,900
Ciparay (▲1,909,456)	135,300
Cirebon (★315,000)	254,477
Denpasar (▲663,390)	209,500
Depok (▲1,812,734) (★Jakarta)	382,000
Dili (▲123,475)	12,900
Dumai (▲904,375)	71,500
Garut (▲1,478,757)	145,900
Genteng (▲1,455,010)	60,900
Gorontalo (▲119,745)	94,058
Gresik (▲856,853)	102,000
Indramayu (▲1,226,609)	32,700
• JAKARTA (★10,200,000)	8,227,746
Jambi	339,786
Jayapura (Sukarnapura) (▲246,389)	101,200
Jember (▲2,062,554)	190,000
Jepara (▲827,657)	36,200
Jombang (▲1,048,805)	65,700
Karawang (▲1,152,405)	143,300
Kebumen (▲1,120,982)	48,300
Kediri	249,538
Kendari (▲488,471)	70,700
Kisaran (▲884,594)	66,600
Klangenang (▲1,035,575)	291,200
Klaten (▲1,056,135)	120,400
Kudus (▲631,322)	182,600
Kuningan (▲739,360)	33,100
Kupang (▲522,944)	111,300
Lumajang (▲924,894)	62,100
Madiun (★200,000)	170,050
Magelang (★180,000)	123,156
Majalaya (▲1,909,459)	176,600
Malang	695,089
Manado	320,600
Mataram (▲859,273)	276,300
Medan	1,730,052
Mojokerto	99,707
Muncar (▲1,455,010)	48,100
Padang (▲631,263)	477,064
Padangsidempuan (▲954,184)	72,100
Palangkaraya	112,511
Palembang	1,144,047
Palu (▲784,647)	56,500
Pangkalpinang	113,129
Pare (▲1,343,125)	51,400
Parepare (▲101,421)	84,093
Pasuruan (★190,000)	152,075
Pati (▲1,064,115)	54,900
Payakumbuh (▲90,838)	50,475
Pekalongan (★430,000)	242,714
Pekanbaru	398,621
Pemalang (▲1,114,228)	86,200
Pematangsiantar (★250,000)	219,316
Perabumulih (▲582,396)	59,500
Ponorogo (▲837,055)	59,500
Pontianak	396,658
Pringsewu (▲1,825,040)	58,300
Probolinggo (▲176,906)	131,077
Purwakarta (▲437,327)	62,300
Purwokerto (▲1,348,825)	158,300
Purworejo (▲700,788)	38,600
Salatiga	98,012
Samarinda (▲407,174)	334,851
Semarang	1,249,230
Serang (▲1,201,742)	84,900
Sibolga	71,559
Sidoarjo (▲1,167,467)	76,800
Singaraja (▲540,150)	59,200
Singkawang (▲574,156)	64,000
Situbondo (▲574,156)	63,800
Sorong (▲199,085)	77,900
Subang (▲1,037,394)	52,700
Sukabumi (★250,000)	119,938
Sumedang (▲718,488)	42,900
Sumenep (▲933,746)	53,300
Surabaya	2,473,272
Surakarta (★590,000)	503,827
Taman (▲1,167,467)	88,100
Tangerang (▲1,244,151)	99,100
Tanjungbalai	107,751
Tanjungkarang-Telukbetung (▲636,418)	457,927
Tanjungpinang	105,820
Tarakan (▲232,494)	61,300
Tasikmalaya (▲1,444,242)	194,000
Tebingtinggi	116,749
Tegal (★510,000)	229,553
Tembilahan (▲4,878,066)	62,700
Tuban (▲977,716)	54,700
Tulungagung (▲890,032)	97,000
Ujungpandang (Makasar)	944,372
Yogyakarta (★540,000)	412,059

IRAN / Īrān

1986 C	49,445,010
Ābādān	21,879
Abhar	62,145
Āghā Jārī	64,102
Ahvāz	579,826
Alīgūdarz	53,843
Āmol	118,242
Andīmeshk	56,288
Arāk	265,349
Ardabīl	281,973
Bābol	115,320
Bākhtarān (Kermānshāh)	560,514
Bam	50,709
Bandar-e 'Abbās	201,642
Bandar-e Anzalī (Bandar-e Pahlavī)	87,063
Bandar-e Būshehr	120,787
Bandar-e Māh Shahr	71,808
Behbahān	78,694
Behshahr	52,461
Bīrjand	81,798
Bojnūrd	93,392
Borāzjān	67,061
Borūjerd	183,879
Dezfūl	151,420
Do Gonbadān	51,107
Do Rūd	62,517
Emāmshahr (Shāhrūd)	78,950
Eṣfahān (★1,175,000)	986,753
Eslāmābād	73,362
Eslāmshahr (★Tehrān)	215,129
Fasā	64,771
Gonbad-e Qābūs	87,100
Gorgān	139,430
Hamadān	272,499
Īlām	89,035
Jahrom	77,174
Karaj (★Tehrān)	275,100
Kāshān	138,599
Kāshmar	49,259
Kāzerūn	73,444
Kermān	257,284
Khomeynīshahr (★Eṣfahān)	104,647
Khorramābād	208,592
Khorramshahr (1976C)	146,706
Khvoy	115,343
Mahābād	75,238
Malāyer	103,640
Marāgheh	100,679
Marand	71,394
Marv Dasht	79,132
Mashhad	1,463,508
Masjed-e Soleymān	104,787
Mīāndoāb	59,551
Mīāneh	65,959
Nahāvand	52,265
Najafābād	129,058
Naqadeh	52,275
Neyshābūr	109,258
Orūmīyeh (Reẕā'īyeh)	300,746
Qā'emshahr	109,288
Qazvīn	248,591
Qom	543,139
Qomsheh	73,367
Qūchān	66,531
Rafsanjān	66,498
Rasht	290,897
Sabzevār	129,103
Salmās	50,573
Sanandaj	204,537
Saqqez	81,351
Sārī	141,020
Sāveh	64,081
Semnān	64,891
Shahr-e Kord	75,080
Shīrāz	848,289
Shīrvān	48,688
Shūshtar	65,840
Sīrjān	90,072
Tabrīz	971,482
• TEHRĀN (★7,500,000)	6,042,584
Torbat-e Heydarīyeh	72,068
Varāmīn	58,311
Yazd	230,483
Zābol	75,105
Zāhedān	281,923
Zanjān	215,261

IRAQ / Al 'Irāq

1985 E	15,584,987
Ad-Dīwānīyah (1970E)	62,300
Al-'Amārah	131,785
Al-Baṣrah	616,700
Al-Hillah	215,249
Al-Kūt	73,022
Al-Mawṣil	570,926
An-Najaf	242,603
An-Nāṣirīyah	138,842
Ar-Ramādī	137,388
As-Samāwah	75,293
As-Sulaymānīyah	279,424
• BAGHDĀD (1987C)	3,841,268
Ba'qūbah	114,516
Irbīl	333,903
Karbalā'	184,574
Kirkūk (1970E)	207,900

IRELAND / Éire

1991 C	3,525,719
Cork (★174,400)	127,253
• DUBLIN (BAILE ĀTHA CLIATH) (★1,150,000)	478,389
Dún Laoghaire (★Dublin)	55,540
Galway	50,853
Limerick (★75,436)	52,083
Waterford (★41,853)	40,328

ISLE OF MAN

1991 C	69,788
• DOUGLAS (★30,000)	22,214

ISRAEL / Isrā'īl / Yisra'el

1994 E	5,182,200
'Akko (Acre) (★Hefa)	45,100
Ashdod	110,300
Ashqelon	73,300
Bat Yam (★Tel Aviv-Yafo)	143,200
Be'ér Sheva'(Beersheba)	141,400
Bene Beraq (★Tel Aviv-Yafo)	125,000
Elat	33,300
Giv'atayim (★Tel Aviv-Yafo)	47,200
Hadera	56,100
Hefa (★460,000)	246,500
Herzliyya (★Tel Aviv-Yafo)	82,700
Holon (★Tel Aviv-Yafo)	162,800
Kefar Sava (★Tel Aviv-Yafo)	65,800
Lod (Lydda) (★Tel Aviv-Yafo)	49,500
Nazerat (Nazareth) (★77,000)	52,200
Netanya (★Tel Aviv-Yafo)	142,700
Petah Tiqwa (★Tel Aviv-Yafo)	151,100
Ra'anana (★Tel Aviv-Yafo)	56,900
Ramat Gan (★Tel Aviv-Yafo)	122,800
Ramla (★Tel Aviv-Yafo)	55,500
Rehovot (★Tel Aviv-Yafo)	83,200
Rishon LeZiyyon (★Tel Aviv-Yafo)	154,300
• Tel Aviv-Yafo (★1,887,200)	357,400
YERUSHALAYIM (AL-QUDS) (JERUSALEM) (★604,000)	567,100

ITALY / Italia

1991 C	56,411,290
Afragola (★Napoli)	59,940
Alessandria (▲93,351)	74,000
Altamura	57,462
Ancona	103,268
Andria	82,556
Arezzo (▲91,623)	74,200
Asti (▲74,497)	62,800
Avellino	54,343
Aversa (★Napoli)	50,361
Bari (★475,000)	341,273
Barletta	86,215
Benevento (▲62,683)	51,900
Bergamo (★345,000)	115,655
Biella	50,993
Bitonto	49,792
Bologna (★525,000)	411,803
Bolzano	100,380
Brescia	196,766
Brindisi	91,778
Busto Arsizio (★Milano)	77,001
Cagliari (★305,000)	211,719
Caltanissetta	62,853
Campobasso (▲51,307)	44,400
Carpi (▲60,794)	49,600
Carrara (★Massa)	68,480
Caserta	68,811
Casoria (▲79,315) (★Napoli)	57,800
Castellammare di Stabia (★Napoli)	68,720
Catania (★550,000)	330,037
Catanzaro	103,802
Cava de' Tirreni (★Salerno)	52,610
Cerignola	54,971
Cesena (▲89,497)	72,200
Chieti	57,535
Cinisello Balsamo (★Milano)	75,606
Civitavecchia	50,856
Collegno (★Torino)	47,192
Cologno Monzese (★Milano)	50,853
Como (★165,000)	85,955
Cosenza (★150,000)	104,483
Cremona	75,160
Crotone (▲61,813)	54,300
Cuneo (▲55,838)	47,900
Empoli (▲42,790)	32,300
Ercolano (★Napoli)	60,869
Ferrara (▲140,600)	110,700
Firenze (★640,000)	402,316
Foggia	155,042
Foligno (▲53,518)	42,500
Forlì (▲109,755)	90,600
Gela	79,718
Genova (Genoa) (★805,000)	675,639
Giugliano in Campania (★Napoli)	59,091
Grosseto (▲71,373)	57,000
Imola (▲62,352)	48,800
Imperia	41,278
L'Aquila (▲67,818)	43,100
La Spezia (★185,000)	101,701
Latina (▲105,543)	72,700
Lecce	102,344
Lecco	45,859
Legnano (★Milano)	50,068
Livorno	171,265
Lucca	86,437
Manfredonia	58,157
Mantova (▲54,228)	46,800
Marsala	77,218
Massa (★145,000)	67,779
Matera	54,872
Messina	274,846
Mestre (▲317,837) (★Venezia)	181,900
• Milano (Milan) (★3,750,000)	1,371,008
Modena	177,501
Molfetta	66,658
Moncalieri (★Torino)	58,433
Monopoli (▲43,019)	33,100
Monza (★Milano)	121,151
Napoli (Naples) (★2,875,000)	1,024,601
Nicastro (▲69,660)	53,700
Nocera Inferiore	49,021
Novara	103,349
Padova (★270,000)	218,186
Palermo	697,162
Parma	173,991
Pavia	80,073
Perugia (▲150,576)	109,500
Pesaro (▲90,341)	78,700
Pescara	128,553
Piacenza	102,252
Pisa	101,500
Pistoia (▲87,275)	73,900
Pordenone	50,222
Portici (★Napoli)	67,824
Potenza (▲68,499)	58,800
Pozzuoli (▲75,706) (★Napoli)	67,100
Prato (★215,000)	165,364
Quartu Sant'Elena	60,852
Ragusa	69,423
Ravenna (▲136,724)	87,000
Reggio di Calabria	178,496
Reggio nell'Emilia (▲131,880)	108,800
Rho (★Milano)	51,646
Rimini (▲130,896)	114,800
Rivoli (★Torino)	51,884
ROMA (★3,175,000)	2,693,383
Salerno (★250,000)	153,436
San Benedetto del Tronto	45,220
San Giorgio a Cremano (★Napoli)	62,168
San Remo	59,247
San Severo	55,376
Sassari	120,011
Savona (★112,000)	68,997
Scandicci (★Firenze)	53,264
Sesto Fiorentino (★Firenze)	46,899
Sesto San Giovanni (★Milano)	85,175
Siena	57,745
Siracusa	125,444
Taranto	232,200
Teramo (▲52,490)	36,100
Terni (▲109,809)	93,400
Torino (★1,550,000)	961,916
Torre Annunziata (★Napoli)	50,346
Torre del Greco (★Napoli)	101,456
Trani	49,337
Trapani (▲69,273)	59,700
Trento (▲102,124)	83,100
Treviso	83,886
Trieste (Triest) (Trst)	231,047
Udine (★126,000)	98,322
Varese	85,461
Venezia (Venice) (★420,000)	85,100
Vercelli	50,207
Verona	258,946
Viareggio (▲60,559)	51,500
Vicenza	109,333
Vigevano	61,380
Viterbo (▲60,213)	48,700
Vittoria	56,970

JAMAICA

1991 C	2,366,067
• KINGSTON (★890,000)	587,798
Montego Bay	83,446
Portmore (★Kingston)	90,138
Spanish Town (★Kingston)	92,383

JAPAN / Nihon

1990 C	123,611,167
Abiko (★Tōkyō)	120,628
Ageo (★Tōkyō)	194,947
Aizu-wakamatsu	119,080
Akashi (★Ōsaka)	270,722
Akigawa (★Tōkyō)	50,387
Akishima (★Tōkyō)	105,372
Akita	302,362
Akō	51,131
Amagasaki (★Ōsaka)	498,999
Anan (▲59,044)	47,000
Anjō	142,251
Aomori	287,808
Arao (★Ōmuta)	59,507
Asahikawa	359,071
Asaka (★Tōkyō)	103,617
Ashikaga	167,686
Ashiya (★Ōsaka)	87,524
Atami	47,291
Atsugi (★Tōkyō)	197,282
Ayase (★Tōkyō)	77,926
Beppu	130,334
Bisai (★Nagoya)	55,880
Chiba (★Tōkyō)	829,455
Chichibu	60,915
Chigasaki (★Tōkyō)	201,675
Chikushino (★Fukuoka)	70,303
Chiryū (★Nagoya)	54,059
Chita (★Nagoya)	75,433
Chitose	78,946
Chōfu (★Tōkyō)	197,677
Chōshi	85,138
Daitō (★Ōsaka)	126,460
Dazaifu (★Fukuoka)	62,402
Ebetsu (★Sapporo)	97,201
Ebina (★Tōkyō)	105,822
Eniwa	55,615
Fuchū	45,739
Fuchū	50,060
Fuchū (★Tōkyō)	209,396
Fuji (★370,000)	222,490
Fujieda (★Shizuoka)	119,815
Fujiidera (★Ōsaka)	65,922
Fujimi (★Tōkyō)	94,864
Fujinomiya (★Fuji)	117,092
Fujioka (▲60,981)	50,100
Fujisawa (★Tōkyō)	350,330
Fuji-yoshida	54,804
Fukaya (▲94,017)	75,600
Fukuchiyama (▲66,506)	56,700
Fukui	252,743
Fukuoka (★1,750,000)	1,237,062
Fukushima	277,528
Fukuyama	365,612
Funabashi (★Tōkyō)	533,270
Furukawa (▲64,230)	51,200
Fussa (★Tōkyō)	58,062
Gamagōri	84,819
Gifu	410,324
Ginowan	75,905
Gotemba	79,557
Gushikawa	54,018
Gyōda	83,181
Habikino (★Ōsaka)	115,049
Hachinohe	241,057
Hachiōji (★Tōkyō)	466,347
Hadano (★Tōkyō)	155,620
Hagi	50,618
Hakodate	307,249
Hamada	49,135
Hamakita	81,157
Hamamatsu	534,620
Hanamaki (▲70,514)	55,000
Handa (★Nagoya)	99,550
Hannō (★Tōkyō)	73,214
Hashima	61,460
Hasuda (★Tōkyō)	59,706
Hatogaya (★Tōkyō)	56,440
Hatsukaichi (★Hiroshima)	63,441
Hekinan	65,899
Higashihiroshima (★Hiroshima)	94,209
Higashikurume (★Tōkyō)	113,818
Higashimatsuyama	84,394
Higashimurayama (★Tōkyō)	134,002
Higashiōsaka (★Ōsaka)	518,319
Higashiyamato (★Tōkyō)	75,132

▲ Population of an entire municipality, commune, or district, including rural area.
• Largest city in country.
★ Population or designation of the metropolitan area, including suburbs.
C Census. E Official estimate. U Unofficial estimate.

▲ Bevölkerung eines ganzen städtischen Verwaltungsgebietes, eines Kommunalbezirkes oder eines Distrikts, einschliesslich ländlicher Gebiete.
• Grösste Stadt des Landes.
★ Bevölkerung oder Bezeichnung der Stadtregion einschliesslich Vororte.
C Volkszählung. E Offizielle Schätzung. U Inoffizielle Schätzung.

Hikari (★Tokuyama)	47,611
Hikone	99,519
Himeji (★660,000)	454,360
Himi (▲60,766)	51,400
Hino (★Tōkyō)	165,928
Hirakata (★Ōsaka)	390,788
Hiratsuka (★Tōkyō)	245,950
Hirosaki (▲174,704)	133,800
Hiroshima (★1,575,000)	1,085,705
Hita (▲64,695)	57,100
Hitachi	202,141
Hōfu	117,634
Honjō	59,098
Hōya (★Tōkyō)	95,146
Hyūga	58,442
Ibaraki (★Ōsaka)	254,078
Ichihara (★Tōkyō)	257,716
Ichikawa (★Tōkyō)	436,596
Ichinomiya (★Nagoya)	262,434
Ichinoseki (▲61,967)	50,100
Iida (▲91,859)	64,700
Iizuka (★110,000)	83,131
Ikeda (★Ōsaka)	104,218
Ikoma (★Ōsaka)	99,604
Imabari	123,114
Imari (▲60,882)	50,000
Ina (▲60,062)	49,500
Inagi (★Tōkyō)	58,635
Inazawa (★Nagoya)	96,274
Inuyama (★Nagoya)	69,801
Iruma (★Tōkyō)	137,585
Isahaya	90,683
Ise (Uji-yamada)	104,164
Isehara (★Tōkyō)	89,567
Isesaki	115,938
Ishinomaki	121,976
Itami (★Ōsaka)	186,134
Itō	71,223
Iwaki (Taira)	355,812
Iwakuni	109,530
Iwamizawa	80,417
Iwata	83,521
Iwatsuki (★Tōkyō)	106,462
Izumi (★Sendai)	124,216
Izumi (★Ōsaka)	146,127
Izumi-ōtsu (★Ōsaka)	67,035
Izumi-sano (★Ōsaka)	88,866
Izumo (▲82,679)	69,600
Joetsu	130,116
Jōyō (★Ōsaka)	84,770
Kadoma (★Ōsaka)	142,297
Kaga	69,196
Kagoshima	536,752
Kainan (★Wakayama)	48,596
Kaizuka (★Ōsaka)	79,234
Kakamigahara	129,680
Kakegawa (▲72,795)	59,000
Kakogawa (★Ōsaka)	239,803
Kamagaya (★Tōkyō)	95,052
Kamaishi	52,484
Kamakura (★Tōkyō)	174,307
Kameoka	85,283
Kamifukuoka (★Tōkyō)	58,761
Kanazawa	442,868
Kani (★Nagoya)	80,012
Kanoya (▲77,655)	61,500
Kanuma (▲90,043)	74,900
Karatsu (▲79,207)	70,500
Kariya (★Nagoya)	120,126
Kasai	51,784
Kasaoka (▲59,619)	52,700
Kashihara (★Ōsaka)	115,554
Kashiwa (★Tōkyō)	305,058
Kashiwara (★Ōsaka)	76,819
Kashiwazaki (▲88,309)	75,300
Kasuga (★Fukuoka)	88,699
Kasugai (★Nagoya)	266,599
Kasukabe (★Tōkyō)	188,823
Katano (★Ōsaka)	65,308
Katsuta	109,825
Kawachi-nagano (★Ōsaka)	108,767
Kawagoe (★Tōkyō)	304,854
Kawaguchi (★Tōkyō)	438,680
Kawanishi (★Ōsaka)	141,253
Kawasaki (★Tōkyō)	1,173,603
Kesennuma	65,578
Kimitsu (▲89,242)	76,100
Kiryū	126,446
Kisarazu	123,433
Kishiwada (★Ōsaka)	188,563
Kitaibaraki	51,093
Kitakyūshū (★1,525,000)	1,026,455
Kitami	107,247
Kitamoto (★Tōkyō)	63,929
Kiyose (★Tōkyō)	67,539
Kōbe (★Ōsaka)	1,477,410
Kōchi	317,069
Kodaira (★Tōkyō)	164,013
Kōfu	200,626
Koga (★Tōkyō)	58,231
Koganei (★Tōkyō)	105,899
Kokubunji (★Tōkyō)	100,982
Komae (★Tōkyō)	74,189
Komaki (★Nagoya)	124,441
Komatsu	106,075
Kōnan (★Nagoya)	93,837
Kōnosu (★Tōkyō)	72,435
Kōriyama	314,642
Koshigaya (★Tōkyō)	285,259
Kudamatsu (★Tokuyama)	53,030
Kuki (★Tōkyō)	66,852
Kumagaya	152,124
Kumamoto	579,306
Kunitachi (★Tōkyō)	65,833
Kurashiki	414,693
Kure (★Hiroshima)	216,723
Kuroiso (▲52,344)	41,900
Kurume	228,347
Kusatsu (★Ōsaka)	94,767
Kushiro	205,639
Kuwana (★Nagoya)	97,909
Kyōto (★Ōsaka)	1,461,103
Machida (★Tōkyō)	349,050
Maebashi	286,261
Maizuru	96,333
Marugame	75,606
Matsubara (★Ōsaka)	135,919
Matsudo (★Tōkyō)	456,210
Matsue	142,956
Matsumoto	200,715
Matsusaka	118,725
Matsuyama	443,322
Mihara	85,518
Miki (★Ōsaka)	76,501
Minō (★Ōsaka)	122,120
Misato (★Tōkyō)	128,376
Mishima (★Numazu)	105,418
Mitaka (★Tōkyō)	165,564
Mito	234,968
Miura (★Tōkyō)	52,440
Miyako	58,503
Miyakonojō (▲130,153)	106,200
Miyazaki	287,352
Mobara	83,437
Moriguchi (★Ōsaka)	157,372
Morioka	235,434
Moriyama	58,561
Mukō (★Ōsaka)	52,928
Munakata	68,265
Muroran (★195,000)	117,855
Musashimurayama (★Tōkyō)	65,562
Musashino (★Tōkyō)	139,077
Mutsu	48,470
Nabari	68,933
Nagahama	55,485
Nagano	347,026
Nagaoka	185,938
Nagaokakyō (★Ōsaka)	77,191
Nagareyama (★Tōkyō)	140,059
Nagasaki	444,599
Nagoya (★4,800,000)	2,154,793
Naha	304,836
Nakama (★Kitakyūshū)	49,216
Nakatsu	66,388
Nakatsugawa	53,722
Nanao	50,103
Nara (★Ōsaka)	349,349
Narashino (★Tōkyō)	151,471
Narita	86,708
Naruto	64,575
Naze	46,306
Neyagawa (★Ōsaka)	256,524
Niigata	486,097
Niihama	129,149
Niitsu (▲63,999)	55,700
Niiza (★Tōkyō)	138,919
Nishinomiya (★Ōsaka)	426,909
Nishio	95,197
Nobeoka	130,624
Noboribetsu (★Muroran)	55,571
Noda (★Tōkyō)	114,475
Nōgata	62,530
Noshiro (▲55,915)	47,800
Numazu (★495,000)	211,732
Obihiro	167,384
Ōbu (★Nagoya)	69,720
Ōdate (▲68,195)	58,500
Odawara	193,417
Ōgaki	148,281
Ōita	408,501
Ōkawa	45,704
Okaya	59,849
Okayama	593,730
Okazaki	306,822
Okegawa (★Tōkyō)	69,029
Okinawa	105,845
Ōme (★Tōkyō)	125,960
Ōmi-hachiman (★Ōsaka)	66,066
Ōmiya (★Tōkyō)	403,776
Ōmura	73,435
Ōmuta (★225,000)	150,453
Ōnojō (★Fukuoka)	75,214
Onomichi	97,103
Ōsaka (★16,900,000)	2,623,801
Ōta	139,801
Otaru (★Sapporo)	163,211
Ōtsu (★Ōsaka)	260,018
Owariashi (★Nagoya)	65,675
Oyama (▲142,262)	120,000
Sabae	62,283
Saga	169,963
Sagamihara (★Tōkyō)	531,542
Saijō	56,821
Saiki	52,323
Sakado (★Tōkyō)	95,740
Sakai (★Ōsaka)	807,765
Sakaide	63,876
Sakata	100,811
Saku (▲62,003)	50,000
Sakura (★Tōkyō)	144,688
Sakurai	60,262
Sanda (▲64,560) (★Ōsaka)	54,500
Sanjō	85,823
Sano	83,484
Sapporo (★1,900,000)	1,671,742
Sasebo	244,677
Satte	54,342
Sayama (★Tōkyō)	157,309
Sayama (★Ōsaka)	54,319
Seki	68,386
Sendai, Kagoshima pref. (▲71,735)	58,000
Sendai, Miyagi pref. (★1,175,000)	918,398
Sennan (★Ōsaka)	60,065
Seto	126,340
Settsu (★Ōsaka)	87,453
Shibata (▲78,170)	63,600
Shijōnawate (★Ōsaka)	50,035
Shiki (★Tōkyō)	63,491
Shimada (▲73,810)	64,500
Shimizu (★Shizuoka)	241,523
Shimodate (▲66,028)	54,100
Shimonoseki (★Kitakyūshū)	262,635
Shiogama (★Sendai)	62,025
Shizuoka (★975,000)	472,196
Sōka (★Tōkyō)	206,132
Suita (★Ōsaka)	345,206
Suwa	52,464
Suzuka	174,105
Tachikawa (★Tōkyō)	152,824
Tagajō (★Sendai)	58,456
Tagawa	57,700
Tajimi (★Nagoya)	94,036
Takaishi (★Ōsaka)	65,086
Takamatsu	329,684
Takaoka (★220,000)	175,466
Takarazuka (★Ōsaka)	201,862
Takasago (★Ōsaka)	93,273
Takasaki	236,461
Takatsuki (★Ōsaka)	359,867
Takayama	65,243
Takefu	70,187
Takikawa	49,591
Tama (★Tōkyō)	144,489
Tamano	73,238
Tanabe (▲69,859)	59,100
Tanashi (★Tōkyō)	75,144
Tatebayashi	76,221
Tenri	68,815
Tochigi	86,216
Toda (★Tōkyō)	87,599
Tōkai (★Nagoya)	97,358
Toki	64,946
Tokoname (★Nagoya)	51,784
Tokorozawa (★Tōkyō)	303,040
Tokushima	263,356
Tokuyama (★250,000)	110,900
• TŌKYŌ (★30,300,000)	8,163,573
Tomakomai	160,118
Tondabayashi (★Ōsaka)	110,447
Toride (★Tōkyō)	81,665
Tosu	55,877
Tottori	142,467
Toyama	321,254
Toyoake (★Nagoya)	62,160
Toyohashi	337,982
Toyokawa	111,730
Toyonaka (★Ōsaka)	409,837
Toyota	332,336
Tsu	157,177
Tsuchiura	127,471
Tsuruga	68,041
Tsuruoka	99,889
Tsushima (★Nagoya)	59,343
Tsuyama	89,400
Ube (★230,000)	175,053
Ueda	119,435
Ueno (▲60,242)	51,400
Uji (★Ōsaka)	177,010
Uozu	49,514
Urasoe	89,994
Urawa (★Tōkyō)	418,271
Urayasu (★Tōkyō)	115,675
Usa (▲50,829)	38,600
Ushiku	60,693
Utsunomiya	426,795
Uwajima	68,034
Wakayama (★495,000)	396,553
Wakkanai	48,232
Wakō (★Tōkyō)	56,890
Warabi (★Tōkyō)	73,620
Yachiyo (★Tōkyō)	148,615
Yaizu (★Shizuoka)	112,186
Yamagata	249,487
Yamaguchi	129,461
Yamato (★Tōkyō)	194,866
Yamato-kōriyama (★Ōsaka)	92,949
Yamato-takada (★Ōsaka)	68,237
Yao (★Ōsaka)	277,568
Yashio (★Tōkyō)	72,473
Yatsushiro (▲108,135)	88,300
Yawata (★Ōsaka)	75,758
Yokkaichi	274,180
Yokohama (★Tōkyō)	3,220,331
Yokosuka (★Tōkyō)	433,358
Yonago	131,453
Yonezawa	94,760
Yono (★Tōkyō)	79,060
Yotsukaidō (★Tōkyō)	72,157
Yukuhashi	65,711
Zama (★Tōkyō)	112,102
Zushi (★Tōkyō)	56,704

JERSEY

1991 C	84,082
• SAINT HELIER (★46,500)	28,123

JORDAN / Al-Urdun

1989 E	3,111,000
Al-Baqʿah (★ʿAmmān)	63,985
• ʿAMMĀN (★1,625,000)	936,300
Ar-Ruṣayfah (★ʿAmmān)	72,580
As-Salṭ	47,585
Az-Zarqāʾ (★ʿAmmān)	318,055
Irbid	167,785

KAZAKHSTAN

1991 E	16,793,100
Akmola	286,000
Aktau	169,000
Akt'ubinsk	266,600
• ALMATY (★1,190,000)	1,156,200
Arkalyk	64,900
Atyrau	156,700
Balchaš	87,600
Džetygara	48,900
Ekibastuz	138,900
Karaganda	608,600
Kentau	65,100
Kokčetav	143,300
Kustanaj	233,900
Kzyl-Orda	158,200
Leninogorsk	69,500
Leninsk	73,000
Pavlodar	342,500
Petropavlovsk	248,300
Rudnyj	128,800
Šachtinsk	65,300
Šaran'	62,600
Šatpajev	61,400
Ščučinsk	56,000
Semipalatinsk	344,700
Šymkent	438,800
Taldykorgan	136,100
Temirtau	213,100
Turkestan	81,200
Ural'sk	214,000
Ust'-Kamenogorsk	332,900
Žambyl	312,300
Žanatas	53,000
Žezkazgan	111,100
Zyr'anovsk	53,800

KENYA

1989 C	21,397,000
Eldoret	104,900
Kakamega	47,300
Kisii	44,000
Kisumu	185,100
Kitale	53,000
Machakos	116,100
Meru	78,100
Mombasa (1990E)	537,000
• NAIROBI (1990E)	1,505,000
Nakuru	162,800
Nyeri	88,600
Thika	57,100

KIRIBATI

1990 C	72,298
BAIRIKI	2,226
• Bikenibeu	5,055

KOREA, NORTH / Chosŏn-minjujuŭi-inmīn-konghwaguk

1981 E	18,317,000
Ch'ŏngjin	490,000
Haeju (1983E)	213,000
Hamhŭng (1970E)	150,000
Hŭngnam (1976E)	260,000
Kaesŏng	259,000
Kanggye (1967E)	130,000
Kimch'aek (Sŏngjin) (1967E)	265,000
Namp'o	241,000
• P'YŎNGYANG	2,355,000
Sinŭiju	305,000
Songnim (1944C)	53,035
Wŏnsan	398,000

KOREA, SOUTH / Taehan-min'guk

1990 C	43,520,199
Andong	116,932
Ansan (★Sŏul)	252,157
Anyang (★Sŏul)	480,668
Bucheon (★Sŏul)	667,777
Changsŭngp'o	48,614
Changwŏn (★Masan)	323,138
Chech'on	102,037
Cheju	232,687
Chinhae	120,207
Chinju	258,365
Chŏmch'on	47,802
Ch'ŏnan	211,382
Ch'ŏngju	497,429
Chŏnju	86,850
Chŏnju	517,104
Ch'unch'ŏn	174,153
Ch'ungju	129,994
Ch'ungmu	92,159
Hanam (★Sŏul)	101,278
Inch'ŏn (★Sŏul)	1,818,293
Iri	203,401
Kangnŭng	152,605
Kimch'ŏn	81,349
Kimhae	106,166
Kimje	55,136
Kongju	65,195
Kumi	206,101
Kŭmsŏng (1985C)	58,897
Kunp'o (★Sŏul)	99,956
Kunsan	218,216
Kwachŏn (★Sŏul)	72,328
Kwangju	1,144,695
Kwangmyŏng (★Sŏul)	328,803
Kyŏngju	141,895
Kyŏngsan	60,524
Masan (★625,000)	496,639
Mikŭm (★Sŏul)	74,688
Miryang	52,995
Mokp'o	253,423
Naju	55,306
Namwŏn	63,121
Ŏnyang	66,379
Osan	59,492
P'ohang	318,595
Pusan (★3,800,000)	3,797,566
P'yŏngt'aek	79,238
Samch'ŏnp'o	62,824
Sangju	51,875
Shihŭng (★Sŏul)	107,190
Sŏgwipo	88,292
Sŏkch'o	73,796
Sŏngnam (★Sŏul)	540,764
Songtan	77,460
Sŏsan	55,930
• SŎUL (★15,850,000)	10,627,790
Sunch'ŏn	167,209
Suwŏn (★Sŏul)	644,968
T'aebaek	89,770
Taech'ŏn	56,922
Taegu	2,228,834
Taejŏn	1,062,084
Tongduchŏn	71,448
Tonghae	89,162
Tongkwang	70,118
Ŭijŏngbu (★Sŏul)	212,368
Ŭiwang	96,892
Ulsan	682,978
Wŏnju	173,013
Yŏch'ŏn	63,802
Yŏngch'ŏn	48,890
Yŏngju	84,335
Yŏsu	173,164

KUWAIT / Al-Kuwayt

1985 C	1,697,301
Abraq Khīṭān (★Al-Kuwayt)	45,120
Al-Aḥmadī (★285,000)	26,899
Al-Farwānīyah (★Al-Kuwayt)	68,701
Al-Fuḥayḥīl (★Al-Aḥmadī)	50,081
Al-Jahrah (★Al-Kuwayt)	111,222
• AL-KUWAYT (★1,375,000)	44,335
As-Sālimīyah (★Al-Kuwayt)	153,359
Aṣ-Ṣulaybīyah (★Al-Kuwayt)	51,314
Ḥawallī (★Al-Kuwayt)	145,126
Qalīb ash-Shuyūkh (★Al-Kuwayt)	114,771
South Khīṭān (★Al-Kuwayt)	69,256
Subahiya (★Al-Aḥmadī)	60,787

KYRGYZSTAN

1991 E	4,422,200
• BIŠKEK	631,300
Džalal-Abad	79,900
Kara-Balta	55,000
Karakol (Prževal'sk)	64,300
Oš	238,200
Tokmak	71,200

LAOS / Lao

1985 C	3,584,803
Savannakhét (1975E)	53,000
• VIANGCHAN (VIENTIANE)	377,409

LATVIA / Latvija

1991 E	2,680,500
Daugavpils	129,000
Jelgava	74,500
Jūrmala (★Rīga)	66,500
Liepāja	114,900
• RĪGA (★1,005,000)	910,200
Ventspils	50,400

LEBANON / Lubnān

1982 E	2,637,000
• BAYRŪT (★1,675,000)	509,000
Ṣaydā	105,000
Ṣūr (Tyre) (1970E)	12,500
Ṭarābulus (Tripoli)	198,000

LESOTHO

1986 C	1,577,536
• MASERU	109,382

LIBERIA

1986 E	2,221,000
• MONROVIA	465,000

▲ Población de un municipio, comuna o distrito entero, incluyendo sus áreas rurales.
• Ciudad más grande de un país.
★ Población o designación de un área metropolitana, incluyendo los suburbios.
C Censo. **E** Estimado oficial. **U** Estimado no oficial.

▲ Population d'une municipalité, d'une commune ou d'un district, zone rurale incluse.
• Ville la plus peuplée du pays.
★ Population de l'agglomération (ou nom de la zone métropolitaine englobante).
C Recensement. **E** Estimation officielle. **U** Estimation non officielle.

▲ População de um municipio, comuna ou distrito, inclusive as respectivas áreas rurais.
• Maior cidade de um país.
★ População ou indicação de uma área metropolitana.
C Censo. **E** Estimativa oficial. **U** Estimativa não oficial.

LIBYA / Lībiyā

1988 E	3,772,500
Al-Bayḍā (Beida) (1984C)	67,120
Banghāzī (★472,000)	446,250
Darnah (1984C)	62,179
Misrāṭah (★160,000)	121,669
• ṬARĀBULUS (TRIPOLI) (★960,000)	591,062
Ṭubruq (Tobruk) (1984C)	75,282

LIECHTENSTEIN

1992 E	29,386
• VADUZ	4,887

LITHUANIA / Lietuva

1992 C	3,746,400
Alytus	77,500
Kaunas	423,000
Klaipėda (Memel)	208,300
Marijampole	52,300
Panevėžys	132,300
Šiauliai	149,000
• VILNIUS	596,900

LUXEMBOURG

1991 C	384,062
Esch-sur-Alzette (★83,000)	24,012
• LUXEMBOURG (★136,000)	75,377

MACAU

1991 C	403,038
• MACAU	342,548

MACEDONIA / Makedonija

1994 C	1,936,877
Bitola	75,386
Kumanovo	66,237
Ohrid	41,213
Prilep	67,371
• SKOPJE	440,577
Štip	41,637

MADAGASCAR / Madagasikara

1988 E	11,238,000
• ANTANANARIVO	1,250,000
Antsirabe	100,000
Antsiranana	220,000
Fianarantsoa	300,000
Mahajanga	200,000
Toamasina	230,000
Toliara	150,000

MALAWI / Malaŵi

1987 C	7,988,507
• Blantyre	333,120
LILONGWE	223,318
Mzuzu	51,904

MALAYSIA

1991 C	17,566,982
Alor Setar (★165,113)	125,026
Batu Pahat (★84,538)	71,132
Butterworth (★94,231) (★George Town)	78,672
George Town (Pinang) (★520,000)	219,376
Ipoh (★468,765)	382,633
Johor Baharu (★442,250) (★Singapore, Singapore)	328,646
Kajang (★99,914)	46,269
Kelang (★368,228)	243,698
Keluang (★98,837)	49,043
Kota Baharu (★234,604)	219,713
Kota Kinabalu (Jesselton) (★160,122)	75,787
• KUALA LUMPUR (★1,800,000)	1,145,075
Kuala Terengganu	228,659
Kuantan	198,356
Kuching (★277,346)	147,729
Melaka (★112,873)	74,962
Miri (★102,969)	87,230
Muar (Bandar Maharani) (★70,637)	63,123
Petaling Jaya (★351,719) (★Kuala Lumpur)	254,849
Port Dickson (★47,962)	25,792
Sandakan (★157,180)	126,092
Seremban (★193,009)	182,584
Shah Alam (★Kuala Lumpur)	101,733
Sibu (★133,471)	126,384
Sungai Petani	115,519
Taiping	183,165
Telok Anson (★62,393)	48,350

MALDIVES

1990 C	213,215
• MALE'	55,130

MALI

1987 C	7,696,348
• BAMAKO	658,275
Gao	55,266
Kayes	50,993
Koutiala	48,698
Mopti	74,771
Ségou	88,135
Sikasso	73,859
Tombouctou (Timbuktu)	31,962

MALTA

1991 E	355,910
• VALLETTA (★215,000)	9,199

MARSHALL ISLANDS

1988 C	43,380
• Jarej-Uliga-Delap	14,649

MARTINIQUE

1990 C	359,579
• FORT-DE-FRANCE (★116,400)	100,072

MAURITANIA / Mauritanie / Mūrītāniyā

1987 E	2,007,000
• NOUAKCHOTT	285,000

MAURITIUS

1989 E	1,081,669
Beau Bassin-Rose Hill (★Port Louis)	94,236
Curepipe (★Port Louis)	66,704
• PORT LOUIS (★525,000)	141,870
Quatre Bornes (★Port Louis)	65,759
Vacoas-Phoenix (★Port Louis)	56,335

MAYOTTE

1985 E	67,205
• DZAOUDZI (★6,979)	5,865

MEXICO / México

1990 C	81,249,645
Acámbaro	52,248
Acapulco de Juárez	515,374
Aguascalientes	440,425
Apatzingán de la Constitución	76,643
Apodaca	103,364
Atlixco	74,233
Buenavista	114,653
Campeche	150,518
Cancún	167,730
Cárdenas	61,017
Celaya	214,856
Chalco (★Ciudad de México)	224,190
Chetumal	94,158
Chicoloapan de Juárz	57,306
Chihuahua	516,153
Chilpancingo de los Bravo	97,165
Chimalhuacán	235,587
Cholula de Rivadabia (★Puebla)	53,673
Ciudad Acuña	52,983
Ciudad del Carmen	83,806
• CIUDAD DE MÉXICO (★14,100,000)	8,235,744
Ciudad Guzmán	72,619
Ciudad Hidalgo	48,476
Ciudad Juárez (★El Paso, Tex., U.S.A.)	789,522
Ciudad Lerdo (★Torreón)	46,593
Ciudad López Mateos	315,059
Ciudad Madero (★Tampico)	160,331
Ciudad Mante	76,799
Ciudad Obregón	219,980
Ciudad Valles	91,402
Ciudad Victoria	194,996
Coacalco	151,255
Coatzacoalcos	198,817
Colima	106,967
Comitan de Dominguez	48,299
Córdoba	130,695
Cortazar	45,579
Cuautitlán Izcalli (★Ciudad de México)	313,238
Cuernavaca	279,187
Culiacán	415,046
Delicias	87,412
Durango	348,036
Ecatepec (★Ciudad de México)	1,218,135
Ensenada	169,426
Fresnillo	75,118
Garza García (★Monterrey)	113,017
General Escobedo	96,962
Gómez Palacio (★Torreón)	164,092
Guadalajara (★2,325,000)	1,650,042
Guadalupe (★Monterrey)	535,332
Guadalupe	46,433
Guamúchil	49,635
Guanajuato	73,108
Guasave	49,338
Guaymas	87,484
Hermosillo	406,417
Heroica Zitácuaro	66,983
Hidalgo del Parral	88,197
Iguala	83,412
Irapuato	265,042
Ixtapaluca	115,711
Jiutepec	82,845
Juchitán de Zaragoza	53,666
Lagos de Moreno	63,646
La Paz	137,641
La Piedad de Cabadas	62,625
Las Choapas	43,868
León	758,279
Los Mochis	162,659
Los Reyes la Paz	134,544
Manzanillo	67,697
Matamoros (★Brownsville, Tex., U.S.A.)	266,055
Matehuala	54,713
Mazatlán	262,705
Mérida	523,422
Metepec	116,203
Mexicali (★460,000)	438,377
Minatitlán	142,060
Monclova	177,792
Monterrey (★2,015,000)	1,068,996
Morelia	428,486
Naucalpan de Juárez (★Ciudad de México)	845,960
Navojoa	82,618
Nezahualcóyotl (★Ciudad de México)	1,255,456
Nogales	105,873
Nuevo Laredo (★Laredo, Tex., U.S.A.)	218,413
Oaxaca de Juárez	212,818
Ocotlán	62,595
Orizaba (★215,000)	114,216
Pachuca	174,013
Papantla de Olarte	46,075
Piedras Negras	96,178
Poza Rica	151,739
Puebla (★1,200,000)	1,007,170
Puerto Vallarta	93,503
Querétaro	385,503
Reynosa	265,663
Río Bravo	67,092
Sahuayo de José María Morelos	50,463
Salamanca	123,190
Salina Cruz	61,656
Saltillo	420,947
San Andrés Tuxtla	49,658
San Cristóbal de las Casas	73,388
San Francisco del Rincón	52,291
San Juan del Río	61,652
San Luis Potosí (★600,000)	489,238
San Luis Río Colorado	95,461
San Martín Texmelucan	57,519
San Miguel de Allende	48,935
San Nicolás de los Garza (★Monterrey)	436,603
San Pablo de las Salinas	84,217
Santa Catarina (★Monterrey)	162,707
Silao	50,828
Soledad de Graciano Sanchez	123,943
Tampico (★440,000)	272,690
Tapachula	138,858
Tecomán	60,938
Tehuacán	139,450
Temixco	65,058
Tepatitlán de Morelos	54,036
Tepic	206,967
Texcoco de Mora (★Ciudad de México)	74,194
Tijuana (★San Diego, Calif., U.S.A.)	698,752
Tlalnepantla (★Ciudad de México)	702,270
Tlaquepaque (★Guadalajara)	328,031
Tlaxcala de Xicotencatl	50,486
Toluca de Lerdo	327,865
Tonalá	151,190
Torreón (★690,000)	439,436
Tulancingo	75,477
Tuxpan	69,224
Tuxtepec	62,788
Tuxtla Gutiérrez	289,626
Uruapan del Progreso	187,623
Valle de Santiago	56,009
Veracruz (★540,000)	438,821
Villa Frontera	58,216
Villahermosa	261,231
Villa Nicolás Romero	148,342
Xalapa	279,451
Zacatecas	100,051
Zamora de Hidalgo	109,751
Zapopan (★Guadalajara)	668,323

MICRONESIA, FEDERATED STATES OF

1985 C	
• KOLONIA	6,169

MOLDOVA

1991 E	4,366,300
Bălţi	164,900
• CHIŞINĂU (KISHINEV)	676,700
Râbniţa (Rybnica)	62,900
Tighina	141,500
Tiraspol	186,000

MONACO

1990 C	29,972
• MONACO (★87,000)	29,972

MONGOLIA / Mongol Ard Uls

1991 E	2,250,000
Darchan	88,600
Erdene	58,200
• ULAANBAATAR	575,000

MONTSERRAT

1980 C	11,606
• PLYMOUTH	1,568

MOROCCO / Al-Magreb

1982 C	20,419,555
Agadir	110,479
Beni-Mellal	95,003
Berkane	60,490
• Casablanca (Dar-el-Beida) (★2,475,000)	2,139,204
El-Jadida (Mazagan)	81,455
Fès (★535,000)	448,823
Kenitra	188,194
Khemisset	58,925
Khouribga	127,181
Ksar-el-Kebir	73,541
Larache	63,893
Marrakech (★535,000)	439,728
Meknès (★375,000)	319,783
Mohammedia (Fedala) (★Casablanca)	105,120
Nador	62,040
Oued-Zem	58,744
Oujda	260,082
RABAT (★980,000)	518,616
Safi	197,309
Salé (★Rabat)	289,391
Settat	65,203
Sidi Kacem	55,833
Sidi Slimane	50,457
Tanger (Tangier) (★370,000)	266,346
Tan-Tan	41,451
Taza	77,216
Temera (★Rabat)	48,644
Tétouan	199,615

MOZAMBIQUE / Moçambique

1989 E	15,326,476
Beira	291,604
Chimoio (1986E)	86,928
Inhambane (1986E)	64,274
• MAPUTO	1,069,727
Nacala	101,615
Nampula	197,379
Pemba (1986E)	50,215
Quelimane	78,520
Tete (1986E)	56,178
Xai-Xai (1986E)	51,620

MYANMAR (BURMA)

1983 C	34,124,908
Bago (Pegu)	150,528
Chauk	51,437
Dawei (Tavoy)	69,882
Henzada	82,005
Kale	52,628
Lashio	88,590
Magway	54,881
Mandalay	532,949
Mawlamyine (Moulmein)	219,961
Maymyo	63,782
Meiktila	96,496
Mergui (Myeik)	88,600
Mogok	49,392
Monywa	106,843
Myingyan	77,060
Myitkyinā	56,427
Nyaunglebin	55,194
Pakokku	71,860
Pathein (Bassein)	144,096
Prome (Pyè)	83,332
Pyinmana	52,962
Sagaing	46,212
Shwebo	52,185
Sittwe (Akyab)	107,621
Taunggyi	108,231
Thaton	61,790
Toungoo	65,861
• YANGON (RANGOON) (★2,650,000)	2,513,023
Yenangyaung	62,582

NAMIBIA

1988 E	1,760,000
Walvis Bay (★22,999) (1991C)	12,383
• WINDHOEK	114,500

NEPAL / Nepāl

1991 C	18,491,097
Bhaktapur	61,405
Bharatpur	54,670
Buṭwal	44,272
Dhangaḍhī	44,753
Dharān	66,457
Heṭauṇḍā	53,836
Janakpur	54,710
• KĀṬHMĀṆḌAŨ (★520,000)	421,258
Lalitpur	115,865
Mahendranagar	62,050
Nepālgañj	47,819
Pokharā	95,286
Wirāṭnagar	129,388
Wīrgañj	69,005

NETHERLANDS / Nederland

1992 E	15,129,150
Alkmaar (★124,000)	91,817
Almelo	63,383
Alphen aan den Rijn	63,573
Amersfoort	104,390
Amstelveen (★Amsterdam)	71,939
• AMSTERDAM (★1,875,000)	713,407
Apeldoorn	148,745
Arnhem (★305,000)	132,928
Assen	50,880
Bergen op Zoom	47,259
Breda (★165,000)	126,709
Delft (★'s-Gravenhage)	90,066
Den Helder	61,225
Deventer	68,004
Dordrecht (★209,000)	111,791
Ede (▲96,044)	50,700
Eindhoven (★384,000)	193,966
Emmen (▲93,107)	37,000
Enschede (★252,000)	147,199
Geleen (★179,000)	33,922
Gouda	67,416
Groningen (★208,000)	169,387
Haarlem (★Amsterdam)	149,788
Haarlemmermeer (▲100,659) (★Amsterdam)	14,000
Heerlen (★267,500)	53,600
Helmond	70,574
Hengelo (★Enschede)	76,726
Hilversum (★Amsterdam)	84,674
Hoorn	59,028
IJmuiden (★Amsterdam)	61,506
Kerkrade (★Heerlen)	53,364
Leeuwarden	86,405
Leiden (★190,000)	112,976
Maastricht (★163,000)	118,152
Nieuwegein (★Utrecht)	58,882
Nijmegen (★242,000)	146,344
Oss	52,132
Purmerend (★Amsterdam)	62,504
Ridderkerk (★Rotterdam)	45,834
Rijswijk (★'s-Gravenhage)	47,456
Roosendaal	61,354
Rotterdam (★1,120,000)	589,707
Schiedam (★Rotterdam)	71,117
'S-GRAVENHAGE (THE HAGUE) (★773,000)	445,287
's-Hertogenbosch (★200,000)	93,171
Soest (★Amersfoort)	41,693
Spijkenisse (★Rotterdam)	69,655
Tilburg (★235,000)	160,618
Utrecht (★528,000)	232,705
Veenendaal	50,791
Venlo (★88,000)	64,890
Vlaardingen (★Rotterdam)	73,893
Vlissingen (Flushing) (▲43,913)	25,000
Zaanstad (★Amsterdam)	131,273
Zeist (★Utrecht)	59,211
Zoetermeer (★'s-Gravenhage)	100,623
Zwolle	97,131

NETHERLANDS ANTILLES / Nederlandse Antillen

1990 E	189,687
• WILLEMSTAD (★130,000) (1981C)	31,883

NEW CALEDONIA / Nouvelle-Calédonie

1989 C	164,173
• NOUMÉA (★97,581)	65,110

NEW ZEALAND

1991 C	3,434,950
• Auckland (★855,571)	315,668
Christchurch (★307,179)	292,858
Dunedin	116,577
Hamilton (★148,625)	101,448
Invercargill	56,148
Lower Hutt (★Wellington)	94,540
Manukau (★Auckland)	226,147
Napier (★110,216)	51,645
Palmerston North (★70,951)	70,318
Rotorua (★53,702)	45,144
Takapuna (★Auckland)	74,360
Tauranga (★70,803)	46,308
Waitemata (★Auckland)	136,716
WELLINGTON (★375,000)	150,301
Whangarei (★44,183)	40,101

NICARAGUA

1985 E	3,272,100
Chinandega	75,000
Granada (1981E)	64,642
León	101,000
• MANAGUA	682,000
Masaya	75,000
Matagalpa	68,000

NIGER

1988 C	7,220,089
Agadez	49,361
Maradi	104,386
• NIAMEY	392,165
Tahoua	49,948
Zinder	119,838

NIGERIA

1987 E	101,907,000
Aba	239,800
Abakaliki	56,800
Abeokuta	341,300

▲ Population of an entire municipality, commune, or district, including rural area.
• Largest city in country.
★ Population or designation of the metropolitan area, including suburbs.
C Census. **E** Official estimate. **U** Unofficial estimate.

▲ Bevölkerung eines ganzen städtischen Verwaltungsgebietes, eines Kommunalbezirkes oder eines Distrikts, einschliesslich ländlicher Gebiete.
• Grösste Stadt des Landes.
★ Bevölkerung oder Bezeichnung der Stadtregion einschliesslich Vororte.
C Volkszählung. **E** Offizielle Schätzung. **U** Inoffizielle Schätzung.

Population of Cities and Towns / Einwohnerzahlen von Grossstädten / Habitantes en las Ciudades y Poblaciones
Population des Grands Centres et des Villes / População dos Centros Urbanos 311

ABUJA (1993U)	250,000
Ado-Ekiti	287,000
Afikpo	65,790
Agege	83,810
Akure	129,600
Amaigbo	53,690
Apomu	49,570
Aramoko	48,280
Asaba	47,410
Awka	88,800
Azare	50,020
Bauchi	68,840
Benin City	183,200
Bida	100,200
Calabar	139,800
Deba	110,600
Duku	52,880
Ede	245,200
Effon-Alaiye	122,300
Ejigbo	84,570
Emure-Ekiti	58,750
Enugu	252,500
Epe	80,560
Erin-Oshogbo	59,940
Eruwa	49,140
Fiditi	49,440
Gboko	49,390
Gbongan	53,990
Gombe	86,120
Gusau	126,200
Ibadan	1,144,000
Idah	50,550
Idanre	56,080
Ife	237,000
Ifon-Oshogbo	65,980
Igbasa-Odo	48,040
Igboho	85,230
Igbo-Ora	68,060
Igede-Ekiti	56,570
Ihiala	73,240
Ijebu-Igbo	78,680
Ijebu-Ode	124,900
Ijero-Ekiti	76,420
Ikare	112,500
Ikerre	195,400
Ikire	94,450
Ikirun	144,900
Ikole	71,860
Ikorodu	147,700
Ikot Ekpene	69,440
Ila	210,800
Ilawe-Ekiti	147,300
Ilesha	302,100
Ilobu	159,000
Ilorin	380,000
Inisa	95,630
Ipoti-Ekiti	53,220
Ise-Ekiti	82,580
Iseyin	173,500
Iwo	289,100
Jega (1985E)	47,000
Jimeta	66,130
Jos	164,700
Kaduna	273,200
Kano	538,300
Katsina	165,000
Kaura Namoda	52,910
Keffi	57,790
Kishi	77,210
Kumo	118,200
Lafia	97,810
Lafiagi	57,580
• LAGOS (★3,800,000)	1,213,000
Lalupon	56,130
Lere	49,670
Maiduguri	255,100
Makurdi	98,350
Minna	109,300
Mubi	51,190
Mushin (★Lagos)	266,100
Nguru	78,770
Nsukka	47,760
Ode-Ekiti	48,910
Offa	157,500
Ogbomosho	582,900
Oka	114,400
Oke-Mesi	55,040
Okwe	52,550
Olupona	65,720
Ondo	135,300
Onitsha	298,200
Opobo	64,620
Oron	62,260
Oshogbo	380,800
Owerri (1985E)	37,000
Owo	146,600
Oyan	50,930
Oyo	204,700
Pindiga	64,130
Port Harcourt	327,300
Potiskum	56,490
Sapele	111,200
Shagamu	93,610
Shaki	139,000
Shomolu (★Lagos)	120,700
Sokoto	163,700
Ugep	81,910
Umuahia	52,550
Uyo	60,500
Warri	100,700
Zaria	302,800

NIUE

1989 C	2,267
• ALOFI	706

NORTHERN MARIANA ISLANDS

1990 C	43,345
Chalan Kanoa	2,549
• Garapan	3,904

NORWAY / Norge

1993 E	4,299,231
Bærum (★Oslo)	89,774
Bergen (▲218,105)	192,747
Drammen (★58,388)	49,300
Fredrikstad (★50,077)	25,748
Hammerfest (▲9,468)	6,717
Kristiansand (▲67,113)	55,129
Narvik (▲18,888)	14,005
• OSLO (★703,896)	470,204
Skien (▲48,454)	29,807
Stavanger (★102,267)	97,721
Tromsø (▲53,382)	44,030
Trondheim (▲140,718)	132,301

▲ Población de un municipio, comuna o distrito entero, incluyendo sus áreas rurales.
• Ciudad más grande de un país.
★ Población o designación de un área metropolitana, incluyendo los suburbios.
C Censo. **E** Estimado oficial. **U** Estimado no oficial.

OMAN / 'Umān

1983 E	1,131,000
• MASQAṬ (MUSCAT)	30,000
Maṭraḥ (1971E)	14,000
Ṣūr	30,000

PAKISTAN / Pākistān

1981 C	84,253,644
Abbottābād (★65,996)	32,188
Ahmadpur East	56,979
Attock (★39,986)	26,233
Bahāwalnagar	74,533
Bahāwalpur (★180,263)	152,009
Bannu (★43,210)	35,170
Bhakkar	41,934
Chārsadda	62,530
Chīchāwatni	50,241
Chiniot	105,559
Chishtiān Mandi	61,959
Daska	55,555
Dera Ghāzi Khān	102,007
Dera Ismāīl Khān (★68,145)	64,358
Drigh Road Cantonment (★Karāchi)	56,742
Faisalabad (Lyallpur)	1,104,209
Gojra	68,000
Gujrānwāla (★658,753)	600,993
Gujrānwāla Cantonment (★Gujrānwāla)	57,760
Gujrāt	155,058
Hāfizābād	83,464
Hyderābād (★800,000)	702,539
Hyderābād Cantonment (★Hyderābād)	48,990
ISLAMABAD (★Rāwalpindi)	204,364
Jacobābād	79,365
Jarānwāla	69,459
Jhang Sadar	195,558
Jhelum (★106,462)	92,646
Kamālia	61,107
Kāmoke	71,097
• Karāchi (★5,300,000)	4,901,627
Karāchi Cantonment (★Karāchi)	181,981
Kasūr	155,523
Khairpur	61,447
Khānewāl	89,090
Khānpur	70,589
Khāriān Cantonment (★51,506)	16,042
Khushāb	56,274
Kohāt (★77,604)	55,832
Lahore (★3,025,000)	2,707,215
Lahore Cantonment (★Lahore)	245,474
Lārkāna	123,890
Leiah	51,482
Malir Cantonment (★Karāchi)	47,588
Mandi Būrewāla	86,311
Mardān (★147,977)	141,842
Miānwāli	59,159
Mingāora	88,078
Mīrpur Khās	124,371
Multān (★732,070)	696,316
Muzaffargarh	53,000
Nawābshāh	102,139
Nowshera (★74,913)	38,875
Okāra (★153,483)	127,455
Pākpattan	69,820
Peshāwar (★566,248)	506,896
Peshāwar Cantonment (★Peshāwar)	59,352
Quetta (★285,719)	244,842
Rahīmyār Khān (★132,635)	119,036
Rāwalpindi (★1,040,000)	457,091
Rāwalpindi Cantonment (★Rāwalpindi)	337,752
Sādiqābād	63,935
Sāhīwal	150,954
Sargodha (★291,362)	231,895
Sargodha Cantonment (★Sargodha)	59,467
Shekhūpura	141,168
Shikārpur	88,138
Shorkot (★50,568)	18,533
Siālkot (★302,009)	258,147
Sukkur	190,551
Tando Ādam	62,744
Turbat	52,337
Vihāri	53,799
Wāh Cantonment	122,335
Wazīrābād	62,725

PALAU / Belau

1990 C	15,122
• KOROR	9,018

PANAMA / Panamá

1990 C	2,315,047
Balboa (★Panamá)	1,214
Colón (★96,000)	54,469
David	65,635
• PANAMÁ (★770,000)	411,549
San Miguelito (★Panamá)	242,529

PAPUA NEW GUINEA

1990 C	3,534,038
Lae	78,265
• PORT MORESBY	193,242
Rabaul	16,883

PARAGUAY

1992 C	4,123,550
• ASUNCIÓN (★700,000)	502,426
Caaguazú	38,200
Capiatá	83,189
Ciudad del Este	133,896
Encarnación	55,359
Fernando de la Mora (★Asunción)	95,287
Lambaré (★Asunción)	99,681
Mariano Roque Alonso	39,240
Pedro Juan Caballero	53,601
San Lorenzo (★Asunción)	133,311

PERU / Perú

1981 C	17,031,221
Arequipa (★446,942)	108,023
Ayacucho (★69,533)	57,432
Barranco (★Lima)	46,478
Breña (★Lima)	112,398
Cajamarca	62,259
Callao (★Lima)	264,133
Cerro de Pasco (★66,373)	55,597
Chiclayo (★279,527)	213,095
Chimbote	223,341
Chorrillos (★Lima)	141,881

▲ Population d'une municipalité, d'une commune ou d'un district, zone rurale incluse.
• Ville la plus peuplée du pays.
★ Population de l'agglomération (ou nom de la zone métropolitaine englobante).
C Recensement. **E** Estimation officielle. **U** Estimation non officielle.

Chosica	65,139
Cusco (★184,550)	89,563
Huacho	43,398
Huancayo (★164,954)	84,845
Huánuco	61,812
Ica	114,786
Iquitos	178,738
Jesús María (★Lima)	83,179
Juliaca	87,651
La Victoria (★Lima)	270,778
• LIMA (★4,608,010)	371,122
Lince (★Lima)	80,456
Magdalena (★Lima)	55,535
Miraflores (★Lima)	103,453
Pisco	55,604
Piura (★207,934)	144,609
Pucallpa	112,263
Pueblo Libre (★Lima)	83,985
Puno	67,397
Rímac (★Lima)	184,484
San Isidro (★Lima)	71,203
San Martin de Porras (★Lima)	404,856
Santiago de Surco (★Lima)	146,636
Sullana	89,037
Surquillo (★Lima)	134,158
Tacna	97,173
Talara	57,351
Trujillo (★354,301)	202,469
Tumbes	47,936
Vitarte (★Lima)	145,504

PHILIPPINES / Pilipinas

1990 C	60,559,116
Angeles	236,685
Antipolo (▲207,842)	83,641
Bacolod	364,180
Bacoor (★Manila)	159,685
Baguio	183,102
Baliuag	89,719
Biñan (★Manila)	134,553
Binangonan	127,561
Bislig (▲103,510)	59,619
Bocaue	67,243
Butuan (▲227,829)	100,940
Cabanatuan (▲173,065)	74,966
Cagayan de Oro (▲339,598)	252,453
Cainta (★Manila)	126,839
Calamba (▲173,453)	97,623
Caloocan (★Manila)	761,011
Calumpit	59,042
Catarman (▲50,965)	21,149
Catbalogan (▲70,470)	29,233
Cavite (★195,000)	91,641
Cebu (★825,000)	610,417
Cotabato	127,065
Dagupan	122,247
Davao (▲849,947)	521,525
Digos (▲96,806)	37,303
Dumaguete	80,262
General Santos (Dadiangas) (▲250,389)	152,907
Guagua	88,290
Iloilo	309,505
Isabela (Basilan) (▲59,482)	13,616
Jolo	53,055
Kawit (★Cavite)	47,755
Koronadal (▲108,708)	44,542
Lapu-Lapu (Opon)	146,194
Las Piñas (★Manila)	296,851
Legaspi (▲121,116)	62,974
Lucena	150,624
Mabalacat (▲121,115)	64,261
Macabebe	55,505
Makati (★Manila)	452,734
Malabon (★Manila)	278,380
Malaybalay (▲94,790)	24,906
Malolos	125,178
Mandaluyong (★Manila)	244,538
Mandaue (★Cebu)	180,285
Mangaldan	65,947
• MANILA (★9,650,000)	1,598,918
Marawi	91,901
Marikina (★Manila)	310,010
Mariveles (▲60,761)	52,000
Mati (▲93,023)	28,504
Meycauayan (★Manila)	123,982
Muntinglupa (★Manila)	276,972
Naga	115,329
Navotas (★Manila)	186,799
Olongapo	193,327
Pagadian (▲106,307)	47,737
Parañaque (★Manila)	307,717
Pasay (★Manila)	366,623
Pasig (★Manila)	397,309
Pateros (★Manila)	51,401
Polomolok (▲89,372)	43,399
Puerto Princesa (▲92,147)	47,461
Pulilan	48,199
Quezon City (★Manila)	1,666,766
Sagay (▲105,713)	47,326
San Fernando	157,851
San Jose	40,267
San Juan del Monte (★Manila)	126,708
San Pablo (▲161,630)	80,671
San Pedro	156,486
Santa Cruz	76,603
Santa Rosa (★Manila)	94,719
Sorsogon (▲72,871)	35,058
Surigao (▲100,379)	38,593
Tacloban	137,190
Tagbilaran	56,363
Tagig (★Manila)	266,080
Tagum (▲135,440)	60,865
Tarlac (▲208,722)	46,993
Taytay (★Manila)	112,403
Valenzuela (★Manila)	340,050
Zamboanga (▲442,345)	99,056

PITCAIRN

1988 C	59
• ADAMSTOWN	59

POLAND / Polska

1993 E	38,418,100
Będzin (★Katowice)	64,100
Bełchatów	58,300
Biała Podlaska	55,000
Białystok	274,100
Bielsko-Biała	179,700
Bydgoszcz	383,600
Bytom (Beuthen) (★Katowice)	229,200
Chełm	68,000
Chorzów (★Katowice)	128,800
Częstochowa	299,500
Dąbrowa Górnicza (★Katowice)	131,600
Dzierżoniów (Reichenbach) (★90,000)	38,400

▲ População de um municipio, comuna ou distrito, inclusive as respectivas áreas rurais.
• Maior cidade de um país.
★ População ou indicação de uma área metropolitana.
C Censo. **E** Estimativa oficial. **U** Estimativa não oficial.

Elbląg (Elbing)	127,300
Ełk	53,800
Gdańsk (Danzig) (★892,000)	461,700
Gdynia (★Gdańsk)	250,200
Gliwice (Gleiwitz) (★Katowice)	214,400
Głogów	73,300
Gniezno	70,600
Gorzów Wielkopolski (Landsberg an der Warthe)	124,600
Grudziądz	103,400
Inowrocław	79,000
Jastrzębie-Zdrój	104,200
Jaworzno (★Katowice)	98,500
Jelenia Góra (Hirschberg)	93,000
Kalisz	106,600
• Katowice (★2,770,000)	359,900
Kędzierzyn Kozle	71,000
Kielce	213,600
Konin	81,500
Koszalin (Köslin)	110,800
Kraków (★823,000)	744,000
Krosno	49,400
Kutno	50,900
Legionowo (★Warszawa)	50,600
Legnica (Liegnitz)	106,600
Leszno	60,200
Łódź (★950,000)	938,400
Łomża	61,500
Lubin	82,800
Lublin (★388,000)	350,400
Mielec	63,700
Mysłowice (★Katowice)	93,200
Nowy Sącz	80,500
Olsztyn (Allenstein)	164,900
Opole (Oppeln)	129,600
Ostrołęka	52,400
Ostrowiec Świętokrzyski	79,300
Ostrów Wielkopolski	74,100
Pabianice (★Łódź)	76,000
Piekary Śląskie (★Katowice)	67,800
Piła (Schneidemühl)	74,400
Piotrków Trybunalski	81,300
Płock	125,000
Poznań (★666,000)	582,900
Pruszków (★Warszawa)	53,000
Przemyśl	68,300
Puławy	54,300
Racibórz (Ratibor)	64,300
Radom	230,400
Radomsko	50,900
Ruda Śląska (★Katowice)	167,700
Rybnik	143,100
Rzeszów	156,700
Siedlce	73,000
Siemianowice Śląskie (★Katowice)	79,600
Skarżysko-Kamienna	51,300
Słupsk (Stolp)	102,000
Sopot (★Gdańsk)	45,000
Sosnowiec (★Katowice)	251,300
Stalowa Wola	71,200
Starachowice	57,300
Stargard Szczeciński (Stargard in Pommern)	72,200
Starogard Gdański	50,100
Suwałki	63,900
Świdnica (Schweidnitz)	64,300
Świętochłowice (★Katowice)	60,200
Świnoujście (Swinemünde)	43,300
Szczecin (Stettin) (★448,000)	416,400
Tarnobrzeg	49,900
Tarnów	121,900
Tarnowskie Góry (★Katowice)	76,900
Tczew	59,900
Tomaszów Mazowiecki	69,900
Toruń	201,800
Tychy (★Katowice)	136,600
Wałbrzych (Waldenburg) (★207,000)	140,600
WARSZAWA (★2,312,000)	1,644,500
Włocławek	122,300
Wodzisław Śląski	88,400
Wrocław (Breslau)	640,700
Zabrze (Hindenburg) (★Katowice)	203,500
Zamość	64,300
Zawiercie	56,500
Zgierz (★Łódź)	59,000
Zielona Góra (Grünberg)	115,100
Żory	66,200

PORTUGAL

1981 C	9,833,014
Amadora (★Lisboa)	95,518
Barreiro (★Lisboa)	50,863
Braga	63,033
Coimbra	74,616
• LISBOA (★2,250,000)	807,167
Ponta Delgada	21,187
Porto (★1,225,000)	327,368
Setúbal	77,885
Vila Nova de Gaia (★Porto)	62,469

PUERTO RICO

1990 C	3,522,037
Arecibo (★160,500)	49,545
Bayamón (▲220,262) (★San Juan)	202,103
Caguas (▲133,447) (★San Juan)	92,429
Carolina (▲177,806) (★San Juan)	162,404
Guaynabo (▲92,886) (★San Juan)	73,385
Mayagüez (★200,600)	83,010
Ponce (★232,700)	159,151
• SAN JUAN (★1,877,000)	426,832

QATAR / Qaṭar

1986 C	369,079
• AD-DAWḤAH (DOHA) (★310,000)	217,294
Ar-Rayyān (★Ad-Dawḥah)	91,996

REUNION / Réunion

1982 C	515,814
• SAINT-DENIS (▲109,072)	84,400

ROMANIA / România

1992 C	22,760,449
Alba Iulia	71,254
Alexandria	58,582
Arad	190,088
Bacău	204,495
Baia Mare	148,815
Bistriṭa	87,793
Botoșani	126,204
Brăila	234,706

• BUCUREȘTI (BUCHAREST) (★2,300,000)	2,064,474
Buzău	148,247
Călărași	76,886
Cluj-Napoca	328,008
Constanța	350,476
Craiova	303,520
Deva	78,366
Drobeta-Turnu Severin	115,526
Focșani	101,296
Galați	325,788
Giurgiu	74,236
Hunedoara	81,198
Iași	342,994
Lugoj	50,983
Medgidia	46,586
Mediaș	64,488
Miercurea-Ciuc	46,029
Onești	59,008
Oradea	220,848
Petroșani (★76,000)	52,532
Piatra Neamț	123,175
Pitești	179,479
Ploiești (★310,000)	252,073
Râmnicu Vâlcea	113,356
Reșița	96,798
Roman	80,192
Satu Mare	131,859
Sfântu Gheorghe	68,070
Sibiu	169,696
Slatina	85,336
Slobozia	55,614
Suceava	114,355
Târgoviște	97,876
Târgu Jiu	98,267
Târgu Mureș	163,625
Tecuci	46,735
Timișoara	334,278
Tulcea	97,500
Turda	61,135
Vaslui	80,151
Zalău	68,322

RUSSIA

1991 E	148,542,700
Abakan	157,300
Achtubinsk	50,800
Ačinsk	122,000
Alapajevsk	50,300
Alatyr'	47,700
Aleksandrov	68,600
Aleksin	74,200
Al'metjevsk	132,700
Amursk	59,600
Anapa	55,900
Angarsk	268,500
Anžero-Sudžensk	107,000
Apatity	88,600
Archangel'sk	420,400
Armavir	162,200
Arsenjev	71,200
Art'om	70,100
Arzamas	111,800
Asbest	84,900
Astrachan'	511,900
Azov	80,700
Balakovo	201,300
Balašicha (★Moskva)	137,600
Balašov	97,300
Barnaul (★673,000)	606,800
Batajsk (★Rostov-na-Donu)	93,300
Belebej	54,500
Belgorod	311,400
Belogorsk	74,300
Belorečensk	51,900
Beloreck	73,100
Belovo	92,900
Berdsk (★Novosibirsk)	80,400
Berezniki	199,700
Ber'ozovskij	51,900
Bijsk	234,600
Birobidžan	86,300
Blagoveščensk	211,000
Bor (★Niňij Novgorod)	64,500
Borisoglebsk	72,100
Boroviči	62,800
Br'ansk	458,900
Bratsk	259,400
Bud'onnovsk	57,500
Bugul'ma	91,100
Buguruslan	54,100
Buj	62,900
Bujnaksk	57,900
Buzuluk	85,100
Čajkovskij	88,300
Čapajevsk	96,000
Čebarkul'	50,700
Čeboksary	436,000
Čechov	60,200
Čel'abinsk (★1,325,000)	1,148,300
Čeremchovo	73,600
Čerepovec	315,900
Čerkessk	117,000
Černogorsk	79,700
Chabarovsk	613,300
Chasavjurt	72,800
Chimki (★Moskva)	135,500
Cholmsk	51,800
Čistopol'	66,600
Čita	376,300
Čusovoj	58,000
Dal'negorsk	50,300
Derbent	81,500
Dimitrovgrad	127,000
Dmitrov	65,600
Dolgoprudnyj (★Moskva)	71,100
Domodedovo (★Moskva)	56,300
Doneck	48,900
Dubna	67,200
Dzeržinsk (★Nižnij Novgorod)	286,700
Elektrostal'	153,000
Elista	92,700
Engel's (★Saratov)	183,600
Fr'azino (★Moskva)	54,000
Furmanov	45,900
Gatčina (★Sankt-Peterburg)	80,600
Gelendžik	48,600
Georgijevsk	63,700
Georgiu-Dež	54,600
Glazov	106,000
Gorno-Altajsk	47,500
Gr'azi	47,700
Groznyj	401,400
Gubkin	76,400
Gukovo	67,700
Gus'-Chrustal'nyj	77,000
Inta	60,900
Irbit	51,300
Irkutsk	640,500
Išim	65,900
Išimbaj	71,000
Iskitim	68,700
Ivanovo	482,200
Ivantejevka (★Moskva)	53,200
Iževsk	646,800
Jakutsk	193,300
Jarcevo	54,000
Jaroslavl'	638,100
Jefremov	56,600
Jegorjevsk	74,200
Jejsk	79,400
Jelec	121,300
Jelizovo	48,700
Jermolajevo	65,600
Jessentuki	86,300
Joškar-Ola	247,800
Jurga	94,000
Južno-Sachalinsk	164,000
Kaliningrad (★Moskva)	161,500
Kaliningrad (Königsberg)	408,100
Kaluga	315,500
Kamensk-Šachtinskij	73,100
Kamensk-Ural'skij	208,700
Kamyšin	124,400
Kanaš	56,100
Kandalakša	54,300
Kansk	109,900
Kaspijsk	61,900
Kazan' (★1,165,000)	1,107,300
Kemerovo	520,700
Kimry	62,000
Kinel'	33,800
Kinešma	104,900
Kingisepp	50,600
Kiriši	53,100
Kirov	491,200
Kirovo-Čepeck	95,600
Kisel'ovsk (★Prokopjevsk)	126,900
Kislovodsk	116,800
Kizel	36,600
Klimovsk (★Moskva)	57,600
Klin	95,100
Klincy	71,200
Kogalym	48,200
Kol'čugino	45,600
Kolomna	163,500
Kolpino (★Sankt-Peterburg)	144,500
Komsomol'sk-na-Amure	318,800
Kopejsk (★Čel'abinsk)	78,300
Korkino	44,800
Korsakov	45,300
Kostroma	281,800
Kotlas	68,900
Kovrov	161,900
Krasnodar	631,200
Krasnogorsk (★Moskva)	91,700
Krasnojarsk	924,400
Krasnokamensk	57,800
Krasnokamsk	67,000
Krasnoturjinsk	67,200
Krasnoufimsk	46,100
Krasnoural'sk	34,800
Krasnyj Sulin	43,200
Kropotkin	76,600
Krymsk	51,100
Kstovo (★Nižnij Novgord)	65,300
Kujbyšev	51,600
Kungur	81,800
Kurgan	363,800
Kursk	433,300
Kušva	43,300
Kuzneck	100,000
Kyzyl	88,000
Labinsk	58,600
Leninogorsk	63,300
Leninsk-Kuzneckij	133,400
Lesosibirsk	69,300
Lipeck	460,100
Livny	52,600
Lobn'a (★Moskva)	61,000
L'ubercy (★Moskva)	164,900
Lys'va	77,800
Lytkarino (★Moskva)	51,700
Machačkala	333,500
Magadan	154,900
Magnitogorsk	443,900
Majkop	152,500
Mcensk	49,200
Meleuz	55,200
Meždurečensk	107,500
Miass	169,700
Michajlovka	58,700
Mičurinsk	109,400
Mineral'nyje Vody	72,500
Minusinsk	74,200
987Mončegorsk	68,100
Moršansk	50,500
• MOSKVA (MOSCOW) (★13,150,000)	8,801,500
Murmansk	472,900
Murom	126,000
Mytišči (★Moskva)	153,900
Nabereżnyje Čelny	510,100
Nachodka	164,500
Nadym	52,200
Nal'čik	240,600
Naro-Fominsk	58,800
Nazarovo	65,200
Neftejugansk	65,500
Ner'ungri	77,200
Nevinnomyssk	123,300
Nikolo-Berjozovka	110,500
Nižnekamsk	196,200
Nižnevartovsk	247,400
Nižnij Novgorod (Gorky) (★2,025,000)	1,445,000
Nižnij Tagil	439,200
Njagan	59,800
Noginsk	122,700
Nojabr'sk	88,900
Noril'sk	169,000
Novgorod	233,800
Novoaltajsk (★Barnaul)	55,200
Novočeboksarsk	119,300
Novočerkassk	188,500
Novodvinsk	50,300
Novokujbyševsk (★Samara)	113,200
Novokuzneck	601,900
Novomoskovsk, Tula oblast' (★365,000)	145,800
Novorossijsk	188,600
Novošachtinsk	107,300
Novosibirsk (★1,600,000)	1,446,300
Novotroick	107,600
Novyj Urengoj	93,600
Obninsk	103,700
Odincovo (★Moskva)	128,400
Okt'abr'skij	106,700
Omsk (★1,190,000)	1,166,800
Orechovo-Zujevo (★205,000)	136,800
Orel	345,200
Orenburg	556,500
Orsk	272,200
Osinniki	63,200
Otradnyj	49,600
Partizansk	50,000
P'atigorsk	131,100
Pavlovo	72,200
Pavlovskij Posad	70,800
Pečora	65,500
Penza	551,100
Perm' (★1,180,000)	1,110,400
Pervoural'sk	143,700
Petrodvorec (★Sankt-Peterburg)	83,800
Petropavlovsk-Kamčatskij	272,900
Petrozavodsk	277,400
Podol'sk (★Moskva)	208,500
Polevskoj	71,900
Prochladnyj	58,500
Prokopjevsk (★410,000)	272,600
Pskov	207,500
Puškin (★Sankt-Peterburg)	95,300
Puškino (★Moskva)	75,800
Ramenskoje	88,800
Rasskazovo	49,800
R'azan'	527,200
Reutov (★Moskva)	68,900
Revda	66,000
Roslavl'	60,700
Rossoš'	58,900
Rostov-na-Donu (★1,165,000)	1,027,600
Rubcovsk	172,500
Ruzajevka	52,100
Rybinsk	252,600
Ržev	70,900
Šachty	227,700
Šadrinsk	87,500
Safonovo	56,300
Sajanogorsk	53,000
Salavat	151,400
Sal'sk	61,700
Samara (★1,505,000)	1,257,300
Sankt-Peterburg (Saint Petersburg) (★5,525,000)	4,466,800
Saransk	319,600
Sarapul	110,600
Saratov (★1,155,000)	911,100
Šatka	51,100
Ščelkovo (★Moskva)	109,600
Ščokino	68,800
Šelechov	48,600
Sergijev Posad (Zagorsk)	115,600
Serov	103,800
Serpuchov	141,200
Severodvinsk	251,500
Severomorsk	66,200
Slav'ansk-Na-Kubani	58,500
Smolensk	349,800
Soči	341,500
Sokol	46,700
Solikamsk	110,200
Solnečnogorsk (★Moskva)	56,700
Sosnovyj Bor	56,700
Spassk-Dal'nij	61,100
Staryj Oskol	181,900
Stavropol'	328,300
Sterlitamak	252,200
Stupino	74,600
Šuja	69,000
Surgut	261,100
Sverdlovsk (★1,620,000)	1,375,400
Svetlogorsk	71,600
Svobodnyj	80,900
Syktyvkar	224,000
Syzran'	174,900
Taganrog	293,600
Talnach	65,600
Tambov	309,600
Tichoreck	67,600
Tichvin	71,800
Tobol'sk	96,800
Toljatti	654,700
Tomsk	505,600
Toržok	50,500
Troick	89,800
Tuapse	63,800
Tujmazy	59,800
Tula (★640,000)	543,600
Tulun	53,700
T'umen'	494,200
Tver'	455,300
Tyndinskij	64,700
Uchta	112,100
Ufa (★1,118,000)	1,097,000
Uglič	40,000
Ulan-Ude	362,400
Uljanovsk	648,300
Usinsk	52,300
Usolje-Sibirskoje	106,800
Ussurijsk	160,200
Ust'-Ilimsk	112,200
Ust'-Kut	61,800
Uzlovaja (★Novomoskovsk)	34,000
V'az'ma	59,900
Velikije Luki	115,400
Verchn'aja Pyšma (★Sverdlovsk)	53,500
Verchn'aja Salda	55,100
Vičuga	49,700
Vidnoje (★Moskva)	56,900
Vladikavkaz	306,000
Vladimir	355,600
Vladivostok	648,000
Volchov	50,100
Volgodonsk	180,700
Volgograd (Stalingrad) (★1,360,000)	1,007,300
Vologda	289,200
Vol'sk	65,500
Volžsk	62,000
Volžskij (★Volgograd)	278,400
Vorkuta	117,400
Voronež	900,000
Voskresensk	81,400
Votkinsk	104,500
Vyborg	81,100
Vyksa	62,200
Vyšnij Voločok	64,600
Zarinsk	51,800
Zelenograd (★Moskva)	162,700
Železnodorožnyj (★Moskva)	99,300
Železnogorsk	89,200
Zel'onodol'sk	97,000
Žigulevsk	45,000
Zlatoust	208,200
Žukovskij	101,300

RWANDA

1991 C	6,762,145
• KIGALI	232,733

SAINT HELENA

1987 C	5,644
• JAMESTOWN	1,413

SAINT KITTS AND NEVIS

1980 C	44,404
• BASSETERRE	14,725
Charlestown	1,771

SAINT LUCIA

1991 C	133,308
• CASTRIES (★13,138)	11,147

SAINT PIERRE AND MIQUELON / Saint-Pierre-et-Miquelon

1982 C	6,041
• SAINT-PIERRE	5,371

SAINT VINCENT AND THE GRENADINES

1991 C	106,499
• KINGSTOWN (★26,223)	15,466

SAN MARINO

1989 E	23,000
• SAN MARINO	2,794

SAO TOME AND PRINCIPE / São Tomé e Príncipe

1991 C	117,504
• SÃO TOMÉ	5,245

SAUDI ARABIA / Al-ʻArabīyah as-Suʻūdīyah

1980 E	9,229,000
Abhā (1974C)	30,150
Ad-Dammām	200,000
Al-Hufūf (1974C)	101,271
Al-Khubar (1974C)	48,817
Al-Madīnah (Medina)	290,000
Al-Mubarraz (1974C)	54,325
AR-RIYĀḌ (RIYADH)	1,250,000
Aṭ-Ṭā'if	300,000
Buraydah (1974C)	69,940
Hā'il (1974C)	40,502
• Jiddah (Jeddah)	1,300,000
Khamīs Mushayṭ (1974C)	49,581
Makkah (Mecca)	550,000
Najran (1974C)	47,501
Tabūk (1974C)	74,825

SENEGAL / Sénégal

1988 C	6,892,720
• DAKAR	1,490,450
Diourbel	77,548
Kaolack	152,007
Louga	52,763
Saint-Louis	160,689
Thiès	184,902
Ziguinchor	124,283

SEYCHELLES

1984 E	64,718
• VICTORIA	23,000

SIERRA LEONE

1985 C	3,515,812
Bo	59,768
• FREETOWN (★525,000)	469,776
Kenema	52,473
Koidu	82,474
Makeni	49,038

SINGAPORE

1990 C	2,690,100
• SINGAPORE (★3,025,000)	2,690,100

SLOVAKIA / Slovenská Republika

1991 C	5,268,935
Banská Bystrica	85,007
• BRATISLAVA	441,453
Komárno	37,370
Košice	234,840
Martin	58,338
Michalovce	38,866
Nitra	89,888
Nové Zámky	42,851
Poprad	52,878
Považská Bystrica	39,801
Prešov	87,788
Prievidza	53,393
Spišská Nová Ves	39,187
Trenčín	56,733
Trnava	71,641
Žilina	83,853
Zvolen	41,935

SLOVENIA / Slovenija

1991 C	1,974,839
Celje	42,041
Kranj	42,988
• LJUBLJANA	292,589
Maribor	124,650

SOLOMON ISLANDS

1986 C	285,176
• HONIARA	30,413

SOMALIA / Somaliya

1984 E	5,423,000
Berbera	65,000
Hargeysa	70,000
Kismaayo	70,000
Marka	60,000
• MUQDISHO	600,000

SOUTH AFRICA / Suid-Afrika

1991 C	30,986,920
Alberton (★Johannesburg)	76,642
Alexandra (★Johannesburg)	124,586
Atteridgeville (★Pretoria)	92,008
Bellville (★Cape Town)	78,822
Benoni (★Johannesburg)	113,501
Bloemfontein (★280,000)	126,867
Blue Downs	60,781
Boksburg (★Johannesburg)	119,890
Botshabelo (★Bloemfontein)	117,926
Brakpan (★Johannesburg)	53,522
CAPE TOWN (KAAPSTAD) (★1,900,000)	854,616
Carletonville (★175,000)	118,699

▲ Population of an entire municipality, commune, or district, including rural area.
• Largest city in country.
★ Population or designation of the metropolitan area, including suburbs.
C Census. **E** Official estimate. **U** Unofficial estimate.

▲ Bevölkerung eines ganzen städtischen Verwaltungsgebietes, eines Kommunalbezirkes oder eines Distrikts, einschliesslich ländlicher Gebiete.
• Grösste Stadt des Landes.
★ Bevölkerung oder Bezeichnung der Stadtregion einschliesslich Vororte.
C Volkszählung. **E** Offizielle Schätzung. **U** Inoffizielle Schätzung.

Daveyton (★Johannesburg)	151,659
Diepmeadow (★Johannesburg)	241,099
Durban (★1,740,000)	715,669
East London (Oos-Londen) (★365,000)	102,325
Edendale (★Pietermaritzburg)	72,063
Elsies River (★Cape Town)	82,045
EMbalenhle	56,502
Evaton (★Vereeniging)	201,026
Galeshewe (★Kimberley)	72,118
Ga-Rankuwa (1980C)	48,300
Germiston (★Johannesburg)	134,005
Grassy Park (★Cape Town)	52,675
Guguletu (★Cape Town)	54,635
Ibhayi (★Port Elizabeth)	257,054
• Johannesburg (★4,000,000)	712,507
Kagiso (★Johannesburg)	61,680
Katlehong (★Johannesburg)	201,785
Kempton Park (★Johannesburg)	106,606
Khayelitsa (★Cape Town)	189,586
Khutsong	55,834
Kimberley (★160,000)	80,082
Klerksdorp (★275,000)	58,923
Krugersdorp (★Johannesburg)	81,584
Kwa Makuta (★Durban)	13,609
Kwa Mashu (★Durban)	156,679
KwaNdengezi (★Durban)	50,835
KwaNobuhle (★Port Elizabeth)	92,381
Kwa-Thema (★Johannesburg)	81,345
Ladysmith (★37,885)	29,589
Lekoa (Shapeville) (★Vereeniging)	217,582
Madadeni (★Newcastle)	95,931
Mafikeng (★16,000) (1980C)	6,500
Mamelodi (★Pretoria)	154,845
Mangaung (★Bloemfontein)	125,545
Mdantsane (★East London) (1986E)	242,823
Midrand (★Pretoria)	51,107
Motherwell (★Port Elizabeth)	72,999
Mpumalanga (★Durban)	62,140
Newtown (★Durban)	60,696
Ntuzuma (★Durban)	102,310
Nyanga (★Cape Town)	92,896
Orange Farm en Omgewing	49,838
Osizweni (★Durban)	78,079
Paarl (★Cape Town)	73,415
Parow (★Cape Town)	68,081
Pietermaritzburg (★265,000)	156,473
Pinetown (★Durban)	70,001
Port Elizabeth (★810,000)	303,353
PRETORIA (★1,100,000)	525,583
Randburg (★Johannesburg)	90,557
Randfontein (★Johannesburg)	90,557
Roodepoort-Maraisburg (★Johannesburg)	162,632
Sandton (★Johannesburg)	101,197
Soshanguve (★Pretoria)	146,334
Soweto (★Johannesburg)	596,632
Springs (★Johannesburg)	72,647
Tembisa (★Johannesburg)	209,238
Thabong (★Welkom)	88,547
Uitenhage (★Port Elizabeth)	67,581
Umlazi (★Durban)	299,275
Umtata (1978E)	30,000
Vanderbijlpark (★Vereeniging)	67,291
Vereeniging (★675,000)	71,255
Verwoerdburg (★Pretoria)	80,552
Vosloosrus (★Johannesburg)	76,015
Welkom (★240,000)	68,111
Westonaria (★Johannesburg)	57,117

SPAIN / España

1988 E	39,217,804
Alacant (Alicante)	261,051
Albacete	125,997
Alcalá de Guadaira	50,935
Alcalá de Henares (★Madrid)	150,021
Alcobendas (★Madrid)	73,455
Alcoi (Alcoy)	66,074
Alcorcón (★Madrid)	139,796
Algeciras	99,528
Almería	157,644
Avilés (★131,000)	87,811
Badajoz (▲122,407)	106,400
Badalona (★Barcelona)	225,229
Baracaldo (★Bilbao)	113,502
Barcelona (★4,040,000)	1,714,355
Bilbao (★985,000)	384,733
Burgos	160,561
Cáceres	71,598
Cádiz (★240,000)	156,591
Cartagena (▲172,710)	70,000
Castelló de la Plana	131,809
Ciudad Real	56,300
Córdoba	302,301
Cornellà de Llobregat (★Barcelona)	86,866
Coslada (★Madrid)	68,765
Donostia (San Sebastián) (★285,000)	177,622
Dos Hermanas (▲68,456)	60,600
Elda	56,756
El Prat de Llobregat (★Barcelona)	64,193
El Puerto de Santa María (▲62,285)	49,900
Elx (Elche) (▲180,256)	158,300
Ferrol (★129,000)	86,503
Fuenlabrada (★Madrid)	128,872
Gernikao (Guernica) (▲17,836) (1981C)	12,214
Getafe (★Madrid)	135,367
Gijón	262,156
Granada	263,334
Granollers (★Barcelona)	49,045
Guadalajara	61,309
Huelva	137,826
Irún	54,886
Jaén	106,435
Jerez de la Frontera (▲183,007)	156,200
La Coruña	248,862
La Línea	60,956
Las Palmas de Gran Canaria (▲366,347)	319,000
Leganés (★Madrid)	168,403
León (★159,000)	136,558
L'Hospitalet de Llobregat (★Barcelona)	278,449
Linares	58,622
Lleida (Lérida) (▲109,795)	91,500
Logroño	119,038
Lugo (▲78,795)	68,700
• MADRID (★4,650,000)	3,102,846
Málaga	574,456
Manresa	65,607
Mataró	100,817
Mérida	52,368
Móstoles (★Madrid)	181,648

▲ Población de un municipio, comuna o distrito entero, incluyendo sus áreas rurales.
• Ciudad más grande de un país.
★ Población o designación de un área metropolitana, incluyendo los suburbios.
C Censo. **E** Estimado oficial. **U** Estimado no oficial.

Murcia (▲314,124)	149,800
Ourense	106,042
Oviedo (▲190,073)	168,900
Palencia	76,692
Palma (▲314,608)	249,000
Pamplona	180,598
Parla (★Madrid)	66,253
Portugalete (★Bilbao)	57,813
Puertollano	52,284
Reus	83,800
Rubí (★Barcelona)	48,807
Sabadell (★Barcelona)	189,489
Salamanca	159,342
San Baudilio de Llobrega (★Barcelona)	77,502
San Cristóbal de la Laguna (▲111,533)	25,900
San Fernando (★Cádiz)	81,975
San Sebastián de los Reyes (★Madrid)	51,653
Santa Coloma de Gramanet (★Barcelona)	136,042
Santa Cruz de Tenerife	215,228
Santander (▲190,795)	166,800
Santiago de Compostela (▲88,110)	68,800
Santurce-Antiguo (★Bilbao)	52,334
Segovia	54,402
Sevilla (★945,000)	663,132
Talavera de la Reina	68,158
Tarragona (▲109,586)	63,500
Tarrasa (★Barcelona)	161,410
Toledo	59,551
Torrejón de Ardoz (★Madrid)	83,267
Torrent (★València)	55,751
València (★1,270,000)	743,933
Valladolid	331,461
Vigo (▲271,128)	179,500
Vitoria (Gasteiz)	204,264
Zamora	62,047
Zaragoza	582,239

SPANISH NORTH AFRICA / Plazas de Soberanía en el Norte de África

1988 E	122,905
• Ceuta	67,188
Melilla	55,717

SRI LANKA

1989 E	16,806,000
Battaramulla (★Colombo) (1981C)	56,535
Batticaloa	50,000
• COLOMBO (★2,050,000)	612,000
Dehiwala-Mount Lavinia (★Colombo)	193,000
Galle	83,000
Jaffna	128,000
Kandy	103,000
Moratuwa (★Colombo)	166,000
Negombo	64,000
SRI JAYAWARDENEPURA (KOTTE) (★Colombo)	108,000
Trincomalee	49,000

SUDAN / As-Sūdān

1983 C	20,594,197
Al-Fāshir	84,298
• AL-KHARṬŪM (★1,450,000)	473,597
Al-Kharṭūm Baḥrī (★Al-Kharṭūm)	340,857
Al-Qaḍārif	116,876
Al-Ubayyiḍ	137,582
'Aṭbarah	72,836
Būr Sūdān (Port Sudan)	206,038
Jūbā	84,377
Kassalā	141,429
Kūstī	89,135
Nyala	111,693
Umm Durmān (Omdurman) (★Al-Kharṭūm)	526,192
Wad Madanī	145,015
Wāw	90,960

SURINAME

1988 E	392,000
• PARAMARIBO (★296,000)	241,000
Wanica (★Paramaribo)	55,000

SWAZILAND

1986 C	712,131
LOBAMBA	
Manzini (★30,000)	18,084
• MBABANE	38,290

SWEDEN / Sverige

1991 E	8,590,630
Borås (▲101,766)	59,400
Eskilstuna (▲89,765)	59,800
Gävle (▲88,568)	67,300
Göteborg (★710,894)	433,042
Halmstad (▲80,061)	48,900
Helsingborg (▲109,267)	82,000
Huddinge (★Stockholm)	73,829
Järfälla (★Stockholm)	56,359
Jönköping (▲111,486)	76,300
Karlstad (▲76,467)	53,100
Linköping (▲122,268)	82,700
Luleå (▲68,412)	42,700
Lund (▲87,681) (★Malmö)	63,700
Malmö (★475,224)	233,887
Mölndal (★Göteborg)	52,028
Nacka (★Stockholm)	64,056
Norrköping (▲120,522)	82,600
Örebro (▲120,944)	86,000
Södertälje (▲81,786) (★Stockholm)	58,100
Sollentuna (★Stockholm)	51,377
Solna (★Stockholm)	51,841
• STOCKHOLM (★1,491,726)	674,452
Sundsvall (▲93,808)	50,300
Täby (★Stockholm)	56,714
Trollhättan (▲51,047)	41,000
Tumba (★Stockholm)	68,542
Umeå (▲91,258)	61,300
Uppsala (▲167,508)	110,000
Västerås (▲119,761)	98,300
Växjö (▲69,547)	48,000

SWITZERLAND / Schweiz / Suisse / Svizzera

1990 C	6,873,687
Aarau (★59,500)	16,481
Arbon (★41,400)	11,043
Baden (★73,200)	15,718
Basel (Bâle) (★587,000)	178,428

▲ Population d'une municipalité, d'une commune ou d'un district, zone rurale incluse.
• Ville la plus peuplée du pays.
★ Population de l'agglomération (ou nom de la zone métropolitaine englobante).
C Recensement. **E** Estimation officielle. **U** Estimation non officielle.

BERN (BERNE) (★300,400)	136,338
Biel (Bienne) (★83,100)	51,893
Fribourg (Freiburg) (★62,500)	36,355
Genève (Geneva) (★470,000)	171,042
Lausanne (★265,000)	128,112
Locarno (★42,200)	13,796
Lugano (★94,700)	25,344
Luzern (★165,000)	61,034
Neuchâtel (★67,500)	33,579
Sankt Gallen (★127,000)	75,237
Schaffhausen (★53,800)	34,225
Thun (★79,500)	38,211
Vevey (★65,900)	15,968
Winterthur (★110,500)	86,959
Zug (★69,000)	21,705
• Zürich (★870,000)	365,043

SYRIA / Sūrīyah

1994 E	13,844,000
Al-Ḥasakah (1981C)	73,426
Al-Kiswah	99,050
Al-Lādhiqīyah (Latakia)	306,535
Al-Qāmishlī (1988E)	126,236
Ar-Raqqah	219,016
At-Tall	66,248
Az-Zabadānī	49,398
Dar'ā	180,093
Dārayyā (★Dimashq) (1988E)	53,204
Dayr az-Zawr	174,085
• DIMASHQ (DAMASCUS) (★2,230,000)	1,549,932
Dūmā (★Dimashq)	131,158
Ḥalab (Aleppo) (★1,640,000)	1,591,400
Ḥamāh (1988E)	222,000
Ḥimṣ	644,204
Idlib	113,360
Jaramānah (★Dimashq)	138,469
Kābir aṣ Ṣaghīr (1988E)	47,728
Madīnat ath Thawrah (1988E)	58,151
Salamīyah (1988E)	46,844
Ṭarṭūs	136,812

TAIWAN / T'aiwan

1991 E	20,352,966
Changhua (▲215,224)	165,000
Chiai (1992E)	258,713
Chilung (1992E)	357,000
Chungho (★T'aipei)	374,339
Chungli	269,804
Chutung (1988E)	104,797
Fangshan (★Kaohsiung)	290,777
Fengyüan (▲151,642)	121,100
Hsichih (★T'aipei) (1980C)	70,031
Hsinchu (1992E)	330,576
Hsinchuang (★T'aipei)	299,174
Hsintien (★T'aipei)	225,517
Hualien	107,552
Ilan (▲81,751) (1980C)	70,900
Kangshan (1980C)	78,049
Kaohsiung (★1,845,000) (1992E)	1,401,239
Lotung (1980C)	57,925
Lukang (1980C)	72,019
Miaoli (1980C)	81,500
Nant'ou (1980C)	84,038
P'ingchen (★T'aipei)	147,030
P'ingtung (▲210,801)	172,400
Sanchung (★T'aipei)	375,996
Shulin (★T'aipei)	111,993
Tach'i (1980C)	67,209
T'aichung (1992E)	785,182
T'ainan (1992E)	692,116
• T'AIPEI (★6,130,000) (1992E)	2,706,453
T'aipeihsien (★T'aipei)	538,954
T'aitung (▲108,196)	79,100
Taoyüan	241,263
T'oufen (1980C)	66,536
T'uch'eng (▲136,928) (★T'aipei)	80,300
Yangmei (1980C)	84,353
Yüanlin (▲121,251)	53,200
Yungho (★T'aipei)	249,736
Yungkang (▲136,705)	70,900

TAJIKISTAN

1991 E	5,358,300
Chudžand (Leninabad)	164,500
• DUŠANBE	582,400
Kul'ab	79,300
Kurgan-T'ube	58,400

TANZANIA

1985 E	21,733,000
Arusha (1984E)	69,000
• DAR ES SALAAM	1,096,000
DODOMA	85,000
Iringa (1984E)	67,000
Kigoma (1978C)	50,044
Mbeya	194,000
Morogoro (1984E)	72,000
Moshi (1984E)	62,000
Mtwara (1978C)	48,510
Mwanza	252,000
Tabora	214,000
Tanga	172,000
Ujiji (1967C)	21,369
Zanzibar	133,000

THAILAND / Prathet Thai

1991 E	56,961,030
Chiang Mai	161,541
Chon Buri	45,763
Hat Yai	142,351
Khon Kaen	131,478
• KRUNG THEP (BANGKOK) (★7,060,000)	5,620,591
Nakhon Ratchasima	202,503
Nakhon Sawan	108,569
Nakhon Si Thammarat	74,219
Nonthaburi (★Krung Thep)	264,201
Pattaya	64,731
Phitsanulok	77,672
Phra Nakhon Si Ayutthaya	60,561
Phuket	42,913
Sakon Nakhon	47,869
Samut Prakan (★Krung Thep)	71,538
Samut Sakhon	55,509
Saraburi	64,915
Songkhla	82,167
Trang	48,589
Ubon Ratchathani	98,950
Udon Thani	78,489
Yala	68,834

TOGO

1987 E	3,148,000
• LOMÉ	500,000
Sokodé	55,000

▲ População de um municipio, comuna ou distrito, inclusive as respectivas áreas rurais.
• Maior cidade de um país.
★ População ou indicação de uma área metropolitana.
C Censo. **E** Estimativa oficial. **U** Estimativa não oficial.

TONGA

1986 C	94,535
• NUKU'ALOFA	21,265

TRINIDAD AND TOBAGO

1990 C	1,234,388
• PORT OF SPAIN (★370,000)	50,878
San Fernando (★75,000)	30,092

TUNISIA / Tunis / Tunisie

1984 C	6,975,450
Ariana (★Tunis)	98,655
Bardo (★Tunis)	65,669
Ben Arous (★Tunis)	52,105
Bizerte	94,509
Gabès	92,258
Gafsa	60,970
Hammam Lif (★Tunis)	47,009
Houmt Essouk	92,269
Kairouan	72,254
Kasserine	47,606
La Goulette (★Tunis)	61,609
Menzel Bourguiba	51,399
Sfax (★310,000)	231,911
Sousse (★160,000)	83,509
• TUNIS (★1,225,000)	596,654
Zarzis	49,063

TURKEY / Türkiye

1990 C	56,473,035
Adana	916,150
Adıyaman	100,045
Afyon	95,643
Ağrı	58,038
Akhisar	73,944
Aksaray	90,698
Akşehir	51,746
Alanya	52,460
Amasya	57,288
ANKARA (★2,650,000)	2,559,471
Antalya	378,208
Aydın	107,011
Bafra	65,600
Balıkesir	170,589
Bandırma	77,444
Batman	147,347
Bilecik	23,273
Bolu	60,789
Burdur	56,432
Bursa	834,576
Çanakkale	53,995
Ceyhan	85,308
Cizre	50,023
Çorlu	74,681
Çorum	116,810
Darıca	53,560
Denizli	204,118
Diyarbakır	381,144
Düzce	61,878
Edirne	102,345
Elazığ	204,603
Elbistan	54,741
Ereğli, Konya prov.	74,283
Ereğli, Zonguldak prov.	63,987
Erzincan	91,772
Erzurum	242,391
Esenyurt (★İstanbul)	70,280
Eskişehir	413,082
Gaziantep	603,434
Gebze (★İstanbul)	159,116
Gelibolu	18,670
Gemlik	50,237
Giresun	67,604
Gölcük	64,911
Gümüşhane	26,014
Hakkâri	30,407
Hatay (Antioch)	123,871
İçel (Mersin)	422,357
İnegöl	71,120
İskenderun	154,807
Isparta	112,117
• İstanbul (★7,550,000)	6,620,241
İzmir (★1,900,000)	1,757,414
İzmit	256,882
Kadirli	55,061
Kahramanmaraş	228,129
Karabük	105,373
Karaman	76,525
Kars	78,455
Kastamonu	51,560
Kayseri	421,362
Kilis	82,882
Kırıkkale	185,431
Kırşehir	73,538
Kızıltepe	60,134
Konya	513,346
Körfez	65,786
Kozan	54,451
Kütahya	130,994
Lüleburgaz	52,384
Malatya	281,776
Manisa	158,928
Mardin	53,005
Muş	44,019
Nazilli	80,277
Nevşehir	52,719
Niğde	55,035
Nizip	58,604
Nusaybin	49,671
Ödemiş	51,620
Ordu	102,107
Osmaniye	123,307
Polatlı	60,158
Rize	52,031
Sakarya	171,225
Salihli	70,861
Samsun	303,979
Şanlıurfa	276,528
Siirt	68,320
Silvan (Miyafarkin)	59,865
Sinop	25,537
Sivas	221,512
Siverek	63,049
Söke	50,866
Soma	49,977
Sultanbeyli (★İstanbul)	82,298
Tarsus	187,508
Tatvan	54,071
Tekirdağ	80,442
Tokat	83,058
Trabzon	143,941
Tunceli	24,513
Turgutlu	73,634
Turhal	68,384
Uşak	105,270

Van	153,111
Viranşehir	57,461
Yalova (★İstanbul)	65,823
Yozgat	50,335
Zonguldak (★220,000)	116,725

TURKMENISTAN

1991 E	3,714,100
• AŠCHABAD (ASHGABAT)	412,200
Čardžou	166,400
Krasnovodsk	59,500
Mary	94,900
Nebit-Dag	89,100
Tašauz	117,000

TURKS AND CAICOS ISLANDS

1990 C	11,465
• GRAND TURK	3,691

TUVALU

1979 C	7,349
• FUNAFUTI	2,191

UGANDA

1991 C	16,582,700
Jinja	60,979
• KAMPALA	773,463
Masaka	49,070
Mbale	53,634

UKRAINE / Ukrayina

1991 E	51,944,400
Alchevs'k	126,000
Antratsyt (★Krasnyy Luch)	72,800
Artemivs'k	90,800
Berdyans'k	138,700
Berdychiv	93,400
Bila Tserkva	204,400
Bilhorod-Dnistrovs'kyy	56,800
Boryspil' (★Kyyiv)	52,700
Brovary (★Kyyiv)	84,800
Bryanka (★Stakhanov)	64,500
Cherkasy	302,200
Chernihiv	305,700
Chernivtsi	258,800
Chervonohrad	74,000
Dniprodzerzhyns'k (★Dnipropetrovs'k)	284,400
Dnipropetrovs'k (★1,600,000)	1,189,300
Donets'k (★2,125,000)	1,121,300
Drohobych	79,200
Druzhkivka (★Kramators'k)	74,400
Dymytrov (★Krasnoarmiys'k)	371,800
Dzerzhyns'k (★Horlivka)	50,500
Dzhankoy	54,500
Enerhodar	51,500
Fastiv	54,400
Feodosiya	85,600
Horlivka (★700,000)	336,600
Illichivs'k (★Odesa)	56,000
Ivano-Frankivs'k	241,000
Izmayil	95,100
Izyum	64,800
Kalush	69,400
Kam'yanets'-Podil's'kyy	104,900
Kerch	178,300
Kharkiv (Kharkov) (★2,050,000)	1,622,800
Khartsyz'k (★Donets'k)	69,300
Kherson	365,400
Khmel'nyts'kyy	244,500
Kirovohrad	277,900
Kolomyya	66,200
Komsomol's'k	56,000
Konotop	97,700
Korosten'	67,500
Kostyantynivka	107,800
Kovel'	69,700
Kramators'k (★515,000)	201,300
Krasnoarmiys'k (★180,000)	73,300
Krasnodon (★165,000)	54,800
Krasnyy Luch (★320,000)	113,400
Kremenchuk	240,600
Kryvyy Rih	724,000
• KYYIV (KIEV) (★3,250,000)	2,635,000
Lozova	74,100
Lubny	60,300
Luhans'k (★650,000)	503,900
Luts'k	209,500
L'viv	802,200
Lysychans'k (★415,000)	126,400
Makiyivka (★Donets'k)	423,900
Marhanets'	54,700
Mariupol' (Ždanov)	521,800
Melitopol'	176,900
Mukacheve	88,000
Mykolayiv	511,600
Nikopol'	159,000
Nizhyn	82,000
Nova Kakhovka	59,000
Novohrad-Volyns'kyy	56,100
Novomoskovs'k	76,600
Novovolyns'k	56,400
Odesa (★1,185,000)	1,100,700
Okhtyrka	52,300
Oleksandriya	104,900
Pavlohrad	134,300
Pervomays'k (★Stakhanov)	52,000
Pervomays'k	83,800
Poltava	320,100
Pryluky	72,900
Rivne	239,300
Romny	57,700
Roven'ky	58,500
Rubizhne (★Lysyscans'k)	75,100
Sevastopol'	366,200
Shakhtars'k (★Torez)	73,100
Shepetivka	51,900
Shostka	95,200
Simferopol'	352,600
Slov'yans'k (★Kramators'k)	137,100
Smila	81,200
Snizhne (★Torez)	68,900
Stakhanov (★700,000)	112,700
Stryy	68,200
Sumy	303,300
Sverdlovs'k (★145,000)	83,700
Svitlovods'k	57,900
Syeverodonets'k (★Lysychans'k)	133,300
Ternopil'	219,200
Torez (★320,000)	88,100
Uman'	97,700
Uzhhorod	122,600
Vinnytsya	380,900
Yalta	89,300
Yenakiyeve (★Horlivka)	120,100
Yevpatoriya	110,500
Zaporizhzhya	896,600
Zhovti Vody	64,900
Zhytomyr	297,500

UNITED ARAB EMIRATES / Al-Imārāt al-'Arabīyah al-Muttaḥidah

1980 C	980,000
ABŪ ZABY (ABU DHABI)	242,975
Al-'Ayn	101,663
Ash-Shāriqah	125,149
• Dubayy	265,702
Ra's al-Khaymah	42,000

UNITED KINGDOM

1981 C	55,678,079

UNITED KINGDOM: ENGLAND

1981 C	46,220,955
Aldershot (★London)	53,665
Ashton-under-Lyne (★Manchester)	43,605
Aylesbury	51,999
Barnsley	76,783
Barrow-in-Furness	50,174
Basildon (★London)	94,800
Basingstoke	73,027
Bath	84,283
Bebington (★Liverpool)	62,618
Bedford	75,632
Beeston and Stapleford (★Nottingham)	64,785
Benfleet (★London)	50,783
Birkenhead (★Liverpool)	99,075
Birmingham (★2,675,000)	1,013,995
Blackburn (★221,900)	109,564
Blackpool (★280,000)	146,297
Bognor Regis	50,323
Bolton (★Manchester)	143,960
Bootle	70,860
Bournemouth (★315,000)	142,829
Bracknell (★London)	52,257
Bradford (★Leeds)	293,336
Brentwood (★London)	51,212
Brighton (★420,000)	134,581
Bristol (★630,000)	413,861
Burnley (★160,000)	76,365
Burton upon Trent	59,040
Bury (★Manchester)	61,785
Bury Saint Edmunds	30,563
Cambridge	87,111
Cannock (★Birmingham)	54,503
Canterbury	34,546
Carlisle	72,206
Carlton (★Nottingham)	46,053
Chatham (★London)	65,835
Cheadle and Gatley (★Manchester)	59,478
Chelmsford (★London)	91,109
Cheltenham	87,188
Cheshunt (★London)	49,616
Chester	80,154
Chesterfield (★127,000)	73,352
Clacton-on-Sea	39,618
Colchester	87,476
Corby	48,704
Coventry (★645,000)	318,718
Crawley (★London)	80,113
Crewe	59,097
Crosby (★Liverpool)	54,103
Darlington	85,519
Dartford (★London)	62,032
Derby (★275,000)	218,026
Dewsbury (★Leeds)	49,612
Doncaster	74,727
Dover	33,461
Dudley (★Birmingham)	186,513
Dunstable (★Luton)	48,436
Durham	38,105
Eastbourne	86,715
Eastleigh (★Southampton)	58,585
Ellesmere Port (★Liverpool)	65,829
Epsom and Ewell (★London)	65,830
Esher / Molesey (★London)	46,688
Exeter	88,235
Fareham / Portchester (★Portsmouth)	55,563
Farnborough (★London)	48,063
Folkestone	42,949
Frimley and Camberley (★London)	45,108
Gateshead (★Newcastle)	91,429
Gillingham (★London)	92,531
Gloucester (★115,000)	106,526
Gosport (★Portsmouth)	69,664
Gravesend (★London)	53,450
Grays (★London)	45,881
Greasby / Moreton (★Liverpool)	56,410
Great Yarmouth	54,777
Grimsby (★145,000)	91,532
Guildford (★London)	61,509
Halesowen (★Birmingham)	57,533
Halifax	76,675
Harlow (★London)	79,150
Harrogate	63,637
Hartlepool (★Middlesbrough)	91,749
Hastings	74,979
Havant (★Portsmouth)	50,098
Hemel Hempstead (★London)	80,110
Hereford	48,277
Hertford (★London)	21,350
High Wycombe (▲156,800)	69,575
Hove (★Brighton)	65,587
Huddersfield (▲377,400)	147,825
Huyton-with-Roby (★Liverpool)	62,011
Ipswich	129,661
Keighley (★Leeds)	49,188
Kidderminster	50,385
Kingston upon Hull (★350,000)	322,144
Kingswood (★Bristol)	54,736
Kirkby (★Liverpool)	52,825
Lancaster	43,902
Leeds (★1,540,000)	445,242
Leicester (★495,000)	324,394
Lincoln	79,980
Littlehampton	46,028
Liverpool (★1,525,000)	538,809
• LONDON (★11,100,000)	6,574,009
Loughborough	44,895
Lowestoft	59,430
Luton (★220,000)	163,209
Macclesfield	47,525
Maidenhead (★London)	59,809
Maidstone	86,067
Manchester (★2,775,000)	437,612
Mansfield (★198,000)	71,325
Margate	53,137
Middlesbrough (★580,000)	158,516
Middleton (★Manchester)	51,373
Milton Keynes	36,886
Newcastle-under-Lyme (★Stoke-on-Trent)	73,208
Newcastle upon Tyne (★1,300,000)	199,064
Northampton	154,172
Norwich (★230,000)	169,814
Nottingham (★655,000)	273,300
Nuneaton (★Coventry)	60,337
Oldbury / Smethwick (★Birmingham)	153,268
Oldham (★Manchester)	107,095
Oxford (★230,000)	113,847
Penzance	18,501
Peterborough	113,404
Plymouth (★290,000)	238,583
Poole (★Bournemouth)	122,815
Portsmouth (★485,000)	174,218
Preston (★250,000)	166,675
Ramsgate	36,678
Reading (★200,000)	194,727
Redditch (★Birmingham)	61,639
Reigate / Redhill (★London)	48,241
Rochdale (★Manchester)	97,292
Rotherham (★Sheffield)	122,374
Royal Leamington Spa (★Coventry)	56,552
Royal Tunbridge Wells	57,699
Rugby	59,039
Runcorn (★Liverpool)	63,995
Saint Albans (★London)	76,709
Saint Helens	114,397
Sale (★Manchester)	57,872
Salford (★Manchester)	96,525
Salisbury	36,890
Scarborough	36,665
Scunthorpe	79,043
Sheffield (★710,000)	470,685
Shrewsbury	57,731
Slough (★London)	106,341
Solihull (★Birmingham)	93,940
Southampton (★415,000)	211,321
Southend-on-Sea (★London)	155,720
Southport (★Liverpool)	88,596
South Shields (★Newcastle)	86,488
Stafford	60,915
Staines (★London)	51,949
Stevenage	74,757
Stockport (★Manchester)	135,489
Stockton-on-Tees (★Middlesbrough)	86,699
Stoke-on-Trent (★440,000)	272,446
Stourbridge (★Birmingham)	55,136
Stratford-upon-Avon	20,941
Stretford (★Manchester)	47,522
Sunderland (★Newcastle)	195,064
Sutton Coldfield (★Birmingham)	102,572
Swindon	127,348
Tamworth	63,260
Taunton	47,793
Torquay (★112,400)	54,430
Wakefield (★Leeds)	74,764
Wallasey (★Liverpool)	62,465
Walsall (★Birmingham)	177,923
Walton and Weybridge (★London)	50,031
Warrington	81,366
Washington (★Newcastle)	48,856
Waterlooville (★Portsmouth)	57,296
Watford (★London)	109,503
West Bromwich (★Birmingham)	153,725
Weston-super-Mare	60,821
Widnes	55,973
Wigan (★Manchester)	88,725
Woking (★London)	92,667
Wolverhampton (★Birmingham)	263,501
Worcester	75,466
Worthing (★Brighton)	90,687
York (★145,000)	123,126

UNITED KINGDOM: NORTHERN IRELAND

1990 E	1,589,400
Bangor (★Belfast)	72,600
Belfast (★685,000)	295,100
Castlereagh (★Belfast)	58,100
Londonderry (Derry)	100,500
Lurgan (★63,000) (1981C)	20,991
Newtownabbey (★Belfast)	72,900

UNITED KINGDOM: SCOTLAND

1990 E	5,102,400
Aberdeen	211,080
Ayr (★100,000) (1981C)	48,493
Clydebank (★Glasgow) (1981C)	51,832
Coatbridge (1981C)	50,831
Cumbernauld (★Glasgow)	50,700
Dundee	172,860
Dunfermline (★125,817) (1981C)	52,105
East Kilbride (★Glasgow)	70,500
Edinburgh (★630,000)	434,520
Falkirk (★148,171) (1981C)	36,372
Glasgow (★1,800,000)	689,210
Greenock (★101,000) (1981C)	58,436
Hamilton (★Glasgow) (1981C)	51,666
Irvine (★94,000)	56,000
Kilmarnock (★84,000) (1981C)	51,799
Kirkcaldy (★148,171) (1981C)	46,356
Motherwell (★Glasgow) (1981C)	30,616
Paisley (★Glasgow) (1981C)	84,330
Perth (1981C)	41,916
Stirling (★61,000) (1981C)	36,640

UNITED KINGDOM: WALES

1981 C	2,790,462
Cardiff (★625,000)	262,313
Cwmbran (★Newport)	44,592
Llanelli	45,336
Merthyr Tydfil	38,893
Neath (★Swansea)	48,687
Newport (★310,000)	115,896
Pontypool (★Newport)	36,064
Port Talbot (★130,000)	40,078
Rhondda (★Cardiff)	70,980
Swansea (★275,000)	172,433
Wrexham	39,929

UNITED STATES

1990 C	248,709,462

UNITED STATES: ALABAMA

1990 C	4,040,587
Anniston (★116,034)	26,623
Auburn (★61,100)	33,830
Birmingham (★907,810)	265,968
Decatur (★131,556)	48,761
Dothan (★130,964)	53,589
Florence (★131,327)	36,426
Gadsden (★99,840)	42,523
Huntsville (★238,912)	159,789
Mobile (★476,923)	196,278
Montgomery (★292,517)	187,106
Tuscaloosa (★150,522)	77,759

UNITED STATES: ALASKA

1990 C	550,043
Anchorage (★248,400)	226,338
Fairbanks (★59,500)	30,843
Juneau	26,751

UNITED STATES: ARIZONA

1990 C	3,665,228
Chandler (★Phoenix)	90,533
Glendale (★Phoenix)	148,134
Mesa (★Phoenix)	288,091
Nogales (★Nogales, Mexico)	19,489
Phoenix (★2,122,101)	983,403
Scottsdale (★Phoenix)	130,069
Tempe (★Phoenix)	141,865
Tucson (★666,880)	405,390
Yuma (★106,895)	54,923

UNITED STATES: ARKANSAS

1990 C	2,350,725
Fayetteville (★113,409)	42,099
Fort Smith (★175,911)	72,798
Hot Springs National Park (★56,500)	32,462
Jonesboro (★49,300)	46,535
Little Rock (★513,117)	175,795
North Little Rock (★Little Rock)	61,741
Pine Bluff (★85,487)	57,140

UNITED STATES: CALIFORNIA

1990 C	29,760,021
Alameda (★Oakland)	76,459
Alhambra (★Los Angeles)	82,106
Anaheim (★2,410,556) (★Los Angeles)	266,406
Antioch (★Oakland)	62,195
Arden (★Sacramento)	62,900
Bakersfield (★543,477)	174,820
Baldwin Park (★Los Angeles)	69,330
Bellflower (★Los Angeles)	61,815
Berkeley (★Oakland)	102,724
Buena Park (★Anaheim)	68,784
Burbank (★Los Angeles)	93,643
Calexico (★Mexicali, Mexico)	18,633
Camarillo (★Oxnard)	52,303
Carlsbad (★San Diego)	63,126
Carmichael (★Sacramento)	48,702
Carson (★Los Angeles)	83,995
Cerritos (★Los Angeles)	53,240
Chico (★182,120)	40,079
Chino (★Riverside)	59,682
Chula Vista (★San Diego)	135,163
Citrus Heights (★Sacramento)	107,439
Clovis (★Fresno)	50,323
Compton (★Los Angeles)	90,454
Concord (★Oakland)	111,348
Corona (★Riverside)	76,095
Costa Mesa (★Anaheim)	96,357
Cucamonga (★Riverside)	101,409
Daly City (★San Francisco)	92,311
Diamond Bar (★Los Angeles)	53,672
Downey (★Los Angeles)	91,444
East Los Angeles (★Los Angeles)	126,379
El Cajon (★San Diego)	88,693
El Monte (★Los Angeles)	106,209
El Toro (★Anaheim)	62,685
Escondido (★San Diego)	108,635
Eureka (★89,800)	27,025
Fairfield (★Vallejo)	77,211
Fontana (★Riverside)	87,535
Fountain Valley (★Anaheim)	53,691
Fremont (★Oakland)	173,339
Fresno (★667,490)	354,202
Fullerton (★Anaheim)	114,144
Gardena (★Los Angeles)	49,847
Garden Grove (★Anaheim)	143,050
Glendale (★Los Angeles)	180,038
Hacienda Heights (★Los Angeles)	52,354
Hawthorne (★Los Angeles)	71,349
Hayward (★Oakland)	111,498
Hemet (★Riverside)	36,094
Huntington Beach (★Anaheim)	181,519
Huntington Park (★Los Angeles)	56,065
Inglewood (★Los Angeles)	109,602
Irvine (★Anaheim)	110,330
La Habra (★Anaheim)	51,266
Lakewood (★Los Angeles)	73,557
La Mesa (★San Diego)	52,931
Lancaster (★189,300) (★Los Angeles)	97,291
Livermore (★Oakland)	56,741
Lodi (★Stockton)	51,874
Lompoc (★Santa Barbara)	37,649
Long Beach (★Los Angeles)	429,433
Los Angeles (★14,531,529)	3,485,398
Lynwood (★Los Angeles)	61,945
Merced (★178,403)	56,216
Milpitas (★San Jose)	50,686
Mission Viejo (★Anaheim)	72,820
Modesto (★370,522)	164,730
Montebello (★Los Angeles)	59,564
Monterey (★Salinas)	31,954
Monterey Park (★Los Angeles)	60,738
Mountain View (★San Jose)	67,460
Napa (★Vallejo)	61,842
National City (★San Diego)	54,249
Newport Beach (★Anaheim)	66,643
Norwalk (★Los Angeles)	94,279
Oakland (★2,082,914) (★San Francisco)	372,242
Oceanside (★San Diego)	128,398
Ontario (★Riverside)	133,179
Orange (★Anaheim)	110,658
Oxnard (★669,016) (★Los Angeles)	142,216
Palm Springs (★Riverside)	40,181
Palo Alto (★San Jose)	55,900
Pasadena (★Los Angeles)	131,591
Pico Rivera (★Los Angeles)	59,177
Pleasanton (★Oakland)	50,553
Pomona (★Los Angeles)	131,723
Porterville (★Visalia)	29,563
Rancho Cordova (★Sacramento)	48,731
Redding (★147,036)	66,462
Redlands (★Riverside)	60,394
Redondo Beach (★Los Angeles)	60,167
Redwood City (★San Francisco)	66,072
Rialto (★Riverside)	72,388
Richmond (★Oakland)	87,425
Riverside (★2,588,793) (★Los Angeles)	226,505

▲ Population of an entire municipality, commune, or district, including rural area.
• Largest city in country.
★ Population or designation of the metropolitan area, including suburbs.
C Census. **E** Official estimate. **U** Unofficial estimate.

▲ Bevölkerung eines ganzen städtischen Verwaltungsgebietes, eines Kommunalbezirkes oder eines Distrikts, einschliesslich ländlicher Gebiete.
• Grösste Stadt des Landes.
★ Bevölkerung oder Bezeichnung der Stadtregion einschliesslich Vororte.
C Volkszählung. **E** Offizielle Schätzung. **U** Inoffizielle Schätzung.

Rosemead (★Los Angeles)	51,638
Sacramento (★1,481,102)	369,365
Salinas (★355,660)	108,777
San Bernardino (★Riverside)	164,164
San Diego (★2,949,000)	1,110,549
San Francisco (★6,253,311)	723,959
San Jose (★1,497,577) (★San Francisco)	782,248
San Leandro (★Oakland)	68,223
San Mateo (★San Francisco)	85,486
Santa Ana (★Anaheim)	293,742
Santa Barbara (★369,608)	85,571
Santa Clara (★San Jose)	93,613
Santa Cruz (★229,734) (★San Francisco)	49,040
Santa Maria (★Santa Barbara)	61,284
Santa Monica (★Los Angeles)	86,905
Santa Rosa (★388,222) (★San Francisco)	113,313
Santee (★San Diego)	52,902
Simi Valley (★Oxnard)	100,217
South Gate (★Los Angeles)	86,284
South San Francisco (★San Francisco)	54,312
South Whittier (★Los Angeles)	51,100
Spring Valley (★San Diego)	54,600
Stockton (★480,628)	210,943
Sunnyvale (★San Jose)	117,229
Thousand Oaks (★Oxnard)	104,352
Torrance (★Los Angeles)	133,107
Tustin (★Anaheim)	50,689
Union City (★Oakland)	53,762
Upland (★Riverside)	63,374
Vacaville (★Vallejo)	71,479
Vallejo (★451,186) (★San Francisco)	109,199
Ventura (San Buenaventura) (★Oxnard)	92,575
Visalia (★311,921)	75,636
Vista (★San Diego)	71,872
Walnut Creek (★Oakland)	60,569
Watsonville (★Santa Cruz)	31,099
West Covina (★Los Angeles)	96,086
Westminster (★Anaheim)	78,118
Whittier (★Los Angeles)	77,671
Yorba Linda (★Anaheim)	52,422
Yuba City (★122,643)	27,437

UNITED STATES: COLORADO

1990 C	3,294,394
Arvada (★Denver)	89,235
Aurora (★Denver)	222,103
Boulder (★225,339) (★Denver)	83,312
Colorado Springs (★397,014)	281,140
Denver (★1,848,319)	467,610
Fort Collins (★186,136)	87,758
Grand Junction (★85,200)	29,034
Greeley (★131,821)	60,536
Lakewood (★Denver)	126,481
Longmont (★Boulder)	51,555
Loveland (★Fort Collins)	37,352
Pueblo (★123,051)	98,640
Thornton (★Denver)	55,031
Westminster (★Denver)	74,625

UNITED STATES: CONNECTICUT

1990 C	3,287,116
Bridgeport (★443,722) (★New York, N.Y.)	141,686
Bristol (★79,488) (★Hartford)	60,640
Danbury (★187,867) (★New York, N.Y.)	65,585
East Hartford (★Hartford)	50,452
Fairfield (★Bridgeport)	53,418
Greenwich (★Stamford)	58,441
Hamden (★New Haven)	52,434
Hartford (★1,085,837)	139,739
Manchester (★Hartford)	51,618
Meriden (★New Haven)	59,479
Milford (★Bridgeport)	48,168
New Britain (★148,188) (★Hartford)	75,491
New Haven (★530,180)	130,474
New London (★266,819)	28,540
Norwalk (★127,378) (★New York, N.Y.)	78,331
Stamford (★202,557) (★New York, N.Y.)	108,056
Stratford (★Bridgeport)	49,389
Torrington (★58,800)	33,687
Waterbury (★221,629)	108,961
West Hartford (★Hartford)	60,110
West Haven (★New Haven)	54,021

UNITED STATES: DELAWARE

1990 C	666,168
Dover (★78,900)	27,630
Wilmington (★Philadelphia, Pa.)	71,529

UNITED STATES: DISTRICT OF COLUMBIA

1990 C	606,900
WASHINGTON (★3,923,574)	606,900

UNITED STATES: FLORIDA

1990 C	12,937,926
Boca Raton (★West Palm Beach)	61,492
Brandon (★Tampa)	57,985
Cape Coral (★Fort Myers)	74,991
Carol City (★Miami)	53,331
City of Sunrise (★Fort Lauderdale)	64,407
Clearwater (★Tampa)	98,784
Daytona Beach (★370,712)	61,921
De Land (★Daytona Beach)	16,491
Fort Lauderdale (★1,255,488) (★Miami)	149,377
Fort Myers (★335,113)	45,206
Fort Pierce (★251,071)	36,830
Fort Walton Beach (★143,776)	21,471
Gainesville (★204,111)	84,770
Hialeah (★Miami)	188,004
Hollywood (★Fort Lauderdale)	121,697
Jacksonville (★906,727)	635,230
Kendall (★Miami)	87,271
Lakeland (★405,382)	70,576
Largo (★Tampa)	65,674
Melbourne (★398,978)	59,646
Miami (★3,192,582)	358,548
Miami Beach (★Miami)	92,639
Naples (★152,099)	19,505
Ocala (★194,833)	42,045
Orlando (★1,072,748)	164,693
Panama City (★126,994)	34,378
Pembroke Pines (★Fort Lauderdale)	65,452
Pensacola (★344,406)	58,165
Plantation (★Fort Lauderdale)	66,692
Pompano Beach (★Fort Lauderdale)	72,411
Saint Petersburg (★Tampa)	238,629
Sarasota (★277,776)	50,961
Tallahassee (★233,598)	124,773
Tampa (★2,067,959)	280,015
Venice (★Sarasota)	16,922
West Palm Beach (★863,518)	67,643
Winter Haven (★Lakeland)	24,725

UNITED STATES: GEORGIA

1990 C	6,478,216
Albany (★112,561)	78,122
Athens (★156,267)	45,734
Atlanta (★2,833,511)	394,017
Augusta (★396,809)	44,639
Columbus (★243,072)	178,681
Macon (★281,103)	106,612
Rome (★74,900)	30,326
Savannah (★242,622)	137,560
Valdosta (★64,000)	39,806
Warner Robins (★Macon)	43,726

UNITED STATES: HAWAII

1990 C	1,108,229
Hilo (★47,600)	37,808
Honolulu (★836,231)	365,272

UNITED STATES: IDAHO

1990 C	1,006,749
Boise (★205,775)	125,738
Idaho Falls (★72,700)	43,929
Lewiston (★44,300)	28,082
Nampa (★70,500)	28,365
Pocatello (★56,700)	46,080

UNITED STATES: ILLINOIS

1990 C	11,430,602
Arlington Heights (★Chicago)	75,460
Aurora (★356,884) (★Chicago)	99,581
Bloomington (★129,180)	51,972
Champaign (★173,025)	63,502
Chicago (★8,065,633)	2,783,726
Cicero (★Chicago)	67,436
Danville (★68,000)	33,828
Decatur (★117,206)	83,885
De Kalb (★52,200)	34,925
Des Plaines (★Chicago)	53,223
East Saint Louis (★Saint Louis, Mo.)	40,944
Elgin (★Aurora)	77,010
Evanston (★Chicago)	73,233
Galesburg (★40,600)	33,530
Joliet (★389,650) (★Chicago)	76,836
Kankakee (★96,255)	27,575
Mount Prospect (★Chicago)	53,170
Naperville (★Chicago)	85,351
Oak Lawn (★Chicago)	56,182
Oak Park (★Chicago)	53,648
Peoria (★339,172)	113,504
Quincy (★50,600)	39,681
Rockford (★283,719)	139,426
Schaumburg (★Chicago)	68,586
Skokie (★Chicago)	59,432
Springfield (★189,550)	105,227
Waukegan (★Chicago)	69,392
Wheaton (★Chicago)	51,464

UNITED STATES: INDIANA

1990 C	5,544,159
Anderson (★130,669)	59,459
Bloomington (★108,978)	60,633
Columbus (★59,000)	31,802
Elkhart (★156,198)	43,627
Evansville (★278,990)	126,272
Fort Wayne (★363,811)	173,072
Gary (★604,526) (★Chicago, Il.)	116,646
Hammond (★Gary)	84,236
Indianapolis (★1,249,822)	731,327
Kokomo (★96,946)	44,962
Lafayette (★130,598)	43,764
Marion (★76,900)	32,618
Michigan City (★55,600)	33,822
Muncie (★119,659)	71,035
Richmond (★64,100)	38,705
South Bend (★247,052)	105,511
Terre Haute (★130,812)	57,483

UNITED STATES: IOWA

1990 C	2,776,755
Ames (★65,400)	47,198
Cedar Rapids (★168,767)	108,751
Clinton (★39,600)	29,201
Council Bluffs (★Omaha, Ne.)	54,315
Davenport (★350,861)	95,333
Des Moines (★392,928)	193,187
Dubuque (★86,403)	57,546
Iowa City (★96,119)	59,738
Mason City	29,040
Sioux City (★115,018)	80,505
Waterloo (★146,611)	66,467

UNITED STATES: KANSAS

1990 C	2,477,574
Hutchinson (★46,800)	39,308
Kansas City (★Kansas City, Mo.)	149,767
Lawrence (★81,798)	65,608
Manhattan (★47,400)	37,712
Olathe (★Kansas City, Mo.)	63,352
Overland Park (★Kansas City, Mo.)	111,790
Salina (★42,700)	42,303
Topeka (★160,976)	119,883
Wichita (★485,270)	304,011

UNITED STATES: KENTUCKY

1990 C	3,685,296
Bowling Green (★59,100)	40,641
Covington (★Cincinnati, Oh.)	43,264
Frankfort	25,968
Lexington (★348,428)	225,366
Louisville (★952,662)	269,063
Owensboro (★87,189)	53,549
Paducah (★63,000)	27,256

UNITED STATES: LOUISIANA

1990 C	4,219,973
Alexandria (★131,556)	49,188
Baton Rouge (★528,264)	219,531
Bossier City (★Shreveport)	52,721
Houma (★182,842)	96,982
Kenner (★New Orleans)	72,033
Lafayette (★208,740)	94,440
Lake Charles (★168,134)	70,580
Metairie (★New Orleans)	149,428
Monroe (★142,191)	54,909
New Iberia (★49,000)	31,828
New Orleans (★1,238,816)	496,938
Shreveport (★334,341)	198,525

UNITED STATES: MAINE

1990 C	1,227,928
Augusta (★56,700)	21,325
Bangor (★88,745)	33,181
Lewiston (★88,141)	39,757
Portland (★215,281)	64,358

UNITED STATES: MARYLAND

1990 C	4,781,468
Annapolis (★Baltimore)	33,187
Baltimore (★2,382,172)	736,014
Bethesda (★Washington, D.C.)	62,936
Columbia (★Baltimore)	75,883
Cumberland (★101,643)	23,706
Dundalk (★Baltimore)	65,800
Hagerstown (★121,393)	35,445
Salisbury (★72,400)	20,592
Silver Spring (★Washington, D.C.)	76,046
Towson (★Baltimore)	49,445
Wheaton (★Washington, D.C.) (1989)	58,300

UNITED STATES: MASSACHUSETTS

1990 C	6,016,425
Amherst (★44,700)	17,824
Boston (★4,171,643)	574,283
Brockton (★189,478) (★Boston)	92,788
Brookline (★Boston)	54,718
Cambridge (★Boston)	95,802
Chicopee (★Springfield)	56,632
Fall River (★157,272) (★Providence, R.I.)	92,703
Fitchburg (★102,797)	41,194
Framingham (★Boston)	64,994
Haverhill (★Lawrence)	51,418
Lawrence (★393,516) (★Boston)	70,207
Lowell (★273,067) (★Boston)	103,439
Lynn (★Salem)	81,245
Malden (★Boston)	53,884
Medford (★Boston)	57,407
New Bedford (★175,641)	99,922
Newton (★Boston)	82,585
Northampton (★Springfield)	29,289
Pittsfield (★79,250)	48,622
Quincy (★Boston)	84,985
Somerville (★Boston)	76,210
Springfield (★529,519)	156,983
Taunton (★59,700)	49,832
Waltham (★Boston)	57,878
Weymouth (★Boston)	54,063
Worcester (★436,905)	169,759

UNITED STATES: MICHIGAN

1990 C	9,295,297
Ann Arbor (★282,937) (★Detroit)	109,592
Battle Creek (★135,982)	53,540
Benton Harbor (★161,378)	12,818
Clinton Township (★Detroit)	85,866
Dearborn (★Detroit)	89,286
Dearborn Heights (★Detroit)	60,838
Detroit (★4,665,236)	1,027,974
East Lansing (★Lansing)	50,677
Farmington Hills (★Detroit)	74,652
Flint (★430,459)	140,761
Grand Rapids (★688,399)	189,126
Holland (★Grand Rapids)	30,745
Jackson (★149,756)	37,446
Kalamazoo (★223,411)	80,277
Lansing (★432,674)	127,321
Livonia (★Detroit)	100,850
Monroe (★62,600) (★Detroit)	22,902
Muskegon (★158,983)	40,283
Pontiac (★Detroit)	71,166
Port Huron (★Sarnia, Canada)	33,694
Redford Township (★Detroit)	54,387
Roseville (★Detroit)	51,412
Royal Oak (★Detroit)	65,410
Saginaw (★399,320)	69,512
Saint Clair Shores (★Detroit)	68,107
Sault Sainte Marie	14,689
Southfield (★Detroit)	75,728
Sterling Heights (★Detroit)	117,810
Taylor (★Detroit)	70,811
Troy (★Detroit)	72,884
Warren (★Detroit)	144,864
Westland (★Detroit)	84,724
Wyoming (★Grand Rapids)	63,891

UNITED STATES: MINNESOTA

1990 C	4,375,099
Bloomington (★Minneapolis)	86,335
Brooklyn Park (★Minneapolis)	56,381
Burnsville (★Minneapolis)	51,288
Coon Rapids (★Minneapolis)	52,978
Duluth (★239,971)	85,493
Mankato (★48,400)	31,477
Minneapolis (★2,464,124)	368,383
Plymouth (★Minneapolis)	50,889
Rochester (★106,470)	70,745
Saint Cloud (★190,921)	48,812
Saint Paul (★Minneapolis)	272,235

UNITED STATES: MISSISSIPPI

1990 C	2,573,216
Biloxi (★197,125)	46,319
Columbus (★52,100)	23,799
Greenville (★48,500)	45,226
Gulfport (★Biloxi)	40,775
Hattiesburg (★71,600)	41,882
Jackson (★395,396)	196,637
Laurel (★47,300)	18,827
Meridian (★60,600)	41,036
Natchez (★45,700)	19,460
Pascagoula (★115,243)	25,899
Vicksburg (★43,500)	20,908

UNITED STATES: MISSOURI

1990 C	5,117,073
Cape Girardeau (★59,100)	34,438
Columbia (★112,379)	69,101
Florissant (★Saint Louis)	51,206
Independence (★Kansas City)	112,301
Jefferson City (★60,100)	35,481
Joplin (★134,910)	40,961
Kansas City (★1,566,280)	435,146
Saint Charles (★Saint Louis)	54,555
Saint Joseph (★83,083)	71,852
Saint Louis (★2,444,099)	396,685
Springfield (★240,593)	140,494

UNITED STATES: MONTANA

1990 C	799,065
Billings (★113,419)	81,151
Butte (★33,900)	33,336
Great Falls (★77,691)	55,097
Helena	24,569
Missoula (★65,700)	42,918

UNITED STATES: NEBRASKA

1990 C	1,578,385
Grand Island (★42,200)	39,386
Lincoln (★213,641)	191,972
Omaha (★618,262)	335,795

UNITED STATES: NEVADA

1990 C	1,201,833
Carson City	40,443
Henderson (★Las Vegas)	64,942
Las Vegas (★741,459)	258,295
Paradise (★Las Vegas)	124,682
Reno (★254,667)	133,850
Sparks (★Reno)	53,367
Sunrise Manor (★Las Vegas)	95,362

UNITED STATES: NEW HAMPSHIRE

1990 C	1,109,252
Concord (★73,300)	36,006
Manchester (★147,809)	99,567
Nashua (★180,557) (★Boston, Ma.)	79,662
Portsmouth (★223,578)	25,925

UNITED STATES: NEW JERSEY

1990 C	7,730,188
Atlantic City (★319,416)	37,986
Bayonne (★Jersey City)	61,444
Bloomfield (★Newark)	45,061
Brick Township (★New York, N.Y.)	66,473
Camden (★Philadelphia, Pa.)	87,492
Cherry Hill (★Philadelphia, Pa.)	69,319
Clifton (★New York, N.Y.)	71,742
East Orange (★Newark)	73,552
Edison (★New York, N.Y.)	88,680
Elizabeth (★Newark)	110,002
Irvington (★Newark)	59,774
Jersey City (★553,099) (★New York, N.Y.)	228,537
Middletown (★New York, N.Y.)	62,298
Newark (★1,824,321) (★New York, N.Y.)	275,221
Passaic (★New York, N.Y.)	58,041
Paterson (★New York, N.Y.)	140,891
Trenton (★325,824) (★Philadelphia, Pa.)	88,675
Union (★Newark)	50,024
Union City (★Jersey City)	58,012
Vineland (★138,053) (★Philadelphia, Pa.)	54,780

UNITED STATES: NEW MEXICO

1990 C	1,515,069
Albuquerque (★480,577)	384,736
Farmington (★50,300)	33,997
Las Cruces (★135,510)	62,126
Roswell (★50,600)	44,654
Santa Fe (★117,043)	55,859

UNITED STATES: NEW YORK

1990 C	17,990,455
Albany (★874,304)	101,082
Auburn (★52,900)	31,258
Binghamton (★264,497)	53,008
Buffalo (★1,189,288)	328,123
Cheektowaga (★Buffalo)	84,387
Elmira (★95,195)	33,724
Glens Falls (★118,539)	15,023
Hempstead (★New York)	49,453
Irondequoit (★Rochester)	52,322
Ithaca (★82,700)	29,541
Jamestown (★141,895)	34,681
Kingston (★88,200)	23,095
Levittown (★New York)	53,286
Lockport (★57,500) (★Buffalo)	24,426
Mount Vernon (★New York)	67,153
Newburgh (★102,300) (★New York)	26,454
New Rochelle (★New York)	67,265
• New York (★18,087,251)	7,322,564
Niagara Falls (★220,756) (★Buffalo)	61,840
Poughkeepsie (★259,462)	28,844
Rochester (★1,002,410)	231,636
Schenectady (★Albany)	65,566
Syracuse (★659,864)	163,860
Troy (★Albany)	54,269
Utica (★316,633)	68,637
West Seneca (★Buffalo)	47,866
Yonkers (★New York)	188,082

UNITED STATES: NORTH CAROLINA

1990 C	6,628,637
Asheville (★174,821)	61,607
Burlington (★108,213)	39,498
Charlotte (★1,162,093)	395,934
Durham (★Raleigh)	136,611
Fayetteville (★274,566)	75,695
Gastonia (★Charlotte)	54,732
Goldsboro (★94,200)	40,709
Greensboro (★942,091)	183,521
Hickory (★221,700)	28,301
High Point (★Greensboro)	69,496
Jacksonville (★149,838)	30,013
Kannapolis (★Charlotte)	29,696
Raleigh (★735,480)	207,951
Rocky Mount (★83,400)	48,997
Salisbury (★Charlotte)	23,087
Wilmington (★120,284)	55,530
Winston-Salem (★Greenboro)	143,485

UNITED STATES: NORTH DAKOTA

1990 C	638,800
Bismarck (★83,831)	49,256
Fargo (★153,296)	74,111
Grand Forks (★70,683)	49,425
Minot (★39,800)	34,544

▲ Población de un municipio, comuna o distrito entero, incluyendo sus áreas rurales.
• Ciudad más grande de un país.
★ Población o designación de un área metropolitana, incluyendo los suburbios.
C Censo. **E** Estimado oficial. **U** Estimado no oficial.

▲ Population d'une municipalité, d'une commune ou d'un district, zone rurale incluse.
• Ville la plus peuplée du pays.
★ Population de l'agglomération (ou nom de la zone métropolitaine englobante).
C Recensement. **E** Estimation officielle. **U** Estimation non officielle.

▲ População de um municipio, comuna ou distrito, inclusive as respectivas áreas rurais.
• Maior cidade de um país.
★ População ou indicação de uma área metropolitana.
C Censo. **E** Estimativa oficial. **U** Estimativa não oficial.

UNITED STATES: OHIO

1990 C	10,347,115
Akron (★657,575) (★Cleveland)	223,019
Alliance (★Canton)	23,376
Ashtabula (★40,900)	21,633
Brunswick (★Cleveland)	28,230
Canton (★394,106)	84,161
Cincinnati (★1,744,124)	364,040
Cleveland (★2,759,823)	505,616
Cleveland Heights (★Cleveland)	54,052
Columbus (★1,377,419)	632,910
Dayton (★951,270)	182,044
East Liverpool (★44,400)	13,654
Elyria (★Lorain)	56,746
Euclid (★Cleveland)	54,875
Hamilton (★291,479) (★Cincinnati)	61,368
Kettering (★Dayton)	60,569
Lakewood (★Cleveland)	59,718
Lancaster (★Columbus)	34,507
Lima (★154,340)	45,549
Lorain (★271,126) (★Cleveland)	71,245
Mansfield (★126,137)	50,627
Marion (★53,900)	34,075
Middletown (★107,200) (★Cincinnati)	46,022
Newark (★Columbus)	44,389
Parma (★Cleveland)	87,876
Portsmouth (★64,300)	22,676
Sandusky (★79,800)	29,764
Springfield (★Dayton)	70,487
Steubenville (★142,523)	22,125
Toledo (★614,128)	332,943
Warren (★Youngstown)	50,793
Youngstown (★492,619)	95,732
Zanesville (★67,800)	26,778

UNITED STATES: OKLAHOMA

1990 C	3,145,585
Broken Arrow (★Tulsa)	58,043
Edmond (★Oklahoma City)	52,315
Enid (★56,735)	45,309
Lawton (★111,486)	80,561
Midwest City (★Oklahoma City)	52,267
Muskogee (★49,500)	37,708
Norman (★Oklahoma City)	80,071
Oklahoma City (★958,839)	444,719
Tulsa (★708,954)	367,302

UNITED STATES: OREGON

1990 C	2,842,321
Beaverton (★Portland)	53,310
Corvallis (★98,700)	44,757
Eugene (★282,912)	112,669
Gresham (★Portland)	68,235
Medford (★146,389)	46,951
Portland (★1,477,895)	437,319
Salem (★278,024)	107,786

UNITED STATES: PENNSYLVANIA

1990 C	11,881,643
Abington (★Philadelphia)	59,300
Allentown (★686,688)	105,090
Altoona (★130,542)	51,881
Bensalem (★Philadelphia)	56,788
Bethlehem (★Allentown)	71,428
Bristol (★Philadelphia)	57,129
Butler (★86,500)	15,714
Coatesville (★93,400) (★Philadelphia)	11,038
Erie (★275,572)	108,718
Hanover (★York)	14,399
Harrisburg (★587,986)	52,376
Haverford (★Philadelphia)	49,848
Hazleton (★Scranton)	24,730
Johnstown (★241,247)	28,134
Lancaster (★422,822)	55,551
Lebanon (★Harrisburg)	24,800
Lower Merion Township (★Philadelphia)	58,003
New Castle (★68,400)	28,334
Oil City (★42,000)	11,949
Penn Hills (★Pittsburgh)	51,430
Philadelphia (★5,899,345)	1,585,577
Pittsburgh (★2,242,798)	369,879
Pottstown (★88,300) (★Philadelphia)	21,831
Pottsville (★54,200)	16,603
Reading (★336,523)	78,380
Scranton (★734,175)	81,805
Sharon (★121,003)	17,493
State College (★123,786)	38,923
Uniontown (★53,200) (★Pittsburgh)	12,034
Upper Darby (★Philadelphia)	84,054
Washington (★66,000) (★Pittsburgh)	15,864
Wilkes-Barre (★Scranton)	47,523
Williamsport (★118,710)	31,933
York (★417,848)	42,192

UNITED STATES: RHODE ISLAND

1990 C	1,003,464
Cranston (★Providence)	76,060
East Providence (★Providence)	50,380
Newport (★64,500)	28,227
Pawtucket (★329,384) (★Providence)	72,644
Providence (★1,141,510)	160,728
Warwick (★Providence)	85,427

UNITED STATES: SOUTH CAROLINA

1990 C	3,486,703
Anderson (★145,196)	26,184
Charleston (★506,875)	80,414
Columbia (★453,331)	98,052
Florence (★114,344)	29,813
Greenville (★640,861)	58,282
North Charleston (★Charleston)	70,218
Rock Hill (★Charlotte, N.C.)	41,643
Spartanburg (★Greenville)	43,467
Sumter (★90,300)	41,943

UNITED STATES: SOUTH DAKOTA

1990 C	696,004
Pierre	12,906
Rapid City (★81,343)	54,523
Sioux Falls (★123,809)	100,814

UNITED STATES: TENNESSEE

1990 C	4,877,185
Bristol (★Johnson City)	23,421
Chattanooga (★433,210)	152,466
Clarksville (★169,439)	75,494
Jackson (★77,982)	48,949
Johnson City (★436,047)	49,381
Kingsport (★Johnson City)	36,365
Knoxville (★604,816)	165,121
Memphis (★981,747)	610,337
Murfreesboro (★Nashville)	44,922
Nashville (★985,026)	487,969

UNITED STATES: TEXAS

1990 C	16,986,510
Abilene (★119,655)	106,654
Amarillo (★187,547)	157,615
Arlington (★Fort Worth)	261,721
Austin (★781,572)	465,622
Baytown (★Houston)	63,850
Beaumont (★361,226)	114,323
Brownsville (★469,000)	98,962
Bryan (★121,862)	55,002
Carrollton (★Dallas)	82,169
College Station (★Bryan)	52,456
Corpus Christi (★349,894)	257,453
Dallas (★3,885,415)	1,006,877
Denton (★Dallas)	66,270
El Paso (★1,211,300)	515,342
Fort Worth (★1,332,053) (★Dallas)	447,619
Freeport (★88,600) (★Houston)	11,389
Galveston (★217,399) (★Houston)	59,070
Garland (★Dallas)	180,650
Grand Prairie (★Dallas)	99,616
Harlingen (★Brownsville)	48,735
Houston (★3,711,043)	1,630,553
Irving (★Dallas)	155,037
Killeen (★255,301)	63,535
Laredo (★356,000)	122,899
Longview (★162,431)	70,311
Lubbock (★222,636)	186,206
Lufkin (★56,000)	30,206
McAllen (★383,545)	84,021
Mesquite (★Dallas)	101,484
Midland (★106,611)	89,443
Odessa (★118,934)	89,699
Pasadena (★Houston)	119,363
Plano (★Dallas)	128,713
Port Arthur (★Beaumont)	58,724
Richardson (★Dallas)	74,840
San Angelo (★98,458)	84,474
San Antonio (★1,302,099)	935,933
Sherman (★95,021)	31,601
Temple (★Killeen)	46,109
Texarkana (★120,132)	31,656
Tyler (★151,309)	75,450
Victoria (★74,361)	55,076
Waco (★189,123)	103,590
Wichita Falls (★122,378)	96,259

UNITED STATES: UTAH

1990 C	1,722,850
Logan (★60,300)	32,762
Ogden (★Salt Lake City)	63,909
Orem (★Provo)	67,561
Provo (★263,590)	86,835
Salt Lake City (★1,072,227)	159,936
Sandy (★Salt Lake City)	75,058
West Valley City (★Salt Lake City)	86,976

UNITED STATES: VERMONT

1990 C	562,758
Burlington (★131,439)	39,127
Montpelier (★52,800)	8,247
Rutland (★53,000)	18,230

UNITED STATES: VIRGINIA

1990 C	6,187,358
Alexandria (★Washington, D.C.)	111,183
Annandale (★Washington, D.C.)	50,975
Arlington (★Washington, D.C.)	170,936
Charlottesville (★131,107)	40,341
Chesapeake (★Norfolk)	151,976
Danville (★108,711)	53,056
Hampton (★Norfolk)	133,793
Lynchburg (★142,199)	66,049
Martinsville (★67,100)	16,162
Newport News (★Norfolk)	170,045
Norfolk (★1,396,107)	261,229
Portsmouth (★Norfolk)	103,907
Richmond (★865,640)	203,056
Roanoke (★224,477)	96,397
Suffolk (★Norfolk)	52,141
Virginia Beach (★Norfolk)	393,069

UNITED STATES: WASHINGTON

1990 C	4,866,692
Bellevue (★Seattle)	86,874
Bellingham (★127,780)	52,179
Bremerton (★189,731)	38,142
Everett (★Seattle)	69,961
Lakes District (★Tacoma)	58,412
Longview (★67,100)	31,499
Olympia (★161,238)	33,840
Pasco (★Richland)	20,337
Seattle (★2,559,164)	516,259
Spokane (★361,364)	177,196
Tacoma (★586,203) (★Seattle)	176,664
Yakima (★188,823)	54,827

UNITED STATES: WEST VIRGINIA

1990 C	1,793,477
Beckley (★64,300)	18,296
Charleston (★250,454)	57,287
Clarksburg (★53,800)	18,059
Fairmont (★53,700)	20,210
Huntington (★312,529)	54,844
Morgantown (★71,500)	25,879
Parkersburg (★149,169)	33,862
Wheeling (★159,301)	34,882

UNITED STATES: WISCONSIN

1990 C	4,891,769
Appleton (★315,121)	65,695
Beloit (★Janesville)	35,573
Eau Claire (★137,543)	56,856
Fond du Lac (★52,400)	37,757
Green Bay (★194,594)	96,466
Janesville (★139,510)	52,133
Kenosha (★128,181) (★Chicago, Il.)	80,352
La Crosse (★97,904)	51,003
Madison (★367,085)	191,262
Manitowoc (★57,300)	32,520
Milwaukee (★1,607,183)	628,088
Oshkosh (★Appleton)	55,006
Racine (★175,034) (★Milwaukee)	84,298
Sheboygan (★103,877)	49,676
Waukesha (★Milwaukee)	56,958
Wausau (★115,400)	37,060
Wauwatosa (★Milwaukee)	49,366
West Allis (★Milwaukee)	63,221

UNITED STATES: WYOMING

1990 C	453,588
Casper (★61,226)	46,742
Cheyenne (★73,142)	50,008

URUGUAY

1985 C	2,955,241
Las Piedras (★Montevideo)	58,288
Melo	42,615
Mercedes	36,702
Minas	34,661
• MONTEVIDEO (★1,550,000)	1,251,647
Paysandú	76,191
Rivera	57,316
Salto	80,823

UZBEKISTAN

1991 E	20,708,200
Almalyk	116,400
Andižan	298,300
Angren	132,600
Bekabad	82,800
Buchara	249,600
Chodžejli	61,200
Čirčik (★Taškent)	158,400
Denau	49,300
Džizak	110,900
Fergana	226,500
Gulistan	56,900
Jangijul'	56,900
Kagan	49,800
Karši	168,000
Kattakurgan	59,600
Kokand	175,000
Margilan	124,900
Namangan	319,200
Navoi	111,600
Nukus	179,600
Šachrichan	47,600
Šachrisabz	53,200
Samarkand	370,500
• TAŠKENT (TASHKENT) (★2,325,000)	2,113,300
Termez	90,400
Urgenč	130,400

VANUATU

1989 C	142,944
• PORT VILA (★23,000)	18,905

VATICAN CITY / Città del Vaticano

1988 E	766

VENEZUELA

1990 C	18,105,265
Acarigua	116,551
Anaco	61,386
Araure	55,299
Barcelona	221,792
Barinas	153,630
Barquisimeto	625,450
Baruta (★Caracas)	182,941
Cabimas	165,755
Cagua	73,465
Calabozo	79,578
• CARACAS (★4,000,000)	1,822,465
Carora	70,715
Carúpano	92,333
Catia La Mar (★Caracas)	100,104
Chacao (★Caracas)	66,897
Ciudad Bolívar	225,340
Ciudad Guayana	453,047
Ciudad Ojeda (Lagunillas)	73,473
Coro	124,506
Cumaná	212,432
El Limón	90,030
El Tigre	93,229
Guacara	100,766
Guanare	84,904
Guarenas (★Caracas)	134,158
La Asunción	16,552
La Victoria	77,326
Los Dos Caminos (★Caracas)	59,141
Los Teques (★Caracas)	140,617
Maiquetía (★Caracas)	62,834
Maracaibo	1,249,670
Maracay	354,196
Mariara	69,404
Maturín	206,654
Mérida	170,902
Palo Negro	50,718
Petare (★Caracas)	338,417
Porlamar	62,732
Pozuelos (1981C)	80,342
Puerto Ayacucho	36,107
Puerto Cabello	128,825
Puerto la Cruz	115,731
Punto Fijo	88,681
San Carlos	50,708
San Cristóbal	220,675
San Felipe	65,509
San Fernando	72,716
San Juan de los Morros	67,791
Trujillo	33,241
Tucupita	41,117
Turmero	174,280
Valencia	903,621
Valera	97,012
Valle de la Pascua	67,100
Villa de Cura	51,096

VIETNAM / Viet Nam

1989 C	64,411,668
Bac Giang	50,879
Bac Lieu	83,483
Bien Hoa	273,879
Buon Me Thuot	97,044
Ca Mau	81,901
Cam Pha	105,336
Can Tho	208,078
Chau Doc	50,935
Da Lat	102,583
Da Nang	369,734
Hai Duong	53,370
Hai Phong (▲1,447,523)	351,919
HA NOI (★1,275,000)	905,939
Hoa Binh	69,323
Hon Gai	123,102
Hue	211,718
Long Xuyen	128,814
Minh Hai (1979C)	72,517
My Tho	104,724
Nam Dinh	165,629
Nha Trang	213,460
Phan Rang	71,111
Phan Thiet	114,236
Play Cu	76,991
Qui Nhon	159,852
Rach Gia	137,784
Sa Dec	50,733
Soc Trang	87,899
Soc Trang	87,899
Tan An	50,288
Thai Binh	57,640
Thai Nguyen	124,871
Thanh Hoa	84,951
• Thanh Pho Ho Chi Minh (Saigon) (★3,300,000)	2,796,229
Tra Vinh	47,785
Tuy Hoa	54,081
Uong Bi	49,595
Viet Tri	73,347
Vinh	110,793
Vinh Long	81,620
Vung Tau	123,528
Yen Bai	58,645

VIRGIN ISLANDS OF THE UNITED STATES

1990 C	101,809
• CHARLOTTE AMALIE (★32,000)	12,331

WALLIS AND FUTUNA / Wallis et Futuna

1983 E	12,408
• MATĀ'UTU	815
Oro (1976C)	624

WEST BANK

1992 E	1,653,000
• Al-Quds (Jerusalem) (★Yerushalayim, Isreal)	285,000
Bayt Lahm (Bethlehem) (1971E)	25,000
Nābulus (1971E)	64,000

WESTERN SAHARA

1982 E	142,000
• EL AAIÚN	93,875

WESTERN SAMOA / Samoa i Sisifo

1991 C	161,298
• APIA	34,126

YEMEN / Al-Yaman

1990 E	15,267,000
'Adan (★318,000) (1984E)	176,100
Al-Hudaydah (1986C)	155,110
Al-Mukallā (1984E)	58,000
• SAN'Ā' (1986C)	427,150
Ta'izz (1986C)	178,043

YUGOSLAVIA / Jugoslavija

1991 C	10,337,920
• BEOGRAD (★1,554,826)	1,136,786
Čačak	72,392
Kragujevac	146,607
Kraljevo	56,616
Kruševac	58,114
Leskovac	61,963
Niš	175,555
Novi Pazar	51,906
Novi Sad	178,896
Pančevo (★Beograd)	72,717
Podgorica	118,059
Priština (▲244,830) (1987E)	125,400
Šabac	54,829
Smederevo	64,257
Sombor	48,789
Subotica	100,219
Užice	53,666
Valjevo	58,324
Vranje	51,695
Zrenjanin	81,382

ZAMBIA

1990 C	7,818,447
Chililabombwe (Bancroft) (★76,848)	35,200
Chingola	167,954
Kabwe (Broken Hill)	166,519
Kalulushi	75,197
Kitwe (★338,207)	247,100
Livingstone	82,218
Luanshya (★146,275)	79,500
• LUSAKA	982,362
Mufulira (★152,944)	85,000
Ndola	376,311

ZIMBABWE

1983 E	7,740,000
Bulawayo	429,000
Chitungwiza (★Harare)	202,000
Gweru (1982C)	78,940
• HARARE (★955,000)	681,000
Mutare (1982C)	75,358

▲ Population of an entire municipality, commune, or district, including rural area.

• Largest city in country.
★ Population or designation of the metropolitan area, including suburbs.
C Census. E Official estimate.
U Unofficial estimate.

▲ Bevölkerung eines ganzen städtischen Verwaltungsgebietes, eines Kommunalbezirkes oder eines Distrikts, einschliesslich ländlicher Gebiete.
• Grösste Stadt des Landes.
★ Bevölkerung oder Bezeichnung der Stadtregion einschliess lich Vororte.
C Volkszählung. E Offizielle Schätzung.
U Inoffizielle Schätzung.

▲ Población de un municipio, comuna o distrito entero, incluyendo sus áreas rurales.

• Ciudad más grande de un país.
★ Población o designación de un área metropolitana, incluyendo los suburbios.
C Censo. E Estimado oficial.
U Estimado no oficial.

▲ Population d'une municipalité, d'une commune ou d'un district, zone rurale incluse.

• Ville la plus peuplée du pays.
★ Population de l'agglomération (ou nom de la zone métropolitaine englobante).
C Recensement. E Estimation officielle.
U Estimation non officielle.

▲ População de um município, comuna ou distrito, inclusive as respectivas áreas rurais.

• Maior cidade de um país.
★ População ou indicação de uma área metropolitana.
C Censo. E Estimativa oficial.
U Estimativa não oficial.

The index includes in a single alphabetical list some 170,000 names appearing on the maps. Each name is followed by a page reference to one or more maps and by the location of the feature on the map, in coordinates of latitude and longitude. If a page contains several maps, a lowercase letter identifies the particular map. The page reference for two-page maps is always to the left-hand page.

Most map features are indexed to the largest-scale map on which they appear. However, a feature usually is not indexed to a Metropolitan Area map if it is also shown on another map where it can be seen in a broader setting. Countries, mountain ranges, and other extensive features are generally indexed to the largest-scale map that shows them in their entirety.

The order in which index information is presented is shown in the English, German, Spanish, French, and Portuguese headings at the center of each two-page spread.

For example:

ENGLISH

Name	Page	Lat.°′	Long.°′

The features indexed are of three types: *point, areal,* and *linear*. For *point* features (for example, cities, mountain peaks, dams), latitude and longitude coordinates give the location of the point on the map. For *areal* features (countries, mountain ranges, etc.), the coordinates generally indicate the approximate center of the feature. For *linear* features (rivers, canals, aqueducts), the coordinates locate a terminating point—for example, the mouth of a river, or the point at which a feature reaches the map margin.

Name Forms Names in the index, as on the maps, are generally in the local language and insofar as possible are spelled according to official practice. Diacritical marks are included, except that those used to indicate tone, as in Vietnamese, are usually not shown. Most features that extend beyond the boundaries of one country have no single official name, and these are usually named in English. Many English, German, Spanish, French, and Portuguese names, which may not be shown on the maps, appear in the index as cross references. All cross references are indicated by the symbol →. A name that appears in a shortened version on the map due to space limitations is given in full in the index, with the portion that is omitted on the map enclosed in brackets, for example, Acapulco [de Juárez].

Transliteration For names in languages not written in the Roman alphabet, the locally official transliteration system has been used where one exists. Thus, names in Russia and Bulgaria have been transliterated according to the systems adopted by the academies of science of these countries. Similarly, the transliteration for mainland Chinese names follows the Pinyin system, which has been officially adopted in mainland China. For languages with no one locally accepted transliteration system, notably Arabic, transliteration in general follows closely a system adopted by the United States Board on Geographic Names.

Alphabetization Names are alphabetized in the order of the letters of the English alphabet. Spanish *ll* and *ch*, for example, are not treated as distinct letters. Furthermore, diacritical marks are disregarded in alphabetization—German or Scandinavian *ä* or *ö* are treated as *a* or *o*.

The names of physical features may appear inverted, since they are always alphabetized under the proper, not the generic, part of the name, thus: "Gibraltar, Strait of ɥ." Otherwise every entry, whether consisting of one word or more, is alphabetized as a single continuous entity. "Lakeland," for example, appears after "La Crosse" and before "La Salle." Names beginning with articles (Le Havre, Den Helder, Al-Qāhirah, As-Suways) are not inverted. Names beginning with "St." and "Sainte" are alphabetized as though spelled "Saint."

In the case of identical names, towns are listed first, then political divisions, then physical features. Entries that are completely identical (including symbols, discussed below) are distinguished by abbreviations of their official country names and are sequenced alphabetically by country name. The many duplicate names in Canada, the United Kingdom, and the United States are further distinguished by abbreviations of the names of their primary subdivisions. (See list of abbreviations on pages 319-320).

Abbreviation and Capitalization Abbreviation and styling have been standardized for all languages. A period is used after every abbreviation even when this may not be the local practice. The abbreviation "St." is used only for "Saint." "Sankt" and other forms of the term are spelled out.

All names are written with an initial capital letter except for a few Dutch names, such as 's-Gravenhage. Capitalization of noninitial words in a name generally follows local practice.

Symbols The symbols that appear in the index represent graphically the broad categories of the features named, for example, ᴧ for mountain (Everest, Mount ᴧ). An abbreviated key to the symbols, in the five atlas languages, appears at the foot of each pair of index pages. Superior numbers following some symbols in the index indicate finer distinctions, for example, ᴧ¹ for volcano (Fuji-san ᴧ¹). A complete list of the symbols and superior numbers is given on page I•1.

Das Register umfasst in alphabetischer Anordnung etwa 170 000 in den Karten erscheinende Namen. Nach jedem Namen folgt die Seitenangabe zu einer oder mehreren Karten und die Lageangabe des Objektes in der Karte mit geographischer Länge und Breite. Enthält eine Seite mehrere Karten, so wird die betreffende Karte durch einen Kleinbuchstaben gekennzeichnet. Die Seitenangabe für Doppelseiten bezieht sich immer auf die linke Seite.

Die Verweise für die meisten Objekte in den Karten beziehen sich auf die Karte mit dem grössten Massstab. Normalerweise werden jedoch Verweise auf Objekte in den Karten der Stadtregionen nicht gegeben, wenn sie auf einer anderen Karte in grösserem Zusammenhang dargestellt sind. Die Lageangaben für Länder, Gebirgszüge und andere ausgedehnte Objekte beziehen sich allgemein auf die Karte grössten Massstabes, die sie in ihrer ganzen Ausdehnung zeigt.

Die Anordnung, in welcher die Lageangabe erfolgt, geht aus den englischen, deutschen, spanischen, französischen und portugiesischen Überschriften in der Mitte jeder Doppelseite hervor.

Zum Beispiel:

DEUTSCH

Name	Seite	Breite°′	Länge°′ E = Ost

Die aufgeführten Objekte gliedern sich in drei Gruppen: *punkt-, flächen-* und *linienförmige* Objekte. Bei *punktförmigen* Objekten (z.B. Städte, Berge, Dämme) beziehen sich die Angaben nach Länge und Breite auf die Signatur in der Karte. Bei *flächenhaften* Objekten (Länder, Gebirgszüge usw.) verweisen die Koordinaten im allgemeinen auf das ungefähre Zentrum des Objektes. Bei *linienhaften* Objekten (Flüsse, Kanäle, Wasserleitungen) beziehen sich die Koordinaten auf einen bestimmten Punkt, z.B. die Mündung eines Flusses oder den Punkt, an dem das Objekt den Kartenrand schneidet.

Namengebung Wie in den Karten so sind auch im Register die Namen im allgemeinen in der örtlichen Namensform wiedergegeben und soweit als möglich in der amtlichen Schreibweise. Diakritische Zeichen wurden gesetzt; sie wurden nur dort weggelassen, wo sie, wie im Vietnamesischen, Tonhöhen kennzeichnen. Meist haben Objekte, die sich über die Grenzen eines Landes hinaus erstrecken, keinen einzelnen offiziellen Namen; normalerweise sind sie daher englisch beschriftet. Viele englische, deutsche, spanische, französische und portugiesische Namensformen, die nicht in den Karten enthalten sind, erscheinen im Register als Kreuzverweis. Alle Kreuzverweise werden durch das Symbol → gekennzeichnet. Namen, die aus Platzgründen in abgekürzter Form in der Karte erscheinen, sind im Register voll ausgeschrieben, wobei der auf der Karte weggelassene Teil in Klammern gesetzt ist, z.B. Acapulco [de Juárez].

Transkription Für die Transkription von Namen aus Sprachen, die nicht im lateinischen Alphabet geschrieben werden, wurde das offizielle Transkriptionssystem benutzt, sofern ein solches vorhanden ist. So wurden die Namen in Russland und in Bulgarien nach dem von den wissenschaftlichen Akademien dieser Länder angewandten System transkribiert. Entsprechend wurden die Namen auf dem chinesischen Festland nach dem Pinyin-System übertragen, das offiziell in der Volksrepublik China eingeführt wurde. Bei Sprachen, für die ein allgemein anerkanntes Transkriptionssystem nicht vorliegt, vor allem für Arabisch, erfolgte die Transkription in enger Anlehnung an das vom United States Board on Geographic Names angewandte System.

Alphabetische Ordnung Die alphabetische Ordnung der Namen entspricht der Reihenfolge der Buchstaben im englischen Alphabet. So werden z.B. das spanische *ll* und *ch* nicht als besondere Buchstaben behandelt. Ferner wurden diakritische Zeichen beim Alphabetisieren nicht berücksichtigt, das deutsche oder skandinavische *ä* oder *ö* als *a* oder *o* behandelt.

Physische Objekte können umgestellt erscheinen, da sie immer nach dem Eigennamen und nicht nach dem Gattungsbegriff eingeordnet wurden, z.B. "Gibraltar, Strait of ɥ." Ansonsten wurde jeder Eintrag, ob er aus einem Wort oder aus mehreren besteht, als eine einzige Einheit behandelt. So ist z.B. "Lakeland" nach "La Crosse," aber vor "La Salle" aufgeführt. Namen, die mit einem Artikel beginnen, wurden nicht umgestellt (Le Havre, Den Helder, Al-Qāhirah, As-Suways). Namen, die mit "St." und "Sainte" beginnen, sind der Schreibweise "Saint" nach eingeordnet.

Wo Namensgleichheit besteht, werden zunächst die Städte aufgeführt, dann politische Einheiten und schliesslich physische Objekte. Eintragungen, die vollkommen identisch sind (einschliesslich der weiter unten erläuterten Symbole), werden durch Hinzufügung der Abkürzung des offiziellen Ländernamens unterschieden und sind den Ländernamen nach alphabetisch geordnet. Die zahlreichen identischen Namen in Kanada, dem Vereinigten Königreich und den Vereinigten Staaten sind darüber hinaus noch durch Abkürzungen der obersten Verwaltungseinheit unterschieden. (Siehe Verzeichnis der Abkürzungen, Seite 319-320).

Abkürzungen und Grossschreibung Abkürzung und Schreibweise wurden für alle Sprachen vereinheitlicht. Nach jeder Abkürzung steht ein Punkt, auch wenn dies nicht der jeweiligen Gepflogenheit entspricht. Die Abkürzung "St." wird ausschliesslich für "Saint" gebraucht. "Sankt" und andere Formen dieses Begriffes werden ausgeschrieben.

Der erste Buchstabe eines Namens wird gross geschrieben, ausgenommen einige holländische Namen wie 's-Gravenhage. Die Grossschreibung der weiteren Worte eines zusammengesetzten Namens folgt im allgemeinen der landesüblichen Schreibweise.

Symbole Die im Register verwendeten Symbole veranschaulichen graphisch die zahlreichen Kategorien der benannten Objekte, z.B. ᴧ = Berg (Everest, Mount ᴧ). Eine kurzgefasste Erläuterung der Symbole erscheint in jeder der fünf Sprachen des Atlas am Fusse jeder Doppelseite des Registers. Hochgestellte Ziffern hinter Symbolen im Register bezeichnen feinere Unterscheidungen, z.B. ᴧ¹ = Vulkan (Fuji-san ᴧ¹). Eine vollständige Übersicht der Symbole und hochgestellten Ziffern findet sich auf Seite I•1.

El índice contiene en una sola lista alfabética, alrededor de 170 000 nombres que aparecen en los mapas. Después de cada nombre está indicada la página o las páginas de referencia, en los cuales se encuentran los mismos, y las coordinadas de la latitud y la longitud del lugar del rasgo. Si una página contiene various mapas, letras minúsculas identifican el mapa correspondiente. Para mapas que ocupan dos páginas, la página de referencia siempre es la de la izquierda.

La mayoría de los nombres que figuran en el índice, se efiere a los mapas en la escala más grande. Sin embargo, un nombre no se refiere en un mapa metropolitano si ya aparece en otro mapa, donde se muestra en un marco de mayor proporción. Los países, sierras y otros rasgos extensivos se refieren generalmente en el índice en los mapas de escalas mayores en que se muestran completos.

En orden en que la información del índice se presenta, aparece en un encabezamiento al centro de cada par de páginas, en inglés, alemán, español, francés y portugués.

Por ejemplo:

ESPAÑOL

Nombre	Página	Lat.°′	Long.°′ W = Oeste

Los rasgos anotados en el índice son de tres tipos: *el punto, el área y la extensión linear.* Para rasgos que indican *el punto* (como por ejemplo, las ciudades, picos de montañas, presas), las coordinadas de latitud y longitud indican la posición exacta del punto sobre el mapa. Respecto a *las áreas* (como países, sierras, etc.), las coordinadas indican usualmente el centro aproximado del rasgo particular. En cuanto a *los rasgos lineares* (ríos, canales, acueductos) las coordinadas indican los puntos terminales, por ejemplo, la boca de un río, o el punto en que un rasgo físico alcanza el margen del mapa.

Las Formas de los Nombres Los nombres que aparecen en el índice, así como también en los mapas, se dan en general en el idioma local, y en tanto que es posible siguen la ortografía oficialmente aceptada. Incluímos también marcas diacríticas, excepto las que se usan para indicar tono, como en la lengua vietnamita. A causa de que la mayoría de los rasgos que se extienden más allá de las fronteras de un país no tienen un solo nombre oficial, éstos se denominan usualmente en inglés. Muchos nombres, en inglés, alemán, español, francés y portugués, que pueden no figurar en el mapa, se dan como referencia de una página a otra en el índice. Todas las referencias que pasan a otras páginas se indican con el símbolo →. Un nombre que aparece en el mapa en forma abreviada, debido a la limitación de espacio, en el índice figura en su forma completa, poniendo entre paréntesis angulares la parte omitida en el mapa, por ejemplo Acapulco [de Juárez].

"Trasliteración" Para los nombres escritos en los idiomas que no usan el alfabeto latino, el sistema oficial de trasliteración ha sido utilizado donde localmente existe. Así, los nombres de Rusia y de Bulgaria se trasliteran conforme a los sistemas aceptados por las academias de las ciencias de sus respectivos países. De la misma manera, la trasliteración de los nombres en chino continental siguen el sistema Pinyin que ha sido oficialmente adoptado en este país. Para idiomas sin ningún sistema localmente aceptado de trasliteración, particularmente para el árabe, éstos se trasliteran usando por lo general un sistema adoptado por el United States Board on Geographic Names.

Alfabetización Los nombres se han ordenado de acuerdo con el alfabeto inglés. Las letras del alfabeto en español *ll* y *ch* por ejemplo, no se han considerado letras separadas. Además, los signos diacríticos no se toman en cuenta en la alfabetización — en alemán o escadinavo letras *ä* u *ö* se tratan como *a* u *o*.

Los nombres de los rasgos físicos algunas veces se invierten, ya que se ordenan alfabéticamente según la parte propia y no genérica del nombre. Así por ejemplo, en el caso del Estrecho de Gibraltar aparece: Gibraltar, Strait of ʉ. Por lo demás, cada renglón, sea una palabra o una frase, se alfabetiza como una unidad. Por ejemplo, "Lakeland" aparece después de "La Crosse" y antes de "La Salle." Los nombres que comienzan con artículos (Le Havre, Den Helder, Al-Qāhirah, As-Suways) no están invertidos. Nombres que empiezan con "St." y "Sainte" se alfabetizan como "Saint".

En los casos de nombres idénticos, las poblaciones aparecen primero, las divisiones políticas después y finalmente los rasgos físicos. En caso de ser completamente idénticos (incluyendo los símbolos, discutidos más abajo) se distinguen por medio de abreviaciones de los nombres oficiales de los países a que pertenecen y son puestos en orden alfabético, de acuerdo al nombre de cada país. Hay muchos nombres duplicados en Canadá, el Reino Unido y los Estados Unidos de América, y éstos se distinguen además, por sus subdivisiones primarias. (Vease abajo, la lista de abreviaciones en las páginas 319-320).

Abreviaciones y Mayúsculas Las abreviaciones y el uso de las mayúsculas se han hecho uniformes para todos los idiomas. Se usa un punto al final de la abreviación, aun cuando en algunos casos no sea ésta la práctica local. La abreviación "St." se usa sólo para "Saint." Las otras formas del mismo término, como "Sankt," se escriben completas.

La mayúscula se usa al comienzo de todos los nombres a excepción de algunos holandeses, como 's-Gravenhage. Las palabras que no son iniciales, se dan con mayúscula o minúscula, según la práctica local.

Símbolos Los símbolos que aparecen en el índice representan gráficamente las grandes categorías de los rasgos que se han ido nombrando, por ejemplo, ▲ para montaña (Everest, Mount ▲). Una clave abreviada para los símbolos aparece en los cinco idiomas del atlas al pie de cada par de páginas del índice. Los números que siguen más arriba del símbolo indican alguna diferencia más precisa, pro ejemplo, ▲¹ para un volcán (Fuji- san ▲¹). Una lista completa de símbolos y números superiores aparece en la página I•1.

L'index rassemble en une seule liste alphabétique, quelque 170 000 noms qui figurent sur les cartes. Chaque nom est suivi d'un renvoi à une ou plusieurs pages de cartes et de coordonnées géographiques qui permettent de localiser ce qu'il désigne. Si une page contient plusieurs cartes, une lettre minuscule permet d'identifier chaque carte. Pour les cartes en double page, la référence indiquée est toujours celle de la page de gauche.

En général, l'index renvoie aux cartes où l'information recherchée est reproduite à la plus grande échelle; cependant, les cartes de zones métropolitaines ne sont pas utilisées si le terme géographique figure sur une autre carte dans un contexte plus large. Pour les éléments de grande dimension comme les pays et les chaînes de montagnes, l'index renvoie généralement à la carte à grande échelle qui les représente en entier.

L'ordre des informations de l'index est rappelé en tête de chaque double page dans les cinq langues: anglais, allemand, espagnol, français et portugais.

Par exemple:

FRANÇAIS			
Nom	Page	Lat.°′	Long.°′ W = Ouest

Les termes de l'index désignent des réalités géographiques de type *ponctuel, spatial* ou *linéaire*. Leur position est déterminée par les coordonnées géographiques du lieu quand les données sont de type *ponctuel* (villes, sommets, barrages, etc.), quand elles sont de type *spatial* (pays, chaînes de montagnes, etc.) par les coordonnées du centre approximatif de la zone considérée, et, quand elles sont du type *linéaire* (aqueducs, canaux, etc.) par les coordonnées soit d'un point terminal comme l'embouchure d'un cours d'eau, soit du point où les limites de la carte les interrompent.

Forme des Toponymes Les noms de l'index comme ceux des cartes sont généralement reproduits dans la langue locale et, dans la mesure du possible, selon leur orthographe officielle. Les signes diacritiques sont conservés, à l'exclusion de ceux qui servent à indiquer le ton, comme en vietnamien. La plupart des données géographiques qui s'étendent au-delà des frontières d'un pays sont nommées souvent en anglais, car elles n'ont pas de nom officiel unique. Beaucoup de noms anglais, allemands, espagnols, français et portugais, qui ne se trouvent pas sur les cartes, sont cités dans l'index sous forme de renvois. Tous les renvois sont signalés par le symbole (→). Un nom écrit sur la carte sous forme abrégée, par manque de place, figure en entier dans l'index; la partie omise est entre crochets, par exemple: Acapulco [de Juárez].

Transcription des Noms Pour les noms qui viennent de langues n'utilisant pas l'alphabet romain, le système local et officiel de transcription a été utilisé là où il existait. Ainsi, les noms russes et bulgares ont été transcrits selon les systèmes adoptés par les académies des sciences de ces pays. De même, pour la transcription des noms de la Chine continentale, on a employé le système Pinyin, officiellement adopté en Chine continentale. Pour les langues qui n'ont pas de système officiel de transcription en alphabet romain, notamment l'arabe, la transcription suit généralement de près le système adopté par le United States Board on Geographic Names (Comité américain pour les noms géographiques).

Ordre Alphabétique Les noms sont classés dans l'ordre de l'alphabet anglais. Les *ll* et *ch* espagnols, par exemple, ne sont pas traités comme des lettres séparées. De plus, on ne tient pas compte des signes diacritiques: le *ä* et le *ö* allemand ou scandinave correspondent au *a* et *o* sans tréma.

Les noms des données physiques peuvent se trouver inversés car ils sont toujours classés suivant le nom propre. Exemple: "Gibraltar, Strait of ʉ." Par ailleurs, les noms composés d'un ou plusieurs mots sont considérés comme une seule entité. Exemple: "Lakeland" est inscrit après "La Crosse" et avant "La Salle." Les noms qui commencent par un article (Le Havre, Den Helder, Al-Qāhirah, As-Suways) ne sont pas inversés. Les noms qui commencent par "St." ou "Sainte" sont classés comme s'ils s'écrivaient "Saint."

Dans le cas de noms identiques, les villes sont inscrites d'abord, puis les divisions politiques, et ensuite les données physiques. Les noms qui sont tout à fait identiques (y compris les symboles qui s'y rapportent) se distinguent par leur pays d'origine, noté en abrégé dans l'ordre alphabétique. Les noms que l'on rencontre plusieurs fois, au Canada, au Royaume-Uni et aux Etats-Unis se distinguent grâce à l'abréviation de la première subdivision administrative de ce pays (voir la liste des abréviations de la page 319-320).

Abréviations et Majuscules L'usage des abréviations a été standardisé pour toutes les langues. Un point suit chaque abréviation, même quand ce n'est pas l'usage dans certaines langues. L'abréviation "St." sert uniquement pour le mot "Saint." "Sankt" et les autres formes du mot "Saint" sont écrites en entier.

Tous les noms commencent par une majuscule, sauf quelques noms des Pays-Bas comme 's-Gravenhage. Certains noms prennent une majuscule, même s'ils ne se trouvent pas au début du terme; on a adopté, en général, l'orthographe locale.

Symboles Les symboles utilisés dans l'index donnent une représentation graphique des réalités géographiques mentionnées. Par exemple, ▲ pour une montagne (Everest, Mount ▲). Une explication abrégée des symboles dans les cinq langues de l'Atlas se trouve au bas de chaque double page de l'index. Les indices qui accompagnent certains symboles permettent une distinction plus précise. Par exemple, ▲¹ pour volcan (Fujisan ▲¹). Une liste complète des symboles et indices est donnée à la page I•1.

O Índice contém, numa só lista alfabética, cerca de 170,000 nomes que figuram nos mapas. Segue-se a cada nome a referência a um ou mais mapas e a localização do acidente geográfico no mapa pelas respectivas coordenadas de latitude e longitude. A referência a mapas que ocupam duas páginas fica sempre na página da esquerda. A maior parte dos acidentes geográficos estão indexados no mapa em que aparecem em escala maior. No entanto, um acidente geográfico não é geralmente indexado num mapa de Área Metropolitana se também figura em outro mapa em que aparece em contexto mais amplo. Os países, cordilheiras e outros acidentes geográficos de maior extensão estão geralmente indexados no mapa em escala maior que os apresente em seu todo.

A ordem em que as informações são apresentadas no Índice figura no cabeçalho, a cada duas páginas, em inglês, alemão, espanhol, francês e PORTUGUÊS.

Por exemplo:

PORTUGUÊS			
Nome	Página	Lat.°′	Long.°′ W = Oeste

Os acidentes indexados são de três tipos: *Ponto, espacial* (área) e *linear* (extensão). Para acidentes que indicam *pontos* (como, por exemplo, cidades, picos de montanhas, represas), as coordenadas de latitude e longitude indicam a posição exata do ponto no mapa. No que se refere aos *acidentes espaciais* (como países, cordilheiras etc.), as coordenadas geralmente indicam o centro aproximado do acidente específico. Quanto aos *acidentes lineares* (rios, canais, aquedutos), as coordenadas localizam os pontos terminais, como, por exemplo, a foz de um rio, ou o ponto em que um acidente físico atinge a margem do mapa.

Formas dos nomes Os nomes que aparecem no Índice, assim como também nos mapas, são geralmente apresentados na língua local, e tanto quanto possível, seguem a ortografia oficial. Usam-se, também, os sinais diacríticos, exceto os que indicam tom, como na língua vietnamita. A maioria dos acidentes geográficos que se estendem além das fronteiras de um só país não possuem um nome oficial único; nesses casos, estão geralmente indicados em inglês. Muitos nomes em inglês, alemão, espanhol, português e francês podem não figurar nos mapas, mas aparecem no Índice como referências remissivas. Todas essas referências são indicadas pelo símbolo (→). Um nome que aparece no mapa em forma abreviada devido a limitações de espaço, figura no Índice em sua forma completa, com a parte omitida no mapa entre chaves (por exemplo, Acapulco [de Juárez]).

Transliteração Para os nomes escritos em línguas que não usam o alfabeto latino, foi utilizado o sistema oficial de transliteração, sempre que este existia. Assim, os nomes da Rússia e da Bulgária foram transliterados de acordo com os sistemas adotados pelas academias de ciências desses países. Do mesmo modo, a transliteração dos nomes da China continental seguem o sistema Pinyin, que foi oficialmente adotado nesse país. Para as línguas que não possuem um sistema de transliteração adotado oficialmente, em especial o árabe, a transliteração geralmente segue de perto o sistema adotado pelo Conselho de Nomes Geográficos dos Estados Unidos (United States Board on Geographic Names).

Alfabetação Os nomes foram ordenados de acordo com o alfabeto inglês. Por exemplo, o espanhol *ll* e *ch* não foram considerados como letras separadas. Além disso, os sinais diacríticos não foram considerados na alfabetação. Por exemplo, em alemão ou escandinavo as letras *ä* ou *ö* foram tratradas como *a* ou *o*.

Os nomes dos acidentes físicos podem aparecer, às vezes, invertidos, já que foram sempre alfabetados pela parte especifica e não genérica do nome, como, por exemplo, *Gibraltar, estreito de* ʉ. Por outro lado, cada entrada do Índice, quer constituída por uma só palavra ou mais de uma, foi alfabetada como uma unidade contínua. Por exemplo, "Lakeland" aparece depois de "La Grosse" e antes de "La Salle". Os nomes que começam por artigo (Le Havre, Den Helder, Al-Qāhirah, As-Suways) não são invertidos. Os nomes que começam por "St." e "Sainte" são alfabetados como se fossem soletrados "Saint".

Nos casos de nomes idênticos, as cidades estão relacionadas em primeiro lugar; depois as divisões políticas e em seguida os acidentes físicos. As entradas completamente idênticas (inclusive símbolos, mencionados mais abaixo), distinguem-se pelas abreviaturas dos nomes oficiais dos países a que pertencem e são arrolados na ordem alfabética do nome do país. Os muitos nomes repetidos no Canadá, no Reino Unido e nos Estados Unidos, são ainda diferenciados pelas abreviaturas dos nomes das respectivas subdivisões primárias (Ver a lista de abreviaturas, das páginas 319-320).

Abreviações e uso de maiúsculas As abreviaturas e o estilo foram normalizados em todas as línguas. Usa-se um ponto depois de cada abreviatura, mesmo que não seja essa a prática local. A abreviatura "St." só é usada para "Saint". As outras formas do termo, tal como "Sankt", são escritas por extenso.

Todos os nomes são escritos com a inicial maiúscula exceto em alguns nomes holandeses, como 's-Gravenhage. O uso de maiúsculas em palavras não iniciais de um nome segue geralmente a prática local.

Símbolos Os símbolos que aparecem no Índice representam graficamente as grandes categorias dos acidentes indicados, por exemplo, ▲ para montanha (Everest, Mount ▲). Uma chave abreviada dos símbolos nas cinco línguas do Atlas figura no pé de cada par de páginas do Índice. Os números altos que acompanham certos símbolos do Índice indicam diferenças mais precisas, como, por examplo, ▲¹ para vulcão (Fuji-san ▲¹). Uma lista completa de símbolos e números altos aparece à pág. I•1.

	LOCAL NAME	ENGLISH	DEUTSCH	ESPAÑOL	FRANÇAIS	PORTUGUÊS
Ab., Can.	Alberta	Alberta	Alberta	Alberta	Alberta	Alberta
Afg.	Afghānestān	Afghanistan	Afghanistan	Afganistán	Afghanistan	Afeganistão
Afr.	. . .	Africa	Afrika	Africa	Afrique	África
Ak., U.S.	Alaska	Alaska	Alaska	Alaska	Alaska	Alasca
Al., U.S.	Alabama	Alabama	Alabama	Alabama	Alabama	Alabama
Alg.	Algérie / Djazaïr	Algeria	Algerien	Argelia	Algérie	Argélia
Am. Sam.	American Samoa / Amerika Samoa	American Samoa	Amerikanisch-Samoa	Samoa Americana	Samoa américaines	Samoa Americana
And.	Andorra	Andorra	Andorra	Andorra	Andorre	Andorra
Ang.	Angola	Angola	Angola	Angola	Angola	Angola
Anguilla	Anguilla	Anguilla	Anguilla	Anguilla	Anguilla	Anguilla
Ant.	. . .	Antarctica	Antarktis	Antártida	Antarctique	Antártida
Antig.	Antigua and Barbuda	Antigua and Barbuda	Antigua und Barbuda	Antigua y Barbuda	Antigua-et-Barbuda	Antígua e Barbuda
Ar., U.S.	Arkansas	Arkansas	Arkansas	Arkansas	Arkansas	Arkansas
Arg.	Argentina	Argentina	Argentinien	Argentina	Argentine	Argentina
Ar. Su.	Al-ʿArabīyah as-Suʿūdīyah	Saudi Arabia	Saudi-Arabien	Arabia Saudita	Arabie saoudite	Arábia Saudita
Aruba	Aruba	Aruba	Aruba	Aruba	Aruba	Aruba
Asia	. . .	Asia	Asien	Asia	Asie	Ásia
Austl.	Australia	Australia	Australien	Australia	Australie	Austrália
Az., U.S.	Arizona	Arizona	Arizona	Arizona	Arizona	Arizona
Azer.	Azerbaijan	Azerbaijan	Aserbaidschan	Azerbaiján	Azerbaïdjan	Azerbaijão
Ba.	Bahamas	Bahamas	Bahamas	Bahamas	Bahamas	Bahamas
Bahr.	Al-Baḥrayn	Bahrain	Bahrain	Bahrein	Bahreïn	Bahrein
Barb.	Barbados	Barbados	Barbados	Barbados	Barbade	Barbados
B.C., Can.	British Columbia / Colombie-Britannique	British Columbia	Britisch Kolumbien	Columbia Británica	Colombie britannique	Colúmbia Britânica
Bdi.	Burundi	Burundi	Burundi	Burundi	Burundi	Burundi
Bel.	Belgique / België	Belgium	Belgien	Bélgica	Belgique	Bélgica
Belize	Belize	Belize	Belize	Belice	Bélize	Belize
Bela.	Belarus	Belarus	Belorussland	Bielorrusia	Biélorussie	Bielorrússia
Bénin	Bénin	Benin	Benin	Benin	Bénin	Benin
Ber.	Bermuda	Bermuda	Bermuda	Bermudas	Bermudes	Bermudas
B.I.O.T.	British Indian Ocean Territory	British Indian Ocean Territory	Britisch-Indien Ozean-Territorium	Territorio Británico del Océano Indico	Territoire britannique de l'océan Indien	Território Britânico do Oceano Indico
Blg.	Bâlgarija	Bulgaria	Bulgarien	Bulgaria	Bulgarie	Bulgária
Bngl.	Bangladesh	Bangladesh	Bangladesch	Bangladesh	Bangladesh	Bangladesh
Bol.	Bolivia	Bolivia	Bolivien	Bolivia	Bolivie	Bolívia
Bos.	Bosna i Hercegovina	Bosnia and Hercegovina	Bosnien und Herzegowina	Bosnia y Herzegovina	Bosnie et Herzégovine	Bósnia e Herzegovina
Bots.	Botswana	Botswana	Botswana	Botswana	Botswana	Botsuana
Bra.	Brasil	Brazil	Brasilien	Brasil	Brésil	Brasil
Bru.	Brunei	Brunei	Brunei	Brunei	Brunéi	Brunei
Br. Vir. Is.	British Virgin Islands	British Virgin Islands	Britische Jungferninseln	Islas Vírgenes Británicas	Îles Vierges britanniques	Virgens Britânicas, Ilhas
Burkina	Burkina Faso	Burkina Faso	Burkina Faso	Burkina Faso	Burkina Faso	Burkina Faso
Ca., U.S.	California	California	Kalifornien	California	Californie	Califórnia
Cam.	Cameroun / Cameroon	Cameroon	Kamerun	Camerún	Cameroun	Camarão
Can.	Canada	Canada	Kanada	Canadá	Canada	Canadá
Cay. Is.	Cayman Islands	Cayman Islands	Caiman-Inseln	Islas Caimán	Îles Caïmanes	Cayman, Ilhas
Centraf.	République centrafricaine	Central African Republic	Zentralafrikanische Republik	República Centroafricana	République centrafricaine	Centro-Africana, República
Česká Rep.	Česká Republika	Czech Republic	Tschechische Republik	República Checa	République Tcheque	República Tcheca
Chile	Chile	Chile	Chile	Chile	Chili	Chile
Christ. I.	Christmas Island	Christmas Island	Weihnachtsinsel	Isla Christmas	Île Christmas	Christmas, Ilha
C. Iv.	Côte d'Ivoire	Cote d'Ivoire	Côte d'Ivoire	Côte d'Ivoire	Côte d'Ivoire	Côte d'Ivoire
C.M.I.K.	Chosŏn-minjujuŭi-inmīn-konghwaguk	Korea, North	Nordkorea	Corea del Norte	Corée du Nord	Coréia do Norte
Co., U.S.	Colorado	Colorado	Colorado	Colorado	Colorado	Colorado
Cocos Is.	Cocos (Keeling) Islands	Cocos (Keeling) Islands	Cokos-Inseln	Islas Cocos (Keeling)	Îles Cocos (Keeling)	Cocos (Keeling), Ilhas
Col.	Colombia	Colombia	Kolumbien	Colombia	Colombie	Colômbia
Comores	Comores / Al-Qumur	Comoros	Komoren	Comoras	Comores	Comores
Congo	Congo	Congo	Kongo	Congo	Congo	Congo
Cook Is.	Cook Islands	Cook Islands	Cook-Inseln	Islas Cook	Îles Cook	Cook, Ilhas
C.R.	Costa Rica	Costa Rica	Costa Rica	Costa Rica	Costa Rica	Costa Rica
Ct., U.S.	Connecticut	Connecticut	Connecticut	Connecticut	Connecticut	Connecticut
Cuba	Cuba	Cuba	Kuba	Cuba	Cuba	Cuba
C.V.	Cabo Verde	Cape Verde	Kap Verde	Cabo Verde	Cap-Vert	Cabo Verde
Dan.	Danmark	Denmark	Dänemark	Dinamarca	Danemark	Dinamarca
D.C., U.S.	District of Columbia	District of Columbia	District of Columbia	District of Columbia	District of Columbia	Distrito de Columbia
De., U.S.	Delaware	Delaware	Delaware	Delaware	Delaware	Delaware
Dji.	Djibouti	Djibouti	Djibouti	Djibouti	Djibouti	Djibouti
Dom.	Dominica	Dominica	Dominica	Dominica	Dominique	Dominica
Dtsch.	Deutschland	Germany	Deutschland	Alemania	Allemagne	Alemanha
D.Y.	Druk-Yul	Bhutan	Bhutan	Bhután	Bhoutan	Butã
Ec.	Ecuador	Ecuador	Ecuador	Ecuador	Équateur	Equador
Eesti	Eesti	Estonia	Estland	Estonia	Estonie	Estónia
Ellás	Ellás	Greece	Griechenland	Grecia	Grèce	Grécia
El Sal.	El Salvador	El Salvador	El Salvador	El Salvador	El Salvador	El Salvador
Eng., U.K.	England	England	England	Inglaterra	Angleterre	Inglaterra
Erit.	Eritrea	Eritrea	Eritrea	Eritrea	Erythrée	Eritréia
Esp.	España	Spain	Spanien	España	Espagne	Espanha
Europe	. . .	Europe	Europa	Europa	Europe	Europa
Falk. Is.	Falkland Islands	Falkland Islands	Falkland-Inseln	Islas Malvinas	Îles Falkland	Falkland, Ilhas
Fiji	Fiji	Fiji	Fidschi	Fiji	Fidji	Fiji (Fidji)
Fl., U.S.	Florida	Florida	Florida	Florida	Floride	Flórida
Før.	Føroyar	Faeroe Islands	Färöer	Islas Feroe	Îles Féroé	Faeroe, Ilhas
Fr.	France	France	Frankreich	Francia	France	França
Ga., U.S.	Georgia	Georgia	Georgia	Georgia	Georgie	Geórgia
Gabon	Gabon	Gabon	Gabun	Gabón	Gabon	Gabão
Gam.	Gambia	Gambia	Gambia	Gambia	Gambie	Gâmbia
Gaza	. . .	Gaza Strip	Gazastreifen	Franja de Gaza	Bande de Gaza	Faixa de Gaza
Ghana	Ghana	Ghana	Ghana	Ghana	Ghana	Gana
Gib.	Gibraltar	Gibraltar	Gibraltar	Gibraltar	Gibraltar	Gibraltar
Golan	. . .	Golan Heights	Golan-Höhen	Alturas de Golán	Hauteurs de Golan	Colinas de Golan
Gren.	Grenada	Grenada	Grenada	Granada	Grenade	Grenada
Guad.	Guadeloupe	Guadeloupe	Guadeloupe	Guadalupe	Guadeloupe	Guadalupe
Guam	Guam	Guam	Guam	Guam	Guam	Guam
Guat.	Guatemala	Guatemala	Guatemala	Guatemala	Guatemala	Guatemala
Guernsey	Guernsey	Guernsey	Guernsey	Guernsey	Guernesey	Guernsey
Gui.-B.	Guiné-Bissau	Guinea-Bissau	Guinea-Bissau	Guinea-Bissau	Guinée-Bissau	Guiné-Bissau
Gui. Ecu.	Guinea Ecuatorial	Equatorial Guinea	Äquatorial-guinea	Guinea Ecuatorial	Guinée équatoriale	Guiné Equatorial
Guinée	Guinée	Guinea	Guinea	Guinea	Guinée	Guiné
Guy.	Guyana	Guyana	Guyana	Guyana	Guyane	Guiana

	LOCAL NAME	ENGLISH	DEUTSCH	ESPAÑOL	FRANÇAIS	PORTUGUÊS
Guy. fr.	Guyane française	French Guiana	Französisch-Guayana	Guayana Francesa	Guyane française	Guiana Francesa
Haï.	Haïti	Haiti	Haiti	Haití	Haïti	Haiti
Haya.	Hayastan	Armenia	Armenien	Armenia	Arménie	Arménia
Hi., U.S.	Hawaii	Hawaii	Hawaii	Hawaii	Hawaii	Havaí
Hond.	Honduras	Honduras	Honduras	Honduras	Honduras	Honduras
Hrv.	Hrvatska	Croatia	Kroatien	Croacia	Croatie	Croácia
Ia., U.S.	Iowa	Iowa	Iowa	Iowa	Iowa	Iowa
I.A.M.	Al-Imārāt al-ʿArabīyah al-Muttaḥidah	United Arab Emirates	Vereinigte Arabische Emirate	Emiratos Arabes Unidos	Émirats arabes unis	Emirados Árabes Unidos
Id., U.S.	Idaho	Idaho	Idaho	Idaho	Idaho	Idaho
Il., U.S.	Illinois	Illinois	Illinois	Illinois	Illinois	Illinois
In., U.S.	Indiana	Indiana	Indiana	Indiana	Indiana	Indiana
India	India / Bharat	India	Indien	India	Inde	Índia
Indon.	Indonesia	Indonesia	Indonesien	Indonesia	Indonésie	Indonésia
I. of Man	Isle of Man	Isle of Man	Insel Man	Isla de Man	Île de Man	Man, Ilha de
Īrān	Īrān	Iran	Iran	Irán	Iran	Irã
ʿĪrāq	Al-ʿĪrāq	Iraq	Irak	Iraq	Iraq	Iraque
Ire.	Ireland / Éire	Ireland	Irland	Irlanda	Irlande	Irlanda
Ísland	Ísland	Iceland	Island	Islandia	Islande	Islândia
It.	Italia	Italy	Italien	Italia	Italie	Itália
Ityo.	Ityopiya	Ethiopia	Äthiopien	Etiopía	Éthiopie	Etiópia
Jam.	Jamaica	Jamaica	Jamaika	Jamaica	Jamaïque	Jamaica
Jersey	Jersey	Jersey	Jersey	Jersey	Jersey	Jersey
Jugo.	Jugoslavija	Yugoslavia	Jugoslawien	Yugoslavia	Yougoslavie	Iugoslávia
Kal. Nun.	Kalaallit Nunaat / Grønland	Greenland	Grönland	Groenlandia	Groenland	Groenlândia
Kâm.	Kâmpŭchéa	Cambodia	Kambodscha	Camboya	Cambodge	Camboja
Kaz.	Kazachstan	Kazakhstan	Kasachstan	Kazajstán	Kazakhstan	Cazaquistão
Kenya	Kenya	Kenya	Kenia	Kenya	Kenya	Quênia
Kıbrıs	Kuzey Kıbrıs	Cyprus, North	Türkische Republik Nordzypern	República Turca de Chipre del Norte	République turque du Nord de Chypre	República Turca do Norte de Chipre
Kípros	Kípros / Kıbrıs	Cyprus	Zypern	Chipre	Chypre	Chipre
Kiribati	Kiribati	Kiribati	Kiribati	Kiribati	Kiribati	Kiribati
Ks., U.S.	Kansas	Kansas	Kansas	Kansas	Kansas	Kansas
Kuwayt	Al-Kuwayt	Kuwait	Kuwait	Kuwait	Koweït	Kuwait
Ky., U.S.	Kentucky	Kentucky	Kentucky	Kentucky	Kentucky	Kentucky
Kyrg.	Kyrgyzstan	Kyrgyzstan	Kirgisistan	Kirguizia	Kirghizistan	Quirguistão
La., U.S.	Louisiana	Louisiana	Louisiana	Luisiana	Louisiane	Louisiana
Lao	Lao	Laos	Laos	Laos	Laos	Lao
Lat.	Latvija	Latvia	Lettland	Letonia	Lettonie	Letónia
Leso.	Lesotho	Lesotho	Lesotho	Lesotho	Lesotho	Lesoto
Liber.	Liberia	Liberia	Liberia	Liberia	Libéria	Libéria
Lībiyā	Lībiyā	Libya	Libyen	Libia	Libye	Líbia
Liech.	Liechtenstein	Liechtenstein	Liechtenstein	Liechtenstein	Liechtenstein	Liechtenstein
Liet.	Lietuva	Lithuania	Litauen	Lituania	Lithuanie	Lituânia
Lubnān	Lubnān	Lebanon	Libanon	Líbano	Liban	Líbano
Lux.	Luxembourg	Luxembourg	Luxemburg	Luxemburgo	Luxembourg	Luxemburgo
Ma., U.S.	Massachusetts	Massachusetts	Massachusetts	Massachusetts	Massachusetts	Massachusetts
Macau	Macau	Macao	Macao	Macao	Macao	Macau
Madag.	Madagasikara / Madagascar	Madagascar	Madagaskar	Madagascar	Madagascar	Madagascar
Magreb	Al-Magreb	Morocco	Marokko	Marruecos	Maroc	Marrocos
Magy.	Magyarország	Hungary	Ungarn	Hungría	Hongrie	Hungria
Mak.	Makedonija	Macedonia	Makedonien	Macedonia	Macédoine	Macedonia
Malaŵi	Malaŵi	Malawi	Malawi	Malawi	Malawi	Malaui
Malay.	Malaysia	Malaysia	Malaysia	Malasia	Malaisie	Malásia
Mald.	Maldives	Maldives	Malediven	Maldivas	Maldives	Maldivas
Mali	Mali	Mali	Mali	Malí	Mali	Mali
Malta	Malta	Malta	Malta	Malta	Malte	Malta
Marsh. Is.	Marshall Islands	Marshall Islands	Marshall Islands	Islas Marshall	Îles Marshall	Marshall Islands
Mart.	Martinique	Martinique	Martinique	Martinica	Martinique	Martinica
Maur.	Mauritanie / Mūrītāniyā	Mauritania	Mauretanien	Mauritania	Mauritanie	Mauritânia
Maus.	Mauritius	Mauritius	Mauritius	Mauricio	Maurice	Maurício
Mayotte	Mayotte	Mayotte	Mayotte	Mayotte	Mayotte	Mayotte
Mb., Can.	Manitoba	Manitoba	Manitoba	Manitoba	Manitoba	Manitoba
Md., U.S.	Maryland	Maryland	Maryland	Maryland	Maryland	Maryland
Me., U.S.	Maine	Maine	Maine	Maine	Maine	Maine
Méx.	México	Mexico	Mexiko	México	Mexique	México
Mi., U.S.	Michigan	Michigan	Michigan	Michigan	Michigan	Michigan
Micron.	Federated States of Micronesia	Micronesia, Federated States of	Federated States of Micronesia	Estado Federal de Micronesia	États fédérés de Micronésie	Federated States of Micronesia
Mid. Is.	Midway Islands	Midway Islands	Midway-Inseln	Islas Midway	Îles Midway	Midway, Ilhas
Miṣr	Miṣr	Egypt	Ägypten	Egipto	Égypte	Egito
Mn., U.S.	Minnesota	Minnesota	Minnesota	Minnesota	Minnesota	Minnesota
Mo., U.S.	Missouri	Missouri	Missouri	Misuri	Missouri	Missouri
Moç.	Moçambique	Mozambique	Mosambik	Mozambique	Mozambique	Moçambique
Mol.	Moldova	Moldova	Moldawien	Moldavia	Moldavie	Moldávia
Monaco	Monaco	Monaco	Monaco	Mónaco	Monaco	Mônaco
Mong.	Mongol Ard Uls	Mongolia	Mongolei	Mongolia	Mongolie	Mongólia
Monts.	Montserrat	Montserrat	Montserrat	Montserrat	Montserrat	Montserrat
Ms., U.S.	Mississippi	Mississippi	Mississippi	Misisipi	Mississippi	Mississippi
Mt., U.S.	Montana	Montana	Montana	Montana	Montana	Montana
Mya.	Myanmar	Myanmar	Myanmar	Myanmar	Myanmar	Myanmar
N.A.	. . .	North America	Nordamerika	América del Norte	Amérique du Nord	América do Norte
Namibia	Namibia	Namibia	Namibia	Namibia	Namibie	Namíbia
Nauru	Nauru / Naoero	Nauru	Nauru	Nauru	Nauru	Nauru
N.B., Can.	New Brunswick / Nouveau-Brunswick	New Brunswick	Neubraunschweig	Nueva Brunswick	Nouveau-Brunswick	Nova Brunswick
N.C., U.S.	North Carolina	North Carolina	Nord Karolina	Carolina del Norte	Caroline du Nord	Carolina do Norte
N. Cal.	Nouvelle-Calédonie	New Caledonia	Neukaledonien	Nueva Caledonia	Nouvelle Calédonie	Nova Caledônia
N.D., U.S.	North Dakota	North Dakota	Nord Dakota	Dakota del Norte	Dakota du Nord	Dakota do Norte
Ne., U.S.	Nebraska	Nebraska	Nebraska	Nebraska	Nebraska	Nebraska
Ned.	Nederland	Netherlands	Niederlande	Países Bajos	Pays-Bas	Países Baixos
Ned. Ant.	Nederlandse Antillen	Netherlands Antilles	Niederländische Antillen	Antillas Neerlandesas	Antilles néerlandaises	Antilhas Holandesas
Nepāl	Nepāl	Nepal	Nepal	Nepal	Népal	Nepal
Nf., Can.	Newfoundland / Terre-Neuve	Newfoundland	Neufundland	Terranova	Terre-Neuve	Terra Nova
N.H., U.S.	New Hampshire	New Hampshire	New Hampshire	Nuevo Hampshire	New Hampshire	Nova Hampshire
Nic.	Nicaragua	Nicaragua	Nicaragua	Nicaragua	Nicaragua	Nicarágua
Nig.	Nigeria	Nigeria	Nigeria	Nigeria	Nigéria	Nigéria
Niger	Niger	Niger	Niger	Níger	Niger	Níger
Nihon	Nihon	Japan	Japan	Japón	Japon	Japão
N. Ire., U.K.	Northern Ireland	Northern Ireland	Nordirland	Irlanda del Norte	Irlande du Nord	Irlanda do Norte
Niue	Niue	Niue	Niue	Niue	Nioué	Niue
N.J., U.S.	New Jersey	New Jersey	New Jersey	Nueva Jersey	New Jersey	Nova Jersey

	LOCAL NAME	ENGLISH	DEUTSCH	ESPAÑOL	FRANÇAIS	PORTUGUÊS
N.M., U.S.	New Mexico	New Mexico	New Mexico	Nuevo México	Nouveau-Mexique	Nova México
N. Mar. Is.	Northern Mariana Islands	Northern Mariana Islands	Northern Mariana Islands	Islas Marianas	Îles Mariannes du Nord	Northern Mariana Islands
Nor.	Norge	Norway	Norwegen	Noruega	Norvège	Noruega
Norf. I.	Norfolk Island	Norfolk Island	Norfolk-Insel	Isla Norfolk	Île Norfolk	Norfolk, Ilha
N.S., Can.	Nova Scotia / Nouvelle-Écosse	Nova Scotia	Neu Schottland	Nueva Escocia	Nouvelle-Écosse	Nova Scotia
N.T., Can.	Northwest Territories / Territoires du Nord-Ouest	Northwest Territories	Nord-West Territorien	Territorios del Noroeste	Territoires du Nord-Ouest	Territórios do Noroeste
Nv., U.S.	Nevada	Nevada	Nevada	Nevada	Nevada	Nevada
N.Y., U.S.	New York	New York	New York	Nueva York	New York	Nova York
N.Z.	New Zealand	New Zealand	Neuseeland	Nueva Zelanda	Nouvelle-Zélande	Nova Zelândia
Oc.	...	Oceania	Ozeanien	Oceanía	Océanie	Oceania
Oh., U.S.	Ohio	Ohio	Ohio	Ohio	Ohio	Ohio
Ok., U.S.	Oklahoma	Oklahoma	Oklahoma	Oklahoma	Oklahoma	Oklahoma
On., Can.	Ontario	Ontario	Ontario	Ontario	Ontario	Ontário
Or., U.S.	Oregon	Oregon	Oregon	Oregón	Oregon	Oregon
Öst.	Österreich	Austria	Österreich	Austria	Autriche	Austria
Pa., U.S.	Pennsylvania	Pennsylvania	Pennsylvanien	Pensilvania	Pennsylvanie	Pennsylvania
Päk.	Päkistän	Pakistan	Pakistan	Pakistán	Pakistan	Paquistão
Palau	Palau / Belau	Palau	Palau	Palau	Palau (Belau)	Palau
Pan.	Panamá	Panama	Panama	Panamá	Panamá	Panamá
Pap. N. Gui.	Papua New Guinea	Papua New Guinea	Papua-Neuguinea	Papua Nueva Guinea	Papouasie-Nouvelle Guinée	Papua-Nova Guiné
Para.	Paraguay	Paraguay	Paraguay	Paraguay	Paraguay	Paraguai
P.E., Can.	Prince Edward Island / Île-du-Prince-Édouard	Prince Edward Island	Prinz Edward-Insel	Isla Príncipe Eduardo	Île-du-Prince Édouard	Príncipe Eduardo, Ilha do
Perú	Perú	Peru	Peru	Perú	Pérou	Peru
Pil.	Pilipinas / Philippines	Philippines	Philippinen	Filipinas	Philippines	Filipinas
Pit.	Pitcairn	Pitcairn	Pitcairn	Pitcairn	Pitcairn	Pitcairn
Pol.	Polska	Poland	Polen	Polonia	Pologne	Polônia
Poly. fr.	Polynésie française	French Polynesia	Französisch-Polynesien	Polinesia Francesa	Polynésie française	Polinésia Francesa
Port.	Portugal	Portugal	Portugal	Portugal	Portugal	Portugal
P.Q., Can.	Québec	Quebec	Quebec	Quebec	Québec	Québec
P.R.	Puerto Rico	Puerto Rico	Puerto Rico	Puerto Rico	Porto Rico	Porto Rico
P.S.N.Á.	Plazas de Soberanía en el Norte de África	Spanish North Africa	Spanisch-Nordafrika	Plazas de Soberanía en el Norte de África	Afrique du Nord espagnole	África do Norte Espanhola
Qatar	Qatar	Qatar	Katar	Qatar	Qatar	Qatar
R.D.C.	République démocratique du Congo	Democratic Republic of the Congo	Demokratische Republik Kongo	República Democrática del Congo	République démocratique du Congo	República Democrático do Congo
Rep. Dom.	República Dominicana	Dominican Republic	Dominikanische Republik	República Dominicana	République dominicaine	República Dominicana
Réu.	Réunion	Reunion	Réunion	Reunión	Réunion	Reunião
R.I., U.S.	Rhode Island	Rhode Island	Rhode Island	Rhode Island	Rhode Island	Rhode Island
Rom.	România	Romania	Rumänien	Rumanía	Roumanie	Romênia
Ross.	Rossija	Russia	Russland	Rusia	Russie	Rússia
Rw.	Rwanda	Rwanda	Ruanda	Rwanda	Rwanda	Ruanda
S.A.	...	South America	Südamerika	América del Sur	Amérique du Sud	América do Sul
S. Afr.	South Africa / Suid-Afrika	South Africa	Südafrika	Sudáfrica	Afrique du Sud	África do Sul
Sak.	Sakartvelo	Georgia	Georgien	Georgia	Géorgie	Geórgia
S.C., U.S.	South Carolina	South Carolina	Süd Karolina	Carolina del Sur	Caroline du Sud	Carolina do Sul
Schw.	Schweiz / Suisse / Svizzera	Switzerland	Schweiz	Suiza	Suisse	Suíça
Scot., U.K.	Scotland	Scotland	Schottland	Escocia	Écosse	Escócia
S.D., U.S.	South Dakota	South Dakota	Süd Dakota	Dakota del Sur	Dakota du Sud	Dakota do Sul
Sén.	Sénégal	Senegal	Senegal	Senegal	Sénégal	Senegal
Sey.	Seychelles	Seychelles	Seschellen	Seychelles	Seychelles	Seychelles
Shq.	Shqipëri	Albania	Albanien	Albania	Albanie	Albânia
Sing.	Singapore	Singapore	Singapur	Singapur	Singapour	Cingapura
Sk., Can.	Saskatchewan	Saskatchewan	Saskatchewan	Saskatchewan	Saskatchewan	Saskatchewan
S.L.	Sierra Leone	Sierra Leone	Sierra Leone	Sierra Leona	Sierra Leone	Serra Leoa
S. Lan.	Sri Lanka	Sri Lanka	Sri Lanka	Sri Lanka	Sri Lanka	Sri Lanka
Slvk.	Slovensko	Slovakia	Slowakei	Eslovaquia	Slovaquie	Eslováquia
Slvn.	Slovenija	Slovenia	Slowenien	Eslovenia	Slovénie	Eslovênia
S. Mar.	San Marino	San Marino	San Marino	San Marino	Saint-Marin	San Marino
Sol. Is.	Solomon Islands	Solomon Islands	Salomonen	Islas Salomón	Îles Salomon	Salomão, Ilhas
Som.	Somaliya	Somalia	Somalia	Somalia	Somalie	Somália
St. Hel.	St. Helena	St. Helena	Sankt Helena	Santa Elena	Sainte-Hélène	Santa Helena

	LOCAL NAME	ENGLISH	DEUTSCH	ESPAÑOL	FRANÇAIS	PORTUGUÊS
St. K./N.	St. Kitts and Nevis	St. Kitts and Nevis	Sankt Kitts und Nevis	San Kitts y Nevis	Saint-Kitts-et-Nevis	São Kitts e Nevis
St. Luc.	St. Lucia	St. Lucia	Sankt Lucia	Santa Lucía	Sainte-Lucie	Santa Lúcia
S. Tom./P.	São Tomé e Príncipe	Sao Tome and Principe	São Tomé und Principe	Santo Tomé y Príncipe	Sao Tomé-et-Principe	São Tomé e Príncipe
St. P./M.	Saint-Pierre-et-Miquelon	St. Pierre and Miquelon	Saint-Pierre und Miquelon	San Pedro y Miquelón	Saint-Pierre-et-Miquelon	São Pedro e Miquelon
St. Vin.	St. Vincent and the Grenadines	St. Vincent and the Grenadines	Sankt Vincent und die Grenadinen	San Vicente y las Granadinas	Saint-Vincent-et-Grenadines	São Vicente e Granadinas
Süd.	As-Sūdān	Sudan	Sudan	Sudán	Soudan	Sudão
Suomi	Suomi / Finland	Finland	Finnland	Finlandia	Finlande	Finlândia
Sur.	Suriname	Suriname	Suriname	Suriname	Suriname	Suriname
Sūrīy.	Sūrīyah	Syria	Syrien	Siria	Syrie	Síria
Sve.	Sverige	Sweden	Schweden	Suecia	Suéde	Suécia
Swaz.	Swaziland	Swaziland	Swasiland	Swazilandia	Swaziland	Suazilândia
T.a.a.f.	Terres australes et antarctiques françaises	French Southern and Antarctic Territories	Französische Süd- und Antarktis-Gebiete	Tierras Australes y Antárticas Francesas	Terres australes et antarctiques françaises	Terras Austrais e Antárticas Francesas
Taehan	Taehan-min'guk	Korea, South	Südkorea	Corea del Sur	Corée du Sud	Coréia do Sul
T'aiwan	T'aiwan	Taiwan	Taiwan	Taiwán	Taïwan	Taiwan (Formosa)
Taj.	Tajikistan	Tajikistan	Tadschikistan	Tadjikistán	Tadjikistan	Tajiquistão
Tan.	Tanzania	Tanzania	Tansania	Tanzanía	Tanzanie	Tanzânia
Tchad	Tchad	Chad	Tschad	Chad	Tchad	Tchad
T./C. Is.	Turks and Caicos Islands	Turks and Caicos Islands	Turks- und Caicos-Inseln	Islas Turcas y Caicos	Îles Turques et Caïques	Turcas e Caicos, Ilhas
Thai	Prathet Thai	Thailand	Thailand	Tailandia	Thaïlande	Tailândia
Tn., U.S.	Tennessee	Tennessee	Tennessee	Tennessee	Tennessee	Tennessee
Togo	Togo	Togo	Togo	Togo	Togo	Togo
Tok.	Tokelau	Tokelau	Tokelau	Tokelau	Tokélaou	Tokelau
Tonga	Tonga	Tonga	Tonga	Tonga	Tonga	Tonga
Trin.	Trinidad and Tobago	Trinidad and Tobago	Trinidad und Tobago	Trinidad y Tabago	Trinité-et-Tobago	Trinidad e Tobago
Tun.	Tunisie / Tunis	Tunisia	Tunesien	Túnez	Tunisie	Tunísia
Tür.	Türkiye	Turkey	Türkei	Turquía	Turquie	Turquia
Turk.	Turkmenistan	Turkmenistan	Turkmenistan	Turkmenia	Turkmenistan	Turquemenistão
Tuvalu	Tuvalu	Tuvalu	Tuvalu	Tuvalu	Tuvalu	Tuvalu
Tx., U.S.	Texas	Texas	Texas	Texas	Texas	Texas
Ug.	Uganda	Uganda	Uganda	Uganda	Ouganda	Uganda
U.K.	United Kingdom	United Kingdom	Vereinigtes Königreich	Reino Unido	Royaume-Uni	Reino Unido
Ukr.	Ukraina	Ukraine	Ukraine	Ucrania	Ukraine	Ucrânia
'Umān	'Umān	Oman	Oman	Omán	Oman	Omã
Ur.	Uruguay	Uruguay	Uruguay	Uruguay	Uruguay	Uruguai
Urd.	Al-Urdun	Jordan	Jordanien	Jordania	Jordanie	Jordânia
U.S.	United States	United States	Vereinigte Staaten	Estados Unidos	États-Unis	Estados Unidos
Ut., U.S.	Utah	Utah	Utah	Utah	Utah	Utah
Uzb.	Uzbekistan	Uzbekistan	Usbekistan	Uzbekistán	Ouzbekistan	Usbequistão
Va., U.S.	Virginia	Virginia	Virginia	Virginia	Virginie	Virgínia
Vanuatu	Vanuatu	Vanuatu	Vanuatu	Vanuatu	Vanuatu	Vanuatu
Vat.	Città del Vaticano	Vatican City	Vatikanstadt	Ciudad del Vaticano	Cité du Vatican	Vaticano
Ven.	Venezuela	Venezuela	Venezuela	Venezuela	Venezuela	Venezuela
Viet	Viet Nam	Viet Nam	Vietnam	Viet Nam	Viet Nam	Vietnam
Vir. Is., U.S.	Virgin Islands (U.S.)	Virgin Islands (U.S.)	Amerikanische Jungferninseln	Islas Vírgenes (americanas)	Îles Vierges (américaines)	Virgens Americanas, Ilhas
Vt.	Vermont	Vermont	Vermont	Vermont	Vermont	Vermont
Wa., U.S.	Washington	Washington	Washington	Washington	Washington	Washington
Wake I.	Wake Island	Wake Island	Wake Island	Isla Wake	Île Wake	Wake
Wales, U.K.	Wales	Wales	Wales	Gales	Galles	Gales
Wal./F.	Wallis et Futuna	Wallis and Futuna	Wallis und Futuna	Wallis y Futuna	Wallis et Futuna	Wallis e Futuna
W.B.	...	West Bank	Westufer	Ribera Oeste	Cisjordanie	Margem Oeste
Wi., U.S.	Wisconsin	Wisconsin	Wisconsin	Wisconsin	Wisconsin	Wisconsin
W. Sah.	...	Western Sahara	Westliche Sahara	Sahara Occidental	Sahara occidental	Saara Ocidental
W. Sam.	Western Samoa / Samoa i Sisifo	Western Samoa	Westsamoa	Samoa Occidental	Samoa-Occidental	Samoa Ocidental
W.V., U.S.	West Virginia	West Virginia	West Virginia	Virginia Occidental	Virginie Occidentale	Virgínia Ocidental
Wy., U.S.	Wyoming	Wyoming	Wyoming	Wyoming	Wyoming	Wyoming
Yaman	Al-Yaman	Yemen	Jemen	Yemen	Yémen	Iêmen
Yis.	Yisra'el / Isrā'īl	Israel	Israel	Israel	Israël	Israel
Yk., Can.	Yukon Territory	Yukon Territory	Yukon	Yukón	Yukon	Yukon
Zam.	Zambia	Zambia	Sambia	Zambia	Zambie	Zâmbia
Zhg.	Zhongguo	China	China	China	Chine	China
Zimb.	Zimbabwe	Zimbabwe	Simbabwe	Zimbabwe	Zimbabwe	Zimbabwe

Key to Index Symbols

The symbols below represent the categories into which the physical and cultural features are classified in the Index. Broad categories appear in **boldface** type. Symbols with superior numbers identify subcategories.

Schlüssel zu den Symbolen des Registers

Die folgenden Symbole veranschaulichen die Kategorien, nach denen physische und kulturgeographische Objekte im Register geordnet sind. Die Oberbegriffe sind in **Fettdruck** hervorgehoben. Symbole mit hochgestellten Nummern kennzeichnen Unterbegriffe.

Clave de los Símbolos del Índice

Los símbolos abajo representan las categorías dentro de las cuales están clasificados los rasgos físicos y culturales que están incluídos en el Índice. Las grandes categorías aparecen en **negrilla**. Los símbolos que tienen números en su parte superior identifican las subcategorías.

Signification des Symboles de l'Index

Les symboles ci-dessous représentent les catégories sous lesquelles les données physiques et culturelles sont classées dans l'index. Les symboles en caractèter **gras** correspondent aux catégories principales. Ceux suivis d'un indice désignent les subdivisions d'une même catégorie.

Chave dos Símbolos do Índice

Os símbolos abaixo representam as categorias em que estão classificados os acidentes físicos e culturais no Índice. As grandes categorias aparecem em **negrito**. Os símbolos acompanhados de números altos identificam as subcategorias.

ENGLISH	DEUTSCH	ESPAÑOL	FRANÇAIS	PORTUGUÊS
Mountain	**Berg**	**Montaña**	**Montagne**	**Montanha**
Volcano	Vulkan	Volcán	Volcan	Vulcão
Hill	Hügel	Colina	Colline	Colina
Mountains	**Gebirge**	**Montañas**	**Montagnes**	**Montanhas**
Plateau	Hochebene	Meseta	Plateau	Planalto
Hills	Hügel	Colinas	Collines	Colinas
Pass	**Paß**	**Paso**	**Col**	**Passo**
Valley, Canyon	**Tal, Cañon**	**Valle, Cañón**	**Vallée, Canyon**	**Vale, Canhão**
Plain	**Ebene**	**Llano**	**Plaine**	**Planície**
Basin	Becken	Cuenca	Bassin	Bacia
Delta	Delta	Delta	Delta	Delta
Cape	**Kap**	**Cabo**	**Cap**	**Cabo**
Peninsula	Halbinsel	Península	Péninsule	Península
Spit, Sand Bar	Landzunge, Sandbarre	Lengua de Tierra, Bajo	Flèche, Banc de sable	Ponta de Terra, Banco de Areia
Island	**Insel**	**Isla**	**Île**	**Ilha**
Atoll	Atoll	Atolón	Atcll	Atol
Rock	Fels	Roca	Rocher	Rochedo
Islands	**Inseln**	**Islas**	**Îles**	**Ilhas**
Rocks	Felsen	Rocas	Rochers	Rochedos
Other Topographic Features	**Andere Topographische Objekte**	**Otros Elementos Topográficos**	**Autres données topographiques**	**Outros Acidentes Topográficos**
Continent	Erdteil	Continente	Continent	Continente
Coast, Beach	Küste, Strand	Costa, Playa	Côte, Plage	Costa, Praia
Isthmus	Landenge	Istmo	Isthme	Istmo
Cliff	Kliff	Risco	Falaise	Falésia
Cave, Caves	Höhle, Höhlen	Cueva, Cuevas	Caverne, Cavernes	Caverna, Cavernas
Crater	Krater	Cráter	Cratère	Cratera
Depression	Senke	Depresión	Dépression	Depressão
Dunes	Dünen	Dunas	Dunes	Dunas
Lava Flow	Lavastrom	Corriente de Lava	Couiée de lave	Corrente de Lava
River	**Fluß**	**Río**	**Rivière, Fleuve**	**Rio**
River Channel	Flussarm	Brazo de Río	Bras de rivière	Canal de Rio
Canal	**Kanal**	**Canal**	**Canal**	**Canal**
Aqueduct	Aquädukt	Acueducto	Aqueduc	Aqueduto
Waterfall, Rapids	**Wasserfall, Stromschnellen**	**Cascada, Rápidos**	**Chute d'eau, Rapides**	**Quedas d'água, Rápidos**
Strait	**Meeresstraße**	**Estrecho**	**Détroit**	**Estreito**
Bay, Gulf	**Bucht, Golf**	**Bahía, Golfo**	**Baie, Golfe**	**Baía, Golfo**
Estuary	Trichtermündung	Estuario	Estuaire	Estuário
Fjord	Fjord	Fiordo	Fjord	Fiorde
Bight	Bucht	Bahía	Baie	Enseada
Lake, Lakes	**See, Seen**	**Lago, Lagos**	**Lac, Lacs**	**Lago, Lagos**
Reservoir	Stausee	Embalse	Réservoir, Retenue	Reservatório
Swamp	**Sumpf**	**Pantano**	**Marais**	**Pântano**
Ice Features, Glacier	**Eis- und Gletscherformen**	**Accidentes Glaciales, Glaciar**	**Formes glaciaires, Glacier**	**Acidentes Glaciares, Geleira**
Other Hydrographic Features	**Andere Hydrographische Objekte**	**Otros Elementos Hidrográficos**	**Autres données hydrographiques**	**Outros Acidentes Hidrográficos**
Ocean	Ozean	Océano	Océan	Oceano
Sea	Meer	Mar	Mer	Mar
Anchorage	Ankerplatz	Ancladero	Ancrage	Ancoradouro
Oasis, Well, Spring	Oase, Brunnen, Quelle	Oasis, Pozo, Manantial	Oasis, Puits, Source	Oásis, Poço, Fonte, Manancial

ENGLISH	DEUTSCH	ESPAÑOL	FRANÇAIS	PORTUGUÊS
Submarine Features	**Untermeerische Objekte**	**Accidentes Submarinos**	**Formes de relief sous-marin**	**Acidentes Submarinos**
Depression	Senke	Depresión	Dépression	Depressão
Reef, Shoal	Riff, Untiefe	Arrecife, Bajo	Récif, Haut-fond	Recife, Baixio
Mountain, Mountains	Berg, Gebirge	Montaña, Montañas	Montagne, Montagnes	Montanha, Montanhas
Slope, Shelf	Abhang, Schelf	Talud, Plataforma	Talus, Plateau continental	Talude, Plataforma
Political Unit	**Politische Einheit**	**Unidad Política**	**Entité politique**	**Unidade Política**
Independent Nation	Unabhängiger Staat	Nación Independiente	État indépendant	País Independente
Dependency	Abhängiges Gebiet	Dependencia	Dépendance	Dependência
State, Canton, Republik	Land, Kanton, Republik	Estado, Cantón, República	État, Canton, République	Estado, Cantão, República
Province, Region, Oblast	Provinz, Landschaft, Oblast	Provincia, Región, Oblast	Province, Région, Oblast	Província, Região, Oblast
Department, District, Prefecture	Département, Distrikt, Präfektur	Departamento, Distrito, Prefectura	Département, District, Préfecture	Departamento, Distrito, Prefeitura
County	Grafschaft	Condado	Comté	Condado
City, Municipality	Stadt, Stadtkreis	Ciudad, Municipalidad	Ville, Municipalité	Cidade, Municipalidade
Miscellaneous	Verschiedenes	Misceláneo	Divers	Diversos
Historical	Historisch	Histórico	Historique	Sítio Histórico
Cultural Institution	**Kulturelle Institution**	**Institución Cultural**	**Institution culturelle**	**Instituição Cultural**
Religious Institution	Religiöse Institution	Institución Religiosa	Institution religieuse	Instituição Religiosa
Educational Institution	Erziehungsinstitution	Institución Educacional	Établissement d'éducation	Estabelecimento de Ensino
Scientific, Industrial Facility	Wissenschaftliche, Industrielle Anlage	Institución Científica o Industrial	Établissement scientifique ou industriel	Estabelecimento Científico ou Industrial
Historical Site	**Historische Stätte**	**Sitio Histórico**	**Site historique**	**Sítio Histórico**
Recreational Site	**Erholungs- und Ferienort**	**Sitio de Recreo**	**Centre de loisirs**	**Área de Lazer**
Airport	**Flughafen**	**Aeropuerto**	**Aéroport**	**Aeroporto**
Military Installation	**Militäranlage**	**Instalación Militar**	**Installation militaire**	**Instalação Militar**
Miscellaneous	**Verschiedenes**	**Misceláneo**	**Divers**	**Diversos**
Region	Region	Región	Région	Região
Desert	Wüste	Desierto	Désert	Deserto
Forest, Moor	Wald, Moor	Bosque, Páramo	Forêt, Lande	Floresta, Pântano
Reserve, Reservation	Reservat	Reserva, Reservación	Réserve	Reserva
Transportation	Verkehr	Transporte	Transport	Transporte
Dam	Damm	Presa	Barrage	Represa
Mine, Quarry	Bergwerk, Steinbruch	Mina, Cantera	Mine, Carrière	Mina, Pedreira
Neighborhood	Nachbarschaft	Barrio	Quartier	Arredores, Vizinhança
Shopping Center	Einkaufszentrum	Mercado	Centre commercial	Shopping Center

---

A

			Abacou, Pointe	238	18.03 N	73.47 W	Abashiri	92a	44.01 N 144.17 E	Abbeyfeale	48	52.24 N	9.18 W
			Abadab, Jabal ▲	140	18.53 N	35.59 E	Abasolo, Méx.	196	27.12 N 101.24 W	Abbey Head	44	54.46 N	3.58 W
			Ābādān	128	30.20 N	48.16 E	Abasolo, Méx.	196	25.57 N 100.24 W	Abbeyleix	48	52.55 N	7.20 W
			Ābādeh	128	31.10 N	52.37 E	Abasolo, Méx.	204	22.39 N 115.21 W	Abbey Peak ▲	164	14.18 S 144.29 E
Aa ≃	50	51.01 N	2.06 E	Abadia dos Dourados	255	18.28 S	47.24 W	Abasolo, Méx.	232	25.18 N 104.40 W	Abbey Wood ·⁸	260	51.29 N	0.08 E
Aach	58	47.50 N	8.51 E	Abadiânia	255	16.06 S	48.48 W	Abasolo, Méx.	232	24.04 N 98.22 W	Abbiategrasso	62	45.24 N	8.54 E
Aachen	56	50.47 N	6.05 E	Abadla	148	31.01 N	2.44 W	Abasolo, Méx.	234	20.27 N 101.32 W	Abbot, Mount ▲	166	20.03 S 147.45 E
Aach-Linz	58	47.54 N	9.11 E	Abaeté	255	19.09 S	45.27 W	Abasolo del Valle	234	17.44 N 95.29 W	Abbots Bromley	42	52.48 N	1.52 W
Aadorf	58	47.30 N	8.54 E	Abaetetuba	250	1.42 S	48.54 W	Abasto	258	34.58 S 58.06 W	Abbotsbury	42	50.40 N	2.36 W
Aaiun				Abagaljtuj	88	49.35 N 117.49 E	Abastumani	84	41.46 N 42.50 E	Abbotsford, Austl.	274a	33.51 S 151.08 E
— El Aaiún	148	27.09 N	13.12 W	Abagnar Qi	102	43.58 N 116.04 E	Abate Aloria, Lago di			Abbotsford, B.C., Can.	224	49.03 N 122.17 W
Aalen	56	48.50 N 10.05 E	Abag Qi	102	43.53 N 114.33 E		68	41.01 N 15.45 E	Abbotsford, Wi., U.S.	190	44.56 N 90.18 W
A'alī an-Nīl □¹	140	9.30 N 31.00 E	Abai	252	26.01 S 55.57 W	Abatimbo el Gumas	144	14.30 N 35.13 E	Abbots Langley	42	51.43 N 0.25 W
Aalsmeer	52	52.16 N	4.45 E	Abaj, Kaz.	86	49.38 N 72.52 E	Abatskij	86	56.18 N 70.28 E	Abbott, Arg.	258	35.17 S 58.48 W
Aalst (Alost), Bel.	52	50.56 N	4.02 E	Abaj, Ross.	86	50.44 N 69.30 E	Abau	164	10.11 S 148.42 E	Abbott, Tx., U.S.	222	31.53 N 97.04 W
Aalst, Ned.	52	51.23 N	5.29 E	Abaj, Ross.	86	50.27 N 85.05 E	Abava ≃	76	57.06 N 21.54 E	Abbottābād	123	34.09 N 73.13 E
Aalten	52	51.56 N	6.35 E	Abaji	150	8.28 N 6.57 E	Abay			Abbott Butte ▲	202	42.57 N 122.33 W
Aalter	52	51.05 N	3.27 E	Abajo Mountains ⫝̸	200	37.50 N 109.25 W	— Blue Nile ≃	140	15.38 N 32.31 E	Abbottstown	208	39.53 N 76.59 W
Aalwynsfontein	158	30.27 S 18.38 E	Abajo Peak ▲	200	37.51 N 109.28 W	Abaya, Lake ⊜	144	6.20 N 37.55 E	Abchazskaja Respublika □³	84	43.10 N 41.00 E
Äänekoski	26	62.36 N 25.44 E	Abak	150	4.57 N 7.47 E	Abayuda	258	34.51 S 56.14 W	Abcoude	52	52.16 N 4.58 E
Aansluit	158	26.44 S 22.28 E	Abakaliki	150	6.21 N 8.06 E	Abaza	86	52.39 N 90.06 E	Abdallah		
Aar ≃	56	50.23 N	8.00 E	Abakan	86	53.43 N 91.26 E	Abba	152	5.20 N 15.11 E	'Abd al-'Azīz, Jabal ⫝̸	130	36.25 N 40.20 E
Aarau	58	47.23 N	8.03 E	Abakan ≃	86	53.43 N 91.30 E	Abbach	263	51.28 N 7.41 E			
Aarberg	58	47.03 N	7.16 E	Abakanskij chrebet ⫝̸	86	59.18 N 37.39 E	Abbadia San Salvatore	66	42.53 N 11.41 E	'Abd al-Hafiz, Qārat ▲²	142	28.53 N 30.08 E
Aarburg	58	47.19 N	7.54 E	Abakanskoje	86	52.20 N 88.50 E	'Abbāsābād ·⁸	267d	35.44 N 51.25 E	'Abd al-Kūrī I	118	12.12 N 52.13 E
Aardenburg	52	51.16 N	3.27 E	Abala, Congo	152	1.21 S 15.30 E	Abbasanta	71	40.08 N 8.49 E	'Abd Allāh □³	130	30.33 N 23.02 E
Aare ≃	58	47.37 N	8.13 E	Abala, Niger	150	14.56 N 3.26 E				'Abd Allāh, Khawr ⫝	128	29.50 N 48.20 E
Aareschlucht ⫝	58	46.44 N	8.12 E	Abalak, Niger	150	15.27 N 6.17 E	Abbeganj ≃	114	21.33 N 86.10 W	'Abd ash-Shāhīd	273c	29.51 N 31.13 E
Aargau □³	58	47.30 N	8.10 E	Abalak, Ross.	86	58.08 N 68.36 E	'Abd Allāh, Étang de l'	261	48.41 N 1.56 E	Ābdānān	128	32.58 N 47.26 E
Aarle-Rixtel	52	51.31 N	5.38 E	Abalemma, Vallée d'			Abbé, Lac (Lake Abe)			Ābdêra ⫝̸	38	40.59 N 24.58 E
Aaronsburg	210	40.54 N 77.27 W	𝖵	150	15.34 N 6.23 E	Abbasanta	244	11.06 N 41.50 E	Abdrachmanovo	54	54.46 N 52.30 E
Aarschot	56	50.59 N	4.50 E	Abalessa	148	22.54 N 4.50 E	Abbehausen	52	53.29 N 8.26 E	Abduazirja	144	6.20 N 33.36 E
Aarwangen	58	47.15 N	7.46 E	Aban	88	56.41 N 96.04 E	Abbekås	41	55.24 N 13.36 E	Abdul Hakīm	123	30.33 N 72.07 E
Aazanèn	34	33.13 N	3.10 W	Abancay	248	13.35 S 72.55 W	Abbenden	52	52.23 N 10.11 E	Abdulino	80	53.42 N 53.40 E
Aba, Nig.	150	5.06 N	7.21 E	Abanga ≃	152	0.20 S 10.30 E	Abbert ≃	48	53.25 N 8.53 W	Abdulovo	80	54.16 N 53.27 E
Aba, D.R.C.	154	3.52 N 30.14 E	Abano Terme	64	45.21 N 11.47 E	Abbess Roding	260	51.47 N 0.17 E	Abe ▲	94	34.56 N 138.24 E
Aba, Zhg.	102	33.06 N 101.59 E	Abaokoro	174t	1.29 N 173.02 E	Abbeville, Fr.	50	50.06 N 1.50 E	Abe, Lake (Lac Abbé)		
Abā al-Bawl, Qurayn			Abar Irir	144	4.43 N 46.10 E	Abbeville, La., U.S.	192	31.59 N 83.18 W	⊜	144	11.06 N 41.50 E
▲²	128	24.56 N 51.13 E	Abar Kūh	128	31.08 N 53.17 E	Abbeville, La., U.S.	194	29.58 N 92.08 W	Abéché	146	13.49 N 20.49 E
Abā al-Waqf	142	28.35 N 30.46 E	Abarra	144	5.23 N 39.58 E	Abbeville, S.C., U.S.	192	34.11 N 82.23 W	Abejar	60	41.48 N 2.47 W
Abā as-Su'ūd	144	17.29 N 44.08 E	Abarracamento	255	22.12 S 43.30 W	Abbeville, S.C., U.S.	192	34.10 N 82.20 W	Abejorral, Cerro ▲	238	13.39 N 86.10 W
Abacaxis ≃	242	3.54 S 58.47 W	Abašа	84	42.12 N 42.13 E	Abbey ≃	184	50.43 N 108.45 W	Abejorral	246	5.47 N 75.26 W
Abaco I	238	26.28 N 77.05 W	Abascay, Arroyo ≃	258	35.17 S 58.07 W	Abbeydorney	48	52.19 N 9.41 W	Abekr	140	12.43 N 28.55 E

Abelek	140	7.23 N 28.46 E	Aberdeen Lake ⊜¹	194	33.55 N 88.30 W			
Abel Tasman National Park ♦	172	40.55 S 173.00 E	Aberdeen Proving Ground ■	208	39.25 N 76.10 W			
Abelti	144	8.10 N 37.34 E	Aberdour	46	56.03 N 3.19 W			
Aberama I¹	14	0.21 N 173.51 E	Aberdulais	42	51.41 N 3.48 W			
Abenberg	58	49.14 N 10.57 E	Aberdyfi	42	52.33 N 4.02 W			
Abengourou	150	6.44 N 3.29 W	Aberfeldy	46	56.37 N 3.54 W			
Abeno ·⁸	270	34.38 N 135.32 E	Aberfoyle	46	56.11 N 4.23 W			
Åbenjår	34	35.43 N 4.21 W	Abergavenny	42	51.50 N 3.00 W			
Åbenrå	41	55.02 N 9.26 E	Abergele	44	53.17 N 3.34 W			
Åbenrå Fjord c	41	55.03 N 9.34 E	Abergwynfi	42	51.40 N 3.35 W			
Abens ≃	60	48.51 N 11.46 E	Abergynolwyn	42	52.40 N 3.58 W			
Abensberg	58	48.49 N 11.51 E	Aberjona ≃	283	42.27 N 71.08 W			
Abeokuta	150	7.10 N 3.26 E	Abermain	170	32.49 S 151.25 E			
Aber	154	2.12 N 32.21 E	Abernathy	196	33.50 N 101.51 W			
Aberaeron	42	52.15 N 4.15 W	Abernethy, Sk., Can.	184	50.45 N 103.25 W			
Aberaman	42	51.42 N 3.25 W	Abernethy, Scot., U.K.	46	56.20 N 3.19 W			
Aberavon			Aberporth	42	52.09 N 4.33 W			
— Port Talbot	42	51.36 N 3.47 W	Abersoch	42	52.50 N 4.29 W			
Aberchirder	46	57.33 N 2.38 W	Abersychan	42	51.44 N 3.04 W			
Abercorn, P.Q., Can.	206	45.02 N 72.40 W	Abert, Lake ⊜	202	42.38 N 120.13 W			
Abercorn			Abertillery	42	51.45 N 3.09 W			
— Mbala, Zam.	154	8.50 S 31.22 E	Aberuthven	46	56.19 N 3.39 W			
Abercrombie ≃	170	34.09 S 149.40 E	Aberystwyth	42	52.25 N 4.05 W			
Aberdare	42	51.43 N 3.27 W	Abessinien, Hochland von					
Aberdare National Park ♦	154	0.30 S 36.45 E	— Ethiopian Plateau ▲¹	144	9.00 N 38.00 E			
Aberdare Range ⫝̸	154	0.25 S 36.38 E	Abetone	66	44.08 N 10.40 E			
Aberdaron	42	52.49 N 4.43 W	Abez'	24	66.32 N 61.42 E			
Åbdânân	128	32.58 N 47.26 E	Abhā	144	18.13 N 42.30 E			
Aberdeen (Xianggangzi), Zhg.	271d	22.15 N 114.09 E	Abhar	126	36.09 N 49.13 E			
Aberdeen, S. Afr.	158	32.29 S 24.05 E	Abharrud ≃	126	37.05 N 50.00 E			
Aberdeen, Scot., U.K.	46	57.10 N 2.04 W	Abhayāpuri	124	26.20 N 90.40 E			
Aberdeen, Id., U.S.	202	42.56 N 112.50 W	Abhaynagar	126	23.01 N 89.28 E			
Aberdeen, Md., U.S.	208	39.30 N 76.09 W	Abiaca Creek ≃	194	33.20 N 90.15 W			
Aberdeen, Ms., U.S.	194	33.49 N 88.33 W	Abid, Oued el ≃	148	32.18 N 7.03 W			
Aberdeen, N.C., U.S.	192	35.07 N 79.25 W	'Ābidīn	140	13.33 N 29.38 E			
Aberdeen, S.D., U.S.	218	45.27 N 98.29 W	'Abīdīyah	140	18.14 N 33.57 E			
Aberdeen, Wa., U.S.	224	46.58 N 123.48 W	Abidjan	150	5.19 N 4.02 W			
Aberdeen Lake ⊜	176	64.27 N 99.00 W	'Abid Mār, Tall ▲	132	36.46 N 42.30 E			
			Abiego	60	42.06 N 0.06 W			
			Abiekwasputs ⫝̸	158	27.40 S 20.10 E			
			Abiemnhom	140	9.20 N 28.35 E			
			Abiko	94	35.52 N 140.03 E			

≃ River	Fluß	Río	Rivière	Rio
⫶ Canal	Kanal	Canal	Canal	Canal
∪ Waterfall, Rapids	Wasserfall, Stromschnellen	Cascada, Rápidos	Chute d'eau, Rapides	Cascata, Rápidos
⫝ Strait	Meeresstraße	Estrecho	Détroit	Estreito
c Bay, Gulf	Bucht, Golf	Bahía, Golfo	Baie, Golfe	Baía, Golfo
⊜ Lake, Lakes	See, Seen	Lago, Lagos	Lac, Lacs	Lago, Lagos
☶ Swamp	Sumpf	Pantano	Marais	Pântano
⊠ Ice Features, Glacier	Eis- und Gletscherformen	Accidentes Glaciales	Formes glaciaires	Acidentes glaciares
�774 Other Hydrographic Features	Andere Hydrographische Objekte	Otros Elementos Hidrográficos	Autres données hydrographiques	Outros acidentes hidrográficos
✛ Submarine Features	Untermeerische Objekte	Accidentes Submarinos	Formes de relief sous-marin	Acidentes submarinos
□ Political Unit	Politische Einheit	Unidad Política	Entité politique	Unidade política
ṿ Cultural Institution	Kulturelle Institution	Institución Cultural	Institution culturelle	Instituição cultural
⊥ Historical Site	Historische Stätte	Sitio Histórico	Site historique	Sítio histórico
✦ Recreational Site	Erholungs- und Ferienort	Sitio de Recreo	Centre de loisirs	Área de Lazer
⊠ Airport	Flughafen	Aeropuerto	Aéroport	Aeroporto
■ Military Installation	Militäranlage	Instalación Militar	Installation militaire	Instalação militar
·⁸ Miscellaneous	Verschiedenes	Misceláneo	Divers	Diversos

	ENGLISH			DEUTSCH		Länge°′
	Name	Page	Lat.°′	Long.°′	Name	Seite	Breite°′	E = Ost

▲ Mountain	Berg	Montaña	Montagne	Montanha
⋊ Mountains	Gebirge	Montañas	Montagnes	Montanhas
⋊ Pass	Paß	Paso	Col	Passo
V Valley, Canyon	Tal, Cañon	Valle, Cañón	Vale, Cañon	Vale, Canhão
☰ Plain	Ebene	Llano	Plaine	Planície
⊁ Cape	Kap	Cabo	Cap	Cabo
I Island	Insel	Isla	Île	Ilha
II Islands	Inseln	Islas	Îles	Ilhas
⊥ Other Topographic Features	Andere Topographische Objekte	Otros Elementos Topográficos	Autres données topographiques	Outros acidentes topográficos

ESPAÑOL — Nombre, Página, Lat.°′, Long.°′ W = Oeste
FRANÇAIS — Nom, Page, Lat.°′, Long.°′ W = Ouest
PORTUGUÊS — Nome, Página, Lat.°′, Long.°′ W = Oeste

Nombre	Página	Lat.°′	Long.°′ W = Oeste
Afyonkarahisar → Afyon	130	38.45 N	30.33 E
Afzalgarh	124	29.24 N	78.41 E
Aga, Nor.	26	60.18 N	6.36 E
Aga, Ross.	88	51.12 N	115.10 E
Aga ≃	88	51.30 N	115.50 E
Agačag	85	44.03 N	71.58 E
Ağaçören	130	38.52 N	33.56 E
Agadez	150	16.58 N	7.59 E
Agadez □[5]	146	19.45 N	12.00 E
Agadez, Ighazer oua-n- V	150	17.28 N	6.26 E
Agadir	148	30.26 N	9.36 W
Agadir □[4]	148	30.40 N	8.55 W
Agâdîr, Râs ›	148	20.34 N	16.32 W
Agadyr'	86	48.17 N	72.53 E
Agafonovka	80	50.36 N	47.26 E
Agāhpur	272a	28.34 N	77.22 E
Agaie	150	9.03 N	6.18 E
Ägäisches Meer → Aegean Sea ⍑[2]	38	38.30 N	25.00 E
Agalak	140	11.01 N	32.42 E
Agalega Islands II	138	10.24 S	56.37 E
Agal Terara ∧	144	6.57 N	40.08 E
Agan ≃	72	61.23 N	74.35 E
Agana	174p	13.28 N	144.45 E
Agana Heights	174p	13.28 N	144.45 E
Agano ≃	92	37.57 N	139.08 E
Agapa	74	71.27 N	89.15 E
Aga Point ›	174p	13.15 N	144.43 E
Agapovka	86	53.18 N	59.28 E
Agar	120	23.42 N	76.01 E
Agara	84	42.03 N	43.49 E
Agâraktem ⍑[4]	148	23.11 N	6.20 W
Ågård	41	55.35 N	9.26 E
Agaro	144	7.50 N	36.40 E
Agartala	120	23.49 N	91.16 E
Agartu	80	49.49 N	47.06 E
Agaru	140	10.59 N	34.44 E
Agaruut	102	43.10 N	109.26 E
Agasan	272c	19.11 N	73.04 E
Agassiz	224	49.14 N	121.46 W
Agassiz, Cape ›	9	68.29 S	62.56 W
Agassiz Pool ⊜	198	48.20 N	95.58 W
Agat	174p	13.24 N	144.39 E
Agat Bay c	174p	13.24 N	144.39 E
Agate	198	39.27 N	103.56 W
Agate Beach	202	44.40 N	124.03 W
Agate Fossil Beds National Monument ♠	198	42.25 N	103.43 W
Agathonísion I	38	37.28 N	27.00 E
Agats	164	5.33 S	138.08 E
Agatsuma	94	36.34 N	138.50 E
Agatsuma ≃	94	36.30 N	139.01 E
Agatti Island I	122	10.50 N	72.12 E
Agattu Island I	181a	52.25 N	173.35 E
Agattu Strait Ʉ	181a	52.35 N	173.25 E
Agawa	96	33.34 N	133.10 E
Agawa ≃	190	47.21 N	84.38 W
Agawa Bay c	190	47.20 N	84.42 W
Agawa Canyon V	190	47.27 N	84.29 W
Agawam, Ma., U.S.	207	42.04 N	72.36 W
Agawam, Mt., U.S.	182	48.00 N	112.10 W
Agay	62	43.26 N	6.51 E
Agazzano	62	44.57 N	9.31 E
Agbaja	150	7.58 N	6.38 E
Agbede	273a	6.40 N	3.29 E
Agbélouvé	150	6.40 N	1.10 E
Agboju	273a	6.28 N	3.17 E
Agboville	150	5.56 N	4.13 W
Agboyi Creek ≃	273a	6.34 N	3.25 E
Ağcabädi	84	40.03 N	47.28 E
Agcawayan	116	13.46 N	120.16 E
Ağdam	84	39.59 N	46.57 E
Ağdärä	84	40.12 N	46.48 E
Ağdaş	84	40.38 N	47.28 E
Agde	32	43.19 N	3.28 E
Agde, Cap d' ›	32	43.16 N	3.30 E
Agege	273a	6.37 N	3.20 E
Agejevo	82	54.10 N	36.29 E
Agematsu	94	35.47 N	137.42 E
Agen	32	44.12 N	0.37 E
Agency	190	40.59 N	92.18 W
Agency Lake ⊜	202	42.32 N	121.58 W
Ageo	94	35.58 N	139.36 E
Agepsta, gora ∧	84	43.32 N	40.30 E
Ager ≃	60	48.05 N	13.51 E
Agerbæk	41	55.36 N	8.48 E
Agerskov	41	55.07 N	9.08 E
Agersø I	41	55.12 N	11.12 E
Agery	168b	34.10 S	137.44 E
Ágfalva	61	47.41 N	16.31 E
Aggeneis	158	29.03 S	18.51 E
Agger ≃	56	50.48 N	7.11 E
Aggherar	144	4.03 N	42.40 E
Aggius	71	40.56 N	9.04 E
Aggstein ⊥	61	48.18 N	15.25 E
Aggteleki Nemzeti Park ♠	30	48.30 N	20.32 E
Āghā Jārī	128	30.42 N	49.50 E
Aghleam	48	54.08 N	10.07 W
Aghzoumal, Sabkhat ⊜	148	24.21 N	12.52 W
Agia	124	26.05 N	90.32 E
Agidingbi	273a	6.38 N	3.21 E
Agimont	56	50.10 N	4.48 E
Ağın	130	38.57 N	38.43 E
Agincourt ◆[8]	275b	43.48 N	79.17 W
Aginskoje, Ross.	86	55.15 N	94.55 E
Aginskoje, Ross.	88	51.06 N	114.32 E
Agira	70	37.39 N	14.31 E
Aglasterhausen	56	49.21 N	8.59 E
Ağlasun	130	37.40 N	30.32 E
Agliana	66	43.54 N	11.00 E
Agliano	62	44.47 N	8.15 E
Aglientu	71	41.05 N	9.07 E
Agly ≃	32	42.47 N	3.02 E
Agna	64	45.10 N	11.58 E
Agnadello	62	45.26 N	9.33 E
Agnes, Mount ∧	162	26.51 S	128.59 E
Agnes Lake ⊜	190	48.13 N	91.21 W
Agnew	162	28.01 S	120.30 E
Agnew Lake ⊜[1]	190	46.22 N	81.45 W
Agnews Hill ∧[2]	48	54.51 N	5.56 W
Agnibilékrou	150	7.08 N	3.12 W
Agnije-Afanasjevskij	89	51.57 N	138.45 E
Agnita	38	45.59 N	24.38 E
Agno, Pil.	116	16.07 N	119.48 E
Agno, Schw.	58	46.00 N	8.54 E
Agno ≃, It.	64	45.31 N	11.22 E
Agno ≃, Pil.	116	16.02 N	120.08 E
Agnone	66	41.48 N	14.22 E
Agnone Bagni ◆[8]	70	37.18 N	15.06 E
Ago	92	34.20 N	136.51 E
Agogna ≃	62	45.04 N	8.54 E
Agogo, Ghana	150	6.47 N	1.04 W
Agogo, Süd.	140	7.49 N	28.52 E
Agoo	116	16.20 N	120.22 E
Agordat → Akordat	144	15.33 N	37.53 E
Agordo	64	46.17 N	12.02 E
Agostinho Pôrto	287a	22.47 S	43.23 W
Agostitlán	234	19.33 N	100.41 W
Agou, Mont ∧	150	6.52 N	0.46 E
Agouna	150	7.34 N	1.42 E
Agoura Hills	228	34.08 N	118.44 W
Agout ≃	32	43.47 N	1.41 E
Agoza ⊥	146	18.30 N	23.45 E
Āgra	124	27.11 N	78.01 E
Āgra Canal ≊	272a	28.34 N	77.18 E
Agrachanskij poluostrov ›[1]	84	43.42 N	47.36 E
Agraciada	258	33.48 S	58.15 W
Agrado	246	2.15 N	75.46 W
Agraf'novka	83	47.45 N	39.29 E
Agram → Zagreb	36	45.48 N	15.58 E
Agramonte	240p	22.41 N	81.07 W
Agrate Brianza	62	45.34 N	9.21 E
Agreda	34	41.51 N	1.56 W
Ağrı	84	39.44 N	43.03 E
Ağrı □[4]	84	39.30 N	43.15 E
Agri ≃	68	40.13 N	16.44 E
Agri Bavnehøj ∧[2]	41	56.14 N	10.33 E
Ağrı Dağı (Mount Ararat) ∧	84	39.42 N	44.18 E
Agrigento	70	37.18 N	13.35 E
Agrigento □[4]	70	37.27 N	13.30 E
Agrihan I	108	18.46 N	145.40 E
Agrínion	38	38.37 N	21.24 E
Agrio ≃	252	38.21 S	69.43 W
Agropoli	68	40.21 N	15.00 E
Agro Pontino ◆[1]	66	41.25 N	12.55 E
Agryz	80	56.33 N	53.00 E
Ağstafa	84	41.08 N	45.28 E
Ağsu	84	40.34 N	48.24 E
Agtuuganon, Mount ∧	116	7.48 N	126.12 E
Agua, Ilha d' I	287a	22.49 S	43.10 W
Agua, Volcán de ∧[1]	236	14.28 N	90.45 W
Água Branca, Bra.	250	9.17 S	37.55 W
Água Branca, Bra.	250	7.31 S	37.40 W
Água Branca, Bra.	250	5.53 S	42.38 W
Agua Brava, Laguna c	234	22.10 N	105.32 W
Agua Caliente, Méx.	232	27.27 N	108.32 W
Agua Caliente, Méx.	234	23.20 N	105.20 W
Agua Caliente Creek ≃	282	37.29 N	121.56 W
Agua Caliente Grande	232	26.31 N	108.22 W
Aguacate	240p	22.59 N	81.49 W
Aguachica	246	8.19 N	73.38 W
Água Clara	255	20.27 S	52.52 W
Aguada	240m	18.23 N	67.11 W
Aguada, Zanjón de la ≃	286e	33.30 S	70.47 W
Aguada Cecilio	254	40.51 S	65.51 W
Aguada de Guerra	254	41.04 S	68.25 W
Aguada de Pasajeros	240p	22.23 N	80.51 W
Aguadas	246	5.37 N	75.27 W
Aguadilla	240m	18.26 N	67.09 W
Água Doce	252	27.00 S	51.33 W
Agua Dulce, Méx.	234	18.08 N	94.08 W
Aguadulce, Pan.	236	8.15 N	80.33 W
Agua Dulce, Ca., U.S.	228	34.30 N	118.23 W
Agua Dulce, Tx., U.S.	196	27.47 N	97.54 W
Agua Fria ≃	200	33.23 N	112.21 W
Agua Fria Creek ≃	282	37.28 N	121.56 W
Aguaí	256	22.04 S	46.58 W
Agualeguas	232	26.18 N	99.34 W
Água Limpa	255	18.06 S	48.46 W
Agualva-Cacém	266c	38.46 N	9.18 W
Aguán ≃	236	15.57 N	85.44 W
Aguanaval ≃	232	25.28 N	102.53 W
Agua Negra	286c	10.28 N	67.01 W
Aguanish	186	50.13 N	62.05 W
Aguanus ≃	186	50.13 N	62.05 W
Aguapeí ≃, Bra.	248	15.53 S	58.25 W
Aguapeí ≃, Bra.	255	21.03 S	51.47 W
Aguapey ≃	252	29.07 S	56.36 W
Água Preta, Igarapé ≃	246	1.41 S	63.48 W
Agua Prieta	232	31.18 N	109.34 W
Aguaragüe, Serranía de ⋏	248	21.30 S	63.40 W
Aguaray	252	22.16 S	63.44 W
Aguaray-Guazú ≃, Para.	252	24.47 S	57.19 W
Aguaray-Guazú ≃, Para.	252	24.05 S	56.40 W
A Guardia	34	41.54 N	8.53 W
Aguarico ≃	246	0.59 S	75.11 W
Aguaro-Guariquito, Parque Nacional ♠	246	8.10 N	66.50 W
Aguaruto	232	24.47 N	107.29 W
Aguas ≃	34	37.09 N	1.49 W
Águas, Serra das ∧	256	21.55 S	45.25 W
Aguasabon ≃	190	48.46 N	87.07 W
Águas Belas	250	9.07 S	37.07 W
Aguas Buenas	240m	18.15 N	66.06 W
Aguascalientes, Méx.	200	32.18 N	115.10 W
Aguascalientes, Méx.	234	21.53 N	102.18 W
Aguascalientes □[3]	234	22.00 N	102.30 W
Aguascalientes, Río de ≃	234	21.23 N	102.28 W
Aguas Corrientes	258	34.31 S	56.24 W
Águas da Prata	256	21.56 S	46.43 W
Águas de Contendas	256	21.54 S	45.01 W
Águas de Lindóia	256	22.29 S	46.39 W
Águas Formosas	255	17.05 S	40.57 W
Aguasvivas ≃	34	41.20 N	0.25 W
Agua Tibia ∧	228	33.24 N	116.59 W
Água Vermelha, Represa de ⊜[1]	255	20.00 S	50.00 W
Agua-Viva	256	21.41 S	42.33 W
Aguayo	252	31.40 S	65.54 W
Aguaytía ≃	248	8.08 S	74.37 W
Agua Zarca	200	31.10 N	110.59 W
Agu Bay c	176	70.18 N	86.30 W
A Gudiña	34	42.04 N	7.08 W
Agudos	255	22.28 S	49.00 W
Águeda	34	40.34 N	8.27 W
Águeda ≃	34	41.02 N	6.56 W
Aguelhok	150	19.28 N	0.52 E
Aguema	152	12.03 S	21.49 E
Aguenier, Lac ⊜	186	50.43 N	68.13 W
Agugliano	66	43.32 N	13.23 E
Agui	94	34.55 N	136.55 E
Aguié	150	13.30 N	7.47 E
Aguijan I	108	14.51 N	145.34 E
Aguila	200	33.56 N	113.10 W
Aguilar, Esp.	34	37.31 N	4.39 W
Aguilar, Co., U.S.	198	37.24 N	104.39 W
Aguilares, Arg.	252	27.26 S	65.37 W
Aguilares, El Sal.	236	13.58 N	89.12 W
Águilas	34	37.24 N	1.35 W
Aguililla	234	18.44 N	102.44 W
Aguirre ≃	246	8.28 N	61.02 W
Aguirre, Arroyo ≃	288	34.46 S	58.35 W
Aguirre, Bahía c	254	54.57 S	65.50 W
Aguit	102	41.52 N	112.56 E
Aguita Zarc	234	23.10 N	104.28 W
Aguja, Cerro ∧	254	42.11 S	71.51 W
Aguja, Punta ›	248	5.48 S	81.06 W
Aguja Point ›	116	12.42 N	123.23 E
Agujas, Cabo de las → Agulhas, Cape ›	158	34.52 S	20.00 E
Agujereada, Punta ›	240m	18.31 N	67.08 W
Agujita	196	27.53 N	101.09 W
Agul ≃	88	55.44 N	95.41 E
Agulai	144	13.41 N	39.35 E
Agulhas	158	34.50 S	20.00 E
Agulhas, Cape ›	158	34.52 S	20.00 E
Agulhas Basin ✣[1]	8	47.00 S	27.00 E
Agulhas Negras	256	22.28 S	44.27 W
Agulhas Negras, Pico das ∧	256	22.23 S	44.38 W
Agulhas Plateau ✣[3]	10	40.00 S	26.00 E
Agung, Gunung ∧	115b	8.21 S	115.30 E
Aguni-jima I	93b	26.35 N	127.14 E
Agusan ≃	116	9.00 N	125.31 E
Agusan del Norte □[4]	116	9.00 N	125.30 E
Agusan del Sur □[4]	116	8.30 N	125.40 E
Agustín Codazzi	246	10.02 N	73.14 W
Agutaya	116	11.09 N	120.56 E
Agutaya Island I	116	11.09 N	120.58 E
Ağva	130	41.09 N	29.50 E
Agvali	84	42.33 N	46.06 E
Agwarra	150	10.42 N	4.35 E
Ägypten → Egypt □[1]	140	27.00 N	30.00 E
Aha	174m	26.43 N	128.17 E
Ahaggar (Hoggar) ⋏	148	23.00 N	6.30 E
Ahaggar, Tassili ta-n- ⋏[1]	148	21.00 N	6.00 E
Aha Hills ⋏[2]	156	19.45 S	21.10 E
Aha-kō c	174m	26.43 N	128.18 E
Aham	60	48.32 N	12.28 E
Ahar	128	38.28 N	47.04 E
Ahar ≃	128	38.32 N	47.31 E
Ahascragh	48	53.24 N	8.20 W
Ahaura	172	42.21 S	171.32 E
Ahaura ≃	172	42.21 S	171.31 E
Ahaus	52	52.04 N	7.00 E
Aheggar ∧	148	24.43 N	5.39 E
Ahfir	148	34.57 N	2.17 W
Ahimanawa Range ⋏	172	39.00 S	176.27 E
Ahipara	172	35.10 S	173.10 E
Ahipara Bay c	172	35.10 S	173.07 E
'Āhirah	132	32.53 N	36.28 E
Ahırlı	130	37.14 N	32.08 E
Ahklun Mountains ⋏	180	59.15 N	161.00 W
Ahlat, Tür.	128	38.45 N	42.29 E
Ahlat, Tür.	130	38.45 N	42.29 E
Ahlbeck, Dtsch.	54	53.40 N	14.11 E
Ahlbeck, Dtsch.	54	53.56 N	14.11 E
Ahlem	52	52.23 N	9.40 E
Ahlen	52	51.46 N	7.53 E
Ahlenberg	263	51.25 N	7.28 E
Ahlenmoor ◆[3]	52	53.40 N	8.45 E
Ahlerstedt	52	53.24 N	9.27 E
Ahlhorn	52	52.54 N	8.14 E
Ahlsdorf	54	51.32 N	11.28 E
Ahmadābād	120	23.02 N	72.37 E
Ahmadābād-e Sarjām	128	35.51 N	59.36 E
Ahmad al-Bāqir, Jabal ∧	132	29.36 N	35.08 E
Ahmadgarh	123	30.41 N	75.50 E
Ahmadnagar	122	19.05 N	74.44 E
Ahmadpur, India	124	23.31 N	77.13 E
Ahmadpur, India	126	23.50 N	87.42 E
Ahmadpur East	123	29.09 N	71.16 E
Ahmadpur Siāl	123	30.41 N	71.46 E
Ahmad Wāl	120	29.25 N	65.56 E
Ahmar, Al-Bahr al- → Red Sea ⍑[2]	136	20.00 N	38.00 E
Ahmar, 'Erg el ◆[2]	148	23.30 N	4.54 W
Ahmar, Jabal al- ∧	132	29.40 N	35.09 E
Ahmar Mountains ⋏	144	9.15 N	41.00 E
Ahmedabad → Ahmadābād	120	23.02 N	72.37 E
Ahmetli	130	38.31 N	27.57 E
Ahmic Lake ⊜	190	45.37 N	79.42 W
Ahnatal	56	51.22 N	9.24 E
Ahnet ⋏	148	24.58 N	2.57 E
Ahnet, Tanezrouft n- ◆[2]	148	22.15 N	1.30 E
Ahoada	150	5.05 N	6.38 E
Ahoghill	48	54.51 N	6.22 W
Ahome	232	25.55 N	109.11 W
Ahon, Tarso ∧	146	20.23 N	18.18 E
Ahornspitz ∧	64	47.08 N	11.56 E
Ahoskie	192	36.17 N	76.59 W
Ahousat	182	49.17 N	126.04 W
Ahr ≃	56	50.33 N	7.17 E
Ahram	128	28.52 N	51.16 E
Ahrāmāt Dahshūr (North and Bent Pyramids) ⊥	142	29.48 N	31.13 E
Ahrāmāt Maydūm (Maydūm Pyramid) ⊥	142	29.23 N	31.10 E
Ahraura	124	25.01 N	83.01 E
Ahrensbök	54	54.00 N	10.34 E
Ahrensburg	52	53.40 N	10.14 E
Ahrensdorf, Dtsch.	54	52.10 N	14.05 E
Ahrensdorf, Dtsch.	264a	52.19 N	13.12 E
Ahrensfelde	264a	52.35 N	13.35 E
Ahrgebirge ⋏	56	50.30 N	6.50 E
Ahtanum	224	46.34 N	120.37 W
Ahtanum Creek ≃	202	46.32 N	120.31 W
Ahtanum Ridge ∧	224	46.30 N	120.50 W
Ähtäri	26	62.34 N	24.06 E
Ähtärinjärvi ⊜	26	62.40 N	24.03 E
Ähtävänjoki ≃	26	63.38 N	22.48 E
Ahtopol	38	42.06 N	27.57 E
Ahu	98	34.27 N	118.39 E
Ahuacatlán, Méx.	234	21.03 N	104.29 W
Ahuacatlán, Méx.	234	20.00 N	97.52 W
Ahuachapán	236	13.55 N	89.51 W
Ahuacuotzingo	234	17.42 N	98.56 W
Ahualulco de Mercado	234	20.42 N	103.59 W
Ahuijullo	234	19.05 N	103.05 W
Ahuijullo ≃	234	18.49 N	103.37 W
Ahumada, Méx.	204	32.30 N	115.30 W
Ahumada, Méx.	232	30.37 N	106.31 W
Ahun	32	46.05 N	2.05 E
Ahuntsic ◆[8]	275a	45.33 N	73.39 W
Ahunui I[1]	14	19.39 S	140.25 W
Ahuriri ≃	172	44.33 S	170.11 E
Åhus	26	55.55 N	14.17 E
Ahuzhen	98	34.27 N	118.39 E
Ahvāz	128	31.19 N	48.42 E
Ahvenanmaa □[4]	26	60.15 N	20.00 E
Ahwahnee	226	37.21 N	119.43 W
Ahwar	144	13.31 N	46.42 E
Ahwa-ri	98	35.54 N	129.02 E
Ai ≃	98	40.13 N	124.30 E
Aialik Cape ›	180	59.42 N	149.31 W
Aiándion	267c	37.55 N	23.28 E
Aiapuá	246	4.29 S	62.04 W
Aiapuá, Lago ⊜	246	4.27 S	62.08 W
Aibag ≃	102	42.40 N	110.42 E
Aibonito	240m	18.08 N	66.16 W
Aich	64	47.25 N	13.49 E
Aichach	60	48.28 N	11.08 E
Aicha vorm Wald	60	48.41 N	13.18 E
Aichhalden	58	48.16 N	8.24 E
Aichi □[5]	94	35.00 N	137.15 E
Aichi-kōgen-kokutei-kōen ♠	94	35.10 N	137.25 E
Aichi-yōsui ≊	94	34.42 N	136.57 E
Aichstetten	58	47.54 N	10.04 E
Aichtal	56	48.38 N	9.16 E
Aidenbach	60	48.34 N	13.06 E
Aidomaggiore	71	40.10 N	8.51 E
Aidone	70	37.25 N	14.27 E
Aidong	102	24.46 N	107.21 E
Aiduma, Pulau I	164	3.58 S	134.06 E
Aiea	229c	21.22 N	157.56 W
Aiello Calabro	68	39.07 N	16.10 E
Aigáleo Óros ∧[2]	267c	38.00 N	23.37 E
Aigburth ◆[8]	262	53.22 N	2.55 W
Aigen im Mühlkreis	60	48.39 N	13.58 E
Aigenmiao	89	43.36 N	120.50 E
Aigle	58	46.19 N	6.58 E
Aigle, Île à l' I	275a	45.42 N	73.28 W
Aigle, Lac à l' ⊜	186	51.12 N	65.25 W
Aignay-le-Duc	58	47.40 N	4.44 E
Aigre	32	45.54 N	0.01 E
Aiguá	252	34.12 S	54.45 W
Aiguebelette, Lac d' ⊜	62	45.33 N	5.48 E
Aiguebelette-le-Lac	62	45.32 N	5.49 E
Aiguebelle	62	45.32 N	6.18 E
Aiguebelle, Réserve ♠	190	48.33 N	78.45 W
Aigueperse	32	46.01 N	3.12 E
Aigues ≃	62	44.07 N	4.43 E
Aigues-Mortes	62	43.34 N	4.11 E
Aigues-Mortes, Golfe d' c	62	43.31 N	4.03 E
Aigüestortes, Parc National d' ♠	34	42.30 N	1.01 E
Aigues-Vives	62	43.44 N	4.10 E
Aiguilles	62	44.47 N	6.52 E
Aiguines	62	43.46 N	6.15 E
Aigurande	32	46.26 N	1.50 E
Aihui (Heihe)	89	50.16 N	127.28 E
Aija	248	9.46 S	77.38 W
Aikawa, Nihon	92	38.02 N	138.15 E
Aikawa, Nihon	94	35.32 N	139.17 E
Aiken	192	33.33 N	81.43 W
Aikens Lake ⊜	184	51.12 N	95.20 W
Ailao Shan ⋏	102	24.08 N	101.25 E
Ailefroide	62	44.53 N	6.27 E
Aileron	162	22.39 S	133.20 E
Ailette ≃	50	49.35 N	3.10 E
Aileu	112	8.43 S	125.34 E
Ailimutou Shan ∧	104	42.19 N	121.25 E
Ailingen	58	47.41 N	9.29 E
Ailinglapalap I[1]	14	7.23 N	168.46 E
Ailinzhuang	105	39.27 N	117.36 E
Aillant-sur-Tholon	50	47.52 N	3.21 E
Aille ≃	62	43.26 N	6.30 E
Ailly-le-Haut-Clocher	50	50.05 N	2.00 E
Ailly-sur-Noye	50	49.45 N	2.22 E
Ailly-sur-Somme	50	49.55 N	2.12 E
Ailo	164	4.50 S	151.40 E
Ailsa Craig	190	43.08 N	81.33 W
Ailsa Craig I	44	55.16 N	5.07 W
Ailuk I[1]	14	10.20 N	169.56 E
Aim	74	58.50 N	134.12 E
Aimargues	62	43.41 N	4.12 E
Aime	62	45.33 N	6.39 E
Aimere	115b	8.50 S	120.52 E
Aimi	96	35.22 N	133.22 E
Aimogasta	252	28.33 S	66.49 W
Aimorés	255	19.30 S	41.04 W
Aimoto	270	34.59 N	135.10 E
Ain □[5]	32	46.10 N	5.20 E
Ain ≃	58	45.48 N	5.10 E
Aïn Arnat	34	36.11 N	5.19 E
Aïn Azel	34	35.49 N	5.31 E
Ainaži	76	57.52 N	24.21 E
'Aïn Belbela, Sebkha ⩦	148	27.30 N	5.20 W
Aïn Benian	148	36.48 N	2.55 E
Aïn Ben Tili	148	26.00 N	9.32 W
Aïn Berda	36	36.39 N	7.35 E
Aïn Bessem	34	36.18 N	3.40 E
Aincourt	261	49.04 N	1.47 E
Aïn Defla	34	36.16 N	1.58 E
Aïn Deheb	148	34.51 N	1.33 E
Aïn Draham	148	36.47 N	8.42 E
Aine ≃	56	50.23 N	5.31 E
Aïn el Beïda	148	35.48 N	7.24 E
Aïn el Hadjel	34	35.40 N	3.53 E
Aïn el Kebira	34	36.22 N	5.30 E
Aïn Milia	148	36.02 N	6.34 E
Aino	270	34.57 N	135.10 E
Aino-shima I, Nihon	96	33.59 N	130.50 E
Aino-shima I, Nihon	96	33.45 N	130.23 E
Aïn Oulmène	34	35.55 N	5.18 E
Ainring	64	47.48 N	12.56 E
Ainsdale	44	53.36 N	3.02 W
Aïn Sefra	148	32.45 N	0.35 W
Ain Shams University ʊ[2]	273c	30.03 N	31.17 E
Ainslie, Mount ∧	171b	35.16 S	149.10 E
Ainslie Lake ⊜	186	46.08 N	61.12 W
Ainsworth, Eng., U.K.	262	53.35 N	2.22 W
Ainsworth, Ne., U.S.	198	42.33 N	99.51 W
Aïn Taghrout	34	36.08 N	5.05 E
Aïn Tedelès	148	36.00 N	0.18 E
Aïn Témouchent	148	35.18 N	1.08 W
Aïn Touta	148	35.23 N	5.54 E
Aintree	262	53.29 N	2.56 W
Aintree Race Course ♠	262	53.28 N	2.56 W
Aïn Wessara	148	35.27 N	2.54 E
Aïn Yagout	148	35.47 N	6.25 E
Aio	96	34.00 N	131.26 E
Aioi	96	34.48 N	134.28 E
Aiome	164	5.10 S	144.45 E
Aiora	34	39.04 N	1.03 W
Aipe	246	3.13 N	75.15 W
Aiquara	255	14.07 S	39.52 W
Aiquile	248	18.10 S	65.10 W
Aïr ⋏	150	18.00 N	8.30 E
Airabu, Pulau I	112	2.46 N	106.14 E
Airai Airport ⊠	175b	7.22 N	134.33 E
Airaines	50	49.58 N	1.57 E
Airão	246	1.56 S	61.22 W
Airasca	62	44.55 N	7.29 E
Airbangis	110	0.12 N	99.23 E
Airdikit	112	2.40 S	101.15 E
Airdrie, Ab., Can.	182	51.18 N	114.02 W
Airdrie, Scot., U.K.	46	55.52 N	3.59 W
Aire ≃, Fr.	56	49.19 N	4.49 E
Aire ≃, Eng., U.K.	44	53.44 N	0.54 W
Aire-sur-l'Adour	32	43.42 N	0.16 W
Aire-sur-la-Lys	50	50.38 N	2.24 E
Air Force Island I	176	67.55 N	74.10 W
Airgegas	112	2.42 S	106.25 E
Airgin Sum	102	42.58 N	111.08 E
Airhaji	112	1.57 S	100.53 E
Airjamban	114	1.13 N	101.14 E
Airlie	166	20.16 S	148.43 E
Airmolek	112	0.22 S	102.17 E
Airmont	276	41.06 N	74.06 W
Airola	68	41.04 N	14.33 E
Airole	62	43.52 N	7.33 E
Airolo	58	46.32 N	8.37 E
Airor	46	57.04 N	5.46 W
Airport West	274b	37.44 S	144.53 E
Airtenang	112	3.08 S	101.43 E
Airterjun	114	1.20 N	100.27 E
Airuno	62	45.45 N	9.25 E
Airvault	32	46.50 N	0.08 W
Aisch ≃	56	49.46 N	11.01 E
Aisega	164	5.44 S	148.21 E
Aisén del General Carlos Ibáñez del Campo □[4]	254	46.30 S	73.30 W
Aisey-sur-Seine	58	47.45 N	4.35 E
Aishihik	180	61.35 N	137.30 W
Aishihik Lake ⊜	180	61.25 N	137.06 W
Ai-shima I	96	34.30 N	131.17 E
Aisinaike	85	39.47 N	75.47 E
Aislingen	56	48.30 N	10.27 E
Aisne □[5]	50	49.30 N	3.30 E
Aisne ≃	32	49.26 N	2.50 E
Aisne à la Marne, Canal de l' ≊	50	49.24 N	3.55 E
Aïssa, Djebel ∧	148	32.51 N	0.30 W
Aïssey	58	47.16 N	6.20 E
Aist ≃	61	48.14 N	14.35 E
Aisy-sur-Armançon	50	47.39 N	4.13 E
Aitana, Serra d' ∧	34	38.44 N	0.16 W
Aitape	164	3.08 S	142.21 E
Aiterach ≃	60	48.54 N	12.38 E
Aiterhofen	60	48.51 N	12.37 E
Aith	46a	60.16 N	1.23 W
Aitkin	190	46.31 N	93.42 W
Aït-Melloul	148	30.21 N	9.31 W
Aitolikón	38	38.27 N	21.22 E
Aït-Ourir	148	31.38 N	7.42 W
Aitrach	58	47.56 N	10.05 E
Aitutaki I[1]	14	18.52 S	159.45 W
Ait Youssef ou Ali	34	35.13 N	3.55 W
Aiuaba	250	6.38 S	40.07 W
Aiud	38	46.19 N	23.44 E
Aiún → El Aaiún	148	27.09 N	13.12 W
Aiuruoca	256	21.58 S	44.36 W
Aiuruoca ≃, Bra.	256	21.42 S	44.22 W
Aiuruoca ≃, Bra.	256	21.32 S	44.26 W
Aiva	287a	22.42 S	43.28 W
Aiviekste ≃	76	56.37 N	25.45 E
Aix, Mount ∧	224	46.47 N	121.15 W
Aix-en-Othe	50	48.13 N	3.44 E
Aix-en-Provence	62	43.32 N	5.26 E
Aix-la-Chapelle → Aachen	56	50.47 N	6.05 E
Aix-les-Bains	62	45.42 N	5.55 E
Aiyáleo	267c	37.59 N	23.41 E
Aiyang, Mount ∧	164	5.05 S	141.19 E
Aiyansh	182	55.17 N	129.03 W
Aíyina	38	37.44 N	23.27 E
Aíyina I	38	37.46 N	23.26 E
Aiyínion	38	40.30 N	22.33 E
Aíyion	38	38.15 N	22.05 E
Āīzawl	120	23.44 N	92.43 E
Aizhaipuzi	104	40.57 N	124.01 E
Aizkraukle	76	56.38 N	25.13 E
Aizpute	76	56.43 N	21.38 E
Aizu-bange	92	37.34 N	139.49 E
Aizu-wakamatsu	92	37.30 N	139.56 E
Aj ≃	86	56.08 N	57.40 E
Ajā	142	30.57 N	31.17 E
Ajā', Jabal ⋏	128	27.20 N	41.45 E
'Ajab Shīr	128	37.28 N	45.54 E
Ajaccio	36	41.55 N	8.44 E
Ajaguz	86	47.56 N	80.23 E
Ajaguz ≃	86	46.42 N	79.15 E
Ajajú ≃	246	0.59 N	72.20 W
Ajalpan	234	18.22 N	97.15 W
'Ajaltūn	132	33.58 N	35.41 E
Ajalvir	266a	40.32 N	3.29 W
'Ajamī	130	36.28 N	37.42 E
Ajan, Ross.	74	56.27 N	138.10 E
Ajan, Ross.	88	54.43 N	110.55 E
Ajan ≃	74	70.10 N	95.50 E
Ajana	162	27.57 S	114.38 E
Ajanta	122	20.32 N	75.45 E
Ajanta Range ⋏	122	20.30 N	76.00 E
Ajaokuta	150	7.28 N	6.39 E
Ajarani ≃	246	1.33 N	61.16 W
Ajasse	150	8.17 N	4.48 E
Ajasso	150	5.52 N	8.52 E
Ajat ≃	86	52.54 N	63.02 E
Ajax	212	43.51 N	79.02 W
Ajay ≃	126	23.39 N	88.08 E
Ajbas	80	47.51 N	49.37 E
Ajdābiyā	146	30.48 N	20.14 E
Ajdabul'	86	52.42 N	68.59 E
Ajdar	78	50.03 N	38.56 E
Ajdarkul', ozero ⊜[1]	72	40.45 N	67.20 E
Ajdarly	86	44.32 N	65.50 E
Ajdovščina	36	45.53 N	13.53 E
Ajdyrlinskij	86	52.03 N	59.50 E
Ajegunle	273a	6.36 N	3.17 E
Ajgurka ≃	80	45.46 N	43.12 E
Ajgyrkol', ozero ⊜	80	48.15 N	52.50 E
Ajhūr al-Kubrā	142	30.18 N	31.09 E
Aji	96	34.23 N	134.08 E
Ajibar	144	10.52 N	38.40 E
Ajibarang	115a	7.25 S	109.04 E
Ajigasawa	92	40.47 N	140.12 E
'Ajīj, Wādī al- V	130	35.19 N	41.09 E
Ajijic	234	20.18 N	103.17 W
Ajil	114	5.05 N	103.05 E
Ājimganj	126	24.14 N	88.15 E
Ajimu	96	33.26 N	131.21 E
Ajipuzicun	104	42.16 N	123.33 E
Ajisu	96	34.00 N	131.22 E
Ajjer, Tassili-n- ⋏[1]	148	25.10 N	8.00 E
Ajka	30	47.07 N	17.34 E
Ajke, ozero ⊜	86	50.57 N	61.36 E
Ajkino	24	62.15 N	49.56 E
'Ajlūn	132	32.20 N	35.45 E
Ajlune	224	46.31 N	122.26 W
'Ajmah, Jabal al- ⋏	140	29.12 N	34.02 E
Ajmer	120	26.27 N	74.38 E
Ajnāla	123	31.51 N	74.48 E
Ajni	85	39.23 N	68.32 E
Ajo	200	32.22 N	112.51 W
Ajo, Cabo de ›	34	43.31 N	3.35 W
Ajok	140	9.15 N	28.27 E
Ajon, ostrov I	74	69.50 N	168.40 E
Ajoya	232	24.04 N	106.22 W
Ajrag nuur ⊜	88	48.54 N	93.28 E
'Ajramīyah, Bi'r al- ⍑[4]	142	29.39 N	31.50 E
Ajrum	84	41.13 N	44.53 E
Ajryk	86	50.30 N	76.48 E
Ajtos	38	42.42 N	27.15 E
Ajuchitlán del Progreso	234	18.09 N	100.29 W
Ajuda ◆[8]	266c	38.43 N	9.12 W
Ajusco	204	31.35 N	116.25 W
Ajusco ◆[8]	286a	19.14 N	99.12 W
Ajuta ≃	83	47.34 N	40.07 E
Ajuterique	236	14.20 N	87.43 W
Ajutinskij	83	47.46 N	40.08 E
Ajuy	116	11.10 N	123.01 E
Ajuy Bay c	116	11.10 N	123.02 E
Aka ≃	92	38.54 N	139.50 E
Akaba	150	7.57 N	1.03 E
Akabane	94	34.37 N	137.12 E
Akabira	92a	43.34 N	142.03 E
Akabli	148	26.42 N	1.22 E
Akabori	94	36.22 N	139.14 E
Akademii, zaliv c	89	54.15 N	138.05 E
Akagera (Kagera) ≃	154	0.57 S	31.47 E
Akagera, Parc National de l' ♠	154	1.30 S	30.35 E
Akagi, Nihon	94	36.33 N	139.03 E
Akagi, Nihon	96	35.00 N	132.43 E
Akagi-san ∧	94	36.33 N	139.11 E
Akaishi-dake ∧	94	35.27 N	138.09 E
Akaishi-sammyaku ⋏	94	35.18 N	138.07 E
Akaka Falls State Park ♠	229d	19.52 N	155.09 W
Akaki Beseka	144	8.52 N	38.47 E
Akālgarh	123	32.16 N	73.49 E
Akalkot	122	17.32 N	76.13 E
Akamaruno-misaki ›	174m	26.44 N	128.09 E
Akámas, Akrotírion ›	130	35.06 N	32.17 E
Akan	92a	43.06 N	144.10 E
Akana-tōge)(	96	34.57 N	132.44 E
Akan-kokuritsu-kōen ♠	92a	43.30 N	144.15 E
Akaoka	96	33.32 N	133.43 E
Ak-Aral	86	49.10 N	90.57 E
Akaroa	172	43.48 S	172.58 E
Akaroa Harbour c	172	43.50 S	172.56 E
Åkarp	41	55.39 N	13.07 E
Akarsu, Tür.	130	37.14 N	41.04 E
Akarsu, Tür.	130	39.56 N	38.38 E
Akasaki	96	35.31 N	133.38 E
'Akasha East	140	21.05 N	30.43 E
Akashat	130	33.45 N	39.58 E
Akashi	96	34.38 N	134.59 E
Akashi ≃	270	34.38 N	134.59 E
Akashi-kaikyō Ʉ	96	34.37 N	135.02 E
Akashina	94	36.21 N	137.56 E
Akatani-ko ⊜[1]	94	36.43 N	138.54 E
Akatjevo	82	54.59 N	38.45 E
Akatova	76	55.09 N	31.48 E
Akatsuka ◆[8]	268	35.46 N	139.39 E
Akatsutsumi ◆[8]	268	35.39 N	139.39 E
Akbaba ◆[8]	267b	41.09 N	29.06 E
Akbaba Dağı ∧	130	40.12 N	40.51 E
Akbajtal	85	38.32 N	73.49 E
Akbajtal, pereval)(	85	38.32 N	73.40 E
Akbarpur, India	124	24.39 N	83.58 E
Akbarpur, India	124	26.25 N	82.33 E
Akbeit	86	51.38 N	70.02 E
Akbou	148	36.28 N	4.32 E
Akbulak, Kaz.	86	49.26 N	80.28 E
Akbulak, Ross.	86	51.01 N	55.37 E
Akbura ≃	85	40.39 N	72.36 E
Akçaabat	130	41.02 N	39.34 E
Akçadağ	130	38.21 N	37.59 E
Akçakale	130	36.41 N	38.56 E
Akcakışla	130	39.33 N	36.22 E
Akçakoca	130	41.05 N	31.09 E
Akçakoyunlu	130	36.46 N	37.38 E
Akçaova, Tür.	130	37.30 N	28.02 E
Akçaova, Tür.	130	41.03 N	29.57 E
Akçapınar	130	38.57 N	38.57 E
Akčatau	86	47.59 N	74.02 E
Akçay	130	36.36 N	29.45 E
Akçay ≃	130	37.50 N	28.15 E
Akchâr ◆[1]	150	20.00 N	14.30 W
Akcjabr'ski	76	52.38 N	28.53 E
Akdağ	130	40.43 N	36.00 E
Akdağ ∧	130	39.29 N	41.54 E
Akdağmadeni	130	39.40 N	35.54 E
Akdala	86	45.02 N	74.35 E
Akdoğan	130	35.06 N	33.41 E
Ak-Dovurak	86	51.16 N	90.31 E
Akechi	94	35.18 N	137.23 E
Akehama	96	33.19 N	132.26 E
Akeley	190	47.00 N	94.43 W
Aken	54	51.51 N	12.02 E
Akeno, Nihon	94	36.15 N	140.02 E
Akeno, Nihon	94	35.46 N	138.26 E
Åker	40	59.15 N	17.05 E
Åkerby	40	60.25 N	17.46 E
Åkersberga	40	59.29 N	18.18 E
Akershus □[6]	26	60.00 N	11.10 E
Akersloot	52	52.34 N	4.44 E
Akespe	86	46.48 N	60.31 E
Aketi	152	2.44 N	23.46 E
Aketilepa	85	39.57 N	74.03 E
Aketu-Oja	273a	6.41 N	3.23 E
Åkforsån ≃	40	58.54 N	16.28 E
Akgöl ⊜	130	38.58 N	31.48 E
Akharnaí	38	38.05 N	23.44 E
Akhḍar, Al-Jabal al- ⋏, Lībiyā	146	32.30 N	21.30 E
Akhḍar, Al-Jabal al- ⋏, 'Umān	128	23.15 N	57.20 E
Akhelóös ≃	38	38.36 N	21.14 E
Akh Gol ⊜	84	39.33 N	44.47 E
Akhiok	180	56.57 N	154.10 W
Akhisar	130	38.55 N	27.51 E
Akhmīm	140	26.34 N	31.44 E
Akhnūr	123	32.54 N	74.44 E
Akhtarīn	130	36.31 N	37.20 E
Aki, Nihon	96	33.30 N	133.54 E
Aki, Nihon	96	33.28 N	131.43 E
Aki ≃, Nihon	94	35.41 N	139.21 E
Aki ≃, Nihon	96	33.30 N	133.55 E
Akiachak	180	60.55 N	161.27 W
Akiak	180	60.55 N	161.12 W
Akiéni	152	1.11 S	13.53 E
Akima	88	53.06 N	115.44 E
Akimiski Island I	176	53.00 N	81.20 W
Aki-nada ⍑[2]	96	34.05 N	132.48 E
Akıncı	130	37.10 N	40.52 E
Akıncı Burun ›	130	36.19 N	35.47 E
Akıncılar, Tür.	130	40.06 N	38.21 E
Akıncılar, Tür.	130	37.45 N	38.50 E
Akiode	273a	6.38 N	3.21 E
Åkirkeby	26	55.04 N	14.56 E
Akishima	94	35.41 N	139.22 E
Akišma ≃	89	52.08 N	132.40 E
Akita	92	39.43 N	140.07 E
Akita-heiya ⩦	92	39.45 N	140.10 E
Akitan	273a	6.39 N	3.16 E
Akitipa	150	8.17 N	6.16 E
Akitkan, chrebet ⋏	88	57.05 N	109.05 E
Akitsu, Nihon	96	34.19 N	132.50 E
Akitsu, Nihon	270	34.56 N	135.06 E
Akiyama	94	35.34 N	139.05 E
Akiyoshi-dai ⋏[1]	96	34.15 N	131.15 E
Akiyoshi-dai-kokutei-kōen ♠	96	34.15 N	131.17 E
Akiyoshi-do ±[5]	96	34.14 N	131.19 E
Akjar	86	51.50 N	58.14 E
Akjoujt	150	19.45 N	14.23 W
Akka	148	29.22 N	8.14 W
Akkala	86	43.43 N	59.31 E
Akkani	180	65.30 N	171.10 W
Akkense	86	46.49 N	68.20 E
Akkerman → Bilhorod-Dnistrovs'kyy	78	46.12 N	30.20 E
Akkermanovka	86	51.11 N	58.12 E
Akkerwoude	52	53.17 N	5.58 E
Akkeshi	92a	43.02 N	144.51 E
Akkışla	130	39.00 N	36.11 E
'Akko (Acre)	132	32.55 N	35.05 E
Akkol', Kaz.	85	43.25 N	70.47 E
Akkol', Kaz.	86	45.02 N	75.40 E
Akkol', Kaz.	86	52.12 N	75.05 E
Akkol', ozero ⊜	85	43.24 N	70.40 E
Akköy	130	37.29 N	27.15 E
Akkra → Accra	150	5.33 N	0.13 W
Akkrum	52	53.03 N	5.50 E
Ak-Kul'	85	41.41 N	74.16 E
Akkuş	130	40.49 N	37.01 E
Aklan □[4]	116	11.40 N	122.20 E
Aklan ≃	116	11.44 N	122.20 E
Aklan Point ›	116	11.44 N	122.22 E
Aklavik	180	68.12 N	135.00 W
'Aklé 'Aouâna ◆[1]	150	18.00 N	5.30 W
Akmeņrags ›	76	56.51 N	21.03 E
Akmeqit	120	37.01 N	76.59 E
Akmeşe	130	40.51 N	30.12 E
Akmola	86	51.10 N	71.30 E
Akmola □[8]	86	51.00 N	70.00 E
Akmuz	85	41.16 N	76.09 E
Ākna	272b	22.59 N	88.21 E
Aknet, gora ∧	86	50.51 N	75.40 E
Aknīste	76	56.10 N	25.45 E
Aknoul	148	34.43 N	3.49 W
Ako, Nig.	146	10.17 N	10.58 E
Akō, Nihon	96	34.45 N	134.24 E
Akoba	80	49.28 N	47.25 E
Akobo	140	7.47 N	33.01 E
Akobo (Akūbū) ≃	140	7.47 N	33.03 E
Akodiya	124	23.23 N	76.36 E
Akok, Cam.	152	2.46 N	10.18 E
Akok, Gabon	152	0.31 N	9.45 E
Akola	122	20.44 N	77.00 E
Akonolinga	152	3.47 N	12.15 E
Akop	140	8.21 N	29.05 E
Akor	150	14.53 N	6.58 W
Akora	123	34.00 N	72.08 E
Akordat	144	15.33 N	37.53 E
Akören	130	37.27 N	32.23 E
Akosombo Dam ◆[6]	150	6.16 N	0.03 E
Akot, India	120	21.11 N	77.04 E
Akot, Süd.	140	6.33 N	30.03 E
Akoupé	150	6.23 N	3.54 W
Akowonjo	273a	6.37 N	3.19 E
Akpatok Island I	176	60.25 N	68.00 W
Akpınar, Tür.	130	37.34 N	38.13 E
Akpınar, Tür.	130	39.17 N	33.40 E
Akqi	85	40.52 N	77.58 E
Åkrafjorden c[2]	26	59.46 N	6.06 E
Akranes	24a	64.18 N	22.02 W
Åkrehamn	26	59.16 N	5.11 E
Akrítas, Ákra ›	38	36.43 N	21.54 E
Akrofuom	150	6.07 N	1.39 W
Akrokórinthos ⊥	38	37.54 N	22.56 E
Akron, Co., U.S.	198	40.09 N	103.12 W
Akron, In., U.S.	216	41.02 N	86.01 W
Akron, Ia., U.S.	198	42.49 N	96.33 W
Akron, N.Y., U.S.	210	43.01 N	78.29 W
Akron, Oh., U.S.	214	41.04 N	81.31 W
Akron, Pa., U.S.	208	40.09 N	76.12 W
Akron-Canton Regional Airport ⊠	214	40.55 N	81.27 W
Akron City Reservoir ⊜[1]	214	41.20 N	81.17 W
Akrotíri	130	34.36 N	32.57 E
Akša	88	50.16 N	113.17 E
Aksa ◆[8]	272c	19.10 N	72.48 E
Aksaj, Kaz.	80	51.09 N	53.00 E
Aksaj, Ross.	80	47.58 N	43.59 E
Aksaj, Ross.	83	47.15 N	39.52 E
Aksaj (Toxkan) ≃, Asia	85	40.55 N	78.16 E
Aksaj ≃, Ross.	83	47.15 N	39.53 E
Aksaj ≃, Ross.	84	43.32 N	46.51 E
Aksakovo	80	54.02 N	54.09 E
Aksaray	130	38.23 N	34.03 E
Aksaray □[4]	130	38.30 N	34.00 E
Aksarka	74	66.36 N	67.46 E
Akšatau	86	49.23 N	54.36 E
Aksaut ≃	84	43.55 N	41.42 E
Aksay	102	39.28 N	94.15 E
Aksayqin Hu ⊜	120	35.12 N	79.50 E
Akşehir	130	38.21 N	31.25 E
Akşehir Gölü ⊜	130	38.30 N	31.28 E
Akseki	130	37.02 N	31.48 E
Aksengir ≃	85	43.40 N	76.14 E
Aksenkino	80	53.59 N	53.06 E
Aksenovo	82	55.40 N	38.15 E
Aksentjevo	82	55.25 N	35.54 E

≃ River	Fluß	Río	Rivière	Rio	
≊ Canal	Kanal	Canal	Canal	Canal	
⌞ Waterfall, Rapids	Wasserfall, Stromschnellen	Cascada, Rápidos	Chute d'eau, Rapides	Cascata, Rápidos	
Ʉ Strait	Meeresstraße	Estrecho	Détroit	Estreito	
c Bay, Gulf	Bucht, Golf	Bahía, Golfo	Baie, Golfe	Baía, Golfo	
⊜ Lake, Lakes	See, Seen	Lago, Lagos	Lac, Lacs	Lago, Lagos	
⩦ Swamp	Sumpf	Pantano	Marais	Pântano	
⍓ Ice Features, Glacier	Eis- und Gletscherformen	Accidentes Glaciales	Formes glaciaires	Acidentes glaciares	
⍑ Other Hydrographic Features	Andere Hydrographische Objekte	Otros Elementos Hidrográficos	Autres données hydrographiques	Outros acidentes hidrográficos	

✣ Submarine Features	Untermeerische Objekte	Accidentes Submarinos	Formes de relief sous-marin	Acidentes submarinos
□ Political Unit	Politische Einheit	Unidad Politica	Entité politique	Unidade política
ʊ Cultural Institution	Kulturelle Institution	Institución Cultural	Institution culturelle	Institução cultural
⊥ Historical Site	Historische Stätte	Sitio Histórico	Site historique	Sitio histórico
♠ Recreational Site	Erholungs- und Ferienort	Sitio de Recreo	Centre de loisirs	Area de Lazer
⊠ Airport	Flughafen	Aeropuerto	Aéroport	Aeroporto
■ Military Installation	Militäranlage	Instalación Militar	Installation militaire	Instalação militar
◆ Miscellaneous	Verschiedenes	Misceláneo	Divers	Diversos

Name	Page	Lat.°'	Long.°'
Akšij, Kaz.	85	44.00 N	76.20 E
Akšij, Kaz.	86	47.37 N	55.56 E
Akšijrak, chrebet ⩘	85	41.20 N	74.15 E
Aksinjino, Ross.	82	55.44 N	36.59 E
Aksinjino, Ross.	82	56.02 N	38.12 E
Aks'onovo	88	58.51 N	101.43 E
Aks'onovo-Zilovskoje	88	53.04 N	117.32 E
Aksoran, gora ⋀	86	48.27 N	75.32 E
Akstafa ⩘	84	41.15 N	45.26 E
Aksu, Kaz.	80	50.56 N	53.06 E
Aksu, Kaz.	86	52.28 N	71.59 E
Aksu, Kaz.	86	45.37 N	79.30 E
Aksu, Tür.	130	36.58 N	30.50 E
Aksu, Zhg.	90	41.10 N	80.20 E
Aksu ⩘, Asia	85	43.22 N	73.54 E
Aksu ⩘, Kaz.	86	46.20 N	78.15 E
Aksu ⩘, Tür.	130	37.25 N	36.54 E
Aksu ⩘, Tür.	130	36.51 N	30.54 E
Aksu-Ajuly	86	48.47 N	73.40 E
Aksuat, Kaz.	86	51.32 N	64.34 E
Aksuat, Kaz.	86	47.45 N	82.40 E
Aksuat, Kaz.	86	48.16 N	83.50 E
Aksubajevo	80	54.52 N	50.50 E
Aksu-Džabaglinskij zapovednik ♦	85	42.20 N	70.35 E
Aksum	144	14.08 N	38.43 E
Aktag ⋀	120	36.45 N	84.40 E
Aktal	85	41.25 N	75.03 E
Aktanyš	80	55.43 N	54.05 E
Aktas, Kaz.	82	42.57 N	70.04 E
Aktas, Kaz.	86	48.02 N	66.21 E
Aktas, Kaz.	86	49.47 N	72.59 E
Aktaš, Ross.	86	50.18 N	87.44 E
Aktaš, Uzb.	85	41.38 N	69.44 E
Aktas Gölü ⊘	85	41.15 N	43.12 E
Aktasty, Kaz.	86	50.06 N	76.40 E
Aktasty, Kaz.	86	50.44 N	61.43 E
Aktau, Kaz.	72	43.35 N	51.05 E
Aktau, Kaz.	86	50.16 N	73.02 E
Aktau, gora ⋀	86	48.00 N	71.45 E
Aktepe	130	36.44 N	36.27 E
Akterek, Kaz.	85	43.22 N	75.18 E
Akterek, Kyrg.	85	42.14 N	77.45 E
Akto	85	39.08 N	75.57 E
Aktobe	85	43.13 N	67.46 E
Aktogaj, Kaz.	86	44.27 N	76.42 E
Aktogaj, Kaz.	86	48.18 N	74.58 E
Aktogaj, Kaz.	86	46.57 N	79.40 E
Aktubek	86	48.58 N	71.06 E
Akt'ubinsk	86	50.17 N	57.10 E
Akt'ubinsk ⁸	86	48.30 N	58.30 E
Akt'ubinskij	80	54.49 N	52.47 E
Aktuluk	130	39.03 N	39.32 E
Aktumsyk	86	46.40 N	57.19 E
Akt'uz	85	42.54 N	76.07 E
Aku	150	6.42 N	7.20 E
Akūbū (Akobo) ⩘	140	7.47 N	33.03 E
Akui ⩘	96	34.06 N	134.33 E
Akula	152	2.22 N	20.11 E
Akuliči Pervyje	76	53.11 N	33.13 E
Akulovo, Ross.	82	55.31 N	36.42 E
Akulovo, Ross.	82	56.05 N	38.59 E
Akumadan	150	7.24 N	1.57 W
Akune	92	32.01 N	130.11 E
Akun Island I	180	54.12 N	165.35 W
Akure	150	7.15 N	5.12 E
Akureyri	24a	65.44 N	18.08 W
Akurli	272c	19.01 N	73.06 E
Akuša	84	42.17 N	47.21 E
Akuse	150	6.06 N	0.08 E
Akuseki-jima I	93b	29.27 N	129.37 E
Akutan	180	54.08 N	165.46 W
Akutan Island I	180	54.10 N	165.55 W
Akutan Pass ⨄	180	54.06 N	166.10 W
Akuticha	86	52.27 N	84.29 E
Akwanga	150	8.55 N	8.23 E
Akwatia	150	6.04 N	0.49 W
Akwawa ⩘²	150	6.27 N	0.25 W
Akwaya	152	6.30 N	9.40 E
Akyab — Sittwe	110	20.09 N	92.54 E
Akyazi	130	40.41 N	30.37 E
Akyel	144	12.33 N	37.04 E
Akyrtobe	85	42.59 N	72.07 E
Akyurt	130	40.08 N	33.06 E
Akžajkyn, ozero ⊘	86	44.55 N	67.46 E
Akžal, Kaz.	86	47.47 N	74.02 E
Akžal, Kaz.	86	49.13 N	81.25 E
Akžar, Kaz.	85	43.08 N	71.38 E
Akžar, Kaz.	86	48.34 N	75.30 E
Akžaryk	86	48.34 N	75.30 E
Al	26	60.38 N	8.34 E
Ala	85	45.45 N	11.00 E
Ala ⩘, Bela.	76	52.41 N	29.39 E
Ala ⩘, Zhg.	86	42.42 N	89.12 E
Alā, Monti di ⋀	71	40.40 N	9.14 E
Al-Ab'ādīyah	142	31.22 N	31.07 E
Alabama	210	43.06 N	78.23 W
Alabama ⩘³, U.S.	178	32.50 N	87.00 W
Alabama ⩘, U.S.	194	31.08 N	87.57 W
Alabama and Coushatta Indian Reservation ⨀⁴	222	30.43 N	94.42 W
Alabaster	194	33.14 N	86.48 W
Alabat Island I	116	14.07 N	122.03 E
Al-'Abbāsah ash-Sharqīyah	142	30.32 N	31.43 E
Al-'Abbāsīyah	140	12.10 N	31.18 E
Al-'Abbāsīyah ⁸	273c	30.04 N	31.17 E
Alabino	82	55.31 N	37.01 E
Āl-i-'Ābīs	144	18.04 N	43.10 E
Alabuga ⩘	85	41.26 N	74.41 E
Ala-Buka	85	41.22 N	71.31 E
Alaca	130	40.10 N	34.51 E
Alacahan	130	39.37 N	37.37 E
Alaçam	130	41.11 N	29.27 E
Alaçam Dağları ⩘	130	41.37 N	35.37 E
Alacant	34	38.21 N	0.29 W
Alacant ⩘²	34	38.16 N	26.23 E
Alachadży	130	41.14 N	40.18 E
Alachua	192	29.47 N	82.29 W
Alacrán, Arrecife ⩘²	232	22.24 N	89.42 W
Alacranes, Presa @¹	240p	22.45 N	80.40 W
Aladağ	130	37.02 N	32.41 E
Aladağ ⩘, Tür.	84	40.11 N	42.49 E
Aladağ ⩘, Tür.	130	37.45 N	35.09 E
Aladağlar ⩘, Tür.	130	39.20 N	43.35 E
Aladağlar ⋀, Tür.	132	37.55 N	35.13 E
Al-'Adasīyah	132	32.40 N	35.37 E
Alā dei Sardi	71	40.39 N	9.20 E
Aladino	86	54.24 N	38.12 E
Aladinskij, porog ⨄	86	58.24 N	95.29 E
Ala di Stura	45	45.19 N	7.19 E
Aladjino	82	56.21 N	37.04 E
Aladža manastir ⩘¹	38	43.17 N	28.01 E
Alafia ⩘	220	27.52 N	82.27 W
Alafia, South Prong ⩘	220	27.51 N	82.08 W
Alagbado	273a	6.40 N	3.18 E
Alagna Valsesia	62	45.51 N	7.56 E
Alag nuur ⊘	102	45.09 N	94.28 E
Alagoa	250	22.10 S	44.38 W
Alagoa Grande	252	7.04 S	35.37 W
Alagoa Nova	250	7.03 S	36.06 W
Alagoas ⩘³	250	9.30 S	36.00 W
Alagón	34	41.46 N	1.07 W
Alagón ⩘	34	39.44 N	7.30 W
Alaguntan	273a	6.26 N	3.50 E
Ala ⩘	144	14.30 N	40.30 E
Alahanpanjang	118	1.05 S	100.47 E
Alahärmä	26	63.14 N	22.51 E
Alaior	34	39.56 N	4.08 E
Al-Ait	140	12.42 N	27.27 E
Al-'Ajnūn	142	30.55 N	32.18 E
Alajärvi	26	63.00 N	23.49 E
Alajku	85	40.18 N	74.27 E
Alajōe	76	59.01 N	27.26 E

Name	Page	Lat.°'	Long.°'
Alajskaja dolina ⩗	85	39.30 N	73.00 E
Alajskij chrebet ⩘	85	39.45 N	72.00 E
Al'Azīzah	142	31.11 N	31.57 E
Alajuela	236	10.01 N	84.13 W
Alajuela ⩘⁴	236	10.30 N	84.30 W
Alajuela, Lago @¹	236	9.15 N	79.35 W
Ālājūjeh	84	38.57 N	46.41 E
Alakai Swamp ⩘	229b	22.05 N	159.35 W
Alakamisy	157b	21.19 S	47.14 E
Alakanuk	180	62.41 N	164.37 W
Alaköl, ozero ⊘	86	46.10 N	81.45 E
Al-'Akrīshah	142	31.08 N	30.09 E
Alaktara	124	22.01 N	82.26 E
Alak'ul'a	265a	59.44 N	29.56 E
Al-'Āl	132	32.48 N	35.44 E
Alalakeiki Channel ⨄	229a	20.35 N	156.30 W
Al-'Alamayn	140	30.49 N	28.57 E
Al-'Alāqimah	142	30.37 N	31.38 E
Alalaú ⩘	246	0.30 S	61.09 W
Al-'Amādīyah	128	37.06 N	43.29 E
Alamagan I	108	17.36 N	145.50 E
Al-'Amārah	128	31.50 N	47.09 E
Al-'Amār al-Kubrā	142	30.21 N	31.08 E
Alamata	144	12.25 N	39.33 E
Alamdānga	124	23.46 N	88.57 E
Alameda, Esp.	34	37.12 N	4.39 W
Alameda, Ca., U.S.	226	37.45 N	122.14 W
Alameda, N.M., U.S.	200	35.11 N	106.37 W
Alameda, Ca., U.S.	226	37.35 N	121.55 W
Alameda, Estación ⩘⁵	286e	33.27 S	70.41 W
Alameda Creek ⩘	226	37.35 N	122.09 W
Alameda Naval Air Station ⩘	226	37.47 N	122.18 W
Alamedin ⩘	85	42.54 N	74.37 E
Alamein — Al-'Alamayn	140	30.49 N	28.57 E
Alaminos	200	31.02 N	110.35 W
Alaminos	116	16.10 N	119.59 E
Al-'Āmirīyah	142	31.01 N	29.48 E
'Alam Lek	128	37.02 N	65.57 E
Álamo, Mér.	234	20.55 N	97.41 W
Álamo, Ca., U.S.	226	37.51 N	122.02 W
Álamo, Ga., U.S.	192	32.08 N	82.46 W
Álamo, Mi., U.S.	216	42.22 N	85.43 W
Álamo, Nv., U.S.	204	37.21 N	115.09 W
Álamo, Tn., U.S.	194	35.47 N	89.07 W
Álamo ⩘	204	33.14 N	115.39 W
Alamo Creek ⩘	226	37.42 N	121.55 W
Alamo Creek, West Branch ⩘	282	37.45 N	121.55 W
Alamogordo	200	32.53 N	105.57 W
Alamogordo Creek ⩘	196	34.40 N	104.23 W
Alamo Heights	196	29.29 N	98.27 W
Alamo Indian Reservation ⨀⁴	200	34.30 N	107.30 W
Alamo Lake @¹	200	34.20 N	113.30 W
Alamo Oaks	282	37.51 N	121.59 W
Álamor	246	4.02 S	80.02 W
Álamos, Méx.	196	26.25 N	100.25 W
Álamos, Méx.	232	27.01 N	108.56 W
Álamos, Río de los ⩘	196	27.53 N	101.12 W
Alamosa	200	37.28 N	105.52 W
Alamosa ⩘	200	37.28 N	105.46 W
Alamosa Creek ⩘, N.M., U.S.	196	34.26 N	103.58 W
Alamosa Creek ⩘, N.M., U.S.	200	33.20 N	107.21 W
Alamosa East	200	37.28 N	105.49 W
Álamos de Márquez	232	28.40 N	103.30 W
Ālampur, Bngl.	126	23.49 N	89.06 E
Alampur, India	272b	22.25 N	88.08 E
Alanäs	26	64.10 N	15.42 E
Al-'Anāt	132	32.06 N	35.18 E
Al-Anbār ⩘⁴	128	33.45 N	41.45 E
Al-'Anz	132	17.34 N	76.34 E
Alaotra, Lac @	157b	17.30 S	48.30 E
Alapaha	192	31.23 N	83.13 W
Alapaha ⩘	192	30.26 N	83.06 W
Alapajevsk	86	57.52 N	61.42 E
Alapli	130	41.11 N	31.24 E
'Alaqah, Jabal ⋀	142	29.59 N	32.53 E
Alaquines	234	22.08 N	99.36 W
Al-'Arabīyah as-Su'ūdīyah — Saudi Arabia ⩘¹	118	25.00 N	45.00 E
Alarcón	34	39.33 N	2.05 W
Alarcón, Embalse de @¹	34	39.36 N	2.10 W
Al-'Armah ⩘¹	128	25.30 N	46.30 E
Alarobia Vohiposa	157b	20.59 S	47.09 E
Alas ⩘, Indon.	114	3.05 N	97.55 E
Alas, Selat ⨄	115b	8.40 S	116.40 E
Alasan	124	1.45 S	123.19 E
Alasdair, Sgurr ⋀	46	57.12 N	6.14 W
Alashanyouqi	130	38.21 N	28.32 E
Al-'Ashūrīyah	128	33.01 N	43.15 E
Al-'Ashūrīyah @¹	128	30.00 N	103.33 E
Al-'Ashūrīyah	140	34.55 N	40.34 E
Al-'Ashmūnayn	142	27.47 N	30.49 E
Alaska ⩘³	216	65.00 N	153.00 W
Alaska, Gulf of ⲥ	16	58.00 N	146.00 W
Alaska Peninsula ⩘¹	180	57.00 N	158.00 W
Alaska Range ⩘¹	180	62.30 N	150.00 W
Al-'Assāfīyah	128	28.31 N	39.08 E
Alasso	62	44.00 N	8.10 E
Alastaro	26	60.56 N	22.55 E
Alastuey	34	34.25 S	59.13 W
Ālāt, Azer.	84	39.57 N	49.25 E
Alat, Uzb.	85	39.26 N	63.48 E
Al-'Atāminah	142	27.30 N	30.50 E
Alatna ⩘	180	66.34 N	152.34 W
Al-'Atrūn	140	18.11 N	26.36 E
Alatyr'	80	54.51 N	46.36 E
Alatyr' ⩘	80	54.52 N	46.36 E
Alausí	246	2.12 S	78.50 W
Alava, Cape ⩟	204	48.10 N	124.44 W
Alaverdi	84	41.08 N	44.39 E
Alawa	116	4.10 N	121.39 E
Alaw, Llyn @¹	50	53.23 N	4.30 W
Alawa	150	10.00 N	6.39 E
Al-'Awjā'	142	30.37 N	30.32 E
'Alayh	132	33.48 N	35.32 E
Al-'Ayn	128	24.13 N	55.46 E
Al-'Ayyāḍ	142	30.45 N	31.02 E
Al-'Ayyāṭ	142	29.37 N	31.15 E
Alazani ⩘	84	41.05 N	46.40 E
Alazeja ⩘	74	70.51 N	153.34 E

Name	Page	Lat.°'	Long.°'
Al-Azhar University ⩘²	273c	30.03 N	31.16 E
Al'Azīzah	142	31.11 N	31.57 E
Al-'Azīzīyah, Lībiyā	146	32.32 N	13.01 E
Al-'Azīzīyah, Misr	142	30.29 N	31.18 E
Al-'Azīzīyah, Misr	273c	29.52 N	31.15 E
Al-Azraq ⩘¹	132	31.52 N	36.50 E
Alb ⩟	58	47.35 N	8.08 E
Alba, It.	62	44.42 N	8.02 E
Alba, Mi., U.S.	190	44.58 N	84.58 W
Alba, Pa., U.S.	210	41.42 N	76.50 W
Alba, Tx., U.S.	222	32.48 N	95.38 W
Alba ⩘⁶	38	46.15 N	23.30 E
Alba, Foum de ⵏ	148	20.27 N	3.36 W
Al-Bāb	130	36.22 N	37.31 E
Albacete	34	38.59 N	1.51 W
Albacete ⩘⁴	34	38.50 N	1.50 W
Albacina	66	43.21 N	13.01 E
Al-Bad¹	128	28.25 N	35.04 E
Al-Badārī	140	26.59 N	31.25 E
Alba de Tormes	34	40.49 N	5.31 W
Al-Badrashayn	142	29.51 N	31.16 E
Albæk	26	57.36 N	10.25 E
Al-Bahnasā	142	28.32 N	30.39 E
Al-Bahr al-Abyad ⩘¹	140	13.15 N	32.25 E
Al-Bahr al-Ahmar ⩘⁴, Misr	142	28.45 N	32.00 E
Al-Bahr al-Ahmar ⩘⁴, Süd.	140	20.00 N	35.15 E
Al-Bahrayn — Bahrain ⩘¹	128	26.00 N	50.30 E
Albaida	34	38.51 N	0.31 W
Albairate	266b	45.25 N	8.56 E
Alba Iulia	38	46.04 N	23.35 E
Al-Bajalāt	142	31.10 N	31.37 E
Al-Bājūr	142	30.26 N	31.02 E
Al-Bakātūsh	142	31.03 N	30.48 E
Al-Ballāhūn	142	30.49 N	31.26 E
Al-Ballāshūn	142	30.26 N	31.26 E
Al-Ballah	142	30.46 N	32.19 E
Al-Ballās	140	26.01 N	32.46 E
Al-Balqā' ⩘⁸	132	32.00 N	35.40 E
Al-Balqā'ah ⩘³⁰	130	35.55 N	36.28 E
Al-Balyanā	140	26.14 N	32.00 E
Alban ⩘	82	43.54 N	2.28 E
Albanel, Lac @	175	50.55 N	73.12 W
Albanella	68	40.30 N	15.08 E
Albani, Colli ⩘²	66	41.45 N	12.45 E
Albano, Col.	202	42.24 N	113.34 W
Albino, Il., U.S.	194	38.22 N	88.03 W
Albion, In., U.S.	216	41.23 N	85.25 W
Albion, Ia., U.S.	190	42.06 N	92.59 W
Albion, Mi., U.S.	216	42.14 N	84.45 W
Albion, Ne., U.S.	198	41.41 N	98.00 W
Albion, N.J., U.S.	285	39.47 N	74.56 W
Albion, N.Y., U.S.	210	43.14 N	78.11 W
Albion, Pa., U.S.	214	41.53 N	80.22 W
Albion, R.I., U.S.	207	41.57 N	71.27 W
Albion, Wa., U.S.	202	46.47 N	117.14 W
Albion Airstrip ⩘	285	39.46 N	74.58 W
Albion Park	170	34.34 S	150.47 E
Al-Biqā' ⩘¹	130	34.00 N	36.00 E
Al-Biqā' ⩘⁴	132	33.50 N	36.00 E
Al-Bīrah	132	31.54 N	35.13 E
Al-Birīqāt	142	30.30 N	30.49 E
Al-Birk	128	18.13 N	41.33 E
Al-Birkah	142	30.24 N	30.49 E
Al-Birkah ⩘⁴	144	22.12 N	40.43 E
Albisola Marina	62	44.20 N	8.31 E
Albisola Superiore	62	44.20 N	8.31 E
Albizzate	62	45.43 N	8.44 E
Alblasserdam	52	51.52 N	4.40 E
Albo, Monte ⩘	71	40.31 N	9.35 E
Albocàsser	34	40.21 N	0.02 E
Albogas	266c	38.51 N	9.15 W
Alboran, Isla de I	34	35.56 N	3.02 W
Alborán Sea ⩘²	34	36.00 N	3.00 W
Álborg	26	57.03 N	9.56 E
Álborg Bugt ⲥ	26	56.45 N	10.30 E
Alborz, Reshteh-ye Kūhhā-ye (Elburz Mountains) ⩘	128	36.00 N	53.00 E
Albright-Knox Art Gallery ⩘	284a	42.56 N	78.53 W
Albrighton	42	52.38 N	2.16 W
Albstadt	58	48.13 N	9.01 E
Albuch ⩘	58	48.45 N	10.07 E
Albufeira	116	10.55 N	124.42 E
Albufeira	34	37.05 N	8.15 W
Albū Gharz, Sabkhat ⊘	130	35.10 N	38.40 E
Albuñol	34	36.48 N	3.12 W
Al-Buḥayrah ⩘³	142	30.30 N	30.12 E
Al-Buḥayrah ⩘⁴, Süd.	140	7.30 N	29.20 E
Albula ⩘	58	46.42 N	9.27 E
Al-Bunbah	146	32.24 N	23.08 E
Albuquerque	200	35.05 N	106.39 W
Albuquerque, N.M., U.S.	200	35.05 N	106.39 W
Albuquerque, Cayos de II	236	12.10 N	81.50 W
Al-Buraymī	128	24.15 N	55.45 E
Alburg	206	44.58 N	73.18 W
Al-Burjāyah	142	30.59 N	30.59 E
Alburno, Monte ⋀	68	40.31 N	15.17 E
Alburquerque	34	39.13 N	7.00 W
Alburtis	208	40.31 N	75.36 W
Al-Burumbul	142	31.12 N	31.45 E
Albury, Austl.	162	36.05 S	146.55 E
Albury, N.Z.	172	44.14 S	170.52 E
Albury, Eng., U.K.	50a	51.13 N	0.30 W
Al-Busayr	142	31.20 N	30.24 E
Al-Busaylī	142	31.08 N	30.45 E
Al-Buṭāḥ ⩘¹	128	29.30 N	38.45 E
Al-Butnah ⩘	132	32.30 N	35.40 E
Al-Buṭnān ⩘¹	146	31.30 N	25.00 E
Al-Butanah	132	31.50 N	35.50 E
Al-Buwaydah	142	30.42 N	30.52 E
Al-Buzūn	128	15.35 N	50.55 E
Al-Buzzanco	62	45.11 N	16.32 E
Alby, Fr.	62	45.49 N	6.01 E
Alby, Sve.	26	62.30 N	15.28 E
Alca	248	15.15 S	72.46 W
Alcácer do Sal	266c	38.22 N	8.31 W
Alcains	116	39.56 N	7.27 W
Alcalá de Guadaira	34	37.20 N	5.50 W
Alcalá de Henares	34	40.28 N	3.22 W
Alcalá la Real	34	37.27 N	3.56 W
Alcamo	71	37.59 N	12.58 E
Alcañices	34	41.42 N	6.21 W
Alcañiz	34	41.03 N	0.08 W
Alcántara, Esp.	34	39.43 N	6.53 W
Alcántara, Pil.	116	12.16 N	123.08 E
Alcántara I, Embalse de @¹	34	39.49 N	6.25 W
Alcantarilla	34	37.58 N	1.13 W
Alcantilado	255	16.23 S	53.31 W
Alcaraz	34	38.40 N	2.29 W
Alcatraz Island I	282	37.50 N	122.25 W
Alcaudete	34	37.36 N	4.05 W
Alcázar de San Juan	34	39.24 N	3.12 W
Alcester, Austl.	170	36.50 S	140.41 E
Alcester, Eng., U.K.	42	52.13 N	1.52 W
Alcester, S.D., U.S.	198	43.00 N	96.37 W
Alchevs'k	64	48.30 N	38.47 E
Alcira (Gigena)	255	33.12 S	64.32 W
Alcoa	192	35.47 N	83.58 W

Name	Page	Lat.°'	Long.°'
Albertirsa	30	47.15 N	19.38 E
Albert Kanaal (Canal Albert) ⩘	56	50.39 N	5.37 E
Albert Lea	190	43.38 N	93.22 W
Albert Markham, Mount ⋀	9	81.23 S	158.12 E
Albert Nile ⩘	154	3.36 N	32.02 E
Alberto, Lago @ — Albert, Lake @	154	1.40 N	31.00 E
Alberto Eduardo — Albert Edward, Mount ⋀	164	8.23 S	147.24 E
Alberton, P.E., Can.	186	46.49 N	64.04 W
Alberton, S. Afr.	273d	26.16 S	28.08 E
Alberton, Mt., U.S.	202	47.00 N	114.29 W
Albert Park ♦	274b	37.51 S	144.57 E
Albert Peak ♦	182	51.02 N	117.51 W
Albertshof	264a	52.42 N	13.40 E
Albertson	276	40.46 N	73.38 W
Albertson Brook ⩘	285	39.41 N	74.43 W
Albertson Brook, Blue Anchor Branch ⩘	285	39.42 N	74.49 W
Albertson Brook, Pump Branch ⩘	285	39.42 N	74.49 W
Albertville, Fr.	62	45.41 N	6.23 E
Albertville, Al., U.S.	194	34.16 N	86.12 W
Albertville — Kalemie, R.D.C.	154	5.56 S	29.12 E
Albestroff	54	48.59 N	6.51 E
Albettone	64	45.21 N	11.35 E
Albi	32	43.56 N	2.09 E
Albia, Ia., U.S.	190	41.01 N	92.48 W
Albia, N.Y., U.S.	210	42.43 N	73.39 W
Albidona	68	39.55 N	16.28 E
Al Bidia	146	10.33 N	20.13 E
Albidona	68	39.55 N	16.28 E
Albignasego	64	45.21 N	11.52 E
Albina	246	5.30 N	54.03 W
Albina, Ponta ⵜ	152	15.51 S	11.44 E
Albinea	64	44.37 N	10.36 E
Albino	62	45.46 N	9.47 E
Albion, B.C., Can.	224	49.11 N	122.33 W
Albion, Al., U.S.	194	32.28 N	87.25 W
Albion, Il., U.S.	194	38.22 N	88.03 W
Albion, In., U.S.	216	41.23 N	85.25 W
Albion, Ia., U.S.	190	42.06 N	92.59 W
Albion, Mi., U.S.	216	42.14 N	84.45 W
Albion, Ne., U.S.	198	41.41 N	98.00 W
Albion, N.J., U.S.	285	39.47 N	74.56 W
Albion, N.Y., U.S.	210	43.14 N	78.11 W
Albion Center	221	42.55 N	78.32 W
Albion, Pa., U.S.	214	41.53 N	80.22 W
Al-Bīrah	132	31.54 N	35.13 E
Al-Birīqāt	142	30.30 N	30.49 E
Alberley Edge	44	53.18 N	2.15 W
Aldermaston	42	51.23 N	1.09 W
Alderney I	43b	49.43 N	2.12 W
Alder Peak ⋀	226	35.53 N	121.22 W
Aldershot	42	51.15 N	0.47 W
Alderson	192	37.44 N	80.38 W
Alderton	192	37.04 N	4.28 W
Alder, Ben ⋀	46	56.48 N	4.28 W
Alder Creek ⩘	202	45.50 N	119.56 W
Alderwood Manor	224	47.49 N	122.17 W
Aldine	222	29.54 N	95.23 W
Aldinga	168b	35.17 S	138.28 E
Aldinga Bay ⲥ	168b	35.18 S	138.27 E
Aldinga Beach	168b	35.18 S	138.27 E
Aldo Bonzi	286f	34.42 S	58.31 W
Aldridge	42	52.36 N	1.55 W
Aldwell, Lake @¹	224	48.05 N	123.34 W
Alechovščina	76	60.25 N	33.58 E
Aled ⩘	44	53.14 N	3.34 W
Aledo, Il., U.S.	190	41.11 N	90.45 W
Aledo, Tx., U.S.	222	32.42 N	97.36 W
Alefa	144	11.57 N	36.52 E
Aleg	150	17.03 N	13.55 W
Alegranza, Isla I	148	29.23 N	13.30 W
Alegre	255	20.46 S	41.32 W
Alegre ⩘	248	15.01 S	59.57 W
Alegres Mountain ⋀	200	34.09 N	108.11 W
Alegrete	255	29.46 S	55.46 W
Alejandría	244	33.45 N	41.15 E
Alejandría — Al-Iskandarīyah	142	31.12 N	29.54 E
Alejandro, Isla de I — Alexander Island	9	71.00 S	70.00 W
Alejandro Roca	255	33.21 S	63.43 W
Alejandro Selkirk, Isla (Isla Más Afuera) I	244	33.45 S	80.46 W
Alejo Ledesma	255	33.37 S	62.37 W
Alejsk	86	52.28 N	82.45 E
Aleknagik	180	59.17 N	158.38 W
Aleknagik, Lake @	180	59.17 N	158.37 W
Aleksandr-Nevskaja	82	55.14 N	36.59 E
Aleksandr-Nevskij	82	53.27 N	40.08 E
Aleksandrov	82	56.24 N	38.43 E
Aleksandrovka Gaj	80	50.09 N	48.34 E
Aleksandrovka, Kaz.	85	50.47 N	52.58 E
Aleksandrovka, Ross.	82	52.30 N	41.48 E
Aleksandrovka, Ross.	86	50.26 N	77.50 E
Aleksandrovskaja, Ross.	265a	60.03 N	29.59 E
Aleksandrovskaja, Ross.	265a	59.44 N	30.23 E
Aleksandrovskij Šl'uz ⩘	265a	59.49 N	30.50 E
Aleksandrovskij Zavod	88	50.55 N	117.57 E
Aleksandrovskoje, Ross.	84	44.42 N	43.02 E
Aleksandrovskoje, Ross.	86	60.26 N	77.52 E
Aleksandrovsk-Sachalinskij	74	50.54 N	142.10 E
Aleksandrów Kujawski	30	52.52 N	18.43 E
Aleksandrów Łódzki	30	51.49 N	19.18 E
Aleksandróv	76	51.49 N	19.18 E
Aleksandrówka	76	48.40 N	38.44 E
Aleksandrup	66	48.27 N	38.41 E
Aleksandroúpolis	40	40.50 N	25.52 E
Alexis Creek	182	52.05 N	123.17 W
Alexis Indian Reserve ⩘⁴	182	53.46 N	114.30 W
Alf	56	50.00 N	7.07 E
Alfādānga	124	23.20 N	89.42 E
Alfafar	34	39.22 N	0.23 W
Alfalfa ⩘³	200	36.45 N	98.20 W
Alfambra ⩘	34	40.55 N	1.00 W
Alfānt	208	40.35 N	74.53 W
Alfaro	34	42.11 N	1.45 W
Alfatar	38	43.57 N	27.17 E
Alfdorf	58	48.50 N	9.44 E
Alfeld	58	51.59 N	9.50 E
Alfeld	58	49.27 N	12.10 E
Alfenas	255	21.26 S	45.57 W
Alfiós ⩘	40	37.37 N	21.27 E
Alfold	42	51.07 N	0.34 W
Alföld ⩘	30	47.00 N	20.00 E
Alfonsine	64	44.30 N	12.03 E

Alcoa Center	279b	40.33 N	79.39 W
Alcoa Lake @¹	222	30.34 N	97.03 W
Alcobaça, Bra.	255	17.30 S	39.13 W
Alcobaça, Port.	34	39.33 N	8.59 W
Alcobaça ⩘	255	17.32 S	39.12 W
Alcobendas	34	40.32 N	3.38 W
Alcochete	266c	38.45 N	8.58 W
Alcockspruit ⩘	158	27.55 S	30.01 E
Alcoi	34	38.42 N	0.28 W
Alcoleda del Pinar	34	41.02 N	2.28 W
Alcolu	192	33.45 N	80.12 W
Alcomunga	234	18.25 N	97.02 W
Alconbury Brook ⩘	42	52.19 N	0.12 W
Alconchel	34	38.31 N	7.04 W
Alcorny	218	40.11 N	84.04 W
Alcorcón	286a	40.21 S	3.50 W
Alcorn ⩘³	194	31.52 N	91.09 W
Alcorta	252	33.32 S	61.07 W
Alcoutim	34	37.28 N	7.28 W
Alcova Reservoir @¹	200	42.32 N	106.45 W
Alcove	210	42.28 N	73.55 W
Alcove Reservoir @¹	210	42.29 N	73.57 W
Alcoy ⩘	116	9.42 N	123.30 E
Alcubierre	34	41.48 N	0.27 W
Alcúdia	34	39.52 N	3.07 E
Alcúdia, Badia d' ⲥ	34	39.48 N	3.13 E
Alcyon Lake @	285	39.44 N	75.08 W
Aldabra Island I	138	9.25 S	46.22 E
Aldama, Méx.	232	28.51 N	105.54 W
Aldama, Méx.	234	22.55 N	98.04 W
Aldama, Arroyo ⩘	286b	23.05 N	82.15 W
Aldan, Ross.	74	58.37 N	125.24 E
Aldan, Pa., U.S.	285	39.55 N	75.17 W
Aldan ⩘	74	63.28 N	129.35 E
Aldanskoje nagorje ⩘	74	57.00 N	127.00 E
Aldbourne	42	51.31 N	1.37 W
Aldbrough	44	53.50 N	0.07 W
Aldbury	42	51.48 N	0.36 W
Alde ⩘	42	52.03 N	1.28 E
Aldea Apeleg	254	44.41 S	70.51 W
Aldeburgh	42	52.09 N	1.35 E
Aldeia de Paio Pires	266c	38.38 N	9.05 W
Aldeia Nova de Santo Aleixo ⩘	266c	39.12 N	8.20 W
Aldeia Velha	256	22.47 S	42.55 W
Aldemha	287b	23.45 S	46.53 W
Alden, Il., U.S.	216	42.27 N	88.31 W
Alden, Ia., U.S.	190	42.31 N	93.22 W
Alden, Mn., U.S.	190	43.40 N	93.34 W
Alden, N.Y., U.S.	210	42.54 N	78.29 W
Alden Center	221	42.55 N	78.32 W
Aldenhoven	56	50.53 N	6.16 E
Aldenrade ⩘⁸	263	51.31 N	6.44 E
Alder, Ben ⋀	46	56.48 N	4.28 W
Alder Creek ⩘	202	45.50 N	119.56 W
Alderney I	43b	49.43 N	2.12 W
Alderley Edge	44	53.18 N	2.15 W
Aldershot	42	51.15 N	0.47 W
Alderson	192	37.44 N	80.38 W
Aleksandrovka	82	55.14 N	36.59 E
Aleksin	82	54.30 N	37.05 E

ESPAÑOL

Nombre	Página	Lat.°′	Long.°′ W = Oeste
Alford, Austl.	168b	33.49 S	137.49 E
Alford, Eng., U.K.	44	53.16 N	0.10 E
Alford, Scot., U.K.	46	57.13 N	2.42 W
Alfortville	261	48.49 N	2.25 E
Ålfotbreen ⍓	26	61.45 N	5.40 E
Alfred, On., Can.	206	45.34 N	74.53 W
Alfred, Me., U.S.	188	43.28 N	70.43 W
Alfred, N.Y., U.S.	210	42.15 N	77.47 W
Alfred National Park ♠	166	37.35 S	149.20 E
Alfredo M. Terrazas	234	21.28 N	98.51 W
Alfreton	44	53.06 N	1.23 W
Alfriston	42	50.48 N	0.10 E
Alfta	26	61.21 N	16.05 E
Alfter	56	50.44 N	7.01 E
Al-Fujayrah	128	25.06 N	56.21 E
Al-Fuqahā'	146	27.50 N	16.22 E
Al-Furzul	132	33.52 N	35.56 E
Alga	86	49.46 N	57.20 E
Algabas, Kaz.	80	50.39 N	52.07 E
Algabas, Kaz.	86	44.41 N	78.06 E
Algabas, Kaz.	86	48.21 N	81.39 E
Algači	88	50.43 N	117.47 E
Älgarås	40	58.48 N	14.14 E
Ålgård	26	58.46 N	5.51 E
Al-Garef	140	12.03 N	34.19 E
Algarrobal	252	28.08 S	70.39 W
Algarrobo, Arg.	252	38.53 S	63.08 W
Algarrobo, Arg.	252	31.44 S	68.18 W
Algarrobo, Chile	252	33.22 S	71.40 W
Algarrobo del Águila	252	36.26 S	67.09 W
Algarve □[9]	34	37.10 N	8.15 W
Algás ≃	34	41.13 N	0.16 E
Algasovo	76	53.41 N	41.40 E
Al-Gebir	140	13.43 N	29.49 E
Algeciras, Col.	246	2.35 N	75.18 W
Algeciras, Esp.	34	36.08 N	5.30 W
Algemesí	34	39.11 N	0.26 W
Algena	144	17.19 N	38.31 E
Alger → El Djazaïr, Alg.	148	36.47 N	3.03 E
Alger, Oh., U.S.	216	40.42 N	83.50 W
Alger, Baie d' c	34	36.50 N	3.15 E
Algeria (Algérie) □[1], Afr.	134	28.00 N	3.00 E
Algeria (Algérie) □[1], Afr.	148	28.00 N	3.00 E
Algérie → Algeria □[1]	148	28.00 N	3.00 E
Algerien → Algeria □[1]	148	28.00 N	3.00 E
Algermissen	52	52.15 N	9.58 E
Algés	266c	38.42 N	9.13 W
Al-Ghāb ⊜	130	35.30 N	36.18 E
Al-Gharaq as-Sulṭānī	142	29.08 N	30.42 E
Al-Gharbīyah □[4]	142	30.45 N	31.00 E
Al-Ghāriyah	132	32.23 N	36.39 E
Al-Ghāṭ	128	26.00 N	45.03 E
Al-Ghawr V	132	31.50 N	35.30 E
Al-Ghayatah	142	30.57 N	30.06 E
Al-Ghayḍah	118	16.12 N	52.15 E
Al-Ghazālah	128	26.48 N	41.19 E
Al-Ghazālī	142	30.49 N	31.49 E
Al-Ghāzīyah	132	33.31 N	35.22 E
Alghero	71	40.34 N	8.19 E
Al-Ghurayfah	128	24.00 N	56.29 E
Al-Ghurdaqah	140	27.14 N	33.50 E
Algier → El Djazaïr	148	36.47 N	3.03 E
Algiers → El Djazaïr	148	36.47 N	3.03 E
Alginet	34	39.16 N	0.28 W
Algoa	222	29.24 N	95.11 W
Algoabaai c	158	33.50 S	25.50 E
Algodão, Ilha do I	256	23.13 S	44.36 W
Algodón ≃	246	2.23 S	71.56 W
Algodones	200	35.22 N	106.28 W
Algodor ≃	34	39.55 N	3.53 W
Algoma	190	44.36 N	87.25 W
Algoma Mills	190	46.10 N	82.50 W
Algona, Ia., U.S.	190	43.04 N	94.13 W
Algona, Wa., U.S.	224	47.16 N	122.15 W
Algonac	214	42.37 N	82.31 W
Algonquin	216	42.09 N	88.17 W
Algonquin Lake ⊜	216	42.40 N	85.20 W
Algonquin Provincial Park ♠	190	45.45 N	78.26 W
Algood	194	36.11 N	85.26 W
Algorta, Esp.	34	43.22 N	3.01 W
Algorta, Ur.	252	32.25 S	57.23 W
Alguierão-Mem Martins	266c	38.48 N	9.20 W
Al-Ḥaddādī	142	31.20 N	30.47 E
Al-Ḥaddayn	142	30.44 N	30.38 E
Al-Ḥadīthah	128	34.07 N	42.23 E
Al-Ḥaḍr	128	35.35 N	42.44 E
Al-Ḥaffah	130	35.35 N	36.02 E
Al-Ḥafīr Al-Fawqānī	132	33.42 N	36.28 E
Al-Ḥajālīj	140	14.36 N	31.54 E
Al-Ḥajarah ●[1]	128	30.00 N	44.00 E
Al-Ḥajar al-Gharbī ⩘	128	24.10 N	56.15 E
Al-Ḥajar ash-Sharqī ⩘	128	22.45 N	59.00 E
Al Hajeb	148	33.43 N	5.13 W
Al-Ḥājir	142	30.41 N	31.49 E
Al-Ḥalfāyah	128	31.49 N	47.26 E
Al-Ḥamād ≚	128	32.00 N	39.30 E
Alhama de Granada	34	37.00 N	3.59 W
Alhama de Murcia	34	37.51 N	1.25 W
Al-Ḥamal ●[1]	128	23.30 N	49.45 E
Alhambra, Ca., U.S.	228	34.05 N	118.07 W
Alhambra, Il., U.S.	219	38.53 N	89.44 W
Al-Ḥamīdīyah	130	34.43 N	35.56 E
Al-Ḥammām	140	30.50 N	29.23 E
Al-Ḥamrā', Ar. Su.	128	23.57 N	38.52 E
'Al-Ḥamrā', Lubnān	132	33.42 N	35.27 E
Al-Ḥamrah	142	31.10 N	30.52 E
Al-Ḥāmūl	142	31.19 N	31.10 E
Alhandra	250	7.26 S	34.54 W
Alhandra, Mouchão de I	266c	38.54 N	9.00 W
Al-Ḥarāk	132	32.44 N	36.18 E
Al-Ḥarīq	128	23.37 N	46.31 E
Al-Ḥārrah	132	33.03 N	36.00 E
Al-Ḥarrah ≛[9]	128	31.00 N	38.30 E
Al-Harūj al-Aswad ⩘[2]	146	27.00 N	17.10 E
Al-Ḥasakah	130	36.29 N	40.45 E
Al-Ḥasakah □[8]	130	36.30 N	41.00 E
Al-Ḥasānī I	128	24.58 N	37.05 E
Alhaurín el Grande	34	36.38 N	4.41 W
Al-Ḥawāmidīyah	273c	29.54 N	31.15 E
Al-Ḥawātah	140	13.25 N	34.38 E
Al-Ḥawātikah	142	27.16 N	31.01 E
Al-Ḥawrah	144	13.49 N	47.37 E
Al-Ḥawṭah	144	15.50 N	48.27 E
Al-Ḥawwārīyah	142	30.58 N	29.41 E
Al-Ḥayy, 'Irāq	128	32.10 N	46.03 E
Al-Ḥayy, Miṣr	142	29.39 N	31.18 E
Al-Ḥayyānīyah	128	28.38 N	42.45 E
Al-Ḥayz	140	28.02 N	28.39 E
Al-Ḥībah	142	28.45 N	30.55 E
Al-Ḥījānah	132	33.21 N	36.33 E
Al-Ḥijāz ●[1]	118	24.30 N	38.30 E
Al-Ḥillah, 'Irāq	128	32.29 N	44.25 E
Al-Ḥillah, Sūd.	140	13.27 N	27.08 E
Al-Ḥilmīyah ●[8]	273c	30.07 N	31.19 E
Al-Hindīyah	128	32.33 N	44.13 E
Al-Hirmil	130	34.23 N	36.23 E
Al-Ḥiṣn	132	32.29 N	35.52 E
Al-Hoceïma	148	35.15 N	3.55 W
Al-Hoceïma □[4]	148	35.00 N	4.30 W
Al Hoceïma, Baie d' c	34	35.20 N	3.50 W
Alhos Vedros	266c	38.39 N	9.02 W
Alhucemas, Peñón de I	34	35.13 N	3.53 W
Al-Ḥudayb	140	13.00 N	32.50 E
Al-Ḥudaydah	144	14.48 N	42.57 E
Al-Ḥufrah	146	29.10 N	18.02 E
Al-Ḥufrah ●[1]	128	28.40 N	38.30 E
Al-Hufūf	128	25.22 N	49.34 E

FRANÇAIS

Nom	Page	Lat.°′	Long.°′ W = Ouest
Al-Ḥulwah	128	23.27 N	46.47 E
Al-Ḥumayshah	144	13.41 N	45.52 E
Al-Ḥumrah ●[1]	128	23.20 N	54.30 E
Al-Ḥuṣayḥiṣah	140	14.44 N	33.18 E
Al-Ḥusaynīyah	142	30.52 N	31.55 E
Al-Ḥusaynīyah ⫧[4]	144	17.48 N	44.27 E
Al-Ḥuwaylizah	132	33.02 N	35.51 E
Al-Ḥuwaymī	144	14.05 N	47.44 E
Al-Ḥuwayyiṭ	128	25.36 N	40.23 E
Alì	70	38.02 N	15.25 E
Ali ●[8]	272a	28.31 N	77.18 E
'Alī, As-Sadd al- (Aswān High Dam) ●[6]	140	23.58 N	32.52 E
Alía, Esp.	34	39.27 N	5.13 W
Alia, It.	70	37.47 N	13.43 E
Äliabad, Azer.	84	41.29 N	46.37 E
'Alīābād, Īrān	128	36.57 N	54.59 E
Alīābād, Pāk.	123	36.18 N	74.37 E
Aliade	150	7.16 N	8.28 E
Aliaga, Esp.	34	40.40 N	0.42 W
Aliağa, Tür.	130	38.48 N	26.59 E
Aliákmon ≃	38	40.30 N	22.36 E
Aliákmonos, Tekhnití Límni ⊜[1]	38	40.15 N	22.00 E
Aliaksin, Cape ›	180	55.30 N	160.43 W
'Alī al-Gharbī	128	32.27 N	46.41 E
Aliança	250	7.35 S	35.13 W
Aliano	68	40.19 N	16.14 E
Alībāg	122	18.39 N	72.54 E
Alibahadır ●[8]	267b	41.11 N	29.12 E
Alibardak	130	38.06 N	40.25 E
Alibates Flint Quarries National Monument ♠	196	35.35 N	101.39 W
Älibäyli	84	41.23 N	46.49 E
Äli Bayramlı	84	39.56 N	48.56 E
Alibey ≃	267b	41.03 N	28.56 E
Alibey, ozero ⊜	78	45.48 N	30.02 E
Alibey Adası I	130	39.20 N	26.38 E
Alibey Barajı ⊜[1]	267b	41.07 N	28.55 E
Alibeyköy ●[8]	267b	41.04 N	28.56 E
Alibijaban Island I	116	13.20 N	122.43 E
Alibori ≃	150	11.56 N	3.17 E
Al-Ibrāhīmīyah	142	30.57 N	31.35 E
Alibunar	38	45.05 N	20.58 E
Alicante → Alacant	34	38.21 N	0.29 W
Alice, S. Afr.	158	32.47 S	26.50 E
Alice, Tx., U.S.	196	27.45 N	98.04 W
Alice ≃, Austl.	164	15.22 S	141.58 E
Alice ≃, Austl.	166	24.02 S	144.50 E
Alice, Punta ›	68	39.24 N	17.10 E
Alice Arm	182	55.29 N	129.29 W
Alicedale	158	33.19 S	26.05 E
Alice Downs	162	17.45 S	127.56 E
Alice Springs	162	23.42 S	133.53 E
Alice Superiore	62	45.28 N	7.47 E
Alice Town	238	25.44 N	79.17 W
Aliceville	194	33.07 N	88.09 W
Alicia, Pil.	116	16.45 N	121.42 E
Alicia, Pil.	116	7.30 N	122.55 E
Alıcık	130	40.49 N	35.21 E
Alick Creek ≃	166	20.25 S	142.00 E
Alicudi, Isola I	70	38.32 N	14.21 E
Alicurá, Embalse de ⊜[1]	254	40.40 S	71.00 W
Al-'Idwah	142	29.21 N	30.55 E
Alief	222	29.43 N	95.35 W
Alife	68	41.20 N	14.20 E
Al-Ifranj	132	31.11 N	35.41 E
Alīganj, India	124	28.07 N	80.36 E
Alīganj, India	124	27.30 N	79.11 E
Alīgarh	124	27.53 N	78.05 E
Alignements de Carnac ⊥	32	47.35 N	3.05 W
Alīgūdarz	128	33.24 N	49.41 E
Alijos, Islas II	232	24.57 N	115.44 W
'Alī Kheyl	120	33.57 N	69.43 E
Al-Ikhṣāṣ al-Qiblīyah	142	29.42 N	31.17 E
Al-Ikhwān II	118	12.08 N	53.10 E
Alikovo	80	55.45 N	46.45 E
Alima ≃	152	1.36 S	16.36 E
Al-Imām ●[8]	273c	30.01 N	31.10 E
Al-Imārāt al-'Arabīyah al-Muttaḥidah → United Arab Emirates □[1]	128	24.00 N	54.00 E
Al-'Imārīyah	142	27.37 N	30.53 E
Alimena	70	37.42 N	14.07 E
Alimini Grande ⊜	68	40.12 N	18.27 E
Alimini Piccolo ⊜	68	40.10 N	18.27 E
Aliminusa	70	37.52 N	13.47 E
Alim Island I	164	2.55 S	147.05 E
Alimkent	85	40.58 N	69.11 E
Alimodian	116	10.49 N	122.26 E
Alindao	152	5.02 N	21.13 E
Alingsås	26	57.56 N	12.31 E
Ālipur, India	272b	22.43 N	88.12 E
Alipur, India	272b	22.55 N	88.11 E
Alīpur, Pāk.	123	29.23 N	70.55 E
Ālīpur ●[8]	126	22.31 N	88.20 E
Ālīpur Duār	124	26.29 N	89.44 E
Alīpur Janūbi	123	30.13 N	71.18 E
Aliquippa	214	40.38 N	80.14 W
Aliquippa-Hopewell Airport ⊠	279b	40.35 N	80.17 W
Alīrājpur	120	22.19 N	74.21 E
Al-'Irāq	132	31.05 N	35.39 E
Al-'Irāq → Iraq □[1]	128	33.00 N	44.00 E
Al-'Irqah	144	13.30 N	47.22 E
Ali-Sabieh	144	11.09 N	42.42 E
Al-'Īsāwīyah	128	30.38 N	37.53 E
Aliseda	34	39.26 N	6.41 W
Alise-Sainte-Reine	58	47.32 N	4.29 E
Alīshārī	84	39.02 N	47.15 E
Al-Iskandarīyah (Alexandria)	142	31.12 N	29.54 E
Al-Iskandarīyah □[4]	142	31.10 N	29.53 E
Al-Ismā'īlīyah (Ismailia)	142	30.35 N	32.16 E
Al-Ismā'īlīyah □[4]	142	30.30 N	32.15 E
Al-Ismā'īlīyah Military Base ■	142	30.35 N	32.14 E
Aliso Canyon V, Ca., U.S.	280	33.53 N	117.40 W
Aliso Canyon V, Ca., U.S.	280	34.18 N	118.33 W
Aliso Creek ≃	228	33.31 N	117.45 W
Al-Istiwā'īyah al-Gharbīyah □[4]	140	5.55 N	28.15 E
Al-Istiwā'īyah ash-Sharqīyah □[4]	154	4.30 N	33.00 E
Alistráti	38	41.04 N	23.57 E
Alitak, Cape ›	180	56.51 N	154.21 W
Alitak Bay c	180	57.00 N	154.05 W
Alitanguo	120	35.10 N	83.30 E
Alì Terme	70	38.01 N	15.26 E
Alivérion	38	38.24 N	24.02 E
Aliwal North	158	30.45 S	26.45 E
Alix	182	52.24 N	113.11 W
Al-'Izzīyah	142	27.13 N	30.59 E
Al-Jabal al-Abyaḍ ∧[2]	142	28.46 N	31.00 E
Al-Jabal al-Aḥmar ∧[2]	142	28.19 N	31.07 E
Al-Jabalayn	140	12.36 N	32.48 E
Al-Jadīdah	140	25.34 N	28.51 E
Al-Jafādūn	142	28.50 N	30.48 E
Al-Jafr	132	30.18 N	36.13 E
Al-Jāfūrah ●[2]	128	24.14 N	50.00 E
Al-Jaghbūb	146	29.45 N	24.31 E
Al-Jaghbūb ⫧[4]	146	29.40 N	24.43 E
Al-Jahrah	128	29.20 N	47.40 E
Al-Jamālīyah	142	31.11 N	31.51 E
Al-Jarnūs	142	28.36 N	30.43 E
Al-Jawf, Ar. Su.	128	29.50 N	39.52 E
Al-Jawf, Lībiyā	146	24.11 N	23.19 E
Al-Jawsh	146	32.00 N	11.40 E
Al-Jaylī	140	16.01 N	32.36 E

PORTUGUÊS

Nome	Página	Lat.°′	Long.°′ W = Oeste
Al-Jazā'ir → Algeria □[1]	148	28.00 N	3.00 E
Al-Jazīrah □[4]	140	14.30 N	33.20 E
Al-Jazīrah ●[1]	140	14.25 N	33.00 E
Aljezur, Bra.	287a	22.40 S	43.36 W
Aljezur, Port.	34	37.19 N	8.48 W
Al-Jibāb	132	33.06 N	36.15 E
Al-Jifārah	128	23.59 N	45.11 E
Al-Jifārah (Jeffara) ≚	146	32.30 N	11.45 E
Al-Jīzah (Giza), Miṣr	142	30.01 N	31.13 E
Al-Jīzah, Urd.	132	31.43 N	35.58 E
Al-Jīzah □[4]	142	29.46 N	31.18 E
Al-Jubayl	128	27.01 N	49.40 E
Al-Jubayn	140	12.07 N	35.10 E
Al-Judaydah	132	33.54 N	35.34 E
Al-Judayyidah, Urd.	132	31.32 N	35.39 E
Al-Judayyidah, Urd.	132	31.15 N	35.49 E
Al-Jufrah ⫧[4]	146	29.10 N	16.00 E
Al-Julaydah ⫧[4]	128	29.03 N	45.38 E
Al-Junaynah, Miṣr	142	31.06 N	31.41 E
Al-Junaynah, Sūd.	140	13.27 N	22.27 E
Al-Junaynah, Sūrīy.	132	32.54 N	36.44 E
Al-Jundīyah	142	28.34 N	30.50 E
Aljustrel	34	37.52 N	8.10 W
Al-Kāb	142	30.57 N	32.18 E
Al-Kabrit Military Base ■	142	30.15 N	32.29 E
Al-Kafr	132	32.38 N	36.38 E
Al-Kafr ash-Sharqī	142	31.17 N	31.10 E
Al-Kahfah	128	27.04 N	43.02 E
Alkali Creek ≃, Ab., Can.	184	50.52 N	110.30 W
Alkali Creek ≃, Wy., U.S.	202	43.16 N	107.40 W
Alkali Lake	182	51.47 N	122.14 W
Alkali Lake ⊜, Nv., U.S.	204	41.42 N	119.50 W
Alkali Lake ⊜, Or., U.S.	202	42.58 N	120.02 W
Alkamari	146	13.24 N	11.07 E
Al-Kāmilīn	140	15.05 N	33.11 E
Al-Karabah	140	18.33 N	33.42 E
Al-Karak	132	31.11 N	35.42 E
Al-Karak □[8]	132	31.10 N	35.45 E
Al-Karnak	140	25.43 N	32.39 E
Al-Kawah	140	13.44 N	32.30 E
Al-Kawd	144	13.05 N	45.22 E
Al-Kawm	130	35.11 N	38.52 E
Al-Kawm al-Akhḍar	142	30.58 N	30.17 E
Al-Kawm Aṭ-Ṭawīl	142	31.12 N	31.05 E
Alken	56	50.15 N	7.26 E
Al-Khabrā'	128	26.04 N	43.33 E
Al-Khābūrah	128	23.59 N	57.08 E
Al-Khafaqān ⊜	128	23.24 N	40.24 E
Al-Khalīl (Hebrón)	132	31.32 N	35.06 E
Al-Khālis	128	33.49 N	44.32 E
Al-Khandaq	140	18.36 N	30.34 E
Al-Khānkah	142	30.13 N	31.21 E
Al-Kharaqānīyah	273c	30.10 N	31.10 E
Al-Khārijah	140	25.26 N	30.33 E
Al-Kharṭūm (Khartoum)	140	15.36 N	32.32 E
Al-Kharṭūm □[4]	140	15.45 N	32.30 E
Al-Kharṭūm Baḥrī	140	15.38 N	32.33 E
Al-Khaṣab	128	26.12 N	56.15 E
Al-Khatam ●[1]	128	24.00 N	55.10 E
Al-Khirbah as-Samrā'	132	32.11 N	36.10 E
Al-Khiyām	132	33.19 N	35.36 E
Al-Khubar	128	26.17 N	50.12 E
Al-Khums (Homs)	146	32.39 N	14.16 E
Al-Khuraybah, Urd.	132	32.40 N	35.52 E
Al-Khuraybah, Yaman	144	15.06 N	48.19 E
Al-Khurmah	144	21.54 N	42.03 E
Al-Khushnīyah	132	33.00 N	35.48 E
Al-Khuṣūṣ	273c	30.09 N	31.19 E
Al-Kifl	128	32.14 N	44.22 E
Al-Kiswah	132	33.21 N	36.14 E
Alkmaar	52	52.37 N	4.44 E
Alkoven	61	48.17 N	14.06 E
Al-Kūbrī	142	30.02 N	32.33 E
Al-Kūfah	128	32.02 N	44.24 E
Al-Kufrah (Cufra) ⫧[4]	146	24.20 N	23.15 E
Al-Kunayyisah	273c	29.59 N	31.11 E
Al-Kuntillah	140	30.00 N	34.41 E
Al-Kūt	128	32.25 N	45.49 E
Al-Kuwayt	128	29.20 N	47.59 E
Al-Kuwayt → Kuwait □[1]	128	29.30 N	47.45 E
Alkvettern ⊜	40	59.25 N	14.21 E
Allaben	210	42.07 N	74.22 W
Al-Labwah	130	34.12 N	36.21 E
Allacapan	116	18.15 N	121.35 E
Allach-Jun'	74	61.08 N	138.03 E
Allada	150	6.39 N	2.09 E
Al-Lādhiqīyah (Latakia)	130	35.31 N	35.47 E
Al-Lādhiqīyah □[8]	130	35.30 N	36.00 E
Allagash ≃	186	47.05 N	69.02 W
Allagen	56	51.28 N	8.14 E
Al-Lagowa	140	11.24 N	29.08 E
Allahābād, India	124	25.27 N	81.51 E
Allāhābād, Pāk.	123	28.57 N	70.53 E
Allāhbās	272a	28.31 N	77.25 E
Allahüekber Dağları ⩘	130	40.35 N	42.32 E
Al-Lāhūn	142	29.13 N	30.59 E
Allāhwardipur	272a	28.33 N	77.26 E
Allaines	50	48.12 N	1.50 E
Allaire State Park ♠	208	40.08 N	74.08 W
Allakaket	180	66.34 N	152.41 W
Allaman	58	46.28 N	6.24 E
Allamuchy	210	40.55 N	74.48 W
Allan	184	51.53 N	106.04 W
Allan, Pointe ›	275a	45.26 N	73.45 W
Allanche	32	45.14 N	2.56 E
Alland	61	48.03 N	16.05 E
Allan Island I	224	48.28 N	122.42 W
Allanmyo	110	19.22 N	95.13 E
Allanridge	158	27.55 S	26.44 E
Allanson	168a	33.20 S	116.06 E
Allanton	46	55.47 N	3.51 W
Allan Water ≃	46	56.08 N	3.56 W
Allapattah Flats ⩩	220	27.08 N	80.27 W
'Allāq, Bi'r ⫧[4]	146	31.05 N	11.42 E
'Allāqī, Wādī al- V	140	22.42 N	33.12 E
Allard, Lac ⊜	186	50.32 N	63.31 W
Allardt	194	36.22 N	84.53 W
Allariz	34	42.11 N	7.48 W
Allatoona Lake ⊜[1]	192	34.08 N	84.38 W
Allauch	62	43.20 N	5.29 E
Al-Layyah	140	16.16 N	35.25 E
Alldays	156	22.44 S	29.04 E
Alle, Bel.	56	49.51 N	4.58 E
Alle, Schw.	58	47.26 N	7.08 E
Ålleberg ∧[2]	26	58.08 N	13.36 E
Allegan	216	42.31 N	85.51 W
Allegan □[6]	216	42.35 N	85.53 W
Allegan, Lake ⊜	216	42.33 N	85.55 W
Allegany	210	42.05 N	78.29 W
Allegany □[6]	210	42.13 N	78.02 W
Allegany Indian Reservation ●[4]	210	42.10 N	78.47 W
Allegany State Park ♠	210	42.04 N	78.44 W
Alleghany	226	39.28 N	120.51 W
Alleghe	64	46.24 N	12.01 E
Allegheny □[6]	214	40.26 N	79.59 W
Allegheny ≃	214	40.27 N	80.00 W
Allegheny Acres	279b	40.37 N	79.53 W
Allegheny Center ʊ	279b	40.27 N	80.01 W
Allegheny County Airport ⊠	279b	40.21 N	79.56 W
Allegheny County Park ♠	279b	40.34 N	79.55 W
Allegheny Mountains ⩘	188	38.30 N	80.00 W
Allegheny Observatory ʊ[3]	279b	40.29 N	80.01 W
Allegheny Plateau ⩘[1]	188	41.30 N	78.00 W
Allegheny Portage Railroad National Historic Site ⊥	214	40.28 N	78.32 W

Allegheny Reservoir ⊜[1]	214	42.00 N	78.56 W
Allègre	62	45.12 N	3.42 E
Allègre, Pointe ›	241o	16.22 N	61.45 W
Allemagne → Germany □[1]	30	51.00 N	10.00 E
Allemands, Lac Des ⊜	194	29.55 N	90.35 W
Allemanskraaldam ⊜[1]	158	28.16 S	27.07 E
Allemant	261	48.45 N	1.37 E
Allemont	62	45.08 N	6.02 E
Allen, Arg.	252	38.58 S	67.50 W
Allen, Pil.	116	12.30 N	124.17 E
Allen, Md., U.S.	208	38.17 N	75.41 W
Allen, Mi., U.S.	216	41.57 N	84.46 W
Allen, Ne., U.S.	198	42.24 N	96.50 W
Allen, Ok., U.S.	196	34.52 N	96.24 W
Allen, Pa., U.S.	208	40.10 N	77.05 W
Allen, S.D., U.S.	198	43.16 N	101.55 W
Allen, Tx., U.S.	222	33.06 N	96.40 W
Allen, Wa., U.S.	224	48.31 N	122.23 W
Allen □[6], In., U.S.	216	41.04 N	85.09 W
Allen □[6], Oh., U.S.	216	40.46 N	84.06 W
Allen ≃	44	54.58 N	2.19 W
Allen, Lough ⊜	48	54.08 N	8.08 W
Allen, Mount ∧, N.Z.	172	47.05 S	167.48 E
Allen, Mount ∧, Ak., U.S.	180	62.14 N	142.13 W
Allenby Bridge ●[5]	132	31.52 N	35.52 E
Allendale, Il., U.S.	194	38.32 N	87.43 W
Allendale, Mi., U.S.	216	42.58 N	85.57 W
Allendale, N.J., U.S.	276	41.02 N	74.07 W
Allendale, S.C., U.S.	192	33.00 N	81.18 W
Allendale Town	44	54.54 N	2.15 W
Allende, Méx.	232	28.20 N	100.51 W
Allende, Méx.	234	18.09 N	94.16 W
Allendorf	56	51.02 N	8.38 E
Allenfarm	222	30.24 N	96.14 W
All England Lawn Tennis Club ♠	260	51.26 N	0.13 W
Allen Grove	216	42.35 N	88.41 W
Allen Park	216	42.15 N	83.12 W
Allenport, Pa., U.S.	214	40.20 N	77.53 W
Allenport, Pa., U.S.	214	40.06 N	79.51 W
Allensbach	58	47.43 N	9.03 E
Allenstein → Olsztyn	30	53.48 N	20.29 E
Allensville	214	40.32 N	77.49 W
Allenton, Mi., U.S.	214	42.55 N	82.57 W
Allenton, R.I., U.S.	207	41.32 N	71.28 W
Allentown, N.J., U.S.	208	40.10 N	74.35 W
Allentown, N.Y., U.S.	210	42.05 N	78.03 W
Allentown, Oh., U.S.	216	40.46 N	84.12 W
Allentown, Pa., U.S.	208	40.36 N	75.28 W
Allentsteig	61	48.42 N	15.20 E
Allenwood, N.J., U.S.	208	40.12 N	74.13 W
Allenwood, N.Y., U.S.	276	40.48 N	73.44 W
Allenwood, Pa., U.S.	210	41.07 N	76.54 W
Alleppey	122	9.29 N	76.19 E
Aller ≃	30	52.57 N	9.11 E
Allerona	66	42.49 N	11.58 E
Allersberg	60	49.15 N	11.15 E
Allershausen	60	48.26 N	11.36 E
Allerslev	41	55.05 N	12.03 E
Allerton, Ia., U.S.	190	40.42 N	93.21 W
Allerton, Ma., U.S.	283	42.18 N	70.53 W
Allerton ●[8]	262	53.22 N	2.53 W
Allerton, Point ›	207	42.18 N	70.53 W
Allestree	42	52.57 N	1.29 W
Allevard	62	45.24 N	6.04 E
Alley Park ♠	276	40.45 N	73.44 W
Alleyton	222	29.43 N	96.29 W
Allgäu ●[1]	58	47.35 N	10.10 E
Allgäuer Alpen ⩘	58	47.20 N	10.25 E
Allhallows	260	51.28 N	0.39 E
Alli ≃	68	38.51 N	16.40 E
Alliance, Ab., Can.	182	52.26 N	111.47 W
Alliance, Ne., U.S.	198	42.12 N	102.58 W
Alliance, Oh., U.S.	214	40.54 N	81.06 W
Allibaudières	50	48.35 N	4.07 E
Al-Lidām	144	20.29 N	44.50 E
Allier □[5]	32	46.25 N	3.00 E
Allier ≃	32	46.58 N	3.04 E
Alligator ≃	192	35.58 N	75.58 W
Alligator Creek ≃, Ga., U.S.	192	31.58 N	82.22 W
Alligator Creek ≃, Tx., U.S.	222	30.42 N	97.07 W
Alligator Lake ⊜	220	28.13 N	81.13 W
Alligator Pond	241q	17.52 N	77.34 W
Alligny-en-Morvan	50	47.12 N	4.10 E
Allihies	48	51.38 N	10.03 W
Allinagaram	122	10.02 N	77.30 E
Allinge	26	55.16 N	14.49 E
Allington Castle ⊥	260	51.17 N	0.31 E
Al-Lisān ›[1]	132	31.17 N	35.28 E
Al-Lisht	142	29.34 N	31.14 E
Allison	190	42.45 N	92.47 W
Allison, Mount ∧	282	37.30 N	121.52 W
Allison Gulch V	280	34.16 N	117.44 W
Allison Park	214	40.34 N	79.57 W
Alliste	68	39.57 N	18.05 E
Alliston	212	44.09 N	79.52 W
Al-Līth	144	20.09 N	40.16 E
Allmendingen	58	48.20 N	9.43 E
Alloa	46	56.07 N	3.49 W
Allochio, Galleria degli ●[5]	66	44.03 N	11.30 E
Allogny	50	47.13 N	2.19 E
Allonby	44	54.46 N	3.25 W
Alloné Abba	132	32.44 N	35.10 E
Allonnes, Fr.	50	48.20 N	1.40 E
Allonnes, Fr.	50	47.58 N	0.09 E
Allora	171a	28.02 S	151.59 E
Allos	62	44.14 N	6.38 E
Allos, Col d')(	62	44.18 N	6.36 E
Allott, Mount ∧[2]	162	26.06 S	124.46 E
Allouez	190	44.28 N	88.00 W
Alloway	208	39.33 N	75.21 W
Alloway Creek ≃	208	39.27 N	75.30 W
Allport	214	40.58 N	78.12 W
Allred Peak ∧	200	40.32 N	108.33 W
All Saints	240c	17.03 N	61.48 W
Allschwil	58	47.33 N	7.33 E
Allstedt	54	51.24 N	11.23 E
Allston ●[8]	283	42.22 N	71.08 W
Alluets, Forêt des ♠	261	48.55 N	1.55 E
Al-Luḥayyah	144	15.42 N	42.42 E
Allumette Lake ⊜	190	45.53 N	77.13 W
Allumettes, Île des I	190	45.50 N	77.05 W
Allumiere	66	42.09 N	11.54 E
Allview Estates	208	39.12 N	76.51 W
Allyn	224	47.23 N	122.49 W
Alm ≃	60	48.05 N	13.55 E
Alma, N.B., Can.	186	45.36 N	64.57 W
Alma, P.Q., Can.	186	48.33 N	71.39 W
Alma, Ar., U.S.	194	35.28 N	94.13 W
Alma, Ga., U.S.	192	31.32 N	82.27 W
Alma, Il., U.S.	219	38.43 N	88.55 W
Alma, Ks., U.S.	198	39.01 N	96.17 W
Alma, Mi., U.S.	190	43.22 N	84.39 W
Alma, Ne., U.S.	198	40.05 N	99.21 W
Alma, N.Y., U.S.	210	42.01 N	78.03 W
Alma, Wi., U.S.	190	44.19 N	91.54 W
Al-Ma'ābidah	142	27.20 N	31.01 E
Al-Ma'ādī ●[8]	142	29.58 N	31.15 E
Alma-Ata → Almaty	85	43.15 N	76.57 E
Alma-Atinskij zapovednik ♠	85	43.10 N	77.25 E
Alma Center	190	44.26 N	90.54 W
Almada	34	38.41 N	9.09 W
Almaden, Austl.	166	17.20 S	144.41 E
Almadén, Esp.	34	38.46 N	4.50 W
Almadén de la Plata	34	37.52 N	6.04 W
Al-Madīnah (Medina)	128	24.28 N	39.36 E
Al-Madīnah al-Fikrīyah	142	27.56 N	30.49 E
Al-Madwar	132	32.17 N	36.00 E
Al-Mafāzah	140	13.36 N	34.33 E

Al-Mafraq	132	32.21 N	36.12 E
Al-Mafraq □[8]	132	32.15 N	36.30 E
Almafuerte	252	32.12 S	64.15 W
Al-Maghārīm	144	15.01 N	47.51 E
Al-Maghrah ⫧[4]	140	30.14 N	28.56 E
Almagor	132	32.55 N	35.36 E
Almagre, Laguna c	234	23.48 N	97.48 W
Al-Magreb → Morocco □[1]	148	32.00 N	5.00 W
Almagro	34	38.53 N	3.43 W
Almagro Island I	116	11.56 N	124.18 E
Al-Maḥallah al-Kubrā	142	30.58 N	31.10 E
Al-Maḥārīq	140	25.37 N	30.39 E
Al Mahbas	148	27.13 N	9.44 W
Alma Hill ∧[2]	210	42.03 N	78.01 W
Al-Maḥmūdīyah	142	31.11 N	30.32 E
Al-Maḥraṣ	142	27.49 N	30.48 E
Al-Maḥsamah	142	30.34 N	32.01 E
Al-Majdal	132	32.47 N	36.30 E
Al-Majma'ah	128	25.54 N	45.20 E
Almăjului, Munții ⩘	38	44.43 N	22.12 E
Al-Maks ●[8]	142	31.09 N	29.51 E
Al-Mālikīyah	130	37.10 N	42.08 E
Almalyk	85	40.50 N	69.35 E
Al-Ma'mūrah ●[8]	142	31.18 N	30.03 E
Al-Manāmah	128	26.13 N	50.35 E
Al-Manāqil	140	14.15 N	32.59 E
Al-Manāṣif ●[1]	130	35.17 N	40.50 E
Al-Manāwāt	273c	29.55 N	31.14 E
Almanor, Lake ⊜	204	40.15 N	121.08 W
Almansa	34	38.52 N	1.05 W
Al-Manshāh	140	26.28 N	31.48 E
Al-Manṣūrah, Golan	132	33.08 N	35.48 E
Al-Manṣūrah, Miṣr	142	31.03 N	31.23 E
Al-Manṣūrīyah	142	30.08 N	31.05 E
Almanza	34	42.39 N	5.02 W
Al-Manzilah	142	31.09 N	31.56 E
Almanzor ∧	34	40.15 N	5.18 W
Almanzora ≃	34	37.14 N	1.46 W
Almar ≃	34	40.54 N	5.29 W
Al-Marāghah	140	26.42 N	31.36 E
Almargem do Bispo	266c	38.51 N	9.16 W
Al-Marj	146	32.30 N	20.54 E
Al-Marj ●[8]	273c	30.09 N	31.20 E
Almas	250	11.33 S	47.09 W
Almaş ≃	38	47.14 N	23.19 E
Almas, Pico das ∧	255	13.33 S	41.56 W
Al-Ma'ṣarah, Miṣr	142	27.42 N	30.52 E
Al-Ma'ṣarah, Miṣr	142	31.13 N	31.19 E
Al-Ma'sarah ●[8]	142	29.54 N	31.17 E
Al-Mashqūq	132	32.24 N	36.43 E
Al-Mashrafah	130	34.50 N	36.52 E
Al-Masīd	140	15.15 N	32.57 E
Almassora	34	39.57 N	0.03 W
Al-Matammah	140	16.43 N	33.22 E
Al-Maṭarīyah	142	31.11 N	32.02 E
Al-Maṭarīyah ●[8]	142	30.07 N	31.19 E
Al-Matnah	140	13.47 N	35.03 E
Almaty (Alma-Ata)	85	43.15 N	76.57 E
Almaty □[8]	86	44.00 N	77.00 E
Al-Mawṣil (Mosul)	128	36.20 N	43.08 E
Al-Mayādīn	130	35.01 N	40.27 E
Al-Maymūn	142	29.14 N	31.12 E
Almazán	34	41.29 N	2.32 W
Al-Mazār, Urd.	132	31.04 N	35.42 E
Almazar, Uzb.	85	40.59 N	68.54 E
Almaznyj	83	48.02 N	40.03 E
Almazovo	265b	55.51 N	38.02 E
Al-Mazra'ah	132	31.16 N	35.31 E
Al-Mazzah	132	33.30 N	36.15 E
Alme	56	51.28 N	8.37 E
Almeer	52	52.20 N	5.14 E
Almeida	34	40.43 N	6.54 W
Almeirim, Bra.	250	1.32 S	52.34 W
Almeirim, Port.	34	39.12 N	8.38 W
Almelo	52	52.21 N	6.39 E
Almena	198	39.53 N	99.42 W
Almenara	255	16.11 S	40.42 W
Almenar de Soria	34	41.41 N	2.12 W
Almendares ≃	286b	23.08 N	82.25 W
Almendra, Embalse de ⊜[1]	34	41.15 N	6.10 W
Almendralejo	34	38.41 N	6.24 W
Almenêches	50	48.42 N	0.07 E
Al'menevo	86	54.57 N	63.34 E
Almenno San Salvatore	62	45.45 N	9.35 E
Almería	34	36.50 N	2.27 W
Almería □[4]	34	37.10 N	2.25 W
Almería, Golfo de c	34	36.46 N	2.30 W
Al'metjevsk	80	54.53 N	52.20 E
Al'mež	24	60.03 N	48.03 E
Älmhult	26	56.33 N	14.08 E
Al-Midhnab	128	25.54 N	44.14 E
Al-Mīnā'	130	34.27 N	35.49 E
Almina, Punta de ›	34	35.53 N	5.15 W
Almino Afonso	250	6.09 S	37.46 W
Al-Minshāt al-Kubrā	142	31.03 N	30.54 E
Al-Minūfīyah □[4]	142	30.30 N	31.00 E
Al-Minyā, Miṣr	142	28.06 N	30.45 E
Al-Minyā, Miṣr	142	29.45 N	31.18 E
Al-Minyā, Miṣr	142	29.14 N	30.45 E
Al-Minyā □[4]	142	28.26 N	30.42 E
Al-Miqdādīyah	128	33.59 N	44.56 E
Almira	202	47.42 N	118.56 W
Almirantazgo, Islas → Admiralty Islands II	164	2.10 S	147.00 E
Almirantazgo, Montes → Admiralty Mountains ⩘	9	71.45 S	168.30 E
Almirante	236	9.18 N	82.24 W
Almirante, Bahía de c	236	9.20 N	82.18 W
Almirante Brown	258	34.48 S	58.23 W
Almirante Brown □[5]	288	34.50 S	58.20 W
Almirante Guillermo Brown, Parque ♠	288	34.40 S	58.28 W
Almirante Latorre	252	29.38 S	70.58 W
Almirante Montt, Golfo ⋓	254	51.55 S	72.45 W
Almirós	38	39.11 N	22.46 E
Almiroú, Kólpos c	38	35.23 N	24.20 E
Al-Mismīyah	132	33.08 N	36.23 E
Almo	202	42.06 N	113.37 W
Almoçageme	266c	38.48 N	9.28 W
Almodôvar	34	37.31 N	8.04 W
Almodóvar del Campo	34	38.43 N	4.10 W
Almolonga	236	14.49 N	91.30 W
Almond, N.Y., U.S.	210	42.19 N	77.44 W
Almond, Wi., U.S.	190	44.15 N	89.24 W
Almond ≃, Scot., U.K.	46	56.25 N	3.27 W
Almond ≃, Scot., U.K.	46	55.58 N	3.18 W
Almondbank	46	56.24 N	3.33 W
Almondsbury	42	51.34 N	2.34 W
Almonesson	208	39.49 N	75.06 W
Almont	214	42.55 N	83.02 W
Almont ≃	261	48.32 N	2.40 E
Almonte, On., Can.	212	45.14 N	76.12 W
Almonte, Esp.	34	37.15 N	6.31 W
Almonte, Ca., U.S.	282	37.53 N	122.32 W
Almonte ≃	34	39.42 N	6.28 W
Almora	124	29.37 N	79.40 E
Almsee ⊜	64	47.45 N	13.57 E
Älmsta	40	59.58 N	18.48 E
Al-Mu'aḍḍamīyah	132	33.45 N	36.39 E
Al-Mubarraz, Ar. Su.	128	25.25 N	49.35 E
Al-Mubarraz, Ar. Su.	144	22.17 N	46.44 E
Al-Mudawwarah	128	29.19 N	35.59 E
Almudévar	34	42.03 N	0.35 W
Al-Muglad	140	11.02 N	27.44 E
Al-Muḥarraq	128	26.16 N	50.37 E
Al-Mukallā	144	14.32 N	49.08 E
Al-Mukhā (Mocha)	144	13.19 N	43.15 E
Al-Munājāt al-Kubrā	142	30.50 N	32.01 E
Almuñécar	34	36.43 N	3.41 W
Almunge	40	59.53 N	18.03 E
Al-Muntazah ●[8]	142	31.17 N	30.01 E

Almus	130	40.23 N	36.55 E
Al-Musallamīyah	140	14.34 N	33.21 E
Al-Musayfirah	132	32.37 N	36.20 E
Al-Musayjīd	128	24.05 N	39.06 E
Al-Musayyib	128	32.47 N	44.18 E
Almus Barajı ⊜[1]	130	40.20 N	37.00 E
Al-Mushannaf	132	32.44 N	36.46 E
Al-Musharrak Qiblī	142	29.23 N	30.34 E
Al-Mutā'iyah	132	32.29 N	36.17 E
Al-Mu'tamadīyah	142	31.02 N	31.05 E
Al-Mutayn	132	33.54 N	35.44 E
Al-Muthannā □[4]	128	30.30 N	45.15 E
Al-Muṭī'ah	142	27.08 N	31.18 E
Al-Muwaqqar ⊥	132	31.49 N	36.06 E
Al-Muwassam	144	16.25 N	42.20 E
Al-Muwayh	144	22.45 N	41.36 E
Al-Muwayliḥ	128	27.41 N	35.27 E
Aln ≃	44	55.23 N	1.37 W
Alnarp	41	55.39 N	13.05 E
Al-Narrānīyah	273c	29.58 N	31.10 E
Al'n'aš	80	56.44 N	54.43 E
Alnaši	80	56.11 N	52.28 E
Al-Nasser	140	24.32 N	32.55 E
Alne ≃	42	52.13 N	1.52 W
Alness	46	57.41 N	4.15 W
Alnmouth	44	55.23 N	1.36 W
Alnön I	26	62.25 N	17.26 E
Alnor	41	54.55 N	9.36 E
Alnwick	44	55.25 N	1.42 W
Alnwick Indian Reserve ●[4]	212	44.10 N	78.06 W
Alo	146	11.47 N	20.53 E
Aloândia	255	17.43 S	49.29 W
Alofau	174u	14.16 S	170.36 W
Alofi	174v	19.01 S	169.55 W
Alofi, Île I	14	14.21 S	178.02 W
Alofi Bay c	174v	19.01 S	169.56 W
Aloha	224	45.29 N	122.51 W
Aloha, Lake ⊜	226	38.52 N	120.09 W
Aloi	154	2.17 N	33.10 E
Aloja	76	57.46 N	24.53 E
Alondra	280	33.55 N	118.15 W
Along	120	28.18 N	94.39 E
Alónnisos	38	39.08 N	23.50 E
Alónnisos I	38	39.13 N	23.55 E
Alor, Kepulauan II	112	8.15 S	124.30 E
Alor, Pulau I	112	8.15 S	124.45 E
Alor, Selat ⋓	112	8.20 S	123.48 E
Álora	34	36.48 N	4.42 W
Alor Gajah	114	2.23 N	102.13 E
Alor Setar	114	6.07 N	100.22 E
Alor Star → Alor Setar	114	6.07 N	100.22 E
Alorton	219	38.36 N	90.08 W
Al'oškino	88	58.35 N	100.32 E
Al'ošn'a, Ross.	76	53.38 N	33.29 E
Al'ošn'a, Ross.	82	54.14 N	37.16 E
Alosno	34	37.33 N	7.07 W
Alost → Aalst	50	50.56 N	4.02 E
Alotau	164	10.14 S	150.30 E
Alouette ≃	224	49.16 N	122.42 W
Alouette Lake ⊜	224	49.19 N	122.28 W
Alovo	80	54.38 N	46.27 E
Aloxe-Corton	58	47.04 N	4.52 E
Aloysius, Mount ∧	162	26.01 S	128.34 E
Alpachiri	252	37.22 S	63.46 W
Alpaugh	226	35.53 N	119.29 W
Alpen	52	51.35 N	6.30 E
Alpen → Alps ⩘	32	46.25 N	10.00 E
Alpena, Ar., U.S.	194	36.17 N	93.17 W
Alpena, Mi., U.S.	190	45.03 N	83.25 W
Alpena, S.D., U.S.	198	44.10 N	98.21 W
Alpercatas ≃	250	6.02 S	44.19 W
Alpes → Alps ⩘	32	46.25 N	10.00 E
Alpes-de-Haute-Provence □[5]	62	44.10 N	6.00 E
Alpes Dináricos → Dinara ⩘	36	43.50 N	16.35 E
Alpes-Maritimes □[5]	62	44.00 N	7.10 E
Alpes Marítimos → Maritime Alps ⩘	62	44.15 N	7.10 E
Alpes Transilvanos → Carpații Meridionali ⩘	38	45.30 N	24.15 E
Alpha, Austl.	166	23.39 S	146.38 E
Alpha, Il., U.S.	190	41.12 N	90.23 W
Alpha, Mi., U.S.	190	46.02 N	88.22 W
Alpha, N.J., U.S.	210	40.40 N	75.09 W
Alpharetta	192	34.04 N	84.17 W
Alphen aan den Rijn	52	52.07 N	4.40 E
Alphington	42	50.42 N	3.31 W
Alphin Pike ∧[2]	262	53.31 N	2.00 W
Alphonse Island I	138	7.00 S	52.45 E
Alpi → Alps ⩘	32	46.25 N	10.00 E
Alpi, Monte ∧	68	40.07 N	15.59 E
Alpiarça	34	39.15 N	8.35 W
Alpi Dinariche → Dinara ⩘	36	43.50 N	16.35 E
Alpignano	62	45.06 N	7.31 E
Alpilles, Chaîne des ⩘[2]	62	43.45 N	4.50 E
Alpine, Az., U.S.	200	33.50 N	109.08 W
Alpine, Ca., U.S.	204	32.50 N	116.47 W
Alpine, N.J., U.S.	276	40.57 N	73.55 W
Alpine, N.Y., U.S.	210	42.19 N	76.44 W
Alpine, Tx., U.S.	196	30.21 N	103.39 W
Alpine □[6]	226	38.41 N	119.47 W
Alpine Creek ≃	282	37.19 N	122.17 W
Alpine National Park ♠	166	37.00 S	147.15 E
Alpinópolis	255	20.52 S	46.23 W
Alpi Retiche → Rhaetian Alps ⩘	58	46.30 N	10.00 E
Alpirsbach	58	48.21 N	8.23 E
Alplaus Kill ≃	210	42.51 N	73.54 W
Alpnachstad	58	46.57 N	8.17 E
Alps ⩘	22	46.25 N	10.00 E
Alpsee ⊜	58	47.34 N	10.10 E
Alpu	130	39.47 N	30.58 E
Al-Qābil	128	23.57 N	55.48 E
Al-Qābūn	132	33.33 N	36.20 E
Al-Qadam	132	33.28 N	36.17 E
Al-Qaḍārif	140	14.02 N	35.24 E
Al-Qadīmah	144	22.21 N	39.09 E
Al-Qādisīyah □[4]	128	31.55 N	45.00 E
Al-Qāhirah (Cairo), Miṣr	142	30.03 N	31.15 E
Al-Qāhirah (Cairo), Miṣr	273c	30.03 N	31.15 E
Al-Qāhirah □[4]	142	30.02 N	31.17 E
Al-Qāhirah West Military Base ■	142	30.06 N	30.56 E
Al-Qaḥmah	144	18.00 N	41.41 E
Al-Qā'im	128	34.21 N	41.07 E
Al-Qā'īyah ⫧[4]	128	26.27 N	45.35 E
Al-Qāiyāt	142	28.40 N	30.41 E
Al-Qalaj	142	30.11 N	31.21 E
Al-Qalībah	128	28.32 N	37.42 E
Al-Qalyūbīyah □[4]	142	30.18 N	31.18 E
Al-Qāmishlī	130	37.02 N	41.14 E
Al-Qanāṭir al-Khayrīyah	142	30.12 N	31.08 E
Al-Qanāyāt	142	30.37 N	31.28 E
Al-Qanṭarah	142	30.52 N	32.19 E
Al-Qaryah ash-Sharqīyah	146	30.24 N	13.36 E
Al-Qaryatayn	130	34.14 N	37.14 E
Al-Qaṣabāt	146	32.35 N	14.03 E
Al-Qaṣābī	142	31.16 N	30.41 E
Al-Qaṣr, Miṣr	140	25.42 N	28.53 E
Al-Qaṣr, Urd.	132	31.19 N	35.45 E
Al-Qaṣṣāṣīn	142	30.34 N	31.56 E
Al-Qaṭīf	128	26.33 N	50.00 E
Al-Qaṭrānah	132	31.15 N	36.03 E
Al-Qaṭrūn	146	24.56 N	14.38 E
Al-Qaṭṭā	142	30.13 N	30.58 E

≃	River	Fluß	Río	Rivière	Rio
≊	Canal	Kanal	Canal	Canal	Canal
ʟ	Waterfall, Rapids	Wasserfall, Stromschnellen	Cascada, Rápidos	Chute d'eau, Rapides	Cascata, Rápidos
⋓	Strait	Meeresstraße	Estrecho	Détroit	Estreito
c	Bay, Gulf	Bucht, Golf	Bahía, Golfo	Baie, Golfe	Baía, Golfo
⊜	Lake, Lakes	See, Seen	Lago, Lagos	Lac, Lacs	Lago, Lagos
⩩	Swamp	Sumpf	Pantano	Marais	Pântano
⍓	Ice Features, Glacier	Eis- und Gletscherformen	Accidentes Glaciales	Formes glaciaires	Acidentes glaciares
⫧	Other Hydrographic Features	Andere Hydrographische Objekte	Otros Elementos Hidrográficos	Autres données hydrographiques	Outros acidentes hidrográficos
✣	Submarine Features	Untermeerische Objekte	Accidentes Submarinos	Formes de relief sous-marin	Acidentes submarinos
□	Political Unit	Politische Einheit	Unidad Politica	Entité politique	Unidade política
ʊ	Cultural Institution	Kulturelle Institution	Institución Cultural	Institution culturelle	Institução cultural
⊥	Historical Site	Historische Stätte	Sitio Histórico	Site historique	Sitio histórico
♠	Recreational Site	Erholungs- und Ferienort	Sitio de Recreo	Centre de loisirs	Area de Lazer
⊠	Airport	Flughafen	Aeropuerto	Aéroport	Aeroporto
■	Military Installation	Militäranlage	Instalación Militar	Installation militaire	Instalação militar
●	Miscellaneous	Verschiedenes	Misceláneo	Divers	Diversos

Name	Page	Lat.°′	Long.°′
Al-Qaṭṭāwīyah	142	30.33 N	31.40 E
Al-Qays	142	28.29 N	30.47 E
Al-Qayṣūmah	128	28.16 N	46.03 E
Al-Qir'awn	132	33.34 N	35.43 E
Al-Qiṣfah	132	32.38 N	35.52 E
Al-Quds → Yerushalayim	132	31.46 N	35.14 E
Alquízar	240p	22.48 N	82.35 W
Al-Qun'abah	132	33.08 N	35.40 E
Al-Qunayṭirah	132	33.07 N	35.49 E
Al-Qunayṭirah ▫[8]	132	33.00 N	35.50 E
Al-Qunfudhah	144	19.08 N	41.05 E
Al-Qurayn	142	30.37 N	31.44 E
Al-Qurayyah	132	32.32 N	36.36 E
Al-Qurnah	128	31.00 N	47.26 E
Al-Quṣaymah	132	30.40 N	34.22 E
Al-Quṣayr, Miṣr	128	26.06 N	34.17 E
Al-Quṣayr, Miṣr	142	27.27 N	30.52 E
Al-Quṣayr, Sūrīy.	130	34.31 N	36.35 E
Al-Qūṣīyah	142	27.26 N	30.49 E
Al-Quṭayfah	132	33.44 N	36.36 E
Al-Quṭaynah	140	14.52 N	32.21 E
Al-Quway'īyah	128	24.03 N	45.15 E
Al-Quwaysī	140	13.20 N	34.05 E
Alrø I	41	55.51 N	10.05 E
Alroy Downs	162	19.18 S	136.04 E
Als I	41	54.59 N	9.55 E
Alsace ▫[9]	58	48.30 N	7.30 E
Alsace, Ballon d' ∧	58	47.50 N	6.51 E
Alsager	44	53.06 N	2.17 W
Al'šany	78	52.05 N	27.20 E
Alsask	184	51.23 N	109.59 W
Alsasua	34	42.54 N	2.10 W
Alsdorf	56	50.53 N	6.10 E
Alsea	202	44.22 N	123.35 W
Alsea ≃	202	44.26 N	124.05 W
Alsek ≃	180	59.10 N	138.10 W
Alsen	198	48.37 N	98.42 W
Alseno	64	44.54 N	9.59 E
Alsenz	56	49.43 N	7.49 E
Alsenz ≃	56	49.49 N	7.51 E
Alsey	219	39.34 N	90.25 W
Alsfeld	56	50.45 N	9.16 E
Als Fjord ⊂[2]	41	55.02 N	9.38 E
Alsh, Loch ⊂	46	57.15 N	5.39 W
Al-Shallūfa Military Base ■	142	30.03 N	32.32 E
Alsike	40	59.45 N	17.45 E
Alsina	252	33.54 S	59.23 W
Alsip	216	41.40 N	87.44 W
Alsleben	54	51.42 N	11.41 E
Alsónémedi	264c	47.19 N	19.10 E
Alstaden ◆[8]	263	51.28 N	6.50 E
Alstäket	40	59.20 N	18.28 E
Alstätte	52	52.08 N	6.55 E
Alstead ≃	184	55.50 N	107.26 W
Alster	40	59.24 N	13.36 E
Alster ≃	52	53.36 N	9.59 E
Alsterbro	26	56.57 N	15.55 E
Alstern ⊜	40	59.40 N	13.55 E
Alston	44	54.49 N	2.26 W
Alsunga	76	56.59 N	21.34 E
Alswede	52	52.20 N	8.33 E
Alt ≃	44	53.32 N	3.03 W
Alta, Nor.	24	69.55 N	23.12 E
Älta, Sve.	40	59.16 N	18.11 E
Alta, Ca., U.S.	226	39.12 N	120.49 W
Alta, Ia., U.S.	198	42.40 N	95.17 W
Alta, Cachoeira L	250	5.46 S	54.28 W
Alta, Mount ∧	172	44.30 S	168.58 E
Altadena	228	34.11 N	118.07 W
Alta Floresta	250	9.57 S	56.06 W
Alta Gracia, Arg.	252	31.40 S	64.26 W
Altagracia, Nic.	236	11.34 N	85.35 W
Altagracia, Ven.	246	10.43 N	71.32 W
Altagracia de Orituco	246	9.52 N	66.23 W
Alta Hill	226	39.14 N	121.04 W
Altai ⛰	90	48.00 N	90.00 E
Altair	222	29.34 N	96.28 W
Altaj, Mong.	86	48.18 N	89.35 E
Altaj (Jesönbulag), Mong.	90	46.20 N	96.18 E
Altaj, Ross.	86	53.27 N	91.48 E
Altaj ▫[3]	86	51.00 N	86.00 E
Altajskij	86	51.58 N	85.22 E
Alta Loma	222	29.22 N	95.04 W
Altamaha ≃	192	31.19 N	81.17 W
Altamira, Arg.	258	34.40 S	59.22 W
Altamira, Bra.	250	3.12 S	52.12 W
Altamira, Chile	252	25.47 S	69.51 W
Altamira, C.R.	236	10.30 N	84.23 W
Altamira, Méx.	234	22.24 N	97.55 W
Altamira, Las Cuevas de ±[5]	34	43.18 N	4.08 W
Altamirano, Arg.	258	35.21 S	58.09 W
Altamirano, Méx.	196	25.55 N	97.47 W
Altamont, Il., U.S.	219	39.03 N	88.44 W
Altamont, Ks., U.S.	198	37.11 N	95.17 W
Altamont, N.Y., U.S.	210	42.42 N	74.02 W
Altamont, Or., U.S.	202	42.12 N	121.44 W
Altamont, Tn., U.S.	194	35.25 N	85.43 W
Altamonte Springs	220	28.39 N	81.21 W
Altamont Pass)(	226	37.45 N	121.40 W
Altamura	68	40.50 N	16.33 E
Altamura, Isla I	232	25.00 N	108.10 W
Altan, Ross.	88	49.31 N	111.32 E
Altan, Ross.	88	49.53 N	109.04 E
Altanbulag, Mong.	88	50.19 N	106.30 E
Altanbulag, Mong.	88	47.41 N	106.22 E
Altan-Cögor	86	49.03 N	90.27 E
Altanširee	102	45.35 N	110.27 E
Altar	232	30.43 N	111.44 W
Altar ≃	232	30.39 N	111.53 W
Altar, Desierto de ◆[2]	232	31.50 N	114.15 W
Altar de Los Sacrificios ⊥	232	16.28 N	90.32 W
Altare	62	44.20 N	8.20 E
Altario	184	51.55 N	110.09 W
Altarnun	42	50.37 N	4.30 W
Altar of the Earth ʊ[1]	271a	39.57 N	116.24 E
Altar of the Moon ʊ[1]	271a	39.55 N	116.20 E
Altar of the Sun ʊ[1]	271a	39.54 N	116.27 E
Altar Wash V	200	32.05 N	111.19 W
Altaskij Kraj ▫[8]	86	52.30 N	83.00 E
Altastenberg	56	51.11 N	8.28 E
Altata, Méx.	232	24.38 N	107.55 W
Altata, Ross.	80	51.07 N	48.44 E
Alta Verapaz ▫[5]	236	15.40 N	90.00 W
Altavilla Irpina	68	41.00 N	14.47 E
Altavilla Milicia	70	38.02 N	13.32 E
Altavilla Silentina	68	40.32 N	15.08 E
Alta Vista, Ks., U.S.	198	38.51 N	96.29 W
Altavista, Va., U.S.	192	37.06 N	79.17 W
Altay, Ross.	86	60.20 N	68.58 E
Altay, Zhg.	86	47.52 N	88.07 E
Altay → Altaj ▫[3]	86	51.00 N	86.00 E
Alt Buchhorst	264a	52.26 N	13.51 E
Altdöbern	54	51.39 N	14.02 E
Altdorf, Dtsch.	60	48.34 N	12.07 E
Altdorf, Schw.	58	46.53 N	8.39 E
Altdorf bei Nürnberg	60	49.23 N	11.21 E
Alte Donau ⊜	264b	48.14 N	16.26 E
Alteelva ≃	24	69.58 N	23.23 E
Altefähr	54	54.20 N	13.07 E
Alteglofsheim	60	48.55 N	12.12 E
Alte Grund	264a	52.28 N	13.47 E
Altena	56	51.17 N	7.40 E
Altenahr	56	50.31 N	6.59 E
Altenau	52	51.48 N	10.26 E
Altenbeken	52	51.46 N	8.56 E
Altenberg	54	50.46 N	13.45 E
Altenberge	52	52.03 N	7.27 E
Altenbruch	52	53.49 N	8.46 E
Altenbüren	56	51.23 N	8.30 E
Altenburg, Dtsch.	54	50.59 N	12.26 E
Altenburg, Öst.	61	48.38 N	15.35 E
Altenderne Oberbecker ◆[8]	263	51.35 N	7.33 E
Altendorf	263	51.29 N	7.40 E
Altendorf ◆[8]	263	51.25 N	7.06 E
Altendorf-Ulfkotte	263	51.38 N	7.00 E
Altenesch	52	53.08 N	8.37 E
Altenessen ◆[8]	263	51.29 N	7.00 E
Altenfelden	60	48.29 N	13.58 E
Altengamme ◆[8]	52	53.25 N	10.16 E
Altenglan	56	49.33 N	7.28 E
Altenhagen, Dtsch.	52	52.03 N	8.38 E
Altenhagen, Dtsch.	54	53.45 N	13.06 E
Altenhagen ◆[8]	263	51.22 N	7.28 E
Altenhof	54	52.55 N	13.43 E
Altenholz	41	54.24 N	10.07 E
Altenkirchen, Dtsch.	54	54.38 N	13.20 E
Altenkirchen (Westerwald), Dtsch.	56	50.41 N	7.38 E
Altenkrempe	54	54.08 N	10.49 E
Altenkunstadt	54	50.07 N	11.14 E
Altenmarkt an der Alz	60	48.00 N	12.32 E
Altenmünster	58	48.28 N	10.35 E
Altenoythe	52	53.02 N	7.52 E
Altenpleen	54	54.21 N	12.57 E
Altenstadt an der Waldnaab	60	49.48 N	12.10 E
Altensteig	56	48.35 N	8.37 E
Altentreptow	54	53.42 N	13.14 E
Altenvoerde	263	51.18 N	7.22 E
Altenwalde	52	53.49 N	8.40 E
Altenweddingen	54	52.00 N	11.31 E
Alte Oder ≃	54	52.52 N	14.09 E
Alter do Chão	34	39.12 N	7.40 W
Alterosa	256	21.15 S	46.08 W
Alter Rhein ≃	263	51.35 N	6.36 E
Altes Land ◆[1]	52	53.33 N	9.38 E
Altevatnet ⊜	24	68.32 N	19.30 E
Altfraunhofen	60	48.27 N	12.10 E
Altfriedland	54	52.38 N	14.12 E
Altglashütten	58	47.51 N	8.06 E
Alt-Glienicke ◆[8]	264a	52.25 N	13.32 E
Altgruland	263	51.27 N	7.41 E
Altha	192	30.34 N	85.07 W
Altham	262	53.47 N	2.21 W
Alt-Hartmannsdorf	264a	52.21 N	13.50 E
Althea Lake ⊜	283	42.40 N	71.23 W
Altheim	60	48.15 N	13.13 E
Altheimer	194	34.19 N	91.50 W
Althofen	61	46.54 N	14.27 E
Altıağaç	84	40.50 N	48.54 E
Altınekin	130	38.19 N	32.53 E
Altinho	250	8.29 S	36.04 W
Altınoluk	130	39.34 N	26.44 E
Altinópolis	255	21.02 S	47.23 W
Altınova	130	39.13 N	26.47 E
Altınözü	130	36.08 N	36.12 E
Altıntaş	130	39.04 N	30.07 E
Altınyaka	130	36.34 N	30.21 E
Altiplano ⛰[1]	248	18.00 S	68.00 W
Alt Käbelich	54	53.29 N	13.29 E
Altkirch	58	47.37 N	7.15 E
Altkirchen	54	50.56 N	12.21 E
Altlandsberg	54	52.33 N	13.43 E
Altlangerwisch	264a	52.19 N	13.04 E
Altlewin	54	52.42 N	14.16 E
Altlüdersdorf	54	53.02 N	13.11 E
Altlünen	52	51.38 N	7.31 E
Altmannsdorf ◆[8]	264b	48.10 N	16.20 E
Altmannstein	60	48.54 N	11.39 E
Altmar	212	43.31 N	76.00 W
Altmark ◆[1]	54	52.40 N	11.20 E
Alt Meteln	54	53.45 N	11.21 E
Altmittweida	54	50.58 N	12.57 E
Altmühl ≃	60	48.54 N	11.54 E
Altmünster	64	47.54 N	13.45 E
Altnaharra	46	58.16 N	4.27 W
Alto, Mi., U.S.	216	42.51 N	85.22 W
Alto, Tx., U.S.	222	31.39 N	95.04 W
Alto, Cerro ∧, Méx.	234	20.50 N	100.22 W
Alto, Cerro ∧, Ca., U.S.	226	35.25 N	120.43 W
Alto Anapu ≃	250	2.15 S	51.27 W
Alto Araguaia	255	17.19 S	53.12 W
Alto Cauale	152	7.34 S	16.16 E
Alto Cedro	240p	20.31 N	75.58 W
Alto Chicapa	152	10.53 S	19.14 E
Alto Coité	255	15.47 S	54.20 W
Alto Cuito	152	13.27 S	18.49 E
Alto da Moóca ◆[8]	287b	23.34 S	46.35 W
Alto da Serra	256	22.53 S	44.14 W
Alto de las Vizcachas, Cerro ∧	286e	33.25 S	70.26 W
Alto del Carmen	252	28.46 S	70.30 W
Alto de Ña Paula	286c	10.24 N	66.48 W
Alto do Rio Doce	255	21.02 S	43.25 W
Altofonte	70	38.03 N	13.18 E
Alto Garças	255	16.56 S	53.32 W
Alto Ligonha	154	15.30 S	38.20 E
Alto Longá	250	5.15 S	42.12 W
Alto Lucero	234	19.37 N	96.43 W
Alto Molócuè	154	15.38 S	37.42 E
Altomonte	68	39.42 N	16.08 E
Altomünster	60	48.23 N	11.15 E
Alton, On., Can.	212	43.52 N	80.04 W
Alton, Eng., U.K.	42	51.09 N	0.59 W
Alton, Il., U.S.	219	38.53 N	90.11 W
Alton, Ia., U.S.	198	42.59 N	96.00 W
Alton, Ks., U.S.	198	39.28 N	98.56 W
Alton, Ky., U.S.	218	38.04 N	84.55 W
Alton, Mo., U.S.	194	36.41 N	91.23 W
Alton, N.H., U.S.	188	43.27 N	71.13 W
Alton, N.Y., U.S.	210	43.13 N	76.59 W
Alton, R.I., U.S.	207	41.26 N	71.43 W
Altona, Austl.	162	27.34 S	120.00 E
Altona, Austl.	169	37.52 S	144.50 E
Altona, Mb., Can.	184	49.06 N	97.33 W
Altona, In., U.S.	216	41.21 N	85.09 W
Altona ◆[8]	52	53.32 N	9.56 E
Altona Bay ⊂	274b	37.53 S	144.51 E
Altona North	274b	37.50 S	144.51 E
Altona Sports Park ♦	274b	37.52 S	144.52 E
Altoona, Al., U.S.	194	34.01 N	86.19 W
Altoona, Fl., U.S.	220	28.57 N	81.38 W
Altoona, Ia., U.S.	190	41.39 N	93.28 W
Altoona, Ks., U.S.	198	37.31 N	95.39 W
Altoona, Pa., U.S.	214	40.31 N	78.23 W
Altoona, Wa., U.S.	224	46.16 N	123.39 W
Altoona, Wi., U.S.	190	44.48 N	91.26 W
Alto Pacajá ≃	250	3.07 S	50.20 W
Alto Paraguai	248	14.30 S	56.31 W
Alto Paraguay ▫[5]	248	21.00 S	58.45 W
Alto Paraíso de Goiás	255	14.07 S	47.31 W
Alto Paraná ▫[5]	252	25.00 S	54.50 W
Alto Parnaíba	250	9.06 S	45.57 W
Alto Purús ≃	248	9.34 S	70.36 W
Alto Río Mayo	254	45.35 S	71.06 W
Alto Río Senguer	254	45.02 S	70.50 W
Altos	250	5.03 S	42.28 W
Alto Santo	250	5.31 S	38.15 W
Alto Sucuriú	255	19.19 S	52.47 W
Altotonga	234	19.46 N	97.14 W
Altötting	60	48.13 N	12.40 E
Alto Volta → Burkina Faso ▫[1]	150	13.00 N	1.30 W
Alto Yurua ≃	248	9.24 S	72.43 W
Altrincham	44	53.24 N	2.21 W
Alt Rüdersdorf	264a	52.28 N	13.49 E
Alt Ruppin	54	52.56 N	12.50 E
Altshausen	58	47.56 N	9.32 E
Alt Stahnsdorf	264a	52.17 N	13.53 E
Altstätten	58	47.23 N	9.33 E
Alt Töplitz	264a	52.26 N	12.55 E
Altuchovo	76	52.40 N	34.20 E
Āltūn Kūprī	128	35.45 N	44.09 E
Altun Shan ⛰	90	38.00 N	88.00 E
Alturas	204	41.29 N	120.32 W
Altus, Ar., U.S.	194	35.26 N	93.45 W
Altus, Ok., U.S.	196	34.38 N	99.20 W
Altus, Lake ⊜[1]	196	34.56 N	99.18 W
Altus Air Force Base ■	196	34.40 N	99.16 W
Altusried	58	47.48 N	10.13 E
Altyaryk	85	40.23 N	71.30 E
Altykarasu	86	49.12 N	55.52 E
Altynaj	86	57.04 N	62.00 E
Altynasar ⊥	86	45.10 N	63.07 E
Altynivka	78	51.27 N	33.10 E
Altynkul'	85	40.48 N	72.10 E
Altyntau	86	44.08 N	68.03 E
Altyn-Topkan	85	40.38 N	69.35 E
Alu I	175e	7.02 S	155.47 E
Al-Ubayyiḍ	140	13.11 N	30.13 E
Alubijid	116	8.35 N	124.29 E
Alucra	130	40.20 N	38.46 E
Al-'Udaysāt	140	25.35 N	32.29 E
Al-Uḍayyah	140	12.03 N	28.17 E
Aluk	140	8.26 N	27.27 E
Alūksne	76	57.25 N	27.03 E
Al-'Ulā	128	26.37 N	37.52 E
Alum Bank	214	40.14 N	78.34 W
Alum Creek ≃	218	39.53 N	82.54 W
Alum Creek Lake ⊜[1]	214	40.15 N	82.58 W
Aluminé	254	39.13 S	70.57 W
Aluminé ≃	254	39.50 S	70.53 W
Aluminé, Lago ⊜	252	38.55 S	71.09 W
Alum Rock Park ♦	282	37.24 N	121.49 W
Alunda	40	60.04 N	18.05 E
Alunitdağ	84	40.32 N	46.03 E
Alupka	78	44.26 N	34.03 E
Al-'Uqaylah	146	30.16 N	19.12 E
Al-'Uqayr	128	25.39 N	50.12 E
Al-Uqṣur (Luxor)	140	25.41 N	32.39 E
Al-'Urayq ±[8]	128	29.10 N	39.15 E
Al-'Urayq ◆[1]	128	24.47 N	42.55 E
Al-Urdun → Jordan ▫[1]	128	31.00 N	36.00 E
Alushta	78	44.42 N	34.24 E
Al-'Uṭayshān ⊤[4]	140	16.25 N	34.30 E
Al-'Uwaynāt	146	25.46 N	10.34 E
Al-'Uwaynidhīyah I	128	26.37 N	36.05 E
Al-'Uyaynah	128	24.54 N	46.23 E
Alva, Scot., U.K.	46	56.09 N	3.48 W
Alva, Fl., U.S.	220	26.42 N	81.36 W
Alva, Ok., U.S.	196	36.48 N	98.39 W
Alva ≃	34	40.18 N	8.15 W
Alvada	214	41.03 N	83.24 W
Alvaiázere	34	39.49 N	8.23 W
Alvaneu-Bad	58	46.40 N	9.39 E
Älvängen	26	57.58 N	12.07 E
Alvanley	262	53.16 N	2.45 W
Alvarado, Méx.	234	18.46 N	95.46 W
Alvarado, Tx., U.S.	222	32.24 N	97.12 W
Alvarado, Lake ⊜[1]	222	32.23 N	97.15 W
Alvarães	246	3.12 S	64.50 W
Álvarez Jonte	258	35.19 S	57.28 W
Alvarinhos	266c	38.54 N	9.22 W
Álvaro Obregón	234	19.50 N	101.05 W
Álvaro Obregón ◆[8]	286a	19.21 N	99.12 W
Álvaro Obregón, Presa ⊜[1]	232	27.55 N	109.52 W
Alvastra ⊥	26	58.18 N	14.39 E
Alvdal	26	62.07 N	10.39 E
Älvdalen	26	61.14 N	14.02 E
Alvear	252	29.06 S	56.33 W
Alvechurch	42	52.21 N	1.57 W
Alverca	34	38.54 N	9.02 W
Alverda	214	40.38 N	78.52 W
Alvernia, Mount ∧[2]	238	24.15 N	75.24 W
Alverton	214	40.08 N	79.35 W
Alves	46	57.38 N	3.27 W
Alvesta	26	56.54 N	14.33 E
Alveston	42	51.36 N	2.32 W
Alviano, Lago di ⊜[1]	66	42.36 N	12.15 E
Ålvik, Nor.	26	60.26 N	6.26 E
Alvik, Sve.	26	62.25 N	17.24 E
Alvin, Il., U.S.	216	40.19 N	87.37 W
Alvin, Tx., U.S.	222	29.25 N	95.14 W
Alvinópolis	255	20.06 S	43.03 W
Alvinston	214	42.49 N	81.52 W
Alviso ◆[8]	282	37.26 N	121.58 W
Alviso Slough ≃	282	37.27 N	122.02 W
Alvito, It.	66	41.41 N	13.45 E
Alvito, Port.	34	38.15 N	7.59 W
Älvkarleby	40	60.34 N	17.27 E
Älvkarleö bruk	40	60.32 N	17.24 E
Alvord	196	33.22 N	97.42 W
Alvord Desert ◆[2]	202	42.30 N	118.25 W
Alvord Lake ⊜	202	42.23 N	118.36 W
Alvordton	216	41.40 N	84.26 W
Alvra, Pass d')(	58	46.35 N	9.50 E
Älvros	26	62.03 N	14.39 E
Älvsborgs Län ▫[6]	26	58.00 N	12.30 E
Älvsbyn	24	65.39 N	20.59 E
Älvsnabben ⊥	40	58.59 N	18.10 E
Al-Wafā'īyah	142	30.46 N	30.36 E
Al-Wajh	128	26.15 N	36.26 E
Al-Wakrah	128	25.10 N	51.36 E
Al-Walīdīyah	142	27.12 N	31.10 E
Alwar	124	27.34 N	76.36 E
Alwar Hills ⛰[2]	124	27.20 N	76.15 E
Al-Wāṣifīyah	142	30.35 N	32.10 E
Al-Wāsiṭah	142	29.20 N	31.12 E
Alwaye	122	10.07 N	76.21 E
Al-Wazīrīyah	142	31.11 N	30.57 E
Al-Wazz	140	15.01 N	30.10 E
Alwen ≃	44	52.58 N	3.24 W
Al-Widy	142	29.31 N	31.16 E
Alxa Zuoqi	102	38.50 N	105.32 E
Al-Yamāmah → As-Sulaymānīyah	128	24.09 N	47.19 E
Al-Yaman → Yemen ▫[1]	144	15.00 N	47.00 E
Al Yāmūn	132	32.29 N	35.14 E
Alygdžer	88	53.38 N	98.16 E
Alyn and Deeside ▫[8]	262	53.16 N	3.02 W
Alypsatar	86	48.03 N	80.21 E
Alyth	46	56.37 N	3.13 W
Alytus	76	54.24 N	24.03 E
Alz ≃	60	48.16 N	12.49 E
Alzamaj	88	55.33 N	98.39 E
Alzano Lombardo	62	45.44 N	9.43 E
Al-Zarqa	142	31.13 N	31.38 E
Alzenau	56	50.05 N	9.04 E
Alzette ≃	56	49.52 N	6.07 E
Alzey	56	49.45 N	8.07 E
Alzira (Alcira)	34	39.09 N	0.26 W
Amab, Khawr V	140	17.08 N	34.51 E
Amacayacu, Parque Nacional ♦	246	3.45 S	70.10 W
Amacuro ≃	246	8.32 N	60.28 W
Amacuzac ≃	234	17.53 N	99.12 W
Amadeus, Lake ⊜	162	24.50 S	130.45 E
Āmādi, Bngl.	126	22.28 N	89.19 E
Amadi, R.D.C.	154	3.35 N	26.47 E
Amadjuak Lake ⊜	176	65.00 N	71.00 W
Amador ▫[6]	226	38.21 N	120.46 W
Amadora	266c	38.45 N	9.14 W
Amador City	226	38.25 N	120.56 W
Amador Valley V	282	37.41 N	121.51 W
Amagansett	207	40.58 N	72.08 W
Amagasaki	96	34.43 N	135.25 E
Amagase	96	33.15 N	131.02 E
Amager I	41	55.37 N	12.37 E
Amagi	96	33.25 N	130.39 E
Amagi-san ∧	94	34.51 N	139.00 E
Amagi-yugashima	94	34.53 N	138.56 E
Amagoi-dake ∧	94	35.01 N	136.23 E
Amagunze	150	6.20 N	7.40 E
Amahai	164	3.20 S	128.55 E
Amaichá del Valle	252	26.36 S	65.55 W
Amaimon	164	5.10 S	145.25 E
Amajac ≃	234	21.15 N	98.46 W
Amaka ≃	236	14.14 N	85.07 W
Ama Keng	271c	1.24 N	103.42 E
Amak Island I	180	55.25 N	163.07 W
Amakusa-nada ⊤[2]	92	32.35 N	130.05 E
Amakusa-shotō II	92	32.20 N	130.15 E
Amakuso-Shimo-shima I	92	32.20 N	130.05 E
Amal, Lībiyā	146	29.25 N	21.10 E
Åmål, Sve.	26	59.03 N	12.42 E
Amalāpuram	122	16.35 N	82.01 E
Amalat ≃	88	54.49 N	115.12 E
Amalfi, Col.	246	6.55 N	75.04 W
Amalfi, It.	68	40.38 N	14.36 E
Amalia	158	27.16 S	25.03 E
Amaliás	38	37.49 N	21.23 E
Amalner	120	21.03 N	75.04 E
Amamaki-zan ∧	94	36.25 N	140.09 E
Amambaí	255	23.05 S	55.13 W
Amambaí ≃	255	23.22 S	53.56 W
Amambay ▫[5]	252	23.00 S	56.00 W
Amami-Ō-shima I	93b	28.15 N	129.20 E
Amami-shotō II	93b	28.16 N	129.21 E
Amamula	154	0.18 S	27.50 E
Amana	190	41.48 N	91.52 W
Amanã ≃, Bra.	250	4.25 S	57.34 W
Amana ≃, Ven.	238	9.45 N	62.39 W
Amanã, Lago ⊜	246	2.35 S	64.40 W
Amanab	164	3.35 S	141.13 E
Amanave	174u	14.19 S	170.49 W
Amance	58	47.48 N	6.04 E
Amancey	58	47.02 N	6.05 E
Amancio	240p	20.49 N	77.35 W
Amanda	188	39.38 N	82.44 W
Amanda Park	224	47.28 N	123.54 W
Amandola	66	42.59 N	13.21 E
Amānganj	124	24.26 N	80.02 E
Amangel'dy, Kaz.	85	43.43 N	71.07 E
Amangel'dy, Kaz.	86	50.10 N	65.13 E
Amangel'dy, Kaz.	86	49.52 N	59.00 E
Åmänningen ⊜	40	59.57 N	15.56 E
Amano	270	34.26 N	135.33 E
Amanotkel'	86	46.07 N	61.34 E
Amantea	68	39.08 N	16.05 E
Amantogaj	86	50.22 N	65.33 E
Amanu I[1]	14	17.48 S	140.46 W
Amanzimtoti	158	30.03 S	30.53 E
Amapá	250	2.03 N	50.48 W
Amapá ▫[3]	250	1.00 N	52.00 W
Amapa ≃	234	18.18 N	96.19 W
Amapala	236	13.17 N	87.40 W
Amapala, Punta de >	236	13.10 N	87.54 W
Amapari ≃	250	0.43 N	51.32 W
Amaraji	250	8.24 S	35.27 W
Amaral	287a	22.42 S	43.29 W
Amaramba, Lago ⊜	154	14.30 S	35.55 E
Amarante	250	6.14 S	42.50 W
Amarante do Maranhão	250	5.36 S	46.45 W
Amaranth	184	50.36 N	98.43 W
Amarapura	110	21.54 N	96.03 E
Amărăștii de Jos	38	43.59 N	24.10 E
'Amārat Abū Sinn	140	15.21 N	35.45 E
Amarāvati ≃	122	10.51 N	78.11 E
Amarda	126	21.47 N	87.08 E
Amareleja	34	38.12 N	7.14 W
Amares	34	41.38 N	8.21 W
Amargosa	255	13.02 S	39.36 W
Amargosa ≃	204	36.13 N	116.48 W
Amargosa Range ⛰	204	36.15 N	116.45 W
Amarillo	196	35.13 N	101.49 W
Amarillo, Mar → Yellow Sea ⊤[2]	90	36.00 N	123.00 E
'Amar Jadīd	140	14.28 N	25.14 E
Amarkantak	124	22.40 N	81.45 E
Amarnāth	122	19.11 N	73.10 E
Amarnāth Cave ±[5]	123	34.13 N	75.31 E
Amaro, Monte ∧	66	42.05 N	14.05 E
Amaroni	68	38.47 N	16.27 E
Amaroúsion	267c	38.03 N	23.49 E
Amarpātan	124	24.19 N	80.59 E
Amarube-saki >	96	35.40 N	134.32 E
Amarume	92	38.50 N	139.55 E
Amarwāra	124	22.18 N	79.10 E
Amasa	190	46.13 N	88.26 W
Amaseno ≃	66	41.19 N	13.11 E
Amasija	84	40.58 N	43.46 E
Amasra	130	41.45 N	32.24 E
Amasya	130	40.39 N	35.51 E
Amasya ▫[4]	130	40.45 N	35.30 E
Amataurá	246	3.29 S	68.06 W
Amatignak Island I	181a	51.15 N	179.08 W
Amatikulu	158	29.06 S	31.27 E
Amatique, Bahía de ⊂	236	15.55 N	88.45 W
Amatitán	234	20.50 N	103.43 W
Amatitlán	236	14.29 N	90.37 W
Amatitlán, Lago de ⊜	236	14.27 N	90.34 W
Amatlán de Cañas	234	20.52 N	104.27 W
Amatlán de los Reyes	234	18.50 N	96.55 W
Amatrice	66	42.38 N	13.17 E
Amatsu-kominato	94	35.07 N	140.10 E
Amau	164	10.02 S	148.34 E
Amausi	124	26.46 N	80.51 E
Amawalk	210	41.17 N	73.46 W
Amay	56	50.33 N	5.19 E
Ama-zaki >	94	37.08 N	136.40 E
Amazar	89	53.54 N	120.53 E
Amazon (Solimões) (Amazonas) ≃	242	0.10 S	49.00 W
Amazonas ▫[3]	242	5.00 S	63.00 W
Amazonas ▫[5], Col.	246	1.00 S	72.00 W
Amazonas ▫[5], Perú	248	5.30 S	78.00 W
Amazonas ▫[8]	246	3.30 N	66.00 W
Amazonas → Amazon ≃	242	0.10 S	49.00 W
Amazônia, Parque Nacional da ♦	250	4.30 S	56.30 W
Amb	123	34.19 N	72.51 E
Ambāh	124	26.43 N	78.14 E
Ambahikily	157b	21.36 S	43.41 E
Ambahita	157b	24.01 S	45.16 E
Ambaí	287a	22.43 S	43.28 W
Ambājogāi	122	18.44 N	76.23 E
Ambakaka	157b	24.10 S	46.17 E
Ambāla	124	30.21 N	76.50 E
Ambāla Airport ⊠	123	30.22 N	76.50 E
Ambalabe	157b	18.24 S	49.10 E
Ambalafany	157b	22.32 S	47.36 E
Ambalangoda	122	6.14 N	80.03 E
Ambalanjanakomby	157b	16.42 S	47.05 E
Ambalavao	157b	21.50 S	46.56 E
Ambam	152	2.23 N	11.17 E
Amba Maryam	144	11.26 N	39.17 E
Ambanja	157b	13.41 S	48.27 E
Ambar	248	10.44 S	77.16 W
Ambararata	157b	15.03 S	48.33 E
Ambarawa	115a	7.15 S	110.24 E
Ambarčik, Ross.	74	69.39 N	162.20 E
Ambarčik, Ross.	88	55.09 N	95.46 E
Ambargasta, Salinas de ≃	252	29.15 S	64.30 W
Ambarijeby	157b	14.56 S	47.41 E
Ambarnyj	24	65.56 N	33.43 E
Ambaro, Baie d' ⊂	157b	13.23 S	48.38 E
Ambāsamudram	122	8.42 N	77.28 E
Ambassador Bridge ◆[5]	281	42.20 N	83.05 W
Ambato, Ec.	246	1.15 S	78.37 W
Ambato, Madag.	157b	13.24 S	48.29 E
Ambato Boeny	157b	16.28 S	46.43 E
Ambatofinandrahana	157b	20.33 S	46.48 E
Ambatolampy	157b	19.23 S	47.25 E
Ambatomainty	157b	17.41 S	45.40 E
Ambatomanoina	157b	18.18 S	47.37 E
Ambatondrazaka	157b	17.50 S	48.25 E
Ambatosoratra	157b	17.34 S	48.32 E
Ambeláki	267c	37.57 N	23.32 E
Ambelau, Pulau I	164	3.51 S	127.12 E
Ámbelos, Ákra >	38	39.56 N	23.55 E
Ambenja	157b	15.17 S	46.58 E
Amber ≃	44	53.04 N	1.29 W
Amberes → Antwerpen	50	51.13 N	4.25 E
Amberg, Dtsch.	60	49.27 N	11.52 E
Amberg, Wi., U.S.	190	45.30 N	87.59 W
Ambergris Cay I	232	18.03 N	87.56 W
Ambérieu-en-Bugey	58	45.57 N	5.21 E
Amberley	172	43.10 S	172.44 E
Amberley Royal Australian Air Force Base ■	171a	27.37 S	152.41 E
Amberson	214	40.10 N	77.41 W
Ambert	62	45.33 N	3.45 E
Ambevongo	157b	15.27 S	47.27 E
Ambia	216	40.29 N	87.31 W
Ambidédi	150	14.35 N	11.47 W
Ambikānagar	126	22.57 N	86.46 E
Ambikāpur	124	23.07 N	83.12 E
Ambil	116	13.49 N	120.20 E
Ambil Island I	116	13.48 N	120.18 E
Ambilobe	157b	13.12 S	49.04 E
Ambinanindrano	157b	20.20 S	48.19 E
Ambinanitelo	157b	15.21 S	49.35 E
Ambinda	157b	16.25 S	45.52 E
Ambivy	157b	21.31 S	44.02 E
Ambjörby	26	60.30 N	13.10 E
Ambla	76	59.11 N	25.51 E
Amble	44	55.20 N	1.34 W
Ambler, Ak., U.S.	180	67.05 N	157.52 W
Ambler, Pa., U.S.	208	40.09 N	75.13 W
Ambleside	44	54.26 N	2.58 W
Ambleteuse	50	50.49 N	1.36 E
Amblève ≃	56	50.28 N	5.36 E
Ambo	248	10.07 S	76.10 W
Amboahangy	157b	24.15 S	46.22 E
Amboasary, Madag.	157b	18.26 S	48.16 E
Amboasary, Madag.	157b	25.02 S	46.23 E
Ambodifototra	157b	16.59 S	49.52 E
Ambodilazana	157b	18.06 S	49.10 E
Ambodiriana	157b	17.55 S	49.18 E
Ambohibary	157b	19.20 S	46.17 E
Ambohidratrimo	157b	18.50 S	47.26 E
Ambohidray	157b	18.36 S	48.18 E
Ambohimahamasina	157b	21.56 S	47.11 E
Ambohimahasoa	157b	21.07 S	47.13 E
Ambohimanga du Sud	157b	20.52 S	47.36 E
Ambohimitombo	157b	20.43 S	47.26 E
Amboina → Ambon	164	3.43 S	128.12 E
Amboise	50	47.25 N	0.59 E
Amboíva	152	11.32 S	14.44 E
Ambon	164	3.43 S	128.12 E
Ambon, Pulau I	164	3.40 S	128.10 E
Ambondro	157b	25.13 S	45.44 E
Ambonnay	50	49.04 N	4.10 E
Amboseli, Lake ⊜	154	2.37 S	37.08 E
Amboseli National Park ♦	154	2.30 S	37.15 E
Amboshe	272c	19.09 N	73.08 E
Ambositra	157b	20.31 S	47.15 E
Ambovombe	157b	25.11 S	46.05 E
Amboy, Il., U.S.	190	41.42 N	89.19 W
Amboy, In., U.S.	216	40.36 N	85.55 W
Amboy, Mn., U.S.	190	43.53 N	94.09 W
Amboy, Wa., U.S.	224	45.54 N	122.26 W
Ambre, Cap d' >	157b	11.57 S	49.17 E
Ambre, Montagne d' ∧	157b	12.30 S	49.10 E
Ambridge	214	40.35 N	80.13 W
Ambridge Heights	279b	40.36 N	80.13 W
Ambridge Reservoir ⊜[1]	214	40.34 N	80.21 W
Ambrières	32	48.24 N	0.38 W
Ambriz	152	7.50 S	13.06 E
Ambrolauri	84	42.31 N	43.09 E
Ambronay	58	46.00 N	5.21 E
Ambrose	198	48.57 N	103.28 W
Ambrose Brook ≃	276	40.33 N	74.32 W
Ambrose Channel ɥ	276	40.32 N	74.02 W
Ambrosia Lake	200	35.25 N	107.49 W
Ambrym ▫[8]	175f	16.15 S	168.12 E
Ambrym I	175f	16.15 S	168.10 E
Ambuklao Dam ◆[6]	116	16.28 N	120.45 E
Ambulong Island I	116	12.12 N	121.01 E
Ambulu	115a	8.21 S	113.36 E
Ambuntentimur	115a	6.54 S	113.45 E
Ambunti	164	4.14 S	142.50 E
Āmbūr	122	12.47 N	78.42 E
Amburambur	115b	8.15 S	116.18 E
Amburayan Nabunga ≃	116	16.55 N	120.27 E
Amby	56	50.53 N	5.44 E
Amchitka Island I	181a	51.30 N	179.00 E
Amchitka Pass ɥ	181a	51.30 N	179.30 W
'Amd	144	15.18 N	48.00 E
Am-Dam	146	12.46 N	20.29 E
Āmdānga	272b	22.49 N	88.31 E
Amded, Oued V	148	22.09 N	3.15 E
Amden	58	47.09 N	9.11 E
Amderma	72	69.45 N	61.39 E
Amdo	120	32.18 N	91.04 E
Ameagle	188	37.56 N	81.25 W
Ameca	234	20.33 N	104.02 W
Ameca ≃	234	20.41 N	105.18 W
Amecameca [de Juárez]	234	19.07 N	98.46 W
Ameghino	252	34.50 S	62.27 W
Ameglia	64	44.04 N	9.57 E
Ameisberg ∧	60	48.33 N	13.50 E
Ameixoeira ◆[8]	266c	38.47 N	9.10 W
Ameland I	52	53.25 N	5.45 E
Amele	164	5.16 S	145.42 E
Amelia, It.	66	42.33 N	12.25 E
Amelia, Oh., U.S.	218	39.01 N	84.13 W
Amelia, Passo d')(	66	42.36 N	12.32 E
Amelia Court House	192	37.20 N	77.58 W
Amelia Earhart Peak ∧	226	37.47 N	119.17 W
Amelia Island I	192	30.37 N	81.27 W
Amelinghausen	52	53.08 N	10.13 E
Amelsbüren	52	51.53 N	7.37 E
Amendolara	68	39.57 N	16.35 E
Ameng	102	23.50 N	104.32 E
Amenia	210	41.50 N	73.33 W
Amenucourt	261	49.06 N	1.39 E
Āmer	120	26.59 N	75.52 E
Amerang	60	48.00 N	12.18 E
Amerevo	265b	55.55 N	38.03 E
America	52	51.26 N	5.59 E
América del Norte → North America ±[1]	16	45.00 N	100.00 W
América del Sur → South America ±[1]	18	15.00 S	60.00 W
American ≃, Ca., U.S.	226	38.36 N	121.30 W
American ≃, Wa., U.S.	224	46.58 N	121.08 W
American, Middle Fork ≃	226	38.55 N	121.02 W
American, North Fork ≃	226	38.43 N	121.09 W
American, South Fork ≃	226	38.43 N	121.09 W
Americana	255	22.45 S	47.20 W
American Canyon	226	38.10 N	122.15 W
American Cemetery and Memorial ◆	269f	14.33 N	121.03 E
American Falls	202	42.47 N	112.51 W
American Falls L	284a	43.05 N	79.04 W
American Falls Reservoir ⊜[1]	202	42.45 N	112.45 W
American Fork	200	40.22 N	111.47 W
American Highland ⛰[1]	9	72.30 S	78.00 E
American Lake ⊜	224	47.07 N	122.34 W
American Museum of Natural History ʊ	276	40.47 N	73.59 W
Americano	250	1.19 S	48.04 W
American River	168b	35.47 S	137.47 E
American Samoa ▫[2], Oc.	14	14.20 S	170.00 W
American Samoa ▫[2], Oc.	175a	14.20 S	170.00 W
American University ʊ[2]	284c	38.56 N	77.05 W
Américas, Hipódromo de las ♦	286a	19.26 N	99.13 W
Americus, Ga., U.S.	192	32.04 N	84.13 W
Americus, Ks., U.S.	198	38.30 N	96.15 W
Amerikanisches Hochland → American Highland ⛰[1]	9	72.30 S	78.00 E
Ameringkogel ∧	61	47.04 N	14.48 E
Amérique du Nord → North America ±[1]	16	45.00 N	100.00 W
Amern	56	51.14 N	6.15 E
Amerongen	52	52.00 N	5.27 E
Amersfoort, Ned.	52	52.09 N	5.24 E
Amersfoort, S. Afr.	158	27.01 S	29.51 E
Amersham	42	51.40 N	0.38 W
Amery, Austl.	162	31.09 S	117.05 E
Amery, Mb., Can.	184	56.34 N	94.03 W
Amery, Wi., U.S.	190	45.18 N	92.21 W
Amery Ice Shelf ⊓	9	69.30 S	72.00 E
Ames, Ia., U.S.	190	42.02 N	93.37 W
Ames, N.Y., U.S.	210	42.50 N	74.36 W
Ames, Tx., U.S.	222	30.03 N	94.46 W
Amesbury, Eng., U.K.	42	51.10 N	1.45 W
Amesbury, Ma., U.S.	207	42.51 N	70.55 W
Ames Long Pond ⊜	283	42.05 N	71.07 W
Ames Nowell State Park ♦	283	42.07 N	70.59 W
Ames Pond ⊜	283	42.38 N	71.13 W
Ames Research Center ʊ[3]	282	37.25 N	122.04 W
Amet Sound ɥ	186	45.47 N	63.13 W
Amfíklia	38	38.38 N	22.35 E
Amfilokhía	38	38.51 N	21.10 E
Ámfissa	38	38.31 N	22.24 E
Amfreville-la-Campagne	50	49.13 N	0.57 E
Amfreville-les-Champs	50	49.19 N	1.19 E
Amga	74	60.53 N	132.00 E
Amga ≃	74	62.38 N	134.32 E
Am Géréda	146	12.52 N	21.10 E
Amguema	180	66.58 N	179.16 W
Amguema ≃	180	68.10 N	177.40 W
Amguid	148	26.26 N	5.22 E
Amgun' ≃	89	52.56 N	139.40 E
Amherst, N.S., Can.	186	45.49 N	64.14 W
Amherst, Ma., U.S.	207	42.22 N	72.31 W
Amherst, N.H., U.S.	207	42.51 N	71.37 W
Amherst, N.Y., U.S.	210	42.58 N	78.48 W
Amherst, Oh., U.S.	214	41.23 N	82.13 W
Amherst, Tx., U.S.	196	34.01 N	102.25 W
Amherst, Va., U.S.	192	37.35 N	79.03 W
Amherst, Wi., U.S.	190	44.27 N	89.17 W
Amherst, Mount ∧	162	18.11 S	126.59 E
Amherstburg	214	42.06 N	83.06 W
Amherstdale	188	37.47 N	81.48 W
Amherst Island I	212	44.08 N	76.45 W
Amherstview	212	44.13 N	76.38 W
Ami	94	36.02 N	140.14 E
Amianan Island I	108	21.07 N	121.57 E
Amiata, Monte ∧	66	42.53 N	11.37 E
Amicalola Falls State Park ♦	192	34.33 N	84.15 W
Amidon	198	46.28 N	103.19 W
Amiens, Austl.	166	28.35 S	151.49 E
Amiens, Fr.	50	49.54 N	2.18 E
Amili, India	120	28.26 N	95.52 E
Amili, Zhg.	120	28.25 N	95.52 E
Amīn as-Samālūsī, Bi'r ⊤[4]	142	29.52 N	30.02 E
Amīndīvi Islands II	122	11.23 N	72.23 E
Aminga	252	28.50 S	66.54 W
Amini Island I	122	11.07 N	72.44 E
Amino, Ityo.	144	4.31 N	41.49 E
Amino, Nihon	96	35.41 N	135.02 E
Aminuis	156	23.43 S	19.21 E
Amīrābād	128	36.04 N	54.10 E
Amīrābād ◆[8]	267d	35.43 N	51.23 E
Amirante Islands II	138	6.00 S	53.10 E
Amirauté, Îles de l' → Admiralty Islands II	164	2.10 S	147.00 E
Amisk	182	52.33 N	111.04 W
Amisk Lake ⊜	184	54.35 N	102.13 W
Amistad, Parque Internacional de la ♦	236	9.25 N	83.10 W
Amistad, Presa de la (Amistad Reservoir) ⊜[1]	196	29.34 N	101.15 W
Amistad National Recreation Area ♦	196	29.32 N	101.12 W
Amistad Reservoir (Presa de la Amistad) ⊜[1]	196	29.34 N	101.15 W
Amite	194	30.43 N	90.30 W
Amite ≃	194	30.12 N	90.35 W
Amite, East Fork ≃	194	30.58 N	90.51 W
Amiterno ⊥	66	42.21 N	13.19 E
Amitori	175d	24.18 N	123.41 E
Amity, Ar., U.S.	194	34.15 N	93.27 W
Amity, Oh., U.S.	214	40.03 N	83.17 W
Amity, Or., U.S.	224	45.06 N	123.12 W
Amity Point >	171a	27.24 S	153.27 E
Amityville	276	40.40 N	73.25 W
Amixtlán	234	20.03 N	97.48 W
Amizmiz	148	31.14 N	8.14 W
Āmjhori ∧	126	21.51 N	86.19 E
Āmjhupi	126	23.45 N	88.42 E
Āmla, Bngl.	126	23.54 N	88.56 E
Amla, India	124	21.56 N	78.07 E
Āmlāgora	126	22.50 N	87.20 E
Amlekhgañj	124	27.17 N	84.59 E
Åmli	26	58.47 N	8.30 E
Amlia Island I	180	52.06 N	173.30 W
Amloh	124	30.37 N	76.14 E
Am Loubia	146	13.39 N	20.08 E
Amlwch	44	53.25 N	4.20 W
'Amm-Adām	140	16.22 N	36.06 E
Ammagan	85	38.56 N	67.15 E
'Ammān	132	31.57 N	35.56 E
'Ammān ▫[8]	132	31.45 S	36.15 E
Ammanford	42	51.48 N	3.59 W
Ämmänsaari	26	64.53 N	28.55 E
Ammansville	222	29.47 N	96.51 W
'Ammār, Tall ∧[2]	132	32.53 N	36.29 E
Ammarnäs	24	65.56 N	16.09 E
Ammaroo	162	21.45 S	135.15 E
Åmmeberg	40	58.52 N	15.00 E
Ammeloe	52	52.05 N	6.47 E
Ammer ≃	64	47.57 N	11.08 E
Ammerån ≃	26	63.09 N	16.13 E
Ammerbuch	56	48.33 N	8.58 E
Ammer Gebirge ⛰	64	47.35 N	10.55 E
Ammerland ◆[1]	52	53.15 N	8.00 E
Ammerman Mountain ∧	180	68.21 N	141.03 W
Ammersbek	52	53.42 N	10.12 E
Ammerschwihr	58	48.07 N	7.17 E
Ammersee ⊜	60	48.00 N	11.08 E
Ammerthal	60	49.26 N	11.45 E
Ammon	202	43.28 N	111.57 W
Ammonoosuc ≃	188	44.10 N	72.02 W
Amnān	272b	22.56 N	88.18 E
Amnat Charoen	110	15.51 N	104.38 E
Amnay ≃	116	12.58 N	120.46 E
Amne Machin Shan → A'nyêmaqên Shan ⛰	102	34.30 N	100.00 E
Amnicon ≃	190	46.41 N	91.52 W
Amnok-kang (Yalu) ≃	98	39.55 N	124.22 E
Amo ≃, Asia	124	26.16 N	89.36 E
Amo ≃, Zhg.	102	22.58 N	101.44 E
Āmol	128	36.23 N	52.20 E
Amolar	248	18.01 S	57.30 W
Amöneburg	56	50.48 N	8.55 E
Amorbach	56	49.39 N	9.13 E
Amorgós	38	36.50 N	25.54 E
Amorgós I	38	36.50 N	25.59 E
Amorim, Morro ∧[2]	287a	23.00 S	43.26 W
Amorinópolis	255	16.36 S	51.08 W
Amorosi	68	41.12 N	14.28 E
Amory	194	33.59 N	88.29 W

Symbols in the index entries represent the broad categories identified in the key at the right. Symbols with superior numbers (⛰[1]) identify subcategories (see complete key on page *I · 1).*

Symbole im Register stellen die rechts im Schlüssel erklärten Kategorien dar. Symbole mit hochgestellten Ziffern (⛰[1]) bezeichnen Unterabteilungen einer Kategorie (vgl. vollständiger Schlüssel auf Seite *I · 1).*

Los símbolos incluídos en el texto del índice representan las grandes categorías identificadas con la clave a la derecha. Los símbolos con numeros en su parte superior (⛰[1]) identifican las subcategorías (véase la clave completa en la página *I · 1).*

Les symboles de l'index représentent les catégories indiquées dans la légende à droite. Les symboles suivis d'un indice (⛰[1]) représentent des sous-catégories (voir légende complète à la page *I · 1).*

Os símbolos incluídos no texto do índice representam as grandes categorias identificadas com a chave à direita. Os símbolos com números em sua parte superior (⛰[1]) identificam as subcategorias (veja-se a chave completa à página *I · 1).*

English	Deutsch	Español	Français	Português
∧ Mountain	Berg	Montaña	Montagne	Montanha
⛰ Mountains	Gebirge	Montañas	Montagnes	Montanhas
)(Pass	Paß	Paso	Col	Passo
V Valley, Canyon	Tal, Cañon	Valle, Cañón	Vallée, Canyon	Vale, Canhão
≃ Plain	Ebene	Llano	Plaine	Planície
> Cape	Kap	Cabo	Cap	Cabo
I Island	Insel	Isla	Île	Ilha
II Islands	Inseln	Islas	Îles	Ilhas
± Other Topographic Features	Andere Topographische Objekte	Otros Elementos Topográficos	Autres données topographiques	Outros acidentes topográficos

ESPAÑOL

Nombre	Página	Lat.°'	Long.°' W = Oeste
Amos	190	48.35 N	78.07 W
Amose ≃	41	55.35 N	11.18 E
Åmot, Nor.	26	59.35 N	8.00 E
Åmot, Nor.	26	59.54 N	9.54 E
Åmotfors	26	59.46 N	12.22 E
Amour	228	33.50 N	1.00 E
— Amur ≃	74	52.56 N	141.10 E
Amour, Djebel ⋏	148	34.00 N	2.15 E
Amoy			
— Xiamen	100	24.28 N	118.07 E
Amozoc	234	19.02 N	98.03 W
Ampana	112	0.51 S	121.32 E
Ampanavoana	157b	15.41 S	50.22 E
Ampang	115b	8.47 S	118.00 E
Ampanihy	157b	24.42 S	44.45 E
Ampaqid, Mount ⋏	118	7.57 N	125.41 E
Amparafaravola	157b	17.35 S	48.13 E
Amparihy, Madag.	157b	16.40 S	44.49 E
Amparihy, Madag.	157b	23.57 S	47.20 E
Amparo	256	22.42 S	46.45 W
Ampasibe	157b	22.56 S	46.58 E
Ampasinambo	157b	20.31 S	48.00 E
Ampasindava, Baie d' ≃	157b	13.16 S	48.43 E
Ampasindava, Presqu'île d' ⊁¹	157b	13.45 S	48.00 E
Ampato, Nevado ⋏	248	15.50 S	71.52 W
Ampel	115a	7.27 S	110.32 E
Amper	150	9.20 N	9.43 E
Ampezzo	64	46.25 N	12.48 E
Ampezzo, Valle d' V	64	46.30 N	12.10 E
Ampfing	60	48.16 N	12.25 E
Ampflwang	64	48.15 N	13.34 E
Amphion-les-Bains	58	46.23 N	6.32 E
Ampisikina	157b	12.57 S	49.08 E
Ampleforth	44	54.12 N	1.06 W
Ampollino, Lago ⊜	68	39.12 N	16.37 E
Ampombiantambo	157b	12.42 S	48.57 E
Amposta	34	40.43 N	0.35 E
Ampotaka	157b	25.03 S	44.41 E
Ampoza	157b	22.20 S	44.44 E
Ampthill	42	52.02 N	0.30 W
Ampuis	62	45.29 N	4.49 E
Ampus	62	43.36 N	6.23 E
Amqui	186	48.28 N	67.26 W
Āmr, Jabal al- ⋏	132	30.45 N	34.20 E
Amraoti			
— Amrāvati	120	20.56 N	77.45 E
Amrāvati	120	20.56 N	77.45 E
Am-Raya	146	14.00 N	16.35 E
Amreli	120	21.37 N	71.14 E
Āmreswar	272b	22.28 N	88.34 E
Amriswil	58	47.33 N	9.18 E
Amritsar	123	31.35 N	74.53 E
Amroha	123	28.55 N	78.28 E
Amrūka	123	30.19 N	73.53 E
Amrum I	30	54.39 N	8.21 E
Amsdell Heights	284a	42.45 N	78.54 W
Amsden	214	41.13 N	83.20 W
Amsel	148	22.37 N	5.26 E
Åmsele	26	64.32 N	19.20 E
Am Sigan	146	11.41 N	19.51 E
Amsoldingen	58	46.43 N	7.35 E
Amstel ≃	52	52.22 N	4.54 E
Amstelveen	52	52.22 N	4.54 E
Amstelmeer ⊜	52	52.52 N	4.45 E
Amstetten, Ned.	52	52.22 N	4.54 E
Amsterdam, S. Afr.	158	26.35 S	30.45 E
Amsterdam, N.Y., U.S.	210	42.56 N	74.11 W
Amsterdam, Oh., U.S.	214	40.28 N	80.55 W
Amsterdam, Île I	6	37.52 S	77.32 E
Amsterdam-Rijnkanaal ≅	52	51.57 N	5.20 E
Amstetten	61	48.07 N	14.53 E
Amston	207	41.37 N	72.20 W
Ämta	126	22.35 N	88.01 E
Amt'ae-do I	98	34.50 N	126.07 E
Amtala	126	23.55 N	88.27 E
Amtāli	126	22.08 N	90.14 E
Am Timan	146	11.02 N	20.17 E
Amtrak Station ⊷⁵	281	42.19 N	83.04 W
Amubri	236	9.31 N	82.56 W
'Āmūdah	130	37.05 N	40.54 E
Amu-Darja	128	37.53 N	65.15 E
Amu Darya ≃	72	43.40 N	59.01 E
Amudat	154	1.57 N	34.57 E
Amugulang			
— Xin Barag Zuoqi	88	48.14 N	118.18 E
Amukta Island I	180	52.29 N	171.15 W
Amukta Pass ⋃	180	52.25 N	172.00 W
Amulree	46	56.30 N	3.47 W
Amun	175e	5.57 S	154.45 E
Amundsen Bay ⊂	9	66.55 S	50.00 E
Amundsen Gulf ⊂	178	71.00 N	124.00 W
Amundsen-Scott ⊼⁸	9	90.00 S	0.00
Amundsen Sea ⊽²	9	72.30 S	112.00 W
Amung, Mount ⋏	164	7.26 S	146.36 E
Amungen ⊜	26	61.09 N	15.39 E
Amuntai	112	2.26 S	115.15 E
Amur (Heilong) ≃	74	52.56 N	141.10 E
'Amūr, Wādī V	140	18.56 N	33.34 E
Amurang	112	1.11 N	124.35 E
Amuria	154	2.01 N	33.38 E
Amursk	89	50.13 N	136.52 E
Amurskaja Oblast' ⊡⁸	89	53.00 N	129.00 E
Amurskij liman ⊂	89	52.45 N	141.40 E
Amursko-Zejskaja ravnina ⊼	89	52.30 N	128.30 E
Amurzet	89	47.42 N	131.05 E
Amutag	116	12.23 N	123.16 E
Amuwo	273a	6.28 N	3.18 E
Amuyimusu	98	42.25 N	113.21 E
Amuzhong	120	30.33 N	84.28 E
Amvang	152	1.45 N	10.29 E
Amvrakikós Kólpos ⊂	38	39.00 N	21.00 E
Amvrosiyivka	83	47.47 N	38.29 E
Amwom, Khawr V	140	7.50 N	31.13 E
Amyl ≃	88	53.47 N	92.54 E
Amyûn	130	34.18 N	35.49 E
Amz'a	100	34.15 N	105.40 E
Amzi, Oued ti-n- V	148	20.30 N	4.35 E
An	110	19.47 N	94.02 E
Anaa I	18	17.25 S	145.30 W
Anabanua	112	3.57 S	120.04 E
Anabar	174b	0.30 S	166.57 E
Anabar ≃	74	73.08 N	113.36 E
'Ānabtā	132	32.19 N	35.07 E
Anabuki	98	34.02 N	134.11 E
Anacapri	68	40.33 N	14.13 E
Anaco	246	9.27 N	64.28 W
Anacoco	194	31.15 N	93.20 W
Anacoco, Bayou ≃	194	30.52 N	93.34 W
Anaconda	202	46.07 N	112.56 W
Anaconda Range ⋀	202	45.55 N	113.30 W
Anacortes	224	48.30 N	122.36 W
Anacostia ≃	284c	38.52 N	76.59 W
Anacostia, Little Paint Branch ≃	284c	39.01 N	76.56 W
Anacostia, Northeast Branch ≃	284c	38.57 N	76.57 W
Anacostia, Paint Branch ≃	284c	38.54 N	76.58 W
Anacostia Park ♦	284c	38.54 N	76.58 W
Anacuao, Mount ⋏	116	16.16 N	121.53 E
Anadarko	196	35.04 N	98.14 W
Anadia	250	9.42 S	36.18 W
Anadolufeneri ⊷⁸	257	41.12 N	29.09 E
Anadoluhisari ≃	267h	41.04 N	29.03 E
Anadyr'	180	64.45 N	177.29 E
Anadyr' ≃	74	64.55 N	176.05 E
Anadyrskij nizmennost' ≃	180	65.30 N	176.00 E
Anadyrskij zaliv ⊂	180	64.00 N	179.00 E

FRANÇAIS

Nom	Page	Lat.°'	Long.°' W = Ouest
Anadyrskoje ploskogorje ⊼¹	180	67.00 N	174.00 E
Anáfi I	38	36.21 N	25.50 E
Anagni	66	41.44 N	13.09 E
'Ānah	128	34.28 N	41.56 E
Anaheim	228	33.50 N	117.54 W
Anaheim Arena ♦	280	33.48 N	117.52 W
Anaheim Shopping Center ⊷⁹	280	33.51 N	117.56 W
Anaheim Stadium ♦	280	33.51 N	117.57 W
Anaheim Union Canal ≅	280	33.54 N	117.52 W
Anahi, Baie ⊂	174x	9.45 S	138.56 W
Anahim Lake	182	52.28 N	125.18 W
Anahola	229b	22.08 N	159.18 W
Anahola Bay ⊂	229b	22.09 N	159.18 W
Anáhuac, Méx.	196	25.48 N	97.45 W
Anáhuac, Méx.	232	27.14 N	100.09 W
Anáhuac, Méx.	232	28.25 N	106.40 W
Anahuac, Tx., U.S.	222	29.46 N	94.41 W
Anahuac, Lake ⊜	222	29.48 N	94.41 W
Anaimala	122	10.10 N	77.04 E
Anajás	250	0.59 S	49.57 W
Anajás, Ilha I	250	0.20 S	50.30 W
Anajatuba	250	3.16 S	44.37 W
Anakāpalle	122	17.41 N	83.01 E
Anaklia	84	42.24 N	41.33 E
Anaktuvuk ≃	180	69.32 N	151.30 W
Anaktuvuk Pass	180	68.10 N	151.50 W
Analalava	157b	14.38 S	47.45 E
Analalapatsy	157b	25.10 S	46.42 E
Analavoka	157b	22.33 S	46.30 E
Analomink	210	41.03 N	75.13 W
Anamã, Lago ⊜	246	3.35 S	61.22 W
Anamã, Lago ⊜	246	3.32 S	61.35 W
Anama Bay	184	51.56 N	98.05 W
Ana María, Cayos de I			
Ana María, Golfo de ⊂	240p	21.29 N	78.46 W
Anambas, Kepulauan II	240p	21.25 N	78.40 W
Anambra ≃	112	3.00 N	106.00 E
Anambra ≃	150	6.11 N	6.46 E
Anamizu	94	37.14 N	136.54 E
Anamoose	198	47.52 N	100.14 W
Anamosa	190	42.06 N	91.17 W
Anamur	250	0.56 N	57.03 W
Anamur	130	36.06 N	32.50 E
Anamur Burnu ⊁	130	36.03 N	32.48 E
Anan, Nihon	94	35.19 N	137.49 E
Anan, Nihon	96	33.55 N	134.39 E
Anand	120	22.34 N	72.56 E
Ananda	94	7.17 N	4.16 W
Anandanagar	272b	22.51 N	88.16 E
Anandapur, India	120	21.14 N	86.07 E
Anandpur, India	126	22.34 N	87.25 E
Anandpur Sahib	123	31.15 N	76.30 E
Anane	248	14.42 S	63.39 W
Ananindeua	250	1.22 S	48.23 W
Ananjevo	85	42.45 N	77.40 E
Anantapur	122	14.41 N	77.36 E
Anantnāg (Islāmābād)	123	33.44 N	75.09 E
Anan'yiv	78	47.40 N	29.55 E
Anao-aon	116	9.47 N	125.26 E
Anapa	78	44.53 N	37.19 E
Anápolis	255	16.20 S	48.58 W
Anapu ≃	250	1.53 S	50.53 W
Anapurus	250	3.40 S	43.06 W
Anār, Īrān	128	30.53 N	55.18 E
Anar, Kaz.	86	50.38 N	72.27 E
Anārak	128	33.20 N	53.42 E
Anārbay	85	44.20 N	75.15 E
Anār Darreh	128	32.46 N	61.39 E
Anaš	86	54.52 N	91.00 E
Anasagasti	258	35.01 S	59.24 W
Añasco	240m	18.17 N	67.08 W
Anastácio	255	21.31 S	54.08 W
Anastasia Island I	192	29.48 N	81.16 W
Anastasijevka	83	47.34 N	38.31 E
Anastasijevskaja	78	45.13 N	37.53 E
'Anātā	132	31.49 N	35.16 E
Anatahan I	108	16.22 N	145.40 E
Anatoliki Makedhonia kaí Thráki ⊡⁸	38	41.00 N	25.00 E
Anatolikón	78	46.48 N	31.13 E
Anatom I	175f	20.12 S	169.45 E
Añatuya	252	28.28 S	62.50 W
Anauá ≃	246	0.58 N	61.21 W
Anaurilândia	255	22.03 S	52.45 W
Anavilhanas, Arquipélago das II	246	2.42 S	60.45 W
Anbanjing	102	37.20 N	81.26 W
Anbanjing	102	23.57 N	100.55 E
Anbei, Zhg.	102	40.45 N	96.06 E
Anbei, Zhg.	102	40.49 N	108.55 E
Anbianbu	102	37.39 N	108.11 E
Anbo	100	39.51 N	122.19 E
Anbu	100	23.28 N	116.44 E
Anbyŏn	98	39.03 N	127.32 E
Ancarano	66	42.50 N	13.44 E
Ancash ⊡⁸	248	9.30 S	77.45 W
Ancaster, Ont., Can.	212	43.12 N	80.00 W
Ancaster, Eng., U.K.	44	52.59 N	0.32 W
Ancasti	252	28.49 S	65.30 W
Ancasti, Sierra de ⋀	252	28.50 S	65.39 W
Ance ≃, Fr.	62	45.17 N	4.08 E
Ance ≃, Fr.	62	44.58 N	3.40 E
Ancenis	32	47.22 N	1.11 W
Ancerville	58	48.38 N	5.02 E
Anchang	100	30.09 N	120.30 E
Anchieta	250	20.49 S	40.39 W
Anchieta, Ilha I	256	23.33 S	45.04 W
Anch'ing			
— Anqing	100	30.31 N	117.02 E
Ancho, Canal ⋃	254	49.54 S	74.23 W
Ancholme ≃	44	53.41 N	0.32 W
Anchor	216	40.34 N	88.32 W
Anchorage	180	61.13 N	149.54 W
Anchor Bay ⊂	214	42.39 N	82.49 W
Anchor Bay Gardens	214	42.39 N	82.49 W
Anchor Point	180	59.46 N	151.52 W
Anchor Point ⊁	180	59.47 N	151.52 W
Anchorville	214	42.42 N	82.41 W
Anchuras	34	39.29 N	4.50 W
Anci (Langfang)	98	39.31 N	116.42 E
Ancien Ekalla	152	1.17 N	14.00 E
Ancien Goubéré	146	5.51 N	26.46 E
Ancienne-Lorette	206	46.48 N	71.21 W
Anciferovo, Ross.	76	58.58 N	34.01 E
Anciferovo, Ross.	82	55.53 N	38.49 E
Ancipa, Lago di ⊜	70	37.50 N	14.34 E
Anclote, Cayo I	240p	22.24 N	84.03 W
Anclote Keys II	228	28.12 N	82.51 W
Anclote ≃	234	22.35 N	101.11 W
Ancón, Méx.	248	11.47 S	77.11 W
Ancona, S. Afr.	158	27.40 S	26.32 E
Ancón de Sardinas, Bahía de ⊂	248	1.30 N	79.00 W
Ancora	34	41.49 N	8.49 W
Ancram	210	42.03 N	73.38 W
Ancre ≃	50	49.54 N	2.28 E
Ancud	254	41.52 S	73.50 W
Ancud, Golfo de ⊂	254	42.05 S	73.00 W
Ancy-le-Franc	50	47.46 N	4.10 E
Ancy-sur-Moselle	58	49.03 N	6.04 E
Anda, Pil.	116	16.17 N	119.57 E
'Anda, Zhg.	88	46.24 N	125.19 E
Andacollo, Arg.	252	37.11 S	70.41 W
Andacollo, Chile	252	30.14 S	71.06 W

PORTUGUÊS

Nome	Página	Lat.°'	Long.°' W = Oeste
Andahuaylas	248	13.39 S	73.23 W
Andaingo	157b	18.12 S	48.17 E
Andal	124	23.36 N	87.12 E
Andalgalá	252	27.36 S	66.19 W
Andalo	64	46.10 N	11.00 E
Andalsnes	26	62.34 N	7.42 E
Andalucía ⊡³	34	37.30 N	4.30 W
Andalusia, Al., U.S.	194	31.19 N	86.29 W
Andalusia, Pa., U.S.	285	40.04 N	74.58 W
Andaman and Nicobar Islands ⊡⁸	110	11.00 N	93.00 E
Andaman Basin ⊽¹	12	10.00 N	94.00 E
Andamanen			
— Andaman Islands II	110	12.00 N	92.45 E
Andaman Islands II	110	12.00 N	92.45 E
Andaman Sea ⊽²	110	10.00 N	95.00 E
Andamarca, Bol.	248	18.49 S	67.31 W
Andamarca, Perú	248	11.46 S	74.44 W
Andamooka	166	30.27 S	137.12 E
Andance	62	45.14 N	4.47 E
Andapa	157b	14.39 S	49.39 E
Andara	152	18.03 S	21.27 E
Andaraí	255	12.48 S	41.20 W
Andaraí ≃	287a	22.58 S	43.15 W
Andaray	248	15.49 S	72.50 W
Andau	61	47.46 N	17.02 E
Andechs, Kloster ⊻¹	64	47.58 N	11.10 E
Andeer	58	46.36 N	9.26 E
Andelfingen	58	47.36 N	8.41 E
Andelle ≃	50	49.19 N	1.14 E
Andelot	58	48.15 N	5.18 E
Andelot-en-Montagne	58	46.51 N	5.56 E
Andelu	261	48.53 N	1.50 E
Anden			
— Andes ⋏	18	20.00 S	67.00 W
Andenes	26	69.16 N	16.08 E
Andenne	56	50.29 N	5.06 E
Andéranboukane	150	15.26 N	3.02 E
Anderdalen Nasjonalpark ♦	24	69.14 N	17.17 E
Anderlecht	50	50.50 N	4.18 E
Anderlues	50	50.24 N	4.16 E
Andermatt	58	46.38 N	8.36 E
Andernach	56	50.26 N	7.24 E
Andersen Air Force Base ♦	174p	13.35 N	144.56 E
Anderslöv	41	55.26 N	13.22 E
Anderson, Al., U.S.	194	34.55 N	87.15 W
Anderson, Ak., U.S.	180	64.21 N	149.10 W
Anderson, Ca., U.S.	204	40.26 N	122.17 W
Anderson, In., U.S.	218	40.06 N	85.40 W
Anderson, Mo., U.S.	196	36.39 N	94.26 W
Anderson, S.C., U.S.	192	34.30 N	82.39 W
Anderson, Tx., U.S.	222	30.29 N	95.59 W
Anderson ⊡⁶, Ky., U.S.	218	38.05 N	84.55 W
Anderson ⊡⁶, Tx., U.S.	222	31.47 N	95.40 W
Anderson ≃	180	69.43 N	128.58 W
Anderson, Mount ⋏	224	47.43 N	123.20 W
Anderson Creek ≃	194	33.18 N	94.26 W
Anderson Dam	202	43.30 N	115.30 W
Anderson Inlet ⊂	168	38.39 S	145.48 E
Anderson Island I	182	60.11 N	122.07 W
Anderson Lake ⊜	226	37.11 N	121.37 W
Anderson Peak ⋏	228	34.08 N	116.53 W
Anderson Ranch Reservoir ⊜¹	202	43.25 N	115.20 W
Andersonville	218	39.30 N	85.17 W
Andersonville National Historic Site ♦	192	32.12 N	84.07 W
Anderstorp	26	57.17 N	13.38 E
Andertlen	56	52.21 N	9.51 E
Anderton	262	53.17 N	2.32 W
Andes, Col.	246	5.40 N	75.53 W
Andes, N.Y., U.S.	210	42.12 N	74.47 W
Andes ⋏	18	20.00 S	67.00 W
Andes, Lake ⊜	198	43.11 N	98.27 W
Andeville	50	49.15 N	2.10 E
Andevoranto	157b	18.57 S	49.06 E
Andfjorden ⋃	24	69.10 N	16.20 E
Andheri ⊷⁸	272c	19.07 N	72.51 E
Andhra Pradesh ⊡³	122	16.00 N	79.00 E
Andíjan	128	40.45 N	72.22 E
Andíjan ⊡⁸	85	40.45 N	72.15 E
Andikíthira I	38	35.52 N	23.18 E
Andilamena	157b	17.01 S	48.35 E
Andímákhia	38	36.48 N	27.07 E
Andingpu	102	38.27 N	107.02 E
Anding Zhan	98	39.38 N	116.29 E
Andiparos I	38	37.00 N	25.03 E
Andirá ≃	250	2.45 S	56.49 W
Andirá, Riozinho do ≃			
Andmn	130	37.34 N	36.20 E
Andirlang	102	37.36 N	83.50 E
Àndlssa	54	39.03 N	127.32 E
Àndissa	38	39.14 N	25.59 E
Andižan	85	40.45 N	72.22 E
Andižan ⊡⁸	85	40.45 N	72.15 E
Andkhvoy	128	36.56 N	65.08 E
Andlau-eu-Val	58	48.23 N	7.25 E
Ando	270	34.37 N	135.46 E
Andoas	246	2.50 S	76.30 W
Andoga ≃	76	59.10 N	37.27 E
Andogskaja gr'ada ⋀	76	59.15 N	37.30 E
Andolsheim	58	48.04 N	7.25 E
Andomskij Pogost	76	61.14 N	36.36 E
Andong, Taehan	98	36.35 N	128.44 E
Andong, Zhg.	98	40.07 N	124.23 E
Andong-chósuji ⊜¹	98	39.28 N	127.27 E
Andong-ni	98	39.28 N	127.27 E
Andonno	76	55.57 N	62.30 W
Andorra ⊡¹	62	43.59 N	9.08 E
Andorf	60	48.23 N	13.35 E
Andorno Micca	62	45.37 N	8.03 E
Andorra ⊡¹, Europe	22	42.30 N	1.30 E
Andorra ⊡¹, Europe	34	42.30 N	1.30 E
Andorra la Vella	34	42.30 N	1.31 E
Andover, Eng., U.K.	42	51.13 N	1.28 W
Andover, Ct., U.S.	207	41.44 N	72.22 W
Andover, Me., U.S.	188	44.38 N	70.45 W
Andover, Ma., U.S.	207	42.39 N	71.08 W
Andover, N.J., U.S.	210	41.00 N	74.45 W
Andover, N.Y., U.S.	210	42.09 N	77.47 W
Andover, Oh., U.S.	210	41.36 N	80.34 W
Andover, S.D., U.S.	198	45.24 N	97.54 W
Andowj	123	37.02 N	71.27 E
Andoya I	26	69.08 N	15.54 E
Andradas	256	22.04 S	46.34 W
Andrade Pinto	258	22.23 S	43.35 W
Andradina	255	20.54 S	51.23 W
Andramasina	157b	19.11 S	47.35 E
Andranopasy	157b	21.17 S	43.44 E
Andranovory	157b	23.08 S	44.10 E
Andratx	34	39.35 N	2.25 E
Andravida	38	37.54 N	21.17 E
Andreafsky, East Fork ≃	180	62.03 N	163.07 W
Andreanof Islands II	180	51.40 N	176.00 W
Andreapol'	76	56.39 N	32.15 E
Andreas, I. of Man	44	54.22 N	4.26 W
Andreas, Tx., U.S.	208	40.45 N	76.55 W
Andreatta	208		
Andrejevka, Kaz.	86	52.59 N	67.23 E
Andrejevka, Ross.	80	53.15 N	49.58 E
Andrejevka, Ross.	82	55.55 N	37.08 E
Andrejevsk	88	58.06 N	114.08 E

Symbols in the index entries represent the broad categories identified in the key at the right. Symbols with superior numbers (↗ 1) identify subcategories (see complete key on page *I · 1*).

Symbole im Register stellen die rechts im Schlüssel erklärten Kategorien dar. Symbole mit hochgestellten Ziffern (↗ 1) bezeichnen Unterabteilungen einer Kategorie (vgl. vollständiger Schlüssel auf Seite *I · 1*).

Los símbolos incluidos en el texto del índice representan las grandes categorías identificadas con la clave a la derecha. Los símbolos con numeros en su parte superior (↗ 1) identifican las subcategorías (véase la clave completa en la página *I · 1*).

Les symboles de l'index représentent les catégories indiquées dans la légende à droite. Les symboles suivis d'un indice (↗ 1) représentent des sous-catégories (voir légende complète à la page *I · 1*).

Os símbolos incluídos no texto do índice representam as 'grandes categorias identificadas com a chave à direita. Os símbolos com números em sua parte superior (↗ 1) identificam as subcategorias (veja-se a chave completa à página *I · 1*).

↗ Mountain	Berg	Montaña	Montagne	Montanha
↗ Mountains	Gebirge	Montañas	Montagnes	Montanhas
)(Pass	Paß	Paso	Col	Passo
✓ Valley, Canyon	Tal, Cañon	Valle, Cañón	Vallée, Canyon	Vale, Canhão
> Cape	Kap	Cabo	Cap	Cabo
I Island	Insel	Isla	Île	Ilha
II Islands	Inseln	Islas	Îles	Ilhas
⊥ Other Topographic Features	Andere Topographische Objekte	Otros Elementos Topográficos	Autres données topographiques	Outros acidentes topográficos

ESPAÑOL Nombre	Página	Lat.°′	Long.°′ W = Oeste
Arborg	184	50.55 N	97.15 W
Arbrå	26	61.29 N	16.23 E
Arbroath	46	56.34 N	2.35 W
Arbu, Monte ∧	71	39.15 N	9.27 E
Arbuckle	226	39.01 N	122.03 W
Arbuckle, Lake ⊜	220	27.41 N	81.24 W
Arbuckle Creek ≃	220	27.26 N	81.17 W
Arbuckle Mountains ⩘	196	34.25 N	97.20 W
Arbuckles, Lake of the ⊜[1]	196	34.25 N	97.00 W
Arbury Hills	216	41.33 N	87.51 W
Arbus	71	39.32 N	8.36 E
Arbutus Lake ⊜	276	40.31 N	74.10 W
Arbuzovo	76	56.21 N	32.27 E
Arbuzynka	78	47.53 N	31.19 E
Arc ≃, Fr.	62	43.31 N	5.07 E
Arc ≃, Fr.	62	45.34 N	6.12 E
Arc, Bayou des ≃	194	35.00 N	91.30 W
Arcachon	32	44.37 N	1.12 W
Arcachon, Bassin d' c	32	44.40 N	1.10 W
Arcadas	256	22.42 S	46.52 W
Arcade, It.	64	45.47 N	12.13 E
Arcade, Ca., U.S.	226	34.02 N	118.15 W
Arcade, N.Y., U.S.	210	42.32 N	78.25 W
Arcadia, Ca., U.S.	228	34.08 N	118.02 W
Arcadia, Fl., U.S.	220	27.12 N	81.51 W
Arcadia, In., U.S.	218	40.10 N	86.01 W
Arcadia, Ia., U.S.	198	42.01 N	95.02 W
Arcadia, Ks., U.S.	198	37.38 N	94.37 W
Arcadia, La., U.S.	194	32.32 N	92.55 W
Arcadia, Mi., U.S.	190	44.29 N	86.13 W
Arcadia, Mo., U.S.	194	37.35 N	90.37 W
Arcadia, Ne., U.S.	198	41.25 N	99.07 W
Arcadia, Oh., U.S.	216	41.06 N	83.31 W
Arcadia, Pa., U.S.	214	40.47 N	78.51 W
Arcadia, S.C., U.S.	192	34.57 N	81.59 W
Arcadia, Tx., U.S.	222	29.23 N	95.07 W
Arcadia, Wi., U.S.	190	44.15 N	91.30 W
Arcângelo	256	21.18 S	44.19 W
Arcanum	218	39.59 N	84.33 W
Arcas, Cayos II	232	20.12 N	91.58 W
Arcata	204	40.52 N	124.04 W
Arcatao	236	14.05 N	88.45 W
Arc de Triomphe ⊥	261	48.53 N	2.17 E
Arc Dome ∧	204	38.50 N	117.21 W
Arce	66	41.35 N	13.34 E
Arceburgo	256	21.22 S	46.56 W
Arčeda ≃	80	49.52 N	43.10 E
Arčedinsko-Donskije peski ◆[2]	80	49.33 N	43.15 E
Arcelia	234	18.17 N	100.16 W
Arcen	52	51.29 N	6.11 E
Arc-en-Barrois	58	47.57 N	5.00 E
Arces	50	48.05 N	3.36 E
Arc-et-Senans	58	47.02 N	5.46 E
Arcevia	66	43.30 N	12.56 E
Archambault, Lac ⊜	206	46.18 N	74.15 W
Archangaj □[8]	88	48.00 N	101.30 E
Archangel → Archangel'sk	24	64.34 N	40.32 E
Archangel'sk	24	64.34 N	40.32 E
Archangel'skaja	78	45.41 N	40.15 E
Archangel'sk Oblast' □[4]	24	63.00 N	42.00 E
Archangel'skoje, Ross.	76	53.16 N	37.42 E
Archangel'skoje, Ross.	78	51.27 N	40.55 E
Archangel'skoje, Ross.	80	55.13 N	44.05 E
Archangel'skoje, Ross.	80	54.26 N	48.40 E
Archangel'skoje, Ross.	82	55.19 N	35.58 E
Archangel'skoje, Ross.	84	44.37 N	44.05 E
Archangel'skoje, Ross.	265b	55.47 N	37.18 E
Archara	89	49.27 N	130.07 E
Archara ≃	89	49.13 N	129.53 E
Archbald	210	41.29 N	75.32 W
Archbold	216	41.31 N	84.18 W
Archdale	192	35.54 N	79.58 W
Archer	192	29.31 N	82.31 W
Archer ≃	164	13.28 S	141.41 E
Archer, Lake ⊜	283	42.04 N	71.20 W
Archer, Mount ∧	166	23.20 S	150.34 E
Archer Bay c	164	13.25 S	141.43 E
Archer Bend National Park ♠	164	13.30 S	142.20 E
Archer City	196	33.35 N	98.37 W
Archer's Post	154	0.39 N	37.41 E
Arches	58	48.07 N	6.32 E
Arches National Park ♠	200	38.42 N	109.45 W
Archi	66	42.05 N	14.23 E
Archiac	32	45.31 N	0.18 W
Archidona	34	37.05 N	4.23 W
Archipo-Osipovka	78	44.22 N	38.33 E
Archipovka	80	56.38 N	41.14 E
Archipovo	24	66.26 N	45.52 E
Archonskaja	84	43.07 N	44.30 E
Archshofen	56	49.27 N	10.04 E
Archville	276	41.07 N	73.52 W
Arci, Monte ∧	71	39.47 N	8.44 E
Arcidosso	66	42.52 N	11.33 E
Arcille	66	42.48 N	11.15 E
Arcinazzo Romano	66	41.48 N	13.12 E
Arcisate	62	45.54 N	8.52 E
Arcis-sur-Aube	50	48.32 N	4.08 E
Arckaringa	162	27.56 S	134.45 E
Arckaringa Creek ≃	162	28.10 S	135.22 E
Arc-les-Gray	58	47.27 N	5.35 E
Arco, It.	64	45.55 N	10.53 E
Arco, Id., U.S.	202	43.38 N	113.17 W
Arco de Baúlhe	34	41.29 N	7.58 W
Arcola, Sk., Can.	184	49.37 N	102.30 W
Arcola, It.	64	44.07 N	9.54 E
Arcola, Il., U.S.	194	39.41 N	88.18 W
Arcola, In., U.S.	216	41.06 N	85.17 W
Arcola, Ms., U.S.	194	33.16 N	90.52 W
Arcola, Pa., U.S.	285	40.09 N	75.27 W
Arcola, Tx., U.S.	222	29.31 N	95.27 W
Arconate	266b	45.32 N	8.51 E
Arcore	266b	45.38 N	9.19 E
Arcos	255	20.17 S	45.32 W
Arcos de la Frontera	34	36.45 N	5.48 W
Arcot	122	12.54 N	79.20 E
Arcoverde	250	8.25 S	37.04 W
Arctic Bay	176	73.02 N	85.11 W
Arctic Ocean ⊤[1]	16	85.00 N	170.00 E
Arctic Red ≃	180	67.27 N	133.46 W
Arctic Red River	180	67.27 N	133.46 W
Arctic Village	180	68.08 N	145.19 W
Arctique, Océan Glacial → Arctic Ocean ⊤[1]	16	85.00 N	170.00 E
Arctowski ℧[3]	9	62.09 S	58.28 W
Arcturus	154	17.47 S	31.20 E
Arcueil	261	48.48 N	2.20 E
Arcuentu, Monte ∧	71	39.35 N	8.33 E
Arcvašen	84	40.38 N	45.32 E
Arcy-sur-Cure	50	47.36 N	3.45 E
Ard, Loch ⊜	46	56.11 N	4.28 W
Arḍ, Ra's al- ›	128	29.21 N	48.05 E
Arda ≃, Europe	38	41.39 N	26.29 E
Arda ≃, It.	64	45.02 N	10.02 E
Ardabīl	128	38.15 N	48.18 E
Ardagger	61	48.11 N	14.50 E
Ardagh	48	52.28 N	9.04 W
Ardahan	130	41.07 N	42.41 E
Ardakān, Īrān	128	30.16 N	52.01 E
Ardakān, Īrān	128	32.19 N	53.59 E
Ardal	128	31.59 N	50.39 E
Ardalanish, Rubh' ›	46	56.17 N	6.18 W
Årdalsfjorden c[2]	26	61.12 N	7.30 E
Årdalstangen	26	61.14 N	7.43 E

FRANÇAIS Nom	Page	Lat.°′	Long.°′ W = Ouest
Ardanuç	130	41.08 N	42.04 E
Ardara, Ire.	48	54.46 N	8.25 W
Árdara, It.	71	40.37 N	8.48 E
Ardara, Pa., U.S.	279b	40.22 N	79.44 W
Ardarroch	46	57.25 N	5.38 W
Ardatov, Ross.	80	55.15 N	43.06 E
Ardatov, Ross.	80	54.51 N	46.13 E
Ardbeg	46	55.39 N	6.05 W
Ardcharnich	46	57.51 N	5.05 W
Ardea	66	41.36 N	12.33 E
Ardèche □[5]	62	44.40 N	4.20 E
Ardèche ≃	62	44.16 N	4.39 E
Ardee	48	53.52 N	6.33 W
Ardélik	146	12.26 N	21.25 E
Arden, Mb., Can.	184	50.17 N	99.14 W
Arden, Ca., U.S.	226	38.36 N	121.23 W
Arden, De., U.S.	208	39.48 N	75.29 W
Arden, Forest of ◆[3]	42	52.23 N	1.42 W
Arden, Mount ∧	166	32.09 S	137.59 E
Ardenay-sur-Mérize	50	48.00 N	0.25 E
Arden Mines	279b	40.12 N	80.17 W
Ardennes □[5]	32	49.40 N	4.40 E
Ardennes ◆[1]	56	50.10 N	5.45 E
Ardennes, Canal des ≍	50	49.26 N	4.02 E
Ardenno	58	46.10 N	9.39 E
Ardentinny	46	56.03 N	4.55 W
Ardenza	66	43.31 N	10.19 E
Arderin ∧[2]	48	53.02 N	7.40 W
Ardersier	46	57.34 N	4.02 W
Ardeşen	130	41.12 N	41.00 E
Ardestān	128	33.22 N	52.23 E
Ardey	263	51.28 N	7.43 E
Ardeygebirge ⩘[2]	263	51.25 N	7.23 E
Ardez	58	46.46 N	10.11 E
Ardfern	46	56.10 N	5.32 W
Ardglass	48	54.16 N	5.37 W
Ardgroom	48	51.42 N	9.52 W
Ardıçlı	130	40.40 N	37.00 E
Ardila ≃	34	38.12 N	7.28 W
Ardill	184	49.53 N	105.49 W
Ardino	38	41.35 N	25.08 E
Ardlethan	166	34.21 S	146.54 E
Ardlui	46	56.18 N	4.43 W
Ardlussa	46	56.02 N	5.47 W
Ardmolich	46	56.49 N	5.41 W
Ardmore, Ire.	48	51.57 N	7.43 W
Ardmore, Al., U.S.	194	34.59 N	86.50 W
Ardmore, In., U.S.	216	41.41 N	86.19 W
Ardmore, Md., U.S.	284c	38.56 N	76.51 W
Ardmore, Ok., U.S.	196	34.10 N	97.08 W
Ardmore, Pa., U.S.	208	40.01 N	75.18 W
Ardmore Point ›, Scot., U.K.	46	56.39 N	6.07 W
Ardmore Point ›, Scot., U.K.	46	55.42 N	6.01 W
Ardnamurchan ›[1]	46	56.43 N	6.00 W
Ardnamurchan, Point of ›	46	56.44 N	6.13 W
Ardnaree	48	54.06 N	9.08 W
Ardnave Point ›	46	55.54 N	6.20 W
Ardoch	166	27.26 S	144.08 E
Ardon, Ross.	84	43.12 N	44.18 E
Ardon, Schw.	58	46.13 N	7.15 E
Ardon ≃	84	43.17 N	44.18 E
Ardon, Har ∧	132	30.38 N	34.57 E
Ardooie	50	50.59 N	3.12 E
Ardore	68	38.11 N	16.10 E
Ardoux ≃	50	47.42 N	1.35 E
Ardoz, Arroyo de ≃	266a	40.26 N	3.27 W
Ardres	50	50.51 N	1.59 E
Ardres ≃	50	49.18 N	3.40 E
Ardrishaig	46	56.01 N	5.27 W
Ardrossan, Austl.	168b	34.25 S	137.55 E
Ardrossan, Scot., U.K.	46	55.39 N	4.49 W
Ardsley, Eng., U.K.	44	53.32 N	1.23 W
Ardsley, N.Y., U.S.	276	41.00 N	73.50 W
Ardtalnaig	46	56.31 N	4.06 W
Arduan Island I	140	19.55 N	30.22 E
Ardusson ≃	50	48.30 N	3.32 E
Ardvasar	46	57.04 N	5.54 W
Åre	26	63.24 N	13.04 E
Areado	256	21.21 S	46.09 W
Areal	256	22.14 S	43.07 W
Arèches	62	45.41 N	6.34 E
Arecibo	240m	18.28 N	66.43 W
Arecibo, Observatorio de ℧[3]	240m	18.20 N	66.46 W
Areco ≃	258	33.56 S	59.16 W
Areeiro	266c	38.39 N	9.12 W
Arefjevo	86	57.01 N	90.40 E
Areguá	252	25.18 S	57.25 W
Arèhausk	76	54.41 N	30.30 E
Areia, Bra.	250	6.58 S	35.42 W
Areia, Port.	266c	38.43 N	9.08 W
Areia, Ribeirão da ≃	255	16.07 S	45.52 W
Areia Branca, Bra.	250	4.56 S	37.07 W
Areia Branca, Bra.	287a	22.44 S	43.25 W
Areias	256	22.35 S	44.42 W
Arena	68	38.34 N	16.13 E
Arena, Point ›	204	38.57 N	123.44 W
Arena, Punta ›	232	23.33 N	109.28 W
Arena de la Ventana, Punta ›	232	24.04 N	109.52 W
Arena Island I	116	9.14 N	120.46 E
Arenal, C.R.	236	10.29 N	84.53 W
Arenal, P.R.	240m	17.59 N	66.19 W
Arenal, Laguna de ⊜	236	10.32 N	84.56 W
Arenal, Volcán ∧[1]	236	10.28 N	84.44 W
Arenápolis	248	14.26 S	56.49 W
Arenas, Cayo I	232	22.08 N	91.24 W
Arenas, Punta ›	240m	18.07 N	65.35 W
Arenas, Punta de ›	254	53.09 S	68.13 W
Arenas de San Pedro	34	40.12 N	5.05 W
Arendal	26	58.27 N	8.48 E
Arendonk	56	51.19 N	5.05 E
Arendsee	54	52.53 N	11.30 E
Arendsee ⊜	54	52.53 N	11.30 E
Arendtsville	208	39.55 N	77.18 W
Arenes, Riera de les ≃	266d	41.29 N	2.02 E
Arenig Fawr ∧	42	52.55 N	3.45 W
Arenillas	246	3.33 S	80.04 W
Arenosa Creek ≃	196	28.52 N	96.44 W
Arenys de Mar	34	41.35 N	2.33 E
Arenzano	62	44.24 N	8.41 E
Arenzville	219	39.53 N	90.22 W
Arequipa	248	16.24 S	71.33 W
Arequipa □[5]	248	16.00 S	72.15 W
Arequito	252	33.09 S	61.28 W
Arero	144	4.45 N	38.49 E
Arês, Bra.	250	6.11 S	35.09 W
Arès, Fr.	32	44.46 N	1.08 W
Arèsa ≃	76	52.33 N	28.45 E
Arese	266b	45.33 N	9.05 E
Aresing	60	48.32 N	11.18 E
Åreskutan ∧	26	63.26 N	13.06 E
Areuse ≃	58	46.56 N	6.53 E
Arévalo	34	41.04 N	4.43 W
Arezzo	66	43.25 N	11.53 E
Arezzo □[4]	66	43.32 N	11.50 E
Arfa', Jabal ∧	132	29.51 N	35.27 E
'Arfā', Wādī al- V	132	30.16 N	36.34 E
Arga ≃	34	42.18 N	1.47 W
Argada	88	54.14 N	110.41 E
Argadargada	166	21.40 S	136.40 E
Argajaš	86	55.29 N	60.52 E
Argamasilla de Alba	34	39.07 N	3.06 W
Arganda	34	40.18 N	3.26 W
Argao	116	9.52 N	123.36 E
Arga-Sala ≃	74	68.30 N	112.12 E
Argedeb	144	6.10 N	41.10 E
Argegno	58	45.56 N	9.08 E
Argel → El Djazaïr	148	36.47 N	3.03 E
Argelès-Gazost	32	43.01 N	0.06 W
Argelès-sur-Mer	32	42.33 N	3.01 E
Argelia → Algeria □[1]	148	28.00 N	3.00 E

PORTUGUÊS Nome	Página	Lat.°′	Long.°′ W = Oeste
Argen ≃	58	47.35 N	9.33 E
Argenbühl	58	47.40 N	9.56 E
Argens ≃	62	43.24 N	6.44 E
Argent	158	26.04 S	28.50 E
Argenta, It.	66	44.37 N	11.50 E
Argenta, Il., U.S.	219	39.58 N	88.49 W
Argentan	32	48.45 N	0.01 W
Argentat	32	45.06 N	1.56 E
Argentera	62	44.24 N	6.57 E
Argentera ∧	62	44.10 N	7.18 E
Argenteuil	50	48.57 N	2.15 E
Argenteuil □[6]	206	45.45 N	74.30 W
Argentia	186	47.18 N	53.59 W
Argentiera	71	40.44 N	8.09 E
Argentière	58	45.59 N	6.56 E
Argentières	261	48.39 N	2.52 E
Argentina □[1]	244	34.00 S	64.00 W
Argentina ≃	62	43.50 N	7.51 E
Argentine	216	42.47 N	83.51 W
Argentine → Argentina □[1]	244	34.00 S	64.00 W
Argentine Basin ✢[1]	18	45.00 S	45.00 W
Argentinien → Argentina □[1]	244	34.00 S	64.00 W
Argentino, Hipódromo ♠	288	34.34 S	58.26 W
Argentino, Lago ⊜	254	50.13 S	72.25 W
Argentona	266d	41.33 N	2.24 E
Argentona, Riera d' ≃	266d	41.31 N	2.26 E
Argenton-Château	32	46.59 N	0.27 W
Argenton-sur-Creuse	32	46.35 N	1.31 E
Argentré	32	48.05 N	0.39 W
Argent-sur-Sauldre	50	47.33 N	2.27 E
Argeș □[6]	38	45.00 N	24.45 E
Argeș ≃	38	44.04 N	26.37 E
Arghandāb ≃	128	31.27 N	64.23 E
Arghastān ≃	120	31.23 N	65.45 E
Argirita	256	21.37 S	42.50 W
Argıthanı	130	38.17 N	31.43 E
Argo	140	19.31 N	30.25 E
Argoal	126	21.58 N	87.38 E
Argo Island I	140	19.25 N	30.27 E
Argolikós Kólpos c	38	37.33 N	22.45 E
Argonia	198	37.15 N	97.45 W
Argonne	190	45.39 N	88.52 W
Argonne ◆[1]	56	49.30 N	5.00 E
Argonne National Laboratory ℧[3]	216	41.43 N	87.58 W
Argopuro, Gunung ∧	115a	7.57 S	113.33 E
Árgos, Ellás	38	37.39 N	22.44 E
Argos, In., U.S.	216	41.14 N	86.15 W
Árgos Orestikón	38	40.28 N	21.16 E
Argostólion	38	38.10 N	20.30 E
Argoules	50	50.21 N	1.50 E
Argueil	50	49.32 N	1.31 E
Arguello, Point ›	204	34.35 N	120.39 W
Argun	84	43.16 N	45.52 E
Argun ≃	84	43.22 N	45.55 E
Argun' (Ergun) ≃, Asia	74	53.20 N	121.28 E
Argungu	150	12.45 N	4.31 E
Arguni, Teluk c	164	3.06 S	133.42 E
Ārgur	272b	22.48 N	88.13 E
Argut	86	49.51 N	87.03 E
Argut ≃	86	50.16 N	86.43 E
Arguvan	130	38.47 N	38.17 E
Argyle, Austl.	162	33.32 S	115.46 E
Argyle, Mn., U.S.	198	48.19 N	96.49 W
Argyle, Mo., U.S.	219	38.18 N	92.02 W
Argyle, N.Y., U.S.	210	43.14 N	73.30 W
Argyle, Tx., U.S.	222	33.07 N	97.11 W
Argyle, Lake ⊜[1]	164	16.15 S	128.45 E
'Arhāb, Wādī V	142	28.55 N	31.09 E
Arhavi	130	41.22 N	41.16 E
Arhéa Epídavros ⊥	38	37.37 N	23.02 E
Århus	41	56.09 N	10.13 E
Århus □[6]	41	56.15 N	10.05 E
Århus Bugt c	41	56.09 N	10.18 E
Aria	172	38.33 S	174.59 E
Aria ≃	164	5.45 S	149.15 E
Ariadnoje	89	45.08 N	134.25 E
Ariah	126	23.33 N	86.20 E
Ariake-kai c	92	33.00 N	130.20 E
Ariāl Khān ≃	126	23.56 N	90.46 E
Ariamácina, Lago di ⊜[1]	68	39.20 N	16.32 E
Ariamsvlei	156	28.07 S	19.49 E
Ariana	36	36.52 N	10.12 E
Ariano, Isola d' I	64	45.00 N	12.10 E
Ariano Irpino	68	41.09 N	15.05 E
Ariano nel Polesine	64	44.56 N	12.07 E
Ariari ≃	246	2.35 N	72.47 W
Arias	252	33.38 S	62.25 W
Arias, Arroyo de ≃	258	34.17 S	56.06 W
Arias, Cañada ≃	258	34.39 S	58.59 W
Ariaú	250	3.11 S	57.14 W
Aribinda	150	14.14 N	0.52 W
Arica, Chile	248	18.29 S	70.20 W
Arica, Col.	246	2.08 S	71.47 W
Arıcak	130	38.33 N	39.48 E
Aricanduva, Ribeirão ≃	287b	23.32 S	46.33 W
Ariccia	66	41.43 N	12.40 E
Arichat	186	45.31 N	61.01 W
Arichuna	246	7.42 N	67.08 W
Arid, Cape ›	162	34.00 S	123.09 E
Arida, Nig.	273a	6.34 N	3.16 E
Arida, Nihon	96	34.05 N	135.07 E
Arida ≃	96	34.05 N	135.06 E
Aridal, Sabkhat ⊜	148	26.12 N	14.05 W
Aridhaía	38	40.59 N	22.03 E
Ariège □[5]	32	43.00 N	1.30 E
Ariège ≃	32	43.31 N	1.25 E
Ariel, Wa., U.S.	224	45.57 N	122.34 W
Ari'el, W.B.	132	32.06 N	35.06 E
Arienzo	68	41.01 N	14.30 E
Arieș ≃	38	46.26 N	23.59 E
'Arif, Har ∧	132	30.26 N	34.44 E
Ārifwāla	123	30.17 N	73.04 E
Ariguanabo, Laguna de ⊜	286b	22.56 N	82.33 W
Ariguaní ≃	246	9.35 N	73.46 W
Arīḥā (Jericho), Ariha	132	31.52 N	35.27 E
Arīḥā, Sūrīy.	130	35.48 N	36.36 E
Arīḥā, Urd.	132	31.25 N	35.47 E
Arikaree ≃	198	40.01 N	101.56 W
Arikaree, North Fork ≃	198	39.39 N	102.57 W
Arikawa	92	32.59 N	129.07 E
Arikha, Har ∧[2]	132	30.39 N	34.47 E
Arild	41	56.16 N	12.34 E
Arima	241r	10.38 N	61.17 W
Arima ◆[8]	270	34.48 N	135.15 E
Arima ≃	270	34.52 N	135.15 E
Arima-fuji ∧[2]	270	34.55 N	135.14 E
Arimine-dam ◆[6]	94	36.29 N	137.27 E
Arinagour	46	56.37 N	6.31 W
Aringay	116	16.26 N	120.21 E
Arino ◆[8]	270	34.50 N	135.14 E
Arinos ≃	248	10.25 S	58.20 W
Arinthod	58	46.23 N	5.34 E
Ario de Rosales	234	19.12 N	101.43 W
Ariogala	76	55.16 N	23.30 E
Aripeka	220	28.25 N	82.39 W
Ariporo ≃	246	6.03 N	69.54 W
Aripuanã	248	9.10 S	60.38 W
Aripuanã ≃	248	5.07 S	60.24 W
Ariquemes	248	9.56 S	63.04 W
Arisa ≃	246	7.32 N	64.00 W
Arisaig	46	56.51 N	5.51 W
Arisaig, Sound of c	46	56.51 N	5.51 W
'Arīsh, Wādī al- V	140	31.09 N	33.49 E
Arismendi	246	8.29 N	68.22 W
Aristazabal Island I	182	52.30 N	129.05 W
Aristes	210	40.49 N	76.20 W
Aristizábal, Cabo ›	254	45.13 S	66.31 W
Aristovo	82	54.37 N	36.40 E
Arıt	130	41.41 N	32.39 E
Aritao	116	16.18 N	121.02 E

Ariton	194	31.36 N	85.43 W
Aritzo	71	39.57 N	9.12 E
Arivonimamo	157b	19.01 S	47.15 E
Ariyalūr	122	11.08 N	79.05 E
Arizaro, Salar de ≡	252	24.42 S	67.45 W
Arizgoiti	34	43.13 N	2.54 W
Arizona	252	35.43 S	65.18 W
Arizona □[3], U.S.	178	34.00 N	112.00 W
Arizona □[3], U.S.	200	34.00 N	112.00 W
Arizpe	232	30.20 N	110.10 W
Arja	80	57.30 N	46.00 E
Årjäng	26	59.23 N	12.08 E
Arjasa	112	6.51 S	115.16 E
Arjawinangun	115a	6.39 S	108.24 E
Arjay	192	36.48 N	83.38 W
Arjeplog	24	66.00 N	17.58 E
Arjona, Col.	246	10.15 N	75.21 W
Arjona, Esp.	34	37.56 N	4.03 W
Arka	74	60.03 N	142.12 E
Arkabutla Lake ⊜[1]	194	34.45 N	90.06 W
Arkadak	80	51.58 N	43.28 E
Arkadelphia	194	34.07 N	93.03 W
Arkaig, Loch ⊜	46	56.58 N	5.08 W
Arkalyk	86	50.13 N	66.50 E
Arkansas □[3], U.S.	178	34.50 N	92.30 W
Arkansas □[3], U.S.	194	34.50 N	92.30 W
Arkansas ≃	178	33.48 N	91.04 W
Arkansas, Salt Fork ≃	196	36.36 N	97.03 W
Arkansas City, Ar., U.S.	194	33.36 N	91.12 W
Arkansas City, Ks., U.S.	198	37.03 N	97.02 W
Arkansas Post National Memorial ⊥	194	33.55 N	91.26 W
Arkanū, Jabal ∧	146	22.13 N	24.41 E
Arkatag Shan ⩘	120	36.48 N	89.10 E
Arken-Ahon ∧	146	20.05 N	18.25 E
Arkhangélos	38	36.12 N	28.08 E
Arkhangel'sk → Archangel'sk	24	64.34 N	40.32 E
Arki	123	31.09 N	76.58 E
Árki I	38	37.22 N	26.45 E
Arkit	85	41.47 N	71.58 E
Arklow	48	52.48 N	6.09 W
Arkoma	194	35.21 N	94.26 W
Arkona, Kap ›	54	54.41 N	13.26 E
Arkösund	26	58.30 N	16.56 E
Arkport	210	42.23 N	77.41 W
Arktičeskij, mys ›	74	81.15 N	95.45 E
Arktičeskogo Instituta, ostrova II	74	75.20 N	81.55 E
Arkul'	80	57.17 N	50.03 E
Arkville	210	42.08 N	74.37 W
Arkwright	207	41.43 N	71.33 W
Ärla	40	59.17 N	16.40 E
Arlan	80	55.58 N	54.15 E
Arlan, gora ∧	128	39.40 N	54.33 E
Arlanc	62	45.25 N	3.44 E
Arlanda flygplats ⊠	40	59.37 N	17.55 E
Arlanza ≃	34	42.06 N	4.09 W
Arlanzón ≃	34	42.03 N	4.17 W
Arlbergpass)(	64	47.08 N	10.12 E
Arlberg-Tunnel ◆[5]	64	47.08 N	10.12 E
Arlee	202	47.09 N	114.05 W
Arles	62	43.40 N	4.38 E
Arles à Port de Bouc, Canal d' ≍	62	43.40 N	4.37 E
Arlesey	42	52.01 N	0.14 W
Arlesheim	58	47.30 N	7.37 E
Arleta ◆[8]	280	34.15 N	118.26 W
Arleux	50	50.17 N	3.06 E
Arley	262	53.19 N	2.30 W
Arli	150	11.35 N	1.28 E
Arli, Parc National de l' ♠	150	11.35 N	1.30 E
Arlington, S. Afr.	158	28.06 S	27.54 E
Arlington, Ga., U.S.	192	31.26 N	84.43 W
Arlington, In., U.S.	218	39.38 N	85.34 W
Arlington, Ia., U.S.	190	42.44 N	91.40 W
Arlington, Ks., U.S.	198	37.53 N	98.10 W
Arlington, Ky., U.S.	194	36.47 N	89.00 W
Arlington, Ma., U.S.	207	42.24 N	71.09 W
Arlington, Mn., U.S.	190	44.36 N	94.04 W
Arlington, Ne., U.S.	198	41.27 N	96.21 W
Arlington, N.Y., U.S.	210	41.41 N	73.53 W
Arlington, Oh., U.S.	216	40.53 N	83.39 W
Arlington, Or., U.S.	202	45.43 N	120.11 W
Arlington, S.D., U.S.	198	44.21 N	97.07 W
Arlington, Tn., U.S.	194	35.18 N	89.40 W
Arlington, Tx., U.S.	222	32.44 N	97.06 W
Arlington, Vt., U.S.	210	43.04 N	73.09 W
Arlington, Va., U.S.	208	38.52 N	77.06 W
Arlington, Wa., U.S.	224	48.11 N	122.07 W
Arlington □[6]	284c	38.50 N	77.10 W
Arlington, Lake ⊜[1]	222	32.42 N	97.13 W
Arlington Heights, Il., U.S.	216	42.05 N	87.58 W
Arlington Heights, Ma., U.S.	283	42.25 N	71.11 W
Arlington International Race Course ♠	278	42.05 N	88.00 W
Arlington Memorial Bridge ◆[5]	284c	38.53 N	77.03 W
Arlington Mill Reservoir ⊜[1]	283	42.48 N	71.13 W
Arlington National Cemetery ◆	284c	38.53 N	77.04 W
Arlit	150	19.00 N	7.38 E
Arlod	58	46.06 N	5.49 E
Arlon	56	49.41 N	5.49 E
Arlöv	41	55.39 N	13.05 E
Arltunga	162	23.26 S	134.41 E
Arl'uk	86	55.26 N	84.50 E
Arluno	62	45.30 N	8.56 E
Arly ≃	62	45.40 N	6.23 E
Arlyn Oaks	276	40.40 N	73.27 W
Arm ≃	184	50.46 N	105.00 W
Arma	198	37.32 N	94.42 W
Armação, Ponta da ›	287a	22.53 S	43.08 W
Armada	214	42.50 N	82.53 W
Armadale, Austl.	168a	32.09 S	116.00 E
Armadale, On., Can.	275b	43.50 N	79.15 W
Armadale, S. Afr.	273d	26.17 S	27.57 E
Armadale, Scot., U.K.	46	55.54 N	3.42 W
Arma di Taggia	62	43.50 N	7.51 E
Armageddon → Tel Megiddo ⊥	132	32.35 N	35.11 E
Armagh, N. Ire., U.K.	48	54.21 N	6.39 W
Armagh, Pa., U.S.	214	40.27 N	79.02 W
Armagnac □[9]	32	43.45 N	0.10 E
Armah, Wādī V	144	18.12 N	51.02 E
Armainvilliers, Étang d' ⊜	261	48.45 N	2.44 E
Armainvilliers, Forêt d' ♠	261	48.45 N	2.45 E
Armance ≃	50	47.59 N	3.43 E
Armançon ≃, Fr.	50	47.57 N	3.30 E
Armançon ≃, Fr.	58	47.33 N	4.17 E
Armant	140	25.37 N	32.32 E
Armavir	72	45.00 N	41.08 E
Armazém	252	28.16 S	49.01 W
Armbrust	214	40.13 N	79.33 W
Armells Creek ≃	202	47.37 N	108.40 W
Armenia	246	4.31 N	75.41 W
Armenia □[9]	84	40.30 N	43.30 E
Armenia □[1], Asia	72	40.00 N	45.00 E
Armenia (Hayastan) □[1], Asia	84	40.00 N	45.00 E
Armenija → Armenia □[1]	72	40.00 N	45.00 E
Armeniș	38	45.12 N	22.19 E
Armenistís	38	37.36 N	26.08 E
Armeniya → Armenia □[1]	72	40.00 N	45.00 E
Armeno	62	45.49 N	8.26 E
Armenonville-les-Gâtineaux	261	48.33 N	1.39 E
Armentières	50	50.41 N	2.53 E

Armento	68	40.18 N	16.04 E
Armería	234	18.56 N	103.58 W
Armería ≃	234	18.52 N	103.59 W
Armero	246	4.58 N	74.54 W
Armidale	166	30.31 S	151.39 E
Armijo	200	35.03 N	106.40 W
Armitage	42	52.44 N	1.53 W
Armit Lake ⊜	176	64.10 N	91.32 W
Armizonskoje	86	55.57 N	67.42 E
Armona	226	36.19 N	119.42 W
Armonk	276	41.07 N	73.42 W
Armor	210	42.44 N	78.48 W
Armori	122	20.28 N	79.59 E
Armour	198	43.19 N	98.20 W
Armoy, Fr.	58	46.21 N	6.31 E
Armoy, N. Ire., U.K.	48	55.07 N	6.20 W
Armstrong, Arg.	252	32.47 S	61.36 W
Armstrong, B.C., Can.	182	50.27 N	119.12 W
Armstrong, Il., U.S.	216	40.18 N	87.53 W
Armstrong, Ia., U.S.	198	43.23 N	94.28 W
Armstrong, Mo., U.S.	194	39.16 N	92.42 W
Armstrong □[6]	214	40.49 N	79.32 W
Armstrong ≃	164	16.46 S	131.12 E
Armstrong, Mount ∧	180	63.12 N	133.16 W
Armstrong Station	176	50.18 N	89.02 W
Armthorpe	44	53.32 N	1.03 W
Ārmūr	122	18.48 N	78.17 E
Armutlu	130	40.31 N	28.50 E
Armyans'k	78	46.07 N	33.41 E
Arnå ≃	41	54.57 N	8.53 E
Arnaccio	66	43.40 N	10.27 E
Arnaía	38	40.29 N	23.35 E
Arnarfjörður c[2]	24a	65.45 N	23.40 W
Arnäs	40	58.41 N	13.35 E
Arnaud ≃	176	59.59 N	69.46 W
Arnaudville	194	30.24 N	91.56 W
Arnavad, gora ∧	85	38.33 N	71.31 E
Arnavutköy ≃	267b	41.13 N	29.12 E
Arnay-le-Duc	58	47.08 N	4.29 E
Arnaz	62	45.38 N	7.43 E
Arnborg	41	56.01 N	8.59 E
Arnbruck	60	49.08 N	13.00 E
Arncliffe	274a	33.56 S	151.09 E
Arneburg	54	52.40 N	12.00 E
Arnedo	34	42.13 N	2.06 W
Arneiro dos Marinheiros	266c	38.51 N	9.25 W
Arneiroz	250	6.20 S	40.08 W
Arnejevo	82	54.58 N	37.35 E
Arnemuiden	52	51.30 N	3.41 E
Årnes	26	60.09 N	11.28 E
Arnett	196	36.08 N	99.46 W
Arney ≃	48	54.16 N	7.37 W
Arnhem	52	51.59 N	5.55 E
Arnhem, Cape ›	164	12.21 S	136.21 E
Arnhem Bay c	164	12.20 S	136.12 E
Arnhem Land ◆[1]	164	13.10 S	134.30 E
Arnhem Land Aboriginal Reserve ◆[4]	164	13.10 S	134.30 E
Arni	64	44.04 N	10.15 E
Arnis	41	54.38 N	9.56 E
Árnissa	38	40.48 N	21.50 E
Arno I[1]	14	7.05 N	171.41 E
Arno ≃	66	43.41 N	10.17 E
Arno, Torrente ≃	266b	45.42 N	8.48 E
Arno Bay	166	33.54 S	136.34 E
Arnoia ≃	34	42.15 N	8.09 W
Arnold, B.C., Can.	224	49.08 N	122.03 W
Arnold, Eng., U.K.	44	53.00 N	1.08 W
Arnold, Ca., U.S.	204	38.15 N	120.21 W
Arnold, Md., U.S.	208	39.01 N	76.30 W
Arnold, Mn., U.S.	190	46.52 N	92.05 W
Arnold, Mo., U.S.	219	38.25 N	90.22 W
Arnold, Ne., U.S.	198	41.25 N	100.11 W
Arnold, Pa., U.S.	214	40.34 N	79.46 W
Arnold ≃	164	15.19 S	134.06 E
Arnold Arboretum ♠	283	42.18 N	71.08 W
Arnold Mills	283	41.58 N	71.23 W
Arnold Mills Reservoir ⊜[1]	283	41.59 N	71.25 W
Arnolds Park	198	43.22 N	95.08 W
Arnoldstein	64	46.33 N	13.43 E
Arnon ≃	50	47.13 N	2.01 E
Arnos Vale Airport ⊠	241h	13.09 N	61.13 W
Arnot	210	41.39 N	77.07 W
Arnouville-lès-Gonesse	261	49.00 N	2.25 E
Arnouville-lès-Mantes	261	48.55 N	1.44 E
Arnprior	212	45.26 N	76.21 W
Arnsberg	56	51.24 N	8.03 E
Arnsberg □[5]	52	51.20 N	8.00 E
Arnsdorf	54	51.05 N	13.59 E
Arnside	44	54.12 N	2.50 W
Arnstadt	54	50.50 N	10.57 E
Arnstein	56	49.58 N	9.58 E
Arnstorf	60	48.34 N	12.49 E
Arnum	41	55.15 N	8.59 E
Ærø I	41	55.15 N	9.45 E
Aro ≃	246	8.01 N	64.11 W
Aroa	246	10.26 N	68.54 W
Aroa ≃	246	10.40 N	68.19 W
Aroa, Pointe ›	174s	17.28 S	149.46 W
Aroab	156	26.47 S	19.40 E
Aroali	126	24.03 N	87.56 E
Arochukwu	150	5.23 N	7.55 E
Aroeiras	250	7.31 S	35.41 W
Ar'ofino	80	58.16 N	39.15 E
Arolla	58	46.02 N	7.29 E
Arolsen	56	51.23 N	9.01 E
Aroma	140	15.49 N	36.08 E
Aroma Park	216	41.04 N	87.48 W
Aromas	226	36.53 N	121.39 W
Aromaševo	86	56.52 N	68.39 E
Arona, It.	62	45.46 N	8.34 E
Arona, Pap. N. Gui.	164	6.20 S	146.00 E
Arona, Pa., U.S.	279b	40.16 N	79.39 W
Aroostook ≃	186	46.48 N	67.45 W
Arop Island I	164	5.20 S	147.05 E
Aropuk Lake ⊜	180	61.12 N	163.50 W
Arorae I	14	2.38 S	176.49 E
Arorangi	174k	21.13 S	159.49 W
Aroroy	116	12.31 N	123.24 E
Aros ≃	232	29.09 N	109.40 W
Arosa	58	46.47 N	9.41 E
Arosbaya	115a	6.56 S	112.51 E
Årøsund	41	55.16 N	9.45 E
Arousa, Ría de c[1]	34	42.28 N	8.57 W
Aro Usu, Tanjung ›	164	8.20 S	130.45 E
Arowhana ∧	172	38.07 S	177.52 E
Arp	222	32.13 N	95.03 W
Arpa ≃	84	39.28 N	44.57 E
Arpaçay	84	40.52 N	43.20 E
Arpaçay (Achur'an) ≃	84	40.06 N	43.39 E
Arpačin	83	47.14 N	40.11 E
Arpaia	68	41.02 N	14.33 E
Arpajon	50	48.35 N	2.15 E
Ārpāra	126	23.23 N	89.23 E
Arpino	66	41.39 N	13.36 E
Arpoador, Ponta do ›	287a	22.59 S	43.12 W
Arquà Petrarca	64	45.16 N	11.43 E
Arquà Polesine	64	45.01 N	11.45 E
Arquata del Tronto	66	42.46 N	13.18 E
Arquata Scrivia	62	44.41 N	8.53 E
Arque	248	17.48 S	66.23 W
Arques	50	50.44 N	2.17 E
Arques-la-Bataille	50	49.53 N	1.08 E
Ar-Rabad	128	23.11 N	39.32 E
Ar-Rabbah	132	31.16 N	35.44 E
Arracourt	58	48.44 N	6.32 E
Ar-Radīsīyah Baḥrī	140	24.57 N	32.53 E
Ar-Rafīd	132	32.57 N	35.53 E
Arraga	252	28.04 S	64.14 W
Arrah	150	6.40 N	3.58 W
Ar-Rahad	140	12.43 N	30.39 E
Ar-Raḥāminah	142	31.18 N	31.45 E
Ar-Raḥmānīyah	142	31.06 N	30.38 E
Arraial do Cabo	255	22.58 S	42.01 W

Arraias	255	12.56 S	46.57 W
Arraias ≃, Bra.	250	11.10 S	53.35 W
Arraias ≃, Bra.	255	12.28 S	47.18 W
'Arrām, Wādī V	132	32.55 N	36.10 E
Ar-Ramādī	128	33.25 N	43.17 E
Ar-Ramthā	132	32.34 N	36.00 E
Arran, Island of I	46	55.35 N	5.15 W
Ar-Rank	140	11.45 N	32.48 E
Arran Lake ⊜	212	44.29 N	81.16 W
Ar-Raqqah	130	35.56 N	39.01 E
Ar-Raqqah □[8]	130	36.00 N	39.00 E
Arras	50	50.17 N	2.47 E
Arras, Nuraghe ⊥	71	39.40 N	9.25 E
Ar-Rāshidah	140	25.35 N	28.56 E
Ar-Rass	128	25.52 N	43.28 E
Ar-Rastan	130	34.55 N	36.44 E
Arrats ≃	32	44.06 N	0.52 E
Ar-Rawḍah, Ar. Su.	128	26.05 N	40.37 E
Ar-Rawḍah, Miṣr	142	27.48 N	30.52 E
Ar-Rawḍah, Miṣr	142	29.27 N	31.00 E
Ar-Rawḍah, Yaman	144	14.28 N	47.17 E
Ar-Rāwuk	144	15.45 N	48.54 E
Ar-Rayramūn	142	27.45 N	30.52 E
Ar-Rayyāḥ ar-Minūfīya ≍	142	30.20 N	31.00 E
Ar-Rayyāḥ at-Tawfīqī ≍	142	30.11 N	31.07 E
Ar-Rayyān	128	25.18 N	51.27 E
Arrecife	148	28.57 N	13.32 W
Arrecifes	252	34.03 S	60.07 W
Arrée, Montagnes d' ⩘	32	48.26 N	3.55 W
Arregui, Laguna ⊜	258	35.05 S	57.33 W
Arrentela	266c	38.38 N	9.06 W
Arresø ⊜	41	55.58 N	12.08 E
Arrey	200	32.50 N	107.19 W
Arriaga	234	16.14 N	93.54 W
Arriba	198	39.17 N	103.16 W
Arrild	41	55.09 N	8.58 E
Ar-Riyāḍ (Riyadh)	128	24.38 N	46.43 E
Arrochar	46	56.12 N	4.44 W
Arroio Grande	252	32.14 S	53.05 W
Arrojado ≃	255	13.24 S	44.20 W
Arronches	34	39.07 N	7.17 W
Arrone ≃, It.	66	41.52 N	12.11 E
Arrone ≃, It.	66	42.18 N	11.38 E
Arros ≃	32	43.40 N	0.02 W
Arroscia ≃	62	44.03 N	8.11 E
Arroux ≃	32	46.29 N	3.58 E
Arrow ≃, Eng., U.K.	42	52.12 N	2.43 W
Arrow ≃, Eng., U.K.	42	52.09 N	1.53 W
Arrow, Lough ⊜	48	54.04 N	8.21 W
Arrow Creek ≃	202	47.43 N	109.50 W
Arrowhead, Lake ⊜[1], Ca., U.S.	228	34.15 N	117.11 W
Arrowhead, Lake ⊜[1], Tx., U.S.	196	33.40 N	98.20 W
Arrowhead Peak ∧	228	34.13 N	117.16 W
Arrowhead Provincial Park ♠	212	45.24 N	79.13 W
Arrowhead Village	208	40.04 N	74.07 W
Arrow Lake ⊜	190	48.08 N	90.18 W
Arrowrock Reservoir ⊜[1]	202	43.36 N	115.51 W
Arrowsmith	216	40.27 N	88.38 W
Arrowsmith, Mount ∧, Austl.	166	30.09 S	141.50 E
Arrowsmith, Mount ∧, B.C., Can.	224	49.13 N	124.36 W
Arrowsmith, Mount ∧, N.Z.	172	43.21 S	170.59 E
Arrowtown	172	44.56 S	168.50 E
Arrowwood	182	50.44 N	113.09 W
Arroyan, Arroyo ≃[1]	288	34.24 S	58.32 W
Arroyito	252	31.25 S	63.03 W
Arroyo	240m	17.58 N	66.04 W
Arroyo de la Luz	34	39.29 N	6.35 W
Arroyo Grande, Ca., U.S.	204	35.07 N	120.35 W
Arroyo Grande → Ismael Cortinas, Ur.	258	33.58 S	57.06 W
Arroyo Hondo	200	36.32 N	105.40 W
Arroyo Naranjo ◆[8]	286b	23.02 N	82.23 W
Arroyo Seco	252	33.14 S	60.50 W
Arroyo Seco Park ♠	280	34.06 N	118.12 W
Arroyos y Esteros	252	25.04 S	57.06 W
Arrozal	256	22.37 S	44.03 W
Ar-Ru'at	140	12.21 N	32.17 E
Ar-Rub' al-Khālī ◆[2]	118	20.00 N	51.00 E
Ar-Rubayqī	142	30.10 N	31.46 E
Ar-Ruḥaybah	132	33.45 N	36.42 E
Ar-Rukhaymīyah ⊤[4]	128	29.14 N	45.35 E
Ar-Rumaythah	128	31.32 N	45.12 E
Ar-Rummān	132	32.10 N	35.50 E
Ar-Ruqayyah ⊥	132	32.47 N	37.05 E
Ar-Ruṣāfah ⊥	130	35.37 N	38.45 E
Ar-Ruṣayfah	132	32.01 N	36.03 E
Ar-Ruṣayriṣ	140	11.51 N	34.23 E
Ar-Rushaydah	132	32.40 N	36.50 E
Ar-Ruṭbah	128	33.02 N	40.17 E
Ar-Rū'ūs	142	29.21 N	31.04 E
Ar-Ruways	128	26.08 N	51.13 E
Års	26	56.48 N	9.32 E
Aršan, Ross.	88	51.54 N	102.27 E
Aršan, Ross.	88	53.54 N	99.54 E
Arsanjān	128	29.56 N	53.18 E
Aršan'-Zel'men'	80	47.36 N	44.36 E
Ārsāpota	272b	22.55 N	88.18 E
Arsbeck	56	51.08 N	6.12 E
Arsenal de Marinha ■	266c	38.39 N	9.09 W
Arsenal Football Club ♠	260	51.33 N	0.06 W
Arsenault Lake ⊜	184	55.06 N	108.30 W
Arsenjev	89	44.10 N	133.15 E
Arsenjevka ≃	89	44.54 N	133.35 E
Arsenjevo	76	53.44 N	36.40 E
Ars-en-Ré	32	46.12 N	1.31 W
Arsi □[4]	144	8.00 N	39.40 E
Arsiè	64	45.59 N	11.45 E
Arsiero	64	45.48 N	11.21 E
Arsikere	122	13.20 N	76.15 E
Arsin	130	40.58 N	39.56 E
Arsintsevo	78	45.17 N	36.25 E
Arsk	80	56.06 N	49.54 E
Arslanbob	85	41.21 N	72.56 E
Årslev	41	55.18 N	10.29 E
Arso	164	2.56 S	140.47 E
Arsoli	66	42.02 N	13.01 E
Ársos	130	34.50 N	32.46 E
Ars-sur-Formans	58	45.59 N	4.49 E
Ars-sur-Moselle	56	49.05 N	6.04 E
Årsta havsbad	40	59.05 N	18.10 E
Arsufhsa ≃	84	39.08 N	46.50 E
Årsunda	40	60.32 N	16.44 E
Art, Île I	175f	19.43 S	163.38 E
Árta, Ellás	38	39.09 N	20.59 E
Artà, Esp.	34	39.42 N	3.21 E
Artarmon	274a	33.49 S	151.11 E
Artašat	84	39.59 N	44.33 E
Arta Terme	64	46.28 N	13.01 E
Arteaga	234	18.28 N	102.25 W
Arteche	116	12.17 N	125.22 E
Arte Contemporânea, Museu de ℧	287b	23.32 S	46.38 W
Artegna	64	46.14 N	13.09 E
Artemare	62	45.52 N	5.42 E
Artemisa	240p	22.49 N	82.46 W
Artemivka	78	49.46 N	35.04 E
Artemivs'k, Ukr.	83	48.27 N	38.42 E
Artemivs'k, Ukr.	83	48.35 N	38.00 E
Artemón	38	36.59 N	24.43 E
Artémou	150	15.31 N	12.16 W
Artemove	83	48.22 N	37.53 E
Artemovsk → Artemivs'k	83	48.35 N	38.00 E
Artèn	64	46.00 N	11.50 E
Artenay	50	48.05 N	1.53 E
Artern	54	51.22 N	11.17 E

≃ River	Fluß	Río	Rivière	Rio	
≍ Canal	Kanal	Canal	Canal	Canal	
⌊ Waterfall, Rapids	Wasserfall, Stromschnellen	Cascada, Rápidos	Chute d'eau, Rapides	Cascata, Rápidos	
⋓ Strait	Meeresstraße	Estrecho	Détroit	Estreito	
c Bay, Gulf	Bucht, Golf	Bahía, Golfo	Baie, Golfe	Baía, Golfo	
⊜ Lake, Lakes	See, Seen	Lago, Lagos	Lac, Lacs	Lago, Lagos	
≡ Swamp	Sumpf	Pantano	Marais	Pântano	
⩍ Ice Features, Glacier	Eis- und Gletscherformen	Accidentes Glaciales	Formes glaciaires	Acidentes glaciares	
⊤ Other Hydrographic Features	Andere Hydrographische Objekte	Otros Elementos Hidrográficos	Autres données hydrographiques	Outros acidentes hidrográficos	

✢ Submarine Features	Untermeerische Objekte	Accidentes Submarinos	Formes de relief sous-marin	Acidentes submarinos
□ Political Unit	Politische Einheit	Unidad Politica	Entité politique	Unidade política
℧ Cultural Institution	Kulturelle Institution	Institución Cultural	Institution culturelle	Instituição cultural
⊥ Historical Site	Historische Stätte	Sitio Histórico	Site historique	Sitio histórico
♠ Recreational Site	Erholungs- und Ferienort	Sitio de Recreo	Centre de loisirs	Area de Lazer
⊠ Airport	Flughafen	Aeropuerto	Aéroport	Aeroporto
■ Military Installation	Militäranlage	Instalación Militar	Installation militaire	Instalação militar
◆ Miscellaneous	Verschiedenes	Misceláneo	Divers	Diversos

ENGLISH — Name | Page | Lat.°′ | Long.°′
DEUTSCH — Name | Seite | Breite°′ | Länge°′ E = Ost

Artesia
→ Mosomane, Bots. 156 24.04 S 26.15 E
Artesia, Ca., U.S. 280 33.51 N 118.04 W
Artesia, Ms., U.S. 194 33.24 N 88.38 W
Artesia, N.M., U.S. 196 32.50 N 104.24 W
Artesia Lake ⊜ 226 38.57 N 119.22 W
Artesian 198 44.00 N 97.55 W
Arth 58 47.04 N 8.31 E
Arthabaska 206 46.02 N 71.55 W
Arthabaska □[6] 206 46.05 N 72.00 W
Arthal 123 33.16 N 76.11 E
Arthala 272a 28.40 N 77.24 E
Arthies 261 49.06 N 1.48 E
Arthonnay 50 47.56 N 4.13 E
Arthur, On., Can. 212 43.50 N 80.32 W
Arthur, Il., U.S. 194 39.43 N 88.28 W
Arthur, Ne., U.S. 198 41.34 N 101.41 W
Arthur, N.D., U.S. 198 47.06 N 97.13 W
Arthur, Tn., U.S. 192 36.32 N 83.40 W
Arthur ≃, Austl. 166 41.03 S 144.40 E
Arthur ≃, Austl. 168a 33.31 S 116.50 E
Arthur, Lake ⊜[1] 214 40.57 N 80.05 W
Arthur Creek ≃ 162 22.55 S 136.45 E
Arthur Kill ⊔ 276 40.30 N 74.15 W
Arthurs Pass 172 42.57 S 171.34 E
Arthurs Pass)(172 42.54 S 171.34 E
Arthur's Pass National Park ♦ 172 42.50 S 171.40 E
Arthurs Seat ∧[2] 169 38.21 S 144.57 E
Arthur's Town 238 24.38 N 75.42 W
Arthurton 168b 34.16 S 137.45 E
Arti 86 56.26 N 58.32 E
Artibonite ≃ 238 19.15 N 72.47 W
Artico, Océano → Arctic Ocean ⊤[1] 16 85.00 N 170.00 E
Artigas 252 30.24 S 56.28 W
Artigas ◆[8] 286c 10.30 N 66.56 W
Artigas, Casa de ⊥ 258 34.39 S 56.03 W
Artik 84 40.37 N 43.59 E
Artilleros 258 34.22 S 57.34 W
Artilleros, Punta › 258 34.28 S 57.32 W
Artillery Lake ⊜ 176 63.09 N 107.52 W
Artlenburg 52 53.22 N 10.29 E
Artney, Glen V 46 56.20 N 4.04 W
Artois □[9] 50 50.30 N 2.30 E
Artois, Collines de l' ⋏[2] 50 50.25 N 2.10 E
Art'om 89 43.22 N 132.13 E
Art'omovsk 86 54.21 N 93.26 E
Art'omovskij, Ross. 86 57.21 N 61.54 E
Art'omovskij, Ross. 88 58.12 N 114.45 E
Art'omovskij, Ross. 89 43.27 N 132.22 E
Artova 130 40.03 N 36.19 E
Artpark ♦ 284a 43.10 N 79.03 W
Artrutx, Cap d' › 34 39.56 N 3.48 E
Artsyz 78 46.00 N 29.26 E
Artuby ≃ 62 43.44 N 6.22 E
Artur Nogueira 256 22.35 S 47.09 W
Arturo Merino Benítez, Aeropuerto ⊠ 286e 33.23 S 70.49 W
Arturo Segui ◆[8] 258 34.51 S 58.09 W
Artvin 130 41.11 N 41.49 E
Artvin □[4] 130 41.05 N 42.00 E
Artybaš 86 51.48 N 87.16 E
Artyk 74 64.12 N 145.06 E
Artyom 84 40.28 N 50.20 E
Aru, Kepulauan II 164 6.00 S 134.30 E
Aru, Tanjung › 112 2.10 S 116.34 E
Aru, Teluk ⊂ 114 4.09 N 98.12 E
Arua 154 3.01 N 30.55 E
Aruã ≃ 250 2.39 S 55.38 W
Aruaddin 144 16.15 N 38.43 E
Aruanã 255 14.54 S 51.05 W
Aruângua (Luangwa) ≃ 154 15.36 S 30.25 E
Aruba □[2], N.A. 230 12.30 N 69.58 W
Aruba □[2], N.A. 241s 12.30 N 69.58 W
Aru Basin ✢[1] 14 5.00 S 134.00 E
Arucas 148 28.07 N 15.31 W
Arue 174s 17.32 S 149.32 W
Arufu 150 7.50 N 9.14 E
Arujá 256 23.24 S 46.20 W
Arujá □[7] 287b 23.24 S 46.20 W
Arumanduba 250 1.29 S 52.29 W
Arume 174m 26.36 N 128.07 E
Arume-wan ⊂ 174m 26.35 N 128.08 E
Arun (Pong) ≃, Asia 124 26.49 N 87.09 E
Arun ≃, Eng., U.K. 42 50.48 N 0.33 W
Arunāchal Pradesh □[3] 120 28.30 N 95.00 E
Arundel, P.Q., Can. 206 45.58 N 74.37 W
Arundel, Eng., U.K. 42 50.51 N 0.34 W
Arun Qi 89 48.07 N 123.28 E
Århus 41 55.23 N 10.04 E
Aruppukkottai 122 9.31 N 78.06 E
Arurandeua ≃ 250 3.43 S 48.50 W
Arusha 154 3.22 S 36.41 E
Arusha □[4] 154 4.00 S 36.15 E
Arusha Chini 154 3.35 S 37.20 E
Arusha National Park ♦ 154 3.17 S 36.56 E
Arut ≃ 112 2.42 S 111.34 E
Aruvi ≃ 122 8.49 N 79.55 E
Aruwimi ≃ 138 1.13 N 23.36 E
Arvada 200 39.48 N 105.05 W
Arvagh 48 53.55 N 7.34 W
Arvajcheer 90 46.15 N 102.48 E
Arve ≃ 58 46.12 N 6.08 E
Arverne ◆[8] 276 40.35 N 73.48 W
Arves, Les Aiguilles d' ∧ 62 45.08 N 6.21 E
Arvi 120 20.59 N 78.14 E
Arvida 186 48.25 N 71.11 W
Arvidsjaur 24 65.35 N 19.07 E
Arvier 62 45.42 N 7.11 E
Arvieux 62 44.46 N 6.44 E
Arvika 26 59.39 N 12.36 E
Arvillard 62 45.27 N 6.07 E
Arvin 228 35.12 N 118.49 W
Arvo, Lago ⊜ 68 39.14 N 16.29 E
Arvon, Mount ∧ 190 46.45 N 88.09 W
Arvonia 192 37.40 N 78.20 W
Arvorezinha 252 28.53 S 52.10 W
Arwal 124 25.15 N 84.41 E
Arwala 112 7.41 S 126.49 E
Arxan 89 47.11 N 119.57 E
Aryamūn 142 31.11 N 30.54 E
Aryiroúpolis 267c 37.54 N 23.45 E
Arys' 85 42.26 N 68.48 E
Arys ≃ 85 42.48 N 68.12 E
Arys, ozero ⊜ 86 45.50 N 66.20 E
Arys-Turkestanskij kanal ≊ 85 42.44 N 69.00 E
Arzachena 71 41.05 N 9.23 E
Arzamas 80 55.23 N 43.50 E
Arzana 71 39.55 N 9.31 E
Arzano 68 40.55 N 14.16 E
Arzberg, Dtsch. 54 51.32 N 13.08 E
Arzberg, Dtsch. 60 50.04 N 12.12 E
Arzew, Golfe d' ⊂ 34 35.50 N 0.10 W
Arzew, Salines d' ⊜ 34 35.40 N 0.15 W
Arzfeld 56 50.05 N 6.16 E
Arzignano 64 45.31 N 11.20 E
Arziw 148 35.51 N 0.19 W
Arz Lubnān ◆[3] 130 34.14 N 36.03 E
Arzni 84 40.19 N 44.36 E
Arzon ≃ 62 45.11 N 3.54 E
Arzúa 34 42.56 N 8.09 W
As, Bel. 56 51.01 N 5.35 E
Aš, Česká Rep. 54 50.10 N 12.10 E
Ås, Nor. 26 59.40 N 10.48 E
Asa, Nihon 96 34.33 N 132.26 E
Aša, Ross. 86 55.00 N 57.16 E
Asa ≃, Nihon 94 35.39 N 139.26 E
Asa ≃, Nihon 96 34.01 N 131.09 E
Asa ≃, Ven. 246 6.50 N 63.18 W
Asab 156 25.29 S 17.59 E
Asaba, Nig. 150 6.12 N 6.44 E
Asaba, Nihon 94 34.42 N 137.56 E
Asad, Buḥayrat al- ⊜[1] 130 36.00 N 38.10 E
Asadābād, Afg. 120 34.52 N 71.09 E
Asadābād, Īrān 128 34.47 N 48.07 E
Asafo 150 6.11 N 0.28 W
Asaga Strait ⊔ 174y 14.11 S 169.40 W
Asagaya ◆[8] 268 35.42 N 139.38 E
Aşağibostancı 130 35.10 N 33.00 E
Aşağıçiğil 130 38.03 N 31.52 E
Aşağı Dağ ∧ 84 40.01 N 43.11 E
Aşağı Köynük 84 41.18 N 47.00 E
Aşağı Kuluşağı 130 38.39 N 38.39 E
Aşağılahan 130 38.50 N 39.59 E
Aşağı Mestikân 130 38.25 N 38.46 E
Asahan 114 2.23 N 102.33 E
Asahan ≃ 114 3.02 N 99.52 E
Asahi, Nihon 94 35.14 N 137.22 E
Asahi, Nihon 94 35.43 N 140.39 E
Asahi, Nihon 94 35.59 N 136.07 E
Asahi, Nihon 94 36.05 N 137.21 E
Asahi, Nihon 94 36.14 N 140.31 E
Asahi, Nihon 94 35.02 N 136.40 E
Asahi, Nihon 94 36.07 N 137.52 E
Asahi, Nihon 94 36.57 N 137.34 E
Asahi, Nihon 96 34.59 N 133.50 E
Asahi, Nihon 96 34.51 N 132.16 E
Asahi, Nihon 96 34.17 N 131.28 E
Asahi ◆[8], Nihon 268 35.29 N 139.33 E
Asahi ◆[8], Nihon 270 34.44 N 135.34 E
Asahi ≃ 96 34.36 N 133.58 E
Asahi-dake ∧, Nihon 92a 43.40 N 142.51 E
Asahi-dake ∧, Nihon 94 37.14 N 139.21 E
Asahigawa → Asahikawa 92a 43.46 N 142.22 E
Asahi-gawa-daiichi-dam ◆[6] 96 34.53 N 133.22 E
Asahikawa 92a 43.46 N 142.22 E
Asahikawa-chūtonchi, Rikujō-Jieitai- ■ 92a 43.49 N 142.25 E
Asahi-ko ⊜[1] 96 34.56 N 133.51 E
Asahi-sanchi ⋏ 92 38.25 N 139.50 E
Asaka 94 35.48 N 139.36 E
Asaka, Camp ■ 268 35.47 N 139.36 E
Asakanskij Golec, gora ∧ 88 50.18 N 109.55 E
Asakawa 94 37.05 N 140.25 E
Asake ≃ 94 35.00 N 136.41 E
Asako 96 35.14 N 134.48 E
Asakura 96 33.23 N 130.44 E
Asakusa ◆[8] 268 35.43 N 139.49 E
Asālafpur ◆[8] 272a 28.38 N 77.05 E
Asale 144 14.22 N 40.32 E
Asale, Lake ⊜ 144 14.19 N 40.18 E
Asamankese 150 5.52 N 0.42 W
Asama-yama ∧ 94 36.24 N 138.31 E
Asanbani, India 126 22.43 N 86.20 E
Asanbāni, India 126 24.07 N 87.27 E
Asani 154 4.25 S 29.05 E
Asankrangwa 150 5.48 N 2.26 W
Asan-man ⊂ 98 36.56 N 126.51 E
Āsānsol, India 126 24.14 N 87.17 E
Āsānsol, India 126 23.41 N 86.59 E
Ašap 86 57.07 N 56.30 E
Asar 88 47.56 N 117.38 E
Åsarna 26 62.39 N 14.21 E
Asarum 26 56.12 N 14.50 E
Asashina 94 36.16 N 138.25 E
Āsāsuni 126 22.32 N 89.10 E
Asati 272b 22.29 N 88.14 E
Asa-yama ∧ 96 34.47 N 132.23 E
Asayita 144 11.33 N 41.30 E
Asbach 56 50.40 N 7.25 E
Asbeck 263 51.21 N 7.18 E
Asberg 263 51.26 N 6.40 E
Asbesberg ⋏ 158 28.55 S 23.15 E
Asbest 86 57.00 N 61.30 E
Asbestos 206 45.46 N 71.57 W
Asbestos Range National Park ♦ 166 41.08 S 146.39 E
Asbe Teferi 144 9.02 N 40.58 E
Åsbro 40 59.00 N 15.03 E
Asbury 210 40.41 N 75.00 W
Asbury Park 208 40.13 N 74.01 W
Ascea 68 40.08 N 15.11 E
Ascensión 232 31.06 N 107.59 W
Ascension I 10 7.57 S 14.22 W
Ascent 158 27.12 S 29.03 E
Aščerino 265b 55.36 N 37.46 E
Asch 58 47.57 N 10.49 E
Aschabad (Ashgabat) 128 37.57 N 58.23 E
Aschach an der Donau 61 48.22 N 14.02 E
Aschaffenburg 56 49.59 N 9.09 E
Aschbach Markt 61 48.04 N 14.45 E
Ascheberg, Dtsch. 52 51.47 N 7.37 E
Ascheberg, Dtsch. 54 54.08 N 10.20 E
Aschendorf 52 53.04 N 7.22 E
Aschersleben 54 51.45 N 11.27 E
Asciano 66 43.14 N 11.33 E
Aščikol', ozero ⊜ 86 45.05 N 67.15 E
Aščitastysor, ozero ⊜ 86 49.19 N 63.59 E
Ascoli Piceno 66 42.51 N 13.34 E
Ascoli Piceno □[4] 66 43.01 N 13.34 E
Ascoli Satriano 68 41.12 N 15.34 E
Ascona 58 46.09 N 8.46 E
Ascope 248 7.43 S 79.07 W
Ascot, Austl. 171a 27.26 S 153.04 E
Ascot, Eng., U.K. 42 51.25 N 0.41 W
Ascot ≃ 206 45.21 N 71.51 W
Ascotán 252 21.44 S 68.18 W
Ascros 62 43.55 N 7.01 E
Aščykol', ozero ⊜ 85 43.32 N 70.35 E
Aščyozek ≃ 80 49.12 N 48.06 E
Aščysu ≃ 86 49.54 N 78.58 E
Aseb 144 13.00 N 42.45 E
Åseda 26 57.10 N 15.20 E
Asedjrad ⋏[1] 148 24.28 N 1.52 E
Asekejevo 80 53.36 N 52.49 E
Asela 144 7.59 N 39.08 E
Åsele 26 64.10 N 17.20 E
Asem ≃ 115a 6.14 S 107.42 E
Asembagus 115a 7.45 S 114.14 E
Asembourg 56 49.43 N 6.02 E
Åsen 26 63.36 N 11.03 E
Asendabo 144 9.50 N 37.33 E
Asendorf 52 52.46 N 9.00 E
Asenovgrad 38 42.01 N 24.52 E
Åsensbruk 26 58.48 N 12.25 E
Aseri 76 59.27 N 26.52 E
Aşfar, Jabal al- ∧ 132 32.12 N 36.54 E
Asfordby 42 52.46 N 0.57 W
Aşfūn al-Maṭā'inah 140 25.23 N 32.32 E
Åsgårdstrand 26 59.21 N 10.28 E
Ash, Eng., U.K. 42 51.17 N 1.16 E
Ash, Eng., U.K. 42 51.15 N 0.44 W
Ashalim 132 30.58 N 34.40 E
Åshammar 40 60.39 N 16.32 E
Ashanti □[4] 150 6.45 N 1.30 W
'Asharah, Wādī al- V 142 30.21 N 32.15 E
Asharoken 276 40.56 N 73.22 W
Ashaway 207 41.25 N 71.47 W
Ashbourne, Ire. 48 53.31 N 6.24 W
Ashbourne, Eng., U.K. 44 53.02 N 1.44 W
Ash Brook Swamp Reservation ♦ 276 40.37 N 74.21 W
Ashburn, Ga., U.S. 192 31.42 N 83.39 W
Ashburn, Mo., U.S. 219 39.33 N 91.10 W
Ashburn, Va., U.S. 208 39.02 N 77.29 W
Ashburnham 207 42.38 N 71.54 W
Ashburton, Austl. 274b 37.52 S 145.05 E
Ashburton, N.Z. 172 43.55 S 171.45 E
Ashburton, Eng., U.K. 42 50.31 N 3.45 W
Ashburton ≃, Austl. 162 21.40 S 114.56 E
Ashburton ≃, N.Z. 172 44.04 S 171.48 E
Ashburton, North Branch ≃ 172 43.54 S 171.44 E
Ashburton, South Branch ≃ 172 43.44 S 171.32 E
Ashburton Downs 162 23.24 S 117.04 E
Ashby 207 42.40 N 71.49 W
Ashby, Lake ⊜ 220 28.56 N 81.07 W
Ashby-de-la-Zouch 42 52.46 N 1.28 W
Ashchurch 42 52.00 N 2.07 W
Ash Creek ≃, Ca., U.S. 204 41.05 N 121.08 W
Ash Creek ≃, Ct., U.S. 276 41.08 N 73.14 W
Ashcroft 182 50.43 N 121.17 W
Ashdod, Ma., U.S. 283 42.04 N 70.45 W
Ashdod, Yis. 132 31.49 N 34.40 E
Ashdod, Tel ⊥ 132 31.45 N 34.40 E
Ashdot Ya'aqov 132 32.40 N 35.35 E
Ashdown 194 33.40 N 94.07 W
Asheboro 192 35.42 N 79.48 W
Ashern 184 51.11 N 98.21 W
Asherton 196 28.26 N 99.45 W
Asheville 192 35.36 N 82.33 W
Ashewat Ziārat 120 31.22 N 68.32 E
Asheweig ≃ 176 54.17 N 87.12 W
Ashfield, Austl. 274a 33.53 S 151.08 E
Ashfield, Ma., U.S. 207 42.31 N 72.47 W
Ash Flat 194 36.13 N 91.36 W
Ashford, Austl. 166 29.20 S 151.06 E
Ashford, Eng., U.K. 42 51.08 N 0.53 E
Ashford, Eng., U.K. 260 51.26 N 0.27 W
Ashford, Al., U.S. 194 31.10 N 85.14 W
Ashford, Wa., U.S. 224 46.46 N 122.02 W
Ashford Airport ⊠ 42 51.04 N 1.01 E
Ash Fork 200 35.13 N 112.28 W
Ash Grove 194 37.18 N 93.35 W
Ashhurst 172 40.18 S 175.45 E
Ashibe 92 33.48 N 129.46 E
Ashibetsu 92a 43.31 N 142.11 E
Ashida ≃ 96 34.26 N 133.25 E
Ashikaga 94 36.20 N 139.27 E
Ashikagga-gakkō ⊥ 94 36.22 N 139.30 E
Ashingdon 260 51.36 N 0.42 E
Ashington 44 55.12 N 1.35 W
Ashino-ko ⊜ 94 35.13 N 139.00 E
Ashio 94 36.38 N 139.27 E
Ashio-sanchi ⋏ 94 36.35 N 139.30 E
Ashippun 216 43.14 N 88.31 W
Ashippun ≃ 216 43.10 N 88.33 W
Ashitaka-yama ∧ 94 35.12 N 138.49 E
Ashiya, Nihon 96 33.53 N 130.40 E
Ashiya, Nihon 96 34.43 N 135.17 E
Ashiya ≃ 270 34.43 N 135.18 E
Ashiyasu 94 35.38 N 138.23 E
Ashiyoro 92a 43.15 N 143.30 E
Ashizuri-misaki › 92 32.44 N 133.01 E
Ashizuri-Uwakai-kokuritsu-kōen ♦, Nihon 92 32.45 N 132.45 E
Ashizuri-Uwakai-kokuritsu-kōen ♦, Nihon 96 33.07 N 132.27 E
Ashkhabad → Aščhabad 128 37.57 N 58.23 E
Ashkum 216 40.53 N 87.57 W
Ashland, Al., U.S. 194 33.16 N 85.50 W
Ashland, Ca., U.S. 226 37.41 N 122.06 W
Ashland, Il., U.S. 219 39.53 N 90.00 W
Ashland, Ks., U.S. 198 37.11 N 99.45 W
Ashland, Ky., U.S. 188 38.28 N 82.38 W
Ashland, Me., U.S. 186 46.37 N 68.24 W
Ashland, Ma., U.S. 207 42.15 N 71.27 W
Ashland, Ms., U.S. 194 34.49 N 89.10 W
Ashland, Mo., U.S. 219 38.46 N 92.15 W
Ashland, Mt., U.S. 202 45.35 N 106.16 W
Ashland, Ne., U.S. 198 41.02 N 96.22 W
Ashland, N.H., U.S. 188 43.41 N 71.37 W
Ashland, N.J., U.S. 285 39.51 N 75.00 W
Ashland, N.Y., U.S. 210 42.18 N 74.20 W
Ashland, Oh., U.S. 214 40.52 N 82.19 W
Ashland, Or., U.S. 202 42.11 N 122.42 W
Ashland, Pa., U.S. 210 40.46 N 76.20 W
Ashland, Va., U.S. 208 37.45 N 77.28 W
Ashland, Wi., U.S. 190 46.35 N 90.53 W
Ashland □[6] 214 40.52 N 82.19 W
Ashland, Mount ∧ 202 42.05 N 122.43 W
Ashland City 194 36.16 N 87.03 W
Ashley, Austl. 166 29.19 S 149.49 E
Ashley, Eng., U.K. 262 53.21 N 2.20 W
Ashley, Il., U.S. 219 38.20 N 89.11 W
Ashley, In., U.S. 216 41.32 N 85.04 W
Ashley, Mi., U.S. 190 43.11 N 84.28 W
Ashley, Mo., U.S. 219 39.15 N 91.14 W
Ashley, N.D., U.S. 198 46.01 N 99.22 W
Ashley, Oh., U.S. 214 40.24 N 82.57 W
Ashley, Pa., U.S. 210 41.12 N 75.53 W
Ashley ≃ 172 43.16 S 172.43 E
Ashley Creek ≃ 200 40.21 N 109.22 W
Ashley Falls 207 42.03 N 73.20 W
Ashley Green 260 51.44 N 0.35 W
Ashmore 194 39.32 N 88.01 W
Ashmore Islands II 160 12.14 S 123.05 E
Ashmūn 142 30.18 N 30.58 E
Ashokan Reservoir ⊜[1] 210 41.58 N 74.10 W
Ashoknagar 120 24.34 N 77.43 E
Ashqelon 132 31.40 N 34.35 E
Ashridge Park ♦ 260 51.48 N 0.34 W
Ash-Shabakah 128 30.49 N 43.39 E
Ash-Shabb ⊤[4] 140 22.19 N 29.46 E
Ash-Shaddādah 130 36.02 N 40.45 E
Ash-Shāgūr 132 31.50 N 35.39 E
Ash-Shā'ib ∧[2] 142 29.50 N 30.56 E
Ash-Shajarah 132 32.39 N 35.56 E
Ash-Shallūfah 142 30.07 N 32.34 E
Ash-Shamāl □[4] 130 34.30 N 36.00 E
Ash-Shamālīyah □[4] 140 19.15 N 29.00 E
Ash-Shāmīyah 128 31.57 N 44.36 E
Ash-Shanāwīyah 142 29.08 N 31.08 E
Ash-Sharāh ◆[1] 132 30.20 N 35.30 E
Ash-Shāriqah 128 25.22 N 55.23 E
Ash-Sharmah 128 28.01 N 35.18 E
Ash-Sharqāṭ 128 35.27 N 43.16 E
Ash-Sharqīyah □[4] 142 30.48 N 31.48 E
Ash-Sharqīyah ◆[1] 128 27.00 N 49.00 E
Ash-Shaṭrah 128 31.25 N 46.10 E
Ash-Shawāshinah 142 29.22 N 30.36 E
Ash-Shawbak 132 30.32 N 35.34 E
Ash-Shawmarah 132 33.07 N 35.08 E
Ash-Shaykh Faḍl 142 28.29 N 30.50 E
Ash-Shaykh 'Ibādah 142 27.48 N 30.52 E
Ash-Shaykh Sa'd 132 32.50 N 36.02 E
Ash-Shaykh Timay 142 27.53 N 30.51 E
Ash-Shiḥr 144 14.44 N 49.35 E
Ash-Shīn 142 31.01 N 30.53 E
Ash-Shināfīyah 128 31.35 N 44.39 E
Ash-Shīyāḥ 132 33.51 N 35.30 E
Ash-Shufayyah 128 23.50 N 39.08 E
Ash-Shuhadā' 142 30.36 N 30.54 E
Ash-Shumlul 128 26.31 N 47.19 E
Ash-Shuqayq 144 17.43 N 42.01 E
Ash-Shurayf 128 25.43 N 39.14 E
Ash-Shurayk 140 18.48 N 33.34 E
Ash-Shuwayfāt 132 33.49 N 35.31 E
Ash Slough ≃ 226 37.02 N 120.32 W
Ashta, India 122 16.57 N 74.24 E
Ashta, India 124 23.01 N 76.43 E
Ashtabula 214 41.51 N 80.47 W
Ashtabula □[6] 214 41.44 N 80.46 W
Ashtabula ≃ 214 41.55 N 80.47 W
Ashtabula, East Branch ≃ 214 41.48 N 80.37 W
Ashtabula, Lake ⊜[1] 198 47.11 N 97.58 W
Ashtabula, West Branch ≃ 214 41.48 N 80.37 W
Ashtead 42 51.19 N 0.18 W
Ashton, S. Afr. 158 33.50 S 20.05 E
Ashton, Eng., U.K. 262 53.13 N 2.45 W
Ashton, Id., U.S. 202 44.04 N 111.26 W
Ashton, Il., U.S. 190 41.51 N 89.13 W
Ashton, Ia., U.S. 198 43.18 N 95.47 W
Ashton, Md., U.S. 208 39.08 N 77.00 W
Ashton, Ne., U.S. 198 41.14 N 98.47 W
Ashton, R.I., U.S. 207 41.46 N 71.25 W
Ashton-in-Makerfield 44 53.29 N 2.39 W
Ashton-under-Lyne 44 53.29 N 2.06 W
Ashton upon Mersey 262 53.26 N 2.19 W
Ashuanipi Lake ⊜ 176 52.35 N 66.10 W
Ashuelot ≃ 188 42.46 N 72.29 W
Ashurst's Beacon ∧[2] 262 53.34 N 2.45 W
Ashville, Al., U.S. 194 33.52 N 86.17 W
Ashville, N.Y., U.S. 214 42.06 N 79.23 W
Ashville, Oh., U.S. 218 39.42 N 82.57 W
Ashville, Pa., U.S. 214 40.34 N 78.33 W
Ashwater 42 50.44 N 4.16 W
Ashwaubenon 190 44.30 N 88.06 W
Ashworth Moor Reservoir ⊜[1] 262 53.38 N 2.16 W
Asi (Nahr al-'Āṣī) ≃ 130 36.02 N 35.58 E
Asia ⊥[1] 4 50.00 N 100.00 E
Asia ⊥[1] 12 50.00 N 100.00 E
Asia, Kepulauan II 108 1.03 N 131.18 E
Asiago 64 45.52 N 11.30 E
Asia Menor → Asia Minor □[9] 22 39.00 N 32.00 E
Asia Minor □[9] 22 39.00 N 32.00 E
Asid Gulf ⊂ 116 12.07 N 123.30 E
Asie → Asia ⊥[1] 12 50.00 N 100.00 E
Asie Mineure → Asia Minor □[9] 22 39.00 N 32.00 E
Asien → Asia ⊥[1] 12 50.00 N 100.00 E
āsika 120 19.36 N 84.39 E
Asikuma 150 5.35 N 1.00 W
Asilah 148 35.32 N 6.00 W
Asinara, Golfo dell' ⊂ 71 41.00 N 8.32 E
Asinara, Isola I 71 41.04 N 8.16 E
Asinaro ≃ 70 36.53 N 15.08 E
Asino 86 57.00 N 86.09 E
Asintorf 76 54.42 N 30.39 E
Asipoquobah Lake ⊜ 184 53.40 N 91.15 W
Asipovičy 76 53.18 N 28.38 E
'Asīr ◆[1] 144 19.00 N 42.00 E
Ašitkovo 82 55.26 N 38.36 E
Aşkale 130 39.55 N 40.42 E
Askam in Furness 44 54.11 N 3.13 W
Askaniya-Nova 78 46.27 N 33.52 E
Askarovo 86 53.21 N 58.30 E
Askeaton 48 52.36 N 8.58 W
Asker 26 59.50 N 10.26 E
Askern 44 53.37 N 1.09 W
Askersund 40 58.53 N 14.54 E
Askham 158 26.59 S 20.47 E
Askim 26 59.35 N 11.10 E
Askino 86 56.05 N 56.34 E
Askira 146 10.39 N 12.55 E
Askival ∧ 46 56.59 N 6.17 W
Askiz 86 53.08 N 90.32 E
Askja ∧[1] 24a 65.00 N 16.48 W
Askø I 41 54.54 N 11.30 E
Äsköping 40 59.09 N 16.04 E
Askov 41 55.28 N 9.06 E
Askraal 158 34.09 S 20.52 E
Askrigg 44 54.19 N 2.04 W
Askvoll 26 61.21 N 5.04 E
Aslanapa 130 39.13 N 29.52 E
Aslan-Sara 84 39.02 N 48.16 E
Aslantaş Barajı ⊜[1] 130 37.20 N 36.15 E
Asleigh 284c 39.01 N 77.10 W
Åsljunga 41 56.19 N 13.22 E
Ašlyk 86 57.33 N 68.40 E
Ašlyk ≃ 86 57.50 N 69.12 E
Asmār 120 35.02 N 71.22 E
Asmara → Asmera 144 15.20 N 38.53 E
Asmera 144 15.20 N 38.53 E
Ašmjanskae uzvyšša ⋏[1] 76 54.20 N 26.00 E
Ašmjany 76 54.25 N 25.56 E
Asmundtorp 41 55.53 N 12.56 E
Asnæs 41 55.49 N 11.31 E
Asnæs ›[1] 41 55.40 N 11.00 E
Asnebumskit Hill ∧[2] 207 42.18 N 71.54 W
Åsnen ⊜ 26 56.38 N 14.42 E
Asni 148 31.14 N 7.55 W
Asnières [-sur-Seine] 50 48.55 N 2.17 E
Asō, Nihon 94 35.59 N 140.29 E
Aso, Nihon 96 32.58 N 131.02 E
Aso ≃ 66 43.06 N 13.51 E
Asoc 152 1.26 N 11.18 E
Aso-kokuritsu-kōen ♦ 92 33.00 N 131.07 E
Asola 64 45.13 N 10.24 E
Asolo 64 45.48 N 11.54 E
Asomante 240m 18.23 N 66.36 W
Ason 273a 6.34 N 3.31 E
Asosa 144 10.03 N 34.32 E
Aso-san ∧ 92 32.53 N 131.06 E
Asoteriba, Jabal ∧ 140 21.51 N 36.30 E
Asotin 202 46.20 N 117.02 W
Asouf, Oued V 148 25.51 N 1.33 E
Asowsches Meer → Azov, Sea of ⊤[2] 78 46.00 N 36.00 E
Asp 34 38.21 N 0.46 W
Aspach, Dtsch. 56 48.58 N 9.24 E
Aspach, Öst. 60 48.11 N 13.18 E
Aspach-le-Bas 58 47.46 N 7.09 E
Aspang Markt 61 47.33 N 16.06 E
Aspara ≃ 85 43.17 N 73.28 E
Aspatria 44 54.46 N 3.20 W
Aspe, Gave d' ≃ 32 43.12 N 0.36 W
Aspen 200 39.11 N 106.49 W
Aspen Butte ∧ 202 42.19 N 122.05 W
Aspendale 274b 38.02 S 145.07 E
Aspendos ⊥ 130 37.00 N 31.10 E
Aspen Hill 284c 39.04 N 77.04 W
Aspen Knolls 284c 39.05 N 77.05 W
Aspen Lake ⊜ 202 42.18 N 122.00 W
Asperg 56 48.54 N 9.07 E
Aspermont 196 33.08 N 100.13 W
Aspern ◆[8] 264b 48.13 N 16.29 E
Aspers 208 39.59 N 77.13 W
Asperup 41 55.29 N 9.55 E
Aspid, Mount ∧ 180 53.30 N 167.33 W
Aspindza 84 41.36 N 43.15 E
Aspinwall → Colón, Pan. 236 9.22 N 79.54 W
Aspinwall, Pa., U.S. 279b 40.29 N 79.54 W
Aspiring, Mount ∧ 172 44.23 S 168.44 E
Aspö 40 59.29 N 17.02 E
Aspres-sur-Buëch 62 44.31 N 5.45 E
Aspromonte ⋏ 68 38.10 N 15.55 E
Aspropírgos 267c 38.04 N 23.35 E
Aspull 262 53.34 N 2.35 W
Aspy Bay ⊂ 186 46.55 N 60.25 W
Asquins 50 47.29 N 3.45 E
Asquith, Austl. 274a 33.41 S 151.06 E
Asquith, Sk., Can. 184 52.08 N 107.13 W
Asralt chajrchan ∧ 88 48.29 N 107.24 E
Asrāni 123 29.31 N 72.07 E
Assa, Kaz. 85 43.02 N 71.10 E
Assa, Magreb 148 28.34 N 9.27 W
Assa ≃, Kaz. 85 43.55 N 70.25 E
Assa ≃, Ross. 84 43.13 N 45.25 E
As-Sa'ata 140 13.37 N 29.59 E
Assab → Aseb 144 13.00 N 42.45 E
Assabet ≃ 283 42.28 N 71.21 W
As-Sabkhah 130 35.48 N 39.15 E
Aş-Şadārah 144 14.30 N 48.04 E
As-Sa'dīyah 128 34.11 N 45.07 E
Aş-Şaff 140 29.34 N 31.17 E
As-Saffānīyah 128 27.58 N 48.47 E
Aş-Şāfī 132 31.02 N 35.28 E
As-Safīrah 130 36.04 N 37.22 E
Aş-Şāfiyah 140 15.31 N 30.07 E
Assago 266b 45.24 N 9.08 E
Assaí 255 23.22 S 50.49 W
Aş-Şa'īd □[9] 140 26.00 N 32.00 E
Assaikwatamo ≃ 184 56.52 N 95.50 W
Assal, Lac ⊜ 144 11.41 N 42.25 E
'Assāl al-Ward 132 33.52 N 36.24 E
Aş-Şāliḥīyah 142 30.47 N 31.59 E
As-Salīmah 144 14.02 N 45.46 E
As-Sallūm 140 31.34 N 25.09 E
As-Salmān 128 30.30 N 44.32 E
As-Salṭ 132 32.03 N 35.44 E
Assam □[3] 120 26.00 N 93.00 E
As-Samāwah 128 31.18 N 45.17 E
As-Samū' 132 31.24 N 35.04 E
Assam Valley V 124 26.30 N 90.30 E
'Assān 130 36.05 N 37.14 E
Aş-Şanāfīn Al-Qiblīyah 142 30.27 N 31.18 E
Aş-Şanamayn 132 33.05 N 36.10 E
As-Santah 142 30.45 N 31.08 E
Assaq, Oued V 148 25.41 N 14.40 W
Aş-Şaqlabiyah 130 35.22 N 36.23 E
Aş-Şarafand 132 33.27 N 35.18 E
Assaré 250 6.52 S 39.52 W
Aş-Şarīḥ 132 32.30 N 35.54 E
As-Sarīrīyah 142 28.20 N 30.45 E
Assateague Island I 208 38.05 N 75.10 W
Assateague Island National Seashore ♦ 208 38.00 N 75.15 W
Assawoman Bay ⊂ 208 38.25 N 75.05 W
Assawoman Canal ≊ 208 38.31 N 75.04 W
Assawompset Pond ⊜ 207 41.50 N 70.55 W
Asse 50 50.55 N 4.12 E
Asse ≃ 62 43.53 N 5.53 E
Assean Lake ⊜ 184 56.13 N 96.30 W
Assebroek 50 51.12 N 3.16 E
Assekaifaf 148 27.08 N 8.50 E
Assel 52 53.41 N 9.25 E
Asseln ◆[8] 263 51.32 N 7.35 E
Assembleia Nacional, Palacio da ᵾ 266c 38.43 N 9.09 W
Assemini 71 39.17 N 9.00 E
Assen 52 52.59 N 6.34 E
Assendelft 52 52.27 N 4.45 E
Assenede 50 51.14 N 3.45 E
Assens 41 55.16 N 9.55 E
Asserbo 41 56.01 N 12.01 E
Assergi 66 42.25 N 13.30 E
Asseria ⊥ 36 44.02 N 15.39 E
As-Sīb 128 23.41 N 58.11 E
As-Sidr 128 23.27 N 39.45 E
As-Sijn 132 32.47 N 36.28 E
As-Simākīyah 132 31.18 N 35.48 E
As-Sinbillāwayn 142 30.53 N 31.27 E
Assíni ⊥ 38 37.36 N 22.48 E
Assiniboia 184 49.38 N 105.59 W
Assiniboine ≃ 184 49.53 N 97.08 W
Assiniboine, Mount ∧ 182 50.52 N 115.39 W
Assiniboine Indian Reserve ◆[4] 184 50.21 N 103.28 W
Assinika ≃ 184 52.37 N 96.10 W
Assinippi 283 42.09 N 70.51 W
Assis, Bra. 252 22.40 S 50.25 W
Assis, Bra. 255 22.40 S 50.25 W
Assis Chateaubriand 252 24.29 S 53.32 W
Assiscunk Creek ≃ 208 40.05 N 74.51 W
Assisi 66 43.04 N 12.37 E
Asslar 56 50.35 N 8.28 E
Assling 60 48.00 N 12.00 E
Asso 62 45.52 N 9.16 E
Assodé ⊤[4] 150 18.26 N 8.28 E
Assomada 150a 15.06 N 23.41 W
Assonet 207 41.47 N 71.04 W
Assoro 70 37.37 N 14.25 E
As-Subū' ⊥ 140 22.45 N 32.34 E
As-Sūdān → Sudan □[1] 140 15.00 N 30.00 E
As-Sudd ◆[1] 140 8.00 N 31.00 E
As-Sufāl 144 14.06 N 48.42 E
Aş-Şufayyah 140 15.30 N 34.42 E
Aş-Şūfīyah 142 30.55 N 31.46 E
As-Sukhnah, Sūrīy. 130 34.52 N 38.52 E
As-Sukhnah, Urd. 132 32.08 N 36.04 E
As-Sulaymānīyah, Ar. Su. 128 24.09 N 47.19 E
As-Sulaymānīyah, 'Irāq 128 35.33 N 45.26 E
As-Sulaymānīyah □[4] 128 35.30 N 45.25 E
As-Sulaymī 128 26.17 N 41.21 E
As-Sulayyil 144 20.27 N 45.34 E
As-Sulṭān 146 31.07 N 17.10 E
As-Sumayh 140 9.49 N 27.39 E
Aş-Şummān ◆[1] 128 25.00 N 47.00 E
As-Summāqīyāt 132 32.26 N 36.24 E
Assumption, Il., U.S. 219 39.31 N 89.02 W
Assumption, Oh., U.S. 216 41.40 N 83.54 W
Assumption Island I 138 9.45 S 46.30 E
Assunpink Creek ≃ 285 40.13 N 74.46 W
As-Su'ūdīyah 142 29.33 N 31.14 E
Aş-Şuwār 130 35.30 N 40.39 E
As-Suwaydā' 132 32.42 N 36.34 E
As-Suwaydā' □[8] 132 32.45 N 36.45 E
As-Suways (Suez) 142 29.58 N 32.33 E
As-Suways □[4] 142 30.12 N 32.30 E
Assynt, Loch ⊜ 46 58.11 N 5.06 W
Ašt 85 40.41 N 70.20 E
Asta, Cima d' ∧ 64 46.10 N 11.36 E
Astaffort 32 44.04 N 0.40 E
Astakós 38 38.32 N 21.05 E
Āstāneh, Īrān 128 37.17 N 49.59 E
Āstāneh, Īrān 128 33.53 N 49.22 E
Astara, Azer. 84 38.28 N 48.52 E
Āstārā, Īrān 128 38.26 N 48.52 E
Aštarak 84 40.18 N 44.22 E
Astaškovo 82 55.32 N 38.38 E
Astatula 220 28.43 N 81.44 W
Asten, Ned. 52 51.24 N 5.45 E
Asten, Öst. 61 48.13 N 14.25 E
Asti 62 44.54 N 8.12 E
Asti □[4] 62 44.55 N 8.10 E
Astica 252 30.56 S 67.23 W
Astico ≃ 64 45.37 N 11.37 E
Astipálaia 38 36.30 N 26.30 E
Astipálaia I 38 36.35 N 26.25 E
Astley Bridge 262 53.36 N 2.26 W
Astley Green 262 53.29 N 2.27 W
Astley Hall ⊥ 262 53.39 N 2.38 W
Astola Island I 128 25.07 N 63.51 E
Astolfo Dutra 256 21.19 S 42.52 W
Aston, Eng., U.K. 262 53.18 N 2.40 W
Aston, Pa., U.S. 285 39.52 N 75.26 W
Aston Clinton 42 51.48 N 0.44 W
Aston-on-Trent 42 52.52 N 1.23 W
Astor 123 35.22 N 74.51 E
Astor ≃ 123 35.34 N 74.41 E
Astorga, Bra. 255 23.13 S 51.40 W
Astorga, Esp. 34 42.27 N 6.03 W
Astorga, Pil. 116 6.54 N 125.27 E
Astoria, Il., U.S. 219 40.13 N 90.21 W
Astoria, Or., U.S. 224 46.11 N 123.49 W
Astoria ◆[8] 276 40.46 N 73.55 W
Astoria Bridge ◆[5] 224 46.13 N 123.52 W
Astoria Column ⊥ 224 46.11 N 123.50 W
Åstorp 41 56.08 N 12.57 E
Astove Island I 138 10.06 S 47.45 E
Astra 254 45.44 S 67.30 W
Astrachan' 80 46.21 N 48.03 E
Astrachanka 86 51.33 N 69.47 E
Astrachan' Oblast' □[4] 80 47.00 N 47.30 E
Astrachanskij 80 46.12 N 47.16 E
Astrachanskij zapovednik ◆[4] 80 46.00 N 48.32 E
Astrakhan → Astrachan' 80 46.21 N 48.03 E
Astrašycki Haradok 76 54.04 N 27.42 E
Astravec 76 54.37 N 25.57 E
Astrodome ♦ 222 29.41 N 95.25 W
Astrolabe, Cape › 175e 8.20 S 160.34 E
Astrolabe, Récifs de l' ✢[2] 175f 19.48 S 165.37 E
Astrolabe Bay ⊂ 164 5.20 S 145.50 E
Astrouna 76 55.08 N 29.53 E
Astryna 76 53.44 N 24.32 E
Astudillo 34 42.12 N 4.18 W
Astura, Torre ⊥ 66 41.24 N 12.46 E
Asturias 116 10.34 N 123.43 E
Asturias □[3] 34 43.20 N 6.00 W
Asturias □[4] 34 43.20 N 6.00 W
Astwood Bank 42 52.15 N 1.56 W
Asubulak 86 49.31 N 83.03 E
Asuisui, Cape › 175a 13.47 S 172.29 W
Asuka 96 34.28 N 135.50 E
Asuka ᵾ[3] 9 71.32 S 24.08 E
Asuke 94 35.08 N 137.19 E
Asunción 252 25.16 S 57.40 W
Asunción, Bahía ⊂ 232 27.06 N 114.11 W
Asuncion Island I 108 19.40 N 145.24 E
Asunción Ixtaltepec 234 16.30 N 95.03 W
Asunción Mita 236 14.20 N 89.43 W
Asunción Nochixtlán 234 17.28 N 97.14 W
Åsunden ⊜, Sve. 26 57.58 N 15.50 E
Åsunden ⊜, Sve. 26 57.44 N 13.22 E
Asunga, Wādī V 146 13.21 N 22.17 E
Asuni 71 39.52 N 8.56 E
'Āṣūr, Tall ∧ 132 31.59 N 35.17 E
Asuwa 94 36.01 N 136.16 E
Asuwa ≃ 94 36.04 N 136.11 E
Asveja 76 56.01 N 28.06 E
Asvejskae, vozero ⊜ 76 56.03 N 28.03 E
Aswad, Ar-Ra's al- › 144 21.22 N 39.03 E
Aswān 140 24.05 N 32.53 E
Aswān High Dam → 'Āli, As-Sadd al- ◆[6] 140 23.58 N 32.52 E
Aswatthaberia 272b 22.26 N 88.32 E
Asy ≃ 85 43.31 N 78.20 E
Asyūṭ 142 27.11 N 31.11 E
Asyūṭ □[4] 142 27.20 N 30.50 E
Asyūṭī, Wādī al- V 142 27.11 N 31.16 E
Aszód 30 47.39 N 19.31 E
'Ata I, Tonga 14 22.20 S 176.12 W
Ata I, Tonga 174w 21.03 S 175.00 W
Atabaj 85 43.30 N 68.20 E
Atabapo ≃ 246 4.03 N 67.42 W
Atabasca → Athabasca ≃ 176 58.40 N 110.50 W
Atabasca, Lago → Athabasca, Lake ⊜ 176 59.07 N 110.00 W
Atabey 130 37.57 N 30.39 E
Atacama □[4] 252 27.30 S 70.00 W
Atacama, Desierto de ◆[2] 18 24.30 S 69.15 W
Atacama, Puna de ⋏[1] 252 24.30 S 67.30 W
Atacama, Salar de ⩳ 252 23.30 S 68.15 W
Ataco 246 3.35 N 75.23 W
Atacora, Chaîne de l' ⋏ 150 10.45 N 1.30 E
Atacuari ≃ 246 3.47 S 70.44 W
Atafu I[1] 14 8.33 S 172.30 W
Atagaj 88 55.06 N 99.23 E
Atago-yama ∧, Nihon 94 35.07 N 139.59 E
Atago-yama ∧, Nihon 96 35.03 N 135.37 E
Ātāi ≃[1] 126 22.51 N 89.33 E
'Aṭā'iṭah, Jabal al- ∧ 132 30.40 N 35.39 E
Atakakup Indian Reserve ◆[4] 184 53.24 N 106.55 W
Atakano-seki ⊥ 94 36.24 N 136.25 E
Atakora □[5] 150 10.00 N 1.35 E
Atakora, Réserve d' ◆[4] 150 11.30 N 2.10 E
Atakpamé 150 7.32 N 1.08 E
Atalaia, Bra. 250 9.31 S 36.02 W
Atalaia, Port. 266c 38.42 N 8.55 W
Atalándi 38 38.39 N 23.00 E
Atalanka 88 54.50 N 103.05 E
Atalaya, Arg. 258 35.02 S 57.32 W
Atalaya, Pan. 236 8.03 N 80.56 W
Atalaya, Perú 248 10.44 S 73.45 W
Atalaya, Cerro ∧, Chile 254 52.45 S 72.42 W
Atalaya, Cerro ∧, Perú 248 12.38 S 71.56 W
Atalaya, Punta › 258 35.01 S 57.31 W
Atamanovka 88 51.56 N 113.37 E
Atamanovo 86 56.24 N 93.36 E
Atambua 112 9.07 S 124.54 E
Atami 94 35.05 N 139.04 E
Atapupu 112 9.00 S 124.51 E
'Atāq 144 14.33 N 46.48 E
'Atāqah, Jabal ⋏ 142 29.58 N 32.20 E
Atâr 150 20.31 N 13.03 W
Ataram, 'Erg n- ◆[2] 148 23.46 N 1.44 E
Atarés, Castillo de ⊥ 286b 23.08 N 82.21 W
Atāri 123 31.36 N 74.35 E
Atary 80 57.32 N 49.18 E
Atascadero 226 35.29 N 120.40 W
Atascosa ≃ 196 28.26 N 98.12 W
At'aševo 80 54.36 N 46.06 E
Atasu 86 48.42 N 71.38 E
Atas uul ∧ 102 43.18 N 96.36 E
Atata I 174w 21.03 S 175.15 W
Atatürk Barajı ⊜[1] 130 37.30 N 38.30 E
Ataturk Tower ⊥ 267b 41.00 N 28.59 E
Ataur 272a 28.43 N 77.24 E
Atauro, Pulau I 112 8.13 S 125.35 E
Atbara ('Aṭbarah) ≃ 140 17.40 N 33.56 E
'Aṭbarah 140 17.42 N 33.59 E
'Aṭbarah (Atbara) ≃ 140 17.40 N 33.56 E
Atbasar 86 51.48 N 68.20 E
At-Baši 85 41.10 N 75.48 E
Atbaši ≃ 85 41.24 N 75.38 E
Atbaši, chrebet ⋏ 85 40.55 N 75.40 E
Atchafalaya ≃ 194 29.53 N 91.28 W
Atchafalaya Bay ⊂ 194 29.25 N 91.20 W
Atchison 198 39.33 N 95.07 W
Atco 208 39.46 N 74.53 W
Ate 286d 12.03 S 76.58 W
Atebubu 150 7.45 N 0.59 W
Ateca 34 41.20 N 1.47 W
Atelchu ≃ 255 12.05 S 53.46 W
Ateleta 66 41.51 N 14.12 E
Ateli 124 28.06 N 76.17 E
Atella 68 40.52 N 15.39 E
Atemajac de Brizuela 234 20.11 N 103.42 W
Atemar 80 54.11 N 45.24 E
Atemble 164 5.05 S 144.45 E
Atena Lucana 68 40.27 N 15.33 E
Atenango del Río 234 18.05 N 99.06 W
Atenas → Athínai 38 37.58 N 23.43 E
Atencingo 234 18.30 N 98.36 W
Atengo ≃ 234 21.50 N 104.43 W
Atenguillo 234 20.25 N 104.31 W
Atenguillo ≃ 234 20.55 N 104.38 W
Atenquique 234 19.31 N 103.30 W
Atepcevo 82 55.20 N 36.46 E
Aterno ≃ 66 42.11 N 13.51 E
Aterrado, Ribeirão do ≃ 256 22.09 S 45.03 W
Atessa 66 42.04 N 14.27 E
Aṭfīḥ 142 29.24 N 31.15 E
Aṭfīḥī, Wādī al- V 142 29.23 N 31.16 E
Ātgharia 126 24.06 N 89.14 E
Atglen 208 39.57 N 75.58 W
Ath 50 50.38 N 3.47 E
Athabasca 182 54.43 N 113.17 W
Athabasca ≃ 176 58.40 N 110.50 W
Athabasca, Lake ⊜ 176 59.07 N 110.00 W
Athalmer 182 50.32 N 116.02 W
Athapapuskow Lake ⊜ 184 54.33 N 101.40 W
Athārabānki ≃[1] 126 22.49 N 89.39 E
Athārān Hazāri 123 31.11 N 72.06 E
Athboy 48 53.37 N 6.55 W
Athea 48 52.28 N 9.17 W
Athen → Athínai 38 37.58 N 23.43 E
Athena 202 45.48 N 118.29 W
Athènes → Athínai 38 37.58 N 23.43 E
Athenry 48 53.18 N 8.45 W
Athens, On., Can. 212 44.38 N 75.57 W
Athens → Athínai, Ellás 38 37.58 N 23.43 E
Athens, Al., U.S. 194 34.48 N 86.58 W
Athens, Ga., U.S. 192 33.57 N 83.22 W
Athens, Il., U.S. 219 39.57 N 89.43 W

Symbols in the index entries represent the broad categories identified in the key at the right. Symbols with superior numbers (⋏[1]) identify subcategories (see complete key on page I · 1).

Symbole im Register stellen die rechts im Schlüssel erklärten Kategorien dar. Symbole mit hochgestellten Ziffern (⋏[1]) bezeichnen Unterabteilungen einer Kategorie (vgl. vollständiger Schlüssel auf Seite I · 1).

Los símbolos incluídos en el texto del índice representan las grandes categorías identificadas con la clave a la derecha. Los símbolos con numeros en su parte superior (⋏[1]) identifican las subcategorías (véase la clave completa en la página I · 1).

Les symboles de l'index représentent les catégories indiquées dans la légende à droite. Les symboles suivis d'un indice (⋏[1]) représentent des sous-catégories (voir légende complète à la page I · 1).

Os símbolos incluídos no texto do índice representam as grandes categorias identificadas com a chave à direita. Os símbolos com números em sua parte superior (⋏[1]) identificam as subcategorias (veja-se a chave completa à página I · 1).

∧	Mountain	Berg	Montaña	Montagne	Montanha
⋏	Mountains	Gebirge	Montañas	Montagnes	Montanhas
)(	Pass	Paß	Paso	Col	Passo
V	Valley, Canyon	Tal, Cañon	Valle, Cañón	Vallée, Canyon	Vale, Canhão
≐	Plain	Ebene	Llano	Plaine	Planície
›	Cape	Kap	Cabo	Cap	Cabo
I	Island	Insel	Isla	Île	Ilha
II	Islands	Inseln	Islas	Îles	Ilhas
◆	Other Topographic Features	Andere Topographische Objekte	Otros Elementos Topográficos	Autres données topographiques	Outros acidentes topográficos

Athe-Aydo I · 11

ESPAÑOL

Nombre	Página	Lat.°′	Long.°′ W = Oeste
Athens, La., U.S.	194	32.39 N	93.01 W
Athens, Mi., U.S.	216	42.05 N	85.14 W
Athens, N.Y., U.S.	210	42.15 N	73.48 W
Athens, Oh., U.S.	188	39.19 N	82.06 W
Athens, Pa., U.S.	210	41.57 N	76.31 W
Athens, Tn., U.S.	192	35.26 N	84.35 W
Athens, Tx., U.S.	222	32.12 N	95.51 W
Athens, W.V., U.S.	192	37.25 N	81.00 W
Athens, Wi., U.S.	190	45.01 N	90.04 W
Athens, Lake ⊜ [1]	222	32.14 N	95.45 W
Athenstedt	54	51.56 N	10.55 E
Athens University ʊ [2]	267c	37.59 N	23.44 E
Atherley	212	44.36 N	79.22 W
Atherstone	42	52.35 N	1.31 W
Atherton, Austl.	166	17.16 S	145.29 E
Atherton, Eng., U.K.	44	53.31 N	2.31 W
Atherton, Ca., U.S.	226	37.27 N	122.11 W
Athi ≃	154	2.59 S	38.31 E
Athiaínou	130	35.04 N	33.32 E
Athiémé	150	6.35 N	1.40 E
Athies-sous-Laon	50	49.34 N	3.41 E
Athínai (Athens), Ellás	38	37.58 N	23.43 E
Athínai (Athens), Ellás	267c	37.58 N	23.43 E
Äthiopien → Ethiopia □ [1]	144	9.00 N	39.00 E
Athi River	154	1.27 S	36.59 E
Athis-Mons	261	48.43 N	2.24 E
Athlat al-Bāshā ∧ [2]	142	27.31 N	32.20 E
Athleague	48	53.34 N	8.15 W
Athlone	48	53.25 N	7.56 W
Athni	122	16.44 N	75.04 E
Athok	110	17.12 N	95.05 E
Athol, N.Z.	172	45.31 S	168.35 E
Athol, Ma., U.S.	207	42.35 N	72.13 W
Athol Bay c	212	43.53 N	77.15 W
Athol Island I	240b	25.05 N	77.16 W
Atholl, Forest of ◆ [3]	46	56.50 N	4.00 W
Athol Springs	210	42.46 N	78.52 W
Áthos ∧	38	40.09 N	24.19 E
Ath-Thaʿlah	132	32.42 N	36.26 E
Ath-Thamad	140	29.41 N	34.18 E
Ath-Thanīyah	132	31.10 N	35.43 E
Athus	56	49.34 N	5.50 E
Athy	48	53.00 N	7.00 W
Ati	146	13.13 N	18.20 E
Atiak	154	3.15 N	32.07 E
Atibaia	256	23.07 S	46.33 W
Atibainha ≃	256	22.42 S	47.17 W
Atibainha, Reservatório ⊜ [1]	256	23.10 S	46.20 W
Atico	248	16.14 S	73.39 W
Aticonipi, Lac ⊜	186	51.52 N	59.22 W
Atienza	34	41.12 N	2.52 W
Atigun Pass)(	180	68.08 N	149.29 W
Atik Lake ⊜	184	55.16 N	96.00 W
Atikokan	190	48.45 N	91.37 W
Atikonak Lake ⊜	176	52.40 N	64.30 W
Atil	200	30.50 N	111.35 W
Atimari ≃	248	9.04 S	67.23 W
Atimonan	116	14.00 N	121.55 E
Atina	66	41.37 N	13.48 E
Atiparaná ≃ [1]	246	1.51 S	65.37 W
Atiquizaya	236	13.58 N	89.46 W
Atirāmpattinam	122	10.21 N	79.24 E
Atitlán, Lago de ⊜	236	14.42 N	91.12 W
Atitlán, Volcán ∧ [1]	236	14.35 N	91.11 W
Atiu I	14	20.02 S	158.07 W
Atka, Ross.	74	60.50 N	151.48 E
Atka, Ak., U.S.	180	52.12 N	174.12 W
Atka Island I	180	52.15 N	174.30 W
Atkaracalar	130	40.50 N	33.04 E
Atkarsk	80	51.52 N	45.00 E
Atkins	194	35.14 N	92.56 W
Atkinson, Il., U.S.	190	41.25 N	90.00 W
Atkinson, Ne., U.S.	198	42.31 N	98.58 W
Atkinson, N.H., U.S.	207	42.50 N	71.08 W
Atkinson, N.C., U.S.	192	34.31 N	78.10 W
Atkinson Island I	222	29.40 N	94.58 W
Atkinson Lake ⊜	184	55.59 N	94.48 W
Atkri	164	1.44 S	130.04 E
Atlacomulco	234	19.48 N	99.53 W
Atlanta, Ga., U.S.	192	33.44 N	84.23 W
Atlanta, Il., U.S.	194	40.15 N	89.14 W
Atlanta, Mi., U.S.	190	45.00 N	84.08 W
Atlanta, Mo., U.S.	194	39.53 N	92.28 W
Atlanta, N.Y., U.S.	210	42.33 N	77.28 W
Atlanta, Oh., U.S.	218	39.34 N	83.11 W
Atlanta, Tx., U.S.	194	33.06 N	94.09 W
Atlantic, Ia., U.S.	198	41.24 N	95.00 W
Atlantic, N.C., U.S.	192	34.53 N	76.20 W
Atlantic, Pa., U.S.	214	41.30 N	80.21 W
Atlantic, Va., U.S.	208	37.54 N	75.30 W
Atlantic □ [6]	208	39.27 N	74.44 W
Atlantic Beach, Fl., U.S.	192	30.20 N	81.23 W
Atlantic Beach, N.Y., U.S.	276	40.35 N	73.44 W
Atlantic City	208	39.21 N	74.25 W
Atlantic Highlands	208	40.24 N	74.02 W
Atlantic-Indian Basin ✢ [1]	6	60.00 S	15.00 E
Atlantic-Indian Ridge ✢ [3]	4	53.00 S	15.00 E
Atlántico □ [5]	246	10.45 N	75.00 W
Atlántico, Océano → Atlantic Ocean ⊤ [1]	8	5.00 S	25.00 W
Atlantic Ocean ⊤ [1]	4	5.00 S	25.00 W
Atlantic Ocean ⊤ [1]	8	5.00 S	25.00 W
Atlantic Peak ∧	200	42.37 N	109.00 W
Atlántida	252	34.46 S	55.45 W
Atlántida □ [5]	236	15.40 N	87.00 W
Atlantique	276	40.39 N	73.10 W
Atlantique □ [5]	150	6.35 N	2.15 E
Atlantique, Océan → Atlantic Ocean ⊤ [1]	8	5.00 S	25.00 W
Atlantischer Ozean → Atlantic Ocean ⊤ [1]	8	5.00 S	25.00 W
Atlas, Mi., U.S.	216	42.56 N	83.32 W
Atlas, Pa., U.S.	208	40.48 N	76.26 W
Atlasburg	214	40.20 N	80.23 W
Atlas Mountains ⋀	148	33.00 N	2.00 W
Atlasova, ostrov I	74	50.53 N	155.27 E
Atlasovo	92a	46.01 N	142.09 E
Atlas Saharien ⋀	148	33.25 N	1.20 E
Atlas Tellien ⋀	148	36.00 N	3.00 E
Atlin	180	59.35 N	133.42 W
Atlin Lake ⊜	180	59.20 N	133.45 W
ʿAtlit	132	32.41 N	34.56 E
Atlixco	234	18.54 N	98.26 W
Ātmakūr	122	15.53 N	78.35 E
Atmanov Ugol	80	53.07 N	41.23 E
Atmis	80	53.28 N	43.57 E
Atmore	194	31.01 N	87.29 W
Ätna → Etna, Monte ∧ [1]	70	37.46 N	15.00 E
Atna ≃	26	61.44 N	10.49 E
Atna Peak ∧	182	53.57 N	128.03 W
Atnarko ≃	182	52.22 N	126.04 W
Atnis	86	58.48 N	69.38 E
Atnosen	26	61.44 N	10.49 E
Atō	96	34.24 N	131.43 E
Atocha	248	20.56 S	66.14 W
Atocha, Estación de ◆ [5]	266a	40.24 N	3.41 W
Atocongo	286d	12.08 S	76.56 W
Atocongo ⊥	286d	12.12 S	76.55 W
Atoka	196	34.23 N	96.07 W
Atotonilco	232	24.15 N	102.45 W
Atotonilco, Cerro ∧	196	26.08 N	104.43 W
Atotonilco, Lago ⊜	234	20.22 N	103.39 W
Atotonilco de Tula	234	20.00 N	99.13 W
Atotonilco El Alto	234	20.33 N	102.31 W
Atoui, Khaṭṭ V	150	20.04 N	15.59 W
Atoyac	234	20.01 N	103.32 W
Atoyac ≃, Méx.	234	17.05 N	100.29 W
Atoyac ≃, Méx.	234	18.10 N	98.31 W
Atoyac ≃, Méx.	234	16.30 N	97.31 W

FRANÇAIS

Nom	Page	Lat.°′	Long.°′ W = Ouest
Atoyac ≃, Méx.	234	19.02 N	96.08 W
Atoyac de Álvarez	234	17.12 N	100.26 W
Atoyaquillo ≃	234	16.37 N	97.41 W
Atpur	272b	22.50 N	88.23 E
Atrå	26	59.59 N	8.45 E
ʿAṭrah, Jabal ∧	132	29.40 N	35.34 E
Atrai ≃	124	24.29 N	89.03 E
Atrak (Atrek) ⊜	128	37.28 N	53.57 E
Ätran ≃	26	56.53 N	12.30 E
Atrato ≃	246	8.17 N	76.58 W
Atrauli	124	28.02 N	78.17 E
Atrek (Atrak) ≃	128	37.28 N	53.57 E
Atri	66	42.35 N	13.58 E
Atripalda	68	40.55 N	14.50 E
Atrisco	200	34.59 N	106.41 W
Atrop ◆ [8]	263	51.24 N	6.43 E
Atsion Lake ⊜	285	39.44 N	74.44 W
Atsugi	94	35.27 N	139.22 E
Atsugi-hikōjō ■	94	35.28 N	139.27 E
Atsumi, Nihon	92	38.37 N	139.35 E
Atsumi, Nihon	94	34.37 N	137.07 E
Atsumi-hantō › [1]	94	34.39 N	137.15 E
Atta	272a	28.34 N	77.20 E
At-Tabbīn	142	29.47 N	31.18 E
Aṭ-Ṭafīlah	132	30.50 N	35.36 E
Aṭ-Ṭafīlah □ [8]	132	30.45 N	35.45 E
At-Tahrīr □ [4]	142	30.40 N	30.15 E
Aṭ-Ṭāʾif	144	21.16 N	40.24 E
Attainville	261	49.03 N	2.21 E
At-Tāj	146	24.13 N	23.18 E
Aṭ-Ṭalibīyah	273c	30.00 N	31.11 E
At-Tall	132	33.36 N	36.18 E
Attalla	194	34.01 N	86.05 W
At-Tall al-Kabīr	142	30.34 N	31.47 E
At-Taʾmīm □ [4]	128	35.25 N	44.20 E
At-Tamīmī	146	32.20 N	23.04 E
Attapu	110	14.48 N	106.50 E
Attar, Oued el V	148	33.27 N	5.26 E
At-Taṭāīyah	142	27.20 N	30.50 E
Attáviros ∧	38	36.12 N	27.52 E
Attawapiskat	176	52.55 N	82.26 W
Attawapiskat ≃	176	52.57 N	82.18 W
Attawapiskat Lake ⊜	176	52.18 N	87.54 W
Attawaugan	207	41.52 N	71.52 W
At-Ṭawd	142	30.47 N	30.37 E
Aṭ-Ṭawīl ⋀	128	29.20 N	39.35 E
Aṭ-Ṭayrīyah	142	30.39 N	30.46 E
At-Taysīyah ≚	128	28.00 N	44.00 E
Aṭ-Ṭayyibah, Miṣr	142	28.16 N	30.39 E
Aṭ-Ṭayyibah, Sūrīy.	132	32.33 N	36.14 E
Aṭ-Ṭayyibah, Sūrīy.	132	32.48 N	36.46 E
Aṭ-Ṭayyibah, Urd.	132	32.33 N	35.43 E
Attel ≃	64	48.01 N	12.11 E
Attendorn	56	51.07 N	7.54 E
Attenhausen	58	47.59 N	10.20 E
Attenkirchen	60	48.30 N	11.46 E
Atterbury	219	40.04 N	89.55 W
Attersee	64	47.55 N	13.33 E
Attersee ⊜	64	47.52 N	13.33 E
Attert ≃	56	49.52 N	6.05 E
Attica, In., U.S.	216	40.17 N	87.14 W
Attica, Ks., U.S.	198	37.14 N	98.13 W
Attica, N.Y., U.S.	210	42.51 N	78.16 W
Attica, Oh., U.S.	214	41.03 N	82.53 W
Attica → Attikí □ [9]	38	38.10 N	23.20 E
Attichy	50	49.25 N	3.03 E
Attigliano	66	42.31 N	12.17 E
Attigny	56	49.29 N	4.35 E
Attikí □ [4]	38	38.00 N	23.45 E
Attikí □ [9]	38	38.10 N	23.20 E
ʿAttīl	132	32.22 N	35.04 E
Attimis	64	46.11 N	13.16 E
Aṭ-Ṭīnah	142	31.03 N	32.18 E
Attingal	122	8.41 N	76.50 E
Attir	140	6.04 N	30.50 E
Attleboro	207	41.56 N	71.17 W
Attleborough	42	52.31 N	1.01 E
Attnang	60	48.01 N	13.43 E
Attock	123	33.54 N	72.15 E
Attoyac ≃	194	31.29 N	94.18 W
Attu	181a	52.56 N	173.14 E
At-Tubah	144	12.40 N	43.30 E
Attu Island I	181a	52.55 N	173.00 E
Aṭ-Ṭunayb	132	31.48 N	35.57 E
Āttūr, India	122	11.36 N	78.37 E
Aṭ-Ṭūr, Miṣr	140	28.14 N	33.37 E
Aṭ-Ṭuwayshah	140	12.21 N	26.32 E
Aṭ-Ṭuwayyah	128	27.36 N	41.13 E
Attymon	48	53.19 N	8.35 W
Atucatiquini ≃	248	7.44 S	67.57 W
Atucha	258	33.58 S	59.18 W
Atuel ≃	252	36.17 S	66.50 W
Atuel, Bañados del ≡	252	36.30 S	66.55 W
Atuntaqui	246	0.20 N	78.13 W
Atuona	174x	9.48 S	139.02 W
At'urjevo	80	54.21 N	43.19 E
Ątushi	85	39.43 N	76.08 E
Åtvidaberg	26	58.12 N	16.00 E
Atwater, Sk., Can.	184	50.47 N	102.10 W
Atwater, Ca., U.S.	226	37.20 N	120.36 W
Atwater, Il., U.S.	219	39.20 N	89.44 W
Atwater, Mn., U.S.	198	45.08 N	94.46 W
Atwater, Oh., U.S.	214	41.01 N	81.10 W
Atwood, On., Can.	212	43.40 N	81.01 W
Atwood, Ca., U.S.	280	33.52 N	117.50 W
Atwood, Il., U.S.	194	39.48 N	88.28 W
Atwood, In., U.S.	216	41.15 N	85.58 W
Atwood, Ks., U.S.	198	39.48 N	101.02 W
Atwood, Tn., U.S.	194	35.58 N	88.40 W
Atwood Lake ⊜ [1]	214	40.33 N	81.13 W
Atyrau (Gurjev)	80	47.07 N	51.56 E
Atyrau □ [4]	80	47.30 N	51.00 E
Atzalpur	272a	28.43 N	77.21 E
Atzendorf	54	51.55 N	11.35 E
Atzgersdorf ◆ [8]	264b	48.09 N	16.18 E
Au	58	47.19 N	9.59 E
Auagrām	126	23.31 N	87.41 E
Auaiá-Miçu ≃	250	10.51 S	53.08 W
Aua Island I	164	1.27 S	143.04 E
Aual Edo	144	4.14 N	40.37 E
Auari ≃	246	3.33 N	63.48 W
Auau Channel ⊔	229a	20.51 N	156.45 W
Aub	56	49.33 N	10.04 E
Aubá	112	9.02 S	125.22 E
Aubagne	62	43.17 N	5.34 E
Aubange	56	49.35 N	5.48 E
Aube □ [5]	32	48.15 N	4.05 E
Aube ≃	32	48.34 N	3.43 E
Aubenas	62	44.37 N	4.23 E
Aubenton	50	49.50 N	4.12 E
Aubepierre	261	48.38 N	2.53 E
Aubergenville	261	48.58 N	1.51 E
Auberive	58	47.47 N	5.03 E
Auberry	226	37.04 N	119.29 W
Aubervilliers	50	48.55 N	2.23 E
Aubetin ≃	50	48.49 N	3.01 E
Aubette ≃	261	49.00 N	1.54 E
Aubigny-en-Artois	50	50.21 N	2.35 E
Aubigny-sur-Nère	50	47.29 N	2.26 E
Aubin	32	44.32 N	2.14 E
Aubinadong ≃	190	46.51 N	83.22 W
Aubonne	58	46.28 N	6.24 E
Auboué	56	49.13 N	5.59 E
Aubrac ⋀	32	44.40 N	3.00 E
Aubrey Cliffs ▴ [4]	200	35.45 N	113.00 W
Aubrey Lake ⊜ [1]	190	46.54 N	83.11 W
Aubrives	56	50.06 N	4.46 E
Aubry Lake ⊜	180	67.23 N	126.30 W
Auburn, Austl.	168b	34.01 S	138.41 E
Auburn, Austl.	274a	33.51 S	151.02 E
Auburn, Al., U.S.	194	32.36 N	85.28 W
Auburn, Ca., U.S.	226	38.53 N	121.04 W
Auburn, Il., U.S.	219	39.35 N	89.44 W
Auburn, In., U.S.	216	41.22 N	85.03 W
Auburn, Ky., U.S.	194	37.02 N	86.54 W
Auburn, Me., U.S.	188	44.05 N	70.13 W
Auburn, Ma., U.S.	207	42.11 N	71.50 W
Auburn, Mi., U.S.	190	43.36 N	84.04 W
Auburn, Ne., U.S.	198	40.23 N	95.50 W

PORTUGUÊS

Nome	Página	Lat.°′	Long.°′ W = Oeste
Auburn, N.J., U.S.	285	39.42 N	75.22 W
Auburn, N.Y., U.S.	210	42.55 N	76.33 W
Auburn, Pa., U.S.	208	40.35 N	76.05 W
Auburn, Wa., U.S.	224	47.18 N	122.13 W
Auburn ≃	166	25.38 S	151.12 E
Auburndale, Fl., U.S.	220	28.03 N	81.47 W
Auburndale, Ma., U.S.	283	42.21 N	71.22 W
Auburn Hills	214	42.38 N	83.13 W
Auburn Hills, Palace of ♠	281	42.41 N	83.14 W
Auburn Range ⋀	166	25.10 S	150.30 E
Auburn Ravine V	226	38.51 N	121.31 W
Auburn Southeast	210	42.54 N	76.32 W
Aubusson	32	45.57 N	2.11 E
Auby-sur-Semois	56	49.49 N	5.10 E
Auca Mahuida	252	37.53 S	68.31 W
Auca Mahuida, Cerro ∧	252	37.45 S	68.56 W
Aucará	248	14.15 S	74.05 W
Auce	76	56.28 N	22.53 E
Auch	32	43.39 N	0.35 E
Auchel	50	50.30 N	2.28 E
Auchenblae	46	56.54 N	2.26 W
Auchencairn	44	54.51 N	3.53 W
Auchi	150	7.02 N	6.14 E
Auchinleck	44	55.28 N	4.17 W
Auchterarder	46	56.18 N	3.43 W
Auchterderran	46	56.09 N	3.16 W
Auchtermuchty	46	56.17 N	3.15 W
Aucilla ≃	192	30.05 N	83.59 W
Auckland	172	36.52 S	174.46 E
Auckland Islands II	9	50.40 S	166.30 E
Auckland Park ◆ [8]	273d	26.11 S	28.00 E
Auckland Park Race Course ♠	273d	26.11 S	28.00 E
Aude □ [5]	32	43.05 N	2.30 E
Aude ≃	32	43.13 N	3.14 E
Audenge	32	44.41 N	1.00 W
Audenshaw	262	53.28 N	2.08 W
Audenshaw Reservoirs ⊜ [1]	262	53.28 N	2.08 W
Auderghem	50	50.49 N	4.26 E
Audeux	58	47.16 N	5.53 E
Audierne	32	48.01 N	4.32 W
Audincourt	58	47.29 N	6.50 E
Audley	44	53.03 N	2.18 W
Audo Range ⋀	144	6.30 N	41.30 E
Audrain □ [6]	219	39.12 N	91.50 W
Audresselles	50	50.49 N	1.36 E
Audruicq	50	50.53 N	2.05 E
Audubon, Ia., U.S.	198	41.43 N	94.55 W
Audubon, N.J., U.S.	208	39.53 N	75.04 W
Audubon, Pa., U.S.	285	40.07 N	75.27 W
Audubon Lake ⊜ [1]	198	47.35 N	101.10 W
Audubon Park, Ky., U.S.	218	38.12 N	85.43 W
Audubon Park, N.J., U.S.	285	39.54 N	75.05 W
Audun-le-Roman	56	49.22 N	5.53 E
Aue	54	50.35 N	12.42 E
Aue ≃	52	53.11 N	7.41 E
Auer → Ora	64	46.21 N	11.18 E
Auerbach, Dtsch.	54	50.41 N	12.54 E
Auerbach, Dtsch.	54	50.30 N	12.23 E
Auerbach, Dtsch.	60	48.48 N	13.06 E
Auerbach in der Oberpfalz	60	49.42 N	11.38 E
Auersberg ∧	54	50.27 N	12.39 E
Auerswalde	54	50.54 N	12.55 E
Auezov	86	49.46 N	81.38 E
Auf dem Kreinberge	263	51.27 N	7.36 E
Auffargis	261	48.42 N	1.53 E
Auffay	50	49.43 N	1.06 E
Aufsess	60	49.54 N	11.13 E
Augarten ♠	264b	48.14 N	16.23 E
Augathella	166	25.48 S	146.35 E
Augher	48	54.26 N	7.09 W
Aughnacloy	48	54.25 N	6.58 W
Aughrim	48	52.51 N	6.17 W
Aughton, Eng., U.K.	44	53.22 N	1.18 W
Aughton, Eng., U.K.	262	53.32 N	2.56 W
Aughton Park	262	53.33 N	2.53 W
Aughwick Creek ≃	214	40.22 N	77.50 W
Auglaize □ [6]	216	40.34 N	84.12 W
Auglaize ≃	216	41.17 N	84.21 W
Augrabies	158	28.37 S	20.20 E
Augrabies Falls National Park ♠	158	28.35 S	20.19 E
Augrabiesvalle ʟ	158	28.35 S	20.19 E
Au Gres	190	44.02 N	83.41 W
Au Gres ≃	190	44.02 N	83.40 W
Au Gres, East Branch ≃	190	44.05 N	83.41 W
Augsburg	58	48.23 N	10.53 E
Augšlīgatne	76	57.14 N	25.02 E
Augusta, Austl.	162	34.19 S	115.10 E
Augusta, It.	70	37.13 N	15.13 E
Augusta, Ar., U.S.	194	35.16 N	91.21 W
Augusta, Ga., U.S.	192	33.28 N	82.01 W
Augusta, Il., U.S.	194	40.13 N	90.57 W
Augusta, Ks., U.S.	198	37.41 N	97.58 W
Augusta, Ky., U.S.	218	38.46 N	84.00 W
Augusta, Me., U.S.	188	44.18 N	69.46 W
Augusta, Mi., U.S.	216	42.20 N	85.21 W
Augusta, Mo., U.S.	219	38.34 N	90.53 W
Augusta, Mt., U.S.	202	47.29 N	112.23 W
Augusta, N.J., U.S.	210	41.07 N	74.43 W
Augusta, Oh., U.S.	214	40.41 N	81.01 W
Augusta, Wi., U.S.	190	44.40 N	91.07 W
Augusta, Golfo di c	70	37.12 N	15.13 E
Augustdorf	52	51.53 N	8.43 E
Augustenborg	41	54.57 N	9.53 E
Augustine Island I	180	59.22 N	153.28 W
Augusto Severo	250	5.52 S	37.19 W
Augustów	30	53.51 N	22.59 E
Augustowski, Kanał ≅	76	53.54 N	23.26 E
Augustus, Mount ∧	162	24.20 S	116.50 E
Augustusburg	54	50.49 N	13.06 E
Augustus Downs	166	18.33 S	139.52 E
Augustus Island I	164	15.20 S	124.30 E
Auila, Ribeirão ≃	255	12.09 S	53.20 W
Au in der Hallertau	60	48.33 N	11.45 E
Aujon ≃	58	48.09 N	4.48 E
Auki	175e	8.46 S	160.42 E
Aulander	192	36.13 N	77.06 W
Aulanko	26	61.02 N	24.27 E
Auld, Lake ⊜	162	22.32 S	123.44 E
Auldearn	46	57.34 N	3.49 W
Aulendorf	58	47.57 N	9.38 E
Aulestad	26	61.13 N	10.17 E
Auletta	68	40.34 N	15.25 E
Aulla	64	44.12 N	9.58 E
Aulnay	32	46.01 N	0.21 W
Aulnay-sous-Bois	50	48.57 N	2.31 E
Aulnay-sur-Mauldre	261	48.56 N	1.51 E
Aulne ≃	32	48.17 N	4.16 W
Aulneau Peninsula › [1]	184	49.23 N	94.29 W
Aulnois-sur-Seille	56	48.52 N	6.19 E
Aulnoye-Aymeries	50	50.12 N	3.50 E
Ault, Fr.	50	50.06 N	1.27 E
Ault, Co., U.S.	200	40.34 N	104.43 W
Ault, Ky., U.S.	218	38.12 N	83.14 W
Aultbea	46	57.50 N	5.35 W
Aultman	214	40.34 N	79.16 W
Aultshire	216	40.13 N	85.19 W
Auma	54	50.42 N	11.54 E
Aumale	50	49.46 N	1.45 E
Auma Point ›	164	7.55 S	145.25 E
Aumetz	56	49.25 N	5.56 E
Aumont-Aubrac	32	44.43 N	3.17 E
Aumühle	52	53.31 N	10.19 E
Auna	150	10.12 N	4.45 E
Auneau	50	48.27 N	1.46 E
Auneuil	50	49.22 N	2.00 E
Auning	26	56.26 N	10.23 E
Auno	146	11.50 N	12.53 E
Aunuu I	174u	14.17 S	170.33 W

Auob ≃	156	26.25 S	20.35 E
Auponhia	112	1.56 S	125.29 E
Aups	62	43.37 N	6.14 E
Aur, Pulau I	112	2.27 N	104.31 E
Aura	26	60.36 N	22.34 E
Aurach	56	49.15 N	10.25 E
Aurach ≃, Dtsch.	56	49.34 N	10.59 E
Aurach ≃, Dtsch.	56	49.51 N	10.56 E
Aurachmat	85	41.34 N	70.07 E
Auraiya	124	26.28 N	79.31 E
Aurangābād, India	122	19.53 N	75.20 E
Aurangābād, India	124	24.45 N	84.22 E
Auray	32	47.40 N	2.59 W
Aurdal	26	60.56 N	9.24 E
Aure	26	63.16 N	8.32 E
Aurelia	198	42.42 N	95.26 W
Aurelius	216	42.31 N	84.31 W
Aurès, Massif de l' ⋀	148	35.08 N	6.30 E
Auri, Kepulauan II	164	1.59 S	134.42 E
Aurich	52	53.28 N	7.29 E
Auriesville Shrine ʊ [1]	210	42.54 N	74.19 W
Auriflama	255	20.41 S	50.34 W
Aurigny → Alderney I	43b	49.43 N	2.12 W
Aurilândia	255	16.44 S	50.28 W
Aurillac	32	44.56 N	2.26 E
Aurina, Valle V	64	47.00 N	12.00 E
Aurine, Alpi (Zillertaler Alpen) ⋀	64	47.00 N	11.55 E
Aurino ≃	64	46.48 N	11.55 E
Auriol	62	43.23 N	5.38 E
Aurisina	64	45.45 N	13.41 E
Aurlandsfjorden c [2]	26	61.05 N	7.02 E
Aurlandsvangen	26	60.54 N	7.11 E
Aurolzmünster	60	48.15 N	13.27 E
Auron	62	44.14 N	6.56 E
Auronzo di Cadore	64	46.33 N	12.26 E
Aurora, Bra.	250	6.57 S	38.58 W
Aurora, Bra.	287a	22.46 S	43.24 W
Aurora, On., Can.	212	44.00 N	79.28 W
Aurora, S. Afr.	158	32.42 S	18.29 E
Aurora, Co., U.S.	200	39.43 N	104.49 W
Aurora, Il., U.S.	216	41.45 N	88.19 W
Aurora, In., U.S.	218	39.03 N	84.54 W
Aurora, Me., U.S.	188	44.51 N	68.19 W
Aurora, Mn., U.S.	190	47.31 N	92.14 W
Aurora, Mo., U.S.	194	36.58 N	93.43 W
Aurora, Ne., U.S.	198	40.52 N	98.00 W
Aurora, N.Y., U.S.	210	42.45 N	76.42 W
Aurora, N.C., U.S.	192	35.18 N	76.47 W
Aurora, Oh., U.S.	214	41.19 N	81.20 W
Aurora, Or., U.S.	224	45.13 N	122.45 W
Aurora, Ut,. U.S.	200	38.55 N	111.56 W
Aurora, W.V., U.S.	188	39.19 N	79.33 W
Aurora □ [4]	116	16.00 N	121.40 E
Aurora ʊ	265a	59.57 N	30.21 E
Aurora do Norte	255	12.43 S	46.24 W
Aurora Pond ⊜	279a	41.20 N	81.23 W
Auroux	62	44.45 N	3.44 E
Aursunden ⊜	26	62.40 N	11.40 E
Aurukun	164	13.19 S	141.45 E
Aurukun Aboriginal Land Trust ◆ [4]	164	13.45 S	141.45 E
Aurunci, Monti ⋀	66	41.22 N	13.40 E
Aus	156	26.40 S	16.15 E
Ausable ≃, On., Can.	190	43.19 N	81.46 W
Au Sable ≃, Mi., U.S.	190	44.25 N	83.20 W
Au Sable, North Branch ≃	190	44.40 N	84.23 W
Au Sable, South Branch ≃	190	44.40 N	84.23 W
Au Sable Forks	188	44.26 N	73.40 W
Au Sable Point ›	190	44.20 N	83.20 W
Auschwitz → Oświęcim	30	50.03 N	19.12 E
Ausevik ⊥	26	61.32 N	5.16 E
Auskerry I	46	59.02 N	2.34 W
Ausleben	54	52.05 N	11.07 E
Ausoni, Monti ⋀	66	41.25 N	13.20 E
Ausserferrera	58	46.33 N	9.26 E
Ausserfragant	64	46.56 N	13.06 E
Aussig → Ústí nad Labem	54	50.40 N	14.02 E
Aussois	62	45.14 N	6.45 E
Aust-Agder □ [6]	26	58.50 N	8.00 E
Austerlitz → Slavkov u Brna, Česká Rep.	61	49.09 N	16.52 E
Austerlitz, Ned.	52	52.05 N	5.19 E
Austerlitz, N.Y., U.S.	210	42.19 N	73.28 W
Austerlitz, Gare ◆ [5]	261	48.50 N	2.22 E
Austin, Bra.	287a	22.43 S	43.32 W
Austin, Mb., Can.	184	49.57 N	98.56 W
Austin, In., U.S.	218	38.45 N	85.48 W
Austin, Mn., U.S.	190	43.40 N	92.58 W
Austin, Nv., U.S.	204	39.29 N	117.04 W
Austin, Pa., U.S.	214	41.37 N	78.05 W
Austin, Tx., U.S.	222	30.16 N	97.44 W
Austin □ [6]	222	29.53 N	96.15 W
Austin ◆ [8]	278	41.54 N	87.45 W
Austin, Lake ⊜	162	27.40 S	118.00 E
Austin, Lake ⊜ [1]	222	30.19 N	97.46 W
Austin Bayou ≃	222	29.07 N	95.18 W
Austinburg	214	41.46 N	80.51 W
Austin Channel ⊔	176	75.35 N	103.25 W
Austin Lake ⊜	216	42.11 N	85.33 W
Austinmer	170	34.18 S	150.56 E
Austin's Post	158	29.32 S	25.49 E
Austintown	214	41.06 N	80.45 W
Austinville	192	36.51 N	80.54 W
Austnes	26	62.38 N	6.16 E
Austonio	222	31.11 N	95.38 W
Austonley	262	53.34 N	1.50 W
Austral	274a	33.56 S	150.48 E
Australes, Îles II	14	23.00 S	150.00 W
Australia □ [1]	160	25.00 S	135.00 E
Australia Mountain ∧	180	63.36 N	138.08 W
Australian Capital Territory □ [8]	171b	35.30 S	149.00 E
Australian War Memorial ⊥	171b	35.17 S	149.09 E
Australia Plains	168b	34.06 S	139.09 E
Australie → Australia □ [1]	160	25.00 S	135.00 E
Australien → Australia □ [1]	160	25.00 S	135.00 E
Australind	168a	33.16 S	115.44 E
Austral Seamounts ✢ [3]	14	22.40 S	152.45 W
Austråt	26	63.43 N	9.45 E
Austria (Österreich) □ [1], Europe	22	47.20 N	13.20 E
Austria (Österreich) □ [1], Europe	30	47.20 N	13.20 E
Austvågøya I	24	68.20 N	14.36 E
Autazes	246	3.35 S	59.08 W
Auteuil, Fr.	50	49.21 N	2.05 E
Auteuil, Fr.	261	48.50 N	1.49 E
Autheuil	50	49.06 N	1.17 E
Authie ≃	50	50.21 N	1.38 E
Authon	62	44.14 N	6.08 E
Authon-du-Perche	50	48.12 N	0.55 E
Authon-la-Plaine	50	48.27 N	1.57 E
Auth Village	284c	38.49 N	76.55 W
Autlán de Navarro	234	19.46 N	104.22 W
Autore, Monte ∧	66	41.58 N	13.12 E
Autrey-lès-Gray	58	47.29 N	5.30 E
Autriche → Austria □ [1]	30	47.20 N	13.20 E
Autumn Hill	284b	39.16 N	76.48 W
Autun	32	46.57 N	4.18 E
Auve	56	49.02 N	4.42 E
Auvergne	164	15.41 S	130.01 E
Auvergne □ [9]	32	45.25 N	2.30 E
Auvernaux	261	48.32 N	2.30 E
Auvers-sur-Oise	50	49.04 N	2.10 E
Auvézère ≃	32	45.12 N	0.51 E
Aux Cayes → Les Cayes	238	18.12 N	73.45 W
Auxerre	50	47.48 N	3.34 E

Auxier	192	37.44 N	82.45 W
Auxi-le-Château	50	50.14 N	2.07 E
Auxon	50	48.06 N	3.55 E
Auxonne	58	47.12 N	5.23 E
Aux Sable Creek ≃	216	41.23 N	88.20 W
Auxvasse	219	39.01 N	91.53 W
Auxvasse Creek ≃	219	38.41 N	91.49 W
Auxy	58	46.57 N	4.24 E
Auyamita, Quebrada ≃	286c	10.30 N	66.46 W
Auyán Tepuy ∧	246	5.55 N	62.32 W
Auzances	32	46.02 N	2.30 E
Auzangate, Nevado ∧	248	13.48 S	71.14 W
Auzon ≃, Fr.	58	48.30 N	4.20 E
Auzon ≃, Fr.	62	44.02 N	4.54 E
Ava, Il., U.S.	194	37.53 N	89.29 W
Ava, Mo., U.S.	194	36.57 N	92.39 W
Avadchara	84	43.31 N	40.39 E
Avadh Plains ≚	124	26.20 N	82.00 E
Avaí	255	22.08 S	49.22 W
Āvaj	128	35.34 N	49.13 E
Avakubi	154	1.20 N	27.34 E
Aval'	85	40.19 N	71.50 E
Aval, Falaise d' ▴ [4]	50	49.45 N	0.10 E
Avala ⊥	38	44.45 N	20.35 E
Avaldsnes	26	59.21 N	5.16 E
Avallon	50	47.29 N	3.54 E
Avaloirs, Les ∧ [2]	32	48.28 N	0.07 W
Avalon, Ca., U.S.	228	33.20 N	118.19 W
Avalon, N.J., U.S.	208	39.06 N	74.43 W
Avalon, Pa., U.S.	214	40.30 N	80.04 W
Avalon, Tx., U.S.	222	32.12 N	96.48 W
Avalon, Wi., U.S.	216	42.38 N	88.52 W
Avalon Peninsula › [1]	186	47.30 N	53.30 W
Ávalos	232	28.35 N	106.00 W
Avana ≃	174k	21.14 S	159.43 W
Avanos	130	38.43 N	34.51 E
Avant	196	36.29 N	96.03 W
Avaré, Bra.	252	23.05 S	48.55 W
Avaré, Bra.	255	23.05 S	48.55 W
Avarskoje Kojsu ≃	84	42.47 N	46.48 E
Avarua	174k	21.12 S	159.46 W
Avarua Harbour c	174k	21.11 S	159.46 W
Avatanak Island I	180	54.03 N	165.19 W
Avatele	174v	19.06 S	169.55 W
Avatele Bay c	174v	19.05 S	169.56 W
Avatiu	174k	21.12 S	159.47 W
Avatiu Harbour c	174k	21.11 S	159.47 W
Avčala	84	41.48 N	44.48 E
Avdiyivka	83	48.08 N	37.46 E
Ave ≃	34	41.20 N	8.45 W
Avebury	42	51.27 N	1.51 W
Avebury Stone Circle ⊥	42	51.28 N	1.51 W
ʿAvedat, Ḥorvot ⊥	132	30.48 N	34.46 E
Avegbadje ∧	150	7.14 N	0.38 E
Aveiro, Bra.	250	3.15 S	55.10 W
Aveiro, Port.	34	40.38 N	8.39 W
Aveiro, Ria de ≃ [1]	34	40.38 N	8.44 W
Avelar	256	22.20 S	43.25 W
Avelengo	64	46.38 N	11.13 E
Aveley	260	51.30 N	0.16 E
Avelgem	50	50.46 N	3.26 E
Avella, It.	68	40.58 N	14.36 E
Avella, Pa., U.S.	214	40.16 N	80.27 W
Avellaneda, Arg.	252	34.39 S	58.23 W
Avellaneda, Arg.	252	29.07 S	59.40 W
Avellaneda, Arg.	258	34.39 S	58.23 W
Avellaneda □ [5]	288	34.40 S	58.20 W
Avellaneda, Estacion ◆ [5]	288	34.41 S	58.22 W
Avelle, Île I	275a	45.24 N	74.00 W
Avellino	68	40.54 N	14.47 E
Avellino □ [4]	68	41.00 N	15.10 E
Avenal	226	36.00 N	120.07 W
Avenal Creek ≃	226	35.47 N	120.04 W
Aven Armand ▴ [5]	32	44.15 N	3.22 E
Avenas	58	46.12 N	4.37 E
Avenches	58	46.53 N	7.02 E
Avenel	276	40.34 N	74.17 W
Aventureiro, Rio do ≃	256	21.52 S	42.39 W
Avenue	208	38.15 N	76.46 W
Averbode	56	51.02 N	4.59 E
Averbode, Abbaye d' ʊ [1]	56	51.02 N	4.59 E
Averill Lake ⊜	206	44.59 N	71.44 W
Averill Park	210	42.38 N	73.33 W
Avern ⊜	40	58.54 N	15.32 E
Avernakø I	41	55.01 N	10.17 E
Avernes	261	49.05 N	1.52 E
Avernes, Ru des ≃	261	49.04 N	2.51 E
Averøya I	26	63.01 N	7.34 E
Aversa	68	40.58 N	14.12 E
Avery, Ca., U.S.	226	38.13 N	120.22 W
Avery, Id., U.S.	202	47.15 N	115.48 W
Avery, Tx., U.S.	194	33.33 N	94.47 W
Avery Island	194	29.54 N	91.54 W
Aves, Isla de I	238	15.42 N	63.38 W
Avesnelles	50	50.07 N	3.57 E
Avesnes-le-Comte	50	50.17 N	2.32 E
Avesnes-lès-Aubert	50	50.12 N	3.23 E
Avesnes-sur-Helpe	50	50.07 N	3.56 E
Avesta	40	60.09 N	16.12 E
Aveto ≃	62	44.42 N	9.23 E
Avetrana	68	40.21 N	17.43 E
Aveyron □ [5]	32	44.15 N	2.40 E
Aveyron ≃	32	44.05 N	1.16 E
Avezzano	66	42.02 N	13.25 E
Avgustovka	80	52.16 N	50.44 E
Aviano	64	46.04 N	12.36 E
Avich, Loch ⊜	46	56.16 N	5.20 W
Aviemore	46	57.12 N	3.50 W
Avigliana	62	45.05 N	7.23 E
Avigliano	68	40.44 N	15.44 E
Avignon	62	43.57 N	4.49 E
Ávila	34	40.39 N	4.42 W
Ávila □ [4]	34	40.35 N	5.00 W
Avila Beach	226	35.10 N	120.43 W
Avilés	34	43.33 N	5.55 W
Avilla	216	41.22 N	85.14 W
Avilley	58	47.26 N	6.16 E
Aviña	34	43.36 N	8.08 W
Avinger	222	32.54 N	94.33 W
Avinurme	76	58.59 N	26.51 E
Avio	64	45.44 N	10.56 E
Avion	50	50.24 N	2.50 E
Avioth	56	49.34 N	5.24 E
Avis	210	41.11 N	77.18 W
Avisio ≃	64	46.07 N	11.05 E
Avispa, Cerro ∧	246	1.16 N	65.51 W
Aviston	219	38.36 N	89.36 W
Aviz	34	39.03 N	7.53 W
Avize	50	48.58 N	4.01 E
Avlan Gölü ⊜	130	36.34 N	29.57 E
Avlum	41	56.16 N	8.48 E
Avnbøl	41	54.58 N	9.39 E
Avnik	130	38.39 N	40.20 E
Avoca, Austl.	169	37.05 S	143.28 E
Avoca, Ia., U.S.	198	41.28 N	95.20 W
Avoca, N.Y., U.S.	210	42.24 N	77.25 W
Avoca, Pa., U.S.	210	41.20 N	75.44 W
Avoca ≃, Austl.	166	35.42 S	143.44 E
Avoca ≃, Ire.	48	52.48 N	6.09 W
Avoca, Mount ∧	169	37.07 S	143.21 E
Avoca Beach	170	33.29 S	151.29 E
Avocado Heights	280	34.08 N	117.54 W
Avola, B.C., Can.	182	51.47 N	119.19 W
Avola, It.	70	36.54 N	15.08 E
Avon, Austl.	168b	34.17 S	138.20 E
Avon, Fr.	50	48.24 N	2.43 E
Avon, Ct., U.S.	207	41.48 N	72.49 W
Avon, Il., U.S.	190	40.39 N	90.26 W
Avon, Ma., U.S.	207	42.07 N	71.02 W
Avon, Mn., U.S.	190	45.36 N	94.27 W
Avon, Mt., U.S.	202	46.35 N	112.36 W
Avon, N.Y., U.S.	210	42.54 N	77.44 W
Avon, N.C., U.S.	192	35.21 N	75.30 W
Avon, Oh., U.S.	214	41.27 N	82.02 W
Avon, Pa., U.S.	208	40.22 N	76.23 W

Avon, S.D., U.S.	198	43.00 N	98.03 W
Avon □ [6]	42	51.30 N	2.40 W
Avon ≃, Austl.	168a	31.40 S	116.07 E
Avon ≃, N.S., Can.	186	45.10 N	64.15 W
Avon ≃, On., Can.	212	43.18 N	81.11 W
Avon ≃, Eng., U.K.	42	51.30 N	2.43 W
Avon ≃, Eng., U.K.	42	50.17 N	3.52 W
Avon ≃, Eng., U.K.	42	50.43 N	1.46 W
Avon ≃, Eng., U.K.	42	52.25 N	1.31 W
Avon ≃, Eng., U.K.	42	51.59 N	2.10 W
Avon ≃, Scot., U.K.	46	56.01 N	3.40 W
Avon ≃, Scot., U.K.	46	57.25 N	3.23 W
Avon, Ben ∧	46	57.05 N	3.27 W
Avon, Ru d' ≃	261	48.39 N	2.46 E
Avon Basin c	279a	41.30 N	82.03 W
Avon by the Sea	208	40.11 N	74.00 W
Avondale, Az., U.S.	200	33.26 N	112.20 W
Avondale, Co., U.S.	198	38.14 N	104.21 W
Avondale, Md., U.S.	284c	38.56 N	76.59 W
Avondale, Oh., U.S.	214	39.47 N	84.08 W
Avondale Heights	274b	37.46 S	144.51 E
Avon Downs	166	20.05 S	137.30 E
Avondrust	158	34.21 S	21.51 E
Avon Lake	214	41.30 N	82.01 W
Avonlea	184	50.00 N	105.04 W
Avonmore, On., Can.	206	45.10 N	74.58 W
Avonmore, Pa., U.S.	214	40.31 N	79.27 W
Avonmore ≃	48	52.50 N	6.13 W
Avonmouth	42	51.31 N	2.42 W
Avon Park	220	27.35 N	81.30 W
Avon Reservoir ⊜ [1]	170	34.24 S	150.40 E
Avontuur	158	33.44 S	23.11 E
Avon Valley National Park ♠	168a	31.41 S	116.06 E
Avon Water ≃	46	55.47 N	4.01 W
Avoudrey	58	47.08 N	6.26 E
Avrainville	261	48.34 N	2.15 E
Avranches	32	48.41 N	1.22 W
Avranlo	84	41.39 N	43.52 E
Avre ≃, Fr.	50	49.53 N	2.20 E
Avre ≃, Fr.	50	48.47 N	1.22 E
Avrieux	62	45.13 N	6.43 E
Avroult	50	50.38 N	2.09 E
Avtatkuul' ≃	180	64.06 N	178.10 E
Avtovo ◆ [8]	265a	59.52 N	30.15 E
Avu Avu	175e	9.50 S	160.23 E
Awa, Nihon	96	34.04 N	134.12 E
Awa, Nihon	174m	26.36 N	127.56 E
Awaba	170	33.01 S	151.33 E
Aʿwaj, Nahr al- ≃	132	33.20 N	36.34 E
Awaji	96	34.35 N	135.01 E
Awaji-shima I	96	34.21 N	134.51 E
Awakino	172	38.39 S	174.38 E
ʿAwālī	128	26.05 N	50.33 E
Awang	115b	8.54 S	116.24 E
Awano	94	36.31 N	139.41 E
Awanui	172	35.03 S	173.15 E
Awar	164	4.09 S	144.51 E
Awara	94	36.13 N	136.12 E
Awarawar, Tanjung ›	115a	6.45 S	111.56 E
Aware	144	8.15 N	44.10 E
Awarua Point ›	172	44.15 S	168.03 E
Awasa	144	6.45 N	38.15 E
Awasa, Lake ⊜	144	7.05 N	38.25 E
Awasan Bay c	116	9.56 N	125.36 E
Awash	144	8.59 N	40.10 E
Awash ≃	144	11.45 N	41.05 E
Awa-shima I, Nihon	92	38.27 N	139.14 E
Awa-shima I, Nihon	96	34.16 N	133.38 E
Awash National Park ♠	144	9.05 N	40.00 E
Awaso	150	6.14 N	2.16 W
Awatere ≃	172	41.37 S	174.10 E
Awbārī	146	26.35 N	12.46 E
Awbārī, Ṣaḥrā' ▴ [8]	146	28.00 N	11.30 E
Awdheegle	144	1.59 N	44.50 E
Awe	150	8.09 N	9.07 E
Awe, Loch ⊜	46	56.15 N	5.17 W
Awegyun	110	12.44 N	98.44 E
Awgu	150	6.04 N	7.29 E
Awīsh al-Ḥajar	142	31.01 N	31.19 E
ʿAwjā', Wādī al- V	132	31.56 N	35.31 E
Awjilah	146	29.09 N	21.15 E
Awka	150	6.12 N	7.05 E
Awlād Mūsā	142	30.48 N	31.44 E
Awled Djellal	148	34.28 N	5.02 E
Awlef	148	26.58 N	1.05 E
Aworo Kit	140	10.59 N	32.38 E
Aworro	164	7.45 S	143.10 E
Awosting	276	41.09 N	74.20 W
Awsīm	273c	30.07 N	31.08 E
Awul	164	6.00 S	151.00 E
Awuna ≃	180	69.04 N	155.30 W
Awwal, Ash-Shallāl al- (First Cataract) ʟ	140	24.01 N	32.52 E
Awwalī, Nahr al- ≃	132	33.35 N	35.23 E
Axamilpa ≃	234	18.35 N	98.11 W
Axams	64	47.14 N	11.18 E
Axat	32	42.48 N	2.14 E
Axbridge	42	51.18 N	2.49 W
Axe ≃, Eng., U.K.	42	51.19 N	2.59 W
Axe ≃, Eng., U.K.	42	50.42 N	3.03 W
Axe Creek ≃	169	36.46 S	144.30 E
Axedale	169	36.47 S	144.30 E
Axe Edge ⋀ [2]	262	53.14 N	1.57 W
Axel	52	51.16 N	3.55 E
Axel Heiberg Island I	16	79.45 N	91.00 W
Axim	150	4.52 N	2.14 W
Axinim	246	4.02 S	59.22 W
Axiós (Vardar) ≃	38	40.35 N	22.50 E
Axis	194	30.55 N	88.01 W
Axixá	250	2.51 S	44.04 W
Ax-les-Thermes	32	42.43 N	1.50 E
Axminster	42	50.47 N	3.00 W
Axmouth	42	50.42 N	3.02 W
Axochiapan	234	18.30 N	98.46 W
Axtell, Ks., U.S.	198	39.52 N	96.15 W
Axtell, Ne., U.S.	198	40.28 N	99.07 W
Axtell, Tx., U.S.	222	31.39 N	96.58 W
Aÿ	50	49.03 N	4.00 E
Ayabaca	246	4.38 S	79.43 W
Ayabe	96	35.18 N	135.15 E
Ayachi, Ari n' ∧	148	32.29 N	4.57 W
Ayacucho, Arg.	252	37.09 S	58.29 W
Ayacucho, Bol.	248	17.51 S	63.20 W
Ayacucho, Perú	248	13.07 S	74.13 W
Ayacucho □ [5]	248	14.00 S	74.00 W
Ayakkum Hu ⊜	120	37.30 N	89.20 E
Ayamé	150	5.37 N	3.11 W
Ayamiken	152	2.07 N	10.01 E
Ayamonte	34	37.13 N	7.24 W
Āyān	272b	22.43 N	88.09 E
Ayancık	130	41.57 N	34.36 E
Ayangba	150	7.30 N	7.08 E
Ayapel	246	8.19 N	75.09 W
Ayarza, Laguna de ⊜	236	14.25 N	90.08 W
Ayas, It.	62	45.50 N	7.41 E
Ayaş, Tür.	130	40.01 N	32.21 E
Ayase	94	35.26 N	139.26 E
Ayase ≃	268	35.45 N	139.49 E
Ayauta	96	34.13 N	133.53 E
Ayaviri	248	14.52 S	70.35 W
Ayaviri ≃	248	15.01 S	70.22 W
ʿAybaāl, Jabal ∧	132	32.14 N	35.16 E
Aybastı, Tür.	130	39.42 N	39.02 E
Aybastı, Tür.	130	40.41 N	37.24 E
Aydar ≃	78	48.42 N	39.13 E
Aydar-Mykolayivka	83	48.58 N	38.58 E
Ayden	192	35.28 N	77.24 W
Aydere	128	38.24 N	56.45 E
Aydın	130	37.51 N	27.51 E
Aydın □ [4]	130	37.45 N	28.00 E
Aydıncık, Tür.	130	36.08 N	33.19 E
Aydıncık, Tür.	130	40.08 N	35.18 E
Aydın Dağları ⋀	130	38.00 N	28.00 E
Aydınkent	130	37.06 N	31.36 E
Aydıntepe	130	40.24 N	40.09 E
Aydin Ula ∧	86	42.55 N	87.35 E
Aydosdağı ∧	267b	40.56 N	29.15 E

Symbol	English	Deutsch	Español	Français	Português
≃	River	Fluß	Río	Rivière	Rio
≅	Canal	Kanal	Canal	Canal	Canal
ʟ	Waterfall, Rapids	Wasserfall, Stromschnellen	Cascada, Rápidos	Chute d'eau, Rapides	Cascata, Rápidos
⊔	Strait	Meeresstraße	Estrecho	Détroit	Estreito
c	Bay, Gulf	Bucht, Golf	Bahía, Golfo	Baie, Golfe	Baía, Golfo
⊜	Lake, Lakes	See, Seen	Lago, Lagos	Lac, Lacs	Lago, Lagos
≡	Swamp	Sumpf	Pantano	Marais	Pântano
⊓	Ice Features, Glacier	Eis- und Gletscherformen	Accidentes Glaciales	Formes glaciaires	Acidentes glaciares
⊤	Other Hydrographic Features	Andere Hydrographische Objekte	Otros Elementos Hidrográficos	Autres données hydrographiques	Outros acidentes hidrográficos
✢	Submarine Features	Untermeerische Objekte	Accidentes Submarinos	Formes de relief sous-marin	Acidentes submarinos
□	Political Unit	Politische Einheit	Unidad Politica	Entité politique	Unidade política
ʊ	Cultural Institution	Kulturelle Institution	Institución Cultural	Institution culturelle	Institução cultural
⊥	Historical Site	Historische Stätte	Sitio Histórico	Site historique	Sitio histórico
♠	Recreational Site	Erholungs- und Ferienort	Sitio de Recreo	Centre de loisirs	Area de Lazer
⊠	Airport	Flughafen	Aeropuerto	Aéroport	Aeroporto
■	Military Installation	Militäranlage	Instalación Militar	Installation militaire	Instalação militar
◆	Miscellaneous	Verschiedenes	Misceláneo	Divers	Diversos

ENGLISH

Name	Page	Lat.°′	Long.°′
Ayelu ∧	144	10.04 N	40.46 E
Ayer, Schw.	58	46.11 N	7.36 E
Ayer, Ma., U.S.	207	42.33 N	71.35 W
Ayer Baloi	114	1.35 N	103.20 E
Ayer Chawan, Pulau I	271c	1.17 N	103.42 E
Ayer Hitam, Malay.	114	1.55 N	103.11 E
Ayer Hitam, Malay.	114	2.56 N	102.24 E
Ayer Jerneh	114	4.24 N	103.24 E
Ayer Kuning Selatan	114	2.30 N	102.28 E
Ayer Merbau, Pulau I	271c	1.16 N	103.43 E
Ayers Cliff	206	45.10 N	72.03 W
Ayers Rock (Uluru) ∧	162	25.23 S	131.05 E
Ayersville	216	41.14 N	84.17 W
Ayeyarwady □[8]	110	17.00 N	95.00 E
Ayeyarwady (Irrawaddy) ≃	110	15.50 N	95.06 E
Aygün	130	38.26 N	41.17 E
Ayía Marína	38	37.09 N	26.52 E
Ayía Paraskeví, Ellás	38	39.15 N	26.16 E
Ayía Paraskeví, Ellás	267c	38.01 N	23.50 E
Ayiássos	38	39.05 N	26.23 E
Ayía Varvára	267c	37.59 N	23.39 E
Ayina ≃	152	1.48 N	13.10 E
Aying	64	47.58 N	11.47 E
Áyioi Anáryiroi	267c	38.02 N	23.43 E
Áyion Óros □[8]	38	40.15 N	24.15 E
Áyion Óros ›[1]	38	40.15 N	24.15 E
Áyios Dhimítrios	267c	37.56 N	23.44 E
Áyios Evstrátios I	38	39.31 N	25.00 E
Áyios Ioánnis Réndis	267c	37.58 N	23.40 E
Áyios Kírikos	38	37.37 N	26.14 E
Áyios Nikólaos	38	35.11 N	25.42 E
Ayiou Nikolaou Monastery ✝[1]	267c	37.53 N	23.27 E
Ayíou Órous, Kólpos c	38	40.12 N	24.03 E
Ayl	132	30.13 N	35.32 E
Aylesbury	42	51.50 N	0.50 W
Aylesford	42	51.18 N	0.29 E
Aylesham	42	51.13 N	1.13 E
Aylmer	188	45.26 N	75.50 W
Aylmer, Lake ◎	206	45.50 N	71.22 W
Aylmer, Mount ∧	182	51.19 N	115.26 W
Aylmer-East	212	45.26 N	75.50 W
Aylmer Lake ◎	176	64.05 N	108.30 W
Aylmer West	212	42.46 N	80.59 W
Aylsham, Sk., Can.	184	53.11 N	103.49 W
Aylsham, Eng., U.K.	42	52.49 N	1.15 E
ʻAyn al-ʻArab	130	36.54 N	38.21 E
ʻAyn Dār	128	25.59 N	49.23 E
ʻAyn Dīwār	130	37.17 N	42.11 E
ʻAynīn ⊤[4]	144	20.48 N	41.39 E
Aynor	192	33.59 N	79.11 W
ʻAynūnah	128	28.05 N	35.08 E
Ayo	248	15.41 S	72.16 W
Ayo Ayo	248	17.05 S	68.00 W
Ayod	140	8.07 N	31.26 E
Ayodhya	124	26.48 N	82.12 E
Ayo El Chico	234	20.32 N	102.21 W
Ayom	140	7.52 N	28.23 E
Ayorou	150	14.44 N	0.55 E
Ayos	152	3.54 N	12.31 E
ʻAyoûn el ʻAtroûs	150	16.40 N	9.37 W
Ay-Petri, hora ∧	78	44.27 N	34.03 E
Ayr, Austl.	166	19.35 S	147.24 E
Ayr, On., Can.	212	43.17 N	80.27 W
Ayr, Scot., U.K.	44	55.28 N	4.38 W
Ayr ≃	44	55.29 N	4.28 W
ʻAyrah	132	32.37 N	36.32 E
Ayrancı	130	37.22 N	33.42 E
Ayre, Point of ›	44	54.26 N	4.22 W
Aysgarth	44	54.17 N	2.00 W
Aysha	144	10.46 N	42.37 E
ʻAytā al-Fakhkhār	132	33.38 N	35.54 E
ʻAytanīt	132	33.34 N	35.40 E
Ayton, Austl.	164	15.56 S	145.22 E
Ayton, On., Can.	212	44.03 N	80.56 W
Ayton, Eng., U.K.	44	54.14 N	0.29 W
Ayu, Kepulauan II	108	0.28 N	131.03 E
Ayubnagar	126	23.46 N	90.23 E
Ayulhai	102	44.36 N	115.36 E
Ayuñgon	116	9.51 N	123.08 E
Ayuquila ≃	234	19.23 N	103.51 W
Ayutla	234	20.07 N	104.22 W
Ayutla de los Libres	234	16.54 N	99.13 W
Ayvacık, Tür.	130	39.36 N	26.24 E
Ayvacık, Tür.	130	41.00 N	36.39 E
Ayvalı	130	38.44 N	37.38 E
Ayvalık	130	39.18 N	26.41 E
Aywaille	56	50.28 N	5.40 E
Azabarabān, Ra's ›	142	28.51 N	32.43 E
Azacualpa, Hond.	236	14.27 N	86.09 W
Azacualpa, Hond.	236	15.19 N	88.33 W
Azādpur ⊕[8]	272a	28.43 N	77.11 E
Azai	94	35.26 N	136.18 E
Azaila	34	41.17 N	0.29 W
Azalea Park	220	28.32 N	81.18 W
Azama	174m	26.11 N	127.49 E
Azamatovo	80	53.18 N	53.28 E
Azambuja	34	39.04 N	8.52 W
Āzamgarh	124	26.04 N	83.11 E
Azamiga-dake ∧	96	34.20 N	131.47 E
Azángaro	248	14.55 S	70.13 W
Azángaro ≃	248	15.17 S	70.10 W
Azanka	86	58.02 N	64.48 E
Azao ∧	148	25.12 N	8.08 E
Azaouâd ⊕[1]	150	19.00 N	3.00 W
Azaouagh, Vallée de l' V	150	15.30 N	3.18 E
Azapa, Quebrada de ≃	248	18.30 S	70.17 W
Azar V	150	16.02 N	4.04 E
Azara	150	8.21 N	9.12 E
Āzārbāyjān-e Gharbī □[4]	128	37.40 N	45.00 E
Āzārbāyjān-e Sharqī □[4]	128	38.00 N	47.00 E
Azare	150	11.40 N	10.11 E
Āzar Shahr	128	37.45 N	45.59 E
Azaryčy	76	52.28 N	29.16 E
Azas ≃	88	52.26 N	96.15 E
Azat, gora ∧[2]	86	46.55 N	69.00 E
Azay-le-Rideau	50	47.16 N	0.28 E
Azay-sur-Cher	50	47.21 N	0.51 E
Azay-sur-Indre	50	47.12 N	0.57 E
Aʻzāz	130	36.35 N	37.03 E
Azazga	148	36.44 N	4.22 E
Azcuénaga	258	34.23 S	59.21 W
Aždaak, gora ∧	84	40.13 N	44.56 E
Azdavay	130	41.39 N	33.18 E
Azdzjacičy	76	54.06 N	28.50 E
Azeffâl ⊥[8]	148	21.00 N	14.45 W
Azeffoun	148	36.53 N	4.25 E
Azejevo	80	54.41 N	42.02 E
Azemmour	148	33.20 N	8.25 W
Azenhas do Mar	266c	38.50 N	9.28 W
Azennezal, ʻErg V	148	22.50 N	0.25 E
Azerbaidzhan → Azerbaijan □[1]	22	40.30 N	47.30 E
Azerbaijan (Azärbaycan) □[1], Asia	72	40.30 N	47.30 E
Azerbaijan (Azärbaycan) □[1], Asia	84	40.30 N	47.30 E
Azerbajdžan → Azerbaijan □[1]	72	40.30 N	47.30 E
Azerbaydzan → Azerbaijan □[1]	72	40.30 N	47.30 E
Azergues ≃	58	45.56 N	4.44 E
Azëry	76	53.43 N	24.11 E
Azezo	144	12.35 N	37.28 E
Azgir	80	47.50 N	47.54 E
Azhikode	122	11.59 N	75.21 E
Azilal	148	31.58 N	6.34 W
Azilal □[4]	148	31.55 N	6.30 W
Azile	154	3.32 N	29.52 E
Azincourt	50	50.28 N	2.08 E
Azle	222	32.53 N	97.32 W
Aznakajevo	80	54.53 N	53.04 E
Aznapuquio	286d	11.59 S	77.04 W
Azogues	246	2.44 S	78.50 W
Azoia	266c	38.46 N	9.29 W
Azor	132	32.01 N	34.48 E
Azores → Açores II	148a	38.30 N	28.00 W
Azores-Gibraltar Ridge ✦[3]	10	37.00 N	16.00 W
Azores Plateau ✦[3]	10	39.00 N	30.00 W
Azoum, Bahr (Wādī ʻAzūm) V	146	10.53 N	20.15 E
Azov	83	47.07 N	39.25 E
Azov, Sea of ⊤[2]	78	46.00 N	36.00 E
Azovs'ke	78	45.34 N	34.34 E
Azovskij kanal ≊	83	47.07 N	39.27 E
Azoyú	234	16.43 N	98.44 W
Azpeitia	34	43.11 N	2.16 W
Azraq, Al-Baḥr al- → Blue Nile ≃	140	15.38 N	32.31 E
Azraq, Bahr ≃	146	10.52 N	20.35 E
Azraq, Wādī al- V	140	10.33 N	28.40 E
Azraq ash-Shīshān	132	31.50 N	36.48 E
Azrou	148	33.27 N	5.14 W
Aztalan State Park ♦	216	43.04 N	88.51 W
Aztec	200	36.49 N	107.59 W
Azteca, Estadio ♦	286a	19.18 N	99.09 W
Aztec Peak ∧	200	33.48 N	110.55 W
Aztec Ruins National Monument ♦	200	36.51 N	108.10 W
Azua	238	18.27 N	70.44 W
Azuaga	34	38.16 N	5.41 W
Azuay □[4]	246	3.00 S	79.00 W
Azucena	252	37.29 S	59.18 W
Azuchi	94	35.09 N	136.08 E
Azuchi-jō ⊥	94	35.10 N	136.08 E
Azuer ≃	34	39.08 N	3.36 W
Azuero, Península de ›[1]	246	7.40 N	80.35 W
Azufre, Volcán ∧[1]	252	25.11 S	68.31 W
Azuga	38	45.27 N	25.33 E
Azul	252	36.47 S	59.51 W
Azul, Cerro ∧, C.R.	236	9.54 N	85.14 W
Azul, Cerro ∧, Ec.	246a	0.54 S	91.21 W
Azul, Cerro ∧, Hond.	236	14.32 N	88.23 W
Azul, Cordillera ∧∧	248	8.30 S	76.10 W
Azul Casa, Cerro ∧	252	22.29 S	65.20 W
ʻAẓūm, Wādī (Bahr Azoum) V	146	10.53 N	20.15 E
Azuma, Nihon	94	36.31 N	139.19 E
Azuma, Nihon	94	36.33 N	138.54 E
Azuma, Nihon	94	35.56 N	140.28 E
Azuma, Nihon	94	36.36 N	138.20 E
Azumaya-san ∧	94	36.32 N	138.25 E
Azumazaka	270	34.26 N	135.39 E
Azumi	94	36.11 N	137.47 E
Azur, Côte d' ⊥[2]	62	43.30 N	7.00 E
Azurduy	248	19.59 S	64.29 W
Azure Clouds, Temple of the ✝[1]	271a	40.00 N	116.11 E
Azure Lake ◎	182	52.23 N	120.00 W
Azusa	228	34.08 N	117.54 W
Azusa ≃	94	36.17 N	137.56 E
Ažu-Tajga, gora ∧	86	51.35 N	88.45 E
Az-Zabābidah	132	32.23 N	35.20 E
Az-Zabadānī	132	33.43 N	36.05 E
Az-Zāb al-Kabīr → Great Zab ≃	128	36.00 N	43.21 E
Az-Zāb aṣ-Ṣaghīr → Little Zab ≃	128	35.12 N	43.25 E
Aẓ-Ẓāhirīyah	132	31.25 N	34.58 E
Aẓ-Ẓahrān (Dhahran)	128	26.18 N	50.08 E
Az-Zamālik ⊕[8]	273c	30.04 N	31.13 E
Azzanello	64	45.18 N	9.55 E
Az-Zankalūn	142	30.33 N	31.27 E
Azzano Decimo	64	45.53 N	12.43 E
Az-Zaqāzīq	142	30.35 N	31.31 E
Az-Zarbah	130	36.04 N	36.59 E
Az-Zarqāʼ	132	32.05 N	36.06 E
Az-Zarqāʼ □[8]	132	32.00 N	36.45 E
Az-Zawāmil	142	30.21 N	31.26 E
Az-Zāwiyah	146	32.45 N	12.44 E
Az-Zaydāb	140	17.26 N	33.53 E
Az-Zaydīyah	144	15.18 N	43.04 E
Az-Zaytīyah ⊕[8]	142	29.58 N	32.31 E
Az-Zaytūn ⊕[8]	273c	30.06 N	31.19 E
Azzel Matti, Sebkha ≚	148	25.55 N	0.56 E
Az-Zilfī	128	26.18 N	44.48 E
Az-Zrārīyah	132	33.21 N	35.20 E
Az-Zubayr	128	30.23 N	47.43 E
ʻAzzūn	132	32.11 N	35.03 E
Azzurra, Grotta (Blue Grotto) ⊥[5]	68	40.35 N	14.14 E

B

Name	Page	Lat.°′	Long.°′
Ba ≃, Viet	110	13.02 N	109.03 E
Ba ≃, Zhg.	100	30.25 N	115.02 E
Ba ≃, Zhg.	102	31.03 N	107.08 E
Ba ≃, Zhg.	271a	39.57 N	116.38 E
Ba, Loch ◎	46	56.36 N	4.44 W
Baa	112	10.43 S	123.03 E
Baaba, Île I	175f	20.03 S	163.59 E
Baacagaan	102	45.35 N	99.27 E
Baad	58	47.19 N	10.07 E
Baah	112	10.28 S	121.59 E
Baak	263	51.25 N	7.10 E
Baal	56	51.02 N	6.17 E
Baao	116	13.27 N	123.22 E
Baar	58	47.12 N	8.32 E
Baar ⊕[1]	58	48.00 N	8.30 E
Baarbach ≃	263	51.27 N	7.39 E
Baardheere (Bardera)	144	2.20 N	42.17 E
Baardskeerdersbos	158	34.34 S	19.35 E
Baargaal	144	11.17 N	51.04 E
Baarle-Hertog	56	51.27 N	4.56 E
Baarle-Nassau	52	51.27 N	4.53 E
Baarlo	52	51.20 N	6.05 E
Baarn	52	52.13 N	5.16 E
Baasrode	50	51.02 N	4.10 E
Baba	246	1.47 S	79.40 W
Baba ≃	152	6.25 N	17.07 E
Baba Burnu ›, Tür.	130	39.29 N	26.04 E
Baba Burnu ›, Tür.	130	41.17 N	31.24 E
Babaçulândia	250	7.13 S	47.46 W
Babadag, Rom.	38	44.54 N	28.43 E
Babadağ, Tür.	130	37.48 N	28.52 E
Babadağ ∧	84	41.02 N	48.19 E
Babaeski	130	41.26 N	27.06 E
Babahoyo	246	1.49 S	79.31 W
Babaī (Sarju) ≃	124	27.42 N	81.16 E
Babailiqiao	100	32.26 N	118.57 E
Babajevo	76	59.23 N	35.56 E
Babajurt	84	43.36 N	46.47 E
Babak	112	7.08 N	125.41 E
Babakin	162	32.07 S	118.01 E
Babana	150	10.26 N	3.50 E
Babanango	158	28.30 S	31.00 E
Babanka	78	48.43 N	30.26 E
Babanūsah	140	11.20 N	27.48 E
Babar, Kepulauan II	164	7.50 S	129.45 E
Babar, Pulau I	164	7.55 S	129.45 E
Bābarpur ⊕[8]	272a	28.41 N	77.17 E
Babat, Indon.	112	2.45 S	103.38 E
Babat, Indon.	115a	7.06 S	112.10 E
Babatag, chrebet ∧∧	85	38.15 N	68.20 E
Babati	154	4.13 S	35.45 E
Bābā Valī Ṣāḥeb	120	31.40 N	65.40 E
Babaykivka	78	49.01 N	34.32 E
Babb	182	48.51 N	113.26 W
Babbacombe Bay c	42	50.30 N	3.25 W
Babb Creek ≃	210	41.33 N	77.23 W
Babbitt, Mn., U.S.	190	47.43 N	91.57 W
Babbitt, Nv., U.S.	204	38.32 N	118.38 W
Bʻabdā	132	33.50 N	35.32 E
Bʻabdāt	132	33.53 N	35.40 E
Babel, Mont de ∧	186	51.27 N	68.42 W
Babelijamun	164	2.04 S	137.43 E
Bab el Mandeb → Mandeb, Bab el ᛘ	144	12.40 N	43.20 E
Babelsberg ⊕[8]	264a	52.24 N	13.05 E
Babelsberg, Schloss ⊥	264a	52.24 N	13.05 E
Babelthuap I	175b	7.30 N	134.36 E
Babenhausen, Dtsch.	56	49.57 N	8.56 E
Babenhausen, Dtsch.	58	48.09 N	10.15 E
Babenki	82	55.21 N	37.11 E
Babeyru	154	1.52 N	27.27 E
Babi, Pulau I	114	2.05 N	96.39 E
Babia, Arroyo de la ≃	196	28.25 N	101.45 W
Babian ≃	102	22.58 N	101.44 E
Babičy	76	52.17 N	30.00 E
Bābil	142	30.41 N	31.00 E
Bābil □[4]	128	32.40 N	44.35 E
Bābil, Aṭlāl (Babylon) ⊥	128	32.33 N	44.24 E
Babile	144	9.15 N	42.19 E
Babilônia	256	22.33 S	44.28 W
Babimost	30	52.10 N	15.51 E
Babīna	124	25.15 N	78.28 E
Babina Greda	38	45.07 N	18.33 E
Babinda	166	17.20 S	145.55 E
Babine	182	55.19 N	126.37 W
Babine ≃	182	55.42 N	127.40 W
Babine Lake ◎	182	54.45 N	126.00 W
Babine Range ∧∧	182	55.00 N	126.25 W
Babino, Ross.	76	59.50 N	40.49 E
Babino, Ross.	76	56.44 N	34.17 E
Babino, Ross.	76	59.14 N	31.26 E
Babino, Ross.	80	57.22 N	48.45 E
Babiogórski Park Narodowy ♦	30	49.35 N	19.30 E
Babo	164	2.33 S	133.25 E
Bābol	128	36.34 N	52.42 E
Bābol Sar	128	36.43 N	52.39 E
Baboon Point ›	158	32.19 S	18.20 E
Baboquivari Mountains ∧∧	200	31.45 N	111.35 W
Baboquivari Peak ∧	200	31.46 N	111.35 W
Babor, Djebel ∧	34	36.30 N	5.28 E
Baborów	30	50.09 N	17.59 E
Babošino	82	54.13 N	37.08 E
Baboua	152	5.48 N	14.49 E
Babrongan Tower ∧[2]	162	18.36 S	123.33 E
Babrujsk	76	53.09 N	29.14 E
Babson Park, Fl., U.S.	220	27.49 N	81.31 W
Babson Park, Ma., U.S.	283	42.18 N	71.23 W
Babson Reservoir ◎[1]	283	42.38 N	70.40 W
Babstovo	89	48.07 N	132.27 E
Bab-Taza	148	35.03 N	5.14 W
Bābu Bheri	272b	22.51 N	88.14 E
Bābupur, India	126	24.01 N	87.10 E
Bābūpur, India	272a	28.30 N	76.59 E
Babura	150	12.46 N	9.01 E
Bābūsar Pass)(	123	35.09 N	74.03 E
Babuškin	88	51.41 N	105.54 E
Babuškin ⊕[8]	265b	55.52 N	37.42 E
Babuyan	116	10.00 N	118.54 E
Babuyan Channel ᛘ	116	18.44 N	121.40 E
Babuyan Island I	108	19.32 N	121.57 E
Babuyan Islands II	108	19.15 N	121.40 E
Babylon	210	40.41 N	73.19 W
Babylon → Bābil, Aṭlāl ⊥	128	32.33 N	44.24 E
Babynino	76	54.23 N	35.43 E
Bača ≃	64	46.09 N	13.48 E
Bacaadweeyn	144	7.12 N	47.32 E
Bacabal	250	4.14 S	44.47 W
Bacacay	116	13.18 N	123.47 E
Bacadéhuachi	232	29.44 N	109.10 W
Bacajaí ≃	250	3.27 S	51.53 W
Bacalhau, Canal do ≊	287a	23.03 S	43.35 W
Bacaligo	84	42.33 N	44.57 E
Bačalino	86	57.46 N	67.17 E
Bacan, Pulau I	164	0.35 S	127.30 E
Bacao	116	10.27 N	119.48 E
Bacarra	116	18.15 N	120.35 E
Bacatuba	250	5.40 S	43.42 W
Bacău	38	46.34 N	26.55 E
Bacău □[6]	38	46.30 N	26.45 E
Baccalieu Island I	186	48.08 N	52.48 W
Bac Can	110	22.08 N	105.50 E
Baccarat	58	48.27 N	6.45 E
Bacchiglione ≃	64	45.11 N	12.14 E
Bacchus Marsh	169	37.41 S	144.27 E
Bačėjkava	76	55.01 N	29.09 E
Baceno	58	46.16 N	8.19 E
Bacerac	232	30.18 N	108.50 W
Bacevičy	76	53.24 N	29.14 E
Bac Giang	110	21.16 N	106.12 E
Bach	58	47.16 N	10.24 E
Bachagou	98	40.36 N	122.54 E
Bachaquero	246	9.56 N	71.08 W
Bacharach	56	50.04 N	7.46 E
Bacharden	128	38.26 N	57.25 E
Bachardok	128	38.46 N	58.30 E
Bachauan	116	12.28 N	122.06 E
Bache	106	31.05 N	120.40 E
Bacheng	106	31.27 N	120.52 E
Bachi	100	24.48 N	115.49 E
Bachiniva	232	28.45 N	107.15 W
Bach Ma	110	16.12 N	107.52 E
Bachmetjevka	80	51.06 N	44.46 E
Bachmutovo	76	56.22 N	34.03 E
Bacho	114	6.37 N	101.39 E
Bachok	114	6.04 N	102.24 E
Bacht	85	40.43 N	68.42 E
Bachta, Ross.	74	62.28 N	89.00 E
Bachta, Ross.	86	55.45 N	92.26 E
Bachtemir ≃	80	45.43 N	47.38 E
Bachten-Berg ∧[2]	264a	52.20 N	12.54 E
Bachty	86	46.39 N	82.42 E
Bachu	90	39.50 N	78.20 E
Bachuma	144	6.48 N	35.53 E
Back ≃, N.T., Can.	176	67.15 N	95.15 W
Back ≃, Va., U.S.	208	37.06 N	76.17 W
Bačka ⊕[1]	38	45.50 N	19.30 E
Bačka Palanka	38	45.15 N	19.24 E
Bačka Topola	38	45.49 N	19.38 E
Back Bay ⊕[8]	283	42.21 N	71.05 W
Back Bay c, India	272c	18.56 N	72.49 E
Back Bay c, Va., U.S.	208	36.35 N	75.57 W
Backberg	40	60.37 N	16.37 E
Backbone Ranges ∧∧	180	63.30 N	129.00 W
Back Branch ≃	284c	38.50 N	76.48 W
Back Brook ≃	276	40.26 N	74.39 W
Back Channel ≃[1]	279b	40.30 N	80.05 W
Back Creek ≃	188	38.02 N	79.54 W
Backe	26	63.49 N	16.24 E
Bäckefors	26	58.48 N	12.10 E
Bäckehagen	40	60.39 N	15.34 E
Backford	262	53.15 N	2.54 W
Bäckhammar	40	59.10 N	14.11 E
Bački Petrovac	38	45.22 N	19.35 E
Backnang	56	48.56 N	9.25 E
Back River c	208	39.16 N	76.27 W
Back River Neck ›[1]	284b	39.18 N	76.26 W
Backstairs Passage ᛘ	168b	35.42 S	138.05 E
Bac Lieu	110	9.17 N	105.44 E
Bacliff	222	29.31 N	94.59 W
Bac Ninh	110	21.11 N	106.03 E
Baco, Mount ∧	116	12.49 N	121.10 E
Bacoachi	232	30.38 N	109.56 W
Bacoli	68	40.48 N	14.05 E
Bacolod	116	10.40 N	122.57 E
Bacon	116	13.03 N	124.03 E
Baconga ⊕[8]	273b	4.18 S	15.16 E
Bacon Peak ∧	224	48.39 N	121.31 W
Bacons Run ≃	285	40.06 N	74.41 W
Baconton	192	31.22 N	84.09 W
Bacoor	116	14.28 N	120.56 E
Bacoor Bay c	269f	14.28 N	120.54 E
Bac Phan □[9]	110	22.00 N	105.00 E
Bac Quang	110	22.29 N	104.52 E
Bacqueville-en-Caux	50	49.47 N	1.00 E
Bácsalmás	30	46.08 N	19.20 E
Bács-Kiskun □[6]	30	46.30 N	19.25 E
Bacton	42	52.52 N	1.28 E
Bâcu ≃	38	46.55 N	29.28 E
Bacuag	116	9.37 N	125.38 E
Bacuit Bay c	116	11.07 N	119.23 E
Bácum	232	27.33 N	110.05 W
Bacungan	116	9.56 N	118.42 E
Bacup	44	53.43 N	2.12 W
Bacuranao ≃	286b	23.10 N	82.14 W
Bacuranao, Presa ◎[1]	286b	23.07 N	82.13 W
Bacuri, Cachoeira do ⌊	250	5.29 S	54.18 W
Bacuri, Ilha do I	250	2.55 S	49.43 W
Bacuri, Lago do ◎	250	3.16 S	42.15 W
Bačurka	24	68.32 N	56.57 E
Bacuyangan	116	9.39 N	122.27 E
Bād	128	33.41 N	52.01 E
Bad ≃, Mi., U.S.	190	43.18 N	84.06 W
Bad ≃, S.D., U.S.	198	44.22 N	100.22 W
Bad ≃, Wi., U.S.	190	46.38 N	90.40 W
Badʻ, Wādī V	142	29.41 N	32.20 E
Bada	88	51.23 N	109.54 E
Bad Abbach	60	48.56 N	12.03 E
Badagara	122	11.36 N	75.35 E
Badagri	150	6.27 N	2.55 E
Badagri Creek c	273a	6.25 N	3.18 E
Badahl	142	28.56 N	30.54 E
Bad Aibling	64	47.52 N	12.00 E
Bada Jāmda	124	22.09 N	85.23 E
Badajia	100	33.57 N	120.17 E
Badajós ≃	246	3.15 S	63.02 W
Badajós, Lago ◎	246	3.15 S	62.47 W
Badajoz	34	38.53 N	6.58 W
Badajoz □[4]	34	38.40 N	6.00 W
Badakani	152	4.46 S	14.52 E
Badakhshān □[4]	120	36.45 N	72.00 E
Badal Khān Goth	120	26.31 N	67.06 E
Badalona	34	41.27 N	2.15 E
Badalucco	62	43.55 N	7.51 E
Badam	85	42.23 N	69.15 E
Bādāmi	122	15.55 N	75.41 E
Bādāmpahār	124	22.06 N	86.06 E
Badana, Lach V	144	0.50 S	42.04 E
Badanah	128	30.59 N	41.02 E
Badanga	146	11.36 N	17.26 E
Badanganj	126	22.54 N	87.33 E
Badaohao	104	41.47 N	121.57 E
Badaohe, Zhg.	98	40.24 N	118.42 E
Badaohe, Zhg.	98	40.02 N	122.17 E
Badarīnāth	124	30.44 N	79.29 E
Badarma	88	57.46 N	102.36 E
Badas	112	4.36 N	114.27 E
Badas, Kepulauan II	112	0.35 N	107.06 E
Badata, gora ∧	88	51.55 N	111.35 E
Bad Aussee	64	47.36 N	13.47 E
Bad Axe	190	43.48 N	83.00 W
Badaying	98	41.22 N	117.28 E
Badazhou	102	24.36 N	105.04 E
Bad Bentheim	52	52.19 N	7.10 E
Badbergen	52	52.38 N	7.59 E
Bad Bergzabern	56	49.07 N	8.00 E
Bad Berka	54	50.54 N	11.17 E
Bad Berleburg	56	51.03 N	8.23 E
Bad Berneck	60	50.03 N	11.40 E
Bad Bertrich	56	50.04 N	7.02 E
Bad Bevensen	52	53.05 N	10.34 E
Bad Bibra	54	51.12 N	11.35 E
Bad Birnbach	60	48.27 N	13.01 E
Bad Blankenburg	54	50.41 N	11.16 E
Bad Bocklet	56	50.16 N	10.05 E
Bad Brambach	54	50.13 N	12.19 E
Bad Bramstedt	52	53.55 N	9.53 E
Bad Breisig	56	50.31 N	7.18 E
Bad Brückenau	56	50.18 N	9.47 E
Bad Buchau	58	48.03 N	9.36 E
Bad Camberg	56	50.18 N	8.16 E
Bad Creek ≃	216	41.25 N	83.57 W
Baddā	132	33.41 N	36.26 E
Badda Rogghie ∧	144	8.43 N	37.41 E
Baddeck	186	46.07 N	60.45 W
Bad Ditzenbach	56	48.35 N	9.41 E
Baddo ≃	128	27.59 N	64.21 E
Bad Doberan	54	54.06 N	11.53 E
Baddomalhi	123	31.59 N	74.40 E
Bad Dreibergen	52	53.12 N	8.01 E
Bad Driburg	52	51.44 N	9.01 E
Bad Düben	54	51.36 N	12.34 E
Bad Dürkheim	56	49.28 N	8.10 E
Bad Dürrenberg	54	51.18 N	12.04 E
Bad Dürrheim	58	48.01 N	8.32 E
Badé, Centraf.	152	6.41 N	17.07 E
Bade, Indon.	164	7.10 S	139.35 E
Badeggi	150	9.05 N	6.08 E
Badéguichéri	150	14.31 N	5.22 E
Bad Eilsen	52	52.14 N	9.06 E
Bad Elster	54	50.17 N	12.14 E
Bad Ems	56	50.20 N	7.43 E
Baden, On., Can.	212	43.24 N	80.39 W
Baden, Dtsch.	52	53.00 N	9.04 E
Baden, Erit.	144	17.00 N	38.00 E
Baden, Öst.	61	48.00 N	16.14 E
Baden, Schw.	58	47.29 N	8.18 E
Baden, Pa., U.S.	214	40.38 N	80.13 W
Baden-Baden	56	48.46 N	8.14 E
Bad Endbach	56	50.45 N	8.32 E
Bad Endorf	64	47.54 N	12.18 E
Badenoch □[9]	46	56.57 N	4.19 W
Baden-Powell, Mount ∧	228	34.21 N	117.46 W
Badenweiler	58	47.48 N	7.40 E
Baden-Württemberg □[3]	30	48.30 N	9.00 E
Badenyon	46	57.15 N	3.05 W
Baderna	64	45.12 N	13.46 E
Badersleben	54	51.59 N	10.53 E
Bad Essen	52	52.19 N	8.20 E
Bad Feilnbach	64	47.46 N	12.00 E
Badfish Creek ≃	216	42.50 N	89.10 W
Bad Frankenhausen	54	51.21 N	11.06 E
Bad Freienwalde	54	52.47 N	14.01 E
Bad Friedrichshall	56	49.14 N	9.11 E
Bad Fusch	64	47.12 N	12.51 E
Bad Füssingen	60	48.22 N	13.17 E
Badgam	123	34.01 N	74.43 E
Bad Gandersheim	52	51.52 N	10.01 E
Badgastein	64	47.07 N	13.08 E
Badger, Nf., Can.	186	48.59 N	56.02 W
Badger, Mn., U.S.	198	48.46 N	96.00 W
Badger Creek ≃, Co., U.S.	198	40.17 N	103.42 W
Badger Creek ≃, Co., U.S.	200	38.28 N	105.52 W
Badger Creek ≃, Or., U.S.	224	45.16 N	121.11 W
Badger Pass)(	226	37.40 N	119.39 W
Badger's Mount	260	51.20 N	0.09 E
Badgery's Creek	274a	33.53 S	150.44 E
Badgerys Creek ≃	274a	33.51 S	150.46 E
Bādghīs □[4]	128	35.00 N	63.45 E
Bad Gleichenberg	61	46.52 N	15.54 E
Bad Godesberg	56	50.41 N	7.10 E
Bad Goisern	64	47.38 N	13.37 E
Bad Gottleuba	54	50.51 N	13.56 E
Bad Grund	52	51.48 N	10.14 E
Bad Hall	61	48.02 N	14.13 E
Bad Harzburg	54	51.53 N	10.33 E
Bad Heilbrunn	64	47.45 N	11.28 E
Badhela ⊕[8]	272a	28.38 N	77.04 E
Bad Helmstedt	54	52.14 N	11.03 E
Bad Herrenalb	56	48.48 N	8.26 E
Bad Hersfeld	56	50.52 N	9.42 E
Badhoevedorp	52	52.21 N	4.46 E
Bad Hofgastein	64	47.10 N	13.06 E
Bad Homburg vor der Höhe	56	50.13 N	8.37 E
Bad Honnef	56	50.39 N	7.13 E
Bad Hönningen	56	50.31 N	7.19 E
Bāḍī ≃	124	27.55 N	83.27 E
Badia (Abtei)	64	46.37 N	11.54 E
Badia, Val V	64	46.40 N	11.53 E
Badia Calavena	64	45.34 N	11.09 E
Badia Polesine	64	45.05 N	11.29 E
Badia Prataglia	66	43.47 N	11.52 E
Badia Tedalda	66	43.42 N	12.11 E
Bad Iburg	52	52.09 N	8.02 E
Badile Camuno, Pizzo ∧	58	46.01 N	10.25 E
Badīn	120	24.39 N	68.50 E
Bādinan	272b	22.54 N	88.14 E
Badinko ≃	150	13.42 N	9.35 W
Badin Lake ◎[1]	192	35.27 N	80.06 W
Badiraguato	232	25.22 N	107.31 W
Bad Ischl	64	47.43 N	13.37 E
Bad Karlshafen	52	51.38 N	9.27 E
Bad Kissingen	56	50.12 N	10.04 E
Bad Kleinen	54	53.46 N	11.28 E
Bad Kleinkirchheim	64	46.49 N	13.49 E
Bad Klosterlausnitz	54	50.55 N	11.52 E
Bad Kohlgrub	64	47.40 N	11.03 E
Bad König	56	49.45 N	9.01 E
Bad Königshofen im Grabfeld, Dtsch.	54	50.18 N	10.29 E
Bad Königshofen im Grabfeld, Dtsch.	56	50.18 N	10.29 E
Bad Kösen	54	51.08 N	11.43 E
Bad Köstritz	54	50.56 N	12.01 E
Bad Kreuznach	56	49.52 N	7.51 E
Bad Krozingen	58	47.55 N	7.43 E
Bādkulla	126	23.17 N	88.32 E
Bad Laasphe	56	50.56 N	8.24 E
Bad Laer	52	52.06 N	8.05 E
Badlands ∧∧[2], U.S.	198	46.45 N	103.30 W
Badlands ∧∧[2], S.D., U.S.	198	43.30 N	102.20 W
Badlands National Park ♦	198	43.47 N	102.15 W
Bad Langensalza	56	51.06 N	10.38 E
Bad Lauchstädt	54	51.23 N	11.52 E
Bad Lausick	54	51.08 N	12.38 E
Bad Lauterberg [im Harz]	52	51.38 N	10.28 E
Bad Leonfelden	61	48.33 N	14.19 E
Bādli ⊕[8]	272a	28.45 N	77.09 E
Bad Liebenstein	54	50.49 N	10.21 E
Bad Liebenwerda	54	51.31 N	13.23 E
Bad Liebenzell	56	48.46 N	8.44 E
Bad Lippspringe	52	51.46 N	8.49 E
Bad Marienberg	56	50.39 N	7.57 E
Bad Meinberg	52	51.53 N	8.58 E
Bad Mergentheim	56	49.30 N	9.46 E
Bad Mitterndorf	60	47.33 N	13.55 E
Bad Mukran	54	54.26 N	13.35 E
Bad Münder	52	52.12 N	9.27 E
Bad Münster am Stein-Ebernburg	56	49.49 N	7.51 E
Bad Münstereifel	56	50.33 N	6.46 E
Bad Muskau	54	51.32 N	14.43 E
Bad Nauheim	56	50.22 N	8.44 E
Bad Nenndorf	52	52.20 N	9.22 E
Badnera	122	20.52 N	77.44 E
Badner Lindkogel ∧	264b	48.01 N	16.11 E
Bad Neuenahr-Ahrweiler	56	50.33 N	7.08 E
Bad Neustadt an der Saale	56	50.19 N	10.13 E
Bad Niedernau	58	48.27 N	8.53 E
Bad Oeynhausen	52	52.12 N	8.48 E
Badogo	150	11.02 N	8.13 W
Badolato	68	38.34 N	16.31 E
Bad Oldesloe	52	53.48 N	10.22 E
Ba Dong, Viet	110	9.40 N	106.34 E
Badong, Zhg.	102	31.02 N	110.20 E
Badonviller	58	48.30 N	6.54 E
Bad Orb	56	50.14 N	9.20 E
Badou, Togo	150	7.35 N	0.36 E
Badou, Zhg.	98	36.27 N	117.55 E
Badouling	100	32.10 N	117.36 E
Badoumbé	150	13.38 N	10.13 W
Bad Peterstal-Griesbach	58	48.26 N	8.12 E
Badplaas	158	25.57 S	30.35 E
Bad Pyrmont	52	51.59 N	9.15 E
Badr	142	30.33 N	30.43 E
Bad Radkersburg	61	46.41 N	15.59 E
Bad Ragaz	58	47.00 N	9.30 E
Bad Rappenau	56	49.14 N	9.06 E
Bad Rehburg	52	52.26 N	9.13 E
Bad Reichenhall	64	47.43 N	12.52 E
Badr Ḥunayn	128	23.44 N	38.46 E
Bad Rippoldsau	58	48.26 N	8.19 E
Bad River Indian Reservation ⊕[4]	190	46.33 N	90.40 W
Bad Rothenfelde	52	52.06 N	8.09 E
Bad Saarow	54	52.17 N	14.03 E
Bad Sachsa	54	51.36 N	10.32 E
Bad Säckingen	58	47.33 N	7.56 E
Bad Salzdetfurth	52	52.03 N	10.01 E
Bad Salzig	56	50.12 N	7.38 E
Bad Salzschlirf	56	50.37 N	9.29 E
Bad Salzuflen	52	52.05 N	8.44 E
Bad Salzungen	56	50.48 N	10.13 E
Bad Sankt Leonhard im Lavanttal	61	46.58 N	14.48 E
Bad Sassendorf	52	51.35 N	8.10 E
Bad Schandau	54	50.55 N	14.10 E
Bad Schmiedeberg	54	51.41 N	12.44 E
Bad Schönborn	56	49.13 N	8.39 E
Bad Schwalbach	56	50.08 N	8.04 E
Bad Schwartau	54	53.55 N	10.40 E
Bad Segeberg	52	53.56 N	10.17 E
Bādshāhpur	124	25.47 N	82.49 E
Bad Soden	56	50.08 N	8.30 E
Bad Soden-Salmünster	56	50.17 N	9.22 E
Bad Sooden-Allendorf	56	51.16 N	9.58 E
Bad Steben	54	50.22 N	11.38 E
Bad Stuer	54	53.22 N	12.19 E
Bad Suderode	54	51.44 N	11.07 E
Bad Sulza	54	51.05 N	11.37 E
Bad Sülze	54	54.06 N	12.38 E
Bad Tatzmannsdorf	61	47.20 N	16.13 E
Bad Teinach	56	48.41 N	8.41 E
Bad Tennstedt	54	51.09 N	10.50 E
Bad Tölz	64	47.46 N	11.34 E
Badu, Bra.	287a	22.54 S	43.04 W
Badu, Zhg.	100	26.51 N	119.35 E
Badu, Zhg.	100	28.32 N	117.57 E
Badu, Zhg.	102	24.15 N	105.41 E
Badu Island I	164	10.07 S	142.08 E
Badulla	122	6.59 N	81.03 E
Badung, Selat ᛘ	115b	8.40 S	115.22 E
Badupi	120	21.36 N	93.25 E
Bādura	126	22.16 N	90.21 E
Bad Urach	58	48.29 N	9.23 E
Bāduria	126	22.44 N	88.47 E
Badvel	122	14.45 N	79.03 E
Bad Vellach	61	46.26 N	14.33 E
Bad Vilbel	56	50.12 N	8.42 E
Bad Vöslau	61	47.57 N	16.16 E
Bad Waldsee	58	47.55 N	9.45 E
Badwater Creek ≃	202	43.17 N	108.08 W
Bad Westernkotten	52	51.38 N	8.21 E
Bad Wiessee	64	47.43 N	11.43 E
Bad Wildbad im Schwarzwald	56	48.45 N	8.32 E
Bad Wildungen	56	51.07 N	9.07 E
Bad Wilsnack	54	52.57 N	11.57 E
Bad Wimpfen	56	49.14 N	9.09 E
Bad Windsheim	56	49.31 N	10.25 E
Bad Wörishofen	58	48.00 N	10.36 E
Bad Wurzach	58	47.54 N	9.54 E
Badžalskij chrebet ∧∧	89	50.40 N	134.50 E
Bad Zwesten	56	51.03 N	9.10 E
Bad Zwischenahn	52	53.11 N	8.00 E
Baediam	150	15.03 N	11.51 W
Bække	41	55.34 N	9.09 E
Baena	34	37.37 N	4.19 W
Baependi	256	21.57 S	44.53 W

DEUTSCH

Name	Seite	Breite°′	Länge°′ E = Ost
Baependi ≃	256	21.52 S	45.04 W
Baer Field ⊠	216	40.59 N	85.11 W
Baerl ⊕[8]	263	51.29 N	6.41 E
Baesweiler	56	50.54 N	6.11 E
Báez	240p	22.13 N	79.45 W
Baeza, Ec.	246	0.27 S	77.53 W
Baeza, Esp.	34	37.59 N	3.28 W
Baezaeko ≃	182	53.09 N	123.48 W
Bafang	152	5.09 N	10.11 E
Bafatá	150	12.10 N	14.40 W
Bafelé	150	10.09 N	10.08 W
Baffa	123	34.26 N	73.13 E
Baffin Basin ✦[1]	16	73.15 N	67.00 W
Baffin Bay c, N.A.	16	73.00 N	66.00 W
Baffin Bay c, Tx., U.S.	196	27.15 N	97.33 W
Baffin Island I	176	68.00 N	70.00 W
Bafia	152	4.44 N	11.16 E
Bafilo	150	9.21 N	1.16 E
Bafing ≃, Afr.	150	13.49 N	10.50 W
Bafing ≃, Mali	150	12.27 N	7.07 W
Bafing Makana	150	12.33 N	10.15 W
Bafoulabé	150	13.48 N	10.50 W
Bafoussam	152	5.29 N	10.24 E
Bāfq	128	31.35 N	55.24 E
Bafra	130	41.34 N	35.56 E
Bafra Burnu ›	130	41.44 N	35.58 E
Bāft	128	29.14 N	56.38 E
Bafuku	154	4.15 N	27.54 E
Bafwabaka	154	2.07 N	27.40 E
Bafwabalinga	154	0.51 N	27.04 E
Bafwaboli	154	0.39 N	26.10 E
Bafwangbe	154	1.39 N	26.51 E
Bafwapada	154	0.56 N	26.57 E
Bafwasende	154	1.05 N	27.16 E
Bafwasomboli	154	1.27 N	27.01 E
Baga	126	22.26 N	90.28 E
Bagabag	116	16.37 N	121.15 E
Bagabag Island I	164	4.50 S	146.15 E
Baga-Burul	80	46.00 N	44.36 E
Bagac	116	14.36 N	120.23 E
Bagacay Point ›	116	8.58 N	124.48 E
Bagac Bay c	116	14.36 N	120.22 E
Bagaces	236	10.31 N	85.15 W
Baga Chentej nuruu ∧∧	88	48.30 N	107.30 E
Bagage ∧	154	3.23 N	40.12 E
Bagagem ≃, Bra.	250	11.37 S	48.12 W
Bagagem ≃, Bra.	255	13.58 S	48.21 W
Bagaha	124	27.06 N	84.05 E
Bagahak ∧	116	5.03 N	118.44 E
Bagajevskij	78	47.19 N	40.23 E
Bāgalkot	122	16.11 N	75.42 E
Bagamanoc	116	13.57 N	124.17 E
Bagamoyo	154	6.26 S	38.54 E
Bagan	86	54.06 N	77.40 E
Bagana	80	54.22 N	51.25 E
Bagana, Mount ∧	175e	6.09 S	155.12 E
Bagan Datoh	114	3.59 N	100.47 E
Bagañga	116	7.35 N	126.34 E
Bagan Serai	114	5.01 N	100.32 E
Bagansiapiapi	114	2.09 N	100.49 E
Bagansinembah	114	1.46 N	100.29 E
Bagansitukang	114	2.38 N	100.15 E
Baganza ≃	64	44.47 N	10.19 E
Bagara	85	40.55 N	68.26 E
Bağarası	130	37.42 N	27.33 E
Bagaroua	150	14.38 N	4.21 E
Bagasra	120	21.29 N	70.57 E
Bagata	152	3.44 S	17.57 E
Bāgātipāra	126	24.18 N	88.57 E
Bagawi	140	12.19 N	34.21 E
Bagband	52	53.21 N	7.36 E
Bagbe ≃	150	8.42 N	11.15 W
Bagbele	154	4.21 N	29.17 E
Bāgda	126	23.13 N	86.41 E
Bagdad → Baghdād, ʻĪrāq	128	33.21 N	44.25 E
Bagdad, Az., U.S.	200	34.34 N	113.12 W
Bagdad, Fl., U.S.	194	30.35 N	87.01 W
Bagdad, Ky., U.S.	218	38.15 N	85.03 W
Bagdaha	126	23.13 N	88.53 E
Bagdanga	126	24.02 N	88.32 E
Bagdarin	88	54.26 N	113.36 E
Bagdati	84	42.06 N	42.48 E
Bağdere	130	38.07 N	40.44 E
Bagé	252	31.20 S	54.06 W
Bagehadu	120	35.25 N	84.50 E
Bâgé-le-Châtel	58	46.18 N	4.56 E
Bagenkop	41	54.45 N	10.41 E
Bāgerhāt	124	22.40 N	89.48 E
Bages et de Sigean, Étang de c	32	43.05 N	3.03 E
Bāgevādi	122	16.35 N	75.58 E
Baggao	116	17.56 N	121.46 E
Baggeryd	24	57.30 N	14.07 E
Baggetorp	40	59.01 N	16.04 E
Baggio ⊕[8]	266b	45.27 N	9.06 E
Bağgöze	130	37.43 N	41.55 E
Baggs	200	41.02 N	107.39 W
Baggy Point ›	42	51.09 N	4.16 W
Bāgh	123	33.59 N	73.47 E
Baghdād	128	33.21 N	44.25 E
Baghdād □[4]	128	33.30 N	44.30 E
Baghdobā	126	22.08 N	87.54 E
Baghelkhand Plateau ∧∧[1]	124	23.45 N	82.20 E
Bāgh-e Malek	128	31.32 N	49.55 E
Bagheria	70	38.05 N	13.30 E
Bāgherpāra	126	23.14 N	89.21 E
Bāghia	126	23.27 N	90.29 E
Baghia Bīl ≡	126	23.07 N	90.03 E
Bāghīn	128	30.12 N	56.48 E
Baghlān	120	36.13 N	68.46 E
Baghlān □[4]	120	35.45 N	69.00 E
Bāghmundi	124	23.12 N	86.03 E
Bāghpat	124	28.57 N	77.13 E
Baghrān Khowleh	120	33.01 N	64.58 E
Bagillt	262	53.16 N	3.10 W
Bağırpaşa Dağı ∧	130	39.30 N	40.06 E
Bağırsak (Sājūr) ≃	130	36.40 N	38.05 E
Bağkonak	130	38.12 N	31.17 E
Bagley	198	47.31 N	95.23 W
Bāgli	124	22.39 N	76.21 E
Bağlıca	130	37.53 N	41.46 E
Bağlum	130	40.03 N	32.51 E
Bāgmāri ⊕[8]	272b	22.34 N	88.25 E
Bāgmatī □[8]	124	27.45 N	85.30 E
Bāgmatī ≃	124	25.31 N	86.44 E
Bagn	26	60.49 N	9.34 E
Bagnacavallo	66	44.25 N	12.00 E
Bagnaia	66	42.25 N	12.09 E
Bāgnān	126	22.28 N	87.59 E
Bagnara Calabra	68	38.18 N	15.49 E
Bagnara di Romagna	66	44.23 N	11.49 E
Bag Narin	102	38.57 N	94.08 E
Bagnasco	62	44.18 N	8.02 E
Bagnell Dam ⊕[6]	194	38.11 N	92.39 W
Bagnères-de-Bigorre	32	43.04 N	0.09 E
Bagnères-de-Luchon	32	42.47 N	0.36 E
Bagnes, Vallée de V	58	46.03 N	7.18 E
Bagneux	261	48.48 N	2.18 E
Bagni Acque Albule	66	41.57 N	12.43 E
Bagni del Masino	58	46.15 N	9.36 E
Bagni di Lucca	66	44.01 N	10.35 E
Bagni di Rabbi	64	46.24 N	10.48 E
Bagno a Ripoli	66	43.45 N	11.19 E
Bagno di Romagna	66	43.50 N	11.57 E
Bagnolet	261	48.52 N	2.25 E
Bagnoli del Trigno	66	41.42 N	14.27 E
Bagnoli di Sopra	64	45.11 N	11.53 E
Bagnoli Irpino	68	40.50 N	15.04 E
Bagnolo in Piano	64	44.46 N	10.40 E
Bagnolo Mella	64	45.26 N	10.10 E
Bagnols-en-Forêt	62	43.32 N	6.42 E
Bagnols-les-Bains	62	44.30 N	3.40 E
Bagnols-sur-Cèze	62	44.10 N	4.37 E
Bagñon	116	13.44 N	122.50 E
Bagnone	64	44.19 N	10.00 E
Bagnoregio	66	42.37 N	12.05 E
Bagno Vignoni	66	43.02 N	11.39 E

Symbols in the index entries represent the broad categories identified in the key at the right. Symbols with superior numbers (∧∧[1]) identify subcategories (see complete key on page *I · 1).*

Symbole im Register stellen die rechts im Schlüssel erklärten Kategorien dar. Symbole mit hochgestellten Ziffern (∧∧[1]) bezeichnen Unterabteilungen einer Kategorie (vgl. vollständiger Schlüssel auf Seite *I · 1).*

Los símbolos incluídos en el texto del índice representan las grandes categorías identificadas con la clave a la derecha. Los símbolos con numeros en su parte superior (∧∧[1]) identifican las subcategorías (véase la clave completa en la página *I · 1).*

Les symboles de l'index représentent les catégories indiquées dans la légende à droite. Les symboles suivis d'un indice (∧∧[1]) représentent des sous-catégories (voir légende complète à la page *I · 1).*

Os símbolos incluídos no texto do índice representam as grandes categorias identificadas com a chave à direita. Os símbolos com números em sua parte superior (∧∧[1]) identificam as subcategorias (veja-se a chave completa à página *I · 1).*

	English	Deutsch	Español	Français	Português
∧	Mountain	Berg	Montaña	Montagne	Montanha
∧∧	Mountains	Gebirge	Montañas	Montagnes	Montanhas
)(	Pass	Paß	Paso	Col	Passo
V	Valley, Canyon	Tal, Cañon	Valle, Cañón	Vallée, Canyon	Vale, Canhão
≚	Plain	Ebene	Llano	Plaine	Planície
›	Cape	Kap	Cabo	Cap	Cabo
I	Island	Insel	Isla	Île	Ilha
II	Islands	Inseln	Islas	Îles	Ilhas
⊥	Other Topographic Features	Andere Topographische Objekte	Otros Elementos Topográficos	Autres données topographiques	Outros acidentes topográficos

Bago-Ball *I* · *13*

ESPAÑOL — Nombre | Página | Lat.°′ | Long.°′ W = Oeste
FRANÇAIS — Nom | Page | Lat.°′ | Long.°′ W = Ouest
PORTUGUÊS — Nome | Página | Lat.°′ | Long.°′ W = Oeste

Nombre / Nom / Nome	Página / Page	Lat.°′	Long.°′
Bago (Pegu)	110	17.20 N	96.29 E
Bago □[8]	110	18.00 N	96.00 E
Bågø I	41	55.18 N	9.49 E
Bago ≃	116	10.33 N	122.50 E
Bagod	61	46.53 N	16.45 E
Bagodar	124	24.05 N	85.52 E
Bagodo	152	6.25 N	13.23 E
Bagoé ≃	150	12.36 N	6.34 W
Bagolino	64	45.49 N	10.28 E
Bagoni	146	7.53 N	10.43 E
Bagot □[6]	206	45.40 N	72.45 W
Bagotville, Base des Forces canadiennes ■	186	48.20 N	70.58 W
Bağpınar	130	37.35 N	38.19 E
Bagrationovsk	76	54.23 N	20.39 E
Bagraula ◆[8]	272a	28.34 N	77.04 E
Bagre	250	1.54 S	50.12 W
Bagshot	42	51.22 N	0.42 W
Bag Tal	89	43.20 N	122.16 E
Bāguiati	272b	22.36 N	88.26 E
Baguio	116	16.25 N	120.36 E
Bagula	126	23.19 N	88.39 E
Bagumbayan	269f	14.28 N	121.03 E
Bagyrlaj ≃	80	48.08 N	51.14 E
Bāh	124	26.53 N	78.36 E
Bāhādurābād Ghāt	124	25.09 N	89.42 E
Bahādurgarh	124	28.41 N	76.56 E
Bāhādurpur	126	23.25 N	88.28 E
Bahaia, Monte ∧	144	11.20 N	49.45 E
Baha'i Temple ⊽[1]	278	42.05 N	87.41 W
Bahamas □[1], N.A.	230	24.15 N	76.00 W
Bahamas □[1], N.A.	238	24.15 N	76.00 W
Bahār	128	34.54 N	48.26 E
Baharāgora	126	22.17 N	86.43 E
Baharampur	126	24.06 N	88.15 E
Baharpur	126	23.41 N	89.34 E
Bahata Cherneshchyna	78	48.59 N	35.35 E
Bahau	114	2.49 N	102.25 E
Bahau ≃	112	2.34 N	116.20 E
Bahāwalnagar	123	29.59 N	73.16 E
Bahāwalpur	123	29.24 N	71.41 E
Bahçe	130	37.14 N	36.34 E
Bahçeköy ◆[8]	267b	41.11 N	28.59 E
Bahçeköy su kemeri ≍[1]	267b	41.03 N	28.59 E
Bahechuan	98	40.59 N	124.49 E
Baheri	124	28.47 N	79.30 E
Baherove	78	45.23 N	36.17 E
Bahi, Pil.	116	13.53 N	123.38 E
Bahi, Tan.	154	5.59 S	35.19 E
Bahia → Salvador	255	12.59 S	38.31 W
Bahia □[3]	250	11.00 S	42.00 W
Bahía, Islas de la II	236	16.20 N	86.30 W
Bahía Azul	236	9.11 N	81.54 W
Bahía Blanca	252	38.43 S	62.17 W
Bahía Bustamante	254	45.08 S	66.32 W
Bahía Erasmo, Parque Nacional ♠	254	46.05 S	73.35 W
Bahia Honda	240p	22.54 N	83.10 W
Bahia Honda Key I	220	24.40 N	81.16 W
Bahia Honda Point ≻	116	9.24 N	118.07 E
Bahía Kino	232	28.50 N	111.55 W
Bahía Laura	254	48.24 S	66.29 W
Bahīj	142	30.56 N	29.35 E
Bahir Dar	144	11.35 N	37.28 E
Bahi Swamp ⩸	154	6.05 S	35.10 E
Bahjoi	124	28.24 N	78.37 E
Bahl	123	28.38 N	75.38 E
Bahlolpur	272a	28.37 N	77.24 E
Bahn	150	7.05 N	8.45 W
Bahnāy	142	30.23 N	31.04 E
Bahnayā	142	30.41 N	31.23 E
Baḥrah	144	21.24 N	39.29 E
Bahraich	124	27.35 N	81.36 E
Bahrain (Al-Baḥrayn) □[1], Asia	118	26.00 N	50.30 E
Bahrain (Al-Baḥrayn) □[1], Asia	128	26.00 N	50.30 E
Baḥr al-Ghazāl □[4]	140	8.30 N	26.00 E
Bahrām Chāh	128	29.26 N	64.03 E
Baḥrānī, Ḥālat al- I	128	24.23 N	54.14 E
Bahranivtsi	78	49.17 N	27.56 E
Baḥrayn, Khalīj al ⊂	128	25.45 N	50.40 E
Bahrdorf	54	52.23 N	11.00 E
Bahrein → Bahrain □[1]	128	26.00 N	50.30 E
Baḥrīyah, Al-Wāḥāt al- ⊤[4]	140	28.15 N	28.57 E
Bahser	130	37.57 N	39.18 E
Bahtīm	142	30.08 N	31.17 E
Bahṭīṭ	142	30.29 N	31.38 E
Bāhū Kalāt	128	25.43 N	61.25 E
Bāhū Kalāt ≃	128	25.11 N	61.31 E
Bahulu, Pulau I	112	3.33 S	122.18 E
Bahu-mbelu	112	2.13 S	121.41 E
Bahušèųsk	76	54.51 N	30.13 E
Bahūt	142	31.10 N	31.19 E
Baï	150	13.38 N	3.22 W
Bai ≃, Zhg.	102	32.10 N	112.20 E
Bai ≃, Zhg.	105	40.43 N	116.33 E
Baia	68	40.49 N	14.04 E
Baia de Aramă	38	45.00 N	22.49 E
Baía dos Tigres	152	16.36 S	11.43 E
Baía Farta	152	12.40 S	13.11 E
Baia Mare	38	47.40 N	23.35 E
Baiano	68	40.57 N	14.37 E
Baião	250	2.41 S	49.41 W
Baiardo	62	43.54 N	7.43 E
Baía Rica ≃	248	12.40 S	63.04 W
Baia Sprie	38	47.40 N	23.42 E
Baibao	105	39.04 N	115.31 E
Baibei	100	27.47 N	115.53 E
Baïbokoum	146	7.46 N	15.43 E
Baibuting	106	30.33 N	120.46 E
Baicang	124	30.14 N	90.44 E
Baicao	98	41.13 N	116.07 E
Baicaochang	102	32.08 N	103.59 E
Baicao Ling ⋏	102	26.10 N	101.20 E
Baicha	100	29.11 N	115.37 E
Baicheng, Zhg.	89	45.38 N	122.46 E
Baicheng, Zhg.	90	41.46 N	81.52 E
Baidian	106	30.47 N	119.14 E
Baidiao	102	28.07 N	101.28 E
Baidoa → Baydhabo	144	3.07 N	43.39 E
Baidunzi	102	43.11 N	95.19 E
Baidyabāti	126	22.47 N	88.20 E
Baidyanāth	124	24.29 N	86.42 E
Baidyer Bāzār	126	23.39 N	90.37 E
Baie-Comeau	186	49.13 N	68.10 W
Baie-Comeau-Hauterive, Réserve ♠	186	50.05 N	68.00 W
Baie-des-Ha! Ha!	186	50.56 N	58.56 W
Baie-de-Shawinigan	206	46.34 N	72.45 W
Baie-des-Moutons	186	50.47 N	59.02 W
Baie-du-Renard	186	49.17 N	61.50 W
Baie-d'Urfé	206	45.25 N	73.55 W
Baie-Johan-Beetz	186	50.17 N	62.48 W
Baie-Mahault	241o	16.16 N	61.35 W
Baienfurt	64	47.49 N	9.38 E
Baiersbronn	58	48.30 N	8.22 E
Baiersdorf	60	49.39 N	11.01 E
Baies, Lac des ⊜	190	47.18 N	77.40 W
Baie-Sainte-Claire	186	49.54 N	64.30 W
Baie-Saint-Paul	186	47.27 N	70.30 W
Baie-Trinité	186	49.25 N	67.18 W
Baie Verte	186	49.56 N	56.11 W
Baieville	206	46.08 N	72.43 W
Baigezhuang	105	39.54 N	118.09 E
Baigneux-les-Juifs	58	47.36 N	4.38 E
Baigong	100	24.18 N	116.14 E
Baigou	105	39.07 N	116.01 E
Baigou ≃	105	39.06 N	116.00 E
Baiguoshu	106	30.45 N	119.07 E
Baigusi	102	33.10 N	103.52 E
Baihāli Jot ∧	123	32.51 N	76.32 E
Baihar	124	22.06 N	80.33 E
Baihe, Zhg.	100	29.12 N	120.55 E
Baihe, Zhg.	102	32.17 N	110.02 E
Baihebu	105	40.39 N	116.10 E
Baihegang	106	31.16 N	121.08 E
Baihekou	102	31.46 N	110.13 E
Baihou	100	24.18 N	116.48 E
Baihua	107	29.07 N	104.37 E
Baihua Shan ∧	105	39.50 N	115.35 E
Baijala	272b	22.51 N	88.16 E
Baijian	105	39.36 N	115.16 E
Baijiang	100	29.51 N	119.20 E
Baijiawu	105	39.30 N	116.28 E
Baijie	107	29.17 N	106.31 E
Baijietan	107	28.44 N	105.30 E
Baijnāth	124	29.55 N	79.37 E
Baiju	100	33.04 N	120.20 E
Baikal, Lago → Bajkal, ozero ⊜	88	53.00 N	107.40 E
Baikal, Lake → Bajkal, ozero ⊜	88	53.00 N	107.40 E
Baikal-See → Bajkal, ozero ⊜	88	53.00 N	107.40 E
Baikeshu	106	30.26 N	118.55 E
Baikonur → Bajkonyr	86	47.50 N	66.03 E
Baikunthapur	272b	22.59 N	88.13 E
Baikunthpur	124	23.15 N	82.33 E
Bailadores	246	8.15 N	71.50 W
Bailaiqiao	100	32.40 N	118.23 E
Bailang	89	46.57 N	120.05 E
Baildon	44	53.52 N	1.46 W
Baile	105	39.55 N	114.51 E
Baile Átha Luain → Athlone	48	53.25 N	7.56 W
Băile Govora	38	45.05 N	24.11 E
Băile Herculane	38	44.54 N	22.25 E
Bailén	34	38.06 N	3.46 W
Băile Olănești	38	45.11 N	24.16 E
Băilești	38	44.02 N	23.21 E
Bailey	192	35.46 N	78.07 W
Bailey Lakes	214	40.57 N	82.21 W
Bailey Run ≃	279b	40.35 N	79.47 W
Baileys Crossroads	284c	38.51 N	77.08 W
Bail Hongal	122	15.49 N	74.52 E
Bailian	102	24.09 N	112.22 E
Bailicun	102	25.45 N	110.33 E
Bailieborough	48	53.54 N	6.59 W
Bailin, Zhg.	100	27.12 N	120.10 E
Bailin, Zhg.	100	26.20 N	113.18 E
Bailin, Zhg.	107	29.11 N	105.57 E
Bailin, Zhg.	107	28.45 N	106.26 E
Bailingmiao → Darhan Muminggan Lianheqi	102	41.50 N	110.27 E
Bailique	250	0.58 N	50.04 W
Bailique, Ilha I	250	1.02 N	49.58 W
Bailleau-sous-Gallardon	261	48.32 N	1.39 E
Bailleul	50	50.44 N	2.44 E
Ba Illi	146	10.30 N	16.34 E
Baillie ≃	176	65.10 N	104.24 W
Baillie Islands II	176	70.33 N	128.10 W
Baillif	241o	16.01 N	61.45 W
Bailly-Romainvilliers	261	48.50 N	2.49 E
Bailong ≃	102	32.18 N	105.42 E
Bailonggang	106	31.15 N	121.44 E
Bailu ≃	100	32.25 N	115.34 E
Bailuchang	107	28.56 N	105.57 E
Bailu Hu ⊜	100	30.03 N	113.06 E
Bailundo	152	12.12 S	15.52 E
Bailuoji	100	29.37 N	113.15 E
Baima, Zhg.	106	31.35 N	119.10 E
Baima, Zhg.	107	30.03 N	103.44 E
Baima, Zhg.	107	29.09 N	104.16 E
Baimachang, Zhg.	102	29.18 N	107.30 E
Baimachang, Zhg.	104	41.59 N	122.30 E
Baimachang, Zhg.	107	29.40 N	103.54 E
Baimaguan	105	40.41 N	116.52 E
Baimakou	102	25.55 N	102.06 E
Baimamiao, Zhg.	102	36.58 N	108.08 E
Baimamiao, Zhg.	107	29.33 N	104.59 E
Baimao, Zhg.	106	31.39 N	120.52 E
Baimao, Zhg.	106	31.35 N	120.54 E
Baima Shan ∧	102	27.12 N	110.32 E
Baimashi	100	29.15 N	118.42 E
Baimazhai	100	28.06 N	115.50 E
Baimiaozi, Zhg.	89	46.18 N	123.35 E
Baimiaozi, Zhg.	98	40.34 N	120.36 E
Baimiaozi, Zhg.	104	41.55 N	122.12 E
Baimiaozi, Zhg.	107	29.47 N	106.29 E
Baimuqiao	106	32.01 N	120.19 E
Baimuru	164	7.30 S	144.49 E
Bain ≃	44	53.05 N	0.12 W
Baïna Bondio	152	5.10 N	16.33 E
Bainang	120	29.11 N	89.12 E
Bainbridge, Ga., U.S.	192	30.54 N	84.34 W
Bainbridge, N.Y., U.S.	210	42.17 N	75.28 W
Bainbridge, Oh., U.S.	218	39.13 N	83.16 W
Bainbridge, Pa., U.S.	208	40.05 N	76.40 W
Bainbridge Island I	224	47.37 N	122.33 W
Bainchi	126	23.07 N	88.14 E
Bainchipota	272b	22.52 N	88.16 E
Bain-de-Bretagne	32	47.50 N	1.41 W
Baindt	58	47.51 N	9.40 E
Baing	115b	10.14 S	120.34 E
Bainiqiao	100	29.35 N	114.09 E
Bains-les-Bains	58	48.00 N	6.16 E
Bainville	198	48.08 N	104.13 W
Bainyik	164	3.40 S	143.00 E
Baio Grande	34	43.09 N	8.58 W
Baiona	34	42.07 N	8.51 W
Baipeng	102	24.09 N	109.25 E
Baipu	106	32.15 N	120.46 E
Baiqibao	104	41.48 N	122.30 E
Baiqiu	100	32.44 N	112.38 E
Baiquan, Zhg.	89	47.36 N	126.07 E
Baiquan, Zhg.	100	30.06 N	122.08 E
Baiqueyuan	100	31.48 N	115.05 E
Bair, Pa., U.S.	208	39.54 N	76.50 W
Bā'ir, Urd.	132	30.46 N	36.41 E
Bā'ir, Wādī V	132	30.58 N	37.09 E
Bairab Co ⊜	120	35.00 N	83.03 E
Baird	196	32.23 N	99.23 W
Baird, Mount ∧	202	43.22 N	111.06 W
Bairdford	214	40.37 N	79.52 W
Baird Inlet ⊂	180	60.45 N	164.00 W
Baird Mountains ⋏	180	67.35 N	161.30 W
Baire	240p	20.19 N	76.20 W
Bairiki	174t	1.20 N	173.01 E
Bairin Zuoqi	90	44.00 N	119.00 E
Bair Island I	282	37.32 N	122.13 W
Bairkum	85	42.05 N	68.11 E
Bairnsdale	166	37.50 S	147.38 E
Bairoil	200	42.14 N	107.33 W
Bairrinho	256	22.36 S	47.06 W
Bairro Alto	256	23.29 S	45.21 W
Bairuopu	100	28.12 N	112.46 E
Bais, Fr.	32	48.15 N	0.22 W
Bais, Pil.	116	9.35 N	123.07 E
Baïse ≃	32	44.17 N	0.18 E
Baisha, Zhg.	100	29.26 N	119.16 E
Baisha, Zhg.	100	25.40 N	118.59 E
Baisha, Zhg.	100	25.24 N	117.16 E
Baisha, Zhg.	100	34.22 N	112.32 E
Baisha, Zhg.	100	26.58 N	115.22 E
Baisha, Zhg.	100	24.39 N	113.31 E
Baisha, Zhg.	100	34.20 N	113.14 E
Baisha, Zhg.	107	28.55 N	105.45 E
Baisha, Zhg.	107	29.04 N	106.07 E
Baisha, Zhg.	110	19.17 N	109.27 E
Baishaba	107	30.03 N	106.21 E
Bai Shan I	106	30.35 N	121.43 E
Baishanji	100	33.48 N	116.40 E
Baishantu	104	42.21 N	122.35 E
Baishapu	100	29.58 N	115.04 E
Baishatan	98	36.52 N	121.38 E
Baishe	100	27.02 N	116.20 E
Baishecun	105	40.10 N	116.18 E
Baishi, Zhg.	100	27.18 N	119.45 E
Baishi, Zhg.	100	26.48 N	119.46 E
Baishi, Zhg.	102	22.36 N	110.55 E
Baishidu	100	25.26 N	113.01 E
Baishiyi	107	29.29 N	106.22 E
Baishizhai	104	40.57 N	122.58 E
Baishui, Zhg.	100	28.42 N	113.04 E
Baishui, Zhg.	106	30.34 N	119.39 E
Baishui, Zhg.	107	30.06 N	105.38 E
Baishuifan	100	30.17 N	115.43 E
Baishuijiang	102	33.29 N	106.01 E
Baishun	100	25.12 N	114.01 E
Baishuxia	100	27.22 N	113.41 E
Baisinga	126	21.39 N	86.54 E
Baisley Pond ⊜	276	40.41 N	73.47 W
Baisogala	76	55.38 N	23.43 E
Bāisrasi	126	23.27 N	90.02 E
Baita, India	272b	22.27 N	88.11 E
Baita, Zhg.	106	31.48 N	119.35 E
Baitaḍī	124	29.32 N	80.26 E
Baital	126	22.57 N	87.28 E
Baitazi	98	42.19 N	120.19 E
Baitazibeigou	104	42.17 N	120.48 E
Bai Thuong	110	19.54 N	105.23 E
Baitings Reservoir ⊜[1]	262	53.40 N	1.59 W
Baitou	107	30.37 N	103.36 E
Baitoutan	102	32.30 N	106.56 E
Baitu	106	31.59 N	119.21 E
Baitugang	100	33.28 N	112.22 E
Baiwang	102	24.14 N	108.32 E
Baiwen	102	38.15 N	111.06 E
Baixa da Banheira	266c	38.39 N	9.03 W
Baixa Grande	255	11.57 S	40.11 W
Baixi	107	29.39 N	106.28 E
Baixiang	98	37.32 N	114.34 E
Baixingt	89	43.08 N	121.03 E
Baixio	250	6.44 S	38.43 W
Baixo Longa	152	15.42 S	18.50 E
Baiyan, Zhg.	100	28.04 N	120.02 E
Baiyan, Zhg.	106	31.08 N	119.38 E
Baiyang	100	34.25 N	112.12 E
Baiyang Dian ⊜	98	38.53 N	116.00 E
Baiyanghe	86	43.13 N	88.28 E
Baiyan Shan ∧	100	26.05 N	118.25 E
Baiyer River	164	5.35 S	144.10 E
Baiyin	102	36.47 N	104.07 E
Baiyinheshuo	89	44.31 N	119.51 E
Baiyintaohai	89	43.12 N	120.23 E
Baiyu, Zhg.	102	31.18 N	98.49 E
Baiyu, Zhg.	105	40.01 N	115.37 E
Baiyundu	100	26.10 N	118.47 E
Baiyunguan	271a	39.54 N	116.19 E
Baizhongpu	100	33.22 N	114.50 E
Baizi	107	30.06 N	105.43 E
Baja	30	46.11 N	18.57 E
Baja, Punta ≻	232	29.58 N	115.49 W
Baja California	200	32.18 N	115.12 W
Baja California □[3]	232	30.00 N	115.00 W
Baja California ≻[1]	232	28.00 N	113.30 W
Baja California Seamount Province ✣	16	26.00 N	124.00 W
Baja California Sur □[3]	232	26.00 N	112.00 W
Bajada del Agrio	252	38.23 S	70.02 W
Baján	196	26.32 N	101.15 W
Bajan Adraga	88	48.32 N	111.03 E
Bajan Agt	88	49.02 N	102.05 E
Bajanaul	86	50.47 N	75.42 E
Bajancagaan	102	45.00 N	98.59 E
Bajan Chajrchan	88	49.18 N	96.20 E
Bajanchongor	90	46.08 N	100.43 E
Bajanchongor □[4]	102	45.00 N	99.30 E
Bajancogt	88	45.54 N	106.10 E
Bajandaj	88	53.04 N	105.30 E
Bajandalaj	102	43.28 N	103.28 E
Bajandelger, Mong.	88	47.44 N	108.07 E
Bajandelger, Mong.	102	45.40 N	112.20 E
Bajan Dün	88	49.13 N	113.23 E
Bajandžargalan	102	45.40 N	107.59 E
Bajan Dzürch	88	50.12 N	98.58 E
Bajan-Enger	86	48.25 N	90.50 E
Bajango	88	48.55 N	106.06 E
Bajangol, Ross.	88	50.44 N	103.27 E
Bajan-Gol, Ross.	88	52.49 N	99.54 E
Bajangov'	102	44.44 N	100.24 E
Bajanleg	102	44.33 N	100.50 E
Bajan Nuur	86	48.54 N	91.14 E
Bajanölgij □[4]	86	48.20 N	89.50 E
Bajan-Öndör	102	44.47 N	98.39 E
Bajan-Ovoo, Mong.	88	47.47 N	112.05 E
Bajan-Ovoo, Mong.	102	42.57 N	106.07 E
Bajánsenye	30	46.48 N	16.23 E
Bajan Tümen	88	48.04 N	114.24 E
Bajan Uul, Mong.	88	47.40 N	101.30 E
Bajan Uul, Mong.	88	49.10 N	112.50 E
Bajan Uul, Mong.	88	49.41 N	96.20 E
Bājaur □[9]	123	34.50 N	71.30 E
Baja Verapaz □[5]	236	15.05 N	90.20 W
Bajawa	115b	8.47 S	120.59 E
Bajbičetau ⋏	85	41.12 N	75.15 E
Baj-Chak	88	51.13 N	94.34 E
Bajčunas	80	47.14 N	52.55 E
Bajčurovo	80	51.20 N	42.41 E
Bajdarackaja guba ⊂	72	69.00 N	67.30 E
Bajdonovo	88	54.17 N	104.38 E
Bajdrag ≃	102	45.38 N	99.15 E
Bājegūn, Kūh-e ∧	128	31.28 N	55.51 E
Bājengdoba	124	25.54 N	90.31 E
Bāje Phukura	126	23.09 N	89.45 E
Bajer	88	55.44 N	99.30 E
Bajestān	128	34.31 N	58.10 E
Bajevo	86	53.17 N	80.46 E
Bajganin	86	48.43 N	55.53 E
Bajgekum	86	44.18 N	66.28 E
Bajghera	272a	28.32 N	77.01 E
Bājgīrān	128	37.36 N	58.24 E
Bajgul	80	48.49 N	49.08 E
Bajiaotai	104	41.14 N	121.14 E
Bajiazi, Zhg.	104	42.17 N	122.37 E
Bajiazi, Zhg.	104	42.21 N	121.27 E
Bajiazi, Zhg.	104	41.36 N	123.53 E
Bājil	144	15.04 N	43.16 E
Bajimba, Mount ∧	166	29.18 S	152.07 E
Bajina Bašta	38	43.58 N	19.34 E
Bajkadam	85	43.44 N	69.55 E
Bajkal	88	51.53 N	104.47 E
Bajkal, ozero (Lake Baikal) ⊜	88	53.00 N	107.40 E
Bajkalovo, Ross.	86	57.24 N	63.46 E
Bajkalovo, Ross.	86	57.45 N	67.40 E
Bajkal'sk	88	51.33 N	104.05 E
Bajkal'skij chrebet ⋏	88	55.00 N	108.40 E
Bajkal'skij zapovednik ♠	88	51.25 N	105.10 E
Bajkal'skoje	88	55.21 N	109.12 E
Bajkit	74	61.41 N	96.25 E
Bajkonur	86	47.50 N	66.03 E
Bajkovo	80	54.47 N	44.51 E
Bajmak	86	52.36 N	58.19 E
Bajmok	38	45.58 N	19.25 E
Bajnazar	86	48.32 N	73.42 E
Bajo, Indon.	112	0.27 N	120.48 E
Bajo, Indon.	115b	8.35 S	119.01 E
Bajo, Canal ≍	266a	40.27 N	3.43 W
Bajo Baudó	246	4.58 N	77.22 W
Bajo Boquete	236	8.47 N	82.26 W
Bajool	166	23.39 S	150.39 E
Bajos de Haina	238	18.25 N	70.02 W
Bajos del Balsamar	234	17.34 N	100.48 W
Bajr'aki	80	54.43 N	53.24 E
Bajram-Ali	128	37.37 N	62.10 E
Bajsa	88	53.58 N	113.33 E
Bajseit	85	43.35 N	78.20 E
Baj-Sot	88	51.42 N	95.22 E
Bajsun	85	38.14 N	67.12 E
Bajtajlak	86	45.15 N	75.00 E
Bajulmati	115a	7.56 S	114.23 E
Bajžansaj	85	43.13 N	69.56 E
Bak	61	46.43 N	16.51 E
Bakacak	130	40.12 N	27.06 E
Bakal	86	54.56 N	58.48 E
Bakala	152	6.11 N	20.22 E
Bakaldy	80	55.39 N	44.44 E
Bakali ≃	152	4.34 S	17.06 E
Bakaly	80	55.10 N	53.48 E
Bakambe	152	5.39 S	23.37 E
Bakanas	86	44.50 N	76.15 E
Bakanas ≃	86	47.05 N	79.18 E
Bakap	114	4.26 N	101.04 E
Bakar	116	7.09 N	125.42 E
Bākarganj	124	22.33 N	90.21 E
Bakaruma	124	22.32 N	83.25 E
Bakau, Pulau I	271c	1.16 N	103.43 E
Bakbakty	86	44.35 N	76.40 E
Bakčar	86	57.01 N	82.05 E
Bakčar ≃	86	57.37 N	82.18 E
Bake	112	3.03 S	100.16 E
Bakebe	152	5.35 N	9.33 E
Bakel	150	14.54 N	12.27 W
Bakem	112	1.58 S	105.54 E
Bakenkop	158	28.01 S	23.02 E
Bakeoven Creek ≃	224	45.12 N	121.05 W
Baker, Ca., U.S.	204	35.15 N	116.04 W
Baker, Fl., U.S.	194	30.47 N	86.40 W
Baker, La., U.S.	194	30.35 N	91.10 W
Baker, Mt., U.S.	198	46.22 N	104.17 W
Baker, Or., U.S.	202	44.46 N	117.49 W
Baker ≃, Chile	254	47.49 S	73.37 W
Baker ≃, Wa., U.S.	224	48.38 N	121.41 W
Baker, Canal ⊍	254	48.00 S	74.00 W
Baker, Mount ∧	224	48.47 N	121.49 W
Baker Butte ∧	200	34.27 N	111.22 W
Baker Canyon V	280	33.47 N	117.38 W
Baker Creek ≃, B.C., Can.	182	52.59 N	122.30 W
Baker Creek ≃, Oh., U.S.	279a	41.21 N	81.54 W
Baker Creek ≃, Or., U.S.	224	45.15 N	123.14 W
Baker Island I, Oc.	14	0.15 N	176.27 W
Baker Island I, Ak., U.S.	182	55.20 N	133.36 W
Baker Lake	176	64.15 N	96.00 W
Baker Lake ⊜, Austl.	162	26.54 S	126.05 E
Baker Lake ⊜, N.T., Can.	176	64.10 N	95.30 W
Baker Lake ⊜, Il., U.S.	278	42.08 N	88.07 W
Baker Lake ⊜[1]	224	48.43 N	121.37 W
Bakersfield	226	35.22 N	119.01 W
Bakersfield South	228	35.20 N	119.03 W
Bakers Hill	168a	31.45 S	116.27 E
Bakers Island I	283	42.32 N	70.47 W
Bakerstown	214	40.39 N	79.56 W
Baker Street	260	51.30 N	0.21 E
Bakersville, N.C., U.S.	192	36.00 N	82.09 W
Bakersville, Oh., U.S.	214	40.21 N	81.39 W
Bakerville	158	26.00 S	26.06 E
Bakeshu	98	42.26 N	124.37 E
Bâ Kêv	110	13.42 N	107.12 E
Bakewell	44	53.13 N	1.40 W
Bakhchysaray	78	44.45 N	33.51 E
Bakhmach	78	51.13 N	32.46 E
Bakhmut ≃	83	48.56 N	38.03 E
Bakhmutivka	83	48.52 N	39.03 E
Bakhra	126	22.24 N	88.11 E
Bākhrābād	126	23.43 N	90.53 E
Bakhri	124	25.35 N	86.16 E
Bākhtarān (Kermānshāh)	128	34.19 N	47.04 E
Bakhtarān □[4]	128	34.30 N	47.00 E
Bakhtegān, Daryācheh-ye ⊜	128	29.20 N	54.05 E
Bakhtiyārpur	124	25.28 N	85.31 E
Bakhuis	250	4.42 N	56.49 W
Bakı (Baku)	84	40.23 N	49.51 E
Bakile	154	13.58 S	35.15 E
Bakino	82	56.20 N	38.59 E
Bakinskaja	78	44.46 N	39.18 E
Bakır ≃	130	38.55 N	27.00 E
Bakitabu	154	1.29 S	35.34 E
Bakkafjörður	24a	66.04 N	14.45 W
Bakkaflói ⊂	24a	66.10 N	14.45 W
Bakkagerði	24a	65.32 N	13.48 W
Bakkeswar	272b	22.25 N	88.22 E
Bakkeveen	52	53.05 N	6.15 E
Baklan	130	37.58 N	29.36 E
Baklanka	76	58.43 N	40.06 E
Bakloh	123	32.28 N	75.55 E
Bakluši	80	52.07 N	43.22 E
Bako, C. Iv.	150	9.09 N	7.37 W
Bako, Ityo.	144	5.50 N	36.40 E
Bakony ⋏	30	47.15 N	17.50 E
Bakool □[4]	144	4.00 N	44.00 E
Bakoondfontein	158	32.43 S	22.30 E
Bakori	150	11.34 N	7.27 E
Bakou → Bakı	84	40.23 N	49.51 E
Bakouma	152	5.42 N	22.47 E
Bakovka	265b	55.41 N	37.20 E
Bakoy ≃	150	13.49 N	10.50 W
Bakruz'ak	86	52.59 N	58.42 E
Baksan	84	43.40 N	43.32 E
Baksan ≃	84	43.42 N	43.32 E
Bakšejevo, Ross.	80	55.44 N	39.53 E
Bakšejevo, Ross.	86	57.26 N	73.00 E
Baksir Chāndpur	126	23.30 N	89.44 E
Bakšty	76	53.56 N	26.11 E
Baksuk ≃	86	51.50 N	69.30 E
Baku → Bakı	84	40.23 N	49.51 E
Bakulin Point ≻	116	8.33 N	126.22 E
Bakum	52	52.45 N	8.11 E
Bakumpai	112	1.26 S	113.05 E
Bakun	120	32.32 N	80.26 E
Bakung, Pulau I	112	0.04 N	104.27 E
Bakungan	114	2.56 N	97.30 E
Bakuriani	84	41.46 N	43.32 E
Bakury	80	52.22 N	44.42 E
Bakwa-Kenge	152	4.51 S	22.04 E
Bakwanga → Mbuji-Mayi	152	6.09 S	23.38 E
Bakyrly	86	44.21 N	67.48 E
Bal ≃	126	21.58 N	89.21 E
Bala, On., Can.	212	45.01 N	79.37 W
Bala, Sén.	150	14.02 N	13.10 W
Balâ, Tür.	130	39.34 N	33.08 E
Bala, Wales, U.K.	42	52.54 N	3.35 W
Balabac	116	7.59 N	117.04 E
Balabac Island I	116	7.57 N	117.01 E
Balabac Strait ⊍	112	7.35 N	117.00 E
Bālā Bāgh	120	34.24 N	70.14 E
Ba'labakk	130	34.00 N	36.12 E
Balabalagan, Kepulauan II	112	2.20 S	117.25 E
Balaban	130	38.28 N	37.36 E
Balabanovo	82	55.11 N	36.40 E
Balabio, Île I	175f	20.07 S	164.11 E
Balabyne	78	47.44 N	35.13 E
Balachčin	86	54.09 N	89.23 E
Balachna	80	56.30 N	43.36 E
Balachta	86	55.24 N	91.37 E
Balachtison, gora ∧	86	54.36 N	93.50 E
Balaci	38	44.21 N	24.55 E
Bala-Cynwyd	285	40.00 N	75.14 W
Balad	128	34.01 N	44.09 E
Baladbandh	272b	22.52 N	88.07 E
Balad'ok	89	53.41 N	133.07 E
Balagansk	88	53.57 N	103.02 E
Bālāghāt	120	21.48 N	80.11 E
Bālāghāt Range ⋏	122	18.45 N	76.30 E
Balagny-sur-Thérain	50	49.18 N	2.20 E
Balaguer	34	41.47 N	0.49 E
Balaikarangan	112	0.50 N	110.26 E
Balaiselasa	112	1.48 S	100.50 E
Balaisepuah	112	0.27 N	111.13 E
Balaj	86	55.52 N	93.59 E
Balaka	152	4.51 S	19.57 E
Balakän	84	41.43 N	46.26 E
Balakété	152	6.56 N	19.54 E
Balakirevo	82	56.30 N	38.51 E
Balaklava, Austl.	168b	34.09 S	138.25 E
Balaklava, Ukr.	78	44.30 N	33.36 E
Balakliya, Ukr.	78	49.14 N	31.44 E
Balakliya, Ukr.	78	49.27 N	36.52 E
Bālākot	123	34.33 N	73.21 E
Balakovo	80	52.02 N	47.47 E
Balal, Laga ≃	154	3.25 N	37.15 E
Balallan	46	58.05 N	6.35 W
Balama, Moç.	154	13.20 S	38.30 E
Bal'amā, Urd.	132	32.14 N	36.05 E
Balamban	116	10.30 N	123.42 E
Balambangan, Pulau I	112	7.15 N	116.55 E
Bālā Morghāb	128	35.35 N	63.20 E
Bālandi	272b	22.58 N	88.32 E
Balanga	116	14.41 N	120.32 E
Balangala	152	0.24 N	19.45 E
Ba Lang An, Mui ≻	110	15.14 N	108.56 E
Balangero	62	45.16 N	7.31 E
Balangiga	116	11.07 N	125.23 E
Balāngīr	122	20.43 N	83.29 E
Balanguingui Island I	116	6.01 N	121.41 E
Bālān Ṣafar 'Ali	128	38.59 N	47.27 E
Balanṣūrah	142	27.55 N	30.41 E
Balantak, Gunung ∧	112	0.45 S	123.20 E
Balapulang	115a	7.03 S	109.05 E
Bālāpur	122	20.40 N	76.46 E
Balaqs	273c	30.10 N	31.17 E
Balaqṭar	142	31.05 N	30.13 E
Balaraja	115a	6.12 S	106.27 E
Balarāmbāti	272b	22.48 N	88.13 E
Balarāmpota	272b	22.31 N	88.08 E
Balarāmpur	126	23.07 N	86.13 E
Balaruc-le-Vieux	62	43.27 N	3.41 E
Balaši	80	51.24 N	49.55 E
Balašicha	82	55.49 N	37.58 E
Balašov	80	51.32 N	43.08 E
Balassagyarmat	30	48.05 N	19.18 E
Balāṭ	140	25.33 N	29.16 E
Balatan, Indon.	164	6.05 S	134.45 E
Balatan, Pil.	116	13.20 N	123.10 E
Balatina	38	47.42 N	27.21 E
Balaton	198	44.14 N	95.52 W
Balaton ⊜	30	46.50 N	17.45 E
Balaurin	112	8.15 S	123.43 E
Balavé	150	12.23 N	4.09 W
Balaxanı	84	40.29 N	49.54 E
Balayan	116	13.57 N	120.44 E
Balayan Bay ⊂	116	13.51 N	120.47 E
Balazote	34	38.53 N	2.08 W
Balbi, Mount ∧[1]	175e	5.55 S	154.59 E
Balbieriškis	76	54.32 N	23.52 E
Balbigny	62	45.49 N	4.11 E
Balbina, Represa ⊜[1]	246	1.20 S	59.40 W
Balboa	236	8.57 N	79.34 W
Balbriggan	48	53.37 N	6.11 W
Balcad	144	2.23 N	45.23 E
Balcanoona	166	30.31 S	139.18 E
Balcarce	252	37.50 S	58.15 W
Balcarres	184	50.48 N	103.33 W
Bălcești	38	44.37 N	23.56 E
Balchaš	86	46.49 N	74.59 E
Balchaš, ozero (Lake Balkhash) ⊜	86	46.00 N	74.00 E
Balch Springs	222	32.43 N	96.37 W
Balcı	130	38.43 N	34.06 E
Balčik	38	43.25 N	28.10 E
Balclutha	172	46.14 S	169.44 E
Balcombe	42	51.04 N	0.08 W
Balcones Escarpment ⊥[4]	196	29.30 N	99.15 W
Balde	252	33.20 S	66.38 W
Baldeador	287a	22.53 S	43.02 W
Bald Eagle	214	40.42 N	78.12 W
Bald Eagle Creek ≃	210	41.08 N	77.24 W
Bald Eagle Mountain ∧	214	41.00 N	77.45 W
Bald Eagle State Park ♠	214	41.00 N	77.40 W
Baldegger See ⊜	58	47.12 N	8.16 E
Baldeneysee ⊜	263	51.24 N	7.03 E
Balderschwang	58	47.28 N	10.06 E
Balderstone	262	53.47 N	2.34 W
Balderton	44	53.03 N	0.47 W
Bald Head ≻	162	35.07 S	118.01 E
Bald Hill ∧[2]	166	20.18 S	144.06 E
Bald Hill Branch ≃	284c	18.55 N	76.49 W
Baldhill Creek ≃	198	47.09 N	98.03 W
Bald Hills	171a	27.19 S	153.01 E
Baldichieri d'Asti	62	44.54 N	8.07 E
Baldim	255	19.17 S	43.57 W
Bald Island I	162	34.55 S	118.27 E
Bald Knob	194	35.18 N	91.34 W
Bald Knob ∧, Ca., U.S.	282	37.25 N	122.21 W
Bald Knob ∧, Va., U.S.	192	37.56 N	79.51 W
Bald Knoll ∧	200	42.24 N	110.29 W
Bald Mountain ∧, Ct., U.S.	207	41.59 N	72.25 W
Bald Mountain ∧, Nv., U.S.	226	38.33 N	119.07 W
Bald Mountain ∧, Or., U.S.	202	43.16 N	121.21 W
Bald Mountain ∧, Or., U.S.	202	44.36 N	117.53 W
Bald Mountain ∧, Or., U.S.	202	44.48 N	123.33 W
Bald Mountain ∧, Vt., U.S.	210	42.55 N	73.09 W
Bald Mountain State Recreation Area ♠	216	42.46 N	83.14 W
Baldo, Monte ∧	64	45.47 N	10.48 E
Baldock	42	51.59 N	0.12 W
Baldock Lake ⊜	184	56.33 N	97.57 W
Baldone	76	56.45 N	24.24 E
Baldovino, Arroyo ≃	288	34.46 S	58.07 W
Baldoyle	48	53.24 N	6.08 W
Baldpate Pond ⊜	283	42.42 N	71.00 W
Balduinstein	56	50.20 N	7.58 E
Baldur	184	49.23 N	99.15 W
Baldwin, Fl., U.S.	192	30.18 N	81.58 W
Baldwin, La., U.S.	194	29.50 N	91.32 W
Baldwin, Mi., U.S.	190	43.54 N	85.51 W
Baldwin, N.Y., U.S.	210	40.39 N	73.36 W
Baldwin, Pa., U.S.	214	40.23 N	79.57 W
Baldwin, Wi., U.S.	190	44.58 N	92.22 W
Baldwin Bay ⊂	276	40.38 N	73.35 W
Baldwin City	198	38.46 N	95.11 W
Baldwin Creek ≃	279a	41.22 N	81.51 W
Baldwin Hills ⋏[2]	280	34.00 N	118.22 W
Baldwin Lake ⊜	279a	41.21 N	81.51 W
Baldwin Park	228	34.05 N	117.57 W
Baldwin Peninsula ≻[1]	180	66.44 N	162.15 W
Baldwinsville	210	43.09 N	76.19 W
Baldwinville	207	42.36 N	72.04 W
Baldwin-Wallace College ⊽[2]	279a	41.23 N	81.51 W
Baldwyn	194	34.31 N	88.38 W
Baldy Mountain ∧, B.C., Can.	182	51.28 N	120.02 W
Baldy Mountain ∧, Mb., Can.	184	51.28 N	100.44 W
Baldy Mountain ∧, Mt., U.S.	202	48.09 N	109.39 W
Baldy Mountain ∧, N.M., U.S.	200	36.38 N	105.13 W
Baldy Peak ∧	200	33.55 N	109.35 W
Bale, Hrv.	64	45.02 N	13.48 E
Bale, India	272c	19.08 N	73.06 E
Bâle → Basel, Schw.	58	47.33 N	7.35 E
Bale □[4]	144	6.20 N	41.30 E
Bale-Akiosi	273a	6.41 N	3.21 E
Balearen → Balears, Illes II	34	39.30 N	3.00 E
Baléares, Îles → Balears, Illes II	34	39.30 N	3.00 E
Balearic Islands → Balears, Illes II	34	39.30 N	3.00 E
Balears □[3]	34	39.30 N	3.00 E
Balears, Illes (Balearic Islands) II	34	39.30 N	3.00 E
Balease, Gunung ∧	112	2.24 S	120.33 E
Balegane	158	26.04 S	31.34 E
Baleh ≃	112	2.01 N	113.01 E
Baleia, Ponta da ≻	255	17.40 S	39.07 W
Baleine, Grande rivière de la ≃	176	55.16 N	77.47 W
Baleine, Petite rivière de la ≃	176	56.00 N	76.45 W
Baleine, Rivière à la ≃	176	58.15 N	67.40 W
Balej	88	51.36 N	116.38 E
Balelasberg ⋏	158	27.30 S	30.07 E
Bale Mountains National Park ♠	144	7.00 N	39.40 E
Bâle-Mulhouse, Aéroport ⊠	58	47.35 N	7.32 E
Balen	56	51.10 N	5.09 E
Balena	152	0.55 N	20.00 E
Baleno	116	12.28 N	123.30 E
Baler	116	15.46 N	121.34 E
Baler Bay ⊂	116	15.50 N	121.35 E
Baleshare I	46	57.31 N	7.22 W
Bāleshwar	126	21.30 N	86.56 E
Balesin Island I	116	14.26 N	122.02 E
Balestrand	26	61.12 N	6.32 E
Balestrate	70	38.03 N	13.00 E
Baléya	150	9.15 N	10.29 W
Baléyara	150	13.47 N	2.57 E
Balezino	80	57.58 N	53.00 E
Balfate	236	15.48 N	86.25 W
Balfes Creek	166	20.13 S	145.55 E
Balfour, N.Z.	172	45.50 S	168.35 E
Balfour, S. Afr.	158	26.44 S	28.31 E
Balfour, Scot., U.K.	46	59.01 N	2.55 W
Balfour, N.C., U.S.	192	35.20 N	82.28 W
Balfour Downs	162	22.50 S	120.50 E
Balfour Park ♠	273d	26.08 S	28.06 E
Balfron	46	56.04 N	4.20 W
Balgach	58	47.25 N	9.35 E
Bălgarija → Bulgaria □[1]	38	43.00 N	25.00 E
Balgazyn	88	51.08 N	95.00 E
Balgo	162	20.09 S	127.48 E
Balgowlah	274a	33.48 S	151.16 E
Balguerie, Cap ≻	174x	9.45 S	138.47 W
Balhannah	168b	35.00 S	138.50 E
Bāli	120	25.11 N	73.17 E
Bali □[4]	115b	8.30 S	115.00 E
Bali I	115b	8.20 S	115.00 E
Bali, Laut (Bali Sea) ⊤[2]	112	7.45 S	115.30 E
Bali, Selat ⊍	112	8.18 S	114.25 E
Bāliākāndi	126	23.38 N	89.33 E
Baliangao	116	8.40 N	123.36 E
Bāliāpāl	126	21.40 N	87.17 E
Bāliāti	126	23.59 N	90.03 E
Balibago	116	13.37 N	121.18 E
Bali Barat National Park ♠	115b	8.15 S	114.40 E
Baliceaux I	241h	12.57 N	61.08 W
Bāli Chak	126	22.22 N	87.33 E
Balicuatro Islands II	116	12.39 N	124.24 E
Balicuatro Point ≻	116	12.35 N	124.16 E
Balidianzi	98	41.13 N	124.49 E
Bālidiha	126	21.58 N	86.38 E
Balige	114	2.20 N	99.04 E
Bālighai	126	21.52 N	87.35 E
Balihan	98	41.29 N	118.41 E
Bālihāti	272b	22.44 N	88.19 E
Balıkesir	130	39.39 N	27.53 E
Balıkesir □[4]	130	39.45 N	27.50 E
Balık Gölü ⊜	84	39.47 N	43.34 E
Balīkh ≃	130	35.52 N	39.12 E
Balıklıtohma ≃	130	38.50 N	37.41 E
Balikpapan	112	1.17 S	116.50 E
Balikumbat	152	5.54 N	10.23 E
Balimbing, Indon.	112	5.55 S	104.34 E
Balimbing, Pil.	116	5.05 N	119.58 E
Balimo	164	8.03 S	142.56 E
Balin	89	48.19 N	122.19 E
Balincollig	48	51.53 N	8.35 W
Balindong (Watu)	116	7.55 N	124.12 E
Baling	114	5.40 N	100.55 E
Balingasag	116	8.45 N	124.47 E
Balingen	58	48.16 N	8.51 E
Balingian	112	2.55 N	112.32 E
Balingup	162	33.48 S	115.58 E
Balintang Channel ⊍	108	19.49 N	121.40 E
Balintore	46	57.45 N	3.54 W
Balipu	105	39.53 N	117.48 E
Balışeyh	130	39.56 N	33.43 E
Baliuag	116	14.57 N	120.54 E
Baliung ≃	115a	6.50 S	105.52 E
Baliungan Island I	116	5.09 N	120.12 E
Baliyingzi	104	41.59 N	121.14 E
Baliza	255	16.15 S	52.25 W
Balizhuang, Zhg.	105	39.16 N	116.28 E
Balizhuang, Zhg.	271a	39.52 N	116.28 E
Balk	52	52.54 N	5.34 E
Balkach, Lago → Balchaš, ozero ⊜	86	46.00 N	74.00 E
Balkan □[8]	128	39.30 N	55.00 E
Balkan Mountains → Stara Planina ⋏	38	42.45 N	25.00 E
Balkan Peninsula ≻[1]	10	44.00 N	23.00 E
Balkaria → Kabardino-Balkarija □[3]	84	43.30 N	43.30 E
Balkašino	86	52.31 N	68.46 E
Balkbrug	52	52.36 N	6.24 E
Balkh	120	36.46 N	66.54 E
Balkh □[4]	120	36.30 N	67.00 E
Balkh ≃	120	36.39 N	66.56 E
Balkhash → Balchaš	86	46.49 N	74.59 E
Balkhash, Lake → Balchaš, ozero ⊜	86	46.00 N	74.00 E
Balky	78	47.23 N	34.57 E
Ball	194	31.24 N	92.24 W
Balla	48	53.48 N	9.09 W
Balla Balla	154	20.26 S	29.02 E
Ballabhpur	272b	22.44 N	88.21 E
Ballachulish	46	56.40 N	5.10 W
Balladonia	162	32.27 S	123.51 E
Ballagh	48	52.35 N	7.59 W
Ballaghaderreen	48	53.55 N	8.36 W
Ballālpur	122	19.50 N	79.22 E
Ballan	169	37.36 S	144.14 E
Ballancourt	50	48.31 N	2.23 E
Ballangen	24	68.20 N	16.50 E
Ballantine	202	45.56 N	108.08 W
Ballantrae	44	55.06 N	5.00 W
Ballao	71	39.33 N	9.22 E
Ballarat, Austl.	166	37.34 S	143.52 E
Ballarat, Austl.	169	37.34 S	143.52 E
Ballard, Lake ⊜	162	29.27 S	120.55 E
Ballardvale	207	42.37 N	71.09 W
Ballata	70	37.58 N	12.41 E
Ballater	46	57.03 N	3.03 W
Ballaugh	44	54.20 N	4.32 W
Ball Bay ⊂	174c	29.03 S	167.59 E
Ballé	150	15.20 N	8.35 W
Ballen	41	55.49 N	10.39 E
Ballenas, Bahía de ⊂	232	26.45 N	113.26 W
Ballenato, Punta ≻	286b	23.06 N	82.30 W
Ballengeich	158	27.52 S	29.59 E
Ballenita, Punta ≻	252	25.46 S	70.44 W
Ballenstedt	54	51.43 N	11.14 E
Balleny Basin ✣[1]	9	67.00 S	170.00 E
Balleny Islands II	9	66.35 S	162.50 E
Balleroy	32	49.11 N	0.50 W

Symbol	English	Deutsch	Español	Français	Português
≃	River	Fluß	Río	Rivière	Rio
≍	Canal	Kanal	Canal	Canal	Canal
∟	Waterfall, Rapids	Wasserfall, Stromschnellen	Cascada, Rápidos	Chute d'eau, Rapides	Cascata, Rápidos
⊍	Strait	Meeresstraße	Estrecho	Détroit	Estreito
⊂	Bay, Gulf	Bucht, Golf	Bahía, Golfo	Baie, Golfe	Baía, Golfo
⊜	Lake, Lakes	See, Seen	Lago, Lagos	Lac, Lacs	Lago, Lagos
⩸	Swamp	Sumpf	Pantano	Marais	Pântano
⊓	Ice Features, Glacier	Eis- und Gletscherformen	Accidentes Glaciales	Formes glaciaires	Acidentes glaciares
⊤	Other Hydrographic Features	Andere Hydrographische Objekte	Otros Elementos Hidrográficos	Autres données hydrographiques	Outros acidentes hidrográficos
✣	Submarine Features	Untermeerische Objekte	Accidentes Submarinos	Formes de relief sous-marin	Acidentes submarinos
□	Political Unit	Politische Einheit	Unidad Politica	Entité politique	Unidade política
⊽	Cultural Institution	Kulturelle Institution	Institución Cultural	Institution culturelle	Instituição cultural
⊥	Historical Site	Historische Stätte	Sitio Histórico	Site historique	Sitio histórico
♠	Recreational Site	Erholungs- und Ferienort	Sitio de Recreo	Centre de loisirs	Area de Lazer
⊠	Airport	Flughafen	Aeropuerto	Aéroport	Aeroporto
■	Military Installation	Militäranlage	Instalación Militar	Installation militaire	Instalação militar
◆	Miscellaneous	Verschiedenes	Misceláneo	Divers	Diversos

▲ Mountain	Berg	Montaña	Montagne	Montanha
▲ Mountains	Gebirge	Montañas	Montagnes	Montanhas
᙭ Pass	Paß	Paso	Col	Passo
⩔ Valley, Canyon	Tal, Cañon	Valle, Cañón	Vallée, Canyon	Vale, Canhão
≃ Plain	Ebene	Llano	Plaine	Planicie
⟩ Cape	Kap	Cabo	Cap	Cabo
I Island	Insel	Isla	Île	Ilha
II Islands	Inseln	Islas	Îles	Ilhas
⊥ Other Topographic Features	Andere Topographische Objekte	Otros Elementos Topográficos	Autres données topographiques	Outros acidentes topográficos

ESPAÑOL: Nombre · Página · Lat.°′ · Long.°′ W = Oeste
FRANÇAIS: Nom · Page · Lat.°′ · Long.°′ W = Ouest
PORTUGUÊS: Nome · Página · Lat.°′ · Long.°′ W = Oeste

Nombre / Nom / Nome	Página / Page	Lat.°′	Long.°′
Baptistown	208	40.31 N	75.00 W
Bāqa el Gharbīya	132	32.25 N	35.03 E
Baqar, Maṣrif Baḥr al- ≍	142	31.05 N	32.08 E
Baqar, Wādī al- V	146	27.49 N	18.37 E
Baqên	120	31.56 N	94.00 E
Baqing	120	32.15 N	93.30 E
B'aqlīn	132	33.41 N	35.33 E
Ba'qūbah	128	33.45 N	44.38 E
Baquedano	252	23.20 S	69.51 W
Ba Queo	269c	10.48 N	106.38 E
Bar, Jugo.	38	42.05 N	19.05 E
Bar, Ross.	88	51.17 N	107.33 E
Bar, Ukr.	78	49.04 N	27.40 E
Bar ≃	56	49.42 N	4.50 E
Bāra, India	124	25.13 N	87.22 E
Bara, India	272b	22.43 N	88.31 E
Bara, India	272b	22.46 N	88.17 E
Bara, Nig.	146	10.22 N	10.44 E
Baraawe	144	1.06 N	44.03 E
Barabai	112	2.35 S	115.23 E
Bara Bāngurda	126	22.57 N	86.24 E
Bāra Banki	124	26.55 N	81.12 E
Barabanovo	82	54.43 N	38.10 E
Barābhūm	126	23.02 N	86.22 E
Barabinsk	86	55.21 N	78.21 E
Barabinskaja step' ≋	86	55.00 N	79.00 E
Baraboo	190	43.28 N	89.44 W
Baraboo ≃	190	43.29 N	89.26 W
Baraboulé	150	14.12 N	1.51 W
Baracaju ≃	255	12.21 S	51.00 W
Barachit	144	14.39 N	39.27 E
Barachois Pond Provincial Park ♠	186	48.30 N	58.14 W
Baracoa, Cuba	240p	20.21 N	74.30 W
Baracoa, Hond.	236	15.43 N	87.52 W
Baradā ≃	132	33.30 N	36.28 E
Baradero	258	33.48 S	59.30 W
Baradero ≃	258	33.55 S	59.16 W
Baradili	71	39.43 N	8.54 E
Baradine	166	30.56 S	149.04 E
Bara Doāni	126	22.06 N	89.59 E
Baraga	190	46.46 N	88.29 W
Baragaon → Nālanda	124	25.07 N	85.25 E
Baragarh	120	21.20 N	83.37 E
Baragiano	68	40.41 N	15.35 E
Baragoi	154	1.47 N	36.47 E
Baraguá	240p	21.41 N	78.38 W
Baragwanath Aerodrome ⊠	273d	26.15 S	27.59 E
Baragwanath Military Hospital ᵾ	273d	26.16 S	27.56 E
Bārah	140	13.42 N	30.22 E
Barahānuddin	126	22.30 N	90.43 E
Barahona	238	18.12 N	71.06 W
Barāigrām	126	24.19 N	89.10 E
Bara Issa ≃	150	16.09 N	3.28 W
Barajas, Aeropuerto ⊠	266a	40.28 N	3.34 W
Barajas de Madrid ⬥[8]	266a	40.28 N	3.35 E
Bara Jorda	126	23.10 N	86.50 E
Barak	130	36.51 N	37.59 E
Barāk ≃	120	24.52 N	92.30 E
Baraka	154	4.06 S	29.06 E
Baraka (Khawr Barakah) V	144	18.13 N	37.35 E
Barakah	140	10.58 N	27.59 E
Barakah, Khawr (Baraka) V	144	18.13 N	37.35 E
Barakaldo	34	43.18 N	2.59 W
Barākar	126	24.07 N	86.14 E
Barākar ≃	126	23.42 N	86.48 E
Bara Khunta	126	21.43 N	86.38 E
Baraki	120	33.56 N	68.55 E
Barakloj	86	52.12 N	67.49 E
Bārākpur, Bngl.	126	22.55 N	89.32 E
Bārākpur, India	126	22.46 N	88.21 E
Bārākpur Cantonment	272b	22.46 N	88.22 E
Barakula	166	26.26 S	150.31 E
Barāl	272b	22.27 N	88.22 E
Baral ≃	126	24.10 N	89.27 E
Baralaba	166	24.11 S	149.49 E
Barām	126	22.57 N	86.18 E
Baram ≃	112	4.36 N	113.59 E
Baram, Tanjong ›	112	4.35 N	113.59 E
Barama ≃	246	7.40 N	59.15 W
Barāmāria	126	21.42 N	87.04 E
Bārāmati	122	18.09 N	74.35 E
Bāramūla	123	34.12 N	74.21 E
Baran', Bela.	76	54.30 N	28.40 E
Baran', Bela.	76	54.29 N	30.18 E
Bārān, India	124	25.06 N	76.31 E
Baranagar	126	22.38 N	88.22 E
Baranakovo	86	58.08 N	82.58 E
Baranavičy	76	53.08 N	26.02 E
Barancevo	82	55.04 N	37.38 E
Baranello	66	41.32 N	14.34 E
Barangbarang	112	6.24 S	120.28 E
Barangeon ≃	50	47.12 N	2.10 E
Barani	150	13.10 N	3.53 W
Baraniki	80	46.31 N	41.50 E
Baranivka	78	50.18 N	27.40 E
Baranoa	246	10.48 N	74.55 W
Barano d'Ischia	68	40.42 N	13.55 E
Baranof	180	57.05 N	134.50 W
Baranof Island I	180	57.00 N	135.00 W
Baranovskoje	82	55.25 N	38.45 E
Barany, Ross.	76	57.20 N	29.09 E
Barany, Ross.	80	57.38 N	52.16 E
Baranya ▫[6]	30	46.05 N	18.15 E
Baranykivka	83	49.10 N	39.50 E
Barão Ataliba Nogueira	256	22.24 S	46.45 W
Barão de Geraldo	256	22.49 S	47.06 W
Barão de Grajaú	250	6.45 S	43.01 W
Barão de Juparanã	256	22.21 S	43.41 W
Barão de Melgaço	248	16.13 S	55.58 W
Barão de Tromaí	250	1.29 S	45.36 W
Baraolt	38	46.05 N	25.36 E
Baraque de Fraiture ∧	56	50.15 N	5.44 E
Baras	116	13.40 N	124.22 E
Barasāhi	126	21.43 N	86.44 E
Bārāsat, India	126	22.43 N	88.29 E
Bārasat, India	272b	22.51 N	88.22 E
Baraševo	80	54.32 N	42.53 E
Barashi	78	50.43 N	28.01 E
Baraški	24	65.40 N	52.10 E
Barat, Lintasan ʮ	115a	7.08 S	112.40 E
Baratā	266c	38.48 N	9.19 W
Baratang Island I	110	12.13 N	92.45 E
Barataria	194	29.43 N	90.07 W
Barataria Bay c	194	29.22 N	89.57 W
Barat Daya, Kepulauan II	108	7.25 S	128.00 E
Barate	112	9.54 S	123.38 E
Bar'atino, Ross.	76	54.19 N	34.31 E
Bar'atino, Ross.	82	54.43 N	36.49 E
Baratolia	126	22.25 N	86.37 E
Baratta	166	31.59 S	139.06 E
Barauana ≃	246	1.14 N	60.41 W
Baraula	272a	28.34 N	77.22 E
Barauni	124	25.29 N	85.59 E
Baraut	124	29.06 N	77.16 E
Baravuha	76	55.36 N	28.37 E
Baraya	246	3.10 N	75.04 W
Barbacena	256	21.14 S	43.46 W
Barbacoas	246	1.41 N	78.09 W
Barbades → Barbados ▫[1]	241g	13.10 N	59.32 W
Barbadillo del Mercado	34	42.02 N	3.21 W
Barbadoes Island I	285	40.07 N	75.22 W
Barbados ▫[1], N.A.	230	13.10 N	59.32 W
Barbados ▫[1], N.A.	241g	13.10 N	59.32 W
Barbagia ⬥[1]	71	39.55 N	9.12 E
Barbalha	250	7.19 S	39.17 W
Barbar	140	18.01 N	33.59 E
Barbarano Vicentino	64	45.24 N	11.32 E
Barbarasco	64	44.14 N	9.56 E
Barbareta, Isla I	236	16.26 N	86.09 W
Barbaria, Cap de ›	34	38.38 N	1.23 E
Barbaros	130	40.54 N	27.27 E
Barbas, Cap ›	148	22.18 N	16.41 W
Barbaši	76	57.42 N	28.24 E
Barbastro	34	42.02 N	0.08 E
Barbate	34	36.12 N	5.55 W
Barbate ≃	34	36.11 N	5.55 W
Barbeau Peak ∧	16	81.54 N	75.01 W
Barbentane	62	43.54 N	4.45 E
Barberà del Vallès	266d	41.31 N	2.08 E
Barber Booth	262	53.22 N	1.50 W
Barberena	236	14.18 N	90.22 W
Barberena ≃	234	22.34 N	97.52 W
Barberino di Mugello	66	44.00 N	11.15 E
Barberino Val d'Elsa	66	43.32 N	11.10 E
Barbers Point ›	229c	21.18 N	158.07 W
Barbers Point Naval Air Station ■	229c	21.19 N	158.04 W
Barberton, S. Afr.	156	25.48 S	31.03 E
Barberton, Oh., U.S.	214	41.00 N	81.36 W
Barbezieux	32	45.28 N	0.09 W
Bar Bigha	124	25.13 N	85.44 E
Barbil	124	22.06 N	85.20 E
Barbis	54	51.37 N	10.25 E
Barbizon	50	48.27 N	2.36 E
Barbosa, Col.	246	6.26 N	75.20 W
Barbosa, Col.	246	5.57 N	73.37 W
Barboursville	188	38.24 N	82.17 W
Barbourville	192	36.51 N	83.53 W
Barbuda I	238	17.38 N	61.48 W
Barbuise ≃	50	48.33 N	3.58 E
Barby	54	51.58 N	11.53 E
Bârca	38	43.58 N	23.37 E
Barčadiv	85	38.19 N	72.29 E
Barca Grande ≃	258	34.09 S	58.23 W
Barcaldine	166	23.33 S	145.17 E
Barcarena	266c	38.44 N	9.17 W
Barcarena, Ribeira de ≃	266c	38.42 N	9.27 W
Barcarrota	34	38.31 N	6.51 W
Barcău (Berettyó) ≃	38	46.59 N	21.07 E
Barce → Al-Marj	146	32.30 N	20.54 E
Barcellona Pozzo di Gotto	70	38.09 N	15.13 E
Barcelona, Esp.	34	41.23 N	2.11 E
Barcelona, Esp.	266d	41.23 N	2.11 E
Barcelona, Méx.	232	26.12 N	103.25 W
Barcelona, Pil.	116	12.52 N	124.09 E
Barcelona, Ven.	246	10.08 N	64.42 W
Barcelona ▫[4]	34	41.40 N	2.00 E
Barcelona, Aeropuerto Transoceánico de ⊠	266d	41.18 N	2.05 E
Barcelone → Barcelona	34	41.23 N	2.11 E
Barceloneta	240m	18.27 N	66.32 W
Barcelonnette	62	44.23 N	6.39 E
Barcelos, Bra.	246	0.58 S	62.57 W
Barcelos, Port.	34	41.32 N	8.37 W
Barchaticha	80	57.34 N	45.13 E
Barchyn ≃	88	48.43 N	110.17 E
Barcillonnette	62	44.26 N	5.55 E
Barcin	30	52.52 N	17.57 E
Barcis	64	46.11 N	12.33 E
Barclay	208	39.08 N	75.51 W
Barclay Brook ≃	276	40.19 N	74.22 W
Barcoo ≃	166	25.30 S	142.50 E
Barcroft, Lake ⊜[1]	284c	38.51 N	77.09 W
Barcs	30	45.58 N	17.28 E
Barcy	261	49.01 N	2.53 E
Barczewo	30	53.50 N	20.42 E
Bard	62	45.36 N	7.45 E
Bärdä, Azer.	84	40.23 N	47.08 E
Barda, Ross.	86	56.54 N	55.38 E
Barda del Medio	252	38.43 S	68.10 W
Bardagué, Enneri V	146	22.06 N	16.28 E
Bardai, Sūd.	140	12.43 N	21.53 E
Bardaï, Tchad	146	21.22 N	16.59 E
Bardawīl, Sabkhat al- ≋	140	31.10 N	33.10 E
Barddhamān	126	23.15 N	87.51 E
Bardejov	30	49.18 N	21.16 E
Bardenas Reales ≁[1]	34	42.10 N	1.25 W
Bardeskan	128	35.12 N	57.58 E
Bardi	62	44.38 N	9.44 E
Bardīyah	146	31.46 N	25.06 E
Bardız	130	40.26 N	42.20 E
Bardney	44	53.12 N	0.21 W
Bardo	36	36.50 N	10.06 E
Bardoc	162	30.20 S	121.17 E
Bārdoli	120	21.07 N	73.07 E
Bardolino	64	45.33 N	10.43 E
Bardonecchia	62	45.05 N	6.42 E
Bardonia	276	41.07 N	74.00 W
Bardoux, Lac ⊜	186	51.09 N	67.50 W
Bardowick	52	53.18 N	10.23 E
Bardsey Island I	42	52.45 N	4.45 W
Bardsey Sound ʮ	42	52.47 N	4.45 W
Bardstown	194	37.48 N	85.28 W
Bardu	24	68.52 N	18.21 E
Bardufoss	24	69.04 N	18.30 E
Bardwell, Ky., U.S.	194	36.52 N	89.00 W
Bardwell, Tx., U.S.	222	32.16 N	96.42 W
Bardwell Lake ⊜[1]	222	32.16 N	96.39 W
Bare	144	4.42 N	42.47 E
Bareggio	266b	45.29 N	9.00 E
Barei, Wādī V	140	13.27 N	23.57 E
Bareilly	124	28.21 N	79.25 E
Bareli	124	23.00 N	78.14 E
Barenburg	52	52.37 N	8.47 E
Barendrecht	52	51.51 N	4.32 E
Bärenklau	54	51.56 N	14.34 E
Bärenstein, Dtsch.	54	50.30 N	13.02 E
Bärenstein, Dtsch.	54	50.48 N	13.47 E
Barentin	50	49.33 N	0.57 E
Barents Sea ⊤[2]	12	74.00 N	36.00 E
Barents Trough ✢[1]	12	75.00 N	29.00 E
Barentu	144	15.04 N	37.37 E
Bareo	112	3.45 N	115.27 E
Baresville	208	39.48 N	76.57 W
Bareta	123	29.52 N	75.42 E
Barfleur	32	49.40 N	1.15 W
Barfleur, Pointe de ›	32	49.42 N	1.16 W
Barga	64	44.04 N	10.29 E
Bargāchia, India	126	22.39 N	88.07 E
Bargāchia, India	272b	22.48 N	88.27 E
Bargagli	62	44.27 N	9.05 E
Bargaintown	208	39.22 N	70.35 W
Bargara	166	24.49 S	152.27 E
Bargas	34	39.56 N	4.03 W
Barge, It.	62	44.43 N	7.20 E
Barge, Ityo.	144	6.14 N	36.58 E
Barg-e Maṯāl	120	35.40 N	71.21 E
Bargemon	62	43.37 N	6.32 E
Bargen	58	47.48 N	8.37 E
Bargersville	218	39.31 N	86.10 W
Barghanak	128	33.56 N	62.26 E
Bargnop	140	9.30 N	28.28 E
Bargo	170	34.18 S	150.35 E
Bargoed	42	51.43 N	3.15 W
Bargteheide	52	53.44 N	10.16 E
Bārguna	126	22.09 N	90.07 E
Barguzin	88	53.37 N	109.37 E
Barguzin ≃	88	53.27 N	109.00 E
Barguzinskij chrebet ≁	88	54.30 N	110.20 E
Barguzinskij zapovednik ♠	88	54.25 N	109.40 E
Bārh	124	25.29 N	85.43 E
Barhaj	124	26.17 N	83.44 E
Bar Harbor	188	44.23 N	68.12 W
Barharwa	124	24.52 N	87.47 E
Barhau	112	5.19 S	102.10 E
Barhi	124	24.18 N	85.25 E
Bar Hill	42	52.15 N	0.01 E
Barhiya	124	25.17 N	86.02 E
Bāri, India	124	23.03 N	78.05 E
Bāri, India	124	26.39 N	77.36 E
Bari, It.	68	41.07 N	16.52 E
Bari, R.D.C.	152	3.19 N	19.23 E
Bari ▫[4], It.	68	40.56 N	16.40 E
Bari ▫[4], Som.	144	10.00 N	50.00 E
Baria ≃	246	1.56 N	66.35 W
Baricella	64	44.39 N	11.32 E
Barichara	246	6.38 N	73.14 W
Barīdī, Ra's ›	128	24.17 N	37.31 E
Bāri Doāb ≁[1]	123	30.25 N	73.00 E
Barī Gāv	120	33.52 N	67.49 E
Barigazzo	64	44.16 N	10.39 E
Barigua, Salina de ≋	241s	12.08 N	69.59 W
Barika	34	35.23 N	5.22 E
Barika, Oued ≃	34	35.22 N	5.18 E
Barikiwa	154	9.28 S	37.54 E
Barīkowṯ	120	35.18 N	71.32 E
Barile	68	40.57 N	15.40 E
Barillas	236	15.48 N	91.18 W
Bariloche → San Carlos de Bariloche	254	41.09 S	71.18 W
Barilo-Krepinskaja	83	47.45 N	39.32 E
Barīm (Perim) I	144	12.39 N	43.25 E
Barima ≃	246	8.33 N	60.25 W
Barima-Waini ▫[4]	246	7.45 N	59.30 W
Barin	84	39.13 N	44.28 E
Barinas, P.R.	240m	18.01 N	66.51 W
Barinas, Ven.	246	8.38 N	70.12 W
Barinas ▫[3]	246	8.10 N	69.50 W
Baring	224	47.46 N	121.29 W
Baring, Cape ›	176	70.05 N	117.20 W
Baringa, R.D.C.	152	6.17 S	16.55 E
Baringa, R.D.C.	152	0.45 N	20.52 E
Baringo, Lake ⊜	154	0.38 N	36.05 E
Båring Vig c	41	55.32 N	9.56 E
Barinitas	246	8.45 N	70.25 W
Bāripada	126	21.56 N	86.43 E
Bariri	255	22.04 S	48.44 W
Bārīs	140	24.40 N	30.36 E
Barisacho	84	42.28 N	44.54 E
Bari Sādri	120	24.25 N	74.28 E
Barisāl	124	22.42 N	90.22 E
Barisan, Pegunungan ≁	112	3.00 S	102.15 E
Bari Sardo	71	39.50 N	9.38 E
Barisciano	66	42.19 N	13.35 E
Bariti Bil ⊜	272b	22.48 N	88.26 E
Barito ≃	112	3.32 S	114.29 E
Baritú, Parque Nacional ♠	252	22.30 S	64.35 W
Barjā	132	33.39 N	35.26 E
Barjac	62	44.18 N	4.21 E
Barjols	62	43.33 N	6.00 E
Barjora	126	23.26 N	87.17 E
Barjūj, Wādī V	146	25.57 N	13.12 E
Bark ≃	216	42.55 N	88.50 W
Barka Kāna	124	23.37 N	85.29 E
Barkal	120	22.44 N	92.23 E
Barkam	102	31.50 N	102.40 E
Barkava	76	56.43 N	26.36 E
Barkelsby	41	54.30 N	9.50 E
Barker, N.Y., U.S.	210	43.19 N	78.33 W
Barker, Ur.	258	34.16 S	57.27 W
Barker Point ›	276	40.51 N	73.44 W
Barker Reservoir ⊜[1]	222	29.44 N	95.44 W
Barkers Brook ≃	285	40.03 N	74.45 W
Barkerville	182	53.04 N	121.31 W
Barkerville Historic Park ♠	182	53.04 N	121.30 W
Barkeyville	214	41.12 N	79.58 W
Barkhamsted Reservoir ⊜[1]	207	41.57 N	72.57 W
Bārkhān	120	29.54 N	69.31 E
Barkhanpur	126	23.50 N	89.33 E
Barking ⬥[8]	42	51.33 N	0.06 E
Barkingside ⬥[8]	260	51.36 N	0.05 E
Barki Saraiya	124	24.10 N	85.53 E
Barkisland	262	53.41 N	1.55 W
Bark Lake ⊜, On., Can.	190	46.54 N	82.28 W
Bark Lake ⊜, On., Can.	212	45.27 N	77.51 W
Barkley, Lake ⊜[1]	194	36.40 N	87.55 W
Barkley Sound ʮ	182	48.53 N	125.20 W
Barkly ≃	169	37.32 S	146.32 E
Barkly, Mount ∧[2]	162	21.34 S	132.28 E
Barkly East	158	30.58 S	27.33 E
Barkly Tableland ≁[1]	162	18.00 S	136.00 E
Barkly West	158	28.05 S	24.31 E
Barkol	90	43.50 N	93.30 E
Barksdale	196	29.44 N	100.02 W
Barkuni	124	22.13 N	78.42 E
Barla	130	38.01 N	30.47 E
Bârlad	38	46.14 N	27.40 E
Bârlad ≃	38	45.36 N	27.31 E
Barlassina	266b	45.39 N	9.08 E
Barlaston	42	52.57 N	2.10 W
Barlby	44	53.48 N	1.03 W
Barleben	54	52.12 N	11.37 E
Bar-le-Duc	56	48.47 N	5.10 E
Barlee, Lake ⊜	162	29.10 S	119.30 E
Barlee, Mount ∧[2]	162	24.37 S	128.06 E
Barlee Range ≁	162	23.35 S	116.00 E
Barles	62	44.16 N	6.16 E
Barletta	68	41.19 N	16.17 E
Barlin	50	50.27 N	2.37 E
Barlinek	30	53.00 N	15.12 E
Barling	194	35.19 N	94.18 W
Barlow	194	37.03 N	89.02 W
Barluk	88	54.32 N	101.43 E
Barma	164	1.54 S	133.00 E
Barmancak, ozero ⊜	80	48.02 N	44.40 E
Barmashove	78	47.07 N	32.26 E
Barmedman	166	34.09 S	147.23 E
Barmen ⬥[8]	263	51.17 N	7.13 E
Bārmer	120	25.45 N	71.23 E
Barmera	166	34.15 S	140.28 E
Barmouth	42	52.43 N	4.03 W
Barmouth Bay c	42	52.42 N	4.08 W
Barmstedt	52	53.47 N	9.46 E
Barnaby Manor Oaks	284c	38.50 N	76.58 W
Barnagar	120	23.03 N	75.22 E
Barnāla	123	30.23 N	75.33 E
Barnard Castle	44	54.33 N	1.55 W
Barnasht	142	29.41 N	31.15 E
Bärnau	60	49.49 N	12.26 E
Barnaul	86	53.22 N	83.45 E
Bärnbach	61	47.05 N	15.06 E
Barn Bluff ∧	166	41.43 S	145.56 E
Barneberg	54	52.08 N	11.03 E
Barnegat	208	39.45 N	74.13 W
Barnegat Bay c	208	39.52 N	74.07 W
Barnegat Light	208	39.45 N	74.06 W
Barne Inlet c	9	80.15 S	160.15 E
Barnes	214	41.40 N	79.01 W
Barnes ⬥[8]	260	51.28 N	0.15 W
Barnesboro	214	40.39 N	78.46 W
Barnes Corners	212	43.49 N	75.49 W
Barnes Ice Cap ⊓	176	70.00 N	73.15 W
Barnes Lake ⊜	184	56.23 N	98.06 W
Barnes Sound ʮ	220	25.14 N	80.23 W
Barnesville, Ga., U.S.	192	33.03 N	84.09 W
Barnesville, Mn., U.S.	198	46.39 N	96.25 W
Barnesville, Oh., U.S.	188	39.59 N	81.10 W
Barnet ⬥[8]	42	51.40 N	0.13 W
Barnetby le Wold	44	53.35 N	0.25 W
Barnett	219	39.16 N	89.42 W
Barnetts	208	37.22 N	77.09 W
Barneveld, Ned.	52	52.08 N	5.35 E
Barneveld, N.Y., U.S.	210	43.16 N	75.12 W
Barneville-Carteret	32	49.23 N	1.47 W
Barnhart, Mo., U.S.	219	38.20 N	90.23 W
Barnhart, Tx., U.S.	196	31.08 N	101.10 W
Barnhill	214	40.27 N	81.21 W
Barnim ⬥[1]	54	52.40 N	13.45 E
Barnoldswick	44	53.55 N	2.11 W
Barnówko	54	52.48 N	14.45 E
Barnsboro	285	39.46 N	75.09 W
Barnsdall	196	36.33 N	96.09 W
Barnsley	44	53.34 N	1.28 W
Barnstable	207	41.42 N	70.18 W
Barnstable ▫[6]	207	41.42 N	70.18 W
Barnstable Harbor c	207	41.43 N	70.18 W
Barnstaple	42	51.05 N	4.04 W
Barnstaple Bay c	42	51.05 N	4.20 W
Barnston	262	53.21 N	3.05 W
Barnstorf	52	52.42 N	8.30 E
Barnt Green	42	52.22 N	1.59 W
Barnton	262	53.16 N	2.33 W
Barntrup	52	51.59 N	9.06 E
Barnum Island	276	40.36 N	73.39 W
Barnwell, Ab., Can.	182	49.46 N	112.15 W
Barnwell, S.C., U.S.	192	33.14 N	81.21 W
Baro	150	8.37 N	6.25 E
Baro ≃	144	8.26 N	33.13 E
Barobo	116	8.33 N	126.07 E
Baroda → Vadodara, India	122	22.18 N	73.12 E
Baroda, India	124	25.30 N	76.39 E
Baroda, Mi., U.S.	216	41.57 N	86.29 W
Baroe	158	33.13 S	24.33 E
Barometer ∧	172	41.50 S	173.39 E
Baron Bluff ⊥[4]	241n	17.47 N	64.47 W
Baronissi	68	40.44 N	14.45 E
Baron'ki	76	53.09 N	32.08 E
Barons	182	50.00 N	113.05 W
Barora Fa Island I	175e	7.30 S	158.20 E
Barora Ite Island I	175e	7.35 S	158.24 E
Barossa Reservoir ⊜[1]	168b	34.39 S	138.51 E
Barotac Nuevo	116	10.54 N	122.42 E
Barotac Viejo	116	11.03 N	122.51 E
Barouéli	150	13.04 N	6.50 W
Barpathār	120	26.17 N	93.53 E
Barpeta	120	26.19 N	91.00 E
Bar Point ›	214	42.03 N	83.06 W
Barqa	120	30.57 N	81.20 E
Barqah (Cyrenaica) ▫[9]	146	31.00 N	22.30 E
Barqah, Jabal al- ∧	132	30.25 N	34.18 E
Barq al-'Izz	142	31.01 N	31.26 E
Barque Canada Reef ✢[2]	108	8.12 N	113.19 E
Barques, Pointe aux ›	190	44.04 N	82.58 W
Barquisimeto	246	10.04 N	69.19 W
Barr	58	48.24 N	7.27 E
Barra, Bra.	250	11.05 S	43.10 W
Barra, Gam.	150	13.20 N	16.36 W
Barra I	46	56.58 N	7.29 W
Barra, Ponta da ›	156	23.47 S	35.32 E
Barra, Sound of ʮ	46	57.05 N	7.25 W
Barraba	166	30.22 S	150.36 E
Barracas ⬥[8]	288	34.38 S	58.22 W
Barrackpore → Bārākpur	126	22.46 N	88.21 E
Barrackpore Airport ⊠	272b	22.47 N	88.22 E
Barrackville	188	39.30 N	80.10 W
Barracouta, Cape ›	158	34.26 S	21.22 E
Barra da Estiva	255	13.38 S	41.19 W
Barra de Santo Antônio	250	9.24 S	35.30 W
Barra de São Francisco	256	21.58 S	42.42 W
Barra do Bugres	248	15.05 S	57.11 W
Barra do Corda	250	5.30 S	45.15 W
Barra do Cuanza	152	9.09 S	13.00 E
Barra do Dande	152	8.28 S	13.22 E
Barra do Garças	255	15.53 S	52.15 W
Barra do Mendes	255	11.43 S	42.04 W
Barra do Piraí	256	22.28 S	43.49 W
Barra do Ribeiro	252	30.18 S	51.18 W
Barra dos Coqueiros	250	10.54 S	37.03 W
Barra Falsa, Ponta da ›	156	22.55 S	35.37 E
Barrafranca	70	37.22 N	14.12 E
Barra Funda ⬥[8]	287b	23.31 S	46.39 W
Barra Head ›	46	56.46 N	7.38 W
Barrali	71	39.28 N	9.06 E
Barra Mansa	256	22.32 S	44.11 W
Barranca, Perú	248	10.45 S	77.46 W
Barranca, Perú	248	4.50 S	76.42 W
Barrancabermeja	246	7.03 N	73.52 W
Barrancas, Col.	246	10.57 N	72.50 W
Barrancas, Ven.	246	8.46 N	70.06 W
Barrancas, Ven.	246	8.42 N	62.11 W
Barrancas ≃	252	36.52 S	69.45 W
Barranco	286d	12.09 S	77.02 W
Barranco Azul	196	29.21 N	104.17 W
Barranco de Guadalupe	196	30.02 N	104.44 W
Barranco do Velho	34	37.14 N	7.56 W
Barrancos	34	38.08 N	6.59 W
Barrânia	256	21.33 S	46.32 W
Barranqueras	252	27.29 S	58.56 W
Barranquilla	246	10.59 N	74.48 W
Barranquitas	240m	18.11 N	66.18 W
Barras	250	4.15 S	42.18 W
Barrax	34	39.03 N	2.12 W
Barre, Ma., U.S.	207	42.25 N	72.06 W
Barre, Vt., U.S.	188	44.11 N	72.30 W
Barrea	66	41.45 N	13.59 E
Barreal	252	31.38 S	69.28 W
Barree	214	40.35 N	78.06 W
Barre Falls Dam ⬥[6]	207	42.26 N	72.02 W
Barreiras	255	12.08 S	45.00 W
Barreirinha	250	2.47 S	57.03 W
Barreirinhas	250	2.45 S	42.50 W
Barreiro	34	38.40 N	9.05 W
Barreiro ≃, Bra.	255	15.43 S	52.45 W
Barreiro ≃, Bra.	287a	22.52 S	43.34 W
Barreiros	250	8.49 S	35.12 W
Barrême	62	43.57 N	6.22 E
Barren ≃	194	37.11 N	86.37 W
Barren, Nosy II	157b	18.25 S	43.40 E
Barren Island I	110	12.16 N	93.51 E
Barren Islands II	180	58.55 N	152.15 W
Barrenjoey Head ›	170	33.34 S	151.20 E
Barren River Lake ⊜[1]	194	36.45 N	86.02 W
Barren Run ≃	279b	40.09 N	79.42 W
Barre Plains	207	42.22 N	72.06 W
Barret-le-Bas	62	44.16 N	5.44 E
Barretos	255	20.33 S	48.33 W
Barrett	222	29.53 N	95.04 W
Barrett, Mount ∧	162	18.10 S	127.33 E
Barrhead, Ab., Can.	182	54.08 N	114.24 W
Barrhead, Scot., U.K.	46	55.48 N	4.24 W
Barrhill	44	55.07 N	4.46 W
Barrie	212	44.24 N	79.40 W
Barriefield	212	44.14 N	76.28 W
Barrie Island I	190	45.55 N	82.40 W
Barrien	52	52.56 N	8.49 E
Barrier, Cape ›	172	36.21 S	175.31 E
Barrière	182	51.11 N	120.07 W
Barrier Range ≁	166	31.25 S	141.25 E
Barrier Reef ✢[2]	164	11.36 S	153.00 E
Barrigada	174p	13.28 N	144.48 E
Barrilla Draw V	196	31.21 N	103.23 W
Barr Ilyās	132	33.46 N	35.54 E
Barrington, N.S., Can.	186	43.34 N	65.34 W
Barrington, Il., U.S.	216	42.09 N	88.08 W
Barrington, N.J., U.S.	285	39.51 N	75.03 W
Barrington, R.I., U.S.	207	41.44 N	71.18 W
Barrington Hills	216	42.07 N	88.09 W
Barrington Lake ⊜	184	56.55 N	100.15 W
Barrington Tops ∧	166	32.00 S	151.28 E
Barrington Woods	278	42.09 N	88.04 W
Barringun	166	29.01 S	145.43 E
Barrio de la Soledad	234	16.48 N	95.15 W
Barrita Vieja	236	13.55 N	90.54 W
Barrīyat al-Uṣayfir	142	31.18 N	30.40 E
Barro, Bra.	250	7.11 S	38.47 W
Barro, Gui.-B.	150	12.24 N	15.30 W
Barro Alto	255	15.04 S	48.58 W
Barron	190	45.24 N	91.50 W
Barron Creek ≃	282	37.27 N	122.05 W
Barron Lake	216	41.51 N	86.11 W
Barrouallie	241h	13.14 N	61.17 W
Barrow, Arg.	252	38.18 S	60.14 W
Barrow, Ak., U.S.	180	71.17 N	156.34 W
Barrow ≃	48	52.15 N	7.00 W
Barrow, Point ›	180	71.23 N	156.30 W
Barrow Bay c	212	44.58 N	81.13 W
Barrow Creek	162	21.33 S	133.53 E
Barrowford	44	53.52 N	2.13 W
Barrow-in-Furness	44	54.07 N	3.14 W
Barrow Island I	162	20.48 S	115.23 E
Barrows	184	52.49 N	101.27 W
Barrow Strait ʮ	176	74.21 N	94.10 W
Barrowsville	207	41.56 N	71.12 W
Barrow upon Humber	44	53.41 N	0.23 W
Barry, Wales, U.K.	42	51.24 N	3.18 W
Barry, Il., U.S.	219	39.41 N	91.02 W
Barry, Tx., U.S.	222	32.06 N	96.38 W
Barry ▫[6]	216	42.35 N	85.18 W
Barrydale	158	33.55 S	20.43 E
Barrys Bay	212	45.29 N	77.41 W
Barrys Bay c	212	45.28 N	77.42 W
Barryton	190	43.45 N	85.08 W
Barrytown	210	42.00 N	73.56 W
Barryville	210	41.28 N	74.54 W
Barsakel'mes, ostrov I	86	45.40 N	59.58 E
Barsalpur	120	28.10 N	72.15 E
Baršatas	86	48.13 N	78.21 E
Barsbüttel	52	53.34 N	10.10 E
Bårse	41	55.07 N	11.58 E
Bārsi	122	18.14 N	75.42 E
Barsinghausen	52	52.18 N	9.27 E
Baršino	86	49.45 N	69.36 E
Barskaun	85	42.10 N	77.37 E
Barsø I	41	55.07 N	9.34 E
Barssel	52	53.10 N	7.44 E
Barst	56	49.04 N	6.50 E
Barstow, Ca., U.S.	228	34.53 N	117.01 W
Barstow, Tx., U.S.	196	31.28 N	103.24 W
Barsuki	82	54.15 N	37.30 E
Bar-sur-Aube	58	48.14 N	4.43 E
Bar-sur-Seine	50	48.07 N	4.22 E
Bart	208	39.56 N	76.05 W
Bārta ≃	76	56.24 N	21.03 E
Bartala	272b	22.33 N	88.16 E
Bartang ≃	120	37.56 N	71.34 E
Bartazuga, Jabal ∧	140	21.44 N	33.33 E
Bartelso	219	38.32 N	89.28 W
Bartenheim	58	47.38 N	7.28 E
Bartenstein	56	49.21 N	9.53 E
Barter Island I	180	70.08 N	143.35 W
Barth	54	54.22 N	12.43 E
Barthe ≃	54	54.22 N	12.41 E
Barthélemy, Deo ⟩⟨	110	19.26 N	104.06 E
Bartholomew ▫[6]	218	39.13 N	85.55 W
Bartholomew, Bayou ≃	194	32.43 N	92.04 W
Bartibougou	150	12.52 N	0.48 E
Bartica	246	6.24 N	58.37 W
Bartın	130	41.38 N	32.21 E
Bartle Frere ∧	166	17.23 S	145.49 E
Bartlesville	196	36.44 N	95.58 W
Bartlett, Il., U.S.	216	41.59 N	88.11 W
Bartlett, Ne., U.S.	198	41.53 N	98.33 W
Bartlett, N.H., U.S.	188	44.04 N	71.17 W
Bartlett, Tn., U.S.	194	35.12 N	89.52 W
Bartlett, Tx., U.S.	222	30.48 N	97.26 W
Bartlett Brook ≃	283	42.42 N	71.13 W
Bartlett Cove	180	58.27 N	135.55 W
Bartlett Reservoir ⊜[1]	200	33.52 N	111.37 W
Bartletts ∧[2]	168a	32.19 S	116.43 E
Bartletts Harbour	186	50.57 N	57.00 W
Bartley	198	40.14 N	100.18 W
Bartolomé Bavio → General Mansilla	258	35.05 S	57.45 W
Bartolomé de las Casas	252	25.24 S	59.34 W
Bartolomeu de Gusmão, Aeroporto ⊠	256	22.56 S	43.43 W
Bartolomeu Dias	156	21.10 S	35.09 E
Barton, Austl.	162	30.31 S	132.39 E
Barton, N.Y., U.S.	210	42.03 N	76.27 W
Barton, Oh., U.S.	214	40.06 N	80.50 W
Barton, Vt., U.S.	188	44.44 N	72.10 W
Barton Aerodrome ⊠	262	53.28 N	2.23 W
Barton Lake	216	42.06 N	85.35 W
Barton Lake ⊜	184	52.00 N	94.06 W
Barton-le-Clay	42	51.57 N	0.25 W
Barton Mills	42	52.20 N	0.31 E
Barton Park ♠	274a	33.57 S	151.09 E
Barton Run ≃	285	39.53 N	74.51 W
Barton-under-Needwood	42	52.45 N	1.43 W
Barton-upon-Humber	44	53.41 N	0.27 W
Bartonville	190	40.39 N	89.39 W
Barton Water Swing Bridge ⬥[5]	262	53.28 N	2.21 W
Bartoszyce	30	54.16 N	20.49 E
Bartow, Fl., U.S.	220	27.53 N	81.50 W
Bartow, Ga., U.S.	192	32.52 N	82.28 W
Baru, Kali ≍	269e	6.10 S	106.51 E
Barú, Volcán ∧[1]	236	8.48 N	82.33 W
Barueri	256	23.31 S	46.53 W
Barugo	116	11.20 N	124.44 E
Bāruipāra	272b	22.46 N	88.14 E
Bāruipur	126	22.21 N	88.27 E
Bārūk, Jabal al- ∧	132	33.43 N	35.45 E
Barumini	71	39.42 N	9.00 E
Barumun ≃	114	2.30 N	100.09 E
Barun Bogd uul ∧	90	44.57 N	100.15 E
Barung, Nusa I	115a	8.28 S	113.20 E
Barun Su	102	42.27 N	111.01 E
Barun-Torej, ozero ⊜	88	50.10 N	115.30 E
Baruntse ∧	124	27.51 N	86.59 E
Barus	114	2.00 N	98.24 E
Baruta	286c	10.26 N	66.53 W
Baruth	54	52.03 N	13.30 E
Baruun Bajan-Ulaan	102	45.10 N	101.24 E
Baruun bogd uul ∧	102	44.57 N	100.15 E
Baruun-Urt	90	46.42 N	113.15 E
Barva, Volcán ∧[1]	236	10.08 N	84.06 W
Barvas	46	58.22 N	6.32 W
Barver	52	52.37 N	8.35 E
Barvicha	265b	55.44 N	37.16 E
Barview	202	43.21 N	124.18 W
Barvinkove	78	48.54 N	37.02 E
Barwa	126	23.51 N	86.26 E
Barwāh	120	22.16 N	76.03 E
Barwāla ⬥[8]	272a	28.46 N	77.04 E
Barwāni	120	22.02 N	74.54 E
Barwa Sāgar	124	25.23 N	78.44 E
Barwell	42	52.32 N	1.21 W
Barwice	30	53.45 N	16.22 E
Barwick	192	30.54 N	83.44 W
Barwidgee	162	27.02 S	120.54 E
Barwon ≃, Austl.	166	30.00 S	148.05 E
Barwon ≃, Austl.	169	38.13 S	144.25 E
Barwon Heads (South Barwon)	169	38.17 S	144.30 E
Barybino, Ross.	82	55.16 N	37.54 E
Barybino, Ross.	82	54.56 N	37.47 E
Barycz ≃	30	51.42 N	16.15 E
Barykova, mys ›	180	63.02 N	179.29 E
Barykovo	82	54.38 N	38.48 E
Barynino	82	55.47 N	36.21 E
Baryš	80	53.39 N	47.08 E
Baryš ≃	80	54.35 N	46.48 E
Barysau	76	54.15 N	28.30 E
Baryševo	86	54.58 N	83.11 E
Baryshivka	78	50.22 N	31.19 E
Baryšniki	80	56.57 N	46.33 E
Barzah	132	33.34 N	36.19 E
Barzas	86	55.43 N	86.19 E
Barzio	58	45.57 N	9.27 E
Basacato del Este	152	3.37 N	8.54 E
Basai Dārāpur ⬥[8]	272a	28.40 N	77.08 E
Bāsa' Īdū	128	26.39 N	55.17 E
Basail, Arg.	252	27.52 S	59.18 W
Bāsāil, Bngl.	126	24.14 N	90.04 E
Basakin	80	48.11 N	42.18 E
Basāl	123	33.33 N	72.15 E
Basalt ≃	166	19.38 S	145.52 E
Basalt Island I	271d	22.19 N	114.22 E
Basaluzzo	62	44.46 N	8.42 E
Basandīlah	142	31.12 N	31.26 E
Basankusu	152	1.14 N	19.48 E
Bašanta	80	46.05 N	41.56 E
Basanti	126	22.12 N	88.42 E
Basarabeasca	78	46.20 N	28.58 E
Basarabi	38	44.10 N	28.24 E
Basatongwula Shan ∧	120	33.05 N	91.30 E
Basavakalyān	122	17.52 N	76.57 E
Basavilbaso	252	32.22 S	58.53 W
Baščelakskij chrebet ≁	86	51.15 N	84.30 E
Baschi	66	42.40 N	12.13 E
Basco	108	20.27 N	121.58 E
Bascom	214	41.07 N	83.17 W
Bascuñán, Cabo ›	252	28.51 S	71.30 W
Basdahl	52	53.26 N	8.59 E
Basdorf	54	52.44 N	13.26 E
Basekpio	154	4.44 N	24.40 E
Basel (Bâle)	58	47.33 N	7.35 E
Baselga di Pinè	64	46.08 N	11.14 E
Baselice	68	41.24 N	14.58 E
Basel-Land ▫[3]	58	47.30 N	7.50 E
Basel-Stadt ▫[3]	58	47.38 N	7.40 E
Basen ≃	96	34.48 N	132.51 E
Bas-en-Basset	62	45.18 N	4.06 E
Basentello ≃	68	40.40 N	16.23 E
Basento ≃	68	40.21 N	16.50 E
Başeu ≃	38	47.44 N	27.15 E
Basey	116	11.17 N	125.04 E
Bashaw	182	52.35 N	112.58 W
Basher Kill ≃	210	41.27 N	74.35 W
Bashi Channel ʮ	108	22.00 N	121.00 E
Bashikejike	120	37.30 N	85.50 E
Bashiqiao	106	31.40 N	120.22 E
Bashkortostan → Baškirija ▫[3]	86	54.00 N	56.00 E
Bashtanka	78	47.24 N	32.25 E
Bashtīl	273c	30.05 N	31.11 E
Basi, India	123	30.36 N	76.50 E
Basi, India	123	30.41 N	76.24 E
Basiad Bay c	116	14.16 N	122.19 E
Basiano	112	1.16 S	122.50 E
Basibasy	157b	22.10 S	43.40 E
Başıbüyük ⬥[8]	267b	40.57 N	29.08 E
Basicò	70	38.04 N	15.04 E
Basid	85	38.07 N	72.09 E
Basilaki Island I	164	10.35 S	151.00 E
Basilan ▫[4]	116	6.35 N	121.55 E
Basilan Island I	116	6.34 N	122.03 E
Basilan Peak ∧	116	6.33 N	122.04 E
Basilan Strait ʮ	116	6.49 N	122.05 E
Basildon	42	51.35 N	0.25 E
Basildon ▫[8]	260	51.35 N	0.29 E
Basile	194	30.29 N	92.35 W
Basiliano	64	46.01 N	13.06 E
Basilicata ▫[4]	68	40.30 N	16.10 E
Basiluzzo, Isola I	70	38.39 N	15.07 E
Basin, Mt., U.S.	202	46.16 N	112.15 W
Basin, Wy., U.S.	202	44.22 N	108.02 W
Bäsingen ⊜	40	60.09 N	16.20 E
Basinger	220	27.24 N	81.01 W
Basingstoke	42	51.15 N	1.05 W
Basingstoke Canal ≍	260	51.21 N	0.29 W
Basingwerk Abbey ᵾ[1]	262	53.17 N	3.12 W
Basin Lake ⊜	184	52.38 N	105.18 W
Basīrhāt	126	22.40 N	88.53 E
Basīrpur	123	30.35 N	73.50 E
Basīṭ, Ra's al- ›	130	35.51 N	35.48 E
Basiyingzi	104	42.05 N	121.37 E
Basja ≃	76	53.46 N	31.01 E
Basjanovskij	86	58.19 N	60.44 E
Baška	36	44.58 N	14.46 E
Baskahegan Lake ⊜	188	45.30 N	67.48 W
Baskakovka	76	54.36 N	34.19 E
Başkale	128	38.02 N	44.00 E
Baskatong, Réservoir ⊜[1]	190	46.48 N	75.50 W
Baškaus ≃	86	51.09 N	87.43 E
Basket Lake ⊜	184	49.43 N	92.00 W
Basking Ridge	276	40.42 N	74.32 W
Baškino	82	55.18 N	36.41 E
Baškirija ▫[3], Ross.	72	54.00 N	56.00 E
Baškirija ▫[3], Ross.	86	54.00 N	56.00 E
Baškirskij zapovednik ♠	86	53.30 N	57.58 E
Baskomutan Milli Parkı ♠	130	38.50 N	30.05 E
Başköy	84	39.53 N	44.32 E
Baskuduk	86	49.43 N	61.32 E
Baš-Kugandy	85	42.00 N	74.39 E
Baskunčak, ozero ⊜	80	48.12 N	46.54 E
Baslow	44	53.15 N	1.38 W
Başmakçı	130	37.54 N	30.01 E
Bašmakovo	80	53.12 N	43.02 E
Basmat	122	19.19 N	77.10 E
Bäsna	40	60.32 N	15.12 E
Bāsoda	124	23.51 N	77.56 E
Basoko	152	1.14 N	23.36 E
Basoko ≃	273b	4.19 S	15.16 E
Basoli	123	32.30 N	75.49 E
Basom	210	43.04 N	78.24 W
Basongo	152	4.20 S	20.24 E
Basora, Punt ›	241s	12.25 N	69.52 W
Basovizza	64	45.38 N	13.52 E
Başpınar	130	39.12 N	38.42 E
Basque Lands → Euskal Herriko ▫[3]	34	43.00 N	2.30 W
Basra → Al-Baṣrah	128	30.30 N	47.47 E
Bas-Rhin ▫[5]	32	48.35 N	7.40 E
Bass ≃	169	38.30 S	145.26 E
Bassano	182	50.47 N	112.28 W
Bassano del Grappa	64	45.46 N	11.44 E
Bassari	150	9.15 N	0.47 E
Bassas da India ✢[2]	138	21.25 S	39.42 E
Bass Creek ≃	216	42.37 N	89.04 W
Basse-Californie → Baja California ›[1]	232	28.00 N	113.30 W
Bassecourt	58	47.20 N	7.15 E
Bassein → Pathein	110	16.47 N	94.44 E
Bassein ≃[1]	110	15.56 N	94.18 E
Basse-Kotto ▫[5]	152	5.00 N	21.30 E
Bassella	34	42.01 N	1.18 E
Bassen	52	53.04 N	9.04 E
Bassendean	168a	31.55 S	115.56 E
Bassenthwaite	44	54.41 N	3.12 W
Bassenthwaite Lake ⊜	44	54.38 N	3.13 W
Basse-Pointe	240e	14.52 N	61.07 W
Basses, Pointe des ›	241o	15.52 N	61.17 W
Basse Santa Su	150	13.19 N	14.13 W
Basse-Terre, Guad.	241o	16.00 N	61.44 W
Basseterre, St. K.-N.	238	17.18 N	62.43 W
Basse Terre, Trin.	241r	10.08 N	61.18 W
Basse-Terre I	241o	16.10 N	61.40 W
Bassett, Ne., U.S.	198	42.35 N	99.32 W
Bassett, Va., U.S.	192	36.45 N	79.59 W
Bassett Creek ≃	194	31.25 N	87.56 W
Bassett Peak ∧	200	32.30 N	110.17 W
Bassfield	194	31.30 N	89.44 W
Bass Harbor	188	44.14 N	68.20 W
Bass Hill	274a	33.54 S	151.00 E
Bassignana	62	45.00 N	8.44 E
Bassikounou	150	15.52 N	5.57 W
Bassila	150	9.01 N	1.40 E
Bassin des Aghlabites ⊥	36	35.43 N	10.10 E
Bassingbourn	42	52.04 N	0.03 W
Bass Lake, Ca., U.S.	226	37.19 N	119.33 W

Symbol	English	Deutsch	Español	Français	Português
≃	River	Fluß	Río	Rivière	Rio
≍	Canal	Kanal	Canal	Canal	Canal
∟	Waterfall, Rapids	Wasserfall, Stromschnellen	Cascada, Rápidos	Chute d'eau, Rapides	Cascata, Rápidos
ʮ	Strait	Meeresstraße	Estrecho	Détroit	Estreito
c	Bay, Gulf	Bucht, Golf	Bahía, Golfo	Baie, Golfe	Baía, Golfo
⊜	Lake, Lakes	See, Seen	Lago, Lagos	Lac, Lacs	Lago, Lagos
≋	Swamp	Sumpf	Pantano	Marais	Pântano
⊓	Ice Features, Glacier	Eis- und Gletscherformen	Accidentes Glaciales	Formes glaciaires	Acidentes glaciares
⊤	Other Hydrographic Features	Andere Hydrographische Objekte	Otros Elementos Hidrográficos	Autres données hydrographiques	Outros acidentes hidrográficos
✢	Submarine Features	Untermeerische Objekte	Accidentes Submarinos	Formes de relief sous-marin	Acidentes submarinos
▫	Political Unit	Politische Einheit	Unidad Politica	Entité politique	Unidade política
ᵾ	Cultural Institution	Kulturelle Institution	Institución Cultural	Institution culturelle	Instituição cultural
⊥	Historical Site	Historische Stätte	Sitio Histórico	Site historique	Sitio histórico
♠	Recreational Site	Erholungs- und Ferienort	Sitio de Recreo	Centre de loisirs	Area de Lazer
⊠	Airport	Flughafen	Aeropuerto	Aéroport	Aeroporto
■	Military Installation	Militäranlage	Instalación Militar	Installation militaire	Instalação militar
⬥	Miscellaneous	Verschiedenes	Misceláneo	Divers	Diversos

Column 1

Bass Lake, In., U.S. 216 41.12 N 86.36 W
Bass Lake ⊜, On., Can. 212 44.49 N 76.08 W
Bass Lake ⊜, In., U.S. 216 41.13 N 86.36 W
Bass Lake ⊜¹ 216 37.19 N 119.34 W
Bass Point ▸ 170 34.36 S 150.54 E
Bass River 186 45.25 N 63.47 W
Bass Strait ⊔ 166 39.20 S 145.30 E
Bassum 52 52.51 N 8.43 E
Basswood Lake ⊜, On., Can. 190 46.20 N 83.23 W
Basswood Lake ⊜, N.A. 190 48.06 N 91.40 W
Basta 126 21.41 N 87.03 E
Båstad 26 56.26 N 12.51 E
Bastah 132 30.14 N 35.32 E
Bastak 128 27.14 N 54.22 E
Bastām 128 36.29 N 55.04 E
Bastei ♦ 54 50.58 N 14.04 E
Bastelica 36 42.00 N 9.02 E
Basti 124 26.48 N 82.43 E
Bastia, Fr. 36 42.42 N 9.27 E
Bastia, It. 66 43.04 N 12.33 E
Bastian 192 37.09 N 81.09 W
Bastiglia 64 44.43 N 11.00 E
Bastimentos 236 9.21 N 82.12 W
Bastimentos, Isla I 236 9.18 N 82.08 W
Bastogne 56 50.06 N 5.43 E
Bastrop, La., U.S. 194 32.46 N 91.54 W
Bastrop, Tx., U.S. 222 30.06 N 97.18 W
Bastrop □⁶ 222 33.00 N 97.18 W
Bastrop, Lake ⊜¹ 222 30.09 N 97.18 W
Bastrop Bay c 222 29.06 N 95.11 W
Bastrop State Park ♦ 222 30.07 N 97.17 W
Basturträsk 26 64.47 N 20.02 E
Basu, Pulau I 112 0.18 S 103.36 E
Basubäti 272b 22.47 N 88.12 E
Bāsudebpur, India 126 21.49 N 87.38 E
Bāsudebpur, India 272b 22.49 N 88.25 E
Basuo → Dongfang 110 19.05 N 108.39 E
Bāsūs 273c 30.08 N 31.13 E
Baswa 126 24.08 N 87.52 E
Basyūn 142 30.57 N 30.49 E
Bas-Zaïre □⁴ 152 5.30 S 14.30 E
Bata 152 1.51 N 9.45 E
Bataan □⁴ 116 14.40 N 120.25 E
Bataan, Mount ⋀ 116 14.40 N 120.25 E
Bataan Peninsula ⋗¹ 116 14.40 N 120.25 E
Batabanó 240p 22.43 N 82.17 W
Batabanó, Golfo de c 240p 22.15 N 82.30 W
Batac 116 18.05 N 120.35 E
Batad 116 11.25 N 123.06 E
Batagaj 74 67.38 N 134.38 E
Batagaj-Alyta 74 67.48 N 130.25 E
Batag Island I 116 12.38 N 125.04 E
Batagol 88 52.22 N 100.45 E
Bataguassu 255 21.42 S 52.22 W
Bataiporã 255 22.20 S 53.17 W
Batajsk 83 47.10 N 39.44 E
Batak 38 41.57 N 24.13 E
Batak, Jazovir ⊜¹ 38 41.59 N 24.11 E
Batakan 112 4.05 S 114.38 E
Batala 123 31.48 N 75.12 E
Batalha, Bra. 250 9.41 S 37.08 W
Batalha, Bra. 250 4.01 S 42.05 W
Batalha, Port. 34 39.39 N 8.50 W
Bataly 86 52.52 N 62.00 E
Batam, Pulau I 112 1.05 N 104.03 E
Batama, Ross. 88 53.53 N 101.36 E
Batama, R.D.C. 154 0.56 N 26.39 E
Batamaj 74 63.31 N 129.27 E
Batamšinskij 86 50.36 N 58.16 E
Batan, Pil. 116 11.35 N 122.30 E
Batan, Zhg. 98 34.10 N 104.59 E
Batanagar 126 22.31 N 88.15 E
Batang, Indon. 115a 6.55 S 109.45 E
Batang, Zhg. 102 30.02 N 99.02 E
Batangas 152 7.18 N 18.18 E
Batangas 116 13.45 N 121.03 E
Batangas □⁴ 116 13.45 N 121.00 E
Batangas Bay c 116 13.43 N 121.00 E
Batangbatangdaya 115a 6.56 S 113.59 E
Batang Berjuntai 114 3.23 N 101.25 E
Batang Kali 114 3.28 N 101.38 E
Batangoru 114 1.29 N 99.03 E
Batan Island I, Pil. 108 20.26 N 121.58 E
Batan Island I, Pil. 116 13.15 N 124.00 E
Batan Islands II 108 20.30 N 121.50 E
Batanta, Pulau I 164 0.50 S 130.40 E
Batas 287a 22.44 S 43.24 W
Batas Island I 116 11.10 N 119.36 E
Bátaszék 30 46.12 N 18.44 E
Batatais 255 20.53 S 47.37 W
Batatuba 256 23.04 S 46.25 W
Batavia, Arg. 252 34.47 S 65.41 W
Batavia, Il., U.S. 216 45.18 N 88.18 W
Batavia, N.Y., U.S. 190 40.59 N 92.10 W
Batavia, Mi., U.S. 216 41.53 N 85.03 W
Batavia, N.Y., U.S. 210 42.59 N 78.11 W
Batavia, Oh., U.S. 218 39.04 N 84.10 W
Batawa 212 44.10 N 77.36 W
Batbatan Island I 116 11.28 N 121.55 E
Batcengel 88 47.47 N 101.58 E
Batchawana ⋍ 190 46.55 N 84.32 W
Batchawana Mountain ⋀ 190 47.04 N 84.24 W
Batchawana Island I 190 46.53 N 84.30 W
Batchelor 164 36.53 N 131.01 E
Bátdâmbâng 110 13.06 N 103.12 E
Bate Bay c 170 34.04 S 151.12 E
Bateckij 22 58.39 N 30.19 E
Batéké, Plateaux ⋌¹ 152 3.30 S 15.45 E
Batemans Bay 166 35.43 S 150.11 E
Batenbrock ⋗⁸ 263 51.30 N 6.57 E
Batepito ▸ 263 19.09 N 109.11 W
Bates, Mount ⋀ 174c 29.01 S 167.56 E
Batesburg 192 33.54 N 81.32 W
Bates Creek ≏ 200 42.48 N 106.37 W
Bates Range ⋀ 162 27.25 S 121.13 E
Batesville, Ar., U.S. 194 35.46 N 91.38 W
Batesville, In., U.S. 218 39.18 N 85.13 W
Batesville, Ms., U.S. 194 34.18 N 89.56 W
Batesville, Tx., U.S. 196 28.57 N 99.37 W
Bath, N.B., Can. 186 46.31 N 67.36 W
Bath, Eng., U.K. 42 44.11 N 76.47 W
Bath, Eng., U.K. 42 51.23 N 2.22 W
Bath, Me., U.S. 188 43.54 N 69.49 W
Bath, Mi., U.S. 216 42.49 N 84.26 W
Bath, N.Y., U.S. 210 42.20 N 77.19 W
Bath, Pa., U.S. 210 40.43 N 75.23 W
Bath □⁶ 218 38.18 N 83.48 W
Batha ⊔⁶ 146 14.00 N 19.00 E
Batha ⋍ 146 12.47 N 17.34 E
Bath Addition 285 40.06 N 74.52 W
Bathgate, Scot., U.K. 46 55.55 N 3.39 W
Bathgate, N.D., U.S. 198 48.52 N 97.28 W
Bathinda 241g 30.12 N 74.57 E
Bathsheba 241g 13.13 N 59.31 W
Bathurst, Austl. 166 33.25 S 149.35 E
Bathurst 186 47.36 N 65.39 W
Bathurst → Banjul, Gam. 150 13.28 N 16.39 W
Bathurst, S. Afr. 158 33.30 S 26.50 E
Bathurst, Cape ▸ 170 35.04 S 149.44 E
Bathurst 160 66.50 N 108.01 W
Bathurst Inlet 176 68.10 N 108.50 W
Bathurst Island I, Austl. 164 11.37 S 130.23 E
Bathurst Island I, N.T., Can. 16 76.00 N 100.30 W
Bathurst Island Aboriginal Reserve ⋋ 164 11.37 S 130.23 E
Bati 144 11.10 N 40.02 E
Batia 150 10.54 N 1.29 E

Column 2

Batiãgarh 124 24.07 N 79.21 E
Batié 150 9.53 N 2.55 W
Bâtin, Wâdî al- ⋁ 128 29.35 N 47.00 E
Batina 38 45.51 N 18.51 E
Batiquitos Lagoon c 228 33.05 N 117.18 W
Batif 132 31.16 N 35.42 E
Batiscan ≏ 206 46.31 N 72.15 W
Batiste Creek ≏ 222 30.04 N 94.28 W
Batkanu 150 9.05 N 12.25 W
Batken 85 40.03 N 70.50 E
Batley 44 53.44 N 1.37 W
Batlow 171b 35.31 S 148.09 E
Batman □⁴ 130 37.52 N 41.07 E
Batman ⋍⁴ 130 38.00 N 41.15 E
Batna 188 35.34 N 6.11 E
Batn al-Ghūl 132 29.44 N 35.52 E
Batnorov 88 47.55 N 111.30 E
Batō, Nihon 94 36.44 N 140.10 E
Bato, Pil. 116 10.20 N 124.47 E
Ba To, Viet 110 14.46 N 108.44 E
Bato, Lake ⊜ 116 13.19 N 123.21 E
Batoala 112 0.48 N 13.27 E
Batoche Rectory National Historic Site ⋋ 184 52.41 N 106.02 W
Batoka 154 16.47 S 27.15 E
Baton Rouge 194 30.27 N 91.09 W
Batopilas 123 33.06 N 75.19 E
Batorampon Point ▸ 116 7.07 N 121.54 E
Batouri 152 4.26 N 14.22 E
Batpajsagyr, peski ⋍² 80 47.20 N 48.40 E
Batrā (Petra) I 132 30.20 N 35.26 E
Batrā', Jibāl al- ⋀ 132 29.53 N 35.38 E
Batrah 142 31.10 N 31.27 E
Ba Tri 110 10.02 N 106.36 E
Batsawul 120 34.15 N 70.52 E
Batson 222 30.15 N 94.37 W
Batsto ≏ 285 39.39 N 74.39 W
Batsto, Skit Branch ≏ 285 39.46 N 74.41 W
Batsto State Historic Site ♦ 285 39.39 N 74.39 W
Bat Sümber 88 48.29 N 106.42 E
Battaglia Terme 64 45.17 N 11.47 E
Battambang → Bâtdâmbâng 110 13.06 N 103.12 E
Battenberg 56 51.01 N 8.38 E
Batten Kill ≏ 188 43.06 N 73.35 W
Batterie, Pointe de la ⋗ 240e 14.44 N 60.54 W
Bätterkinden 58 47.08 N 7.32 E
Battersea ⋗⁸ 260 51.28 N 0.10 W
Battersea Park ♦ 260 51.29 N 0.09 W
Batticaloa 122 7.43 N 81.42 E
Battice 56 50.39 N 5.49 E
Battin 224 45.29 N 122.34 W
Battiglia 68 40.37 N 14.58 E
Battle 42 50.55 N 0.29 E
Battle ≏ 176 52.43 N 108.15 W
Battle Creek, Ia., U.S. 198 42.18 N 95.35 W
Battle Creek, Mi., U.S. 216 42.19 N 85.10 W
Battle Creek, Ne., U.S. 198 41.59 N 97.35 W
Battle Creek ≏, N.A. 202 48.36 N 109.11 W
Battle Creek ≏, Ca., U.S. 204 40.21 N 122.11 W
Battle Creek ≏, Id., U.S. 202 42.14 N 116.32 W
Battle Creek ≏, Tx., U.S. 216 42.19 N 85.12 W
Battle Creek, North Fork ≏ 204 40.26 N 122.00 W
Battle Creek, South Fork ≏ 204 40.26 N 122.00 W
Battlefields 154 18.31 S 29.52 E
Battle Green I 283 42.27 N 71.14 W
Battle Ground, In., U.S. 216 40.30 N 86.50 W
Battle Ground, Wa., U.S. 224 45.46 N 122.31 W
Battle Harbour 176 52.16 N 55.35 W
Battle Lake 198 46.16 N 95.42 W
Battlement Mesa ⋀ 200 39.20 N 108.00 W
Battle Mountain 204 40.38 N 116.56 W
Battle Mountain ⋀ 200 41.02 N 107.16 W
Battleshridge 290 51.37 N 0.34 E
Battonya 30 46.17 N 21.00 E
Batu, Bukit ⋀ 115b 8.20 S 115.05 E
Batu, Kepulauan II 112 0.18 N 115.01 E
Batuan 114 3.19 N 101.28 E
Batuata, Pulau I 112 6.12 S 122.42 E
Batuata, Tanjung ▸ 115b 9.37 S 120.29 E
Batu-Batu 114 4.09 S 119.52 E
Batu Berinchang, Gunong ⋀ 114 4.30 N 101.24 E
Batubetumpang 112 2.53 S 106.09 E
Batubrok, Bukit ⋀ 112 1.10 N 114.36 E
Batu Caves 114 3.14 N 101.40 E
Batudaka, Pulau I 112 0.28 S 121.48 E
Batu Enam 114 2.35 N 102.43 E
Batu Gajah 114 4.28 N 101.03 E
Batuku 112 1.15 S 122.10 E
Batu, Pegunungan ⋀ 112 1.15 S 102.10 E
Batuku 112 10.38 S 123.25 E
Batukau, Bukit ⋀ 115b 8.20 S 115.05 E
Batukelau 112 0.48 N 115.01 E
Batu Laut 112 2.41 N 101.31 E
Batu-Batu 112 3.27 S 116.00 E
Batumata Point ⋗ 112 10.17 S 148.57 E
Batuan 84 41.38 N 41.38 E
Batumundan 114 1.17 N 98.50 E
Batu Pahat (Bandar Penggaram) 114 1.51 N 102.56 E
Batupanjang 114 1.43 N 101.31 E
Batu Puteh, Gunong ⋀ 114 4.13 N 101.27 E
Batuputih 112 1.24 N 118.29 E
Baturaja 112 4.08 S 104.10 E
Batu Rakit 114 5.29 N 103.03 E
Baturetno 115a 7.59 S 110.56 E
Baturino, Ross. 88 57.48 N 85.12 E
Baturino, Ross. 265b 55.35 N 37.31 E
Baturinskaja 78 45.47 N 39.22 E
Baturité 250 4.20 S 38.53 W
Baturotok 115b 8.42 S 117.10 E
Batutinggi 112 2.02 S 106.07 E
Baturyn 78 51.21 N 32.54 E
Batusangkar 112 0.27 S 100.35 E
Batutinggi 112 1.55 S 113.19 E
Batyrevo 54 55.04 N 47.38 E
Batyr-Mala, ozero ⊜ 80 45.01 N 44.45 E
Baú ≏ 250 1.25 N 10.08 E
Baú ⋍ 250 7.26 S 54.47 W
Baubašata, gory ⋗ 85 40.31 N 72.45 E
Baucau 164 8.28 S 126.27 E
Baud 32 47.52 N 3.01 W
Bauda 36 50.29 N 3.49 E
Bauernschaft ⋗⁸ 263 51.34 N 6.33 E
Bauerstown 279b 40.31 N 79.57 W
Baugo Creek ≏ 216 41.40 N 86.04 W
Baukau 112 8.27 S 126.27 E
BAuland ⋗ 56 49.31 N 9.29 E
Bauld, Cape ▸ 186 51.38 N 55.25 W

Column 3

Baulkham Hills 274a 33.46 S 151.00 E
Baulmes 58 46.48 N 6.32 E
Bauma 58 47.23 N 8.53 E
Baumberg 263 51.07 N 6.54 E
Baume ⋍ 62 44.26 N 4.20 E
Baume-les-Dames 58 47.21 N 6.22 E
Baumholder 56 49.37 N 7.20 E
Baumschulenweg ⋗⁸ 264a 52.28 N 13.29 E
Baun 112 10.18 S 123.43 E
Baunach 56 49.59 N 10.50 E
Baunach ≏ 56 49.59 N 10.51 E
Baunatal 56 51.16 N 9.25 E
Baunei 71 40.02 N 9.40 E
Baunt 88 55.16 N 113.08 E
Baunt, ozero ⊜ 88 55.12 N 113.00 E
Bauphal 126 22.25 N 90.33 E
Baure 150 12.50 N 8.45 E
Baures 255 22.19 S 49.04 W
Baús 255 18.19 S 53.10 W
Bausendorf 56 50.01 N 6.59 E
Bausenhagen 263 51.31 N 7.48 E
Bauska 76 56.24 N 24.14 E
Bauta 240p 22.59 N 82.33 W
Bauta □⁷ 286b 22.59 N 82.33 W
Bautino 84 44.33 N 50.15 E
Bautzen 54 51.11 N 14.26 E
Bauxite 194 34.33 N 92.31 W
Bauya 150 8.11 N 12.34 W
Bavani 58 47.29 N 6.44 E
Bavari 62 44.26 N 9.01 E
Bavaria — Bayern □³ 30 49.00 N 11.30 E
Bavarian Alps — Bayerische Alpen ⋀ 64 47.30 N 11.00 E
Båven ⊜ 40 59.01 N 16.56 E
Baveno 58 45.55 N 8.30 E
Bavilliers 58 47.37 N 6.50 E
Bavispe 232 30.24 N 108.50 W
Bavispe ≏ 232 29.15 N 109.11 W
Bavleny 80 56.24 N 39.34 E
Bavly 80 54.25 N 53.17 E
Bawnhöj ⋀² 41 55.55 N 10.07 E
Bavtugaj 84 43.11 N 46.49 E
Baw 110 23.19 N 95.50 E
Bawal 124 28.05 N 76.35 E
Bawal, Pulau I 112 2.44 S 110.06 E
Båwäli 272b 22.25 N 88.12 E
Bawang 115a 7.06 S 109.55 E
Baw Baw, Mount ⋀ 169 37.50 S 146.17 E
Baw Baw National Park ♦ 169 37.55 S 146.22 E
Baw Beese Lake ⊜ 216 41.54 N 84.36 W
Bawdeswell 42 52.45 N 1.01 E
Bawdwin 110 23.06 N 97.18 E
Bawean, Pulau I 115a 5.46 S 112.40 E
Baweigang 106 31.57 N 120.14 E
Bawinkel 52 52.36 N 7.25 E
Bawku 150 11.05 N 0.14 W
Bawlake 110 19.11 N 97.21 E
Bawmi 117 17.19 N 94.35 E
Bawria 126 22.29 N 88.10 E
Bawtry 44 53.26 N 1.01 W
Baxdo 144 5.46 N 47.15 E
Baxenden 262 53.44 N 2.20 W
Baxian, Zhg. 105 39.06 N 116.23 E
Baxian (Yudongxi), Zhg. 107 29.23 N 106.32 E
Baxian, Zhg. 192 31.46 N 82.20 W
Baxley, Ga., U.S. 192 31.46 N 82.20 W
Baxter, Ia., U.S. 198 41.49 N 93.09 W
Baxter, Mn., U.S. 190 46.20 N 94.17 W
Baxter, Tn., U.S. 194 36.09 N 85.38 W
Baxter Estates 276 40.50 N 73.42 W
Baxter Springs 198 37.02 N 94.44 W
Baxter State Park ♦ 188 46.00 N 69.00 W
Baxterville 194 31.05 N 89.35 W
Bay 194 35.44 N 90.33 W
Bay, Laguna de ⊜ 116 14.23 N 121.15 E
Baya, R.D.C. 152 4.57 N 19.43 E
Baya, R.D.C. 154 11.52 S 27.27 E
Bayādah, Wādī al- ⋁ 146 26.08 N 18.35 E
Bayād an-Naşārā 142 29.04 N 31.08 E
Bayaga 116 18.16 N 121.02 E
Bay al-Kabīr, Wādī ⋁ 146 31.15 N 15.57 E
Bayamamang 116 15.49 N 120.27 E
Bayamo 240p 20.23 N 76.39 W
Bayamo ≏ 240m 20.21 N 76.28 W
Bayamón 240m 18.24 N 66.09 W
Bayan, Azer. 106 40.34 N 46.09 E
Bayan, Indon. 115b 8.16 S 116.26 E
Bayan, Zhg. 89 46.05 N 127.24 E
Bãyan, Band-e ⋀ 120 34.20 N 65.30 E
Bayanai 124 26.54 N 77.17 E
Bayanbayanan 269f 44.39 N 121.06 E
Bayanchagan 98 44.19 N 114.03 E
Bayang 116 7.48 N 124.12 E
Bayanga 152 2.53 N 16.19 E
Bayange 102 39.19 N 100.37 E
Bayan Har Shan ⋀ 102 33.48 N 98.10 E
Bayanhushuomiao 98 48.51 N 119.46 E
Bayanle 89 46.39 N 124.37 E
Bayanlü 98 50.52 N 119.33 E
Bayannaobao 102 39.44 N 107.40 E
Bayano, Lago ⊜¹ 246 9.10 N 78.40 W
Bayan Obo 98 41.58 N 110.02 E
Bayan Tal 89 43.44 N 123.16 E
Bayard, Ia., U.S. 198 41.51 N 94.33 W
Bayard, Ne., U.S. 198 41.45 N 103.20 W
Bayard, N.M., U.S. 200 32.46 N 108.07 W
Bayard, Oh., U.S. 214 40.46 N 81.04 W
Bayard, W.V., U.S. 188 39.16 N 79.21 W
Bayard, Col ⋊ 62 44.37 N 6.05 E
Bayard Cutting Arboretum State Park ♦ 276 40.45 N 73.10 W
Bayat, Indon. 112 2.06 S 103.38 E
Bayat, Tür. 130 38.59 N 30.56 E
Bayat, Tür. 130 40.39 N 34.15 E
Bayawan 116 9.22 N 122.48 E
Bayawan ≏ 116 9.22 N 122.49 E
Baybay 116 10.41 N 124.48 E
Bayberry 285 43.08 N 76.13 W
Baybora 192 35.08 N 76.46 W
Bay Bulls 186 47.19 N 52.49 W
Bayburt 84 40.15 N 40.15 E
Bay Center 224 46.37 N 124.00 W
Bay City, Mi., U.S. 190 43.35 N 83.53 W
Bay City, Or., U.S. 224 45.31 N 123.53 W
Bay City, Tx., U.S. 222 28.58 N 95.58 W
Bay City ⊜, Il., U.S. 194 37.16 N 88.31 W
Bay Creek ≏, Il., U.S. 194 37.16 N 88.31 W
Baydā, Bi'r ⊤⁴ 132 29.45 N 32.13 E
Bay de Verde 186 48.05 N 52.54 W
Baydhabo (Baidoa) 144 3.07 N 43.39 E
Bay du Nord ≏ 186 47.44 N 55.25 W
Bayel 58 48.12 N 4.47 E
Bayerisch Eisenstein 56 49.07 N 13.12 E
Bayerischer Wald, Nationalpark ♦ 60 48.56 N 13.26 E
Bayern □³ 30 49.00 N 11.00 E
Bayes, Cap ⋗ 175f 20.57 S 165.25 E
Bayeux, Bra. 250 7.08 S 34.56 W
Bayeux, Fr. 32 49.16 N 0.42 W
Bay Farm Island I 282 37.43 N 122.14 W
Bayfield, Co., U.S. 200 37.13 N 107.36 W
Bayfield, Wi., U.S. 190 46.49 N 90.49 W
Bayfield, Île I 186 51.13 N 58.41 W
Bayford 260 51.46 N 0.06 W
'Bayh 132 33.44 N 35.31 E

Column 4

Bayḥān al-Qaşāḍ 144 14.48 N 45.43 E
Bay Harbor Islands 220 25.53 N 80.08 W
Bayhead, Scot., U.K. 46 57.33 N 7.24 W
Bay Head, N.J., U.S. 208 40.04 N 74.03 W
Bayiji 98 34.18 N 117.41 E
Bayindir 130 38.13 N 27.40 E
Bayingzi 104 41.28 N 120.46 E
Baykan 130 38.09 N 41.47 E
Baykonur → Bajkonyr 86 47.50 N 66.03 E
Beagle, Canal ⊔ 254 54.53 S 68.10 W
Beagle Bay 162 16.58 S 122.40 E
Bay L'Argent 186 47.33 N 54.54 W
Bayley Point ▸ 164 16.56 S 139.02 E
Baylis 219 39.44 N 90.54 W
Bay Meadows Race Track ♦ 282 37.32 N 122.18 W
Bay Minette 194 30.52 N 87.46 W
Baynūnah ⋍¹ 128 23.50 N 52.50 E
Bayombong 116 16.29 N 121.09 E
Bayon 58 48.29 N 6.19 E
Bayonne, Fr. 32 43.29 N 1.29 W
Bayonne, N.J., U.S. 208 40.40 N 74.06 W
Bayonne, N.J., U.S. 206 46.05 N 73.10 W
Bayonne Bridge ⋗⁸ 276 40.38 N 74.09 W
Bayons 62 44.20 N 6.10 E
Bayou Bodcau ≏ 194 32.45 N 93.30 W
Bayou Cane 194 29.37 N 90.45 W
Bayou D'Arbonne Lake ⊜¹ 194 32.45 N 92.25 W
Bayou La Batre 194 30.24 N 88.14 W
Bayovar 248 5.50 S 81.03 W
Bay Park 164 40.38 N 73.40 W
Bayport, Fl., U.S. 176 75.47 N 87.00 W
Bayport, Mn., U.S. 190 45.01 N 92.46 W
Bayport, N.Y., U.S. 210 40.44 N 73.03 W
Bayramiç 130 39.48 N 26.37 E
Bayramören 130 40.57 N 33.12 E
Bayreuth 60 49.57 N 11.35 E
Bay Ridge 188 43.05 N 71.26 W
Bay Ridge ⋗⁸ 276 40.37 N 74.02 W
Bay Ridge Channel ⊔ 276 40.39 N 74.02 W
Bayrischzell 60 47.40 N 12.00 E
Bay Roberts 186 47.36 N 53.16 W
Bayrūt (Beirut) 130 33.53 N 35.30 E
Bayrūt □⁴ 130 33.56 N 35.30 E
Bays, Lake of ⊜ 212 45.15 N 79.04 W
Bay Saint Louis 194 30.18 N 89.19 W
Bay Shore 210 40.43 N 73.14 W
Bayshore Gardens 220 27.25 N 82.35 W
Bayside, On., Can. 212 44.07 N 77.30 W
Bayside, Ca., U.S. 283 42.18 N 70.53 W
Bayside, Wi., U.S. 216 43.10 N 87.54 W
Bayside ⋗⁸ 276 40.46 N 73.46 W
Bay Springs 194 31.58 N 89.17 W
Bay Springs Lake ⊜¹ 194 34.35 N 88.20 W
Bayston Hill 42 52.40 N 2.45 W
Bayswater 162 31.54 N 115.56 E
Bayswater North 274b 37.51 S 145.17 E
Bayt ad-Dīn 132 33.42 N 35.35 E
Bayt Hānūn 132 31.32 N 34.33 E
Bayt Jālā 132 31.43 N 35.11 E
Bayt Jinn 132 33.19 N 35.53 E
Bayt Lahm (Bethlehem) 132 31.43 N 35.12 E
Bayt Mirī 132 33.52 N 35.36 E
Baytown 222 29.44 N 94.58 W
Bayt Şāḥūr 132 31.43 N 35.13 E
Bayt Şīrā 132 31.54 N 35.03 E
Bayunglecir 112 2.03 S 103.41 E
Bayview, Austl. 274a 33.40 S 151.18 E
Bay View, N.Z. 172 39.25 S 176.53 E
Bay View, N.Y., U.S. 210 42.47 N 78.51 W
Bay View, Oh., U.S. 214 41.28 N 82.50 W
Bayville, N.J., U.S. 208 39.54 N 74.09 W
Bayville, N.Y., U.S. 210 40.54 N 73.33 W
Baywater 168a 31.55 S 115.56 E
Baywood Park 228 35.20 N 120.50 W
Bayyāḍ Iyah al-Kabīrah 130 35.42 N 37.09 E
Bayyūdah ⋍⁴ 150 17.32 N 32.07 E
Baza 34 37.29 N 2.46 W
Bazai 188 24.32 N 114.10 E
Bazainville 261 48.48 N 1.40 E
Bazardüzü dağ ⋀ 84 41.13 N 47.51 E
Bãzãr-e Panjvā'ī 120 31.32 N 65.28 E
Bazargic → Dobrič 38 34.20 N 27.50 E
Bazar-Kurgan 85 41.02 N 72.45 E
Bazarnyy Mataki 80 54.53 N 50.10 E
Bazarny Karabulak 80 52.16 N 46.25 E
Bazarnyj Syzgan 80 53.45 N 46.46 E
Bazarovo 82 54.47 N 38.10 E
Bazartobe 82 49.23 N 51.50 E
Bazas 32 44.26 N 0.13 W
Bazaruk ⋍ 78 47.34 N 34.04 E
Bazdār 120 26.21 N 65.03 E
Bazeilles 261 49.40 N 4.59 E
Bazemont 261 48.56 N 1.52 E
Bazhong 102 31.52 N 106.39 E
Baziège 32 43.27 N 1.37 E
Bazitan 102 40.34 N 104.00 E
Bazine 198 38.26 N 99.41 W
Bazkovskaja 83 49.36 N 41.43 E
Bazmān 120 27.49 N 60.12 E
Bazmān, Kūh-e ⋀ 128 28.04 N 60.01 E
Bazoches-les-Gallerandes 58 48.10 N 2.03 E
Bazoches-sur-Hoëne 58 48.35 N 0.28 E
Bazoj 144 5.45 N 49.45 E
Bazzano 64 44.30 N 11.05 E
Be, Nosy I 157b 13.20 S 48.15 E
Beach, N.D., U.S. 198 46.55 N 104.00 W
Beach, N.D., U.S. 222 35.08 N 95.29 W
Beach Channel ≏ 276 40.35 N 73.50 W
Beach City 214 40.39 N 81.34 W
Beach City Lake ⊜¹ 214 40.39 N 81.36 W
Beach Glen 276 40.56 N 74.29 W
Beach Haven, N.J., U.S. 208 39.33 N 74.14 W
Beach Haven, Pa., U.S. 210 41.04 N 76.11 W
Beach Haven Terrace 208 39.36 N 74.13 W
Beach Lake 210 41.36 N 75.09 W
Beach Pond State Park ♦ 207 41.35 N 71.45 W
Beachport 166 37.30 S 140.01 E
Beach Run ≏ 214 40.05 N 80.49 W
Beachville 212 43.05 N 80.49 W
Beachwood, N.J., U.S. 208 39.56 N 74.11 W
Beachwood, Oh., U.S. 214 41.28 N 81.30 W
Beachy Head ⋗ 42 50.44 N 0.16 E
Beacon, Austl. 162 30.26 S 117.51 E
Beacon, N.Y., U.S. 210 41.30 N 73.58 W
Beacon Falls 207 41.26 N 73.03 W
Beacon Hill, Austl. 274a 33.45 S 151.15 E
Beacon Hill ⋗, Zhg. 271d 22.21 N 114.09 E
Beacon Hill ⋗, Wales, U.K. 271 53.19 N 3.12 W
Beacon Rock State Park ♦ 224 45.38 N 122.03 W

Column 5

Beasley 222 29.30 N 95.55 W
Beasley Bay c 208 37.51 N 75.44 W
Beason 219 40.09 N 89.12 W
Beata, Cabo ▸ 238 17.36 N 71.25 W
Beata, Isla I 238 17.35 N 71.31 W
Beatenberg 58 46.42 N 7.48 E
Beato ⋗⁸ 266c 38.44 N 9.06 W
Beaton 182 50.44 N 117.44 W
Beatrice, Ne., U.S. 198 40.16 N 96.44 W
Beatrice, Zimb. 154 18.15 S 30.55 E
Beatrice, Cape ▸ 164 14.15 S 136.59 E
Beattie 198 39.51 N 96.25 W
Beattock 44 55.18 N 3.28 W
Beatton ≏ 176 56.10 N 120.25 W
Beatty, Nv., U.S. 204 36.54 N 116.45 W
Beatty, Oh., U.S. 218 39.53 N 83.50 W
Beatty Saugeen ≏ 212 44.08 N 81.02 W
Beattyville 192 37.34 N 83.42 W
Beaubru 58 49.46 N 5.05 E
Beaucaire 62 43.48 N 4.38 E
Beauce ⋗¹ 58 48.22 N 1.50 E
Beauceville 188 46.12 N 70.46 W
Beauchamp 261 49.01 N 2.12 E
Beauchamp Roding 260 51.44 N 0.18 E
Beauchêne Island I 254 52.55 S 59.12 W
Beaucoup Creek ≏, Il., U.S. 194 37.47 N 89.17 W
Beaucoup Creek ≏, Il., U.S. 219 38.13 N 89.20 W
Beaucourt 58 47.29 N 6.55 E
Beaudesert 171a 27.59 S 153.00 E
Beaudry, Lac ⊜ 206 47.44 N 78.55 W
Beauduc, Pointe de ⋗ 62 43.22 N 4.34 E
Beaufays 56 50.34 N 5.38 E
Beaufort, Austl. 166 37.26 S 143.23 E
Beaufort, Fr. 58 46.34 N 5.26 E
Beaufort, Fr. 62 45.43 N 6.35 E
Beaufort, Lux. 56 49.51 N 6.18 E
Beaufort, Malay. 112 5.20 N 115.45 E
Beaufort, Mo., U.S. 219 38.26 N 91.12 W
Beaufort, N.C., U.S. 192 34.43 N 76.39 W
Beaufort, S.C., U.S. 192 32.25 N 80.40 W
Beaufort, Cape ▸ 162 34.26 S 115.32 E
Beaufort, Massif de ⋀ 62 45.44 N 6.35 E
Beaufort Castle — Qal'at ash-Shaqīf ⋍ 132 33.19 N 35.32 E
Beaufort Island I 271d 22.11 N 114.15 E
Beaufort Marine Corps Air Station ⋈ 192 32.30 N 80.44 W
Beaufort Sea ⊤² 16 73.00 N 140.00 W
Beaufort West 158 32.18 S 22.38 E
Beaugency 58 47.47 N 1.38 E
Beauharnois 206 45.19 N 73.52 W
Beauharnois ⋍⁶ 206 45.15 N 74.00 W
Beauharnois, Barrage de ⋗⁶ 275a 45.19 N 73.55 W
Beauharnois, Canal de ⋍ 206 45.19 N 73.54 W
Beaujeu 58 46.09 N 4.36 E
Beaujolais ⋗ 62 46.05 N 4.10 E
Beaulieu 42 50.49 N 1.27 W
Beaulieu-les-Loches 58 47.07 N 1.01 E
Beaulieu-sur-Mer 63 43.42 N 7.20 E
Beauly 46 57.28 N 4.28 W
Beauly Firth c¹ 46 57.30 N 4.23 W
Beaumaris, Austl. 274b 37.59 S 145.02 E
Beaumaris, Wales, U.K. 198 46.10 N 98.06 W
Beaumaris Bay c 274b 38.00 S 145.03 E
Beaumes-de-Venise 62 44.07 N 5.02 E
Beaumesnil 58 49.04 N 0.43 E
Beaumont-les-Loges 58 50.14 N 2.39 E
Beaumont, Bel. 56 50.14 N 4.14 E
Beaumont, Nf., Can. 186 49.37 N 55.41 W
Beaumont, Fr. 32 45.12 N 1.51 W
Beaumont, N.Z. 172 45.49 S 169.32 E
Beaumont, Ca., U.S. 228 33.55 N 116.58 W
Beaumont, Ms., U.S. 194 31.10 N 88.55 W
Beaumont, Tx., U.S. 194 30.05 N 94.06 W
Beaumont-du-Gâtinais 58 48.08 N 2.29 E
Beaumont-en-Argonne 56 49.32 N 5.03 E
Beaumont-Hague ⋍² 166 31.33 S 145.13 E
Beaumont-la-Ronce 58 47.34 N 0.40 E
Beaumont-le-Roger 58 49.05 N 0.47 E
Beaumont Place 222 29.50 N 95.14 W
Beaumont-sur-Oise 261 49.08 N 2.17 E
Beaumont-sur-Sarthe 58 48.14 N 0.08 E
Beaune 58 47.02 N 4.50 E
Beaune-la-Rolande 58 48.04 N 2.26 E
Beauport 206 46.52 N 71.12 W
Beaupré 188 47.03 N 70.54 W
Beaupré Island I 212 44.26 N 76.19 W
Beauraing 56 50.07 N 4.58 E
Beaurepaire 62 45.20 N 5.03 E
Beaurepaire-en-Bresse 58 46.40 N 5.23 E
Beaurivage ≏ 206 46.35 N 5.33 W
Beaurivage 206 46.42 N 71.14 W
Beauséjour, Mb., Can. 184 50.04 N 96.33 W
Beausoleil 62 16.18 N 61.04 W
Beausoleil Island I 212 44.52 N 79.52 W
Beautor 58 49.39 N 3.20 E
Beauvais, Fr. 58 49.26 N 2.05 E
Beauvais, Fr. 261 48.22 N 2.03 E
Beauvais Creek ≏ 202 45.29 N 107.45 W
Beauvais-Tillé, Aéroport ⋈ 261 49.28 N 2.07 E
Beauval, Sk., Can. 184 55.06 N 107.37 W
Beauval, Fr. 58 50.06 N 2.20 E
Beauvezer 62 44.08 N 6.36 E
Beauvoir 58 44.17 N 0.52 E
Beauvoir-sur-Mer 58 46.11 N 2.03 W
Beauvoir-sur-Niort 32 46.11 N 0.28 W
Beaux Arts 224 47.35 N 122.11 W
Beaver, Ak., U.S. 180 66.22 N 147.24 W
Beaver, Oh., U.S. 196 35.16 N 100.31 W
Beaver, Ut., U.S. 196 38.16 N 112.38 W
Beaver, Pa., U.S. 214 40.42 N 80.18 W
Beaver ≏ 190 55.25 N 107.45 W
Beaver ≏, Pa., U.S. 214 40.40 N 80.18 W
Beaver ≏, Pa., U.S. 214 40.42 N 80.18 W
Beaver □⁶ 214 40.40 N 80.25 W
Beaver, Can. 186 55.26 N 107.45 W
Beaver Brook ≏, On., Can. 212 45.25 N 75.10 W
Beaver Brook ≏, N.J., U.S. 276 44.02 N 74.03 W
Beaver Brook ≏, Co., U.S. 200 39.40 N 105.00 W
Beaver City 198 40.08 N 99.49 W
Beaver Creek, Yk., Can. 180 62.22 N 140.52 W
Beaver Creek ≏, Ak., U.S. 180 62.52 N 106.20 W
Beaver Creek ≏, Ct., U.S. 207 41.39 N 73.24 W
Beaver Creek ≏, Ca., U.S. 204 39.44 N 121.53 W
Beaver Creek ≏, N.D., U.S. 198 48.07 N 121.53 W
Beaver Creek ≏, Oh., U.S. 214 41.45 N 78.04 W
Beaver Creek ≏, Or., U.S. 202 44.06 N 120.46 W
Beaver Creek ≏, Pa., U.S. 214 40.21 N 78.50 W
Beaver Creek ≏, Wy., U.S. 198 41.41 N 104.13 W
Beaver Creek, South Fork ≏ 219 40.09 N 91.18 W
Beaver Creek, West Fork ≏ 280 34.16 N 117.53 W
Bearden 194 33.43 N 92.36 W
Beardmore 176 49.36 N 87.57 W
Beardmore Glacier ⊠ 83 83.45 S 171.00 E
Beardsley Lake ⊜¹ 226 38.13 N 120.03 W
Beardstown, Il., U.S. 219 40.01 N 90.25 W
Beardstown, In., U.S. 219 40.46 N 85.60 W
Beardy and Okemasis Indian Reserves ⋋ 184 52.48 N 106.20 W
Bearfort Mountain ⋀ 276 41.09 N 74.23 W
Bear Head Lake ⋀ 190 30.18 N 93.35 W
Bear Head Lake State Park ♦ 190 47.49 N 92.04 W
Bearhead Mountain ⋀ 224 47.02 N 121.53 W
Bear Hill ⋀², U.S. 207 41.39 N 73.24 W
Bear Hill ⋀², N.Y., U.S. 207 41.39 N 74.00 W
Bearhead 120 27.49 N 60.12 E
Bear Island I, Ant. 9 74.30 S 110.45 W
Bear Island I, Ire. 48 51.38 N 9.50 W
Bear Island I, Va., U.S. 192 37.03 N 75.40 W
Bear Island I → Bjørnøya I, Nor. 12 74.25 N 19.00 E
Bear Lake, Mi., U.S. 216 44.26 N 86.09 W
Bear Lake, Pa., U.S. 214 41.59 N 79.30 W
Bear Lake ⊜, Ab., Can. 182 55.16 N 119.00 W
Bear Lake ⊜, B.C., Can. 176 56.06 N 126.45 W
Bear Lake ⊜, Mb., Can. 184 55.08 N 96.00 W
Bear Mountain ⋀, N.J., U.S. 276 41.11 N 74.38 W
Bear Mountain ⋀, S.D., U.S. 198 43.51 N 103.49 W
Bear Mountain ⋀, N.Y., U.S. 276 41.18 N 74.00 W
Bear Mountain State Park ♦ 276 41.17 N 74.01 W
Béarn ⋗⁹ 32 43.25 N 0.45 W
Bear Pond ⊜ 276 40.58 N 74.44 W
Bear River 186 44.34 N 65.39 W
Bear River Range ⋀ 200 41.30 N 111.30 W
Bear Run ≏ 214 40.03 N 80.49 W
Bears Paw Mountains ⋀ 202 48.08 N 109.30 W
Bearstead 260 51.16 N 0.35 E
Bear Swamp ⋍ 207 41.30 N 73.44 W
Bear Swamp Brook ≏ 276 40.53 N 74.47 W
Beartooth Mountains ⋀ 202 45.00 N 109.30 W
Beartooth Pass ⋊ 202 44.58 N 109.28 W
Bear Town 194 31.13 N 90.27 W
Beãs 123 31.10 N 75.17 E
Beasain 36 43.03 N 2.12 W
Beas de Segura 34 38.15 N 2.53 W

Column 6 (DEUTSCH · Name / Seite / Breite / Länge)

Beasley 222 29.30 N 95.55 W
Beasley Bay c 208 37.51 N 75.44 W
Beason 219 40.09 N 89.12 W
Beata, Cabo ▸ 238 17.36 N 71.25 W
Beata, Isla I 238 17.35 N 71.31 W
Beatenberg 58 46.42 N 7.48 E
Beato ⋗⁸ 266c 38.44 N 9.06 W
Beaton 182 50.44 N 117.44 W
Beatrice, Ne., U.S. 198 40.16 N 96.44 W
Beatrice, Zimb. 154 18.15 S 30.55 E
Beatrice, Cape ▸ 164 14.15 S 136.59 E
Beattie 198 39.51 N 96.25 W
Beattock 44 55.18 N 3.28 W
Beatton ≏ 176 56.10 N 120.25 W
Beatty, Nv., U.S. 204 36.54 N 116.45 W
Beatty, Oh., U.S. 218 39.53 N 83.50 W
Beatty Saugeen ≏ 212 44.08 N 81.02 W
Beattyville 192 37.34 N 83.42 W
Beaubru 58 49.46 N 5.05 E
Beaucaire 62 43.48 N 4.38 E
Beauce ⋗¹ 58 48.22 N 1.50 E
Beauceville 188 46.12 N 70.46 W
Beauchamp 261 49.01 N 2.12 E
Beauchamp Roding 260 51.44 N 0.18 E
Beauchêne Island I 254 52.55 S 59.12 W
Beaucoup Creek ≏, Il., U.S. 194 37.47 N 89.17 W
Beaucoup Creek ≏, Il., U.S. 219 38.13 N 89.20 W
Beaucourt 58 47.29 N 6.55 E
Beaudesert 171a 27.59 S 153.00 E
Beaudry, Lac ⊜ 206 47.44 N 78.55 W
Beauduc, Pointe de ⋗ 62 43.22 N 4.34 E
Beaufays 56 50.34 N 5.38 E
Beaufort, Austl. 166 37.26 S 143.23 E
Beaufort, Fr. 58 46.34 N 5.26 E
Beaufort, Fr. 62 45.43 N 6.35 E
Beaufort, Lux. 56 49.51 N 6.18 E
Beaufort, Malay. 112 5.20 N 115.45 E
Beaufort, Mo., U.S. 219 38.26 N 91.12 W
Beaufort, N.C., U.S. 192 34.43 N 76.39 W
Beaufort, S.C., U.S. 192 32.25 N 80.40 W
Beaufort, Cape ▸ 162 34.26 S 115.32 E
Beaufort, Massif de ⋀ 62 45.44 N 6.35 E
Beaufort Castle — Qal'at ash-Shaqīf ⋍ 132 33.19 N 35.32 E
Beaufort Island I 271d 22.11 N 114.15 E
Beaufort Marine Corps Air Station ⋈ 192 32.30 N 80.44 W
Beaufort Sea ⊤² 16 73.00 N 140.00 W
Beaufort West 158 32.18 S 22.38 E
Beaugency 58 47.47 N 1.38 E
Beauharnois 206 45.19 N 73.52 W
Beauharnois ⋍⁶ 206 45.15 N 74.00 W
Beauharnois, Barrage de ⋗⁶ 275a 45.19 N 73.55 W
Beauharnois, Canal de ⋍ 206 45.19 N 73.54 W
Beaujeu 58 46.09 N 4.36 E
Beaujolais ⋗ 62 46.05 N 4.10 E
Beaulieu 42 50.49 N 1.27 W
Beaulieu-les-Loches 58 47.07 N 1.01 E
Beaulieu-sur-Mer 63 43.42 N 7.20 E
Beauly 46 57.28 N 4.28 W
Beauly Firth c¹ 46 57.30 N 4.23 W
Beaumaris, Austl. 274b 37.59 S 145.02 E
Beaumaris, Wales, U.K. 198 46.10 N 98.06 W
Beaumaris Bay c 274b 38.00 S 145.03 E
Beaumes-de-Venise 62 44.07 N 5.02 E
Beaumesnil 58 49.04 N 0.43 E
Beaumetz-les-Loges 58 50.14 N 2.39 E
Beaumont, Bel. 56 50.14 N 4.14 E
Beaumont, Nf., Can. 186 49.37 N 55.41 W
Beaumont, Fr. 32 45.12 N 1.51 W
Beaumont, N.Z. 172 45.49 S 169.32 E
Beaumont, Ca., U.S. 228 33.55 N 116.58 W
Beaumont, Ms., U.S. 194 31.10 N 88.55 W
Beaumont, Tx., U.S. 194 30.05 N 94.06 W
Beaumont-du-Gâtinais 58 48.08 N 2.29 E
Beaumont-en-Argonne 56 49.32 N 5.03 E
Beaumont Hill ⋀² 166 31.33 S 145.13 E
Beaumont-la-Ronce 58 47.34 N 0.40 E
Beaumont-le-Roger 58 49.05 N 0.47 E
Beaumont Place 222 29.50 N 95.14 W
Beaumont-sur-Oise 261 49.08 N 2.17 E
Beaumont-sur-Sarthe 58 48.14 N 0.08 E
Beaune 58 47.02 N 4.50 E
Beaune-la-Rolande 58 48.04 N 2.26 E
Beauport 206 46.52 N 71.12 W
Beaupré 188 47.03 N 70.54 W
Beaupré Island I 212 44.52 N 76.19 W
Beauraing 56 50.07 N 4.58 E
Beaurepaire 62 45.20 N 5.03 E
Beaurepaire-en-Bresse 58 46.40 N 5.23 E
Beaurivage ≏ 206 46.35 N 5.33 W
Beaurivage 206 46.42 N 71.14 W
Beauséjour, Mb., Can. 184 50.04 N 96.33 W
Beausoleil 240l 16.18 N 61.04 W
Beausoleil Island I 212 44.52 N 79.52 W
Beautor 58 49.39 N 3.20 E
Beauvais, Fr. 261 49.26 N 2.05 E
Beauvais, Fr. 261 48.22 N 2.03 E
Beauvais Creek ≏ 202 45.29 N 107.45 W
Beauvais-Tillé, Aéroport ⋈ 261 49.28 N 2.07 E
Beauval, Sk., Can. 184 55.06 N 107.37 W
Beauval, Fr. 58 50.06 N 2.20 E
Beauvezer 62 44.08 N 6.36 E
Beauvoir 58 44.17 N 0.52 E
Beauvoir-sur-Mer 58 46.55 N 2.03 W
Beauvoir-sur-Niort 32 46.11 N 0.28 W
Beaux Arts 224 47.35 N 122.11 W
Beaver, Ak., U.S. 180 66.22 N 147.24 W
Beaver, Ok., U.S. 196 36.48 N 100.31 W
Beaver, Ut., U.S. 196 38.16 N 112.38 W
Beaver, Pa., U.S. 214 40.42 N 80.18 W
Beaver ≏, Can. 176 55.26 N 107.45 W
Beaver ≏, Pa., U.S. 214 40.40 N 80.18 W
Beaver ≏, Pa., U.S. 214 40.42 N 80.18 W
Beaver □⁶ 214 40.40 N 80.25 W
Beaver Brook ≏, N.J., U.S. 207 44.02 N 74.03 W
Beaver Brook ≏, Ma., U.S. 283 42.23 N 71.14 W
Beaver City 198 40.08 N 99.49 W

Symbols in the index entries represent the broad categories identified in the key at the right. Symbols with superior numbers (⋌¹) identify subcategories (see complete key on page *I · 1*).

Symbole im Register stellen die rechts im Schlüssel erklärten Kategorien dar. Symbole mit hochgestellten Ziffern (⋌¹) bezeichnen Unterteilungen einer Kategorie (vgl. vollständiger Schlüssel auf Seite *I · 1*).

Los símbolos incluídos en el texto del índice representan las grandes categorías identificadas con la clave a la derecha. Los símbolos con numeros en su parte superior (⋌¹) identifican las subcategorías (véase la clave completa en la página *I · 1*).

Os símbolos incluídos no texto do índice representam as grandes categorias identificadas na chave à direita. Os símbolos com números em sua parte superior (⋌¹) identificam as subcategorias (veja-se a chave completa na página *I · 1*).

Les symboles de l'index représentent les grandes catégories indiquées dans la légende à droite. Les symboles suivis d'un indice (⋌¹) représentent des sous-catégories (voir légende complète à la page *I · 1*).

⋀ Mountain	Berg	Montaña	Montagne	Montanha
⋀⋀ Mountains	Gebirge	Montañas	Montagnes	Montanhas
⋊ Pass	Paß	Paso	Col	Passo
⋁ Valley, Canyon	Tal, Cañon	Valle, Cañón	Vallée, Canyon	Vale, Canhão
⌿ Plain	Ebene	Llano	Plaine	Planície
▸ Cape	Kap	Cabo	Cap	Cabo
I Island	Insel	Isla	Île	Ilha
II Islands	Inseln	Islas	Îles	Ilhas
⋍ Other Topographic Features	Andere Topographische Objekte	Otros Elementos Topográficos	Autres données topographiques	Outros acidentes topográficos

ESPAÑOL			FRANÇAIS			PORTUGUÊS		
Nombre	Página	Lat.°′ Long.°′ W=Oeste	Nom	Page	Lat.°′ Long.°′ W=Ouest	Nome	Página	Lat.°′ Long.°′ W=Oeste

---

ENGLISH   DEUTSCH

Name	Page	Lat.ᵒʳ	Long.ᵒʳ	Name	Seite	Breiteᵒʳ	Längeᵒʳ E = Ost

The main body of this page consists of a multi-column alphabetical atlas index (place names Bellinzona through Bero-... with page numbers, latitude and longitude coordinates), which is too dense to reproduce entry-by-entry with full accuracy.

Bero-Bigh *I* · *19*

ESPAÑOL / FRANÇAIS / PORTUGUÊS

Nombre / Nom / Nome	Página / Page	Lat.°'	Long.°' W = Oeste / W = Ouest
Ber'ozovo, Ross.	82	54.03 N	36.24 E
Ber'ozovo, Ross.	82	54.19 N	38.17 E
Ber'ozovskaja	80	50.16 N	43.59 E
Ber'ozovskij	86	55.39 N	86.16 E
Ber'ozovskij R'adok	76	58.06 N	34.29 E
Ber'ozovskoje	86	55.50 N	89.36 E
Berra	64	44.59 N	11.58 E
Berras, Arroyo los ≃	288	34.34 S	58.40 W
Berre ≃	62	44.24 N	4.40 E
Berre, Étang de ⊂	62	43.27 N	5.08 E
Berrechid	148	33.17 N	7.35 W
Berre-des-Alpes	62	43.50 N	7.19 E
Berre-l'Étang	62	43.28 N	5.11 E
Ber Remad, Oued V	148	31.45 N	1.10 E
Berri	166	34.17 S	140.36 E
Berridale	171b	36.22 S	148.50 E
Berriedale	46	58.11 N	3.29 W
Berrien □[6]	216	41.59 N	86.30 W
Berrien Springs	216	41.56 N	86.20 W
Berrigan	166	35.40 S	145.49 E
Berrima	170	34.30 S	150.20 E
Berriozábal	234	16.48 N	93.16 W
Berriyyane	148	32.50 N	3.46 E
Berrouaghia	34	36.08 N	2.55 E
Berrugosa Point ▸	116	10.23 N	125.33 E
Berry, Austl.	170	34.47 S	150.42 E
Berry, Al., U.S.	194	33.39 N	87.36 W
Berry, Ky., U.S.	218	38.31 N	84.23 W
Berry □[9]	50	47.20 N	2.10 E
Berry, Canal du ≅	50	47.17 N	1.25 E
Berry-au-Bac	50	49.24 N	3.54 E
Berry Creek ≃, Ab., Can.	182	50.50 N	111.36 W
Berry Creek ≃, Tx., U.S.	222	30.40 N	97.36 W
Berryessa, Lake ◎[1]	226	38.35 N	122.14 W
Berryessa Creek ≃	282	37.24 N	121.53 W
Berryessa Peak ∧	226	38.40 N	122.11 W
Berry Islands II	238	25.34 N	77.45 W
Berry Mountain ∧	208	40.31 N	77.02 W
Berrysburg	208	40.36 N	76.49 W
Berrys Creek ≃	276	40.47 N	74.05 W
Berryville	194	36.21 N	93.34 W
Berseba	156	26.00 S	17.46 E
Bersenbrück	52	52.33 N	7.56 E
Bershad'	78	48.23 N	29.30 E
Bersut	80	55.32 N	50.54 E
Berta ≃	130	41.09 N	41.53 E
Bertam	114	5.09 N	102.03 E
Berté, Lac ◎	186	50.48 N	68.30 W
Bertha	198	46.16 N	95.03 W
Berthåga	40	59.52 N	17.35 E
Berthelsdorf	54	51.05 N	14.13 E
Berthier □[6]	206	46.30 N	73.45 W
Berthierville	206	46.05 N	73.10 W
Berthold	198	48.18 N	101.44 W
Berthoud	200	40.18 N	105.04 W
Berthoud Pass)(	200	39.45 N	105.45 W
Bertincourt	50	50.05 N	2.59 E
Bertinoro	66	44.09 N	12.08 E
Bertioga	256	23.51 S	46.09 W
Bertioga, Enseada da ⊂	256	23.50 S	46.08 W
Bertkow	54	52.43 N	11.54 E
Bertlich	263	51.37 N	7.04 E
Bertogne	56	50.05 N	5.40 E
Bertolínia	250	7.38 S	43.57 W
Bertoua	152	4.35 N	13.41 E
Bertram	196	30.45 N	98.03 W
Bertrand, Mi., U.S.	216	41.46 N	86.15 W
Bertrand, Ne., U.S.	198	40.31 N	99.38 W
Bertrix	56	49.51 N	5.15 E
Bertry	50	50.05 N	3.27 E
Beru I	14	1.20 S	176.00 E
Beruas	114	4.30 N	100.47 E
Beruri	246	3.54 S	61.22 W
Berville	214	42.55 N	82.53 W
Berville-sur-Mer	50	49.26 N	0.22 E
Berwang	58	47.24 N	10.45 E
Berwick, Austl.	169	38.02 S	145.21 E
Berwick, N.S., Can.	186	45.03 N	64.44 W
Berwick, La., U.S.	194	29.41 N	91.13 W
Berwick, Me., U.S.	188	43.15 N	70.51 W
Berwick, Pa., U.S.	210	41.03 N	76.14 W
Berwick-upon-Tweed	44	55.46 N	2.00 W
Berwyn, Il., U.S.	216	41.51 N	87.47 W
Berwyn, Pa., U.S.	208	40.02 N	75.26 W
Berwyn ⋀	42	52.53 N	3.24 W
Berwyn Heights	284c	38.59 N	76.54 W
Beryslav	78	46.51 N	33.26 E
Bērze ≃	76	56.41 N	23.37 E
Berzé-la-Ville	58	46.22 N	4.42 E
Berz-Macomb Airport ⊠	281	42.40 N	82.58 W
Bès ≃	62	44.08 N	6.14 E
Besalampy	157b	16.45 S	44.30 E
Besana in Brianza	62	45.42 N	9.17 E
Besançon	58	47.15 N	6.02 E
Besani	124	24.08 N	80.17 E
Bešankovičy	76	55.03 N	29.27 E
Besar, Gunong ∧, Malay.	114	5.10 N	101.18 E
Besar, Gunong ∧, Malay.	114	2.30 N	103.10 E
Besar, Gunung ∧	112	2.43 S	115.37 E
Besar, Pulau I	115b	8.28 S	122.22 E
Besar Hantu, Gunong ∧	114	3.12 N	102.02 E
Besaya ≃	34	43.21 N	4.04 W
Besbes	36	36.42 N	7.51 E
Besedino	78	51.42 N	36.28 E
Besedy	265b	55.37 N	37.47 E
Besedz' ≃	76	52.38 N	31.09 E
Besenfeld	56	48.35 N	8.25 E
Beserah	114	3.52 N	103.22 E
Besigheim	56	49.00 N	9.08 E
Besikama	112	9.36 S	124.57 E
Beşiktaş ◆[8]	267b	41.03 N	29.01 E
Beşiri	130	37.55 N	41.18 E
Besitang	114	4.02 N	98.12 E
Beškent	128	38.49 N	65.39 E
Beskid Mountains ⋀	30	49.40 N	20.00 E
Beşkonak	130	37.08 N	31.12 E
Beskra	148	34.51 N	5.44 E
Beškube	85	39.50 N	68.18 E
Beskudnikovo ◆[8]	265b	55.52 N	37.34 E
Beslan	84	43.12 N	44.33 E
Beslenej	84	44.14 N	41.44 E
Besnard Lake ◎	184	55.24 N	106.05 W
Besni	130	37.41 N	37.52 E
Besor, Naḥal V	132	31.28 N	34.22 E
Besós ≃	266d	41.25 N	2.04 E
Besozzo	62	45.51 N	8.39 E
Besp'atovo	82	54.45 N	38.54 E
Beşpınar, Tür.	130	41.09 N	35.14 E
Beşpınar, Tür.	130	37.51 N	41.36 E
Besputa ≃	82	54.50 N	37.58 E
Bessacarr	44	53.30 N	1.04 W
Bessancourt	261	49.02 N	2.13 E
Bessans	62	45.19 N	7.00 E
Bessarabia □[9]	38	47.00 N	28.30 E
Bessarabka	86	53.37 N	73.17 E
Bessaz, gora ∧	85	43.49 N	68.40 E
Bessbrook	48	54.12 N	6.25 W
Besse, Dtsch.	56	51.13 N	9.23 E
Besse, Nig.	150	11.15 N	4.30 E
Bessèges	62	44.17 N	4.06 E
Bessemer, Al., U.S.	194	33.24 N	86.57 W
Bessemer, Mi., U.S.	190	46.28 N	90.03 W
Bessemer, Pa., U.S.	214	40.58 N	80.29 W
Bessemer City	192	35.17 N	81.17 W
Besser	41	55.52 N	10.39 E
Bessé-sur-Braye	50	47.50 N	0.45 E
Bessheim	26	61.31 N	8.51 E
Besshiyama	96	33.50 N	133.23 E
Bessho	270	34.27 N	135.31 E
Bessonovka	80	53.18 N	45.03 E
Best	52	51.31 N	5.24 E
Best'ach	74	61.52 N	129.55 E
Bestamak, Kaz.	86	49.43 N	55.07 E
Bestamak, Kaz.	86	49.13 N	78.21 E
Beštau, gora ∧	84	44.06 N	43.01 E
Besten	263	51.39 N	6.54 E
Bestensee	54	52.15 N	13.37 E
Bestfield	285	39.43 N	75.36 W
Bestobe	86	52.30 N	73.05 E
Beštor, gora ∧	85	42.03 N	70.50 E
Bestuževo	24	61.37 N	43.58 E
Bestwig, Dtsch.	52	51.22 N	8.24 E
Bestwig, Dtsch.	56	51.22 N	8.24 E
Besuki	115a	7.45 S	113.41 E
Besut ≃	114	5.48 N	102.35 E
Beswick Aboriginal Reserve ◆[4]	164	14.30 S	133.10 E
Betā	272b	22.55 N	88.14 E
Betafo	157b	19.50 S	46.51 E
Betāgi	126	22.25 N	90.11 E
Bet Alfa	132	32.31 N	35.26 E
Beta Main Canal ≅	226	36.34 N	120.11 W
Betamba	152	2.13 S	21.23 E
Betang Melaka	114	2.28 N	102.25 E
Betano	112	9.10 S	125.43 E
Betanzos, Bol.	248	19.34 S	65.27 W
Betanzos, Esp.	34	43.17 N	8.12 W
Betanzos, Ría de ⊂[1]	34	43.23 N	8.15 W
Betaré Oya	152	5.36 N	14.05 E
Betarsjön ◎	26	63.44 N	16.52 E
Bet Bet Creek ≃	169	36.52 S	143.52 E
Betbetti	140	15.06 N	24.12 E
Betchworth	260	51.14 N	0.16 W
Bet Dagan	132	32.00 N	34.50 E
Bete Hor	144	11.37 N	39.02 E
Betém	256	22.52 S	44.17 W
Bétera	34	39.35 N	0.27 W
Bétérou	150	9.12 N	2.16 E
Bet Guvrin	132	31.36 N	34.54 E
Bet Ha'arava	132	31.48 N	35.32 E
Bethal	158	26.27 S	29.28 E
Bethalto	219	38.54 N	90.02 W
Bethanien	156	26.32 S	17.11 E
Bethany, Ct., U.S.	207	41.25 N	72.59 W
Bethany, Il., U.S.	219	39.38 N	88.44 W
Bethany, Mo., U.S.	194	40.16 N	94.01 W
Bethany, N.Y., U.S.	210	42.55 N	78.08 W
Bethany, Ok., U.S.	196	35.31 N	97.37 W
Bethany, Pa., U.S.	210	41.37 N	75.21 W
Bethany, W.V., U.S.	214	40.12 N	80.33 W
Bethany Reservoir ◎[1]	226	37.47 N	121.37 W
Bet HaShitta	132	32.33 N	35.26 E
Bethel, Ak., U.S.	180	60.48 N	161.46 W
Bethel, Ct., U.S.	207	41.22 N	73.24 W
Bethel, De., U.S.	208	38.27 N	75.21 W
Bethel, Ky., U.S.	218	38.14 N	83.52 W
Bethel, Me., U.S.	188	44.24 N	70.47 W
Bethel, Mo., U.S.	219	39.52 N	92.01 W
Bethel, N.Y., U.S.	210	41.41 N	74.52 W
Bethel, N.C., U.S.	192	35.48 N	77.22 W
Bethel, Oh., U.S.	218	38.57 N	84.04 W
Bethel, Pa., U.S.	208	40.28 N	76.18 W
Bethel, Wa., U.S.	224	47.32 N	122.38 W
Bethel Acres	196	35.19 N	97.00 W
Bethel Island	226	38.01 N	121.39 W
Bethel Manor	208	37.06 N	76.25 W
Bethel Park	214	40.18 N	80.02 W
Bethelsdorp	158	33.52 S	25.34 E
Bethel Springs	194	35.14 N	88.36 W
Béthencourt-sur-Mer	50	50.05 N	1.30 E
Bethersden	42	51.08 N	0.48 E
Bethesda, Wales, U.K.	44	53.11 N	4.03 W
Bethesda, Md., U.S.	208	38.58 N	77.06 W
Bethesda, Oh., U.S.	188	40.00 N	81.04 W
Bethesdaweg	158	31.55 S	24.45 E
Bethford	284a	42.48 N	78.48 W
Bethgate	284b	39.18 N	76.51 W
Béthisy-Saint-Pierre	50	49.18 N	2.49 E
Bethlehem, S. Afr.	156	28.15 S	28.15 E
Bethlehem, S. Afr.	158	27.10 S	24.00 E
Bethlehem, S. Afr.	158	28.15 S	28.15 E
Bethlehem, Ct., U.S.	207	41.38 N	73.12 W
Bethlehem, In., U.S.	218	38.32 N	85.25 W
Bethlehem, Ky., U.S.	218	38.24 N	85.04 W
Bethlehem, Pa., U.S.	210	40.37 N	75.22 W
Bethlehem, W.V., U.S.	188	40.02 N	80.41 W
Bethlehem → Bayt Laḥm, W.B.	132	31.43 N	35.12 E
Bethlehem Center	210	42.40 N	73.42 W
Bethlehem Steel Corporation ⊍[3], Md., U.S.	284b	39.13 N	76.29 W
Bethlehem Steel Corporation (Lackawanna Plant) ⊍[3], N.Y., U.S.	284a	42.49 N	78.52 W
Bethnal Green ◆[8]	260	51.32 N	0.03 W
Bethoncourt	58	47.32 N	6.48 E
Bethpage	210	40.44 N	73.28 W
Bethpage State Park ♣	210	40.45 N	73.27 W
Bethulie	158	30.32 S	25.59 E
Bethune, Sk., Can.	184	50.43 N	105.08 W
Béthune, Fr.	50	50.32 N	2.38 E
Bethune, S.C., U.S.	192	34.24 N	80.20 W
Béthune ≃	50	49.53 N	1.09 E
Betijoque	246	9.23 N	70.44 W
Betil	126	24.14 N	89.43 E
Betio	174t	1.21 N	172.56 E
Betioky	157b	23.42 S	44.22 E
Betis ≃	114	4.53 N	101.48 E
Betlica	76	54.01 N	33.57 E
Betna ≃	126	22.34 N	89.12 E
Bet Netofa, Biq'at ≅	132	32.49 N	35.19 E
Betnoti	126	21.44 N	86.51 E
Beton-Bazoches	50	48.42 N	3.15 E
Betong, Malay.	112	1.24 N	111.31 E
Betong, Thai	110	5.45 N	101.05 E
Betoota	166	25.42 S	140.44 E
Bétou	152	3.03 N	18.31 E
Betpak-Dala ◆[2]	86	46.00 N	70.00 E
Betroka	157b	23.16 S	46.06 E
Betsham	260	51.25 N	0.19 E
Bet Sh'ean	132	32.30 N	35.30 E
Bet She'arim, Ḥorbat ⊥	132	32.42 N	35.08 E
Bet Shemesh	132	31.45 N	35.00 E
Betsiamites	186	48.56 N	68.38 W
Betsiamites ≃	186	48.56 N	68.38 W
Betsiamites, Barrage ◆[6]	186	49.22 N	69.47 W
Betsiamites, Pointe de ▸	186	48.55 N	68.37 W
Betsiamites, Réserve indienne de ◆[4]	186	49.05 N	68.37 W
Betsiboka ≃	157b	16.03 S	46.36 E
Betsie, Point ▸	190	44.42 N	86.16 W
Betsioky	157b	21.31 S	44.28 E
Betsukai	92a	43.23 N	145.17 E
Betsy Layne	192	37.33 N	82.38 W
Betsy Ross Bridge ◆[5]	285	39.59 N	75.04 W
Bettembourg	56	49.32 N	6.02 E
Bettendorf	190	41.31 N	90.30 W
Betterton	208	39.21 N	76.03 W
Bettiah	124	26.48 N	84.30 E
Bettie	222	32.48 N	94.58 W
Bettles Field	180	66.55 N	151.30 W
Bettola	62	44.47 N	9.36 E
Bettona	66	43.01 N	12.29 E
Bettrath ◆[8]	263	51.13 N	6.26 E
Bettsville	214	41.14 N	83.14 W
Bettyhill	46	58.32 N	4.14 W
Betty's Bay	158	34.22 S	18.52 E
Betūl	124	21.55 N	77.54 E
Betumbe-Bongo	152	2.11 S	18.46 E
Betung, Indon.	112	1.52 S	103.16 E
Betung, Indon.	112	2.50 S	104.14 E
Betuwe ◆[1]	52	51.55 N	5.30 E
Betwa ≃	124	25.55 N	80.12 E
Betws-y-Coed	44	53.05 N	3.48 W
Betz	50	49.09 N	2.57 E
Betz ≃	50	48.09 N	2.45 E
Betzdorf	56	50.47 N	7.53 E
Betzenstein	60	49.41 N	11.25 E
Béu	152	6.14 S	15.28 E
Beucha	54	51.19 N	12.34 E
Beugneux	50	49.14 N	3.25 E
Beuil	62	44.06 N	6.59 E
Beulah, Austl.	166	35.56 S	142.26 E
Beulah, Co., U.S.	200	38.04 N	104.59 W
Beulah, Mi., U.S.	190	44.37 N	86.05 W
Beulah, Ms., U.S.	194	33.47 N	90.58 W
Beulah, N.D., U.S.	198	47.15 N	101.46 W
Beulah, Lake ◎	216	42.49 N	88.23 W
Beulah Beach	214	41.25 N	82.22 W
Beulah Reservoir ◎[1]	202	43.56 N	118.09 W
Beulaville	192	34.55 N	77.46 W
Beult ≃	42	51.14 N	0.25 E
Beure	58	47.12 N	6.00 E
Beureunun	114	5.18 N	95.59 E
Beuron	58	48.03 N	8.58 E
Beuthen → Bytom	30	50.22 N	18.54 E
Beuvron ≃, Fr.	50	47.28 N	3.31 E
Beuvron ≃, Fr.	50	47.29 N	1.15 E
Beuvronne ≃	261	48.56 N	2.44 E
Beuvry	50	50.31 N	2.41 E
Beuzeville	50	49.20 N	0.21 E
Bevagna	66	42.56 N	12.36 E
Bever ≃	52	52.01 N	7.46 E
Bevera ≃	62	43.49 N	7.34 E
Beveren	50	51.13 N	4.15 E
B. Everett Jordan Lake ◎[1]	192	35.45 N	79.00 W
Beverino	62	44.14 N	9.47 E
Beverley, Austl.	168a	32.06 S	116.56 E
Beverley, Eng., U.K.	44	53.52 N	0.26 W
Beverley Minster ⊍[1]	44	53.50 N	0.27 W
Beverley Springs	162	16.43 S	125.28 E
Beverlo	56	51.05 N	5.12 E
Beverly, Ma., U.S.	207	42.33 N	70.52 W
Beverly, N.J., U.S.	208	40.03 N	74.55 W
Beverly, Tx., U.S.	222	31.30 N	97.10 W
Beverly ◆[8]	278	41.43 N	87.41 W
Beverly Farms, Md., U.S.	284c	39.04 N	77.11 W
Beverly Farms, Ma., U.S.	283	42.34 N	70.49 W
Beverly Harbor ⊂	283	42.32 N	70.53 W
Beverly Hills, Austl.	274a	33.57 S	151.05 E
Beverly Hills, Ca., U.S.	228	34.04 N	118.23 W
Beverly Hills, Fl., U.S.	220	28.56 N	82.28 W
Beverly Hills, Mi., U.S.	216	42.31 N	83.13 W
Beverly Lake ◎	176	64.36 N	100.30 W
Beverly Municipal Airport ⊠	283	42.35 N	70.55 W
Beverly Run ≃	208	37.55 N	77.11 W
Beverly Shores	216	41.41 N	86.58 W
Bevern	52	51.51 N	9.29 E
Beverstausee ◎[1]	263	51.09 N	7.23 E
Beverstedt	52	53.26 N	8.49 E
Beverungen	52	51.39 N	9.22 E
Beverwijk	52	52.28 N	4.40 E
Bevier	194	39.45 N	92.34 W
Bevin, Lac ◎	206	45.57 N	74.35 W
Bevoalavo	157b	25.13 S	45.26 E
Bewani	164	3.02 S	141.10 E
Bewani Mountains ⋀	164	3.10 S	141.25 E
Bewār	124	27.13 N	79.18 E
Bewdley, On., Can.	212	44.05 N	78.19 W
Bewdley, Eng., U.K.	42	52.22 N	2.19 W
Bewl Water ◎[1]	42	51.04 N	0.24 E
Bex	58	46.15 N	7.01 E
Bexbach	56	49.21 N	7.16 E
Bexhill	42	50.50 N	0.29 E
Bexley, Austl.	274a	33.57 S	151.08 E
Bexley, Oh., U.S.	218	39.58 N	82.56 W
Bexley ◆[8]	42	51.26 N	0.10 E
Beyazköy	130	41.21 N	27.42 E
Beybach ≃	56	50.13 N	7.23 E
Beyçayırı	130	40.15 N	26.55 E
Beycuma	130	41.19 N	31.59 E
Bey Dağları ⋀	130	36.40 N	30.15 E
Beydağları Olimpos Milli Parkı ♣	130	36.40 N	30.25 E
Beydili	130	40.10 N	31.01 E
Beyenburg ◆[8]	263	51.15 N	7.18 E
Beykoz ◆[8]	267b	41.08 N	29.05 E
Beyla	150	8.41 N	8.37 W
Beyläqan	84	39.47 N	47.37 E
Beylerbeyi ◆[8]	267b	41.03 N	29.03 E
Beylikahır	130	39.42 N	31.13 E
Beylul	144	13.10 N	42.26 E
Beynes	261	48.51 N	1.53 E
Beynes-Thiverval, Aérodrome de ⊠	261	48.51 N	1.54 E
Beyoğlu ◆[8]	267b	41.02 N	28.59 E
Beypazarı	130	40.10 N	31.56 E
Beypınarı	130	39.31 N	37.44 E
Beypore	122	11.11 N	75.49 E
Beyra	144	6.57 N	47.19 E
Beyrouth → Bayrūt	130	33.53 N	35.30 E
Beyşehir	130	37.41 N	31.43 E
Beyşehir Gölü ◎	130	37.40 N	31.30 E
Beytüşşebap	128	37.34 N	43.10 E
Bezaha	157b	23.30 S	44.31 E
Bežanickaja vozvyšennost' ⋀[1]	76	56.54 N	29.20 E
Bežanicy	76	56.58 N	29.53 E
Bezau	58	47.23 N	9.54 E
Bezavona ∧	157b	15.02 S	49.52 E
Bezděz ∧	54	50.32 N	14.43 E
Bezděz ⊥	54	50.32 N	14.46 E
Bezdzež	76	52.19 N	25.18 E
Bèze	58	47.28 N	5.16 E
Bežeck	76	57.47 N	36.39 E
Bežeckij Verch ⋀[1]	76	57.36 N	36.54 E
Bezenčuk	80	52.59 N	49.26 E
Bezerra ≃	255	13.16 S	47.31 W
Bezerros	250	8.14 S	35.45 W
Bezet	132	33.05 N	35.08 E
Béziers	32	43.21 N	3.15 E
Bezimenne	83	47.06 N	37.56 E
Bezmein	128	38.05 N	58.12 E
Bezmenšur	80	56.29 N	51.17 E
Bezno	54	50.22 N	14.48 E
Bezons	261	48.56 N	2.13 E
Bežta	84	42.08 N	46.08 E
Bezwada → Vijayawāda	122	16.31 N	80.37 E
Bezym'anka	80	49.56 N	43.15 E
Bezym'annaja	80	51.20 N	46.26 E
Bezzecca	64	45.55 N	10.43 E
Bezzubovo	82	55.27 N	38.55 E
Bhabānipur, India	272b	22.57 N	88.27 E
Bhabānipur, India	272b	22.56 N	88.13 E
Bhabhua	124	25.03 N	83.37 E
Bhābta	126	23.59 N	88.15 E
Bhadarwāh	123	32.59 N	75.43 E
Bhadaur	123	30.29 N	75.19 E
Bhādgāon → Bhaktapur	124	27.42 N	85.27 E
Bhadohi	124	25.25 N	82.34 E
Bhādra	123	29.07 N	75.10 E
Bhadra ≃[1]	126	22.19 N	89.31 E
Bhadrāchalam	122	17.40 N	80.53 E
Bhadrak	120	21.03 N	86.30 E
Bhadrapur	124	26.32 N	88.06 E
Bhadra Reservoir ◎[1]	122	13.40 N	75.35 E
Bhadrāvati	122	13.52 N	75.43 E
Bhadreswar	126	22.50 N	88.21 E
Bhādua	272b	22.41 N	88.12 E
Bhāg	120	29.02 N	67.49 E
Bhagaiya	124	25.12 N	87.29 E
Bhāgalpur	124	25.15 N	87.00 E
Bhāgīrathi ≃, India	124	30.08 N	78.35 E
Bhāgīrathi ≃, India	126	23.25 N	88.23 E
Bhagirathpur	126	24.05 N	88.29 E
Bhagwānpur	126	22.07 N	87.45 E
Bhainsa	122	19.06 N	77.58 E
Bhāi Pheru	123	31.12 N	73.57 E
Bhairab ≃[1]	126	22.51 N	89.34 E
Bhairab Bāzār	120	24.04 N	90.58 E
Bhairhawā	124	27.31 N	83.24 E
Bhaironghāti	120	31.01 N	78.53 E
Bhakkar	123	31.38 N	71.04 E
Bhākra Dam ◆[6]	123	31.24 N	76.30 E
Bhaktapur	124	27.42 N	85.27 E
Bhal	272c	19.11 N	73.08 E
Bhālki	122	18.02 N	77.13 E
Bhalswa ◆[8]	272a	28.44 N	77.10 E
Bhalwāl	123	32.16 N	72.54 E
Bhamdūn	132	33.48 N	35.39 E
Bhamo	110	24.16 N	97.14 E
Bhandāra	120	21.10 N	79.39 E
Bhandārdaha	272b	22.37 N	88.13 E
Bhandāria	126	22.29 N	90.04 E
Bhānder	124	25.44 N	78.45 E
Bhander Plateau ⋀[1]	124	24.10 N	80.20 E
Bhāndup ◆[8]	272c	19.09 N	72.57 E
Bhānga	126	23.22 N	89.59 E
Bhāngar	126	22.31 N	88.37 E
Bhāngar Kāta Khāl ≃	272b	22.31 N	88.33 E
Bhanvad	120	21.56 N	69.47 E
Bhārat → India □[1]	118	20.00 N	77.00 E
Bharatpur, India	124	27.13 N	77.29 E
Bharatpur, India	126	23.53 N	88.05 E
Bharatpur, Nepāl	124	27.14 N	84.21 E
Bharthana	124	26.45 N	79.14 E
Bharūch	120	21.42 N	72.58 E
Bhātai	126	23.36 N	89.11 E
Bhātāpāra	120	21.44 N	81.56 E
Bhātār	126	23.25 N	87.54 E
Bhatgaon → Bhaktapur	124	27.42 N	85.27 E
Bhātghar Lake ◎[1]	122	18.12 N	73.49 E
Bhātiāpāra Ghāt	124	23.13 N	89.42 E
Bhatkal	122	13.58 N	74.34 E
Bhātpāra	126	22.52 N	88.24 E
Bhātpur	272b	22.43 N	88.25 E
Bhātsāla	126	22.33 N	90.30 E
Bhattapratāp	126	22.45 N	89.48 E
Bhattiprolu	122	16.06 N	80.47 E
Bhātua	272b	22.57 N	88.22 E
Bhaun	123	32.52 N	72.45 E
Bhaunja	272a	28.40 N	77.25 E
Bhavāni	122	11.27 N	77.41 E
Bhāvnagar	122	21.46 N	72.09 E
Bhawānīgarh	124	30.16 N	76.02 E
Bhawani Mandi	120	24.25 N	75.50 E
Bhawānipatna	122	19.54 N	83.10 E
Bhedia	126	23.36 N	87.42 E
Bheigeir, Beinn ∧[2]	46	55.44 N	6.05 W
Bhendkhal	272c	18.53 N	72.59 E
Bhera	123	32.29 N	72.55 E
Bheramara	126	24.02 N	88.58 E
Bherī □[8]	124	28.30 N	81.45 E
Bherī ≃	124	28.44 N	81.16 E
Bheula, Beinn ∧	46	56.08 N	4.58 W
Bhīkampur	272a	28.45 N	77.27 E
Bhīkangaon	120	21.52 N	75.57 E
Bhilai	120	21.13 N	81.26 E
Bhilainagar → Bhilai	120	21.13 N	81.26 E
Bhīlwāra	120	25.21 N	74.38 E
Bhīma ≃	122	16.24 N	77.18 E
Bhīmavaram	122	16.32 N	81.32 E
Bhimbar	123	32.59 N	74.04 E
Bhīmphedī	124	27.32 N	85.07 E
Bhīmpur, India	126	22.37 N	87.08 E
Bhimpur, India	272b	22.46 N	88.08 E
Bhind	124	26.34 N	78.48 E
Bhinga	124	27.43 N	81.56 E
Bhīnmāl	120	25.00 N	72.15 E
Bhiwandi	122	19.18 N	73.04 E
Bhiwāni	124	28.47 N	76.08 E
Bhoāgāchi	272b	22.57 N	88.20 E
Bhojpur	124	27.10 N	87.03 E
Bhojudih	126	23.38 N	86.27 E
Bhokardan	122	20.16 N	75.46 E
Bhola	124	22.41 N	90.39 E
Bhola ≃[1]	126	22.04 N	89.49 E
Bhongaon	124	27.15 N	79.11 E
Bhongīr	122	17.31 N	78.53 E
Bhonrāsa	124	22.59 N	76.12 E
Bhopāl	124	23.16 N	77.24 E
Bhopar	272c	19.12 N	73.05 E
Bhopura	272a	28.42 N	77.20 E
Bhoutan → Bhutan □[1]	120	27.30 N	90.30 E
Bhowali	124	29.23 N	79.31 E
Bhuāpur	272a	28.43 N	77.26 E
Bhuban	120	20.53 N	85.50 E
Bhubaneshwar	120	20.14 N	85.50 E
Bhucho	123	30.13 N	75.06 E
Bhuj	120	23.16 N	69.40 E
Bhunarheri	124	30.13 N	76.27 E
Bhunya	158	26.32 S	31.01 E
Bhusāwal	120	21.03 N	75.46 E
Bhūshana	126	23.24 N	89.40 E
Bhutali	272c	19.07 N	73.04 E
Bhutan (Druk-Yul) □[1], Asia	118	27.30 N	90.30 E
Bhutan (Druk-Yul) □[1], Asia	120	27.30 N	90.30 E
Bia ≃, Afr.	150	5.21 N	3.11 W
Biá ≃, Bra.	246	3.28 S	67.23 W
Bia, Phou ∧	110	18.59 N	103.09 E
Biābānak	128	32.11 N	64.11 E
Biabo ≃	248	6.58 S	76.23 W
Biacesa	64	45.56 N	10.47 E
Biache-Saint-Vaast	50	50.18 N	2.57 E
Biadene	64	45.47 N	12.04 E
Biafra, Bight of ⊂[3]	134	4.00 N	8.00 E
Biak I	164	1.00 S	136.00 E
Biała	30	50.23 N	17.40 E
Biała ≃	30	50.03 N	20.55 E
Biała Piska	30	53.37 N	22.04 E
Biała Podlaska	30	52.02 N	23.06 E
Biała Podlaska □[4]	30	52.00 N	23.00 E
Biała Rawska	30	51.49 N	20.29 E
Białobrzegi	30	51.40 N	20.57 E
Białogard	30	54.01 N	16.00 E
Białowieski Park Narodowy ♣	30	52.40 N	23.50 E
Biały Bór	30	53.54 N	16.51 E
Białystok	30	53.09 N	23.09 E
Białystok □[4]	30	53.00 N	23.00 E
Bian ≃	164	8.07 S	139.56 E
Bian, Bidean nam ∧	46	56.38 N	5.02 W
Biancavilla	70	37.38 N	14.52 E
Bianchi	68	39.06 N	16.24 E
Bianco	68	38.05 N	16.09 E
Bianco, Canale ≅	64	45.02 N	12.05 E
Bianco, Capo ▸	70	37.23 N	13.16 E
Bianco, Monte (Mont Blanc) ∧	62	45.50 N	6.52 E
Bian'er	102	31.14 N	101.28 E
Bianga	152	4.51 N	20.25 E
Bian'gezhuang	105	39.28 N	115.53 E
Biankouma	150	7.44 N	7.37 W
Bianlinzhen	98	37.26 N	116.32 E
Bianminchang	107	29.41 N	105.04 E
Bianniulupucun	104	41.30 N	123.42 E
Bianquanwopu	104	41.21 N	120.48 E
Bianzè	62	45.18 N	8.07 E
Biaora	124	23.55 N	76.54 E
Biaro, Pulau I	112	2.05 N	125.20 E
Biarritz	32	43.29 N	1.34 W
Biasca	58	46.22 N	8.58 E
Bias Fortes	256	21.36 S	43.46 W
Biassono	62	45.37 N	9.16 E
Biaza	86	56.38 N	78.18 E
Bibā	142	28.55 N	30.59 E
Bibai	92a	43.19 N	141.52 E
Bibala	152	14.46 S	13.21 E
Bībān	142	30.47 N	30.40 E
Bibane, Bahiret el ⊂	148	33.16 N	11.19 E
Bibanga	152	6.15 S	23.56 E
Bibban, Khawr V	140	11.00 N	32.41 E
Bibb City	192	32.30 N	84.59 W
Bibbiano	64	44.40 N	10.28 E
Bibbiena	66	43.42 N	11.49 E
Bibbona	66	43.16 N	10.35 E
Bibei ≃	34	42.24 N	7.13 W
Bibémi	146	9.19 N	13.53 E
Biberach	58	48.20 N	8.02 E
Biberach an der Riss	58	48.06 N	9.47 E
Biberbach	56	48.31 N	10.48 E
Biberonne ≃	261	48.59 N	2.41 E
Bibert ≃	56	49.27 N	10.59 E
Bibertal	58	48.24 N	10.12 E
Bibiani	150	6.28 N	2.20 W
Bībi Chīni	126	22.28 N	90.12 E
Bibione	64	45.38 N	13.00 E
Bibir'ovo	76	54.28 N	33.08 E
Biblián	246	2.42 S	78.52 W
Biblis	56	49.41 N	8.27 E
Bibo	102	29.02 N	99.20 E
Bibrka	78	49.38 N	24.18 E
Bic	186	48.22 N	68.42 W
Biča	86	57.53 N	70.37 E
Bicas	256	21.43 S	43.04 W
Bicaz	38	46.54 N	26.05 E
Biccari	68	41.24 N	15.11 E
Bicester	42	51.54 N	1.09 W
Bičevinka	76	59.44 N	37.40 E
Biche, Lac la ◎	182	54.50 N	112.03 W
Bichena	144	10.27 N	38.12 E
Bicheno	166	41.53 S	148.18 E
Bichhia	124	22.27 N	80.42 E
Bichl	64	47.43 N	11.24 E
Bichlbach	58	47.25 N	10.47 E
Bichota Canyon V	280	34.16 N	117.48 W
Biči ≃	89	52.10 N	139.50 E
Bičigt	88	47.06 N	95.05 E
Bickerstaffe	262	53.32 N	2.50 W
Bickerton, Cape ▸	9	66.20 S	136.56 E
Bickerton Island I	164	13.45 S	136.12 E
Bickle Knob ∧	188	38.56 N	79.44 W
Bickley ◆[8]	260	51.24 N	0.03 E
Bicknacre, Eng., U.K.	42	51.41 N	0.35 E
Bicknacre, Eng., U.K.	260	51.41 N	0.35 E
Bicknell, In., U.S.	194	38.46 N	87.18 W
Bicknell, Ut,. U.S.	200	38.20 N	111.32 W
Bicknor	260	51.18 N	0.40 E
Bicol ≃	116	13.44 N	123.07 E
Bicske	30	47.29 N	18.37 E
Bicudo ≃	255	18.04 S	44.33 W
Bičura	88	50.36 N	107.35 E
Bičurina	86	56.51 N	55.25 E
Bīd	122	18.59 N	75.46 E
Bida, Nig.	146	12.20 N	13.25 E
Bida, Nig.	150	9.05 N	6.01 E
Bīdar	122	17.54 N	77.33 E
Bidde	144	0.58 N	42.37 E
Biddeford	188	43.29 N	70.27 W
Biddenden	42	51.07 N	0.39 E
Biddiyā	132	32.07 N	35.05 E
Biddulph	44	53.08 N	2.10 W
Bideford	42	51.01 N	4.13 W
Bidente ≃	66	44.24 N	12.12 E
Bidford-on-Avon	42	52.10 N	1.51 W
Bidhūna	124	26.49 N	79.31 E
Bidian	100	32.38 N	113.03 E
Bīdokht	128	34.21 N	58.46 E
Bidoni	71	40.07 N	8.56 E
Bidor	114	4.07 N	101.17 E
Bidston	262	53.24 N	3.05 W
Bidwell	188	38.55 N	82.17 W
Bidwell, Mount ∧	204	41.58 N	120.10 W
Bidya ≃[1]	126	21.56 N	88.42 E
Bidyādhari ≃	272b	22.23 N	88.35 E
Bidyādharpur	272b	22.50 N	88.24 E
Bidžan	89	47.58 N	131.58 E
Bidžan ≃	89	47.44 N	132.19 E
Bie	40	59.05 N	16.12 E
Bié □[5]	152	12.30 S	17.15 E
Biebelried	56	49.46 N	10.04 E
Bieber, Dtsch.	56	50.09 N	9.19 E
Bieber, Ca., U.S.	204	41.07 N	121.08 W
Biebrza ≃	30	53.13 N	22.25 E
Biecz	30	49.44 N	21.14 E
Biedenkopf	56	50.55 N	8.32 E
Biederitz	54	52.09 N	11.43 E
Biedermannsdorf	264b	48.05 N	16.21 E
Bieguzhuang	105	39.19 N	116.39 E
Biei	92a	43.35 N	142.28 E
Biel (Bienne)	58	47.10 N	7.12 E
Bielawa	30	50.41 N	16.38 E
Bielawski, Mount ∧	226	37.13 N	122.06 W
Bielefeld	52	52.01 N	8.31 E
Bieler Lake ◎	176	70.20 N	73.00 W
Bielersee ◎	58	47.05 N	7.10 E
Bielin	54	52.47 N	14.28 E
Biella	62	45.34 N	8.03 E
Biella □[4]	62	45.35 N	8.50 E
Bielsk	30	52.40 N	19.49 E
Bielsko-Biała	30	49.49 N	19.02 E
Bielsko-Biała □[4]	30	49.40 N	19.10 E
Bielsk Podlaski	30	52.47 N	23.12 E
Biemenhorst	52	51.49 N	6.36 E
Bienenbüttel	52	53.08 N	10.29 E
Bienfait	184	49.08 N	102.47 W
Bien Hoa	110	10.57 N	106.49 E
Bienne → Biel	58	47.10 N	7.12 E
Bienne ≃, Fr.	50	48.15 N	0.04 E
Bienne ≃, Fr.	58	46.20 N	5.38 E
Bienno	64	45.56 N	10.18 E
Bientina	66	43.42 N	10.37 E
Bienville	194	32.21 N	92.58 W
Bienville, Lac ◎	176	55.05 N	72.40 W
Biere, Dtsch.	54	51.58 N	11.39 E
Bière, Schw.	58	46.33 N	6.20 E
Bierné	28	47.49 N	0.32 W
Bieruń Stary	30	50.06 N	19.06 E
Bierutów	30	51.08 N	17.32 E
Bierwart	56	50.34 N	5.01 E
Biesbos ◆[1]	52	51.45 N	4.50 E
Biesdorf ◆[8]	264a	52.31 N	13.33 E
Biese ≃	54	52.45 N	11.37 E
Biesel ◆[8]	263	51.10 N	6.29 E
Biesenthal	54	52.46 N	13.37 E
Bieshan	105	39.58 N	117.29 E
Biesiesvlei	158	26.22 S	25.55 E
Biesles	58	48.05 N	5.18 E
Biessenhofen, Dtsch.	58	47.50 N	10.38 E
Biessenhofen, Dtsch.	64	47.50 N	10.38 E
Bieszczadzki Park Narodowy ♣	30	49.05 N	22.45 E
Bieteluobaoluosika	89	48.35 N	119.56 E
Bietigheim	56	48.54 N	8.14 E
Bietigheim-Bissingen	56	48.58 N	9.07 E
Bietschhorn ∧	58	46.24 N	7.51 E
Bièvre	56	49.56 N	5.01 E
Bièvre ≃	261	48.47 N	2.20 E
Bièvres	261	48.45 N	2.13 E
Biferno ≃	66	41.59 N	15.02 E
Bifoun	152	0.22 S	10.23 E
Bifuka	92a	44.29 N	142.21 E
Bifurcación	258	34.19 S	56.48 W
Big ≃, Austl.	169	37.18 S	146.02 E
Big ≃, N.T., Can.	176	72.30 N	125.14 W
Big ≃, Sk., Can.	184	53.50 N	107.02 W
Big ≃, Ak., U.S.	180	63.00 N	154.56 W
Big ≃, Mo., U.S.	219	38.28 N	90.37 W
Biga	130	40.13 N	27.14 E
Bigadiç	130	39.23 N	28.08 E
Big A Mountain ∧	192	37.03 N	82.02 W
Big Annemessex River ⊂	208	38.03 N	75.50 W
Big Antelope Creek ≃	202	42.28 N	117.13 W
Big Bald Mountain ∧, N.B., Can.	186	47.12 N	66.25 W
Big Bald Mountain ∧, Ga., U.S.	192	34.45 N	84.19 W
Big Baldy ∧	202	44.47 N	115.13 W
Big Baldy Mountain ∧	202	46.58 N	110.37 W
Big Bar Creek	182	51.12 N	122.06 W
Big Basin Redwoods State Park ♣	226	37.09 N	122.17 W
Big Bay	190	46.49 N	87.44 W
Big Bay ⊂, N.Z.	172	44.18 S	168.05 E
Big Bay ⊂, Vanuatu	175f	15.06 S	166.54 E
Big Bay De Noc ⊂	190	45.46 N	86.43 W
Big Bay Point ▸	212	44.24 N	79.31 W
Big Bear City	228	34.15 N	116.50 W
Big Bear Lake	228	34.15 N	116.53 W
Big Bear Lake ◎	228	34.15 N	116.55 W
Big Beaver, Sk., Can.	184	49.08 N	105.10 W
Big Beaver, Pa., U.S.	214	40.50 N	80.20 W
Big Beaver Airport ⊠	281	42.33 N	83.06 W
Big Beaver Creek ≃, Mi., U.S.	281	42.32 N	83.01 W
Big Beaver Creek ≃, Oh., U.S.	218	39.01 N	83.03 W
Big Beaver Creek ≃, Wa., U.S.	224	48.40 N	121.08 W
Big Bell	162	27.21 S	117.40 E
Big Belt Mountains ⋀	202	46.40 N	111.25 W
Big Bend, Swaz.	158	26.50 S	31.57 E
Big Bend, Wi., U.S.	216	42.52 N	88.12 W
Big Bend National Park ♣	196	29.12 N	103.12 W
Big Bend Reservoir ◎[1]	182	52.57 N	115.37 W
Big Black ≃	194	32.00 N	91.05 W
Big Blue ≃, U.S.	198	39.11 N	96.32 W
Big Blue ≃, In., U.S.	218	39.20 N	85.59 W
Big Blue, West Fork ≃	198	40.42 N	96.59 W
Big Bone Lick State Park ♣	218	38.53 N	84.45 W
Big Bonito Creek ≃	200	33.34 N	109.56 W
Big Brook ≃	276	40.19 N	74.10 W
Big Brushy Creek ≃, Tx., U.S.	222	32.32 N	96.20 W
Big Brushy Creek ≃, Tx., U.S.	222	29.12 N	96.55 W
Big Bureau Creek ≃	194	41.17 N	89.21 W
Bigbury Bay ⊂	42	50.16 N	3.48 W
Big Cabin Creek ≃	194	36.26 N	95.08 W
Big Canyon V	196	30.05 N	101.55 W
Big Carlos Pass ⊂	220	26.24 N	81.52 W
Big Cedar Lake ◎	212	44.37 N	78.10 W
Big Chino Wash V	200	34.52 N	112.28 W
Big Clear Lake ◎	212	44.43 N	76.55 W
Big Clifty	194	37.32 N	86.09 W
Big Coulee Creek ≃	202	46.17 N	108.56 W
Big Cow Creek ≃	194	30.34 N	93.44 W
Big Creek, B.C., Can.	182	51.44 N	123.03 W
Big Creek, Ca., U.S.	226	37.12 N	119.14 W
Big Creek ≃, B.C., Can.	182	51.40 N	122.50 W
Big Creek ≃, On., Can.	214	42.19 N	82.27 W
Big Creek ≃, On., Can.	214	42.36 N	80.27 W
Big Creek ≃, Ar., U.S.	194	34.21 N	91.03 W
Big Creek ≃, Ca., U.S.	226	37.12 N	119.19 W
Big Creek ≃, Ca., U.S.	226	36.53 N	119.15 W
Big Creek ≃, Id., U.S.	202	45.06 N	114.44 W
Big Creek ≃, Il., U.S.	219	39.07 N	88.52 W
Big Creek ≃, In., U.S.	216	40.38 N	86.46 W
Big Creek ≃, In., U.S.	218	38.48 N	85.39 W
Big Creek ≃, Ks., U.S.	198	38.47 N	98.55 W
Big Creek ≃, La., U.S.	194	32.10 N	91.53 W
Big Creek ≃, Mo., U.S.	194	40.02 N	94.07 W
Big Creek ≃, Mo., U.S.	219	38.52 N	90.50 W
Big Creek ≃, Oh., U.S.	279a	41.27 N	81.41 W
Big Creek ≃, Or., U.S.	224	46.11 N	123.35 W
Big Creek ≃, Tx., U.S.	222	29.22 N	95.34 W
Big Creek ≃, Tx., U.S.	222	31.09 N	96.52 W
Big Creek ≃, Wa., U.S.	224	47.15 N	121.10 W
Big Creek, East Fork ≃	194	40.16 N	94.03 W
Big Creek, West Fork ≃	194	40.16 N	94.03 W
Big Creek Parkway ♣	279a	41.24 N	81.45 W
Big Creek Peak ∧	202	44.28 N	113.32 W
Big Crow Island I	276	40.37 N	73.33 W
Big Cypress Creek ≃	222	33.00 N	94.51 W
Big Cypress Indian Reservation ◆[4]	220	26.14 N	80.49 W
Big Cypress National Preserve ♣	220	25.55 N	81.10 W
Big Cypress Swamp ≡	220	26.10 N	81.38 W
Big Dalton Canyon V	280	34.10 N	117.48 W
Big Dalton Wash V	280	34.04 N	117.58 W
Big Darby Creek ≃	218	39.37 N	82.58 W
Big Delta	180	64.09 N	145.50 W
Big Desert ◆[2]	166	35.40 S	141.00 E
Big Diomede Island → Ratmanova, ostrov I	180	65.46 N	169.02 W
Big Ditch ≅	216	40.13 N	88.22 W
Big Dry Creek ≃	202	47.30 N	106.19 W
Big Dubbo Hill ∧	171b	35.25 S	148.36 E
Big Eau Pleine ≃	190	44.48 N	90.00 W
Big Elk Creek ≃	208	39.35 N	75.52 W
Big Elkhart Creek ≃	222	31.22 N	95.41 W
Big Elm Creek ≃	222	30.53 N	96.56 W
Bigelow Bight ⊂[3]	188	43.15 N	70.30 W
Big Escambia Creek ≃	194	30.58 N	87.14 W
Big Falls	190	48.11 N	93.48 W
Big Flat	194	36.00 N	92.24 W
Big Flat Creek ≃	194	31.33 N	87.31 W
Big Flats	210	42.08 N	76.56 W
Bigfork, Mn., U.S.	190	47.44 N	93.39 W
Bigfork, Mt., U.S.	202	48.04 N	114.04 W
Big Fork ≃	190	48.31 N	93.43 W
Big Four Ditch ≅	216	40.27 N	88.10 W
Big Frog Mountain ∧	192	35.00 N	84.32 W
Biggar, Sk., Can.	184	52.04 N	108.00 W
Biggar, Scot., U.K.	46	55.38 N	3.32 W
Biggarsberg ⋀	158	28.12 S	29.48 E
Bigge	56	51.21 N	8.28 E
Bigge Island I	164	14.35 S	125.10 E
Biggers	194	36.19 N	90.48 W
Biggestausee ◎[1]	56	51.05 N	7.55 E
Biggin Hill ◆[8]	42	51.18 N	0.04 E
Biggin Hill Aerodrome ⊠	260	51.19 N	0.03 E
Biggleswade	42	52.05 N	0.17 W
Biggs, Ca., U.S.	226	39.24 N	121.42 W
Biggs, Or., U.S.	224	45.40 N	120.50 W
Big Gull Lake ◎	212	44.50 N	76.58 W
Big Gully Creek ≃	184	53.13 N	109.03 W
Bighāi ≃[1]	126	22.10 N	90.13 E
Big Hawk Lake ◎	212	45.10 N	78.44 W
Bighead ≃	212	44.36 N	80.35 W
Big Hole ≃	202	45.34 N	112.20 W
Big Hole National Battlefield ⊥	202	45.35 N	113.35 W
Bighorn ≃	202	46.09 N	107.28 W

≃	River	Fluß	Río	Rivière	Rio
≅	Canal	Kanal	Canal	Canal	Canal
⌊	Waterfall, Rapids	Wasserfall, Stromschnellen	Cascada, Rápidos	Chute d'eau, Rapides	Cascata, Rápidos
)(	Strait	Meeresstraße	Estrecho	Détroit	Estreito
⊂	Bay, Gulf	Bucht, Golf	Bahía, Golfo	Baie, Golfe	Baía, Golfo
◎	Lake, Lakes	See, Seen	Lago, Lagos	Lac, Lacs	Lago, Lagos
≡	Swamp	Sumpf	Pantano	Marais	Pântano
⊓	Ice Features, Glacier	Eis- und Gletscherformen	Accidentes Glaciales	Formes glaciaires	Acidentes glaciares
⊤	Other Hydrographic Features	Andere Hydrographische Objekte	Otros Elementos Hidrográficos	Autres données hydrographiques	Outros acidentes hidrográficos
✢	Submarine Features	Untermeerische Objekte	Accidentes Submarinos	Formes de relief sous-marin	Acidentes submarinos
□	Political Unit	Politische Einheit	Unidad Politica	Entité politique	Unidade política
⊍	Cultural Institution	Kulturelle Institution	Institución Cultural	Institution culturelle	Instituição cultural
⊥	Historical Site	Historische Stätte	Sitio Histórico	Site historique	Sitio histórico
♣	Recreational Site	Erholungs- und Ferienort	Sitio de Recreo	Centre de loisirs	Area de Lazer
⊠	Airport	Flughafen	Aeropuerto	Aéroport	Aeroporto
■	Military Installation	Militäranlage	Instalación Militar	Installation militaire	Instalação militar
◆	Miscellaneous	Verschiedenes	Misceláneo	Divers	Diversos

ENGLISH / DEUTSCH

Name	Page	Lat.°′	Long.°′
Bighorn Basin ≚¹	202	44.15 N	108.10 W
Bighorn Canyon National Recreation Area ♦	202	45.00 N	108.15 W
Big Horn Lake ⊜¹	202	45.06 N	108.08 W
Bighorn Mountains ⋏	202	44.00 N	107.30 W
Bight, Head of c	162	31.30 S	131.10 E
Big Huckleberry Mountain ∧	224	45.51 N	121.47 W
Big Island	192	37.32 N	79.21 W
Big Island I, N.T., Can.	176	62.43 N	70.43 W
Big Island I, On., Can.	184	49.10 N	94.40 W
Big Island I, On., Can.	212	44.33 N	78.30 W
Big Knob ∧	192	36.40 N	82.31 W
Big Koniuji Island I	180	55.06 N	159.33 W
Big Lake, Ak., U.S.	180	61.33 N	149.52 W
Big Lake, Mn., U.S.	190	45.19 N	93.44 W
Big Lake, Tx., U.S.	196	31.11 N	101.27 W
Big Lake, Wa., U.S.	224	48.24 N	122.14 W
Big Lake ⊜, Me., U.S.	188	45.10 N	67.40 W
Big Lake ⊜, Wa., U.S.	224	48.23 N	122.12 W
Bigler	214	40.59 N	78.19 W
Biglerville	208	39.55 N	77.14 W
Big Lick Creek ≃	216	40.22 N	85.27 W
Big Lookout Mountain ∧	202	44.37 N	117.17 W
Big Lost ≃	202	43.50 N	112.44 W
Big Monon Ditch ≋	216	40.52 N	86.46 W
Big Mossy Point ›	184	53.41 N	97.57 W
Big Mountain ∧, B.C., Can.	180	56.53 N	131.31 W
Big Mountain ∧, Nv., U.S.	204	41.17 N	119.04 W
Big Mountain Creek ≃	182	55.04 N	118.39 W
Big Muddy ≃	194	37.35 N	89.31 W
Big Muddy, Casey Fork ≃	194	38.06 N	88.57 W
Big Muddy Creek ≃, Mt., U.S.	198	48.08 N	104.36 W
Big Muddy Creek ≃, N.D., U.S.	198	46.37 N	101.24 W
Big Muddy Lake ⊜	184	49.08 N	104.54 W
Big Muscamoot Bay c	281	42.33 N	82.40 W
Bignasco	58	46.20 N	8.36 E
Big Nasty Creek ≃	198	45.41 N	102.51 W
Big Nemaha, North Fork ≃	198	40.04 N	95.43 W
Bignona	150	12.49 N	16.14 W
Big Oak Flat	226	37.49 N	120.16 W
Bigot, Morne ∧²	240e	14.31 N	61.04 W
Big Otter ≃	192	37.07 N	79.23 W
Big Otter Creek ≃	212	42.38 N	80.48 W
Big Ox Creek ≃	218	38.44 N	85.52 W
Big Pine	204	37.09 N	118.17 W
Big Pine Creek ≃	216	40.18 N	87.15 W
Big Pine Key	220	24.40 N	81.21 W
Big Pine Key I	220	24.42 N	81.23 W
Big Pine Mountain ∧	204	34.42 N	119.39 W
Big Piney	200	42.32 N	110.06 W
Big Piney ≃	194	37.53 N	92.04 W
Big Piney Creek ≃	194	35.20 N	93.20 W
Big Pipe Creek ≃	208	39.36 N	77.17 W
Big Plain	218	39.50 N	83.17 W
Big Pocono State Park ♦	210	41.03 N	75.19 W
Bigpoint	194	30.35 N	88.28 W
Big Pond	210	41.53 N	76.43 W
Big Porcupine Creek ≃	202	46.16 N	106.43 W
Big Porcupine Lake ⊜	212	45.27 N	78.36 W
Big Prairie	214	40.40 N	82.06 W
Big Prairie Creek ≃	194	32.35 N	87.45 W
Big Quilcene ≃	224	47.49 N	122.52 W
Big Quill Lake ⊜	184	51.55 N	104.22 W
Big Raccoon Creek ≃	194	39.46 N	87.22 W
Big Rapids	190	43.41 N	85.29 W
Bigras, Île I	275a	45.31 N	73.51 W
Big Rib ≃	190	44.56 N	89.41 W
Big Rideau Lake ⊜	212	44.45 N	76.14 W
Big River	184	53.50 N	107.01 W
Big River Indian Reserve ⊸⁴	184	53.33 N	107.10 W
Big Rock	216	41.46 N	88.33 W
Big Rock Creek ≃	216	41.38 N	88.32 W
Big Rocky Creek ≃	222	29.34 N	96.50 W
Big Run	214	40.58 N	78.52 W
Big Sable ≃	190	44.02 N	86.31 W
Big Sable Point ›	190	44.03 N	86.31 W
Big Salmon ≃	180	61.52 N	134.56 W
Big Salmon Range ⋏	180	61.10 N	133.45 W
Big Sand Lake ⊜	176	57.45 N	99.42 W
Big Sandy, Mt., U.S.	202	48.10 N	110.06 W
Big Sandy, Tn., U.S.	194	36.14 N	88.05 W
Big Sandy, Tx., U.S.	222	32.35 N	95.07 W
Big Sandy ≃, U.S.	188	38.25 N	82.36 W
Big Sandy ≃, Az., U.S.	200	34.19 N	113.31 W
Big Sandy ≃, Tn., U.S.	194	36.15 N	88.06 W
Big Sandy ≃, Wy., U.S.	202	41.51 N	109.47 W
Big Sandy Creek ≃, Ca., U.S.	226	35.47 N	120.43 W
Big Sandy Creek ≃, Co., U.S.	198	38.06 N	102.29 W
Big Sandy Creek ≃, Ga., U.S.	192	32.42 N	82.57 W
Big Sandy Creek ≃, Mt., U.S.	202	48.34 N	109.48 W
Big Sandy Creek ≃, Ne., U.S.	198	40.13 N	97.18 W
Big Sandy Creek ≃, Tx., U.S.	196	33.11 N	97.40 W
Big Sandy Creek ≃, Tx., U.S.	222	32.33 N	95.05 W
Big Sandy Creek ≃, Tx., U.S.	222	30.31 N	94.28 W
Big Sandy Lake ⊜, Sk., Can.	184	54.26 N	104.04 W
Big Sandy Lake ⊜, Mn., U.S.	190	46.45 N	93.17 W
Big Sandy Reservoir ⊜¹	200	42.16 N	109.26 W
Big Satilla Creek ≃	192	31.27 N	82.03 W
Bigsby Island I	184	49.04 N	94.35 W
Big Sewickley Creek ≃	279b	40.35 N	80.13 W
Big Shawnee Creek ≃	216	40.15 N	87.18 W
Big Sheep Mountain ∧	202	47.03 N	105.43 W
Big Signal Peak ∧	204	39.31 N	123.06 W
Big Sinking Creek ≃	194	37.55 N	86.31 W
Big Sioux ≃	198	42.30 N	96.25 W
Big Sixmile Creek ≃	284a	43.02 N	79.01 W
Big Sky	202	45.17 N	111.17 W
Big Slough ≃	192	30.56 N	84.33 W
Big Smoky Valley V	204	38.30 N	117.15 W
Big Snowy Mountains ⋏	202	46.50 N	109.30 W
Big Southern Butte ∧	202	43.23 N	113.01 W
Big Spanish Channel ʯ	220	24.44 N	81.20 W
Bigspring, Mo., U.S.	219	38.38 N	91.28 W
Big Spring, Tx., U.S.	196	32.15 N	101.28 W
Big Springs	198	41.03 N	102.04 W
Big Spruce Knob ∧	188	38.16 N	80.12 W
Big Squaw Mountain ∧	188	45.30 N	69.45 W
Bigstick Lake ⊜	184	50.16 N	109.20 W
Bigstone ≃	184	55.55 N	94.36 W
Big Stone City	198	45.17 N	96.27 W
Big Stone Gap	192	36.52 N	82.44 W
Bigstone Lake ⊜, Mb., Can.	184	53.42 N	95.44 W
Big Stone Lake ⊜, U.S.	198	45.25 N	96.40 W
Big Sunflower ≃	194	32.40 N	90.40 W
Big Sur	226	36.16 N	121.48 W
Big Sur ≃	226	36.17 N	121.51 W
Big Sur ⊸¹	226	35.45 N	121.20 W
Big Swamp Creek ≃	194	32.19 N	86.49 W
Big Swan Creek ≃	194	35.46 N	87.24 W
Big Thicket National Preserve ♦	222	32.35 N	94.40 W
Big Thompson ≃	200	40.21 N	104.45 W
Big Timber	202	45.50 N	109.57 W
Big Timber Creek ≃	285	39.53 N	75.08 W
Big Timber Creek, North Branch ≃	285	39.50 N	75.05 W
Big Timber Creek, South Branch ≃	285	39.50 N	75.05 W
Big Torch Key I	220	24.43 N	81.26 W
Big Tree	210	42.46 N	78.49 W
Big Trout Lake ⊜, On., Can.	176	53.45 N	90.00 W
Big Trout Lake ⊜, On., Can.	212	44.56 N	78.56 W
Big Tujunga Canyon V	228	34.16 N	118.18 W
Big Tujunga Dam ⊸⁶	280	34.18 N	118.12 W
Biguaçu	252	27.30 S	48.40 W
Big Valley	182	52.02 N	112.46 W
Bigwa	154	7.13 S	39.09 E
Big Walnut Creek ≃, In., U.S.	194	39.30 N	86.57 W
Big Walnut Creek ≃, Oh., U.S.	218	39.48 N	83.01 W
Big Warrambool ≃	166	30.05 S	147.33 E
Big Water	200	37.05 N	111.41 W
Big Wells	196	28.34 N	99.34 W
Big White Mountain ∧	182	49.42 N	118.58 W
Big Wills Creek ≃	194	33.59 N	86.00 W
Big Wood ≃	202	42.52 N	114.54 W
Bihać	36	44.49 N	15.52 E
Bīhar	124	25.11 N	85.31 E
Bihār □³	124	25.00 N	86.00 E
Biharamulo	154	2.38 S	31.20 E
Bihārīganj	124	25.44 N	86.59 E
Bihor □⁶	38	47.00 N	22.15 E
Bihor, Vârful ∧	38	46.27 N	22.42 E
Bihoro	92a	43.49 N	144.07 E
Bihosava	76	55.49 N	27.43 E
Bihu	100	28.21 N	119.48 E
Bihun	78	51.24 N	28.17 E
Bija ≃	86	52.25 N	85.05 E
Bijagós, Arquipélago dos II	150	11.25 N	16.20 W
Bijainagar	120	25.56 N	74.38 E
Bijaipur	124	26.03 N	77.22 E
Bijaipura	124	24.46 N	77.48 E
Bijāpur	122	16.50 N	75.42 E
Bījār	128	35.52 N	47.36 E
Bijāwar	124	24.38 N	79.30 E
Bijbān Chāh	128	26.54 N	64.42 E
Bījbiāra	123	33.48 N	75.06 E
Bijeljina	38	44.45 N	19.13 E
Bijelo Polje	38	43.02 N	19.44 E
Bijiang	110	26.30 N	98.55 E
Bijia Shan ∧	105	40.17 N	116.50 E
Bijie	102	27.18 N	105.20 E
Bijlikol', ozero ⊜	85	43.03 N	70.41 E
Bijna	272b	22.55 N	88.27 E
Bijni	124	26.31 N	90.40 E
Bijnor	124	29.22 N	78.08 E
Bijōki	268	35.49 N	139.39 E
Bijou Creek ≃	198	40.17 N	103.52 W
Bijpur	126	22.56 N	88.26 E
Bijsk	86	52.34 N	85.15 E
Bijwāsan ⊸⁸	272a	28.32 N	77.03 E
Bīkāner	120	28.01 N	73.18 E
Bīkaner Canal ≋	123	30.08 N	73.57 E
Bikar I¹	14	12.15 N	170.06 E
Bikbulovo	80	55.39 N	53.26 E
Bike	144	9.30 N	41.18 E
Bikeman Island I	174t	1.22 N	173.00 E
Bikenibeu	174t	1.21 N	173.07 E
Bikeqi	102	40.45 N	111.17 E
Bikeru	112	5.15 S	120.07 E
Bikfayyā	132	33.55 N	35.41 E
Bikié	152	3.06 S	13.52 E
Bikin	89	46.48 N	134.16 E
Bikin ≃	89	46.51 N	134.02 E
Bikini I¹	14	11.35 N	165.23 E
Bikita	154	20.06 S	31.41 E
Bīkkū Bīttī ∧	146	22.00 N	19.12 E
Bikl'an'	80	55.37 N	52.10 E
Bikoro	152	0.45 S	18.07 E
Bikuar, Parque Nacional do ♦	152	15.12 S	14.42 E
Bila ≃, Indon.	114	2.30 N	100.08 E
Bila ≃, Ukr.	83	49.18 N	38.52 E
Bila ≃, Ukr.	83	48.35 N	39.10 E
Bilaa Point ›	116	9.49 N	125.26 E
Bilac	255	21.24 S	50.28 W
Bilād Zahrān ⊸¹	144	20.16 N	41.14 E
Bílá hora ⊥	54	50.05 N	14.20 E
Bila Krynytsya, Ukr.	78	47.21 N	33.10 E
Bila Krynytsya, Ukr.	78	50.38 N	29.29 E
Bilang, Teluk c	112	1.15 N	121.25 E
Bilanga	150	12.32 N	0.02 E
Bilāra	120	26.10 N	73.42 E
Bilāri	124	28.38 N	78.48 E
Bil'arsk	80	54.58 N	50.22 E
Bilāsipāra	124	26.14 N	90.14 E
Bilāspur, India	123	31.20 N	76.45 E
Bilāspur, India	124	28.53 N	79.16 E
Bilāspur, India	124	22.05 N	82.09 E
Biläsuvar, Azer.	84	39.24 N	48.24 E
Biläsuvar (Pushkino), Azer.	84	39.27 N	48.33 E
Bilatan Island I	116	4.59 N	120.00 E
Bilato	112	0.32 N	122.38 E
Bila Tserkva	78	49.49 N	30.07 E
Bilauktaung Range ⋏	110	13.00 N	99.00 E
Bilbao	34	43.15 N	2.58 W
Bilbays	142	30.25 N	31.34 E
Bilbays Military Base ■	142	30.24 N	31.36 E
Bilbilis ⊥	34	41.25 N	1.39 W
Bil'čir	88	51.02 N	110.34 E
Bile	83	48.31 N	39.04 E
Bileća	38	42.53 N	18.26 E
Bilecik	130	40.09 N	29.59 E
Bilecik □⁴	130	40.10 N	30.10 E
Bilen'ka ≃	83	48.53 N	38.29 E
Bilen'ke, Ukr.	78	47.37 N	35.03 E
Bilen'ke, Ukr.	83	48.46 N	37.38 E
Biles Island I	285	40.10 N	74.45 W
Biłgoraj	30	50.34 N	22.43 E
Bilgrām	124	27.11 N	80.02 E
Bilhorod-Dnistrovs'kyy	78	46.12 N	30.20 E
Bili	154	4.09 N	25.10 E
Bili ≃	136	4.09 N	22.29 E
Bilian	100	28.21 N	120.33 E
Bilifyā	142	29.07 N	31.03 E
Bilimora	120	20.45 N	72.57 E
Bilin	110	17.14 N	97.15 E
Bilin ≃	110	17.05 N	97.08 E
Bílina	54	50.35 N	13.45 E
Bílina ≃	54	50.40 N	14.02 E
Bilioso ≃	68	40.39 N	16.24 E
Biliran Island I	116	11.35 N	124.28 E
Biliran Strait ʯ	116	11.30 N	124.28 E
Biliri	146	9.52 N	11.13 E
Biliu ≃	98	39.30 N	122.36 E
Bilk ⊸⁸	263	51.12 N	6.47 E
Bilky	78	50.49 N	28.11 E
Billabong Creek ≃	166	35.06 S	144.02 E
Billeberga	41	55.53 N	13.00 E
Billerbeck	52	51.59 N	7.17 E
Billerica	207	42.33 N	71.16 W
Billericay	42	51.38 N	0.25 E
Billesdon	42	52.37 N	0.55 W
Billesholm	41	56.03 N	13.00 E
Billiat	58	46.04 N	5.47 E
Billigheim	56	49.21 N	9.15 E
Billiluna	162	19.37 S	127.41 E
Billinge, Sve.	41	55.58 N	13.21 E
Billinge, Eng., U.K.	262	53.30 N	2.42 W
Billingen ⋏²	26	58.24 N	13.45 E
Billingham	44	54.36 N	1.17 W
Billings, Mo., U.S.	194	37.04 N	93.33 W
Billings, Mt., U.S.	202	45.46 N	108.30 W
Billings, Ok., U.S.	196	36.31 N	97.26 W
Billings, Reprêsa ⊜¹	256	23.47 S	46.37 W
Billingsfors	26	58.59 N	12.15 E
Billings Heights	202	45.50 N	108.32 W
Billingshurst	42	51.01 N	0.28 W
Billmerich	263	51.30 N	7.41 E
Billolo ≃	273b	4.07 S	15.19 E
Billom	32	45.44 N	3.21 E
Billund	41	55.44 N	9.07 E
Bill Williams ≃	200	34.17 N	114.03 W
Bill Williams Mountain ∧	200	35.12 N	112.12 W
Billy Chinook, Lake ⊜¹	202	44.33 N	121.20 W
Billy-Montigny	50	50.25 N	2.52 E
Bilma	146	18.41 N	12.56 E
Biloela	166	24.24 S	150.30 E
Bilo Gora ⋏	36	46.06 N	16.46 E
Bilohirs'k	78	45.03 N	34.36 E
Bilohir'ya	78	50.01 N	26.25 E
Bilohorivka	83	48.55 N	38.15 E
Bilohorodka	78	50.00 N	26.39 E
Bilokurakine	83	49.33 N	38.44 E
Biloluts'k	83	49.41 N	39.02 E
Bilopillya	78	51.09 N	34.18 E
Bilousivka	78	49.57 N	32.20 E
Bilovods'k	83	49.12 N	39.35 E
Biloxi	194	30.23 N	88.53 W
Biloxi ≃	194	30.26 N	89.00 W
Biloxi Creek ≃	222	31.05 N	94.37 W
Bilozerka	78	46.37 N	32.27 E
Bilozers'ke	78	48.33 N	37.04 E
Bilozir'ya, Ukr.	78	49.29 N	31.35 E
Bilozir'ya, Ukr.	78	49.18 N	31.54 E
Bilpa Morea Claypan ≚	166	25.00 S	140.00 E
Bilpin	170	33.30 S	150.31 E
Bilqās Qism Awwal	142	31.13 N	31.21 E
Bilsārā	126	23.05 N	88.10 E
Bil'sha Kam'yanka ≃	83	48.22 N	40.04 E
Bilshausen	52	51.37 N	10.10 E
Bil'shivtsi	78	49.12 N	24.44 E
Bilsi	124	28.08 N	78.55 E
Bil's'ka Volya	78	51.27 N	25.49 E
Bilston	42	52.34 N	2.04 W
Biltāj	142	31.00 N	30.59 E
Bilthoven	52	52.07 N	5.17 E
Biltine	146	14.32 N	20.55 E
Biltine □⁵	146	15.00 N	21.00 E
Biltmore Forest	192	35.32 N	82.31 W
Bilugyun Island I	110	16.24 N	97.32 E
Bilwaskarma	236	14.45 N	83.53 W
Bilyayivka	78	46.29 N	30.12 E
Bilychi	78	50.29 N	30.19 E
Bilyky	78	49.15 N	34.16 E
Bilyts'ke	83	48.25 N	37.13 E
Bilyy Kolodyaz'	78	50.12 N	37.08 E
Bilzen	56	50.52 N	5.31 E
Bima	115b	8.28 S	118.43 E
Bimbān	140	24.26 N	32.53 E
Bimbe	152	11.49 S	15.49 E
Bimberi Peak ∧	171b	35.40 S	148.47 E
Bimbila	150	8.51 N	0.04 E
Bimbo	152	4.18 N	18.33 E
Bimbowrie	166	32.03 S	140.09 E
Bimé	273b	4.09 S	15.11 E
Bimini Islands II	192	25.42 N	79.15 W
Bin ≃	100	23.40 N	112.58 E
Bina	175e	8.55 S	160.46 E
Bīna-Etāwa	124	24.11 N	78.11 E
Binaiya, Gunung ∧	164	3.11 S	129.26 E
Binalbagan	116	10.12 N	122.50 E
Binalbagan ≃	116	10.12 N	122.51 E
Bin'an	89	45.50 N	127.45 E
Binanga	114	1.24 N	99.46 E
Binangonan	116	14.28 N	121.11 E
Binas	50	47.54 N	1.28 E
Binasco	62	45.20 N	9.06 E
Binau	56	49.22 N	9.04 E
Binche	50	50.24 N	4.10 E
Binchuan	102	25.46 N	100.33 E
Bindal	24	65.06 N	12.30 E
Binder, Mong.	88	48.35 N	110.36 E
Binder, Tchad	146	9.58 N	14.28 E
Bindki	124	26.02 N	80.36 E
Bindlach	60	49.59 N	11.37 E
Bindloss	184	50.52 N	110.16 W
Bindo, Mount ∧	170	33.40 S	150.01 E
Bindow	264a	52.17 N	13.45 E
Bindura	154	17.19 S	31.20 E
Bine-el-Ouidane	148	32.07 N	6.26 W
Binéfar	34	41.51 N	0.18 E
Binford	198	47.33 N	98.20 W
Binga, Pil.	116	10.45 N	119.19 E
Binga, R.D.C.	152	2.23 N	20.30 E
Binga, Monte ∧	156	19.45 S	33.04 E
Bingara	166	29.52 S	150.34 E
Bingaram Island I	122	10.56 N	72.17 E
Bingay Point ›	116	13.04 N	124.11 E
Bingcha	100	32.30 N	120.52 E
Bingen, Dtsch.	56	49.57 N	7.54 E
Bingen, Wa., U.S.	224	45.42 N	121.27 W
Binger	196	35.18 N	98.20 W
Bingerbrück	56	49.58 N	7.53 E
Bingerville	150	5.21 N	3.54 W
Bingfang	106	32.15 N	121.20 E
Bingham, Eng., U.K.	42	52.57 N	0.57 W
Bingham, Me., U.S.	188	45.03 N	69.52 W
Bingham ≃	168a	33.20 S	116.16 E
Bingham Farms	281	42.32 N	83.16 W
Binghamton	210	42.05 N	75.55 W
Bin Ghashīr	146	32.41 N	13.11 E
Bin Ghunaymah, Jabal ⋏	146	25.00 N	15.30 E
Bingi	154	0.24 S	29.05 E
Bingley	44	53.51 N	1.50 W
Bingöl	130	38.53 N	40.29 E
Bingöl □⁴	130	39.00 N	40.40 E
Bingöl Dağları ⋏	130	39.20 N	41.20 E
Binhai (Dongkan)	100	34.03 N	119.51 E
Binh Ca	110	21.48 N	105.18 E
Binh Chanh	269c	10.40 N	106.34 E
Binh Gia	110	21.59 N	106.21 E
Binh Hung Hoa	269c	10.49 N	106.37 E
Binh Khe	110	13.57 N	108.51 E
Binh Kieu	110	15.35 N	108.04 E
Bin-Houyé	150	6.47 N	8.19 W
Binh Son	110	15.18 N	108.46 E
Binh Trung	269c	10.47 N	106.46 E
Binigsian Point ›	116	9.50 N	122.23 E
Bining	56	49.02 N	7.15 E
Binjai, Indon.	112	3.48 N	108.14 E
Binjai, Indon.	114	3.36 N	98.30 E
Binjohara	114	2.12 N	98.12 E
Binlūd, Kūh-e ⋏	128	36.28 N	58.49 E
Binna Burra	171a	28.13 S	153.14 E
Binnah, Ras ›	144	11.08 N	51.10 E
Binnaway	166	31.33 S	149.23 E
Binnian, Slieve ∧	48	54.08 N	5.58 W
Binningen	58	47.32 N	7.34 E
Binodepur	126	23.26 N	89.30 E
Binongko, Pulau I	112	5.57 S	124.02 E
Binpur	126	22.36 N	86.55 E
Binscarth	184	50.37 N	101.16 W
Binsheim ⊸⁸	263	51.31 N	6.42 E
Bintan, Pulau I	112	1.05 N	104.30 E
Bintang	150	13.10 N	16.08 W
Bintang, Gunong ∧	114	5.25 N	100.52 E
Bintauna	112	0.53 N	123.33 E
Bint Goda	140	13.17 N	31.33 E
Bintimani ∧	150	9.13 N	11.07 W
Bint Jubayl	132	33.07 N	35.26 E
Bintuhan	112	4.48 S	103.22 E
Bintulu	112	3.10 N	113.02 E
Bintuni	164	2.07 S	133.32 E
Bintuni, Teluk c	164	2.20 S	133.30 E
Binxian, Zhg.	89	45.44 N	127.29 E
Binxian, Zhg.	98	37.28 N	117.56 E
Binxian, Zhg.	102	35.00 N	108.08 E
Binyamina	132	32.31 N	34.57 E
Binyang	102	23.18 N	108.46 E
Bin Yauri	150	10.47 N	4.50 E
Binz	54	54.24 N	13.36 E
Binza	273b	4.21 S	15.14 E
Binza ⊸⁸	273b	4.20 S	15.14 E
Binza ≃	273b	4.21 S	15.14 E
Bio Addo	144	8.18 N	49.48 E
Bíobío □⁴	252	37.00 S	72.30 W
Biobío ≃, Chile	252	36.49 S	73.10 W
Bíobío ≃, Chile	252	31.38 S	71.34 W
Biodi	154	3.19 N	28.35 E
Biograd	36	43.56 N	15.27 E
Biogradska Gora Nacionalni Park ♦	38	42.57 N	19.40 E
Bioko □⁴	152	3.30 N	8.40 E
Bioko I	152	3.30 N	8.40 E
Biola	226	36.48 N	120.00 W
Bionaz	62	45.52 N	7.25 E
Biondo	154	0.23 S	25.13 E
Biondo Monument ⊥	146	31.25 N	10.15 E
Biot	62	43.38 N	7.06 E
Bipindi	152	3.05 N	10.25 E
Bippen	52	52.35 N	7.44 E
Bippus	216	40.56 N	85.37 W
Biqiao	106	31.02 N	119.02 E
Bir, Ras ›	144	11.59 N	43.22 E
Bira, India	272b	22.47 N	88.34 E
Bira, Ross.	89	49.15 N	137.16 E
Bira, Ross.	89	49.02 N	132.30 E
Bira ≃	89	48.07 N	133.21 E
Birab	164	6.12 S	138.25 E
Bīraba	126	23.51 N	90.34 E
Birāk	146	27.32 N	14.16 E
Birakan	89	49.01 N	131.42 E
Bi'r 'Alī	144	14.01 N	48.19 E
Bi'r al-Uzam	146	31.54 N	23.58 E
Birandža	89	54.35 N	136.18 E
Birao	146	10.17 N	22.47 E
Birati	272b	22.39 N	88.27 E
Birava	154	2.21 S	28.54 E
Bircao → Buur Gaabo	144	1.12 S	41.51 E
Birch	262	53.34 N	2.13 W
Birch ≃, Ab., Can.	176	58.30 N	112.15 W
Birch ≃, W.V., U.S.	188	38.35 N	80.53 W
Birch Bay	224	48.55 N	122.45 W
Birch Bay c	224	48.53 N	122.47 W
Birch Bay State Park ♦	224	49.54 N	123.47 W
Birch Cliff ⊸⁸	275b	43.41 N	79.17 W
Birch Creek ≃, Ak., U.S.	180	66.30 N	146.30 W
Birch Creek ≃, Id., U.S.	202	43.51 N	112.43 W
Birch Creek ≃, Mt., U.S.	202	48.26 N	112.15 W
Birch Creek ≃, Mt., U.S.	202	47.45 N	109.34 W
Birch Hill Dam ⊸⁶	207	42.38 N	72.09 W
Birch Hills	184	52.59 N	105.25 W
Birchington	42	51.23 N	1.19 E
Birch Island	182	51.36 N	119.55 W
Birch Island I	184	52.25 N	99.55 W
Birch Lake ⊜, Ab., Can.	182	53.19 N	111.35 W
Birch Lake ⊜, On., Can.	184	51.24 N	92.20 W
Birch Lake ⊜, Sk., Can.	184	53.28 N	108.07 W
Birch Mountains ⋏²	176	57.30 N	112.30 W
Bir Chouhada	34	35.53 N	6.18 E
Birch Pond ⊜	283	42.28 N	71.00 W
Birch Reservoir ⊜¹	196	36.31 N	96.12 W
Birch River	184	52.23 N	101.06 W
Birch Run	190	43.15 N	83.47 W
Birch Run ≃	285	40.09 N	75.37 W
Birchrunville	285	40.08 N	75.39 W
Birch Tree	194	36.59 N	91.29 W
Birch Vale	262	53.23 N	1.57 W
Birchwood, Eng., U.K.	44	53.13 N	0.36 W
Birchwood, Ak., U.S.	180	61.28 N	149.22 W
Birchwood, Wi., U.S.	190	45.39 N	91.33 W
Birchwood City	284c	38.49 N	76.59 W
Birchwood Park, De., U.S.	285	39.22 N	75.39 W
Birchwood Park, N.J., U.S.	208	40.06 N	74.09 W
Birchy Bay	186	49.21 N	54.44 W
Bird City	198	39.45 N	101.31 W
Bird Creek ≃	196	36.13 N	95.44 W
Bird Island	198	44.46 N	94.53 W
Bird Island I, S. Afr.	158	33.51 S	26.18 E
Bird Island I, S. Geor.	244	54.00 S	38.05 W
Bird Island ʊ³	9	54.00 S	38.03 W
Bird Islet I	160	22.10 S	155.28 E
Bird River c	284b	39.23 N	76.23 W
Birdsall	210	42.23 N	77.55 W
Birdsboro	208	40.15 N	75.48 W
Birds Landing	282	38.08 N	121.52 W
Birdsview	224	48.32 N	121.52 W
Birdsville	166	25.54 S	139.22 E
Birdtail Creek ≃	184	50.16 N	101.12 W
Birdum	164	15.39 S	133.13 E
Birdum Creek ≃	164	15.14 S	133.00 E
Birdwood	168b	34.49 S	138.57 E
Birecik	130	37.02 N	37.58 E
Bire Kpatua Game Reserve ⊸⁴	154	5.12 N	27.36 E
Bir el Ater	148	34.44 N	8.03 E
Bir Enzaran	148	23.56 N	14.33 W
Bireuen	114	5.12 N	96.41 E
Bir Ghbalou	34	36.16 N	3.35 E
Birgi	126	22.42 N	86.41 E
Birgi Vecchi	70	37.53 N	12.29 E
Biri	116	12.41 N	124.22 E
Birigui	255	21.18 S	50.19 W
Biri Island I	116	12.40 N	124.22 E
Birikčul'	86	53.20 N	89.56 E
Biril'ussy	86	57.07 N	90.32 E
Birimbāl	142	31.21 N	30.30 E
Birimbāl al-Qadīmah	142	31.10 N	31.44 E
Birimşe	130	38.03 N	38.32 E
Biritiba-Mirim	256	23.35 S	46.02 W
Bīrjand	128	32.53 N	59.13 E
Birkat as-Sab'	142	30.38 N	31.05 E
Birkat Ghiṭās	142	31.07 N	30.16 E
Birkdale	262	53.37 N	3.02 W
Birkeland	26	58.20 N	8.14 E
Birken	182	50.29 N	122.36 W
Birkenau	56	49.34 N	8.43 E
Birkendorf	58	47.45 N	8.18 E
Birkenfeld, Dtsch.	56	48.52 N	8.38 E
Birkenfeld, Dtsch.	56	49.51 N	9.42 E
Birkenfeld, Dtsch.	56	49.39 N	7.10 E
Birkenfeld, Or., U.S.	224	45.59 N	123.20 W
Birkenhead	44	53.24 N	3.02 W
Birkenhead Park ♦	262	53.24 N	3.02 W
Birkenwerder bei Berlin	54	52.41 N	13.16 E
Birkerød	41	55.50 N	12.26 E
Birket Fatimé	146	12.54 N	19.05 E
Birkfeld	61	47.21 N	15.42 E
Birkholz	264a	52.38 N	13.34 E
Birkkarspitze ∧	64	47.25 N	11.25 E
Birk-Nack ›	41	54.48 N	9.55 E
Birksgate Range ⋏	162	27.10 S	129.45 E
Birky	78	49.42 N	36.02 E
Birla Museum ʊ	272b	22.32 N	88.22 E
Birlik, Kaz.	80	47.28 N	50.32 E
Birlik, Kaz.	86	44.05 N	73.31 E
Birling	260	51.19 N	0.25 E
Birling ∧²	274a	33.57 S	150.43 E
Birmā	142	30.51 N	30.54 E
Birmania → Myanmar □¹	110	22.00 N	98.00 E
Birmanie → Myanmar □¹	110	22.00 N	98.00 E
Birmingham, Eng., U.K.	42	52.28 N	1.55 W
Birmingham, Al., U.S.	194	33.31 N	86.48 W
Birmingham, Ia., U.S.	190	40.52 N	91.56 W
Birmingham, Mi., U.S.	216	42.32 N	83.12 W
Birmingham, N.J., U.S.	285	39.58 N	74.42 W
Birmingham, Oh., U.S.	214	41.20 N	82.21 W
Birmingham, Pa., U.S.	214	40.38 N	78.13 W
Birmingham Airport ⊠	42	52.27 N	1.45 W
Birmitrapur	124	22.24 N	84.46 E
Bîr Mogreïn (Fort-Trinquet)	148	25.14 N	11.35 W
Birnagar	126	23.14 N	88.33 E
Birnamwood	190	44.56 N	89.12 W
Birnbaum	64	46.41 N	12.54 E
Birni	150	10.00 N	1.31 E
Birnie I¹	14	3.35 S	171.31 W
Birni Ngaouré	150	13.05 N	2.54 E
Birnin Gwari	150	11.01 N	6.48 E
Birnin Kebbi	150	12.32 N	4.12 E
Birni Nkonni	150	13.48 N	5.15 E
Birnin Kudu	150	11.27 N	9.30 E
Birobidžan	89	48.48 N	132.57 E
Birobijan → Jevrej □³	89	48.30 N	132.00 E
Birofel'd	89	48.26 N	132.47 E
Birome	222	31.49 N	96.58 W
Birqāsh	142	30.10 N	31.02 E
Birr	48	53.05 N	7.54 W
Birregurra	169	38.20 S	143.48 E
Birrie ≃	166	29.43 S	146.37 E
Birrindudu	162	18.22 S	129.27 E
Birs (Birse) ≃	58	47.22 N	7.22 E
Birsk	86	55.25 N	55.32 E
Birstall	42	52.41 N	1.07 W
Birstein	56	50.21 N	9.19 E
Birštonas	76	54.37 N	24.02 E
Birten	263	51.38 N	6.29 E
Birtle	184	50.25 N	101.03 W
Birtley	44	54.54 N	1.34 W
Biru	120	31.30 N	93.51 E
Bir'učij	83	46.53 N	39.33 E
Bir'učja ≃	83	47.23 N	39.07 E
Birufu	164	5.52 S	138.24 E
Bir'ul'ka	88	53.52 N	106.21 E
Bir'ul'ovo ⊸⁸	265b	55.35 N	37.40 E
Birungu, Parc des ♦	154	1.25 S	29.30 E
Birūr	122	13.37 N	75.58 E
Bir'usa	88	57.10 N	96.30 E
Bir'usa (Ona) ≃	88	57.43 N	95.24 E
Bir'usinsk	88	55.57 N	97.49 E
Biryukove	83	47.57 N	39.44 E
Biržai	76	56.12 N	24.45 E
Bîrzava ≃	38	45.16 N	20.49 E
Birżebbuġa	36	35.49 N	14.32 E
Bisa, Pulau I	164	1.15 S	127.28 E
Bisaccia	68	41.01 N	15.22 E
Bisacquino	70	37.42 N	13.15 E
Bisāi, India	126	22.10 N	86.24 E
Bisai, Nihon	94	35.16 N	136.44 E
Bīsalpur	124	28.18 N	79.48 E
Bisamberg	264b	48.20 N	16.22 E
Bisamberg ∧²	264b	48.19 N	16.22 E
Bisan-shotō II	96	34.24 N	133.50 E
Bisbee, Az., U.S.	200	31.26 N	109.55 W
Bisbee, N.D., U.S.	198	48.37 N	99.22 W
Biscarrosse	32	44.24 N	1.10 W
Biscarrosse et de Parentis, Lac de c	32	44.20 N	1.10 W
Biscay, Bay of c	32	44.00 N	4.00 W
Biscayne, Key I	220	25.42 N	80.10 W
Biscayne Bay c	220	25.33 N	80.15 W
Biscayne National Park ♦	220	25.25 N	80.12 W
Bisceglie	68	41.14 N	16.31 E
Bischheim	58	48.37 N	7.45 E
Bischofsgrün	60	50.03 N	11.47 E
Bischofsheim, Dtsch.	56	50.24 N	10.01 E
Bischofsheim, Dtsch.	56	49.59 N	8.22 E
Bischofshofen	64	47.25 N	13.13 E
Bischofsmais	60	48.55 N	13.05 E
Bischofswerda	54	51.07 N	14.10 E
Bischofswiesen	64	47.39 N	12.57 E
Bischofszell	58	47.29 N	9.15 E
Bischwald, Étang de ⊜	56	49.00 N	6.42 E
Bischwiller	56	48.46 N	7.52 E
Biscoe, Ar., U.S.	194	34.49 N	91.24 W
Biscoe, N.C., U.S.	192	35.21 N	79.46 W
Biscoe Islands II	9	66.00 S	66.30 W
Biscotasi Lake ⊜	190	47.19 N	82.07 W
Biscucuy	246	9.22 N	69.59 W
Bise	174m	26.42 N	127.54 E
Bisei	96	34.41 N	133.33 E
Bisentina, Isola I	66	42.35 N	11.54 E
Bisenzio ≃	66	43.46 N	11.06 E
Biser	86	58.25 N	58.53 E
Biserovo	265b	55.47 N	38.07 E
Biserovskoje, ozero ⊜	265b	55.46 N	38.07 E
Bisert' ≃	86	56.39 N	57.55 E
Bise-zaki ›	174m	26.43 N	127.53 E
Bisha	144	15.28 N	37.34 E
Bīshah, Wādī V	144	21.24 N	43.26 E
Bishahari	126	23.10 N	89.01 E
Bishan	107	29.37 N	106.13 E
Bishanga	152	4.31 S	21.02 E
Bishaykhāli	126	23.28 N	89.09 E
Bishkek → Biškek	85	42.54 N	74.36 E
Bishkhāli ≃¹	126	21.59 N	89.59 E
Bishkin' ≃	83	49.15 N	39.35 E
Bishnāh	123	32.37 N	74.52 E
Bishnupur, India	120	24.38 N	93.46 E
Bishnupur, India	126	22.23 N	88.16 E
Bishnupur, India	126	23.05 N	87.19 E
Bishnupur, India	272b	22.37 N	88.31 E
Bisho	158	32.50 S	27.20 E
Bishop, Ca., U.S.	204	37.21 N	118.23 W
Bishop, Pa., U.S.	279b	40.19 N	80.12 W
Bishop, Tx., U.S.	196	27.35 N	97.47 W
Bishop Airport ⊠	216	42.58 N	83.44 W
Bishop Auckland	44	54.40 N	1.40 W
Bishop Rock I²	42a	49.52 N	6.27 W
Bishop's Castle	42	52.29 N	3.00 W
Bishop's Cleeve	42	51.57 N	2.04 W
Bishop's Falls	186	49.01 N	55.30 W
Bishops Frome	42	52.08 N	2.29 W
Bishops Head	208	38.16 N	76.04 W
Bishops Lydeard	42	51.04 N	3.12 W
Bishop's Stortford	42	51.53 N	0.09 E
Bishopsteignton	42	50.34 N	3.31 W
Bishopstoke	42	50.59 N	1.19 W
Bishopston	42	51.35 N	4.03 W
Bishop's Waltham	42	50.58 N	1.12 W
Bishopthorpe	44	53.55 N	1.06 W
Bishopton	206	45.35 N	71.35 W
Bishopville, Md., U.S.	208	38.26 N	75.11 W
Bishopville, S.C., U.S.	192	34.13 N	80.14 W
Bishrah, Ma'ṭan ⫪⁴	146	22.58 N	22.39 E
Bishrī, Jabal ∧	130	35.20 N	39.20 E
Bisignano	68	39.31 N	16.17 E
Bisina, Lake ⊜	154	1.38 N	33.56 E
Bisinadi Game Reserve ⊸⁴	154	0.10 N	38.20 E
Bisingen	58	48.18 N	8.55 E
Biskamža	86	53.30 N	89.30 E

Name	Seite	Breite°′	Länge°′ E = Ost
Biskaya, Golf von → Biscay, Bay of c	32	44.00 N	4.00 W
Biškek (Frunze)	85	42.54 N	74.36 E
Biskintā	132	33.57 N	35.43 E
Biskupiec	30	53.52 N	20.58 E
Bisley, Eng., U.K.	42	51.45 N	2.08 W
Bisley, Eng., U.K.	260	51.20 N	0.38 W
Bislich	263	51.41 N	6.29 E
Bislig	116	8.13 N	126.19 E
Bislig Bay c	116	8.14 N	126.22 E
Bismarck, Il., U.S.	216	40.16 N	87.37 W
Bismarck, Mo., U.S.	194	37.46 N	90.37 W
Bismarck, N.D., U.S.	198	46.48 N	100.47 W
Bismarck Archipelago II	164	5.00 S	150.00 E
Bismarck Range ⋏	164	5.30 S	144.45 E
Bismarck Sea ⫪²	164	4.00 S	148.00 E
Bismark	54	52.39 N	11.32 E
Bismil	130	37.51 N	40.40 E
Bismo	26	61.53 N	8.16 E
Bismuna, Laguna c	236	14.45 N	83.20 W
Biso	154	1.46 N	31.25 E
Bison	198	45.31 N	102.27 W
Bison Peak ∧	200	39.14 N	105.30 W
Bispberg	40	60.22 N	15.47 E
Bispgården	26	63.02 N	16.37 E
Bispingen	52	53.05 N	10.00 E
Bisrakh	272a	28.34 N	77.26 E
Bisrāmpur	124	24.15 N	83.56 E
Bissa, Djebel ∧	34	36.26 N	1.28 E
Bissau	150	11.51 N	15.35 W
Bissaula	146	7.00 N	10.27 E
Bissegem	50	50.49 N	3.13 E
Bissendorf, Dtsch.	52	52.14 N	8.10 E
Bissendorf, Dtsch.	52	52.31 N	9.45 E
Bissett	184	51.02 N	95.40 W
Bissigh, Lach ≃	144	0.45 N	41.33 E
Bissikrima	150	10.51 N	10.56 W
Bissingen	56	48.43 N	10.37 E
Bissingheim ⊸⁸	263	51.21 N	7.31 E
Bissorã	150	12.14 N	15.31 W
Bistcho Lake ⊜	176	59.40 N	118.40 W
Bistineau, Lake ⊜¹	194	32.25 N	93.22 W
Bistra ≃	38	45.29 N	22.11 E
Bistreț	38	43.54 N	23.30 E
Bistrica	61	46.33 N	16.16 E
Bistrița	38	47.08 N	24.30 E
Bistrița ≃	38	46.30 N	26.57 E
Bistrița-Năsăud □⁶	38	47.15 N	24.30 E
Biswān	124	27.30 N	81.00 E
Bisztynek	30	54.06 N	20.55 E
Bitadton	116	11.30 N	122.05 E
Bitam	152	2.05 N	11.29 E
Bitam, Oued ≃	34	35.15 N	5.11 E
Bitatolo ≃	273b	4.09 S	15.19 E
Bitburg	56	49.58 N	6.31 E
Bitca	265b	55.34 N	37.37 E
Bitca ≃	265b	55.34 N	37.37 E
Bitche	56	49.03 N	7.26 E
Bitchū	96	34.47 N	133.27 E
Bitéa, Ouadi V	146	13.11 N	20.10 E
Bitetto	68	41.02 N	16.45 E
Bithia ⊥	71	38.53 N	8.52 E
Bithlo	220	28.33 N	81.06 W
Bithynia □⁹	130	40.10 N	30.15 E
Bitia, Wādī V	140	17.34 N	32.15 E
Bitik	80	50.09 N	50.30 E
Bitkine	146	11.59 N	18.13 E
Bitlis	130	38.22 N	42.06 E
Bitlis □⁴	128	38.30 N	42.10 E
Bitola	38	41.01 N	21.20 E
Bitolj → Bitola	38	41.01 N	21.20 E
Bitonto	68	41.06 N	16.42 E
Bitou	150	11.16 N	0.18 W
Bitra Island I	122	11.33 N	72.09 E
Bitritto	68	41.03 N	16.50 E
Bitschwiller-lès-Thann	58	47.50 N	7.05 E
Bitter Creek ≃, Ut,. U.S.	200	39.58 N	109.25 W
Bitter Creek ≃, Wy., U.S.	200	41.31 N	109.27 W
Bitterfeld	54	51.37 N	12.20 E
Bitterfontein	158	31.00 S	18.32 E
Bitter Lake ⊜	184	50.08 N	109.48 W
Bittermark ⊸⁸	263	51.27 N	7.28 E
Bitterness, Mount ∧	172	44.45 S	170.18 E
Bittern Lake ⊜	184	53.55 N	105.50 W
Bitterroot ≃	202	46.52 N	114.06 W
Bitterroot, East Fork ≃	202	45.57 N	114.08 W
Bitterroot, West Fork ≃	202	45.57 N	114.08 W
Bitterroot Range ⋏	202	47.06 N	115.10 W
Bitterwater Creek ≃	226	35.41 N	119.58 W
Bitti	71	40.29 N	9.23 E
Bit'ug ≃	78	50.37 N	39.55 E
Bitung	112	1.27 N	125.11 E
Bitupitá	250	2.54 S	41.16 W
Bituruna	252	26.10 S	51.34 W
Biu	146	10.35 N	12.13 E
Bivalve	208	38.18 N	75.53 W
Bivins	194	33.01 N	94.12 W
Bivio	58	46.28 N	9.38 E
Bivona	70	37.37 N	13.26 E
Bivongi	68	38.28 N	16.27 E
Biwabik	190	47.31 N	92.20 W
Biwa-ko ⊜	94	35.15 N	136.05 E
Biwa-ko-kokutei-kōen ♦	94	35.10 N	136.00 E
Biwa-ko-ōhashi ⊸⁵	94	35.08 N	135.56 E
Bixby	196	35.56 N	95.52 W
Biyalā	142	31.10 N	31.13 E
Biyang	100	32.44 N	113.20 E
Biysk → Bijsk	86	52.34 N	85.15 E
Biyuk-Karasu ≃	78	45.27 N	34.47 E
Bi Yun Si (Temple of the Azure Clouds) ʊ¹	105	40.00 N	116.11 E
Biz'aki	80	55.56 N	52.28 E
Bizana	158	30.58 S	29.52 E
Biz'ar	86	57.31 N	56.09 E
Bizard, Île I	275a	45.29 N	73.54 W
Bižbul'ak	80	53.43 N	54.16 E
Bizcocho, Cuchilla del ⋏²	258	33.45 S	57.30 W
Bizen	96	34.44 N	134.09 E
Bizerte	148	37.17 N	9.52 E
Bizerte, Lac de ⊜	36	37.12 N	9.52 E
Bīzhanābād	128	27.55 N	58.03 E
Bizkaiko □⁴	34	43.20 N	2.45 W
Bjæverskov	41	55.27 N	12.02 E
Bjahoml'	76	54.44 N	28.04 E
Bjala, Blg.	38	42.53 N	27.53 E
Bjala, Blg.	38	43.27 N	25.44 E
Bjala Slatina	38	43.28 N	23.56 E
Bjalyničy	76	53.59 N	29.42 E
Bjalynkavičy	76	53.15 N	32.08 E
Bjarèzina ≃, Bela.	76	52.33 N	30.14 E
Bjarèzina ≃, Bela.	76	53.48 N	25.59 E
Bjarezinski Bijasferny zapavednik ♦	76	54.40 N	28.15 E
Bjargtangar ›	24a	65.31 N	24.32 W
Bjärnum	41	56.17 N	13.42 E
Bjaroza	76	52.32 N	24.59 E
Bjarozauka	76	53.43 N	25.30 E
Bjärred	41	55.43 N	13.01 E
Bjärsjölagård	41	55.44 N	13.41 E
Bjästa	26	63.12 N	18.30 E
Bjelaja → Belaja ≃	72	55.54 N	53.33 E
Bjelovar	36	45.54 N	16.51 E
Bjernede	41	55.27 N	11.38 E
Bjerre Skov ∧²	41	55.47 N	9.53 E
Bjerringbro	26	56.23 N	9.40 E
Björbo	40	60.28 N	14.42 E
Bjørkelangen	26	59.53 N	11.34 E
Björklinge	40	60.02 N	17.33 E
Björknäs	40	59.19 N	18.14 E

Symbols in the index entries represent the broad categories identified in the key at the right. Symbols with superior numbers (⋏¹) identify subcategories (see complete key on page *I · 1*).

Symbole im Register stellen die rechts im Schlüssel erklärten Kategorien dar. Symbole mit hochgestellten Ziffern (⋏¹) bezeichnen Unterabteilungen einer Kategorie (vgl. vollständiger Schlüssel auf Seite *I · 1*).

Los símbolos incluídos en el texto del índice representan las grandes categorías identificadas con la clave a la derecha. Los símbolos con numeros en su parte superior (⋏¹) identifican las subcategorías (véase la clave completa en la página *I · 1*).

Les symboles de l'index représentent les catégories indiquées dans la légende à droite. Les symboles suivis d'un indice (⋏¹) représentent des sous-catégories (voir légende complète à la page *I · 1*).

Os símbolos incluídos no texto do índice representam as grandes categorias identificadas com a chave à direita. Os símbolos com números em sua parte superior (⋏¹) identificam as subcategorias (veja-se a chave completa à página *I · 1*).

∧	Mountain	Berg	Montaña	Montagne	Montanha
⋏	Mountains	Gebirge	Montañas	Montagnes	Montanhas
)(	Pass	Paß	Paso	Col	Passo
V	Valley, Canyon	Tal, Cañon	Valle, Cañón	Vallée, Canyon	Vale, Canhão
≚	Plain	Ebene	Llano	Plaine	Planície
›	Cape	Kap	Cabo	Cap	Cabo
I	Island	Insel	Isla	Île	Ilha
II	Islands	Inseln	Islas	Îles	Ilhas
⊥	Other Topographic Features	Andere Topographische Objekte	Otros Elementos Topográficos	Autres données topographiques	Outros acidentes topográficos

ESPAÑOL Nombre / FRANÇAIS Nom / PORTUGUÊS Nome	Página / Page / Página	Lat.°′	Long.°′ W = Oeste / W = Ouest / W = Oeste
Björkö I	40	59.53 N	19.00 E
Björköby	26	63.21 N	21.19 E
Björköfjärden ⊂	40	59.53 N	18.56 E
Björkvik	40	58.50 N	16.31 E
Björna	26	63.34 N	18.33 E
Bjørnafjorden ⊂[2]	26	60.06 N	5.22 E
Björndammen	40	59.12 N	16.49 E
Björneborg → Pori, Suomi	26	61.29 N	21.47 E
Björneborg, Sve.	40	59.15 N	14.15 E
Bjornesfjorden ⊜	26	60.10 N	7.41 E
Björnlunda	40	59.04 N	17.09 E
Bjørnøya (Bear Island) I	12	74.25 N	19.00 E
Bjurholm	26	63.56 N	19.13 E
Bjuv	41	56.05 N	12.54 E
Bkāsīn	132	33.34 N	35.35 E
Bla	150	12.57 N	5.46 W
Blaby	42	52.34 N	1.09 W
Blace	38	43.17 N	21.18 E
Black (Lixian) (Da) ≃, Asia	110	21.15 N	105.20 E
Black ≃, Mb., Can.	184	50.49 N	96.20 W
Black ≃, On., Can.	190	48.42 N	80.38 W
Black ≃, On., Can.	190	48.36 N	86.16 W
Black ≃, On., Can.	212	44.32 N	77.22 W
Black ≃, On., Can.	212	44.20 N	79.20 W
Black ≃, On., Can.	212	44.42 N	79.19 W
Black ≃, U.S.	194	35.38 N	91.19 W
Black ≃, Ak., U.S.	180	66.39 N	144.50 W
Black ≃, Az., U.S.	200	33.44 N	110.13 W
Black ≃, La., U.S.	194	31.16 N	91.50 W
Black ≃, Mi., U.S.	190	43.00 N	82.25 W
Black ≃, Mi., U.S.	190	45.39 N	84.29 W
Black ≃, Mi., U.S.	190	46.40 N	90.03 W
Black ≃, Mi., U.S.	214	43.00 N	82.25 W
Black ≃, N.M., U.S.	196	32.14 N	104.03 W
Black ≃, N.Y., U.S.	188	43.59 N	76.04 W
Black ≃, N.C., U.S.	192	34.35 N	78.16 W
Black ≃, Oh., U.S.	214	41.28 N	82.11 W
Black ≃, S.C., U.S.	192	33.24 N	79.15 W
Black ≃, Vt., U.S.	188	43.16 N	72.27 W
Black ≃, Vt., U.S.	188	44.55 N	72.13 W
Black ≃, Wa., U.S.	224	46.49 N	123.13 W
Black ≃, Wi., U.S.	190	43.57 N	91.22 W
Black, East Branch ≃	214	41.22 N	82.07 W
Black, East Fork ≃	190	44.26 N	90.42 W
Black, Middle Branch ≃	216	42.25 N	86.14 W
Black, South Branch ≃	216	42.25 N	86.15 W
Black, West Branch ≃	214	41.22 N	82.07 W
Blackadder Water ≃	46	55.46 N	2.15 W
Blackall	166	24.25 S	145.28 E
Black Bay ⊂	190	48.40 N	88.30 W
Black Bay Peninsula ›[1]	190	48.38 N	88.21 W
Black Bear Creek ≃	196	36.25 N	96.38 W
Black Bear Island Lake ⊜	184	55.38 N	105.40 W
Blackberry Creek ≃	216	41.38 N	88.27 W
Blackberry Heights	216	41.45 N	88.23 W
Black Birch Lake ⊜	184	56.54 N	107.45 W
Black Brook ≃, Ma., U.S.	283	41.59 N	71.03 W
Black Brook ≃, Ma., U.S.	283	42.38 N	71.21 W
Black Brook ≃, N.J., U.S.	276	40.42 N	74.31 W
Black Bullock Hill ∧[2]	168b	35.37 S	138.12 E
Blackburn, Austl.	274b	37.49 S	145.09 E
Blackburn, Eng., U.K.	44	53.45 N	2.29 W
Blackburn, Scot., U.K.	46	55.52 N	3.38 W
Blackburn □[8]	262	53.42 N	2.28 W
Blackburn, Mount ∧	180	61.44 N	143.26 W
Blackbutt	171a	26.53 S	152.06 E
Black Butte ∧, Ca., U.S.	228	34.33 N	117.43 W
Black Butte ∧, Mt., U.S.	202	44.54 N	111.51 W
Black Butte ∧, Mt., U.S.	202	46.47 N	110.56 W
Black Butte Lake ⊜[1]	204	39.45 N	122.20 W
Blackbutt Range ⩚	171a	27.00 S	152.00 E
Black Canyon of the Gunnison National Monument ♠	200	38.32 N	107.42 W
Blackcraig Hill ∧	44	55.20 N	4.08 W
Black Creek, B.C., Can.	182	49.50 N	125.08 W
Black Creek, On., Can.	284a	43.00 N	79.01 W
Black Creek, N.Y., U.S.	210	42.17 N	78.14 W
Black Creek ≃, On., Can.	214	42.43 N	82.21 W
Black Creek ≃, On., Can.	275b	43.41 N	79.32 W
Black Creek ≃, On., Can.	284a	42.59 N	79.01 W
Black Creek ≃, Az., U.S.	200	35.16 N	109.14 W
Black Creek ≃, Mi., U.S.	216	41.49 N	83.54 W
Black Creek ≃, Mi., U.S.	216	43.11 N	86.14 W
Black Creek ≃, Ms., U.S.	194	33.01 N	90.21 W
Black Creek ≃, Ms., U.S.	194	30.39 N	88.39 W
Black Creek ≃, Mo., U.S.	219	39.41 N	91.55 W
Black Creek ≃, N.Y., U.S.	210	43.19 N	75.04 W
Black Creek ≃, N.Y., U.S.	210	43.06 N	77.41 W
Black Creek ≃, N.Y., U.S.	284a	43.03 N	78.42 W
Black Creek ≃, N.Y., U.S.	284a	43.05 N	78.57 W
Black Creek ≃, Pa., U.S.	210	41.00 N	76.10 W
Black Creek ≃, S.C., U.S.	192	34.18 N	79.37 W
Black Creek Park ♠	275b	43.46 N	79.31 W
Black Creek Pioneer Village ♠	275b	43.47 N	79.32 W
Black Cypress Creek ≃	222	32.53 N	94.26 W
Blackden Heath	262	53.14 N	2.20 W
Black Devon ≃	46	56.06 N	3.47 W
Black Diamond, Ab., Can.	182	50.42 N	114.14 W
Black Diamond, Wa., U.S.	224	47.18 N	122.00 W
Black Donald Lake ⊜[1]	212	45.13 N	76.55 W
Black Down Hills ⩚[2]	42	50.57 N	3.09 W
Blackdown Tableland National Park ♠	166	23.43 S	149.05 E
Blackduck	190	47.43 N	94.32 W
Black Duck ≃	176	56.51 N	89.02 W
Black Eagle	202	47.31 N	111.16 W
Black Esk ≃	44	55.12 N	3.10 W
Blackfalds	182	52.23 N	113.47 W
Blackfeet Indian Reservation ◆[4]	202	48.40 N	113.00 W
Blackfoot, Id., U.S.	202	43.11 N	112.20 W
Blackfoot, Mt., U.S.	182	48.34 N	112.52 W
Blackfoot ≃, Id., U.S.	202	43.08 N	112.30 W
Blackfoot ≃, Mt., U.S.	202	46.52 N	113.53 W
Blackfoot, North Fork ≃	202	46.59 N	113.07 W
Blackfoot Indian Reserve ◆[4]	182	50.45 N	113.00 W
Blackfoot Reservoir ⊜[1]	202	42.55 N	111.35 W
Blackford	46	56.15 N	3.46 W
Blackford □[6]	216	40.27 N	85.22 W
Black Forest → Schwarzwald ⩚	58	48.00 N	8.15 E
Blackhall Colliery	44	54.44 N	1.14 W
Blackhall Mountain ∧	200	41.02 N	106.41 W
Black Hameldon ∧[2]	262	53.44 N	2.08 W
Black Hawk	184	48.48 N	93.59 W
Black Hawk Creek ≃	190	42.30 N	92.21 W
Black Head ›, Ire.	48	53.08 N	9.17 W
Black Head ›, Eng., U.K.	42	50.01 N	5.06 W
Blackhead Bay ⊂	186	48.34 N	53.15 W
Blackheath, Austl.	170	33.38 S	150.17 E
Blackheath, S. Afr.	273d	26.08 S	27.58 E
Blackheath, Eng., U.K.	260	51.12 N	0.31 W
Black Hill ∧[2], Eng., U.K.	262	53.20 N	2.01 W
Black Hill ∧[2], Eng., U.K.	262	53.33 N	1.53 W
Black Hills ⩚	198	44.00 N	104.00 W
Black Hills ⩚[2]	282	37.50 N	121.52 W
Blackhope Scar ∧	46	55.44 N	3.05 W
Black Horse, Oh., U.S.	214	41.09 N	81.18 W
Black Horse, Pa., U.S.	285	39.55 N	75.25 W
Black Horse, Pa., U.S.	285	40.06 N	75.19 W
Black Horse Creek ≃	285	40.05 N	75.43 W
Black Island I	184	51.10 N	96.30 W
Black Isle ›[1]	46	57.35 N	4.15 W
Black Jack	219	38.47 N	90.16 W
Black Jack Mountain ∧	228	33.23 N	118.24 W
Black-Lake	206	46.03 N	71.21 W
Black Lake ⊜, On., Can.	212	44.46 N	76.18 W
Black Lake ⊜, Sk., Can.	176	59.10 N	105.20 W
Black Lake ⊜, Mi., U.S.	190	45.28 N	84.15 W
Black Lake ⊜, N.Y., U.S.	212	44.31 N	75.35 W
Black Lake ⊜, Wa., U.S.	224	47.00 N	122.58 W
Black Lake Bayou ≃	194	32.01 N	93.09 W
Blacklegs Creek ≃	214	40.30 N	79.27 W
Blackley ◆[8]	262	53.31 N	2.13 W
Black Lick	214	40.28 N	79.11 W
Blacklick Creek ≃	214	40.28 N	79.13 W
Blacklick Creek, North Branch ≃	214	40.29 N	78.55 W
Blacklick Estates	218	39.54 N	83.22 W
Blacklog Mountain ∧	214	40.20 N	77.45 W
Blacklunans	46	56.44 N	3.22 W
Black Mesa ∧, U.S.	196	37.05 N	103.10 W
Black Mesa ∧, Az., U.S.	200	36.35 N	110.20 W
Blackmoor ⩚[1]	42	50.24 N	4.46 W
Blackmoorfoot Reservoir ⊜[1]	262	53.37 N	1.51 W
Blackmoor Vale V	42	50.56 N	2.25 W
Blackmore	260	51.41 N	0.19 E
Blackmore, Mount ∧	202	45.27 N	111.01 W
Black Moshannon State Park ♠	214	40.54 N	78.03 W
Black Mountain	192	35.37 N	82.19 W
Black Mountain ∧, D.Y.	124	27.17 N	90.23 E
Black Mountain ∧, Wales, U.K.	42	51.52 N	3.46 W
Black Mountain ∧, U.S.	192	36.54 N	82.54 W
Black Mountain ∧, Az., U.S.	200	32.46 N	110.57 W
Black Mountain ∧, Ca., U.S.	226	35.24 N	120.21 W
Black Mountain ∧, Ca., U.S.	228	35.08 N	117.14 W
Black Mountain ∧, Ca., U.S.	282	37.19 N	122.09 W
Black Mountain ∧, Id., U.S.	202	46.53 N	115.33 W
Black Mountain ∧, Mt., U.S.	202	46.44 N	112.31 W
Black Mountain ∧, Or., U.S.	202	45.13 N	119.17 W
Black Mountain ∧, Wy., U.S.	202	44.45 N	107.22 W
Black Mountain ∧[2], Austl.	166	21.08 S	139.41 E
Black Mountain ∧[2], Ca., U.S.	228	32.59 N	117.07 W
Black Mountain ∧[2], Tx., U.S.	222	31.09 N	97.44 W
Black Mountains ⩚, Wales, U.K.	42	51.57 N	3.08 W
Black Mountains ⩚, Az., U.S.	200	35.30 N	114.30 W
Black Nossob ≃	156	23.05 S	18.45 E
Black Peak ∧	200	34.08 N	114.13 W
Black Pine Peak ∧	202	42.08 N	113.08 W
Black Pipe Creek ≃	198	43.47 N	101.14 W
Black Point	226	38.07 N	122.31 W
Black Point ›, Austl.	168b	34.37 S	137.54 E
Black Point ›, Austl.	170	34.47 S	150.50 E
Black Point ›, Ak., U.S.	180	57.00 N	153.18 W
Blackpool	44	53.50 N	3.03 W
Blackpool □[8]	262	53.47 N	3.02 W
Blackpool (Squire's Gate) Airport ⊠	262	53.47 N	3.02 W
Blackpool Football Ground ♠	262	53.49 N	3.03 W
Blackpool Tower ᵿ	262	53.49 N	3.03 W
Black Range ⩚	200	33.20 N	107.50 W
Black River, Jam.	241q	18.01 N	77.51 W
Black River, N.Y., U.S.	212	44.00 N	75.47 W
Black River Bay ⊂	212	43.58 N	76.07 W
Black River Falls	190	44.17 N	90.51 W
Black Rock, Austl.	274b	37.59 S	145.01 E
Black Rock, Ar., U.S.	194	36.06 N	91.05 W
Black Rock, Ma., U.S.	283	42.14 N	70.49 W
Black Rock I[2], Ire.	48	54.05 N	10.22 W
Black Rock I[2], S. Geor.	244	53.39 S	41.48 W
Black Rock Desert ◆[2]	204	41.10 N	119.00 W
Blackrod	262	53.35 N	2.35 W
Blacksburg, S.C., U.S.	192	35.07 N	81.30 W
Blacksburg, Va., U.S.	192	37.13 N	80.24 W
Blacks Creek ≃	285	40.08 N	74.43 W
Black Sea ⊤[2]	22	43.00 N	35.00 E
Blacks Fork ≃	200	41.24 N	109.38 W
Blacks Harbour	186	45.03 N	66.47 W
Blackshear	192	31.18 N	82.14 W
Blackshear, Lake ⊜[1]	192	31.56 N	83.56 W
Blacksod Bay ⊂	48	54.08 N	10.00 W
Black Springs, Austl.	170	33.52 S	149.42 E
Black Springs, Austl.	274b	37.46 S	145.19 E
Black Springs Hill ∧[2]	274b	37.46 S	145.19 E
Black Star Canyon V	280	33.47 N	117.39 W
Blackstone, Ma., U.S.	207	42.01 N	71.32 W
Blackstone, Va., U.S.	192	37.04 N	77.59 W
Blackstone ≃, Ab., Can.	182	52.50 N	116.07 W
Blackstone ≃, Yk., Can.	180	65.51 N	137.12 W
Blackstone Lake ⊜	212	45.14 N	79.53 W
Black Sugarloaf Mountain ∧	166	31.20 S	151.33 E
Black Thunder Creek ≃	198	43.33 N	104.41 W
Blacktown	170	33.46 S	150.55 E
Blackville	192	33.21 N	81.16 W
Black Volta (Volta Noire) ≃	150	8.41 N	1.33 W
Blackwall Tunnel ◆[5]	260	51.30 N	0.01 E
Blackwalnut Point ›	208	38.40 N	76.20 W
Black Warrior ≃	194	32.32 N	87.51 W
Blackwatch Hills	210	43.05 N	77.27 W
Blackwater, Austl.	166	23.35 S	148.53 E
Blackwater, Ire.	48	52.26 N	6.21 W
Blackwater ≃, Europe	48	54.31 N	6.34 W
Blackwater ≃, Ire.	48	51.51 N	7.50 W
Blackwater ≃, Ire.	48	53.39 N	6.43 W
Blackwater ≃, Eng., U.K.	42	51.45 N	1.00 E
Blackwater ≃, U.S.	194	30.36 N	87.02 W
Blackwater ≃, Md., U.S.	208	38.21 N	76.01 W
Blackwater ≃, Mo., U.S.	194	38.56 N	92.51 W
Blackwater ≃, Va., U.S.	208	36.33 N	76.55 W
Blackwater Creek ≃, Austl.	166	25.56 S	144.20 E
Black Water Creek ≃, Fl., U.S.	220	28.51 N	81.24 W
Blackwater Draw V	196	33.35 N	101.50 W
Blackwaterfoot	46	55.30 N	5.19 W
Blackwater Lake ⊜	180	64.00 N	123.05 W
Blackwater Reservoir ⊜[1], Scot., U.K.	46	56.41 N	4.46 W
Blackwater Reservoir ⊜[1], Scot., U.K.	46	56.44 N	3.14 W
Blackwater Sound ʊ	220	25.10 N	80.25 W
Blackwell, Ok., U.S.	196	36.48 N	97.16 W
Blackwell, Tx., U.S.	196	32.05 N	100.19 W
Blackwood, Austl.	168b	35.02 S	138.37 E
Blackwood, Austl.	169	37.29 S	144.19 E
Blackwood, N.J., U.S.	285	39.48 N	75.03 W
Blackwood ≃	162	34.19 S	115.11 E
Blackwood, Cape ›	164	7.50 S	144.30 E
Blackwood Terrace	285	39.48 N	75.05 W
Bladel	52	51.23 N	5.13 E
Bladenboro	192	34.32 N	78.47 W
Bladensburg, Md., U.S.	284c	38.56 N	76.56 W
Bladensburg, Oh., U.S.	214	40.17 N	82.17 W
Blades	208	38.38 N	75.36 W
Bladgrond	158	28.52 S	19.57 E
Bladnoch ≃	44	54.51 N	4.25 W
Bladworth	184	51.18 N	106.09 W
Blaenau Ffestiniog	42	52.59 N	3.56 W
Blaenavon	42	51.48 N	3.05 W
Bláfell ∧	24a	64.32 N	19.53 W
Blagaj	36	43.15 N	17.50 E
Blagdon	42	51.20 N	2.43 W
Blagodarnoje	86	47.03 N	82.10 E
Blagodarnyj	72	45.06 N	43.27 E
Blagodatnoje, Kaz.	86	51.18 N	72.49 E
Blagodatnoje, Ross.	78	51.32 N	34.54 E
Blagodatovka	80	52.14 N	50.27 E
Blagoevgrad	38	42.01 N	23.06 E
Blagoveščenka, Kaz.	85	43.18 N	74.12 E
Blagoveščenka, Kaz.	86	54.22 N	66.58 E
Blagoveščenka, Ross.	80	51.19 N	44.03 E
Blagoveščenka, Ross.	86	52.50 N	79.52 E
Blagoveščensk, Ross.	86	55.01 N	55.59 E
Blagoveščensk, Ross.	89	50.17 N	127.32 E
Blagoveščenskoje	86	58.08 N	62.58 E
Blåhø ∧	26	62.45 N	9.19 E
Blahodatne, Ukr.	83	47.42 N	37.25 E
Blahodatne, Ukr.	83	47.53 N	38.29 E
Blåhøj	41	55.51 N	9.01 E
Blaichach	58	47.34 N	10.15 E
Blaikfjället ∧	26	64.33 N	16.12 E
Blain, Fr.	32	47.29 N	1.46 W
Blain, Pa., U.S.	208	40.20 N	77.31 W
Blaina	42	51.46 N	3.10 W
Blain City	214	40.45 N	78.34 W
Blaine, Mn., U.S.	190	45.09 N	93.14 W
Blaine, Wa., U.S.	224	48.59 N	122.44 W
Blaine Creek ≃	188	38.11 N	82.37 W
Blaine Hill	279b	40.16 N	79.53 W
Blaine Lake	184	52.50 N	106.54 W
Blaineys	224	48.53 N	123.47 W
Blainville	206	45.40 N	73.52 W
Blainville-sur-l'Eau	58	48.33 N	6.24 E
Blair, On., Can.	212	43.23 N	80.23 W
Blair, Ne., U.S.	198	41.32 N	96.07 W
Blair, Ok., U.S.	196	34.46 N	99.20 W
Blair, Wi., U.S.	190	44.18 N	91.14 W
Blair □[6]	214	40.30 N	78.25 W
Blair Athol	166	22.42 S	147.33 E
Blair Atholl	46	56.46 N	3.51 W
Blairgowrie	46	56.36 N	3.21 W
Blairs Mills	214	40.17 N	77.43 W
Blairstown, Ia., U.S.	190	41.54 N	92.05 W
Blairstown, N.J., U.S.	210	40.59 N	74.57 W
Blairsville, Ga., U.S.	192	34.52 N	83.57 W
Blairsville, Pa., U.S.	214	40.25 N	79.15 W
Blaise ≃, Fr.	50	48.46 N	1.25 E
Blaise ≃, Fr.	58	48.38 N	4.43 E
Blaisy-Bas	58	47.22 N	4.44 E
Blaj	38	46.11 N	23.55 E
Blakehurst	274a	33.59 S	151.07 E
Blakeley Canal ≚	226	36.09 N	119.48 W
Blakely, Ga., U.S.	192	31.22 N	84.56 W
Blakely, Pa., U.S.	210	41.28 N	75.35 W
Blakely Island I	224	48.33 N	122.50 W
Blakeney, Eng., U.K.	42	52.58 N	1.00 E
Blakeney, Eng., U.K.	42	51.46 N	2.29 W
Blake Plateau ✢[4]	16	31.00 N	79.00 W
Blake Point ›	190	48.12 N	88.25 W
Blake Ridge ✢[3]	16	29.00 N	73.30 W
Blakes	208	37.30 N	76.22 W
Blakesburg	190	40.57 N	92.38 W
Blakeslee, Oh., U.S.	216	41.31 N	84.44 W
Blakeslee, Pa., U.S.	210	41.06 N	75.36 W
Blalock Island I	202	45.53 N	119.41 W
Blâmont, Fr.	58	48.35 N	6.51 E
Blamont, Fr.	58	47.23 N	6.51 E
Blanc, Cap → Nouâdhibou, Râs ›, Afr.	148	20.46 N	17.03 W
Blanc, Cap ›, Tun.	36	37.20 N	9.51 E
Blanc, Mont ∧, P.Q., Can.	186	48.47 N	66.52 W
Blanc, Mont (Monte Bianco) ∧, Europe	62	45.50 N	6.52 E
Blanca	200	37.27 N	105.31 W
Blanca, Bahía ⊂	252	38.55 S	62.10 W
Blanca, Isla I	248	9.06 S	78.38 W
Blanca, Laguna ⊜	254	52.25 S	71.10 W
Blanca, Punta ›, Arg.	258	34.57 S	57.40 W
Blanca, Punta ›, Chile	252	25.06 S	70.30 W
Blanca, Sierra ∧	200	31.15 N	105.26 W
Blanca Lake ⊜	224	47.53 N	121.21 W
Blanca Peak ∧	200	37.35 N	105.29 W
Blancas, Peñas ⩚	236	13.15 N	85.41 W
Blanc du Cheilon, Mont ∧	58	45.59 N	7.25 E
Blanchard, Ok., U.S.	196	35.08 N	97.39 W
Blanchard, Pa., U.S.	210	41.04 N	77.36 W
Blanchard, Wa., U.S.	224	48.35 N	122.24 W
Blanchard ≃	216	41.02 N	84.18 W
Blanchardville	190	42.48 N	89.51 W
Blanche ≃, On., Can.	190	47.34 N	79.32 W
Blanche ≃, P.Q., Can.	206	46.40 N	72.08 W
Blanche, Cape ›	162	33.01 S	134.09 E
Blanche, Dent ∧	58	46.03 N	7.36 E
Blanche, Lake ⊜, Austl.	162	22.25 S	123.17 E
Blanche, Lake ⊜, Austl.	166	29.15 S	139.39 E
Blanche, Mer → Beloje more ⊤[2]	24	65.30 N	38.00 E
Blanche Channel ʊ	175e	8.30 S	157.30 E
Blancheface	261	48.32 N	2.06 E
Blanche Marie Val ⌊	250	4.44 N	56.53 W
Blanchester	218	39.17 N	83.59 W
Blanchisseuse	241r	10.47 N	61.18 W
Blanco, S. Afr.	158	33.57 S	22.24 E
Blanco, Tx., U.S.	196	30.06 N	98.25 W
Blanco ≃, Arg.	252	30.12 S	69.05 W
Blanco ≃, Arg.	254	47.22 S	71.12 W
Blanco ≃, Bol.	248	13.09 S	63.46 W
Blanco ≃, Ec.	246	0.28 N	79.25 W
Blanco ≃, Tx., U.S.	196	29.51 N	97.55 W
Blanco, Cabo → Nouâdhibou, Râs ›, Afr.	148	20.46 N	17.03 W
Blanco, Cabo ›, C.R.	236	9.34 N	85.07 W
Blanco, Cañon V	200	35.20 N	105.05 W
Blanco, Cape ›	202	42.50 N	124.34 W
Blanco, Lago ⊜	254	54.03 S	69.00 W
Blanco, Mar → Beloje more ⊤[2]	24	65.30 N	38.00 E
Blanco, Monte → Blanc, Mont ∧	62	45.50 N	6.52 E
Blanco, Rio ≃	200	37.07 N	107.03 W
Blanco Creek ≃	196	28.19 N	97.19 W
Blanc-Sablon	186	51.25 N	57.07 W
Bland, Mo., U.S.	219	38.18 N	91.37 W
Bland, Va., U.S.	192	37.06 N	81.06 W
Blanda ≃	24a	65.39 N	20.18 W
Blandburg	214	40.41 N	78.24 W
Blandford	207	42.10 N	72.55 W
Blandford Forum	42	50.52 N	2.11 W
Blanding	200	37.37 N	109.28 W
Blandinsville	190	40.33 N	90.51 W
Blandon	208	40.26 N	75.53 W
Blandy	261	48.34 N	2.47 E
Blanes	34	41.41 N	2.48 E
Blangkejeren	114	3.59 N	97.20 E
Blangpidie	114	3.45 N	96.51 E
Blangy-le-Château	50	49.14 N	0.17 E
Blangy-sur-Bresle	50	49.56 N	1.38 E
Blanice ≃	61	49.05 N	14.03 E
Blankenberg	56	50.45 N	7.22 E
Blankenberge	50	51.19 N	3.08 E
Blankenburg	54	51.48 N	10.58 E
Blankenburg ◆[8]	264a	52.35 N	13.28 E
Blankenese ◆[8]	52	53.33 N	9.48 E
Blankenfelde	54	52.20 N	13.23 E
Blankenfelde ◆[8]	264a	52.37 N	13.23 E
Blankenhain	54	50.51 N	11.21 E
Blankenheim, Dtsch.	54	51.31 N	11.25 E
Blankenheim, Dtsch.	56	50.26 N	6.39 E
Blankensee	54	52.14 N	13.08 E
Blankenstein	263	51.24 N	7.14 E
Blanket	196	31.49 N	98.47 W
Blanquilla, Isla I	246	11.51 N	64.37 W
Blansko	30	49.22 N	16.39 E
Blanský Les ◆[3]	61	48.52 N	14.16 E
Blantyre	154	15.47 S	35.00 E
Blanzac	62	45.07 N	3.51 E
Blanzy	58	46.42 N	4.23 E
Blaricum	52	52.16 N	5.15 E
Blarney	48	51.56 N	8.34 W
Blarney Castle ⊥	48	51.56 N	8.34 W
Blasdell	210	42.47 N	78.49 W
Blasheim	52	52.18 N	8.34 E
Błaszki	30	51.39 N	18.27 E
Blatná	60	49.26 N	13.53 E
Blatten	58	46.25 N	7.50 E
Blau ≃	58	48.23 N	9.49 E
Blaubeuren	58	48.24 N	9.47 E
Blauen ∧	58	47.47 N	7.42 E
Blauer Nil → Blue Nile ≃	140	15.38 N	32.31 E
Blaufelden	56	49.18 N	9.58 E
Blaustein	58	48.25 N	9.53 E
Blauvelt	276	41.03 N	73.57 W
Blauvelt State Park ♠	276	41.04 N	73.56 W
Blawenburg	276	40.24 N	74.42 W
Blawnox	279b	40.29 N	79.51 W
Blaxland	170	33.45 S	150.36 E
Blaxland Creek ≃	274a	33.48 S	150.46 E
Blaydon	44	54.58 N	1.42 W
Blaye-et-Sainte-Luce	32	45.08 N	0.39 W
Blayney	166	33.32 S	149.15 E
Blaze, Point ›	164	12.56 S	130.12 E
Błażowa	30	49.54 N	22.05 E
Bleaker Island I	254	52.13 S	58.53 W
Bleaklow Head ∧	262	53.28 N	1.50 W
Blean	42	51.19 N	1.02 E
Bleckede	54	53.17 N	10.44 E
Bled	36	46.22 N	14.06 E
Bledsoe	196	33.38 N	103.01 W
Bleecker	210	43.07 N	74.22 W
Blefjell ∧	26	59.48 N	9.10 E
Blega	115a	7.08 S	113.03 E
Bleiberg ob Villach	64	46.37 N	13.41 E
Bleiburg	61	46.35 N	14.48 E
Bleicherode	54	51.26 N	10.34 E
Blekendorf	54	54.16 N	10.38 E
Blekinge □[9]	26	56.20 N	15.05 E
Blekinge Län □[6]	26	56.20 N	15.20 E
Bléneau	50	47.42 N	2.57 E
Blenheim, Austl.	171a	27.39 S	152.20 E
Blenheim, On., Can.	214	42.20 N	82.00 W
Blenheim, N.Z.	172	41.31 S	173.57 E
Blenheim, N.J., U.S.	285	39.48 N	75.05 W
Blenheim Palace ᵿ	42	51.47 N	1.21 W
Blenio, Val V	58	46.27 N	8.58 E
Blénod-lès-Pont-à-Mousson	56	48.53 N	6.03 E
Blénod-lès-Toul	58	48.36 N	5.50 E
Bléone ≃	62	44.03 N	6.00 E
Blérancourt	50	49.31 N	3.09 E
Bléré	50	47.20 N	1.00 E
Blerick	52	51.23 N	6.10 E
Blériot-Plage	50	50.57 N	1.50 E
Blesbokspruit ≃	273d	26.14 S	28.29 E
Blessing	222	28.52 N	96.13 W
Blessington	48	53.10 N	6.32 W
Bletchingley	260	51.14 N	0.06 W
Bletchley	42	52.00 N	0.46 W
Bletterans	58	46.45 N	5.27 E
Bleu → Chang ≃	90	31.48 N	121.10 E
Bleue, Mer ≡	212	45.24 N	75.30 W
Bleury	261	48.31 N	1.45 E
Bleus, Monts ⩚	154	1.30 N	30.30 E
Blevio	62	45.50 N	9.05 E
Blewett Falls Lake ⊜[1]	192	35.03 N	79.54 W
Blexen	52	53.32 N	8.32 E
Blidö I	40	59.37 N	18.54 E
Blidworth	44	53.06 N	1.07 W
Bliedinghausen ◆[8]	263	51.09 N	7.12 E
Bliersheim ◆[8]	263	51.23 N	6.43 E
Blies ≃	56	49.07 N	7.04 E
Blieskastel	56	49.14 N	7.16 E
Bligh Sound ʊ	172	44.50 S	167.32 E
Bligh Water ʊ	175g	17.00 S	178.00 E
Bligny	50	49.11 N	3.52 E
Bligny-sur-Ouche	58	47.06 N	4.40 E
Blik, Mount ∧	116	6.58 N	124.15 E
Blina	162	17.46 S	124.32 E
Blind ≃	276	40.57 N	73.42 W
Blind Creek ≃	274b	37.54 S	145.12 E
Blindley Heath	260	51.12 N	0.04 W
Blind River	190	46.10 N	82.58 W
Blinman	166	31.06 S	138.41 E
Blinnenhorn ∧	58	46.26 N	8.19 E
Blinovskij	80	49.23 N	42.19 E
Bliss	210	42.34 N	78.15 W
Blissfield, Mi., U.S.	216	41.49 N	83.51 W
Blissfield, Oh., U.S.	214	40.24 N	81.58 W
Blitar	115a	8.06 S	112.09 E
Blithe ≃	42	52.45 N	1.50 W
Blithfield Reservoir ⊜[1]	42	52.48 N	1.53 W
Blitta	150	8.19 N	0.59 E
Blocher	218	38.43 N	85.39 W
Block Dam ◆[6]	212	45.12 N	76.54 W
Block Island	207	41.10 N	71.33 W
Block Island I	207	41.11 N	71.35 W
Block Island Sound ʊ	207	41.10 N	71.45 W
Blockley	42	52.01 N	1.45 W
Blockton	198	40.36 N	94.28 W
Blodgett Mills	210	42.34 N	76.08 W
Bloed ≃	158	28.15 S	30.30 E
Bloedel	182	50.07 N	125.23 W
Bloedrivier, S. Afr.	158	28.06 S	30.33 E
Bloedrivier, S. Afr.	158	27.53 S	30.30 E
Bloekomspruit	158	26.45 S	28.21 E
Bloemendaal	52	52.24 N	4.37 E
Bloemfontein	158	29.12 S	26.07 E
Bloemhof	158	27.38 S	25.32 E
Bloemhofdam ⊜[1]	158	27.40 S	25.40 E
Blois	50	47.35 N	1.20 E
Blokhus	26	57.15 N	9.35 E
Blokzijl	52	52.44 N	5.57 E
Blombacher Bach ◆[8]	263	51.15 N	7.14 E
Blombacka	40	59.37 N	13.47 E
Blomberg	52	51.56 N	9.05 E
Blomstermåla	26	56.59 N	16.20 E
Blonay	58	46.28 N	6.54 E
Blönduós	24a	65.39 N	20.15 W
Blongas	115b	8.53 S	116.02 E
Blonville-sur-Mer	50	49.19 N	0.02 E
Blood Indian Creek ≃	184	50.55 N	111.03 W
Blood Indian Reserve ◆[4]	182	49.30 N	113.10 W
Blood Mountain ∧	192	34.44 N	83.56 W
Blood River ⊥	158	28.20 S	30.35 E
Bloodsworth Island I	208	38.10 N	76.03 W
Bloodvein ≃	184	51.45 N	96.44 W
Bloody Foreland ›	48	55.09 N	8.17 W
Bloomdale	216	41.10 N	83.33 W
Bloomer	190	45.06 N	91.29 W
Bloomfield, On., Can.	212	43.59 N	77.14 W
Bloomfield, Ct., U.S.	207	41.49 N	72.43 W
Bloomfield, In., U.S.	194	39.01 N	86.56 W
Bloomfield, Ia., U.S.	190	40.45 N	92.24 W
Bloomfield, Ky., U.S.	194	37.54 N	85.19 W
Bloomfield, Mo., U.S.	194	36.53 N	89.55 W
Bloomfield, Ne., U.S.	198	42.35 N	97.38 W
Bloomfield, N.J., U.S.	210	40.48 N	74.11 W
Bloomfield, N.M., U.S.	200	36.42 N	107.59 W
Bloomfield, Oh., U.S.	214	40.03 N	81.44 W
Bloomfield ◆[8]	279b	40.27 N	79.56 W
Bloomfield Glens	281	42.33 N	83.20 W
Bloomfield Highlands	281	42.36 N	83.16 W
Bloomfield Hills	216	42.35 N	83.14 W
Bloomfield Village	216	42.33 N	83.15 W
Bloomingburg, N.Y., U.S.	210	41.33 N	74.26 W
Bloomingburg, Oh., U.S.	218	39.36 N	83.23 W
Bloomingdale, Il., U.S.	278	41.57 N	88.04 W
Bloomingdale, Mi., U.S.	216	42.22 N	85.57 W
Bloomingdale, N.J., U.S.	210	41.00 N	74.19 W
Bloomingdale, Oh., U.S.	214	40.21 N	80.49 W
Blooming Glen	208	40.22 N	75.15 W
Blooming Grove, In., U.S.	218	39.30 N	85.04 W
Blooming Grove, N.Y., U.S.	210	41.25 N	74.11 W
Blooming Grove, Pa., U.S.	210	41.21 N	75.09 W
Blooming Grove, Tx., U.S.	222	32.06 N	96.43 W
Blooming Prairie	190	43.52 N	93.03 W
Bloomington, Ca., U.S.	228	34.04 N	117.23 W
Bloomington, Il., U.S.	216	40.29 N	88.59 W
Bloomington, In., U.S.	218	39.09 N	86.31 W
Bloomington, Mn., U.S.	190	44.50 N	93.17 W
Bloomington, N.Y., U.S.	210	41.53 N	74.03 W
Bloomington, Tx., U.S.	196	28.38 N	96.53 W
Bloomington, Wi., U.S.	190	42.53 N	90.55 W
Bloomington, Lake ⊜[1]	216	40.37 N	88.55 W
Blooming Valley	214	41.40 N	80.03 W
Bloomsburg	210	41.00 N	76.27 W
Bloomsbury, Austl.	166	20.43 S	148.35 E
Bloomsbury, N.J., U.S.	210	40.39 N	75.05 W
Bloomsdale Gardens	285	40.07 N	74.52 W
Bloomville, N.Y., U.S.	210	42.20 N	74.48 W
Bloomville, Oh., U.S.	214	41.03 N	83.00 W
Blora	115a	6.57 S	111.25 E
Bloserville	208	40.12 N	77.24 W
Blossburg	210	41.40 N	77.03 W
Blossom	196	33.39 N	95.23 W
Blossom Hill	208	40.05 N	76.19 W
Blötberget	40	60.07 N	15.04 E
Blotzheim	58	47.36 N	7.29 E
Blouberg	156	23.08 S	28.56 E
Blouberg ∧	156	23.01 S	28.59 E
Bloubergstrand	158	33.47 S	18.28 E
Blouin, Lac ⊜	190	48.10 N	77.44 W
Bloumet	148	23.27 N	6.06 E
Blountstown	192	30.26 N	85.02 W
Blountsville	194	34.04 N	86.35 W
Blountville	192	36.31 N	82.19 W
Blovice	60	49.35 N	13.33 E
Blovstrød	41	55.52 N	12.24 E
Blowering Reservoir ⊜[1]	171b	35.30 S	148.15 E
Blowing Rock	192	36.08 N	81.40 W
Bloxham	42	52.02 N	1.22 W
Bloxom	208	37.49 N	75.37 W
Blšanka ≃	54	50.10 N	13.34 E
Blšany	54	50.10 N	13.29 E
Bludenz	58	47.09 N	9.49 E
Bludnaja ≃	88	51.24 N	110.39 E
Blue ≃, Az., U.S.	200	33.13 N	109.11 W
Blue ≃, Co., U.S.	200	40.03 N	106.24 W
Blue ≃, In., U.S.	216	41.07 N	85.30 W
Blue ≃, In., U.S.	218	38.11 N	86.19 W
Blue ≃, Ok., U.S.	196	33.53 N	95.56 W
Blue, Middle Fork ≃	218	38.33 N	86.07 W
Blue, South Fork ≃	218	38.26 N	86.11 W
Blue, West Fork ≃	218	38.33 N	86.07 W
Blue Anchor	285	39.41 N	74.52 W
Blue Anchor Brook ≃	285	39.42 N	74.49 W
Blue Ash	218	39.13 N	84.22 W
Blue Ball	218	39.29 N	84.21 W
Blue Bell	208	40.09 N	75.16 W
Bluebell Hill	260	51.20 N	0.30 E
Blue Bonnets, Champ de Course ♠	275a	45.29 N	73.39 W
Blue Brook ≃	276	40.40 N	74.25 W
Blue Buck Knob ∧[2]	194	36.57 N	92.07 W
Bluebush Swamp ≡	162	20.30 S	137.25 E
Blue Creek, Oh., U.S.	218	38.47 N	83.20 W
Blue Creek, Wa., U.S.	182	48.19 N	117.49 W
Blue Creek, Wa., U.S.	202	48.19 N	117.49 W
Blue Creek ≃, Ca., U.S.	226	38.28 N	120.22 W
Blue Creek ≃, Id., U.S.	202	42.02 N	116.08 W
Blue Creek ≃, Ne., U.S.	198	41.19 N	102.10 W
Blue Creek ≃, Oh., U.S.	216	41.07 N	84.26 W
Blue Creek ≃, Ut,. U.S.	200	41.31 N	112.24 W
Blue Cypress Lake ⊜	220	27.44 N	80.45 W
Blue Earth	190	43.38 N	94.06 W
Blue Earth ≃	190	44.09 N	94.02 W
Bluefield, Va., U.S.	192	37.15 N	81.16 W
Bluefield, W.V., U.S.	192	37.16 N	81.13 W
Bluefields	236	12.00 N	83.45 W
Bluefields, Bahía de ⊂	236	12.02 N	83.44 W
Bluefields Bay ⊂	241q	18.10 N	78.03 W
Blue Grass Airport ⊠	218	38.02 N	84.36 W
Blue Grotto → Azzurra, Grotta ⊥[5]	68	40.35 N	14.14 E
Blue Hill, Me., U.S.	188	44.24 N	68.35 W
Blue Hill, Ne., U.S.	198	40.19 N	98.26 W
Blue Hill Bay ⊂	188	44.15 N	68.30 W
Blue Hills	207	41.40 N	72.56 W
Blue Hills of Couteau ⩚[2]	186	47.59 N	57.43 W
Blue Hills Reservation ♠	283	42.13 N	71.05 W
Blue Island	216	41.39 N	87.40 W
Blue Jay	228	34.15 N	117.13 W
Bluejoint Lake ⊜	202	42.35 N	119.40 W
Blue Knob ∧	214	40.17 N	78.34 W
Blue Knob State Park ♠	214	40.16 N	78.35 W
Blue Lagoon National Park ♠	154	15.30 S	27.25 E
Blue Lake National Park ♠	171a	27.31 S	153.29 E
Blue Licks Battlefield State Park ♠	218	38.26 N	84.00 W
Blue Marsh Lake ⊜[1]	208	40.25 N	76.05 W
Blue Mesa Reservoir ⊜[1]	200	38.27 N	107.10 W
Blue Mosque ᵿ[1]	273c	30.02 N	31.15 E
Blue Mound, Il., U.S.	219	39.42 N	89.07 W
Blue Mound, Ks., U.S.	198	38.05 N	95.00 W
Blue Mound, Tx., U.S.	222	32.51 N	97.19 W
Blue Mountain, Ms., U.S.	194	34.40 N	89.01 W
Blue Mountain, N.Y., U.S.	210	42.07 N	74.01 W
Blue Mountain ∧, N.B., Can.	186	47.49 N	66.19 W
Blue Mountain ∧, Nf., Can.	186	50.24 N	57.10 W
Blue Mountain ∧, Ar., U.S.	194	34.41 N	94.03 W
Blue Mountain ∧, Mt., U.S.	198	47.16 N	104.10 W
Blue Mountain ∧, N.H., U.S.	188	44.47 N	71.28 W
Blue Mountain ∧, Pa., U.S.	188	40.15 N	77.30 W
Blue Mountain ∧[2], On., Can.	190	48.15 N	80.07 W
Blue Mountain ∧[2], On., Can.	212	44.40 N	77.58 W
Blue Mountain Peak ∧	241q	18.03 N	76.35 W
Blue Mountains ⩚, Austl.	170	33.37 S	150.17 E
Blue Mountains ⩚, Jam.	241q	18.06 N	76.40 W
Blue Mountains ⩚, U.S.	202	45.30 N	118.15 W
Blue Mountains ⩚, Me., U.S.	188	44.50 N	70.35 W
Blue Mountains National Park ♠	170	33.40 S	150.25 E
Blue Mud Bay ⊂	164	13.26 S	135.56 E
Blue Nile (Al-Baḥr al-Azraq) (Abay) ≃	140	15.38 N	32.31 E
Bluenose Lake ⊜	180	68.25 N	119.45 W
Blue Point	276	40.45 N	73.02 W
Blue Point ›	276	40.44 N	73.02 W
Blue Rapids	198	39.40 N	96.39 W
Blue Ridge, Ab., Can.	182	54.08 N	115.22 W
Blue Ridge, Ga., U.S.	192	34.51 N	84.19 W
Blue Ridge, Il., U.S.	216	40.17 N	88.29 W
Blue Ridge ⩚	178	37.00 N	82.00 W
Blue Ridge Summit	208	39.43 N	77.28 W
Blue River	182	52.05 N	119.17 W
Blue Rock Springs Park ♠	282	38.08 N	122.12 W
Bluesky	182	56.04 N	118.14 W
Blue Springs	198	40.08 N	96.39 W
Blue Stack Mountains ⩚	48	54.45 N	8.05 W
Bluestone ≃	192	37.34 N	80.59 W
Bluestone Dam ◆[6]	192	37.36 N	80.53 W
Bluestone Lake ⊜[1]	192	37.30 N	80.50 W
Bluestone State Park ♠	192	37.37 N	80.56 W
Bluewater	200	35.15 N	107.59 W
Blue Water Bridge ◆[5]	214	43.00 N	82.25 W
Bluff, N.Z.	172	46.36 S	168.20 E
Bluff, Ut,. U.S.	200	37.17 N	109.33 W
Bluff Cape ›	110	18.00 N	94.26 E
Bluff City, Il., U.S.	219	38.57 N	89.02 W
Bluff City, Tn., U.S.	192	36.28 N	82.15 W
Bluff Cove ⊂	280	33.48 N	118.24 W
Bluff Creek ≃, U.S.	196	36.58 N	97.26 W
Bluff Creek ≃, Ks., U.S.	198	37.02 N	99.29 W
Bluff Dale	196	32.21 N	98.01 W
Bluff Head ›	271d	22.11 N	114.12 E
Bluff Island I	271d	22.19 N	114.21 E
Bluff Knoll ∧	162	34.23 S	118.20 E
Bluff Park	194	33.24 N	86.51 W
Bluff Point ›	162	27.50 S	114.06 E
Bluffs	219	39.45 N	90.32 W
Bluff Springs	219	39.59 N	90.21 W
Bluffton, In., U.S.	216	40.44 N	85.10 W
Bluffton, Oh., U.S.	216	40.53 N	83.53 W
Bluffton, S.C., U.S.	192	32.14 N	80.51 W
Bluffy Lake ⊜	184	50.47 N	92.55 W
Bluford	219	38.20 N	88.45 W
Blum	222	32.09 N	97.24 W
Blumberg, Dtsch.	54	52.36 N	13.37 E
Blumberg, Dtsch.	58	47.50 N	8.31 E
Blumenau	252	26.56 S	49.03 W
Blumenhof	184	50.01 N	107.41 W
Blumenthal	54	53.05 N	12.22 E
Blümlisalp ∧	58	46.30 N	7.47 E
Blunt	198	44.30 N	99.59 W
Blup Blup Island I	164	3.30 S	144.37 E
Bly	202	42.23 N	121.02 W
Blying Sound ʊ	180	59.50 N	149.15 W
Blyth, Austl.	168b	33.51 S	138.29 E
Blyth, On., Can.	190	43.44 N	81.26 W
Blyth, Eng., U.K.	44	55.07 N	1.30 W
Blyth ≃, Austl.	164	12.04 S	134.35 E
Blyth ≃, Eng., U.K.	42	52.18 N	1.40 E
Blyth ≃, Eng., U.K.	44	55.08 N	1.31 W
Blyth Bridge	46	55.42 N	3.24 W
Blythe	204	33.36 N	114.35 W
Blythedale	214	40.15 N	79.48 W
Blytheswood	214	42.07 N	82.36 W
Blytheville	194	35.55 N	89.55 W
Blytheville Air Force Base ■	194	35.57 N	89.57 W
Blyth Range ⩚	162	26.50 S	129.00 E
Blyznyuky	78	48.52 N	36.33 E
Bnei Braq → Bene Beraq	132	32.05 N	34.50 E
Bø, Nor.	24	68.37 N	14.33 E
Bø, Nor.	26	59.25 N	9.04 E
Bo, S.L.	150	7.56 N	11.21 W
Boa	154	10.32 S	28.06 E
Boac	116	13.27 N	121.50 E

Symbol	English	Deutsch	Español	Français	Português
≃	River	Fluß	Río	Rivière	Rio
≚	Canal	Kanal	Canal	Canal	Canal
⌊	Waterfall, Rapids	Wasserfall, Stromschnellen	Cascada, Rápidos	Chute d'eau, Rapides	Cascata, Rápidos
ʊ	Strait	Meeresstraße	Estrecho	Détroit	Estreito
⊂	Bay, Gulf	Bucht, Golf	Bahía, Golfo	Baie, Golfe	Baía, Golfo
⊜	Lake, Lakes	See, Seen	Lago, Lagos	Lac, Lacs	Lago, Lagos
≡	Swamp	Sumpf	Pantano	Marais	Pântano
⊓	Ice Features, Glacier	Eis- und Gletscherformen	Accidentes Glaciales	Formes glaciaires	Acidentes glaciares
⊤	Other Hydrographic Features	Andere Hydrographische Objekte	Otros Elementos Hidrográficos	Autres données hydrographiques	Outros acidentes hidrográficos
✢	Submarine Features	Untermeerische Objekte	Accidentes Submarinos	Formes de relief sous-marin	Acidentes submarinos
□	Political Unit	Politische Einheit	Unidad Politica	Entité politique	Unidade política
ᵿ	Cultural Institution	Kulturelle Institution	Institución Cultural	Institution culturelle	Instituição cultural
⊥	Historical Site	Historische Stätte	Sitio Histórico	Site historique	Sitio histórico
♠	Recreational Site	Erholungs- und Ferienort	Sitio de Recreo	Centre de loisirs	Area de Lazer
⊠	Airport	Flughafen	Aeropuerto	Aéroport	Aeroporto
■	Military Installation	Militäranlage	Instalación Militar	Installation militaire	Instalação militar
◆	Miscellaneous	Verschiedenes	Misceláneo	Divers	Diversos

Name	Page	Lat.°′	Long.°′
Boaco	236	12.28 N	85.40 W
Boaco □[5]	236	12.30 N	85.30 W
Boadilla del Monte	266a	40.24 N	3.53 W
Boa Esperança, Bra.	255	21.05 S	45.34 W
Boa Esperança, Bra.	256	22.48 S	42.34 W
Boa Esperança, Bra.	256	22.24 S	43.05 W
Boa Esperança, Represa ⊜[1]	250	6.50 S	44.00 W
Bo'ai	102	35.10 N	113.04 E
Boali	152	4.48 N	18.07 E
Boalia	126	23.35 N	88.57 E
Boalsburg	214	40.46 N	77.48 W
Boane	156	26.06 S	32.19 E
Boano, Pulau I	164	2.56 S	127.56 E
Boa Nova	255	14.22 S	40.10 W
Bo'ao	110	19.14 N	110.34 E
Boara Pisani	64	45.08 N	11.47 E
Boara Polesine	64	45.07 N	11.48 E
Board Camp Mountain ∧	204	40.42 N	123.43 W
Boardman	214	41.01 N	80.39 W
Boardman ≃	190	44.46 N	85.38 W
Boarhills	46	56.19 N	2.42 W
Boario Terme	64	45.54 N	10.10 E
Boat Basin	182	49.29 N	126.25 W
Boat Channel ʊ	212	44.10 N	76.31 W
Boath	46	57.44 N	4.23 W
Boat Lake ⊜	212	44.44 N	81.13 W
Boatman	166	27.16 S	146.55 E
Boat of Garten	46	57.20 N	3.44 W
Boa Viagem	250	5.07 S	39.44 W
Boa Vista, Bra.	246	2.49 N	60.40 W
Boa Vista, Bra.	256	21.25 S	45.35 W
Boa Vista I	150a	16.05 N	22.50 W
Boa Vista, Morro ∧[2]	287a	22.53 S	43.06 W
Boavita	246	6.20 N	72.35 W
Boawai	115b	8.46 S	121.10 E
Boayan Island I	116	10.34 N	119.09 E
Boaz	194	34.12 N	86.09 W
Boba	115b	8.57 S	121.04 E
Bobai	102	22.12 N	109.52 E
Bobbau	54	51.41 N	12.16 E
Bobbili	122	18.34 N	83.22 E
Bobbing	260	51.21 N	0.43 E
Bobbingworth	260	51.44 N	0.13 E
Bobbin Head	274a	33.39 S	151.08 E
Bobbio	62	44.46 N	9.23 E
Bobbio Pellice	62	44.48 N	7.07 E
Bobbys Run ≃	285	39.58 N	74.48 W
Bobcaygeon	212	44.33 N	78.33 W
Bobenheim-Roxheim	56	49.35 N	8.21 E
Bobigny	50	48.54 N	2.27 E
Böbingen, Dtsch.	56	48.49 N	9.54 E
Bobingen, Dtsch.	58	48.16 N	10.50 E
Bobitz	54	53.47 N	11.20 E
Bob Lake ⊜	212	44.55 N	78.47 W
Böblingen	56	48.41 N	9.01 E
Boblo Island Amusement Park ♠	281	42.06 N	83.07 W
Bobo Dioulasso	150	11.12 N	4.18 W
Boboiob, gora ∧	85	40.52 N	70.21 E
Bobo Island I	164	9.08 S	143.14 E
Bobolice	30	53.57 N	16.36 E
Bobonaza ≃	246	2.36 S	76.38 W
Bobonong	156	21.58 S	28.17 E
Bobos ≃	234	20.15 N	96.47 W
Bobotsari	115a	7.18 S	109.22 E
Bobr	76	54.20 N	29.16 E
Bobr ≃, Bela.	76	54.03 N	28.51 E
Bóbr ≃, Pol.	30	52.04 N	15.04 E
Bobrov	78	51.06 N	40.02 E
Bobrovytsya	78	50.44 N	31.22 E
Bobrujsk → Babrujsk	76	53.09 N	29.14 E
Bobryk ≃	76	52.08 N	26.46 E
Bobrykove	83	47.56 N	39.13 E
Bobrynets'	78	48.03 N	32.09 E
Bob Sandlin, Lake ⊜[1]	222	33.05 N	95.03 W
Bobs Creek ≃	219	38.57 N	90.42 W
Bobs Lake ⊜	212	44.40 N	76.35 W
Bobtown	188	39.45 N	79.58 W
Bobuk	140	11.30 N	34.05 E
Bobures	246	9.15 N	71.11 W
Boby, Pic ∧	157b	22.12 S	46.55 E
Boca •[8]	288	34.38 S	58.21 W
Bôca, Cachoeira da L	250	5.27 S	54.24 W
Boca Brava, Isla I	236	8.13 N	82.16 W
Boca Chica	240m	17.59 N	66.32 W
Boca Chica Key I	220	24.34 N	81.42 W
Bôca da Mata	250	9.41 S	36.11 W
Boca del Monte	236	8.21 N	82.07 W
Boca del Río	234	19.06 N	96.06 W
Boca del Rosario	258	34.26 S	57.17 W
Boca de Pozo	246	11.00 N	64.23 W
Boca de Quadra ʊ	182	55.08 N	130.50 W
Boca do Acre	248	8.45 S	67.23 W
Bôca do Jari	250	1.07 S	51.58 W
Bocage, Cap ≻	175f	21.12 S	165.35 E
Boca Grande	220	26.44 N	82.15 W
Boca Grande Channel ʊ	220	24.34 N	82.03 W
Boca Grande Key I	220	24.32 N	82.00 W
Bocaina ≃	256	22.40 S	45.00 W
Bocaina, Parque Nacional de ♠	256	23.00 S	44.15 W
Bocaina, Serra da ⛰	256	22.43 S	44.40 W
Bocaina de Minas	256	22.10 S	44.24 W
Bocaiúva	255	17.07 S	43.49 W
Bocanda	150	7.04 N	4.30 W
Bocanegra	286d	12.01 S	77.07 W
Bocaranga	152	6.59 N	15.39 E
Boca Raton	220	26.21 N	80.05 W
Boca Reservoir ⊜[1]	226	39.24 N	120.06 W
Bocas del Toro	236	9.20 N	82.15 W
Bocas del Toro □[4]	236	8.50 N	82.10 W
Bocas del Toro, Archipiélago de II	236	9.20 N	82.10 W
Bocaue	116	14.48 N	120.55 E
Bocay	236	14.19 N	85.10 W
Bocay ≃	236	14.20 N	85.10 W
Boccaleone	66	44.39 N	11.48 E
Boccea •[8]	267a	41.58 N	12.19 E
Bocchigliero	68	39.25 N	16.45 E
Bocconi	64	44.01 N	11.46 E
Bochan	88	53.09 N	103.48 E
Bochil	234	16.59 N	92.55 W
Böch Möron	86	49.40 N	90.20 E
Bochnia	30	49.58 N	20.26 E
Bocholt, Bel.	56	51.10 N	5.35 E
Bocholt, Dtsch.	52	51.50 N	6.36 E
Bocholtz	56	50.49 N	6.00 E
Bochov	54	50.06 N	13.02 E
Bochum, Dtsch.	56	51.28 N	7.13 E
Bochum, Dtsch.	263	51.28 N	7.13 E
Bochum, S. Afr.	156	23.17 S	29.07 E
Bockel	52	53.12 N	9.17 E
Böckel •[8]	263	51.13 N	7.12 E
Bockenem	52	52.00 N	10.07 E
Bockhorn	52	53.23 N	8.01 E
Böckstein	64	47.05 N	13.07 E
Bockum •[8], Dtsch.	263	51.21 N	6.38 E
Bockum •[8], Dtsch.	263	51.20 N	6.44 E
Bockum-Hövel	52	51.42 N	7.46 E
Bocognano	36	42.05 N	9.03 E
Bocón, Caño ≃	246	3.42 N	67.53 W
Boconó	246	9.15 N	70.16 W
Bocq ≃	56	50.20 N	4.53 E
Bocșa	38	45.23 N	21.47 E
Boczów	54	52.19 N	14.58 E
Boda, Centraf.	152	4.19 N	17.28 E
Böda, Sve.	26	57.15 N	17.03 E
Boda, Sve.	26	61.01 N	15.13 E
Bodafors	26	57.30 N	14.42 E
Boda Glasbruk	26	56.44 N	15.40 E
Bodāi	272b	22.48 N	88.29 E
Bodajbo	88	57.51 N	114.10 E
Bodalangi	152	3.14 N	22.14 E
Bodalla	166	36.05 S	150.03 E
Bodallin	162	31.22 S	118.52 E
Bodåsgruvan	40	60.25 N	16.26 E
Bodcau Creek ≃	194	33.01 N	93.31 W
Boddam, Scot., U.K.	46	57.28 N	1.47 W
Boddam, Scot., U.K.	46a	59.55 N	1.17 W
Boddington	168a	32.48 S	116.28 E
Bode	198	42.52 N	94.17 W
Bode ≃	54	51.50 N	11.46 E
Bodega Bay ⊂	204	38.15 N	123.00 W
Bodegraven	52	52.05 N	4.45 E
Bodélé •[1]	146	16.30 N	16.30 E
Bodelschwingh •[8]	263	51.33 N	7.22 E
Bodelshausen	58	48.24 N	8.58 E
Boden → Fleres, It.	64	46.58 N	11.21 E
Boden, Sve.	26	65.50 N	21.42 E
Bodenburg	52	52.01 N	10.01 E
Bodenfelde	52	51.38 N	9.33 E
Bodenheim	56	49.56 N	8.18 E
Bodenmais	60	49.04 N	13.06 E
Bodensee (Lake Constance) ⊜	58	47.35 N	9.25 E
Bodenteich	54	52.50 N	10.41 E
Bodenwerder	52	51.59 N	9.31 E
Bodenwies ∧	61	47.45 N	14.34 E
Bodenwöhr	60	49.16 N	12.19 E
Boderg, Lough ⊜	48	53.52 N	7.58 W
Bode Sadu	150	9.00 N	4.47 E
Bodhan	122	18.40 N	77.54 E
Bodh Gaya	124	24.42 N	84.59 E
Bodiam	42	51.00 N	0.33 E
Bodināyakkanūr	122	10.01 N	77.21 E
Bodine, Mount ∧	182	55.37 N	125.49 W
Bodjoki	152	2.59 N	22.18 E
Bodjokola	152	3.54 N	20.17 E
Bodmin	42	50.29 N	4.43 W
Bodmin Moor •[3]	42	50.33 N	4.33 W
Bodø	24	67.17 N	14.23 E
Bodocó	250	7.47 S	39.55 W
Bodoquena, Serra da ⛰[1]	248	21.00 S	56.50 W
Bodoukpa	152	5.43 N	17.36 E
Bodri ≃	115a	6.52 S	110.10 E
Bodrog ≃	30	48.07 N	21.25 E
Bodrum	130	37.02 N	27.26 E
Bodstedt	54	54.22 N	12.37 E
Bo Duc	110	11.58 N	106.48 E
Bodzentyn	30	50.56 N	20.57 E
Boè, Piz ∧	64	46.31 N	11.48 E
Boëge	58	46.13 N	6.25 E
Boekelo	52	52.13 N	6.47 E
Boele •[8]	263	51.24 N	7.28 E
Boémbé	152	2.54 S	15.39 E
Boende	152	0.13 S	20.52 E
Bœng Lvea	110	12.36 N	105.34 E
Boeni	157a	12.55 S	45.06 E
Boën-sur-Lignon	62	45.44 N	3.59 E
Boeo, Capo ≻	70	37.48 N	12.25 E
Boerboonfontein	158	33.43 S	20.32 E
Boerne	196	29.47 N	98.43 W
Boeslunde	41	55.18 N	11.17 E
Boesmans ≃, S. Afr.	158	28.46 S	30.09 E
Boesmans ≃, S. Afr.	158	33.42 S	26.39 E
Boesmansriviermond	158	33.42 S	26.39 E
Boetsap	158	27.59 S	24.30 E
Boeuf ≃	194	31.52 N	91.47 W
Boeuf Creek ≃	219	38.36 N	91.09 W
Boffa	150	10.10 N	14.02 W
Boffalora	266b	45.28 N	8.50 E
Boffzen	52	51.45 N	9.23 E
Bofoku	152	0.57 S	20.53 E
Bofors	40	59.20 N	14.32 E
Bofosso	150	8.40 N	9.42 W
Bōfu → Hōfu	96	34.03 N	131.34 E
Boga	154	1.03 N	29.56 E
Bogachiel ≃	224	47.55 N	124.28 W
Bogadjim	164	5.25 S	145.45 E
Bogal, Lagh ≃	154	0.45 N	40.50 E
Bogale	110	16.17 N	95.24 E
Bogalusa	194	30.47 N	89.50 W
Bogan ≃	166	29.57 S	146.21 E
Bogandé	150	12.59 N	0.08 W
Bog and Vly Meadows ≡	276	40.56 N	74.19 W
Bogan Gate	166	33.07 S	147.48 E
Bogangolo	152	5.34 N	18.15 E
Bogantungan	166	23.39 S	147.18 E
Bogart, Mount ∧	182	50.55 N	115.14 W
Bogastow Brook ≃	283	42.12 N	71.22 W
Bogata	196	33.28 N	95.13 W
Bogatiščevo-Jepišino	82	54.47 N	38.25 E
Bogatoje	80	53.04 N	51.24 E
Bogatyje Saby	80	56.01 N	50.27 E
Bogatynia	54	50.53 N	15.00 E
Bogatyr'	80	53.25 N	50.02 E
Bogatyrevo	80	50.22 N	48.46 E
Boğazkale	130	40.02 N	34.37 E
Boğazkaya	130	41.27 N	35.54 E
Boğazköy •[8]	267b	41.11 N	28.46 E
Boğazköy ≃	267b	41.10 N	28.49 E
Boğazlıyan	130	39.12 N	35.15 E
Bogbonga	152	1.35 N	19.25 E
Bogcang ≃	120	31.56 N	87.24 E
Bogd	102	45.11 N	100.43 E
Bogdanovič	86	56.47 N	62.01 E
Bogdanovka, Ross.	80	52.42 N	50.46 E
Bogdanovka, Ross.	80	52.10 N	52.37 E
Bogda Shan ⛰	90	43.30 N	89.45 E
Bogdo Ula ∧	86	43.50 N	88.20 E
Bogel	56	50.11 N	7.48 E
Bogembaj	86	52.29 N	72.20 E
Bogen	60	48.55 N	12.43 E
Bogense	41	55.34 N	10.06 E
Boger City	192	35.29 N	81.12 W
Bogess Creek ≃	282	37.18 N	122.19 W
Boget	80	49.40 N	47.59 E
Boggabilla	166	28.37 S	150.21 E
Boggabri	166	30.42 S	150.02 E
Boggeragh Mountains ⛰	48	52.03 N	8.55 W
Boggola, Mount ∧	162	23.48 S	117.40 E
Boggs Run ≃	279b	40.32 N	80.14 W
Boggstown	218	39.34 N	85.55 W
Boggy Creek ≃	222	31.07 N	95.46 W
Boggy Peak ∧	240c	17.03 N	61.51 W
Bogia	164	4.15 S	144.55 E
Bogie Lake ⊜	281	42.37 N	83.31 W
Bogilima	152	3.34 N	19.16 E
Bogliasco	62	44.23 N	9.04 E
Bognanco Fonti	58	46.07 N	8.12 E
Bognes	24	68.10 N	16.00 E
Bognor Regis	42	50.47 N	0.41 W
Bogny-sur-Meuse	56	49.51 N	4.46 E
Bogo, Cam.	146	10.44 N	14.36 E
Bogo, Pil.	116	11.03 N	124.00 E
Bogø I	41	54.56 N	12.04 E
Bogo Bay ⊂	116	11.05 N	124.01 E
Bogol Manyo	144	4.31 N	41.32 E
Bogol'ubovo, Ross.	76	55.32 N	32.57 E
Bogol'ubovo, Ross.	80	56.13 N	40.31 E
Bogomila	38	41.36 N	21.28 E
Bogong, Mount ∧	166	36.45 S	147.18 E
Bogong Peaks ⛰	171b	35.34 S	148.28 E
Bogor	115a	6.35 S	106.47 E
Bogoria, Lake ⊜	154	0.15 N	36.06 E
Bogoro	154	1.24 N	30.17 E
Bogorodick	76	53.46 N	38.08 E
Bogorodickoje	80	46.20 N	41.10 E
Bogorodsk, Ross.	24	62.16 N	52.28 E
Bogorodsk, Ross.	80	56.06 N	43.31 E
Bogorodskoje, Ross.	80	57.51 N	50.45 E
Bogorodskoje, Ross.	80	46.20 N	43.53 E
Bogorodskoje, Ross.	82	55.02 N	38.29 E
Bogorodskoje, Ross.	82	55.26 N	36.14 E
Bogorodskoje, Ross.	89	52.22 N	140.30 E
Bogorodskoje •[8]	265b	55.49 N	37.44 E
Bogoso	150	5.34 N	2.01 W
Bogosskij chrebet ⛰	84	42.15 N	46.05 E
Bogotá → Santa Fe de Bogotá, Col.	246	4.36 N	74.05 W
Bogota, N.J., U.S.	276	40.52 N	74.01 W
Bogotol	86	56.12 N	89.33 E
Bogou	150	10.39 N	0.11 E
Bogovarovo	24	58.59 N	47.01 E
Bogra	124	24.51 N	89.22 E
Bograd	86	54.13 N	90.51 E
Bogrie Hill ∧[2]	44	55.08 N	3.55 W
Bogučany	88	58.23 N	97.29 E
Bogučar	78	49.57 N	40.33 E
Bogučar ≃	78	49.57 N	40.39 E
Bogué	150	16.35 N	14.16 W
Bogue Chitto	194	31.26 N	90.27 W
Bogue Chitto ≃	194	30.35 N	89.49 W
Bogue Chitto Creek ≃	194	32.10 N	87.14 W
Bogue Phalia ≃	194	33.15 N	90.44 W
Bogues Bay ⊂	208	37.52 N	75.29 W
Böğürtlen	130	37.10 N	38.04 E
Bogustan	85	41.41 N	70.05 E
Bo Hai (Gulf of Chihli) ⊂	98	38.30 N	120.00 E
Bohai Haixia ʊ	98	38.15 N	121.00 E
Bohain-en-Vermandois	50	49.59 N	3.27 E
Bohai Wan ⊂	98	38.40 N	118.20 E
Bohan	56	49.52 N	4.53 E
Bohannon	208	37.24 N	76.22 W
Böheimkirchen	61	48.12 N	15.46 E
Bohemia	210	40.46 N	73.06 W
Bohemia → Čechy □[9]	30	49.50 N	14.00 E
Bohemia ≃	208	39.29 N	75.55 W
Bohemia Downs	162	18.53 S	126.14 E
Bohemian Forest ⛰	30	49.15 N	12.45 E
Bohetai	104	42.01 N	123.13 E
Bohicon	150	7.12 N	2.04 E
Bohin	144	11.44 N	51.15 E
Bohinjska Bistrica	36	46.17 N	13.57 E
Bohinjsko Jezero ⊜	64	46.17 N	13.50 E
Böhlen	54	51.12 N	12.23 E
Böhlitz-Ehrenberg	54	51.21 N	12.17 E
Böhme ≃	52	52.46 N	9.28 E
Böhmen → Čechy □[9]	30	49.50 N	14.00 E
Böhmenkirch	56	48.41 N	9.55 E
Böhmerwald → Bohemian Forest ⛰	30	49.15 N	12.45 E
Bohmte	52	52.22 N	8.19 E
Bohners Lake	216	42.37 N	88.17 W
Böhnsdorf •[8]	264a	52.24 N	13.33 E
Bohodou	150	9.46 N	9.04 W
Bohodukhiv	78	50.10 N	35.30 E
Bohol	144	5.45 N	46.09 E
Bohol □[4]	116	9.50 N	124.10 E
Bohol I	116	9.50 N	124.10 E
Bohol Sea ⊤[2]	116	9.10 N	124.25 E
Bohongou	150	12.30 N	0.42 E
Bohorg	152	6.23 N	15.37 E
Bohorodchany	78	48.48 N	24.32 E
Bohorok	114	3.30 N	98.12 E
Bohuslän □[9]	26	58.15 N	11.50 E
Bohuslav	78	49.33 N	30.53 E
Bohušovice nad Ohří	54	50.29 N	14.07 E
Bohutín	60	49.40 N	13.55 E
Boi	150	9.34 N	9.27 E
Boi, Ponta do ≻	256	23.58 S	45.15 W
Boiaçu	246	0.27 S	61.46 W
Boiano	66	41.29 N	14.29 E
Boiceville	210	41.59 N	74.15 W
Boiestown	186	46.27 N	66.25 W
Boigu Island I	164	9.16 S	142.12 E
Boila	154	16.10 S	39.50 E
Boiling Springs, N.C., U.S.	192	35.30 N	81.37 W
Boiling Springs, Pa., U.S.	208	40.08 N	77.07 W
Boim	250	2.49 S	55.10 W
Boinville-en-Mantois	261	48.56 N	1.46 E
Boinvilliers	261	48.55 N	1.40 E
Boipeba, Ilha de I	255	13.39 S	38.55 W
Boiro	34	42.39 N	8.54 W
Bois, Lac des ⊜, N.T., Can.	180	66.40 N	125.15 W
Bois, Lac des → Woods, Lake of the ⊜, N.A.	184	49.15 N	94.45 W
Bois, Rio dos ≃	255	18.35 S	50.02 W
Bois Blanc Island I	190	45.45 N	84.28 W
Boisbriand	275a	45.37 N	73.51 W
Bois Brule ≃	190	46.45 N	91.37 W
Boischâtel	206	46.54 N	71.08 W
Bois-Colombes	261	48.55 N	2.16 E
Boisdale, Loch ⊂	46	57.08 N	7.19 W
Bois d'Arc Creek ≃	196	33.50 N	95.50 W
Bois-d'Arcy	261	48.48 N	2.01 E
Bois-des-Filion	206	45.40 N	73.45 W
Bois de Sioux ≃	198	46.16 N	96.36 W
Boise	202	43.36 N	116.12 W
Boise ≃	202	43.49 N	117.01 W
Boise, Middle Fork ≃	202	43.42 N	115.38 W
Boise, North Fork ≃	202	43.42 N	115.38 W
Boise, South Fork ≃	202	43.36 N	115.51 W
Boise City	196	36.43 N	102.30 W
Boisemont	261	49.01 N	2.00 E
Bois-Guillaume	50	49.28 N	1.08 E
Bois-le-Roi	50	48.28 N	2.42 E
Boissettes	261	48.31 N	2.37 E
Boissevain	184	49.14 N	100.03 W
Boissise-la-Bertrand	261	48.32 N	2.35 E
Boissy-l'Aillerie	261	49.05 N	2.02 E
Boissy-Saint-Léger	50	48.45 N	2.31 E
Boissy-sous-Saint-Yon	261	48.34 N	2.13 E
Boistfort Peak ∧	224	46.29 N	123.12 W
Boitzenburg	54	53.15 N	13.37 E
Boizenburg	54	53.22 N	10.43 E
Boja	115a	7.06 S	110.16 E
Bojadła	30	51.57 N	15.50 E
Bojarkino	82	54.57 N	38.31 E
Bojarsk	88	56.19 N	106.04 E
Bojayá ≃	246	6.35 N	76.54 W
Bojeador, Cape ≻	116	18.30 N	120.34 E
Bojelebung	116	6.31 N	122.11 E
Bojevo	78	51.24 N	39.19 E
Boji Plain ⌣	154	1.30 N	39.45 E
Bojizhang	98	41.49 N	117.46 E
Bojnūrd	128	37.28 N	57.19 E
Bojonegoro	115a	7.09 S	111.52 E
Boju	150	7.25 N	7.52 E
Boju Ega	150	7.24 N	8.04 E
Bojuru	252	31.38 S	51.26 W
Bokad	272c	18.53 N	72.58 E
Bokada	152	4.08 N	19.23 E
Bokal	168a	33.29 S	116.54 E
Bokala, R.D.C.	152	3.07 S	17.02 E
Bokala, R.D.C.	152	2.03 N	18.59 E
Bokani	150	9.26 N	5.13 E
Bokāro Steel City	124	23.45 N	86.07 E
Bokatola	152	0.38 S	18.46 E
Bokchito	196	34.01 N	96.08 W
Boké, Guinée	150	10.56 N	14.18 W
Boke, Kaz.	86	49.05 N	81.38 E
Bokeelia	220	26.42 N	82.09 W
Bokel	52	53.23 N	8.46 E
Bokela	152	1.08 S	21.56 E
Bokes Creek ≃	188	40.19 N	83.10 W
Bokfontein	158	32.48 S	19.16 E
Bokhara	158	27.57 S	20.30 E
Bokhara ≃	166	29.55 S	146.42 E
Boki	146	8.48 N	13.32 E
Bokino	80	52.38 N	41.26 E
Bokkol ∧	154	1.50 N	37.02 E
Bok Koŭ	110	10.37 N	104.03 E
Böklund	41	54.36 N	9.34 E
Boknafjorden ⊂[2]	26	59.10 N	5.35 E
Boko	152	4.47 S	14.38 E
Bokod	116	16.30 N	120.50 E
Bokode	152	3.58 N	19.29 E
Bokolako	150	13.36 N	12.33 W
Bokonbajevskoje	85	42.07 N	77.00 E
Bokondji	152	2.22 N	18.42 E
Bokondo	152	0.15 N	22.32 E
Bokong	112	9.58 S	124.04 E
Bokoro	146	12.23 N	17.03 E
Boko Songo	152	4.26 S	13.37 E
Bokota	152	0.51 S	22.18 E
Bokote	152	0.05 S	20.08 E
Bokovo-Antratsit → Antratsyt	83	48.06 N	39.06 E
Bokovskaja	80	49.15 N	41.49 E
Bokpunt ≻	158	33.34 S	18.19 E
Bokpyin	110	11.16 N	98.46 E
Boksburg	158	26.12 S	28.14 E
Boksburg □[5]	273d	26.12 S	28.14 E
Boksburg-Noord	273d	26.12 S	28.15 E
Boksburg South	273d	26.14 S	28.15 E
Boksburg-West	273d	26.13 S	28.14 E
Boksitogorsk	76	59.28 N	33.51 E
Bokungu	152	0.41 S	22.19 E
Bol, Hrv.	36	43.16 N	16.40 E
Bol, Tchad	146	13.28 N	14.43 E
Bolaang Mongondow	112	0.56 N	124.10 E
Bolama, Gui.-B.	150	11.35 N	15.28 W
Bolama, R.D.C.	152	1.57 N	22.58 E
Bolaman	130	41.03 N	37.37 E
Bolān ≃	120	28.38 N	67.42 E
Bolanda, Jabal ∧	140	7.44 N	25.28 E
Bol'andkiik ≃	85	39.11 N	72.17 E
Bolangum	166	36.46 S	142.53 E
Bolaños	234	21.41 N	103.47 W
Bolaños ≃	234	21.14 N	104.08 W
Bolaños de Calatrava	34	38.54 N	3.40 W
Bolān Pass)(	120	29.45 N	67.35 E
Bolans	240c	17.02 N	61.53 W
Bolay I	152	4.20 N	17.21 E
Bolayır	130	40.31 N	26.45 E
Bolbec	50	49.34 N	0.29 E
Bolçalı	84	40.38 N	46.18 E
Bolčary	86	59.49 N	68.48 E
Bolchov	76	53.27 N	36.01 E
Bolchuny	80	47.59 N	46.25 E
Bolda ≃	80	46.10 N	48.14 E
Boldasevo	80	54.43 N	45.33 E
Boldekow	54	53.43 N	13.35 E
Bolderslev	41	54.59 N	9.18 E
Bold Heath	262	53.24 N	2.42 W
Boldon	44	54.57 N	1.27 W
Bol'džuan	85	38.19 N	69.40 E
Bole, Ghana	150	9.02 N	2.29 W
Bole, Zhg.	86	44.53 N	82.05 E
Bolekhiv	78	49.04 N	23.52 E
Boleko	152	1.31 S	19.53 E
Bolero	154	10.59 S	33.45 E
Boles	194	34.46 N	94.02 W
Bolesławiec	30	51.16 N	15.34 E
Boleszkowice	30	52.44 N	14.36 E
Boletice nad Labem	54	50.45 N	14.13 E
Boley	196	35.29 N	96.29 W
Bolgart	162	31.16 S	116.30 E
Bolgatanga	150	10.46 N	0.52 W
Bolhrad	78	45.41 N	28.36 E
Boli, Sūd.	140	6.01 N	28.43 E
Boli, Tchad	146	10.50 N	18.43 E
Boli, Zhg.	89	45.46 N	130.31 E
Bolia	152	1.36 S	18.23 E
Boliden	26	64.52 N	20.23 E
Boligee	194	32.45 N	88.01 W
Boligeqiu	104	42.14 N	121.40 E
Bolíkov	61	49.02 N	15.22 E
Bolinao	116	16.23 N	119.54 E
Bolinas	226	37.54 N	122.42 W
Boling	222	29.15 N	95.56 W
Bolingbrook	216	41.41 N	88.04 W
Bolinger Creek ≃	282	37.47 N	122.00 W
Bolingo	152	3.30 S	21.43 E
Bolishan	89	43.50 N	123.31 E
Bolivar, Austl.	168b	34.46 S	138.36 E
Bolívar, Col.	246	5.50 N	76.01 W
Bolívar, Col.	246	1.50 N	76.58 W
Bolívar, Col.	246	4.21 N	76.10 W
Bolívar, Perú	248	7.18 S	77.48 W
Bolivar, Mo., U.S.	194	37.36 N	93.24 W
Bolivar, N.Y., U.S.	210	42.04 N	78.10 W
Bolivar, Oh., U.S.	214	40.39 N	81.27 W
Bolivar, Pa., U.S.	214	40.23 N	79.09 W
Bolivar, Tn., U.S.	194	35.15 N	88.59 W
Bolívar □[3]	246	6.20 N	63.30 W
Bolívar □[4]	246	1.35 S	79.00 W
Bolívar □[5]	246	9.00 N	74.40 W
Bolívar, Cerro ∧	246	7.28 N	63.25 W
Bolívar, Pico ∧	246	8.30 N	71.02 W
Bolivar Peninsula ≻[1]	196	29.27 N	94.39 W
Bolivar Run	214	41.59 N	78.39 W
Bolivia □[1], S.A.	242	17.00 S	65.00 W
Bolivia □[1], S.A.	248	17.00 S	65.00 W
Bolivie → Bolivia □[1]	248	17.00 S	65.00 W
Bolivien → Bolivia □[1]	248	17.00 S	65.00 W
Boljarovo	38	42.09 N	26.49 E
Boljoon	116	9.38 N	123.29 E
Bolkar Dağları ⛰	130	37.15 N	34.20 E
Bölkenbusch	263	51.21 N	7.06 E
Boll	56	48.38 N	9.37 E
Bolladello	266b	45.41 N	8.50 E
Bollate	62	45.33 N	9.07 E
Böllberg ∧[2]	263	51.23 N	7.19 E
Bollendorf	56	49.51 N	6.22 E
Bollène	62	44.17 N	4.45 E
Bollensdorf	264a	52.31 N	13.43 E
Bolles Canal ≋	220	26.38 N	80.34 W
Bolles Harbor	216	41.51 N	83.24 W
Bollin ≃	44	53.23 N	2.28 W
Bolling Air Force Base ■	284c	38.51 N	77.02 W
Bollington, Eng., U.K.	44	53.18 N	2.06 W
Bollington, Eng., U.K.	262	53.22 N	2.25 W
Bollnäs	26	61.21 N	16.25 E
Bollon	166	28.05 S	147.15 E
Bollstabruk	26	63.00 N	17.39 E
Bollstanäs	40	59.30 N	17.56 E
Bollullos par del Condado	34	37.20 N	6.32 W
Bollwerk	263	51.10 N	7.35 E
Bolmen ⊜	26	56.55 N	13.40 E
Bolnisi	84	41.28 N	44.33 E
Bolo	144	8.50 N	39.22 E
Bolobo	152	2.10 S	16.14 E
Bolochovo	82	54.05 N	37.50 E
Bologna	64	44.29 N	11.20 E
Bologna □[4]	64	44.28 N	11.26 E
Bologne, Fr.	58	48.12 N	5.08 E
Bologne → Bologna, It.	64	44.29 N	11.20 E
Bolognesi	248	6.35 S	73.10 W
Bolognetta	70	37.58 N	13.27 E
Bolognola	66	42.59 N	13.14 E
Bologoje	76	57.54 N	34.02 E
Bologovo	76	56.54 N	31.42 E
Bololo	152	3.50 S	21.08 E
Bolomba	152	0.29 N	19.12 E
Bolombo	152	3.59 S	21.22 E
Bolombo ≃	152	1.32 N	21.14 E
Bolon'	89	49.55 N	136.07 E
Bolon', ozero ⊜	89	49.51 N	136.22 E
Bolonchén de Rejón	232	20.00 N	89.49 W
Bolondo	152	0.27 N	20.01 E
Bolondrón	240p	22.46 N	81.27 W
Bolong ≃	170	34.15 S	149.36 E
Bolonia → Bologna	64	44.29 N	11.20 E
Bolótana	71	40.20 N	8.57 E
Bolotnoje	86	55.41 N	84.23 E
Boloto	82	54.10 N	36.20 E
Bolotovskoje	86	58.33 N	62.28 E
Bolovens, Plateau des ⛰[1]	110	15.20 N	106.20 E
Bolpur	126	23.40 N	87.43 E
Bolqār (Bolqarçay) ≃	84	39.28 N	48.36 E
Bolqarçay (Bolqār) ≃	84	39.28 N	48.36 E
Bol'šaja	76	59.36 N	41.48 E
Bol'šaja ≃	80	48.36 N	41.00 E
Bol'šaja Atn'a	80	56.15 N	49.27 E
Bol'šaja Balachn'a ≃	74	73.37 N	107.05 E
Bol'šaja Brembola	82	56.45 N	38.55 E
Bol'šaja Bukon'	86	48.53 N	82.43 E
Bol'šaja Čalykla ≃	80	51.51 N	49.34 E
Bol'šaja Černigovka	80	52.07 N	50.52 E
Bol'šaja Chalan'	78	50.56 N	37.26 E
Bol'šaja Cheta ≃	74	69.33 N	84.15 E
Bol'šaja Chobda ≃	86	50.56 N	54.34 E
Bol'šaja Chundala	76	60.04 N	34.18 E
Bol'šaja Čuja ≃	88	58.56 N	112.13 E
Bol'šaja Čurakovka	86	53.03 N	64.20 E
Bol'šaja Dmitrijevka	80	51.21 N	45.15 E
Bol'šaja Dora	76	59.05 N	37.38 E
Bol'šaja Džalga	80	45.59 N	42.41 E
Bol'šaja Glušica	80	52.24 N	50.28 E
Bol'šaja Ižora	76	59.56 N	29.34 E
Bol'šaja Ižorka ≃	265a	59.48 N	30.36 E
Bol'šaja Kakša ≃	80	57.53 N	45.28 E
Bol'šaja Kamenka	80	53.39 N	50.31 E
Bol'šaja Kandala	80	54.32 N	49.22 E
Bol'šaja Kaskara	86	57.11 N	65.58 E
Bol'šaja Ket'	86	57.39 N	91.45 E
Bol'šaja Kinel' ≃	80	53.14 N	50.30 E
Bol'šaja Kirsanovka	83	47.40 N	38.54 E
Bol'šaja Kokšaga ≃	80	56.08 N	47.47 E
Bol'šaja Konkudera ≃	88	57.34 N	112.30 E
Bol'šaja Kugul'ta ≃	80	45.45 N	41.57 E
Bol'šaja Kuonamka ≃	74	70.45 N	113.24 E
Bol'šaja Laba ≃	84	44.16 N	40.53 E
Bol'šaja Lipovica	80	52.33 N	41.20 E
Bol'šaja Martynovka	80	47.17 N	41.40 E
Bol'šaja Murta	86	56.55 N	93.07 E
Bol'šaja Neva ≃	265a	59.58 N	30.13 E
Bol'šaja Norja	80	56.41 N	52.43 E
Bol'šaja Ochta •[8]	265a	59.57 N	30.25 E
Bol'šaja Ol'šanka	80	51.32 N	44.17 E
Bol'šaja Orlovka	80	47.20 N	41.16 E
Bol'šaja Osinovaja ≃	180	66.30 N	174.00 E
Bol'šaja Pas'ma	80	58.38 N	43.53 E
Bol'šaja Rečka	88	51.57 N	104.44 E
Bol'šaja Ržaksa	80	52.08 N	42.13 E
Bol'šaja Sestra ≃	82	56.16 N	35.56 E
Bol'šaja Smedva ≃	82	54.50 N	38.34 E
Bol'šaja Sosnova	80	57.40 N	54.36 E
Bol'šaja Talovaja	78	46.58 N	40.37 E
Bol'šaja Tarel'	88	53.45 N	106.40 E
Bol'šaja Tavoložka	80	52.07 N	49.04 E
Bol'šaja Uča	80	56.37 N	52.05 E
Bol'šaja Usa	86	56.44 N	55.06 E
Bol'šaja Ussurka ≃	89	45.57 N	133.42 E
Bol'šaja Višera	76	58.55 N	32.08 E
Bol'šaja Vladimirovka	86	50.53 N	79.31 E
Bolsa Knolls	226	36.44 N	121.38 W
Bol'šakovo, Ross.	76	54.53 N	21.40 E
Bol'šakovo, Ross.	265b	55.54 N	37.17 E
Bol'šekrepinskaja	83	47.36 N	39.22 E
Bol'šelig	24	62.07 N	52.25 E
Bolsena	66	42.39 N	11.59 E
Bolsena, Lago di ⊜	66	42.36 N	11.56 E
Bol'šenarymskoje	86	49.16 N	84.32 E
Bol'šerečje	86	56.06 N	74.38 E
Bol'šereck	74	52.25 N	156.24 E
Bol'šetroickoje	78	50.33 N	37.17 E
Bol'šeustjikinskoje	86	55.57 N	58.16 E
Bol'ševik, Ross.	74	62.44 N	147.30 E
Bol'ševik, Ross.	265a	59.49 N	30.30 E
Bol'ševik, ostrov I	74	78.40 N	102.30 E
Bol'šezemel'skaja Tundra •[1]	72	67.30 N	56.00 E
Bolshoi Theatre ℧	265b	55.46 N	37.37 E
Bol'šije Algaši	80	55.22 N	46.29 E
Bol'šije Belyniči	82	54.38 N	38.50 E
Bol'šije Berezniki	80	54.11 N	45.58 E
Bol'šije Gorki, Ross.	82	56.28 N	35.51 E
Bol'šije Gorki, Ross.	265a	59.42 N	29.51 E
Bol'šije Kajbicy	80	55.25 N	48.13 E
Bol'šije Kizi, ozero ⊜	89	51.38 N	140.20 E
Bol'šije Kl'uči	80	55.59 N	48.47 E
Bol'šije Kl'učišči	80	54.08 N	48.14 E
Bol'šije Liachvi ≃	84	41.58 N	44.06 E
Bol'šije Michalicyny	80	58.29 N	48.14 E
Bol'šije Ozerki	80	52.36 N	46.33 E
Bol'šije Pom'aly	80	56.42 N	46.40 E
Bol'šije Ručji	82	56.36 N	36.58 E
Bol'šije Saly	83	47.24 N	39.41 E
Bol'šije Tarchany	80	54.42 N	48.34 E
Bol'šije Ugli	88	57.47 N	112.51 E
Bol'šije Uki	86	56.57 N	72.37 E
Bol'šije Ždanovy	80	58.40 N	49.05 E
Bol'šoj	80	50.13 N	43.26 E
Bol'šoj Aksuat, ozero ⊜	86	51.24 N	64.28 E
Bol'šoj An'uj ≃	74	68.30 N	160.49 E
Bol'šoj Ažbulat, ozero ⊜	86	53.17 N	77.25 E
Bol'šoj Begičev, ostrov I	74	74.20 N	112.30 E
Bol'šoj Bogdo, gora ∧[2]	80	48.08 N	46.52 E
Bol'šoj Boktybaj, gora ∧	86	48.27 N	58.30 E
Bol'šoj Čeremšan ≃	80	54.11 N	49.39 E
Bol'šoj Civil' ≃	80	55.54 N	47.28 E
Bol'šoje, ozero ⊜	265a	60.04 N	30.39 E
Bol'šoje Aksu	86	43.20 N	79.35 E
Bol'šoje Aleksejevskoje	82	55.14 N	38.12 E
Bol'šoje Boldino	80	54.59 N	45.19 E
Bol'šoje Bun'kovo	82	55.51 N	38.37 E
Bol'šoje Goloustnoje	88	52.01 N	105.25 E
Bol'šoje Gorodišče, Ross.	76	57.17 N	30.31 E
Bol'šoje Gorodišče, Ross.	78	50.37 N	37.06 E
Bol'šoje Ignatovo	80	55.02 N	45.34 E
Bol'šoje Jarovoje, ozero ⊜	86	52.53 N	78.36 E
Bol'šoje Jašaltinskoje, ozero ⊜	80	46.17 N	42.27 E
Bol'šoje Kibejevo	80	56.55 N	47.05 E
Bol'šoje Korovino	82	54.30 N	39.02 E
Bol'šoje Manuškino	265a	59.53 N	30.49 E
Bol'šoje Michajlovskoje	82	56.47 N	38.04 E
Bol'šoje Mikuškino	80	53.56 N	51.42 E
Bol'šoje Muraškino	80	55.47 N	44.46 E
Bol'šoje Nagatkino	80	54.31 N	47.58 E
Bol'šoje Nurkejevo	80	55.22 N	52.40 E
Bol'šoje Nyrsy	80	55.44 N	50.19 E
Bol'šoje Ogar'ovo	76	53.33 N	37.43 E
Bol'šoje Pikino	80	56.25 N	44.22 E
Bol'šoje Polpino	76	53.14 N	34.30 E
Bol'šoje Ramenje	76	58.21 N	36.40 E
Bol'šoje Rybuškino	80	55.25 N	45.48 E
Bol'šoje Sazonovo	80	58.06 N	53.21 E
Bol'šoje Selo	76	57.43 N	38.56 E
Bol'šoje Šem'akino	80	55.03 N	48.38 E
Bol'šoje Soldatskoje	78	51.21 N	35.31 E
Bol'šoje Sudačje	80	50.49 N	44.05 E
Bol'šoje Topol'noje, ozero ⊜	86	53.20 N	78.00 E
Bol'šoje Uro	88	53.32 N	109.48 E
Bol'šoje Zagorje	76	57.51 N	28.57 E
Bol'šoje Žokovo	82	54.35 N	38.57 E
Bol'šoj Gašun ≃	80	47.22 N	42.43 E
Bol'šoj Golec, gora ∧	88	51.52 N	119.24 E
Bol'šoj Irgiz ≃	80	52.01 N	47.24 E
Bol'šoj Jenisej (Bij-Chem) ≃	88	51.43 N	94.26 E
Bol'šoj Jugan ≃	86	60.55 N	73.40 E
Bol'šoj Kamen'	89	43.06 N	132.21 E
Bol'šoj Kandarat'	80	54.25 N	47.00 E
Bol'šoj Kanym, gora ∧	86	54.13 N	88.20 E
Bol'šoj Karagaj	86	57.57 N	70.15 E
Bol'šoj Karaman ≃	80	51.40 N	46.38 E
Bol'šoj Ketmen'	86	43.27 N	80.24 E
Bol'šoj Kujaš	86	55.50 N	61.06 E
Bol'šoj Kundyš ≃	80	56.32 N	47.23 E
Bol'šoj Kuvaj	80	54.37 N	47.05 E
Bol'šoj Kymynej, gora ∧	180	66.34 N	172.32 W
Bol'šoj L'achovskij, ostrov I	74	73.35 N	142.00 E
Bol'šoj Lug	88	52.07 N	104.10 E
Bol'šoj Matačynaj, gora ∧	180	66.28 N	179.25 W
Bol'šoj Melik	80	51.38 N	43.18 E
Bol'šoj Nesvetaj ≃	83	47.27 N	39.54 E
Bol'šoj Onguren	88	53.38 N	107.36 E
Bol'šoj Patom ≃	88	59.15 N	113.56 E
Bol'šoj Pit ≃	86	59.01 N	91.44 E
Bol'šoj Porog	86	52.35 N	92.18 E
Bol'šoj Šagan	80	50.57 N	51.08 E
Bol'šoj Sajan ⛰	88	52.00 N	99.30 E
Bol'šoj Salym ≃	86	60.55 N	70.25 E
Bol'šoj Šantar, ostrov I	89	55.00 N	137.42 E
Bol'šoj Šatan, gora ∧	86	53.41 N	57.36 E
Bol'šoj Simonogont	265a	59.50 N	29.49 E
Bol'šoj Sorokino	86	56.38 N	69.53 E
Bol'šoj Sundyr'	80	56.07 N	46.46 E
Bol'šoj Tal'cy	76	59.13 N	33.00 E
Bol'šoj Tolkaj	80	53.30 N	51.57 E
Bol'šoj T'uters, ostrov I	76	59.51 N	27.13 E
Bol'šoj Uluj	86	56.39 N	90.36 E
Bol'šoj Uran ≃	80	52.24 N	53.15 E
Bol'šoj Uvat, ozero ⊜	86	57.35 N	70.30 E
Bol'šoj Uzen' ≃	80	48.50 N	49.40 E
Bol'šoj Uzigont	265a	59.48 N	29.53 E
Bol'šoj Vjass	80	53.48 N	45.30 E
Bol'šoj Vlasjevo	89	53.24 N	140.55 E
Bol'šoj Zelenčuk ≃	84	44.36 N	41.56 E
Bolsover	44	53.14 N	1.18 W
Bolsward	52	53.03 N	5.31 E
Boltaña	34	42.27 N	0.04 E
Boltigen	58	46.38 N	7.24 E
Boltino	265b	55.58 N	37.41 E
Bolton, On., Can.	212	43.53 N	79.44 W
Bolton, Eng., U.K.	44	53.35 N	2.26 W
Bolton, Ct., U.S.	207	41.46 N	72.26 W
Bolton, Ms., U.S.	194	32.20 N	90.27 W
Bolton, N.C., U.S.	192	34.19 N	78.24 W
Bolton □[8]	262	53.34 N	2.28 W
Bolton Abbey	44	53.59 N	1.53 W
Bolton Abbey ℧[1]	44	53.59 N	1.54 W
Bolton Center	207	41.47 N	72.26 W
Bolton Creek ≃	212	44.58 N	76.23 W
Bolton Lake ⊜	184	54.16 N	95.47 W
Bolton-le-Sands	44	54.06 N	2.47 W
Bolton upon Dearne	44	53.31 N	1.19 W
Bolton Wanderers Football Ground ♠	262	53.34 N	2.25 W
Bolu	130	40.44 N	31.37 E
Bolu □[4]	130	40.40 N	31.30 E
Bölükyazı	130	38.18 N	42.10 E
Boluntay	120	36.34 N	92.38 E
Boluo, Zhg.	100	23.11 N	114.17 E
Boluo, Zhg.	100	24.27 N	113.03 E
Boluochi	98	41.24 N	119.56 E
Boluokeng	100	24.05 N	113.22 E
Bolus Head ≻	48	51.46 N	10.21 W
Bolva ≃	76	53.17 N	34.20 E
Bolvadin	130	38.42 N	31.04 E
Bolwarra	166	17.24 S	144.11 E
Bóly	30	45.58 N	18.32 E
Bolyčevo	82	55.46 N	35.43 E
Bolzaneto	62	44.27 N	8.54 E
Bolzano (Bozen)	64	46.31 N	11.22 E
Bolzano □[4]	64	46.43 N	11.30 E
Boma	152	5.51 S	13.03 E
Bomaderry	170	34.51 S	150.37 E
Bomal	56	50.23 N	5.32 E
Bomandjokou	152	0.34 N	14.23 E
Bomaneh	152	1.18 N	23.47 E
Bomarsund	26	60.13 N	20.15 E
Bomate	152	1.10 S	19.41 E
Bomba	66	42.02 N	14.22 E
Bombakabo	152	3.04 N	19.42 E
Bombala	166	36.54 S	149.14 E
Bombarral	34	39.16 N	9.09 W
Bombat	130	38.08 N	42.14 E
Bombay → Mumbai, India	122	18.58 N	72.50 E
Bombay, N.Y., U.S.	206	44.56 N	74.34 W
Bombay, University of ℧[2]	272c	18.57 N	72.50 E
Bombay Harbour ⊂	272c	18.57 N	72.53 E
Bomberai, Semenanjung ≻[1]	164	3.00 S	133.00 E
Bombetoka, Baie de ⊂	157b	15.50 S	46.17 E
Bombimba	152	0.31 N	19.24 E
Bombo	154	0.35 N	32.32 E
Bombo ≃	152	3.58 S	15.59 E
Bombo-Kasanji	152	5.54 S	21.51 E
Bomboma	152	2.25 N	18.54 E
Bombo-Makuka	152	5.26 S	16.19 E
Bombombwa	154	1.21 N	25.30 E
Bombon	261	48.34 N	2.52 E
Bomboyo	146	12.01 N	15.28 E
Bom Conselho	250	9.10 S	36.41 W
Bom Despacho	255	19.43 S	45.15 W
Bomdila	120	27.27 N	92.17 E
Bomei	100	22.57 N	115.46 E
Bom Fim do Bom Jesus	256	23.17 S	47.02 W
Bomhus	40	60.41 N	17.13 E
Bomili	154	1.40 N	27.01 E
Bom Jardim, Ilha do I	287a	23.02 S	43.35 W
Bom Jardim de Goiás	255	16.17 S	52.07 W
Bom Jardim de Minas	256	21.57 S	44.11 W
Bom Jesus, Ang.	152	9.09 S	13.34 E
Bom Jesus, Bra.	250	9.04 S	44.22 W
Bom Jesus da Lapa	255	13.15 S	43.25 W
Bom Jesus de Goiás	255	18.12 S	49.44 W
Bom Jesus dos Perdões	256	23.08 S	46.28 W
Bømlafjorden ⊂[2]	26	59.39 N	5.20 E
Bomlitz	52	52.54 N	9.37 E
Bømlo I	26	59.46 N	5.12 E
Bommerholz	263	51.23 N	7.18 E
Bommern	263	51.25 N	7.20 E
Bomnak	89	54.46 N	128.51 E
Bomokandi ≃	154	3.39 N	26.08 E
Bomongiri	152	1.57 S	21.13 E
Bomongo	152	1.22 N	18.21 E
Bompata	150	6.38 N	1.04 W
Bompensiere	70	37.28 N	13.47 E
Bompietro	70	37.44 N	14.06 E
Bomputu	152	0.20 S	20.06 E
Bom Repouso	256	22.28 S	46.09 W
Bom Retiro	252	27.48 S	49.31 W
Bom Retiro •[8]	287b	23.32 S	46.38 W
Bom Sucesso, Bra.	248	15.43 S	56.07 W
Bom Sucesso, Bra.	255	23.42 S	51.45 W
Bom Sucesso, Bra.	256	22.17 S	42.49 W
Bom Sucesso, Bra.	287b	23.25 S	46.24 W
Bomu (Mbomou) ≃	136	4.08 N	22.26 E
Bon, Cap ≻	36	37.05 N	11.03 E
Bona	40	58.34 N	15.03 E
Bona Bona Island I	164	10.30 S	149.50 E
Bon Accord	158	25.38 S	28.11 E
Bonaduz	58	46.49 N	9.25 E
Bonaero Park	273d	26.07 S	28.16 E
Bonai	114	1.16 N	100.52 E
Bonaigarh	120	21.50 N	84.57 E
Bon Air	208	37.31 N	77.33 W
Bon Aire	214	40.54 N	79.55 W
Bonaire I	241s	12.10 N	68.15 W
Bonampak ⊥	232	16.44 N	91.05 W
Bönan	40	60.44 N	17.18 E
Bonandolok	114	1.47 N	98.48 E
Bonanza, Nic.	236	14.01 N	84.35 W
Bonanza, Or., U.S.	202	42.11 N	121.24 W
Bonanza, Ut,. U.S.	200	40.01 N	109.10 W

Symbols in the index entries represent the broad categories identified in the key at the right. Symbols with superior numbers (⛰[1]) identify subcategories (see complete key on page *I · 1).*

Symbole im Register stellen die rechts im Schlüssel erklärten Kategorien dar. Symbole mit hochgestellten Ziffern (⛰[1]) bezeichnen Unterabteilungen einer Kategorie (vgl. vollständiger Schlüssel auf Seite *I · 1).*

Los símbolos incluídos en el texto del índice representan las grandes categorías identificadas con la clave a la derecha. Los símbolos con numeros en su parte superior (⛰[1]) identifican las subcategorías (véase la clave completa en la página *I · 1).*

Les symboles de l'index représentent les catégories indiquées dans la légende à droite. Les symboles suivis d'un indice (⛰[1]) représentent des sous-catégories (voir légende complète à la page *I · 1).*

Os símbolos incluídos no texto do índice representam as grandes categorias identificadas com a chave à direita. Os símbolos com números em sua parte superior (⛰[1]) identificam as subcategorias (veja-se a chave completa à página *I · 1).*

	English	Deutsch	Español	Français	Português
∧	Mountain	Berg	Montaña	Montagne	Montanha
⛰	Mountains	Gebirge	Montañas	Montagnes	Montanhas
)(	Pass	Paß	Paso	Col	Passo
∨	Valley, Canyon	Tal, Cañon	Valle, Cañón	Vallée, Canyon	Vale, Canhão
⌣	Plain	Ebene	Llano	Plaine	Planície
≻	Cape	Kap	Cabo	Cap	Cabo
I	Island	Insel	Isla	Île	Ilha
II	Islands	Inseln	Islas	Îles	Ilhas
⊥	Other Topographic Features	Andere Topographische Objekte	Otros Elementos Topográficos	Autres données topographiques	Outros acidentes topográficos

ESPAÑOL

Nombre	Página	Lat. °′	Long. °′ W = Oeste
Bonanza Peak ∧	224	48.14 N	120.52 W
Bonao	238	18.56 N	70.25 W
Bonaparte	190	40.41 N	91.48 W
Bonaparte ≃	182	50.46 N	121.17 W
Bonaparte, Lake ⊜	212	44.09 N	75.23 W
Bonaparte, Mount ∧	202	48.45 N	119.08 W
Bonaparte Archipelago II	160	14.17 S	125.18 E
Bonaparte Lake ⊜	182	51.16 N	120.35 W
Bonar Bridge	46	57.53 N	4.21 W
Bonarcado	71	40.04 N	8.38 E
Bonasila Dome ∧	180	62.19 N	160.30 W
Bonasse	241r	10.05 N	61.52 W
Bonassola	62	44.11 N	9.35 E
Bonaventure	186	48.03 N	65.29 W
Bonaventure ≃	186	48.02 N	65.28 W
Bonaventure, Île I	186	48.30 N	64.10 W
Bonavista	186	48.39 N	53.07 W
Bonavista, Cape ›	186	48.42 N	53.05 W
Bonavista Bay c	186	48.45 N	53.20 W
Bonawe	46	56.26 N	5.13 W
Bonawon	116	9.08 N	122.55 E
Bonbeach	274b	38.04 S	145.08 E
Bonboillon	58	47.20 N	5.42 E
Bon Bon	162	30.26 S	135.28 E
Bonbonon Point ›	116	9.03 N	123.08 E
Bonchester Bridge	44	55.24 N	2.40 W
Boncourt	58	47.30 N	6.56 E
Boncuk Dağı ∧	130	36.53 N	29.17 E
Bond	194	30.54 N	89.10 W
Bond □[6]	219	38.53 N	89.25 W
Bondari	80	52.57 N	42.04 E
Bondarivka	83	49.23 N	39.37 E
Bondeno	64	44.53 N	11.25 E
Bondi	274a	33.53 S	151.17 E
Bondo, R.D.C.	152	1.22 S	23.53 E
Bondo, R.D.C.	152	3.49 N	23.40 E
Bondoc Peninsula ›[1]	116	13.30 N	122.30 E
Bondoc Point ›	116	13.10 N	122.36 E
Bondorf	58	48.31 N	8.49 E
Bondoufle	261	48.37 N	2.23 E
Bondoukou	150	8.02 N	2.48 W
Bondowoso	115a	7.55 S	113.49 E
Bondsville	207	42.12 N	72.20 W
Bonduel	190	44.44 N	88.26 W
Bondues	50	50.42 N	3.06 E
Bondy	261	48.54 N	2.28 E
Bondy, Forêt de ♦	261	48.55 N	2.35 E
Bône → Annaba, Alg.	148	36.54 N	7.46 E
Bone, Indon.	112	4.46 S	122.52 E
Bone → Watampone, Indon.	112	4.32 S	120.20 E
Bone, Indon.	112	5.09 S	122.37 E
Bone, Teluk c	112	4.00 S	120.40 E
Bonebone	112	2.36 S	120.33 E
Bon Echo Provincial Park ♦	212	44.52 N	77.15 W
Bonefro	66	41.42 N	14.56 E
Bone Island I	212	44.56 N	79.51 W
Bonelipu	112	4.50 S	123.11 E
Bonelohe	112	5.48 S	120.27 E
Bönen	52	51.36 N	7.44 E
Boneogeh	112	7.16 S	120.48 E
Bonerate, Pulau I	112	7.22 S	121.08 E
Bon Espérance, Cap de → Good Hope, Cape of ›	158	34.24 S	18.30 E
Bo'ness	46	56.01 N	3.37 W
Bonesteel	198	43.04 N	98.56 W
Bonete, Cerro ∧	252	27.51 S	68.47 W
Bonete Chico, Cerro ∧	252	28.01 S	68.45 W
Bonětice	60	49.41 N	12.49 E
Bonfield	216	41.09 N	88.03 W
Bonfinópolis de Minas	255	16.28 S	45.59 W
Bonfol	58	47.29 N	7.09 E
Bonga	144	7.17 N	36.15 E
Bongabon	116	15.38 N	121.08 E
Bongabon ≃	116	12.40 N	121.33 E
Bongabong	116	12.45 N	121.29 E
Bongaigaon	124	26.28 N	90.34 E
Bongak	140	7.27 N	33.14 E
Bongandanga	152	1.30 N	21.03 E
Bongao Island I	116	5.01 N	119.46 E
Bongaree	171a	27.05 S	153.10 E
Bonggaw	116	5.02 N	119.46 E
Bongka	112	0.58 S	121.27 E
Bongka ≃	112	0.59 S	121.05 E
Bong Mieu	110	15.25 N	108.24 E
Bongo, Ang.	152	8.48 S	17.49 E
Bongo, Gabon	152	2.10 S	10.12 E
Bongo, Massif des ⩘	146	8.40 N	22.25 E
Bongo I	152	3.01 N	20.06 E
Bongo II	152	1.47 S	17.41 E
Bongo Island I	116	7.20 N	124.02 E
Bongolu	152	2.48 N	22.29 E
Bongon	112	6.35 N	116.52 E
Bongor	146	10.17 N	15.22 E
Bongou ≃	140	6.42 N	22.04 E
Bongouanou	150	6.39 N	4.12 W
Bong Range ⩘	150	6.50 N	10.00 W
Bong Son	110	14.26 N	109.01 E
Bonham	196	33.34 N	96.10 W
Bonheiden	56	51.02 N	4.32 E
Bonhomme, Col du)(	58	48.10 N	7.06 E
Bonhomme, Morne ∧	238	19.05 N	72.18 W
Bonhomme Island I	219	38.42 N	90.36 W
Bonifacio, Fr.	36	41.23 N	9.10 E
Bonifacio, Pil.	116	8.03 N	123.37 E
Bonifacio, Strait of Ʉ	36	41.20 N	9.15 E
Bonifacio Monument ⊥	269f	14.39 N	120.59 E
Bonifati	68	39.35 N	15.54 E
Bonifati, Capo ›	68	39.35 N	15.52 E
Bonifay	194	30.47 N	85.40 W
Bonifica del Volturno ⩸	68	41.01 N	14.00 E
Bonilla Island I	182	53.29 N	130.36 W
Bonin Islands → Ogasawara-guntō II	14	27.00 N	142.10 E
Bonita	194	32.55 N	91.40 W
Bonita, Point ›	282	37.49 N	122.32 W
Bonita Springs	220	26.20 N	81.46 W
Bonito, Bra.	248	21.08 S	56.28 W
Bonito, Bra.	250	8.29 S	35.44 W
Bonito, It.	68	41.06 N	15.00 E
Bonito ≃, Bra.	255	16.31 S	51.23 W
Bonito ≃, Bra.	256	22.12 S	43.02 W
Bonito ≃, Bra.	256	22.09 S	43.40 W
Bonito, Pico ∧	236	15.38 N	86.55 W
Bonito, Rio ≃	200	33.23 N	105.16 W
Bonito de Santa Fé	250	7.19 S	38.31 W
Bonjol	112	0.01 S	100.13 E
Bonkoukou	150	14.01 N	3.13 E
Bon Meade	279b	40.33 N	80.14 W
Bonn	56	50.44 N	7.05 E
Bonnanaro	71	40.32 N	8.45 E
Bonndorf im Schwarzwald	58	47.49 N	8.20 E
Bonneauville	208	39.46 N	77.10 W
Bonne Bay (Woody Point)	186	49.30 N	57.56 W
Bonne Bay c	186	49.33 N	57.55 W
Bonnebosq	50	49.12 N	0.05 E
Bonnechere ≃	190	45.31 N	76.33 W
Bonneia	144	5.41 N	37.45 E
Bonnelles	261	48.37 N	2.02 E
Bonner	202	46.52 N	113.51 W
Bonners Ferry	202	48.41 N	116.18 W
Bonne-sur-Ménoge	58	46.10 N	6.20 E
Bonnet, Lac du ⊜	184	50.22 N	95.55 W
Bonnétable	50	48.11 N	0.26 E
Bonne Terre	194	37.55 N	90.33 W
Bonnet Plume ≃	180	65.55 N	134.58 W
Bonneuil-sur-Marne	261	48.46 N	2.29 E

FRANÇAIS

Nom	Page	Lat. °′	Long. °′ W = Ouest
Bonneval	50	48.11 N	1.24 E
Bonneval-sur-Arc	62	45.22 N	7.03 E
Bonnevaux	58	46.18 N	6.40 E
Bonneville, Fr.	58	46.05 N	6.25 E
Bonneville, Or., U.S.	224	45.38 N	121.57 W
Bonneville Dam ◆[6]	224	45.39 N	121.56 W
Bonneville Peak ∧	202	42.46 N	112.08 W
Bonneville Salt Flats ⩸	200	40.45 N	113.52 W
Bonney, Lake ⊜	166	37.48 S	140.22 E
Bonney Lake	224	47.10 N	122.11 W
Bonnie Doone	192	35.05 N	78.57 W
Bonnières	50	49.02 N	1.35 E
Bonnie Rock	162	30.32 S	118.21 E
Bonnieux	62	43.49 N	5.18 E
Bonnievale	158	33.57 S	20.06 E
Bönnigheim	56	49.03 N	9.06 E
Bönninghardt	263	51.35 N	6.28 E
Bonnots Mill	219	38.34 N	91.58 W
Bonny	150	4.27 N	7.10 E
Bonny ≃[1]	150	4.20 N	7.10 E
Bonnyrigg, Austl.	274a	33.54 S	150.54 E
Bonnyrigg, Scot., U.K.	46	55.52 N	3.08 W
Bonny-sur-Loire	50	47.34 N	2.50 E
Bonnyville	182	54.16 N	110.44 W
Bono, It.	71	40.25 N	9.02 E
Bono, Ar., U.S.	194	35.54 N	90.48 W
Bono, Oh., U.S.	214	41.38 N	83.16 W
Bonoi	164	1.51 S	137.48 E
Bonorva	71	40.25 N	8.46 E
Bonoua	150	5.16 N	3.36 W
Bonpas Creek ≃	194	38.16 N	87.59 W
Bonriki	174t	1.23 N	173.09 E
Bonriki Airport ⊠	174t	1.22 N	173.10 E
Bons	58	46.16 N	6.23 E
Bonsall	228	33.17 N	117.13 W
Bonsari	272c	19.04 N	73.02 E
Bon Secour	194	30.18 N	87.43 W
Bon-Secours, Bel.	50	50.30 N	3.36 E
Bonsecours, Fr.	50	49.26 N	1.08 E
Bonshaw	186	46.12 N	63.21 W
Bonsucesso ◆[8]	287a	22.52 S	43.15 W
Bontang	112	0.08 N	117.30 E
Bontberg ∧	158	32.21 S	21.04 E
Bontebok National Park ♦	158	34.07 S	20.23 E
Bonthe	150	7.32 N	12.30 W
Bontoc	116	17.05 N	120.58 E
Bon Wier	194	30.44 N	93.39 W
Bonyhád	30	46.19 N	18.32 E
Boo, Kepulauan II	164	1.12 S	129.24 E
Booby Point ›	284b	39.17 N	76.23 W
Boock	54	53.29 N	14.15 E
Boody	219	39.46 N	89.03 W
Boogardie	162	28.02 S	117.47 E
Booischot	56	51.03 N	4.46 E
Bookabie	162	31.50 S	132.41 E
Bookaloo	166	31.55 S	137.22 E
Book Cliffs ⊓[4]	200	39.20 N	109.00 W
Booke	152	2.33 S	22.00 E
Booker	196	36.27 N	100.32 W
Booker T. Washington National Monument ♦	192	37.01 N	79.45 W
Bookwalter	218	39.42 N	83.32 W
Boola	150	8.22 N	8.43 W
Boolaloo	162	22.35 S	115.51 E
Booleroo Centre	166	32.53 S	138.21 E
Booligal	166	33.52 S	144.53 E
Boologooro	162	24.21 S	114.02 E
Boom	50	51.05 N	4.22 E
Boomarra	166	19.33 S	140.20 E
Boomer	188	38.09 N	81.17 W
Boomi	166	28.44 S	149.35 E
Boomrivier	158	29.33 S	20.27 E
Boonah	171a	28.00 S	152.41 E
Böön cagaan nuur ⊜	102	45.35 N	99.09 E
Boone, Ia., U.S.	190	42.03 N	93.52 W
Boone, N.C., U.S.	192	36.13 N	81.40 W
Boone □[6], Il., U.S.	216	42.15 N	88.50 W
Boone □[6], In., U.S.	218	40.03 N	86.28 W
Boone □[6], Ky., U.S.	218	38.57 N	84.45 W
Boone □[6], Mo., U.S.	219	38.55 N	92.15 W
Boone ≃	190	42.19 N	93.56 W
Boone Draw ∨	196	33.51 N	103.42 W
Boone Grove	216	41.21 N	87.08 W
Boone Lake ⊜[1]	192	36.25 N	82.25 W
Boone Reservoir ⊜[1]	279b	40.15 N	80.08 W
Boones Mill	192	37.06 N	79.57 W
Booneville, Ar., U.S.	194	35.08 N	93.55 W
Booneville, Ky., U.S.	192	37.28 N	83.40 W
Booneville, Ms., U.S.	194	34.39 N	88.34 W
Boon Point ›	240c	17.10 N	61.50 W
Boons	158	25.59 S	27.13 E
Boonsboro	208	39.30 N	77.39 W
Boonsville	222	33.04 N	97.52 W
Boonton	210	40.54 N	74.24 W
Boonton Reservoir ⊜[1]	276	40.53 N	74.25 W
Boonville, Ca., U.S.	204	39.00 N	123.21 W
Boonville, In., U.S.	194	38.02 N	87.16 W
Boonville, Mo., U.S.	194	38.58 N	92.44 W
Boonville, N.Y., U.S.	212	43.29 N	75.20 W
Boopi ≃	248	15.41 S	67.15 W
Boorabbin National Park ♦	162	31.13 S	120.10 E
Boorama	144	9.56 N	43.11 E
Boorindal	166	30.21 S	146.08 E
Booroorban	166	34.56 S	144.46 E
Boorowa	166	34.26 S	148.43 E
Boos	50	49.23 N	1.12 E
Boosaaso	144	11.17 N	49.11 E
Boossen	54	52.22 N	14.29 E
Boot	44	54.24 N	3.17 W
Bootahnie Indian Reserve ◆[4]	182	50.24 N	121.31 W
Booth	194	32.30 N	86.34 W
Booth, Lac ⊜	190	46.45 N	78.34 W
Boothbay Harbor	188	43.51 N	69.37 W
Boothby, Cape ›	9	66.34 S	57.16 E
Booth Corner	285	39.51 N	75.29 W
Boothia, Gulf of c	176	71.00 N	91.00 W
Boothia Peninsula ›[1]	176	70.30 N	95.00 W
Boothstown	262	53.30 N	2.25 W
Boothville	194	29.20 N	89.25 W
Booth Wood Reservoir ⊜[1]	262	53.38 N	1.58 W
Boothwyn	285	39.49 N	75.26 W
Bootle	44	53.28 N	3.00 W
Boot Reefs ✢[2]	164	10.00 S	144.40 E
Booué	152	0.06 S	11.56 E
Booysens ◆[8]	273d	26.14 S	28.01 E
Booze Creek ≃	284c	38.59 N	77.07 W
Bopfingen	56	48.51 N	10.21 E
Bo Phloi	110	14.19 N	99.31 E
Bophuthatswana □[9]	156	26.00 S	25.35 E
Boping	98	36.36 N	116.07 E
Boping Ling ⩘	100	25.00 N	117.00 E
Bopo	150	7.37 N	7.52 E
Bopolu	150	7.03 N	10.32 W
Boppard	56	50.14 N	7.35 E
Boqér, Har ∧	132	30.52 N	34.43 E
Boqueirão, Ilha do I	287a	22.46 S	43.09 W
Boqueirão, Serra do ⩘[2]	250	11.30 S	43.45 W
Boquerón	236	8.30 N	82.34 W
Boquerón □[5]	252	21.30 S	60.00 W
Boquerón, Bahía de c	240m	18.01 N	67.12 W
Boquerón, Túnel ◆[5]	286c	10.34 N	67.00 W
Boquet	279b	40.23 N	79.36 W
Boquilla, Presa de la ⊜[1]	232	27.30 N	105.30 W
Boquilla del Refugio	196	25.33 N	102.28 W
Boquillas del Carmen	232	29.17 N	102.53 W
Boquim	250	11.09 S	37.37 W
Bor, Česká Rep.	60	49.43 N	12.47 E
Bor, Jugo.	38	44.05 N	22.07 E

PORTUGUÊS

Nome	Página	Lat. °′	Long. °′ W = Oeste
Bor, Ross.	24	63.00 N	42.38 E
Bor, Ross.	80	56.22 N	44.05 E
Bor, Sūd.	140	6.12 N	31.33 E
Bor, Tür.	130	37.54 N	34.34 E
Bor, Lak ≃	154	1.18 N	40.40 E
Bora-Bora I	14	16.30 S	151.45 W
Borabu	110	16.02 N	103.07 E
Boracay Island I	116	11.59 N	121.55 E
Boraha, Nosy I	157b	16.50 S	49.55 E
Borah Peak ∧	202	44.08 N	113.48 W
Boraldaj ≃	85	42.33 N	69.07 E
Borale	144	9.10 N	42.35 E
Borambola	171b	35.12 S	147.41 E
Borang, Tanjung ›	164	5.16 S	133.07 E
Borås	26	57.43 N	12.55 E
Borāzjān	128	29.16 N	51.12 E
Borba, Bra.	246	4.24 S	59.35 W
Borba, Port.	34	38.48 N	7.27 W
Borbeck ◆[8]	263	51.29 N	6.57 E
Borbera ≃	62	44.42 N	8.52 E
Borca di Cadore	64	46.26 N	12.13 E
Borcea, Brațul ≃	38	44.40 N	27.53 E
Borchen	52	51.39 N	8.44 E
Borçka	130	41.22 N	41.40 E
Borculo, Ned.	52	52.07 N	6.31 E
Borculo, Mi., U.S.	216	42.53 N	86.01 W
Borda, Cape ›	166	35.45 S	136.34 E
Borda da Mata	256	22.16 S	46.10 W
Bordeaux, Fr.	32	44.50 N	0.34 W
Bordeaux, S. Afr.	273d	26.06 S	28.01 E
Bordeaux ◆[8]	275a	45.33 N	73.41 W
Bordeaux Mountain ∧[2]	240m	18.20 N	64.44 W
Borden, Austl.	162	34.05 S	118.16 E
Borden, Sk., Can.	184	52.25 N	107.13 W
Borden, Eng., U.K.	260	51.20 N	0.42 E
Borden, In., U.S.	218	38.28 N	85.57 W
Borden, Canadian Forces Base ■	212	44.17 N	79.55 W
Borden Lake ⊜	190	47.50 N	83.18 W
Borden Peninsula ›[1]	176	73.00 N	83.00 W
Bordentown	208	40.08 N	74.42 W
Border Mountains ⩘	164	3.40 S	141.05 E
Borders □[4]	46	55.37 N	3.15 W
Bordertown	166	36.19 S	140.47 E
Bordesholm	30	54.11 N	10.01 E
Bordeyri	24a	65.15 N	21.10 W
Bordighera	62	43.46 N	7.39 E
Bording	41	56.12 N	9.17 E
Bording Kirkeby	41	56.10 N	9.15 E
Bordino, Fiume di ≃	70	37.53 N	12.37 E
Bordj Bou Arreridj	148	36.04 N	4.46 E
Bordj Bounaama	34	35.51 N	1.36 E
Bordj Menaïel	148	36.44 N	3.43 E
Bordj Omar Idriss	148	28.09 N	6.43 E
Bordj Sidi Toui	148	32.44 N	11.22 E
Bordunskij	85	42.40 N	75.37 E
Bore, It.	62	44.43 N	9.47 E
Bore, Ityo.	144	4.40 N	37.40 E
Boré, Mali	150	15.08 N	3.29 W
Boreda	144	6.32 N	37.48 E
Boreham	260	51.46 N	0.33 E
Borehamwood	42	51.40 N	0.16 W
Borel Hill ∧	282	37.19 N	122.12 W
Borello	66	44.03 N	12.11 E
Borensberg	26	58.34 N	15.17 E
Boreray I	46	57.42 N	7.18 W
Boretto	64	44.54 N	10.33 E
Borgå → Porvoo	26	60.24 N	25.40 E
Borgallo, Galleria del ◆[5]	62	44.25 N	9.53 E
Borgarnes	24a	64.35 N	21.53 W
Borgata Costiera	70	37.43 N	12.39 E
Børgefjell Nasjonalpark ♦	24	65.10 N	14.00 E
Borgentreich	52	51.34 N	9.14 E
Börger, Dtsch.	52	52.54 N	7.32 E
Borger, Ned.	52	52.55 N	6.46 E
Borger, Tx., U.S.	196	35.40 N	101.23 W
Borgerhout	50	51.13 N	4.26 E
Borgetto	70	38.03 N	13.08 E
Borggård	40	58.44 N	15.32 E
Borghetto	64	45.41 N	10.56 E
Borghetto di Vara	62	44.13 N	9.43 E
Borghetto Lodigiano	62	45.13 N	9.30 E
Borghetto Santo Spirito	62	44.06 N	8.14 E
Borgholm	26	56.53 N	16.39 E
Borgholzhausen	52	52.06 N	8.18 E
Borghorst	52	52.07 N	7.23 E
Borgia	68	38.49 N	16.30 E
Borgio-Verezzi	62	44.10 N	8.18 E
Borgloon	56	50.48 N	5.20 E
Borg Mountain ∧	9	72.42 S	3.30 W
Borgne, Lake c	194	30.05 N	89.40 W
Borgnesse, Pointe ›	240e	14.27 N	60.54 W
Borgo	64	46.03 N	11.27 E
Borgo alla Collina	66	43.45 N	11.43 E
Borgo a Mozzano	66	43.59 N	10.33 E
Borgo Cerreto	66	42.49 N	12.54 E
Borgo d'Ale	62	45.21 N	8.03 E
Borgoforte	64	45.03 N	10.45 E
Borgofranco d'Ivrea	62	45.30 N	7.51 E
Borgolavezzaro	62	45.19 N	8.42 E
Borgomanero	62	45.42 N	8.28 E
Borgomaro	62	43.58 N	7.56 E
Borgonovo Val Tidone	62	45.01 N	9.26 E
Borgo Pace	66	43.39 N	12.17 E
Borgoricco	64	45.32 N	11.58 E
Borgorose	66	42.11 N	13.13 E
Borgo San Dalmazzo	62	44.20 N	7.30 E
Borgo San Giacomo	64	45.21 N	9.58 E
Borgo San Lorenzo	66	43.57 N	11.23 E
Borgosatollo	64	45.28 N	10.14 E
Borgosesia	62	45.43 N	8.16 E
Borgo Tossignano	66	44.16 N	11.35 E
Borgou □[5]	150	10.30 N	2.50 E
Borgo Val di Taro	62	44.29 N	9.46 E
Borgo Vercelli	62	45.21 N	8.28 E
Borgsdorf	54	52.42 N	13.14 E
Borgsdorf, Forst ◆[3]	264a	52.42 N	13.19 E
Borgu Game Reserve ◆[4]	150	10.15 N	4.10 E
Borgund ʊ[1]	26	61.03 N	7.49 E
Bori	150	4.42 N	7.21 E
Borig Delijn els ◆[2]	88	50.00 N	94.00 E
Borikhan	110	18.33 N	103.43 E
Borilovo	76	53.22 N	35.58 E
Borinage □[9]	50	50.30 N	4.00 E
Boring, Md., U.S.	208	39.31 N	76.49 W
Boring, Or., U.S.	224	45.25 N	122.22 W
Borinskoje	76	52.27 N	39.22 E
Borisoglebsk	80	51.23 N	42.06 E
Borisoglebskij	80	57.16 N	39.09 E
Borisovka, Ross.	76	52.50 N	39.58 E
Borisovka, Ross.	78	50.36 N	36.01 E
Borisovo	82	55.25 N	36.03 E
Borisovo ◆[8]	265b	55.38 N	37.45 E
Borisovo-Sudskoje	76	59.54 N	36.01 E
Borisovskaja	76	60.12 N	39.48 E
Borivs'ke	83	48.51 N	38.34 E
Borja, Esp.	34	41.50 N	1.32 W
Borja, Perú	246	4.26 S	77.33 W
Bork	52	51.40 N	7.28 E
Borkavičy	76	55.40 N	28.20 E
Borken, Dtsch.	52	51.51 N	6.51 E
Borken, Dtsch.	56	51.03 N	9.16 E
Borkenwirthe	52	51.53 N	6.50 E
Borki	86	59.08 N	82.15 E
Borkoldoj, chrebet ⩘	85	41.25 N	77.50 E
Børkop	41	55.39 N	9.39 E
Borkou ◆[1]	146	18.15 N	18.50 E
Borkou-Ennedi-Tibesti □[5]	146	18.15 N	18.50 E
Borkum	52	53.35 N	6.40 E
Borkum I	52	53.35 N	6.41 E
Borland Manor	279b	40.15 N	80.09 W
Borlänge	40	60.29 N	15.25 E

Borle ◆[8]	272c	19.02 N	72.55 E
Borlu	130	38.44 N	28.27 E
Bormes-les-Mimosas	62	43.09 N	6.20 E
Bormida ≃	62	44.56 N	8.40 E
Bormida di Millesimo ≃	62	44.40 N	8.20 E
Bormida di Spigno ≃	62	44.40 N	8.20 E
Bormio	64	46.28 N	10.22 E
Born, Dtsch.	54	52.22 N	11.28 E
Born, Dtsch.	54	54.23 N	12.32 E
Borna, Dtsch.	54	51.19 N	13.11 E
Borna, Dtsch.	54	51.07 N	12.30 E
Borndiep c	52	53.25 N	5.35 E
Borne	52	52.18 N	6.45 E
Borne ≃	62	45.03 N	3.54 E
Borneo (Kalimantan) I	112	0.30 N	114.00 E
Bornheim	56	50.46 N	6.59 E
Bornholm I	26	55.10 N	15.00 E
Bornholte	52	51.52 N	8.29 E
Bornhöved	54	54.04 N	10.16 E
Börnicke, Dtsch.	54	52.41 N	12.56 E
Börnicke, Dtsch.	264a	52.40 N	13.38 E
Börnig ◆[8]	263	51.33 N	7.16 E
Bornim ◆[8]	264a	52.26 N	13.00 E
Borno	64	45.56 N	10.12 E
Bornos, Embalse de ⊜[1]	34	36.50 N	5.30 W
Bornsdorf	54	51.46 N	13.41 E
Bornstedt ◆[8]	264a	52.25 N	13.02 E
Boro ≃	140	8.52 N	26.11 E
Borobudur ⊥	115a	7.36 S	110.12 E
Borodarou	150	10.59 N	2.53 E
Borodino, Ross.	82	55.32 N	35.50 E
Borodino, Ross.	82	56.53 N	37.00 E
Borodino, Ross.	88	55.55 N	94.55 E
Borodino, Ukr.	78	46.18 N	29.13 E
Borodulicha	86	50.43 N	80.55 E
Borodulino	80	57.59 N	54.20 E
Borodyanka	78	50.39 N	29.56 E
Borogoncy	74	62.42 N	131.08 E
Borohoro Shan ⩘	86	44.06 N	83.10 E
Boroko	112	0.55 N	123.16 E
Boromlya	78	50.37 N	34.59 E
Boromo	150	11.45 N	2.56 W
Boron, Mali	150	14.01 N	7.30 W
Boron, Ca., U.S.	228	34.59 N	117.38 W
Boronga Islands II	110	19.58 N	93.06 E
Borongan	116	11.37 N	125.26 E
Boronia	274b	37.52 S	145.17 E
Borore	71	40.13 N	8.48 E
Borotou	150	8.44 N	7.30 W
Boroughbridge	44	54.06 N	1.23 W
Borough Green	42	51.17 N	0.19 E
Borough Park ◆[8]	276	40.38 N	74.00 W
Borova, Ukr.	78	50.12 N	30.07 E
Borova, Ukr.	83	49.24 N	37.40 E
Borova ≃	83	48.58 N	38.24 E
Borovan	38	43.26 N	23.45 E
Borovany	61	48.54 N	14.39 E
Borove	78	51.06 N	27.13 E
Boroviči	76	58.24 N	33.55 E
Borovka ≃	80	52.54 N	52.00 E
Borovl'anka	86	52.38 N	84.29 E
Borovoj	24	59.55 N	51.38 E
Borovoje	86	53.04 N	70.19 E
Borovsk	82	55.12 N	36.30 E
Borovskaja	24	60.46 N	41.06 E
Borovskij	86	57.03 N	65.44 E
Borovskoj	86	53.48 N	64.12 E
Borovskoje	86	52.39 N	82.08 E
Borovy	60	49.33 N	13.18 E
Borovyk ≃	83	49.11 N	38.33 E
Borozdino	82	54.07 N	38.22 E
Borraan	144	10.14 N	48.44 E
Borrachudo ≃	255	18.12 S	45.16 W
Borrazópolis	255	23.56 S	51.36 W
Borrby	26	55.27 N	14.10 E
Borre	41	55.00 N	12.28 E
Borre ⊥	26	59.23 N	10.28 E
Borreby	41	55.14 N	11.19 E
Borriana, Esp.	34	39.53 N	0.05 W
Borriana, It.	62	45.30 N	8.02 E
Borris	48	52.35 N	6.55 W
Borrisokane	48	52.59 N	8.07 W
Borrisoleigh	48	52.45 N	7.57 W
Borroloola	164	16.04 S	136.17 E
Borroloola Aboriginal Reserve ◆[4]	164	16.00 S	136.15 E
Borrowdale	44	54.31 N	3.10 W
Börry	52	52.01 N	9.27 E
Borş	38	47.07 N	21.49 E
Borşa, Rom.	38	47.39 N	24.40 E
Borşa, Rom.	38	46.56 N	23.40 E
Borsad	120	22.25 N	72.54 E
Borsano	266b	45.35 N	8.51 E
Borschemich	263	51.04 N	6.25 E
Borščovo	82	56.30 N	36.51 E
Borščovočnyj chrebet ⩘	88	52.00 N	117.00 E
Borsdorf	54	51.21 N	12.32 E
Borshchiv	78	48.48 N	26.03 E
Borskoje	80	53.02 N	51.43 E
Borsod-Abaúj-Zemplén □[6]	30	48.15 N	21.00 E
Börssum	54	52.04 N	10.35 E
Borstendorf	54	50.46 N	13.10 E
Bortala ≃	86	44.50 N	82.45 E
Borth, Dtsch.	52	51.36 N	6.33 E
Borth, Wales, U.K.	42	52.29 N	4.03 W
Borthwick Water ≃	44	55.24 N	2.50 W
Bortigali	71	40.17 N	8.50 E
Bortigiadas	71	40.53 N	9.02 E
Bort-les-Orgues	32	45.24 N	2.30 E
Bortnychi	78	50.22 N	30.41 E
Borto	88	53.35 N	111.53 E
Bortondale	285	39.54 N	79.24 W
Boru	164	10.14 S	148.50 E
Boruca	236	9.00 N	83.20 W
Borūjen	128	31.59 N	51.18 E
Borūjerd	128	33.54 N	48.46 E
Bor Ul Shan ⩘	102	41.20 N	98.55 E
Borve	46	56.58 N	7.32 W
Borysiv	78	50.11 N	26.31 E
Boryslav	78	49.16 N	23.27 E
Boryspil'	78	50.21 N	30.57 E
Borz'a	88	50.24 N	116.31 E
Borz'a ≃	88	50.38 N	115.38 E
Borzna	78	51.15 N	32.25 E
Boržomi	84	41.50 N	43.21 E
Boržomskij zapovednik ♦	84	41.50 N	43.10 E
Borzonasca	62	44.25 N	9.23 E
Borzyszkowy	30	54.03 N	17.22 E
Bosa	71	40.18 N	8.30 E
Bosaga	86	47.55 N	72.58 E
Bosambi	152	2.24 N	22.39 E
Bosanska Dubica	36	45.11 N	16.49 E
Bosanska Gradiška	36	45.09 N	17.15 E
Bosanska Krupa	36	44.53 N	16.10 E
Bosanski Novi	36	45.03 N	16.23 E
Bosanski Petrovac	36	44.33 N	16.22 E
Bosanski Šamac	38	45.03 N	18.28 E
Bosansko Grahovo	36	44.11 N	16.22 E
Bősárkány	61	47.41 N	17.14 E
Bosau	54	54.06 N	10.25 E
Bosavi, Mount ∧	164	6.35 S	142.50 E
Boscastle	42	50.41 N	4.42 W
Bosco, It.	66	44.53 N	12.14 E
Bosco, It.	66	43.08 N	12.28 E
Boscobel	190	43.08 N	90.42 W
Bosco Chiesanuova	64	45.37 N	11.02 E
Bosco Marengo	62	44.49 N	8.41 E
Boscoreale	68	40.46 N	14.28 E
Bose	102	23.54 N	106.37 E
Bösel	52	53.00 N	7.58 E
Bosencheve, Parque Nacional ♦	234	19.36 N	100.15 W
Bosenge	152	1.18 N	22.19 E

Bósforo, Estrecho del → İstanbul Boğazı Ʉ	130	41.06 N	29.04 E
Bosham	42	50.49 N	0.52 W
Boshan	98	36.29 N	117.50 E
Boshkung Lake ⊜	212	45.04 N	78.44 W
Boshoek	156	25.30 S	27.09 E
Boshof	158	28.34 S	25.04 E
Boshrūyeh	128	33.53 N	57.26 E
Bosilegrad	38	42.29 N	22.28 E
Bösingen	58	48.14 N	8.34 E
Bosjökloster	41	55.54 N	13.31 E
Boškajnar	85	38.13 N	68.51 E
Boskol'	86	53.45 N	61.12 E
Boskop	158	26.34 S	27.08 E
Boskop ∧	273d	26.05 S	27.57 E
Boskovice	30	49.29 N	16.40 E
Boskuil	158	27.23 S	25.51 E
Bosman	164	4.10 S	144.40 E
Bosna	272b	22.37 N	88.30 E
Bosna ≃	36	45.04 N	18.29 E
Bosna-Hercegovina → Bosnia and Herzegovina □[1]	36	44.15 N	17.30 E
Bošn'akovo	89	49.38 N	142.10 E
Bosnia and Herzegovina □[1]	22	44.15 N	17.30 E
Bosnik	164	1.10 S	136.14 E
Boso	272b	22.58 N	88.08 E
Bosobolo	152	4.11 N	19.54 E
Boso-Djafo	152	1.06 N	19.14 E
Bosogo	85	41.09 N	76.25 E
Bōsō-hantō ›[1]	94	35.18 N	140.10 E
Bōsō-kyūryō ⩘[2]	268	35.08 N	139.56 E
Bososama	152	4.18 N	20.00 E
Bösperde	263	51.28 N	7.46 E
Bosphore, Détroit du → İstanbul Boğazı Ʉ	130	41.06 N	29.04 E
Bosporus → İstanbul Boğazı Ʉ	130	41.06 N	29.04 E
Bosque □[6]	222	31.55 N	97.35 W
Bosque, Paseo del ♦	288	34.55 S	57.56 W
Bosque Farms	200	34.53 N	106.40 W
Bosques	288	34.49 S	58.14 W
Bosques Petrificados, Monumento Natural ♦	254	47.39 S	68.07 W
Bosqueville	222	31.38 N	97.13 W
Bossangoa	152	6.29 N	17.27 E
Bossdorf	54	51.59 N	12.40 E
Bossé Bangou	150	13.21 N	1.18 E
Bossembélé	152	5.16 N	17.39 E
Bossentele	152	5.41 N	16.38 E
Bossert Estates	285	40.09 N	74.44 W
Bossier City	194	32.30 N	93.43 W
Bossley Park	274a	33.52 S	150.54 E
Bosso	146	13.42 N	13.19 E
Bosso, Dallol ∨	150	12.25 N	2.50 E
Bossolasco	62	44.32 N	8.02 E
Bossut, Cape ›	162	18.43 S	121.38 E
Bostān, Īrān	128	31.43 N	48.00 E
Bostān, Pāk.	120	30.26 N	67.02 E
Bostancı ◆[8]	267b	40.57 N	29.05 E
Bostandyk	80	49.38 N	48.54 E
Bosten Hu ⊜	90	42.00 N	87.00 E
Bostock Green	262	53.13 N	2.30 W
Boston, Pil.	116	7.52 N	126.22 E
Boston, Eng., U.K.	44	52.59 N	0.01 W
Boston, Ga., U.S.	192	30.47 N	83.47 W
Boston, In., U.S.	218	39.44 N	84.51 W
Boston, Ma., U.S.	207	42.21 N	71.03 W
Boston, Ma., U.S.	283	42.21 N	71.03 W
Boston, N.Y., U.S.	210	42.38 N	78.44 W
Boston, Pa., U.S.	279b	40.18 N	79.49 W
Boston Bar	182	49.52 N	121.26 W
Boston Bay c	283	42.22 N	70.54 W
Boston Brook ≃	283	42.37 N	71.00 W
Boston College ʊ[2]	283	42.20 N	71.10 W
Boston Common ♦	283	42.21 N	71.05 W
Boston Corners	210	42.03 N	73.31 W
Boston Creek ≃	212	43.02 N	79.56 W
Boston Harbor	224	47.08 N	122.54 W
Boston Harbor c	283	42.20 N	70.58 W
Boston Heights	214	41.15 N	81.30 W
Boston Mill	214	41.16 N	81.34 W
Boston Mountains ⩘	194	35.50 N	93.20 W
Boston Spa	44	53.54 N	1.21 W
Boston University ʊ[2]	283	42.21 N	71.07 W
Bosumtwi, Lake ⊜	150	6.30 N	1.25 W
Bosut ≃	38	44.57 N	19.22 E
Boswell, In., U.S.	216	40.31 N	87.22 W
Boswell, Ok., U.S.	196	34.01 N	95.52 W
Boswell, Pa., U.S.	214	40.09 N	79.01 W
Boswell Bay	180	60.24 N	146.08 W
Bosworth	194	39.28 N	93.20 W
Bosworth Airport ⊠	279a	41.26 N	82.00 W
Bosworth Field ⊥	42	52.36 N	1.25 W
Botād	120	22.10 N	71.40 E
Botafogo ◆[8]	287a	22.57 S	43.11 W
Botafogo, Enseada de c	287a	22.57 S	43.10 W
Botany	274a	33.57 S	151.12 E
Botany Bay ◆[8]	260	51.41 N	0.07 W
Botany Bay c	170	33.59 S	151.12 E
Botelhos	256	21.39 S	46.24 W
Botera	152	11.37 S	14.17 E
Botersleegte	158	30.35 S	21.22 E
Botesdale	42	52.20 N	1.01 E
Boteti ≃	156	20.08 S	23.23 E
Botev ∧	38	42.43 N	24.55 E
Botevgrad	38	42.54 N	23.47 E
Botha's Hill	158	29.45 S	30.45 E
Bothaville	158	27.27 S	26.36 E
Bothel	52	53.04 N	9.30 E
Bothell	224	47.45 N	122.12 W
Bothe-Napa Valley State Park ♦	226	38.32 N	122.32 W
Bothnia, Gulf of c	26	63.00 N	20.00 E
Bothwell, Austl.	166	42.23 S	147.00 E
Bothwell, On., Can.	214	42.38 N	81.52 W
Boticas	34	41.41 N	7.40 W
Botija, Ilha da I	246	3.58 S	62.53 W
Botija, Isla I	258	33.52 S	59.02 W
Botiyeve	78	46.41 N	35.52 E
Botkins	216	40.28 N	84.10 W
Botkul', ozero ⊜	80	48.46 N	46.40 E
Botkyrka	40	59.14 N	17.49 E
Botlich	84	42.39 N	46.14 E
Bot Makak	152	4.00 N	10.55 E
Botnia, Golfo de → Bothnia, Gulf of c	26	63.00 N	20.00 E
Botola	152	1.17 S	18.13 E
Botolan	116	15.17 N	120.01 E
Botoșani	38	47.45 N	26.40 E
Botoșani □[6]	38	48.00 N	26.45 E
Botoșanița	38	47.53 N	26.07 E
Botou	150	12.40 N	2.03 E
Botovo	82	56.03 N	38.26 E
Bo Trach	110	17.35 N	106.32 E
Botrange ∧	56	50.30 N	6.08 E
Botricello	68	38.56 N	16.51 E
Botro	150	7.51 N	5.19 W
Botsford	210	41.21 N	73.15 W
Botswana □[1], Afr.	138	22.00 S	24.00 E
Botswana □[1], Afr.	156	22.00 S	24.00 E
Botte Donato, Monte ∧	68	39.17 N	16.26 E
Bottenhavet (Selkämeri) c	26	62.00 N	20.00 E
Bottenviken (Perämeri) c	26	65.00 N	23.00 E
Bottesford	42	52.56 N	0.48 W
Bottineau	198	48.49 N	100.26 W
Bottisham	42	52.13 N	0.16 E

Bottnischer Meerbusen → Bothnia, Gulf of c	26	63.00 N	20.00 E
Bottoms Reservoir ⊜[1]	262	53.28 N	1.58 W
Bottrop	52	51.31 N	6.55 E
Botucatu	255	22.52 S	48.26 W
Botwood	186	49.09 N	55.21 W
Boty	88	52.24 N	118.32 E
Bötzingen	58	48.04 N	7.44 E
Bötzow	54	52.39 N	13.08 E
Bötzsee ⊜	264a	52.34 N	13.50 E
Bouaflé, C. Iv.	150	6.59 N	5.45 W
Bouafle, Fr.	261	48.58 N	1.54 E
Bou Ahmed	148	35.25 N	5.00 W
Bouaké	150	7.41 N	5.02 W
Bou Ali, Oued ∨	148	31.14 N	4.16 E
Bouânane	148	32.03 N	3.03 W
Bouandougou	150	8.13 N	5.40 W
Bouar	152	5.57 N	15.36 E
Bou Arada	36	36.20 N	9.38 E
Bou Areg, Sebkha c	34	35.10 N	2.45 W
Bouârfa	148	32.30 N	1.59 W
Bouaye	32	47.09 N	1.42 W
Boubandjidah, Parc National de ♦	146	8.45 N	14.45 E
Bou Bernous	148	27.18 N	2.59 W
Boubín ∧	60	48.59 N	13.51 E
Bouca	152	6.30 N	18.17 E
Bouchain	50	50.17 N	3.19 E
Bouchegouf	36	36.28 N	7.44 E
Boucher ≃	186	49.10 N	69.06 W
Boucher, Lac ⊜	186	51.07 N	59.35 W
Boucherville	206	45.36 N	73.27 W
Boucherville, Îles de II	275a	45.37 N	73.28 W
Bouches-du-Rhône □[5]	62	43.30 N	5.00 E
Bouchoir	50	49.45 N	2.41 E
Bouclans	58	47.14 N	6.15 E
Boucle du Baoulé, Parc National de la ♦	150	13.50 N	9.00 W
Bouddi National Park ♦	170	33.31 S	131.24 E
Boudjellil	34	36.20 N	4.21 E
Boudnib	148	31.57 N	4.38 W
Boudouaou	34	36.43 N	3.25 E
Boudry	58	46.57 N	6.50 E
Boué	50	50.01 N	3.42 E
Bouenza □[5]	152	4.00 S	13.45 E
Boufarik	148	36.34 N	2.55 E
Bouffémont	261	49.03 N	2.18 E
Bou Ficha	36	36.18 N	10.29 E
Bougaa	34	36.20 N	5.05 E
Bougainville I	175e	6.00 S	155.00 E
Bougainville, Cape ›	164	13.54 S	126.06 E
Bougainville, Détroit de Ʉ	175f	15.50 S	167.10 E
Bougainville Reef ✢[2]	164	15.30 S	147.06 E
Bougainville Strait Ʉ	175e	6.40 S	156.10 E
Bougar'oûn, Cap ›	34	37.06 N	6.28 E
Bough Beech Reservoir ⊜[1]	260	51.13 N	0.08 E
Boughton	44	53.12 N	1.00 W
Boughton Green	260	51.14 N	0.32 E
Boughton Malherbe	260	51.13 N	0.42 E
Boughton Place ʊ	260	51.13 N	0.32 E
Bougie → Bejaïa	148	36.45 N	5.05 E
Bougou	152	3.45 S	11.12 E
Bougouni	150	11.25 N	7.29 W
Bougouriba ≃	150	10.42 N	2.56 W
Bougzoul	34	35.42 N	2.51 E
Bou Hadjar	36	36.30 N	8.06 E
Bou Hajar	36	35.42 N	10.48 E
Bouillante	241o	16.06 N	61.45 W
Bouillon	56	49.48 N	5.04 E
Bouilly	50	48.12 N	4.00 E
Bouïra	148	36.23 N	3.54 E
Bouisy, Ru de ≃	261	48.34 N	2.45 E
Bou Izakarn	148	29.09 N	9.44 W
Boujad	148	32.48 N	6.26 W
Boujailles	58	46.53 N	6.05 E
Boujdour, Cap ›	148	26.08 N	14.30 W
Bouka ≃	150	11.00 N	10.50 W
Bou Kadir	148	36.04 N	1.07 E
Bou Khadra	36	35.45 N	8.02 E
Boukiéro	273b	4.12 S	15.18 E
Boukiéro, Mont ∧[2]	273b	4.11 S	15.17 E
Boukombé	150	10.11 N	1.06 E
Boula Ibib	146	9.34 N	13.46 E
Boulaide	56	49.54 N	5.49 E
Boularderie Island I	186	46.15 N	60.30 W
Boulay-Moselle	56	49.11 N	6.30 E
Boulbon	62	43.52 N	4.41 E
Boulder, Co., U.S.	200	40.00 N	105.16 W
Boulder, Mt., U.S.	202	46.14 N	112.07 W
Boulder ≃	202	45.52 N	111.57 W
Boulder City	204	35.58 N	114.49 W
Boulder Creek	226	37.07 N	122.07 W
Boulder Creek ≃	200	37.47 N	111.22 W
Boulder Hill	216	41.41 N	88.25 W
Bouleaux, Lac des ⊜	275a	45.33 N	73.19 W
Bouli ≃	150	13.15 N	0.03 E
Boulia	166	22.54 S	139.54 E
Bouligny	56	49.17 N	5.45 E
Boullay-les-Troux	261	48.41 N	2.03 E
Boulmane	148	33.22 N	4.45 W
Boulmane □[4]	148	33.00 N	4.00 W
Boulogne ◆[8]	258	34.31 S	58.34 W
Boulogne, Bois de ♦	261	48.50 N	2.15 E
Boulogne-Billancourt	50	48.50 N	2.15 E
Boulogne-sur-Gesse	32	43.18 N	0.39 E
Boulogne-sur-Mer	50	50.43 N	1.37 E
Bouloire	50	47.58 N	0.33 E
Boulouli	150	15.34 N	9.21 W
Bouloupari	175f	21.52 S	166.04 E
Boulouris-sur-Mer	62	43.25 N	6.48 E
Boulsa	150	12.39 N	0.34 W
Boulsworth Hill ∧	44	53.48 N	2.06 W
Bouly	150	15.19 N	11.48 W
Bou Maad, Djebel ∧	34	36.26 N	2.08 E
Boumalne	148	31.32 N	5.27 W
Boumba ≃	152	2.02 N	15.12 E
Boumbé I ≃	152	4.04 N	15.23 E
Boumbé II ≃	152	4.08 N	15.08 E
Boumboum	150	15.01 N	1.42 W
Boûmdeïd	150	17.26 N	9.50 W
Bou Medfaa	34	36.22 N	2.28 E
Boumentana	152	6.59 N	16.56 E
Boumnyebe	152	3.52 N	10.49 E
Boumou	146	9.02 N	16.26 E
Bouna	150	9.16 N	3.00 W
Boundary	180	64.04 N	141.06 W
Boundary Bay c	224	49.00 N	122.58 W
Boundary Peak ∧	204	37.51 N	118.21 W
Boundary Ranges ⩘	180	59.00 N	134.00 W
Bound Brook	210	40.34 N	74.32 W
Bound Brook ≃, Ma., U.S.	283	42.13 N	70.47 W
Bound Brook ≃, N.J., U.S.	276	40.35 N	74.30 W
Boundiali	150	9.31 N	6.29 W
Boun Nua	110	21.38 N	101.54 E
Bountiful	200	40.53 N	111.52 W
Bounty Bay c	174e	25.04 S	130.05 W
Bounty Islands II	14	47.42 S	179.04 E
Bounty Trough ✢[1]	14	46.00 S	178.00 E
Bouqteb	148	34.02 N	0.05 E
Bouquet Reservoir ⊜[1]	228	34.35 N	118.24 W
Bouqueval	261	49.01 N	2.26 E
Boura	150	12.25 N	4.33 W
Bouradière	62	43.58 N	5.19 E
Bourail	175f	21.34 S	165.30 E
Bouray-sur-Juine	261	48.31 N	2.18 E
Bourbeuse ≃	194	38.24 N	90.53 W
Bourbeuse, Dry Fork ≃	194	38.16 N	91.26 W

≃ River	Fluß	Río	Rivière	Rio	✢ Submarine Features	Untermeerische Objekte	Accidentes Submarinos	Formes de relief sous-marin	Acidentes submarinos
≊ Canal	Kanal	Canal	Canal	Canal	□ Political Unit	Politische Einheit	Unidad Política	Entité politique	Unidade política
∟ Waterfall, Rapids	Wasserfall, Stromschnellen	Cascada, Rápidos	Chute d'eau, Rapides	Cascata, Rápidos	ʊ Cultural Institution	Kulturelle Institution	Institución Cultural	Institution culturelle	Instituição cultural
Ʉ Strait	Meeresstraße	Estrecho	Détroit	Estreito	⊥ Historical Site	Historische Stätte	Sitio Histórico	Site historique	Sitio histórico
c Bay, Gulf	Bucht, Golf	Bahía, Golfo	Baie, Golfe	Baía, Golfo	♦ Recreational Site	Erholungs- und Ferienort	Sitio de Recreo	Centre de loisirs	Area de Lazer
⊜ Lake, Lakes	See, Seen	Lago, Lagos	Lac, Lacs	Lago, Lagos	⊠ Airport	Flughafen	Aeropuerto	Aéroport	Aeroporto
⩸ Swamp	Sumpf	Pantano	Marais	Pântano	■ Military Installation	Militäranlage	Instalación Militar	Installation militaire	Instalação militar
⊓ Ice Features, Glacier	Eis- und Gletscherformen	Accidentes Glaciales	Formes glaciaires	Acidentes glaciares	◆ Miscellaneous	Verschiedenes	Misceláneo	Divers	Diversos
⊤ Other Hydrographic Features	Andere Hydrographische Objekte	Otros Elementos Hidrográficos	Autres données hydrographiques	Outros acidentes hidrográficos					

Name	Page	Lat.°'	Long.°'
Bourbon, In., U.S.	216	41.17 N	86.06 W
Bourbon, Mo., U.S.	194	38.09 N	91.14 W
Bourbon ≈⁶	218	38.14 N	84.14 W
Bourbon ≈	206	46.17 N	71.55 W
Bourbon-Lancy	32	46.38 N	3.46 E
Bourbonnais	216	41.08 N	87.52 W
Bourbonnais ⊡⁹	32	46.20 N	3.00 E
Bourbonne-les-Bains	58	47.57 N	5.45 E
Bourbourg	50	50.57 N	2.12 E
Bourbre ≈	62	45.47 N	5.11 E
Bourdeaux	62	44.35 N	5.08 E
Bourdon, Île I	275a	45.43 N	73.29 W
Bourdon, Réservoir du ⊜¹	50	47.36 N	3.07 E
Bourdonné	261	48.45 N	1.40 E
Bou Regreg, Oued ≈	148	34.03 N	6.50 W
Bourem	150	16.57 N	0.21 W
Bourg	194	29.33 N	90.36 W
Bourg-Achard	50	49.21 N	0.49 E
Bourganeuf	32	45.57 N	1.46 E
Bourg-Argental	62	45.18 N	4.33 E
Bourg-de-Péage	62	45.02 N	5.03 E
Bourg-en-Bresse	58	46.12 N	5.13 E
Bourges	32	47.05 N	2.24 E
Bourget	206	45.26 N	75.09 W
Bourget, Lac du ⊜	62	45.44 N	5.52 E
Bourg-la-Reine	261	48.47 N	2.19 E
Bourg-Lastic	32	45.39 N	2.33 E
Bourg-lès-Valence	62	44.57 N	4.53 E
Bourgneuf	261	48.36 N	2.00 E
Bourgneuf-en-Retz	32	47.02 N	1.57 W
Bourgogne	50	49.21 N	4.04 E
Bourgogne (Burgundy) ⊡⁹	32	47.00 N	4.30 E
Bourgogne, Canal de ≈	32	47.58 N	3.30 E
Bourgoin-Jallieu	62	45.35 N	5.17 E
Bourg-Saint-Andéol	62	44.22 N	4.39 E
Bourg-Saint-Maurice	62	45.37 N	6.46 E
Bourg-Saint-Pierre	58	45.57 N	7.12 E
Bourgtheroulde	50	49.18 N	0.53 E
Bourgueil	50	47.17 N	0.10 E
Bou Rjeïmât ⊽⁴	150	19.04 N	15.08 W
Bourke	166	30.05 S	145.56 E
Bourmont	58	48.12 N	5.35 E
Bourne	42	52.46 N	0.23 W
Bourne ≈, Fr.	62	45.04 N	5.15 E
Bourne ≈, Eng., U.K.	42	51.02 N	1.47 W
Bournebridge	260	51.38 N	0.11 E
Bourne End	260	51.45 N	0.32 W
Bournemouth	42	50.43 N	1.54 W
Bourneville, Fr.	50	49.23 N	0.37 E
Bourneville, Oh., U.S.	218	39.17 N	83.09 W
Bourn Vincent Memorial Park ♦	48	52.01 N	9.30 W
Bouroum	150	13.37 N	0.39 E
Bourron-Marlotte	58	48.20 N	2.42 E
Bourscheid	56	49.55 N	6.04 E
Bourtange	52	53.00 N	7.11 E
Bourtanger Moor ≈³	52	52.50 N	7.06 E
Bourton-on-the-Water	42	51.53 N	1.45 W
Bourzanga	150	13.41 N	1.33 W
Bou Saâda	148	35.12 N	4.11 E
Bou Salem	36	36.36 N	8.59 E
Bousbecque	50	50.46 N	3.05 E
Bouse	200	33.55 N	114.00 W
Bou Sellam, Oued ≈	34	36.26 N	4.34 E
Bouse Wash V	200	34.02 N	114.20 W
Bou Smaïl	148	36.38 N	2.41 E
Boussac	32	46.21 N	2.13 E
Boussé, Burkina	150	12.39 N	1.53 W
Bousse, Fr.	56	49.17 N	6.12 E
Boussières	58	47.09 N	5.54 E
Bousso	146	10.29 N	16.43 E
Boussois	50	50.17 N	4.03 E
Boussouma	150	12.55 N	1.16 W
Boussu	50	50.26 N	3.48 E
Boussy-Saint-Antoine	261	48.41 N	2.32 E
Bout, Pointe du ➤	240e	14.34 N	61.03 W
Bouteille, Lac de la ⊜	206	46.42 N	73.41 W
Bouteldja	36	36.47 N	8.12 E
Bou Temezguida ≈	148	29.21 N	9.55 W
Boutilimit	150	17.33 N	14.42 W
Bouttencourt	50	49.56 N	1.38 E
Bouvard, Cape ➤	168a	32.41 S	115.37 E
Bouvetøya I	9	54.26 S	3.24 E
Bouvier Bay C	281	42.39 N	82.38 W
Bouvières	62	44.30 N	5.13 E
Bouvières-aux-Dames	56	48.45 N	6.16 E
Bouxwiller	56	48.49 N	7.29 E
Bouyon	62	43.50 N	7.07 E
Bouza	150	14.25 N	6.02 E
Bou Zadjar	34	35.05 N	1.09 W
Bouzonville	56	49.18 N	6.32 E
Bov	41	54.50 N	9.23 E
Bova	68	38.00 N	15.56 E
Bøvågen	26	60.40 N	4.58 E
Bovalino Marina	68	38.10 N	16.11 E
Bova Marina	68	37.56 N	15.55 E
Bovard	279b	40.19 N	79.30 W
Bovec	66	46.20 N	13.33 E
Bovegno	64	45.48 N	10.16 E
Bovenden	52	51.32 N	9.55 E
Bovenkarspel	52	52.42 N	5.15 E
Bøverdal	26	61.43 N	8.21 E
Boves, Fr.	50	49.51 N	2.23 E
Boves, It.	64	44.19 N	7.33 E
Bovey ≈	42	50.36 N	3.40 W
Bovey	192	47.18 N	93.25 W
Bovey Tracey	42	50.34 N	3.37 W
Bovill	202	46.51 N	116.23 W
Bovina Center	196	34.31 N	102.53 W
Bovingdon	260	51.44 N	0.32 W
Bovinghausen ≈⁸	263	51.31 N	7.19 E
Bovington Camp	42	50.42 N	2.14 E
Bovino	68	41.15 N	15.20 E
Bovisio Masciago	266b	45.37 N	9.08 E
Bovolenta	64	45.16 N	11.56 E
Bovolone	64	45.15 N	11.07 E
Bovril	252	31.21 S	59.26 W
Bovrup	41	54.59 N	9.36 E
Bow	224	48.33 N	122.23 W
Bow ≈, Austl.	162	16.32 S	128.39 E
Bow ≈, Mb., Can.	166	18.53 S	138.29 E
Bow ≈, Ab., Can.	184	50.56 N	111.42 W
Bo-Wadrif	158	32.26 S	20.07 E
Bowang	106	31.34 N	118.52 E
Bowbells	192	48.48 N	102.14 W
Bowburn	44	54.43 N	1.31 W
Bow Creek ≈	198	39.35 N	99.14 W
Bowden	182	51.55 N	114.02 W
Bowdle	192	45.27 N	99.39 W
Bowdoin, Lake ⊜	202	48.24 N	107.41 W
Bowdon, Eng., U.K.	44	53.23 N	2.22 W
Bowdon, Ga., U.S.	222	33.32 N	85.15 W
Bowdon, N.D., U.S.	198	47.28 N	99.42 W
Bowelling	168a	33.25 S	116.27 E
Bowen, Arg.	252	35.00 S	67.31 W
Bowen, Austl.	166	20.01 S	148.15 E
Bowen ≈	166	20.24 S	147.21 E
Bowenfels	170	33.28 S	150.05 E
Bowens Creek ≈	170	33.21 S	150.35 E
Bowers	208	39.04 N	75.23 W
Bowers Gifford	260	51.34 N	0.32 E
Bowers Marshes ≈	260	51.33 N	0.32 E
Bowers Ridge ⊽³	5	53.00 N	179.00 W
Bowerston	218	40.25 N	81.11 W
Bowersville	218	39.34 N	83.43 W
Bowgreave	44	53.52 N	2.46 W
Bowie, Az., U.S.	200	32.19 N	109.29 W
Bowie, Md., U.S.	208	39.00 N	76.46 W
Bowie, Tx., U.S.	196	33.33 N	97.50 W
Bowie Creek ≈	194	31.26 N	89.19 W
Bow Island	184	49.52 N	111.22 W

Name	Page	Lat.°'	Long.°'
Bowland, Forest of ⫟³	44	53.58 N	2.32 W
Bowles Creek ≈	222	32.02 N	94.59 W
Bowley Bar ➤²	284b	39.18 N	76.23 W
Bowleys Quarters	284b	39.19 N	76.24 W
Bowling Green, Fl., U.S.	220	27.38 N	81.49 W
Bowling Green, Ky., U.S.	194	36.59 N	86.26 W
Bowling Green, Mo., U.S.	219	39.20 N	91.11 W
Bowling Green, Oh., U.S.	216	41.22 N	83.39 W
Bowling Green, S.C., U.S.	285	39.55 N	75.23 W
Bowling Green, Va., U.S.	208	38.02 N	77.20 W
Bowling Green, Cape ➤	166	19.19 S	147.25 E
Bowling Green Bay National Park ♦	166	19.17 S	147.14 E
Bowman, Ca., U.S.	226	38.57 N	121.03 W
Bowman, Ga., U.S.	192	34.12 N	83.01 W
Bowman, N.D., U.S.	198	46.10 N	103.23 W
Bowman, S.C., U.S.	192	33.20 N	80.40 W
Bowman, Mount ▲	182	51.10 N	121.55 W
Bowman Creek ≈, Pa., U.S.	210	41.31 N	75.58 W
Bowman Creek ≈, Wa., U.S.	224	45.50 N	121.03 W
Bowman-Haley Lake ⊜¹	198	46.00 N	103.20 W
Bowman Island I	9	65.17 S	103.08 E
Bowman Lake ⊜¹	226	39.27 N	120.38 W
Bowmans	168b	34.09 S	138.16 E
Bowmansdale	208	40.10 N	76.59 W
Bowmanstown	208	40.48 N	75.40 W
Bowmansville, N.Y., U.S.	212	42.56 N	78.41 W
Bowmansville, Pa., U.S.	208	40.10 N	76.04 W
Bowmanville	212	43.55 N	78.41 W
Bowmanville Creek ≈	212	43.53 N	78.40 W
Bowmont Water ≈	44	55.34 N	2.09 W
Bowmore	46	55.45 N	6.17 W
Bowness-on-Windermere	44	54.22 N	2.55 W
Bowokan, Kepulauan II	112	2.05 S	123.35 E
Bowral	170	34.28 S	150.25 E
Bowraville	166	30.39 S	152.51 E
Bowron ≈	182	54.04 N	121.48 W
Bowron Lake Provincial Park ♦	182	53.10 N	121.06 W
Bowsman	184	52.14 N	101.14 W
Bowwood	154	17.07 S	26.17 E
Box	42	51.26 N	2.15 W
Boxberg, Dtsch.	54	51.24 N	14.34 E
Boxberg, Dtsch.	56	49.29 N	9.38 E
Box Butte Creek ≈	198	40.24 N	102.37 W
Box Creek ≈, Tx., U.S.	222	31.33 N	95.10 W
Box Creek ≈, Tx., U.S.	222	31.35 N	95.10 W
Box Elder	202	48.19 N	110.00 W
Box Elder Creek ≈, Co., U.S.	198	45.59 N	103.57 W
Box Elder Creek ≈, Co., U.S.	198	40.23 N	104.28 W
Box Elder Creek ≈, Co., U.S.	198	40.33 N	105.00 W
Box Elder Creek ≈, Mt., U.S.	202	46.57 N	108.04 W
Box Elder Creek ≈, S.D., U.S.	198	44.01 N	102.27 W
Boxford, Eng., U.K.	42	51.48 N	1.45 W
Boxford, Eng., U.K.	260	51.57 N	0.57 E
Boxholm	26	58.12 N	15.03 E
Boxing	100	33.53 N	115.45 E
Boxing	98	37.08 N	118.07 E
Boxley	260	51.18 N	0.33 E
Boxmeer	52	51.39 N	5.57 E
Boxmoor	260	51.45 N	0.29 W
Boxodoi	98	42.34 N	115.18 E
Boxtel	52	51.35 N	5.20 E
Boyabat	130	41.28 N	34.47 E
Boyacá	152	3.43 N	18.46 E
Boyacá ◻⁵	246	5.30 N	73.30 W
Boyacı́köy ≈	267b	41.06 N	29.02 E
Boyali	130	41.28 N	33.19 E
Boyalık	130	41.15 N	28.37 E
Boyang	100	28.59 N	116.40 E
Boyarka	168a	33.29 S	115.44 E
Boyarka	78	50.19 N	30.19 E
Boyasengese	152	3.29 N	20.33 E
Boyce	194	31.23 N	92.40 W
Boyd, Mn., U.S.	190	45.02 N	92.02 W
Boyd, Tx., U.S.	222	33.05 N	97.34 W
Boyd ≈	168	29.51 S	152.35 E
Boyd's Cove	186	49.27 N	54.39 W
Boydton	192	36.40 N	78.23 W
Boyenge	152	0.36 N	18.51 E
Boyer ≈	198	41.28 N	95.55 W
Boyer Ahmadī va Kohkīlūyeh ◻⁴	128	30.40 N	50.40 E
Boyer Run ≈	279b	40.13 N	79.32 W
Boyer's Creek ≈	284a	43.00 N	79.02 W
Boyes Hot Springs	226	38.19 N	122.29 W
Boyertown	208	40.20 N	75.38 W
Boykin, Al., Can.	48	54.35 N	112.49 W
Boyle, Ire.	48	53.58 N	8.18 W
Boyle, Ms., U.S.	194	33.42 N	90.50 W
Boyle Heights ≈⁸	280	34.02 N	118.13 W
Boylston, Al., U.S.	222	32.26 N	86.17 W
Boylston, Ma., U.S.	207	42.23 N	71.42 W
Boyne ≈	275b	43.29 N	79.50 W
Boyne ≈, Austl.	166	23.56 S	151.21 E
Boyne ≈, Mb., Can.	184	49.34 N	97.30 W
Boyne ≈, On., Can.	212	44.10 N	79.49 W
Braemar	46	57.01 N	3.23 W
Braeside, Austl.	274b	37.59 S	145.07 E
Braeside, On., Can.	206	45.28 N	76.24 W

Name	Page	Lat.°'	Long.°'
Bozkurt, Tür.	130	37.49 N	29.37 E
Bozkurt, Tür.	130	41.57 N	34.01 E
Bozman	208	38.46 N	76.16 W
Bozoğlak	130	39.38 N	38.49 E
Bozok	130	37.18 N	40.22 E
Bozoum	152	6.19 N	16.23 E
Bozova, Tür.	130	37.22 N	38.31 E
Bozova, Tür.	130	37.13 N	30.18 E
Bozovici	38	44.15 N	21.59 E
Bozšakov'	86	51.50 N	74.20 E
Bozurn	52	53.05 N	5.42 E
Bozüyük	130	39.54 N	30.03 E
Bozzolo	64	45.06 N	10.29 E
Bra	62	44.42 N	7.51 E
Braan ≈	46	56.33 N	3.35 W
Bråås	26	57.04 N	15.03 E
Brabant ≈⁴	56	50.45 N	4.30 E
Brabante, Isla de — Brabant Island I	9	64.15 S	62.20 W
Brabant Island I	9	64.15 S	62.20 W
Brabant Lake	184	56.00 N	103.43 W
Brabrand	41	56.09 N	10.07 E
Brač, Otok I	36	43.20 N	16.40 E
Bracadale, Loch C	46	57.19 N	6.30 W
Bracciano	66	42.06 N	12.10 E
Bracciano, Lago di ⊜	66	42.07 N	12.14 E
Bracco, Passo del ⋉	64	44.15 N	9.34 E
Bracebridge	212	45.02 N	79.19 W
Bracebridge Heath	44	53.13 N	0.33 W
Braceville, Il., U.S.	216	41.14 N	88.16 W
Braceville, Oh., U.S.	214	41.14 N	80.58 W
Brachfield	222	32.03 N	94.39 W
Bracieux	50	47.33 N	1.33 E
Bracigliano	68	40.49 N	14.42 E
Bracigovo	38	42.01 N	24.22 E
Bräcke	26	62.43 N	15.27 E
Brackel ≈⁸	263	51.32 N	7.33 E
Bracken ≈⁶	218	38.40 N	84.06 W
Brackendale	182	49.46 N	123.09 W
Brackenheim	56	49.05 N	9.03 E
Brackenhurst	273d	26.19 S	28.06 E
Bracken Lake ⊜	184	53.37 N	99.50 W
Brackenridge	214	40.36 N	79.44 W
Brackett Field ◇	280	34.05 N	117.47 W
Brackettville	196	29.18 N	100.25 W
Brački Kanal ʊ	36	43.24 N	16.40 E
Brackley	42	52.02 N	1.09 W
Bracknell	42	51.26 N	0.45 W
Bracton	218	38.04 N	84.31 W
Brackwede	52	51.59 N	8.31 E
Braco	46	56.15 N	3.53 W
Braço do Norte	252	28.17 S	49.11 W
Bracuí ≈	256	22.57 S	44.24 W
Bradano ≈	68	40.23 N	16.51 E
Bradbury	280	34.08 N	117.59 W
Bradbury Heights	284c	38.52 N	76.56 W
Braddock, N.J., U.S.	285	39.42 N	74.53 W
Braddock, Pa., U.S.	214	40.24 N	79.52 W
Braddock Acres	284c	38.49 N	77.10 W
Braddock Heights, Md., U.S.	208	39.25 N	77.30 W
Braddock Heights, N.Y., U.S.	210	43.19 N	77.42 W
Braddock Hills	279b	40.25 N	79.51 W
Braddock Point ➤	210	43.19 N	77.43 W
Braddocks Millpond ≈	285	39.49 N	74.51 W
Braden ≈	220	27.30 N	82.32 W
Bradenton	220	27.29 N	82.34 W
Bradenton Beach	220	27.28 N	82.42 W
Bradenville	214	40.23 N	79.20 W
Braderup	41	54.50 N	8.53 E
Bradford, On., Can.	212	44.07 N	79.34 W
Bradford, Eng., U.K.	44	53.48 N	1.45 W
Bradford, Ar., U.S.	194	35.25 N	91.27 W
Bradford, Il., U.S.	190	41.10 N	89.39 W
Bradford, N.Y., U.S.	210	42.22 N	77.07 W
Bradford, Oh., U.S.	218	40.08 N	84.26 W
Bradford, Pa., U.S.	214	41.57 N	78.38 W
Bradford, R.I., U.S.	207	41.23 N	71.44 W
Bradford, Tn., U.S.	194	36.04 N	88.48 W
Bradford, Vt., U.S.	188	58.12 N	15.03 E
Bradford ◻³	42	53.47 N	1.52 W
Bradford Hills	285	40.01 N	75.39 W
Bradford Mountain ▲	207	41.59 N	73.18 W
Bradford-on-Avon	42	51.20 N	2.15 W
Bradford Regional Airport ◇	214	41.48 N	78.38 W
Bradfordwoods	214	40.38 N	80.05 W
Brading	42	50.41 N	1.09 W
Bradley, Ar., U.S.	194	33.05 N	93.39 W
Bradley, Ca., U.S.	226	35.51 N	120.47 W
Bradley, Fl., U.S.	220	27.48 N	81.59 W
Bradley, Il., U.S.	216	41.08 N	87.51 W
Bradley, Me., U.S.	188	45.05 N	97.38 W
Bradley, S.D., U.S.	198	45.05 N	97.38 W
Bradley Beach	208	40.12 N	74.01 W
Bradley Farms	284c	39.00 N	77.11 W
Bradley Gardens	276	40.34 N	74.40 W
Bradley Institute	154	17.02 S	31.27 E
Bradley International Airport ◇	207	41.55 N	72.40 W
Bradley Reefs ➤²	175e	6.52 S	160.48 E
Bradley Woods Reservation ♦	279a	41.21 N	81.58 W
Bradley W. Palmer State Park ♦	283	42.39 N	70.54 W
Bradner, B.C., Can.	214	41.59 N	83.26 W
Bradner, Oh., U.S.	214	41.20 N	83.26 W
Bradore-Bay	186	51.28 N	57.14 W
Bradshaw, Eng., U.K.	262	53.36 S	2.24 W
Bradshaw, Md., U.S.	208	39.29 N	76.22 W
Bradshaw, W.V., U.S.	192	37.21 N	81.47 W

Name	Page	Lat.°'	Long.°'
Brainard, N.Y., U.S.	210	42.30 N	73.31 W
Braine	50	49.20 N	3.32 E
Braine-l'Alleud	50	50.41 N	4.22 E
Braine-le-Château	50	50.41 N	4.16 E
Braine-le-Comte	50	50.36 N	4.08 E
Brainerd	190	46.21 N	94.12 W
Braint ≈	44	53.08 N	4.19 W
Braintree, Eng., U.K.	42	51.53 N	0.32 E
Braintree, Ma., U.S.	207	42.13 N	71.00 W
Braintree ≈⁸	260	51.47 N	0.36 E
Brak ≈, S. Afr.	158	31.32 S	21.33 E
Brak ≈, S. Afr.	158	29.35 S	22.55 E
Brake, Dtsch.	52	53.19 N	8.28 E
Brake, Dtsch.	52	52.04 N	8.35 E
Brake, Dtsch.	52	52.01 N	8.55 E
Brakel, Bel.	50	50.48 N	3.46 E
Brakel, Dtsch.	52	51.43 N	9.10 E
Brakna ◻⁴	150	17.30 N	13.30 W
Brakpan	158	26.14 S	28.22 E
Brakpan ◻⁵	273d	26.16 S	28.21 E
Brakpoort	158	31.20 S	23.22 E
Brakputs	158	29.29 S	18.24 E
Brakwater	156	22.24 S	17.06 E
Brålanda	26	58.34 N	12.22 E
Bralorne	182	50.47 N	122.49 W
Bramalea	212	43.44 N	79.43 W
Bramall Hall ⊥	262	53.23 N	2.09 W
Braman	196	36.55 N	97.20 W
Brambauer	263	51.35 N	7.27 E
Bramberg am Wildkogel	64	47.16 N	12.21 E
Bramble Bay C	171a	27.17 S	153.05 E
Bramble Cay I	164	9.08 S	143.52 E
Bramdrupdam	41	55.31 N	9.28 E
Bramey-Lenningsen	263	51.34 N	7.46 E
Bramfeld ≈⁸	52	53.37 N	10.04 E
Bramford	42	52.04 N	1.06 E
Bramhope	44	53.53 N	1.37 W
Bramley	260	51.12 N	0.34 W
Bramley ≈⁸	273d	26.08 S	28.05 E
Bramley Mountain ▲	210	42.18 N	74.49 W
Bramming	41	55.28 N	8.42 E
Brampton, On., Can.	212	43.41 N	79.46 W
Brampton, Eng., U.K.	42	52.19 N	0.14 W
Brampton, Eng., U.K.	44	54.57 N	2.44 W
Brampton Airfield ◇	275b	43.40 N	79.47 W
Bramsche	52	52.24 N	7.58 E
Bramsöfjärden ⊜	40	60.20 N	17.10 E
Bramstedt	52	53.22 N	8.41 E
Brancaleone Marina	68	37.58 N	16.06 E
Brancaster	42	52.58 N	0.39 E
Brancaster Roads ⊽³	42	53.00 N	0.41 E
Branch	186	46.53 N	53.57 W
Branch ◻⁶	41	41.55 N	85.03 W
Branch Brook Park ♦	276	40.46 N	74.10 W
Branch Dale	208	40.41 N	76.20 W
Branchport	210	42.36 N	77.09 W
Branchville, Ct., U.S.	207	41.16 N	73.26 W
Branchville, N.J., U.S.	210	41.08 N	74.45 W
Branchville, S.C., U.S.	192	33.15 N	80.48 W
Branchville, Va., U.S.	208	36.34 N	77.14 W
Branco ≈, Bra.	248	1.24 S	61.51 W
Branco ≈, Bra.	248	10.03 S	67.51 W
Branco ≈, Bra.	248	7.44 S	61.46 W
Branco ≈, Bra.	248	9.12 S	64.22 W
Branco ≈, Bra.	248	9.37 S	60.33 W
Branco ≈, Bra.	248	21.00 S	57.48 W
Branco ≈, Bra.	250	7.01 S	51.42 W
Branco, Clear Fork ≈	196	33.01 N	99.10 W
Branco, Double Mountain Fork ≈	196	33.01 N	100.00 W
Branco, Salt Fork ≈	196	33.59 N	100.00 W
Branco Sur (del Rio Coig) ≈	254	51.32 S	70.04 W
Brazzaville, Congo	152	4.16 S	15.17 E
Brazzaville, Congo ◻⁵	273b	4.15 S	15.15 E

Name	Page	Lat.°'	Long.°'
Br'anta ≈	89	54.27 N	127.42 E
Brantas ≈	115a	7.28 S	112.25 E
Brantford	212	43.08 N	80.16 W
Brantingham Lake ⊜	212	43.42 N	75.17 W
Brant Lake	188	43.40 N	73.45 W
Brantley	194	31.34 N	86.15 W
Brantôme	32	45.22 N	0.39 E
Brantville	186	47.22 N	64.58 W
Branxholme	166	37.51 S	141.47 E
Branxton	170	32.39 S	151.22 E
Branzi	64	46.00 N	9.46 E
Brás ≈⁸	287b	23.32 S	46.36 W
Brás Cubas	256	23.32 S	46.13 W
Bras d'Or Lake ⊜	186	45.52 N	60.50 W
Brashear	222	33.07 N	95.44 W
Brasil			
— Brazil ◻¹	242	10.00 S	55.00 W
Brasilândia ◻⁸	287b	23.28 S	46.41 W
Brasiléia	248	11.00 S	68.44 W
Brasília	255	15.47 S	47.55 W
Brasília, Parque Nacional de ♦	255	15.36 S	48.08 W
Brasília de Minas	255	16.12 S	44.26 W
Brasília Legal	250	3.49 S	55.36 W
Brasilien			
— Brazil ◻¹	242	10.00 S	55.00 W
Braslaw	76	55.38 N	27.02 E
Brasopolis	256	22.28 S	45.37 W
Braşov	38	45.39 N	25.37 E
Braşov ◻⁶	38	45.45 N	25.15 E
Brass	150	4.19 N	6.14 E
Brass Castle	164	44.47 N	74.58 W
Brasschaat	50	51.17 N	4.27 E
Brassert	263	51.40 N	7.05 E
Brassey, Banjaran ▲	112	4.54 N	117.30 E
Brassey, Mount ▲	162	23.05 S	134.38 E
Brass Islands II	240m	18.24 N	64.58 W
Brasstown Bald ▲	192	34.52 N	83.48 W
Brastad	26	58.23 N	11.29 E
Brasted	260	51.16 N	0.06 E
Brasted Chart	260	51.16 N	0.06 E
Břasy	60	49.50 N	13.35 E
Bratca	38	46.56 N	22.37 E
Bratenahl	279a	41.31 N	81.37 W
Brateş, Lacul ⊜	38	45.30 N	28.05 E
Bratislava	30	48.09 N	17.07 E
Bratol'ubovka	88	51.13 N	66.46 E
Bratsk	88	56.05 N	101.48 E
Bratskaja Kada	88	55.02 N	102.06 E
Bratsk'e	88	52.06 N	2.03 W
Bratslav	78	48.50 N	28.55 E
Brattfors	40	59.40 N	14.01 E
Brattleboro	207	42.51 N	72.33 W
Bratto	64	45.55 N	10.04 E
Brattvåg	26	62.36 N	6.27 E
Braubach	56	50.16 N	7.40 E
Braúlio Carrillo, Parque Nacional ♦	236	10.10 N	84.00 W
Braúnas	256	19.04 S	42.43 W
Braunau am Inn	60	48.15 N	13.02 E
Braunfels	56	50.31 N	8.23 E
Braunlage	52	51.44 N	10.37 E
Bräunlingen	58	47.55 N	8.26 E
Braunsbedra	54	51.15 N	11.49 E
Braunschweig, S. Afr.	158	32.48 S	27.22 E
Braunschweig ◻⁵	52	52.00 N	10.30 E
Braunschweig, Dtsch.	52	52.16 N	10.31 E
Brava, Costa ≈²	34	41.45 N	3.04 E
Brava, Laguna ⊜	252	28.22 S	68.50 W
Brava, Punta ➤	248	34.56 S	56.10 W
Braviecea	38	47.29 N	27.56 E
Bråviken C	40	58.38 N	16.32 E
Bravo, Cerro ▲, Bol.	252	21.00 S	67.43 W
Bravo, Cerro ▲, Perú	248	5.32 S	79.15 W
Bravo del Norte (Rio Grande) ≈	178	25.55 N	97.09 W
Brawley	204	33.58 N	115.31 W
Brawley Peaks ▲	226	38.20 N	118.41 W
Brawley Wash V	200	32.35 N	111.36 W
Bray, Bel.	50	50.31 N	5.36 E
Bray, Ire.	48	53.12 N	6.06 W
Bray, Pays de ◻¹	50	49.46 N	1.26 E
Bray-Dunes	50	51.05 N	2.31 E
Bray Head ➤¹	42	54.46 N	1.39 W
Bray Head ➤²	48	51.52 N	10.26 W
Brayiliv	78	49.00 N	28.12 E
Braymer	194	39.36 N	93.47 W
Braye-sur-Seine	50	48.25 N	3.28 E
Bray-sur-Somme	50	49.56 N	2.43 E
Brazeau, Mount ▲	182	52.34 N	117.21 W
Brazeau, Dam ≈⁶	182	52.55 N	115.30 W
Brazen Head ➤	48	53.14 N	10.15 W
Brazey-en-Plaine	58	47.08 N	5.16 E
Brazil (Brasil) ◻¹	242	10.00 S	55.00 W
Brazil Basin ⊽¹	8	15.00 S	25.00 W
Brazo Chico, Arroyo ≈	252	33.47 S	58.36 W
Brazo Largo, Arroyo ≈	252	33.43 S	58.56 W
Brazoria	222	29.03 N	95.34 W
Brazoria ◻⁶	222	29.12 N	95.30 W
Brazos ≈	196	28.53 N	95.23 W
Brazos, Clear Fork ≈	196	33.01 N	99.10 W
Brazos, Double Mountain Fork ≈	196	33.01 N	100.00 W
Brazos, Salt Fork ≈	196	33.59 N	100.00 W
Brazos Bay C	222	28.53 N	95.23 W
Brazos Island I	196	26.04 N	97.09 W
Brazzaville, Congo	152	4.16 S	15.17 E
Brazzaville, Maya Airport ◇	273b	4.15 S	15.15 E
Brčko	38	44.52 N	18.49 E
Brda ≈	30	53.07 N	18.08 E
Brdy ⫟	60	49.40 N	13.50 E
Bré — Bray	48	53.12 N	6.06 W
Brea, Punta ➤	240m	17.56 N	66.58 W
Brea Canyon V	280	33.55 N	117.53 W
Brea Creek ≈	280	33.51 N	117.57 W

Name	Page	Lat.°'	Long.°'
Bréau	261	48.34 N	2.53 E
Breaux Bridge	194	30.16 N	91.53 W
Breaza	38	45.11 N	25.40 E
Brebes	115a	6.53 S	109.03 E
Brécey	32	48.44 N	1.10 W
Brechen	56	50.20 N	8.14 E
Brechfa	42	51.57 N	4.09 W
Brechin	46	56.44 N	2.40 W
Brecht	56	51.21 N	4.38 E
Brechten ≈⁸	263	51.35 N	7.28 E
Breckenridge, Co., U.S.	200	39.28 N	106.02 W
Breckenridge, Mi., U.S.	190	43.24 N	84.28 W
Breckenridge, Mn., U.S.	198	46.15 N	96.35 W
Breckenridge, Mo., U.S.	194	39.45 N	93.48 W
Breckenridge, Tx., U.S.	196	32.45 N	98.54 W
Breckerfeld	56	51.16 N	7.28 E
Brecknock	42	52.28 N	0.37 E
Brecknock, Península ➤¹	254	54.35 S	71.50 W
Brecksville	214	41.19 N	81.37 W
Břeclav	30	48.46 N	16.53 E
Brecon	42	51.57 N	3.24 W
Brecon Beacons ▲	42	51.53 N	3.31 W
Brecon Beacons National Park ♦	42	51.52 N	3.25 W
Bred	41	55.22 N	10.07 E
Breda, Ned.	52	51.35 N	4.46 E
Breda, Ia., U.S.	198	42.10 N	94.58 W
Bredaryd	26	57.10 N	13.44 E
Bredasdorp	158	34.32 S	20.02 E
Bredbo	171b	35.57 S	149.10 E
Bredbo ≈	171b	35.58 S	149.08 E
— Bredow	38	35.39 N	25.37 E
Bredbury	262	53.25 N	2.08 E
Breddin	54	52.52 N	12.13 E
Brede ≈	42	55.09 N	8.42 E
Bredebro	41	55.03 N	8.48 E
Bredell	273d	26.05 S	23.17 E
Bredenbeck	52	52.16 N	22.37 E
Bredenbruch	263	51.21 N	7.41 E
Bredenbury	184	50.57 N	102.03 W
Bredene	50	51.14 N	2.58 E
Bredeney ≈⁸	263	51.24 N	6.59 E
Bredenscheid-Stüter	263	51.22 N	7.11 E
Bredereiche	54	53.08 N	13.14 E
Bredgar	260	51.18 N	0.42 E
Bredhurst	260	51.20 N	0.35 E
Bredon Hill ▲²	42	52.06 N	2.03 W
Bredsjö	40	59.50 N	14.44 E
Bredsjön	60	60.13 N	13.55 E
Bredstedt	41	54.37 N	8.59 E
Bredsten	41	55.42 N	9.24 E
Bredy	86	52.26 N	60.21 E
Bree	52	51.08 N	5.36 E
Breech	260	51.16 N	5.36 E
Breeches, Lac ⊜	206	46.54 N	71.28 W
Breedi	48	53.55 N	8.27 W
Breeds Pond ⊜	283	42.28 N	70.59 W
Breedsville	216	42.21 N	86.08 W
Breese	219	38.36 N	89.31 W
Breeport	222	42.10 N	76.44 W
Breeza Plains	164	15.27 S	143.32 E
Breezewood	279b	40.34 N	80.03 W
Bregalnica ≈	38	41.43 N	22.09 E
Breganze	64	45.42 N	11.34 E
Bregenz	30	47.30 N	9.46 E
Bregenzer Wald ⫟	58	47.20 N	10.00 E
Breginje, Dan.	41	55.19 N	11.19 E
Brehna	54	51.33 N	12.12 E
Breiðafjörður C	24a	65.15 N	23.15 W
Breidbach	158	32.54 S	27.27 E
Breidenbach, Dtsch.	56	50.53 N	8.27 E
Breidenbach, Fr.	56	49.08 N	7.25 E
Breisach	58	48.02 N	7.37 E
Breithardt	261	50.16 N	8.07 E
Breitenbach, Schw.	58	47.22 N	7.33 E
Breitenbrunn	60	47.56 N	16.44 E
Breitenfelde	52	53.36 N	10.37 E
Breitenfurt bei Wien	60	48.08 N	16.08 E
Breitengüßbach	54	49.57 N	10.53 E
Breitenworbis	54	51.31 N	10.36 E
Breithorn ▲	58	45.56 N	7.38 E
Breitnau	58	47.55 N	8.03 E
Breitscheid, Dtsch.	56	50.41 N	8.11 E
Breitscheid, Dtsch.	263	51.18 N	6.53 E
Breitungen	54	50.45 N	10.21 E
Brejetuba	256	20.09 S	41.20 W
Brejinho de Nazaré	250	11.01 S	48.34 W
Brejo	250	3.41 S	42.47 W
Brejões	255	13.06 S	39.50 W
Brejo Grande	255	10.26 S	36.26 W
Brejo Santo	250	7.29 S	39.00 W
Brejtovo	76	58.18 N	37.58 E
Brekke	26	61.00 N	5.25 E
Brekkvasselv	24	64.49 N	13.50 E
Brekstad	24	63.41 N	9.40 E
— Bremen	52	53.05 N	8.49 E
Bremelau	58	48.18 N	9.32 E
Bremen, Dtsch.	52	53.05 N	8.49 E
Bremen, Ga., U.S.	216	33.43 N	85.09 W
Bremen, In., U.S.	216	41.26 N	86.09 W
Bremen, Oh., U.S.	218	39.42 N	82.26 W
Bremen, Flughafen ◇	52	53.03 N	8.47 E
Bremen ◻⁵	52	53.05 N	8.48 E
Bremer ≈	171a	27.39 S	152.46 E
Bremer Bay C	168a	34.23 S	119.22 E
Bremerhaven	52	53.33 N	8.35 E
Bremersdorp			
— Manzini	158	26.30 S	31.24 E
Bremerton	224	47.34 N	122.38 W
Bremervörde	52	53.29 N	9.08 E
Bremgarten	58	47.21 N	8.20 E
Bremke	263	51.20 N	8.12 E
Bremm	56	50.06 N	7.08 E
Bremnes	26	59.47 N	5.09 E
Brémoy	261	48.59 N	0.51 W
Brenna	24b	69.04 N	18.05 E
Brennbergbánya	60	47.40 N	16.29 E
Brenner Pass ⋉	60	47.00 N	11.30 E
Brennero (Brenner)	60	47.00 N	11.30 E
Breno	64	45.57 N	10.18 E
Brenod	62	46.04 N	5.36 E
Brent, Al., U.S.	194	32.56 N	87.09 W
Brent, Fl., U.S.	194	30.28 N	87.14 W

Symbol	English	Deutsch	Español	Français	Português
▲	Mountain	Berg	Montaña	Montagne	Montanha
▲	Mountains	Gebirge	Montañas	Montagnes	Montanhas
⋉	Pass	Paß	Paso	Col	Passo
V	Valley, Canyon	Tal, Cañon	Valle, Cañón	Vallée, Canyon	Vale, Carhão
≈	Plain	Ebene	Llano	Plaine	Planície
➤	Cape	Kap	Cabo	Cap	Cabo
I	Island	Insel	Isla	Île	Ilha
II	Islands	Inseln	Islas	Îles	Ilhas
⊥	Other Topographic Features	Andere Topographische Objekte	Otros Elementos Topográficos	Autres données topographiques	Outros acidentes topográficos

ESPAÑOL — Nombre · Página · Lat.°′ · Long.°′ W = Oeste
FRANÇAIS — Nom · Page · Lat.°′ · Long.°′ W = Ouest
PORTUGUÊS — Nome · Página · Lat.°′ · Long.°′ W = Oeste

Brent ✦⁸ 42 51.34 N 0.17 W
Brent ≃ 260 51.28 N 0.18 W
Brenta ≃ 64 45.11 N 12.18 E
Brenta, Gruppo di ∧ 64 46.11 N 10.54 E
Brentford ✦⁸ 260 51.29 N 0.18 W
Brenthurst 273d 26.16 S 28.23 E
Brentino 64 45.40 N 10.55 E
Brentonico 64 45.49 N 10.57 E
Brent Reservoir ◎¹ 260 51.35 N 0.15 W
Brentwood, Eng., U.K. 42 51.38 N 0.18 E
Brentwood, Eng., U.K. 260 51.38 N 0.18 E
Brentwood, Ca., U.S. 226 37.55 N 121.41 W
Brentwood, Md., U.S. 208 38.56 N 76.57 W
Brentwood, N.Y., U.S. 210 40.46 N 73.14 W
Brentwood, Oh., U.S. 218 39.13 N 84.31 W
Brentwood, Pa., U.S. 214 40.22 N 79.58 W
Brentwood, Tn., U.S. 194 36.01 N 86.46 W
Brentwood □⁸ 260 51.37 N 0.20 E
Brentwood Bay 224 48.35 N 123.28 W
Brentwood Estates 214 40.25 N 80.45 W
Brentwood Heights ✦⁸ 280 34.04 N 118.30 W
Brentwood Lake 214 41.19 N 82.05 W
Brentwood Park 273d 26.08 S 28.18 E
Brenz ≃ 56 48.34 N 10.24 E
Breo 62 44.23 N 7.49 E
Bréon, Ruisseau du ≃ 261 48.40 N 2.49 E
Brera, Palazzo di ✦ 266b 45.28 N 9.11 E
Brereton Park 158 26.55 S 30.30 E
Brescello 64 44.54 N 10.31 E
Brescia 64 45.33 N 10.15 E
Brescia □⁴ 64 45.38 N 10.18 E
Bresewitz 54 54.24 N 12.40 E
Brésil
 → Brazil □¹ 242 10.00 S 55.00 W
Breskens 52 51.24 N 3.34 E
Breslau, On., Can. 212 43.28 N 80.25 W
Breslau
 → Wrocław, Pol. 30 51.06 N 17.00 E
Breslau, Tx., U.S. 222 29.31 N 97.00 W
Bresle ≃ 50 50.04 N 1.22 E
Bresles 50 49.25 N 2.15 E
Bresnahan, Mount ∧ 162 23.50 S 117.55 E
Bressanone (Brixen) 64 46.43 N 11.39 E
Bressay I 46a 60.08 N 1.05 W
Bressay Sound ꓤ 46a 60.07 N 1.09 W
Bresse ✦¹ 58 46.30 N 5.15 E
Bresso 266b 45.32 N 9.11 E
Bressuire 32 46.51 N 0.30 W
Brest, Blg. 38 43.38 N 24.35 E
Brèst, Bela. 76 52.06 N 23.42 E
Brest, Fr. 32 48.24 N 4.29 W
Brest' □⁸ 76 52.30 N 25.30 E
Brestanica 36 45.59 N 15.29 E
Bretagne (Brittany) □⁹ 32 48.00 N 3.00 W
Bretenoux 32 44.55 N 1.50 E
Breteuil 50 49.38 N 2.18 E
Breteuil-sur-Iton 50 48.50 N 0.55 E
Bréthencourt 261 48.30 N 1.55 E
Bretherton 262 53.41 N 2.48 W
Brétigny ■ 261 48.35 N 2.20 E
Brétigny-sur-Orge 50 48.37 N 2.19 E
Bretnig 54 51.08 N 14.04 E
Breton 182 53.07 N 114.28 W
Bretón, Canal de ꓤ 240p 21.10 N 79.30 W
Breton, Pertuis ꓤ 32 46.25 N 1.20 W
Breton Bay ⊂ 208 38.16 N 76.39 W
Breton Islands II 194 29.28 N 89.11 W
Breton Sound ꓤ 194 29.30 N 89.30 W
Breton Woods 208 40.02 N 74.06 W
Brett ≃ 42 51.58 N 0.58 E
Brett, Cape ⊱ 172 35.10 S 174.20 E
Bretten 56 49.02 N 8.42 E
Breu, Rio do ≃ 246 3.29 S 66.20 W
Breuberg 56 49.49 N 9.03 E
Breueh, Pulau I 110 5.41 N 95.05 E
Breuil-Bois-Robert 261 48.57 N 1.43 E
Breuil-Cervinia 58 45.56 N 7.38 E
Breuillet 261 48.34 N 2.10 E
Breuilpont 50 48.58 N 1.26 E
Breukelen 52 52.10 N 5.00 E
Breux 261 48.34 N 2.11 E
Brevard 192 35.14 N 82.44 W
Brevard □⁶ 220 28.18 N 80.42 W
Brevenne ≃ 62 45.51 N 4.42 E
Brevens bruk 40 59.01 N 15.35 E
Breves 250 1.40 S 50.29 W
Brevig Mission 180 65.20 N 166.29 W
Brevik, Nor. 26 59.04 N 9.42 E
Brevik, Sve. 40 59.21 N 18.12 E
Brevoort Island I 176 63.30 N 64.20 W
Brewarrina 166 29.57 S 146.52 E
Brewer 188 44.47 N 68.45 W
Brewer Island I 287 37.33 N 122.16 W
Brewersville 218 39.05 N 85.37 W
Brewerton 210 43.14 N 76.08 W
Brewerville 150 6.26 N 10.47 W
Brewongle 170 33.29 S 149.43 E
Brewood 42 52.41 N 2.10 W
Brewster, Ks., U.S. 198 39.22 N 101.22 W
Brewster, Ma., U.S. 207 41.45 N 70.05 W
Brewster, Mn., U.S. 198 43.41 N 95.28 W
Brewster, Ne., U.S. 198 41.56 N 99.51 W
Brewster, N.Y., U.S. 210 41.23 N 73.37 W
Brewster, Oh., U.S. 214 40.42 N 81.35 W
Brewster, Wa., U.S. 202 48.05 N 119.46 W
Brewster, Kap ⊱ 16 70.19 N 22.05 W
Brewster, Lake ◎ 166 33.28 S 146.00 E
Brewster, Mount ∧ 172 44.04 S 169.27 E
Brewton 194 31.06 N 87.04 W
Breyten 158 26.16 S 30.00 E
Březany 61 48.52 N 16.20 E
Brežice 54 45.54 N 15.36 E
Brezina 148 33.04 N 1.14 E
Brézins 62 45.21 N 5.19 E
Breznice 60 49.33 N 13.57 E
Breznik 38 42.44 N 22.54 E
Březno, Česká Rep. 54 50.24 N 13.26 E
Brezno, Slvk. 30 48.50 N 19.39 E
Brézolles 50 48.41 N 1.04 E
Brezová 54 50.06 N 12.39 E
Brezové Hory 60 49.41 N 13.58 E
Bria 152 6.32 N 21.59 E
Brian Boru Peak ∧ 182 55.05 N 127.35 W
Briançon 62 44.54 N 6.39 E
Brian Head ∧ 200 37.41 N 112.50 W
Brianza ✦⁹ 64 45.40 N 9.10 E
Briar 222 33.00 N 97.34 W
Briarcliff Manor 210 41.08 N 73.49 W
Briar Creek 210 40.10 N 76.46 W
Briar Creek ≃ 222 32.06 N 96.22 W
Briare 50 47.38 N 2.44 E
Briare, Canal de ≅ 50 48.02 N 2.43 E
Briarres-sur-Essonne 50 48.14 N 2.25 E
Briarwood Beach 214 41.06 N 81.54 W
Briarwood Center ✦⁹ 281 42.14 N 83.45 W
Briatico 68 38.43 N 16.02 E
Bribano 64 46.06 N 12.05 E
Bribie Island I 171a 27.00 S 153.07 E
Bricelyn 190 43.33 N 93.48 W
Briceni 78 48.22 N 27.04 E
Brice Run ≃ 284b 39.19 N 76.50 W
Brices Cross Roads National Battlefield Site ⊥ 194 34.31 N 88.41 W
Briceville 192 36.10 N 84.11 W
Bricherasio 62 44.49 N 7.18 E
Bricht 263 51.41 N 6.51 E
Brickebacken 40 59.15 N 15.15 E
Brick Lake ◎ 220 28.10 N 81.12 W
Brick Township 208 40.04 N 74.08 W
Briçonnet, Lac ◎ 186 51.27 N 60.11 W
Bricquebec 50 49.28 N 1.38 W
Bridal Veil 224 45.33 N 122.10 W
Bridalveil Fall ∟ 226 37.43 N 119.39 W
Bride 44 54.22 N 4.22 W
Bride ≃ 48 52.04 N 7.52 W
Bridesburg ✦⁸ 285 40.00 N 75.04 W
Brides-les-Bains 62 45.27 N 6.34 E
Bridge 42 51.14 N 1.07 E
Bridge ≃ 182 50.45 N 121.55 W
Bridge City 194 30.01 N 93.50 W
Bridge Creek ≃ 224 48.26 N 120.52 W
Bridgehampton 207 40.56 N 72.18 W
Bridge Lake 182 51.29 N 120.43 W
Bridgend, Scot., U.K. 46 55.48 N 6.16 W
Bridgend, Scot., U.K. 46 56.48 N 2.45 W
Bridgend, Wales, U.K. 42 51.31 N 3.35 W
Bridgenorth 212 44.23 N 78.23 W
Bridge of Allan 46 56.09 N 3.57 W
Bridge of Gaur 46 56.41 N 4.27 W
Bridge of Orchy 46 56.30 N 4.46 W
Bridge of Weir 46 55.52 N 4.35 W
Bridgeport, Al., U.S. 194 34.56 N 85.42 W
Bridgeport, Ca., U.S. 226 38.10 N 119.13 W
Bridgeport, Ct., U.S. 207 41.10 N 73.12 W
Bridgeport, Il., U.S. 194 38.42 N 87.45 W
Bridgeport, Mi., U.S. 190 43.21 N 83.52 W
Bridgeport, Ne., U.S. 198 41.39 N 103.05 W
Bridgeport, N.J., U.S. 285 39.48 N 75.20 W
Bridgeport, N.Y., U.S. 210 43.09 N 75.58 W
Bridgeport, Oh., U.S. 214 40.04 N 80.44 W
Bridgeport, Pa., U.S. 285 40.06 N 75.21 W
Bridgeport, Tx., U.S. 222 33.12 N 97.45 W
Bridgeport, Wa., U.S. 202 48.00 N 119.40 W
Bridgeport, W.V., U.S. 188 39.17 N 80.15 W
Bridgeport ✦⁸ 278 41.51 N 87.39 W
Bridgeport, Lake ◎¹ 222 33.13 N 97.48 W
Bridgeport, University of ✦² 276 41.10 N 73.12 W
Bridgeport Airport ✈ 285 39.47 N 75.20 W
Bridgeport Harbor ⊂ 276 41.10 N 73.11 W
Bridgeport Municipal Airport ✈ 276 41.10 N 73.08 W
Bridgeport Reservoir ◎¹ 226 38.22 N 119.14 W
Bridger 202 45.17 N 108.54 W
Bridge River Indian Reserve ✦⁴ 182 50.45 N 122.00 W
Bridger Peak ∧ 200 41.12 N 107.02 W
Bridges Point ⊱ 174o 1.58 N 157.28 W
Bridgeton, Mo., U.S. 219 38.44 N 90.24 W
Bridgeton, N.J., U.S. 208 39.25 N 75.14 W
Bridgetown, Austl. 162 33.57 S 116.08 E
Bridgetown, Barb. 241g 13.06 N 59.37 W
Bridgetown, N.S., Can. 186 44.51 N 65.18 W
Bridgetown, Oh., U.S. 218 39.09 N 84.38 W
Bridge Trafford 262 53.14 N 2.49 W
Bridgeview 278 41.45 N 87.48 W
Bridgeville, De., U.S. 208 38.44 N 75.36 W
Bridgeville, Pa., U.S. 214 40.21 N 80.06 W
Bridgewater, Austl. 166 42.44 S 147.14 E
Bridgewater, Austl. 168b 35.02 S 138.47 E
Bridgewater, N.S., Can. 186 44.23 N 64.31 W
Bridgewater, Ct., U.S. 210 41.32 N 73.22 W
Bridgewater, Me., U.S. 186 46.25 N 67.50 W
Bridgewater, Ma., U.S. 207 41.59 N 70.58 W
Bridgewater, N.Y., U.S. 210 42.58 N 75.15 W
Bridgewater, Pa., U.S. 285 40.05 N 74.55 W
Bridgewater, S.D., U.S. 198 43.33 N 97.30 W
Bridgewater, Va., U.S. 188 38.22 N 78.58 W
Bridgewater Canal ≅ 262 53.20 N 2.45 W
Bridgewater State College ✦² 283 41.59 N 70.58 W
Bridgman 216 41.57 N 86.33 W
Bridgnorth 42 52.33 N 2.25 W
Bridgton 188 44.03 N 70.42 W
Bridgwater 42 51.08 N 3.00 W
Bridgwater Bay ⊂ 42 51.16 N 3.12 W
Bridlington 44 54.05 N 0.12 W
Bridlington Bay ⊂ 44 54.04 N 0.08 W
Bridport 42 50.44 N 2.46 W
Brie ✦¹ 50 48.40 N 3.20 E
Briec 32 48.06 N 4.00 W
Brie-Comte-Robert 50 48.41 N 2.37 E
Brie Française ✦¹ 261 48.48 N 2.46 E
Brieg
 → Brzeg 30 50.52 N 17.27 E
Brielle, Ned. 52 51.54 N 4.10 E
Brielle, N.J., U.S. 208 40.06 N 74.03 W
Brienne-le-Château 58 48.24 N 4.32 E
Brienne-sur-Aisne 50 49.26 N 4.03 E
Brienno 58 45.55 N 9.07 E
Brienon-sur-Armançon 50 48.00 N 3.37 E
Brien Run ≃ 284b 39.20 N 76.28 W
Brienz 58 46.46 N 8.03 E
Brienza 68 40.29 N 15.37 E
Brienzer Rothorn ∧ 58 46.48 N 8.04 E
Brienzersee ◎ 58 46.43 N 7.57 E
Brier Creek ≃ 192 32.47 N 81.26 W
Brierfield 44 53.50 N 2.14 W
Brier Hill 212 44.32 N 75.40 W
Brier Island I 186 44.16 N 66.22 W
Brierley Hill 42 52.29 N 2.07 W
Brier Mountain ∧ 210 41.37 N 77.02 W
Briese 264a 52.42 N 13.18 E
Briese ≃ 264a 52.41 N 13.15 E
Brieselang 54 52.35 N 13.00 E
Briesen 54 52.20 N 14.16 E
Brieske 54 51.29 N 13.57 E
Brieskow-Finkenheerd 54 52.16 N 14.35 E
Briey 56 49.15 N 5.56 E
Brig 58 46.19 N 8.00 E
Brigach ≃ 58 47.58 N 8.30 E
Brigantine 208 39.24 N 74.21 W
Brig Bay 186 51.04 N 56.55 W
Brigden 214 42.49 N 82.17 W
Brigg 44 53.34 N 0.30 W
Briggs 196 30.53 N 97.56 W
Brigham City 200 41.30 N 112.00 W
Brighouse 44 53.42 N 1.47 W
Brighstone 42 50.38 N 1.24 W
Bright 166 36.44 S 146.58 E
Brightlingsea 42 51.49 N 1.02 E
Brightmoor ✦⁸ 281 42.24 N 83.14 W
Brighton, Austl. 168b 35.01 S 138.31 E
Brighton, Austl. 169 37.55 S 145.00 E
Brighton, On., Can. 212 44.02 N 77.44 W
Brighton, N.Z. 172 45.57 S 170.21 E
Brighton, Eng., U.K. 42 50.50 N 0.08 W
Brighton, Co., U.S. 200 39.59 N 104.49 W
Brighton, Fl., U.S. 220 27.14 N 81.06 W
Brighton, Il., U.S. 219 39.02 N 90.08 W
Brighton, Md., U.S. 284b 39.21 N 76.43 W
Brighton, Mi., U.S. 216 42.31 N 83.46 W
Brighton, N.Y., U.S. 210 43.08 N 77.33 W
Brighton ✦⁸ 283 42.21 N 71.08 W
Brighton Airport ✈ 281 42.34 N 83.47 W
Brighton Downs 166 23.22 S 141.34 E
Brighton Indian Reservation ✦⁴ 220 27.04 N 81.05 W
Brighton-Le-Sands 274a 33.58 S 151.09 E
Brighton Park ✦⁸ 278 41.49 N 87.42 W
Brighton State Recreation Area ♦ 216 42.30 N 83.48 W
Brightsand Lake ◎ 184 53.36 N 108.52 W
Brightwater 172 41.23 S 173.07 E
Brightwaters 276 40.43 N 73.16 W
Brightwood 224 45.23 N 122.01 W
Brightwood ✦⁸ 284c 38.58 N 77.02 W
Brigittenau ✦⁸ 264b 48.14 N 16.22 E
Brignoles 62 43.24 N 6.04 E
Brignoud 62 45.15 N 5.54 E
Brig o'Turk 46 56.13 N 4.22 W
Brigstock 42 52.27 N 0.36 W
Brigus 186 47.32 N 53.13 W
Brihuega 34 40.45 N 2.52 W
Briis-sous-Forges 261 48.38 N 2.07 E
Brijuni (Brioni) 64 44.55 N 13.46 E
Brijuni I 64 44.55 N 13.46 E
Brikama 150 13.15 N 16.39 W
Brilhante ≃ 255 21.58 S 54.18 W
Brill 42 51.49 N 1.03 W
Brilliant, B.C., Can. 182 49.19 N 117.38 W
Brilliant, Al., U.S. 194 34.01 N 87.45 W
Brilliant, Oh., U.S. 214 40.15 N 80.37 W
Brillion 190 44.10 N 88.03 W
Brilon 56 51.24 N 8.34 E
Brilyn Park 284c 38.54 N 77.10 W
Brimfield, Eng., U.K. 42 52.18 N 2.42 W
Brimfield, In., U.S. 216 41.27 N 85.24 W
Brimfield, Ma., U.S. 207 42.07 N 72.12 W
Brimfield, Oh., U.S. 214 41.06 N 81.21 W
Brimington 44 53.16 N 1.23 W
Brindabella 171b 35.23 S 148.45 E
Brindisi 68 40.38 N 17.56 E
Brindisi □⁴ 68 40.35 N 17.40 E
Brindisi Montagna 68 40.37 N 15.57 E
Brindle 262 53.43 N 2.36 W
Bringelly 170 33.56 S 150.44 E
Bringelly Creek ≃ 274a 33.58 S 150.38 E
Brinje 36 45.00 N 15.08 E
Brinkerton 279b 40.13 N 79.32 W
Brinkhaven 214 40.28 N 82.12 W
Brinkleigh 284b 39.18 N 76.50 W
Brinkley, Austl. 168b 35.14 S 139.13 E
Brinkley, Ar., U.S. 194 34.53 N 91.11 W
Brinkum 52 53.00 N 8.47 E
Brinkworth 166 33.42 S 138.24 E
Brinnon 224 47.40 N 122.53 W
Brinon-sur-Beuvron 50 47.17 N 3.30 E
Brins, Ābār al- ✦⁴ 142 30.29 N 30.05 E
Brinscall 262 53.41 N 2.34 W
Brinyan 46 59.07 N 2.59 W
Brion, Île I 186 47.48 N 61.28 W
Brione 58 46.18 N 8.47 E
Briones Hills ∧² 282 37.56 N 122.08 W
Briones Regional Park ♦ 282 37.56 N 122.08 W
Briones Reservoir ◎¹ 282 37.55 N 122.12 W
Brionne 50 49.12 N 0.43 E
Brion-sur-Ource 58 47.55 N 4.39 E
Brioude 32 45.18 N 3.23 E
Briouze 32 48.42 N 0.22 W
Brisbane, Austl. 171a 27.28 S 153.02 E
Brisbane, Ca., U.S. 226 37.41 N 122.24 W
Brisbane ≃ 171a 27.24 S 153.09 E
Brisbane, Mount ∧ 171a 27.05 S 152.52 E
Brisbane International Airport ✈ 171a 27.27 S 153.11 E
Brisbane Ranges National Park ♦ 169 37.52 S 144.14 E
Brisbane Water ⊂ 170 33.28 S 151.20 E
Brisbane Water National Park ♦ 170 33.30 S 151.15 E
Brisben 210 42.22 N 75.41 W
Brisbin 214 40.50 N 78.21 W
Briseñas 234 20.16 N 102.33 W
Brisighella 66 44.13 N 11.46 E
Brissac 62 43.52 N 3.42 E
Brissago 58 46.07 N 8.43 E
Bristol, Eng., U.K. 42 51.27 N 2.35 W
Bristol, Ct., U.S. 207 41.41 N 72.57 W
Bristol, Fl., U.S. 192 30.25 N 84.58 W
Bristol, Il., U.S. 216 41.39 N 88.27 W
Bristol, In., U.S. 216 41.43 N 85.49 W
Bristol, N.H., U.S. 188 43.35 N 71.44 W
Bristol, Pa., U.S. 208 40.06 N 74.51 W
Bristol, R.I., U.S. 207 41.40 N 71.16 W
Bristol, S.D., U.S. 198 45.20 N 97.44 W
Bristol, Tn., U.S. 192 36.35 N 82.11 W
Bristol, Vt., U.S. 188 44.08 N 73.04 W
Bristol, Va., U.S. 192 36.35 N 82.11 W
Bristol, Wi., U.S. 216 42.33 N 88.02 W
Bristol □⁶, Ma., U.S. 207 41.54 N 71.06 W
Bristol □⁶, R.I., U.S. 207 41.42 N 71.18 W
Bristol (Lulsgate) Airport ✈ 42 51.23 N 2.43 W
Bristol Bay ⊂ 180 58.00 N 159.00 W
Bristol-Blake Reservation ♦ 283 42.06 N 71.19 W
Bristol Center 210 42.49 N 77.23 W
Bristol Channel ꓤ 42 51.20 N 4.00 W
Bristol Lake ◎ 204 34.28 N 115.41 W
Bristolville 214 41.23 N 80.52 W
Bristow 196 35.49 N 96.23 W
Britânia 255 15.14 S 51.09 W
Britânicas, Ilhas
 → British Isles II 4 54.00 N 4.00 W
Britannia, On., Can. 275b 43.37 N 79.41 W
Britannia, Eng., U.K. 262 53.41 N 2.11 W
Britannia Beach 182 49.38 N 123.12 W
Britische Jungfern-Inseln
 → British Virgin Islands □² 240m 18.30 N 64.30 W
British Columbia □⁴, Can. 176 54.00 N 125.00 W
British Columbia □⁴, Can. 182 54.00 N 125.00 W
British Honduras
 → Belize □¹ 232 17.15 N 88.45 W
British Indian Ocean Territory □² 12 7.00 S 72.00 E
British Isles II 4 54.00 N 4.00 W
British Mountains ∧ 180 69.00 N 140.20 W
British Museum ✦ 260 51.31 N 0.08 W
British Solomon Islands
 → Solomon Islands □¹ 175e 8.00 S 159.00 E
British Virgin Islands □², N.A. 230 18.30 N 64.30 W
British Virgin Islands □², N.A. 240m 18.30 N 64.30 W
Britland Edge Hill ∧² 262 53.31 N 1.50 W
Briton Ferry 42 51.38 N 3.49 W
Brits 158 25.42 S 27.45 E
Britstown 158 30.37 S 23.30 E
Britt 190 43.05 N 93.48 W
Brittany
 → Bretagne □⁹ 32 48.00 N 3.00 W
Brittas 48 53.14 N 6.27 W
Britten 158 27.42 S 25.17 E
Brittingham 196 25.45 N 103.24 W
Britton, Mi., U.S. 216 41.59 N 83.49 W
Britton, S.D., U.S. 198 45.47 N 97.45 W
Britton, Tx., U.S. 222 32.33 N 97.02 W
Britton, Mount ∧² 162 26.31 S 134.43 E
Britz 54 52.53 N 13.49 E
Britz ✦⁸ 264a 52.27 N 13.26 E
Brive-la-Gaillarde 32 45.10 N 1.32 E
Briviesca 34 42.33 N 3.19 W
Brivio 62 45.44 N 9.27 E
Brixen im Thale 64 47.27 N 12.15 E
Brixham 42 50.24 N 3.30 W
Brixlegg 64 47.25 N 11.53 E
Brixton 166 23.32 S 144.57 E
Brixworth 42 52.20 N 0.54 W
Brlik 85 43.40 N 73.49 E
Brloh 60 48.56 N 14.13 E
Brno 30 49.12 N 16.37 E
Bro 40 59.31 N 17.38 E
Broa, Ensenada de la ⊂ 240p 22.35 N 82.00 W
Broad ≃, Can. 192 34.00 N 81.04 W
Broad ≃, Fl., U.S. 220 25.28 N 81.09 W
Broad ≃, Ga., U.S. 192 33.59 N 82.39 W
Broadalbin 210 43.03 N 74.11 W
Broad Arrow 162 30.20 S 121.27 E
Broad Axe 285 40.10 N 75.15 W
Broadback ≃ 176 51.21 N 78.52 W
Broad Bay ⊂ 46 58.15 N 6.15 W
Broadbottom 262 53.26 N 2.01 W
Broad Brook 207 41.54 N 72.32 W
Broad Chalke 42 51.02 N 1.57 W
Broadclyst 42 50.46 N 3.26 W
Broad Creek ⊂ 208 38.45 N 76.15 W
Broad Creek ≃ 208 39.42 N 76.14 W
Broadford, Austl. 169 37.13 S 145.03 E
Broadford, Scot., U.K. 46 57.14 N 5.54 W
Broad Haven ⊂ 48 54.18 N 9.55 W
Broadheath 262 53.24 N 2.21 W
Broadhurst Range ∧ 162 22.23 S 122.09 E
Broadkill ≃ 208 38.47 N 75.10 W
Broad Law ∧ 46 55.30 N 3.22 W
Broadley Common 260 51.45 N 0.04 E
Broadmeadows 169 37.40 S 144.54 E
Broadmoor 226 37.41 N 122.29 W
Broad Neck ⊱¹ 208 39.03 N 76.27 W
Broad Oak 42 50.57 N 0.36 E
Broad Pass ⟩⟨ 180 63.18 N 149.09 W
Broad Run ≃, Pa., U.S. 285 39.56 N 75.41 W
Broad Run ≃, Pa., U.S. 285 39.59 N 75.40 W
Broad Run ≃, Va., U.S. 208 38.41 N 77.29 W
Broad Sound ꓤ, Austl. 166 22.10 S 149.45 E
Broad Sound ꓤ, Ma., U.S. 283 42.25 N 70.58 W
Broad Sound Channel ꓤ 166 22.05 S 150.20 E
Broadstairs 42 51.22 N 1.27 E
Broad Street 260 51.17 N 0.38 E
Broad Top 214 40.12 N 78.08 W
Broadus 198 45.26 N 105.24 W
Broadview, Sk., Can. 184 50.20 N 102.30 W
Broadview, Il., U.S. 216 41.51 N 87.51 W
Broadview, In., U.S. 218 39.10 N 87.33 W
Broadview Heights 214 41.18 N 81.41 W
Broadwater 198 41.35 N 102.51 W
Broadway, Eng., U.K. 42 52.02 N 1.51 W
Broadway, Oh., U.S. 214 40.20 N 83.24 W
Broadway, Va., U.S. 188 38.38 N 78.46 W
Broadwell 219 40.04 N 89.27 W
Broadwindsor 42 50.49 N 2.48 W
Broadwood 172 35.16 S 173.23 E
Broager 41 54.53 N 9.41 E
Brobo 150 7.43 N 4.42 W
Broby 26 56.15 N 14.05 E
Brobyværk 41 55.14 N 10.15 E
Broc 58 46.36 N 7.06 E
Broceni 76 56.42 N 22.35 E
Brochel 46 57.26 N 6.01 W
Brochet 176 57.53 N 101.40 W
Brochet, Lac au ◎ 186 49.40 N 69.37 W
Brochterbeck 52 52.13 N 7.44 E
Brock 184 51.27 N 108.42 W
Brock ≃ 44 53.52 N 2.47 W
Brock Creek ≃ 285 40.15 N 74.50 W
Brocken ∧ 54 51.48 N 10.36 E
Brockenhurst 42 50.49 N 1.34 W
Brockenscheidt 263 51.38 N 7.25 E
Brockhagen 52 51.59 N 8.20 E
Brockham 260 51.14 N 0.17 W
Brockman ≃ 168a 31.41 S 116.07 E
Brockman, Mount ∧ 162 22.28 S 117.18 E
Brock Monument ⊥ 284a 43.09 N 79.04 W
Brockport, N.Y., U.S. 210 43.12 N 77.56 W
Brockport, Pa., U.S. 214 41.15 N 78.44 W
Brocks Beach 212 44.27 N 80.06 W
Brocks Creek 164 13.28 S 131.25 E
Brockton, Ma., U.S. 207 42.05 N 71.01 W
Brockton, Mt., U.S. 198 48.09 N 104.54 W
Brockton, Pa., U.S. 208 40.45 N 76.04 W
Brockton Reservoir ◎¹ 283 42.07 N 71.03 W
Brock University ✦² 284a 43.07 N 79.15 W
Brockville 212 44.35 N 75.41 W
Brockway 214 41.15 N 78.47 W
Brockworth 42 51.51 N 2.09 W
Brocoió, Ilha de I 287a 22.45 S 43.07 W
Brocton 214 42.23 N 79.26 W
Brod, Česká Rep. 60 49.51 N 12.50 E
Brod, Mak. 38 41.31 N 21.12 E
Broddbo 40 59.59 N 16.28 E
Brodenbach 56 50.14 N 7.26 E
Brodeur Peninsula ⊱¹ 176 73.00 N 88.00 W
Brodhead, Ky., U.S. 192 37.24 N 84.24 W
Brodhead, Wi., U.S. 190 42.37 N 89.22 W
Brodhead Creek ≃ 210 40.59 N 75.08 W
Brodheadsville 210 40.55 N 75.24 W
Brodick 46 55.35 N 5.09 W
Brodnax 192 36.42 N 78.01 W
Brodnica 30 53.16 N 19.23 E
Brodokalmak 86 55.35 N 62.06 E
Brody, Pol. 30 51.45 N 14.45 E
Brody, Ukr. 78 50.06 N 25.10 E
Broedersput 158 26.49 S 25.08 E
Broek [op Langendijk] 52 52.40 N 4.48 E
Brogan 202 44.14 N 117.30 W
Broglie 50 49.01 N 0.32 E
Brohlbach ≃ 56 50.29 N 7.20 E
Broich ✦⁸ 263 51.25 N 6.51 E
Broichweiden 56 50.49 N 6.09 E
Brok 30 52.43 N 21.52 E
Brok ∧ 123 34.32 N 76.35 E
Brokdorf 52 53.52 N 9.19 E
Broke 170 32.45 S 151.06 E
Broke Inlet ⊂ 162 34.55 S 116.25 E
Broken ≃ 169 36.41 S 146.00 E
Broken Arrow 196 36.03 N 95.47 W
Broken Bay ⊂ 170 33.34 S 151.18 E
Broken Bow, Ne., U.S. 198 41.24 N 99.38 W
Broken Bow, Ok., U.S. 194 34.01 N 94.44 W
Broken Bow Lake ◎¹ 194 34.10 N 94.40 W
Broken Cross, Eng., U.K. 262 53.15 N 2.29 W
Broken Cross, Eng., U.K. 262 53.15 N 2.10 W
Brokenhead ≃ 184 50.25 N 96.40 W
Broken Hill, Austl. 166 31.57 S 141.27 E
Broken Hill
 → Kabwe, Zam. 154 14.27 S 28.27 E
Broken Ridge ✦³ 12 31.30 S 95.00 E
Brokenstraw Creek ≃ 214 41.51 N 79.09 W
Broken Sword Creek ≃ 214 40.46 N 83.11 W
Brokopondo 250 5.04 N 54.58 W
Brokopondo □⁵ 250 4.40 N 55.00 W
Brokopondo Stuwmeer ◎¹ 250 4.45 N 55.00 W
Brölbach ≃ 56 50.47 N 7.18 E
Brolo 70 38.09 N 14.50 E
Bromberg
 → Bydgoszcz 30 53.08 N 18.00 E
Bromborough 262 53.19 N 2.59 W
Brome, P.Q., Can. 206 45.12 N 72.34 W
Brome, Dtsch. 54 52.36 N 10.56 E
Brome □⁶ 206 45.10 N 72.30 W
Brome, Lac ◎ 206 45.15 N 72.30 W
Brome, Mount ∧ 206 45.17 N 72.38 W
Bromham 42 52.09 N 0.31 W
Bromley ✦⁸ 260 51.24 N 0.02 E
Bromley Common ✦⁸ 260 51.22 N 0.03 E
Bromley Plateau ✦³ 18 32.00 S 35.00 W
Bromma ✦⁸ 40 59.21 N 17.55 E
Bromma flygplats ✈ 40 59.21 N 17.55 E
Brommö I 40 58.50 N 13.41 E
Bromo, Gunung ∧ 115a 7.57 S 112.57 E
Bromölla 26 56.04 N 14.28 E
Brompton, Eng., U.K. 44 54.22 N 1.25 W
Brompton, Eng., U.K. 260 51.23 N 0.33 E
Brompton, Lac ◎ 206 45.27 N 72.09 W
Bromptonville 206 45.28 N 71.57 W
Bromsgrove 42 52.20 N 2.03 W
Bromyard 42 52.11 N 2.30 W
Bron 62 45.44 N 4.55 E
Brønderslev 26 57.16 N 9.58 E
Bronevskaja 24 61.43 N 39.10 E
Brong-Ahafo □⁴ 150 7.45 N 1.30 W
Broni 62 45.04 N 9.16 E
Bronkhorstspruit 158 25.48 S 28.44 E
Bronkhorstspruitdam ◎¹ 158 25.55 S 28.42 E
Bronkow 54 51.40 N 13.55 E
Bronllys 42 52.01 N 3.16 W
Bronlund Peak ∧ 176 57.26 N 126.38 W
Bronn 60 49.44 N 11.28 E
Bronnae 76 52.19 N 30.29 E
Bronnicy 82 55.25 N 38.16 E
Bronnikovo 86 58.32 N 68.25 E
Brønnøysund 24 65.30 N 12.10 E
Bronnzell 56 50.31 N 9.41 E
Brøns 41 55.11 N 8.44 E
Bronson, Fl., U.S. 192 29.26 N 82.38 W
Bronson, Ks., U.S. 198 37.54 N 95.04 W
Bronson, Mi., U.S. 216 41.52 N 85.11 W
Bronson, Tx., U.S. 194 31.21 N 94.01 W
Bronson Lake ◎ 184 53.52 N 109.43 W
Bronte, It. 70 37.47 N 14.50 E
Bronte, Tx., U.S. 196 31.53 N 100.18 W
Bronte Creek ≃ 212 43.23 N 79.43 W
Bronwood 192 31.49 N 84.21 W
Bronx □⁶ 210 40.49 N 73.56 W
Bronx ✦⁸ 276 40.49 N 73.56 W
Bronx ≃ 276 40.49 N 73.52 W
Bronx Park ♦ 276 40.52 N 73.53 W
Bronxville 276 40.56 N 73.49 W
Bronx-Whitestone Bridge ✦⁵ 276 40.48 N 73.50 W
Bronx Zoo ♦ 276 40.51 N 73.53 W
Bronyts'ka Huta 78 50.56 N 27.19 E
Bronzolo (Branzoll) 64 46.24 N 11.19 E
Brooch, Lac ◎ 186 50.44 N 67.58 W
Broodsnyersplaas 158 26.03 S 29.29 E
Brook 216 40.51 N 87.21 W
Brooke 208 38.23 N 77.22 W
Brooke □⁶ 214 40.18 N 80.33 W
Brookeborough 48 54.19 N 7.24 W
Brookeland 194 31.09 N 94.00 W
Brooker 192 29.53 N 82.19 W
Brooke's Point 116 8.47 N 117.50 E
Brookfield, N.S., Can. 186 45.15 N 63.17 W
Brookfield, Ct., U.S. 207 41.28 N 73.24 W
Brookfield, Il., U.S. 216 41.49 N 87.51 W
Brookfield, Ma., U.S. 207 42.12 N 72.06 W
Brookfield, Mi., U.S. 216 42.27 N 84.47 W
Brookfield, Mo., U.S. 194 39.47 N 93.04 W
Brookfield, N.Y., U.S. 210 42.48 N 75.19 W
Brookfield, Oh., U.S. 214 41.14 N 80.34 W
Brookfield, Wi., U.S. 216 43.03 N 88.06 W
Brookfield Center 207 41.27 N 73.23 W
Brookfield Zoo ♦ 278 41.50 N 87.50 W
Brookford 192 35.42 N 81.20 W
Brookhaven, De., U.S. 285 39.42 N 75.41 W
Brookhaven, Ms., U.S. 194 31.34 N 90.26 W
Brookhaven, Pa., U.S. 285 39.52 N 75.22 W
Brookhaven National Laboratory ✦³ 207 40.54 N 72.52 W
Brookings, Or., U.S. 202 42.03 N 124.16 W
Brookings, S.D., U.S. 198 44.18 N 96.47 W
Brookland, Eng., U.K. 42 50.59 N 0.50 E
Brookland, Ar., U.S. 194 35.54 N 90.34 W
Brookland ✦⁸ 284c 38.56 N 76.59 W
Brooklands 214 42.38 N 83.06 W
Brookland Terrace 285 39.44 N 75.37 W
Brooklandville 284b 39.25 N 76.40 W
Brooklawn 285 39.52 N 75.07 W
Brooklet 192 32.22 N 81.39 W
Brooklin 212 43.57 N 78.57 W
Brookline, Ma., U.S. 207 42.21 N 71.07 W
Brookline, N.H., U.S. 207 42.44 N 71.39 W
Brooklyn, N.S., Can. 186 44.03 N 64.42 W
Brooklyn, Ct., U.S. 207 41.47 N 71.57 W
Brooklyn, Il., U.S. 219 38.39 N 90.10 W
Brooklyn, In., U.S. 218 39.32 N 86.22 W
Brooklyn, Ia., U.S. 190 41.44 N 92.26 W
Brooklyn, Mi., U.S. 216 42.06 N 84.14 W
Brooklyn, Ms., U.S. 194 31.03 N 89.11 W
Brooklyn, Oh., U.S. 214 41.26 N 81.44 W
Brooklyn, Pa., U.S. 210 41.45 N 75.48 W
Brooklyn, Wa., U.S. 224 46.47 N 123.31 W
Brooklyn, Wi., U.S. 216 42.51 N 89.22 W
Brooklyn ✦⁸, Md., U.S. 284b 39.14 N 76.36 W
Brooklyn ✦⁸, N.Y., U.S. 210 40.42 N 74.00 W
Brooklyn Battery Tunnel ✦⁵ 276 40.42 N 74.01 W
Brooklyn Bridge ✦⁵ 276 40.42 N 74.00 W
Brooklyn Center 190 45.04 N 93.19 W
Brooklyn Heights 279a 41.24 N 81.40 W
Brooklyn Marine Park ♦ 276 40.35 N 73.55 W
Brooklyn Museum ✦ 276 40.40 N 73.58 W
Brookmans Park 260 51.43 N 0.12 W
Brookmere 182 49.49 N 120.53 W
Brookmont 284c 38.57 N 77.07 W
Brookneal 192 37.03 N 78.56 W
Brook Park 214 41.23 N 81.48 W
Brookport 194 37.07 N 88.37 W
Brooks, Ab., Can. 182 50.35 N 111.53 W
Brooks, Ca., U.S. 226 38.45 N 122.09 W
Brooks, Me., U.S. 188 44.33 N 69.07 W
Brooks, Or., U.S. 224 45.02 N 122.57 W
Brooks, Mount ∧ 180 63.11 N 150.40 W
Brooks Air Force Base ■ 196 29.21 N 98.25 W
Brooks Bay ⊂ 182 50.13 N 127.55 W
Brooksburg 218 38.44 N 85.15 W
Brookshire 222 29.47 N 95.57 W
Brookside, De., U.S. 285 39.40 N 75.43 W
Brookside, N.J., U.S. 276 40.48 N 74.34 W
Brookside, Pa., U.S. 214 42.08 N 80.00 W
Brookside, Tx., U.S. 222 29.35 N 95.18 W
Brookside Park ♦ 279a 41.27 N 81.43 W
Brooks Island I 282 37.54 N 122.21 W
Brooks Mountain ∧ 180 65.33 N 167.09 W
Brooks Place 283 42.02 N 71.01 W
Brooks Range ∧ 180 68.00 N 154.00 W
Brookston 216 40.36 N 86.52 W
Brook Street 260 51.37 N 0.17 E
Brooksville, Fl., U.S. 220 28.33 N 82.23 W
Brooksville, Ky., U.S. 218 38.40 N 84.03 W
Brooksville, Ms., U.S. 194 33.14 N 88.34 W
Brookton 162 32.22 S 117.01 E
Brooktondale 210 42.23 N 76.24 W
Brookvale 274a 33.46 S 151.17 E
Brookview 210 42.32 N 73.43 W
Brookville, In., U.S. 218 39.25 N 85.00 W
Brookville, Ma., U.S. 207 42.07 N 71.00 W
Brookville, N.Y., U.S. 276 40.48 N 73.34 W
Brookville, Oh., U.S. 218 39.50 N 84.24 W
Brookville, Pa., U.S. 214 41.09 N 79.05 W
Brookville Lake ◎¹ 218 39.30 N 85.00 W
Brookwood 260 51.18 N 0.38 W
Brooloo 166 26.29 S 152.42 E
Broom, Little Loch ⊂ 46 57.54 N 5.22 W
Broom, Loch ⊂ 46 57.52 N 5.08 W
Broomall 285 39.58 N 75.21 W
Broome 162 17.58 S 122.14 E
Broome □⁶ 210 42.08 N 75.54 W
Broome County Airport ✈ 210 42.13 N 75.59 W
Broomes Island 208 38.25 N 76.32 W
Broomfield, Eng., U.K. 260 51.46 N 0.28 E
Broomfield, Eng., U.K. 260 51.14 N 0.38 E
Broomfield, Co., U.S. 200 39.55 N 105.05 W
Broons 32 48.19 N 2.16 W
Brooten 198 45.30 N 95.07 W
Brophy, Mount ∧² 162 19.11 S 128.51 E
Brora 46 58.01 N 3.51 W
Brora ≃ 46 58.01 N 3.52 W
Brørup 41 55.29 N 9.01 E
Broseley 42 52.37 N 2.29 W
Brosewere Bay ⊂ 276 40.37 N 73.42 W
Broshniv-Osada 78 49.00 N 24.13 E
Brosna ≃ 48 53.13 N 7.58 W
Brossac 32 45.20 N 0.03 W
Brossard 206 45.26 N 73.29 W
Brossasco 62 44.34 N 7.21 E
Brosso 62 45.30 N 7.48 E
Brotas de Macaúbas 255 12.00 S 42.38 W
Brothers Brook ≃ 276 41.02 N 73.36 W
Brötjärna 40 60.30 N 15.01 E
Broto 34 42.36 N 0.06 W
Brotton 44 54.34 N 0.56 W
Brou 50 48.13 N 1.11 E
Brough, Eng., U.K. 44 54.32 N 2.19 W
Brough, Eng., U.K. 44 53.44 N 0.35 W
Brough, Scot., U.K. 46 58.39 N 3.20 W
Brougham 212 43.55 N 79.06 W
Brough Head ⊱ 46 59.08 N 3.17 W
Broughshane 48 54.54 N 6.12 W
Broughton, Eng., U.K. 42 52.23 N 0.46 W
Broughton, Eng., U.K. 44 53.34 N 0.33 W
Broughton, Eng., U.K. 44 53.49 N 2.44 W
Broughton, Eng., U.K. 262 53.49 N 2.44 W
Broughton, Scot., U.K. 46 55.37 N 3.25 W
Broughton, Wales, U.K. 44 53.10 N 2.59 W
Broughton, Pa., U.S. 214 40.21 N 79.59 W
Broughton in Furness 44 54.17 N 3.12 W
Broughton Island I 176 67.35 N 63.50 W
Broughtown 46 59.15 N 2.36 W
Broughty Ferry 46 56.28 N 2.53 W
Broumov 30 50.35 N 16.20 E
Brousseval 58 48.29 N 4.58 E
Brou-sur-Chantereine 261 48.53 N 2.38 E
Brouvelieures 58 48.14 N 6.44 E
Brouwersdam ✦⁶ 52 51.46 N 3.51 E
Brouwershaven 52 51.44 N 3.54 E
Brovary 78 50.31 N 30.46 E
Brovst 26 57.06 N 9.32 E
Broward □⁶ 220 26.09 N 80.29 W
Browerville 198 46.05 N 94.51 W
Brown □⁶, Il., U.S. 219 39.59 N 90.45 W
Brown □⁶, In., U.S. 218 39.12 N 86.15 W
Brown □⁶, Oh., U.S. 218 38.52 N 83.54 W
Brown, Mount ∧ 202 48.52 N 111.09 W
Brown, Point ⊱ 224 46.56 N 124.10 W
Brownbacks 285 40.11 N 75.37 W
Brown City 190 43.12 N 82.59 W
Brown Clee Hill ∧² 42 52.28 N 2.35 W
Brown County State Park ♦ 218 39.09 N 86.14 W
Brown Creek ≃ 276 40.43 N 73.04 W
Browndale 210 41.40 N 75.27 W
Brown Deer 216 43.09 N 87.57 W
Browne Bay ⊂ 176 73.08 N 97.30 W
Brownfield 196 33.10 N 102.16 W
Brown Gelly ∧² 42 50.32 N 4.32 W
Brownhills 42 52.39 N 1.55 W
Browning, Il., U.S. 219 40.08 N 90.22 W
Browning, Mo., U.S. 194 40.02 N 93.09 W
Browning, Mt., U.S. 202 48.33 N 113.00 W
Browning Entrance ⊂ 182 53.41 N 130.32 W
Browning Island I 212 45.00 N 79.25 W
Brown Lake ◎ 176 65.55 N 91.15 W
Brownlee Park 216 42.18 N 85.05 W
Brownlee Reservoir ◎¹ 202 44.40 N 117.05 W
Brown Mountain ∧, Ca., U.S. 204 35.41 N 117.01 W
Brown Mountain ∧, Ca., U.S. 280 34.14 N 118.08 W
Brown Mountain ∧² 222 31.51 N 97.39 W
Brown Point ⊱ 276 40.43 N 73.04 W
Brownsberg, Natuurpark ♦ 250 4.50 N 55.10 W
Brownsboro 222 32.18 N 95.37 W
Browns Brook ≃ 276 41.09 N 73.17 W
Brownsburg, P.Q., Can. 206 45.41 N 74.25 W
Brownsburg, In., U.S. 218 39.50 N 86.23 W
Browns Canyon ∨ 280 34.18 N 118.35 W
Brownsdale 190 43.44 N 92.52 W
Browns Island I 282 38.02 N 121.52 W
Browns Lake 216 42.42 N 88.14 W
Brownsmead 224 46.13 N 123.32 W
Browns Mills 208 39.58 N 74.35 W
Browns Point 224 47.18 N 122.21 W
Browns Town, Jam. 241q 18.24 N 77.22 W
Brownstown, Il., U.S. 219 38.59 N 88.57 W
Brownstown, In., U.S. 218 38.52 N 86.02 W
Brownstown, Pa., U.S. 208 40.08 N 76.13 W
Brownstown Creek ≃ 281 42.06 N 83.13 W
Browns Valley, Ca., U.S. 226 39.15 N 121.23 W
Browns Valley, Mn., U.S. 198 45.35 N 96.49 W
Brownsville, On., Can. 212 42.52 N 80.50 W
Brownsville, Ca., U.S. 226 39.28 N 121.16 W
Brownsville, Fl., U.S. 220 25.50 N 80.17 W
Brownsville, In., U.S. 218 39.39 N 85.00 W
Brownsville, Ky., U.S. 194 37.11 N 86.16 W
Brownsville, La., U.S. 194 32.30 N 92.10 W
Brownsville, Or., U.S. 202 44.23 N 122.59 W
Brownsville, Pa., U.S. 214 40.01 N 79.53 W
Brownsville, Tn., U.S. 194 35.35 N 89.15 W
Brownsville, Tx., U.S. 196 25.54 N 97.29 W
Brownton 190 44.43 N 94.21 W
Browntown 276 40.24 N 74.19 W
Brownvale 182 56.08 N 117.53 W
Brownville, Al., U.S. 194 33.25 N 87.45 W
Brownville, Me., U.S. 188 45.18 N 69.02 W
Brownville, Ne., U.S. 198 40.23 N 95.39 W
Brownville, N.Y., U.S. 212 44.00 N 75.59 W
Brownville Junction 188 45.21 N 69.03 W
Brown Willy ∧² 42 50.35 N 4.36 W
Brownwood 196 31.42 N 98.59 W
Brownwood, Lake ◎¹ 196 31.51 N 99.02 W
Browse Island I 160 14.07 S 123.33 E
Broxbourne 260 51.45 N 0.01 W
Broxbourne □⁸ 260 51.44 N 0.04 W
Broxton 192 31.37 N 82.53 W
Broye ≃ 58 46.55 N 7.02 E
Broyhill Park 284c 38.51 N 77.11 W
Broža 76 52.57 N 29.07 E
Brozas 34 39.37 N 6.46 W
Brozzo 64 45.43 N 10.14 E
Brtonigla 64 45.23 N 13.38 E
Brû 58 48.21 N 6.41 E
Bruay-en-Artois 50 50.29 N 2.33 E
Bruay-sur-l'Escaut 50 50.23 N 3.32 E
Bruce, Ms., U.S. 194 33.59 N 89.20 W
Bruce, S.D., U.S. 198 44.26 N 96.53 W
Bruce, Wi., U.S. 190 45.27 N 91.16 W
Bruce □⁶ 212 44.10 N 81.25 W
Bruce, Mount ∧ 162 22.36 S 118.08 E
Bruce Bay ⊂ 172 43.35 S 169.41 E
Bruce Creek ≃ 275b 43.52 N 79.18 W
Bruce Lake 184 50.49 N 93.24 W
Bruce Lake ◎ 184 50.49 N 93.20 W

≃	River	Fluß	Río	Rivière	Rio
≅	Canal	Kanal	Canal	Canal	Canal
∟	Waterfall, Rapids	Wasserfall, Stromschnellen	Cascada, Rápidos	Chute d'eau, Rapides	Cascata, Rápidos
ꓤ	Strait	Meeresstraße	Estrecho	Détroit	Estreito
⊂	Bay, Gulf	Bucht, Golf	Bahía, Golfo	Baie, Golfe	Baía, Golfo
◎	Lake, Lakes	See, Seen	Lago, Lagos	Lac, Lacs	Lago, Lagos
≋	Swamp	Sumpf	Pantano	Marais	Pântano
❄	Ice Features, Glacier	Eis- und Gletscherformen	Accidentes Glaciales	Formes glaciaires	Acidentes glaciares
✦	Other Hydrographic Features	Andere Hydrographische Objekte	Otros Elementos Hidrográficos	Autres données hydrographiques	Outros acidentes hidrográficos

✦	Submarine Features	Untermeerische Objekte	Accidentes Submarinos	Formes de relief sous-marin	Acidentes submarinos
□	Political Unit	Politische Einheit	Unidad Política	Entité politique	Unidade política
✦	Cultural Institution	Kulturelle Institution	Institución Cultural	Institution culturelle	Instituição cultural
⊥	Historical Site	Historische Stätte	Sitio Histórico	Site historique	Sitio histórico
♦	Recreational Site	Erholungs- und Ferienort	Sitio de Recreo	Centre de loisirs	Área de Lazer
✈	Airport	Flughafen	Aeropuerto	Aéroport	Aeroporto
■	Military Installation	Militäranlage	Instalación Militar	Installation militaire	Instalação militar
✦	Miscellaneous	Verschiedenes	Misceláneo	Divers	Diversos

ESPAÑOL

Nombre	Página	Lat.°′	Long.°′ W = Oeste
Bully Creek ≃	202	43.58 N	117.15 W
Bully Hill	214	41.22 N	79.50 W
Bully-les-Mines	50	50.26 N	2.43 E
Bulmke-Hüllen •[8]	263	51.31 N	7.06 E
Bulnaj nuruu ⋌	88	49.05 N	98.30 E
Bulnes	252	36.44 S	72.18 W
Bulo Ghedudo	144	2.52 N	43.01 E
Bulolo	164	7.10 S	146.40 E
Bulpham	260	51.33 N	0.22 E
Bulpitt	219	39.35 N	89.26 W
Bulsār	122	20.38 N	72.56 E
Bulstrode ≃	206	46.02 N	72.15 W
Bultei	71	40.27 N	9.03 E
Bultfontein	158	28.20 S	26.05 E
Buluan	116	6.44 N	124.47 E
Buluan ≃	116	6.47 N	124.47 E
Buluan, Lake ⊜	116	6.40 N	124.49 E
Buluduku	114	2.20 N	98.14 E
Bulugansk	88	52.24 N	110.23 E
Bulukumba	112	5.33 S	120.11 E
Bulukuto	152	0.12 S	21.42 E
Bululawang	115a	8.05 S	112.38 E
Bulungu, R.D.C.	152	6.04 S	21.54 E
Bulungu, R.D.C.	152	4.33 S	18.36 E
Bulupayung	114	1.38 N	99.11 E
Bulusan	116	12.45 N	124.08 E
Bulusan Volcano ∧	116	12.46 N	124.03 E
Bulwater	158	32.29 S	21.48 E
Bulwer	158	29.46 S	29.47 E
Bulyčevo	82	55.06 N	37.15 E
Bulyee	162	32.22 S	117.31 E
Bumba	152	2.11 N	22.28 E
Bumbah, Khalīj al- ⊂	146	32.20 N	23.10 E
Bumbire Island I	154	1.40 S	31.53 E
Bumbles Green	260	51.44 N	0.02 E
Bumbo	152	6.55 S	19.16 E
Bumbu ≃	273b	4.23 S	15.18 E
Bumbulan	112	0.29 N	122.04 E
Bumbun, Pulau I	112	4.27 N	118.40 E
Bumbuna	150	9.03 N	11.44 W
Bumbunga Lake ⊜	168b	33.54 S	138.11 E
Bumiayu	115a	7.15 S	109.00 E
Bumijawa	115a	7.10 S	109.07 E
Bumkin Island I	283	42.17 N	70.54 W
Bumping ≃	224	46.59 N	121.06 W
Bumping Lake ⊜	224	46.52 N	121.19 W
Bumpus, Mount ∧[2]	176	69.33 N	112.40 W
Bumtang ≃	124	26.56 N	90.51 E
Bumu Hu ⊜	120	31.15 N	91.10 E
Buna, Kenya	154	2.47 N	39.31 E
Buna, Pap. N. Gui.	164	8.40 S	148.25 E
Buna, Tx., U.S.	194	30.26 N	93.58 W
Buna, R.D.C.	152	3.15 S	18.59 E
Bunagāti	126	23.19 N	89.25 E
Bunai	164	2.11 S	147.14 E
Bunaj	85	38.26 N	71.32 E
Bun'atino	82	56.24 N	37.15 E
Bunavista	196	35.39 N	101.28 W
Bunawan	116	8.12 N	125.57 E
Bunazi	154	1.13 S	31.24 E
Bunbeg	48	55.03 N	8.18 W
Bunbury	168a	33.19 S	115.38 E
Bunceton	194	38.47 N	92.47 W
Bunclody	48	52.38 N	6.40 W
Buncrana	48	55.08 N	7.27 W
Bundaberg	166	24.52 S	152.21 E
Bundanoon	170	34.39 S	150.18 E
Bundarra	166	30.10 S	151.05 E
Bunde, Dtsch.	52	53.11 N	7.16 E
Bünde, Dtsch.	52	52.12 N	8.35 E
Bunde, Ned.	56	50.54 N	5.45 E
Bundeena	274a	34.05 S	151.09 E
Bundey ≃	162	21.46 S	135.37 E
Bündheim	54	51.53 N	10.32 E
Būndi, India	120	25.27 N	75.39 E
Bundi, Pap. N. Gui.	164	5.40 S	145.15 E
Bundick Creek ≃	194	30.36 N	92.57 W
Bundoora	274b	37.42 S	145.04 E
Bundoran	48	54.28 N	8.17 W
Būndu, India	124	23.11 N	85.35 E
Bundu, S. Afr.	158	29.45 S	22.02 E
Bunduqiyah	154	5.06 N	30.53 E
Bund'ur	86	57.32 N	82.01 E
Buner □[9]	123	34.35 N	72.35 E
Bunessan	46	56.19 N	6.14 W
Bunga	150	11.04 N	9.38 E
Bunga ≃	150	11.23 N	9.56 E
Bungamas	112	3.42 S	102.23 E
Bungay	42	52.28 N	1.26 E
Bungbulang	115a	7.27 S	107.35 E
Bunge	26	57.51 N	19.01 E
Bungegep	164	7.48 S	139.52 E
Bungendore	171b	35.15 S	149.27 E
Bunger Hills ⋌[2]	9	66.17 S	100.47 E
Bung Kan	110	18.23 N	103.37 E
Bungku	112	2.33 S	121.58 E
Bungo	152	7.26 S	15.23 E
Bungoma	154	0.34 N	34.34 E
Bungonia	170	34.51 S	149.57 E
Bungo-suidō ⋓	92	33.00 N	132.13 E
Bungo-takada	96	33.33 N	131.27 E
Bungsberg ∧[2]	54	54.12 N	10.43 E
Bungtlang	120	22.20 N	92.46 E
Bungu	154	7.38 S	39.03 E
Buni ≃	115a	7.26 S	106.47 E
Bunia	154	1.34 N	30.15 E
Bunianga	152	3.34 S	20.06 E
Būnīken, Kūh-e ∧	128	26.46 N	58.12 E
Buninyong	169	37.39 S	143.53 E
Buninyong, Mount ∧	169	37.39 S	143.56 E
Bunji	123	35.40 N	74.36 E
Bunkeflo strand	41	55.33 N	12.57 E
Bunker	194	37.27 N	91.12 W
Bunker Group II	166	23.48 S	152.20 E
Bunker Hill, Il., U.S.	219	39.02 N	89.57 W
Bunker Hill, In., U.S.	216	40.40 N	86.06 W
Bunker Hill, Or., U.S.	202	43.21 N	124.12 W
Bunker Hill, Tx., U.S.	222	29.46 N	95.32 W
Bunker Hill ∧	204	39.15 N	117.08 W
Bunker Hill Monument ⊥	283	42.22 N	71.04 W
Bunkeya	154	10.07 S	27.17 E
Bunkie	194	30.57 N	92.10 W
Bunkyō •[8]	268	35.43 N	139.45 E
Bunnahowen	48	54.11 N	9.54 W
Bunnell	192	29.27 N	81.15 W
Bunnik	52	52.04 N	5.12 E
Bünningstedt	52	53.41 N	10.13 E
Bunola	214	40.14 N	79.56 W
Bun Plains ≚	154	0.44 N	40.42 E
Bunratty Castle ⊥	48	52.42 N	8.48 W
Bunschoten	52	52.14 N	5.22 E
Bunsuru ≃	150	13.21 N	6.23 E
Bunta	112	0.48 S	122.10 E
Buntine	162	29.59 S	116.34 E
Buntingford	42	51.57 N	0.01 W
Buntok	112	1.42 S	114.48 E
Bununu Dass	150	10.00 N	9.31 E
Bunut	112	0.46 N	112.30 E
Bunyambili	154	2.21 S	29.25 E
Bünyan	130	38.51 N	35.52 E
Bunyip	169	38.06 S	145.43 E
Bunyip ≃	169	38.13 S	145.27 E
Bunyolo	34	39.25 N	0.47 W
Bunyrevo	82	54.34 N	37.09 E
Bunyu, Pulau I	112	3.30 N	117.50 E
Bunza	150	12.08 N	4.00 E
Buochs	58	46.58 N	8.22 E
Buol	112	1.10 N	121.26 E
Buolkalach	74	72.56 N	119.50 E
Buonalbergo	68	41.13 N	14.59 E
Buona Vista	271c	1.16 N	103.47 E
Buon Bu N'jang	110	12.06 N	107.40 E
Buonconvento	66	43.08 N	11.29 E
Buon Me Thuot	110	12.40 N	108.03 E
Buon Mrong	110	12.48 N	108.28 E
Buon Ngo	110	12.30 N	108.28 E
Buon Thach Hom	110	12.17 N	108.48 E
Buon Ya Soup	110	13.05 N	107.52 E
Buor-Chaja, guba ⊂	74	71.30 N	131.00 E

FRANÇAIS

Nom	Page	Lat.°′	Long.°′ W = Ouest
Buor-Chaja, mys ≻	74	71.56 N	132.40 E
Bupul	164	7.31 S	140.52 E
Buqay'āwīyah, Qā' al- ≚	132	32.03 N	37.07 E
Buqayq	128	25.56 N	49.40 E
Buqda Koosaar	144	4.31 N	44.49 E
Buqde Caqable	144	4.04 N	45.15 E
Buquira ≃	256	23.10 S	45.54 W
Buquirivu ≃	287b	23.28 S	46.28 W
Buqūm, Ḥarrat al- ⩡[9]	144	20.54 N	42.00 E
Bur	88	58.47 N	107.01 E
Bura, Kenya	154	3.30 S	38.18 E
Bura, Kenya	154	1.06 S	39.57 E
Bura Gaurānga ≃[1]	126	22.00 N	90.33 E
Burakin	162	30.31 S	117.10 E
Buraly	80	55.04 N	52.52 E
Buram	140	10.49 N	25.10 E
Buran	86	48.04 N	85.15 E
Burangulovo	86	53.26 N	58.23 E
Buranhém ≃	255	16.27 S	39.04 W
Burankol'	86	46.14 N	54.12 E
Burannoje	86	50.59 N	54.28 E
Burano ≃	66	43.37 N	12.40 E
Burao Kibir	144	8.42 N	45.29 E
Burāq	132	33.10 N	36.29 E
Burāri •[8]	272a	28.46 N	77.12 E
Buras	194	29.21 N	89.31 W
Buraševo	82	56.44 N	35.52 E
Burauen	116	10.58 N	124.53 E
Burayd, Bi'r ⊤[4]	142	29.08 N	32.07 E
Buraydah	128	26.20 N	43.59 E
Burayk	146	26.33 N	13.08 E
Buraykah	132	32.50 N	36.34 E
Burbach	56	50.45 N	8.05 E
Burbage, Eng., U.K.	42	51.20 N	1.40 W
Burbage, Eng., U.K.	262	53.15 N	1.56 W
Burbank, Ca., U.S.	226	37.19 N	121.55 W
Burbank, Ca., U.S.	228	34.10 N	118.18 W
Burbank, Il., U.S.	216	41.45 N	87.45 W
Burbank, Il., U.S.	278	41.45 N	87.46 W
Burbank, Oh., U.S.	214	40.59 N	81.59 W
Burbank, Wa., U.S.	202	46.12 N	119.00 W
Burbank Studios ⊌[3]	280	34.09 N	118.21 W
Burbure	50	50.32 N	2.28 E
Burç	130	37.02 N	37.10 E
Burcei	71	39.21 N	9.21 E
Burcevo	82	55.02 N	38.09 E
Burcher	166	33.32 S	147.18 E
Burcin	62	45.26 N	5.26 E
Burco	144	9.31 N	45.34 E
Burda	124	25.50 N	77.35 E
Burdalyk	128	38.25 N	64.20 E
Burdekin ≃	166	19.39 S	147.30 E
Burdekin Falls ∟	166	20.39 S	147.09 E
Burden	198	37.18 N	96.45 W
Burdeos → Bordeaux, Fr.	32	44.50 N	0.34 W
Burdeos, Pil.	116	14.51 N	121.58 E
Burdeos Bay ⊂	116	14.44 N	122.06 E
Burdett, Ab., Can.	182	49.50 N	111.32 W
Burdett, Ks., U.S.	198	38.11 N	99.31 W
Burdett, N.Y., U.S.	210	42.25 N	76.50 W
Burdul	272c	19.07 N	73.07 E
Burdur	130	37.43 N	30.17 E
Burdur □[4]	130	37.30 N	30.00 E
Burdur Gölü ⊜	130	37.44 N	30.12 E
Burdwood Bank ⊹[3]	18	54.15 S	59.00 W
Bure, Ityo.	144	8.15 N	35.09 E
Bure, Ityo.	144	10.47 N	37.06 E
Bure ≃	42	52.37 N	1.43 E
Bure, Pic de ∧	62	44.38 N	5.56 E
Bureå	26	64.37 N	21.12 E
Bureälven ≃	26	64.37 N	21.13 E
Bureg Changaj	88	48.14 N	103.57 E
Bureinskij chrebet ⋌	89	50.35 N	133.35 E
Bureja	89	49.52 N	129.48 E
Bureja ≃	89	49.25 N	129.35 E
Burekup	168a	33.19 S	115.49 E
Büren, Dtsch.	52	51.33 N	8.33 E
Büren, Mong.	88	47.13 N	95.54 E
Büren an der Aare	58	47.08 N	7.23 E
Büren Chaan	88	49.29 N	99.14 E
Bürengijn nuruu ⋌	88	49.15 N	104.30 E
Bures	261	48.57 N	1.58 E
Bures-sur-Yvette	261	48.42 N	2.10 E
Burey-en-Vaux	58	48.34 N	5.40 E
Burfjord	24	69.56 N	22.00 E
Burford, On., Can.	212	43.06 N	80.26 W
Burford, Eng., U.K.	42	51.49 N	1.38 W
Būr Fu'ād •[8]	142	31.15 N	32.19 E
Burg, Dtsch.	54	51.49 N	14.08 E
Burg, Dtsch.	54	52.16 N	11.51 E
Burg, Dtsch.	56	50.42 N	8.19 E
Burg •[8]	263	51.08 N	7.09 E
Burg, Schloss ⊥	263	51.08 N	7.10 E
Burga	76	58.45 N	32.29 E
Burgas	38	42.30 N	27.28 E
Burgas □[4], Blg.	38	42.36 N	26.41 E
Burgas □[4], Blg.	130	42.10 N	27.00 E
Burgaski Zaliv ⊂	38	42.30 N	27.33 E
Burgau	58	48.26 N	10.25 E
Burg [auf Fehmarn]	54	54.26 N	11.12 E
Burgaw	192	34.33 N	77.55 W
Burgaz •[8]	267b	40.53 N	29.03 E
Burgaz Adası I	267b	40.53 N	29.04 E
Burgbernheim	56	49.27 N	10.19 E
Burgdorf, Dtsch.	52	52.27 N	10.00 E
Burgdorf, Schw.	58	47.04 N	7.37 E
Burgebrach	56	49.50 N	10.44 E
Bürgel	54	50.56 N	11.45 E
Burgenland □[3]	61	47.30 N	16.20 E
Burgeo	186	47.37 N	57.37 W
Burgersdorp	158	31.00 S	26.20 E
Burger Township	273d	26.05 S	27.46 E
Burges, Mount ∧[2]	162	30.50 S	121.06 E
Burgess	208	37.53 N	76.21 W
Burgess Hill	42	50.57 N	0.07 W
Burgessville	212	43.01 N	80.39 W
Burgettstown	214	40.22 N	80.23 W
Burggrafenberg ∧[2]	263	51.13 N	7.07 E
Burghaun	56	50.42 N	9.44 E
Burghausen	60	48.09 N	12.49 E
Burghead	46	57.42 N	3.30 W
Burgheim	60	48.42 N	11.01 E
Burgh Heath	260	51.18 N	0.13 W
Burghill	214	41.22 N	80.34 W
Burgh le Marsh	44	53.09 N	0.15 E
Burghūth, Sabkhat al- ⊜	130	34.58 N	41.06 E
Burgin	194	37.45 N	84.46 W
Burgio	70	37.36 N	13.17 E
Burgjoss	56	50.12 N	9.29 E
Burgkirchen, Dtsch.	64	48.10 N	12.44 E
Burgkirchen, Öst.	60	48.12 N	13.06 E
Burgkunstadt	54	50.08 N	11.14 E
Bürglen, Schw.	58	46.53 N	8.40 E
Bürglen, Schw.	58	47.33 N	9.09 E
Burglengenfeld	60	49.13 N	12.03 E
Burgo de Osma	34	41.35 N	3.04 W
Burgoon	214	41.16 N	83.15 W
Burgos, Esp.	34	42.21 N	3.42 W
Burgos, It.	71	40.23 N	8.59 E
Burgos, Méx.	232	24.57 N	98.47 W
Burgos, Pil.	116	16.04 N	119.52 E
Burgos, Pil.	116	15.30 N	120.24 E
Burgos □[4]	34	42.20 N	3.40 W
Burgsinn	56	50.09 N	9.38 E
Burgstädt	54	50.55 N	12.49 E
Burgstall, Dtsch.	54	52.24 N	11.41 E
Burgstall → Postal, It.	64	46.36 N	11.11 E
Burg Stargard	54	53.29 N	13.18 E
Burgsvik	26	57.03 N	18.16 E
Burgueño, Arroyo ≃	288	34.24 S	58.47 W
Burgund → Bourgogne □[9]	32	47.00 N	4.30 E
Burgundy → Bourgogne □[9]	32	47.00 N	4.30 E
Burgusio (Burgeis)	64	46.42 N	10.31 E
Burgwedel	52	52.29 N	9.51 E

PORTUGUÊS

Nome	Página	Lat.°′	Long.°′ W = Oeste
Burgwindheim	56	49.49 N	10.35 E
Burhābalang ≃	126	21.28 N	87.04 E
Burham	260	51.20 N	0.29 E
Burhan Budai Shan ⋌	102	36.00 N	96.00 E
Burhaniye, Tür.	130	37.57 N	28.45 E
Burhaniye, Tür.	130	39.30 N	26.58 E
Burhānpur	120	21.18 N	76.14 E
Burhar	124	23.13 N	81.32 E
Burhave	52	53.34 N	8.21 E
Burholme •[8]	285	40.03 N	75.05 W
Buri	255	23.48 S	48.35 W
Burias Island I	116	12.57 N	123.08 E
Burias Pass ⋓	116	13.00 N	123.15 E
Buribaj	86	51.57 N	58.11 E
Būr Ibrāhīm •[8]	142	29.57 N	32.34 E
Burica, Punta ≻	236	8.03 N	82.53 W
Burien	224	47.28 N	122.20 W
Burigi, Lake ⊜	154	2.05 S	31.15 E
Burila Mare	38	44.27 N	22.34 E
Burin	186	47.02 N	55.10 W
Burin Peninsula ≻[1]	186	47.00 N	55.40 W
Buri Ram	110	15.00 N	103.07 E
Buriswar ≃[1]	126	21.58 N	90.02 E
Buritama	255	21.03 S	50.08 W
Buriti, Bra.	250	3.55 S	42.57 W
Buriti, Bra.	255	16.27 S	53.27 W
Buriti ≃	248	12.50 S	58.28 W
Buriti Alegre	255	18.09 S	49.03 W
Buriti Bravo	250	5.50 S	43.50 W
Buriticupu ≃	250	4.13 S	46.33 W
Buriti dos Lopes	250	3.10 S	41.52 W
Buritizeiro	255	17.21 S	44.58 W
Būriya	124	30.09 N	77.21 E
Burj al-'Arab	140	30.55 N	29.32 E
Burjassot	34	39.31 N	0.25 W
Burjatija □[3], Ross.	74	53.00 N	109.00 E
Burjatija □[3], Ross.	88	53.00 N	109.00 E
Burji	144	5.20 N	37.57 E
Burj Islām	130	35.41 N	35.48 E
Burj Mughayzil	142	31.27 N	30.23 E
Burkan ≃	85	41.43 N	76.46 E
Burkau	54	51.10 N	14.10 E
Burkburnett	196	34.05 N	98.34 W
Burke, S.D., U.S.	198	43.10 N	99.17 W
Burke, Tx., U.S.	222	31.14 N	94.46 W
Burke, Va., U.S.	284c	38.47 N	77.16 W
Burke ≃	166	23.12 S	139.33 E
Burke Channel ⋓	182	52.07 N	127.38 W
Burke Island I	9	73.15 S	104.35 W
Burke Lake ⊜[1]	284c	38.46 N	77.18 W
Burke Lake County Park ♠	284c	38.45 N	77.18 W
Burke Lakefront Airport ⊠	279a	41.31 N	81.41 W
Burkesville	194	36.47 N	85.22 W
Burket	216	41.09 N	85.58 W
Burketown	166	17.43 S	139.34 E
Burkett Gardens	226	37.57 N	121.15 W
Burkettsville	216	40.21 N	84.39 W
Burkhardtsdorf	54	50.44 N	12.55 E
Burkina Faso □[1], Afr.	134	13.00 N	1.30 W
Burkina Faso □[1], Afr.	150	13.00 N	1.30 W
Burkit	80	47.03 N	50.42 E
Burksville	219	38.16 N	90.09 W
Burla	86	53.19 N	78.21 E
Burla ≃	86	53.20 N	78.02 E
Burladingen	58	48.17 N	9.07 E
Burleigh	208	39.02 N	74.51 W
Burleigh Falls	212	44.34 N	78.13 W
Burleigh Heads	171a	28.06 S	153.27 E
Burleson	222	32.32 N	97.19 W
Burleson □[6]	222	30.30 N	96.43 W
Burley, Id., U.S.	202	42.32 N	113.47 W
Burley, Wa., U.S.	224	47.25 N	122.37 W
Burley Griffin, Lake ⊜	171b	35.13 S	149.05 E
Burli	86	53.36 N	61.55 E
Burlin	80	51.25 N	52.44 E
Burlingame, Ca., U.S.	226	37.35 N	122.21 W
Burlingame, Ks., U.S.	198	38.45 N	95.00 W
Burlingame State Park ♠	207	41.22 N	71.43 W
Burlington, Nf., Can.	186	49.45 N	56.02 W
Burlington, On., Can.	212	43.19 N	79.47 W
Burlington, Co., U.S.	198	39.18 N	102.16 W
Burlington, Ct., U.S.	207	41.46 N	72.57 W
Burlington, Il., U.S.	216	42.03 N	88.33 W
Burlington, In., U.S.	216	40.29 N	86.24 W
Burlington, Ia., U.S.	190	40.48 N	91.06 W
Burlington, Ks., U.S.	198	38.11 N	95.44 W
Burlington, Ky., U.S.	218	39.01 N	84.43 W
Burlington, Ma., U.S.	207	42.30 N	71.11 W
Burlington, Mi., U.S.	216	42.06 N	85.05 W
Burlington, N.J., U.S.	208	40.04 N	74.51 W
Burlington, N.C., U.S.	192	36.05 N	79.26 W
Burlington, N.D., U.S.	198	48.16 N	101.25 W
Burlington, Pa., U.S.	210	41.47 N	76.37 W
Burlington, Tx., U.S.	222	31.01 N	96.60 W
Burlington, Vt., U.S.	188	44.28 N	73.12 W
Burlington, Wa., U.S.	224	48.28 N	122.19 W
Burlington, Wi., U.S.	216	42.40 N	88.16 W
Burlington, Wy., U.S.	202	44.26 N	108.25 W
Burlington □[6]	208	39.50 N	74.47 W
Burlington Beach	216	41.30 N	87.03 W
Burlington County Airpark ⊠	285	39.56 N	74.50 W
Burlington Island I	285	40.05 N	74.51 W
Burlington Junction	194	40.26 N	95.03 W
Burlington Mall •[9]	283	42.29 N	71.13 W
Burlit	89	46.33 N	134.14 E
Burluk	80	50.34 N	44.33 E
Burma → Myanmar □[1]	110	22.00 N	98.00 E
Burmā, Tall ∧	132	30.38 N	35.50 E
Burmakino	80	57.27 N	40.20 E
Burn ≃	44	54.12 N	1.38 W
Burnaby	224	49.15 N	122.57 W
Burnaby Island I	182	52.24 N	131.20 W
Burnage	262	53.26 N	2.12 W
Burnas, ozero ⊜	78	45.52 N	30.08 E
Burnet	196	30.45 N	98.13 W
Burnett ≃	166	24.46 S	152.25 E
Burnett Bay ⊂	176	73.53 N	124.00 W
Burnett Brook ≃	276	40.46 N	74.38 W
Burnett Heads	166	24.46 S	152.25 E
Burnettsville	216	40.46 N	86.36 W
Burney, Ca., U.S.	204	40.52 N	121.39 W
Burney, In., U.S.	218	39.19 N	85.38 W
Burnham, Eng., U.K.	42	51.33 N	0.39 W
Burnham, Il., U.S.	278	41.39 N	87.34 W
Burnham, Pa., U.S.	208	40.38 N	77.34 W
Burnham Beeches •[3]	260	51.34 N	0.38 W
Burnham Market	42	52.57 N	0.44 E
Burnham-on-Crouch	42	51.38 N	0.49 E
Burnham-on-Sea	42	51.15 N	3.00 W
Burnhamthorpe	275b	43.37 N	79.36 W
Burnhaven	46	57.29 N	1.47 W
Burnie	166	41.04 S	145.54 E
Burning Tree Estates	284c	39.01 N	77.12 W
Burnips	216	42.44 N	85.50 W
Burniston	44	54.19 N	0.26 W
Burnley	44	53.48 N	2.14 W
Burnley □[8]	262	53.46 N	2.15 W
Burnley Creek ≃	212	44.13 N	77.51 W
Burnley Football Ground ♠	262	53.48 N	2.14 W
Burnmouth	46	55.50 N	2.04 W
Burnoje	85	42.37 N	70.46 E
Burnookt'abr'skoje	85	42.42 N	70.49 E
Burnpur	126	23.40 N	86.57 E
Burns, Ks., U.S.	198	38.05 N	96.53 W
Burns, Or., U.S.	202	43.35 N	119.03 W
Burns, Tn., U.S.	194	36.03 N	87.18 W
Burns, Wy., U.S.	198	41.11 N	104.21 W
Burns Creek ≃	198	47.22 N	104.25 W
Burns Flat	196	35.20 N	99.10 W
Burns Harbor	216	41.37 N	87.10 W
Burnside, Austl.	168b	34.57 S	138.40 E
Burnside, Ky., U.S.	192	36.59 N	84.36 W
Burnside, Pa., U.S.	214	40.49 N	78.47 W

Burnside ≃	176	66.51 N	108.04 W
Burnside, Lake ⊜	162	25.33 S	123.02 E
Burns Lake	182	54.14 N	125.46 W
Burnsville, Al., U.S.	194	32.28 N	86.53 W
Burnsville, Ms., U.S.	194	34.50 N	88.18 W
Burnsville, N.C., U.S.	192	35.55 N	82.18 W
Burnsville, W.V., U.S.	188	38.51 N	80.39 W
Burnt ≃, On., Can.	212	44.35 N	78.46 W
Burnt ≃, Or., U.S.	202	44.22 N	117.14 W
Burnt Cabins	214	40.05 N	77.54 W
Burnt Corn Creek ≃	194	31.06 N	87.04 W
Burnt Hills	210	42.54 N	73.53 W
Burnt Island, Nf., Can.	186	47.36 N	58.53 W
Burntisland, Scot., U.K.	46	56.03 N	3.15 W
Burnt Meadow Brook ≃	276	41.05 N	74.18 W
Burnt Mills, Lake ⊜	208	36.50 N	76.38 W
Burnt Mills Hills	284c	39.02 N	77.00 W
Burnt Mills Manor	284c	39.02 N	77.00 W
Burnt Mountain ∧	228	33.12 N	117.04 W
Burntop	158	26.49 S	30.54 E
Burnt Pine	174c	29.02 S	167.56 E
Burnt Pond ⊜	186	48.11 N	57.24 W
Burntwick Island I	260	51.25 N	0.41 E
Burntwood	42	52.41 N	1.56 W
Burntwood ≃	184	56.08 N	96.30 W
Burntwood Lake ⊜	184	55.29 N	100.07 W
Burnyj, porog ∟	86	57.43 N	95.18 E
Buro	144	11.28 N	49.41 E
Buron	84	42.48 N	44.03 E
Buronzo	62	45.29 N	8.16 E
Burow	54	53.46 N	13.16 E
Burpengary	171a	27.10 S	152.57 E
Burpham	260	51.15 N	0.33 W
Burqin	86	47.43 N	86.53 E
Burqin ≃	86	47.40 N	86.55 E
Burra	166	33.40 S	138.56 E
Burra Burra Creek ≃	170	34.10 S	149.38 E
Burracoppin	162	31.23 S	118.29 E
Burra Creek ≃	168b	33.51 S	139.18 E
Burrage	283	42.02 N	70.51 W
Burrage Pond ⊜	283	42.01 N	70.52 W
Burragorang, Lake ⊜[1]	170	33.57 S	150.26 E
Burramurra	166	20.30 S	137.20 E
Burravoe	46a	60.32 N	1.28 W
Burrawang	170	34.36 S	150.31 E
Burray I	46	58.51 N	2.54 W
Burrel, Shq.	38	41.37 N	20.00 E
Burrel, Ca., U.S.	226	36.30 N	119.59 W
Burrendong Reservoir ⊜[1]	166	32.39 S	149.15 E
Burren Junction	166	30.06 S	148.58 E
Burrill Lake ⊂	170	35.23 S	150.27 E
Burrinjuck Reservoir ⊜[1]	166	35.00 S	148.45 E
Burro, Serranías del ⋌	196	29.10 N	102.05 W
Burr Oak, In., U.S.	216	41.15 N	86.25 W
Burr Oak, Ks., U.S.	198	39.51 N	98.18 W
Burr Oak, Mi., U.S.	216	41.50 N	85.19 W
Burro Burro ≃	246	4.48 N	58.51 W
Burro Creek ≃	200	34.32 N	113.35 W
Burro Peak ∧	200	32.35 N	108.26 W
Burrowa, Mount ∧	171b	36.05 S	147.42 E
Burrowa-Pine Mountain National Park ♠	171b	36.06 S	147.44 E
Burrow Head ≻	44	54.41 N	4.24 W
Burrowhill	260	51.21 N	0.36 W
Burrows	216	40.40 N	86.30 W
Burrows Island I	224	48.29 N	122.42 W
Burr Ridge	278	41.46 N	87.55 W
Burrs Mill Brook ≃	285	39.53 N	74.42 W
Burrton	198	38.01 N	97.40 W
Burrumbeet, Lake ⊜	169	37.30 S	143.39 E
Burrundie	164	13.32 S	131.42 E
Burruyacú	252	26.30 S	64.45 W
Burrwood	194	28.58 N	89.22 W
Burry Holms I	42	51.37 N	4.18 W
Burry Port	42	51.42 N	4.15 W
Bürs	58	47.09 N	9.48 E
Bursa	130	40.11 N	29.04 E
Bursa □[4]	130	40.10 N	29.00 E
Būr Safājah	140	26.44 N	33.56 E
Būr Sa'īd (Port Said)	142	31.16 N	32.18 E
Būr Sa'īd □[4]	142	30.36 N	32.15 E
Burscheid	56	51.05 N	7.06 E
Burscough	262	53.35 N	2.51 W
Burscough Bridge	44	53.36 N	2.52 W
Bursey, Mount ∧	9	76.00 S	132.40 W
Burshtyn	78	49.17 N	24.37 E
Bursol'	86	53.11 N	78.27 E
Bürstadt	56	49.38 N	8.27 E
Burstall	184	50.40 N	109.54 W
Būr Sūdān (Port Sudan)	140	19.37 N	37.14 E
Burt, Ia., U.S.	190	43.11 N	94.13 W
Burt, N.Y., U.S.	210	43.19 N	78.43 W
Būr Tawfīq •[8]	128	29.57 N	32.34 E
Burtenbach	58	48.20 N	10.26 E
Burt Lake ⊜	190	45.27 N	84.40 W
Burtnieks ezers ⊜	76	57.45 N	25.16 E
Burton, B.C., Can.	182	49.59 N	117.54 W
Burton, Eng., U.K.	42	50.44 N	1.45 W
Burton, Eng., U.K.	262	53.16 N	3.01 W
Burton, Il., U.S.	219	39.55 N	91.15 W
Burton, Mi., U.S.	216	43.01 N	84.16 W
Burton, Mi., U.S.	216	43.02 N	83.36 W
Burton, Oh., U.S.	214	41.28 N	81.08 W
Burton, Tx., U.S.	222	30.11 N	96.36 W
Burton, Wa., U.S.	224	47.23 N	122.27 W
Burton, Lake ⊜[1]	192	34.50 N	83.33 W
Burton Fleming	44	54.08 N	0.20 W
Burton Latimer	42	52.23 N	0.41 W
Burtons Bridge	216	42.17 N	88.14 W
Burton Seamount ⊹[3]	14	32.00 S	171.45 W
Burtonsville	208	39.07 N	76.56 W
Burton upon Stather	44	53.39 N	0.41 W
Burton upon Trent	42	52.49 N	1.36 W
Burtonwood	262	53.26 N	2.39 W
Burtonwood Airfield ⊠	262	53.24 N	2.39 W
Burträsk	26	64.31 N	20.39 E
Burtundy	166	33.44 S	142.16 E
Burṭus	142	30.09 N	31.08 E
Buru I	108	3.24 S	126.40 E
Buruanga	116	11.51 N	121.53 E
Burukan	89	53.02 N	136.03 E
Buruldaj	85	42.48 N	75.52 E
Burullus, Buḥayrat al- ⊜	142	31.30 N	30.50 E
Burūm	144	14.22 N	48.57 E
Burundaj	85	43.23 N	76.51 E
Burundi □[1], Afr.	138	3.15 S	30.00 E
Burundi □[1], Afr.	154	3.15 S	30.00 E
Burundučicha	80	58.21 N	46.07 E
Burun-Šibertuj, gora ∧	88	49.42 N	109.59 E
Bururi	154	3.57 S	29.37 E
Burutu	150	5.21 N	5.31 E
Buruz Bāgān	126	23.03 N	89.00 E
Burwash	190	46.19 N	80.48 W
Burwash Landing	180	61.21 N	139.00 W
Burwell, Eng., U.K.	42	52.16 N	0.19 E
Burwell, Ne., U.S.	198	41.46 N	99.07 W
Burwell Bay ⊂	208	37.04 N	76.38 W
Burwick	46	58.44 N	2.57 W
Burwood, Austl.	274a	33.53 S	151.06 E
Burwood, Austl.	274b	37.51 S	145.06 E
Bury, P.Q., Can.	206	45.28 N	71.30 W
Bury, Eng., U.K.	42	50.54 N	0.34 W
Bury, Eng., U.K.	44	53.36 N	2.17 W
Bury □[8]	262	53.35 N	2.19 W
Buryatia → Burjatija □[3]	88	53.00 N	109.00 E
Buryn'	78	51.13 N	33.49 E
Bury Saint Edmunds	42	52.15 N	0.43 E
Burzaco	258	34.49 S	58.24 W
Burzet	62	44.44 N	4.15 E
Burzil	123	34.52 N	75.07 E
Burzil Pass)(	123	34.54 N	75.06 E
Būṣ, Ghubbat al- ⊂	142	29.36 N	32.22 E
Busa, Mount ∧	116	6.08 N	124.39 E
Busachi	71	40.02 N	8.54 E
Busalla	62	44.34 N	8.57 E
Busambra, Rocca ∧	70	37.51 N	13.24 E
Busan → Pusan	98	35.06 N	129.03 E
Busana	64	44.22 N	10.19 E
Busanga	152	0.51 S	22.04 E
Busanga Swamp ⩩	154	14.10 S	25.50 E
Busangu	154	8.32 S	25.31 E
Buṣayrah	130	35.09 N	40.26 E
Busby, Austl.	274a	33.54 S	150.53 E
Busby, Mt., U.S.	202	45.32 N	106.57 W
Busca	62	44.31 N	7.29 E
Buscate	266b	45.32 N	8.49 E
Buscbusc ≃	144	1.08 S	41.49 E
Buschberg ∧[2]	61	48.34 N	16.23 E
Busche	64	46.02 N	11.59 E
Busch Gardens ♠	280	34.13 N	118.28 W
Buschhausen •[8]	263	51.30 N	6.51 E
Busdorf	41	54.29 N	9.32 E
Buseck	56	50.36 N	8.47 E
Buseto Palizzolo	70	38.01 N	12.43 E
Būsh	142	29.09 N	31.08 E
Bush ≃, N. Ire., U.K.	44	55.13 N	6.32 W
Bush ≃, S.C., U.S.	192	34.08 N	81.36 W
Būshehr □[4]	128	28.50 N	51.20 E
Bushenyi	154	0.32 S	30.11 E
Bushey	42	51.39 N	0.22 W
Bushey Heath	260	51.38 N	0.20 W
Bushi	268	35.50 N	139.22 E
Bushimaie ≃	152	6.02 S	23.45 E
Bushiribana	241s	12.33 N	69.58 W
Bushkill	210	41.06 N	75.00 W
Bush Kill ≃	210	41.05 N	74.59 W
Bushkill Falls ∟	210	41.09 N	75.01 W
Bushland	196	35.11 N	102.04 W
Bush Lot	246	6.12 N	57.16 W
Bushman Land □[9]	158	29.15 S	20.00 E
Bushmills	48	55.12 N	6.32 W
Bushnell, Fl., U.S.	220	28.39 N	82.06 W
Bushnell, Il., U.S.	190	40.33 N	90.30 W
Bush River ≃	208	39.21 N	76.14 W
Bushton	198	38.30 N	98.23 W
Bushtyna	78	48.04 N	23.27 E
Bū Shubayrim, Wādī V	146	27.07 N	19.30 E
Bushwick •[8]	276	40.42 N	73.55 W
Bushy Park	166	21.16 S	139.43 E
Bushy Park ♠	260	51.25 N	0.20 W
Bushy Run ≃	279b	40.20 N	79.40 W
Bushy Run Battlefield ⊥	279b	40.21 N	79.38 W
Busia	154	0.28 N	34.05 E
Busigny	50	50.02 N	3.28 E
Busing, Pulau I	271c	1.14 N	103.45 E
Businga	152	3.20 N	20.53 E
Büsingen	58	47.42 N	8.41 E
Busira ≃	152	0.15 S	18.59 E
Busjön ⊜, Sve.	40	60.06 N	13.28 E
Busjön ⊜, Sve.	40	60.31 N	13.58 E
Bus'k	78	49.58 N	24.37 E
Buskerud □[6]	26	60.25 N	9.12 E
Buskhyttan	40	58.40 N	16.56 E
Busko Zdrój	30	50.28 N	20.44 E
Busle	144	5.28 N	44.25 E
Busoga □[5]	154	0.40 N	33.30 E
Busovača	36	44.06 N	17.53 E
Buṣrā al-Ḥarīrī (Bosor)	132	32.50 N	36.20 E
Buṣrá ash-Shām	132	32.31 N	36.29 E
Bussana	62	43.49 N	7.51 E
Bussang	58	47.53 N	6.51 E
Bussang, Col de)(	58	47.54 N	6.54 E
Busselton	162	33.39 S	115.20 E
Busseri ≃	140	7.41 N	28.03 E
Busseto	64	44.59 N	10.02 E
Bussey	190	41.12 N	92.52 W
Bussières	62	45.50 N	4.16 E
Bussi sul Tirino	66	42.12 N	13.49 E
Busskoje	84	43.50 N	44.37 E
Bussolengo	64	45.28 N	10.51 E
Bussoleno	62	45.08 N	7.09 E
Bussum	52	52.16 N	5.10 E
Bussy-Rabutin, Château de ⊥	58	47.35 N	4.31 E
Bussy-Saint-Georges	261	48.51 N	2.42 E
Bustamante, Méx.	232	26.33 N	100.30 W
Bustamante, Méx.	234	23.26 N	99.47 W
Bustān, Wādī al- V	142	28.24 N	30.49 E
Buštěhrad	54	50.09 N	14.10 E
Bușteni	38	45.25 N	25.32 E
Busti	214	42.02 N	79.17 W
Bustleton •[8]	285	40.05 N	75.02 W
Busto Arsizio	62	45.37 N	8.51 E
Busto Garolfo	62	45.33 N	8.53 E
Buston, Taj.	85	40.31 N	69.19 E
Buston, Uzb.	128	40.04 N	64.49 E
Busu-Adula	152	2.05 N	21.40 E
Busuanga	116	12.10 N	119.55 E
Busuanga Island I	116	12.05 N	120.05 E
Busu-Djanoa	152	1.43 N	21.23 E
Bušuicha	76	59.02 N	40.26 E
Bušulej	88	52.45 N	117.13 E
Büsum	30	54.08 N	8.51 E
Busu-Melo	152	1.48 N	20.15 E
Bū Sunbul, Jabal ⋌[2]	146	23.10 N	22.21 E
Buta, Ross.	80	55.02 N	51.57 E
Buta, R.D.C.	154	2.48 N	24.44 E
Butag	116	12.38 N	123.56 E
Butajira	144	8.07 N	38.22 E
Butala	164	6.42 S	147.37 E
Butan	38	43.39 N	23.45 E
Bután → Bhutan □[1]	120	27.30 N	90.30 E
Butand State Park ♠	226	37.13 N	122.20 W
Butantã •[8]	287b	23.34 S	46.43 W
Butantã, Instituto ⊌[3]	287b	23.34 S	46.43 W
Buta Ranquil	252	37.03 S	69.50 W
Butare	154	2.36 S	29.44 E
Butaritari I[1]	14	3.07 N	172.48 E
Butarque, Arroyo de ≃	266a	40.19 N	3.39 W
Butauanan Island I	116	14.07 N	123.17 E
Butchart Gardens ♠	224	48.33 N	123.28 W
Butcher Island (Dia Deva) I	272c	18.58 N	72.54 E
Bute	168b	33.52 S	138.01 E
Bute, Island of I	46	55.50 N	5.06 W
Bute, Kyles of ⋓	46	55.53 N	5.13 W
Bute, Sound of ⋓	46	55.44 N	5.12 W
Büteelijn nuruu ⋌	88	50.00 N	104.50 E
Bute Giarti	144	4.33 N	37.45 E
Bute Inlet ⊂	182	50.37 N	124.53 W
Butemba	154	1.09 N	31.36 E
Butembo	154	0.09 N	29.17 E
Butera	70	37.11 N	14.11 E
Butere	154	0.13 N	34.30 E
Bütgenbach	56	50.26 N	6.12 E
Butha Buthe	158	28.45 S	28.15 E
Butha Qi (Zalantun)	89	48.02 N	122.43 E
Buthidaung	110	20.52 N	92.32 E
Buthier ≃	62	45.44 N	7.22 E
Buthroton ⊥	38	39.46 N	20.00 E
Buti	66	43.44 N	10.35 E
Butiá	252	30.07 S	51.58 W
Butiaba	154	1.49 N	31.19 E
Butig Mountains ⋌	116	7.39 N	124.20 E
Butka	86	56.47 N	63.47 E
Butler, Al., U.S.	194	32.05 N	88.13 W
Butler, Ga., U.S.	192	32.33 N	84.14 W
Butler, Il., U.S.	219	39.12 N	89.32 W
Butler, In., U.S.	216	41.25 N	84.52 W
Butler, Ky., U.S.	218	38.47 N	84.22 W
Butler, Mo., U.S.	194	38.15 N	94.19 W
Butler, N.J., U.S.	210	41.00 N	74.20 W
Butler, Oh., U.S.	214	40.35 N	82.25 W
Butler, Ok., U.S.	196	35.38 N	99.11 W
Butler, Pa., U.S.	214	40.51 N	79.53 W
Butler, Tx., U.S.	222	30.19 N	97.18 W
Butler, Wi., U.S.	216	43.06 N	88.04 W
Butler □[6], Oh., U.S.	218	39.26 N	84.30 W
Butler □[6], Pa., U.S.	214	40.52 N	79.54 W
Butler, Lake ⊜	220	28.28 N	81.33 W
Butler Lake ⊜	278	42.17 N	87.58 W
Butler Point ≻	207	41.40 N	70.43 W
Butler Reservoir ⊜[1]	276	40.59 N	74.23 W
Butlers Bridge	48	54.02 N	7.22 W
Butlerville	218	39.02 N	85.30 W
Butmīyah	132	32.56 N	35.53 E
Butnau Lake ⊜	184	56.13 N	95.20 W
Butner	192	36.07 N	78.45 W
Buto	152	15.46 S	15.09 E
Buton, Pulau I	112	5.00 S	122.55 E
Butong	112	1.06 S	114.50 E
Butru	166	21.30 S	139.43 E
Butsha	154	0.57 N	29.13 E
Buttapietra	64	45.20 N	11.00 E
Butte, Mt., U.S.	202	46.00 N	112.32 W
Butte, Ne., U.S.	198	42.54 N	98.50 W
Butte □[6]	226	39.27 N	121.30 W
Butte City	226	39.28 N	121.59 W
Butte Creek ≃, Ca., U.S.	204	39.12 N	121.56 W
Butte Creek ≃, Or., U.S.	224	45.09 N	122.46 W
Butte du Lion ⊥	50	50.40 N	4.24 E
Butte Falls	202	42.32 N	122.33 W
Buttelstedt	54	51.05 N	11.20 E
Butte Mountains ⋌	204	39.50 N	115.05 W
Butten	56	48.58 N	7.13 E
Butter Brook ≃	283	42.31 N	71.24 W
Butter Creek ≃	202	45.52 N	119.19 W
Butterfield, Il., U.S.	278	41.50 N	88.02 W
Butterfield, Mn., U.S.	198	43.57 N	94.47 W
Butterfield Creek ≃	278	41.33 N	87.37 W
Butterfield Lake ⊜	212	44.19 N	75.46 W
Butterley Reservoir ⊜[1]	262	53.35 N	1.56 W
Buttermere	44	54.33 N	3.17 W
Butternut	190	46.00 N	90.29 W
Butternut Creek ≃, N.Y., U.S.	210	42.25 N	75.22 W
Butternut Creek ≃, N.Y., U.S.	210	43.06 N	76.00 W
Butterwick	44	52.59 N	0.05 E
Butterworth, Malay.	114	5.25 N	100.24 E
Butterworth, S. Afr.	158	32.23 S	28.04 E
Buttevant	48	52.14 N	8.40 W
Büttgen	56	51.12 N	6.36 E
Buttlar	56	50.45 N	9.57 E
Buttle Lake ⊜	182	49.46 N	125.36 W
Button Islands II	176	60.35 N	64.45 W
Buttonville	275b	43.52 N	79.22 W
Buttonville Airfield ⊠	275b	43.52 N	79.23 W
Buttonwillow	226	35.24 N	119.28 W
Buttrio	64	46.01 N	13.20 E
Buttstädt	54	51.07 N	11.25 E
Butty Head ≻	162	33.54 S	121.38 E
Buttzville	210	40.49 N	75.00 W
Butuan	116	8.57 N	125.33 E
Butuan Bay ⊂	116	9.06 N	125.20 E
Butuj	88	53.27 N	112.22 E
Bū Tumayyim, Wādī V	146	26.56 N	19.13 E
Buṭūris	142	31.00 N	30.15 E
Buturlino, Ross.	80	55.34 N	44.55 E
Buturlino, Ross.	82	54.55 N	37.29 E
Buturlinovka	78	50.50 N	40.36 E
Buṭwal	124	27.42 N	83.27 E
Butylicy	80	55.32 N	41.31 E
Butzbach	56	50.26 N	8.40 E
Bützfleth	52	53.39 N	9.28 E
Bützow	54	53.50 N	11.59 E
Bützsee ⊜	54	52.49 N	12.53 E
Butztown	208	40.39 N	75.22 W
Buuhoodle	144	8.15 N	46.20 E
Buulo Berde	144	3.51 N	45.34 E
Buur Gaabo	144	1.12 S	41.51 E
Buurgplaatz ∧	56	50.10 N	6.01 E
Buur Hakaba	144	2.47 N	44.05 E
Buur Haybe	144	3.57 N	45.07 E
Buwarah, Sabkhat al- ⩩	130	35.09 N	41.12 E
Buwayḍān	132	33.12 N	36.26 E
Buxar	124	25.35 N	83.59 E
Buxheim, Dtsch.	58	48.00 N	10.08 E
Buxheim, Dtsch.	64	48.00 N	10.08 E
Buxtehude	52	53.28 N	9.41 E
Buxton, Guy.	246	6.47 N	58.02 W
Buxton, S. Afr.	158	27.38 S	24.42 E
Buxton, Eng., U.K.	44	53.15 N	1.55 W
Buxton, N.C., U.S.	192	35.16 N	75.32 W
Buxton, N.D., U.S.	198	47.36 N	97.05 W
Buxton, Or., U.S.	224	45.41 N	123.11 W
Buxton, Mount ∧	182	51.35 N	127.55 W
Buxy	58	46.43 N	4.41 E
Buye	154	4.38 N	27.30 E
Buyiqiao	106	31.47 N	119.48 E
Buyo	150	6.16 N	7.03 W
Buyo, Barrage de •[6]	150	6.15 N	7.05 W
Buyuan ≃	102	21.51 N	101.13 E
Büyükada	130	40.52 N	29.07 E
Büyükada I	267b	40.52 N	29.07 E
Büyükarmutlu	130	39.35 N	38.26 E
Büyükbakkal •[8]	267b	40.59 N	29.11 E
Büyükçeçeli	130	39.43 N	33.52 E
Büyükçekmece	130	41.01 N	28.34 E
Büyükdere •[8]	267b	41.09 N	29.02 E
Büyükeceli	130	36.11 N	33.40 E
Büyükkale	130	38.01 N	27.34 E
Büyükkarıştıran	130	41.18 N	27.32 E
Büyükkemikli Burnu ≻	130	40.18 N	26.14 E
Büyükmenderes ≃	130	37.28 N	27.11 E
Büyükzap → Great Zab ≃	128	36.00 N	43.21 E
Buyun Shan ∧	98	40.06 N	122.42 E
Buyun Uzun	128	39.13 N	63.19 E
Buzan ≃	80	46.18 N	49.06 E
Buzanaj, peski •[2]	80	47.30 N	49.50 E
Buzançais	32	46.53 N	1.25 E
Buzancy	56	49.25 N	4.57 E
Bužaninovo	82	56.23 N	38.18 E
Bužarovo	82	55.59 N	36.47 E
Buzău	38	45.09 N	26.49 E
Buzău □[6]	38	45.15 N	26.45 E
Buzău ≃	38	45.26 N	27.44 E
Buzen	96	33.37 N	131.08 E
Búzi ≃	156	19.50 S	34.43 E
Buziaș	38	45.39 N	21.36 E
Buziji	100	33.49 N	118.14 E
Buzinovka	80	48.32 N	43.53 E
Búzios, Ilha dos I	256	23.48 S	45.08 W
Búzios, Ponta dos ≻	255	22.44 S	41.53 W
Buz'kyy lyman ⊂[1]	78	46.45 N	31.55 E
Buzlanovo	265b	55.46 N	37.13 E
Buzovna	84	40.31 N	50.04 E
Buzuluk, Kaz.	86	51.55 N	66.16 E
Buzuluk, Ross.	80	52.47 N	52.15 E
Buzuluk ≃, Ross.	80	50.13 N	42.12 E
Buzuluk ≃, Ross.	80	52.47 N	52.16 E
Buzzards Bay	207	41.44 N	70.37 W
Buzzards Bay ⊂	207	41.33 N	70.47 W
Bwana Mkubwa	154	13.01 S	28.42 E
Bwasa	152	3.53 S	18.25 E
Bwendi	154	4.01 N	26.41 E
Bwlch	42	51.54 N	3.15 W
By	40	60.12 N	16.28 E
Byādgi	122	14.41 N	75.29 E
Byam Channel ⋓	176	75.20 N	105.20 W
Byam Martin Channel ⋓	176	75.45 N	104.00 W
Byam Martin Island I	176	75.15 N	104.00 W
Byberry Creek ≃	285	40.04 N	74.59 W

≃	River	Fluß	Río	Rivière	Rio
≍	Canal	Kanal	Canal	Canal	Canal
∟	Waterfall, Rapids	Wasserfall, Stromschnellen	Cascada, Rápidos	Chute d'eau, Rapides	Cascata, Rápidos
⋓	Strait	Meeresstraße	Estrecho	Détroit	Estreito
⊂	Bay, Gulf	Bucht, Golf	Bahía, Golfo	Baie, Golfe	Baía, Golfo
⊜	Lake, Lakes	See, Seen	Lago, Lagos	Lac, Lacs	Lago, Lagos
⩩	Swamp	Sumpf	Pantano	Marais	Pântano
⍓	Ice Features, Glacier	Eis- und Gletscherformen	Accidentes Glaciales	Formes glaciaires	Acidentes glaciares
⊤	Other Hydrographic Features	Andere Hydrographische Objekte	Otros Elementos Hidrográficos	Autres données hydrographiques	Outros acidentes hidrográficos

⊹	Submarine Features	Untermeerische Objekte	Accidentes Submarinos	Formes de relief sous-marin	Acidentes submarinos
□	Political Unit	Politische Einheit	Unidad Politica	Entité politique	Unidade política
⊌	Cultural Institution	Kulturelle Institution	Institución Cultural	Institution culturelle	Instituição cultural
⊥	Historical Site	Historische Stätte	Sitio Histórico	Site historique	Sitio histórico
♠	Recreational Site	Erholungs- und Ferienort	Sitio de Recreo	Centre de loisirs	Area de Lazer
⊠	Airport	Flughafen	Aeropuerto	Aéroport	Aeroporto
■	Military Installation	Militäranlage	Instalación Militar	Installation militaire	Instalação militar
•	Miscellaneous	Verschiedenes	Misceláneo	Divers	Diversos

ENGLISH: Name | Page | Lat.°′ | Long.°′
DEUTSCH: Name | Seite | Breite°′ | Länge°′ E = Ost

Byblos — Jubayl 130 34.07 N 35.39 E
Bycen' 76 52.54 N 25.29 E
Bychawa 30 51.01 N 22.32 E
Bychok ≏ 83 48.26 N 37.47 E
Byčki, Ross. 76 54.15 N 34.39 E
Byčki, Ross. 80 53.38 N 40.54 E
Byculla ✦8 272c 18.58 N 72.49 E
Byčyha 76 55.41 N 29.58 E
Byczyna 30 51.07 N 18.11 E
Bydalen 26 63.06 N 13.47 E
Bydgoszcz 30 53.08 N 18.00 E
Bydgoszcz □4 30 53.15 N 18.00 E
Byelorussia — Belarus □1 72 53.50 N 28.00 E
Byers, Pa., U.S. 285 40.05 N 75.41 W
Byers, Tx., U.S. 196 34.04 N 98.11 W
Byersdale 279b 40.37 N 80.13 W
Byers Run ≏ 279b 40.24 N 79.42 W
Byesville 188 39.58 N 81.32 W
Byfang ✦8 263 51.24 N 7.06 E
Byfield, Eng., U.K. 42 52.11 N 1.14 W
Byfield, Ma., U.S. 207 42.45 N 70.56 W
Byfleet 42 51.20 N 0.29 W
Byford 168a 32.13 S 116.00 E
Byforde 284c 39.01 N 77.05 W
Bygdeå 26 64.04 N 20.51 E
Bygdeträsket ⊜ 26 64.26 N 20.32 E
Bygdin 26 61.20 N 8.48 E
Bygdin ⊜ 26 61.21 N 8.36 E
Bygi 80 57.13 N 53.44 E
Byglandsfjord 26 58.41 N 7.48 E
Byglandsfjorden ⊜ 26 58.48 N 7.50 E
Byhalia 194 34.52 N 89.41 W
Byhau 76 53.32 N 30.12 E
Bykivka 78 50.17 N 27.58 E
Bykle 26 59.21 N 7.20 E
Bykov 89 47.21 N 142.32 E
Bykovka 82 55.29 N 37.40 E
Bykovo, Ross. 80 49.47 N 45.22 E
Bykovo, Ross. 82 54.01 N 37.54 E
Bykovo, Ross. 82 55.37 N 38.04 E
Bykovo Airport ⊠ 265b 55.38 N 38.05 E
Bylas 200 33.08 N 110.07 W
Bylbasivka 83 48.51 N 37.30 E
Bylderup 41 54.57 N 9.07 E
Byley 262 53.13 N 2.25 W
Bylkyldak 86 48.38 N 75.16 E
Bylnice 30 49.04 N 18.01 E
Bylot Island I 176 73.13 N 78.34 W
Byng Inlet 190 45.46 N 80.33 W
Bynum, Mt., U.S. 182 47.58 N 112.18 W
Bynum, N.C., U.S. 192 35.46 N 79.08 W
Bynum, Tx., U.S. 222 31.58 N 97.00 W
Byōdōin Temple ⊕1 270 34.53 N 135.48 E
Byram ≏ 276 40.59 N 73.39 W
Byramgore Reef ✧2 122 11.54 N 71.49 E
Byram Lake Reservoir ⊜1 276 41.10 N 73.41 W
Byrd, Lac ⊜ 190 47.01 N 76.56 W
Byrdstown 194 36.34 N 85.07 W
Byrka 88 50.39 N 118.31 E
Byrne Arena ♦ 276 40.49 N 74.05 W
Byrnedale 214 41.17 N 78.30 W
Byro 162 26.05 S 116.09 E
Byrock 166 30.40 S 146.24 E
Byron, Ca., U.S. 226 37.52 N 121.38 W
Byron, Ga., U.S. 192 32.39 N 83.45 W
Byron, Il., U.S. 190 42.07 N 89.15 W
Byron, Mi., U.S. 216 42.49 N 83.57 W
Byron, N.Y., U.S. 210 43.04 N 78.03 W
Byron, Wy., U.S. 202 44.47 N 108.30 W
Byron, Cape > 166 28.39 S 153.38 E
Byron, Isla I 254 47.47 S 75.12 W
Byron Bay 166 28.39 S 153.37 E
Byron Center 216 42.49 N 85.42 W
Byrranga, gory ⩚ 74 75.00 N 104.00 E
Byryuchyy Ostriv, kosa >2 78 46.08 N 35.05 E
Byšice-Liblice 54 50.19 N 14.38 E
Bysjön ⊜ 40 60.23 N 14.30 E
Byske 26 64.57 N 21.12 E
Byskeälven ≏ 26 64.57 N 21.13 E
Bystraja ≏ 80 47.58 N 41.00 E
Bystřany 54 50.38 N 13.51 E
Bystrica ≏ 80 58.38 N 49.05 E
Bystřice 30 49.45 N 14.41 E
Bystřice pod Hostýnem 30 49.24 N 17.40 E
Bystrij Tanyp ≏ 86 55.46 N 54.35 E
Bystrovka 85 42.47 N 75.43 E
Bystryj 86 57.50 N 73.58 E
Bystryj Istok 86 52.23 N 84.24 E
Bystrzyca Kłodzka 30 50.18 N 16.39 E
Bytantaj ≏ 74 68.46 N 134.20 E
Bytča, Bela. 76 54.18 N 28.24 E
Bytča, Slvk. 30 49.14 N 18.36 E
Bytkiv 78 48.38 N 24.26 E
Bytom (Beuthen) 30 50.22 N 18.54 E
Bytoš' 76 53.50 N 34.06 E
Bytów 30 54.11 N 17.30 E
Byumba 154 1.35 S 30.04 E
Byval'ki 78 51.51 N 30.37 E
Byxelkrok 26 57.20 N 17.00 E
Bzyb' ≏ 84 43.12 N 40.18 E
Bzybskij chrebet ⩚ 84 43.18 N 40.41 E

C

Ça ≏ 110 18.46 N 105.47 E
Caa-Chol' 86 51.32 N 92.23 E
Caacupé 252 25.23 S 57.09 W
Čaadajevka 80 53.09 N 45.56 E
Čaadajevo 80 55.40 N 42.02 E
Caaguazú 252 25.26 S 56.02 W
Caaguazú □5 252 25.00 S 55.45 W
Caála 152 12.51 S 15.33 E
Caamaño Sound ʊ 182 52.49 N 129.28 W
Caapiranga 246 3.18 S 61.13 W
Caapucú 252 26.13 S 57.12 W
Caarapó 255 22.38 S 54.48 W
Caatinga 255 17.10 S 45.53 W
Caazapá 252 26.09 S 56.24 W
Caazapá □5 252 26.10 S 56.00 W
Cabaçal ≏ 248 16.00 S 57.42 W
Cabadbaran 116 9.10 N 125.38 E
Cabadiangan Plateau ⩚1 116 9.50 N 122.36 E
Cabagan 116 17.26 N 121.46 E
Cabaiguán 240p 22.05 N 79.30 W
Cabalete Island I 116 14.17 N 121.50 E
Cabalian 116 10.16 N 125.10 E
Cabaliana, Lago ⊜ 246 3.20 S 60.50 W
Cabalian Bay ⊂ 116 10.13 N 125.10 E
Cabalian Point > 116 12.06 N 122.01 E
Caballero Creek ≏ 280 34.11 N 118.32 W
Caballito ✦8 288 34.37 S 58.27 W
Caballones, Cayo I 240p 20.52 N 79.00 W
Caballo Reservoir ⊜1 200 32.58 N 107.18 W
Cabana 248 8.24 S 78.02 W
Cabanaconde 248 15.37 S 71.59 W
Cabañas 240p 22.58 N 82.55 W
Cabanatuan 116 15.29 N 120.58 E
Cabangan 116 15.10 N 120.03 E
Cabano 186 47.41 N 68.53 W
Cabarroguis 116 16.33 N 121.32 E
Cabarruyan Island I 116 16.18 N 119.59 E
Cabaun Island I 116 12.34 N 124.30 E
Cabeceiras 255 15.48 S 46.59 W
Cabeço de Montachique 266c 38.54 N 9.11 W
Cabellera, Sierra de la ⩚ 200 30.55 N 109.07 W
Cabery 216 41.00 N 88.12 W
Cabeza del Buey 34 38.43 N 5.13 W
Cabeza de Tigre 286c 10.28 N 66.46 W
Cabezas 248 18.46 S 63.24 W
Cabiao 116 15.15 N 120.51 E
Cabiate 266b 45.40 N 9.10 E
Cabildo, Arg. 252 38.29 S 61.54 W
Cabildo, Chile 252 32.26 S 71.05 W
Cabimas 246 10.23 N 71.28 W
Cabin Branch ≏, Md., U.S. 284b 39.13 N 76.35 W
Cabin Branch ≏, Md., U.S. 284c 38.51 N 76.48 W
Cabin Creek ≏ 198 46.55 N 104.52 W
Cabinda 152 5.33 S 12.12 E
Cabinda □5 152 5.00 S 12.30 E
Cabinet Mountains ⩚ 202 48.20 N 116.00 W
Cabingaan Island I 116 5.41 N 121.03 E
Cabin John 208 38.58 N 77.09 W
Cabin John Creek ≏ 284b 38.58 N 77.09 W
Cabin John Creek Park ♦ 284c 38.59 N 77.09 W
Cabin John Regional Park ♦ 284c 39.02 N 77.09 W
Cabiri 152 8.52 S 13.39 E
Cabixi ≏ 248 13.41 S 60.44 W
Cable 190 46.12 N 91.17 W
Cable Airport ⊠ 280 34.08 N 117.41 W
Cables 162 27.59 S 123.23 E
Cabo 250 8.17 S 35.02 W
Cabo Blanco 254 47.12 S 65.45 W
Cabo de Hornos, Parque Nacional ♦ 250 55.45 S 67.25 W
Cabo Delgado □5 154 12.35 S 39.00 E
Cabo Frio 255 22.53 S 42.01 W
Cabo Gracias a Dios 236 14.59 N 83.10 W
Cabo Ledo 152 9.39 S 13.17 E
Cabonga, Réservoir ⊜1 190 47.20 N 76.35 W
Cabool 194 37.07 N 92.06 W
Caboolture 166 27.05 S 152.57 E
Cabo Orange, Parque Nacional do ♦ 250 3.00 N 51.00 W
Cabo Raso 254 44.21 S 65.14 W
Caborca 232 30.37 N 112.06 W
Cabo Rojo 240m 18.05 N 67.09 W
Cabot, Ar., U.S. 194 34.58 N 92.00 W
Cabot, Pa., U.S. 214 40.46 N 79.46 W
Cabot, Mount ∧ 188 44.31 N 71.24 W
Cabot Head > 212 45.14 N 81.17 W
Cabot Strait ʊ 186 47.20 N 59.30 W
Cabo Verde 256 21.28 S 46.24 W
Cabo Verde — Cape Verde □1 150a 16.00 N 24.00 W
Cabo Verde ≏ 256 21.28 S 46.17 W
Cabra 34 37.28 N 4.27 W
Cabra Corral, Embalse ⊜1 252 25.15 S 65.25 W
Cabra Island I 116 13.53 N 120.02 E
Cabramatta 274a 33.54 S 150.56 E
Cabramatta Creek ≏ 274a 33.54 S 150.57 E
Cabramurra 171b 35.58 S 148.23 E
Cabras 71 39.56 N 8.32 E
Cabras, Stagno di ⊜ 71 39.57 N 8.29 E
Cabras Island I 174p 13.27 N 144.40 E
Cabrayil 84 39.23 N 47.02 E
Cabrel 234 20.06 N 105.14 W
Cabrera ≏, Col. 246 3.26 N 75.07 W
Cabrera ≏, Esp. 34 42.25 N 6.49 W
Cabrera, Illa de I 34 39.09 N 2.56 E
Cabrera de Mar 266d 41.32 N 2.24 E
Cabreúva 256 23.18 S 47.08 W
Cabri 184 50.37 N 108.28 W
Cabria 64 45.54 N 13.35 E
Cabriel ≏ 34 39.14 N 1.03 W
Cabrillo National Monument ♦ 228 32.41 N 117.15 W
Cabrils 266d 41.32 N 2.22 E
Cabrobó 250 8.31 S 39.19 W
Cabruta 246 7.38 N 66.15 W
Cabucgayan 116 11.29 N 124.34 E
Cabuçu 256 22.50 S 42.55 W
Cabuçu ≏, Bra. 287a 22.59 S 43.37 W
Cabuçu ≏, Bra. 287a 22.48 S 43.27 W
Cabuçu de Cima ≏ 287b 23.31 S 46.33 W
Cabugao 116 17.48 N 120.27 E
Cabulauan Island I 116 11.23 N 120.06 E
Cabullones, Punta > 240m 17.58 N 66.35 W
Cabulo 152 10.15 S 16.40 E
Cabure 246 11.08 N 69.38 W
Cabusy 76 52.49 N 28.06 E
Cabuta 152 9.50 S 19.04 E
Cabuya 236 9.36 N 85.06 W
Cabuyal 236 10.40 N 85.40 W
Cabuyaro 246 4.18 N 72.49 W
Caca 80 48.11 N 44.40 E
Caçador 252 26.47 S 51.00 W
Čačak 38 43.53 N 20.21 E
Cacaohatán 236 14.59 N 92.10 W
Cacaoui, Lac ⊜ 186 50.53 N 66.58 W
Caçapava 256 23.06 S 45.42 W
Caçapava do Sul 252 30.30 S 53.30 W
Caçapava Velha 256 23.07 S 45.39 W
Cacapon ≏ 188 39.37 N 78.16 W
Cacapon State Park ♦ 188 39.32 N 78.23 W
Cacas 130 38.23 N 41.17 E
Caccamo 70 37.56 N 13.40 E
Caccia, Capo > 71 40.34 N 8.09 E
Caccuri 68 39.14 N 16.47 E
Čačenka ≏ 265b 55.46 N 37.18 E
Cacequi 252 29.53 S 54.49 W
Cáceres, Bra. 248 16.04 S 57.41 W
Cáceres, Col. 246 7.35 N 75.20 W
Cáceres, Esp. 34 39.29 N 6.22 W
Cáceres □4 34 39.40 N 6.05 E
Čačersk 76 52.55 N 30.55 E
Čačevičy 76 53.31 N 29.51 E
Cachan 261 48.48 N 2.20 E
Cachari 252 36.24 S 59.32 W
Cache 196 34.37 N 98.37 W
Cache ≏, Ar., U.S. 194 34.42 N 91.20 W
Cache ≏, Il., U.S. 194 37.04 N 89.10 W
Cache, Lac ⊜ 206 46.21 N 74.39 W
Cache Creek 182 50.48 N 121.19 W
Cache Creek ≏, Ca., U.S. 226 38.42 N 121.42 W
Cache Creek ≏, Ca., U.S. 228 35.06 N 117.58 W
Cache Creek, North Fork ≏ 226 38.59 N 122.30 W
Cache la Poudre ≏ 200 40.25 N 104.36 W
Cache la Poudre, North Fork ≏ 198 40.54 N 105.22 W
Cache Mountain ∧ 180 65.31 N 147.20 W
Cache Peak ∧, Ca., U.S. 228 35.13 N 118.15 W
Cache Peak ∧, Id., U.S. 198 42.11 N 113.40 W
Cache Slough ≏ 226 38.13 N 121.40 W
Cacheu 150 12.16 N 16.10 W
Cacheu ⊂1 150 12.10 N 16.21 W
Cachí 252 25.06 S 66.11 W
Cachimbo 250 9.24 S 54.56 W
Cachimbo, Serra do ⩚ 250 8.30 S 55.50 W
Cachimo 152 8.21 S 21.20 E
Cachingues 152 13.05 S 16.43 E
Cachir 88 48.06 N 98.52 E
Cachkadzor 84 40.33 N 44.43 E
Cachoeira ≏ 256 23.06 S 46.29 W
Cachoeira, Reservatório ⊜1 256 23.03 S 46.15 W
Cachoeira, Rio da ≏ 287a 23.00 S 43.18 W
Cachoeira Alta 255 18.48 S 50.58 W
Cachoeira de Goiás 255 16.44 S 50.38 W
Cachoeira de Manteiga 255 16.39 S 45.16 W
Cachoeira de Minas 256 22.21 S 45.47 W
Cachoeira do Arari 250 1.01 S 48.58 W
Cachoeira do Sul 252 30.02 S 52.54 W
Cachoeira Grande, Alto da ∧ 256 21.54 S 44.06 W
Cachoeira Paulista 256 22.40 S 45.01 W
Cachoeiras 287a 22.39 S 43.28 W
Cachoeiras de Macacu 256 22.28 S 42.39 W
Cachoeirinha 250 8.29 S 36.14 W
Cachoeiro de Itapemirim 255 20.51 S 41.06 W
Cachos, Punta > 252 27.39 S 71.02 W
Cachos, Rio dos ≏ 287b 23.36 S 46.26 W
Čachrov 60 49.16 N 13.18 E
Cachuela Esperanza 248 10.32 S 65.38 W
Cachuma, Lake ⊜1 204 34.35 N 119.55 W
Cacilhas 266c 38.41 N 9.09 W
Cacine 150 11.08 N 14.57 W
Caciporé ≏ 250 3.51 N 51.08 W
Caciporé, Cabo > 250 3.55 N 51.07 W
Căciulați 38 44.38 N 26.10 E
Cacnipa Island I 116 10.30 N 119.04 E
Cacocum 240p 20.44 N 76.23 W
Cacólo 152 10.07 S 19.17 E
Caconda 152 13.43 S 15.06 E
Caconde 256 21.33 S 46.38 W
Cacra 248 12.48 S 75.48 W
Cactus 196 36.04 N 102.00 W
Cactus Flat ≚ 204 37.45 N 116.45 W
Cactus Peak ∧ 204 37.47 N 116.53 W
Caçu 255 18.37 S 51.04 W
Cacuaco 152 8.47 S 13.22 E
Cacula 152 14.29 S 14.10 E
Caculé 255 14.30 S 42.13 W
Caculuvar ≏ 152 16.46 S 14.36 E
Cacuri, Ang. 152 8.14 S 18.20 E
Cacuri, Ven. 246 4.48 N 65.21 W
Cacuso 152 9.26 S 15.43 E
Çadale 144 2.45 N 46.19 E
Čadan 86 51.17 N 91.35 E
Cadaqués 34 42.17 N 3.17 E
Cadariri ≏ 248 6.20 S 57.46 W
Čadca 30 49.26 N 18.48 E
Caddington 42 51.51 N 0.27 W
Caddo, Ok., U.S. 196 34.07 N 96.15 W
Caddo, Tx., U.S. 196 32.38 N 98.40 W
Caddo ≏ 194 34.10 N 93.03 W
Caddo Creek ≏, Ok., U.S. 196 34.14 N 96.59 W
Caddo Creek ≏, Tx., U.S. 222 32.02 N 95.26 W
Caddo Creek Lake ⊜1 222 32.05 N 95.39 W
Caddo Lake ⊜1 194 32.42 N 94.01 W
Caddo Mills 222 33.04 N 96.14 W
Caddo Peak ∧ 222 32.29 N 97.24 W
Caddy Vista 216 42.50 N 87.54 W
Cadell ≏ 166 22.51 S 141.55 E
Cadena, Arroyo de la ≏ 196 26.17 N 104.00 W
Cadena, Cerro ∧ 196 25.50 N 104.04 W
Cadena, Punta > 240m 18.18 N 67.14 W
Cadenberge 52 53.46 N 9.04 E
Cadenet 62 43.44 N 5.22 E
Cadeo 62 44.58 N 9.48 E
Cadereyta de Jiménez 232 25.36 N 100.00 W
Cader Idris ∧ 42 52.42 N 3.54 W
Cadibarrawirracanna, Lake ⊜ 162 28.52 S 135.27 E
Cadig, Mount ∧ 116 14.09 N 122.27 E
Cadillac, Sk., Can. 184 49.44 N 107.43 W
Cadillac, Fr. 32 44.38 N 0.19 W
Cadillac, Mi., U.S. 190 44.15 N 85.24 W
Cadipietra (Steinhaus) 64 46.59 N 11.59 E
Cadishead 262 53.25 N 2.26 W
Cadix — Cádiz 34 36.32 N 6.18 W
Cádiz, Esp. 34 36.32 N 6.18 W
Cadiz, Pil. 116 10.57 N 123.18 E
Cadiz, In., U.S. 218 39.57 N 85.30 W
Cadiz, Ky., U.S. 194 36.51 N 87.50 W
Cadiz, Oh., U.S. 214 40.16 N 80.59 W
Cádiz □4 34 36.35 N 5.50 W
Cádiz, Bahía de ⊂ 34 36.32 N 6.16 W
Cádiz, Golfo de ⊂ 34 36.50 N 7.10 W
Cadiz Lake ⊜ 204 34.18 N 115.24 W
Cadlao Island I 116 11.13 N 119.21 E
Cadnam 42 50.55 N 1.35 W
Čadobec 88 58.40 N 98.51 E
Čadobec ≏ 88 58.40 N 98.50 E
Cadogan 214 40.45 N 79.34 W
Cadolzburg 56 49.28 N 10.51 E
Cadomin 182 53.02 N 117.20 W
Cadoneghe 64 45.26 N 11.55 E
Cadore ✦1 64 46.30 N 12.20 E
Cadosia 210 41.58 N 75.16 W
Cadott 190 44.56 N 91.09 W
Cadoux 162 30.47 S 117.08 E
Caduruan Point > 116 11.45 N 124.05 E
Caduta, Fosso delle ≏ 267a 41.56 N 12.12 E
Cadwell 192 32.20 N 83.02 W
Cady Marsh Ditch ≊ 278 41.33 N 87.29 W
Cady Mountain ∧2 224 48.33 N 123.07 W
Cadzand 52 51.22 N 3.25 E
Caen 32 49.11 N 0.21 W
Caengo (Kwenge) ≏ 152 4.50 S 18.42 E
Caerano di San Marco 64 45.47 N 12.00 E
Caere ⊥ 66 42.02 N 12.07 E
Caergwrle 44 53.07 N 3.03 W
Caerleon 42 51.37 N 2.57 W
Caernarfon 44 53.08 N 4.16 W
Caernarfon Bay ⊂ 44 53.05 N 4.30 W
Caernarfon Castle ⊥ 44 53.08 N 4.16 W
Caerphilly 42 51.35 N 3.14 W
Caerphilly Castle ⊥ 42 51.34 N 3.14 W
Caersws 42 52.31 N 3.25 W
Caesar Creek ≏ 218 39.29 N 84.06 W
Caesar Creek, Anderson Fork ≏ 218 39.33 N 83.58 W
Caesar Creek Lake ⊜1 218 39.30 N 84.00 W
Cæsarea — Qesari, Horbat ⊥ 132 32.30 N 34.53 E
Caetanópolis 255 19.18 S 44.24 W
Caeté 255 19.54 S 43.40 W
Caeté ≏ 248 9.03 S 68.39 W
Caeté, Morro ∧2 287a 23.03 S 43.31 W
Caetité 255 14.04 S 42.29 W
Cafayate 252 26.05 S 65.58 W
Cafelândia do Leste 255 16.40 S 53.25 W
Cafima 152 16.39 S 16.27 E
Cafu 152 16.27 S 15.14 E
Cafuini ≏ 246 1.17 N 57.11 W
Cagaan Chajrchan 88 49.25 N 94.15 E
Cagaan Gol 86 48.57 N 89.07 E
Cagaan Nuur, Mong. 86 49.32 N 89.42 E
Cagaannuur, Mong. 88 50.20 N 105.03 E
Cagaan-Ovoo 102 45.51 N 105.17 E
Cagaan Uul 88 49.28 N 98.30 E
Cagaan-Üür 88 50.32 N 101.30 E
Çágado ≏ 256 22.02 S 43.09 W
Čagan ≏ 80 51.12 N 51.20 E
Cagan-Aman 80 47.34 N 46.43 E
Cagan-Churtej, chrebet ⩚ 88 51.32 N 110.00 E
Cagarras, Ilhas II 287a 23.02 S 43.12 W
Cagayan □4 116 18.00 N 121.50 E
Cagayan ≏ 116 18.22 N 121.37 E
Cagayancillo 116 9.34 N 121.12 E
Cagayan de Oro 116 8.29 N 124.39 E
Cagayan de Tawi-Tawi 116 7.01 N 118.30 E
Cagayan Island I 116 9.36 N 121.14 E
Cagayan Islands II 116 9.40 N 121.16 E
Cagayan Sulu Island I 116 7.01 N 118.30 E
Čagda 74 58.45 N 130.37 E
Cageri 84 42.39 N 42.45 E
Caggiano 68 40.34 N 15.29 E
Çağış 130 39.30 N 28.01 E
Çağlarca 130 39.05 N 39.10 E
Cagli 66 43.33 N 12.39 E
Cagliari 71 39.13 N 9.07 E
Cagliari □4 71 39.30 N 8.45 E
Cagliari, Golfo di ⊂ 71 39.08 N 9.11 E
Cagliari, Stagno di ⊜ 71 39.13 N 9.02 E
Čaglinka ≏ 86 53.59 N 69.47 E
Cagnano Varano 68 41.49 N 15.47 E
Cagnes-sur-Mer 62 43.40 N 7.09 E
Čagoda 76 59.10 N 35.17 E
Čagoda ≏ 76 59.05 N 35.18 E
Čagodošča ≏ 76 58.57 N 36.35 E
Čagojan 89 52.08 N 128.15 E
Čagra ≏ 80 52.37 N 48.15 E
Cagraray Island I 116 13.18 N 123.52 E
Cagua 246 10.11 N 67.27 W
Caguán ≏ 246 0.08 S 74.18 W
Caguas 240m 18.14 N 66.02 W
Cagveri 84 41.48 N 43.29 E
Cagwait 116 8.55 N 126.18 E
Cahaba ≏ 194 32.20 N 87.05 W
Cahabón 236 15.34 N 89.49 W
Cahabón ≏ 236 15.25 N 89.36 W
Cahama 152 16.17 S 14.19 E
Caha Mountains ⩚ 48 51.45 N 9.45 W
Caher 48 52.21 N 7.56 W
Caherdaniel 48 51.45 N 10.05 W
Cahersiveen 48 51.57 N 10.13 W
Cahokia 219 38.34 N 90.11 W
Cahokia Creek ≏ 219 38.47 N 90.01 W
Cahokia Mounds State Park ♦ 219 38.39 N 90.03 W
Cahoon Creek ≏ 279a 41.29 N 81.55 W
Cahoon Park ♦ 279a 41.29 N 81.56 W
Cahoonzie 210 41.26 N 74.43 W
Cahora Bassa 154 15.35 S 32.48 E
Cahora Bassa, Albufeira de ⊜1 154 15.40 S 31.40 E
Cahore Point > 48 52.34 N 6.11 W
Cahors 32 44.27 N 1.26 E
Cahto Peak ∧ 204 39.41 N 123.35 W
Cahuilla Indian Reservation ✦4 204 33.30 N 116.43 W
Cahuinari ≏ 246 1.21 S 70.44 W
Cahuita, Punta > 236 9.45 N 82.49 W
Cahul 38 45.54 N 28.11 E
Caí ≏ 252 29.56 S 51.16 W
Caia ≏ 34 38.50 N 7.05 W
Caianda 152 11.02 S 23.31 E
Caiapó ≏, Bra. 250 8.52 S 49.36 W
Caiapó ≏, Bra. 255 15.49 S 51.53 W
Caiapó, Serra do ⩚ 255 17.00 S 52.00 W
Caiapônia 255 16.57 S 51.49 W
Caiazzo 68 41.11 N 14.22 E
Caibarién 240p 22.31 N 79.28 W
Cai Bau, Dao I 110 21.10 N 107.27 E
Caibiran 116 11.34 N 124.35 E
Caiçara, Bra. 250 6.36 S 35.29 W
Caiçara, Bra. 255 15.34 S 50.12 W
Caicara, Caño ≏ 246 7.44 N 69.04 W
Caicara de Maturín 246 9.49 N 63.36 W
Caicara de Orinoco 246 7.37 N 66.10 W
Caicedonia 246 4.20 N 75.50 W
Caicó 250 6.27 S 37.06 W
Caicos Bank ✧4 238 21.35 N 71.55 W
Caicos Islands II 238 21.56 N 71.58 W
Caicos Passage ʊ 238 22.00 N 72.30 W
Caieiras 256 23.22 S 46.44 W
Caieiras □7 287b 23.23 S 46.41 W
Caigou 100 33.16 N 114.32 E
Caiguna 162 32.17 S 125.25 E
Caihuaping 100 26.54 N 113.23 E
Caijiachang 107 29.44 N 106.29 E
Caijiagang 107 28.55 N 106.21 E
Caijialou 104 41.24 N 121.06 E
Caijiapo 102 34.17 N 107.39 E
Caijiazhuang 105 40.48 N 114.44 E
Caille 62 43.46 N 6.44 E
Cailloma 248 15.12 S 71.46 W
Caillou Bay ⊂ 194 29.06 N 90.56 W
Caima Bay ⊂ 116 13.42 N 122.48 E
Caimán, Islas — Cayman Islands □2 238 19.30 N 80.40 W
Caimanera 240p 19.59 N 75.09 W
Caïmanes — Cayman Islands □2 238 19.30 N 80.40 W
Caiman Point > 116 15.55 N 119.46 E
Caimbambo 152 12.58 S 14.01 E
Cain ≏ 42 52.46 N 3.08 W
Cain Creek ≏ 198 44.17 N 98.10 W
Cainde 152 15.42 S 13.12 E
Caine ≏ 248 18.23 S 65.21 W
Caino 64 45.38 N 10.18 E
Cains ≏ 186 46.40 N 65.47 W
Cainsdorf 54 50.41 N 12.29 E
Cainsville 194 40.28 N 93.59 W
Cainta 269f 14.35 N 121.07 E
Cai Nuoc 110 8.56 N 105.01 E
Cairano 68 40.54 N 15.22 E
Cairari 250 2.33 S 49.07 W
Caird Coast ⊥2 9 76.00 S 24.30 W
Caire, Le — Al-Qāhirah 142 30.03 N 31.15 E
Cairnbrook 214 40.07 N 78.49 W
Cairn Curran Reservoir ⊜1 169 37.04 S 143.59 E
Cairndow 46 56.15 N 4.56 W
Cairngorm Mountains ⩚ 46 57.04 N 3.50 W
Cairn Mountain ∧ 180 61.10 N 155.20 W
Cairnryan 44 54.58 N 5.02 W
Cairns 166 16.55 S 145.46 E
Cairns Lake ⊜ 184 51.42 N 94.30 W
Cairnsmore of Carsphairn ∧ 44 55.15 N 4.12 W
Cairnsmore of Fleet ∧ 44 54.59 N 4.20 W
Cairn Table ∧ 44 55.29 N 4.02 W
Cairn Water ≏ 44 55.07 N 3.45 W
Cairo — Al-Qāhirah, Mișr 142 30.03 N 31.15 E
Cairo, Ga., U.S. 192 30.52 N 84.12 W
Cairo, Il., U.S. 194 37.00 N 89.10 W
Cairo, Ne., U.S. 198 41.00 N 98.36 W
Cairo, N.Y., U.S. 210 42.17 N 73.59 W
Cairo, Oh., U.S. 216 40.49 N 84.05 W
Cairo, W.V., U.S. 188 39.12 N 81.09 W
Cairo (Almaza) Airport ⊠, Mișr 273c 30.06 N 31.22 E
Cairo (Imbābah) Airport ⊠, Mișr 273c 30.04 N 31.12 E
Cairo, University of ⊕2 273c 30.02 N 31.12 E
Cairoçu, Pico do ∧ 256 23.18 S 44.36 W
Cairofa 152 14.05 S 12.54 E
Cairo International Airport ⊠ 142 30.08 N 31.24 E
Cairo Main Station ✦5 273c 30.04 N 31.15 E
Cairo Montenotte 62 44.24 N 8.16 E
Cairu 255 13.30 S 39.03 W
Caister-on-Sea 42 52.39 N 1.44 E
Caistor 44 53.30 N 0.20 W
Caitingqiao 105 39.54 N 117.39 E
Caitou 152 14.28 S 13.06 E
Caiundo 152 15.46 S 17.28 E
Caivano 68 40.57 N 14.18 E
Caiwan 102 25.50 N 110.50 E
Caixi 100 25.15 N 116.28 E
Caiyu 105 39.39 N 116.37 E
Caizhuang 98 34.17 N 114.08 E
Caizi Hu ⊜ 100 30.48 N 117.05 E
Čaja ≏, Ross. 86 58.08 N 82.57 E
Čaja ≏, Ross. 88 58.15 N 109.35 E
Cajabamba, Ec. 246 1.42 S 78.45 W
Cajabamba, Perú 248 7.37 S 78.03 W
Cajacay 248 10.10 S 77.26 W
Caja de Muertos, Isla I 240m 17.54 N 66.32 W
Cajamar 256 23.21 S 46.53 W
Cajamarca 248 7.10 S 78.31 W
Cajamarca □5 248 6.15 S 78.50 W
Čajan 85 43.02 N 69.23 E
Čajan ≏ 85 42.52 N 68.56 E
Cajapió 250 2.58 S 44.48 W
Cajarc 32 44.29 N 1.50 E
Cajari 250 3.20 S 45.01 W
Cajari ≏ 250 0.48 S 51.43 W
Cajatambo 248 10.29 S 77.02 W
Čajatyn, chrebet ⩚ 89 52.25 N 138.25 E
Cajàzeiras 250 6.54 S 38.34 W
Čajek 85 41.56 N 74.30 E
Čajkovskij 80 56.47 N 54.09 E
Čajniče 38 43.33 N 19.04 E
Cajones ≏ 234 17.45 N 95.55 W
Cajones, Cayos ✧2 236 16.05 N 83.12 W
Cajon Mountain ∧ 228 34.16 N 117.25 W
Cajon Pass)(228 34.19 N 117.26 W
Cajon Summit)(228 34.21 N 117.27 W
Caju ✦8 287a 22.53 S 43.13 W
Cajuru 255 21.17 S 47.18 W
Caka 102 36.48 N 99.19 E
Caka Yanhu ⊜ 102 36.40 N 99.20 E
Čakčar, chrebet ⩚ 85 38.35 N 67.28 E
Cakeni 152 17.48 S 19.27 E
Cakir 88 50.27 N 103.35 E
Çakıralan 130 41.10 N 35.47 E
Çakırgöl Dağı ∧ 130 40.34 N 39.42 E
Çakırhüyük 130 37.34 N 37.50 E
Çakmak 130 37.37 N 34.19 E
Çakmak Dağı ∧ 130 39.46 N 42.12 E
Čakovec 61 46.23 N 16.26 E
Čakovice ✦8 54 50.08 N 14.31 E
Cakung ≏ 269e 6.06 S 106.56 E
Çal 130 38.05 N 29.24 E
Čala, S. Afr. 158 31.30 S 27.37 E
Cala, Tür. 84 41.05 N 43.21 E
Cala, Embalse de ⊜1 34 37.50 N 6.00 W
Calabacillas 234 23.13 N 99.45 W
Calabanga 116 13.42 N 123.12 E
Calabar 150 4.57 N 8.19 E
Calabasas 228 34.09 N 118.38 W
Calabasas, Arroyo ≏ 280 34.12 N 118.36 W
Calabazar ✦8 286b 23.01 N 82.22 W
Calabazas Creek ≏ 282 37.25 N 121.58 W
Calabernardo 70 36.52 N 15.08 E
Calabogie 212 45.18 N 76.43 W
Calabogie Lake ⊜ 212 45.16 N 76.45 W
Calabozo 246 8.56 N 67.26 W
Calabozo, Ensenada de ⊂ 246 11.30 N 71.45 W
Calabria □4 68 39.00 N 16.30 E
Calabria, Parco Nazionale di ♦ 68 38.09 N 15.54 E
Calabritto 68 40.47 N 15.13 E
Calabro ≏ 70 37.53 N 14.11 E
Calabugdong Island I 116 11.06 N 119.41 E
Calaca 116 13.56 N 120.49 E
Calacuccia 36 42.20 N 9.03 E
Caladang, Mount ∧ 116 14.49 N 121.21 E
Caladesi Island I 220 28.02 N 82.49 W
Caladesi Island State Park ♦ 220 28.02 N 82.48 W
Cala d'Oliva 71 41.05 N 8.20 E
Calafat 38 43.59 N 22.56 E
Calafquén, Lago ⊜ 254 39.31 S 72.10 W
Calagnaan Island I 116 11.29 N 123.13 E
Cala Gonone 71 40.18 N 9.38 E
Calagua Islands II 116 14.27 N 122.55 E
Calahorra 34 42.18 N 1.58 W
Calais, Fr. 50 50.57 N 1.50 E
Calais, Me., U.S. 188 45.11 N 67.16 W
Calais, Canal de ≊ 50 50.57 N 1.51 E
Calais, Pas de (Strait of Dover) ʊ 50 51.00 N 1.30 E
Calala 152 12.59 S 23.30 E
Calalaste, Sierra de ⩚ 252 25.30 S 67.30 W
Calalzo di Cadore 64 46.27 N 12.23 E
Calama 252 22.28 S 68.56 W
Calamar, Col. 246 10.15 N 74.55 W
Calamar, Col. 246 1.58 N 72.41 W
Calamarca 248 16.55 S 68.09 W
Calamba, Pil. 116 14.13 N 121.10 E
Calamba, Pil. 116 8.35 N 123.39 E
Calamian Group II 116 12.00 N 120.00 E
Calamity Creek ≏ 196 29.41 N 103.42 W
Calamocha 34 40.55 N 1.18 W
Calamonaci 70 37.31 N 13.17 E
Calamus ≏ 198 41.48 N 99.09 W
Calañas 34 37.39 N 6.53 W
Calanca, Val V 58 46.22 N 9.07 E
Calanda 34 40.56 N 0.14 W
Calandagan Island I 116 10.39 N 120.15 E
Calang 114 4.38 N 95.34 E
Calangianus 71 40.56 N 9.11 E
Calanna 68 38.11 N 15.43 E
Calapan 116 13.25 N 121.10 E
Calape 116 9.54 N 123.52 E
Calapooia ≏ 202 44.38 N 123.08 W
Calapooya Mountains ⩚ 202 43.30 N 122.50 W
Calar Alto ∧ 34 37.15 N 2.25 W
Călărași, Mol. 38 47.16 N 28.19 E
Călărași, Rom. 38 44.11 N 27.20 E
Călărași □6 38 44.20 N 27.10 E
Calarcá 246 4.31 N 75.38 W
Calascibetta 70 37.35 N 14.16 E
Calasetta 71 39.07 N 8.22 E
Calatabiano 70 37.49 N 15.14 E
Calatafimi 70 37.55 N 12.52 E
Calatagan 116 13.50 N 120.38 E
Calatayud 34 41.21 N 1.38 W
Calau 54 51.45 N 13.56 E
Calauag Bay ⊂ 116 14.02 N 122.13 E
Calavà, Capo > 70 38.11 N 14.55 E
Calaveras □6 226 38.12 N 120.41 W
Calaveras ≏ 226 37.58 N 121.22 W
Calaveras, North Fork ≏ 226 38.12 N 120.43 W
Calaveras Big Trees State Park ♦ 226 38.16 N 120.19 W
Calaveras Point > 282 37.28 N 122.03 W
Calaveras Reservoir ⊜1 226 37.28 N 121.49 W
Calaveritas Creek ≏ 226 38.10 N 120.40 W
Calavino 64 46.03 N 10.59 E
Calavite, Cape > 116 13.27 N 120.18 E
Calavite, Mount ∧ 116 13.29 N 120.24 E
Calavite Passage ʊ 116 13.36 N 120.25 E
Calavon ≏ 62 43.52 N 5.35 E
Calawah ≏ 224 47.56 N 124.27 W
Calawah, North Fork ≏ 224 47.58 N 124.20 W
Calawah, South Fork ≏ 224 47.58 N 124.20 W
Calayan 116 19.16 N 121.28 E
Calayan Island I 116 19.20 N 121.27 E
Čalba 89 52.43 N 131.27 E
Calbayog 116 12.04 N 124.36 E
Calbe 54 51.54 N 11.46 E
Calberlah 54 52.25 N 10.37 E
Calbiga 116 11.38 N 125.01 E
Calbuco 254 41.46 S 73.08 W
Calca 248 13.20 S 71.57 W
Calçado ≏ 256 22.05 S 43.04 W
Calcasieu ≏ 194 30.05 N 93.20 W
Calcasieu Lake ⊜ 194 29.50 N 93.17 W
Calceta 246 0.51 S 80.10 W
Calcha 248 21.06 S 67.31 W
Calchaquí 252 29.54 S 60.18 W
Calchaquí ≏ 252 26.03 S 65.50 W
Calciano 68 40.35 N 16.11 E
Calcinaia 66 43.41 N 10.37 E
Calcinato 64 45.27 N 10.24 E
Calcio 62 45.30 N 9.50 E
Calcium 212 44.01 N 75.51 W
Calçoene 250 2.30 N 50.57 W
Calçoene ≏ 250 2.30 N 50.50 W
Calcutta, India 126 22.32 N 88.22 E
Calcutta, India 272b 22.32 N 88.22 E
Calcutta, Oh., U.S. 214 40.40 N 80.34 W
Calcutta University ⊕2 272b 22.35 N 88.22 E
Caldaro (Kaltern) 64 46.25 N 11.14 E
Caldarola 66 43.08 N 13.13 E
Caldas, Bra. 256 21.56 S 46.23 W
Caldas, Col. 246 6.05 N 75.38 W
Caldas □5 246 5.15 N 75.30 W
Caldas da Rainha 34 39.24 N 9.08 W
Caldas de Reis 34 42.36 N 8.38 W
Caldas Novas 255 17.45 S 48.38 W
Caldè 58 45.57 N 8.38 E
Caldecott Tunnel ✦5 282 37.52 N 122.12 W
Calden 56 51.25 N 9.24 E
Calder ≏, Eng., U.K. 44 53.44 N 1.21 W
Calder ≏, Eng., U.K. 262 53.49 N 2.24 W
Calder, Loch ⊜ 46 58.31 N 3.36 W
Caldera 252 27.04 S 70.50 W
Caldera de Taburiente, Parque Nacional de la ♦ 148 28.48 N 17.52 W
Calder and Hebble Navigation Canal ≊ 262 53.43 N 1.54 W
Calder Bridge 44 54.27 N 3.29 W
Calderbrook 262 53.39 N 2.05 W
Calderdale □8 262 53.44 N 2.00 W
Calderstones Park ♦ 262 53.23 N 2.54 W
Caldes 64 46.22 N 10.56 E
Caldes ≏ 266d 41.31 N 2.13 E
Caldew ≏ 44 54.54 N 2.56 W
Caldey Island I 42 51.38 N 4.41 W
Caldicot 42 51.36 N 2.45 W
Caldiero 64 45.22 N 11.11 E
Çaldıran 84 39.09 N 43.55 E
Čaldonazzo 64 45.59 N 11.16 E
Caldonazzo, Lago di ⊜ 64 46.01 N 11.15 E
Čaldonka 88 53.47 N 119.12 E
Caldwell, Id., U.S. 202 43.39 N 116.41 W
Caldwell, Ks., U.S. 198 37.01 N 97.36 W
Caldwell, N.J., U.S. 276 40.51 N 74.17 W
Caldwell, Oh., U.S. 188 39.44 N 81.31 W
Caldwell, Tx., U.S. 222 30.31 N 96.41 W
Caldwell □6 222 29.50 N 97.40 W
Caldwell Creek ≏ 214 41.37 N 79.37 W
Caldwell-Wright Airport ⊠ 276 40.53 N 74.17 W
Caldy 262 53.21 N 3.10 W
Cale ≏ 42 50.59 N 2.20 W
Caledon, On., Can. 212 43.52 N 80.00 W
Caledon, S. Afr. 158 34.12 S 19.23 E
Caledon (Mohokare) ≏ 158 30.31 S 26.05 E
Caledon East 212 43.52 N 79.52 W
Caledonia, Belize 232 18.14 N 88.29 W
Caledonia, N.S., Can. 186 44.22 N 65.02 W
Caledonia, On., Can. 212 43.04 N 79.56 W
Caledonia, Il., U.S. 216 42.22 N 88.53 W
Caledonia, Mi., U.S. 216 42.47 N 85.31 W
Caledonia, Mn., U.S. 190 43.38 N 91.29 W
Caledonia, Ms., U.S. 194 33.40 N 88.19 W
Caledonia, N.Y., U.S. 210 42.58 N 77.51 W
Caledonia, Oh., U.S. 214 40.38 N 82.58 W
Caledonia, Pa., U.S. 214 41.17 N 78.27 W
Caledonian Canal ≊ 46 56.50 N 5.06 W
Caledonia State Park ♦ 208 39.56 N 77.29 W
Calego 152 12.10 S 23.36 E
Calella 34 41.37 N 2.40 E
Calemba 152 16.04 S 15.44 E
Calen 166 20.54 S 148.46 E
Calendžicha 84 42.37 N 42.04 E
Calenzano 66 43.51 N 11.09 E
Calera, Al., U.S. 194 33.06 N 86.45 W
Calera, Ok., U.S. 196 33.56 N 96.25 W
Calera Creek ≏ 282 37.27 N 121.54 W
Caleta, Punta > 240p 20.04 N 74.18 W
Caleta Olivia 254 46.26 S 67.32 W
Caleufú 252 35.35 S 64.33 W
Calexico 204 32.40 N 115.29 W
Calf Island I 283 42.20 N 70.54 W
Calf Islands II 276 40.59 N 73.38 W
Calfkiller ≏ 194 35.49 N 85.29 W
Calf of Man I 44 54.03 N 4.48 W
Calfpasture ≏ 188 37.58 N 79.28 W
Calf Pasture Point > 276 41.05 N 73.24 W
Calgary 182 51.03 N 114.05 W
Calhan 198 39.02 N 104.17 W
Calhariz ✦8 266c 38.44 N 9.12 W
Calhoun, Al., U.S. 194 32.03 N 86.32 W
Calhoun, Ga., U.S. 192 34.30 N 84.57 W
Calhoun, Ky., U.S. 194 37.32 N 87.15 W
Calhoun, Mo., U.S. 194 38.28 N 93.37 W
Calhoun, Tn., U.S. 192 35.17 N 84.44 W
Calhoun □6, Il., U.S. 219 39.09 N 90.37 W
Calhoun □6, Mi., U.S. 216 42.14 N 85.00 W
Calhoun City 194 33.51 N 89.18 W
Calhoun Falls 192 34.05 N 82.35 W
Cali, Col. 246 3.27 N 76.31 W
Çalı, Tür. 130 40.10 N 28.54 E
Calian Point > 116 6.07 N 125.42 E
Calicoan Island I 116 10.59 N 125.48 E
Calico Ghost Town ⊥ 228 34.57 N 116.52 W
Calico Rock 194 36.07 N 92.08 W
Calicut — Kozhikode 122 11.15 N 75.46 E
Caliente 204 37.36 N 114.30 W
Caliente Creek ≏ 228 35.17 N 118.48 W
Califon 210 40.43 N 74.50 W
California, Mo., U.S. 194 38.37 N 92.33 W
California, Pa., U.S. 214 40.03 N 79.53 W
California □3, U.S. 178 37.30 N 119.30 W
California □3, U.S. 204 37.30 N 119.30 W
California, Golfo de ⊂ 232 28.00 N 112.00 W
California, University of ⊕2 282 37.52 N 122.15 W
California Aqueduct ≊1 204 33.52 N 117.12 W
California City 228 35.08 N 117.58 W
California Creek ≏ 196 33.05 N 99.33 W
California Institute of Technology ⊕2 280 34.08 N 118.08 W
California Institution for Men ⊕ 280 33.59 N 117.40 W
California Institution for Women ⊕ 280 33.57 N 117.38 W
California-Los Angeles, University of (U.C.L.A.) ⊕2 280 34.04 N 118.26 W
California State Polytechnic University ⊕2 280 34.04 N 117.49 W
California State University (Northridge) ⊕2, Ca., U.S. 280 34.14 N 118.32 W
California State University (Los Angeles) ⊕2, Ca., U.S. 280 34.04 N 118.10 W
California State University (Dominguez Hills) ⊕2, Ca., U.S. 280 33.52 N 118.17 W
California State University (Fullerton) ⊕2, Ca., U.S. 280 33.53 N 117.53 W
California State University (Long Beach) ⊕2, Ca., U.S. 280 33.47 N 118.06 W
California State University (Hayward) ⊕2, Ca., U.S. 282 37.39 N 122.04 W
Calihualá 234 17.35 N 98.10 W
Călilabad 84 39.14 N 48.31 E
Calilegua 252 23.47 S 64.47 W
Calilegua, Parque Nacional ♦ 252 23.40 S 64.50 W
Călimănești 38 45.14 N 24.20 E
Călimani, Munții ⩚ 38 47.07 N 25.03 E
Calimera 68 40.15 N 18.17 E
Calimere, Point > 122 10.18 N 79.52 E

Symbols in the index entries represent the broad categories identified in the key at the right. Symbols with superior numbers (⩚1) identify subcategories (see complete key on page I · 1).

Symbole im Register stellen die rechts im Schlüssel erklärten Kategorien dar. Symbole mit hochgestellten Ziffern (⩚1) bezeichnen Unterabteilungen einer Kategorie (vgl. vollständiger Schlüssel auf Seite I · 1).

Los símbolos incluídos en el texto del índice representan las grandes categorías identificadas con la clave a la derecha. Los símbolos con numeros en su parte superior (⩚1) identifican las subcategorías (véase la clave completa en la página I · 1).

Les symboles de l'index représentent les catégories indiquées dans la légende à droite. Les symboles suivis d'un indice (⩚1) représentent des sous-catégories (voir légende complète à la page I · 1).

Os símbolos incluídos no texto do índice representam as grandes categorias identificadas com a chave à direita. Os símbolos com números em sua parte superior (⩚1) identificam as subcategorias (veja-se a chave completa à página I · 1).

English	Deutsch	Español	Français	Português
∧ Mountain	Berg	Montaña	Montagne	Montanha
⩚ Mountains	Gebirge	Montañas	Montagnes	Montanhas
)(Pass	Paß	Paso	Col	Passo
V Valley, Canyon	Tal, Cañon	Valle, Cañón	Vallée, Canyon	Vale, Canhão
≚ Plain	Ebene	Llano	Plaine	Planície
> Cape	Kap	Cabo	Cap	Cabo
I Island	Insel	Isla	Île	Ilha
II Islands	Inseln	Islas	Îles	Ilhas
⊥ Other Topographic Features	Andere Topographische Objekte	Otros Elementos Topográficos	Autres données topographiques	Outros acidentes topográficos

ESPAÑOL · FRANÇAIS · PORTUGUÊS

Nombre / Nom / Nome	Página / Page	Lat.°′	Long.°′ W = Oeste / W = Ouest
Calimesa	228	34.00 N	117.03 W
Calindó ≃	255	14.26 S	43.51 W
Calingasta	252	31.19 S	69.25 W
Calingiri	162	31.06 S	116.27 E
Calinog	116	11.07 N	122.32 E
Calintaan	116	12.35 N	120.56 E
Calion	194	33.19 N	92.32 W
Calipatria	204	33.07 N	115.30 W
Calispell Peak ʌ	202	48.26 N	117.30 W
Calistoga	226	38.34 N	122.34 W
Calitri	68	40.54 N	15.27 E
Calitzdorp	158	33.33 S	21.42 E
Calizzano	62	44.14 N	8.07 E
Calka	84	41.37 N	44.05 E
Calkinskoje vodochranilišče ⊜[1]	84	41.38 N	44.03 E
Čalkojdy	85	40.44 N	73.39 E
Calla	226	37.46 N	121.11 W
Callabonna, Lake ⊜	166	29.45 S	140.04 E
Callabonna Creek ≃	166	29.38 S	140.08 E
Callac	32	48.24 N	3.26 W
Callaghan, Mount ʌ	204	39.42 N	116.57 W
Callahan	192	30.33 N	81.49 W
Callahan, Mount ʌ	200	39.26 N	108.07 W
Callahans	276	40.58 N	74.37 W
Callan	48	52.33 N	7.23 W
Callander, On., Can.	190	46.13 N	79.23 W
Callander, Scot., U.K.	46	56.15 N	4.14 W
Callang	116	17.02 N	121.38 E
Callanish	46	58.12 N	6.43 W
Callanmarca	248	12.52 S	74.38 W
Callanna	166	29.38 S	137.55 E
Callantsoog	52	52.49 N	4.41 E
Callao, Perú	248	12.04 S	77.09 W
Callao, Va., U.S.	208	37.58 N	76.33 W
Callao □[4]	286d	12.04 S	77.09 W
Callaquén, Volcán ʌ[1]	252	37.54 S	71.26 W
Callas	62	43.35 N	6.32 E
Callaway	198	41.17 N	99.55 W
Callaway □[6]	219	38.50 N	91.52 W
Callaway Gardens ♦	192	32.51 N	84.52 W
Calle	56	51.20 N	8.13 E
Callensburg	214	41.08 N	79.33 W
Callery	214	40.45 N	80.02 W
Call Hill ʌ[2]	210	42.13 N	77.40 W
Calliano, It.	62	45.00 N	8.15 E
Calliano, It.	64	45.56 N	11.05 E
Calliaqua	241h	13.08 N	61.12 W
Callicoon	210	41.46 N	75.03 W
Callicoon Center	210	41.50 N	74.57 W
Calliham	196	28.29 N	98.21 W
Calling Lake	182	55.15 N	113.12 W
Calling Lake ⊜	182	55.13 N	113.15 W
Callington, Austl.	168b	35.07 S	139.02 E
Callington, Eng., U.K.	42	50.30 N	4.18 W
Calliope	166	24.00 S	151.12 E
Callosa d'En Sarrià	34	38.39 N	0.07 W
Callosa de Segura	34	38.08 N	0.52 W
Calloway Canal ≊	226	35.24 N	119.01 W
Calmar, Ab., Can.	182	53.16 N	113.49 W
Calmar → Kalmar, Sve.	26	56.40 N	16.22 E
Calmar, Ia., U.S.	190	43.11 N	91.51 W
Călmățui ≃	38	44.50 N	27.50 E
Calmazzo	66	43.40 N	12.46 E
Calmbach	56	48.46 N	8.35 E
Calm Lake ⊜	190	48.46 N	92.04 W
Čal'mny-Varre	24	67.10 N	37.33 E
Čalna	24	61.55 N	34.01 E
Calnali	234	20.55 N	98.35 W
Calne	42	51.27 N	2.00 W
Calobre	236	8.19 N	80.51 W
Calola	152	16.30 S	17.51 E
Calolbon	116	13.36 N	124.06 E
Calólo	152	10.00 S	14.53 E
Calolziocorte	62	45.48 N	9.26 E
Calonne-Ricouart	50	50.29 N	2.29 E
Caloocan	116	14.39 N	120.58 E
Caloosahatchee ≃	220	26.31 N	82.01 W
Caloosahatchee Canal ≊	220	26.46 N	81.27 W
Caloote	168b	34.58 S	139.16 E
Calore ≃, It.	68	40.31 N	15.01 E
Calore ≃, It.	68	41.11 N	14.28 E
Caloundra	166	26.48 S	153.09 E
Calouste-Gulbenkian, Museu de ʋ	266c	38.44 N	9.08 W
Caloveto	68	39.30 N	16.45 E
Calp	34	38.39 N	0.03 E
Calpulalpan	234	19.35 N	98.35 W
Čalpy	80	55.05 N	53.06 E
Calshot	42	50.49 N	1.19 W
Calstock	42	50.30 N	4.12 W
Caltabellotta	70	37.34 N	13.13 E
Caltagirone	70	37.14 N	14.31 E
Caltagirone ≃	70	37.21 N	14.42 E
Caltanissetta	70	37.29 N	14.04 E
Caltanissetta □[4]	70	37.29 N	14.04 E
Caltavuturo	70	37.49 N	13.53 E
Çaltılıbük	130	39.57 N	28.36 E
Caltra	48	53.26 N	8.25 W
Čaltyr'	83	47.17 N	39.30 E
Caluango	152	8.21 S	19.40 E
Calubian	116	11.27 N	124.26 E
Calucinga	152	11.18 S	16.12 E
Călugăreni	38	44.07 N	26.01 E
Caluire-et-Cuire	62	45.48 N	4.51 E
Calumbolaca	152	9.09 S	13.48 E
Calumet, Mi., U.S.	190	47.14 N	88.27 W
Calumet, Mn., U.S.	190	47.19 N	93.16 W
Calumet, Pa., U.S.	214	40.13 N	79.28 W
Calumet ≃	278	41.44 N	87.32 W
Calumet, Lake ⊜	216	41.41 N	87.35 W
Calumet City	216	41.36 N	87.31 W
Calumet Harbor ⊂	278	41.44 N	87.32 W
Calumet Park	278	41.39 N	87.39 W
Calumet Park ♦	278	41.43 N	87.32 W
Calumet Sag Channel ≊	278	41.42 N	87.57 W
Calumpit	116	14.55 N	120.46 E
Calunda	152	12.06 S	23.23 E
Caluquembe	152	13.47 S	14.44 E
Calusa Island I	116	9.37 N	121.01 E
Caluso	62	45.18 N	7.53 E
Caluula	144	11.58 N	50.45 E
Caluula, Raasiga ›	144	11.59 N	50.47 E
Caluya Island I	116	11.55 N	121.34 E
Calvados □[5]	32	49.10 N	0.30 W
Calvello	68	40.28 N	15.51 E
Calver	44	53.16 N	1.38 W
Calvera	68	40.09 N	16.09 E
Calvert, Al., U.S.	194	31.09 N	88.01 W
Calvert, Tx., U.S.	222	30.58 N	96.40 W
Calvert □[6]	208	38.33 N	76.35 W
Calvert ≃	164	16.17 S	137.44 E
Calvert, Lough ⊜	169	38.11 S	143.42 E
Calvert City	194	37.02 N	88.21 W
Calvert Hills	166	17.15 S	137.20 E
Calvert Island I	182	51.35 N	128.00 W
Calverton, Eng., U.K.	44	53.02 N	1.05 W
Calverton, Md., U.S.	284c	39.03 N	76.56 W
Calverton, N.Y., U.S.	207	40.55 N	72.45 W
Calvi	36	42.34 N	8.45 E
Calvi, Monte ʌ	66	43.05 N	10.37 E
Calvia	34	39.34 N	2.31 E
Calvi dell'Umbria	66	42.24 N	12.34 E
Calvillo	234	21.51 N	102.43 W
Calvin, Ok., U.S.	196	34.58 N	96.14 W
Calvin, Pa., U.S.	214	40.20 N	78.02 W
Calvinia	158	31.25 S	19.45 E
Calvisano	64	45.20 N	10.20 E
Calvo, Monte ʌ	68	41.44 N	15.46 E
Calvörde	54	52.23 N	11.17 E
Calw	56	48.43 N	8.44 E
Calwa	226	36.42 N	119.45 W
Calypso	192	35.09 N	78.06 W
Calzada	248	6.02 S	77.02 W
Cam ≃	42	52.21 N	0.15 E
Camabatela	152	8.11 S	15.22 E
Camaçã ≃	248	6.35 S	66.27 W
Camaçari	255	12.41 S	38.18 W
Camachigama, Lac ⊜	190	47.50 N	76.19 W
Camacupa	152	12.03 S	17.30 E
Camaguán	246	8.06 N	67.36 W
Camagüey	240p	21.23 N	77.55 W
Camagüey □[4]	240p	21.30 N	78.00 W
Camagüey, Archipiélago de II	240p	22.30 N	78.10 W
Camaiore	64	43.56 N	10.18 E
Camaiú ≃	248	5.30 S	59.42 W
Camajuaní	240p	22.28 N	79.44 W
Camaldoli, Eremo di ʋ[1]	66	43.46 N	11.47 E
Camamu	255	13.57 S	39.07 W
Camaná	248	16.37 S	72.42 W
Camaná ≃	248	16.39 S	72.46 W
Camanaú ≃	246	1.51 S	61.14 W
Camanche	190	41.47 N	90.15 W
Camanche Reservoir ⊜[1]	226	38.13 N	120.58 W
Camandag Island I	116	11.59 N	124.25 E
Camanducaia	256	22.46 S	46.09 W
Camanducaia ≃, Bra.	256	22.39 S	46.58 W
Camanducaia ≃, Bra.	256	22.55 S	46.25 W
Camano Island I	224	48.10 N	122.30 W
Camaoí ≃	250	3.12 S	48.04 W
Camapuã	255	19.30 S	54.05 W
Camaquã	252	30.51 S	51.49 W
Camaquã ≃	252	31.17 S	51.47 W
Camará	246	3.55 S	62.44 W
Camarajibe	250	8.01 S	34.58 W
Camararé ≃	248	12.15 S	58.55 W
Camarat, Cap ›	62	43.12 N	6.41 E
Camarda	66	42.23 N	13.29 E
Çamardı	130	37.50 N	35.00 E
Camarès	32	43.49 N	2.53 E
Camargo, Bol.	248	20.39 S	65.13 W
Camargo, Méx.	232	27.40 N	105.10 W
Camargos, Reprêsa de ⊜[1]	256	21.25 S	44.30 W
Camargue ✦[1]	62	43.34 N	4.34 E
Camargue, Parc Naturel Regional de ♦	62	43.30 N	4.28 E
Camarillo	228	34.12 N	119.02 W
Camarillo Heights	228	34.14 N	119.02 W
Camarina ⊥	70	36.52 N	14.27 E
Camariñas	34	43.07 N	9.10 W
Camarines Norte □[4]	116	14.10 N	122.40 E
Camarines Sur □[4]	116	13.35 N	123.20 E
Camarón, Arroyo ≃	196	27.08 N	100.00 W
Camarón, Cabo ›	236	16.00 N	85.05 W
Camarones	254	44.48 S	65.42 W
Camarones, Bahía ⊂	254	44.45 S	65.34 W
Camas, Esp.	34	37.24 N	6.02 W
Çamaş, Tür.	130	40.55 N	37.32 E
Camas, Wa., U.S.	224	45.35 N	122.23 W
Camas Creek ≃, Id., U.S.	202	43.20 N	114.24 W
Camas Creek ≃, Id., U.S.	202	44.53 N	114.44 W
Camas Creek ≃, Id., U.S.	202	43.53 N	112.21 W
Camas Creek ≃, Or., U.S.	202	45.01 N	118.59 W
Camastra	70	37.15 N	13.47 E
Camatagua, Embalse de ⊜[1]	246	9.50 N	67.00 W
Camatambo	152	6.30 S	15.18 E
Ca Mau	110	9.11 N	105.08 E
Ca Mau, Mui ›	110	8.38 N	104.44 E
Camaxilo	152	8.21 S	18.56 E
Camba	112	4.54 S	119.50 E
Camba Cassai	152	9.40 S	19.18 E
Cambados	34	42.30 N	8.48 W
Cambará	255	23.03 S	50.05 W
Čambarak	84	40.36 N	45.21 E
Camberley	42	51.21 N	0.45 W
Camberwell	169	37.50 S	145.04 E
Camberwell ✦[8]	260	51.28 N	0.05 W
Cambiano	62	44.58 N	7.47 E
Cambo	44	55.10 N	1.57 W
Cambo ≃	152	7.40 S	17.17 E
Cambodia (Kâmpŭchéa) □[1], Asia	108	13.00 N	105.00 E
Cambodia (Kâmpŭchéa) □[1], Asia	110	13.00 N	105.00 E
Cambois	44	55.10 N	1.31 W
Cambonda, Serra ⌃	152	12.06 S	14.00 E
Camboon	166	25.03 S	150.26 E
Cambooya	171a	27.42 S	151.52 E
Camboriú	252	27.01 S	48.38 W
Camborne	42	50.12 N	5.19 W
Cambra	210	41.11 N	76.18 W
Cambrai, Austl.	168b	34.39 S	139.17 E
Cambrai, Fr.	50	50.10 N	3.14 E
Cambremer	50	49.09 N	0.03 E
Cambria, Ca., U.S.	226	35.33 N	121.04 W
Cambria, In., U.S.	216	40.22 N	86.33 W
Cambria, Mi., U.S.	216	41.49 N	84.39 W
Cambria, Wi., U.S.	190	43.32 N	89.06 W
Cambria □[6]	214	40.29 N	79.16 W
Cambria Ice Field ⍓	182	55.55 N	129.30 W
Cambrian Mountains ⌃	28	52.35 N	3.35 W
Cambrian Park	226	37.15 N	121.55 W
Cambridge (Galt), On., Can.	212	43.22 N	80.19 W
Cambridge, N.Z.	172	37.53 S	175.28 E
Cambridge, Eng., U.K.	42	52.13 N	0.08 E
Cambridge, Id., U.S.	202	44.34 N	116.41 W
Cambridge, Il., U.S.	190	41.18 N	90.11 W
Cambridge, Ia., U.S.	190	41.53 N	93.31 W
Cambridge, Md., U.S.	208	38.33 N	76.04 W
Cambridge, Ma., U.S.	207	42.22 N	71.06 W
Cambridge, Mn., U.S.	190	45.34 N	93.13 W
Cambridge, Ne., U.S.	198	40.16 N	100.09 W
Cambridge, N.Y., U.S.	210	43.01 N	73.22 W
Cambridge, Oh., U.S.	188	40.02 N	81.35 W
Cambridge, Wi., U.S.	216	43.00 N	89.01 W
Cambridge Bay	176	69.03 N	105.05 W
Cambridge City	218	39.48 N	85.10 W
Cambridge Fiord ⊂[2]	176	71.20 N	74.44 W
Cambridge Gulf ⊂	164	14.55 S	128.15 E
Cambridge Park	274a	33.45 S	150.43 E
Cambridge Reservoir ⊜[1]	283	42.24 N	71.16 W
Cambridgeshire □[6]	42	52.20 N	0.05 E
Cambridge Springs	214	41.48 N	80.03 W
Cambrils	34	41.04 N	1.03 E
Cambriú, Ponta de ›	252	25.10 S	47.55 W
Cambuci ✦[8]	287b	23.34 S	46.37 W
Cambuí	256	22.37 S	46.04 W
Cambulo	152	7.48 S	21.14 E
Cambundi-Catembo	152	10.09 S	17.31 E
Cambuquira	256	21.51 S	45.18 W
Cambural	286c	10.26 N	66.59 W
Camburg	54	51.03 N	11.42 E
Camburú ≃	256	23.41 S	45.28 W
Çamby	218	39.40 N	86.19 W
Čamčakly	128	37.56 N	63.06 E
Camden, Austl.	170	34.03 S	150.42 E
Camden, S. Afr.	158	26.38 S	30.07 E
Camden, Al., U.S.	194	31.59 N	87.17 W
Camden, Ar., U.S.	194	33.35 N	92.50 W
Camden, De., U.S.	208	39.06 N	75.32 W
Camden, Il., U.S.	219	40.09 N	90.46 W
Camden, In., U.S.	216	40.36 N	86.32 W
Camden, Me., U.S.	188	44.12 N	69.03 W
Camden, Mi., U.S.	216	41.45 N	84.45 W
Camden, Ms., U.S.	194	32.46 N	89.50 W
Camden, N.J., U.S.	208	39.55 N	75.07 W
Camden, N.Y., U.S.	210	43.20 N	75.44 W
Camden, N.C., U.S.	192	36.19 N	76.10 W
Camden, Oh., U.S.	218	39.37 N	84.38 W
Camden, S.C., U.S.	192	34.14 N	80.36 W
Camden, Tn., U.S.	194	36.03 N	88.05 W
Camden, Tx., U.S.	222	30.55 N	94.44 W
Camden □[6], N.J., U.S.	208	39.57 N	75.07 W
Camden □[6], N.C., U.S.	208	36.28 N	76.21 W
Camden ✦[8]	260	51.33 N	0.10 W
Camden, Grupo II	254	54.40 S	71.58 W
Camden Aerodrome ⊠	274a	34.03 S	150.41 E
Camden Bay ⊂	180	70.00 N	145.00 W
Camden Hills State Park ♦	188	44.17 N	69.05 W
Camden Lake ⊜	212	44.25 N	76.52 W
Camden Station ✦[5]	284b	39.17 N	76.37 W
Camdenton	194	38.00 N	92.44 W
Camedo	58	46.09 N	8.37 E
Cameia, Parque Nacional da ♦	152	11.45 S	21.20 E
Camel ≃	42	50.33 N	4.55 W
Camel, Mount ʌ[2]	169	36.45 S	144.43 E
Camelback Mountain ʌ, Ak., U.S.	180	62.33 N	157.20 W
Camelback Mountain ʌ, Pa., U.S.	210	41.03 N	75.21 W
Camelford	42	50.37 N	4.41 W
Çameli	130	37.05 N	29.20 E
Camels Hump ʌ	188	44.19 N	72.53 W
Camenca	38	48.03 N	28.42 E
Cameo Acres	282	37.51 N	121.58 W
Camerano	66	43.32 N	13.33 E
Cameri	62	45.30 N	8.39 E
Cameri, Aeroporto di ⊠	266b	45.32 N	8.40 E
Camerino	66	43.08 N	13.04 E
Cameron, La., U.S.	194	29.47 N	93.19 W
Cameron, Mo., U.S.	194	39.44 N	94.14 W
Cameron, N.Y., U.S.	210	42.12 N	77.24 W
Cameron, Pa., U.S.	214	41.27 N	78.10 W
Cameron, S.C., U.S.	192	33.33 N	80.42 W
Cameron, Tx., U.S.	222	30.51 N	96.58 W
Cameron, W.V., U.S.	188	39.49 N	80.34 W
Cameron, Wi., U.S.	190	45.24 N	91.44 W
Cameron □[6]	214	41.31 N	78.14 W
Cameron ≃	224	49.17 N	124.38 W
Cameron, Lac ⊜	206	46.06 N	74.50 W
Cameron Highlands	114	4.29 N	101.27 E
Cameron Hills ⌃[2]	176	59.48 N	118.00 W
Cameron Lake ⊜, B.C., Can.	224	49.17 N	124.37 W
Cameron Lake ⊜, On., Can.	212	44.34 N	78.45 W
Cameron Mills	210	42.11 N	77.22 W
Cameron Mountains ⌃	172	46.00 S	167.00 E
Cameron Park	226	38.39 N	120.56 W
Cameron Run ≃	284c	38.48 N	77.04 W
Cameroon (Cameroun) □[1]	134	6.00 N	12.00 E
Cameroon Mountain ʌ	152	4.12 N	9.11 E
Camerota	68	40.02 N	15.23 E
Cameroun → Cameroon □[1]	134	6.00 N	12.00 E
Camerún → Cameroon □[1]	134	6.00 N	12.00 E
Cametá	250	2.15 S	49.30 W
Camfield	164	17.09 S	131.21 E
Çamiçi Gölü ⊜	130	37.30 N	27.25 E
Camiguin □[4]	116	9.15 N	124.40 E
Camiguin Island I, Pil.	116	18.56 N	121.55 E
Camiguin Island I, Pil.	116	9.11 N	124.42 E
Camiling	116	15.42 N	120.24 E
Camilla	192	31.13 N	84.12 W
Camillus	210	43.02 N	76.19 W
Camin	54	53.27 N	10.58 E
Camiña	248	19.18 S	69.26 W
Caminha	34	41.52 N	8.50 W
Camino	226	38.44 N	120.40 W
Camiranga	250	1.48 S	46.17 W
Camiri	248	20.03 S	63.31 W
Camisano Vicentino	64	45.31 N	11.43 E
Camisea ≃	248	11.35 S	72.58 W
Camissombo	152	8.10 S	20.39 E
Čamjarysy	78	51.42 N	30.24 E
Camlad ≃	42	52.36 N	3.10 W
Çamlıbel	130	40.05 N	36.29 E
Çamlıdere, Tür.	130	37.08 N	39.03 E
Çamlıdere, Tür.	130	40.30 N	32.29 E
Çamlıyayla	130	37.09 N	34.36 E
Cam Lo	110	16.49 N	106.59 E
Čamlyk ≃	84	44.45 N	40.45 E
Cammal	210	41.24 N	77.28 W
Cammarata	70	37.38 N	13.38 E
Cammarta, Monte ʌ	70	37.37 N	13.36 E
Camoapa	236	12.23 N	85.31 W
Camocim	250	2.54 S	40.50 W
Camogli	62	44.21 N	9.09 E
Çamoluk	130	40.08 N	38.45 E
Camonica, Val V	64	46.00 N	10.20 E
Camooweal	166	19.55 S	138.07 E
Camopi ≃	250	3.11 S	52.20 W
Camorim ≃	287a	22.59 S	43.25 W
Camorim, Reprêsa do ⊜[1]	287a	22.58 S	43.27 W
Camorta Island I	110	8.08 N	93.30 E
Camote, Cerro ʌ	286d	11.57 S	77.06 W
Camotes Islands II	116	10.40 N	124.24 E
Camotes Sea ⍑[2]	116	10.30 N	124.15 E
Camotlán ≃	234	22.01 N	104.15 W
Camowen ≃	48	54.36 N	7.18 W
Camp □[6]	222	33.00 N	94.58 W
Campagna	68	40.40 N	15.08 E
Campagna di Roma ✦[1]	66	41.50 N	12.35 E
Campagna Lupia	64	45.21 N	12.06 E
Campagnano di Roma	66	42.08 N	12.23 E
Campagnatico	66	42.53 N	11.16 E
Campagne-lès-Hesdin	50	50.24 N	1.52 E
Campaign	194	35.46 N	85.37 W
Campamento	236	14.33 N	86.42 W
Campana, Arg.	258	34.10 S	58.57 W
Campana, It.	68	39.24 N	16.50 E
Campana, Isla I	254	48.20 S	75.15 W
Campanario	34	38.52 N	5.37 W
Campanario, Cerro de ʌ	248	5.57 S	77.31 W
Campanella, Punta ›	68	40.34 N	14.19 E
Campanero, Cerro ʌ	246	5.54 N	65.12 W
Campanha	256	21.50 S	45.24 W
Campania □[4]	68	40.55 N	14.50 E
Campania Island I	182	53.05 N	129.30 W
Camparada	266b	45.39 N	9.19 E
Campaspe ≃, Austl.	166	21.00 S	146.24 E
Campaspe ≃, Austl.	169	36.41 S	144.31 E
Campbell, S. Afr.	158	28.48 S	23.44 E
Campbell, Ca., U.S.	226	37.17 N	121.56 W
Campbell, Mn., U.S.	198	46.05 N	96.24 W
Campbell, Mo., U.S.	194	36.29 N	90.04 W
Campbell, Ne., U.S.	198	40.18 N	98.44 W
Campbell, N.Y., U.S.	210	42.13 N	77.11 W
Campbell, Oh., U.S.	214	41.04 N	80.35 W
Campbell, Tx., U.S.	222	33.09 N	95.57 W
Campbell □[6]	218	38.55 N	84.20 W
Campbell, Cape ›	172	41.44 S	174.17 E
Campbell Airport ⊠	279b	40.21 N	80.11 W
Campbellfield	274b	37.41 S	144.57 E
Campbellford	212	44.18 N	77.48 W
Campbell Hall	210	41.27 N	74.16 W
Campbell Hill ʌ[2]	216	40.22 N	83.43 W
Campbell Island	182	52.10 N	128.09 W
Campbell Island I	9	52.30 S	169.05 E
Campbell Lake ⊜	182	50.01 N	125.27 W
Campbell Plateau ✤[3]	9	51.00 S	170.00 E
Campbell Point ›	171a	27.22 S	153.55 E
Campbellpore	123	33.46 N	72.22 E
Campbell Range ⌃	180	61.08 N	129.45 W
Campbell River	182	50.01 N	125.15 W
Campbells ≃	170	33.42 S	149.37 E
Campbell's Airport ⊠	278	42.20 N	88.04 W
Campbell's-Bay	188	45.44 N	76.36 W
Campbellsburg, In., U.S.	218	38.39 N	86.15 W
Campbellsburg, Ky., U.S.	218	38.31 N	85.12 W
Campbell Slough ≃	226	39.22 N	121.51 W
Campbellsport	190	43.35 N	88.16 W
Campbells River	170	33.54 S	149.37 E
Campbells Run ≃	279b	40.24 N	80.05 W
Campbellsville	194	37.20 N	85.20 W
Campbellton, N.B., Can.	186	48.00 N	66.40 W
Campbellton, Nf., Can.	186	49.17 N	54.56 W
Campbellton, P.E., Can.	186	46.47 N	64.18 W
Campbellton, Fl., U.S.	192	30.56 N	85.24 W
Campbell Town, Austl.	166	41.56 S	147.29 E
Campbelltown, Austl.	168b	34.53 S	138.40 E
Campbelltown, Austl.	170	34.04 S	150.49 E
Campbelltown, Pa., U.S.	208	40.17 N	76.35 W
Campbellville	212	43.29 N	79.59 W
Campbeltown	46	55.26 N	5.36 W
Camp Creek ≃, Ca., U.S.	226	38.38 N	120.40 W
Camp Creek ≃, Mo., U.S.	219	39.02 N	91.12 W
Camp Creek Lake ⊜[1]	222	31.03 N	96.19 W
Camp David ʋ	208	39.38 N	77.28 W
Camp de Frileuse ■	261	48.52 N	1.55 E
Camp de Satory ■	261	48.47 N	2.06 E
Camp Dix	218	38.29 N	83.17 W
Camp Douglas	190	43.55 N	90.16 W
Campeche	232	19.51 N	90.32 W
Campeche □[3], Méx.	232	19.00 N	90.30 W
Campeche □[3], Méx.	232	19.00 N	90.30 W
Campeche, Bahía de ⊂	232	20.00 N	94.00 W
Campeche Bank ✤[4]	16	22.00 N	90.00 W
Campechuela	240p	20.14 N	77.17 W
Campegine	64	44.45 N	10.32 E
Campello Monti	58	45.56 N	8.15 E
Câmpeni	38	46.22 N	23.03 E
Camperdown, Austl.	169	38.14 S	143.09 E
Camperdown, S. Afr.	158	29.42 S	30.33 E
Camperville	184	51.59 N	100.09 W
Campestre	256	21.43 S	46.15 W
Cam Pha	110	21.01 N	107.19 E
Camp Hill, Al., U.S.	194	32.48 N	85.39 W
Camp Hill, Pa., U.S.	208	40.14 N	76.55 W
Câmpia Turzii	38	46.33 N	23.54 E
Campi Bisenzio	66	43.49 N	11.08 E
Campidano ✦[1]	71	39.30 N	8.47 E
Campiglia dei Fosci	66	43.27 N	11.03 E
Campiglia Marittima	66	43.03 N	10.37 E
Campillo de Llerena	34	38.30 N	5.50 W
Campillos	34	37.03 N	4.51 W
Câmpina	38	45.08 N	25.44 E
Campina ✦[1]	34	37.45 N	4.45 W
Campina Grande	250	7.13 S	35.53 W
Campinas	256	22.54 S	47.05 W
Campina Verde	255	19.31 S	49.28 W
Campinho, Rio do ≃	287a	22.52 S	43.37 W
Campione	58	45.58 N	8.58 E
Campione del Garda	64	45.45 N	10.45 E
Campi Salentina	68	40.24 N	18.01 E
Campitello	64	46.28 N	11.44 E
Camp King	150	4.55 N	7.58 W
Camp Lake	216	42.32 N	88.09 W
Camp Lake ⊜	212	45.27 N	78.54 W
Camp Leger ■	261	48.34 N	2.34 E
Camp Lejeune Marine Corps Base ■	192	34.40 N	77.21 W
Campli	66	42.43 N	13.41 E
Camplong	112	10.02 S	123.55 E
Campo, Cam.	152	2.22 N	9.49 E
Campo, Moç.	156	17.44 S	36.21 E
Campo, Co., U.S.	198	37.06 N	102.34 W
Campo, Réserve de ✦[4]	152	2.35 N	9.57 E
Campoalegre	246	2.41 N	75.20 W
Campo Alegre ≃	250	9.19 S	50.06 W
Campo Alegre de Goiás	255	17.39 S	47.45 W
Campobasso	66	41.34 N	14.39 E
Campobasso □[4]	66	41.38 N	14.35 E
Campobello di Licata	70	37.15 N	13.55 E
Campobello di Mazara	70	37.38 N	12.45 E
Campobello Island I	186	44.53 N	66.55 W
Campo Belo	255	20.53 S	45.16 W
Campo Blenio	58	46.34 N	8.56 E
Campocologno	58	46.13 N	10.08 E
Campodarsego	64	45.30 N	11.54 E
Campo de Criptana	34	39.24 N	3.07 W
Campo de la Cruz	246	10.23 N	74.53 W
Campo de Marte ♦	286d	12.04 S	77.03 W
Campo de Marte ■	287b	23.30 S	46.37 W
Campo de Mayo ■	288	34.32 S	58.38 W
Campo di Giove	66	42.01 N	14.03 E
Campo di Trens (Trens)	64	46.52 N	11.29 E
Campo do Coelho	256	22.15 S	42.39 W
Campodolcino	58	46.24 N	9.21 E
Campo Erê	252	26.23 S	53.03 W
Campofelice di Fitalia	70	37.50 N	13.29 E
Campofelice di Roccella	70	37.59 N	13.53 E
Campofiorito	70	37.45 N	13.16 E
Campo Florido	255	19.47 S	48.35 W
Campoformido	64	46.01 N	13.09 E
Campo Formoso	250	10.31 S	40.20 W
Campofranco	70	37.30 N	13.43 E
Campogalliano	64	44.41 N	10.50 E
Campo Gallo	252	26.35 S	62.51 W
Campo Grande, Arg.	252	27.13 S	54.58 W
Campo Grande, Bra.	255	20.27 S	54.37 W
Campo Grande ✦[8], Bra.	256	22.54 S	43.34 W
Campo Grande ✦[8], Port.	266c	38.45 N	9.09 W
Campo Indian Reservation ✦[4]	204	32.40 N	116.20 W
Campo Largo, Arg.	252	26.48 S	60.50 W
Campo Largo, Bra.	252	25.26 S	49.32 W
Campolaro	64	45.55 N	10.20 E
Campolasta (Astfeld)	64	46.40 N	11.22 E
Campolato, Capo ›	70	37.17 N	15.12 E
Campo Libertad ■	286b	23.05 N	82.26 W
Campolide	256	21.36 S	43.53 W
Campolieto	66	41.38 N	14.46 E
Campo Ligure	62	44.32 N	8.42 E
Campo Limpo Paulista	256	23.12 S	46.48 W
Campo Maior, Bra.	250	4.49 S	42.10 W
Campo Maior, Port.	34	39.01 N	7.04 W
Campomarino	66	41.57 N	15.02 E
Campo Militar Número Uno ■	286a	19.27 N	99.14 W
Campomorone	62	44.30 N	8.53 E
Campo Mourão	255	24.03 S	52.22 W
Campo Novo	252	27.42 S	53.48 W
Campo Pequeno ♦	266c	38.44 N	9.08 W
Campo Quijano	252	24.55 S	65.39 W
Campora	68	40.19 N	15.17 E
Camporeale	70	37.54 N	13.06 E
Camporgiano	64	44.09 N	10.20 E
Camporredondo	248	6.07 S	78.21 W
Campos	255	21.45 S	41.18 W
Campos Altos	255	19.41 S	46.10 W
Camposampiero	64	45.34 N	11.56 E
Campo Santo, Arg.	252	24.40 S	65.06 W
Camposanto, It.	64	44.47 N	11.08 E
Campos Belos	255	13.03 S	46.53 W
Campos de Cunha	256	22.55 S	44.49 W
Campos do Jordão	256	22.44 S	45.35 W
Campos Elisios	256	22.42 S	43.17 W
Campos Gerais	256	21.14 S	45.46 W
Campos Novos	252	27.24 S	51.12 W
Campos Sales	250	7.04 S	40.23 W
Campo Tencia, Pizzo ʌ	58	46.26 N	8.43 E
Campotosto	66	42.33 N	13.22 E
Campotosto, Lago di ⊜	66	42.32 N	13.22 E
Campo Tures (Sand in Taufers)	64	46.55 N	11.57 E
Campovalano	66	42.44 N	13.40 E
Camp Parks Communications Annex ■	282	37.44 N	121.54 W
Camp Pendleton Marine Corps Base ■	228	33.19 N	117.18 W
Camp Point	219	40.02 N	91.04 W
Camp Ruby	222	30.42 N	94.45 W
Campsie	274a	33.55 S	151.06 E
Campsie Fells ⌃[2]	46	56.02 N	4.12 W
Camp Springs	208	38.48 N	76.54 W
Campti	194	31.53 N	93.07 W
Campton	192	37.44 N	83.32 W
Camptonville	226	39.27 N	121.03 W
Camptown	210	41.43 N	76.14 W
Câmpulung	38	45.16 N	25.03 E
Câmpulung Moldovenesc	38	47.31 N	25.34 E
Campus	216	41.01 N	88.18 W
Campuya ≃	246	1.43 S	73.30 W
Camp Verde	200	34.33 N	111.51 W
Campville	210	42.06 N	76.09 W
Camp Wood	196	29.40 N	100.01 W
Cam Ranh	110	11.54 N	109.09 E
Cam Ranh, Vinh ⊂	110	11.53 N	109.10 E
Camrose, Ab., Can.	182	53.01 N	112.50 W
Camrose, Wales, U.K.	42	51.51 N	5.01 W
Camsell ≃	176	65.40 N	118.07 W
Camu ≃	250	1.15 N	57.09 W
Camucia	66	43.16 N	11.58 E
Camucuio	152	14.12 S	13.20 E
Camurí Chiquito, Quebrada ≃	286c	10.37 N	66.52 W
Çamurlu Dağ ʌ	130	40.21 N	42.26 E
Camuy	240m	18.29 N	66.51 W
Cam Xuyen	110	18.15 N	106.00 E
Čamyndy	85	41.37 N	74.20 E
Čamzinka	80	54.24 N	45.47 E
Çan, Tür.	130	40.02 N	27.03 E
Çan, Tür.	130	39.09 N	40.13 E
Can ≃	42	51.44 N	0.28 E
Canaan, Ct., U.S.	207	42.01 N	73.19 W
Canaan, Fl., U.S.	220	28.48 N	81.14 W
Canaan, In., U.S.	218	38.52 N	85.25 W
Canaan, N.Y., U.S.	210	42.25 N	73.27 W
Canaan, Vt., U.S.	206	44.59 N	71.32 W
Canaan ≃	186	45.55 N	65.47 W
Canaan Lake ⊜	276	40.47 N	73.01 W
Canaan Valley State Park ♦	188	39.02 N	79.32 W
Cana-brava ≃, Bra.	255	13.11 S	48.11 W
Cana-brava ≃, Bra.	255	12.12 S	48.40 W
Cañacao Bay ⊂	269f	14.29 N	120.55 E
Canaçarí, Lago ⊜	250	2.57 S	58.15 W
Canada □[1]	176	60.00 N	95.00 W
Cañada, Loma la ʌ[2]	240p	21.41 N	82.57 W
Canada Bay ⊂	186	50.43 N	56.10 W
Cañada de Caracheo	234	20.22 N	100.57 W
Cañada de Gómez	252	32.49 S	61.24 W
Cañada Honda	252	31.59 S	68.33 W
Canada Lake ⊜	210	43.10 N	74.32 W
Cañada Nieto	258	33.43 S	58.05 W
Canadarago Lake ⊜	210	42.48 N	75.01 W
Canada's Wonderland ♦	275b	43.51 N	79.33 W
Cañada Verde → Villa Huidobro	252	34.50 S	64.35 W
Canadaway Creek ≃	214	42.28 N	79.22 W
Canadensis	210	41.11 N	75.15 W
Canadian	196	35.54 N	100.22 W
Canadian ≃, U.S.	196	35.27 N	95.03 W
Canadian ≃, Co., U.S.	200	40.53 N	106.20 W
Canadian, Deep Fork ≃	196	35.28 N	95.50 W
Canadian Forces Base Trenton ■	212	44.07 N	77.33 W
Canadice Lake ⊜	210	42.43 N	77.34 W
Cañadón Seco	254	46.33 S	67.35 W
Canaguá ≃	246	7.57 N	69.36 W
Canaima	246	6.14 N	62.52 W
Canaima, Parque Nacional ♦	246	4.27 N	62.00 W
Canajoharie	210	42.54 N	74.34 W
Çanakkale	130	40.09 N	26.24 E
Çanakkale □[4]	130	40.10 N	26.45 E
Çanakkale Boğazı (Dardanelles) ꭒ	130	40.15 N	26.25 E
Canal, Islas del → Channel Islands II	28	49.20 N	2.20 W
Canala	175f	21.32 S	165.57 E
Canale	62	44.48 N	8.00 E
Canale, Val V	64	46.29 N	13.30 E
Canalejas	234	19.57 N	99.39 W
Canal Flats	182	50.09 N	115.48 W
Canal Fulton	214	40.53 N	81.35 W
Canal Lake ⊜	212	44.34 N	79.03 W
Canal Lewisville	214	40.18 N	81.50 W
Canal Point	220	26.51 N	80.38 W
Canals	252	33.33 S	62.53 W
Canal Winchester	188	39.51 N	82.48 W
Canamã ≃	248	8.45 S	59.15 W
Canandaigua	210	42.52 N	77.20 W
Canandaigua Lake ⊜	210	42.49 N	77.16 W
Canandaigua Outlet ≃	210	43.04 N	77.00 W
Cananea	232	30.57 N	110.18 W
Cananéia	252	25.01 S	47.57 W
Canan Station	214	40.28 N	78.26 W
Canapine, Forca)(	66	42.45 N	13.12 E
Canápolis	255	18.44 S	49.13 W
Canapville	50	49.19 N	0.08 E
Cañar	246	2.33 S	78.56 W
Cañar □[4]	246	2.30 S	79.00 W
Canard ≃	214	42.09 N	83.06 W
Canard, Lac au ⊜	206	45.48 N	71.31 W
Canarias, Islas (Canary Islands) II	148	28.00 N	15.30 W
Canaries	241f	13.55 N	61.04 W
Canaro	64	44.56 N	11.40 E
Canarreos, Archipiélago de los II	240p	21.50 N	82.30 W
Canarsie ✦[8]	276	40.38 N	73.53 W
Canarsie Park ♦	276	40.38 N	73.53 W
Canarsie Polder I	276	40.37 N	73.52 W
Canary Basin ✤[1]	10	30.00 N	25.00 W
Canary Islands → Canarias, Islas II	148	28.00 N	15.30 W
Cañas	236	10.25 N	85.07 W
Canaseraga	210	42.27 N	77.46 W
Canaseraga Creek ≃	210	42.45 N	77.50 W
Cañasgordas	246	6.45 N	76.01 W
Canastota	210	43.04 N	75.45 W
Canatlán	232	24.31 N	104.47 W
Canaveral, Cape ›	220	28.27 N	80.32 W
Canaveral Bight ⊂[3]	220	28.26 N	80.33 W
Canaveral National Seashore ♦	220	28.45 N	80.45 W
Canaveral Peninsula ›[1]	220	28.28 N	80.34 W
Cañaveras	34	40.22 N	2.24 W
Canavese □[9]	62	45.20 N	7.40 E
Canavieiras	255	15.39 S	38.57 W
Cañazas	236	8.19 N	81.13 W
Canazei	64	46.28 N	11.46 E
Canbelego	166	31.33 S	146.19 E
Canberra	171b	35.17 S	149.08 E
Canberra Wildlife Gardens ♦	171b	35.20 S	149.09 E
Canby, Ca., U.S.	204	41.26 N	120.52 W
Canby, Mn., U.S.	198	44.42 N	96.16 W
Canby, Or., U.S.	224	45.15 N	122.41 W
Cancajanang, Mount ʌ	116	11.04 N	124.47 E
Cancale	32	48.41 N	1.51 W
Cancano, Lago di ⊜	64	46.31 N	10.18 E
Cance ≃	62	45.12 N	4.48 E
Cancellara	68	40.44 N	15.56 E
Cancello e Arnone	68	41.04 N	14.03 E
Canchaque	248	5.24 S	79.36 W
Canche ≃	50	50.31 N	1.39 E
Cancon	32	44.32 N	0.38 E
Cancún	232	21.05 N	86.46 W
Čančur	88	53.49 N	106.59 E
Canda	64	45.03 N	11.30 E
Candala → Qandala	144	11.28 N	49.52 E
Candarave	248	17.16 S	70.15 W
Çandarlı	130	38.56 N	26.56 E
Çandarlı Körfezi ⊂	130	38.52 N	26.55 E
Candás	34	43.35 N	5.46 W
Candé	32	47.34 N	1.02 W
Candeias, Bra.	255	12.40 S	38.33 W
Candeias, Bra.	255	20.47 S	45.16 W
Candeias ≃	248	8.39 S	63.31 W
Candela, It.	68	41.08 N	15.31 E
Candela, Méx.	232	26.50 N	100.40 W
Candela, Río de ≃	196	27.16 N	100.18 W
Candelaria, Arg.	252	27.28 S	55.44 W
Candelaria, Arg.	252	32.04 S	65.49 W
Candelária, Bra.	252	29.40 S	52.48 W
Candelaria, Col.	246	3.25 N	76.20 W
Candelaria, Cuba	240p	22.44 N	82.58 W
Candelaria, Pil.	116	15.38 N	119.56 E
Candelaria ≃	232	18.37 N	91.14 W
Candelaria Loxicha	234	15.54 N	96.31 W
Candelaro ≃	68	41.34 N	15.53 E
Candeleda	34	40.09 N	5.14 W
Candelo, Austl.	166	36.46 S	149.42 E
Candelo, It.	62	45.33 N	8.07 E
Candia → Iráklion	38	35.20 N	25.09 E
Candiac	206	45.23 N	73.31 W
Candia Canavese	62	45.20 N	7.53 E
Candia Lomellina	62	45.11 N	8.36 E
Cándido Aguilar	232	25.30 N	98.02 W
Cândido de Abreu	252	24.35 S	51.20 W
Cândido Mendes	250	1.27 S	45.43 W
Candies Creek ≃	192	35.18 N	84.51 W
Candijay	116	9.49 N	124.30 E
Çandır, Tür.	130	40.16 N	33.29 E
Çandır, Tür.	130	39.15 N	35.32 E
Candle	180	65.55 N	161.56 W
Candle Lake ⊜	184	53.50 N	105.18 W
Candlemas Islands II	18	57.03 S	26.40 W
Candlestick	194	32.15 N	90.20 W
Candlestick Park ♦	282	37.43 N	122.23 W
Candlewood, Lake ⊜	207	41.32 N	73.27 W
Candlewood Isle	207	41.29 N	73.27 W
Candlewood Knolls	207	41.28 N	73.27 W
Candlewood Shores	207	41.28 N	73.26 W
Çandman', Mong.	86	50.02 N	92.03 E
Čandman', Mong.	102	45.20 N	97.59 E
Cando, Ang.	152	16.30 S	18.19 E
Cando, Sk., Can.	184	52.23 N	108.14 W
Cando, N.D., U.S.	198	48.29 N	99.12 W
Candombé ≃	152	16.54 S	21.52 E
Candon	116	17.12 N	120.27 E
Candon Point ›	116	17.13 N	120.24 E
Candor, N.Y., U.S.	210	42.13 N	76.20 W
Candor, N.C., U.S.	192	35.17 N	79.44 W
Candover	158	27.28 S	31.57 E
Cane ≃, Austl.	162	21.33 S	115.23 E
Cane ≃, La., U.S.	194	31.31 N	92.43 W
Cane ≃, N.C., U.S.	192	36.00 N	82.16 W
Canea → Khaniá	38	35.31 N	24.02 E
Caneadea	210	42.23 N	78.09 W
Caneças	266c	38.49 N	9.14 W
Cane Creek ≃	194	36.29 N	90.28 W
Canegrate	266b	45.34 N	8.56 E
Canela	252	29.22 S	50.50 W
Canelas	232	25.06 N	106.34 W
Canelles, Embalse de ⊜[1]	34	42.10 N	0.30 E
Canelli	62	44.43 N	8.17 E
Canelones	258	34.32 S	56.17 W
Canelones □[5]	258	34.35 S	56.15 W
Canelón Grande, Arroyo ≃	258	34.30 S	56.24 W
Cane Run ≃	218	38.13 N	84.37 W
Cañete, Chile	252	37.48 S	73.24 W
Cañete, Esp.	34	40.03 N	1.35 W
Caneva	64	45.58 N	12.26 E
Caney	198	37.00 N	95.56 W
Caney ≃	196	36.20 N	95.42 W
Caney Brook ≃	276	41.07 N	73.50 W
Caney Creek ≃, Ar., U.S.	194	33.46 N	93.07 W
Caney Creek ≃, Tx., U.S.	196	28.46 N	95.39 W
Caney Creek ≃, Tx., U.S.	222	32.48 N	95.33 W
Caney Creek ≃, Tx., U.S.	222	30.28 N	95.38 W
Caney Creek ≃, Tx., U.S.	222	30.04 N	96.08 W
Caney Creek ≃, Tx., U.S.	222	31.52 N	96.13 W
Caney Creek ≃, Tx., U.S.	222	31.03 N	94.33 W
Caney Creek ≃, Tx., U.S.	222	30.53 N	95.48 W
Caney Creek ≃, Tx., U.S.	222	30.07 N	95.10 W
Canfield	214	41.01 N	80.45 W
Canfield Island I	276	41.06 N	73.23 W
Canfranc-Estación	34	42.43 N	0.31 W
Cangaíba ✦[8]	287b	23.30 S	46.31 W
Cangallo	248	13.33 S	74.12 W
Cangamba	152	13.40 S	19.54 E
Cangandala	152	9.45 S	16.33 E
Cangandala, Parque Nacional da ♦	152	9.45 S	16.50 E
Cangas, Bra.	248	16.05 S	56.33 W
Cangas, Esp.	34	42.16 N	8.47 W
Cangas de Narcea	34	43.11 N	6.33 W
Cangas de Onís	34	43.21 N	5.07 W
Cangbu	100	30.49 N	114.35 E
Can Gioc ≃	269c	10.42 N	106.37 E
Cangkuang, Tanjung ›	115a	6.51 S	105.15 E
Cangniutun	105	39.23 N	115.54 E
Cango Caves ⫠[5]	158	33.23 S	22.14 E
Cangola	152	7.58 S	15.52 E
Cangombe	152	14.24 S	19.59 E
Cangongo	152	9.24 S	17.30 E
Cangqian, Zhg.	106	30.17 N	120.25 E
Cangqian, Zhg.	106	30.18 N	120.00 E
Cangshangtun	105	40.03 N	117.32 E
Canguaretama	250	6.24 S	35.08 W
Canguçu	252	31.24 S	52.41 W
Canguera	256	23.36 S	47.09 W
Cangumbe	152	12.00 S	19.17 E
Cangwu	102	23.22 N	111.13 E
Çangxi	102	31.48 N	105.57 E
Čangyrtas	85	40.53 N	72.50 E
Cangyuan	102	23.12 N	99.16 E
Cangzhou	98	38.19 N	116.51 E
Canhoca	152	9.15 S	14.41 E
Canhotinho	250	8.53 S	36.12 W
Caniapiscau ≃	176	57.40 N	69.30 W
Caniapiscau, Lac ⊜	176	54.10 N	69.55 W
Canicanian	116	14.46 N	122.01 E

Symbol	English	Deutsch	Español	Français	Português
≃	River	Fluß	Río	Rivière	Rio
≊	Canal	Kanal	Canal	Canal	Canal
ʟ	Waterfall, Rapids	Wasserfall, Stromschnellen	Cascada, Rápidos	Chute d'eau, Rapides	Cascata, Rápidos
ꭒ	Strait	Meeresstraße	Estrecho	Détroit	Estreito
⊂	Bay, Gulf	Bucht, Golf	Bahía, Golfo	Baie, Golfe	Baía, Golfo
⊜	Lake, Lakes	See, Seen	Lago, Lagos	Lac, Lacs	Lago, Lagos
≡	Swamp	Sumpf	Pantano	Marais	Pântano
⍓	Ice Features, Glacier	Eis- und Gletscherformen	Accidentes Glaciales	Formes glaciaires	Acidentes glaciares
⍑	Other Hydrographic Features	Andere Hydrographische Objekte	Otros Elementos Hidrográficos	Autres données hydrographiques	Outros acidentes hidrográficos
✤	Submarine Features	Untermeerische Objekte	Accidentes Submarinos	Formes de relief sous-marin	Acidentes submarinos
□	Political Unit	Politische Einheit	Unidad Política	Entité politique	Unidade política
ʋ	Cultural Institution	Kulturelle Institution	Institución Cultural	Institution culturelle	Instituição cultural
⊥	Historical Site	Historische Stätte	Sitio Histórico	Site historique	Sitio histórico
♦	Recreational Site	Erholungs- und Ferienort	Sitio de Recreo	Centre de loisirs	Area de Lazer
⊠	Airport	Flughafen	Aeropuerto	Aéroport	Aeroporto
■	Military Installation	Militäranlage	Instalación Militar	Installation militaire	Instalação militar
✦	Miscellaneous	Verschiedenes	Misceláneo	Divers	Diversos

Name	Page	Lat.	Long.
Canicattì	70	37.21 N	13.51 E
Canicattini Bagni	70	37.02 N	15.04 E
Canigao Channel ⥬	116	10.15 N	124.42 E
Canigou, Pic du ▲	32	42.31 N	2.27 E
Canillas ◆⁸	266a	40.28 N	3.38 W
Canillejas ◆⁸	266a	40.27 N	3.37 W
Canim Lake	182	51.46 N	120.54 W
Canim Lake ◎	182	51.52 N	120.45 W
Canim Lake Indian Reserve ◆⁴	182	51.47 N	121.00 W
Canindé	250	4.22 S	39.19 W
Canindé ≃	250	6.15 S	42.52 W
Canindeyú ◻⁵	252	24.15 S	55.15 W
Canino	66	42.28 N	11.45 E
Canipaan	116	8.35 N	117.16 E
Canipo Island I	116	10.59 N	120.57 E
Canisius College ∨²	284a	42.55 N	78.52 W
Canisp ▲	46	58.07 N	5.03 W
Canistear Reservoir ◎¹	276	41.08 N	74.29 W
Canisteo	210	42.16 N	77.36 W
Canisteo ≃	210	42.07 N	77.08 W
Canistota	198	43.35 N	97.17 W
Cañitas de Felipe Pescador	234	23.36 N	102.43 W
Canjáyar	34	37.00 N	2.44 W
Canjinge	152	10.12 S	21.17 E
Cankhor	144	10.46 N	46.13 E
Çankiri	130	40.36 N	33.37 E
Çankiri ◻⁴	130	40.45 N	33.25 E
Canlaon	116	10.22 N	123.12 E
Canlaon Volcano ▲¹	116	10.25 N	123.08 E
Canley Vale	274a	33.53 S	150.57 E
Canmore	182	51.05 N	115.21 W
Canna I	68	40.05 N	16.30 E
Canna I	46	57.04 N	6.34 W
Canna, Sound of ⥬	46	57.03 N	6.25 W
Cannanore	122	11.51 N	75.22 E
Cannara	66	43.00 N	12.35 E
Canne ≖	68	41.18 N	16.09 E
Cannel City	192	37.47 N	83.16 W
Cannelton	194	37.54 N	86.44 W
Canner ≃	56	49.24 N	6.16 E
Cannero-Riviera	58	46.01 N	8.41 E
Cannes	62	43.33 N	7.01 E
Cannes, Bayou des ≃	194	30.12 N	92.35 W
Canneto, It.	66	43.12 N	10.44 E
Canneto, It.	70	38.29 N	14.58 E
Canneto sull'Oglio	64	45.09 N	10.25 E
Cannich	46	57.21 N	4.46 W
Cannich ≃	46	57.21 N	4.44 W
Cannifton	212	44.12 N	77.23 W
Canning, Arg.	284	34.53 S	58.30 W
Canning, Austl.	168a	32.02 S	115.56 E
Canning, N.S., Can.	186	45.09 N	64.25 W
Canning ≃, Austl.	168a	32.01 S	115.51 E
Canning ≃, Ak., U.S.	180	70.05 N	145.30 W
Canning Hill ▲²	162	28.50 S	117.49 E
Canning Lake	212	44.56 N	78.38 W
Canning Reservoir ◎¹	168a	32.10 S	116.09 E
Cannington, On., Can.	212	44.21 N	79.02 W
Cannington, Eng., U.K.	42	51.09 N	3.04 W
Cannobio	58	46.04 N	8.42 E
Cannock	42	52.42 N	2.09 W
Cannock Chase ◆¹	42	52.43 N	2.00 W
Cannon ≃	42	44.35 N	92.33 W
Cannon Air Force Base ■	196	44.23 N	103.18 W
Cannon Ball	198	46.23 N	100.35 W
Cannonball ≃	198	46.26 N	100.38 W
Cannon Beach	224	45.53 N	123.57 W
Cannondale	207	41.12 N	73.25 W
Cannon Falls	190	44.30 N	92.54 W
Cannonsburg	216	43.03 N	85.28 W
Cannonsville Reservoir ◎¹	210	42.08 N	75.19 W
Cannonvale	166	20.17 S	148.42 E
Cann River	166	37.34 S	149.10 E
Caño, Isla del I	236	8.44 N	83.53 W
Canoas	256	25.56 S	51.11 W
Canoas ≃, Bra.	252	27.36 S	51.25 W
Canoas ≃, Bra.	256	21.30 S	47.09 W
Canobie Lake	283	42.48 N	71.14 W
Canobie Lake ◎	283	42.49 N	71.15 W
Canobie Lake Park ◆	283	42.48 N	71.15 W
Canoe	182	50.45 N	119.13 W
Canoe ≃, B.C., Can.	182	52.33 S	119.27 W
Canoe ≃, Ma., U.S.	283	41.58 N	71.08 W
Canoe Brook ≃	276	40.45 N	74.22 W
Canoe Brook Reservoirs ◎¹	276	40.45 N	74.21 W
Canoe Creek Indian Reserve ◆⁴	182	51.32 N	122.15 W
Canoe Lake ◎	184	55.11 N	108.15 W
Canoe Lake Indian Reserve ◆⁴	184	55.08 N	108.12 W
Canoga Park ◆⁸	280	34.12 N	118.35 W
Canoinhas	252	26.10 S	50.24 W
Canol	180	65.14 N	126.56 W
Canon	192	34.21 N	83.07 W
Canon	224	46.36 N	123.53 W
Canonie	44	55.05 N	2.57 W
Canon City	200	38.24 N	105.13 W
Cañón del Sumidero, Parque Nacional ◆	234	16.45 N	93.05 W
Caño Negro	236	10.54 N	84.44 W
Canonsburg	216	40.15 N	80.11 W
Canonsburg Lake ◎	279b	40.16 N	80.13 W
Canonchee ≃	192	31.59 N	81.18 W
Canoole Cise	144	2.02 N	42.19 E
Canopus ▲¹	142	31.18 N	30.03 E
Canora	184	51.37 N	102.26 W
Canosa di Puglia	68	41.13 N	16.04 E
Canossa ⊥	64	44.35 N	10.27 E
Canot, Pointe ➤	241o	16.12 N	61.28 W
Canouan I	238	12.43 N	61.20 W
Canova	198	43.52 N	97.30 W
Canova Beach	280	28.08 N	80.34 W
Cañoves ≃	266d	41.37 N	2.22 E
Canow	54	53.12 N	12.54 E
Canowindra	166	33.34 S	148.38 E
Can Quer, Torrente de ≃	266d	41.31 N	2.17 E
Cansado	146	20.51 N	17.02 W
Cansanção	250	10.41 S	39.31 W
Canso	186	45.20 N	61.00 W
Canso, Strait of ⥬	186	45.37 N	61.25 W
Canta	234	11.25 S	76.38 W
Cantabria	234	19.50 N	101.44 W
Cantabria ◻³	34	43.15 N	4.00 W
Cantabria (Santander) ◻⁴	34	43.15 N	4.00 W
Cantábrica, Cordillera ⊶	34	43.00 N	5.00 W
Cantabriques ⊶ →Cantábrica, Cordillera ⊶	34	43.00 N	5.00 W
Cantagalo, Bra.	255	21.58 S	42.22 W
Cantagalo, Cachoeira ⌇	255	21.58 S	42.22 W
Cantal ◻⁵	32	45.05 N	2.45 E
Cantalejo	34	41.15 N	3.55 W
Cantalupo in Sabina	66	42.18 N	12.39 E
Cantalupo nel Sannio	66	41.33 N	14.24 E
Cant'vejergum ≖	68	41.21 N	15.48 E
Cantanhede, Bra.	250	3.39 S	44.24 W
Cantanhede, Port.	34	40.21 N	8.36 W
Cantareira ◆⁸	287b	23.27 S	46.37 W
Cantareira, Serra da ⊶	287b	23.25 S	46.39 W
Cantaura	248	10.19 N	64.21 W
Cant Clough Reservoir ◎	262	53.46 N	2.09 W
Cantelleu ◻⁵	50	49.27 N	1.07 E
Canterbury, Austl.	274a	33.55 S	151.07 E
Canterbury, Austl.	287b	37.49 S	145.05 E
Canterbury, N.B., Can.	186	45.53 N	67.29 W
Canterbury, Eng., U.K.	42	51.17 N	1.05 E
Canterbury Bight c³	172	44.15 S	171.38 E
Canterbury Cathedral ⌂¹	42	51.17 N	1.05 E
Canterbury Park Racecourse ◆	274a	33.54 S	151.07 E
Canterbury Plains ⥾	172	44.00 S	171.45 E
Canterbury Woods	286a	38.49 N	77.15 W
Can Tho	110	10.02 N	105.47 E
Cantiano	66	43.28 N	12.38 E
Cantil	228	35.18 N	117.58 W
Cantiles, Cayo I	240p	21.36 N	82.02 W
Cantin Lake ◎	184	53.27 N	95.10 W
Canto do Buriti	250	8.07 S	42.58 W
Canto do Pontes	287a	22.58 S	43.04 W
Canto Grande, Quebrada ∨	286d	11.59 S	77.01 W
Cantoira	62	45.21 N	7.23 E
Canton, Ct., U.S.	207	41.49 N	72.53 W
Canton, Ga., U.S.	192	34.14 N	84.29 W
Canton, Il., U.S.	190	40.33 N	90.02 W
Canton, Ks., U.S.	198	38.23 N	97.25 W
Canton, Ma., U.S.	207	42.09 N	71.08 W
Canton, Mn., U.S.	190	43.31 N	91.55 W
Canton, Mo., U.S.	190	40.07 N	91.37 W
Canton, Ms., U.S.	194	32.36 N	90.02 W
Canton, N.J., U.S.	208	39.28 N	75.10 W
Canton, N.Y., U.S.	188	44.35 N	75.10 W
Canton, N.C., U.S.	192	35.31 N	82.50 W
Canton, Oh., U.S.	214	40.47 N	81.22 W
Canton, Ok., U.S.	196	36.03 N	98.35 W
Canton, Pa., U.S.	210	41.39 N	76.51 W
Canton, S.D., U.S.	198	43.18 N	96.35 W
Canton, Tx., U.S.	222	32.33 N	95.51 W
Canton →Guangzhou, Zhg.	100	23.06 N	113.16 E
Canton →Kanton I	174h	2.50 S	171.40 W
Canton Airport ★	174h	2.46 S	171.43 W
Canton Lake ◎¹	196	36.08 N	98.36 W
Canton Lake State Recreational Area ◆	196	36.08 N	98.39 W
Cantonment	194	30.36 N	87.20 W
Cantorbéry →Canterbury	42	51.17 N	1.05 E
Cantrall	219	39.56 N	89.41 W
Cantril	266c	38.53 N	9.25 W
Cantù	62	45.44 N	9.08 E
Cantua Creek	226	36.33 N	120.22 W
Cantua Creek ≃	226	36.28 N	120.17 W
Cantwell	180	63.23 N	148.57 W
Cañuelas	258	35.03 S	58.44 W
Cañuelas ≃	258	34.56 S	58.41 W
Cañuelas, Arroyo ≃	258	34.55 S	58.38 W
Canumã	246	4.02 S	59.04 W
Canumã ≃	246	3.55 S	59.10 W
Canungra	171a	28.02 S	153.10 E
Canungra Creek ≃	171a	27.55 S	153.06 E
Canungra Jungle Training Ground ■	171a	28.02 S	153.10 E
Canutama	248	6.32 S	64.20 W
Canutillo	200	31.54 N	106.35 W
Canvastown	172	41.18 S	173.40 E
Canvey Island	42	51.32 N	0.36 E
Canvey Island I	42	51.33 N	0.34 E
Cany, ozero ◎	86	54.50 N	77.30 E
Cany-Barville	50	49.47 N	0.38 E
Canyon, Yk., Can.	180	60.52 N	137.02 W
Canyon, Ca., U.S.	282	37.49 N	122.09 W
Canyon, Tx., U.S.	196	34.58 N	101.55 W
Canyon City	202	44.23 N	118.56 W
Canyon Creek	182	55.22 N	115.05 W
Canyon Creek ≃, Az., U.S.	200	33.49 N	110.40 W
Canyon Creek ≃, Id., U.S.	202	42.59 N	115.59 W
Canyon Creek ≃, Wa., U.S.	224	45.57 N	122.22 W
Canyon Creek ≃, Wa., U.S.	224	48.43 N	120.55 W
Canyon de Chelly National Monument ◆	200	36.01 N	109.26 W
Canyon Ferry Lake ◎¹	202	46.33 N	111.37 W
Canyon Lake ◎¹	196	29.52 N	98.16 W
Canyonlands National Park ◆	200	38.10 N	110.00 W
Canyonville	203	42.55 N	123.16 W
Canzar	152	7.38 S	21.32 E
Canzo	62	45.51 N	9.16 E
Cao ≃, Zhg.	98	40.29 N	124.08 E
Cao ≃, Zhg.	105	38.52 N	115.46 E
Cao Bang	110	22.40 N	106.15 E
Caocun	106	31.42 N	118.58 E
Caodian, Zhg.	100	28.39 N	120.23 E
Caodian, Zhg.	100	33.21 N	112.39 E
Cao'e	100	30.01 N	120.52 E
Cao'e ≃	100	30.06 N	120.46 E
Caofang	100	26.04 N	116.35 E
Caogezhai	105	39.00 N	117.50 E
Caohe, Zhg.	105	38.57 N	115.52 E
Caohe, Zhg.	269b	31.09 N	121.25 E
Caohecheng	104	40.46 N	124.02 E
Caohekou	104	40.54 N	123.53 E
Caohezhang	104	41.04 N	124.03 E
Caojian	102	25.38 N	99.07 E
Caojiawopeng	104	40.46 N	122.20 E
Caojiawopu	104	42.37 N	122.59 E
Caojiawu	105	39.24 N	116.31 E
Caojiazhen	106	31.55 N	121.38 E
Caojiezi	107	31.55 N	106.24 E
Caojing	100	30.47 N	121.24 E
Caojun	104	41.16 N	116.17 E
Cao Lanh	110	10.27 N	105.38 E
Caolaoji	100	33.06 N	117.22 E
Caolisport, Loch c	46	55.54 N	5.37 W
Caomaji	98	34.52 N	116.17 E
Caombo	152	8.43 S	16.51 E
Caonao ≃	240p	22.00 N	78.05 W
Caonian	100	32.56 N	120.20 E
Caonillas, Lago ◎	240m	18.16 N	66.30 W
Caopeng	106	31.44 N	121.17 E
Caoping	106	28.48 N	118.22 E
Caopu	106	34.34 N	118.52 E
Caoqiao	106	31.32 N	119.59 E
Caotang	100	36.28 N	116.48 E
Caoxi	106	31.16 N	117.18 E
Caoyangxi	100	34.53 N	118.47 E
Cao Town →Cape Town	158	33.55 S	18.22 E
Cap, Pointe du ➤	241l	14.07 N	60.57 W
Capac	190	43.00 N	82.55 W
Capaccio	68	40.25 N	15.05 E
Capaci	70	38.10 N	13.14 E
Çapage	152	11.23 S	21.05 E
Capajevka ≃	82	54.38 N	35.50 E
Capajevo	80	53.08 N	49.37 E
Capajevo	80	50.12 N	51.10 E
Capajevsk	78	53.00 N	49.41 E
Capajevo ◻⁵	80	52.58 N	49.41 E
Capala	152	13.37 S	14.45 E
Capalbio	66	42.27 N	11.26 E
Capalonga	116	14.20 N	122.30 E
Capanaparo ≃	246	7.01 N	67.07 W
Capanema, Bra.	250	1.12 S	47.11 W
Capanema, Bra.	252	25.40 S	53.48 W
Capanema ≃	252	15.05 S	13.08 E
Capanne, Monte ▲	66	42.46 N	10.10 E
Capannoli	66	43.35 N	10.41 E
Capannori	66	43.50 N	10.34 E
Capão Bonito	255	24.01 S	48.20 W
Capão Doce, Morro do ▲	252	26.43 S	51.25 W
Capão Redondo ◆⁸	287b	23.40 S	46.46 W
Capaotigamau, Lac ◎	186	50.18 N	68.14 W
Caparaó, Parque Nacional do ◆	255	20.33 S	41.45 W
Caparica	266c	38.40 N	9.12 W
Caparo Viejo ≃	250	8.07 S	42.58 W
Capas	116	15.20 N	120.35 E
Capatárida	246	11.11 N	70.37 W
Cap-aux-Meules (Grindstone Island)	186	47.23 N	61.52 W
Cap aux Meules, Île du I	186	47.23 N	61.54 W
Capay	226	38.32 N	122.03 W
Cap-Chat	186	49.06 N	66.42 W
Cap-de-la-Madeleine	206	46.22 N	72.31 W
Cape ≃	166	20.49 S	146.51 E
Cape Arid National Park ◆	162	33.40 S	123.25 E
Cape Barren Island I	166	40.25 S	148.12 E
Cape Basin ⊶¹	8	37.00 S	7.00 E
Cape Bougainville Aboriginal Reserve ◆⁴	164	14.10 S	126.30 E
Cape Breton Highlands National Park ◆	186	46.45 N	60.45 W
Cape Breton Island I	186	46.00 N	60.30 W
Cape Broyle	186	47.06 N	52.57 W
Cape Canaveral	220	28.24 N	80.36 W
Cape Canaveral Air Force Station ■	220	28.29 N	80.35 W
Cape Charles	208	37.16 N	76.01 W
Cape Coast	150	5.05 N	1.15 W
Cape Cod Bay c	207	41.52 N	70.22 W
Cape Cod Canal ⌇	207	41.47 N	70.30 W
Cape Cod National Seashore ◆	207	41.56 N	70.00 W
Cape Comorin →Kanniyākumari	122	8.05 N	77.34 E
Cape Coral	220	26.33 N	81.56 W
Cape Croker Indian Reserve ◆⁴	212	44.55 N	81.01 W
Cape Dorset	176	64.14 N	76.32 W
Cape Elizabeth	188	43.33 N	70.12 W
Cape Fear ≃	192	33.53 N	78.00 W
Cape Girardeau	194	37.18 N	89.31 W
Cape Hatteras National Seashore ◆	192	35.30 N	76.35 W
Cape Henlopen State Park ◆	208	38.45 N	75.06 W
Cape Jervis	168b	35.36 S	138.06 E
Cape Johnson Tablemount ⊶³	14	17.08 N	177.15 W
Cape Krusenstern National Monument ◆	180	67.30 N	163.40 W
Capela	250	10.30 S	37.04 W
Cape LaHave Island I	186	44.12 N	64.22 W
Cape la Hune	186	47.33 N	56.52 W
Capel Curig	44	53.06 N	3.54 W
Capelengue	152	9.12 S	19.43 E
Capelinha	255	17.42 S	42.31 W
Capelinha do Embirazal	256	22.02 S	45.26 W
Capel Lisburne	180	68.52 N	166.05 W
Capel'ka	76	58.03 N	28.59 E
Capella	166	23.05 S	148.02 E
Capella ▲	164	5.00 S	141.05 E
Capelle [aan de IJssel]	52	51.55 N	4.35 E
Capellen	56	49.38 N	5.59 E
Capelongo	152	14.54 S	15.08 E
Cape Lookout National Seashore ◆	192	34.40 N	76.23 W
Cape Lookout State Park ◆	224	45.21 N	123.59 W
Capel Saint Mary	42	52.00 N	1.04 E
Cape May	208	38.56 N	74.54 W
Cape May ◆⁸	208	38.56 N	74.55 W
Cape May Coast Guard Air Station ■	208	38.57 N	74.53 W
Cape May Court House	208	39.04 N	74.49 W
Cape May Point	208	38.56 N	74.58 W
Capemole ≃	152	16.10 S	21.00 E
Cape Melville National Park ◆	164	14.20 S	144.30 E
Capenda Camulemba	152	9.24 S	18.27 E
Capenga ≃	287a	22.49 S	43.37 W
Capenhurst	262	53.15 N	2.57 W
Cape of Good Hope Nature Reserve ◆	158	34.18 S	18.26 E
Cape Pole	180	55.58 N	133.48 W
Cape Pond	283	42.38 N	70.38 W
Cape Porpoise	188	43.22 N	70.26 W
Cape Range National Park ◆	162	22.10 S	113.55 E
Capernaum →Kefar Naḥum ⊥	132	32.53 N	35.34 E
Cape Romanzof	180	61.49 N	165.56 W
Capertee	166	33.09 S	149.59 E
Capertee ≃	170	33.12 S	150.28 E
Cape Sable Island I	186	43.25 N	65.37 W
Cape Scott Provincial Park ◆	182	50.45 N	128.20 W
Capesterre	241o	15.54 N	61.13 W
Capesterre-Belle-Eau	241o	16.03 N	61.33 W
Capesthorne Hall ⌂¹	262	53.15 N	2.14 W
Capetão ≃	66	42.54 N	11.56 E
Capetinga	255	20.37 S	47.04 W
Cape Tormentine	186	46.08 N	63.47 W
Cape Town (Kaapstad)	158	33.55 S	18.22 E
Cape Verde (Cabo Verde) ◻¹, Afr.	134	16.00 N	24.00 W
Cape Verde (Cabo Verde) ▪¹, Islands	150a	16.00 N	24.00 W
Cape Verde Basin ⊶¹	8	15.00 N	30.00 W
Cape Verde Islands →Cape Verde ◻¹	150a	16.00 N	24.00 W
Cape Verde Terrace ⊶	10	18.00 N	20.00 W
Capeville	208	37.17 N	75.57 W
Cape Vincent	212	44.07 N	76.19 W
Cape Yakataga	180	60.04 N	142.26 W
Cape York Peninsula ⊶¹	164	14.00 S	142.30 E
Cap-Haïtien	238	19.45 N	72.12 W
Capilla de Farruco	258	33.07 S	55.01 W
Capilla del Señor	258	34.18 S	59.06 W
Capim Melado, Morro do ▲	287b	21.05 S	44.23 W
Capinas Point ➤	116	11.05 N	125.14 E
Capinópolis	255	18.41 S	49.35 W
Capinota	248	17.43 S	66.14 W
Capinzal	252	27.20 S	51.36 W
Capira	236	8.45 N	79.53 W
Capira ≃	236	8.45 N	79.45 W
Cap Island I	116	5.57 N	120.06 E
Capistrano, It.	250	4.39 S	38.55 W
Capistrano, It.	68	38.41 N	16.17 E
Capit ≃	116	11.30 N	122.45 E
Capiz ◻⁴	116	11.30 N	122.30 E
Capizzi	70	37.51 N	14.29 E
Caplan	186	48.06 N	65.41 W
Caples Lake ◎¹	226	38.42 N	120.03 W
Caplina ≃	248	18.14 S	70.33 W
Çaplino	180	64.25 N	172.15 W
Čapljina	72	43.06 N	17.41 E
Capljone, Monte ▲	66	45.48 N	10.38 E
Çaplygin	76	53.14 N	39.58 E
Cap Mountain ▲	180	63.25 N	123.29 W
Capnoyan Island I	116	14.00 N	120.54 E
Capoche ≃	154	15.23 S	32.53 E
Capodichino, Aeroporto di ★	68	40.50 N	14.17 E
Capodimonte	66	42.33 N	11.55 E
Capo di Ponte	64	46.02 N	10.21 E
Capo d'Orlando	70	38.10 N	14.53 E
Capoeira, Corredeira ⌇	250	6.48 S	58.21 W
Capologo	58	45.55 N	8.59 E
Capoliveri	66	42.45 N	10.22 E
Capoo ≃	152	12.56 S	13.00 E
Caposele	68	40.49 N	15.13 E
Capostrada	66	43.57 N	10.54 E
Capot ≃	240e	14.51 N	61.05 W
Capoterra	71	39.11 N	8.58 E
Capoti-an, Mount ▲	116	11.45 N	125.15 E
Capotoan, Mount ▲	116	12.09 N	124.57 E
Cappadocia ◻⁹	130	38.36 N	34.00 E
Cappamore	48	52.37 N	8.20 W
Cap-Pelé	186	46.13 N	64.18 W
Cappella Islands II	240m	18.17 N	64.54 W
Cappelle	68	42.03 N	13.22 E
Cappelle sul Tavo	66	42.28 N	14.06 E
Cappeln	52	52.48 N	8.07 E
Cappenberg	263	51.39 N	7.32 E
Cappenberg, Schloss ⌂¹	263	51.39 N	7.32 E
Cappercleuch	44	55.29 N	3.12 W
Cappoquin	48	52.08 N	7.50 W
Capracotta	68	41.50 N	14.16 E
Capraia	68	43.03 N	9.50 E
Capraia, Isola I	66	42.08 N	15.31 E
Capraia, Isola di I	66	43.03 N	9.50 E
Capranica	66	42.15 N	12.11 E
Caprara, Punta ➤	71	41.07 N	8.19 E
Caprarola	66	42.19 N	12.14 E
Capreol	190	46.43 N	80.56 W
Caprera, Isola I	71	41.12 N	9.28 E
Caprese Michelangelo	66	43.39 N	11.59 E
Capri	68	40.33 N	14.14 E
Capri, Isola di I	68	40.33 N	14.13 E
Capriati a Volturno	68	41.28 N	14.08 E
Capricorn, Cape ➤	166	23.00 S	151.13 E
Capricorn Channel ⥬	166	23.00 S	152.20 E
Capricorn Group II	166	23.28 S	152.00 E
Caprino Veronese	64	45.36 N	10.47 E
Caprivi ◻⁴	156	18.00 S	23.00 E
Caprivi Zipfel (Caprivi Strip) ⊶⁹	156	17.59 S	23.00 E
Caproláce, Lago di ◎	66	41.21 N	12.58 E
Capron, Va., U.S.	216	36.42 N	77.12 W
Cap-Saint Jacques →Vung Tau	110	10.21 N	107.04 E
Cap-Santé	206	46.40 N	71.47 W
Capstone	260	51.21 N	0.34 E
Captain Anthony Meldahl Dam ◆⁶	218	38.48 N	84.11 W
Captain Cook	229d	19.29 N	155.55 W
Captain Cook Bridge ◆	274a	34.00 S	151.08 E
Captain Cook Landing Place Park ◆	274a	34.00 S	151.14 E
Captain Cook Monument ⊥	174c	29.00 S	167.56 E
Captain Daniel Wright Woods ◆	278	42.13 N	87.56 W
Captain Harbor c	276	40.59 N	73.36 W
Captain Pond ◎	283	42.47 N	71.10 W
Captains Flat	171b	35.35 S	149.27 E
Captieux	32	44.17 N	0.16 W
Captina Creek ≃	188	39.50 N	80.48 W
Captiva	220	26.31 N	82.11 W
Captiva Island I	220	26.31 N	82.11 W
Captree Island I	276	40.39 N	73.16 W
Captree State Park ◆	276	40.38 N	73.16 W
Capua	68	41.06 N	14.12 E
Capual Island I	116	6.02 N	121.24 E
Capúava ◆⁸	287b	23.39 S	46.29 W
Capucapu ≃	246	1.37 S	62.07 W
Capucapu ≃	246	1.15 S	61.28 W
Capucin ➤	240d	15.38 N	61.28 W
Capulin, Río del ≃	196	27.31 N	101.33 W
Capulin Mountain National Monument ◆	196	36.48 N	103.55 W
Capunda	152	12.26 N	124.10 E
Capurro	258	34.25 S	56.28 W
Capuru ≃	116	15.38 S	19.43 E
Caputh	54	52.21 N	12.58 E
Cap-Vert →Cape Verde ◻¹	150a	16.00 N	24.00 W
Caquetá (Japurá) ≃	246	3.08 S	64.46 W
Çaqu ≃	130	50.22 N	80.55 E
Cara, Ityo.	248	29.57 S	69.38 W
Cara, Ross.	74	56.54 N	118.12 E
Carà, Ilha do I	250	3.08 S	60.13 W
Caraballeda	266c	10.37 N	66.50 W
Caraballo, Punta ➤	250	4.38 N	38.55 W
Carabanchel Alto ◆⁸	266a	40.22 N	3.45 W
Carabanchel Bajo ◆⁸	266a	40.23 N	3.47 W

Name	Page	Lat.	Long.
Capitachouane ≃	190	47.36 N	76.54 W
Capitachouane, Lac ◎	190	48.05 N	75.55 W
Capital Airport ★	219	39.51 N	89.41 W
Capital Centre ◆	284c	38.54 N	76.51 W
Capital City Airport ★	216	42.47 N	84.35 W
Capitan	200	33.32 N	105.34 W
Capitan I	255	54.10 S	71.20 W
Capitán Arturo Prat □	9	62.30 S	59.41 W
Capitán Bado	252	23.16 S	55.32 W
Capitán Bermúdez	252	32.49 S	60.43 W
Capitán Meza	252	26.55 S	55.15 W
Capitan Peak ▲	200	33.36 N	105.16 W
Capitán Sarmiento	252	34.10 S	59.48 W
Capitão de Campos	250	4.28 S	41.57 W
Capitão Enéas	255	16.21 S	43.43 W
Capitola	226	36.58 N	121.57 W
Capitol Heights	208	38.53 N	76.54 W
Capitol Park	208	39.08 N	75.30 W
Capitol Peak ▲	204	41.50 N	117.18 W
Capitol Reef National Park ◆	200	38.11 N	111.20 W
Capitol View	192	33.36 N	80.56 W
Capivara	255	23.00 S	47.31 W
Capivari ≃, Bra.	248	19.16 S	57.10 W
Capivari ≃, Bra.	255	12.30 S	39.55 W
Capivari ≃, Bra.	256	24.09 S	46.48 W
Capivari ≃, Bra.	256	22.14 S	44.57 W
Capivari ≃, Bra.	255	21.53 S	46.15 W
Capivari ≃, Bra.	256	22.26 S	45.47 W
Capivari ≃, Bra.	256	22.56 S	47.16 W
Capivari ≃, Bra.	256	21.30 S	44.20 W
Capivari ≃, Bra.	256	21.12 S	44.52 W
Capivari, Canal ⌇	287a	22.42 S	43.21 W
Capiz	116	11.35 N	122.45 E
—Roxas	116	11.35 N	122.45 E
Capiz ◻⁴	116	11.30 N	122.30 E
Capizzi	70	37.51 N	14.29 E
Caplen	222	29.29 N	94.33 W
Caplina ≃	248	18.14 S	70.33 W
Çaplino	180	64.25 N	172.15 W
Çaplygin	76	53.14 N	39.58 E
Capo Mountain ▲	180	63.25 N	123.29 W
Capnoyan Island I	116	14.00 N	120.54 E
Capoche ≃	154	15.23 S	32.53 E
Capodichino, Aeroporto di ★	68	40.50 N	14.17 E
Capodimonte	66	42.33 N	11.55 E
Capo di Ponte	64	46.02 N	10.21 E
Capo d'Orlando	70	38.10 N	14.53 E
Capoeira, Corredeira ⌇	250	6.48 S	58.21 W
Capologo	58	45.55 N	8.59 E
Capoliveri	66	42.45 N	10.22 E
Capoo ≃	152	12.56 S	13.00 E
Caposele	68	40.49 N	15.13 E
Capostrada	66	43.57 N	10.54 E
Capot ≃	240e	14.51 N	61.05 W
Capoterra	71	39.11 N	8.58 E
Capoti-an, Mount ▲	116	11.45 N	125.15 E
Capotoan, Mount ▲	116	12.09 N	124.57 E
Cappadocia ◻⁹	130	38.36 N	34.00 E
Cappamore	48	52.37 N	8.20 W
Cap-Pelé	186	46.13 N	64.18 W
Cappella Islands II	240m	18.17 N	64.54 W
Cappelle	68	42.03 N	13.22 E
Cappelle sul Tavo	66	42.28 N	14.06 E
Cappeln	52	52.48 N	8.07 E
Cappenberg	263	51.39 N	7.32 E
Cappenberg, Schloss ⌂¹	263	51.39 N	7.32 E
Cappercleuch	44	55.29 N	3.12 W
Cappoquin	48	52.08 N	7.50 W
Capracotta	68	41.50 N	14.16 E
Capraia	68	43.03 N	9.50 E
Capraia, Isola I	66	42.08 N	15.31 E
Capraia, Isola di I	66	43.03 N	9.50 E
Capranica	66	42.15 N	12.11 E
Caprara, Punta ➤	71	41.07 N	8.19 E
Caprarola	66	42.19 N	12.14 E
Capreol	190	46.43 N	80.56 W
Caprera, Isola I	71	41.12 N	9.28 E
Caprese Michelangelo	66	43.39 N	11.59 E
Capri	68	40.33 N	14.14 E
Capri, Isola di I	68	40.33 N	14.13 E
Capriati a Volturno	68	41.28 N	14.08 E
Capricorn, Cape ➤	166	23.00 S	151.13 E
Capricorn Channel ⥬	166	23.00 S	152.20 E
Capricorn Group II	166	23.28 S	152.00 E
Caprino Veronese	64	45.36 N	10.47 E
Caprivi ◻⁴	156	18.00 S	23.00 E
Caprivi Zipfel (Caprivi Strip) ⊶⁹	156	17.59 S	23.00 E
Caproláce, Lago di ◎	66	41.21 N	12.58 E
Capron, Va., U.S.	216	36.42 N	77.12 W
Cap-Saint Jacques →Vung Tau	110	10.21 N	107.04 E
Cap-Santé	206	46.40 N	71.47 W
Capstone	260	51.21 N	0.34 E
Captain Anthony Meldahl Dam ◆⁶	218	38.48 N	84.11 W
Captain Cook	229d	19.29 N	155.55 W
Captain Cook Bridge ◆	274a	34.00 S	151.08 E
Captain Cook Landing Place Park ◆	274a	34.00 S	151.14 E
Captain Cook Monument ⊥	174c	29.00 S	167.56 E
Captain Daniel Wright Woods ◆	278	42.13 N	87.56 W
Captain Harbor c	276	40.59 N	73.36 W
Captain Pond ◎	283	42.47 N	71.10 W
Captains Flat	171b	35.35 S	149.27 E
Captieux	32	44.17 N	0.16 W
Captina Creek ≃	188	39.50 N	80.48 W
Captiva	220	26.31 N	82.11 W
Captiva Island I	220	26.31 N	82.11 W
Captree Island I	276	40.39 N	73.16 W
Captree State Park ◆	276	40.38 N	73.16 W
Capua	68	41.06 N	14.12 E
Capual Island I	116	6.02 N	121.24 E
Capúava ◆⁸	287b	23.39 S	46.29 W
Capucapu ≃	246	1.37 S	62.07 W
Capucapu ≃	246	1.15 S	61.28 W
Capucin ➤	240d	15.38 N	61.28 W
Capulin, Río del ≃	196	27.31 N	101.33 W
Capulin Mountain National Monument ◆	196	36.48 N	103.55 W
Capunda	152	12.26 N	124.10 E
Capurro	258	34.25 S	56.28 W
Capuru ≃	116	15.38 S	19.43 E
Caputh	54	52.21 N	12.58 E
Cap-Vert →Cape Verde ◻¹	150a	16.00 N	24.00 W

Bilingual equivalence index (ENGLISH / DEUTSCH):

English Name	Page	Lat.	Long.	Deutsch Name	Seite	Breite	Länge E = Ost
Carabao Island I	116	12.04 N	121.56 E	Čardarinskoje vodochranilišče ◎¹	85	41.10 N	68.15 E
Carabaya	248	14.43 S	70.17 W	Cardeña	34	38.13 N	4.19 W
Carabaya, Cordillera de ⊶	248	13.50 S	70.45 W	Cárdenas, Cuba	240p	23.02 N	81.12 W
Carabayllo	286d	11.52 S	77.02 W	Cárdenas, Méx.	234	22.00 N	99.40 W
Carabelas Grande ≃	258	34.15 S	58.43 W	Cárdenas, Méx.	234	17.59 N	93.22 W
Carabinani ≃	246	1.58 S	61.31 W	Cárdenas, Nic.	236	11.12 N	85.31 W
Caraboio ◻³	246	10.10 N	68.05 W	Cárdenas, Bahía de c	240p	23.05 N	81.10 W
Carabost	171b	35.36 S	147.44 E	Cardener ≃	34	41.41 N	1.51 E
Caracal	34	44.07 N	24.21 E	Carderock Springs	284c	38.59 N	77.10 W
Caracalla, Terme di ⊥	266d	41.53 N	12.29 E	Cardiel, Lago ◎	254	48.55 S	71.15 W
Caracaraí	246	1.50 N	61.08 W	Cardiff, Austl.	170	32.57 S	151.41 E
Caracas, Ven.	246	10.30 N	66.56 W	Cardiff, Wales, U.K.	42	51.29 N	3.13 W
Caracas, Ven.	266c	10.30 N	66.56 W	Cardiff, Md., U.S.	208	39.43 N	76.20 W
Çarach	86	59.03 N	62.15 E	Cardiff, N.J., U.S.	208	39.24 N	74.35 W
Carache	246	9.38 N	70.14 W	Cardigan, Wales, U.K.	42	52.06 N	4.40 W
Caracol, Bra.	250	9.17 S	43.20 W	Cardigan ◻¹	42	52.06 N	4.40 W
Caracol, Bra.	252	22.01 S	57.02 W	Cardigan Bay c, P.E., Can.	186	46.10 N	62.30 W
Caracollo	248	17.39 S	67.10 W	Cardigan Bay c, Wales, U.K.	42	52.30 N	4.20 W
Caracorum →Karakoram Range ⊶	120	35.30 N	77.00 E	Cardigan Island I	42	52.08 N	4.41 W
Carácuaro de Morelos	234	18.46 N	101.02 W	Cardigan State Park ◆	188	43.38 N	71.54 W
Caradoc Indian Reserve ◆⁴	214	42.48 N	81.29 W	Cardinal	212	44.47 N	75.23 W
Caraffa di Catanzaro	68	38.53 N	16.29 E	Cardinale	68	38.38 N	16.23 E
Caraga	116	7.20 N	126.34 E	Cardinal Heights	212	42.45 N	77.57 W
Caraga ≃	116	7.20 N	126.34 E	Cardinal Lake ◎	182	56.14 N	117.44 W
Caragh, Lough ◎	48	52.03 N	9.52 W	Cardington, S. Afr.	158	27.11 S	23.30 E
Caraghnan Mountain ▲	166	31.20 S	149.03 E	Cardington, Oh., U.S.	214	40.30 N	82.53 W
Caraglio	62	44.25 N	7.26 E	Cardinia Creek ≃	274b	38.12 S	145.23 E
Caraguata, Arroyo ≃	288	34.24 S	58.38 W	Cardona	169	37.58 S	145.25 E
Caraguatatuba	256	23.37 S	45.25 W	Cardonal, Punta ➤	232	28.28 N	111.45 W
Caraguatatuba, Enseada de c	256	23.40 S	45.20 W	Cardoso	255	20.04 S	49.54 W
Caraguatay	252	25.16 S	56.52 W	Cardoso ≃	255	20.38 S	56.21 W
Caraí	255	17.12 S	41.42 W	Cardston	182	49.12 N	113.18 W
Caraíbamba	248	14.23 S	73.09 W	Cardwell, Austl.	166	18.16 S	146.02 E
Caraíbes, Îles des →West Indies II	230	19.00 N	70.00 W	Cardwell, Mo., U.S.	194	36.02 N	90.17 W
Caraïbes, Mer des →Caribbean Sea ≃²	230	15.00 N	73.00 W	Cardwell Mountain ▲	154	35.41 N	85.41 W
Caraigres, Cerro ▲	236	9.43 N	84.05 W	Cardžou	128	39.06 N	63.34 E
Caraíva ≃	255	16.48 S	39.08 W	Careaçu	256	22.02 S	45.42 W
Carajari ≃	250	4.45 S	54.20 W	Careen Lake ◎	184	57.00 N	108.10 W
Carajás	250	5.50 S	51.20 W	Carega, Cima ▲	64	45.44 N	11.08 E
Carajás, Serra dos ⊶	250	5.50 S	51.20 W	Carei	38	47.42 N	22.28 E
Caraúbe Bluff ➤¹	168	33.26 S	136.16 E	Careiro	246	3.12 S	59.45 W
Caramagna-Piemonte	62	44.46 N	7.44 E	Careiro, Ilha do I	246	3.10 S	59.44 W
Caramanico Terme	66	42.09 N	14.00 E	Carèja	76	54.37 N	29.17 E
Caramay	116	10.10 N	119.14 E	Carén	252	30.50 S	70.47 W
Caramoan	116	13.46 N	123.52 E	Carencro	194	30.19 N	92.02 W
Caramoan Peninsula ➤¹	116	13.48 N	123.40 E	Carentan	32	49.18 N	1.14 W
Caramoran	116	13.59 N	124.08 E	Cares ≃	34	43.19 N	4.36 W
Caramy ≃	62	43.26 N	6.12 E	Caresana	62	45.13 N	8.33 E
Caranavi	248	15.46 S	67.36 W	Caretta	192	37.20 N	81.40 W
Čaravčina	80	50.57 S	43.48 W	Carevščina	84	52.27 N	46.43 E
Carandayti	248	20.57 S	63.04 W	Carey	214	40.57 N	83.22 W
Carangola	255	20.44 S	42.02 W	Carey, Lake ◎	162	29.05 S	122.15 E
Carano	64	46.16 N	11.27 E	Carey Downs	162	25.38 S	115.27 E
Caransebeş	38	45.25 S	22.13 E	Careysburg	150	6.30 N	10.32 W
Carapá ≃	252	24.30 S	54.20 W	Cargados Carajos Shoals II	12	16.38 S	59.38 E
Carapachay ≃¹	288	34.25 S	58.35 W	Çargh	86	56.30 N	3.22 E
Carapajó	250	2.16 S	49.22 W	Carhaix-Plouguer	32	48.17 N	3.35 W
Cara-Paraná ≃	246	1.45 S	73.13 W	Carhuamayo	248	10.55 S	76.02 W
Carapeguá	252	25.48 S	57.14 W	Carhuaz	248	9.16 S	77.38 W
Carapicuíba	256	23.31 S	46.53 W	Carhué	252	37.11 S	62.44 W
Carapicuíba ◻⁷	287b	23.31 S	46.53 W	Caria ◻⁹	130	37.30 N	28.00 E
Carapo ≃	246	7.30 N	64.02 W	Cariaco	246	10.30 N	63.33 W
Caraquet	186	47.48 N	64.57 W	Cariaco, Golfo de c	246	10.30 N	64.00 W
Carare ≃	246	6.46 N	74.06 W	Cariamanga	246	4.20 S	79.35 W
Carasco	62	44.21 N	9.21 E	Cariango	152	10.37 S	15.20 E
Caraş-Severin ◻⁶	38	45.30 N	22.00 E	Cariati	68	39.30 N	16.56 E
Caratasca, Laguna de c	236	15.23 N	83.55 W	Caribana, Punta ➤	246	8.37 N	76.52 W
Caratinga	255	19.47 S	42.08 W	Caribbean Sea ≃²	230	15.00 N	73.00 W
Carauari	246	4.52 S	66.54 W	Caribe, Mar →Caribbean Sea ≃²	230	15.00 N	73.00 W
Caraúbas	250	5.47 S	37.34 W	Cariboo ≃	182	52.40 N	121.40 W
Caravaca de la Cruz	34	38.06 N	1.51 W	Cariboo Mountains ⊶	182	53.00 N	121.00 W
Caravaggio	62	45.30 N	9.38 E	Caribou, N.S., Can.	186	45.44 N	62.42 W
Caravela I	150	11.30 N	16.20 W	Caribou, Me., U.S.	176	46.52 N	68.00 W
Caravelas	255	17.45 S	39.15 W	Caribou ≃	176	59.20 N	94.44 W
Caravelle, Presqu'île de la ➤¹	240e	14.45 N	60.55 W	Caribou, Lac du ◎	186	50.15 N	69.45 W
Caravius, Monte is ▲	71	39.05 N	8.49 E	Caribou Island I	190	47.22 N	85.49 W
Caraway	194	35.46 N	90.19 W	Caribou Mountain ▲, Id., U.S.	202	43.06 N	111.18 W
Carayaó	252	25.15 S	56.26 W	Caribou Mountain ▲, Me., U.S.	188	45.26 N	70.38 W
Carazinho	252	28.18 S	52.48 W	Caribou Mountains ⊶	182	59.12 N	115.40 W
Carazo ◻⁵	236	11.45 N	86.15 W	Caribou River ◆	222	27.56 N	107.03 W
Carballiño	34	42.26 N	8.05 W	Carichic	232	27.56 N	107.03 W
Carballo	34	43.13 N	8.41 W	Caricuao	286c	10.26 N	66.59 W
Carbery	184	49.52 N	99.21 W	Caricyn →Volgograd	78	48.44 N	44.25 E
Carbet, Pitons du ▲	240e	14.42 N	61.07 W	Caridad, Pil.	116	10.50 N	124.45 E
Carbo	232	29.42 N	110.58 W	Caridade	250	4.13 S	39.12 W
Carbon, Ab., Can.	182	51.29 N	113.09 W	Carife	68	41.01 N	15.11 E
Carbon, Pa., U.S.	279b	40.10 N	79.34 W	Carigara	116	11.18 N	124.41 E
Carbon, Tx., U.S.	196	32.16 N	98.50 W	Carigara Bay c	116	11.18 N	124.45 E
Carbon ≃	210	40.55 N	75.48 W	Carignan, Fr.	56	49.37 N	5.10 E
Carbon, Cap ➤	34	36.47 N	5.06 E	Carignan, P.Q., Can.	275a	45.27 N	73.18 W
Carbonado	224	47.07 N	122.03 W	Carignano	62	44.54 N	7.40 E
Carbonara, Capo ➤	71	39.06 N	9.31 E	Carini	70	38.08 N	13.11 E
Carbonara, Pizzo ▲	70	37.54 N	14.02 E	Carini, Golfo di c	70	38.10 N	13.08 E
Carbonare	64	45.56 N	11.13 E	Cariño	34	43.44 N	7.52 W
Carbonate	266b	38.23 S	147.41 E	Carinhanha	255	14.18 S	43.47 W
Carbon-Blanc	32	44.53 N	0.31 W	Carinhanha ≃	255	14.20 S	43.47 W
Carbon Canyon Dam ◆⁶	280	33.49 N	118.04 W	Carini	70	38.08 N	13.11 E
Carbon Creek ≃	280	33.49 N	118.04 W	Caripe	246	10.12 N	63.29 W
Carbondale, Il., U.S.	200	39.24 N	107.12 W	Caripito	246	10.08 N	63.06 W
Carbondale, Il., U.S.	194	37.43 N	89.13 W	Cariré	250	3.56 N	51.27 W
Carbondale, Ks., U.S.	198	38.49 N	95.41 W	Carira	250	10.21 S	37.42 W
Carbondale, Pa., U.S.	210	41.34 N	75.30 W	Cariri ≃	250	3.52 S	40.25 W
Carbonear	186	47.45 N	53.13 W	Cariús	250	6.32 S	39.30 W
Carbonia de Guadazoan	34	39.53 N	1.48 W	Carlópolis	256	23.26 S	49.44 W
Carbon Hill	194	33.53 N	87.32 W	Carlos Barbosa	252	29.18 S	51.30 W
Carbonia	71	39.10 N	8.31 E	Carmo	256	21.56 S	42.37 W
Carbonia (Schuderbach)	64	46.32 N	12.13 E	Carlisbrook	166	36.58 S	143.49 E
Carbost	46	57.18 N	6.22 W	Carlisle	46	54.54 N	2.55 W
Carcaixent	34	39.08 N	0.27 W	Carleton, Mi., U.S.	216	42.03 N	83.23 W
Carcajou	182	65.37 N	128.43 W	Carleton, Mount ▲	186	47.23 N	66.53 W
Carcalong Hill ▲	170	32.52 S	149.41 E	Carlet	34	39.14 N	0.32 W
Carcans, Lac de ◎	32	45.08 N	1.08 W	Carleton Place	212	45.08 N	76.09 W
Carcar	116	10.07 N	123.38 E	Carleton University ∨	277	45.23 N	75.42 W
Carcar Point ➤	116	10.05 N	123.41 E	Carlentini	70	37.16 N	15.01 E
Carcassonne	32	43.13 N	2.21 E	Carley Place	170	37.19 S	149.57 E
Carcastillo	34	42.22 N	1.26 W	Carleses	34	41.30 N	0.49 E
Carcavelos, Port.	266c	38.53 N	9.14 W	Carlet	34	39.14 N	0.32 W
Carceri, Eremo delle ⊥	66	43.04 N	12.38 E	Cârlibaba	38	47.35 N	25.07 E
Carces	62	43.28 N	6.11 E	Carling	212	49.10 N	6.43 E
Carchi ◻³	246	0.40 N	78.00 W	Carlin	204	40.43 N	116.06 W
Çardaba	130	38.57 N	35.06 E	Carlingford Lough c	48	54.04 N	6.10 W
Cardak, Tür.	130	37.49 N	29.41 E	Carlingwark Lake ◎	44	54.55 N	3.55 W
Cardak, Uzb.	128	38.06 N	66.49 E	Carlisle, Eng., U.K.	46	54.54 N	2.55 W
Cardal	258	34.18 S	56.24 W	Carlisle, Ar., U.S.	194	34.46 N	91.44 W
Cárdeno al Campo	266b	38.53 N	9.14 W	Carlisle, In., U.S.	218	38.58 N	87.24 W
Çardara	85	41.17 N	67.55 E	Carlisle, Ky., U.S.	218	38.18 N	84.01 W
Çardara, step' ⥾	85	41.30 N	67.45 E				

ESPAÑOL

Nombre	Página	Lat.°′	Long.°′ W = Oeste
Carlisle, Ma., U.S.	283	42.31 N	71.21 W
Carlisle, N.Y., U.S.	210	42.45 N	74.27 W
Carlisle, Oh., U.S.	218	39.35 N	84.20 W
Carlisle, Pa., U.S.	208	40.12 N	77.11 W
Carlisle Barracks ■	208	40.13 N	77.11 W
Carlisle Bay ⊂	241g	13.05 N	59.37 W
Carlisle Gardens	210	43.11 N	78.39 W
Carlisle Island I	180	52.52 N	170.02 W
Carlisle Springs	208	40.16 N	77.10 W
Carl Junction	194	37.10 N	94.33 W
Carlls ≃	276	40.41 N	73.20 W
Carloforte	71	39.08 N	8.18 E
Carlopoli	68	39.03 N	16.27 E
Carlópolis	255	23.25 S	49.41 W
Carlos, Isla I	254	54.03 S	73.20 W
Carlos Alves	256	21.37 S	43.07 W
Carlos Barbosa	252	29.18 S	51.30 W
Carlos Beguerie	258	35.29 S	59.06 W
Carlos Casares	252	35.38 S	61.21 W
Carlos Chagas	255	17.43 S	40.45 W
Carlos City	218	40.02 N	85.02 W
Carlos Forseca Amador	236	11.59 N	86.31 W
Carlos Keen	258	34.29 S	59.14 W
Carlos Manuel de Céspedes	240p	21.35 N	78.17 W
Carlos Pellegrini	252	32.03 S	61.48 W
Carlos Reyles	252	33.03 S	56.29 W
Carlos Sampaio	287a	22.42 S	43.31 W
Carlos Tejedor	252	35.23 S	62.25 W
Carlow, Dtsch.	54	53.46 N	10.56 E
Carlow, Ire.	48	52.50 N	6.55 W
Carlow □[6]	48	52.40 N	6.50 W
Carloway	46	58.17 N	6.48 W
Carl Sandburg Home National Historic Site ⊥	192	35.16 N	82.27 W
Carlsbad → Karlovy Vary, Česká Rep.	54	50.11 N	12.52 E
Carlsbad, Ca., U.S.	228	33.09 N	117.20 W
Carlsbad, N.M., U.S.	196	32.25 N	104.13 W
Carlsbad, Tx., U.S.	196	31.36 N	100.38 W
Carlsbad Caverns National Park ♠	196	32.08 N	104.35 W
Carlsberg Ridge ✦[3]	12	6.00 N	61.00 E
Carlsborg	224	48.05 N	123.10 W
Carlsfeld	54	50.26 N	12.35 E
Carlstadt	276	40.50 N	74.05 W
Carlton, Austl.	274a	33.58 S	151.08 E
Carlton, Eng., U.K.	42	52.58 N	1.05 W
Carlton, Eng., U.K.	44	53.42 N	1.01 W
Carlton, Mn., U.S.	190	46.39 N	92.25 W
Carlton, Or., U.S.	224	45.18 N	123.11 W
Carlton, Tx., U.S.	196	31.55 N	98.10 W
Carlton Gardens ♠	274b	37.48 S	144.59 E
Carlton Lake ⊜	224	45.18 N	123.11 W
Carluke	46	55.45 N	3.51 W
Carlyle, Sk., Can.	184	49.38 N	102.16 W
Carlyle, Il., U.S.	219	38.36 N	89.22 W
Carlyle Lake ⊜[1]	219	38.40 N	89.18 W
Carmacks	180	62.05 N	136.18 W
Carmagnola	62	44.51 N	7.43 E
Carman	184	49.32 N	98.00 W
Carmanah Creek ≃	224	48.37 N	124.44 W
Carmangay	182	50.08 N	113.07 W
Carmanville	186	49.24 N	54.17 W
Carmarthen	42	51.52 N	4.19 W
Carmarthen Bay ⊂	42	51.40 N	4.30 W
Carmaux	32	44.03 N	2.09 E
Carmel, Wales, U.K.	262	53.17 N	3.15 W
Carmel, Ca., U.S.	226	36.33 N	121.55 W
Carmel, In., U.S.	218	39.58 N	86.07 W
Carmel, N.J., U.S.	208	39.26 N	75.07 W
Carmel, N.Y., U.S.	210	41.26 N	73.41 W
Carmel ≃	226	36.32 N	121.56 W
Carmel, Mount ∧, Ca., U.S.	226	36.23 N	121.47 W
Carmel, Mount → Karmel, Har ∧, Yis.	132	32.44 N	35.02 E
Carmel Bay ⊂	226	36.33 N	121.57 W
Carmel Head ›	44	53.24 N	4.34 W
Carmel Highlands	226	36.30 N	121.56 W
Carmel Hills	226	36.32 N	121.53 W
Carmel Mountain ∧[2]	228	32.55 N	117.13 W
Carmelo	258	34.00 S	58.17 W
Carmel Point	226	36.31 N	122.55 W
Carmel Valley	226	36.29 N	121.43 W
Carmel Woods	226	36.34 N	121.54 W
Carmen → Ciudad del Carmen, Méx.	232	18.38 N	91.50 W
Carmen, Pil.	116	8.59 N	125.17 E
Carmen, Pil.	116	9.50 N	124.12 E
Carmen, Pil.	116	10.35 N	124.01 E
Carmen, Pil.	116	12.37 N	122.07 E
Carmen, Ok., U.S.	196	36.34 N	98.27 W
Carmen, Ur.	252	33.15 S	56.01 W
Carmen, Isla I	232	25.57 N	111.12 W
Carmen, Isla del I	232	18.42 N	91.40 W
Carmen, Río del ≃	252	28.45 S	70.30 W
Carmen Alto	252	23.11 S	69.40 W
Carmen de Apicalá	246	4.09 N	74.44 W
Carmen de Areco	252	34.22 S	59.49 W
Carmen de Huechuraba	286e	33.21 S	70.40 W
Carmen de Patagones	254	40.48 S	62.59 W
Carmer Hill ∧[2]	214	41.54 N	77.58 W
Carmi	194	38.05 N	88.09 W
Carmi, Lake ⊜	206	44.58 N	72.53 W
Carmiano	68	40.21 N	18.03 E
Carmichael	226	38.37 N	121.19 W
Carmignano di Brenta	64	45.38 N	11.42 E
Carmila	166	21.55 S	149.25 E
Carmine	222	30.09 N	96.41 W
Carmo	256	21.56 S	42.37 W
Carmo, Monte ∧	62	44.11 N	8.11 E
Carmo, Ribeirão do ≃	256	21.20 S	45.10 W
Carmo, Rio do ≃	250	5.02 S	37.12 W
Carmo da Cachoeira	256	21.28 S	45.13 W
Carmo de Minas	256	22.07 S	45.08 W
Carmo do Paranaíba	255	18.59 S	46.21 W
Carmo do Rio Verde	255	15.21 S	49.42 W
Carmody Hills	284c	38.54 N	76.54 W
Carmona, Esp.	34	37.28 N	5.38 W
Carmona, Pil.	116	14.19 N	121.03 E
Carmópolis de Minas	255	20.33 S	44.38 W
Carmzow	54	53.23 N	14.02 E
Carnaíba	250	7.48 S	37.49 W
Carnamah	162	29.42 S	115.53 E
Carnarvon, Austl.	162	24.53 S	113.40 E
Carnarvon, S. Afr.	158	30.56 S	22.08 E
Carnarvon → Caernarfon, Wales, U.K.	44	53.08 N	4.16 W
Carnarvon National Park ♠	166	25.00 S	148.00 E
Carnatic □[9]	118	12.30 N	78.15 E
Carnation	224	47.38 N	121.54 W
Carnaval, Arroyo ≃	288	34.52 S	58.02 W
Carnaxide	266c	38.43 N	9.15 W
Carncastle	48	54.54 N	5.53 W
Carndonagh	48	55.15 N	7.15 W
Carnduff	184	49.10 N	101.50 W
Carnedd Llewelyn ∧	44	53.10 N	3.58 W
Carnedd Wen ∧	42	52.41 N	3.35 W
Carnegie, Austl.	162	25.43 S	122.59 E
Carnegie, N.Y., U.S.	210	42.45 N	78.51 W
Carnegie, Ok., U.S.	196	35.06 N	98.36 W
Carnegie, Pa., U.S.	214	40.24 N	80.05 W
Carnegie, Lake ⊜	162	26.10 S	122.30 E
Carnegie Institute ʋ[2]	279b	40.27 N	79.57 W
Carnegie-Mellon University ʋ[2]	279b	40.27 N	79.57 W
Carnegie Ridge ✦[3]	18	1.00 S	85.00 W
Carnelian Bay	226	39.14 N	120.05 W
Carnetin	261	48.54 N	2.42 E

FRANÇAIS

Nom	Page	Lat.°′	Long.°′ W = Ouest
Carnew	48	52.43 N	6.30 W
Carneys Point	208	39.42 N	75.28 W
Carnforth	44	54.08 N	2.46 W
Carnia	64	46.22 N	13.08 E
Carnia ◆[1]	64	46.25 N	13.00 E
Carniche, Alpi (Karnische Alpen) ⩕	64	46.40 N	13.00 E
Car Nicobar Island I	110	9.10 N	92.47 E
Carnide ◆[8]	266c	38.46 N	9.11 W
Carnières	50	50.10 N	3.21 E
Carniques → Karnische Alpen ⩕	64	46.40 N	13.00 E
Carnlough	48	54.59 N	6.00 W
Carno	42	52.33 N	3.31 W
Carnon-Plage	62	43.32 N	3.59 E
Carnot, Centraf.	152	4.56 N	15.52 E
Carnot, Pa., U.S.	214	40.31 N	80.13 W
Carnot, Cape ›	166	34.57 S	135.38 E
Carnoules	62	43.18 N	6.11 E
Carnoustie	46	56.30 N	2.44 W
Carnsore Point ›	48	52.10 N	6.22 W
Carnwath	46	55.43 N	3.38 W
Carnwath ≃	180	68.26 N	128.50 W
Caro	190	43.29 N	83.23 W
Caroga Creek ≃	210	42.58 N	74.38 W
Caroga Lake	210	43.08 N	74.29 W
Carol Beach Estates	216	42.31 N	87.49 W
Carol City	220	25.56 N	80.14 W
Carole Acres	284c	39.04 N	77.00 W
Caroleen	192	35.16 N	81.47 W
Carole Highlands	284c	38.58 N	76.59 W
Carolei	68	39.15 N	16.13 E
Carolina, Bra.	250	7.20 S	47.28 W
Carolina, Col.	246	6.43 N	75.17 W
Carolina, El Sal.	236	13.51 N	88.19 W
Carolina, P.R.	240m	18.23 N	65.57 W
Carolina, S. Afr.	158	26.05 S	30.06 E
Carolina, R.I., U.S.	207	41.27 N	71.39 W
Carolina Beach	192	34.02 N	77.53 W
Carolinas, Puntan ›	174n	14.55 N	145.38 E
Caroline □[6], Md., U.S.	208	38.53 N	75.50 W
Caroline □[6], Va., U.S.	208	38.00 N	77.20 W
Caroline I[1]	14	9.58 S	150.13 W
Caroline du Nord → North Carolina □[3]	192	35.30 N	80.00 W
Caroline du Sud → South Carolina □[3]	192	34.00 N	81.00 W
Caroline Islands II	14	8.00 N	147.00 E
Caroline Livermore, Mount ∧[2]	282	37.52 N	122.26 W
Caroline Peak ∧	172	45.56 S	167.13 E
Carol Stream	216	41.54 N	88.08 W
Caron	184	50.28 N	105.52 W
Caron, Lac ⊜	190	48.00 N	78.53 W
Çarona	64	46.01 N	9.47 E
Čaronda	76	60.34 N	38.59 E
Caroní ≃	246	8.21 N	62.43 W
Caronia	70	38.01 N	14.26 E
Caronia ≃	70	38.03 N	14.26 E
Caronno Pertusella	266b	45.36 N	9.03 E
Carora	246	10.11 N	70.05 W
Carosino	68	40.27 N	17.23 E
Carouge	58	46.11 N	6.09 E
Car'ov	80	48.40 N	45.22 E
Carovigno	68	40.42 N	17.39 E
Carovilli	66	41.43 N	14.17 E
Çar'ovščina	80	53.37 N	44.45 E
Čarozero	76	60.28 N	38.39 E
Carp	212	45.21 N	76.02 W
Carp ≃, On., Can.	212	45.29 N	76.14 W
Carp ≃, Mi., U.S.	190	46.02 N	84.42 W
Carpaneto Piacentino	62	44.55 N	9.47 E
Carpanzano	68	39.09 N	16.18 E
Carpates → Carpathian Mountains ⩕	22	48.00 N	24.00 E
Carpathian Mountains ⩕	22	48.00 N	24.00 E
Carpații Meridionali ⩕	38	45.30 N	24.15 E
Cárpatos → Carpathian Mountains ⩕	22	48.00 N	24.00 E
Carpegna	66	43.47 N	12.20 E
Carpenedolo	64	45.22 N	10.26 E
Carpentaria, Gulf of ⊂	164	14.00 S	139.00 E
Carpenter	198	41.02 N	104.21 W
Carpenter Creek ≃	216	40.54 N	87.12 W
Carpenter Lake ⊜	182	50.50 N	122.30 W
Carpentersville	216	42.07 N	88.15 W
Carpentertown	279b	40.11 N	79.31 W
Carpentras	62	44.03 N	5.03 E
Carpet Museum ʋ	267d	35.43 N	51.24 E
Carpi	64	44.47 N	10.53 E
Carpignano Sesia	62	45.32 N	8.25 E
Carpina	250	7.51 S	35.15 W
Cărpineni	38	46.47 N	28.22 E
Carpineti	64	44.28 N	10.31 E
Carpineto Romano	66	41.36 N	13.05 E
Carpino	68	41.51 N	15.51 E
Carpinone	66	41.35 N	14.19 E
Carpinteria	204	34.23 N	119.31 W
Carpio	198	48.26 N	101.42 W
Carp Lake ⊜	182	54.45 N	123.20 W
Carpolac	166	36.44 S	141.19 E
Carquefou	32	47.18 N	1.30 W
Carqueiranne	62	43.05 N	6.05 E
Carquinez Bridge ◆[5]	282	38.04 N	122.14 W
Carquinez Strait ⩆	282	38.02 N	122.12 W
Carra, Lough ⊜	48	53.42 N	9.16 W
Carrabelle	192	29.51 N	84.39 W
Carradale	46	55.35 N	5.28 W
Carramar	274a	33.53 S	150.58 E
Carrancas	256	21.30 S	44.39 W
Carr and Craggs Moor ◆[3]	262	53.43 N	2.09 W
Carranglan	116	15.58 N	121.04 E
Carranza, Cabo ›	252	35.36 S	72.38 W
Carrao ≃	246	6.17 N	62.51 W
Carrara	64	44.05 N	10.06 E
Carrascal	116	9.22 N	125.56 E
Carrasco ◆[8]	258	34.54 S	56.05 W
Carrasco, Aeropuerto Nacional de ⊠	258	34.52 S	56.02 W
Carrathool	166	34.24 S	145.26 E
Carrauntoohil ∧	48	51.59 N	9.45 W
Carrazedo	250	1.36 S	51.54 W
Carrboro	192	35.54 N	79.04 W
Carr Bridge	46	57.17 N	3.49 W
Carrcroft	285	39.47 N	75.30 W
Carrcroft Crest	285	39.47 N	75.30 W
Carrefour Pompadour ♠	261	48.46 N	2.26 E
Carregueira, Serra da ⩕[2]	266c	38.48 N	9.15 W
Carreria	252	21.59 S	58.35 W
Carreta, Punta ›	248	14.13 S	76.18 W
Carreta Quemada, Arroyo ≃	258	34.21 S	56.41 W
Carriacou I	238	12.30 N	61.27 W
Carrick ◆[8]	279b	40.23 N	79.59 W
Carrick ◆[1]	44	55.12 N	4.38 W
Carrickart	48	55.10 N	7.47 W
Carrickfergus	48	54.43 N	5.49 W
Carrickmacross	48	53.58 N	6.43 W
Carrick on Shannon	48	53.57 N	8.05 W
Carrick on Suir	48	52.21 N	7.25 W
Carrie, Mount ∧	224	47.53 N	123.39 W
Carriere	194	30.37 N	89.39 W
Carrière, Lac ⊜	190	47.14 N	77.12 W
Carrières, Pointe aux ›	275a	45.31 N	73.54 W
Carrières-sous-Bois	261	48.57 N	2.07 E
Carrières-sous-Poissy	261	48.57 N	2.03 E
Carrières-sur-Seine	261	48.55 N	2.11 E
Carriers Mills	194	37.41 N	88.38 W

PORTUGUÊS

Nome	Página	Lat.°′	Long.°′ W = Oeste
Carrieton	166	32.26 S	138.32 E
Carrigahorig	48	53.04 N	8.09 W
Carrigaline	48	51.48 N	8.24 W
Carrigallen	48	53.59 N	7.39 W
Carrillo, C.R.	236	9.52 N	85.30 W
Carrillo, Méx.	232	26.54 N	103.55 W
Carrington, Eng., U.K.	262	53.26 N	2.24 W
Carrington, N.D., U.S.	198	47.26 N	99.07 W
Carrington Island I	202	41.00 N	112.37 W
Carrington Moss ◆[3]	262	53.25 N	2.23 W
Carr Inlet ⊂	224	47.17 N	122.42 W
Carrión ≃	34	41.53 N	4.32 W
Carrión de los Condes	34	42.20 N	4.36 W
Carrizal ≃	234	23.03 N	97.46 W
Carrizal, Cerro ∧	196	26.43 N	100.36 W
Carrizal Bajo	252	28.05 S	71.10 W
Carrizo	34	42.35 N	5.50 W
Carrizo Creek ≃, U.S.	196	36.05 N	102.36 W
Carrizo Creek ≃, N.M., U.S.	196	35.40 N	103.43 W
Carrizo Mountain ∧	200	33.41 N	105.42 W
Carrizo Mountains ⩕	200	36.45 N	109.10 W
Carrizo Plain ≚	226	35.25 N	120.00 W
Carrizo Springs	196	28.31 N	99.51 W
Carrizo Wash V, U.S.	200	34.36 N	109.26 W
Carrizo Wash V, Ca., U.S.	204	33.05 N	115.56 W
Carrizozo	200	33.38 N	105.52 W
Carro	62	43.20 N	5.02 E
Carrodano	62	44.14 N	9.39 E
Carroll, Ia., U.S.	198	42.03 N	94.52 W
Carroll, Ne., U.S.	198	42.16 N	97.11 W
Carroll □[6], In., U.S.	216	40.36 N	86.41 W
Carroll □[6], Ky., U.S.	218	38.39 N	85.06 W
Carroll □[6], Md., U.S.	208	39.35 N	77.00 W
Carroll □[6], Oh., U.S.	214	40.34 N	81.05 W
Carroll Lake ⊜	184	51.07 N	95.05 W
Carroll Park ♠	284b	39.17 N	76.39 W
Carrolls	224	46.05 N	122.52 W
Carrollton, Al., U.S.	194	33.10 N	88.06 W
Carrollton, Ga., U.S.	192	33.35 N	85.05 W
Carrollton, Il., U.S.	219	39.18 N	90.24 W
Carrollton, Ky., U.S.	218	38.40 N	85.10 W
Carrollton, Mi., U.S.	190	43.27 N	83.55 W
Carrollton, Ms., U.S.	194	33.30 N	89.55 W
Carrollton, Mo., U.S.	194	39.21 N	93.29 W
Carrollton, Oh., U.S.	214	40.34 N	81.05 W
Carrollton, Tx., U.S.	222	32.57 N	96.53 W
Carrollton Manor	208	39.05 N	76.35 W
Carrolltown	214	40.36 N	78.43 W
Carrollwood	284b	39.20 N	76.23 W
Carron ≃, Austl.	166	17.42 S	141.06 E
Carron ≃, Scot., U.K.	46	57.25 N	5.27 W
Carron ≃, Scot., U.K.	46	57.53 N	4.21 W
Carron ≃, Scot., U.K.	46	56.02 N	3.44 W
Carron, Loch ⊂	46	57.22 N	5.31 W
Carronbridge	44	55.16 N	3.48 W
Carron Valley Reservoir ⊜[1]	46	56.02 N	4.05 W
Carros	62	43.48 N	7.11 E
Carrot ≃	184	53.50 N	101.17 W
Carrot River	184	53.17 N	103.35 W
Carrouges	28	48.34 N	0.09 W
Carrowmore Lake ⊜	48	54.12 N	9.47 W
Carrsville	208	36.43 N	76.50 W
Carrù	62	44.29 N	7.52 E
Carrum	169	38.05 S	145.08 E
Carrum Downs	274b	38.06 S	145.11 E
Carrum North	274b	38.03 S	145.09 E
Carrville	194	32.32 N	85.52 W
Carryduff	48	54.31 N	5.53 W
Carry Falls Reservoir ⊜[1]	188	44.25 N	74.45 W
Carry-le-Rouet	62	43.20 N	5.09 E
Carsaig	46	56.17 N	6.00 W
Çarşamba	130	41.12 N	36.44 E
Čaršanga	128	37.30 N	66.01 E
Carseland	182	50.51 N	113.28 W
Çarshalton ◆[8]	260	51.22 N	0.10 W
Čarsk	86	49.35 N	81.05 E
Carsoli	66	42.06 N	13.05 E
Carson, Ca., U.S.	228	33.49 N	118.16 W
Carson, N.D., U.S.	198	46.25 N	101.33 W
Carson, Va., U.S.	208	37.02 N	77.23 W
Carson, Wa., U.S.	224	45.43 N	121.49 W
Carson ≃	204	39.45 N	118.40 W
Carson, East Fork ≃	226	38.59 N	119.49 W
Carson, West Fork ≃	226	38.59 N	119.49 W
Carson City, Mi., U.S.	190	43.10 N	84.50 W
Carson City, Nv., U.S.	226	39.10 N	119.46 W
Carsondale	284c	38.57 N	76.50 W
Carson Lake ⊜, On., Can.	212	45.31 N	77.46 W
Carson Lake ⊜, Nv., U.S.	204	39.19 N	118.43 W
Carson Range ⩕	226	39.15 N	119.50 W
Carson Sink ⊜	204	39.45 N	118.30 W
Carson Valley V	226	39.00 N	119.48 W
Carstairs, Ab., Can.	182	51.34 N	114.06 W
Carstairs, Scot., U.K.	46	55.42 N	3.42 W
Carstensz-Toppen → Jaya, Puncak ∧	164	4.05 S	137.11 E
Carswell Air Force Base ■	222	32.47 N	97.26 W
Cartagena, Chile	252	33.33 S	71.37 W
Cartagena, Col.	246	10.25 N	75.32 W
Cartagena, Esp.	34	37.36 N	0.59 W
Cartago, Col.	246	4.45 N	75.55 W
Cartago, C.R.	236	9.52 N	83.55 W
Çartago □[4]	236	9.50 N	83.45 W
Čartak	85	41.05 N	71.50 E
Cartaxo	34	39.09 N	8.47 W
Cartaxos ∧[2]	266c	38.54 N	9.20 W
Cartaya	34	37.17 N	7.09 W
Carter	196	35.13 N	99.30 W
Carter □[6]	218	38.20 N	83.05 W
Carter Bridge ◆[5]	273a	6.28 N	3.23 E
Carter Caves State Resort Park ♠	218	38.22 N	83.10 W
Carteret	210	40.34 N	74.13 W
Carter Lake	198	41.17 N	95.55 W
Carter Mountain ∧	202	44.12 N	109.25 W
Carters Lake ⊜[1]	192	34.35 N	84.35 W
Cartersville	192	34.09 N	84.48 W
Carterton, N.Z.	172	41.02 S	175.31 E
Carterton, Eng., U.K.	42	51.45 N	1.35 W
Carterville	194	37.45 N	89.04 W
Carthage, Tun.	148	36.51 N	10.21 E
Carthage, Ar., U.S.	194	34.04 N	92.33 W
Carthage, Il., U.S.	190	40.24 N	91.08 W
Carthage, In., U.S.	218	39.44 N	85.34 W
Carthage, Ms., U.S.	194	32.43 N	89.32 W
Carthage, Mo., U.S.	194	37.10 N	94.18 W
Carthage, N.Y., U.S.	212	43.58 N	75.36 W
Carthage, N.C., U.S.	192	35.20 N	79.25 W
Carthage, S.D., U.S.	198	44.10 N	97.42 W
Carthage, Tn., U.S.	194	36.15 N	85.57 W
Carthage, Tx., U.S.	194	32.09 N	94.20 W
Carthage ⊥	36	36.52 N	10.20 E
Cartier Islands II	160	12.32 S	123.32 E
Cartierville ◆[8]	275a	45.32 N	73.42 W
Cartierville, Aéroport de ⊠	275a	45.31 N	73.43 W
Cartridge Hill ∧[2]	262	53.41 N	2.30 W
Cartura	64	45.16 N	11.50 E
Cartwright, Mb., Can.	184	49.06 N	99.20 W
Cartwright, Nf., Can.	176	53.42 N	57.01 W
Caruaru	250	8.17 S	35.58 W
Caruban	115a	7.33 S	111.39 E
Çarumas	248	16.49 S	70.43 W
Čarüngol	88	49.14 N	106.29 E
Carunjamba ≃	152	13.57 S	12.25 E
Carúpano	246	10.40 N	63.14 W
Caruray	116	10.20 N	119.00 E
Carutapera	250	1.13 S	46.01 W
Caruthers	226	36.32 N	119.50 W
Caruthersville	194	36.11 N	89.39 W
Carutu ≃	246	5.05 N	63.28 W
Carvalhopolis	256	21.47 S	46.51 W
Carvalhos	256	22.00 S	44.28 W
Carver	207	41.53 N	70.45 W
Carversville	208	40.23 N	75.04 W
Carvin	50	50.29 N	2.58 E
Carvoeiro	246	1.24 S	61.59 W
Carvoeiro, Cabo ›	34	39.21 N	9.24 W
Carwitzer See ⊜	54	53.18 N	13.28 E
Cary, Il., U.S.	216	42.12 N	88.14 W
Cary, Ms., U.S.	194	32.48 N	90.55 W
Cary, N.C., U.S.	192	35.47 N	78.46 W
Cary ≃	42	51.09 N	2.59 W
Caryčelekskij zapovednik ♠	85	41.50 N	71.55 E
Çaryk, ozero ⊜	80	46.13 N	42.43 E
Çarymovo	86	58.31 N	77.42 E
Çaryn	86	43.46 N	79.24 E
Čaryš ≃	86	52.22 N	83.45 E
Čaryšskoje	86	51.24 N	83.35 E
Caryville, Fl., U.S.	194	30.46 N	85.48 W
Caryville, Tn., U.S.	192	36.17 N	84.13 W
Casablanca (Dar-el-Beida)	148	33.39 N	7.35 W
Casablanca □[4]	148	33.35 N	7.30 W
Casablanca ◆[8]	286b	23.09 N	82.20 W
Casabona	68	39.15 N	16.57 E
Casa Branca	256	21.46 S	47.04 W
Casacalenda	68	41.44 N	14.51 E
Casa de la Torrecilla	266a	40.19 N	3.37 W
Casa del Campo ♠	266a	40.32 N	3.47 W
Casa de Piedra, Embalse ⊜[1]	252	38.15 S	67.20 W
Casa Grande	200	32.52 N	111.45 W
Casa Grande National Monument ♠	200	32.59 N	111.32 W
Casainhos	266c	38.53 N	9.10 W
Casalanguida	66	42.03 N	14.30 E
Casalattico	66	41.37 N	13.43 E
Casalbordino	66	42.09 N	14.35 E
Casalbuono	68	40.13 N	15.41 E
Casalbuttano	64	45.15 N	9.58 E
Casal di Principe	68	41.00 N	14.08 E
Casale Abbruciato ◆[8]	267a	41.44 N	12.33 E
Casalecchio di Reno	64	44.28 N	11.16 E
Casale Monferrato	62	45.08 N	8.27 E
Casale sul Sile	64	45.36 N	12.19 E
Casaletto Spartano	68	40.09 N	15.37 E
Casalmaggiore	64	44.59 N	10.26 E
Casalmorano	62	45.17 N	9.54 E
Casalnuovo Monterotaro	68	41.37 N	15.06 E
Casa Loma ʋ	275b	43.41 N	79.25 W
Casalone ◆[8]	267a	41.56 N	12.41 E
Casalotti ◆[8]	267a	41.55 N	12.22 E
Casalpusterlengo	62	45.11 N	9.39 E
Casal Velino	68	40.11 N	15.06 E
Casalvieri	66	41.38 N	13.43 E
Casamance ≃	150	12.33 N	16.46 W
Casamari, Abbazia di ʋ[1]	66	41.41 N	13.29 E
Casamassima	68	40.57 N	16.55 E
Casamicciola Terme	68	40.45 N	13.54 E
Casanare □[3]	246	5.45 N	72.00 W
Casanare ≃	246	6.02 N	69.51 W
Casanay	246	10.30 N	63.25 W
Casa Nova	250	9.07 S	40.58 W
Casarano	68	40.00 N	18.10 E
Casar de Cáceres	34	39.34 N	6.25 W
Casarsa della Delizia	64	45.57 N	12.50 E
Casas	234	23.44 N	98.45 W
Casas Adobes	200	32.19 N	110.59 W
Casas Grandes ≃	232	31.22 N	107.31 W
Casas-Ibáñez	34	39.17 N	1.28 W
Casasimarro	34	39.22 N	2.02 W
Casauman ≃	116	7.16 N	126.31 E
Casa Verde ◆[8]	287b	23.30 S	46.39 W
Casavieja	34	40.17 N	4.46 W
Casbas	252	36.45 S	62.30 W
Casca	252	28.34 S	51.59 W
Casca, Rio da ≃	248	14.52 S	55.52 W
Cascadas Basaseachic, Parque Nacional ♠	232	28.10 N	108.22 W
Cascade, B.C., Can.	182	49.01 N	118.13 W
Cascade, Id., U.S.	202	44.30 N	116.02 W
Cascade, Ia., U.S.	190	42.17 N	91.00 W
Cascade, Mi., U.S.	216	42.55 N	85.30 W
Cascade, Mt., U.S.	202	47.16 N	111.41 W
Cascade, Wi., U.S.	190	43.39 N	88.00 W
Cascade ≃, N.Z.	172	44.02 S	168.22 E
Cascade ≃, Wa., U.S.	224	48.32 N	121.26 W
Cascade Bay ⊂	174c	29.01 S	167.58 E
Cascade Locks	224	45.40 N	121.53 W
Cascade Mountains (Cascade Range) ⩕	202	45.00 N	121.30 W
Cascade Park ♠	279a	41.23 N	82.06 W
Cascade Point ›	172	44.00 S	168.22 E
Cascade Range ⩕	178	45.00 N	121.30 W
Cascade Reservoir ⊜[1]	202	44.35 N	116.06 W
Cascade Tunnel ◆[5]	224	47.40 N	121.03 W
Cascadura ◆[8]	287a	22.53 S	43.20 W
Cascais	34	38.42 N	9.25 W
Cascalho Rico	255	18.34 S	47.52 W
Cascapédia ≃	186	48.11 N	65.54 W
Cascatinha	256	22.29 S	43.09 W
Cascavel, Bra.	250	4.07 S	38.14 W
Cascavel, Bra.	252	24.57 S	53.28 W
Cascia	66	42.43 N	13.01 E
Casciana Terme	66	43.31 N	10.32 E
Cascina	66	43.41 N	10.33 E
Casco Bay ⊂	188	43.40 N	70.00 W
Çascumpec Bay ⊂	186	46.45 N	64.03 W
Čascy	82	55.37 N	36.52 E
Casei Gerola	62	45.00 N	8.55 E
Case Inlet ⊂	224	47.19 N	122.53 W
Casekow	54	53.12 N	14.12 E
Casella	62	44.32 N	9.00 E
Caselle, Aeroporto di ⊠	62	45.13 N	7.40 E
Caselle in Pittari	68	40.10 N	15.33 E
Caselle Torinese	62	45.10 N	7.39 E
Cà Selva, Lago di ⊜[1]	64	46.16 N	12.40 E
Casenove	66	42.58 N	12.50 E
Casentino V	66	43.40 N	11.50 E
Casenuove	266b	45.38 N	8.42 E
Case-Pilote	240e	14.38 N	61.08 W
Caseros	258	34.36 S	58.33 W
Caserta	68	41.04 N	14.20 E
Caserta □[4]	68	41.14 N	14.10 E
Caseville	190	43.56 N	83.16 W
Case Western Reserve University ʋ[2]	279a	41.30 N	81.36 W
Casey, Il., U.S.	194	39.17 N	87.59 W
Casey, Ia., U.S.	198	41.30 N	94.31 W
Casey ʋ[3]	9	66.17 S	110.32 E
Casey, Mount ∧	202	48.26 N	116.42 W
Casey Bay ⊂	9	67.20 S	48.00 E
Casey Key I	220	27.10 N	82.29 W
Caseyville	219	38.38 N	90.02 W
Cash	222	32.59 N	96.07 W
Cashel, Ire.	48	52.31 N	7.53 W
Cashel, Ire.	48	53.25 N	9.48 W
Cashie ≃	192	35.53 N	76.49 W
Cashiers	192	35.06 N	83.05 W
Cashmere	202	47.31 N	120.28 W
Cashmere Downs	162	28.58 S	119.35 E
Cashton	190	43.44 N	90.46 W
Cashtown	208	39.53 N	77.22 W
Casigua	246	8.46 N	72.30 W
Casiguran, Pil.	116	16.17 N	122.07 E
Casiguran, Pil.	116	12.52 N	124.00 E
Casiguran Sound ⩆	116	16.06 N	121.58 E
Casilda, Arg.	252	33.03 S	61.10 W
Casilda, Cuba	240p	21.46 N	79.59 W
Casimcea	38	44.43 N	28.23 E
Casimiro Castillo	234	19.38 N	104.28 W
Casina	64	44.30 N	10.30 E
Casino	166	28.52 S	153.03 E
Casiquiare ≃	246	2.01 N	67.07 W
Casita	200	31.00 N	110.53 W
Çasitas Springs	228	34.22 N	119.18 W
Čáslav	30	49.54 N	15.23 E
Çasma	248	9.28 S	78.19 W
Čašniki	76	54.52 N	29.08 E
Čašnikovo	265b	55.59 N	37.25 E
Časnočor, gora ∧	24	67.45 N	33.25 E
Casola in Lunigiana	64	44.14 N	10.10 E
Casola Valsenio	66	44.13 N	11.37 E
Casole d'Elsa	66	43.20 N	11.02 E
Casoli	66	42.07 N	14.18 E
Cason	222	33.02 N	94.49 W
Casorate Primo	62	45.19 N	9.01 E
Casorate Sempione	62	45.40 N	8.44 E
Casorezzo	266b	45.31 N	8.54 E
Çasoria	68	40.54 N	14.17 E
Časovo	24	62.01 N	50.36 E
Caspe	34	41.14 N	0.02 W
Casper	200	42.52 N	106.18 W
Casper Creek, Middle Fork ≃	200	43.01 N	106.29 W
Caspian	190	46.03 N	88.37 W
Caspian Sea ⊤[2]	72	42.00 N	50.30 E
Caspienne, Mer → Caspian Sea ⊤[2]	72	42.00 N	50.30 E
Caspio, Depresión del → Prikaspijskaja nizmennost' ≚	80	48.00 N	52.00 E
Caspio, Mar → Caspian Sea ⊤[2]	72	42.00 N	50.30 E
Caspoggio	64	46.16 N	9.52 E
Cass □[6], Il., U.S.	219	39.57 N	90.13 W
Cass □[6], In., U.S.	216	40.45 N	86.21 W
Cass □[6], Mi., U.S.	216	41.55 N	86.01 W
Cass □[6], Tx., U.S.	222	33.05 N	94.32 W
Cass ≃	190	43.23 N	83.59 W
Cassadaga	214	42.20 N	79.18 W
Cassadaga Creek ≃	214	42.05 N	79.08 W
Cassadaga Lakes ⊜	214	42.21 N	79.19 W
Cassaday Point ›	284a	42.52 N	79.13 W
Cassagnas	62	44.16 N	3.45 E
Cassai	152	10.33 S	21.59 E
Cassai (Kasai) ≃	152	3.02 S	16.57 E
Cassamba	152	13.06 S	20.18 E
Cassandra	214	40.24 N	78.38 W
Cassanje ≃	248	17.06 S	57.23 W
Cassano allo Ionio	68	39.47 N	16.20 E
Cassano d'Adda	62	45.32 N	9.31 E
Cassano delle Murge	68	40.53 N	16.46 E
Cassano Magnago	62	45.41 N	8.50 E
Cassaro	70	37.07 N	14.56 E
Cass Benton Parkway ♠	281	42.25 N	83.28 W
Cass City	190	43.36 N	83.10 W
Cassel	50	50.48 N	2.29 E
Casselberry	220	28.40 N	81.19 W
Cassella	216	40.25 N	84.34 W
Casselman	206	45.19 N	75.05 W
Casselton	198	46.54 N	97.12 W
Cássia, Bra.	255	20.36 S	46.56 W
Cassia, Fl., U.S.	220	28.53 N	81.28 W
Cássia dos Coqueiros	256	21.17 S	47.10 W
Cassiar	180	59.16 N	129.40 W
Cassiar Mountains ⩕	176	59.00 N	129.00 W
Cassibile ≃	70	36.57 N	15.11 E
Cassidy	224	49.04 N	123.53 W
Cassidy Airfield ⊠	174o	1.57 N	157.18 W
Cassilândia	255	19.09 S	51.45 W
Cassimbazar	126	24.07 N	88.16 E
Cassine	62	44.45 N	8.31 E
Cassinetta di Lugagnano	266b	45.25 N	8.54 E
Cassinga	152	15.08 S	16.05 E
Cassino, Bra.	252	32.11 S	52.10 W
Cassino, It.	66	41.30 N	13.49 E
Cassio	64	44.35 N	10.02 E
Cassipore ◆[8]	272b	22.37 N	88.22 E
Cassis	62	43.13 N	5.32 E
Cass Lake	190	47.22 N	94.36 W
Cass Lake ⊜, Mi., U.S.	281	42.36 N	83.22 W
Cass Lake ⊜, Mn., U.S.	190	47.25 N	94.32 W
Cassley ≃	46	57.58 N	4.35 W
Cassoalala	152	9.30 S	14.22 E
Cassoango	152	13.42 S	20.56 E
Cassolnovo	62	45.22 N	8.48 E
Cassone	64	45.44 N	10.46 E
Cassongue	152	11.51 S	15.03 E
Cassopolis	216	41.54 N	86.00 W
Casstown	218	40.03 N	84.07 W
Cassumba, Ilha I	255	17.46 S	39.17 W
Cassunda	152	10.57 S	21.03 E
Cassununga	255	16.03 S	53.38 W
Cassville, In., U.S.	216	40.33 N	86.08 W
Cassville, Mo., U.S.	194	36.40 N	93.52 W
Cassville, N.Y., U.S.	210	42.57 N	75.15 W
Cassville, Pa., U.S.	214	40.18 N	78.02 W
Cassville, Wi., U.S.	190	42.42 N	90.59 W
Castac Lake ⊜	228	34.50 N	118.51 W
Castagnaro	64	45.07 N	11.24 E
Castagneto Carducci	66	43.10 N	10.36 E
Castaic	228	34.30 N	118.37 W
Castaic Creek ≃	228	34.25 N	118.37 W
Castaic Lake ⊜[1]	228	34.32 N	118.37 W
Castalia	214	41.24 N	82.48 W
Castanea	210	41.07 N	77.25 W
Castanhal	250	1.18 S	47.55 W
Castanheira de Pêra	34	40.00 N	8.13 W
Castaños	196	26.47 N	101.25 W
Castañones, Punta ›	236	12.28 N	87.11 W
Castano Primo	62	45.33 N	8.47 E
Casteggio	62	45.00 N	9.07 E
Castel	43b	49.28 N	2.34 W
Castelar	258	34.40 S	58.40 W
Castel Baronia	68	41.03 N	15.11 E
Castel Bolognese	66	44.19 N	11.48 E
Castelbuono	70	37.56 N	14.05 E
Castelcivita	68	40.30 N	15.15 E
Casteldaccia	70	38.03 N	13.32 E
Castel d'Ario	64	45.11 N	10.58 E
Casteldarne (Ehrenburg)	64	46.48 N	11.50 E
Casteldelfino	62	44.35 N	7.04 E
Castel del Monte	66	42.22 N	13.43 E
Castel del Piano	66	42.53 N	11.32 E
Castel del Rio	66	44.12 N	11.30 E
Castel di Decima ◆[8]	267a	41.45 N	12.26 E
Castel di Guido ◆[8]	267a	41.54 N	12.17 E
Castel di Ieri	66	42.06 N	13.44 E
Castel di Iudica	70	37.30 N	14.38 E
Castel di Leva ◆[8]	267a	41.47 N	12.32 E
Castel di Lucio	70	37.53 N	14.19 E
Castel di Sangro	66	41.47 N	14.06 E
Castel di Tora	66	42.13 N	12.58 E
Castelfidardo	66	43.28 N	13.33 E
Castelfiorentino	66	43.36 N	10.58 E
Castelfondo	64	46.27 N	11.07 E
Castelforte	66	41.18 N	13.49 E
Castelfranco Emilia	64	44.37 N	11.03 E
Castelfranco in Miscano	68	41.18 N	15.05 E
Castelfranco Veneto	64	45.40 N	11.55 E
Castel Frentano	66	42.12 N	14.22 E
Castel Fusano ◆[8]	267a	41.44 N	12.19 E
Castel Gandolfo	66	41.45 N	12.39 E
Castel Giorgio	66	42.42 N	11.59 E
Castelgrande	68	40.47 N	15.26 E
Castelhanos, Baía de ⊂	256	23.51 S	45.15 W
Castelhanos, Ponta dos ›	256	23.10 S	44.06 W
Castellabate	68	40.17 N	14.57 E
Castell'Alfero	62	44.59 N	8.13 E
Castellalto	66	42.40 N	13.49 E
Castellammare, Golfo di ⊂	70	38.08 N	12.54 E
Castellammare del Golfo	70	38.01 N	12.53 E
Castellammare di Stabia	68	40.42 N	14.29 E
Castellamonte	62	45.23 N	7.42 E
Castellana, Grotte di ⩊[5]	68	40.53 N	17.07 E
Castellana Grotte	68	40.53 N	17.11 E
Castellana Sicula	70	37.47 N	14.02 E
Castellane	62	43.51 N	6.31 E
Castellaneta	68	40.37 N	16.57 E
Castellanza	62	45.37 N	8.54 E
Castellarano	64	44.30 N	10.44 E
Castell'Arquato	62	44.51 N	9.52 E
Castell'Azzara	66	42.46 N	11.42 E
Castellazzo Bormida	62	44.51 N	8.34 E
Castellbisbal	266d	41.29 N	1.59 E
Castelldefels	266d	41.17 N	1.59 E
Castelleone	62	45.18 N	9.46 E
Castelletto	266b	45.30 N	8.48 E
Castelletto di Brenzone	64	45.41 N	10.45 E
Castelli, Arg.	252	36.06 S	57.47 W
Castelli, It.	66	42.29 N	13.43 E
Castellina in Chianti	66	43.28 N	11.17 E
Castellina Marittima	66	43.25 N	10.35 E
Castelli Romani ◆[1]	267a	41.48 N	12.42 E
Castelló □[4]	34	40.10 N	0.10 W
Castello, Monte ∧[2]	66	43.03 N	9.49 E
Castello d'Annone	62	44.53 N	8.19 E
Castello di Fiemme	64	46.17 N	11.26 E
Castello Lavazzo	64	46.17 N	12.18 E
Castellón de la Plana	34	39.59 N	0.02 W
Castellote	34	40.48 N	0.19 W
Castello Tesino	64	46.04 N	11.38 E
Castellucchio	64	45.09 N	10.39 E
Castelluccio	68	40.00 N	15.58 E
Castell'Umberto	70	38.05 N	14.48 E
Castelluzzo	70	38.06 N	12.44 E
Castel Madama	66	41.58 N	12.52 E
Castel Maggiore	64	44.34 N	11.22 E
Castelmagno	62	44.24 N	7.13 E
Castelmassa	64	45.01 N	11.18 E
Castelmauro	66	41.50 N	14.43 E
Castelmezzano	68	40.32 N	16.03 E
Castelmoron-sur-Lot	32	44.24 N	0.30 E
Castelnaudary	32	43.19 N	1.57 E
Castelnau-Montratier	32	44.16 N	1.21 E
Castelnovo di Sotto	64	44.49 N	10.34 E
Castelnovo ne'Monti	64	44.26 N	10.24 E
Castelnuovo	64	45.26 N	10.47 E
Castelnuovo Berardenga	66	43.21 N	11.30 E
Castelnuovo dell'Abate	66	43.00 N	11.31 E
Castelnuovo della Daunia	68	41.35 N	15.07 E
Castelnuovo di Garfagnana	64	44.06 N	10.24 E
Castelnuovo di Porto	66	42.07 N	12.30 E
Castelnuovo di Val di Cecina	66	43.12 N	10.59 E
Castelnuovo Don Bosco	62	45.03 N	7.58 E
Castelnuovo Nigra	62	45.26 N	7.41 E
Castelnuovo Rangone	64	44.33 N	10.56 E
Castelnuovo Scrivia	62	44.59 N	8.53 E
Castelo	255	20.36 S	41.12 W
Castelo Branco	34	39.49 N	7.30 W
Castelo do Piauí	250	5.20 S	41.33 W
Castel Pagano	68	41.24 N	14.48 E
Castel Porziano ◆[8]	267a	41.44 N	12.24 E
Castelraimondo	66	43.12 N	13.04 E
Castel Romano ◆[8]	267a	41.44 N	12.27 E
Castel San Gimignano	66	43.24 N	11.00 E
Castel San Giorgio	68	40.47 N	14.42 E
Castel San Giovanni	62	45.04 N	9.26 E
Castel San Lorenzo	68	40.25 N	15.14 E
Castel San Pietro Terme	66	44.24 N	11.35 E
Castel Sant'Elia	66	42.15 N	12.22 E
Castelsaraceno	68	40.10 N	16.00 E
Castelsardo	71	40.55 N	8.43 E
Castelsarrasin	32	44.02 N	1.06 E
Castelsilano	68	39.16 N	16.46 E
Casteltermini	70	37.32 N	13.39 E
Castelvecchio Subequo	66	42.08 N	13.44 E
Castelvetere in Val Fortore	68	41.27 N	14.56 E
Castelvetrano	70	37.41 N	12.47 E
Castelvetro di Modena	64	44.30 N	10.57 E
Castelvetro Piacentino	64	45.05 N	9.59 E
Castel Viscardo	66	42.45 N	12.00 E
Castel Volturno	68	41.02 N	13.56 E
Castenaso	64	44.30 N	11.28 E
Castenedolo	64	45.28 N	10.18 E
Casterton	166	37.35 S	141.24 E
Castets	32	43.53 N	1.09 W
Castiglioncello	66	43.24 N	10.24 E
Castiglione Chiavarese	62	44.16 N	9.21 E
Castiglione d'Adda	62	45.13 N	9.41 E
Castiglione dei Pepoli	66	44.08 N	11.09 E
Castiglione del Lago	66	43.07 N	12.03 E
Castiglione della Pescaia	66	42.46 N	10.53 E
Castiglione delle Stiviere	64	45.23 N	10.29 E
Castiglione di Sicilia	70	37.53 N	15.07 E
Castiglione d'Orcia	66	43.00 N	11.37 E
Castiglione d'Ossola	58	46.03 N	8.13 E
Castiglione Messer Marino	66	41.52 N	14.27 E
Castiglione Olona	62	45.46 N	8.52 E
Castiglion Fibocchi	66	43.32 N	11.46 E
Castiglion Fiorentino	66	43.20 N	11.55 E
Castile	210	42.37 N	78.03 W
Castilho	255	20.52 S	51.29 W
Castilla	248	5.12 S	80.38 W
Castilla, Playa de ⩊[2]	34	37.00 N	6.33 W
Castilla-La Mancha □[3]	34	39.30 N	3.00 W
Castilla la Nueva □[9]	34	40.00 N	3.45 W
Castilla la Vieja □[9]	34	41.30 N	4.00 W
Castilla-León □[3]	34	41.30 N	5.00 W
Castillo	258	33.53 S	57.40 W
Castillo, Cerro ∧	254	43.03 S	71.57 W
Castillo, Pampa del ≚	254	45.58 S	68.24 W
Castillo de San Marcos National Monument ♠	192	29.44 N	81.20 W
Castillo Incaico de Ingapirca ⊥	246	2.34 S	78.50 W
Castillon-la-Bataille	32	44.51 N	0.03 W
Castillos	252	34.12 S	53.50 W
Castillos, Laguna de ⊜	252	34.20 S	53.54 W
Castine	188	44.23 N	68.48 W
Castione della Presolana	64	45.54 N	10.04 E
Castions di Strada	64	45.54 N	13.11 E
Castle Acre	42	52.42 N	0.41 E
Castle Air Force Base ■	226	37.22 N	120.34 W
Castlebar	48	53.52 N	9.17 W
Castlebay	46	56.57 N	7.28 W

Symbol	English	Deutsch	Español	Français	Português
≃	River	Fluß	Río	Rivière	Rio
≊	Canal	Kanal	Canal	Canal	Canal
⌞	Waterfall, Rapids	Wasserfall, Stromschnellen	Cascada, Rápidos	Chute d'eau, Rapides	Cascata, Rápidos
⩆	Strait	Meeresstraße	Estrecho	Détroit	Estreito
⊂	Bay, Gulf	Bucht, Golf	Bahía, Golfo	Baie, Golfe	Baía, Golfo
⊜	Lake, Lakes	See, Seen	Lago, Lagos	Lac, Lacs	Lago, Lagos
≋	Swamp	Sumpf	Pantano	Marais	Pântano
⍓	Ice Features, Glacier	Eis- und Gletscherformen	Accidentes Glaciales	Formes glaciaires	Acidentes glaciares
⊤	Other Hydrographic Features	Andere Hydrographische Objekte	Otros Elementos Hidrográficos	Autres données hydrographiques	Outros acidentes hidrográficos
✦	Submarine Features	Untermeerische Objekte	Accidentes Submarinos	Formes de relief sous-marin	Acidentes submarinos
□	Political Unit	Politische Einheit	Unidad Politica	Entité politique	Unidade política
ʋ	Cultural Institution	Kulturelle Institution	Institución Cultural	Institution culturelle	Institução cultural
⊥	Historical Site	Historische Stätte	Sitio Histórico	Site historique	Sitio histórico
♠	Recreational Site	Erholungs- und Ferienort	Sitio de Recreo	Centre de loisirs	Area de Lazer
⊠	Airport	Flughafen	Aeropuerto	Aéroport	Aeroporto
■	Military Installation	Militäranlage	Instalación Militar	Installation militaire	Instalação militar
◆	Miscellaneous	Verschiedenes	Misceláneo	Divers	Diversos

Castlebellingham 48 53.54 N 6.23 W
Castleberry 194 31.17 N 87.01 W
Castleblayney 48 54.07 N 6.44 W
Castle Bruce 240d 15.26 N 61.16 W
Castle Cape ≻ 180 56.15 N 158.06 W
Castle Cary 42 51.06 N 2.31 W
Castlecliff 172 39.57 S 174.59 E
Castlecomer 48 52.48 N 7.12 W
Castleconnell 48 52.43 N 8.30 W
Castlecrag 274a 33.48 S 151.13 E
Castle Crags State Park ♦ 204 41.10 N 122.20 W
Castle Creek 210 42.14 N 75.55 W
Castle Creek ≃, Austl. 169 36.41 S 145.29 E
Castle Creek ≃, Id., U.S. 202 43.06 N 116.16 W
Castle Dale 200 39.23 N 110.27 W
Castledawson 48 54.47 N 6.33 W
Castlederg 48 54.42 N 7.36 W
Castledermot 48 52.55 N 6.50 W
Castle Dome Peak ʌ 200 33.05 N 114.08 W
Castle Donington 42 52.51 N 1.19 W
Castle Douglas 44 54.57 N 3.56 W
Castlefinn 48 54.47 N 7.35 W
Castleford 44 53.44 N 1.21 W
Castlegar 182 49.19 N 117.40 W
Castle Harbour ⊂ 240a 32.21 N 64.40 W
Castle Hill 274a 33.44 S 151.00 E
Castle Hills, De., U.S. 208 39.41 N 75.33 W
Castle Hills, Tx., U.S. 196 29.32 N 98.31 W
Castleisland 48 52.14 N 9.27 W
Castlemaine, Austl. 169 37.04 S 144.13 E
Castlemaine, Ire. 48 52.09 N 9.43 W
Castlemartyr 48 51.55 N 8.03 W
Castlemore 275b 43.47 N 79.41 W
Castle Mountain ʌ, Ab., Can. 182 51.18 N 115.55 W
Castle Mountain ʌ, Yk., Can. 180 64.32 N 135.25 W
Castle Mountain ʌ, Ca., U.S. 226 35.56 N 120.20 W
Castle Neck ≻[1] 283 42.41 N 70.45 W
Castle Neck ≃ 283 42.40 N 70.44 W
Castle Park 228 32.36 N 117.04 W
Castle Peak ʌ, Co., U.S. 200 39.01 N 106.52 W
Castle Peak ʌ, Id., U.S. 202 44.02 N 114.35 W
Castle Peak ʌ, Wa., U.S. 224 48.58 N 120.51 W
Castlepoint 172 40.54 S 176.13 E
Castle Point □[8] 260 51.33 N 0.35 E
Castlepollard 48 53.40 N 7.17 W
Castlerea 48 53.46 N 8.29 W
Castlereagh ≃ 166 30.12 S 147.32 E
Castle Rock, Co., U.S. 200 39.22 N 104.51 W
Castle Rock, Pa., U.S. 285 39.58 N 75.26 W
Castle Rock, Wa., U.S. 224 46.16 N 122.54 W
Castle Rock ʌ, Or., U.S. 202 44.02 N 118.11 W
Castle Rock ʌ, Va., U.S. 192 37.57 N 78.44 W
Castle Rock Butte ʌ 198 45.00 N 103.27 W
Castle Rock Lake ⊜[1] 190 43.56 N 89.58 W
Castle Shannon 279b 40.21 N 80.01 W
Castleshaw Moor ◆[3] 262 53.36 N 2.00 W
Castleside 44 54.50 N 1.52 W
Castleton, Eng., U.K. 44 53.21 N 1.46 W
Castleton, Eng., U.K. 44 54.28 N 0.56 W
Castleton, Eng., U.K. 262 53.35 N 2.11 W
Castleton, In., U.S. 218 39.54 N 86.03 W
Castleton, Vt., U.S. 188 43.36 N 73.10 W
Castleton on Hudson 210 42.32 N 73.45 W
Castletown, I. of Man 44 54.04 N 4.40 W
Castletown, Scot., U.K. 46 58.35 N 3.23 W
Castletown Bearhaven (Castletown Bere) 48 51.39 N 9.55 W
Castletown Bere → Castletown Bearhaven 48 51.39 N 9.55 W
Castletown Geoghegan 48 53.26 N 7.38 W
Castletownroche 48 52.10 N 8.28 W
Castletownshend 48 51.32 N 9.11 W
Castlewellan 48 54.16 N 5.57 W
Castlewood, Ky., U.S. 218 38.04 N 84.27 W
Castlewood, S.D., U.S. 198 44.43 N 97.01 W
Castlewood, Va., U.S. 192 36.53 N 82.16 W
Častoje 82 54.11 N 37.47 E
Častooz'ornoje 86 55.34 N 67.53 E
Castor 182 52.13 N 111.53 W
Castor ≃, On., Can. 212 45.18 N 75.10 W
Castor ≃, Mo., U.S. 194 36.51 N 89.44 W
Castorano 66 42.54 N 13.43 E
Castor Creek ≃ 194 31.47 N 92.22 W
Castorland 212 43.53 N 75.30 W
Castra Vetera ⊥ 263 51.39 N 6.28 E
Castres 32 43.36 N 2.15 E
Castricum 52 52.33 N 4.39 E
Castries, Fr. 62 43.40 N 3.59 E
Castries, St. Luc. 241f 14.01 N 61.00 W
Castries, Port ⊂ 241f 14.01 N 61.01 W
Castro, Bra. 252 24.47 S 50.00 W
Castro, Chile 254 42.29 S 73.46 W
Castro, It. 64 45.48 N 10.04 E
Castro, Arroyo de ≃ 258 33.37 S 56.10 W
Castro, Punta ≻ 254 43.22 S 65.03 W
Castro Barros 252 30.35 S 65.44 W
Castrocaro Terme 66 44.10 N 11.57 E
Castrocielo 66 41.32 N 13.42 E
Castro Daire 34 40.54 N 7.56 W
Castro dei Volsci 66 41.30 N 13.24 E
Castro del Río 34 37.41 N 4.28 W
Castrofilippo 70 37.21 N 13.46 E
Castrojeriz 34 42.17 N 4.08 W
Castro Marim 34 37.13 N 7.26 W
Castronuño 34 41.23 N 5.16 W
Castronuovo di Sant'Andrea 68 40.11 N 16.11 E
Castronuovo di Sicilia 70 37.41 N 13.36 E
Castropol 34 43.32 N 7.02 W
Castrop-Rauxel 52 51.34 N 7.18 E
Castroreale 70 38.06 N 15.12 E
Castro-Urdiales 34 43.23 N 3.13 W
Castro Valley 226 37.41 N 122.05 W
Castro Verde 34 37.42 N 8.05 W
Castrovillari 68 39.49 N 16.13 E
Castroville, Ca., U.S. 226 36.45 N 121.45 W
Castroville, Tx., U.S. 196 29.21 N 98.52 W
Castrovirreyna 248 13.16 S 75.19 W
Castuera 34 38.43 N 5.33 W
Čast uul ʌ 86 48.40 N 90.45 E
Častyje 80 57.19 N 54.59 E
Casummit Lake 184 51.28 N 92.24 W
Casupá 252 34.07 S 55.39 W
Caswell Sound ʮ 172 45.00 S 167.10 E
Çat 130 39.40 N 41.00 E
Cat ≃ 184 51.07 N 91.25 W
Catabola 152 12.09 S 17.16 E
Cataby 162 30.43 S 115.31 E
Catacamas 236 14.48 N 85.54 W
Catacaos 248 5.16 S 80.41 W
Catacocha 246 4.04 S 79.38 W
Cataguarino 256 21.18 S 42.43 W
Cataguases 256 21.24 S 42.41 W
Catahoula Lake ⊜ 194 31.30 N 92.06 W
Çatak 128 38.01 N 43.07 E
Çatakköprü 130 38.09 N 41.12 E
Catalaban Island I 116 11.51 N 125.28 E
Çatalan 130 37.14 N 35.16 E
Catalão 255 18.10 S 47.57 W
Catalão, Ponta do ≻ 287a 22.51 S 43.13 W
Çatalca 130 41.09 N 28.27 E
Çatalçam 130 40.00 N 38.51 E
Catalfaro ≃ 70 37.22 N 14.43 E
Catalina, Nf., Can. 186 48.31 N 53.05 W
Catalina, Chile 252 25.13 S 69.43 W
Catalina → Santa Catalina Island I 228 33.23 N 118.24 W
Catalina, Punta ≻ 254 52.32 S 68.47 W
Catalonia → Catalunya □[4] 34 41.40 N 1.30 E
Catalunya □[3] 34 41.40 N 1.30 E
Catalzeytin 130 41.57 N 34.13 E
Catamarca □[4] 252 27.00 S 67.00 W
Catamare 286c 10.36 N 67.02 W
Catamayo 246 3.59 S 79.21 W
Catamayo ≃ 246 4.18 S 80.09 W
Catanauan 116 13.36 N 122.19 E
Catanduanes □[4] 116 13.47 N 124.16 E
Catanduanes Island I 116 13.45 N 124.15 E
Catanduva 255 21.08 S 48.58 W
Catane → Catania 70 37.30 N 15.06 E
Catania 70 37.30 N 15.06 E
Catania □[4] 70 37.23 N 14.40 E
Catania, Golfo di ⊂ 70 37.24 N 15.09 E
Catania, Piana di ≚ 70 37.25 N 14.51 E
Cataño 240m 18.27 N 66.07 W
Catanzaro 68 38.54 N 16.36 E
Catanzaro □[4] 68 38.54 N 16.36 E
Catanzaro Lido 68 38.49 N 16.36 E
Cataonia □[9] 130 38.00 N 35.00 E
Catára ≃ 152 13.34 S 12.35 E
Cataract Canyon V 200 36.03 N 112.35 W
Cataract Reservoir ⊜[1] 170 34.16 S 150.48 E
Catarama 246 1.35 S 79.28 W
Cataraqui 212 44.16 N 76.32 W
Cataraqui ≃ 212 44.13 N 76.28 W
Catarina 250 6.12 S 39.54 W
Catarman, Pil. 116 9.08 N 124.40 E
Catarman, Pil. 116 12.30 N 124.38 E
Catarroja 34 39.24 N 0.24 W
Catasauqua 208 40.39 N 75.29 W
Catatumbo ≃ 246 9.22 N 71.45 W
Catawba 218 40.00 N 83.37 W
Catawba ≃ 192 34.36 N 80.54 W
Catawba Island 214 41.35 N 82.50 W
Catawissa, Mo., U.S. 219 38.25 N 90.47 W
Catawissa, Pa., U.S. 210 40.57 N 76.27 W
Catawissa Creek ≃ 210 40.57 N 76.28 W
Cataxa 154 15.58 S 33.12 E
Cat Ba, Dao I 110 20.50 N 107.00 E
Catbalogan 116 11.46 N 124.53 E
Catchabutan, Punta ≻ 236 15.50 N 86.32 W
Catchacoma Lake ⊜ 212 44.45 N 78.20 W
Cateco Cangola 152 8.27 S 15.48 E
Catedral, Cerro ʌ[2] 252 34.23 S 54.40 W
Cateel 116 7.48 N 126.27 E
Cateel ≃ 116 7.47 N 126.27 E
Cateel Bay ⊂ 116 7.54 N 126.25 E
Catemaco 234 18.25 N 95.07 W
Catemaco, Laguna ⊜ 234 18.25 N 95.05 W
Catembe 156 26.00 S 32.33 E
Catenanuova 70 37.34 N 14.41 E
Caterham 42 51.17 N 0.04 W
Caterino Rodriguez 232 24.51 N 100.19 W
Catete 152 9.06 S 13.43 E
Catete ◆[8] 287a 22.55 S 43.10 W
Catete ≃ 250 6.04 S 54.09 W
Catfish Creek ≃, On., Can. 212 42.39 N 81.01 W
Catfish Creek ≃, N.Y., U.S. 212 43.31 N 76.19 W
Catfish Creek ≃, Tx., U.S. 222 31.47 N 95.56 W
Catford ◆[8] 260 51.27 N 0.01 W
Catharine Creek ≃ 210 42.21 N 76.51 W
Cathcart 158 32.18 S 27.09 E
Cathead Mountain ʌ 210 43.17 N 74.17 W
Cathedral City 204 33.46 N 116.27 W
Cathedral Gorge State Park ♦ 204 37.50 N 114.30 W
Cathedral Mountain ʌ 196 30.10 N 103.40 W
Cathedral of the Pines ʊ[1] 207 42.47 N 71.58 W
Cathedral Provincial Park ♦ 202 49.05 N 120.10 W
Cathedral Range ⋀ 226 37.47 N 119.21 W
Catherines Peak ʌ 241q 18.04 N 76.42 W
Catheys Valley 226 37.25 N 120.06 W
Cathlamet 224 46.12 N 123.22 W
Catholic University ʊ[2] 284c 38.56 N 77.00 W
Catia ◆[8] 286c 10.31 N 66.57 W
Catia La Mar 286c 10.36 N 67.02 W
Ca' Tiepolo 66 44.56 N 12.22 E
Catignano 66 42.21 N 13.57 E
Catió 150 11.13 N 15.10 W
Catirina, Punta ʌ 71 40.29 N 9.32 E
Cat Island I, Ba. 238 24.27 N 75.30 W
Cat Island I, Ma., U.S. 283 42.31 N 70.49 W
Cat Island I, Ms., U.S. 194 30.13 N 89.06 W
Čatkal ≃ 85 41.38 N 70.01 E
Čatkal'skij chrebet ⋀ 85 41.40 N 71.05 E
Cat Lake ⊜ 184 51.40 N 91.50 W
Catlettsburg 188 38.24 N 82.36 W
Catlin 194 40.03 N 87.42 W
Catlins ≃ 172 46.29 S 169.43 E
Catlodge 46 57.00 N 4.15 W
Catnip Mountain ʌ 204 41.52 N 119.23 W
Cato 210 43.10 N 76.34 W
Catoche, Cabo ≻ 232 21.35 N 87.05 W
Catoctin Creek ≃ 208 39.18 N 77.33 W
Catoctin Mountain ʌ 208 39.26 N 77.31 W
Cato Island I 166 23.15 S 155.32 E
Catolé do Rocha 250 6.21 S 37.45 W
Católica, Universidad ʊ[2], Chile 286e 33.27 S 70.39 W
Católica, Universidad ʊ[2], Perú 286d 12.04 S 77.05 W
Caton 44 54.04 N 2.43 W
Catonsville 208 39.16 N 76.43 W
Catonsville Manor 284b 39.18 N 76.44 W
Catoosa 196 36.11 N 95.44 W
Catorce 234 23.42 N 100.54 W
Catorce, Sierra de ⋀ 234 23.36 N 100.52 W
Catota 152 13.52 S 17.15 E
Catria, Monte ʌ 66 43.28 N 12.42 E
Catriló 252 36.26 S 63.24 W
Catrimani ≃ 246 0.28 N 61.44 W
Catrine 46 55.30 N 4.20 W
Cats, Mont des ʌ[2] 50 50.47 N 2.40 E
Catshill 42 52.22 N 2.03 W
Catskill 210 42.13 N 73.51 W
Catskill Aqueduct ≃ 276 41.11 N 73.48 W
Catskill Creek ≃ 210 42.12 N 73.51 W
Catskill Game Farm ♦ 210 42.15 N 74.01 W
Catskill Mountains ⋀ 210 42.10 N 74.30 W
Catskill Park ♦ 210 42.00 N 74.30 W
Cat Spring 222 29.51 N 96.20 W
Catt, Mount ʌ 182 54.21 N 128.47 W
Cattai Creek ≃ 274a 33.40 S 150.56 E
Cattaraugus 210 42.19 N 78.52 W
Cattaraugus □[6] 214 42.15 N 78.45 W
Cattaraugus Creek ≃ 214 42.35 N 79.10 W
Cattaraugus Creek, South Branch ≃ 214 42.26 N 78.53 W
Cattaraugus Indian Reservation ◆[4] 210 42.33 N 78.56 W
Cattenom 56 49.25 N 6.15 E
Catterick 44 54.22 N 1.38 W
Catterick Garrison 44 54.22 N 1.43 W
Cattle Canyon V 280 34.14 N 117.46 W
Cattolica 66 43.58 N 12.44 E
Cattolica del Sacro Cuore, Università ʊ[2] 266b 45.27 N 9.11 E
Cattolica Eraclea 70 37.26 N 13.24 E
Catton 44 54.55 N 2.15 W
Catu 255 12.21 S 38.23 W
Catuala 152 16.29 S 19.03 E
Catuane 156 26.48 S 32.18 E
Catubig 116 12.24 N 125.03 E
Catubig ≃ 116 12.34 N 125.01 E
Catuçaba 256 23.15 S 45.12 W
Catumbela 152 12.25 S 13.34 E
Catumbela ≃ 152 12.27 S 13.29 E
Catur 154 13.45 S 35.30 E
Catus 32 44.34 N 1.20 E
Çatwick, Îles II 110 10.00 N 109.00 E
Čatyr-K'ol', ozero ⊜ 85 40.38 N 75.17 E
Čatyrtaš 85 40.55 N 76.26 E
Cau ≃ 110 21.07 N 106.18 E
Cau, Rach ≃ 269c 10.51 N 106.49 E
Cauaburi ≃ 246 0.17 S 65.56 W
Cauayan, Pil. 116 16.56 N 121.46 E
Cauayan, Pil. 116 9.58 N 122.37 E
Caubvick, Mount (Mont d'Iberville) ʌ 176 58.53 N 63.43 W
Cauca □[5] 246 2.30 N 76.50 W
Cauca ≃ 246 8.54 N 74.28 W
Caucaia 250 3.42 S 38.39 W
Caucaia do Alto 256 23.41 S 47.02 W
Caucase, Monts du → Caucasus ⋀ 84 42.30 N 45.00 E
Caucasia 246 8.00 N 75.12 W
Caucaso → Caucasus ⋀ 84 42.30 N 45.00 E
Caucasus (Bol'šoj Kavkaz) ⋀ 84 42.30 N 45.00 E
Caucete 252 31.39 S 68.17 W
Cauchari, Salar de ≚ 252 23.50 S 66.50 W
Cauchon Lake ⊜ 184 55.25 N 96.30 W
Caudebec-en-Caux 50 49.32 N 0.44 E
Caudebec-lès-Elbeuf 50 49.17 N 1.02 E
Caudry 50 50.08 N 3.25 E
Caughdenoy 210 43.16 N 76.12 W
Caughnawaga 275a 45.25 N 73.41 W
Caughnawaga Indian Reserve ◆[4] 206 45.23 N 73.41 W
Cauitan, Mount ʌ 116 17.16 N 121.00 E
Cauit Point ≻, Pil. 116 12.16 N 122.38 E
Cauit Point ≻, Pil. 116 9.18 N 126.12 E
Cauldcleuch Head ʌ 44 55.18 N 2.51 W
Caulfield 169 37.53 S 145.03 E
Caulfield Racecourse ♦ 274b 37.53 S 145.02 E
Caulkerbush 44 54.54 N 3.40 W
Caulonia 68 38.23 N 16.25 E
Caumont-sur-Durance 62 43.54 N 4.57 E
Caumsett State Park ♦ 276 40.55 N 73.28 W
Caúngula 152 8.25 S 18.40 E
Čaunskaja guba ⊂ 74 69.20 N 170.00 E
Cauquenes 252 35.58 S 72.21 W
Caura ≃ 246 7.38 N 64.53 W
Caurés ≃ 246 1.21 S 62.20 W
Caurimare ≃ 286c 10.28 N 66.48 W
Căușani 38 46.38 N 29.25 E
Causapscal 186 48.22 N 67.14 W
Čausovo 82 54.49 N 36.55 E
Caussade 32 44.10 N 1.32 E
Cautário ≃ 248 12.13 S 64.34 W
Caution, Cape ≻ 182 51.10 N 127.47 W
Cauto ≃ 240p 20.33 N 77.14 W
Čauvaj 85 40.08 N 72.13 E
Caux, Pays de ◆[1] 50 49.40 N 0.40 E
Cava 256 22.41 S 43.26 W
Cava de' Tirreni 68 40.42 N 14.42 E
Cávado ≃ 34 41.32 N 8.48 W
Cavaglià 62 45.24 N 8.05 E
Cavaillon 62 43.50 N 5.02 E
Cavalaire-sur-Mer 62 43.10 N 6.32 E
Cavalcante 255 13.48 S 47.30 W
Cavalese 64 46.17 N 11.27 E
Cavalheiro 255 17.15 S 48.02 W
Cavalier 198 48.47 N 97.37 W
Cavalière 62 43.09 N 6.26 E
Cavalla (Cavally) ≃ 150 4.22 N 7.32 W
Cavalleria, Cap de ≻ 34 40.05 N 4.05 E
Cavallermaggiore 62 44.43 N 7.41 E
Cavalli Islands II 172 35.02 S 173.58 E
Cavallino, Litorale di ⊥[2] 64 45.27 N 12.30 E
Cavallo, Île I 71 41.21 N 9.16 E
Cavallo, Monte ʌ 64 46.08 N 12.30 E
Cavally (Cavalla) ≃ 150 4.22 N 7.32 W
Cavalos, Ribeirão dos ≃ 256 21.29 S 44.13 W
Cava Manara 62 45.08 N 9.07 E
Cavan 48 54.00 N 7.21 W
Cavan □[6] 48 53.55 N 7.15 W
Cavanaugh, Lake ⊜ 224 48.23 N 122.00 W
Čavan'ga 24 66.06 N 37.47 E
Cavarzere 64 45.08 N 12.05 E
Cavaso del Tomba 64 45.51 N 11.52 E
Çavdır 130 37.09 N 29.42 E
Cave, It. 66 41.49 N 12.56 E
Cave, N.Z. 172 44.19 S 170.57 E
Cave City, Ar., U.S. 194 35.56 N 91.32 W
Cave City, Ky., U.S. 194 37.08 N 85.57 W
Cave Creek ≃ 200 33.34 N 112.07 W
Cave del Predil 64 46.26 N 13.34 E
Cavedine 64 45.59 N 10.59 E
Cave In Rock 194 37.29 N 88.10 W
Caveiras ≃ 252 27.35 S 50.56 W
Cavelo 152 17.33 S 19.21 E
Cavendish 166 37.31 S 142.02 E
Cavernago 62 45.38 N 9.46 E
Cavertitz 54 51.23 N 13.08 E
Cave Run Lake ⊜[1] 188 38.03 N 83.30 W
Cave Spring 192 34.14 N 85.20 W
Cavettsville 279b 40.22 N 79.46 W
Cavezzo 64 44.50 N 11.02 E
Cavi 62 44.17 N 9.22 E
Caviana de Fora, Ilha I 250 0.10 N 50.10 W
Cavili Island I 116 9.17 N 120.50 E
Cavinzas, Isla I 286d 12.07 S 77.13 W
Cavite 116 14.29 N 120.55 E
Cavite □[4] 116 14.15 N 120.50 E
Čavka 84 41.44 N 41.45 E
Čavlisaj 85 41.08 N 69.44 E
Cavo, Monte ʌ 267a 41.45 N 12.42 E
Cavoli, Isola dei I 71 39.05 N 9.33 E
Cavonne ≃ 68 40.17 N 16.47 E
Cavour 62 44.47 N 7.22 E
Cavour, Canale ≋ 62 45.11 N 7.54 E
Cavriago 64 44.42 N 10.31 E
Cavriana 64 45.21 N 10.36 E
Cavtat 38 42.35 N 18.13 E
Çavuş 130 37.36 N 31.56 E
Çavuşbaşı ≃ 267b 40.58 N 28.51 E
Çavuşçu Gölü ⊜ 130 38.25 N 31.53 E
Čavusy 76 53.48 N 30.58 E
Cawatose, Lac ⊜ 190 47.20 N 77.07 W
Cawayan 116 11.56 N 123.46 E
Cawdor 46 57.31 N 3.56 W
Cawker City 198 39.30 N 98.26 W
Cawnpore → Kānpur 124 26.28 N 80.21 E
Cawood, Eng., U.K. 44 53.50 N 1.07 W
Cawood, Ky., U.S. 192 36.47 N 83.13 W
Cawston, B.C., Can. 182 49.11 N 119.45 W
Cawston, Eng., U.K. 42 52.46 N 1.10 E
Cawthon 222 30.25 N 96.14 W
Caxambu 256 21.59 S 44.56 W
Caxias, Bra. 250 4.50 S 43.21 W
Caxias, Port. 266c 38.42 N 9.16 W
Caxias do Sul 252 29.10 S 51.11 W
Caxinas, Punta ≻ 236 16.01 N 86.02 W
Caxito 152 8.33 S 13.36 E
Caxiuana, Baía de ⊂ 250 1.45 S 51.20 W
Caxopa 152 11.52 S 20.52 E
Çay 130 38.35 N 31.02 E
Çayacal, Punta ≻ 234 17.56 N 102.11 W
Çayağzı ◆[8] 267b 41.13 N 29.12 E
Çayağzı ≃ 267b 41.14 N 29.12 E
Çayambe 246 0.03 N 78.08 W
Cayambe ʌ[1] 246 0.00 77.59 W
Cayapoñga 116 5.48 N 125.33 E
Çaybaşı 130 41.02 N 37.06 E
Cayce 192 33.57 N 81.04 W
Çaycuma 130 41.25 N 32.05 E
Caycuse 224 48.53 N 124.22 W
Caycuse ≃ 224 48.48 N 124.41 W
Cay Duong, Vinh ⊂ 110 10.10 N 104.45 E
Cayenne 250 4.56 N 52.20 W
Cayenne □[8] 250 4.00 N 52.30 W
Cayes → Les Cayes 238 18.12 N 73.45 W
Cayeux-sur-Mer 50 50.11 N 1.29 E
Cayey 240m 18.07 N 66.10 W
Cayey, Sierra de ⋀ 240m 18.07 N 66.02 W
Çayıralan 130 39.18 N 35.40 E
Çayırbaşı 130 40.53 N 42.36 E
Çayırhan 130 40.06 N 31.37 E
Çayırlı 130 39.48 N 40.01 E
Çaylarbası 130 37.41 N 39.00 E
Caylus 32 44.14 N 1.46 E
Cayman Brac I 238 19.43 N 79.49 W
Cayman Islands □[2], N.A. 230 19.30 N 80.40 W
Cayman Islands □[2], N.A. 238 19.30 N 80.40 W
Cayman Trench ⊹[1] 16 19.00 N 80.00 W
Cayna 248 10.11 S 76.20 W
Caynabo 144 8.57 N 46.26 E
Cayo Agua, Isla I 236 9.09 N 82.02 W
Çayözü 130 39.36 N 38.11 E
Cay Point ≻ 240b 24.59 N 77.25 W
Çayra 130 40.41 N 39.06 E
Cayres 62 44.55 N 3.48 E
Cay Sal Bank ⊹[2] 238 23.45 N 80.00 W
Çaytepe 130 38.48 N 40.41 E
Cayucos 226 35.27 N 120.54 W
Cayuga, In., U.S. 194 39.56 N 87.27 W
Cayuga, N.Y., U.S. 210 42.55 N 76.44 W
Cayuga, N.D., U.S. 198 46.04 N 97.23 W
Cayuga, Tx., U.S. 222 31.57 N 95.57 W
Cayuga □[6] 210 42.56 N 76.34 W
Cayuga and Seneca Canal ≋ 210 42.56 N 76.44 W
Cayuga Creek ≃, N.Y., U.S. 210 42.52 N 78.47 W
Cayuga Creek ≃, N.Y., U.S. 284a 43.04 N 78.57 W
Cayuga Heights 210 42.27 N 76.29 W
Cayuga Lake ⊜ 210 42.45 N 76.45 W
Cayuta 210 42.17 N 76.42 W
Cayuta Creek ≃ 210 41.59 N 76.30 W
Cazaclia 38 46.00 N 28.37 E
Cazage 152 11.02 S 20.45 E
Cazalla de la Sierra 34 37.56 N 5.45 W
Căzănești 38 44.37 N 27.01 E
Cazaux et de Sanguinet, Lac de ⊂ 32 44.30 N 1.10 W
Cazenovia 210 42.55 N 75.51 W
Cazenovia Creek ≃ 210 42.52 N 78.50 W
Cazenovia Creek, East Branch ≃ 210 42.46 N 78.38 W
Cazenovia Creek, West Branch ≃ 210 42.46 N 78.39 W
Cazenovia Lake ⊜ 210 42.57 N 75.53 W
Cazenovia Park ♦ 284a 42.51 N 78.48 W
Cazères 32 43.13 N 1.05 E
Cazhai 269b 31.12 N 121.34 E
Cazin 36 44.58 N 15.57 E
Çazis 58 46.43 N 9.25 E
Čazma 36 45.45 N 16.37 E
Cazombo 152 11.54 S 22.52 E
Cazones ≃ 234 20.44 N 97.12 W
Cazones, Golfo de ⊂ 240p 21.55 N 81.20 W
Cazorla, Esp. 34 37.55 N 3.00 W
Cazorla, Ven. 246 8.01 N 67.00 W
Cazula 154 15.25 S 33.40 E
Ccapi 248 13.52 S 72.05 W
Cchaltubo 84 42.20 N 42.35 E
Cchenisckali ≃ 84 42.07 N 42.18 E
Çchinvali 84 42.13 N 43.56 E
Čchorocku 84 42.32 N 42.07 E
Cchunkuri 84 42.23 N 42.34 E
Cea ≃ 34 42.00 N 5.36 W
Ceanannus Mór (Kells) 48 53.44 N 6.53 W
Ceará → Fortaleza 250 3.43 S 38.30 W
Ceará □[3] 250 5.00 S 40.00 W
Ceará-Mirim 250 5.38 S 35.26 W
Ceará-Mirim ≃ 250 5.40 S 35.13 W
Ceatharlach → Carlow 48 52.50 N 6.55 W
Cebaco, Isla De I 246 7.32 N 81.09 W
Çeballos 232 26.32 N 104.09 W
Čebarkul' 86 54.58 N 60.25 E
Çebeci ◆[8] 267b 41.07 N 28.52 E
Čeboksarskoje vodochranilišče ⊜[1] 24 56.10 N 46.00 E
Čeboksary 80 56.09 N 47.15 E
Cebolla Creek ≃ 200 38.29 N 107.13 W
Cebollar 252 29.06 S 66.33 W
Cebollas 234 23.23 N 104.50 W
Cebollatí 252 33.16 S 53.47 W
Cebollatí ≃ 252 33.09 S 53.38 W
Cebollita Peak ʌ 200 34.43 N 107.51 W
Céboruco, Volcán ʌ[1] 234 21.09 N 104.30 W
Čebotovka, Ross. 83 48.42 N 39.51 E
Čebotovka, Ross. 83 48.41 N 40.00 E
Çebreros 34 40.27 N 4.28 W
Čebsara 76 59.12 N 38.50 E
Cebu 116 10.18 N 123.54 E
Cebu □[4] 116 10.20 N 123.45 E
Çebu I 116 10.20 N 123.45 E
Čeburgol' 78 45.34 N 38.07 E
Cebu Strait ʮ 116 9.45 N 123.40 E
Ceccano 66 41.34 N 13.20 E
Cecchignola ◆[8] 267a 41.49 N 12.29 E
Çeceda 196 26.04 N 103.25 W
Čečen', ostrov I 84 43.58 N 47.45 E
Cecer Chaan → Öndörchaan 88 47.19 N 110.39 E
Cecerleg, Mong. 88 48.52 N 101.14 E
Cecerleg, Mong. 88 47.30 N 101.27 E
Cecerleg, Mong. 88 49.30 N 97.36 E
Çecheng 105 39.06 N 116.48 E
Čechov, Ross. 82 55.09 N 37.27 E
Čechov, Ross. 89 47.28 N 141.59 E
Čechova, gora ʌ 89 47.03 N 142.50 E
Čechtice 30 49.37 N 15.03 E
Čechy □[9] 30 49.50 N 14.00 E
Cecil, Ga., U.S. 192 31.02 N 83.23 W
Cecil, Oh., U.S. 216 41.13 N 84.35 W
Cecil, Pa., U.S. 214 40.19 N 80.10 W
Cecil □[6] 208 39.36 N 75.50 W
Cecil Field Naval Air Station ■ 192 30.12 N 81.52 W
Cecilia 194 37.39 N 85.57 W
Cecilia, Mount ʌ[2] 162 20.45 S 120.55 E
Cecil Park 274a 33.52 S 150.51 E
Cecil Plains 166 27.32 S 151.12 E
Cecil Rhodes, Mount ʌ 162 25.26 S 121.26 E
Cecilton 208 39.24 N 75.52 W
Cecina 66 43.19 N 10.31 E
Cecina ≃ 66 43.18 N 10.29 E
Çecita, Lago di ⊜ 68 39.24 N 16.30 E
Čečnja-Ingušetija □[3] 84 43.15 N 45.40 E
Čečuj ≃ 88 58.12 N 109.18 E
Čečujsk 88 58.05 N 108.42 E
Cedar ≃, U.S. 190 41.17 N 91.21 W
Cedar ≃, Mi., U.S. 190 43.53 N 84.29 W
Cedar ≃, Mi., U.S. 190 45.25 N 87.21 W
Cedar ≃, Ne., U.S. 198 41.22 N 97.57 W
Cedar ≃, N.Y., U.S. 188 43.51 N 74.11 W
Cedar ≃, Wa., U.S. 224 47.30 N 122.12 W
Cedar, Middle Branch ≃ 216 42.38 N 84.05 W
Cedar, West Branch ≃ 216 42.41 N 84.09 W
Cedar, West Fork ≃ 190 42.37 N 92.29 W
Cedar Bayou ≃ 222 29.41 N 94.56 W
Cedar Beach 284b 39.17 N 76.25 W
Cedar Bluff Reservoir ⊜[1] 198 38.47 N 99.47 W
Cedar Bluffs 198 41.23 N 96.36 W
Cedar Breaks National Monument ♦ 200 37.29 N 112.53 W
Cedar Brook 208 39.42 N 74.54 W
Cedar Brook ≃, N.J., U.S. 276 40.19 N 74.33 W
Cedar Brook ≃, N.J., U.S. 276 40.23 N 74.23 W
Cedar Brook ≃, N.J., U.S. 285 39.40 N 74.43 W
Cedar Brook Park ♦ 275b 43.45 N 79.14 W
Cedarburg 190 43.17 N 87.59 W
Cedar City, Mo., U.S. 219 38.35 N 92.10 W
Cedar City, Ut,. U.S. 200 37.40 N 113.03 W
Cedar Creek 222 30.05 N 97.30 W
Cedar Creek ≃, Al., U.S. 194 32.13 N 87.06 W
Cedar Creek ≃, Az., U.S. 200 33.48 N 110.18 W
Cedar Creek ≃, Ct., U.S. 276 41.09 N 73.13 W
Cedar Creek ≃, De., U.S. 208 38.55 N 75.20 W
Cedar Creek ≃, Ga., U.S. 194 34.08 N 85.19 W
Cedar Creek ≃, Id., U.S. 202 42.24 N 114.49 W
Cedar Creek ≃, In., U.S. 216 41.12 N 85.02 W
Cedar Creek ≃, Ia., U.S. 190 40.58 N 91.40 W
Cedar Creek ≃, Ia., U.S. 198 42.24 N 94.59 W
Cedar Creek ≃, Ky., U.S. 218 38.25 N 84.53 W
Cedar Creek ≃, Mo., U.S. 219 38.38 N 92.13 W
Cedar Creek ≃, N.D., U.S. 198 46.07 N 101.18 W
Cedar Creek ≃, Oh., U.S. 214 41.38 N 83.17 W
Cedar Creek ≃, Pa., U.S. 279b 40.10 N 79.47 W
Cedar Creek ≃, Tx., U.S. 196 32.53 N 98.37 W
Cedar Creek ≃, Tx., U.S. 222 30.51 N 96.12 W
Cedar Creek ≃, Tx., U.S. 222 32.04 N 96.05 W
Cedar Creek ≃, Tx., U.S. 222 30.02 N 97.17 W
Cedar Creek ≃, Wa., U.S. 224 45.56 N 122.37 W
Cedar Creek Reservoir ⊜[1], Tx., U.S. 222 32.20 N 96.10 W
Cedar Creek Reservoir ⊜[1], Tx., U.S. 222 29.56 N 96.44 W
Cedar Crest Manor 285 39.41 N 75.28 W
Cedaredge 200 38.54 N 107.55 W
Cedar Falls 190 42.31 N 92.26 W
Cedar Grove, On., Can. 275b 43.52 N 79.12 W
Cedar Grove, In., U.S. 218 39.21 N 84.56 W
Cedar Grove, N.J., U.S. 276 40.51 N 74.13 W
Cedar Grove, W.V., U.S. 188 38.13 N 81.25 W
Cedar Grove, Wi., U.S. 190 43.34 N 87.49 W
Cedar Grove Reservoir ⊜[1] 276 40.52 N 74.13 W
Cedar Heights, Md., U.S. 284c 38.54 N 76.54 W
Cedar Heights, Pa., U.S. 285 40.05 N 75.17 W
Cedar Hill, Mo., U.S. 219 38.21 N 90.39 W
Cedar Hill, N.Y., U.S. 210 42.33 N 73.47 W
Cedar Hill, Tn., U.S. 194 36.33 N 86.59 W
Cedar Hill, Tx., U.S. 222 32.35 N 96.57 W
Cedar Hills 224 45.30 N 122.47 W
Cedar Hollow 285 40.04 N 75.31 W
Cedarhurst, Md., U.S. 208 39.07 N 76.41 W
Cedarhurst, N.Y., U.S. 276 40.37 N 73.43 W
Cedar Island I, Md., U.S. 208 37.56 N 75.52 W
Cedar Island I, N.Y., U.S. 276 40.38 N 73.21 W
Cedar Island I, Va., U.S. 208 37.39 N 75.36 W
Cedar Island Lake ⊜ 281 42.38 N 83.28 W
Cedar Key 192 29.08 N 83.02 W
Cedar Knolls 276 40.49 N 74.26 W
Cedar Lake, In., U.S. 216 41.21 N 87.26 W
Cedar Lake, Tx., U.S. 222 28.54 N 95.35 W
Cedar Lake ⊜, On., Can. 190 46.02 N 78.30 W
Cedar Lake ⊜, In., U.S. 216 41.22 N 87.26 W
Cedar Lake ⊜, N.J., U.S. 276 40.55 N 74.28 W
Cedar Lake ⊜, Tx., U.S. 196 32.49 N 102.17 W
Cedar Lake ⊜[1] 184 53.15 N 100.10 W
Cedar Lake Creek ≃ 222 28.50 N 95.35 W
Cedar Lane 222 28.54 N 95.38 W
Cedar Mill 224 45.32 N 122.51 W
Cedarmont 158 26.50 S 29.01 E
Cedar Mountain ʌ 204 41.36 N 120.16 W
Cedar Point 216 41.16 N 89.08 W
Cedar Point ≻, Ct., U.S. 276 41.06 N 73.22 W
Cedar Point ≻, Oh., U.S. 214 41.42 N 83.20 W
Cedar Point ≻, Oh., U.S. 214 41.30 N 82.41 W
Cedar Pond ⊜ 276 41.07 N 74.06 W
Cedar Rapids, Ia., U.S. 190 41.59 N 91.40 W
Cedar Rapids, Ne., U.S. 198 41.34 N 98.09 W
Cedar Ridge 226 39.12 N 121.01 W
Cedar Run ≃ 208 38.41 N 77.29 W
Cedars 285 40.13 N 75.22 W
Cedars of Lebanon → Arz Lubnān ◆[3] 130 34.14 N 36.03 E
Cedar Springs, On., Can. 214 42.17 N 82.02 W
Cedar Springs, Mi., U.S. 190 43.13 N 85.33 W
Cedar Swamp ≡, Ma., U.S. 283 42.33 N 71.05 W
Cedar Swamp ≡, N.J., U.S. 285 39.48 N 75.20 W
Cedartown 192 34.03 N 85.15 W
Cedarvale, B.C., Can. 182 55.01 N 128.20 W
Cedar Vale, Ks., U.S. 198 37.06 N 96.30 W
Cedarville, S. Afr. 158 30.23 S 29.03 E
Cedarville, Ca., U.S. 204 41.31 N 120.10 W
Cedarville, In., U.S. 216 41.12 N 85.01 W
Cedarville, Ma., U.S. 207 41.48 N 70.33 W
Cedarville, Mi., U.S. 190 46.00 N 84.22 W
Cedarville, N.J., U.S. 208 39.19 N 75.12 W
Cedarville, N.Y., U.S. 210 42.56 N 75.07 W
Cedarville, Oh., U.S. 218 39.44 N 83.48 W
Cedarville, Pa., U.S. 285 40.14 N 75.40 W
Cedarville Reservoir ⊜[1] 216 41.12 N 85.01 W
Cedar Wash V 200 35.53 N 111.25 W
Cedarwood Park 208 40.03 N 74.08 W
Cedegolo 64 46.05 N 10.21 E
Çedeira 34 43.39 N 8.03 W
Čeder 88 51.25 N 94.45 E
Cedillo, Embalse de ⊜[1] 34 39.40 N 7.25 W
Cedral 234 23.48 N 100.44 W
Cedrino ≃ 71 40.23 N 9.44 E
Cedro 250 6.36 S 39.03 W
Cedro, Cerro ʌ 234 18.35 N 99.42 W
Cedros, Hond. 236 14.35 N 87.08 W
Cedros, Méx. 232 24.41 N 101.47 W
Cedros, Isla I 232 28.12 N 115.15 W
Ceduna 162 32.07 S 133.40 E
Cedynia 30 52.50 N 14.14 E
Ceel 102 45.36 N 95.51 E
Ceelaayo 144 11.15 N 48.54 E
Ceel Afweyne 144 9.55 N 47.15 E
Ceel Berdaale 144 3.14 N 43.11 E
Ceel Berde 144 4.50 N 43.39 E
Ceel Buur 144 4.40 N 46.37 E
Ceel Dhaab 144 8.56 N 46.30 E
Ceel Dheere, Som. 144 3.51 N 47.12 E
Ceeldheere, Som. 144 5.22 N 46.11 E
Ceel Doofaar 144 10.38 N 49.02 E
Ceel Waaq 144 2.44 N 41.01 E
Ceel Xamurre 144 7.13 N 48.54 E
Ceemadle 144 5.14 N 46.56 E
Ceepeecee 182 49.52 N 126.43 W
Ceerigaabo 144 10.37 N 47.22 E
Cefalà Diana 70 37.54 N 13.28 E
Cefalonia → Kefallinía I 38 38.15 N 20.35 E
Cefalú 70 38.02 N 14.01 E
Cefni ≃ 44 53.12 N 4.23 W
Cefn-mawr 42 52.58 N 3.04 W
Ceg 144 8.58 N 45.20 E
Çega ≃ 34 41.33 N 4.46 W
Čeganly 80 53.54 N 53.34 E
Čegdomyn 89 51.07 N 133.05 E
Čegem ≃ 84 43.38 N 43.48 E
Čegem Pervyj 84 43.34 N 43.35 E
Čegitun' 180 66.34 N 171.06 W
Cegléd 30 47.10 N 19.48 E
Ceglie Messapico 68 40.39 N 17.31 E
Cehegín 34 38.06 N 1.48 W
Ceheng 102 25.10 N 105.48 E
Cehnice 60 49.12 N 14.02 E
Cehu Silvaniei 38 47.25 N 23.11 E
Ceiba 240m 18.16 N 65.39 W
Ceibo ≃ 258 33.57 S 58.27 W
Ceilán → Sri Lanka □[1] 122 7.00 N 81.00 E
Ceiriog ≃ 42 52.57 N 3.02 W
Çeirw ≃ 44 52.59 N 3.27 W
Čejč 61 48.57 N 16.57 E
Čekalin 82 54.06 N 36.15 E
Čekan 80 54.51 N 53.34 E
Čekanovskij 88 56.13 N 101.25 E
Çekerek 130 40.04 N 35.31 E
Çekerek ≃ 130 40.34 N 35.46 E
Čekmaguš 86 55.08 N 54.40 E
Çekme ◆[8] 267b 41.03 N 29.10 E
Čekšino 76 59.39 N 40.33 E
Čekujevo 24 63.34 N 38.56 E
Čekunda 89 50.48 N 132.10 E
Čel'abinsk 86 55.10 N 61.24 E
Čel'abinsk Oblast' □[4] 86 54.30 N 60.30 E
Čelákovice 54 50.10 N 14.46 E
Celâlli 130 39.42 N 37.26 E
Celano 66 42.05 N 13.33 E
Celanova 34 42.09 N 7.58 W
Çelaya 234 20.31 N 100.49 W
Čelbas ≃ 78 46.06 N 38.59 E
Čelbasskaja 78 45.59 N 39.22 E
Celbridge 48 53.20 N 6.33 W
Celebes → Sulawesi I 112 2.00 S 121.00 E
Celebes Basin ⊹[1] 14 4.00 N 122.00 E
Çelebes Sea ⊤[2] 112 3.00 N 122.00 E
Čeleken 128 39.26 N 53.07 E
Celendín 248 6.52 S 78.09 W
Celenza sul Trigno 66 41.52 N 14.35 E
Celenza Valfortore 68 41.34 N 14.58 E
Celerina 58 46.31 N 9.51 E
Celeryville 214 41.02 N 82.45 W
Celeste 196 33.18 N 96.12 W
Celestún 232 20.52 N 90.24 W
Celica 246 4.07 S 79.59 W
Celico 68 39.19 N 16.20 E
Çelikhan 130 38.02 N 38.15 E
Čelina, Ross. 80 46.32 N 41.02 E
Celina, Oh., U.S. 216 40.32 N 84.34 W
Celina, Tn., U.S. 194 36.33 N 85.30 W
Celina, Tx., U.S. 196 33.19 N 96.47 W
Celinnoje, Ross. 86 53.04 N 85.40 E
Celinnoje, Ross. 86 54.31 N 63.39 E
Celinnyj 80 46.40 N 44.32 E
Celinograd → Akmola 86 51.10 N 71.30 E
Celjahany 76 52.31 N 25.51 E
Çelje 36 46.14 N 15.16 E
Čelkar, Kaz. 80 50.32 N 51.51 E
Čelkar, Kaz. 86 47.50 N 59.36 E
Cellar Head ≻ 46 58.26 N 6.10 W
Celldömölk 30 47.16 N 17.09 E
Celle 52 52.37 N 10.05 E
Celle, Ruisseau la ≃ 261 48.35 N 2.01 E
Celle Ligure 62 44.20 N 8.33 E
Celles 56 50.14 N 5.01 E
Celles-sur-Plaine 58 48.28 N 6.57 E
Cellettes 50 47.32 N 1.23 E
Cellina ≃ 64 46.02 N 12.47 E
Cellino Attanasio 66 42.36 N 13.52 E
Çellino San Marco 68 40.28 N 17.58 E
Čelmozero 24 64.18 N 31.48 E
Čelno-Veršiny 80 54.26 N 51.06 E
Čelobitjevo 265b 55.55 N 37.40 E
Celone ≃ 68 41.36 N 15.41 E
Celorico da Beira 34 40.38 N 7.23 W
Celoron 214 42.06 N 79.17 W
Celtic Sea ⊤[2] 28 51.00 N 6.30 W
Celtic Shelf ⊹[4] 10 49.15 N 7.00 W
Çeltikçi, Tür. 130 40.20 N 32.28 E
Çeltikçi, Tür. 130 37.32 N 30.29 E
Čel'uš 86 51.32 N 87.46 E
Čel'uskin, mys ≻ 74 77.45 N 104.20 E
Čel'uskincev park ♦ 265a 60.01 N 30.19 E
Çemaes Head ≻ 42 52.07 N 4.44 W
Čemal 86 51.25 N 86.01 E
Čembilej 80 55.19 N 45.43 E
Cembra 64 46.10 N 11.13 E
Cembra, Val di V 64 46.10 N 11.13 E
Cement 196 34.55 N 98.08 W
Cement City 216 42.04 N 84.19 W
Cementon, N.Y., U.S. 210 42.09 N 73.55 W
Çementon, Pa., U.S. 208 40.41 N 75.30 W
Čemerno 36 43.11 N 18.37 E
Cemesskaja buchta ⊂ 78 44.40 N 37.50 E
Cemilbey 130 40.21 N 35.04 E
Çemişkezek 130 39.04 N 38.55 E
Çemmaes 42 52.37 N 3.42 W
Čemolgan 85 43.23 N 76.37 E
Cempi, Teluk ⊂ 115b 8.44 S 118.25 E
Cenajo, Embalse de ⊜[1] 34 38.25 N 2.00 W
Čenča 88 55.57 N 110.59 E
Cencenighe 64 46.21 N 11.58 E
Çenchermandal 88 47.37 N 109.05 E
Čency 82 56.03 N 36.01 E
Cenderawasih, Teluk ⊂ 164 2.30 S 135.20 E
Cendras 62 44.09 N 4.04 E
Cene 62 45.47 N 9.49 E
Cenepa ≃ 246 4.35 S 78.12 W
Çengel 86 48.56 N 89.10 E
Čengel'dy 85 41.51 N 68.59 E
Çengelköy ◆[8] 267b 41.03 N 29.03 E
Čengerli 130 39.48 N 38.52 E
Cengles, Croda di ʌ 64 46.34 N 10.38 E
Ceno ≃ 36 44.41 N 10.05 E
Cenovo 38 43.32 N 25.39 E

Symbols in the index entries represent the broad categories identified in the key at the right. Symbols with superior numbers (⋀[1]) identify subcategories (see complete key on page *I · 1)*.

Symbole im Register stellen die rechts im Schlüssel erklärten Kategorien dar. Symbole mit hochgestellten Ziffern (⋀[1]) bezeichnen Unterabteilungen einer Kategorie (vgl. vollständiger Schlüssel auf Seite *I · 1)*.

Los símbolos incluídos en el texto del índice representan las grandes categorías identificadas con la clave a la derecha. Los símbolos con numeros en su parte superior (⋀[1]) identifican las subcategorías (véase la clave completa en la página *I · 1)*.

Les symboles de l'index représentent les catégories indiquées dans la légende à droite. Les symboles suivis d'un indice (⋀[1]) représentent des sous-catégories (voir légende complète à la page *I · 1)*.

Os símbolos incluídos no texto do índice representam as grandes categorias identificadas com a chave à direita. Os símbolos com números em sua parte superior (⋀[1]) identificam as subcategorias (veja-se a chave completa à página *I · 1)*.

ʌ	Mountain	Berg	Montaña	Montagne	Montanha
⋀	Mountains	Gebirge	Montañas	Montagnes	Montanhas
)(	Pass	Paß	Paso	Col	Passo
V	Valley, Canyon	Tal, Cañon	Valle, Cañón	Vallée, Canyon	Vale, Canhão
≚	Plain	Ebene	Llano	Plaine	Planície
≻	Cape	Kap	Cabo	Cap	Cabo
I	Island	Insel	Isla	Île	Ilha
II	Islands	Inseln	Islas	Îles	Ilhas
⊥	Other Topographic Features	Andere Topographische Objekte	Otros Elementos Topográficos	Autres données topographiques	Outros acidentes topográficos

Cenr-Cham I · 33

ESPAÑOL

Nombre	Página	Lat.°′	Long.°′ W = Oeste
Cenrana	112	3.18 S	118.50 E
Censeau	58	46.49 N	6.04 E
Centallo	62	44.30 N	7.35 E
Centenario	252	38.48 S	68.08 W
Centenário do Sul	255	22.48 S	51.37 W
Centennial Lake ⊜	285	39.50 N	74.51 W
Centennial Lake ⊜[1]	212	45.10 N	72.05 W
Centennial Mountains ⋏	202	44.35 N	111.55 W
Centennial Park ♠, Austl.	274a	33.54 S	151.14 E
Centennial Park ♠, On., Can.	275b	43.39 N	79.35 W
Centennial Wash V	200	33.14 N	112.46 W
Centeno	66	42.48 N	11.49 E
Center, Co., U.S.	200	37.45 N	106.06 W
Center, In., U.S.	216	40.26 N	86.04 W
Center, Mo., U.S.	219	39.30 N	91.31 W
Center, Ne., U.S.	198	42.36 N	97.52 W
Center, N.D., U.S.	198	47.06 N	101.17 W
Center, Tx., U.S.	194	31.47 N	94.10 W
Centerbrook	207	41.21 N	72.24 W
Center Brunswick	210	42.45 N	73.37 W
Centerburg	214	40.18 N	82.41 W
Center City	190	45.23 N	92.48 W
Center Cross	208	37.48 N	76.46 W
Centereach	210	40.51 N	73.06 W
Centerfield	218	38.21 N	83.24 W
Center Hill	220	28.38 N	81.59 W
Center Hill Lake ⊜[1]	194	36.00 N	85.45 W
Center Line	214	42.29 N	83.01 W
Center Moriches	188	40.48 N	72.47 W
Center Mountain ∧	202	45.06 N	115.13 W
Center Point, Al., U.S.	194	33.37 N	86.41 W
Center Point, Ia., U.S.	190	42.11 N	91.47 W
Center Point, Tx., U.S.	196	29.57 N	99.02 W
Centerport, N.Y., U.S.	210	40.54 N	73.22 W
Centerport, Pa., U.S.	208	40.29 N	76.01 W
Center Square, N.J., U.S.	285	39.46 N	75.23 W
Center Square, Pa., U.S.	208	40.10 N	75.18 W
Centerton, In., U.S.	218	39.30 N	86.23 W
Centerton, N.J., U.S.	285	39.31 N	75.10 W
Center Valley	208	40.32 N	75.24 W
Centerville, De., U.S.	285	39.49 N	75.37 W
Centerville, In., U.S.	218	39.49 N	84.59 W
Centerville, Ia., U.S.	190	40.43 N	92.52 W
Centerville, Ma., U.S.	207	41.38 N	70.20 W
Centerville, Mo., U.S.	194	37.26 N	90.57 W
Centerville, N.Y., U.S.	210	42.29 N	78.15 W
Centerville, Oh., U.S.	218	39.37 N	84.09 W
Centerville, Pa., U.S.	188	40.02 N	79.58 W
Centerville, S.D., U.S.	198	43.07 N	96.57 W
Centerville, Tn., U.S.	194	35.46 N	87.28 W
Centerville, Tx., U.S.	222	31.15 N	95.58 W
Centerville, Ut,. U.S.	200	40.55 N	111.52 W
Centerville, Wa., U.S.	224	45.45 N	120.54 W
Centinela	196	28.47 N	100.34 W
Cento	64	44.43 N	11.17 E
Centocelle ◆[8]	267a	41.53 N	12.34 E
Cento Croci, Passo di)(	62	44.25 N	9.37 E
Centola	68	40.04 N	15.19 E
Central, Bra.	250	11.08 S	42.08 W
Central, Ak., U.S.	180	65.34 N	144.48 W
Central, Az., U.S.	200	32.52 N	109.47 W
Central, N.M., U.S.	200	32.46 N	108.08 W
Central, S.C., U.S.	192	34.43 N	82.46 W
Central, Tx., U.S.	222	31.26 N	94.49 W
Central ▫[4], Ghana	150	5.30 N	1.00 W
Central ▫[4], Kenya	154	0.45 S	37.00 E
Central ▫[4], Malaŵi	154	13.00 S	34.00 E
Central ▫[4], Sol.Is.	175e	9.10 S	159.50 E
Central ▫[4], Scot., U.K.	46	56.05 N	4.20 W
Central ▫[4], Zam.	154	14.30 S	29.00 E
Central ▫[5], Bots.	156	21.30 S	26.00 E
Central ▫[5], Pap. N. Gui.	164	9.00 S	147.00 E
Central ▫[5], Para.	252	25.30 S	57.30 W
Central ▫[5], Ug.	154	0.10 N	32.00 E
Central, Cordillera ⋏, Col.	246	5.00 N	75.00 W
Central, Cordillera ⋏, C.R.	236	10.10 N	84.05 W
Central, Cordillera ⋏, Pan.	236	8.30 N	81.30 W
Central, Cordillera ⋏, Perú	248	8.00 S	77.00 W
Central, Cordillera ⋏, Pil.	116	17.20 N	120.57 E
Central, Cordillera ⋏, P.R.	240m	18.10 N	66.35 W
Central, Macizo → Central, Massif ⋏	32	45.00 N	3.10 E
Central, Massif ⋏	32	45.00 N	3.10 E
Central, Planalto ⋏[1]	242	18.00 S	47.00 W
Central, Sistema ⋏	34	40.30 N	5.00 W
Central African Republic ▫[1]	136	7.00 N	21.00 E
Central Aguirre	240m	17.57 N	66.13 W
Central Arizona Project ≋[1]	200	32.25 N	111.08 W
Central Barren	218	38.22 N	86.06 W
Central Brāhui Range ⋏	120	29.20 N	66.55 E
Central Bridge	210	42.42 N	74.20 W
Central Butte	184	50.47 N	106.30 W
Central City, Il., U.S.	219	38.32 N	89.07 W
Central City, Ia., U.S.	190	42.12 N	91.31 W
Central City, Ky., U.S.	194	37.17 N	87.07 W
Central City, Ne., U.S.	198	41.06 N	98.00 W
Central City, Pa., U.S.	214	40.06 N	78.48 W
Central Division ▫[5]	175g	18.05 S	178.30 E
Centrale, Stazione ◆[5]	266b	45.29 N	9.12 E
Central Falls	207	41.53 N	71.23 W
Central Heights	200	33.24 N	110.48 W
Central Highlands	279b	40.16 N	79.50 W
Centralia, Il., U.S.	219	38.31 N	89.08 W
Centralia, Ks., U.S.	198	39.43 N	96.07 W
Centralia, Mo., U.S.	219	39.12 N	92.08 W
Centralia, Tx., U.S.	222	31.16 N	95.02 W
Centralia, Wa., U.S.	224	46.42 N	122.57 W
Centralia, Lake ⊜	219	38.32 N	88.59 W
Centralia Draw V	196	31.27 N	101.16 W
Centralia Reservoir ⊜[1]	219	38.32 N	89.08 W
Centralina	255	18.34 S	49.13 W
Central Intelligence Agency ʊ	284c	38.57 N	77.09 W
Central Island I	154	3.30 N	36.03 E
Central Islip	210	40.47 N	73.12 W
Central Kalahari Game Reserve ◆[4]	156	22.15 S	23.45 E
Central Lake	190	45.04 N	85.15 W
Central Makrān Range ⋏	128	26.40 N	64.30 E
Central'nolesnoj zapovednik ◆[4]	76	56.32 N	32.50 E
Central Nyack	276	41.06 N	73.57 W
Central'nyj, Ross.	76	53.41 N	39.38 E
Central'nyj, Ross.	86	55.12 N	87.40 E
Central'nyj, Ross.	86	58.45 N	84.28 E
Central'nyj, Ross.	86	57.41 N	80.57 E
Central'nyj, Ross.	265b	55.53 N	37.52 E
Central'nyje Karakumy ◆[2]	128	39.00 N	60.00 E
Central Pacific Basin ✣[1]	14	5.00 N	175.00 W

FRANÇAIS

Nom	Page	Lat.°′	Long.°′ W = Ouest
Central Park, N.J., U.S.	276	40.26 N	74.18 W
Central Park, Wa., U.S.	224	46.58 N	123.41 W
Central Park ♠	276	40.47 N	73.58 W
Central Point	202	42.22 N	122.54 W
Central Railroad Station ◆[5]	272c	18.58 N	72.50 E
Central Range ⋏, Leso.	158	29.35 S	28.35 E
Central Range ⋏, Pap. N. Gui.	164	5.00 S	142.30 E
Central Square	210	43.17 N	76.08 W
Central Utah Canal ≋	200	39.35 N	112.12 W
Central Valley, Ca., U.S.	204	40.40 N	122.22 W
Central Valley, N.Y., U.S.	210	41.19 N	74.07 W
Central Village	207	41.43 N	71.54 W
Centre	194	34.09 N	85.40 W
Centre ▫[6]	210	40.55 N	77.47 W
Centre, Canal du ≋	32	46.27 N	4.07 E
Centre Atomique de Marcoule ʊ[3]	62	44.08 N	4.42 E
Centre City	285	39.46 N	75.10 W
Centre d'Énergie de Pierrelatte ʊ[3]	62	44.21 N	4.44 E
Centre Hall	214	40.50 N	77.41 W
Centre Island	276	40.54 N	73.32 W
Centre Island I	172	46.28 S	167.51 E
Centre Island Park ♠	275b	43.37 N	79.23 W
Centre Lake ⊜	212	44.36 N	75.51 W
Centre Peak ∧	182	55.41 N	126.26 W
Centre-Sud ▫[4]	152	4.10 N	12.00 E
Centreville, Al., U.S.	194	32.56 N	87.08 W
Centreville, Il., U.S.	219	38.35 N	90.07 W
Centreville, Ky., U.S.	218	38.13 N	84.24 W
Centreville, Md., U.S.	208	39.02 N	76.04 W
Centreville, Mi., U.S.	216	41.55 N	85.31 W
Centreville, Ms., U.S.	194	31.05 N	91.04 W
Centreville, Va., U.S.	208	38.50 N	77.25 W
Centro Puntas	240m	18.22 N	67.16 W
Centro Simón Bolívar ◆[9]	286c	10.30 N	66.55 W
Centuripe	70	37.37 N	14.44 E
Century, Fl., U.S.	194	30.58 N	87.15 W
Century, W.V., U.S.	188	39.05 N	80.11 W
Century City ◆[8]	280	34.03 N	118.26 W
Century III Mall ◆[9]	279b	40.21 N	79.57 W
Century Village	220	26.42 N	80.05 W
Cenxi	102	22.59 N	111.00 E
Čepca	80	57.54 N	53.25 E
Čepca ≃	80	58.36 N	50.04 E
Čepeckij	80	58.29 N	51.12 E
Čepelare	38	41.44 N	24.41 E
Čepel'ovo	82	55.11 N	37.30 E
Čepovan	64	46.03 N	13.47 E
Cepoy	50	48.03 N	2.44 E
Ceprano	66	41.33 N	13.31 E
Čepřovice	60	49.10 N	13.59 E
Ceptia	152	12.56 S	17.35 E
Cepu	115a	7.09 S	111.35 E
Čerahouka	76	52.13 N	31.27 E
Ceraino	64	45.35 N	10.50 E
Ceram → Seram I	164	3.00 S	129.00 E
Cerami	70	37.49 N	14.30 E
Cerami ≃	70	37.42 N	14.29 E
Ceram Sea → Seram, Laut ⊤[2]	108	2.30 S	128.00 E
Cerano, It.	62	45.25 N	8.47 E
Cerano, Méx.	234	20.07 N	101.23 W
Ceraso	68	40.11 N	15.15 E
Cerbicale, Îles II	71	41.34 N	9.24 E
Čerčany	30	49.51 N	14.43 E
Cerchiara di Calabria	68	39.51 N	16.23 E
Čerchov ∧	60	49.23 N	12.47 E
Cercié	58	46.07 N	4.40 E
Cerco, Alto do ∧	256	22.38 S	45.22 W
Cerda	70	37.54 N	13.49 E
Čerdakly	80	54.23 N	48.51 E
Cerdanyola del Vallès	266d	41.30 N	2.09 E
Cerdas	248	20.48 S	66.29 W
Cerdeña, Isla de → Sardegna I	71	40.00 N	9.00 E
Čerdojak	86	48.48 N	84.00 E
Cerdon, Fr.	50	47.38 N	2.22 E
Cerdon, Fr.	58	46.05 N	5.28 E
Čerdyn'	24	60.23 N	56.24 E
Cère ≃	32	44.55 N	1.53 E
Cerea	64	45.12 N	11.13 E
Cereal	184	51.25 N	110.48 W
Cereales	252	36.49 S	63.51 W
Čerecha ≃	76	57.46 N	28.21 E
Cereglio	64	44.18 N	11.04 E
Čerek ≃	84	43.42 N	44.03 E
Čeremchovo	88	53.09 N	103.05 E
Čeremisinovo	78	51.54 N	37.15 E
Čeremšan, Ross.	80	55.15 N	48.07 E
Čeremšan, Ross.	80	54.40 N	51.30 E
Čeremšanka, Ross.	86	59.10 N	76.51 E
Čeremšanka, Ross.	86	56.07 N	60.19 E
Čeremšany	89	44.42 N	135.43 E
Cerenti	112	0.30 S	101.52 E
Čerepanovka	80	57.07 N	54.10 E
Čerepanovo	86	54.13 N	83.22 E
Čerepaška, ostrov I	83	47.11 N	38.59 E
Čerepet'	82	54.07 N	36.23 E
Čerepkovo ◆[8]	265b	55.46 N	37.23 E
Čerepovec	76	59.08 N	37.54 E
Ceres, Arg.	252	29.53 S	61.57 W
Ceres, Bra.	255	15.17 S	49.35 W
Ceres, It.	62	45.19 N	7.23 E
Ceres, S. Afr.	158	33.21 S	19.18 E
Ceres, Ca., U.S.	226	37.35 N	120.57 W
Ceres, N.Y., U.S.	210	42.00 N	78.16 W
Ceresco, Mi., U.S.	216	42.16 N	85.04 W
Ceresco, Ne., U.S.	198	41.03 N	96.38 W
Ceresole Reale	62	45.26 N	7.15 E
Céreste	62	43.51 N	5.35 E
Céret	32	42.29 N	2.45 E
Cereté	246	8.53 N	75.48 W
Čerevkovo	24	61.46 N	45.12 E
Cereweh	115b	8.52 S	116.51 E
Cerf Island I	138	9.32 S	50.59 E
Čerga	86	51.35 N	85.38 E
Cergy	261	49.02 N	2.04 E
Ceri ≃	42	52.03 N	4.29 W
Ceriale	62	44.06 N	8.14 E
Ceriana	62	43.53 N	7.46 E
Ceriano	266b	45.38 N	9.05 E
Cerignola	68	41.16 N	15.54 E
Cérilly	32	46.37 N	2.49 E
Cerisano	68	39.16 N	16.11 E
Cerisiers	50	48.08 N	3.29 E
Čerkašina	88	58.37 N	108.30 E
Čerkasovo	82	54.33 N	36.48 E
Čerkasskoje	80	52.26 N	47.13 E
Čerkassy	76	52.41 N	38.43 E
Çerkeş	130	40.50 N	32.54 E
Čerkesovskij	80	50.41 N	42.34 E
Čerkessk	84	44.14 N	42.04 E
Çerkezköy	130	41.17 N	28.00 E
Čerkizovo, Ross.	82	55.12 N	38.45 E
Čerkizovo, Ross.	265b	55.58 N	37.48 E
Čerkizovo, Ross.	265b	55.57 N	37.22 E
Cerknica	36	45.48 N	14.22 E
Čerkovišče	76	55.54 N	30.51 E
Čerlak	86	54.09 N	74.48 E
Čerlakskij	86	53.47 N	74.31 E
Cermei	38	46.33 N	21.51 E
Čermen	84	43.11 N	44.42 E
Cermignano	66	42.35 N	13.47 E
Çermik	130	38.09 N	39.27 E
Čermoz	86	58.53 N	56.08 E
Čern'	76	53.27 N	36.55 E
Cerna, Hrv.	38	45.11 N	18.42 E
Cerna, Rom.	38	45.04 N	28.18 E
Čern'achovsk (Insterburg)	76	54.38 N	21.49 E

PORTUGUÊS

Nome	Página	Lat.°′	Long.°′ W = Oeste
Černá hora ∧	60	48.58 N	13.48 E
Černaja Rečka	85	43.00 N	74.55 E
Čern'ajevo	89	52.45 N	126.00 E
Černak	85	43.24 N	68.02 E
Čern'anka	78	50.55 N	37.49 E
Černaučycy	76	52.13 N	23.44 E
Cernăuţi → Chernivtsi	78	48.18 N	25.56 E
Černava	76	53.37 N	39.09 E
Černavka, Ross.	80	52.18 N	47.14 E
Černavka, Ross.	80	52.11 N	42.25 E
Cernavodă	38	44.21 N	28.01 E
Černá v Pošumavi	61	48.44 N	14.07 E
Cernay	58	47.49 N	7.10 E
Cernay-la-Ville	50	48.40 N	1.58 E
Cerne Abbas	42	50.49 N	2.29 W
Černeckoje	82	55.15 N	37.20 E
Cernei, Munţii ⋏	38	45.02 N	22.31 E
Černigovka, Kaz.	86	50.28 N	71.27 E
Černigovka, Ross.	89	49.37 N	129.57 E
Černigovka, Ross.	89	44.21 N	132.33 E
Černigovskaja	78	44.41 N	39.40 E
Černi Vrăh ∧	38	42.34 N	23.17 E
Cernobbio	62	45.50 N	9.04 E
Černogolovka	82	56.00 N	38.22 E
Černogorsk	86	53.49 N	91.18 E
Černokol'skaja	86	56.42 N	72.49 E
Černorečje	84	43.15 N	45.41 E
Černoreckoje	86	52.45 N	76.40 E
Černošín	60	49.49 N	12.53 E
Čerňovice	60	49.49 N	13.06 E
Černovka, Ross.	86	56.47 N	76.28 E
Černovka, Ross.	89	51.43 N	128.12 E
Čern'ovo, Ross.	76	58.39 N	28.14 E
Čern'ovo, Ross.	82	54.43 N	38.36 E
Čern'ovo, Ross.	265b	55.50 N	37.18 E
Černovskije Kopi	88	52.00 N	113.15 E
Černovskoje, Ross.	80	58.42 N	47.23 E
Černovskoje, Ross.	80	57.29 N	54.36 E
Černucha	80	55.36 N	43.46 E
Cernusco sul Naviglio	62	45.31 N	9.19 E
Černuška, Ross.	86	56.29 N	56.03 E
Černuška, Ross.	88	52.58 N	101.55 E
Cerny-en-Laonnois	50	49.27 N	3.40 E
Černyševsk	88	52.35 N	117.00 E
Černyševskij	74	63.00 N	112.15 E
Černyškovskij	80	48.27 N	42.14 E
Černyšova, gr'ada ⋏	24	66.30 N	59.00 E
Čer'omuchova	80	54.57 N	51.09 E
Čer'omuški ◆[8]	265b	55.41 N	37.35 E
Cerralvo	232	26.06 N	99.37 W
Cerralvo, Isla I	232	24.15 N	109.55 W
Cerreto, Passo del)(	64	44.18 N	10.13 E
Cerreto d'Esi	66	43.19 N	12.59 E
Cerreto Guidi	66	43.45 N	10.53 E
Cerreto Sannita	68	41.17 N	14.33 E
Cerrigydrudion	44	53.02 N	3.33 W
Cërrik	38	41.02 N	19.57 E
Cerrillos, Arg.	252	24.54 S	65.29 W
Cerrillos, Chile	286e	33.30 S	70.43 W
Cerrillos, N.M., U.S.	200	35.26 N	106.07 W
Cerrina	62	45.07 N	8.13 E
Cerritos, Méx.	234	22.26 N	100.17 W
Cerritos, Ca., U.S.	280	33.52 N	118.05 W
Cerro	58	45.54 N	8.36 E
Cerro, Forca di)(	66	42.45 N	12.47 E
Cerro Azul, Arg.	252	27.38 S	55.29 W
Cerro Azul, Bra.	252	24.50 S	49.15 W
Cerro Azul, Méx.	234	21.12 N	97.44 W
Cerro Azul, Perú	248	13.02 S	76.30 W
Cerro Chato	252	33.06 S	55.08 W
Cerro Colorado	252	33.52 S	55.33 W
Cerro Corá	250	6.03 S	36.21 W
Cerro de las Mesas ⊥	234	18.47 N	96.05 W
Cerro de los Angeles ʊ[1]	266a	40.19 N	3.41 W
Cerro de Pasco	248	10.41 S	76.16 W
Cerro Gordo	219	39.53 N	88.43 W
Cerro Grande ≃	286c	10.37 N	66.49 W
Cerro Largo	252	28.09 S	54.45 W
Cerro Maggiore	266b	45.36 N	8.58 E
Cerro Moreno	252	23.28 S	70.25 W
Cerrón, Cerro ∧	246	10.19 N	70.39 W
Cerro Navia	286e	33.25 S	70.43 W
Cerrón Grande, Embalse ⊜[1]	236	14.00 N	89.00 W
Cerro Prieto	204	32.27 N	115.17 W
Cerros Colorados, Embalse ⊜[1]	252	38.35 S	68.40 W
Cerros de Amotape, Parque Nacional ♠	246	4.10 S	80.30 W
Cerro Tololo, Observatorio ʊ[3]	252	30.05 S	71.00 W
Cerro Vera	252	33.11 S	57.28 W
Čerskij	74	68.45 N	161.45 E
Čerskogo, chrebet ⋏, Ross.	74	65.00 N	144.00 E
Čerskogo, chrebet ⋏, Ross.	88	52.00 N	114.00 E
Čerskogo, gora ∧	88	55.05 N	108.40 E
Cersosimo	68	40.03 N	16.21 E
Certaldo	66	43.33 N	11.02 E
Čertanovka ≃	265b	55.38 N	37.47 E
Čertanovo ◆[8]	265b	55.38 N	37.37 E
Čertkovo	83	49.23 N	40.10 E
Čertolino	76	56.12 N	33.54 E
Certosa (Karthaus)	64	46.42 N	10.54 E
Certosa di Pavia	62	45.15 N	9.09 E
Čerusti	76	55.33 N	40.01 E
Červ'anka	88	57.41 N	99.33 E
Cervantes, Austl.	162	30.30 S	115.04 E
Cervantes, Pil.	116	16.59 N	120.44 E
Cervarezza	64	44.23 N	10.20 E
Cervaro	66	41.29 N	13.54 E
Cervaro ≃	68	41.30 N	15.52 E
Cervati, Monte ∧	68	40.17 N	15.29 E
Cervelló	266d	41.24 N	1.57 E
Cervello, Cozzo ∧	68	39.24 N	16.05 E
Cervelló, Riera de ≃	266d	41.24 N	2.01 E
Čèrven'	76	53.42 N	28.26 E
Červen Brjag	38	43.16 N	24.06 E
Červený Kostelec	30	50.29 N	16.06 E
Cervera	34	41.40 N	1.17 E
Cervera del Río Alhama	34	42.01 N	1.57 W
Cervera de Pisuerga	34	42.52 N	4.30 W
Cerveteri	66	42.00 N	12.06 E
Cervi, Monte dei ∧	70	37.53 N	13.58 E
Cervia	66	44.15 N	12.22 E
Cervialto, Monte ∧	68	40.47 N	15.08 E
Cervignano del Friuli	64	45.49 N	13.20 E
Cervin, Mont → Matterhorn ∧	58	45.59 N	7.43 E
Cervinara	68	41.01 N	14.37 E
Cervino (Matterhorn) ∧	58	45.59 N	7.43 E
Cervione	36	42.20 N	9.31 E
Červl'onnaja	84	43.30 N	45.54 E
Cervo, Esp.	34	43.40 N	7.25 W
Cervo, It.	62	43.55 N	8.07 E
Cervo ≃	62	45.22 N	8.24 E
Cervo, Capo ›	62	43.55 N	8.08 E
Cervo, Rio do ≃, Bra.	256	21.12 S	45.10 W
Cervo, Rio do ≃, Bra.	256	22.07 S	45.49 W
Cervo, Serra do ∧	256	22.06 S	46.07 W
Čèrykaŭ	76	53.34 N	31.23 E
Cesana Torinese	62	44.57 N	6.47 E
Cesano, It.	66	42.07 N	12.21 E
Cesano, It.	66	43.45 N	13.10 E
Cesano ≃	66	43.45 N	13.10 E
Cesano Boscone	266b	45.27 N	9.06 E
Cesano Maderno	62	45.38 N	9.08 E
Cesar ▫[5]	246	9.20 N	73.30 W
Cesar ≃	246	9.00 N	73.58 W
Cesarò	70	37.50 N	14.43 E
Cesate	266b	45.36 N	9.05 E
Cesena	66	44.08 N	12.15 E
Cesenatico	66	44.12 N	12.24 E

Cesi, Poggio ∧[2]	267a	42.02 N	12.44 E
Cesiomaggiore	64	46.05 N	11.59 E
Cēsis	76	57.18 N	25.15 E
Česká Kamenice	54	50.47 N	14.26 E
Česká Kublice	60	49.22 N	12.52 E
Česká Lípa	54	50.42 N	14.32 E
Česká Třebová	30	49.54 N	16.27 E
České Budějovice	61	48.59 N	14.28 E
České středohoří ⋏	54	50.35 N	14.09 E
Českomoravská vrchovina ⋏[1]	30	49.20 N	15.30 E
Český Brod	54	50.02 N	14.58 E
Český Krumlov	61	48.49 N	14.19 E
Česma	86	53.50 N	60.40 E
Çeşme	130	38.18 N	26.19 E
Cessalto	64	45.42 N	12.36 E
Češskaja guba ⊂	24	67.30 N	46.30 E
Cessnock	170	32.50 S	151.21 E
Cesson	261	48.34 N	2.36 E
Cestos ≃	150	5.40 N	9.10 W
Cesvaine	76	56.58 N	26.19 E
Čet' ≃	86	56.51 N	86.48 E
Cetara	68	40.39 N	14.42 E
Cetate	38	44.06 N	23.03 E
Cetatea Albă → Bilhorod-Dnistrovs'kyy	78	46.12 N	30.20 E
Četbulak	85	41.17 N	73.58 E
Cetian	100	25.44 N	116.22 E
Cetina ≃	36	43.26 N	16.42 E
Cetinje	38	42.23 N	18.55 E
Çetinkaya	130	39.15 N	37.38 E
Cetona	66	42.58 N	11.54 E
Cetona, Monte ∧	66	42.56 N	11.52 E
Cetraro	68	39.31 N	15.56 E
Cetronia	208	40.35 N	75.31 W
Céüse, Montagne de ∧	62	44.31 N	5.57 E
Ceuta	34	35.53 N	5.19 W
Ceva	62	44.23 N	8.02 E
Cevedale, Monte (Zufallspitze) ∧	64	46.27 N	10.37 E
Cevennen → Cévennes ◆[1]	32	44.00 N	3.30 E
Cévennes ◆[1]	32	44.00 N	3.30 E
Cévennes, Parc National des ♠	32	44.15 N	3.40 E
Cevins	62	45.35 N	6.28 E
Cevio	58	46.19 N	8.36 E
Cevizli	130	37.12 N	31.45 E
Ceyhan	130	37.04 N	35.47 E
Ceyhan ≃	130	36.45 N	35.41 E
Ceylanpınar	130	36.51 N	40.02 E
Çeyldağ	84	40.17 N	49.18 E
Ceylon, Sk., Can.	184	49.28 N	104.36 W
Ceylon, Mn., U.S.	198	43.32 N	94.37 W
Ceylon → Sri Lanka ▫[1]	122	7.00 N	81.00 E
Ceyzériat	58	46.10 N	5.19 E
Cèze ≃	62	44.06 N	4.42 E
Chaam, Ned.	52	51.31 N	4.52 E
Cha-am, Thai	110	12.48 N	99.58 E
Chaanling	100	29.39 N	113.49 E
Chaatl Island I	182	53.00 N	132.25 W
Chabanais	32	45.52 N	0.43 E
Chabang Tiga	114	5.19 N	103.08 E
Chabaricha	24	65.50 N	52.16 E
Chabařovice	54	50.40 N	13.56 E
Chabarovo	72	69.39 N	60.24 E
Chabarovsk	89	48.27 N	135.06 E
Chabarovsk Kraj ▫[8]	89	52.00 N	138.00 E
Chabarowsk → Chabarovsk	89	48.27 N	135.06 E
Chabary	86	53.37 N	79.33 E
Chabás	252	33.15 S	61.22 W
Chabeuil	62	44.54 N	5.01 E
Chabez	84	44.02 N	41.47 E
Chābi	124	22.49 N	80.41 E
Chabjuwardoo Bay ⊂	162	22.57 S	113.48 E
Chablais ◆[1]	58	46.18 N	6.39 E
Chablis	50	47.49 N	3.48 E
Chabogongba	120	31.47 N	81.14 E
Chaboje	265a	59.53 N	30.46 E
Chabot, Lake ⊜, Ca., U.S.	282	38.08 N	122.14 W
Chabot, Lake ⊜, Ca., U.S.	282	37.43 N	122.07 W
Chabris	50	47.15 N	1.39 E
Chabuchaer	86	43.42 N	81.04 E
Chabu-Rabot, pereval)(	85	38.40 N	70.43 E
Chacabuco	252	34.38 S	60.29 W
Chacaito, Quebrada ≃	286c	10.29 N	66.52 W
Chacaltianguis	234	18.20 N	95.50 W
Chacao	286c	10.30 N	66.51 W
Chácara	256	21.41 S	43.13 W
Chacarita, Cementerio de la ◆	288	34.33 S	58.28 W
Chacarrão, Cachoeira do ∟	250	6.32 S	58.12 W
Chacayán	248	10.24 S	76.25 W
Chachani, Nevado ∧	248	16.12 S	71.33 W
Chachapoyas, Perú	242	6.13 S	77.51 W
Chachapoyas, Perú	248	6.13 S	77.51 W
Chachas	248	15.30 S	72.16 W
Chachoengsao	110	13.42 N	101.05 E
Chāchora	124	24.10 N	76.59 E
Chāchro	120	25.07 N	70.15 E
Chachu	120	33.16 N	81.41 E
Chaclacyo	248	11.59 S	76.46 W
Chaco ▫[4]	252	26.25 S	60.30 W
Chaco ▫[5]	248	20.00 S	60.30 W
Chaco ≃	200	36.46 N	108.39 W
Chaco Austral ◆[1]	252	26.30 S	61.30 W
Chaco Boreal ◆[1]	252	23.00 S	60.00 W
Chaco Central ◆[1]	252	25.00 S	59.45 W
Chaco Culture National Historical Park ♠	200	36.06 N	108.00 W
Chaco Mesa ∧	200	35.47 N	107.35 W
Chacón, Arroyo ≃	288	34.53 S	58.39 W
Chacon, Cape ›	182	54.42 N	132.00 W
Chacra Cerro	286d	11.55 S	77.04 W
Chacuaco Creek ≃	196	37.34 N	103.38 W
Chad (Tchad) ▫[1], Afr.	136	15.00 N	19.00 E
Chad (Tchad) ▫[1], Afr.	146	15.00 N	19.00 E
Chad, Lake (Lac Tchad) ⊜	146	13.20 N	14.00 E
Chada-Bulak	88	50.38 N	116.18 E
Chadbourn	192	34.19 N	78.49 W
Chadderton	44	53.33 N	2.08 W
Chadds Ford	285	39.52 N	75.35 W
Chādegān	128	32.46 N	50.39 E
Chadian, Zhg.	102	26.48 N	105.48 E
Chadian, Zhg.	105	39.14 N	117.45 E
Chadian, Zhg.	107	30.14 N	105.56 E
Chadianzi	107	30.31 N	104.22 E
Chadiza	154	14.05 S	32.28 E
Chadron	198	42.49 N	103.00 W
Chadstone	274b	37.53 S	145.05 E
Chadwell Saint Mary	260	51.29 N	0.22 E
Chadwick	190	42.01 N	89.53 W
Chadwick Manor	284b	39.19 N	76.46 W
Chadwick Pond ⊜	283	42.44 N	71.05 W
Chadwicks	210	43.01 N	75.16 W
Chadyžensk	78	44.25 N	39.33 E
Chadžalmachi	84	42.26 N	47.13 E
Chae Hom	110	18.43 N	99.35 E
Chaem ≃	110	18.11 N	98.38 E
Chaersen	89	46.19 N	121.54 E
Chaeryŏng	98	38.24 N	125.36 E
Chafarinas, Islas II	34	35.11 N	2.26 W
Chafe	150	11.56 N	6.55 E
Chaffee	194	37.10 N	89.39 W
Chaffins	207	42.21 N	71.51 W
Chāgai	128	29.18 N	64.42 E
Chāgai Hills ⋏[2]	128	29.30 N	64.15 E
Chagandianlisu	102	41.47 N	103.29 E

Chagang Do ▫[4]	98	40.50 N	126.30 E
'Chaghcharān	120	34.32 N	65.15 E
Chagny	58	46.55 N	4.45 E
Chagos Archipelago II	12	6.00 S	72.00 E
Chagos-Laccadive Plateau ✣[3]	12	3.00 N	73.00 E
Chagrin ≃	214	41.40 N	81.27 W
Chagrin, Aurora Branch ≃	279a	41.25 N	81.25 W
Chagrin Falls	214	41.26 N	81.24 W
Chagrin Falls Park	214	41.21 N	81.32 W
Chagrin Valley Parkway ♠	279a	41.26 N	81.25 W
Chaguanas	241r	10.31 N	61.25 W
Chaguaramas	246	9.20 N	66.16 W
Chahaignes	50	47.44 N	0.31 E
Chāhak	128	33.17 N	58.54 E
Chahal	236	15.45 N	89.34 W
Chahancheluo	98	41.39 N	114.22 E
Chahanwusu → Dulan	102	36.16 N	98.28 E
Chahār Borjak	128	30.17 N	62.03 E
Chahār Deh-ye Ghowrband	120	34.59 N	68.44 E
Chahār Maḥāl va Bakhtīārī ▫[4]	128	32.00 N	51.00 E
Chahayang	89	48.24 N	124.15 E
Chahe, Zhg.	100	33.16 N	119.02 E
Chahe, Zhg.	102	33.48 N	97.22 E
Chahe, Zhg.	105	39.50 N	115.21 E
Chāh Gheybī, Hāmūn-e ☷	128	28.06 N	60.50 E
Chahuamiao	100	33.00 N	115.56 E
Chahuites	234	16.17 N	94.11 W
Chai ≃	104	42.20 N	123.52 E
Chai Badan	110	15.04 N	101.05 E
Chāībāsa	124	22.34 N	85.49 E
Chaigou	98	36.15 N	119.36 E
Chaihe	89	44.47 N	129.42 E
Chaijiawan	100	29.10 N	113.06 E
Chaillé-les-Marais	32	46.24 N	1.01 W
Chailley	50	48.05 N	3.42 E
Chailly-en-Bière	50	48.28 N	2.35 E
Chai Nat	110	15.11 N	100.08 E
Chainhurst	260	51.12 N	0.29 E
Chain O'Lakes State Park ♠, Il., U.S.	216	42.27 N	88.11 W
Chain O'Lakes State Park ♠, In., U.S.	216	41.20 N	85.26 W
Chainpur	124	23.08 N	84.15 E
Chaipudyrskaja guba ⊂	24	68.30 N	59.30 E
Chaiqiao	100	29.51 N	121.56 E
Chairel, Laguna de ⊂	234	22.17 N	97.57 W
Chaishudian	105	40.46 N	116.30 E
Chaiši	84	42.57 N	42.12 E
Chait	85	39.11 N	70.53 E
Chaital	126	22.31 N	88.47 E
Chaitén	254	42.55 S	72.43 W
Chaiwopu	86	43.33 N	87.59 E
Chaiya	110	9.23 N	99.14 E
Chaiyaphum	110	15.48 N	102.02 E
Chajarí	252	30.46 S	57.59 W
Chajdarken	85	39.57 N	71.21 E
Chajia	107	29.37 N	104.27 E
Chajian	100	32.40 N	118.46 E
Chajianling	98	39.14 N	114.36 E
Chajiaqiao	100	34.00 N	120.07 E
Chajrchan	88	48.35 N	101.56 E
Chajrchandulaan	102	45.57 N	102.03 E
Chajul	236	15.30 N	91.02 W
Chaka	154	4.49 N	31.14 E
Chakachamna Lake ⊜	180	61.13 N	152.35 W
Chakāltor	126	23.14 N	86.22 E
Chak Amru	123	32.22 N	75.11 E
Chakari	154	18.05 S	29.51 E
Chakaria	120	21.45 N	92.05 E
Chakarnaba	146	14.13 N	20.51 E
Chakasija ▫[3], Ross.	72	53.00 N	90.00 E
Chakasija ▫[3], Ross.	86	53.00 N	90.00 E
Chākdaha, India	126	23.05 N	88.31 E
Chakdaha, India	272b	22.20 N	88.20 E
Chake Chake	154	5.15 S	39.46 E
Chakhānsūr	128	31.10 N	62.04 E
Chākia	124	26.25 N	85.03 E
Chakkarat	110	15.00 N	102.16 E
Chakou, Zhg.	98	38.03 N	113.36 E
Chakou, Zhg.	105	38.53 N	116.41 E
Chakradharpur	124	22.42 N	85.38 E
Chakrāta	120	30.42 N	77.51 E
Chāksu	120	26.36 N	75.57 E
Chākulia	126	22.29 N	86.43 E
Chakwadām	102	27.29 N	98.31 E
Chakwāl	123	32.56 N	72.52 E
Chal	272c	19.06 N	73.08 E
Chala	248	15.52 S	74.16 W
Chalabesa	154	11.22 S	31.01 E
Chalais	32	45.16 N	0.02 E
Chālakuda	122	10.18 N	76.20 E
Chalamont	58	46.00 N	5.10 E
Chalampé	58	47.49 N	7.33 E
Chalan Kanoa	174n	15.08 N	145.43 E
Chalatenango	236	14.03 N	88.56 W
Chalaua	154	16.06 S	39.11 E
Chalaux ≃	50	47.23 N	3.54 E
Chalaxung	102	34.10 N	97.44 E
Chalbi Desert ◆[2]	154	3.00 N	37.20 E
Chalchgol	88	48.11 N	114.54 E
Chalchihuites	234	23.29 N	103.53 W
Chalchis Terara ∧	144	9.08 N	36.44 E
Chalchuapa	236	13.59 N	89.41 W
Chalchyn ≃	88	47.55 N	117.47 E
Chalcis → Khalkís	38	38.28 N	23.36 E
Chalco ≃	286a	19.19 N	99.08 W
Chaldon	260	51.17 N	0.07 W
Chaleine	261	48.36 N	1.43 E
Chalengkou	120	38.02 N	93.54 E
Châlette-sur-Loing	50	48.01 N	2.44 E
Chaleur Bay ⊂	186	48.00 N	65.45 W
Chalfant	279b	40.25 N	79.52 W
Chalfant Run ≃	279b	40.25 N	79.48 W
Chalfont	208	40.17 N	75.13 W
Chalfont Common	260	51.38 N	0.33 W
Chalfonte	285	39.49 N	75.31 W
Chalfont Saint Giles	260	51.38 N	0.34 W
Chalfont Saint Peter	42	51.37 N	0.33 W
Chalford	42	51.45 N	2.09 W
Chalhuanca	248	14.17 S	73.15 W
Chalía ≃	254	49.35 S	69.34 W
Chalifert	261	48.53 N	2.46 E
Chalilovo	86	51.24 N	58.04 E
Chalindrey	58	47.48 N	5.26 E
Chaling	100	26.47 N	113.33 E
Chālisgaon	122	20.28 N	75.01 E
Chalisi	102	32.55 N	102.04 E
Chaliun	88	48.50 N	103.59 E
Chalk	260	51.26 N	0.25 E
Chalkabad	86	42.42 N	59.43 E
Chalk Draw V	196	29.36 N	103.15 W
Chalk River	190	46.01 N	77.27 W
Chalkyitsik	180	66.39 N	143.43 W
Challakere	122	14.19 N	76.39 E
Challans	32	46.51 N	1.53 W
Challapata	248	18.54 S	66.47 W
Challenge	226	39.29 N	121.13 W
Challenger, Mount ∧	224	48.50 N	121.20 W
Challenger Deep ✣[1]	14	11.21 N	142.12 E
Challes-les-Eaux	62	45.33 N	5.59 E
Challis	202	44.30 N	114.13 W
Challviri, Salar de ☷	248	22.32 S	67.34 W
Chal'mer-Ju	24	67.58 N	64.50 E
Chalmers	216	40.39 N	86.52 W
Chalmette	194	29.56 N	89.57 W
Chalone Creek ≃	226	36.21 N	121.14 W
Chalonnes-sur-Loire	32	47.21 N	0.46 W
Châlons-sur-Marne	50	48.57 N	4.22 E
Chalon-sur-Saône	58	46.47 N	4.51 E

Chalosse ◆[1]	32	43.45 N	0.30 W
Chalt	123	36.15 N	74.20 E
Chaltel, Cerro (Monte Fitzroy) ∧	254	49.17 S	73.05 W
Chaluhe	89	43.43 N	126.00 E
Châlus, Fr.	32	45.39 N	0.59 E
Chālūs, Īrān	128	36.38 N	51.26 E
Cham, Dtsch.	60	49.13 N	12.41 E
Cham, Schw.	58	47.11 N	8.28 E
Cham ≃	60	49.13 N	12.42 E
Chama	200	36.54 N	106.34 W
Chama ≃	246	9.03 N	71.40 W
Chama, Rio ≃	200	36.03 N	106.05 W
Chamah, Gunong ∧	114	5.13 N	101.33 E
Chamaicó	252	35.03 S	64.58 W
Chamama	154	12.55 S	33.43 E
Chamamat'urt	84	43.36 N	46.30 E
Chaman	120	30.55 N	66.27 E
Chamangonge	152	11.16 S	20.24 E
Chamao, Khao ∧	110	12.57 N	101.45 E
Chamarande	261	48.31 N	2.13 E
Chamar-Daban, chrebet ⋏	88	51.15 N	105.00 E
Chāmārpāra	272b	22.35 N	88.08 E
Chamaya ≃	248	5.44 S	78.39 W
Chamba, India	123	32.34 N	76.08 E
Chamba, Moç.	154	12.07 S	36.57 E
Chamba, Tan.	154	11.35 S	36.58 E
Chambal ≃	120	26.30 N	79.15 E
Chambaran, Plateau de ⋏[1]	62	45.15 N	5.15 E
Chambas	240p	22.12 N	78.55 W
Chamberlain, Sk., Can.	184	50.50 N	105.34 W
Chamberlain, S.D., U.S.	198	43.48 N	99.19 W
Chamberlain ≃	164	15.08 S	128.06 E
Chamberlain Lake ⊜	186	46.17 N	69.20 W
Chamberlin, Mount ∧	180	69.16 N	144.55 W
Chamberry, Ruisseau ≃	275a	45.20 N	73.58 W
Chambers, Az., U.S.	200	35.11 N	109.25 W
Chambers, Ne., U.S.	198	42.12 N	98.44 W
Chambers, N.Y., U.S.	210	42.16 N	76.57 W
Chambers ▫[6]	222	29.42 N	94.40 W
Chambers Brook ≃	276	40.35 N	74.41 W
Chambersburg, Il., U.S.	219	39.49 N	90.39 W
Chambersburg, In., U.S.	218	38.31 N	86.24 W
Chambersburg, Pa., U.S.	208	39.56 N	77.39 W
Chambers Corner	285	40.01 N	74.44 W
Chambers Creek ≃	222	31.58 N	96.10 W
Chambers Creek, North Fork ≃	222	32.16 N	96.58 W
Chambers Creek, South Fork ≃	222	32.16 N	96.58 W
Chambers Island I	190	45.11 N	87.21 W
Chambéry	62	45.34 N	5.56 E
Chambeshi ≃	154	11.21 S	30.37 E
Chambi, Jebel ∧	148	35.11 N	8.42 E
Chambira ≃, Perú	246	4.28 S	74.50 W
Chambira ≃, Perú	246	3.55 S	73.45 W
Chamblee	192	33.53 N	84.17 W
Chambley-Bussières	56	49.03 N	5.54 E
Chambly, P.Q., Can.	206	45.27 N	73.17 W
Chambly, Fr.	50	49.10 N	2.15 E
Chambly ▫[6]	206	45.30 N	73.20 W
Chambly, Bassin de ⊜	206	45.27 N	73.17 W
Chambly, Canal de ≋	275a	45.25 N	73.15 W
Chambois	50	48.48 N	0.07 E
Chambon-sur-Dolore	62	45.30 N	3.37 E
Chambon-sur-Voueize	32	46.11 N	2.25 E
Chambord, Château de ⊥	50	47.37 N	1.31 E
Chambourcy	261	48.54 N	2.03 E
Chambri Lake ⊜	164	4.16 S	143.08 E
Chambry	261	49.00 N	2.54 E
Chamburi Kalāt	128	26.09 N	64.43 E
Chamdo → Qamdo	102	31.11 N	97.15 E
Chāme, Nepāl	124	28.33 N	84.15 E
Chame, Pan.	236	8.35 N	79.53 W
Chame, Punta ›	236	8.39 N	79.42 W
Chamela	234	19.32 N	105.05 W
Chamelecón	236	15.24 N	88.01 W
Chamelecón ≃	236	15.51 N	87.49 W
Chamical	252	30.21 S	66.19 W
Chamizo	258	34.10 S	56.41 W
Chamizo, Arroyo ≃	258	34.15 S	56.44 W
Chamkanī	120	33.48 N	69.49 E
Chāmlūjā ≃	124	29.38 N	80.24 E
Chamo, Lake ⊜	144	5.50 N	37.33 E
Chamois, It.	62	45.50 N	7.37 E
Chamois, Mo., U.S.	219	38.40 N	91.46 W
Chamojie	89	49.25 N	124.45 E
Chamoli	124	30.24 N	79.21 E
Chamonix-Mont-Blanc	58	45.55 N	6.52 E
Chamousset	62	45.33 N	6.12 E
Chamoux-sur-Gelon	62	45.32 N	6.13 E
Chāmpa	124	22.03 N	82.39 E
Champagne, Yk., Can.	180	60.47 N	136.29 W
Champagne, Fr.	62	45.16 N	4.48 E
Champagne ▫[9]	32	49.00 N	4.30 E
Champagne Castle ∧	158	29.06 S	29.20 E
Champagne-en-Valromay	58	45.54 N	5.41 E
Champagner-Berg ∧[2]	264a	52.31 N	13.05 E
Champagne-sur-Seine	50	48.24 N	2.48 E
Champagney	58	47.42 N	6.41 E
Champagnole	58	46.45 N	5.55 E
Champagny	62	45.27 N	6.42 E
Chāmpāhāti	126	22.23 N	88.29 E
Champaign	194	40.06 N	88.14 W
Champaign ▫[6], Il., U.S.	216	40.07 N	88.12 W
Champaign ▫[6], Oh., U.S.	218	40.07 N	83.45 W
Champapur	126	24.02 N	86.31 E
Champaquí, Cerro ∧	252	31.59 S	64.56 W
Champasak	110	14.53 N	105.52 E
Champāwat	124	29.20 N	80.06 E
Champcueil	261	48.31 N	2.27 E
Champdāni	126	22.48 N	88.21 E
Champdeniers	32	46.29 N	0.24 W
Champdepraz	62	45.41 N	7.39 E
Champdeuil	261	48.37 N	2.44 E
Champdor	58	46.01 N	5.36 E
Champdoré, Lac ⊜	176	55.55 N	65.49 W
Champeaux	50	48.35 N	2.48 E
Champeix	32	45.36 N	3.08 E
Champerico	236	14.18 N	91.55 W
Champéry	58	46.10 N	6.52 E
Champex	58	46.02 N	7.07 E
Champier	62	45.27 N	5.17 E
Champigneulles	56	48.44 N	6.10 E
Champigny-sur-Marne	261	48.49 N	2.31 E
Champion, Ab., Can.	182	50.14 N	113.09 W
Champion, Mi., U.S.	190	46.30 N	87.57 W
Champion, Oh., U.S.	214	41.17 N	80.51 W
Champion, Pa., U.S.	214	40.05 N	79.21 W
Champions	222	29.59 N	95.31 W
Champlain	206	44.59 N	73.26 W
Champlain ▫[6]	206	46.45 N	72.35 W
Champlain ≃	206	46.27 N	72.17 W
Champlain, Lake ⊜	188	44.45 N	73.15 W
Champlain, Pont ◆[5]	206	45.28 N	73.32 W
Champlain Canal ≋	210	43.20 N	73.34 W
Champlan	261	48.43 N	2.16 E
Champlin Creek ≃	276	40.43 N	73.12 W
Champlitte-et-le-Prélot	58	47.37 N	5.31 E
Champlon	56	50.07 N	5.28 E

≃ River	Fluß	Río	Rivière	Rio
≋ Canal	Kanal	Canal	Canal	Canal
∟ Waterfall, Rapids	Wasserfall, Stromschnellen	Cascada, Rápidos	Chute d'eau, Rapides	Cascata, Rápidos
⊔ Strait	Meeresstraße	Estrecho	Détroit	Estreito
⊂ Bay, Gulf	Bucht, Golf	Bahía, Golfo	Baie, Golfe	Baía, Golfo
⊜ Lake, Lakes	See, Seen	Lago, Lagos	Lac, Lacs	Lago, Lagos
☷ Swamp	Sumpf	Pantano	Marais	Pântano
⌂ Ice Features, Glacier	Eis- und Gletscherformen	Accidentes Glaciales	Formes glaciaires	Acidentes glaciares
⊤ Other Hydrographic Features	Andere Hydrographische Objekte	Otros Elementos Hidrográficos	Autres données hydrographiques	Outros acidentes hidrográficos

✣ Submarine Features	Untermeerische Objekte	Accidentes Submarinos	Formes de relief sous-marin	Acidentes submarinos
▫ Political Unit	Politische Einheit	Unidad Política	Entité politique	Unidade política
ʊ Cultural Institution	Kulturelle Institution	Institución Cultural	Institution culturelle	Instituição cultural
⊥ Historical Site	Historische Stätte	Sitio Histórico	Site historique	Sitio histórico
♠ Recreational Site	Erholungs- und Ferienort	Sitio de Recreo	Centre de loisirs	Area de Lazer
⊠ Airport	Flughafen	Aeropuerto	Aéroport	Aeroporto
■ Military Installation	Militäranlage	Instalación Militar	Installation militaire	Instalação militar
◆ Miscellaneous	Verschiedenes	Misceláneo	Divers	Diversos

ENGLISH — DEUTSCH (Name / Seite / Breite°′ / Länge°′ E = Ost)

Name	Page	Lat.°′	Long.°′
Champoluc	62	45.50 N	7.44 E
Champotón	232	19.21 N	90.43 W
Champrond-en-Gâtine	50	48.24 N	1.05 E
Champs	50	47.44 N	3.36 E
Champs-sur-Marne	261	48.51 N	2.36 E
Chāmpua	124	22.05 N	85.40 E
Champvans	58	47.06 N	5.26 E
Chāmrāil	272b	22.38 N	88.18 E
Chāmrājnagar Rāmasamudram	122	11.55 N	76.57 E
Chamrousse	62	45.08 N	5.52 E
Chamsara ≃	88	52.42 N	95.46 E
Chamusca	34	39.21 N	8.29 W
Chamza Chakimzada	85	40.26 N	71.30 E
Chana	110	6.55 N	100.44 E
Chanabadskij	85	40.49 N	72.58 E
Chanakyapuri □[9]	272a	28.36 N	77.11 E
Chañar	252	30.32 S	65.58 W
Chañaral	252	26.21 S	70.37 W
Chañaral, Isla I	252	29.02 S	71.35 W
Chanas	62	45.18 N	4.49 E
Chānasma	120	23.43 N	72.07 E
Chanbogd	102	43.12 N	107.10 E
Chancay	248	11.35 S	77.16 W
Chancay ≃	248	11.37 S	77.15 W
Chance	208	38.10 N	75.56 W
Chanceaux	58	47.31 N	4.42 E
Chanceaux-sur-Choisille	50	47.28 N	0.42 E
Chanch	88	51.30 N	100.40 E
Chanchelulla Peak ∧	204	40.28 N	122.59 W
Chanchiang → Zhanjiang	102	21.16 N	110.28 E
Chanchöchij uul ⋏	88	49.30 N	94.30 E
Chanchongor	102	43.50 N	104.25 E
Chanco	252	35.44 S	72.32 W
Chancy	58	46.08 N	6.00 E
Chanda → Chandrapur, India	122	19.57 N	79.18 E
Chanda, Ross.	88	55.00 N	107.14 E
Chanda ≃	88	55.00 N	107.14 E
Chāndābila	126	22.05 N	87.00 E
Chandagajty	86	50.44 N	92.03 E
Chandalar	180	67.30 N	148.30 W
Chandalar ≃	180	66.36 N	145.48 W
Chandalar, East Fork ≃	180	67.05 N	147.16 W
Chandalar, Middle Fork ≃	180	67.10 N	148.19 W
Chandalar, North Fork ≃	180	67.10 N	148.19 W
Chandan Chauki	124	28.33 N	80.47 E
Chandankiāri	126	23.34 N	86.22 E
Chandannagar	126	22.51 N	88.21 E
Chandanpratāp	126	23.33 N	89.24 E
Chāndar	126	23.54 N	89.58 E
Chandausi	124	28.27 N	78.46 E
Chāndbāli	120	20.47 N	86.46 E
Chandeleur Islands II	194	29.48 N	88.51 W
Chandeleur Sound ⋓	194	29.55 N	89.10 W
Chanderi	124	24.43 N	78.08 E
Chandernagore → Chandannagar	126	22.51 N	88.21 E
Chandīgarh	123	30.44 N	76.55 E
Chandīgarh □[8]	123	30.45 N	76.50 E
Chāndil	124	22.58 N	86.03 E
Chandīpur	126	23.59 N	89.01 E
Chanditala	272b	22.41 N	88.16 E
Chandla	124	25.05 N	80.12 E
Chandler, P.Q., Can.	186	48.21 N	64.41 W
Chandler, Az., U.S.	200	33.18 N	111.50 W
Chandler, In., U.S.	194	38.02 N	87.22 W
Chandler, Ok., U.S.	196	35.42 N	96.52 W
Chandler, Tx., U.S.	222	32.18 N	95.29 W
Chandler ≃	180	69.27 N	151.30 W
Chandler, Mount ∧[2]	162	27.00 S	133.20 E
Chandler Lake ⊜	180	68.15 N	152.43 W
Chandler Park ♠	281	42.24 N	82.58 W
Chandler's Cross	260	51.40 N	0.27 W
Chandler's Ford	42	50.59 N	1.23 W
Chandlers Valley	214	41.56 N	79.18 W
Chandlerville	219	40.02 N	90.09 W
Chandless ≃	248	9.08 S	69.51 W
Chāndor Hills ⋏[2]	122	20.30 N	74.00 E
Chandos Lake ⊜	212	44.49 N	78.00 W
Chāndpara	126	22.58 N	88.47 E
Chāndpur, Bngl.	120	22.08 N	91.55 E
Chāndpur, Bngl.	124	23.13 N	90.39 E
Chāndpur, India	124	29.09 N	78.16 E
Chāndpur ◆[8]	272a	28.45 N	77.01 E
Chāndra	126	22.28 N	87.09 E
Chandrabhāga ≃	123	32.59 N	76.25 E
Chandra Dighalia	126	23.04 N	89.46 E
Chandrakona	126	22.44 N	87.31 E
Chandrakona Road	126	22.44 N	87.21 E
Chandrapur	122	19.57 N	79.18 E
Chāndvad	122	20.20 N	74.15 E
Chandyga	74	62.40 N	135.36 E
Chanfang	105	39.56 N	115.55 E
Chang (Yangtze) ≃, Zhg.	90	31.48 N	121.10 E
Chang ≃, Zhg.	100	28.59 N	116.42 E
Chang ≃, Zhg.	100	26.53 N	119.41 E
Chang, Ko I	110	12.05 N	102.20 E
Changa	84	44.27 N	50.36 E
Changaj	88	47.52 N	99.28 E
Changajn nuruu ⋏	90	47.30 N	100.00 E
Changal	88	49.19 N	104.24 E
Changalane	156	26.17 S	32.11 E
Chang'an, Zhg.	102	26.00 N	109.34 E
Changan → Xi'an, Zhg.	102	34.15 N	108.52 E
Changanācheri	122	9.28 N	76.33 E
Changane ≃	156	24.43 S	33.32 E
Chang'anzhen	106	30.28 N	120.27 E
Changara	154	16.54 S	33.14 E
Changarul'skij chrebet ⋏	88	51.10 N	103.00 E
Changbai	98	41.26 N	128.11 E
Changbai Shan ⋏	98	41.40 N	128.00 E
Changbu	100	23.48 N	115.26 E
Changcaocun	105	39.49 N	115.47 E
Changchaoling	106	31.00 N	119.40 E
Changcheng, Zhg.	100	31.49 N	116.54 E
Changcheng, Zhg.	110	19.24 N	108.42 E
Chang Cheng (Great Wall) ⊥	98	40.30 N	116.30 E
Chang Chenmo ≃	120	34.17 N	78.19 E
Changchiak'ou → Zhangjiakou	105	40.50 N	114.53 E
Ch'angchih → Changzhi	102	36.11 N	113.08 E
Changchou → Zhangzhou	100	24.33 N	117.39 E
Changchow → Changzhou	106	31.47 N	119.57 E
Changchun	89	43.53 N	125.19 E
Changchunling	89	45.22 N	125.28 E
Changdan	98	37.56 N	126.45 E
Changdang Hu ⊜	106	31.35 N	119.35 E
Changdao (Sihou)	98	37.56 N	120.42 E
Changde	102	29.02 N	111.41 E
Changdian	105	40.01 N	116.32 E
Ch'angdo	98	38.30 N	127.40 E
Ch'ang-dong	98	39.03 N	126.34 E
Change Islands	186	49.40 N	54.25 W
Changeon ≃	50	47.16 N	0.05 E
Changfeng	100	32.27 N	117.09 E
Changgang	100	24.38 N	113.05 E
Changgangzi	104	41.26 N	122.41 E
Changge	100	34.15 N	113.50 E
Changgi-ap ›	98	36.05 N	129.34 E
Changgi-li	271b	37.35 N	126.44 E
Changgi-ri	271b	37.38 N	126.41 E
Changgou	105	39.34 N	115.53 E
Changgouyu	105	39.44 N	115.52 E
Changguandian	100	32.58 N	115.16 E
Changguowei	100	29.15 N	121.56 E
Changgye-ri	98	34.33 N	126.49 E
Changgyong Palace ʊ	271b	37.36 N	127.00 E
Changhai, Zhg.	98	39.18 N	122.35 E
Chang-hai → Shanghai, Zhg.	106	31.14 N	121.28 E
Changhang	98	36.01 N	126.40 E
Changhe	106	30.11 N	120.11 E
Changhowŏn	98	37.08 N	127.39 E
Chang Hu ⊜	100	30.15 N	112.35 E
Changhua, T'aiwan	100	24.05 N	120.32 E
Changhua, Zhg.	100	30.11 N	119.13 E
Changhŭng	98	34.41 N	126.52 E
Changhŭng-ni	98	40.24 N	128.19 E
Changi	271c	1.23 N	103.59 E
Changi, Tanjong ›	271c	1.23 N	104.00 E
Changi International Airport ⊠	271c	1.22 N	103.59 E
Changi Prison ʊ	271c	1.22 N	103.58 E
Changji	86	44.01 N	87.19 E
Changjiang, Zhg.	100	25.19 N	113.56 E
Changjiang, Zhg.	110	19.17 N	109.02 E
Changjiangbu	100	30.52 N	113.43 E
Changjiapuzi	104	40.51 N	123.43 E
Changjiazhuang	105	40.35 N	115.24 E
Changjie	100	29.16 N	121.40 E
Changjing	106	31.45 N	120.29 E
Changjin-gang ≃	98	41.24 N	127.45 E
Changjin-ŭp	98	40.23 N	127.15 E
Changkai	100	28.04 N	116.18 E
Changkalajier	85	40.09 N	76.59 E
Changkeng	106	30.19 N	121.57 E
Changkiakow → Zhangjiakou	105	40.50 N	114.53 E
Changlapod Pass)(	124	30.08 N	87.06 E
Changle, Zhg.	98	36.42 N	118.49 E
Changle, Zhg.	100	29.25 N	120.37 E
Changle, Zhg.	100	26.00 N	119.31 E
Changlejie	100	28.52 N	113.19 E
Changleqiao	106	30.21 N	119.51 E
Changlezhen	106	31.56 N	121.15 E
Changli, Zhg.	98	39.43 N	119.11 E
Changli, Zhg.	98	36.57 N	119.45 E
Changling	89	44.15 N	123.58 E
Changlingfeng	105	40.11 N	118.24 E
Changlingji	100	32.30 N	114.54 E
Changlingzi, Zhg.	98	39.47 N	122.43 E
Changlingzi, Zhg.	98	39.33 N	121.19 E
Changlinhe	100	31.40 N	117.29 E
Changlun	114	6.26 N	100.26 E
Changmar	120	34.15 N	79.45 E
Changmong-ni	98	34.58 N	128.41 E
Changning, Zhg.	102	26.19 N	112.21 E
Changning, Zhg.	102	24.55 N	99.35 E
Changning (Anningqiao), Zhg.	102	28.21 N	104.53 E
Changning, Zhg.	105	39.59 N	114.55 E
Ch'angnyŏng	98	35.33 N	128.29 E
Changnyŏn-ni	98	38.37 N	125.16 E
Changokurt	72	61.58 N	64.18 E
Ch'angpin	100	23.19 N	121.27 E
Changping	105	40.14 N	116.14 E
Changputong	102	28.05 N	98.29 E
Ch'angp'yŏng-dong	98	41.27 N	127.31 E
Changqiao, Zhg.	100	24.15 N	117.39 E
Changqiao, Zhg.	100	26.49 N	118.50 E
Changqing	98	36.34 N	116.43 E
Changsa	102	19.51 N	110.53 E
Changsan-got ›	98	38.08 N	124.39 E
Changsha, Zhg.	100	28.12 N	112.58 E
Changsha, Zhg.	100	24.13 N	116.07 E
Changshaba Shuiku ⊜[1]	107	29.42 N	104.40 E
Changshageng	107	30.00 N	104.35 E
Changshan, Zhg.	98	36.54 N	117.50 E
Changshan, Zhg.	100	28.55 N	118.30 E
Changshan, Zhg.	107	29.30 N	104.13 E
Changshan ≃	100	28.57 N	118.50 E
Changshan Qundao II	98	39.00 N	122.45 E
Changsheng	100	26.16 N	116.01 E
Changshengqiao	107	29.31 N	106.39 E
Changshitai	104	42.33 N	120.43 E
Changshitou	102	35.03 N	99.11 E
Changshou	102	29.51 N	107.06 E
Changshoudian	100	31.26 N	112.35 E
Changshoujie	100	28.44 N	113.57 E
Changshu	106	31.39 N	120.45 E
Changshui	102	34.21 N	111.29 E
Changsŏng	98	35.20 N	126.49 E
Changsŏng-ni	98	40.58 N	127.04 E
Changsu	98	35.40 N	127.32 E
Changtai, Zhg.	100	28.34 N	118.37 E
Changtai, Zhg.	100	24.40 N	117.46 E
Changtai, Zhg.	104	41.34 N	122.00 E
Changtancun	104	41.33 N	123.02 E
Ch'angte → Changde	102	29.02 N	111.41 E
Changteh → Anyang	98	36.06 N	114.21 E
Changting, Zhg.	89	44.32 N	128.47 E
Changting, Zhg.	100	25.52 N	116.20 E
Changtumiao	102	43.30 N	114.34 E
Changuinola	236	9.25 N	82.32 W
Changuinola ≃	236	9.28 N	82.27 W
Changwu, Zhg.	89	46.00 N	125.36 E
Changwu, Zhg.	102	35.09 N	107.42 E
Changxindianzhen	105	39.49 N	116.12 E
Changxing	106	31.01 N	119.54 E
Changxing Dao I, Zhg.	98	39.34 N	121.23 E
Changxing Dao I, Zhg.	106	31.24 N	121.42 E
Changxingdian, Zhg.	104	41.27 N	121.44 E
Changxingdian, Zhg.	104	41.33 N	123.23 E
Changxingzhen	104	41.40 N	122.14 E
Changxuanling	100	31.08 N	114.20 E
Changyi	98	36.51 N	119.23 E
Changyŏn	98	38.15 N	125.06 E
Changyuan	98	35.13 N	114.39 E
Changyukou	105	40.46 N	115.08 E
Changzhi	102	36.11 N	113.08 E
Changzhou (Changchow)	106	31.47 N	119.57 E
Chanhanga	152	16.04 S	14.07 E
Chanh Hung	269c	10.44 N	106.41 E
Chani	88	57.05 N	120.58 E
Chani ≃	88	57.02 N	120.59 E
Chanino	76	54.13 N	36.37 E
Chanka, ozero (Xingkai Hu) ⊜	89	45.00 N	132.24 E
Chankiang → Zhanjiang	102	21.16 N	110.28 E
Chankou	102	35.52 N	104.27 E
Channagiri	122	14.02 N	75.56 E
Channahon	216	41.26 N	88.14 W
Channapatna	122	12.39 N	77.13 E
Channel Country ◆[1]	166	24.45 S	141.00 E
Channel Islands II, Europe	43b	49.20 N	2.20 W
Channel Islands II, Ca., U.S.	204	33.30 N	119.15 W
Channel Islands National Park ♠	204	33.28 N	119.02 W
Channel Lake	216	42.29 N	88.08 W
Channel-Port-aux-Basques	186	47.34 N	59.09 W
Channel Tunnel ◆[5]	50	51.00 N	1.35 E
Channelview	222	29.46 N	95.06 W
Channing, Mi., U.S.	190	46.08 N	88.05 W
Channing, Tx., U.S.	196	35.41 N	102.20 W
Chānpādānga	126	22.50 N	87.58 E
Chantada	34	42.37 N	7.46 W
Chantajskoje, ozero ⊜	74	68.20 N	91.00 E
Chantajskoje vodochranilišče ⊜[1]	72	68.00 N	88.00 E
Chantang	100	33.41 N	117.37 E
Chantau	86	44.13 N	73.51 E
Chanteloup	261	48.51 N	2.44 E
Chanteloup-les-Vignes	261	48.59 N	2.02 E
Chan-Tengri, pik ∧	72	42.15 N	80.10 E
Chanthaburi	110	12.36 N	102.09 E
Chantilly	50	49.12 N	2.28 E
Chantraine	58	48.10 N	6.26 E
Chantrans	58	47.03 N	6.09 E
Chantrey Inlet ⊂	176	67.48 N	96.20 W
Chanty-Mansijsk	74	61.00 N	69.06 E
Chanty-Mansijskij Avtonomnyj Okrug □[8]	86	60.15 N	70.45 E
Chanujn ≃	88	49.22 N	102.22 E
Chanumla	110	8.19 N	93.05 E
Chanute	198	37.40 N	95.27 W
Chanute Air Force Base ■	216	40.18 N	88.09 W
Chanuwāla	123	32.44 N	73.08 E
Chao ≃	105	40.36 N	117.08 E
Chao, Isla I	248	8.45 S	78.47 W
Chao'an	100	23.41 N	116.38 E
Chaobai ≃	105	39.48 N	117.08 E
Chaobai Xinhe ≃	105	39.37 N	117.26 E
Chaocheng	98	36.05 N	115.35 E
Ch'aochou, T'aiwan	100	22.33 N	120.32 E
Ch'aochou → Chao'an, Zhg.	100	23.41 N	116.38 E
Chao Hu ⊜	100	31.31 N	117.33 E
Chaomidian	105	39.04 N	117.01 E
Chao Phraya ≃	110	13.32 N	100.36 E
Chaor ≃	89	46.48 N	123.37 E
Chaoshui, Zhg.	89	49.44 N	127.21 E
Chaoshui, Zhg.	98	37.42 N	120.55 E
Chaouen	148	35.10 N	5.16 W
Chaouen □[4]	148	35.15 N	5.00 W
Chaource	50	48.04 N	4.08 E
Chaoxian	100	31.36 N	117.52 E
Chaoyang, Zhg.	89	44.34 N	126.20 E
Chaoyang, Zhg.	100	23.17 N	116.37 E
Chaoyang, Zhg.	104	41.35 N	120.28 E
Chaoyangchuan	98	42.54 N	129.21 E
Chaoyangcun	89	50.02 N	124.16 E
Chaoyanggou	104	42.07 N	121.04 E
Chaoyangpo	89	43.37 N	124.42 E
Chaoyangshan	89	43.02 N	125.40 E
Chaozhuang	98	34.18 N	114.56 E
Chapada dos Guimarães	248	15.26 S	55.45 W
Chapada dos Veadeiros, Parque Nacional da ♠	255	13.58 S	47.30 W
Chapadinha	250	3.44 S	43.21 W
Chapala	234	20.18 N	103.12 W
Chapala, Laguna de ⊜	234	20.15 N	103.00 W
Chapare ≃, Bol.	248	15.58 S	64.42 W
Chapare ≃, Bol.	248	16.25 S	64.35 W
Chapareillan	62	45.28 N	5.58 E
Chāparmukh	120	26.12 N	92.32 E
Chaparra, Bahía de ⊂	240p	21.13 N	76.31 W
Chaparral	246	3.43 N	75.28 W
Chapayeve	78	49.21 N	35.54 E
Chapayevka, Ukr.	78	49.33 N	32.06 E
Chapayevka, Ukr.	78	47.29 N	36.20 E
Chapčeranga	88	49.42 N	112.24 E
Chapeauroux	62	44.50 N	3.44 E
Chapecó	252	27.06 S	52.36 W
Chapel-en-le-Frith	44	53.20 N	1.54 W
Chapelfell Top ∧	44	54.41 N	2.13 W
Chapelhall	46	55.50 N	3.56 W
Chapel Hill, De., U.S.	285	39.42 N	75.44 W
Chapel Hill, N.C., U.S.	192	35.54 N	79.03 W
Chapel Hill, Tn., U.S.	194	35.37 N	86.41 W
Chapel Hill Channel ⋓	276	40.32 N	74.02 W
Chapelle Creek ≃	198	44.16 N	99.55 W
Chapellerie	261	49.02 N	2.26 E
Chapel Oaks	284c	38.54 N	76.55 W
Chapel Point ›	42	50.16 N	4.46 W
Chapel Saint Leonards	44	53.13 N	0.19 E
Chapelton	241q	18.05 N	77.16 W
Chapeltown, Eng., U.K.	44	53.28 N	1.28 W
Chapeltown, Eng., U.K.	262	53.38 N	2.24 W
Chapet	261	48.58 N	1.56 E
Chapéu, Morro do ∧	255	14.55 S	42.31 W
Chapéu, Ribeirão do ≃	256	23.14 S	45.18 W
Chapicuy	252	31.39 S	57.54 W
Chapimarca	248	13.58 S	73.04 W
Chapin	219	39.46 N	90.24 W
Chapin, Lake ⊜	216	41.56 N	86.21 W
Chaplain, Lake ⊜[1]	224	47.57 N	121.51 W
Chapleau	190	47.50 N	83.24 W
Chapleau ≃	190	48.29 N	82.57 W
Chapleau, Lac ⊜	206	46.14 N	74.57 W
Chaplin, Sk., Can.	184	50.28 N	106.40 W
Chaplin, Ct., U.S.	207	41.47 N	72.07 W
Chaplin ≃	194	37.50 N	85.11 W
Chaplin Lake ⊜	184	50.18 N	106.35 W
Chapliyivka	78	51.43 N	33.12 E
Chaplyne	78	48.09 N	36.14 E
Chaplynka	78	46.23 N	33.32 E
Chapman, Ks., U.S.	198	38.58 N	97.01 W
Chapman, Ne., U.S.	198	41.01 N	98.09 W
Chapman, Pa., U.S.	208	40.46 N	75.24 W
Chapman, Cape ›	176	69.12 N	88.59 W
Chapman, Mount ∧	182	51.50 N	118.20 W
Chapman College ʊ[2]	280	33.47 N	117.51 W
Chapman Creek ≃	198	38.58 N	97.00 W
Chapman Lake ⊜	184	56.58 N	98.12 W
Chapman's (Okwa) ≃	156	22.30 S	23.00 E
Chapmanville	188	37.58 N	82.01 W
Chapman Woods	280	34.08 N	118.05 W
Chapo	196	29.17 N	104.20 W
Chaponval	261	49.04 N	2.09 E
Chappaqua	210	41.09 N	73.45 W
Chappell	198	41.05 N	102.28 W
Chappell Hill	222	30.09 N	96.16 W
Chāpra	126	23.32 N	88.33 E
Chapry	83	47.14 N	39.31 E
Chaptico Bay ⊂	208	38.21 N	76.49 W
Chapultepec, Méx.	204	31.50 N	116.38 W
Chapultepec, Méx.	204	32.22 N	115.05 W
Chapultepec, Bosque de ♠	286a	19.25 N	99.12 W
Chapultepec, Castillo de ⊥	286a	19.25 N	99.11 W
Chá Pungana	152	13.44 S	18.39 E
Chaqui	248	19.36 S	65.32 W
Chaquiago	252	27.32 S	66.21 W
Char ≃	42	50.44 N	2.53 W
Char ⍑[4]	148	21.31 N	12.51 W
Charaa ≃	88	49.38 N	105.49 E
Charabali	80	47.24 N	47.16 E
Chara-Chužar	88	52.30 N	99.39 E
Charadai	252	27.38 S	59.54 W
Charagauli	84	42.01 N	43.12 E
Charagua	248	19.48 S	63.13 W
Charagun	88	51.36 N	111.05 E
Char-Ajrag	102	45.49 N	109.17 E
Charal	88	51.58 N	96.39 E
Charalá	246	6.17 N	73.10 W
Charām	128	30.45 N	50.44 E
Charaña	248	17.36 S	69.28 W
Charanor	88	50.05 N	116.40 E
Charanpur	126	23.45 N	87.02 E
Charapán	234	19.41 N	102.06 W
Charapucu, Ilha I	250	0.18 S	50.48 W
Charata	252	27.13 S	61.12 W
Charauz	88	52.16 N	106.17 E
Charavines-les-Bains	62	45.26 N	5.31 E
Charazani → Amarete	248	15.14 S	68.58 W
Charazargaj	88	52.57 N	104.41 E
Charbala	74	64.07 N	120.19 E
Char Bansi	126	22.59 N	90.43 E
Charbatovo	88	53.46 N	106.00 E
Charbon	170	32.54 S	149.58 E
Charcana	248	15.15 S	73.04 W
Charcas	234	23.08 N	101.07 W
Charco Azul, Bahía de ⊂	236	8.15 N	82.45 W
Charco Hondo	240m	18.25 N	66.43 W
Charcos de Figueroa	232	27.45 N	102.11 W
Charcos de Risa	232	26.15 N	103.10 W
Charcot Island I	9	69.45 S	75.15 W
Chard	42	50.53 N	2.58 W
Chardon	214	41.36 N	81.08 W
Charduār	120	26.52 N	92.46 E
Chardzhou → Čardžou	128	39.06 N	63.34 E
Charef, Oued V	148	34.07 N	2.05 W
Charente □[5]	32	45.40 N	0.10 E
Charente ≃	32	45.57 N	1.05 W
Charente-Maritime □[5]	32	45.30 N	0.45 W
Charenton-du-Cher	32	46.44 N	2.38 E
Charenton-le-Pont	261	48.49 N	2.25 E
Charentonne ≃	50	49.07 N	0.44 E
Charest ≃	206	46.36 N	72.14 W
Chārghāt	126	24.17 N	88.45 E
Char Hāim	126	23.04 N	90.38 E
Chari ≃	146	12.58 N	14.31 E
Chariāl Canal ≊	272b	22.28 N	88.11 E
Chari-Baguirmi □[5]	146	11.30 N	16.30 E
Charik	88	54.15 N	101.39 E
Chārīkār	120	35.01 N	69.11 E
Charing	42	51.13 N	0.48 E
Charing Cross	214	42.20 N	82.06 W
Charino, Ross.	76	59.57 N	43.44 E
Charino, Ross.	82	54.33 N	37.52 E
Charistvala	84	42.26 N	43.02 E
Chariton	190	41.00 N	93.18 W
Chariton ≃	194	39.19 N	92.57 W
Chariton, Mussel Fork ≃	194	39.24 N	92.55 W
Charitonovo, Ross.	24	61.27 N	47.28 E
Charitonovo, Ross.	82	56.52 N	36.44 E
Charity	246	7.24 N	58.36 W
Charkhāri	124	25.24 N	79.45 E
Charkhi Dādri	124	28.37 N	76.16 E
Char'kin	80	48.46 N	51.49 E
Charkop ◆[8]	272c	19.13 N	72.49 E
Charkow → Kharkiv	78	50.00 N	36.15 E
Char Lākhpur	126	24.04 N	90.40 E
Charland, Lac ⊜	206	46.52 N	74.11 W
Charlbury	42	51.53 N	1.29 W
Charl Cilliers	158	26.39 S	29.12 E
Charlemagne	206	45.43 N	73.29 W
Charlemont	207	42.37 N	72.52 W
Charleroi, Bel.	50	50.25 N	4.26 E
Charleroi, Pa., U.S.	214	40.08 N	79.53 W
Charleroi à Bruxelles, Canal de ≊	50	50.51 N	4.19 E
Charles □[6]	208	38.32 N	76.59 W
Charles ≃	207	42.22 N	71.03 W
Charles, Cape ›	208	37.08 N	75.58 W
Charles, Lake ⊜	278	42.15 N	87.58 W
Charles, Peak ∧	162	32.52 S	121.11 E
Charlesbourg	206	46.51 N	71.16 W
Charles Branch ≃	284c	38.47 N	76.48 W
Charles City, Ia., U.S.	190	43.03 N	92.40 W
Charles City, Va., U.S.	208	37.20 N	77.04 W
Charles City □[6]	208	37.20 N	77.02 W
Charles de Gaulle, Aéroport ⊠	50	49.01 N	2.33 E
Charles Island I	176	62.40 N	74.15 W
Charles Lee Tilden Regional Park ♠	282	37.54 N	122.15 W
Charles Mill Lake ⊜[1]	214	40.45 N	82.22 W
Charles Mound ∧[2]	190	42.30 N	90.14 W
Charles Point ›	164	12.23 S	130.36 E
Charles Sound ⋓	172	45.02 S	167.04 E
Charleston, Austl.	168b	34.55 S	138.54 E
Charleston, N.Z.	172	41.54 S	171.26 E
Charleston, Ar., U.S.	194	35.17 N	94.02 W
Charleston, Il., U.S.	194	39.29 N	88.10 W
Charleston, Ms., U.S.	194	34.00 N	90.03 W
Charleston, Mo., U.S.	194	36.55 N	89.21 W
Charleston, S.C., U.S.	192	32.46 N	79.55 W
Charleston, W.V., U.S.	188	38.20 N	81.37 W
Charleston Air Force Base ■	192	32.55 N	80.03 W
Charleston Lake ⊜	212	44.32 N	76.00 W
Charleston Peak ∧	204	36.16 N	115.42 W
Charlestown, Austl.	170	32.58 S	151.42 E
Charlestown, Ire.	48	53.57 N	8.49 W
Charlestown, St. K.-N.	238	17.08 N	62.37 W
Charlestown, S. Afr.	158	27.30 S	29.55 E
Charlestown, In., U.S.	218	38.27 N	85.40 W
Charlestown, Md., U.S.	208	39.34 N	75.58 W
Charlestown, N.H., U.S.	188	43.14 N	72.25 W
Charlestown, Pa., U.S.	285	40.06 N	75.33 W
Charlestown, R.I., U.S.	207	41.22 N	71.38 W
Charles Town, W.V., U.S.	188	39.17 N	77.51 W
Charlestown ◆[8]	283	42.23 N	71.04 W
Charlestown of Aberlour	46	57.28 N	3.14 W
Charlesworth	262	53.26 N	1.59 W
Charleville, Austl.	166	26.24 S	146.15 E
Charleville → Ráth Luirc, Ire.	48	52.21 N	8.41 W
Charleville-Mézières	56	49.46 N	4.43 E
Charlevoix	190	45.19 N	85.15 W
Charlevoix, Lake ⊜	190	45.15 N	85.08 W
Charley ≃	180	65.20 N	142.49 W
Charlie Bluff	216	42.50 N	88.58 W
Charlie Creek ≃	220	27.21 N	81.49 W
Charlie Lake	182	56.16 N	120.57 W
Charlieu	32	46.10 N	4.10 E
Charlotte, Mi., U.S.	216	42.33 N	84.50 W
Charlotte, N.C., U.S.	192	35.13 N	80.50 W
Charlotte, Tn., U.S.	194	36.10 N	87.20 W
Charlotte, Tx., U.S.	196	28.51 N	98.42 W
Charlotte □[6]	220	26.54 N	81.58 W
Charlotte Amalie	240m	18.21 N	64.56 W
Charlotte Court House	192	37.03 N	78.39 W
Charlotte Creek ≃	210	42.27 N	75.01 W
Charlotte Harbor	220	26.57 N	82.04 W
Charlotte Harbor ⊂	220	26.45 N	82.12 W
Charlotte Lake ⊜	182	52.11 N	125.20 W
Charlottenberg	26	59.53 N	12.17 E
Charlottenburg ◆[8]	264a	52.31 N	13.16 E
Charlottenburg, Schloss ⊥	264a	52.31 N	13.14 E
Charlottesburg Reservoir ⊜[1]	276	41.02 N	74.26 W
Charlottes Pass ♠	171b	36.25 S	145.20 E
Charlottesville, In., U.S.	218	39.47 N	85.36 W
Charlottesville, Va., U.S.	192	38.01 N	78.28 W
Charlottetown	186	46.14 N	63.08 W
Charlotteville	210	42.33 N	74.40 W
Charlovka	24	68.47 N	37.15 E
Charlton, Austl.	166	36.16 S	143.21 E
Charlton, Ma., U.S.	207	42.08 N	71.58 W
Charlton ◆[8]	260	51.29 N	0.02 E
Charlton City	207	42.08 N	71.59 W
Charlton Island I	176	52.00 N	79.30 W
Charlton Kings	42	51.53 N	2.03 W
Charlu	24	61.48 N	30.52 E
Charly-sur-Marne	50	48.58 N	3.17 E
Charm	214	40.30 N	81.47 W
Charmentray	261	48.57 N	2.47 E
Charmes	58	48.22 N	6.17 E
Charmes-sur-Rhône	62	44.52 N	4.50 E
Charmey	58	46.38 N	7.10 E
Charminster	42	50.43 N	2.28 W
Charmois-l'Orgueilleux	58	48.06 N	6.16 E
Charmont-en-Beauce	50	48.14 N	2.06 E
Charmouth	42	50.45 N	2.55 W
Charnay-lès-Mâcon	58	46.18 N	4.47 E
Charneca	266c	38.44 N	9.27 W
Charneca ◆[8]	266c	38.47 N	9.08 W
Charnley ≃	164	16.25 S	124.57 E
Charnock Richard	262	53.38 N	2.41 W
Char nuur ⊜, Mong.	88	48.06 N	93.12 E
Char nuur ⊜, Mong.	88	48.20 N	96.05 E
Charnwood Forest ◆[3]	42	52.43 N	1.15 W
Charny, P.Q., Can.	206	46.43 N	71.16 W
Charny, Fr.	50	47.53 N	3.06 E
Charny, Fr.	261	48.58 N	2.46 E
Charny-sur-Meuse	56	49.12 N	5.22 E
Charo	234	19.45 N	101.03 W
Charolles	32	46.26 N	4.17 E
Charouine	148	29.01 N	0.16 W
Charovsk	76	59.59 N	40.11 E
Charpi ≃	89	49.40 N	136.10 E
Charquemont	58	47.13 N	6.49 E
Charred Oak Estates	284c	39.00 N	77.10 W
Charrette Creek ≃	219	38.37 N	91.03 W
Charron Lake ⊜	184	52.45 N	95.15 W
Charroux	32	46.09 N	0.24 E
Chars	50	49.10 N	1.56 E
Chārsadda	123	34.09 N	71.44 E
Charter Oak, Ca., U.S.	280	34.06 N	117.52 W
Charter Oak, Ia., U.S.	198	42.04 N	95.35 W
Charters Towers	166	20.05 S	146.16 E
Charterwood	279b	40.33 N	80.00 W
Chartiers Creek ≃	214	40.28 N	80.03 W
Chartiers Run ≃, Pa., U.S.	279b	40.36 N	79.43 W
Chartiers Run ≃, Pa., U.S.	279b	40.15 N	80.12 W
Chartley	207	41.56 N	71.13 W
Chartres	50	48.27 N	1.30 E
Chartrettes	50	48.29 N	2.42 E
Chartridge	260	51.44 N	0.39 W
Chart Sutton	260	51.13 N	0.35 E
Chartwell ⊥	260	51.14 N	0.05 E
Char Us nuur ⊜	90	48.00 N	92.10 E
Charutajuvom	24	66.49 N	59.30 E
Chās	126	23.38 N	86.10 E
Chasav'urt	84	43.15 N	46.37 E
Chascomús	258	35.34 S	58.01 W
Chascomús, Laguna ⊜	258	35.36 S	58.01 W
Chašdala	85	39.42 N	67.07 E
Chase, B.C., Can.	182	50.49 N	119.41 W
Chase, Ak., U.S.	180	62.27 N	150.07 W
Chase, Ks., U.S.	198	38.21 N	98.20 W
Chase, Md., U.S.	208	39.21 N	76.22 W
Chase, Mount ∧	188	46.07 N	68.29 W
Chase Brook ≃	283	42.48 N	71.27 W
Chase City	192	36.47 N	78.27 W
Chase Field Naval Air Station ■	196	28.21 N	97.40 W
Chasefu	154	11.55 S	33.08 E
Chase Lake	212	43.46 N	75.19 W
Chase River	224	49.08 N	123.55 W
Chashma Barrage ◆[6]	123	32.26 N	71.23 E
Chasicó	254	40.18 S	68.58 W
Chasidaba	104	42.19 N	121.19 E
Chasiv Yar	83	48.35 N	37.50 E
Chaska	190	44.47 N	93.36 W
Chaslands Mistake ›	172	46.38 S	169.22 E
Chasŏng	98	41.27 N	126.37 E
Chasŏngganggu	98	41.34 N	126.36 E
Chassahowitzka	220	28.43 N	82.34 W
Chassahowitzka Bay ⊂	220	28.41 N	82.40 W
Chassahowitzka Swamp ≡	220	28.38 N	82.37 W
Chasseron, Mont ∧	58	46.51 N	6.33 E
Chasse-sur-Rhône	62	45.34 N	4.49 E
Chassezac ≃	62	44.26 N	4.19 E
Chašuri	84	42.00 N	43.36 E
Chasurta	88	52.17 N	108.52 E
Chasuta	248	6.35 S	76.11 W
Chāt	128	37.59 N	55.16 E
Chatanbulag	102	43.09 N	109.08 E
Chatanga	74	71.58 N	102.30 E
Chatanga ≃	74	72.55 N	106.00 E
Chatangskij zaliv ⊂	74	73.30 N	109.00 E
Chatanika	180	65.07 N	147.31 W
Chatanika ≃	180	65.04 N	149.18 W
Château-Arnoux	62	44.06 N	6.00 E
Chateaubelair	241h	13.17 N	61.15 W
Châteaubriant	32	47.43 N	1.23 W
Château-Chinon	32	47.04 N	3.56 E
Château d'Oex	58	46.28 N	7.08 E
Château-du-Loir	50	47.42 N	0.25 E
Châteaudun	50	48.05 N	1.20 E
Châteaufort	261	48.44 N	2.06 E
Chateaugay	206	44.55 N	74.04 W
Château-Gontier	32	47.50 N	0.42 W
Châteauguay	206	45.23 N	73.45 W
Châteauguay □[6]	206	45.15 N	73.45 W
Châteauguay ≃	188	45.24 N	73.45 W
Châteauguay-Centre	206	45.21 N	73.45 W
Châteauguay Heights	275a	45.23 N	73.44 W
Château-Landon	50	48.09 N	2.42 E
Château-la-Vallière	50	47.33 N	0.19 E
Châteaulin	32	48.12 N	4.05 W
Châteaumeillant	32	46.34 N	2.12 E
Châteauneuf	62	43.23 N	5.10 E
Châteauneuf-de-Randon	62	44.39 N	3.40 E
Châteauneuf-du-Pape	62	44.03 N	4.50 E
Châteauneuf-du-Rhône	62	44.29 N	4.43 E
Châteauneuf-en-Thymerais	50	48.35 N	1.15 E
Châteauneuf-sur-Charente	32	45.36 N	0.03 W
Châteauneuf-sur-Loire	50	47.52 N	2.14 E
Châteauneuf-sur-Sarthe	32	47.41 N	0.30 W
Châteauneuf-Val-de-Bargis	50	47.17 N	3.14 E
Château-Porcien	50	49.32 N	4.15 E
Château-Queyras	62	44.45 N	6.47 E
Châteauredon	62	44.01 N	6.13 E
Châteaurenard, Fr.	50	47.56 N	2.56 E
Châteaurenard, Fr.	62	43.53 N	4.51 E
Château-Renault	50	47.35 N	0.55 E
Château-Richer	186	46.58 N	71.01 W
Châteauroux	32	46.49 N	1.42 E
Château-Salins	56	48.49 N	6.30 E
Château-Thierry	50	49.03 N	3.24 E
Châteauvillain	58	48.02 N	4.55 E
Châtel	58	46.17 N	6.50 E
Châtel-Censoir	50	47.31 N	3.38 E
Châtelet	50	50.24 N	4.31 E
Châtelineau	56	50.25 N	4.31 E
Châtellerault	32	46.49 N	0.33 E
Châtel-Saint-Denis	58	46.32 N	6.54 E
Châtel-sur-Moselle	58	48.18 N	6.24 E
Châtelus-Malvaleix	32	46.18 N	2.01 E
Châtenay-en-France	261	49.04 N	2.27 E
Châtenay-Malabry	261	48.46 N	2.17 E
Châtenois, Fr.	58	48.18 N	5.50 E
Châtenois, Fr.	58	48.16 N	7.24 E
Châtenois-les-Forges	58	47.34 N	6.51 E
Chater ≃	42	52.38 N	0.32 W
Chatfield, Mn., U.S.	190	43.50 N	92.11 W
Chatfield, Oh., U.S.	214	40.57 N	82.56 W
Chatgal	88	50.26 N	100.09 E
Chatham, N.B., Can.	186	47.02 N	65.28 W
Chatham, On., Can.	214	42.24 N	82.11 W
Chatham, Eng., U.K.	42	51.23 N	0.32 E
Chatham, Il., U.S.	219	39.40 N	89.42 W
Chatham, La., U.S.	194	32.18 N	92.27 W
Chatham, Ma., U.S.	207	41.40 N	69.57 W
Chatham, N.J., U.S.	210	40.44 N	74.23 W
Chatham, N.Y., U.S.	210	42.21 N	73.35 W
Chatham, Oh., U.S.	214	41.06 N	82.01 W
Chatham, Pa., U.S.	208	39.51 N	75.49 W
Chatham, Va., U.S.	192	36.49 N	79.23 W
Chatham ◆[8]	278	41.45 N	87.37 W
Chatham ≃	220	25.42 N	81.17 W
Chatham, Isla I	254	50.40 S	74.20 W
Chatham Head	186	47.00 N	65.33 W
Chatham Islands II	14	43.55 S	176.30 W
Chatham Rise ✦[3]	14	43.30 S	178.00 W
Chatham Sound ⋓	182	54.32 N	130.35 W
Chatham Strait ⋓	180	57.30 N	134.45 W
Chatian	100	27.54 N	118.58 E
Châtillon, Fr.	261	48.48 N	2.17 E
Châtillon, It.	62	45.45 N	7.37 E
Châtillon-Coligny	50	47.50 N	2.51 E
Châtillon-en-Bazois	32	47.03 N	3.40 E
Châtillon-en-Diois	62	44.41 N	5.28 E
Châtillon-la-Borde	261	48.33 N	2.49 E
Châtillon-sur-Chalaronne	58	46.07 N	4.58 E
Châtillon-sur-Indre	32	46.59 N	1.11 E
Châtillon-sur-Loire	50	47.35 N	2.45 E
Châtillon-sur-Marne	50	49.06 N	3.45 E
Châtillon-sur-Seine	58	47.51 N	4.33 E
Chating	106	31.21 N	119.25 E
Chātmohar	126	24.13 N	89.15 E
Chat Moss ◆[3]	262	53.27 N	2.27 W
Chato, Cerro ∧	254	42.29 S	72.01 W
Chatom	194	31.27 N	88.15 W
Chatonville	261	48.33 N	1.52 E
Chatou	261	48.54 N	2.09 E
Chatpur ◆[8]	272b	22.36 N	88.22 E
Chatra, India	124	24.13 N	84.52 E
Chatra, India	272b	22.46 N	88.20 E
Châtres	261	48.43 N	2.49 E
Chats, Lac des ⊜	212	45.28 N	76.23 W
Chatsquot Mountain ∧	182	53.08 N	127.30 W
Chatswood	274a	33.48 S	151.12 E
Chatsworth, Austl.	166	21.58 S	140.19 E
Chatsworth, On., Can.	212	44.27 N	80.54 W
Chatsworth, Ga., U.S.	192	34.45 N	84.46 W
Chatsworth, Il., U.S.	216	40.45 N	88.17 W
Chatsworth, N.J., U.S.	208	39.49 N	74.32 W
Chatsworth, Zimb.	154	19.38 S	31.13 E
Chatsworth ◆[8]	280	34.15 N	118.36 W
Chatsworth House ʊ	44	53.13 N	1.36 W
Chatsworth Reservoir ⊜[1]	228	34.14 N	118.37 W
Chattahoochee	192	30.42 N	84.50 W
Chattahoochee ≃	192	30.52 N	84.57 W
Chattanooga, Oh., U.S.	216	40.38 N	84.47 W
Chattanooga, Tn., U.S.	194	35.02 N	85.18 W
Chattaroy	192	37.42 N	82.16 W
Chattenden	260	51.25 N	0.32 E
Chatteris	42	52.27 N	0.03 E
Châttillon-de-Michaille	58	46.08 N	5.47 E
Chattolanee	284b	39.24 N	76.45 W
Chatton	44	55.33 N	1.55 W
Chatun'	82	55.00 N	37.50 E
Chaturat	110	15.34 N	101.51 E
Chatwood	208	39.58 N	75.35 W
Chatyrka	74	62.03 N	175.15 E
Chaubaria	126	22.59 N	88.40 E
Chaubourg, Mount ∧[2]	241f	14.02 N	60.57 W
Chauconin	261	48.58 N	2.51 E
Chaudes-Aigues	32	44.51 N	3.00 E
Chaudfontaine	56	50.35 N	5.38 E
Chaudière ≃	186	46.45 N	71.17 W
Chau Doc	110	10.42 N	105.07 E
Chauekuktuli, Lake ⊜	180	60.03 N	158.45 W
Chauffayer	62	44.45 N	6.01 E
Chaugācha, Bngl.	126	23.16 N	89.01 E
Chaugācha, Bngl.	126	23.16 N	89.01 E
Chauhtan	120	25.29 N	71.04 E
Chauk	110	20.54 N	94.50 E
Chaukhandi	272a	28.37 N	77.24 E
Chaullay	248	12.57 S	72.39 W
Chaulnes	50	49.49 N	2.48 E
Chaumergy	58	46.51 N	5.29 E
Chaumes-en-Brie	261	48.40 N	2.51 E
Chaumont, Fr.	58	48.07 N	5.08 E
Chaumont, N.Y., U.S.	212	44.04 N	76.07 W
Chaumont ≃	212	44.04 N	76.08 W
Chaumont Bay ⊂	212	44.02 N	76.13 W
Chaumont-en-Vexin	50	49.16 N	1.53 E
Chaumont-Porcien	50	49.39 N	4.15 E
Chaumont-sur-Aire	56	48.56 N	5.15 E
Chaumont-sur-Loire	50	47.29 N	1.11 E
Chaumont-sur-Tharonne	50	47.37 N	1.54 E
Chaumua	272b	22.39 N	88.33 E
Chauncey	188	39.23 N	82.07 W
Chaŭn-do I	98	34.53 N	126.03 E
Chaungwabyin	110	13.41 N	98.22 E
Chaungzon	110	16.22 N	97.32 E
Chauny	50	49.37 N	3.13 E
Chaupāran	124	24.23 N	85.15 E
Chaussin	58	46.58 N	5.25 E
Chausu-yama ∧	94	35.14 N	137.39 E
Chausuyama-kofun ⊥	94	36.25 N	139.50 E
Chautārā	124	27.46 N	85.42 E
Chautauqua	214	42.12 N	79.28 W
Chautauqua □[6]	214	42.15 N	79.30 W
Chautauqua Creek ≃	214	42.20 N	79.36 W
Chautauqua Lake ⊜	214	42.12 N	79.27 W
Chautengo, Laguna ⊂	234	16.37 N	99.07 W
Chauvigny	32	46.34 N	0.39 E
Chauvin, Ab., Can.	184	52.42 N	110.07 W
Chauvin, La., U.S.	194	29.26 N	90.35 W
Chauvirey-le-Châtel	58	47.47 N	5.45 E
Chauvry	261	49.03 N	2.16 E
Chavakkad	122	10.32 N	76.06 E
Chaval	250	3.02 S	41.15 W
Chavanges	58	48.31 N	4.34 E
Chavannes, Lac ⊜	190	46.51 N	77.10 W
Chavarría, Arg.	252	28.57 S	58.35 W
Chavarría, Perú	286d	12.01 S	77.05 W
Chavast	85	40.13 N	68.50 E
Chavenay	261	48.51 N	1.59 E
Chavenay-Villepreux, Aérodrome de ⊠	261	48.51 N	1.58 E
Chavertovo	82	54.17 N	39.12 E
Chaves, Bra.	250	0.10 S	49.55 W
Chaves, Port.	34	41.44 N	7.28 W
Chaville	261	48.48 N	2.10 E
Chaviña	248	14.59 S	73.50 W
Cháviva	246	4.22 N	72.20 W
Chavki	82	54.20 N	38.13 E
Chavornay	58	46.43 N	6.34 E
Chavuma	152	13.05 S	22.40 E
Chawa'nanake	120	31.36 N	89.41 E
Chawang	110	8.25 N	99.30 E
Chawinda	123	32.21 N	74.42 E
Chay ≃	110	21.39 N	105.12 E
Chayanta	248	18.27 S	66.30 W
Chayuan, Zhg.	100	29.20 N	121.34 E
Chayuan, Zhg.	100	27.40 N	112.57 E
Chayue	106	30.49 N	119.21 E
Chazay-d'Azergues	62	45.53 N	4.37 E
Chazelles-sur-Lyon	62	45.38 N	4.23 E
Chazratišoch, chrebet ⋏	85	38.30 N	70.15 E
Chazy	188	44.53 N	73.26 W
Chbar ≃	110	13.19 N	107.05 E
Cheadle, Eng., U.K.	42	52.59 N	1.59 W
Cheadle, Eng., U.K.	44	53.24 N	2.13 W
Cheadle Hulme	262	53.22 N	2.12 W
Cheaha Mountain ∧	194	33.30 N	85.47 W
Cheakamus Indian Reserve ◆[4]	182	49.48 N	123.11 W
Cheam ◆[8]	260	51.21 N	0.13 W
Cheam View	224	49.15 N	121.41 W
Cheapside	222	29.17 N	97.24 W
Cheat ≃	188	39.45 N	79.54 W
Cheat, Shavers Fork ≃	188	39.06 N	79.33 W

Symbols in the index entries represent the broad categories identified in the key at the right. Symbols with superior numbers (⋏[1]) identify subcategories (see complete key on page *I · 1).*

Symbole im Register stellen die rechts im Schlüssel erklärten Kategorien dar. Symbole mit hochgestellten Ziffern (⋏[1]) bezeichnen Unterabteilungen einer Kategorie (vgl. vollständiger Schlüssel auf Seite *I · 1).*

Los símbolos incluídos en el texto del índice representan las grandes categorías identificadas con la clave a la derecha. Los símbolos con numeros en su parte superior (⋏[1]) identifican las subcategorías (véase la clave completa en la página *I · 1).*

Les symboles de l'index représentent les catégories indiquées dans la légende à droite. Les symboles suivis d'un indice (⋏[1]) représentent des sous-catégories (voir légende complète à la page *I · 1).*

Os símbolos incluídos no texto do índice representam as grandes categorias identificadas com a chave à direita. Os símbolos com números em sua parte superior (⋏[1]) identificam as subcategorias (veja-se a chave completa à página *I · 1).*

∧ Mountain	Berg	Montaña	Montagne	Montanha
⋏ Mountains	Gebirge	Montañas	Montagnes	Montanhas
)(Pass	Paß	Paso	Col	Passo
V Valley, Canyon	Tal, Cañon	Valle, Cañón	Vallée, Canyon	Vale, Canhão
≚ Plain	Ebene	Llano	Plaine	Planície
› Cape	Kap	Cabo	Cap	Cabo
I Island	Insel	Isla	Île	Ilha
II Islands	Inseln	Islas	Îles	Ilhas
⊥ Other Topographic Features	Andere Topographische Objekte	Otros Elementos Topográficos	Autres données topographiques	Outros acidentes topográficos

ESPAÑOL				FRANÇAIS				PORTUGUÊS			
Nombre	Página	Lat.° ′	Long.° ′ W = Oeste	Nom	Page	Lat.° ′	Long.° ′ W = Ouest	Nome	Página	Lat.° ′	Long.° ′ W = Oeste

Legend (bottom of page):

Symbol	English	Deutsch	Español/Français/Portuguese
☈	River	Fluß	Rio / Rivière / Rio
☰	Canal	Kanal	Canal / Canal / Canal
☩	Waterfall, Rapids	Wasserfall, Stromschnellen	Cascada, Rápidos / Chute d'eau, Rapides / Cascata, Rápidos
☩	Strait	Meeresstraße	Estrecho / Détroit / Estreito
c	Bay, Gulf	Bucht, Golf	Bahía, Golfo / Baie, Golfe / Baía, Golfo
☺	Lake, Lakes	See, Seen	Lago, Lagos / Lac, Lacs / Lago, Lagos
☈	Swamp	Sumpf	Pantano / Marais / Pântano
⋈	Ice Features, Glacier	Eis- und Gletscherformen	Accidentes Glaciales / Formes glaciaires / Acidentes glaciares
❖	Other Hydrographic Features	Andere Hydrographische Objekte	Otros Elementos Hidrográficos / Autres données hydrographiques / Outros acidentes hidrográficos

◆	Submarine Features	Untermeerische Objekte	Accidentes Submarinos / Formes de relief sous-marin / Acidentes submarinos
◻	Political Unit	Politische Einheit	Unidad Política / Entité politique / Unidade política
◀	Cultural Institution	Kulturelle Institution	Institución Cultural / Institution culturelle / Instituição cultural
⊥	Historical Site	Historische Stätte	Sitio Histórico / Site historique / Sítio histórico
♦	Recreational Site	Erholungs- und Ferienort	Sitio de Recreo / Centre de loisirs / Área de Lazer
▹	Airport	Flughafen	Aeropuerto / Aéroport / Aeroporto
▪	Military Installation	Militäranlage	Instalación Militar / Installation militaire / Instalação militar
◆	Miscellaneous	Verschiedenes	Misceláneo / Divers / Diversos

Name	Page	Lat.°′	Long.°′
Chikodi	122	16.26 N	74.36 E
Chikou	100	30.44 N	117.32 E
Chikrêng ≃	110	12.51 N	104.14 E
Ch'iku	100	23.08 N	120.07 E
Chikugo	96	33.12 N	130.30 E
Chikugo ≃	92	33.09 N	130.21 E
Chikujō-kichi, Kōkū-jieitai- ■	96	33.41 N	131.03 E
Chikuma ≃	94	36.59 N	138.35 E
Chikuminuk Lake ⊜	180	60.14 N	159.00 W
Chikura	94	34.57 N	139.57 E
Chikusa	96	35.09 N	134.26 E
Chikusa ≃	96	34.44 N	134.24 E
Chikushino	96	33.29 N	130.31 E
Chikwawa	154	16.03 S	34.48 E
Chi-kyaw	110	20.17 N	93.54 E
Chikyu-misaki ⲻ	92a	42.18 N	141.00 E
Chila	152	12.04 S	14.29 E
Chilacachapa	234	18.17 N	99.43 W
Chilakalūrupet	122	16.05 N	80.10 E
Chilako ≃	182	53.54 N	122.59 W
Chilam Chauki	123	35.03 N	75.07 E
Chilanga	154	15.34 S	28.17 E
Chilanko Forks	182	52.06 N	124.10 W
Chilapa de Álvarez	234	17.36 N	99.10 W
Chilās	123	35.26 N	74.05 E
Chilaw	122	7.34 N	79.47 E
Chilca, Perú	248	12.32 S	76.44 W
Chilca, Perú	248	12.09 S	75.11 W
Chilca, Punta ⲻ	248	12.27 S	76.48 W
Chilchota	234	19.51 N	102.08 W
Chilcotin ≃	182	51.45 N	122.24 W
Chilcott Island I	166	16.58 S	149.58 E
Childers	166	25.14 S	152.17 E
Childersburg	194	33.16 N	86.21 W
Childer Thornton	262	53.17 N	2.57 W
Childress	196	34.25 N	100.12 W
Childs	210	41.34 N	75.32 W
Chile □[1]	244	30.00 S	71.00 W
Chile, Hipódromo ♦	286e	33.24 S	70.41 W
Chile, Universidad de ʊ[2]	286e	33.27 S	70.40 W
Chile Basin ✣[1]	18	33.00 S	80.00 W
Chile Chico	254	46.33 S	71.44 W
Chilecito, Arg.	252	29.10 S	67.30 W
Chilecito, Arg.	252	33.53 S	69.03 W
Chilengue, Serra do ⋏	152	13.10 S	15.18 E
Chileno, Arroyo ≃, Ur.	258	33.55 S	58.08 W
Chileno, Arroyo ≃, Ur.	288	34.22 S	57.54 W
Chile Rise ✣[3]	18	40.00 S	90.00 W
Chilete	248	7.14 S	78.51 W
Chilham	42	51.15 N	0.57 E
Chilhowie	192	36.47 N	81.40 W
Chili	216	40.52 N	86.02 W
Chili → Chile □[1]	244	30.00 S	71.00 W
Chili ≃	248	16.23 S	71.46 W
Chili, Ouadi V	146	16.44 N	20.53 E
Chilia, Braţul ≃[1]	78	45.18 N	29.40 E
Chili Center	210	43.06 N	77.44 W
Chilika Lake ⊜	122	19.45 N	85.25 E
Chililabombwe (Bancroft)	154	12.18 S	27.43 E
Chilin → Jilin	89	43.51 N	126.33 E
Chilingchang	107	28.58 N	105.31 E
Chilivani	71	40.36 N	8.56 E
Chilkat Pass)(	180	59.43 N	136.35 W
Chilko ≃	182	52.08 N	123.30 W
Chilko Lake ⊜	182	51.20 N	124.05 W
Chilko Lake Indian Reserve ⬥[4]	182	51.25 N	124.07 W
Chillagoe	166	17.09 S	144.32 E
Chillán	252	36.36 S	72.07 W
Chillar	252	37.18 S	59.59 W
Chilla Saroda ⬥[8]	272a	28.36 N	77.18 E
Chillicothe, Il., U.S.	190	40.55 N	89.29 W
Chillicothe, Mo., U.S.	194	39.47 N	93.33 W
Chillicothe, Oh., U.S.	218	39.19 N	82.58 W
Chillicothe, Tx., U.S.	196	34.15 N	99.30 W
Chilliwack	224	49.10 N	121.57 W
Chilliwack ≃	224	49.05 N	121.57 W
Chilliwack Lake ⊜	224	49.03 N	121.25 W
Chillón	286d	11.55 S	77.05 W
Chillón ≃	248	11.57 S	77.09 W
Chillon, Château de ⊥	58	46.25 N	6.56 E
Chillum	284c	38.58 N	76.59 W
Chilly-Mazarin	261	48.42 N	2.19 E
Chilmāri	124	25.33 N	89.43 E
Chilmark	207	41.20 N	70.44 W
Chilo	218	38.48 N	84.08 W
Chiloane, Ilha I	156	20.40 S	34.55 E
Chiloé, Isla Grande de I	254	42.30 S	73.55 W
Chilok	88	51.21 N	110.28 E
Chilok ≃	88	51.19 N	106.59 E
Chilón	232	17.14 N	92.25 W
Chilonga	154	12.03 S	31.21 E
Chilongo	152	13.55 S	16.35 E
Chiloquin	202	42.34 N	121.51 W
Chilovo	76	57.46 N	29.23 E
Chilpancingo de los Bravo	234	17.33 N	99.30 W
Chilpi	124	22.15 N	81.33 E
Chilston Park ♦	260	51.12 N	0.42 E
Chiltern □[8]	260	51.40 N	0.37 W
Chiltern Hills ⋏[2]	42	51.42 N	0.48 W
Chilton, Eng., U.K.	44	54.39 N	1.33 W
Chilton, Tx., U.S.	222	31.16 N	97.03 W
Chilton, Wi., U.S.	190	44.01 N	88.09 W
Chiluage	152	9.30 S	21.47 E
Chilubula Mission	154	10.09 S	31.00 E
Chilumba	154	10.28 S	34.12 E
Chilung	100	25.08 N	121.44 E
Chilung ≃	269d	25.07 N	121.27 E
Chilung Kang c	269d	25.09 N	121.45 E
Chilung Shih □[7]	269d	25.08 N	121.45 E
Chiluvya	154	12.18 S	34.01 E
Chilwa, Lake ⊜	154	15.12 S	35.50 E
Chilwell	169	38.10 S	144.21 E
Chimaco	152	15.12 S	21.56 E
Chimacum	224	48.00 N	122.46 W
Chimacum Creek ≃	224	48.03 N	122.45 W
Chimakela	152	15.24 S	16.58 E
Chimaltenango	236	14.40 N	90.49 W
Chimaltenango □[5]	236	14.40 N	90.55 W
Chimaltitán	234	21.46 N	103.50 W
Chimán	246	8.42 N	78.37 W
Chimanimani National Park ♦	154	19.48 S	33.56 E
Chimay	50	50.03 N	4.19 E
Chimayo	200	36.00 N	105.55 W
Chimbarongo	252	34.42 S	71.03 W
Chimbas	252	31.29 S	68.32 W
Chimborazo □[4]	246	2.00 S	78.40 W
Chimborazo ∧	236	13.05 N	85.58 W
Chimborazo ∧[1]	246	1.28 S	78.48 W
Chimbote	248	9.05 S	78.36 W
Chimbua	152	16.32 S	15.08 E
Ch'imei Yü I	100	23.13 N	119.26 E
Chimichagua	246	9.15 N	73.49 W
Chimkent → Šymkent	85	42.18 N	69.36 E
Chimki	82	55.54 N	37.26 E
Chimki-Chovrino ⬥[8]	265b	55.51 N	37.30 E
Chimkinskoje vodochranilišče ⊜[1]	265b	55.51 N	37.28 E
Chimney Reservoir ⊜[1]	204	41.25 N	117.10 W
Chimney Rock National Historic Site ⊥	198	41.39 N	103.20 W
Chimoio	156	19.08 S	33.29 E
Chimon Island I	276	41.04 N	73.23 W
Chimpay	252	39.10 S	66.09 W
Chimpembe	154	9.31 S	29.33 E
Chimpôro ≃	152	17.20 S	17.17 E
Chin □[8]	110	22.00 N	93.30 E
China, Méx.	232	25.42 N	99.14 W
Chinā, Nihon	174m	26.24 N	127.46 E
China (Zhongguo) □[1]	90	35.00 N	105.00 E
China, Tanjong ⲻ	271c	1.14 N	103.51 E
Chinácota	246	7.37 N	72.36 W
China Grove	192	35.34 N	80.34 W
China Lake ⊜	204	35.46 N	117.39 W
China Lake Naval Weapons Center ■	204	35.35 N	117.10 W
Chinameca	236	13.30 N	88.21 W
China Meridional, Mar de → South China Sea ⩫[2]	108	10.00 N	113.00 E
Chinan, Taehan	98	35.48 N	127.25 E
Chinan → Jinan, Zhg.	98	36.40 N	116.57 E
Chinandega	236	12.37 N	87.09 W
Chinandega □[5]	236	12.45 N	87.05 W
China Spring	222	31.39 N	97.18 W
Chinati Peak ∧	196	29.57 N	104.29 W
Chinatown ⬥[8]	282	37.48 N	122.26 W
Chincha Alta	248	13.27 S	76.08 W
Chinchaga ≃	176	58.50 N	118.20 W
Chincheros	248	13.27 S	73.44 W
Chinchiang → Quanzhou	100	24.54 N	118.35 E
Chinchilla, Austl.	166	26.45 S	150.38 E
Chinchilla, Pa., U.S.	210	41.28 N	75.41 W
Chinchilla de Monte-Aragón	34	38.55 N	1.43 W
Chinchiná	246	4.58 N	75.36 W
Chincholi	272c	19.10 N	73.08 E
Chinchón, Esp.	34	40.08 N	3.25 W
Chinch'ŏn, Taehan	98	36.52 N	127.26 E
Chinchorro, Banco ✣[4]	232	18.35 N	87.22 W
Chinchou → Jinzhou	104	41.07 N	121.08 E
Chincolco	252	32.13 S	70.50 W
Chincoteague	208	37.55 N	75.22 W
Chincoteague Bay c	208	38.06 N	75.15 W
Chincoteague Inlet c	208	37.53 N	75.25 W
Chinde	156	18.37 S	36.24 E
Chindo	98	34.28 N	126.15 E
Chin-do I	98	34.25 N	126.15 E
Chindong	98	35.07 N	128.29 E
Chindwinn ≃	110	21.26 N	95.15 E
Chine (la République populaire de) → China □[1], Asia	90	35.00 N	105.00 E
Chine (nationaliste) → Taiwan □[1], Asia	100	23.30 N	121.00 E
Chinen	174m	26.09 N	127.49 E
Chineni	123	33.02 N	75.17 E
Chine Orientale, Mer de → East China Sea ⩫[2]	90	30.00 N	126.00 E
Chinese Camp	226	37.52 N	120.26 W
Chinese Cemetery ⬥	269f	14.38 N	120.59 E
Chinese University ʊ[2]	271d	22.26 N	114.12 E
Chingamba	152	12.49 S	18.20 E
Chingansk	89	49.07 N	131.11 E
Chingarora Creek ≃	276	40.27 N	74.12 W
Ch'ingchiang → Qingjiang	100	33.35 N	119.02 E
Chingford ⬥[8]	260	51.38 N	0.01 E
Chingleput	122	12.42 N	79.59 E
Chingmei ⬥[8]	269d	24.59 N	121.32 E
Chingola	154	12.32 S	27.52 E
Chingoni	157a	12.48 S	45.08 E
Chingoroi	152	13.37 S	14.01 E
Chingshih → Jinshi	102	29.39 N	111.52 E
Ch'ingtao → Qingdao	98	36.06 N	120.19 E
Chingtechen → Jingdezhen	100	29.16 N	117.11 E
Ch'ingt'ung	269d	25.02 N	121.43 E
Chinguar	152	12.36 S	16.20 E
Chinguetti	150	20.27 N	12.22 W
Chingune	156	20.38 S	34.55 E
Chinhae	98	35.09 N	128.40 E
Chinhae-man c	98	35.01 N	128.34 E
Chin Hills ⋏[2]	110	22.30 N	93.30 E
Chinhoyi	154	17.22 S	30.12 E
Chinhsien → Jinxian	98	39.04 N	121.40 E
Chinhua → Jinhua	100	29.07 N	119.39 E
Ch'inhuangtao → Qinhuangdao	98	39.56 N	119.36 E
Chīni	120	31.32 N	78.15 E
Chiniak, Cape ⲻ	180	57.36 N	152.08 W
Chining → Jining, Zhg.	98	35.25 N	116.36 E
Chining → Jining, Zhg.	102	40.57 N	113.02 E
Chiniot	123	31.43 N	72.59 E
Chinit ≃	110	12.55 N	105.35 E
Chinitna Point ⲻ	180	59.43 N	153.02 W
Chinizíua	156	19.00 S	35.09 E
Chinjan	120	30.34 N	67.58 E
Chinju	98	35.11 N	128.05 E
Chinkiang → Zhenjiang	106	32.13 N	119.26 E
Chinko ≃	136	4.50 N	23.53 E
Chinkuashih	100	25.07 N	121.51 E
Chin Lakes ⊜	182	49.37 N	112.13 W
Chinle	200	36.09 N	109.33 W
Chinle Creek ≃	200	37.12 N	109.43 W
Chinle Wash V	200	36.54 N	109.45 W
Chinley	262	53.20 N	1.56 W
Chinley Churn ∧[2]	262	53.21 N	1.57 W
Chinmen	100	24.27 N	118.21 E
Chinmen Tao I	100	24.27 N	118.23 E
Chinnampo → Namp'o	98	38.45 N	125.23 E
Chinnor	42	51.43 N	0.56 W
Chino, Nihon	94	35.59 N	138.09 E
Chino, Ca., U.S.	228	34.00 N	117.41 W
Chino Airport ⊠	280	33.59 N	117.38 W
Chino Creek ≃	280	33.53 N	117.38 W
Chino Hills	228	34.01 N	117.43 W
Chino Hills ⋏[2]	280	33.56 N	117.45 W
Chinon	50	47.10 N	0.15 E
Chinook, Ab., Can.	184	51.27 N	110.56 W
Chinook, Mt., U.S.	202	48.35 N	109.13 W
Chinook, Wa., U.S.	224	46.16 N	123.56 W
Chinook Cove	182	51.14 N	120.10 W
Chino Valley	200	34.45 N	112.27 W
Chinpāi	126	23.50 N	87.28 E
Chinquapin	192	34.49 N	77.49 W
Chinsali	154	10.34 S	32.03 E
Chinshan	100	25.13 N	121.38 E
Chinshui	100	24.36 N	120.53 E
Chintāmani	122	13.24 N	78.04 E
Chintembwe	154	13.25 S	33.59 E
Chintheche	154	11.52 S	34.09 E
Chinú	246	9.06 N	75.24 W
Chinunje	154	11.19 S	37.19 E
Chinwangtao → Qinhuangdao	98	39.56 N	119.36 E
Chiny	56	49.44 N	5.20 E
Chinyama Litapi	152	13.31 S	22.21 E
Chioco	154	16.25 S	32.50 E
Chioggia	64	45.13 N	12.17 E
Chiomonte	62	45.07 N	6.59 E
Chios → Khíos	38	38.22 N	26.08 E
Chios → Khíos I	38	38.22 N	26.00 E
Chipamanu (Xipamanu) ≃	248	10.43 S	67.50 W
Chipao	248	14.15 S	73.57 W
Chipata (Fort Jameson)	154	13.39 S	32.40 E
Chipei Tao I	100	23.45 N	119.37 E
Chipera	154	15.28 S	32.30 E
Chiperceni	38	47.32 N	28.50 E
Chiperone ∧	154	16.28 S	35.12 E
Chipili	154	10.44 S	29.04 E
Chiping	98	36.37 N	116.16 E
Chipinge	154	20.12 S	32.38 E
Chip Lake ⊜	182	53.40 N	115.20 W
Chipley	194	30.46 N	85.32 W
Chiplūn	122	17.32 N	73.31 E
Chipman	186	46.11 N	65.53 W
Chipogolo	154	6.52 S	36.02 E
Chipoka	154	14.00 S	34.31 E
Chipola ≃	192	30.01 N	85.05 W
Chippawa ⬥[8]	284a	43.04 N	79.03 W
Chippawa Channel ≃[1]	284a	43.04 N	79.01 W
Chippego Lake ⊜	212	44.34 N	76.49 W
Chippenham	42	51.28 N	2.07 W
Chipperfield	260	51.42 N	0.29 W
Chippewa ≃, Mi., U.S.	190	43.35 N	84.17 W
Chippewa ≃, Mn., U.S.	198	44.56 N	95.44 W
Chippewa ≃, Wi., U.S.	190	44.25 N	92.10 W
Chippewa, East Branch ≃	198	45.20 N	95.36 W
Chippewa, East Fork ≃	190	45.53 N	91.05 W
Chippewa, Lake ⊜	190	45.56 N	91.13 W
Chippewa Bay c	212	44.27 N	75.47 W
Chippewa Creek ≃	212	44.27 N	75.46 W
Chippewa Falls	190	44.56 N	91.23 W
Chippewa Lake	214	41.04 N	81.54 W
Chippewanuck Creek ≃	216	41.07 N	86.12 W
Chipping Campden	42	52.03 N	1.46 W
Chipping Norton	42	51.56 N	1.32 W
Chipping Ongar	42	51.43 N	0.15 E
Chipping Sodbury	42	51.33 N	2.24 W
Chippis	58	46.17 N	7.33 E
Chippokes Plantation State Park ♦	208	37.08 N	76.44 W
Chipps Island I	282	38.03 N	121.55 W
Chipre → Cyprus □[1]	130	35.00 N	33.00 E
Chipstead, Eng., U.K.	260	51.17 N	0.09 E
Chipstead, Eng., U.K.	260	51.18 N	0.10 W
Chipuriro	154	16.39 S	30.42 E
Chiquelequele	152	16.40 S	19.06 E
Chiquián	248	10.09 S	77.11 W
Chiquihuitlán	234	17.59 N	96.48 W
Chiquimula	236	14.48 N	89.33 W
Chiquimula □[5]	236	14.40 N	89.25 W
Chiquimulilla	236	14.05 N	90.23 W
Chiquinquirá	246	5.37 N	73.50 W
Chiquintirca	248	13.09 S	73.41 W
Chiquita	152	8.38 S	17.05 E
Chiquito ≃	234	18.29 N	101.07 W
Chiquito Creek ≃	226	37.20 N	119.20 W
Chira ≃	246	4.54 S	81.08 W
Chira, Isla I	236	10.06 N	85.09 W
Chirad	272c	19.09 N	73.07 E
Chiradzulu	154	15.42 S	35.10 E
Chirāgh Delhi ⬥[8]	272a	28.32 N	77.14 E
Chīrāla	122	15.49 N	80.21 E
Chiramba	154	16.55 S	34.39 E
Chirape	156	21.18 S	33.33 E
Chirāwa	120	28.15 N	75.38 E
Chirchik → Čirčik	85	41.29 N	69.35 E
Chire (Shire) ≃	154	17.42 S	35.19 E
Chiredzi	154	21.03 S	31.45 E
Chireno	194	31.30 N	94.21 W
Chirens	62	45.25 N	5.33 E
Chirfa	146	20.57 N	12.21 E
Chīrgaon	124	25.35 N	78.49 E
Chiriaco ≃	248	5.05 S	78.19 W
Chiricahua Mountains ⋏	200	31.50 N	109.15 W
Chiricahua National Monument ♦	200	32.02 N	109.19 W
Chiricahua Peak ∧	200	31.52 N	109.20 W
Chiriguaná	246	9.22 N	73.36 W
Chirikof Island I	180	55.50 N	155.35 W
Chirilagua	236	13.13 N	88.08 W
Chirinos	248	5.16 S	78.52 W
Chiriquí	236	8.24 N	82.19 W
Chiriquí □[4]	236	8.30 N	82.00 W
Chiriquí, Golfo de c	246	8.00 N	82.20 W
Chiriquí, Laguna de c	236	9.03 N	82.00 W
Chiriquí Grande	236	8.57 N	82.07 W
Chiriquí Viejo ≃	236	8.20 N	82.41 W
Chirk	42	52.56 N	3.03 W
Chirki	126	24.03 N	86.09 E
Chirle	272c	18.56 N	73.02 E
Chirmiri	124	23.12 N	82.21 E
Chirnside	46	55.48 N	2.13 W
Chiromo	154	16.33 S	35.08 E
Chirovo	76	58.56 N	33.24 E
Chirripó ≃	236	10.41 N	83.41 W
Chirripó, Cerro ∧	236	9.29 N	83.30 W
Chirripó, Parque Nacional ♦	236	9.30 N	83.30 W
Chirsa	84	41.31 N	46.06 E
Chirundu	154	15.59 S	28.54 E
Chirvosti	265a	59.57 N	30.37 E
Chiryū	94	35.00 N	137.02 E
Chisago City	190	45.22 N	92.53 W
Chisamba	154	14.58 S	28.23 E
Chisana	180	62.09 N	142.10 W
Chisasibi	176	53.50 N	79.00 W
Chiscas	246	6.33 N	72.29 W
Chisec	236	15.49 N	90.17 W
Chiseldon	42	51.31 N	1.44 W
Chisenga	154	9.56 S	33.26 E
Chisep'o	98	34.50 N	128.42 E
Ch'ishan	100	22.53 N	120.28 E
Chishanji	98	36.56 N	122.23 E
Chishi	100	27.42 N	117.58 E
Chishisi	100	25.32 N	113.11 E
Chisholm, Al., U.S.	194	32.25 N	86.15 W
Chisholm, Me., U.S.	188	44.28 N	70.12 W
Chisholm, Mn., U.S.	190	47.29 N	92.53 W
Chisholm, Tx., U.S.	222	32.51 N	96.22 W
Chisholm Mills	182	54.55 N	114.08 W
Chishtiān Mandi	123	29.48 N	72.52 E
Chishui	102	28.29 N	105.38 E
Chishui ≃, Zhg.	102	28.53 N	105.48 E
Chishui ≃, Zhg.	107	28.49 N	105.50 E
Chishuihe	102	27.50 N	105.32 E
Chišig-Öndör	88	48.19 N	103.25 E
Chisimaio → Kismaayo	144	0.22 N	42.32 E
Chişinău (Kishinev)	38	47.00 N	28.50 E
Chişineu-Criş	38	46.31 N	21.31 E
Chislaviči	76	54.11 N	32.10 E
Chislehurst ⬥[8]	260	51.25 N	0.04 E
Chisone ≃	62	44.49 N	7.25 E
Chisone, Valle del V	62	45.01 N	7.07 E
Chisos Mountains ⋏	196	29.15 N	103.20 W
Chisseaux	50	47.20 N	1.05 E
Chissengue	152	9.14 S	20.42 E
Chissilo	152	13.34 S	16.30 E
Chistochina	180	62.34 N	144.40 W
Chistopol → Čistopol'	80	55.21 N	50.37 E
Chiswellgreen	260	51.44 N	0.22 W
Chiswick ⬥[8]	260	51.29 N	0.16 W
Chita, Bol.	248	20.06 S	66.57 W
Chita, Col.	246	6.11 N	72.28 W
Chita, Nihon	94	35.00 N	136.51 E
Chita → Čita, Ross.	88	52.03 N	113.30 E
Chitado	152	17.20 S	13.54 E
Chitagá	246	7.09 N	72.40 W
Chita-hantō ⲻ[1]	94	34.50 N	136.53 E
Chitambo	154	12.55 S	30.39 E
Chitanda ≃	152	16.01 S	15.12 E
Chitarda	126	21.50 N	86.57 E
Chitata	152	13.47 S	15.43 E
Chitato	152	7.20 S	20.47 E
Chita-wan c	94	34.47 N	136.58 E
Chiţcani	38	46.47 N	29.36 E
Chitek ≃	184	54.06 N	108.16 W
Chitek Lake ⊜, Mb., Can.	184	52.26 N	99.25 W
Chitek Lake ⊜, Sk., Can.	184	53.44 N	107.47 W
Chitembo	152	13.34 S	16.40 E
Chitina	180	61.31 N	144.27 W
Chitina ≃	180	61.30 N	144.28 W
Chitipa	154	9.43 S	33.16 E
Chitokoloki	152	13.50 S	23.13 E
Chitose	92a	42.49 N	141.39 E
Chitose-chūtonchi, Rikujō-jieitai- ■	92a	42.46 N	141.40 E
Chitou Shan I	100	27.40 N	120.50 E
Chitra ≃[1]	126	22.53 N	89.40 E
Chitradurga	122	14.14 N	76.24 E
Chitrakūt Dham	124	25.11 N	80.52 E
Chitrāl	123	35.51 N	71.47 E
Chitrasāli	272b	22.52 N	88.09 E
Chitrāvati ≃	122	14.48 N	78.14 E
Chitré	236	7.58 N	80.26 W
Chittagong	120	22.20 N	91.50 E
Chittagong □[5]	120	23.00 N	91.00 E
Chīttāpur	122	17.07 N	77.05 E
Chittaranjan	126	23.52 N	86.52 E
Chittaurgarh	120	24.53 N	74.38 E
Chittenango	210	43.02 N	75.52 W
Chittenango Creek ≃	210	43.11 N	76.00 W
Chittenango Falls	210	42.59 N	75.50 W
Chittering	162	31.29 S	116.06 E
Chittoor	122	13.12 N	79.07 E
Chittūr	122	10.42 N	76.45 E
Chitu, Ityo.	144	8.36 N	37.59 E
Ch'itu, T'aiwan	269d	25.06 N	121.43 E
Chitungwiza	154	17.45 S	31.16 E
Chiuchiang → Jiujiang	100	29.44 N	115.59 E
Chíuchíu	252	22.21 S	68.39 W
Chiuduno	62	45.40 N	9.51 E
Chiumbe	152	12.29 S	16.08 E
Chiumbe ≃	152	7.00 S	21.12 E
Chiúme	152	15.03 S	21.14 E
Chiuppano	64	45.46 N	11.28 E
Chiuro	64	46.10 N	9.59 E
Chiusa (Klausen)	64	46.38 N	11.34 E
Chiusa di Pesio	62	44.19 N	7.40 E
Chiusa di San Michele	62	45.06 N	7.19 E
Chiusaforte	64	46.24 N	13.18 E
Chiusa Sclafani	70	37.41 N	13.16 E
Chiusella ≃	62	45.24 N	7.55 E
Chiusi	66	43.01 N	11.57 E
Chiusi, Lago di ⊜	66	43.03 N	11.58 E
Chiúta	154	15.34 S	33.17 E
Chiuta, Lake ⊜	154	14.55 S	35.50 E
Chiv	84	41.46 N	47.54 E
Chiva	72	41.24 N	60.22 E
Chivacoa	246	10.10 N	68.54 W
Chivasso	62	45.11 N	7.53 E
Chivato, Punta ⲻ	232	27.05 N	111.59 W
Chivay	248	15.40 S	71.35 W
Chivhu	154	19.01 S	30.53 E
Chivilcoy	252	34.53 S	60.01 W
Chivirira Falls ∟	154	21.14 S	32.20 E
Chiwanda	154	11.22 S	34.54 E
Chiwawa ≃	224	47.47 N	120.40 W
Chixi	100	28.22 N	116.22 E
Chixoy (Salinas) ≃	232	16.28 N	90.33 W
Chixoy, Embalse ⊜[1]	236	15.15 N	90.30 W
Chiyoda, Nihon	94	36.12 N	139.26 E
Chiyoda, Nihon	94	36.11 N	140.14 E
Chiyoda, Nihon	96	34.41 N	132.32 E
Chiyoda ⬥[8]	268	35.41 N	139.44 E
Chizarira National Park ♦	154	17.45 S	28.00 E
Chizhen	100	31.55 N	118.12 E
Chizizhen	100	32.22 N	115.11 E
Chizu	96	35.16 N	134.14 E
Chjargas	88	49.32 N	93.48 E
Chjargas nuur ⊜	88	49.12 N	93.24 E
Chkalov → Orenburg	86	51.54 N	55.06 E
Chkalove	78	46.28 N	34.11 E
Chlebnikovo, Ross.	80	56.38 N	49.56 E
Chlebnikovo, Ross.	265b	55.58 N	37.31 E
Chlebodarnyj	80	46.41 N	40.50 E
Chlevnoje	76	52.12 N	39.05 E
Chloride	200	35.24 N	114.11 W
Chlum	60	48.52 N	13.55 E
Chlum ∧	61	48.42 N	14.04 E
Chmelevicy	80	57.45 N	46.22 E
Chmelevo	82	56.09 N	39.08 E
Chmelita	76	55.25 N	33.53 E
Chmel'niki, Ross.	82	56.52 N	38.13 E
Chmel'niki, Ross.	82	56.53 N	38.39 E
Chmielnik	30	50.37 N	20.46 E
Chmost' ≃	76	54.45 N	32.34 E
Choa Chu Kang	271c	1.22 N	103.41 E
Choāli	272b	22.24 N	88.24 E
Chŏâm Khsant	110	14.13 N	104.56 E
Choba	154	2.26 N	38.03 E
Chobe □[5]	156	18.30 S	25.00 E
Chobe ≃	156	17.50 S	25.05 E
Chobeju	24	64.53 N	60.10 E
Chobe National Park ♦	156	18.45 S	24.15 E
Chobham	260	51.21 N	0.36 W
Chobham Common ♦	260	51.23 N	0.37 W
Chobi	84	42.21 N	41.53 E
Chocamán	234	18.59 N	97.01 W
Choccolocco Creek ≃	194	33.33 N	86.11 W
Choceň	30	50.00 N	16.13 E
Chocenice	60	49.33 N	13.31 E
Chochis, Cerro ∧	248	18.04 S	60.03 W
Choch'iwŏn	98	36.37 N	127.18 E
Chochloma	80	56.58 N	43.54 E
Chŏchmor't	88	47.21 N	94.33 E
Chochol'skij	78	51.34 N	38.45 E
Cho Chu	110	21.54 N	105.39 E
Chocianów	30	51.25 N	15.55 E
Chociwel	30	53.28 N	15.19 E
Chocó □[5]	246	6.00 N	77.00 W
Chocolate Bay c	222	29.11 N	95.09 W
Chocolate Bayou ≃	222	29.13 N	95.13 W
Chocolate Mountains ⋏	204	33.20 N	115.15 W
Chocontá	246	5.09 N	73.41 W
Chocope	248	7.47 S	79.13 W
Choctawhatchee, East Fork ≃	194	31.21 N	85.33 W
Choctawhatchee, West Fork ≃	194	31.21 N	85.33 W
Choctawhatchee Bay c	194	30.25 N	86.21 W
Choctaw Lake ⊜[1]	218	39.58 N	83.29 W
Chodarus	88	52.36 N	99.19 E
Chodavaram	122	17.50 N	82.57 E
Chodecz	30	52.24 N	19.01 E
Ch'o-do I, C.M.I.K.	98	38.32 N	124.50 E
Ch'o-do I, Taehan	98	34.14 N	127.15 E
Chodoi	114	2.50 N	101.27 E
Chodov	54	50.11 N	12.43 E
Chodovaja Griva	80	57.08 N	50.16 E
Chodovaricha	24	68.57 N	53.40 E
Chodz' ≃	84	44.43 N	40.45 E
Chodžaimetk	85	39.37 N	69.14 E
Chodžakala	128	38.43 N	56.20 E
Chodžejli	72	42.48 N	59.25 E
Chodzież	30	52.59 N	16.56 E
Choele-Choel	252	39.16 S	65.41 W
Chofombo	154	14.35 S	31.50 E
Chōfu	94	35.39 N	139.33 E
Chofu Airport ⊠	268	35.40 N	139.32 E
Chogo Lungma Glacier ⊓	123	35.52 N	75.19 E
Chogot	88	53.15 N	105.52 E
Choiceland	184	53.27 N	104.25 W
Choichuff, Laga ≃	154	1.34 N	39.24 E
Choire, Loch ⊜	46	58.13 N	4.21 W
Choisel	261	48.41 N	2.01 E
Choiseul	241f	13.47 N	61.03 W
Choiseul □[4]	175e	6.40 S	157.15 E
Choiseul I	175e	7.05 S	157.00 E
Choiseul Sound ʯ	254	51.57 S	58.35 W
Choisy	58	45.59 N	6.03 E
Choisy-le-Roi	261	48.46 N	2.25 E
Choix	232	26.43 N	108.17 W
Chojna	30	52.58 N	14.28 E
Chojnice	30	53.42 N	17.34 E
Chojnów	30	51.17 N	15.56 E
Chōkai-san ∧	92	39.06 N	140.03 E
Choke ⋏	144	10.45 N	37.35 E
Choke Canyon Lake ⊜[1]	196	28.30 N	98.20 W
Chokio	198	45.34 N	96.10 W
Chokoloskee	220	25.48 N	81.21 W
Chokwé	156	24.36 S	33.00 E
Cholame	226	35.43 N	120.17 W
Cholame Creek ≃	226	35.39 N	120.22 W
Cholame Hills ⋏[2]	226	35.45 N	120.30 W
Cholbon	88	51.53 N	116.15 E
Choldarkipčak	85	39.51 N	68.52 E
Cholet	32	47.04 N	0.53 W
Cholila	254	42.31 S	71.27 W
Chŏlla Namdo □[4]	98	34.45 N	127.00 E
Chŏlla Pukdo □[4]	98	35.45 N	127.15 E
Cholm	76	57.09 N	31.11 E
Cholmec	76	56.21 N	33.21 E
Cholmogorovka	86	44.25 N	78.31 E
Cholmogorskaja	24	63.49 N	40.39 E
Cholmogory	24	64.15 N	41.40 E
Cholmsk	89	47.03 N	142.03 E
Cholmskij	78	44.52 N	38.24 E
Cholmy	82	54.56 N	38.33 E
Cholm-Žirkovskij	76	55.31 N	33.29 E
Choloj ≃	88	53.12 N	112.47 E
Choloma	236	15.34 N	87.56 W
Chölönbujr	88	47.55 N	112.57 E
Ch'ŏlsan	98	39.46 N	124.40 E
Cholsey	42	51.34 N	1.10 W
Choltobino	82	54.11 N	38.28 E
Choltoson	88	50.20 N	103.20 E
Choluj, Ross.	80	56.34 N	41.53 E
Choluj, Ross.	80	56.04 N	42.08 E
Cholula de Rivadabia	234	19.04 N	98.18 W
Choluteca	236	13.18 N	87.12 W
Choluteca □[5]	236	13.20 N	87.10 W
Choluteca ≃	236	13.07 N	87.19 W
Choma	154	16.48 S	26.59 E
Chomedey ⬥[8]	275a	45.32 N	73.44 W
Chomen Swamp ≡	144	9.25 N	37.20 E
Chomérac	62	44.42 N	4.39 E
Chomičev	80	48.11 N	45.01 E
Chomiomo ∧	124	28.01 N	88.31 E
Cho Moi, Viet	110	10.33 N	105.24 E
Cho Moi, Viet	269c	10.51 N	106.38 E
Chomo Lhāri ∧	124	27.50 N	89.15 E
Chom Thong	110	18.25 N	98.41 E
Chomūm	120	27.10 N	75.44 E
Chomutov	54	50.28 N	13.26 E
Chomutovka	78	51.56 N	34.33 E
Chomutovka ≃	54	50.11 N	13.37 E
Chomutovo, Ross.	76	52.51 N	37.27 E
Chomutovo, Ross.	88	52.28 N	104.25 E
Chomutovskaja	83	47.03 N	40.04 E
Chōnan, Nihon	94	35.24 N	140.14 E
Ch'ŏnan, Taehan	98	36.48 N	127.09 E
Chon'atino	82	55.11 N	38.07 E
Chon Buri	110	13.22 N	100.59 E
Chonchi	254	42.38 S	73.47 W
Choncholoj	88	51.08 N	108.14 E
Chon Daen	110	16.11 N	100.51 E
Chone	246	0.41 S	80.06 W
Chone ≃	246	0.35 S	80.25 W
Chong'an	100	27.45 N	118.02 E
Ch'ŏngch'ŏn-gang ≃	98	39.35 N	125.28 E
Ch'ŏngdan	98	37.58 N	125.56 E
Chongde	106	30.32 N	120.26 E
Ch'ŏngdo	98	35.38 N	128.43 E
Chonggu	106	31.12 N	121.10 E
Ch'ŏngha	98	36.13 N	129.20 E
Ch'onghak-ni	271b	37.43 N	127.05 E
Chonghe	89	44.43 N	127.45 E
Ch'ŏngjin	98	41.47 N	129.50 E
Chŏngju, C.M.I.K.	98	39.41 N	125.13 E
Ch'ŏngju, Taehan	98	36.39 N	127.31 E
Chŏng Kal	110	13.57 N	103.35 E
Chongkanzhen	107	30.09 N	105.37 E
Chongli (Xiwanzi)	98	40.54 N	115.16 E
Chongming	106	31.37 N	121.24 E
Chongming Dao I	106	31.36 N	121.33 E
Chongoene	156	25.00 S	33.47 E
Chongor	102	45.59 N	112.45 E
Chongos Bajo	248	12.07 S	75.16 W
Chongoyape	248	6.39 S	79.24 W
Chong Pang	271c	1.26 N	103.50 E
Chŏngp'yŏng-chŏsuji ⊜[1]	98	37.40 N	127.30 E
Chongqing, Zhg.	107	30.39 N	103.41 E
Chongqing (Chungking), Zhg.	107	29.34 N	106.35 E
Chongren, Zhg.	100	29.37 N	120.43 E
Chongren, Zhg.	100	27.46 N	116.01 E
Chongru	100	27.01 N	120.10 E
Ch'ŏngsan	98	36.22 N	127.46 E
Ch'ŏngsan-do I	98	34.11 N	126.54 E
Chongshi	100	25.24 N	115.28 E
Chŏngsŏn	98	37.22 N	128.38 E
Ch'ŏngsong	98	41.47 N	129.48 E
Chŏngŭp	98	35.36 N	126.51 E
Chongwe ≃	154	15.43 S	29.20 E
Chongwu	100	24.53 N	118.55 E
Chongxi	98	42.07 N	128.59 E
Chongxin	102	35.13 N	107.29 E
Ch'ŏngyang, Taehan	98	36.27 N	126.48 E
Chongyang, Zhg.	100	29.33 N	114.00 E
Chongyang ≃	100	27.18 N	118.08 E
Chongyi	100	25.44 N	114.18 E
Chongzuo	102	22.21 N	107.26 E
Choni	84	42.20 N	42.25 E
Chŏnju	98	35.49 N	127.08 E
Chonkham	120	27.48 N	96.02 E
Ch'ŏnma	98	40.03 N	125.01 E
Chonobad	85	40.48 N	72.58 E
Chonos, Archipiélago de los II	254	45.00 S	74.00 W
Ch'ŏnsu-ri	98	41.43 N	128.45 E
Chontaleña, Cordillera ⋏	236	11.50 N	84.50 W
Chontales □[5]	236	12.05 N	85.10 W
Chon Thanh	110	11.24 N	106.36 E
Chŏnŭi	98	36.42 N	127.11 E
Chonuu	74	66.27 N	143.06 E
Chonzie, Ben ∧	46	56.27 N	3.59 W
Cho Oyu → Chopu ∧	124	28.06 N	86.39 E
Chop	78	48.26 N	22.10 E
Chopda	120	21.15 N	75.18 E
Cho Phuoc Hai	110	10.26 N	107.18 E
Chopim ≃	252	25.35 S	53.05 W
Chopinzinho	252	25.51 S	52.30 W
Chopon	124	24.31 N	83.02 E
Chop'or ≃	80	49.36 N	42.19 E
Chop'orskij zapovednik ⬥[4]	80	51.15 N	41.48 E
Chopovychi	78	50.49 N	27.58 E
Choptank ≃	208	38.38 N	76.13 W
Chopu ∧	124	28.06 N	86.39 E
Chopwell	44	54.55 N	1.49 W
Chor	89	47.53 N	134.58 E
Chor ≃	89	47.48 N	134.43 E
Chora Saādatpur	272a	28.36 N	77.21 E
Chordil sar'dag ⋏	88	50.50 N	99.40 E
Chorejver	24	67.25 N	58.03 E
Chorges	62	44.33 N	6.17 E
Chorin ⊥	54	52.54 N	13.52 E
Chorinsk	88	52.10 N	109.46 E
Chorley	44	53.39 N	2.39 W
Chorley □[8]	262	53.38 N	2.38 W
Chorleywood	260	51.39 N	0.31 W
Chorlovo	82	55.20 N	38.49 E
Chorlton-cum-Hardy ⬥[8]	262	53.27 N	2.17 W
Chorna	78	47.37 N	29.20 E
Chornobay	78	49.41 N	32.19 E
Chornobayivka	78	46.42 N	32.32 E
Chornobyl'	78	51.16 N	30.14 E
Chornomors'ke, Ukr.	78	45.30 N	32.42 E
Chornomors'ke, Ukr.	78	45.03 N	35.58 E
Chornukhy	78	50.16 N	32.57 E
Chornukhyne	83	48.19 N	38.30 E
Chornyy Ostriv	78	49.32 N	26.46 E
Chornyy Tashlyk ≃	78	48.11 N	30.51 E
Chorog	120	37.31 N	71.33 E
Chorol'	89	44.25 N	132.04 E
Chorolque, Cerro ∧	248	20.56 S	66.01 W
Choros, Isla I	252	29.16 S	71.33 W
Chorošovo	82	55.08 N	38.47 E
Chorošovo ⬥[8]	265b	55.47 N	37.28 E
Choroszcz	30	53.09 N	22.59 E
Chorreras	232	28.50 N	105.18 W
Chorrillos	286d	12.10 S	77.02 W
Chorrochó	250	8.59 S	39.06 W
Chorro Creek ≃	226	35.20 N	120.50 W
Chort'ak, gora ∧	88	53.15 N	110.45 E
Chortkiv	78	49.01 N	25.48 E
Chortomlyk	78	47.37 N	34.09 E
Ch'ŏrwŏn	98	38.16 N	127.12 E
Chorzele	30	53.16 N	20.55 E
Ch'osan	98	40.50 N	125.47 E
Chosanch'am	98	40.22 N	126.11 E
Chosedachard	24	67.02 N	59.22 E
Chosen	220	26.42 N	80.41 W
Chošeutovo	80	47.02 N	47.50 E
Chōshi	94	35.44 N	140.50 E
Choshi-ōhashi ⬥[5]	94	35.44 N	140.50 E
Chōshi-zuka-kofun ⊥	94	34.42 N	137.50 E
Choshui ≃	100	24.03 N	120.24 E
Chosica	248	11.54 S	76.42 W
Chos Malal	252	37.23 S	70.16 W
Chosŏn Minjujuŭi In'min Konghwaguk → Korea, North □[1]	98	40.00 N	127.00 E
Chosrech	84	41.59 N	47.18 E
Chosta	84	43.33 N	39.53 E
Choszczno	30	53.10 N	15.26 E
Chota	248	6.33 S	78.39 W
Chotanāgpur Plateau ⋏[1]	124	23.30 N	84.30 E
Chotča ≃	82	56.54 N	37.35 E
Choteau	202	47.48 N	112.10 W
Choteau Creek ≃	198	42.51 N	98.09 W
Chotěboř	30	49.43 N	15.40 E
Chotěšov	60	49.39 N	13.12 E
Chotila	120	22.25 N	71.11 E
Chotilovo	76	57.44 N	34.05 E
Chotisino	82	54.24 N	36.33 E
Chot'kovo, Ross.	76	53.46 N	35.14 E
Chot'kovo, Ross.	76	52.56 N	35.23 E
Chot'kovo, Ross.	82	56.15 N	38.00 E
Chotuš'	82	54.32 N	37.44 E
Chotynec	76	53.08 N	35.24 E
Chotyrboky	78	50.02 N	27.01 E
Chouchiak'ou → Shangshui	100	33.33 N	114.34 E
Chouk'ou → Shangshui	100	33.33 N	114.34 E
Choûm	148	21.18 N	13.01 W
Chouteau	196	36.11 N	95.20 W
Chovaling	85	38.21 N	69.58 E
Chovd, Mong.	86	49.16 N	90.55 E
Chovd, Mong.	86	48.08 N	91.23 E
Chovd, Mong.	86	48.01 N	91.38 E
Chovd, Mong.	102	44.42 N	102.24 E
Chovd □[4]	86	48.00 N	91.30 E
Chovd ≃	90	48.06 N	92.11 E
Chövsgöl	102	43.36 N	109.39 E
Chövsgöl □[4]	88	50.00 N	100.00 E
Chövsgöl nuur ⊜	88	51.00 N	100.30 E
Chovu-Aksy	88	51.11 N	93.53 E
Chowan ≃	192	36.00 N	76.40 W
Chowchilla	226	37.07 N	120.15 W
Chowchilla ≃	226	37.07 N	120.32 W
Chowchilla, East Fork ≃	226	37.20 N	119.50 W
Chowchilla, West Fork ≃	226	37.20 N	119.50 W
Chowkay	123	34.41 N	70.56 E
Chown, Mount ∧	182	53.24 N	119.22 W
Ch'owŏn-ni	98	39.40 N	127.17 E
Choya	252	28.30 S	64.52 W
Choyak-to I	98	34.22 N	126.54 E
Chr'aščevka	80	53.48 N	49.06 E
Chrást	60	49.48 N	13.29 E
Chrebtovo	82	56.35 N	38.16 E
Chrenovoje	80	51.07 N	40.17 E
Chreščatij	83	49.37 N	39.42 E
Chřibská	54	50.50 N	14.29 E
Chříč	60	49.57 N	13.39 E
Chriesman	222	30.36 N	96.46 W
Chrisman	194	39.48 N	87.40 W
Chrissiesmeer	158	26.16 S	30.13 E
Chrissiesmeer ⊜	158	26.19 S	30.13 E
Christanshåb (Qasigiannguit)	176	68.50 N	51.12 W
Christchurch, N.Z.	172	43.32 S	172.38 E
Christchurch, Eng., U.K.	42	50.44 N	1.45 W
Christ Church Cathedral ʊ[1]	273a	6.27 N	3.23 E
Christian □[6]	219	39.33 N	89.18 W
Christian ≃	180	66.36 N	145.49 W
Christian, Cape ⲻ	176	70.31 N	68.18 W
Christian, Point ⲻ	174e	25.04 S	130.07 W
Christiana, Jam.	241q	18.10 N	77.29 W
Christiana, S. Afr.	158	27.52 S	25.08 E
Christiana, De., U.S.	285	39.39 N	75.39 W
Christiana, Pa., U.S.	208	39.57 N	75.59 W
Christiana Creek ≃	216	41.41 N	85.59 W
Christianburg	218	38.17 N	85.06 W
Christian Channel ʯ	212	44.47 N	80.08 W
Christian Island I	212	44.50 N	80.13 W
Christian Island Indian Reserve ⬥[4]	212	44.50 N	80.10 W
Christiansburg, Oh., U.S.	218	40.03 N	84.01 W
Christiansburg, Va., U.S.	192	37.07 N	80.24 W
Christiansfeld	41	55.21 N	9.29 E
Christiansø I	26	55.19 N	15.12 E
Christian Sound ʯ	180	55.56 N	134.40 W
Christiansted	241n	17.45 N	64.42 W
Christie, Mount ∧	180	63.01 N	129.40 W
Christie, Mount ∧[2]	216	42.53 N	83.20 W
Christie Bay c	176	62.32 N	111.10 W
Christie Lake ⊜, Mb., Can.	184	56.54 N	96.56 W
Christie Lake ⊜, On., Can.	212	44.48 N	76.26 W
Christina ≃, Ab., Can.	184	56.40 N	111.03 W
Christina ≃, De., U.S.	285	39.43 N	75.31 W
Christina Lake ⊜, Ab., Can.	182	55.38 N	110.55 W
Christina Lake ⊜, B.C., Can.	182	49.05 N	118.14 W
Christmas	220	28.32 N	81.01 W
Christmas Bay c	222	29.03 N	95.11 W
Christmas Creek	162	18.53 S	125.55 E
Christmas Creek ≃	162	18.29 S	125.23 E
Christmas Island □[2], Oc.	108	10.30 S	105.40 E
Christmas Island □[2], Oc.	112	10.30 S	105.40 E
Christmas Island → Kiritimati I[1]	174o	1.52 N	157.20 W
Christmas Mountain ∧	180	64.34 N	160.34 W
Christmas Ridge ✣[3]	14	5.00 N	160.00 W
Christoforovo	24	60.53 N	47.13 E

Symbols in the index entries represent the broad categories identified in the key at the right. Symbols with superior numbers (⋏[1]) identify subcategories (see complete key on page *I · 1*).

Symbole im Register stellen die rechts im Schlüssel erklärten Kategorien dar. Symbole mit hochgestellten Ziffern (⋏[1]) bezeichnen Unterabteilungen einer Kategorie (vgl. vollständiger Schlüssel auf Seite *I · 1*).

Los símbolos incluídos en el texto del índice representan las grandes categorías identificadas con la clave a la derecha. Los símbolos con numeros en su parte superior (⋏[1]) identifican las subcategorías (véase la clave completa en la página *I · 1*).

Les symboles de l'index représentent les catégories indiquées dans la légende à droite. Les symboles suivis d'un indice (⋏[1]) représentent des sous-catégories (voir légende complète à la page *I · 1*).

Os símbolos incluídos no texto do índice representam as grandes categorias identificadas com a chave à direita. Os símbolos com números em sua parte superior (⋏[1]) identificam as subcategorias (veja-se a chave completa à página *I · 1*).

	English	Deutsch	Español	Français	Português
∧	Mountain	Berg	Montaña	Montagne	Montanha
⋏	Mountains	Gebirge	Montañas	Montagnes	Montanhas
)(	Pass	Paß	Paso	Col	Passo
V	Valley, Canyon	Tal, Cañon	Valle, Cañón	Vallée, Canyon	Vale, Canhão
≃	Plain	Ebene	Llano	Plaine	Planície
ⲻ	Cape	Kap	Cabo	Cap	Cabo
I	Island	Insel	Isla	Île	Ilha
II	Islands	Inseln	Islas	Îles	Ilhas
⊥	Other Topographic Features	Andere Topographische Objekte	Otros Elementos Topográficos	Autres données topographiques	Outros acidentes topográficos

ESPAÑOL — Nombre | Página | Lat.°′ | Long.°′ W = Oeste
FRANÇAIS — Nom | Page | Lat.°′ | Long.°′ W = Ouest
PORTUGUÊS — Nome | Página | Lat.°′ | Long.°′ W = Oeste

Nombre	Página	Lat.°′	Long.°′ W = Oeste
Christ of the Andes → Cristo Redentor ⊥	252	32.50 S	70.05 W
Christoph Columbus-Spitze → Cristóbal Colón, Pico ∧	246	10.50 N	73.41 W
Christopher	194	37.58 N	89.03 W
Christopher, Lake ⊜	162	24.49 S	127.42 E
Christoval	196	31.12 N	100.30 W
Chroma ≃	74	71.36 N	144.49 E
Chromtau	86	50.17 N	58.27 E
Chrudim	30	49.57 N	15.48 E
Chrustal'nyj	89	44.24 N	135.06 E
Chrzanów	30	50.09 N	19.24 E
Chu (Xam) ≃, Asia	110	19.53 N	105.45 E
Chu ≃, Zhg.	100	32.08 N	118.43 E
Chu ≃, Zhg.	106	32.15 N	119.03 E
Chuādanga	124	23.38 N	88.51 E
Chualar	226	36.34 N	121.31 W
Chuanbu	106	31.17 N	119.49 E
Chuanchang ≊	100	33.46 N	119.51 E
Chuanergu	105	39.20 N	117.43 E
Chuan'gang	106	31.57 N	121.04 E
Chuangjiapuzi	104	40.50 N	124.06 E
Chuanliao	100	28.17 N	120.13 E
Chuansha	106	31.12 N	121.42 E
Chuanshan	100	29.53 N	121.57 E
Chuanxindian	104	41.25 N	120.30 E
Chuanyao Gang ᴄ	106	32.12 N	121.25 E
Chuathbaluk	180	61.40 N	159.15 W
Chubbuck	202	42.55 N	112.27 W
Chūbu-Sangaku-kokuritsu-kōen ♠	94	36.30 N	137.41 E
Chubut □[4]	254	44.00 S	69.00 W
Chubut ≃	254	43.20 S	65.03 W
Ch'üchiang → Shaoguan	100	24.50 N	113.37 E
Chuchi Lake ⊜	182	55.10 N	124.33 W
Chuchou → Zhuzhou	100	27.50 N	113.09 E
Chu Chua	182	51.21 N	120.10 W
Chuchuwayha Indian Reserve -◆-[4]	182	49.21 N	120.06 W
Chuckatuck	208	36.52 N	76.35 W
Chučni	84	41.57 N	47.55 E
Chucuito	248	15.53 S	69.53 W
Chucun	100	33.04 N	116.32 E
Chucunaque ≃	246	8.09 N	77.44 W
Chudan ≃	88	52.08 N	109.40 E
Chudanskij chrebet ⛰	88	52.00 N	110.00 E
Chudeč	60	49.58 N	13.05 E
Chudleigh	42	50.36 N	3.38 W
Chudniv	78	50.04 N	28.06 E
Chudojelan'	88	54.42 N	99.37 E
Chudžand (Leninabad)	85	40.17 N	69.37 E
Chudžand □[4]	85	39.15 N	69.30 E
Chudzirt	86	47.05 N	91.10 E
Chuen Lung	271d	22.24 N	114.06 E
Chugach Islands II	180	59.06 N	151.42 W
Chugach Mountains ⛰	180	61.00 N	145.00 W
Chuginadak Island I	180	52.49 N	169.50 W
Chūgoku-sanchi ⛰	96	34.58 N	132.57 E
Chugwater	200	41.45 N	104.49 W
Chugwater Creek ≃	198	42.07 N	104.51 W
Chugyn-ri	271b	37.39 N	126.50 E
Chūhar Kāna	123	31.45 N	73.48 E
Chuhe	100	34.03 N	113.35 E
Chuhuichupa	232	29.38 N	108.22 W
Chuhuyiv	78	49.50 N	36.41 E
Chuhynka	83	48.55 N	39.39 E
Chuí	252	33.41 S	53.27 W
Chuius Mountain ∧	182	54.51 N	124.30 W
Chukai	114	4.15 N	103.25 E
Chukchi Sea ⫧[2]	16	69.00 N	171.00 W
Chuke Hu ⊜	120	31.40 N	88.00 E
Chukou	100	25.44 N	113.22 E
Chulalongkorn University ʋ[2]	269a	13.44 N	100.33 E
Chula Vista	228	32.38 N	117.05 W
Chuld	102	45.04 N	105.35 E
Chulga ≃	24	64.20 N	61.00 E
Chullora	274a	33.54 S	151.04 E
Chulmleigh	42	50.55 N	3.52 W
Chulo	84	41.41 N	42.18 E
Chulp'o	98	35.37 N	126.40 E
Chulucanas	248	5.06 S	80.10 W
Chulumani	248	16.24 S	67.31 W
Chuluota	220	28.38 N	81.10 W
Chuma	248	15.24 S	68.56 W
Chumalag	84	43.14 N	44.28 E
Chumbicha	252	28.52 S	66.14 W
Chummi, ozero ⊜	89	50.18 N	137.17 E
Chum Phae	110	16.32 N	102.06 E
Chumphon	110	10.30 N	99.10 E
Chumphon Buri	110	15.21 N	103.24 E
Chumpi	248	15.06 S	73.46 W
Chum Saeng	110	15.54 N	100.19 E
Chumunjin	98	37.54 N	128.49 E
Chunal	262	53.25 N	1.57 W
Chunan, T'aiwan	100	24.41 N	120.52 E
Chun'an, Zhg.	100	29.35 N	118.58 E
Chunār	124	25.08 N	82.54 E
Chuncheon → Ch'unch'ŏn	98	37.52 N	127.43 E
Chunchi, Ec.	246	2.17 S	78.55 W
Chunchi, Zhg.	100	27.22 N	119.20 E
Ch'unch'ŏn	98	37.52 N	127.43 E
Chunchula	194	30.55 N	88.12 W
Chūnd	123	31.26 N	72.16 E
Chung-ang University ʋ[2]	271b	37.30 N	126.58 E
Chungari ≃	89	50.04 N	136.55 E
Ch'ungch'ŏng Namdo □[4]	98	36.30 N	127.00 E
Ch'ungch'ŏng Pukdo □[4]	98	36.45 N	128.00 E
Chunggang-ni	98	40.52 N	127.20 E
Chung Hau	271d	22.16 N	114.00 E
Chungho	269d	25.00 N	121.30 E
Chung Hsing Bridge -◆-[5]	269d	25.03 N	121.29 E
Chunghwa	98	38.52 N	125.47 E
Ch'ungju	98	36.58 N	127.58 E
Chungking → Chongqing	107	29.34 N	106.35 E
Chungli	100	24.57 N	121.13 E
Chungliao	100	22.41 N	121.28 E
Ch'ungmu	98	34.51 N	128.25 E
Chungp'u	100	23.25 N	120.31 E
Chungp'yŏngjang	98	41.11 N	128.03 E
Chungsam-ni	98	38.34 N	127.09 E
Chŭngsan	98	39.06 N	125.22 E
Chŭngsanha-ri -◆-[8]	271b	37.35 N	126.54 E
Chungshan → Zhongshan	100	22.31 N	113.22 E
Chungshan Bridge -◆-[5]	269d	25.05 N	121.31 E
Chunguj ≃	88	48.51 N	93.32 E
Chungyang Shanmo ⛰	100	23.30 N	121.00 E
Chunheji	100	32.12 N	115.22 E
Chunhua, Zhg.	102	34.50 N	108.31 E
Chunhua, Zhg.	106	31.56 N	118.56 E
Chunhuhux	232	19.12 N	88.55 W
Chūniān	123	30.58 N	73.59 E
Chuntuquí	232	17.31 N	90.09 W
Chünüj ≃	88	48.48 N	102.00 E
Chunya	154	8.32 S	33.25 E
Ch'unyang, Taehan	98	36.56 N	128.54 E
Chunyang, Zhg.	89	43.43 N	129.28 E
Chunzach	84	42.33 N	46.43 E
Chūō	96	35.00 N	133.58 E
Chūō -◆-[8], Nihon	268	35.40 N	139.47 E
Chūō -◆-[8], Nihon	270	34.42 N	135.11 E
Chuŏr Phnum Krâvanh ⛰	110	12.00 N	103.15 E
Chuosijia	102	31.53 N	101.59 E
Chupaca	248	12.04 S	75.19 W
Chupadera Arroyo V	200	33.47 N	106.37 W
Chupadero, Cerro ∧	200	31.01 N	111.37 W
Chupakhivka	78	50.23 N	34.36 E
Chupara Point ›	241r	10.48 N	61.22 W
Chuquibamba	248	15.50 S	72.39 W
Chuquibambilla	248	14.07 S	72.43 W
Chuquicamata	252	22.19 S	68.56 W
Chuquisaca □[5]	248	20.00 S	64.20 W
Chuquitanta	286d	11.58 S	77.06 W
Chur	58	46.51 N	9.32 E
Churach ≃	88	48.37 N	110.42 E
Churāchāndpur	120	24.20 N	93.40 E
Churāmankāti	126	23.14 N	89.09 E
Churcampa	248	12.42 S	74.24 W
Church	262	53.45 N	2.24 W
Churchdown	42	51.53 N	2.10 W
Church Hill	192	36.31 N	82.42 W
Churchill, Mb., Can.	176	58.46 N	94.10 W
Churchill, Oh., U.S.	214	41.09 N	80.39 W
Churchill, Pa., U.S.	279b	40.27 N	79.51 W
Churchill, Va., U.S.	284c	38.54 N	77.10 W
Churchill ≃, Can.	176	58.47 N	94.12 W
Churchill ≃, Nf., Can.	176	53.30 N	60.10 W
Churchill, Cape ›	176	58.46 N	93.12 W
Churchill, Mount ∧, B.C., Can.	182	49.58 N	123.51 W
Churchill, Mount ∧, Ak., U.S.	180	61.25 N	141.43 W
Churchill Downs ♠	218	38.12 N	85.46 W
Churchill Falls ʟ	176	53.35 N	64.27 W
Churchill Lake ⊜	184	55.55 N	108.20 W
Churchill National Park ♠	169	37.58 S	145.17 E
Church Point	194	30.24 N	92.12 W
Church Rock	200	35.32 N	108.35 W
Church Street	260	51.26 N	0.28 E
Church Stretton	42	52.32 N	2.49 W
Churchton	208	38.48 N	76.32 W
Churchtown, Eng., U.K.	262	53.40 N	2.58 W
Churchtown, Pa., U.S.	208	40.08 N	75.58 W
Church View	208	37.41 N	76.41 W
Churchville, On., Can.	275b	43.38 N	79.45 W
Churchville, Md., U.S.	208	39.33 N	76.14 W
Churchville, N.Y., U.S.	210	43.06 N	77.53 W
Churchville, Pa., U.S.	285	40.11 N	75.01 W
Churdan	198	42.09 N	94.28 W
Churen Himāl ∧	124	28.44 N	83.12 E
Chure Śringklā ⛰	124	27.40 N	83.40 E
Churfirsten ⛰	58	47.08 N	9.17 E
Chürmen	102	43.20 N	104.05 E
Churmuli	89	51.00 N	136.50 E
Churn ≃	42	51.38 N	1.53 W
Churn Creek ≃	182	51.30 N	122.17 W
Churnet ≃	44	52.55 N	1.50 W
Churni ≃[1]	126	23.08 N	88.30 E
Chursdorf	54	50.46 N	12.15 E
Chūru	120	28.18 N	74.57 E
Churubusco, In., U.S.	216	41.13 N	85.19 W
Churubusco, N.Y., U.S.	206	44.57 N	73.56 W
Churuguara	246	10.49 N	69.32 W
Churumuco de Morelos	234	18.37 N	101.38 W
Churwalden	58	46.47 N	9.33 E
Chušenga	88	51.27 N	110.55 E
Chushan	100	23.45 N	120.40 E
Chushul	120	33.36 N	78.39 E
Chuska Mountains ⛰	200	36.15 N	108.50 W
Chuska Peak ∧	200	35.53 N	108.50 W
Chusovoy → Čusovoj	86	58.17 N	57.49 E
Chusuut uul ∧	88	47.45 N	105.45 E
Chūta	174m	26.32 N	127.58 E
Chutag	88	49.23 N	102.43 E
Chutag Uul	102	43.23 N	110.13 E
Chute-à-Blondeau	206	45.35 N	74.29 W
Chute-Panet	206	46.51 N	71.51 W
Chutorskoj	80	46.52 N	42.59 E
Chutove	78	49.43 N	35.10 E
Chutu ≃	89	49.27 N	140.02 E
Chutung	100	24.44 N	121.05 E
Chuuk (Truk Islands) II	175c	7.25 N	151.47 E
Chuŭl	98	41.33 N	129.34 E
Chuvashia → Čuvašija □[3]	80	55.30 N	47.00 E
Chuwang	98	36.02 N	114.52 E
Chuwang-san Kukrip Kongwŏn ♠	98	36.26 N	129.10 E
Chuwei	269d	25.08 N	121.27 E
Chuxian	100	32.19 N	118.17 E
Chuxiong	102	25.02 N	101.30 E
Chuy	252	33.41 S	53.27 W
Chuzenji-ko ⊜	94	36.44 N	139.29 E
Chuzhai	100	33.22 N	113.37 E
Chužir	88	53.11 N	107.20 E
Chūzu	94	35.06 N	136.00 E
Chvalynsk	80	52.30 N	48.07 E
Chvančkara	84	42.34 N	43.01 E
Chvastoviči	76	53.28 N	35.06 E
Chvatovka	80	52.21 N	46.34 E
Chvojnaja	76	58.54 N	34.32 E
Chvorost'anka	80	52.36 N	48.59 E
Chvostovo	92a	46.08 N	142.14 E
Chwefru ≃	42	52.09 N	3.25 W
Ch'wiya-ri	98	38.03 N	125.32 E
Chychykliya ≃	78	47.23 N	31.34 E
Chyhyryn	78	49.04 N	32.40 E
Chynadiyeve	78	48.30 N	22.50 E
Chypre → Cyprus □[1]	130	35.00 N	33.00 E
Chystovodivka	83	49.24 N	37.20 E
Ci ≃, Zhg.	98	38.19 N	115.23 E
Ci ≃, Zhg.	100	33.27 N	115.31 E
Ciadâr Lunga	38	46.03 N	28.47 E
Ciago	64	46.12 N	12.46 E
Ciagola, Monte ∧	68	39.54 N	15.53 E
Ciales	240m	18.20 N	66.28 W
Ciamis	115a	7.20 S	108.21 E
Ciampino	66	41.48 N	12.36 E
Ciampino, Aeroporto di ⊠	267a	41.48 N	12.36 E
Cianciana	70	37.31 N	13.26 E
Ciandur	115a	6.24 S	105.59 E
Cianjur	115a	6.49 S	107.08 E
Ciano d'Enza	64	44.36 N	10.24 E
Cianorte	255	23.37 S	52.37 W
Cians, Gorges du V	62	43.57 N	6.59 E
Čiatura	84	42.17 N	43.17 E
Ciavolo	70	37.46 N	12.33 E
Ciawi, Indon.	115a	7.10 S	108.09 E
Ciawi, Indon.	115a	6.40 S	106.50 E
Ciawigebang	115a	6.58 S	108.34 E
Ciba	107	29.07 N	105.55 E
Cibadak	115a	6.53 S	106.46 E
Cibaliung	115a	6.46 S	105.51 E
Čibargata	85	41.08 N	69.48 E
Cibatu	115a	7.06 S	107.59 E
Cibeber	115a	6.56 S	107.07 E
Cibecue	200	34.02 N	110.29 W
Cibiana	64	46.23 N	12.17 E
Cibinong	115a	6.27 S	106.51 E
Čibisovka	78	50.47 N	40.05 E
Čibižek	86	54.27 N	93.40 E
Cibolo Creek ≃, Tx., U.S.	196	28.57 N	97.53 W
Cibolo Creek ≃, Tx., U.S.	196	29.34 N	104.24 W
Cibolo Creek ≃, Tx., U.S.	196	28.27 N	98.54 W
Cibuta	200	31.04 N	110.54 W
Cicagna	62	44.25 N	9.14 E
Cicala	68	39.01 N	16.29 E
Cicalengka	115a	6.59 S	107.50 E
Čićarija ⛰	36	45.30 N	13.54 E
Čičatka	89	54.03 N	121.18 E
Cicciano	68	40.58 N	14.32 E
Cicero, Il., U.S.	216	41.50 N	87.45 W
Cicero, In., U.S.	218	40.07 N	86.00 W
Cicero, N.Y., U.S.	210	43.10 N	76.07 W
Cicero Creek ≃	194	40.01 N	86.01 W
Cícero Dantas	250	10.36 S	38.23 W
Čichačovo, Ross.	76	57.17 N	29.54 E
Čichačovo, Ross.	89	51.50 N	141.07 E
Čichareši	84	42.48 N	43.03 E
Ciche, Sgurr na ∧	46	57.01 N	5.27 W
Cicheng	100	30.00 N	121.22 E
Čičkajul ≃	86	57.34 N	85.44 E
Cícladas, Islas → Kikládhes II	38	37.30 N	25.00 E
Cicolano -◆-[1]	66	42.12 N	13.12 E
Cicurug	115a	6.47 S	106.47 E
Cidacos ≃	34	42.19 N	1.55 W
Cidade, Rio da ≃	256	22.25 S	43.09 W
Cidade Universitária ʋ[2], Bra.	287a	22.52 S	43.14 W
Cidade Universitária ʋ[2], Bra.	287b	23.33 S	46.43 W
Cide	130	41.54 N	33.00 E
Cidra	240m	18.11 N	66.10 W
Cidra, Lago de ⊜[1]	240m	18.12 N	66.08 W
Ciechanów	30	52.53 N	20.38 E
Ciechanów □[4]	30	53.00 N	20.20 E
Ciechanowiec	30	52.42 N	22.31 E
Ciechocinek	30	52.52 N	18.49 E
Ciego de Ávila	240p	21.51 N	78.46 W
Ciego de Ávila □[4]	240p	22.00 N	78.40 W
Ciempozuelos	34	40.10 N	3.37 W
Ciénaga	246	11.01 N	74.15 W
Ciénaga de Oro	246	8.53 N	75.37 W
Ciénega de Flores	196	25.57 N	100.11 W
Cienfuegos	240p	22.09 N	80.27 W
Cienfuegos □[4]	240p	22.10 N	80.25 W
Cienfuegos, Bahía de ᴄ	240p	22.07 N	80.29 W
Čierna [nad Tisou]	30	48.25 N	22.05 E
Čierny Balog	30	48.45 N	19.40 E
Cíes, Illas II	34	42.13 N	8.54 W
Cieszanów	30	50.16 N	23.08 E
Cieszyn	30	49.45 N	18.38 E
Cieza	34	38.14 N	1.25 W
Çiftalan -◆-[8]	267b	41.15 N	28.54 E
Çiftehan	130	37.31 N	34.46 E
Çifteler	130	39.22 N	31.03 E
Çiftlik	130	38.11 N	34.30 E
Cifuentes, Cuba	240p	22.39 N	80.03 W
Cifuentes, Esp.	34	40.47 N	2.37 W
Čiganak, Kaz.	86	45.06 N	73.58 E
Čiganak, Ross.	80	51.47 N	43.18 E
Čiganaki	80	47.57 N	43.05 E
Cigliano	62	45.18 N	8.01 E
Čigorak	80	51.26 N	42.09 E
Cigou	100	33.51 N	113.35 E
Cigüela ≃	34	39.08 N	3.44 W
Cihanbeyli	130	38.40 N	32.56 E
Cihara	115a	6.52 S	106.06 E
Cihuatlán	234	19.14 N	104.35 W
Čiili	86	44.10 N	66.45 E
Cijara, Embalse de ⊜[1]	34	39.18 N	4.52 W
Čijen	85	43.08 N	75.55 E
Cijiawu	105	39.48 N	115.59 E
Čijirčik, pereval)(	85	40.15 N	73.20 E
Čijli ≃	85	40.17 N	72.38 E
Cijulang	115a	7.44 S	108.27 E
Čik	86	55.01 N	82.27 E
Cikajang	115a	7.22 S	107.47 E
Cikalong-kulon	115a	6.42 S	107.12 E
Cikampek	115a	6.24 S	107.27 E
Čikan	88	54.54 N	105.39 E
Cikarang	115a	6.15 S	107.09 E
Cikatomas	115a	7.37 S	108.15 E
Čikišl'ar	128	37.34 N	53.55 E
Čikoj	88	50.16 N	106.54 E
Čikoj ≃	88	51.02 N	106.39 E
Čikola	84	43.12 N	43.55 E
Cikou	100	29.42 N	114.46 E
Cıksı	130	38.30 N	40.55 E
Cilacap	115a	7.44 S	109.00 E
Cilamaya	115a	6.15 S	107.35 E
Cilavegna	62	45.19 N	8.44 E
Çıldır	84	41.08 N	43.07 E
Çıldır Gölü ⊜	84	41.04 N	43.15 E
Ciledug	115a	6.54 S	108.44 E
Cilegon	115a	6.01 S	106.03 E
Čilekovo	80	47.50 N	43.30 E
Cilento -◆-[1]	68	40.15 N	15.15 E
Čil'gaz	85	40.10 N	70.39 E
Cili	102	29.17 N	111.00 E
Cilicia □[9]	130	36.40 N	34.20 E
Čilik, Kaz.	85	43.36 N	78.15 E
Čilik, Kaz.	86	51.07 N	54.07 E
Čilik ≃, Kaz.	85	43.05 N	78.28 E
Čilik ≃, Kaz.	85	43.50 N	78.06 E
Cililin	115a	6.56 S	107.26 E
Cilimus	115a	6.52 S	108.29 E
Cilincing -◆-[8]	269e	6.06 S	106.56 E
Cill Airne → Killarney	48	52.03 N	9.30 W
Cill Chainnigh → Kilkenny	48	52.39 N	7.15 W
Cilleruelo de Bezana	34	42.58 N	3.51 W
Cil'ma ≃	24	65.27 N	52.06 E
Čilov ada I	84	40.19 N	50.36 E
Cimabanche (Schluderbach)	64	46.37 N	12.11 E
Cima Gogna	64	46.31 N	12.28 E
Cimahi	115a	6.53 S	107.32 E
Cimalaka	115a	6.49 S	107.56 E
Cimalmotto	58	46.17 N	8.29 E
Cimarron, Ks., U.S.	198	37.48 N	100.20 W
Cimarron, N.M., U.S.	200	36.30 N	104.54 W
Cimarron ≃, U.S.	196	36.10 N	96.17 W
Cimarron ≃, N.M., U.S.	196	36.20 N	104.31 W
Cimarron, North Fork ≃	196	37.25 N	101.13 W
Čimbaj	86	42.57 N	59.47 E
Čimčinej gora ∧[2]	180	63.37 N	178.04 E
Cimini, Monti ⛰	66	42.20 N	12.10 E
Ciminna	70	37.54 N	13.34 E
Cimino, Monte ∧	66	42.24 N	12.12 E
Čimion	85	40.16 N	71.31 E
Cimişlia	38	46.32 N	28.44 E
Cimitile	68	40.56 N	14.31 E
Čimkavičy	76	53.03 N	27.00 E
Čimkent → Šymkent	85	42.18 N	69.36 E
Čimkorgon	85	42.50 N	75.30 E
Cimla ≃	80	48.01 N	42.24 E
Ciml'ansk	80	47.38 N	42.04 E
Ciml'anskoje vodochranilišče ⊜[1]	80	48.00 N	43.00 E
Cimolais	64	46.17 N	12.26 E
Cimone, Monte ∧	64	44.12 N	10.42 E
Cimpu	112	3.25 S	120.22 E
Čimtarga, gora ∧	85	39.12 N	68.10 E
Čina ≃	88	54.20 N	112.24 E
Cina, Tanjung ›	112	5.56 S	104.45 E
Činabad	85	40.52 N	71.58 E
Cinandali	84	41.53 N	45.34 E
Çınar	130	37.44 N	40.25 E
Çınarcık	130	40.39 N	29.06 E
Cinaruco ≃	246	6.41 N	67.07 W
Činaz	85	40.56 N	68.45 E
Cinca ≃	34	41.26 N	0.21 E
Cincar ∧	36	43.54 N	17.04 E
Cincinnati, Ia., U.S.	190	40.37 N	92.55 W
Cincinnati, Oh., U.S.	218	39.09 N	84.27 W
Cincinnatus	210	42.32 N	75.53 W
Cinco, Canal Numero ≊	252	37.35 S	57.20 W
Cinco Balas, Cayos II	240p	21.06 N	79.20 W
Cinco de Mayo	196	25.46 N	104.19 W
Cinco Pinos	236	13.14 N	86.52 W
Cinco Saltos	252	38.49 S	68.04 W
Cinderella	273d	26.15 S	28.16 E
Cinderella Dam ⊜[1]	273d	26.15 S	28.14 E
Cinderford	42	51.50 N	2.29 W
Cinder Island I	276	40.36 N	73.36 W
Çine	130	37.36 N	28.04 E
Cinebar	224	46.36 N	122.32 W
Cinecittà ʋ[3]	267a	41.51 N	12.34 E
Cinema	182	53.14 N	122.27 W
Ciney	56	50.18 N	5.06 E
Cinfães	34	41.04 N	8.05 W
Čingaly	86	60.13 N	69.45 E
Čingis	86	54.08 N	81.41 E
Cingoli	66	43.22 N	13.13 E
Cinigiano	66	42.53 N	11.24 E
Cinisello Balsamo	62	45.33 N	9.13 E
Cinişeuţi	38	47.42 N	28.52 E
Cinisi	70	38.09 N	13.06 E
Činja-Voryk	24	63.13 N	52.38 E
Cinkota -◆-[8]	264c	47.31 N	19.14 E
Cinnaminson	285	40.00 N	74.59 W
Cínovec	54	50.43 N	13.45 E
Cinq, Lac des ⊜	206	46.51 N	72.59 W
Cinq Doigts, Lac ⊜	206	46.36 N	74.32 W
Cinquefrondi	68	38.25 N	16.06 E
Cinquemiglia, Piano delle ≚	66	41.50 N	14.00 E
Cinqueterre □[9]	62	44.10 N	9.45 E
Cintalapa	234	16.44 N	93.43 W
Cinto, Monte ∧	36	42.23 N	8.56 E
Cinto Euganeo	64	45.16 N	11.40 E
Cintra → Sintra	34	38.48 N	9.23 W
Cintra, Golfe de ᴄ	148	23.00 N	16.20 W
Ciocăneşti	38	44.12 N	27.04 E
Ciociaria -◆-[1]	66	41.45 N	13.15 E
Ciomas	115a	6.12 S	106.01 E
Čiovo, Otok I	36	43.30 N	16.20 E
Cipa ≃	88	55.23 N	115.55 E
Ciparay	115a	7.03 S	107.43 E
Cipatujah	115a	7.45 S	108.00 E
Cipikan	88	54.55 N	113.21 E
Cipikan ≃	88	55.14 N	113.05 E
Cipó	250	11.06 S	38.31 W
Cipó ≃	255	18.40 S	43.59 W
Cipolândia	255	20.08 S	55.24 W
Cipolletti	252	38.56 S	67.59 W
Ciqikou	107	29.35 N	106.26 E
Čir	80	48.29 N	43.10 E
Čir ≃	80	48.35 N	42.51 E
Ciraadhame	144	10.30 N	49.22 E
Čirachčaj ≃	84	41.40 N	48.11 E
Ciragidzor	84	40.27 N	46.19 E
Ciranjang	115a	6.49 S	107.14 E
Circeo, Monte ∧	66	41.14 N	13.03 E
Circeo, Parco Nazionale del ♠	66	41.17 N	13.05 E
Čirčik	85	41.29 N	69.35 E
Čirčik ≃	85	40.54 N	68.41 E
Çırçır	130	40.04 N	36.48 E
Circle, Ak., U.S.	180	65.50 N	144.04 W
Circle, Mt., U.S.	202	47.20 N	105.35 W
Circle Hot Springs	180	65.28 N	144.39 W
Circleville, N.Y., U.S.	210	41.31 N	75.23 W
Circleville, Oh., U.S.	218	39.36 N	82.56 W
Circleville, Pa., U.S.	279b	40.20 N	79.44 W
Circleville, Ut,. U.S.	200	38.10 N	112.16 W
Circleville Mountain ∧	200	38.12 N	112.24 W
Circular Reef ✣[2]	164	3.25 S	147.47 E
Circus World ♠	220	28.14 N	81.38 W
Cirebon	115a	6.44 S	108.34 E
Cireglio	66	43.59 N	10.51 E
Ciremay, Gunung ∧	115a	6.54 S	108.24 E
Cirencester	42	51.44 N	1.59 W
Cirey-sur-Vezouze	58	48.35 N	6.57 E
Čirgalandy	88	50.36 N	97.20 E
Ciriè	62	45.14 N	7.36 E
Cirigliano	68	40.24 N	16.10 E
Čirikovo	82	55.23 N	37.14 E
Ciriquiri ≃	248	8.05 S	65.18 W
Cirk, gora ∧	180	64.33 N	175.25 E
Cirò	68	39.23 N	17.04 E
Cirò Marina	68	39.22 N	17.08 E
Ciro Redondo	240p	22.01 N	78.43 W
Čirpan	38	42.12 N	25.20 E
Ciruas	115a	6.06 S	106.13 E
Cisa, Passo della)(	64	44.28 N	9.55 E
Cisano	64	45.32 N	10.43 E
Cisarua	115a	6.40 S	106.59 E
Cisco, Il., U.S.	219	40.01 N	88.43 W
Cisco, Tx., U.S.	196	32.23 N	98.58 W
Cishan	98	36.37 N	114.07 E
Cishangang	106	30.55 N	119.31 E
Ciskei □[9]	158	32.50 S	27.00 E
Cislago	62	45.39 N	8.58 E
Cisliano	266b	45.27 N	8.59 E
Cismar	54	54.11 N	10.59 E
Čismena	82	56.02 N	36.13 E
Cismon ≃	64	45.55 N	11.43 E
Cismon del Grappa	64	45.55 N	11.44 E
Čišmy	86	54.35 N	55.20 E
Cisnădie	38	45.43 N	24.09 E
Cisne	194	38.31 N	88.26 W
Cisneros	246	6.33 N	75.04 W
Cisnes ≃	254	44.45 S	72.42 W
Cisolok	115a	6.57 S	106.26 E
Cison di Valmarino	64	45.58 N	12.10 E
Cispus ≃	224	46.25 N	122.10 W
Cisse ≃	50	47.25 N	0.47 E
Cissna Park	216	40.33 N	87.53 W
Čistá, Česká Rep.	54	50.06 N	12.44 E
Čistá, Česká Rep.	60	50.02 N	13.35 E
Cisterna di Latina	66	41.35 N	12.49 E
Cisternino	68	40.44 N	17.25 E
Cistern Point ›	238	23.43 N	77.35 W
Cistierna	34	42.48 N	5.07 W
Čistoje	80	56.32 N	43.02 E
Čistooz'ornoje	86	54.43 N	76.33 E
Čistopol'	80	55.21 N	50.37 E
Čistopolje, Kaz.	86	52.34 N	67.15 E
Čistopolje, Ross.	83	47.31 N	39.27 E
Čita	88	52.03 N	113.30 E
Čita ≃	88	52.00 N	113.30 E
Citac, Nevado ∧	248	12.48 S	75.14 W
Čita Oblast' □[4]	88	52.00 N	117.00 E
Citaré ≃	250	1.11 N	54.41 W
Cité Universitaire ʋ[2]	261	48.49 N	2.20 E
Citlaltépetl, Volcán → Orizaba, Pico de ∧[1]	234	19.01 N	97.16 E
Citra	192	29.24 N	82.06 W
Citronelle	194	31.05 N	88.13 W
Citrus □[6]	220	28.52 N	82.28 W
Citrusdal	158	32.36 S	19.00 E
Citrus Heights	226	38.42 N	121.16 W
Citrus Springs	220	29.00 N	82.27 W
Citrus Tower ʋ	220	28.33 N	81.44 W
Cittadella	64	45.39 N	11.47 E
Città della Pieve	66	42.57 N	12.00 E
Città del Vaticano → Vatican City □[1]	66	41.54 N	12.27 E
Città di Castello	66	43.27 N	12.14 E
Cittaducale	66	42.23 N	12.57 E
Cittanova	68	38.21 N	16.05 E
Cittareale	66	42.37 N	13.10 E
Città Sant'Angelo	66	42.31 N	14.03 E
Città Universitaria ʋ[2]	267a	41.55 N	12.31 E
City Beach	168a	31.56 S	115.45 E
City Bell -◆-[8]	258	34.52 S	58.05 W
City Island -◆-[8]	276	40.51 N	73.47 W
City Mills	283	42.06 N	71.21 W
City of Hope National Medical Center ʋ	280	34.08 N	117.58 W
City Of Industry	280	34.01 N	117.57 W
City of London -◆-[8]	260	51.31 N	0.05 W
City of Refuge → Pu'uhonua o Honaunau National Historic Site ⊥	229d	19.25 N	155.54 W
City of Sunrise	220	26.08 N	80.14 W
City Point	220	28.24 N	80.45 W
City University of New York Brooklyn College ʋ[2]	276	40.38 N	73.57 W
City University of New York City College ʋ[2]	276	40.49 N	73.57 W
City University of New York Queens College ʋ[2]	276	40.44 N	73.49 W
City University of New York York College ʋ[2]	276	40.42 N	73.48 W
Ciucaş, Vârful ∧	38	45.31 N	25.55 E
Ciuciuleni	38	47.02 N	28.22 E
Ciudad Acuña	232	29.18 N	100.55 W
Ciudad Altamirano	234	18.20 N	100.40 W
Ciudad Barrios	236	13.46 N	88.16 W
Ciudad Bolívar	246	8.08 N	63.33 W
Ciudad Bolivia	246	8.21 N	70.34 W
Ciudad Camargo	232	26.19 N	98.50 W
Ciudad Constitución	232	24.59 N	111.39 W
Ciudad Cortés	236	8.58 N	83.32 W
Ciudad Cuauhtémoc	234	22.28 N	102.20 W
Ciudad Darío	236	12.43 N	86.08 W
Ciudad de Carangas	248	17.53 S	66.11 W
Ciudad de Guayana → Ciudad Guayana	246	8.22 N	62.40 W
Ciudad de la Habana □[4]	240p	23.08 N	82.22 W
Ciudad del Cabo → Cape Town	158	33.55 S	18.22 E
Ciudad del Carmen	232	18.38 N	91.50 W
Ciudad del Este	252	25.30 S	54.36 W
Ciudad del Maíz	234	22.24 N	99.36 W
Ciudad de los Deportes ♠	286a	19.23 N	99.11 W
Ciudad del Vaticano → Vatican City □[1]	66	41.54 N	12.27 E
Ciudad de México (Mexico City), Méx.	234	19.24 N	99.09 W
Ciudad de México (Mexico City), Méx.	286a	19.24 N	99.09 W
Ciudad de Nutrias	246	8.05 N	69.18 W
Ciudad Deportiva ♠, Cuba	286b	23.07 N	82.22 W
Ciudad Deportiva ♠, Méx.	286a	19.24 N	99.06 W
Ciudadela, Parque de la ♠	266d	41.23 N	2.11 E
Ciudad General Belgrano	288	34.43 S	58.32 W
Ciudad Guayana	246	8.22 N	62.40 W
Ciudad Guzmán	234	19.41 N	103.29 W
Ciudad Hidalgo, Méx.	234	19.41 N	100.34 W
Ciudad Hidalgo, Méx.	236	14.41 N	92.09 W
Ciudad Juárez	232	31.44 N	106.29 W
Ciudad Lerdo	196	25.32 N	103.32 W
Ciudad Lerdo de Tejada	234	18.37 N	95.31 W
Ciudad Lineal -◆-[8]	266a	40.27 N	3.40 W
Ciudad López Mateos	286a	19.33 N	99.15 W
Ciudad Madero	234	22.16 N	97.50 W
Ciudad Mante	234	22.44 N	98.57 W
Ciudad Manuel Doblado	234	20.44 N	101.56 W
Ciudad Mendoza	234	18.48 N	97.11 W
Ciudad Miguel Alemán	232	26.23 N	99.01 W
Ciudad Morelos	232	32.38 N	114.52 W
Ciudad Obregón	232	27.29 N	109.56 W
Ciudad Ojeda (Lagunillas)	246	10.12 N	71.19 W
Ciudad Piar	246	7.27 N	63.19 W
Ciudad Real	34	38.59 N	3.56 W
Ciudad Real □[4]	34	38.50 N	3.45 W
Ciudad Rodrigo	34	40.36 N	6.32 W
Ciudad Sahagún	234	19.47 N	98.33 W
Ciudad Sandino	236	13.43 N	86.08 W
Ciudad Serdán	234	18.59 N	97.27 W
Ciudad Tecún Umán	236	14.40 N	92.09 W
Ciudad Trujillo → Santo Domingo	238	18.28 N	69.54 W
Ciudad Universitaria -◆-[8]	266a	40.27 N	3.44 W
Ciudad Universitaria ʋ[2], Esp.	266a	40.27 N	3.43 W
Ciudad Universitaria ʋ[2], Méx.	286a	19.20 N	99.11 W
Ciudad Universitaria ʋ[2], Ven.	286c	10.29 N	66.53 W
Ciudad Valles	234	21.59 N	99.01 W
Ciudad Victoria, Méx.	204	32.20 N	115.06 W
Ciudad Victoria, Méx.	234	23.44 N	99.08 W
Ciudad Vieja	236	14.31 N	90.46 W
Ciuma	152	13.14 S	15.40 E
Ciutadella	34	40.02 N	3.50 E
Civa Burnu ›	130	41.22 N	36.35 E
Civate	62	45.50 N	9.21 E
Civenna	58	45.56 N	9.16 E
Civetta, Monte ∧	64	46.23 N	12.03 E
Civezzano	64	46.05 N	11.11 E
Cividale del Friuli	64	46.06 N	13.25 E
Cividate al Piano	62	45.33 N	9.50 E
Cividate Camuno	64	45.57 N	10.17 E
Civil' ≃	80	56.08 N	47.35 E
Civil'sk	80	55.53 N	47.29 E
Civita	68	39.49 N	16.18 E
Civitacampomarano	66	41.47 N	14.41 E
Civita Castellana	66	42.17 N	12.25 E
Civita di Bagno	66	42.18 N	13.26 E
Civitanova Alta	66	43.19 N	13.40 E
Civitanova del Sannio	66	41.40 N	14.24 E
Civitanova Marche	66	43.18 N	13.44 E
Civitaquana	66	42.19 N	13.54 E
Civitavecchia	66	42.06 N	11.48 E
Civitella del Tronto	66	42.46 N	13.40 E
Civitella di Romagna	66	44.00 N	11.56 E
Civitella in Val di Chiana	66	43.25 N	11.43 E
Civitella Marittima	66	43.00 N	11.17 E
Civitella Roveto	66	41.54 N	13.25 E
Civray	32	46.09 N	0.18 E
Çivril	130	38.18 N	29.45 E
Ciwidey	115a	7.06 S	107.27 E
Cixerri ≃	71	39.17 N	8.59 E
Cixi	100	30.11 N	121.15 E
Cixian	98	36.22 N	114.23 E
Ciyutuo	104	41.31 N	122.53 E
Čiža	24	67.06 N	44.19 E
Čižapka ≃	86	59.01 N	79.36 E
Čiža Vtoraja	80	50.52 N	49.40 E
Cize	58	46.12 N	5.26 E
Cizhuping	107	29.11 N	103.36 E
Čižinskije razlivy ≡	80	50.25 N	49.40 E
Cizre	130	37.20 N	42.12 E
Cjahcin	76	53.51 N	29.44 E
Cjaluša	76	53.03 N	29.31 E
C.J. Strike Reservoir ⊜[1]	202	42.57 N	115.53 W
Čkalov → Orenburg	86	51.54 N	55.06 E
Čkalovo	86	53.38 N	70.24 E
Čkalovsk, Kaz.	85	41.15 N	68.00 E
Čkalovsk, Ross.	80	56.46 N	43.16 E
Čkalovsk, Taj.	85	40.13 N	69.50 E
Čkalovskij	265b	55.54 N	38.04 E
C K Creek ≃	202	47.36 N	108.29 W
Čkyně	60	49.07 N	13.49 E
Čl'a, ozero ⊜	89	53.27 N	140.03 E
Clachan	46	55.45 N	5.34 W
Clackamas	224	45.24 N	122.34 W
Clackamas □[6]	224	45.10 N	122.16 W
Clackamas ≃	224	45.22 N	122.36 W
Clackamas, Oak Grove Fork ≃	224	45.05 N	122.03 W
Clackamas Heights	224	45.23 N	122.34 W
Clackline	168a	31.43 S	116.31 E
Clackmannan	46	56.06 N	3.46 W
Clacton-on-Sea	42	51.48 N	1.09 E
Cladich	46	56.21 N	5.05 W
Claerwen ≃	42	52.16 N	3.35 W
Claerwen Reservoir ⊜[1]	42	52.17 N	3.43 W
Claflin	198	38.31 N	98.32 W
Claiborne	194	31.32 N	87.31 W
Clain ≃	32	46.47 N	0.32 E
Claire, Lake ⊜	176	58.35 N	112.05 W
Claire, Pointe ›	275a	45.25 N	73.50 W
Clairefontaine-en-Yvelines	50	48.37 N	1.55 E
Clair Engle Lake ⊜[1]	204	40.52 N	122.43 W
Claireville	275b	43.45 N	79.38 W
Claireville Reservoir ⊜[1]	275b	43.44 N	79.39 W
Clairis ≃	50	48.07 N	2.45 E
Clairmarais	50	50.46 N	2.18 E
Clairmont	182	55.16 N	118.47 W
Clairton	214	40.17 N	79.52 W
Clairvaux-les-Lacs	58	46.34 N	5.45 E
Claix	62	45.07 N	5.40 E
Clallam □[6]	224	48.10 N	123.49 W
Clallam Bay	224	48.15 N	124.15 W
Clam ≃, Mi., U.S.	190	44.05 N	85.00 W
Clam ≃, Wi., U.S.	190	45.57 N	92.33 W
Clam, North Fork ≃	190	45.46 N	92.18 W
Clamart	261	48.48 N	2.16 E
Clamecy	50	47.27 N	3.31 E
Clam Gulch	180	60.15 N	151.22 W
Clam Lake ⊜	184	55.19 N	105.43 W
Clampton	162	29.56 S	119.06 E
Clan Alpine Mountains ⛰	204	39.40 N	117.55 W
Clandonald	182	53.34 N	110.44 W
Clandon Park ♠	260	51.15 N	0.30 W
Clandulla	170	32.55 S	149.57 E
Clane	48	53.18 N	6.41 W
Clans	62	44.00 N	7.09 E
Clanton	194	32.50 N	86.37 W
Clanwilliam	158	32.11 S	18.54 E
Claonaig	46	55.46 N	5.22 W
Clapham	42	52.09 N	0.29 W
Clapier, Mont ∧	62	44.07 N	7.25 E
Clapperton Island I	190	46.02 N	82.13 W
Clapp Farm	214	41.24 N	79.32 W
Clàr, Loch nan ⊜	46	58.17 N	4.08 W
Clara, Arg.	252	31.50 S	58.49 W
Clara, Ire.	48	53.20 N	7.36 W
Clara, Ms., U.S.	194	31.34 N	88.41 W
Clara ≃	166	18.30 S	141.18 E
Clara City	198	44.57 N	95.21 W
Clara Island I	110	10.54 N	97.55 E
Claraz	252	37.54 S	59.17 W
Clare, Austl.	166	33.25 S	143.55 E
Clare, Austl.	168b	33.50 S	138.36 E
Clare, Eng., U.K.	42	52.05 N	0.35 E
Clare, Mi., U.S.	190	43.49 N	84.46 W
Clare □[6]	48	52.50 N	9.00 W
Clare ≃, On., Can.	212	44.28 N	77.17 W
Clare ≃, Ire.	48	53.20 N	9.03 W
Clarecastle	48	52.49 N	8.57 W
Claregalway	48	53.21 N	8.57 W
Clare Island I	48	53.48 N	10.00 W
Claremont, On., Can.	212	43.58 N	79.07 W
Claremont, Eng., U.K.	260	51.21 N	0.22 W
Claremont, Ca., U.S.	228	34.05 N	117.43 W
Claremont, N.H., U.S.	188	43.22 N	72.20 W
Claremont, S.D., U.S.	198	45.40 N	98.00 W
Claremont, Va., U.S.	208	37.13 N	76.57 W
Claremont ∧	204	39.53 N	120.57 W
Claremore	196	36.18 N	95.36 W
Claremorris	48	53.44 N	9.00 W
Clarence, N.Z.	172	42.10 S	173.56 E
Clarence, Il., U.S.	216	40.28 N	87.58 W
Clarence, Ia., U.S.	190	41.53 N	91.03 W
Clarence, Mo., U.S.	219	39.44 N	92.15 W
Clarence, N.Y., U.S.	210	42.59 N	78.35 W
Clarence, Pa., U.S.	214	41.03 N	77.56 W
Clarence ≃, Austl.	166	29.25 S	153.22 E
Clarence ≃, N.Z.	172	42.10 S	173.57 E
Clarence, Isla I	254	54.10 S	71.50 W
Clarence, Port ᴄ	180	65.15 N	166.40 W
Clarence Cannon Dam -◆-[6]	219	39.31 N	91.39 W
Clarence Center	210	43.00 N	78.35 W
Clarence Creek	206	45.30 N	75.13 W
Clarence Fahnestock Memorial State Park ♠	210	41.26 N	73.50 W
Clarence Island I	9	61.09 S	54.06 W
Clarence J. Brown Reservoir ⊜[1]	218	39.58 N	83.44 W
Clarence Strait ʯ, Austl.	164	12.00 S	131.00 E
Clarence Strait ʯ, Ak., U.S.	180	55.25 N	132.00 W
Clarence Town, Austl.	170	32.35 S	151.47 E
Clarence Town, Ba.	238	23.06 N	74.59 W
Clarenceville, P.Q., Can.	206	45.04 N	73.15 W
Clarenceville, Mi., U.S.	281	42.27 N	83.19 W
Clarendon, Austl.	168b	35.07 S	138.38 E
Clarendon, Ar., U.S.	194	34.41 N	91.18 W
Clarendon, N.Y., U.S.	210	43.11 N	78.04 W
Clarendon, Pa., U.S.	214	41.46 N	79.05 W
Clarendon, Tx., U.S.	196	34.56 N	100.53 W
Clarendon Hills	278	41.47 N	87.57 W
Clarens	158	28.30 S	28.29 E
Clarenville	186	48.10 N	53.58 W
Claresholm	182	50.02 N	113.35 W
Claret	62	43.52 N	3.54 E
Clarholz	52	51.54 N	8.11 E
Claridge	214	40.21 N	79.37 W
Clarie Coast ±[2]	9	66.30 S	133.00 E
Clarin	116	9.58 N	124.01 E
Clarinda	198	40.44 N	95.02 W
Clarines	246	9.56 N	65.10 W
Clarington	214	41.20 N	79.07 W
Clarion, Ia., U.S.	190	42.43 N	93.43 W
Clarion, Pa., U.S.	214	41.12 N	79.23 W
Clarion □[6]	214	41.13 N	79.24 W
Clarion ≃	214	41.07 N	79.41 W
Clarión, Isla I	232	18.22 N	114.44 W
Clarion, West Branch ≃	214	41.29 N	78.41 W
Clarion Fracture Zone ✣	16	18.00 N	122.00 W
Clarissa	198	46.07 N	94.56 W
Clark, N.J., U.S.	276	40.38 N	74.18 W
Clark, Oh., U.S.	214	40.27 N	81.54 W
Clark, S.D., U.S.	198	44.52 N	97.43 W
Clark, Tx., U.S.	222	30.23 N	94.46 W
Clark □[6], In., U.S.	218	38.17 N	85.44 W
Clark □[6], Oh., U.S.	218	39.56 N	83.49 W
Clark □[6], Wa., U.S.	224	45.48 N	122.31 W
Clark, Lake ⊜	180	60.15 N	154.15 W
Clark, Mount ∧	180	64.25 N	124.12 W
Clark, Point ›	190	44.04 N	81.45 W
Clark Air Base (U.S.) ■	116	15.11 N	120.32 E
Clark Branch ≃	285	39.43 N	74.45 W
Clark Canyon Reservoir ⊜[1]	202	44.58 N	112.51 W
Clark Creek ≃	208	40.22 N	76.58 W
Clarkdale	200	34.46 N	112.03 W
Clarke ≃	166	19.12 S	145.30 E
Clarke City	186	50.12 N	66.38 W
Clarke Island I	166	40.33 S	148.10 E
Clarke Lake ⊜	184	54.25 N	106.51 W
Clarke Range ⛰	166	20.50 S	148.33 E
Clarkesville	192	34.36 N	83.31 W
Clarkfield	198	44.47 N	95.48 W
Clark Fork	202	48.08 N	116.10 W
Clark Fork ≃	202	48.09 N	116.15 W
Clark Hill	218	38.18 N	83.12 W
Clarklake	216	42.04 N	84.21 W
Clark Lake ⊜	216	42.07 N	84.19 W
Clark Mills	210	43.06 N	75.22 W

≃ River	Fluß	Río	Rivière	Rio
≊ Canal	Kanal	Canal	Canal	Canal
ʟ Waterfall, Rapids	Wasserfall, Stromschnellen	Cascada, Rápidos	Chute d'eau, Rapides	Cascata, Rápidos
ʯ Strait	Meeresstraße	Estrecho	Détroit	Estreito
ᴄ Bay, Gulf	Bucht, Golf	Bahía, Golfo	Baie, Golfe	Baía, Golfo
⊜ Lake, Lakes	See, Seen	Lago, Lagos	Lac, Lacs	Lago, Lagos
≡ Swamp	Sumpf	Pantano	Marais	Pântano
⊼ Ice Features, Glacier	Eis- und Gletscherformen	Accidentes Glaciales	Formes glaciaires	Acidentes glaciares
⫧ Other Hydrographic Features	Andere Hydrographische Objekte	Otros Elementos Hidrográficos	Autres données hydrographiques	Outros acidentes hidrográficos

✣ Submarine Features	Untermeerische Objekte	Accidentes Submarinos	Formes de relief sous-marin	Acidentes submarinos
□ Political Unit	Politische Einheit	Unidad Politica	Entité politique	Unidade política
ʋ Cultural Institution	Kulturelle Institution	Institución Cultural	Institution culturelle	Institução cultural
⊥ Historical Site	Historische Stätte	Sitio Histórico	Site historique	Sitio histórico
♠ Recreational Site	Erholungs- und Ferienort	Sitio de Recreo	Centre de loisirs	Area de Lazer
⊠ Airport	Flughafen	Aeropuerto	Aéroport	Aeroporto
■ Military Installation	Militäranlage	Instalación Militar	Installation militaire	Instalação militar
-◆- Miscellaneous	Verschiedenes	Misceláneo	Divers	Diversos

Name	Page	Lat.°′	Long.°′
Clark Mountain ∧, Ca., U.S.	204	35.32 N	115.35 W
Clark Mountain ∧, Wa., U.S.	224	48.03 N	120.57 W
Clarks, La., U.S.	194	32.01 N	92.08 W
Clarks, Ne., U.S.	198	41.12 N	97.50 W
Clarks ≃	194	37.03 N	88.33 W
Clarks, West Fork ≃	194	36.59 N	88.31 W
Clarksboro	285	39.47 N	75.13 W
Clarksburg, On., Can.	212	44.43 N	80.27 W
Clarksburg, Ca., U.S.	226	38.25 N	121.32 W
Clarksburg, Il., U.S.	219	39.20 N	88.44 W
Clarksburg, In., U.S.	218	39.26 N	85.20 W
Clarksburg, Md., U.S.	208	39.14 N	77.16 W
Clarksburg, N.J., U.S.	208	40.11 N	74.26 W
Clarksburg, Oh., U.S.	218	39.30 N	83.09 W
Clarksburg, W.V., U.S.	188	39.16 N	80.20 W
Clarksburg State Park ♦	207	42.43 N	73.06 W
Clarks Creek ≃, Ks., U.S.	198	39.05 N	96.42 W
Clarks Creek ≃, Ky., U.S.	218	38.40 N	84.44 W
Clarksdale	194	34.12 N	90.34 W
Clarks Green	210	41.30 N	75.42 W
Clark's Harbour	186	43.26 N	65.38 W
Clarks Hill	216	40.14 N	86.43 W
Clarks Hill Lake ⊜[1]	192	33.50 N	82.20 W
Clarks Island I	283	42.01 N	70.38 W
Clarks Mills	214	41.24 N	80.11 W
Clarkson, On., Can.	275b	43.31 N	79.37 W
Clarkson, Ky., U.S.	194	37.29 N	86.13 W
Clarkson, Ne., U.S.	198	41.43 N	97.07 W
Clarkson, N.Y., U.S.	210	43.14 N	77.56 W
Clarks Point	180	58.51 N	158.30 W
Clarks Summit	210	41.29 N	75.42 W
Clarkston, Mi., U.S.	216	42.44 N	83.25 W
Clarkston, Wa., U.S.	202	46.24 N	117.02 W
Clark's Town	241q	18.25 N	77.34 W
Clarksville, Ar., U.S.	194	35.28 N	93.27 W
Clarksville, De., U.S.	208	38.32 N	75.08 W
Clarksville, In., U.S.	218	38.15 N	85.47 W
Clarksville, Ia., U.S.	190	42.47 N	92.40 W
Clarksville, Md., U.S.	208	39.12 N	76.56 W
Clarksville, Mi., U.S.	216	42.50 N	85.14 W
Clarksville, Mo., U.S.	219	39.22 N	90.54 W
Clarksville, N.Y., U.S.	210	42.35 N	73.58 W
Clarksville, Oh., U.S.	218	39.24 N	83.58 W
Clarksville, Tn., U.S.	194	36.31 N	87.21 W
Clarksville, Tx., U.S.	196	33.36 N	95.03 W
Clarksville, Va., U.S.	192	36.37 N	78.33 W
Clarksville City	222	32.32 N	94.34 W
Clarkton, Mo., U.S.	194	36.27 N	89.58 W
Clarkton, N.C., U.S.	192	34.29 N	78.39 W
Claro ≃, Bra.	248	13.25 S	56.35 W
Claro ≃, Bra.	255	15.28 S	51.43 W
Claro ≃, Bra.	255	19.06 S	47.52 W
Claro ≃, Bra.	255	19.08 S	50.40 W
Claro, Arroyo ≃	288	34.25 S	58.41 W
Claro, Ribeirão ≃	287b	23.40 S	46.17 W
Clary	50	50.05 N	3.24 E
Claryville	210	41.55 N	74.34 W
Clashmore	48	52.00 N	7.48 W
Clatskanie	224	46.06 N	123.12 W
Clatskanie ≃	224	46.08 N	123.14 W
Clatsop □[6]	224	46.01 N	123.41 W
Clatsop Spit ≻[2]	224	46.13 N	124.01 W
Clatteringshaws Lake ⊜	44	55.05 N	4.17 W
Claude	196	35.07 N	101.22 W
Claudy	48	54.54 N	7.09 W
Claughton	44	54.06 N	2.40 W
Claussnitz	54	50.56 N	12.53 E
Clausthal-Zellerfeld	52	51.48 N	10.20 E
Claver	116	9.35 N	125.44 E
Claverack	210	42.13 N	73.44 W
Claveria, Pil.	116	18.37 N	121.05 E
Claveria, Pil.	116	8.38 N	124.55 E
Clavet	184	52.00 N	106.23 W
Clavey ≃	226	37.52 N	120.07 W
Clawit, Mount ∧	116	16.58 N	120.58 E
Clawson, Mi., U.S.	281	42.32 N	83.08 W
Clawson, Tx., U.S.	222	31.24 N	94.47 W
Claxton	192	32.09 N	81.54 W
Clay, Ky., U.S.	194	37.28 N	87.49 W
Clay, Tx., U.S.	222	30.23 N	96.21 W
Clay, W.V., U.S.	188	38.27 N	81.05 W
Clay □[6]	219	38.45 N	88.40 W
Claybank Creek ≃	194	31.10 N	85.44 W
Clay Center, Ks., U.S.	198	39.22 N	97.07 W
Clay Center, Ne., U.S.	198	40.31 N	98.03 W
Clay Center, Oh., U.S.	214	41.33 N	83.21 W
Clay City, Il., U.S.	194	38.41 N	88.21 W
Clay City, In., U.S.	194	39.16 N	87.06 W
Clay City, Ky., U.S.	192	37.51 N	83.55 W
Clay Creek ≃	198	38.06 N	102.31 W
Clay Cross	44	53.10 N	1.24 W
Claydon	42	52.06 N	1.07 E
Claye-Souilly	50	48.57 N	2.42 E
Claygate	260	51.22 N	0.20 W
Claygate Cross	260	51.16 N	0.19 E
Clayhole Wash V	200	36.59 N	113.17 W
Clayhurst	182	56.15 N	120.01 W
Claymont	208	39.48 N	75.27 W
Clayoquot Sound ʉ	182	49.11 N	126.08 W
Claypole	288	34.48 S	58.20 W
Claypool, Az., U.S.	200	33.24 N	110.50 W
Claypool, In., U.S.	216	41.07 N	85.52 W
Claysburg	214	40.17 N	78.27 W
Clay Springs	200	34.21 N	110.17 W
Claysville	214	40.07 N	80.24 W
Clayton, Austl.	274b	37.56 S	145.07 E
Clayton, Eng., U.K.	262	53.47 N	1.50 W
Clayton, Al., U.S.	194	31.52 N	85.26 W
Clayton, Ca., U.S.	282	37.57 N	121.56 W
Clayton, De., U.S.	208	39.17 N	75.38 W
Clayton, Ga., U.S.	192	34.52 N	83.24 W
Clayton, Il., U.S.	219	40.01 N	90.57 W
Clayton, In., U.S.	218	39.41 N	86.31 W
Clayton, La., U.S.	194	31.43 N	91.32 W
Clayton, Mi., U.S.	216	41.52 N	84.14 W
Clayton, Mo., U.S.	219	38.38 N	90.19 W
Clayton, N.J., U.S.	208	39.39 N	75.05 W
Clayton, N.M., U.S.	196	36.27 N	103.11 W
Clayton, N.Y., U.S.	212	44.14 N	76.05 W
Clayton, N.C., U.S.	192	35.39 N	78.27 W
Clayton, Ok., U.S.	196	34.35 N	95.21 W
Clayton, Tx., U.S.	222	32.06 N	94.28 W
Clayton, Wa., U.S.	182	48.00 N	117.33 W
Clayton ≃	166	29.06 S	138.05 E
Claytonia	214	41.00 N	79.58 W
Clayton-le-Moors	262	53.47 N	2.23 W
Clayton-le-Woods	262	53.41 N	2.38 W
Clayton Park ♦	285	39.52 N	75.29 W
Clayton Valley V	282	37.58 N	121.58 W
Claytonville	216	40.34 N	87.49 W
Clay Village	218	38.11 N	85.07 W
Clayville	210	42.59 N	75.15 W
Clear ≃	182	56.11 N	119.42 W
Clear, Cape ≻, Ire.	48	51.24 N	9.30 W
Clear, Cape ≻, Ak., U.S.	180	59.48 N	147.54 W
Clear, Lake ⊜	212	45.26 N	77.12 W
Clear, Mount ∧	171b	35.52 S	149.04 E
Clear Boggy Creek ≃	196	34.03 N	95.47 W
Clearbrook, B.C., Can.	224	49.08 N	122.26 W
Clearbrook, Mn., U.S.	198	47.41 N	95.25 W
Clear Creek	218	39.07 N	86.32 W
Clear Creek ≃, Al., U.S.	194	34.00 N	87.19 W
Clear Creek ≃, Az., U.S.	200	34.59 N	110.38 W
Clear Creek ≃, Ca., U.S.	204	40.31 N	122.22 W
Clear Creek ≃, Ca., U.S.	280	34.17 N	118.12 W
Clear Creek ≃, Ca., U.S.	282	37.20 N	122.21 W
Clear Creek ≃, Ky., U.S.	218	38.10 N	85.17 W
Clear Creek ≃, Mo., U.S.	194	38.00 N	93.56 W
Clear Creek ≃, Mt., U.S.	202	48.46 N	109.25 W
Clear Creek ≃, Ne., U.S.	198	41.08 N	99.06 W
Clear Creek ≃, Oh., U.S.	218	39.33 N	84.20 W
Clear Creek ≃, Or., U.S.	224	45.09 N	121.31 W
Clear Creek ≃, Or., U.S.	224	45.23 N	122.29 W
Clear Creek ≃, Tn., U.S.	192	36.05 N	84.42 W
Clear Creek ≃, Tx., U.S.	196	33.16 N	97.03 W
Clear Creek ≃, Tx., U.S.	222	29.33 N	95.05 W
Clear Creek ≃, Tx., U.S.	222	29.09 N	97.23 W
Clear Creek ≃, Wa., U.S.	224	46.07 N	122.00 W
Clear Creek ≃, Wy., U.S.	202	44.53 N	106.04 W
Clear Creek State Park ♦	214	41.20 N	79.05 W
Clearfield, Ia., U.S.	198	40.48 N	94.28 W
Clearfield, Ky., U.S.	218	38.09 N	83.25 W
Clearfield, Pa., U.S.	214	41.01 N	78.26 W
Clearfield, Ut,. U.S.	200	41.06 N	112.01 W
Clearfield □[6]	214	41.02 N	78.27 W
Clearfield Creek ≃	214	41.02 N	78.24 W
Clear Fork Reservoir ⊜[1]	214	40.42 N	82.38 W
Clearing ⬥[8]	278	41.47 N	87.47 W
Clear Island I	48	51.26 N	9.30 W
Clearlake, Ca., U.S.	226	38.57 N	122.38 W
Clear Lake, Ia., U.S.	190	43.08 N	93.22 W
Clear Lake, S.D., U.S.	198	44.44 N	96.40 W
Clearlake, Wa., U.S.	224	48.28 N	122.14 W
Clear Lake, Wi., U.S.	190	45.15 N	92.16 W
Clear Lake ⊜, Mb., Can.	184	50.42 N	100.00 W
Clear Lake ⊜, On., Can.	212	45.14 N	79.57 W
Clear Lake ⊜, On., Can.	212	44.30 N	78.13 W
Clear Lake ⊜, On., Can.	212	44.59 N	79.33 W
Clear Lake ⊜, In., U.S.	216	41.44 N	84.50 W
Clear Lake ⊜[1], Ca., U.S.	204	39.02 N	122.50 W
Clear Lake ⊜[1], La., U.S.	194	31.55 N	93.05 W
Clearlake Oaks	226	39.07 N	122.40 W
Clear Lake Reservoir ⊜[1]	204	41.52 N	121.08 W
Clear Lake Shores	222	29.33 N	95.02 W
Clearmont	202	44.38 N	106.22 W
Clear Run	214	41.08 N	78.45 W
Clear Site	180	64.19 N	149.11 W
Clearview, Oh., U.S.	214	41.25 N	82.10 W
Clearview, Wa., U.S.	224	47.45 N	122.06 W
Clearview, W.V., U.S.	214	40.09 N	80.41 W
Clearview Estates	279b	40.34 N	80.16 W
Clearwater, B.C., Can.	182	51.38 N	120.02 W
Clearwater, Mb., Can.	184	49.08 N	99.01 W
Clearwater, Fl., U.S.	220	27.57 N	82.48 W
Clearwater, Ks., U.S.	198	37.30 N	97.30 W
Clearwater, Ne., U.S.	198	42.10 N	98.11 W
Clearwater, S.C., U.S.	192	33.29 N	81.53 W
Clearwater, Wa., U.S.	224	47.34 N	124.17 W
Clearwater ≃, Can.	184	56.44 N	111.23 W
Clearwater ≃, Ab., Can.	182	52.23 N	114.50 W
Clearwater ≃, B.C., Can.	182	51.42 N	120.00 W
Clearwater ≃, Id., U.S.	202	46.25 N	117.02 W
Clearwater ≃, Mn., U.S.	198	47.54 N	96.16 W
Clearwater ≃, Mt., U.S.	202	46.58 N	113.23 W
Clearwater ≃, Wa., U.S.	224	47.33 N	124.21 W
Clearwater, Middle Fork ≃	202	46.09 N	115.59 W
Clearwater, North Fork ≃	202	46.30 N	116.19 W
Clearwater, South Fork ≃	202	46.09 N	115.59 W
Clear Water Bay c	271d	22.17 N	114.18 E
Clearwater Beach Island I	220	27.59 N	82.49 W
Clearwater Lake ⊜, B.C., Can.	182	52.15 N	120.13 W
Clearwater Lake ⊜, Mb., Can.	184	54.05 N	101.00 W
Clearwater Lake Provincial Park ♦	184	54.03 N	101.10 W
Clearwater Mountains ⋀	202	46.00 N	115.30 W
Cleator Moor	44	54.31 N	3.30 W
Clebit	196	34.21 N	94.52 W
Cleburne	222	32.20 N	97.23 W
Cleckheaton	44	53.43 N	1.43 W
Cle Elum	224	47.11 N	120.56 W
Cle Elum ≃	224	47.11 N	121.01 W
Cle Elum Lake ⊜[1]	224	47.18 N	121.06 W
Cleethorpes	44	53.34 N	0.02 W
Cleeve Cloud ∧[2]	42	51.54 N	2.00 W
Clefmont	58	48.06 N	5.31 E
Cleggan	48	53.33 N	10.09 W
Cleland Conservation Park ♦	168b	34.59 S	138.44 E
Cleland Heights	285	39.44 N	75.34 W
Clelles	62	44.50 N	5.37 E
Clementon	285	39.48 N	74.59 W
Clementsport	186	44.40 N	65.37 W
Clemson	192	34.41 N	82.50 W
Clemville	222	29.00 N	96.08 W
Clendenin	188	38.29 N	81.20 W
Clendening Lake ⊜[1]	214	40.16 N	81.13 W
Clenze	54	52.56 N	10.58 E
Cleobury Mortimer	42	52.23 N	2.29 W
Cleona	208	40.20 N	76.28 W
Cléon-d'Andran	62	44.37 N	4.56 E
Cleopatra Needle ∧	116	10.07 N	118.58 E
Clères	50	49.36 N	1.07 E
Clerke Rocks II[1]	244	55.01 S	34.41 W
Clermont, Austl.	166	22.49 S	147.39 E
Clermont, P.Q., Can.	186	47.41 N	70.14 W
Clermont, Fr.	50	49.23 N	2.24 E
Clermont, Fl., U.S.	220	28.32 N	81.46 W
Clermont, N.J., U.S.	285	39.59 N	74.48 W
Clermont, Pa., U.S.	214	41.41 N	78.29 W
Clermont □[6]	218	39.05 N	84.11 W
Clermont-en-Argonne	56	49.06 N	5.04 E
Clermont-Ferrand	32	45.47 N	3.05 E
Clermont State Park ♦	210	42.05 N	73.55 W
Clerval	58	47.24 N	6.30 E
Clervaux	56	50.04 N	6.01 E
Cléry-Saint-André	50	47.49 N	1.45 E
Cles	64	46.22 N	11.02 E
Cleve	166	33.42 S	136.30 E
Clevedon	42	51.27 N	2.51 W
Cleveland, Austl.	171a	27.32 S	153.17 E
Cleveland, Al., U.S.	194	33.59 N	86.34 W
Cleveland, Fl., U.S.	220	26.57 N	82.00 W
Cleveland, Ga., U.S.	192	34.35 N	83.45 W
Cleveland, Ms., U.S.	194	33.44 N	90.43 W
Cleveland, N.Y., U.S.	210	43.14 N	75.53 W
Cleveland, N.C., U.S.	192	35.43 N	80.40 W
Cleveland, Oh., U.S.	214	41.29 N	81.41 W
Cleveland, Oh., U.S.	279a	41.29 N	81.41 W
Cleveland, Ok., U.S.	196	36.18 N	96.27 W
Cleveland, Tn., U.S.	194	35.09 N	84.52 W
Cleveland, Tx., U.S.	222	30.20 N	95.05 W
Cleveland, Va., U.S.	192	36.56 N	82.09 W
Cleveland □[6]	44	54.35 N	1.15 W
Cleveland, Cape ≻	166	19.11 S	147.01 E
Cleveland, Mount ∧, Austl.	166	41.25 S	145.23 E
Cleveland, Mount ∧, Mt., U.S.	202	48.56 N	113.51 W
Cleveland Heights	214	41.31 N	81.33 W
Cleveland Hills ⋀[2]	44	54.23 N	1.05 W
Cleveland-Hopkins International Airport ⊠	279a	41.25 N	81.51 W
Clevelândia	252	26.24 S	52.21 W
Clevelândia do Norte	250	3.49 N	51.52 W
Cleveland Museum of Art ⊌	279a	41.31 N	81.37 W
Cleveland National Forest ♦	280	33.47 N	117.38 W
Cleveland Park ⬥[8]	284c	38.56 N	77.04 W
Cleveland Peninsula ≻[1]	182	55.45 N	132.00 W
Cleveland Pond ⊜	283	42.07 N	70.58 W
Cleveland State University ⊌[2]	279a	41.30 N	81.40 W
Cleveland Zoo ♦	279a	41.27 N	81.43 W
Cleveleys	44	53.53 N	3.03 W
Cleversburg	208	40.02 N	77.28 W
Cleves → Kleve, Dtsch.	52	51.48 N	6.09 E
Cleves, Oh., U.S.	218	39.10 N	84.45 W
Clew Bay c	48	53.50 N	9.50 W
Clewer	158	25.55 S	29.07 E
Clewiston	220	26.45 N	80.56 W
Cley next the Sea	42	52.58 N	1.03 E
Clichy	50	48.54 N	2.18 E
Clichy-sous-Bois	261	48.55 N	2.33 E
Clifden	48	53.29 N	10.01 W
Clifden Bay c	48	53.28 N	10.05 W
Cliffdale Creek ≃	166	16.56 S	138.48 E
Cliffdell	224	46.44 N	120.42 W
Cliffe	42	51.28 N	0.30 E
Cliffe Marshes ⩨	260	51.28 N	0.30 E
Cliffe Woods	260	51.26 N	0.30 E
Clifford, On., Can.	212	43.58 N	80.58 W
Clifford, S. Afr.	158	31.04 S	27.28 E
Clifford, In., U.S.	218	39.16 N	85.52 W
Clifford, Pa., U.S.	210	41.39 N	75.36 W
Clifford Park ♦	274b	37.43 S	145.16 E
Cliffside	210	42.31 N	74.59 W
Cliffside Park	276	40.58 N	73.57 W
Cliffwood	276	40.26 N	74.14 W
Cliffwood Beach	276	40.26 N	74.13 W
Clifton, Austl.	171a	27.56 S	151.54 E
Clifton, Eng., U.K.	262	53.46 N	2.49 W
Clifton, Az., U.S.	200	33.03 N	109.17 W
Clifton, Il., U.S.	216	40.56 N	87.56 W
Clifton, Ks., U.S.	198	39.34 N	97.16 W
Clifton, N.J., U.S.	210	40.51 N	74.09 W
Clifton, N.Y., U.S.	210	43.03 N	77.49 W
Clifton, Or., U.S.	224	46.12 N	123.27 W
Clifton, Tn., U.S.	194	35.23 N	87.59 W
Clifton, Tx., U.S.	222	31.46 N	97.34 W
Clifton, Lake ⊜	168a	32.49 S	115.41 E
Clifton Court Forebay ⊜[1]	226	37.50 N	121.35 W
Clifton Forge	192	37.48 N	79.49 W
Clifton Gorge V	42	51.28 N	2.37 W
Clifton Heights, N.Y., U.S.	284a	42.44 N	78.56 W
Clifton Heights, Pa., U.S.	285	39.55 N	75.17 W
Clifton Hills	166	26.52 S	138.50 E
Clifton Knolls	210	42.52 N	73.46 W
Clifton Park ♦	284b	39.19 N	76.35 W
Clifton Point ≻	240b	25.01 N	77.34 W
Clifton Springs	210	42.57 N	77.08 W
Clifty, Mount ∧	224	47.07 N	121.10 W
Clifty Creek ≃	218	39.09 N	85.54 W
Clifty Falls State Park ♦	218	38.45 N	85.26 W
Clignon ≃	50	49.07 N	3.04 E
Climax, Sk., Can.	184	49.13 N	108.23 W
Climax, Co., U.S.	200	39.22 N	106.10 W
Climax, Ga., U.S.	192	30.52 N	84.25 W
Climax, Mi., U.S.	216	42.14 N	85.20 W
Climax, Pa., U.S.	214	40.59 N	79.23 W
Clinch ≃	192	35.53 N	84.29 W
Clinchco	192	37.09 N	82.21 W
Clingen	54	51.14 N	10.55 E
Clingmans Dome ∧	192	35.35 N	83.30 W
Clinton, B.C., Can.	182	51.05 N	121.35 W
Clinton, On., Can.	190	43.37 N	81.32 W
Clinton, N.Z.	172	46.12 S	169.22 E
Clinton, Al., U.S.	194	32.55 N	88.00 W
Clinton, Ar., U.S.	194	35.35 N	92.27 W
Clinton, Ct., U.S.	207	41.16 N	72.31 W
Clinton, Il., U.S.	219	40.09 N	88.57 W
Clinton, In., U.S.	194	39.39 N	87.23 W
Clinton, Ia., U.S.	190	41.50 N	90.11 W
Clinton, Ky., U.S.	194	36.40 N	88.59 W
Clinton, La., U.S.	194	30.51 N	91.00 W
Clinton, Me., U.S.	188	44.38 N	69.30 W
Clinton, Md., U.S.	208	38.45 N	76.53 W
Clinton, Ma., U.S.	207	42.25 N	71.41 W
Clinton, Mi., U.S.	216	42.04 N	83.58 W
Clinton, Mn., U.S.	198	45.27 N	96.26 W
Clinton, Ms., U.S.	194	32.20 N	90.19 W
Clinton, Mo., U.S.	194	38.22 N	93.46 W
Clinton, N.J., U.S.	210	40.38 N	74.54 W
Clinton, N.Y., U.S.	210	43.02 N	75.22 W
Clinton, N.C., U.S.	192	34.59 N	78.19 W
Clinton, Oh., U.S.	214	40.56 N	81.42 W
Clinton, Ok., U.S.	196	35.30 N	98.58 W
Clinton, Pa., U.S.	214	40.29 N	80.18 W
Clinton, S.C., U.S.	192	34.28 N	81.52 W
Clinton, Tn., U.S.	192	36.06 N	84.07 W
Clinton, Tx., U.S.	222	33.06 N	96.14 W
Clinton, Wa., U.S.	224	47.58 N	122.21 W
Clinton, Wi., U.S.	216	42.33 N	88.51 W
Clinton □[6], Il., U.S.	219	38.37 N	89.22 W
Clinton □[6], In., U.S.	216	40.17 N	86.31 W
Clinton □[6], Mi., U.S.	216	42.56 N	84.36 W
Clinton □[6], N.Y., U.S.	206	44.57 N	73.42 W
Clinton □[6], Oh., U.S.	218	39.27 N	83.50 W
Clinton □[6], Pa., U.S.	210	41.08 N	71.26 W
Clinton ≃	214	42.36 N	82.48 W
Clinton, Cape ≻	166	22.32 S	150.47 E
Clinton, Lake ⊜[1]	194	40.10 N	88.50 W
Clinton, Middle Branch ≃	281	42.36 N	82.54 W
Clinton, North Branch ≃	214	42.36 N	82.54 W
Clinton-Colden Lake ⊜	176	63.58 N	107.27 W
Clintondale	210	41.01 N	77.29 W
Clinton Lake ⊜[1]	198	38.55 N	95.25 W
Clinton Park	210	42.36 N	73.43 W
Clinton Reservoir ⊜[1]	276	41.05 N	74.27 W
Clinton Township	214	42.33 N	82.53 W
Clintonville, Mi., U.S.	281	42.43 N	83.22 W
Clintonville, Pa., U.S.	214	41.12 N	79.53 W
Clintonville, Wi., U.S.	190	44.37 N	88.45 W
Clintwood	192	37.09 N	82.27 W
Clio, Al., U.S.	194	31.42 N	85.36 W
Clio, Mi., U.S.	190	43.10 N	83.44 W
Clio, S.C., U.S.	192	34.34 N	79.32 W
Clipperton, Île I[1]	230	10.17 N	109.13 W
Clipperton Fracture Zone ✣	16	10.00 N	115.00 W
Clisham ∧	46	57.57 N	6.49 W
Clisson	32	47.05 N	1.17 W
Clitheroe	44	53.53 N	2.23 W
Clitunno ≃	66	42.56 N	12.37 E
Clive	172	39.35 S	176.55 E
Cloates, Point ≻	162	22.43 S	113.40 E
Clock Face	262	53.25 N	2.43 W
Clocolan	158	29.00 S	27.30 E
Clodomira	252	27.35 S	64.08 W
Cloe	214	40.56 N	78.56 W
Cloete	196	27.55 N	101.10 W
Cloghan, Ire.	48	54.51 N	7.56 W
Cloghan, Ire.	48	53.13 N	7.53 W
Cloghane	48	52.13 N	10.12 W
Clogheen	48	52.16 N	8.00 W
Clogher	48	54.25 N	7.12 W
Clogher Head ≻	48	53.48 N	6.12 W
Cloghjordan	48	52.57 N	8.02 W
Clonakilty	48	51.37 N	8.54 W
Clonakilty Bay c	48	51.35 N	8.50 W
Cloncurry	166	20.42 S	140.30 E
Cloncurry ≃	166	18.37 S	140.40 E
Clondalkin	48	53.19 N	6.24 W
Clonee	48	53.25 N	6.26 W
Clones	48	54.11 N	7.15 W
Clonfert	48	53.14 N	8.05 W
Clonmacnois ⊥	48	53.20 N	7.59 W
Clonmany	48	55.14 N	7.25 W
Clonmel	48	52.21 N	7.42 W
Clonroche	48	52.27 N	6.43 W
Clontarf	274a	33.48 S	151.16 E
Cloone	48	53.57 N	7.46 W
Clo-oose	224	48.40 N	124.49 W
Cloppenburg	52	52.50 N	8.02 E
Cloquallum Creek ≃	224	46.58 N	123.24 W
Cloquet	190	46.43 N	92.27 W
Cloquet ≃	190	46.52 N	92.35 W
Clorinda	252	25.17 S	57.43 W
Closter	276	40.58 N	73.57 W
Cloudcroft	200	32.57 N	105.44 W
Cloud Peak ∧, Ak., U.S.	180	68.24 N	148.26 W
Cloud Peak ∧, Wy., U.S.	202	44.25 N	107.10 W
Cloudy Bay c	172	41.27 S	174.10 E
Cloudy Mountain ∧	180	63.11 N	156.05 W
Clough	48	54.18 N	5.50 W
Clough Foot	262	53.43 N	2.08 W
Clova	46	56.50 N	3.06 W
Clova, Glen V	46	56.49 N	3.04 W
Clove Lakes Park ♦	276	40.37 N	74.07 W
Clovelly, Austl.	274a	33.55 S	151.16 E
Clovelly, Eng., U.K.	42	51.00 N	4.24 W
Clover	192	35.06 N	81.13 W
Clover Bank	210	42.45 N	78.53 W
Clover Creek ≃, Id., U.S.	202	43.00 N	115.11 W
Clover Creek ≃, Id., U.S.	202	42.34 N	115.38 W
Cloverdale, B.C., Can.	224	49.06 N	122.44 W
Cloverdale, Al., U.S.	194	34.56 N	87.46 W
Cloverdale, Ca., U.S.	204	38.48 N	123.00 W
Cloverdale, Il., U.S.	278	41.56 N	88.07 W
Cloverdale, In., U.S.	194	39.30 N	86.47 W
Cloverdale, Ky., U.S.	218	38.10 N	84.53 W
Cloverdale, Mi., U.S.	216	42.32 N	85.23 W
Cloverdale, Oh., U.S.	216	41.01 N	84.18 W
Cloverdale, Or., U.S.	224	45.12 N	123.53 W
Cloverdale Mall ⬥[9]	275b	43.38 N	79.34 W
Cloverdene	273d	26.09 S	28.22 E
Cloverleaf	222	29.46 N	95.10 W
Clover Pass	182	55.28 N	131.47 W
Cloverport	194	37.50 N	86.37 W
Cloverville	216	43.11 N	86.10 W
Clovis, Ca., U.S.	226	36.49 N	119.42 W
Clovis, N.M., U.S.	196	34.24 N	103.12 W
Clowbridge Reservoir ⊜[1]	262	53.45 N	2.16 W
Clowne	44	53.18 N	1.16 W
Cloyes-sur-le-Loir	50	48.00 N	1.14 E
Cloyne	48	51.51 N	8.08 W
Cluain Meala → Clonmel	48	52.21 N	7.42 W
Cluanie, Loch ⊜	46	57.07 N	5.05 W
Cluj □[6]	38	46.45 N	23.45 E
Cluj-Napoca	38	46.47 N	23.36 E
Clun	42	52.26 N	3.00 W
Clun ≃	42	52.22 N	2.53 W
Clune	214	40.34 N	79.18 W
Clunes	169	37.18 S	143.47 E
Clun Forest ⬥[3]	42	52.28 N	3.07 W
Clunie Water ≃	46	57.00 N	3.24 W
Cluny, Austl.	166	24.31 S	139.35 E
Cluny, Fr.	58	46.26 N	4.39 E
Cluses	58	46.04 N	6.36 E
Clusone	64	45.53 N	9.57 E
Clute	222	29.01 N	95.23 W
Clutha ≃	172	46.21 S	169.48 E
Clwyd □[6]	44	53.05 N	3.20 W
Clwyd ≃	44	53.20 N	3.30 W
Clwyd, Vale of V	44	53.12 N	3.24 W
Clwydian Range ⋀	44	53.10 N	3.20 W
Clydach	42	51.43 N	3.50 W
Clyde, Austl.	274a	33.50 S	151.00 E
Clyde, Ab., Can.	182	54.09 N	113.39 W
Clyde, N.Z.	172	45.11 S	169.19 E
Clyde, Ca., U.S.	226	38.02 N	122.02 W
Clyde, Ks., U.S.	198	39.35 N	97.23 W
Clyde, Mi., U.S.	281	42.41 N	83.37 W
Clyde, N.Y., U.S.	210	43.05 N	76.52 W
Clyde, N.C., U.S.	192	35.32 N	82.54 W
Clyde, Oh., U.S.	214	41.18 N	82.58 W
Clyde, Tx., U.S.	196	32.24 N	99.30 W
Clyde ≃, Austl.	170	35.23 S	150.15 E
Clyde ≃, N.S., Can.	186	43.35 N	65.25 W
Clyde ≃, On., Can.	212	44.58 N	76.22 W
Clyde ≃, Scot., U.K.	46	55.44 N	4.55 W
Clyde ≃, N.Y., U.S.	210	43.04 N	77.00 W
Clyde ≃, Vt., U.S.	188	44.56 N	72.12 W
Clyde, Firth of c[1]	46	55.42 N	5.00 W
Clydebank	46	55.54 N	4.24 W
Clydegale Lake ⊜	212	45.25 N	78.23 W
Clyde Lake ⊜	182	55.18 N	111.28 W
Clyde No. 3	214	39.59 N	80.03 W
Clyde Park	202	45.53 N	110.36 W
Clyde Potts Reservoir ⊜[1]	276	40.48 N	74.35 W
Clyde River	176	70.25 N	68.30 W
Clydesdale	158	26.54 S	27.55 E
Clydesdale V	46	55.42 N	3.50 W
Clymer, N.Y., U.S.	214	42.01 N	79.37 W
Clymer, Pa., U.S.	214	40.40 N	79.00 W
Clynnog-fawr	44	53.01 N	4.23 W
Clywedog ≃	42	52.27 N	3.32 W
Ćmielów	30	50.53 N	21.31 E
Cna ≃, Bela.	76	52.10 N	27.03 E
Cna ≃, Ross.	76	57.33 N	34.36 E
Cna ≃, Ross.	80	54.32 N	42.05 E
Cna ≃, Ross.	82	55.03 N	39.09 E
Cnori	84	41.37 N	45.59 E
Cnossus → Knossós ⊥	38	35.20 N	25.10 E
Côa ≃	34	41.05 N	7.06 W
Coacalco	286a	19.37 N	99.05 W
Coachella	204	33.40 N	116.10 W
Coachella Canal ≍	204	33.34 N	116.00 W
Coachford	48	51.53 N	8.48 W
Coacoyole	232	24.31 N	106.34 W
Coacuilco	234	21.07 N	98.35 W
Coahoma	196	32.18 N	101.18 W
Coahuayana	234	18.44 N	103.41 W
Coahuayutla de Guerrero	234	18.19 N	101.49 W
Coahuila	200	32.12 N	114.59 W
Coahuila □[3]	232	27.20 N	102.00 W
Coal ≃	180	59.39 N	126.57 W
Coalbrook	158	26.51 S	27.53 E
Coalbrookdale	42	52.38 N	2.30 W
Coalburg	214	41.11 N	80.36 W
Coalburn	46	55.36 N	3.54 W
Coal City	216	41.17 N	88.17 W
Coalcomán ≃	234	18.11 N	103.08 W

ENGLISH

Name	Page	Lat.°′	Long.°′
Coalcomán de Matamoros	234	18.47 N	103.09 W
Coal Creek	180	65.22 N	143.10 W
Coal Creek ≃, Co., U.S.	198	40.30 N	104.26 W
Coal Creek ≃, In., U.S.	194	39.57 N	87.25 W
Coal Creek ≃, Wa., U.S.	202	47.19 N	118.36 W
Coal Creek Flat	172	45.29 S	169.18 E
Coaldale, Ab., Can.	182	49.43 N	112.37 W
Coaldale, Pa., U.S.	210	40.49 N	75.54 W
Coal Fire Creek ≃	194	33.15 N	88.18 W
Coal Fork	188	38.19 N	81.32 W
Coalgate, N.Z.	172	43.29 S	171.58 E
Coalgate, Ok., U.S.	196	34.32 N	96.13 W
Coal Grove	188	38.30 N	82.38 W
Coal Harbour	182	50.36 N	127.35 W
Coal Hill	194	35.26 N	93.40 W
Coal Hill Park ♦	271a	39.56 N	116.23 E
Coalhurst	182	49.45 N	112.56 W
Coalinga	226	36.08 N	120.21 W
Coalisland	48	54.33 N	6.42 W
Coal Island I	172	46.07 S	166.38 E
Coalmont	182	49.31 N	120.41 W
Coalpit Heath	42	51.32 N	2.28 W
Coalport	214	40.44 N	78.32 W
Coal River	180	59.45 N	126.55 W
Coal Run ≃	279b	40.21 N	80.07 W
Coalspur	182	53.11 N	117.01 W
Coalton	219	39.17 N	89.19 W
Coaltown	214	41.02 N	80.20 W
Coal Valley V	204	38.00 N	115.05 W
Coalville, S. Afr.	158	26.01 S	29.10 E
Coalville, Eng., U.K.	42	52.44 N	1.20 W
Coalville, Ut,. U.S.	200	40.55 N	111.23 W
Coamo	240m	18.05 N	66.22 W
Coamo, Lago ⊜[1]	240m	18.01 N	66.23 W
Coapilla	234	17.08 N	93.10 W
Coaraci	255	14.38 S	39.32 W
Coari	246	4.05 S	63.08 W
Coari ≃	246	4.30 S	63.33 W
Coari, Lago de ⊜	246	4.15 S	63.22 W
Coarsegold	226	37.16 N	119.42 W
Coast □[4]	154	3.00 S	39.30 E
Coast Mountains ⋀	176	55.00 N	129.00 W
Coast Ranges ⋀	178	41.00 N	123.30 W
Coatán ≃	236	14.48 N	92.31 W
Coatbridge	46	55.52 N	4.01 W
Coatepec	234	19.27 N	96.58 W
Coatepec Harinas	234	18.54 N	99.43 W
Coatepeque	236	14.42 N	91.52 W
Coatepeque, Lago de ⊜	236	13.52 N	89.33 W
Coates Creek ≃	212	44.24 N	79.54 W
Coatesville	208	39.58 N	75.49 W
Coaticook	206	45.08 N	71.48 W
Coaticook ≃	206	45.20 N	71.53 W
Coatsburg	219	40.02 N	91.10 W
Coats Island I	176	62.30 N	83.00 W
Coats Land ⬥[1]	9	77.00 S	28.00 W
Coatzacoalcos	234	18.09 N	94.25 W
Coatzacoalcos ≃	234	18.10 N	94.27 W
Coatzintla	234	20.29 N	97.27 W
Coayllo	248	12.44 S	76.28 W
Coazze	62	45.03 N	7.18 E
Cobá ⊥	232	20.36 N	87.35 W
Cobadin	38	44.04 N	28.13 E
Coballo Cocha	246	3.54 S	70.32 W
Cobalt, On., Can.	190	47.24 N	79.41 W
Cobalt, Ct., U.S.	207	41.33 N	72.33 W
Cobán	236	15.29 N	90.19 W
Çobanlar	130	38.41 N	30.47 E
Cobar	166	31.30 S	145.49 E
Cobargo	166	36.23 S	149.53 E
Cobb	226	38.49 N	122.43 W
Cobb Creek ≃	196	35.05 N	98.25 W
Cobberas, Mount ∧	166	36.52 S	148.10 E
Cobbetts Pond ⊜	283	42.48 N	71.17 W
Cobbin's Brook ≃	260	51.41 N	0.01 W
Cobb Island	208	38.16 N	76.51 W
Cobb Island I, Md., U.S.	208	38.16 N	76.51 W
Cobb Island I, Va., U.S.	208	37.20 N	75.44 W
Cobbitty	274a	34.01 S	150.41 E
Cobbitty ∧[2]	274a	33.59 S	150.42 E
Cobble Hill	224	48.41 N	123.36 W
Cobble Mountain Reservoir ⊜[1]	207	42.08 N	72.55 W
Cobblestone Mountain ∧	228	34.37 N	118.52 W
Cobb Neck ≻[1]	208	38.20 N	76.55 W
Cobbs Creek ≃	285	39.54 N	75.15 W
Cobbs Creek Park ♦	285	39.58 N	75.16 W
Cobb Seamount ✣[3]	16	46.46 N	130.49 W
Cobden, Austl.	169	38.20 S	143.05 E
Cobden, On., Can.	190	45.38 N	76.53 W
Cobden, Il., U.S.	194	37.31 N	89.15 W
Cobeña	266a	40.34 N	3.30 W
Cobequid Bay c	186	45.21 N	63.45 W
Cobequid Mountains ⋀	186	45.31 N	64.05 W
Cobh	48	51.51 N	8.17 W
Cobham, Eng., U.K.	42	51.20 N	0.25 W
Cobham, Eng., U.K.	260	51.23 N	0.24 E
Cobham ≃	184	53.15 N	93.58 W
Cobham Hall ⊥	260	51.23 N	0.25 E
Cobija, Bol.	248	11.02 S	68.44 W
Cobija, Chile	252	22.33 S	70.16 W
Coblenz → Koblenz	56	50.21 N	7.35 E
Cobleskill	210	42.40 N	74.29 W
Cobleskill Creek ≃	210	42.43 N	74.20 W
Coboconk	212	44.39 N	78.48 W
Cobo Hall ⊌	281	42.19 N	83.03 W
Cobolgo, gora ∧	84	42.50 N	46.23 E
Coboto, Cerro ∧	200	31.29 N	112.05 W
Čoboty	265b	55.39 N	37.21 E
Cobourg	212	43.58 N	78.10 W
Cobourg Peninsula ≻[1]	164	11.20 S	132.15 E
Cobquecura	252	36.08 S	72.47 W
Cobram	166	35.55 S	145.39 E
Cobras, Ilha das I	287a	22.54 S	43.10 W
Cobras, Ribeirão das ≃	256	23.08 S	46.05 W
Cobre ≃	236	8.01 N	81.18 W
Cobre, Barranca del V	232	27.28 N	107.50 W
Cóbuè	154	12.04 S	34.50 E
Coburg, Austl.	169	37.45 S	144.58 E
Coburg, Dtsch.	56	50.15 N	10.58 E
Coburg Island I	176	76.00 N	79.25 W
Coburn	210	40.52 N	77.28 W
Coburn Mountain ∧	188	45.28 N	70.06 W
Coca ≃	246	0.29 S	76.58 W
Coca, Laguna ⊜	286b	22.57 N	82.27 W
Coca, Pizzo di ∧	64	46.04 N	10.01 E
Cocachacra	248	17.06 S	71.46 W
Cocais, Ribeirão dos ≃	256	21.59 S	47.15 W
Cocal	250	3.28 S	41.34 W
Cocalico Creek ≃	208	40.07 N	76.14 W
Coccaglio	64	45.34 N	9.58 E
Cocconato	62	45.05 N	8.02 E
Cocentaina	34	38.45 N	0.26 W
Cochabamba	248	17.24 S	66.09 W
Cochabamba □[5]	248	17.30 S	65.40 W
Čochatauri	84	42.01 N	42.15 E
Cochato ≃	283	42.10 N	71.01 W
Coche, Isla I	246	10.45 N	63.55 W
Cochem	56	50.11 N	7.09 E
Cochesett	283	42.01 N	71.02 W
Cochetopa Creek ≃	200	38.31 N	106.47 W
Cochichewick, Lake ⊜	283	42.42 N	71.06 W
Cochin → Kochi	122	9.58 N	76.14 E
Cochin China → Nam Phan □[9]	110	11.00 N	107.00 E

DEUTSCH

Name	Seite	Breite°′	Länge°′ E = Ost
Cochinos, Bahía de (Bay of Pigs) c	240p	22.07 N	81.10 W
Cochinos, Cayos II	236	15.57 N	86.33 W
Cochise Head ∧	200	32.03 N	109.18 W
Cochiti Indian Reservation ⬥[4]	200	35.37 N	106.20 W
Cochituate	207	42.19 N	71.21 W
Cochituate, Lake ⊜	283	42.17 N	71.22 W
Cochituate State Park ♦	207	42.20 N	71.22 W
Cochran	192	32.23 N	83.21 W
Cochrane, Ab., Can.	182	51.11 N	114.28 W
Cochrane, On., Can.	176	49.04 N	81.01 W
Cochrane, Chile	254	47.16 S	72.33 W
Cochrane, Wi., U.S.	190	44.13 N	91.50 W
Cochrane ≃	176	57.52 N	101.38 W
Cochrane, Cerro (Monte San Lorenzo) ∧	254	47.37 S	72.19 W
Cochrane, Lago (Lago Pueyrredón) ⊜	254	47.20 S	72.00 W
Cochranton	214	41.31 N	80.02 W
Cochranville	208	39.53 N	75.55 W
Cochstedt	54	51.53 N	11.24 E
Cockatoo-Inseln → Buccaneer Archipelago II	160	16.17 S	123.20 E
Cock Bridge	46	57.09 N	3.14 W
Cockburn	166	32.05 S	141.00 E
Cockburn, Canal ʉ	254	54.20 S	71.30 W
Cockburn, Cape ≻	164	11.20 S	132.52 E
Cockburn, Mount ∧	162	22.46 S	130.36 E
Cockburn Island I	190	45.55 N	83.22 W
Cockburn Sound ʉ	168a	32.12 S	115.42 E
Cockburnspath	46	55.56 N	2.21 W
Cock Clarks	260	51.42 N	0.37 E
Cockenoe Island I	276	41.05 N	73.21 W
Cockenzie	46	55.58 N	2.58 W
Cocker ≃	44	54.39 N	3.22 W
Cockerham	44	53.59 N	2.50 W
Cockermouth	44	54.40 N	3.21 W
Cockeysville	208	39.28 N	76.38 W
Cockfield	44	54.37 N	1.48 W
Cockfosters ⬥[8]	260	51.39 N	0.09 W
Cocklebiddy	162	32.02 S	126.06 E
Cockpit Country ⬥[1]	241q	18.18 N	77.43 W
Cockrell Hill	222	32.44 N	96.53 W
Cockroach Island I	240m	18.24 N	65.04 W
Cockscomb Point ≻	174u	14.14 S	170.40 W
Coclé □[4]	236	8.30 N	80.15 W
Coclé del Norte ≃	236	9.05 N	80.35 W
Coclois	50	48.28 N	4.20 E
Coco ≃	236	15.00 N	83.10 W
Coco, Cayo I	240p	22.30 N	78.28 W
Coco, Isla del I	230	5.32 N	87.04 W
Côco, Rio do ≃	250	9.27 S	50.02 W
Cocoa	220	28.23 N	80.44 W
Cocoa Beach	220	28.19 N	80.36 W
Cocobeach	152	0.59 N	9.36 E
Coco Channel ʉ	110	13.45 N	93.00 E
Cococi	250	6.25 S	40.30 W
Cocodrie Lake ⊜[1]	194	30.58 N	92.25 W
Coco Islands II	110	14.05 N	93.18 E
Coconino Plateau ⋀[1]	200	35.50 N	112.30 W
Cocorocuma, Cayos ✣[2]	236	15.45 N	83.00 W
Cocos	255	14.10 S	44.33 W
Cocos (Keeling) Islands □[2]	14	12.10 S	96.55 E
Cocos Bay c	241r	10.27 N	61.00 W
Cocos Island I	174p	13.14 N	144.39 E
Cocos Lagoon c	174p	13.14 N	144.38 E
Cocos Ridge ✣[3]	16	5.30 N	86.00 W
Cocotá ⬥[8]	287a	22.49 S	43.11 W
Cocuiza ≃	246	10.59 N	71.17 W
Cocula, Méx.	234	18.14 N	99.40 W
Cocula, Méx.	234	20.23 N	103.50 W
Cod ≃	44	54.10 N	1.22 W
Cod, Cape ≻[1]	207	41.42 N	70.15 W
Codăeşti	38	46.52 N	27.46 E
Codajás	246	3.50 S	62.05 W
Codaruina	71	40.56 N	8.49 E
Coddenham	42	52.09 N	1.07 E
Codera, Cabo ≻	246	10.35 N	66.05 W
Coderre	134	50.10 N	106.23 W
Coderre, Ruisseau ≃	275a	45.43 N	73.19 W
Codesa	182	55.45 N	118.04 W
Codfish Island I	172	46.47 S	167.38 E
Codigoro	66	44.49 N	12.08 E
Cod Island I	176	57.45 N	61.50 W
Codlea	38	45.42 N	25.27 E
Codnor	44	53.03 N	1.23 W
Codó	250	4.29 S	43.53 W
Codogno	62	45.09 N	9.42 E
Codorus	208	39.48 N	76.52 W
Codorus Creek ≃	208	40.03 N	76.38 W
Codorus State Park ♦	208	39.48 N	76.54 W
Codòzinho	250	4.46 S	44.10 W
Codpa	248	18.50 S	69.44 W
Codrii ⋀[2]	38	47.10 N	28.25 E
Codro	86	50.50 N	88.34 E
Codroipo	64	45.58 N	12.59 E
Codrongianos	71	40.39 N	8.41 E
Codroy	186	47.53 N	59.24 W
Codroy Pond	186	48.04 N	58.52 W
Codru-Moma, Munţii ⋀	38	46.30 N	22.20 E
Codsall	42	52.38 N	2.12 W
Cody, Ne., U.S.	198	42.56 N	101.14 W
Cody, Wy., U.S.	202	44.31 N	109.03 W
Coeburn	192	36.56 N	82.27 W
Coelemu	252	36.29 S	72.42 W
Coelho da Rocha	256	22.47 S	43.23 W
Coelho Neto	250	4.15 S	43.00 W
Coemba	152	12.08 S	18.05 E
Coen	164	13.56 S	143.12 E
Coen ≃, Austl.	164	13.56 S	142.02 E
Coén ≃, C.R.	236	9.34 N	82.58 W
Coeneo [de la Libertad]	234	19.49 N	101.35 W
Coeroeni ≃	250	3.21 N	57.31 W
Coesfeld	52	51.56 N	7.10 E
Coetivy Island I	138	7.08 S	56.16 E
Coeur d'Alene	202	47.40 N	116.46 W
Coeur d'Alene ≃	202	47.28 N	116.48 W
Coeur d'Alene Indian Reservation ⬥[4]	202	47.18 N	116.45 W
Coeur d'Alene Lake ⊜	202	47.32 N	116.48 W
Coeur d'Alene Mountains ⋀	202	47.50 N	116.05 W
Coevorden	52	52.40 N	6.45 E
Coeymans	210	42.28 N	73.48 W
Coffeen	219	39.05 N	89.24 W
Coffeen Lake ⊜[1]	219	39.03 N	89.20 W
Coffeeville	194	33.58 N	89.40 W
Coffeyville	198	37.02 N	95.36 W
Coffin Bay	162	34.37 S	135.29 E
Coffin Bay c	162	34.27 S	135.19 E
Coffin Bay Peninsula ≻[1]	162	34.32 S	135.15 E
Coffs Harbour	166	30.18 S	153.08 E
Cofimvaba	158	32.00 S	27.35 E
Cofradía	236	15.24 N	88.09 W
Cofre de Perote, Cerro ∧	234	19.29 N	97.08 W
Cofre de Perote, Parque Nacional ♦	234	19.32 N	97.10 W
Cofrents	34	39.14 N	1.04 W
Cogâlnic (Kohyl'nyk) ≃	78	45.51 N	29.38 E
Coggeshall	42	51.52 N	0.41 E
Coggiola	62	45.41 N	8.11 E
Coggon	190	42.16 N	91.31 W
Coghill, Mount ∧	170	35.10 S	149.44 E
Coghinas ≃	71	40.56 N	8.48 E
Coghinas, Lago del ⊜	71	40.45 N	9.02 E
Coglians, Monte (Hohe Warte) ∧	64	46.37 N	12.53 E
Cogliate	266b	45.39 N	9.05 E

Symbols in the index entries represent the broad categories identified in the key at the right. Symbols with superior numbers (⋀[1]) identify subcategories (see complete key on page *I · 1)*.

Symbole im Register stellen die rechts im Schlüssel erklärten Kategorien dar. Symbole mit hochgestellten Ziffern (⋀[1]) bezeichnen Unterabteilungen einer Kategorie (vgl. vollständiger Schlüssel auf Seite *I · 1)*.

Los símbolos incluídos en el texto del índice representan las grandes categorías identificadas con la clave a la derecha. Los símbolos con numeros en su parte superior (⋀[1]) identifican las subcategorías (véase la clave completa en la página *I · 1)*.

Les symboles de l'index représentent les catégories indiquées dans la légende à droite. Les symboles suivis d'un indice (⋀[1]) représentent des sous-catégories (voir légende complète à la page *I · 1)*.

Os símbolos incluídos no texto do índice representam as grandes categorias identificadas com a chave à direita. Os símbolos com números em sua parte superior (⋀[1]) identificam as subcategorias (veja-se a chave completa à página *I · 1)*.

	English	Deutsch	Español	Français	Português
∧	Mountain	Berg	Montaña	Montagne	Montanha
⋀	Mountains	Gebirge	Montañas	Montagnes	Montanhas
x	Pass	Paß	Paso	Col	Passo
V	Valley, Canyon	Tal, Cañon	Valle, Cañón	Vallée, Canyon	Vale, Canhão
≃	Plain	Ebene	Llano	Plaine	Planície
≻	Cape	Kap	Cabo	Cap	Cabo
I	Island	Insel	Isla	Île	Ilha
II	Islands	Inseln	Islas	Îles	Ilhas
⊥	Other Topographic Features	Andere Topographische Objekte	Otros Elementos Topográficos	Autres données topographiques	Outros acidentes topográficos

ESPAÑOL: Nombre | Página | Lat. °′ | Long. °′ W = Oeste
FRANÇAIS: Nom | Page | Lat. °′ | Long. °′ W = Ouest
PORTUGUÊS: Nome | Página | Lat. °′ | Long. °′ W = Oeste

Nombre / Nom / Nome	Página / Page	Lat. °′	Long. °′
Cognac	32	45.42 N	0.20 W
Cogne	62	45.37 N	7.21 E
Cognin	62	45.34 N	5.54 E
Cogo	152	1.05 N	9.42 E
Cogoleto	62	44.23 N	8.39 E
Cogolin	62	43.15 N	6.32 E
Cogollo del Cengio	64	45.47 N	11.25 E
Cogolludo	34	40.57 N	3.05 W
Cogolo	64	46.21 N	10.41 E
Cogoon ≃	166	27.19 S	148.50 E
Čograjuskoje vodochranilišče ⊜¹	80	45.30 N	44.25 E
Cogswell	198	46.06 N	97.46 W
Cogswell Reservoir ⊜¹	280	34.14 N	117.58 W
Cogt	102	45.20 N	96.38 E
Cogtoandman'	102	45.50 N	104.28 E
Cogton Bay c	116	9.51 N	124.33 E
Cogt-Ovoo	102	44.25 N	105.20 E
Çoğun	130	39.20 N	34.08 E
Cohansey ≃	208	39.21 N	75.22 W
Cohasset	207	42.14 N	70.48 W
Cohasset Harbor c	283	42.15 N	70.47 W
Cohengu ≃	248	10.17 S	73.57 W
Cohoctah	216	42.46 N	83.57 W
Cohocton	210	42.30 N	77.30 W
Cohocton ≃	210	42.09 N	77.05 W
Cohoe	180	60.23 N	151.18 W
Cohoes	210	42.46 N	73.42 W
Cohoon, Lake ⊜¹	208	36.45 N	76.38 W
Cohuna	166	35.49 S	144.13 E
Coiba, Isla de I	246	7.27 N	81.45 W
Coig ≃	254	50.58 S	69.11 W
Coigeach, Rubha >	46	58.06 N	5.26 W
Coignières	261	48.45 N	1.55 E
Coihaique	254	45.34 S	72.04 W
Coils Creek ≃	204	39.32 N	116.16 W
Coimbatore	122	11.00 N	76.58 E
Coimbra, Bra.	248	19.55 S	57.47 W
Coimbra, Bra.	255	20.52 S	42.48 W
Coimbra, Port.	34	40.12 N	8.25 W
Coín, Esp.	34	36.40 N	4.45 W
Coin, Ia., U.S.	198	40.39 N	95.13 W
Coina ≃	266c	38.38 N	9.03 W
Coipasa, Lago ⊜	248	19.12 S	68.07 W
Coipasa, Salar de ≚	248	19.26 S	68.09 W
Coire → Chur	58	46.51 N	9.32 E
Čojbalsan, Mong.	88	48.25 N	114.52 E
Čojbalsan, Mong.	88	48.04 N	114.30 E
Čojbalsan uul ʌ	88	47.49 N	107.00 E
Cojedes	246	9.37 N	68.55 W
Cojedes □³	246	9.20 N	68.20 W
Cojímar ◆⁸	286b	23.10 N	82.18 W
Cojímar ≃	286b	23.10 N	82.17 W
Cojudo Blanco, Cerro ʌ	254	47.05 S	69.20 W
Cojumatlán de Régules	234	20.07 N	102.50 W
Cojutepeque	236	13.43 N	88.56 W
Čokak	130	37.45 N	36.19 E
Cokato	190	45.04 N	94.11 W
Cokeburg	214	40.06 N	80.04 W
Coker	273a	6.29 N	3.20 E
Cokeville	200	42.04 N	110.57 W
Čokpar	85	43.49 N	74.21 E
Čoktal	85	42.36 N	76.44 E
Čokurdach	74	70.38 N	147.55 E
Colāba ◆⁸	272c	18.54 N	72.48 E
Colāba Point >	272c	18.53 N	72.48 E
Colac	169	38.20 S	143.35 E
Colac, Lake ⊜	169	38.18 S	143.35 E
Çolaklı	130	38.22 N	38.33 E
Colalao del Valle	252	26.22 S	65.57 W
Colapsin Point >	116	6.38 N	125.25 E
Colares, Bra.	250	0.56 S	48.17 W
Colares, Port.	266c	38.48 N	9.27 W
Colares, Ribeira de ≃	266c	38.49 N	9.28 W
Colatina	255	19.32 S	40.37 W
Cölbe	56	50.51 N	8.48 E
Colbeck, Cape >	9	77.06 S	157.48 W
Colberry Park	281	42.36 N	83.16 W
Colbert	196	33.51 N	96.30 W
Colbinabbin	166	36.35 S	144.49 E
Colbitz	54	52.19 N	11.36 E
Colbitz-Letzlinger Heide ◆³	54	52.27 N	11.35 E
Colborne, On., Can.	212	42.51 N	80.19 W
Colborne, On., Can.	212	44.00 N	77.53 W
Colbún	252	35.42 S	71.25 W
Colbún, Embalse ⊜¹	252	35.40 S	71.20 W
Colburn, Eng., U.K.	44	54.23 N	1.41 W
Colburn, In., U.S.	216	40.31 N	86.42 W
Colby, Ks., U.S.	198	39.23 N	101.03 W
Colby, Wi., U.S.	190	44.54 N	90.18 W
Colca	248	12.18 S	75.13 W
Colca ≃	248	15.51 S	72.26 W
Colcamar	248	6.16 S	77.55 W
Colchester, On., Can.	214	41.59 N	82.56 W
Colchester, Eng., U.K.	42	51.54 N	0.54 E
Colchester, Ct., U.S.	207	41.34 N	72.19 W
Colchester, Il., U.S.	190	40.25 N	90.47 W
Coldbackie	46	58.31 N	4.23 W
Cold Bay	180	55.11 N	162.30 W
Cold Bay c	180	55.13 N	162.33 W
Coldblow ◆⁸	260	51.26 N	0.10 E
Cold Brook	210	43.15 N	75.03 W
Cold Creek ≃	212	44.12 N	77.36 W
Colden	210	42.39 N	78.41 W
Cold Fell ʌ	44	54.54 N	2.36 W
Cold Harbor Battlefield ⊥	208	37.36 N	77.20 W
Coldingham	46	55.53 N	2.10 W
Colditz	54	51.07 N	12.48 E
Cold Lake	184	54.27 N	110.10 W
Cold Lake ⊜	184	54.33 N	110.05 W
Cold Lake, Canadian Forces Base ■	184	54.25 N	110.17 W
Cold Lake Indian Reserve ◆⁴	184	54.33 N	110.10 W
Cold Norton	260	51.40 N	0.40 E
Coldrano	64	46.38 N	10.50 E
Cold Spring, Ky., U.S.	218	39.01 N	84.26 W
Cold Spring, Mn., U.S.	190	45.27 N	94.25 W
Cold Spring, N.J., U.S.	208	38.58 N	74.55 W
Cold Spring, N.Y., U.S.	210	41.25 N	73.57 W
Coldspring, Tx., U.S.	222	30.36 N	95.08 W
Cold Spring Harbor	276	40.52 N	73.27 W
Cold Spring Harbor c	276	40.53 N	73.28 W
Coldsprings, On., Can.	212	44.17 N	78.18 W
Cold Springs, N.Y., U.S.	210	43.08 N	76.15 W
Cold Spring Terrace	276	40.50 N	73.26 W
Coldstream, Austl.	169	37.44 S	145.23 E
Coldstream, Scot., U.K.	46	55.39 N	2.15 W
Cold Stream ≃	226	39.35 N	120.22 W
Coldwater, On., Can.	212	44.42 N	79.40 W
Coldwater, Ks., U.S.	198	37.16 N	99.19 W
Coldwater, Mi., U.S.	216	41.56 N	85.00 W
Coldwater, Ms., U.S.	194	34.41 N	89.58 W
Coldwater, Oh., U.S.	216	40.28 N	84.37 W
Coldwater ≃, On., Can.	212	44.44 N	79.39 W
Coldwater ≃, Mi., U.S.	216	42.04 N	85.08 W
Coldwater ≃, Ms., U.S.	194	34.11 N	90.13 W
Coldwater Canyon ∨	280	34.14 N	117.44 W
Coldwater Creek ≃	196	36.40 N	101.08 W
Coldwater Indian Reserve ◆⁴	182	50.04 N	120.48 W
Coldwater Lake ⊜	216	41.49 N	84.58 W
Cole □⁶	219	38.30 N	92.13 W
Cole ≃, Ang.	152	9.07 S	15.50 E
Cole ≃, Eng., U.K.	42	51.42 N	1.42 W
Coleambally	166	34.49 S	145.52 E
Colebrook, N.H., U.S.	188	44.53 N	71.29 W
Colebrook, Oh., U.S.	214	41.32 N	80.46 W
Colebrook River Lake ⊜¹	207	42.03 N	73.04 W
Cole Camp	194	38.27 N	93.12 W
Coledale	170	34.17 S	150.57 E
Coleen ≃	180	67.05 N	142.31 W
Coleford, Eng., U.K.	42	51.48 N	2.36 W
Coleford, Eng., U.K.	42	51.14 N	2.27 W
Colégio, Morro do ʌ	287b	23.38 S	46.21 W
Coleman, Ab., Can.	182	49.38 N	114.30 W
Coleman, Fl., U.S.	220	28.47 N	82.04 W
Coleman, Md., U.S.	208	39.20 N	76.04 W
Coleman, Mi., U.S.	190	43.45 N	84.35 W
Coleman, Tx., U.S.	196	31.49 N	99.25 W
Coleman, Wi., U.S.	190	45.03 N	88.02 W
Coleman ≃	164	15.06 S	141.38 E
Coleman, Lake ⊜¹	196	32.02 N	99.30 W
Colembert	50	50.45 N	1.50 E
Colen Lakes ⊜	184	54.33 N	95.25 W
Colenso	158	28.50 S	29.44 E
Colerain	214	40.07 N	80.49 W
Coleraine, Austl.	166	37.36 S	141.42 E
Coleraine, N. Ire., U.K.	48	55.08 N	6.40 W
Coleraine, Mn., U.S.	190	47.17 N	93.25 W
Coleridge	198	42.30 N	97.12 W
Coleridge, Lake ⊜	172	43.17 S	171.30 E
Coles	194	31.16 N	91.01 W
Coles, Punta >	248	17.42 S	71.23 W
Colesberg	158	30.45 S	25.05 E
Coles Brook ≃	276	40.55 N	74.02 W
Coleshill, Eng., U.K.	42	52.30 N	1.42 W
Coleshill, Eng., U.K.	260	51.39 N	0.38 W
Coles Point	208	38.09 N	76.38 W
Colesville, Md., U.S.	284c	39.05 N	77.00 W
Colesville, N.J., U.S.	210	41.15 N	74.39 W
Coleto Creek ≃	196	28.41 N	97.01 W
Coleville, Sk., Can.	184	51.43 N	109.16 W
Coleville, Ca., U.S.	226	38.33 N	119.30 W
Colfax, Ca., U.S.	226	39.06 N	120.57 W
Colfax, Il., U.S.	216	40.34 N	88.36 W
Colfax, In., U.S.	194	40.11 N	86.40 W
Colfax, Ia., U.S.	190	41.40 N	93.14 W
Colfax, La., U.S.	194	31.31 N	92.42 W
Colfax, Wa., U.S.	202	46.52 N	117.21 W
Colfax, Wi., U.S.	190	44.59 N	91.43 W
Colfiorito	66	43.02 N	12.55 E
Colgate	216	43.12 N	88.12 W
Colgate Creek ≃	284b	39.15 N	76.32 W
Colgong	124	25.16 N	87.13 E
Colgrave Sound ɥ	46a	60.37 N	0.58 W
Colhué Huapi, Lago ⊜	254	45.30 S	68.48 W
Coliban ≃	169	36.56 S	144.33 E
Colibris, Pointe des >, Guad.	241o	16.15 N	61.11 W
Colibris, Pointe des >, Guad.	241o	16.17 N	61.06 W
Colico	58	46.08 N	9.22 E
Coligny, Fr.	58	46.23 N	5.21 E
Coligny, S. Afr.	158	26.17 S	26.15 E
Colijnsplaat	52	51.46 N	3.51 E
Colima, Méx.	200	32.25 N	115.05 W
Colima, Méx.	234	19.14 N	103.43 W
Colima □³	234	19.10 N	104.00 W
Colima, Nevado de ʌ	234	19.33 N	103.38 W
Colimes ≃	246	1.32 S	80.00 W
Colin ≃	50	47.08 N	2.32 E
Colina	252	33.12 S	70.41 W
Colinas, Bra.	250	6.02 S	44.14 W
Colinas, Bra.	255	14.12 S	48.03 W
Colinet	186	47.13 N	53.33 W
Colinton, Austl.	171b	35.51 S	149.09 E
Colinton, Ab., Can.	182	54.37 N	113.15 W
Coliseum → Colosseo ⊥	267a	41.54 N	12.29 E
Coll I	46	56.38 N	6.34 W
Colla	258	34.04 S	57.21 W
Colla, Arroyo ≃	258	34.19 S	57.20 W
Collagna	64	44.21 N	10.16 E
Collalbo (Klobenstein)	64	46.32 N	11.28 E
Collalto Sabino	66	42.08 N	13.02 E
Collamer	210	43.06 N	76.04 W
Collarenebri	166	29.33 S	148.35 E
Collarmele	66	42.03 N	13.38 E
Collaroy	274a	33.44 S	151.18 E
Collazzone	66	42.54 N	12.26 E
Collbran	200	39.14 N	107.57 W
Collecchio	64	44.45 N	10.13 E
Collecorvino	66	42.27 N	14.01 E
Colle di Tora	66	42.13 N	12.57 E
Colle di Val d'Elsa	66	43.25 N	11.07 E
Colleen Bawn	154	21.00 S	29.13 E
Colleferro	66	41.44 N	12.59 E
College	180	64.51 N	147.47 W
College City	226	39.00 N	122.00 W
College Corner	218	39.30 N	84.36 W
Collegedale	194	35.04 N	85.03 W
College Meadows	218	39.56 N	86.07 W
College Park, Ga., U.S.	192	33.39 N	84.26 W
College Park, Md., U.S.	208	38.58 N	76.56 W
College Park Airport ⊠	284c	38.58 N	76.55 W
College Place	202	46.02 N	118.23 W
College Point ◆⁸	276	40.47 N	73.51 W
College Station, Ar., U.S.	194	34.43 N	92.13 W
College Station, Tx., U.S.	222	30.37 N	96.20 W
Collegeville, In., U.S.	216	40.54 N	87.09 W
Collegeville, Pa., U.S.	208	40.11 N	75.27 W
Collégien	261	48.50 N	2.40 E
Collegno	62	45.05 N	7.34 E
Colle Isarco (Gossensass)	64	46.56 N	11.26 E
Collepardo	66	41.46 N	13.22 E
Collepasso	68	40.04 N	18.10 E
Collepietro	66	42.13 N	13.46 E
Collerina	166	29.41 S	146.38 E
Collesalvetti	66	43.35 N	10.28 E
Colle Sannita	68	41.22 N	14.50 E
Collesano	70	37.55 N	13.56 E
Colletorto	66	41.40 N	14.58 E
Colleymount	182	54.01 N	126.09 W
Colleyville	222	32.52 N	97.09 W
Colliano	68	40.43 N	15.17 E
Colli a Volturno	66	41.36 N	14.06 E
Colli del Tronto	66	42.52 N	13.44 E
Colli di Monte Bove	66	42.06 N	13.09 E
Collie	168a	33.21 S	116.09 E
Collie ≃	168a	33.18 S	115.44 E
Collie East ≃	168a	33.18 S	116.10 E
Collier □⁶	220	26.10 N	81.22 W
Collier Bay c	160	16.10 S	124.15 E
Collier Bridge ◆⁵	220	26.57 N	82.04 W
Collier City	220	26.14 N	80.09 W
Collier Law ʌ²	44	54.46 N	1.58 W
Collier Range ⋏	162	24.43 S	119.12 E
Collier Range National Park ♠	162	24.40 S	119.15 E
Collier Row ◆⁸	260	51.36 N	0.10 E
Colliers	214	40.22 N	80.32 W
Collier-Seminole State Park ♠	220	25.59 N	81.36 W
Colliersville	210	42.29 N	74.59 W
Collierville	194	35.02 N	89.39 W
Collie South ≃	168a	33.18 S	116.10 E
Collieston	46	57.21 N	1.56 W
Colliford Lake Reservoir ⊜¹	42	50.32 N	4.33 W
Colligan ≃	48	52.06 N	7.38 W
Collin □⁶	222	33.07 N	96.35 W
Collingbourne Kingston	42	51.18 N	1.40 W
Collingdale	208	39.54 N	75.16 W
Collingham	44	53.54 N	1.24 W
Collingswood	285	39.55 N	75.04 W
Collingwood, Austl.	274b	37.48 S	145.00 E
Collingwood, On., Can.	212	44.29 N	80.13 W
Collingwood, N.Z.	172	40.40 S	172.41 E
Collingwood Bay c	164	9.20 S	149.30 E
Collins, Ga., U.S.	192	32.10 N	82.06 W
Collins, Ia., U.S.	190	41.54 N	93.18 W
Collins, Ms., U.S.	194	31.38 N	89.33 W
Collins, N.Y., U.S.	210	42.30 N	78.55 W
Collins, Oh., U.S.	214	41.16 N	82.30 W
Collins ≃	194	35.48 N	85.37 W
Collins, Mount ʌ²	190	47.51 N	80.59 W
Collins Bay	212	44.15 N	76.36 W
Collinsburg	214	40.13 N	79.46 W
Collins Center	210	42.30 N	78.51 W
Collins Lake ⊜	212	44.22 N	76.27 W
Collins Park	208	39.41 N	75.33 W
Collinston	194	32.41 N	91.52 W
Collinsville, Austl.	166	20.34 S	147.51 E
Collinsville, Al., U.S.	194	34.15 N	85.51 W
Collinsville, Ca., U.S.	282	38.05 N	121.51 W
Collinsville, Ct., U.S.	207	41.48 N	72.55 W
Collinsville, Il., U.S.	219	38.40 N	89.59 W
Collinsville, Ms., U.S.	194	32.29 N	88.50 W
Collinsville, N.J., U.S.	276	40.49 N	74.28 W
Collinsville, Ok., U.S.	196	36.21 N	95.50 W
Collinsville, Tx., U.S.	196	33.32 N	96.54 W
Collinwood	194	35.10 N	87.44 W
Collio	64	45.48 N	10.20 E
Collipulli	252	37.57 S	72.26 W
Collister	202	43.38 N	116.15 W
Collobrières	62	43.14 N	6.18 E
Collombey	58	46.16 N	6.57 E
Collomsville	210	41.09 N	77.09 W
Collon	48	53.47 N	6.29 W
Collonges	58	46.08 N	5.54 E
Collooney	48	54.11 N	8.29 W
Collserola, Serra de ⋏	266d	41.26 N	2.07 E
Colma	226	37.41 N	122.28 W
Colma Creek ≃	282	37.38 N	122.23 W
Colman	198	43.58 N	96.48 W
Colmar	58	48.05 N	7.22 E
Colmar Manor	284c	38.55 N	76.56 W
Colmars	62	44.11 N	6.38 E
Colmenar	34	36.54 N	4.20 W
Colmenar de Oreja	34	40.06 N	3.23 W
Colmenar Viejo	34	40.40 N	3.46 W
Colmeneros	234	18.06 N	101.40 W
Colmesneil	194	30.54 N	94.25 W
Colmnitz	54	50.54 N	13.31 E
Colmonell	44	55.08 N	4.55 W
Coln ≃	42	51.42 N	1.42 W
Colnbrook	260	51.29 N	0.31 W
Colne	44	53.52 N	2.09 W
Colne ≃, Eng., U.K.	42	51.48 N	1.01 E
Colne ≃, Eng., U.K.	260	51.26 N	0.30 W
Colney Heath	260	51.44 N	0.15 W
Colney Street	260	51.42 N	0.20 W
Colo	190	42.01 N	93.18 W
Colo ≃	170	33.26 S	150.53 E
Colobraro	68	40.11 N	16.25 E
Cologna Veneta	64	45.18 N	11.23 E
Cologne → Köln, Dtsch.	56	50.56 N	6.59 E
Cologne, Mn., U.S.	190	44.46 N	93.46 W
Cologne, N.J., U.S.	208	39.30 N	74.36 W
Cologno al Serio	62	45.37 N	9.42 E
Cologno Monzese	266b	45.32 N	9.17 E
Cololo, Nevado ʌ	248	14.53 S	69.06 W
Coloma, Ca., U.S.	226	38.48 N	120.53 W
Coloma, Mi., U.S.	216	42.11 N	86.18 W
Coloma, Wi., U.S.	190	44.02 N	89.31 W
Colomb-Béchar → Béchar	148	31.37 N	2.13 W
Colombes	50	48.55 N	2.15 E
Colombey-les-Belles	58	48.32 N	5.54 E
Colombey-les-Deux-Églises	58	48.13 N	4.53 E
Colômbia, Bra.	255	20.30 S	48.37 W
Colombia, Col.	246	3.24 N	74.49 W
Colombia, Cuba	240p	20.59 N	77.25 W
Colombia, Méx.	196	27.42 N	99.45 W
Colombia □¹, S.A.	242	4.00 N	72.00 W
Colombia □¹, S.A.	246	4.00 N	72.00 W
Colombian Basin ✧¹	16	13.00 N	76.00 W
Colombie → Colombia □¹	246	4.00 N	72.00 W
Colombie-Britannique → British Columbia □⁴	182	54.00 N	125.00 W
Colombier	58	46.58 N	6.52 E
Colombo, Bra.	252	25.17 S	49.14 W
Colombo, S. Lan.	122	6.56 N	79.51 E
Colome	198	43.15 N	99.42 W
Colomiers	32	43.37 N	1.20 E
Colón, Arg.	252	33.53 S	61.07 W
Colón, Arg.	252	32.13 S	58.08 W
Colón, Cuba	240p	22.43 N	80.54 W
Colón, Méx.	234	20.48 N	100.03 W
Colón, Pan.	236	9.22 N	79.54 W
Colon, Mi., U.S.	216	41.57 N	85.19 W
Colón, Ur.	252	33.53 S	54.43 W
Colón, Ur.	258	34.48 S	56.14 W
Colón □⁴	236	9.00 N	80.20 W
Colón □⁵	236	15.40 N	85.30 W
Colón, Archipiélago de (Galapagos Islands) II	246a	0.30 S	90.30 W
Colón, Cementerio ◆	286b	23.08 N	82.23 W
Colón, Isla I	236	9.24 N	82.17 W
Colón, Montañas de ⋏	236	14.55 N	84.45 W
Colón, Teatro ♠	288	34.36 S	58.23 W
Colona	162	31.38 S	132.05 E
Colonard-Corubert	50	48.25 N	0.39 E
Colonarie ≃	241h	13.14 N	61.06 W
Colonel Danforth Park ♠	275b	43.47 N	79.10 W
Colonelganj	124	27.08 N	81.42 E
Colonești	38	46.34 N	27.18 E
Colonet	204	31.05 N	116.10 W
Colonet, Cabo >	204	30.58 N	116.19 W
Colongulac, Lake ⊜	169	38.10 S	143.11 E
Colonia → Köln, Dtsch.	56	50.56 N	6.59 E
Colonia, Micron.	174q	9.31 N	138.08 E
Colonia, N.J., U.S.	210	40.34 N	74.18 W
Colonia □⁵	258	34.10 S	57.30 W
Colônia ≃	255	15.11 S	39.45 W
Colonia, Aeropuerto ⊠	258	34.28 S	57.49 W
Colonia, Cuchilla de la ⋏²	258	34.15 S	57.35 W
Colonia Alvear	252	35.00 S	67.40 W
Colonia Caroya	252	31.02 S	64.05 W
Colonia del Sacramento	258	34.28 S	57.51 W
Colonia Dora	252	28.36 S	62.57 W
Colonia Elisa	252	26.56 S	59.32 W
Colonia Guadalupe	204	32.04 N	116.37 W
Colonia Hogar Ricardo Gutiérrez	288	34.51 S	58.51 W
Colonia José Mármol	252	26.59 S	60.44 W
Colonial Acres	208	39.31 N	76.20 W
Colonia Lavalleja	252	31.06 S	57.01 W
Colonial Beach	208	38.15 N	76.57 W
Colonial Crest	208	40.20 N	76.50 W
Colônia Leopoldina	250	8.57 S	35.39 W
Colonial Heights	208	37.14 N	77.24 W
Colonial Manor	285	39.51 N	75.09 W
Colonial National Historical Park ♠	208	37.12 N	76.45 W
Colonial Park	208	40.18 N	76.48 W
Colonial Village, N.Y., U.S.	210	43.08 N	78.58 W
Colonial Village, Pa., U.S.	285	40.04 N	75.24 W
Colonial Village Airport ⊠	284a	43.08 N	78.58 W
Colonial Williamsburg ⊥	208	37.16 N	76.42 W
Colonia Morelos	200	30.50 N	109.10 W
Colonia Nicolich	258	34.50 S	56.02 W
Colonia Progreso	204	32.35 N	115.37 W
Colonia Providencia	240m	17.59 N	66.00 W
Colonias Unidas	252	26.42 S	59.38 W
Colonia Valdense	258	34.20 S	57.14 W
Colonia Vicente Guerrero	232	30.45 N	116.00 W
Colonia Villafañe	252	26.12 S	59.05 W
Colonie	210	42.43 N	73.50 W
Colon Koret	152	0.34 N	23.28 E
Colonna	267a	41.50 N	12.45 E
Colonna, Capo >	68	39.02 N	17.11 E
Colonnata	64	44.05 N	10.10 E
Colón Ridge ✧³	18	2.00 N	96.00 W
Colonsay	184	51.59 N	105.53 W
Colonsay I	46	56.04 N	6.13 W
Colony	198	38.04 N	95.21 W
Colora	208	39.40 N	76.06 W
Colorada, Laguna ≅	254	44.50 S	68.15 W
Colorada, Punta >	288	34.45 S	58.06 W
Colorada Grande, Salina ≚	252	38.15 S	63.47 W
Coloradas, Lomas ⋏²	254	43.24 S	67.24 W
Colorado, C.R.	236	10.46 N	83.35 W
Colorado, Hond.	236	15.47 N	87.19 W
Colorado, Ak., U.S.	180	63.09 N	149.26 W
Colorado □⁶	222	29.40 N	96.30 W
Colorado □³	178	39.00 N	105.30 W
Colorado ≃, Arg.	244	39.50 S	62.08 W
Colorado ≃, Bra.	248	13.03 S	62.20 W
Colorado ≃, Méx.	234	16.30 N	97.31 W
Colorado ≃, N.A.	200	31.54 N	114.57 W
Colorado ≃, Tx., U.S.	196	28.36 N	95.58 W
Colorado, Canal do ≅	287a	23.00 S	43.25 W
Colorado, Cerro ʌ, Arg.	254	45.02 S	69.38 W
Colorado, Cerro ʌ, Chile	286e	33.24 S	70.45 W
Colorado, Cerro ʌ, Perú	286d	12.07 S	76.55 W
Colorado, Williams Fork ≃	200	40.03 N	106.11 W
Colorado City, Az., U.S.	200	36.59 N	112.58 W
Colorado City, Co., U.S.	200	37.56 N	104.50 W
Colorado City, Tx., U.S.	196	32.23 N	100.51 W
Colorado de Abajo	196	26.28 N	99.54 W
Colorado National Monument ♠	200	39.04 N	108.25 W
Colorado Plateau ⋏¹	200	36.30 N	108.00 W
Colorado River Aqueduct ≅¹	204	33.50 N	117.23 W
Colorado River Indian Reservation ◆⁴	200	34.00 N	114.25 W
Colorados, Archipiélago de los II	240p	22.36 N	84.20 W
Colorado Springs	200	38.50 N	104.49 W
Colorines	234	19.07 N	100.12 W
Colorno	64	44.56 N	10.23 E
Colosimi	68	39.07 N	16.24 E
Colosseo ⊥	267a	41.54 N	12.29 E
Colotepec ≃	234	15.47 N	97.03 W
Colotlán	234	22.06 N	103.16 W
Colotlán ≃	234	22.06 N	103.42 W
Colotlipa	234	17.25 N	99.09 W
Colo Vale	170	34.24 S	150.29 E
Čolpon	85	42.12 N	75.28 E
Čolpon-Ata	85	42.40 N	77.06 E
Colpoys Bay c	212	44.47 N	81.05 W
Colquechaca	248	18.40 S	66.01 W
Colquencha	248	17.00 S	68.17 W
Colquiri	248	17.25 S	67.08 W
Colquitt	192	31.10 N	84.44 W
Colsterworth	42	52.48 N	0.37 W
Colstrip	202	45.53 N	106.37 W
Colt	194	35.07 N	90.48 W
Colta	248	15.10 S	73.18 W
Coltauco	252	34.18 S	71.06 W
Coltishall	42	52.44 N	1.22 E
Colton, Austl.	162	33.29 S	134.56 E
Colton, Ca., U.S.	228	34.04 N	117.18 W
Colton, Oh., U.S.	216	41.28 N	83.57 W
Colton, Or., U.S.	224	45.10 N	122.26 W
Colton, S.D., U.S.	198	43.47 N	96.55 W
Coltons Point	208	38.13 N	76.45 W
Colts Neck	208	40.17 N	74.10 W
Coltsville Center	214	41.05 N	80.34 W
Columbia, Al., U.S.	192	31.17 N	85.06 W
Columbia, Ca., U.S.	226	38.02 N	120.24 W
Columbia, Ct., U.S.	207	41.42 N	72.18 W
Columbia, Il., U.S.	219	38.26 N	90.12 W
Columbia, In., U.S.	218	39.35 N	85.12 W
Columbia, Ky., U.S.	194	37.06 N	85.18 W
Columbia, La., U.S.	194	32.06 N	92.04 W
Columbia, Md., U.S.	208	39.14 N	76.50 W
Columbia, Ms., U.S.	194	31.15 N	89.50 W
Columbia, Mo., U.S.	219	38.57 N	92.20 W
Columbia, N.J., U.S.	210	40.55 N	75.05 W
Columbia, N.C., U.S.	192	35.55 N	76.15 W
Columbia, Pa., U.S.	208	40.02 N	76.30 W
Columbia, S.C., U.S.	192	34.00 N	81.02 W
Columbia, Tn., U.S.	194	35.36 N	87.02 W
Columbia □⁶, N.Y., U.S.	210	42.15 N	73.47 W
Columbia □⁶, Or., U.S.	224	45.57 N	123.03 W
Columbia □⁶, Pa., U.S.	210	41.00 N	76.28 W
Columbia ≃	176	46.15 N	124.05 W
Columbia, Cape >	16	83.08 N	70.35 W
Columbia, Lake ⊜¹	216	42.05 N	84.18 W
Columbia, Mount ʌ	182	52.09 N	117.25 W
Columbia Airport ⊠	279a	41.19 N	81.58 W
Columbia Basin ≚¹	202	46.45 N	119.05 W
Columbia Center	279a	41.19 N	81.56 W
Columbia City, In., U.S.	216	41.09 N	85.29 W
Columbia City, Or., U.S.	224	45.53 N	122.48 W
Columbia Cross Roads	210	41.50 N	76.48 W
Columbia Falls, Me., U.S.	188	44.39 N	67.43 W
Columbia Falls, Mt., U.S.	202	48.22 N	114.10 W
Columbia Heights	224	46.09 N	122.58 W
Columbia Hills	284b	39.15 N	76.50 W
Columbia Icefield ⊓	182	52.10 N	117.30 W
Columbia Lake ⊜	182	50.15 N	115.57 W
Columbia Lake Indian Reserve ◆⁴	182	50.25 N	115.57 W
Columbia Mountains ⋏	182	52.00 N	119.00 W
Columbiana, Al., U.S.	194	33.10 N	86.36 W
Columbiana, Oh., U.S.	214	40.53 N	80.41 W
Columbiana □⁶	214	40.47 N	80.46 W
Columbia Plateau ⋏¹	202	44.00 N	117.30 W
Columbia Regional Airport ⊠	219	38.50 N	92.13 W
Columbia Road Reservoir ⊜¹	198	45.45 N	98.15 W
Columbia State Historical Park ♠	226	38.02 N	120.25 W
Columbia Station	214	41.20 N	81.57 W
Columbia University ⊌²	276	40.48 N	73.58 W
Columbiaville, Mi., U.S.	190	43.09 N	83.24 W
Columbiaville, N.Y., U.S.	210	42.19 N	73.45 W
Columbine, Cape >	158	32.47 S	17.52 E
Columbrets, Illes II	34	39.52 N	0.40 E
Columbus, Ga., U.S.	192	32.29 N	84.59 W
Columbus, In., U.S.	218	39.12 N	85.55 W
Columbus, Ks., U.S.	198	37.10 N	94.50 W
Columbus, Ms., U.S.	194	33.29 N	88.25 W
Columbus, Mt., U.S.	202	45.38 N	109.15 W
Columbus, Ne., U.S.	198	41.25 N	97.22 W
Columbus, N.J., U.S.	208	40.04 N	74.43 W
Columbus, N.M., U.S.	200	31.49 N	107.38 W
Columbus, N.C., U.S.	192	35.15 N	82.11 W
Columbus, N.D., U.S.	198	48.54 N	102.46 W
Columbus, Oh., U.S.	214	39.57 N	82.59 W
Columbus, Pa., U.S.	214	41.56 N	79.35 W
Columbus, Tx., U.S.	222	29.42 N	96.32 W
Columbus, Wi., U.S.	190	43.20 N	89.00 W
Columbus Air Force Base ■	194	33.38 N	88.26 W
Columbus Grove	216	40.55 N	84.03 W
Columbus Junction	190	41.16 N	91.21 W
Columbus Lake ⊜¹	194	33.35 N	88.30 W
Columbus Park ♠	278	41.53 N	87.47 W
Columbus Point >, Ba.	238	24.08 N	75.16 W
Columbus Point >, Trin.	241r	11.08 N	60.48 W
Columbus Salt Marsh ≚	204	38.04 N	117.58 W
Coluna	255	18.14 S	42.50 W
Colusa	226	39.12 N	122.00 W
Colusa □⁶	226	39.13 N	122.01 W
Colusa Trough ≅	226	39.02 N	121.59 W
Colver	214	40.32 N	78.47 W
Colville, N.Z.	172	36.38 S	175.28 E
Colville, Wa., U.S.	202	48.32 N	117.54 W
Colville ≃, Ak., U.S.	180	70.25 N	150.30 W
Colville ≃, Wa., U.S.	202	48.37 N	118.05 W
Colville, Cape >	172	36.28 S	175.21 E
Colville Channel ɥ	172	36.23 S	175.24 E
Colville Indian Reservation ◆⁴	202	48.15 N	119.00 W
Colville Lake ⊜	180	67.10 N	126.00 W
Colvin Run	284c	38.58 N	77.18 W
Colwell	44	55.04 N	2.04 W
Colwood	224	48.26 N	123.29 W
Colwyn	285	39.55 N	75.15 W
Colwyn Bay	44	53.18 N	3.43 W
Colyton, Austl.	274a	33.47 S	150.48 E
Colyton, Eng., U.K.	42	50.44 N	3.04 W
Comacchio	66	44.42 N	12.11 E
Comacchio, Valli di c	66	44.38 N	12.06 E
Comal	115a	6.55 S	109.31 E
Comala	234	19.19 N	103.45 W
Comalapa, Guat.	236	14.44 N	90.53 W
Comalapa, Nic.	236	12.17 N	85.31 W
Comalcalco	234	18.16 N	93.13 W
Comallo, Arroyo ≃	254	40.29 S	70.12 W
Coman, Mount ʌ	9	74.02 S	65.04 W
Comana	38	43.54 N	28.19 E
Comanche, Ok., U.S.	196	34.22 N	97.57 W
Comanche, Tx., U.S.	196	31.53 N	98.36 W
Comanche Creek ≃, Co., U.S.	198	39.53 N	104.19 W
Comanche Creek ≃, Tx., U.S.	196	31.06 N	102.24 W
Comandante Ferraz ⊌³	9	62.05 S	58.23 W
Comandante Fontana	252	25.20 S	59.41 W
Comandante Leal	252	30.53 S	65.47 W
Comandante Luis Piedrabuena	254	49.59 S	68.54 W
Comandante Nicanor Otamendi	252	38.07 S	57.51 W
Comănești	38	46.25 N	26.26 E
Comanjá de Corona	234	21.19 N	101.42 W
Comarapa	248	17.54 S	64.29 W
Comar Gambon	144	3.10 N	45.47 E
Comas, Perú	248	11.46 S	75.02 W
Comas, Perú	286d	11.57 S	77.04 W
Comayagua	236	14.25 N	87.37 W
Comayagua □⁵	236	14.30 N	87.40 W
Comayagua, Montañas de ⋏	236	14.23 N	87.26 W
Combahee ≃	192	32.30 N	80.31 W
Combarbalá	252	31.11 S	71.02 W
Combault	261	48.48 N	2.36 E
Combeaufontaine	58	47.43 N	5.53 E
Combe Bank ✧³	14	12.32 S	177.35 W
Combe Martin	42	51.13 N	4.02 W
Comber, On., Can.	214	42.14 N	82.33 W
Comber, N. Ire., U.K.	48	54.33 N	5.45 W
Comberbach	262	53.17 N	2.32 W
Combermere Bay c	110	19.37 N	93.34 E
Comberton	42	52.11 N	0.02 E
Combie, Lake ⊜¹	226	39.01 N	121.02 W
Comblain-au-Pont	56	50.28 N	5.35 E
Combles	50	50.01 N	2.52 E
Combloux	62	45.54 N	6.39 E
Combourg	32	48.25 N	1.45 W
Comboyne	166	31.36 S	152.29 E
Comboyuro Point >	171a	27.04 S	153.24 E
Combres	50	48.19 N	1.04 E
Combronde	32	45.59 N	3.05 E
Combs	262	53.18 N	1.57 W
Combs-la-Ville	50	48.40 N	2.34 E
Combs Reservoir ⊜¹	262	53.19 N	1.57 W
Comburg ⊌¹	56	49.06 N	9.44 E
Comb Wash ∨	200	37.13 N	109.42 W
Come by Chance	186	47.51 N	53.58 W
Comeglians	64	46.31 N	12.52 E
Comelico Superiore	64	46.35 N	12.30 E
Comendado Levy Gasparain	256	22.01 S	43.12 W
Comendador	238	18.53 N	71.42 W
Comendador Gomes	255	19.41 S	49.05 W
Comer	192	34.03 N	83.07 W
Comercinho	255	16.19 S	41.47 W
Comerío	240m	18.13 N	66.14 W
Comet	166	23.37 S	148.33 E
Comet ≃	166	23.34 S	148.32 E
Cometela	156	21.51 S	34.29 E
Comfort, N.C., U.S.	192	35.00 N	77.30 W
Comfort, Tx., U.S.	196	29.58 N	98.54 W
Comfort, Cape >	176	65.08 N	83.21 W
Comfort, Point >	276	40.27 N	74.08 W
Comfrey	198	44.06 N	94.54 W
Comilla	124	23.27 N	91.12 E
Comines	50	50.46 N	3.01 E
Comino → Kemmuna I	36	36.00 N	14.20 E
Comino, Capo >	71	40.32 N	9.49 E
Comiskey Park ♠	278	41.50 N	87.38 W
Comiso	70	36.56 N	14.36 E
Comitan de Dominguez	232	16.15 N	92.08 W
Comitini	70	37.24 N	13.39 E
Comloșu Mare	38	45.54 N	20.38 E
Commack	210	40.50 N	73.17 W
Commagene □⁹	130	37.50 N	38.00 E
Commencement Bay c	224	47.17 N	122.28 W
Commentry	32	46.17 N	2.44 E
Commerce, Ca., U.S.	280	34.00 N	118.09 W
Commerce, Ga., U.S.	192	34.12 N	83.27 W
Commerce, Mi., U.S.	216	42.34 N	83.30 W
Commerce, Ok., U.S.	196	36.56 N	94.52 W
Commerce, Tx., U.S.	196	33.14 N	95.53 W
Commerce City	198	39.49 N	104.56 W
Commerciale Luigi Bocconi, Università ⊌²	266b	45.26 N	9.11 E
Commercial Point	218	39.46 N	83.04 W
Commercy	56	48.45 N	5.35 E
Commewijne □⁵	250	5.50 N	55.00 W
Comminges ◆¹	32	43.15 N	0.45 E
Committee Bay c	176	68.30 N	86.30 W
Commodore	214	40.43 N	78.57 W
Commodore Barry Bridge ◆⁵	285	39.49 N	75.22 W
Commondale	158	27.20 S	30.56 E
Common Edge	262	53.47 N	3.02 W
Commonwealth Bay c	9	66.54 S	142.40 E
Commonwealth Range ⋏	9	84.15 S	172.20 E
Commoron Creek ≃	166	28.22 S	150.08 E
Como, Austl.	274a	34.00 S	151.04 E
Como, It.	62	45.47 N	9.05 E
Como, Ms., U.S.	194	34.30 N	89.56 W
Como, N.C., U.S.	208	36.30 N	77.00 W
Como, Tx., U.S.	222	33.03 N	95.28 W
Como, Wi., U.S.	216	42.37 N	88.28 W
Como □⁴	58	45.59 N	9.13 E
Como, Lago di ⊜	58	46.00 N	9.20 E
Como, Lake ⊜	216	42.36 N	88.29 W
Como, Mount ʌ	226	39.02 N	119.28 W
Comodoro Rivadavia	254	45.52 S	67.30 W
Como Lake ⊜	190	47.55 N	83.30 W
Comologno	58	46.12 N	8.34 E
Comonfort	234	20.43 N	100.46 W
Comoras → Comoros □¹	157a	12.10 S	44.15 E
Comores → Comoros □¹	157a	12.10 S	44.15 E
Comores, Archipel des II	157a	12.10 S	44.15 E
Comorin, Cape >	122	8.06 N	77.33 E
Comoros (Comores) □¹, Afr.	138	12.10 S	44.15 E
Comoros (Comores) □¹, Afr.	157a	12.10 S	44.15 E
Comox	182	49.40 N	124.55 W
Comox, Canadian Forces Base ■	182	49.43 N	124.54 W
Companhia Siderúrgica Nacional ⊌³	256	22.31 S	44.07 W
Compans	261	49.00 N	2.40 E
Compatsch	58	46.58 N	10.25 E
Compiègne	50	49.25 N	2.50 E
Compo Cove c	276	41.07 N	73.21 W
Compostela, Méx.	234	21.15 N	104.53 W
Compostela, Pil.	116	7.40 N	126.02 E
Comprida, Ilha I, Bra.	252	24.50 S	47.42 W
Comprida, Ilha I, Bra.	287a	23.02 S	43.12 W
Comps-sur-Artuby	62	43.43 N	6.30 E
Compstall	262	53.25 N	2.03 W
Compton, Eng., U.K.	260	51.13 N	0.38 W
Compton, Ca., U.S.	228	33.53 N	118.13 W
Compton, Il., U.S.	216	41.42 N	89.05 W
Compton □⁶	206	45.20 N	71.25 W
Compton Airport ⊠	280	33.53 N	118.15 W
Compton Creek ≃, Ca., U.S.	280	33.50 N	118.12 W
Compton Creek ≃, N.J., U.S.	276	40.26 N	74.05 W
Comptonville	273d	26.17 S	27.58 E
Comrat	38	46.18 N	28.38 E
Comrie	46	56.22 N	4.00 W
Comstock, Mi., U.S.	216	42.17 N	85.30 W
Comstock, Ne., U.S.	198	41.33 N	99.15 W
Comstock, Tx., U.S.	196	29.41 N	101.11 W
Comstock Park	216	43.02 N	85.40 W
Comunanza	66	42.57 N	13.25 E
Con ≃, Ross.	76	52.54 N	36.00 E
Con ≃, Viet	110	19.02 N	104.58 E
Čona ≃, Ross.	74	62.54 N	111.06 E
Cona ≃, Scot., U.K.	46	56.46 N	5.14 W
Co Nag ⊜	120	32.00 N	91.15 E
Conakry	150	9.31 N	13.43 W
Conambo ≃	246	2.07 S	76.03 W
Conanicut Island I	207	41.32 N	71.21 W
Cona Niyeo	254	41.53 S	67.00 W
Conara Junction	166	41.50 S	147.26 E
Conasauga ≃	192	34.33 N	84.55 W
Conaskonk Point >	276	40.27 N	74.11 W
Conca ≃	66	43.58 N	12.43 E
Concarán	252	32.34 S	65.15 W
Concarneau	32	47.52 N	3.55 W
Conceição, Bra.	248	7.24 S	58.05 W
Conceição, Bra.	250	7.33 S	38.31 W
Conceição, Moç.	156	18.45 S	36.10 E
Conceição, Cachoeira ⌞	248	9.34 S	64.22 W
Conceição, Ilha da I	287a	22.52 S	43.07 W
Conceição da Barra	255	18.35 S	39.45 W
Conceição da Pedra	256	22.09 S	45.27 W
Conceição das Alagoas	255	19.55 S	48.23 W
Conceição de Ipanema	255	19.55 S	41.41 W
Conceição de Jacareí	256	23.02 S	44.09 W
Conceição do Almeida	255	12.48 S	39.12 W
Conceição do Araguaia	250	8.15 S	49.17 W
Conceição do Canindé	250	7.54 S	41.34 W
Conceição do Coité	250	11.33 S	39.16 W
Conceição do Formoso	256	21.25 S	43.21 W
Conceição do Mato Dentro	255	19.01 S	43.25 W
Conceição do Maú	246	3.35 N	59.53 W
Conceição do Norte	255	12.13 S	47.18 W
Conceição do Rio Verde	256	21.53 S	45.05 W
Conceição dos Ouros	256	22.25 S	45.47 W
Concepción, Arg.	252	28.23 S	57.53 W
Concepción, Arg.	252	27.20 S	65.35 W
Concepción, Bol.	248	11.29 S	66.31 W
Concepción, Bol.	248	16.15 S	62.04 W
Concepción, Chile	252	36.50 S	73.03 W
Concepción, Col.	246	6.46 N	72.42 W
Concepción, Para.	252	23.25 S	57.17 W
Concepción, Perú	248	11.55 S	75.17 W
Concepcion, Pil.	116	11.13 N	123.06 E
Concepcion, Pil.	116	10.42 N	123.03 E
Concepcion, Pil.	116	12.24 N	122.06 E
Concepcion, Pil.	116	15.19 N	120.39 E
Concepción □⁵	252	23.00 S	57.00 W
Concepción, Bahía c	232	26.39 N	111.48 W
Concepción, Canal ɥ	254	50.30 S	74.55 W
Concepción, Laguna ⊜	248	17.29 S	61.25 W
Concepción, Volcán ʌ¹	236	11.34 N	85.37 W
Concepcion Bay c	116	11.15 N	123.07 E
Concepción de Ataco	236	13.52 N	89.51 W
Concepción de Buenos Aires	234	19.58 N	103.16 W
Concepción de la Sierra	252	27.59 S	55.31 W
Concepcíon del Oro	232	24.38 N	101.25 W
Concepción del Uruguay	252	32.29 S	58.14 W
Concepción Huista	236	15.37 N	91.41 W
Concepción Quezaltepeque	236	14.06 N	88.58 W
Conception, Point >	204	34.27 N	120.27 W
Conception Bay c, Nf., Can.	186	47.45 N	53.00 W
Conception Bay c, Namibia	156	23.53 S	14.28 E
Concession	154	17.22 S	30.57 E
Conchagua	236	13.19 N	87.52 W
Conchagua, Volcán ʌ¹	236	13.14 N	87.46 W
Conchal	256	22.20 S	47.10 W
Conchalí	286e	33.24 S	70.39 W
Conchalí, Cerros de ⋏	286e	33.20 S	70.38 W
Conchas ≃	196	35.23 N	104.18 W
Conchas Dam	196	35.22 N	104.11 W
Conchas Lake ⊜¹	196	35.25 N	104.14 W
Conche	186	50.53 N	55.54 W
Conches-en-Ouche	50	48.58 N	0.56 E
Conchi	252	22.02 S	68.38 W
Conchillas	258	34.15 S	58.04 W
Conchitas, Arroyo ≃	288	34.45 S	58.09 W

Symbol	English	Deutsch	Español	Français	Português
≃	River	Fluß	Río	Rivière	Rio
≅	Canal	Kanal	Canal	Canal	Canal
⌞	Waterfall, Rapids	Wasserfall, Stromschnellen	Cascada, Rápidos	Chute d'eau, Rapides	Cascata, Rápidos
ɥ	Strait	Meeresstraße	Estrecho	Détroit	Estreito
c	Bay, Gulf	Bucht, Golf	Bahía, Golfo	Baie, Golfe	Baía, Golfo
⊜	Lake, Lakes	See, Seen	Lago, Lagos	Lac, Lacs	Lago, Lagos
≚	Swamp	Sumpf	Pantano	Marais	Pântano
⊓	Ice Features, Glacier	Eis- und Gletscherformen	Accidentes Glaciales	Formes glaciaires	Acidentes glaciares
	Other Hydrographic Features	Andere Hydrographische Objekte	Otros Elementos Hidrográficos	Autres données hydrographiques	Outros acidentes hidrográficos
✧	Submarine Features	Untermeerische Objekte	Accidentes Submarinos	Formes de relief sous-marin	Acidentes submarinos
□	Political Unit	Politische Einheit	Unidad Politica	Entité politique	Unidade política
⊌	Cultural Institution	Kulturelle Institution	Institución Cultural	Institution culturelle	Instituição cultural
⊥	Historical Site	Historische Stätte	Sitio Histórico	Site historique	Sitio histórico
♠	Recreational Site	Erholungs- und Ferienort	Sitio de Recreo	Centre de loisirs	Area de Lazer
⊠	Airport	Flughafen	Aeropuerto	Aéroport	Aeroporto
■	Military Installation	Militäranlage	Instalación Militar	Installation militaire	Instalação militar
◆	Miscellaneous	Verschiedenes	Misceláneo	Divers	Diversos

Symbols in the index entries represent the broad categories identified in the key at the right. Symbols with superior numbers (≃¹) identify subcategories (see complete key on page I · 1).

Symbole im Register stellen die rechts im Schlüssel erklärten Kategorien dar. Symbole mit hochgestellten Ziffern (≃¹) bezeichnen Unterteilungen einer Kategorie (vgl. vollständiger Schlüssel auf Seite I · 1).

Los símbolos incluidos en el texto del índice representan las grandes categorías identificadas con la clave a la derecha. Los símbolos con numeros en su parte superior (≃¹) identifican las subcategorías (véase la clave completa en la página I · 1).

Les symboles de l'index représentent les catégories indiquées dans la légende à droite. Les symboles suivis d'un indice (≃¹) représentent des sous-catégories (voir légende complète à la page I · 1).

Os símbolos incluídos no texto do índice representam as grandes categorias identificadas na chave à direita. Os símbolos com números em sua parte superior (≃¹) identificam as subcategorias (veja-se a chave completa na página I · 1).

Symbol	English	Deutsch	Español	Français	Português
▲	Mountain	Berg	Montaña	Montagne	Montanha
⬈	Mountains	Gebirge	Montañas	Montagnes	Montanhas
⑂	Pass	Paß	Paso	Col	Passo
V	Valley, Canyon	Tal, Cañon	Valle, Cañón	Vallée, Canyon	Vale, Canhão
≃	Plain	Ebene	Llano	Plaine	Planície
➤	Cape	Kap	Cabo	Cap	Cabo
I	Island	Insel	Isla	Île	Ilha
II	Islands	Inseln	Islas	Îles	Ilhas
⊥	Other Topographic Features	Andere Topographische Objekte	Otros Elementos Topográficos	Autres données topographiques	Outros acidentes topográficos

ESPAÑOL — Nombre / Página / Lat.° / Long.° W=Oeste
FRANÇAIS — Nom / Page / Lat.° / Long.° W=Ouest
PORTUGUÊS — Nome / Página / Lat.° / Long.° W=Oeste

Corp-Cres   I · 41

Legend

Symbol	English	Deutsch	Español	Français	Português
≃	River	Fluß	Río	Rivière	Rio
≊	Canal	Kanal	Canal	Canal	Canal
⋓	Waterfall, Rapids	Wasserfall, Stromschnellen	Cascada, Rápidos	Chute d'eau, Rapides	Cascata, Rápidos
⋈	Strait	Meeresstraße	Estrecho	Détroit	Estreito
c	Bay, Gulf	Bucht, Golf	Bahía, Golfo	Baie, Golfe	Baía, Golfo
⊜	Lake, Lakes	See, Seen	Lago, Lagos	Lac, Lacs	Lago, Lagos
⊶	Swamp	Sumpf	Pantano	Marais	Pântano
⊠	Ice Features, Glacier	Eis- und Gletscherschollen	Accidentes Glaciares	Formes glaciaires	Acidentes glaciares
⋰	Other Hydrographic Features	Andere Hydrographische Objekte	Otros Elementos Hidrográficos	Autres données hydrographiques	Outros acidentes hidrográficos
⋆	Submarine Features	Untermeerische Objekte	Accidentes Submarinos	Formes de relief sous-marin	Acidentes submarinos
⊡	Political Unit	Politische Einheit	Unidad Política	Entité politique	Unidade política
†	Cultural Institution	Kulturelle Institution	Institución Cultural	Institution culturelle	Instituição Cultural
⋄	Historical Site	Historische Stätte	Sitio Histórico	Site historique	Sítio histórico
♦	Recreational Site	Erholungs- und Ferienort	Sitio de Recreo	Centre de loisirs	Área de Lazer
⋆	Airport	Flughafen	Aeropuerto	Aéroport	Aeroporto
■	Military Installation	Militäranlage	Instalación Militar	Installation militaire	Instalação militar
⇌	Miscellaneous	Verschiedenes	Misceláneo	Divers	Diversos

I · 42 **Cres-Cumb**

ENGLISH / DEUTSCH

Name / Page / Lat.°′ / Long.°′ — Name / Seite / Breite°′ / Länge°′ E = Ost

Name	Page	Lat.°′	Long.°′
Crescent Ditch ≃	226	36.29 N	120.07 W
Crescent Heights, N.J., U.S.	285	39.58 N	74.43 W
Crescent Heights, Tx., U.S.	222	32.11 N	95.56 W
Crescent Lake ⊜, Fl., U.S.	192	29.28 N	81.30 W
Crescent Lake ⊜, Or., U.S.	202	43.29 N	121.59 W
Crescent Lake Estates	281	42.38 N	83.25 W
Crescent Spur	182	53.35 N	120.41 W
Crescentville ◆[8]	285	40.02 N	75.05 W
Crescenzago ◆[8]	266b	45.30 N	9.15 E
Cresco, Ia., U.S.	190	43.22 N	92.06 W
Cresco, Pa., U.S.	210	41.09 N	75.17 W
Crespano del Grappa	64	45.49 N	11.50 E
Crespian	62	43.53 N	4.06 E
Crespières	261	48.53 N	1.55 E
Crespin	50	50.25 N	3.39 E
Crespino	64	44.59 N	11.53 E
Crespo	252	32.02 S	60.19 W
Cressbrook Creek ≃	171a	27.05 S	152.27 E
Cressely	261	48.43 N	2.05 E
Cressey	226	37.25 N	120.40 W
Cresskill	276	40.56 N	73.57 W
Cresskill Brook ≃	276	40.57 N	73.58 W
Cresson, Pa., U.S.	214	40.27 N	78.35 W
Cresson, Tx., U.S.	222	32.32 N	97.37 W
Cressona	208	40.37 N	76.11 W
Cressy	169	38.02 S	143.38 E
Crest	62	44.44 N	5.02 E
Cresta	58	46.28 N	9.31 E
Crested Butte	200	38.52 N	106.59 W
Cresthaven	220	26.03 N	80.08 W
Crest Hill	216	41.33 N	88.05 W
Crestline, Ca., U.S.	228	34.14 N	117.17 W
Crestline, Oh., U.S.	214	40.47 N	82.44 W
Creston, B.C., Can.	182	49.06 N	116.31 W
Creston, Nf., Can.	186	47.09 N	55.11 W
Creston, Ca., U.S.	226	35.31 N	120.31 W
Creston, Il., U.S.	216	41.56 N	88.58 W
Creston, Ia., U.S.	198	41.03 N	94.21 W
Creston, Oh., U.S.	214	40.59 N	81.53 W
Crestone Peak ∧	200	37.58 N	105.36 W
Crestview, Fl., U.S.	194	30.45 N	86.34 W
Crestview, Wi., U.S.	216	42.49 N	87.49 W
Crestview Heights	210	42.05 N	76.07 W
Crestwood, Il., U.S.	278	41.39 N	87.45 W
Crestwood, Ky., U.S.	218	38.19 N	85.28 W
Crestwood, Mo., U.S.	219	38.33 N	90.22 W
Crestwood Hills	192	35.56 N	84.05 W
Creswell, Eng., U.K.	44	53.16 N	1.12 W
Creswell, Or., U.S.	202	43.55 N	123.01 W
Creswell Bay ⊂	176	72.35 N	93.25 W
Creswell Creek ≃	162	18.10 S	135.11 E
Creswell Downs	162	17.57 S	135.55 E
Creswick	169	37.26 S	143.54 E
Creta → Kriti I	38	35.15 N	25.00 E
Crete, Il., U.S.	216	41.27 N	87.38 W
Crete, Ne., U.S.	198	40.37 N	96.57 W
Crete → Kriti I	38	35.15 N	25.00 E
Crete, Sea of → Kritikón Pélagos ⩡[2]	38	35.46 N	23.54 E
Créteil	50	48.48 N	2.28 E
Crétéville	36	36.40 N	10.20 E
Cretin, Cape ›	164	6.40 S	147.52 E
Creus, Cap de ›	34	42.19 N	3.19 E
Creuse □[5]	32	46.05 N	2.00 E
Creuse ≃	32	47.00 N	0.34 E
Creussen	60	49.51 N	11.37 E
Creutzwald	56	49.12 N	6.41 E
Creuzburg	56	51.03 N	10.15 E
Crevacuore	62	45.41 N	8.15 E
Crevalcore	64	44.43 N	11.09 E
Creve Coeur, Il., U.S.	190	40.38 N	89.35 W
Creve Coeur, Mo., U.S.	219	38.39 N	90.25 W
Crèvecœur-en-Auge	50	49.07 N	0.01 E
Crèvecœur-en-Brie	261	48.45 N	2.55 E
Crèvecœur-le-Grand	50	49.36 N	2.05 E
Crevillent	34	38.15 N	0.48 W
Crevoladossola	58	46.09 N	8.18 E
Crewe, Eng., U.K.	44	53.05 N	2.27 W
Crewe, Va., U.S.	192	37.10 N	78.07 W
Crewkerne	42	50.53 N	2.48 W
Crews Lake ⊜	220	28.23 N	82.31 W
Crewsville	220	27.16 N	81.36 W
Crianlarich	46	56.23 N	4.36 W
Crib Point	169	38.22 S	145.12 E
Cricamola ≃	236	8.59 N	81.54 W
Cricaré ≃	255	18.37 S	40.05 W
Criccieth	42	52.55 N	4.14 W
Crichi	68	38.57 N	16.38 E
Criciúma	252	28.40 S	49.23 W
Crick	42	52.21 N	1.07 W
Cricket	192	36.10 N	81.11 W
Crickhowell	42	51.53 N	3.07 W
Cricklade	42	51.39 N	1.51 W
Cridersville	216	40.39 N	84.09 W
Crieff	46	56.23 N	3.52 W
Criel-sur-Mer	50	50.01 N	1.19 E
Criffell ∧	44	54.57 N	3.38 W
Crikvenica	36	45.11 N	14.42 E
Crillon, Mount ∧	180	58.40 N	137.10 W
Crimean Peninsula → Kryms'kyy pivostriv ›[1]	78	45.00 N	34.00 E
Crimmitschau	54	50.49 N	12.23 E
Crimond	46	57.36 N	1.54 W
Crinan	46	56.05 N	5.35 W
Cringila	170	34.28 S	150.53 E
Cripple Creek	200	38.44 N	105.10 W
Criquetot l'Esneval	50	49.39 N	0.16 E
Criminoso, Monte ∧	256	21.32 S	43.25 W
Crisenoy	261	48.36 N	2.45 E
Crisfield	208	37.59 N	75.51 W
Crisólia	256	22.15 S	46.25 W
Crisóstomo, Ribeirão ≃	250	10.19 S	50.26 W
Crispiano	68	40.36 N	17.14 E
Criss Creek	182	51.03 N	120.44 W
Crissiumal	252	27.30 S	54.07 W
Cristal, Monts de ⋏	152	0.30 N	10.30 E
Cristal, Sierra del ⋏	240p	20.33 N	75.31 W
Cristalândia	250	10.36 S	49.11 W
Cristália	255	16.43 S	42.52 W
Cristalina	255	16.45 S	47.36 W
Cristalino ≃	255	12.38 S	50.40 W
Cristallo ∧	64	46.34 N	12.12 E
Cristianópolis	255	17.13 S	48.45 W
Cristina	256	22.13 S	45.16 W
Cristinápolis	250	11.29 S	37.46 W
Cristino Castro	250	8.49 S	44.13 W
Cristóbal	236	9.21 N	79.55 W
Cristóbal Colón, Pico ∧	246	10.50 N	73.41 W
Cristóbal Obregón	234	16.20 N	93.30 W
Cristoforo Colombo, Aeroporto di ⊠	62	44.25 N	8.49 E
Cristo Redentor ⊥	252	32.50 S	70.05 W
Cristo Redentor, Estatua do ⊍[1]	287a	22.57 S	43.13 W
Cristuru Secuiesc	38	46.17 N	25.02 E
Crișul Alb ≃	38	46.42 N	21.17 E
Crișul Negru ≃	38	46.42 N	21.16 E
Crișul Repede (Sebes Körös) ≃	38	46.55 N	20.59 E
Crittenden	218	38.46 N	84.36 W
Criuleni	38	47.13 N	29.09 E
Crivitz, Dtsch.	54	53.35 N	11.38 E
Crivitz, Wi., U.S.	190	45.13 N	88.00 W
Crixalândia	255	15.18 S	47.15 W
Crixás	255	14.27 S	49.58 W
Crixás ≃	250	11.02 S	48.34 W
Crixás-Açu ≃	255	13.19 S	50.36 W
Crixás-Mirim ≃	255	13.30 S	50.30 W
Črna	61	46.28 N	14.51 E
Crna ≃	38	41.35 N	21.59 E
Crna Gora □[3]	38	42.30 N	19.18 E
Črni vrh ∧	61	46.29 N	15.14 E
Črnomelj	36	45.34 N	15.11 E
Croachy	46	57.19 N	4.14 W
Croagh Patrick ∧	48	53.46 N	9.40 W
Croajingolong National Park ♠	166	37.40 S	149.30 E
Croal ≃	262	53.33 N	2.23 W
Croatia □[1], Europe	22	45.10 N	15.30 E
Croatia (Hrvatska) □[1], Europe	36	45.10 N	15.30 E
Croce dello Scrivano, Passo)(	68	40.34 N	15.50 E
Croce Domini, Passo di)(	64	45.54 N	10.24 E
Crocefieschi	62	44.35 N	9.01 E
Crocetta del Montello	64	45.50 N	12.02 E
Crocheron	208	38.14 N	76.03 W
Crockenhill	260	51.23 N	0.10 E
Crocker	194	37.56 N	92.15 W
Crocker, Banjaran ⋏	112	5.40 N	116.14 E
Crockery Creek ≃	216	43.02 N	86.05 W
Crocketford	44	55.02 N	3.50 W
Crockett, Ca., U.S.	226	38.03 N	122.12 W
Crockett, Tx., U.S.	222	31.19 N	95.27 W
Crockham Hill	260	51.14 N	0.04 E
Crocus Hill → The Valley	238	18.13 N	63.04 W
Croft	262	53.26 N	2.33 W
Crofton, B.C., Can.	224	48.52 N	123.38 W
Crofton, Ky., U.S.	194	37.02 N	87.29 W
Crofton, Md., U.S.	208	39.00 N	76.41 W
Crofton, Ne., U.S.	198	42.43 N	97.29 W
Croft State Park ♠	192	34.49 N	81.52 W
Croggan	46	56.22 N	5.42 W
Croghan	212	43.53 N	75.23 W
Croglin	44	54.49 N	2.39 W
Croick	46	57.53 N	4.35 W
Croil Islands II	206	44.58 N	74.58 W
Croisette, Cap ›	62	43.13 N	5.20 E
Croisilles	50	50.12 N	2.53 E
Croissy-Beaubourg	261	48.50 N	2.40 E
Croissy-sur-Seine	261	48.53 N	2.09 E
Croix	50	50.40 N	3.09 E
Croix, Lac à la ⊜	186	51.16 N	70.13 W
Croix, Lac la ⊜	190	48.21 N	92.05 W
Croker, Cape ›, Austl.	164	10.58 S	132.35 E
Croker, Cape ›, On., Can.	212	44.58 N	80.59 W
Croker Island I	164	11.12 S	132.32 E
Crolles	62	45.17 N	5.53 E
Cromarty	46	57.40 N	4.02 W
Cromarty Firth ⊂[1]	46	57.41 N	4.07 W
Cromby	285	40.09 N	75.32 W
Cromer, Austl.	274a	33.44 S	151.17 E
Cromer, Eng., U.K.	42	52.56 N	1.18 E
Cromford	44	53.06 N	1.34 W
Cromínia	255	17.17 S	49.21 W
Cromore	46	58.09 N	6.29 W
Crompton Point ›	240d	15.35 N	61.19 W
Cromwell, N.Z.	172	45.03 S	169.12 E
Cromwell, Al., U.S.	194	32.13 N	88.16 W
Cromwell, Ct., U.S.	207	41.35 N	72.38 W
Cromwell, In., U.S.	216	41.24 N	85.36 W
Cromwell Park ♠	279a	41.28 N	82.08 W
Cronadun	172	42.02 S	171.52 E
Cronenberg ◆[8]	263	51.12 N	7.08 E
Cronin, Mount ∧	182	54.54 N	126.52 W
Cronton	262	53.23 N	2.46 W
Cronulla	170	34.03 S	151.09 E
Cronulla Beach ⩡[2]	274a	34.02 S	151.11 E
Croob, Slieve ∧[2]	48	54.20 N	5.58 W
Crook, Eng., U.K.	44	54.43 N	1.44 W
Crook, Co., U.S.	198	40.51 N	102.48 W
Crooked ≃, B.C., Can.	182	54.50 N	122.54 W
Crooked ≃, Mo., U.S.	194	39.13 N	93.49 W
Crooked ≃, Or., U.S.	202	44.34 N	121.16 W
Crooked Creek	180	61.52 N	158.08 W
Crooked Creek ≃, U.S.	196	36.57 N	100.06 W
Crooked Creek ≃, Ar., U.S.	194	36.14 N	92.29 W
Crooked Creek ≃, Il., U.S.	219	38.30 N	89.25 W
Crooked Creek ≃, In., U.S.	216	40.45 N	86.30 W
Crooked Creek ≃, Mo., U.S.	219	39.34 N	91.55 W
Crooked Creek ≃, Pa., U.S.	210	41.55 N	77.08 W
Crooked Creek ≃, Pa., U.S.	214	40.45 N	79.33 W
Crooked Creek Lake ⊜[1]	214	40.42 N	79.30 W
Crooked Island I	238	22.45 N	74.13 W
Crooked Island Passage ᛘ	238	22.55 N	74.35 W
Crooked Lake, In., U.S.	216	41.41 N	85.02 W
Crooked Lake, Mi., U.S.	216	42.29 N	85.25 W
Crooked Lake ⊜, Nf., Can.	186	48.24 N	56.17 W
Crooked Lake ⊜, Sk., Can.	184	50.36 N	102.45 W
Crooked Lake ⊜, N.A.	190	48.13 N	91.50 W
Crooked Lake ⊜, Fl., U.S.	220	27.48 N	81.35 W
Crooked Lake ⊜, In., U.S.	216	41.40 N	85.03 W
Crooked River	184	52.51 N	103.44 W
Crookes Point ›	276	40.32 N	74.08 W
Crookham	279b	40.12 N	79.59 W
Crookston	198	47.46 N	96.36 W
Crookstown	48	51.50 N	8.50 W
Crooksville	188	39.46 N	82.05 W
Crookwell	166	34.28 S	149.28 E
Croom	48	52.31 N	8.42 W
Cropalati	68	39.31 N	16.43 E
Cropani	68	38.58 N	16.47 E
Cropper	218	38.18 N	85.06 W
Crosby, Eng., U.K.	44	53.30 N	3.02 W
Crosby, Mn., U.S.	190	46.28 N	93.57 W
Crosby, Ms., U.S.	194	31.17 N	91.03 W
Crosby, N.D., U.S.	198	48.54 N	103.17 W
Crosby, Pa., U.S.	214	41.45 N	78.24 W
Crosby, Tx., U.S.	222	29.55 N	95.04 W
Crosby, Mount ∧	202	43.53 N	109.20 W
Crosby Lake ⊜	212	44.45 N	76.26 W
Crosbyton	196	33.39 N	101.14 W
Crosia	68	39.34 N	16.46 E
Crosne	261	48.43 N	2.28 E
Cross ≃	152	4.42 N	8.21 E
Cross Banks II	283	42.43 N	70.49 W
Cross Bay ⊂	184	53.15 N	99.25 W
Cross Bay Bridge ◆[5]	276	40.35 N	73.49 W
Crossbost	46	58.08 N	6.23 W
Cross City	192	29.38 N	83.07 W
Cross County Center ◆[9]	276	40.56 N	73.51 W
Cross Creek ≃, Ca., U.S.	226	36.08 N	119.38 W
Cross Creek ≃, Oh., U.S.	214	40.18 N	80.36 W
Crossens	262	53.41 N	2.57 W
Crossett	194	33.07 N	91.57 W
Cross Fell ∧	44	54.42 N	2.29 W
Crossfield	182	51.26 N	114.02 W
Crossgar	48	54.24 N	5.45 W
Cross Hands	42	51.48 N	4.04 W
Crosshaven	48	51.48 N	8.17 W
Crosshill	44	55.19 N	4.39 W
Crossinsee ⊜	264a	52.22 N	13.41 E
Cross Island I	272c	18.57 N	72.51 E
Cross Keys	285	39.42 N	75.01 W
Cross Keys Airfield ⊠	285	39.42 N	75.02 W
Cross Lake	184	54.37 N	97.47 W
Cross Lake ⊜, Mb., Can.	184	54.45 N	97.30 W
Cross Lake ⊜, On., Can.	190	46.53 N	79.57 W
Cross Lake ⊜, N.Y., U.S.	210	43.08 N	76.29 W
Crossley, Mount ∧	172	42.50 S	172.04 E
Crossmaglen	48	54.05 N	6.37 W
Crossman	168a	32.47 S	116.36 E
Crossman ≃	168a	32.47 S	116.32 E
Crossman Peak ∧	200	34.32 N	114.07 W
Crossmolina	48	54.06 N	9.20 W
Cross Plains, In., U.S.	218	38.57 N	85.12 W
Cross Plains, Tx., U.S.	196	32.08 N	99.11 W
Cross Plains, Wi., U.S.	190	43.06 N	89.39 W
Cross Roads	222	32.03 N	95.58 W
Cross Sound ᛘ	180	58.10 N	136.30 W
Crossville, Il., U.S.	194	38.09 N	88.03 W
Crossville, Tn., U.S.	194	35.56 N	85.01 W
Crosswicks	285	40.09 N	74.38 W
Crosswicks Creek ≃	208	40.09 N	74.43 W
Crostolo ≃	64	44.55 N	10.38 E
Croston	44	53.39 N	2.46 W
Croswell	190	43.16 N	82.37 W
Crotch Lake ⊜	212	44.55 N	76.48 W
Crotenay	58	46.45 N	5.49 E
Crothersville	218	38.48 N	85.50 W
Croton	214	40.14 N	82.41 W
Crotona Park ♠	276	40.50 N	73.54 W
Croton Creek ≃	196	33.18 N	100.25 W
Crotone	68	39.05 N	17.07 E
Crotone □[4]	68	39.10 N	17.00 E
Croton Falls	210	41.21 N	73.40 W
Croton-on-Hudson	210	41.12 N	73.53 W
Croton Point ›	276	41.10 N	73.54 W
Crottendorf	54	50.30 N	12.56 E
Crouch ≃	42	51.37 N	0.57 E
Crouse Run ≃	279b	40.35 N	79.58 W
Crouy	50	49.24 N	3.22 E
Crow ≃	190	45.15 N	93.31 W
Crow, North Fork ≃	190	45.05 N	93.45 W
Crow, South Fork ≃	190	45.05 N	93.45 W
Crow Agency	202	45.36 N	107.27 W
Crowborough	42	51.03 N	0.09 E
Crow Creek ≃, U.S.	198	40.23 N	104.29 W
Crow Creek ≃, Ca., U.S.	282	37.42 N	122.03 W
Crow Creek ≃, Il., U.S.	194	40.56 N	89.27 W
Crow Creek ≃, Mt., U.S.	198	45.45 N	105.06 W
Crow Creek ≃, Mt., U.S.	202	46.11 N	111.29 W
Crow Creek ≃, S.D., U.S.	198	43.57 N	99.15 W
Crow Creek ≃, Wy., U.S.	202	43.19 N	109.09 W
Crow Creek Indian Reservation ◆[4]	198	44.11 N	99.30 W
Crowder, Ms., U.S.	194	34.10 N	90.08 W
Crowder, Ok., U.S.	196	35.07 N	95.40 W
Crowduck Lake ⊜	184	50.08 N	95.15 W
Crowdy Head ›	166	31.50 S	152.45 E
Crowe ≃	212	44.22 N	77.46 W
Crowe Lake ⊜	212	44.29 N	77.46 W
Crowell	196	33.59 N	99.43 W
Crowfoot, Mount ∧	172	45.33 S	167.03 E
Crow Hill ∧[2]	262	53.42 N	1.58 W
Crowhurst	260	51.12 N	0.01 W
Crow Indian Reservation ◆[4]	202	45.27 N	108.00 W
Crow Lake	184	49.12 N	93.57 W
Crow Lake ⊜	212	44.43 N	76.37 W
Crowland	42	52.41 N	0.11 W
Crowle	44	53.37 N	0.49 W
Crowley, La., U.S.	194	30.12 N	92.22 W
Crowley, Tx., U.S.	222	32.34 N	97.21 W
Crowley, Lake ⊜[1]	204	37.37 N	118.44 W
Crowleys Ridge ∧	194	35.45 N	90.45 W
Crowlin Islands II	46	57.20 N	5.44 W
Crown	214	41.23 N	79.16 W
Crown Hill	212	44.26 N	79.39 W
Crown Island I	164	5.05 S	146.55 E
Crown Memorial Beach ♠	282	37.46 N	122.16 W
Crown Mines ◆[7]	273d	26.13 S	28.00 E
Crown Mountain ∧	240m	18.21 N	64.58 W
Crown Point, In., U.S.	216	41.25 N	87.21 W
Crownpoint, N.M., U.S.	200	35.40 N	108.09 W
Crown Point, N.Y., U.S.	188	43.57 N	73.26 W
Crown Point State Park ♠	224	45.32 N	122.15 W
Crown Prince Frederik Island I	176	70.02 N	86.50 W
Crown Village	276	40.40 N	73.27 W
Crow Peak ∧	202	46.18 N	111.54 W
Crow Rock Creek ≃	202	47.06 N	106.15 W
Crows Fork Creek ≃	219	38.47 N	91.52 W
Crows Landing	226	37.24 N	121.04 W
Crows Nest, Austl.	171a	27.16 S	152.03 E
Crows Nest, Austl.	274a	33.50 S	151.12 E
Crowsnest, Ab., Can.	182	49.38 N	114.41 W
Crows Nest Falls National Park ♠	171a	27.16 S	152.08 E
Crowsnest Pass	182	49.36 N	114.26 W
Crowsnest Pass)(	182	49.39 N	114.45 W
Crows Nest Peak ∧	198	44.03 N	103.58 W
Crowthorne	42	51.23 N	0.49 W
Crowton	262	53.16 N	2.38 W
Crow Wing ≃	198	46.19 N	94.20 W
Croxley Green	42	51.39 N	0.27 W
Croxteth Park ♠	262	53.26 N	2.53 W
Croy	46	57.31 N	4.02 W
Croyde	42	51.07 N	4.13 W
Croydon, Austl.	166	18.12 S	142.14 E
Croydon, Austl.	169	37.48 S	145.17 E
Croydon, Austl.	274a	33.53 S	151.07 E
Croydon, Pa., U.S.	208	40.05 N	74.54 W
Croydon ◆[8]	42	51.23 N	0.06 W
Croydon Park	274a	33.54 S	151.07 E
Croydon Peak ∧	188	43.28 N	72.13 W
Croydon Station	182	53.05 N	119.44 W
Crozet	192	38.04 N	78.42 W
Crozet, Archipel II	6	46.00 S	52.00 E
Crozet Basin ✦[1]	6	39.00 S	60.00 E
Crozon	32	48.15 N	4.29 W
Cruachan, Ben ∧	46	56.25 N	5.08 W
Cruas	62	44.39 N	4.46 E
Crucea	38	44.32 N	28.14 E
Crucero	248	14.21 S	70.00 W
Cruces, Cuba	240p	22.21 N	80.16 W
Cruces, Méx.	232	29.26 N	107.24 W
Crucoli	68	39.25 N	17.00 E
Cruden Bay	46	57.25 N	1.50 W
Crudgington	42	52.46 N	2.33 W
Crudine Creek ≃	170	33.05 S	149.40 E
Cruger	194	33.19 N	90.13 W
Cruillas	232	24.45 N	98.31 W
Crum Creek ≃	285	39.51 N	75.19 W
Crumhorn Mountain ∧	210	42.33 N	74.55 W
Crumlin, On., Can.	212	43.01 N	81.09 W
Crumlin, N. Ire., U.K.	48	54.37 N	6.14 W
Crum Lynne	285	39.52 N	75.20 W
Crummock Water ⊜	44	54.34 N	3.18 W
Crump Lake ⊜	202	42.17 N	119.50 W
Crumpton	208	39.14 N	75.55 W
Crumstown	216	41.38 N	86.25 W
Crupet	56	50.21 N	4.48 E
Cruseilles	58	46.02 N	6.07 E
Cruser Brook ≃	276	40.27 N	74.39 W
Crusheen	48	52.58 N	8.53 W
Crusnes	56	49.26 N	5.55 E
Crusnes ≃	56	49.27 N	5.36 E
Crustepec, Cerro ∧	234	21.15 N	97.53 W
Cruz, Arroyo de la ≃, Ca., U.S.	226	35.42 N	121.09 W
Cruz, Arroyo de la ≃, Ur.	258	34.00 S	56.08 W
Cruz, Cabo ›	240p	19.51 N	77.44 W
Cruz, Cañada de la ≃	258	34.09 S	58.58 W
Cruz, Cayo I	240p	22.15 N	77.49 W
Cruz, Pico de la ∧	148	28.44 N	17.52 W
Cruz Alta, Arg.	252	33.01 S	61.49 W
Cruz Alta, Bra.	252	28.39 S	53.36 W
Cruz Bay	240m	18.20 N	64.48 W
Cruz de Elorza	234	23.49 N	100.29 W
Cruz del Eje	252	30.44 S	64.48 W
Cruz del Marquez, Cerro ∧	286a	19.12 N	99.15 W
Cruzeiro	256	22.34 S	44.58 W
Cruzeiro do Oeste	255	23.46 S	53.04 W
Cruzeiro do Sul	248	7.38 S	72.36 W
Cruzeta	250	6.25 S	36.47 W
Cruz Grande, Chile	252	29.25 S	71.18 W
Cruz Grande, Méx.	234	16.44 N	99.08 W
Cruzília	256	21.50 S	44.48 W
Cruz Machado	252	26.01 S	51.21 W
Cruzy-le-Châtel	50	47.51 N	4.12 E
Crvenka	38	45.39 N	19.28 E
Crymych	42	51.59 N	4.40 W
Crynant	42	51.43 N	3.45 W
Crysler	188	45.13 N	75.09 W
Crystal, Mn., U.S.	190	45.01 N	93.21 W
Crystal, N.D., U.S.	198	48.35 N	97.40 W
Crystal ≃	200	39.25 N	107.14 W
Crystal Bay	226	39.13 N	120.00 W
Crystal Bay ⊂	220	28.55 N	82.43 W
Crystal Beach, On., Can.	284a	42.52 N	79.04 W
Crystal Beach, Fl., U.S.	220	28.05 N	82.46 W
Crystal Beach, Tx., U.S.	222	29.27 N	94.38 W
Crystal Brook	166	33.21 S	138.13 E
Crystal Cave ⩡[5]	208	40.32 N	75.51 W
Crystal City, Mb., Can.	184	49.09 N	98.56 W
Crystal City, Mo., U.S.	219	38.13 N	90.22 W
Crystal City, Tx., U.S.	196	28.40 N	99.49 W
Crystal Creek ≃	278	41.58 N	87.51 W
Crystal Falls	190	46.05 N	88.20 W
Crystal Gardens	216	42.14 N	88.23 W
Crystal Lake, Il., U.S.	216	42.14 N	88.18 W
Crystal Lake, N.Y., U.S.	210	42.31 N	74.12 W
Crystal Lake, N.Y., U.S.	210	42.28 N	78.20 W
Crystal Lake ⊜, On., Can.	212	44.45 N	78.30 W
Crystal Lake ⊜, Ma., U.S.	283	42.29 N	71.05 W
Crystal Lake ⊜, Ma., U.S.	283	42.48 N	71.09 W
Crystal Lake ⊜, Mi., U.S.	190	44.40 N	86.10 W
Crystal Lake ⊜, N.J., U.S.	276	41.02 N	74.15 W
Crystal Lakes	218	39.52 N	84.04 W
Crystal Lawns	216	41.34 N	88.09 W
Crystal Manor	216	42.14 N	88.17 W
Crystal Palace Stadium and Motor Race Track ♠	260	51.25 N	0.04 W
Crystal River	192	28.54 N	82.35 W
Crystal Spring Lake ⊜	285	39.43 N	75.01 W
Crystal Springs, Fl., U.S.	220	28.10 N	82.09 W
Crystal Springs, Ms., U.S.	194	31.59 N	90.21 W
Crystal Springs Dam ◆[6]	282	37.32 N	122.22 W
Crystal Vista	216	42.14 N	88.24 W
Csepel ◆[8]	264c	47.24 N	19.14 E
Csepel-sziget I	30	47.15 N	18.57 E
Csepreg	61	47.24 N	16.43 E
Cserhát ⋏	30	47.55 N	19.30 E
Cserta ≃	61	46.35 N	16.36 E
Csesznek ⊥	30	47.16 N	17.53 E
Csesztreg	61	46.43 N	16.31 E
Csobánka	264c	47.38 N	18.58 E
Csomád	264c	47.40 N	19.15 E
Csömodér	61	46.37 N	16.39 E
Csömör	264c	47.33 N	19.14 E
Csömöri-patak ≃	264c	47.36 N	19.07 E
Csongrád	30	46.43 N	20.09 E
Csongrád □[6]	30	46.25 N	20.15 E
Csorna	30	47.37 N	17.16 E
Csurgó	30	46.16 N	17.06 E
Ču □[4]	85	42.30 N	74.30 E
Ču ≃	86	45.00 N	67.44 E
Cúa	246	10.10 N	66.54 W
Cuacnopalan	234	18.49 N	97.30 W
Cuácua ≃	154	17.54 S	36.48 E
Cuajimalpa ◆[8]	286a	19.21 N	99.18 W
Cuajinicuilapa	234	16.28 N	98.25 W
Cuajone	248	17.00 S	70.43 W
Cuále	152	8.06 S	16.03 E
Cua Lo	110	18.49 N	105.43 E
Cuamato	152	17.05 S	15.09 E
Cuamba	154	14.49 S	36.33 E
Cuambog	116	7.20 N	125.52 E
Cuanavale ≃	152	15.07 S	19.14 E
Cuando	152	16.32 S	22.07 E
Cuando (Kwando) ≃	152	18.27 S	23.32 E
Cuando Cubango □[5]	152	16.00 S	20.00 E
Cuangar	152	17.36 S	18.39 E
Cuango, Ang.	152	14.30 S	18.59 E
Cuango, Ang.	152	9.10 S	17.58 E
Cuango, Ang.	152	6.17 S	16.41 E
Cuango (Kwango) ≃	152	3.14 S	17.23 E
Cuanza ≃	152	9.19 S	13.08 E
Cuanza Norte □[5]	152	8.50 S	14.30 E
Cuanza Sul □[5]	152	10.50 S	14.50 E
Cuao ≃	246	4.55 N	67.40 W
Cuapiaxtla	234	19.18 N	97.46 W
Cuareim (Quaraí) ≃	252	30.12 S	57.36 W
Cuaró	252	30.37 S	56.54 W
Cuartillo, Arroyo ≃	258	33.45 S	59.06 W
Cuarto ≃	252	33.25 S	62.56 W
Cuatir ≃	152	17.01 S	18.09 E
Cuatro Caminos	286b	22.54 N	82.23 W
Cuatro Ciénegas [de Carranza]	196	26.59 N	102.05 W
Cuatro Islands II	116	10.31 N	124.39 E
Cuauhtémoc, Méx.	232	28.25 N	106.52 W
Cuauhtémoc, Méx.	234	19.20 N	103.36 W
Cuauhtémoc, Méx.	234	22.38 N	98.08 W
Cuautepec el Alto ◆[8]	286a	19.34 N	99.08 W
Cuautitlán	234	19.26 N	104.23 W
Cuautitlán ≃	286a	19.41 N	99.13 W
Cuautitlán [de Romero Rubio]	234	19.40 N	99.11 W
Cuautitlán Izcalli	286a	19.39 N	99.13 W
Cuautla, Méx.	234	20.11 N	104.21 W
Cuautla, Méx.	234	18.48 N	98.57 W
Cuautzin, Volcán ∧[1]	286a	19.09 N	99.06 W
Cuba, Port.	34	38.10 N	7.53 W
Cuba, Al., U.S.	194	32.25 N	88.22 W
Cuba, Il., U.S.	190	40.29 N	90.11 W
Cuba, Ks., U.S.	198	39.48 N	97.27 W
Cuba, Mo., U.S.	194	38.03 N	91.24 W
Cuba, N.M., U.S.	200	36.01 N	106.57 W
Cuba, N.Y., U.S.	210	42.13 N	78.16 W
Cuba □[1], N.A.	230	21.30 N	80.00 W
Cuba □[1], N.A.	240p	21.30 N	80.00 W
Cubabi, Cerro ∧	200	31.42 N	112.46 W
Cubadak	112	0.19 N	100.00 E
Cubagua, Isla I	246	10.48 N	64.10 W
Cuba Island I	276	40.38 N	73.32 W
Cubal	152	13.02 S	14.19 E
Cubal ≃, Ang.	152	15.22 S	12.39 E
Cubal ≃, Ang.	152	12.42 S	13.56 E
Cubal ≃, Ang.	152	11.19 S	13.48 E
Cuba Lake ⊜	210	42.15 N	78.18 W
Cubanea	254	41.02 S	70.16 W
Cubango (Okavango) ≃	138	18.50 S	22.25 E
Cubangui ≃	152	14.22 S	19.58 E
Čubaricha	86	57.37 N	68.22 E
Čubarovo	82	55.12 N	36.56 E
Cubatão	256	23.53 S	46.25 W
Cubatão, Serra do ⩡[4]	256	23.52 S	46.28 W
Cubati	250	6.51 S	36.21 W
Cub Hills ⋏[2]	184	54.20 N	104.30 W
Cubia ≃	152	16.01 S	21.50 E
Čublas	24	64.44 N	45.00 E
Cub Run ≃	208	38.48 N	77.28 W
Çubuk	130	40.15 N	33.02 E
Cuc ≃	250	1.22 N	53.33 W
Cucamonga	228	34.06 N	117.35 W
Cucamonga Creek ≃	280	33.57 N	117.37 W
Cucamonga Peak ∧	228	34.14 N	117.36 W
Cuccaro Vetere	68	40.09 N	15.18 E
Cucco, Monte ∧	66	43.22 N	12.45 E
Cucharas ≃	198	37.55 N	104.32 W
Cucharas, Sierra ⋏	234	22.20 N	98.55 W
Cuchi	152	14.36 S	16.58 E
Cuchi ≃	152	15.28 S	17.21 E
Cuchibi ≃	152	15.00 S	20.45 E
Cuchilla Alta, Cerro ∧	236	15.10 N	88.12 W
Cuchillo-Có	252	38.20 S	64.37 W
Cuchillo Negro Creek ≃	200	33.08 N	107.14 W
Cuchivero ≃	246	7.40 N	65.57 W
Čuchloma	76	58.45 N	42.41 E
Čuchlomskoje, ozero ⊜	76	58.46 N	42.35 E
Cuchumatanes, Sierra los ⋏	236	15.35 N	91.25 W
Cuckels Brook ≃	276	40.33 N	74.33 W
Cuckfield	42	51.00 N	0.09 W
Cuckney	44	53.15 N	1.08 W
Cuckold Point ›	284b	39.14 N	76.24 W
Čučkovo, Ross.	76	59.36 N	41.14 E
Čučkovo, Ross.	80	54.17 N	41.26 E
Cucuí	246	1.12 N	66.50 W
Cucumbi	152	10.17 S	19.05 E
Cucuron	62	43.47 N	5.26 E
Cucurpe	232	30.20 N	110.43 W
Cúcuta	246	7.54 N	72.31 W
Cudachar	84	42.21 N	47.11 E
Cudahy, Ca., U.S.	280	33.57 N	118.11 W
Cudahy, Wi., U.S.	216	42.57 N	87.51 W
Cuddalore	122	11.45 N	79.45 E
Cuddapah	122	14.28 N	78.49 E
Cuddeback Lake ⊜	228	35.18 N	117.28 W
Cuddebackville	210	41.28 N	74.36 W
Cuddia ≃	70	37.53 N	12.37 E
Cuddington	44	53.14 N	2.36 W
Cuddle Lake ⊜	184	55.25 N	95.47 W
Cuddy	279b	40.21 N	80.09 W
Cuddy Mountain ∧	202	44.46 N	116.47 W
Cudgegong	170	32.48 S	149.49 E
Cudgegong ≃	170	32.37 S	149.43 E
Cudgewa	171b	36.12 S	147.46 E
Cudgewa Creek ≃	171b	36.03 S	147.55 E
Cudham ◆[8]	260	51.19 N	0.05 E
Cudia Park ♠	275b	43.43 N	79.13 W
Cudjoe Key I	220	24.40 N	81.30 W
Čudovo	76	59.07 N	31.41 E
Čudskoje ozero (Peipsi järv) ⊜	76	58.45 N	27.30 E
Cudworth, Sk., Can.	184	52.30 N	105.45 W
Cudworth, Eng., U.K.	44	53.35 N	1.25 W
Čudzin	76	52.44 N	26.59 E
Cue	162	27.25 S	117.54 E
Cuebe ≃	152	15.48 S	17.30 E
Cueio ≃, Ang.	152	15.27 S	21.21 E
Cueio ≃, Ang.	152	16.17 S	17.46 E
Cuelei ≃	152	15.33 S	17.21 E
Cuéllar	34	41.24 N	4.19 W
Cuenca, Ec.	246	2.53 S	78.59 W
Cuenca, Esp.	34	40.04 N	2.08 W
Cuenca □[4]	34	39.55 N	2.10 W
Cuencamé [de Ceniceros]	232	24.53 N	103.42 W
Cuerámaro	234	20.37 N	101.43 W
Cuernavaca	234	18.55 N	99.15 W
Cuero	222	29.05 N	97.17 W
Cuers	62	43.14 N	6.04 E
Cuervos	204	32.38 N	114.52 W
Cuesmes	50	50.26 N	3.55 E
Cuesta Pass)(	226	35.21 N	120.38 W
Cueto	240p	20.39 N	75.56 W
Cuetzala del Progreso	234	18.07 N	99.50 W
Cuetzalan del Progreso	234	20.02 N	97.31 W
Cuevas del Almanzora	34	37.18 N	1.53 W
Cuevo	248	20.27 S	63.32 W
Čufarovo	80	54.06 N	47.19 E
Cuffley	42	51.42 N	0.07 W
Cufra → Al-Kufrah ⩡[4]	146	24.20 N	23.15 E
Cufré	258	34.12 S	57.06 W
Cufré, Arroyo ≃	258	34.27 S	57.09 W
Cuggiono	62	45.31 N	8.49 E
Cugir	38	45.50 N	23.22 E
Cuglieri	71	40.11 N	8.34 E
Cugo ≃	152	7.18 S	16.39 E
Čugujevka	89	44.08 N	133.53 E
Čugunaš	86	52.52 N	87.46 E
Čuguš, gora ∧	84	43.47 N	40.16 E
Cuiabá	248	15.35 S	56.05 W
Cuiabá ≃	248	17.53 S	57.27 W
Cuiari	246	1.30 N	68.11 W
Cuiari ≃	246	1.30 N	68.11 W
Cuicatlán	234	17.48 N	96.58 W
Cuichapa	234	17.59 N	94.15 W
Cuieiras ≃	246	2.50 S	60.31 W
Cuigezhuang, Zhg.	105	40.01 N	116.28 E
Cuigezhuang, Zhg.	105	40.02 N	117.54 E
Cuihuangkou	105	39.32 N	117.11 E
Cuijiatun	104	40.57 N	121.09 E
Cuijiazhuang	104	40.57 N	122.44 E
Cuilapa	236	14.17 N	90.18 W
Cuilcagh ∧	48	54.10 N	7.48 W
Cuilco	236	15.24 N	91.58 W
Cuillin Hills ⋏[2]	46	57.15 N	6.15 W
Cuilo (Kwilu) ≃, Afr.	152	3.22 S	17.22 E
Cuilo ≃, Afr.	152	5.52 S	16.35 E
Cuilo Futa	152	6.25 S	15.44 E
Cuimba	152	6.08 S	14.38 E
Cuio	152	12.58 S	12.58 E
Cuiqiao	98	34.12 N	114.36 E
Cuiseaux	58	46.30 N	5.24 E
Cuisery	58	46.33 N	5.00 E
Cuisy	261	49.01 N	2.46 E
Cuité	250	6.29 S	36.09 W
Cuitláhuac	234	18.49 N	96.43 W
Cuíto ≃	152	18.01 S	20.48 E
Cuíto-Cuanavale	152	15.10 S	19.10 E
Cuitzeo, Laguna de ⊜	234	19.55 N	101.05 W
Cuitzeo del Porvenir	234	19.59 N	101.09 W
Cuiuni ≃	246	0.45 S	63.07 W
Cuivre ≃	219	38.56 N	90.42 W
Cuivre, North Fork ≃	219	39.02 N	90.59 W
Cuivre, West Fork ≃	219	39.02 N	90.59 W
Cuivre River State Park ♠	219	39.02 N	90.57 W
Čuja	88	59.12 N	112.25 E
Čuja ≃, Ross.	86	50.24 N	86.39 E
Čuja ≃, Ross.	88	59.17 N	112.24 E
Cují	286c	10.28 N	67.02 W
Cukas	112	0.25 S	104.18 E
Čukčagirskoje ozero ⊜	89	52.00 N	136.36 E
Čukotskij, mys ›	180	64.14 N	173.10 W
Čukotskij Avtonomnyj Okrug □[8]	180	66.00 N	178.00 E
Čukotskij poluostrov ›[1]	180	66.00 N	175.00 W
Çukurca	128	37.15 N	43.37 E
Čukurčak	85	41.47 N	71.07 E
Culaba	116	11.40 N	124.32 E
Čulakkurgan	85	43.46 N	69.12 E
Culaman	116	5.58 N	125.40 E
Culari ≃	250	1.27 N	53.42 W
Culasi, Pil.	116	11.26 N	122.03 E
Culasi, Pil.	116	10.43 N	125.43 E
Culasian	116	8.51 N	117.29 E
Culasi Point ›	116	11.37 N	122.42 E
Culbertson, Mt., U.S.	198	48.08 N	104.30 W
Culbertson, Ne., U.S.	198	40.13 N	100.50 W
Culbertson Run ≃	285	40.03 N	75.45 W
Culbin	168a	33.10 S	116.50 E
Culburra	170	34.57 S	150.47 E
Culcairn	166	35.40 S	147.03 E
Culcheth	262	53.27 N	2.32 W
Culdaff	48	55.18 N	7.11 W
Culdaff Bay ⊂	48	55.17 N	7.10 W
Culebra	240m	18.18 N	65.18 W
Culebra, Isla de I	240m	18.19 N	65.17 W
Culebra, Sierra de la ⋏	34	41.54 N	6.20 W
Culebra Peak ∧	200	37.07 N	105.11 W
Culebrinas ≃	240m	18.24 N	67.11 W
Culebrita, Isla I	240m	18.19 N	65.14 W
Culebro, Arroyo del ≃	266a	40.19 N	3.34 W
Culemborg	52	51.56 N	5.13 E
Culfa	84	38.58 N	45.38 E
Culgoa ≃	166	29.56 S	146.20 E
Culham Inlet ⊂	162	33.55 S	120.04 E
Culiacán, Méx.	232	24.48 N	107.24 W
Culiacán, Méx.	232	24.04 N	107.05 W
Culiacán, Cerro ∧	234	20.20 N	100.58 W
Culiacancito	232	24.50 N	107.32 W
Culijón, Nevado ∧	248	14.38 S	69.14 W
Culion	116	11.53 N	120.01 E
Culion Island I	116	11.50 N	119.55 E
Cúllar	34	37.35 N	2.34 W
Cull Creek ≃	282	37.42 N	122.03 W
Cullen, Scot., U.K.	46	57.41 N	2.49 W
Cullen, La., U.S.	194	32.58 N	93.27 W
Cullen Bullen	170	33.18 S	150.01 E
Cullen Point ›	164	11.57 S	141.54 E
Culleoka, Tn., U.S.	194	35.28 N	86.58 W
Culleoka, Tx., U.S.	222	33.08 N	96.29 W
Cullera	34	39.10 N	0.15 W
Cullicudden	46	57.39 N	4.13 W
Cullin, Lough ⊜	48	53.57 N	9.12 W
Cullinan	158	25.40 S	28.31 E
Cullman	194	34.10 N	86.50 W
Culloden Battlesite ⊥	46	57.28 N	4.05 W
Cullom	216	40.53 N	88.16 W
Cullompton	42	50.52 N	3.24 W
Cullowhee	192	35.18 N	83.10 W
Cully	58	46.29 N	6.44 E
Cullybackey	48	54.53 N	6.21 W
Culm ≃	42	50.46 N	3.31 W
Čul'man	74	56.52 N	124.52 E
Cülmen	130	37.19 N	38.48 E
Culmore	284c	38.51 N	77.08 W
Culoz	62	45.51 N	5.47 E
Culpeper	188	38.28 N	77.59 W
Culpina	248	20.50 S	64.58 W
Culrain	46	57.55 N	4.24 W
Cults	46	57.07 N	2.10 W
Cultus Lake	224	49.04 N	121.58 W
Cultus Lake ⊜	224	49.03 N	121.58 W
Cultus Lake Provincial Park ♠	224	49.03 N	121.58 W
Culú-Culú, Arroyo ≃	258	35.19 S	58.57 W
Culú-Culú, Laguna ⊜	258	35.20 S	58.59 W
Culuene ≃	255	12.56 S	52.51 W
Čuluunchoroot	88	49.41 N	114.15 E
Čuluut	102	45.48 N	107.05 E
Čuluutyn ≃	88	49.11 N	100.41 E
Culvain ∧	46	56.56 N	5.17 W
Culver, In., U.S.	216	41.13 N	86.25 W
Culver, Or., U.S.	202	44.31 N	121.12 W
Culver, Point ›	162	32.54 S	124.43 E
Culver City	228	34.01 N	118.23 W
Culverden	172	42.46 S	172.51 E
Culvers Lake	210	41.10 N	74.48 W
Culverstone Green	260	51.20 N	0.21 E
Čulym	86	55.06 N	80.58 E
Čulym ≃, Ross.	86	57.43 N	83.51 E
Čulym ≃, Ross.	86	54.38 N	78.16 E
Čulyšman ≃	86	51.20 N	87.45 E
Čum	24	67.06 N	63.07 E
Cuma	152	12.52 S	15.05 E
Cuma (Cumae) ⊥	68	40.50 N	14.06 E
Čumakovo	86	55.41 N	79.02 E
Cumalı	130	36.42 N	27.27 E
Cumaná	246	10.28 N	64.10 W
Cumanacoa	246	10.15 N	63.55 W
Cumanayagua	240p	22.09 N	80.12 W
Cumaovası	130	38.15 N	27.09 E
Cumare, Cerro ∧[2]	246	0.28 N	73.52 W
Cumari	255	18.16 S	48.11 W
Cumbal	246	0.54 N	77.47 W
Cumbal, Nevado ∧	246	0.57 N	77.52 W
Cumbe	250	10.21 S	37.14 W
Cumbee	220	28.04 N	81.55 W
Cumberland, B.C., Can.	182	49.37 N	125.01 W
Cumberland, Ia., U.S.	198	41.16 N	94.52 W
Cumberland, Ky., U.S.	192	36.58 N	82.59 W
Cumberland, Md., U.S.	188	39.39 N	78.45 W
Cumberland, Va., U.S.	192	37.29 N	78.14 W
Cumberland, Wa., U.S.	224	47.16 N	121.55 W
Cumberland, Wi., U.S.	190	45.31 N	92.01 W
Cumberland □[6], N.J., U.S.	208	39.26 N	75.14 W
Cumberland □[6], Pa., U.S.	208	40.12 N	77.12 W
Cumberland ≃	178	37.09 N	88.25 W
Cumberland, Lake ⊜[1]	194	36.57 N	84.55 W
Cumberland, South Fork ≃	192	36.58 N	84.36 W
Cumberland City	194	36.23 N	87.38 W
Cumberland Falls State Resort Park ♠	192	36.50 N	84.20 W
Cumberland Gap)(	192	36.36 N	83.41 W
Cumberland Gap National Historical Park ♠	192	36.36 N	83.40 W
Cumberland Hill	207	41.58 N	71.27 W
Cumberland House	184	53.58 N	102.16 W
Cumberland Indian Reserve ◆[4]	184	53.04 N	104.50 W
Cumberland Island National Seashore ♠	192	30.50 N	81.27 W
Cumberland Islands II	166	20.40 S	149.09 E
Cumberland Lake ⊜	184	54.02 N	102.17 W
Cumberland Peninsula ›[1]	176	66.50 N	64.00 W
Cumberland Plateau ⋏[1]	192	36.20 N	84.30 W
Cumberland Sound ᛘ	176	65.10 N	65.30 W
Cumbernauld	46	55.58 N	3.59 W
Cumborah	166	29.44 S	147.46 E
Cumbria □[6]	44	54.30 N	3.00 W
Cumbrian Mountains ⋏	44	54.30 N	3.05 W
Čumbur-Kosa	83	46.57 N	38.53 E
Cumby	222	33.08 N	95.50 W

Symbols in the index entries represent the broad categories identified in the key at the right. Symbols with superior numbers (⋏[1]) identify subcategories (see complete key on page *I · 1)*.

Symbole im Register stellen die rechts im Schlüssel erklärten Kategorien dar. Symbole mit hochgestellten Ziffern (⋏[1]) bezeichnen Unterabteilungen einer Kategorie (vgl. vollständiger Schlüssel auf Seite *I · 1)*.

Los símbolos incluídos en el texto del índice representan las grandes categorías identificadas con la clave a la derecha. Los símbolos con numeros en su parte superior (⋏[1]) identifican las subcategorías (véase la clave completa en la página *I · 1)*.

Les symboles de l'index représentent les catégories indiquées dans la légende à droite. Les symboles suivis d'un indice (⋏[1]) représentent des sous-catégories (voir légende complète à la page *I · 1)*.

Os símbolos incluídos no texto do índice representam as grandes categorias identificadas com a chave à direita. Os símbolos com números em sua parte superior (⋏[1]) identificam as subcategorias (veja-se a chave completa à página *I · 1)*.

∧	Mountain	Berg	Montaña	Montagne	Montanha
⋏	Mountains	Gebirge	Montañas	Montagnes	Montanhas
)(	Pass	Paß	Paso	Col	Passo
V	Valley, Canyon	Tal, Cañon	Valle, Cañón	Vallée, Canyon	Vale, Canhão
≚	Plain	Ebene	Llano	Plaine	Planície
›	Cape	Kap	Cabo	Cap	Cabo
I	Island	Insel	Isla	Île	Ilha
II	Islands	Inseln	Islas	Îles	Ilhas
⩡	Other Topographic Features	Andere Topographische Objekte	Otros Elementos Topográficos	Autres données topographiques	Outros acidentes topográficos

ESPAÑOL — Nombre · Página · Lat.°′ · Long.°′ W = Oeste
FRANÇAIS — Nom · Page · Lat.°′ · Long.°′ W = Ouest
PORTUGUÊS — Nome · Página · Lat.°′ · Long.°′ W = Oeste

Cumeral Nuevo 200 30.54 N 110.51 W
Cumiana 62 44.59 N 7.22 E
Čumikan 89 54.42 N 135.19 E
Cuminá
→ Paru de Oeste ≃ 250 1.30 S 56.00 W
Cuminapanema ≃ 250 1.09 S 54.54 W
Cuminestown 46 57.32 N 2.20 W
Cumming 192 34.12 N 84.08 W
Cummings Mountain ∧ 228 35.03 N 118.34 W
Cummington 207 42.27 N 72.53 W
Cummins 166 34.16 S 135.44 E
Cummins, Mount ∧ 182 52.03 N 118.15 W
Cummins Creek ≃ 222 29.43 N 96.31 W
Cummins Range ⋏ 162 19.05 S 127.10 E
Cumnock 44 55.27 N 4.16 W
Cumnor 42 51.44 N 1.20 W
Cumpas 232 30.02 N 109.48 W
Çumra 130 37.34 N 32.48 E
Cumshewa Inlet ⊂ 182 53.03 N 131.45 W
Cumuripa 232 28.08 N 109.53 W
Cumwhinton 44 54.52 N 2.51 W
Čumyš ≃ 86 53.31 N 83.10 E
Čun'a ≃, Ross. 74 61.36 N 96.30 E
Čuna ≃, Ross. 88 57.47 N 95.26 E
Cunani 250 2.52 N 51.06 W
Cunauaru ≃ 246 3.10 S 63.01 W
Cunaviche 246 7.22 N 67.25 W
Cunco 252 38.55 S 72.02 W
Cuncumén 252 31.53 S 70.38 W
Cundeelee Reserve ◆[4] 162 30.30 S 123.25 E
Cunderdin 162 31.39 S 117.15 E
Cundinamarca □[5] 246 5.00 N 74.00 W
Cunduacán 234 18.04 N 93.10 W
Čundža 86 43.32 N 79.28 E
Cunene □[5] 152 16.30 S 15.30 E
Cunene (Kunene) ≃ 152 17.20 S 11.50 E
Cuneo 62 44.23 N 7.32 E
Cuneo □[4] 62 44.31 N 7.34 E
Cunewalde 54 51.06 N 14.30 E
Cuney 222 32.02 N 95.25 W
Cung Hau, Cua ≃[1] 110 9.46 N 106.34 E
Cung Son 110 13.02 N 108.58 E
Çüngüş 130 38.13 N 39.17 E
Cunha 256 23.05 S 44.58 W
Cunhambebe 256 23.00 S 44.20 W
Cunha Porã 252 26.54 S 53.09 W
Cunhinga 152 12.11 S 16.47 E
Cunhinga ≃ 152 10.38 S 16.48 E
Cunhuã, Igarapé ≃ 248 5.46 S 64.36 W
Cunlhat 62 45.38 N 3.35 E
Cunliffe 168b 34.05 S 137.45 E
Cunnamulla 166 28.04 S 145.41 E
Cunningham, Austl. 171a 28.09 S 151.51 E
Cunningham, Ks., U.S. 198 37.38 N 98.25 W
Cunningham, Lake ⊜ 240b 25.04 N 77.26 W
Cunninghame □[9] 46 55.40 N 4.30 W
Cunningham Falls State Park ♠ 208 39.35 N 77.27 W
Cunningham Park ♠, Ma., U.S. 283 42.15 N 71.03 W
Cunningham Park ♠, N.Y., U.S. 276 40.44 N 73.46 W
Čunojar 88 57.27 N 97.18 E
Cunqian 100 28.30 N 115.10 E
Čunskij, Ross. 88 56.05 N 99.41 E
Čunskij, Ross. 88 57.26 N 97.31 E
Cuntan 107 29.37 N 106.36 E
Cunucunuma ≃ 246 3.13 N 65.58 W
Čuny 76 59.39 N 36.04 E
Čuokkaraš'ša ∧ 24 69.57 N 24.32 E
Cuorgnè 62 45.23 N 7.39 E
Čupa 24 66.16 N 33.00 E
Čupalejka 80 55.11 N 42.33 E
Cupar, Sk., Can. 184 50.57 N 104.12 W
Cupar, Scot., U.K. 46 56.19 N 3.01 W
Cupecê, Ribeirão ≃ 287b 23.37 S 46.42 W
Cupello 66 42.04 N 14.40 E
Cuperly 50 49.04 N 4.26 E
Cupertino 226 37.19 N 122.01 W
Cupica, Golfo de ⊂ 246 6.35 N 77.25 W
Cupins 255 19.51 S 51.03 W
Cupra Marittima 66 43.01 N 13.51 E
Cupramontana 66 43.27 N 13.07 E
Ćuprija 38 43.56 N 21.23 E
Čuprovo 24 64.14 N 46.36 E
Cupsaw Lake ⊜ 276 41.07 N 74.15 W
Cuqiao 107 30.36 N 103.59 E
Cuquema ≃ 152 12.03 S 17.40 E
Cuquenán ≃ 246 4.45 N 61.30 W
Cuquío 234 20.55 N 103.02 W
Čur 80 57.07 N 52.58 E
Curaçá 250 8.59 S 39.54 W
Curaçao I 241s 12.11 N 69.00 W
Curacautín 252 38.26 S 71.53 W
Curacaví 252 33.24 S 71.09 W
Čuračiki 80 55.44 N 47.26 E
Curaglia 58 46.41 N 8.51 E
Cural Novo, Ribeirão ≃ 256 21.17 S 43.51 W
Curanilahue 252 37.28 S 73.21 W
Curanipe 252 35.50 S 72.38 W
Curanja ≃ 248 9.58 S 70.58 W
Čurapča 74 62.00 N 132.24 E
Curapi ≃ 250 1.25 N 53.49 W
Curaray ≃ 246 2.20 S 74.05 W
Čurbek 85 39.59 N 69.56 E
Curcani 38 44.12 N 26.35 E
Curdies ≃ 169 38.30 S 142.55 E
Cure ≃ 50 47.40 N 3.41 E
Curecanti National Recreation Area ♠ 200 38.24 N 107.25 W
Curepipe 157c 20.19 S 57.31 E
Curepto 252 35.05 S 72.01 W
Curequetê ≃ 248 8.20 S 65.40 W
Curiapo 246 8.33 N 61.00 W
Curib 84 42.14 N 46.49 E
Curiche Grande (Corixo Grande) ≃ 248 17.43 S 57.43 W
Curicó 252 34.59 S 71.14 W
Curicuriari ≃ 246 0.14 S 66.48 W
Curières, Lac ⊜ 206 46.41 N 74.51 W
Curimatá 250 10.02 S 44.17 W
Curimeo 234 20.01 N 101.42 W
Curinga 68 38.49 N 16.19 E
Curious, Mount ∧ 162 27.28 S 114.20 E
Curisevo ≃ 255 12.14 S 53.17 W
Curitiba 252 25.25 S 49.15 W
Curitibanos 252 27.18 S 50.36 W
Curiuaú ≃ 246 1.51 S 61.14 W
Curiúva 255 24.02 S 50.27 W
Curl Curl 274a 33.46 S 151.18 E
Curlew 182 48.53 N 118.35 W
Curlewis 166 31.07 S 150.16 E
Curnamona 166 31.39 S 139.32 E
Curoca Norte 152 16.18 S 12.58 E
Curone ≃ 62 45.03 N 8.54 E
Curon Venosta (Graun) 64 46.49 N 10.32 E
Čurovići 78 52.10 N 32.01 E
Currais Novos 250 6.15 S 36.31 W
Curralinho 250 1.48 S 49.47 W
Curramulka 168b 34.42 S 137.42 E
Curran 219 39.44 N 89.46 W
Currant Creek ≃, Co., U.S. 200 38.29 N 105.24 W
Currant Creek ≃, Mt., U.S. 202 46.22 N 108.39 W
Currant Mountain ∧ 204 38.55 N 115.25 W
Currarong 170 35.01 S 150.49 E
Currency Creek 168b 35.28 S 138.46 E
Current ≃, On., Can. 190 48.27 N 89.11 W
Current ≃, U.S. 194 36.16 N 90.57 W
Current Islands II 192 25.22 N 76.49 W
Currie, Austl. 166 39.56 S 143.52 E
Currie, Scot., U.K. 46 55.54 N 3.20 W
Currie, Mn., U.S. 198 44.04 N 95.39 W

Currituck 192 36.26 N 76.00 W
Currituck □[6] 208 36.28 N 76.03 W
Currituck Seamount ✤[3] 14 30.00 S 173.30 W
Currituck Sound ⊔ 192 36.20 N 75.52 W
Curry 180 62.37 N 150.01 W
Curry, Lake ⊜[1] 226 38.22 N 122.08 W
Curry Rivel 42 51.02 N 2.52 W
Curryville, Mo., U.S. 219 39.20 N 91.20 W
Curryville, Pa., U.S. 214 40.17 N 78.20 W
Cursi 68 40.09 N 18.18 E
Curslack ◆[8] 52 53.27 N 10.13 E
Curtarolo 64 45.31 N 11.50 E
Curtea de Argeş 38 45.08 N 24.41 E
Curtice 214 41.29 N 82.49 W
Curtina 252 32.09 S 56.07 W
Curtin Springs 162 25.20 S 131.45 E
Curtis, Ar., U.S. 194 33.59 N 93.06 W
Curtis, Ne., U.S. 198 40.37 N 100.30 W
Curtis, Port ⊤[3] 166 24.00 S 151.30 E
Curtis Bay ⊂ 284b 39.13 N 76.35 W
Curtis Channel ⊔ 166 23.30 S 151.45 E
Curtis Creek ⊂ 284b 39.12 N 76.35 W
Curtis Island I, Austl. 166 23.38 S 151.09 E
Curtis Island I, N.Z. 14 30.30 S 178.34 W
Curtis Lake ⊜ 176 66.38 N 89.02 W
Curtisville 214 40.38 N 79.51 W
Curu ≃ 250 3.22 S 39.04 W
Curuá ≃, Bra. 250 5.23 S 54.22 W
Curuá ≃, Bra. 250 1.55 S 55.07 W
Curuá ≃, Bra. 255 13.51 S 51.38 W
Curuá, Ilha do I 250 0.48 N 50.10 W
Curuaés ≃ 250 7.30 S 54.45 W
Curuan 116 7.13 N 122.14 E
Curuá-Una ≃ 250 2.24 S 54.05 W
Curubandé 236 10.43 N 85.26 W
Curuçá 250 0.43 S 47.50 W
Curuçá ◆[8] 287b 23.30 S 46.25 W
Curuçá ≃ 246 4.27 S 71.23 W
Curuçambaba 250 2.08 S 49.18 W
Curug, Indon. 115a 6.15 S 106.33 E
Čurug, Jugo. 38 45.29 N 20.04 E
Curuguaty 252 24.31 S 55.42 W
Curumo 286c 10.27 N 66.52 W
Curumu 250 1.01 S 51.03 W
Curunga 152 12.51 S 21.12 E
Curup 112 3.28 S 102.32 E
Curupá 250 9.54 S 45.54 W
Curupayty, Riacho ≃ 248 22.03 S 58.00 W
Cururu ≃, Bra. 248 7.12 S 58.03 W
Cururu ≃, Bra. 250 0.39 S 50.11 W
Cururu-Açu ≃ 250 8.58 S 57.13 W
Cururupu 250 1.50 S 44.52 W
Curuzú Cuatiá 252 29.47 S 58.03 W
Curva Grande 250 2.37 S 45.27 W
Curvelo 255 18.45 S 44.25 W
Curwensville 214 40.58 N 78.31 W
Curwensville Lake ⊜[1] 214 40.55 N 78.37 W
Curwensville State Park ♠ 214 40.55 N 78.34 W
Cusago 266b 45.27 N 9.02 E
Cusano Milanino 62 45.33 N 9.11 E
Cusano Mutri 68 41.20 N 14.30 E
Cusco 248 13.31 S 71.59 W
Cusco □[5] 248 12.30 S 72.30 W
Cuscuzeiro, Pico do ∧ 256 23.18 S 44.47 W
Cushabatay ≃ 248 7.09 S 75.08 W
Cushendall 48 55.06 N 6.04 W
Cushendun 48 55.07 N 6.03 W
Cushina ≃ 48 53.11 N 7.05 W
Cushing, Ok., U.S. 196 35.59 N 96.46 W
Cushing, Tx., U.S. 222 31.43 N 94.50 W
Cushing Memorial State Park ♠ 283 42.10 N 70.45 W
Cushman 194 35.52 N 91.45 W
Cushman, Lake ⊜[1] 224 47.28 N 123.14 W
Cusiana ≃ 246 4.33 N 71.51 W
Cusick 202 48.20 N 117.17 W
Cusihuiriáchic 232 28.14 N 106.50 W
Cusna, Monte ∧ 64 44.17 N 10.23 E
Čusovaja ≃ 86 58.13 N 56.22 E
Čusovoj 86 58.17 N 57.49 E
Cusset 32 46.08 N 3.28 E
Cusseta 192 32.18 N 84.46 W
Cussewago Creek ≃ 214 41.38 N 80.11 W
Cussey-sur-l'Ognon 58 47.20 N 5.56 E
Cusso ≃ 152 14.16 S 15.36 E
Cust, N.Z. 172 43.19 S 172.22 E
Čust, Uzb. 85 41.00 N 71.15 E
Custar 216 41.17 N 83.51 W
Custer, Mi., U.S. 190 43.57 N 86.13 W
Custer, Mt., U.S. 202 46.07 N 107.33 W
Custer, Ok., U.S. 196 35.40 N 98.53 W
Custer, S.D., U.S. 198 43.46 N 103.35 W
Custer, Wa., U.S. 224 48.55 N 122.38 W
Custer City 214 41.54 N 78.39 W
Custer Creek ≃ 198 46.42 N 105.29 W
Custer State Park ♠ 198 43.43 N 103.23 W
Custines 56 48.48 N 6.09 E
Custódia 250 8.07 S 37.39 W
Custonaci 70 38.04 N 12.41 E
Cut, Nuhu I 164 5.35 S 133.00 E
Cut and Shoot 222 30.19 N 95.25 W
Cutato ≃ 152 10.33 S 16.48 E
Cut Bank 202 48.37 N 112.19 W
Cutbank ≃ 182 54.44 N 118.31 W
Cut Bank Creek ≃, N.A. 198 48.35 N 100.52 W
Cut Bank Creek ≃, Mt., U.S. 202 48.29 N 112.14 W
Cut Beaver Lake ⊜ 184 53.47 N 102.38 W
Čutejevo 80 55.16 N 47.47 E
Cutervo 248 6.22 S 78.51 W
Cutervo, Parque Nacional ♠ 248 6.10 S 78.45 W
Cuthand Creek ≃ 194 33.23 N 94.57 W
Cuthbert 192 31.46 N 84.47 W
Cut Knife 184 52.44 N 109.01 W
Cutler, Ca., U.S. 226 36.31 N 119.17 W
Cutler, Me., U.S. 188 44.39 N 67.12 W
Cutler Ridge 220 25.34 N 80.20 W
Cutlerville 216 42.50 N 85.39 W
Cutral-Có 252 38.56 S 69.14 W
Cutro 68 39.02 N 16.59 E
Cutrofiano 68 40.07 N 18.12 E
Cuttack 120 20.30 N 85.50 E
Cuttyhunk Island I 207 41.25 N 70.56 W
Čutyr' 80 57.24 N 53.17 E
Cutzamala ≃ 234 18.22 N 100.39 W
Cutzamala de Pinzón 234 18.28 N 100.34 W
Cutzio 234 18.39 N 100.54 W
Čuvašija □[3] 80 55.30 N 47.00 E
Cuvette □[5] 152 0.30 S 16.00 E
Cuvier, Cape › 162 24.05 S 113.22 E
Cuvilly 50 49.33 N 2.42 E
Cuvo ≃ 152 10.50 S 13.47 E
Cuxhaven 52 53.52 N 8.42 E
Cuxton 260 51.22 N 0.27 E
Cuyabá
→ Cuiabá 248 15.35 S 56.05 W
Cuyaguateje ≃ 240p 22.05 N 83.58 W
Cuyahoga □[6] 214 41.30 N 81.41 W
Cuyahoga ≃ 214 41.30 N 81.42 W
Cuyahoga County Airport ⊠ 279a 41.34 N 81.29 W
Cuyahoga Falls 214 41.08 N 81.29 W
Cuyahoga Heights 279a 41.26 N 81.39 W
Cuyahoga Valley National Recreation Area ♠ 214 41.20 N 81.35 W
Cuyama ≃ 204 34.54 N 120.18 W
Cuyamaca Peak ∧ 204 32.57 N 116.36 W
Cuyamaca Rancho State Park ♠ 204 32.58 N 116.32 W
Cuyamel 236 15.38 N 88.12 W
Cuyapo 116 15.46 N 120.40 E
Cuyk 52 51.44 N 5.52 E
Cuyler 210 42.44 N 75.57 W
Cuylerville 210 42.47 N 77.52 W

Cuyo 116 10.51 N 121.00 E
Cuyo East Pass ⊔ 116 11.00 N 121.28 E
Cuyo Island I 116 10.51 N 121.02 E
Cuyo Islands II 116 11.04 N 120.57 E
Cuyo West Pass ⊔ 116 11.00 N 120.30 E
Cuyubini ≃ 246 8.20 N 60.20 W
Cuyuni ≃ 246 6.23 N 58.41 W
Cuyuni-Mazaruni □[4] 246 6.00 N 60.00 W
Cuyutlán, Laguna ⊂ 234 19.00 N 104.10 W
Cuzco
→ Cusco 248 13.31 S 71.59 W
Čuzik ≃ 86 58.03 N 80.37 E
Cuzna ≃ 34 38.04 N 4.41 W
Cuzzago 58 46.00 N 8.22 E
Cvetnogorsk 86 54.14 N 90.27 E
Cvikov 54 50.48 N 14.40 E
Cwmbran 42 51.39 N 3.00 W
Cyangugu 154 2.29 S 28.54 E
Cybinka 30 52.12 N 14.48 E
Cyclades
→ Kikládhes II 38 37.30 N 25.00 E
Cyclone 214 41.50 N 78.35 W
Cygnet 216 41.14 N 83.38 W
Cygnet Bay ⊂ 162 16.35 S 123.05 E
Cygnet Lake ⊜ 184 56.47 N 94.54 W
Cygnet River 168b 35.42 S 137.31 E
Cylburn Park ♠ 284b 39.21 N 76.39 W
Cynin ≃ 42 51.48 N 4.29 W
Cynthiana, Ky., U.S. 218 38.23 N 84.17 W
Cynthiana, Oh., U.S. 218 39.10 N 83.21 W
Cynwyl Elfed 42 51.55 N 4.22 W
Cypern
→ Cyprus □[1] 130 35.00 N 33.00 E
Cypress, Ca., U.S. 280 33.49 N 118.02 W
Cypress, La., U.S. 194 31.36 N 93.02 W
Cypress, Tx., U.S. 222 29.58 N 95.42 W
Cypress Bayou ≃ 194 35.03 N 91.42 W
Cypress Creek ≃, Fl., U.S. 220 28.05 N 82.24 W
Cypress Creek ≃, Tx., U.S. 194 30.19 N 93.45 W
Cypress Creek ≃, Tx., U.S. 222 30.02 N 95.19 W
Cypress Gardens ♠ 220 28.00 N 81.42 W
Cypress Hills ⋏[2] 184 49.40 N 109.30 W
Cypress Hills Provincial Park ♠, Ab., Can. 184 49.39 N 110.10 W
Cypress Hills Provincial Park ♠, Sk., Can. 184 49.39 N 109.30 W
Cypress Island I 224 48.35 N 122.42 W
Cypress Lake ⊜, Sk., Can. 184 49.28 N 109.29 W
Cypress Lake ⊜, Fl., U.S. 220 28.05 N 81.19 W
Cypress Point › 226 36.35 N 121.59 W
Cypress Quarters 220 27.15 N 80.48 W
Cypress River 184 49.34 N 99.05 W
Cypress Swamp ≃ 208 37.02 N 76.53 W
Cypress Swamp ⩨ 208 38.30 N 75.17 W
Cyprus □[1], Asia 22 35.00 N 33.00 E
Cyprus □[1], Asia 130 35.00 N 33.00 E
Cyprus, North (Kuzey Kıbrıs) □[1], Asia 22 35.15 N 33.40 E
Cyprus, North (Kuzey Kıbrıs) □[1], Asia 130 35.15 N 33.40 E
Cyrenaica
→ Barqah □[9] 146 31.00 N 22.30 E
Cyrene 219 39.17 N 91.06 W
Cyrene ⊥ 146 32.49 N 21.52 E
Cyril 196 34.53 N 98.12 W
Cyrildene ◆[8] 273d 26.11 S 28.06 E
Cyrus Field Bay ⊂ 176 62.50 N 64.55 W
Čyrvonae, vozero ⊜ 76 52.24 N 27.57 E
Cysoing 50 50.34 N 3.13 E
Cythera
→ Kíthira I 38 36.20 N 22.58 E
Czaplinek 30 53.34 N 16.14 E
Czarna Białostocka 30 53.19 N 23.16 E
Czarna Woda 30 53.51 N 18.06 E
Czarne 30 53.42 N 16.57 E
Czarnków 30 52.55 N 16.34 E
Czech Republic (Česká Republika) □[1], Europe 22 49.40 N 15.10 E
Czech Republic (Česká Republika) □[1], Europe 30 49.40 N 15.10 E
Czempiń 30 52.10 N 16.47 E
Czerniejewo 30 52.26 N 17.30 E
Czernowitz
→ Chernivtsi 78 48.18 N 25.56 E
Czersk 30 53.48 N 18.00 E
Czerwieńsk 30 52.01 N 15.25 E
Częstochowa 30 50.49 N 19.06 E
Częstochowa □[4] 30 50.40 N 19.15 E
Człopa 30 53.06 N 16.08 E
Człuchów 30 53.41 N 17.21 E
Czudec 30 49.57 N 21.50 E

D

Da
→ Black ≃, Asia 110 21.15 N 105.20 E
Da ≃, Zhg. 100 28.10 N 120.14 E
Daaden 56 50.44 N 7.58 E
Da'an, Zhg. 89 45.28 N 124.18 E
Da'an, Zhg. 100 23.05 N 115.37 E
Da'an, Zhg. 107 29.23 N 106.01 E
Da'an, Zhg. 110 23.19 N 110.34 E
Daanbantayan 116 11.14 N 124.00 E
Daba 104 42.06 N 122.00 E
Ḍabāb, Jabal aḍ- ∧ 132 31.02 N 35.38 E
Dabagou 104 42.27 N 122.00 E
Ḍab'ah, Ra's aḍ- › 140 31.05 N 28.26 E
Dabai 150 11.31 N 5.11 E
Dabaizhuang 105 39.27 N 117.23 E
Dabajuro 246 11.02 N 70.40 W
Dabakala 150 8.22 N 4.26 W
Dabali 104 41.51 N 120.37 E
Daba Ling ∧ 100 24.28 N 113.17 E
Dabancheng 86 43.21 N 88.19 E
Dabangdian 100 31.37 N 113.41 E
Dabaojiagangzi 104 42.09 N 123.33 E
Dabaozhuang 105 40.18 N 116.58 E
Dabaozi 105 40.11 N 115.10 E
Daba Shan ⋏ 102 31.55 N 109.05 E
Dabasi 107 28.55 N 105.09 E
Dabat 144 12.58 N 37.48 E
Dabayingzi 104 42.11 N 121.35 E
Dabbāgh, Jabal ∧ 128 27.52 N 35.45 E
Dabbūriya 132 32.41 N 35.22 E
Dabegabis 158 28.07 S 18.36 E
Dabeiba 246 7.01 N 76.16 W
Dabeiwa 105 40.48 N 117.31 E
Dabeiyingzi 104 42.05 N 122.08 E
Dabendorf 54 52.14 N 13.26 E
Daberas 156 25.38 S 18.29 E
Daberg ◆[8] 263 51.40 N 7.47 E
Dabhoi 120 22.11 N 73.26 E
Dābhol 122 17.36 N 73.10 E
Ḍab'ī, Wādī aḍ- V 132 31.42 N 36.42 E
Dąbie 30 52.06 N 18.49 E
Dąbie ◆[8] 54 53.24 N 14.40 E
Dąbie, Jezioro ⊜ 54 53.27 N 14.40 E
Dabie Shan ⋏ 100 31.00 N 115.40 E
Dabilda 146 12.46 N 14.34 E
Dablān 130 34.52 N 40.34 E
Ďáblice ◆[8] 54 50.08 N 14.29 E
Dabnou 150 14.09 N 5.22 E
Dabo 58 48.39 N 7.14 E
Dabob Bay ⊂ 224 47.47 N 122.50 W
Dabobeizhuang 105 39.18 N 117.59 E
Dabola 150 10.45 N 11.07 W
Dabong 114 5.23 N 102.01 E
Daborow 144 6.21 N 48.43 E
Dabou 150 5.19 N 4.23 W

Daboya 150 9.32 N 1.23 W
Dabra 124 25.54 N 78.20 E
Dabraslaŭka 76 52.24 N 26.15 E
Dābri ◆[8] 272a 28.37 N 77.05 E
Dabringhausen 52 51.05 N 7.11 E
Dąbrowa Białostocka 30 53.39 N 23.20 E
Dąbrowa Tarnowska 30 50.11 N 21.00 E
Dabryn' 78 51.46 N 29.12 E
Dabsan Hu ⊜ 102 36.58 N 94.55 E
Dabu, Zhg. 100 23.52 N 116.54 E
Dabu, Zhg. 100 24.20 N 114.35 E
Dabu, Zhg. 100 24.19 N 116.43 E
Dabus ≃ 144 10.48 N 35.10 E
Dabusutu-Ula, gora ∧ 86 50.44 N 92.40 E
Dacaitun 104 41.38 N 121.18 E
Dacangzigou 104 40.59 N 121.01 E
Dacaocun 105 40.34 N 117.07 E
Dacca
→ Dhaka 126 23.43 N 90.25 E
Dachakou 100 29.38 N 118.18 E
Dachang, Zhg. 105 39.53 N 116.59 E
Dachang, Zhg. 106 32.12 N 118.45 E
Dachang, Zhg. 106 31.18 N 121.25 E
Dachang Airport ⊠ 269b 31.18 N 121.25 E
Dachangshan Dao I 98 39.10 N 122.34 E
Dachau 60 48.15 N 11.27 E
Dachauer Moos ⩨ 60 48.12 N 11.25 E
Dacheng 100 28.34 N 115.31 E
Dachengji 100 33.52 N 119.26 E
Dachenjiabao 106 32.11 N 120.22 E
Dachen Shan I 106 30.21 N 121.52 E
Dachixu 100 25.10 N 116.46 E
Dachongyu 105 40.23 N 117.41 E
Dachsberg ∧[2] 263 51.30 N 6.30 E
Dachsteinhöhlen ⏏[5] 64 47.32 N 13.43 E
Dačice 61 49.05 N 15.26 E
Dac Lac, Cao Nguyen ⋏[1] 110 12.50 N 108.05 E
Dačnoje ◆[8] 265a 59.50 N 30.16 E
Dacoma 196 36.39 N 98.33 W
Dacorum □[8] 260 51.45 N 0.30 W
Dac To 110 14.42 N 107.51 E
Dacun, Zhg. 102 27.55 N 101.08 E
Dacun, Zhg. 106 31.12 N 119.40 E
Dadal 88 49.01 N 111.37 E
Dadanawa 246 2.50 N 59.30 W
Dadaolizhuang 105 39.59 N 116.59 E
Dadaotun 104 41.46 N 122.13 E
Dadar ◆[8] 272c 19.01 N 72.50 E
Daday 130 41.28 N 33.28 E
Dadayungou 104 41.23 N 123.25 E
Daddys Creek ≃ 192 36.05 N 84.47 W
Dade □[6] 220 25.33 N 80.32 W
Dade Battlefield Historic Memorial ⊥ 220 28.38 N 82.09 W
Dade City 220 28.21 N 82.11 W
Ḍaḍeldhurā 124 29.18 N 80.35 E
Dadès, Oued ≃ 148 30.55 N 6.47 W
Dadeville 194 32.49 N 85.45 W
Dādhar 120 29.28 N 67.39 E
Dadian 100 33.36 N 117.16 E
Dadiangas
→ General Santos 116 6.07 N 125.11 E
Dadianzi 104 42.11 N 124.02 E
Dadingjiawopu 104 41.13 N 122.16 E
D'adino 88 55.44 N 105.45 E
Dadiya 146 9.37 N 11.26 E
Dadle 144 5.20 N 46.58 E
Ḍadnah 128 25.33 N 56.21 E
Dadonggejiang 105 39.51 N 116.48 E
Dadongzhou 104 41.44 N 124.00 E
Dadou ≃ 32 43.44 N 1.49 E
Dādpur, India 272b 22.42 N 88.33 E
Dādpur, India 272b 22.54 N 88.31 E
Dādra and Nagar Haveli □[8] 122 20.05 N 73.00 E
Dādu 120 26.44 N 67.47 E
Dadu ≃ 102 29.33 N 103.45 E
Dadugang 102 22.23 N 100.55 E
Dadukou, Zhg. 100 25.44 N 119.05 E
Dadukou, Zhg. 107 28.45 N 105.13 E
Dadukou, Zhg. 107 29.28 N 106.29 E
Daegu
→ Taegu 98 35.52 N 128.35 E
Daejeon
→ Taejŏn 98 36.20 N 127.26 E
Daerhanwangfu 89 44.19 N 122.15 E
Da'erhao 98 41.45 N 116.01 E
Daet 116 14.05 N 122.55 E
Daf' 146 28.03 N 19.57 E
Dafan, Zhg. 100 29.41 N 114.40 E
Dafan, Zhg. 104 42.38 N 122.11 E
Dafang 102 27.04 N 105.31 E
Dafangshen, Zhg. 104 42.25 N 123.14 E
Dafangshen, Zhg. 104 42.34 N 123.28 E
Dafangshen, Zhg. 104 42.36 N 123.04 E
Dafanhe 104 42.13 N 123.43 E
Dafanpuzi 104 41.37 N 122.50 E
Dafeng 100 33.12 N 120.30 E
Dafna 132 33.14 N 35.38 E
Dafoe 184 51.46 N 104.32 W
Dafoe ≃ 184 55.55 N 94.48 W
Dafoe Lake ⊜ 184 55.43 N 96.15 W
Da Fo Si (Great Buddha Temple) ♁[1] 106 30.16 N 120.09 E
Dafoutuo 105 40.24 N 115.58 E
Dafu 100 29.55 N 118.35 E
Dafu ≃ 100 30.52 N 113.32 E
Dāfūr al-Janūbīyah □[4] 140 11.45 N 25.25 E
Dagā ≃ 110 16.56 N 94.45 E
Daga Medo 144 7.59 N 43.01 E
Dagana 150 16.31 N 15.30 W
Dagang, Zhg. 100 33.12 N 120.07 E
Dagang, Zhg. 100 22.49 N 113.23 E
Dagang, Zhg. 106 32.12 N 119.39 E
Dagangtou 100 28.18 N 119.44 E
Daganwangzhai 104 40.49 N 122.33 E
Daganzo de Arriba 266a 40.33 N 3.27 W
Dagaokan 104 40.46 N 122.22 E
Dagaolifangcun 104 41.10 N 122.28 E
Dagaolitun 104 42.26 N 123.53 E
Dagaoyang 106 30.35 N 120.26 E
Daga Post 140 9.12 N 33.58 E
Dağardı 130 39.26 N 29.00 E
Dagash 140 19.22 N 33.24 E
Dağbeli 130 37.12 N 30.31 E
Dagcanglhamo 102 34.02 N 102.30 E
Dagda 76 56.06 N 27.32 E
Dageløkke 41 55.04 N 10.53 E
Dagenham ◆[8] 260 51.32 N 0.10 E
Dagestan □[3] 72 43.00 N 47.00 E
Dagestanskije Ogni 84 42.07 N 48.12 E
Daggafontein 273d 26.18 S 28.28 E
Daggafontein Mines ◆[7] 273d 26.18 S 28.29 E
Daggett 228 34.51 N 116.53 W
Dagg Sound ⊔ 172 45.23 S 166.46 E
Daghfalī 140 19.17 N 32.30 E
Dağkızılca 130 38.18 N 27.24 E
Daglung 120 28.54 N 90.33 E
Dagmersellen 58 47.13 N 7.59 E
Dagö
→ Hiiumaa I 76 58.52 N 22.40 E
Dagomys 84 43.40 N 39.41 E
Dagongtun 89 42.48 N 121.58 E
Dagoretti 154 1.18 S 36.46 E
Dagsboro 208 38.32 N 75.14 W
Dagshai 123 30.53 N 77.03 E
Dagu 105 38.59 N 117.41 E
Dagu ≃ 98 36.15 N 120.06 E
Dagua 164 3.25 S 143.20 E
Daguan, Zhg. 100 31.14 N 117.01 E
Daguan, Zhg. 102 27.44 N 104.16 E
Daguan Hu ⊜ 100 30.00 N 116.24 E
Daguao 240m 18.14 N 65.41 W
Dagufen'gou 105 40.41 N 116.20 E
D'Aguilar, Cape › 271d 22.14 N 114.15 E
D'Aguilar, Mount ∧ 171a 27.19 S 152.47 E
D'Aguilar Range ⋏ 171a 27.10 S 152.45 E
Dagujia 98 42.22 N 124.52 E

Dagujiazi 104 42.20 N 123.20 E
Da Guokui Shan ∧ 89 45.17 N 129.30 E
Dagupan 116 16.03 N 120.20 E
Daguragu Aboriginal Reserve ◆[4] 162 17.35 S 130.30 E
Dagushan 104 41.03 N 123.02 E
Dagus Mines 214 41.21 N 78.36 W
Dagutang 100 29.38 N 116.06 E
Dagwin 110 18.04 N 97.41 E
Dagzê Co ⊜ 120 31.55 N 87.35 E
Dahabān 144 21.55 N 39.04 E
Dahalac National Park ♠ 144 15.40 N 40.05 E
Dahanchang 105 39.29 N 117.05 E
Dahaneh-ye Ghowrī 120 35.54 N 68.30 E
Dahaneh-ye Kāshār 120 35.09 N 66.14 E
Dahan-e Qowmghī 120 34.28 N 66.31 E
Dahantun 104 42.10 N 122.41 E
Dahasah, Wādī V 142 28.08 N 31.00 E
Dahao Dao I 100 22.17 N 113.59 E
Dahḍāh, Tall ∧[2] 132 32.36 N 36.03 E
Dahe 106 31.42 N 120.37 E
Dahebei 105 39.10 N 117.39 E
Dahei 120 21.42 N 72.35 E
Daheiding Shan ∧ 89 47.58 N 129.07 E
Daheiyugou 104 41.21 N 121.55 E
Dahekou 106 32.16 N 119.05 E
Dahengdu 100 29.03 N 121.30 E
Dahenqin Dao I 100 22.06 N 113.30 E
Daheqiao 100 29.25 N 115.16 E
Dahijuri 126 22.31 N 86.59 E
Da Hinggan Ling ⋏ 90 49.00 N 122.00 E
Dahīrpur ◆[8] 272a 28.43 N 77.12 E
Dahl 56 51.18 N 7.31 E
Dahlak Archipelago II 144 15.45 N 40.30 E
Dahle 263 51.18 N 7.45 E
Dahlem 56 50.23 N 6.33 E
Dahlem ◆[8] 264a 52.28 N 13.17 E
Dahlem, Museum ♁ 264a 52.27 N 13.18 E
Dahlen 54 51.22 N 12.59 E
Dahlenburg 54 53.11 N 10.44 E
Dahlerau 263 51.13 N 7.19 E
Dahlewitz 54 52.19 N 13.26 E
Dahlgren, Il., U.S. 194 38.12 N 88.41 W
Dahlgren, Va., U.S. 208 38.19 N 77.03 W
Dahlia 154 18.35 S 27.08 E
Dahlonega 192 34.31 N 83.59 W
Dahlonega Plateau ⋏[1] 192 34.10 N 84.20 W
Dahlwitz 264a 52.30 N 13.38 E
Dahlwitz-Hoppegarten 54 52.30 N 13.38 E
Dahmani 36 35.57 N 8.50 E
Dahmarū 142 28.41 N 30.49 E
Dahme, Dtsch. 54 51.52 N 13.25 E
Dahme, Dtsch. 54 54.13 N 11.04 E
Dahme ≃ 54 52.25 N 13.35 E
Dahn 56 49.09 N 7.47 E
Dāhod 120 22.50 N 74.16 E
Dahomey
→ Benin □[1] 150 9.30 N 2.15 E
Dahong 106 31.53 N 121.17 E
Dahongmen 105 39.50 N 116.25 E
Dahongqi 104 41.52 N 122.36 E
Dahong Shan ⋏ 100 31.30 N 113.00 E
Dahongtaizi 104 41.41 N 121.23 E
Dahoucun 105 38.51 N 115.37 E
Dahra 146 29.34 N 17.50 E
Dahra ⋏ 34 36.25 N 1.00 E
Dähre 54 52.48 N 10.54 E
Dahsah, Wādī ad- V 142 27.19 N 31.26 E
Dahshūr 142 29.45 N 31.14 E
Dahu, Zhg. 100 26.22 N 119.06 E
Dahu, Zhg. 100 26.04 N 117.19 E
Dahua 102 23.44 N 107.59 E
Dahuan 100 22.33 N 113.29 E
Dahuangdi 104 42.08 N 122.27 E
Dahuangji 98 35.06 N 115.15 E
Dahuangpu 105 39.26 N 117.16 E
Dahuangshanpu 104 41.16 N 121.23 E
Dahuashan 105 40.17 N 117.04 E
Dahuasi 107 30.05 N 104.08 E
Dahujiang 100 26.10 N 114.57 E
Dahūk 128 36.52 N 43.00 E
Dahūk □[4] 128 37.00 N 43.00 E
Dahuni 164 10.31 S 149.55 E
Dahuofang Shuiku ⊜[1] 98 41.55 N 124.15 E
Dahushan 104 41.37 N 122.09 E
Daḥy, Nafūd ad- ◆[2] 118 22.20 N 45.35 E
Dai I 175e 7.57 S 160.37 E
Dai ≃ 100 26.14 N 119.40 E
Dai, Pulau I 164 7.33 S 129.41 E
Daia 38 44.00 N 25.59 E
Daian 94 35.05 N 136.33 E
Daibosatsu-rei ∧ 94 35.45 N 138.51 E
Daibu, Zhg. 100 32.19 N 117.12 E
Daibu, Zhg. 106 31.18 N 119.30 E
Daibutsu ♁[1] 94 35.19 N 139.32 E
Daiei 96 35.29 N 133.45 E
Daifang 100 27.32 N 115.41 E
Daigo 94 36.46 N 140.21 E
Daigo ◆[8] 270 34.57 N 135.50 E
Daiguantun 105 39.57 N 117.50 E
Dai Hai ⊜ 102 40.31 N 112.43 E
Daihaiyingzi 104 42.30 N 121.26 E
Daiji 100 33.48 N 115.03 E
Daijiagou 107 30.00 N 106.33 E
Daijiayao 100 32.56 N 120.19 E
Daikanbō ∧ 96 33.00 N 131.04 E
Daik-u 110 17.47 N 96.40 E
Dā'il 132 32.45 N 36.08 E
Dailekh 124 28.50 N 81.44 E
Dailing 89 47.01 N 129.02 E
Dailly 44 55.16 N 4.43 W
Daimanji-san ∧ 92 36.15 N 133.19 E
Daimiel 34 39.04 N 3.37 W
Daimon, Nihon 94 36.44 N 137.03 E
Daimon, Nihon 268 35.53 N 139.44 E
Daimuken-zan ∧ 94 35.15 N 138.10 E
Dainan 100 32.43 N 120.06 E
Daingean 48 53.18 N 7.17 W
Daingerfield 222 33.01 N 94.43 W
Dainhāt 126 23.37 N 88.04 E
Dainichiga-take ∧ 94 36.00 N 136.50 E
Dainkog 102 32.31 N 97.59 E
Daintree 164 16.15 S 145.19 E
Daintree National Park ♠ 164 16.15 S 145.10 E
Daiō-zaki › 92 34.17 N 136.54 E
Dāira Dīn Panāh 123 30.34 N 70.56 E
Dairago 266b 45.34 N 8.52 E
Daireaux 252 36.36 S 61.45 W
Dairen
→ Dalian 98 38.53 N 121.35 E
Dairsie 46 56.20 N 2.56 W
Dairy City
→ Cypress 280 33.50 N 118.01 W
Dairy Creek, East Fork ≃ 224 45.34 N 123.09 W
Dairy Creek, West Fork ≃ 224 45.34 N 123.09 W
Dairyland
→ La Palma, Ca., U.S. 280 33.51 N 118.02 W
Dairyland, N.Y., U.S. 210 41.45 N 74.33 W
Dairyland Reservoir ⊜[1] 190 45.30 N 91.00 W
Dairy Valley
→ Cerritos 280 33.51 N 118.05 W
Dai-sen ∧ 96 35.22 N 133.33 E
Daisen-oki-kokuritsu-kōen ♠ 96 35.20 N 133.35 E
Daisen-zan ∧ 96 34.07 N 133.56 E
Daisetsu-zan-kokuritsu-kōen ♠ 92a 43.30 N 142.57 E
Daisetta 222 30.06 N 94.38 W
Daishan 100 30.14 N 122.12 E
Daishin 94 37.12 N 140.15 E
Daishōji ≃ 94 36.18 N 136.15 E

Daisizhen 107 29.14 N 105.09 E
Daitō, Nihon 96 34.42 N 135.38 E
Daitō, Nihon 96 35.19 N 132.58 E
Daiwa, Nihon 96 34.32 N 132.57 E
Daiwa, Nihon 96 34.57 N 132.39 E
Daixi 106 30.40 N 120.01 E
Daixian 102 39.08 N 113.01 E
Daixiqiao 106 31.36 N 120.04 E
Daiya ≃ 94 36.45 N 139.46 E
Daiyun Shan ⋏ 100 25.46 N 118.16 E
Dajabón 238 19.33 N 71.42 W
Dājal 120 29.33 N 70.23 E
Da'jānīyah, Jabal ad- ∧ 132 30.34 N 35.43 E
Dajarra 166 21.41 S 139.31 E
Dajian Shan ∧ 102 26.42 N 103.34 E
Dajidian 105 38.50 N 115.26 E
Dajindian 100 34.24 N 112.58 E
Dajing, Zhg. 100 28.24 N 121.07 E
Dajing, Zhg. 100 28.59 N 113.19 E
Dajin Shan II 106 30.41 N 121.26 E
Dajishan 100 24.38 N 114.26 E
Dajitai 104 42.20 N 121.11 E
Dajiuba 120 36.50 N 89.35 E
Daji Yang ⊔ 100 30.54 N 122.18 E
Daju 105 39.12 N 115.31 E
Da Juh 102 36.36 N 94.04 E
Dak ⊜ 128 32.48 N 61.14 E
Daka ≃ 150 8.19 N 0.13 W
Dakangpu 104 41.32 N 121.06 E
Dakanzi 104 40.52 N 122.53 E
Dakar 150 14.40 N 17.26 W
Dakar □[4] 150 14.45 N 17.25 W
Dākātia ≃[1] 126 22.57 N 90.42 E
Dakeng 100 26.18 N 115.32 E
Dakengkou 100 24.33 N 113.37 E
Daketa ≃ 144 7.16 N 42.13 E
Dak Gle 110 15.11 N 107.48 E
Dakhal, Bi'r ad- ⊤[4] 142 28.40 N 32.24 E
Dakhal, Wādī ad- V 142 28.49 N 32.45 E
Dākhilah, Al-Wāḥāt ad- ⊤[4] 140 25.30 N 29.05 E
Dakhin Shāhbāzpur Island I 126 22.30 N 90.45 E
Dakhla 148 23.43 N 15.57 W
Dakhlet Nouâdhibou □[4] 148 20.40 N 16.00 W
Dakingari 150 11.37 N 4.01 E
Dakka
→ Dhaka 124 23.43 N 90.25 E
Dākoānk 110 7.02 N 93.43 E
Dakongcheng 105 39.30 N 117.09 E
Dakongwan 104 40.51 N 122.19 E
Dakoro 150 14.31 N 6.46 E
Dakota City, Ia., U.S. 190 42.43 N 94.12 W
Dakota City, Ne., U.S. 198 42.24 N 96.25 W
Dakou 100 34.27 N 112.44 E
Dakoutun 105 39.35 N 117.14 E
Đakovica 38 42.23 N 20.25 E
Đakovo 38 45.19 N 18.25 E
Dakshingram 126 24.03 N 87.48 E
Dakumu 89 48.51 N 124.18 E
Dakunlun 98 36.34 N 117.52 E
Dakwa 154 4.00 N 26.26 E
Dakwah, Tall ad- ∧[2] 132 33.25 N 36.56 E
Dala, Ang. 152 11.03 S 20.17 E
Dala, Ang. 152 8.05 S 15.50 E
Dala, Sol.Is. 175e 8.35 S 160.40 E
Dalaas 58 47.07 N 10.00 E
Dalaba 150 10.42 N 12.15 W
Dalabani 150 10.28 N 9.27 W
Dala Cachibo 152 10.28 S 14.39 E
Dalad Qi 102 40.28 N 110.02 E
Dala-Floda 40 60.31 N 14.47 E
Dalaguete 116 9.46 N 123.32 E
Dalahan (Shiqizhan) 89 52.06 N 125.46 E
Dala-Husby 40 60.21 N 16.00 E
Dala-Järna 26 60.33 N 14.21 E
Dalajchöl 86 47.59 N 90.47 E
Dalaji 89 51.38 N 120.06 E
Dalälven ≃ 40 60.38 N 17.27 E
Dalama 130 37.47 N 28.04 E
Dalaman ≃ 130 36.40 N 28.45 E
Dalāmī 140 11.52 N 30.28 E
Dalan 100 23.19 N 114.47 E
Dalan Dzadgad 102 43.37 N 104.29 E
Dalandžargalan 102 45.55 N 109.05 E
Dalane ◆[1] 26 58.35 N 6.20 E
Dalang 100 22.57 N 113.56 E
Dalantuozi 104 41.28 N 122.47 E
Dalao 150 11.29 N 13.40 W
Dalarna □[9] 26 61.01 N 14.04 E
Dalarö 40 59.08 N 18.24 E
Dalat, Malay. 112 2.44 N 111.56 E
Da Lat, Viet 110 11.56 N 108.25 E
Dalayaozi 105 40.49 N 117.41 E
Dālbandin 128 28.53 N 64.25 E
Dalbeattie 44 54.56 N 3.49 W
D'Albertis Dome ∧ 164 5.00 S 142.05 E
Dalbosjön ⊂ 26 58.45 N 12.48 E
Dalby, Austl. 166 27.11 S 151.16 E
Dalby, Sve. 41 55.40 N 13.20 E
Dalby Söderskogs Nationalpark ♠ 41 55.43 N 13.17 E
Dalcahue 254 42.23 S 73.40 W
Dalch ≃ 42 50.52 N 3.47 W
Dale, Nor. 26 60.35 N 5.49 E
Dale, Nor. 26 61.22 N 5.25 E
Dale, Wales, U.K. 42 51.43 N 5.11 W
Dale, In., U.S. 194 38.10 N 86.59 W
Dale, Pa., U.S. 214 40.18 N 78.54 W
Dale, Tx., U.S. 222 29.56 N 97.34 W
Dale ≃ 168a 32.10 S 116.49 E
Dale, Mount ∧ 168a 32.08 S 116.18 E
Dale Bridge 168a 32.05 S 116.49 E
Dalecarlia
→ Dalarna □[9] 26 61.01 N 14.04 E
Dale City 208 38.38 N 77.18 W
Dale Hollow Lake ⊜[1] 192 36.36 N 85.19 W
Dale Lake ⊜ 204 34.08 N 115.42 W
Dalen 26 59.27 N 8.00 E
Dalengtu 98 41.11 N 113.45 E
Dalešice, údolní nádrž ⊜[1] 61 49.09 N 16.05 E
Daleside 158 26.30 S 28.04 E
Dale South ≃ 168a 32.16 S 116.47 E
Dalesville 206 45.42 N 74.24 W
Dalesville ≃ 206 45.40 N 74.24 W
Daleszyce 30 50.48 N 20.48 E
Dalet 110 19.59 N 93.51 E
Daleville, Al., U.S. 194 31.18 N 85.42 W
Daleville, In., U.S. 218 40.07 N 85.33 W
Daleville, Pa., U.S. 210 41.18 N 75.31 W
Dalfsen 52 52.30 N 6.16 E
Dalgaranga 162 27.46 S 117.02 E
Dalgaranger ∧ 162 27.51 S 117.06 E
Dalgety 171b 36.30 S 148.50 E
Dalgety Bay 46 56.02 N 3.20 W
Dalgety Brook ≃ 162 25.07 S 115.47 E
Dalgety Downs 162 25.17 S 116.15 E
Dalgomai 124 26.06 N 90.47 E
Dalhalvaig 46 58.28 N 3.54 W
Dalhart 196 36.03 N 102.30 W
Dalhausen 52 51.37 N 9.17 E
Dalhousie, N.B., Can. 186 48.04 N 66.23 W
Dalhousie, India 123 32.32 N 75.59 E
Dalhousie, Cape › 180 70.14 N 129.42 W
Dalhousie Island I 126 21.35 N 88.45 E
Dalhousie Lake ⊜ 212 44.58 N 76.35 W
Dalhousie Square ♠ 272b 22.33 N 88.22 E
Dali, Zhg. 102 34.47 N 109.57 E
Dali, Zhg. 102 25.38 N 100.09 E
Dalian (Dairen) 98 38.53 N 121.35 E
Dalian Dao I 100 25.40 N 119.42 E
Daliangdi 98 41.54 N 115.45 E
Daliang Shan ⋏ 102 28.00 N 103.00 E
Dalianhe 104 40.57 N 123.15 E
Daliankeng 105 40.54 N 117.45 E
Dalian Wan ⊂ 98 38.57 N 121.45 E

≃ River	Fluß	Río	Rivière	Rio	
⩩ Canal	Kanal	Canal	Canal	Canal	
∟ Waterfall, Rapids	Wasserfall, Stromschnellen	Cascada, Rápidos	Chute d'eau, Rapides	Cascata, Rápidos	
⊔ Strait	Meeresstraße	Estrecho	Détroit	Estreito	
⊂ Bay, Gulf	Bucht, Golf	Bahía, Golfo	Baie, Golfe	Baía, Golfo	
⊜ Lake, Lakes	See, Seen	Lago, Lagos	Lac, Lacs	Lago, Lagos	
⩨ Swamp	Sumpf	Pantano	Marais	Pântano	
⍓ Ice Features, Glacier	Eis- und Gletscherformen	Accidentes Glaciales	Formes glaciaires	Acidentes glaciares	
⊤ Other Hydrographic Features	Andere Hydrographische Objekte	Otros Elementos Hidrográficos	Autres données hydrographiques	Outros acidentes hidrográficos	
✤ Submarine Features	Untermeerische Objekte	Accidentes Submarinos	Formes de relief sous-marin	Acidentes submarinos	
□ Political Unit	Politische Einheit	Unidad Politica	Entité politique	Unidade política	
♁ Cultural Institution	Kulturelle Institution	Institución Cultural	Institution culturelle	Institução cultural	
⊥ Historical Site	Historische Stätte	Sitio Histórico	Site historique	Sitio histórico	
♠ Recreational Site	Erholungs- und Ferienort	Sitio de Recreo	Centre de loisirs	Area de Lazer	
⊠ Airport	Flughafen	Aeropuerto	Aéroport	Aeroporto	
■ Military Installation	Militäranlage	Instalación Militar	Installation militaire	Instalação militar	
◆ Miscellaneous	Verschiedenes	Misceláneo	Divers	Diversos	

Name	Page	Lat.°′	Long.°′
Dalianwukou	106	30.17 N	119.00 E
Daliao ≃	104	40.42 N	122.08 E
Dalías	34	36.49 N	2.52 W
Dälidağ ∧	84	39.55 N	46.02 E
Dalikou	100	26.52 N	118.00 E
Dälimämmadli	84	40.42 N	46.34 E
Dalin, Zhg.	89	43.43 N	122.45 E
Dalin, Zhg.	107	30.17 N	104.07 E
Daling	104	41.27 N	121.15 E
Daling ≃	98	40.56 N	121.43 E
Dalingbeigou	104	40.42 N	123.08 E
Dalipe Point ›	116	10.46 N	121.55 E
Daliushugou	104	40.46 N	122.14 E
Daliutai	104	41.25 N	121.55 E
Daliutun	104	42.14 N	122.46 E
Daliuzhen	105	38.51 N	116.19 E
Daliuzhuang	100	33.04 N	114.03 E
Daliyat et Karmil	132	32.42 N	35.03 E
Daliyya	132	32.35 N	35.04 E
Dalizi	98	41.45 N	126.49 E
Dalj	38	45.29 N	18.59 E
Daljā'	142	27.39 N	30.42 E
Dalkarlsberg	40	59.26 N	14.51 E
Dalkeith	46	55.54 N	3.04 W
Dālkola	124	25.52 N	87.51 E
Dall, Mount ∧	180	62.35 N	152.18 W
Dāllah, ʻAyn ⊤[4]	140	27.19 N	27.20 E
Dallardsville	222	30.38 N	94.38 W
Dallas, Scot., U.K.	46	57.33 N	3.28 W
Dallas, Al., U.S.	194	33.50 N	86.39 W
Dallas, Ga., U.S.	192	33.55 N	84.50 W
Dallas, N.C., U.S.	192	35.18 N	81.10 W
Dallas, Or., U.S.	202	44.55 N	123.18 W
Dallas, Pa., U.S.	210	41.20 N	75.57 W
Dallas, Tx., U.S.	222	32.46 N	96.47 W
Dallas, Wi., U.S.	190	45.15 N	91.48 W
Dallas □[6]	222	32.17 N	96.47 W
Dallas Center	190	41.41 N	93.57 W
Dallas City	190	40.38 N	91.10 W
Dallas-Fort Worth Regional Airport ⊠	222	32.54 N	97.01 W
Dallas Naval Air Station ■	222	32.44 N	96.59 W
Dallastown	208	39.53 N	76.38 W
Dallgow	54	52.32 N	13.05 E
Dallıbahçe	130	39.09 N	39.53 E
Dalli Rājhara	122	20.35 N	81.04 E
Dall Island I	182	54.50 N	132.55 W
Dall Lake ⊜	180	60.18 N	163.35 W
Dalmā I	128	24.30 N	52.20 E
Dalmacija □[9]	36	43.00 N	17.00 E
Dalmacio Vélez Sarsfield	252	32.36 S	63.35 W
Dalmally	46	56.24 N	4.58 W
Dalmatia	208	40.39 N	76.54 W
Dalmatia → Dalmacija □[9]	36	43.00 N	17.00 E
Dalmatovo	86	56.16 N	62.56 E
Dalmau	124	26.04 N	81.02 E
Dalmellington	44	55.19 N	4.24 W
Dalmeny	184	52.20 N	106.46 W
Dalmine	62	45.39 N	9.36 E
Dalmose	41	55.18 N	11.26 E
Dal'n'aja	89	45.56 N	142.04 E
Dal'n'aja Muja	88	54.21 N	103.37 E
Dalnaspidal	46	56.50 N	4.14 W
Dal'negorsk	89	44.35 N	135.35 E
Dal'neje-Konstantinovo	80	55.49 N	44.06 E
Dal'nerečensk	89	45.55 N	133.43 E
Dal'ne-Rusanovo	82	54.15 N	36.45 E
Dal'nyk	78	46.28 N	30.34 E
Daloa	150	6.53 N	6.27 W
Dalongchang	105	39.50 N	116.06 E
Dalonghua	105	39.18 N	115.18 E
Dalongtian	100	24.14 N	115.44 E
Dalovice	54	50.11 N	12.55 E
Dalqū	140	20.07 N	30.37 E
Dalroy	182	51.07 N	113.39 W
Dalry, Scot., U.K.	44	55.07 N	4.10 W
Dalry, Scot., U.K.	46	55.43 N	4.44 W
Dalrymple	44	55.23 N	4.35 W
Dalrymple, Mount ∧	166	21.02 S	148.38 E
Dalrymple Creek ≃	171a	27.59 S	151.46 E
Dalrymple Lake ⊜	212	44.38 N	79.07 W
Dalsbruk (Taalintehdas)	26	60.02 N	22.31 E
Dalsingpara	124	26.47 N	89.22 E
Dalsing Sarai	124	25.40 N	85.50 E
Dalsjöfors	26	57.43 N	13.05 E
Dalsland □[9]	26	58.30 N	12.50 E
Dals-Långed	26	58.55 N	12.18 E
Dal'stroja	180	68.19 N	177.39 W
Dāltenganj	124	24.02 N	84.04 E
Dalton, S. Afr.	158	29.20 S	30.40 E
Dalton, Eng., U.K.	262	53.34 N	2.46 W
Dalton, Ga., U.S.	192	34.47 N	84.58 W
Dalton, Ma., U.S.	207	42.28 N	73.10 W
Dalton, Ne., U.S.	198	41.24 N	102.58 W
Dalton, N.Y., U.S.	210	42.32 N	77.57 W
Dalton, Oh., U.S.	214	40.47 N	81.41 W
Dalton, Pa., U.S.	210	41.32 N	75.44 W
Dalton City	219	39.43 N	88.48 W
Dalton Gardens	202	47.43 N	116.46 W
Dalton-in-Furness	44	54.09 N	3.11 W
Dalu	104	41.27 N	123.19 E
Dalubeikou	105	38.59 N	117.12 E
Daludalu	114	1.05 N	100.15 E
Dalu Dao I	98	39.44 N	123.45 E
Daluis, Gorges de V	62	44.04 N	6.49 E
Dalum, Dan.	41	55.22 N	10.22 E
Dalum, Dtsch.	52	52.35 N	7.14 E
Daluojiazhuang	106	32.09 N	120.08 E
Daluotaozi	104	41.17 N	122.52 E
Daluoxi	100	25.14 N	118.36 E
Daluping	100	26.11 N	114.30 E
Dalupiri Island I, Pil.	116	19.05 N	121.14 E
Dalupiri Island I, Pil.	116	12.25 N	124.16 E
Daluxi	100	24.28 N	117.01 E
Dalview	273d	26.15 S	28.21 E
Dalvík	24a	65.59 N	18.32 W
Dalwallinu	162	30.17 S	116.40 E
Dalwhinnie	46	56.56 N	4.14 W
Dalworthington Gardens	222	32.42 N	97.10 W
Daly ≃	164	13.20 S	130.19 E
Daly Bay c	176	64.00 N	89.40 W
Daly City	226	37.43 N	122.31 W
Daly Lake ⊜	184	56.33 N	105.40 W
Daly Point ›	212	44.53 N	80.14 W
Daly River	164	13.45 S	130.50 E
Daly River Aboriginal Reserve ⊸[4]	164	14.20 S	130.00 E
Daly Waters	164	16.15 S	133.22 E
Dam ≃	120	33.56 N	92.41 E
Dāmā, Sūrīy.	132	32.57 N	36.25 E
Dama, Zhg.	100	32.03 N	118.02 E
Damačava	78	51.44 N	23.37 E
Damagum	146	11.41 N	11.20 E
Damān	122	20.25 N	72.51 E
Damān □[8]	122	20.10 N	73.00 E
Damanhār Shubra	273c	30.07 N	31.14 E
Damanhūr	142	31.02 N	30.28 E
Damanling	105	40.36 N	115.08 E
Damaopu	104	41.16 N	121.07 E
Damar	130	41.15 N	41.34 E
Damar, Pulau I, Indon.	164	7.09 S	128.40 E
Damar, Pulau I, Indon.	164	1.00 S	128.24 E
Damara	152	4.58 N	18.42 E
Damaraland □[9]	156	22.34 S	17.06 E
Damāș, Mișr	142	30.48 N	31.20 E
Damas → Dimashq, Sūrīy.	132	33.30 N	36.18 E
Damasco → Dimashq	132	33.30 N	36.18 E
Damascus → Dimashq, Sūrīy.	132	33.30 N	36.18 E
Damascus, Ar., U.S.	194	35.22 N	92.24 W
Damascus, Ga., U.S.	192	34.33 N	84.56 W
Damascus, Md., U.S.	208	39.17 N	77.12 W
Damascus, Oh., U.S.	214	40.54 N	80.58 W
Damascus, Pa., U.S.	210	41.42 N	75.04 W
Damascus, Va., U.S.	192	36.38 N	81.47 W
Damascus International Airport ⊠	132	33.29 N	36.13 E
Damaskus → Dimashq	132	33.30 N	36.18 E
Damāț	142	30.57 N	30.57 E
Damaturu	146	11.45 N	11.58 E
Damāvand	128	35.43 N	52.04 E
Damāvand, Qolleh-ye ∧	128	35.56 N	52.08 E
Damba, Ang.	152	6.41 S	15.08 E
Damba, Kaz.	80	46.57 N	51.47 E
Dambach-la-Ville	58	48.20 N	7.26 E
Dambarta	150	12.26 N	8.31 E
Dambeck	54	52.48 N	11.09 E
Dâmbovița □[6]	38	45.00 N	25.30 E
Dâmbovița ≃	38	44.14 N	26.27 E
Dambuki	89	54.21 N	127.38 E
Dam Doi	110	8.50 N	105.15 E
Damelevières	58	48.33 N	6.23 E
Damen Dao I	100	27.58 N	121.06 E
Damengjialazi	104	41.04 N	120.53 E
Damengzhuang	105	39.32 N	116.59 E
Damergou ⊸[1]	150	15.00 N	8.55 E
Damerham	42	50.57 N	1.52 W
Dämeritzsee ⊜	264a	52.25 N	13.45 E
Damery	50	49.04 N	3.53 E
Dames Quarter	208	38.11 N	75.53 W
Dam Gamad	140	13.17 N	27.28 E
Dāmghān	128	36.09 N	54.22 E
Damianópolis	255	14.33 S	46.10 W
Damianzhen	107	30.36 N	104.10 E
Damiao, Zhg.	98	42.26 N	118.22 E
Damiao, Zhg.	98	34.20 N	117.23 E
Damiao, Zhg.	102	37.18 N	104.39 E
Damiao, Zhg.	104	42.33 N	122.18 E
Damiaochang	107	29.39 N	106.05 E
Damiaogou	104	41.06 N	123.52 E
Damiaojiang	106	31.00 N	120.28 E
Damiaoshang	105	39.56 N	115.12 E
Dămienești	38	46.44 N	26.59 E
Damietta → Dumyāț	142	31.25 N	31.48 E
Damietta Branch → Dumyāț, Far' ≃	142	31.32 N	31.51 E
Damietta Mouth → Dumyāț, Mașabb ≃[1]	142	31.32 N	31.51 E
Damin	100	28.56 N	120.29 E
Daming	98	36.19 N	115.06 E
Damingzhen	104	42.34 N	123.36 E
Damintun	104	41.52 N	122.56 E
Dāmiyā	132	32.06 N	35.33 E
Damlacık	130	37.56 N	38.39 E
Damm	263	51.40 N	6.48 E
Dammai Island I	116	5.47 N	120.25 E
Dammarie	50	48.21 N	1.30 E
Dammarie-lès-Lys	50	48.31 N	2.39 E
Dammartin-en-Goële	50	49.03 N	2.41 E
Dammartin-en-Serve	50	48.54 N	1.37 E
Dammastock ∧	58	46.39 N	8.25 E
Damme, Bel.	50	51.15 N	3.17 E
Damme, Dtsch.	52	52.31 N	8.12 E
Damme, Dtsch.	54	53.17 N	14.01 E
Dammer Berge ⋏[2]	52	52.32 N	8.10 E
Dāmodar ≃	124	22.17 N	88.05 E
Dāmodar Main Canal ≍	126	23.01 N	87.53 E
Damoh, India	118	23.50 N	79.27 E
Damoh, India	124	23.50 N	79.27 E
Damon	222	29.17 N	95.45 W
Damongo	150	9.05 N	1.49 W
Damotapāda	272c	19.03 N	73.04 E
Damous	34	36.33 N	1.42 E
Damozhuang	105	39.53 N	115.40 E
Dampar, Tasek ⊜	114	3.02 N	102.43 E
Dampelas → Sabang	112	0.11 N	119.51 E
Dampier	162	20.39 S	116.45 E
Dampier, Cape ›	164	6.02 S	151.02 E
Dampier, Selat ⌴	164	0.40 S	130.40 E
Dampier Archipelago II	162	20.35 S	116.35 E
Dampier Land ›[1]	162	17.30 S	122.55 E
Dampierre, Fr.	50	48.42 N	1.59 E
Dampierre, Fr.	58	47.09 N	5.45 E
Dampierre, Château de ⊥	261	48.42 N	1.59 E
Dampierre-en-Burly	50	47.46 N	2.31 E
Dampierre-sur-Linotte	58	47.31 N	6.14 E
Dampierre-sur-Salon	58	47.33 N	5.41 E
Dampier Strait ⌴	164	5.36 S	148.12 E
Dampit	115a	8.13 S	112.45 E
Dampmart	261	48.53 N	2.44 E
Damprichard	58	47.15 N	6.53 E
Dâmrei, Chuŏr Phnum ⋏	110	11.00 N	104.05 E
Damují ≃	240p	22.11 N	80.33 W
Damüls	58	47.17 N	9.53 E
Dāmurhuda	126	23.36 N	88.47 E
Damutougou	98	42.28 N	118.56 E
Damville	50	48.52 N	1.04 E
Damvillers	56	49.20 N	5.24 E
Damxung	120	30.31 N	91.08 E
Dan	132	33.14 N	35.39 E
Dan ≃, U.S.	192	36.42 N	78.45 W
Dan ≃, Zhg.	102	33.02 N	111.20 E
Dana, Cam.	146	10.14 N	15.18 E
Dana, In., U.S.	194	39.48 N	87.29 W
Dana, Mount ∧	226	37.54 N	119.13 W
Dana, Pulau I	112	10.50 S	121.16 E
Danahu	102	42.28 N	93.32 E
Danai	112	0.29 N	103.26 E
Danajon Bank ⊸[4]	116	10.16 N	124.17 E
Danakil → Denakil ⊸[1]	144	13.00 N	41.00 E
Danakil National Park ♣	144	10.50 N	40.45 E
Danané	150	7.16 N	8.09 W
Da Nang	110	16.04 N	108.13 E
Danan'gou	105	40.32 N	117.49 E
Danao, Pil.	116	10.32 N	124.02 E
Danao, Pil.	116	12.29 N	122.39 E
Dana Point	228	33.29 N	117.44 W
Dana Point ›	228	33.28 N	117.43 W
Dānāpur	124	25.38 N	85.03 E
Danba	102	31.00 N	101.50 E
Danboro	208	40.21 N	75.08 W
Danbury, Eng., U.K.	42	51.44 N	0.33 E
Danbury, Ct., U.S.	207	41.23 N	73.27 W
Danbury, Ia., U.S.	198	42.14 N	95.43 W
Danbury, Ne., U.S.	198	40.02 N	100.24 W
Danbury, N.C., U.S.	192	36.24 N	80.12 W
Danbury, Tx., U.S.	222	29.14 N	95.21 W
Danby Lake ⊜	204	34.14 N	115.07 W
Dancheng	100	33.39 N	115.11 E
Danchengji	100	33.47 N	116.17 E
Dancug	144	10.58 N	49.04 E
Dand	120	31.37 N	65.41 E
Dandaragan	162	30.40 S	115.42 E
Dande ≃	152	8.28 S	13.21 E
Dandeli	122	15.15 N	74.37 E
Dandenong	169	37.59 S	145.12 E
Dandenong, Mount ∧	274b	37.50 S	145.21 E
Dandenong Creek ≃	274b	38.01 S	145.05 E
Dandenong Ranges National Park ♣	169	37.53 S	145.20 E
Danderyd	40	59.25 N	18.01 E
Dandīl	142	29.10 N	31.02 E
Dandong	98	40.08 N	124.20 E
Dandot	123	32.39 N	72.58 E
Dandridge	192	36.00 N	83.24 W
Dan Dume	150	11.27 N	7.10 E
Dane □[6]	216	43.04 N	89.15 W
Dane ≃	44	53.15 N	2.31 W
Dane County Regional Airport-Truax Field ⊠	216	43.08 N	89.20 W
Dänemark → Denmark □[1]	26	56.00 N	10.00 E
Dänemark-Strasse → Denmark Strait ⌴	10	67.00 N	25.00 W
Danevang	222	29.03 N	96.13 W
Danewitz	264a	52.44 N	13.40 E
Danfeng	102	33.40 N	110.17 E
Danfengzhen	102	24.50 N	103.56 E
Danforth, Il., U.S.	216	40.49 N	87.59 W
Danforth, Me., U.S.	188	45.39 N	67.52 W
Danforth Hills ⋏	200	40.15 N	108.00 W
Dang ≃	102	40.30 N	94.42 E
Dānga, Bngl.	126	23.54 N	90.36 E
Dānga, India	272b	22.47 N	88.28 E
Danga ≃	271c	1.27 N	103.43 E
Dangādiha	126	21.30 N	86.19 E
Dangan Liedao II	100	22.00 N	114.14 E
Dangara, Taj.	85	38.06 N	69.22 E
Dangara, Uzb.	85	40.35 N	70.54 E
Dangba	98	40.46 N	118.32 E
Dangchang	102	34.03 N	104.23 E
Dangcheng	98	38.46 N	114.34 E
Dange, Ang.	152	7.56 S	15.02 E
Dange, Ang.	152	8.09 S	14.46 E
Dange, Nig.	150	12.52 N	5.21 E
Dange-Iá-Menha	152	9.32 S	14.39 E
Danger, Point ›	171a	28.10 S	153.33 E
Danger Point ›	158	34.40 S	19.17 E
Danggali Conservation Park ♣	166	33.20 S	140.40 E
Danghe Nanshan ⋏	102	38.53 N	96.11 E
Danghui	105	40.03 N	117.04 E
Dangila	144	11.16 N	36.50 E
Dangkou	106	31.32 N	120.34 E
Dango	140	10.00 N	24.45 E
Dan Gora	150	11.30 N	8.09 E
Dāngori	120	27.40 N	95.32 E
Dangriga	232	16.58 N	88.13 W
Dangshan	98	34.26 N	116.21 E
Dangtu	100	31.34 N	118.30 E
Dan Gulbi	150	11.38 N	6.16 E
Dangyang	102	30.50 N	111.38 E
Dangyu	105	40.00 N	118.01 E
Dani	150	13.43 N	0.10 W
Dania	220	26.03 N	80.08 W
Daniel	200	42.51 N	110.04 W
Daniel, Mount ∧	224	47.34 N	121.11 W
Daniel Boone Home ⊥	219	38.39 N	90.52 W
Daniel Boone Homestead State Historic Site ⊥	208	40.21 N	75.49 W
Daniel-Johnson, Barrage ⊸[6]	186	50.39 N	68.44 W
Daniels	284b	39.26 N	77.03 W
Daniel's Harbour	186	50.14 N	57.35 W
Danielskuil	158	28.11 S	23.33 E
Danielson	207	41.48 N	71.53 W
Daniels Pass)(	200	40.18 N	111.15 W
Daniels Run ≃	284c	38.51 N	77.17 W
Danielsville, Ga., U.S.	192	34.07 N	83.13 W
Danielsville, Pa., U.S.	208	40.48 N	75.32 W
Danilov	80	58.12 N	40.12 E
Danilovka, Kaz.	86	52.23 N	70.39 E
Danilovka, Ross.	80	52.33 N	45.23 E
Danilovka, Ross.	80	50.21 N	44.06 E
Danilovo	82	55.40 N	38.46 E
Danilovskaja vozvyšennost' ⋏[1]	80	58.12 N	40.16 E
Danilovskoje	82	56.48 N	35.45 E
Daning, Zhg.	102	24.39 N	111.51 E
Daning, Zhg.	102	36.33 N	110.38 E
Daningbashi	85	38.45 N	75.04 E
Dänisch Nienhof	54	54.28 N	10.07 E
Daniupucun	104	41.23 N	122.37 E
Dänizkänarı	84	40.13 N	49.33 E
Danja	150	11.21 N	7.31 E
Danjiangkou Shuiku ⊜[1]	102	32.37 N	111.30 E
Danjo-guntō II	92	32.02 N	128.23 E
Danjoutin	58	47.37 N	6.52 E
Ḍank	128	23.33 N	56.17 E
Dankama	150	13.20 N	7.44 E
Dankersen	52	52.17 N	8.58 E
Danki	82	54.55 N	37.34 E
Dankov	76	53.15 N	39.08 E
Dankova, Pik ∧	85	41.05 N	77.38 E
Danleng, Zhg.	102	29.58 N	103.31 E
Danleng, Zhg.	102	29.18 N	103.10 E
Danleng, Zhg.	107	30.01 N	103.30 E
Danlí	236	14.00 N	86.35 W
Danmark → Denmark □[1]	26	56.00 N	10.00 E
Dannebrog	198	41.07 N	98.32 W
Dannemare	41	54.45 N	11.12 E
Dannemarie	58	47.38 N	7.08 E
Dannemora, Sve.	40	60.11 N	17.49 E
Dannemora, N.Y., U.S.	188	44.43 N	73.43 W
Dannenberg	54	53.06 N	11.05 E
Dannenreich	264a	52.19 N	13.45 E
Dannenwalde	54	53.04 N	13.11 E
Dannevirke	172	40.12 S	176.07 E
Dannewerk	41	54.29 N	9.31 E
Dannhauser	158	28.04 S	30.04 E
Dano	150	11.09 N	3.04 W
Danompari	112	0.09 N	115.02 E
Dañoso, Cabo ›	254	48.50 S	67.13 W
Dan Ryan Woods ♣	278	41.45 N	87.39 W
Dan Sai	110	17.17 N	101.09 E
Danshan	107	30.06 N	104.54 E
Danshui	100	22.49 N	114.27 E
Dansville, Mi., U.S.	216	42.34 N	84.18 W
Dansville, N.Y., U.S.	210	42.33 N	77.41 W
Dāntan	126	21.57 N	87.16 E
Dante	192	36.58 N	82.17 W
Dantewāra	122	18.54 N	81.21 E
Dantuzhen	106	32.12 N	119.31 E
Danube ≃	22	45.20 N	29.40 E
Danube, Mouths of the ≃[1]	38	45.10 N	29.50 E
Danubio → Danube ≃	22	45.20 N	29.40 E
Danubyu	110	17.15 N	95.35 E
Danvers, Il., U.S.	190	40.31 N	89.10 W
Danvers, Ma., U.S.	207	42.34 N	70.55 W
Danvers ≃	283	42.32 N	70.53 W
Danville, P.Q., Can.	206	45.47 N	72.01 W
Danville, Ar., U.S.	194	35.03 N	93.23 W
Danville, Ca., U.S.	226	37.49 N	121.59 W
Danville, Ga., U.S.	192	32.36 N	83.14 W
Danville, Il., U.S.	194	40.07 N	87.37 W
Danville, In., U.S.	218	39.45 N	86.31 W
Danville, Ky., U.S.	194	37.42 N	84.46 W
Danville, Mo., U.S.	219	38.54 N	91.32 W
Danville, Oh., U.S.	214	40.26 N	82.15 W
Danville, Pa., U.S.	210	40.57 N	76.36 W
Danville, Vt., U.S.	188	44.25 N	72.07 W
Danville, Va., U.S.	192	36.35 N	79.23 W
Danville, Wa., U.S.	182	48.59 N	118.30 W
Danxian (Nada)	110	19.35 N	109.17 E
Danyang, Zhg.	100	26.22 N	119.30 E
Danyang, Zhg.	106	32.00 N	119.35 E
Danylivka	83	49.08 N	39.38 E
Danzig → Gdańsk	30	54.23 N	18.40 E
Dao	116	10.31 N	121.57 E
Dâo ≃, Port.	34	40.20 N	8.11 W
Dao ≃, Zhg.	100	30.44 N	114.39 E
Daocheng	102	29.06 N	100.38 E
Daodemiao	89	43.41 N	120.19 E
Daodi	105	39.32 N	118.11 E
Daoguanhe	100	30.54 N	114.57 E
Daohu	100	29.42 N	117.29 E
Daolazui	105	40.06 N	115.06 E
Daoliban	104	41.52 N	121.37 E
Daolin	100	27.59 N	112.42 E
Daolinggang	98	34.02 N	114.34 E
Daoliupu	107	30.12 N	105.09 E
Daomaguan	98	39.07 N	114.38 E
Daosa	124	26.53 N	76.20 E
Daoshiwu	106	30.18 N	118.57 E
Daoshuqiao	106	31.51 N	119.41 E
Daotiandi	89	48.53 N	130.03 E
Dao Timmi	146	20.32 N	13.33 E
Daotou	98	37.14 N	120.20 E
Daoukro	150	7.03 N	3.58 W
Daoulas	32	48.22 N	4.15 W
Daoura, Oued V	148	28.15 N	3.30 W
Daoxian	102	25.35 N	111.27 E
Daozhen	102	28.42 N	107.56 E
Daozi	89	45.00 N	123.43 E
Dapa	116	9.46 N	126.03 E
Dapango	150	10.52 N	0.12 E
Dapanzhuang	98	37.20 N	115.28 E
Dapaozi	89	45.27 N	122.07 E
Dapchi	146	12.28 N	11.32 E
Dapdap	116	14.14 N	122.15 E
Dapeng	100	22.34 N	114.29 E
Da Peng Wan c	100	22.30 N	114.24 E
Daphne	194	30.36 N	87.54 W
Dapiak, Mount ∧	116	8.15 N	123.28 E
Daping, Zhg.	100	23.11 N	115.49 E
Daping, Zhg.	100	24.24 N	115.58 E
Dapingshan	102	25.30 N	109.39 E
Dapishi	100	26.30 N	112.54 E
Dapitan	116	8.39 N	123.25 E
Dapitan ≃	116	8.38 N	123.25 E
Dapitan Bay c	116	8.40 N	123.23 E
Dapto	170	34.30 S	150.47 E
Dapu, Zhg.	98	40.34 N	124.12 E
Dapu, Zhg.	100	23.16 N	113.32 E
Dapu, Zhg.	106	31.19 N	119.56 E
Dapujie	100	27.01 N	112.46 E
Da Qaidam	102	37.53 N	95.07 E
Da Qaidam Hu ⊜	102	37.50 N	95.00 E
Daqian	106	30.55 N	120.11 E
Daqiangmen	106	31.29 N	120.27 E
Daqiangzi	104	42.21 N	120.29 E
Daqiao, Zhg.	100	29.39 N	121.26 E
Daqiao, Zhg.	100	26.38 N	118.54 E
Daqiao, Zhg.	100	28.11 N	114.16 E
Daqiao, Zhg.	100	32.21 N	119.41 E
Daqiao, Zhg.	100	24.56 N	113.09 E
Daqiao, Zhg.	106	30.59 N	121.14 E
Daqiao, Zhg.	107	28.52 N	105.40 E
Daqiaojie	106	30.46 N	119.14 E
Daqiaokou	100	27.06 N	113.38 E
Daqiaotou	106	30.47 N	120.52 E
Daqiaozhai	102	25.21 N	106.15 E
Daqing	98	39.13 N	118.51 E
Daqing ≃	105	39.04 N	116.55 E
Daqinggou, Zhg.	98	41.16 N	114.10 E
Daqinggou, Zhg.	98	41.12 N	125.07 E
Daqing Shan ∧, Zhg.	89	45.35 N	127.51 E
Daqing Shan ∧, Zhg.	104	42.03 N	123.45 E
Daqing Shan ∧, Zhg.	104	41.47 N	121.15 E
Daqiu	100	25.24 N	119.39 E
Daqqāq	140	12.56 N	26.58 E
Daquan	102	41.21 N	95.17 E
Daquanshan	98	40.14 N	113.47 E
Daquantou	105	39.31 N	114.46 E
Daquanyan	104	42.37 N	123.32 E
Dāqūf	142	28.24 N	30.38 E
Daqu Shan I	100	30.27 N	122.20 E
Dara, Sén.	150	15.21 N	15.29 W
Dar'ā, Sūrīy.	132	32.37 N	36.06 E
Dar'ā □[8]	132	33.00 N	36.10 E
Dārāb	128	28.45 N	54.34 E
Darāban	120	31.44 N	70.20 E
Darabani	38	48.11 N	26.35 E
Darāfisah	140	13.23 N	31.59 E
Daraga	116	11.54 N	123.52 E
Daragodleh	144	10.10 N	44.51 E
Daraina	157b	13.12 S	49.40 E
Darājīl	142	30.39 N	30.52 E
Daram Island I	116	11.38 N	124.47 E
Dārān	128	32.59 N	50.24 E
Daraoli ⊸[8]	272c	19.11 N	72.48 E
Darap	112	1.13 S	112.03 E
Dār as-Salām	273c	29.59 N	31.13 E
Darasun	88	51.40 N	114.00 E
Daraut-Kurgan	85	39.33 N	72.13 E
Darave	272c	19.02 N	73.01 E
Darāw	140	24.25 N	32.56 E
Darawah	142	30.13 N	31.06 E
Dārayyā	132	33.27 N	36.15 E
Darazo	146	11.00 N	10.24 E
Darb Al-Hājj	142	30.10 N	31.33 E
Darb al-Ḥajj, Jabal ∧	132	30.05 N	35.26 E
Darband	123	34.20 N	72.52 E
Darbāsīyah	130	37.04 N	40.39 E
Darbaza	85	41.35 N	69.02 E
Darbėnai	76	56.01 N	21.15 E
Dar-ben-Karriche-el-Bahri	34	35.30 N	5.20 W
Darbhanga	124	26.10 N	85.54 E
Darbod (Taikang)	89	46.52 N	124.27 E
D'Arbonne, Bayou ≃	194	32.34 N	92.09 W
Darburruk	144	9.44 N	44.31 E
Darby, Mt., U.S.	202	46.01 N	114.10 W
Darby, Pa., U.S.	208	39.55 N	75.15 W
Darby, Cape ›	180	64.20 N	162.22 W
Darby Creek ≃	285	39.52 N	75.18 W
Darbydale	218	39.51 N	83.11 W
Darčeli	84	42.27 N	41.42 E
Darchan	88	49.29 N	105.55 E
D'Archiac, Mount ∧	172	43.28 S	170.35 E
D'Arcy	182	50.33 N	122.29 W
D'Arcy Island I	224	48.34 N	123.17 W
Darda	38	45.37 N	18.41 E
Dardadine	168a	33.14 S	116.50 E
Dardanelle, Ar., U.S.	194	35.13 N	93.09 W
Dardanelle, Ca., U.S.	226	38.20 N	119.50 W
Dardanelle Lake ⊜[1]	194	35.25 N	93.20 W
Dardanelles → Çanakkale Boğazı ⌴	130	40.15 N	26.25 E
Dardanup	168a	33.24 S	115.45 E
Dardara	34	35.08 N	5.15 W
Dardenelles Cone ∧	226	38.25 N	119.53 W
Dardenne Creek ≃	219	38.52 N	90.32 W
Dardesheim	54	51.59 N	10.49 E
Dardistān □[9]	123	35.30 N	74.00 E
Dare	208	37.10 N	76.26 W
Darebin Creek ≃	274b	37.47 S	145.02 E
Dareda	154	4.13 S	35.33 E
Dar-el-Beida → Casablanca	148	33.39 N	7.35 W
Darende	130	38.34 N	37.30 E
Darent ≃	42	51.28 N	0.13 E
Daresbury	262	53.21 N	2.38 W
Dar es Salaam	154	6.48 S	39.17 E
Dar es Salaam □[4]	154	6.30 S	39.25 E
Daressalam → Dar es Salaam	154	6.48 S	39.17 E
Darfeld	52	52.01 N	7.16 E
Darfo	64	45.53 N	10.11 E
Dārfūr ash-Shamālīyah □[4]	140	16.00 N	25.25 E
Dargai	123	34.30 N	71.54 E
Dargan-Ata	72	40.29 N	62.10 E
Dargaville	172	35.56 S	173.53 E
Dargeçit	130	37.33 N	41.44 E
Dargol	150	13.55 N	1.15 E
Dargol ≃	150	13.53 N	1.33 E
Dargun	54	53.54 N	12.51 E
Darhan Muminggan Lianheqi	102	41.50 N	110.27 E
Dari	140	5.48 N	30.21 E
Dāriāpur	126	23.36 N	89.27 E
Darıca	130	40.45 N	29.23 E
Darie Hills ⋏	144	8.21 N	47.16 E
Darién, Col.	246	3.56 N	76.31 W
Darien, Ct., U.S.	207	41.04 N	73.28 W
Darien, Ga., U.S.	192	31.22 N	81.26 W
Darien, Il., U.S.	278	41.45 N	87.58 W
Darien, N.Y., U.S.	210	42.54 N	78.21 W
Darien, Wi., U.S.	216	42.36 N	88.42 W
Darien, Parque Nacional ♣	246	7.40 N	77.40 W
Darién, Serranía del ⋏	246	8.20 N	77.22 W
Darien Center	210	42.54 N	78.23 W
Darien Lakes State Park ♣	210	42.55 N	78.25 W
Dariense, Cordillera ⋏	236	12.55 N	85.30 W
Dariganga	102	45.18 N	113.52 E
Darigayos Point ›	116	16.50 N	120.20 E
Dar'inskij	86	49.04 N	72.56 E
Dar'inskoje	80	51.20 N	51.44 E
Dariv	88	46.57 N	93.38 E
Darjevka	83	47.42 N	39.41 E
Dārjiling	124	27.02 N	88.16 E
Darkan	168a	33.20 S	116.44 E
Darke □[6]	218	40.06 N	84.38 W
Darke Peak	166	33.28 S	136.12 E
Darkhāna	123	30.39 N	72.11 E
Dar Khazīneh	128	31.54 N	48.59 E
Dark Head ›	241h	13.17 N	61.16 W
Darkin ≃	168a	32.00 S	116.14 E
Darkūsh	130	35.59 N	36.23 E
Darlag	102	33.48 N	99.52 E
Darley Woods	285	39.49 N	75.28 W
Darling, S. Afr.	158	33.23 S	18.23 E
Darling, Ms., U.S.	194	34.21 N	90.16 W
Darling ≃	166	34.07 S	141.55 E
Darling, Lake ⊜[1]	198	48.35 N	101.40 W
Darling Downs ⊸[1]	166	27.30 S	150.30 E
Darlingford	184	49.12 N	98.22 W
Darling Range ⋏	162	31.25 S	116.00 E
Darlington, Austl.	169	38.00 S	143.03 E
Darlington, Eng., U.K.	44	54.31 N	1.34 W
Darlington, Md., U.S.	208	39.38 N	76.12 W
Darlington, Pa., U.S.	214	40.49 N	80.26 W
Darlington, Pa., U.S.	285	39.54 N	75.28 W
Darlington, S.C., U.S.	192	34.17 N	79.52 W
Darlington, Wi., U.S.	190	42.40 N	90.07 W
Darlington Brook ≃	276	41.05 N	74.11 W
Darlington Corners	285	39.55 N	75.34 W
Darlington Range ⋏	171a	27.50 S	153.15 E
Darlot, Lake ⊜	162	27.48 S	121.35 E
Darłowo	30	54.26 N	16.23 E
Darmagī, Kūh-e ∧	128	26.35 N	58.54 E
Darmstadt	56	49.53 N	8.40 E
Darmstadt □[5]	56	49.45 N	8.40 E
Darnah	146	32.46 N	22.39 E
Darnall	158	29.23 S	31.18 E
Darnétal	50	49.27 N	1.09 E
Darney	58	48.05 N	6.03 E
Darnick	166	32.51 S	143.37 E
Darnley, Cape ›	9	67.43 S	69.30 E
Darnley Bay c	176	69.35 N	123.30 W
Daroca	34	41.07 N	1.25 W
Darodih	126	23.14 N	86.27 E
Daror	144	8.14 N	44.42 E
Dar-Ould-Zidouh	148	32.22 N	6.49 W
Darou Mousti	150	15.03 N	16.03 W
Darovoje	82	54.34 N	38.22 E
Darr ≃	166	23.39 S	143.50 E
Darra	171a	27.34 S	152.58 E
Darragh	279b	40.16 N	79.41 W
Darrah, Mount ∧	182	49.28 N	114.35 W
Darregueira	252	37.42 S	63.10 W
Darreh Gaz	128	37.27 N	59.07 E
Darrington	224	48.15 N	121.36 W
Darrouzett	196	36.27 N	100.20 W
Darryl Gardens	284b	39.25 N	76.25 W
Dārsana	126	23.32 N	88.52 E
Darscheid	56	50.12 N	6.53 E
Darss ›[1]	54	54.25 N	12.31 E
Darsser Ort ›	54	54.29 N	12.31 E
Dart ≃	42	50.20 N	3.33 W
Dart, Cape ›	9	73.06 S	126.20 W
Dār Ta'izzah	130	36.17 N	36.51 E
Dartford	42	51.27 N	0.14 E
Dartford □[8]	260	51.26 N	0.15 E
Dartford Tunnel ⊸[5]	260	51.28 N	0.16 E
Dartmoor	166	37.55 S	141.17 E
Dartmoor ⊸[3]	42	50.35 N	3.55 W
Dartmoor National Park ♣	42	50.37 N	3.52 W
Dartmouth, N.S., Can.	186	44.40 N	63.34 W
Dartmouth, Eng., U.K.	42	50.21 N	3.35 W
Dartmouth ≃	186	48.53 N	64.34 W
Dartmouth, Lake ⊜	166	26.04 S	145.18 E
Dartmouth Woods	285	39.50 N	75.31 W
Darton	44	53.36 N	1.32 W
Daru, Pap. N. Gui.	164	9.04 S	143.21 E
Daru, S.L.	150	7.59 N	10.50 W
Daruvar	36	45.36 N	17.13 E
Darvaza	128	40.11 N	58.24 E
Darvazskij chrebet ⋏	85	38.30 N	71.15 E
Darvel	46	55.37 N	4.18 W
Darvinskij zapovednik ⊸[4]	76	58.50 N	37.40 E
Darwāzahgêy	120	31.48 N	67.44 E
Darwen	44	53.42 N	2.28 W
Darwen ≃	262	53.45 N	2.41 W
Darwendale	154	17.43 S	30.33 E
Dārwha	122	20.19 N	77.46 E
Darwin, Arg.	254	39.12 S	65.46 W
Darwin, Austl.	164	12.28 S	130.50 E
Darwin, Bahía c	254	45.27 S	74.40 W
Darwin, Cordillera ⋏	254	54.40 S	70.00 W
Darwin, Isla I	246a	1.39 N	92.00 W
Darwin, Volcán ∧[1]	246a	0.10 S	91.18 W
Darwin River	164	12.49 S	130.58 E
Daryābād	124	26.53 N	81.33 E
Darya Khān	123	31.48 N	71.06 E
Daryāpur	120	20.56 N	77.20 E
Darzāb	120	35.58 N	65.22 E
Darzo	64	45.51 N	10.33 E
Dār Zubi	140	13.07 N	23.40 E
Dās	123	35.05 N	75.05 E
Dās I	128	25.09 N	52.53 E
Dasanjiazi	104	42.31 N	122.54 E
Daš Balbar	88	49.31 N	114.21 E
Dasburg	56	50.03 N	6.07 E
Daščhovuze □[8]	128	40.15 N	59.00 E
Dase → Dese	144	11.05 N	39.41 E
Dasha ≃	98	38.20 N	115.22 E
Dashafa	105	39.19 N	116.19 E
Dashalitu	104	42.31 N	122.30 E
Dashan	98	38.02 N	117.39 E
Dashankou	105	40.17 N	115.49 E
Dashanpu	107	29.25 N	104.49 E
Dashaping	100	29.24 N	113.51 E
Dashava	78	49.16 N	24.01 E
Dashengfenchang	106	31.53 N	121.34 E
Dashengpu	104	41.13 N	121.02 E
Dashentang	105	39.13 N	117.56 E
Dashetai	102	40.58 N	109.19 E
Dashi	107	30.39 N	105.37 E
Dashi ≃	105	39.35 N	116.05 E
Dashields Dam ⊸[6]	214	40.33 N	80.12 W
Dashiqiao, Zhg.	100	33.57 N	113.53 E
Dashiqiao, Zhg.	104	41.52 N	123.17 E
Dashiqiao, Zhg.	107	30.07 N	106.12 E
Dashiqiao, Zhg.	107	30.28 N	106.29 E
Dashitou, Zhg.	89	43.19 N	128.28 E
Dashitou, Zhg.	102	42.49 N	95.19 E
Dashiv	78	49.00 N	29.26 E
Dashizhai	89	46.16 N	121.25 E
Dashlūț	142	27.34 N	30.42 E
Dash Point	224	47.19 N	122.26 W
Dasht ≃	128	25.10 N	61.40 E
Dashu	106	31.13 N	120.56 E
Dashun	100	28.06 N	119.52 E
Dashutang	102	23.00 N	103.55 E
Dashuwan	105	40.37 N	117.19 E
Dasi (Huangfansi)	102	38.15 N	100.22 E
Dasiji	100	33.48 N	115.55 E
Dašinčilen	88	47.51 N	104.03 E
Dasing	60	48.23 N	11.03 E
Dasizhan	89	45.53 N	130.24 E

Name	Seite	Breite°′	Länge°′ E = Ost
Daska	123	32.20 N	74.21 E
Daṣkäsän	84	40.30 N	46.04 E
Daškauka	76	53.44 N	30.13 E
Daskop	158	33.44 S	22.43 E
Dasmina	126	22.17 N	90.35 E
Dasol	116	15.59 N	119.52 E
Dasol Bay c	116	15.53 N	119.51 E
Dassalan Island I	116	6.45 N	121.28 E
Dassel, Dtsch.	52	51.48 N	9.41 E
Dassel, Mn., U.S.	190	45.04 N	94.18 W
Dasseneiland I	158	33.26 S	18.04 E
Dasserat, Lac ⊜	190	48.16 N	79.25 W
Dassiefontein	158	31.35 S	24.25 E
Dassow	54	53.50 N	10.59 E
Dastakert	84	39.23 N	46.02 E
Dastgardān	128	34.19 N	56.51 E
Daštidžum	85	38.01 N	70.12 E
Daštioburdon	85	39.24 N	69.04 E
Dastjerd	128	34.33 N	50.15 E
Dasūa	123	31.49 N	75.38 E
Dāsuria	126	24.07 N	89.08 E
Datachang	107	28.55 N	104.21 E
Datagenoyang	112	2.03 N	115.10 E
Datai	105	39.58 N	115.54 E
Dataizi	104	41.17 N	121.46 E
Datan, Zhg.	98	41.35 N	116.00 E
Datan, Zhg.	98	39.31 N	122.11 E
Datang, Zhg.	100	24.47 N	113.43 E
Datang, Zhg.	100	25.17 N	114.56 E
Datang, Zhg.	102	22.23 N	108.23 E
Datang, Zhg.	102	24.11 N	109.00 E
Datça	130	36.45 N	27.40 E
Datchet	260	51.29 N	0.34 W
Datchet Reservoir ⊜[1]	260	51.29 N	0.33 W
Date	92a	42.27 N	140.51 E
Date Creek ≃	200	34.13 N	113.29 W
Datia	124	25.40 N	78.28 E
Datian, Zhg.	100	25.42 N	117.49 E
Datian, Zhg.	100	24.06 N	116.19 E
Datian Ding ∧	102	22.17 N	111.13 E
Datianwei	100	25.54 N	115.10 E
Dativli	272c	19.11 N	73.03 E
D'at'kovo	76	53.36 N	34.20 E
D'atlovo	82	56.14 N	36.16 E
Datong, Zhg.	89	46.03 N	124.50 E
Datong, Zhg.	100	30.48 N	117.45 E
Datong, Zhg.	100	32.50 N	118.52 E
Datong, Zhg.	102	37.03 N	101.45 E
Datong, Zhg.	102	40.05 N	113.18 E
Datong ≃	102	36.20 N	102.55 E
Datong Shan ⋏	102	38.00 N	99.30 E
Datongzhen	106	32.12 N	121.19 E
Datoushan	98	41.50 N	117.08 E
Dātra	272b	22.58 N	88.16 E
Datta	89	49.18 N	140.22 E
Dattapāra	126	23.01 N	90.53 E
Dattapukur	126	22.45 N	88.33 E
Dattapulia	126	23.14 N	88.43 E
Datteln	52	51.40 N	7.23 E
Datteln-Hamm-Kanal ≍	263	51.39 N	7.21 E
Dattilo	70	37.58 N	12.39 E
Datu, Tanjung ›	112	2.05 N	109.39 E
Datuan	106	30.58 N	121.44 E
Datumakuta	112	2.32 N	117.51 E
Datun, Zhg.	89	43.49 N	125.12 E
Datun, Zhg.	98	40.37 N	119.57 E
Datun, Zhg.	104	40.59 N	122.55 E
Datuopu	100	28.03 N	112.58 E
Datu Piang	116	7.01 N	124.30 E
Daua (Dawa) ≃	144	4.11 N	42.06 E
Daudkāndi	126	23.32 N	90.43 E
Dāud Khel	123	32.53 N	71.34 E
Daudnagar	124	25.02 N	84.24 E
Daugai	76	54.22 N	24.20 E
Daugård	41	55.44 N	9.43 E
Daugava (Zaḥodnjaja Dzvina) ≃	76	57.04 N	24.03 E
Daugavpils	76	55.53 N	26.32 E
Dauhinava	76	54.39 N	27.29 E
Dauin	116	9.12 N	123.16 E
Daulatabad	126	24.08 N	88.22 E
Daulatkhān	126	22.38 N	90.49 E
Daulatpur, Bngl.	126	24.00 N	88.52 E
Daulatpur, Bngl.	126	22.53 N	89.31 E
Daulatpur, Bngl.	126	23.58 N	89.50 E
Daulatpur, India	272b	22.26 N	88.18 E
Daulatpur, Pāk.	120	26.30 N	67.58 E
Daulatpur ⊸[8]	272a	28.44 N	77.06 E
Daule, Ec.	246	0.24 N	80.00 W
Daule, Ec.	246	1.50 S	79.56 W
Daule, India	272c	19.10 N	73.03 E
Daule ≃	246	2.10 S	79.52 W
Daultāla	123	33.12 N	73.09 E
Daulton Creek ≃	226	37.04 N	119.59 W
Daun	56	50.11 N	6.50 E
Daund	122	18.28 N	74.36 E
Daung Kyun I	110	12.14 N	98.05 E
Dauphin, Mb., Can.	184	51.09 N	100.03 W
Dauphin, Pa., U.S.	208	40.22 N	76.55 W
Dauphin □[6]	208	40.15 N	76.52 W
Dauphin ≃	184	51.58 N	98.04 W
Dauphiné □[9]	62	44.50 N	6.00 E
Dauphin Island	194	30.15 N	88.07 W
Dauphin Island I	194	30.14 N	88.12 W
Dauphin Lake ⊜	184	51.17 N	99.48 W
Daura	150	13.02 N	8.21 E
Daurija	88	49.56 N	116.52 E
Daurskoje	86	55.14 N	92.05 E
Dausenau	56	50.20 N	7.45 E
D'Auteuil, Lac ⊜	186	50.38 N	61.17 W
Dautphetal	56	50.51 N	8.32 E
Däväçi	84	41.12 N	48.59 E
Dāvangere	122	14.28 N	75.55 E
Davant	194	29.37 N	89.51 W
Davao	116	7.04 N	125.36 E
Davao □[4]	116	7.40 N	125.50 E
Davao ≃	116	7.04 N	125.37 E
Davao del Sur □[4]	116	6.50 N	125.20 E
Davao Gulf c	116	6.40 N	125.55 E
Davao Oriental □[4]	116	7.30 N	126.30 E
Dāvar Panāh	128	27.21 N	62.21 E
Dāvarzan	128	36.23 N	56.50 E
Davegoriale	144	8.45 N	44.50 E
Davel	158	26.24 S	29.40 E
Daveluyville	206	46.12 N	72.08 W
Davenda	88	53.33 N	119.18 E
Davenham	262	53.14 N	2.31 W
Davenport, Ca., U.S.	226	37.00 N	122.11 W
Davenport, Fl., U.S.	220	28.09 N	81.36 W
Davenport, Ia., U.S.	190	41.31 N	90.34 W
Davenport, Ne., U.S.	198	40.18 N	97.48 W
Davenport, N.Y., U.S.	210	42.28 N	74.51 W
Davenport, Ok., U.S.	196	35.42 N	96.45 W
Davenport, Wa., U.S.	202	47.39 N	118.08 W
Davenport, Mount ∧	162	22.23 S	130.51 E
Davenport Downs	166	24.08 S	141.07 E
Davenport Range ⋏	162	20.47 S	134.48 E
Daventry	42	52.16 N	1.09 W
Davey, Port c	166	43.19 S	145.55 E
Daveyton	273d	26.09 S	28.25 E
David	236	8.26 N	82.26 W
David City	198	41.15 N	97.07 W
Davids Island I	276	40.53 N	73.46 W
Davidson, Sk., Can.	184	51.16 N	105.59 W
Davidson, N.C., U.S.	192	35.29 N	80.50 W
Davidson, Ok., U.S.	196	34.14 N	99.04 W
Davidson, Mount ∧	170	33.09 S	150.07 E
Davidson Creek ≃	222	30.21 N	96.27 W
Davidson Heights	214	40.35 N	80.15 W
Davidson Lake ⊜	184	53.47 N	99.37 W
Davidson Mountains ⋏	180	68.45 N	142.10 W
Davidson Park ♣	274a	33.45 S	151.12 E
Davidsville	214	40.14 N	78.56 W
Davie	220	26.03 N	80.13 W
Davies, Mount ∧	162	26.14 S	129.16 E
Davignab	158	27.32 S	19.48 E
Davila	116	18.29 N	120.35 E
Davilla	222	30.47 N	97.17 W
Davington	44	55.18 N	3.12 W

Symbols in the index entries represent the broad categories identified in the key at the right. Symbols with superior numbers (⋏[1]) identify subcategories (see complete key on page I · 1).

Symbole im Register stellen die rechts im Schlüssel erklärten Kategorien dar. Symbole mit hochgestellten Ziffern (⋏[1]) bezeichnen Unterabteilungen einer Kategorie (vgl. vollständiger Schlüssel auf Seite I · 1).

Los símbolos incluídos en el texto del índice representan las grandes categorías identificadas con la clave a la derecha. Los símbolos con numeros en su parte superior (⋏[1]) identifican las subcategorías (véase la clave completa en la página I · 1).

Les symboles de l'index représentent les catégories indiquées dans la légende à droite. Les symboles suivis d'un indice (⋏[1]) représentent des souscatégories (voir légende complète à la page I · 1).

Os símbolos incluídos no texto do índice representam as grandes categorias identificadas com a chave à direita. Os símbolos com números em sua parte superior (⋏[1]) identificam as subcategorias (veja-se a chave completa à página I · 1).

	English	Deutsch	Español	Français	Português
∧	Mountain	Berg	Montaña	Montagne	Montanha
⋏	Mountains	Gebirge	Montañas	Montagnes	Montanhas
)(	Pass	Paß	Paso	Col	Passo
V	Valley, Canyon	Tal, Cañon	Valle, Cañón	Vallée, Canyon	Vale, Canhão
≃	Plain	Ebene	Llano	Plaine	Planície
›	Cape	Kap	Cabo	Cap	Cabo
I	Island	Insel	Isla	Île	Ilha
II	Islands	Inseln	Islas	Îles	Ilhas
◆	Other Topographic Features	Andere Topographische Objekte	Otros Elementos Topográficos	Autres données topographiques	Cutros acidentes topográficos

ESPAÑOL — Nombre	FRANÇAIS — Nom	PORTUGUÊS — Nome
Página / Lat. / Long. W=Oeste	Page / Lat. / Long. W=Ouest	Página / Lat. / Long. W=Oeste

Legend (symbols):

Symbol	English	Deutsch	Español	Français	Português
≃	River	Fluß	Río	Rivière	Rio
⨆	Canal	Kanal	Canal	Canal	Canal
L	Waterfall, Rapids	Wasserfall, Stromschnellen	Cascada, Rápidos	Chute d'eau, Rapides	Cascata, Rápidos
⨆	Strait	Meeresstraße	Estrecho	Détroit	Estreito
c	Bay, Gulf	Bucht, Golf	Bahía, Golfo	Baie, Golfe	Baía, Golfo
⊚	Lake, Lakes	See, Seen	Lago, Lagos	Lac, Lacs	Lago, Lagos
≊	Swamp	Sumpf	Pantano	Marais	Pântano
⊠	Ice Features, Glacier	Eis- und Gletscherformen	Accidentes Glaciales	Formes glaciaires	Acidentes glaciares
⊽	Other Hydrographic Features	Andere Hydrographische Objekte	Otros Elementos Hidrográficos	Autres données hydrographiques	Outros acidentes hidrográficos
✦	Submarine Features	Untermeerische Objekte	Accidentes Submarinos	Formes de relief sous-marin	Acidentes submarinos
⊡	Political Unit	Politische Einheit	Unidad Política	Entité politique	Unidade política
☆	Cultural Institution	Kulturelle Institution	Institución Cultural	Institution culturelle	Instituição cultural
⌂	Historical Site	Historische Stätte	Sitio Histórico	Site historique	Sitio Histórico
♦	Recreational Site	Erholungs- und Ferienort	Sitio de Recreo	Centre de loisirs	Area de Lazer
⊡	Airport	Flughafen	Aeropuerto	Aéroport	Aeroporto
■	Military Installation	Militäranlage	Instalación Militar	Installation militaire	Instalação militar
←	Miscellaneous	Verschiedenes	Misceláneo	Divers	Diversos

Name	Page	Lat.	Long.
Dembecha	144	10.35 N	37.30 E
Dembéni	157a	11.50 S	43.24 E
Dembi	144	8.05 N	36.27 E
Dembia, Centraf.	154	5.07 N	24.25 E
Dembia, R.D.C.	154	3.31 N	25.50 E
Dembi Dolo	144	8.32 N	34.48 E
Dembo	152	3.56 S	12.35 E
Dême ≏	50	47.43 N	0.29 E
Demen	54	53.38 N	11.46 E
Demer ≏	56	50.58 N	4.42 E
Demerara ≏	246	6.48 N	58.10 W
Demerara-Mahaica □[4]	246	6.40 N	58.00 W
Demerthin	54	52.58 N	12.17 E
Demidov	76	55.16 N	31.31 E
Demidovo	76	59.17 N	38.17 E
Deming, N.M., U.S.	200	32.16 N	107.45 W
Deming, Wa., U.S.	224	48.49 N	122.12 W
Demini ≏	246	0.46 S	62.56 W
Demirci	130	39.03 N	28.40 E
Demirköprü Barajı ⊜[1]	130	38.40 N	28.20 E
Demirköy	130	41.49 N	27.45 E
Demirtaş	130	40.16 N	29.06 E
Demitz-Thumitz	54	51.09 N	14.14 E
Demjanka ≏	86	59.34 N	69.20 E
Demjanovo	24	60.22 N	47.03 E
Demjanskoje	86	59.36 N	69.18 E
Demjas	80	51.13 N	49.08 E
Demmeltrath ◆[8]	263	51.11 N	7.03 E
Demmin	54	53.54 N	13.02 E
Demmitt	182	55.26 N	119.54 W
Demnate	148	31.44 N	6.59 W
Democracy Monument ⊥	269a	13.45 N	100.30 E
Democrat Point ›	276	40.37 N	73.18 W
Demoiselles, Grotte des ±[5]	62	43.55 N	3.45 E
Demone, Val ◆[1]	70	37.58 N	14.35 E
Demonte	62	44.19 N	7.17 E
De Montigny, Lac ⊜	190	48.08 N	77.54 W
Demopolis	194	32.31 N	87.50 W
Demorest	192	34.33 N	83.32 W
De Mossville	218	38.48 N	84.25 W
Demotte	216	41.12 N	87.12 W
Dempo, Gunung ∧	112	4.02 S	103.09 E
Dempster, Point ›	162	33.39 S	123.52 E
Demsa	146	9.32 N	13.14 E
Demta	164	2.20 S	140.08 E
Demuryne	78	48.10 N	36.29 E
Demydivka	78	50.25 N	25.20 E
De Naauwte	158	30.08 S	21.42 E
Denain	50	50.20 N	3.23 E
Denair	226	37.32 N	120.47 W
Denakil ◆[1]	144	13.00 N	41.00 E
Denali	180	63.11 N	147.28 W
Denali National Park	180	63.44 N	148.54 W
Denali National Park ♠	180	63.15 N	150.30 W
Denan	144	6.30 N	43.30 E
Denare Beach	184	54.40 N	102.05 W
Denau	85	38.16 N	67.54 E
Denbigh, On., Can.	212	45.08 N	77.16 W
Denbigh, Wales, U.K.	44	53.11 N	3.25 W
Denbigh, Cape ›	180	64.23 N	161.31 W
Den Burg	52	53.03 N	4.48 E
Denby Dale	44	53.35 N	1.38 W
Den Chai	110	17.59 N	100.04 E
Dendang	112	3.05 S	107.54 E
Dender (Dendre) ≏	50	51.02 N	4.06 E
Denderleeuw	50	50.53 N	4.04 E
Dendermonde	50	51.02 N	4.07 E
Dendre (Dender) ≏	50	51.02 N	4.06 E
Dendron, S. Afr.	156	23.25 S	29.11 E
Dendron, Va., U.S.	208	37.02 N	76.56 W
Dendy Park ♠	274b	37.56 S	145.00 E
Deneba	144	9.50 N	39.09 E
Denekamp	52	52.23 N	7.00 E
Denenchōfu ◆[8]	268	35.35 N	139.41 E
Deneysville	158	26.53 S	28.06 E
Denezhnykove	83	49.02 N	38.57 E
Denežnikovo	82	55.26 N	38.07 E
Dengcheng	100	33.41 N	114.27 E
Deng Deng	152	5.12 N	13.31 E
Denge	154	3.34 N	28.14 E
Denge Marsh ≡	42	50.57 N	0.55 E
Dengfeng	100	34.29 N	113.04 E
Denggongchang	107	30.24 N	103.49 E
Dengguanzhen	107	29.10 N	104.56 E
Dengkou	102	40.20 N	106.59 E
Denglongshu	98	41.20 N	115.15 E
Dengmingsi	98	37.53 N	116.42 E
Dêngqên	102	31.32 N	95.27 E
Dengshahe	98	39.13 N	122.04 E
Dengta	100	24.01 N	114.49 E
Denguiro	152	5.38 N	23.02 E
Dengxian	102	32.42 N	112.01 E
Dengyoufang	98	41.34 N	114.32 E
Den Haag → 's-Gravenhage	52	52.06 N	4.18 E
Denham, Austl.	162	25.55 S	113.32 E
Denham, Eng., U.K.	260	51.34 N	0.30 W
Denham, In., U.S.	216	41.09 N	86.43 W
Denham, Mount ∧	241q	18.13 N	77.32 W
Denham Aerodrome ⊠	260	51.36 N	0.31 W
Denham Island I	166	16.43 S	139.09 E
Denham Place ♥	260	51.34 N	0.30 W
Denham Range ⋏	166	21.55 S	147.46 E
Denham Sound ʮ	162	25.40 S	113.15 E
Denham Springs	194	30.29 N	90.57 W
Den Helder	52	52.54 N	4.45 E
Denholme	262	53.48 N	1.54 W
Dénia	34	38.51 N	0.07 E
Denial Bay	162	32.06 S	133.32 E
Dénié	150	11.14 N	7.29 W
Deniliquin	166	35.32 S	144.58 E
Deniskoviči	76	52.19 N	31.43 E
Denison, Ia., U.S.	198	42.01 N	95.21 W
Denison, Tx., U.S.	196	33.45 N	96.32 W
Denison, Mount ∧	180	58.25 N	154.27 W
Denison Dam ◆[6]	196	33.50 N	96.34 W
Denisovka	24	66.14 N	55.20 E
Denisōvo	82	54.28 N	37.51 E
Denisy	261	48.33 N	1.56 E
Denizli	130	37.46 N	29.06 E
Denizli □[4]	130	37.40 N	29.15 E
Denkanikota	122	12.32 N	77.48 E
Denkendorf	60	48.56 N	11.27 E
Denkingen	58	47.53 N	9.19 E
Denklingen	58	47.55 N	10.51 E
Den'kovo	82	56.01 N	36.21 E
Denmark, Austl.	162	34.57 S	117.21 E
Denmark, S.C., U.S.	192	33.19 N	81.08 W
Denmark, Wi., U.S.	190	44.20 N	87.49 W
Denmark (Danmark) □[1], Europe	22	56.00 N	10.00 E
Denmark (Danmark) □[1], Europe	26	56.00 N	10.00 E
Denmark, Lake ⊜	276	40.58 N	74.31 W
Denmark Bay C	176	70.33 N	103.20 W
Denmark Strait ʮ	10	67.00 N	25.00 W
Denmead	42	50.54 N	1.04 W
Dennemont	261	49.01 N	1.42 E
Dennery	241f	13.55 N	60.54 W
Dennis	207	41.44 N	70.11 W
Dennis Head ›	46	59.23 N	2.23 W
Dennison	214	40.23 N	81.20 W
Dennis Port	207	41.39 N	70.07 W
Denniston	172	41.44 S	171.48 E
Denniston Creek ≏	282	37.30 N	122.28 W
Dennisville	208	39.11 N	74.49 W
Denny	46	56.02 N	3.55 W
Den Oever	52	52.56 N	5.02 E
Denouval	261	48.58 N	2.03 E
Denpasar	115b	8.39 S	115.13 E
Denshaw	262	53.35 N	2.02 W
Dent Ditch ≖	279a	41.18 N	82.08 W
Denton, Eng., U.K.	44	53.27 N	2.07 W
Denton, Md., U.S.	208	38.53 N	75.49 W
Denton, Mi., U.S.	281	42.20 N	83.03 W
Denton, Mt., U.S.	202	47.19 N	109.56 W
Denton, N.C., U.S.	192	35.38 N	80.06 W
Denton, Tx., U.S.	222	33.12 N	97.07 W
Denton □[6]	222	33.07 N	97.10 W
Denton Creek ≏	196	32.58 N	96.57 W
Dentonia Park ♠	275b	43.42 N	79.17 W
D'Entrecasteaux, Point ›	162	34.50 S	116.00 E
D'Entrecasteaux Islands II	164	9.30 S	150.40 E
D'Entrecasteaux National Park ♠	162	34.41 S	115.58 E
Dents du Midi ⋏	58	46.10 N	6.56 E
Denver, Co., U.S.	200	39.44 N	104.59 W
Denver, In., U.S.	216	40.51 N	86.04 W
Denver, Ia., U.S.	190	42.40 N	92.20 W
Denver, Pa., U.S.	208	40.13 N	76.08 W
Denver City	196	32.57 N	102.49 W
Denville	210	40.53 N	74.28 W
Denzlingen	58	48.04 N	7.52 E
Deoband	124	29.42 N	77.41 E
Deocha	126	24.03 N	87.35 E
Deodoro ◆[8]	287a	22.51 S	43.23 W
Deogarh, India	120	25.32 N	73.54 E
Deogarh, India	122	21.32 N	84.44 E
Deogarh, India	124	24.33 N	78.15 E
Deogarh ∧	124	23.32 N	82.16 E
Deogarh Hills ⋏[2]	124	23.35 N	82.30 E
Deoghar	124	24.29 N	86.42 E
Deogsu Palace ♥	271b	37.35 N	126.58 E
Deolāli	122	19.57 N	73.50 E
Deoli	126	22.03 N	86.49 E
Deoli ◆[8]	272a	28.30 N	77.14 E
Deongwar, Mount ∧	171a	27.12 S	152.16 E
Deopāra	126	22.55 N	90.15 E
Deori, India	124	23.08 N	78.41 E
Deori, India	124	23.24 N	79.01 E
Deoria	124	26.31 N	83.47 E
Deosai Mountains ⋏	123	35.20 N	75.12 E
Deosil	124	23.42 N	82.15 E
Dep ≏	89	52.54 N	127.45 E
Depāl	126	21.44 N	87.33 E
De Panne	50	51.06 N	2.35 E
Depāra	272b	22.53 N	88.34 E
Departure Bay	224	49.12 N	123.58 W
DePaul University ♥[2]	278	41.56 N	87.39 W
Depauville	212	44.08 N	76.04 W
Depauw	218	38.20 N	86.13 W
De Peel ≡	52	51.25 N	6.00 E
De Pere	190	44.26 N	88.03 W
Depew, N.Y., U.S.	210	42.54 N	78.41 W
Depew, Ok., U.S.	196	35.48 N	96.30 W
Deping	98	37.28 N	116.57 E
De Pinte	50	51.00 N	3.39 E
Depoe Bay	202	44.48 N	124.03 W
Depok	115a	6.24 S	106.50 E
Deport	196	33.32 N	95.19 W
Deposit	210	42.03 N	75.25 W
Deptford	285	39.50 N	75.07 W
Deptford ◆[8]	260	51.28 N	0.02 W
Deptford Mall ◆[9]	285	39.50 N	75.06 W
Deptford Terrace	285	39.48 N	75.09 W
Depuch Island I	162	20.38 S	117.43 E
Depue	190	41.19 N	89.18 W
Deputy	218	38.48 N	85.39 W
Dêqên	102	28.38 N	98.52 E
Deqing, Zhg.	102	23.09 N	111.45 E
Deqing, Zhg.	106	30.33 N	120.05 E
De Queen	194	34.02 N	94.20 W
De Quincy	194	30.27 N	93.25 W
Dera ≏	264c	47.39 N	19.05 E
Dera, Lach (Lak Dera) V	144	0.35 N	41.50 E
Dera Bugti	120	29.02 N	69.09 E
Dera Ghāzi Khān	123	30.03 N	70.38 E
Dera Gopipur	123	31.54 N	76.13 E
Dera Ismāīl Khān	123	31.50 N	70.54 E
Derakht-e Yaḥyá	120	31.50 N	68.08 E
Dera Nānak	123	32.02 N	75.01 E
Dera Nawāb	123	29.06 N	71.16 E
Derāwar Fort	123	28.46 N	71.20 E
Derazhnya	78	49.16 N	27.26 E
Derbent	84	42.03 N	48.18 E
Derbeškinskij	80	55.52 N	53.30 E
Derbetovka	80	45.48 N	43.05 E
Der Bodden ʮ	54	54.16 N	13.12 E
Derby, Austl.	162	17.18 S	123.38 E
Derby, Austl.	166	41.09 S	147.47 E
Derby, S. Afr.	158	25.55 S	27.02 E
Derby, Eng., U.K.	42	52.55 N	1.29 W
Derby, Ct., U.S.	207	41.19 N	73.05 W
Derby, Ks., U.S.	198	37.32 N	97.16 W
Derby, Me., U.S.	188	45.14 N	68.58 W
Derby, N.Y., U.S.	210	42.40 N	78.58 W
Derby, Oh., U.S.	218	39.46 N	83.12 W
Derby, Vt., U.S.	206	44.57 N	72.08 W
Derby Acres	226	35.15 N	119.35 W
Derby Line	206	45.00 N	72.05 W
Derbyshire □[6]	44	53.00 N	1.33 W
Der-Chantecoq, Lac du ⊜[1]	58	48.35 N	4.46 E
Derdepoort	156	24.42 S	26.20 E
Dere	130	39.00 N	39.18 E
Derecske	30	47.21 N	21.34 E
Dereköy, Tür.	130	39.16 N	27.19 E
Dereköy, Tür.	130	40.08 N	37.47 E
Dereköy, Tür.	130	41.56 N	27.21 E
Dereli	130	40.45 N	38.27 E
Derenburg	54	51.52 N	10.54 E
Derendorf ◆[8]	263	51.15 N	6.48 E
Derenwu	105	39.40 N	116.46 E
Dereseki ◆[8]	267b	41.08 N	29.08 E
Derev'anka	24	61.34 N	34.27 E
Derg ≏	48	54.44 N	7.25 W
Derg, Lough ⊜, Ire.	48	52.57 N	8.19 W
Derg, Lough ⊜, Ire.	48	54.36 N	7.53 W
Dergači	80	51.14 N	48.46 E
Dergaon	120	26.42 N	93.58 E
Der Grabow C	54	54.23 N	12.50 E
Derhachi	78	50.07 N	36.07 E
De Ridder	194	30.50 N	93.17 W
De Rijp	52	52.34 N	4.50 E
Derik	130	37.22 N	40.17 E
Derinkuyu	130	38.23 N	34.45 E
Der Kanal → English Channel ʮ	28	50.20 N	1.00 W
Derkul	80	51.16 N	51.18 E
Derkul ≏	83	48.35 N	39.41 E
Dermbach	56	50.43 N	10.06 E
Dermentobe	86	45.44 N	63.37 E
Dermott	194	33.31 N	91.26 W
Dermulo	64	46.20 N	11.04 E
Derne	263	51.35 N	7.41 E
Derne ◆[8]	263	51.34 N	7.31 E
Dernieres, Isles II	194	29.02 N	90.47 W
Dernoviči	78	51.36 N	29.43 E
Deroche	224	49.11 N	122.04 W
Dero Eri	144	9.01 N	46.43 E
Dêrong	102	28.47 N	99.14 E
Déroute, Passage de la ʮ	32	49.25 N	2.00 W
Derrame	196	26.19 N	104.23 W
Derravaragh, Lough ⊜	48	53.40 N	7.24 W
Derre	154	16.56 S	36.11 E
Derrick City	214	41.58 N	78.34 W
Derrinallum	169	37.57 S	143.13 E
Derry → Londonderry, N. Ire., U.K.	48	54.59 N	7.20 W
Derry, N.H., U.S.	188	42.52 N	71.19 W
Derry, Pa., U.S.	214	40.20 N	79.18 W
Derrybrien	48	53.04 N	8.36 W
Derrykeighan	48	55.08 N	6.29 W
Derryveagh Mountains ⋏	48	55.00 N	8.05 W
Derry West	275b	43.39 N	79.42 W
Der Sārāi ◆[8]	272a	28.33 N	77.11 E
Dersau	54	54.07 N	10.20 E
Dersingham	42	52.51 N	0.30 E
Derudeb	140	17.32 N	36.06 E
De Rust	158	33.30 S	22.32 E
Deruta	66	42.59 N	12.25 E
De Ruyter	210	42.45 N	75.53 W
DeRuyter Reservoir ⊜[1]	210	42.49 N	75.53 W
Der'uzino	82	56.18 N	38.16 E
Derval	32	47.40 N	1.40 W
Derventa	38	44.58 N	17.55 E
Derwent	182	53.39 N	110.58 W
Derwent ≏, Austl.	166	43.03 S	147.22 E
Derwent ≏, Eng., U.K.	44	54.57 N	1.41 W
Derwent ≏, Eng., U.K.	44	54.38 N	3.34 W
Derwent ≏, Eng., U.K.	44	52.53 N	1.17 W
Derwent ≏, Eng., U.K.	44	53.45 N	0.57 W
Derwent Bridge	166	42.08 S	146.13 E
Derwent Reservoir ⊜[1]	44	54.50 N	2.00 W
Derwent Water ⊜	44	54.34 N	3.08 W
Deržavino	80	53.13 N	52.22 E
Deržavinsk	86	51.03 N	66.19 E
Desaguadero ≏, Arg.	252	34.13 S	66.47 W
Desaguadero ≏, Bol.	248	18.24 S	67.05 W
Desagüe, Canal de ≖	286a	19.29 N	99.05 W
Des Allemands	194	29.49 N	90.28 W
Desamparados	236	9.54 N	84.04 W
Désappointement, Îles du II	14	14.10 S	141.20 W
Des Arc	194	34.58 N	91.29 W
Desborough	42	52.27 N	0.49 W
Descabezado Grande, Volcán ∧[1]	252	35.36 S	70.45 W
Descanso, Bra.	252	26.50 S	53.35 W
Descanso, Ca., U.S.	204	32.51 N	116.37 W
Descanso, Punta ›	204	32.16 N	117.03 W
Descanso Gardens ♠	280	34.12 N	118.13 W
Descartes	32	46.58 N	0.42 E
Deschaillons	206	46.32 N	72.07 W
Deschambault	206	46.39 N	71.56 W
Deschambault Lake	184	54.55 N	103.22 W
Deschambault Lake ⊜	184	54.40 N	103.35 W
Descharme Lake ⊜	184	57.05 N	109.13 W
Deschênes	212	45.23 N	75.48 W
Deschênes, Lac ⊜	212	45.22 N	75.51 W
Deschutes ≏, Or., U.S.	202	45.38 N	120.54 W
Deschutes ≏, Wa., U.S.	224	47.02 N	122.54 W
Descoberto	256	21.27 S	42.58 W
Desdunes	238	19.17 N	72.39 W
Dese	144	11.05 N	39.41 E
Deseado ≏	254	47.45 S	65.54 W
Deseado, Cabo ›	254	52.44 S	74.44 W
Desembarco de los 33 Orientales, Monumento ⊥	258	33.48 S	58.25 W
Desengaño, Punta ›	254	49.15 S	67.37 W
Desenzano del Garda	64	45.28 N	10.32 E
Deseret Peak ∧	200	40.28 N	112.38 W
Deseronto	212	44.12 N	77.03 W
Désert ≏	190	46.23 N	75.58 W
Désert, Lac ⊜	190	46.35 N	76.19 W
Desertas, Ilhas II	148	32.30 N	16.30 W
Desert Creek ≏	226	38.48 N	119.19 W
Desert Hot Springs	204	33.57 N	116.30 W
Desert Lake ⊜, On., Can.	212	44.32 N	76.35 W
Desert Lake ⊜, Nv., U.S.	204	36.58 N	115.05 W
Desert Mountains ⋏	226	39.16 N	119.00 W
Desert Peak ∧	200	41.11 N	113.22 W
Desert Valley V	204	41.15 N	118.20 W
Desert View Highlands	228	34.37 N	118.13 W
Desford	42	52.39 N	1.17 W
Desha	194	35.44 N	91.40 W
Deshaies	241o	16.18 N	61.48 W
Desheng	102	24.45 N	108.28 E
Deshengchang	107	29.06 N	105.25 E
Deshengpo	102	26.58 N	103.59 E
Deshengtai	104	42.14 N	123.45 E
Deshengyingzi	104	41.44 N	123.14 E
Deshler, Ne., U.S.	198	40.08 N	97.43 W
Deshler, Oh., U.S.	216	41.12 N	83.53 W
Deshnok	120	27.48 N	73.21 E
Deshon Manor	214	40.52 N	79.57 W
Deshu	128	30.26 N	63.19 E
Deshun	106	31.58 N	120.29 E
Desiderio Tello	252	31.13 S	66.19 W
Desio	62	45.37 N	9.13 E
Des Lacs ≏	198	48.17 N	101.25 W
Deslinde, Arroyo ≏	258	33.44 S	58.52 W
Desloge	194	37.52 N	90.31 W
Desmarais	182	55.56 N	113.49 W
De Smet	198	44.23 N	97.33 W
De Smet, Lake ⊜[1]	202	44.29 N	106.45 W
Des Moines, Ia., U.S.	190	41.36 N	93.36 W
Des Moines, N.M., U.S.	196	36.45 N	103.50 W
Des Moines, Wa., U.S.	224	47.24 N	122.19 W
Des Moines ≏	178	40.22 N	91.26 W
Des Moines, East Fork ≏	198	42.41 N	94.12 W
Dešná, Česká Rep.	61	48.58 N	15.33 E
Desna, Ukr.	78	50.56 N	30.46 E
Desna ≏, Europe	78	50.33 N	30.32 E
Desna ≏, Ross.	82	55.26 N	37.30 E
Desolación, Isla I	254	53.00 S	74.10 W
Désolation, Cap de la → Disappointment, Cape ›	244	54.53 S	36.07 W
Desolation Point ›	116	10.28 N	125.39 E
Desor, Mount ∧[2]	190	47.58 N	89.01 W
De Soto, Il., U.S.	194	37.49 N	89.13 W
De Soto, In., U.S.	216	40.15 N	85.17 W
De Soto, Mo., U.S.	194	38.08 N	90.33 W
De Soto, Tx., U.S.	222	32.35 N	96.51 W
De Soto □[6]	220	27.11 N	81.48 W
De Soto City	220	27.26 N	81.24 W
De Soto National Memorial ⊥	220	27.31 N	82.40 W
De Soto State Park ♠	194	34.28 N	85.36 W
Despatch	158	33.46 S	25.30 E
Despeñaperros, Desfiladero de)(	34	38.24 N	3.30 W
Des Plaines	216	42.02 N	87.53 W
Des Plaines ≏	216	41.24 N	88.16 W
Despotovac	38	44.05 N	21.33 E
Despujols	116	12.31 N	122.01 E
Desroches, Île I	138	5.41 S	53.41 E
Desruisseaux	241f	13.47 N	60.56 W
Dessau	54	51.50 N	12.14 E
Dessel	56	51.14 N	5.07 E
Deşt	130	39.10 N	39.22 E
Destacado Island I	116	12.16 N	124.06 E
De Steeg	52	52.02 N	6.04 E
Destek	130	40.51 N	36.12 E
Destelbergen	50	51.03 N	3.48 E
Desterro	250	7.17 S	37.06 W
Destin	194	30.23 N	86.29 W
Destruction, Mount ∧[2]	162	24.35 S	127.59 E
Destruction Bay	180	61.15 N	138.48 W
Destruction Island I	224	47.40 N	124.30 W
Desulo	71	40.01 N	9.14 E
Desvres	50	50.40 N	1.50 E
Deta	38	45.24 N	21.13 E
Detčino	82	54.49 N	36.19 E
Dete	154	18.38 S	26.50 E
Dethlingen	52	52.57 N	10.07 E
Detling	260	51.18 N	0.34 E
Detmold	52	51.56 N	8.52 E
Detmold □[5]	52	52.00 N	8.45 E
Detour, Point ›	190	45.36 N	86.37 W
De Tour Village	190	46.00 N	83.54 W
Detrital Wash V	200	36.02 N	114.28 W
Detroit, Il., U.S.	219	39.37 N	90.40 W
Detroit, Mi., U.S.	216	42.20 N	83.03 W
Detroit, Mi., U.S.	281	42.20 N	83.03 W
Detroit, Or., U.S.	202	44.44 N	122.08 W
Detroit, Tx., U.S.	196	33.40 N	95.16 W
Detroit ≏	214	42.06 N	83.08 W
Detroit Beach	216	41.55 N	83.20 W
Detroit City Airport ⊠	281	42.25 N	83.01 W
Detroit Institute of Arts ♥	281	42.22 N	83.04 W
Detroit Lake ⊜[1]	202	44.42 N	122.10 W
Detroit Lakes	198	46.48 N	95.50 W
Detroit Mercy, University Of ♥[2]	281	42.25 N	83.08 W
Detroit Metropolitan-Wayne County Airport ⊠	281	42.13 N	83.22 W
Detroit Race Course ♠	281	42.23 N	83.19 W
Detroit-Windsor Tunnel ◆[5]	281	42.20 N	83.02 W
Detroit Zoological Park ♠	281	42.29 N	83.09 W
Detskosel'skij	265a	59.44 N	30.28 E
Dettelbach	56	49.48 N	10.09 E
Dettifoss L	24a	65.50 N	16.20 W
Dettingen an der Erms	56	48.32 N	9.20 E
Dettwiller	56	48.45 N	7.28 E
Det Udom	110	14.54 N	105.05 E
Detva	30	48.31 N	19.28 E
Deua National Park ♠	166	36.00 S	149.45 E
Deuben	54	51.06 N	12.04 E
Deuels Corners	284a	42.45 N	78.45 W
Deuil-la-Barre	261	48.59 N	2.20 E
Deūlgaon Rāja	122	20.01 N	76.02 E
Deulpur	272b	22.36 N	88.10 E
Deulti	126	22.26 N	87.56 E
Deurne, Bel.	50	51.13 N	4.28 E
Deurne, Ned.	52	51.28 N	5.47 E
Deusen ◆[8]	263	51.33 N	7.26 E
Deutsche Bucht C	30	54.30 N	7.30 E
Deutsch Eylau → Iława	30	53.37 N	19.33 E
Deutschfeistritz	61	47.11 N	15.20 E
Deutschkreutz	61	47.36 N	16.38 E
Deutsch Krone → Wałcz	30	53.17 N	16.28 E
Deutschland → Germany □[1]	30	51.00 N	10.00 E
Deutschlandsberg	61	46.49 N	15.13 E
Deutschneudorf	54	50.38 N	13.27 E
Deutsch Wagram	61	48.18 N	16.34 E
Deutsch Wusterhausen	264a	52.18 N	13.35 E
Deutzen	54	51.06 N	12.26 E
Deux-Montagnes	206	45.32 N	73.53 W
Deux-Montagnes □[6]	206	45.35 N	74.05 W
Deux Montagnes, Lac des ⊜	206	45.28 N	73.59 W
Deux-Sèvres □[5]	32	46.30 N	0.20 W
Deva	38	45.53 N	22.55 E
Devakottai	122	9.57 N	78.49 E
De Valls Bluff	194	34.47 N	91.27 W
Devaprayāg	124	30.09 N	78.37 E
Dev'atern'a	80	56.12 N	53.24 E
Dev'atiny	24	60.56 N	36.46 E
Devault	285	40.05 N	75.32 W
Dévaványa	30	47.02 N	20.58 E
Devecikonağı	130	39.55 N	28.34 E
Devecser	30	47.06 N	17.26 E
Devedağı Tepesi ∧	130	40.34 N	41.21 E
Devegeçidi Barajı ⊜[1]	130	38.05 N	39.55 E
Develi	130	38.23 N	35.30 E
Deventer	52	52.15 N	6.10 E
Deveron ≏	46	57.40 N	2.31 W
Devers	222	30.02 N	94.36 W
Devers Canal, West Branch ≖	222	29.57 N	94.46 W
Deversoir Military Base ■	142	30.25 N	32.20 E
Devès, Monts du ⋏	32	45.00 N	3.45 E
Devgadh Bāriva	120	22.42 N	73.54 E
De View, Bayou ≏	194	34.48 N	91.18 W
Devīkot	120	26.42 N	71.12 E
Devil Lake ⊜	212	44.35 N	76.27 W
Deville	56	49.53 N	4.42 E
Déville-lès-Rouen	50	49.28 N	1.02 E
Devil Peak ∧	226	37.32 N	119.44 W
Devil River Peak ∧	172	40.58 S	172.39 E
Devils ≏	196	29.39 N	100.58 W
Devil's Bridge	42	52.23 N	3.51 W
Devils Brook ≏	276	40.20 N	74.37 W
Devils Canyon V	280	34.16 N	117.58 W
Devil's Den State Park ♠	194	35.46 N	94.16 W
Devils Hole Rapids L	284a	43.08 N	79.03 W
Devils Hopyard State Park ♠	207	41.28 N	72.22 W
Devils Island → Diable, Île du I	250	5.17 N	52.35 W
Devils Lake	198	48.06 N	98.51 W
Devils Lake ⊜, Mi., U.S.	216	41.58 N	84.17 W
Devils Lake ⊜, N.D., U.S.	198	48.01 N	98.52 W
Devils Lake State Park ♠	190	43.24 N	89.44 W
Devils Marbles ♠	162	20.30 S	134.14 E
Devils Paw ∧	180	58.44 N	133.50 W
Devils Postpile National Monument ♠	226	37.37 N	119.05 W
Devils Tower ∧	198	44.31 N	104.57 W
Devils Tower National Monument ♠	198	44.31 N	104.57 W
Devil's Water ≏	44	54.58 N	2.02 W
Devin	38	41.45 N	24.24 E
Devine, B.C., Can.	182	50.32 N	122.30 W
Devine, Tx., U.S.	196	29.08 N	98.54 W
Devizes	42	51.22 N	1.59 W
Devladove	78	48.07 N	33.45 E
Devli	120	25.45 N	75.23 E
De Voe Lake ⊜	276	40.23 N	74.23 W
Devoll ≏	38	40.49 N	19.51 E
Dévoluy ⋏	62	44.39 N	5.53 E
Devon, Ab., Can.	182	53.22 N	113.44 W
Devon, S. Afr.	158	26.21 S	28.48 E
Devon, Pa., U.S.	285	40.02 N	75.25 W
Devon □[6]	42	50.45 N	3.50 W
Devon ≏, Eng., U.K.	42	53.04 N	0.43 W
Devon ≏, Scot., U.K.	46	56.07 N	3.51 W
Devon Island I	16	75.00 N	87.00 W
Devonport, Austl.	166	41.11 S	146.21 E
Devonport, N.Z.	172	36.49 S	174.48 E
Devonport, Eng., U.K.	42	50.22 N	4.10 W
Devonshire	285	39.49 N	75.32 W
Devonshire Plaza ◆[9]	281	42.17 N	83.00 W
Devore	228	34.13 N	117.25 W
Devoto	252	31.24 S	62.19 W
Devrek	130	41.13 N	31.57 E
Devrekâni	130	41.36 N	33.51 E
Devres ≏	130	41.06 N	34.25 E
Devure ≏	154	20.00 S	32.20 E
Dewa, Ujung ›	114	2.55 N	95.48 E
Dewakang-lompo, Pulau I	112	5.24 S	118.25 E
Dewar	196	35.27 N	95.56 W
Dewart	210	41.07 N	76.53 W
Dewart Lake ⊜	216	41.22 N	85.47 W
Dewās	120	22.58 N	76.04 E
Dewa-sanchi ⋏[2]	92	39.05 N	140.10 E
Dewdney	224	49.10 N	122.12 W
Dewetsdorp	158	29.33 S	26.34 E
Dewey, Il., U.S.	216	40.19 N	88.17 W
Dewey, Ok., U.S.	196	36.47 N	95.56 W
Dewey, Wa., U.S.	224	48.25 N	122.37 W
Dewey Beach	208	38.41 N	75.04 W
Deweyville	194	30.18 N	93.45 W
De Witt, Ar., U.S.	194	34.17 N	91.20 W
Dewitt, Il., U.S.	219	40.11 N	88.47 W
De Witt, Ia., U.S.	190	41.49 N	90.32 W
De Witt, Mi., U.S.	216	42.50 N	84.34 W
De Witt, Ne., U.S.	198	40.23 N	96.55 W
De Witt, N.Y., U.S.	210	43.02 N	76.03 W
De Witt □[6], Il., U.S.	216	40.12 N	88.55 W
De Witt □[6], Tx., U.S.	222	29.07 N	97.20 W
Dewittville	214	42.14 N	79.27 W
Dewsbury	44	53.42 N	1.37 W
Dexing	100	28.54 N	117.36 E
Dexingjie	98	39.54 N	122.50 E
Dexter, Me., U.S.	188	45.01 N	69.17 W
Dexter, Mi., U.S.	216	42.20 N	83.53 W
Dexter, Mo., U.S.	194	36.47 N	89.57 W
Dexter, N.M., U.S.	196	33.11 N	104.22 W
Dexter, N.Y., U.S.	212	44.00 N	76.02 W
Dexterity Fiord C[2]	176	71.11 N	73.03 W
Deyang	102	31.14 N	104.22 E
Dey-Dey, Lake ⊜	162	29.12 S	131.04 E
Deyhūk	128	33.17 N	57.30 E
Deyyer	128	27.50 N	51.55 E
Dez ≏	128	31.39 N	48.52 E
Dezfūl	128	32.23 N	48.24 E
Dez Gerd	128	30.45 N	51.57 E
Dezhou	98	37.27 N	116.18 E
Dežneva, mys ›	180	66.06 N	169.45 W
Dezong	120	32.09 N	90.20 E
Dezzo di Scalve	64	45.59 N	10.05 E
Dgâmcha, Sebkhet te-n- ⊜	150	18.45 N	15.48 W
Dhabān Singh	123	31.44 N	73.34 E
Dhāding	124	27.52 N	84.55 E
Dhādkā	126	22.47 N	86.30 E
Dháfna ∧	267c	38.07 N	23.38 E
Dháfni, Ellás	38	37.48 N	22.01 E
Dháfni, Ellás	267c	38.01 N	23.38 E
Dhafnion Monastery ♥[1]	267c	38.01 N	23.38 E
Dhahab	140	28.29 N	34.32 E
Dhahab, Wādī adh- V	132	32.44 N	35.54 E
Dhahran → Aẓ-Ẓahrān	128	26.18 N	50.08 E
Dhaka (Dacca), Bngl.	126	23.43 N	90.25 E
Dhāka, India	124	26.41 N	85.10 E
Dhaka □[5]	120	24.15 N	90.15 E
Dhākauli	124	24.45 N	77.51 E
Dhakuria Lake ⊜	272b	22.31 N	88.22 E
Dhaleswari ≏	126	23.32 N	90.34 E
Dháli	130	35.01 N	33.25 E
Dhamār	144	14.46 N	44.23 E
Dhāmpur	124	29.19 N	78.31 E
Dhāmrai	126	23.55 N	90.13 E
Dhamtari	122	20.41 N	81.34 E
Dhāmura	126	22.53 N	90.12 E
Dhanaula	123	30.17 N	75.35 E
Dhanaura	124	28.58 N	78.15 E
Dhanbād	126	23.48 N	86.27 E
Dhandhuka	120	22.22 N	71.59 E
Dhanera	126	23.25 N	86.39 E
Dhaneswargāti	126	23.25 N	89.20 E
Dhangaḍhī	124	28.41 N	80.36 E
Dhaniakhāli	126	22.58 N	88.06 E
D'Hanis	196	29.20 N	99.17 W
Dhankuṭa	124	26.59 N	87.20 E
Dhansar	272c	19.07 N	73.05 E
Dhānyahānā	272b	22.48 N	88.11 E
Dhār	120	22.36 N	75.18 E
Dharampur	122	20.32 N	73.11 E
Dharān	124	26.49 N	87.17 E
Dharangaon	120	21.01 N	75.16 E
Dhārāpuram	122	10.44 N	77.31 E
Dhāri	120	21.20 N	71.01 E
Dhārīwāl	123	31.57 N	75.19 E
Dharmābād	122	18.54 N	77.51 E
Dharmapuri	122	12.08 N	78.10 E
Dharmavaram	122	14.26 N	77.43 E
Dharmjaygarh	124	22.28 N	83.13 E
Dharmkot	123	30.57 N	75.14 E
Dharmshāla	123	32.13 N	76.19 E
Dharoor, Tog V	144	10.20 N	50.30 E
Dharug National Park ♠	170	33.25 S	151.05 E
Dhasān ≏	124	25.48 N	79.24 E
Dhātrigrām	126	23.15 N	88.20 E
Dhaulpur	124	26.42 N	77.54 E
Dhawalāgiri □[8]	124	28.30 N	83.30 E
Dhawalāgiri ∧	124	28.42 N	83.30 E
Dhebar Lake ⊜	120	24.16 N	74.00 E
Dhelfoí ⊥	38	38.30 N	22.29 E
Dhenkānāl	120	20.40 N	85.36 E
Dhenoúsa I	38	37.06 N	25.49 E
Dherínia	130	35.03 N	33.57 E
Dhërmiu ♥[1]	38	40.08 N	19.42 E
Dherue, Loch an ⊜	46	58.25 N	4.27 W
Dheskáti	38	39.55 N	21.49 E
Dheune ≏	58	46.54 N	5.00 E
Dhiavolítsion	38	37.18 N	21.58 E
Dhībān	132	31.30 N	35.47 E
Dhidhimótikhon	38	41.21 N	26.30 E
Dhiinsoor	144	2.24 N	42.59 E
Dhíkti ∧	38	35.08 N	25.30 E
Dhílos ⊥	38	37.26 N	25.16 E
Dhimitsána	38	37.37 N	22.03 E
Dhiónisos	267c	38.06 N	23.53 E
Dhī Qār □[4]	128	31.00 N	46.15 E
Dhirāsrām	126	23.57 N	90.25 E
Dhirwah, Wādī adh- V	132	31.18 N	36.56 E
Dhodhekánisos (Dodecanese) II	38	36.30 N	27.00 E
Dhodhóni ⊥	38	39.34 N	20.47 E
Dhofar → Ẓufār ◆[1]	118	17.00 N	54.10 E
Dhokra	272b	22.40 N	88.34 E
Dholka	120	22.43 N	72.28 E
Dhomhnuill, Sgurr ∧	46	56.45 N	5.27 W
Dhone	122	15.25 N	77.53 E
Dhopākhola	126	23.08 N	89.10 E
Dhorāji	120	21.44 N	70.27 E
Dhosha	126	22.15 N	88.33 E
Dhowa	126	24.03 N	86.54 E
Dhoxáton	38	41.05 N	24.14 E
Dhrāngadhra	120	22.59 N	71.28 E
Dhrapetsóna	267c	37.57 N	23.37 E
Dhrol	120	22.34 N	70.25 E
Dhron ≏	56	49.52 N	6.54 E
Dhubāb	144	12.56 N	43.25 E
Dhuburi	124	26.01 N	89.59 E
Dhudiāl	123	33.04 N	72.58 E
Dhulāgarh	272b	22.35 N	88.11 E
Dhule	120	20.54 N	74.47 E
Dhulia → Dhule	120	20.54 N	74.47 E
Dhuliān	124	24.41 N	87.58 E
Dhulikhel	124	27.37 N	85.33 E
Dhūlsīrās ◆[8]	272a	28.33 N	77.02 E
Dhünn	56	51.06 N	7.16 E
Dhünn-Stausee ⊜[1]	263	51.05 N	7.16 E
Dhupgāri	124	26.36 N	89.01 E
Dhurbo	144	11.37 N	50.20 E
Dhūri	124	30.22 N	75.52 E
Dhutumkhar ≏	272c	18.54 N	73.00 E
Dhuudo	144	9.20 N	50.12 E
Dhuudo V	144	9.14 N	50.39 E
Dhuusa Mareeb	144	5.31 N	46.24 E
Dhytikí Ellás □[4]	38	38.00 N	21.30 E
Dhytikí Makedhonía □[4]	38	40.30 N	21.30 E
Día I	38	35.27 N	25.13 E
Diabaig	46	57.34 N	5.40 W
Diabakania	150	10.38 N	10.58 W
Diable, Île du (Devils Island) I	250	5.17 N	52.35 W
Diable, Lac du ⊜	206	46.31 N	74.20 W
Diable, Pointe du ›	240e	14.47 N	60.54 W
Diable, Rivière du ≏	206	46.03 N	74.38 W
Diables, Morne aux ∧	240d	15.37 N	61.27 W
Diablo, Ca., U.S.	226	37.50 N	121.58 W
Diablo, Wa., U.S.	224	48.43 N	121.09 W
Diablo, Canyon V	200	35.18 N	110.59 W
Diablo, Isla del → Diable, Île du I	250	5.17 N	52.35 W
Diablo, Mount ∧	226	37.53 N	121.55 W
Diablo, Pico del ∧	232	30.59 N	115.45 W
Diablo, Sierra del ⋏	196	27.20 N	104.05 W
Diablo Lake ⊜[1]	224	48.43 N	121.08 W
Diablo Plateau ⋏[1]	200	31.30 N	105.30 W
Diablo Range ⋏	226	37.00 N	121.20 W
Diablotins, Morne ∧	240d	15.30 N	61.24 W
Diabo	150	7.47 N	5.11 W
Diaca	154	11.30 S	39.59 E
Diadema	256	23.42 S	46.37 W
Diadema □[7]	287b	23.42 S	46.36 W
Diafarabé	150	14.09 N	5.01 W
Diagonal	198	40.48 N	94.20 W
Diaka ≏[1]	150	15.13 N	4.14 W
Dialakoto	150	13.19 N	13.18 W
Dialassagou	150	13.45 N	3.37 W
Diamant, Pointe du ›	240e	14.27 N	61.03 W
Diamante, Arg.	252	32.04 S	60.39 W
Diamante, It.	68	39.41 N	15.49 E
Diamante ≏	252	34.31 S	66.56 W
Diamante, Punta ›	234	16.47 N	99.52 W
Diamante de Ubá	256	21.12 S	42.55 W
Diamantina	255	18.15 S	43.36 W
Diamantina ≏	166	26.45 S	139.10 E
Diamantina Fracture Zone ✦	14	36.00 S	105.00 E
Diamantina Lakes	166	23.46 S	141.09 E
Diamantino	248	14.25 S	56.27 W
Diamantino ≏	255	16.08 S	52.28 W
Diamond, Il., U.S.	216	41.17 N	88.15 W
Diamond, Mo., U.S.	194	37.00 N	94.19 W
Diamond, Oh., U.S.	214	41.06 N	81.01 W
Diamond Bar	228	34.01 N	117.48 W
Diamond Brook ≏	276	40.56 N	74.08 W
Diamond Creek	274b	37.41 S	145.09 E
Diamond Creek ≏	169	37.44 S	145.09 E
Diamond Harbour	126	22.12 N	88.12 E
Diamond Head ±[6]	229c	21.16 N	157.49 W
Diamond Hill	207	41.59 N	71.24 W
Diamond Hill Reservoir ⊜[1]	283	42.00 N	71.24 W
Diamond Hill State Park ♠	283	42.00 N	71.26 W
Diamond Islets II	166	17.25 S	150.58 E
Diamond Lake	278	42.15 N	88.00 W
Diamond Lake ⊜, On., Can.	212	45.04 N	78.02 W
Diamond Lake ⊜, Il., U.S.	278	42.15 N	88.00 W
Diamond Lake ⊜, Mi., U.S.	216	41.54 N	85.59 W
Diamond Lake ⊜, Or., U.S.	202	43.10 N	122.09 W
Diamond Peak ∧, Id., U.S.	202	44.09 N	113.05 W
Diamond Peak ∧, Or., U.S.	202	43.33 N	122.09 W
Diamond Peak ∧, Wa., U.S.	202	46.07 N	117.32 W
Diamond Springs	226	38.41 N	120.48 W
Diamondville	200	41.46 N	110.32 W
Diana	222	32.43 N	94.45 W
Diana Bay C	176	60.50 N	69.50 W
Dianalund	41	55.32 N	11.30 E
Dianbai	102	21.30 N	111.01 E
Dian Chi ⊜	102	24.50 N	102.42 E
Diancun	105	39.55 N	116.14 E
Dianfangba	102	32.54 N	103.35 E
Diangounté Kamara	150	14.33 N	9.31 W
Dianhu	100	33.58 N	119.38 E
Dianji	98	36.32 N	120.27 E
Dianjiang	102	30.21 N	107.23 E
Diano, Vallo di V	68	40.21 N	15.36 E
Diano Marina	62	43.54 N	8.05 E
Dianópolis	250	11.38 S	46.50 W
Dianqianhe	100	30.44 N	116.02 E
Dianra	150	8.45 N	6.14 W
Dianshang	106	31.10 N	118.51 E
Dianshan Hu ⊜	106	31.08 N	120.55 E
Diantou	100	27.18 N	120.11 E
Dianzi	104	41.37 N	122.05 E
Diaobingshan	104	42.28 N	123.33 E
Diao'ecun	105	40.43 N	115.49 E
Diaohetou	105	39.17 N	116.41 E
Diaopu	100	32.22 N	119.54 E
Diaoshuilouzi	104	40.59 N	122.22 E
Diaotai	100	29.40 N	119.39 E
Diaowo	105	39.30 N	116.04 E
Diapaga	150	12.04 N	1.47 E
Diapangou	150	12.07 N	0.11 E
Diapblo, Puntan ›	174n	15.00 N	145.35 E
Dias	256	22.28 S	45.34 W
Diascund Creek Reservoir ⊜[1]	208	37.27 N	76.54 W
Diawala	150	10.07 N	5.28 W
Diaz	194	35.38 N	91.15 W
Diaz Point ›	156	26.38 S	15.05 E
Dibai	124	28.13 N	78.15 E
Dibāng ≏	120	27.50 N	95.32 E
Dibay → Dubayy	128	25.18 N	55.18 E
Dibaya	152	6.30 S	22.57 E
Dibbīn	132	32.26 N	36.34 E
Dibeng	158	27.35 S	22.54 E
D'Iberville	194	30.25 N	88.53 W
Dibete	156	23.45 S	26.26 E
Dibi	144	4.13 N	41.56 E
Dibo	144	6.31 N	41.52 E
Diboll	222	31.11 N	94.46 W
Dibrugarh	120	27.29 N	94.54 E
Dibs	140	12.34 N	24.14 E
Dibs, Bi'r ⍑[4]	140	22.12 N	29.32 E
Dichāon Kalān ◆[8]	272a	28.39 N	76.59 E
Dick, Mount ∧[2]	168a	31.35 S	116.42 E
Dickelsbach ≏	263	51.24 N	6.45 E
Dickens	196	33.37 N	100.50 W
Dickerson	208	39.13 N	77.25 W
Dickey ≏	224	47.55 N	124.37 W
Dickey Lake ⊜, On., Can.	212	44.47 N	77.44 W
Dickey Lake ⊜, Wa., U.S.	224	48.06 N	124.31 W
Dickinson, N.D., U.S.	198	46.52 N	102.47 W
Dickinson, Pa., U.S.	208	40.07 N	77.20 W
Dickinson, Tx., U.S.	222	29.27 N	95.03 W
Dickinson Bayou ≏	222	29.28 N	94.58 W
Dickinson Island I	281	42.37 N	82.38 W
Dickins Seamount ✦[3]	16	54.30 N	137.00 W
Dicks	158	27.43 S	30.10 E
Dickson, Ok., U.S.	196	34.11 N	96.59 W
Dickson, Tn., U.S.	194	36.04 N	87.23 W
Dickson City	210	41.28 N	75.36 W
Dicle, Tür.	130	37.18 N	42.04 E
Dicle, Tür.	130	38.22 N	40.04 E
Dicle → Tigris ≏	128	31.00 N	47.25 E
Dicomano	66	43.53 N	11.31 E
Diculom	116	7.54 N	122.14 E
Dicun	100	33.46 N	117.32 E
Didam	52	51.56 N	6.08 E
Didao	89	45.22 N	130.51 E
Didbiran	89	51.58 N	139.20 E
Didcot	42	51.37 N	1.15 W
Didesa ≏	144	9.56 N	35.45 E
Didiéni	150	13.53 N	8.06 W
Didimbo	152	17.30 S	21.45 E
Didinga Hills ⋏	154	4.20 N	33.35 E
Didsbury	182	51.40 N	114.08 W
Didsbury ◆[8]	262	53.25 N	2.14 W
Diduyon ≏	116	16.36 N	121.42 E
Dīdwāna	120	27.24 N	74.34 E
Didy	157b	18.07 S	48.32 E
Die	62	44.45 N	5.22 E
Die Aue ◆[1]	263	51.40 N	6.35 E
Die Berg ∧	156	25.12 S	30.09 E
Die Boss	158	31.59 S	19.44 E
Diébougou	150	10.58 N	3.15 W
Dieburg	56	49.54 N	8.50 E

Symbols in the index entries represent the broad categories identified in the key at the right. Symbols with superior numbers (⋏[1]) identify subcategories (see complete key on page *I · 1).*

Symbole im Register stellen die rechts im Schlüssel erklärten Kategorien dar. Symbole mit hochgestellten Ziffern (⋏[1]) bezeichnen Unterabteilungen einer Kategorie (vgl. vollständiger Schlüssel auf Seite *I · 1).*

Los símbolos incluídos en el texto del índice representan las grandes categorías identificadas con la clave a la derecha. Los símbolos con numeros en su parte superior (⋏[1]) identifican las subcategorías (véase la clave completa en la página *I · 1).*

Les symboles de l'index représentent les catégories indiquées dans la légende à droite. Les symboles suivis d'un indice (⋏[1]) représentent des sous-catégories (voir légende complète à la page *I · 1).*

Os símbolos incluídos no texto do índice representam as grandes categorias identificadas com a chave à direita. Os símbolos com números em sua parte superior (⋏[1]) identificam as subcategorias (veja-se a chave completa à página *I · 1).*

ENGLISH	DEUTSCH	ESPAÑOL	FRANÇAIS	PORTUGUÊS
∧ Mountain	Berg	Montaña	Montagne	Montanha
⋏ Mountains	Gebirge	Montañas	Montagnes	Montanhas
)(Pass	Paß	Paso	Col	Passo
V Valley, Canyon	Tal, Cañon	Valle, Cañón	Vallée, Canyon	Vale, Canhão
≚ Plain	Ebene	Llano	Plaine	Planície
› Cape	Kap	Cabo	Cap	Cabo
I Island	Insel	Isla	Île	Ilha
II Islands	Inseln	Islas	Îles	Ilhas
± Other Topographic Features	Andere Topographische Objekte	Otros Elementos Topográficos	Autres données topographiques	Outros acidentes topográficos

Diec-Doln I · 47

ESPAÑOL Nombre	Página	Lat.°′	Long.°′ W = Oeste
Dieciocho de Julio	252	33.41 S	53.33 W
Diecke	150	7.21 N	8.58 W
Diedenhofen → Thionville	56	49.22 N	6.10 E
Diedersdorf	264a	52.20 N	13.21 E
Diedorf	58	48.21 N	10.47 E
Die Erpe ≃	264a	52.27 N	13.38 E
Diefenbaker, Lake ⊜[1]	184	51.00 N	106.55 W
Diego de Almagro	252	26.23 S	70.03 W
Diego de Almagro, Isla I	254	51.25 S	75.10 W
Diego de Ocampo, Pico ∧	238	19.35 N	70.45 W
Diego Garcia I	12	7.20 S	72.25 E
Diego Gaynor	258	34.17 S	59.14 W
Diego Pérez, Cayería de II	240p	22.05 N	81.40 W
Diego Ramírez, Islas II	244	56.30 S	68.44 W
Die Haard ◆[1]	263	51.41 N	7.15 E
Diekirch	56	49.53 N	6.10 E
Dieksee ⊜	54	54.10 N	10.30 E
Dieleemu	86	46.22 N	88.43 E
Dielingen	52	52.26 N	8.20 E
Dielsdorf	58	47.29 N	8.27 E
Diéma	150	14.32 N	9.12 W
Diemansputs	158	29.54 S	21.33 E
Diembéring	150	12.28 N	16.47 W
Diemel ≃	52	51.39 N	9.27 E
Diemelstadt	52	51.29 N	9.01 E
Diemel-Talsperre ◆[6]	56	51.22 N	8.43 E
Diemen	52	52.20 N	4.58 E
Diemuchuoke	120	32.42 N	79.29 E
Dien Bien Phu	110	21.23 N	103.01 E
Dien Khanh	110	12.15 N	109.06 E
Diepenau	52	52.25 N	8.44 E
Diepenbeek	56	50.54 N	5.24 E
Diepenheim	52	52.12 N	6.33 E
Diepensee	264a	52.22 N	13.31 E
Diepenveen	52	52.18 N	6.08 E
Diepholz	52	52.35 N	8.21 E
Diepoldsau	58	47.23 N	9.38 E
Dieppe, N.B., Can.	186	46.06 N	64.45 W
Dieppe, Fr.	50	49.56 N	1.05 E
Dierbao	98	40.20 N	114.32 E
Dierdorf	56	50.33 N	7.39 E
Dieren	52	52.03 N	6.06 E
Dierks	194	34.07 N	94.00 W
Diersbach	60	48.25 N	13.34 E
Di'er Songhua ≃	89	45.26 N	124.39 E
Diesdorf	54	52.45 N	10.52 E
Dieskau	54	51.26 N	12.02 E
Diessem ◆[8]	263	51.20 N	6.35 E
Diessen	64	47.56 N	11.06 E
Diessenhofen	58	47.41 N	8.45 E
Diest	56	50.59 N	5.03 E
Dietenheim	58	48.12 N	10.04 E
Dietenhofen	56	49.24 N	10.41 E
Dietersburg	60	48.30 N	12.55 E
Dietersdorf	56	50.13 N	10.49 E
Dietfurt	56	48.57 N	10.56 E
Dietfurt an der Altmühl	60	49.02 N	11.35 E
Dietikon	58	47.24 N	8.24 E
Dietmannsried	58	47.49 N	10.17 E
Dietramszell	64	47.51 N	11.35 E
Dietrich	202	42.54 N	114.15 W
Dietzenbach	56	50.01 N	8.47 E
Dietzhölztal	56	50.50 N	8.19 E
Dieue-sur-Meuse	56	49.04 N	5.25 E
Dieulefit	62	44.31 N	5.04 E
Dieulouard	56	48.51 N	6.04 E
Dieuze	56	48.49 N	6.43 E
Dieveniškės	76	54.12 N	25.37 E
Diever	52	52.52 N	6.19 E
Die Ville ⩘[2]	56	50.40 N	6.55 E
Die Wurzen (Koren))(	64	46.31 N	13.45 E
Diez	56	50.22 N	8.01 E
Diez de Octubre	232	24.44 N	104.39 W
Dif	144	0.59 N	40.57 E
Difang	98	35.23 N	117.52 E
Diffa	146	13.19 N	12.37 E
Diffa □[5]	146	16.00 N	13.30 E
Differdange	56	49.32 N	5.52 E
Difficult Run ≃	284c	38.58 N	77.14 W
Diffun	116	16.34 N	121.33 E
Difuri I	122	5.24 N	73.38 E
Digambar Jain Temple ʋ[1]	272b	22.36 N	88.23 E
Digambarpur	126	21.57 N	88.22 E
Digba	154	4.24 N	25.47 E
Digboi	120	27.23 N	95.38 E
Digby	186	44.37 N	65.46 W
Digby Neck ›[1]	186	44.30 N	66.10 W
Dige	98	34.22 N	114.28 E
Digerberget ∧[2]	40	60.35 N	13.25 E
Digges Islands II	176	62.35 N	77.50 W
Diggle	262	53.34 N	1.59 W
Dighalia	126	23.07 N	89.39 E
Dighipāra	126	21.58 N	88.17 E
Dighode	272c	18.54 N	73.02 E
Dighra	272b	22.47 N	88.32 E
Dighton, Ks., U.S.	198	38.28 N	100.28 W
Dighton, Ma., U.S.	207	41.48 N	71.07 W
Di Giorgio	228	35.15 N	118.51 W
Dīglūr	122	18.33 N	77.36 E
Digmoor	262	53.32 N	2.45 W
Dīgnagar	126	23.27 N	87.41 E
Dignano	64	46.05 N	12.56 E
Digne	62	44.06 N	6.14 E
Digoin	32	46.29 N	3.59 E
Digomi	84	41.47 N	44.44 E
Digong	104	42.11 N	122.03 E
Digor	84	40.23 N	43.24 E
Digora	84	43.10 N	44.09 E
Digos	116	6.45 N	125.20 E
Digra	272b	22.50 N	88.20 E
Digras	122	20.07 N	77.43 E
Digri	120	25.10 N	69.07 E
Digui	152	5.28 N	20.50 E
Digul ≃	164	7.07 S	138.42 E
Dihaer	86	42.35 N	89.49 E
Dihtyari	78	50.35 N	32.45 E
Dihun	144	7.18 N	42.42 E
Dijag	24	65.48 N	57.39 E
Dijlah → Tigris ≃	128	31.00 N	47.25 E
Dijlah, Wādī V	142	29.58 N	31.18 E
Dijle (Dyle) ≃	56	51.04 N	4.25 E
Dijohan Point ›	116	16.19 N	122.14 E
Dijon	58	47.19 N	5.01 E
Dik	146	9.58 N	17.31 E
Dikaja	76	59.15 N	39.30 E
Dikala	154	4.41 N	31.23 E
Dikbıyık	130	41.13 N	36.38 E
Dike	190	42.27 N	92.37 W
Dikhil	144	11.06 N	42.22 E
Dikili	130	39.04 N	26.53 E
Dikirnis	142	31.05 N	31.35 E
Dikli	76	57.35 N	25.06 E
Diklosmta, gora ∧	84	42.29 N	45.47 E
Dikmen	130	39.53 N	32.50 E
Dikodougou	150	9.04 N	5.46 W
Diksmuide (Dixmude)	50	51.02 N	2.52 E
Dikson	74	73.30 N	80.35 E
Dikwa	146	12.02 N	13.56 E
Dila	144	6.21 N	38.17 E
Dilektepe	130	38.04 N	41.49 E
Dile Point ›	116	17.34 N	120.20 E
Dilerpur	272b	22.51 N	88.10 E
Dili	112	8.33 S	125.35 E
Dilia V	146	16.53 N	11.00 E
Diligent Strait ʮ	110	12.11 N	92.57 E
Di Linh	110	11.35 N	108.04 E
Diližan	84	40.45 N	44.52 E
Diližanskij zapovednik ♠	84	40.40 N	45.00 E
Dill ≃	56	50.33 N	8.29 E
Dill City	196	35.16 N	99.08 W
Dillenburg	56	50.44 N	8.17 E

FRANÇAIS Nom	Page	Lat.°′	Long.°′ W = Ouest
Diller	198	40.06 N	96.56 W
Dilley, Or., U.S.	224	45.29 N	123.07 W
Dilley, Tx., U.S.	196	28.40 N	99.10 W
Dilling	140	12.03 N	29.39 E
Dillingen	56	49.21 N	6.44 E
Dillingen an der Donau	56	48.34 N	10.29 E
Dillingham	180	59.02 N	158.29 W
Dillon, Co., U.S.	200	39.37 N	106.02 W
Dillon, Mt., U.S.	202	45.12 N	112.38 W
Dillon, S.C., U.S.	192	34.24 N	79.22 W
Dillon ≃	184	55.56 N	108.57 W
Dillon Cone ∧	172	42.16 S	173.13 E
Dillon Lake ⊜	184	55.45 N	109.30 W
Dillon Lake ⊜[1]	188	40.02 N	82.10 W
Dillon Mountain ∧	200	33.51 N	108.48 W
Dillon Reservoir ⊜[1]	200	39.35 N	106.02 W
Dillon State Park ♠	188	40.03 N	82.08 W
Dillonvale	214	40.11 N	80.46 W
Dillsboro	218	39.01 N	85.03 W
Dillsburg	208	40.06 N	77.02 W
Dilltown	214	40.29 N	79.00 W
Dillwyn	192	37.32 N	78.27 W
Dilly	150	15.01 N	7.40 W
Dilolo	152	10.42 S	22.20 E
Dilsen	56	51.02 N	5.44 E
Dilworth	198	46.52 N	96.42 W
Dilworthtown	285	39.54 N	75.34 W
Dima, Ang.	152	15.27 S	20.10 E
Dima, Indon.	114	1.20 N	97.20 E
Dimāpur	120	25.54 N	93.44 E
Dimaro	64	46.20 N	10.52 E
Dimasalang	116	12.12 N	123.51 E
Dimashq (Damascus)	132	33.30 N	36.18 E
Dimashq □[8]	132	33.30 N	37.00 E
Dimass, Rass ›	36	35.37 N	11.03 E
Dimataling	116	7.32 N	123.22 E
Dimbelenge	152	5.33 S	23.07 E
Dimbokro	150	6.39 N	4.42 W
Dimboola	166	36.27 S	142.02 E
Dimbulah	166	17.09 S	145.07 E
Dime	144	6.16 N	36.20 E
Dime Box	222	30.21 N	96.50 W
Dimitrovgrad, Blg.	38	42.03 N	25.36 E
Dimitrovgrad, Jugo.	38	43.01 N	22.47 E
Dimitrovgrad, Ross.	80	54.14 N	49.39 E
Dimitrovo → Pernik	38	42.36 N	23.02 E
Dimitrovskoje	85	40.16 N	69.03 E
Dimlang ∧	146	8.24 N	11.47 E
Dimmitt	196	34.33 N	102.18 W
Dimo	154	5.19 N	29.10 E
Dimock	210	41.45 N	75.32 W
Dimona	132	31.04 N	35.02 E
Dimondale	216	42.38 N	84.38 W
Dina	123	33.02 N	73.36 E
Dinach	144	9.15 N	50.37 E
Dinagat	116	9.59 N	125.35 E
Dinagat Island I	116	10.12 N	125.35 E
Dinagat Sound ʮ	116	9.59 N	125.50 E
Dinahican Point ›	116	14.42 N	121.44 E
Dinājpur	124	25.38 N	88.38 E
Dinalupihan	116	14.52 N	120.28 E
Dinamarca → Denmark □[1]	26	56.00 N	10.00 E
Dinamarca, Estrecho de → Denmark Strait ʮ	10	67.00 N	25.00 W
Dinami	68	38.31 N	16.09 E
Dinamita	196	25.43 N	103.38 W
Dinamo	80	50.15 N	41.38 E
Dinan	32	48.27 N	2.02 W
Dīnānagar	123	32.09 N	75.28 E
Dinant	56	50.16 N	4.55 E
Dinar	130	38.04 N	30.10 E
Dinara (Dinaric Alps) ⩘	36	43.50 N	16.35 E
Dinard	32	48.38 N	2.04 W
Dinaric Alps → Dinara ⩘	36	43.50 N	16.35 E
Dinarische Alpen → Dinara ⩘	36	43.50 N	16.35 E
Dinas, Pil.	116	7.38 N	123.20 E
Dinas, Wales, U.K.	42	52.00 N	4.54 W
Dinas Head ›	42	52.02 N	4.55 W
Dinas Powys	42	51.26 N	3.14 W
Dindanko	150	14.08 N	9.30 W
Dindar, Nahr ad- (Dinder) ≃	140	14.06 N	33.40 E
Dīndārpur ◆[8]	272a	28.36 N	76.59 E
Dinde	152	14.12 S	13.44 E
Dinder (Nahr ad-Dindar) ≃	140	14.06 N	33.40 E
Dinder National Park ♠	140	12.40 N	35.20 E
Dindi ≃	122	16.21 N	79.13 E
Dindigul	122	10.21 N	77.57 E
Dindima	150	10.18 N	10.12 E
Dindori	124	22.57 N	81.05 E
Dineksaray	130	37.23 N	32.37 E
Dinga, Pāk.	120	25.26 N	67.10 E
Dinga, Pāk.	123	32.38 N	73.43 E
Dinga, R.D.C.	152	5.19 S	16.34 E
Dingalan Bay ᑕ	116	15.18 N	121.25 E
Ding'an	110	19.44 N	110.21 E
Dingba	154	3.24 N	27.55 E
Dingbian	102	37.40 N	107.41 E
Dingbianji	102	36.37 N	108.41 E
Dingbu	106	31.18 N	119.10 E
Dingden	52	51.46 N	6.37 E
Dinge	152	4.58 S	12.22 E
Dingelstädt	54	51.18 N	10.19 E
Dingelstedt	54	51.58 N	10.58 E
Dingeryu	105	39.37 N	114.55 E
Dingfeng	106	31.20 N	121.45 E
Dinggou	100	32.34 N	119.39 E
Dinggyê	124	28.29 N	88.06 E
Dinghai	100	30.02 N	122.06 E
Dingila	154	3.39 N	26.22 E
Dingjia	107	29.24 N	106.09 E
Dingjiagou	104	40.40 N	122.35 E
Dingjiandian	106	32.06 N	120.52 E
Dingjiasuo	100	32.32 N	120.40 E
Dingjiazhuang	106	32.11 N	120.16 E
Dingkouzhen	102	39.55 N	106.40 E
Dingle	48	52.08 N	10.15 W
Dingle ◆[8]	262	53.23 N	2.57 W
Dingle Bay ᑕ	48	52.05 N	10.15 W
Dingley	274b	37.58 S	145.07 E
Dingman Creek ≃	212	42.55 N	81.25 W
Dingmans Ferry	210	41.14 N	74.53 W
Dingnan	100	24.48 N	114.59 E
Dingnan ≃	100	24.28 N	115.26 E
Dingo	166	23.39 S	149.20 E
Dingolfing	60	48.38 N	12.31 E
Dingras	116	18.06 N	120.42 E
Dingshuzhen	106	31.17 N	119.50 E
Dingtao	98	35.04 N	115.34 E
Dingtuna	40	59.34 N	16.22 E
Dinguira	150	14.11 N	11.16 W
Dinguiraye	150	11.18 N	10.43 W
Dingwall, N.S., Can.	186	46.54 N	60.28 W
Dingwall, Scot., U.K.	46	57.35 N	4.29 W
Dingxi	102	35.33 N	104.32 E
Dingxian	98	38.32 N	114.59 E
Dingxiang	102	38.30 N	113.00 E
Dingxiao	102	25.13 N	105.07 E
Dingxing	105	39.17 N	115.46 E
Dingyan	100	32.23 N	120.45 E
Dingyuan	100	32.32 N	117.40 E
Dingzhouying	105	40.20 N	115.43 E
Dingzichang	107	28.54 N	106.08 E
Dingzi Gang ᑕ	98	36.37 N	120.50 E
Dinh, Mui ›	110	11.22 N	109.01 E
Dinhāta	124	26.08 N	89.28 E
Dinh Ca	110	21.45 N	106.03 E
Dinh Lap	110	21.33 N	107.06 E
Dinin ≃	48	52.43 N	7.18 W
Dinkel ≃	52	52.30 N	6.58 E

PORTUGUÊS Nome	Página	Lat.°′	Long.°′ W = Oeste
Dinkelsbühl	56	49.04 N	10.19 E
Dinkelscherben	58	48.21 N	10.35 E
Dinkey Creek ≃	226	36.54 N	119.07 W
Dinklage	52	52.40 N	8.07 E
Dinnebito Wash V	200	35.29 N	111.14 W
Dinner Point ›	220	28.28 N	82.41 W
Dinnet	46	57.03 N	2.54 W
Dinnington	44	53.22 N	1.12 W
Dinokwe	156	23.24 S	26.40 E
Dinorwic	184	49.41 N	92.30 W
Dinorwic Lake ⊜	184	49.37 N	92.33 W
Dinosaur	200	40.14 N	109.00 W
Dinosaur Lake ⊜[1]	182	55.57 N	122.07 W
Dinosaur National Monument ♠	200	40.32 N	108.58 W
Dinosaur Provincial Park ♠	182	50.45 N	111.30 W
Dinskaja	78	45.13 N	39.14 E
Dinslaken	52	51.34 N	6.44 E
Dinslakener Bruch	263	51.35 N	6.43 E
Dinslaken-Schwarze Heide, Flughafen ⊠	263	51.37 N	6.51 E
Dinsmore	184	51.20 N	107.26 W
Dintel ≃	52	51.39 N	4.22 E
Dinteloord	52	51.37 N	4.22 E
Dinuba	226	36.32 N	119.23 W
Dinwiddie, S. Afr.	273d	26.16 S	28.10 E
Dinwiddie, Va., U.S.	208	37.04 N	77.35 W
Dinwiddie □[6]	208	37.10 N	77.20 W
Dinxperlo	52	51.52 N	6.29 E
Diö	26	56.38 N	14.13 E
Diobo	152	2.16 N	20.29 E
Dioïla	150	12.29 N	6.48 W
Diois ◆[1]	62	44.40 N	5.20 E
Diomede	180	65.47 N	169.00 W
Dion ≃	150	10.12 N	8.39 W
Dionísio	255	19.49 S	42.45 W
Dionísio Cerqueira	252	26.15 S	53.38 W
Dionne, Lac ⊜	186	49.26 N	67.55 W
Dions	62	43.56 N	4.19 E
Diorama	255	16.21 S	51.14 W
Dios	175e	5.33 S	154.58 E
Dios, Cayos de II	240p	21.39 N	81.09 W
Diósd	264c	47.25 N	18.57 E
Diouloulou	150	13.03 N	16.36 W
Dioumanténé	150	10.32 N	5.55 W
Dioundiou	150	12.37 N	3.33 E
Diourgani	150	14.19 N	2.44 W
Dioura	150	14.50 N	5.15 W
Diourbel	150	14.40 N	16.15 W
Diourbel □[4]	150	14.45 N	16.30 W
Dipaculao	116	15.51 N	121.32 E
Dipai	100	23.50 N	114.06 E
Dīpālpur	123	30.40 N	73.39 E
Dipignano	68	39.15 N	16.15 E
Dipilo, Pizzo ∧	70	37.57 N	13.59 E
Dipkarpaz	130	35.36 N	34.23 E
Diplo	120	24.28 N	69.35 E
Dipolog	116	8.35 N	123.20 E
Dippoldiswalde	54	50.54 N	13.40 E
Dipton	172	45.54 S	168.22 E
Dipu	106	30.38 N	119.41 E
Diqiyingzi	104	42.11 N	121.29 E
Dique Florentino Ameghino	254	43.40 S	66.25 W
Dīr	123	35.12 N	71.53 E
Dira, Djebel ∧	34	36.05 N	3.38 E
Diré	150	16.16 N	3.24 W
Direction, Cape ›	164	12.51 S	143.32 E
Dire Dawa	144	9.37 N	41.52 E
Direkli	130	39.43 N	36.40 E
Diriamba	236	11.51 N	86.14 W
Dirico	152	17.58 S	20.47 E
Dirillo, Lago ⊜	70	37.08 N	14.42 E
Diriomo	236	11.52 N	86.03 W
Dirj	146	30.09 N	10.26 E
Dirk Hartog Island I	162	25.48 S	113.00 E
Dirkiesdorp	158	27.10 S	30.25 E
Dirkou	146	19.01 N	12.53 E
Dirkshorn	52	52.45 N	4.45 E
Dirksland	52	51.44 N	4.06 E
Dirnaich	60	48.27 N	12.30 E
Dirrah	140	13.37 N	26.06 E
Dirranbandi	166	28.35 S	148.14 E
Dirri	144	4.20 N	46.37 E
Dirs	144	18.32 N	42.05 E
Dirschau → Tczew	30	54.06 N	18.47 E
Dirty Devil ≃	200	37.53 N	110.24 W
Dīsa	120	24.15 N	72.10 E
Dīsah	140	12.02 N	34.19 E
Disappointment, Cape ›, S. Geor.	244	54.53 S	36.07 W
Disappointment, Cape ›, Wa., U.S.	224	46.18 N	124.03 W
Disappointment, Lake ⊜	162	23.30 S	122.50 E
Disappointment, Mount ∧	169	37.25 S	145.18 E
Disappointment Creek ≃	200	38.01 N	108.51 W
Disaster Bay ᑕ	166	37.17 S	150.00 E
Disautel	182	48.22 N	119.14 W
Disbrow Drain ≊	281	42.06 N	83.27 W
Disco	214	42.41 N	83.02 W
Discovery	273d	26.10 S	27.54 E
Discovery Bay ᑕ, Austl.	166	38.12 S	141.07 E
Discovery Bay ᑕ, Zhg.	271d	22.18 N	114.01 E
Discovery Bay ᑕ, Wa., U.S.	224	48.05 N	122.52 W
Discovery Island I	224	48.25 N	123.15 W
Discovery Passage ʮ	182	50.00 N	125.15 W
Discovery Tablemount ✣[3]	8	42.00 S	0.10 E
Disentis	58	46.43 N	8.51 E
Dishāshah	142	28.59 N	30.51 E
Dishergarh	126	23.41 N	86.50 E
Dishman	202	47.39 N	117.16 W
Dishnā	140	26.07 N	32.28 E
Dishna ≃	180	63.37 N	157.18 W
Disihao	89	50.28 N	124.35 E
Disko	216	41.00 N	85.57 W
Disko I	176	69.50 N	53.30 W
Disko Bugt ᑕ	176	69.15 N	52.00 W
Disley	262	53.21 N	2.02 W
Disley Tunnel ◆[5]	262	53.22 N	2.03 W
Dismal ≃	198	41.50 N	100.05 W
Dismal Lakes ⊜	176	67.26 N	117.07 W
Dismal Swamp Canal ≊	208	36.45 N	76.20 W
Disney	196	36.28 N	95.00 W
Disneyland ♠	228	33.48 N	117.55 W
Disneyworld ♠	220	28.27 N	81.28 W
Diso	68	40.00 N	18.23 E
Dispur	120	26.08 N	91.47 E
Disputanta	208	37.07 N	77.13 W
Disraeli	206	45.54 N	71.21 W
Diss	42	52.23 N	1.07 E
Dissimieux, Lac ⊜	186	49.51 N	69.48 W
Distant	214	40.58 N	79.21 W
Disteghil Sār ∧	123	36.19 N	75.12 E
Disteln	263	51.36 N	7.09 E
Distington	44	54.36 N	3.32 W
District Heights	284c	38.51 N	76.53 W
District of Columbia □[3]	208	38.54 N	77.01 W
Distrito Especial □[5]	246	4.15 N	74.15 W
Distrito Federal □[5], Arg.	258	34.36 S	58.26 W
Distrito Federal □[5], Bra.	255	15.45 S	47.45 W
Distrito Federal □[5], Méx.	234	19.15 N	99.10 W
Distrito Federal □[5], Ven.	246	10.30 N	66.55 W
Distroff	56	49.20 N	6.16 E
Disūq	142	31.08 N	30.39 E
Ditfurt	54	51.50 N	11.11 E

Name	Page	Lat.°′	Long.°′
Dithmarschen ◆[1]	30	54.05 N	9.00 E
Dit Island I	116	11.15 N	120.56 E
Dittáino ≃	70	37.25 N	15.00 E
Dittelbrunn	56	50.05 N	10.13 E
Ditton, Eng., U.K.	260	51.18 N	0.27 E
Ditton, Eng., U.K.	262	53.22 N	2.45 W
Ditton ≃	206	45.23 N	71.12 W
Ditton Priors	42	52.30 N	2.35 W
Ditzingen	56	48.49 N	9.03 E
Ditzum	52	53.18 N	7.16 E
Diu	120	20.42 N	70.59 E
Diu □[8]	120	20.42 N	70.59 E
Diuata Mountains ⩘	116	9.10 N	125.47 E
Diuata Point ›	116	9.05 N	125.12 E
Dīva	272c	19.09 N	72.59 E
Divalá	236	8.25 N	82.43 W
Dīvāndarreh	128	35.55 N	47.02 E
Dívčice	61	49.06 N	14.19 E
Dive	272c	19.11 N	73.02 E
Divejevo	80	55.03 N	43.15 E
Divenié	152	2.41 S	12.05 E
Divenskaja	76	59.12 N	30.01 E
Diveria ≃	58	46.09 N	8.19 E
Divernon	219	39.33 N	89.39 W
Dives ≃	32	49.19 N	0.05 W
Dividing Creek	208	39.16 N	75.06 W
Dividing Creek ≃	208	38.05 N	75.32 W
Dividing Ridge ∧	219	39.07 N	90.39 W
Divignano	266b	45.40 N	8.36 E
Divilacan Bay ᑕ	116	17.25 N	122.19 E
Divine Corners	210	41.48 N	74.40 W
Divinhe	156	20.40 S	34.49 E
Divino	255	20.37 S	42.09 W
Divinolândia	256	21.40 S	46.45 W
Divinópolis	255	20.09 S	44.54 W
Divi Point ›	122	15.58 N	81.09 E
Divis ∧[2]	48	54.37 N	6.01 W
Divisa Nova	256	21.31 S	46.12 W
Divisor, Serra do (Cordillera Ultraoriental) ⩘[1]	248	8.20 S	73.30 W
Divnogorsk	86	55.58 N	92.22 E
Divnoje	80	45.55 N	43.22 E
Divo	150	5.50 N	5.22 W
Divodar	120	24.06 N	71.47 E
Divonne-les-Bains	58	46.22 N	6.08 E
Divriği	130	39.23 N	38.07 E
Dīwāl Qol	120	34.19 N	67.54 E
Dix, Il., U.S.	219	38.27 N	88.56 W
Dix, Ne., U.S.	198	41.14 N	103.29 W
Dix ≃	192	37.49 N	84.43 W
Dix, Lac des ⊜	58	46.03 N	7.24 E
Dixboro	216	42.19 N	83.39 W
Dixfield	188	44.32 N	70.27 W
Dix Hills	276	40.49 N	73.22 W
Dixie	275b	43.36 N	79.36 W
Dixie Valley V	204	39.50 N	117.55 W
Dix Milles, Lac ⊜	190	46.46 N	77.45 W
Dixmoor	278	41.38 N	87.40 W
Dixmude → Diksmuide	50	51.02 N	2.52 E
Dixon, Ca., U.S.	226	38.19 N	121.49 W
Dixon, Il., U.S.	190	41.50 N	89.28 W
Dixon, Ky., U.S.	194	37.31 N	87.41 W
Dixon, Mo., U.S.	194	37.59 N	92.05 W
Dixon, N.M., U.S.	200	36.11 N	105.53 W
Dixon, Oh., U.S.	216	40.57 N	84.48 W
Dixon Entrance ʮ	182	54.25 N	132.30 W
Dixons Mills	194	32.04 N	87.47 W
Dixons Pond ⊜	276	40.56 N	74.27 W
Dixonville	214	40.42 N	79.00 W
Dixville	206	45.04 N	71.46 W
Diyā al-Kawm	142	30.38 N	31.05 E
Diyadin	84	39.33 N	43.41 E
Diyālā □[4]	128	34.00 N	45.00 E
Diyālā (Sīrvān) ≃	128	33.14 N	44.31 E
Diyanga	152	1.29 S	11.52 E
Diyarbakır	130	37.55 N	40.14 E
Diyarbakır □[4]	130	38.05 N	40.15 E
Diyarb Najm	142	30.45 N	31.26 E
Diyu al-Wasta	142	30.54 N	31.30 E
Dizangsi	104	41.26 N	120.57 E
Dizhou	102	23.00 N	106.20 E
Dizy	50	49.04 N	3.58 E
Dizzard Point ›	42	50.45 N	4.38 W
Dja ≃	152	2.02 N	15.12 E
Dja, Réserve du ◆[4]	152	3.05 N	13.00 E
Djabalpur → Jabalpur	124	23.10 N	79.57 E
Djabir	152	0.32 N	24.05 E
Djadié ≃	152	0.46 N	12.58 E
Djado	146	21.01 N	12.18 E
Djado, Plateau du ⩘[1]	146	21.45 N	12.50 E
Djaipur → Jaipur	120	26.55 N	75.49 E
Djakarta → Jakarta	269e	6.10 S	106.48 E
Djakonovo	82	54.34 N	38.20 E
Djakovka	80	50.43 N	46.46 E
Djakovo ◆[8]	265b	55.39 N	37.40 E
Djamâa	148	33.32 N	6.00 E
Djamba, Ang.	152	16.46 S	13.59 E
Djamba, R.D.C.	152	9.49 S	22.07 E
Djambala	152	2.33 S	14.45 E
Djamschedpur → Jamshedpur	126	22.48 N	86.11 E
Djanet	148	24.34 N	9.29 E
Djaouro Mbali	152	5.52 N	13.29 E
Djaret, Oued V	148	26.32 N	1.30 E
Djebobo ∧	150	8.20 N	0.35 E
Djébrène	146	11.14 N	19.01 E
Djédaa	146	13.31 N	18.34 E
Djedda → Jiddah	144	21.30 N	39.12 E
Djedi, Oued V	148	34.28 N	6.05 E
Djéké Djéké	146	8.25 N	18.12 E
Djelo-Binza	273b	4.23 S	15.16 E
Djema	140	6.03 N	25.19 E
Djember → Jember, Indon.	115a	8.10 S	113.42 E
Djember, Tchad	146	10.25 N	17.50 E
Djemila ⊥	34	36.25 N	5.44 E
Djénné	150	13.54 N	4.33 W
Djenoun, Garet el ∧	148	25.05 N	5.25 E
Djérem ≃	152	5.20 N	13.24 E
Djibasso	150	13.07 N	4.10 W
Djibo	150	14.06 N	1.38 W
Djibouti	144	11.36 N	43.09 E
Djibouti □[1], Afr.	136	11.30 N	43.00 E
Djibouti □[1], Afr.	144	11.30 N	43.00 E
Djibrouïa	150	13.13 N	11.14 W
Djiri	273b	4.08 S	15.19 E
Djiri ≃	273b	4.11 S	15.20 E
Djohong	152	6.50 N	14.42 E
Djokjakarta → Yogyakarta	115a	7.48 S	110.22 E
Djokoumatombi	152	0.47 N	15.22 E
Djokupunda	152	5.27 S	20.58 E
Djolu	152	0.37 N	22.21 E
Djombo	152	1.21 N	20.22 E
Djoua ≃	152	1.13 N	13.12 E
Djouari ≃	273b	4.13 S	15.08 E
Djoubissi	152	6.12 N	20.45 E
Djoué ≃	273b	4.19 S	15.14 E
Djougou	150	9.42 N	1.40 E
Djoum	152	2.40 N	12.40 E
Djouna	146	10.27 N	20.04 E
Djourab, Erg du ⍓[8]	146	16.40 N	18.50 E
Djugu	154	1.55 N	30.30 E
Djúpivogur	24a	64.40 N	14.10 W
Djura	40	60.37 N	15.00 E
Djurås	40	60.33 N	15.08 E
Djurmo	40	60.33 N	15.10 E
Djurö	40	59.19 N	18.41 E
Djurö I	26	58.52 N	13.28 E
Djursholm	40	59.24 N	18.05 E
Dlouhá Ves	60	49.12 N	13.31 E
Dmanisi	84	41.22 N	44.12 E
Dmitr'ašovka	76	52.09 N	39.04 E

Name	Page	Lat.°′	Long.°′
Dmitrija Lapteva, proliv ʮ	74	73.00 N	142.00 E
Dmitrijevka, Kaz.	85	43.30 N	77.02 E
Dmitrijevka, Ross.	76	52.53 N	40.47 E
Dmitrijevka, Ross.	86	55.10 N	75.36 E
Dmitrijev-L'govskij	78	52.08 N	35.05 E
Dmitrijevskoje, Kaz.	86	49.08 N	57.50 E
Dmitrijevskoje, Ross.	80	45.48 N	41.54 E
Dmitrijevskoje, Ross.	82	54.40 N	37.38 E
Dmitrijev Usad, Ross.	76	54.08 N	43.08 E
Dmitrijev Usad, Ross.	80	54.14 N	43.18 E
Dmitrijevy Gory	80	55.12 N	41.47 E
Dmitrivka	78	45.29 N	35.04 E
Dmitrov	82	56.21 N	37.31 E
Dmitrovcy	82	55.16 N	38.55 E
Dmitrovskij Pogost	76	55.19 N	39.49 E
Dmitrovsk-Orlovskij	76	52.30 N	35.09 E
Dmukhaylivka	78	49.03 N	34.46 E
Dmytrivka, Ukr.	78	46.51 N	36.35 E
Dmytrivka, Ukr.	78	50.56 N	32.58 E
Dmytrivka, Ukr.	78	48.48 N	32.44 E
Dmytrivka, Ukr.	83	48.55 N	39.10 E
Dmytriyivka	83	47.56 N	38.56 E
Dnepropetrovsk → Dnipropetrovs'k	78	48.27 N	34.59 E
Dneprovskoje	76	55.40 N	33.55 E
Dnieper (Dnipro) (Dnjapro) ≃	78	46.30 N	32.18 E
Dniepropetrovsk → Dnipropetrovs'k	78	48.27 N	34.59 E
Dniester (Dnister) (Nistru) ≃	78	46.18 N	30.17 E
Dniprodzerzhyns'k	78	48.30 N	34.37 E
Dniprodzerzhyns'ke vodoskhovyshche ⊜[1]	78	48.45 N	34.00 E
Dnipropetrovs'k	78	48.27 N	34.59 E
Dnipropetrovs'k □[4]	78	48.30 N	35.00 E
Dniprovka	78	47.26 N	34.38 E
Dniprovs'kyy lyman ᑕ[1]	78	46.35 N	31.55 E
Dnipryany	78	46.44 N	33.16 E
Dnistrovs'ke vodoskhovyshche ⊜[1]	78	48.30 N	26.45 E
Dnistrovs'kyy lyman ⊜	78	46.15 N	30.17 E
Dnjaprouska Buhski, kanal ≊	76	52.03 N	25.35 E
Dno	76	57.50 N	29.59 E
Do, Lac ⊜	150	15.54 N	2.45 W
Doa	154	16.44 S	34.32 E
Do Āb-e Mīkh-e Zarrīn	120	35.16 N	68.00 E
Doaktown	186	46.33 N	66.08 W
Doangdoangan-Besar, Pulau I	112	5.24 S	117.55 E
Doany	157b	14.22 S	49.31 E
Doba	146	8.39 N	16.51 E
Dobane	140	6.24 N	24.42 E
Dobbertin	54	53.37 N	12.04 E
Dobbiaco (Toblach)	64	46.44 N	12.14 E
Dobbin	222	30.22 N	95.46 W
Dobbins	226	39.22 N	121.12 W
Dobbins Air Force Base ■	192	33.54 N	84.31 W
Dobbs Ferry	210	41.00 N	73.52 W
Dobczyce	30	49.54 N	20.06 E
Dobel	56	48.48 N	8.29 E
Dobele	76	56.37 N	23.16 E
Döbeln	54	51.07 N	13.07 E
Doberai, Jazirah (Vogelkop) ›[1]	164	1.30 S	132.30 E
Döberitz	264a	52.33 N	13.03 E
Doberlug-Kirchhain	54	51.38 N	13.34 E
Döbern	54	51.37 N	14.36 E
Dobiegniew	30	52.59 N	15.47 E
Döbling ◆[8]	264b	48.15 N	16.22 E
Dobo	164	5.46 S	134.13 E
Doboj	38	44.44 N	18.06 E
Dobra, Pol.	30	51.54 N	18.37 E
Dobra, Pol.	30	53.35 N	15.18 E
Dobra ≃	36	45.33 N	15.31 E
Dobr'anka	86	58.27 N	56.24 E
Dobřany	60	49.40 N	13.18 E
Dobra Stausee ⊜[1]	61	48.35 N	15.20 E
Dobre Miasto	30	53.59 N	20.25 E
Döbriach	64	46.47 N	13.39 E
Dobrič	38	43.34 N	27.50 E
Dobrich → Dobrič	38	43.34 N	27.50 E
Dobrinka, Ross.	80	52.09 N	40.29 E
Dobrinka, Ross.	80	48.49 N	42.58 E
Dobrinka, Ross.	80	50.49 N	41.51 E
Dobříš	30	49.47 N	14.11 E
Dobritz	54	52.01 N	12.13 E
Dobrodzień	30	50.44 N	18.27 E
Dobroje, Ross.	76	57.06 N	32.02 E
Dobroje, Ross.	76	52.52 N	39.48 E
Dobroměřice	54	50.23 N	13.46 E
Dobromyl'	78	49.34 N	22.47 E
Dobropillya	78	48.28 N	37.05 E
Dobroteasa	38	44.47 N	24.23 E
Dobrotvir	78	50.14 N	24.22 E
Dobrovelychkivka	78	48.23 N	31.11 E
Dobrovillya	78	48.41 N	36.37 E
Dobrovol'sk	76	54.46 N	22.31 E
Dobrudžansko plato ⩘[1]	38	43.32 N	27.50 E
Dobruja □[9]	38	44.00 N	28.00 E
Dobruš	76	52.25 N	31.19 E
Dobruška	30	50.17 N	16.10 E
Dobryanka, Ukr.	78	52.04 N	31.11 E
Dobryanka, Ukr.	78	48.21 N	30.54 E
Dobrzany	30	53.22 N	15.25 E
Dobrzyń nad Wisłą	30	52.38 N	19.20 E
Dobšiná	30	48.49 N	20.23 E
Dobson	192	36.23 N	80.43 W
Dobzha	120	28.28 N	88.14 E
Doce ≃, Bra.	255	19.37 S	39.49 W
Doce ≃, Bra.	255	18.28 S	51.05 W
Doce de Octubre	196	25.38 N	97.47 W
Dochart ≃	46	56.28 N	4.20 W
Döčin ≃	88	49.39 N	114.48 E
Docker River	162	24.52 S	129.05 E
Docking	42	52.55 N	0.38 E
Dock Junction	192	31.11 N	81.31 W
Dockton	224	47.22 N	122.27 W
Dockweiler	56	50.15 N	6.46 E
Dockweiler Beach State Park ♠	280	33.55 N	118.26 W
Doctor Arroyo	234	23.40 N	100.11 W
Doctor Cecilio Báez	252	25.03 S	56.19 W
Doctor Coss	196	25.55 N	99.11 W
Doctor Edmund A. Babler Memorial State Park ♠	219	38.36 N	90.43 W
Doctor Hicks Range ⩘	162	28.40 S	124.20 E
Doctor Pedro P. Peña	252	22.26 S	62.22 W
Doctors Creek ≃	208	40.11 N	74.41 W
Doda	123	33.08 N	75.34 E
Dod Ballāpur	122	13.18 N	77.32 E
Doddinghurst	42	51.40 N	0.18 E
Doddridge	194	33.05 N	93.54 W
Dodds Island I	219	38.35 N	91.59 W
Doddsville	194	33.39 N	90.31 W
Dodecanese → Dhodhekánisos II	38	36.30 N	27.00 E
Dodéo	152	7.29 N	12.04 E
Dodge, Ne., U.S.	198	41.43 N	96.52 W
Dodge, Tx., U.S.	222	30.45 N	95.24 W
Dodge □[6]	216	43.14 N	88.40 W
Dodge Brothers State Park Number 4♠, Mi., U.S.	281	42.37 N	83.22 W

Name	Page	Lat.°′	Long.°′
Dodge Brothers State Park Number 8♠, Mi., U.S.	281	42.36 N	83.01 W
Dodge Center	190	44.01 N	92.51 W
Dodge City	198	37.45 N	100.01 W
Dodge Park	284c	38.56 N	76.53 W
Dodger Stadium ♠	280	34.04 N	118.14 W
Dodgeville	190	42.57 N	90.07 W
Dodman Point ›	42	50.13 N	4.48 W
Dodo Goei	140	5.57 N	29.26 E
Dodola	144	7.02 N	39.07 E
Dodoma	154	6.11 S	35.45 E
Dodoma □[4]	154	6.00 S	36.00 E
Dodori ≃	154	1.52 S	41.02 E
Dodsland	184	51.48 N	108.49 W
Dodson, La., U.S.	194	32.04 N	92.39 W
Dodson, Mt., U.S.	202	48.23 N	108.14 W
Dodson, Tx., U.S.	196	34.46 N	100.02 W
Dodurga	130	39.48 N	29.55 E
Doe Lake ⊜	212	45.32 N	79.25 W
Doe River	182	56.00 N	120.05 W
Doerun	192	31.19 N	83.55 W
Doesburg	52	52.01 N	6.09 E
Doetinchem	52	51.58 N	6.17 E
Dog ≃	190	48.51 N	89.37 W
Dogāchia	272b	22.58 N	88.31 E
Dogai Coring ⊜	120	34.30 N	89.15 E
Dōga-mori ∧	96	33.09 N	132.53 E
Doğanbey, Tür.	130	37.37 N	27.11 E
Doğanbey, Tür.	130	38.04 N	26.53 E
Doğanbey, Tür.	130	37.48 N	31.54 E
Doğanca	130	37.49 N	42.20 E
Doğançay	130	40.37 N	30.20 E
Doganella	66	41.34 N	12.56 E
Doğanhisar	130	38.09 N	31.41 E
Doğankent, Tür.	130	40.48 N	38.56 E
Doğankent, Tür.	130	36.52 N	35.18 E
Doğanşehir	130	38.06 N	37.53 E
Doğanyol	130	38.19 N	39.03 E
Doğanyurt, Tür.	130	42.00 N	33.27 E
Doğanyurt, Tür.	130	40.41 N	36.43 E
Dog Creek	182	51.35 N	122.15 W
Dog Creek ≃, B.C., Can.	182	51.35 N	122.17 W
Dog Creek ≃, Mt., U.S.	202	47.44 N	109.36 W
Dog Creek ≃, Oh., U.S.	216	41.03 N	84.23 W
Dog Ear Creek ≃	198	43.42 N	99.59 W
Dog Island I, Anguilla	238	18.17 N	63.16 W
Dog Island I, Fl., U.S.	192	29.48 N	84.35 W
Dog Islands II	240m	18.29 N	64.28 W
Dog Lake ⊜, Mb., Can.	184	51.02 N	98.30 W
Dog Lake ⊜, On., Can.	190	48.46 N	89.32 W
Dog Lake ⊜, On., Can.	190	48.18 N	84.10 W
Dog Lake ⊜, On., Can.	212	44.27 N	76.20 W
Dogliani	62	44.32 N	7.56 E
Dogna	64	46.27 N	13.19 E
Dōgo I	92	36.15 N	133.16 E
Do Gonbadān	128	30.21 N	50.48 E
Dogondoutchi	150	13.38 N	4.02 E
Doğonşar	130	40.14 N	37.33 E
Dōgo-yama ∧	96	35.04 N	133.14 E
Dogpound Creek ≃	182	51.50 N	114.24 W
Dogs, Isle of I	260	51.29 N	0.01 W
D'ogtevo, Ross.	78	49.10 N	40.39 E
D'ogtevo, Ross.	80	49.11 N	40.39 E
Doğubayazıt	84	39.32 N	44.08 E
Doguéraoua	150	13.58 N	5.35 E
Doğu Karadeniz Dağları ⩘	130	40.30 N	40.30 E
Dogura	164	10.05 S	150.05 E
Doha → Ad-Dawḥah	128	25.17 N	51.32 E
Dohār	126	23.35 N	90.09 E
Dohhi	124	24.32 N	84.54 E
Dohna	54	50.57 N	13.51 E
Döhren	52	52.26 N	9.02 E
Dohrgaul	263	51.06 N	7.27 E
Dohrīghāt	124	26.16 N	83.31 E
Doi	96	33.57 N	133.26 E
Doi, Kinh ≊	269c	10.43 N	106.37 E
Doilungdêqên	124	29.48 N	90.47 E
Doiran, Lake ⊜	38	41.13 N	22.44 E
Doiras, Embalse de ⊜[1]	34	43.10 N	6.45 W
Dois de Novembro, Cachoeira ⌊	248	8.52 S	62.16 W
Dois Irmãos, Pico ∧	287a	22.59 S	43.14 W
Dois Irmãos de Goiás	250	9.16 S	49.05 W
Doi Suthep-Pui National Park ♠	110	18.50 N	98.50 E
Dōjō	268	35.51 N	139.37 E
Dōjō ◆[8]	270	34.52 N	135.14 E
Doka, Indon.	164	6.39 S	134.15 E
Doka, Sūd.	140	13.31 N	35.46 E
Doki ≃	96	34.18 N	133.48 E
Dokka	26	60.50 N	10.05 E
Dokkum	52	53.19 N	6.00 E
Dökmetepe	130	40.19 N	36.18 E
Dokri	120	27.23 N	68.06 E
Dokská pahorkatina ⩘[2]	54	50.30 N	14.45 E
Doksy	54	50.35 N	14.38 E
Dokšycy	76	54.54 N	27.46 E
Dokuchayevs'k	83	47.44 N	37.40 E
Dola	216	40.47 N	83.42 W
Dolak ≃	164	7.48 S	139.00 E
Doland	198	44.53 N	98.06 W
Dolany	60	49.27 N	13.15 E
Dolavon	254	43.18 S	65.42 W
Dolayoba	267b	40.54 N	29.15 E
Dolbeau	176	48.53 N	72.14 W
Dolberg	52	51.42 N	7.55 E
Dolceacqua	62	43.51 N	7.37 E
Dolcedorme, Serra ∧	68	39.53 N	16.13 E
Dol-de-Bretagne	32	48.33 N	1.45 W
Dole	58	47.06 N	5.30 E
Dolega	236	8.34 N	82.25 W
Dolen	222	30.26 N	94.54 W
Dolgaja	86	55.49 N	64.15 E
Dolgaja, kosa ›[2]	78	46.43 N	37.41 E
Dolgarrog	44	53.11 N	3.51 W
Dolgelin	54	52.29 N	14.24 E
Dolgellau	42	52.44 N	3.53 W
Dolgeville	210	43.06 N	74.46 W
Dolgij, ostrov I	24	69.15 N	59.04 E
Dolgij Most	88	56.45 N	96.48 E
Dolgoi Island I	180	55.10 N	161.45 W
Dolgoje	78	52.04 N	37.34 E
Dolgoprudnyj	82	55.56 N	37.31 E
Dolgorukovo	76	52.19 N	38.21 E
Dolgoščelje	24	66.03 N	43.24 E
Dolianova	71	39.22 N	9.10 E
Dolinnyj	80	51.16 N	52.11 E
Dolinsk	89	47.21 N	142.48 E
Dolisie	152	4.12 S	12.41 E
Dolj □[6]	38	44.15 N	23.45 E
Döllach	64	46.58 N	12.54 E
Dollar	46	56.09 N	3.40 W
Dollard ᑕ	52	53.17 N	7.10 E
Dollard-des-Ormeaux	206	45.29 N	73.49 W
Dollar Law ∧	46	55.33 N	3.17 W
Döllbach	56	50.26 N	9.44 E
Dolle	54	52.25 N	11.37 E
Dollern	52	53.32 N	9.32 E
Dollerup	41	54.46 N	9.40 E
Döllnitz	54	51.24 N	12.01 E
Dollnstein	60	48.52 N	11.04 E
Döllstädt	54	51.05 N	10.49 E
Dolmabahce Palace ʋ	267b	41.02 N	29.00 E
Dolmativka	78	46.13 N	32.26 E
Dolmatovskij	80	57.29 N	42.18 E
Dolni Dăbnik	38	43.24 N	24.26 E
Dolní Dvořiště	61	48.39 N	14.27 E
Dolní Jiřetín	54	50.35 N	13.33 E

≃	River	Fluß	Río	Rivière	Rio
≊	Canal	Kanal	Canal	Canal	Canal
⌊	Waterfall, Rapids	Wasserfall, Stromschnellen	Cascada, Rápidos	Chute d'eau, Rapides	Cascata, Rápidos
ʮ	Strait	Meeresstraße	Estrecho	Détroit	Estreito
ᑕ	Bay, Gulf	Bucht, Golf	Bahía, Golfo	Baie, Golfe	Baía, Golfo
⊜	Lake, Lakes	See, Seen	Lago, Lagos	Lac, Lacs	Lago, Lagos
≡	Swamp	Sumpf	Pantano	Marais	Pântano
⍓	Ice Features, Glacier	Eis- und Gletscherformen	Accidentes Glaciales	Formes glaciaires	Acidentes glaciares
⍑	Other Hydrographic Features	Andere Hydrographische Objekte	Otros Elementos Hidrográficos	Autres données hydrographiques	Outros acidentes hidrográficos

✣	Submarine Features	Untermeerische Objekte	Accidentes Submarinos	Formes de relief sous-marin	Acidentes submarinos
□	Political Unit	Politische Einheit	Unidad Politica	Entité politique	Unidade política
ʋ	Cultural Institution	Kulturelle Institution	Institución Cultural	Institution culturelle	Instituição cultural
⊥	Historical Site	Historische Stätte	Sitio Histórico	Site historique	Sitio histórico
♠	Recreational Site	Erholungs- und Ferienort	Sitio de Recreo	Centre de loisirs	Area de Lazer
⊠	Airport	Flughafen	Aeropuerto	Aéroport	Aeroporto
■	Military Installation	Militäranlage	Instalación Militar	Installation militaire	Instalação militar
◆	Miscellaneous	Verschiedenes	Misceláneo	Divers	Diversos

I · 48 **Doln-Draa**

ENGLISH — DEUTSCH

Name / Name	Page / Seite	Lat. °′ / Breite °′	Long. °′ / Länge °′ E = Ost
Dolni Lom	38	43.31 N	22.47 E
Dolní Žandov	60	50.02 N	12.34 E
Dolný Kubín	30	49.12 N	19.17 E
Dolo	64	45.25 N	12.05 E
Dolohmwar ∧	174r	6.52 N	158.14 E
Dolokmerawan	114	3.10 N	99.08 E
Dolokparibuan	114	3.01 N	98.39 E
Dolomites → Dolomiti ↗	64	46.25 N	11.50 E
Dolomiti (Dolomiten) ↗	64	46.25 N	11.50 E
Dolon'	86	50.40 N	79.18 E
Dolon ≃	62	45.18 N	4.46 E
Dolon, pereval)(	85	41.52 N	75.45 E
Dolores, Arg.	252	36.20 S	57.40 W
Dolores, Col.	246	3.33 N	74.54 W
Dolores, Guat.	232	16.31 N	89.25 W
Dolores, Méx.	196	26.20 N	101.29 W
Dolores, Co., U.S.	200	37.28 N	108.30 W
Dolores, Ur.	252	33.33 S	58.13 W
Dolores, Ven.	246	8.18 N	69.34 W
Dolores ≃, Pil.	116	12.02 N	125.29 E
Dolores ≃, U.S.	200	38.49 N	109.17 W
Dolores, Mission ʋ[1]	282	37.46 N	122.26 W
Dolores Hidalgo	234	21.10 N	100.56 W
Dolphin, Cape ›	254	51.15 S	58.57 W
Dolphin and Union Strait ʊ	176	69.05 N	114.45 W
Dolphin Head ∧	241q	18.22 N	78.10 W
Dölsach	64	46.49 N	12.51 E
Dolsk	30	52.00 N	17.03 E
Dol'skoje	82	54.47 N	36.26 E
Dolton, Eng., U.K.	42	50.53 N	4.01 W
Dolton, Il., U.S.	216	41.38 N	87.36 W
Dolwyddelan	44	53.03 N	3.53 W
Dolyna, Ukr.	78	48.58 N	24.01 E
Dolyna, Ukr.	83	48.59 N	37.27 E
Dolyns'ka	78	48.07 N	32.44 E
Dolžanskaja	78	46.37 N	37.48 E
Dolzhak	78	48.41 N	26.32 E
Dolžicy, Ross.	76	58.00 N	29.51 E
Dolžicy, Ross.	76	58.31 N	29.08 E
Dom ∧	58	46.06 N	7.50 E
Dom, Gunung ∧	164	2.40 S	136.53 E
D'oma ≃	86	54.42 N	55.57 E
Domacha	76	52.28 N	34.58 E
Domadare	144	1.50 N	41.13 E
Domaine, Pointe du ›	275a	45.23 N	73.54 W
Domaniči	76	53.02 N	33.25 E
Domanico	68	39.13 N	16.12 E
Domanivka	78	47.37 N	30.58 E
Dom Aquino	255	15.48 S	54.53 W
Domar, Enneri V	146	18.11 N	18.04 E
Domariāganj	124	27.13 N	82.40 E
Domart-en-Ponthieu	50	50.04 N	2.07 E
Domasi	154	15.18 S	35.20 E
Domaška	80	53.00 N	50.47 E
Domaso	58	46.09 N	9.19 E
Domat/Ems	58	46.50 N	9.28 E
Domažlice	60	49.27 N	12.56 E
Dombaj	84	43.17 N	41.37 E
Dombaj-Ul'gen, gora ∧	84	43.14 N	41.41 E
Dombarovskij	86	50.46 N	59.32 E
Dombås	26	62.05 N	9.08 E
Dombasle-sur-Meurthe	58	48.38 N	6.21 E
Dombe	156	19.59 S	33.25 E
Dombe Grande	152	12.58 S	13.11 E
Dombes ◆[1]	58	46.00 N	5.03 E
Dombóvár	30	46.23 N	18.08 E
Dombrád	30	48.14 N	21.56 E
Dombresson	58	47.04 N	6.58 E
Domburg	52	51.34 N	3.30 E
Dom Cavati	255	19.23 S	42.06 W
Dôme, Puy de ∧	32	45.47 N	2.58 E
Dome Creek	182	53.44 N	121.01 W
Domegge di Cadore	64	46.27 N	12.25 E
Domène	62	45.12 N	5.50 E
Dome Peak ∧, Pil.	116	5.37 N	125.20 E
Dome Peak ∧, Wa., U.S.	224	48.18 N	121.02 W
Domett	172	42.51 S	173.13 E
Domèvre-en-Haye	56	48.49 N	5.55 E
Domeyko	252	28.57 S	70.54 W
Domeyko, Cordillera ↗	252	24.30 S	69.00 W
Domfront	32	48.36 N	0.39 W
Domiciano Ribeiro	255	16.56 S	47.46 W
Domíngo M. Irala	252	25.54 S	54.43 W
Domingos Martins	255	20.22 S	40.40 W
Dominguez	280	33.50 N	118.13 W
Dominguez Channel ʊ	280	38.47 N	118.15 W
Dominguez Hills ↗[2]	280	33.52 N	118.14 W
Dominica □[1], N.A.	230	15.30 N	61.20 W
Dominica □[1], N.A.	240d	15.30 N	61.20 W
Dominicain (république) → Dominican Republic □[1]	238	19.00 N	70.40 W
Dominical	236	9.13 N	83.51 W
Dominicana, República → Dominican Republic □[1]	238	19.00 N	70.40 W
Dominican Republic (República Dominicana) □[1], N.A.	230	19.00 N	70.40 W
Dominican Republic (República Dominicana) □[1], N.A.	238	19.00 N	70.40 W
Dominica Passage ʊ	238	15.45 N	61.30 W
Dominikanische Republik → Dominican Republic □[1]	238	19.00 N	70.40 W
Dominion	186	46.13 N	60.01 W
Dominion, Cape ›	176	66.13 N	74.28 W
Dominion Astrophysical Observatory ʋ[3]	224	48.31 N	123.25 W
Dominion City	184	49.08 N	97.09 W
Dominique → Dominica □[1]	240d	15.30 N	61.20 W
Domiongo	152	4.37 S	21.15 E
Domitilla, Catacombe di ⊥	267a	41.52 N	12.31 E
Dömitz	54	53.08 N	11.14 E
Dom Joaquim	255	18.57 S	43.16 W
Domleschg V	58	46.44 N	9.28 E
Dommartin-lès-Toul	58	48.40 N	5.54 E
Dommartin-Varimont	56	48.58 N	4.46 E
Dommary-Baroncourt	56	49.17 N	5.42 E
Dommel ≃	52	51.40 N	5.20 E
Dommitzsch	54	51.38 N	12.53 E
Domnarvet	40	60.30 N	15.27 E
Domnești	38	44.25 N	25.56 E
Domnino	82	54.10 N	38.11 E
Dom Noi ≃	110	15.17 N	105.28 E
Domo	144	7.54 N	46.52 E
Domodedovo	82	55.26 N	37.46 E
Domodossola	58	46.07 N	8.17 E
Domohani	124	26.35 N	88.48 E
Domoni	157a	12.15 S	44.32 E
Domont	261	49.02 N	2.20 E
Dompaire	58	48.13 N	6.13 E
Dom Pedrito	252	30.59 S	54.40 W
Dom Pedro	250	4.29 S	44.27 W
Dom Pedro II, Estação ◆[5]	287a	23.54 S	43.12 W
Dompu	115b	8.32 S	118.28 E
Domremy	184	52.47 N	105.44 W
Domrémy-la-Pucelle	58	48.27 N	5.41 E
Domselaar	258	35.04 S	58.18 W
Dom Silvério	255	20.09 S	42.58 W
Domsjö	26	63.15 N	18.43 E
Domus de Maria	71	38.57 N	8.52 E
Domusnovas	71	39.19 N	8.39 E
Domuyo, Volcán ∧[1]	252	36.38 S	70.26 W
Domvast	50	50.12 N	1.55 E
Dom Viçoso	256	22.13 S	45.09 W
Dom Yai ≃	110	15.18 N	105.10 E
Domžale	36	46.08 N	14.36 E
Don ≃, On., Can.	212	43.39 N	79.21 W
Don ≃, India	122	16.17 N	76.27 E
Don ≃, Lao	110	15.07 N	105.48 E
Don ≃, Ross.	72	47.04 N	39.18 E
Don ≃, Eng., U.K.	44	53.39 N	0.59 W
Don ≃, Eng., U.K.	262	53.47 N	2.14 W
Don ≃, Scot., U.K.	46	57.08 N	2.05 W
Don, East Branch ≃, On., Can.	212	43.42 N	79.20 W
Don, East Branch ≃, On., Can.	275b	43.43 N	79.20 W
Don, West Branch ≃	275b	43.43 N	79.20 W
Dona Ana, Moç.	154	17.25 S	35.07 E
Dona Ana, N.M., U.S.	200	32.23 N	106.48 W
Donada	64	45.02 N	12.12 E
Donadeu	252	26.43 S	62.44 W
Dona Euzébia	256	21.18 S	42.48 W
Donaghadee	48	54.39 N	5.33 W
Donaghmore	48	54.32 N	6.49 W
Donahoe Creek ≃	222	30.49 N	97.12 W
Donald	166	36.22 S	143.00 E
Donalda	182	52.35 N	112.34 W
Donaldson, Ar., U.S.	194	34.14 N	92.55 W
Donaldson, In., U.S.	216	41.22 N	86.27 W
Donaldson, Pa., U.S.	208	40.38 N	76.24 W
Donaldson Crossroads	279b	40.16 N	80.07 W
Donaldson Dam ⊜[1]	273d	26.17 S	27.41 E
Donaldsonville	194	30.06 N	90.59 W
Donalsonville	192	31.02 N	84.52 W
Doñana, Parque Nacional de ♠	34	37.00 N	6.30 W
Donard, Slieve ∧	48	54.11 N	5.55 W
Donau → Danube ≃	22	45.20 N	29.40 E
Donaueschingen	58	47.57 N	8.29 E
Donaufeld ◆[8]	264b	48.15 N	16.25 E
Donaukanal ≋	264b	48.10 N	16.30 E
Donaumoos ≡, Dtsch.	58	48.30 N	10.15 E
Donaumoos ≡, Dtsch.	60	48.40 N	11.15 E
Donaupark ♠	264b	48.14 N	16.25 E
Donauried ◆[1]	56	48.35 N	10.40 E
Donaustadt ◆[8]	264b	48.13 N	16.30 E
Donaustauf	60	49.02 N	12.13 E
Donauturm ʋ	264b	48.14 N	16.25 E
Donauwörth	56	48.43 N	10.46 E
Don Benito	34	38.57 N	5.52 W
Dönberg ◆[8]	263	51.18 N	7.10 E
Don Bosco ◆[8]	258	34.42 S	58.18 W
Doncaster, Austl.	274b	37.47 S	145.08 E
Doncaster, On., Can.	275b	43.48 N	79.25 W
Doncaster, Eng., U.K.	44	53.32 N	1.07 W
Doncaster ≃	206	45.58 N	74.06 W
Doncaster East	274b	37.47 S	145.10 E
Doncaster Indian Reserve ◆[4]	206	46.09 N	74.07 W
Donchêry	56	49.42 N	4.52 E
Dondaicha	120	21.20 N	74.34 E
Dondo, Ang.	152	9.38 S	14.25 E
Dondo, Moç.	156	19.36 S	34.44 E
Dondo, Teluk ⊂	112	0.55 N	120.30 E
Dondra Head ›	122	5.55 N	80.35 E
Dondușeni	38	48.15 N	27.37 E
Doneck	83	48.21 N	40.02 E
Donegal, Ire.	48	54.39 N	8.07 W
Donegal, S. Afr.	158	26.10 S	23.58 E
Donegal, Pa., U.S.	214	40.07 N	79.23 W
Donegal □[6]	48	54.50 N	8.00 W
Donegal Bay ⊂	48	54.30 N	8.30 W
Doneraile, Ire.	48	52.13 N	8.35 W
Doneraile, S.C., U.S.	192	34.19 N	79.53 W
Donets'k	83	48.00 N	37.48 E
Donets'k □[4]	78	48.00 N	37.30 E
Donets'kyy ◆[8]	83	48.42 N	38.41 E
Donets'kyy kryazh ∧	83	48.15 N	38.45 E
Dong ≃, Zhg.	100	23.06 N	114.00 E
Dong ≃, Zhg.	100	25.00 N	118.27 E
Dong ≃, Zhg.	100	23.42 N	117.13 E
Dong ≃, Zhg.	102	42.10 N	101.00 E
Donga ≃	146	8.19 N	9.58 E
Dong'an, Zhg.	89	47.20 N	134.10 E
Dongan → Mishan, Zhg.	89	45.33 N	131.52 E
Dong'an, Zhg.	100	33.24 N	114.24 E
Dong'an, Zhg.	102	26.17 N	111.07 E
Dong'an, Zhg.	106	30.30 N	118.48 E
Dong'an, Zhg.	106	31.35 N	119.44 E
Dongao	100	29.12 N	121.25 E
Dongara	162	29.15 S	114.56 E
Dongargarh	120	21.12 N	80.44 E
Dongba, Zhg.	105	39.58 N	116.32 E
Dongba, Zhg.	106	31.18 N	119.03 E
Dongbahe	105	39.58 N	116.27 E
Dongbaimiao	105	40.34 N	116.05 E
Dongbei	100	27.15 N	116.06 E
Dongbeicha	98	41.43 N	127.23 E
Dongbeijipo	98	36.06 N	117.08 E
Dongchan	107	30.20 N	105.20 E
Dongchang	106	31.52 N	121.38 E
Dongchangjie	106	32.04 N	119.18 E
Dongcheng	100	28.56 N	121.16 E
Dongchong	100	26.35 N	119.52 E
Dongchuan (Xincun)	102	26.10 N	103.01 E
Dongcun	106	30.57 N	121.46 E
Dongdaoan	98	38.21 N	117.12 E
Dong Dian ≡	105	39.03 N	116.35 E
Dongduluo	105	39.04 N	115.15 E
Dong'e (Tongcheng)	98	36.14 N	116.16 E
Dongen	52	51.37 N	4.56 E
Dong'ezhen	98	36.11 N	116.16 E
Dongfang (Basuo)	110	19.05 N	108.39 E
Dongfeng, Zhg.	98	42.40 N	125.28 E
Dongfeng, Zhg.	100	27.20 N	118.53 E
Dongfengtai	105	39.34 N	117.45 E
Donggala	112	0.40 S	119.44 E
Donggang	100	22.58 N	115.57 E
Donggangzi	89	45.53 N	129.49 E
Donggi	112	1.33 S	122.15 E
Donggi Cona ⊜	102	37.10 N	96.55 E
Donggong Shan ↗	100	27.36 N	119.26 E
Donggongsuo	106	32.07 N	121.25 E
Donggou, Zhg.	98	39.54 N	124.09 E
Donggou, Zhg.	100	33.38 N	119.40 E
Donggou, Zhg.	106	32.17 N	118.59 E
Donggu	100	26.46 N	115.22 E
Dongguan, Zhg.	100	27.49 N	116.25 E
Dongguan, Zhg.	100	23.03 N	113.46 E
Dongguan, Zhg.	106	30.22 N	119.28 E
Dongguan, Zhg.	107	30.47 N	106.16 E
Dongguang	98	37.53 N	116.30 E
Dongguanpu	106	31.13 N	120.43 E
Dongguanyingzi	104	41.55 N	120.38 E
Donggugang	105	39.10 N	116.49 E
Dong Hai, Viet	110	12.34 N	109.14 E
Donghai (Niushan), Zhg.	98	34.30 N	118.47 E
Dong Hai → East China Sea ⊤[2]	90	30.00 N	126.00 E
Donghai Dao I	102	21.02 N	110.25 E
Dongheng ≋	106	31.54 N	120.17 E
Donghezhen	106	31.08 N	120.17 E
Dong Hoi	110	17.29 N	106.36 E
Donghu	100	26.28 N	113.07 E
Dong Hu ⊜	120	32.10 N	84.40 E
Donghuanggou	104	40.43 N	123.29 E
Dongi	112	2.02 S	121.28 E
Dongio	58	46.27 N	8.58 E
Dongjia	98	37.18 N	118.24 E
Dongjiangkou	102	33.37 N	108.49 E
Dongjie	100	25.53 N	116.22 E
Dongjielang	100	31.03 N	115.57 E
Dongjingcheng	89	44.07 N	129.09 E
Dongjingji	98	40.02 N	114.01 E
Dongjingling	104	41.18 N	123.15 E
Dongjug	120	29.58 N	94.53 E
Dongkaihecheng	104	41.04 N	122.38 E
Dongkalang	112	0.10 N	120.06 E
Dongkeng, Zhg.	100	24.59 N	114.54 E
Dongkeng, Zhg.	100	27.48 N	119.42 E
Dong Khe	110	22.26 N	106.27 E
Dongkou	98	35.29 N	115.20 E
Donglan	102	24.40 N	107.18 E
Donglaohuyu	104	42.28 N	124.17 E
Donglaojunpu	104	41.24 N	121.22 E
Dongli	102	20.50 N	110.20 E
Dongliang	104	42.00 N	121.25 E
Dongliangjia	105	40.52 N	118.17 E
Donglidian	98	36.02 N	118.23 E
Donglinchang	107	29.39 N	104.07 E
Dongling	104	41.50 N	123.35 E
Dongliu, Zhg.	100	30.14 N	116.53 E
Dongliu, Zhg.	106	32.06 N	118.58 E
Dongliujiazi	104	42.21 N	122.44 E
Donglizhuang	105	39.21 N	116.47 E
Donglong	100	23.36 N	116.50 E
Donglucun	89	49.28 N	128.50 E
Dongmen	100	28.29 N	114.02 E
Dongming	98	35.18 N	115.08 E
Dong Nai ≃	110	10.45 N	106.46 E
Dongnangou	104	41.25 N	122.02 E
Dong Nhien, Rach ≃	269c	10.49 N	106.46 E
Dongning	89	44.04 N	131.07 E
Dongo, Ang.	152	14.36 S	15.48 E
Dongo, It.	58	46.07 N	9.17 E
Dongo, R.D.C.	152	2.43 N	18.24 E
Dongobe	152	4.37 N	23.12 E
Dongobesh	154	4.04 S	35.23 E
Dongola → Dunqulah	140	19.10 N	30.29 E
Dongon Point ›	116	12.44 N	120.48 E
Dongou	152	2.02 N	18.04 E
Dongping, Zhg.	98	35.55 N	116.18 E
Dongping, Zhg.	100	27.24 N	118.39 E
Dongping, Zhg.	102	21.43 N	112.15 E
Dongping Hu ⊜	98	36.00 N	116.12 E
Dongpu	100	30.03 N	120.34 E
Dongqian	106	30.52 N	120.23 E
Dongqiao	100	31.12 N	112.48 E
Dongqing	106	31.49 N	120.03 E
Dongqingduizi	104	41.02 N	122.08 E
Dongsanjiazi	104	41.54 N	122.48 E
Dongsanlintang	106	31.09 N	121.31 E
Dongsanpu	100	33.38 N	117.09 E
Dongsha ≃	104	41.07 N	121.50 E
Dongshaer	120	28.41 N	89.09 E
Dongshajiao	100	30.19 N	122.09 E
Dongshan, Zhg.	100	23.42 N	117.24 E
Dongshan, Zhg.	102	19.50 N	110.14 E
Dongshan, Zhg.	106	31.04 N	120.24 E
Dongshan Dao I	100	23.40 N	117.25 E
Dongshanqiao	106	31.52 N	118.46 E
Dongshe	106	32.07 N	121.12 E
Dongsheng	102	39.49 N	109.59 E
Dongsheshanzi	104	42.15 N	123.09 E
Dongshi, Zhg.	100	24.42 N	118.27 E
Dongshi, Zhg.	100	24.43 N	115.59 E
Dongshi, Zhg.	271a	39.49 N	116.34 E
Dongshuiyan	105	39.15 N	115.23 E
Dongtai	100	32.51 N	120.20 E
Dongtai Hu ⊂	106	31.05 N	120.30 E
Dongtaipingzhen	89	45.18 N	122.05 E
Dongtangou	105	39.23 N	118.22 E
Dongtianmu Shan ∧	106	30.22 N	119.31 E
Dongtiao ≃	106	30.51 N	120.06 E
Dongting	98	38.29 N	115.08 E
Dongtinghu	106	30.53 N	119.30 E
Dongting Hu ⊜	102	29.20 N	112.54 E
Dongtingxi	102	28.34 N	110.36 E
Dongtou	100	27.50 N	121.09 E
Dongtou Shan I	100	27.50 N	121.08 E
Dong Trieu	110	21.05 N	106.31 E
Dongtuhulu	104	41.55 N	121.33 E
Dongtuoshanzi	104	42.10 N	123.08 E
Dongtuozi	104	41.17 N	121.53 E
Dong Van	110	23.16 N	105.22 E
Dongwangfu	89	44.47 N	120.53 E
Dongwangzhuang	106	32.16 N	120.32 E
Dongwe ≃	152	13.58 S	23.53 E
Dongwuquan	105	39.20 N	115.43 E
Dongxi, Zhg.	100	28.35 N	120.02 E
Dongxi, Zhg.	102	28.47 N	106.39 E
Dongxi, Zhg.	107	30.24 N	104.33 E
Dongxia	106	31.11 N	119.05 E
Dongxiagaogao	104	42.36 N	122.30 E
Dongxiang	100	28.13 N	116.35 E
Dongxiang Dao I	100	25.36 N	119.48 E
Dongxing	89	46.23 N	127.52 E
Dongxingchang, Zhg.	107	29.16 N	103.55 E
Dongxingchang, Zhg.	107	29.36 N	105.04 E
Dongxinghe	105	39.46 N	114.49 E
Dongxinpu	104	41.00 N	123.18 E
Dongxinzhen	106	31.57 N	121.42 E
Dongyang, Zhg.	89	48.03 N	124.17 E
Dongyang, Zhg.	100	29.16 N	120.14 E
Dongyangqiao	106	30.52 N	120.34 E
Dongyao	98	35.56 N	113.58 E
Dongyian	105	39.22 N	115.46 E
Dongyin ≃	105	39.09 N	117.43 E
Dongyou	100	27.10 N	118.37 E
Dongyuemiao	106	31.36 N	119.14 E
Dongyuezhen	107	30.24 N	103.32 E
Dongzhang	100	25.44 N	119.17 E
Dongzhaocun	105	40.02 N	116.46 E
Dongzhaozhuang	105	39.57 N	118.24 E
Dongzhenbeng	106	30.59 N	121.01 E
Dongzhi	100	30.07 N	116.59 E
Dongzhizhuang	105	40.25 N	116.50 E
Dongzhuangpu	105	40.34 N	115.42 E
Dongziya	105	38.50 N	116.44 E
Donie	222	31.29 N	96.13 W
Doninga	150	10.37 N	1.26 W
Donington	42	52.55 N	0.12 W
Doniphan, Mo., U.S.	194	36.37 N	90.49 W
Doniphan, Ne., U.S.	198	40.46 N	98.22 W
Don Islands II	116	11.05 N	123.38 E
Donja Stubica	36	45.59 N	15.58 E
Donjek ≃	180	62.35 N	140.00 W
Donjezk → Donets'k	83	48.00 N	37.48 E
Donji Vakuf	36	44.09 N	17.25 E
Donk	52	51.33 N	5.37 E
Donkerpoort	158	30.32 S	25.30 E
Donkey Creek ≃	198	44.12 N	104.58 W
Donkey Town	260	51.20 N	0.39 W
Donmānick Islands II	126	22.00 N	90.37 E
Don Martín	196	27.32 N	100.37 W
Don Matías	246	6.30 N	75.22 W
Don Mills ◆[8]	275b	43.44 N	79.20 W
Don Mills Centre ◆[9]	275b	43.44 N	79.21 W
Don Muang Airport ⊠	269a	13.56 N	100.37 E
Donna	196	26.10 N	98.03 W
Donna, Punta sa ∧	71	40.35 N	9.25 E
Donna Buang, Mount ∧	169	37.43 S	145.40 E
Donnacona	206	46.40 N	71.47 W
Donnalucata	70	36.45 N	14.38 E
Donnaz	62	45.36 N	7.46 E
Donnell Lake ⊜[1]	226	38.20 N	119.56 W
Donnellson	219	39.02 N	89.29 W
Donnelly, Ab., Can.	182	55.44 N	117.06 W
Donnelly, Ak., U.S.	180	63.41 N	145.53 W
Donnelly, Id., U.S.	202	44.43 N	116.04 W
Donnellys Crossing	172	35.43 S	173.37 E
Donnemarie-Dontilly	50	48.29 N	3.08 E
Donner	194	29.41 N	90.56 W
Donner Lake ⊜[1]	226	39.20 N	120.16 W
Donner Memorial State Park ♠	226	39.18 N	120.16 W
Donner Pass)(	226	39.19 N	120.20 W
Donnersberg ∧	56	49.38 N	7.55 E
Donner und Blitzen ≃	202	43.17 N	118.49 W
Donnybrook, Austl.	162	33.35 S	115.49 E
Donnybrook, S. Afr.	158	30.00 S	29.48 E
Donora	214	40.10 N	79.51 W
Donostia (San Sebastián)	34	43.19 N	1.59 W
Donovan	216	40.53 N	87.37 W
Don Peninsula ›[1]	182	52.30 N	128.10 W
Donque	152	15.28 S	14.06 E
Donskaja gr'ada ↗[2]	80	49.30 N	42.00 E
Dons'ke	83	47.31 N	37.33 E
Donskoj, Ross.	76	53.58 N	38.20 E
Donskoj, Ross.	83	48.49 N	40.06 E
Donskoj, Ross.	83	47.25 N	40.14 E
Donskoje, Ross.	76	52.37 N	39.00 E
Donskoje, Ross.	80	45.21 N	41.59 E
Donskoje belogorje ↗[1]	78	50.30 N	39.45 E
Donsol	116	12.54 N	123.36 E
Don Torcuato	288	34.30 S	58.38 W
Don Torcuato, Aeródromo ⊠	288	34.30 S	58.36 W
Dontsivka	83	49.35 N	39.16 E
Donuzlav, ozero ⊜	78	45.23 N	33.05 E
Donyztau, čink ↗	86	46.25 N	57.00 E
Donzdorf	56	48.41 N	9.48 E
Donzère	62	44.27 N	4.43 E
Donzy	50	47.22 N	3.08 E
Dooagh	48	53.59 N	10.09 W
Dood nuur ⊜	88	51.20 N	99.20 E
Doogort	48	54.01 N	10.01 W
Doolow	144	4.10 N	42.05 E
Doomadgee	166	17.56 S	138.49 E
Doomadgee Aboriginal Reserve ◆[4]	166	17.43 S	138.36 E
Doon, On., Can.	212	43.23 N	80.26 W
Doon, Ia., U.S.	198	43.16 N	96.13 W
Doon ≃	44	55.26 N	4.38 W
Doon, Loch ⊜	44	55.15 N	4.22 W
Doonbeg	48	52.44 N	9.32 W
Doonbeg ≃	48	52.44 N	9.34 W
Doon Doon Aboriginal Reserve ◆[4]	164	16.15 S	128.15 E
Doonerak, Mount ∧	180	67.56 N	150.37 W
Doonside	274a	33.46 S	150.52 E
Dooralong	170	33.12 S	151.22 E
Doorn	52	52.03 N	5.21 E
Doorndam	158	28.03 S	21.03 E
Doornik → Tournai	50	50.36 N	3.23 E
Door Peninsula ›[1]	190	44.55 N	87.20 W
Dopping Brook ≃	283	42.12 N	71.23 W
Do Qal'eh	128	32.18 N	61.31 E
Dor	132	32.37 N	34.55 E
Dora	194	33.43 N	87.05 W
Dora, Lake ⊜, Austl.	162	22.05 S	122.55 E
Dora, Lake ⊜, Fl., U.S.	220	29.00 N	81.37 W
Dora Baltea ≃	62	45.11 N	8.05 E
Dora di Rhêmes ≃	62	45.42 N	7.11 E
Dorado	240m	18.28 N	66.15 W
Dorāha	123	30.49 N	76.01 E
Dorāh Ān)(	123	36.07 N	71.15 E
Dorain, Beinn ∧	46	56.30 N	4.42 W
Dorândia	256	22.27 S	43.57 W
Dora Riparia ≃	62	45.05 N	7.44 E
Doraville	192	33.53 N	84.17 W
Dorback Burn ≃	46	57.31 N	3.40 W
Dorcheat, Bayou ≃	194	32.30 N	93.21 W
Dorchester, N.B., Can.	186	45.54 N	64.31 W
Dorchester, On., Can.	212	42.59 N	81.04 W
Dorchester, Eng., U.K.	42	50.43 N	2.26 W
Dorchester, Eng., U.K.	42	51.39 N	1.10 W
Dorchester, Il., U.S.	219	39.05 N	89.53 W
Dorchester, Ne., U.S.	198	40.38 N	97.06 W
Dorchester, N.J., U.S.	208	39.16 N	74.58 W
Dorchester, Wi., U.S.	190	45.00 N	90.20 W
Dorchester □[6]	208	38.34 N	76.04 W
Dorchester ◆[8]	283	42.17 N	71.04 W
Dorchester, Cape ›	176	65.29 N	77.30 W
Dorchester Bay ⊂	283	42.19 N	71.02 W
Dorchester Crossing	186	46.10 N	64.34 W
Dorchester Estates	284c	38.47 N	76.55 W
Dorchester Heights National Historic Site ⊥	283	42.20 N	71.03 W
Dorchheim	56	50.30 N	8.04 E
Dordabis	156	22.52 S	17.38 E
Dordives	50	48.09 N	2.46 E
Dordogne □[5]	32	45.10 N	0.45 E
Dordogne ≃	32	45.02 N	0.35 W
Dordon	42	52.36 N	1.37 W
Dordrecht, Ned.	52	51.49 N	4.40 E
Dordrecht, S. Afr.	158	31.20 S	27.03 E
Doré ≃, Sk., Can.	184	54.56 N	107.45 W
Dore ≃, Fr.	62	45.50 N	3.35 E
Dore ≃, Eng., U.K.	42	51.57 N	2.52 W
Dore, Monts ↗	32	45.30 N	2.45 E
Doreissou	146	10.33 N	15.08 E
Doré Lake	184	54.38 N	107.24 W
Doré Lake ⊜	184	54.46 N	107.17 W
Dorena	202	43.43 N	122.51 W
Dörentrup	52	52.03 N	8.59 E
Dores	46	57.22 N	4.15 W
Dores do Indaiá	255	19.27 S	45.36 W
Dores do Paraibuna	256	21.31 S	43.39 W
Dorfen	60	48.17 N	12.08 E
Dorfgastein	64	47.15 N	13.06 E
Dorfmark	52	52.54 N	9.46 E
Dorgali	71	40.17 N	9.35 E
Dörgön nuur ⊜	88	47.40 N	93.30 E
Doring ≃	158	31.54 S	18.39 E
Doringbaai	158	31.48 S	18.15 E
Doringkop ∧	273d	26.15 S	27.50 E
Dorino	82	56.28 N	36.09 E
Dorion-Vaudreuil	206	45.23 N	74.01 W
Dorje Lāpka ∧	124	28.11 N	85.47 E
Dorking	42	51.14 N	0.20 W
Dorloo	210	42.43 N	74.37 W
Dormaa Ahenkro	150	7.17 N	2.53 W
Dormagen	56	51.05 N	6.50 E
Dormans	50	49.04 N	3.38 E
Dormidontovka	89	47.45 N	134.57 E
Dormont	279b	40.23 N	80.02 W
Dornach	58	47.29 N	7.37 E
Dornap ◆[8]	263	51.15 N	7.04 E
Dornbach ◆[8]	264b	48.14 N	16.18 E
Dornbirn	58	47.25 N	9.44 E
Dornburg, Dtsch.	54	51.01 N	11.40 E
Dornburg, Dtsch.	56	50.30 N	8.07 E
Dorndorf	56	50.50 N	10.05 E
Dorndorf-Steudnitz	54	51.00 N	11.40 E
Dornecy	50	47.26 N	3.35 E
Dorney	260	51.30 N	0.40 W
Dornhan	58	48.21 N	8.30 E
Dornie	46	57.17 N	5.31 W
Dorno	62	45.09 N	8.57 E
Dornoch	46	57.52 N	4.02 W
Dornoch Firth ⊂[1]	46	57.53 N	4.00 W
Dornod □[4]	88	48.00 N	115.00 E
Dornogov' □[4]	102	44.30 N	110.00 E
Dornsife	208	40.45 N	76.47 W
Dornstadt	58	48.28 N	9.56 E
Dornstetten	58	48.28 N	8.30 E
Dornumersiel	52	53.40 N	7.28 E
Doro, Indon.	115a	7.02 S	109.41 E
Doro, Mali	150	16.09 N	0.51 W
Dorochovo	82	55.33 N	36.23 E
Dorog	30	47.43 N	18.44 E
Dorogobuž	76	54.55 N	33.18 E
Doroḥ	128	32.17 N	60.30 E
Dorohoi	38	47.57 N	26.24 E
Dorokempo	115b	8.33 S	118.15 E
Doromata	115b	8.46 S	118.13 E
Doromo	154	3.49 N	26.17 E
Dorošata	80	57.21 N	51.08 E
Dorošicha	82	56.52 N	35.50 E
Dorotea	26	64.16 N	16.24 E
Dorothy	208	39.24 N	74.49 W
Dorothy, Lake ⊜	224	47.34 N	121.22 W
Dorotockeys Run ≃	276	40.59 N	73.58 W
Dorpat → Tartu	76	58.23 N	26.43 E
Dörpen	52	52.57 N	7.20 E
Dorr	216	42.43 N	85.43 W
Dorrance	198	38.50 N	98.35 W
Dorre Island I	162	25.09 S	113.07 E
Dorrigo	166	30.21 S	152.43 E
Dorris	204	41.58 N	121.55 W
Dorsale ↗	36	36.00 N	9.50 E
Dorset, Oh., U.S.	214	41.41 N	80.40 W
Dorset, Vt., U.S.	210	43.15 N	73.05 W
Dorset □[6]	42	50.47 N	2.20 W
Dorset Peak ∧	188	43.19 N	73.02 W
Dorsey Run ≃	284b	39.11 N	76.48 W
Dorseyville	279b	40.35 N	79.53 W
Dorsten	52	51.39 N	6.58 E
Dorstfeld ◆[8]	263	51.31 N	7.25 E
Dort → Dordrecht	52	51.49 N	4.40 E
Dortan	58	46.19 N	5.40 E
Dörtdivan	130	40.43 N	32.04 E
Dortmund, Dtsch.	52	51.31 N	7.28 E
Dortmund, Dtsch.	263	51.31 N	7.28 E
Dortmund-Ems-Kanal ≋	52	51.32 N	7.27 E
Dortmunder Rieselfelder ◆[1]	263	51.39 N	7.25 E
Dortmund-Wickede, Flughafen ⊠	263	51.32 N	7.35 E
Dorton	192	37.16 N	82.34 W
Dörtyol	130	36.52 N	36.12 E
Do Rūd	128	33.28 N	49.04 E
Dorum	52	53.41 N	8.34 E
Doruma	154	4.44 N	27.42 E
Dorval	206	45.27 N	73.44 W
Dorval, Île I	275a	45.26 N	73.45 W
Dorval Gardens Centre ◆[9]	275a	45.27 N	73.44 W
Dörverden	52	52.51 N	9.13 E
Dörvöldžin	88	48.08 N	93.58 E
Dörzbach	56	49.23 N	9.42 E
Dos, Canal Numero ≋	252	36.21 S	56.54 W
Dosara	150	12.32 N	6.09 E
Do Sārī	128	28.25 N	57.59 E
Dos Arroyos	234	17.02 N	99.40 W
Dosatuj	88	50.23 N	118.38 E
Dos Bahías, Cabo ›	254	44.55 S	65.32 W
Dos Bocas	240m	18.20 N	66.40 W
Dos Bocas, Lago ⊜[1]	240m	18.19 N	66.40 W
Doščatoje	80	55.23 N	42.07 E
Döşemealtı	130	37.04 N	30.36 E
Dosewallips ≃	224	47.42 N	122.53 W
Dos Hermanas	34	37.17 N	5.55 W
Dos Hermanas, Islas II	258	34.05 S	58.17 W
Dōshi	94	35.32 N	139.02 E
Dōshi ≃	94	35.36 N	139.14 E
Doshisha University ʋ[2]	270	35.02 N	135.46 E
Dosi	164	5.56 S	134.34 E
Dösjebro	41	55.49 N	13.01 E
Do Son	110	20.42 N	106.47 E
Dosoris Island ›[1]	276	40.53 N	73.38 W
Dosoris Pond ⊜	276	40.54 N	73.38 W
Dos Pos	241s	12.15 N	68.20 W
Dos Quebradas	246	4.51 N	75.40 W
Dos Reyes, Punta ›	252	24.33 S	70.35 W
Dosse ≃	54	53.13 N	12.20 E
Dosséo, Bahr ≃	146	9.01 N	19.38 E
Dossin Great Lakes Museum ʋ	281	42.20 N	82.59 W
Dosso	150	13.03 N	3.12 E
Dosso □[5]	150	13.00 N	3.00 E
Dossor	80	47.32 N	53.01 E
Doster	216	42.27 N	85.33 W
Doswell	208	37.51 N	77.27 W
Dothan	194	31.13 N	85.23 W
Doting Cove	186	49.27 N	53.57 W
Dot Lake	180	63.40 N	144.04 W
Dötlingen	52	52.56 N	8.23 E
Dotnuva	76	55.21 N	23.54 E
Dotson	222	32.01 N	94.31 W
Döttingen	58	47.34 N	8.16 E
Doty	224	46.38 N	123.16 W
Dou ≃	105	39.13 N	118.03 E
Douai	50	50.22 N	3.04 E
Douala	152	4.03 N	9.42 E
Douala-Edéa, Réserve de ◆[4]	152	4.30 S	9.50 E
Douarnenez	32	48.06 N	4.20 W
Doubabougou	150	14.13 N	7.59 W
Double, Lac ⊜	186	50.46 N	70.23 W
Doublé, Pointe ›	241o	16.20 N	61.00 W
Double Bayou	222	29.41 N	94.39 W
Double Cone ∧	172	45.04 S	168.48 E
Double Island Point ›	166	25.56 S	153.11 E
Double Mountain ∧	228	35.02 N	118.29 W
Double Point ›	166	17.39 S	146.09 E
Double Springs	194	34.08 N	87.24 W
Doubletop Peak ∧	200	43.21 N	110.17 W
Doubs	58	46.56 N	6.21 E
Doubs □[5]	58	47.10 N	6.25 E
Doubs ≃	58	46.54 N	5.02 E
Doubs, Saut de ∟	58	47.05 N	6.43 E
Doubtful Sound ʊ	172	45.17 S	166.51 E
Doubtless Bay ⊂	172	34.55 S	173.25 E
Douchy	50	47.57 N	3.03 E
Douchy-les-Mines	50	50.18 N	3.23 E
Doudeville	50	49.43 N	0.48 E
Doudian	105	39.39 N	116.03 E
Doué ≃[1]	150	16.38 N	15.02 W
Douentza	150	15.00 N	2.57 W
Dougga ⊥	36	36.25 N	9.13 E
Doughboy	170	35.15 S	149.39 E
Doughboy Bay ⊂	172	47.02 S	167.41 E
Douglas, Austl.	164	16.29 S	145.28 E
Douglas, Mb., Can.	184	49.53 N	99.42 W
Douglas, On., Can.	212	45.31 N	76.56 W
Douglas, I. of Man	44	54.09 N	4.28 W
Douglas, S. Afr.	158	29.04 S	23.46 E
Douglas, Scot., U.K.	46	55.33 N	3.51 W
Douglas, Ak., U.S.	180	58.16 N	134.22 W
Douglas, Az., U.S.	200	31.20 N	109.32 W
Douglas, Ga., U.S.	192	31.30 N	82.51 W
Douglas, Mi., U.S.	216	42.38 N	86.12 W
Douglas, N.D., U.S.	198	47.51 N	101.30 W
Douglas, Wy., U.S.	200	42.45 N	105.22 W
Douglas □[6]	226	38.55 N	119.39 W
Douglas ≃	44	53.43 N	2.50 W
Douglas, Cape ›	180	58.52 N	153.18 W
Douglas, Mount ∧	180	58.52 N	153.31 W
Douglas, Mount ∧[2]	162	28.39 S	123.53 E
Douglas Aircraft Company ʋ[3]	280	33.50 N	118.09 W
Douglas Channel ʊ	182	53.30 N	129.12 W
Douglas Creek ≃	200	40.06 N	108.46 W
Douglas Lake	182	50.10 N	120.12 W
Douglas Lake ⊜[1]	192	36.00 N	83.22 W
Douglas Lake Indian Reserve ◆[4]	182	50.10 N	120.49 W
Douglas Park	170	34.11 S	150.43 E
Douglas Park ♠	278	41.52 N	87.42 W
Douglass, Ks., U.S.	198	37.31 N	97.01 W
Douglass, Tx., U.S.	222	31.40 N	94.53 W
Douglass Run ≃	279b	40.15 N	79.48 W
Douglassville	208	40.15 N	75.44 W
Douglasville	192	33.45 N	84.44 W
Douglas Water ≃	46	55.38 N	3.46 W
Dougouzi, Zhg.	89	49.57 N	127.01 E
Dougouzi, Zhg.	104	41.16 N	122.34 E
Douhutun	98	42.06 N	124.50 E
Douigny	152	3.11 S	10.45 E
Doujiapu	104	41.05 N	122.12 E
Doujiazhuang	105	40.22 N	116.59 E
Doukkane, Djebel ∧	36	35.23 N	8.00 E
Doulaincourt	58	48.19 N	5.12 E
Doulevant-le-Château	58	48.23 N	4.55 E
Doullens	50	50.09 N	2.21 E
Doumanaba	150	11.40 N	5.56 W
Doumanga	152	2.41 S	12.40 E
Doumba Bélo	152	5.05 N	14.18 E
Doumdégué	152	7.29 N	18.58 E
Doumé, Cam.	152	4.14 N	13.27 E
Doumé, Cam.	152	5.32 N	12.19 E
Doumé ≃	152	4.06 N	14.34 E
Doumen, Zhg.	100	22.12 N	113.16 E
Doumen, Zhg.	105	39.18 N	115.53 E
Douna	150	14.39 N	1.44 W
Doune	46	56.12 N	4.05 W
Doune Castle ⊥	46	56.11 N	4.03 W
Dounguila	152	2.53 S	11.58 E
Doupov	54	50.10 N	13.08 E
Doupovské hory ↗	54	50.13 N	13.08 E
Dour	50	50.24 N	3.47 E
Doura	150	13.14 N	5.55 W
Dourada, Serra ↗[1]	255	13.10 S	48.45 W
Douradinho	256	21.45 S	45.46 W
Dourado ≃	256	21.43 S	45.44 W
Dourados	255	22.13 S	54.48 W
Dourados ≃	255	21.58 S	54.18 W
Dourbali	146	11.49 N	15.52 E
Dourdan	50	48.32 N	2.01 E
Dourdou ≃	32	44.00 N	2.41 E
Dourges	50	50.26 N	2.59 E
Dourkoulé	146	14.27 N	22.13 E
Douro ≃, Bra.	287a	22.42 S	43.35 W
Douro (Duero) ≃, Europe	34	41.08 N	8.40 W
Doushanhe	100	31.38 N	114.42 E
Dousman	216	43.00 N	88.28 W
Douthat State Park ♠	192	37.55 N	79.50 W
Douvaine	58	46.19 N	6.18 E
Douvres → Dover	42	51.08 N	1.19 E
Douvres, Falaises de ⊥[4]	273b	4.06 S	15.25 E
Douvrin	50	50.31 N	2.50 E
Doux ≃	62	45.04 N	4.50 E
Douy-la-Ramée	261	49.04 N	2.53 E
Douyu	98	37.53 N	114.30 E
Douz	148	33.28 N	9.01 E
Douze ≃	32	43.54 N	0.30 W
Douzhangzhuang	105	39.23 N	116.55 E
Douzishan	107	29.04 N	104.57 E
Douziyu	105	40.18 N	117.19 E
Douzy	56	49.40 N	5.03 E
Dovadola	66	44.07 N	11.53 E
Dovbysh	78	50.22 N	27.59 E
Dove ≃, Eng., U.K.	44	52.50 N	1.35 W
Dove ≃, Eng., U.K.	44	54.12 N	0.54 W
Dove Creek	200	37.45 N	108.54 W
Dove Creek ≃, Tx., U.S.	196	31.20 N	100.36 W
Dove Creek ≃, Ut,. U.S.	200	41.37 N	113.15 W
Dove Holes	262	53.18 N	1.53 W
Dove Holes Tunnel ◆[5]	262	53.18 N	1.53 W
Dover, Austl.	166	43.19 S	147.01 E
Dover, S. Afr.	158	27.02 S	27.46 E
Dover, Eng., U.K.	42	51.08 N	1.19 E
Dover, Ar., U.S.	194	35.24 N	93.06 W
Dover, De., U.S.	208	39.09 N	75.31 W
Dover, Fl., U.S.	220	27.59 N	82.13 W
Dover, Id., U.S.	202	48.15 N	116.36 W
Dover, Ky., U.S.	218	38.45 N	83.52 W
Dover, Ma., U.S.	283	42.14 N	71.17 W
Dover, N.H., U.S.	188	43.11 N	70.52 W
Dover, N.J., U.S.	210	40.53 N	74.34 W
Dover, N.C., U.S.	192	35.12 N	77.26 W
Dover, Oh., U.S.	214	40.31 N	81.28 W
Dover, Ok., U.S.	196	35.58 N	97.54 W
Dover, Pa., U.S.	208	40.00 N	76.51 W
Dover, Tn., U.S.	194	36.29 N	87.50 W
Dover, Point ›	162	32.32 S	125.32 E
Dover, Strait of (Pas de Calais) ʊ	50	51.00 N	1.30 E
Dover Air Force Base ■	208	39.08 N	75.28 W
Dover-Foxcroft	188	45.11 N	69.13 W
Dover Heights	274a	33.53 S	151.17 E
Dover Hills	276	40.52 N	74.33 W
Dover Plains	210	41.44 N	73.35 W
Dovers Hills ↗[2]	162	23.10 S	128.45 E
Dove Stone Reservoir ⊜[1]	262	53.32 N	1.58 W
Doveton	274b	38.00 S	145.14 E
Dovey Valley V	42	52.35 N	3.50 W
Dovhen'ke	83	49.01 N	37.19 E
Dovol'noje	86	54.30 N	79.40 E
Dovre	26	61.59 N	9.15 E
Dovrefjell ↗	26	62.06 N	9.25 E
Dovrefjell Nasjonalpark ♠	26	62.18 N	9.36 E
Dovsk	76	53.09 N	30.28 E
Dovzhyk	78	50.13 N	35.55 E
Dowa	154	13.40 S	33.58 E
Dowagiac	216	41.59 N	86.06 W
Dowagiac ≃	216	41.51 N	86.16 W
Dowagiac Creek ≃	216	41.49 N	86.10 W
Dowally	46	56.36 N	3.37 W
Dow City	198	41.55 N	95.29 W
Dowden Terrace	284c	38.50 N	77.08 W
Dowell	208	38.20 N	76.27 W
Dowerin	162	31.12 S	117.02 E
Dowi, Tanjung ›	114	1.31 N	97.25 E
Dowker, Île I	275a	45.24 N	73.54 W
Dowlatābād, Afg.	120	36.59 N	66.50 E
Dowlatābād, Afg.	120	36.26 N	64.55 E
Dowlatābād, Īrān	128	28.18 N	56.40 E
Dowlat Yār	120	34.33 N	65.47 E
Dowling Lake ⊜	182	51.44 N	112.00 W
Downderry	42	50.22 N	4.22 W
Downe ◆[8]	260	51.20 N	0.03 E
Down East	285	40.03 N	75.32 W
Downers Grove	216	41.48 N	88.00 W
Downey, Ca., U.S.	228	33.56 N	118.07 W
Downey, Id., U.S.	202	42.25 N	112.07 W
Downey Creek ≃	224	48.16 N	121.14 W
Downham, Eng., U.K.	42	52.26 N	0.15 E
Downham, Eng., U.K.	260	51.38 N	0.30 E
Downham Market	42	52.36 N	0.23 E
Down House ⊥	260	51.20 N	0.03 E
Downieville	226	39.33 N	120.49 W
Downing	194	40.29 N	92.22 W
Downingtown	208	40.00 N	75.42 W
Downingtown Airport ⊠	285	39.59 N	75.45 W
Downpatrick	48	54.20 N	5.43 W
Downpatrick Head ›	48	54.20 N	9.20 W
Downs, Il., U.S.	216	40.24 N	88.52 W
Downs, Ks., U.S.	198	39.30 N	98.32 W
Downs Mountain ∧	200	43.18 N	109.40 W
Downsview Dells Park ♠	275b	43.44 N	79.30 W
Downsville	210	42.04 N	74.59 W
Downsville Dam ◆[6]	210	42.05 N	74.58 W
Downton	42	51.00 N	1.44 W
Downton, Mount ∧	182	52.42 N	124.51 W
Downton Lake ⊜	182	50.51 N	123.00 W
Downwind Acres Airfield ⊠	281	42.09 N	83.34 W
Dows	190	42.39 N	93.30 W
Dowshī	120	35.37 N	68.41 E
Doygaab	144	0.59 N	43.32 E
Doyle	204	40.01 N	120.06 W
Doyles	186	47.50 N	59.12 W
Doylesburg	214	40.13 N	77.42 W
Doylestown, Oh., U.S.	214	40.58 N	81.41 W
Doylestown, Pa., U.S.	208	40.18 N	75.07 W
Doyline	194	32.32 N	93.25 W
Dōzan ≃	96	33.58 N	133.47 E
Dōzen II	92	36.05 N	133.05 E
Dozier	194	31.29 N	86.21 W
Dozois, Réservoir ⊜[1]	190	47.30 N	77.05 W
Dozza	66	44.22 N	11.37 E
Drâa, Cap ›	148	28.44 N	11.08 W

Symbols in the index entries represent the broad categories identified in the key at the right. Symbols with superior numbers (↗[1]) identify subcategories (see complete key on page *I · 1)*.

Symbole im Register stellen die rechts im Schlüssel erklärten Kategorien dar. Symbole mit hochgestellten Ziffern (↗[1]) bezeichnen Unterabteilungen einer Kategorie (vgl. vollständiger Schlüssel auf Seite *I · 1)*.

Los símbolos incluídos en el texto del índice representan las grandes categorías identificadas con la clave a la derecha. Los símbolos con numeros en su parte superior (↗[1]) identifican las subcategorías (véase la clave completa en la página *I · 1)*.

Les symboles de l'index représentent les catégories indiquées dans la légende à droite. Les symboles suivis d'un indice (↗[1]) représentent des sous-catégories (voir légende complète à la page *I · 1)*.

Os símbolos incluídos no texto do índice representam as grandes categorias identificadas com a chave à direita. Os símbolos com números em sua parte superior (↗[1]) identificam as subcategorias (veja-se a chave completa à página *I · 1)*.

∧ Mountain	Berg	Montaña	Montagne	Montanha
↗ Mountains	Gebirge	Montañas	Montagnes	Montanhas
)(Pass	Paß	Paso	Col	Passo
V Valley, Canyon	Tal, Cañon	Valle, Cañón	Vallée, Canyon	Vale, Canhão
≚ Plain	Ebene	Llano	Plaine	Planície
› Cape	Kap	Cabo	Cap	Cabo
I Island	Insel	Isla	Île	Ilha
II Islands	Inseln	Islas	Îles	Ilhas
⊥ Other Topographic Features	Andere Topographische Objekte	Otros Elementos Topográficos	Autres données topographiques	Outros acidentes topográficos

ESPAÑOL Nombre / Página / Lat.°′ / Long.°′ W = Oeste — FRANÇAIS Nom / Page / Lat.°′ / Long.°′ W = Ouest — PORTUGUÊS Nome / Página / Lat.°′ / Long.°′ W = Oeste

Dra'a, Hamada du ◆² 148 29.00 N 6.45 W
Drâa, Oued V 148 28.43 N 11.09 W
Draa el Mizan 34 36.32 N 3.50 E
Drabble — José Enrique Rodó 258 33.41 S 57.34 W
Drabenderhöhe 56 50.57 N 7.27 E
Drabiv 78 49.58 N 32.08 E
Drac ≃ 62 45.13 N 5.41 E
Dracena 255 21.32 S 51.29 W
Drachenfels ⊥ 56 50.40 N 7.12 E
Drachselsried 60 49.06 N 13.01 E
Drachten 52 53.06 N 6.05 E
Dracut 207 42.40 N 71.18 W
Dragalina 38 44.26 N 27.20 E
Drăgănești-Olt 38 44.10 N 24.32 E
Drăgănești-Vlașca 38 44.06 N 25.36 E
Drăgășani 38 44.40 N 24.16 E
Drag Lake ⊜ 212 45.05 N 78.24 W
Dragone ≃ 64 44.23 N 10.37 E
Dragonera I 34 39.35 N 2.19 E
Dragoni 68 41.16 N 14.18 E
Dragonja ≃ 64 45.28 N 13.37 E
Dragons Mouths ʮ 241r 10.43 N 61.46 W
Dragon Swamp ≃ 208 37.33 N 76.34 W
Dragoon 200 32.01 N 110.02 W
Dragør 41 55.36 N 12.41 E
Draguignan 62 43.32 N 6.28 E
Drahičyn 76 52.11 N 25.09 E
Drain 202 43.39 N 123.19 W
Drake, Mo., U.S. 219 38.28 N 91.28 W
Drake, N.D., U.S. 198 47.55 N 100.22 W
Drakenburg 52 52.41 N 9.13 E
Drakensberg ⋀ 156 27.00 S 30.00 E
Drake Passage ʮ 18 58.00 S 70.00 W
Drake Peak ⋀ 202 42.19 N 120.07 W
Drakesboro 194 37.13 N 87.02 W
Drakes Branch 192 36.59 N 78.36 W
Drakes Brook ≃ 276 40.49 N 74.43 W
Drake Well Museum ✝ 214 41.36 N 79.39 W
Drakino 82 54.52 N 37.17 E
Dráma 38 41.09 N 24.08 E
Drammen 26 59.44 N 10.15 E
Dran 110 11.51 N 108.35 E
Drancy 50 48.56 N 2.27 E
Dranda 84 42.53 N 41.09 E
Drang ≃ 110 13.19 N 107.21 E
Drangajökull ⊓ 24a 66.11 N 22.15 W
Drangstedt 52 53.36 N 8.44 E
Dranov, Ostrovul I 38 44.52 N 29.15 E
Dransfeld 52 51.30 N 9.45 E
Dranske 54 54.38 N 13.14 E
Drap 62 43.45 N 7.19 E
Draper, N.C., U.S. 192 36.31 N 79.41 W
Draper, Ut., U.S. 200 40.31 N 111.51 W
Draperstown 48 54.48 N 6.47 W
Drās 123 34.27 N 75.46 E
Drās ≃ 123 34.37 N 75.59 E
Drau (Drava) (Dráva) ≃ 36 45.33 N 18.55 E
Drava (Drau) (Dráva) ≃ 36 45.33 N 18.55 E
Draveil 50 48.41 N 2.25 E
Dravinja ≃ 36 46.22 N 15.57 E
Dravograd 61 46.35 N 15.02 E
Dravosburg 279b 40.21 N 79.51 W
Drawno 30 53.13 N 15.45 E
Drawsko Pomorskie 30 53.32 N 15.48 E
Drayton, On., Can. 212 43.46 N 80.40 W
Drayton, Eng., U.K. 42 51.38 N 1.18 W
Drayton, N.D., U.S. 198 48.34 N 97.10 W
Drayton, S.C., U.S. 192 34.58 N 81.54 W
Drayton Plains 216 42.41 N 83.22 W
Drayton Valley 182 53.13 N 114.59 W
Draženov 60 49.28 N 12.52 E
Drean 36 36.41 N 7.46 E
Drebkau 54 51.39 N 14.13 E
Dreetz 54 52.48 N 12.28 E
Dreieich 56 50.01 N 8.41 E
Dreifelder Weiher ⊜ 56 50.36 N 7.49 E
Dreihausen 56 50.43 N 8.50 E
Dreiherrnspitze (Picco dei Tre Signori) ⋀ 64 47.04 N 12.15 E
Dreikikir 164 3.35 S 142.45 E
Drejø I 41 54.58 N 10.25 E
Dremsel, Mount ⋀ 164 2.10 S 146.55 E
Drena 64 45.58 N 10.56 E
Drenovec 38 43.42 N 22.59 E
Drensteinfurt 52 51.48 N 7.44 E
Drenthe □⁴ 52 52.45 N 6.30 E
Dresde — Dresden 54 51.03 N 13.44 E
Dresden, On., Can. 214 42.35 N 82.11 W
Dresden, Dtsch. 54 51.03 N 13.44 E
Dresden, N.Y., U.S. 210 42.41 N 76.58 W
Dresden, Oh., U.S. 214 40.07 N 82.00 W
Dresden, Tn., U.S. 194 36.17 N 88.42 W
Dresher 285 40.08 N 75.10 W
Drëtun' 76 55.41 N 29.13 E
Dreux 50 48.44 N 1.22 E
Drevenack 263 51.40 N 6.45 E
Drew 194 33.48 N 90.31 W
Drewer 263 51.40 N 7.07 E
Drewitz, Dtsch. 54 52.22 N 13.07 E
Drewitz, Dtsch. 54 52.12 N 12.10 E
Drewitz ◆⁸ 264a 52.22 N 13.08 E
Drewryville 208 36.42 N 77.18 W
Drews Reservoir ⊜¹ 202 42.10 N 120.40 W
Drew University ✝² 276 40.46 N 74.25 W
Drexel 218 39.44 N 84.17 W
Drexel Gardens 218 39.44 N 86.15 W
Drexel Hill 285 39.56 N 75.17 W
Drexel University ✝² 285 39.57 N 75.11 W
Drezdenko 30 52.51 N 15.50 E
Drezna 82 55.44 N 38.51 E
Driebergen 52 52.03 N 5.16 E
Drienov 30 48.53 N 21.17 E
Drifton 210 41.00 N 75.54 W
Driftpile ≃ 182 55.23 N 115.40 W
Drift Pile River Indian Reserve ◆⁴ 182 55.18 N 115.45 W
Driftwood, B.C., Can. 182 55.49 N 126.25 W
Driftwood, Pa., U.S. 214 41.20 N 78.08 W
Driftwood ≃, B.C., Can. 182 55.43 N 126.15 W
Driftwood ≃, In., U.S. 218 39.12 N 85.56 W
Driftwood Creek ≃ 198 40.11 N 100.39 W
Driggs 202 43.43 N 111.06 W
Drimnin 46 56.36 N 6.00 W
Drimoleague 48 51.38 N 9.14 W
Drin ≃ 38 41.45 N 19.34 E
Drina ≃ 38 44.53 N 19.21 E
Dringenberg 52 51.40 N 9.02 E
Drini i Zi ≃ 38 42.00 N 20.21 E
Drinit, Gjiri i c 38 41.45 N 19.28 E
Driorejo 115a 7.21 S 112.37 E
Driscoll 196 27.40 N 97.45 W
Driskill Mountain ⋀² 194 32.25 N 92.54 W
Driver 208 36.49 N 76.30 W
Drizzle Lake ⊜ 212 45.20 N 78.10 W
Drjanovo 38 42.58 N 25.27 E
Drnholec 61 48.52 N 16.29 E
Drniš 36 43.51 N 16.09 E
Dro 64 45.58 N 10.54 E
Drøbak 26 59.39 N 10.39 E
Drobeta-Turnu Severin 38 44.38 N 22.39 E
Drobylevo 82 55.44 N 35.53 E
Drobysheve 83 49.02 N 37.44 E
Drobyšovo 86 53.58 N 74.40 E
Drochia 38 48.03 N 27.48 E
Drochtersen 52 53.42 N 9.23 E
Drocourt 261 49.03 N 1.46 E
Drod Harts ≃ 158 27.35 S 24.41 E
Drogheda (Droichead Átha) 48 53.43 N 6.21 W
Drohiczyn 30 52.24 N 22.41 E
Drohobych 78 49.21 N 23.30 E
Drohobycz — Drohobych 78 49.21 N 23.30 E
Droichead Átha — Drogheda 48 53.43 N 6.21 W
Droichead Nua 48 53.11 N 6.48 W
Droitwich 42 52.16 N 2.09 W
Drolshagen 56 51.01 N 7.46 E
Dromahair 48 54.14 N 8.19 W
Dromana 169 38.21 S 144.58 E
Dromara 48 54.23 N 6.01 W
Dromcolliher 48 52.20 N 8.54 W
Drôme □⁵ 62 44.35 N 5.10 E
Drôme ≃ 62 44.46 N 4.46 E
Drömling ◆¹ 54 52.29 N 11.04 E
Dromod 48 53.51 N 7.55 W
Dromore, N. Ire., U.K. 48 54.31 N 7.28 W
Dromore, N. Ire., U.K. 48 54.25 N 6.09 W
Dromore West 48 54.15 N 8.53 W
Dronero 62 44.28 N 7.22 E
Dronfield 44 53.19 N 1.27 W
Drongan 44 55.26 N 4.27 W
Drongen 50 51.03 N 3.40 E
Dronne ≃ 32 45.02 N 0.09 W
Dronninglund 26 57.09 N 10.18 E
Dronrijp 52 53.11 N 5.38 E
Dröschede 263 51.22 N 7.39 E
Drosendorf Stadt 61 48.52 N 15.37 E
Drosiá 267c 38.07 N 23.52 E
Drösing 61 48.32 N 16.54 E
Droskovo 76 52.31 N 37.05 E
Drottningholm slott ⊥ 40 59.19 N 17.53 E
Droué 50 48.02 N 1.05 E
Droue-sur-Drouette 261 48.36 N 1.42 E
Drouette ≃ 261 48.37 N 1.37 E
Drouin 169 38.08 S 145.51 E
Drov'anaja 88 51.35 N 113.02 E
Droyßig 54 51.02 N 12.01 E
Droylsden 262 53.29 N 2.10 W
Druc' ≃ 76 53.03 N 30.42 E
Druid Hill Park ♦ 284b 39.19 N 76.39 W
Druja 76 55.47 N 27.27 E
Drūkšiai ⊜ 76 55.38 N 26.35 E
Druk-Yul — Bhutan □¹ 120 27.30 N 90.30 E
Drulingen 58 48.52 N 7.11 E
Drum, Mount ⋀ 180 62.07 N 144.35 W
Drumbeg 46 58.14 N 5.12 W
Drumbo 212 43.14 N 80.33 W
Drumcliff 48 54.20 N 8.30 W
Drumheller 182 51.28 N 112.42 W
Drumlish 48 53.48 N 7.46 W
Drummond, N.Z. 172 45.59 S 168.09 E
Drummond, Mt., U.S. 202 46.40 N 113.08 W
Drummond, Wi., U.S. 190 46.20 N 91.15 W
Drummond □⁶ 206 45.50 N 72.20 W
Drummond, Lake ⊜ 208 36.36 N 76.28 W
Drummond Island I 190 46.00 N 83.40 W
Drummond Range ⋀ 166 23.30 S 147.15 E
Drummondville 206 45.53 N 72.29 W
Drummore 44 54.42 N 4.54 W
Drummoyne 274a 33.51 S 151.09 E
Drumquin 48 54.37 N 7.30 W
Drumright 196 35.59 N 96.36 W
Drumshanbo 48 54.02 N 8.02 W
Drunen 52 51.42 N 5.08 E
Drusenheim 56 48.46 N 7.57 E
Druskininkai 76 54.01 N 23.58 E
Druten 52 51.54 N 5.36 E
Druyes-les-Belles-Fontaines 50 47.33 N 3.25 E
Družba, Kaz. 86 45.15 N 82.26 E
Družba, Ross. 265b 55.53 N 37.45 E
Druzhba 78 52.03 N 33.56 E
Druzhkivka 83 48.37 N 37.33 E
Družina 74 68.14 N 145.18 E
Družnaja Gorka 76 59.17 N 30.08 E
Drvar 36 44.22 N 16.24 E
Drwęca ≃ 30 53.00 N 18.42 E
Dry ≃ 164 14.54 S 132.24 E
Dry Arm c 202 47.45 N 106.20 W
Dry Bay c 180 59.08 N 138.25 W
Dryberry Lake ⊜ 184 49.33 N 93.53 W
Drybin 76 54.08 N 31.06 E
Dryburgh Abbey ✝¹ 46 55.34 N 2.40 W
Dry Cimarron ≃ 196 36.54 N 102.59 W
Dry Creek ≃, Ca., U.S. 204 38.35 N 122.51 W
Dry Creek ≃, Ca., U.S. 226 38.39 N 121.28 W
Dry Creek ≃, Ca., U.S. 226 38.22 N 122.18 W
Dry Creek ≃, Ca., U.S. 226 38.58 N 121.32 W
Dry Creek ≃, Ca., U.S. 226 39.13 N 121.25 W
Dry Creek ≃, Ca., U.S. 226 38.14 N 121.24 W
Dry Creek ≃, Ca., U.S. 226 36.58 N 120.13 W
Dry Creek ≃, Ca., U.S. 226 36.47 N 119.46 W
Dry Creek ≃, Ca., U.S. 226 37.27 N 120.37 W
Dry Creek ≃, Ca., U.S. 282 37.22 N 122.23 W
Dry Creek ≃, Or., U.S. 202 43.34 N 117.21 W
Dry Creek ≃, Or., U.S. 224 45.30 N 121.03 W
Dry Creek ≃, Tx., U.S. 222 32.46 N 95.28 W
Dry Creek ≃, Wy., U.S. 202 43.13 N 108.54 W
Dry Creek ≃, Wy., U.S. 202 44.30 N 108.03 W
Dry Creek Mountain ⋀ 204 41.22 N 116.22 W
Dryden, On., Can. 184 49.47 N 92.50 W
Dryden, N.Y., U.S. 210 42.29 N 76.17 W
Dryden, Wa., U.S. 224 47.32 N 120.33 W
Dry Devils ≃, Tx., U.S. 196 30.20 N 100.57 W
Dry Devils ≃, Tx., U.S. 196 29.47 N 100.59 W
Dryfe Water ≃ 44 55.08 N 3.26 W
Dry Fork ≃ 194 37.58 N 91.31 W
Dry Frio ≃ 196 29.17 N 99.39 W
Drygalski Island I 9 65.45 S 92.30 E
Dry Lake ⊜ 198 48.15 N 98.58 W
Drymen 46 56.04 N 4.27 W
Dry Prong 194 31.34 N 92.31 W
Dry Ridge 218 38.40 N 84.35 W
Dry Run 214 40.10 N 77.45 W
Drysa ≃ 76 55.47 N 27.55 E
Drysdale 169 38.11 S 144.34 E
Drysdale ≃ 164 13.59 S 126.51 E
Drysdale River National Park ♦ 164 15.00 S 127.00 E
Dry Tortugas II 220 24.38 N 82.55 W
Dry Tortugas National Park ♦ 220 24.37 N 82.54 W
Drzewica 30 51.27 N 20.28 E
Drzewice 54 52.38 N 14.38 E
Dschang 152 5.27 N 10.04 E
Dschidda — Jiddah 144 21.30 N 39.12 E
Dschuba — Jubba ≃ 144 0.15 S 42.38 E
Du 150 10.30 N 0.59 W
Du ≃ 102 32.48 N 110.38 E
Du ≃ 150 3.20 N 20.53 E
Duabo 150 5.40 N 8.05 W
Duālgaon 126 24.14 N 90.51 E
Duala — Douala 152 4.03 N 9.42 E
Dualchi 71 40.13 N 8.54 E
Du'an 102 24.06 N 108.10 E
Duancun 105 38.52 N 115.56 E
Duane L. Bliss State Park ♦ 226 38.59 N 120.05 W
Duanesburg 210 42.46 N 74.08 W
Duanjialing 105 39.59 N 117.09 E
Duaringa 166 23.43 S 149.40 E
Duarte 228 34.08 N 117.58 W
Duarte, Pico ⋀ 238 19.02 N 70.59 W
Duartina 255 22.24 S 49.25 W
Duas Barras 256 22.02 S 42.32 W
Duayaw Nkwanta 150 7.10 N 2.06 W
Dubā, Ar. Su. 128 27.21 N 35.40 E
Dubá, Česká Rep. 54 50.34 N 14.33 E
Dubach 194 32.41 N 92.39 W
Dubai — Dubayy 128 25.18 N 55.18 E
Dubăsari (Dubesar') 38 47.16 N 29.08 E
Dubăsari, Lacul ⊜¹ 38 47.35 N 29.00 E
Dubawnt ≃ 176 64.33 N 100.06 W
Dubawnt Lake ⊜ 176 63.08 N 101.30 W
Dubayy 128 25.18 N 55.18 E
Dubbeldam 52 51.47 N 4.42 E
Dubbo 166 32.15 S 148.36 E
Dube ≃ 150 5.45 N 8.00 W
Dubele 154 2.54 N 29.33 E
Dübendorf 58 47.25 N 8.38 E
Dübener Heide ◆³ 54 51.40 N 12.40 E
Dubenskij 86 51.27 N 56.38 E
Dubh Artach II¹ 46 56.08 N 6.40 W
Dubí 54 50.42 N 13.45 E
Dubi Bheri 272b 22.53 N 88.17 E
Dubica 36 45.11 N 16.48 E
Dubie 154 8.33 S 28.32 E
Dubinino 82 56.09 N 37.01 E
Dubino 58 46.09 N 9.27 E
Dubjazy 80 56.08 N 49.13 E
Dubki, Ross. 265a 60.00 N 30.00 E
Dubki, Ross. 265b 55.41 N 37.14 E
Dublin, Austl. 168b 34.27 S 138.21 E
Dublin, On., Can. 212 43.31 N 81.17 W
Dublin (Baile Átha Cliath), Ire. 48 53.20 N 6.15 W
Dublin, Ca., U.S. 226 37.42 N 121.56 W
Dublin, Ga., U.S. 192 32.32 N 82.54 W
Dublin, In., U.S. 218 39.48 N 85.12 W
Dublin, Md., U.S. 208 39.39 N 76.16 W
Dublin, Oh., U.S. 214 40.06 N 83.07 W
Dublin, Pa., U.S. 208 40.22 N 75.12 W
Dublin, Tx., U.S. 196 32.05 N 98.20 W
Dublin, Va., U.S. 192 37.06 N 80.41 W
Dublin □⁶ 48 53.20 N 6.15 W
Dublin (Collinstown) Airport ⊠ 48 53.26 N 6.15 W
Dublin Bay c 48 53.20 N 6.06 W
Dublin Canyon V 282 37.42 N 121.59 W
Dublon I 175c 7.23 N 151.53 E
Dubna, Ross. 82 54.09 N 36.58 E
Dubna, Ross. 82 56.44 N 37.10 E
Dubna ≃, Lat. 76 56.22 N 26.10 E
Dubna ≃, Ross. 82 56.47 N 37.15 E
Dubňany 30 48.55 N 17.06 E
Dubnevo 82 55.06 N 38.08 E
Dubnica nad Váhom 30 48.58 N 18.09 E
Dubno 78 50.26 N 25.44 E
Dubois, Id., U.S. 202 44.10 N 112.13 W
Dubois, Il., U.S. 219 38.13 N 89.13 W
Dubois, In., U.S. 194 38.26 N 86.48 W
Du Bois, Ne., U.S. 198 40.02 N 96.02 W
Du Bois, Pa., U.S. 214 41.07 N 78.45 W
Dubois, Wy., U.S. 200 43.32 N 109.37 W
Du Bois Reservoir ⊜¹ 214 41.06 N 78.38 W
Duboistown 210 41.13 N 77.02 W
Dubo'onki 80 54.27 N 46.18 E
Dubovaja Rošča 76 53.11 N 36.04 E
Dubovka, Ross. 78 51.26 N 41.25 E
Dubovka, Ross. 80 49.03 N 44.50 E
Dubovoje 78 53.08 N 40.05 E
Dubovskij 80 56.21 N 46.48 E
Dubovskoje 80 47.25 N 42.46 E
Dubov yazivka 78 51.08 N 33.22 E
Dubovychi 78 51.38 N 33.35 E
Dubovyj Ovrag 80 48.20 N 44.37 E
Dubovyj Umet 80 52.59 N 50.17 E
Dubovweitun 82 50.42 N 120.44 E
Dubra 126 23.32 N 86.31 E
Dubrājpur 126 23.48 N 87.23 E
Dubrar dağ ⋀ 84 40.55 N 48.50 E
Dubréka 150 9.48 N 13.31 W
Dubrouna 76 54.35 N 30.41 E
Dubrova, Bela. 76 52.25 N 29.58 E
Dubrova, Bela. 76 51.47 N 28.13 E
Dubrova, Ross. 80 59.34 N 42.06 E
Dubrova, Ross. 80 57.42 N 55.01 E
Dubroviči 80 54.39 N 39.56 E
Dubrovicy 82 56.46 N 39.10 E
Dubrovino 86 55.28 N 83.17 E
Dubrovka, Ross. 76 59.13 N 36.13 E
Dubrovka, Ross. 76 53.42 N 33.30 E
Dubrovka, Ross. 76 59.51 N 30.56 E
Dubrovka, Ross. 82 54.44 N 36.21 E
Dubrovki 80 53.49 N 43.19 E
Dubrovnik 38 42.38 N 18.07 E
Dubrovnoje, Kaz. 86 54.49 N 68.06 E
Dubrovnoje, Ross. 86 57.58 N 69.25 E
Dubrovo 76 59.51 N 33.34 E
Dubrovskoje 88 58.45 N 111.10 E
Dubrovytsya 78 51.34 N 26.34 E
Dubunskaja 86 43.46 N 80.13 E
Dubuque 190 42.30 N 90.39 W
Dubysa ≃ 76 55.05 N 23.26 E
Duchana 85 38.02 N 68.13 E
Duchang 100 29.15 N 116.13 E
Duchcov 54 50.37 N 13.45 E
Ducherow 54 53.46 N 13.46 E
Duchesne 200 40.09 N 110.24 W
Duchesne ≃ 200 40.05 N 109.41 W
Duchess 166 21.22 S 139.52 E
Duchovnickoje 80 52.28 N 48.15 E
Duchovščina 76 55.12 N 32.25 E
Duck ≃, Austl. 274a 33.50 S 151.02 E
Duck ≃, Tn., U.S. 194 36.02 N 87.52 W
Duckabush ≃ 224 47.38 N 122.56 W
Duck Bay 184 52.10 N 100.09 W
Duck Creek ≃, On., Can. 281 42.18 N 82.41 W
Duck Creek ≃, Ca., U.S. 226 37.55 N 121.16 W
Duck Creek ≃, In., U.S. 218 40.08 N 85.57 W
Duck Creek ≃, Nv., U.S. 204 40.06 N 114.43 W
Duck Creek ≃, N.D., U.S. 198 46.03 N 102.14 W
Duck Creek ≃, Tx., U.S. 196 33.14 N 100.37 W
Duck Creek ≃, Tx., U.S. 222 32.48 N 96.31 W
Duck Creek ≃, Tx., U.S. 222 31.06 N 96.17 W
Duck Creek ≃, Wi., U.S. 190 44.33 N 88.02 W
Duck Hill 194 33.37 N 89.42 W
Duck Island Harbor c 276 40.55 N 73.23 W
Duck Key I 220 24.46 N 80.56 W
Duck Lake, Sk., Can. 184 52.47 N 106.13 W
Duck Lake, Mi., U.S. 216 42.24 N 84.48 W
Duck Lake ⊜, Mb., Can. 184 54.52 N 98.11 W
Duck Lake ⊜, Mi., U.S. 216 42.23 N 84.47 W
Duck Lake ⊜, Mi., U.S. 281 42.40 N 83.35 W
Duck Mountain ⋀ 184 51.35 N 101.00 W
Duck Mountain Provincial Park ♦, Mb., Can. 184 51.36 N 100.55 W
Duck Mountain Provincial Park ♦, Sk., Can. 184 51.38 N 101.53 W
Duck Valley Indian Reservation ◆⁴ 204 42.00 N 116.10 W
Duckwall Mountain ⋀ 226 37.58 N 120.07 W
Duclair 50 49.29 N 0.53 E
Ducos 240e 14.34 N 60.58 W
Du Couedic, Cape > 166 36.04 S 136.42 E
Ducun 106 31.07 N 120.27 E
Duda ≃ 246 2.33 N 74.02 W
Dudačkino 76 59.57 N 32.53 E
Dudchany 78 47.12 N 33.46 E
Duddington 42 52.36 N 0.32 W
Duddon ≃ 44 54.15 N 3.13 W
Dudelange 56 49.28 N 6.05 E
Dudergofka ≃ 265a 59.52 N 30.12 E
Duderstadt 52 51.31 N 10.16 E
Dūdhi 124 24.13 N 83.15 E
Dudhkośī ≃ 124 27.08 N 86.26 E
Dudhnai 124 25.59 N 90.44 E
Dudinka 74 69.25 N 86.15 E
Dudkin 78 47.53 N 40.32 E
Dudley, Eng., U.K. 42 52.30 N 2.05 W
Dudley, Eng., U.K. 44 55.03 N 1.35 W
Dudley, Ma., U.S. 207 42.02 N 71.55 W
Dudley, Pa., U.S. 214 40.12 N 78.10 W
Dudley Pond ⊜ 283 42.20 N 71.22 W
Dudleyville 200 32.58 N 110.47 W
Dudna ≃ 122 19.07 N 76.54 E
Dudorovskij 76 53.40 N 35.22 E
Dūdūwā Śrīngklā ⋀ 124 27.45 N 82.30 E
Dudwa National Park ♦ 124 28.30 N 80.40 E
Dudweiler 56 49.17 N 7.02 E
Dudzele 50 51.17 N 3.14 E
Due 89 50.50 N 142.06 E
Duékoué 150 6.45 N 7.21 W
Dueré 250 11.20 S 49.17 W
Dueré ≃ 250 10.59 S 49.48 W
Duerji 89 45.39 N 121.49 E
Duerna ≃ 34 42.19 N 5.54 W
Duero (Douro) ≃ 34 41.08 N 8.40 W
Duevile 64 45.38 N 11.32 E
Due West 192 34.20 N 82.23 W
Dufault, Lac ⊜ 190 48.19 N 79.00 W
Duff Dunbar 123 32.15 N 77.12 E
Duffel 50 51.06 N 4.31 E
Dufferin □⁶ 212 44.05 N 80.15 W
Duffer Peak ⋀ 204 41.40 N 118.44 W
Duffield, Austl. 162 25.50 S 134.40 E
Duffield, Eng., U.K. 42 52.58 N 1.29 W
Duffins Creek ≃ 212 43.49 N 79.02 W
Dufftown 46 57.26 N 3.08 W
Dufourspitze ⋀ 58 45.55 N 7.52 E
Dufresne ≃ 206 46.16 N 73.59 W
Dufur 224 45.27 N 121.07 W
Dugadda 124 29.48 N 78.37 E
Duga Resa 36 45.27 N 15.30 E
Duga-Zapadnaja, mys > 74 59.09 N 145.59 E
Dugdemona ≃ 194 31.47 N 92.22 W
Dugede 120 30.54 N 90.48 E
Dugger 194 39.04 N 87.16 W
Dugino 83 47.09 N 39.27 E
Dugi Otok I 36 44.00 N 15.04 E
Dugna 82 54.25 N 36.51 E
Dugny-sur-Meuse 56 49.06 N 5.23 E
Dug Pond ⊜ 283 42.17 N 71.22 W
Du Gué ≃ 176 57.21 N 70.45 W
Dugui Qarag 102 39.38 N 108.40 E
Dugway Proving Ground ■ 200 40.10 N 113.15 W
Duhernal Lake ⊜ 276 40.24 N 74.22 W
Duhi 140 7.07 N 28.45 E
Duhnen 52 53.53 N 8.38 E
Duhu 100 22.04 N 112.56 E
Duhūr ash-Shuwayr 132 33.55 N 35.43 E
Duich, Loch c 46 57.14 N 5.30 W
Duida, Cerro ⋀ 246 3.25 N 65.40 W
Duifken Point > 164 12.33 S 141.38 E
Duingen 52 52.00 N 9.42 E
Duingt 62 45.50 N 6.12 E
Duino 64 45.46 N 13.36 E
Duirinish 46 57.19 N 5.41 W
Duisburg, Dtsch. 56 51.25 N 6.46 E
Duisburg, Dtsch. 263 51.25 N 6.46 E
Duissern ◆⁸ 263 51.26 N 6.47 E
Duitama 246 5.50 N 73.02 W
Duitsland — Germany □¹ 30 51.00 N 10.00 E
Duiveland I 52 51.38 N 4.00 E
Duiwelskloof 156 23.42 S 30.06 E
Duji, Zhg. 98 37.44 N 116.50 E
Duji, Zhg. 98 34.11 N 115.48 E
Dujiahang 106 31.03 N 121.29 E
Dujuuma 144 1.15 N 42.34 E
Dukambiya 144 14.47 N 37.28 E
Dukana ⊤⁴ 154 3.59 N 37.16 E
Dukazi 120 30.54 N 92.52 E
Duke 196 34.39 N 99.34 W
Duke Center 214 41.57 N 78.28 W
Duke Island I 182 54.55 N 131.20 W
Duke of York Bay c 176 65.25 N 84.50 W
Duke of York Island I 164 4.10 S 152.26 E
Dukes □⁶ 207 41.23 N 70.31 W
Dukes Brook ≃ 276 40.33 N 74.37 W
Duk Fadiat 140 7.45 N 31.25 E
Duk Faiwil 140 7.30 N 31.29 E
Dukhān 128 25.25 N 50.48 E
Dukhmays 142 31.07 N 31.04 E
Duki 120 30.09 N 68.34 E
Dukinfield 262 53.29 N 2.05 W
Dukla 30 49.34 N 21.41 E
Dukla Pass)(30 49.25 N 21.43 E
Dukou 102 26.40 N 101.39 E
Dūkštas 76 55.32 N 26.20 E
Duku, Nig. 146 10.49 N 10.46 E
Duku, Nig. 150 11.10 N 4.55 E
Dūlā 152 4.41 N 20.22 E
Dūlāb ◆⁸ 267d 35.39 N 51.27 E
Dulag 116 10.57 N 125.02 E
Dulan 124 23.57 N 89.31 E
Dulan (Chahanwusu) 102 36.16 N 98.06 E
Dul'apino 80 57.15 N 40.49 E
Dulas ≃ 42 52.36 N 3.50 W
Dulas Bay c 44 53.23 N 4.15 W
Dulata 86 43.26 N 80.50 E
Dulayb, Khawr V 140 11.45 N 32.47 E
Dulaym 140 25.58 N 14.03 E
Dulce 200 36.56 N 106.59 W
Dulce ≃ 252 30.31 S 62.32 W
Dulce, Arroyo ≃ 258 35.28 S 57.41 W
Dulce, Golfo c 236 8.32 N 83.14 W
Dulce Grande 234 22.59 N 102.14 W
Dulce Nombre de Culmí 236 15.09 N 85.37 W
Dul'durga 88 50.41 N 113.36 E
Duleek 48 53.39 N 6.25 W
Dulgalach ≃ 74 67.44 N 133.12 E
Dulin 98 38.22 N 116.43 E
Duliu, Zhg. 105 39.13 N 116.51 E
Duliu, Zhg. 105 39.01 N 116.54 E
Duliu Jianhe ≃ 105 38.51 N 117.20 E
Duljo Point > 116 8.35 N 123.43 E
Dulkaninna 166 29.01 S 138.27 E
Dülken 56 51.15 N 6.20 E
Dulles International Airport ⊠ 208 38.58 N 77.28 W
Dullstroom 156 25.27 S 30.07 E
Dülmen 52 51.51 N 7.16 E
Dulnain Bridge 46 57.18 N 3.40 W
Dulnan ≃ 46 57.18 N 3.40 W
Dulovka 76 57.31 N 28.10 E
Dulovo 38 43.49 N 27.09 E
Dulq Maghār 130 36.22 N 38.39 E
D'ul'tydag, gora ⋀ 84 41.58 N 46.56 E
Dulung ≃ 126 22.08 N 87.05 E
Duluni 126 26.44 N 94.46 E
Dulunguin Point > 116 7.45 N 122.05 E
Duluth, Ga., U.S. 192 34.00 N 84.08 W
Duluth, Mn., U.S. 190 46.45 N 92.07 W
Dulverton 42 51.03 N 3.33 W
Dulwich ◆⁸ 260 51.26 N 0.05 W
Duma, Bots. 156 18.45 S 22.46 E
Dūmā, Lubnān 130 34.12 N 35.50 E
Dūmā, Sūrīy. 132 33.35 N 36.24 E
Duma, R.D.C. 154 4.57 N 27.19 E
Dumaguete 116 9.18 N 123.18 E
Dumai 114 1.41 N 101.27 E
Dumalag 116 11.18 N 122.37 E
Dumalinao 116 7.49 N 123.23 E
Dumali Point > 116 13.07 N 121.33 E
Dumanjug 116 10.04 N 123.26 E
Dumanlıdağ ⋀ 84 40.31 N 43.25 E
Dumanquilas Bay c 116 7.34 N 123.04 E
Dumaran Channel ʮ 116 10.25 N 119.45 E
Dumaran Island I 116 10.33 N 119.51 E
Dumaresq ≃ 166 28.40 S 150.28 E
Dumaring 112 1.36 N 118.12 E
Dumas, Ar., U.S. 194 33.53 N 91.29 W
Dumas, Tx., U.S. 196 35.51 N 101.58 W
Dumayr 132 33.38 N 36.40 E
Dumbarton 46 55.57 N 4.35 W
Dumbarton Bridge ◆⁵ 282 37.31 N 122.07 W
Dumbarton Point > 282 37.30 N 122.06 W
Ďumbier ⋀ 30 48.57 N 19.37 E
Dumbleyung 162 33.19 S 117.44 E
Dumbo 152 14.06 S 17.24 E
Dumboa 146 11.10 N 12.45 E
Dumbrăveni 38 46.14 N 24.35 E
Dum Dum 126 22.35 N 88.24 E
Dum Dum International Airport ⊠ 126 22.38 N 88.25 E
Dume, Point > 228 34.00 N 118.48 W
Dumei 100 24.47 N 117.21 E
Dumfries, Scot., U.K. 44 55.04 N 3.37 W
Dumfries, Va., U.S. 208 38.34 N 77.19 W
Dumfries and Galloway □⁴ 44 55.00 N 4.00 W
Duminiči 76 53.55 N 35.06 E
Dumjor 272b 22.38 N 88.13 E
Dumka 126 24.16 N 87.15 E
Dumlupinar 130 38.52 N 30.00 E
Dummar 132 33.32 N 36.14 E
Dümmer 54 53.35 N 11.12 E
Dümmer ⊜ 52 52.31 N 8.19 E
Dummer Range ⋀ 162 20.11 S 125.59 E
Dummerstorf 54 54.01 N 12.14 E
Dumoga-Bone National Park ♦ 112 0.30 N 123.25 E
Dumoga Kecil 112 0.31 N 123.55 E
Dumoine ≃ 190 46.13 N 77.51 W
Dumoine, Lac ⊜ 190 46.53 N 77.54 W
Dumont, Ia., U.S. 190 42.45 N 92.58 W
Dumont, N.J., U.S. 210 40.56 N 73.59 W
Dumont, Lac ⊜ 190 46.04 N 76.27 W
Dumont d'Urville ✝³ 9 66.35 S 140.00 E
Dümpelfeld 56 50.27 N 6.56 E
Dümpten ◆⁸ 263 51.27 N 6.54 E
Dumpu 164 5.50 S 145.45 E
Dumra 124 26.34 N 85.31 E
Dumraon 124 25.33 N 84.09 E
Dumuria, Bngl. 126 22.47 N 89.26 E
Dumuriā, India 126 22.11 N 86.20 E
Dumyāṭ (Damietta) 142 31.25 N 31.48 E
Dumyāṭ □⁴ 142 31.20 N 31.45 E
Dumyāṭ, Far' (Damietta Branch) ≃ 142 31.32 N 31.51 E
Dumyāṭ, Maṣabb (Damietta Mouth) ≃¹ 142 31.32 N 31.51 E
Dün ⋀ 54 51.21 N 10.30 E
Duna — Danube ≃ 22 45.20 N 29.40 E
Dünaburg — Daugavpils 76 55.53 N 26.32 E
Dunaff Head > 48 55.17 N 7.33 W
Dunaföldvár 30 46.48 N 18.55 E
Dunaharaszti 30 47.21 N 19.05 E
Dunaj, Ross. 89 42.52 N 132.22 E
Dunaj, Ross. 265a 59.58 N 30.56 E
Dunaj — Danube ≃ 22 45.20 N 29.40 E
Dunaj, ostrova II 74 73.52 N 124.29 E
Dunajec ≃ 30 50.14 N 20.44 E
Dunajevo 88 52.05 N 117.02 E
Dunajská Streda 30 48.01 N 17.35 E
Dunakeszi 30 47.38 N 19.08 E
Dunany Point > 48 53.52 N 6.14 W
Dunărea — Danube ≃ 22 45.20 N 29.40 E
Dunărea Veche, Brațul ≃ 38 45.17 N 28.02 E
Duna-Tisza-csatorna ≅ 264c 47.21 N 19.05 E
Dunaújváros 30 46.58 N 18.57 E
Dunav — Danube ≃ 22 45.20 N 29.40 E
Dunavățu de Sus 38 44.59 N 29.13 E
Duna-Völgyi-főcsatorna ≅ 30 46.12 N 18.56 E
Dunayivtsi 78 48.54 N 26.51 E
Dunback 172 45.23 S 170.38 E
Dunbar, Scot., U.K. 46 56.00 N 2.31 W
Dunbar, W.V., U.S. 188 38.21 N 81.44 W
Dunbarton 275b 43.49 N 79.06 W
Dunbeath 46 58.15 N 3.25 W
Dunblane, Sk., Can. 184 51.11 N 106.52 W
Dunblane, Scot., U.K. 46 56.12 N 3.59 W
Dunboyne 48 53.24 N 6.28 W
Duncan, B.C., Can. 224 48.47 N 123.42 W
Duncan, Az., U.S. 200 32.43 N 109.06 W
Duncan, Ms., U.S. 194 34.02 N 90.44 W
Duncan, Ok., U.S. 196 34.30 N 97.57 W
Duncan ≃ 182 50.11 N 116.57 W
Duncan Lake ⊜¹ 182 50.20 N 117.00 W
Duncannon 208 40.23 N 77.01 W
Duncan Passage ʮ 110 11.00 N 92.30 E
Duncans 241q 18.28 N 77.32 W
Duncansby Head > 46 58.39 N 3.02 W
Duncans Creek ≃ 274a 33.53 S 151.00 E
Duncansville 214 40.25 N 78.26 W
Duncanville 222 32.39 N 96.54 W
Dunchurch 42 52.20 N 1.16 W
Duncormick 48 52.14 N 6.39 W
Dundaga 76 57.31 N 22.21 E
Dundāhera 272a 28.38 N 77.26 E
Dundalk, On., Can. 212 44.10 N 80.24 W
Dundalk (Dún Dealgan), Ire. 48 54.01 N 6.25 W
Dundalk, Md., U.S. 208 39.15 N 76.31 W
Dundalk Bay c 48 53.57 N 6.17 W
Dundas, Austl. 274a 33.48 S 151.02 E
Dundas, On., Can. 212 43.16 N 79.58 W
Dundas, Mn., U.S. 190 44.25 N 93.12 W
Dundas, Cape > 212 44.57 N 81.07 W
Dundas, Lake ⊜ 162 32.35 S 121.50 E
Dundas Island I 182 54.33 N 130.55 W
Dundas Peninsula >¹ 176 74.50 N 111.30 W
Dundas Strait ʮ 164 11.20 S 131.35 E
Dún Dealgan — Dundalk 48 54.01 N 6.25 W
Dundee, S. Afr. 158 28.12 S 30.16 E
Dundee, Scot., U.K. 46 56.28 N 3.00 W
Dundee, Fl., U.S. 220 28.01 N 81.37 W
Dundee, Il., U.S. 216 42.06 N 88.17 W
Dundee, Mi., U.S. 216 41.57 N 83.39 W
Dundee, Ms., U.S. 194 34.31 N 90.27 W
Dundee, N.Y., U.S. 210 42.31 N 76.58 W
Dundee, Oh., U.S. 214 40.35 N 81.37 W
Dundee, Or., U.S. 224 45.16 N 123.00 W
Dundee Creek c 284b 39.21 N 76.22 W
Dundgov' □⁴ 102 45.30 N 106.30 E
Dundit 142 30.41 N 31.18 E
Dundonald 44 55.34 N 4.35 W
Dundoo 166 27.39 S 144.39 E
Dundrum, Ire. 48 52.33 N 8.03 W
Dundrum, N. Ire., U.K. 48 54.16 N 5.51 W
Dundrum Bay c 48 54.13 N 5.45 W
Dundurn 184 51.49 N 106.30 W
Duneaton Water ≃ 46 55.32 N 3.42 W
Dunedin, N.Z. 172 45.52 S 170.30 E
Dunedin, Fl., U.S. 220 28.01 N 82.46 W
Dunedoo 166 32.01 S 149.24 E
Duneland Beach 216 41.35 N 86.50 W
Dunellen 276 40.35 N 74.28 W
Dunewood 276 40.38 N 73.11 W
Dunfanaghy 48 55.11 N 7.59 W
Dunfermline 46 56.04 N 3.29 W
Du Ngae, Khao ⋀ 110 15.10 N 98.47 E
Dungannon, N. Ire., U.K. 48 54.31 N 6.46 W
Dungannon, Va., U.S. 192 36.49 N 82.28 W
Dūngarpur 120 23.50 N 73.43 E
Dungarvan 48 52.05 N 7.37 W
Dungarvan Harbour c 48 52.10 N 7.35 W
Dungas 150 13.04 N 9.20 E
Dungau ◆¹ 60 48.50 N 12.40 E
Dungeness > 42 50.55 N 0.58 E
Dungeness ≃ 224 48.08 N 123.06 W
Dungeness, Punta > 254 52.23 S 68.25 W
Dungeness Bay c 224 48.10 N 123.07 W
Dungeness Spit >² 224 48.10 N 123.09 W
Dungiven 48 54.55 N 6.55 W
Dunglow 48 54.57 N 8.22 W
Dungo, Lagoa do ⊜ 152 17.20 S 18.58 E
Dungog 166 32.24 S 151.46 E
Dungu 154 3.37 N 28.34 E
Dungu ≃ 154 3.37 N 28.34 E
Dungun 114 4.47 N 103.26 E
Dungun ≃ 114 4.47 N 103.23 E
Dunham 206 45.08 N 72.48 W
Dunham Lake ⊜ 281 42.39 N 83.41 W
Dunham-on-the-Hill 262 53.15 N 2.47 W
Dunham Park ♦ 262 53.23 N 2.24 W
Dunham Town 262 53.23 N 2.24 W
Dunheved, Austl. 274a 33.45 S 150.47 E
Dunheved — Launceston, Eng., U.K. 42 50.38 N 4.21 W
Dunholme 44 53.18 N 0.28 W
Dunhou 100 27.02 N 114.58 E
Dunhua 89 43.21 N 128.13 E
Dunhuang 102 40.12 N 94.41 E
Dunières 62 45.13 N 4.20 E
Dunilovo, Ross. 76 57.46 N 38.55 E
Dunilovo, Ross. 80 57.00 N 41.27 E
Dunkeld 46 56.34 N 3.35 W
Dunkeld ◆⁸ 273d 26.09 S 28.03 E
Dunkellin ≃ 48 53.12 N 8.54 W
Dunkelsteinerwald ◆³ 61 48.15 N 15.29 E
Dunkern ⊜ 40 59.09 N 16.52 E
Dunkerque 50 51.03 N 2.22 E
Dunkerrin 48 52.55 N 7.55 W
Dunkery Hill ⋀² 42 51.11 N 3.35 W
Dunkineely 48 54.38 N 8.23 W
Dunkinsville 218 38.51 N 83.30 W
Dunkirk — Dunkerque, Fr. 50 51.03 N 2.22 E
Dunkirk, Eng., U.K. 42 51.17 N 0.59 E
Dunkirk, In., U.S. 216 40.22 N 85.12 W
Dunkirk, N.Y., U.S. 214 42.28 N 79.20 W
Dunkirk, Oh., U.S. 216 40.47 N 83.38 W
Dunk Island I 166 17.57 S 146.10 E
Dunk's Green 260 51.15 N 0.19 E
Dunkuj 140 12.50 N 32.49 E
Dunkwa, Ghana 150 5.58 N 1.46 W
Dunkwa, Ghana 150 5.22 N 1.12 W
Dún Laoghaire 48 53.17 N 6.08 W
Dunlap, In., U.S. 216 41.38 N 85.55 W
Dunlap, Ia., U.S. 198 41.51 N 95.36 W
Dunlap, Tn., U.S. 194 35.22 N 85.23 W
Dunlavin 48 53.02 N 6.41 W
Dunleary — Dún Laoghaire 48 53.17 N 6.08 W
Dunleer 48 53.50 N 6.24 W
Dunleith 285 39.42 N 75.33 W
Dun-le-Palestel 32 46.18 N 1.40 E
Dunlo 214 40.17 N 78.43 W
Dunlop 46 55.43 N 4.32 W
Dunloy 48 55.01 N 6.25 W
Dunmanus Bay c 48 51.35 N 9.45 W
Dunmanway 48 51.43 N 9.06 W
Dunmarra 164 16.42 S 133.25 E
Dunmore, Ire. 48 53.36 N 8.46 W
Dunmore, Pa., U.S. 210 41.25 N 75.37 W
Dunmore Cave ⊥⁵ 48 52.44 N 7.15 W
Dunmore East 48 52.09 N 7.00 W
Dunmore Town 238 25.30 N 76.39 W
Dunmurry 48 54.33 N 6.01 W
Dunn 192 35.18 N 78.36 W
Dunnamanagh 48 54.52 N 7.18 W
Dünnbach ≃ 56 50.10 N 7.18 E
Dunnellon 220 29.02 N 82.27 W
Dunnet 46 58.37 N 3.20 W
Dunnet Bay c 46 58.37 N 3.24 W
Dunnet Head > 46 58.40 N 3.24 W
Dunnigan 226 38.53 N 121.58 W
Dunning 198 41.49 N 100.06 W
Dunning Creek ≃ 214 40.02 N 78.28 W
Dunnington 44 53.57 N 0.59 W
Dunningtown 279b 40.25 N 79.35 W
Dunn Loring 284c 38.53 N 77.14 W
Dunn Loring Woods 284c 38.52 N 77.14 W
Dunnockshaw 262 53.45 N 2.17 W
Dunnottar Castle ⊥ 46 56.57 N 2.11 W
Dunns Bridge 216 41.13 N 86.59 W
Dunnville 212 42.54 N 79.36 W
Dunolly 169 36.52 S 143.44 E
Dunoon 46 55.57 N 4.56 W
Dunqul ⊤⁴ 140 23.26 N 31.37 E
Dunqulah 140 19.10 N 30.29 E
Dunqulah al-Qadīmah 140 18.13 N 30.45 E
Dunqunāb 140 21.06 N 37.05 E
Dunqunāb, Khalīj c 140 21.05 N 37.08 E
Dunrea 184 49.25 N 99.44 W
Dun Rig ⋀ 46 55.34 N 3.10 W
Duns 46 55.47 N 2.20 W
Dunsandel 172 43.40 S 172.11 E
Dunsborough 162 33.36 S 115.06 E
Dunseith 198 48.48 N 100.03 W
Dunsford 42 50.41 N 3.40 W
Dunshaughlin 48 53.31 N 6.32 W
Dunsmuir 204 41.13 N 122.16 W
Dunstable, Eng., U.K. 42 51.53 N 0.32 W
Dunstable, Ma., U.S. 207 42.40 N 71.29 W
Dunstaffnage Castle ⊥ 46 56.26 N 5.32 W
Dunstan Mountains ⋀ 172 44.57 S 169.32 E
Dunster, B.C., Can. 182 53.08 N 119.50 W
Dunster, Eng., U.K. 42 51.12 N 3.27 W
Dun-sur-Auron 32 46.53 N 2.34 E
Dun-sur-Meuse 56 49.23 N 5.11 E
Duntelchaig, Loch ⊜ 46 57.20 N 4.16 W
Dunton Green 42 51.18 N 0.11 E
Dunton Waylets 260 51.35 N 0.24 E
Duntou 100 29.21 N 119.46 E
Duntroon 172 44.52 S 170.41 E
Dunvegan, S. Afr. 273d 26.09 S 28.09 E
Dunvegan, Scot., U.K. 46 57.26 N 6.35 W
Dunvegan, Loch c 46 57.28 N 6.40 W
Dunvegan Castle ⊥ 46 57.26 N 6.35 W
Dunvegan Head > 46 57.31 N 6.43 W
Dunville 186 47.16 N 53.54 W
Dunwich 171a 27.31 S 153.23 E
Dunyāpur 123 29.48 N 71.44 E
Duobukur ≃ 89 49.56 N 125.12 E
Duogu'nao 102 31.32 N 103.14 E
Duojiundian 105 39.22 N 117.31 E
Duolun (Dolonnur) 98 42.15 N 116.18 E
Duolundabohuer 120 33.25 N 93.54 E
Duomo ✝¹ 266b 45.27 N 9.11 E
Duomula 120 34.07 N 82.30 E
Duoyuezhen 107 30.11 N 103.42 E
Duozhu 100 22.59 N 114.43 E
Duozhuang 98 35.25 N 118.12 E
Du Page □⁶ 216 41.52 N 88.06 W

Symbol	English	Deutsch	Español	Français	Português
≃	River	Fluß	Río	Rivière	Rio
≅	Canal	Kanal	Canal	Canal	Canal
⌞	Waterfall, Rapids	Wasserfall, Stromschnellen	Cascada, Rápidos	Chute d'eau, Rapides	Cascata, Rápidos
ʮ	Strait	Meeresstraße	Estrecho	Détroit	Estreito
c	Bay, Gulf	Bucht, Golf	Bahía, Golfo	Baie, Golfe	Baía, Golfo
⊜	Lake, Lakes	See, Seen	Lago, Lagos	Lac, Lacs	Lago, Lagos
≡	Swamp	Sumpf	Pantano	Marais	Pântano
⊓	Ice Features, Glacier	Eis- und Gletscherformen	Accidentes Glaciales	Formes glaciaires	Acidentes glaciares
⊤	Other Hydrographic Features	Andere Hydrographische Objekte	Otros Elementos Hidrográficos	Autres données hydrographiques	Outros acidentes hidrográficos
◆	Submarine Features	Untermeerische Objekte	Accidentes Submarinos	Formes de relief sous-marin	Acidentes submarinos
□	Political Unit	Politische Einheit	Unidad Política	Entité politique	Unidade política
✝	Cultural Institution	Kulturelle Institution	Institución Cultural	Institution culturelle	Instituição cultural
⊥	Historical Site	Historische Stätte	Sitio Histórico	Site historique	Sítio histórico
♦	Recreational Site	Erholungs- und Ferienort	Sitio de Recreo	Centre de loisirs	Area de Lazer
⊠	Airport	Flughafen	Aeropuerto	Aéroport	Aeroporto
■	Military Installation	Militäranlage	Instalación Militar	Installation militaire	Instalação militar
◆	Miscellaneous	Verschiedenes	Misceláneo	Divers	Diversos

ENGLISH | DEUTSCH

Name (Name)	Page (Seite)	Lat.°' (Breite°')	Long.°' (Länge°' E = Ost)
Du Page ≏	216	41.25 N	88.14 W
Du Page, East Branch ≏	278	41.42 N	88.09 W
Dupang Ling ⋆	102	25.32 N	111.11 E
Duparquet, Lac ⊜	190	48.28 N	79.16 W
Dupax	116	16.17 N	121.05 E
Duping	102	27.11 N	108.20 E
Dupl'atka	80	51.07 N	42.20 E
Dupli	82	54.21 N	36.54 E
Dupnica	38	42.16 N	23.07 E
Dupo	219	38.31 N	90.13 W
Dupont, In., U.S.	218	38.53 N	85.31 W
Dupont, Oh., U.S.	216	41.03 N	84.18 W
Dupont, Pa., U.S.	210	41.19 N	75.44 W
Du Pont, Wa., U.S.	224	47.05 N	122.37 W
Dupont Research Center ʊ[3]	285	39.46 N	75.34 W
Düppel, Berliner Forst ⊕[3]	264a	52.25 N	13.08 E
Dupree	198	45.02 N	101.36 W
Duque Bacelar	250	4.09 S	42.57 W
Duque de Caxias	256	22.47 S	43.18 W
Duque de Caxias □[7]	287a	22.45 S	43.16 W
Duque de York, Isla I	254	50.40 S	75.20 W
Duquesne	214	40.22 N	79.51 W
Duquesne University ʊ[2]	279b	40.26 N	79.59 W
DuQuoin	194	37.59 N	89.15 W
Dūrā	132	31.30 N	35.02 E
Durach, Dtsch.	58	47.42 N	10.20 E
Durach, Dtsch.	64	47.42 N	10.20 E
Durack ≏	164	15.33 S	127.52 E
Durack Ranges ⋆	160	17.00 S	128.00 E
Durağan	130	41.25 N	35.04 E
Durak	130	39.42 N	28.17 E
Durak Dağı ∧	84	39.47 N	43.42 E
Dural	170	33.41 S	151.02 E
Duran	200	34.28 N	105.23 W
Durance ≏	62	43.55 N	4.44 E
Durand, Il., U.S.	190	42.26 N	89.19 W
Durand, Mi., U.S.	216	42.54 N	83.59 W
Durand, Wi., U.S.	190	44.37 N	91.57 W
Durand Reef ✢[2]	175f	22.03 S	168.39 E
Duran Durat I	271c	1.15 N	103.51 E
Durango, Esp.	34	43.10 N	2.37 W
Durango, Méx.	234	24.02 N	104.40 W
Durango, Co., U.S.	200	37.16 N	107.52 W
Durango □[3]	232	24.50 N	104.50 W
Duranillin	168a	33.31 S	116.48 E
Durant, Ia., U.S.	190	41.35 N	90.54 W
Durant, Ms., U.S.	194	33.04 N	89.51 W
Durant, Ok., U.S.	196	33.59 N	96.22 W
Duras	32	44.41 N	0.11 E
Duratón ≏	34	41.37 N	4.07 W
Duraur V	144	10.33 N	49.07 E
Durazno	252	33.22 S	56.31 W
Durazzo → Durrës	38	41.19 N	19.26 E
Durbach	58	48.30 N	8.01 E
Durbādānga	126	22.57 N	89.15 E
Durban	158	29.55 S	30.56 E
Durban Roodepoort Deep Gold Mines ⊕[7]	273d	26.10 S	27.51 E
Durbanville	158	33.50 S	18.39 E
Durbe	76	56.35 N	21.21 E
D'urbel'džin	85	41.16 N	74.57 E
Durbet-Daba, pereval)(	86	49.37 N	89.25 E
Durbin	188	38.32 N	79.49 W
Durbuy	56	50.21 N	5.28 E
Durchholz	263	51.23 N	7.17 E
Durdent ≏	50	49.51 N	0.36 E
Đurđevac	36	46.03 N	17.04 E
Durdur V	144	10.34 N	43.58 E
Dureji	120	25.53 N	67.18 E
Düren	56	50.48 N	6.28 E
Durg	120	21.11 N	81.17 E
Durgāpur	126	23.29 N	87.20 E
Durham, On., Can.	212	44.10 N	80.49 W
Durham, Eng., U.K.	44	54.47 N	1.34 W
Durham, Ca., U.S.	204	39.38 N	121.47 W
Durham, Ct., U.S.	207	41.28 N	72.40 W
Durham, Mo., U.S.	219	39.58 N	91.40 W
Durham, N.H., U.S.	188	43.08 N	70.55 W
Durham, N.C., U.S.	192	35.59 N	78.53 W
Durham, Or., U.S.	224	45.25 N	122.46 W
Durham □[6], On., Can.	212	43.56 N	78.53 W
Durham □[6], Eng., U.K.	44	54.45 N	1.45 W
Durham Cathedral ʊ[1]	44	54.46 N	1.36 W
Durham Downs	166	27.05 S	141.54 E
Durham Heights ∧	176	71.08 N	122.56 W
Durham Pond ⊜	276	41.00 N	74.27 W
Durhamville	210	43.07 N	75.40 W
Durian ≏	115a	6.01 S	106.24 E
Durian, Selat ⊔	114	0.42 N	103.42 E
Duriansebatang	112	0.47 S	109.56 E
Durian Tipus	114	3.07 N	102.13 E
D'urinskije razlivy ≡	80	50.25 N	50.20 E
Durlabhpur	272b	22.47 N	88.29 E
Durlești	38	47.02 N	28.45 E
Durmersheim	56	48.56 N	8.16 E
Durmitor ∧	38	43.08 N	19.01 E
Durness	46	58.33 N	4.45 W
Durness, Kyle of c	46	58.34 N	4.49 W
Durneva, ostrova II	80	45.25 N	52.50 E
Durnikino	80	51.39 N	42.49 E
Dürnkrut	61	48.28 N	16.51 E
Dürnstein ⊥	61	48.24 N	15.32 E
Duro ∧	144	5.31 N	37.12 E
Durón	34	40.38 N	2.43 W
Duross Heights	285	39.40 N	75.37 W
Dürre Liesing ≏	264b	48.08 N	16.16 E
Durrell	186	49.40 N	54.44 W
Dürrenboden	58	46.57 N	8.50 E
Durrës	38	41.19 N	19.26 E
Durrie	166	25.38 S	140.16 E
Durrington	42	51.13 N	1.45 W
Durrow	48	52.50 N	7.22 W
Durrus	48	51.36 N	9.31 W
Dürrwangen	56	49.07 N	10.23 E
Dursey Head ›	48	51.35 N	10.14 W
Dursey Island I	48	51.36 N	10.12 W
Dursley	42	51.42 N	2.21 W
Dursunbey	130	39.35 N	28.38 E
D'urt'uli	86	55.29 N	54.52 E
Duru	154	4.14 N	28.45 E
Duru Gölü ⊜	130	41.20 N	28.35 E
Durulova	130	38.17 N	38.01 E
Durunkah	142	27.08 N	31.10 E
Durūz, Jabal ad- ⋆	132	32.40 N	36.44 E
D'Urville, Tanjung ›	164	1.28 S	137.54 E
D'Urville Island I	172	40.50 S	173.52 E
Duryea	210	41.20 N	75.44 W
Dury Voe c	46a	60.20 N	1.08 W
Dušak	128	37.13 N	60.02 E
Dušanbe	85	38.35 N	68.48 E
Dušekan	74	60.39 N	109.03 E
Dušeti	84	42.06 N	44.42 E
Dusetos	76	55.45 N	25.51 E
Dushan, Zhg.	100	31.36 N	116.14 E
Dushan, Zhg.	102	25.53 N	107.30 E
Du Shan ∧	98	40.30 N	118.45 E
Dushanbe → Dušanbe	85	38.35 N	68.48 E
Dushan Hu ⊜	98	35.06 N	116.52 E
Dushantou	106	30.46 N	119.47 E
Dushanzi	86	44.20 N	84.51 E
Dusheng	98	38.23 N	116.33 E
Dushichang	107	29.10 N	106.31 E
Dushikou	98	41.17 N	115.38 E
Dushore	210	41.31 N	76.24 W
Düshorn	52	52.49 N	9.37 E
Dushu	100	33.21 N	113.09 E
Dushu Hu ⊜	106	31.17 N	120.42 E
Dusia ⊜	76	54.18 N	23.42 E
Dusky Sound ⊔	172	45.47 S	166.28 E
Dušocha, gora ∧	85	39.10 N	70.01 E
Duson	194	30.14 N	92.11 W
Dušonovo	82	56.04 N	38.18 E
Düssel	263	51.16 N	7.03 E
Düssel ≏	263	51.13 N	6.45 E
Düsseldorf, Dtsch.	56	51.12 N	6.47 E
Düsseldorf, Dtsch.	263	51.12 N	6.47 E
Düsseldorf □[5]	52	51.15 N	7.00 E
Düsseldorf, Flughafen ⊠	56	51.17 N	6.47 E
Düsseldorf, Universität ʊ[2]	263	51.12 N	6.48 E
Dusslingen	58	48.27 N	9.03 E
Dussnang	58	47.26 N	8.58 E
Dustin	196	35.16 N	96.01 W
Dutch Creek ≏, B.C., Can.	182	50.20 N	115.52 W
Dutch Creek ≏, Ar., U.S.	194	35.03 N	93.24 W
Dutchess □[6]	210	41.42 N	73.56 W
Dutch Harbor	180	53.53 N	166.32 W
Dutch John	200	40.55 N	109.23 W
Dutchman Creek ≏	226	37.11 N	120.28 W
Dutianjie	102	24.38 N	101.31 E
Dutluca	130	39.09 N	38.37 E
Dutlwe	156	23.55 S	23.47 E
Dutoitspiek ∧	158	33.46 S	19.12 E
Dutou, Zhg.	100	22.54 N	115.12 E
Dutou, Zhg.	106	31.19 N	120.54 E
Dutovlje	64	45.46 N	13.50 E
Dutovo	24	63.47 N	56.35 E
Dutsen Wai	150	10.50 N	8.12 E
Dutton, Austl.	168b	34.22 S	139.08 E
Dutton, On., Can.	214	42.39 N	81.30 W
Dutton, Eng., U.K.	262	53.19 N	2.38 W
Dutton, Mi., U.S.	216	42.50 N	85.35 W
Dutton, Mt., U.S.	202	47.50 N	111.42 W
Dutton ≏	166	20.45 S	143.12 E
Dutton, Mount ∧, Ak., U.S.	180	55.10 N	162.15 W
Dutton, Mount ∧, Ut,. U.S.	200	38.01 N	112.13 W
Dutun	105	39.46 N	117.02 E
Dutzow	219	38.37 N	90.59 W
Duut	86	47.30 N	91.40 E
Duval, Lac ⊜	190	46.19 N	76.55 W
Duvall	224	47.44 N	121.59 W
Duvan	86	55.42 N	57.54 E
Duvanka ≏	83	49.35 N	38.10 E
Duved	26	63.24 N	12.52 E
Duvernay ⊕[8]	275a	45.35 N	73.40 W
Duvno	36	43.43 N	17.14 E
Duwamish	224	47.32 N	122.19 W
Duwaydār, Bi'r ad- ⊤[4]	142	30.55 N	32.31 E
Duxbury	207	42.02 N	70.40 W
Duxbury Bay c	207	42.02 N	70.39 W
Duxbury Beach ≗[2]	283	42.03 N	70.38 W
Duxun	100	23.55 N	117.37 E
Duyagan Point ›	116	12.36 N	121.33 E
Duyun	102	26.12 N	107.31 E
Düzce	130	40.50 N	31.10 E
Duze	100	29.07 N	118.56 E
Dve Mogili	38	43.36 N	25.52 E
Dvina Occidental → Zapadnaja Dvina ≏	76	57.04 N	24.03 E
Dvina Septentrional → Severnaja Dvina ≏	24	64.32 N	40.30 E
Dvinje, ozero ⊜	76	56.08 N	31.12 E
Dvinsk → Daugavpils	76	55.53 N	26.32 E
Dvinskaja guba c	24	65.00 N	39.45 E
Dvojnovskij	80	51.03 N	42.27 E
Dvorcy	82	54.37 N	36.00 E
Dvorec	88	58.23 N	99.56 E
Dvorichna	78	49.52 N	37.40 E
Dvoriši	76	58.12 N	35.13 E
Dvornikovo	82	55.30 N	38.38 E
Dvuch Cirkov, gora ∧	74	67.35 N	168.07 E
Dvugorbaja, gora ∧	180	68.30 N	179.20 E
Dvulučnoje	78	50.02 N	38.02 E
Dvůr Králové [nad Labem]	30	50.26 N	15.48 E
Dwangwa ≏	154	12.33 S	34.12 E
Dwarbasini	272b	22.59 N	88.14 E
Dwārka	120	22.14 N	68.58 E
Dwārka ≏	126	23.44 N	88.11 E
Dwārkeswar ≏	126	23.06 N	87.21 E
Dwarli	272c	19.12 N	73.08 E
Dwars Kill ≏	276	40.58 N	73.58 W
Dwellingup	168a	32.43 S	116.02 E
D.W. Field Park ♠	283	42.06 N	71.03 W
Dwight	216	41.05 N	88.25 W
Dwight D. Eisenhower Lock ⊕[5]	206	45.00 N	74.45 W
Dwina-Bucht → Dvinskaja guba c	24	65.00 N	39.45 E
Dwingeloo	52	52.50 N	6.21 E
Dworshak Reservoir ⊜[1]	202	46.40 N	116.00 W
Dwyfor ≏	44	52.55 N	4.17 W
Dwyka	158	33.02 S	21.30 E
Dwyka ≏	158	33.18 S	21.39 E
Dyakove	83	47.57 N	39.09 E
Dyaul Island I	164	2.56 S	150.55 E
Dybbøl	41	54.55 N	9.45 E
Dyberry Creek ≏	210	41.35 N	75.15 W
Dyce	46	57.12 N	2.11 W
Dychtau, gora ∧	84	43.03 N	43.08 E
Dyck, Schloss ⊥	263	51.09 N	6.34 E
Dyer, In., U.S.	216	41.29 N	87.31 W
Dyer, Tn., U.S.	194	36.04 N	88.59 W
Dyer, Cape ›	176	66.37 N	61.18 W
Dyer Bay c	212	45.10 N	81.18 W
Dyer Island I	158	34.41 S	19.25 E
Dyero	150	12.50 N	6.30 W
Dyersburg	194	36.02 N	89.23 W
Dyersville	190	42.29 N	91.07 W
Dyess Air Force Base ■	196	32.25 N	99.51 W
Dyfed □[6]	42	52.00 N	4.30 W
Dyfi ≏	42	52.32 N	4.03 W
Dyje (Thaya) ≏	61	48.37 N	16.56 E
Dykan'ka	78	49.49 N	34.32 E
Dyke	46	57.36 N	3.41 W
Dyke Ackland Bay c	164	9.00 S	148.45 E
Dyken Pond ⊜	210	42.43 N	73.26 W
Dykes Pond ⊜	283	42.36 N	70.44 W
Dyle (Dijle) ≏	56	51.04 N	4.25 E
Dyleň ∧	60	49.58 N	12.30 E
Dylym	84	43.04 N	46.38 E
Dymchurch	42	51.02 N	1.00 E
Dyment	184	49.37 N	92.19 W
Dymer	78	50.47 N	30.18 E
Dymock	42	51.59 N	2.26 W
Dymytrov	83	48.15 N	37.18 E
Dymytrove	78	48.36 N	33.01 E
Dynamo Stadium ♠	265b	55.48 N	37.34 E
Dynów	30	49.49 N	22.14 E
Dyreborg	41	55.04 N	10.13 E
Dyrnesvågen	26	63.26 N	7.51 E
Dyrotz	264a	52.33 N	12.58 E
Dysart, Austl.	166	22.27 S	148.20 E
Dysart, Sk., Can.	184	50.56 N	104.02 W
Dysart, Scot., U.K.	46	56.08 N	3.08 W
Dysart, Ia., U.S.	190	42.10 N	92.18 W
Dysart, Pa., U.S.	214	40.36 N	78.31 W
Dyšina	60	49.46 N	13.29 E
Dysna (Dzisna) ≏	76	55.34 N	28.12 E
Dysnai ⊜	76	55.29 N	26.20 E
Dysselsdorp	158	33.34 S	22.28 E
Dysynni ≏	42	52.36 N	4.05 W
Dyviziya	78	45.57 N	29.59 E
Dzaamar	88	48.10 N	104.50 E
Dzaamaryn uul ∧	88	48.10 N	104.30 E
Džabžur	84	40.54 N	43.58 E
Dzachuj	102	44.59 N	96.37 E
Džagdy, chrebet ⋆	89	53.40 N	131.00 E
Džalagaš	86	45.05 N	64.40 E
Džalal-Abad	85	40.56 N	73.00 E
Džalal-Abad □[4]	85	41.30 N	72.30 E
Džalinda	89	53.29 N	123.54 E
Džamantau, gory ⋆	85	40.55 N	74.40 E
Džamašuj	85	40.52 N	71.28 E
Džambejty	80	50.16 N	52.35 E
Džambul, Kaz.	80	47.34 N	50.12 E
Džambul → Žambyl, Kaz.	85	42.54 N	71.22 E
Džambul, gora ∧	86	44.46 N	73.08 E
Džanga	128	40.00 N	53.03 E
Džangi-Džol	85	41.36 N	72.08 E
Džansugurov	86	45.24 N	79.29 E
Džanybek	80	49.25 N	46.51 E
Dzaoudzi	157a	12.47 S	45.17 E
Džardžan	74	68.43 N	124.02 E
Džargalant → Chovd, Mong.	86	48.01 N	91.39 E
Džargalant, Mong.	88	48.40 N	100.43 E
Džargalant, Mong.	88	46.57 N	115.15 E
Džargalant, Mong.	88	48.33 N	99.20 E
Džargaltchaan	88	47.28 N	109.30 E
Dzaudzhikau → Vladikavkaz	84	43.03 N	44.40 E
Džaur	89	50.02 N	138.30 E
Džava	84	42.24 N	43.54 E
Dzavchan	88	48.48 N	93.07 E
Dzavchan □[4]	88	48.00 N	96.00 E
Dzavchan ≏	88	48.54 N	93.23 E
Dzavchan Mandal	88	48.19 N	95.07 E
Džavchlant → Uliastaj	88	47.45 N	96.49 E
Džazator	86	49.45 N	87.23 E
Džbán ∧	54	50.12 N	13.45 E
Džebel	128	39.38 N	54.14 E
Dzelter ≏	88	50.30 N	105.06 E
Dzemul	232	21.12 N	89.18 W
Dzeng	152	3.45 N	12.00 E
Dženretlen, mys ›	180	67.07 N	173.45 W
Džergetal	85	41.30 N	75.47 E
Džermuk	84	39.51 N	45.41 E
Dzerzhinsk → Dzeržinsk	80	56.15 N	43.24 E
Dzerzhyns'k, Ukr.	78	50.09 N	27.56 E
Dzerzhyns'k, Ukr.	83	48.26 N	37.50 E
Dzeržinsk	80	56.15 N	43.24 E
Dzeržinskij	82	55.38 N	37.50 E
Dzeržinskoje, Kaz.	86	45.50 N	81.07 E
Dzeržinskoje, Ross.	86	56.49 N	95.18 E
Džetim, chrebet ⋆	85	41.35 N	77.05 E
Džetygara	86	52.11 N	61.12 E
Džetyoguz	85	42.27 N	78.14 E
Džetyoguzskij zapovednik ♠	85	42.15 N	78.20 E
Džetysaj	85	40.47 N	68.16 E
Dzhambul → Žambyl	85	42.54 N	71.22 E
Dzhankoy	78	45.43 N	34.24 E
Dzharylhach, ostriv I	78	46.02 N	32.55 E
Dzharylhats'ka zatoka c	78	46.05 N	32.50 E
Dzhuryn	78	48.41 N	28.18 E
Działdowo	30	53.15 N	20.10 E
Działoszyce	30	50.22 N	20.21 E
Dzibalchén	232	19.31 N	89.45 W
Dzibilchaltun ⊥	232	21.05 N	89.36 W
Džida ≏	88	50.37 N	106.14 E
Džidinskij chrebet ⋆	88	50.10 N	102.00 E
Dzierzgoń	30	53.56 N	19.21 E
Dzierżoniów (Reichenbach)	30	50.44 N	16.39 E
Dzilam González	232	21.17 N	88.56 W
Džilav	85	39.19 N	67.45 E
Džinst	102	45.24 N	100.35 E
Dzioua	148	33.14 N	5.14 E
Džirgatal'	85	39.13 N	71.12 E
Dzisna	76	55.33 N	28.10 E
Dzisna (Dysna) ≏	76	55.34 N	28.12 E
Dzitás	232	20.51 N	88.31 W
Dzitbalché	232	20.19 N	90.03 W
Dzivin	76	51.58 N	24.35 E
Dziwna ≏[1]	54	54.01 N	14.44 E
Dziwnów	30	54.03 N	14.45 E
Džizak	85	40.06 N	67.50 E
Džizak □[4]	85	40.30 N	67.45 E
Dzjaniskavičy	76	52.44 N	26.41 E
Dzjarèčyn	76	53.15 N	24.55 E
Dzjaršynskaja, hara ∧[2]	76	53.51 N	27.03 E
Dzjaržynsk	76	53.41 N	27.08 E
Dzjatlava	76	53.28 N	25.24 E
Dzjatlavičy	76	52.20 N	26.50 E
Dzmitravičy	76	53.59 N	29.06 E
Dzodze	150	6.14 N	1.00 E
Džubga	78	44.20 N	38.43 E
Džugdžur, chrebet ⋆	74	58.00 N	136.00 E
Džūkste	76	56.47 N	23.15 E
Džumabazar	85	39.31 N	67.13 E
Džumgoltau, chrebet ⋆	85	42.18 N	74.32 E
Dzungarian Basin → Junggar Pendi ≚[1]	86	45.00 N	88.00 E
Dzungarian Gate (Džungarskije vorota))(	86	45.25 N	82.25 E
Džungarskij Alatau, chrebet ⋆	86	45.00 N	81.00 E
Džungarskije vorota → Dzungarian Gate)(	86	45.25 N	82.25 E
Džurak-Sal ≏	80	47.18 N	43.36 E
Dzürch	88	48.55 N	100.10 E
Džusaly	86	45.28 N	64.05 E
Dzüün Changaj	88	49.17 N	95.14 E
Džüün Charaa	88	48.52 N	106.28 E
Dzüün Gov	88	49.55 N	93.47 E
Dzuunmod	88	47.45 N	106.55 E
Džvari	84	42.43 N	42.04 E
Dzyhivka	78	48.22 N	28.19 E
E			
Eads	198	38.28 N	102.46 W
Eagar	200	34.06 N	109.17 W
Eagle, Ak., U.S.	180	64.46 N	141.16 W
Eagle, Co., U.S.	200	39.39 N	106.49 W
Eagle, N.Y., U.S.	210	42.33 N	78.18 W
Eagle, Wi., U.S.	216	42.52 N	88.28 W
Eagle ≏, Nf., Can.	176	53.35 N	57.25 W
Eagle ≏, Yk., Can.	180	67.20 N	137.10 W
Eagle ≏, Co., U.S.	200	39.39 N	107.04 W
Eagle, Mount ∧[2]	241n	17.46 N	64.49 W
Eagle Bay	182	50.56 N	119.12 W
Eagle Bend	198	46.09 N	95.02 W
Eagle Bridge	210	42.57 N	73.24 W
Eagle Butte	198	45.00 N	101.14 W
Eagle Chief Creek ≏	196	36.22 N	98.27 W
Eagle Creek	224	45.21 N	122.21 W
Eagle Creek ≏, Sk., Can.	184	52.22 N	107.24 W
Eagle Creek ≏, Az., U.S.	200	32.58 N	109.25 W
Eagle Creek ≏, In., U.S.	218	39.43 N	86.12 W
Eagle Creek ≏, Ky., U.S.	218	38.36 N	85.04 W
Eagle Creek ≏, Mt., U.S.	202	48.12 N	111.11 W
Eagle Creek ≏, N.M., U.S.	196	32.47 N	104.20 W
Eagle Creek ≏, Oh., U.S.	214	41.18 N	80.53 W
Eagle Creek ≏, Oh., U.S.	218	38.43 N	83.51 W
Eagle Creek ≏, Or., U.S.	202	44.45 N	117.10 W
Eagle Creek ≏, Or., U.S.	224	45.21 N	122.23 W
Eagle Creek, East Fork ≏	218	38.47 N	83.43 W
Eagle Creek, West Fork ≏	218	38.47 N	83.43 W
Eagle Creek Reservoir ⊜[1]	218	39.50 N	86.18 W
Eagledale	224	47.37 N	122.32 W
Eagle Grove	190	42.39 N	93.54 W
Eagle Harbor	210	43.15 N	78.15 W
Eaglehawk	169	36.43 S	144.15 E
Eagle Hill ≏	283	42.42 N	70.49 W
Eagle Key I	220	25.09 N	80.36 W
Eagle Lake, Fl., U.S.	220	27.59 N	81.45 W
Eagle Lake, Me., U.S.	186	47.02 N	68.35 W
Eagle Lake, Mi., U.S.	216	41.48 N	86.02 W
Eagle Lake, Tx., U.S.	222	29.35 N	96.20 W
Eagle Lake ⊜, B.C., Can.	182	51.55 N	124.25 W
Eagle Lake ⊜, On., Can.	184	50.39 N	94.54 W
Eagle Lake ⊜, On., Can.	184	49.42 N	93.13 W
Eagle Lake ⊜, On., Can.	212	44.41 N	76.43 W
Eagle Lake ⊜, On., Can.	212	45.08 N	78.29 W
Eagle Lake ⊜, Ca., U.S.	204	40.39 N	120.44 W
Eagle Lake ⊜, Me., U.S.	186	46.20 N	69.20 W
Eagle Lake ⊜, Mi., U.S.	216	41.48 N	86.02 W
Eagle Lake ⊜, Tx., U.S.	222	29.34 N	96.21 W
Eagle Lake ⊜, Wi., U.S.	216	42.42 N	88.07 W
Eagle Mountain, Ca., U.S.	204	33.49 N	115.27 W
Eagle Mountain, Tx., U.S.	222	32.52 N	97.30 W
Eagle Mountain ∧	202	46.20 N	115.07 W
Eagle Mountain ∧[2]	190	47.54 N	90.33 W
Eagle Mountain Lake ⊜[1]	222	32.55 N	97.30 W
Eagle Nest Butte ∧	198	43.27 N	101.39 W
Eagle Nest Lake ⊜	222	29.13 N	95.37 W
Eagle Pass	196	28.42 N	100.29 W
Eagle Peak ∧, Ca., U.S.	204	41.17 N	120.12 W
Eagle Peak ∧, Ca., U.S.	228	35.15 N	118.28 W
Eagle Peak ∧, Ca., U.S.	282	37.54 N	121.54 W
Eagle River, Mi., U.S.	190	47.24 N	88.18 W
Eagle River, Wi., U.S.	190	45.55 N	89.14 W
Eagle Rock	192	37.38 N	79.48 W
Eagle Rock ⊕[8]	280	34.09 N	118.12 W
Eagle Rock Reservation ♠	276	40.49 N	74.14 W
Eaglesfield	44	55.03 N	3.12 W
Eaglesham, Ab., Can.	182	55.47 N	117.53 W
Eaglesham, Scot., U.K.	46	55.44 N	4.18 W
Eagles Mere	210	41.25 N	76.35 W
Eagleton Village	192	35.46 N	83.56 W
Eagletown	194	34.02 N	94.34 W
Eagle Village	180	64.47 N	141.07 W
Eagleville, Ct., U.S.	207	41.47 N	72.16 W
Eagleville, Pa., U.S.	285	40.10 N	75.24 W
Eagleville, Wi., U.S.	216	42.52 N	88.26 W
Ealing ⊕[8]	42	51.31 N	0.20 W
Eamont ≏	44	54.40 N	2.39 W
Earaheedy	162	25.34 S	121.39 E
Earby	44	53.56 N	2.08 W
Earcroft	262	53.43 N	2.29 W
Eardisley	42	52.08 N	2.59 W
Eardley Lake ⊜	184	52.32 N	96.05 W
Ear Falls	184	50.38 N	93.13 W
Earle	194	35.16 N	90.28 W
Earlestown	262	53.27 N	2.39 W
Earl Grey	184	50.56 N	104.45 W
Earlham	194	41.29 N	94.07 W
Earlimart	226	35.53 N	119.16 W
Earlington	194	37.16 N	87.30 W
Earlish	46	57.34 N	6.23 W
Earl Park	216	40.40 N	87.24 W
Earl Rowe Provincial Park ♠	212	44.10 N	79.54 W
Earls Barton	42	52.15 N	0.45 W
Earls Colne	42	51.56 N	0.42 E
Earlsferry	46	56.11 N	2.50 W
Earl Shilton	42	52.35 N	1.20 W
Earl Soham	42	52.14 N	1.16 E
Earlston	46	55.39 N	2.40 W
Earlton	210	42.21 N	73.54 W
Earlville, Il., U.S.	216	41.35 N	88.55 W
Earlville, N.Y., U.S.	210	42.44 N	75.33 W
Earlville, Pa., U.S.	208	40.19 N	75.44 W
Earlwood	274a	33.56 S	151.08 E
Early, Ia., U.S.	198	42.27 N	95.09 W
Early, Tx., U.S.	196	31.45 N	98.54 W
Early Winters Creek ≏	224	48.35 N	120.35 W
Earn ≏	46	56.21 N	3.19 W
Earn, Loch ⊜	46	56.23 N	4.14 W
Earnslaw, Mount ∧	172	44.37 S	168.24 E
Earth	196	34.14 N	102.24 W
Eas	175f	16.22 S	168.12 E
Easington, Eng., U.K.	44	54.47 N	1.19 W
Easington, Eng., U.K.	44	53.40 N	0.07 E
Easingwold	44	54.07 N	1.11 W
Easky	48	54.18 N	8.58 W
Easley	192	34.49 N	82.36 W
East ≏, On., Can.	190	45.20 N	79.17 W
East ≏, Co., U.S.	200	38.40 N	106.51 W
East ≏, N.Y., U.S.	276	40.48 N	73.48 W
East, University of the ʊ[2]	269f	14.36 N	120.59 E
East Acton	283	42.28 N	71.24 W
East Allen ≏	44	54.55 N	2.19 W
East Alliance	214	40.55 N	81.04 W
East Alligator ≏	164	12.08 S	132.42 E
East Alton	219	38.52 N	90.06 W
East Amherst	210	43.01 N	78.42 W
East-Angus	206	45.29 N	71.40 W
East Arlington	210	43.03 N	73.08 W
East Atlantic Beach	276	40.35 N	73.43 W
East Aurora	210	42.46 N	78.36 W
East Avon	210	42.55 N	77.42 W
East Baines ≏	164	15.38 S	129.58 E
East Bangor	210	40.52 N	75.11 W
East Barming	260	51.16 N	0.28 E
East Barnet ⊕[8]	260	51.38 N	0.09 W
East Basin c	279a	41.32 N	81.40 W
East Bay c, Fl., U.S.	194	30.05 N	85.32 W
East Bay c, N.Y., U.S.	210	40.38 N	73.32 W
East Bay c, Tx., U.S.	222	29.30 N	94.35 W
East Bedfont ⊕[8]	260	51.27 N	0.26 W
East Bend	192	36.12 N	80.30 W
East Berbice-Corentyne □[4]	246	4.00 N	58.15 W
East Berkshire	206	44.56 N	72.42 W
East Berlin, Ct., U.S.	207	41.37 N	72.42 W
East Berlin, N.J., U.S.	285	39.48 N	74.55 W
East Berlin, Pa., U.S.	208	39.56 N	76.58 W
East Bernard	222	29.32 N	96.04 W
East Bernstadt	192	37.11 N	84.07 W
East Berwick	210	41.03 N	76.13 W
East Bethany	210	42.56 N	78.06 W
East Bhāgīrath Plain ≚	126	23.30 N	88.30 E
East Bijou Creek ≏	198	39.51 N	104.08 W
East Billerica	283	42.34 N	71.14 W
East Blackstone	207	42.02 N	71.31 W
East Bloomfield	210	42.54 N	77.26 W
East Boston ⊕[8]	283	42.23 N	71.02 W
Eastbourne, N.Z.	172	41.18 S	174.54 E
Eastbourne, Eng., U.K.	42	50.46 N	0.17 E
East Brady	214	40.59 N	79.36 W
East Braintree	184	49.37 N	95.38 W
East Branch	210	41.59 N	75.08 W
East Branch Lake ⊜[1]	214	41.35 N	78.35 W
East Brewster	207	41.46 N	70.03 W
East Brewton	194	31.05 N	87.03 W
East Bridgewater	207	42.02 N	70.58 W
East Brimfield Lake ⊜[1]	207	42.06 N	72.10 W
East Brookfield	207	42.13 N	72.02 W
East Brooklyn	207	41.47 N	71.53 W
East Brother I	271d	22.20 N	113.58 E
East Brunswick	208	40.25 N	74.23 W
East Bucas Island I	116	9.43 N	126.02 E
East Burwood	274b	37.51 S	145.09 E
Eastbury	260	51.37 N	0.25 W
East Butler	214	40.53 N	79.51 W
East Cache Creek ≏	196	34.08 N	98.16 W
East Caicos I	238	21.41 N	71.30 W
East Calder	46	55.54 N	3.27 W
East Canaan	207	42.00 N	73.17 W
East Canada Creek ≏	210	43.00 N	74.45 W
East Canton	214	40.47 N	81.17 W
East Cape ›, N.Z.	172	37.41 S	178.33 E
East Cape ›, Ak., U.S.	181a	51.21 N	179.29 E
East Cape ›, Fl., U.S.	220	25.07 N	81.05 W
East Carancahua Creek ≏	222	28.51 N	96.19 W
East Carbon	200	39.32 N	110.24 W
East Carlisle	214	41.19 N	82.05 W
East Caroline Basin ✢[1]	14	4.00 N	146.45 E
East Castor ≏	212	45.16 N	75.17 W
East Catfish Creek ≏	212	42.47 N	81.04 W
East Channel ≏[1]	180	69.20 N	134.00 W
East Chatham	210	42.25 N	73.32 W
East Chelmsford	207	42.36 N	71.18 W
Eastchester	210	40.57 N	73.49 W
Eastchester Bay c	276	40.51 N	73.48 W
East Chicago	216	41.38 N	87.27 W
East Chicago Heights	278	41.30 N	87.35 W
East China Sea ⊤[2]	90	30.00 N	126.00 E
Eastchurch	42	51.25 N	0.52 E
East Clandon	260	51.15 N	0.29 W
East Claridon	214	41.32 N	81.07 W
East Cleddau ≏	42	51.46 N	4.52 W
East Cleveland	214	41.31 N	81.34 W
East Coast Bays	172	36.45 S	174.46 E
East Concord	210	42.33 N	78.38 W
Eastcote ⊕[8]	260	51.35 N	0.24 W
East Cote Blanche Bay c	194	29.35 N	91.40 W
East Coulee	182	51.20 N	112.29 W
East Creek ≏	276	40.27 N	74.09 W
East Cross Creek ≏	212	44.17 N	78.44 W
East Dean	42	50.45 N	0.12 E
East Delaware Aqueduct ≍[1]	210	41.52 N	74.31 W
East Dennis	207	41.44 N	70.09 W
East Dereham	42	52.41 N	0.56 E
East Dismal Swamp ≡	192	35.45 N	76.35 W
East Ditch ≍	276	40.56 N	74.19 W
East Douglas	207	42.04 N	71.42 W
East Dublin	192	32.32 N	82.52 W
East Dubuque	190	42.29 N	90.38 W
East Dundee	216	42.06 N	88.16 W
East Durham	210	42.22 N	74.06 W
East Ely	204	39.15 N	114.53 W
Eastend, Sk., Can.	184	49.31 N	108.48 W
East End, Vir. Is., U.S.	240m	18.21 N	64.40 W
East End Point ›	240b	25.03 N	77.16 W
East Enterprise	218	38.52 N	84.59 W
Easter Island → Pascua, Isla de I	174z	27.07 S	109.22 W
Easterly	222	31.06 N	96.23 W
Eastern □[4], Ghana	150	6.30 N	0.30 W
Eastern □[4], Kenya	154	0.05 N	38.00 E
Eastern □[4], S.L.	150	8.15 N	11.00 W
Eastern □[4], Zam.	154	13.00 S	32.15 E
Eastern □[5]	154	1.25 N	33.50 E
Eastern Bay c	208	38.51 N	76.19 W
Eastern Cape □[4]	158	32.30 S	26.30 E
Eastern Channel → Tsushima-kaikyō ⊔	92	34.00 N	129.00 E
Eastern Cherokee Indian Reservation ⊕[4]	192	35.25 N	83.24 W
Eastern Cove c	168b	35.46 S	137.50 E
Eastern Creek ≏, Austl.	166	20.10 S	141.08 E
Eastern Creek ≏, Austl.	274a	33.39 S	150.51 E
Eastern Division □[5]	175g	19.00 S	180.00 E
Eastern Fields ✢[2]	164	10.20 S	145.45 E
Eastern Ghāts ⋆	122	14.00 N	78.50 E
Eastern Highlands □[5]	164	6.30 S	145.15 E
Eastern Island I	174g	28.12 N	177.20 W
Eastern Isles II	42a	49.57 N	6.15 W
Eastern Michigan University ʊ[2]	281	42.15 N	83.37 W
Eastern Neck Island I	208	39.02 N	76.13 W
Eastern Point ›	283	42.35 N	70.40 W
Eastern Samar □[4]	116	12.00 N	125.00 E
Eastern Sayans → Vostočnyj Sajan ⋆	88	53.00 N	97.00 E
Eastern Shore ⊕[1]	208	38.40 N	75.50 W
Eastern Yamuna Canal ≍	272a	28.40 N	77.15 E
East Falkland I	254	51.55 S	59.00 W
East Falls ⊕[8]	285	40.01 N	75.11 W
East Falmouth	207	41.34 N	70.33 W
East Farleigh	260	51.15 N	0.29 E
East Farmingdale	276	40.44 N	73.26 W
East Faxon	210	41.15 N	76.58 W
East Fayetteville	192	35.05 N	78.51 W
Eastfield	44	54.14 N	0.24 W
East Flat Rock	192	35.16 N	82.25 W
East Foot Hills	226	37.21 N	121.49 W
Eastford	207	41.54 N	72.04 W
East Foxboro	283	42.03 N	71.12 W
East Freedom	214	40.21 N	78.26 W
East Freetown	207	41.46 N	70.57 W
East Frisian Islands → Ostfriesische Inseln II	52	53.44 N	7.25 E
East Gaffney	192	35.04 N	81.37 W
East Gallatin ≏	202	45.53 N	111.20 W
Eastgate	224	47.34 N	122.09 W
East Ghor Canal → Ghawr ash-Sharqīyah, Qanāt al- ≍	132	32.41 N	35.38 E
East Glacier Park	202	48.26 N	113.13 W
East Glenville	210	42.53 N	73.55 W
East Granby	207	41.56 N	72.43 W
East Grand Forks	198	47.55 N	97.01 W
East Grand Rapids	216	42.56 N	85.36 W
East Greenbush	210	42.35 N	73.42 W
East Greenville, Oh., U.S.	214	40.48 N	81.36 W
East Greenville, Pa., U.S.	208	40.24 N	75.30 W
East Greenwich, N.Y., U.S.	210	43.09 N	73.24 W
East Greenwich, R.I., U.S.	207	41.39 N	71.27 W
East Grinstead	42	51.08 N	0.01 W
East Gwillimbury	212	44.08 N	79.25 W
East Haddam	207	41.27 N	72.27 W
East Half Hollow Hills	276	40.57 N	72.11 W
Eastham, Eng., U.K.	262	53.19 N	2.58 W
Eastham, Ma., U.S.	207	41.49 N	69.58 W
East Ham ⊕[8]	260	51.32 N	0.03 E
East Hampton, Ct., U.S.	207	41.34 N	72.30 W
Easthampton, Ma., U.S.	207	42.16 N	72.40 W
East Hampton, N.Y., U.S.	207	40.57 N	72.11 W
East Hanningfield	260	51.41 N	0.34 E
East Hanover	276	40.48 N	74.22 W
East Harbor State Park ♠	214	41.32 N	82.49 W
East Harling	42	52.26 N	0.55 E
East Hartford	207	41.46 N	72.36 W
East Hartland	207	41.59 N	72.54 W
East Harwich	207	41.43 N	70.02 W
East Haven	207	41.16 N	72.52 W
East Hazel Crest	278	41.35 N	87.39 W
East Helena	202	46.35 N	111.54 W
East Hemet	228	33.45 N	116.57 W
East Herkimer	210	43.02 N	74.58 W
East Hertfordshire □[8]	260	51.46 N	0.02 W
East Hickory	214	41.35 N	79.24 W
East Highland Park	208	37.36 N	77.25 W
East Hills, Austl.	274a	33.58 S	150.59 E
East Hills, N.Y., U.S.	276	40.47 N	73.37 W
East Hoathly	42	50.55 N	0.10 E
East Horsley	42	51.15 N	0.26 W
East Humber ≏	212	43.47 N	79.35 W
East Huntington	276	40.52 N	73.24 W
East Ilsley	42	51.32 N	1.17 W
East Irvington	276	41.03 N	73.51 W
East Island ›[1]	276	40.54 N	73.38 W
East Islip	276	40.43 N	73.11 W
East Jewett	210	42.14 N	74.09 W
East Jordan	190	45.09 N	85.07 W
East Keansburg	276	40.26 N	74.07 W
East Kelowna	182	49.51 N	119.25 W
East Kilbride	46	55.46 N	4.10 W
East Killingly	207	41.50 N	71.49 W
East Kingston	210	41.57 N	73.58 W
Eastlake, Mi., U.S.	190	44.15 N	86.18 W
Eastlake, Oh., U.S.	214	41.39 N	81.27 W
East Lake ⊜, On., Can.	184	53.42 N	93.10 W
East Lake ⊜, On., Can.	212	43.55 N	77.12 W
East Lake ⊜, N.J., U.S.	276	40.58 N	74.21 W
East Lake Tohopekaliga ⊜	220	28.18 N	81.17 W
East Lamma Channel ⊔	271d	22.14 N	114.09 E
Eastland	196	32.24 N	98.49 W
Eastland Center ⊕[9]	281	42.27 N	82.56 W
Eastland Shopping Plaza ⊕[9]	279b	40.22 N	79.50 W
East Lansdowne	285	39.56 N	75.16 W
East Lansing	216	42.44 N	84.29 W
East Laurinburg	192	34.46 N	79.26 W
East Leake	42	52.49 N	1.10 W
Eastleigh	42	50.58 N	1.22 W
East Lewistown	214	40.57 N	80.42 W
East Liberty	216	40.19 N	83.34 W
East Liberty ⊕[8]	279b	40.27 N	79.55 W
East Licking Creek ≏	208	40.32 N	77.24 W
East Lindfield	274a	33.46 S	151.11 E
East Linton	46	55.59 N	2.39 W
East Liverpool	214	40.37 N	80.34 W
East London (Oos-Londen)	158	33.00 S	27.55 E
East Longmeadow	207	42.03 N	72.30 W
East Los Angeles	228	34.01 N	118.10 W
East Lyme	207	41.22 N	72.13 W
East Lynn	216	40.28 N	87.48 W
East Lynn Lake ⊜[1]	188	38.05 N	82.20 W
Eastmain	176	52.15 N	78.30 W
Eastmain ≏	176	52.15 N	78.35 W
Eastmain-Opinaca, Réservoir ⊜[1]	176	52.25 N	76.35 W
East Malling	260	51.17 N	0.26 E
Eastman, P.Q., Can.	206	45.18 N	72.19 W
Eastman, Ga., U.S.	192	32.11 N	83.10 W
Eastman Lake ⊜[1]	226	37.14 N	119.58 W
East Mansfield	283	42.01 N	71.10 W
East Mariana Basin ✢[1]	14	12.00 N	153.00 E
East Marin Island I	282	37.58 N	122.27 W
East Markham	44	53.15 N	0.54 W
East McKeesport	279b	40.23 N	79.48 W
East Meadow	210	40.43 N	73.33 W
East Meadow ≏	283	42.47 N	71.02 W
East Meadow Brook ≏	276	40.39 N	73.34 W
East Meadowview	216	41.08 N	87.52 W
East Mecca	214	41.24 N	80.45 W
East Meredith	210	42.25 N	74.53 W
East Midlands Airport ⊠	42	52.50 N	1.20 W
East Millbury	207	42.13 N	71.44 W
East Mill Creek ≏	222	29.55 N	96.17 W
East Millinocket	188	45.37 N	68.34 W
East Millstone	276	40.30 N	74.35 W
East Missoula	202	46.52 N	113.58 W
East Molesey	260	51.24 N	0.21 W
East Moline	190	41.30 N	90.26 W
East Monongahela	279b	40.12 N	79.55 W
East Mountain	222	32.35 N	94.51 W
East Mustang Creek ≏	222	29.03 N	96.27 W
East Naples	220	26.06 N	81.44 W
East Nassau	210	42.30 N	73.30 W
East Newark	276	40.48 N	73.59 W
East New Britain □[5]	164	6.00 S	152.00 E
East New Market	208	38.35 N	75.55 W
East New York ⊕[8]	276	40.40 N	73.53 W
East Nishnabotna ≏	198	40.39 N	95.37 W
East Nodaway ≏	194	40.38 N	95.01 W
East Norriton	208	40.09 N	75.18 W
East Northfield	207	42.43 N	72.27 W
East Northport	210	40.52 N	73.19 W
East Norwich	210	40.50 N	73.32 W
East Novaya Zemlya Trough ✢[1]	12	73.30 N	61.00 E
East Olympia	224	46.58 N	122.50 W
Easton, Eng., U.K.	42	50.32 N	2.26 W
Easton, Ca., U.S.	226	36.39 N	119.47 W
Easton, Ct., U.S.	207	41.15 N	73.17 W
Easton, Il., U.S.	219	40.14 N	89.50 W
Easton, Md., U.S.	208	38.46 N	76.04 W
Easton, Ma., U.S.	283	42.02 N	71.06 W
Easton, Pa., U.S.	208	40.41 N	75.13 W
Easton, Tx., U.S.	222	32.23 N	94.35 W
Easton, Wa., U.S.	224	47.14 N	121.10 W
Eastondale	283	42.02 N	71.04 W
Easton Reservoir ⊜[1]	207	41.16 N	73.16 W
East Orange	210	40.46 N	74.12 W
East Orleans	207	41.47 N	69.58 W
East Otto	210	42.23 N	78.45 W
Eastover	192	33.52 N	80.41 W
East Pacific Rise ✢[3]	6	20.00 S	115.00 W
East Pakistan → Bangladesh □[1]	118	24.00 N	90.00 E
East Palatka	192	29.39 N	81.35 W
East Palestine	214	40.50 N	80.32 W
East Palo Alto	226	37.28 N	122.08 W
East Park Reservoir ⊜[1]	226	39.21 N	122.30 W
East Parkrose	224	45.33 N	122.32 W
East Peak ∧	116	11.13 N	119.29 E
East Peckham	42	51.15 N	0.23 E
East Pecos	200	35.34 N	105.39 W
East Pembroke, Ma., U.S.	283	42.05 N	70.46 W
East Pembroke, N.Y., U.S.	210	42.59 N	78.18 W
East Peoria	190	40.39 N	89.34 W
East Pepperell	207	42.39 N	71.34 W
East Petersburg	208	40.06 N	76.21 W
East Pharsalia	210	42.34 N	75.43 W
East Pine	182	55.43 N	121.13 W
East Pines	284c	38.57 N	76.55 W

Symbols in the index entries represent the broad categories identified in the key at the right. Symbols with superior numbers (⋆[1]) identify subcategories (see complete key on page *I · 1*).

Symbole im Register stellen die rechts im Schlüssel erklärten Kategorien dar. Symbole mit hochgestellten Ziffern (⋆[1]) bezeichnen Unterabteilungen einer Kategorie (vgl. vollständiger Schlüssel auf Seite *I · 1*).

Los símbolos incluídos en el texto del índice representan las grandes categorías identificadas con la clave a la derecha. Los símbolos con numeros en su parte superior (⋆[1]) identifican las subcategorías (véase la clave completa en la página *I · 1*).

Les symboles de l'index représentent les catégories indiquées dans la légende à droite. Les symboles suivis d'un indice (⋆[1]) représentent des sous-catégories (voir légende complète à la page *I · 1*).

Os símbolos incluídos no texto do índice representam as grandes categorias identificadas com a chave à direita. Os símbolos com números em sua parte superior (⋆[1]) identificam as subcategorias (veja-se a chave completa à página *I · 1*).

∧ Mountain	Berg	Montaña	Montagne	Montanha
⋆ Mountains	Gebirge	Montañas	Montagnes	Montanhas
)(Pass	Paß	Paso	Col	Passo
V Valley, Canyon	Tal, Cañon	Valle, Cañón	Vallée, Canyon	Vale, Canhão
≚ Plain	Ebene	Llano	Plaine	Planície
› Cape	Kap	Cabo	Cap	Cabo
I Island	Insel	Isla	Île	Ilha
II Islands	Inseln	Islas	Îles	Ilhas
⊥ Other Topographic Features	Andere Topographische Objekte	Otros Elementos Topográficos	Autres données topographiques	Outros acidentes topográficos

East-Ekol I · 51

ESPAÑOL · FRANÇAIS · PORTUGUÊS

Nombre / Nom / Nome	Página / Page / Página	Lat.°′	Long.°′ W = Oeste / W = Ouest / W = Oeste
East Pittsburgh	279b	40.23 N	79.50 W
Eastpoint, Fl., U.S.	192	29.44 N	84.52 W
East Point, Ga., U.S.	192	33.40 N	84.26 W
East Point >, P.E., Can.	186	46.27 N	61.58 W
East Point >, Ma., U.S.	207	42.25 N	70.54 W
East Point >, Vir. Is., U.S.	241n	17.45 N	64.34 W
Eastpoint ◆ 9	284b	39.18 N	76.31 W
Eastpointe	214	42.28 N	82.57 W
Eastport, Nf., Can.	186	48.39 N	53.45 W
Eastport, Id., U.S.	202	49.00 N	116.10 W
Eastport, Me., U.S.	188	44.54 N	66.59 W
Eastport, N.Y., U.S.	207	40.49 N	72.44 W
East Porterville	204	36.04 N	118.56 W
East Potomac Park ♠	284c	38.52 N	77.01 W
East Prairie	194	36.46 N	89.23 W
East Prairie ≃	182	55.34 N	116.25 W
East Prospect	208	39.58 N	76.31 W
East Providence	207	41.48 N	71.22 W
East Pryor Mountain ∧	202	45.11 N	108.20 W
East Quogue	207	40.51 N	72.35 W
East Rājasthān Uplands ⋏ 1	124	26.40 N	76.35 E
East Randolph	210	42.10 N	78.56 W
East Retford	44	53.19 N	0.56 W
East Richmond	282	37.57 N	122.19 W
Eastridge Center ◆ 9	282	37.20 N	121.49 W
East Rigaud ≃	206	45.27 N	74.22 W
Eastriggs	44	54.59 N	3.10 W
East River c	208	37.24 N	76.21 W
East Rochester, N.Y., U.S.	210	43.06 N	77.29 W
East Rochester, Oh., U.S.	214	40.45 N	81.02 W
East Rockaway	276	40.38 N	73.40 W
East Rockingham	192	34.55 N	79.45 W
East Rockwood	216	42.03 N	83.13 W
East Rosebud Creek ≃	202	45.29 N	109.27 W
East Rudolf National Park ♠	154	3.55 N	36.20 E
East Rutherford	276	40.50 N	74.05 W
Eastry	42	51.15 N	1.18 E
East Saint Louis	219	38.38 N	90.09 W
East Salem	208	40.37 N	77.14 W
East Salt Creek ≃	200	39.13 N	108.54 W
East Sandwich	207	41.44 N	70.27 W
East Sandy Creek ≃	214	41.22 N	79.51 W
East Schodack	210	42.34 N	73.38 W
East Scotia Basin ✦ 1	9	57.00 S	35.00 W
East Sepik □ 5	164	4.00 S	143.30 E
East Setauket	210	40.57 N	73.06 W
East Shoal Lake ⊜	184	50.23 N	97.37 W
East Siberian Sea → Vostočno-Sibirskoje more ⊤ 2	12	74.00 N	166.00 E
East Side	210	41.04 N	75.46 W
Eastside Bypass ≊	226	37.05 N	120.28 W
East Side Canal ≊, Ca., U.S.	226	37.21 N	120.55 W
East Side Canal ≊, Ca., U.S.	226	35.33 N	119.33 W
East Sixteen Mile Creek ≃	275b	43.28 N	79.48 W
East Smethport	214	41.49 N	78.26 W
East Smithfield	210	41.52 N	76.38 W
East Sooke	224	48.22 N	123.43 W
Eastsound	224	48.41 N	122.54 W
East Sound ʯ	224	48.39 N	122.53 W
East Sparta	214	40.40 N	81.21 W
East Spencer	192	35.40 N	80.25 W
East Springbrook	284c	39.04 N	77.00 W
East Springfield, Oh., U.S.	214	40.27 N	80.52 W
East Springfield, Pa., U.S.	214	41.57 N	80.28 W
East Stony Creek ≃	210	43.15 N	74.12 W
East Stour ≃	42	51.08 N	0.53 E
East Stroudsburg	210	40.59 N	75.10 W
East Sudbury	283	42.24 N	71.24 W
East Sussex □ 6	42	50.55 N	0.15 E
East Syracuse	210	43.04 N	76.05 W
East Tawas	190	44.16 N	83.29 W
East Templeton	207	42.33 N	72.02 W
East Texas	210	40.33 N	75.33 W
East Thompson	207	42.00 N	71.48 W
East Tilbury	260	51.28 N	0.26 E
East Troy	216	42.47 N	88.24 W
East Tustin	280	33.46 N	117.49 W
Eastvale	214	40.46 N	80.19 W
East Vandergrift	214	40.36 N	79.34 W
Eastview	218	40.19 N	80.38 W
Eastville	208	37.21 N	75.56 W
East Walker ≃	204	38.53 N	119.10 W
East Walpole	207	42.09 N	71.12 W
East Wareham	207	41.45 N	70.40 W
East Washington	214	40.10 N	80.14 W
East Waterford	208	40.22 N	77.36 W
East Wemyss	46	56.09 N	3.04 W
East Wenatchee	202	47.24 N	120.17 W
East Wenonah	285	39.47 N	75.08 W
East White Plains	276	41.03 N	73.47 W
Eastwick ◆ 8	285	39.55 N	75.14 W
East Wickham ◆ 8	260	51.28 N	0.07 E
East Williamson	210	43.14 N	77.09 W
East Williston	276	40.46 N	73.38 W
East Wilmington	192	34.13 N	77.53 W
East Wittering	42	50.41 N	0.53 W
Eastwood, Austl.	274a	33.48 S	151.05 E
Eastwood, Eng., U.K.	44	53.01 N	1.18 W
Eastwood, Eng., U.K.	260	51.34 N	0.40 E
Eastwood, Eng., U.K.	262	53.43 N	2.03 W
Eastwood, Mi., U.S.	216	42.18 N	85.33 W
Eastwood, Pa., U.S.	279b	40.17 N	79.31 W
East Worcester	210	42.37 N	74.40 W
East Yegua Creek ≃	222	30.19 N	96.45 W
East Yellow Creek ≃	194	39.38 N	93.04 W
East York, On., Can.	212	43.41 N	79.20 W
East York, Pa., U.S.	208	39.58 N	76.43 W
Eaton, Austl.	168a	33.19 S	115.43 E
Eaton, Co., U.S.	200	40.31 N	104.42 W
Eaton, In., U.S.	216	40.20 N	85.21 W
Eaton, N.Y., U.S.	210	42.51 N	75.37 W
Eaton, Oh., U.S.	218	39.44 N	84.38 W
Eaton ≃	206	45.28 N	71.39 W
Eaton Estates	214	41.19 N	82.01 W
Eatonia	184	51.13 N	109.23 W
Eaton Nord ≃	206	45.24 N	71.35 W
Eaton Park	220	28.00 N	81.54 W
Eaton Rapids	216	42.30 N	84.39 W
Eatons Neck	276	40.56 N	73.24 W
Eatons Neck > 1	276	40.57 N	73.23 W
Eatons Neck Point >	210	40.57 N	73.24 W
Eaton Socon	42	52.13 N	0.18 W
Eatonton	192	33.19 N	83.23 W
Eatontown	208	40.17 N	74.03 W
Eatonville	224	46.52 N	122.15 W
Eaton Wash V	280	34.04 N	118.03 W
Eaton Wash Dam ◆ 6	280	34.10 N	118.06 W
Eau ≃	44	53.31 N	0.44 W
Eaubonne	261	49.00 N	2.17 E
Eau Claire, Mi., U.S.	216	41.59 N	86.17 W
Eau Claire, Pa., U.S.	214	41.08 N	79.48 W
Eau Claire, Wi., U.S.	190	44.48 N	91.29 W
Eau Claire ≃, Wi., U.S.	190	44.49 N	91.31 W
Eau Claire ≃, Wi., U.S.	190	44.55 N	89.37 W
Eau Claire, Lac à l' ⊜, P.Q., Can.	176	56.10 N	74.25 W
Eau Claire, Lac à l' ⊜, P.Q., Can.	206	46.33 N	73.04 W
Eau Galle ≃	190	44.37 N	92.00 W
Eau Gallie	220	28.08 N	80.38 W
Eaulne ≃	50	49.54 N	1.07 E
Eauripik I 1	108	6.42 N	143.03 E
Eauripik Rise ✦ 3	14	3.00 N	142.00 E
Eauze	32	43.52 N	0.06 E
Ebabaka	152	2.30 S	18.19 E
Eban	150	9.44 N	4.56 E
Ebanga	152	12.44 S	14.44 E
Ebangalakata	152	0.29 S	21.29 E
Ebano	234	22.13 N	98.22 W
Ebb and Flow Indian Reserve ◆ 4	184	51.05 N	99.05 W
Ebb and Flow Lake ⊜	184	51.05 N	98.56 W
Ebbegebirge ⋏	56	51.08 N	7.46 E
Ebben Creek ≃	283	42.38 N	70.45 W
Ebberup	41	55.15 N	9.59 E
Ebbetts Pass)(	226	38.33 N	119.48 W
Ebbs	64	47.38 N	12.13 E
Ebbw ≃	42	51.33 N	2.59 W
Ebbw Vale	42	51.47 N	3.12 W
Ebebiyín	152	2.09 N	11.20 E
Ebeji (El Beïd) ≃	146	12.32 N	14.11 E
Ebejty, ozero ⊜	86	54.38 N	71.44 E
Ebeleben	54	51.17 N	10.43 E
Ebeltoft	41	56.12 N	10.41 E
Ebeltoft Vig c	41	56.10 N	10.36 E
Ebenau	64	47.47 N	13.11 E
Ebendorf	54	52.11 N	11.34 E
Ebene Reichenau	64	46.51 N	13.54 E
Ebenezer	275b	43.46 N	79.40 W
Ebenezer Ridge ∧	218	39.06 N	84.55 W
Eben Junction	190	46.21 N	86.58 W
Ebensburg	214	40.29 N	78.43 W
Ebensee	64	47.48 N	13.46 E
Ebensfeld	56	50.04 N	10.58 E
Eberbach	56	49.28 N	8.59 E
Ebergassing	264b	48.03 N	16.31 E
Eber Gölü ⊜	130	38.38 N	31.12 E
Ebergötzen	52	51.34 N	10.06 E
Ebermannstadt	60	49.43 N	11.13 E
Ebern	56	50.05 N	10.47 E
Eberndorf	61	46.35 N	14.38 E
Ebersbach, Dtsch.	54	51.15 N	13.37 E
Ebersbach, Dtsch.	54	51.00 N	14.35 E
Ebersbach, Dtsch.	56	48.43 N	9.31 E
Ebersberg	60	48.05 N	11.58 E
Eberschwang	60	48.09 N	13.34 E
Ebersdorf, Dtsch.	52	53.31 N	9.03 E
Ebersdorf, Dtsch.	54	50.29 N	11.40 E
Ebersdorf bei Coburg	56	50.13 N	11.04 E
Eberstein	61	46.48 N	14.34 E
Eberswalde-Finow	54	52.50 N	13.49 E
Ebetsu	92a	43.07 N	141.34 E
Ebian	102	29.10 N	103.20 E
Ebina	94	35.26 N	139.25 E
Ebino	92	32.03 N	130.50 E
Ebinur Hu ⊜	86	44.55 N	82.55 E
Ebi-Sekigahara-Yōrō-kokutei-kōen ♠	94	35.30 N	136.30 E
Ebnat	58	47.15 N	9.08 E
Ebo	152	11.02 S	14.41 E
Ebola ≃	152	3.20 N	20.57 E
Eboli	68	40.37 N	15.04 E
Ebolowa	152	2.54 N	11.09 E
Ebon I 1	14	4.35 N	168.44 E
Ebonda	152	2.12 N	22.21 E
Ebony	156	22.05 S	15.15 E
Eboshi-yama ∧	96	35.04 N	133.04 E
Eboué Stadium ♠	273b	4.17 S	15.18 E
Ebrach	56	49.50 N	10.29 E
Ebre, Delta de l' ≐ 2	34	40.43 N	0.54 E
Ebreichsdorf	61	47.58 N	16.24 E
Ébrié, Lagune c	150	5.14 N	4.26 W
Ebro (Ebre) ≃	34	40.43 N	0.54 E
Ebro, Embalse del ⊜ 1	34	43.00 N	3.58 W
Ebstorf	52	53.01 N	10.25 E
Ebute-Ikorodu	273a	6.37 N	3.30 E
Ebute-Metta ◆ 8	273a	6.29 N	3.23 E
Ecatepec	286a	19.35 N	99.04 W
Écaussinnes-d'Enghien	50	50.34 N	4.10 E
Ecclefechan	44	55.03 N	3.17 W
Eccles, Eng., U.K.	44	53.29 N	2.21 W
Eccles, Eng., U.K.	260	51.19 N	0.29 E
Eccles, W.V., U.S.	192	37.46 N	81.15 W
Eccleshall	42	52.52 N	2.15 W
Eccleston, Eng., U.K.	44	53.38 N	2.43 W
Eccleston, Eng., U.K.	262	53.27 N	2.47 W
Eccleston, Md., U.S.	284b	39.24 N	76.44 W
Eceabat	130	40.11 N	26.21 E
Echabi	89	53.30 N	142.59 E
Echague	116	16.42 N	121.40 E
Echallens	58	46.38 N	6.38 E
Echaporã	255	22.26 S	50.12 W
Echarcon	261	48.34 N	2.24 E
Échauffour	50	48.44 N	0.23 E
Ech Cheliff (Orléansville)	148	36.10 N	1.20 E
Echeconnee Creek ≃	192	32.39 N	83.36 W
Echelon Mall ◆ 9	285	39.51 N	75.00 W
Echeng	100	30.24 N	114.51 E
Échenoz-la-Méline	58	47.36 N	6.08 E
Echi ≃	94	35.13 N	136.07 E
Echigawa	94	35.10 N	136.12 E
Echigo-sammyaku ⋏	92	37.50 N	139.50 E
Echimamish ≃	184	54.20 N	97.27 W
Echizen	94	35.54 N	136.00 E
Echizen-Kaga-kaigan-kokutei-kōen ♠	94	36.08 N	136.05 E
Echizen-misaki >	94	35.59 N	135.57 E
Echo	198	44.37 N	95.25 W
Echo Bay	176	66.05 N	118.02 W
Echo Bay c	276	40.54 N	73.46 W
Echoing ≃	184	55.51 N	92.05 W
Echoing Lake ⊜	184	54.31 N	92.15 W
Echo Lake ⊜, Il., U.S.	278	42.13 N	88.05 W
Echo Lake ⊜, N.J., U.S.	276	41.04 N	74.25 W
Echo Summit ∧	226	38.50 N	120.02 W
Echouani, Lac ⊜	190	47.46 N	75.42 W
Echt, Ned.	52	51.06 N	5.52 E
Echt, Scot., U.K.	46	57.08 N	2.26 W
Echternach	56	49.48 N	6.26 E
Echternacherbrück	56	49.49 N	6.25 E
Echuca	166	36.08 S	144.46 E
Echunga	168b	35.07 S	138.48 E
Écija	34	37.32 N	5.05 W
Ecilda Paullier	258	34.22 S	57.04 W
Eck, Loch ⊜	46	56.05 N	5.00 W
Eckartsberga	54	51.07 N	11.34 E
Eckbolsheim	58	48.35 N	7.41 E
Eckental	60	49.35 N	11.15 E
Eckernförde	41	54.28 N	9.50 E
Eckernförder Bucht c	41	54.30 N	10.02 E
Eckerö I	26	60.14 N	19.35 E
Eckersdorf	60	49.56 N	11.30 E
Eckington	44	53.19 N	1.21 W
Eckley	210	40.59 N	75.51 W
Eckville	182	52.21 N	114.22 W
Eckwarderhörne	52	53.31 N	8.14 E
Eclectic	194	32.38 N	86.02 W
Ecleto	222	29.03 N	97.45 W
Ecleto Creek ≃	196	28.52 N	97.45 W
Eclipse Sound ʯ	176	72.38 N	79.00 W
Ečmiadzin	84	40.10 N	44.18 E
Ecola State Park ♠	224	45.57 N	123.58 W
École ≃	261	48.32 N	2.33 E
École Militaire (Saint-Cyr) ■	261	48.48 N	2.04 E
Écommoy	50	47.50 N	0.16 E
Econfina ≃	192	30.02 N	83.55 W
Econlockhatchee ≃	220	28.42 N	81.02 W
Economy, In., U.S.	218	39.58 N	85.05 W
Economy, Pa., U.S.	214	40.39 N	80.14 W
Economy Park ♠	279b	40.37 N	80.12 W
Ecoporanga	255	18.23 S	40.50 W
Écorce, Lac de l' ⊜ 1	190	47.05 N	76.24 W
Écorces, Lac des ⊜	206	46.00 N	74.32 W
Ecorse	216	42.14 N	83.08 W
Ecorse ≃	281	42.14 N	83.09 W
Ecorse, South Branch ≃	281	42.14 N	83.09 W
Écos	50	49.10 N	1.39 E
Écosse → Scotland □ 8	28	57.00 N	4.00 W
Écouen	50	49.01 N	2.23 E
Écouen, Château d' ⊥	261	49.01 N	2.23 E
Écouis	50	49.19 N	1.26 E
Ecoute, Ru d' ≃	261	48.39 N	2.26 E
Ecquevilly	261	48.57 N	1.55 E
Écrins, Barre des ∧	62	44.55 N	6.22 E
Écrins, Massif des ⋏ 1	62	44.55 N	6.20 E
Écrins, Parc National des ♠	62	44.50 N	6.15 E
Écrosnes	261	48.33 N	1.44 E
Ecru	194	34.21 N	89.01 W
Ecser	264c	47.27 N	19.20 E
Ecstall ≃	182	54.09 N	129.56 W
Ecuador □ 1, S.A.	242	2.00 S	77.30 W
Ecuador □ 1, S.A.	246	2.00 S	77.30 W
Ecuandureo	234	20.10 N	102.11 W
Écueillé	32	47.05 N	1.21 E
Écuisses	58	46.45 N	4.32 E
Ecum Secum	186	44.58 N	62.08 W
Écury-sur-Coole	50	48.54 N	4.20 E
Ed, Erit.	144	13.52 N	41.40 E
Ed, Sve.	26	58.55 N	11.55 E
Eda ◆ 8	268	35.34 N	139.34 E
Edah	162	28.17 S	117.10 E
Edam, Sk., Can.	184	53.12 N	108.46 W
Edam, Ned.	52	52.31 N	5.03 E
Eday I	46	59.11 N	2.47 W
Edderton	46	57.50 N	4.10 W
Eddington Gardens	285	40.06 N	74.57 W
Eddleston	46	55.43 N	3.13 W
Eddrachillis Bay c	46	58.18 N	5.15 W
Eddy	222	31.18 N	97.15 W
Eddystone	208	39.51 N	75.20 W
Eddystone Point >	166	41.00 S	148.21 E
Eddystone Rocks II 1	42	50.12 N	4.15 W
Eddyville, Ia., U.S.	190	41.09 N	92.38 W
Eddyville, Ky., U.S.	194	37.05 N	88.04 W
Eddyville, N.Y., U.S.	210	41.54 N	74.02 W
Ede, Ned.	52	52.03 N	5.40 E
Ede, Nig.	150	7.44 N	4.27 E
Edéa	152	3.48 N	10.08 E
Edebäck	40	60.04 N	13.33 E
Edebo	40	60.01 N	18.34 E
Edegem	52	51.09 N	4.27 E
Edehon Lake ⊜	176	60.25 N	97.15 W
Edéia	255	17.18 S	49.55 W
Edelény	30	48.18 N	20.44 E
Edelsfeld	60	49.34 N	11.42 E
Edelshausen	60	48.37 N	11.17 E
Edelweiss	273d	26.16 S	28.28 E
Edelweiss Spitze ∧	64	47.07 N	12.50 E
Edemissen	52	52.23 N	10.16 E
Eden, Austl.	166	37.04 S	149.54 E
Éden, Bra.	287a	22.48 S	43.24 W
Eden, N. Ire., U.K.	48	54.44 N	5.47 W
Eden, Mi., U.S.	216	42.32 N	84.26 W
Eden, Ms., U.S.	194	32.59 N	90.19 W
Eden, N.Y., U.S.	210	42.39 N	78.53 W
Eden, Tx., U.S.	196	31.12 N	99.50 W
Eden, Wy., U.S.	200	42.03 N	109.26 W
Eden ≃, Eng., U.K.	42	51.10 N	0.11 E
Eden ≃, Eng., U.K.	44	54.57 N	3.01 W
Eden ≃, Scot., U.K.	46	56.22 N	2.50 W
Eden ≃, Wales, U.K.	42	52.48 N	3.53 W
Edenbridge	42	51.12 N	0.04 E
Edenburg	158	29.45 S	25.56 E
Eden Canyon V	282	37.42 N	122.01 W
Edendale, N.Z.	172	46.19 S	168.47 E
Edendale, S. Afr.	158	29.39 S	30.18 E
Edendale, S. Afr.	273d	26.09 S	28.09 E
Edenderry	48	53.20 N	7.03 W
Edenfield	262	53.40 N	2.18 W
Eden Hill ∧ 2	207	41.20 N	73.19 W
Edenkoben	56	49.17 N	8.07 E
Eden Lake ⊜	184	56.38 N	100.15 W
Eden Mills	212	43.35 N	80.09 W
Eden Park ◆ 8	260	51.23 N	0.02 W
Edenside V	44	54.40 N	2.35 W
Edenton	192	36.03 N	76.36 W
Edenvale	273d	26.08 S	28.09 E
Eden Valley, Austl.	168b	34.39 S	139.06 E
Eden Valley, Mn., U.S.	190	45.19 N	94.32 W
Edenville	158	27.37 S	27.34 E
Edeowie	166	31.27 S	138.27 E
Eder ≃	56	51.13 N	9.27 E
Ederkopf ∧	56	50.56 N	8.12 E
Ederny	48	54.32 N	7.39 W
Edersee ⊜ 1	56	51.11 N	9.00 E
Eder-Talsperre ◆ 6	56	51.11 N	9.02 E
Edesheim	56	49.16 N	8.08 E
Edessa → Édhessa	38	40.48 N	22.03 E
Edewecht	52	53.07 N	8.02 E
Edfu → Idfū	140	24.58 N	32.52 E
Edgar, Ne., U.S.	198	40.22 N	97.58 W
Edgar, Wi., U.S.	190	44.55 N	89.57 W
Edgard	194	30.03 N	90.34 W
Edgar Ranges ⋏	162	18.43 S	123.25 E
Edgars Creek ≃	274b	37.44 S	144.58 E
Edgartown	207	41.23 N	70.30 W
Edgartown Harbor c	207	41.24 N	70.30 W
Edgecliff	222	32.39 N	97.22 W
Edgecumbe	172	37.59 S	176.50 E
Edgefield	192	33.47 N	81.55 W
Edge Hill ◆ 8	262	53.24 N	2.57 W
Edge Hill ∧	42	52.08 N	1.27 W
Edgeley, On., Can.	275b	43.48 N	79.31 W
Edgeley, N.D., U.S.	198	46.21 N	98.42 W
Edgely	285	40.07 N	74.50 W
Edgemere	208	39.14 N	76.26 W
Edgemont, Pa., U.S.	285	39.57 N	75.27 W
Edgemont, S.D., U.S.	198	43.18 N	103.49 W
Edgemont Park	216	42.44 N	84.36 W
Edgemoor	285	39.45 N	75.30 W
Edge Mountain ∧	180	58.12 N	152.06 W
Edgeøya I	12	77.45 N	22.30 E
Edgeroi	166	30.07 S	149.48 E
Edgerton, Ab., Can.	184	52.45 N	110.27 W
Edgerton, In., U.S.	216	41.05 N	84.49 W
Edgerton, Mn., U.S.	198	43.52 N	96.07 W
Edgerton, Oh., U.S.	216	41.26 N	84.44 W
Edgerton, Wi., U.S.	216	42.50 N	89.04 W
Edgerton, Wy., U.S.	200	43.24 N	106.14 W
Edgewater, Al., U.S.	194	33.31 N	86.57 W
Edgewater, Fl., U.S.	220	28.59 N	80.54 W
Edgewater, N.J., U.S.	276	40.50 N	73.58 W
Edgewater Park	285	40.04 N	74.54 W
Edgewater Park ♠	279a	41.29 N	81.43 W
Edgewater Point >	276	40.55 N	73.44 W
Edgewood, B.C., Can.	182	49.47 N	118.08 W
Edgewood, Fl., U.S.	220	28.29 N	81.22 W
Edgewood, Il., U.S.	219	38.55 N	88.40 W
Edgewood, In., U.S.	218	40.06 N	85.44 W
Edgewood, Ia., U.S.	190	42.38 N	91.24 W
Edgewood, Md., U.S.	208	39.25 N	76.17 W
Edgewood, Oh., U.S.	214	41.52 N	80.46 W
Edgewood, Pa., U.S.	279b	40.25 N	79.52 W
Edgewood, Tx., U.S.	222	32.42 N	95.53 W
Edgeworth	214	40.33 N	80.11 W
Edgeworthstown → Mostrim	48	53.42 N	7.36 W
Edgware ◆ 8	260	51.37 N	0.17 W
Edgworth	262	53.39 N	2.24 W
Édhessa	38	40.48 N	22.03 E
Ediger-Eller	56	50.06 N	7.09 E
Edimbourg → Edinburgh	46	55.57 N	3.13 W
Edimburgo → Edinburgh	46	55.57 N	3.13 W
Edina, Liber.	150	6.01 N	10.10 W
Edina, Mn., U.S.	190	44.53 N	93.20 W
Edina, Mo., U.S.	219	40.10 N	92.10 W
Edinboro	214	41.52 N	80.07 W
Edinboro Lake ⊜	214	41.53 N	80.08 W
Edinburg, Il., U.S.	219	39.39 N	89.23 W
Edinburg, In., U.S.	218	39.21 N	85.58 W
Edinburg, Ms., U.S.	194	32.47 N	89.20 W
Edinburg, N.Y., U.S.	210	43.13 N	74.07 W
Edinburg, N.D., U.S.	198	48.29 N	97.51 W
Edinburg, Oh., U.S.	214	41.06 N	81.09 W
Edinburg, Tx., U.S.	196	26.18 N	98.09 W
Edinburg, Va., U.S.	188	38.49 N	78.33 W
Edinburgh	46	55.57 N	3.13 W
Edinburgh (Turnhouse) Airport ⊠	46	55.57 N	3.21 W
Edinburgh, Arrecife ✦ 2	236	14.50 N	82.39 W
Edinburgh Castle ⊥	46	55.56 N	3.14 W
Edinburgh Channel ʯ	236	14.45 N	82.40 W
Edinburgh Mountain ∧	224	48.38 N	124.24 W
Edincik	130	40.20 N	27.51 E
Edineț	38	48.10 N	27.19 E
Edingen → Enghien	50	50.42 N	4.02 E
Edirne	130	41.40 N	26.34 E
Edirne □ 4	130	41.20 N	26.40 E
Edison, Ga., U.S.	192	31.33 N	84.44 W
Edison, N.J., U.S.	210	40.27 N	74.18 W
Edison, Oh., U.S.	214	40.33 N	82.51 W
Edison, Pa., U.S.	208	40.17 N	75.07 W
Edison Bridge ◆ 5	214	41.27 N	82.49 W
Edison National Historic Site ⊥	276	40.47 N	74.14 W
Edison Park ◆ 8	278	42.01 N	87.49 W
Edisseja	84	44.03 N	44.33 E
Edisto ≃	192	32.39 N	80.24 W
Edisto, North Fork ≃	192	33.16 N	80.53 W
Edisto, South Fork ≃	192	33.16 N	80.53 W
Edisto Island I	192	32.35 N	80.20 W
Edith	170	33.48 S	149.55 E
Edith, Mount ∧	202	46.26 N	111.11 W
Edithburgh	168b	35.06 S	137.44 E
Edith Cavell, Mount ∧	182	52.40 N	118.03 W
Edith River	164	14.11 S	132.02 E
Edithvale	274b	38.02 S	145.07 E
Edith Weston	42	52.37 N	0.37 W
Edjejou, Oued i-n- V	148	22.46 N	4.05 E
Edjeleh	148	27.38 N	9.50 E
Edjerir ≃	150	18.06 N	0.50 E
Edjudina	162	29.48 S	122.23 E
Edmeston	210	42.41 N	75.14 W
Edmond	196	35.39 N	97.28 W
Edmondbyers	44	54.51 N	1.58 W
Edmonds	224	47.48 N	122.22 W
Edmondson Heights	284b	39.18 N	76.43 W
Edmonston	284c	38.57 N	76.56 W
Edmonton, Austl.	166	17.01 S	145.45 E
Edmonton, Ab., Can.	182	53.33 N	113.28 W
Edmonton, Ky., U.S.	194	36.58 N	85.36 W
Edmonton ◆ 8	260	51.37 N	0.04 W
Edmore, Mi., U.S.	190	43.24 N	85.02 W
Edmore, N.D., U.S.	198	48.24 N	98.27 W
Edmund	162	23.46 S	116.02 E
Edmund Lake ⊜	184	54.45 N	93.15 W
Edmundson Acres	228	35.14 N	118.49 W
Edmundston	186	47.22 N	68.20 W
Edna, Ks., U.S.	198	37.03 N	95.21 W
Edna, Pa., U.S.	279b	40.19 N	79.39 W
Edna, Tx., U.S.	222	28.58 N	96.38 W
Edna Bay	180	55.57 N	133.40 W
Ednor	208	39.09 N	76.59 W
Edo ≃	94	35.37 N	139.53 E
Edogawa ◆ 8	268	35.42 N	139.52 E
Edolo	64	46.11 N	10.20 E
Edom	222	32.22 N	95.37 W
Edon	216	41.33 N	84.46 W
Edosaki	94	35.57 N	140.19 E
Edremit	130	39.35 N	27.01 E
Edremit Körfezi c	130	39.30 N	26.45 E
Edrengijn nuruu ⋏	102	44.15 N	97.45 E
Edsall Park	284c	38.48 N	77.11 W
Edsbro	40	59.54 N	18.29 E
Edsbruk	26	58.02 N	16.28 E
Edsbyn	26	61.23 N	15.49 E
Edsgatan	40	59.26 N	13.33 E
Edson	182	53.35 N	116.26 W
Edson Butte ∧	202	42.52 N	124.20 W
Eduardo Castex	252	35.54 S	64.18 W
Eduardo VII, Península → Edward VII Peninsula > 1	9	77.40 S	155.00 W
Eduni, Mount ∧	180	64.15 N	128.04 W
Edward ≃, Austl.	164	14.44 S	141.35 E
Edward ≃, Austl.	166	35.33 S	144.58 E
Edward, Lake ⊜	154	0.25 S	29.30 E
Edward, Mount ∧	162	23.22 S	131.55 E
Edwardes Park ♠	274b	37.43 S	145.00 E
Edward Island I	190	48.24 N	88.36 W
Edward River Aboriginal Reserve ◆ 4	164	14.30 S	141.45 E
Edwards, Ca., U.S.	228	34.54 N	117.53 W
Edwards, Ms., U.S.	194	32.19 N	90.36 W
Edwards, N.Y., U.S.	212	44.19 N	75.15 W
Edwards ≃	190	41.09 N	90.59 W
Edwards Air Force Base ■	228	34.54 N	117.52 W
Edwards Airport ⊠	276	40.45 N	73.03 W
Edwardsburg	216	41.47 N	86.04 W
Edwards Butte ∧	224	45.23 N	123.41 W
Edwards Gardens ♠	275b	43.44 N	79.22 W
Edwards Plateau ⋏ 1	196	31.20 N	101.00 W
Edwards Point >	169	38.13 S	144.42 E
Edwards Run ≃	285	39.48 N	75.12 W
Edwardsville, Il., U.S.	219	38.48 N	89.57 W
Edwardsville, In., U.S.	218	38.16 N	85.55 W
Edwardsville, Pa., U.S.	210	41.16 N	75.55 W
Edward VIII Bay c	9	66.50 S	57.00 E
Edward VII Peninsula > 1	9	77.40 S	155.00 W
Edwinstowe	44	53.12 N	1.04 W
Edzell	46	56.48 N	2.39 W
Edziza, Mount ∧	180	57.40 N	130.36 W
Eede	52	51.15 N	3.28 E
Eefde	52	52.10 N	6.14 E
Eek	180	60.12 N	162.15 W
Eek ≃	180	60.12 N	162.15 W
Eeklo	50	51.11 N	3.34 E
Eel ≃, Ca., U.S.	204	40.40 N	124.20 W
Eel ≃, In., U.S.	194	39.07 N	86.57 W
Eel ≃, In., U.S.	216	40.45 N	86.22 W
Eel, Middle Fork ≃	204	39.42 N	123.21 W
Eel, North Fork ≃	204	39.57 N	123.26 W
Eel, South Fork ≃	204	40.22 N	123.55 W
Eel Bay c	212	44.19 N	76.02 W
Eelde	52	53.07 N	6.35 E
Eels Creek ≃	212	44.35 N	78.03 W
Eels Lake ⊜	212	44.54 N	78.08 W
Eemskanaal ≊	52	53.15 N	6.45 E
Eerbeek	52	52.07 N	6.04 E
Eersel	52	51.22 N	5.19 E
Eesti → Estonia □ 1	22	59.00 N	26.00 E
Eexta	52	53.10 N	6.59 E
Efate □ 8	175f	17.45 S	168.20 E
Éfaté I	175f	17.40 S	168.25 E
Eferding	61	48.18 N	14.02 E
Efes (Ephesus) ⊥	130	37.55 N	27.17 E
Effigy Mounds National Monument ♠	190	43.06 N	91.13 W
Effingham, Eng., U.K.	260	51.16 N	0.24 W
Effingham, Il., U.S.	194	39.07 N	88.32 W
Effingham, Ks., U.S.	198	39.31 N	95.24 W
Effingham □ 6	219	39.07 N	88.33 W
Effingham Lake ⊜	212	44.59 N	77.22 W
Effort	210	40.56 N	75.26 W
Efiduasi	150	6.51 N	1.24 W
Efkere	130	38.47 N	35.40 E
Eflâni	130	41.26 N	32.57 E
Eforie Nord	38	44.06 N	28.38 E
Eforie Sud	38	44.03 N	28.38 E
Efringen-Kirchen	58	47.39 N	7.34 E
Ega ≃	34	42.19 N	1.55 W
Egadi, Isole II	70	37.58 N	12.16 E
Egan	222	32.28 N	97.17 W
Egaña	252	36.59 S	59.06 W
Egan Range ⋏	204	39.10 N	114.55 W
Eganville	190	45.32 N	77.06 W
Egau ≃	56	48.36 N	10.34 E
Egbe, Nig.	150	8.16 N	5.31 E
Egbe, Nig.	273a	6.33 N	3.17 E
Egbunda	154	2.44 N	27.12 E
Egedesminde (Aasiaat)	176	68.42 N	52.45 W
Égée, Mer → Aegean Sea ⊤ 2	38	38.30 N	25.00 E
Egegik	180	58.13 N	157.22 W
Egeln	54	51.56 N	11.25 E
Egeo, Mar → Aegean Sea ⊤ 2	38	38.30 N	25.00 E
Eger → Cheb, Česká Rep.	54	50.01 N	12.25 E
Eger, Magy.	30	47.54 N	20.23 E
Eger ≃, Dtsch.	56	48.50 N	10.37 E
Eger (Ohře) ≃, Europe	54	50.32 N	14.08 E
Egeria Mountain ∧	182	53.55 N	130.22 W
Egernsund	41	54.54 N	9.37 E
Egerpohl	263	51.07 N	7.27 E
Egersund	26	58.27 N	6.00 E
Egerton	262	53.38 N	2.26 W
Egerton, Mount ∧	9	80.50 S	158.50 E
Egeskov ⊥	41	55.10 N	10.30 E
Egestorf	52	53.11 N	10.04 E
Egestorf [am Süntel]	52	52.17 N	9.31 E
Egg	58	47.26 N	9.54 E
Egg Creek ≃	198	48.22 N	100.47 W
Egge ⋏	52	51.40 N	8.55 E
Eggebek	41	54.37 N	9.22 E
Eggelsberg	60	48.05 N	13.00 E
Eggenberg, Schloss ⊥	61	47.05 N	15.25 E
Eggenburg	61	48.39 N	15.50 E
Eggenfelden	60	48.25 N	12.46 E
Eggerscheid	263	51.19 N	6.53 E
Eggersdorf	54	52.32 N	13.49 E
Eggesin	54	53.41 N	14.05 E
Egg Harbor City	208	39.31 N	74.38 W
Egg Island Point >	208	39.11 N	75.08 W
Egg Lagoon	166	39.39 S	143.58 E
Egg Lake ⊜, Mb., Can.	184	54.21 N	101.26 W
Egg Lake ⊜, Sk., Can.	184	55.05 N	105.30 W
Egglestone Abbey ʊ 1	44	54.32 N	1.54 W
Egglham	60	48.32 N	13.04 E
Egglkofen	60	48.24 N	12.27 E
Eggmühl	60	48.51 N	12.11 E
Eggolsheim	60	49.46 N	11.04 E
Egham	42	51.26 N	0.34 W
Egherta	144	2.04 N	43.11 E
Éghezée	56	50.36 N	4.54 E
Egijn ≃	88	49.24 N	103.36 E
Eğil	130	38.15 N	40.05 E
Egilsay I	46	59.09 N	2.56 W
Egilsstaðir	24a	65.16 N	14.18 W
Eging	60	48.43 N	13.16 E
Egipto → Egypt □ 1	140	27.00 N	30.00 E
Égletons	32	45.24 N	2.03 E
Eglin Air Force Base ■	194	30.29 N	86.30 W
Egling	64	47.56 N	11.31 E
Eglinton	48	55.02 N	7.11 W
Eglisau	58	47.34 N	8.32 E
Egloffstein	60	49.42 N	11.15 E
Egloskerry	42	50.39 N	4.27 W
Égly	261	48.35 N	2.13 E
Egmond aan Zee	52	52.36 N	4.37 E
Egmond-Binnen	52	52.35 N	4.39 E
Egmont, Cape >	172	39.17 S	173.45 E
Egmont, Mount → Taranaki, Mount ∧	172	39.18 S	174.04 E
Egmont Bay c	186	46.35 N	64.12 W
Egmont Channel ʯ	220	27.36 N	82.45 W
Egmont Key I	220	27.35 N	82.46 W
Egmont National Park ♠	172	39.15 S	174.05 E
Egna (Neumarkt)	64	46.19 N	11.16 E
Egnach	58	47.33 N	9.23 E
Egnazia ⊥	68	40.53 N	17.24 E
Egoryevsk → Jegorjevsk	82	55.23 N	39.02 E
Egota ◆ 8	268	35.43 N	139.40 E
Egra	126	21.54 N	87.32 E
Egremont, Ab., Can.	182	54.02 N	113.08 W
Egremont, Eng., U.K.	44	54.29 N	3.33 W
Égreville	50	48.10 N	2.52 E
Eğridir	130	37.52 N	30.51 E
Eğridir Gölü ⊜	130	38.02 N	30.53 E
Eğriköy	130	38.44 N	27.21 E
Egrisskij chrebet ⋏	84	42.49 N	42.24 E
Egton	44	54.26 N	0.45 W
Egtved	41	55.37 N	9.18 E
Éguas, Rio das ≃	255	13.26 S	44.14 W
Éguilles	62	43.34 N	5.22 E
Eguisheim	58	48.03 N	7.18 E
Egum Atoll I 1	164	9.25 S	151.55 E
Egvekinot	180	66.19 N	179.10 W
Egyházasrádóc	61	47.05 N	16.37 E
Egypt, Ma., U.S.	207	42.12 N	70.45 W
Egypt, Pa., U.S.	208	40.41 N	75.32 W
Egypt, Tx., U.S.	222	29.24 N	96.14 W
Egypt (Mișr) □ 1, Afr.	136	27.00 N	30.00 E
Egypt (Mișr) □ 1, Afr.	140	27.00 N	30.00 E
Egypt, Lake of ⊜ 1	194	37.35 N	88.55 W
Égypte → Egypt □ 1	140	27.00 N	30.00 E
Egyptian Museum ʊ	273c	30.03 N	31.14 E
Eha-Amufu	150	6.40 N	7.46 E
Ehekirchen	60	48.38 N	11.06 E
Ehen ≃	44	54.25 N	3.30 W
Ehime □ 5	96	33.40 N	132.50 E
Ehingen	58	48.17 N	9.43 E
Ehingen ◆ 8	263	51.22 N	6.42 E
Ehle ≃	54	52.12 N	11.44 E
Ehlershausen	52	52.31 N	10.01 E
Ehmen	54	52.24 N	10.41 E
Ehra-Lessien	54	52.34 N	10.46 E
Ehrenberg	200	33.36 N	114.31 W
Ehrenberg Range ⋏	162	23.18 S	130.20 E
Ehrenbreitstein, Feste ⊥	56	50.21 N	7.37 E
Ehrenburg ⊥	56	50.12 N	7.27 E
Ehrenfeld	214	40.22 N	78.46 W
Ehrenfriedersdorf	54	50.38 N	12.58 E
Ehrenhausen	61	46.43 N	15.35 E
Ehreshoven	56	50.58 N	7.20 E
Ehrhardt	192	33.05 N	81.00 W
Ehrhorn	52	53.10 N	9.53 E
Ehringhausen	263	51.11 N	7.33 E
Ehringhausen ◆ 8	263	51.09 N	7.11 E
Ehringshausen	56	50.36 N	8.23 E
Ehrwald	64	47.24 N	10.55 E
Ehwa Women's University ʊ 2	271b	37.34 N	126.56 E
Ei	92	31.12 N	130.30 E
Eibar	34	43.11 N	2.28 W
Eibau	54	50.58 N	14.40 E
Eibelstadt	56	49.43 N	10.00 E
Eibenstock	54	50.29 N	12.35 E
Eibergen	52	52.06 N	6.39 E
Eibiswald	61	46.41 N	15.15 E
Eibsee ⊜	64	47.27 N	10.58 E
Eich	56	49.45 N	8.24 E
Eicha	54	50.21 N	10.34 E
Eich-Berg ∧ 2	264a	52.39 N	13.50 E
Eiche, Dtsch.	264a	52.34 N	13.36 E
Eiche, Dtsch.	264a	52.25 N	12.58 E
Eichenau	64	48.10 N	11.19 E
Eichenbarleben	54	52.10 N	11.24 E
Eichenbrandt	264a	52.38 N	13.51 E
Eichendorf	60	48.38 N	12.51 E
Eichenzell	56	50.30 N	9.41 E
Eichgraben	61	48.10 N	15.59 E
Eichigt	54	50.21 N	12.10 E
Eichlinghofen ◆ 8	263	51.29 N	7.24 E
Eichsfeld ◆ 1	56	51.20 N	10.10 E
Eichstädt	264a	52.42 N	13.07 E
Eichstätt	60	48.54 N	11.12 E
Eichtersheim	56	49.14 N	8.46 E
Eichwalde	54	52.22 N	13.37 E
Eickelborn	52	51.39 N	8.13 E
Eicken ◆ 8	263	51.13 N	6.26 E
Eickerend	263	51.13 N	6.34 E
Eickerkopf ∧ 2	263	51.21 N	7.42 E
Eicklingen	52	52.33 N	10.10 E
Eide	26	62.55 N	7.26 E
Eidelstedt ◆ 8	52	53.36 N	9.53 E
Eider ≃	41	54.19 N	8.58 E
Eiderstedt > 1	41	54.22 N	8.50 E
Eidfjord	26	60.28 N	7.05 E
Eidsvåg, Nor.	26	60.27 N	5.21 E
Eidsvåg, Nor.	26	62.47 N	8.03 E
Eidsvold	166	25.22 S	151.07 E
Eidsvoll	26	60.19 N	11.14 E
Eifa	56	50.58 N	8.34 E
Eifel ⋏	56	50.15 N	6.45 E
Eiffel, Tour ⊥	261	48.51 N	2.18 E
Eiffel Flats	154	18.15 S	29.59 E
Eifgenbach ≃	263	51.05 N	7.09 E
Eige, Carn ∧	46	57.17 N	5.07 W
Eigen ◆ 8	263	51.33 N	6.57 E
Eigenji	94	35.04 N	136.18 E
Eigenrieden	54	51.11 N	10.22 E
Eiger ∧	58	46.35 N	8.00 E
Eigg I	46	56.54 N	6.10 W
Eigg, Sound of ʯ	46	56.51 N	6.13 W
Eight Degree Channel ʯ	122	8.00 N	73.00 E
Eighteenmile Creek ≃, N.Y., U.S.	210	42.43 N	78.58 W
Eighteenmile Creek ≃, N.Y., U.S.	210	43.21 N	78.43 W
Eight Mile Creek ≃, On., Can.	284a	43.14 N	79.11 W
Eightmile Creek ≃, In., U.S.	216	40.57 N	85.22 W
Eightmile Creek ≃, Or., U.S.	224	45.36 N	121.05 W
Eights Coast ± 2	9	73.30 S	93.00 W
Eighty Four	279b	40.11 N	80.08 W
Eighty Mile Beach ± 2	162	19.45 S	121.00 E
Eiheiji	94	36.05 N	136.20 E
Eijerlandsche Gat c	52	53.12 N	4.50 E
Eijsden	56	50.47 N	5.43 E
Eikeren ⊜	26	59.38 N	9.58 E
Eikisdalsvatnet ⊜	26	62.34 N	8.11 E
Eildon	169	37.14 S	145.56 E
Eildon, Lake ⊜ 1	169	37.11 S	145.55 E
Eilean Gowan Island I	212	45.02 N	79.25 W
Eileen	216	41.17 N	88.15 W
Eilenburg	54	51.27 N	12.37 E
Eilsleben	54	52.09 N	11.13 E
Eimbeckhausen	52	52.14 N	9.25 E
Eimke	52	52.58 N	10.19 E
Eina	26	60.38 N	10.36 E
Einasleigh	166	18.31 S	144.05 E
Einasleigh ≃	166	17.30 S	142.17 E
Einbeck	52	51.49 N	9.52 E
Eindhoven	52	51.26 N	5.28 E
Eine	50	50.52 N	3.37 E
Einme	110	16.54 N	95.11 E
Einöd	56	49.16 N	7.19 E
Einödriegel ∧	60	48.56 N	13.02 E
Einruhr	56	50.35 N	6.22 E
Einsiedel	54	50.46 N	12.58 E
Einsiedeln	58	47.08 N	8.45 E
Einville-au-Jard	58	48.39 N	6.30 E
Eirauli	272c	19.10 N	72.59 E
Éire → Ireland □ 1	48	53.00 N	8.00 W
Eiru ≃	248	6.42 S	69.52 W
Eirunepé	248	6.40 S	69.52 W
Eisbach ≃	56	49.38 N	8.22 E
Eisch ≃	56	49.45 N	6.07 E
Eiseb ≃	156	20.33 S	20.59 E
Eiselfing	64	48.03 N	12.14 E
Eisenach	54	50.59 N	10.19 E
Eisenberg, Dtsch.	54	50.58 N	11.53 E
Eisenberg, Dtsch.	56	49.38 N	8.05 E
Eisenberg ∧ 2	61	47.12 N	16.24 E
Eisenerz	61	47.33 N	14.53 E
Eisenerzer Alpen ⋏	61	47.28 N	14.45 E
Eisenhower Center ʊ	198	38.54 N	97.12 W
Eisenhower Memorial Park ♠	276	40.44 N	73.34 W
Eisenhüttenstadt	54	52.10 N	14.39 E
Eisenkappel	61	46.29 N	14.35 E
Eisenschmitt	56	50.03 N	6.43 E
Eisenstadt	61	47.51 N	16.32 E
Eisfeld	54	50.26 N	10.54 E
Eisgarn	61	48.54 N	15.06 E
Eishken	46	58.01 N	6.32 W
Eishort, Loch c	46	57.10 N	5.59 W
Eišiškės	76	54.10 N	25.00 E
Eisk → Jejsk	78	46.42 N	38.16 E
Eislingen	56	48.42 N	9.42 E
Eisriesenwelt ± 5	64	47.32 N	13.10 E
Eita	174t	1.21 N	173.05 E
Eiterfeld	56	50.46 N	9.48 E
Eitorf	56	50.46 N	7.26 E
Eivissa	34	38.54 N	1.26 E
Eivissa (Ibiza) I	34	39.00 N	1.25 E
Ejasi → Eyasi, Lake ⊜	154	3.40 S	35.05 E
Ejby, Dan.	41	55.30 N	12.07 E
Ejby, Dan.	41	55.26 N	9.57 E
Ejea de los Caballeros	34	42.08 N	1.08 W
Ejeda	157b	24.20 S	44.31 E
Ejército Rebelde, Presa ⊜ 1	286b	23.01 N	82.20 W
Ejido	246	8.33 N	71.14 W
Ejido Jaboncillos	232	28.57 N	102.39 W
Ejigbo	273a	6.33 N	3.18 E
Ejin Horo Qi	102	39.27 N	109.40 E
Ejin Qi	102	41.50 N	100.50 E
Ejstrup	41	55.59 N	9.17 E
Ejura	150	7.23 N	1.22 W
Ejutla de Crespo	234	16.34 N	96.44 W
Ekalaka	198	45.53 N	104.33 W
Ekáli	267c	38.07 N	23.50 E
Ekanga	152	2.23 S	23.14 E
Ekas	115b	8.53 S	116.27 E
Ekaterinburg → Jekaterinburg	86	56.51 N	60.36 E
Ekaterinodar → Krasnodar	78	45.02 N	39.00 E
Ekaterinoslav → Dnipropetrovs'k	78	48.27 N	34.59 E
Ekeby	41	56.00 N	12.58 E
Ekenäs (Taamisaari)	26	59.58 N	23.26 E
Ekenässjön	26	57.30 N	15.00 E
Ekerö I	40	59.18 N	17.43 E
Eket, Nig.	150	4.39 N	7.56 E
Eket, Sve.	41	56.15 N	13.11 E
Eketahuna	172	40.39 S	175.42 E
Ekhínos	38	41.17 N	24.59 E
Ekibastuz	86	51.42 N	75.22 E
Ekimčan	89	53.04 N	132.58 E
Ekitykskij chrebet ⋏	180	67.45 N	179.00 E
Eko → Lagos	150	6.27 N	3.24 E
Ekoli	152	0.23 S	24.16 E

Symbol	English	Deutsch	Español	Français	Português
≃	River	Fluß	Río	Rivière	Rio
≊	Canal	Kanal	Canal	Canal	Canal
∟	Waterfall, Rapids	Wasserfall, Stromschnellen	Cascada, Rápidos	Chute d'eau, Rapides	Cascata, Rápidos
ʯ	Strait	Meeresstraße	Estrecho	Détroit	Estreito
c	Bay, Gulf	Bucht, Golf	Bahía, Golfo	Baie, Golfe	Baía, Golfo
⊜	Lake, Lakes	See, Seen	Lago, Lagos	Lac, Lacs	Lago, Lagos
≡	Swamp	Sumpf	Pantano	Marais	Pântano
⌂	Ice Features, Glacier	Eis- und Gletscherformen	Accidentes Glaciales	Formes glaciaires	Acidentes glaciares
⊤	Other Hydrographic Features	Andere Hydrographische Objekte	Otros Elementos Hidrográficos	Autres données hydrographiques	Outros acidentes hidrográficos
✦	Submarine Features	Untermeerische Objekte	Accidentes Submarinos	Formes de relief sous-marin	Acidentes submarinos
□	Political Unit	Politische Einheit	Unidad Politica	Entité politique	Unidade política
ʊ	Cultural Institution	Kulturelle Institution	Institución Cultural	Institution culturelle	Instituição cultural
⊥	Historical Site	Historische Stätte	Sitio Histórico	Site historique	Sitio histórico
♠	Recreational Site	Erholungs- und Ferienort	Sitio de Recreo	Centre de loisirs	Area de Lazer
⊠	Airport	Flughafen	Aeropuerto	Aéroport	Aeroporto
■	Military Installation	Militäranlage	Instalación Militar	Installation militaire	Instalação militar
◆	Miscellaneous	Verschiedenes	Misceláneo	Divers	Diversos

Name	Page	Lat.	Long.
Ekoln ⊚	40	59.45 N	17.37 E
Ekolsund	40	59.37 N	17.22 E
Ekolsundsviken c	40	59.35 N	17.24 E
Ekombe	152	1.16 N	21.36 E
Ekonda	74	65.47 N	105.17 E
Ekoungounou	152	0.33 S	15.38 E
Ekovamou	152	0.07 N	16.31 E
Ekpoma	150	6.46 N	6.08 E
Eksära	272b	22.38 N	88.17 E
Eksel	56	51.09 N	5.23 E
Eksjö	26	57.40 N	14.57 E
Ekuk	180	58.49 N	158.34 W
Ekuku	152	0.42 S	21.38 E
Ekuta	152	2.59 N	18.42 E
Ekvyvatapskij chrebet ⋌	180	69.00 N	178.30 E
Ekwan ≈	176	53.14 N	82.13 W
Ekwata	152	0.13 S	9.18 E
Ekwenden	154	11.23 S	33.50 E
Ekwok	180	59.22 N	157.30 W
El-			
— Ad-, Al-, An-, Ar-, As-, Ash-, At-, Az-			
Ela	110	19.37 N	96.13 E
El Aaiún (La'youn)	148	27.09 N	13.12 W
El Abiadh Sidi Cheikh	148	32.56 N	0.42 E
El 'Açâba ⋋¹	150	16.10 N	11.30 W
El 'Açâba ⋋¹	150	16.00 N	12.00 W
El Adde	144	2.35 N	46.09 E
El Adeb Larache	148	27.22 N	8.52 E
El Adelanto	236	14.10 N	89.50 W
El Affroun	34	36.30 N	2.38 E
El Agreb	148	30.48 N	6.59 W
El Aguacate	286c	10.28 N	66.59 W
El Aguacate ≈	234	18.16 N	100.40 W
El Aguilar	252	23.12 S	65.42 W
El Agustino	286d	12.03 S	76.59 W
El Agustino, Cerro ⋋²	286d	12.04 S	77.00 W
Elaine	234	34.18 N	90.51 W
El Alamein			
— Al-'Alamayn	140	30.49 N	28.57 E
El Álamo, Méx.	196	27.32 N	100.52 W
El Álamo, Méx.	196	26.29 N	99.46 W
El Álamo, Méx.	204	31.34 N	116.02 W
El Alia	36	37.10 N	10.03 E
El Alto, Arg.	252	28.18 S	65.22 W
El Alto, Perú	246	4.18 S	81.07 W
Elands ⋋	285	39.51 N	75.32 W
Elamanchili	272	17.33 N	82.52 E
El Amparo de Apure	246	7.06 N	70.45 W
Elan ≈, Rom.	38	46.07 N	28.04 E
Elan ≈, Wales, U.K.	42	52.17 N	3.31 W
Élancourt	261	48.47 N	1.58 E
Elands ≈, S. Afr.	156	25.10 S	29.10 E
Elands ≈, S. Afr.	158	25.31 S	26.39 E
Elandsbaai	158	32.19 S	18.21 E
Elandsfontein	273d	26.10 S	28.12 E
Elandsvlei	158	32.19 S	19.33 E
El Angel	246	0.37 N	77.56 W
Elanora Heights	274a	33.42 S	151.17 E
El Aouiret	36	35.52 N	7.54 E
El Arba	36	37.31 N	3.13 E
El Arco	232	28.00 N	113.25 W
El Arenal	234	20.47 N	103.42 W
El Aricha	148	34.09 N	1.10 W
El Aroussa	36	36.22 N	9.28 E
El Arrayán	286e	33.21 S	70.28 W
Elassón	38	39.54 N	22.11 E
El Astillero	34	34.24 N	3.49 W
Elat	132	29.33 N	34.57 E
Elat, Gulf of			
— Aqaba, Gulf of c	128	29.00 N	34.40 E
Elat, Sede Te'ufa ≈	132	29.34 N	34.55 E
El Avagi	144	3.36 N	46.57 E
El Ávila, Parque Nacional ♦	286c	10.35 N	66.52 W
Elazig	246	10.35 N	66.48 W
Elazig ⋴¹	130	38.41 N	39.14 E
El Azúcar, Presa de ⊞	196	26.10 N	99.00 W
El Azu⋋, Sierra ⋌	234	23.25 N	100.30 W
Elba, Al., U.S.	194	31.24 N	86.04 W
Elba, Id., U.S.	216	43.02 N	83.26 W
Elba, N.Y., U.S.	210	43.04 N	78.11 W
Elba			
— Elbe ⋋	30	53.50 N	9.00 E
Elba, Isola d' I	66	42.46 N	10.17 E
El'ban	89	50.06 N	136.31 E
El Banco	246	9.00 N	73.58 W
El Barco de Ávila	34	40.21 N	5.31 W
El Barreal	200	31.17 N	107.10 W
El Barril	234	23.02 N	102.08 W
Elbasan	38	41.06 N	20.05 E
Elbaşı	130	38.41 N	35.59 E
El Baul	246	8.57 N	68.17 W
El Baul, Cerro ⋋, Méx.	234	16.36 N	94.13 W
El Baúl, Cerro ⋋, Méx.	234	17.38 N	100.19 W
Elbe	224	46.45 N	121.49 W
Elbe, île d'			
— Elba, Isola d' I	66	42.46 N	10.17 E
Elbe-Havel-Kanal ⋌	54	52.24 N	12.23 E
El Béïd (Ebeji) ≈	146	12.32 N	14.11 E
El-Beida			
— Al-Baydâ'	140	32.46 N	21.43 E
Elbe–Lübeck-Kanal ⋌	54	53.50 N	10.36 E
Elberfeld	263	51.16 N	7.09 E
El Djazaïr (Algiers)	148	34.40 N	3.03 E
El Doce	232	17.13 N	94.03 W
Elbert	200	39.13 N	104.32 W
Elbert, Mount ⋋	200	39.07 N	106.27 W
Elberta	190	44.37 N	86.13 W
Elberton	192	34.06 N	82.52 W
Elbeuf	50	49.17 N	1.00 E
Elbeyli	130	36.41 N	37.26 E
El Beyyadh	148	33.40 N	1.01 E
Elblag			
— Elbląg	30	54.10 N	19.25 E
Elbingerode	54	51.45 N	10.46 E
Elbistan	130	38.13 N	37.12 E
Elbląg (Elbing)	30	54.10 N	19.25 E
Elbląg ⋴⁴	30	54.00 N	19.30 E
El Bluff	236	11.59 N	83.40 W
El Bolsón	254	41.58 S	71.31 W
El Bonillo	34	38.57 N	2.32 W
El-Borj	34	35.43 N	5.40 W
El-Boruuj	148	32.30 N	7.10 W
El Bosque, Chile	286e	33.32 S	70.40 W
El Bosque, Méx.	234	17.04 N	92.44 W
El Boulaïda	36	36.28 N	2.50 E
Elbow	58	51.07 N	106.35 W
Elbow Cay I	238	26.18 N	77.20 W
Elbow Cay I	238	23.57 N	80.29 W
Elbow Lake	198	45.59 N	95.58 W
Elbow Lake ⊞	184	54.50 N	100.53 W
Elbridge	210	43.02 N	76.27 W
El'brus, gora (Mount Elbrus) ⋋	84	43.21 N	42.26 E
El'brus, Mount			
— El'brus, gora ⋋	84	43.21 N	42.26 E
El'brusskij	84	43.38 N	42.10 E
Elbsandsteingebirge ⋌	54	50.50 N	14.20 E
Elburg	56	52.27 N	5.50 E
Elburn	216	41.53 N	88.28 W
Elburz Mountains			
— Alborz, Reshteh-ye Kühhā-ye ⋌	128	36.00 N	53.00 E
El'buzd	83	46.10 N	39.41 E
El'ouzd ≈	83	47.15 N	41.30 E
El Cabezo, Arrecífe ⋌	234	19.04 N	95.51 W
El Caburé	252	26.01 S	62.22 W
El Caimanero, Laguna c	234	23.00 N	106.07 W
El Cajon	228	32.47 N	116.57 W

Name	Page	Lat.	Long.
El Cajón, Embalse ⊞¹	236	15.00 N	87.35 W
El Calafate	254	50.20 S	72.18 W
El Callao	246	7.21 N	61.49 W
El Calvario, Col.	246	4.22 N	73.40 W
El Calvario, Ven.	246	8.59 N	67.00 W
El Calvario ≈⁸	286b	23.05 N	82.20 W
El Campamento	240m	18.22 N	66.28 W
El Campamento ⋗⁸	266a	40.24 N	3.46 W
El Campo	222	29.11 N	96.16 W
El Capitan ⋋, Ca., U.S.	226	37.43 N	119.38 W
El Capitan ⋋, Mt., U.S.	202	46.01 N	114.23 W
El Caracol Depósito de Evaporación Solar ⋌³	286a	19.35 N	99.00 W
El Caribe	286c	10.37 N	66.50 W
El Carmen, Arg.	252	24.23 S	65.16 W
El Carmen, Bol.	248	18.49 S	58.33 W
El Carmen, Chile	286e	33.21 S	70.43 W
El Carmen, Col.	246	8.30 N	73.27 W
El Carmen, Méx.	234	15.35 N	93.05 W
El Carmen, Perú	248	13.30 S	76.04 W
El Carmen, Ven.	286c	10.24 N	67.01 W
El Carmen, Ven.	286c	10.24 N	66.50 W
El Carmen ⋋	232	30.42 N	106.29 W
El Carmen, Canal ⋌	286	33.18 S	70.41 W
El Carmen de Bolívar	246	9.43 N	75.08 W
El Carricito	232	28.24 N	103.23 W
El Carril	252	25.05 S	65.28 W
El Casco	196	25.34 N	104.35 W
El Castillo de La Concepción	236	11.01 N	84.24 W
El Cedral	236	16.26 N	90.03 W
El Cedrito	232	29.11 N	101.59 W
El Centinela	204	32.38 N	115.40 W
El Centinela, Cerro ⋋	234	19.13 N	104.17 W
El Centro	204	32.47 N	115.33 W
El Cerrito, Col.	246	3.42 N	76.19 W
El Cerrito, Ca., U.S.	228	37.54 N	122.18 W
El Cerro, Bol.	248	17.31 S	61.34 W
El Cerro, Ur.	258	34.00 S	58.15 W
El Cerro Del Aripo ⋋	241r	10.43 N	61.15 W
El Chamal	232	23.56 N	97.54 W
El Chante	234	19.41 N	104.10 W
Elche	34	38.15 N	0.42 W
Elche de la Sierra	34	38.27 N	2.03 W
El Chichonal, Volcán ⋋¹	234	17.22 N	93.14 W
El'chkakvun ⋌	180	68.42 N	171.00 E
Elchingen	58	48.27 N	10.07 E
Elcho Island I	164	11.55 S	135.45 E
El Chorrillo	252	33.18 S	66.16 W
El Ciprés	204	31.50 N	116.38 W
El Cobre	240p	20.03 N	75.57 W
El Cocuy	246	6.25 N	72.27 W
El Cojo	286c	10.37 N	66.53 W
El Cojo, Quebrada ≈	286c	10.37 N	66.53 W
El Colorado	252	26.18 S	59.22 W
El Cóndor, Cerro ⋋	252	26.38 S	68.22 W
El Congo	236	13.54 N	89.30 W
El Corazón	246	1.12 S	79.06 W
El Corcovado	254	43.32 S	71.36 W
El Corozo	286c	10.35 N	66.58 W
El Corpus	236	13.16 N	87.03 W
El Corte ≈	234	17.03 N	94.54 W
El Corte de Madera Creek ≈	282	37.19 N	122.20 W
El Cortijo	252	33.22 S	70.42 W
El Coto	240m	18.28 N	66.44 W
El Coyote	200	30.50 N	112.40 W
El Coyote ≈	232	30.32 N	113.02 W
El Coyote, Laguna c	196	27.14 N	103.18 W
El Cozón	232	31.18 N	112.29 W
El Cristo	240p	20.07 N	75.45 W
El Cubo			
— Casigua	246	8.46 N	72.30 W
El Cuco	236	13.10 N	88.07 W
El Cuervo, Laguna ⊞	232	29.17 N	105.57 W
El Cuidado	234	22.00 N	103.35 W
El Cuy	254	39.56 S	68.20 W
Elda	34	38.29 N	0.47 W
Eidagsen	52	52.10 N	9.40 E
El Dambahaddo	144	3.17 N	46.40 E
El Dátil	232	30.07 N	112.15 W
Elde ≈	54	53.14 N	11.27 E
Eldekanal ⋌	54	53.24 N	11.36 E
Eldikan, Dtsch.	54	53.13 N	11.25 E
Eldingen	52	52.41 N	10.21 E
Eld Inlet c	224	47.04 N	123.01 W
Eldivan	130	40.32 N	33.31 E
El Diviso	246	1.22 N	78.14 W
El Djelfa	148	34.40 N	3.15 E
El Doce	232	17.13 N	94.03 W
Eldon, Ia., U.S.	190	40.55 N	92.13 W
Eldon, Mo., U.S.	194	38.20 N	92.34 W
Eldon Hazlet State Park ♦	219	38.39 N	89.22 W
Eldora, Ia., U.S.	190	42.21 N	93.05 W
Eldora, Arg.	252	26.24 S	54.38 W
Eldorado, Bra.	252	24.32 S	48.06 W
El Dorado, Méx.	234	24.17 N	107.21 W
El Dorado, Ar., U.S.	194	33.12 N	92.39 W
El Dorado, Il., U.S.	194	37.48 N	88.26 W
El Dorado, Ks., U.S.	198	37.49 N	96.51 W
El Dorado, Tx., U.S.	196	30.51 N	100.36 W
El Dorado, Ven.	246	6.44 N	61.38 W
Eldorado Hills	228	38.43 N	121.02 W
El Dorado Park ♦	280	33.48 N	118.06 W
Eldorado Peak ⋋	224	48.32 N	121.08 W
El Dorado Springs	194	37.52 N	94.01 W
Eldoret	154	0.31 N	35.17 E
Eldred, Il., U.S.	219	39.17 N	90.33 W
Eldred, N.Y., U.S.	210	41.32 N	74.53 W
Eldred, Pa., U.S.	214	41.57 N	78.23 W
Eldredge Hill	285	39.49 N	75.18 W
El Dudu	246	3.41 N	70.54 W
El Durazno, Arroyo ≈	258	34.41 S	58.52 W
Eleanor	198	38.32 N	81.56 W
Eleanor, Lake ⊞¹	282	37.59 N	119.51 W
Electra	158	34.01 S	24.52 E
Electric City	202	47.56 N	119.02 W

Name	Page	Lat.	Long.
Eleja	76	56.26 N	23.42 E
Elektrogorsk	82	55.53 N	38.47 E
Elektrostal'	82	55.47 N	38.28 E
Elektrougli	82	55.43 N	38.13 E
Elektrozavod	80	52.34 N	54.01 E
Elek	150	5.07 N	6.48 E
Elena	38	42.56 N	25.53 E
El Encantado	286c	10.27 N	66.47 W
El Encanto, Col.	246	1.37 S	73.14 W
El Encanto, Guat.	232	17.17 N	89.34 W
Elend	54	51.44 N	10.41 E
Elepete	273a	6.41 N	3.28 E
Elephant, Mount ⋋²	169	37.58 S	143.12 E
Elephanta Caves ⋋⁵	272c	18.58 N	72.56 E
Elephanta Island (Ghārāpuri) I	272c	18.57 N	72.55 E
Elephant Butte Lake State Park ♦	200	33.11 N	107.14 W
Elephant Butte Reservoir ⊞¹	200	33.19 N	107.10 W
Elephant Island I	9	61.10 S	55.14 W
Elephant Lake ⊞	212	45.08 N	78.07 W
Elephant Mountain ⋋	188	44.46 N	70.46 W
Elesbão Veloso	250	6.13 S	42.08 W
Eleşkirt	130	39.48 N	42.42 E
El Espinal	234	16.29 N	95.03 W
El Estor	236	15.32 N	89.21 W
Elets			
— Jelec	76	52.37 N	38.30 E
El Eulma	148	36.08 N	5.40 E
Eleusis			
— Elevsís	38	38.02 N	23.32 E
Eleutéro	256	21.29 S	46.43 W
Eleuthera I	70	38.06 N	13.29 E
Eleuthera ⋋²	238	25.10 N	76.14 W
Eleuthera Point ⋋	238	24.40 N	76.11 W
Eleva	190	44.34 N	91.28 W
Eleven Point ≈	194	36.09 N	91.05 W
Elevsís, Kólpos c	267c	38.02 N	23.34 E
Elevsínos	38	38.02 N	23.32 E
Elevtherúpolis	38	40.55 N	24.16 E
El Fahs	36	36.22 N	9.55 E
El Faro	240m	18.00 N	66.47 W
Elfenbeinküste			
— Côte d'Ivoire □¹	150	8.00 N	5.00 W
Elfers	220	28.13 N	82.43 W
Elfershausen	56	50.09 N	9.58 E
Elfin Cove	180	58.12 N	136.20 W
Elfros	184	51.43 N	103.52 W
El Fud	144	7.20 N	42.52 E
El Fuerte	232	26.25 N	108.39 W
El Galpón	252	25.23 S	64.38 W
El Ghazawet	148	35.06 N	1.51 W
Elgin, Austl.	168a	33.31 S	115.37 E
Elgin, On., Can.	212	44.36 N	76.13 W
Elgin, Scot., U.K.	46	57.39 N	3.20 W
Elgin, Il., U.S.	216	42.02 N	88.16 W
Elgin, Ia., U.S.	190	42.57 N	91.37 W
Elgin, Mn., U.S.	190	44.07 N	92.15 W
Elgin, Ne., U.S.	198	41.59 N	98.05 W
Elgin, N.D., U.S.	198	46.24 N	101.50 W
Elgin, Oh., U.S.	216	40.44 N	84.28 W
Elgin, Oh., U.S.	216	40.34 N	98.17 W
Elgin, Or., U.S.	202	45.33 N	117.54 W
Elgin, Pa., U.S.	214	41.54 N	79.45 W
Elgin, Tx., U.S.	222	30.20 N	97.22 W
Elgin ⋌⁶	214	42.42 N	81.15 W
Elgin, Lake ⊞	206	45.45 N	71.20 W
Elgol	46	57.09 N	6.06 W
El Goloso ⋗⁸	266a	40.33 S	3.42 W
Elgon, Mount ⋋	154	1.08 N	34.33 E
Elgoras, gora ⋋	24	68.06 N	31.30 E
El Granada	226	37.30 N	122.28 W
El Grara	148	32.46 N	4.34 E
El Grullo	234	19.48 N	104.13 W
El Guaje	232	27.52 N	103.18 W
El Guaje, Laguna ⊞	232	27.55 N	103.13 W
El Guamo	246	10.02 N	74.59 W
El Guanábano	286c	10.24 N	67.01 W
El Guapo	286c	10.08 N	66.02 W
El Guarapo	286c	10.36 N	66.58 W
El Guayabo de Abajo	232	26.00 N	107.26 W
El Guayaneco, Parque Nacional ♦	254	48.15 S	75.30 W
El Guettar	36	34.21 N	8.57 E
El gygytgyn, ozero ⊞	180	67.30 N	172.00 E
El Hadjar	36	36.48 N	7.45 E
Elham	42	51.10 N	1.07 E
El Hammâmi ⋋¹	148	23.03 N	11.30 W
El Hank ⋋⁴	148	24.30 N	7.00 W
El Haouaria	36	37.03 N	11.02 E
El Hatillo, Quebrada ≈	286c	10.27 N	66.47 W
El Havre			
— Le Havre	50	49.30 N	0.08 E
El Higo	234	21.46 N	98.28 W
Elhovo	38	42.10 N	26.34 E
El Huecú	252	37.37 S	70.36 W
El Husache	234	22.55 N	100.25 W
Eliase	164	8.21 S	130.47 E
Elías Romero	234	23.58 S	58.52 W
Eliasville	196	32.57 N	98.49 W
Elida, N.M., U.S.	196	33.56 N	103.39 W
Elida, Oh., U.S.	216	40.47 N	84.12 W
El Idolo, Isla I	234	21.34 N	97.25 W
El Idrissia	148	34.30 N	2.37 E
Elila	154	2.43 S	25.53 E
Elim, Namibia	156	17.48 S	15.31 E
Elim, S. Afr.	158	34.35 S	19.45 E
Elim, Ak., U.S.	180	64.37 N	162.15 W
Elim Church ♦	158	34.35 S	19.45 E
El Infiernillo, Canal ⋌	232	29.09 N	112.15 W
Elingampangu	152	2.03 S	24.02 E
Elin Pelin	38	42.40 N	23.36 E
Eliot	188	43.09 N	70.48 W
Elipa	152	0.53 S	24.34 E
Elisabeth-Sophien- Koog	41	54.30 N	8.53 E
Élisabethville, Fr.	261	48.58 N	1.51 E
Élisabethville			
— Lubumbashi, R.D.C.	154	11.40 S	27.28 E
Elisenvaara	24	61.25 N	29.46 E
Eliseu Martins	250	8.13 S	43.42 W
Elista	82	46.16 N	44.14 E
Elizabeth, Austl.	168b	34.43 S	138.40 E
Elizabeth, Il., U.S.	190	42.19 N	90.13 W
Elizabeth, N.J., U.S.	210	40.39 N	74.12 W
Elizabeth, W.V., U.S.	198	39.04 N	81.23 W
Elizabeth □⁸, N.J.	283	40.39 N	74.13 W
Elizabeth, Bahía c	246a	0.38 S	91.27 W
Elizabeth, Cape ⋋	188	43.34 N	70.12 W
Elizabeth, Cape ⋋	224	47.21 N	124.22 W
Elizabeth, West Branch ≈	276	40.42 N	74.14 W
Elizabeth Bay c	156	26.54 S	15.11 E
Elizabeth City	192	36.18 N	76.13 W
Elizabeth Creek ≈	224	41.35 N	73.53 W
Elizabeth Islands II	188	41.27 N	70.47 W
Elizabeth Lake ⊞	280	34.40 N	118.23 W
Elizabeth Reef I ¹	160	29.56 S	159.04 E
Elizabethton	192	36.20 N	82.12 W
Elizabethtown, Il., U.S.	194	37.27 N	88.18 W
Elizabethtown, In., U.S.	218	39.08 N	85.48 W
Elizabethtown, Ky., U.S.	194	37.41 N	85.51 W

Name	Page	Lat.	Long.
Elizabethtown, N.Y., U.S.	188	44.12 N	73.35 W
Elizabethtown, N.C., U.S.	192	34.37 N	78.36 W
Elizabethtown, Pa., U.S.	214	40.09 N	76.36 W
Elizabethville	208	40.32 N	76.49 W
Eliza Howell Park ♦	281	42.24 N	83.16 W
Elizaville, Il., U.S.	218	38.08 N	86.24 W
Elizaville, N.Y., U.S.	210	42.03 N	73.48 W
Elk ≈	54	51.44 N	10.41 E
El-Jadida	148	33.16 N	8.30 W
El-Jadida □⁴	148	33.00 N	8.40 W
El Jaralito	232	26.07 N	104.10 W
El Jebel	200	39.23 N	107.05 W
El-Jebha	34	35.13 N	4.38 W
El Jem	148	35.18 N	10.43 E
El Jícaro ≈	236	13.31 N	86.00 W
El Jobean	220	26.58 N	82.13 W
El Juile	234	17.45 N	94.59 W
Elk	30	53.50 N	22.22 E
Elk ≈, Ab., Can.	182	52.55 N	115.14 W
Elk ≈, B.C., Can.	182	49.11 N	115.14 W
Elk ≈, Pol.	30	53.31 N	22.47 E
Elk ≈, U.S.	194	34.46 N	87.16 W
Elk ≈, Co., U.S.	200	40.29 N	106.58 W
Elk ≈, Ks., U.S.	198	37.15 N	95.41 W
Elk ≈, Mn., U.S.	190	45.18 N	93.34 W
Elk ≈, Mo., U.S.	194	36.38 N	94.38 W
Elk ≈, W.V., U.S.	198	38.21 N	81.38 W
Elk ≈, Wi., U.S.	190	45.42 N	90.37 W
Elkader	190	42.51 N	91.24 W
El Kantara	148	33.41 N	10.55 E
El-Karafab	140	18.10 N	31.36 E
Elk Bayou ≈	282	36.06 N	119.24 W
Elk City, Id., U.S.	202	45.50 N	115.26 W
Elk City, Ok., U.S.	196	35.24 N	99.24 W
Elk City Lake ⊞¹	198	37.15 N	95.55 W
Elk Creek	204	39.36 N	122.32 W
Elk Creek ≈, Ok., U.S.	196	34.48 N	99.09 W
Elk Creek ≈, Or., U.S.	202	43.38 N	123.34 W
Elk Creek ≈, Pa., U.S.	214	42.01 N	80.22 W
Elk Creek ≈, Wa., U.S.	198	44.15 N	102.22 W
Elkedra ≈	162	21.08 S	136.22 E
Elkford	182	50.02 N	114.55 W
Elkhart, In., U.S.	216	41.41 N	85.58 W
Elkhart, Ks., U.S.	196	37.00 N	101.53 W
Elkhart, Tx., U.S.	222	31.38 N	95.35 W
Elkhart ≈	216	41.41 N	85.58 W
Elkhart Lake	190	43.50 N	88.01 W
El Khatt ≈⁴	148	22.40 N	10.05 W
Elkhead Creek ≈	200	40.40 N	107.26 W
Elkhead Mountains ⋌	200	40.50 N	107.05 W
Elk Hills ⋌²	228	35.15 N	119.25 W
El Khnâchîch ⋋⁴	148	21.50 N	3.45 W
Elkhorn, Mb., Can.	184	49.58 N	101.14 W
Elkhorn, Ia., U.S.	190	41.35 N	95.03 W
Elkhorn, Wi., U.S.	190	42.40 N	88.32 W
Elkhorn ≈	198	41.08 N	96.19 W
Elkhorn City	192	37.18 N	82.21 W
Elkhorn Mountain ⋋, B.C., Can.	182	49.41 N	125.50 W
Elkhorn Mountains ⋌, Mo., U.S.	219	39.05 N	91.20 W
Elkin	192	36.14 N	80.50 W
Elkins	198	38.55 N	79.50 W
Elk Island I	184	50.45 N	96.32 W
Elk Island National Park ♦	182	53.37 N	112.45 W
Elkland	214	41.59 N	77.18 W
Elk Mills	208	39.39 N	75.49 W
Elk Mountain	224	48.18 N	121.06 W
Elk Mountain ⋋, Wa., U.S.	224	46.08 N	122.28 W
Elk Mountain ⋋, Wy., U.S.	200	41.38 N	106.32 W
Elk Neck ⋋¹	208	39.35 N	75.55 W
Elk Neck State Park ♦	208	39.30 N	75.58 W
Elko, B.C., Can.	182	49.18 N	115.07 W
Elko, Nv., U.S.	204	40.49 N	115.45 W
El Kouif	36	35.28 N	8.19 E
Elk Peak ⋋	200	46.27 N	110.46 W
Elk Plain	224	47.04 N	122.24 W
Elk Point, Ab., Can.	182	53.54 N	110.54 W
Elk Point, S.D., U.S.	198	42.41 N	96.41 W
El Kra ≈	150	6.39 N	5.24 W
Elk Rapids	190	44.54 N	85.24 W
Elk River, Id., U.S.	202	46.47 N	116.11 W
Elk River, Mn., U.S.	190	45.18 N	93.35 W
Elk River ≈	200	39.31 N	75.55 W
El Kseur	36	36.41 N	4.49 E
Elk State Park ♦	214	41.38 N	78.01 W
Elkton, Ky., U.S.	194	36.48 N	87.09 W
Elkton, Md., U.S.	208	39.36 N	75.50 W
Elkton, Mi., U.S.	216	43.49 N	83.10 W
Elkton, Or., U.S.	202	43.38 N	123.34 W
Elkton, S.D., U.S.	198	44.15 N	96.29 W
Elkton, Va., U.S.	208	38.25 N	78.37 W
El Kure	144	5.41 N	42.33 E
Elkville	218	37.54 N	89.14 W
Ell, Lake ⊞	162	29.13 S	127.46 E
Ellamar	180	60.54 N	146.42 W
Ellás			
— Greece □¹	38	39.00 N	22.00 E
Ellaville	192	32.14 N	84.18 W
El Meco	234	21.15 N	86.48 W
El Médano	232	24.25 N	111.30 W
Elmen	58	47.20 N	10.32 E
El Menia	148	30.35 N	2.50 E
El-Milagro	252	30.59 S	65.59 W

Name	Page	Lat.	Long.
Ellichpur	120	21.16 N	77.31 E
Ellicott City	208	39.16 N	76.47 W
Ellicott Creek ≈	210	43.01 N	78.53 W
Ellicott Creek Park ♦	284a	43.01 N	78.50 W
Ellicottville	210	42.16 N	78.40 W
Ellijay	192	34.41 N	84.28 W
El Limón, Méx.	234	18.05 N	101.59 W
El Limón, Méx.	234	19.49 N	104.11 W
El Limoncito	286c	10.29 N	66.47 W
El Limón de Teachi	232	24.43 N	107.08 W
Ellingen	56	49.04 N	10.58 E
Ellington	222	29.50 N	96.44 W
Ellinghorst ⋗⁸	263	51.34 N	6.57 E
Ellington, Eng., U.K.	44	55.13 N	1.34 W
Ellington, Ct., U.S.	207	41.54 N	72.28 W
Ellington, Mo., U.S.	194	37.14 N	90.58 W
Ellington, N.Y., U.S.	214	42.13 N	79.07 W
Elliniko International Airport ✈	267c	37.54 N	23.44 E
Ellinwood	198	38.21 N	98.34 W
Elliot	158	31.18 S	27.50 E
Elliotdale	158	31.55 S	28.38 E
Elliotganj	126	23.31 N	90.52 E
Elliot Lake	190	46.23 N	82.39 W
Elliott, Austl.	164	17.33 S	133.32 E
Elliott, II., U.S.	216	40.28 N	88.16 W
Elliott, Ia., U.S.	198	41.09 N	95.10 W
Elliott, Ms., U.S.	194	33.36 N	89.45 W
Elliott, Mount ⋋	162	20.29 S	126.37 E
Elliott Bay c	224	47.36 N	122.22 W
Elliott Key I	220	25.27 N	80.11 W
Elliottville	218	38.11 N	83.16 W
Ellis	198	38.56 N	99.33 W
Ellis ⋌⁶	222	32.20 N	96.48 W
Ellisburg	212	43.44 N	76.08 W
Ellis Mountain ⋋	228	48.10 N	124.19 W
Ellison Creek Reservoir ⊞¹	222	32.56 N	94.43 W
Ellisport	224	47.25 N	122.26 W
Ellisras	156	23.40 S	27.46 E
Elliston, Austl.	162	33.39 S	134.55 E
Elliston, Nf., Can.	186	48.38 N	53.03 W
Elliston, Mt., U.S.	202	46.33 N	112.25 W
Elliston, Va., U.S.	208	37.14 N	80.13 W
Ellmau	64	47.31 N	12.18 E
Ellmauer Halt ⋋	64	47.34 N	12.18 E
Ellon	46	57.22 N	2.05 W
Ellora	122	20.01 N	75.10 E
Ellore			
— Elūru	122	16.42 N	81.06 E
Elloree	192	33.31 N	80.34 W
Ellport	214	40.51 N	80.15 W
Ellrich	54	51.35 N	10.40 E
Ellsworth, Il., U.S.	216	40.27 N	88.43 W
Ellsworth, Ks., U.S.	198	38.44 N	98.13 W
Ellsworth, Me., U.S.	188	44.32 N	68.25 W
Ellsworth, Mi., U.S.	190	45.09 N	85.14 W
Ellsworth, Wi., U.S.	190	44.43 N	92.29 W
Ellsworth Air Force Base ✈	198	44.08 N	103.05 W
Ellsworth Land ⋗¹	9	75.30 S	80.00 W
Ellsworth Mountains ⋌	9	79.00 S	85.00 W
Ellwangen	56	48.58 N	10.07 E
Ellwanger Berge ⋌²	56	49.00 N	10.01 E
Ellwood City	214	40.51 N	80.17 W
Elm, Dtsch.	52	53.31 N	9.12 E
Elm, Schw.	58	46.55 N	9.10 E
Elm, Eng., U.K.	42	52.38 N	0.10 E
Elm ≈	64	47.40 N	13.57 E
Elm ⋌²	54	52.09 N	10.53 E
Elma, N.Y., U.S.	210	42.51 N	78.38 W
Elma, Wa., U.S.	224	47.00 N	123.24 W
El Machorro, Punta ⋋	234	21.03 N	114.51 W
Elmadağ (Küçükyozgat)	130	39.55 N	33.15 E
Elmadağ ⋋	130	39.49 N	33.15 E
Elmalı	130	36.44 N	29.55 E
Elmali Bendi ⋗⁶	267b	41.09 N	29.06 E
El Manteco	246	7.27 N	62.32 W
El Mansa el Kebir	148	35.45 N	0.54 W
Elmas	66	39.16 N	9.03 E
Elmas, Aeroporto di ✈	71	39.14 N	9.03 E
Elmas Burnu ⋋	267b	41.13 N	29.13 E
El Masnou	266d	41.29 N	2.19 E
Elmaton	222	28.58 N	96.09 W
El Mayoco	196	27.31 N	107.59 W
Elmbridge ⋌⁶	282	51.23 N	0.23 W
Elmbrook	285	39.52 N	75.10 W
El Médano, Punta ⋋	234	22.41 N	106.29 W
Elm City	192	35.48 N	77.51 W
Elm Creek	198	40.43 N	99.22 W
Elm Creek ≈, Ne., U.S.	198	40.42 N	99.28 W
Elm Creek ≈, S.D., U.S.	198	43.45 N	94.11 W
Elm Creek ≈, Tx., U.S.	222	30.56 N	98.10 W
Elm Creek ≈, Tx., U.S.	196	29.55 N	101.01 W
El Médano, Punta ⋋	196	26.54 N	109.22 W
Elmdale	52	50.29 N	9.41 E
Elmenhorst ⋗⁸	54	54.18 N	10.12 E
Elmsdale	186	44.58 N	63.30 W
Elmsford	210	41.03 N	73.49 W
Elmshorn	52	53.45 N	9.39 E
Elm Springs	194	36.12 N	94.14 W
Elmsta	26	59.58 N	18.48 E
Elmstein	56	49.21 N	7.56 E
Elmswell	42	52.15 N	0.53 E
El Mulato	196	29.22 N	104.10 W
El Multe	232	17.41 N	91.24 W
Elmvale	212	44.35 N	79.52 W
Elmville	285	39.56 N	84.46 W
Elmwood, On., Can.	212	44.14 N	81.03 W
Elmwood, Il., U.S.	190	40.46 N	89.57 W
Elmwood, Md., U.S.	284b	39.21 N	76.32 W
Elmwood, Ne., U.S.	198	40.50 N	96.17 W
Elmwood, Wi., U.S.	190	44.46 N	92.08 W
Elmwood ⋗⁸	285	39.56 N	75.14 W
Elmwood Park, Il., U.S.	216	41.55 N	87.48 W
Elmwood Park, N.J., U.S.	276	40.54 N	74.07 W
Elmwood Park, Wi., U.S.	281	42.41 N	87.50 W
El Naranjo ≈	234	18.41 N	103.45 W
El Naranjo de Chila	234	18.55 N	102.28 W
Elne	32	42.36 N	2.58 E
El Negralejo	266a	40.24 N	3.31 W
El Negrito	236	15.16 N	87.41 W
El Nido, Pil.	116	11.11 N	119.23 E
El Nido, Ca., U.S.	226	37.08 N	120.29 W
El Nihuil	252	35.02 S	68.40 W
El Niybo	144	4.32 N	39.59 E
El Nopal, Cerro ⋋	232	28.15 N	107.36 W
Elnora, Ab., Can.	182	51.59 N	113.12 W
Elnora, In., U.S.	194	38.52 N	87.05 W
El Oasis	286c	10.35 N	66.59 W
El-Obeid			
— Al-Ubayyid	140	13.11 N	30.13 E
Elobey, Islas II	152	0.59 N	9.30 E
El Ocote, Cerro ⋋	232	25.58 N	106.08 W
Elogbatindi	152	3.27 N	10.08 E
Eloida, Lake ⊞	212	44.40 N	75.58 W
El Oued	148	33.22 N	6.53 E

Elro-Erko I · 53

ESPAÑOL

Nombre	Página	Lat.°′	Long.°′ W = Oeste
El Roble, Mesa ʌ	232	31.31 N	115.31 W
El Rom	132	33.11 N	35.46 E
El Rosario, Laguna ⊜	234	17.52 N	93.48 W
El Rosarito	232	28.38 N	114.04 W
Elrose	184	51.13 N	108.01 W
Elroy	190	43.44 N	90.16 W
El Rucio	234	23.23 N	102.05 W
Elsa, Yk., Can.	180	63.55 N	135.28 W
Elsa, Tx., U.S.	196	26.17 N	97.59 W
Elsa ≃	66	43.43 N	10.52 E
Elsah	219	38.57 N	90.22 W
El Sahuaro	200	31.05 N	112.55 W
El Salado	252	26.25 S	70.19 W
El Salado, Parque Nacional ♠	246	2.12 S	80.00 W
El Salitre	246	1.50 S	79.48 W
El Salto, Méx.	234	23.47 N	105.22 W
El Salto, Méx.	234	20.32 N	103.11 W
El Salvador, Chile	252	26.17 S	69.43 W
El Salvador, Pil.	116	8.34 N	124.32 E
El Salvador □ [1], N.A.	230	13.50 N	88.55 W
El Salvador □ [1], N.A.	236	13.50 N	88.55 W
El Samán de Apure	246	7.55 N	68.44 W
El Santo	240p	22.42 N	79.41 W
Elsass → Alsace □ [9]	32	48.30 N	7.30 E
El Sauce, Laguna ⊜	258	35.20 S	58.16 W
El Sauz	232	29.02 N	106.16 W
El Sauzal	232	31.54 N	116.41 W
Elsberry	219	39.10 N	90.46 W
Elsbethen	64	47.45 N	13.05 E
Elsburg	273d	26.15 S	28.12 E
Elsdorf, Dtsch.	52	53.14 N	9.20 E
Elsdorf, Dtsch.	56	50.54 N	6.34 E
El Seco, Laguna ⊜	258	35.31 S	58.42 W
El Segundo	228	33.55 N	118.24 W
El Seibo	238	18.46 N	69.02 W
Elsen	52	51.44 N	8.39 E
Elsenham	42	51.55 N	0.14 E
Elsen Nur ⊜	120	35.11 N	92.15 E
Elsenz ≃	56	49.24 N	8.48 E
Elsfleth	52	53.14 N	8.28 E
El Siasgo, Arroyo ≃	258	35.33 S	58.33 W
Elsie, Mi., U.S.	216	43.05 N	84.23 W
Elsie, Or., U.S.	224	45.52 N	123.35 W
Elsinore → Helsingør, Dan.	41	56.02 N	12.37 E
Elsinore, Ut,. U.S.	200	38.40 N	112.08 W
Elsinore, Lake ⊜ [1]	228	33.39 N	117.21 W
El Sitio	286c	10.28 N	66.46 W
El'sk	78	51.48 N	29.09 E
Elsmere, De., U.S.	208	39.44 N	75.35 W
Elsmere, Ky., U.S.	218	39.00 N	84.36 W
Elsmere, N.Y., U.S.	210	42.37 N	73.49 W
El Sobrante	226	37.58 N	122.17 W
El Socorro	246	8.59 N	65.44 W
El Sombrero	246	9.23 N	67.03 W
Elspark	273d	26.16 S	28.14 E
Elspeet	52	52.17 N	5.46 E
Elst	52	51.55 N	5.50 E
Elstal	54	52.32 N	12.59 E
Elstead	42	51.11 N	0.43 W
Elster	54	51.50 N	12.49 E
Elsterberg	54	50.36 N	12.10 E
Elstergebirge ⩘	54	50.15 N	12.20 E
Elsterwerda	54	51.28 N	13.31 E
Elston, In., U.S.	216	40.22 N	86.55 W
Elston, Mo., U.S.	219	38.37 N	92.19 W
Elstra	54	51.13 N	14.08 E
Elstree	42	51.39 N	0.16 W
Elstree Aerodrome ⊠	260	51.39 N	0.19 W
El Sueco	232	29.54 N	106.24 W
El Tagarete, Cerro ʌ	232	26.31 N	105.56 W
El Tajín ⊥	234	20.27 N	97.23 W
El Tala	252	26.07 S	65.17 W
El Talar	258	34.27 S	58.39 W
El Tamarindo	236	13.11 N	87.54 W
El Tambo, Col.	246	1.26 N	77.23 W
El Tambo, Perú	248	12.04 S	75.13 W
El Tanque	196	26.28 N	99.38 W
El Tapextle	234	23.52 N	105.33 W
El Tarf	36	36.45 N	8.20 E
El Tecuán	232	25.29 N	107.00 W
El Tejocote, Cerro ʌ	234	18.48 N	103.03 W
Elten	52	51.52 N	6.10 E
El Terrero	234	18.58 N	102.28 W
Eltham, Austl.	169	37.44 S	145.09 E
Eltham, N.Z.	172	39.26 S	174.18 E
Eltham ◆ [8]	260	51.27 N	0.04 E
Eltham Palace ʊ	260	51.27 N	0.03 E
El Tigre	246	8.55 N	64.15 W
El Tigre, Isla I	236	13.16 N	87.38 W
El Tigrito → San José de Guanipa	246	8.54 N	64.09 W
El Timbiriche	234	18.38 N	101.31 W
Eltmann	56	49.58 N	10.40 E
El Tocuyo	246	9.47 N	69.48 W
El Tofo	252	29.27 S	71.15 W
El'ton, Ross.	80	49.08 N	46.50 E
Elton, Eng., U.K.	262	53.16 N	2.49 W
Elton, La., U.S.	194	30.28 N	92.41 W
Elton, Pa., U.S.	214	40.17 N	78.48 W
El'ton, ozero ⊜	80	49.16 N	46.35 E
El Toreo ♠	286a	19.27 N	99.13 W
El Toro	228	33.37 N	117.41 W
El Toro ʌ	240m	18.16 N	65.49 W
El Toro, Isla I	234	21.26 N	97.31 W
El Toro Marine Corps Air Station ■	228	33.41 N	117.44 W
El Tránsito, Chile	252	28.52 S	70.17 W
El Tránsito, El Sal.	236	13.22 N	88.21 W
El Trébol	252	32.12 S	61.42 W
El Triunfo, Hond.	236	13.06 N	87.00 W
El Triunfo, Méx.	232	23.47 N	110.08 W
El Triunfo, Cerro ʌ	234	15.40 N	92.49 W
El Triunfo de la Cruz	236	15.46 N	87.26 W
El Tuito	234	20.19 N	105.22 W
El Tulillo	234	22.30 N	104.05 W
El Tunal	252	25.15 S	64.27 W
El Turbio	254	51.41 S	72.05 W
Eltville	56	50.02 N	8.07 E
Eltz, Burg ⊥	56	50.12 N	7.20 E
El-Uarre	144	3.41 N	45.20 E
Elura → Ellora	122	20.01 N	75.10 E
Elūru	122	16.42 N	81.06 E
Elva	76	58.13 N	26.25 E
El Valle	236	8.36 N	80.08 W
El Valle ◆ [8]	286c	10.27 N	66.55 W
Elvas	34	38.53 N	7.10 W
Elvas ≃	256	21.12 S	44.08 W
Elven	32	47.44 N	2.35 W
El Vendrell	34	41.13 N	1.32 E
El Verano	226	38.18 N	122.29 W
El Verde	234	23.21 N	106.09 W
Elverdissen	52	52.05 N	8.38 E
Elverlingsen	263	51.17 N	7.42 E
Elverta	226	38.43 N	121.28 W
Elverum	26	60.53 N	11.34 E
El Viejo	236	12.40 N	87.10 W
El Vigía	246	8.38 N	71.39 W
El Vigía, Cerro ʌ	234	21.19 N	104.03 W
Elvins	194	37.50 N	90.31 W
Elvira	258	35.14 S	59.29 W
Elvo ≃	62	45.23 N	8.21 E
El Volcán	252	33.49 S	70.11 W
El Wad	148	33.20 N	6.58 E
El Wak	154	2.49 N	40.56 E
El Walamo	234	23.07 N	106.15 W
El Wanza	148	35.57 N	8.04 E
Elwell, Lake ⊜ [1]	202	48.22 N	111.17 W
Elwha ≃	224	48.10 N	123.35 W
Elwood, Austl.	274b	37.53 S	144.59 E
Elwood, Il., U.S.	216	41.24 N	88.07 W
Elwood, In., U.S.	216	40.16 N	85.50 W
Elwood, Ks., U.S.	198	39.45 N	94.52 W
Elwood, Ne., U.S.	198	40.35 N	99.51 W
Elwood, N.J., U.S.	208	39.35 N	74.43 W
Elwood, N.Y., U.S.	207	40.50 N	73.20 W

FRANÇAIS

Nom	Page	Lat.°′	Long.°′ W = Ouest
Elwood Park, Fl., U.S.	220	27.28 N	82.30 W
Elwood Park, Pa., U.S.	279b	40.10 N	80.17 W
Elwy ≃	44	53.16 N	3.26 W
Elwyn	285	39.54 N	75.24 W
Elx	34	38.15 N	0.42 W
Elxleben	54	51.02 N	10.56 E
Ely, Eng., U.K.	42	52.24 N	0.16 E
Ely, Mn., U.S.	190	47.54 N	91.52 W
Ely, Mo., U.S.	219	39.41 N	91.39 W
Ely, Nv., U.S.	204	39.14 N	114.53 W
Ely, Isle of ◆ [1]	42	52.24 N	0.10 E
El Yagual	246	7.29 N	68.25 W
Ely Cathedral ʊ [1]	42	52.24 N	0.16 E
Elyria	214	41.22 N	82.06 W
Elyria Airport ⊠	279a	41.20 N	82.06 W
Elysburg	210	40.51 N	76.33 W
Elysian Park ♠	280	34.05 N	118.14 W
El Yunque ʌ	240m	18.19 N	65.48 W
Elywood Park ♠	279a	41.23 N	82.06 W
Elz	56	50.25 N	8.02 E
Elz ≃	58	48.21 N	7.45 E
Elzach	58	48.10 N	8.04 E
El Zamural	286c	10.27 N	67.00 W
El Zapotal	234	15.27 N	93.10 W
Elzbach ≃	56	50.12 N	7.22 E
Elze, Dtsch.	52	52.35 N	9.44 E
Elze, Dtsch.	52	52.07 N	9.44 E
El Zig-Zag	286c	10.33 N	66.58 W
Elztal	56	49.24 N	9.12 E
Émaé I	175f	17.04 S	168.24 E
Emajõgi ≃	76	58.26 N	27.15 E
Emali	154	2.05 S	37.38 E
Emam Khomeyni Mosque ʊ [1]	267d	35.40 N	51.25 E
Emāmshahr (Shāhrūd)	128	36.25 N	55.01 E
Emån ≃	26	57.08 N	16.30 E
Émancé	261	48.35 N	1.44 E
Emas, Parque Nacional das ♠	255	18.08 S	52.48 W
Emba	86	48.50 N	58.08 E
Emba ≃	80	46.38 N	53.14 E
Embarcación	252	23.13 S	64.06 W
Embarras ≃, Ab., Can.	182	53.27 N	116.37 W
Embarras ≃, Il., U.S.	194	38.39 N	87.37 W
Embarras, North Fork ≃	194	38.55 N	87.59 W
Embarrass	190	44.39 N	88.42 W
Embarrass ≃, Mn., U.S.	190	47.24 N	92.25 W
Embarrass ≃, Wi., U.S.	190	44.23 N	88.45 W
Embetsu	92a	44.44 N	141.47 E
Embid	34	40.58 N	1.43 W
Embleton	44	55.30 N	1.37 W
Embo	46	57.54 N	3.59 W
Emboabas	256	21.18 S	44.08 W
Embondo	152	0.15 N	19.38 E
Emborcação, Represa ⊜ [1]	255	18.30 S	47.50 W
Embrach	58	47.30 N	8.36 E
Embreeville, Pa., U.S.	285	39.56 N	75.44 W
Embreeville, Tn., U.S.	192	36.10 N	82.27 W
Embro	212	43.09 N	80.54 W
Embrun, On., Can.	212	45.16 N	75.17 W
Embrun, Fr.	62	44.34 N	6.30 E
Embry	50	50.29 N	1.58 E
Embsay	44	53.58 N	1.59 W
Embu, Bra.	256	23.39 S	46.51 W
Embu, Kenya	154	0.32 S	37.27 E
Embu □ [7]	287b	23.40 S	46.50 W
Embu-Guaçu	256	23.49 S	46.48 W
Embu-Guaçu □ [7]	287b	23.48 S	46.48 W
Embu-mirim ≃	287b	23.39 S	46.51 W
Emden, Dtsch.	52	53.22 N	7.12 E
Emden, Il., U.S.	194	40.18 N	89.29 W
Emden, Mo., U.S.	219	39.48 N	91.52 W
Emei	107	29.36 N	103.31 E
Emeigh	214	40.42 N	78.47 W
Emel' (Emin) ≃	86	46.20 N	81.46 E
Emelle	194	32.43 N	88.18 W
Emerado	198	47.55 N	97.21 W
Émerainville	261	48.49 N	2.37 E
Emerald, Austl.	166	23.32 S	148.10 E
Emerald, Austl.	169	37.56 S	145.26 E
Emerald Bay State Park ♠	226	38.57 N	120.05 W
Emerson, Mb., Can.	184	49.00 N	97.12 W
Emerson, Ar., U.S.	194	33.05 N	93.11 W
Emerson, Ga., U.S.	192	34.07 N	84.45 W
Emerson, Ia., U.S.	198	41.01 N	95.24 W
Emerson, Mo., U.S.	219	39.53 N	91.42 W
Emerson, Ne., U.S.	198	42.17 N	96.44 W
Emerson, N.J., U.S.	276	40.58 N	74.01 W
Emery, S.D., U.S.	198	43.36 N	97.37 W
Emery, Ut,. U.S.	200	38.55 N	111.14 W
Emeryville, On., Can.	214	42.18 N	82.45 W
Emeryville, Ca., U.S.	226	37.50 N	122.17 W
Emet	130	39.20 N	29.15 E
Emgayet	146	29.04 N	12.58 E
Emhouse	222	32.09 N	96.35 W
Emi	88	50.36 N	97.49 E
Emigrant Gap	226	39.17 N	120.40 W
Emigrant Gap)(	226	39.18 N	120.40 W
Emigsville	208	40.01 N	76.44 W
Emiliano Mitre, Canal Ʉ	288	34.36 S	58.18 W
Emiliano Zapata, Méx.	232	17.45 N	91.46 W
Emiliano Zapata, Méx.	234	16.10 N	94.01 W
Emiliano Zapata, Bahía ᑕ	232	19.40 N	87.30 W
Emilia-Romagna □ [4]	36	44.35 N	11.00 E
Emílio de Carvalho	152	5.55 S	12.57 E
Emily Provincial Park ♠	212	44.21 N	78.31 W
Emin	86	46.32 N	83.39 E
Emin (Emel') ≃	86	46.20 N	81.46 E
Eminābād	123	32.02 N	74.16 E
Emine, nos ›	38	42.42 N	27.51 E
Eminence, Ky., U.S.	218	38.22 N	85.10 W
Eminence, Mo., U.S.	194	37.09 N	91.21 W
Emiralem	130	38.36 N	27.09 E
Emiratos Arabes Unidos → United Arab Emirates □ [1]	128	24.00 N	54.00 E
Emirau Island I	164	1.40 S	150.00 E
Emirdağ	130	39.01 N	31.10 E
Emir Dağları ⩘	130	38.50 N	31.15 E
Emirhan	130	39.42 N	37.46 E
Emir Pasha Gulf ᑕ	154	2.32 S	31.52 E
Emissi, Tarso ʌ	146	21.13 N	18.32 E
Emita	166	40.00 S	147.54 E
Emlembe ʌ	158	25.57 S	31.11 E
Emlenton	214	41.11 N	79.43 W
Emlichheim	52	52.36 N	6.50 E
Emmaån ≃	40	58.44 N	15.35 E
Emmaboda	26	56.38 N	15.32 E
Emmaste	76	58.42 N	22.36 E
Emmaus, Ross.	82	56.47 N	36.07 E
Emmaus, Pa., U.S.	208	40.32 N	75.29 W
Emmaville	166	29.26 S	151.36 E
Emme ≃	58	47.13 N	7.34 E
Emmeline Lake ⊜	184	55.00 N	106.22 W
Emmeloord	52	52.43 N	5.45 E
Emmen	52	52.47 N	6.54 E
Emmenbrücke	58	47.04 N	8.17 E
Emmendingen	58	48.07 N	7.50 E
Emmental V	58	46.56 N	7.45 E
Emmer ≃	52	52.03 N	9.23 E
Emmer-Compascuum	52	52.48 N	7.02 E
Emmer-Erfscheidenveen	52	52.48 N	7.01 E
Emmerich	52	51.50 N	6.15 E
Emmerstedt	54	52.15 N	10.58 E

PORTUGUÊS

Nome	Página	Lat.°′	Long.°′ W = Oeste
Emmerthal	52	52.03 N	9.23 E
Emmet, Austl.	166	24.40 S	144.28 E
Emmet, Ar., U.S.	194	33.43 N	93.28 W
Emmetsburg	198	43.06 N	94.40 W
Emmett, Id., U.S.	202	43.52 N	116.29 W
Emmett, Mi., U.S.	214	42.59 N	82.45 W
Emmiganūru	122	15.44 N	77.29 E
Emmingen-Liptingen	58	47.56 N	8.51 E
Emmitsburg	208	39.42 N	77.20 W
Emmonak	180	62.46 N	164.30 W
Emneth	42	52.38 N	0.11 E
Emo	190	48.38 N	93.50 W
Emőd	30	47.56 N	20.49 E
Emory	222	32.52 N	95.46 W
Emory ≃	192	35.56 N	84.29 W
Emory Peak ʌ	196	29.13 N	103.17 W
Empalme	232	27.58 N	110.51 W
Empalme Escobedo	234	20.41 N	100.44 W
Empalme Purísima	234	23.55 N	105.05 W
Empalme San Vicente	258	34.58 S	58.22 W
Empangeni	158	28.50 S	31.48 E
Empedrado, Arg.	252	27.57 S	58.48 W
Empedrado, Chile	252	35.36 S	72.17 W
Emperor Jimmu, Tomb of ⊥	270	34.29 N	135.47 E
Emperor Nintoku, Tomb of ⊥	270	34.34 N	135.29 E
Emperor Range ⩘	175e	5.45 S	154.55 E
Emperor Seamounts ✦ [3]	6	42.00 N	170.00 E
Emperor Tenchi, Tomb of ⊥	270	34.59 N	135.48 E
Empfingen	58	48.24 N	8.42 E
Empire, Ca., U.S.	226	37.38 N	120.54 W
Empire, La., U.S.	194	29.23 N	89.35 W
Empire, Nv., U.S.	204	40.34 N	119.20 W
Empire, Oh., U.S.	214	40.30 N	80.37 W
Empoli	66	43.43 N	10.57 E
Emporia, Ks., U.S.	198	38.24 N	96.10 W
Emporia, Va., U.S.	208	36.41 N	77.32 W
Emporium	214	41.30 N	78.14 W
Empress	184	50.57 N	110.00 W
Empress Augusta Bay ᑕ	175e	6.25 S	155.05 E
Emptinne	56	50.19 N	5.07 E
Empty Quarter → Ar-Rub' al-Khālī ◆ [2]	118	20.00 N	51.00 E
Ems ≃	52	53.20 N	7.06 E
Emsbüren	52	52.24 N	7.17 E
Emscher ≃	263	51.34 N	6.42 E
Emscherbruch ◆ [1]	263	51.34 N	7.09 E
Emsdetten	52	52.10 N	7.31 E
Ems-Jade-Kanal ≊	52	53.19 N	7.10 E
Emskirchen	56	49.33 N	10.43 E
Emsland ◆ [1]	52	52.50 N	7.20 E
Emst ◆ [8]	263	51.21 N	7.30 E
Emstek	52	52.50 N	8.09 E
Emsworth, Eng., U.K.	42	50.51 N	0.56 W
Emsworth, Pa., U.S.	214	40.30 N	80.05 W
Emsworth Dam ◆ [6]	279b	40.30 N	80.05 W
Emu	89	43.45 N	128.10 E
Emu, Mount ʌ [2]	169	37.35 S	143.27 E
Emu Creek ≃	171a	26.56 S	152.19 E
Emu Downs	168b	33.54 S	138.59 E
Emukae	92	33.18 N	129.38 E
Emu Park	166	23.15 S	150.50 E
Emu Plains	274a	33.45 S	150.41 E
Emur ≃	89	53.24 N	124.00 E
Emuren	273a	6.40 N	3.31 E
Emyvale	48	54.20 N	6.59 W
En (Inn) ≃, Europe	32	48.35 N	13.28 E
En ≃, Zhg.	100	27.12 N	115.08 E
Ena	94	35.27 N	137.25 E
Enana	156	17.29 S	16.19 E
Enånger	26	61.32 N	17.00 E
Enard Bay ᑕ	46	58.05 N	5.20 W
Enarotali	164	3.55 S	136.21 E
Ena-san ʌ	94	35.26 N	137.36 E
Ena-san Tunnel ◆ [5]	94	35.30 N	137.40 E
Enbacka	40	60.25 N	15.36 E
Enborne ≃	42	51.24 N	1.06 W
Encampment	200	41.12 N	106.47 W
Encampment ≃	200	41.18 N	106.43 W
Encantado	252	29.15 S	51.53 W
Encantado ◆ [8]	287a	22.54 S	43.18 W
Encanto, Cape ›	116	15.44 N	121.37 E
Encarnação ◆ [8]	266c	38.47 N	9.06 W
Encarnación	252	27.20 S	55.54 W
Encarnación de Díaz	234	21.31 N	102.14 W
Encha	98	37.25 N	115.42 E
Enchenberg	56	49.01 N	7.20 E
Enchi	150	5.49 N	2.49 W
Enchilayas	200	30.50 N	112.50 W
Enchovas, Enseada das ᑕ	256	23.57 S	45.18 W
Enciastraia, Monte ʌ	62	44.22 N	6.53 E
Encinal	196	28.02 N	99.21 W
Encinitas	228	33.02 N	117.17 W
Encino, N.M., U.S.	200	34.39 N	105.27 W
Encino, Tx., U.S.	196	26.57 N	98.08 W
Encino ◆ [8]	280	34.09 N	118.30 W
Encino Reservoir ⊜ [1]	280	34.05 N	118.31 W
Encontrados	246	9.03 N	72.14 W
Encounter Bay ᑕ	168b	35.35 S	138.44 E
Encrucijada, Cuba	240p	22.37 N	79.52 W
Encrucijada, Méx.	234	18.18 N	93.29 W
Encruzilhada	255	15.31 S	40.54 W
Encruzilhada do Sul	252	30.32 S	52.31 W
Encs	30	48.20 N	21.08 E
Endako	182	54.05 N	125.02 W
Endako ≃	182	54.05 N	124.55 W
Endau ≃	114	2.39 N	103.38 E
Ende	115b	8.50 S	121.39 E
Ende, Pulau I	115b	8.53 S	121.32 E
Ende, Teluk ᑕ	115b	8.52 S	121.30 E
Endeavor, Pa., U.S.	214	41.35 N	79.23 W
Endeavor, Wi., U.S.	190	43.42 N	89.27 W
Endeavour	184	52.08 N	102.40 W
Endeavour Strait Ʉ	164	10.50 S	142.15 E
Endelave I	41	55.46 N	10.17 E
Enderbury I [1]	14	3.08 S	171.05 W
Enderby, B.C., Can.	182	50.33 N	119.08 W
Enderby, Eng., U.K.	42	52.36 N	1.12 W
Enderby Land ◆ [1]	9	67.30 S	53.00 E
Enderlin	198	46.37 N	97.36 W
Endicott, N.Y., U.S.	210	42.05 N	76.02 W
Endicott, Wa., U.S.	202	46.55 N	117.40 W
Endicott Mountains ⩘	180	67.50 N	152.00 W
Endimari ≃	248	8.46 S	66.07 W
Endine	64	45.46 N	9.59 E
Endine Gaiano	64	45.48 N	9.59 E
Endingen	58	48.09 N	7.42 E
Endja, Oued ≃	34	36.31 N	6.15 E
Endō	268	35.23 N	139.27 E
Endola	156	17.37 S	15.50 E
'En Dor	132	32.39 N	35.25 E
Endre ≃	62	43.28 N	6.36 E
Endrick ʌ	170	35.12 S	150.12 E
Endrick ≃	170	35.01 S	150.03 E
Endwell	210	42.06 N	76.01 W
Ene ≃	248	11.09 S	74.19 W
Eneabba	162	29.50 S	115.20 E
Enemonzo	64	46.25 N	12.53 E
Enewetak I [1]	14	11.30 N	162.15 E
Enez	130	40.44 N	26.04 E
Enfida	36	36.07 N	10.23 E
Enfield, Austl.	168b	34.53 S	138.35 E
Enfield, Austl.	274a	33.53 S	151.06 E
Enfield, N.Z.	172	45.03 S	170.52 E
Enfield, Ct., U.S.	207	41.58 N	72.35 W
Enfield, N.H., U.S.	188	43.38 N	72.08 W
Enfield, N.C., U.S.	192	36.10 N	77.40 W
Enfield, Va., U.S.	208	37.43 N	77.12 W
Enfield ◆ [8]	42	51.40 N	0.05 W
Enga □ [5]	164	5.30 S	143.30 E
Engadine	170	34.04 S	151.01 E
Engaño, Cabo ›	238	18.37 N	68.20 W
Engaru	92a	44.03 N	143.31 E
Engažimo	88	57.51 N	114.56 E
Engcobo	158	31.37 S	28.00 E
'En Gedi	132	31.27 N	35.23 E
Engelberg	58	46.49 N	8.25 E
Engelhard	192	35.30 N	75.59 W
Engelhartszell	60	48.31 N	13.44 E
Engel's	80	51.30 N	46.07 E
Engelsdorf	54	51.20 N	12.29 E
Engelskirchen	56	50.59 N	7.24 E
Engelsmanplaat I	52	53.28 N	6.02 E
Engen, B.C., Can.	182	54.02 N	124.18 W
Engen, Dtsch.	58	47.51 N	8.46 E
Engenheiro Navarro	255	17.17 S	43.57 W
Engenheiro Passos	256	22.30 S	44.41 W
Engenheiro Paulo de Frontin	256	22.33 S	43.41 W
Engenho	248	15.10 S	56.25 W
Engenho, Ilha do I	287a	22.50 S	43.07 W
Engenho de Dentro ◆ [8]	287a	22.54 S	43.18 W
Engenho do Mato	287a	22.52 S	43.01 W
Éngenho Novo	256	21.49 S	43.00 W
Engenho Nôvo ◆ [8]	287a	22.55 S	43.17 W
Enger	52	52.08 N	8.34 E
Engestofte	41	54.46 N	11.34 E
Engesvang	41	56.10 N	9.21 E
'En Gev	132	32.47 N	35.38 E
Enggano, Pulau I	112	5.24 S	102.16 E
Enghershatu ʌ	144	16.40 N	38.20 E
Enghien (Edingen)	50	50.42 N	4.02 E
Enghien-les-Bains	261	48.58 N	2.19 E
Enghien-Moisselles, Aéroport d' ⊠	261	49.02 N	2.21 E
Engiadina Bassa V	58	46.50 N	10.20 E
Engis	56	50.35 N	5.25 E
Engizek Dağı ʌ	130	37.50 N	37.10 E
Engjan	26	63.09 N	8.32 E
England	194	34.32 N	91.58 W
England □ [8]	28	52.30 N	1.30 W
England Air Force Base ■	194	31.20 N	92.33 W
Englebright Lake ⊜ [1]	226	39.15 N	121.15 W
Englee	186	50.44 N	56.06 W
Englefield, Cape ›	176	69.51 N	85.39 W
Englefield Green	260	51.26 N	0.35 W
Englefontaine	50	50.11 N	3.39 E
Englehart	190	47.49 N	79.52 W
Englehart ≃	190	47.51 N	79.50 W
Engleside	208	38.43 N	77.05 W
Englewood, B.C., Can.	182	50.33 N	126.53 W
Englewood, Co., U.S.	200	39.38 N	104.59 W
Englewood, Fl., U.S.	220	26.57 N	82.21 W
Englewood, In., U.S.	218	38.50 N	86.31 W
Englewood, Ks., U.S.	198	37.02 N	99.58 W
Englewood, N.J., U.S.	210	40.53 N	73.58 W
Englewood, Oh., U.S.	218	39.52 N	84.18 W
Englewood, Tn., U.S.	192	35.25 N	84.29 W
Englewood ◆ [8]	278	41.47 N	87.39 W
Englewood Cliffs	276	40.53 N	73.57 W
Englewood Dam ◆ [6]	218	39.52 N	84.17 W
English, In., U.S.	218	38.20 N	86.27 W
English, Ky., U.S.	218	38.37 N	85.08 W
English ≃, On., Can.	176	50.12 N	95.00 W
English (Rivière des Anglais) ≃, N.A.	206	45.13 N	73.50 W
English ≃, Ia., U.S.	190	41.29 N	91.30 W
English Bay	180	59.22 N	151.55 W
English Bāzār → Ingrāj Bāzār	124	25.00 N	88.09 E
English Center	210	41.26 N	77.17 W
English Channel (La Manche) Ʉ	28	50.20 N	1.00 W
English Coast ≗ [2]	9	73.45 S	73.00 W
English Harbour West	186	47.28 N	55.29 W
Englishman ≃	224	49.22 N	124.18 W
Englishtown	208	40.17 N	74.21 W
Engong	152	0.36 N	10.06 E
Engstingen	58	48.23 N	9.17 E
Engter	52	52.23 N	8.04 E
Énguera	34	38.59 N	0.41 W
Engum	41	55.44 N	9.40 E
Engure	76	57.10 N	23.13 E
Engures ezers ⊜	76	57.16 N	23.06 E
Engwilen	58	47.37 N	9.05 E
'En Harod	132	32.33 N	35.23 E
'En HaShofét	132	32.35 N	35.06 E
Enid	196	36.23 N	97.52 W
Enid Lake ⊜ [1]	194	34.10 N	89.50 W
Enilda	182	55.25 N	116.18 W
Eningen unter Achalm	58	48.29 N	9.16 E
Eniwa	92a	42.45 N	141.33 E
Eniwetok → Enewetak I [1]	14	11.30 N	162.15 E
eNjesuthi ʌ	158	29.09 S	29.23 E
Enka	192	35.32 N	82.39 W
Enkenbach-Alsenborn	56	49.29 N	7.54 E
Enkhuizen	52	52.42 N	5.17 E
Enkirch	56	49.59 N	7.07 E
Enköping	40	59.38 N	17.04 E
Enle	102	24.00 N	101.07 E
Enmedio	196	29.04 N	103.29 W
Enmedio, Cerro de ʌ	234	19.48 N	100.36 W
Enmelen	180	65.01 N	175.54 W
Enna	70	37.34 N	14.16 E
Enna □ [4]	70	37.35 N	14.26 E
Ennadai Lake ⊜	176	60.53 N	101.15 W
Enné, Ouadi V	146	14.24 N	18.45 E
Ennedi ⩘ [1]	146	17.15 N	22.00 E
Ennell, Lough ⊜	48	53.28 N	7.24 W
Ennenda	58	47.01 N	9.05 E
Ennepe ≃	263	51.22 N	7.27 E
Ennepestausee ⊜ [1]	263	51.14 N	7.25 E
Ennepetal	56	51.18 N	7.22 E
Ennerdale Water ⊜	44	54.31 N	3.23 W
Ennery	261	49.05 N	2.06 E
Enngonia	166	29.19 S	145.51 E
Enniger	52	51.50 N	7.56 E
Ennigerloh	52	51.50 N	8.02 E
Ennigloh	52	52.12 N	8.34 E
Ennis, Ire.	48	52.50 N	8.59 W
Ennis, Mt., U.S.	202	45.20 N	111.43 W
Ennis, Tx., U.S.	222	32.19 N	96.37 W
Enniscorthy	48	52.30 N	6.34 W
Enniskillen	48	54.21 N	7.38 W
Ennis Lake ⊜ [1]	202	45.26 N	111.41 W
Ennistimon	48	52.57 N	9.15 W
Enns	61	48.13 N	14.29 E
Enns ≃	61	48.14 N	14.32 E
Ennstaler Alpen ⩘	61	47.37 N	14.35 E
Eno	26	62.48 N	30.09 E
Enø I	41	55.10 N	11.40 E
Eno ≃	96	34.53 N	132.41 E
Enochs	196	33.52 N	102.46 W
Enogera Military Camp ■	171a	27.25 S	152.58 E
Enola	208	40.17 N	76.56 W
Enon	218	39.53 N	83.56 W
Enontekiö	24	68.23 N	23.38 E
Enon Valley	214	40.51 N	80.28 W
Enoree ≃	192	34.26 N	81.25 W
Enosburg Falls	188	44.54 N	72.48 W
Eno-shima I	94	35.18 N	139.29 E
Enping	102	22.11 N	112.17 E
Enrekang	112	3.34 S	119.47 E
Enrile	116	17.34 N	121.42 E
Enrique Fynn	258	34.50 S	59.08 W
Enrique Urien	252	27.34 S	60.32 W
Enriquillo	238	17.54 N	71.14 W
Enriquillo, Lago ⊜	238	18.27 N	71.39 W
Ens	52	52.38 N	5.50 E
Ensay I	46	57.46 N	7.05 W
Enschede	52	52.12 N	6.53 E
Ensdorf	60	49.21 N	11.56 E
Ensenada, Arg.	258	34.51 S	57.55 W
Ensenada, Méx.	232	31.52 N	116.37 W
Ensenada, P.R.	240m	17.58 N	66.56 W
Ensenada □ [5]	288	34.50 S	58.00 W
Enshi	102	30.17 N	109.19 E
Enshū-nada ⫪ [2]	92	34.27 N	137.38 E
Ensisheim	58	47.52 N	7.21 E
Enstaberga	40	58.45 N	16.51 E
Entebbe	154	0.04 N	32.28 E
Entenbühl ʌ	60	49.46 N	12.24 E
Enter	52	52.18 N	6.34 E
Enterprise, Guy.	246	6.56 N	58.24 W
Enterprise, Al., U.S.	194	31.18 N	85.51 W
Enterprise, Ca., U.S.	204	39.32 N	121.22 W
Enterprise, Ks., U.S.	198	38.54 N	97.07 W
Enterprise, Ms., U.S.	194	32.10 N	88.49 W
Enterprise, Or., U.S.	202	45.25 N	117.16 W
Enterprise, Ut,. U.S.	200	37.34 N	113.43 W
Entiat ≃	202	47.40 N	120.14 W
Entiat, Lake ⊜ [1]	202	47.40 N	120.12 W
Entiat Mountains ⩘	224	48.00 N	120.42 W
Entinas, Punta ›	34	36.41 N	2.46 W
Entlebuch	58	47.00 N	8.04 E
Entlebuch V	58	46.58 N	8.00 E
Entracque	62	44.14 N	7.24 E
Entraigues-sur-Sorgue	62	44.00 N	4.55 E
Entrains-sur-Nohain	50	47.27 N	3.15 E
Entrance, Cape ›	164	2.21 S	150.12 E
Entraunes	62	44.11 N	6.45 E
Entraygues	32	44.39 N	2.34 E
Entrechaux	62	44.13 N	5.08 E
Entrée, Île d' I	186	47.17 N	61.42 W
Entremont-le-Vieux	62	45.26 N	5.53 E
Entrepeñas, Embalse de ⊜ [1]	34	40.34 N	2.42 W
Entre Rios, Bol.	248	21.32 S	64.12 W
Entre Rios, Bra.	255	11.56 S	38.05 W
Entre Ríos □ [4]	252	32.00 S	59.00 W
Entre Ríos, Cordillera ⩘	236	14.05 N	85.37 W
Entre-Rios de Minas	255	20.41 S	44.04 W
Entrevaux	62	43.57 N	6.49 E
Entrèves	62	45.49 N	6.57 E
Entriken	214	40.20 N	78.12 W
Entroncamento	34	39.28 N	8.28 W
Entupido	256	22.30 S	44.51 W
Entwistle	182	53.36 N	115.00 W
Enu, Pulau I	164	7.05 S	134.30 E
Enugu	150	6.27 N	7.27 E
Enumclaw	224	47.12 N	121.59 W
Enurmino	180	66.57 N	171.49 W
Envalira, Port d')(	34	42.35 N	1.45 E
Envermeu	50	49.54 N	1.16 E
Envies, Rivière des ≃	206	46.37 N	72.24 W
Envigado	246	6.10 N	75.35 W
Envira	248	7.18 S	70.13 W
Envira ≃	248	6.42 S	69.46 W
'En Yahav	132	30.38 N	35.11 E
Enyamba	154	3.40 S	24.58 E
Enyang	102	31.48 N	106.31 E
Enyellé	152	2.49 N	18.06 E
Enys, Mount ʌ	172	43.14 S	171.38 E
Enz ≃	56	49.01 N	9.07 E
Enza ≃	64	44.54 N	10.31 E
Enzan	94	35.42 N	138.44 E
Enzbach ≃	56	49.54 N	6.25 E
Enzenkirchen	60	48.23 N	13.39 E
Enzesfeld	61	47.55 N	16.10 E
Enzklösterle	56	48.40 N	8.28 E
Eo ≃	34	43.28 N	7.03 W
Eolia	219	39.14 N	91.00 W
Eolie o Lipari, Isole II	70	38.30 N	14.50 E
Epanomí	38	40.26 N	22.56 E
Épars, Bois de l' ♠	261	48.45 N	1.45 E
Epe, Dtsch.	52	52.11 N	7.02 E
Epe, Ned.	52	52.21 N	6.00 E
Epe, Nig.	150	6.37 N	3.59 E
Epecuén, Lago ⊜	252	37.10 S	62.54 W
Épéhy	50	50.02 N	3.10 E
Epéna	152	1.22 N	17.29 E
Épernay	50	49.03 N	3.57 E
Épernon	50	48.37 N	1.41 E
Epes	194	32.41 N	88.07 W
Epfendorf	58	48.15 N	8.36 E
Ephesus → Efes ⊥	130	37.55 N	27.17 E
Ephraim	200	39.21 N	111.35 W
Ephrata, Pa., U.S.	208	40.10 N	76.10 W
Ephrata, Wa., U.S.	202	47.19 N	119.33 W
Ephrata Cloister ⊥	208	40.12 N	76.09 W
Ephratah	210	43.00 N	74.32 W
Epi □ [8]	175f	16.42 S	168.15 E
Épi I	175f	16.43 S	168.15 E
Épiais-lès-Louvres	261	49.02 N	2.33 E
Épila	34	41.36 N	1.17 W
Épinac-les-Mines	58	46.59 N	4.31 E
Épinal	58	48.11 N	6.27 E
Épinay-sous-Sénart	261	48.42 N	2.31 E
Épinay-sur-Orge	261	48.40 N	2.20 E
Épinay-sur-Seine	261	48.57 N	2.19 E
Epirus → Ípeiros □ [9]	38	39.40 N	20.50 E
Episcopia	68	40.04 N	16.06 E
Episkopí	130	34.40 N	32.54 E
Époisses	50	47.30 N	4.10 E
Epokiro	156	21.41 S	19.08 E
Epomeo, Monte ʌ	68	40.44 N	13.54 E
Épône	261	48.57 N	1.49 E
Eport, Loch ᑕ	46	57.33 N	7.11 W
Eppalock, Lake ⊜ [1]	169	36.52 S	144.31 E
Eppelborn	56	49.24 N	6.58 E
Eppendorf	54	50.48 N	13.14 E
Eppendorf ◆ [8]	263	51.27 N	7.11 E
Eppenhausen ◆ [8]	263	51.21 N	7.31 E
Eppeville	50	49.44 N	3.03 E
Epping, Austl.	169	37.39 S	145.02 E
Epping, Austl.	274a	33.46 S	151.05 E
Epping, Eng., U.K.	42	51.43 N	0.07 E
Epping, N.H., U.S.	188	43.02 N	71.04 W
Eppingen	56	49.08 N	8.54 E
Epping Forest □ [8]	260	51.43 N	0.10 E
Epping Forest ◆ [3]	42	51.40 N	0.03 E
Epping Green, Eng., U.K.	260	51.45 N	0.07 W
Epping Green, Eng., U.K.	260	51.44 N	0.05 E
Epping Upland	260	51.43 N	0.06 E
Epsom	42	51.20 N	0.16 W
Epsom and Ewell □ [8]	260	51.20 N	0.16 W
Epsom Downs Race Course ♠	260	51.19 N	0.15 W
Epte ≃	50	49.04 N	1.37 E
Épuisay	50	47.54 N	0.56 E
Epukiro ≃	156	20.45 S	21.05 E
Epupa Falls ⌞	152	16.55 S	13.10 E
Epuyén	254	42.14 S	71.21 W
Epworth	44	53.32 N	0.49 W
Eqlīd	128	30.55 N	52.39 E
Equality	194	37.44 N	88.20 W
Équateur □ [4]	152	1.00 N	20.30 E
Équateur → Ecuador □ [1]	246	2.00 S	77.30 W
Equatorial Guinea (Guinea Ecuatorial) □ [1]	152	2.00 N	9.00 E
Équihen-Plage	50	50.41 N	1.34 E
Equimina ≃	152	13.11 S	12.47 E
Equinox Mountain ʌ	210	43.10 N	73.08 W
Equinunk	210	41.51 N	75.14 W
Equi Terme	64	44.09 N	10.10 E
Era ≃, It.	66	43.40 N	10.38 E
Era ≃, Pap. N. Gui.	164	7.35 S	144.41 E
Erac Creek ≃	166	26.56 S	145.48 E
Eraclea	64	45.35 N	12.40 E
Eraclea ⊥	68	40.13 N	16.40 E
Eraclea Minoa ⊥	70	37.23 N	13.17 E
Eradu	162	28.41 S	115.02 E
Éragny	261	49.01 N	2.06 E
Eramosa ≃	212	43.32 N	80.14 W
Eran Bay ᑕ	116	9.06 N	117.43 E
Eranga	152	1.52 S	18.56 E
Erangal ◆ [8]	272c	19.10 N	72.47 E
Erap	164	6.35 S	146.40 E
Erath	194	29.57 N	92.02 W
Erave	164	6.40 S	143.50 E
Erave ≃	164	6.40 S	143.55 E
Erba	62	45.48 N	9.15 E
Erba, Jabal ʌ, Sūd.	140	19.04 N	36.46 E
Erba, Jabal ʌ, Sūd.	140	20.45 N	36.50 E
Erbaa	130	40.42 N	36.36 E
Erbach, Dtsch.	56	49.40 N	8.59 E
Erbach, Dtsch.	58	48.20 N	9.53 E
Erbendorf	60	49.50 N	12.03 E
Erbeskopf ʌ	56	49.44 N	7.05 E
Erchie	68	40.26 N	17.44 E
Erciş	84	39.02 N	43.22 E
Erciyes Dağı ʌ	130	38.32 N	35.28 E
Ercolano	68	40.48 N	14.21 E
Ercolano (Herculaneum) ⊥	68	40.46 N	14.20 E
Érd	30	47.23 N	18.56 E
Erdao ≃, Zhg.	98	42.39 N	127.35 E
Erdao ≃, Zhg.	104	42.16 N	122.20 E
Erdao Bai ≃	98	42.34 N	128.08 E
Erdaobaihe	98	42.22 N	128.07 E
Erdaofang, Zhg.	104	41.54 N	123.57 E
Erdaofang, Zhg.	104	41.37 N	122.34 E
Erdaofangshen	104	42.09 N	123.17 E
Erdaogangzi, Zhg.	104	41.57 N	122.09 E
Erdaogangzi, Zhg.	104	42.04 N	123.06 E
Erdaohe	89	43.37 N	127.35 E
Erdaohezi, Zhg.	89	45.07 N	127.16 E
Erdaohezi, Zhg.	89	45.08 N	129.39 E
Erdaojingzi	104	41.49 N	122.20 E
Erdaoliangzi, Zhg.	98	40.50 N	119.04 E
Erdaoliangzi, Zhg.	105	40.31 N	118.03 E
Erdaowan	89	47.58 N	124.33 E
Erdek	130	40.24 N	27.48 E
Erdemli	130	36.37 N	34.18 E
Erdene, Mong.	88	47.48 N	107.55 E
Erdene, Mong.	102	44.15 N	111.14 E
Erdene, Mong.	102	45.08 N	97.45 E
Erdene Bulgan	88	50.07 N	101.35 E
Erdene-Büren	86	48.26 N	91.27 E
Erdenedalaj	102	46.02 N	104.55 E
Erdene Mandal	88	48.30 N	101.21 E
Erdenheim	285	40.05 N	75.12 W
Erdevik	38	45.07 N	19.25 E
Erdiao	106	32.12 N	121.12 E
Erding	60	48.18 N	11.54 E
Erdinger Moos ≡	60	48.22 N	11.52 E
Erdnijevskij	80	46.52 N	46.17 E
Erebato ≃	246	5.54 N	64.16 W
Erebus, Mount ʌ	9	77.32 S	167.09 E
Ereğli, Tür.	130	37.31 N	34.04 E
Ereğli, Tür.	130	41.17 N	31.25 E
Eregun	273a	6.36 N	3.22 E
Erei, Monti ⩘	70	37.27 N	14.19 E
Erenas	116	12.25 N	124.19 E
Erenhot	102	43.46 N	112.05 E
Erenköy ◆ [8]	267b	40.58 N	29.04 E
Erepecuru, Lago do ⊜	250	1.20 S	56.35 W
Eresma ≃	34	41.26 N	4.45 W
Eressós	38	39.10 N	25.56 E
Erétria	38	38.24 N	23.48 E
Erexim	252	27.38 S	52.17 W
Erez	132	31.34 N	34.34 E
Érezée	56	50.18 N	5.33 E
Erfa ≃	56	49.43 N	9.15 E
Erfde	41	54.19 N	9.19 E
Erfelek	130	41.53 N	34.55 E
Erfenisdam ⊜ [1]	158	28.33 S	26.50 E
Erfoud	148	31.28 N	4.10 W
Erft ≃	56	51.11 N	6.44 E
Erftstadt	56	50.48 N	6.46 E
Erfurt	54	50.58 N	11.01 E
Ergak-Targak-Tajga, chrebet ⩘	88	53.25 N	95.30 E
Ergani	130	38.17 N	39.46 E
Ergene ≃	130	41.01 N	26.22 E
Ergenzingen	58	48.29 N	8.48 E
Erges (Erjas) ≃	34	39.40 N	7.01 W
Ērgļi	76	56.54 N	25.38 E
Ergolding	60	48.35 N	12.10 E
Ergoldsbach	60	48.41 N	12.12 E
Ergste	56	51.25 N	7.34 E
Erguig, Bahr ≃	146	11.22 N	15.24 E
Ergun (Argun') ≃	74	53.20 N	121.28 E
Ergun Youqi	89	50.14 N	120.10 E
Ergun Zuoqi	89	50.47 N	121.31 E
Erguvejem ≃	180	65.20 N	176.00 W
Er Hai ⊜	102	25.48 N	100.11 E
Erhlin	100	23.54 N	120.22 E
Erhshui	100	23.49 N	120.36 E
Erhulai	98	41.23 N	125.08 E
Eria ≃	34	42.03 N	5.44 W
Erial	208	39.46 N	75.00 W
Eriba	140	16.37 N	36.04 E
Eriboll	46	58.28 N	4.41 W
Eriboll, Loch ᑕ	46	58.31 N	4.41 W
Erica, Austl.	169	37.59 S	146.22 E
Erica, Ned.	52	52.43 N	6.55 E
Erice	70	38.02 N	12.35 E
Ericeira	34	38.59 N	9.25 W
Erichsen Lake ⊜	176	70.38 N	80.21 W
Erichshagen	52	52.40 N	9.14 E
Ericht, Loch ⊜	46	56.48 N	4.24 W
Erick	196	35.12 N	99.51 W
Erickson, B.C., Can.	182	49.05 N	116.28 W
Erickson, Mb., Can.	184	50.30 N	99.55 W
Ericson	198	41.46 N	98.40 W
Erie, Co., U.S.	200	40.03 N	105.03 W
Erie, Il., U.S.	190	41.39 N	90.04 W
Erie, Ks., U.S.	198	37.34 N	95.14 W
Erie, Mi., U.S.	216	41.47 N	83.29 W
Erie, Pa., U.S.	214	42.07 N	80.05 W
Erie □ [6], N.Y., U.S.	210	42.54 N	78.53 W
Erie □ [6], Oh., U.S.	214	41.27 N	82.42 W
Erie □ [6], Pa., U.S.	214	42.08 N	80.04 W
Erie, Lake ⊜	214	42.15 N	81.00 W
Erieau	214	42.16 N	81.56 W
Erie Basin ᑕ	276	40.40 N	74.01 W
Erie Beach, On., Can.	214	42.16 N	82.00 W
Erie Beach, On., Can.	284a	42.53 N	78.57 W
Erie Canal → New York State Barge Canal ≊	210	43.05 N	78.43 W
Erie County Fairgrounds ♠	284a	42.45 N	78.49 W
Erie International Airport ⊠	214	42.05 N	80.11 W
Eriksberg ⊥	40	58.56 N	16.22 E
Eriksdale	184	50.52 N	98.06 W
Erímanthos ʌ	38	37.59 N	21.51 E
Erimo	92a	42.01 N	143.09 E
Erimo-misaki ›	92a	41.55 N	143.15 E
Erin, On., Can.	212	43.45 N	80.07 W
Erin, N.Y., U.S.	210	42.11 N	76.40 W
Erin, Tn., U.S.	194	36.19 N	87.41 W
Erindale	275b	43.32 N	79.39 W
Ering	60	48.18 N	13.09 E
Eriskay I	46	57.04 N	7.18 W
Erisort, Loch ᑕ	46	58.07 N	6.24 W
Eriswil	58	47.05 N	7.51 E
Erith ◆ [8]	260	51.29 N	0.10 E
Erithraí	38	38.13 N	23.19 E
Eritrea □ [1], Afr.	136	15.20 N	39.00 E
Eritrea □ [1], Afr.	144	15.20 N	39.00 E
Erivan → Jerevan	84	40.11 N	44.30 E
Erjas (Erges) ≃	34	39.40 N	7.01 W
Erjiazhen	106	32.02 N	121.13 E
Erkelenz	56	51.05 N	6.19 E
Erken ⊜	40	59.51 N	18.34 E
Erken-Jurt	84	44.27 N	41.54 E
Erkheim	58	48.02 N	10.20 E
Erkilet	130	38.49 N	35.27 E
Erkina ≃	48	52.51 N	7.23 W
Erkner	54	52.25 N	13.45 E
Erkner, Forst ◆ [3]	264a	52.22 N	13.47 E
Erkowit	140	18.46 N	37.07 E

	English	Deutsch	Español	Français	Português
≃	River	Fluß	Río	Rivière	Rio
≊	Canal	Kanal	Canal	Canal	Canal
⌞	Waterfall, Rapids	Wasserfall, Stromschnellen	Cascada, Rápidos	Chute d'eau, Rapides	Cascata, Rápidos
Ʉ	Strait	Meeresstraße	Estrecho	Détroit	Estreito
ᑕ	Bay, Gulf	Bucht, Golf	Bahía, Golfo	Baie, Golfe	Baía, Golfo
⊜	Lake, Lakes	See, Seen	Lago, Lagos	Lac, Lacs	Lago, Lagos
≡	Swamp	Sumpf	Pantano	Marais	Pântano
⍓	Ice Features, Glacier	Eis- und Gletscherformen	Accidentes Glaciales	Formes glaciaires	Acidentes glaciares
⫪	Other Hydrographic Features	Andere Hydrographische Objekte	Otros Elementos Hidrográficos	Autres données hydrographiques	Outros acidentes hidrográficos

	English	Deutsch	Español	Français	Português
✦	Submarine Features	Untermeerische Objekte	Accidentes Submarinos	Formes de relief sous-marin	Acidentes submarinos
□	Political Unit	Politische Einheit	Unidad Politica	Entité politique	Unidade política
ʊ	Cultural Institution	Kulturelle Institution	Institución Cultural	Institution culturelle	Instituição cultural
⊥	Historical Site	Historische Stätte	Sitio Histórico	Site historique	Sitio histórico
♠	Recreational Site	Erholungs- und Ferienort	Sitio de Recreo	Centre de loisirs	Area de Lazer
⊠	Airport	Flughafen	Aeropuerto	Aéroport	Aeroporto
■	Military Installation	Militäranlage	Instalación Militar	Installation militaire	Instalação militar
◆	Miscellaneous	Verschiedenes	Misceláneo	Divers	Diversos

Erkrath 56 51.13 N 6.55 E
Erl 64 47.41 N 12.11 E
Erlach, Öst. 61 47.43 N 16.13 E
Erlach, Schw. 58 47.03 N 7.06 E
Erlands Point 224 47.36 N 122.42 W
Erlangen 60 49.36 N 11.01 E
Erlanger 218 39.01 N 84.36 W
Erlanghe 100 30.19 N 116.04 E
Erlangmiao 100 33.46 N 112.23 E
Erlau ≃ 60 48.34 N 13.36 E
Erlauf ≃ 61 48.12 N 15.11 E
Erlbach 54 50.18 N 12.22 E
Erldunda 162 25.14 S 133.12 E
Erle ✦[8] 263 51.33 N 7.05 E
Erlenbach 56 49.48 N 9.10 E
Erli 62 44.08 N 8.06 E
Erling 106 31.53 N 119.36 E
Erling, Lake ⊜[1] 194 33.05 N 93.35 W
Erlistoun 162 28.20 S 122.08 E
Erlongshan, Zhg. 89 47.20 N 132.28 E
Erlongshan, Zhg. 89 50.04 N 126.47 E
Erlongshantun 89 48.28 N 126.31 E
Erlsbach 64 46.55 N 12.15 E
Erma 208 38.58 N 74.54 W
Ermana, chrebet ⋏ 88 50.00 N 113.30 E
Ermatingen 58 47.41 N 9.06 E
Erme ≃ 42 50.18 N 3.56 W
Ermelindo Matarazo ✦[8] 287b 23.29 S 46.29 W
Ermelo, Ned. 52 52.17 N 5.37 E
Ermelo, S. Afr. 158 26.34 S 29.58 E
Ermendegou 104 42.02 N 121.56 E
Ermenek 130 36.38 N 32.54 E
Ermenek ≃ 130 36.35 N 33.23 E
Ermenonville 50 49.08 N 2.42 E
Ermidas 34 38.00 N 8.23 W
Ermil Post 140 13.37 N 27.36 E
Ermineskin Indian Reserve ✦[4] 182 52.52 N 113.30 W
Ermington 274a 33.48 S 151.04 E
Ermita de Guadalupe 234 22.36 N 103.03 W
Ermita de los Correas 234 22.54 N 103.01 W
Ermont 50 48.59 N 2.16 E
Ermoúpolis 38 37.26 N 24.56 E
Ermsleben 54 51.44 N 11.21 E
Ernaballa 162 26.17 S 132.07 E
Erndtebrück 56 50.59 N 8.15 E
Erne ≃ 48 54.30 N 8.16 W
Erne, Lower Lough ⊜ 48 54.26 N 7.46 W
Erne, Upper Lough ⊜ 48 54.14 N 7.32 W
Ernée 32 48.18 N 0.56 W
Ernest 214 40.41 N 79.10 W
Ernestina 258 35.16 S 59.34 W
Ernest Sound ʮ 182 55.52 N 132.10 W
Ernici, Monti ⋏ 66 41.48 N 13.22 E
Ernstbrunn 61 48.32 N 16.22 E
Ernst Thälmann, Pioneerpark ♦ 264a 52.28 N 13.33 E
Ernst-Thälmann-Stadion ♦ 264a 52.23 N 13.05 E
Ernz Blanche ≃ 56 49.52 N 6.16 E
Erode 122 11.21 N 77.44 E
Eromanga 166 26.40 S 143.16 E
Erongo 156 21.44 S 15.53 E
Erongo □[4] 156 22.00 S 15.00 E
Erongo ⋏ 156 21.45 S 15.37 E
Erota 144 16.14 N 37.55 E
Erp 56 50.46 N 6.43 E
Erpuzi 105 40.29 N 115.33 E
Erquelinnes 50 50.18 N 4.07 E
Err, Piz d' ∧ 58 46.33 N 9.41 E
Errabiddy 162 25.28 S 117.07 E
Er-Rachidia 148 31.58 N 4.25 W
Er-Rachidia □[4] 148 31.15 N 4.05 W
Errego 154 16.02 S 37.14 E
Errer ≃ 144 7.32 N 42.05 E
Er-Riad → Ar-Riyāḍ 128 24.38 N 46.43 E
Errigal Mountain ∧ 48 55.02 N 8.07 W
Errington 224 49.17 N 124.22 W
Erris Head › 48 54.19 N 10.00 W
Errochty, Loch ⊜ 46 56.45 N 4.12 W
Errogie 46 57.16 N 4.22 W
Errol Heights 224 45.28 N 122.36 W
Erromango I 175f 18.45 S 169.05 E
Ersekë 38 40.20 N 20.41 E
Ershijiazi 104 41.17 N 120.32 E
Ershilipu 105 40.07 N 117.24 E
Ershiqizhan 89 53.23 N 123.16 E
Ershiwuzhan 89 53.22 N 123.55 E
Erskine 198 47.40 N 96.00 W
Erskine, Lake ⊜ 276 41.06 N 74.15 W
Erskine Inlet C 176 76.15 N 102.20 W
Erskine Park 274a 33.49 S 150.47 E
Erstein 58 48.26 N 7.40 E
Erste Wiener Hochquellenleitung ≊[1] 61 48.10 N 16.17 E
Erstfeld 58 46.49 N 8.39 E
Ertai, Zhg. 86 46.07 N 90.06 E
Ertai, Zhg. 86 44.14 N 80.52 E
Ertaizi, Zhg. 104 41.52 N 121.56 E
Ertaizi, Zhg. 104 42.05 N 123.35 E
Ertaizi, Zhg. 104 42.35 N 124.00 E
Ertaizi, Zhg. 104 40.47 N 120.54 E
Ertil' 78 51.51 N 40.49 E
Ertingen 58 48.06 N 9.28 E
Ertix (Irtyš) ≃ 74 61.04 N 68.52 E
Erto 64 46.16 N 12.22 E
Ertuğrul 130 39.34 N 27.43 E
Ertvelde 50 51.11 N 3.45 E
Eruar 126 23.28 N 87.52 E
Erudina 166 31.28 S 139.23 E
Eruh 130 37.46 N 42.11 E
Erundu 156 20.36 S 16.25 E
Erunkan 273a 6.37 N 3.24 E
Erva, Ponta da › 266c 38.50 N 8.58 W
Erval 252 32.02 S 53.24 W
Erval d'Oeste 252 27.13 S 51.34 W
Ervalla 40 59.22 N 15.15 E
Erving 207 42.36 N 72.23 W
Ervy-le-Châtel 50 48.02 N 3.55 E
Erwin, N.C., U.S. 192 35.19 N 78.40 W
Erwin, Tn., U.S. 192 36.08 N 82.25 W
Erwitte 52 51.37 N 8.20 E
Erwood 184 52.50 N 102.10 W
Erxleben 54 52.13 N 11.14 E
Érythrée → Eritrea □[1] 144 15.20 N 39.00 E
Eryuan 102 26.06 N 99.55 E
Erzaohang 106 31.05 N 121.49 E
Erzberg ✦[7] 61 47.32 N 14.54 E
Erzgebirge (Krušné hory) ⋏ 54 50.30 N 13.10 E
Erzhan 89 43.58 N 128.44 E
Erzhuang 105 39.24 N 117.22 E
Erzin 88 50.15 N 95.10 E
Erzincan 130 39.44 N 39.29 E
Erzincan □[4] 130 39.40 N 39.30 E
Erzurum 130 39.55 N 41.17 E
Erzurum □[4] 130 40.00 N 41.30 E
Èsa ≃ 76 54.53 N 28.40 E
Esa'ala 164 9.44 S 150.49 E
Esambo 152 3.40 S 23.24 E
Esan-misaki › 92a 41.49 N 141.11 E
Esashi, Nihon 92 41.52 N 140.07 E
Esashi, Nihon 92 39.12 N 141.09 E
Esashi, Nihon 92a 44.56 N 142.35 E
Esbiye 130 40.57 N 38.44 E
Esbjerg 26 55.28 N 8.27 E
Esbly 261 48.54 N 2.49 E
Esbo → Espoo 26 60.13 N 24.40 E
Esborn 263 51.23 N 7.20 E
Esca ≃ 34 42.37 N 1.03 W
Escada 250 8.22 S 35.14 W
Escalada 258 34.10 S 59.07 W
Escalante, Pil. 116 10.50 N 123.33 E
Escalante, Ut,. U.S. 200 37.46 N 111.36 W
Escalante ≃, Ut,. U.S. 200 37.17 N 110.53 W
Escalante ≃, Ven. 246 9.15 N 71.50 W
Escalante Desert ✦[2] 200 37.50 N 113.30 W
Escalaplano 71 39.37 N 9.21 E
Escalón, Méx. 232 26.45 N 104.20 W
Escalon, Ca., U.S. 226 37.47 N 120.59 W
Escalona 34 40.10 N 4.24 W
Escambia ≃ 194 30.32 N 87.11 W
Escanaba 190 45.44 N 87.04 W
Escanaba ≃ 190 45.47 N 87.04 W
Escandón, Puerto)(34 40.17 N 1.00 W
Escárcega 232 18.37 N 90.43 W
Escarpada Point › 116 18.31 N 122.13 E
Escarpado Peak ∧ 116 8.36 N 117.22 E
Escarpment 284a 43.10 N 79.00 W
Escatawpa ≃ 194 30.25 N 88.35 W
Escaudain 50 50.20 N 3.21 E
Escaut (Schelde) ≃ 50 51.22 N 4.15 E
Eschach 58 47.44 N 9.36 E
Eschau, Dtsch. 56 49.49 N 9.15 E
Eschau, Fr. 58 48.29 N 7.43 E
Eschborn 56 50.09 N 8.34 E
Esche ≃ 56 48.54 N 6.04 E
Eschede 52 52.44 N 10.14 E
Eschen 58 47.13 N 9.31 E
Eschenbach 60 49.45 N 11.49 E
Eschenburg 56 50.49 N 8.20 E
Eschenlohe 64 47.36 N 11.11 E
Eschershausen 52 51.56 N 9.38 E
Eschlkam 60 49.18 N 12.55 E
Escholzmatt 58 46.55 N 7.56 E
Eschscholtz Bay C 180 66.18 N 161.25 W
Esch-sur-Alzette 56 49.30 N 5.59 E
Esch-sur-Sûre 56 49.55 N 5.55 E
Eschwege 56 51.11 N 10.04 E
Eschweiler 56 50.49 N 6.16 E
Esclave, Grand Lac de l' → Great Slave Lake ⊜ 176 61.30 N 114.00 W
Escobal 236 9.09 N 79.58 W
Escobar □[5] 288 34.23 S 58.46 W
Escobar, Arroyo ≃ 288 34.21 S 58.44 W
Escobedo, Méx. 196 27.13 N 101.21 W
Escobedo, Méx. 232 29.05 N 102.19 W
Escocesa, Bahía C 238 19.25 N 69.45 W
Escoheag 207 41.36 N 71.45 W
Escondido 228 33.07 N 117.05 W
Escondido ≃, Méx. 196 28.39 N 100.34 W
Escondido ≃, Nic. 236 12.04 N 83.45 W
Escondido Creek ≃ 228 33.01 N 117.15 W
Escorial → San Lorenzo de El Escorial 34 40.35 N 4.09 W
Escoutay ≃ 62 44.29 N 4.42 E
Escravos ≃[1] 150 5.35 N 5.10 E
Escrick 44 53.53 N 1.02 W
Escuadrón 201 ✦[8] 286a 19.22 N 99.06 W
Escudero, Arroyo ≃ 258 34.20 S 57.05 W
Escudo de Veraguas, Isla I 236 9.06 N 81.33 W
Escuinapa de Hidalgo 234 22.51 N 105.48 W
Escuintla, Guat. 236 14.18 N 90.47 W
Escuintla, Méx. 232 15.20 N 92.38 W
Escuintla □[5] 236 14.10 N 91.00 W
Escuminac, Point › 186 47.04 N 64.46 W
Esebi 154 2.57 N 30.39 E
Eséka 152 3.39 N 10.46 E
Eşen 130 36.27 N 29.16 E
Eşen ≃ 130 36.16 N 29.15 E
Esenler ✦[8] 267b 41.02 N 28.51 E
Esens 52 53.39 N 7.37 E
Esera ≃ 34 42.06 N 0.15 E
Esesi 130 39.49 N 39.19 E
Eşfahān (Isfahan) 128 32.40 N 51.38 E
Eşfahān □[4] 128 33.00 N 52.00 E
Esfandaqeh 128 28.38 N 57.12 E
Esfarāyen 128 37.02 N 57.27 E
Esgueva ≃ 34 41.40 N 4.43 W
Eshan 102 24.11 N 102.22 E
Esher ✦[8] 42 51.23 N 0.22 W
Eshkāshem 123 36.42 N 71.34 E
Eshowe 158 28.58 S 31.29 E
Esh-Sham → Dimashq 132 33.30 N 36.18 E
Eshta'ol 132 31.47 N 35.00 E
Esh Winning 44 54.47 N 1.43 W
Esiama 150 4.56 N 2.21 W
Esigodini 154 20.18 S 28.56 E
Esine 64 45.55 N 10.15 E
Esino ≃ 66 43.39 N 13.22 E
Esira 157b 24.20 S 46.42 E
Esk 171a 27.15 S 152.25 E
Esk ≃, N.Z. 172 43.06 S 171.57 E
Esk ≃, U.K. 44 54.58 N 3.04 W
Esk ≃, Eng., U.K. 44 54.29 N 0.37 W
Esk ≃, Eng., U.K. 44 54.21 N 3.23 W
Esk ≃, Scot., U.K. 46 55.57 N 3.03 W
Eskdale, N.Z. 172 39.24 S 176.50 E
Eskdale, W.V., U.S. 188 38.05 N 81.26 W
Eskdale V 44 55.10 N 3.00 W
Eske, Lough ⊜ 48 54.41 N 8.03 W
Eski Dzhumaya → Târgovište 38 43.15 N 26.34 E
Eskifjörður 24a 65.04 N 13.59 W
Eskiikan 85 43.12 N 68.31 E
Eskilstrup 41 54.51 N 11.54 E
Eskilstuna 40 59.22 N 16.30 E
Eskimalatya 130 38.26 N 38.23 E
Eskimo Lakes ⊜ 180 69.15 N 132.17 W
Eskimo Point 176 61.07 N 94.03 W
Eskipazar 130 40.58 N 32.33 E
Eskişehir 130 39.46 N 30.32 E
Eskişehir □[4] 130 39.35 N 31.10 E
Eskridge 198 38.51 N 96.06 W
Esla ≃ 34 41.29 N 6.03 W
Eslāmābād 128 34.06 N 46.31 E
Eslām Qal'eh 128 34.40 N 61.04 E
Eslāmshahr 128 35.40 N 51.10 E
Eslarn 60 49.35 N 12.32 E
Eslohe 56 51.15 N 8.09 E
Eslöv 41 55.50 N 13.20 E
Eşme 130 38.24 N 28.59 E
Esmeralda, Austl. 166 18.50 S 142.34 E
Esmeralda, Cuba 240p 21.51 N 78.07 W
Esmeralda, Méx. 196 25.40 N 103.30 W
Esmeralda, Isla I 254 48.57 S 75.25 W
Esmeraldas 246 0.59 N 79.42 W
Esmeraldas □[4] 246 0.40 N 79.30 W
Esmeraldas ≃ 246 0.58 N 79.38 W
Esmirna → İzmir 130 38.25 N 27.09 E
Esmond, N.D., U.S. 198 48.02 N 99.45 W
Esmond, R.I., U.S. 207 41.52 N 71.29 W
Esnagi Lake ⊜ 190 48.38 N 84.32 W
Esneux 56 50.32 N 5.34 E
Esong 152 2.09 N 10.58 E
Esopus Creek ≃ 210 42.04 N 73.56 W
Espada, Punta › 246 12.05 N 71.07 W
Espagne → Spain □[1] 34 40.00 N 4.00 W
Espalion 32 44.31 N 2.46 E
Espaly-Saint-Marcel 62 45.03 N 3.52 E
España → Spain □[1] 34 40.00 N 4.00 W
Espanola, On., Can. 190 46.15 N 81.46 W
Espanola, N.M., U.S. 200 35.59 N 106.04 W
Española, Isla I 246a 1.25 S 89.42 W
Esparto 226 38.41 N 122.00 W
Esparza 236 9.59 N 84.40 W
Espasingen 58 47.49 N 9.00 E
Espe, Dan. 41 55.12 N 10.25 E
Espe, Kaz. 85 43.52 N 74.10 E
Espejo 34 37.41 N 4.33 W
Espelkamp 52 52.25 N 8.36 E
Espenberg, Cape › 180 66.33 N 163.36 W
Espenhain 54 51.11 N 12.29 E
Espera, Arroyo ≃[1] 288 34.24 S 58.36 W
Espera Feliz 255 20.39 S 41.55 W
Esperança, Bra. 246 4.24 S 69.52 W
Esperança, Bra. 250 7.01 S 35.51 W
Esperance, Austl. 162 33.51 S 121.53 E
Esperance, N.Y., U.S. 210 42.46 N 74.15 W
Esperance Bay C 162 33.51 S 121.53 E
Esperantina 250 3.54 S 42.14 W
Esperantinópolis 250 4.53 S 44.53 W
Esperanza, Arg. 252 31.27 S 60.56 W
Esperanza, Cuba 240p 22.27 N 80.06 W
Esperanza, Méx. 232 27.35 N 109.56 W
Esperanza, Méx. 234 18.52 N 97.24 W
Esperanza, Pil. 116 8.43 N 125.36 E
Esperanza, Pil. 116 11.44 N 124.03 E
Esperanza, P.R. 240m 18.06 N 65.28 W
Esperanza, S. Afr. 158 30.21 S 30.40 E
Esperanza ʋ[3] 9 63.24 S 56.59 W
Esperanza Inlet C 182 49.48 N 126.50 W
Espergærde 41 56.00 N 12.34 E
Esperia 66 41.23 N 13.41 E
Esperito, Arroyo ≃[1] 288 34.23 S 58.36 W
Espevær 26 59.36 N 5.10 E
Espichel, Cabo › 34 38.25 N 9.13 W
Espinal 246 4.09 N 74.53 W
Espinazo 196 26.16 N 101.06 W
Espinazo, Sierra del → Espinhaço, Serra do ⋏ 255 17.30 S 43.30 W
Espingarda ≃ 250 10.03 S 47.13 W
Espinhaço, Serra do ⋏ 255 17.30 S 43.30 W
Espinho 34 41.00 N 8.39 W
Espinillo 252 24.58 S 58.34 W
Espinillo, Arroyo ≃ 258 34.59 S 57.36 W
Espinillo, Punta del › 258 34.50 S 56.26 W
Espino 246 8.34 N 66.01 W
Espinosa 255 14.56 S 42.50 W
Espírito Santo → Vila Velha 250 3.13 N 51.13 W
Espírito Santo □[3] 255 19.30 S 40.30 W
Espírito Santo do Dourado 256 22.03 S 45.58 W
Espiritu Santo I 175f 15.15 S 166.50 E
Espíritu Santo, Isla I 232 24.30 N 110.22 W
Espita 232 21.01 N 88.19 W
Espoir, Bay d' C 186 47.50 N 55.51 W
Espoo (Esbo) 26 60.13 N 24.40 E
Es Port de Pollença 34 39.55 N 3.05 E
Esposende 34 41.32 N 8.47 W
Esposizione Universale di Roma ♦ 267a 41.50 N 12.28 E
Espugues de Llobregat 266d 41.22 N 2.05 E
Espumoso 252 28.44 S 52.51 W
Espungabera 156 20.29 S 32.48 E
Espy 210 41.00 N 76.24 W
Espyville Station 214 41.36 N 80.29 W
Esquatzel Coulee V 202 46.17 N 119.07 W
Esquel 254 42.54 S 71.19 W
Esquimalt 224 48.26 N 123.24 W
Esquina 252 30.01 S 59.32 W
Esquina Negra 258 35.02 S 58.03 W
Esquipulas, Guat. 236 14.34 N 89.21 W
Esquipulas, Nic. 236 12.40 N 85.47 W
Esquiú 252 29.23 S 65.17 W
Esrum Sø ⊜ 41 56.00 N 12.24 E
Essaoui Mellene, Oued V 148 27.26 N 6.40 E
Essaouira (Mogador) 148 31.30 N 9.47 W
Essaouira □[4] 148 31.25 N 9.30 W
Essarts 261 48.30 N 1.46 E
Essé 152 4.05 N 11.53 E
Esse ≃ 66 43.16 N 11.54 E
Esseg → Osijek 38 45.33 N 18.41 E
Es-Sekhira 148 34.17 N 10.06 E
Essen, Bel. 50 51.28 N 4.28 E
Essen, Dtsch. 52 52.43 N 7.57 E
Essen, Dtsch. 56 51.28 N 7.01 E
Essen, Dtsch. 263 51.28 N 7.01 E
Essenbach 60 48.37 N 12.13 E
Essenberg ✦[8] 263 51.26 N 6.42 E
Essendon, Austl. 169 37.46 S 144.55 E
Essendon, Eng., U.K. 260 51.46 N 0.09 W
Essendon, Mount ∧ 162 24.59 S 120.28 E
Essendon Airport ⊠ 169 37.43 S 144.53 E
Essen-Mülheim, Flughafen ⊠ 263 51.24 N 6.58 E
Essentuki → Jessentuki 84 44.03 N 42.51 E
Essequibo ≃ 246 6.59 N 58.23 W
Essequibo Islands-West Demerara □[4] 246 6.40 N 58.30 W
Es Sers 36 36.04 N 9.02 E
Essex, On., Can. 214 42.10 N 82.49 W
Essex, Ct., U.S. 207 41.21 N 72.23 W
Essex, Il., U.S. 216 41.11 N 88.11 W
Essex, Ia., U.S. 198 40.50 N 95.18 W
Essex, Md., U.S. 208 39.18 N 76.28 W
Essex, Ma., U.S. 207 42.37 N 70.47 W
Essex, Mo., U.S. 194 36.48 N 89.51 W
Essex, Mt., U.S. 182 48.16 N 113.36 W
Essex □[6], On., Can. 214 42.10 N 82.50 W
Essex □[6], Eng., U.K. 42 51.48 N 0.40 E
Essex □[6], Ma., U.S. 207 42.40 N 70.55 W
Essex □[6], N.J., U.S. 210 40.48 N 74.12 W
Essex □[6], Vt., U.S. 206 44.57 N 71.43 W
Essex □[6], Va., U.S. 208 37.55 N 76.55 W
Essex ≃ 283 42.39 N 70.46 W
Essex Bay C 283 42.39 N 70.44 W
Essex Fells 276 40.49 N 74.17 W
Essex Junction 188 44.29 N 73.06 W
Essex Skypark ⊠ 284b 39.18 N 76.28 W
Essexville 190 43.36 N 83.50 W
Essing 60 48.56 N 11.47 E
Essington 285 39.52 N 75.18 W
Essling ✦[8] 264b 48.13 N 16.32 E
Esslingen 56 48.45 N 9.16 E
Es Smala es Souassi 36 35.21 N 10.33 E
Esson Lake ⊜ 212 45.02 N 78.16 W
Essonne □[5] 50 48.36 N 2.20 E
Essonne ≃ 50 48.37 N 2.29 E
Essoyes 58 48.04 N 4.32 E
Es-Suki 140 13.20 N 33.54 E
Essvik 26 62.19 N 17.24 E
Est □[4] 152 4.00 N 14.00 E
Est, Canal de l' ≊ 56 48.45 N 5.35 E
Est, Cap › 157b 15.16 S 50.29 E
Est, Gare ✦[5] 261 48.53 N 2.22 E
Est, Île de l' I 186 47.37 N 61.26 W
Est, Pointe de l' › 186 49.08 N 61.41 W
Estacada 224 45.17 N 122.19 W
Estaca de Bares, Punta da la › 34 43.46 N 7.42 W
Estacado, Llano ≚ 196 33.30 N 102.40 W
Estación La Colorado 234 23.52 N 102.26 W
Estado, Parque do ♦ 287b 23.39 S 46.37 W
Estados, Isla de los (Staten Island) I 254 54.47 S 64.15 W
Estados Unidos → United States □[1] 178 38.00 N 97.00 W
Eṣṭahbān 128 29.08 N 54.04 E
Estaires 50 50.38 N 2.43 E
Estambul → İstanbul 130 41.01 N 28.58 E
Estância, Bra. 250 11.16 S 37.26 W
Estancia, Pil. 116 11.28 N 123.09 E
Estancia, S. Afr. 158 26.17 S 29.52 E
Estancia, N.M., U.S. 200 34.45 N 106.03 W
Estancia Los López 234 20.53 N 104.31 W
Estanislao del Campo 252 25.03 S 60.06 W
Estanzuelas 236 13.38 N 88.30 W
Estarreja 34 40.45 N 8.34 W
Estats, Pique d' ∧ 34 42.40 N 1.24 E
Estavayer-le-Lac 58 46.51 N 6.50 E
Estcourt 158 29.01 S 29.52 E
Este 64 45.14 N 11.39 E
Este ≃ 52 53.32 N 9.47 E
Este, Parque Nacional del ♦ 286c 10.30 N 66.50 W
Este, Punta › 240m 18.08 N 65.16 W
Esteban Echeverría 258 34.50 S 58.28 W
Esteban Echeverría □[5] 288 34.51 S 58.32 W
Estefanía, Lago → Stefanie, Lake ⊜ 144 4.40 N 36.50 E
Esteio 252 29.51 S 51.10 W
Estelí 236 13.05 N 86.23 W
Estelí □[5] 236 13.10 N 86.20 W
Estella 34 42.40 N 2.02 W
Estelline, S.D., U.S. 198 44.34 N 96.54 W
Estelline, Tx., U.S. 196 34.33 N 100.26 W
Estell Manor 208 39.24 N 74.44 W
Estenfeld 56 49.50 N 10.01 E
Estèng 62 44.14 N 6.45 E
Estepa 34 37.18 N 4.54 W
Estepas de Kirguises → Kirgizskij chrebet ⋏ 85 42.30 N 74.00 E
Estepona 34 36.26 N 5.08 W
Ester 180 64.51 N 148.01 W
Esterel ⋏ 62 43.30 N 6.50 E
Esterhazy 184 50.40 N 102.08 W
Esterhazy, Schloss ⊥ 61 47.51 N 16.32 E
Estérias, Cap › 152 0.37 N 9.20 E
Esternay 50 48.44 N 3.34 E
Estero 220 26.26 N 81.49 W
Estero Bay C, Ca., U.S. 226 35.24 N 120.53 W
Estero Bay C, Fl., U.S. 220 26.25 N 81.52 W
Estero Island I 220 26.26 N 81.56 W
Estéron ≃ 62 43.49 N 7.11 E
Esteros 252 26.37 S 63.39 W
Esterwegen 52 52.59 N 7.38 E
Estes Park 200 40.22 N 105.31 W
Este Sudeste, Cayos del II 236 12.26 N 81.27 W
Estevan 184 49.08 N 102.59 W
Estevan Group II 182 53.05 N 129.40 W
Estevan Point 182 49.23 N 126.33 W
Esther Island I 180 60.50 N 148.05 W
Estherville 198 43.24 N 94.49 W
Estill 192 32.45 N 81.14 W
Estissac 50 48.16 N 3.49 E
Estiva 256 22.28 S 46.02 W
Estiva, Ribeirão da ≃ 287b 23.44 S 46.23 W
Estiva, Rio da ≃ 255 12.23 S 45.05 W
Estling, Lake ⊜ 276 40.53 N 74.30 W
Estocolmo → Stockholm 40 59.20 N 18.03 E
Eston, Sk., Can. 184 51.10 N 108.46 W
Eston, Eng., U.K. 44 54.34 N 1.07 W
Estonia (Eesti) □[1], Europe 22 59.00 N 26.00 E
Estonia (Eesti) □[1], Europe 76 59.00 N 26.00 E
Estoril 34 38.42 N 9.23 W
Estrasburgo → Strasbourg 58 48.35 N 7.45 E
Estrées-Saint-Denis 50 49.26 N 2.39 E
Estrela 252 29.29 S 51.58 W
Estrela ∧ 34 40.19 N 7.37 W
Estrela ≃ 287a 22.43 S 43.13 W
Estrela, Serra da ⋏ 34 40.20 N 7.38 W
Estrela do Norte 255 13.49 S 49.04 W
Estrela do Sul 255 18.46 S 47.42 W
Estrella ≃ 226 35.45 N 120.41 W
Estremadura □[9] 34 39.15 N 9.10 W
Estremoz 34 38.51 N 7.35 W
Estribo 234 22.26 N 99.17 W
Estrondo, Serra do ⋏[1] 250 9.00 S 48.45 W
Estuaire □[4] 152 0.15 N 10.00 E
Estuary 184 50.56 N 109.46 W
Esumba, Île I 152 2.00 N 21.12 E
Eszék → Osijek 38 45.33 N 18.41 E
Esztergom 30 47.48 N 18.45 E
Étables 32 48.38 N 2.50 W
Etadunna 166 28.43 S 138.38 E
Etah, India 124 27.38 N 78.40 E
Etah, Kal. Nun. 16 78.19 N 72.38 W
Étain 56 49.13 N 5.38 E
Etajima 96 34.15 N 132.30 E
Eta-jima I 96 34.15 N 132.28 E
Étalle 56 49.41 N 5.36 E
Étamaniou ≃ 186 50.17 N 59.58 W
Étampes 50 48.26 N 2.09 E
Etamunbanie, Lake ⊜ 166 26.15 S 139.44 E
Étaples 50 50.31 N 1.39 E
États-Unis → United States □[1] 178 38.00 N 97.00 W
Etāwah 124 26.46 N 79.02 E
Etchemin ≃ 186 46.46 N 71.14 W
Etchojoa 232 26.55 N 109.38 W
Etéké 152 1.29 S 11.35 E
Etembue 152 1.17 N 9.25 E
Etendard, Pic de l' ∧ 62 45.09 N 6.09 E
Ethan 198 43.32 N 97.59 W
Ethel 194 33.07 N 89.27 W
Ethel ≃ 162 24.09 S 118.26 E
Ethel, Mount ∧ 200 40.39 N 106.41 W
Ethelbert 184 51.31 N 100.22 W
Ethel Creek 162 22.54 S 120.09 E
Ethel Lake ⊜ 180 63.21 N 136.00 W
Etherow ≃ 262 53.24 N 2.03 W
Ethiopia (Ityopiya) □[1], Afr. 136 9.00 N 39.00 E
Ethiopia (Ityopiya) □[1], Afr. 144 9.00 N 39.00 E
Ethiopian Plateau ⋏[1] 144 9.00 N 38.00 E
Ethiopie → Ethiopia □[1] 144 9.00 N 39.00 E
Ethridge, Mt., U.S. 202 48.33 N 112.07 W
Ethridge, Tn., U.S. 194 35.19 N 87.18 W
Eticoga 150 11.09 N 16.08 W
Eticuera Creek ≃ 226 38.41 N 122.16 W
Etigo-heiya ≚ 92 37.45 N 139.00 E
Etili 130 39.59 N 26.54 E
Étiolles 261 48.38 N 2.29 E
Etiopía → Ethiopia □[1] 144 9.00 N 39.00 E
Etive, Loch ⊜ 46 56.29 N 5.09 W
Etjo ∧ 156 21.09 S 16.30 E
Etna, Ca., U.S. 204 41.27 N 122.53 W
Etna, N.Y., U.S. 210 42.29 N 76.23 W
Etna, Pa., U.S. 214 40.30 N 79.56 W
Etna, Wy., U.S. 200 43.02 N 111.00 W
Etna, Monte (Mongibello) ∧[1] 70 37.46 N 15.00 E
Etna Green 216 41.17 N 86.03 W
Etne 26 59.40 N 5.56 E
Etobicoke 212 43.42 N 79.32 W
Etobicoke Creek ≃ 212 43.35 N 79.32 W
Etoile 154 11.38 S 27.34 E
Étoile, Chaîne de l' ⋏ 62 43.22 N 5.30 E
Etoka 152 0.10 N 23.23 E
Etolin Island I 180 56.08 N 132.26 W
Etolin Strait ʮ 180 60.20 N 165.15 W
Etomami ≃ 184 52.48 N 102.33 W
Eton, Austl. 166 21.16 S 148.58 E
Eton, Eng., U.K. 42 51.30 N 0.36 W
Eton College ʋ[2] 260 51.30 N 0.36 W
Etondo 152 7.46 S 23.36 E
Etorofu-tō → Iturup, ostrov I 92a 44.54 N 147.30 E
Etosha National Park ♦ 156 19.00 S 15.50 E
Etosha Pan ≚ 156 18.45 S 16.15 E
Etoumbi 152 0.01 S 14.57 E
Etowah 192 35.19 N 84.31 W
Etowah ≃ 192 34.15 N 85.11 W
Étréchy 50 48.30 N 2.12 E
Étrépagny 50 49.18 N 1.37 E
Étretat 50 49.42 N 0.12 E
Etrotroka 157b 22.53 S 47.36 E
Etroubles 62 45.49 N 7.14 E
Etrusca, Necropoli ⊥ 66 42.15 N 11.47 E

ENGLISH

Name Page Lat.°′ Long.°′

Etsch → Adige ≃ 64 45.10 N 12.20 E
Ettal 64 47.34 N 11.05 E
Ettalong 170 33.31 S 151.21 E
Ettelbruck 56 49.52 N 6.05 E
Ettenheim 58 48.15 N 7.49 E
Etten-Leur 52 51.34 N 4.38 E
Etterbeek 56 50.50 N 4.23 E
Etters 208 40.09 N 76.45 W
Et Tîdra I 150 19.44 N 16.24 W
Ettington 42 52.09 N 1.36 W
Ettlingen 56 48.56 N 8.24 E
Ettrema Creek ≃ 170 34.50 S 150.22 E
Ettrick 208 37.14 N 77.25 W
Ettrick Forest ✦[3] 46 55.30 N 3.00 W
Ettrick Pen ∧ 44 55.22 N 3.16 W
Ettrick Water ≃ 46 55.31 N 2.55 W
Ettringen, Dtsch. 56 50.21 N 7.13 E
Ettringen, Dtsch. 58 48.06 N 10.39 E
Etuku 154 3.43 S 25.44 E
Etyka 88 51.00 N 116.50 E
Etzatlán 234 20.46 N 104.05 W
Etzikom Coulee ≃ 184 49.25 N 111.10 W
Etzná ⊥ 232 19.35 N 90.15 W
Eu 50 50.03 N 1.25 E
Eua I 14 21.22 S 174.56 W
Eua Iki I 174w 21.07 S 174.59 W
Eubank Acres 222 30.23 N 97.42 W
Euboea → Évvoia I 38 38.34 N 23.50 E
Euchiniko ≃ 182 53.14 N 123.30 W
Eucla 162 31.43 S 128.52 E
Euclid, Oh., U.S. 214 41.35 N 81.31 W
Euclid, Pa., U.S. 214 41.00 N 79.56 W
Euclid Center 216 42.08 N 86.24 W
Euclid Creek ≃ 279a 41.35 N 81.35 W
Euclid Creek Reservation ♦ 279a 41.33 N 81.32 W
Euclides da Cunha 250 10.31 S 39.01 W
Eucumbene 171b 36.07 S 148.38 E
Eucumbene ≃ 171b 36.21 S 148.38 E
Eucumbene, Lake ⊜[1] 171b 36.05 S 148.45 E
Eudistes, Lac des ⊜ 186 50.30 N 65.15 W
Eudora, Ar., U.S. 194 33.06 N 91.15 W
Eudora, Ks., U.S. 198 38.56 N 95.05 W
Eudunda 168b 34.11 S 139.04 E
Eufaula, Al., U.S. 194 31.53 N 85.08 W
Eufaula, Ok., U.S. 196 35.17 N 95.34 W
Eufaula Lake ⊜[1] 196 35.17 N 95.31 W
Eufrates → Euphrates ≃ 128 31.00 N 47.25 E
Euganei, Colli ⋏[2] 64 45.19 N 11.40 E
Eugendorf 64 47.52 N 13.07 E
Eugene 202 44.03 N 123.05 W
Eugenia, Punta › 232 27.50 N 115.05 W
Eugenia Lake ⊜ 212 44.20 N 80.30 W
Eugenio Bustos 252 33.46 S 69.04 W
Eugênio de Melo 256 23.09 S 45.47 W
Eugmo I 26 63.49 N 22.45 E
Eugowra 166 33.26 S 148.23 E
Euijeongbu → Ŭijŏngbu 98 37.44 N 127.03 E
Euless 222 32.50 N 97.04 W
Eulo 166 28.10 S 145.03 E
Eume ≃ 34 43.25 N 8.08 W
Eumemmerring Creek ≃ 274b 38.03 S 145.10 E
Eumungerie 166 31.57 S 148.37 E
Eunápolis 255 16.22 S 39.35 W
Eungella National Park ♦ 166 21.00 S 148.30 E
Eunice, La., U.S. 194 30.29 N 92.25 W
Eunice, N.M., U.S. 196 32.26 N 103.09 W
Eupen 56 50.38 N 6.02 E
Euphrat → Euphrates ≃ 128 31.00 N 47.25 E
Euphrates (Fırat) (Nahr al-Furāt) ≃ 128 31.00 N 47.25 E
Eupora 194 33.32 N 89.16 W
Eure 208 36.25 N 76.51 W
Eure □[5] 50 49.10 N 1.00 E
Eure ≃ 50 49.18 N 1.12 E
Eure-et-Loir □[5] 50 48.30 N 1.30 E
Eureka, Ak., U.S. 180 61.56 N 147.10 W
Eureka, Ca., U.S. 204 40.48 N 124.09 W
Eureka, Il., U.S. 190 40.43 N 89.16 W
Eureka, Ks., U.S. 198 37.49 N 96.17 W
Eureka, Mo., U.S. 219 38.30 N 90.37 W
Eureka, Mt., U.S. 202 48.52 N 115.03 W
Eureka, Nv., U.S. 204 39.30 N 115.57 W
Eureka, Pa., U.S. 214 40.15 N 78.46 W
Eureka, S.C., U.S. 192 34.42 N 81.11 W
Eureka, S.D., U.S. 198 45.46 N 99.37 W
Eureka, Tx., U.S. 222 32.01 N 96.18 W
Eureka, Ut,. U.S. 200 39.57 N 112.07 W
Eureka, Mount ∧ 162 26.34 S 121.32 E
Eureka Springs 194 36.24 N 93.44 W
Eurialo, Castello ⊥ 70 37.06 N 15.14 E
Eurinilla Creek ≃ 166 30.50 S 140.01 E
Euroa 169 36.45 S 145.35 E
Euro Disney, Parc ♦ 261 48.51 N 2.47 E
Europa, Île I 138 22.20 S 40.22 E
Europabrücke ✦[5] 64 47.11 N 11.23 E
Europa Point › 34 36.10 N 5.22 W
Europe ⊥[1] 4 50.00 N 28.00 E
Europe ⊥[1] 10 50.00 N 28.00 E
Europoort ✦[5] 52 51.57 N 4.07 E
Eursinge 52 52.46 N 6.28 E
Eurville 58 48.35 N 5.02 E
Euseigne 58 46.10 N 7.25 E
Euskal Herriko □[3] 34 43.00 N 2.30 W
Euskirchen 56 50.39 N 6.47 E
Eustace 222 32.18 N 96.01 W
Eustis, Fl., U.S. 220 28.51 N 81.41 W
Eustis, Ne., U.S. 198 40.39 N 100.09 W
Eustis, Lake ⊜ 220 28.50 N 81.44 W
Euston 166 34.35 S 142.44 E
Euston Station ✦[5] 260 51.32 N 0.08 W
Eutaw 194 32.50 N 87.53 W
Eutin 54 54.08 N 10.37 E
Eutsuk Lake ⊜ 182 53.20 N 126.44 W
Eutzsch 54 51.49 N 12.38 E
Euxton 44 53.39 N 2.40 W
Euzet-les-Bains 62 44.04 N 4.14 E
Eva 194 34.20 N 86.46 W
Evadale 194 30.21 N 94.04 W
Eva Downs 162 18.01 S 134.52 E
Evale 152 16.33 S 15.44 E
Evällen ⊜ 40 60.03 N 18.20 E
Evançon ≃ 62 45.40 N 7.41 E
Evandale 166 41.34 S 147.14 E
Evans 200 40.22 N 104.41 W
Evans, Lac ⊜ 176 50.55 N 77.00 W
Evans, Mount ∧ 200 39.35 N 105.38 W
Evansburg, Ab., Can. 182 53.36 N 115.01 W
Evansburg, Pa., U.S. 285 40.11 N 75.26 W
Evans Center 210 42.39 N 79.02 W
Evans City 214 40.46 N 80.03 W
Evans Creek ≃ 202 42.25 N 123.11 W
Evansdale 190 42.28 N 92.16 W
Evans Head › 166 29.07 S 153.26 E
Evans Mills 212 44.05 N 75.48 W
Evansport 216 41.25 N 84.24 W
Evans Strait ʮ 176 63.15 N 82.00 W
Evanston, Il., U.S. 216 42.02 N 87.41 W
Evanston, Pa., U.S. 279b 40.16 N 79.41 W
Evanston, Wy., U.S. 200 41.16 N 110.57 W
Evansville, Il., U.S. 194 38.05 N 89.56 W
Evansville, In., U.S. 194 37.58 N 87.33 W
Evansville, Mn., U.S. 198 46.00 N 95.40 W
Evansville, Wi., U.S. 216 42.46 N 89.17 W
Evansville, Wy., U.S. 200 42.51 N 106.16 W
Evant 196 31.29 N 98.09 W
Evanton 46 57.40 N 4.20 W
Eva Perón → La Plata 258 34.55 S 57.57 W
Evart 190 43.54 N 85.15 W
Evarts 192 36.51 N 83.11 W
Evaz 128 27.46 N 53.59 E
Ève 261 49.05 N 2.42 E
Evecquemont 261 49.02 N 1.57 E

DEUTSCH

Name Seite Breite°′ Länge°′ E = Ost

Eveking 263 51.14 N 7.44 E
Eveleth 190 47.27 N 92.32 W
Evelyn, Mount ∧[2] 164 13.36 S 132.53 E
Evening Shade 194 36.04 N 91.37 W
Evenkamp 263 51.40 N 7.39 E
Evenlode ≃ 42 51.47 N 1.21 W
Evensk 74 61.57 N 159.14 E
Evenwood 44 54.37 N 1.46 W
Even Yehuda 132 32.16 N 34.53 E
Everard, Lake ⊜ 162 31.25 S 135.05 E
Everard, Mount ∧, Austl. 162 26.16 S 132.04 E
Everard, Mount ∧, B.C., Can. 182 51.05 N 125.45 W
Everard Ranges ⋏ 162 27.05 S 132.28 E
Evercreech 42 51.09 N 2.30 W
Evere 56 50.52 N 4.24 E
Everest 198 39.40 N 95.25 W
Everest, Mount (Qomolangma Feng) ∧ 124 27.59 N 86.56 E
Everett, On., Can. 212 44.11 N 79.57 W
Everett, Ma., U.S. 207 42.24 N 71.03 W
Everett, N.J., U.S. 276 40.21 N 74.09 W
Everett, Pa., U.S. 188 40.00 N 78.22 W
Everett, Wa., U.S. 224 47.58 N 122.12 W
Everett, Mount ∧ 207 42.06 N 73.25 W
Evergem 50 51.07 N 3.42 E
Everglades, The ≚ 220 26.00 N 80.40 W
Everglades City 220 25.52 N 81.23 W
Everglades National Park ♦ 220 25.27 N 80.53 W
Evergreen, Al., U.S. 194 31.26 N 86.57 W
Evergreen, Ca., U.S. 204 35.54 N 120.26 W
Evergreen, Mt., U.S. 202 48.13 N 114.18 W
Evergreen, Tx., U.S. 222 30.33 N 95.14 W
Evergreen Lake ⊜[1] 216 40.40 N 89.02 W
Evergreen Park 216 41.43 N 87.42 W
Evergreen Plaza ✦[9] 278 41.43 N 87.41 W
Everly 198 43.09 N 95.19 W
Everman 222 32.37 N 97.17 W
Everman, Volcán ∧[1] 232 18.48 N 110.59 W
Everöd 26 55.54 N 14.06 E
Eversael 263 51.33 N 6.39 E
Eversen 52 52.45 N 10.02 E
Everson, Pa., U.S. 214 40.05 N 79.35 W
Everson, Wa., U.S. 224 48.55 N 122.20 W
Everswinkel 52 51.55 N 7.50 E
Everton 218 39.34 N 85.05 W
Everton ✦[8] 262 53.25 N 2.58 W
Everton Football Ground ♦ 262 53.26 N 2.58 W
Evesen 52 52.17 N 8.59 E
Evesham, Sk., Can. 184 52.24 N 109.50 W
Evesham, Eng., U.K. 42 52.06 N 1.56 W
Evesham, Vale of V 42 52.06 N 1.50 W
Évian-les-Bains 58 46.23 N 6.35 E
Evijärvi 26 63.22 N 23.29 E
Evinayong 152 1.27 N 10.34 E
Eving ✦[8] 263 51.33 N 7.29 E
Evingsen 263 51.18 N 7.44 E
Evionnaz 58 46.11 N 7.01 E
Evisa 36 42.15 N 8.47 E
Evje 26 58.36 N 7.51 E
Evolène 58 46.07 N 7.30 E
Évora 34 38.34 N 7.54 W
Evoron, ozero ⊜ 89 51.28 N 136.30 E
Evpatoria → Yevpatoriya 78 45.12 N 33.22 E
Évrange 56 49.30 N 6.12 E
Évreux 50 49.01 N 1.09 E
Evrieu 62 45.35 N 5.34 E
'Evron 132 32.59 N 35.06 E
Évros (Marica) (Meriç) ≃ 38 40.52 N 26.12 E
Evrótas ≃ 38 36.48 N 22.40 E
Évry 50 48.38 N 2.27 E
Évry-les-Châteaux 261 48.39 N 2.38 E
E. V. Spence Reservoir ⊜[1] 196 31.55 N 100.35 W
Evungu 154 4.27 S 25.12 E
Évvoia I 38 38.34 N 23.50 E
Évzonos ∧ 267c 37.57 N 23.49 E
Ewa 229c 21.20 N 158.02 W
Ewa Beach 229c 21.18 N 158.00 W
Ewan 285 39.42 N 75.11 W
Ewaninga 162 23.58 S 133.58 E
Ewan Lake ⊜ 285 39.42 N 75.11 W
Ewansville 285 39.59 N 74.44 W
Ewbank 158 26.14 S 23.35 E
Ewbank da Câmara 256 21.31 S 43.33 W
Ewe, Loch C 46 57.48 N 5.40 W
Ewell, Eng., U.K. 260 51.21 N 0.15 W
Ewell, Md., U.S. 208 37.59 N 76.02 W
Ewen 190 46.32 N 89.16 W
Ewenkiku Zizhiqi 89 49.07 N 119.40 E
Ewes Water ≃ 44 55.08 N 3.00 W
Ewing, Ky., U.S. 218 38.25 N 83.51 W
Ewing, Mo., U.S. 219 40.00 N 91.42 W
Ewing, Ne., U.S. 198 42.15 N 98.20 W
Ewing, Va., U.S. 192 36.38 N 83.25 W
Ewingsville 279b 40.24 N 80.06 W
Ewing Township 208 40.16 N 74.46 W
Ewo 152 0.53 S 14.49 E
Ewu 273a 6.33 N 3.19 E
Exaltación 248 13.16 S 65.15 W
Excelda 158 32.16 S 22.08 E
Excello 218 39.29 N 84.25 W
Excelsior 158 28.56 S 27.06 E
Excelsior Mountain ∧ 226 38.02 N 119.18 W
Excelsior Park ♦ 274a 33.45 S 151.01 E
Excelsior Springs 194 39.20 N 94.13 W
Excenevex 58 46.21 N 6.21 E
Exchange 210 41.07 N 76.41 W
Exchange Station ✦[5] 262 53.25 N 2.59 W
Excursion Inlet 180 58.25 N 135.27 W
Exe ≃ 42 50.37 N 3.25 W
Executive Committee Range ⋏ 9 76.50 S 126.00 W
Exeter, Austl. 170 34.38 S 150.19 E
Exeter, On., Can. 190 43.21 N 81.29 W
Exeter, Eng., U.K. 42 50.43 N 3.31 W
Exeter, Ca., U.S. 226 36.17 N 119.08 W
Exeter, Ne., U.S. 198 40.38 N 97.27 W
Exeter, N.H., U.S. 188 42.58 N 70.56 W
Exeter, Pa., U.S. 210 41.19 N 75.49 W
Exeter, R.I., U.S. 207 41.34 N 71.32 W
Exeter ≃ 188 43.02 N 70.55 W
Exeter Sound ʮ 176 66.14 N 62.00 W
Exford 42 51.08 N 3.38 W
Exhibition of Economic Achievements ʋ 265b 55.50 N 37.37 E
Exhibition Park ♦ 275b 43.38 N 79.25 W
Exhibition Stadium ♦ 275b 43.38 N 79.25 W
Exincourt 58 47.30 N 6.50 E
Exira 198 41.35 N 94.52 W
Exline Slough ≃ 216 41.05 N 87.47 W
Exmes 50 48.46 N 0.11 E
Exminster 42 50.41 N 3.29 W
Exmoor ⋏[1] 42 51.10 N 3.45 W
Exmoor National Park ♦ 42 51.12 N 3.46 W
Exmore 208 37.31 N 75.49 W
Exmouth, Austl. 162 21.56 S 114.07 E
Exmouth, Eng., U.K. 42 50.37 N 3.25 W
Exmouth Gulf C 162 22.00 S 114.20 E
Exmouth Plateau ✦[3] 14 19.00 S 114.00 E
Exning 42 52.16 N 0.21 E
Expedition Range ⋏ 166 24.30 S 149.05 E
Experiment 192 33.15 N 84.16 W
Exploits ≃ 186 49.05 N 55.20 W
Exploits, Bay of C 186 49.24 N 55.00 W
Exploits Dam ✦[6] 186 48.45 N 56.30 W
Expo Memorial Park ♦ 270 34.48 N 135.32 E
Export 214 40.25 N 79.37 W
Exposition Park ♦ 280 34.01 N 118.17 W
Exshaw 182 51.03 N 115.09 W
Extension 224 49.06 N 123.57 W
Exter 52 52.08 N 8.46 E

Symbols in the index entries represent the broad categories identified in the key at the right. Symbols with superior numbers (⋏[1]) identify subcategories (see complete key on page *I · 1*).

Symbole im Register stellen die rechts im Schlüssel erklärten Kategorien dar. Symbole mit hochgestellten Ziffern (⋏[1]) bezeichnen Unterabteilungen einer Kategorie (vgl. vollständiger Schlüssel auf Seite *I · 1*).

Los símbolos incluídos en el texto del índice representan las grandes categorías identificadas con la clave a la derecha. Los símbolos con numeros en su parte superior (⋏[1]) identifican las subcategorías (véase la clave completa en la página *I · 1*).

Les symboles de l'index représentent les catégories indiquées dans la légende à droite. Les symboles suivis d'un indice (⋏[1]) représentent des sous-catégories (voir légende complète à la page *I · 1*).

Os símbolos incluídos no texto do índice representam as grandes categorias identificadas com a chave à direita. Os símbolos com números em sua parte superior (⋏[1]) identificam as subcategorias (veja-se a chave completa à página *I · 1*).

∧ Mountain	Berg	Montaña	Montagne	Montanha
⋏ Mountains	Gebirge	Montañas	Montagnes	Montanhas
)(Pass	Paß	Paso	Col	Passo
V Valley, Canyon	Tal, Cañon	Valle, Cañón	Vallée, Canyon	Vale, Canhão
≚ Plain	Ebene	Llano	Plaine	Planície
› Cape	Kap	Cabo	Cap	Cabo
I Island	Insel	Isla	Île	Ilha
II Islands	Inseln	Islas	Îles	Ilhas
⊥ Other Topographic Features	Andere Topographische Objekte	Otros Elementos Topográficos	Autres données topographiques	Outros acidentes topográficos

Exte-Faye *I* · 55

ESPAÑOL — Nombre | Página | Lat.°′ | Long.°′ W = Oeste
FRANÇAIS — Nom | Page | Lat.°′ | Long.°′ W = Ouest
PORTUGUÊS — Nome | Página | Lat.°′ | Long.°′ W = Oeste

Externsteine ⊥ 52 51.52 N 8.55 E
Extertal 52 52.04 N 9.07 E
Exton 208 40.02 N 75.37 W
Extoraz ≃ 234 21.06 N 99.23 W
Extrema 256 22.51 S 46.19 W
Extremadura □[3] 34 39.15 N 6.15 W
Exu 250 7.31 S 39.43 W
Exuma Cays II 238 24.15 N 76.30 W
Exuma Sound ⩌ 238 24.15 N 76.00 W
Eyak 180 60.32 N 145.36 W
Eyam 44 53.17 N 1.41 W
Eyasi, Lake ⊜ 154 3.40 S 35.05 E
Eydehavn 26 58.31 N 8.53 E
Eye, Eng., U.K. 42 52.19 N 1.09 E
Eye, Eng., U.K. 42 52.35 N 0.10 W
Eyebrow 184 50.47 N 106.09 W
Eyehill Creek ≃ 184 52.40 N 109.39 W
Eyemouth 46 55.52 N 2.06 W
Eye Peninsula ›[1] 46 58.13 N 6.13 W
Eyers Grove 210 41.05 N 76.31 W
Eye Water ≃ 46 55.53 N 2.06 W
Eygalières 62 43.45 N 4.57 E
Eyguières 62 43.42 N 5.02 E
Eyhorne Street 260 51.16 N 0.38 E
Eyjafjördur c[2] 24a 65.54 N 18.15 W
Eyl 144 7.59 N 49.49 E
Eylar Mountain ∧ 204 37.28 N 121.33 W
Eymet 32 44.40 N 0.24 E
Eymir 130 40.02 N 35.14 E
Eymoutiers 32 45.44 N 1.44 E
Eynesil 130 41.03 N 39.08 E
Eynhallow Sound ⩌ 46 59.08 N 3.06 W
Eynort, Loch c 46 57.13 N 7.18 W
Eynsford 260 51.22 N 0.13 E
Eynsham 42 51.48 N 1.22 W
Eyota 190 43.59 N 92.13 W
Eyrarbakki 24a 63.53 N 21.05 W
Eyre 162 32.15 S 126.18 E
Eyrecourt 48 53.11 N 8.07 W
Eyre Creek ≃ 166 26.40 S 139.00 E
Eyre Mountains ⩕ 172 45.20 S 168.30 E
Eyre North, Lake ⊜ 166 28.40 S 137.10 E
Eyre Peninsula ›[1] 162 34.00 S 135.45 E
Eyre South, Lake ⊜ 166 29.30 S 137.20 E
Eyrieux ≃ 62 44.48 N 4.48 E
Eystrup 52 52.46 N 9.13 E
Eythorne 42 51.11 N 1.17 E
Eyüp ➜[8] 267b 41.03 N 28.55 E
Eyvānekey 128 35.20 N 52.04 E
Eyzaguirre, Canal ≋ 286e 33.36 S 70.41 W
Ézanville 261 49.02 N 2.22 E
Ezbekīyah ➜[8] 273c 30.03 N 31.15 E
Ezeiza, Aeropuerto Internacional de ⊠ 288 34.49 S 58.32 W
Ezequiel Ramos Mexía, Embalse ⊜[1] 254 39.30 S 69.00 W
Ezere 76 56.26 N 22.22 E
Ežerėlis 76 54.53 N 23.37 E
Ezeriș 38 45.24 N 21.53 E
Ezine 130 39.47 N 26.20 E
Ezinepazarı 130 40.34 N 36.09 E
Ezjaryšča 76 55.50 N 29.59 E
Ezop, chrebet ⩕ 89 52.36 N 133.37 E
Ežva 24 61.47 N 50.40 E
Ézy-sur-Eure 50 48.52 N 1.25 E
Ezzell 222 29.17 N 96.58 W

F

Faaa Airport ⊠ 174s 17.33 S 149.36 W
Faafaxdhuun 144 2.13 N 41.37 E
Faal 174q 9.37 N 138.10 E
Faaone 174s 17.40 S 149.18 W
Fabala 150 9.44 N 9.05 W
Fabbrico 64 44.52 N 10.50 E
Fabens 200 31.30 N 106.09 W
Fåberg 26 61.10 N 10.24 E
Faber Lake ⊜ 176 63.56 N 117.15 W
Fabert Seamount ✦[3] 14 24.07 S 158.33 W
Fabius 210 42.50 N 75.59 W
Fåborg 41 55.06 N 10.15 E
Fábrega, Cerro ∧ 236 9.07 N 82.52 W
Fabrègues 62 43.33 N 3.46 E
Fabreville ➜[8] 275a 45.34 N 73.50 W
Fabriano 66 43.20 N 12.54 E
Fabrica di Roma 66 42.20 N 12.18 E
Fabričnyj 85 43.11 N 76.24 E
Fabrizia 68 38.29 N 16.18 E
Facatativá 246 4.49 N 74.22 W
Facha 146 29.27 N 17.18 E
Faches-Thumesnil 50 50.35 N 3.04 E
Fachi 146 18.06 N 11.34 E
Facpi Point › 174p 13.20 N 144.38 E
Factoryville 210 41.34 N 75.47 W
Facundo 254 45.18 S 69.58 W
Fada 146 17.14 N 21.33 E
Fada, Lochan ⊜ 46 57.41 N 5.18 W
Fadalto 64 46.05 N 12.20 E
Fada Ngourma 150 12.04 N 0.21 E
Fadd 30 46.28 N 18.50 E
Faddeja, zaliv c 74 76.40 N 107.20 E
Faddejevskij, ostrov I 74 75.30 N 144.00 E
Faddoi 140 8.07 N 32.07 E
Fadian Point › 174p 13.26 N 144.49 E
Fadiffolu Atoll I[1] 122 5.25 N 73.30 E
Fadit 140 9.58 N 32.13 E
Faedis 64 46.10 N 13.20 E
Fænø I 41 55.29 N 9.42 E
Faenza 66 44.17 N 11.53 E
Faeroe Islands □[2] 22 62.00 N 7.00 W
Faeröerne → Faeroe Islands □[2] 22 62.00 N 7.00 W
Faete, Monte ∧ 267a 41.45 N 12.44 E
Fafa 150 15.20 N 0.43 E
Fafa ≃ 152 7.18 N 18.16 E
Fafakourou 150 13.04 N 14.34 W
Fafe 34 41.27 N 8.10 W
Fafen ≃ 144 5.59 N 44.25 E
Faga ≃ 150 13.15 N 0.55 E
Fagaitua 174u 14.16 S 170.37 W
Fagamalo 175a 13.25 S 172.21 W
Făgăraș 38 45.51 N 24.58 E
Făgărașului, Munții ⩕ 38 45.35 N 25.00 E
Fagasa 174u 14.17 S 170.43 W
Fagatogo 174u 14.17 S 170.41 W
Fagernes 26 60.59 N 9.15 E
Fagersta 40 60.00 N 15.47 E
Fagertärn ➜[4] 40 58.46 N 14.42 E
Fagerviken 40 60.33 N 17.45 E
Făget 38 45.51 N 22.10 E
Faggen Bach ≃ 64 47.05 N 10.40 E
Faggo 150 11.23 N 9.57 E
Fagnano, Lago ⊜ 254 54.35 S 68.00 W
Fagnano Castello 68 39.34 N 16.03 E
Fagnano Olona 62 45.40 N 8.52 E
Fagnières 50 48.58 N 4.19 E
Faguibine, Lac ⊜ 150 16.45 N 3.54 W
Fagundes, Rio do ≃ 256 22.12 S 43.11 W
Fagurhólsmýri 24a 63.54 N 16.38 W
Fagwir 140 9.33 N 30.25 E
Fahan 48 55.05 N 7.28 W
Fahl, Oued el V 148 31.15 N 4.41 E
Fahraj 128 28.58 N 58.52 E
Fährdorf 54 53.58 N 11.28 E
Fahrland 54 52.28 N 13.01 E
Fahrlander See ⊜ 264a 52.27 N 13.01 E
Fahrnau 58 47.39 N 7.50 E
Fahuaqiao 106 30.52 N 121.25 E
Faial I 148a 38.34 N 28.42 W
Faichuk II 175c 7.23 N 151.40 E
Fā'id 142 30.19 N 32.19 E
Fā'id Military Base ■ 142 30.20 N 32.16 E
Faido 58 46.29 N 8.48 E
Faillon, Lac ⊜ 190 48.21 N 76.38 W
Failsworth 44 53.31 N 2.09 W
Fains-les-Sources 56 48.47 N 5.08 E
Fairbairn Airport ⊠ 171b 35.18 S 149.15 E
Fairbairn Park ♣ 274b 37.47 S 144.55 E
Fairbairn Reservoir ⊜[1] 166 23.45 S 148.00 E
Fairbank 190 42.38 N 92.02 W
Fairbanks, Ak., U.S. 180 64.51 N 147.43 W
Fairbanks, La., U.S. 194 30.00 N 92.02 W
Fair Bluff 192 34.18 N 79.02 W
Fairborn 218 39.49 N 84.01 W
Fairbourne 42 52.41 N 4.03 W
Fairburn 192 33.34 N 84.34 W
Fairbury, Il., U.S. 216 40.44 N 88.30 W
Fairbury, Ne., U.S. 198 40.08 N 97.10 W
Fairchance 188 39.49 N 79.45 W
Fairchild 190 44.36 N 90.57 W
Fairchild Air Force Base ■ 202 47.38 N 117.38 W
Fairchild Creek ≃ 212 43.07 N 80.07 W
Fairdale 216 42.06 N 88.56 W
Faire 116 17.53 N 121.34 E
Fairfax, Al., U.S. 194 32.47 N 85.11 W
Fairfax, Ca., U.S. 226 37.59 N 122.35 W
Fairfax, De., U.S. 285 39.47 N 75.32 W
Fairfax, Mn., U.S. 198 44.31 N 94.43 W
Fairfax, Mo., U.S. 194 40.20 N 95.23 W
Fairfax, Ok., U.S. 196 36.34 N 96.42 W
Fairfax, S.C., U.S. 192 32.57 N 81.14 W
Fairfax, S.D., U.S. 198 43.01 N 98.53 W
Fairfax, Vt., U.S. 188 44.39 N 73.00 W
Fairfax, Va., U.S. 208 38.50 N 77.18 W
Fairfax □[6] 208 38.45 N 77.15 W
Fairfax Forest 284c 38.52 N 77.15 W
Fairfax Park 284c 38.47 N 77.14 W
Fairfax State Recreation Area ♣ 218 39.02 N 86.29 W
Fairfax Station 284c 38.48 N 77.19 W
Fairfield, Austl. 170 33.52 S 150.57 E
Fairfield, Al., U.S. 194 33.33 N 86.47 W
Fairfield, Ca., U.S. 226 38.14 N 122.02 W
Fairfield, Ct., U.S. 210 41.08 N 73.15 W
Fairfield, Id., U.S. 202 43.20 N 114.47 W
Fairfield, Il., U.S. 194 38.22 N 88.21 W
Fairfield, Ia., U.S. 190 41.00 N 91.57 W
Fairfield, Me., U.S. 188 44.35 N 69.35 W
Fairfield, Mt., U.S. 202 47.36 N 111.58 W
Fairfield, Ne., U.S. 198 40.25 N 98.06 W
Fairfield, N.J., U.S. 276 40.53 N 74.16 W
Fairfield, N.Y., U.S. 210 43.08 N 74.55 W
Fairfield, Oh., U.S. 218 39.20 N 84.33 W
Fairfield, Pa., U.S. 214 39.47 N 77.22 W
Fairfield, Tx., U.S. 222 31.43 N 96.09 W
Fairfield □[6] 207 41.15 N 73.20 W
Fairfield Lake ⊜[1] 222 31.50 N 96.05 W
Fairfield University ʊ[2] 276 41.09 N 73.15 W
Fairford 42 51.44 N 1.47 W
Fairgrove 190 43.31 N 83.32 W
Fair Harbor 210 40.38 N 73.11 W
Fairhaven, Ma., U.S. 207 41.38 N 70.54 W
Fair Haven, Mi., U.S. 214 42.40 N 82.39 W
Fair Haven, N.J., U.S. 208 40.21 N 74.02 W
Fair Haven, N.Y., U.S. 210 43.18 N 76.42 W
Fairhaven, Oh., U.S. 218 39.38 N 84.47 W
Fair Haven, Vt., U.S. 188 43.35 N 73.15 W
Fair Haven, Va., U.S. 284c 38.47 N 77.05 W
Fairhaven Bay ⊜ 283 42.26 N 71.21 W
Fair Haven Beach State Park ♣, N.Y., U.S. 210 43.21 N 76.41 W
Fair Haven Beach State Park ♣, N.Y., U.S. 212 43.21 N 76.41 W
Fair Head › 48 55.13 N 6.09 W
Fairhope, Al., U.S. 194 30.31 N 87.54 W
Fairhope, Oh., U.S. 214 40.51 N 81.19 W
Fairhope, Pa., U.S. 214 40.07 N 79.50 W
Fair Isle I 46 59.32 N 1.39 W
Fairknoll 284c 39.05 N 76.59 W
Fairland, In., U.S. 218 39.35 N 85.51 W
Fairland, Md., U.S. 284c 39.05 N 76.58 W
Fairland, Ok., U.S. 196 36.45 N 94.50 W
Fairlane Town Center ➜[9] 281 42.19 N 83.13 W
Fair Lawn, N.J., U.S. 210 40.56 N 74.07 W
Fairlawn, Oh., U.S. 214 41.07 N 81.36 W
Fairlee 284c 38.52 N 77.16 W
Fairleigh Dickinson University (Teaneck) ʊ[2], N.J., U.S. 276 40.53 N 74.02 W
Fairleigh Dickinson University ʊ[2], N.J., U.S. 276 40.50 N 74.07 W
Fairleigh Dickinson University (Florham-Madison) ʊ[2], N.J., U.S. 276 40.46 N 74.26 W
Fairless Hills 208 40.10 N 74.51 W
Fairlie, N.Z. 172 44.06 S 170.50 E
Fairlie, Scot., U.K. 46 55.46 N 4.51 W
Fairlight 42 50.53 N 0.40 E
Fairmont, Il., U.S. 216 41.33 N 88.03 W
Fairmont, Mn., U.S. 198 43.39 N 94.27 W
Fairmont, Ne., U.S. 198 40.38 N 97.35 W
Fairmont, N.C., U.S. 192 34.29 N 79.06 W
Fairmont, Pa., U.S. 279b 40.19 N 79.43 W
Fairmont, Wa., U.S. 224 48.54 N 122.16 W
Fairmont, W.V., U.S. 188 39.29 N 80.08 W
Fairmont City 219 38.40 N 90.06 W
Fairmont Hot Springs 182 50.19 N 115.53 W
Fairmont Reservoir ⊜[1] 228 34.43 N 118.26 W
Fairmont Terrace 282 37.43 N 122.07 W
Fairmount, Ga., U.S. 192 34.26 N 84.42 W
Fairmount, Il., U.S. 194 40.03 N 87.56 W
Fairmount, In., U.S. 216 40.24 N 85.39 W
Fairmount, N.Y., U.S. 210 43.02 N 76.14 W
Fairmount, N.D., U.S. 198 46.03 N 96.36 W
Fairmount City 214 41.01 N 79.19 W
Fairmount Heights 208 38.54 N 76.54 W
Fairmount Park ♣ 285 40.00 N 75.12 W
Fair Ness › 176 63.24 N 72.05 W
Fair Oaks, Ca., U.S. 226 38.38 N 121.16 W
Fair Oaks, Ga., U.S. 192 33.54 N 84.32 W
Fair Oaks, In., U.S. 216 41.05 N 87.16 W
Fairoaks, Pa., U.S. 279b 40.34 N 80.13 W
Fairoaks Airport ⊠ 260 51.21 N 0.32 W
Fair Plain 216 42.05 N 86.27 W
Fairplains 192 36.13 N 81.10 W
Fairplay 200 39.13 N 106.00 W
Fairpoint 214 40.07 N 80.55 W
Fairport, On., Can. 275b 43.49 N 79.05 W
Fairport, N.Y., U.S. 210 43.05 N 77.26 W
Fairport Beach 275b 43.48 N 79.06 W
Fairport Harbor 214 41.44 N 81.16 W
Fairseat 260 51.20 N 0.20 E
Fairton 208 39.22 N 75.13 W
Fairview, Austl. 164 15.33 S 144.19 E
Fairview, Ab., Can. 182 56.04 N 118.23 W
Fairview, Ga., U.S. 192 34.56 N 85.17 W
Fairview, Il., U.S. 190 40.38 N 90.10 W
Fairview, In., U.S. 216 40.18 N 85.11 W
Fairview, Ks., U.S. 198 39.50 N 95.43 W
Fairview, Md., U.S. 208 39.09 N 76.29 W
Fairview, Mi., U.S. 190 44.43 N 84.03 W
Fairview, Mt., U.S. 198 47.51 N 104.02 W
Fairview, N.J., U.S. 276 40.51 N 73.58 W
Fairview, N.Y., U.S. 210 41.43 N 73.55 W
Fairview, Oh., U.S. 214 40.03 N 81.14 W
Fairview, Ok., U.S. 196 36.16 N 98.28 W
Fairview, Pa., U.S. 214 42.01 N 80.15 W
Fairview, Tn., U.S. 194 35.58 N 87.07 W
Fairview, Ut,. U.S. 200 39.37 N 111.26 W
Fairview, W.V., U.S. 188 39.35 N 80.14 W
Fairview Heights 219 38.10 N 90.00 W
Fairview Lanes 214 41.23 N 82.40 W
Fairview Mall ➜[9] 275b 43.47 N 79.21 W
Fairview Park, In., U.S. 194 39.40 N 87.25 W
Fairview Park, Oh., U.S. 214 41.26 N 81.51 W
Fairview Park, Pa., U.S. 210 41.10 N 75.53 W
Fairview Peak ∧, Nv., U.S. 204 39.14 N 118.08 W
Fairview Peak ∧, Or., U.S. 202 43.35 N 122.39 W
Fairview Pointe Claire Centre ➜[9] 275a 45.28 N 73.50 W
Fairview Shores 220 28.35 N 81.23 W
Fairview Village 285 40.10 N 75.23 W
Fairvilla 220 28.35 N 81.24 W
Fairville 285 39.51 N 75.38 W
Fairweather Mountain ∧ 180 58.54 N 137.32 W
Fairy Lake ⊜ 212 45.20 N 79.11 W
Fairy Meadow 170 34.23 S 150.54 E
Fairy Stone State Park ♣ 192 36.48 N 80.06 W
Fairy Water ≃ 48 54.37 N 7.20 W
Fais I 108 9.46 N 140.31 E
Faisalabad (Lyallpur) 123 31.25 N 73.05 E
Faison 192 35.06 N 78.08 W
Faistós ⊥ 38 35.01 N 24.48 E
Faith 198 45.01 N 102.02 W
Faiyum → Al-Fayyūm 142 29.19 N 30.50 E
Faizābād 124 26.47 N 82.08 E
Fajansovyj 76 54.04 N 34.24 E
Fajardo 240m 18.20 N 65.39 W
Fajou, Îlet à I 241o 16.21 N 61.35 W
Fajr, Wādī V 128 30.06 N 38.18 E
Fajzabad 85 38.34 N 69.19 E
Fakahatchee Strand ≡ 220 26.10 N 81.35 W
Fakaofo I[1] 14 9.22 S 171.14 W
Fakarava I[1] 14 16.20 S 145.37 W
Fakejev 80 48.57 N 49.56 E
Fakel 80 57.38 N 53.02 E
Fakenham 42 52.50 N 0.51 E
Fakfak 164 2.55 S 132.18 E
Fakılı 130 39.13 N 35.00 E
Fakīrganj 124 25.58 N 90.02 E
Fakī Şādiq 140 12.08 N 23.55 E
Fakrinkotti 140 18.01 N 31.20 E
Fakse 41 55.15 N 12.08 E
Fakse Bugt c 41 55.10 N 12.15 E
Fakse Ladeplads 41 55.13 N 12.11 E
Faku 104 42.30 N 123.24 E
Fal ≃ 42 50.08 N 5.02 W
Falaba 150 9.51 N 11.19 W
Faladyé 150 13.08 N 8.20 W
Falaise 32 48.54 N 0.12 W
Fālākāta 124 26.32 N 89.12 E
Falam 110 22.55 N 93.40 E
Falāvarjān 128 32.33 N 51.30 E
Falcade 64 46.21 N 11.51 E
Falcão 256 22.17 S 44.16 W
Fălciu 38 46.18 N 28.08 E
Falck 56 49.14 N 6.38 E
Falcognana di Sotto ➜[8] 267a 41.45 N 12.33 E
Falcón □[3] 246 11.00 N 69.50 W
Falcon, Cap › 34 35.46 N 0.48 W
Falcon, Cape › 224 45.46 N 123.59 W
Falcón, Presa (Falcon Reservoir) ⊜[1] 196 26.37 N 99.11 W
Falconara Albanese 68 39.16 N 16.05 E
Falconara Alta 66 43.37 N 13.24 E
Falconara Marittima 66 43.37 N 13.24 E
Falconbridge 190 46.35 N 80.48 W
Falconcrest 285 39.58 N 75.33 W
Falcone 70 38.07 N 15.05 E
Falcone, Capo del › 71 40.58 N 8.12 E
Falconer 214 42.07 N 79.11 W
Falcon Heights 202 42.08 N 121.45 W
Falcon Reservoir (Presa Falcón) ⊜[1] 196 26.37 N 99.11 W
Falconwood 210 43.00 N 78.57 W
Faldsled 41 55.09 N 10.09 E
Faléa 150 12.16 N 11.17 W
Faleasao 174y 14.13 S 169.32 W
Falelatai 175a 13.55 S 171.59 W
Falelima 175a 13.32 S 172.41 W
Falémé ≃ 150 14.46 N 12.14 W
Falenki 80 58.22 N 51.35 E
Falerii Novi ⊥ 66 42.16 N 12.20 E
Falerna 68 39.00 N 16.10 E
Falerone 66 43.06 N 13.28 E
Fălești 38 47.34 N 27.43 E
Falfurrias 196 27.13 N 98.08 W
Falher 182 55.44 N 117.12 W
Falicon 62 43.45 N 7.17 E
Fálirou, Órmos c 267c 37.56 N 23.40 E
Falkenberg, Dtsch. 54 52.48 N 13.58 E
Falkenberg, Dtsch. 54 51.35 N 13.14 E
Falkenberg, Dtsch. 60 49.52 N 12.14 E
Falkenberg, Dtsch. 60 48.28 N 12.43 E
Falkenberg, Sve. 26 56.54 N 12.28 E
Falkenberg ➜[8] 264a 52.34 N 13.33 E
Falkenhagen, Dtsch. 54 53.12 N 12.12 E
Falkenhagen, Dtsch. 54 52.26 N 14.19 E
Falkenhagener See ⊜ 264a 52.34 N 13.08 E
Falkenhain 54 51.25 N 12.53 E
Falkenrehde 264a 52.30 N 12.56 E
Falkensee 54 52.33 N 13.04 E
Falkenstein, Dtsch. 54 50.29 N 12.22 E
Falkenstein, Dtsch. 60 49.06 N 12.29 E
Falkenthal 54 52.54 N 13.17 E
Falkirk 46 56.00 N 3.48 W
Falkland, B.C., Can. 182 50.30 N 119.33 W
Falkland, Scot., U.K. 46 56.15 N 3.12 W
Falkland-Inseln → Falkland Islands □[2] 254 51.45 S 59.00 W
Falkland Islands □[2], S.A. 244 51.45 S 59.00 W
Falkland Islands □[2], S.A. 254 51.45 S 59.00 W
Falkland Plateau ✦[3] 18 51.00 S 50.00 W
Falkland Sound ⩌ 254 51.45 S 59.25 W
Falköping 26 58.10 N 13.31 E
Falkville 194 34.22 N 86.54 W
Fall ≃, On., Can. 212 44.59 N 76.22 W
Fall ≃, Ks., U.S. 198 37.24 N 95.40 W
Fall ≃, Wa., U.S. 224 46.47 N 123.30 W
Falla 40 58.41 N 15.45 E
Fallais 56 50.37 N 5.10 E
Fallbach 61 48.39 N 16.25 E
Fallbrook 228 33.22 N 117.15 W
Fallbrook Square ➜[9] 280 34.12 N 118.38 W
Fall City 224 47.34 N 121.53 W
Fall Creek 190 44.45 N 91.16 W
Fall Creek ≃, In., U.S. 218 39.47 N 86.11 W
Fall Creek ≃, N.Y., U.S. 210 42.28 N 76.31 W
Fall Creek Falls State Park ♣, Tn., U.S. 192 35.39 N 85.25 W
Fall Creek Falls State Park ♣, Tn., U.S. 194 35.39 N 85.25 W
Fallen Jerusalem I 240m 18.25 N 64.27 W
Fallen Leaf 226 38.53 N 120.04 W
Fallen Leaf Reservoir ⊜[1] 226 38.54 N 120.03 W
Fallentimber 214 40.41 N 78.30 W
Fallentimber Creek ≃ 182 51.45 N 114.39 W
Fallen Timbers State Memorial ⊥ 216 41.33 N 83.42 W
Fallin 46 56.06 N 3.52 W
Falling ≃ 192 37.01 N 78.55 W
Fallingbostel 52 52.52 N 9.41 E
Falling Creek ≃ 208 37.26 N 77.26 W
Fallon, Mt., U.S. 198 46.50 N 105.07 W
Fallon, Nv., U.S. 204 39.28 N 118.46 W
Fall River, Ks., U.S. 198 37.36 N 96.01 W
Fall River, Ma., U.S. 207 41.42 N 71.09 W
Fall River, Wi., U.S. 190 43.23 N 89.02 W
Fall River Lake ⊜[1] 198 37.42 N 96.08 W
Fall River Mills 204 41.00 N 121.26 W
Falls 210 41.28 N 75.51 W
Falls □[6] 222 31.17 N 96.55 W
Fallsburg 210 41.44 N 74.36 W
Falls Church 208 38.53 N 77.11 W
Falls City, Ne., U.S. 198 40.03 N 95.36 W
Falls City, Or., U.S. 202 44.51 N 123.26 W
Falls Creek, Austl. 170 34.59 S 150.36 E
Falls Creek, Pa., U.S. 214 41.09 N 78.48 W
Falls Creek ≃ 226 37.57 N 119.46 W
Fallsington 208 40.12 N 74.48 W
Falls Lake ⊜[1] 192 36.00 N 78.45 W
Falls Pond ⊜ 283 41.58 N 71.20 W
Falls Run ≃ 284b 39.22 N 76.52 W
Fallston 208 39.31 N 76.25 W
Falls Village 207 41.57 N 73.21 W
Falmer 42 50.51 N 0.04 W
Falmey 150 12.36 N 2.51 E
Falmouth, Jam. 241q 18.30 N 77.39 W
Falmouth, Eng., U.K. 42 50.08 N 5.04 W
Falmouth, Ky., U.S. 218 38.40 N 84.19 W
Falmouth, Me., U.S. 188 43.43 N 70.14 W
Falmouth, Ma., U.S. 207 41.33 N 70.36 W
Falmouth, Va., U.S. 208 38.19 N 77.28 W
Falmouth Bay c 42 50.05 N 5.01 W
Falmouth Heights 207 41.33 N 70.36 W
False Cape ›, Fl., U.S. 220 28.35 N 80.34 W
False Cape ›, Va., U.S. 208 36.39 N 76.51 W
False Divi Point › 122 15.43 N 80.49 E
False Ducks Islands II 212 43.57 N 76.49 W
False Pass 180 54.52 N 163.24 W
Falset 34 41.08 N 0.49 E
Falsino ≃ 250 0.56 N 51.35 W
Fal'šivyj Gelendžik 78 44.31 N 38.09 E
Falso, Cabo ›, Hond. 236 15.12 N 83.20 W
Falso, Cabo ›, Rep. Dom. 238 17.47 N 71.41 W
Falso Cabo de Hornos › 254 55.43 S 68.05 W
Falster I 41 54.48 N 11.58 E
Falsterbo 41 55.24 N 12.50 E
Falstone 44 55.11 N 2.25 W
Fălticeni 38 47.28 N 26.18 E
Falun, Sve. 40 60.36 N 15.38 E
Falun, Zhg. 107 29.58 N 104.29 E
Falzarego, Passo di)(64 46.31 N 12.00 E
Fam, Kepulauan II 164 0.40 S 130.15 E
Fama 256 21.25 S 46.51 W
Fama, Ouadi V 146 15.22 N 20.34 E
Famagusta → Gazimağusa 130 35.07 N 33.57 E
Famaillá 252 27.03 S 65.24 W
Famatina 252 28.55 S 67.31 W
Famatina, Sierra de ⩕ 252 29.00 S 67.51 W
Fameck 56 49.18 N 6.07 E
Famenne ➜[1] 56 50.10 N 5.15 E
Familleureux 50 50.31 N 4.12 E
Family Lake ⊜ 184 51.54 N 95.30 W
Fan ≃ 104 42.16 N 123.40 E
Fana 150 12.47 N 6.57 W
Fanaco, Lago ⊜ 70 37.39 N 13.33 E
Fanad Head › 48 55.16 N 7.38 W
Fanado ≃ 255 17.10 S 42.40 W
Fanambana 157b 13.34 S 50.00 E
Fanan I 175c 7.11 N 151.59 E
Fanano 64 44.12 N 10.47 E
Fanārah 142 30.17 N 32.21 E
Fanchang 100 31.07 N 118.12 E
Fanch'eng → Xiangfan 102 32.03 N 112.01 E
Fancher, Il., U.S. 219 39.16 N 88.47 W
Fancher, N.Y., U.S. 210 43.15 N 66.06 W
Fanchon, Pointe › 238 18.26 N 74.29 W
Fanchuan 100 32.40 N 119.42 E
Fancy 241h 13.22 N 61.11 W
Fancy Creek ≃ 198 39.28 N 96.45 W
Fancy Prairie 219 39.59 N 89.36 W
Fandriana 157b 20.14 S 47.23 E
Fane ≃ 48 53.57 N 6.22 W
Fanepura 123 31.29 N 72.54 E
Faneromenis Monastery ʊ[1] 267c 37.59 N 23.26 E
Fang 110 19.55 N 99.13 E
Fangaga ∧ 144 17.30 N 38.01 E
Fangak 140 9.04 N 30.53 E
Fangbian 106 31.42 N 119.06 E
Fangcheng, Zhg. 100 33.16 N 112.59 E
Fangcheng, Zhg. 102 21.49 N 108.22 E
Fangcheng, Zhg. 105 39.16 N 115.28 E
Fangcun, Zhg. 100 29.04 N 118.36 E
Fangcun, Zhg. 100 26.50 N 118.15 E
Fangdao 100 27.01 N 118.06 E
Fängersee ⊜ 264a 52.35 N 13.50 E
Fangguan 105 39.20 N 115.58 E
Fangji 100 31.54 N 115.35 E
Fangjiachang 107 30.05 N 104.16 E
Fangjiazhuang 106 30.45 N 119.53 E
Fangliao 100 22.22 N 120.35 E
Fangmutun 98 42.34 N 124.34 E
Fangniu 102 27.40 N 100.25 E
Fangshan, T'aiwan 100 22.16 N 120.39 E
Fangshan, Zhg. 98 39.42 N 115.58 E
Fang Shan ∧ 106 31.40 N 119.16 E
Fang Shan ∧[2] 106 31.29 N 119.09 E
Fangshanzhen 104 41.54 N 122.05 E
Fangshen 104 42.02 N 124.04 E
Fangshengpu 107 30.20 N 104.54 E
Fangsi 98 36.56 N 116.29 E
Fangtai 106 31.19 N 121.12 E
Fangxi 100 28.23 N 114.38 E
Fangxian 102 32.02 N 110.45 E
Fangxianzhen 106 32.00 N 119.44 E
Fangzheng 89 45.50 N 128.50 E
Fangzi 98 36.36 N 119.07 E
Fanhões 266c 38.53 N 9.09 W
Fanipal' 76 53.45 N 27.20 E
Fanjakana 157b 21.10 S 46.53 E
Fanjiadai 106 32.04 N 120.15 E
Fanjiadian 104 41.41 N 121.50 E
Fanjiatun 89 43.43 N 125.06 E
Fanjiazhuang 105 39.12 N 117.20 E
Fannaråki ∧ 26 61.31 N 7.55 E
Fannettsburg 214 40.04 N 77.50 W
Fannich, Loch ⊜ 46 57.38 N 5.00 W
Fannrem 26 63.16 N 9.50 E
Fanny, Mount ∧ 202 45.20 N 117.41 W
Fanny Bay 182 49.30 N 124.50 W
Fano 66 43.50 N 13.01 E
Fanø I 26 55.25 N 8.25 E
Fanqiao 100 28.48 N 121.10 E
Fans, Col des)(62 44.56 N 4.47 E
Fanshan, Zhg. 100 27.21 N 120.24 E
Fanshan, Zhg. 105 40.13 N 115.25 E
Fanshang 106 31.40 N 120.01 E
Fanshawe Lake ⊜ 212 43.05 N 81.10 W
Fansher Creek ≃ 214 42.37 N 82.01 W
Fanshui 100 33.07 N 119.25 E
Fan Si Pan ∧ 110 22.15 N 103.46 E
Fantasy Island ♣ 284a 43.02 N 78.58 W
Fanthyttan 40 59.40 N 15.06 E
Fanwood 276 40.38 N 74.23 W
Fanxian 98 35.57 N 115.38 E
Fanzhen 98 36.14 N 117.21 E
Faoileann, Bàgh nam c 46 57.23 N 7.17 W
Faqīrah, Wādī V 142 28.52 N 30.57 E
Faqqū'ah 132 32.30 N 35.24 E
Fāqūs 142 30.44 N 31.48 E
Farab 85 39.14 N 67.28 E
Faraday ʊ[3] 9 65.15 S 64.16 W
Faraday, Mount ∧ 172 42.02 S 171.34 E
Faradje 154 3.44 N 29.43 E
Faradofay 157b 25.02 S 47.00 E
Farafangana 157b 22.49 S 47.50 E
Farāfirah, Al-Wāḥat al- ⫪[4] 140 27.15 N 28.10 E
Farāh 128 32.22 N 62.07 E
Farāh □[4] 128 33.00 N 62.30 E
Farāh ≃ 128 31.29 N 61.24 E
Faraḥābād 267d 35.42 N 51.30 E
Farahalana 157b 14.26 S 50.10 E
Farā'id, Jabal al- ∧ 140 23.31 N 35.20 E
Fara in Sabina 66 42.12 N 12.43 E
Farallón, Paso del ⩌ 288 34.41 S 57.57 W
Farallon de Medinilla I 108 16.01 N 146.04 E
Farallon de Pajaros I 108 20.32 N 144.54 E
Farallon Islands II 204 37.43 N 123.03 W
Faramana 150 12.03 N 4.40 W
Faranah 150 10.02 N 10.44 W
Farángi Samariás (Samaria Gorge) V 38 35.18 N 24.00 E
Fara Novarese 62 45.33 N 8.27 E
Farasān, Jazā'ir II 144 16.48 N 41.54 E
Farasān al-Kabīr I 144 16.42 N 42.00 E
Faratsiho 157b 19.24 S 46.57 E
Faraulep I[1] 108 8.36 N 144.33 E
Farber 219 39.16 N 91.34 W
Farbovane 78 50.09 N 31.51 E
Farcău, Vârful ∧ 38 47.56 N 24.27 E
Farchant 64 47.32 N 11.06 E
Farcy 261 48.31 N 2.37 E
Fardes ≃ 34 37.35 N 3.00 W
Fare ≃ 50 47.39 N 0.14 E
Fareara, Pointe › 174s 17.52 S 149.39 W
Fareham 42 50.51 N 1.10 W
Fårevejle 41 55.48 N 11.27 E
Farewell 180 62.31 N 153.53 W
Farewell, Cape › 172 40.30 S 172.41 E
Farewell Spit ›[2] 172 40.31 S 172.52 E
Färgelanda 26 58.34 N 11.59 E
Fargniers 50 49.39 N 3.19 E
Fargo 198 46.52 N 96.47 W
Far Hills 276 40.41 N 74.38 W
Faria ≃ 287a 22.53 S 43.15 W
Fāri'ah, Wādī al- V 132 32.06 N 35.31 E
Faribault 190 44.17 N 93.16 W
Faribault, Lac ⊜ 176 59.00 N 72.00 W
Farīdābad 124 28.26 N 77.19 E
Farīdganj 126 23.08 N 90.45 E
Farīdkot 123 30.40 N 74.45 E
Farīdnagar 124 28.46 N 77.37 E
Farīdpur, Bngl. 126 24.10 N 89.26 E
Farīdpur, Bngl. 126 23.36 N 89.50 E
Farīdpur, India 124 28.13 N 79.33 E
Farié Haoussa 150 13.48 N 1.38 E
Fārigh, Wādī al- V 146 29.59 N 19.25 E
Färila 26 61.48 N 15.51 E
Farilhões II 34 39.28 N 9.34 W
Farim 150 12.27 N 15.17 W
Farīmān 128 35.43 N 59.53 E
Farina 219 38.50 N 88.46 W
Faringdon 42 51.40 N 1.35 W
Farington 262 53.43 N 2.42 W
Farinha ≃ 250 6.51 S 47.30 W
Farini d'Olmo 62 44.43 N 9.34 E
Fariš 85 40.35 N 66.52 E
Fariske 130 36.37 N 32.38 E
Fārisķūr 142 31.20 N 31.43 E
Farit, Amba ∧ 144 10.56 N 38.58 E
Färjestaden 26 56.39 N 16.27 E
Farkwa 154 5.24 S 35.36 E
Farleigh 260 51.19 N 0.02 W
Farley 190 42.26 N 91.00 W
Farley Green 260 51.12 N 0.29 W
Farmahīn 128 34.30 N 49.41 E
Farmer City 216 40.14 N 88.38 W
Farmers Branch 222 32.55 N 96.53 W
Farmersburg 194 39.14 N 87.22 W
Farmers Fork 208 38.02 N 76.45 W
Farmer's Museum ʊ 210 42.42 N 74.57 W
Farmers Retreat 218 38.58 N 85.06 W
Farmersville, Ca., U.S. 226 36.17 N 119.12 W
Farmersville, Il., U.S. 219 39.26 N 89.39 W
Farmersville, Pa., U.S. 208 40.08 N 76.10 W
Farmersville, Tx., U.S. 222 33.09 N 96.21 W
Farmersville Station 210 42.26 N 78.22 W
Farmerville 194 32.46 N 92.24 W
Farmingdale, N.J., U.S. 208 40.11 N 74.10 W
Farmingdale, N.Y., U.S. 276 40.43 N 73.26 W
Farmington, Ca., U.S. 226 37.56 N 120.59 W
Farmington, Ct., U.S. 207 41.43 N 72.49 W
Farmington, De., U.S. 208 38.52 N 75.34 W
Farmington, Il., U.S. 190 40.41 N 90.00 W
Farmington, Ia., U.S. 190 40.38 N 91.44 W
Farmington, Me., U.S. 188 44.40 N 70.09 W
Farmington, Mi., U.S. 216 42.27 N 83.22 W
Farmington, Mn., U.S. 190 44.38 N 93.08 W
Farmington, Mo., U.S. 194 37.47 N 90.25 W
Farmington, Mt., U.S. 182 47.54 N 112.11 W
Farmington, N.H., U.S. 188 43.23 N 71.03 W
Farmington, N.M., U.S. 200 36.43 N 108.13 W
Farmington, Ut,. U.S. 200 40.58 N 111.53 W
Farmington ≃ 207 41.51 N 72.38 W
Farmington, West Branch ≃ 207 41.52 N 72.57 W
Farmington Flood Control Basin ⊜[1] 226 37.55 N 120.55 W
Farmington Hills 281 42.28 N 83.23 W
Farmingville 210 40.49 N 73.01 W
Farmland 218 40.11 N 85.07 W
Far Mountain ∧ 182 52.46 N 125.17 W
Farm Pond ⊜, Ma., U.S. 283 42.17 N 71.26 W
Farm Pond ⊜, Ma., U.S. 283 42.14 N 71.21 W
Farmville, N.C., U.S. 192 35.35 N 77.35 W
Farmville, Va., U.S. 192 37.18 N 78.23 W
Färna 40 59.47 N 15.51 E
Farnam 198 40.42 N 100.12 W
Farnawā 142 30.59 N 30.39 E
Farnborough 42 51.17 N 0.46 W
Farnborough ➜[8] 260 51.21 N 0.04 E
Farncombe 260 51.12 N 0.36 W
Farndon 44 53.05 N 0.51 W
Färnebofjärden ⊜ 40 60.14 N 16.47 E
Farne Islands II 44 55.38 N 1.38 W
Farnham, P.Q., Can. 206 45.17 N 72.59 W
Farnham, Eng., U.K. 42 51.13 N 0.49 W
Farnham, N.Y., U.S. 214 42.36 N 79.05 W
Farnham, Va., U.S. 208 37.53 N 76.37 W
Farnham, Mount ∧ 182 50.29 N 116.30 W
Farnham Common 260 51.33 N 0.37 W
Farnham Royal 260 51.32 N 0.37 W
Farnhamville 198 42.16 N 94.24 W
Farningham 260 51.23 N 0.13 E
Farnworth, Eng., U.K. 44 53.33 N 2.24 W
Farnworth, Eng., U.K. 262 53.23 N 2.44 W
Faro, Bra. 250 2.11 S 56.44 W
Faro, Port. 34 37.01 N 7.56 W
Faro □[5] 34 37.15 N 8.00 W
Faro ≃ 146 9.21 N 12.55 E
Faro, Punta del › 70 38.16 N 15.39 E
Faro, Réserve du ➜[4] 146 8.10 N 12.35 E
Färöer → Faeroe Islands □[2] 22 62.00 N 7.00 W
Fårön I 26 57.56 N 19.08 E
Fårösund 26 57.52 N 19.03 E
Farquhar, Cape › 162 23.37 S 113.37 E
Farquhar Group II 138 10.10 S 51.10 E
Farr 46 57.21 N 4.12 W
Farra d'Isonzo 64 45.56 N 13.31 E
Farragut 198 40.43 N 95.28 W
Farragut State Recreation Area ♣ 202 47.55 N 116.35 W
Farrandsville 210 41.10 N 77.31 W
Farrar ≃ 46 57.24 N 4.50 W
Farrar Pond ⊜ 283 42.25 N 71.21 W
Farrars Creek ≃ 166 25.35 S 140.43 E
Farrāshband 128 28.53 N 52.06 E
Farrell 214 41.12 N 80.29 W
Farrell Flat 168b 33.50 S 138.47 E
Farrer Park ♣ 271c 1.19 N 103.51 E
Farrington Lake ⊜ 276 40.26 N 74.28 W
Farrington Lake Heights 276 40.26 N 74.27 W
Far Rockaway ➜[8] 276 40.36 N 73.45 W
Farrukhābād 124 27.24 N 79.34 E
Farrukhnagar, India 124 28.27 N 76.49 E
Farrukhnagar, India 272a 28.43 N 77.23 E
Fārs □[4] 128 29.00 N 53.00 E
Fársala 38 39.18 N 22.23 E
Farschviller 56 49.06 N 6.54 E
Fārsī 128 33.47 N 63.15 E
Fārsī, Jazīreh-ye I 128 27.58 N 50.11 E
Farsīs 142 30.40 N 31.14 E
Farsø 26 56.47 N 9.21 E
Farsta 40 59.14 N 18.04 E
Farsund 26 58.05 N 6.48 E
Fartak, Ra's › 118 15.38 N 52.15 E
Farukolu I 122 6.12 N 73.16 E
Farum 41 55.48 N 12.22 E
Fårvang 41 56.16 N 9.44 E
Farvel, Kap › 176 59.45 N 44.00 W
Farwell, Mi., U.S. 190 43.50 N 84.52 W
Farwell, Tx., U.S. 196 30.15 N 103.15 W
Fāryāb □[4] 128 36.00 N 65.00 E
Fasā 128 28.56 N 53.42 E
Fasano 68 40.50 N 17.22 E
Fashchivka 83 48.16 N 38.37 E
Fashkhah, 'Ayn ⫪[4] 132 31.43 N 35.27 E
Fåsjön ⊜ 40 59.36 N 14.58 E
Fassa 150 13.26 N 8.15 W
Fassberg 52 52.54 N 10.10 E
Fasterholt 41 56.01 N 9.07 E
Fastiv 78 50.06 N 29.55 E
Fastnet Rock I[2] 48 51.24 N 9.35 W
Fastoveckaja 78 45.56 N 40.09 E
Fatagar Tuting, Tanjung › 164 2.46 S 131.57 E
Fataki 154 4.46 S 28.11 E
Fatala ≃ 150 10.13 N 14.00 W
Fat Deer Key I 220 24.44 N 81.00 W
Fate 222 32.56 N 96.23 W
Fatehābād, India 123 29.31 N 75.27 E
Fatehābād, India 124 27.01 N 78.19 E
Fatehgarh, India 124 27.22 N 79.38 E
Fatehgarh, India 124 24.48 N 76.58 E
Fatehgarh Chūriān 123 31.52 N 74.58 E
Fatehjang 123 33.34 N 72.39 E
Fatehpur, India 120 27.59 N 74.57 E
Fatehpur, India 124 25.56 N 80.48 E
Fatehpur, India 124 27.10 N 81.13 E
Fatehpur, India 126 22.17 N 88.14 E
Fatehpur, India 126 24.05 N 87.44 E
Fatehpur, Pāk. 123 31.09 N 71.13 E
Fatehpur Sīkri 124 27.06 N 77.40 E
Fathai 140 8.05 N 31.48 E
Fathom Five National Marine Park ♣ 190 45.15 N 81.40 W
Fatick 150 14.20 N 16.25 W
Fatick □[4] 150 14.00 N 16.30 W
Fatigue, Mount ∧ 169 38.34 S 146.18 E
Fatima, Arg. 258 34.26 S 59.00 W
Fátima, Port. 34 39.37 N 8.39 W
Fatima do Sol 255 22.16 S 54.25 W
Fatima do Sul 252 22.16 S 54.22 W
Fāṭimah, Wādī V 144 21.27 N 39.09 E
Fatoto 150 13.26 N 13.52 W
Fat'ož 78 52.07 N 35.52 E
Fatsa 130 41.02 N 37.31 E
Fatshan → Foshan 100 23.03 N 113.09 E
Fat Tong Point › 271d 22.16 N 114.15 E
Fatu-Berlio 112 8.56 S 125.52 E
Fatulla 126 23.38 N 90.29 E
Fatumu 174w 21.13 S 175.07 W
Fatunda 152 4.08 S 17.13 E
Fatwā 124 25.31 N 85.19 E
Fauabu 175e 8.34 S 160.43 E
Faucigny 58 46.07 N 6.22 E
Faucille, Col de la)(58 46.22 N 6.02 E
Faucilles, Monts ⩕ 58 48.07 N 6.16 E
Faucogney 58 47.51 N 6.34 E
Faucon-de-Barcelonnette 62 44.24 N 6.41 E
Fauglia 66 43.34 N 10.31 E
Fauldhouse 46 55.50 N 3.37 W
Faulkton 198 45.02 N 99.07 W
Faulquemont 56 49.03 N 6.36 E
Fauquembergues 50 50.36 N 2.05 E
Fauquier 182 49.53 N 118.05 W
Fauquier □[6] 208 38.35 N 77.35 W
Făurei 38 45.06 N 27.14 E
Faure Island I 162 25.51 S 113.52 E
Fauresmith 158 29.42 S 25.21 E
Fauro Island I 175e 6.55 S 156.04 E
Fauske 24 67.15 N 15.24 E
Faust 182 55.19 N 115.38 W
Faustovo 82 55.26 N 38.29 E
Fauville-en-Caux 50 49.39 N 0.35 E
Fauvillers 56 49.51 N 5.40 E
Faux-Cap 157b 25.33 S 45.32 E
Fåvang 26 61.27 N 10.11 E
Favara 70 37.19 N 13.39 E
Faverges 62 45.45 N 6.18 E
Faverney 58 47.46 N 6.06 E
Faversham 42 51.20 N 0.53 E
Favières 261 48.46 N 2.47 E
Favignana 70 37.56 N 12.20 E
Favignana, Isola I 70 37.56 N 12.19 E
Favoriten ➜[8] 264b 48.11 N 16.23 E
Favourable Lake ⊜ 184 52.53 N 93.56 W
Favrieux 261 48.57 N 1.39 E
Fawcett 182 54.32 N 114.05 W
Fawcett Lake ⊜ 182 55.19 N 113.57 W
Fawkham Green 260 51.22 N 0.17 E
Fawkner 274b 37.43 S 144.58 E
Fawkner Park ♣ 274b 37.50 S 144.59 E
Fawley 42 50.49 N 1.20 W
Fawn ≃, On., Can. 176 55.22 N 88.20 W
Fawn ≃, U.S. 216 41.51 N 85.40 W
Fawn Grove 208 39.44 N 76.27 W
Fawnie Nose ∧ 182 53.16 N 125.08 W
Fawnie Range ⩕ 182 53.10 N 125.00 W
Fawsett Farms 284c 38.59 N 77.14 W
Faxaflói c 24a 64.25 N 23.00 W
Faxälven ≃ 26 63.13 N 17.13 E
Faxinal 255 23.59 S 51.22 W
Faxinal do Soturno 252 29.37 S 53.26 W
Faxon 210 41.15 N 76.58 W
Faya-Largeau 146 17.55 N 19.07 E
Fayd 128 27.07 N 42.27 E
Fayence 62 43.37 N 6.41 E
Fayerweather Island I 276 41.08 N 73.13 W
Fayette, Al., U.S. 194 33.41 N 87.49 W
Fayette, Ia., U.S. 190 42.50 N 91.48 W
Fayette, Ms., U.S. 194 31.42 N 91.03 W
Fayette, Mo., U.S. 194 39.08 N 92.41 W
Fayette, N.Y., U.S. 210 42.49 N 76.49 W
Fayette, Oh., U.S. 216 41.40 N 84.19 W
Fayette □[6], Il., U.S. 219 38.58 N 89.06 W
Fayette □[6], In., U.S. 218 39.39 N 85.08 W
Fayette □[6], Ky., U.S. 218 38.07 N 84.30 W
Fayette □[6], Oh., U.S. 218 39.32 N 83.26 W
Fayette □[6], Pa., U.S. 214 40.05 N 79.39 W
Fayette □[6], Tx., U.S. 222 29.50 N 96.57 W
Fayette City 214 40.06 N 79.50 W
Fayetteville, Ar., U.S. 194 36.03 N 94.09 W
Fayetteville, Ga., U.S. 192 33.26 N 84.27 W
Fayetteville, Il., U.S. 219 38.22 N 89.48 W
Fayetteville, N.Y., U.S. 210 43.02 N 76.00 W
Fayetteville, N.C., U.S. 192 35.03 N 78.52 W
Fayetteville, Oh., U.S. 218 39.11 N 83.55 W
Fayetteville, Pa., U.S. 208 39.54 N 77.33 W
Fayetteville, Tn., U.S. 194 35.09 N 86.34 W
Fayetteville, Tx., U.S. 222 29.54 N 96.41 W

Symbol	English	Deutsch	Español	Français	Português
≃	River	Fluß	Río	Rivière	Rio
≋	Canal	Kanal	Canal	Canal	Canal
⌞	Waterfall, Rapids	Wasserfall, Stromschnellen	Cascada, Rápidos	Chute d'eau, Rapides	Cascata, Rápidos
⩌	Strait	Meeresstraße	Estrecho	Détroit	Estreito
c	Bay, Gulf	Bucht, Golf	Bahía, Golfo	Baie, Golfe	Baía, Golfo
⊜	Lake, Lakes	See, Seen	Lago, Lagos	Lac, Lacs	Lago, Lagos
≡	Swamp	Sumpf	Pantano	Marais	Pântano
⍓	Ice Features, Glacier	Eis- und Gletscherformen	Accidentes Glaciales	Formes glaciaires	Acidentes glaciares
⫪	Other Hydrographic Features	Andere Hydrographische Objekte	Otros Elementos Hidrográficos	Autres données hydrographiques	Outros acidentes hidrográficos
✦	Submarine Features	Untermeerische Objekte	Accidentes Submarinos	Formes de relief sous-marin	Acidentes submarinos
□	Political Unit	Politische Einheit	Unidad Política	Entité politique	Unidade política
ʊ	Cultural Institution	Kulturelle Institution	Institución Cultural	Institution culturelle	Instituição cultural
⊥	Historical Site	Historische Stätte	Sitio Histórico	Site historique	Sitio histórico
♣	Recreational Site	Erholungs- und Ferienort	Sitio de Recreo	Centre de loisirs	Area de Lazer
⊠	Airport	Flughafen	Aeropuerto	Aéroport	Aeroporto
■	Military Installation	Militäranlage	Instalación Militar	Installation militaire	Instalação militar
➜	Miscellaneous	Verschiedenes	Misceláneo	Divers	Diversos

Symbols in the index entries represent the broad categories identified in the key at the right. Symbols with superior numbers (⋀¹) identify subcategories (see complete key on page *I · 1*).

Los símbolos incluidos en el texto del índice representan las grandes categorías identificadas con la clave a la derecha. Los símbolos con números en su parte superior (⋀¹) identifican las subcategorías (véase la clave completa en la página *I · 1*).

Symbole im Register stellen die rechts im Schlüssel erklärten Kategorien dar. Symbole mit hochgestellten Ziffern (⋀¹) bezeichnen Unterabteilungen einer Kategorie (vgl. vollständiger Schlüssel auf Seite *I · 1*).

Os símbolos incluídos no texto do índice representam as grandes categorias identificadas com a chave à direita. Os símbolos com números em sua parte superior (⋀¹) identificam as subcategorias (veja-se a chave completa à página *I · 1*).

Les symboles de l'index représentent les catégories indiquées dans la légende à droite. Les symboles suivis d'un indice (⋀¹) représentent des sous-catégories (voir légende complète à la page *I · 1*).

	English	Deutsch	Español	Français	Português
⋀	Mountain	Berg	Montaña	Montagne	Montanha
⋀⋀	Mountains	Gebirge	Montañas	Montagnes	Montanhas
)(	Pass	Paß	Paso	Col	Passo
V	Valley, Canyon	Tal, Cañon	Valle, Cañón	Vallée, Canyon	Vale, Canhão
=	Plain	Ebene	Llano	Plaine	Planicie
⊁	Cape	Kap	Cabo	Cap	Cabo
I	Island	Insel	Isla	Île	Ilha
II	Islands	Inseln	Islas	Îles	Ilhas
⊔	Other Topographic Features	Andere Topographische Objekte	Otros Elementos Topográficos	Autres données topographiques	Outros acidentes topográficos

ESPAÑOL — Nombre	Página	Lat.°	Long.° W=Oeste
Fish River	166	17.55 S	137.45 E
Fishs Eddy	210	41.58 N	75.10 W
Fisk	194	36.46 N	90.12 W
Fiskårdhon	38	38.27	20.35 E
Fiskdale	207	42.06 N	72.06 W
Fiskebäckskil	26	58.15 N	11.27 E
Fismes	50	49.18 N	3.41 E
Fišt, gora ▲	84	43.58 N	39.54 E
Fisterra, Cabo de ►	34	42.53 N	9.16 W
Fitchburg, Ma., U.S.	207	42.35 N	71.48 W
Fitchburg, Wi., U.S.	216	42.57 N	89.28 W
Fitchville, Ct., U.S.	207	41.33 N	72.09 W
Fitchville, Oh., U.S.	214	41.06 N	82.29 W
Fitful Head ►	46a	59.54 N	1.23 W
Fitiuta	174y	14.13 S	169.27 W
Fito, Mount ▲	175a	13.55 S	171.44 W
Fitri, Lac ◎	146	12.50 N	17.28 E
Fittja	40	59.15 N	17.52 E
Fittleworth	42	50.58 N	0.35 W
Fitzgerald	192	31.42 N	83.15 W
Fitzgerald River National Park ♦	162	34.00 S	119.30 E
Fitz Henry	279b	40.10 N	79.45 W
Fitz Hugh Sound Ṳ	182	51.40 N	127.57 W
Fitzmaurice ≃	164	14.50 S	129.44 E
Fitz Roy, Arg.	254	47.02 S	67.15 W
Fitzroy, Austl.	274b	37.48 S	144.59 E
Fitzroy ≃, Austl.	162	17.31 S	123.35 E
Fitzroy ≃, Austl.	166	23.32 S	150.52 E
Fitzroy, Monte (Cerro Chaltel) ▲	254	49.17 S	73.05 W
Fitzroy Crossing	162	18.11 S	125.35 E
Fitzroy Falls Reservoir ◎[1]	170	34.38 S	150.30 E
Fitzroy Island I	166	16.56 S	146.00 E
Fitzwilliam	207	42.46 N	72.08 W
Fitzwilliam Island I	190	45.30 N	81.45 W
Fiuggi	66	41.48 N	13.13 E
Fiumalbo	64	44.11 N	10.39 E
Fiume — Rijeka	36	45.20 N	14.27 E
Fiumedinisi	70	38.02 N	15.23 E
Fiumefreddo Bruzio	68	39.14 N	16.04 E
Fiumefreddo di Sicilia	70	37.47 N	15.12 E
Fiumesino	66	43.38 N	13.22 E
Fiume Veneto	64	45.56 N	12.44 E
Fiumicino ◄	66	41.46 N	12.14 E
Five Corners	283	42.01 N	71.07 W
Five Cowrie Creek ≃[1]	273a	6.27 N	3.27 E
Five Dock	274a	33.52 S	151.08 E
Five Forks	284c	38.47 N	77.16 W
Five Islands	186	45.25 N	64.02 W
Five Islands Harbour C	240c	17.06 N	61.54 W
Fivemile	276	41.03 N	73.27 W
Fivemile Creek ≃, N.Y., U.S.	210	42.29 N	77.22 W
Fivemile Creek ≃, Or., U.S.	224	45.36 N	121.05 W
Fivemile Creek ≃, Wy., U.S.	262	43.14 N	108.12 W
Fivemile Point	210	42.06 N	75.48 W
Fivemiletown	48	54.23 N	7.18 W
Five Penny Borve	46	58.25 N	6.25 W
Five Points, Ca., U.S.	226	36.26 N	120.06 W
Five Points, In., U.S.	218	39.35 N	86.20 W
Five Points, N.M., U.S.	200	35.03 N	106.39 W
Five Points, Oh., U.S.	218	39.41 N	83.12 W
Five Points, Pa., U.S.	214	40.34 N	80.15 W
Five Points, Pa., U.S.	285	39.50 N	75.42 W
Fivizzano	64	44.14 N	10.08 E
Fiwila Mission	154	13.58 S	29.36 E
Fixin	58	47.15 N	4.58 E
Fix-Saint-Geneys	62	45.08 N	3.40 E
Fizi	154	4.18 S	28.57 E
Fjællebroen	41	55.03 N	10.24 E
Fjærlandsfjorden c[2]	41	61.17 N	6.40 E
Fjällåsen	24	67.29 N	20.10 E
Fjällbacka	26	58.36 N	11.17 E
Fjällsjöälven ≃	26	63.29 N	16.50 E
Fjärdhundra	40	59.47 N	16.56 E
Fjärdhundra ◎[9]	40	59.47 N	16.55 E
Fjenneslev	41	55.26 N	11.40 E
Fjerritslev	26	57.05 N	9.16 E
Fjugesta	40	59.10 N	14.52 E
Fkih-Ben-Salah	148	32.32 N	6.40 W
Flacksta	40	59.23 N	16.27 E
Fladnitz im Raabtal	61	46.59 N	15.47 E
Fladså ≃	41	55.19 N	8.54 E
Fladungen	56	50.31 N	10.08 E
Flag Creek ≃	278	41.43 N	87.55 W
Flagler	198	39.17 N	103.04 W
Flagler Beach	192	29.28 N	81.07 W
Flagstaff, S. Afr.	158	31.05 S	29.29 E
Flagstaff, Az., U.S.	200	35.11 N	111.39 W
Flagstaff Lake ◎[1]	184	45.10 N	70.15 W
Flagtown	276	40.31 N	74.41 W
Flaken-See ◎	264a	52.25 N	13.46 E
Flåm	26	60.50 N	7.07 E
Flambeau	190	45.18 N	91.15 W
Flambeau, South Fork ≃	190	45.39 N	90.48 W
Flamborough, On., Can.	212	43.20 N	79.53 W
Flamborough Head ►, U.K.	44	54.06 N	0.07 W
Flamborough Head ►	54	52.00 N	12.30 E
Fläming ◄[1]			
Flaming Gorge National Recreation Area ♦	200	41.30 N	109.30 W
Flamingo	192	25.09 N	80.56 W
Flamingo, Teluk c	116	5.33 S	138.00 E
Flanagan	216	40.52 N	88.51 W
Flanagan ≃	216	49.42 N	93.28 W
Flanagan Passage Ṳ	240m	18.18 N	64.39 W
Flanders, On., Can.	190	48.44 N	92.05 W
Flanders, N.J., U.S.	276	40.50 N	74.41 W
Flanders, N.Y., U.S.	207	40.49 N	72.36 W
Flanders (Flandre) □[9]	50	51.00 N	3.00 E
Flanders Airport	246	4.18 N	74.49 W
Flandes	246	4.18 N	74.49 W
Flandorf	264d	48.21 N	16.23 E
Flandre — Flanders □[9]	50	51.00 N	3.00 E
Flandreau	198	44.02 N	96.35 W
Flannan Islands II	46	58.18 N	7.36 W
Flåren ◎	26	57.02 N	14.06 E
Flasher	198	46.27 N	101.13 W
Flåsjön ◎	26	64.06 N	15.51 E
Flat, Ak., U.S.	180	62.27 N	158.01 W
Flat, Tx., U.S.	222	31.19 N	97.38 W
Flat ≃, N.T., Can.	180	61.51 N	128.00 W
Flat ≃, Mi., U.S.	190	42.56 N	85.20 W
Flat ≃, N.C., U.S.	192	36.05 N	78.49 W
Flat Bay	186	48.24 N	58.36 W
Flat Branch ≃	219	39.33 N	89.16 W
Flatbush ◄[9]	283	40.39 N	73.56 W
Flat Creek ≃, Ky., U.S.	218	38.17 N	83.48 W
Flat Creek ≃, Mo., U.S.	194	36.45 N	93.31 W
Flat Creek ≃, Mt., U.S.	202	47.43 N	109.50 W
Flat Creek ≃, N.J., U.S.	276		
Flatey	24a	65.19 N	23.07 W
Flateyri	24	66.04 N	23.30 W
Flathead ≃	202	47.22 N	114.07 W
Flathead, Middle Fork ≃	202	48.28 N	114.04 W
Flathead, North Fork ≃	202	48.28 N	114.04 W
Flathead, South Fork ≃	202	48.23 N	114.04 W

FRANÇAIS — Nom	Page	Lat.°	Long.° W=Ouest
Flathead Indian Reservation ◄[4]	202	47.30 N	114.25 W
Flathead Lake ◎	202	47.52 N	114.08 W
Flat Holm I	42	51.23 N	3.08 W
Flat Lake ◎	182	54.39 N	112.55 W
Flat Lick	192	36.49 N	83.46 W
Flatonia	222	29.41 N	97.06 W
Flatow	264a	52.44 N	12.57 E
Flat River, P.E., Can.	186	46.01 N	62.52 W
Flat River, Mo., U.S.	194	37.51 N	90.31 W
Flat River Reservoir ◎[1]	207	41.42 N	71.37 W
Flat Rock, Al., U.S.	194	34.46 N	85.42 W
Flat Rock, Il., U.S.	194	38.54 N	87.40 W
Flat Rock, In., U.S.	218	39.22 N	85.50 W
Flat Rock, Mi., U.S.	216	42.05 N	83.17 W
Flat Rock, Oh., U.S.	214	41.14 N	82.51 W
Flatrock ≃	218	39.12 N	85.56 W
Flatrock ≃	216	41.10 N	84.27 W
Flat Rock Lake ◎	184	55.37 N	100.47 W
Flatruet ᴴ[2]	26	62.45 N	12.50 E
Flats	222	32.50 N	95.53 W
Flattery, Cape ►, Austl.	164	14.58 S	145.21 E
Flattery, Cape ►, Wa., U.S.	224	48.23 N	124.43 W
Flatts	264a	32.19 N	64.44 W
Flatwillow Creek ≃	202	46.56 N	107.55 W
Flatwood	194	32.27 N	86.15 W
Flatwoods	188	38.31 N	82.43 W
Flaugherty Run ≃	279b	40.33 N	80.13 W
Flauden	260	51.42 N	0.32 W
Flavigny-sur-Moselle	58	48.34 N	6.11 E
Flavigny-sur-Ozerain	58	47.30 N	4.32 E
Flavy-le-Martel	50	49.43 N	3.12 E
Flawil	58	47.24 N	9.12 E
Flaxcombe	184	51.29 N	109.36 W
Flaxman Island I	180	70.13 N	146.00 W
Flax Pond ◎, Ma., U.S.	283	42.29 N	70.57 W
Flax Pond ◎, N.Y., U.S.	276	40.58 N	73.08 W
Flaxton	198	48.53 N	102.23 W
Flaxville	198	48.48 N	105.10 W
Flechas Point ►	116	10.22 N	119.54 E
Flechtingen	54	52.20 N	11.14 E
Fleckeby	41	54.29 N	9.41 E
Flecken Zechlin	54	53.09 N	12.46 E
Fleesensee ◎	54	53.30 N	12.29 E
Fleet	42	51.16 N	0.50 W
Fleet ≃	46	57.57 N	4.05 W
Fleetmark	54	52.48 N	11.23 E
Fleets Bay c	208	37.40 N	76.19 W
Fleetville	210	41.36 N	75.43 W
Fleetwing Estates	285	40.07 N	74.51 W
Fleetwood, Eng., U.K.	44	53.56 N	3.01 W
Fleetwood, Pa., U.S.	208	40.27 N	75.49 W
Fleringen	263	51.12 N	6.47 E
Fleisingen	58	49.05 N	8.46 E
Fleischmanns	210	42.09 N	74.31 W
Fleischmann Village	284c	38.51 N	76.57 W
Flekkefjord	26	58.17 N	6.41 E
Fleming, Co., U.S.	198	40.40 N	102.50 W
Fleming, Pa., U.S.	214	40.55 N	77.52 W
Fleming ◎[6]	218	38.21 N	83.42 W
Fleming Creek ≃, On., Can.	214	42.38 N	81.47 W
Fleming Creek ≃, Ky., U.S.	218	38.22 N	83.57 W
Fleming Creek ≃, Mi., U.S.	281	42.16 N	83.40 W
Fleming-Neon	192	37.11 N	82.42 W
Flemingsburg	218	38.25 N	83.44 W
Flemington, N.J., U.S.	210	40.30 N	74.51 W
Flemington, Pa., U.S.	210	41.07 N	77.28 W
Flemington Racecourse ♦	274a	37.47 S	144.55 E
Flemish Cap ◄[4]	16	47.00 N	45.00 W
Flemsdorf	54	53.02 N	14.10 E
Flen	40	59.04 N	16.35 E
Flensburg	41	54.47 N	9.26 E
Flensburger Förde c	41	54.49 N	9.45 E
Fleres (Boden)	64	46.58 N	11.21 E
Flers	32	48.45 N	0.34 W
Flers-sur-Noye	50	49.44 N	2.15 E
Flesherton	212	44.16 N	80.33 W
Flesko, Tanjung ►	112	0.29 N	124.30 E
Flessau	54	52.46 N	11.40 E
Fletcher, On., Can.	214	42.18 N	82.18 W
Fletcher, N.C., U.S.	192	35.25 N	82.30 W
Fletcher, Oh., U.S.	218	40.08 N	84.06 W
Fletcher, Ok., U.S.	196	34.49 N	98.14 W
Fletcher Islands II	9	72.40 S	94.10 W
Fletcher Moss Museum ♦	262	53.25 N	2.14 W
Fletcher Pond ◎[1]	190	44.58 N	83.52 W
Fletchers Creek ≃	275b	43.50 N	0.40 E
Fleurance	32	43.50 N	0.40 E
Fleur-de-Lys	186	50.07 N	56.08 W
Fleurier	58	46.54 N	6.35 E
Fleurus	50	50.29 N	4.33 E
Fleurville	58	46.27 N	4.53 E
Fleury-les-Aubrais	50	47.56 N	1.55 E
Fleury-Mérogis	261	48.38 N	2.22 E
Fleury-sur-Andelle	50	49.22 N	1.22 E
Fleuth ≃	263	51.32 N	6.26 E
Flevoland □	52	52.26 N	5.30 E
Flexanville	261	48.51 N	1.44 E
Flexaspass Ṳ	58	47.09 N	10.10 E
Fley ◄[9]	263	51.23 N	7.30 E
Flieden	56	50.25 N	9.33 E
Flierich	263	51.35 N	7.48 E
Flight Locks ᵥ[3]	284a	43.08 N	79.12 W
Flimby	44	54.41 N	3.31 W
Flims	58	46.50 N	9.17 E
Flinders ≃	164	17.36 S	140.36 E
Flinders Bay c	162	34.23 S	115.19 E
Flinders Chase National Park ♦	166	36.00 S	136.45 E
Flinders Island I, Austl.	162	33.44 S	134.31 E
Flinders Island I, Austl.	166	40.00 S	148.00 E
Flinders Peak ▲	171a	27.49 S	152.49 E
Flinders Peak ▲[2]	169	37.51 S	144.24 E
Flinders Ranges ≃	166	31.20 S	138.45 E
Flinders Reefs ◄[2]	166	17.37 S	148.31 E
Flinders Street ♦	274c	37.49 S	144.58 E
Flinesjön ◎	40	60.23 N	16.06 E
Flines-léz-Râches	50	50.25 N	3.11 E
Flin Flon	184	54.46 N	101.53 W
Flingern ◄[9]	263	51.14 N	6.48 E
Flins-sur-Seine	261	48.58 N	1.52 E
Flint, Wales, U.K.	44	53.15 N	3.07 W
Flint, Mi., U.S.	216	43.00 N	83.41 W
Flint, Tx., U.S.	222	32.12 N	95.21 W
Flint ≃	14	11.26 S	151.48 W
Flint ≃, Ga., U.S.	192	30.52 N	84.38 W
Flint ≃, Mi., U.S.	190	43.21 N	84.03 W
Flint, South Branch ≃	281	43.10 N	83.23 W
Flint Castle ᴸ	262	53.15 N	3.07 W
Flint Creek ≃, Al., U.S.	194	34.30 N	86.57 W
Flint Creek ≃, Mt., U.S.	202	46.39 N	113.08 W
Flint Creek ≃, N.Y., U.S.	210	42.57 N	77.03 W
Flint Creek Range ▲	202	46.20 N	113.05 W
Flinthill	219	38.53 N	90.52 W
Flint Hills ▲[2]	198	37.50 N	96.40 W
Flint Lake ◎	278	41.34 N	87.10 W

PORTUGUÊS — Nome	Página	Lat.°	Long.° W=Oeste
Flint Lake ◎, In., U.S.	216	41.31 N	87.03 W
Flinton, Austl.	166	27.54 S	149.34 E
Flinton, Pa., U.S.	214	40.43 N	78.31 W
Flint Peak ▲	280	34.10 N	118.12 W
Flint Pond ◎	283	42.40 N	71.26 W
Flintränran ᴸ	41	55.34 N	12.52 E
Flintridge	228	34.11 N	118.11 W
Flintsbach	64	47.43 N	12.08 E
Flints Pond ◎	283	42.26 N	71.19 W
Flintville	194	35.03 N	86.25 W
Flipper Point ►	174a	19.18 N	166.35 E
Flippin	194	36.16 N	92.35 W
Flirey	56	48.53 N	5.50 E
Flirsch	64	47.09 N	10.24 E
Flisa	26	60.34 N	12.06 E
Flitwick	42	52.00 N	0.29 W
Flix, Pantà de ◎[1]	34	41.15 N	0.25 E
Flixecourt	50	50.01 N	2.05 E
Flize	50	49.42 N	4.46 E
Flobecq (Vloesberg)	50	50.44 N	3.44 E
Floby	26	58.08 N	13.20 E
Floda, Sve.	26	57.48 N	12.22 E
Floda, Sve.	40	59.04 N	16.21 E
Flodden	44	55.38 N	2.10 W
Flodden Field Battlesite ᴸ	44	55.38 N	2.13 W
Flogny	50	47.57 N	3.52 E
Flöha	54	50.51 N	13.04 E
Flöha ≃	54	50.51 N	13.04 E
Floing	56	49.43 N	4.56 E
Flomaton	194	31.00 N	87.15 W
Flomborn	56	49.41 N	8.08 E
Flomot	196	34.14 N	100.59 W
Floodwood	190	46.55 N	92.55 W
Flora, Il., U.S.	194	38.40 N	88.29 W
Flora, In., U.S.	216	40.32 N	86.31 W
Flora, Ms., U.S.	194	32.32 N	90.18 W
Flora ≃	62	44.19 N	3.36 E
Florala	194	31.00 N	86.19 W
Floral City	220	28.45 N	82.17 W
Floral Park, Mt., U.S.	202	45.57 N	112.26 W
Floral Park, N.Y., U.S.	210	40.43 N	73.42 W
Florange	56	49.20 N	6.07 E
Florânia	250	6.08 S	36.49 W
Flora Vista	200	36.47 N	108.04 W
Flore, Piton ▲	241f	13.58 N	60.57 W
Floreffe	56	50.26 N	4.45 E
Florence — Firenze, It.	66	43.46 N	11.15 E
Florence, Al., U.S.	194	34.47 N	87.40 W
Florence, Az., U.S.	200	33.02 N	111.23 W
Florence, Co., U.S.	228	33.58 N	118.14 W
Florence, Co., U.S.	200	38.23 N	105.07 W
Florence, Ky., U.S.	218	38.59 N	84.37 W
Florence, N.J., U.S.	285	40.07 N	74.49 W
Florence, Or., U.S.	202	43.58 N	124.05 W
Florence, S.C., U.S.	192	34.11 N	79.45 W
Florence, Tx., U.S.	222	30.51 N	97.48 W
Florence, Wi., U.S.	190	45.55 N	88.15 W
Florencia, Col.	246	1.36 N	75.36 W
Florencia — Firenze, It.	66	43.46 N	11.15 E
Florencio Sánchez	258	33.53 S	57.24 W
Florencio Varela	258	34.49 S	58.17 W
Florencio Varela ◄[5]	288	34.52 S	58.15 W
Florennes	56	50.15 N	4.37 E
Florentia	273d	26.16 S	28.08 E
Florentino Ameghino, Embalse ◎[1]	254	43.55 S	66.20 W
Florenville	56	49.42 N	5.18 E
Florenz — Firenze	66	43.46 N	11.15 E
Flores	258	7.51 S	37.59 W
Flores □[5]	258	33.48 S	56.50 W
Flores ≃	288	34.38 S	58.28 W
Flores I, Indon.	115b	8.30 S	121.00 E
Flores, I, Port.	148a	39.26 N	31.13 W
Flores, Laut (Flores Sea) ᵀ[2]	112	8.00 S	120.00 E
Flores, Rio das ≃	256	22.05 S	43.34 W
Flores, Selat Ṳ	115b	8.25 S	122.55 E
Flores da Cunha	252	29.02 S	51.11 W
Flores de Goiás	255	14.34 S	47.04 W
Flores Island I	182	49.20 N	126.10 W
Flores Sea — Flores, Laut ᵀ[2]	112	8.00 S	120.00 E
Floresta, Bra.	250	8.36 S	38.34 W
Floresta, It.	70	37.59 N	14.55 E
Floresta ◄[8]	288	34.38 S	58.29 W
Floresta Azul	255	14.51 S	39.41 W
Florestal de Monsanto, Parque ♦	266c	38.43 N	9.11 W
Florești	38	47.53 N	28.17 E
Floresville	222	29.08 N	98.09 W
Florham Park	276	40.47 N	74.23 W
Floriano, Bra.	250	6.47 S	43.01 W
Floriano, Bra.	256	22.27 S	44.18 W
Floriano Peixoto	248	9.03 S	67.24 W
Florianópolis	252	27.35 S	48.34 W
Florida, Col.	246	3.20 N	76.15 W
Florida, Cuba	240p	21.32 N	78.14 W
Florida, Hond.	236	15.01 N	88.50 W
Florida, Perú	248	5.50 S	77.55 W
Florida, P.R.	240m	18.14 N	65.47 W
Florida, S. Afr.	273d	26.11 S	27.55 E
Florida, Ur.	258	34.06 S	56.13 W
Florida □	192	28.00 N	82.00 W
Florida, N.Y., U.S.	210	41.20 N	74.21 W
Florida, Oh., U.S.	216	41.20 N	84.12 W
Florida, Ur.	258	34.06 S	56.13 W
Florida ◄[8]	288	34.31 S	58.30 W
Florida □[3], Ur.	258	34.00 S	56.15 W
Floridablanca	246	7.04 N	73.06 W
Florida Caverns State Park ♦	192	30.50 N	85.18 W
Florida City	192	25.26 N	80.28 W
Florida Keys II	175e	24.45 N	81.00 W
Florida Lake ◎[1]	273d	26.11 N	27.54 E
Florida Ridge	220	27.35 N	80.23 W
Florido ≃	234	27.28 N	105.10 W
Florido ≃[1]	232	27.43 N	105.10 W
Floridsdorf ◄[8]	264b	48.16 N	16.25 E
Floridsdorfer Brücke ᵛ[5]	264b	48.14 N	16.23 E
Florien	194	31.26 N	93.27 W
Florin	226	38.29 N	121.24 W
Florina	36	40.48 N	21.24 E
Florissant	219	38.47 N	90.19 W
Florissant Fossil Beds National Monument ♦	200	38.54 N	105.16 W
Floriston	226	39.24 N	120.01 W
Florø	26	61.36 N	5.00 E
Florsheim	56	50.00 N	8.26 E
Floss	60	49.44 N	12.17 E
Flossenbürg	60	49.44 N	12.21 E
Flotantes, Jardines ▲	286a	19.16 N	99.06 W
Flöthbach ≃	263	51.17 N	6.26 E
Flotte, Cap de I	175f	21.10 S	167.25 E
Flour Lake ◎	186	53.15 N	66.42 W
Flourtown	285	40.06 N	75.12 W
Flower Hill	276	40.48 N	73.40 W
Flower Mound	222	33.02 N	97.04 W

Name	Page	Lat.°	Long.° W
Flower's Cove	186	51.18 N	56.44 W
Flowery Branch	192	34.11 N	83.55 W
Floyd, N.M., U.S.	200	34.13 N	103.35 W
Floyd, Tx., U.S.	222	33.09 N	96.15 W
Floyd, Va., U.S.	188	36.54 N	80.19 W
Floydada	196	33.59 N	101.20 W
Floyds Fork ≃	218	38.16 N	85.44 W
Floyds Knobs	218	38.21 N	85.54 W
Fluchthorn ▲	64	46.53 N	10.13 E
Flüela Pass Ṵ	58	46.45 N	9.57 E
Flüelen	58	46.54 N	8.38 E
Fluessen ◎	52	52.57 N	5.30 E
Flühli	58	46.53 N	8.01 E
Flumen ≃	34	41.43 N	0.09 W
Flumendosa ≃	71	39.26 N	9.37 E
Flumendosa, Lago Alto del ◎	71	39.56 N	9.26 E
Flumendosa, Lago del ◎[1]	71	39.40 N	9.17 E
Flumeri	68	41.05 N	15.09 E
Fons-Outre-Gardon	62	13.10 N	87.40 W
Flumet	62	45.49 N	6.31 E
Fluminimaggiore	71	39.26 N	8.30 E
Flums	58	47.05 N	9.20 E
Flüren	263	51.41 N	6.33 E
Flushing — Vlissingen, Ned.	52	51.26 N	3.35 E
Flushing, Mi., U.S.	216	43.03 N	83.51 W
Flushing, Oh., U.S.	214	40.08 N	81.03 W
Flushing ◄[8]	276	40.45 N	73.49 W
Flushing Airport ◄	276	40.47 N	73.50 W
Flushing Bay c	276	40.47 N	73.51 W
Flushing Meadow-Corona Park ♦	276	40.45 N	73.51 W
Fluvanna, N.Y., U.S.	214	42.07 N	79.18 W
Fluvanna, Tx., U.S.	196	32.53 N	101.09 W
Fluvià ≃	34	42.12 N	3.07 E
Fluvanna, Wi., U.S.	216	42.33 N	88.14 W
Fly Creek	210	42.43 N	74.59 W
Fly Creek ≃	202	45.59 N	107.59 W
Flyinge	41	55.45 N	13.21 E
Flying Fish Cove	112	10.25 S	105.43 E
Flynn	222	31.09 N	96.08 W
Foam Lake	184	51.39 N	103.33 W
Fobbing	260	51.32 N	0.29 E
Fobello	62	45.53 N	8.10 E
Foča, Bos.	38	43.31 N	18.46 E
Foça, Tür.	130	38.39 N	26.46 E
Focene ◄[8]	267a	41.48 N	12.14 E
Fochabers	46	57.37 N	3.05 W
Fochville	158	26.30 S	27.30 E
Fockbek	41	54.22 N	9.35 E
Focșani	38	45.41 N	27.11 E
Fodda, Oued ≃	34	36.14 N	1.33 E
Fodé	152	5.29 N	23.18 E
Fodécontea	152	10.50 N	14.22 W
Foding Shan ▲	102	27.08 N	108.02 E
Fodorovka, Kaz.	82	51.09 N	51.59 E
Fodorovka, Kaz.	86	53.22 N	76.18 E
Fodorovka, Ross.	82	53.28 N	49.38 E
Fodorovka, Ross.	82	52.21 N	52.55 E
Fodorovka, Ross.	82	56.15 N	37.14 E
Fodorovskoje, Ross.	83	47.20 N	38.23 E
Fodorovskoje, Ross.	82	53.11 N	55.11 E
Fodorovskoje, Ross.	82	56.05 N	78.49 E
Fodorovskoje, Ross.	82	56.44 N	36.58 E
Fodorovskoje, Ross.	82	56.07 N	38.52 E
Foëcy	50	47.10 N	2.10 E
Foelsche ≃	164	16.03 S	136.50 E
Foeni	58	45.30 N	20.53 E
Fogang (Shijiao)	100	23.52 N	113.32 E
Fogdön ◎[1]	40	59.25 N	16.52 E
Fogelevo	85	47.05 N	38.53 E
Fogelsville	208	40.35 N	75.38 W
Foggaret el Arab	148	27.03 N	2.59 E
Foggaret ez Zoua	148	27.20 N	3.00 E
Foggia	68	41.27 N	15.34 E
Foggo	158	41.30 N	15.30 E
Foggy Island Bay c	180	70.15 N	147.30 W
Foglianise	68	41.12 N	14.36 E
Fogliano, Lago di c	66	41.24 N	12.54 E
Foglizzo	62	45.17 N	7.49 E
Fogo	186	49.43 N	54.17 W
Fogo I	150a	14.55 N	24.25 W
Fogo, Cape ►	186	49.43 N	54.17 W
Fogolawa	140	12.19 N	8.41 E
Fogoteiro	266c	38.37 N	9.07 W
Fohnsdorf	61	47.13 N	14.41 E
Föhr I	54	54.43 N	8.30 E
Foia ▲	34	37.19 N	8.36 W
Foiano della Chiana	64	43.15 N	11.49 E
Foiano di Val Fortore	68	41.30 N	15.00 E
Foinaven ▲	46	58.25 N	4.53 W
Foins, Lac aux ◎	190	47.05 N	78.11 W
Foivre ≃	56	49.39 N	5.44 E
Foix	32	42.58 N	1.36 E
Fojnica	38	43.58 N	17.54 E
Foki	80	44.14 N	41.58 E
Fokino	76	53.27 N	34.24 E
Fokku	140	11.40 N	4.31 E
Folakara	157b	18.20 S	45.02 E
Folamasi	104	6.36 N	121.27 E
Folarskardnuten ▲	26	60.37 N	7.45 E
Folcroft	285	39.53 N	75.17 W
Folda c[2]	24	67.36 N	14.50 E
Foldingbro	41	55.26 N	9.01 E
Folembray	50	49.33 N	3.17 E
Foley, Al., U.S.	194	30.24 N	87.41 W
Foley, Mn., U.S.	190	45.40 N	93.54 W
Foley I	178	68.35 N	75.10 W
Foleyet	190	48.15 N	82.27 W
Foleyville ◄[1]	284c	38.53 N	76.46 W
Folgaria	64	45.55 N	11.10 E
Folgefonni ◉	26	60.03 N	6.20 E
Folger Hill ▲[2]	207	41.17 N	70.01 W
Foligno	66	42.57 N	12.42 E
Folkärna	40	60.16 N	16.16 E
Folkestone	42	51.05 N	1.11 E
Folkingham	44	52.54 N	0.24 W
Folkston	192	30.50 N	82.00 W
Folkmuseum ♦	263	50.59 N	7.06 E
Folldal	26	62.08 N	10.00 E
Follafoss	24	63.59 N	11.06 E
Follébu	26	61.14 N	10.17 E
Folletts Island I	222	29.03 N	95.16 W
Follett	196	36.26 N	100.08 W
Follina	64	45.57 N	12.07 E
Föllinge	24	63.40 N	14.37 E
Follonica	66	42.55 N	10.45 E
Follonica, Golfo di c	66	42.54 N	10.44 E
Folly Branch ≃	284b	38.56 N	76.49 W
Folschviller	56	49.04 N	6.41 E
Folsom, Ca., U.S.	226	38.40 N	121.11 W
Folsom, Pa., U.S.	285	39.53 N	75.20 W
Folsom Lake ◎	226	38.43 N	121.06 W
Folsom Lake State Recreation Area ♦	226	38.43 N	121.06 W
Fombio	64	45.08 N	9.41 E
Fomboni	157a	12.16 S	43.45 E
Fomento, Cuba	240p	22.06 N	79.43 W
Fomento, Ur.	258	34.26 S	57.14 W
Fomin	80	47.48 N	41.41 E
Fominiči	76	54.07 N	34.11 E
Fominskoje, Ross.	24	62.05 N	42.05 E

Name	Page	Lat.°	Long.° W
Fominskoje, Ross.	76	58.59 N	39.06 E
Fomkino	80	54.25 N	50.30 E
Foncine-le-Bas	58	46.38 N	6.03 E
Fonda, Ia., U.S.	198	42.34 N	94.50 W
Fonda, N.Y., U.S.	210	42.57 N	74.22 W
Fondachelli	70	37.58 N	15.11 E
Fond du Lac, Sk., Can.	176	59.19 N	107.10 W
Fond du Lac, Wi., U.S.	190	43.46 N	88.26 W
Fond du Lac ≃	176	59.17 N	106.00 W
Fond du Lac Indian Reservation ◄[4]	190	46.45 N	92.37 W
Fondi	66	41.21 N	13.25 E
Fondi, Lago di c	66	41.19 N	13.22 E
Fondo	64	46.26 N	11.08 E
Fondouk el Aouareb	36	35.34 N	9.46 E
Fongfong	140	12.56 N	23.14 E
Fonni	71	40.07 N	9.15 E
Fonseca	246	10.54 N	72.51 W
Fonseca, Golfo de c	236	13.10 N	87.40 W
Font	44	55.10 N	1.44 W
Fontaine, Fr.	58	47.40 N	7.00 E
Fontaine, Fr.	62	45.11 N	5.40 E
Fontainebleau, Fr.	50	48.24 N	2.42 E
Fontainebleau, S. Afr.	273d	26.07 S	27.59 E
Fontaine-Française	58	47.31 N	5.22 E
Fontaine-le-Dun	50	49.49 N	0.51 E
Fontaine-lès-Dijon	58	47.21 N	5.01 E
Fontaine-lès-Grès	58	48.25 N	3.54 E
Fontaine-lès-Luxeuil	58	47.51 N	6.20 E
Fontaines	58	46.51 N	4.46 E
Fontaines-sur-Saône	62	45.49 N	4.51 E
Fontan	62	43.59 N	7.33 E
Fontana, Arg.	252	27.25 S	59.02 W
Fontana, Ca., U.S.	228	34.05 N	117.26 W
Fontanafredda	64	45.58 N	12.34 E
Fontana Lake ◎[1]	192	35.26 N	83.38 W
Fontanarosa	68	41.01 N	15.01 E
Fontanarossa, Aeroporto di ◄	70	37.29 N	15.03 E
Fontanelas	266c	38.51 N	9.26 W
Fontanelice	66	44.13 N	11.34 E
Fontanellato	64	44.53 N	10.10 E
Fontanelle	198	41.17 N	94.33 W
Fontanetto Po	62	45.12 N	8.11 E
Fontanigorda	62	44.33 N	9.19 E
Fontariabie, Lac ◎	186	51.50 N	66.25 W
Fonte, Bra.	287b	23.25 S	46.21 W
Fonte, It.	64	45.47 N	11.53 E
Fonte Avellana, Monastero di ♦[1]	66	43.29 N	12.45 E
Fonte Blanda	66	42.34 N	11.10 E
Fonte Boa	246	2.32 S	66.01 W
Fonte Colombo, Convento de I	67	42.23 N	12.50 E
Fontelo	34	40.58 N	7.47 W
Fontenay, Abbaye de ♦[1]	50	47.39 N	4.24 E
Fontenay-aux-Roses	261	48.47 N	2.17 E
Fontenay-en-Parisis	261	49.03 N	2.27 E
Fontenay-le-Comte	32	46.28 N	0.48 W
Fontenay-le-Fleury	261	48.49 N	2.03 E
Fontenay-lès-Briis	261	48.37 N	2.09 E
Fontenay-le-Vicomte	261	48.33 N	2.24 E
Fontenay-sous-Bois	261	48.51 N	2.29 E
Fontenay-Trésigny	261	48.42 N	2.52 E
Fonteneau, Lac ◎	186	51.55 N	61.30 W
Fontevraud	50	47.11 N	0.03 E
Fontem	150	5.40 N	9.57 E

Name	Page	Lat.°	Long.° W
Fora ▲	34	37.19 N	8.36 W
Forbach, Fr.	56	49.11 N	6.54 E
Forbach, Dtsch.	58	48.41 N	8.22 E
Forbes	166	33.23 S	148.01 E
Forbes, Mount ▲	182	51.51 N	116.56 W
Forbes Reef	157c	26.10 S	31.05 E
Forbes Road	216	40.10 N	79.32 W
Forbestown	226	39.31 N	121.16 W
Forchheim, Dtsch.	60	49.43 N	11.04 E
Forchtenberg	56	49.17 N	9.34 E
Forclaz, Col de la Ṵ	58	46.03 N	7.03 E
Ford, Scot., U.K.	46	56.10 N	5.26 W
Ford, Ks., U.S.	198	37.38 N	99.45 W
Ford ≃	190	45.40 N	87.10 W
Ford, Cape ►	164	13.26 S	129.52 E
Ford City, Ca., U.S.	226	35.09 N	119.27 W
Ford City, Pa., U.S.	214	40.46 N	79.32 W
Ford Dry Lake ◎	200	33.38 N	115.06 W
Forde, Nor.	26	61.27 N	5.52 E
Fordham University ♦	276	40.51 N	73.53 W
Fordingbridge	42	50.56 N	1.47 W
Ford Lake ◎	281	42.13 N	83.33 W
Fordland	194	37.08 N	92.56 W
Fordon	27	53.10 N	18.14 E
Foreman	194	33.43 N	94.24 W
Foremost	182	49.29 N	111.25 W
Forepaugh Airport ◄	279a	41.21 N	81.30 W

Name	Page	Lat.°	Long.° W
Foresman	216	40.52 N	87.18 W
Forest, Bel.	50	50.48 N	4.19 E
Forest, On., Can.	190	43.06 N	82.00 W
Forest, In., U.S.	216	40.22 N	86.19 W
Forest, Ms., U.S.	194	32.21 N	89.28 W
Forest, Oh., U.S.	216	40.48 N	83.30 W
Forest ◄[9]	214	41.29 N	79.27 W
Forest, Middle Branch ≃	198	48.13 N	97.48 W
Forest Acres	192	34.01 N	80.59 W
Forestburg	182	50.35 N	112.04 W
Forest City, Ia., U.S.	190	43.15 N	93.38 W
Forest City, N.C., U.S.	192	35.20 N	81.51 W
Forest City, Pa., U.S.	210	41.39 N	75.28 W
Forest Creek ≃	226	39.13 N	120.28 W
Forest Gate ◄[8]	260	51.33 N	0.02 E
Forest Glade	222	31.39 N	96.31 W
Forest Grove, B.C., Can.	182	51.46 N	121.06 W
Forest Grove, Or., Can.		45.31 N	123.06 W
Forest Grove, Pa., U.S.			
Forest Heights	279b	40.18 N	75.04 W
Forest Hill, Austl.	171a	27.35 S	152.22 E
Forest Hill, Austl.	171b	35.05 S	147.27 E
Forest Hill, Austl.	274b	37.50 S	145.11 E
Foresthill, Ca., U.S.	226	39.01 N	120.49 W
Forest Hill, Md., U.S.	208	39.35 N	76.23 W
Forest Hill, Tx., U.S.	222	32.40 N	97.16 W
Forest Hill Park ♦	279a	41.31 N	81.35 W
Forest Hill Parkway ♦	279a	41.31 N	81.36 W
Forest Hills	279b	40.25 N	79.51 W
Forest Hills ◄[8]	276	40.42 N	73.51 W
Forest Home	194	31.52 N	86.50 W
Forestier Peninsula ►	166	42.57 S	147.55 E
Forest Knolls	284c	39.02 N	77.01 W
Forest Lake, Il., U.S.	216	42.13 N	88.03 W
Forest Lake, Mn., U.S.	190	45.16 N	92.59 W
Forest Lake ◎, Il., U.S.	282	42.13 N	88.03 W
Forest Lake ◎, Ma., U.S.	283	42.43 N	71.15 W
Forest Lawn Memorial Park ◄	280	34.09 N	118.19 W
Forest Manor	284c	38.50 N	76.53 W
Forest Park, Ga., U.S.	192	33.37 N	84.22 W
Forest Park, Il., U.S.	278	41.52 N	87.48 W
Forest Park, Oh., U.S.	218	39.16 N	84.34 W
Forest Park ♦	276	39.19 N	76.41 W
Forest River	276	40.42 N	73.51 W
Forest River ≃	198	42.05 N	87.54 W
Forest Row	42	51.06 N	0.02 E
Forest View	278	41.49 N	87.47 W
Forestville, Austl.	274a	33.45 S	151.12 E
Forestville, P.Q., Can.	188	48.45 N	69.06 W
Forestville, Md., U.S.	284c	38.50 N	76.52 W
Forestville, N.Y., U.S.	214	42.28 N	79.10 W
Forestville, Wi., U.S.	190	44.41 N	87.28 W
Forêt l'Orient, Lac de ◎	50	48.17 N	4.20 E
Forêt-Noire — Schwarzwald ▲	58	48.00 N	8.15 E
Forez, Monts du ▲	32	45.35 N	3.48 E
Forfar	46	56.38 N	2.54 W
Forffry	261	49.03 N	2.51 E
Forgan	196	36.54 N	100.32 W
Forgaria	64	46.13 N	12.58 E
Forge ≃	284b	39.25 N	76.27 W
Forge Acres	284b	39.25 N	76.25 W
Forges-les-Bains	261	48.37 N	2.06 E
Forges-les-Eaux	50	49.37 N	1.33 E
Forget, Pointe ►	275a	42.57 S	73.58 W
Forge Village	207	42.34 N	71.29 W
Forggensee ◎	58	47.36 N	10.44 E
Forino	68	40.52 N	14.44 E
Foristell	219	38.49 N	90.57 W
Fork	208	36.11 N	76.27 W
Forked Creek ≃	216	41.19 N	88.09 W
Forked Deer ≃	194	36.50 N	89.35 W
Forked Deer, Middle Fork ≃	194	36.01 N	89.13 W
Forked Deer, North Fork ≃	194	36.04 N	89.13 W
Forked Deer, South Fork ≃	194	36.00 N	89.20 W
Forked River	276	39.50 N	74.11 W
Forks	224	47.57 N	124.23 W
Forkston	210	41.30 N	76.06 W
Forks of Salmon	226	41.15 N	123.15 W
Forlì	66	44.13 N	12.03 E
Forlimpopoli	66	44.11 N	12.07 E
Formby	44	53.34 N	3.05 W
Formby Hills ▲[2]	262	53.33 N	3.06 W
Formby Point ►	262	53.34 N	3.07 W
Formentera I	34	38.42 N	1.28 E
Formentor, Cap de ►	34	39.58 N	3.13 E
Formerie	50	49.39 N	1.44 E
Formia	66	41.15 N	13.37 E
Formiga	255	20.27 S	45.25 W
Formigine	64	44.34 N	10.51 E
Formigliana	62	45.27 N	8.22 E
Formignana	64	44.50 N	11.51 E
Formosa, Arg.	252	26.11 S	58.11 W
Formosa, Bra.	255	15.32 S	47.20 W
Formosa □	252	25.00 S	60.00 W
Formosa — Taiwan □[1]	100	23.30 N	121.00 E
Formosa, Ilha I	152	11.29 N	15.48 W
Formosa, Serra ▲[1]	248	12.00 S	55.00 W
Formosa Strait Ṳ — Taiwan Strait Ṳ	100	24.00 N	119.00 E
Formoso ≃	255	11.44 S	49.08 W
Fornalutx	34	39.48 N	2.44 E
Forni Avoltri	64	46.35 N	12.46 E
Forni di sopra	64	46.25 N	12.34 E
Forni di sotto	64	46.24 N	12.40 E
Forni di Val d'Astico	64	45.52 N	11.37 E
Forno	62	45.24 N	7.45 E
Forno Alpi Graie	62	45.21 N	7.13 E
Forno di Zoldo	64	46.21 N	12.11 E
Fornos	34	40.38 N	7.30 W
Fornovo di Taro	64	44.42 N	10.06 E
Foroyar — Faeroe Islands	22	62.00 N	7.00 W

Symbol	English	Deutsch	Español	Français	Português
≃	River	Fluß	Río	Rivière	Rio
≖	Canal	Kanal	Canal	Canal	Canal
Ṿ	Waterfall, Rapids	Wasserfall, Stromschnellen	Cascada, Rápidos	Chute d'eau, Rapides	Cascata, Rápidos
Ṳ	Strait	Meeresstraße	Estrecho	Détroit	Estreito
c	Bay, Gulf	Bucht, Golf	Bahía, Golfo	Baie, Golfe	Baía, Golfo
◎	Lake, Lakes	See, Seen	Lago, Lagos	Lac, Lacs	Lago, Lagos
ᵂ	Swamp	Sumpf	Pantano	Marais	Pântano
◉	Ice Features, Glacier	Eis- und Gletscherformen	Accidentes Glaciales	Formes glaciaires	Acidentes glaciares
ᵀ	Other Hydrographic Features	Andere Hydrographische Objekte	Otros Elementos Hidrográficos	Autres données hydrographiques	Outros acidentes hidrográficos
◄	Submarine Features	Untermeerische Objekte	Accidentes Submarinos	Formes de relief sous-marin	Acidentes submarinos
□	Political Unit	Politische Einheit	Unidad Política	Entité politique	Unidade política
ᴸ	Cultural Institution	Kulturelle Institution	Institución Cultural	Institution culturelle	Instituição cultural
♦	Recreational Site	Erholungs- und Ferienort	Sitio de Recreo	Centre de loisirs	Área de Lazer
ᴸ	Historical Site	Historische Stätte	Sitio histórico	Site historique	Sitio histórico
◄	Airport	Flughafen	Aeropuerto	Aéroport	Aeroporto
ᵢ	Military Installation	Militäranlage	Instalación Militar	Installation militaire	Instalação militar
◄	Miscellaneous	Verschiedenes	Misceláneo	Divers	Diversos

Forreston, Tx., U.S. 222 32.16 N 96.52 W
Forrest River Aboriginal Reserve ◆4 164 15.00 S 127.40 E
Fors 40 60.13 N 16.18 E
Forsan 196 32.07 N 101.22 W
Forsayth 166 18.35 S 143.36 E
Forsbacka 40 60.37 N 16.53 E
Forsby 26 60.30 N 25.56 E
Forserum 26 57.42 N 14.28 E
Forshaga 40 59.32 N 13.28 E
Forsmark 40 60.22 N 18.09 E
Forssa 26 60.49 N 23.38 E
Forst 54 51.44 N 14.39 E
Förste 52 51.44 N 10.10 E
Forster 166 32.11 S 152.31 E
Forstwald ◆8 263 51.18 N 6.30 E
Forsyth, Ga., U.S. 192 33.02 N 83.56 W
Forsyth, Il., U.S. 219 39.56 N 88.57 W
Forsyth, Mo., U.S. 194 36.41 N 93.07 W
Forsyth, Mt., U.S. 202 46.15 N 106.40 W
Forsyth Island I 164 16.50 S 139.06 E
Forsyth Range ⋏ 166 22.45 S 143.15 E
Fort ◆8 272c 18.56 N 72.50 E
Fort Abbās 123 29.12 N 72.52 E
Fort Adams 194 31.05 N 91.32 W
Fort Albany 176 52.15 N 81.37 W
Fort Alexander Indian Reserve ◆4 184 50.27 N 96.15 W
Fortaleza 250 3.43 S 38.30 W
Fortaleza ≃ 248 10.40 S 77.52 W
Fortaleza de Santa Teresa ⊥ 252 33.59 S 53.32 W
Fortaleza do Ituxi 248 7.29 S 66.20 W
Fortaleza dos Nogueiras 250 6.54 S 46.09 W
Fort Amherst National Historic Park ♦ 186 46.12 N 63.09 W
Fort Ancient State Memorial ⊥ 218 39.24 N 84.06 W
Fort Anne National Historic Park ♦ 186 44.44 N 65.26 W
Fort Apache Indian Reservation ◆4 200 34.01 N 110.28 W
Fort-Archambault → Sarh 146 9.09 N 18.23 E
Fort Assiniboine 182 54.20 N 114.46 W
Fort Atkinson 216 42.55 N 88.50 W
Fort Augusta ⊥ 210 40.53 N 76.46 W
Fort Augustus 46 57.09 N 4.41 W
Fort Baker ■ 282 37.50 N 122.29 W
Fort Battleford National Historic Park ♦ 184 52.42 N 108.15 W
Fort Bayard → Zhanjiang 102 21.16 N 110.28 E
Fort Beaufort 158 32.46 S 26.40 E
Fort Beauséjour National Historic Park ♦ 186 45.51 N 64.18 W
Fort Belknap Agency 202 48.28 N 108.45 W
Fort Belknap Indian Reservation ◆4 202 48.16 N 108.38 W
Fort Belvoir ■ 208 38.44 N 77.10 W
Fort Bend □6 222 29.32 N 95.47 W
Fort Benjamin Harrison ■ 218 39.52 N 86.01 W
Fort Benning ■ 192 32.22 N 84.50 W
Fort Benton 202 47.49 N 110.40 W
Fort Berthold Indian Reservation ◆4 198 47.40 N 102.25 W
Fort Bidwell 204 41.51 N 120.09 W
Fort Bliss ■ 200 32.15 N 106.00 W
Fort Bowie National Historic Site ⊥ 200 32.09 N 109.24 W
Fort Bragg 204 39.26 N 123.48 W
Fort Bragg ■ 192 35.09 N 78.59 W
Fort Branch 194 38.15 N 87.34 W
Fort Bridger 200 41.19 N 110.23 W
Fort Calhoun 198 41.27 N 96.01 W
Fort Campbell ■ 194 36.39 N 87.29 W
Fort Canby State Park ♦ 224 46.17 N 124.04 W
Fort-Carnot 157b 21.53 S 47.28 E
Fort Caroline National Memorial ⊥ 192 30.20 N 81.30 W
Fort Carson ■ 200 38.44 N 104.48 W
Fort Casey Historical State Park ♦ 224 48.10 N 122.40 W
Fort Chambly National Historic Park ♦ 206 45.27 N 73.17 W
Fort Chipewyan 176 58.42 N 111.08 W
Fort Churchill Historic State Monument ⊥ 226 39.18 N 119.17 W
Fort Clatsop National Memorial ⊥ 224 46.08 N 123.54 W
Fort Cobb 196 35.05 N 98.26 W
Fort Cobb Reservoir ⊜1 196 35.12 N 98.29 W
Fort Collins 200 40.35 N 105.05 W
Fort Columbia Historical State Park ♦ 224 46.15 N 123.56 W
Fort Constantine 166 20.28 S 140.37 E
Fort-Coulonge 188 45.51 N 76.44 W
Fort Covington 206 44.59 N 74.29 W
Fort Custer State Recreation Area ♦ 216 42.18 N 85.20 W
Fort Davis, Al., U.S. 194 32.14 N 85.42 W
Fort Davis, Tx., U.S. 196 30.35 N 103.53 W
Fort Davis National Historic Site ⊥ 196 30.33 N 103.53 W
Fort de Douaumont ⊥ 56 49.13 N 5.25 E
Fort Defiance 200 35.44 N 109.04 W
Fort-de-France 240e 14.36 N 61.05 W
Fort-de-France, Baie de ⊂ 240e 14.34 N 61.04 W
Fort-de-France-Lamentin, Aérodrome de ✈ 240e 14.35 N 61.00 W
Fort Deposit 194 31.59 N 86.34 W
Fort Detrick ■ 208 39.27 N 77.26 W
Fort de Vaux ⊥ 56 49.12 N 5.28 E
Fort Devens ■ 207 42.32 N 71.37 W
Fort Dix ■ 208 40.00 N 74.33 W
Fort Dodge 190 42.29 N 94.10 W
Fort Donelson National Military Park ♦ 194 36.26 N 87.49 W
Fort Duchesne 200 40.17 N 109.51 W
Fort Dupont Park ♦ 284c 38.53 N 76.57 W
Forte, Monte ⋏2 71 40.43 N 8.15 E
Forteau 186 51.28 N 56.58 W
Forte dei Marmi 64 43.57 N 10.10 E
Forte de Magoito 266c 38.52 N 9.27 W
Fort Edward 210 43.16 N 73.35 W
Forte República 152 7.45 S 16.23 E
Fort Erie 212 42.54 N 78.56 W
Fort Erie Race Track ♦ 284a 42.55 N 78.56 W
Fortescue ≃ 162 21.00 S 116.06 E
Fort Eustis ■ 208 37.09 N 76.35 W
Fortevoit 46 56.20 N 3.32 W
Fortezza (Franzensfeste) 64 46.47 N 11.37 E
Fort Fairfield 186 46.46 N 67.50 W
Fort Fitzgerald 176 59.53 N 111.37 W
Fort Foote Village 284c 38.46 N 77.01 W
Fort-Foureau 146 12.05 N 15.02 E
Fort Frances 190 48.36 N 93.24 W
Fort Franklin 180 65.11 N 123.46 W
Fort Fraser 182 54.04 N 124.33 W
Fort Frederica National Monument ♦ 192 31.12 N 81.26 W
Fort Gaines 192 31.36 N 85.02 W
Fort Garland 200 37.25 N 105.26 W
Fort Gay 188 38.06 N 82.35 W
Fort George ⊥ 284a 43.15 N 79.04 W
Fort George G. Meade ■ 208 39.05 N 76.50 W
Fort Gibson 196 35.47 N 95.15 W
Fort Gibson Lake ⊜1 196 36.00 N 95.18 W
Fort Good Hope 180 66.15 N 128.38 W
Fort Gordon ■ 192 33.25 N 82.11 W
Fort-Gouraud → Fdérik 148 22.41 N 12.43 W
Fort Green 220 27.36 N 81.56 W
Forth 46 55.47 N 3.41 W
Forth ≃ 46 56.03 N 3.44 W
Forth, Carse of ∨ 46 56.08 N 4.05 W
Forth, Firth of ⊂ 46 56.10 N 2.45 W
Förtha 56 50.56 N 10.14 E
Fort Hall 202 43.02 N 112.26 W
Fort Hall Indian Reservation ◆4 202 43.10 N 112.10 W
Fort Hamilton ■ 276 40.37 N 74.02 W
Forth Bridge ◆5 46 56.00 N 3.25 W
Fort Hertz → Putao 102 27.21 N 97.24 E
Fort Hill → Chitipa 154 9.43 S 33.16 E
Fort Hill ■ 188 38.04 N 77.19 W
Fort Hill State Memorial ⊥ 218 39.07 N 83.25 W
Fort Hood ■ 222 31.08 N 97.46 W
Fort Howard 208 39.12 N 76.27 W
Fort Huachuca ■ 200 31.33 N 110.20 W
Fort Hunter 210 42.57 N 74.17 W
Fort Hunter Liggett ■ 226 35.55 N 121.15 W
Fortierville 206 46.29 N 72.02 W
Fortín 234 18.54 N 97.00 W
Fortin, Lac ⊜ 186 50.50 N 67.46 W
Fortín Ayacucho 248 19.58 S 59.47 W
Fortín Coroneles Sanchez 248 19.20 S 59.58 W
Fortine 182 48.45 N 114.54 W
Fortín Florida 248 20.45 S 59.17 W
Fortín Garrapatal 248 21.27 S 61.30 W
Fortín Teniente Montanía 252 22.04 S 59.57 W
Fortín Uno 252 38.51 S 65.17 W
Fort Jackson ■ 192 34.01 N 80.57 W
Fort Jameson → Chipata 154 13.39 S 32.40 E
Fort Jennings 216 40.54 N 84.17 W
Fort Jeudy, Point of ≻ 241k 12.00 N 61.42 W
Fort Johnson 210 42.57 N 74.14 W
Fort Johnston → Mangochi 154 14.28 S 35.16 E
Fort Jones 204 41.36 N 122.50 W
Fort Kent 186 47.15 N 68.35 W
Fort Klamath 202 42.42 N 121.59 W
Fort Knox ■ 194 37.54 N 85.57 W
Fort-Lamy → N'Djamena 146 12.07 N 15.03 E
Fort Langley 224 49.10 N 122.35 W
Fort Langley National Historic Park ♦ 224 49.10 N 122.35 W
Fort Laramie 200 42.12 N 104.31 W
Fort Laramie National Historic Site ⊥ 198 42.09 N 104.41 W
Fort Larned National Historic Site ⊥ 198 38.10 N 99.12 W
Fort Lauderdale 220 26.07 N 80.08 W
Fort Lauderdale-Hollywood International Airport ✈ 220 26.04 N 80.09 W
Fort Laurens State Memorial ⊥ 214 40.38 N 81.27 W
Fort Leavenworth ■ 198 39.21 N 94.55 W
Fort Le Boeuf ⊥ 214 41.56 N 79.59 W
Fort Lee 210 40.51 N 73.58 W
Fort Lee ■ 208 37.14 N 77.20 W
Fort Lennox National Historic Park ♦ 206 45.06 N 73.16 W
Fort Leonard Wood ■ 194 37.45 N 92.07 W
Fort Lewis ■ 224 47.05 N 122.37 W
Fort Liard 176 60.15 N 123.28 W
Fort-Liberté 238 19.39 N 71.49 W
Fort Lincoln State Park ♦ 198 46.45 N 100.52 W
Fort Littleton 214 40.04 N 77.58 W
Fort Loramie 216 40.21 N 84.22 W
Fort Loudoun Lake ⊜1 192 35.45 N 84.10 W
Fort Lupton 200 40.05 N 104.48 W
Fort Lyon Canal ≚ 198 38.11 N 102.31 W
Fort Macleod 182 49.43 N 113.25 W
Fort Madison 190 40.37 N 91.18 W
Fort-Mahon-Plage 50 50.21 N 1.34 E
Fort Malden National Historic Park ♦ 281 42.06 N 83.07 W
Fort Matanzas National Monument ♦ 192 29.40 N 81.18 W
Fort McClellan ■ 194 33.43 N 85.47 W
Fort McDermitt Indian Reservation ◆4 202 42.00 N 117.32 W
Fort McDowell Indian Reservation ◆4 200 33.38 N 111.41 W
Fort McHenry National Monument and Historic Shrine ♦ 208 39.16 N 76.35 W
Fort Mckinley 218 39.47 N 84.15 W
Fort McMurray 184 56.44 N 111.23 W
Fort McNair ■ 284c 38.52 N 77.04 W
Fort McPherson 180 67.27 N 134.53 W
Fort Meade 220 27.45 N 81.48 W
Fort Mill 192 35.00 N 80.56 W
Fort Miller 210 43.10 N 73.35 W
Fort Mitchell, Al., U.S. 192 32.21 N 85.01 W
Fort Mitchell, Ky., U.S. 218 39.03 N 84.32 W
Fort Mojave Indian Reservation ◆4 200 34.55 N 114.35 W
Fort Monmouth ■ 208 40.19 N 74.02 W
Fort Monroe ■ 208 37.00 N 76.18 W
Fort Montgomery 210 41.20 N 73.59 W
Fort Morgan 198 40.15 N 103.47 W
Fort Myer ■ 284c 38.53 N 77.05 W
Fort Myers 220 26.38 N 81.52 W
Fort Myers Beach 220 26.27 N 81.56 W
Fort Myers Shores 220 26.43 N 81.45 W
Fort Myers Villas 220 26.34 N 81.52 W
Fort Necessity National Battlefield ⊥ 188 39.47 N 79.39 W
Fort Neck ≻1 276 40.39 N 73.28 W
Fort Nelson 176 58.49 N 122.43 W
Fort Nelson ≃ 176 59.30 N 124.00 W
Fort Niagara Beach 284a 43.16 N 79.03 W
Fort Niagara State Park ♦, N.Y., U.S. 210 43.16 N 79.03 W
Fort Niagara State Park ♦, N.Y., U.S. 284a 43.16 N 79.03 W
Fort Nonsense ⊥ 276 40.48 N 74.29 W
Fort Norman 180 64.54 N 125.34 W
Fort Nottingham 158 29.25 S 29.55 E
Fort Ogden 220 27.05 N 81.57 W
Fort Ord ■ 226 36.40 N 121.48 W
Fortore ≃ 68 41.55 N 15.17 E
Fort Parker State Park ♦ 222 31.36 N 96.33 W
Fort Payne 194 34.26 N 85.43 W
Fort Peck 202 48.00 N 106.26 W
Fort Peck Dam ◆6 202 47.52 N 106.38 W
Fort Peck Indian Reservation ◆4 202 48.22 N 105.40 W
Fort Peck Lake ⊜1 202 47.45 N 106.50 W
Fort Pierce 220 27.26 N 80.19 W
Fort Pierce Inlet ⊂ 220 27.28 N 80.18 W
Fort Pierre 198 44.21 N 100.22 W
Fort Pitt Tunnels ◆5 279b 40.26 N 80.00 W
Fort Plain 210 42.55 N 74.37 W
Fort Point National Historic Site ⊥ 282 37.48 N 122.28 W
Fort Polk ■ 194 31.04 N 93.11 W
Fort Portal 154 0.40 N 30.17 E
Fort Providence 176 61.21 N 117.39 W
Fort Pulaski National Monument ♦ 192 32.01 N 80.59 W
Fort Qu'Appelle 184 50.46 N 103.48 W
Fort Raleigh National Historic Site ⊥ 192 35.55 N 75.40 W
Fort Randall Dam ◆6 198 42.48 N 98.35 W
Fort Recovery 216 40.24 N 84.46 W
Fort Resolution 176 61.10 N 113.40 W
Fortress Mountain ▲ 202 44.20 N 109.47 W
Fortress of Louisbourg National Historic Park ♦ 186 45.56 N 59.57 W
Fort Riley ■ 198 39.04 N 96.47 W
Fort Ritchie ■ 208 39.43 N 77.30 W
Fort Rixon 154 20.01 S 29.18 E
Fort Robinson State Park ♦ 198 42.41 N 103.30 W
Fort Rodd Hill National Historic Park ♦ 224 48.26 N 123.28 W
Fortrose, N.Z. 172 46.34 S 168.48 E
Fortrose, Scot., U.K. 46 57.34 N 4.09 W
Fort Rosebery → Mansa 154 11.12 S 28.53 E
Fort Rucker ■ 194 31.20 N 85.42 W
Fort Saint James 182 54.26 N 124.15 W
Fort Saint John 182 56.15 N 120.51 W
Fort Salonga 276 40.55 N 73.18 W
Fort Sam Houston ■ 196 29.27 N 98.27 W
Fort Saskatchewan 182 53.43 N 113.13 W
Fort Scott 198 37.50 N 94.42 W
Fort Seneca 214 41.13 N 83.10 W
Fort-Ševčenko 84 44.31 N 50.16 E
Fort Severn 176 56.00 N 87.38 W
Fort Shawnee 216 40.41 N 84.08 W
Fort Sill ■ 196 34.40 N 98.25 W
Fort Simcoe Historical State Park ♦ 224 46.21 N 120.50 W
Fort Simpson 176 61.52 N 121.23 W
Fort Sisseton State Park ♦ 198 45.39 N 97.32 W
Fort Smith, N.T., Can. 176 60.00 N 111.53 W
Fort Smith, Ar., U.S. 194 35.23 N 94.23 W
Fort Steele 182 49.37 N 115.38 W
Fort Stevens State Park ♦ 224 46.10 N 124.00 W
Fort Stewart ■ 192 31.52 N 81.37 W
Fort Stockton 196 30.53 N 102.52 W
Fort Sumner 196 34.28 N 104.14 W
Fort Sumter National Monument ♦ 192 32.44 N 79.46 W
Fort Supply 196 36.34 N 99.34 W
Fort Tejon State Historical Park ♦ 228 34.52 N 118.53 W
Fort Thomas, Az., U.S. 200 33.02 N 109.57 W
Fort Thomas, Ky., U.S. 218 39.04 N 84.26 W
Fort Thompson 198 44.04 N 99.26 W
Fort Tilden ■ 276 40.33 N 73.53 W
Fort Totten 198 47.58 N 98.59 W
Fort Totten Indian Reservation ◆4 198 47.53 N 98.50 W
Fort Totten Park ♦ 284c 38.57 N 77.00 W
Fort Towson 196 34.01 N 95.15 W
Fort-Trinquet → Bîr Mogreïn 148 25.14 N 11.35 W
Fortuna, Arg. 252 35.07 S 65.23 W
Fortuna, C.R. 236 10.30 N 84.35 W
Fortuna, Ca., U.S. 204 40.35 N 124.09 W
Fortuna, Río de la ≃ 248 16.36 S 58.46 W
Fortuna Ledge (Marshall) 180 61.53 N 162.05 W
Fortune 186 47.04 N 55.50 W
Fortune Bay ⊂ 186 47.25 N 55.25 W
Fortune Ditch ≚ 279a 41.20 N 82.03 W
Fortune Harbour 186 49.31 N 55.15 W
Fortuneswell 42 50.34 N 2.27 W
Fort Union National Monument ♦ 200 35.55 N 105.01 W
Fort Union Trading Post National Historic Site ⊥ 198 48.00 N 104.03 W
Fort Valley 192 32.33 N 83.53 W
Fort Vancouver National Historic Site ⊥ 224 45.38 N 122.37 W
Fort Vermilion 176 58.24 N 116.00 W
Fortville 218 39.55 N 85.50 W
Fort Walton Beach 194 30.24 N 86.37 W
Fort Washakie 200 43.00 N 108.52 W
Fort Washington 208 40.08 N 75.12 W
Fort Washington Forest 208 38.43 N 76.59 W
Fort Washington State Park ♦ 285 40.07 N 75.14 W
Fort Wayne 216 41.07 N 85.07 W
Fort Wayne Military Museum ∨ 281 42.18 N 83.06 W
Fort Wellington 246 6.24 N 57.36 W
Fort Wellington National Historic Park ♦ 212 44.44 N 75.31 W
Fort White 192 29.55 N 82.42 W
Fort William → Thunder Bay, On., Can. 190 48.23 N 89.15 W
Fort William, Scot., U.K. 46 56.49 N 5.07 W
Fort Worth 222 32.43 N 97.19 W
Fort Yates 198 46.05 N 100.37 W
Forty Foot Drain ≚ 42 52.28 N 0.05 W
Forty Fort 210 41.16 N 75.52 W
Fortymile ≃ 180 64.26 N 140.32 W
Fort Yukon 180 66.34 N 145.17 W
Fort Yuma Indian Reservation ◆4 204 32.48 N 114.34 W
Forum ♦ 275a 45.29 N 73.35 W
Forūr, Jazīreh-ye I 128 26.17 N 54.32 E
Forza d'Agrò 70 37.55 N 15.20 E
Forcagno, Passo di)(64 46.30 N 10.08 E
Fosdinovo 64 44.08 N 10.01 E
Fosforescente, Bahía ⊂ 240m 17.59 N 67.01 W
Fosforitnyj 82 55.19 N 38.54 E
Foshan 100 23.03 N 113.09 E
Fosna ≻1, Nor. 24 64.00 N 10.30 E
Fosna ≻1, Nor. 26 63.45 N 10.25 E
Fosnavåg 26 62.21 N 5.39 E
Foso 150 5.42 N 1.17 W
Foss 46 56.41 N 3.58 W
Foss ≃, Eng., U.K. 44 53.57 N 1.06 W
Foss ≃, Wa., U.S. 224 47.43 N 121.18 W
Fossacesia 66 42.15 N 14.29 E
Fossacesia Marina 66 42.15 N 14.30 E
Fossa Eugeniana ≚ 263 51.33 N 6.36 E
Fossano 62 44.33 N 7.43 E
Fossato, Colle di)(66 43.19 N 12.47 E
Fossé 56 49.27 N 5.00 E
Fosse-Martin 261 49.05 N 2.54 E
Fosses 261 49.06 N 2.29 E
Fosses-la-Ville 56 50.24 N 4.42 E
Fossil 202 44.59 N 120.12 W
Fossil Butte National Monument ♦ 202 41.50 N 110.40 W
Fossil Downs 162 18.08 S 125.38 E
Fossil Lake ⊜ 202 43.18 N 120.15 W
Fossombrone 66 43.41 N 12.48 E
Fosston 198 47.34 N 95.45 W
Fos-sur-Mer 62 43.26 N 4.57 E
Foster, Austl. 169 38.39 S 146.12 E
Foster, Ky., U.S. 218 38.47 N 84.12 W
Foster, R.I., U.S. 207 41.51 N 71.45 W
Foster ≃ 184 55.47 N 105.49 W
Foster, Mount ▲ 180 59.48 N 135.29 W
Foster Brook 214 41.59 N 78.37 W
Foster City 226 37.33 N 122.16 W
Foster Creek ≃ 198 44.34 N 98.12 W
Fosterdale 210 41.42 N 74.58 W
Foster Joseph Sayers Reservoir ⊜1 214 41.02 N 77.40 W
Fosters 194 33.05 N 87.41 W
Fosters Pond ⊜ 283 42.37 N 71.08 W
Foster Street 260 51.46 N 0.09 E
Foster Village 229c 21.21 N 157.55 W
Fostoria 214 41.09 N 83.25 W
Fót 264c 47.37 N 19.12 E
Fotadrevo 157b 24.03 S 45.01 E
Fotan 100 24.12 N 117.53 E
Fóti-Somlyó ▲2 264c 47.38 N 19.13 E
Foucarmont 50 49.51 N 1.34 E
Fou-Chouen → Fushun 104 41.52 N 123.53 E
Fouesnant 32 47.54 N 4.01 W
Foug 56 48.41 N 5.47 E
Fougamou 152 1.13 S 10.36 E
Fougères 32 48.21 N 1.12 W
Fougères-sur-Bièvre 50 47.27 N 1.21 E
Fougerolles 58 47.53 N 6.24 E
Fouhsin → Fuxin 104 42.03 N 121.46 E
Fouju 261 48.35 N 2.47 E
Fouke 194 33.16 N 93.53 W
Foula I 46a 60.08 N 2.05 W
Foulain 58 48.02 N 5.13 E
Foulalaba 150 10.41 N 7.22 W
Foula Mori 150 12.10 N 13.51 W
Foulatari 146 13.41 N 12.03 E
Foul Bay ⊂ 140 23.30 N 35.39 E
Fouling → Fuling 102 29.42 N 107.21 E
Foulness ≻ 44 53.47 N 0.43 W
Foulness Island I 44 51.36 N 0.55 E
Foulness Point ≻ 44 51.38 N 0.57 E
Foulpointe 157b 17.41 S 49.31 E
Foulsham 42 52.48 N 1.01 E
Foulwind, Cape ≻ 172 41.45 S 171.28 E
Foumban 152 5.43 N 10.55 E
Foumbot 152 5.30 N 10.38 E
Foumbouni 157a 11.50 S 43.30 E
Foum-el-Hisn 148 28.59 N 8.55 W
Foum-Zguid 148 30.04 N 6.54 W
Foundiougne 150 14.08 N 16.28 W
Fountain, Co., U.S. 198 38.40 N 104.42 W
Fountain, Fl., U.S. 192 30.09 N 85.38 W
Fountain □6 216 40.17 N 87.13 W
Fountain City, In., U.S. 218 39.57 N 84.55 W
Fountain City, Wi., U.S. 190 44.07 N 91.43 W
Fountain Creek ≃, Co., U.S. 198 38.15 N 104.35 W
Fountain Creek ≃, Il., U.S. 219 38.20 N 90.22 W
Fountain Green 200 39.37 N 111.38 W
Fountain Hill 208 40.36 N 75.23 W
Fountain Inn 192 34.41 N 82.11 W
Fountain Park 216 41.50 N 84.32 W
Fountain Peak ▲ 204 34.57 N 115.32 W
Fountain Place 194 30.31 N 91.09 W
Fountains Abbey ∨1 44 54.07 N 1.34 W
Fountains Creek ≃ 208 36.33 N 77.21 W
Fountaintown 218 39.41 N 85.46 W
Fountain Valley 228 33.42 N 117.57 W
Fourche LaFave ≃ 194 34.58 N 92.35 W
Fourche Maline ≃ 194 34.55 N 94.55 W
Fourchu 186 45.43 N 60.15 W
Four Corners 204 44.55 N 122.58 W
Four Elms 260 51.13 N 0.06 E
Four Hole Swamp ≃ 192 33.03 N 80.24 W
Fouriesburg 158 28.38 S 28.14 E
Fourmies 50 50.00 N 4.03 E
Four Mile Creek ≃, On., Can. 284a 43.15 N 79.08 W
Fourmile Creek ≃, N.Y., U.S. 284a 43.17 N 79.00 W
Four Mile Creek ≃, Oh., U.S. 218 39.26 N 84.32 W
Four Mile Creek State Park ♦ 284a 43.16 N 79.00 W
Fourmile Draw ∨ 196 32.40 N 104.18 W
Four Mile Lake ⊜ 212 44.40 N 78.44 W
Four Mile Run ≃ 284c 38.50 N 77.02 W
Four Mountains, Islands of II 180 52.50 N 170.00 W
Fournaise, Piton de la ▲ 157c 21.14 S 55.43 E
Fourneau, Pointe à ≻ 275a 45.22 N 73.51 W
Fourneaux, Fr. 50 47.53 N 1.48 E
Fourneaux, Fr. 62 45.11 N 6.39 E
Fournier, Lac ⊜ 186 51.33 N 65.25 W
Fournière, Lac ⊜ 190 48.04 N 78.03 W
Foúrnoi I 38 37.34 N 26.30 E
Four Oaks 192 35.26 N 78.25 W
Fourqueux 261 48.53 N 2.04 E
Fours 32 46.49 N 3.43 E
Fourteenmile Creek ≃ 218 38.26 N 85.37 W
Fourth Cataract → Rābi', Ash-Shallāl ar- ⊥ 140 18.47 N 32.03 E
Fourth Cliff ≻4 283 42.09 N 70.42 W
Four Towns 281 42.37 N 83.25 W
Fous, Pointe des ≻ 240d 15.12 N 61.20 W
Foussard ≃ 50 48.16 N 1.17 E
Fouta Djalon ◆1 150 11.30 N 12.30 W
Fou-Tcheou → Fuzhou 100 26.06 N 119.17 E
Foux, Cap à ≻ 238 19.41 N 73.27 W
Fouyang → Fuyang 100 32.54 N 115.49 E
Fouzon ≃ 50 47.16 N 1.27 E
Foveaux Strait IJ 172 46.35 S 168.00 E
Foveran 46 57.18 N 2.02 W
Fowey 42 50.20 N 4.38 W
Fowler, Ca., U.S. 226 36.37 N 119.40 W
Fowler, Co., U.S. 198 38.07 N 104.01 W
Fowler, In., U.S. 216 40.37 N 87.19 W
Fowler, Ks., U.S. 198 37.23 N 100.11 W
Fowler, Mi., U.S. 216 43.00 N 84.44 W
Fowler, Oh., U.S. 214 41.19 N 80.40 W
Fowler, Lake ⊜ 168b 35.06 S 137.37 E
Fowler, Point ≻ 162 32.02 S 132.29 E
Fowler Creek ≃ 281 42.17 N 83.30 W
Fowlers Bay 162 31.59 S 132.27 E
Fowlerton 196 28.28 N 98.48 W
Fowlerville 216 42.39 N 84.04 W
Fowliang → Jingdezhen 100 29.16 N 117.11 E
Fowman 128 37.13 N 49.19 E
Fox 180 64.51 N 147.46 W
Fox ≃, Mb., Can. 184 56.03 N 93.18 W
Fox ≃, U.S. 190 40.18 N 91.30 W
Fox ≃, U.S. 216 41.21 N 88.50 W
Fox ≃, Il., U.S. 194 38.32 N 88.08 W
Fox ≃, Wi., U.S. 190 44.32 N 88.01 W
Foxboro, On., Can. 212 44.15 N 77.26 W
Foxboro, Ma., U.S. 207 42.03 N 71.15 W
Foxboro Raceway ♦ 283 42.06 N 71.16 W
Foxboro Stadium ♦ 283 42.05 N 71.16 W
Fox Brook ≃ 276 41.03 N 74.13 W
Foxburg 214 41.09 N 79.41 W
Fox Chapel 279b 40.30 N 79.55 W
Fox Chase ◆8 285 40.04 N 75.05 W
Fox Chase Manor 285 40.05 N 75.06 W
Fox Creek ≃, Ky., U.S. 218 38.16 N 83.41 W
Fox Creek ≃, N.Y., U.S. 210 42.41 N 74.18 W
Foxe Basin ⊂ 176 68.25 N 77.00 W
Foxe-Becken → Foxe Basin ⊂ 176 68.25 N 77.00 W
Foxe Channel IJ 176 64.30 N 80.00 W
Foxen ⊜ 26 59.23 N 11.52 E
Foxe Peninsula ≻1 176 65.00 N 76.00 W
Foxford 48 53.58 N 9.08 W
Fox Glacier 172 43.28 S 170.00 E
Foxhall 284c 39.04 N 77.03 W
Fox Harbour 186 47.19 N 53.55 W
Fox Hills 284c 39.02 N 77.11 W
Foxhole 42 50.21 N 4.52 W
Foxholes 44 54.08 N 0.28 W
Fox Hollow Lake ⊜ 276 41.02 N 74.40 W
Fox Island I, On., Can. 212 44.28 N 78.24 W
Fox Island I, Wa., U.S. 224 47.16 N 122.37 W
Fox Islands II 180 53.30 N 168.00 W
Fox Lake, Il., U.S. 216 42.23 N 88.11 W
Fox Lake, Wi., U.S. 190 43.33 N 88.54 W
Fox Lake ⊜ 216 42.25 N 88.09 W
Fox Mountain ▲ 180 61.55 N 133.22 W
Foxpark 200 41.05 N 106.09 W
Fox Point 216 43.09 N 87.54 W
Fox Point ≻ 276 40.54 N 73.35 W
Fox River Estates 216 41.58 N 88.20 W
Fox River Grove 216 42.12 N 88.12 W
Foxton 172 40.28 S 175.18 E
Foxton Beach 172 40.28 S 175.13 E
Foxvale 283 42.02 N 71.14 W
Fox Valley, Austl. 274a 33.45 S 151.06 E
Fox Valley, Sk., Can. 184 50.29 N 109.28 W
Foxwells 208 37.38 N 76.18 W
Foxwist Green 262 53.12 N 2.34 W
Foxworth 194 31.14 N 89.52 W
Foyedong 98 40.41 N 119.12 E
Foyers 46 57.14 N 4.29 W
Foyle ≃ 48 54.59 N 7.18 W
Foyle, Lough ⊂ 48 55.06 N 7.08 W
Foynes 48 52.37 N 9.06 W
Foza 64 45.54 N 11.38 E
Foz do Areia, Represa de ⊜1 252 26.00 S 51.35 W
Foz do Cunene 152 17.16 S 11.50 E
Foz do Iguaçu 252 25.33 S 54.35 W
Foz do Jordão 248 9.23 S 71.56 W
Foz Giraldo 34 40.00 N 7.43 W
Foziling 100 31.20 N 116.17 E
Frabosa Soprana 62 44.17 N 7.48 E
Frackville 208 40.47 N 76.13 W
Fraction Run ≃ 278 41.34 N 88.04 W
Fraga, Arg. 252 33.30 S 65.48 W
Fraga, Esp. 34 41.31 N 0.21 E
Fragagnano 68 40.26 N 17.28 E
Fragneto Monforte 68 41.15 N 14.46 E
Fragoso, Cayo I 240p 22.44 N 79.30 W
Fragrant Hills Park ♦ 271a 39.59 N 116.11 E
Fragua, Sierra de la ⋏ 196 26.41 N 102.13 W
Fraile Muerto 252 32.31 S 54.32 W
Fraïn, Chott el ⊜ 34 35.57 N 5.38 E
Fraire 50 50.16 N 4.30 E
Fraisans 58 47.09 N 5.46 E
Fraisse 62 45.23 N 4.15 E
Fraize 58 48.11 N 7.00 E
Fram 61 46.27 N 15.38 E
Frameries 50 50.24 N 3.54 E
Framingham 207 42.16 N 71.25 W
Framingham State College ∨2 283 42.18 N 71.26 W
Framlingham 42 52.13 N 1.21 E
Frammersbach 56 50.04 N 9.28 E
Framnes Mountains ⋏ 9 67.50 S 62.35 E
Frampol 30 50.41 N 22.40 E
Frampton Cotterell 42 51.32 N 2.29 W
Frampton on Severn 42 51.46 N 2.22 W
França, Bra. 250 11.34 S 40.36 W
Franca, Bra. 255 20.32 S 47.24 W
Franca-Iosifa, Zeml'a (Franz Josef Land) II 12 81.00 N 55.00 E
Français, Récif des ◆2 175f 19.40 S 163.20 E
Francavilla al Mare 66 42.25 N 14.17 E
Francavilla Angitola 68 38.46 N 16.16 E
Francavilla d'Ete 66 43.11 N 13.32 E
Francavilla di Sicilia 70 37.54 N 15.08 E
Francavilla Fontana 68 40.31 N 17.35 E
Francavilla in Sinni 68 40.05 N 16.12 E
Francavilla Marittima 68 39.49 N 16.23 E
France □1, Europe 22 46.00 N 2.00 E
France □1, Europe 32 46.00 N 2.00 E
Frances 180 60.12 N 129.02 W
Francés, Cabo ≻, Cuba 240p 21.54 N 84.02 W
Francés, Cabo ≻, Cuba 240p 21.38 N 83.12 W
Frances Creek 164 13.35 S 131.52 E
Francês dos Carvalhos 256 22.05 S 44.29 W
Frances Lake ⊜ 180 61.25 N 129.30 W
Francés Viejo, Cabo ≻ 238 19.39 N 69.55 W
Francesville 216 40.59 N 86.52 W
Franceville 152 1.38 S 13.35 E
Francfort-sur-Main → Frankfurt am Main 56 50.07 N 8.40 E
Franche-Comté □9 58 47.00 N 6.00 E
Franchère, Lac ⊜ 206 46.47 N 74.58 W
Franches-Montagnes ⋏ 58 47.12 N 7.00 E
Francia 252 32.33 S 56.37 W
Francia → France □1 32 46.00 N 2.00 E
Francia, Estación de ◆5 266d 41.23 N 2.11 E
Francis 184 50.05 N 103.55 W
Francis, Lake ⊜ 206 45.02 N 71.20 W
Francis Case, Lake ⊜1 198 43.15 N 99.00 W
Francisco A. Berra 258 35.23 S 58.51 W
Francisco Álvarez 258 34.38 S 58.52 W
Francisco Beltrão 252 26.05 S 53.04 W
Francisco I. Madero, Méx. 232 25.45 N 103.21 W
Francisco I. Madero, Méx. 232 24.32 N 104.22 W
Francisco I. Madero, Méx. 234 21.36 N 104.49 W
Francisco José, Tierra → Franca-Iosifa, Zeml'a II 12 81.00 N 55.00 E
Francisco Morato 256 23.16 S 46.45 W
Francisco Morazán □5 236 14.15 N 87.15 W
Francisco Murguía 234 24.00 N 103.01 W
Francisco Perito Moreno, Parque Nacional ♦ 254 47.50 S 72.08 W
Francisco Sá 255 16.28 S 43.30 W
Francisco Zarco 204 32.06 N 116.30 W
Francis E. Warren Air Force Base ■ 198 41.09 N 104.52 W
Francistown 156 21.11 S 27.32 E
Francitas 222 28.52 N 96.20 W
Franco da Rocha 256 23.20 S 46.43 W
Francofonte 70 37.14 N 14.53 E
François 186 47.35 N 56.45 W
François, Lacs à ⊜ 186 51.40 N 65.49 W
François-Joseph, Îles du → Franca-Iosifa, Zeml'a II 12 81.00 N 55.00 E
François Lake 182 54.04 N 125.44 W
François Lake ⊜ 182 54.00 N 125.40 W
Francolise 68 41.11 N 14.03 E
Franconia Notch State Park ♦ 188 44.06 N 71.43 W
Franconville 261 48.59 N 2.14 E
Francs Peak ▲ 202 43.58 N 109.20 W
Francueil 50 47.19 N 1.05 E
Franeker 52 53.11 N 5.32 E
Frangy 58 46.01 N 5.56 E
Frank 279b 40.16 N 79.48 W
Frank and Poet Drain ≚ 281 42.06 N 83.12 W
Frankby 262 53.22 N 3.08 W
Frankel City 196 32.23 N 102.47 W
Franken □9 30 50.00 N 10.00 E
Frankenau 56 51.05 N 8.56 E
Frankenberg 54 50.54 N 13.01 E
Frankenberg-Eder 56 51.03 N 8.48 E
Frankenburg 60 48.05 N 13.30 E
Frankenheim 56 50.32 N 10.04 E
Frankenhöhe ⋏ 56 49.15 N 10.15 E
Frankenmarkt 64 47.59 N 13.25 E
Frankenmuth 190 43.19 N 83.44 W
Frankenstein 56 49.26 N 7.58 E
Frankenthal 56 49.32 N 8.21 E
Frankenwald ⋏ 56 50.18 N 11.36 E
Frankfield 241q 18.09 N 77.22 W
Frankford, On., Can. 212 44.12 N 77.36 W
Frankford, De., U.S. 208 38.31 N 75.14 W
Frankford, Mo., U.S. 219 39.29 N 91.19 W
Frankford ◆8 285 40.01 N 75.05 W
Frankford Arsenal ■ 285 40.00 N 75.04 W
Frankfort, S. Afr. 158 32.44 S 27.28 E
Frankfort, S. Afr. 158 27.17 S 28.30 E
Frankfort, Il., U.S. 216 41.29 N 87.50 W
Frankfort, In., U.S. 216 40.16 N 86.30 W
Frankfort, Ks., U.S. 198 39.42 N 96.25 W
Frankfort, Ky., U.S. 218 38.12 N 84.52 W
Frankfort, Mi., U.S. 190 44.38 N 86.14 W
Frankfort, N.Y., U.S. 210 43.02 N 75.04 W
Frankfort, Oh., U.S. 218 39.24 N 83.10 W
Frankfort, S.D., U.S. 198 44.52 N 98.18 W
Frankfort Springs 214 40.30 N 80.25 W
Frankfurt 54 52.20 N 14.33 E
Frankfurt am Main 56 50.07 N 8.40 E
Frankfurt am Main, Flughafen ✈ 56 50.02 N 8.33 E
Frank G. Bonelli Regional County Park ♦ 280 34.05 N 117.49 W
Frank Hann National Park ♦ 162 32.50 S 120.25 E
Fränkische Alb ⋏2 60 49.20 N 11.30 E
Fränkische Rezat ≃ 56 49.11 N 11.01 E
Fränkische Saale ≃ 56 50.03 N 9.42 E
Fränkische Schweiz ◆1 60 49.45 N 11.25 E
Frank Key I 220 25.07 N 80.54 W
Frankland ≃ 162 34.58 S 116.49 E
Frankleben 54 51.18 N 11.56 E
Franklin, S. Afr. 158 30.18 S 29.30 E
Franklin, Az., U.S. 200 32.40 N 109.04 W
Franklin, Ga., U.S. 192 33.16 N 85.05 W
Franklin, Id., U.S. 202 42.00 N 111.48 W
Franklin, Il., U.S. 219 39.37 N 90.03 W
Franklin, In., U.S. 218 39.28 N 86.03 W
Franklin, Ky., U.S. 194 36.43 N 86.34 W
Franklin, La., U.S. 194 29.47 N 91.30 W
Franklin, Me., U.S. 188 44.35 N 68.13 W
Franklin, Ma., U.S. 207 42.05 N 71.23 W
Franklin, Mi., U.S. 281 42.31 N 83.18 W
Franklin, Mn., U.S. 198 44.31 N 94.52 W
Franklin, Ne., U.S. 198 40.05 N 98.57 W
Franklin, N.H., U.S. 188 43.26 N 71.38 W
Franklin, N.J., U.S. 210 41.07 N 74.34 W
Franklin, N.Y., U.S. 210 42.20 N 75.09 W
Franklin, N.C., U.S. 192 35.10 N 83.22 W
Franklin, Oh., U.S. 218 39.33 N 84.18 W
Franklin, Pa., U.S. 214 41.24 N 79.50 W
Franklin, Tn., U.S. 194 35.55 N 86.52 W
Franklin, Tx., U.S. 222 31.01 N 96.29 W
Franklin, Vt., U.S. 206 44.58 N 72.55 W
Franklin, Va., U.S. 208 36.40 N 76.55 W
Franklin, W.V., U.S. 188 38.39 N 79.20 W
Franklin, Wi., U.S. 216 42.54 N 88.03 W
Franklin □6, In., U.S. 218 39.25 N 85.01 W
Franklin □6, Ky., U.S. 218 38.14 N 84.52 W
Franklin □6, Ma., U.S. 207 42.36 N 72.36 W
Franklin □6, Mo., U.S. 219 38.25 N 91.03 W
Franklin □6, N.Y., U.S. 206 44.57 N 74.18 W
Franklin □6, Oh., U.S. 218 39.57 N 83.00 W
Franklin □6, Pa., U.S. 208 39.56 N 77.40 W
Franklin □6, Tx., U.S. 222 33.07 N 95.13 W
Franklin □6, Vt., U.S. 206 44.57 N 72.52 W
Franklin, Mount ▲ 171b 35.29 S 148.47 E
Franklin, Point ≻ 180 70.54 N 158.48 W
Franklin Bay ⊂ 176 69.45 N 126.00 W
Franklin Canyon Reservoir ⊜1 280 34.06 N 118.25 W
Franklin Delano Roosevelt National Historic Site ⊥ 210 41.46 N 73.56 W
Franklin Delano Roosevelt Park ♦ 285 39.54 N 75.11 W
Franklin D. Roosevelt Lake ⊜1 202 48.20 N 118.10 W
Franklin Farms 279b 40.10 N 80.16 W
Franklin Grove 216 41.50 N 89.18 W
Franklin Harbor ⊂ 166 33.42 S 136.56 E
Franklin Institute ∨ 285 39.57 N 75.11 W
Franklin Island I 212 45.24 N 80.20 W
Franklin Lake ⊜, N.T., Can. 176 66.56 N 96.03 W
Franklin Lake ⊜, Nv., U.S. 204 40.24 N 115.12 W
Franklin Lake ⊜, N.J., U.S. 276 40.59 N 74.13 W
Franklin Lakes 276 41.01 N 74.12 W
Franklin-Lower Gordon Wild Rivers National Park ♦ 166 42.46 S 145.45 E
Franklin Mountains ⋏, N.T., Can. 180 63.00 N 123.50 W
Franklin Mountains ⋏, N.Z. 172 44.55 S 167.45 E
Franklin Park, Il., U.S. 216 41.56 N 87.51 W
Franklin Park, Md., U.S. 284c 39.03 N 77.06 W
Franklin Park, N.J., U.S. 276 40.26 N 74.32 W
Franklin Park, N.Y., U.S. 210 43.05 N 76.05 W
Franklin Park, Pa., U.S. 214 40.35 N 80.06 W
Franklin Park, Va., U.S. 284c 38.55 N 77.09 W
Franklin Park ♦ 283 42.18 N 71.06 W
Franklin Pond ⊜ 276 41.06 N 74.35 W
Franklin Ridge ▲ 282 38.00 N 122.10 W
Franklin River 224 49.06 N 124.49 W
Franklin Roosevelt Park ◆8 273d 26.09 S 27.59 E
Franklin Springs 210 43.02 N 75.24 W
Franklin Square 210 40.42 N 73.40 W
Franklin State Forest ♦ 283 42.04 N 71.26 W
Franklin Strait IJ 176 72.00 N 96.00 W
Franklinton, La., U.S. 194 30.50 N 90.09 W
Franklinton, N.C., U.S. 192 36.06 N 78.27 W
Franklintown 208 40.05 N 77.02 W
Franklinville, N.J., U.S. 208 39.37 N 75.04 W
Franklinville, N.Y., U.S. 210 42.20 N 78.27 W
Frankreich → France □1 32 46.00 N 2.00 E
Frankston, Austl. 169 38.08 S 145.07 E
Frankston, Tx., U.S. 222 32.03 N 95.30 W
Franksville 216 42.45 N 87.54 W
Frankton 216 40.13 N 85.46 W
Frankville 194 31.38 N 88.08 W
Frånö 26 62.54 N 17.50 E
Fr'anovo 82 56.08 N 38.27 E
Franschhoek 158 33.55 S 19.09 E
Fransfontein 156 20.12 S 15.01 E
Fränsta 26 62.30 N 16.09 E
Františkovy Lázně 54 50.04 N 12.21 E

Symbols in the index entries represent the broad categories identified in the key at the right. Symbols with superior numbers (⋏1) identify subcategories (see complete key on page I · 1).

Symbole im Register stellen die rechts im Schlüssel erklärten Kategorien dar. Symbole mit hochgestellten Ziffern (⋏1) bezeichnen Unterabteilungen einer Kategorie (vgl. vollständiger Schlüssel auf Seite I · 1).

Los símbolos incluídos en el texto del índice representan las grandes categorias identificadas con la clave a la derecha. Los símbolos con numeros en su parte superior (⋏1) identifican las subcategorias (véase la clave completa en la página I · 1).

Les symboles de l'index représentent les catégories indiquées dans la légende à droite. Les symboles suivis d'un indice (⋏1) représentent des sous-catégories (voir légende complète à la page I · 1).

Os símbolos incluídos no texto do índice representam as grandes categorias identificadas com a chave à direita. Os símbolos com números em sua parte superior (⋏1) identificam as subcategorias (veja-se a chave completa à página I · 1).

	English	Deutsch	Español	Français	Português
▲	Mountain	Berg	Montaña	Montagne	Montanha
⋏	Mountains	Gebirge	Montañas	Montagnes	Montanhas
)(	Pass	Paß	Paso	Col	Passo
∨	Valley, Canyon	Tal, Cañon	Valle, Cañón	Vallée, Canyon	Vale, Canhão
≐	Plain	Ebene	Llano	Plaine	Planície
≻	Cape	Kap	Cabo	Cap	Cabo
I	Island	Insel	Isla	Île	Ilha
II	Islands	Inseln	Islas	Îles	Ilhas
◆	Other Topographic Features	Andere Topographische Objekte	Otros Elementos Topográficos	Autres données topographiques	Outros acidentes topográficos

ESPAÑOL: Nombre · Página · Lat.°′ · Long.°′ W = Oeste
FRANÇAIS: Nom · Page · Lat.°′ · Long.°′ W = Ouest
PORTUGUÊS: Nome · Página · Lat.°′ · Long.°′ W = Oeste

Nombre	Página	Lat.°′	Long.°′ W = Oeste
Franvillers	50	49.58 N	2.30 E
Franzburg	54	54.11 N	12.52 E
Franzensburg ⊥	264b	48.04 N	16.22 E
Franzensfeste → Fortezza	64	46.47 N	11.37 E
Franz Josef	172	43.24 S	170.11 E
Franz Josef Land → Franca Iosifa, Zeml'a II	12	81.00 N	55.00 E
Franz-Josefs-Bahnhof ◆[5]	264b	48.13 N	16.21 E
Franz-Josefs-Höhe ♠	64	47.04 N	12.45 E
Französische Süd- und Antarktis-Gebiete → French Southern and Antarctic Ter □[2]	6	49.30 S	69.30 E
Französisch-Polynesien → French Polynesia □[2]	14	15.00 S	140.00 W
Frasca, Capo della ›	71	39.46 N	8.27 E
Frascati	66	41.48 N	12.41 E
Frascineto	68	39.50 N	16.16 E
Frasdorf	64	47.48 N	12.16 E
Fraser, Co., U.S.	200	39.56 N	105.49 W
Fraser, Mi., U.S.	281	42.32 N	82.56 W
Fraser ≃, B.C., Can.	182	49.09 N	123.12 W
Fraser ≃, Nf., Can.	176	56.35 N	61.55 W
Fraser ≃, Co., U.S.	200	40.06 N	105.58 W
Fraser, Mount ∧	162	25.39 S	118.23 E
Fraserburg	158	31.55 S	21.30 E
Fraserburgh	46	57.42 N	2.00 W
Fraser Island I	166	25.15 S	153.10 E
Fraser Lake	182	54.04 N	124.51 W
Fraser Lake ⊜	182	54.05 N	124.35 W
Fraser National Park ♠	169	37.10 S	145.50 E
Fraser Plateau ⋏[1]	182	52.00 N	123.00 W
Fraser Range	162	32.03 S	122.48 E
Frasertown	172	38.58 S	177.24 E
Frasne	58	46.51 N	6.10 E
Frasnes-lez-Anvaing	50	50.40 N	3.36 E
Frassine ≃	64	45.18 N	11.37 E
Frassinoro	64	44.18 N	10.34 E
Frati, Monte dei ∧	66	43.40 N	12.10 E
Fratres	61	48.59 N	15.21 E
Frattamaggiore	68	40.57 N	14.16 E
Frattócchie	267a	41.46 N	12.37 E
Frauenfeld	58	47.34 N	8.54 E
Frauenkirchen	61	47.50 N	16.56 E
Frauenstein	54	50.48 N	13.32 E
Frauental an der Lassnitz	61	46.48 N	15.14 E
Frauenwald	54	50.35 N	10.51 E
Fray Bentos	252	33.08 S	58.18 W
Fray Jorge, Parque Nacional ♠	252	30.40 S	71.45 W
Fray Luis Beltrán	252	39.19 S	65.46 W
Fray Marcos	252	34.11 S	55.44 W
Frazee	198	46.43 N	95.42 W
Frazer, Mt., U.S.	202	48.03 N	106.02 W
Frazer, Pa., U.S.	208	40.02 N	75.33 W
Frazeysburg	214	40.07 N	82.07 W
Frazier Mountain ∧	228	34.47 N	118.58 W
Frazier Park	228	34.49 N	118.56 W
Fr'azino	82	55.58 N	38.04 E
Frazzanò	70	38.04 N	14.44 E
Frechen	56	50.54 N	6.49 E
Frechilla	34	42.08 N	4.50 W
Freckenhorst	52	51.55 N	7.58 E
Freckleton	262	53.45 N	2.52 W
Freddo ≃	70	38.01 N	12.54 E
Fredeburg	56	51.11 N	8.18 E
Fredelsloh	52	51.44 N	9.47 E
Freden	52	51.56 N	9.54 E
Fredenbeck	52	53.32 N	9.24 E
Fredensborg	41	55.58 N	12.24 E
Fredensborg ⊥	41	55.58 N	12.23 E
Frederic	190	45.39 N	92.28 W
Frederica	208	39.00 N	75.27 W
Fredericia	41	55.35 N	9.46 E
Frederick, Il., U.S.	219	40.04 N	90.26 W
Frederick, Md., U.S.	208	39.24 N	77.24 W
Frederick, Ok., U.S.	196	34.23 N	99.01 W
Frederick, S.D., U.S.	198	45.49 N	98.30 W
Frederick □[6]	208	39.25 N	77.25 W
Frederick Hills ⋏[2]	164	12.41 S	136.00 E
Frederick House ≃	190	49.06 N	81.10 W
Frederick House Lake ⊜	190	48.40 N	80.55 W
Frederick Island I	162	34.04 S	122.00 E
Frederick Reef ✢[2]	166	20.58 S	154.23 E
Fredericksburg, In., U.S.	218	38.26 N	86.11 W
Fredericksburg, Ia., U.S.	190	42.57 N	92.11 W
Fredericksburg, Oh., U.S.	214	40.40 N	81.52 W
Fredericksburg, Pa., U.S.	214	40.27 N	76.26 W
Fredericksburg, Tx., U.S.	196	30.16 N	98.52 W
Fredericksburg, Va., U.S.	208	38.18 N	77.27 W
Fredericksburg Battlefield ⊥	208	38.17 N	77.28 W
Frederick Sound ⊔	180	57.00 N	133.00 W
Fredericktown, Mo., U.S.	194	37.33 N	90.17 W
Fredericktown, Oh., U.S.	214	40.28 N	82.32 W
Frederico Westphalen	252	27.22 S	53.24 W
Fredericton	186	45.58 N	66.39 W
Fredericton Junction	186	45.40 N	66.37 W
Frederik Hendrikeiland → Yos Sudarso, Pulau I	164	7.50 S	138.30 E
Frederiksberg, Dan.	41	55.25 N	11.34 E
Frederiksberg, Dan.	41	55.41 N	12.32 E
Frederiksborg □[6]	41	55.56 N	12.18 E
Frederiksborg ⊥	41	55.56 N	12.19 E
Frederikshåb (Paamiut)	176	62.00 N	49.43 W
Frederikshavn	26	57.26 N	10.32 E
Frederikssund	41	55.50 N	12.04 E
Frederiksted	241n	17.43 N	64.53 W
Frederiksværk	41	55.58 N	12.02 E
Frederik Willem IV Vallen ∟	250	3.28 N	57.37 W
Fredersdorf	54	52.31 N	13.44 E
Fredonia, Col.	246	5.55 N	75.41 W
Fredonia, Az., U.S.	200	36.03 N	112.08 W
Fredonia, Ks., U.S.	198	37.32 N	95.49 W
Fredonia, N.Y., U.S.	214	42.26 N	79.19 W
Fredonia, N.D., U.S.	198	46.19 N	99.05 W
Fredonia, Pa., U.S.	214	41.20 N	80.14 W
Fredrika	26	64.05 N	18.24 E
Fredriksberg	40	60.08 N	14.23 E
Fredrikstad	26	59.13 N	10.57 E
Freeburg, Il., U.S.	219	38.25 N	89.54 W
Freeburg, Mo., U.S.	219	38.18 N	91.55 W
Freeburg, Pa., U.S.	208	40.46 N	76.57 W
Freedom, Ca., U.S.	226	36.56 N	121.46 W
Freedom, Pa., U.S.	214	40.40 N	80.14 W
Freehold, N.J., U.S.	208	40.15 N	74.16 W
Freehold, N.Y., U.S.	210	42.22 N	74.03 W
Freeland, Mi., U.S.	190	43.31 N	84.07 W
Freeland, Pa., U.S.	210	41.01 N	75.53 W
Freeland, Wa., U.S.	224	48.01 N	122.32 W
Freeland Park	216	40.37 N	87.30 W
Freeling, Mount ∧	162	22.35 S	133.06 E
Freel Peak ∧	226	38.52 N	119.54 W
Freels, Cape ›, Nf., Can.	186	46.37 N	53.33 W
Freels, Cape ›, Nf., Can.	186	49.15 N	53.28 W
Freeman	198	43.21 N	97.26 W
Freeman ≃	182	54.20 N	114.47 W
Freeman, Lake ⊜	216	40.42 N	86.45 W
Freemansburg	210	40.37 N	75.20 W
Freemount	48	52.16 N	8.53 W
Freeport, Ba.	238	26.30 N	78.45 W
Freeport, N.S., Can.	186	44.17 N	66.19 W
Freeport, On., Can.	212	43.25 N	80.25 W
Freeport, Fl., U.S.	194	30.29 N	86.08 W
Freeport, Il., U.S.	190	42.17 N	89.37 W
Freeport, Me., U.S.	188	43.51 N	70.06 W
Freeport, Mi., U.S.	216	42.45 N	85.18 W
Freeport, N.Y., U.S.	210	40.39 N	73.35 W
Freeport, Oh., U.S.	214	40.12 N	81.15 W
Freeport, Pa., U.S.	210	40.40 N	79.41 W
Freeport, Tx., U.S.	222	28.57 N	95.21 W
Freer	196	27.52 N	98.37 W
Freest	54	54.08 N	13.43 E
Freeston	222	31.32 N	96.15 W
Freestone	171a	28.08 S	152.08 E
Freestone □[6]	222	31.44 N	96.10 W
Freetown, Antig.	240c	17.03 N	61.42 W
Freetown, S.L.	150	8.30 N	13.15 W
Freetown, In., U.S.	218	38.58 N	86.07 W
Freetown, N.Y., U.S.	207	40.58 N	72.11 W
Freeville	210	42.30 N	76.20 W
Freewood Acres	208	40.10 N	74.15 W
Freezeout Lake ⊜	202	47.40 N	112.03 W
Fregenal de la Sierra	34	38.10 N	6.39 W
Fregene ◆[8]	66	41.51 N	12.12 E
Freiamt	58	48.10 N	7.55 E
Freiberg, Dtsch.	54	50.54 N	13.20 E
Freiberg, Dtsch.	56	48.56 N	9.12 E
Freiberger Mulde ≃	54	51.10 N	12.48 E
Freiburg, Dtsch.	52	53.49 N	9.17 E
Freiburg → Fribourg, Schw.	58	46.48 N	7.09 E
Freiburg □[5]	58	48.00 N	8.25 E
Freiburg im Breisgau	58	47.59 N	7.51 E
Freienbach	58	47.12 N	8.45 E
Freienhufen	54	51.35 N	13.58 E
Freiensteinau	56	50.26 N	9.24 E
Freie Universität ʊ[2]	264a	52.26 N	13.16 E
Freigericht	56	50.08 N	9.07 E
Freihung	60	49.37 N	11.55 E
Freiland	61	47.58 N	15.34 E
Freilassing	64	47.50 N	12.59 E
Freilingen	56	50.33 N	7.50 E
Freinberg	60	48.34 N	13.31 E
Freinsheim	56	49.30 N	8.13 E
Freirina	252	28.30 S	71.06 W
Freisen	56	49.33 N	7.14 E
Freisenbruch ◆[8]	263	51.27 N	7.06 E
Freising	60	48.23 N	11.44 E
Freistadt	61	48.31 N	14.31 E
Freital	54	51.00 N	13.39 E
Freiwalde	54	51.58 N	13.44 E
Freixial	266c	38.54 N	9.09 W
Fréjus	62	43.26 N	6.44 E
Fréjus, Tunnel du ◆[5]	62	45.08 N	6.40 E
Frémainville	261	49.04 N	1.52 E
Fremantle	168a	32.03 S	115.45 E
Fremdingen	56	48.58 N	10.27 E
Fremington	42	51.04 N	4.07 W
Fremont, Ca., U.S.	226	37.32 N	121.59 W
Fremont, In., U.S.	216	41.43 N	84.55 W
Fremont, Ia., U.S.	190	41.12 N	92.26 W
Fremont, Mi., U.S.	190	43.28 N	85.56 W
Fremont, Ne., U.S.	198	41.26 N	96.29 W
Fremont, N.C., U.S.	192	35.32 N	77.58 W
Fremont, Oh., U.S.	214	41.21 N	83.07 W
Fremont, Wi., U.S.	190	44.15 N	88.51 W
Fremont ≃	200	38.24 N	110.42 W
Fremont Canyon V	280	33.48 N	117.42 W
Fremont Island I	200	41.09 N	112.20 W
Fremont Lake ⊜	202	42.57 N	109.49 W
Fremont Peak ∧, Ca., U.S.	226	36.46 N	121.30 W
Fremont Peak ∧, Ca., U.S.	228	35.12 N	117.27 W
Fremont Valley V	228	35.10 N	118.00 W
French ≃	190	45.56 N	80.54 W
French Broad ≃	192	35.57 N	83.51 W
Frenchburg	192	37.57 N	83.37 W
French Camp	226	37.53 N	121.16 W
Frenchcap Cay I	240m	18.14 N	64.51 W
French Creek ≃, Mb., Can.	184	57.02 N	92.12 W
French Creek ≃, U.S.	214	41.25 N	79.50 W
French Creek ≃, Oh., U.S.	279a	41.27 N	82.07 W
French Creek ≃, Pa., U.S.	208	40.08 N	75.31 W
French Creek ≃, S.D., U.S.	198	43.38 N	102.55 W
French Creek, South Branch ≃, Pa., U.S.	214	41.54 N	79.54 W
French Creek, South Branch ≃, Pa., U.S.	285	40.10 N	75.42 W
French Creek, West Branch ≃	214	41.58 N	79.52 W
French Creek State Park ♠	208	40.13 N	75.47 W
French Frigate Shoals ✢[2]	14	23.45 N	166.10 W
French Guiana (Guyane français) □[2], S.A.	242	4.00 N	53.00 W
French Guiana (Guyane français) □[2], S.A.	250	4.00 N	53.00 W
French Island I	169	38.21 S	145.21 E
French Lick	194	38.32 N	86.37 W
Frenchman (Frenchman Creek) ≃	202	48.24 N	107.05 W
Frenchman Bay ⊂	188	44.25 N	68.10 W
Frenchman Butte	184	53.35 N	109.38 W
Frenchman Creek (Frenchman) ≃, N.A.	202	48.24 N	107.05 W
Frenchman Creek ≃, U.S.	198	40.13 N	100.50 W
Frenchman Lake ⊜	204	36.48 N	116.56 W
Frenchman Point ›	212	44.35 N	81.18 W
Frenchman's Bay ⊂	275b	43.49 N	79.05 W
Frenchmans Cap ∧	166	42.16 S	145.50 E
Frenchman's Creek ≃, On., Can.	284a	42.56 N	78.56 W
Frenchmans Creek ≃, Ca., U.S.	282	37.29 N	122.27 W
French Meadows Reservoir ⊜[1]	226	39.07 N	120.25 W
Frenchpark	48	53.52 N	8.26 W
French Pass	172	40.56 S	173.50 E
French Polynesia □[2]	14	15.00 S	140.00 W
Frenchs Forest	274a	33.45 S	151.14 E
French Stream ≃	283	42.07 N	70.53 W
Frenchtown	210	40.31 N	75.03 W
Frenda	148	35.02 N	1.01 E
Freneuse	261	49.03 N	1.36 E
Frensdorferhaar	52	52.25 N	7.03 E
Frenštát pod Radhoštěm	30	49.33 N	18.14 E
Frentani, Monti dei ⋏	66	41.54 N	14.37 E
Frépillon	261	49.03 N	2.12 E
Frere	158	28.52 S	29.47 E
Freren	52	52.29 N	7.32 E
Fresco	150	5.05 N	5.34 W
Fresco ≃	250	6.39 S	51.59 W
Freshfield	262	53.34 N	3.04 W
Freshfield, Mount ∧	182	51.44 N	116.57 W
Freshford	48	52.43 N	7.24 W
Fresh Meadows ◆[8]	276	40.44 N	73.48 W
Fresh Pond ⊜, Ma., U.S.	283	42.23 N	71.09 W
Fresh Pond ⊜, N.Y., U.S.	276	40.55 N	73.18 W
Freshwater	42	50.40 N	1.30 W
Freshwater Creek ≃	226	39.12 N	122.04 W
Fresia	254	41.09 S	73.27 W
Fresnes	261	48.45 N	2.19 E
Fresne-Saint-Mamès	58	47.33 N	5.52 E
Fresnes-en-Woëvre	56	49.08 N	5.39 E
Fresnes-sur-Escaut	50	50.26 N	3.35 E
Fresnes-sur-Marne	261	48.56 N	2.45 E
Fresnillo	234	23.10 N	102.53 W
Fresno, Col.	246	5.09 N	75.01 W
Fresno, Ca., U.S.	226	36.44 N	119.46 W
Fresno, Oh., U.S.	214	40.20 N	81.44 W
Fresno, Tx., U.S.	222	29.32 N	95.27 W
Fresno □[6]	226	36.38 N	119.45 W
Fresno ≃	226	37.05 N	120.33 W
Fresno, Lewis Fork ≃	226	37.20 N	119.39 W
Fresno Air Terminal ⊠	226	36.46 N	119.43 W
Fresno Reservoir ⊜[1]	202	48.41 N	109.57 W
Fresno Slough ≃	226	36.47 N	120.22 W
Fresnoy-Folny	50	49.53 N	1.26 E
Fresnoy-le-Grand	50	49.57 N	3.25 E
Fressenneville	50	50.04 N	1.34 E
Fressin	50	50.27 N	2.03 E
Freswick	46	58.35 N	3.05 W
Fréteval	50	47.53 N	1.13 E
Frétigney-et-Velloreille	58	47.29 N	5.56 E
Fretin	50	50.33 N	3.08 E
Frettes	58	47.41 N	5.34 E
Freu, Cap des ›	34	39.45 N	3.27 E
Freudenberg, Dtsch.	56	49.44 N	9.19 E
Freudenberg, Dtsch.	56	50.54 N	7.52 E
Freudenberg, Dtsch.	60	49.29 N	11.59 E
Freudenberg, Dtsch.	264a	52.42 N	13.49 E
Freudenstadt	58	48.28 N	8.25 E
Frévent	50	50.16 N	2.17 E
Frew ≃	162	20.00 S	135.38 E
Frewena	162	19.25 S	135.25 E
Frewsburg	214	42.03 N	79.09 W
Freyburg	54	51.13 N	11.46 E
Freycinet, Cape ›	162	34.06 S	114.59 E
Freycinet Estuary ⊂[1]	162	26.25 S	113.45 E
Freycinet National Park ♠	166	42.10 S	148.20 E
Freycinet Peninsula ›[1]	166	42.13 S	148.18 E
Freyenstein	54	53.17 N	12.20 E
Freyming-Merlebach	56	49.09 N	6.48 E
Freyre	252	31.10 S	62.06 W
Freystadt	60	49.12 N	11.20 E
Freyung	60	48.48 N	13.33 E
Fria	150	10.05 N	13.32 W
Fria, Cape ›	152	18.30 S	12.01 E
Friant	226	36.59 N	119.42 W
Friant Dam ◆[6]	226	37.00 N	119.43 W
Friant-Kern Canal ≅	226	35.22 N	119.06 W
Friars Point	194	34.22 N	90.38 W
Frías, Arg.	252	28.39 S	65.09 W
Frías, Perú	248	4.52 S	79.57 W
Fribourg (Freiburg)	58	46.48 N	7.09 E
Fribourg (Freiburg) □[3]	58	46.45 N	7.05 E
Frick	58	47.31 N	8.01 E
Frick Park ♠	279b	40.26 N	79.54 W
Friday	222	31.07 N	95.15 W
Friday Harbor	224	48.32 N	123.00 W
Fridaythorpe	44	54.01 N	0.40 W
Fridingen an der Donau	58	48.01 N	8.56 E
Fridley	190	45.05 N	93.15 W
Fridolfing	60	48.00 N	12.49 E
Fridtjof Nansen, Mount ∧	9	85.21 S	167.33 W
Friedberg, Dtsch.	56	50.20 N	8.45 E
Friedberg, Dtsch.	58	48.21 N	10.58 E
Friedberg, Öst.	61	47.27 N	16.03 E
Friedeburg [/Saale]	54	51.37 N	11.44 E
Friedenau ◆[8]	264a	52.28 N	13.20 E
Friedens	214	40.03 N	79.00 W
Friedensburg	208	40.36 N	76.14 W
Friedersdorf, Dtsch.	54	52.17 N	13.47 E
Friedersdorf, Dtsch.	54	51.01 N	14.34 E
Friedersdorf, Dtsch.	54	51.39 N	12.21 E
Friedesheim	158	27.55 S	26.43 E
Friedland, Dtsch.	54	52.06 N	14.16 E
Friedland, Dtsch.	54	53.40 N	13.33 E
Friedland, Dtsch.	56	51.25 N	9.55 E
Friedrich-Ebert-Brücke ◆[5]	263	51.28 N	6.43 E
Friedrich Krupp-Aktiengesellschaft ʊ[3]	263	51.28 N	7.00 E
Friedrichroda	54	50.52 N	10.34 E
Friedrichsbrunn	54	51.41 N	11.02 E
Friedrichsdorf	56	50.15 N	8.38 E
Friedrichsfeld	263	51.38 N	6.39 E
Friedrichsfelde ◆[8]	264a	52.31 N	13.31 E
Friedrichshafen	58	47.39 N	9.28 E
Friedrichshagen ◆[8]	264a	52.27 N	13.38 E
Friedrichshain ◆[8]	264a	52.31 N	13.25 E
Friedrichshof	264a	52.19 N	13.46 E
Friedrichsort ◆[8]	54	54.24 N	10.11 E
Friedrichsruh, Schloss ⊥	52	53.32 N	10.20 E
Friedrichsruhe	54	53.31 N	11.45 E
Friedrichstadt	41	54.22 N	9.05 E
Friedrichsthal, Dtsch.	54	52.48 N	13.16 E
Friedrichsthal, Dtsch.	56	49.19 N	7.06 E
Friedrichstrasse, Bahnhof ◆[5]	264a	52.31 N	13.24 E
Friedrichswalde	54	53.02 N	13.42 E
Frielas	266c	38.49 N	9.09 W
Frielendorf	56	50.58 N	9.19 E
Friemersheim ◆[8]	263	51.23 N	6.42 E
Friend, Ne., U.S.	198	40.39 N	97.17 W
Friend, Or., U.S.	224	45.21 N	121.16 W
Friends Colony ◆[8]	272a	28.34 N	77.16 E
Friendship, N.Y., U.S.	210	42.12 N	78.08 W
Friendship, Tn., U.S.	194	35.54 N	89.14 W
Friendship, Wi., U.S.	190	43.58 N	89.49 W
Friendship Creek ≃	285	39.55 N	74.43 W
Friendship Shoal ✢[2]	112	5.58 N	112.31 E
Friends Meeting House State Memorial ⊥	214	40.09 N	80.47 W
Friendswood	222	29.31 N	95.12 W
Friern Barnet ◆[8]	260	51.37 N	0.10 W
Fries	192	36.42 N	80.58 W
Friesach	61	46.57 N	14.24 E
Friesack	54	52.44 N	12.34 E
Friesenheim	58	48.22 N	7.53 E
Friesenhofen	58	47.45 N	10.04 E
Friesenried	58	47.52 N	10.31 E
Friesland □[4]	52	53.03 N	5.45 E
Friesland □[9]	30	53.00 N	5.40 E
Fries Mills	285	39.39 N	75.03 W
Friesoythe	52	53.01 N	7.51 E
Frigate Point ›	174g	28.11 N	177.24 W
Frigento	68	41.01 N	15.06 E
Frignano	68	41.00 N	14.10 E
Frignano ◆[1]	64	44.20 N	10.51 E
Friguia	150	12.03 N	10.56 W
Friitala	26	61.26 N	21.52 E
Frillendorf ◆[8]	263	51.28 N	7.05 E
Frindsbury	260	51.24 N	0.30 E
Frinsted	260	51.17 N	0.43 E
Frinton-on-Sea	42	51.50 N	1.14 E
Frintrop ◆[8]	263	51.29 N	6.55 E
Frío ≃, N.A.	236	11.08 N	84.46 W
Frio ≃, Tx., U.S.	196	28.30 N	98.10 W
Frio, Cabo ›	255	22.53 S	42.00 W
Friockheim	46	56.38 N	2.38 W
Frio Draw V	196	34.50 N	102.19 W
Friona	196	34.38 N	102.43 W
Frisa, Loch ⊜	46	56.34 N	6.05 W
Frisange	56	49.32 N	6.12 E
Frisches Haff → Vislinskij zaliv ⊂	30	54.27 N	19.40 E
Frisco, Pa., U.S.	214	40.51 N	80.16 W
Frisco, Tx., U.S.	222	33.09 N	96.49 W
Frisco City	194	31.26 N	87.24 W
Frisco Creek ≃	196	36.34 N	101.23 W
Frisian Islands II	30	53.35 N	6.40 E
Friskney	44	53.04 N	0.11 E
Fristad	26	57.50 N	13.01 E
Fritch	196	35.38 N	101.36 W
Fritsla	26	57.33 N	12.47 E
Fritzlar	56	51.08 N	9.16 E
Friuli □[9]	64	46.00 N	13.00 E
Friuli-Venezia Giulia □[4]	64	46.00 N	13.00 E
Friza, proliv ⊔	74	45.30 N	149.10 E
Frizington	44	54.32 N	3.30 W
Frobisher	184	49.12 N	102.26 W
Frobisher Bay ⊂	176	62.30 N	66.00 W
Frobisher Lake ⊜	184	56.25 N	108.20 W
Frodsham, Eng., U.K.	44	53.18 N	2.44 W
Frodsham, Eng., U.K.	262	53.18 N	2.44 W
Frog Lake ⊜	184	53.55 N	110.18 W
Frohavet ⊔	24	63.52 N	9.26 E
Frohburg	54	51.03 N	12.33 E
Frohlinde ◆[8]	263	51.32 N	7.21 E
Frohnau ◆[8]	264a	52.38 N	13.18 E
Frohnhausen	263	51.29 N	7.48 E
Frohnhausen ◆[8]	263	51.27 N	6.58 E
Frohnleiten	61	47.16 N	15.20 E
Froid	198	48.20 N	104.30 W
Froid, Lac ⊜	206	46.40 N	74.32 W
Froid, Ruisseau ≃	206	46.23 N	74.46 W
Froidmont-Cohartille	50	49.41 N	3.42 E
Froidos	56	49.03 N	5.07 E
Froissy	50	49.34 N	2.13 E
Froitzheim	56	50.42 N	6.34 E
Frolišči, Ross.	80	56.25 N	42.39 E
Frolišči, Ross.	82	56.18 N	39.13 E
Frolovo	80	49.47 N	43.39 E
Froman Run ≃	279b	40.12 N	80.00 W
Fromberg	202	45.23 N	108.54 W
Frombork	30	54.22 N	19.41 E
Frome	42	51.14 N	2.20 W
Frome ≃, Austl.	166	29.06 S	137.52 E
Frome ≃, Eng., U.K.	42	52.03 N	2.38 W
Frome ≃, Eng., U.K.	42	50.41 N	2.04 W
Frome, Lake ⊜	166	30.48 S	139.48 E
Frome Downs	166	31.13 S	139.46 E
Fromelennes	56	50.08 N	4.52 E
Fromentières	50	48.54 N	3.43 E
Frömern	263	51.30 N	7.44 E
Frommern	58	48.15 N	8.52 E
Fröndenberg	56	51.28 N	7.46 E
Fronhausen	56	50.42 N	8.42 E
Fronreute	58	47.52 N	9.35 E
Frönsberg	263	51.21 N	7.46 E
Fronteiras	250	7.05 S	40.37 W
Frontenac, Fl., U.S.	220	28.27 N	80.46 W
Frontenac, Ks., U.S.	198	37.27 N	94.41 W
Frontenac □[6], On., Can.	212	44.40 N	76.45 W
Frontenac □[6], P.Q., Can.	206	45.42 N	71.15 W
Frontenard	58	46.55 N	5.10 E
Frontenex-Villard-Rosset	62	45.38 N	6.19 E
Frontenhausen	60	48.33 N	12.32 E
Frontera, Méx.	232	26.56 N	101.27 W
Frontera, Méx.	234	18.32 N	92.38 W
Fronteras	200	30.56 N	109.31 W
Frontier, Sk., Can.	184	49.12 N	108.34 W
Frontier, Mi., U.S.	216	41.47 N	84.36 W
Frontier, Wy., U.S.	200	41.48 N	110.32 W
Frontignan	62	43.27 N	3.45 E
Frontino	246	6.46 N	76.08 W
Frontino, Páramo ∧	246	6.28 N	76.04 W
Frontón, Isla I	286d	12.07 S	77.11 W
Front Range ⋏, Leso.	158	29.05 S	28.20 E
Front Range ⋏, Co., U.S.	200	39.45 N	105.45 W
Front Royal	188	38.55 N	78.11 W
Frose	54	51.48 N	11.23 E
Frosinone	66	41.38 N	13.19 E
Frosinone □[4]	66	41.37 N	13.27 E
Frosolone	66	41.36 N	14.27 E
Frösön	26	63.11 N	14.32 E
Frost	222	32.05 N	96.48 W
Frostavallen	41	55.58 N	13.30 E
Frostburg	188	39.39 N	78.55 W
Frostproof	220	27.44 N	81.31 W
Frotheim	52	52.21 N	8.40 E
Frouard	56	48.46 N	6.08 E
Frövi	40	59.28 N	15.22 E
Frøya I	24	63.43 N	8.42 E
Fruges	50	50.31 N	2.08 E
Fruita	200	39.09 N	108.43 W
Fruitdale, Al., U.S.	194	31.20 N	88.24 W
Fruitdale, Or., U.S.	202	42.24 N	123.20 W
Fruithurst	194	33.43 N	85.26 W
Fruitland, Id., U.S.	202	44.00 N	116.54 W
Fruitland, Md., U.S.	208	38.19 N	75.37 W
Fruitland Park	220	28.51 N	81.54 W
Fruitport	216	43.07 N	86.09 W
Fruitvale, B.C., Can.	182	49.07 N	117.33 W
Fruitvale, Tx., U.S.	222	32.41 N	95.48 W
Fruitvale, Wa., U.S.	202	46.37 N	120.33 W
Fruitville	192	27.19 N	82.27 W
Frumușița	38	45.40 N	28.04 E
Frunze, Kyrg.	85	40.07 N	71.44 E
Frunze → Biškek, Kyrg.	85	42.54 N	74.36 E
Frunze, Ukr.	78	46.16 N	34.52 E
Frunze, Ukr.	83	48.40 N	38.45 E
Frunzivka	78	47.20 N	29.44 E
Frutal	255	20.02 S	48.55 W
Frutigen	58	46.35 N	7.39 E
Frutillar	254	41.07 S	73.03 W
Fryburg	214	41.21 N	79.26 W
Frýdek-Místek	30	49.41 N	18.22 E
Frýdlant	30	50.56 N	15.05 E
Frye	279b	40.11 N	79.56 W
Fryeburg	188	44.00 N	70.58 W
Fryerning	260	51.41 N	0.22 E
Fryingpan ≃	200	39.22 N	107.02 W
Fu ≃, Zhg.	100	29.52 N	115.28 E
Fu ≃, Zhg.	100	28.36 N	116.04 E
Fu ≃, Zhg.	102	29.59 N	106.16 E
Fuaʻamotu	174w	21.16 S	175.08 W
Fua'amotu International Airport ⊠	174w	21.17 S	175.08 W
Fu'an, Zhg.	100	27.08 N	119.40 E
Fu'an, Zhg.	100	32.41 N	120.41 E
Fuanjie	100	25.29 N	117.53 E
Fubao	107	28.47 N	106.05 E
Fubine	62	44.58 N	8.26 E
Fucecchio	66	43.44 N	10.48 E
Fuchang	100	30.06 N	113.08 E
Fucheng	98	37.52 N	116.07 E
Fuchikou	100	29.51 N	115.27 E
Fuchow → Fuzhou	100	28.01 N	116.20 E
Fuchs-Berg ∧[2]	264a	52.27 N	13.51 E
Fuchskaute ∧	56	50.40 N	8.06 E
Fuchsmühl	60	49.56 N	12.09 E
Füchtorf	52	52.03 N	8.02 E
Fuchū, Nihon	94	35.40 N	139.29 E
Fuchū, Nihon	94	36.39 N	137.10 E
Fuchū, Nihon	96	34.24 N	132.30 E
Fuchū, Nihon	96	34.34 N	133.14 E
Fuchun ≃	106	30.10 N	120.09 E
Fucine	64	46.18 N	10.44 E
Fucino, Conca del ⩧	66	42.01 N	13.31 E
Fudan University ʊ[2]	269b	31.17 N	121.29 E
Fuday I	46	57.03 N	7.23 W
Fuding	100	27.21 N	120.12 E
Fudu ≃	107	29.52 N	106.10 E
Fuefuki ≃	94	35.33 N	138.28 E
Fuego, Volcán de ∧[1]	236	14.29 N	90.53 W
Fuelbeckestausee ⊜[1]	263	51.15 N	7.40 E
Fuencaliente	34	38.24 N	4.18 W
Fuencarral ◆[8]	266a	40.30 N	3.41 W
Fuengirola	34	36.32 N	4.37 W
Fuenlabrada	266a	40.17 N	3.48 W
Fuensalida	34	40.03 N	4.12 W
Fuensanta, Embalse de ⊜[1]	34	38.23 N	2.13 W
Fuente	196	28.40 N	100.32 W
Fuente de Cantos	34	38.15 N	6.18 W
Fuente de Oro	246	3.28 N	73.37 W
Fuente Obejuna	34	38.16 N	5.25 W
Fuentesaúco	34	41.14 N	5.30 W
Fuentes de Ebro	34	41.31 N	0.38 W
Fuerli	105	39.40 N	116.41 E
Fuerte ≃	232	25.54 N	109.22 W
Fuerte Olimpo	248	21.02 S	57.54 W
Fuerteventura I	148	28.20 N	14.00 W
Fuerza, Castillo de la ⊥	286b	23.09 N	82.21 W
Fufeng	102	34.20 N	107.51 E
Fuga Island I	116	18.52 N	121.22 E
Fugama, Wādī V	140	14.43 N	24.36 E
Fügen	64	47.21 N	11.51 E
Fuglebjerg	41	55.18 N	11.34 E
Fugløysund ⊔	24	70.12 N	20.20 E
Fugong	102	27.09 N	98.52 E
Fugou	98	34.04 N	114.24 E
Fuhai	86	47.06 N	87.23 E
Fuhe	100	23.22 N	113.37 E
Fuhlenbrock ◆[8]	263	51.32 N	6.54 E
Fuhrberg	52	52.34 N	9.50 E
Fuhse ≃	52	52.37 N	10.03 E
Fuhsien → Fuxian	98	39.37 N	122.01 E
Fuhu	100	29.11 N	118.04 E
Fuji, Nihon	94	35.09 N	138.39 E
Fuji, Zhg.	98	34.24 N	114.48 E
Fuji, Zhg.	107	29.09 N	105.23 E
Fuji ≃	94	35.07 N	138.39 E
Fuji, Mount → Fuji-san ∧[1]	94	35.22 N	138.44 E
Fujiafeng	105	39.11 N	117.32 E
Fujian (Fukien) □[4]	100	26.00 N	118.00 E
Fujiatun	104	41.42 N	123.44 E
Fujiawopu	104	40.58 N	122.14 E
Fujiazhen	107	29.57 N	104.18 E
Fujiazhuangcun	104	41.15 N	122.20 E
Fujie	106	31.09 N	119.27 E
Fujieda	94	34.52 N	138.16 E
Fuji-Hakone-Izu-kokuritsu-kōen ♠	94	35.21 N	138.44 E
Fujiidera	96	34.34 N	135.36 E
Fujikawa	94	35.08 N	138.37 E
Fujikubo	268	35.50 N	139.32 E
Fujimi, Nihon	94	36.27 N	139.05 E
Fujimi, Nihon	94	35.55 N	138.15 E
Fujimi, Nihon	94	35.51 N	139.33 E
Fujin	89	47.14 N	132.00 E
Fujino	94	35.37 N	139.10 E
Fujinomiya	94	35.12 N	138.38 E
Fujioka, Nihon	94	35.12 N	137.12 E
Fujioka, Nihon	94	36.15 N	139.05 E
Fujioka, Nihon	94	36.15 N	139.39 E
Fuji-san ∧[1]	94	35.22 N	138.44 E
Fujisawa	94	35.21 N	139.29 E
Fujishiro	94	35.55 N	140.07 E
Fujiwara, Nihon	94	35.09 N	136.30 E
Fujiwara, Nihon	94	36.51 N	139.44 E
Fujiwara-dam ◆[6]	94	36.49 N	139.02 E
Fujiyama → Fuji-san ∧[1]	94	35.22 N	138.44 E
Fuji-yoshida	94	35.29 N	138.48 E
Fukagawa	92a	43.43 N	142.03 E
Fukagawa ◆[8]	268	35.40 N	139.48 E
Fukami	268	35.28 N	139.28 E
Fukane I	174w	21.05 S	175.02 W
Fukang	86	44.10 N	87.59 E
Fukasaka-tunnel ◆[5]	94	35.35 N	136.10 E
Fuka Shan ∧	89	47.55 N	120.53 E
Fukaya	94	36.12 N	139.17 E
Fukiage	94	36.06 N	139.27 E
Fukiai ◆[8]	270	34.42 N	135.12 E
Fukien → Fujian □[4]	100	26.00 N	118.00 E
Fukou, Zhg.	100	25.45 N	118.28 E
Fukou, Zhg.	100	26.28 N	117.40 E
Fukube	96	35.33 N	134.18 E
Fukuchiyama	96	35.18 N	135.07 E
Fukude	94	34.40 N	137.53 E
Fukue	92	32.41 N	128.50 E
Fukuei Chiao ›	100	25.18 N	121.32 E
Fukue-jima I	92	32.40 N	128.45 E
Fukui, Nihon	94	36.04 N	136.13 E
Fukui, Nihon	270	34.51 N	135.34 E
Fukui □[5]	92	36.00 N	136.15 E
Fukuma	96	33.46 N	130.28 E
Fukumitsu	94	36.33 N	136.52 E
Fukuno	94	36.35 N	136.55 E
Fukuoka, Nihon	94	35.34 N	137.27 E
Fukuoka, Nihon	94	36.42 N	136.56 E
Fukuoka, Nihon	96	33.35 N	130.24 E
Fukuoka □[5]	96	33.45 N	130.30 E
Fukuoka-chūtonchi, Rikujō-jieitai- ■	96	33.32 N	130.28 E
Fukuroda-no-taki ∟	94	36.46 N	140.25 E
Fukuroi	94	34.45 N	137.55 E
Fukushima, Nihon	92	37.45 N	140.28 E
Fukushima, Nihon	92a	41.29 N	140.15 E
Fukushima □[5]	94	37.08 N	140.00 E
Fukushima ◆[8]	270	34.42 N	135.29 E
Fukusumi	270	34.37 N	135.56 E
Fukutani ◆[8]	270	34.43 N	135.02 E
Fukuyama	96	34.29 N	133.22 E
Fukuzaki	96	34.57 N	134.45 E
Fulacunda	150	11.44 N	15.03 W
Fūlādī, Kūh-e ∧	120	34.38 N	67.32 E
Fūlād Maḥalleh	128	36.02 N	53.44 E
Fulanga Island I	175g	19.08 S	178.34 W
Fulanga Passage ⊔	175g	19.00 S	178.40 W
Fulbourn	42	52.11 N	0.13 E
Fulda, Dtsch.	56	50.33 N	9.41 E
Fulda, Mn., U.S.	198	43.52 N	95.36 W
Fulda ≃	30	51.25 N	9.39 E
Fuldatal, Dtsch.	52	51.21 N	9.32 E
Fuldatal, Dtsch.	56	51.22 N	9.31 E
Fuldera	58	46.37 N	10.22 E
Fule	102	25.27 N	104.19 E
Fulerum ◆[8]	263	51.26 N	6.57 E
Fulford Harbour	224	48.46 N	123.27 W
Fulgatore	70	37.57 N	12.42 E
Fulham ◆[8]	260	51.29 N	0.12 W
Fuli	100	23.11 N	121.14 E
Fuliji	100	33.46 N	116.58 E
Fuling	102	29.42 N	107.21 E
Fulitun	89	46.42 N	131.10 E
Fullarton ≃	166	20.15 S	141.10 E
Fullen ⊜	40	60.31 N	16.09 E
Fuller Springs	222	31.18 N	94.41 W
Fullerton, Ca., U.S.	228	33.52 N	117.55 W
Fullerton, Ky., U.S.	218	38.43 N	82.58 W
Fullerton, Md., U.S.	284b	39.22 N	76.31 W
Fullerton, Ne., U.S.	198	41.21 N	97.58 W
Fullerton, Pa., U.S.	208	40.38 N	75.28 W
Fullerton Municipal Airport ⊠	280	33.52 N	117.59 W
Fullerton Point ›	240c	17.06 N	61.54 W
Fulmer	260	51.33 N	0.34 W
Fulong	102	22.57 N	107.41 E
Fulongchang	107	30.03 N	103.38 E
Fulongquan	89	44.22 N	124.36 E
Fulpmes	64	47.10 N	11.21 E
Fulshear	222	29.41 N	95.54 W
Fulton, Al., U.S.	194	31.47 N	87.43 W
Fulton, Ar., U.S.	194	33.36 N	93.48 W
Fulton, Il., U.S.	190	41.52 N	90.09 W
Fulton, In., U.S.	216	40.56 N	86.15 W
Fulton, Ks., U.S.	198	38.00 N	94.43 W
Fulton, Ky., U.S.	194	36.30 N	88.52 W
Fulton, Md., U.S.	208	39.09 N	76.55 W
Fulton, Mi., U.S.	216	47.17 N	88.21 W
Fulton, Ms., U.S.	194	34.16 N	88.24 W
Fulton, Mo., U.S.	219	38.50 N	91.56 W
Fulton, N.Y., U.S.	210	43.19 N	76.25 W
Fulton, Oh., U.S.	214	40.27 N	82.49 W
Fulton, Tx., U.S.	196	28.04 N	97.02 W
Fulton □[6], Il., U.S.	219	40.13 N	90.17 W
Fulton □[6], In., U.S.	216	41.04 N	86.13 W
Fulton □[6], N.Y., U.S.	210	43.00 N	74.22 W
Fulton □[6], Oh., U.S.	216	41.33 N	84.09 W
Fulton □[6], Pa., U.S.	214	40.06 N	78.04 W
Fulton ≃	182	54.48 N	126.07 W
Fultondale	194	33.36 N	86.47 W
Fultonham	210	42.31 N	75.03 W
Fultonville	210	42.57 N	74.22 W
Fuluchang	107	29.38 N	106.08 E
Fulufjället ∧	26	61.33 N	12.43 E
Fuluzhen	107	29.18 N	103.40 E
Fulwood	44	53.47 N	2.41 W
Fumaça	256	22.17 S	44.19 W
Fumahashi	94	36.42 N	137.19 E
Fumane	156	24.29 S	33.58 E
Fumay	56	49.59 N	4.42 E
Fumel	32	44.29 N	0.57 E
Fumin, Zhg.	102	25.16 N	102.26 E
Fumin, Zhg.	106	31.54 N	121.10 E
Fumintun	98	42.29 N	126.22 E
Fuminzhen	106	31.37 N	121.39 E
Funa ≃	273b	4.23 S	15.19 E
Funabashi	94	35.42 N	139.59 E
Funafuti I	14	8.31 S	179.13 E
Funagawa → Oga	92	39.53 N	139.51 E
Funakuyā	175d	24.30 N	124.17 E
Funan	100	32.39 N	115.32 E
Funan Gaba	144	4.25 N	37.57 E
Funaoka	96	35.23 N	134.14 E
Funasaka	270	34.48 N	135.17 E
Funäsdalen	26	62.32 N	12.33 E
Funchal	148	32.38 N	16.54 W
Funchal □[5]	148	32.40 N	16.55 W
Fundación	246	10.31 N	74.11 W
Fundão	34	40.08 N	7.30 W
Fundão, Ilha do I	287a	22.51 S	43.14 W
Funde	272c	18.54 N	72.58 E
Fundo ≃	250	10.12 S	44.39 W
Fundo, Arroio ≃	287a	22.58 S	43.22 W
Fundy, Bay of ⊂	186	45.00 N	66.00 W
Fundy National Park ♠	186	45.38 N	65.00 W
Fünfkirchen → Pécs	30	46.05 N	18.13 E
Funhalouro	156	23.03 S	34.25 E
Funil, Reprêsa do ⊜[1]	256	22.33 S	44.35 W
Funil, Ribeirão do ≃	256	22.02 S	43.46 W
Funil, Rio do ≃	256	22.58 S	44.34 W
Funing, Zhg.	98	39.54 N	119.14 E
Funing, Zhg.	100	33.47 N	119.48 E
Funing, Zhg.	102	23.33 N	105.35 E
Funiuchang	107	29.03 N	106.33 E
Funiu Shan ⋏	100	33.40 N	112.30 E
Funk Island I	186	49.46 N	53.10 W
Funks Creek ≃	226	39.19 N	122.11 W
Funkturm ʊ	264a	52.31 N	13.16 E
Funne ≃	263	51.42 N	7.36 E
Funnel Creek ≃	166	22.18 S	148.57 E
Funnel Hill ∧[2]	272c	18.54 N	73.07 E
Funo	96	34.53 N	132.47 E
Funshinagh, Lough ⊜	48	53.31 N	8.07 W
Funsi	150	10.17 N	1.58 W
Funtana Coberta ⊥	71	39.34 N	9.21 E
Funtua	150	11.31 N	7.17 E
Funza	246	4.40 N	74.09 W
Fuorn, Pass dal (Ofenpass))(	58	46.37 N	10.15 E
Fuping	102	34.47 N	109.07 E
Fuqiao	106	31.36 N	121.12 E
Fuqikou	100	29.44 N	117.48 E
Fuqing	100	25.44 N	119.22 E
Fuquay-Varina	192	35.35 N	78.48 W
Füramoos	58	48.00 N	9.53 E
Furancungo	154	14.55 S	33.35 E
Furano	92a	43.21 N	142.24 E
Furāt, Nahr al- → Euphrates ≃	128	31.00 N	47.25 E
Furci Siculo	70	37.57 N	15.23 E
Furculești	38	43.52 N	25.09 E
Fures	62	45.19 N	5.30 E
Fūrg	128	28.18 N	55.13 E
Furkapass)(	58	46.34 N	8.25 E
Furka-Tunnel ◆[5]	58	46.33 N	8.26 E
Furlong	208	40.18 N	75.05 W
Furmanov	80	57.15 N	41.07 E
Furmanovka	86	44.17 N	72.57 E
Furmanovo	80	49.42 N	49.28 E
Furn, Wādī al- V	142	30.13 N	31.40 E
Furnace	46	56.09 N	5.10 W
Furnace Brook ≃	283	42.06 N	70.43 W
Furnace Creek ≃	284b	39.11 N	76.35 W
Furnace Pond ⊜	283	42.03 N	70.49 W
Furnari	70	38.07 N	15.08 E
Furnas, Reprêsa de ⊜[1]	255	20.45 S	46.00 W
Furn ash-Shubbāk	132	33.52 N	35.31 E
Furneaux Group II	166	40.10 S	148.05 E
Furnes → Veurne	50	51.04 N	2.40 E
Furness Abbey ʊ[1]	44	54.07 N	3.12 W
Furness Fells ⋏[2]	44	54.18 N	3.07 W
Furong Shan ∧	100	27.30 N	115.52 E
Furqlus	130	34.36 N	37.05 E
Fürstenau, Dtsch.	52	51.50 N	9.19 E
Fürstenau, Dtsch.	52	52.31 N	7.40 E
Fürstenberg	52	51.44 N	9.24 E
Fürstenberg/Havel	54	53.11 N	13.08 E
Fürstenfeld	61	47.03 N	16.05 E
Fürstenfeldbruck	60	48.10 N	11.15 E
Fürstenhagen	56	51.12 N	9.41 E
Fürstenstein	60	48.43 N	13.20 E
Fürstenwalde	54	52.21 N	14.04 E
Fürstenwerder	54	53.24 N	13.34 E
Fürstenzell	60	48.32 N	13.19 E
Furtei	71	39.34 N	8.57 E
Fürth, Dtsch.	56	49.28 N	10.59 E
Fürth, Dtsch.	56	49.39 N	8.47 E
Furth, Dtsch.	60	48.35 N	12.02 E
Furth im Wald	60	49.18 N	12.51 E
Furtwangen	58	48.03 N	8.12 E
Furuba ≃	256	23.21 S	44.57 W
Furubō-san ∧[2]	270	34.53 N	135.19 E
Furudal	26	61.10 N	15.08 E
Furudono	94	37.05 N	140.34 E
Furukawa, Nihon	92	38.34 N	140.58 E
Furukawa, Nihon	94	36.14 N	137.11 E
Furulund	41	55.46 N	13.04 E
Furusund	40	59.40 N	18.55 E
Furu-tone ≃	94	35.48 N	139.51 E
Furuvik	40	60.39 N	17.20 E
Furuyakami	268	35.55 N	139.32 E
Fürwiggestausee ⊜[1]	263	51.09 N	7.41 E
Fury and Hecla Strait ⊔	176	69.56 N	84.00 W
Fusagasugá	246	4.21 N	74.22 W
Fusain ≃	50	48.09 N	2.45 E
Fusan → Pusan	98	35.06 N	129.03 E
Fuscaldo	68	39.25 N	16.02 E
Fusch	64	47.13 N	12.49 E
Fuschl am See	64	47.48 N	13.18 E
Fuschun → Fushun	104	41.52 N	123.53 E
Fuse → Higashiōsaka, Nihon	96	34.39 N	135.35 E
Fuse, Nihon	268	35.53 N	140.00 E
Fushan, Zhg.	98	37.29 N	121.16 E
Fushan, Zhg.	102	35.58 N	111.51 E
Fushan, Zhg.	106	31.49 N	120.46 E
Fushimi ◆[8]	270	34.55 N	135.46 E
Fushino ≃	96	34.03 N	131.24 E
Fushuigang	100	31.21 N	113.40 E
Fushun (Funan), Zhg.	104	41.52 N	123.53 E
Fushun, Zhg.	107	29.11 N	105.00 E
Fushuncheng	104	41.53 N	123.51 E
Fusignano	66	44.28 N	11.57 E

≃	River	Fluß	Río	Rivière	Rio
≅	Canal	Kanal	Canal	Canal	Canal
∟	Waterfall, Rapids	Wasserfall, Stromschnellen	Cascada, Rápidos	Chute d'eau, Rapides	Cascata, Rápidos
⊔	Strait	Meeresstraße	Estrecho	Détroit	Estreito
⊂	Bay, Gulf	Bucht, Golf	Bahía, Golfo	Baie, Golfe	Baía, Golfo
⊜	Lake, Lakes	See, Seen	Lago, Lagos	Lac, Lacs	Lago, Lagos
⩧	Swamp	Sumpf	Pantano	Marais	Pântano
⍓	Ice Features, Glacier	Eis- und Gletscherformen	Accidentes Glaciales	Formes glaciaires	Acidentes glaciares
⍑	Other Hydrographic Features	Andere Hydrographische Objekte	Otros Elementos Hidrográficos	Autres données hydrographiques	Outros acidentes hidrográficos
✢	Submarine Features	Untermeerische Objekte	Accidentes Submarinos	Formes de relief sous-marin	Acidentes submarinos
□	Political Unit	Politische Einheit	Unidad Politica	Entité politique	Unidade política
ʊ	Cultural Institution	Kulturelle Institution	Institución Cultural	Institution culturelle	Institução cultural
⊥	Historical Site	Historische Stätte	Sitio Histórico	Site historique	Sitio histórico
♠	Recreational Site	Erholungs- und Ferienort	Sitio de Recreo	Centre de loisirs	Area de Lazer
⊠	Airport	Flughafen	Aeropuerto	Aéroport	Aeroporto
■	Military Installation	Militäranlage	Instalación Militar	Installation militaire	Instalação militar
◆	Miscellaneous	Verschiedenes	Misceláneo	Divers	Diversos

ENGLISH — Name | Page | Lat.°′ | Long.°′

DEUTSCH — Name | Seite | Breite°′ | Länge°′ E = Ost

Name	Page	Lat.°′	Long.°′
Fusilier	184	51.51 N	109.46 W
Fusin → Fuxin	104	42.03 N	121.46 E
Fusine in Valromana	64	46.30 N	13.39 E
Fusio	58	46.27 N	8.40 E
Fusō	94	35.21 N	136.55 E
Fusong	98	42.18 N	127.20 E
Fussa	94	35.45 N	139.20 E
Füssen	64	47.34 N	10.42 E
Fuste, Picacho del ∧	196	27.35 N	102.47 W
Fusui	102	22.32 N	107.56 E
Futa, Passo della)(	66	44.05 N	11.17 E
Futaba	94	35.41 N	138.30 E
Futago-san ∧	96	33.35 N	131.36 E
Futamata → Tenryū	94	34.52 N	137.49 E
Futamatagawa ◆[8]	268	35.28 N	139.33 E
Futami, Nihon	94	34.30 N	136.47 E
Futami, Nihon	96	33.41 N	132.38 E
Futang, Zhg.	102	24.26 N	112.09 E
Futang, Zhg.	106	30.40 N	119.35 E
Futaoi-jima I	96	34.06 N	130.47 E
Futatabi-yama ∧	270	34.43 N	135.11 E
Futatsubashi ◆[8]	268	35.28 N	139.30 E
Futatsu-ne I[2]	174f	24.46 N	141.18 E
Fu Tau Pun Chau I	271d	22.21 N	114.22 E
Futian	100	27.26 N	114.56 E
Futianhe	100	31.30 N	115.05 E
Futianpu	100	27.22 N	112.47 E
Futjāni ≃	126	24.06 N	90.09 E
Futschou → Fuzhou	100	26.06 N	119.17 E
Futtsu, Nihon	94	35.19 N	139.49 E
Futtsu, Nihon	94	35.13 N	139.52 E
Futtsu-misaki ›	268	35.19 N	139.46 E
Futun ≃	100	26.51 N	117.46 E
Futuna I	175f	19.32 S	170.14 E
Futuna, Île I	14	14.15 S	178.09 W
Futuyu	105	39.18 N	114.50 E
Fuveau	62	43.27 N	5.34 E
Fuwah	142	31.12 N	30.33 E
Fuwen	86	47.13 N	89.39 E
Fuxi, Zhg.	100	27.14 N	119.50 E
Fuxi, Zhg.	100	25.14 N	113.52 E
Fuxi ≃	107	29.09 N	104.57 E
Fuxian (Wafangdian), Zhg.	98	39.37 N	122.01 E
Fuxian, Zhg.	102	36.02 N	109.13 E
Fuxian Hu ⊜	102	24.30 N	102.55 E
Fuxin, Zhg.	104	42.08 N	121.45 E
Fuxin, Zhg.	104	42.03 N	121.46 E
Fuxing, Zhg.	107	30.27 N	106.04 E
Fuxing, Zhg.	107	30.24 N	104.53 E
Fuxing, Zhg.	107	29.54 N	105.43 E
Fuxingchang	107	29.40 N	105.13 E
Fuxing Dao I	269b	31.17 N	121.23 E
Fuxinghao	104	42.35 N	120.32 E
Fuyang, Zhg.	100	32.54 N	115.49 E
Fuyang, Zhg.	100	30.03 N	119.57 E
Fuyang, Zhg.	100	23.36 N	116.37 E
Fuyang ≃	98	38.14 N	116.05 E
Fuyouertuo Shan ∧	89	45.52 N	119.48 E
Fuyu, Zhg.	89	47.49 N	124.27 E
Fuyu, Zhg.	89	45.10 N	124.50 E
Fuyuan, Zhg.	89	48.21 N	134.18 E
Fuyuan, Zhg.	102	25.39 N	104.12 E
Fuzhai	100	29.32 N	120.02 E
Fuzhong	102	24.28 N	111.22 E
Fuzhou, Zhg.	100	28.01 N	116.20 E
Fuzhou (Foochow), Zhg.	100	26.06 N	119.17 E
Fuzhoucheng	98	39.45 N	121.47 E
Fuzhuang	98	34.57 N	118.17 E
Fuzhuangyi	98	38.02 N	116.08 E
Füzuli	84	39.37 N	47.08 E
Fyfield	42	51.45 N	0.16 E
Fylde □[8]	262	53.46 N	2.53 W
Fylde ›[1]	44	53.47 N	2.56 W
Fyn □[6]	41	55.20 N	10.25 E
Fyn I	41	55.20 N	10.30 E
Fyne, Loch c	46	56.00 N	5.24 W
Fyns Hoved ›	41	55.37 N	10.36 E
Fyresvatn ⊜	26	59.06 N	8.12 E
Fyrisån ≃	40	59.47 N	17.39 E
Fysingen ⊜	40	59.34 N	17.55 E
Fyvie	46	57.25 N	2.23 W
Fzâra, Gara'et ⊜	36	36.47 N	7.30 E

G

Name	Page	Lat.°′	Long.°′
Ga	150	9.47 N	2.30 W
Gaaden	264b	48.03 N	16.12 E
Gaalkacyo	144	6.47 N	47.26 E
Gaanderen	52	51.56 N	6.21 E
Gabah	144	8.08 N	50.02 E
Gabai	146	11.05 N	11.39 E
Gabaldon	116	15.28 N	121.19 E
Gabare	38	43.19 N	23.55 E
Gabarus	186	45.50 N	60.09 W
Gabarus Bay c	186	45.51 N	60.07 W
Gabas ≃	32	43.46 N	0.42 W
Gabbs	204	38.52 N	117.55 W
Gabby Heights	214	40.09 N	80.15 W
Gabela	152	10.48 S	14.20 E
Gaberones → Gaborone	156	24.45 S	25.55 E
Gabès	148	33.53 N	10.07 E
Gabès, Golfe de c	148	34.00 N	10.25 E
Gabia	152	4.34 S	17.07 E
Gabiarra	255	16.15 S	39.41 W
Gabicce Mare	66	43.58 N	12.46 E
Gabii ⊥	267a	41.54 N	12.43 E
Gabil	146	11.09 N	18.12 E
Gabilan Creek ≃	226	36.41 N	121.38 W
Gabilan Range ⋏	226	36.30 N	121.15 W
Gąbin	30	52.25 N	19.44 E
Gabir	140	8.35 N	24.40 E
Gable Mountain ∧	182	54.30 N	121.40 W
Gablenz	54	51.41 N	14.31 E
Gablingen	58	48.27 N	10.49 E
Gablitz	61	48.14 N	16.09 E
Gablonz → Jablonec nad Nisou	30	50.44 N	15.10 E
Gabon □[1], Afr.	138	1.00 S	11.45 E
Gabon □[1], Afr.	152	1.00 S	11.45 E
Gabon, Estuaire du c[1]	152	0.25 N	9.20 E
Gaborone	156	24.45 S	25.55 E
Gabras	140	10.16 N	26.14 E
Gabria	64	45.52 N	13.34 E
Gabriel	250	11.14 S	41.53 W
Gabriel Strait ʊ	176	61.45 N	65.30 W
Gabriel y Galan, Embalse de ⊜[1]	34	40.15 N	6.15 W
Gabriel Zamora	234	19.05 N	102.05 W
Gābrīk	128	25.44 N	58.28 E
Gabriola	224	49.12 N	123.50 W
Gabriola Island I	224	49.10 N	123.47 W
Gabrovo	38	42.52 N	25.19 E
Gabun → Gabon □[1]	152	1.00 S	11.45 E
Gaby	62	45.43 N	7.53 E
Gacé	50	48.48 N	0.18 E
Gachetá	246	4.49 N	73.36 W
Gachpar	174q	9.33 N	138.10 E
Gachsārān	128	30.12 N	50.47 E
Gackle	198	46.37 N	99.08 W
Gacko	38	43.10 N	18.32 E
Gädäbäy	84	40.34 N	45.49 E
Gadag	122	15.25 N	75.37 E
Gadamai	140	17.09 N	36.06 E
Gādarwāra	124	22.55 N	78.47 E
Gadbjerg	41	55.46 N	9.20 E
Gäddede	26	64.30 N	14.09 E
Gadderbaum	52	52.00 N	8.31 E
Gade ≃	260	51.38 N	0.28 W
Gadebusch	54	53.42 N	11.07 E
Gadein	140	8.11 N	28.44 E
Gadera ≃	64	46.47 N	11.54 E
Gadevang	41	55.58 N	12.18 E
Gadis ≃	114	1.03 N	98.55 E
Gadmen	58	46.44 N	8.21 E
Gado Bravo, Ilha do I	250	10.54 S	42.52 W
Gádor	34	36.57 N	2.29 W
Gadra	120	25.40 N	70.37 E
Gadsden, Al., U.S.	194	34.00 N	86.00 W
Gadsden, Az., U.S.	200	32.33 N	114.47 W
Gadwāl	122	16.14 N	77.48 E
Gadzi	152	4.47 N	16.42 E
Gaerwen	44	53.13 N	4.16 W
Găești	38	44.43 N	25.19 E
Gaeta	66	41.12 N	13.35 E
Gaeta, Golfo di c	66	41.06 N	13.30 E
Gaferut I	108	9.14 N	145.23 E
Gaffney	192	35.04 N	81.39 W
Gafour	36	36.18 N	9.19 E
Gafsa	148	34.25 N	8.48 E
Gafurov	85	40.14 N	69.44 E
Gag, Pulau I	164	0.27 S	129.52 E
Gagal	146	9.01 N	15.08 E
Gagarawa	150	12.25 N	9.32 E
Gagarin	76	55.33 N	35.00 E
Gage	196	36.18 N	99.45 W
Gägelow	54	53.55 N	11.25 E
Gagere ≃	150	13.21 N	6.23 E
Gages Lake	278	42.21 N	87.59 W
Gages Lake ⊜	278	42.21 N	88.00 W
Gagetown	186	45.47 N	66.09 W
Gagetown, Canadian Forces Base ■	186	45.43 N	66.15 W
Gaggenau	56	48.48 N	8.19 E
Gaggi	70	37.51 N	15.13 E
Gaggiano	62	45.24 N	9.02 E
Gaghamni	140	11.41 N	28.19 E
Gagil Tamil I	174q	9.32 N	138.10 E
Gagino	80	55.14 N	45.02 E
Gagliano Castelferrato	70	37.43 N	14.32 E
Gagliano del Capo	68	39.50 N	18.22 E
Gagnef	40	60.35 N	15.04 E
Gagnia	152	1.28 S	16.02 E
Gagnoa	150	6.08 N	5.56 W
Gagnon	176	51.53 N	68.10 W
Gagnon, Lac ⊜	206	46.07 N	75.07 W
Gagny	261	48.53 N	2.32 E
Gagra	84	43.20 N	40.15 E
Gagret	123	31.40 N	76.04 E
Gahanna	218	40.01 N	82.52 W
Gahlen	52	51.40 N	6.52 E
Gaiarine	64	45.52 N	12.29 E
Gaibandha	124	25.19 N	89.33 E
Gaichtpass)(	58	47.27 N	10.37 E
Gaigalava	76	56.40 N	27.18 E
Gaighāta	126	22.56 N	88.44 E
Gaijiatun	104	40.50 N	122.37 E
Gail	196	32.46 N	101.27 W
Gail ≃	64	46.36 N	13.53 E
Gailberg Sattel)(	64	46.43 N	12.58 E
Gail Creek ≃	222	31.07 N	95.23 W
Gaildorf	56	49.00 N	9.46 E
Gaillac	32	43.54 N	1.55 E
Gaillard, Château ⊥	50	49.13 N	1.25 E
Gaillard, Lac ⊜	186	50.06 N	68.47 W
Gaillard, Lake ⊜	207	41.21 N	72.46 W
Gaillefontaine	50	49.39 N	1.37 E
Gaillimh → Galway	48	53.16 N	9.03 W
Gaillon, Fr.	50	49.10 N	1.20 E
Gaillon, Fr.	261	49.02 N	1.54 E
Gailtaler Alpen ⋏	64	46.42 N	13.00 E
Gaima	164	8.20 S	142.55 E
Gaimán	254	43.17 S	65.29 W
Gaimersheim	60	48.49 N	11.22 E
Gaines, Mi., U.S.	216	42.52 N	83.54 W
Gaines, Pa., U.S.	210	41.45 N	77.34 W
Gainesboro	194	36.21 N	85.39 W
Gainesville, Fl., U.S.	192	29.39 N	82.19 W
Gainesville, Ga., U.S.	192	34.17 N	83.49 W
Gainesville, Mo., U.S.	194	36.36 N	92.25 W
Gainesville, N.Y., U.S.	210	42.38 N	78.08 W
Gainesville, Tx., U.S.	196	33.37 N	97.07 W
Gainford	44	54.32 N	1.44 W
Gainsborough, Sk., Can.	184	49.10 N	101.26 W
Gainsborough, Eng., U.K.	44	53.24 N	0.46 W
Gainsborough Creek ≃	184	49.10 N	101.02 W
Gaiole in Chianti	66	43.28 N	11.26 E
Gairatganj	124	23.24 N	78.13 E
Gairdner ≃	162	34.17 S	119.28 E
Gairdner, Lake ⊜	162	31.35 S	136.00 E
Gairloch	46	57.42 N	5.40 W
Gairloch, Loch c	46	57.44 N	5.44 W
Gairn ≃	46	57.03 N	3.05 W
Gais, It.	64	46.50 N	11.57 E
Gais, Schw.	58	47.22 N	9.27 E
Gaisberg ∧	64	47.48 N	13.07 E
Gaisbeuren	58	47.54 N	9.43 E
Gaital, Cerro ∧	236	8.37 N	80.07 W
Gaither	208	39.21 N	76.59 W
Gaithersburg	208	39.08 N	77.12 W
Gaixian	98	40.24 N	122.22 E
Gaizina Kalns ∧[2]	76	56.52 N	25.57 E
Gaj, Hrv.	36	45.29 N	17.02 E
Gaj, Ross.	86	51.27 N	58.27 E
Gajā	272b	22.52 N	88.10 E
Gajahmungkur, Waduk ⊜[1]	115a	7.55 S	110.55 E
Gajendragarh	122	15.44 N	75.59 E
Gajiram	146	12.30 N	13.12 E
Gajny	24	60.15 N	54.15 E
Gājol	124	25.13 N	88.12 E
Gajsinghpur	123	29.40 N	73.27 E
Gajuapara ≃	250	4.17 S	47.25 W
Gajutino	76	58.42 N	38.32 E
Gakarosa ∧	158	27.54 S	23.33 E
Gakona	180	62.18 N	145.18 W
Gākuch	123	36.10 N	73.45 E
Gakugsa	24	61.34 N	36.26 E
Gāla, Bngl.	126	24.18 N	89.54 E
Gala, Zhg.	124	28.16 N	89.23 E
Galaassija	128	39.52 N	64.27 E
Galāchipa	126	22.10 N	90.25 E
Galahad	182	52.31 N	111.56 W
Galamares	266c	38.48 N	9.25 W
Galán, Cerro ∧	252	25.55 S	66.52 W
Galana ≃	154	3.09 S	40.08 E
Galangue	152	13.48 S	16.09 E
Galanovo	80	56.09 N	54.07 E
Galanta	30	48.12 N	17.43 E
Galápagos □[4]	246a	0.30 S	90.30 W
Galápagos, Parque Nacional de ♦	246a	0.15 S	90.15 W
Galapagos Islands → Colón, Archipiélago de II	246a	0.30 S	90.30 W
Galaroza	34	37.55 N	6.42 W
Galas ≃	114	5.31 N	102.12 E
Galashiels	46	55.37 N	2.49 W
Galata ◆[8]	267b	41.01 N	28.58 E
Galata Köprüsü ◆[5]	267b	41.00 N	28.57 E
Galata Tower ʋ	267b	41.01 N	28.58 E
Galatea	172	38.25 S	176.45 E
Galați	38	45.26 N	28.03 E
Galați □[6]	38	45.45 N	27.45 E
Galatia	194	37.50 N	88.36 W
Galatia □[9]	130	39.30 N	32.40 E
Galatina	68	40.10 N	18.10 E
Galatone	68	40.09 N	18.04 E
Galatro	68	38.28 N	16.06 E
Galátsion	267c	38.01 N	23.45 E
Galatz → Galați	38	45.26 N	28.03 E
Galaure ≃	62	45.11 N	4.49 E
Gala Water ≃	46	55.37 N	2.48 W
Galax	192	36.39 N	80.55 W
Galaxídhion	38	38.22 N	22.23 E
Galbyn gov' ◆[2]	102	42.30 N	107.00 E
Galdhøpiggen ∧	26	61.37 N	8.17 E
Gale, Lac ⊜	190	46.46 N	76.51 W
Galeairy Lake ⊜	212	45.29 N	78.17 W
Galeana, Méx.	232	30.07 N	107.38 W
Galeana, Méx.	232	24.50 N	100.04 W
Galeão, Aeroporto do ⊠	256	22.50 S	43.15 W
Galeata	66	44.00 N	11.55 E
Galegu	140	12.36 N	35.02 E
Galeh Dār	128	27.38 N	52.42 E
Galela	108	1.50 N	127.50 E
Galena, Austl.	162	27.50 S	114.41 E
Galena, Ak., U.S.	180	64.44 N	156.57 W
Galena, Il., U.S.	190	42.25 N	90.25 W
Galena, In., U.S.	218	38.21 N	85.56 W
Galena, Ks., U.S.	198	37.04 N	94.38 W
Galena, Md., U.S.	208	39.20 N	75.52 W
Galena, Mo., U.S.	194	36.48 N	93.27 W
Galena, Oh., U.S.	214	40.12 N	82.52 W
Galena Park	222	29.43 N	95.13 W
Galenbecker See ⊜	54	53.38 N	13.43 E
Galeota Point ›	241r	10.08 N	60.59 W
Galera ≃	248	14.25 S	60.07 W
Galera, Punta ›, Chile	254	39.59 S	73.43 W
Galera, Punta ›, Ec.	246	0.49 N	80.03 W
Galera, Punta de ›	34	39.06 N	1.31 E
Galera Point ›	241r	10.49 N	60.55 W
Galeras, Volcán ∧[1]	246	1.13 N	77.22 W
Galeria ⊥	267a	42.02 N	12.18 E
Galeria, Fosso la ≃	267a	41.48 N	12.21 E
Galesburg, Il., U.S.	190	40.56 N	90.22 W
Galesburg, Mi., U.S.	216	42.17 N	85.25 W
Gales Creek	224	45.35 N	123.12 W
Gales Creek ≃	224	45.29 N	123.06 W
Gales Ferry	207	41.25 N	72.04 W
Gales Point ›	283	42.33 N	70.47 W
Galesville, Md., U.S.	208	38.50 N	76.32 W
Galesville, Wi., U.S.	190	44.04 N	91.20 W
Galeton	214	41.43 N	77.38 W
Galeville	210	43.05 N	76.10 W
Galgasc	144	0.11 N	41.38 E
Galgate	44	54.00 N	2.47 W
Galguduud □[4]	144	5.00 N	46.30 E
Galheiros	255	13.18 S	46.25 W
Gali	84	42.38 N	41.44 E
Gali, Torrente de ≃	266d	41.28 N	2.00 E
Galiano	224	48.52 N	123.21 W
Galiano Island I	224	48.56 N	123.29 W
Galibier, Col du)(	62	45.04 N	6.24 E
Galič	80	58.23 N	42.21 E
Galicia □[3]	34	42.45 N	8.00 W
Galicia □[9]	22	49.00 N	22.00 E
Galičskaja vozvyšennost' ⋏[2]	24	58.25 N	42.20 E
Galičskoje, ozero ⊜	80	58.24 N	42.18 E
Galien	216	41.47 N	86.29 W
Galien ≃	216	41.48 N	86.45 W
Galilee	207	41.22 N	71.30 W
Galilee → HaGalil □[9]	132	32.54 N	35.20 E
Galilee, Lake ⊜	166	22.21 S	145.48 E
Galilee, Sea of → Kinneret, Yam ⊜	132	32.48 N	35.35 E
Galiléia	255	19.00 S	41.33 W
Galim	152	7.06 N	12.29 E
Galina Point ›	241q	18.24 N	76.53 W
Galindo Creek ≃	282	37.58 N	122.02 W
Galion	214	40.44 N	82.47 W
Galion, Baie du c	240e	14.44 N	60.57 W
Galis	115a	7.08 S	113.33 E
Galisteo Creek ≃	200	35.31 N	106.22 W
Galite, Canal de la ʊ	36	37.20 N	9.00 E
Galiuro Mountains ⋏	200	32.40 N	110.20 W
Galiwinku	164	12.02 S	135.34 E
Galižana	64	44.56 N	13.52 E
Galka'yo	144	6.47 N	47.26 E
Galkhausen	263	51.05 N	6.58 E
Galkino, Kaz.	86	52.14 N	78.20 E
Galkino, Ross.	82	54.46 N	35.49 E
Galkino, Ross.	86	55.36 N	62.55 E
Gall'aaral	85	40.02 N	67.35 E
Gallan Head ›	46	58.14 N	7.03 W
Gallarate	62	45.40 N	8.47 E
Gallardon	50	48.32 N	1.42 E
Gallatin, Mo., U.S.	194	39.54 N	93.57 W
Gallatin, Pa., U.S.	279b	40.12 N	79.53 W
Gallatin, Tn., U.S.	194	36.23 N	86.26 W
Gallatin, Tx., U.S.	222	31.54 N	95.09 W
Gallatin □[6]	218	38.45 N	84.51 W
Gallatin ≃	202	45.56 N	111.29 W
Gallatin Range ⋏	202	45.15 N	111.05 W
Galle	122	6.02 N	80.13 E
Gállego ≃	34	41.39 N	0.51 W
Gallegos ≃	254	51.36 S	68.59 W
Galles → Wales □[8]	28	52.30 N	3.30 W
Galleyend	260	51.42 N	0.29 E
Galley Head ›	48	51.30 N	8.57 W
Galleywood	260	51.42 N	0.28 E
Galliano	194	29.26 N	90.17 W
Galliate	62	45.29 N	8.42 E
Gallicano	64	44.04 N	10.26 E
Gallicano nel Lazio	267a	41.52 N	12.49 E
Gallicchio	68	40.17 N	16.08 E
Gallico	68	38.10 N	15.41 E
Galliera Veneta	64	45.39 N	11.49 E
Gallinara I	62	44.02 N	8.14 E
Gallinas ≃	196	35.10 N	104.55 W
Gallinas, Punta ›	246	12.28 N	71.40 W
Gallinas Creek ≃	282	38.01 N	122.30 W
Gallinas Peak ∧	200	34.13 N	105.45 W
Gallio	64	45.53 N	11.33 E
Gallipoli, Austl.	166	19.10 S	137.55 E
Gallipoli, It.	68	40.03 N	17.58 E
Gallipoli → Gelibolu, Tür.	130	40.24 N	26.40 E
Gallipoli Peninsula → Gelibolu Yarımadası ›[1]	130	40.20 N	26.30 E
Gallipolis	188	38.48 N	82.12 W
Gallitzin	214	40.28 N	78.33 W
Gallivaggio	58	46.21 N	9.21 E
Gällivare	24	67.07 N	20.45 E
Gallneukirchen	61	48.21 N	14.25 E
Gällö	26	62.55 N	15.14 E
Gallo, Capo ›	70	38.13 N	13.19 E
Gallo, Laguna ⊜	258	35.30 S	58.28 W
Gallo Arroyo V	200	33.55 N	105.00 W
Galloo Island I	212	43.54 N	76.25 W
Galloupes Point ›	283	42.28 N	70.53 W
Galloway □[9]	44	55.00 N	4.25 W
Galloway, Mull of ›	44	54.38 N	4.50 W
Galloway Creek ≃, Md., U.S.	284b	39.18 N	76.23 W
Galloway Creek ≃, Mi., U.S.	281	42.39 N	83.12 W
Galluis	261	48.48 N	1.48 E
Gallup	200	35.31 N	108.44 W
Gallupville	210	42.40 N	74.14 W
Gallur	34	41.52 N	1.19 W
Gallura ◆[1]	71	41.00 N	9.13 E
Gally, Ru de ≃	261	48.53 N	1.53 E
Gälnan ʊ	40	59.31 N	18.45 E
Gålö I	40	59.05 N	18.17 E
Galop Island I	212	44.46 N	75.24 W
Galoppo, Ippodromo del ♦	266b	45.28 N	9.07 E
Galougo	150	13.50 N	11.04 W
Galsi	126	23.20 N	87.42 E
Galston	46	55.36 N	4.24 W
Galt, Mong.	88	48.46 N	99.53 E
Galt, Ca., U.S.	226	38.15 N	121.17 W
Gal Tardo	144	3.34 N	45.58 E
Galtat Zemmour	148	25.15 N	12.20 W
Galtelli	71	40.23 N	9.37 E
Galten	41	56.09 N	9.55 E
Galten c	40	59.27 N	16.09 E
Galtür	58	46.58 N	10.11 E
Galtymore Mountain ∧	48	52.22 N	8.10 W
Galty Mountains ⋏	48	52.25 N	8.10 W
Galūgāh-e Āsīyeh	128	34.01 N	59.55 E
Galugur	114	2.34 N	99.39 E
Galula	154	8.36 S	33.02 E
Galunggung, Gunung ∧	115a	7.15 S	108.03 E
Galuut	88	48.33 N	113.12 E
Galva, Il., U.S.	190	41.10 N	90.02 W
Galva, Ia., U.S.	198	42.30 N	95.25 W
Galva, Ks., U.S.	198	38.22 N	97.32 W
Galvarino	252	38.24 S	72.47 W
Galveston, In., U.S.	216	40.34 N	86.11 W
Galveston, Tx., U.S.	222	29.17 N	94.47 W
Galveston □[6]	222	29.20 N	94.53 W
Galveston Bay c	222	29.36 N	94.57 W
Galveston Island I	222	29.13 N	94.55 W
Gálvez	252	32.02 S	61.13 W
Gálvez ≃	248	5.12 S	72.53 W
Galvin, Austl.	274b	37.51 S	144.49 E
Galvin, Wa., U.S.	224	46.44 N	123.01 W
Galway (Gaillimh), Ire.	48	53.16 N	9.03 W
Galway, N.Y., U.S.	210	43.01 N	74.02 W
Galway □[6]	48	53.20 N	9.00 W
Galway Bay c	48	53.10 N	9.15 W
Gam (Jin) ≃	110	21.55 N	105.12 E
Gam, Pulau I	164	0.27 S	130.36 E
Gama, Isla I	254	40.29 S	62.12 W
Gamaches	50	49.59 N	1.33 E
Gamagōri	94	34.50 N	137.14 E
Gamalejevka	80	52.16 N	53.26 E
Gamaliel	194	36.38 N	85.47 W
Ga-Mankoeng	156	23.57 S	29.42 E
Gamare, Lake ⊜	144	11.30 N	41.40 E
Gamarra	246	8.20 N	73.45 W
Gamawa	146	12.08 N	10.32 E
Gamay	116	12.23 N	125.18 E
Gamay Bay c	116	12.21 N	125.21 E
Gamba	120	28.17 N	88.32 E
Gambach	56	50.28 N	8.44 E
Gambaga	150	10.32 N	0.26 W
Gambais	261	48.46 N	1.40 E
Gambaiseuil	261	48.45 N	1.44 E
Gambang	114	3.43 N	103.06 E
Gambara, It.	64	45.15 N	10.18 E
Gámbara, Méx.	234	18.55 N	102.05 W
Gambarie	68	38.10 N	15.50 E
Gambassi	66	43.32 N	10.57 E
Gambatesa	66	41.30 N	14.54 E
Gambela	144	8.18 N	34.37 E
Gambell	180	63.46 N	171.46 W
Gambellara	64	45.28 N	11.20 E
Gamber	208	39.27 N	76.56 W
Gambia □[1], Afr.	134	13.30 N	15.30 W
Gambia □[1], Afr.	150	13.30 N	15.30 W
Gambia (Gambie) ≃	150	13.28 N	16.34 W
Gambi Aṭrash	140	10.03 N	33.47 E
Gambie → Gambia □[1]	150	13.30 N	15.30 W
Gambie (Gambia) ≃	150	13.28 N	16.34 W
Gambier	214	40.22 N	82.23 W
Gambier, Îles II	6	21.20 S	136.30 W
Gamble Mansion State Historic Site ⊥	220	27.32 N	82.32 W
Gambo, Nf., Can.	186	48.46 N	54.14 W
Gambo, Centraf.	152	4.39 N	22.16 E
Gamboa	236	9.07 N	79.42 W
Gamboli	120	29.50 N	68.26 E
Gambolò	62	45.15 N	8.51 E
Gamboma	152	1.53 S	15.51 E
Gamboula	152	4.08 N	15.09 E
Gambrill State Park ♦	208	39.30 N	77.30 W
Gamchab ≃	156	28.15 S	17.26 E
Gamé	150	6.44 N	1.11 E
Game Creek ≃	285	39.41 N	75.28 W
Gamensee ⊜	264a	52.40 N	13.51 E
Gaming	61	47.56 N	15.06 E
Gamış dağ ∧	84	40.18 N	46.23 E
Gamka ≃	158	33.18 S	21.39 E
Gamlakarleby → Kokkola	26	63.50 N	23.07 E
Gamla Uppsala	40	59.54 N	17.38 E
Gamleby	26	57.54 N	16.24 E
Gamlitz	61	46.43 N	15.33 E
Gammel Estrup ⊥	26	56.26 N	10.21 E
Gammelstad ʋ[1]	26	65.38 N	22.01 E
Gammertingen	58	48.15 N	9.13 E
Gammon ≃	184	51.07 N	95.09 W
Gammon, Point ›	207	41.36 N	70.16 W
Gammon Ranges National Park ♦	166	30.29 S	139.10 E
Gamō, Nihon	94	35.03 N	136.11 E
Gamō, Nihon	268	35.52 N	139.48 E
Gamoep	158	29.55 S	18.25 E
Ga-Mogara ≃	158	27.07 S	22.57 E
Gamo Gofa □[4]	144	5.45 N	37.00 E
Gamon	150	13.20 N	12.55 W
Gamova, mys ›	89	42.35 N	131.12 E
Gamph, Slieve ⋏	48	54.05 N	9.00 W
Gampoko	273b	4.16 S	15.10 E
Gampola	122	7.10 N	80.34 E
Gampongbatak	114	4.48 N	97.39 E
Gampoui	273b	4.08 S	15.22 E
Gams	58	47.12 N	9.28 E
Gamsfeld ∧	64	47.37 N	13.29 E
Gamtoos ≃	158	33.58 S	25.01 E
Gamud ∧	144	4.05 N	38.03 E
Gan ≃, Zhg.	89	49.12 N	125.14 E
Gan ≃, Zhg.	100	29.12 N	116.00 E
Ganado, Az., U.S.	200	35.42 N	109.32 W
Ganado, Tx., U.S.	222	29.02 N	96.31 W
Ganano ≃	116	16.45 N	121.44 E
Gananoque	212	44.20 N	76.10 W
Gananoque ≃	212	44.19 N	76.09 W
Gananoque Lake ⊜	212	44.27 N	76.09 W
Ganaraska ≃	212	43.57 N	78.18 W
Ganargua Creek ≃	210	43.04 N	77.00 W
Ganassi	116	7.49 N	124.06 E
Ganāveh	128	29.34 N	50.31 E
Gäncä	84	40.40 N	46.22 E
Gäncäçay ≃	84	40.54 N	46.28 E
Ganchangba	107	28.52 N	103.41 E
Ganči	85	39.58 N	69.08 E
Gand → Gent	50	51.03 N	3.43 E
Ganda, Ang.	152	13.02 S	14.40 E
Ganda, R.D.C.	152	4.05 N	23.32 E
Gandadiwata, Bulu ∧	112	2.42 S	119.27 E
Gandajika	152	6.45 S	23.57 E
Gandak (Nārāyaṇi) ≃	124	25.39 N	85.13 E
Gaṇḍakī □[8]	124	28.15 N	84.15 E
Gandara, Arg.	258	35.26 S	58.06 W
Gándara, Esp.	34	43.32 N	8.10 W
Ganda Singhwāla	123	31.02 N	74.31 E
Gandāva	120	28.37 N	67.29 E
Gandavaroyi Falls ⌊	154	17.17 S	29.07 E
Gānde	126	24.10 N	86.26 E
Gander	186	48.57 N	54.37 W
Gander ≃	186	49.15 N	54.30 W
Gander Bay	186	49.18 N	54.29 W
Gander Bay c	186	49.25 N	54.28 W
Ganderkesee	52	53.02 N	8.32 E
Gander Lake ⊜	186	48.55 N	54.40 W
Gandesa	34	41.03 N	0.26 E
Gândești	38	47.53 N	28.23 E
Gandevi	120	20.49 N	72.59 E
Gāndhinagar	120	23.12 N	72.40 E
Gāndhi Sāgar ⊜[1]	120	24.18 N	75.21 E
Gandi	150	12.55 N	5.49 E
Gandi, Wādī V	140	11.23 N	24.31 E
Gandia	34	38.58 N	0.11 W
Gandino	62	45.49 N	9.54 E
Gando	152	12.30 S	17.25 E
Gandole	146	8.26 N	11.34 E
Gandou	152	2.24 N	17.27 E
Gandrange	56	49.16 N	6.08 E
Gandria	58	46.01 N	9.00 E
Gandu	255	13.45 S	39.30 W
Gandy Bridge ◆[5]	220	27.53 N	82.34 W
Ganfang	100	28.40 N	114.51 E
Ganfosi	107	29.36 N	104.03 E
Ganga → Ganges ≃	124	23.22 N	90.32 E
Gangādharpur	272b	22.36 N	88.11 E
Gangafani	150	14.23 N	2.24 W
Gangājalghāti	126	23.25 N	87.07 E
Gangala-Na-Bodio	154	3.41 N	29.08 E
Gangalingolo	273b	4.20 S	15.09 E
Gan Gan	254	42.30 S	68.16 W
Gangānagar	123	29.55 N	73.53 E
Gangāpur, India	120	25.13 N	74.16 E
Gangāpur, India	122	19.41 N	75.01 E
Gangāpur, India	124	26.29 N	76.43 E
Gangara, Niger	150	14.36 N	8.30 E
Gangara, Niger	150	13.33 N	7.14 E
Gāngārāmpur	124	25.24 N	88.31 E
Ganga Sāgar	126	21.38 N	88.05 E
Gangaw	110	22.11 N	94.07 E
Gangāwati	122	15.26 N	76.32 E
Gangaw Range ⋏	110	24.50 N	96.40 E
Ganga-Yamuna Doāb ⋏[1]	124	26.40 N	79.30 E
Gangcheng	98	35.52 N	116.52 E
Gangdaba, Tchabal ∧	152	7.44 N	12.45 E
Gangdhār	120	23.57 N	75.37 E
Gangdisê Shan ⋏	120	31.00 N	82.00 E
Gangelt	56	50.59 N	5.59 E
Ganges, B.C., Can.	224	48.51 N	123.30 W
Ganges, Fr.	62	43.56 N	3.42 E
Ganges (Ganga) (Padma) ≃	124	23.22 N	90.32 E
Ganges, Mouths of the ≃[1]	120	22.00 N	89.00 E
Ganges Delta ≚[2]	124	23.00 N	89.00 E
Ganghu	120	32.05 N	86.45 E
Gangi	70	37.49 N	14.13 E
Gangkofen	60	48.26 N	12.34 E
Gangkou, Zhg.	100	29.12 N	113.19 E
Gangkou, Zhg.	100	29.45 N	115.44 E
Gangkou, Zhg.	100	29.21 N	117.58 E
Gangkou, Zhg.	100	22.38 N	113.22 E
Gangkou, Zhg.	100	22.36 N	114.54 E
Gangkou, Zhg.	106	30.44 N	118.54 E
Gangkouzhen	106	31.45 N	120.40 E
Gangmar Co ⊜	120	33.46 N	84.15 E
Gang Mills	210	42.08 N	77.06 W
Gāngnāpur	126	23.09 N	88.38 E
Gangneung → Kangnŭng	98	37.45 N	128.54 E
Gango ≃	152	9.48 S	15.40 E
Gangoa	102	37.15 N	100.28 E
Gangoh	124	29.46 N	77.15 E
Gangotri, India	120	30.56 N	79.02 E
Gangotri, India	120	31.01 N	78.27 E
Gangou	98	40.30 N	119.27 E
Gangoumen	98	41.40 N	116.35 E
Gangouyi	102	36.01 N	105.03 E
Gangqiao	107	30.13 N	105.22 E
Gang Ranch	182	51.33 N	122.20 W
Gangshangji	100	28.06 N	116.30 E
Gangtok	124	27.20 N	88.37 E
Gangtou	98	38.04 N	113.56 E
Gangtouli	106	31.42 N	119.02 E
Gangu	102	34.45 N	105.20 E
Gangwa, R.D.C.	152	3.30 S	20.55 E
Gangwa, Zhg.	105	39.48 N	116.10 E
Gangwei	100	24.20 N	118.01 E
Ganhezi	86	44.08 N	88.32 E
Ganhu	102	44.33 N	94.09 E
Gani	164	0.47 S	128.13 E
Ganišob	85	39.03 N	70.47 E
Ganj Dundwara	124	27.44 N	78.57 E
Ganjiang	107	29.42 N	103.38 E
Ganlan Shan ∧	124	29.54 N	90.02 E
Ganlu	106	31.32 N	120.35 E
Ganluchang	107	29.54 N	104.47 E
Ganluo	102	29.03 N	102.59 E
Gannahoek	158	26.44 S	24.08 E
Gannan	89	47.54 N	123.30 E
Gannano, Lago di ⊜	68	40.19 N	16.26 E
Gannapan	158	30.23 S	22.12 E
Gannat	32	46.06 N	3.12 E
Gannett Peak ∧	200	43.11 N	109.39 W
Gannvalley	198	44.02 N	98.59 W
Ganpingsi	102	35.13 N	102.30 E
Ganpu	106	30.24 N	120.53 E
Ganq	120	37.25 N	92.15 E
Ganquan	102	36.25 N	109.16 E
Gansbaai	158	34.35 S	19.22 E
Gänsbrunnen	58	47.16 N	7.28 E
Gänserndorf	61	48.20 N	16.43 E
Gansevoort	210	43.12 N	73.39 W
Ganshoren	56	50.52 N	4.18 E
Ganspan	158	27.57 S	24.47 E
Gansu (Kansu) □[4]	102	37.00 N	103.00 E
Ganta	150	7.15 N	8.59 W
Gantan	100	29.37 N	119.34 E
Gantang, Zhg.	100	26.56 N	119.40 E
Gantang, Zhg.	102	22.58 N	109.00 E
Gantao ≃	98	38.01 N	114.07 E
Gante → Gent	50	51.03 N	3.43 E
Gantheaume, Cape ›	166	36.05 S	137.27 E
Gantheaume Bay c	162	27.44 S	114.07 E
Gantheaume Point ›	162	17.59 S	122.10 E
Gantiadi	84	43.24 N	40.06 E
Gantian	100	27.30 N	113.10 E
Gantt	194	31.24 N	86.29 W
Gantung	112	2.58 S	108.09 E
Gantung, Mount ∧	116	8.57 N	117.48 E
Gan'uškino	80	46.36 N	49.16 E
Ganwo	150	11.13 N	4.42 E
Ganxi, Zhg.	100	28.08 N	118.06 E
Ganxi, Zhg.	102	29.02 N	109.32 E
Ganyanchi	102	36.39 N	105.18 E
Ganyesa	158	26.35 S	24.10 E
Ganyu (Qing Kou)	98	34.52 N	119.10 E
Ganzê	102	31.40 N	100.01 E
Ganzhenyi	100	30.33 N	113.21 E
Ganzhou, Zhg.	100	25.54 N	114.55 E
Ganzhou, Zhg.	100	28.49 N	115.25 E
Ganzhou → Zhangye, Zhg.	102	38.56 N	100.27 E
Ganzhuermiao	88	48.24 N	118.08 E
Ganzlin	54	53.23 N	12.15 E
Ganzo Azul	248	8.51 S	74.44 W
Gao	150	16.16 N	0.03 W
Gao □[4]	150	18.00 N	1.30 E
Gao'an	100	28.25 N	115.22 E
Gaobaita	271a	39.53 N	116.30 E
Gaobei	100	26.37 N	114.38 E
Gaobeidian	271a	39.54 N	116.33 E
Gaobu	100	27.48 N	117.01 E
Gaochang	107	28.49 N	104.24 E
Gaocheng, Zhg.	98	38.04 N	114.49 E
Gaocheng, Zhg.	100	31.57 N	113.25 E
Gaocheng, Zhg.	106	31.28 N	119.48 E
Gaochengzhai	104	41.24 N	123.43 E
Gaochun	106	31.20 N	118.52 E
Gaocun	98	37.05 N	122.12 E
Gaodianzi	102	30.40 N	110.01 E
Gao Feng ∧	106	30.34 N	118.40 E
Gaogongmiao	100	33.25 N	115.53 E
Gaogou	100	34.03 N	119.15 E
Gaohe	100	22.47 N	112.57 E
Gaohebu	100	30.44 N	116.50 E
Gaoil, Sliabh ∧	46	55.55 N	5.28 W
Gaojiabu	102	38.30 N	110.11 E
Gaojiadi	98	41.33 N	114.58 E
Gaojiadian	98	42.40 N	124.28 E
Gaojian	100	29.04 N	121.14 E
Gaojiapuzi	104	41.22 N	123.36 E
Gaojiaqiao	106	30.43 N	120.38 E
Gaojiatun	104	41.06 N	121.19 E
Gaojiawopeng	104	41.28 N	122.10 E
Gaojiawopu	104	41.50 N	122.47 E
Gaojiazhai	269b	31.23 N	121.33 E
Gaojiazhen	102	30.05 N	107.51 E
Gaokan	104	40.46 N	122.23 E
Gaokeng	100	27.40 N	113.58 E
Gaolan	102	36.25 N	103.56 E
Gaolan Dao I	100	21.55 N	113.15 E
Gaolao	104	41.54 N	120.59 E
Gaoli	105	39.17 N	115.38 E
Gaoliang	107	29.45 N	105.15 E
Gaoliban	104	41.39 N	121.58 E
Gaolifangshen	104	42.27 N	123.21 E
Gaolimen	98	40.22 N	124.02 E
Gaoling	105	40.32 N	117.01 E
Gaolinying	105	39.06 N	115.38 E
Gaoliying	105	40.10 N	116.29 E
Gaoliyingzi	104	41.56 N	124.17 E
Gaolong	100	26.56 N	113.45 E
Gaolou	105	39.59 N	116.50 E
Gaolouchang, Zhg.	107	29.51 N	104.41 E
Gaolouchang, Zhg.	107	30.03 N	105.58 E
Gaoluo	98	37.27 N	113.55 E
Gaomi	98	36.23 N	119.44 E
Gaona	252	25.12 S	64.05 W
Gaopi	100	24.14 N	116.39 E
Gaoping, Zhg.	102	35.48 N	112.52 E
Gaoping, Zhg.	107	30.28 N	105.45 E
Gaopingba	107	30.47 N	106.06 E
Gaoqiao, Zhg.	100	30.08 N	119.56 E
Gaoqiao, Zhg.	100	26.36 N	117.46 E
Gaoqiao, Zhg.	102	28.06 N	106.36 E
Gaoqiao, Zhg.	106	32.14 N	119.38 E
Gaoqiao, Zhg.	106	31.21 N	121.34 E
Gaoqiaomen	106	32.01 N	118.51 E
Gaoqiaozhen	104	40.55 N	121.00 E
Gaoqing (Tianzhen)	98	37.11 N	117.47 E
Gaoqipu	104	41.32 N	121.40 E
Gaosha	100	26.27 N	117.56 E
Gaoshaling	105	38.51 N	117.36 E
Gaoshan, Zhg.	100	25.29 N	119.34 E
Gaoshan, Zhg.	107	29.26 N	104.28 E
Gaoshanbao	105	40.40 N	117.29 E
Gaoshangbao	98	39.11 N	118.30 E
Gaoshanpu	102	27.10 N	105.14 E
Gaoshantai	104	42.22 N	122.28 E
Gaoshanzi	104	41.34 N	122.02 E
Gaoshengchang	107	29.59 N	105.31 E
Gaoshengzhen	104	41.20 N	122.12 E
Gaoshi	107	29.36 N	104.44 E
Gaoshikan	107	29.12 N	105.04 E
Gaosichang	107	30.17 N	104.52 E
Gaotai	102	39.20 N	99.58 E
Gaotaishan	104	42.02 N	122.52 E
Gaotan, Zhg.	100	30.23 N	117.23 E
Gaotan, Zhg.	100	23.12 N	115.22 E
Gaotan, Zhg.	102	32.22 N	108.36 E
Gaotang	98	36.54 N	116.14 E
Gaotangji	100	32.24 N	116.01 E
Gaotingsi	100	26.05 N	112.53 E
Gaotuozi	104	41.08 N	122.40 E
Gaoua	150	10.20 N	3.11 W
Gaoual	150	11.45 N	13.12 W
Gaoxian	102	28.20 N	104.38 E
Gaoxingru	100	26.28 N	115.14 E
Gaoxinji	98	34.11 N	115.33 E
Gaoya	98	36.22 N	118.49 E
Gaoyang	98	34.30 N	114.40 E
Gaoyapu	107	29.14 N	106.19 E
Gaoyi	98	37.36 N	114.36 E
Gaoyou, Zhg.	100	32.47 N	119.27 E
Gaoyou, Zhg.	100	28.25 N	115.31 E
Gaoyou Hu ⊜	100	32.50 N	119.20 E
Gaozhangjia	102	36.06 N	107.18 E
Gaozhou	102	21.55 N	110.50 E
Gaozi	106	32.11 N	119.18 E
Gaoziba	107	29.01 N	106.00 E
Gaozuo	100	33.57 N	118.03 E
Gap, Fr.	62	44.34 N	6.05 E
Gap, Pa., U.S.	208	39.59 N	76.01 W
Gapālnagar	272b	22.49 N	88.08 E
Gapan	116	15.19 N	120.57 E
Gapeau ≃	62	43.07 N	6.11 E
Gapern ⊜	40	59.31 N	13.40 E
Gar	120	32.11 N	79.59 E
Gar ≃	120	32.28 N	79.44 E
Gara, Lough ⊜	48	53.55 N	8.25 W
Garacad	144	6.57 N	49.19 E
Garachiné	246	8.04 N	78.22 W
Garadag	144	9.26 N	46.52 E
Gārādāha	126	24.14 N	89.34 E
Garagoa	246	5.05 N	73.21 W
Garaguso	68	40.33 N	16.14 E
Garah	166	29.04 S	149.38 E
Garai ≃[1]	126	23.32 N	89.31 E
Garaina	164	7.50 S	147.10 E
Gārākhola Madhukhāli	126	23.33 N	89.38 E
Garamba ≃	154	3.53 N	29.12 E
Garamba, Parc National de la ♦	154	4.10 N	29.30 E
Gara Muleta ∧	144	9.17 N	41.47 E
Garānberia	272b	22.24 N	88.34 E
Garancières	261	48.49 N	1.46 E
Garango	150	11.48 N	0.34 W
Garanhuns	250	8.54 S	36.29 W
Garapan	174n	15.12 N	145.43 E
Garara	164	8.37 S	148.17 E
Garautha	124	25.34 N	79.18 E
Garba	146	9.12 N	20.30 E
Garbagna	266b	45.23 N	8.39 E
Garbagnate Milanese	266b	45.35 N	9.05 E
Garbahaarrey	144	3.19 N	42.13 E
Garbatella ◆[8]	267a	41.52 N	12.29 E
Garba Tula	154	0.32 N	38.31 E
Garber	196	36.26 N	97.35 W
Garberville	204	40.06 N	123.47 W
Garbokaraj	88	54.09 N	99.52 E
Garboldisham	42	52.24 N	0.56 E
Gârbova	38	46.50 N	29.21 E
Gârbovu	38	44.44 N	23.21 E
Garbsen	52	52.25 N	9.34 E
Garça	255	22.14 S	49.37 W
Garças, Rio das ≃	255	15.54 S	52.16 W
Garcevo	76	52.45 N	32.59 E
Garches	261	48.51 N	2.11 E
Garching	60	48.15 N	11.39 E
Garching an der Alz	60	48.08 N	12.34 E
Garchitorena	116	13.52 N	123.40 E
García	232	29.59 N	108.20 W
García, Laguna ⊜	288	34.58 S	58.09 W
García de la Cadena	234	21.09 N	103.28 W
García de Sola, Embalse de ⊜[1]	34	39.15 N	5.05 W
Garcia Hernandez	116	9.37 N	124.18 E
Garcias	255	20.34 S	52.13 W
Garcitas Creek ≃	222	28.51 N	96.46 W
Gard □[5]	32	44.00 N	4.00 E
Gard ≃	62	43.51 N	4.37 E
Gard, Pont du ◆[5]	62	43.56 N	4.36 E
Garda	64	45.34 N	10.42 E
Garda, Lago di ⊜	64	45.40 N	10.41 E
Gardabani	84	41.28 N	45.06 E
Gardanne	62	43.27 N	5.28 E
Garde, Lac la ⊜	190	46.46 N	78.14 W
Gardelegen	54	52.31 N	11.23 E
Garden ≃	190	46.32 N	84.09 W
Gardena	228	33.53 N	118.18 W
Gardena, Val V	64	46.35 N	11.35 E
Garden Acres	226	37.58 N	121.13 W
Garden City, Ga., U.S.	192	32.06 N	81.09 W
Garden City, Ks., U.S.	198	37.58 N	100.52 W
Garden City, Mi., U.S.	216	42.19 N	83.19 W
Garden City, Mo., U.S.	194	38.33 N	94.11 W
Garden City, N.Y., U.S.	210	40.43 N	73.38 W
Garden City, Tx., U.S.	196	31.52 N	101.29 W
Garden City → Qasr al-Dubārā ◆[8]	273c	30.02 N	31.14 E
Garden City Park	276	40.44 N	73.39 W

Symbols in the index entries represent the broad categories identified in the key at the right. Symbols with superior numbers (⋏[1]) identify subcategories (see complete key on page *I · 1).*

Symbole im Register stellen die rechts im Schlüssel erklärten Kategorien dar. Symbole mit hochgestellten Ziffern (⋏[1]) bezeichnen Unterabteilungen einer Kategorie (vgl. vollständiger Schlüssel auf Seite *I · 1).*

Los símbolos incluídos en el texto del índice representan las grandes categorías identificadas con la clave a la derecha. Los símbolos con numeros en su parte superior (⋏[1]) identifican las subcategorías (véase la clave completa en la página *I · 1).*

Les symboles de l'index représentent les catégories indiquées dans la légende à droite. Les symboles suivis d'un indice (⋏[1]) représentent des sous-catégories (voir légende complète à la page *I · 1).*

Os símbolos incluídos no texto do índice representam as grandes categorias identificadas com a chave à direita. Os símbolos com números em sua parte superior (⋏[1]) identificam as subcategorias (veja-se a chave completa à página *I · 1).*

	English	Deutsch	Español	Français	Português
∧	Mountain	Berg	Montaña	Montagne	Montanha
⋏	Mountains	Gebirge	Montañas	Montagnes	Montanhas
)(	Pass	Paß	Paso	Col	Passo
V	Valley, Canyon	Tal, Cañon	Valle, Cañón	Vallée, Canyon	Vale, Canhão
≚	Plain	Ebene	Llano	Plaine	Planície
›	Cape	Kap	Cabo	Cap	Cabo
I	Island	Insel	Isla	Île	Ilha
II	Islands	Inseln	Islas	Îles	Ilhas
♦	Other Topographic Features	Andere Topographische Objekte	Otros Elementos Topográficos	Autres données topographiques	Outros acidentes topográficos

ESPAÑOL

Nombre	Página	Lat.°′	Long.°′ W = Oeste
Garden City Raceway ♠	284a	43.09 N	79.11 W
Gardendale	194	33.39 N	86.48 W
Garden Farms	226	35.24 N	120.07 W
Garden Gate Village	282	37.20 N	122.02 W
Garden Grove, Ca., U.S.	228	33.46 N	117.56 W
Garden Grove, Ia., U.S.	190	40.50 N	93.36 W
Garden Home	224	45.27 N	122.45 W
Garden Island I, Austl.	168a	32.13 S	115.41 E
Garden Island I, Mi., U.S.	190	45.49 N	85.30 W
Garden Lakes	192	34.17 N	85.16 W
Garden Peninsula ›[1]	190	45.45 N	86.35 W
Garden Plain	198	37.39 N	97.41 W
Garden Prairie	216	42.15 N	88.44 W
Garden Reach	126	22.33 N	88.17 E
Gardenside	218	38.03 N	84.33 W
Garden State Arts Center ɤ	276	40.24 N	74.11 W
Garden State Park Race Track ♠, N.J., U.S.	285	39.55 N	75.02 W
Garden State Park Race Track ♠, Pa., U.S.	285	39.55 N	75.02 W
Garden State Plaza ✦[9]	276	40.55 N	74.05 W
Gardenton	184	49.05 N	96.40 W
Garden Valley	226	38.51 N	120.51 W
Garden View	210	41.16 N	77.03 W
Gardenville	208	40.22 N	75.07 W
Gardermoen	26	60.13 N	11.06 E
Gardey	252	37.17 S	59.21 W
Gardeyz	120	33.37 N	69.07 E
Gardinas → Hrodna	76	53.41 N	23.50 E
Gardiner, Me., U.S.	188	44.13 N	69.46 W
Gardiner, Mt., U.S.	202	45.01 N	110.42 W
Gardiner, N.Y., U.S.	210	41.41 N	74.09 W
Gardiner, Or., U.S.	202	43.43 N	124.06 W
Gardiner, Wa., U.S.	224	48.03 N	122.55 W
Gardiner Dam ✦[6]	184	51.17 N	106.51 W
Gardiner Range ⩚	162	23.50 S	131.46 E
Gardiners Bay ⊂	207	41.08 N	72.10 W
Gardiners Creek ≃	274b	37.50 S	145.02 E
Gardiners Island I	207	41.05 N	72.07 W
Garding	41	54.20 N	8.46 E
Gardner, Il., U.S.	216	41.11 N	88.18 W
Gardner, Ks., U.S.	198	38.48 N	94.55 W
Gardner, Ma., U.S.	207	42.34 N	71.59 W
Gardner Canal ⊂	182	53.28 N	128.15 W
Gardner Lake ⊜	207	41.31 N	72.13 W
Gardner Pinnacles II[1]	14	25.00 N	167.55 W
Gardnersville	218	38.46 N	84.30 W
Gardnertown	210	41.32 N	74.04 W
Gardnerville	226	38.56 N	119.44 W
Gardno	54	53.15 N	14.38 E
Gardolo	64	46.07 N	11.05 E
Gardon d'Alès ≃	62	44.02 N	4.08 E
Gardon d'Anduze ≃	62	44.02 N	4.08 E
Gardone Riviera	64	45.37 N	10.34 E
Gardone Val Trompia	64	45.41 N	10.11 E
Gårdsjö	40	58.52 N	14.19 E
Gårdskär	40	60.37 N	17.35 E
Gare Loch ⊂	46	56.01 N	4.48 W
Garelochhead	46	56.05 N	4.50 W
Gareloi Island I	181a	51.47 N	178.48 W
Garenfeld ✦[8]	263	51.24 N	7.31 E
Garenin	46	58.21 N	6.50 W
Gare Simon	273b	4.15 S	15.11 E
Garešnica	36	45.35 N	16.56 E
Garessio	62	44.12 N	8.02 E
Garet, Mont ∧[1]	175f	14.16 S	167.30 E
Garfield, Ks., U.S.	198	38.04 N	99.14 W
Garfield, N.J., U.S.	210	40.52 N	74.06 W
Garfield, N.M., U.S.	200	32.45 N	107.15 W
Garfield, Wa., U.S.	202	47.00 N	117.08 W
Garfield Heights	214	41.25 N	81.36 W
Garfield Mountain ∧	202	44.31 N	112.37 W
Garfield Park	285	39.42 N	75.33 W
Garfield Park ♠, Il., U.S.	278	41.53 N	87.43 W
Garfield Park ♠, Oh., U.S.	279a	41.26 N	81.36 W
Garfield Peak ∧	200	42.47 N	107.18 W
Garforth	44	53.48 N	1.22 W
Garga	88	54.26 N	110.33 E
Gargaliánoi	38	37.04 N	21.39 E
Gargano, Promontorio del ›	68	41.50 N	16.00 E
Gargano, Testa del ›	68	41.49 N	16.12 E
Gargantua, Cape ›	190	47.36 N	85.02 W
Garga Sarali	152	5.11 N	14.00 E
Gargazzone (Gargazon)	64	46.35 N	11.12 E
Gargellen	58	46.58 N	9.56 E
Gargenville	261	49.00 N	1.49 E
Garges-lès-Gonesse	261	48.58 N	2.25 E
Gargnano	64	45.41 N	10.40 E
Gargouna	150	15.56 N	0.13 E
Gargrave	44	53.59 N	2.06 W
Gargždai	76	55.43 N	21.24 E
Garhākota	124	23.46 N	79.09 E
Garhbeta	126	22.51 N	87.19 E
Garhdīwāla	123	31.44 N	75.45 E
Garhi Habībullāh Khān	123	34.24 N	73.23 E
Garhi Jasaya	272a	28.46 N	77.16 E
Garhi Katiya	272a	28.45 N	77.16 E
Garhi Khairo	120	28.04 N	67.59 E
Garhi Malehra	124	25.02 N	79.40 E
Garhjāt Hills ⩚[2]	126	21.47 N	86.20 E
Garhmuktesar	124	28.48 N	78.06 E
Garhshankar	123	31.13 N	76.08 E
Garhwa	124	24.11 N	83.49 E
Gari	86	59.26 N	62.21 E
Garibaldi, Bra.	252	29.15 S	51.32 W
Garibaldi, B.C., Can.	182	49.58 N	123.09 W
Garibaldi, Or., U.S.	224	45.34 N	123.55 W
Garibaldi, Casa di ⊥	71	41.13 N	9.27 E
Garibaldi, Mount ∧	182	49.51 N	123.01 W
Garibaldi Provincial Park ♠	182	50.00 N	122.50 W
Garies	158	30.30 S	18.00 E
Garigliano ≃	66	41.13 N	13.45 E
Gariglione, Monte ∧	68	39.09 N	16.41 E
Garín	258	34.26 S	58.44 W
Garín, Arroyo ≃	288	34.23 S	58.43 W
Garin Regional Park ♠	282	37.38 N	122.03 W
Garipçe Burnu ›	267b	41.13 N	29.07 E
Garissa	154	0.28 S	39.38 E
Garita Palmera	236	13.44 N	90.05 W
Gariya	272b	22.28 N	88.23 E
Gārji	272b	22.51 N	88.19 E
Garkida	146	10.25 N	12.36 E
Garko	150	11.38 N	8.48 E
Garland, Al., U.S.	194	31.33 N	86.49 W
Garland, Md., U.S.	284b	39.11 N	76.39 W
Garland, Pa., U.S.	214	41.49 N	79.27 W
Garland, Tx., U.S.	222	32.54 N	96.38 W
Garland, Ut,. U.S.	200	41.44 N	112.09 W
Garland Park ♠	275b	43.44 N	79.35 W
Garland Peak ∧	224	48.01 N	120.43 W
Garlasco	62	45.12 N	8.55 E
Garlate	62	45.49 N	9.23 E
Garlate, Lago di ⊜	58	45.49 N	9.24 E
Garliava	76	54.49 N	23.52 E
Garlieston	44	54.48 N	4.22 W
Garlin	32	43.34 N	0.15 W
Garm	85	39.02 N	70.22 E
Garm Āb	120	32.14 N	65.01 E
Garmal	144	8.35 N	50.19 E
Gärmersdorf	60	49.26 N	11.54 E
Garmī	128	39.01 N	48.03 E
Garmisch-Partenkirchen	64	47.29 N	11.05 E

FRANÇAIS

Nom	Page	Lat.°′	Long.°′ W = Ouest
Garmouth	46	57.40 N	3.07 W
Garmsār	128	35.20 N	52.13 E
Garnavillo	190	42.52 N	91.14 W
Garne	261	48.41 N	1.58 E
Garner, Ia., U.S.	190	43.06 N	93.36 W
Garner, N.C., U.S.	192	35.42 N	78.36 W
Garnet Range ⩚	202	46.45 N	113.15 W
Garnett	198	38.16 N	95.14 W
Garnijskij zapovednik ♠	84	40.00 N	44.55 E
Garnish	186	47.14 N	55.22 W
Garnock ≃	46	55.38 N	4.42 W
Garnpung, Lake ⊜	166	33.30 S	143.12 E
Gāro Hills ⩚[2]	124	25.30 N	90.30 E
Garona → Garonne ≃	32	45.02 N	0.36 W
Garonne ≃	32	45.02 N	0.36 W
Garoowe	144	8.24 N	48.29 E
Garou, Lac ⊜	150	16.04 N	2.45 W
Garoua, Cam.	146	9.18 N	13.24 E
Garoua, Niger	146	13.53 N	13.11 E
Garoua Boulaï	152	5.53 N	14.33 E
Garove Island I	164	4.40 S	149.30 E
Garpenberg	40	60.19 N	16.12 E
Garphyttan	40	59.19 N	14.56 E
Garphyttans Nationalpark ♠	40	59.17 N	14.51 E
Garqu Yan, Zhg.	118	34.29 N	92.35 E
Garqu Yan, Zhg.	120	33.50 N	92.28 E
Garraf, Costa de ⊥[2]	266d	41.16 N	2.02 E
Garrattsville	210	42.39 N	75.10 W
Garrel	52	52.57 N	8.01 E
Garret Mountain Reservation ♠	276	40.54 N	74.11 W
Garretson	198	43.43 N	96.30 W
Garrett, In., U.S.	216	41.20 N	85.08 W
Garrett, Ky., U.S.	192	37.28 N	82.49 W
Garrett Creek ≃	222	32.57 N	95.44 W
Garrett Park	208	39.02 N	77.05 W
Garrett Park Estates	284c	39.02 N	77.06 W
Garrettsville	214	41.17 N	81.06 W
Garrison, N. Ire., U.K.	48	54.25 N	8.05 W
Garrison, Ky., U.S.	218	38.36 N	83.10 W
Garrison, Md., U.S.	208	39.24 N	76.45 W
Garrison, Mt., U.S.	202	46.31 N	112.48 W
Garrison, N.Y., U.S.	210	41.23 N	73.56 W
Garrison, N.D., U.S.	198	47.39 N	101.24 W
Garrison, Tx., U.S.	222	31.49 N	94.30 W
Garrison Dam ✦[6]	198	47.22 N	101.25 W
Garron Point ›	48	55.03 N	5.57 W
Garros	46	57.37 N	6.11 W
Garrovillas	34	39.43 N	6.33 W
Garry ≃	46	56.43 N	3.47 W
Garry, Loch ⊜	206	45.15 N	74.43 W
Garry Bay ⊂	176	68.55 N	85.05 W
Garry Lake ⊜	176	66.00 N	100.00 W
Gars am Kamp	61	48.36 N	15.40 E
Garsdale Head	44	54.19 N	2.20 W
Garsen	154	2.16 S	40.07 E
Garskolk	158	30.41 S	22.02 E
Gårslev	41	55.38 N	9.43 E
Garson	190	46.34 N	80.52 W
Garson Lake ⊜	184	56.19 N	110.02 W
Garstang	44	53.55 N	2.47 W
Garstedt	52	53.41 N	9.58 E
Garstedterheide ✦[3]	52	53.17 N	8.43 E
Garsten	61	48.01 N	14.24 E
Garston	260	51.41 N	0.23 W
Garston ✦[8]	262	53.21 N	2.53 W
Garswood	262	53.29 N	2.40 W
Gartempe ≃	32	46.48 N	0.50 E
Gartenstadt ✦[8]	263	51.30 N	7.26 E
Garthby Station (Beaulac)	206	45.50 N	71.23 W
Gartow	54	53.02 N	11.29 E
Gärtringen	58	48.39 N	8.54 E
Gartrop-Bühl	263	51.40 N	6.49 E
Gartz	54	53.12 N	14.23 E
Garu	150	10.51 N	0.11 W
Garub	156	26.33 S	16.00 E
Garubhāsa	124	26.33 N	90.22 E
Gārulia	126	22.49 N	88.22 E
Garut	115a	7.13 S	107.54 E
Garve	46	57.37 N	4.42 W
Garvellachs II	46	56.14 N	5.47 W
Garvey Reservoir ⊜[1]	280	34.13 N	118.07 W
Garvie Mountains ⩚	172	45.30 S	168.50 E
Garwin	190	42.05 N	92.40 W
Garwolin	30	51.54 N	21.37 E
Garwood, N.J., U.S.	276	40.39 N	74.19 W
Garwood, Tx., U.S.	222	29.27 N	96.24 W
Gary, In., U.S.	216	41.35 N	87.20 W
Gary, S.D., U.S.	198	44.47 N	96.27 W
Gary, Tx., U.S.	194	32.07 N	94.22 W
Gary, W.V., U.S.	192	37.21 N	81.33 W
Garyarsa	120	31.44 N	80.21 E
Gary Harbor ⊂	278	41.38 N	87.20 W
Garyi	102	30.54 N	98.56 E
Gary Municipal Airport ⊠	278	41.37 N	87.25 W
Garysburg	208	36.27 N	77.33 W
Garz	54	54.19 N	13.20 E
Garza	252	28.09 S	63.32 W
Garza Ayala	196	26.29 N	100.02 W
Garza García	196	25.40 N	100.24 W
Garzas Creek ≃	226	37.13 N	120.57 W
Garzeno	58	46.08 N	9.15 E
Garzón, Col.	246	2.12 N	75.38 W
Garzón, Ur.	252	34.36 S	54.33 W
Gas	261	48.34 N	1.40 E
Gasan	116	13.19 N	121.51 E
Gasan-Kuli	128	37.27 N	53.59 E
Gas City	216	40.29 N	85.36 W
Gascogne □[9]	32	44.00 N	0.05 E
Gascogne, Golfe de → Biscay, Bay of ⊂	32	44.00 N	4.00 W
Gasconade	219	38.40 N	91.33 W
Gasconade □[6]	219	38.27 N	91.30 W
Gasconade ≃	194	38.40 N	91.33 W
Gasconade, Osage Fork ≃	194	37.45 N	92.26 W
Gascoyne ≃	162	24.52 S	113.37 E
Gascoyne, Mount ∧	162	24.58 S	116.38 E
Gascoyne Junction	162	25.03 S	115.12 E
Gash (Nahr al-Qāsh) ≃	140	16.48 N	35.51 E
Gashaka	146	7.21 N	11.27 E
Gasherbrum I ∧	123	35.43 N	76.43 E
Gas Hu ⊜	120	38.10 N	90.42 E
Gashua	146	12.54 N	11.00 E
Gasline	284a	42.53 N	79.11 W
Gasny	50	49.05 N	1.36 E
Gaspar	252	26.56 S	48.58 W
Gaspard Creek ≃	182	51.34 N	122.17 W
Gasparilla Island I	220	26.46 N	82.16 W
Gasparilla Sound ⩌	220	26.48 N	82.15 W
Gaspé	186	48.50 N	64.29 W
Gaspé, Baie de ⊂	186	48.46 N	64.17 W
Gaspé, Cap ›	186	48.45 N	64.10 W
Gaspé Peninsula → Gaspésie, Péninsule de la ›[1]	186	48.30 N	65.00 W
Gaspereau Lake ⊜	186	44.57 N	64.34 W
Gasperina	68	38.44 N	16.30 E
Gaspésie, Parc Provincial de la ♠	186	48.55 N	66.00 W
Gaspésie, Péninsule de la ›[1]	186	48.30 N	65.00 W
Gaspoltshofen	60	48.08 N	13.46 E
Gasport	210	43.11 N	78.34 W
Gassan	150	12.49 N	3.12 W
Gas-san ∧	92	38.32 N	140.01 E
Gassaway	188	38.40 N	80.46 W
Gasse	64	47.23 N	11.09 E
Gasselte	52	52.57 N	6.46 E
Gassin	62	43.13 N	6.35 E
Gassino Torinese	62	45.08 N	7.49 E
Gassol	146	8.32 N	10.28 E

PORTUGUÊS

Nome	Página	Lat.°′	Long.°′ W = Oeste
Gastein → Badgastein	64	47.07 N	13.08 E
Gasteiner Tal V	64	47.11 N	13.06 E
Gasteiz → Vitoria	34	42.51 N	2.40 W
Gastello	89	49.07 N	142.58 E
Gaston, In., U.S.	216	40.18 N	85.30 W
Gaston, N.C., U.S.	192	36.30 N	77.38 W
Gaston, Or., U.S.	224	45.26 N	123.08 W
Gaston, Lake ⊜[1]	192	36.35 N	78.00 W
Gastonia, N.C., U.S.	192	35.15 N	81.11 W
Gastonia, Tx., U.S.	222	32.37 N	96.24 W
Gastonville	279b	40.15 N	79.59 W
Gastoúni	38	37.51 N	21.16 E
Gastre	254	42.17 S	69.14 W
Gästrikland □[9]	40	60.30 N	16.27 E
Gat	132	31.37 N	34.47 E
Gata, Cabo de ›	34	36.43 N	2.12 W
Gata, Sierra de ⩚	34	40.14 N	6.45 W
Gătaia	38	45.26 N	21.26 E
Gátas, Akrotírion ›	130	34.34 N	33.02 E
Gatčina	76	59.34 N	30.08 E
Gate	196	36.51 N	100.03 W
Gateacre ✦[8]	262	53.23 N	2.51 W
Gate City	192	36.38 N	82.34 W
Gatehouse of Fleet	44	54.53 N	4.11 W
Gatersleben	54	51.49 N	11.17 E
Gates, N.Y., U.S.	210	43.09 N	77.41 W
Gates, N.C., U.S.	208	36.30 N	76.46 W
Gates □[6]	208	36.28 N	76.43 W
Gateshead	44	54.58 N	1.37 W
Gateshead Island I	176	70.22 N	100.27 W
Gates Mills	279a	41.31 N	81.24 W
Gates of the Arctic National Park ♠	180	67.45 N	153.30 W
Gatesville, N.C., U.S.	192	36.24 N	76.45 W
Gatesville, Tx., U.S.	222	31.26 N	97.44 W
Gateway	200	38.40 N	108.58 W
Gateway Arch ɤ	219	38.37 N	90.12 W
Gateway National Recreation Area ♠	276	40.34 N	74.06 W
Gateway of India ⊥	272c	18.55 N	72.50 E
Gateway Stadium ♠	279a	41.30 N	81.41 W
Gaths Mine	154	20.00 S	30.31 E
Gathurst	262	53.34 N	2.42 W
Gatié Loumo	150	15.28 N	4.37 W
Gatineau	212	45.29 N	75.38 W
Gatineau □[6]	212	45.25 N	75.45 W
Gatineau ≃	176	45.27 N	75.40 W
Gatineau, Parc de la ♠	188	45.30 N	76.05 W
Gatley	262	53.23 N	2.14 W
Gatlinburg	192	35.42 N	83.30 W
Gato, Arroyo del ≃, Arg.	288	34.51 S	57.56 W
Gato, Arroyo del ≃, Arg.	288	34.55 S	58.37 W
Ga'ton	132	33.00 N	35.13 E
Gato Negro	286c	10.33 N	66.57 W
Gatow ✦[8]	54	52.29 N	13.11 E
Gatow, Flugplatz ⊠	264a	52.28 N	13.08 E
Gattendorf	61	48.01 N	16.59 E
Gattières	62	43.46 N	7.11 E
Gattinara	62	45.37 N	8.22 E
Gatton	171a	27.33 S	152.17 E
Gattorna	62	44.26 N	9.11 E
Gatún, Esclusas de ✦[5]	236	9.16 N	79.55 W
Gatún, Lago ⊜[1]	236	9.12 N	79.55 W
Gatvand	128	32.15 N	48.50 E
Gau-Algesheim	56	49.57 N	8.01 E
Gauchy	50	49.49 N	3.16 E
Gaucín	34	36.31 N	5.19 W
Gauer Lake ⊜	184	57.00 N	97.50 W
Gauguin, Musée ɤ	174s	17.45 S	149.23 W
Gauja ≃	76	57.09 N	24.16 E
Gaujiena	76	57.30 N	26.40 E
Gaukler Point ›	281	42.27 N	82.52 W
Gaula ≃	26	63.21 N	10.14 E
Gauley ≃	188	38.10 N	81.12 W
Gauley Bridge	188	38.10 N	81.11 W
Gaultois	186	47.36 N	55.54 W
Gaunless ≃	44	54.40 N	1.41 W
Gau-Odernheim	56	49.47 N	8.11 E
Gaur	124	26.46 N	85.17 E
Gaurain-Ramecroix	50	50.35 N	3.29 E
Gaurambha	126	22.39 N	89.34 E
Gaurela	124	22.45 N	81.54 E
Gaurhāti	126	22.46 N	87.48 E
Gauribaradia	126	23.45 N	89.52 E
Gauribidanūr	122	13.37 N	77.31 E
Gauri Phānta	124	28.41 N	80.33 E
Gauripur	124	26.05 N	89.58 E
Gaurīśaṅgkar ∧	124	27.57 N	86.21 E
Gaurnadi	126	22.58 N	90.14 E
Gause	222	30.47 N	96.43 W
Gausta ∧	26	59.50 N	8.35 E
Gauteng □[4]	156	26.00 S	28.15 E
Gauthiot, Chutes ⌞	146	9.43 N	14.34 E
Gauting	60	48.04 N	11.23 E
Gavà	34	41.18 N	2.01 E
Gāvanpāda	272c	18.57 N	73.01 E
Gavardo	64	45.35 N	10.26 E
Gávdhos I	38	34.50 N	24.06 E
Gávea ✦[8]	287a	22.58 S	43.14 W
Gávea, Hipódromo da ♠	287a	22.58 S	43.13 W
Gávea, Pedra da ∧	287a	23.00 S	43.17 W
Gavel-Långsjön ⊜	40	59.50 N	18.18 E
Gavello	64	45.01 N	11.55 E
Gavet	62	45.04 N	5.52 E
Gavi	62	44.41 N	8.49 E
Gavia, Arroyo de la ≃	266a	40.21 N	3.40 W
Gavião ≃	255	14.06 S	41.01 W
Gavião, Pico do ∧	256	21.37 S	44.50 W
Gavien	164	3.54 S	144.07 E
Gavilán	286c	10.24 N	66.51 W
Gavinana	66	44.05 N	10.45 E
Gavins Point Dam ✦[6]	198	42.48 N	97.40 W
Gaviões	256	22.34 S	42.33 W
Gavirate	62	45.50 N	8.43 E
Gāv Khūnī, Bāṭlāq-e ⩸	128	32.10 N	52.50 E
Gävle	40	60.40 N	17.10 E
Gävleborgs Län □[6]	26	61.30 N	16.15 E
Gävlebukten ⊂	40	60.42 N	17.20 E
Gavnø	41	55.11 N	11.44 E
Gavoi	71	40.10 N	9.12 E
Gavorrano	66	42.55 N	10.54 E
Gavrilov-Jam	80	57.18 N	39.51 E
Gavrilovka Vtoraja	80	52.53 N	42.46 E
Gavrilov Posad	80	56.33 N	40.07 E
Gávrion	38	37.52 N	24.46 E
Gavry	76	56.55 N	27.53 E
Gawachab	156	27.03 S	17.50 E
Gāwān	124	24.37 N	85.55 E
Gaweinstal	61	48.28 N	16.35 E
Gāwīlgarh Hills ⩚[2]	122	21.20 N	77.00 E
Gawler	168b	34.37 S	138.44 E
Gawler ≃	168b	34.41 S	138.27 E
Gawler Ranges ⩚	162	32.30 S	136.00 E
Gawso	150	6.48 N	2.31 W
Gawsworth	262	53.13 N	2.10 W
Gawthorpe Hall ⊥	262	53.48 N	2.18 W
Gaxun Nur (Juyanhai) ⊜	102	42.22 N	100.34 E
Gaya, India	124	24.47 N	85.00 E
Gaya, Niger	150	11.53 N	3.27 E
Gaya, Nig.	150	11.53 N	9.02 E
Gay City State Park ♠	207	41.42 N	72.28 W
Gayéri	150	12.39 N	0.29 E
Gay Head	207	41.20 N	70.48 W
Gay Hill	222	30.16 N	96.30 W
Gaylord, Mi., U.S.	190	45.01 N	84.40 W
Gaylord, Mn., U.S.	190	44.33 N	94.13 W
Gaylordsville	207	41.38 N	73.29 W
Gayndah	166	25.37 S	151.36 E
Gays Mills	190	43.19 N	90.50 W
Gayton, Eng., U.K.	42	52.45 N	0.34 E
Gayton, Eng., U.K.	262	53.19 N	3.06 W
Gaza → Ghazzah	132	31.30 N	34.28 E
Gaza □[5]	156	23.30 S	32.45 E
Gazalkent	85	41.33 N	69.47 E
Gazaoua	150	13.32 N	7.55 E
Gaza Strip □[9]	132	31.25 N	34.20 E
Gazelle Channel ⩌	164	2.50 S	150.55 E
Gazelle Peninsula ›[1]	164	4.40 S	152.00 E
Gazeran	261	48.38 N	1.46 E
Gazeran, Bois de ♠	261	48.40 N	1.45 E
Gazi, Kenya	154	4.25 S	39.30 E
Gazi, R.D.C.	154	1.04 N	24.31 E
Gaziantep	130	37.05 N	37.22 E
Gaziantep □[4]	130	37.00 N	37.20 E
Gazimağusa (Famagusta)	130	35.07 N	33.57 E
Gazimağusa Körfezi ⊂	130	35.15 N	34.10 E
Gazimur ≃	88	52.57 N	120.22 E
Gazimurskij Zavod	88	51.33 N	118.22 E
Gazipaşa	130	36.17 N	32.20 E
Gazira Sporting Club ♠	273c	30.04 N	31.13 E
Gazivoda Jezero ⊜[1]	38	42.55 N	20.40 E
Gaznau	85	40.10 N	71.02 E
Gazoldo degli Ippoliti	64	45.12 N	10.35 E
Gazos Creek ≃	226	37.10 N	122.22 W
Gazzada	62	45.47 N	8.51 E
Gazzaniga	62	45.48 N	9.50 E
Gazzuolo	64	45.04 N	10.35 E
Gbangbatok	150	7.48 N	12.23 W
Gbanhala ≃	150	10.14 N	8.38 W
Gbaoui Bodanga	152	5.33 N	16.45 E
Gbarnga	150	7.00 N	9.29 W
Gbogbo	273a	6.36 N	3.31 E
Gboko	150	7.20 N	8.57 E
Gbon	150	9.50 N	6.27 W
Gbwado	152	3.54 N	20.46 E
Gcoverega	156	19.08 S	24.15 E
Gdańsk (Danzig)	30	54.23 N	18.40 E
Gdańsk □[4]	30	54.15 N	18.25 E
Gdansk, Gulf of ⊂	30	54.40 N	19.15 E
Gdov	76	58.44 N	27.48 E
Gdyel	34	35.48 N	0.26 W
Gdynia	30	54.32 N	18.33 E
Gearhart	224	46.01 N	123.54 W
Gearhart Mountain ∧	202	42.30 N	120.53 W
Gearhartville	214	40.53 N	78.15 W
Geary, N.B., Can.	186	45.46 N	66.29 W
Geary, Ok., U.S.	196	35.43 N	98.22 W
Geauga □[6]	214	41.35 N	81.12 W
Geauga Lake Park ♠	279a	41.21 N	81.23 W
Geba ≃	150	11.46 N	15.36 W
Gebaberg ∧	56	50.36 N	10.16 E
Gebe, Pulau I	164	0.05 S	129.20 E
Gebeit Mine	140	21.03 N	36.19 E
Gebenbach	60	49.32 N	11.53 E
Gebesee	54	51.07 N	10.56 E
Gebi	84	42.46 N	43.30 E
Gebilu	144	10.35 N	41.28 E
Gebiz	130	37.06 N	30.56 E
Gebra	54	51.24 N	10.35 E
Gebweiler → Guebwiller	58	47.55 N	7.12 E
Gebze	130	40.48 N	29.25 E
Gecha	144	7.31 N	35.22 E
Gechang	106	31.05 N	119.27 E
Geçitkale	130	35.15 N	33.45 E
Gecun	106	32.10 N	119.37 E
Geddes, Mi., U.S.	281	42.16 N	83.40 W
Geddes, S.D., U.S.	198	43.15 N	98.41 W
Gede, Gunung ∧	115a	6.47 S	106.59 E
Gedera	132	31.49 N	34.46 E
Gedern	56	50.25 N	9.12 E
Gedian	100	30.32 N	114.38 E
Gedikler	130	39.06 N	38.49 E
Gediksaray	130	40.27 N	35.38 E
Gedi National Monument ♠	154	3.19 S	40.03 E
Gedinne	56	49.59 N	4.56 E
Gediz	130	39.02 N	29.25 E
Gediz ≃	130	38.35 N	26.48 E
Gedlegube	144	6.52 N	45.02 E
Gedo	144	8.58 N	37.27 E
Gedo □[4]	144	3.00 N	42.00 E
Gedongdalem	112	5.04 S	105.25 E
Gedongtataan	115a	5.23 S	105.05 E
Gedser	41	54.35 N	11.57 E
Gedser Odde ›	41	54.34 N	11.59 E
Geduld	273d	26.15 S	28.25 E
Gedun	100	27.39 N	118.26 E
Geebung	171a	27.22 S	153.03 E
Gee Cross	262	53.26 N	2.04 W
Geehi	171b	36.24 S	148.11 E
Geehi ≃	171b	36.11 S	148.02 E
Geel	56	51.10 N	5.00 E
Geelong	169	38.08 S	144.21 E
Geelong West	169	38.08 S	144.20 E
Geelvink Channel ⩌	162	28.30 S	114.10 E
Geer ≃	56	50.51 N	5.42 E
Geeste	52	52.36 N	7.16 E
Geeste ≃	52	53.32 N	8.35 E
Geesthacht	52	53.26 N	10.22 E
Geeveston	166	43.10 S	146.55 E
Gefell	54	50.26 N	11.52 E
Gefle → Gävle	40	60.40 N	17.10 E
Gefrees	54	50.06 N	11.44 E
Gegang	100	30.04 N	117.38 E
Gegenmiao	89	45.58 N	122.15 E
Gegong	100	30.05 N	117.11 E
Gegou	98	35.24 N	118.32 E
Gegu	105	38.59 N	117.30 E
Gehackte Berge ⩚[2]	264a	52.41 N	13.30 E
Gehrden	52	52.18 N	9.36 E
Gehren	54	50.39 N	10.59 E
Gehu	100	27.46 N	119.16 E
Ge Hu ⊜	106	31.36 N	119.51 E
Gehua	164	10.20 S	150.25 E
Geidam	146	12.57 N	11.57 E
Geiger	194	32.52 N	88.18 W
Geigertown	208	40.13 N	75.50 W
Geihoku	96	34.44 N	132.17 E
Geikie ≃	176	57.45 N	103.52 W
Geilenkirchen	56	50.57 N	6.07 E
Geilo	26	60.31 N	8.12 E
Geinō	94	34.48 N	136.25 E
Geiranger	26	62.06 N	7.12 E
Geisa	56	50.43 N	9.57 E
Geisberg ∧	60	49.53 N	11.03 E
Geisecke	263	51.27 N	7.37 E
Geisei	96	33.31 N	133.49 E
Geiselhöring	60	48.50 N	12.23 E
Geiselwind	56	49.46 N	10.28 E
Geisenfeld	60	48.41 N	11.37 E
Geisenhausen	60	48.28 N	12.15 E
Geisenheim	56	49.59 N	7.58 E
Geising	54	50.46 N	13.47 E
Geisingen	58	47.55 N	8.38 E
Geislingen	58	48.17 N	8.49 E
Geislingen an der Steige	56	48.36 N	9.50 E
Geismar	52	51.31 N	9.57 E
Geispolsheim	58	48.31 N	7.39 E
Geisstein ∧	64	47.20 N	12.30 E
Geistenbeck ✦[8]	263	51.09 N	6.27 E
Geistown	214	40.17 N	78.52 W
Geist Reservoir ⊜[1], In., U.S.	218	39.56 N	85.56 W
Geist Reservoir ⊜[1], Pa., U.S.	285	39.57 N	75.24 W
Geisweid	56	50.55 N	8.01 E
Geita	154	2.52 S	32.10 E
Geithain	54	51.03 N	12.41 E
Geiyō-shotō II	96	34.10 N	132.45 E
Gejah	272a	28.31 N	77.23 E
Gejiatun	98	40.27 N	119.55 E
Gejiu (Kokiu)	102	23.22 N	103.06 E
Geka, mys ›	180	64.26 N	178.10 E
Gela	70	37.04 N	14.15 E
Gela ≃	70	37.03 N	14.15 E
Gela, Golfo di ⊂	70	37.03 N	14.10 E
Geladandong ∧	120	33.16 N	91.27 E
Geladi	144	6.57 N	46.25 E
Gelai ∧[1]	154	2.33 S	36.05 E
Gelan	102	30.03 N	107.04 E
Gelang, Tanjong ›	114	3.58 N	103.26 E
Gelaochang	107	29.36 N	103.39 E
Gelasa, Selat ⩌	112	2.40 S	107.15 E
Gelbensande	54	54.12 N	12.18 E
Gelber Fluss → Huang ≃	90	37.32 N	118.19 E
Gelbes Meer → Yellow Sea ⍑[2]	90	36.00 N	123.00 E
Gelderland □[4]	52	52.10 N	5.50 E
Geldermalsen	52	51.53 N	5.17 E
Geldern	52	51.31 N	6.20 E
Geldrop	52	51.25 N	5.33 E
Geleen	56	50.58 N	5.52 E
Gelembe	130	39.10 N	27.50 E
Gelemso	144	8.48 N	40.35 E
Gelenau	54	50.42 N	12.58 E
Gelendost	130	38.07 N	31.01 E
Gelendžik	78	44.33 N	38.06 E
Gelfingen	58	47.13 N	8.16 E
Gelgaudiškis	76	55.05 N	23.00 E
Gelib → Jilib	144	0.29 N	42.46 E
Gelibolu	130	40.24 N	26.40 E
Gelibolu Yarımadası (Gallipoli Peninsula) ›[1]	130	40.20 N	26.30 E
Gelibolu Yarımadası Milli Parkı ♠	130	40.05 N	26.10 E
Gelinden	56	50.46 N	5.15 E
Gélise ≃	32	44.11 N	0.17 E
Geliting	115b	8.39 S	122.18 E
Geliting, Teluk ⊂	115b	8.36 S	122.17 E
Gellénháza	61	46.46 N	16.47 E
Gellenstrom ⩌	54	54.28 N	13.03 E
Gellep-Stratum ✦[8]	263	51.20 N	6.41 E
Gellibrand ≃	169	38.41 S	143.09 E
Gellibrand, Mount ∧[2]	169	38.14 S	143.48 E
Gellibrand, Point ›	274b	37.52 S	144.54 E
Gellibrand River	169	38.32 S	143.32 E
Gellingen → Ghislenghien	50	50.39 N	3.52 E
Gellinsoor	144	6.26 N	46.42 E
Gelnhausen	56	50.11 N	9.11 E
Gelså ≃	41	55.19 N	8.54 E
Gelsdorf	56	50.35 N	7.02 E
Gelsenkirchen	52	51.31 N	7.07 E
Gelsenkirchen-Horst, Galopprennbahn ♠	263	51.32 N	7.02 E
Gelsted	41	55.24 N	9.59 E
Gelt ≃	44	54.56 N	2.47 W
Gelterkinden	58	47.28 N	7.51 E
Gelting	41	54.45 N	9.53 E
Geltow	54	52.22 N	12.58 E
Geltsa	144	6.14 N	37.05 E
Geluji	98	37.08 N	121.50 E
Geluksburg	158	28.30 S	29.33 E
Geluwe	50	50.48 N	3.04 E
Gemas	114	2.35 N	102.37 E
Gembloux	56	50.34 N	4.41 E
Gembrook	169	37.57 S	145.33 E
Gemen	52	51.51 N	6.52 E
Gemena	152	3.15 N	19.46 E
Gémenos	62	43.18 N	5.38 E
Gemerek	130	39.11 N	36.05 E
Gemert	52	51.34 N	5.40 E
Gemla	26	56.52 N	14.38 E
Gemlik	130	40.26 N	29.09 E
Gemlik Körfezi ⊂	130	40.25 N	28.55 E
Gemolong	115a	7.24 S	110.50 E
Gemona del Friuli	64	46.16 N	13.09 E
Gemonio	62	45.53 N	8.40 E
Gemsbok National Park ♠	156	25.15 S	21.10 E
Gemünd	56	50.34 N	6.30 E
Gemünden, Dtsch.	56	50.03 N	9.41 E
Gemünden, Dtsch.	56	50.58 N	8.58 E
Gemünden, Dtsch.	56	49.54 N	7.28 E
Gen ≃	89	50.16 N	119.22 E
Genadendal	158	34.02 S	19.33 E
Genaibashi	268	35.21 N	140.04 E
Genale (Jubba) ≃	144	0.15 S	42.38 E
Genappe	50	50.36 N	4.27 E
Genarp	41	55.36 N	13.23 E
Genazzano	66	41.50 N	12.58 E
Genç	130	38.46 N	40.35 E
Gençay	32	46.23 N	0.24 E
Gencek	130	37.27 N	31.33 E
Gencsapáti	61	47.17 N	16.36 E
Gending	115a	7.48 S	113.18 E
Gendrey	58	47.12 N	5.41 E
Gendringen	52	51.52 N	6.22 E
Gendt	52	51.53 N	5.59 E
Genegantslet Creek ≃	210	42.18 N	75.48 W
Genemuiden	52	52.37 N	6.07 E
General ≃	236	8.59 N	83.11 W
General Acha	252	37.23 S	64.36 W
General Alvear, Arg.	252	36.03 S	60.01 W
General Alvear, Arg.	252	34.58 S	67.42 W
General Aquino	252	24.26 S	56.42 W
General Arenales	252	34.18 S	61.18 W
General Belgrano	252	35.46 S	58.30 W
General Bernardo O'Higgins ɤ[3]	9	63.19 S	57.54 W
General Bravo	232	25.48 N	99.10 W
General Butler State Resort Park ♠	218	38.40 N	85.10 W
General Cabrera	252	32.48 S	63.52 W
General Campos	252	31.32 S	58.24 W
General Carneiro	255	15.42 S	52.45 W
General Carrera, Lago (Lago Buenos Aires) ⊜	254	46.35 S	72.00 W
General Cepeda	232	25.23 N	101.27 W
General Conesa, Arg.	252	36.30 S	57.20 W
General Conesa, Arg.	254	40.06 S	64.26 W
General Daniel Cerri	252	38.42 S	62.24 W
General del Sur, Cementerio ✦	286c	10.28 N	66.55 W
General Elizardo Aquino	252	26.53 S	56.17 W
General Enrique Martínez	252	33.12 S	53.48 W
General Enrique Mosconi	252	22.36 S	63.49 W
General Escobedo, Méx.	196	25.49 N	100.20 W
General Escobedo, Méx.	232	25.30 N	105.15 W
General Eugenio A. Garay, Para.	248	20.31 S	62.08 W
General Eugenio A. Garay, Para.	252	25.55 S	56.11 W
General Galarza	252	32.43 S	59.24 W
General Güemes	252	24.40 S	65.03 W
General Guido	252	36.40 S	57.46 W
General Hornos	258	34.53 S	58.56 W
General Island I	116	9.25 N	126.00 E
General José de San Martín	252	26.33 S	59.21 W
General Juan José Ríos	232	25.40 N	108.40 W
General Juan Madariaga	252	37.00 S	57.09 W
General La Madrid	252	37.16 S	61.17 W
General Las Heras	258	34.56 S	58.57 W
General Las Heras □[5]	288	34.56 S	58.51 W
General Lavalle	252	36.24 S	56.58 W
General Leonidas Plaza Gutiérrez	246	2.58 S	78.25 W
General Levalle	252	34.01 S	63.56 W
General Lorenzo Vintter	254	40.44 S	64.29 W
General Luna	116	9.47 N	126.09 E
General MacArthur (Pambuhan Sur)	116	11.15 N	125.32 E
General Mansilla (Bartolomé Bavio)	258	35.05 S	57.45 W
General Manuel Belgrano, Cerro ∧	252	29.01 S	67.49 W
General Mitchell Field ⊠	216	42.57 N	87.54 W
General Motors Corporation (Pontiac Division) ɤ[3]	281	42.49 N	83.17 W
General Motors Proving Grounds ɤ[3]	281	42.35 N	83.41 W
General Motors Technical Center ɤ[3]	281	42.31 N	83.02 W
General'nyj ≃	265a	60.00 N	30.32 E
General O'Brien	252	34.54 S	60.45 W
General Pacheco	288	34.28 S	58.38 W
General Pánfilo Natera	234	22.40 N	102.06 W
General Paz	258	35.31 S	58.19 W
General Pico	252	35.40 S	63.44 W
General Pinedo	252	27.19 S	61.17 W
General Pinto	252	34.46 S	61.53 W
General Pizarro	252	24.13 S	64.01 W
General Roca	252	39.02 S	67.35 W
General Rodríguez	258	34.36 S	58.57 W
General San Martín, Arg.	252	37.59 S	63.34 W
General San Martín, Arg.	258	34.34 S	58.32 W
General San Martín □[5]	288	34.34 S	58.34 W
General Santos (Dadiangas)	116	6.07 N	125.11 E
General Sarmiento	258	34.33 S	58.43 W
General Sarmiento □[5]	288	34.32 S	58.43 W
General'skoje	83	47.28 N	39.35 E
General Terán	232	25.16 N	99.41 W
General Tinio	116	15.21 N	121.03 E
General Toševo	38	43.42 N	28.02 E
General Treviño	196	26.14 N	99.29 W
General Viamonte (Los Toldos)	252	35.01 S	61.01 W
General Villegas	252	35.02 S	63.01 W
General Vintter, Lago (Lago Palena) ⊜	254	43.55 S	71.40 W
General Warren Village	285	40.02 N	75.32 W
General Zuazua	196	25.54 N	100.07 W
Gênes → Genova	62	44.25 N	8.57 E
Genesee, Id., U.S.	202	46.33 N	116.55 W
Genesee, Pa., U.S.	214	41.59 N	77.52 W
Genesee, Wi., U.S.	216	42.58 N	88.21 W
Genesee □[6], Mi., U.S.	216	42.56 N	83.41 W
Genesee □[6], N.Y., U.S.	210	43.00 N	78.11 W
Genesee ≃	210	43.16 N	77.36 W
Geneseo, Il., U.S.	190	41.26 N	90.09 W
Geneseo, Ks., U.S.	198	38.30 N	98.09 W
Geneseo, N.Y., U.S.	210	42.47 N	77.49 W
Geneva → Genève, Schw.	58	46.12 N	6.09 E
Geneva, S. Afr.	158	27.50 S	27.08 E
Geneva, Al., U.S.	194	31.01 N	85.51 W
Geneva, Fl., U.S.	220	28.44 N	81.07 W
Geneva, Il., U.S.	216	41.53 N	88.18 W
Geneva, In., U.S.	216	40.35 N	84.57 W
Geneva, Ne., U.S.	198	40.31 N	97.35 W
Geneva, N.Y., U.S.	210	42.52 N	77.00 W
Geneva, Oh., U.S.	214	41.48 N	80.56 W
Geneva, Pa., U.S.	214	41.35 N	80.14 W
Geneva, Wa., U.S.	224	48.45 N	122.24 W
Geneva, Lake (Lac Léman) (Lac de Gèneve) ⊜, Europe	58	46.25 N	6.30 E
Geneva, Lake ⊜, Wi., U.S.	216	42.34 N	88.30 W
Geneva-on-the-Lake	214	41.52 N	80.57 W
Genève (Geneva)	58	46.12 N	6.09 E
Genève □[3]	58	46.15 N	6.10 E
Genève, Lac de → Geneva, Lake ⊜	58	46.25 N	6.30 E
Genève-Cointrin, Aéroport ⊠	58	46.14 N	6.06 E
Genevois ✦[1]	58	46.03 N	6.14 E
Genévriers, Île des I	186	51.15 N	58.26 W
Genf → Genève	58	46.12 N	6.09 E
Genga	66	43.26 N	12.56 E
Gengenbach	58	48.24 N	8.01 E
Genghis Khan, Wall of ⊥, Asia	88	49.00 N	115.00 E
Genghis Khan, Wall of ⊥, Mong.	88	49.00 N	116.00 E
Gengji	100	33.47 N	112.47 E
Gengma	102	23.34 N	99.06 E
Gengputou	106	31.12 N	119.55 E
Gengzhuang	104	40.59 N	122.42 E
Génicourt	261	49.05 N	2.04 E
Génicourt-sur-Meuse	56	49.02 N	5.26 E
Genil ≃	34	37.42 N	5.19 W
Génissiat	58	46.03 N	5.47 E
Genk	56	50.58 N	5.30 E
Genkai	96	33.51 N	130.30 E
Genkai-kokutei-kōen ♠	96	33.54 N	130.31 E
Genkai-nada ⍑[2]	92	34.00 N	130.00 E
Genkanyj, chrebet ⩚	180	66.15 N	172.20 W
Genlis	58	47.14 N	5.13 E
Gennach ≃	58	48.10 N	10.43 E
Gennargentu, Monti del ⩚	71	40.01 N	9.19 E
Gennebreck	263	51.19 N	7.12 E
Gennep	52	51.42 N	5.58 E
Genner	41	55.07 N	9.26 E
Gennes	32	47.20 N	0.14 W
Gennevilliers	261	48.56 N	2.18 E
Genoa, Austl.	166	37.29 S	149.35 E
Genoa → Genova, It.	62	44.25 N	8.57 E
Genoa, Il., U.S.	216	42.05 N	88.41 W
Genoa, Ne., U.S.	198	41.26 N	97.43 W
Genoa, Nv., U.S.	226	39.00 N	119.50 W
Genoa, N.Y., U.S.	210	42.40 N	76.32 W
Genoa, Oh., U.S.	214	41.31 N	83.21 W
Genoa, Wi., U.S.	190	43.34 N	91.13 W
Genoa, Arroyo ≃	254	44.58 S	70.06 W
Genoa City	216	42.29 N	88.19 W
Genoa Peak ∧	226	39.03 N	119.53 W
Genola	62	44.35 N	7.39 E
Génolhac	62	44.21 N	3.57 E
Genova (Genoa)	62	44.25 N	8.57 E
Genova □[4]	62	44.30 N	9.04 E
Genova, Golfo di ⊂	62	44.10 N	8.55 E
Genova, Val V	64	46.11 N	10.40 E
Genovesa, Isla I	246a	0.20 N	89.58 W
Genrijetty, ostrov I	74	77.06 N	156.30 E
Gensan → Wŏnsan	98	39.09 N	127.25 E
Gens de Terre ≃	190	46.53 N	76.00 W
Genshagen	264a	52.19 N	13.19 E
Genshagener Heide ✦[3]	264a	52.20 N	13.18 E
Genshiryoku-kenkyūsho ɤ[3]	94	36.27 N	140.36 E
Gensingen	56	49.53 N	7.55 E
Gensungen	56	51.08 N	9.26 E
Gent (Gand)	50	51.03 N	3.43 E
Gentbrugge	50	51.03 N	3.45 E
Gent-Brugge, Kanaal ≍	50	51.03 N	3.43 E

≃ River	Fluß	Río	Rivière	Rio	⟡ Submarine Features	Untermeerische Objekte	Accidentes Submarinos	Formes de relief sous-marin	Acidentes submarinos
≍ Canal	Kanal	Canal	Canal	Canal	□ Political Unit	Politische Einheit	Unidad Politica	Entité politique	Unidade política
⌞ Waterfall, Rapids	Wasserfall, Stromschnellen	Cascada, Rápidos	Chute d'eau, Rapides	Cascata, Rápidos	ɤ Cultural Institution	Kulturelle Institution	Institución Cultural	Institution culturelle	Institução cultural
⩌ Strait	Meeresstraße	Estrecho	Détroit	Estreito	⊥ Historical Site	Historische Stätte	Sitio Histórico	Site historique	Sitio histórico
⊂ Bay, Gulf	Bucht, Golf	Bahía, Golfo	Baie, Golfe	Baía, Golfo	♠ Recreational Site	Erholungs- und Ferienort	Sitio de Recreo	Centre de loisirs	Area de Lazer
⊜ Lake, Lakes	See, Seen	Lago, Lagos	Lac, Lacs	Lago, Lagos	⊠ Airport	Flughafen	Aeropuerto	Aéroport	Aeroporto
⩸ Swamp	Sumpf	Pantano	Marais	Pântano	▪ Military Installation	Militäranlage	Instalación Militar	Installation militaire	Instalação militar
⊓ Ice Features, Glacier	Eis- und Gletscherformen	Accidentes Glaciales	Formes glaciaires	Acidentes glaciares	✦ Miscellaneous	Verschiedenes	Misceláneo	Divers	Diversos
⍑ Other Hydrographic Features	Andere Hydrographische Objekte	Otros Elementos Hidrográficos	Autres données hydrographiques	Outros acidentes hidrográficos					

ENGLISH | DEUTSCH

Name / Name	Page / Seite	Lat.°′ / Breite°′	Long.°′ / Länge°′ E = Ost
Genteng	115a	8.22 S	114.09 E
Genteng, Gili I	115a	7.12 S	113.54 E
Genteng, Tanjung ≻	115a	7.23 S	106.24 E
Genthin	54	52.24 N	12.09 E
Gentilly	261	48.49 N	2.21 E
Gentilly ≃	206	46.24 N	72.21 W
Genting	114	3.42 N	98.10 E
Gentio do Ouro	250	11.25 S	42.30 W
Gentioux	32	45.47 N	1.59 E
Gentofte	41	55.45 N	12.33 E
Gentry	194	36.16 N	94.29 W
Gentry, Lake ⊜	220	28.08 N	81.15 W
Genua → Genova	62	44.25 N	8.57 E
Genuang	114	2.29 N	102.53 E
Genval	50	50.43 N	4.29 E
Genyem	164	2.46 S	140.12 E
Genzano di Lucania	68	40.51 N	16.02 E
Genzano di Roma	66	41.42 N	12.41 E
Geographe Bay ⊂	162	33.35 S	115.15 E
Geographe Channel Ʉ	162	24.40 S	113.20 E
Geok-Tepe	128	38.09 N	57.58 E
Geonkhāli	126	22.12 N	88.03 E
George, S. Afr.	158	33.58 S	22.24 E
George, Ia., U.S.	198	43.20 N	96.00 W
George, Tx., U.S.	222	30.59 N	96.07 W
George ≃, Austl.	162	20.50 S	117.28 E
George ≃, P.Q., Can.	176	58.49 N	66.10 W
George, Cape ≻	186	45.53 N	61.53 W
George, Lake ⊜, Austl.	162	22.37 S	123.38 E
George, Lake ⊜, Austl.	166	35.05 S	149.25 E
George, Lake ⊜, N.A.	190	46.28 N	84.10 W
George, Lake ⊜, Ug.	154	0.02 N	30.12 E
George, Lake ⊜, U.S.	216	41.45 N	85.00 W
George, Lake ⊜, Fl., U.S.	192	29.17 N	81.36 W
George, Lake ⊜, In., U.S.	216	41.40 N	87.30 W
George, Lake ⊜, N.Y., U.S.	188	43.35 N	73.35 W
George Air Force Base ■	228	34.35 N	117.22 W
George B. Stevenson Dam ⟡ 6	214	41.25 N	78.01 W
George Gill Range ⋏	162	24.15 S	131.36 E
George H. Crosby Manitou State Park ♠	190	47.29 N	91.10 W
George Island I	254	52.19 S	59.45 W
George Mason University ʊ 2	284c	38.50 N	77.17 W
Georgensgmünd	56	49.11 N	11.00 E
Georgenthal	54	50.49 N	10.40 E
Georges ≃	170	33.57 S	150.58 E
Georges Bank ✢ 4	16	41.15 N	67.30 W
Georges Island I	283	42.19 N	70.56 W
George Sound Ʉ	172	44.50 S	167.23 E
Georges River Bridge ⟡ 5	274a	34.00 S	151.07 E
Georges Run	214	40.21 N	80.37 W
Georges Run ≃	279b	40.23 N	80.06 W
Georgetown, Austl.	166	18.18 S	143.33 E
George Town, Austl.	166	41.06 S	146.50 E
Georgetown → Halton Hills, On., Can.	190	43.37 N	79.56 W
Georgetown, P.E., Can.	186	46.11 N	62.32 W
George Town, Cay. Is.	238	19.18 N	81.23 W
Georgetown, Gam.	150	13.30 N	14.47 W
Georgetown, Guy.	246	6.48 N	58.10 W
George Town (Pinang), Malay.	114	5.25 N	100.20 E
Georgetown, St. Vin.	241h	13.16 N	61.08 W
Georgetown, Ca., U.S.	226	38.54 N	120.50 W
Georgetown, Co., U.S.	200	39.42 N	105.41 W
Georgetown, Ct., U.S.	207	41.15 N	73.26 W
Georgetown, De., U.S.	208	38.41 N	75.23 W
Georgetown, Fl., U.S.	192	29.23 N	81.38 W
Georgetown, Ga., U.S.	192	31.53 N	85.06 W
Georgetown, Id., U.S.	202	42.29 N	111.22 W
Georgetown, Il., U.S.	194	39.58 N	87.38 W
Georgetown, In., U.S.	218	38.17 N	85.58 W
Georgetown, Ky., U.S.	218	38.12 N	84.33 W
Georgetown, Ma., U.S.	207	42.43 N	70.59 W
Georgetown, Ms., U.S.	194	31.52 N	90.09 W
Georgetown, N.J., U.S.	285	40.04 N	74.39 W
Georgetown, N.Y., U.S.	210	42.46 N	75.44 W
Georgetown, Oh., U.S.	218	38.51 N	83.54 W
Georgetown, Pa., U.S.	214	40.39 N	80.30 W
Georgetown, S.C., U.S.	192	33.22 N	79.17 W
Georgetown, Tx., U.S.	222	30.37 N	97.40 W
Georgetown ⟡ 8	284c	38.54 N	77.03 W
Georgetown, Lake ⊜ 1	222	30.40 N	97.45 W
Georgetown Lake ⊜	202	46.11 N	113.17 W
Georgetown Rowley State Forest ♠	283	42.42 N	70.58 W
Georgetown University ʊ 2	284c	38.54 N	77.04 W
George V Coast ⫠ 2	9	68.30 S	147.30 E
George VI Sound Ʉ	9	71.00 S	68.00 W
George Washington Birthplace National Monument ♠	208	38.11 N	76.56 W
George Washington Bridge ⟡ 5	276	40.51 N	73.57 W
George Washington Carver National Monument ♠	194	37.00 N	94.19 W
George West	196	28.19 N	98.07 W
Georg Forster ʊ 3	9	70.47 S	11.51 E
Georgia □ 1, Asia	72	42.00 N	44.00 E
Georgia □ 1, Asia	84	42.00 N	44.00 E
Georgia □ 3, U.S.	178	32.50 N	83.15 W
Georgia □ 3, U.S.	192	32.50 N	83.15 W
Georgia, Strait of Ʉ	182	49.20 N	124.00 W
Georgia del Sur, Isla de → South Georgia I	244	54.15 S	36.45 W
Georgiana	194	31.38 N	86.44 W
Georgian Bay ⊂	190	45.15 N	80.50 W
Georgian Bay Islands National Park ♠	190	44.54 N	79.52 W
Géorgie du Sud → South Georgia I	244	54.15 S	36.45 W
Georgijevka, Kaz.	85	43.03 N	74.43 E
Georgijevka, Kaz.	85	42.11 N	70.00 E
Georgijevka, Kaz.	86	49.19 N	81.35 E
Georgijevka, Ross.	80	53.18 N	51.01 E
Georgijevsk	84	44.09 N	43.28 E
Georgina ≃	166	23.30 S	139.47 E
Georgina Island I	212	44.23 N	79.17 W
Georgina Island Indian Reserve ⟡ 4	212	44.22 N	79.19 W
Georgsmarienhütte	52	52.12 N	8.02 E
Gera	54	50.52 N	12.04 E
Gera ≃	54	51.08 N	10.56 E
Geraardsbergen	50	50.46 N	3.52 E
Geraberg	54	50.43 N	10.50 E
Gerabronn	56	49.15 N	9.55 E
Gerace	68	38.16 N	16.13 E
Geraci Siculo	70	37.51 N	14.09 E
Geral, Serra ⫠ 4, Bra.	250	11.15 S	46.30 W
Geral, Serra ⫠ 4, Bra.	252	26.30 S	50.30 W
Gerald	219	38.23 N	91.19 W
Geral de Goiás, Serra ⫠ 4	242	13.00 S	46.15 W
Geraldine, N.Z.	172	44.05 S	171.14 E
Geraldine, Mt., U.S.	202	47.36 N	110.15 W
Geraldton, Austl.	162	28.46 S	114.36 E
Geraldton, On., Can.	176	49.44 N	86.57 W
Gerar, Naḥal V	132	31.24 N	34.26 E
Gerard, Lake ⊜	276	41.06 N	74.33 W
Gerard, Mount ∧	162	27.13 S	122.41 E
Gérardmer	58	48.04 N	6.53 E
Geras	61	48.48 N	15.40 E
Gerasa ⊥	132	32.17 N	35.53 E
Gerasdorf	61	48.18 N	16.28 E
Gerasimovka	86	58.37 N	71.53 E
Gerber	204	40.03 N	122.08 W
Gerber Reservoir ⊜ 1	202	42.12 N	121.06 W
Gerbéviller	58	48.30 N	6.31 E
Gerblingerode	52	51.29 N	10.15 E
Gerbstedt	54	51.38 N	11.37 E
Gerchsheim	56	49.42 N	9.47 E
Gercüş	130	37.34 N	41.23 E
Gerdau	158	26.28 S	26.06 E
Gerdine, Mount ∧	180	61.35 N	152.26 W
Gerdview	273d	26.10 S	28.11 E
Gère ≃	62	45.32 N	4.54 E
Gerede	130	40.48 N	32.12 E
Gereja Cathedral ʊ 1	269e	6.10 S	106.49 E
Gerenzano	266b	45.38 N	9.00 E
Gereshk	120	31.48 N	64.34 E
Geretsried	64	47.51 N	11.28 E
Gérgal	34	37.07 N	2.33 W
Gerge'bil	84	42.31 N	47.05 E
Gerger	130	37.57 N	39.01 E
Geria Nij	126	23.56 N	86.55 E
Gerik	114	5.25 N	101.08 E
Gering	198	41.49 N	103.39 W
Geringswalde	54	51.04 N	12.54 E
Geriş	130	36.58 N	31.44 E
Gerlachovský štít ∧	30	49.12 N	20.08 E
Gerlafingen	58	47.10 N	7.34 E
Gerli ⟡ 8	288	34.41 S	58.23 W
Gerlingen	56	48.48 N	9.03 E
Gerlos	64	47.14 N	12.02 E
Gerlospass)(	64	47.14 N	12.08 E
Gerlova Hut'	60	49.10 N	13.17 E
Germa (Jarmah) ⊥	146	26.33 N	13.04 E
Germagnano	62	45.15 N	7.28 E
Germain, Grand lac ⊜	186	51.12 N	66.41 W
Germania	214	41.39 N	77.40 W
Germano	214	40.25 N	80.57 W
Germansen, Mount ∧	182	55.37 N	124.50 W
Germansen Lake ⊜	182	55.41 N	124.53 W
Germansen Landing	182	55.47 N	124.43 W
Germansville	208	40.42 N	75.42 W
Germantown, Il., U.S.	219	38.33 N	89.32 W
Germantown, Ky., U.S.	218	38.39 N	83.57 W
Germantown, N.Y., U.S.	210	42.08 N	73.54 W
Germantown, Oh., U.S.	218	39.37 N	84.22 W
Germantown, Tn., U.S.	194	35.05 N	89.48 W
Germantown, Wi., U.S.	216	43.13 N	88.06 W
Germantown ⟡ 8	285	40.03 N	75.11 W
Germantown Dam ⟡ 6	218	39.38 N	84.24 W
Germany (Deutschland) □ 1, Europe	22	51.00 N	10.00 E
Germany (Deutschland) □ 1, Europe	30	51.00 N	10.00 E
Germany Flats ≚	276	41.05 N	74.39 W
Germaringen	58	47.56 N	10.40 E
Germay	58	48.25 N	5.21 E
Germencik	130	37.51 N	27.37 E
Germendorf	54	52.45 N	13.10 E
Germering	60	48.08 N	11.22 E
Germersheim	56	49.13 N	8.22 E
Germfask	190	46.14 N	85.55 W
Germiston	158	26.13 S	28.11 E
Germiston □ 5	273d	26.15 S	28.10 E
Germiston South	273d	26.15 S	28.10 E
Gernikao (Guernica)	34	43.19 N	2.41 W
Gernrode	54	51.43 N	11.08 E
Gernsbach	56	48.46 N	8.19 E
Gernsheim	56	49.44 N	8.29 E
Gero	94	35.48 N	137.14 E
Geroda	56	50.17 N	9.53 E
Gerola Alta	58	46.03 N	9.32 E
Geroldsgrün	54	50.20 N	11.35 E
Geroldstein	56	50.06 N	7.56 E
Gerolsbach	60	48.30 N	11.22 E
Gerolstein	56	50.13 N	6.40 E
Gerolzhofen	56	49.54 N	10.21 E
Gerona → Girona, Esp.	34	41.59 N	2.49 E
Gerona, Pil.	116	15.36 N	120.36 E
Geronimo	196	34.28 N	98.22 W
Gerpinnes	50	50.20 N	4.31 E
Gerrards Cross	260	51.35 N	0.34 W
Gerrei ⫠ 1	71	39.28 N	9.17 E
Gerresheim ⟡ 8	263	51.14 N	6.52 E
Gerringong	170	34.45 S	150.50 E
Gerry	214	42.12 N	79.15 W
Gers □ 5	32	43.40 N	0.30 E
Gers ≃	32	44.09 N	0.39 E
Gersau	58	47.00 N	8.32 E
Gersdorf	54	50.45 N	12.42 E
Gersfeld	56	50.27 N	9.55 E
Gershøj	41	55.43 N	11.59 E
Gersprenz ≃	56	49.59 N	9.04 E
Gerstetten	56	48.37 N	10.01 E
Gersthofen	58	48.25 N	10.53 E
Gerstungen	56	50.58 N	10.04 E
Gerswalde	54	53.10 N	13.46 E
Gertak Sanggul, Tanjong ≻	114	5.15 N	100.11 E
Gerthe ⟡ 8	263	51.31 N	7.17 E
Gerufa	156	19.17 S	26.02 E
Gervais	224	45.06 N	122.53 W
Gerwisch	54	52.10 N	11.44 E
Gerza	142	29.26 N	31.11 E
Gerze, Tür.	130	41.48 N	35.12 E
Gêrzê, Zhg.	120	32.16 N	84.12 E
Gerzen	60	48.31 N	12.25 E
Gerzensee	58	46.51 N	7.33 E
Gescher	52	51.57 N	6.59 E
Geschriebenstein (Írottkő) ∧	61	47.21 N	16.26 E
Geschwenda	54	50.44 N	10.49 E
Gesees	60	49.54 N	11.32 E
Geseke	52	51.38 N	8.31 E
Geser	164	3.53 S	130.54 E
Gesher HaZiw	132	33.02 N	35.06 E
Gesi	115a	7.20 S	111.01 E
Gesoa	164	8.25 S	143.35 E
Gespunsart	56	49.49 N	4.50 E
Gessertshausen	58	48.20 N	10.44 E
Gesso ≃	62	44.24 N	7.33 E
Gessopalena	66	42.03 N	14.16 E
Gesten	41	55.31 N	9.12 E
Gesualdo	68	41.00 N	15.04 E
Geta	26	60.23 N	19.50 E
Getafe	34	40.18 N	3.43 W
Getafe, Aeropuerto ⊠	266a	40.18 N	3.43 W
Gete ≃	56	50.57 N	5.07 E
Gethaoli	272c	19.08 N	73.01 E
Geti	154	1.13 N	30.12 E
Getinge	26	56.49 N	12.44 E
Gettorf	41	54.24 N	9.58 E
Gettysburg, Oh., U.S.	218	40.06 N	84.29 W
Gettysburg, Pa., U.S.	208	39.49 N	77.13 W
Gettysburg, S.D., U.S.	198	45.00 N	99.57 W
Gettysburg National Military Park ♠	208	39.49 N	77.15 W
Getulândia	256	22.40 S	44.06 W
Getulina	255	21.49 S	49.55 W
Getulio	116	10.45 N	122.40 E
Getúlio Vargas	252	27.50 S	52.16 W
Getz Ice Shelf ⊼	9	75.00 S	129.00 W
Getzville	210	43.01 N	78.46 W
Geumpang	114	4.48 N	96.09 E
Geureudong, Gunung ∧	114	4.48 N	96.48 E
Gevān	128	26.03 N	57.17 E
Gevaş	128	38.16 N	43.07 E
Gevelsberg	56	51.19 N	7.20 E
Gevgelija	38	41.08 N	22.30 E
Gévora ≃	34	38.53 N	6.57 W
Gevrey-Chambertin	58	47.14 N	4.57 E
Gewane	144	10.10 N	40.39 E
Geweke ⟡ 8	263	51.22 N	7.25 E
Gex	58	46.20 N	6.04 E
Geyer	54	50.37 N	12.55 E
Geyer Ditch ≊	216	41.36 N	86.25 W
Geyikli	130	39.48 N	26.12 E
Geysdorp	158	26.32 S	25.18 E
Geyser	202	47.15 N	110.29 W
Geyserville	204	38.42 N	122.54 W
Geyshtasar, Kūh-e ∧	84	38.51 N	47.14 E
Geyuan	100	28.31 N	117.44 E
Geyve	130	40.30 N	30.18 E
Gézenti	146	21.41 N	18.18 E
Gezer	132	31.52 N	34.55 E
Gföhl	61	48.31 N	15.30 E
Ghaapplato ⋏ 1	158	27.30 S	24.00 E
Ghabāghib	132	33.10 N	36.13 E
Ghābat al-ʿArab	140	9.02 N	29.29 E
Ghadaf, Wādī al- V	132	31.46 N	36.50 E
Ghadāmis	146	30.08 N	9.30 E
Ghaddūwah	146	26.26 N	14.18 E
Ghafe	272c	19.05 N	73.07 E
Ghagghar ≃	123	29.30 N	74.53 E
Ghāghara ≃	124	25.47 N	84.37 E
Ghaghar Reservoir ⊜ 1	124	24.38 N	83.11 E
Ghāghra	124	23.17 N	84.33 E
Ghakhar	123	32.18 N	74.09 E
Ghallah, Wādī al- V	140	10.25 N	27.32 E
Ghammāzah al-Kubrā	142	29.43 N	31.18 E
Ghamrīn	142	30.30 N	30.55 E
Ghana □ 1, Afr.	134	8.00 N	1.00 W
Ghana □ 1, Afr.	150	8.00 N	1.00 W
Ghansoli	272c	19.08 N	72.59 E
Ghanzi	156	21.38 S	21.45 E
Ghanzi □ 5	156	22.00 S	23.00 E
Ghārāpuri	272c	18.54 N	72.56 E
Gharaunda	124	29.33 N	76.58 E
Gharbah, Wādī V	142	29.40 N	31.58 E
Gharbi, Chott ⊜	148	33.50 N	1.30 W
Gharbi, Oued el V	148	31.50 N	0.51 E
Gharbīyah, Aṣ-Ṣaḥrā' al- (Western Desert) ⟡ 2	140	27.00 N	27.00 E
Ghardaïa	148	32.31 N	3.37 E
Ghardimaou	36	36.26 N	8.27 E
Gharghoda	124	22.10 N	83.21 E
Gharībwāl	123	32.41 N	73.10 E
Gharīfah	132	33.38 N	35.33 E
Gharig	140	10.47 N	27.33 E
Ghārīyat al-Gharbīyah	132	32.41 N	36.13 E
Ghārīyat ash-Sharqīyah	132	32.40 N	36.16 E
Gharo	120	24.44 N	67.35 E
Gharrāf, Shaṭṭ al- ≃	128	32.30 N	45.48 E
Gharroli ⟡ 8	272a	28.37 N	77.20 E
Gharsa, Chott el ⊜	148	34.06 N	7.50 E
Gharw, Jazīrat I	142	31.21 N	30.06 E
Gharyān	146	32.10 N	13.01 E
Ghaṣm	132	32.33 N	36.22 E
Ghāt	146	24.58 N	10.11 E
Ghātāl	126	22.40 N	87.43 E
Ghatampur	272b	22.54 N	88.10 E
Ghatere, Mount ∧	175e	7.49 S	158.54 E
Ghates Occidentales → Western Ghāts ⋏	122	14.00 N	75.00 E
Ghates Orientales → Eastern Ghāts ⋏	122	14.00 N	78.50 E
Ghātkopar ⟡ 8	272c	19.05 N	72.54 E
Ghātprabha ≃	122	16.20 N	75.48 E
Ghātsīla	126	22.36 N	86.29 E
Għawdex (Gozo) I	36	36.03 N	14.15 E
Ghawr ash-Sharqīyah, Qanāt al- (East Ghor Canal) ≊	132	32.41 N	35.38 E
Ghaylah ∧ 1	132	33.11 N	37.05 E
Ghayl Bā Wazīr	144	14.48 N	49.21 E
Ghayl Bin Yumayn ⫪ 4	144	15.33 N	49.23 E
Ghayth, Wādī V	132	30.59 N	36.00 E
Ghazāl, Baḥr al- ≃	140	9.31 N	30.25 E
Ghazal, Bahr el V	146	13.01 N	15.28 E
Ghazālat al-Khīs	142	30.34 N	31.34 E
Ghāziābād	123	28.40 N	77.26 E
Ghāzīpur, India	124	25.35 N	83.34 E
Ghazipur, India	272b	22.36 N	88.34 E
Ghāzipur ⟡ 8	272a	28.38 N	77.19 E
Ghazīr	130	34.01 N	35.40 E
Ghazlūna	120	31.24 N	67.49 E
Ghaznī	120	33.33 N	68.26 E
Ghaznī □ 4	120	33.15 N	67.45 E
Ghaznī ≃	120	32.35 N	67.58 E
Ghazni Khel	123	32.33 N	70.44 E
Ghazzah (Gaza), Gaza	132	31.30 N	34.28 E
Ghazzah, Lubnān	132	33.40 N	35.49 E
Gheā ≃	272b	22.52 N	88.19 E
Ghedi	64	45.24 N	10.16 E
Ghemme	62	45.37 N	8.25 E
Ghennes Heights	279b	40.09 N	79.56 W
Ghent → Gent, Bel.	50	51.03 N	3.43 E
Ghent, Ky., U.S.	218	38.44 N	85.03 W
Ghent, N.Y., U.S.	210	42.19 N	73.36 W
Ghent, Oh., U.S.	214	41.09 N	81.38 W
Gheora ⟡ 8	272a	28.42 N	77.01 E
Gheorgheni	38	46.43 N	25.36 E
Gherla	38	47.02 N	23.55 E
Ghesar	272c	19.09 N	73.05 E
Ghigo	62	44.53 N	7.03 E
Ghilarza	71	40.07 N	8.50 E
Ghilizane	148	35.44 N	0.30 E
Ghīn, Tall ∧	132	32.39 N	36.43 E
Ghior	126	23.54 N	89.53 E
Ghislenghien (Gellingen)	50	50.39 N	3.52 E
Ghisonaccia	36	42.00 N	9.25 E
Ghizar ≃	123	36.15 N	73.25 E
Ghizunabeana Islands II	175e	7.31 S	158.42 E
Ghlin	50	50.28 N	3.53 E
Ghlò, Beinn a' ∧	46	56.50 N	3.43 W
Ghogha	120	21.41 N	72.17 E
Gholson	222	31.43 N	97.12 W
Ghonda ⟡ 8	272a	28.41 N	77.16 E
Ghondi ⟡ 8	272a	28.42 N	77.16 E
Ghorāsahan	124	26.50 N	85.08 E
Ghoshpur, Bngl.	126	23.27 N	89.39 E
Ghoshpur, India	272b	22.23 N	88.29 E
Ghotki	120	28.01 N	69.19 E
Ghowr □ 4	128	34.00 N	65.00 E
Ghubaysh	140	12.09 N	27.21 E
Ghudāf, Wādī al- V	128	32.56 N	43.30 E
Ghulayfiqah	144	14.27 N	43.02 E
Ghunthur	130	34.23 N	37.09 E
Ghurāb, Jabal ∧ 2	142	28.58 N	31.16 E
Ghurayrah	144	18.37 N	42.41 E
Ghūrīān	128	34.21 N	61.30 E
Ghushuri	272b	22.37 N	88.22 E
Ghuwaybah, Wādī V	142	29.36 N	32.20 E
Ghuwayr, ʿAyn al- ⫪ 4	132	31.37 N	35.25 E
Ghuzzayil, Sabkhat ⊜	146	29.50 N	19.35 E
Giaginskaja	78	44.53 N	40.05 E
Gianh ≃	110	17.40 N	106.30 E
Giannutri, Isola di I	66	42.15 N	11.06 E
Giano, Monte ∧	66	42.25 N	13.06 E
Giano dell'Umbria	66	42.50 N	12.35 E
Giant City State Park ♠	194	37.39 N	89.12 W
Giant Mountain ∧	188	44.10 N	73.44 W
Giant's Castle ∧	158	29.21 S	29.27 E
Giant's Castle Game Reserve ⟡ 4	158	29.16 S	29.30 E
Giant's Causeway ♠	48	55.14 N	6.30 W
Giants Neck	207	41.18 N	72.13 W
Giants Stadium ♠	276	40.49 N	74.05 W
Giants Tomb Island I	212	44.55 N	80.00 W
Gianyar	115b	8.32 S	115.20 E
Gia Rai	110	9.14 N	105.28 E
Giardinello	70	38.05 N	13.09 E
Giardinetto	68	41.19 N	15.24 E
Giardini	70	37.50 N	15.17 E
Giarratana	70	37.03 N	14.48 E
Giarre	70	37.43 N	15.11 E
Giaveno	62	45.02 N	7.21 E
Giazza	64	45.39 N	11.07 E
Giba	71	39.04 N	8.38 E
Gibara	240p	21.07 N	76.08 W
Gibbon, Mn., U.S.	190	44.32 N	94.31 W
Gibbon, Ne., U.S.	198	40.44 N	98.50 W
Gibbons	182	53.50 N	113.20 W
Gibbons Creek Lake ⊜ 1	222	30.38 N	96.04 W
Gibbonsville	202	45.33 N	113.55 W
Gibb River	164	16.25 S	126.22 E
Gibbs, Mount ∧	162	32.55 S	120.00 E
Gibbsboro	285	39.50 N	74.58 W
Gibbstown	208	39.49 N	75.17 W
Gibellina	70	37.47 N	12.58 E
Gibeon	156	25.09 S	17.43 E
Gibilmanna, Santuario di ʊ 1	70	37.59 N	14.02 E
Gibraleón	34	37.23 N	6.58 W
Gibraltar, Gib.	34	36.08 N	5.21 W
Gibraltar, Mi., U.S.	216	42.06 N	83.12 W
Gibraltar, Pa., U.S.	208	40.17 N	75.52 W
Gibraltar □ 2, Europe	22	36.08 N	5.21 W
Gibraltar □ 2, Europe	34	36.08 N	5.21 W
Gibraltar, Strait of (Estrecho de Gibraltar) Ʉ	34	35.57 N	5.36 W
Gibraltar Point ≻, On., Can.	275b	43.36 N	79.23 W
Gibraltar Point ≻, Eng., U.K.	44	53.05 N	0.19 E
Gibsland	194	32.32 N	93.03 W
Gibson, Austl.	162	33.39 S	121.48 E
Gibson, Ga., U.S.	192	33.14 N	82.35 W
Gibson, N.Y., U.S.	210	42.08 N	76.59 W
Gibson, Pa., U.S.	210	41.44 N	75.38 W
Gibson ≃	212	44.58 N	79.51 W
Gibson, Lake ⊜ 1	284a	43.06 N	79.14 W
Gibsonburg	214	41.23 N	83.19 W
Gibson City	216	40.27 N	88.22 W
Gibson Desert ⟡ 2	162	24.30 S	126.00 E
Gibson Hill ∧ 2	214	41.51 N	80.10 W
Gibsonia, Fl., U.S.	220	28.06 N	81.58 W
Gibsonia, Pa., U.S.	214	40.38 N	79.59 W
Gibson Indian Reserve ⟡ 4	212	45.01 N	79.44 W
Gibson Island I	208	39.05 N	76.26 W
Gibsons	182	49.24 N	123.30 W
Gibsonton	220	27.51 N	82.22 W
Gicäki dağ ∧	84	40.25 N	49.01 E
Gidajevo	24	59.57 N	52.22 E
Gidami	144	9.58 N	34.37 E
Gidda	144	9.34 N	35.23 E
Giddalūr	122	15.21 N	78.55 E
Giddarbāha	123	30.12 N	74.40 E
Giddings	222	30.10 N	96.56 W
Gideälven ≃	26	63.20 N	19.08 E
Gidea Park ⟡ 8	260	51.35 N	0.12 E
Gideåvallen	26	63.29 N	18.58 E
Gideon	194	36.27 N	89.55 W
Gidgee	162	27.16 S	119.22 E
Gidgi, Lake ⊜	162	29.16 S	126.03 E
Gidhni	126	22.29 N	86.51 E
Gidole	144	5.38 N	37.30 E
Gidrotorf	80	56.28 N	43.33 E
Giebelstadt	56	49.39 N	9.56 E
Gieboldehausen	52	51.36 N	10.13 E
Giedraičiai	76	55.05 N	25.15 E
Gielow	54	53.42 N	12.44 E
Gielsdorf	264a	52.36 N	13.52 E
Gien	50	47.42 N	2.38 E
Giengen	56	48.37 N	10.14 E
Giens	62	43.02 N	6.08 E
Gier ≃	62	45.35 N	4.46 E
Gierath	263	51.07 N	6.33 E
Gierle	56	51.16 N	4.51 E
Gieselwerder	52	51.36 N	9.33 E
Giesen	52	52.12 N	9.54 E
Giesenkirchen ⟡ 8	263	51.09 N	6.30 E
Giessbachfälle ∟	58	46.42 N	8.03 E
Giessen	56	50.35 N	8.40 E
Giessen □ 5	56	50.40 N	8.40 E
Gieten	52	53.00 N	6.46 E
Giethoorn	52	52.43 N	6.05 E
Gièvres	50	47.16 N	1.40 E
Giez	62	45.45 N	6.15 E
Giffone	68	38.27 N	16.10 E
Gifford, Scot., U.K.	46	55.54 N	2.45 W
Gifford, Fl., U.S.	220	27.40 N	80.24 W
Gifford, Il., U.S.	216	40.18 N	88.01 W
Gifford, In., U.S.	216	41.06 N	87.01 W
Gifford, Pa., U.S.	214	41.51 N	78.36 W
Gifford ≃	176	70.21 N	83.05 W
Gifford Creek	162	24.05 S	116.11 E
Gifford Pinchot State Park ♠	208	40.04 N	76.53 W
Giffre ≃	58	46.05 N	6.30 E
Gifhorn	52	52.29 N	10.33 E
Giflitz	56	51.09 N	9.07 E
Gif-sur-Yvette	261	48.42 N	2.08 E
Gifu	94	35.25 N	136.45 E
Gifu □ 5	94	35.45 N	137.00 E
Gigant	80	46.30 N	41.20 E
Giganta, Sierra de la ⋏	232	26.00 N	111.30 W
Gigante	246	2.23 N	75.33 W
Gigante Islands II	116	11.36 N	123.20 E
Gigen	38	43.42 N	24.29 E
Gigena → Alcira	252	32.45 S	64.20 W
Giggleswick	44	54.04 N	2.17 W
Gigha, Sound of Ʉ	46	55.41 N	5.42 W
Gigha Island I	46	55.41 N	5.46 W
Gig Harbor	224	47.19 N	122.34 W
Giglio, Isola del I	66	42.21 N	10.54 E
Giglio Castello	66	42.22 N	10.54 E
Gigliola	66	44.51 N	12.14 E
Giglio Porto	66	42.22 N	10.55 E
Gigmoto	116	13.47 N	124.23 E
Gignod	62	45.46 N	7.17 E
Gihu → Gifu	94	35.25 N	136.45 E
Gijón	34	43.32 N	5.40 W
Gikongoro	154	2.29 S	29.34 E
Gila ≃	200	32.43 N	114.33 W
Gila, Middle Fork ≃	200	33.14 N	108.14 W
Gila Bend	200	32.56 N	112.42 W
Gila Bend Indian Reservation ⟡ 4	200	33.00 N	112.46 W
Gila Bend Mountains ⋏	200	33.10 N	113.10 W
Gila Cliff Dwellings National Monument ♠	200	33.02 N	108.16 W
Gila Mountains ⋏	200	33.05 N	109.50 W
Gīlān □ 4	128	37.15 N	49.30 E
Gīlān-e Gharb	128	34.08 N	45.55 E
Gila River Indian Reservation ⟡ 4	200	33.12 N	112.00 W
Gilātala	126	22.36 N	89.41 E
Giläzi Dili burnu ≻	84	40.50 N	49.33 E
Gilberdyke	44	53.45 N	0.44 W
Gilbert, La., U.S.	194	32.02 N	91.39 W
Gilbert, Mn., U.S.	190	47.29 N	92.27 W
Gilbert ≃, Austl.	166	16.35 S	141.15 E
Gilbert ≃, Austl.	168b	34.22 S	138.40 E
Gilbert, Mount ∧	182	50.51 N	124.20 W
Gilbert Airport ⊠	279a	41.22 N	81.58 W
Gilbert Island I	219	39.35 N	91.11 W
Gilbert Islands → Kiribati □ 1	14	5.00 S	170.00 W
Gilbert Lake ⊜	281	42.34 N	83.17 W
Gilbert Lake State Park ♠	210	42.36 N	75.08 W
Gilberton	210	40.48 N	76.13 W
Gilbertown	194	31.52 N	88.19 W
Gilbert Peak ∧	224	46.30 N	121.25 W
Gilbert Plains	184	51.09 N	100.29 W
Gilbert River	166	18.09 S	142.52 E
Gilbert Seamount ✢ 3	16	52.50 N	150.10 W
Gilbertsville, N.Y., U.S.	210	42.28 N	75.19 W
Gilbertsville, Pa., U.S.	208	40.19 N	75.37 W
Gilbertville	207	42.18 N	72.12 W
Gilbjerg Hoved ≻	41	56.08 N	12.17 E
Gilboa	216	41.01 N	83.55 W
Gilboaʿ, Haré ⋏ 2	132	32.30 N	35.23 E
Gilbués	250	9.50 S	45.21 W
Gilching	60	48.07 N	11.17 E
Gildehaus	52	52.18 N	7.06 E
Gildford	202	48.34 N	110.17 W
Gilead	216	41.48 N	85.09 W
Giles, Arroyo de ≃	258	34.20 S	59.23 W
Giles Meteorological Station ʊ 3	162	25.02 S	128.18 E
Giles Point ≻	168b	35.03 S	137.45 E
Gilette	62	43.51 N	7.10 E
Gilford	48	54.23 N	6.22 W
Gilford Island I	182	50.45 N	126.25 W
Gilford Park	208	39.58 N	74.08 W
Gilgai	162	31.15 S	119.56 E
Gilgandra	166	31.42 S	148.39 E
Gilgil	154	0.30 S	36.19 E
Gil Gil Creek ≃	166	29.10 S	148.51 E
Gilgit	123	35.55 N	74.18 E
Gilgit ≃	123	35.44 N	74.38 E
Gilgo Island I	276	40.38 N	73.25 W
Gilgo State Park ♠	276	40.38 N	73.22 W
Gilima	154	3.55 N	28.22 E
Gilimanuk	115a	8.10 S	114.26 E
Gilirang	112	3.55 S	120.09 E
Gil Island I	182	53.13 N	129.15 W
Gill, Lough ⊜	48	54.16 N	8.24 W
Gillam	184	56.21 N	94.43 W
Gilleland Creek ≃	222	30.13 N	97.32 W
Gilleleje	41	56.07 N	12.19 E
Gillen, Lake ⊜	162	26.11 S	124.38 E
Gilles, Lake ⊜	166	32.50 S	136.45 E
Gillespie	219	39.07 N	89.49 W
Gillespies Point ≻	172	43.24 S	169.50 E
Gillett, Ar., U.S.	194	34.07 N	91.22 W
Gillett, Pa., U.S.	210	41.57 N	76.48 W
Gillett, Wi., U.S.	190	44.53 N	88.18 W
Gillette, N.J., U.S.	276	40.41 N	74.28 W
Gillette, Wy., U.S.	198	44.17 N	105.30 W
Gillette Castle State Park ♠	207	41.26 N	72.25 W
Gillian, Lake ⊜	176	69.32 N	75.23 W
Gillingham, Eng., U.K.	42	51.24 N	0.33 E
Gillingham, Eng., U.K.	42	51.02 N	2.17 W
Gillingham □ 8	260	51.22 N	0.35 E
Gills Rock	190	45.17 N	87.01 W
Gilman, Ct., U.S.	207	41.34 N	72.11 W
Gilman, Il., U.S.	216	40.46 N	87.59 W
Gilman, Ia., U.S.	190	41.52 N	92.47 W
Gilman, Wi., U.S.	190	45.10 N	90.48 W
Gilman Hot Springs	228	33.50 N	116.59 W
Gilman Lake	285	39.41 N	75.11 W
Gilmer, Il., U.S.	278	42.14 N	88.02 W
Gilmer, Tx., U.S.	222	32.43 N	94.56 W
Gilmer Park	216	41.36 N	86.15 W
Gilmore	171b	35.20 S	148.11 E
Gilmore City	198	42.44 N	94.27 W
Gilmore Creek ≃	171b	35.18 S	148.13 E
Gilo ≃	144	8.10 N	33.15 E
Gilroy	226	37.00 N	121.34 W
Gilserberg	56	50.57 N	9.04 E
Gilsizer Slough ≃	226	38.58 N	121.44 W
Gilston Park ♠	260	51.48 N	0.04 E
Giltner	198	40.46 N	98.09 W
Gil'uj ≃	89	53.58 N	127.30 E
Giluwe, Mount ∧	164	6.05 S	143.50 E
Gilwern	42	51.51 N	3.06 W
Gilze	52	51.33 N	4.57 E
Gimån ≃	26	62.28 N	16.20 E
Gimbi	144	9.10 N	35.42 E
Gimborn	52	51.03 N	7.28 E
Gimcheon → Kimch'ŏn	98	36.07 N	128.05 E
Gimie, Mount ∧	241f	13.52 N	61.01 W
Gimigliano	68	38.58 N	16.32 E
Gimlet	218	38.13 N	83.09 W
Gimli	184	50.38 N	96.59 W
Gimo	40	60.11 N	18.11 E
Gimoly	24	63.03 N	32.19 E
Gimone ≃	32	44.00 N	1.06 E
Gimont	32	43.38 N	0.53 E
Gimpu	112	1.36 S	120.02 E
Ginderich	263	51.39 N	6.32 E
Ginebra → Genève	58	46.12 N	6.09 E
Gineste, Col de la)(	62	43.15 N	5.27 E
Gingell	216	42.43 N	83.17 W
Gingera, Mount ∧	171b	35.35 S	148.47 E
Ginger Hill	279b	40.12 N	80.00 W
Ginger Island I	240m	18.24 N	64.28 W
Gingin, Austl.	162	31.21 S	115.42 E
Gin Gin, Austl.	166	25.00 S	151.58 E
Gingindlovu	158	29.02 S	31.30 E
Gingoog	116	8.50 N	125.07 E
Gingoog Bay ⊂	116	8.59 N	125.05 E
Gingst	54	54.27 N	13.16 E
Ginir	144	7.07 N	40.46 E
Ginkakuji Temple ʊ 1	270	35.03 N	135.47 E
Ginkgo State Park ♠	202	46.59 N	120.01 W
Ginnosar	132	32.51 N	35.31 E
Ginosa	68	40.35 N	16.46 E
Ginostra	70	38.47 N	15.11 E
Ginowan	174m	26.17 N	127.46 E
Ginoza	174m	26.28 N	127.57 E
Ginter	214	40.46 N	78.23 W
Ginza ⟡ 8	268	35.40 N	139.47 E
Gioi	68	40.17 N	15.13 E
Gioia, Golfo di ⊂	68	38.30 N	15.45 E
Gioia dei Marsi	66	41.57 N	13.42 E
Gioia del Colle	68	40.48 N	16.56 E
Gioia Tauro	68	38.26 N	15.54 E
Gioia Vecchio	66	41.54 N	13.44 E
Gioiosa Ionica	68	38.20 N	16.18 E
Gioiosa Marea	70	38.10 N	14.54 E
Giong Rieng	110	9.55 N	105.19 E
Giornico	58	46.24 N	8.52 E
Giovi, Passo dei)(	62	44.33 N	8.57 E
Giovinazzo	68	41.11 N	16.40 E
Giporlos	116	11.07 N	125.27 E
Gipping ≃	42	52.04 N	1.10 E
Gipsy	214	40.48 N	78.53 W
Gipuzkoako □ 4	34	43.10 N	2.10 W
Giraglia, Île de la I	62	43.02 N	9.24 E
Giralia	162	22.41 S	114.21 E
Giraltovce	30	49.07 N	21.31 E
Girard, Il., U.S.	219	39.26 N	89.46 W
Girard, Ks., U.S.	198	37.30 N	94.50 W
Girard, Mi., U.S.	216	42.02 N	85.00 W
Girard, Oh., U.S.	214	41.09 N	80.42 W
Girard, Pa., U.S.	214	42.00 N	80.19 W
Girard, Tx., U.S.	196	33.22 N	100.40 W
Girardot	246	4.18 N	74.48 W
Girardville	208	40.47 N	76.17 W
Giraud, Pointe ≻	240d	15.19 N	61.15 W
Giraul ≃	152	15.04 S	12.08 E
Giraumont	56	49.10 N	5.55 E
Girdletree	208	38.05 N	75.23 W
Giresun	130	40.55 N	38.24 E
Giresun □ 4	130	40.30 N	38.30 E
Giresun Dağları ⋏	130	40.30 N	39.00 E
Girgarre	166	36.24 S	144.59 E
Girgaum ⟡ 8	272c	18.57 N	72.48 E
Girgenti → Agrigento	70	37.18 N	13.35 E
Girgir, Cape ≻	164	3.50 S	144.34 E
Giri ≃	152	0.28 N	17.59 E
Girīdīh	126	24.11 N	86.18 E
Girifalco	68	38.49 N	16.25 E
Girilambone	166	31.15 S	146.54 E
Girmeli	130	37.07 N	41.26 E
Girna ≃	122	21.08 N	75.19 E
Gir National Park ♠	120	21.00 N	70.50 E
Girne (Kyrenia)	130	35.20 N	33.19 E
Giro, Nig.	150	11.06 N	4.46 E
Giro, R.D.C.	154	3.08 N	29.15 E
Giromagny	58	47.45 N	6.50 E
Girón, Ec.	246	3.10 S	79.08 W
Giron, Fr.	58	46.14 N	5.46 E
Girona	34	41.59 N	2.49 E
Girona □ 4	34	42.00 N	2.40 E
Gironde □ 5	32	44.45 N	0.35 W
Gironde ⊂ 1	32	45.20 N	0.45 W
Gironville-sous-les-Côtes	56	48.48 N	5.40 E
Girou ≃	32	43.46 N	1.23 E
Girouxville	182	55.45 N	117.20 W
Gīr Range ⋏	120	21.18 N	71.00 E
Girton	42	52.14 N	0.05 E
Girtys Run ≃	279b	40.28 N	79.58 W
Giru	166	19.31 S	147.06 E
Giruá	252	28.02 S	54.21 W
Girvan	44	55.15 N	4.51 W
Girvan, Water of ≃	44	55.15 N	4.51 W
Girvas	24	62.30 N	33.40 E
Gisborne, Austl.	169	37.29 S	144.35 E
Gisborne, N.Z.	172	38.40 S	178.01 E
Gisborne Lake ⊜	186	47.48 N	54.50 W
Giscome	182	54.04 N	122.22 W
Gisenyi	154	1.42 S	29.15 E
Gishyita	154	2.11 S	29.18 E
Gislaved	26	57.18 N	13.32 E
Gislev	41	55.13 N	10.37 E
Gislinge	41	55.44 N	11.33 E
Gislövs läge	41	55.21 N	13.14 E
Gisors	50	49.17 N	1.47 E
Gissar	85	38.33 N	68.35 E
Gissarskij chrebet ⋏	85	39.00 N	68.40 E
Gisselfeld	41	55.18 N	11.59 E
Gissi	66	42.01 N	14.33 E
Gisslarbo	40	59.38 N	15.49 E
Gistel	50	51.10 N	2.57 E
Giswil	58	46.50 N	8.11 E
Gitambo	154	4.21 N	24.45 E
Gitarama	154	2.07 S	29.45 E
Gitega	154	3.26 S	29.56 E
Gittelde	52	51.48 N	10.10 E
Giuba, Isole II	144	0.45 S	42.19 E
Giudicarie, Valli V	64	45.58 N	10.45 E
Giugliano in Campania	68	40.56 N	14.12 E
Giuliana	70	37.40 N	13.14 E
Giulianova	66	42.45 N	13.57 E
Giulie, Alpi → Julian Alps ⋏	36	46.00 N	14.00 E
Giumbo → Jumboo	144	0.15 S	42.38 E
Giurgiu	38	43.53 N	25.57 E
Giurgiu □ 6	38	44.10 N	26.00 E
Giussano	62	45.42 N	9.14 E
Giuvala, Pasul)(	38	45.26 N	25.17 E
Givʿatayim	132	32.04 N	34.48 E
Givʿat Brenner	132	31.52 N	34.48 E
Give	41	55.51 N	9.15 E
Giverny	50	49.04 N	1.32 E
Givet	56	50.08 N	4.50 E
Givors	62	45.35 N	4.46 E
Givrine, Col de la)(	58	46.27 N	6.05 E
Givry	58	46.47 N	4.45 E
Givry-en-Argonne	56	48.57 N	4.53 E
Giyon	144	8.30 N	38.00 E
Giza → Al-Jīzah	142	30.01 N	31.13 E
Gīzāb	120	33.23 N	66.16 E
Giždduvan	128	40.06 N	64.41 E
Gizen	140	10.49 N	34.48 E
Gizeux	50	47.24 N	0.12 E
Gižiga	74	62.03 N	160.30 E
Gižiginskaja guba ⊂	74	61.30 N	158.00 E
Gizo	175e	8.06 S	156.51 E
Gizo Island I	175e	8.04 S	156.48 E
Giżycko	30	54.03 N	21.47 E
Gizzeria	68	38.59 N	16.12 E
Gjedved	41	55.56 N	9.51 E
Gjern	41	56.14 N	9.45 E
Gjirokastër	38	40.05 N	20.10 E
Gjoa Haven	176	68.38 N	95.57 W
Gjøvik	26	60.48 N	10.42 E
Gjuesevo	38	42.14 N	22.28 E
Gjuhëzës, Kep i ≻	38	40.25 N	19.18 E
Glace Bay	186	46.12 N	59.57 W
Glacier, B.C., Can.	182	51.16 N	117.31 W
Glacier, Wa., U.S.	224	48.53 N	121.56 W
Glacier Bay ⊂	180	58.40 N	136.00 W
Glacier Bay National Park ♠	180	58.45 N	136.30 W
Glacier Hills	276	40.51 N	74.28 W
Glacier National Park ♠, B.C., Can.	182	51.15 N	117.35 W
Glacier National Park ♠, Mt., U.S.	202	48.35 N	113.40 W
Glacier Peak ∧	224	48.07 N	121.07 W
Glad'	76	59.07 N	32.06 E
Gl'ad'anskoje	86	54.54 N	65.06 E
Gladbach → Mönchengladbach	56	51.12 N	6.28 E
Gladbeck	52	51.34 N	6.59 E
Gladbrook	190	42.11 N	92.42 W
Gladden	279b	40.21 N	80.11 W
Gladden Heights	279b	40.22 N	80.15 W
Glade Creek ≃	202	45.54 N	119.42 W
Gladenbach	56	50.46 N	8.34 E
Glades □ 6	220	26.59 N	81.12 W
Glade Spring	192	36.47 N	81.46 W
Gladesville	274a	33.50 S	151.08 E
Gladewater	222	32.32 N	94.56 W
Gladewater, Lake ⊜ 1	222	32.35 N	94.57 W
Gladsakse	41	55.44 N	12.29 E
Gladstone, Austl.	166	23.51 S	151.16 E
Gladstone, Austl.	166	33.17 S	138.22 E
Gladstone, Mb., Can.	184	50.13 N	98.57 W
Gladstone, Mi., U.S.	190	45.51 N	87.01 W
Gladstone, Mo., U.S.	194	39.12 N	94.33 W
Gladstone, N.J., U.S.	210	40.43 N	74.39 W
Gladstone, Or., U.S.	224	45.22 N	122.35 W
Gladstone Brook ≃	276	40.43 N	74.40 E
Gladwin	190	43.58 N	84.29 W
Gladwyne	285	40.02 N	75.17 W
Gladys Lake ⊜	180	59.55 N	132.55 W
Glænø I	41	55.12 N	11.28 E
Glafsfjorden ⊜	26	59.34 N	12.37 E
Glåma ≃	26	59.12 N	10.57 E
Glamis	46	56.36 N	3.00 W
Glamis Castle ⊥	46	56.37 N	3.00 W
Glamoč	36	44.03 N	16.51 E
Glamor Lake ⊜	212	44.58 N	78.23 W
Glamsbjerg	41	55.16 N	10.07 E
Glan	116	5.49 N	125.10 E
Glan ⊜	40	58.37 N	15.58 E
Glan ≃, Dtsch.	56	49.47 N	7.43 E
Glan ≃, Öst.	61	46.36 N	14.25 E
Glan ≃, Pil.	116	5.50 N	125.12 E
Glanamman	42	51.48 N	3.54 W

Symbols in the index entries represent the broad categories identified in the key at the right. Symbols with superior numbers (⋏ 1) identify subcategories (see complete key on page *I · 1*).

Symbole im Register stellen die rechts im Schlüssel erklärten Kategorien dar. Symbole mit hochgestellten Ziffern (⋏ 1) bezeichnen Unterabteilungen einer Kategorie (vgl. vollständiger Schlüssel auf Seite *I · 1*).

Los símbolos incluídos en el texto del índice representan las grandes categorías identificadas con la clave a la derecha. Los símbolos con numeros en su parte superior (⋏ 1) identifican las subcategorías (véase la clave completa en la página *I · 1*).

Les symboles de l'index représentent les catégories indiquées dans la légende à droite. Les symboles suivis d'un indice (⋏ 1) représentent des sous-catégories (voir légende complète à la page *I · 1*).

Os símbolos incluídos no texto do índice representam as grandes categorias identificadas com a chave à direita. Os símbolos com números em sua parte superior (⋏ 1) identificam as subcategorias (veja-se a chave completa à página *I · 1*).

	English	Deutsch	Español	Français	Português
∧	Mountain	Berg	Montaña	Montagne	Montanha
⋏	Mountains	Gebirge	Montañas	Montagnes	Montanhas
)(	Pass	Paß	Paso	Col	Passo
V	Valley, Canyon	Tal, Cañon	Valle, Cañón	Vallée, Canyon	Vale, Canhão
≚	Plain	Ebene	Llano	Plaine	Planície
≻	Cape	Kap	Cabo	Cap	Cabo
I	Island	Insel	Isla	Île	Ilha
II	Islands	Inseln	Islas	Îles	Ilhas
⫠	Other Topographic Features	Andere Topographische Objekte	Otros Elementos Topográficos	Autres données topographiques	Outros acidentes topográficos

ESPAÑOL Nombre	Página	Lat.	Long. W=Oeste	FRANÇAIS Nom	Page	Lat.	Long. W=Ouest	PORTUGUÊS Nome	Página	Lat.	Long. W=Oeste
Gland	58	46.26 N	6.16 E	Gleneden Beach	202	44.53 N	124.02 W	G. L. Martin State Airport	284b	39.20 N	76.25 W
Gland ≈	50	49.55 N	4.05 E	Glen Elder	198	39.29 N	98.18 W	Globe, Az., U.S.	200	33.23 N	110.47 W
Glandon, Col du ⋊	62	45.14 N	6.11 E	Glenelg, Austl.	168b	34.59 S	138.31 E	Globe, Ky., U.S.	218	38.17 N	83.14 W
Glandorf, Dtsch.	52	52.05 N	7.59 E	Glenelg, Scot., U.K.	46	57.13 N	5.38 W	Glodeanu-Siliștea	38	44.50 N	26.48 E
Glandorf, Oh., U.S.	216	41.01 N	84.04 W	Glenelg ≈	166	38.03 S	141.00 E	Glodeni	38	47.47 N	27.31 E
Gläne ≈	58	46.47 N	7.08 E	Glen Ellen	226	38.22 N	122.31 W	Glodok ⋆◦⁸	269e	6.08 S	106.48 E
Glanegg	61	46.44 N	14.11 E	Glenely ≈	48	54.44 N	7.18 W	Głogau			
Glanerbrug	52	52.13 N	6.58 E	Glen Ellyn	278	41.52 N	88.04 W	— Głogów	30	51.40 N	16.05 E
Glanmire	48	51.55 N	8.24 W	Glen Ellyn				Glogovac	126	23.45 N	89.12 E
Glanshammar	40	59.19 N	15.24 E	Countryside	278	41.55 N	88.04 W	Gogur	154	4.20 N	31.04 E
Glanum ⊥	62	43.49 N	4.47 E	Glenfarg	46	56.16 N	3.24 W	Gölcük, Tür.	130	39.18 N	27.59 E
Glan-y-Don	262	53.19 N	3.15 W	Glenfarne	48	54.17 N	7.59 W	Gölcük, Tür.	130	40.44 N	29.48 E
Glaris				Glenfield, Austl.	274a	33.58 S	150.54 E	Göçbeyli	130	39.13 N	27.25 E
— Glarus	58	47.02 N	9.04 E	Glenfield, Eng., U.K.	42	52.39 N	1.12 W	Goceano, Catena del			
Glarner Alpen ⋌	58	46.55 N	9.00 E	Glenfield, N.Y., U.S.	212	43.43 N	75.24 W	∧	71	40.28 N	9.02 E
Glärnisch ⋌	58	47.00 N	9.00 E	Glenfield, Pa., U.S.	279b	40.31 N	80.08 W	Goce Delčev	38	41.34 N	23.44 E
Glarus	58	47.02 N	9.04 E	Glenfinnan	46	56.52 N	5.27 W	Goch	52	51.41 N	6.10 E
Glarus □³	58	47.00 N	9.03 E	Glen Flora	222	29.21 N	96.12 W	Gochas	156	24.55 S	18.55 E
Glascarnoch, Loch ⊜	46	57.40 N	4.50 W	Glen Florrie	162	22.55 S	115.59 E	Gochsheim	56	50.01 N	10.16 E
Glasco, Ks., U.S.	198	39.21 N	97.50 W	Glenford	210	42.00 N	74.07 W	Go Cong	269c	10.50 N	106.50 E
Glasco, N.Y., U.S.	210	42.03 N	73.56 W	Glen Forest	168a	31.54 S	116.06 E	Gloria, Bahía de la ⊂	240p	21.50 N	77.40 W
Glasgow, Scot., U.K.	46	55.53 N	4.15 W	Glengallan Creek ≈	171a	28.09 S	151.53 E	Gloria de Dourados	255	22.21 S	54.13 W
Glasgow, Il., U.S.	219	39.33 N	90.29 W	Glen Gardner	210	40.41 N	74.56 W	Gloria Glens Park	214	41.03 N	81.54 W
Glasgow, Ky., U.S.	194	36.59 N	85.54 W	Glengarriff	48	51.45 N	9.33 W	Glorieta	200	35.34 N	105.46 W
Glasgow, Mo., U.S.	198	39.14 N	92.50 W	Glengarry Range ⋌	162	26.13 S	118.59 E	Glóriões, Îles II	157	11.30 S	47.20 E
Glasgow, Mt., U.S.	202	48.11 N	106.38 W	Glengyle	166	24.48 S	139.37 E	Glôristaussee ⊜¹	263	51.14 N	7.29 E
Glasgow, Pa., U.S.	214	40.42 N	78.27 W	Glenham	210	41.31 N	73.55 W	Glos-la-Ferrière	50	48.51 N	0.36 E
Glasgow, Va., U.S.	192	37.38 N	79.27 W	Glenhaven	274a	33.42 S	151.00 E	Glossop	44	53.27 N	1.57 W
Glasgow (Abbotsinch)				Glen Head	276	40.50 N	73.37 W				
Airport	46	55.52 N	4.26 W	Glen Helen	162	23.43 S	132.40 E	Gnas	9	84.44 S	113.51 W
Glashütte ⋆◦⁸	263	51.13 N	6.52 E	Glen Hills	208	39.04 N	77.12 W	Gloster	194	31.11 N	91.01 W
Glashyn	184	53.21 N	108.22 W	Glenhope	177	41.39 S	172.39 E	Glostrup	41	55.40 N	12.24 E
Glaslyn ≈	44	52.56 N	4.06 W	Glenhuntly	274b	37.54 S	145.03 E	Glotovka	80	53.57 N	46.42 E
Glas Maol ⋀	46	56.52 N	3.22 W	Glen Innes	166	29.44 S	151.44 E	Glotovc	24	63.30 N	49.23 E
Glasow	54	52.20 N	13.28 E	Glen Island I	276	40.53 N	73.47 W	Gloucester, Austl.	166	31.59 S	151.58 E
Glass, Loch ⊜	46	57.43 N	4.30 W	Glen Lake ⊜	224	44.48 N	85.59 W	Gloucester, On., Can.	212	45.22 N	75.35 W
Glassan	48	53.28 N	7.52 W	Glenluce	44	54.53 N	4.49 W	Gloucester, Eng., U.K.	42	51.53 N	2.14 W
Glassboro	208	39.42 N	75.06 W	Glenluce Abbey ⋀¹	44	54.53 N	4.50 W	Gloucester, Ma., U.S.	207	42.36 N	70.39 W
Glassboro State				Glen Lyon	210	41.10 N	76.04 W	Gloucester, Va., U.S.	208	37.24 N	76.31 W
College ⋅²	285	39.42 N	75.07 W	Glen Mills	208	39.55 N	75.30 W	Gloucester □⁶, N.J.,			
Glass House				Glenmont, N.Y., U.S.	210	42.36 N	73.46 W	U.S.	208	39.50 N	75.10 W
Mountains	171a	26.53 S	152.58 E	Glenmont, Oh., U.S.	214	40.31 N	82.06 W	Gloucester □⁶, Va.,			
Glassmanor	284c	38.49 N	76.59 W	Glenmoor	214	40.40 N	80.37 W	U.S.	208	37.25 N	76.30 W
Glass Mountains ⋌	196	30.25 N	103.15 W	Glenmoore, Pa., U.S.	208	40.05 N	75.46 W	Gloucester, Cape ►	164	5.27 S	148.25 E
Glassport	214	40.19 N	79.53 W	Glen Moore, Pa.,				Gloucester, Vale of			
Glastonbury, Eng.,				U.S.	208	40.03 N	76.18 W	⊻	42	51.55 N	2.10 W
U.K.	42	51.06 N	2.43 W	Glenmora	194	30.58 N	92.35 W	Gloucester City	285	39.53 N	75.07 W
Glastonbury, Ct.,				Glenmore	284b	39.11 N	76.36 W	Gloucester Fisherman			
U.S.	207	41.42 N	72.36 W	Glenmorgan	166	27.15 S	149.41 E	⊥	283	42.36 N	70.40 W
Glatt ≈	58	47.34 N	8.28 E	Glenn, Ca., U.S.	226	39.31 N	122.01 W	Gloucester Harbor ⊂	207	42.36 N	70.40 W
Glatten	58	48.26 N	8.31 E	Glenn, Mi., U.S.	216	42.31 N	86.13 W	Gloucester Island I	166	20.01 S	148.27 E
Glattfelden	58	47.33 N	8.30 E	Glenn □⁶	226	39.29 N	122.18 W	Gloucester Point	208	37.15 N	76.29 W
Glatz				Glennallen	180	62.07 N	145.33 W	Gloucester Pool ⊜	212	44.51 N	79.43 W
— Kłodzko	30	50.27 N	16.39 E	Glennamaddy	48	53.37 N	8.35 W	Gloucestershire □⁶	42	51.47 N	2.15 W
Glaubitz	54	51.19 N	13.22 E	Glen-Colusa Canal				Glover	188	39.30 N	82.05 W
Glauchau	54	50.49 N	12.32 E	⟁¹	226	39.07 N	122.08 W	Glover Creek ≈	194	34.02 N	94.56 W

...

| (legend, bottom) | | | | | | | | | | | |

ENGLISH Name / DEUTSCH Name	Page / Seite	Lat.°′ / Breite°′	Long.°′ / Länge°′ E = Ost
Gōnoura	92	33.45 N	129.41 E
Gonubie Mouth	158	32.57 S	28.01 E
Gonža	89	53.36 N	125.19 E
Gonzaga, It.	64	44.57 N	10.49 E
Gonzaga, Pil.	116	18.16 N	122.00 E
Gonzales, Ca., U.S.	226	36.30 N	121.26 W
Gonzales, La., U.S.	194	30.14 N	90.55 W
Gonzales, Tx., U.S.	222	29.30 N	97.27 W
Gonzales □[6]	222	29.28 N	97.30 W
González, Méx.	234	22.50 N	98.27 W
González, Ur.	258	34.14 S	56.52 W
González, Riacho ≃	252	22.48 S	57.54 W
González Catán	258	34.46 S	58.39 W
González Chaves	252	38.02 S	60.06 W
González Moreno	252	35.33 S	63.22 W
González Ortega, Méx.	204	32.40 N	115.23 W
González Ortega, Méx.	234	23.11 N	102.29 W
González Ortega, Méx.	234	23.59 N	103.27 W
González Risos	258	34.52 S	59.13 W
Gonzanamá	246	4.15 S	79.27 W
Goobarragandra ≃	171b	35.20 S	148.15 E
Goochland	192	37.41 N	77.53 W
Good Easter	260	51.47 N	0.21 E
Goodells	214	42.59 N	82.40 W
Goode Mountain ∧	224	48.29 N	120.55 W
Goodenough, Mount ∧	180	67.56 N	135.31 W
Goodenough Bay c	164	9.55 S	150.00 E
Goodenough Island I	164	9.20 S	150.15 E
Gooderham	212	44.54 N	78.23 W
Goodeve	184	51.04 N	103.10 W
Goodfellow Air Force Base ■	196	31.26 N	100.25 W
Good Hope, S. Afr.	158	31.51 S	21.55 E
Good Hope, Oh., U.S.	218	39.26 N	83.21 W
Good Hope, Cape of (Kaap die Gooie Hoop) ›	158	34.24 S	18.30 E
Goodhope Bay c	180	66.10 N	163.45 W
Good Hope Mountain ∧	182	51.09 N	124.10 W
Goodhouse	158	28.57 S	18.13 E
Goodhue	190	44.24 N	92.37 W
Gooding	202	42.56 N	114.42 W
Goodison	214	42.44 N	83.10 W
Goodland, Fl., U.S.	220	25.55 N	81.38 W
Goodland, In., U.S.	216	40.45 N	87.17 W
Goodland, Ks., U.S.	198	39.21 N	101.42 W
Goodlands	184	49.05 N	100.35 W
Goodlow Park	222	32.07 N	96.14 W
Goodman, Ms., U.S.	194	32.58 N	89.54 W
Goodman, Wi., U.S.	190	45.37 N	88.21 W
Goodna	171a	27.37 S	152.54 E
Goodnews Bay	180	59.07 N	161.35 W
Goodnight	200	38.14 N	104.43 W
Goodooga	166	29.07 S	147.27 E
Goodradigbee ≃	171b	35.08 S	148.41 E
Goodrich, Mi., U.S.	216	42.55 N	83.30 W
Goodrich, N.D., U.S.	198	47.28 N	100.07 W
Goodrich, Tx., U.S.	222	30.36 N	94.57 W
Good Spirit Lake ⊜	184	51.34 N	102.40 W
Good Spirit Lake Provincial Park ♦	184	51.36 N	102.45 W
Good Thunder	190	44.00 N	94.03 W
Goodview	190	44.03 N	91.41 W
Goodville	208	40.08 N	76.00 W
Goodwater	194	33.03 N	86.03 W
Goodwell	196	36.35 N	101.38 W
Goodwick	42	52.00 N	5.00 W
Goodwin, Lake ⊜	224	48.08 N	122.18 W
Goodwives ≃	276	41.04 N	73.28 W
Goodwood	212	44.02 N	79.12 W
Goodyear	200	33.26 N	112.21 W
Goof, Webi ≃	144	1.10 N	43.43 E
Googong Reservoir ⊜[1]	171b	35.27 S	149.16 E
Gooie Hoop, Kaap die → Good Hope, Cape of ›	158	34.24 S	18.30 E
Goole	44	53.42 N	0.52 W
Goolgowi	166	33.59 S	145.42 E
Goolwa	168b	35.31 S	138.47 E
Goomalling	162	31.19 S	116.49 E
Goombalie	166	29.59 S	145.23 E
Goombungee	171a	27.18 S	151.51 E
Goomburra	171a	28.03 S	152.07 E
Goonda	156	19.51 S	34.00 E
Goondiwindi	166	28.32 S	150.19 E
Goongarrie	162	30.03 S	121.09 E
Goongarrie National Park ♦	162	29.58 S	121.34 E
Goonyella	166	21.45 S	147.55 E
Goor	52	52.14 N	6.35 E
Goose ≃, Ab., Can.	182	54.58 N	117.11 W
Goose ≃, N.D., U.S.	198	47.28 N	96.52 W
Goose Bay → Happy Valley-Goose Bay	176	53.20 N	60.25 W
Goose Bay c	281	42.35 N	82.41 W
Gooseberry Creek ≃	202	43.55 N	108.04 W
Goose Creek	192	32.58 N	80.01 W
Goose Creek ≃, U.S.	202	42.33 N	113.46 W
Goose Creek ≃, Ne., U.S.	198	42.02 N	100.03 W
Goose Creek ≃, N.Y., U.S.	214	42.06 N	79.22 W
Goose Creek ≃, Va., U.S.	208	39.06 N	77.29 W
Goose Island I	182	51.55 N	128.25 W
Goose Lake ⊜, Mb., Can.	184	54.26 N	101.30 W
Goose Lake ⊜, On., Can.	184	51.46 N	93.00 W
Goose Lake ⊜, On., Can.	212	44.25 N	78.52 W
Goose Lake ⊜, On., Can.	214	42.31 N	82.31 W
Goose Lake ⊜, Sk., Can.	184	51.45 N	107.23 W
Goose Lake ⊜, U.S.	204	41.57 N	120.25 W
Goose Lake Canal ≊	226	35.50 N	119.37 W
Goose Lake Prairie State Park ♦	216	41.21 N	88.18 W
Gooseprairie	224	46.54 N	121.15 W
Goostrey	262	53.13 N	2.20 W
Gooty	122	15.07 N	77.38 E
Gopālganj, Bngl.	124	23.01 N	89.50 E
Gopālganj, India	124	26.28 N	84.26 E
Gopālnagar, India	126	23.03 N	88.45 E
Gopālnagar, India	272b	22.50 N	88.14 E
Gopālpur, Bngl.	124	24.33 N	89.56 E
Gopālpur, India	272b	22.38 N	88.27 E
Gopeng	114	4.28 N	101.10 E
Göpfritz an der Wild	61	48.43 N	15.24 E
Gopiballabhpur	126	22.13 N	86.54 E
Gopichettipālaiyam	122	11.28 N	77.27 E
Gopinagar	272b	22.50 N	88.07 E
Goppenstein	58	46.22 N	7.45 E
Göppingen	56	48.42 N	9.40 E
Goqên	102	29.15 N	96.59 E
Go Quao	110	9.43 N	105.17 E
Gor	123	35.32 N	74.31 E
Góra, Pol.	30	51.40 N	16.33 E
Gora, Ross.	76	60.02 N	41.43 E
Gor'ačegorsk	86	55.24 N	88.55 E
Gor'ačij Kl'uč	84	44.37 N	39.07 E
Gor'ačinsk	88	52.59 N	108.18 E
Goradit	144	11.25 N	38.25 E
Góra Kalwaria	30	51.59 N	21.12 E
Gorakhpur	124	26.45 N	83.22 E
Goranboy	84	40.36 N	46.47 E
Goras	124	25.32 N	76.56 E
Goražde	38	43.40 N	18.56 E
Gorbatov	80	56.08 N	43.04 E
Gorbatovka	80	56.15 N	43.45 E
Gorbica	88	53.06 N	119.13 E
Gorčucha	80	57.43 N	43.43 E
Gorda, Punta ›, Chile	248	19.18 S	70.18 W
Gorda, Punta ›, Cuba	240p	22.24 N	82.10 W
Gorda, Punta ›, Nic.	236	11.26 N	83.48 W
Gorda, Punta ›, Nic.	236	14.21 N	83.12 W
Gorda, Punta ›, Ca., U.S.	204	40.16 N	124.22 W
Gordejevka	76	52.59 N	31.58 E
Gordes, Fr.	62	43.54 N	5.12 E
Gördes, Tür.	130	38.54 N	28.18 E
Gordil	146	9.44 N	21.35 E
Gørding	41	55.29 N	8.48 E
Gordion ⊥	130	39.41 N	32.01 E
Gordo	194	33.19 N	87.54 W
Gordo, Cerro ∧	234	20.46 N	102.35 W
Gordola	58	46.11 N	8.52 E
Gordon, Scot., U.K.	46	55.41 N	2.34 W
Gordon, Ga., U.S.	192	32.52 N	83.19 W
Gordon, Ne., U.S.	198	42.48 N	102.12 W
Gordon, Oh., U.S.	218	39.56 N	84.31 W
Gordon, Pa., U.S.	208	40.45 N	76.21 W
Gordon, Wi., U.S.	190	46.14 N	91.47 W
Gordon ≃	224	48.35 N	124.24 W
Gordon, Isla I	254	54.58 S	69.35 W
Gordon, Lake ⊜[1]	166	42.42 S	146.12 E
Gordon Creek ≃	198	42.49 N	100.40 W
Gordon Downs	162	18.44 S	128.35 E
Gordon Heights	207	40.51 N	72.58 W
Gordon Horne Peak ∧	182	51.46 N	118.50 W
Gordon Indian Reserve ◆[4]	184	51.16 N	104.16 W
Gordon Lake ⊜, Ab., Can.	184	56.30 N	110.25 W
Gordon Lake ⊜, Sk., Can.	184	55.50 N	106.26 W
Gordon Lakes	276	41.03 N	74.22 W
Gordon Pass c	220	26.06 N	81.48 W
Gordon River	224	48.47 N	124.21 W
Gordon's Bay	158	34.10 S	18.52 E
Gordonsville	188	38.08 N	78.11 W
Gordonton	172	37.40 S	175.18 E
Gordonvale	166	17.05 S	145.47 E
Gordonville	220	27.57 N	81.49 W
Gore, Austl.	166	28.17 S	151.29 E
Gore, N.S., Can.	186	45.07 N	63.43 W
Gore, Ityo.	144	8.08 N	35.33 E
Gore, N.Z.	172	46.06 S	168.58 E
Goré, Tchad	146	7.53 N	16.40 E
Gore Bay	190	45.55 N	82.28 W
Gorebridge	46	55.51 N	3.02 W
Goreda	164	3.39 S	134.58 E
Goree	196	33.28 N	99.31 W
Gore Hill	274a	33.49 S	151.11 E
Görele	130	41.02 N	39.00 E
Gorelki	82	54.15 N	37.37 E
Goreloje	80	52.57 N	41.28 E
Gorelovo	265a	59.47 N	30.08 E
Gorelovo Airport ⊠	265a	59.47 N	30.05 E
Gorelyj ≃	265a	59.58 N	30.28 E
Göreme Milli Parkı ♦	130	38.26 N	34.54 E
Gore Mountain ∧	188	44.55 N	71.48 W
Gorenki	265b	55.48 N	37.55 E
Gore Point ›, Austl.	166	17.38 S	139.56 E
Gore Point ›, Ak., U.S.	180	59.12 N	151.00 W
Gore Range ϰ	200	40.00 N	106.30 W
Goretovka ≃	265b	55.56 N	37.20 E
Goreville	194	37.33 N	88.58 W
Gorey, Ire.	48	52.40 N	6.18 W
Gorey, Jersey	43b	49.12 N	2.02 W
Gorfoundurei	144	4.30 N	46.41 E
Gorgān	128	36.50 N	54.29 E
Gorgān ≃	128	36.59 N	54.00 E
Gorge Lake ⊜[1]	224	48.42 N	121.13 W
Görgeshausen	56	50.24 N	7.56 E
Gorgoglione	68	40.23 N	16.09 E
Gorgol □[4]	150	16.00 N	13.00 W
Gorgol el Abiod ≃	150	16.14 N	12.58 W
Gorgol el Akhdar ≃	150	16.13 N	12.58 W
Gorgona, Isla I	246	2.59 N	78.12 W
Gorgona, Isola di I	36	43.26 N	9.54 E
Gorgonzola	62	45.32 N	9.24 E
Gorgor	248	10.35 S	77.02 W
Gorgora	144	12.13 N	37.16 E
Gorgoram	146	12.38 N	10.43 E
Gorgota	38	44.47 N	26.05 E
Gorgova	38	45.11 N	29.10 E
Gorham, Me., U.S.	188	43.40 N	70.26 W
Gorham, N.H., U.S.	188	44.23 N	71.10 W
Gorham, N.Y., U.S.	210	42.47 N	77.07 W
Gorhambury House ⊥	260	51.47 N	0.24 W
Gori	84	41.58 N	44.07 E
Goria	272b	22.24 N	88.29 E
Gorica → Gorizia	64	45.57 N	13.38 E
Goričan	61	46.23 N	16.41 E
Goricy	76	57.09 N	36.44 E
Gorinchem	52	51.50 N	5.00 E
Goring	42	51.32 N	1.09 W
Goring-by-Sea	42	50.49 N	0.25 W
Goring Gap V	42	51.32 N	1.08 W
Goris	84	39.31 N	46.23 E
Göritz	54	53.24 N	13.54 E
Göritzhain	54	50.58 N	12.47 E
Gorizia	64	45.57 N	13.38 E
Gorizia □[4]	64	45.55 N	13.30 E
Gorj □[6]	38	45.00 N	23.20 E
Gorjani	38	45.24 N	18.21 E
Gor'kaja Balka	84	44.17 N	43.59 E
Gor'kaja balka ≃	84	44.38 N	45.00 E
Görke	54	53.51 N	13.38 E
Gorkhā	124	28.00 N	84.37 E
Gorki, Ross.	80	57.38 N	45.05 E
Gorki → Nižnij Novgorod, Ross.	80	56.20 N	44.00 E
Gorki, Ross.	82	54.18 N	36.08 E
Gorki, Ross.	82	55.32 N	37.45 E
Gorki, Ross.	82	56.54 N	38.51 E
Gorki, Ross.	265b	55.57 N	37.55 E
Gor'kij → Nižnij Novgorod	80	56.20 N	44.00 E
Gorki Vtoryje	265b	55.44 N	37.11 E
Gor'koje, ozero ⊜	86	52.30 N	81.20 E
Gor'ko-Solenoje, ozero ⊜	80	49.20 N	46.05 E
Gor'kovskoje	86	55.22 N	74.24 E
Gor'kovskoje vodochranilišče ⊜[1]	80	57.00 N	43.10 E
Gorky → Nižnij Novgorod	80	56.20 N	44.00 E
Gorky Park ♦	265b	55.44 N	37.36 E
Gorlago	62	45.40 N	9.49 E
Gorla Maggiore	266b	45.40 N	8.53 E
Gorla Minore	266b	45.39 N	8.54 E
Gorleston on Sea	42	52.36 N	1.43 E
Gørlev	41	55.32 N	11.14 E
Gorlice	30	49.40 N	21.10 E
Görlitz	54	51.09 N	14.59 E
Gorlosen	54	53.11 N	11.27 E
Gorlovka, Sak.	84	41.14 N	43.42 E
Gorlovka → Horlivka, Ukr.	83	48.18 N	38.03 E
Gorlovo	76	53.50 N	39.02 E
Gorm, Loch ⊜	46	55.48 N	6.25 W
Gorman, Ca., U.S.	228	34.48 N	118.51 W
Gorman, Tx., U.S.	196	32.12 N	98.40 W
Gorman Creek ≃	228	34.38 N	118.45 W
Görmin	54	53.59 N	13.16 E
Gorn'ackij, Ross.	24	67.32 N	64.03 E
Gorn'ackij, Ross.	78	48.17 N	40.55 E
Gorna Dzhumaya → Blagoevgrad	38	42.01 N	23.06 E
Gornaja Prolejka	80	49.24 N	44.59 E
Gorn'ak, Ross.	76	53.36 N	39.29 E
Gorn'ak, Ross.	86	51.00 N	81.29 E
Gornalunga ≃	70	37.24 N	15.03 E
Gorna Orjahovica	38	43.07 N	25.41 E
Gornergrat ♦	58	45.59 N	7.47 E
Gornja Radgona	36	46.41 N	16.00 E
Gornji Grad	36	46.18 N	14.49 E
Gornji Milanovac	38	44.01 N	20.27 E
Gornji Vakuf	36	43.56 N	17.35 E
Gorno-Altajsk	86	51.58 N	85.58 E
Gorno-Altay → Altaj □[3]	86	51.00 N	86.00 E
Gorno-Badachšanskaja Avtonomnaja Respublika □[3]	85	38.30 N	73.00 E
Gornoje	86	48.29 N	85.00 E
Gorno-Lesnoj zapovednik ♦	85	41.10 N	69.55 E
Gornopravdinsk	86	60.07 N	69.54 E
Gorno-Vod'anoje	80	49.16 N	44.56 E
Gornovodnoje	89	43.42 N	134.44 E
Gornozavodsk, Ross.	86	58.20 N	58.32 E
Gornozavodsk, Ross.	89	46.34 N	141.49 E
Gornyj, Ross.	80	51.46 N	48.34 E
Gornyj, Ross.	89	50.48 N	136.29 E
Gornyj, Ross.	89	44.57 N	133.59 E
Gornyj Balyklej	80	49.34 N	45.04 E
Gornyje Kl'uči	89	45.12 N	133.31 E
Goro, Ityo.	144	6.56 N	40.32 E
Goro, N. Cal.	175f	22.16 S	167.02 E
Gorochan ∧	144	9.22 N	37.04 E
Gorochovec	80	56.12 N	42.40 E
Gorochovje	76	56.31 N	30.29 E
Gorodec, Ross.	76	58.32 N	29.47 E
Gorodec, Ross.	80	56.38 N	43.30 E
Gorodišče, Ross.	76	59.38 N	32.08 E
Gorodišče, Ross.	78	51.09 N	38.04 E
Gorodišče, Ross.	80	53.17 N	45.42 E
Gorodišče, Ross.	80	48.48 N	44.29 E
Gorodišče, Ross.	82	54.53 N	38.13 E
Gorodišče, Ross.	82	56.47 N	38.52 E
Gorodišči	82	55.52 N	39.05 E
Gorodn'a, Ross.	82	54.57 N	38.49 E
Gorodn'a, Ross.	82	56.43 N	36.19 E
Gorodn'a ≃	265b	55.38 N	37.48 E
Gorodno	76	57.32 N	29.35 E
Goroka	164	6.05 S	145.25 E
Gorokan	170	33.16 S	151.30 E
Gorom-Gorom	150	14.26 N	0.14 W
Gorong, Pulau I	164	3.59 S	131.25 E
Gorongosa, Parque Nacional da ♦	156	18.45 S	34.15 E
Gorongosa, Serra da ∧	154	18.30 S	34.03 E
Gorongose ≃	156	20.30 S	34.40 E
Gorontalo	112	0.33 N	123.03 E
Goronyo	150	13.29 N	5.39 E
Goroubi ≃	150	12.54 N	2.23 E
Gorouol ≃	150	14.42 N	0.53 E
Górowo Iławeckie	30	54.17 N	20.30 E
Gorple Reservoirs ⊜[1]	262	53.47 N	2.06 W
Gorran ⊜	40	59.43 N	17.32 E
Gorredijk	52	53.00 N	6.05 E
Gorron	28	48.25 N	0.49 W
Görsdorf	54	51.54 N	13.29 E
Goršečnoje	78	51.32 N	38.02 E
Gorsedd	262	53.17 N	3.16 W
Gorseinon	42	51.40 N	4.02 W
Gorskaja	265a	60.03 N	29.59 E
Gorškovo	82	54.26 N	37.59 E
Gorst	224	47.32 N	122.42 W
Gort	48	53.04 N	8.50 W
Gortahork	48	55.08 N	8.09 W
Gorton ◆[8]	262	53.27 N	2.10 W
Görtschitz ≃	61	46.45 N	14.32 E
Goru, Vârful ∧	38	45.48 N	26.25 E
Görükle	130	40.14 N	28.50 E
Gorumna Island I	48	53.14 N	9.40 W
Gor'un ≃	89	50.45 N	137.50 E
Gorutuba ≃	255	14.57 S	43.33 W
Görwihl	58	47.39 N	8.04 E
Gory, Bela.	76	54.16 N	31.13 E
Gory, Kaz.	80	48.38 N	51.46 E
Görz → Gorizia	64	45.57 N	13.38 E
Gorzano, Monte ∧	66	42.37 N	13.24 E
Gorze	56	49.03 N	6.00 E
Görzig	54	51.40 N	12.00 E
Görzke	54	52.10 N	12.22 E
Górzno	30	53.13 N	19.38 E
Gorzów Śląski	30	51.02 N	18.24 E
Gorzów Wielkopolski (Landsberg an der Warthe)	30	52.44 N	15.15 E
Gorzów Wielkopolski □[4]	30	52.45 N	15.20 E
Górzyca	54	52.29 N	14.40 E
Gosāba	126	22.10 N	88.48 E
Gosairhāt	126	23.05 N	90.26 E
Gosaldo	64	46.13 N	11.58 E
Gosau	64	47.34 N	13.31 E
Gosauseen ⊜	64	47.32 N	13.31 E
Gosberton	42	52.51 N	0.09 W
Göschenen	58	46.40 N	8.35 E
Goschen Strait ⋈	164	10.09 S	150.56 E
Gose	96	34.27 N	135.44 E
Gosen, Dtsch.	264a	52.24 N	13.43 E
Gosen, Nihon	92	37.44 N	139.11 E
Gosford	170	33.26 S	151.21 E
Gosforth, Eng., U.K.	44	55.01 N	1.37 W
Gosforth, Eng., U.K.	44	54.26 N	3.27 W
Gosforth Park ♦	273d	26.14 S	28.10 E
Gosforth Park Race Course ♦	273d	26.14 S	28.08 E
Goshabi	140	17.58 N	31.06 E
Goshen, N.S., Can.	186	45.23 N	61.59 W
Goshen, Ca., U.S.	226	36.21 N	119.25 W
Goshen, Ct., U.S.	207	41.49 N	73.13 W
Goshen, In., U.S.	216	41.34 N	85.50 W
Goshen, Ma., U.S.	207	42.26 N	72.48 W
Goshen, N.J., U.S.	208	39.08 N	74.51 W
Goshen, N.Y., U.S.	210	41.24 N	74.19 W
Goshen, Oh., U.S.	218	39.14 N	84.10 W
Goshiki	96	34.24 N	134.47 E
Goshogawara	92	40.48 N	140.27 E
Goshute Indian Reservation ◆[4]	200	39.53 N	114.08 W
Goshute Lake ⊜	204	40.08 N	114.38 W
Goshute Valley V	204	40.40 N	114.30 W
Goslar	52	51.54 N	10.25 E
Gosnells	168a	32.04 S	116.00 E
Gospić	36	44.33 N	15.23 E
Gosport, Eng., U.K.	42	50.48 N	1.08 W
Gosport, In., U.S.	194	39.21 N	86.40 W
Gossa	54	51.40 N	12.26 E
Gossas	150	14.30 N	16.04 W
Gossau	58	47.25 N	9.15 E
Gosse ◆[8]	263	51.08 N	7.01 E
Gosse Bluff ∧	162	23.49 S	132.19 E
Gosselies	56	50.28 N	4.25 E
Gössenheim	56	50.01 N	9.46 E
Gossensass → Colle Isarco	64	46.56 N	11.26 E
Gosser Hill	279b	40.37 N	79.37 W
Gossi	150	15.49 N	1.17 W
Gossinga	140	8.39 N	25.59 E
Gössnitz	54	50.53 N	12.26 E
Gossolengo	62	44.59 N	9.37 E
Gössweinstein	60	49.46 N	11.20 E
Gostagajevskaja	78	45.01 N	37.30 E
Gostilovo	82	55.18 N	38.36 E
Gostiščevo	78	50.47 N	36.39 E
Gostivar	38	41.47 N	20.54 E
Göstling an der Ybbs	61	47.48 N	14.55 E
Gostyń	30	51.53 N	17.00 E
Gostynin	30	52.26 N	19.29 E
Göta älv ≃	26	57.42 N	11.52 E
Göta kanal ≊	40	58.50 N	13.58 E
Gotchen Creek ≃	224	46.00 N	121.30 W
Got Creek ≃	284a	43.03 N	78.42 W
Gotebo	196	35.04 N	98.52 W
Göteborg (Gothenburg)	26	57.43 N	11.58 E
Göteborgs och Bohus län □[6]	26	58.30 N	11.30 E
Gotel Mountains ϰ	152	6.55 N	11.15 E
Gotemba	94	35.18 N	138.56 E
Götene	26	58.32 N	13.29 E
Gotești	38	46.09 N	28.10 E
Gotha, Dtsch.	54	50.57 N	10.41 E
Gotha, Fl., U.S.	220	28.32 N	81.31 W
Gothem	26	57.35 N	18.43 E
Gothenburg → Göteborg, Sve.	26	57.43 N	11.58 E
Gothenburg, Ne., U.S.	198	40.55 N	100.09 W
Gothèye	150	13.52 N	1.34 E
Gotland I	26	57.30 N	18.33 E
Gotlands Län □[6]	26	57.30 N	18.30 E
Gotoputovo	86	56.46 N	70.10 E
Gotō-rettō II	92	32.50 N	129.00 E
Gotska Sandön I	26	58.23 N	19.16 E
Gōtsu	96	35.00 N	132.14 E
Gottenheim	58	48.03 N	7.44 E
Götterswickerhamm	263	51.35 N	6.40 E
Gottesbrücke	264a	52.25 N	13.49 E
Gotthard Tunnel ◆[5]	58	46.35 N	8.35 E
Göttin	264a	52.27 N	12.54 E
Göttingen, Dtsch.	52	51.32 N	9.55 E
Göttingen, Dtsch.	56	50.52 N	8.46 E
Göttin See ⊜	264a	52.28 N	12.54 E
Gottmadingen	58	47.44 N	8.47 E
Gottolengo	64	45.17 N	10.16 E
Gottorf, Schloss ⊥	41	54.30 N	9.32 E
Gottsbüren	52	51.35 N	9.30 E
Gottvaterkapelle ✝[1]	60	49.42 N	11.41 E
Götzendorf	264b	48.01 N	16.35 E
Götzis	58	47.20 N	9.38 E
Gouarec	32	48.13 N	3.11 W
Goubangzi	104	41.22 N	121.46 E
Goubone	146	20.43 N	17.08 E
Gouda, Ned.	52	52.01 N	4.43 E
Gouda, S. Afr.	158	33.19 S	19.04 E
Goudet	62	44.53 N	3.55 E
Goudge	252	34.40 S	68.08 W
Goudhurst	42	51.07 N	0.28 E
Goudiry	150	14.11 N	12.43 W
Goudoumaria	146	13.42 N	11.10 E
Goudswaard	52	51.47 N	4.16 E
Gouéké	150	8.02 N	8.43 W
Goûfi, Djebel el ∧	34	36.57 N	6.27 E
Gougezhuang	105	38.53 N	116.11 E
Gough Island I	10	40.20 S	10.00 W
Gough Lake ⊜	182	52.02 N	112.28 W
Gouin, Réservoir ⊜[1]	176	48.38 N	74.54 W
Goujiaozhen	107	30.36 N	106.33 E
Goukou	89	48.39 N	122.06 E
Goulais ≃	190	46.43 N	84.27 W
Goulburn	170	34.45 S	149.43 E
Goulburn ≃	169	36.41 S	145.12 E
Goulburn Islands II	164	11.33 S	133.26 E
Goulburn Weir ⊜[1]	169	36.45 S	145.08 E
Gould	194	33.59 N	91.33 W
Gould City	190	46.05 N	85.41 W
Gould Park	214	40.04 N	82.53 W
Goulds	220	25.33 N	80.22 W
Gouldsboro	210	41.44 N	75.28 W
Gouldsboro State Park ♦	210	41.13 N	75.28 W
Goulet Lake ⊜	184	55.23 N	96.18 W
Goulia	150	10.01 N	7.11 W
Goulicun	106	31.40 N	120.00 E
Goulimime	148	28.56 N	10.04 W
Goulimine □[4]	148	28.30 N	9.45 W
Goulmima	148	31.02 N	5.00 W
Goumbati ∧[2]	150	13.08 N	12.06 W
Goumbou	150	14.59 N	7.27 W
Gouménissa	38	40.57 N	22.27 E
Goumois	58	47.16 N	6.57 E
Gouna	146	8.32 N	13.34 E
Gounda ≃	146	9.25 N	20.57 E
Goundam	150	16.25 N	3.40 W
Goundi	146	9.22 N	17.22 E
Gounou-Gaya	146	9.38 N	15.31 E
Gouougang, Mount ∧	170	33.53 S	150.07 E
Goupillières	261	48.53 N	1.46 E
Gouraya	34	36.34 N	1.55 E
Gourbassi	150	13.24 N	11.38 W
Gourbeyre	241o	16.00 N	61.42 W
Gourcy	150	13.13 N	2.21 W
Gourdhead Run ≃	279b	40.33 N	79.57 W
Gourdon, Fr.	32	44.44 N	1.23 E
Gourdon, Fr.	62	43.43 N	6.59 E
Gouré	150	13.58 N	10.18 E
Gouri ⊥	124	24.53 N	88.07 E
Gourin	32	48.08 N	3.36 W
Gouripur	124	24.46 N	90.34 E
Gourits ≃	158	34.21 S	21.52 E
Gourlay Lake ⊜	190	48.52 N	84.54 W
Gourma Rharous	150	16.53 N	1.55 W
Gournay-en-Bray	50	49.29 N	1.44 E
Gournay-sur-Marne	261	48.52 N	2.34 E
Gouro	146	19.33 N	19.33 E
Gourock	46	55.58 N	4.49 W
Goussainville	50	49.01 N	2.28 E
Goussonville	261	48.55 N	1.46 E
Goutou	105	39.49 N	117.11 E
Gouveia, Bra.	255	18.27 S	43.44 W
Gouveia, Port.	266c	38.50 N	9.26 W
Gouverneur	212	44.20 N	75.27 W
Gouyadong	100	25.10 N	112.55 E
Gouyave	241k	12.10 N	61.44 W
Gov'altaj □[4]	102	45.30 N	96.00 E
Govan	184	51.18 N	105.00 W
Go Vap	269c	10.49 N	106.41 E
Govardhan	124	27.30 N	77.28 E
Gove	198	38.57 N	100.29 W
Govea ≃	286b	22.56 N	82.30 W
Govena, mys ›	74	59.48 N	166.06 E
Govenlock	184	49.15 N	109.48 W
Gove Peninsula ›[1]	164	12.20 S	136.50 E
Governador, Ilha do I	287a	22.48 S	43.12 W
Governador Portela	256	22.29 S	43.30 W
Governador Valadares	255	18.51 S	41.56 W
Government Camp	224	45.18 N	121.45 W
Governor Bond Lake ⊜[1]	219	38.56 N	89.23 W
Governor Dodge State Park ♦	190	43.00 N	90.07 W
Governor Generoso	116	6.39 N	126.05 E
Governor Head ›	170	35.07 S	150.46 E
Governor Nice Memorial Bridge ◆[5]	208	38.22 N	77.00 W
Governor Printz Park ♦	285	39.52 N	75.18 W
Governor's Harbour	238	25.10 N	76.14 W
Governors Island I	276	40.41 N	74.01 W
Govind Ballabh Pant Sāgar ⊜[1]	124	24.05 N	82.50 E
Govindgarh	124	24.23 N	81.18 E
Govind Sāgar ⊜[1]	123	31.20 N	76.45 E
Gov'-Ugtaal	102	46.04 N	107.30 E
Gowan ≃	184	55.49 N	94.08 W
Gowanda	210	42.27 N	78.56 W
Gowan Range ϰ	166	25.00 S	145.00 E
Gowen City	208	40.45 N	76.32 W
Gower	194	39.36 N	94.35 W
Gower ›[1]	42	51.36 N	4.10 W
Gowerton	42	51.39 N	4.01 W
Gowienica ≃	54	53.40 N	14.38 E
Gowmal (Gumal) ≃	120	31.56 N	70.22 E
Gowmal Kalay	120	32.29 N	68.55 E
Gowna, Lough ⊜	48	53.51 N	7.34 W
Gowrie	198	42.16 N	94.17 W
Gowy ≃	44	53.17 N	2.51 W
Goya	252	29.08 S	59.16 W
Goyania → Goiânia	255	16.40 S	49.16 W
Goyatz-Guhlen	54	52.01 N	14.09 E
Goyave	241o	16.08 N	61.34 W
Goyaves, Grande Rivière à ≃	241o	16.18 N	61.37 W
Goyaves, Îlets à II	241o	16.10 N	61.48 W
Göyçay	84	40.39 N	47.44 E
Göyçay ≃	84	40.39 N	47.45 E
Goyder ≃	164	12.38 S	135.11 E
Goyder Creek ≃	162	25.39 S	134.47 E
Goyelle, Lac ⊜	186	50.47 N	60.45 W
Goyeneche	258	35.20 S	58.43 W
Goyer, Île I	275a	45.29 N	73.17 W
Goyerkāta	124	26.42 N	89.02 E
Göynücek	130	40.24 N	35.32 E
Göynük, Tür.	130	39.08 N	40.53 E
Göynük, Tür.	130	40.24 N	30.47 E
Göynük ≃, Tür.	130	40.20 N	30.05 E
Göynük ≃, Tür.	130	38.53 N	40.34 E
Goyt ≃	262	53.24 N	2.09 W
Göytäpä	84	39.08 N	48.36 E
Goz-Beïda	146	12.13 N	21.25 E
Gozdnica	30	51.26 N	15.06 E
Gozdowice	54	52.45 N	14.18 E
Göze Dağı ∧	130	41.24 N	42.30 E
Gözeli	130	38.25 N	39.04 E
Gozen-yama	94	36.32 N	140.20 E
Gozha Co ⊜	120	34.59 N	81.06 E
Gözne	130	36.59 N	34.34 E
Gozo → Għawdex I	36	36.03 N	14.15 E
Göz Tepe ∧[2]	267b	41.06 N	29.06 E
Gozzano	62	45.45 N	8.26 E
Graaff-Reinet	158	32.14 S	24.32 E
Graafwater	158	32.00 S	18.37 E
Graauw	52	51.20 N	4.05 E
Grabc'ovo	82	54.34 N	36.22 E
Graben-Neudorf	56	49.09 N	8.29 E
Grabenstätt	64	47.51 N	12.32 E
Grabill	216	41.12 N	84.58 W
Grabo	150	4.55 N	7.30 W
Grabouw	158	34.09 S	19.02 E
Grabovo	86	53.07 N	74.52 E
Grabow	54	53.16 N	11.34 E
Grabowhöfe	54	53.34 N	12.36 E
Grabowiec	30	50.50 N	23.33 E
Grabów nad Prosną	30	51.31 N	18.06 E
Gračac	36	44.18 N	15.51 E
Gračanica	38	44.42 N	18.19 E
Gračanica, Manastir ✝[1]	38	42.36 N	21.09 E
Graçay	50	47.08 N	1.51 E
Grace	202	42.34 N	111.43 W
Gracefield	188	46.06 N	76.03 W
Graceham	208	39.36 N	77.22 W
Graceton	214	40.30 N	79.10 W
Graceville, Fl., U.S.	192	30.57 N	85.31 W
Graceville, Mn., U.S.	198	45.34 N	96.26 W
Gračevka	82	55.06 N	36.49 E
Grächen	58	46.12 N	7.50 E
Grachovo	80	56.04 N	51.58 E
Grači	80	49.49 N	43.33 E
Gracia ◆[8]	266d	41.23 N	2.09 E
Gracias	236	14.35 N	88.35 W
Gracias a Dios □[5]	236	15.10 N	84.20 W
Gracias a Dios, Cabo ›	236	15.00 N	83.10 W
Gračiki ≃	83	48.30 N	39.52 E
Graciosa I	148a	39.04 N	28.00 W
Graciosa, Isla I	148	29.15 N	13.30 W
Gračov	80	49.26 N	41.32 E
Gračovka, Ross.	80	52.07 N	40.01 E
Gračovka, Ross.	80	52.57 N	52.52 E
Gračov Kust	80	51.59 N	49.50 E
Gradačac	38	44.53 N	18.26 E
Gradara	66	43.57 N	12.46 E
Gradaús	250	7.43 S	51.11 W
Gr'adcy	76	56.24 N	31.55 E
Gräddö	40	59.46 N	19.02 E
Gradisca d'Isonzo	64	45.53 N	13.30 E
Grado, Esp.	34	43.23 N	6.04 W
Grado, It.	64	45.40 N	13.23 E
Grado, Laguna di c	64	45.43 N	13.20 E
Gradoli	66	42.39 N	11.51 E
Grad Sofija □[4]	38	42.41 N	23.19 E
Grady, Ar., U.S.	194	34.04 N	91.42 W
Grady, N.M., U.S.	196	34.49 N	103.19 W
Gradyville	285	39.57 N	75.28 W
Graemsay I	46	58.56 N	3.17 W
Græsted	41	56.04 N	12.17 E
Graettinger	198	43.14 N	94.45 W
Gräfelfing	60	48.07 N	11.25 E
Grafenau	60	48.52 N	13.25 E
Gräfenberg	60	49.39 N	11.15 E
Grafenberg ◆[8]	263	51.14 N	6.50 E
Gräfenhainichen	54	51.44 N	12.27 E
Gräfenroda	54	50.45 N	10.48 E
Gräfenthal	54	50.31 N	11.18 E
Gräfentonna	54	51.05 N	10.44 E
Grafenwöhr	60	49.43 N	11.54 E
Graffignano	66	42.34 N	12.12 E
Grafham Water ⊜	42	52.17 N	0.20 W
Gräfinau-Angstedt	54	50.42 N	11.01 E
Grafing bei München	60	48.02 N	11.59 E
Gråfjell ∧	26	60.16 N	9.29 E
Grafling	60	48.54 N	12.59 E
Graford	196	32.56 N	98.14 W
Grafrath	64	48.07 N	11.10 E
Gräfrath ◆[8]	263	51.13 N	7.04 E
Grafschaft Bentheim □[9]	52	52.30 N	7.00 E
Grafton, Austl.	166	29.41 S	152.56 E
Grafton, On., Can.	212	44.00 N	78.01 W
Grafton, Il., U.S.	219	38.58 N	90.25 W
Grafton, Ma., U.S.	207	42.12 N	71.41 W
Grafton, N.Y., U.S.	210	42.46 N	73.27 W
Grafton, N.D., U.S.	198	48.24 N	97.24 W
Grafton, Oh., U.S.	214	41.16 N	82.03 W
Grafton, W.V., U.S.	188	39.20 N	80.01 W
Grafton, Wi., U.S.	190	43.19 N	87.57 W
Grafton, Cape ›	164	16.52 S	145.55 E
Grafton Lakes State Park ♦	210	42.48 N	73.28 W
Grafty Green	260	51.12 N	0.41 E
Graglia	62	45.33 N	7.59 E
Gragnano	68	40.41 N	14.31 E
Gragnano Trebbiense	62	45.01 N	9.34 E
Graham, Ca., U.S.	280	34.15 N	118.31 W
Graham, N.C., U.S.	192	36.04 N	79.24 W
Graham, Tx., U.S.	196	33.06 N	98.35 W
Graham, Wa., U.S.	224	47.03 N	122.17 W
Graham, Mount ∧	200	32.42 N	109.52 W
Graham Cave State Park ♦	219	38.55 N	91.32 W
Graham Creek ≃	218	38.49 N	85.39 W
Graham Hill County Park ♦	276	41.07 N	73.48 W
Graham Island I	182	53.40 N	132.30 W
Graham Lake ⊜, On., Can.	212	44.34 N	75.53 W
Graham Lake ⊜, Me., U.S.	188	44.40 N	68.25 W
Graham Land ◆[1]	9	66.00 S	63.30 W
Graham Memorial Park ♦	284b	39.25 N	76.30 W
Graham Moore, Cape ›	176	72.52 N	76.04 W
Graham Moore Bay c	176	75.26 N	101.25 W
Grahamstad → Grahamstown	158	33.19 S	26.31 E
Grahamstown	158	33.19 S	26.31 E
Grahamsville	210	41.51 N	74.33 W
Grahn	218	38.17 N	83.04 W
Graie, Alpi (Alpes Grées) ϰ	62	45.30 N	7.10 E
Graiguenarmanagh	48	52.32 N	6.57 W
Grain	42	51.28 N	0.43 E
Grain, Isle of I	42	51.27 N	0.41 E
Grain Coast ⏚[2]	150	5.00 N	9.00 W
Grainfield	198	39.06 N	100.27 W
Grajagan	115a	8.35 S	114.13 E
Grajagan, Teluk c	115a	8.40 S	114.18 E
Grajaú	250	5.49 S	46.08 W
Grajaú ≃	250	3.41 S	44.48 W
Grajewo	30	53.39 N	22.27 E
Grajvoron	78	50.28 N	35.39 E
Gram	41	55.17 N	9.04 E
Gramacho	287a	22.44 S	43.18 W
Gramada	38	43.50 N	22.39 E
Gramado	252	29.24 S	50.54 W
Gramalote	246	7.53 N	72.48 W
Gramastetten	61	48.23 N	14.12 E
Gramat	32	44.47 N	1.43 E
Gramatneusiedl	264b	48.02 N	16.29 E
Grambling	194	32.31 N	92.42 W
Grambow	54	53.25 N	14.20 E
Gramilla	252	27.18 S	64.37 W
Gramínea	256	22.10 S	46.38 W
Graminha, Reprêsa ⊜[1]	256	21.40 S	46.35 W
Grammer	218	39.09 N	85.43 W
Grammichele	70	37.13 N	14.38 E
Grammont → Geraardsbergen	50	50.46 N	3.52 E
Gramoteino	86	54.31 N	86.22 E
Grampian	214	40.57 N	78.36 W
Grampian □[4]	46	57.15 N	2.45 W
Grampian Mountains ϰ	46	56.55 N	4.00 W
Grampians National Park ♦	166	37.20 S	142.30 E
Gramschatz	56	49.56 N	9.58 E
Gramsh	38	40.52 N	20.11 E
Gramzow	54	53.12 N	14.00 E
Gran → Esztergom	30	47.48 N	18.45 E
Grana ≃	62	44.25 N	7.27 E
Granaatboskolk	158	30.02 S	19.51 E
Granada, Col.	246	3.34 N	73.45 W
Granada, Esp.	34	37.13 N	3.41 W
Granada, Nic.	236	11.56 N	85.57 W
Granada, Pil.	116	10.40 N	123.02 E
Granada, Co., U.S.	198	38.03 N	102.18 W
Granada, Mn., U.S.	190	43.41 N	94.20 W
Granada □[4]	34	37.15 N	3.15 W
Granada □[5]	236	11.50 N	86.00 W
Granada → Grenada □[1]	241k	12.07 N	61.40 W
Granada Hills ◆[8]	280	34.16 N	118.31 W
Granado	286d	12.04 S	76.57 W
Granaglione	66	44.07 N	10.58 E
Gran Altiplanicie Central ϰ[1]	254	48.55 S	69.45 W
Granard	48	53.47 N	7.30 W
Granarolo dell'Emilia	64	44.33 N	11.27 E
Granatello	70	37.53 N	12.32 E
Gran Bahía Australiana → Great Australian Bight c[3]	162	35.00 S	135.00 E
Gran Bajo de San Julián V	254	49.30 S	68.30 W
Gran Barrera de Arrecifes → Great Barrier Reef ✣[2]	160	18.00 S	145.50 E
Granbergsdal	40	59.24 N	14.35 E
Granbury	222	32.26 N	97.47 W
Granbury, Lake ⊜[1]	222	32.25 N	97.45 W
Granby, P.Q., Can.	206	45.24 N	72.44 W
Granby, Co., U.S.	200	40.05 N	105.56 W
Granby, Ct., U.S.	207	41.57 N	72.47 W
Granby, Ma., U.S.	207	42.15 N	72.31 W
Granby, Mo., U.S.	194	36.55 N	94.15 W
Granby ≃	182	49.03 N	118.25 W
Granby, Lake ⊜[1]	200	40.09 N	105.50 W
Gran Canaria I	148	28.00 N	15.36 W
Grancey-le-Château	58	47.40 N	5.02 E
Gran Chaco ◆[1]	18	23.00 S	60.00 W
Grand	58	48.23 N	5.29 E
Grand ≃, On., Can.	212	42.51 N	79.34 W
Grand ≃, U.S.	194	39.23 N	93.06 W
Grand ≃, Mi., U.S.	216	43.04 N	86.15 W
Grand ≃, Oh., U.S.	214	41.46 N	81.17 W
Grand ≃, S.D., U.S.	198	45.40 N	100.32 W
Grand ≃, Wi., U.S.	190	43.45 N	89.16 W
Grand, East Fork ≃	194	40.12 N	94.21 W
Grand, Lac ⊜	190	47.10 N	76.57 W
Grand, North Fork ≃	198	45.47 N	102.16 W
Grand, South Fork ≃	198	45.43 N	102.17 W
Grandas	34	43.13 N	6.52 W
Grand Bahama I	238	26.38 N	78.25 W
Grand Ballon ∧	58	47.55 N	7.08 E
Grand Bank	186	47.06 N	55.46 W
Grand Banks of Newfoundland ✣[4]	16	45.00 N	53.00 W
Grand-Bassam	150	5.12 N	3.44 W
Grand Bay, N.B., Can.	186	45.18 N	66.12 W
Grand Bay, Al., U.S.	194	30.28 N	88.20 W
Grand Beach	184	50.35 N	96.40 W
Grand Bend	190	43.15 N	81.45 W
Grand Béréby	150	4.38 N	6.55 W
Grand Blanc	216	42.55 N	83.37 W
Grand-Bourg	241o	15.53 N	61.19 W
Grand Bruit	186	47.41 N	58.13 W
Grand Caille Point ›	241f	13.52 N	61.05 W
Grand Calumet ≃	278	41.38 N	87.34 W
Grand Calumet, Île du I	190	45.44 N	76.41 W
Grand Canal ≊, Ire.	48	53.21 N	6.14 W
Grand Canal → Da Yunhe ≊, Zhg.	90	32.12 N	119.31 E
Grand Cane	194	32.05 N	93.48 W
Grand Cañon du Verdon ♦	62	43.47 N	6.27 E
Grand Canyon	200	36.03 N	112.08 W
Grand Canyon V	200	36.10 N	112.45 W
Grand Canyon National Park ♦	200	36.15 N	112.58 W
Grand Canyon of Pennsylvania ♦	210	41.43 N	77.28 W
Grand Cayman I	238	19.20 N	81.15 W
Grand Central Terminal ◆[5]	276	40.45 N	73.59 W
Grand Centre	184	54.25 N	110.13 W
Grand Cess	150	4.36 N	8.10 W
Grandchamp, Fr.	58	47.43 N	5.27 E
Grandchamp, Fr.	261	48.43 N	1.37 E
Grand-Charmont	58	47.32 N	6.50 E
Grand Chenier	194	29.46 N	92.58 W
Grand Combin ∧	58	45.56 N	7.18 E
Grand Coulee	202	47.56 N	119.00 W
Grand Coulee V	202	47.45 N	119.15 W
Grand Coulee Dam ◆[6]	202	47.57 N	118.59 W
Grand-Couronne	50	49.21 N	1.00 E
Grand Cul-de-Sac Marin c	241o	16.20 N	61.35 W
Grande ≃, Arg.	252	36.52 S	69.45 W
Grande ≃, Arg.	252	24.12 S	64.42 W
Grande ≃, Bol.	248	15.51 S	64.39 W
Grande ≃, Bra.	242	11.05 S	43.09 W
Grande ≃, Bra.	255	20.06 S	51.04 W
Grande ≃, Bra.	287a	22.55 S	43.25 W
Grande ≃, Bra.	287b	23.45 S	46.22 W
Grande ≃, Chile	252	30.35 S	71.11 W
Grande ≃, Esp.	34	39.07 N	0.44 W
Grande ≃, It.	70	37.55 N	13.13 E
Grande ≃, Méx.	234	17.43 N	96.56 W
Grande ≃, Méx.	234	18.50 N	102.05 W
Grande ≃, Nic.	236	12.28 N	86.21 W
Grande ≃, Pan.	236	8.18 N	80.24 W
Grande ≃, Perú	248	14.59 S	75.29 W
Grande ≃, S.A.	254	53.48 S	67.40 W
Grande ≃, Ven.	246	8.39 N	60.59 W
Grande, Arroyo ≃, Arg.	258	34.37 S	59.25 W
Grande, Arroyo ≃, Arg.	288	34.45 S	58.08 W
Grande, Arroyo ≃, Méx.	234	23.55 N	98.44 W
Grande, Arroyo ≃, Ur.	252	33.08 S	57.09 W
Grande, Arroyo ≃, Ur.	258	33.37 S	57.09 W
Grande, Bahía c[3]	254	50.45 S	68.45 W
Grande, Boca c	220	26.43 N	82.16 W
Grande, Boca ≃[1]	246	8.38 N	60.30 W

Symbols in the index entries represent the broad categories identified in the key at the right. Symbols with superior numbers (ϰ[1]) identify subcategories (see complete key on page *I · 1)*.

Symbole im Register stellen die rechts im Schlüssel erklärten Kategorien dar. Symbole mit hochgestellten Ziffern (ϰ[1]) bezeichnen Unterabteilungen einer Kategorie (vgl. vollständiger Schlüssel auf Seite *I · 1)*.

Los símbolos incluídos en el texto del índice representan las grandes categorías identificadas con la clave a la derecha. Los símbolos con numeros en su parte superior (ϰ[1]) identifican las subcategorías (véase la clave completa en la página *I · 1)*.

Les symboles de l'index représentent les catégories indiquées dans la légende à droite. Les symboles suivis d'un indice (ϰ[1]) représentent des sous-catégories (voir légende complète à la page *I · 1)*.

Os símbolos incluídos no texto do índice representam as grandes categorias identificadas com a chave à direita. Os símbolos com números em sua parte superior (ϰ[1]) identificam as subcategorias (veja-se a chave completa à página *I · 1)*.

∧	Mountain	Berg	Montaña	Montagne	Montanha
ϰ	Mountains	Gebirge	Montañas	Montagnes	Montanhas
⋈	Pass	Paß	Paso	Col	Passo
V	Valley, Canyon	Tal, Cañon	Valle, Cañón	Vallée, Canyon	Vale, Canhão
⩦	Plain	Ebene	Llano	Plaine	Planície
›	Cape	Kap	Cabo	Cap	Cabo
I	Island	Insel	Isla	Île	Ilha
II	Islands	Inseln	Islas	Îles	Ilhas
⏚	Other Topographic Features	Andere Topographische Objekte	Otros Elementos Topográficos	Autres données topographiques	Outros acidentes topográficos

Gran-Gree *I* · 65

ESPAÑOL — Nombre | Página | Lat.°′ | Long.°′ W = Oeste

Grande, Cañada ≃, Arg. 258 35.19 S 57.48 W
Grande, Cañada ≃, Arg. 258 35.15 S 59.23 W
Grande, Cayo I 240p 20.59 N 79.09 W
Grande, Cerro ∧, Méx. 232 28.46 N 107.32 W
Grande, Cerro ∧, Méx. 234 23.22 N 103.35 W
Grande, Cerro ∧, Méx. 234 21.45 N 103.05 W
Grande, Cerro ∧, Méx. 234 20.43 N 101.12 W
Grande, Cerro ∧, Méx. 234 23.39 N 100.51 W
Grande, Corixa (Curiche Grande) ≡ 248 17.10 S 58.20 W
Grande, Cuchilla ∧ 252 33.15 S 55.07 W
Grande, Curiche (Corixa Grande) ≃ 248 17.10 S 58.20 W
Grande, Igarapé ≃ 250 3.37 S 48.53 W
Grande, Ilha I, Bra. 252 23.45 S 54.03 W
Grande, Ilha I, Bra. 256 23.09 S 44.14 W
Grande, Isola I 70 37.53 N 12.26 E
Grande, Lago ⊜, Arg. 254 47.44 S 68.04 W
Grande, Lago ⊜, Bra. 250 2.16 S 54.17 W
Grande, Laguna ⊜, Arg. 258 34.14 S 58.53 W
Grande, Laguna ⊜, Méx. 234 20.06 N 96.40 W
Grande, Mare ⊂ 68 40.27 N 17.12 E
Grande, Naviglio ≅ 266b 45.35 N 8.42 E
Grande, Ponta › 255 16.22 S 39.01 W
Grande, Praia ⩡² 256 24.05 S 46.30 W
Grande, Punta › 252 21.54 S 70.12 W
Grande, Ribeirão ≃ 256 21.24 S 44.29 W
Grande, Rio (Bravo del Norte) ≃ 178 25.55 N 97.09 W
Grande, Salina ≡ 68 40.26 N 17.18 E
Grande, Serra ⋀ 250 6.00 S 40.52 W
Grande, Sierra ⋀ 196 29.40 N 104.55 W
Grande-Anse 186 47.48 N 65.11 W
Grande Anse, La ⊂ 275a 45.23 N 73.53 W
Grande Anse Bay ⊂ 241k 12.02 N 61.45 W
Grande Baie, La ⊂ 275a 45.29 N 74.00 W
Grande Cache 182 53.53 N 119.08 W
Grande Casse, Pointe de la ∧ 62 45.24 N 6.50 E
Grande Cayemite I 238 18.37 N 73.45 W
Grande Chartreuse, Couvent de la ⊍¹ 62 45.22 N 5.50 E
Grande de Añasco ≃ 240m 18.16 N 67.11 W
Grande de Arecibo ≃ 240m 18.29 N 66.42 W
Grande de Jutaí, Ilha I 250 3.15 S 49.37 W
Grande de Lipez ≃ 248 20.47 S 67.14 W
Grande de Loíza ≃ 240m 18.27 N 65.53 W
Grande de Manacapuru, Lago ⊜ 246 3.04 S 61.25 W
Grande de Manatí ≃ 240m 18.29 N 66.32 W
Grande de Matagalpa ≃ 236 12.54 N 83.32 W
Grande de Santiago ≃ 234 21.36 N 105.26 W
Grande de Tarija ≃ 248 22.53 S 64.21 W
Grande de Térraba ≃ 236 8.59 N 83.37 W
Grande do Curuaí, Lago ⊜ 250 2.15 S 55.20 W
Grande do Gurupá, Ilha I 250 1.00 S 51.30 W
Grande do Tapará, Ilha I 250 2.14 S 54.39 W
Grande Île de Criques I 273b 4.20 S 15.25 E
Grande Inferior, Cuchilla ⋀² 258 33.50 S 56.27 W
Grand-Entrée 186 47.33 N 61.34 W
Grande-Prairie 182 55.10 N 118.48 W
Grand Erg de Bilma ◆² 146 18.30 N 14.00 E
Grand Erg Occidental ◆² 148 30.30 N 0.30 E
Grand Erg Oriental ◆² 148 30.30 N 7.00 E
Grande-Rivière 186 48.24 N 64.30 W
Grande Rivière, La ≃ 176 53.50 N 79.00 W
Grande Ronde ≃ 202 46.05 N 116.59 W
Grandes, Salinas ≚, Arg. 252 23.43 S 66.00 W
Grandes, Salinas ≚, Arg. 252 30.05 S 65.05 W
Grandes Antillas, Islas → Greater Antilles II 238 20.00 N 74.00 W
Grandes Antilles, Îles → Greater Antilles II 238 20.00 N 74.00 W
Grande Sassière, Aiguille de la ∧ 62 45.30 N 7.00 E
Grande Sauldre ≃ 50 47.26 N 2.05 E
Gran Desierto de Arena → Great Sandy Desert ◆² 162 21.30 S 125.00 E
Gran Desierto Victoria → Great Victoria Desert ◆² 162 28.30 S 127.45 E
Grandes-Piles 206 46.41 N 72.44 W
Grande-Synthe 50 51.01 N 2.19 E
Grand-Étang 186 46.33 N 61.02 W
Grande-Terre I 241o 16.20 N 61.25 W
Grande Vigie, Pointe de la › 241o 16.31 N 61.28 W
Grand Eyvia ≃ 62 45.42 N 7.14 E
Grand Falls, N.B., Can. 186 47.03 N 67.44 W
Grand Falls, Nf., Can. 186 48.56 N 55.40 W
Grandfalls, Tx., U.S. 196 31.20 N 102.51 W
Grandfather Mountain ∧ 192 36.07 N 81.48 W
Grandfield 196 34.13 N 98.41 W
Grand Forks, B.C., Can. 182 49.02 N 118.27 W
Grand Forks, N.D., U.S. 198 47.55 N 97.01 W
Grand Forks Air Force Base ■ 198 47.57 N 97.25 W
Grand-Fort-Philippe 50 51.00 N 2.06 E
Grand-Fougeray 32 47.44 N 1.44 W
Grand-Gallargues 62 43.43 N 4.10 E
Grand Gorge 210 42.21 N 74.29 W
Grand-Halleux 56 50.19 N 5.54 E
Grand Haven 216 43.03 N 86.13 W
Grand Haven State Park ♦ 216 43.02 N 86.13 W
Grand Hers ≃ 32 43.47 N 1.20 E
Grandin, Lac ⊜ 176 63.59 N 119.00 W
Grandioznyj, pik ∧ 88 53.50 N 96.11 E
Grand Island, Fl., U.S. 220 28.53 N 81.44 W
Grand Island, Ne., U.S. 198 40.55 N 98.20 W
Grand Island, N.Y., U.S. 212 43.01 N 78.58 W
Grand Island I, On., Can. 212 44.34 N 78.50 W
Grand Island I, Mi., U.S. 190 46.30 N 86.40 W
Grand Island I, N.Y., U.S. 210 43.02 N 78.58 W
Grand Isle 194 29.14 N 89.59 W
Grand Isle □⁶ 206 44.57 N 73.17 W
Grand Junction, Co., U.S. 200 39.03 N 108.33 W
Grand Junction, Ia., U.S. 198 42.01 N 94.14 W

FRANÇAIS — Nom | Page | Lat.°′ | Long.°′ W = Ouest

Grand Junction, Mi., U.S. 216 42.24 N 86.04 W
Grand Junction, Tn., U.S. 194 35.02 N 89.11 W
Grand Lac Salé → Great Salt Lake ⊜ 200 41.10 N 112.30 W
Grand lac Victoria ⊜ 190 47.31 N 77.30 W
Grand-Lahou 150 5.08 N 5.01 W
Grand Lake 200 40.15 N 105.49 W
Grand Lake ⊜, N.B., Can. 186 45.55 N 66.05 W
Grand Lake ⊜, Nf., Can. 186 49.00 N 57.25 W
Grand Lake ⊜, N.A. 186 45.43 N 67.50 W
Grand Lake ⊜, La., U.S. 194 29.55 N 91.25 W
Grand Lake ⊜, La., U.S. 194 29.55 N 92.47 W
Grand Lake ⊜, Mi., U.S. 190 45.18 N 83.30 W
Grand Lake ⊜, Oh., U.S. 216 40.30 N 84.32 W
Grand Lake Saint Marys State Park ♦ 216 40.33 N 84.27 W
Grand Ledge 216 42.45 N 84.44 W
Grand Lieu, Lac de ⊜ 32 47.06 N 1.40 W
Grand'Maison, Barrage de ◆⁶ 62 45.12 N 6.07 E
Grand Manan Channel Ʉ 186 44.45 N 66.52 W
Grand Manan Island I 186 44.40 N 66.50 W
Grand Marais, Mi., U.S. 190 46.40 N 85.59 W
Grand Marais, Mn., U.S. 190 47.45 N 90.20 W
Grand Meadow 190 43.42 N 92.34 W
Grand-Mère 206 46.37 N 72.41 W
Grand Mesa ∧ 200 39.00 N 108.00 W
Grandmesnil, Lac ⊜ 186 51.19 N 67.33 W
Grand Morin ≃ 50 48.54 N 2.50 E
Grand Muveran ∧ 58 46.14 N 7.08 E
Grandola, It. 58 46.02 N 9.13 E
Grândola, Port. 34 38.10 N 8.34 W
Grand Pabos, Rivière du ≃ 186 48.21 N 64.43 W
Grand Palace ⊍ 269a 13.45 N 100.30 E
Grand Passage Ʉ 175f 18.45 S 163.10 E
Grand-Popo 150 6.17 N 1.50 E
Grand Portage 190 47.57 N 89.41 W
Grand Portage Indian Reservation ◆⁴ 190 47.55 N 89.45 W
Grand Portage National Monument ♦ 190 48.02 N 89.38 W
Grand Prairie 222 32.44 N 96.59 W
Grandpré 56 49.20 N 4.52 E
Grand Pré National Historic Park ♦ 186 45.08 N 64.18 W
Grand Prix Airport ⊠ 281 42.33 N 83.11 W
Grand Rapids, Mb., Can. 184 53.08 N 99.20 W
Grand Rapids, Mi., U.S. 216 42.58 N 85.40 W
Grand Rapids, Mn., U.S. 190 47.14 N 93.31 W
Grand Rapids, Oh., U.S. 216 41.24 N 83.51 W
Grand Rhône ≃ 62 43.20 N 4.50 E
Grand Ridge 216 41.14 N 88.50 W
Grandrieu, Bel. 50 50.12 N 4.10 E
Grandrieu, Fr. 62 44.47 N 3.38 E
Grand River 214 41.44 N 81.17 W
Grand' Rivière 240e 14.52 N 61.11 W
Grand Ronde 224 45.03 N 123.36 W
Grand Roy 241k 12.08 N 61.45 W
Grand Ruisseau, Le ≃ 275a 45.39 N 73.12 W
Grand-Saint-Bernard, Col du)(58 45.50 N 7.10 E
Grand-Saint-Bernard, Tunnel du ◆⁵ 58 45.51 N 7.11 E
Grand Saline 222 32.40 N 95.42 W
Grand Saline Creek ≃ 222 32.41 N 95.36 W
Grand-Santi 250 4.19 N 54.24 W
Grandson 58 46.49 N 6.38 E
Grand Terrace 228 34.02 N 117.18 W
Grand Teton ∧ 202 43.44 N 110.48 W
Grand Teton National Park ♦ 202 43.30 N 110.45 W
Grand Tower 194 37.37 N 89.29 W
Grand Traverse Bay ⊂ 190 45.02 N 85.30 W
Grand Traverse Bay, East Arm ⊂ 190 44.52 N 85.28 W
Grand Traverse Bay, West Arm ⊂ 190 44.52 N 85.35 W
Grandtully 46 56.39 N 3.46 W
Grand Turk 238 21.28 N 71.08 W
Grand Union Canal ≅ 260 51.30 N 0.02 W
Grand Valley, On., Can. 212 43.54 N 80.19 W
Grand Valley, Pa., U.S. 214 41.43 N 79.32 W
Grandview, Mb., Can. 184 51.10 N 100.42 W
Grandview, Il., U.S. 219 39.48 N 89.37 W
Grandview, Mo., U.S. 194 38.53 N 94.31 W
Grandview, Pa., U.S. 279b 40.10 N 79.52 W
Grandview, Tx., U.S. 222 32.16 N 97.11 W
Grandview, Wa., U.S. 202 46.15 N 119.54 W
Grand View, Wi., U.S. 190 46.22 N 91.06 W
Grandview Beach 216 41.50 N 83.24 W
Grandview Heights, Oh., U.S. 218 39.58 N 83.02 W
Grandview Heights, Pa., U.S. 208 40.03 N 76.17 W
Grandview Homes 216 40.44 N 84.04 W
Grand View-on-Hudson 276 41.44 N 73.55 W
Grandvillars 58 47.33 N 6.58 E
Grandville 216 42.54 N 85.45 W
Grandvilliers 50 49.40 N 1.56 E
Grand Wash Cliffs ⩡⁴ 200 35.40 N 113.50 W
Grandyle Village 210 43.00 N 78.57 W
Grâne 62 44.44 N 4.55 E
Grañén 34 41.56 N 0.22 W
Graneros 252 34.04 S 70.44 W
Graney, Lough ⊜ 48 52.59 N 8.40 W
Grangärde 40 60.16 N 14.59 E
Grange, Austl. 168b 34.54 S 138.30 E
Grange, Eng., U.K. 262 53.23 N 3.09 W
Grange, Bois de la ♦ 261 48.45 N 2.30 E
Grange-Bléneau, Château de la ⊥ 50 48.41 N 2.55 E
Grange Hill 260 51.37 N 0.05 E
Grangemouth 46 56.02 N 3.45 W
Grängen ⊜ 40 59.45 N 14.47 E
Grangent, Lac de ⊜¹ 62 45.25 N 4.15 E
Grange-over-Sands 44 54.12 N 2.55 W
Granger, In., U.S. 216 41.45 N 86.06 W
Granger, Tx., U.S. 222 30.43 N 97.26 W
Granger, Wa., U.S. 202 46.20 N 120.11 W
Granger, Wy., U.S. 200 41.35 N 109.58 W
Granger Draw V 196 30.20 N 100.57 W
Granger Lake ⊜¹ 222 30.42 N 97.22 W
Granges → Grenchen 58 47.11 N 7.24 E
Grängesberg 40 60.05 N 14.59 E
Granges-sur-Vologne 58 48.09 N 6.47 E
Grangeville, Id., U.S. 202 45.55 N 116.07 W
Grangeville, Pa., U.S. 208 39.47 N 76.58 W
Grangousier Hill ∧² 190 47.35 N 84.56 W
Gran Guardia 252 25.52 S 58.53 W
Granite, Md., U.S. 284b 39.21 N 76.51 W
Granite, Ok., U.S. 196 34.57 N 99.22 W
Granite City 219 38.42 N 90.08 W
Granite Creek ≃ 224 48.43 N 120.55 W

PORTUGUÊS — Nome | Página | Lat.°′ | Long.°′ W = Oeste

Granite Dome ∧ 226 38.13 N 119.44 W
Granite Downs 162 26.57 S 133.30 E
Granite Falls, Mn., U.S. 198 44.48 N 95.32 W
Granite Falls, N.C., U.S. 192 35.47 N 81.25 W
Granite Falls, Wa., U.S. 224 48.05 N 121.58 W
Granite Lake ⊜¹ 186 48.08 N 57.05 W
Granite Mountain ∧, Austl. 171b 35.44 S 148.13 E
Granite Mountain ∧, Ak., U.S. 180 65.26 N 161.14 W
Granite Mountain ∧, Ak., U.S. 182 55.30 N 132.35 W
Granite Mountains ⋀ 202 42.35 N 107.30 W
Granite Pass)(202 44.38 N 107.30 W
Granite Peak 162 25.38 S 121.21 E
Granite Peak ∧, Mt., U.S. 202 45.10 N 109.48 W
Granite Peak ∧, Mt., U.S. 202 45.34 N 112.02 W
Granite Peak ∧, Nv., U.S. 204 41.40 N 117.35 W
Granite Peak ∧, Nv., U.S. 204 40.48 N 119.25 W
Granite Range ⋀ 204 41.00 N 119.35 W
Graniteville, Ma., U.S. 207 42.35 N 71.27 W
Graniteville, S.C., U.S. 192 33.33 N 81.48 W
Graniteville, Vt., U.S. 188 44.09 N 72.29 W
Graniti 70 37.53 N 15.14 E
Granitogorsk 85 42.44 N 73.27 E
Granitola, Capo › 70 37.34 N 12.41 E
Granitola Torretta 70 37.34 N 12.40 E
Granity 172 41.38 S 171.51 E
Granitzenbach ≃ 61 47.11 N 14.46 E
Granja, Bra. 250 3.06 S 40.50 W
Granja, Port. 266c 38.51 N 9.06 W
Gran Khingan → Da Hinggan Ling ⋀ 90 49.00 N 122.00 E
Granki 76 54.51 N 31.27 E
Grankulla (Kauniainen) 26 60.13 N 24.45 E
Gran Lago Salado → Great Salt Lake ⊜ 200 41.10 N 112.30 W
Gran Laguna Salada ⊜ 254 44.24 S 67.23 W
Granma □⁴ 240p 21.20 N 76.50 W
Gränna 26 58.01 N 14.28 E
Grannoch, Loch ⊜ 44 55.00 N 4.17 W
Granollers 34 41.37 N 2.18 E
Granön 26 64.15 N 19.19 E
Gran Pajonal ⋀ 248 10.45 S 74.30 W
Gran Paradiso ∧ 62 45.32 N 7.16 E
Gran Paradiso, Parco Nazionale del ♦ 62 45.34 N 7.18 E
Gran Pilastro (Hochfeiler) ∧ 64 46.58 N 11.44 E
Gran Rio ≃ 250 4.01 N 55.31 W
Gran Sasso d'Italia ⋀ 66 42.27 N 13.42 E
Gransee 54 53.00 N 13.09 E
Grant, Fl., U.S. 220 27.55 N 80.31 W
Grant, Mi., U.S. 190 43.20 N 85.48 W
Grant, Ne., U.S. 198 40.50 N 101.43 W
Grant □⁶, In., U.S. 216 40.33 N 85.40 W
Grant □⁶, Ky., U.S. 218 38.39 N 84.39 W
Grant ≃ 190 42.40 N 90.45 W
Grant, Lake ⊜ 218 39.00 N 83.53 W
Grant, Mount ∧ 204 38.34 N 118.48 W
Grant, Point › 169 38.31 S 145.07 E
Granta ≃ 42 52.10 N 0.06 E
Grant Birthplace ⊥ 218 38.54 N 84.14 W
Grant City 194 40.29 N 94.24 W
Grantham, Austl. 171a 27.34 S 152.12 E
Grantham, Eng., U.K. 42 52.55 N 0.39 W
Grantham, Pa., U.S. 208 40.09 N 77.00 W
Grant-Kohrs Ranch National Historic Site ⊥ 202 46.25 N 112.40 W
Grant Lake ⊜¹ 226 37.50 N 119.07 W
Grantley Adams International Airport ⊠ 241g 13.04 N 59.29 W
Grant Mills 283 41.57 N 71.26 W
Granton 46 55.59 N 3.14 W
Grantorto 64 45.36 N 11.43 E
Grantown-on-Spey 46 57.19 N 3.37 W
Grant Park 216 41.14 N 87.39 W
Grant Park ♦ 278 41.52 N 87.37 W
Grant Point › 176 68.19 N 98.53 W
Grant Range ⋀ 204 38.25 N 115.30 W
Grants 200 35.09 N 107.50 W
Grantsburg, In., U.S. 218 38.17 N 86.28 W
Grantsburg, Wi., U.S. 190 45.46 N 92.40 W
Grantshouse 46 55.53 N 2.19 W
Grants Pass 202 42.26 N 123.19 W
Grants Patch 162 30.27 S 121.07 E
Grant-Suttie Bay ⊂ 176 69.47 N 77.15 W
Grantsville, Ut,. U.S. 200 40.36 N 112.27 W
Grantsville, W.V., U.S. 188 38.55 N 81.05 W
Grantville, Ga., U.S. 192 33.14 N 84.50 W
Grantville, Pa., U.S. 208 40.23 N 76.39 W
Granum 182 49.52 N 113.30 W
Granville, Austl. 274a 33.50 S 151.01 E
Granville, Fr. 32 48.50 N 1.36 W
Granville, Il., U.S. 190 41.15 N 89.13 W
Granville, Ma., U.S. 207 42.04 N 72.51 W
Granville, Mo., U.S. 219 39.34 N 92.06 W
Granville, N.Y., U.S. 188 43.24 N 73.15 W
Granville, N.D., U.S. 198 48.16 N 100.50 W
Granville, Oh., U.S. 214 40.04 N 82.31 W
Granville, Pa., U.S. 208 40.33 N 77.38 W
Granville, W.V., U.S. 188 39.38 N 79.59 W
Granville Lake ⊜ 184 56.18 N 100.30 W
Granvin 26 60.33 N 6.43 E
Granzin, Dtsch. 54 53.25 N 12.53 E
Granzin, Dtsch. 54 53.30 N 11.56 E
Grão Mogol 255 16.34 S 42.54 W
Grão-Mogol ≃ 256 21.46 S 43.40 W
Grape Creek ≃ 200 38.26 N 105.16 W
Grape Island I 283 42.16 N 70.55 W
Grapeland 222 31.29 N 95.28 W
Grapeview 224 47.19 N 122.50 W
Grapeville 214 40.19 N 79.36 W
Grapevine 222 32.56 N 97.04 W
Grapevine Lake ⊜¹ 222 32.59 N 97.06 W
Grapevine Peak ∧ 204 36.57 N 117.09 W
Grappa, Monte ∧ 64 45.52 N 11.48 E
Grappenhall 262 53.22 N 2.32 W
Grarem 34 36.31 N 6.19 E
Gras, Lac de ⊜ 176 64.30 N 110.30 W
Grasberg 52 53.11 N 8.59 E
Grasbult 158 30.52 S 21.47 E
Graskop 156 24.58 S 30.49 E
Grasleben 54 52.18 N 11.01 E
Grasmere, S. Afr. 158 26.26 S 27.52 E
Grasmere, Eng., U.K. 44 54.28 N 3.02 W
Grasmere Lake ⊜ 276 40.36 N 74.05 W
Gräsö 40 60.21 N 18.28 E
Gräsö I 40 60.24 N 18.25 E
Grasonville 208 38.57 N 76.12 W
Grass ≃, Mb., Can. 184 56.03 N 96.33 W
Grass ≃, N.Y., U.S. 188 44.59 N 74.46 W
Grass, North Branch ≃ 188 44.25 N 75.06 W
Grass, South Branch ≃ 188 44.22 N 75.05 W
Grassano 68 40.38 N 16.18 E
Grassau 64 47.47 N 12.27 E
Grass Creek 202 43.56 N 108.39 W
Grass Creek ≃ 202 43.52 N 108.22 W
Grasscroft 262 53.32 N 2.02 W
Grasse 62 43.40 N 6.55 E
Grassendale ◆⁸ 262 53.21 N 2.54 W
Grassflat 214 41.00 N 78.07 W

Grass Hassock Channel Ʉ 276 40.36 N 73.48 W
Grasshopper Creek ≃ 202 45.06 N 112.47 W
Grassington 44 54.04 N 2.00 W
Grass Island I 276 40.39 N 73.18 W
Grässjön ⊜ 40 59.52 N 13.43 E
Grass Lake 216 42.15 N 84.13 W
Grass Lake ⊜ 216 42.27 N 88.10 W
Grassmere, Lake ⊜ 172 41.44 S 174.10 E
Grass Patch 162 33.14 S 121.43 E
Grass Range 202 47.01 N 108.48 W
Grassridge Dam ⊜¹ 158 31.45 S 25.29 E
Grass River Provincial Park ♦ 184 54.40 N 100.50 W
Grass Valley, Austl. 168a 31.38 S 116.48 E
Grass Valley, Ca., U.S. 226 39.13 N 121.03 W
Grass Valley, Or., U.S. 224 45.21 N 120.47 W
Grassy 166 40.03 S 144.04 E
Grassy ≃ 190 48.22 N 81.27 W
Grassy Bay ⊂ 276 40.38 N 73.48 W
Grassy Brook ≃ 284a 43.03 N 79.07 W
Grassy Creek ≃, In., U.S. 216 40.55 N 86.30 W
Grassy Creek ≃, Mo., U.S. 219 39.54 N 91.37 W
Grassy Hill ∧ 271d 22.25 N 114.09 E
Grassy Island I 276 41.04 N 73.23 W
Grassy Island Lake ⊜ 184 51.50 N 110.20 W
Grassy Key I 220 24.46 N 80.57 W
Grassy Lake 182 49.49 N 111.43 W
Grassy Lake ⊜ 220 27.13 N 81.20 W
Grassy Plains 182 53.57 N 125.54 W
Grassy Sprain Reservoir ⊜¹ 276 40.58 N 73.51 W
Gråsten 41 54.55 N 9.36 E
Grästorp 26 58.20 N 12.40 E
Graterford 285 40.13 N 75.27 W
Graterford State Correctional Institution ⊍ 285 40.14 N 75.26 W
Grates Point › 186 48.10 N 52.57 W
Gratis 218 39.38 N 84.31 W
Gratitunon 115a 7.43 S 113.00 E
Gratkorn 61 47.08 N 15.21 E
Gratwein 61 47.07 N 15.19 E
Gratz, Ky., U.S. 218 38.28 N 84.57 W
Gratz, Pa., U.S. 208 40.37 N 76.43 W
Gratztown 279b 40.14 N 79.47 W
Graubünden (Grischun) □³ 58 46.45 N 9.30 E
Graudenz → Grudziądz 30 53.29 N 18.45 E
Graue Hörner ∧ 58 46.57 N 9.23 E
Graukogel ∧ 64 47.06 N 13.10 E
Graulhet 32 43.46 N 2.00 E
Graulinster 56 49.45 N 6.18 E
Graun → Curon Venosta 64 46.49 N 10.32 E
Graupa 54 51.00 N 13.54 E
Gravatá 250 8.12 S 35.34 W
Gravatá ≃ 255 16.53 S 42.10 W
Grave 52 51.45 N 5.44 E
Grave Creek ≃ 202 42.39 N 123.35 W
Gravedona 58 46.09 N 9.18 E
Gravelbourg 184 49.53 N 106.34 W
Gravelines 50 50.59 N 2.07 E
Gravellona-Toce 58 45.55 N 8.26 E
Gravell Point › 176 67.10 N 76.43 W
Gravelly Bay ⊂ 284a 42.52 N 79.15 W
Gravelly Brook ≃ 276 40.25 N 74.13 W
Gravelly Pond ⊜ 283 42.36 N 70.48 W
Gravelotte, Fr. 56 49.07 N 6.01 E
Gravelotte, S. Afr. 156 23.56 S 30.34 E
Gravenhurst 212 44.55 N 79.22 W
Grävenwiesbach 56 50.23 N 8.27 E
Grave Peak ∧ 202 46.24 N 114.44 W
Gravesend, Austl. 166 29.35 S 150.19 E
Gravesend, Eng., U.K. 42 51.27 N 0.24 E
Gravesend Bay ⊂ 276 40.36 N 74.01 W
Gravesham □⁸ 260 51.25 N 0.24 E
Gravette 194 36.25 N 94.27 W
Gravigny 50 49.03 N 1.10 E
Gravina 70 37.34 N 15.03 E
Gravina di Matera ≃ 68 40.29 N 16.43 E
Gravina in Puglia 68 40.49 N 16.25 E
Gravina Island I 182 55.17 N 131.45 W
Gray, Fr. 58 47.27 N 5.35 E
Gray, Ga., U.S. 192 33.00 N 83.32 W
Gray, Ky., U.S. 192 36.56 N 84.00 W
Gray, Pa., U.S. 214 40.08 N 79.05 W
Grayback Mountain ∧, Ak., U.S. 180 57.08 N 153.54 W
Grayback Mountain ∧, Or., U.S. 202 42.07 N 123.18 W
Grayland 224 46.48 N 124.05 W
Grayling, Ak., U.S. 180 62.57 N 160.03 W
Grayling, Mi., U.S. 190 44.39 N 84.42 W
Graylyn Crest 285 39.48 N 75.31 W
Grays 42 51.29 N 0.20 E
Grays ≃ 224 46.18 N 123.41 W
Grays Harbor □⁶ 224 47.09 N 123.45 W
Grays Harbor ⊂ 224 46.56 N 124.05 W
Grayshott 42 51.11 N 0.45 W
Grayslake 216 42.21 N 88.03 W
Grays Lake ⊜ 278 42.21 N 88.03 W
Grays Lake ≡ 202 43.04 N 111.26 W
Grays Lake Outlet ≃ 202 43.22 N 111.46 W
Grayson, Sk., Can. 184 50.44 N 102.40 W
Grayson, Al., U.S. 194 34.16 N 87.19 W
Grayson, Ca., U.S. 226 37.33 N 121.10 W
Grayson, Ky., U.S. 218 38.19 N 82.56 W
Grayson, La., U.S. 194 32.02 N 92.06 W
Grayson Lake ⊜¹ 218 38.13 N 83.00 W
Grayson Lake State Park ♦ 218 38.13 N 83.02 W
Grays Peak ∧ 200 39.37 N 105.45 W
Grays Point 274a 34.04 S 151.05 E
Grays River 224 46.21 N 123.36 W
Gray Summit 219 38.29 N 90.49 W
Graysville 194 35.26 N 85.05 W
Graytown 214 41.33 N 83.16 W
Grayville 194 37.57 N 88.10 W
Gray Wolf ≃ 224 47.55 N 123.07 W
Graz 61 47.05 N 15.27 E
Grazalema 34 36.46 N 5.22 W
Graždanka ◆⁸ 265a 60.00 N 30.24 E
Gr'azeva ≃ 265b 55.51 N 37.08 E
Gr'azi 80 52.29 N 39.57 E
Grazierville 214 40.40 N 78.16 W
Gr'aznoje 82 54.02 N 39.07 E
Gr'aznovo, Ross. 82 54.18 N 36.49 E
Gr'aznovo, Ross. 265b 55.57 N 37.34 E
Gr'aznyj Irtek 80 51.56 N 53.11 E
Gr'azovec 76 58.53 N 40.14 E
Grdelica 38 42.54 N 22.04 E
Greåker 26 59.16 N 11.02 E
Greasby 262 53.23 N 3.07 W
Great ≃ 241k 12.08 N 61.36 W
Great Adventure ♦ 208 40.09 N 74.27 W
Great Altcar 262 53.33 N 3.01 W
Great America ♦ 282 37.24 N 121.59 W
Great Amwell 260 51.48 N 0.01 W
Great Artesian Basin ≚¹ 166 25.00 S 143.00 E
Great Australian Bight ⊂³ 162 35.00 S 130.00 E
Great Ayton 44 54.30 N 1.08 W
Great Baddow 42 51.43 N 0.29 E
Great Bahama Bank ✣⁴ 238 23.15 N 78.00 W
Great Barford 42 52.09 N 0.21 W
Great Barrier Island I 172 36.10 S 175.25 E
Great Barrier Reef ✣² 160 18.00 S 146.50 E
Great Barrier Reef Marine Park ♦ 166 21.00 S 151.00 E

Great Barrington 207 42.11 N 73.21 W
Great Barrow 262 53.12 N 2.48 W
Great Basin ≚¹ 178 40.00 N 117.00 W
Great Basin National Park ♦ 204 38.55 N 114.14 W
Great Bay ⊂ 208 39.30 N 74.23 W
Great Bear ≃ 180 64.54 N 125.35 W
Great Bear Lake ⊜ 176 66.00 N 120.00 W
Great Beaver Lake ⊜ 182 54.25 N 123.45 W
Great Belt → Storebælt Ʉ 41 55.30 N 11.00 E
Great Bend, Ks., U.S. 198 38.21 N 98.45 W
Great Bend, N.Y., U.S. 212 44.02 N 75.43 W
Great Bend, Pa., U.S. 210 41.58 N 75.44 W
Great Bernera I 46 58.13 N 6.49 W
Great Bitter Lake → Murrah al-Kubrā, Al-Buḥayrah al- ⊜ 142 30.20 N 32.23 E
Great Blasket Island I 48 52.05 N 10.32 W
Great Blue Hill ∧² 207 42.13 N 71.07 W
Great Bookham 260 51.16 N 0.22 W
Great Braxted 260 51.48 N 0.42 E
Great Brewster Island I 283 42.20 N 70.53 W
Great Britain I 22 54.00 N 2.00 W
Great Brook ≃ 276 40.42 N 74.31 W
Great Buddha ⊍¹ 268 35.19 N 139.32 E
Great Budworth 262 53.18 N 2.30 W
Great Burnt Lake ⊜ 186 48.20 N 56.13 W
Great Burstead 260 51.36 N 0.25 E
Great Camanoe I 240m 18.29 N 64.32 W
Great Captain Island I 276 40.59 N 73.38 W
Great Central 182 49.19 N 124.59 W
Great Central Lake ⊜ 182 49.27 N 125.12 W
Great Channel Ʉ 110 6.25 N 94.20 E
Great Chazy ≃ 188 44.56 N 73.23 W
Great Clifton 44 54.39 N 3.29 W
Great Coco Island I 110 14.05 N 93.24 E
Great Coharie Creek ≃ 192 34.50 N 78.22 W
Great Cove ⊂ 276 40.43 N 73.14 W
Great Crosby 262 53.29 N 3.01 W
Great Crossing 218 38.08 N 84.38 W
Great Cumbrae Island I 46 55.46 N 4.55 W
Great Dismal Swamp ≡ 192 36.30 N 76.30 W
Great Ditch ≅ 276 40.24 N 74.31 W
Great Divide Basin ≚¹ 202 42.00 N 108.10 W
Great Dividing Range ⋀ 160 25.00 S 147.00 E
Great Driffield 44 54.00 N 0.27 W
Great Duck Island I 190 45.40 N 82.58 W
Great Dunmow 42 51.53 N 0.22 E
Great Eau ≃ 44 53.25 N 0.13 E
Great Egg Harbor ≃ 208 39.18 N 74.40 W
Great Egg Harbor Bay ⊂ 208 39.18 N 74.37 W
Great Egg Harbor Inlet ⊂ 208 39.20 N 74.34 W
Greater Antilles II 238 20.00 N 74.00 W
Greater Buffalo International Airport ⊠ 210 42.56 N 78.44 W
Greater Cincinnati Airport ⊠ 218 39.03 N 84.40 W
Greater Khingan Range → Da Hinggan Ling ⋀ 90 49.00 N 122.00 E
Greater London □⁶ 42 51.30 N 0.10 W
Greater Manchester □⁶ 44 53.30 N 2.20 W
Greater Pittsburgh International Airport ⊠ 214 40.29 N 80.14 W
Greater Sunda Islands II 108 2.00 S 110.00 E
Greater Wilmington Airport ⊠ 208 39.41 N 75.36 W
Greater Wollongong → Wollongong 170 34.25 S 150.54 E
Great Escape ♦ 210 43.22 N 73.42 W
Great Exuma I 238 23.32 N 75.50 W
Great Falls, Mb., Can. 184 50.27 N 96.02 W
Great Falls, Mt., U.S. 202 47.30 N 111.17 W
Great Falls, S.C., U.S. 192 34.34 N 80.54 W
Great Falls, Va., U.S. 284c 39.00 N 77.17 W
Great Falls ∟ 284c 39.00 N 77.16 W
Great Falls Park ♦ 284c 39.00 N 77.15 W
Great Fish Point › 158 33.30 S 27.10 E
Great Gable ∧ 44 54.28 N 3.12 W
Great Gaddesden 260 51.47 N 0.30 W
Great Grimsby → Grimsby 44 53.35 N 0.05 W
Great Guana Cay I 238 24.00 N 76.20 W
Great Hameldon ∧² 262 53.45 N 2.19 W
Great Harwood 44 53.48 N 2.24 W
Great Haywood 42 52.48 N 2.00 W
Great Himalaya Range ⋀ 120 29.00 N 83.00 E
Greathouse Peak ∧ 202 46.46 N 109.21 W
Great Inagua I 238 21.05 N 73.18 W
Great Indian Desert (Thar Desert) ◆² 120 27.00 N 71.00 E
Great Island I, Ire. 48 51.52 N 8.17 W
Great Island I, N.Y., U.S. 276 40.38 N 73.30 W
Great Island I, N.Y., U.S. 276 41.05 N 73.44 W
Great Karroo (Groot Karroo) ⋀¹ 158 32.25 S 22.40 E
Great Kills ◆⁸ 276 40.33 N 74.10 W
Great Kills Harbor ⊂ 276 40.32 N 74.08 W
Great Kills Park ♦ 276 40.33 N 74.08 W
Great La Cloche Island I 190 46.01 N 81.52 W
Great Lake ⊜ 166 41.52 S 146.45 E
Great Lakes Naval Training Center ■ 216 42.18 N 87.50 W
Great Lakes Steel Works ⊍³ 281 42.15 N 83.08 W
Great Machipongo Inlet ⊂ 208 37.22 N 75.43 W
Great Malvern 42 52.07 N 2.19 W
Great Marsh ≡ 208 36.32 N 75.57 W
Great Marton 262 53.48 N 3.02 W
Great Massingham 42 52.46 N 0.40 E
Great Meadows 210 40.52 N 74.54 W
Great Meadows National Wildlife Refuge ◆⁴ 283 42.29 N 71.20 W
Great Mercury Island I 172 36.37 S 175.48 E
Great Meteor Tablemount ✣³ 18 30.00 N 28.30 W
Great Miami ≃ 188 39.06 N 84.49 W
Great Mills 208 38.14 N 76.30 W
Great Misery Island I 283 42.33 N 70.48 W
Great Missenden 42 51.43 N 0.43 W
Great Mis Tor ∧ 42 50.34 N 4.01 W
Great Mosque ⊍¹ 146 32.46 N 22.40 E
Great Namaqualand □⁹ 156 25.00 S 17.00 E
Great Neck 276 40.48 N 73.43 W
Great Neck ›¹, Ma., U.S. 283 42.42 N 70.48 W
Great Neck ›¹, N.Y., U.S. 276 40.50 N 73.45 W
Great Neck Estates 276 40.47 N 73.44 W
Great Nicobar I 110 7.00 N 93.50 E
Great North East Channel Ʉ 164 9.30 S 143.25 E
Great Notch Reservoir ⊜¹ 276 40.53 N 74.12 W

Great Ormes Head › 44 53.21 N 3.52 W
Great Ouse ≃ 42 52.47 N 0.22 E
Great Oxney Green 260 51.44 N 0.25 E
Great Palm Island I 166 18.43 S 146.37 E
Great Parndon 260 51.45 N 0.05 E
Great Patchogue Lake ⊜ 276 40.46 N 73.01 W
Great Peconic Bay ⊂ 207 40.56 N 72.30 W
Great Pee Dee ≃ 192 33.21 N 79.16 W
Great Piece Meadows ≡ 276 40.54 N 74.19 W
Great Plain of the Koukdjuak ≚ 176 66.00 N 73.00 W
Great Plains ≚ 16 42.00 N 100.00 W
Great Point › 207 41.23 N 70.03 W
Great Pubnico Lake ⊜ 186 43.42 N 65.43 W
Great Quittacas Pond ⊜ 207 41.48 N 70.54 W
Great River 276 40.45 N 73.10 W
Great Ruaha ≃ 154 7.56 S 37.52 E
Great Sacandaga Lake ⊜ 210 43.08 N 74.10 W
Great Saint Bernard Pass → Grand-Saint-Bernard, Col du)(58 45.50 N 7.10 E
Great Sale Cay I 192 27.00 N 78.12 W
Great Salt Lake ⊜ 200 41.10 N 112.30 W
Great Salt Lake Desert ◆² 200 40.40 N 113.30 W
Great Salt Plains Lake ⊜¹ 196 36.44 N 98.12 W
Great Sand Dunes National Monument ♦ 200 37.43 N 105.36 W
Great Sand Hills ⋀² 184 50.35 N 109.05 W
Great Sandy Desert ◆² 162 21.30 S 125.00 E
Great Sandy National Park ♦ 166 24.59 S 153.17 E
Great Sankey 44 53.23 N 2.37 W
Great Santa Cruz Island I 116 6.52 N 122.03 E
Great Scarcies (Kolenté) ≃ 150 8.55 N 13.08 W
Great Sea Reef ✣² 175g 16.15 S 179.00 E
Great Seneca Creek ≃ 208 39.08 N 77.20 W
Great Shelford 42 52.09 N 0.09 E
Great Sitkin Island I 180 52.03 N 176.07 W
Great Slave Lake ⊜ 176 61.30 N 114.00 W
Great Smoky Mountains ⋀ 192 35.35 N 83.30 W
Great Smoky Mountains National Park ♦ 192 35.39 N 83.30 W
Great Sound Ʉ, Ber. 240a 32.17 N 64.51 W
Great Sound Ʉ, N.J., U.S. 208 39.06 N 74.47 W
Great South Bay ⊂ 210 40.40 N 73.17 W
Great Stour ≃ 42 51.19 N 1.15 E
Great Sutton 262 53.17 N 2.56 W
Great Swamp ≡ 276 40.43 N 74.28 W
Great Swamp National Wildlife Refuge ◆⁴ 276 40.43 N 74.28 W
Great Tenasserim ≃ 110 12.24 N 98.37 E
Great Tobago I 240m 18.27 N 64.48 W
Great Torrington 42 50.57 N 4.08 W
Great Totham 260 51.47 N 0.43 E
Great Usutu (Maputo) (Lusutfu) ≃ 158 26.11 S 32.42 E
Great Valley 210 42.13 N 78.38 W
Great Victoria Desert ◆² 162 28.30 S 127.45 E
Great Wall ⊍³ 9 62.13 S 58.58 W
Great Wall → Chang Cheng ⊥ 98 40.30 N 116.30 E
Great Waltham 260 51.48 N 0.28 E
Great Warley 260 51.35 N 0.17 E
Great Western Forum ♦ 280 33.57 N 118.20 W
Great Whernside ∧ 44 54.09 N 1.59 W
Great Wicomico ≃ 208 37.48 N 76.18 W
Great Wyrley 42 52.41 N 2.01 W
Great Yarmouth 42 52.37 N 1.44 E
Great Zab (Büyükzap) (Az-Zāb al-Kabīr) ≃ 128 36.00 N 43.21 E
Great Zimbabwe Ruins National Park ♦ 154 20.17 S 30.57 E
Grebbestad 26 58.42 N 11.15 E
Grebenau 56 50.45 N 9.28 E
Grebenhain 56 50.29 N 9.19 E
Grebenstein 56 51.26 N 9.24 E
Grebnevo 265b 55.58 N 38.05 E
Gréboun ∧ 150 20.00 N 8.35 E
Grèce → Greece □¹ 38 39.00 N 22.00 E
Grecia 236 10.05 N 84.18 W
Grecia → Greece □¹ 38 39.00 N 22.00 E
Grecken ⊜ 40 59.35 N 14.44 E
Greco 252 32.48 S 57.03 W
Greco ◆⁸ 266b 45.30 N 9.13 E
Greco, Monte ∧ 66 41.48 N 14.00 E
Greco Island I 282 37.31 N 122.11 W
Greding 60 49.03 N 11.21 E
Gredos, Sierra de ⋀ 34 40.18 N 5.05 W
Gredstedbro 41 55.24 N 8.45 E
Greece 210 43.12 N 77.41 W
Greece (Ellás) □¹, Europe 22 39.00 N 22.00 E
Greece (Ellás) □¹, Europe 38 39.00 N 22.00 E
Greeley, Co., U.S. 200 40.25 N 104.42 W
Greeley, Ks., U.S. 198 38.19 N 95.26 W
Greeley, Ne., U.S. 198 41.33 N 98.32 W
Greeley, Pa., U.S. 210 41.25 N 75.00 W
Greeleyville 192 33.34 N 79.59 W
Green □⁶ 216 42.48 N 89.25 W
Green ≃, N.B., Can. 186 47.18 N 68.09 W
Green ≃, U.S. 200 38.11 N 109.53 W
Green ≃, U.S. 207 42.10 N 73.22 W
Green ≃, U.S. 207 42.35 N 72.36 W
Green ≃, Il., U.S. 190 41.28 N 90.23 W
Green ≃, Il., U.S. 216 41.46 N 89.10 W
Green ≃, Ky., U.S. 194 37.55 N 87.30 W
Green ≃, N.D., U.S. 198 46.52 N 102.35 W
Green ≃, Vt., U.S. 210 43.06 N 73.13 W
Green ≃, Wa., U.S. 224 47.33 N 122.20 W
Green ≃, Wa., U.S. 224 46.20 N 122.34 W
Greenacres, Ca., U.S. 226 35.23 N 119.07 W
Green Acres, De., U.S. 285 39.47 N 75.30 W
Greenacres, Wa., U.S. 202 47.39 N 117.06 W
Green Acres ◆⁹ 276 40.40 N 73.43 W
Greenacres City 220 26.37 N 80.07 W
Greenbackville 208 38.00 N 75.23 W
Greenbank 224 48.06 N 122.34 W
Green Bay 190 44.31 N 88.01 W
Green Bay ⊂, Nf., Can. 186 49.43 N 55.58 W
Green Bay ⊂, On., Can. 212 44.38 N 76.36 W
Green Bay ⊂, U.S. 190 45.00 N 87.30 W
Greenbelt 284c 39.00 N 76.52 W
Greenbelt Park ♦ 284c 38.59 N 76.54 W
Greenbo Lake ⊜ 218 38.29 N 82.54 W
Greenbo Lake State Resort Park ♦ 218 38.29 N 82.54 W
Greenbooth Reservoir ⊜¹ 262 53.38 N 2.13 W
Greenbrae 226 37.57 N 122.31 W
Greenbrier, Ar., U.S. 194 35.14 N 92.23 W
Green Brier, Tn., U.S. 194 36.25 N 86.48 W

Symbol	English	Deutsch	Español	Français	Português
≃	River	Fluß	Río	Rivière	Rio
≅	Canal	Kanal	Canal	Canal	Canal
∟	Waterfall, Rapids	Wasserfall, Stromschnellen	Cascada, Rápidos	Chute d'eau, Rapides	Cascata, Rápidos
Ʉ	Strait	Meeresstraße	Estrecho	Détroit	Estreito
⊂	Bay, Gulf	Bucht, Golf	Bahía, Golfo	Baie, Golfe	Baía, Golfo
⊜	Lake, Lakes	See, Seen	Lago, Lagos	Lac, Lacs	Lago, Lagos
≡	Swamp	Sumpf	Pantano	Marais	Pântano
⊓	Ice Features, Glacier	Eis- und Gletscherformen	Accidentes Glaciales	Formes glaciaires	Acidentes glaciares
≈	Other Hydrographic Features	Andere Hydrographische Objekte	Otros Elementos Hidrográficos	Autres données hydrographiques	Outros acidentes hidrográficos
✣	Submarine Features	Untermeerische Objekte	Accidentes Submarinos	Formes de relief sous-marin	Acidentes submarinos
□	Political Unit	Politische Einheit	Unidad Politica	Entité politique	Unidade política
⊍	Cultural Institution	Kulturelle Institution	Institución Cultural	Institution culturelle	Instituição cultural
⊥	Historical Site	Historische Stätte	Sitio Histórico	Site historique	Sitio histórico
♦	Recreational Site	Erholungs- und Ferienort	Sitio de Recreo	Centre de loisirs	Area de Lazer
⊠	Airport	Flughafen	Aeropuerto	Aéroport	Aeroporto
■	Military Installation	Militäranlage	Instalación Militar	Installation militaire	Instalação militar
◆	Miscellaneous	Verschiedenes	Misceláneo	Divers	Diversos

I · 66 **Gree-Grov**

ENGLISH / DEUTSCH

Name	Page	Lat. °′	Long. °′
Greenbrier ≃	192	37.39 N	80.53 W
Greenbrier State Park ♦	208	39.33 N	77.38 W
Green Brook	276	40.36 N	74.27 W
Green Brook ≃	276	40.33 N	74.32 W
Greenburg	194	30.51 N	90.40 W
Greenbush, Ma., U.S.	207	42.11 N	70.45 W
Greenbush, Mn., U.S.	198	48.42 N	96.10 W
Greenbush, Va., U.S.	208	37.45 N	75.41 W
Greenbushes	162	33.51 S	116.03 E
Green Camp	214	40.31 N	83.12 W
Green Cape ›	166	37.15 S	150.03 E
Greencastle, Ire.	48	55.12 N	6.59 W
Greencastle, In., U.S.	194	39.38 N	86.51 W
Greencastle, Pa., U.S.	188	39.47 N	77.43 W
Green City	194	40.16 N	92.57 W
Green Cove Springs	192	29.59 N	81.40 W
Green Creek	208	39.02 N	74.54 W
Green Creek ≃, Oh., U.S.	214	41.26 N	83.01 W
Green Creek ≃, Pa., U.S.	285	39.53 N	75.28 W
Greencrest Park	214	41.23 N	80.24 W
Greendale, Austl.	274a	33.55 S	150.39 E
Greendale, In., U.S.	218	39.06 N	84.51 W
Greendale, Wi., U.S.	216	42.56 N	87.59 W
Greene, Dtsch.	52	51.52 N	9.56 E
Greene, Ia., U.S.	190	42.53 N	92.48 W
Greene, N.Y., U.S.	210	42.19 N	75.46 W
Greene, R.I., U.S.	207	41.41 N	71.44 W
Greene □[6], Il., U.S.	219	39.18 N	90.24 W
Greene □[6], N.Y., U.S.	210	42.13 N	73.52 W
Greene □[6], Oh., U.S.	218	39.41 N	83.56 W
Greeneville	192	36.06 N	82.42 W
Greenfield, Eng., U.K.	262	53.32 N	2.01 W
Greenfield, Wales, U.K.	44	53.18 N	3.13 W
Greenfield, Ca., U.S.	226	36.19 N	121.14 W
Greenfield, Il., U.S.	219	39.20 N	90.12 W
Greenfield, In., U.S.	218	39.47 N	85.46 W
Greenfield, Ia., U.S.	198	41.18 N	94.27 W
Greenfield, Ma., U.S.	207	42.35 N	72.36 W
Greenfield, Mo., U.S.	194	37.24 N	93.50 W
Greenfield, Oh., U.S.	218	39.21 N	83.22 W
Greenfield, Tn., U.S.	194	36.09 N	88.48 W
Greenfield, Wi., U.S.	216	42.58 N	88.02 W
Greenfield-Park, P.Q., Can.	275a	45.29 N	73.29 W
Greenfield Park, N.Y., U.S.	210	41.44 N	74.29 W
Greenfields Village	285	75.10 N	39.49 W
Greenfield Village ⊥	281	42.18 N	83.14 W
Greenford ✦[8]	260	51.32 N	0.21 W
Green Forest	194	36.20 N	93.26 W
Green Harbor	207	42.04 N	70.39 W
Green Harbor ≃	283	42.05 N	70.39 W
Green Head ›	162	30.05 S	114.58 E
Green Hill	285	39.59 N	75.36 W
Greenhill ✦[8]	260	51.35 N	0.20 W
Greenhills, S. Afr.	273d	26.10 S	27.40 E
Greenhills, Oh., U.S.	218	39.16 N	84.31 W
Greenhithe	260	51.27 N	0.17 E
Greenhorn Creek ≃	198	38.08 N	104.38 W
Greenhurst	214	42.07 N	79.19 W
Green Hut Park	276	40.50 N	74.39 W
Green Island, N.Z.	172	45.54 S	170.26 E
Greenisland, N. Ire., U.K.	48	54.42 N	5.52 W
Green Island, N.Y., U.S.	210	42.44 N	73.41 W
Green Island I	241k	12.14 N	61.35 W
Green Island Bay c	116	10.12 N	119.22 E
Green Islands II	14	4.30 S	154.10 E
Green Knoll	276	40.36 N	74.36 W
Green Lake, Sk., Can.	184	54.17 N	107.47 W
Green Lake, Wi., U.S.	190	43.50 N	88.57 W
Green Lake ⊜, B.C., Can.	182	51.24 N	121.15 W
Green Lake ⊜, Sk., Can.	184	54.10 N	107.43 W
Green Lake ⊜, Mi., U.S.	281	42.36 N	83.25 W
Green Lake ⊜, N.Y., U.S.	284a	42.45 N	78.45 W
Green Lake ⊜, Wi., U.S.	190	43.41 N	88.57 W
Green Lakes State Park ♦	212	43.03 N	75.58 W
Greenlal (Saint-Grégoire-de-Greenlay)	206	45.34 N	72.01 W
Greenland, Ar., U.S.	194	35.59 N	94.10 W
Greenland, Mi., U.S.	190	46.46 N	89.06 W
Greenland (Kalaallit Nunaat) □[2]	16	70.00 N	40.00 W
Greenland Basin ✢[1]	16	73.30 N	5.00 W
Greenland-Iceland Rise ✢[3]	10	67.00 N	27.00 W
Greenlands	158	27.07 S	27.40 E
Greenland Sea ✢[2]	16	77.00 N	1.00 W
Green Lane	208	40.20 N	75.28 W
Green Lane Reservoir ⊜[1]	208	40.22 N	75.29 W
Greenlaw	46	55.43 N	2.28 W
Greenlawn	276	40.52 N	73.21 W
Greenlawn Park	285	40.07 N	74.51 W
Greenleaf	198	39.43 N	96.58 W
Green Lookout Mountain ∧	224	45.52 N	122.08 W
Green Manorville	207	42.00 N	72.32 W
Green Meadows	284c	38.58 N	76.57 W
Greenmount, Austl.	171a	27.47 S	151.54 E
Greenmount, Eng., U.K.	262	53.37 N	2.20 W
Greenmount, Md., U.S.	208	39.37 N	76.51 W
Green Mountains ⋏	188	43.45 N	72.45 W
Green Oak Lake ⊜	281	42.27 N	83.43 W
Green Oaks	278	42.18 N	87.55 W
Greenock, Austl.	168b	34.27 S	138.55 E
Greenock, Scot., U.K.	46	55.57 N	4.45 W
Greenock, Pa., U.S.	279b	40.19 N	79.48 W
Greenodd	44	54.14 N	3.04 W
Greenore Point ›	48	52.15 N	6.18 W
Greenough	162	28.57 S	114.44 E
Greenough ≃	162	28.51 S	114.38 E
Greenough, Mount ∧	180	69.10 N	141.35 W
Green Park	208	40.23 N	77.19 W
Green Peter Lake ⊜[1]	202	44.28 N	122.30 W
Green Point ›	276	40.43 N	73.06 W
Green Pond, Al., U.S.	194	33.13 N	87.07 W
Green Pond, N.J., U.S.	276	41.01 N	74.29 W
Green Pond ⊜	276	41.00 N	74.30 W
Green Pond Brook ≃	276	40.53 N	74.34 W
Greenport	207	41.06 N	72.21 W
Green Ridge	285	39.51 N	75.25 W
Green River, Pap. N. Gui.	164	3.55 S	141.10 E
Green River, Ut,. U.S.	200	38.59 N	110.09 W
Green River, Wy., U.S.	200	41.31 N	109.27 W
Green River Lake ⊜[1]	194	37.15 N	85.15 W
Greensboro, Al., U.S.	194	32.42 N	87.35 W
Greensboro, Fl., U.S.	192	30.34 N	84.44 W
Greensboro, Ga., U.S.	192	33.34 N	83.10 W
Greensboro, Md., U.S.	208	38.58 N	75.48 W
Greensboro, N.C., U.S.	192	36.04 N	79.47 W
Greensborough	274b	37.42 S	145.06 E
Greensburg, In., U.S.	218	39.20 N	85.29 W
Greensburg, Ks., U.S.	198	37.36 N	99.17 W
Greensburg, Ky., U.S.	194	37.15 N	85.29 W
Greensburg, Oh., U.S.	214	40.56 N	81.28 W
Greensburg, Pa., U.S.	214	40.18 N	79.32 W
Greens Farms	276	41.07 N	73.19 W
Greens Fork	218	39.53 N	85.02 W
Greens Fork ≃	218	39.45 N	85.07 W
Greenside ✦[8]	273d	26.09 S	28.01 E
Greens Lake c	222	29.16 N	94.59 W
Greens Peak ∧	200	34.07 N	109.35 W
Greenspond	186	49.04 N	53.34 W
Green Springs	214	41.15 N	83.03 W
Greenstead	260	51.42 N	0.14 E
Greenstone	208	39.45 N	77.27 W
Greenstone Point ›	46	57.55 N	5.38 W
Green Street	260	51.40 N	0.16 W
Green Street Green ✦[8]	260	51.21 N	0.04 E
Greensville □[6]	208	36.40 N	77.30 W
Green Swamp ≋, Fl., U.S.	220	28.20 N	81.48 W
Green Swamp ≋, N.C., U.S.	192	34.10 N	78.20 W
Greentown, In., U.S.	216	40.28 N	85.58 W
Greentown, Oh., U.S.	214	40.56 N	81.28 W
Greentown, Pa., U.S.	210	41.19 N	75.18 W
Green Tree	279b	40.24 N	80.02 W
Greenup, Il., U.S.	194	39.14 N	88.09 W
Greenup, Ky., U.S.	218	38.34 N	82.49 W
Greenup □[6]	218	38.33 N	83.00 W
Greenup Dam ✦[6]	218	38.39 N	82.52 W
Greenvale, Austl.	166	18.59 S	145.07 E
Greenvale, N.Y., U.S.	276	40.49 N	73.38 W
Green Valley, On., Can.	206	45.16 N	74.36 W
Green Valley, Az., U.S.	200	31.52 N	110.59 W
Green Valley, Il., U.S.	190	40.24 N	89.38 W
Green Valley Creek ≃	226	38.13 N	122.08 W
Greenview	219	40.04 N	89.44 W
Green Village, N.J., U.S.	276	40.44 N	74.27 W
Greenvillage, Pa., U.S.	208	40.00 N	77.36 W
Greenville, Liber.	150	5.01 N	9.03 W
Greenville, Al., U.S.	194	31.49 N	86.37 W
Greenville, Ca., U.S.	204	40.08 N	120.57 W
Greenville, Fl., U.S.	192	30.28 N	83.37 W
Greenville, Ga., U.S.	192	33.01 N	84.42 W
Greenville, Il., U.S.	219	38.53 N	89.24 W
Greenville, In., U.S.	218	38.22 N	85.59 W
Greenville, Ky., U.S.	194	37.12 N	87.10 W
Greenville, Me., U.S.	188	45.28 N	69.35 W
Greenville, Mi., U.S.	190	43.10 N	85.15 W
Greenville, Ms., U.S.	194	33.24 N	91.03 W
Greenville, Mo., U.S.	194	37.08 N	90.27 W
Greenville, N.H., U.S.	207	42.46 N	71.48 W
Greenville, N.Y., U.S.	210	40.59 N	73.49 W
Greenville, N.Y., U.S.	276	40.59 N	73.49 W
Greenville, N.C., U.S.	192	35.36 N	77.22 W
Greenville, Oh., U.S.	218	40.06 N	84.37 W
Greenville, Pa., U.S.	214	41.24 N	80.23 W
Greenville, R.I., U.S.	207	41.52 N	71.33 W
Greenville, S.C., U.S.	192	34.51 N	82.23 W
Greenville, Tx., U.S.	222	33.08 N	96.06 W
Greenville Creek ≃	218	40.07 N	84.22 W
Greenville Place	285	39.46 N	75.36 W
Greenwater ≃	224	47.09 N	121.39 W
Greenwater Lake ⊜	190	48.34 N	90.26 W
Greenwater Lake Provincial Park ♦	184	52.33 N	103.33 W
Greenwell Point	170	34.55 S	150.44 E
Greenwich, Austl.	274a	33.50 S	151.11 E
Greenwich, Ct., U.S.	207	41.01 N	73.37 W
Greenwich, N.J., U.S.	208	39.23 N	75.20 W
Greenwich, N.Y., U.S.	210	43.05 N	73.29 W
Greenwich, Oh., U.S.	214	41.01 N	82.30 W
Greenwich ✦[8]	42	51.28 N	0.02 E
Greenwich Cove c	276	41.01 N	73.35 W
Greenwich Creek ≃	276	41.02 N	73.37 W
Greenwich Observatory ʊ[3]	260	51.28 N	0.00
Greenwich Point ›	276	41.00 N	73.34 W
Greenwich Village ✦[8]	276	40.44 N	74.00 W
Greenwood, B.C., Can.	182	49.05 N	118.41 W
Greenwood, Ar., U.S.	194	35.12 N	94.15 W
Greenwood, Ca., U.S.	226	38.54 N	120.55 W
Greenwood, De., U.S.	208	38.48 N	75.35 W
Greenwood, In., U.S.	218	39.36 N	86.06 W
Greenwood, Ma., U.S.	283	42.29 N	71.04 W
Greenwood, Ms., U.S.	194	33.30 N	90.10 W
Greenwood, Ne., U.S.	198	40.57 N	96.26 W
Greenwood, N.Y., U.S.	210	42.08 N	77.38 W
Greenwood, Pa., U.S.	214	40.32 N	78.21 W
Greenwood, S.C., U.S.	192	34.11 N	82.09 W
Greenwood, Wi., U.S.	190	44.46 N	90.35 W
Greenwood, Lake ⊜[1]	192	34.15 N	82.02 W
Greenwood Cemetery ✦	276	40.39 N	73.59 W
Greenwood Lake	210	41.13 N	74.17 W
Greenwood Lake ⊜, U.S.	210	41.11 N	74.19 W
Greenwood Lake ⊜, Ma., U.S.	283	42.00 N	71.17 W
Greenwood Race Track ♦	275b	43.40 N	79.19 W
Greer, Oh., U.S.	214	40.31 N	82.13 W
Greer, S.C., U.S.	192	34.56 N	82.13 W
Greers Ferry Lake ⊜[1]	194	35.30 N	92.10 W
Greerton	172	37.43 S	176.08 E
Grées, Alpes (Alpi Graie) ⋏	62	45.30 N	7.10 E
Greeson, Lake ⊜[1]	194	34.10 N	93.45 W
Greet ≃	44	53.03 N	0.53 W
Greetland	262	53.41 N	1.52 W
Greetsiel	52	53.30 N	7.05 E
Greffiers	261	48.37 N	1.51 E
Grefrath, Dtsch.	56	51.20 N	6.20 E
Grefrath, Dtsch.	263	51.10 N	6.38 E
Gregadoo	171b	35.14 S	147.27 E
Gregbe	150	6.48 N	6.43 W
Gregg	279b	40.24 N	80.10 W
Gregg □[6]	222	32.30 N	94.50 W
Greggio	62	45.27 N	8.23 E
Greg Greg	171b	36.03 S	148.02 E
Gregoire Lake Indian Reserve ✦[4]	184	56.28 N	111.10 W
Gregório ≃	248	6.50 S	70.46 W
Gregory, Mi., U.S.	216	42.27 N	84.05 W
Gregory, S.D., U.S.	198	43.13 N	99.25 W
Gregory, Tx., U.S.	196	27.55 N	97.17 W
Gregory ≃	166	17.53 S	139.17 E
Gregory, Lake ⊜, Austl.	162	25.38 S	119.58 E
Gregory, Lake ⊜, Austl.	162	20.10 S	127.20 E
Gregory, Lake ⊜, Austl.	166	28.55 S	139.00 E
Gregory National Park ♦	164	16.30 S	130.30 E
Gregory Range ⋏	166	19.00 S	143.05 E
Grégy-sur-Yerre	261	48.40 N	2.37 E
Greifenburg	64	46.45 N	13.11 E
Greifendorf	54	51.01 N	13.06 E
Greifensee	58	47.22 N	8.41 E
Greifensee ⊜	58	47.21 N	8.41 E
Greifenstein, Dtsch.	56	50.37 N	8.18 E
Greifenstein, Öst.	264b	48.21 N	16.15 E
Greiffenberg	54	53.05 N	13.58 E
Greiffenburg ⊥	263	51.20 N	6.38 E
Greifswald	54	54.05 N	13.23 E
Greifswalder Bodden c	54	54.15 N	13.35 E
Greifswalder Oie I	54	54.14 N	13.55 E
Greim ∧	61	47.15 N	14.09 E
Grein	61	48.14 N	14.51 E
Greiz	54	50.39 N	12.12 E
Grejdernoje	80	46.53 N	45.01 E
Grejsdal	41	55.45 N	9.32 E
Grekov	80	47.24 N	43.41 E
Grekovo	83	48.54 N	40.14 E
Grem'ačevo	82	54.14 N	36.15 E
Grem'ačij	88	57.01 N	108.12 E
Grem'ačinsk, Ross.	86	58.34 N	57.51 E
Grem'ačinsk, Ross.	88	52.48 N	107.57 E
Grem'ačje	78	51.29 N	39.00 E
Gremersdorf	54	54.20 N	10.55 E
Gremicha	24	68.03 N	39.27 E
Grenå	26	56.25 N	10.53 E
Grenada	194	33.46 N	89.48 W
Grenada □[1], N.A.	230	12.07 N	61.40 W
Grenada □[1], N.A.	241k	12.07 N	61.40 W
Grenada Lake ⊜[1]	194	33.50 N	89.40 W
Grenade → Grenada □[1]	241k	12.07 N	61.40 W
Grenadier Island I	212	44.03 N	76.22 W
Grenadier Pond ⊜	275b	43.38 N	79.28 W
Grenadines II	238	12.40 N	61.15 W
Grenagh	48	52.00 N	8.37 W
Grenay	50	50.27 N	2.44 E
Grenchen	58	47.11 N	7.24 E
Grenell	212	44.16 N	76.04 W
Grenen ›[2]	26	57.44 N	10.40 E
Grenfell, Austl.	166	33.54 S	148.10 E
Grenfell, Sk., Can.	184	50.25 N	102.56 W
Grenloch	285	39.47 N	75.03 W
Grenoble	62	45.10 N	5.43 E
Grenola	198	37.20 N	96.27 W
Grenora	198	48.37 N	103.56 W
Grenville, P.Q., Can.	206	45.37 N	74.36 W
Grenville, Gren.	241k	12.07 N	61.37 W
Grenville, Cape ›	164	11.58 S	143.14 E
Grenville, Point ›	224	47.18 N	124.17 W
Grenville Bay	206	45.38 N	74.36 W
Grenville Bay c	241k	12.07 N	61.36 W
Grenville Channel U	182	53.40 N	129.40 W
Grenzaa ≃	52	52.39 N	6.45 E
Grenzach-Wyhlen	58	47.33 N	7.41 E
Grenz-Berge ∧[2]	264a	52.27 N	13.44 E
Grenzlandring ♦	56	51.11 N	6.17 E
Gréolières	62	43.48 N	6.57 E
Gréoux-les-Bains	62	43.45 N	5.53 E
Greppin	54	51.39 N	12.18 E
Gresenhorst	54	54.09 N	12.26 E
Gresham	224	45.29 N	122.25 W
Gresham Park	192	33.42 N	84.19 W
Gresik, Indon.	112	2.18 S	103.57 E
Gresik, Indon.	115a	7.09 S	112.38 E
Gressåmoen Nasjonalpark ♦	26	64.15 N	13.08 E
Gresse-en-Vercors	62	44.54 N	5.34 E
Gressey	261	48.50 N	1.37 E
Gressitt	208	37.29 N	76.43 W
Gressoney, Val di V	62	45.47 N	7.49 E
Gressoney-la-Trinité	62	45.50 N	7.49 E
Gressoney-Saint-Jean	62	45.47 N	7.49 E
Gressy	261	48.58 N	2.41 E
Gresten	61	48.00 N	15.02 E
Grésy-sur-Aix	62	45.43 N	5.57 E
Grésy-sur-Isère	62	45.36 N	6.15 E
Greta	170	32.41 S	151.24 E
Greta ≃, Eng., U.K.	44	54.09 N	2.36 W
Greta ≃, Eng., U.K.	44	54.32 N	1.53 W
Greta ≃, Eng., U.K.	44	54.36 N	3.10 W
Gretna, Mb., Can.	184	49.02 N	97.35 W
Gretna, Scot., U.K.	44	54.59 N	3.04 W
Gretna, La., U.S.	194	29.54 N	90.03 W
Gretna, Va., U.S.	192	36.57 N	79.21 W
Gretz-Armainvilliers	50	48.44 N	2.44 E
Greussen	54	51.14 N	10.57 E
Greve, Dan.	41	55.36 N	12.15 E
Greve, It.	66	43.35 N	11.19 E
Greve ≃	66	43.46 N	11.13 E
Grevel ✦[8]	263	51.34 N	7.33 E
Grevelingen U	52	51.45 N	4.00 E
Grevelingendam ✦[5]	52	51.40 N	4.10 E
Greven	52	52.05 N	7.36 E
Grevená	38	40.05 N	21.25 E
Grevenbroich	56	51.05 N	6.35 E
Greven-Granzin	54	53.29 N	10.48 E
Grevenmacher	56	49.42 N	6.20 E
Grevesmühlen	54	53.51 N	11.10 E
Greve Strand	41	55.35 N	12.14 E
Greville Bay c	186	45.22 N	64.38 W
Grevinge	41	55.48 N	11.34 E
Grey □[6]	212	44.20 N	80.45 W
Grey ≃, Nf., Can.	186	47.38 N	57.05 W
Grey ≃, N.Z.	172	42.27 S	171.12 E
Grey, Cape ›	164	13.00 S	136.40 E
Grey, Point ›, Austl.	169	38.34 S	143.59 E
Grey, Point ›, B.C., Can.	224	49.16 N	123.16 W
Greyabbey	48	54.32 N	5.33 W
Greybull	202	44.29 N	108.03 W
Greybull ≃	202	44.28 N	108.03 W
Grey Eagle	190	45.49 N	94.44 W
Grey Islands II	186	50.50 N	55.37 W
Greylingstad	158	26.44 S	28.45 E
Greylock, Mount ∧	207	42.38 N	73.10 W
Greymouth	172	42.28 S	171.12 E
Grey Range ⋏	166	27.00 S	143.35 E
Grey River	186	47.35 N	57.06 W
Greys ≃	202	43.10 N	111.00 W
Greystanes	274a	33.49 S	150.55 E
Greystoke	44	54.40 N	2.52 W
Greystones	48	53.09 N	6.04 W
Greyton	158	34.04 S	19.38 E
Greytown, N.Z.	172	41.05 S	175.27 E
Greytown → San Juan del Norte, Nic.	236	10.55 N	83.42 W
Greytown, S. Afr.	158	29.07 S	30.30 E
Grez-Doiceau	56	50.44 N	4.42 E
Grez-sur-Loing	50	48.19 N	2.42 E
Grezzana	64	45.31 N	11.01 E
Gribanovskij	80	51.27 N	41.58 E
Gribbel Island I	182	53.25 N	129.00 W
Gribbin Head ›	42	50.19 N	4.40 W
Gribingui □[5]	152	7.00 N	19.15 E
Gribingui ≃	146	8.33 N	19.05 E
Gribingui-Bamingui, Réserve de Faune du ✦[4]	146	8.00 N	19.10 E
Gribovka	82	54.19 N	38.27 E
Gridley, Ca., U.S.	226	39.21 N	121.41 W
Gridley, Il., U.S.	216	40.44 N	88.52 W
Grieben	54	52.26 N	11.58 E
Griebnitz See ⊜	264a	52.24 N	13.06 E
Griechenland → Greece □[1]	38	39.00 N	22.00 E
Griekwastad	158	28.49 S	23.15 E
Grier City	210	40.50 N	76.04 W
Gries am Brenner	64	47.03 N	11.29 E
Griesbach im Rottal	60	48.28 N	13.11 E
Griesen	64	47.29 N	10.56 E
Griesheim	56	49.50 N	8.34 E
Gries im Sellrain	64	47.12 N	11.09 E
Grieskirchen	60	48.14 N	13.50 E
Griessem	52	52.00 N	9.12 E
Griesspitzen ∧	64	47.22 N	10.58 E
Griffen	61	46.42 N	14.44 E
Griffin, Sk., Can.	184	49.40 N	103.26 W
Griffin, Ga., U.S.	192	33.14 N	84.15 W
Griffin, Lake ⊜	220	28.52 N	81.51 W
Griffin Bay c	224	48.30 N	122.58 W
Griffiss Air Force Base ■	210	43.14 N	75.26 W
Griffith, Austl.	166	34.17 S	146.03 E
Griffith, In., U.S.	216	41.31 N	87.25 W
Griffith Airport ⊠	278	41.31 N	87.23 W
Griffith Island I, N.T., Can.	176	74.35 N	95.30 W
Griffith Island I, On., Can.	212	44.51 N	80.54 W
Griffith Park ♦	280	34.09 N	118.17 W
Grifton	192	35.22 N	77.26 W
Griggs Drain ≍	281	42.11 N	83.26 W
Griggs Reservoir ⊜[1]	214	40.03 N	83.06 W
Griggstown	276	40.26 N	74.36 W
Griggsville	219	39.42 N	90.43 W
Grignan	62	44.25 N	4.54 E
Grignano	64	45.42 N	13.43 E
Grignasco	62	45.41 N	8.20 E
Grigno	64	46.01 N	11.38 E
Grignols	32	44.23 N	0.03 W
Grignon	261	48.51 N	1.57 E
Grigny, Fr.	62	45.37 N	4.47 E
Grigny, Fr.	261	48.40 N	2.24 E
Grigoriopol	38	47.10 N	29.18 E
Grigorjevka, Kyrg.	85	42.43 N	77.30 E
Grigorjevka, Ross.	83	47.27 N	38.23 E
Grigorjevskoje, Ross.	82	54.49 N	37.59 E
Grigorjevskoje, Ross.	82	54.48 N	39.15 E
Grigorovka	82	54.38 N	36.20 E
Grigorovo	82	56.42 N	37.35 E
Grigorovskoje	82	54.17 N	36.21 E
Grijalva ≃, Méx.	232	18.36 N	92.39 W
Grijalva (Cuilco) ≃, N.A.	232	17.01 N	93.22 W
Grijpskerk	52	53.15 N	6.18 E
Grillby	40	59.37 N	17.15 E
Grim, Cape ›	166	40.41 S	144.41 E
Grima	152	3.59 N	17.06 E
Grimaldi	68	39.08 N	16.14 E
Grimari	152	5.44 N	20.03 E
Grimaud	62	43.16 N	6.31 E
Grimbergen	50	50.56 N	4.23 E
Grimeford Village	262	53.36 N	2.34 W
Grimes	226	39.04 N	121.54 W
Grimes □[6]	222	30.35 N	96.00 W
Grimlinghausen	263	51.10 N	6.44 E
Grimma	54	51.14 N	12.43 E
Grimmen	54	54.07 N	13.02 E
Grimmenstein	61	47.38 N	16.06 E
Grimmialp	58	46.34 N	7.29 E
Grimnitzsee ⊜	54	52.58 N	13.47 E
Grimsargh	262	53.48 N	2.38 W
Grimsby, On., Can.	212	43.12 N	79.34 W
Grimsby, Eng., U.K.	44	53.35 N	0.05 W
Grimselpass)(	58	46.34 N	8.21 E
Grimselsee ⊜	58	46.34 N	8.18 E
Grímsey I	24a	66.34 N	18.00 W
Grimshaw	182	56.11 N	117.36 W
Grímsstaðir	24a	65.40 N	16.01 W
Grimstad	26	58.20 N	8.36 E
Grimstead	208	37.30 N	76.18 W
Grímsvötn ∧	24a	64.24 N	17.22 W
Grindavík	24a	63.52 N	22.27 W
Grindelwald	58	46.37 N	8.02 E
Grindsted	41	55.45 N	8.56 E
Grindstone Island → Cap-aux-Meules	186	47.23 N	61.52 W
Grindstone Island I	212	44.16 N	76.07 W
Grinnell	190	41.44 N	92.43 W
Grinnell, Lake ⊜	276	41.06 N	74.38 W
Grinnell Peninsula ›[1]	176	76.40 N	95.00 W
Grin'ovo	76	52.35 N	33.04 E
Grintavec ∧	61	46.21 N	14.32 E
Grinzing ✦[8]	264b	48.15 N	16.21 E
Grip	26	63.14 N	7.37 E
Gripsholm slott ⊥	40	59.15 N	17.13 E
Gripsholmsviken c	40	59.17 N	17.20 E
Griqualand East □[9]	158	30.30 S	29.00 E
Griqualand West □[9]	158	28.20 S	23.30 E
Grisdale	224	47.22 N	123.37 W
Grisee → Gresik	115a	7.09 S	112.38 E
Grišino	82	56.13 N	37.40 E
Gris-Nez, Cap ›	50	50.52 N	1.35 E
Grisolia	68	39.43 N	15.51 E
Grisons → Graubünden □[3]	58	46.45 N	9.30 E
Grisslehamn	40	60.06 N	18.50 E
Grissom Air Force Base ■	216	40.40 N	86.08 W
Gristow	54	54.10 N	13.20 E
Griswold, Mb., Can.	184	49.45 N	100.25 W
Griswold, Ia., U.S.	198	41.14 N	95.08 W
Griswold Creek ≃	279a	41.27 N	81.23 W
Griswoldville	207	42.39 N	72.42 W
Grisy-Suisnes	261	48.41 N	2.40 E
Grivaï Pamia	152	7.03 N	19.26 E
Grivenskaja	78	45.38 N	38.09 E
Grizzana	64	44.15 N	11.09 E
Grizzly Bay c	226	38.07 N	122.01 W
Grizzly Bear Mountain ∧	176	65.22 N	121.00 W
Grizzly Bear's Head and Lead Man Indian Reserve ✦[4]	184	52.33 N	108.16 W
Grizzly Creek ≃	282	37.52 N	122.06 W
Grizzly Flats	226	38.38 N	120.31 W
Grizzly Island I	282	38.08 N	121.58 W
Grizzly Mountain ∧, Id., U.S.	202	47.43 N	116.06 W
Grizzly Mountain ∧, Or., U.S.	202	44.26 N	120.57 W
Grizzly Mountain ∧, Wa., U.S.	202	48.25 N	118.30 W
Grizzly Slough ≃	282	38.06 N	121.53 W
Grmeč ⋏	36	44.40 N	16.30 E
Groaíras	250	3.53 S	40.23 W
Groais Island I	186	50.57 N	55.35 W
Grobbendonk	56	51.12 N	4.43 E
Gröben	264a	52.17 N	13.10 E
Gröbener-See ⊜	264a	52.17 N	13.11 E
Gröbenzell	60	48.11 N	11.22 E
Gröbers	54	51.26 N	12.07 E
Grobiņa	76	56.33 N	21.10 E
Groblersdal	156	25.15 S	29.25 E
Groblershoop	158	28.55 S	20.59 E
Gröbming	64	47.26 N	13.54 E
Grobogan	115a	7.01 S	110.55 E
Gröbzig	54	51.41 N	11.52 E
Grödig	64	47.44 N	13.02 E
Grodikovo	85	42.49 N	71.29 E
Gröditsch	54	52.03 N	13.59 E
Gröditz	54	51.24 N	13.27 E
Grodków	30	50.43 N	17.22 E
Grodno → Hrodna	76	53.41 N	23.50 E
Grodzisk Mazowiecki	30	52.07 N	20.37 E
Grodzisk [Wielkopolski]	30	52.14 N	16.22 E
Groede	52	51.23 N	3.30 E
Groen ≃, S. Afr.	158	30.40 S	23.17 E
Groen ≃, S. Afr.	158	29.00 S	22.10 E
Groënland → Greenland □[2]	16	70.00 N	40.00 W
Groenlandia → Greenland □[2]	16	70.00 N	40.00 W
Groenlo	52	52.03 N	6.38 E
Groenvlei	158	27.27 S	30.13 E
Groesbeck, Oh., U.S.	218	39.13 N	84.35 W
Groesbeck, Tx., U.S.	222	31.31 N	96.32 W
Groesbeek	52	51.47 N	5.55 E
Grofa, hora ∧	78	48.37 N	23.56 E
Grogol, Kali ≃	269e	6.10 S	106.47 E
Grogol-hilir ✦[8]	269e	6.13 S	106.47 E
Grohnde	52	52.01 N	9.25 E
Groitzsch	54	51.09 N	12.16 E
Groix	32	47.38 N	3.28 W
Groix, Île de I	32	47.38 N	3.27 W
Grójec	30	51.52 N	20.52 E
Grokgak	115a	8.11 S	114.47 E
Grolley	58	46.50 N	7.05 E
Grombalia	148	36.36 N	10.30 E
Grömitz	54	54.09 N	10.58 E
Gromo	64	45.58 N	9.56 E
Gromoslavka	80	48.12 N	43.37 E
Gronau, Dtsch.	52	52.13 N	7.00 E
Gronau, Dtsch.	52	52.05 N	9.46 E
Grondines (Saint-Charles-des-Grondines)	206	46.36 N	72.03 W
Grondneus	158	28.06 S	20.48 E
Grone	52	51.32 N	9.53 E
Grönenbach	58	47.52 N	10.13 E
Grong	24	64.28 N	12.18 E
Gröningen, Dtsch.	54	51.56 N	11.13 E
Groningen, Ned.	52	53.13 N	6.33 E
Groningen, Sur.	250	5.48 N	55.28 W
Groningen □[4]	52	53.15 N	6.45 E
Grønland → Greenland □[2]	16	70.00 N	40.00 W
Gronlid	184	53.06 N	104.28 W
Grønsund U	41	54.53 N	12.08 E
Grönwohld	52	53.39 N	10.25 E
Groom	196	35.12 N	101.06 W
Groom Lake ⊜	204	37.15 N	115.48 W
Groot ≃, S. Afr.	158	33.54 S	21.39 E
Groot ≃, S. Afr.	158	33.45 S	24.36 E
Groot-Berg ≃	158	32.47 S	18.08 E
Groot-Brakrivier	158	34.02 S	22.14 E
Grootdraaidam ⊜[1]	158	26.56 S	29.20 E
Grootebroek	52	52.43 N	5.13 E
Groote Eylandt I	164	14.00 S	136.40 E
Groote Eylandt Aboriginal Reserve ✦[4]	164	14.00 S	136.40 E
Grootfontein	156	19.32 S	18.05 E
Groot Karasberge ⋏	158	27.20 S	18.40 E
Groot Karroo → Great Karroo ⋏[1]	158	32.25 S	22.40 E
Groot-Kei ≃	158	32.41 S	28.22 E
Groot Laagte ≃	156	20.37 S	21.37 E
Groot-Letaba ≃	156	23.58 S	31.50 E
Groot-Marico	156	25.37 S	26.26 E
Grootpan	158	25.58 S	26.33 E
Groot-Swartberge ⋏	158	33.22 S	22.20 E
Groot-Vis ≃	158	33.30 S	27.08 E
Grootvlei	158	26.44 S	28.32 E
Grootvloer ≚	158	30.00 S	20.40 E
Gröpelingen ✦[8]	52	53.07 N	8.46 E
Gropello Cairoli	62	45.11 N	9.00 E
Gropeni	38	45.04 N	27.53 E
Grosbliederstroff	56	49.09 N	7.01 E
Gros Bois, Parc de ♦	261	48.44 N	2.32 E
Groscavallo	62	45.22 N	7.15 E
Grose ≃	170	33.36 S	150.41 E
Grosio	64	46.18 N	10.16 E
Gros Islet	241f	14.05 N	60.58 W
Groslay	261	48.59 N	2.21 E
Gros Mécatina, Cap du ›	186	50.45 N	59.00 W
Gros-Morne	240e	14.43 N	61.01 W
Gros Morne ∧	186	49.36 N	57.48 W
Gros Morne National Park ♦	186	49.40 N	57.45 W
Grosne ≃	58	46.42 N	4.56 E
Grosnez Point ›	43b	49.16 N	2.15 W
Grosotto	64	46.17 N	10.15 E
Gros Piton ∧	241f	13.49 N	61.04 W
Grosrouvre	261	48.47 N	1.46 E
Grossa, Ponta ›, Bra.	256	23.35 S	45.13 W
Grossa, Ponta ›, Bra.	287a	22.47 S	43.11 W
Grossache (Tiroler Ache) ≃	60	47.51 N	12.30 E
Grossaitingen	58	48.14 N	10.47 E
Grossalmerode	56	51.15 N	9.46 E
Grossalsleben	54	51.59 N	11.13 E
Gross Ammensleben	54	52.14 N	11.31 E
Grossarl	64	47.14 N	13.12 E
Gross-Beeren	54	52.21 N	13.18 E
Gross Berkel	52	52.04 N	9.19 E
Grossbodungen	54	51.28 N	10.28 E
Gross Börnecke	54	51.50 N	11.29 E
Grossbothen	54	51.11 N	12.44 E
Grossbottwar	56	49.00 N	9.17 E
Grossbreitenbach	54	50.35 N	11.02 E
Grossdeuben	54	51.14 N	12.23 E
Grossdubrau	54	51.15 N	14.28 E
Gross Düngen	52	52.06 N	10.01 E
Grosse Antillen → Greater Antilles II	238	20.00 N	74.00 W
Grosse Aue ≃	52	52.37 N	9.10 E
Grosse Australische Bucht → Great Australian Bight c[3]	162	35.00 S	135.00 E
Grossebersdorf	54	50.47 N	11.57 E
Grosse Ebene → Great Plains ≚	16	42.00 N	100.00 W
Grossefehn	52	53.24 N	7.36 E
Grosse Herrenwiese ≋	264a	52.17 N	13.20 E
Grosse Ile	216	42.08 N	83.09 W
Grosse Ile I	216	42.08 N	83.09 W
Grosse Île, La I	186	47.37 N	61.31 W
Grosse Laber ≃	60	48.56 N	12.30 E
Grosse Mühl ≃	61	48.25 N	13.59 E
Grossenbaum ✦[8]	263	51.22 N	6.47 E
Grossenbrode	54	54.22 N	11.05 E
Grossenehrich, Dtsch.	54	51.15 N	10.50 E
Grossenehrich, Dtsch.	56	51.15 N	10.52 E
Grossengottern	54	51.09 N	10.34 E
Grossenhain	54	51.17 N	13.31 E
Grossenkneten	52	52.56 N	8.16 E
Grossenlüder	56	50.35 N	9.32 E
Grossenwiehe	41	54.43 N	9.15 E
Gross-Enzersdorf	61	48.12 N	16.33 E
Grosse Pointe	214	42.23 N	82.54 W
Grosse Pointe ›	241o	16.01 N	61.16 W
Grosse Pointe Farms	214	42.25 N	82.53 W
Grosse Pointe Park	214	42.22 N	82.56 W
Grosse Pointe Shores	214	42.26 N	82.53 W
Grosse Pointe Woods	214	42.26 N	82.54 W
Grosser Arber ∧	60	49.07 N	13.07 E
Grosser Bären-See → Great Bear Lake ⊜	176	66.00 N	120.00 W
Grosser Beerberg ∧	54	50.37 N	10.44 E
Grosser Bösenstein ∧	61	47.26 N	14.24 E
Grosser Buchstein ∧	61	47.36 N	14.35 E
Grosser Chingan → Da Hinggan Ling ⋏	90	49.00 N	122.00 E
Grosser Feldberg ∧	56	50.14 N	8.26 E
Grosser Galtenberg ∧	64	47.20 N	11.58 E
Grosser Gleichberg ∧	54	50.23 N	10.35 E
Grosser Heuberg ⋏[1]	58	48.06 N	8.55 E
Grosser Inselsberg ∧	54	50.52 N	10.28 E
Grosser Jasmunder Bodden c	54	54.31 N	13.29 E
Grosser Knallstein ∧	61	47.19 N	13.58 E
Grosser Königstuhl ∧	64	46.57 N	13.47 E
Grosser Müggelsee ⊜	54	52.26 N	13.39 E
Grosse Röder ≃	54	51.30 N	13.25 E
Grosser oder Kaiser-Kanal → Da Yunhe ≍	90	32.12 N	119.31 E
Grosse Rodl ≃	61	48.20 N	14.09 E
Grosser Peilstein ∧	61	48.18 N	15.06 E
Grosser Plessower See ⊜	264a	52.23 N	12.54 E
Grosser Plöner See ⊜	54	54.06 N	10.25 E
Grosser Priel ∧	61	47.43 N	14.04 E
Grosser Rachel ∧	60	48.59 N	13.24 E
Grosser Ravens-Berg ∧[2]	264a	52.21 N	13.04 E
Grosser Salz-See → Great Salt Lake ⊜	200	41.10 N	112.30 W
Grosser Seddiner See ⊜	264a	52.17 N	13.02 E
Grosser Selchower See ⊜	54	52.14 N	13.53 E
Grosser Sklaven-See → Great Slave Lake ⊜	176	61.30 N	114.00 W
Grosser Speikkogel ∧	61	46.47 N	14.58 E
Grosser Walfisch-Fluss → Baleine, Grande rivière de la ≃	176	55.16 N	77.47 W
Grosser Wannsee ⊜	264a	52.26 N	13.11 E
Grosser Winterberg ∧[2]	54	50.54 N	14.16 E
Grosser Zern-See ⊜	264a	52.24 N	12.56 E
Grosse Sandspitze ∧	64	46.46 N	12.49 E
Grosse Sandwüste → Great Sandy Desert ✦[2]	162	21.30 S	125.00 E
Grosses Barrier-Riff → Great Barrier Reef ✢[2]	160	18.00 S	145.50 E
Grosses Meer ⊜	52	53.25 N	7.17 E
Grosses Moor ✦[3], Dtsch.	52	52.35 N	8.45 E
Grosses Moor ✦[3], Dtsch.	52	52.40 N	8.20 E
Grosses Schulerloch ♦	60	48.55 N	11.48 E
Grosse Sundainseln → Greater Sunda Islands II	108	2.00 S	110.00 E
Grosses Walsertal V	58	47.14 N	9.56 E
Grosse Syrte → Surt, Khalīj c	146	31.30 N	18.00 E
Grosseto	66	42.46 N	11.08 E
Grosseto □[4]	66	42.50 N	11.15 E
Grosseto, Formiche di I	66	42.39 N	10.53 E
Grosse Tulln ≃	61	48.20 N	16.02 E
Grossevičі	89	47.59 N	139.30 E
Grosse Windgällen ∧	58	46.49 N	8.44 E
Gross-Gerau	56	49.55 N	8.29 E
Gross-Gerungs	61	48.34 N	14.57 E
Gross Gleidingen	54	52.14 N	10.25 E
Gross Glienicke	264a	52.28 N	13.07 E
Gross-Glienicker See ⊜	264a	52.28 N	13.06 E
Grossglockner ∧	64	47.04 N	12.42 E
Grossgmain	64	47.43 N	12.55 E
Grossgörschen	54	51.13 N	12.11 E
Gross Grönau	54	53.46 N	10.44 E
Grosshansdorf	52	53.40 N	10.17 E
Grosshartmannsdorf	54	50.48 N	13.19 E
Gross-Hehlen	52	52.39 N	10.03 E
Grossheide	52	53.35 N	7.20 E
Grosshennersdorf	54	50.59 N	14.47 E
Grosshöchstetten	58	46.55 N	7.38 E
Grossjedlersdorf ✦[8]	264b	48.17 N	16.25 E
Grosskarolinenfeld, Dtsch.	64	47.53 N	12.05 E
Grosskarolinenfeld, Dtsch.	64	47.53 N	12.05 E
Grosskayna	54	51.17 N	11.56 E
Gross Kienitz	264a	52.19 N	13.28 E
Gross Kiesow	54	54.01 N	13.29 E
Gross-Kollmar	52	53.44 N	9.30 E
Grosskorbetha	54	51.16 N	12.01 E
Gross Kreutz	54	52.24 N	12.46 E
Grosskrut	61	48.38 N	16.43 E
Grosslehna	54	51.18 N	12.10 E
Gross Leine	54	52.00 N	14.03 E
Gross Leuthen, Dtsch.	54	52.05 N	14.05 E
Gross Leuthen, Dtsch.	54	52.05 N	14.05 E
Grosslittgen	56	50.02 N	6.47 E
Gross-Machnow	264a	52.16 N	13.28 E
Grossmehring	60	48.46 N	11.32 E
Gross Miltzow, Dtsch.	54	53.32 N	13.36 E
Gross Miltzow, Dtsch.	54	53.32 N	13.36 E
Grossmont	228	32.47 N	116.59 W
Gross Muckrow	54	52.04 N	14.26 E
Gross Nemerow, Dtsch.	54	53.28 N	13.14 E
Gross Nemerow, Dtsch.	54	53.28 N	13.14 E
Gross Oesingen	52	52.38 N	10.29 E
Grossörner	54	51.37 N	11.29 E
Grossos	250	4.59 S	37.09 W
Grossostheim	56	49.55 N	9.04 E
Grosspetersdorf	61	47.14 N	16.19 E
Grosspostwitz	54	51.07 N	14.26 E
Grossquenstedt	54	51.56 N	11.07 E
Grossraming	61	47.53 N	14.33 E
Grossräschen	54	51.35 N	14.00 E
Grossrinderfeld	56	49.39 N	9.44 E
Gross Rodensleben	54	52.08 N	11.25 E
Grossröhrsdorf	54	51.08 N	14.01 E
Gross Rosenburg	54	51.55 N	11.53 E
Grossrückerswalde	54	50.38 N	13.07 E
Grossrudestedt	54	51.05 N	11.06 E
Gross Sankt Florian	61	46.49 N	15.19 E
Gross-Sarau	54	53.45 N	10.44 E
Gross Schacksdorf, Dtsch.	54	51.42 N	14.38 E
Gross Schacksdorf, Dtsch.	54	51.42 N	14.38 E
Grossschirma	54	50.58 N	13.17 E
Grossschönau	54	50.54 N	14.40 E
Gross Schönebeck	54	52.54 N	13.32 E
Gross-Schulzendorf	264a	52.16 N	13.21 E
Gross-Siegharts	61	48.48 N	15.24 E
Grosssölk	64	47.25 N	13.58 E
Gross Stieten, Dtsch.	54	53.49 N	11.27 E
Gross Stieten, Dtsch.	54	53.49 N	11.27 E
Gross-Umstadt	56	49.52 N	8.55 E
Grossvenediger ∧	64	47.06 N	12.21 E
Grosswardein → Oradea	38	47.03 N	21.57 E
Grossweil	64	47.41 N	11.18 E
Grossweissenbach	61	48.33 N	15.10 E
Gross Wittensee	41	54.24 N	9.46 E
Gross Ziethen, Dtsch.	264a	52.24 N	13.27 E
Gross Ziethen, Dtsch.	264a	52.44 N	13.01 E
Gross-Zimmern	56	49.52 N	8.50 E
Grostenquin	56	48.59 N	6.44 E
Grosvenor, Lake ⊜	180	58.40 N	155.15 W
Grosvenor Dale	207	41.58 N	71.53 W
Gros Ventre ≃	202	43.33 N	110.46 W
Groswater Bay c	176	54.20 N	57.30 W
Grote Nete ≃	56	51.07 N	4.34 E
Groton, Ct., U.S.	207	41.21 N	72.04 W
Groton, Ma., U.S.	207	42.36 N	71.34 W
Groton, N.Y., U.S.	210	42.35 N	76.22 W
Groton, S.D., U.S.	198	45.26 N	98.05 W
Grottaferrata	66	41.47 N	12.40 E
Grottaglie	68	40.32 N	17.26 E
Grottaminarda	68	41.04 N	15.02 E
Grottammare	66	42.59 N	13.52 E
Grotte	70	37.24 N	13.42 E
Grotte di Castro	66	42.40 N	11.52 E
Grotteria	68	38.22 N	16.17 E
Grottoes	188	38.16 N	78.49 W
Grottole	68	40.36 N	16.23 E
Grou, Oued V	148	33.56 N	6.45 W
Grouard Mission	182	55.31 N	116.09 W
Groundbirch	182	55.47 N	120.55 W
Groundhog ≃	176	49.43 N	81.58 W
Grouse Creek ≃, Ks., U.S.	198	37.00 N	96.55 W
Grouse Creek ≃, Ut,. U.S.	200	41.22 N	113.55 W
Grouse Creek Mountain ∧	202	44.22 N	113.54 W
Grouw	52	53.05 N	5.45 E
Grove, Eng., U.K.	42	51.36 N	1.25 W
Grove, Ok., U.S.	196	36.35 N	94.46 W

Symbols in the index entries represent the broad categories identified in the key at the right. Symbols with superior numbers (⋏[1]) identify subcategories (see complete key on page *I · 1*).

Symbole im Register stellen die rechts im Schlüssel erklärten Kategorien dar. Symbole mit hochgestellten Ziffern (⋏[1]) bezeichnen Unterabteilungen einer Kategorie (vgl. vollständiger Schlüssel auf Seite *I · 1*).

Los símbolos incluídos en el texto del índice representan las grandes categorías identificadas con la clave a la derecha. Los símbolos con numeros en su parte superior (⋏[1]) identifican las subcategorías (véase la clave completa en la página *I · 1*).

Les symboles de l'index représentent les catégories indiquées dans la légende à droite. Les symboles suivis d'un indice (⋏[1]) représentent des sous-catégories (voir légende complète à la page *I · 1*).

Os símbolos incluídos no texto do índice representam as grandes categorias identificadas com a chave à direita. Os símbolos com números em sua parte superior (⋏[1]) identificam as subcategorias (veja-se a chave completa à página *I · 1*).

	English	Deutsch	Español	Français	Português
∧	Mountain	Berg	Montaña	Montagne	Montanha
⋏	Mountains	Gebirge	Montañas	Montagnes	Montanhas
)(	Pass	Paß	Paso	Col	Passo
V	Valley, Canyon	Tal, Cañon	Valle, Cañón	Vallée, Canyon	Vale, Canhão
≚	Plain	Ebene	Llano	Plaine	Planície
›	Cape	Kap	Cabo	Cap	Cabo
I	Island	Insel	Isla	Île	Ilha
II	Islands	Inseln	Islas	Îles	Ilhas
⊥	Other Topographic Features	Andere Topographische Objekte	Otros Elementos Topográficos	Autres données topographiques	Outros acidentes topográficos

Grov-Gull I · 67

ESPAÑOL: Nombre · Página · Lat.°′ · Long.°′ W = Oeste — FRANÇAIS: Nom · Page · Lat.°′ · Long.°′ W = Ouest — PORTUGUÊS: Nome · Página · Lat.°′ · Long.°′ W = Oeste

Nombre	Página	Lat.°′	Long.°′ W = Oeste
Grove, Pa., U.S.	285	40.01 N	75.38 W
Grove City, Fl., U.S.	220	26.54 N	82.19 W
Grove City, Mn., U.S.	198	45.09 N	94.40 W
Grove City, Oh., U.S.	218	39.52 N	83.05 W
Grove City, Pa., U.S.	214	41.09 N	80.05 W
Grove Hill	194	31.42 N	87.46 W
Groveland, Ca., U.S.	226	37.50 N	120.13 W
Groveland, Fl., U.S.	220	28.33 N	81.51 W
Groveland, Ma., U.S.	207	42.45 N	71.01 W
Groveland, N.Y., U.S.	210	42.39 N	77.46 W
Grovely Ridge ʌ	42	51.08 N	2.04 W
Grove Mountains ⋏	9	72.53 S	74.53 E
Grove Park ◆[8]	260	51.26 N	0.01 E
Groveport	218	39.52 N	82.53 W
Grover	210	41.37 N	76.52 W
Grover City	204	35.07 N	120.37 W
Grover Cleveland Birthplace ⊥	276	40.50 N	74.16 W
Grover Cleveland Park ♠	284a	42.57 N	78.49 W
Grover Hill	216	41.01 N	84.28 W
Grovers Mills	276	40.19 N	74.37 W
Groves	194	29.56 N	93.55 W
Groveton, N.H., U.S.	188	44.35 N	71.30 W
Groveton, Pa., U.S.	279b	40.30 N	80.06 W
Groveton, Tx., U.S.	222	31.03 N	95.07 W
Groveton, Va., U.S.	284c	38.46 N	77.05 W
Grovetown	192	33.27 N	82.11 W
Groveville	208	40.10 N	74.40 W
Growa Point ›	150	4.21 N	7.37 W
Growler Peak ʌ	200	32.24 N	113.07 W
Growler Wash V	200	32.35 N	113.30 W
Groznoje	85	42.36 N	71.12 E
Groznyj	84	43.20 N	45.42 E
Groznyy → Groznyj	84	43.20 N	45.42 E
Grube, Dtsch.	54	54.14 N	11.01 E
Grube, Dtsch.	264a	52.26 N	12.57 E
Grubišno Polje	36	45.42 N	17.10 E
Grudziądz	30	53.29 N	18.45 E
Gruesa, Punta ›	248	20.22 S	70.11 W
Gruetli-Laager	194	35.22 N	85.40 W
Grugapark ♠	263	51.26 N	7.00 E
Grugliasco	62	45.04 N	7.35 E
Gruia	38	44.16 N	22.42 E
Gruinard Bay ⊂	46	57.53 N	5.31 W
Gruinart, Loch ⊂	46	55.52 N	6.20 W
Gruiten	56	51.14 N	7.01 E
Gruitrode	56	51.05 N	5.35 E
Grulla	196	26.16 N	98.39 W
Grumello del Monte	62	45.38 N	9.52 E
Grumento Nova	68	40.17 N	15.53 E
Grumentum ⊥	68	40.17 N	15.55 E
Grumman-Bethpage Airport ⊠	276	40.45 N	73.29 W
Grumman Corporation ʋ[3]	276	40.45 N	73.30 W
Grumme ◆[8]	263	51.30 N	7.14 E
Grumo Appula	68	41.01 N	16.42 E
Grums	26	59.21 N	13.06 E
Grüna	54	50.49 N	12.47 E
Grünau	156	27.44 S	18.23 E
Grünau ◆[8]	264a	52.25 N	13.34 E
Grünau im Almtal	64	47.51 N	13.57 E
Grunavat, Loch ⊜	46	58.10 N	6.55 W
Grünbach	54	50.26 N	12.22 E
Grünberg, Dtsch.	56	50.35 N	8.58 E
Grünberg → Zielona Góra, Pol.	30	51.56 N	15.31 E
Grünburg	61	47.57 N	14.15 E
Grundlsee ⊜	64	47.38 N	13.52 E
Grundy	192	37.16 N	82.05 W
Grundy □[6]	216	41.22 N	88.26 W
Grundy Center	190	42.21 N	92.46 W
Grundy Lake Provincial Park ♠	190	45.48 N	80.34 W
Grüneberg	54	52.52 N	13.14 E
Grünefeld	264a	52.41 N	12.58 E
Grünenplan	52	51.57 N	9.44 E
Grünewald, Dtsch.	54	51.24 N	14.00 E
Grünewald, Dtsch.	263	51.13 N	7.37 E
Grunewald ◆[8]	264a	52.30 N	13.17 E
Grunewald, Berliner Forst ◆[3]	264a	52.28 N	13.13 E
Grunewald, Jagdschloss ⊥	264a	52.28 N	13.16 E
Grünhain	54	50.35 N	12.48 E
Grünhainichen	54	50.46 N	13.08 E
Grünheide	54	52.25 N	13.49 E
Grünsfeld	56	49.36 N	9.44 E
Grünstadt	56	49.34 N	8.10 E
Grüntal	264a	52.45 N	13.44 E
Grunthal	184	49.25 N	96.52 W
Grünwald	60	48.02 N	11.31 E
Gruševka	78	47.55 N	40.40 E
Gruševka ≃	83	47.26 N	40.00 E
Gruševskaja	83	47.26 N	39.57 E
Grušino	76	59.27 N	44.09 E
Gruting	46a	60.14 N	1.30 W
Gruver	196	36.16 N	101.24 W
Gruyère, Lac de la ⊜	58	46.38 N	7.06 E
Gruyères	58	46.35 N	7.05 E
Gruzdžiai	76	56.06 N	23.16 E
Gruzija → Georgia □[1]	72	42.00 N	44.00 E
Gruziya → Georgia □[1]	72	42.00 N	44.00 E
Gruznovka	88	55.09 N	105.12 E
Gruzskaja Balka	78	46.25 N	40.19 E
Grybów	30	49.38 N	20.56 E
Grycken ⊜	40	60.27 N	16.13 E
Gryfice	30	53.56 N	15.12 E
Gryfino	30	53.12 N	14.30 E
Grytgöl	40	58.48 N	15.33 E
Grythyttan	40	59.42 N	14.32 E
Gschnitz	64	47.03 N	11.22 E
Gschütt, Pass)(	64	47.35 N	13.30 E
Gschwend	56	48.56 N	9.44 E
Gstaad	58	46.28 N	7.17 E
Gsteig	58	46.23 N	7.16 E
Gu ≃	100	27.02 N	115.03 E
Gua	124	22.12 N	85.23 E
Guabaria ≃[1]	126	22.10 N	90.30 E
Guabito	236	9.30 N	82.37 W
Guabu	106	32.16 N	118.53 E
Guacanayabo, Golfo de ⊂	240p	20.28 N	77.30 W
Guacara	246	10.14 N	67.53 W
Guacarí	246	3.46 N	76.20 W
Gu Achi	200	32.19 N	112.02 W
Guachinango	234	20.32 N	104.24 W
Guachiría ≃	246	5.27 N	70.36 W
Guachochi	232	26.51 N	107.05 W
Guaçuí	255	20.46 S	41.41 W
Guadajoz ≃	34	37.50 N	4.51 W
Guadalajara, Esp.	34	40.38 N	3.10 W
Guadalajara, Méx.	234	20.40 N	103.20 W
Guadalajara □[4]	34	40.50 N	2.30 W
Guadalaviar ≃	34	40.21 N	1.08 W
Guadalcanal	34	38.06 N	5.49 W
Guadalcanal □[4]	175e	9.50 S	160.00 E
Guadalcanal I	175e	9.32 S	160.12 E
Guadalcázar	234	22.37 N	100.24 W
Guadalén ≃	34	38.05 N	3.32 W
Guadalén, Embalse de ⊜[1]	34	38.25 N	3.15 W
Guadalentin ≃	34	37.59 N	1.04 W
Guadalete ≃	34	36.35 N	6.13 W
Guadalhorce ≃	34	36.41 N	4.27 W
Guadalimar ≃	34	38.01 N	3.45 W
Guadalmena ≃	34	38.19 N	2.56 W
Guadalmez ≃	34	38.46 N	5.04 W
Guadalope ≃	34	41.15 N	0.03 W
Guadalquivir ≃	34	36.47 N	6.22 W
Guadalupe, Bol.	248	18.33 S	64.05 W
Guadalupe, Col.	246	2.01 N	75.45 W
Guadalupe, C.R.	236	9.57 N	84.03 W
Guadalupe, Méx.	196	28.09 N	100.36 W
Guadalupe, Méx.	232	25.41 N	100.15 W
Guadalupe, Méx.	234	22.45 N	102.31 W
Guadalupe, Perú	248	7.15 S	79.29 W
Guadalupe, Ca., U.S.	204	34.58 N	120.34 W
Guadalupe □[6]	222	29.37 N	97.45 W
Guadalupe ◆[8]	287a	22.50 S	43.23 W
Guadalupe → Guadeloupe □[2]	241o	16.15 N	61.35 W
Guadalupe ≃, Méx.	204	32.05 N	116.53 W
Guadalupe ≃, Ca., U.S.	282	37.25 N	121.58 W
Guadalupe ≃, Tx., U.S.	196	28.30 N	96.53 W
Guadalupe, Basílica de ʋ[1]	286a	19.29 N	99.07 W
Guadalupe, Isla I	178	29.00 N	118.16 W
Guadalupe, Presa de ⊜[1]	286a	19.37 N	99.16 W
Guadalupe, Sierra de ⋏, Esp.	34	39.26 N	5.25 W
Guadalupe, Sierra de ⋏, Méx.	286a	19.35 N	99.08 W
Guadalupe [Bravos]	232	31.23 N	106.07 W
Guadalupe del Norte ≍	286a	19.34 N	99.01 W
Guadalupe de Ramírez	234	17.45 N	98.10 W
Guadalupe Mountains ⋏	196	32.20 N	105.00 W
Guadalupe Mountains National Park ♠	196	31.55 N	104.55 W
Guadalupe Peak ʌ	196	31.50 N	104.52 W
Guadalupe Seamount ✣[3]	14	27.50 N	168.45 E
Guadalupe Slough ≃	282	37.27 N	122.02 W
Guadalupe Victoria, Méx.	196	27.47 N	101.04 W
Guadalupe Victoria, Méx.	232	24.27 N	104.07 W
Guadalupe Victoria, Méx.	234	19.17 N	97.21 W
Guadalupe Victoria, Presa ⊜[1]	234	23.50 N	104.46 W
Guadalupita	200	36.08 N	105.14 W
Guadarrama, Puerto de)(	34	40.43 N	4.10 W
Guadarrama, Sierra de ⋏	34	40.55 N	4.00 W
Guadazaón ≃	34	39.42 N	1.36 W
Guadeloupe □[2], N.A.	230	16.15 N	61.35 W
Guadeloupe □[2], N.A.	241o	16.15 N	61.35 W
Guadeloupe Passage ʯ	238	16.45 N	61.30 W
Guadiana ≃	34	37.14 N	7.22 W
Guadiana, Bahía de ⊂	240p	22.05 N	84.24 W
Guadiana Menor ≃	34	37.56 N	3.15 W
Guadiaro ≃	34	36.17 N	5.17 W
Guadiato ≃	34	37.48 N	5.03 W
Guadiela ≃	34	40.22 N	2.49 W
Guadix	34	37.18 N	3.08 W
Guafo, Isla I	254	43.36 S	74.43 W
Guagnano	68	40.24 N	17.57 E
Guagua	116	14.58 N	120.38 E
Guahe	105	39.12 N	115.00 E
Guaianases ◆[8]	287b	23.33 S	46.25 W
Guaíba	252	30.06 S	51.19 W
Guaíba ⊂[1]	252	30.15 S	51.12 W
Guaicaipuro □[5]	286c	10.25 N	66.57 W
Guaihe	100	33.28 N	112.59 E
Guaimaca	236	14.32 N	86.51 W
Guáimaro	240p	21.03 N	77.21 W
Guaimoreto, Laguna de ⊂	236	15.58 N	85.55 W
Guaimozi	98	41.31 N	125.26 E
Guainía □[5]	246	2.30 N	69.00 W
Guainía ≃	246	2.01 N	67.07 W
Guaió ≃	287b	23.31 S	46.19 W
Guaipava	256	21.40 S	45.43 W
Guaiquinima, Cerro ʌ	246	5.49 N	63.40 W
Guaíra, Bra.	252	24.04 S	54.15 W
Guaíra, Bra.	255	20.19 S	48.18 W
Guairá □[5]	252	25.45 S	56.30 W
Guaire ≃	286c	10.25 N	66.46 W
Guáitara ≃	246	1.34 N	77.27 W
Guaitecas, Archipiélago de las II	254	43.57 S	73.50 W
Guajaba, Cayo I	240p	21.50 N	77.30 W
Guajará ≃	250	1.48 S	53.02 W
Guajará-Açu	250	1.38 S	48.07 W
Guajará-Miri	250	1.29 S	48.17 W
Guajará-Mirim	248	10.48 S	65.22 W
Guajataca ≃	240m	18.29 N	66.57 W
Guajataca, Lago de ⊜[1]	240m	18.23 N	66.55 W
Guajiasi	104	41.15 N	120.54 E
Gualaca	236	8.32 N	82.18 W
Gualaceo	246	2.54 S	78.47 W
Gualala	204	38.45 N	123.31 W
Gualán	236	15.08 N	89.22 W
Gualaquiza	246	3.24 S	78.33 W
Gualdo Tadino	66	43.14 N	12.47 E
Gualeguay	252	33.09 S	59.20 W
Gualeguay ≃	252	33.19 S	59.39 W
Gualeguaychú	252	33.01 S	58.31 W
Gualicho, Salina del ⊻	254	40.24 S	65.15 W
Gualjaina	254	42.42 S	70.30 W
Gualtieri	64	44.54 N	10.38 E
Guam □[2], Oc.	14	13.28 N	144.47 E
Guam □[2], Oc.	174p	13.28 N	144.47 E
Guamá ≃, Bra.	250	1.29 S	48.30 W
Guamá ≃, Cuba	240p	22.11 N	83.41 W
Guamal, Col.	246	9.09 N	74.14 W
Guamal, Col.	246	3.52 N	73.44 W
Guamal, Quebrada ≃	286c	10.31 N	66.59 W
Guamblín, Isla I	254	44.51 S	75.05 W
Guaminí	252	37.02 S	62.25 W
Guam International Airport ⊠	174p	13.29 N	144.48 E
Guamo	246	4.02 N	74.58 W
Guamo Embarcadero	240p	20.37 N	76.58 W
Guamote	246	1.56 S	78.43 W
Guamúchil, Méx.	232	25.28 N	108.06 W
Guamúchil, Méx.	234	25.28 N	108.06 W
Guamués ≃	246	0.32 N	76.33 W
Gua Musang	114	4.53 N	101.58 E
Gu'an	105	39.26 N	116.18 E
Guan ≃, Zhg.	100	34.29 N	119.49 E
Guan ≃, Zhg.	100	32.16 N	115.42 E
Guanábana	240m	18.01 N	67.07 W
Guanabara, Baía de ⊂	287a	22.50 S	43.10 W
Guanabara, Palácio ʋ	287a	22.56 S	43.11 W
Guanacaste □[4]	236	10.30 N	85.15 W
Guanacaste, Cordillera de ⋏	236	10.45 N	85.05 W
Guanacaste, Parque Nacional ♠	236	10.50 N	85.30 W
Guanacaure, Cerro ʌ	236	13.14 N	87.07 W
Guanaceví	232	25.56 N	105.57 W
Guanache ≃	248	5.53 S	74.21 W
Guanahacabibes, Golfo de ⊂	240p	22.08 N	84.35 W
Guanahacabibes, Península de ›[1]	240p	21.57 N	84.35 W
Guana Island I	240m	18.29 N	64.34 W
Guanaja	236	16.27 N	85.54 W
Guanaja, Isla de I	236	16.30 N	85.55 W
Guanajay	240p	22.55 N	82.42 W
Guanajibo ≃	240m	18.10 N	67.11 W
Guanajibo, Punta ›	240m	18.10 N	67.11 W
Guanajuato	234	21.01 N	101.15 W
Guanajuato □[3]	234	21.00 N	101.00 W
Guanambi	255	14.13 S	42.47 W
Guanaparo, Caño ≃	246	8.19 N	68.10 W
Guañape, Islas II	248	8.33 S	78.57 W
Guanare	246	9.03 N	69.45 W
Guanare ≃	246	8.13 N	67.46 W
Guanarito	246	8.42 N	69.12 W
Guanay	248	15.28 S	67.52 W
Guanay, Cerro ʌ	246	5.51 N	66.18 W
Guanay, Cerro ʌ[2]	286d	12.07 S	77.13 W
Guanbuqiao	100	29.56 N	114.21 E
Guanchao	100	26.41 N	114.58 E
Guancheng, Zhg.	100	30.11 N	121.25 E
Guancheng, Zhg.	107	30.01 N	103.54 E
Guancun	106	31.30 N	119.43 E
Guandacol	252	29.31 S	68.32 W
Guandanghu	100	30.06 N	113.37 E
Guandi, Zhg.	98	41.48 N	116.52 E
Guandi, Zhg.	98	42.37 N	118.27 E
Guandian	100	32.40 N	118.04 E
Guandu, Zhg.	100	24.17 N	113.53 E
Guandu, Zhg.	107	30.04 N	106.25 E
Guane	240p	22.12 N	84.05 W
Guang'an	107	30.28 N	106.39 E
Guang'anmen Station ◆[5]	271a	39.53 N	116.20 E
Guangchang	100	26.50 N	116.14 E
Guangde	106	30.54 N	119.26 E
Guangdong (Kwangtung) □[4]	90	23.00 N	113.00 E
Guangfeng	100	28.25 N	118.11 E
Guangfu, Zhg.	106	31.18 N	120.23 E
Guangfu, Zhg.	107	30.13 N	104.41 E
Guangfu, Zhg.	269b	31.21 N	121.19 E
Guangfuyingzi	104	42.14 N	120.58 E
Guanghua	102	32.25 N	111.36 E
Guangji	100	29.52 N	115.34 E
Guangling, Zhg.	98	39.47 N	114.17 E
Guangling, Zhg.	106	32.06 N	120.13 E
Guanglu Dao I	98	39.09 N	122.21 E
Guangmao Shan ʌ	102	27.02 N	100.58 E
Guangming Ding ʌ	100	30.07 N	118.10 E
Guangnan	102	24.10 N	105.06 E
Guangningsi, Zhg.	98	39.08 N	121.45 E
Guangningsi, Zhg.	98	40.27 N	118.31 E
Guangping	98	36.30 N	114.57 E
Guangrao	98	37.02 N	118.25 E
Guangsbunchang	107	29.22 N	105.31 E
Guangshan	100	32.02 N	114.52 E
Guangshui	100	31.40 N	114.00 E
Guangxing	107	29.04 N	106.33 E
Guangxi Zhuangzu Zizhiqu (Kwangsi Chuang) □[4]	102	24.00 N	109.00 E
Guangyuan	102	32.26 N	105.52 E
Guangyuanzhen	107	30.37 N	104.47 E
Guangze	100	27.32 N	117.20 E
Guangzhen	106	30.45 N	121.07 E
Guangzhou (Canton)	100	23.06 N	113.16 E
Guangzong	98	37.06 N	115.08 E
Guanhães	255	18.46 S	42.53 W
Guanhu	98	34.26 N	117.59 E
Guánica	240m	17.58 N	66.55 W
Guánica, Laguna de ⊜	240m	18.00 N	66.56 W
Guaniguanico, Cordillera de ⋏	240p	22.35 N	83.45 W
Guanipa ≃	246	9.56 N	62.26 W
Guanjian	107	29.59 N	105.59 E
Guanjian ≃	107	30.00 N	106.01 E
Guankou, Zhg.	100	30.35 N	115.20 E
Guankou, Zhg.	107	30.39 N	103.26 E
Guanlin	106	31.32 N	119.42 E
Guanling	102	25.57 N	105.29 E
Guanlipu	104	41.37 N	123.18 E
Guanmenshan	89	47.23 N	122.20 E
Guannan (Xin'anzhen)	98	34.07 N	119.23 E
Guano	246	1.35 S	78.38 W
Guano Creek ≃	202	42.12 N	119.31 W
Guanputou	105	38.58 N	117.04 E
Guanqian, Zhg.	100	30.42 N	117.39 E
Guanqian, Zhg.	100	27.48 N	118.31 E
Guanqian, Zhg.	100	25.57 N	116.33 E
Guanqian, Zhg.	100	26.12 N	117.57 E
Guanqiao, Zhg.	98	34.58 N	117.14 E
Guanqiao, Zhg.	100	25.03 N	118.06 E
Guanqiaopu	100	31.08 N	112.54 E
Guanshanchang	107	28.46 N	103.42 E
Guanshi	100	26.43 N	112.53 E
Guanshui	98	40.55 N	124.33 E
Guanta	246	10.14 N	64.36 W
Guantánamo	240p	20.08 N	75.12 W
Guantánamo □[4]	240p	20.20 N	75.00 W
Guantánamo ≃	240p	19.55 N	75.12 W
Guantánamo, Bahía de ⊂	240p	20.00 N	75.08 W
Guantanamo Bay Naval Station ■	240p	19.55 N	75.10 W
Guantang	106	31.37 N	119.06 E
Guantangqiao	106	32.09 N	119.27 E
Guantao (Nanguantao)	98	36.35 N	115.19 E
Guanting, Zhg.	100	34.19 N	113.47 E
Guanting, Zhg.	105	40.13 N	115.37 E
Guanting Shuiku ⊜[1]	105	40.20 N	115.38 E
Guantou, Zhg.	100	28.03 N	120.41 E
Guantou, Zhg.	100	26.08 N	119.33 E
Guantunpu	98	40.28 N	113.24 E
Guanxian, Zhg.	98	36.30 N	115.27 E
Guanxian, Zhg.	102	31.00 N	103.40 E
Guanxun	100	24.19 N	117.45 E
Guanyin	107	30.16 N	103.51 E
Guanyinchang, Zhg.	107	29.15 N	104.02 E
Guanyinchang, Zhg.	107	30.28 N	105.16 E
Guanyingzicun	104	41.52 N	121.53 E
Guanyinpu	107	28.58 N	104.53 E
Guanyinqiao, Zhg.	107	29.05 N	104.46 E
Guanyinqiao, Zhg.	107	29.46 N	104.12 E
Guanyinshan	106	32.01 N	120.58 E
Guanyinsi	106	31.48 N	118.57 E
Guanyintan	107	29.35 N	105.14 E
Guanyintang, Zhg.	100	31.01 N	112.35 E
Guanyintang, Zhg.	105	39.52 N	116.31 E
Guanyintang, Zhg.	106	32.09 N	121.09 E
Guanyinzhen	107	29.06 N	104.24 E
Guanyinzhou	100	29.30 N	113.09 E
Guanyun (Dayishan)	98	34.20 N	119.17 E
Guanzhuang, Zhg.	98	37.12 N	114.30 E
Guanzhuang, Zhg.	100	32.49 N	114.16 E
Guanzhuang, Zhg.	100	28.58 N	117.24 E
Guapí	246	2.36 N	77.54 W
Guapiaçu ≃	256	22.40 S	42.55 W
Guapiara	255	24.10 S	48.32 W
Guápiles	236	10.13 N	83.46 W
Guapimirim	256	22.32 S	42.59 W
Guapimirim ≃	256	22.40 S	42.58 W
Guapo Bay ⊂	241r	10.12 N	61.40 W
Guaporé	252	28.51 S	51.54 W
Guaporé (Itenes) ≃	248	11.54 S	65.01 W
Guaqui	248	16.35 S	68.51 W
Guará ≃	255	12.59 S	44.49 W
Guarabira	250	6.51 S	35.29 W
Guaraçaí	255	21.02 S	51.11 W
Guaracarumbo	286c	10.34 N	66.59 W
Guaraci	255	20.29 S	48.57 W
Guaraciaba do Norte	250	4.10 S	40.46 W
Guaraciana	255	17.03 S	43.41 W
Guaraguara, Punta ›	241r	10.31 N	62.19 W
Guaraí ≃	287a	22.42 S	43.02 W
Guaramirim	252	26.27 S	49.00 W
Guaranda	246	1.36 S	79.00 W
Guaranésia	256	21.18 S	46.48 W
Guarani	256	21.22 S	43.03 W
Guaraniaçu	252	25.06 S	52.52 W
Guarani das Missões	252	28.08 S	54.34 W
Guarani de Goiás	255	13.59 S	46.31 W
Guarapari	255	20.40 S	40.30 W
Guarapiranga, Reprêsa ⊜[1]	256	23.44 S	46.44 W
Guarapuava	252	25.23 S	51.27 W
Guaraqueçaba	252	25.17 S	48.21 W
Guarará	256	21.43 S	43.02 W
Guarará ≃	287b	23.39 S	46.30 W
Guararé	246	7.49 N	80.17 W
Guararema	256	23.25 S	46.02 W
Guaratiba, Morro de ʌ	287a	23.04 S	43.33 W
Guaratinga	255	16.34 S	39.34 W
Guaratinguetá	256	22.49 S	45.13 W
Guaratinguetá ≃	256	22.49 S	45.13 W
Guaratuba	252	25.54 S	48.34 W
Guar Chempedak	114	5.52 N	100.28 E
Guarcino	66	41.48 N	13.19 E
Guarda	34	40.32 N	7.16 W
Guardado de Abajo	196	26.22 N	98.57 W
Guardafui, Cape → Gwardafuy, Gees ›	144	11.49 N	51.15 E
Guardavalle	68	38.30 N	16.30 E
Guardea	66	42.37 N	12.18 E
Guardia Escolta	252	28.59 S	62.08 W
Guardiagrele	66	42.11 N	14.13 E
Guardia Lombardi	68	40.57 N	15.12 E
Guardia Mitre	254	40.26 S	63.41 W
Guardia Sanframondi	68	41.15 N	14.36 E
Guardo	34	42.47 N	4.50 W
Guareña	34	38.51 N	6.06 W
Guareña ≃	34	41.29 N	5.23 W
Guarenas	246	10.28 N	66.37 W
Guarenas ≃	286c	10.30 N	66.45 W
Guariba ≃	248	7.41 S	60.18 W
Guarico	246	9.32 N	69.48 W
Guárico □[3]	246	8.40 N	66.35 W
Guárico ≃	246	7.55 N	67.23 W
Guárico, Embalse del ⊜[1]	246	9.05 N	67.25 W
Guarico, Punta ›	240p	20.37 N	74.44 W
Guariquito ≃	246	7.40 N	66.18 W
Guarizama	236	14.55 N	86.20 W
Guarujá	256	24.00 S	46.16 W
Guarulhos	256	23.28 S	46.32 W
Guarulhos □[7]	287b	23.26 S	46.29 W
Guasare ≃	246	11.03 N	72.02 W
Guasave	232	25.34 N	108.27 W
Guasdualito	246	7.15 N	70.44 W
Guasila	71	39.34 N	9.03 E
Guasipati	246	7.28 N	61.54 W
Guastalla	64	44.55 N	10.39 E
Guastatoya	236	14.51 N	90.04 W
Guāsuba ≃[1]	126	21.38 N	88.53 E
Guatajiagua	236	13.40 N	88.13 W
Guatemala, Cuba	240p	20.46 N	75.39 W
Guatemala, Guat.	236	14.38 N	90.31 W
Guatemala □[5]	236	14.40 N	90.30 W
Guatemala □[1], N.A.	230	15.30 N	90.15 W
Guatemala □[1], N.A.	236	15.30 N	90.15 W
Guatemala Basin ✣[1]	16	11.00 N	95.00 W
Guateque	246	5.00 N	73.28 W
Guatimozín	252	33.27 S	62.27 W
Guatopo, Parque Nacional ♠	246	10.05 N	66.25 W
Guatraché	252	37.40 S	63.32 W
Guatuaro Point ›	241r	10.20 N	60.59 W
Guaugurina	164	10.37 S	150.28 E
Guavi ≃	164	7.49 S	143.15 E
Guaviare □[8]	246	2.00 N	72.00 W
Guaviare ≃	246	4.03 N	67.44 W
Guaxindiba ≃	287a	22.44 S	43.02 W
Guaxupé	256	21.18 S	46.42 W
Guayabal, Cuba	240p	20.42 N	77.36 W
Guayabal, Ven.	246	8.00 N	67.24 W
Guayabal, Lago ⊜[1]	240m	18.06 N	66.30 W
Guayabero ≃	246	2.36 N	72.47 W
Guayacán	252	29.58 S	71.22 W
Guayaguayare	241r	10.08 N	61.02 W
Guayalejo ≃	234	22.27 N	98.29 W
Guayama	240m	17.59 N	66.07 W
Guayambre ≃	236	14.26 N	86.02 W
Guayameo	234	18.12 N	101.19 W
Guayana → Ciudad Guayana	246	8.22 N	62.40 W
Guayana → Guyana □[1]	246	5.00 N	59.00 W
Guayaneco, Archipiélago II	254	47.45 S	75.10 W
Guayanés, Punta ›	240m	18.04 N	65.48 W
Guayanilla	240m	18.01 N	66.47 W
Guayanilla, Bahía de ⊂	240m	18.00 N	66.46 W
Guayape	236	14.45 N	86.52 W
Guayape ≃	236	14.26 N	85.58 W
Guayapo ≃	246	4.30 N	67.35 W
Guayaquil	246	2.10 S	79.50 W
Guayaquil, Golfo de ⊂	246	3.00 S	80.30 W
Guayaramerín	248	10.48 S	65.23 W
Guayas □[4]	246	2.00 S	80.00 W
Guayas ≃, Col.	246	1.23 N	74.50 W
Guayas ≃, Ec.	246	2.36 S	79.52 W
Guayatayoc, Laguna de ⊜	252	23.25 S	65.51 W
Guaycora	232	28.50 N	109.21 W
Guaycurú, Arroyo ≃	258	34.00 S	56.50 W
Guaymas	232	27.56 N	110.54 W
Guaynabo	240m	18.22 N	66.07 W
Guayquiraró ≃	252	30.10 S	58.34 W
Guayuriba ≃	246	3.55 N	73.05 W
Guazacapán	236	14.04 N	90.25 W
Guazapares	232	27.22 N	108.15 W
Guazárachi	232	26.57 N	106.43 W
Guazhou	106	32.15 N	119.23 E
Guazunamby, Arroyo ≃	288	34.24 S	58.38 W
Guba, Ityo.	144	10.16 N	35.17 E
Guba, R.D.C.	154	10.40 S	26.26 E
Gubacha	86	58.52 N	57.36 E
Gubam	164	8.40 S	141.55 E
Gubany	76	56.37 N	30.40 E
Gubari	80	51.32 N	42.33 E
Gubat	116	12.55 N	124.07 E
Gubavica ʟ	36	43.26 N	16.54 E
Gubbi	122	13.19 N	76.56 E
Gubbio	66	43.21 N	12.35 E
Gubeikou	105	40.42 N	117.09 E
Guben	54	51.57 N	14.43 E
Gubentaoligai	104	42.16 N	122.13 E
Gubin	30	51.56 N	14.45 E
Gubino, Ross.	80	53.19 N	48.44 E
Gubino, Ross.	82	55.42 N	39.07 E
Gubio	146	12.29 N	12.48 E
Gubkin	78	51.18 N	37.32 E
Gubug	115a	7.03 S	110.40 E
Gucheng (Zhengjiakou), Zhg.	98	37.22 N	115.56 E
Gucheng, Zhg.	100	33.59 N	117.29 E
Gucheng, Zhg.	100	25.53 N	116.11 E
Gucheng, Zhg.	100	32.46 N	118.32 E
Gucheng, Zhg.	102	32.18 N	111.35 E
Gucheng, Zhg.	105	40.32 N	116.02 E
Gucheng, Zhg.	105	39.08 N	115.42 E
Gucheng, Zhg.	106	30.29 N	119.46 E
Guchengcang	100	32.34 N	115.20 E
Gucheng Hu ⊜	106	31.17 N	118.54 E
Guchengzi, Zhg.	104	42.33 N	123.45 E
Guchengzi, Zhg.	104	40.58 N	122.36 E
Guchengzi, Zhg.	104	40.40 N	120.31 E
Guchengzi, Zhg.	104	41.44 N	123.35 E
Gučin-Us	102	45.27 N	102.25 E
Gücük	130	38.12 N	37.29 E
Gūdalūr	122	9.41 N	77.16 E
Gúdar, Sierra de ⋏	34	40.27 N	0.42 W
Gudauta	84	43.06 N	40.37 E
Gudbrandsdalen V	26	61.30 N	10.00 E
Gudenå ≃	26	56.29 N	10.13 E
Gudensberg	56	51.10 N	9.22 E
Gudermes	84	43.20 N	46.08 E
Guderup	41	54.59 N	9.53 E
Gudgenby ≃	171b	35.39 S	149.04 E
Gudhjem	26	55.13 N	14.59 E
Gudianzi	100	31.49 N	116.05 E
Gudivāda	122	16.27 N	80.59 E
Gudiyāttam	122	12.57 N	78.52 E
Gudme	41	55.09 N	10.43 E
Gudow	54	53.33 N	10.46 E
Güdül	130	40.13 N	32.15 E
Gūdūr	122	14.08 N	79.51 E
Gudvangen	26	60.52 N	6.50 E
Guebwiller (Gebweiler)	58	47.55 N	7.12 E
Guéckédou	150	8.33 N	10.09 W
Gué-de-Longroi	261	48.30 N	1.43 E
Gué-d'Hossus	50	49.57 N	4.32 E
Guédi, Mont ʌ	146	12.14 N	18.58 E
Guéguen, Lac ⊜	190	48.06 N	77.13 W
Guéherville	261	48.32 N	1.53 E
Güejar ≃	246	2.55 N	73.14 W
Guélendeng	146	10.56 N	15.32 E
Guelma	148	36.28 N	7.26 E
Guelph	212	43.33 N	80.15 W
Guéméné-sur-Scorff	32	48.04 N	3.12 W
Güemes	234	23.56 N	99.00 W
Guemes Island I	224	48.33 N	122.37 W
Guené	150	11.44 N	3.13 E
Guenguel ≃	254	45.41 S	70.20 W
Guer	32	47.54 N	2.07 W
Guéra □[5]	146	11.30 N	18.30 E
Guéra, Massif de ʌ	146	11.55 N	18.12 E
Guérande	32	47.20 N	2.26 W
Guercif	148	34.15 N	3.21 W
Guerdjoumane, Djebel ʌ	34	36.25 N	2.51 E
Güere ≃	246	9.50 N	65.08 W
Guéréda	146	14.31 N	22.05 E
Guéret	32	46.10 N	1.52 E
Guérin Kouka	150	9.41 N	0.37 E
Guerla Mandata Shan ʌ	120	30.26 N	81.20 E
Guermantes	261	48.51 N	2.42 E
Guerne	214	40.46 N	81.54 W
Guernes	261	49.01 N	1.38 E
Guerneville	204	38.30 N	123.00 W
Guernica, Arg.	258	34.56 S	58.25 W
Guernica → Gernika, Esp.	34	43.19 N	2.41 W
Guernsey	200	42.16 N	104.44 W
Guernsey □[6]	214	40.08 N	81.30 W
Guernsey □[2], Europe	22	49.28 N	2.35 W
Guernsey □[2], Europe	43b	49.28 N	2.35 W
Guernsey Reservoir ⊜[1]	198	42.19 N	104.48 W
Guernsey State Park ♠	198	42.20 N	104.50 W
Guerrero, Méx.	196	28.20 N	100.23 W
Guerrero, Méx.	232	28.33 N	107.30 W
Guerrero □[3]	234	17.40 N	100.00 W
Guerrero Negro	232	27.56 N	114.08 W
Guerville	261	48.57 N	1.44 E
Guerzim	148	29.45 N	1.47 W
Guesle ≃	261	48.36 N	1.40 E
Guessou-Sud	150	10.03 N	2.38 E
Guest Peninsula ›[1]	9	76.18 S	148.00 W
Gueydan	194	30.01 N	92.30 W
Guéyo	150	5.49 N	6.36 W
Gufang	100	29.04 N	119.32 E
Guffin Bay ⊂	212	44.01 N	76.09 W
Guga	89	52.43 N	137.35 E
Gugang	100	28.17 N	113.46 E
Guge ʌ	144	6.10 N	37.26 E
Gugera	123	30.58 N	73.19 E
Gugging	264b	48.19 N	16.15 E
Güglia, Pass dal)(	58	46.28 N	9.44 E
Güglingen	56	49.04 N	9.00 E
Guglionesi	66	41.55 N	14.55 E
Gugu ʌ	144	8.12 N	39.58 E
Guguan	102	40.27 N	99.13 E
Guguan I	108	17.19 N	145.51 E
Guhe	100	31.54 N	117.58 E
Gui ≃	102	23.28 N	111.18 E
Guia	248	15.22 S	56.14 W
Guia de Pacobaíba	256	22.43 S	43.10 W
Guia Lopes da Laguna	248	21.26 S	56.07 W
Guiana Basin ✣[1]	18	11.00 N	52.00 W
Guiana Island I	240c	17.07 N	61.44 W
Guibéroua	150	6.14 N	6.10 W
Guibes	156	26.41 S	16.42 E
Güicán	246	6.28 N	72.25 W
Guichen	32	47.58 N	1.48 W
Guichi	100	30.40 N	117.28 E
Guichón	252	32.21 S	57.12 W
Guicun	100	33.37 N	114.11 E
Guidan Roumji	150	13.40 N	6.42 E
Guidari	146	9.17 N	16.40 E
Guide	102	36.03 N	101.28 E
Guide, Mount ʌ[2]	162	22.36 S	136.54 E
Guide Post	44	55.10 N	1.35 W
Guider	146	9.56 N	13.57 E
Guide Rock	198	40.04 N	98.19 W
Guidexiang	107	29.51 N	104.47 E
Guidigri	146	13.40 N	9.51 E
Guidimaka □[4]	150	15.30 N	12.10 W
Guidimouni	150	13.42 N	9.30 E
Guiding	102	26.34 N	107.14 E
Guidizzolo	64	45.19 N	10.35 E
Guidong	100	26.05 N	113.57 E
Guidonia	66	42.01 N	12.45 E
Guidouma	152	1.37 S	10.41 E
Guiers ≃	62	45.37 N	5.37 E
Guiers, Lac de ⊜	150	16.12 N	15.50 W
Guifujie	100	27.20 N	120.01 E
Guiglia	64	44.26 N	10.58 E
Guiglo	150	6.33 N	7.29 W
Guignes-Rabutin	50	48.38 N	2.48 E
Guihuayuan	107	30.37 N	105.25 E
Guihulngan	116	10.07 N	123.16 E
Güija, Lago de ⊜	236	14.17 N	89.31 W
Guijalo	116	13.44 N	123.52 E
Guiji	100	32.51 N	116.33 E
Guijingqiao	106	31.21 N	119.40 E
Guijuelo	34	40.33 N	5.40 W
Guil ≃	62	44.40 N	6.36 E
Guilarte, Monte ʌ	240m	18.09 N	66.46 W
Guilderland	210	42.42 N	73.54 W
Guildford, Austl.	274a	33.51 S	150.59 E
Guildford, Eng., U.K.	42	51.14 N	0.35 W
Guildford □[8]	260	51.16 N	0.32 W
Guildford Cathedral ʋ[1]	260	51.14 N	0.35 W
Guildhall	188	44.33 N	71.33 W
Guildtown	46	56.28 N	3.24 W
Guiler	89	46.11 N	121.45 E
Guilford, Ct., U.S.	207	41.17 N	72.40 W
Guilford, In., U.S.	218	39.10 N	84.55 W
Guilford, Me., U.S.	188	45.10 N	69.23 W
Guilford, N.Y., U.S.	210	42.24 N	75.29 W
Guilford Courthouse National Military Park ♠	192	36.01 N	79.45 W
Guilherand	62	44.56 N	4.52 E
Guilin (Kweilin)	102	25.17 N	110.17 E
Guilinchang	107	30.13 N	105.50 E
Guilinzhen	107	30.15 N	104.53 E
Guillaume-Delisle, Lac ⊜	176	56.15 N	76.17 W
Guillaumes	62	44.05 N	6.51 E
Guillermo E. Hudson	288	34.47 S	58.10 W
Guillestre	62	44.40 N	6.39 E
Guillon	50	47.31 N	4.06 E
Guilsfield	42	52.42 N	3.09 W
Guilvinec	32	47.47 N	4.17 W
Guimarães, Bra.	250	2.08 S	44.36 W
Guimarães, Port.	34	41.27 N	8.18 W
Guimaras Island I	116	10.35 N	122.37 E
Guimaras Strait ʯ	116	10.30 N	122.44 E
Guimba	116	15.40 N	120.46 E
Guimbal	116	10.40 N	122.19 E
Guimeishan	100	24.44 N	114.52 E
Guimu Zhang ʌ	100	24.40 N	116.48 E
Guin	194	33.57 N	87.54 W
Guinan	102	35.24 N	100.57 E
Guinayang	269f	14.42 N	121.08 E
Guinayangan	116	13.54 N	122.27 E
Guinda	226	38.50 N	122.12 W
Guindulman	116	9.46 N	124.29 E
Guindulman Bay ⊂	116	9.44 N	124.29 E
Guiné → Guinea-Bissau □[1]	150	12.00 N	15.00 W
Guinea	208	38.08 N	77.26 W
Guinea (Guinée) □[1], Afr.	134	11.00 N	10.00 W
Guinea (Guinée) □[1], Afr.	150	11.00 N	10.00 W
Guinea, Gulf of ⊂	10	2.00 N	2.30 E
Guinea Basin ✣[1]	10	0.00	5.00 W
Guinea-Bissau (Guiné-Bissau) □[1], Afr.	134	12.00 N	15.00 W
Guinea-Bissau (Guiné-Bissau) □[1], Afr.	150	12.00 N	15.00 W
Guineacor Creek ≃	170	34.21 S	150.05 E
Guinea Ecuatorial → Equatorial Guinea □[1]	152	2.00 N	9.00 E
Guinea Rise ✣[3]	10	8.00 S	0.00
Guiné-Bissau → Guinea-Bissau □[1]	150	12.00 N	15.00 W
Guinecourt, Lac ⊜	186	50.55 N	69.16 W
Guinée → Guinea □[1]	150	11.00 N	10.00 W
Guinée-Bissau → Guinea-Bissau □[1]	150	12.00 N	15.00 W
Guinée équitoriale → Equatorial Guinea □[1]	152	2.00 N	9.00 E
Güines, Cuba	240p	22.50 N	82.02 W
Guînes, Fr.	50	50.52 N	1.52 E
Guingamp	32	48.33 N	3.11 W
Guinguinéo	150	14.16 N	15.57 W
Guinobatan	116	13.11 N	123.36 E
Güinope	236	13.51 N	86.55 W
Guintacan Island I	116	11.19 N	123.54 E
Guintinguintin, Mount ʌ	116	12.25 N	122.24 E
Guintinua Island I	116	14.26 N	122.51 E
Guiones, Punta ›	236	9.54 N	85.41 W
Guiong	116	6.25 N	122.01 E
Guiperreux	261	48.40 N	1.42 E
Guiperreux, Étang de ⊜	261	48.40 N	1.43 E
Guiping	102	23.20 N	110.09 E
Guir, Hammada du ◆[2]	148	30.45 N	3.15 W
Guir, Oued V	148	30.29 N	2.17 W
Güira de Melena	240p	22.48 N	82.30 W
Guiraí ≃	255	22.40 S	53.34 W
Guiratinga	255	16.21 S	53.45 W
Guiren	100	33.42 N	118.12 E
Güiria	246	10.34 N	62.18 W
Guiricema	255	21.00 S	42.43 W
Guisachan Forest ◆[3]	46	57.17 N	4.55 W
Guisanbourg	250	4.25 N	51.56 W
Guisborough	44	54.32 N	1.04 W
Guiscard	50	49.39 N	3.03 E
Guise	50	49.54 N	3.38 E
Guiseley	44	53.53 N	1.42 W
Guisijan	116	11.05 N	122.03 E
Güisisil ʌ	236	12.37 N	86.13 W
Guist Creek ≃	218	38.09 N	85.13 W
Guitiriz	34	43.11 N	7.54 W
Guitou	100	24.58 N	113.25 E
Guitrancourt	261	49.01 N	1.47 E
Guîtres	32	45.03 N	0.11 W
Guitry	150	5.31 N	5.14 W
Guiuan	116	11.02 N	125.43 E
Guixi	100	28.16 N	117.10 E
Guixian	102	23.06 N	109.39 E
Guiyang, Zhg.	100	25.46 N	112.43 E
Guiyang (Kweiyang), Zhg.	102	26.35 N	106.43 E
Güiza ≃	246	1.22 N	78.36 W
Guizhou (Kweichow) □[4]	102	27.00 N	107.00 E
Gujarāt □[3]	118	22.00 N	72.00 E
Gūjar Khān	123	33.16 N	73.19 E
Gujba	146	11.30 N	11.55 E
Gujiabeng	106	30.45 N	120.59 E
Gujiang	100	27.11 N	114.49 E
Gujiatun	104	40.39 N	124.08 E
Gujiatuo	107	29.14 N	106.12 E
Gujiazhai	269b	31.22 N	121.28 E
Gujiazi, Zhg.	104	42.02 N	123.01 E
Gujiazi, Zhg.	104	41.44 N	124.11 E
Gujrānwāla	123	32.09 N	74.11 E
Gujrāt	123	32.34 N	74.05 E
Gukas'an	84	41.03 N	43.52 E
Gukou	100	26.27 N	118.38 E
Gukovo	83	48.03 N	39.56 E
Gul, Tanjong ›	271c	1.17 N	103.39 E
Gul'a	88	54.41 N	121.01 E
Gul'aj-Borisovka	78	46.38 N	40.13 E
Gul'ajevskije Koški, ostrova II	24	68.55 N	55.10 E
Gulang	102	37.36 N	102.58 E
Gulaothi	124	28.36 N	77.47 E
Gulargambone	166	31.20 S	148.28 E
Gulbarga	122	17.20 N	76.50 E
Gulbene	76	57.11 N	26.45 E
Gul'ča	85	40.19 N	73.26 E
Gul'ča ≃	85	40.20 N	73.26 E
Guldasteh	267d	35.36 N	51.16 E
Guldborg	41	54.52 N	11.45 E
Guldborg Sund ʯ	41	54.48 N	11.48 E
Guldsmedshyttan	40	59.42 N	15.06 E
Güldüzü	130	36.52 N	37.07 E
Gülebağdı	130	39.52 N	39.50 E
Guledagudda	122	16.03 N	75.48 E
Guleitou	100	23.47 N	117.36 E
Gülek Boğazı)(	130	37.16 N	34.48 E
Gulf □[5]	164	7.00 S	145.00 E
Gulf Gate Estates	220	27.15 N	82.31 W
Gulf Hammock	192	29.15 N	82.43 W
Gulf Harbors	220	28.14 N	82.45 W
Gulf Islands National Seashore ♠	194	30.14 N	88.42 W
Gulf of Alaska Seamount Province ✣	16	56.00 N	147.00 W
Gulfport, Fl., U.S.	220	27.45 N	82.40 W
Gulfport, Ms., U.S.	194	30.22 N	89.05 W
Gulf Shores	194	30.14 N	87.42 W
Gulf State Park ♠	194	30.16 N	87.40 W
Gulf Stream ≃	212	43.51 N	75.56 W
Gulgong	166	32.22 S	149.32 E
Guli	106	31.38 N	120.50 E
Gulian	89	52.55 N	122.19 E
Gulicun	106	31.52 N	118.41 E
Gul Imām	123	32.16 N	70.32 E
Gulistān, Pāk.	120	30.36 N	66.35 E
Gulistan, Uzb.	85	40.30 N	68.46 E
Guliya Shan ʌ	89	49.48 N	122.25 E
Guljanci	38	43.38 N	24.42 E
Gulkana	180	62.16 N	145.23 W
Gull ≃	212	44.37 N	78.49 W
Gulland Rock II[1]	42	50.34 N	4.59 W
Gullane	46	56.02 N	2.50 W
Gullfoss ʟ	24a	64.24 N	20.08 W
Gullholmen	26	58.11 N	11.24 E
Gullion, Slieve ʌ[2]	48	54.08 N	6.27 W
Gull Island I	281	42.32 N	82.41 W
Gullivan Bay ⊂	220	25.52 N	81.38 W
Gull Lake	184	50.08 N	108.27 W
Gull Lake ⊜, Ab., Can.	182	52.35 N	114.00 W
Gull Lake ⊜, On., Can.	184	51.18 N	91.58 W
Gull Lake ⊜, On., Can.	212	44.51 N	78.47 W
Gull Lake ⊜, Mi., U.S.	216	42.24 N	85.25 W
Gull Lake ⊜, Mn., U.S.	190	46.25 N	94.20 W
Gullrock Lake ⊜	184	50.58 N	93.40 W

≃ River	Fluß	Río	Rivière	Rio	✣ Submarine Features	Untermeerische Objekte	Accidentes Submarinos	Formes de relief sous-marin	Acidentes submarinos
≍ Canal	Kanal	Canal	Canal	Canal	□ Political Unit	Politische Einheit	Unidad Politica	Entité politique	Unidade política
ʟ Waterfall, Rapids	Wasserfall, Stromschnellen	Cascada, Rápidos	Chute d'eau, Rapides	Cascata, Rápidos	ʋ Cultural Institution	Kulturelle Institution	Institución Cultural	Institution culturelle	Instituição cultural
ʯ Strait	Meeresstraße	Estrecho	Détroit	Estreito	⊥ Historical Site	Historische Stätte	Sitio Histórico	Site historique	Sitio histórico
⊂ Bay, Gulf	Bucht, Golf	Bahía, Golfo	Baie, Golfe	Baía, Golfo	♠ Recreational Site	Erholungs- und Ferienort	Sitio de Recreo	Centre de loisirs	Area de Lazer
⊜ Lake, Lakes	See, Seen	Lago, Lagos	Lac, Lacs	Lago, Lagos	⊠ Airport	Flughafen	Aeropuerto	Aéroport	Aeroporto
≡ Swamp	Sumpf	Pantano	Marais	Pântano	■ Military Installation	Militäranlage	Instalación Militar	Installation militaire	Instalação militar
⍓ Ice Features, Glacier	Eis- und Gletscherformen	Accidentes Glaciales	Formes glaciaires	Acidentes glaciares	◆ Miscellaneous	Verschiedenes	Misceláneo	Divers	Diversos
⊤ Other Hydrographic Features	Andere Hydrographische Objekte	Otros Elementos Hidrográficos	Autres données hydrographiques	Outros acidentes hidrográficos					

Gullspång 40 58.59 N 14.06 E
Güllük 130 37.14 N 27.36 E
Güllük Körfezi c 130 37.12 N 27.20 E
Gulmarg 123 34.03 N 74.23 E
Gulnam 140 6.55 N 29.30 E
Gülnar 130 36.20 N 33.25 E
Gulong 89 45.51 N 124.14 E
Gulpen 56 50.48 N 5.54 E
Gülper See ⊜ 54 52.44 N 12.14 E
Gulph Mills 285 40.04 N 75.21 W
Gülpınar 130 39.32 N 26.07 E
Gul'ripš 84 42.57 N 41.06 E
Gul'šad 86 46.39 N 74.24 E
Gülşehir 130 38.45 N 34.38 E
Gulshan 126 23.49 N 90.27 E
Gulsvik 26 60.23 N 9.35 E
Gulu, Ug. 154 2.47 N 32.18 E
Gulu, Zhg. 120 28.06 N 89.17 E
Gulukguluk 115a 7.04 S 113.40 E
Guluogongba 120 34.20 N 84.50 E
Guluy 144 14.44 N 36.43 E
Gulwe 154 6.30 S 36.29 E
Gumaca 116 13.55 N 122.06 E
Gumahang 116 12.35 N 123.16 E
Gumal (Gowmal) ≃ 120 31.56 N 70.22 E
Gumare 156 19.21 S 22.12 E
Gumba, Ang. 152 11.40 S 16.34 E
Gumba, R.D.C. 152 2.57 N 21.26 E
Gumbinnen → Gusev 76 54.36 N 22.12 E
Gumbiro 154 10.16 S 35.39 E
Gumel 150 12.39 N 9.22 E
Gumeracha 168b 34.49 S 138.53 E
Gumiao 100 32.26 N 113.16 E
Gumieńce -•- [8] 54 53.25 N 14.30 E
Gumistskij zapovednik ♦ 84 43.15 N 41.05 E
Gumla 124 23.03 N 84.33 E
Gumma □ [5] 94 36.30 N 139.00 E
Gummersbach 56 51.02 N 7.34 E
Gummi 150 12.09 N 5.09 E
Gumpas Pond ⊜ 283 42.44 N 71.22 W
Gumpas Pond Brook ≃ 283 42.42 N 71.21 W
Gumpoldskirchen 264b 48.03 N 16.17 E
Gum Swamp Creek ≃ 192 32.08 N 82.55 W
Gumti ≃ 126 23.32 N 90.43 E
Gümüşçay 130 40.16 N 27.17 E
Gümüşhacıköy 130 40.53 N 35.14 E
Gümüşhane 130 40.27 N 39.29 E
Gümüşhane □ [4] 130 40.15 N 39.45 E
Gümüşkent 130 38.50 N 34.32 E
Gümüşköy -•- [8] 267b 41.14 N 28.58 E
Gümüşova 130 40.51 N 30.57 E
Gümüşsü 130 38.14 N 30.01 E
Gun ≃ 216 42.28 N 85.40 W
Guna, India 124 24.39 N 77.19 E
Guna, Ityo. 144 8.19 N 39.51 E
Guna ∧ 144 11.42 N 38.12 E
Gunbar 166 34.01 S 145.25 E
Gun Barrel City 222 32.20 N 96.10 W
Gun Creek ≃ 284a 43.03 N 78.55 W
Gunda 88 52.47 N 111.44 E
Gundagai 166 35.04 S 148.07 E
Gundelfingen 56 48.33 N 10.22 E
Gundelsheim 56 49.17 N 9.09 E
Gundik 115a 7.12 S 110.54 E
Gundji 152 2.05 N 21.27 E
Gundlakamma ≃ 122 15.32 N 80.14 E
Gundlupet 122 11.48 N 76.41 E
Gündoğdu 130 40.15 N 27.07 E
Gündoğmuş 130 36.48 N 32.01 E
Guneh Ghar ∧ 123 35.19 N 71.47 E
Güney 130 38.09 N 29.05 E
Gungartan ∧ 171b 36.18 S 148.24 E
Gungi 152 6.21 S 19.15 E
Gungo 152 11.48 S 14.08 E
Güngören -•- [8] 267b 41.01 N 28.53 E
Gungu 152 5.44 S 19.19 E
Gunib 84 42.25 N 46.57 E
Gunisao ≃ 184 53.54 N 97.58 W
Gunisao Lake ⊜ 184 53.33 N 96.15 W
Gunjrauliya 124 26.35 N 84.34 E
Gun Lake ⊜ 216 42.37 N 85.32 W
Gunma 94 36.24 N 139.00 E
Gunnar 176 59.23 N 108.53 W
Günnarijn 102 45.38 N 102.01 E
Gunnarn 26 65.00 N 17.40 E
Gunnbjørn Fjeld ∧ 16 68.55 N 29.53 W
Gunnebo 26 57.43 N 16.32 E
Gunnedah 166 30.59 S 150.15 E
Gunning Island I 276 40.22 N 73.59 W
Gunnislake 42 50.31 N 4.12 W
Gunnison, Co., U.S. 200 38.32 N 106.55 W
Gunnison, Ut,. U.S. 200 39.09 N 111.49 W
Gunnison ≃ 200 39.03 N 108.35 W
Gunnison, Lake Fork ≃ 200 38.28 N 107.19 W
Gunnison, North Fork ≃ 200 38.47 N 107.50 W
Gunn Peak ∧ 224 47.49 N 121.27 W
Gunong Mulu National Park ♦ 112 4.10 N 114.55 E
Gunpowder Creek ≃, Austl. 166 19.14 S 139.58 E
Gunpowder Creek ≃, Ky., U.S. 218 38.53 N 84.47 W
Gunpowder Falls ≃ 208 39.24 N 76.22 W
Gunpowder Falls State Park ♦ 208 39.37 N 76.40 W
Gunpowder River c 208 39.22 N 76.22 W
Gunsan → Kunsan 98 35.58 N 126.41 E
Gunskirchen 60 48.08 N 13.57 E
Gunston Cove c 208 38.40 N 77.09 W
Guntakal 122 15.10 N 77.23 E
Güntersberge 54 51.38 N 10.59 E
Guntersblum 56 49.47 N 8.21 E
Guntersdorf 61 48.39 N 16.03 E
Guntersville 194 34.21 N 86.17 W
Guntersville Dam -•- [6] 194 34.13 N 86.23 W
Guntersville Lake ⊜ [1] 194 34.45 N 86.03 W
Guntingsaga 114 2.33 N 99.39 E
Guntramsdorf 61 48.03 N 16.19 E
Guntung 114 1.38 N 101.34 E
Guntūr 122 16.18 N 80.27 E
Gunungkencana 115a 6.34 S 106.04 E
Gunungmegang 112 3.27 S 103.52 E
Gunungsahilan 112 0.06 N 101.18 E
Gunungsitoli 114 1.17 N 97.37 E
Gunungtua 114 1.30 N 99.37 E
Gunupur 122 19.05 N 83.49 E
Gunyidi 162 30.08 S 116.04 E
Günyüzü 130 39.24 N 31.50 E
Günz ≃ 58 48.27 N 10.16 E
Gunza ≃ 152 11.10 S 13.50 E
Günzburg 58 48.27 N 10.16 E
Gunzenhausen 56 49.07 N 10.45 E
Gunzigou 104 41.31 N 123.58 E
Guo ≃ 100 32.57 N 117.14 E
Guobei 107 29.33 N 105.08 E
Guodian 106 30.27 N 120.33 E
Guoji 100 32.59 N 113.06 E
Guojiadian 104 41.51 N 121.30 E
Guojiajiang 106 32.17 N 120.50 E
Guojiatun, Zhg. 98 41.31 N 117.02 E
Guojiatun, Zhg. 104 42.00 N 122.51 E
Guojiatun, Zhg. 104 40.52 N 122.04 E
Guojiawopeng 104 42.03 N 122.46 E
Guojiayao 105 40.37 N 115.39 E
Guojiayuan 106 32.10 N 120.35 E
Guojiga 86 43.47 N 80.48 E
Guoleizhuang 98 40.44 N 114.36 E
Guolutan 100 32.04 N 115.40 E
Guosu 98 38.24 N 114.00 E
Guoyang 100 33.32 N 116.12 E
Guoyangzhen 102 38.54 N 112.50 E
Guozhuang 98 35.25 N 117.10 E
Guozhuangmiao 106 31.49 N 119.01 E
Gupei 98 34.09 N 117.54 E
Gupis 123 36.14 N 73.26 E
Gura 80 57.18 N 51.25 E
Gura, Wādī V 140 17.28 N 35.10 E
Gurabo 240m 18.16 N 65.58 W
Guraferda 144 6.51 N 35.04 E
Gura Galbehei 38 46.43 N 28.42 E
Gurage ∧ 144 8.24 N 38.24 E
Gurahonț 38 46.16 N 22.21 E
Gura Humorului 38 47.33 N 25.54 E
Gurais 123 34.38 N 74.50 E
Guran 88 54.46 N 100.38 E
Gurara ≃ 150 8.12 N 6.41 E
Gurban Anggir 102 37.45 N 97.30 E
Gurban Obo 102 43.14 N 112.28 E
Gurdāspur 123 32.02 N 75.31 E
Gurdon 194 33.55 N 93.09 W
Gurdžaani 84 41.43 N 45.48 E
Güre 130 38.39 N 29.10 E
Gurejev 80 47.21 N 43.16 E
Gürgan 84 40.23 N 50.19 E
Gurgaon 124 28.28 N 77.02 E
Gurgei, Jabal ∧ 140 13.50 N 24.19 E
Gurghiului, Munții ⋏ 38 46.41 N 25.12 E
Gurgó ∧ [2] 61 46.31 N 16.50 E
Gurgueia ≃ 250 6.50 S 43.24 W
Gurgur 144 7.48 N 41.32 E
Gurha 120 25.11 N 71.40 E
Guri 144 7.27 N 40.36 E
Guri, Embalse de ⊜ [1] 246 7.30 N 62.50 W
Gurig National Park ♦ 164 11.25 S 132.15 E
Gurjevo 82 54.42 N 36.28 E
Gurjevsk, Ross. 76 54.47 N 20.38 E
Gurjevsk, Ross. 86 54.17 N 85.56 E
Gurk 61 46.52 N 14.18 E
Gurk ≃ 61 46.36 N 14.31 E
Gurk ⊍ [1] 61 46.52 N 14.15 E
Gurktaler Alpen ⋏ 64 46.55 N 14.00 E
Gūr Kūh ∧ 128 26.06 N 58.28 E
Gurla Mandhata → Guerla Mandata Shan ∧ 120 30.26 N 81.20 E
Gurlevo 76 59.28 N 28.54 E
Gurnee 216 42.22 N 87.54 W
Gurnet Point › 283 42.01 N 70.34 W
Gürpınar 128 38.18 N 43.25 E
Gurror 174q 9.27 N 138.04 E
Gursarai 124 25.37 N 79.11 E
Gurskoje 89 50.21 N 138.12 E
Gurskøy I 26 62.15 N 5.41 E
Gürsu 130 40.13 N 29.12 E
Gurué 154 15.25 S 36.58 E
Guru Har Sahāi 123 30.43 N 74.25 E
Gurumeti ≃ 154 2.05 S 33.57 E
Gurun, Malay. 114 5.49 N 100.29 E
Gürün, Tür. 130 38.43 N 37.17 E
Gurupá 250 1.25 S 51.39 W
Gurupi 250 11.43 S 49.04 W
Gurupi ≃ 250 1.13 S 46.06 W
Guru Sikhar ∧ 120 24.39 N 72.46 E
Gurvanbulag 88 47.38 N 103.31 E
Gurvansajchan 102 45.32 N 107.00 E
Gurvan Sajchan uul ⋏ 102 43.50 N 103.30 E
Gurvantes 102 43.26 N 101.36 E
Gus' ≃ 80 55.00 N 41.11 E
Gusar 85 39.28 N 67.50 E
Gušari 85 38.55 N 68.51 E
Gusau 150 12.12 N 6.40 E
Gus'-Chrustal'nyj 80 55.37 N 40.40 E
Guselka 80 50.27 N 45.09 E
Güsen 54 52.21 N 11.59 E
Gusen ≃ 61 48.15 N 14.30 E
Gusev, Ross. 76 54.36 N 22.12 E
Gusev, Ross. 78 48.27 N 40.32 E
Gusevo 76 56.06 N 33.21 E
Gusevskij 80 55.40 N 40.34 E
Gushan, Zhg. 98 39.53 N 123.36 E
Gushan, Zhg. 98 36.30 N 116.53 E
Gushan, Zhg. 106 31.44 N 120.33 E
Gu Shan ∧, Zhg. 100 26.05 N 119.22 E
Gu Shan ∧, Zhg. 104 41.18 N 120.35 E
Gushanbeizifu 104 42.10 N 120.30 E
Gushankou 105 39.38 N 115.49 E
Gushantun 89 48.18 N 123.47 E
Gushanzi, Zhg. 98 40.22 N 120.03 E
Gushanzi, Zhg. 104 41.03 N 123.03 E
Gushi, Zhg. 100 28.34 N 119.24 E
Gushi, Zhg. 100 32.12 N 115.41 E
Gushiago 150 9.55 N 0.12 W
Gushikami 174m 26.07 N 127.45 E
Gushikawa 174m 26.21 N 127.52 E
Gushu, Zhg. 104 42.36 N 123.26 E
Gushu, Zhg. 105 39.55 N 117.35 E
Gushuji 98 34.15 N 115.48 E
Gusi 112 6.07 N 117.08 E
Gusino 76 54.44 N 31.22 E
Gusinoje, ozero ⊜ 88 51.12 N 106.24 E
Gusinoje Ozero 88 51.09 N 106.10 E
Gusinoozersk 88 51.17 N 106.30 E
Guskef 85 39.02 N 69.20 E
Guskhara 126 23.30 N 87.45 E
Gus'-Khrustal'nyy → Gus'-Chrustal'nyj 80 55.37 N 40.40 E
Guskube 175d 24.45 N 125.26 E
Gusong 102 28.18 N 105.14 E
Gusow 54 52.34 N 14.21 E
Guspini 71 39.32 N 8.37 E
Gussago 64 45.35 N 10.09 E
Gusselby 40 59.39 N 15.14 E
Güssing 61 47.04 N 16.20 E
Gussola 64 45.00 N 10.20 E
Gusswerk 61 47.45 N 15.18 E
Gustav Holm, Kap › 176 67.00 N 34.00 W
Gustavo A. Madero -•- [8] 286a 19.29 N 99.07 W
Gustavo Díaz Ordaz 234 17.44 N 94.23 W
Gustavsberg 40 59.19 N 18.23 E
Gustavus 180 58.25 N 135.44 W
Güsten 54 51.49 N 11.35 E
Gustia 272b 22.59 N 88.26 E
Gustine, Ca., U.S. 226 37.15 N 120.59 W
Gustine, Tx., U.S. 196 31.51 N 98.24 W
Gustorf 56 51.04 N 6.34 E
Güstrow 54 53.48 N 12.10 E
Gusum 26 58.16 N 16.29 E
Gus'-Železnyj 80 55.03 N 41.10 E
Gutach 58 48.15 N 8.13 E
Gutaj 88 49.59 N 108.12 E
Gutanggou 104 42.02 N 124.10 E
Gutara ≃ 88 54.50 N 97.23 E
Gutarskij chrebet ⋏ 88 54.30 N 97.40 E
Gutau 61 48.25 N 14.37 E
Gutcher 46a 60.40 N 1.00 W
Gutenfels, Burg ⊥ 56 50.07 N 7.46 E
Guten Hoffnung, Kap der → Good Hope, Cape of › 158 34.24 S 18.30 E
Güterfelde 264a 52.22 N 13.12 E
Gütersloh 52 51.54 N 8.23 E
Guthrie, In., U.S. 218 38.59 N 86.31 W
Guthrie, Ky., U.S. 194 36.38 N 87.09 W
Guthrie, Ok., U.S. 196 35.52 N 97.25 W
Guthrie, Tx., U.S. 196 33.37 N 100.19 W
Guthrie Center 198 41.40 N 94.30 W
Guthrie Lake ⊜ 184 55.17 N 100.38 W
Gutian, Zhg. 100 26.36 N 118.46 E
Gutian, Zhg. 100 25.15 N 116.46 E
Gutian, Zhg. 100 25.43 N 116.57 E
Gutian ≃ 100 26.22 N 118.42 E
Gutierrez 248 19.25 S 63.34 W
Gutiérrez Zamora 234 20.27 N 97.05 W
Gutland -•- [1] 56 49.40 N 6.10 E
Gutob Bay c 116 12.09 N 119.54 E
Guton, gora ∧ 84 41.51 N 46.45 E
Gutorfölde 61 46.39 N 16.44 E
Guttannen 58 46.39 N 8.18 E
Guttau 54 51.15 N 14.34 E
Guttenberg, Ia., U.S. 190 42.47 N 91.05 W
Guttenberg, N.J., U.S. 276 40.47 N 74.00 W
Gutu 154 19.38 S 31.10 E
Gutujevskij, ostrov I 265a 59.54 N 30.14 E
Gutulia Nasjonalpark ♦ 26 62.02 N 12.12 E
Gützkow 54 53.56 N 13.24 E
Güvem 130 40.36 N 32.40 E
Guwāhāti 120 26.10 N 91.45 E
Guxhagen 56 51.12 N 9.28 E
Guxi 107 30.18 N 105.52 E
Guxian, Zhg. 98 37.35 N 121.09 E
Guxian, Zhg. 100 32.26 N 113.37 E
Guxian, Zhg. 100 27.09 N 115.31 E
Guxiandu 100 29.06 N 116.50 E
Guxiansi 100 32.01 N 116.20 E
Guxiong 106 31.55 N 118.38 E
Guy 222 29.21 N 95.47 W
Guyana □ [1], S.A. 242 5.00 N 59.00 W
Guyana □ [1], S.A. 246 5.00 N 59.00 W
Guyancourt 261 48.46 N 2.04 E
Guyancourt, Aéroport de ⊠ 261 48.45 N 2.05 E
Guyandotte ≃ 188 38.26 N 82.23 W
Guyane → Guyana □ [1] 246 5.00 N 59.00 W
Guyane française → French Guiana □ [2] 250 4.00 N 53.00 W
Guyang, Zhg. 98 34.58 N 114.58 E
Guyang, Zhg. 102 41.03 N 110.03 E
Guye 105 39.44 N 118.25 E
Guy Fawkes River National Park ♦ 166 30.02 S 152.18 E
Guyi, Zhg. 100 25.38 N 118.47 E
Guyi, Zhg. 107 30.22 N 103.33 E
Guyin 102 23.58 N 105.47 E
Guymon 196 36.40 N 101.28 W
Guyonne, Ruisseau la ≃ 261 48.49 N 1.52 E
Guyot, Mount ∧ 192 35.42 N 83.15 W
Guyra 166 30.14 S 151.40 E
Guysborough 186 45.23 N 61.30 W
Guys Mills 214 41.38 N 79.59 W
Guyton 192 32.20 N 81.23 W
Guyuan (Pingdingbu), Zhg. 98 41.40 N 115.41 E
Guyuan, Zhg. 102 36.01 N 106.17 E
Guzar 72 38.36 N 66.15 E
Güzel ≃ 84 39.44 N 43.01 E
Güzelbahçe 130 38.21 N 26.54 E
Güzelsu 130 36.54 N 31.53 E
Güzelyurt, Kıbrıs 130 35.12 N 32.59 E
Güzelyurt, Tür. 130 38.17 N 34.23 E
Güzelyurt Körfezi c 130 35.10 N 32.50 E
Guzhang 102 28.31 N 109.57 E
Guzhen, Zhg. 100 22.37 N 113.11 E
Guzhen, Zhg. 100 33.19 N 117.21 E
Guzhu 100 26.58 N 116.16 E
Guzmán, Méx. 232 31.13 N 107.27 W
Guzmán → Ciudad Guzmán, Méx. 234 19.41 N 103.29 W
Guzmán, Laguna de ⊜ 200 31.20 N 107.30 W
Gvardejsk 76 54.39 N 21.05 E
Gvazda 78 50.44 N 40.30 E
Gwa 110 17.36 N 94.35 E
Gwabegar 166 30.36 S 148.58 E
Gwadabawa 150 13.20 N 5.15 E
Gwādar 128 25.07 N 62.19 E
Gwagwada 150 10.14 N 7.14 E
Gwai 154 19.15 S 27.42 E
Gwai ≃ 154 17.59 S 26.52 E
Gwalangu 152 2.19 N 18.11 E
Gwalchmai 44 53.15 N 4.25 W
Gwāl Haidarzai 120 30.44 N 68.48 E
Gwalia 162 28.55 S 121.20 E
Gwalior 124 26.13 N 78.10 E
Gwambygine 168a 31.59 S 116.48 E
Gwanda 154 20.57 S 29.01 E
Gwandu 150 12.30 N 4.41 E
Gwane 154 4.43 N 25.50 E
Gwangjang Bridge -•- [5] 271b 37.33 N 127.05 E
Gwangju → Kwangju 98 35.09 N 126.54 E
Gwardafuy, Gees › 144 11.49 N 51.15 E
Gwarzo 150 11.56 N 7.56 E
Gwasero 150 9.29 N 3.30 E
Gwash ≃ 42 52.39 N 0.27 W
Gwātar Bay c 128 25.04 N 61.36 E
Gwatt 58 46.43 N 7.38 E
Gwaun ≃ 42 52.00 N 4.58 W
Gwda ≃ 30 53.04 N 16.44 E
Gweebarra ≃ 48 54.50 N 8.20 W
Gweebarra Bay c 48 54.52 N 8.20 W
Gweedore 48 55.03 N 8.14 W
Gweesalia 48 54.07 N 9.54 W
Gwelo ≃ 154 18.45 S 28.36 E
Gwembe 154 16.30 S 27.35 E
Gwendraeth Fâch ≃ 42 51.44 N 4.18 W
Gwendraeth Fawr ≃ 42 51.43 N 4.18 W
Gwent □ [6] 42 51.43 N 2.57 W
Gweru 154 19.27 S 29.49 E
Gweta 156 20.10 S 25.18 E
Gwinhurst 285 39.47 N 75.29 W
Gwinn 190 46.16 N 87.26 W
Gwinner 198 46.13 N 97.39 W
Gwobu 154 2.37 N 26.13 E
Gwongorella National Park ♦ 171a 28.10 S 153.17 E
Gwydir ≃ 166 29.27 S 149.48 E
Gwynedd 285 40.12 N 75.15 W
Gwynedd □ [6] 28 53.00 N 4.00 W
Gwynedd Square 285 40.13 N 75.18 W
Gwynedd Valley 285 40.11 N 75.15 W
Gwynn 208 37.30 N 76.17 W
Gwynneville 218 39.39 N 85.38 W
Gwynn Island I 208 37.30 N 76.17 W
Gwynns Falls ≃ 284b 39.16 N 76.37 W
Gwynns Falls Park ♦ 284b 39.18 N 76.41 W
Gy 58 47.24 N 5.49 E
Gyál 264c 47.23 N 19.14 E
Gya La)(124 28.44 N 84.40 E
Gyáli-patak ≃ 264c 47.24 N 19.07 E
Gyangtse → Gyangzê 120 28.57 N 89.35 E
Gyangzê 120 28.57 N 89.35 E
Gyaring Co ⊜ 120 31.10 N 88.15 E
Gyaring Hu ⊜ 102 34.53 N 97.58 E
Gybdan 80 56.33 N 51.39 E
Gyda 74 70.52 N 78.30 E
Gydanskaja guba c 74 71.20 N 76.30 E
Gydanskij poluostrov › [1] 74 70.50 N 79.00 E
Gyebu 164 3.03 S 133.51 E
Gyemo Chen ∧ 124 27.20 N 88.52 E
Gyeongbog Palace ⊍ 271b 37.36 N 126.57 E
Gyeongju → Kyŏngju 98 35.51 N 129.14 E
Gyhum 52 53.13 N 9.19 E
Gyirong, Zhg. 120 28.29 N 85.20 E
Gyirong, Zhg. 120 28.57 N 85.15 E
Gyldenløves Fjord c [2] 176 64.30 N 41.30 W
Gyldenløveshøj ∧ [2] 41 55.33 N 11.52 E
Gylling 41 55.53 N 10.11 E
Gymea Bay 274a 34.02 S 151.05 E
Gym Peak ∧ 200 32.04 N 107.35 W
Gympie 166 26.11 S 152.40 E
Gyobingauk 110 18.13 N 95.39 E
Gyōda 94 36.08 N 139.28 E
Gyoma 30 46.56 N 20.50 E
Gyöngyös 30 47.47 N 19.56 E
Gyöngyös ≃ 61 47.14 N 16.55 E
Győr 30 47.42 N 17.38 E
Győr-Moson-Sopron □ [6] 30 47.35 N 17.15 E
Gypsey Race ≃ 44 54.05 N 0.12 W
Gypsum, Co., U.S. 200 39.38 N 106.57 W
Gypsum, Ks., U.S. 198 38.42 N 97.25 W
Gypsum, Oh., U.S. 214 41.29 N 82.52 W
Gypsum Creek ≃, U.S. 200 37.09 N 109.52 W
Gypsum Creek ≃, Ks., U.S. 198 38.51 N 97.25 W
Gypsum Hills ⋏ [2] 196 36.25 N 99.20 W
Gypsum Point › 176 61.53 N 114.35 W
Gypsumville 184 51.45 N 98.35 W
Gysinge 40 60.17 N 16.53 E
Gyttorp 40 59.31 N 14.58 E
Gyula 30 46.39 N 21.17 E
Gyulafehérvár → Alba Iulia 38 46.04 N 23.35 E
Gžat' ≃ 76 55.56 N 34.33 E
Gžatsk 86 55.42 N 78.11 E
Gžel' 82 55.36 N 38.24 E
Gzhatsk → Gagarin 76 55.33 N 35.00 E

H

Haag → 's-Gravenhage, Ned. 52 52.06 N 4.18 E
Haag, Öst. 61 48.07 N 14.34 E
Haag am Hausruck 60 48.11 N 13.38 E
Haagen 58 47.38 N 7.40 E
Haag in Oberbayern 60 48.10 N 12.11 E
Haaksbergen 52 52.09 N 6.44 E
Haalenberg 156 26.52 S 15.30 E
Haaltert 50 50.54 N 4.00 E
Haamstede 52 51.43 N 3.45 E
Haan 56 51.11 N 7.00 E
Haapajärvi 26 63.45 N 25.20 E
Haapajärvi ⊜ 26 63.33 N 27.00 E
Haapamäki 26 62.15 N 24.28 E
Haapavesi 26 64.08 N 25.22 E
Haapiti 174s 17.34 S 149.52 W
Haapsalu 76 58.56 N 23.33 E
Haar 60 48.06 N 11.44 E
Haar -•- [8] 263 51.26 N 7.13 E
Ha'Arava (Wādī al-'Arabah) V, Asia 132 30.10 N 35.10 E
Ha'Arava (Wādī al-Jayb) V, Asia 132 30.58 N 35.24 E
Haarbach 60 48.30 N 13.09 E
Haardt ⋏ 56 49.15 N 8.00 E
Haaren, Dtsch. 52 51.34 N 8.44 E
Haaren, Ned. 52 51.36 N 5.12 E
Haarlem, Ned. 52 52.23 N 4.38 E
Haarlem, S. Afr. 158 33.44 S 23.20 E
Haarlemmermeer -•- [1] 52 52.15 N 4.38 E
Haarstrang ∧ 52 51.35 N 8.10 E
Haarzopf -•- [8] 263 51.25 N 6.58 E
Haast 172 43.53 S 169.03 E
Haast ≃ 172 43.50 S 169.02 E
Haast Bluff 162 23.30 S 131.50 E
Haast Pass)(172 44.06 S 169.21 E
Haasts Bluff Reserve -•- [4] 162 23.30 S 130.30 E
Haatinao, Pointe › 174x 9.47 S 138.51 W
Haava, Canal ʊ 174x 9.53 S 139.04 W
Hab ≃ 120 24.53 N 66.41 E
Habahe 86 47.53 N 86.12 E
Habana, Bahía de la c 286b 23.08 N 82.20 W
Habaqi, Zhg. 104 42.38 N 122.02 E
Habaqi, Zhg. 104 42.36 N 122.52 E
Habaqila 102 42.01 N 106.02 E
Habartov 54 50.08 N 12.33 E
Ḩabashīyah, Jabal ⋏ 144 16.40 N 49.40 E
Habaswein 154 1.01 N 39.29 E
Ḩabawnah, Wādī V 144 17.51 N 44.59 E
Habay-la-Neuve 56 49.44 N 5.39 E
Ḩabbān 144 14.21 N 47.05 E
Ḩabbānīyah, Hawr al- ⊜ 128 33.17 N 43.29 E
Habbūsh 132 33.24 N 35.29 E
Hab Chauki 120 25.01 N 66.53 E
Habère-Poche 58 46.15 N 6.29 E
Haberfield 274a 33.53 S 151.08 E
Haberli 130 37.19 N 41.38 E
Habermehl Peak ∧ 9 71.49 S 6.38 E
Ḩabīb, Wādī V 142 27.20 N 31.30 E
Habiganj 120 24.23 N 91.25 E
Habikino 96 34.33 N 135.37 E
Habīlah 140 12.41 N 22.33 E
Habinghorst 263 51.35 N 7.18 E
Habo 26 57.55 N 14.04 E
Habob, Wādī V 140 18.07 N 35.01 E
Habomai-shotō → Malaja Kuril'skaja Gr'ada II 92a 43.30 N 146.10 E
Haboro 92a 44.22 N 141.42 E
Hābra 126 22.50 N 88.38 E
Habsburg ⊥ 58 47.28 N 8.13 E
Habsheim 58 47.44 N 7.25 E
Habu 270 34.27 N 135.24 E
Habur (Nahr al-Khābūr) ≃ 130 35.08 N 40.26 E
Habutaki 270 34.25 N 135.26 E
Hache, Lac la ⊜ 182 51.50 N 121.30 W
Hachen 56 51.22 N 7.59 E
Hachenburg 56 50.39 N 7.50 E
Hachi 120 27.46 N 94.01 E
Hachijō 270 34.37 N 135.48 E
Hachijō-jima I 90 33.05 N 139.48 E
Hachiman → Ōmi-hachiman, Nihon 94 35.08 N 136.06 E
Hachiman, Nihon 94 35.45 N 136.57 E
Hachiman-misaki › 94 35.08 N 140.19 E
Hachinohe 92 40.30 N 141.29 E
Hachiōji 94 35.39 N 139.20 E
Hachmühlen 52 52.10 N 9.28 E
Hacıbektaş 130 38.57 N 34.35 E
Hacienda Heights 228 34.00 N 117.57 W
Hacienda Miravalles 236 10.41 N 85.14 W
Hacienda Murciélago 236 10.55 N 85.44 W
Hacıhamza 130 41.05 N 34.28 E
Hacıkänd 84 40.31 N 46.21 E
Hacılar 130 38.39 N 35.27 E
Hacı Zeynalabdin 84 40.37 N 49.34 E
Hack, Mount ∧ 166 30.46 S 138.48 E
Hackås 26 62.55 N 14.31 E
Hackberry, Az., U.S. 200 35.22 N 113.43 W
Hackberry, La., U.S. 194 29.59 N 93.20 W
Hackberry Creek ≃, Ks., U.S. 198 38.48 N 100.03 W
Hackberry Creek ≃, Tx., U.S. 222 31.53 N 97.12 W
Hackensack 210 40.53 N 74.02 W
Hackensack ≃ 276 40.43 N 74.06 W
Hacketstown 48 52.52 N 6.33 W
Hackett, Ar., U.S. 194 35.11 N 94.24 W
Hackett, Pa., U.S. 279b 40.15 N 80.01 W
Hacketts 260 51.45 N 0.05 W
Hackettstown 210 40.52 N 74.48 W
Hacking ≃ 274a 34.04 S 151.06 E
Hacking, Port c 274a 34.05 S 151.09 E
Hackleburg 194 34.16 N 87.49 W
Hackney -•- [8] 260 51.33 N 0.03 W
Hack Point 208 39.27 N 75.52 W
Håckren ⊜ 26 63.11 N 13.35 E
Haco 152 10.12 S 15.44 E
Hacreş Dağları ⋏ 130 38.38 N 41.37 E
Hadāli 123 32.18 N 72.12 E
Hadalīya 140 16.10 N 36.06 E
Hadamar 56 50.27 N 8.02 E
Ḩaḑan, Ḩarrat ⊻ [9] 144 21.30 N 41.23 E
Hadano 94 35.22 N 139.14 E
Ḩadāribah, Ra's al- › 140 22.04 N 36.54 E
HaDarom □ [5] 132 30.40 N 34.50 E
Hadat 89 49.40 N 119.40 E
Hadayingzi 104 42.22 N 121.40 E
Ḩadd, Ra's al- › 118 22.32 N 59.48 E
Haddad, Ouadi V 146 14.40 N 18.46 E
Ḩaddādīn, Qārat al- ∧ [2] 142 30.04 N 30.58 E

ENGLISH

Name | Page | Lat.°′ | Long.°′

Haddam, Ct., U.S. 207 41.28 N 72.30 W
Haddam, Ks., U.S. 198 39.51 N 97.18 W
Haddenham, Eng., U.K. 42 51.46 N 0.56 W
Haddenham, Eng., U.K. 42 52.22 N 0.09 E
Haddington 46 55.58 N 2.47 W
Haddock 192 33.01 N 83.25 W
Haddon Downs 166 26.21 S 140.50 E
Haddonfield 208 39.53 N 75.02 W
Haddon Heights 208 39.52 N 75.03 W
Haddon Hills 285 39.54 N 75.03 W
Hadejia 150 12.30 N 9.59 E
Hadejia ≃ 134 12.50 N 10.51 E
Hadeln, Land -•- [1] 52 53.45 N 8.45 E
Haden 171a 27.14 S 151.53 E
Ḩadera 132 32.26 N 34.55 E
Ḩadera ≃ 132 32.27 N 34.53 E
Hadersdorf -•- [8] 264b 48.13 N 16.14 E
Hadersfeld 264b 48.20 N 16.15 E
Haderslev 41 55.15 N 9.30 E
Haderslev Fjord c 41 55.17 N 9.40 E
Hadfield, Austl. 274b 37.42 S 144.56 E
Hadfield, Eng., U.K. 262 53.28 N 1.58 W
Hadībū 118 12.38 N 54.02 E
Ḩadīd, Jabal ∧ [2] 142 30.20 N 30.06 E
Ḩadīd, Jabal al- ∧ [2] 142 28.47 N 31.04 E
Hadım 130 36.59 N 32.28 E
Hadjout 34 36.31 N 2.25 E
Hadleigh, Eng., U.K. 42 52.03 N 0.58 E
Hadleigh, Eng., U.K. 260 51.33 N 0.37 E
Hadleigh Castle ⊥ 260 51.33 N 0.36 E
Hadley, Eng., U.K. 42 52.42 N 2.29 W
Hadley, Ma., U.S. 207 42.20 N 72.35 W
Hadley, Mi., U.S. 216 42.57 N 83.24 W
Hadley, N.Y., U.S. 210 43.19 N 73.50 W
Hadley, Pa., U.S. 214 41.25 N 80.14 W
Hadley Bay c 176 72.30 N 107.45 W
Hadley Creek ≃ 219 39.37 N 91.12 W
Hadlock 224 48.01 N 122.45 W
Hadlow 42 51.14 N 0.20 E
Hadlyme 207 41.25 N 72.24 W
Hadmersleben 54 51.59 N 11.18 E
Hadong, Taehan 98 35.05 N 127.44 E
Ha Dong, Viet 110 20.58 N 105.46 E
Ḩaḑramawt -•- [1] 144 15.00 N 50.00 E
Hadrian's Wall ⊥ 44 54.59 N 2.26 W
Hadrut 84 39.32 N 47.02 E
Hadsten 41 56.20 N 10.03 E
Hadsund 26 56.43 N 10.07 E
Hadyach 78 50.22 N 34.00 E
Hadyai → Hat Yai 110 7.01 N 100.28 E
Hadzilavičy 76 53.05 N 30.16 E
Haeju 98 38.02 N 125.42 E
Haemgon-ni -•- [8] 271b 37.35 N 126.49 E
Haena 229b 22.14 N 159.34 W
Haenam 98 34.34 N 126.35 E
Haena Point › 229b 22.14 N 159.34 W
Haenertsburg 156 24.00 S 29.50 E
Haengyŏng-ni 98 42.33 N 129.56 E
Haernao 104 41.46 N 120.28 E
Hafeïra, Oued el V 148 25.18 N 10.48 W
Hafelekarspitze ∧ 64 47.19 N 11.23 E
Haffen-Mehr 52 51.44 N 6.28 E
Hafford 184 52.43 N 107.21 W
Haffouz 36 35.38 N 9.41 E
Hafik 130 39.52 N 37.24 E
Ḩafīra, Qā' al- ≚ 132 31.06 N 36.14 E
Ḩafīrat al-'Ayda 128 26.26 N 39.10 E
Ḩafīt, Jabal ∧ 128 24.03 N 55.46 E
Ḩāfiẓ, Bi'r ⊤ [4] 142 30.51 N 29.40 E
Ḩāfizābād 123 32.04 N 73.41 E
Hāflong 120 25.11 N 93.02 E
Hafnarfjörður 24a 64.03 N 21.56 W
Haft Gel 128 31.27 N 49.27 E
Haga, Nihon 94 36.32 N 140.04 E
Haga, Nihon 96 35.09 N 134.33 E
Hagachi-zaki › 94 34.41 N 138.45 E
HaGadol, HaMakhtésh ⊻ [7] 132 30.56 N 34.59 E
Haga-Haga 158 32.46 S 28.14 E
Hagal 98 40.23 N 127.15 E
HaGalil (Galilee) □ [9] 132 32.54 N 35.20 E
Hagaman 210 42.59 N 74.09 W
Hagan 192 32.09 N 81.56 W
Hagari ≃ 122 15.45 N 76.56 E
Hagar Shores 216 42.13 N 86.22 W
Hagarstown 219 38.57 N 89.10 W
Hage 52 53.36 N 7.17 E
Hagelberg ∧ [2] 54 52.08 N 12.32 E
Hagemeister Island I 180 58.40 N 161.00 W
Hagen, Dtsch. 52 52.34 N 9.26 E
Hagen, Dtsch. 52 52.12 N 7.59 E
Hagen, Dtsch. 56 51.22 N 7.28 E
Hagenbach 56 49.01 N 8.15 E
Hagenbrunn 264b 48.20 N 16.25 E
Hagengebirge ⋏ 64 47.32 N 13.07 E
Hagenow 54 53.26 N 11.11 E
Hagensborg 182 52.23 N 126.33 W
Hagenwerder 54 51.04 N 14.58 E
Hagere Hiywet 144 8.59 N 37.51 E
Hagere Selam 144 6.29 N 38.31 E
Hagerman, Id., U.S. 202 42.48 N 114.53 W
Hagerman, N.M., U.S. 196 33.06 N 104.19 W
Hagerman Corners 275b 43.50 N 79.18 W
Hagerstown, In., U.S. 218 39.54 N 85.09 W
Hagerstown, Md., U.S. 188 39.38 N 77.43 W
Hagersville 212 42.58 N 80.03 W
Hagetmau 32 43.40 N 0.35 W
Hagfors 40 60.02 N 13.42 E
Haggen ⊜ 40 60.06 N 15.13 E
Haggetts Pond ⊜ 283 42.39 N 71.12 W
Haggin, Mount ∧ 202 46.05 N 113.05 W
Hagi 96 34.24 N 131.25 E
Ha Giang 110 22.50 N 104.59 E
Hagitani 270 34.54 N 135.35 E
Hagiwara 94 35.52 N 137.12 E
Hagley 42 52.26 N 2.08 W
Hagley Museum ⊍ 285 39.46 N 75.35 W
Hagondange 56 49.15 N 6.10 E
HaGosherim 132 33.13 N 35.37 E
Hags Head › 48 52.57 N 9.30 W
Hague, Sk., Can. 184 52.30 N 106.25 W
Hague, N.D., U.S. 198 46.01 N 99.59 W
Hague, Cap de la › 32 49.43 N 1.57 W
Haguenau 56 48.49 N 7.47 E
Hagues Peak ∧ 200 40.29 N 105.38 W
Hahaïa 157a 11.33 S 43.17 E
Hahajima-rettō II 14 26.37 N 142.10 E
Haharro, Uebi ≃ 144 1.37 N 44.13 E
Hāhipur 272b 22.47 N 88.10 E
Hahira 192 30.59 N 83.22 W
Hahlen 52 52.18 N 8.50 E
Hahn am See 56 50.31 N 7.53 E
Hahnbach 60 49.32 N 11.48 E
Hahndorf 168b 35.03 S 138.49 E
Hahnenberg 263 51.12 N 7.24 E
Hahnenkamm ∧ 64 47.25 N 12.22 E
Hahnenklee-Bockswiese 52 51.51 N 10.20 E
Hahnerberg -•- [8] 263 51.13 N 7.09 E
Hahnstätten 56 50.18 N 8.04 E
Hahntown 279b 40.19 N 79.44 W
Haho ≃ 150 6.17 N 1.23 E
Hahyŏn-ni 98 38.33 N 127.57 E
Hai ≃ 105 39.00 N 117.43 E
Hai'an 100 32.34 N 120.28 E
Haian Shanmo ⋏ 100 23.25 N 121.25 E
Haibara, Nihon 94 34.32 N 135.57 E
Haibara, Nihon 94 34.44 N 138.13 E
Haibatpur 272a 28.37 N 77.26 E
Haibei 89 47.39 N 126.51 E
Haicheng, Zhg. 100 24.25 N 117.51 E
Haicheng, Zhg. 104 40.52 N 122.45 E
Haicheng ≃ 104 40.56 N 122.21 E
Haidargarh 124 26.37 N 81.22 E
Haidārpur -•- [8] 272a 28.43 N 77.09 E
Haidenaab ≃ 60 49.36 N 12.08 E

DEUTSCH

Name | Seite | Breite°′ | Länge°′ E = Ost

Haiderabad → Hyderābād, India 122 17.23 N 78.29 E
Haiderabad → Hyderābād, Pāk. 120 25.22 N 68.22 E
Haidershofen 61 48.05 N 14.28 E
Haidian 105 39.59 N 116.18 E
Haiding 60 48.13 N 13.58 E
Haidmühle 60 48.50 N 13.46 E
Haïdra 36 35.34 N 8.27 E
Haidstein ∧ 60 49.13 N 12.48 E
Haidun 100 29.36 N 121.49 E
Hai Duong 110 20.56 N 106.19 E
Haifa → Ḩefa 132 32.50 N 35.00 E
Haifa, Bay of → Ḩefa, Mifraẕ c 132 32.52 N 35.03 E
Haifeng 100 22.59 N 115.21 E
Haifengzheng 106 31.53 N 121.46 E
Haifuzhen 106 31.59 N 121.42 E
Haig 162 31.01 S 126.05 E
Haig, Mount ∧ 182 49.17 N 114.29 W
Haiger 56 50.44 N 8.13 E
Haigerloch 58 48.22 N 8.48 E
Haigh 262 53.35 N 2.36 W
Haigler 198 40.00 N 101.56 W
Haihezhen 100 33.44 N 120.02 E
Haijima 268 35.42 N 139.21 E
Haikang 102 20.56 N 110.04 E
Haikou, Zhg. 100 28.20 N 120.06 E
Haikou, Zhg. 100 25.43 N 119.28 E
Haikou, Zhg. 100 29.04 N 117.46 E
Haikou, Zhg. 102 20.03 N 110.19 E
Haiku 229a 20.55 N 156.19 W
Ḩā'il 128 27.33 N 41.42 E
Hailākāndi 120 24.41 N 92.34 E
Hailar 89 49.12 N 119.42 E
Hailar ≃ 90 49.35 N 117.55 E
Hailasen 89 46.13 N 121.00 E
Hailesboro 212 44.18 N 75.27 W
Hailey, Eng., U.K. 260 51.46 N 0.01 W
Hailey, Id., U.S. 202 43.31 N 114.18 W
Haileybury 190 47.27 N 79.38 W
Haileyville 196 34.51 N 95.34 W
Hailin 89 44.35 N 129.22 E
Hailing Dao I 102 21.37 N 111.55 E
Haillicourt 50 50.28 N 2.35 E
Hailong (Meihekou) 98 42.32 N 125.38 E
Hailsham 42 50.52 N 0.16 E
Hailun 89 47.28 N 126.58 E
Hailuoto 26 65.00 N 24.43 E
Hailuoto I 26 65.02 N 24.42 E
Haiman Tepesi ∧ [2] 267b 41.12 N 29.15 E
Haimen, Zhg. 100 28.41 N 121.27 E
Haimen, Zhg. 100 23.14 N 116.38 E
Haimen, Zhg. 106 31.55 N 121.10 E
Haimen Wan c 100 23.09 N 116.34 E
Haimhausen 60 48.19 N 11.34 E
Haimiao 98 37.13 N 119.51 E
Haiming 64 47.15 N 10.53 E
Haina 56 51.02 N 8.58 E
Hainan □ [4] 110 19.00 N 109.30 E
Hainan → Hainan Dao I 110 19.00 N 109.30 E
Hainan Dao I 110 19.00 N 109.30 E
Hainault -•- [8] 260 51.36 N 0.06 E
Hainaut □ [4] 50 50.30 N 3.50 E
Hainaut □ [9] 50 50.15 N 3.45 E
Hainburg an der Donau 61 48.09 N 16.57 E
Hainchen 56 50.51 N 8.12 E
Haines, Ak., U.S. 180 59.14 N 135.27 W
Haines, Or., U.S. 202 44.54 N 117.56 W
Haines City 220 28.06 N 81.37 W
Haines Falls 210 42.11 N 74.05 W
Haines Junction 180 60.45 N 137.30 W
Hainesport 208 39.59 N 74.49 W
Hainesville 278 42.21 N 88.04 W
Hainewalde 54 50.54 N 14.41 E
Hainfeld 61 48.02 N 15.46 E
Hainich ⋏ 54 51.05 N 10.27 E
Hainichen 54 50.58 N 13.07 E
Haining (Xiashi) 106 30.32 N 120.41 E
Hainleite ⋏ 54 51.20 N 10.48 E
Hainzenberg 64 47.13 N 11.54 E
Hai Phong 110 20.52 N 106.41 E
Haiqiao 106 31.47 N 121.19 E
Haiqing 89 47.53 N 134.40 E
Haitangxi 107 29.33 N 106.35 E
Haitan Xia ʊ 100 25.27 N 119.38 E
Haiterbach 58 48.32 N 8.39 E
Haiti (Haïti) □ [1], N.A. 230 19.00 N 72.25 W
Haiti (Haïti) □ [1], N.A. 238 19.00 N 72.25 W
Haitou, Zhg. 98 34.56 N 119.10 E
Haitou, Zhg. 110 19.34 N 108.58 E
Haitouji 98 35.23 N 115.19 E
Haitun 102 38.50 N 96.41 E
Haiwee Reservoirs ⊜ [1] 204 36.10 N 117.57 W
Haiyan, Zhg. 102 36.54 N 101.12 E
Haiyan, Zhg. 106 30.31 N 120.57 E
Haiyang (Dongcun) 98 36.46 N 121.10 E
Haiyang Dao I 98 39.02 N 123.14 E
Haiyuan 102 36.35 N 105.40 E
Haizhou, Zhg. 98 34.34 N 119.11 E
Haizhou, Zhg. 100 22.40 N 113.10 E
Haizhoumiao 104 42.00 N 121.39 E
Haizhou Wan c 98 35.00 N 119.30 E
Haizhouyingzi 104 42.07 N 121.46 E
Ḩajar, Tall al- ∧ [2] 132 33.21 N 37.03 E
Hajar Banga 140 11.30 N 23.00 E
Hajdú-Bihar □ [6] 30 47.25 N 21.30 E
Hajdúböszörmény 30 47.41 N 21.30 E
Hajdúnánás 30 47.51 N 21.26 E
Hajdúszoboszló 30 47.27 N 21.24 E
Hajeb el Ayoun 36 35.24 N 9.33 E
Hajiadian 98 41.32 N 117.10 E
Hājīganj 126 23.15 N 90.50 E
Hajiki-saki › 92 38.19 N 138.31 E
Haji Langar 120 35.52 N 79.21 E
Hājīpur, India 124 25.41 N 85.13 E
Hājīpur, India 126 22.49 N 87.38 E
Hajipur, India 272b 22.57 N 88.19 E
Ḩājj, Wādī al- V 142 30.03 N 32.45 E
Hajnówka 30 52.45 N 23.36 E
Hajo-do I 98 34.17 N 126.03 E
Ḩajr, Wādī V 144 14.04 N 48.40 E
Ḩajūl, Wādī V 142 29.42 N 32.22 E
Häkäri ≃ 84 39.09 N 46.51 E
Hakata 96 34.12 N 133.07 E
Hakata-jima I 96 34.13 N 133.05 E
Hakataramea ≃ 172 44.44 S 170.29 E
Hakendover 56 50.48 N 4.59 E
Hakha 110 22.39 N 93.37 E
Haki 96 33.20 N 130.50 E
Ḩakīm, Abyār al- ⊤ [4] 146 31.36 N 23.29 E
Hakkâri 128 37.34 N 43.45 E
Hakkâri □ [4] 128 37.20 N 43.45 E
Hakken-san ∧ 92 34.10 N 135.54 E
Hakkōda-san ∧ 92 40.40 N 140.53 E
Hako-dake ∧ 92a 44.40 N 142.25 E
Hakodate 92a 41.45 N 140.43 E
Hakone 94 35.12 N 139.06 E
Hakone-no-seki-ato ⊥ 94 35.10 N 139.02 E
Hakone-tōge)(94 35.11 N 139.01 E
Hakone-yama ∧ 94 35.14 N 139.02 E
Håksberg 40 60.11 N 15.12 E
Hakskeenpan ≚ 158 26.48 S 20.12 E
Haktanır 130 36.51 N 38.50 E
Hakuba 94 36.42 N 137.52 E
Hakui 94 36.53 N 136.47 E
Hakupu 174v 19.06 S 169.50 W
Hakusan 94 34.38 N 136.21 E
Haku-san ∧ 94 36.09 N 136.46 E
Haku-san-kokuritsu-kōen ♦ 94 36.12 N 136.47 E
Hakushū 94 35.48 N 138.20 E
Hakuta 96 35.21 N 133.17 E
Hakuta ≃ 96 35.26 N 133.15 E
Hāla 120 25.49 N 68.25 E

Symbols in the index entries represent the broad categories identified in the key at the right. Symbols with superior numbers (⋏ [1]) identify subcategories (see complete key on page *I · 1).*

Symbole im Register stellen die rechts im Schlüssel erklärten Kategorien dar. Symbole mit hochgestellten Ziffern (⋏ [1]) bezeichnen Unterabteilungen einer Kategorie (vgl. vollständiger Schlüssel auf Seite *I · 1).*

Los símbolos incluídos en el texto del índice representan las grandes categorías identificadas con la clave a la derecha. Los símbolos con numeros en su parte superior (⋏ [1]) identifican las subcategorías (véase la clave completa en la página *I · 1).*

Les symboles de l'index représentent les catégories indiquées dans la légende à droite. Les symboles suivis d'un indice (⋏ [1]) représentent des sous-catégories (voir légende complète à la page *I · 1).*

Os símbolos incluídos no texto do índice representam as grandes categorias identificadas com a chave à direita. Os símbolos com números em sua parte superior (⋏ [1]) identificam as subcategorias (veja-se a chave completa à página *I · 1).*

∧	Mountain	Berg	Montaña	Montagne	Montanha
⋏	Mountains	Gebirge	Montañas	Montagnes	Montanhas
)(	Pass	Paß	Paso	Col	Passo
V	Valley, Canyon	Tal, Cañon	Valle, Cañón	Vallée, Canyon	Vale, Canhão
≚	Plain	Ebene	Llano	Plaine	Planície
›	Cape	Kap	Cabo	Cap	Cabo
I	Island	Insel	Isla	Île	Ilha
II	Islands	Inseln	Islas	Îles	Ilhas
⊻	Other Topographic Features	Andere Topographische Objekte	Otros Elementos Topográficos	Autres données topographiques	Outros acidentes topográficos

ESPAÑOL Nombre	Página	Lat.°′	Long.°′ W = Oeste
Halaaobao	102	42.11 N	107.20 E
Halab (Aleppo)	130	36.12 N	37.10 E
Halab □⁸	130	36.00 N	37.30 E
Halabjah	128	35.10 N	45.59 E
Halachö	232	20.29 N	90.05 W
Halaerjige	104	42.24 N	122.11 E
Halagetu	104	42.34 N	122.40 E
Halahai	89	44.39 N	125.07 E
Halahushao	104	42.11 N	121.44 E
Halä'ib	140	22.13 N	36.38 E
Halalii Lake ⊜	229	21.52 N	160.11 W
Halamutai	86	46.10 N	84.52 E
Halangingie Point ⋗	174	19.03 S	169.57 W
Halasa	140	14.26 N	30.39 E
Halas-patak ≃	264c	47.24 N	19.20 E
Halataojie	104	42.30 N	122.06 E
Halatieke Shan ⩲	85	40.30 N	77.05 E
Halaula	229d	20.14 N	155.48 W
Hålaveden ⩲²	26	58.05 N	14.45 E
Halawa, Cape ⋗	229a	21.10 N	156.43 W
Halawa Bay ⊂	229a	21.10 N	156.44 W
Halawa Heights	229c	21.22 N	157.55 W
Halawotelake	120	37.17 N	90.20 E
Halbach ⩲⁸	263	51.12 N	7.12 E
Halba Deset I	144	12.56 N	42.55 E
Halbe	54	52.06 N	13.42 E
Halberstadt	54	51.54 N	11.02 E
Halbert, Lake ⊜¹	222	32.04 N	96.25 W
Halberton	42	50.55 N	3.25 W
Halbiech, Dtsch.	58	47.38 N	10.49 E
Halblech, Dtsch.	64	47.38 N	10.49 E
Halbrite	184	40.33 N	103.33 W
Halbün	132	33.40 N	36.15 E
Halbury	168b	34.05 S	138.31 E
Halcombe	172	40.09 S	175.30 E
Halcon, Mount ⩲	116	13.16 N	121.00 E
Halcottsville	210	42.12 N	74.36 W
Haldeman	218	38.15 N	83.19 W
Halden	26	59.09 N	11.23 E
Halden ⩲⁸	263	51.23 N	7.31 E
Haldensleben	54	52.18 N	11.26 E
Haldern	52	51.46 N	6.27 E
Haldī	126	22.03 N	88.05 E
Haldī ≃	126	22.01 N	88.03 E
Haldībāri	124	26.20 N	88.46 E
Haldibunia	126	22.26 N	89.38 E
Haldimand	212	43.00 N	79.50 W
Haldimand-Norfolk □⁶	212	42.48 N	80.10 W
Haldwāni	124	29.13 N	79.31 E
Hale, Eng., U.K.	44	53.23 N	2.21 W
Hale, Eng., U.K.	262	53.20 N	2.48 W
Hale, Eng., U.K.	194	39.36 N	93.20 W
Hale ⩲	162	24.56 S	135.53 E
Haleakala Crater ⩲⁶	229a	20.43 N	156.13 W
Haleakala National Park ♦	229a	20.44 N	156.13 W
Haleb			
— Halab	130	36.12 N	37.10 E
Haleburns	262	53.22 N	2.19 W
Hale Center	198	34.03 N	101.50 W
Hale Creek ≃	282	37.23 N	122.06 W
Haledon	276	40.56 N	74.11 W
Haledon Reservoir ⊜¹	276	40.59 N	74.12 W
Hale Eddy	210	42.00 N	75.23 W
Hale Head ⋗	262	53.19 N	2.48 W
Haleiwa	229c	21.35 N	158.06 W
Halekii-Pihana Heiaus State Monument ⊥	229a	20.54 N	156.29 W
Halenkov	30	49.19 N	18.08 E
Hales Corners	216	42.56 N	88.02 W
Halesite	207	40.52 N	73.25 W
Halesowen	52	52.26 N	2.05 W
Hale Street	250	51.13 N	0.24 E
Halesworth	42	52.21 N	1.30 E
Halewood	262	53.22 N	2.49 W
Haleyville	194	34.13 N	87.37 W
Half Assini	150	5.03 N	2.53 W
Halfâyah, Naqb al- (Halfaya Pass) ⋋	140	31.30 N	25.11 E
Halfaya Pass			
— Halfâyah, Naqb al- ⋋	140	31.30 N	25.11 E
Half Day	278	42.12 N	87.56 W
Halfeti	130	37.15 N	37.52 E
Half Hollow Hills	276	40.48 N	73.21 W
Halfing	64	47.57 N	12.16 E
Halfmoon Bay, B.C., Can.	182	49.31 N	123.54 W
Halfmoon Bay, N.Z.	172	46.54 S	168.08 E
Half Moon Bay, Ca., U.S.	282	37.27 N	122.25 W
Halfmoon Bay c, Austl.	274b	37.58 S	145.00 E
Half Moon Bay c, Ca., U.S.	282	37.29 N	122.28 W
Half Moon Bay Airport ⇄	282	37.31 N	122.30 W
Half Moon Bay State Beach ♦	282	37.29 N	122.27 W
Halfway, Md., U.S.	188	39.37 N	77.45 W
Halfway, Or., U.S.	202	44.52 N	117.06 W
Halfway ≃	176	56.10 N	121.35 W
Halfway Lake ⊜	184	55.03 N	98.24 W
Halgān ⩲	40	60.16 N	13.27 E
Halhül	132	31.35 N	35.07 E
Halī ⊤⁴	144	18.42 N	41.20 E
Haliburton	212	45.03 N	78.31 W
Haliburton □⁶	212	44.10 N	78.30 W
Haliburton Lake ⊜	212	45.12 N	78.24 W
Halibut Point ⋗	283	42.42 N	70.38 W
Halic (Golden Horn) c	267b	41.02 N	28.58 E
Halicarnassus ⊥	130	37.03 N	27.23 E
Halifax, Austl.	166	18.35 S	146.18 E
Halifax, N.S., Can.	184	44.39 N	63.36 W
Halifax, Eng., U.K.	44	53.44 N	1.52 W
Halifax, Ma., U.S.	207	41.59 N	70.51 W
Halifax, N.C., U.S.	216	36.19 N	77.35 W
Halifax, Pa., U.S.	208	40.28 N	76.55 W
Halifax, Va., U.S.	192	36.45 N	78.55 W
Halifax, Canadian Forces Base ■	184	44.43 N	63.38 W
Halifax Bay c	166	18.50 S	146.30 E
Halifax Citadel National Historic Site ⊥	186	44.36 N	63.39 W
Halifax Harbour c	186	44.35 N	63.31 W
Haliimaile	229a	20.52 N	156.20 W
Halli ⩲	128	27.38 N	84.04 E
Halimatazi	104	42.37 N	122.35 E
Halim Perdanakusuma Airport ⇄	269e	6.16 S	106.54 E
Halimun, Gunung ⩲	116a	6.42 S	106.26 E
Halingen	263	51.27 N	7.44 E
Hälisahar	126	22.56 N	88.25 E
Haliyāl	128	15.20 N	74.46 E
Halja	76	53.09 N	24.25 E
Halkali ⩲⁸	267b	41.02 N	28.47 E
Halkapinar	130	37.25 N	34.13 E
Halkett, Cape ⋗	180	70.49 N	152.12 W
Halkirk	46	58.30 N	3.30 W
Halkyn	262	53.14 N	3.11 W
Halkyn Mountain ⩲	262	53.14 N	3.13 W
Hall, Austl.	171b	35.10 S	149.04 E
Hall, In., U.S.	218	40.33 N	86.40 W
Hall, N.Y., U.S.	210	42.48 N	77.04 W
Hälleböhl ⩲	58	49.07 N	11.12 E
Halladale ≃	46	58.33 N	3.55 W
Hallam	274b	38.01 S	145.06 E
Hallam Peak ⩲	182	52.11 N	118.46 W
Halland	58	57.00 N	12.40 E
Hallandale	220	25.58 N	80.08 W
Hallands Län □⁶	56	56.45 N	13.00 E
Hallands Väderö I	56	56.26 N	12.33 E
Hallau	58	47.42 N	8.27 E
Hällberga	40	59.19 N	16.26 E
Hallbergmoos	64	48.19 N	11.45 E
Hällbybrunn	40	59.24 N	16.25 E

FRANÇAIS Nom	Page	Lat.°′	Long.°′ W = Ouest
Hällbymagasinet ⊜¹	26	63.56 N	17.13 E
Halle, Bel.	50	50.44 N	4.13 E
Halle, Dtsch.	52	52.04 N	8.22 E
Halle, Dtsch.	52	51.59 N	9.33 E
Halle, Dtsch.	54	51.29 N	11.58 E
Halleberg ⩲²	58	58.23 N	12.27 E
Hällefors	40	59.47 N	14.30 E
Hälleforsnäs	40	59.10 N	16.30 E
Hallein	64	47.41 N	13.06 E
Hällekis	58	58.38 N	13.25 E
Hallen	26	63.11 N	14.05 E
Hallenberg	56	51.06 N	8.37 E
Hallencourt	50	49.59 N	1.53 E
Halle-Neustadt	54	51.29 N	11.56 E
Hallertau ⩲¹	60	48.35 N	11.45 E
Hällestad	40	58.44 N	15.34 E
Hallett, Cape ⋗	9	72.19 S	170.18 E
Hallettsville	222	29.26 N	96.56 W
Halley ⩲³, Ant.	9	75.35 S	26.15 W
Halley ⩲³, Ant.	9	75.36 S	26.46 W
Halliday	198	47.21 N	102.20 W
Halligen II	54	54.35 N	8.35 E
Halling	260	51.21 N	0.27 E
Hallingdalselvi ≃	26	60.24 N	9.35 E
Hällingsåfallet ⌊	26	64.20 N	14.20 E
Hall in Tirol	180	60.40 N	173.05 W
Hall Island I	180	60.40 N	173.05 W
Hall Islands II	14	8.37 N	152.00 E
Halliste ≃	76	58.31 N	25.03 E
Hall-i'-th'-Wood ♦	262	53.36 N	2.26 W
Hall Lake ⊜	176	68.41 N	82.17 W
Hall Meadow Brook Reservoir ⊜¹	207	41.52 N	73.10 W
Hall Mountain ⩲	202	48.49 N	116.57 W
Hällnäs	26	64.19 N	19.38 E
Hallock	198	48.46 N	96.56 W
Hall Peninsula ⋗¹	176	63.30 N	66.00 W
Halls Bayou ≃	222	29.12 N	95.07 W
Hallsberg	40	59.04 N	15.07 E
Halls Brook ≃	283	42.00 N	70.43 W
Halls Creek	162	18.16 S	127.46 E
Halls Creek ≃	200	37.18 N	110.45 W
Halls Gap	166	37.08 S	142.31 E
Hallstätter See ⊜	64	47.33 N	13.39 E
Hallstead	210	41.57 N	75.44 W
Hallstahammar	40	59.37 N	16.13 E
Hallstavik	26	60.03 N	18.36 E
Hallstadt	54	49.55 N	10.52 E
Hallsta	40	59.18 N	16.27 E
Hallsville, Mo., U.S.	219	39.07 N	92.13 W
Hallsville, Tx., U.S.	222	32.30 N	94.34 W
Halluin	50	50.47 N	3.08 E
Hallwiler See ⊜	58	47.18 N	8.13 E
Hallwood	208	37.52 N	75.35 W
Halma	56	50.05 N	5.08 E
Halmahera, Laut ⊤²	108	1.00 N	128.00 E
Halmahera, Laut (Halmahera Sea) ⊤²	108	1.00 S	129.00 E
Halmstad	26	56.39 N	12.50 E
Halopeničy	76	54.31 N	28.58 E
Haloučyn	76	54.04 N	29.55 E
Halpine Village	284c	39.05 N	77.07 W
Hals	26	57.00 N	10.19 E
Halsafjorden c²	26	63.03 N	8.11 E
Halsall	262	53.35 N	2.57 W
Hal'šany	76	54.15 N	26.01 E
Halsbrücke	54	50.57 N	13.21 E
Halsey, Ne., U.S.	198	41.54 N	100.16 W
Halsey, Or., U.S.	202	44.23 N	123.06 W
Halsey Harbor c	176	11.45 N	119.56 E
Halsey Valley	210	42.08 N	76.27 W
Halsingborg			
— Helsingborg	41	56.03 N	12.42 E
Hälsingland ⩲¹	26	61.30 N	17.00 E
Halstad	198	47.21 N	96.49 W
Halstead, Eng., U.K.	42	51.57 N	0.38 E
Halstead, Eng., U.K.	260	51.20 N	0.08 E
Halstead, Ks., U.S.	198	38.00 N	97.30 W
Halsteren	52	51.32 N	4.16 E
Halstow Marshes ⊜	260	51.29 N	0.33 E
Haltang ≃	102	39.00 N	94.40 E
Halten ≃	52	51.46 N	7.10 E
Haltiatunturi ⩲	24	69.18 N	21.16 E
Haltom City	222	32.47 N	97.16 W
Halton, Eng., U.K.	44	54.05 N	2.46 W
Halton, Eng., U.K.	262	53.20 N	2.41 W
Halton □⁶	212	43.30 N	79.53 W
Halton □⁶	262	53.20 N	2.49 W
Halton Hills	212	43.39 N	79.55 W
Haltwhistle	44	54.58 N	2.27 W
Halura, Pulau I	115b	10.19 S	120.11 E
Haluza, Holot ⩲⁸	132	31.05 N	34.28 E
Halüzoril̄, Wādī al- ⩲⁸	273c	30.05 N	31.24 E
Halvarsgårdarna	40	60.24 N	15.23 E
Halvarsnoren ⊜	40	59.49 N	14.36 E
Halvay ≃	56	51.11 N	7.30 E
Halvorson, Mount ⩲	182	53.15 N	120.33 W
Halwell	42	50.22 N	3.43 W
Halych	78	49.08 N	24.43 E
Halyna ≃	42	50.56 N	1.04 W
Ham, Fr.	50	49.45 N	3.04 E
Ham, Tchad	144	10.00 N	15.41 E
Ham □⁶	50	49.45 N	3.04 E
Ham, Oued el ≃	34	35.42 N	4.52 E
Hamad	140	15.19 N	33.43 E
Hamada	98	34.53 N	132.05 E
Hamadān	128	34.48 N	48.30 E
Hamadān □⁴	130	35.00 N	48.40 E
Hamadān □⁸	130	34.30 N	48.00 E
Hamada-jima I	174m	26.19 N	127.57 E
Hamakaze	98	34.48 N	137.47 E
Hamakita	94	34.48 N	137.47 E
Hamale	150	10.59 N	2.44 W
Hamamatsu	94	34.42 N	137.44 E
Hamamatsukita-kichi, Kökū-jieitai- ■	98	34.45 N	137.42 E
Hamamözü	98	40.48 N	35.02 E
Hamana ≃	98	35.15 N	128.24 E
Hamana-ko c	94	34.45 N	137.34 E
Hamanaka	98	35.33 N	140.08 E
Hamaoka	94	34.39 N	138.08 E
Hamar	26	60.48 N	11.06 E
Hamasaka	98	35.38 N	134.27 E
Hamatak, Jabal ⩲	140	24.12 N	35.00 E
Hama-tombetsu	92a	45.07 N	142.23 E
Hambach	56	49.04 N	7.02 E
Hambaek-san ⩲	98	37.09 N	128.55 E
Hamber Provincial Park ♦	182	52.25 N	117.40 W
Hamble	42	50.52 N	1.19 W
Hambleton ⩲	44	54.05 N	1.12 W
Hambleton Hills ⩲²	44	54.16 N	1.14 W
Hambourg			
— Hamburg	52	53.33 N	9.59 E
Hamburg, Dtsch.	52	53.38 N	9.59 E
Hamburg, S. Afr.	158	33.17 S	27.28 E
Hamburg, Ar., U.S.	194	33.13 N	91.47 W
Hamburg, II., U.S.	198	40.36 N	95.39 W
Hamburg, Mi., U.S.	204	42.27 N	83.48 W
Hamburg, N.J., U.S.	210	41.09 N	74.34 W
Hamburg, N.Y., U.S.	210	42.43 N	78.49 W
Hamburg, Pa., U.S.	208	40.33 N	75.58 W
Hämburg □⁸	52	53.30 N	10.00 E

PORTUGUÊS Nome	Página	Lat.°′	Long.°′ W = Oeste
Hamburg, Flughafen ⇄	52	53.38 N	10.00 E
Hamburg Airport ⇄	284a	42.42 N	78.55 W
Hamburg Ditch ≃	208	36.31 N	76.33 W
Hamburger Hallig ⋗¹	41	54.36 N	8.49 E
Hamburg Mountains ⩲	276	41.08 N	74.32 W
Hamburgo			
— Hamburg	52	53.33 N	9.59 E
Hamburgsund	58	58.33 N	11.16 E
Hamd, Wādī al- V	128	25.54 N	36.38 E
Hamdah	144	19.02 N	43.36 E
Hamdallay Timbou	150	12.03 N	10.37 W
Hamdam Āb, Dasht-e ≃	128	34.45 N	61.30 E
Hamdänah	144	19.58 N	40.35 E
Harnden, Ct., U.S.	207	41.23 N	72.53 W
Harnden, N.Y., U.S.	210	42.12 N	75.00 W
Hamden, Oh., U.S.	188	39.09 N	82.31 W
Hamdibey	130	39.50 N	27.15 E
Häne ⩲¹	26	61.45 N	25.10 E
Häreenkangas ⩲³	26	61.45 N	22.40 E
Häreenkylä	26	60.16 N	24.47 E
Häreen lääni □⁴	26	61.30 N	24.32 E
Häreenlinna	26	61.00 N	24.27 E
HaMelah, Yam — Dead Sea ⊜	132	31.30 N	35.30 E
Hameln	162	26.25 S	114.11 E
Hamelin Pool c	162	26.15 S	114.05 E
Hameln	52	52.06 N	9.21 E
HaMerkaz □⁵	132	32.05 N	34.55 E
Hamer Koke	144	5.12 N	36.45 E
Hamero Hadad	144	7.34 N	42.18 E
Hamersleben	54	52.04 N	11.05 E
Hamersley Range ⩲	162	21.53 S	116.46 E
Hamersley Range National Park ♦	162	22.40 S	118.15 E
Hamersville	218	38.55 N	83.59 W
Hames Creek ≃	226	33.53 N	120.50 W
Hamgyöng Namdo □⁴	98	40.00 N	127.30 E
Hamgyöng Pukdo □⁴	98	41.45 N	129.50 E
Hamgyöng-sanmaek ⩲	98	41.00 N	128.30 E
Ham House ⊥	260	51.27 N	0.19 W
Hamhüng	98	39.54 N	127.32 E
Hami (Kumul)	102	42.48 N	93.27 E
Hamidiye	130	41.09 N	26.40 E
Hamiguitan, Mount ⩲	116	6.44 N	126.11 E
Hamilton, Austl.	166	37.45 S	142.02 E
Hamilton, Ber.	240a	32.17 N	64.46 W
Hamilton, On., Can.	212	43.15 N	79.51 W
Hamilton, N.Z.	172	37.47 S	175.17 E
Hamilton, Scot., U.K.	46	55.47 N	4.03 W
Hamilton, Al., U.S.	194	34.08 N	87.59 W
Hamilton, Ak., U.S.	180	62.54 N	163.53 W
Hamilton, In., U.S.	218	41.32 N	84.54 W
Hamilton, Mi., U.S.	204	42.40 N	86.00 W
Hamilton, Mi., U.S.	204	42.37 N	70.52 W
Hamilton, Mt., U.S.	202	46.14 N	114.09 W
Hamilton, N.Y., U.S.	210	42.49 N	75.32 W
Hamilton, N.C., U.S.	192	35.56 N	77.12 W
Hamilton, Oh., U.S.	218	39.23 N	84.33 W
Hamilton, R.I., U.S.	207	41.32 N	71.26 W
Hamilton, Tx., U.S.	196	31.42 N	98.07 W
Hamilton, Va., U.S.	208	39.08 N	77.39 W
Hamilton ≃	162	23.30 S	139.47 E
Hamilton ⩲⁸	210	43.24 N	74.25 W
Harrilton □⁶, Oh., U.S.	210	43.24 N	74.25 W
Hamilton, Lake ⊜	220	28.03 N	81.39 W
Hamilton, Lake ⊜	194	34.30 N	93.05 W
Harrilton, Mount ⩲, Ak., U.S.	180	61.10 N	159.46 W
Harrilton, Mount ⩲, Ca., U.S.	226	37.21 N	121.38 W
Hamilton, Mount ⩲, Nv., U.S.	204	39.14 N	115.32 W
Hamilton Air Force Base ■	282	38.03 N	122.31 W
Hamilton City	204	39.44 N	122.00 W
Hamilton Creek ≃	162	26.40 S	135.19 E
Hamilton Dome	200	43.46 N	108.34 W
Hamilton Harbour c	212	43.17 N	79.50 W
Hamilton Hill	168a	32.05 S	115.46 E
Hamilton Hotel	168	22.50 S	140.35 E
Hamilton Inlet c	176	54.00 N	57.30 W
Hamilton Island I	216	20.22 S	148.57 E
Hamilton Lake ⊜	216	41.33 N	84.55 W
Hamilton Mountain ⩲	188	43.25 N	74.42 W
Hamilton Park, In., U.S.	278	40.17 N	85.19 W
Hamilton Park, Pa., U.S.	208	40.17 N	76.20 W
Hamilton Sound u	186	49.30 N	54.30 W
Hamilton Square	208	40.13 N	74.39 W
Hamilton-Wentworth □⁶			
Hamîm, Wādî al- V	128	43.15 N	80.00 W
Hamina	26	60.34 N	27.12 E
Hamiota	184	50.11 N	100.38 W
Hamîrpur, India	123	31.41 N	76.31 E
Hamīrpur, India	124	25.57 N	80.09 E
Hamer	28	61.45 N	25.10 E
Hamlet, In., U.S.	218	41.23 N	86.34 W
Hamlet, N.C., U.S.	192	34.53 N	79.41 W
Hamlet, Oh., U.S.	218	39.01 N	84.12 W
Hamlin	228	20.53 N	156.42 W
Hamlin, N.Y., U.S.	210	43.18 N	77.55 W
Hamlin, Tx., U.S.	196	32.53 N	100.08 W
Hamlin, W.V., U.S.	188	38.16 N	82.06 W
Hamlin Beach State Park ♦	210	43.22 N	77.58 W
Hamlin Valley Wash V	200	38.53 N	114.01 W
Hamm	52	51.41 N	7.49 E
Hamm ⩲⁸, Dtsch.	263	51.41 N	6.44 E
Hamm ⩲⁸, Dtsch.	263	51.23 N	7.03 E
Hamma, Wādī V	142	29.45 N	32.24 E
Hamma Hamma ≃	224	47.33 N	123.03 W
Hammâffjell ⩲	62	62.27 N	11.17 E
Hammah, al- Turkumān	130	36.32 N	39.03 E
Hammâm, al-	138	35.27 N	7.58 E
Hammam, Tun.	138	36.24 N	10.37 E
Hammamet, Golfe de c	138	36.05 N	10.40 E
Hammâm Lif	138	36.44 N	10.20 E
Hammâmât	132	33.49 N	35.44 E
Hammāmät, Hawr al- ⊜	128	30.50 N	47.10 E
Hammânô ≃	88	60.33 N	16.34 E
Hammel	26	56.15 N	9.52 E
Hammelburg	54	50.07 N	9.53 E
Hamme-Mille	56	50.47 N	4.43 E
Hammerdal	26	63.36 N	15.21 E
Hammerfest	24	70.39 N	23.42 W
Hämmern	263	51.08 N	7.21 E

PORTUGUÊS Nome	Página	Lat.°′	Long.°′ W = Oeste
Hammershus ⊥	26	55.16 N	14.45 E
Hammersley Inlet c	224	47.12 N	123.00 W
Hammersmith ⩲⁸	260	51.30 N	0.14 W
Hammersmith □⁸	41	56.08 N	9.04 E
Hammerun	52	51.44 N	6.35 E
Hamminkeln	196	35.37 N	99.22 W
Hammon	207	41.16 N	72.33 W
Hammonasset ≃	216	41.35 N	87.30 W
Hammond, In., U.S.	194	30.30 N	90.27 W
Hammond, La., U.S.	212	44.26 N	75.41 W
Hammond, N.Y., U.S.	128	25.54 N	36.38 E
Hammond, Or., U.S.	190	44.58 N	92.26 W
Hammond, Wi., U.S.			
Hammond Island I, Austl.	164	10.35 S	142.13 E
Hammond Island I, Ca., U.S.	282	38.06 N	121.57 W
Hammond Pond Park ♦	283	42.19 N	71.11 W
Hammondsport	210	42.24 N	77.13 W
Hammondsville	214	40.33 N	80.43 W
Hammonton	184a	33.57 S	150.57 E
Hamneda	158	28.43 S	27.49 E
Hammonton	208	39.38 N	74.48 W
Hamnvik	24	70.31 N	30.37 E
Hamoir	56	50.26 N	5.32 E
Hamont	56	51.15 N	5.33 E
HaMore, Giv'at ⩲	132	32.37 N	35.21 E
Hamorton	285	39.52 N	75.39 W
Hamoyet, Jabal ⩲	144	17.33 N	38.02 E
Hampden, Austl.	168b	34.09 S	139.03 E
Hampden, N.Z., Can.	186	49.33 N	56.51 W
Hampden, N.Z.	172	45.19 S	170.49 E
Hampden, Me., U.S.	188	44.44 N	68.50 W
Hampden, Ma., U.S.	207	42.03 N	72.24 W
Hampden, N.D., U.S.	198	48.32 N	98.39 W
Hampden □⁶	207	42.07 N	72.36 W
Hampden Sydney	192	37.15 N	78.29 W
Hamperterp	40	59.09 N	15.40 E
Hampi	122	15.24 N	76.37 E
Hampshire	216	42.05 N	88.31 W
Hampshire □⁶, Eng., U.K.	42	51.05 N	1.15 W
Hampshire □⁶, Ma., U.S.	207	42.20 N	72.38 W
Hampshire Downs ⩲²	42	51.15 N	1.17 W
Hampshire Heights	279b	40.20 N	79.33 W
Hampstead, P.Q., Can.	254a	45.29 N	73.38 W
Hampstead, Md., U.S.	208	39.36 N	76.51 W
Hampstead, N.C., U.S.	192	34.22 N	77.42 W
Hampstead ⩲⁸	260	51.33 N	0.10 W
Hampstead Heath ♦	260	51.34 N	0.10 W
Hampton, Austl.	274b	37.56 S	145.00 E
Hampton, On., Can.	212	43.58 N	78.45 W
Hampton, N.B., Can.	186	45.32 N	65.51 W
Hampton, Eng., U.K.	260	51.25 N	0.22 W
Hampton, Ct., U.S.	207	41.47 N	72.03 W
Hampton, Fl., U.S.	192	29.51 N	82.07 W
Hampton, Ga., U.S.	192	33.23 N	84.16 W
Hampton, Ia., U.S.	198	42.44 N	93.12 W
Hampton, N.H., U.S.	207	42.56 N	70.50 W
Hampton, N.J., U.S.	210	40.42 N	74.57 W
Hampton, S.C., U.S.	192	32.52 N	81.06 W
Hampton, Tn., U.S.	192	36.17 N	82.10 W
Hampton, Va., U.S.	208	37.01 N	76.20 W
Hampton □⁶	192	32.46 N	81.06 W
Hampton, Mount ⩲	9	76.29 S	125.48 W
Hampton Bays	207	40.52 N	72.31 W
Hampton Butte ⩲	202	43.46 N	120.17 W
Hampton Court Palace ♦	42	51.24 N	0.20 W
Hampton Harbour c	162	20.40 S	116.30 E
Hampton National Historic Site ⊥	284b	39.25 N	76.35 W
Hampton Park	274b	38.02 S	145.15 E
Hampton Roads ⊤³	208	36.58 N	76.20 W
Hampton Roads Bridge-Tunnel ⩲⁵	208	37.00 N	76.18 W
Hampton Tableland ⩲¹	162	32.10 S	126.10 E
Hamp'yŏng	98	35.05 N	126.30 E
Hamra	54	50.35 N	13.35 E
Hamra □⁸	26	61.39 N	15.00 E
Hamra', Al-Hamādah al- ⩲²	146	30.00 N	12.00 E
Hamra, As Saquia al ≃	148	27.15 N	13.21 W
Hamra, Ouadi V	146	12.52 N	21.15 E
Hamrah, Jabal al- ⩲	132	29.39 N	34.47 E
Hamrā, Har ⩲	132	30.14 N	34.34 E
Hamra Nabraahi ⋖	26	61.45 N	14.55 E
Hamrat ash-Shaykh	140	14.35 N	27.58 E
Hams Bluff ⩲²	241n	17.46 N	64.52 W
Hams Fork ≃	200	41.35 N	109.59 W
Hamselhalten ⩲	42	51.04 N	0.51 E
Hamta	123	32.15 N	77.22 E
Hamu ≃	144	7.34 N	28.01 E
Hamūn ⊜	128	31.00 N	61.15 E
Hamur	130	39.36 N	42.39 E
Hämün, Daryächeh-ye ⊜	128	31.00 N	61.15 E
Hamyang	98	35.32 N	127.42 E
Hamzali	70	41.22 N	22.46 E
Han	150	10.54 N	2.27 W
Han, Zhg.	100	32.35 N	115.02 E
Han, Grottes de ⩲⁵	56	50.08 N	5.15 E
Han, Nong ⊜	116	17.12 N	104.11 E
Hanabä ≃	229a	20.45 N	155.59 W
Hanahan	192	32.55 N	80.01 W
Hanak	130	41.12 N	42.50 E
Hanakapiai ≃	229	22.10 N	159.35 W
Hanalei Bay c	229b	22.12 N	159.31 W
Hanamaulu	229b	21.59 N	159.19 W
Hanamenu, Baie c	174x	9.46 S	139.04 W
Hanam-ni	98	38.23 N	126.43 E
Hanapepe	229b	21.54 N	159.35 W
Hänär Char	144	8.55 N	37.56 E
Hanateten	174x	9.58 S	139.06 W
Hanau	52	50.08 N	8.55 E
Hanauma Bay c	229c	21.16 N	157.41 W
Hanbury ≃	176	63.37 N	104.33 W
Hänceşti	58	46.49 N	28.34 E
Hanceville, B.C., Can.	182	51.55 N	123.03 W
Hanceville, Al., U.S.	194	34.03 N	86.46 W
Hancheng, Zhg.	100	35.22 N	110.27 E
Hancheng, Zhg.	104	43.28 N	125.32 E
Hanchuan	100	30.39 N	113.48 E
Hanch'ŏn	98	37.33 N	127.02 E
Hanchŏng	100	34.49 N	105.28 E
Hancock, Md., U.S.	188	39.41 N	78.10 W
Hancock, Mn., U.S.	198	45.30 N	95.48 W
Hancock, N.Y., U.S.	210	41.57 N	75.17 W
Hancock, Wi., U.S.	216	44.08 N	89.31 W
Hancock □⁶, Ga., U.S.	192	33.15 N	83.00 W
Hancock □⁶, Oh., U.S.	218	41.01 N	83.39 W

Hancock □⁶, W.V., U.S.	214	40.30 N	80.33 W
Hancock, Lake ⊜	220	27.58 N	81.50 W
Hancocks Bridge	208	39.30 N	75.27 W
Hancun	105	39.24 N	116.36 E
Handa, Nihon	94	34.53 N	136.56 E
Handa, Nihon	96	34.02 N	134.02 E
Handa, Som.	144	10.40 N	51.07 E
Handa I	46	58.22 N	5.12 W
Handan	98	36.37 N	114.29 E
Handaokou	98	44.36 N	116.24 E
Handawor	123	34.24 N	74.17 E
Handen	40	59.10 N	18.08 E
Handeni	154	5.26 S	38.01 E
Handforth	262	53.21 N	2.13 W
Handlová	30	48.44 N	18.46 E
Handöl	26	63.16 N	12.26 E
Hanford	226	36.19 N	119.38 W
Hanford Site ⩲³	202	46.35 N	119.30 W
Hang-gang ≃	98	34.39 N	114.38 E
Han-gang ≃	98	37.45 N	126.11 E
Hanga Roa	174z	27.09 S	109.26 W
Hangatiki	172	38.15 S	175.10 E
Hangbu	100	28.53 N	118.49 E
Hangchow			
— Hangzhou	106	30.15 N	120.10 E
Hangchow Bay			
— Hangzhou Wan c	100	30.25 N	121.00 E
Hanger ≃	144	9.35 N	36.02 E
Hanggin Houqi	102	40.55 N	107.15 E
Hanggin Qi	102	39.56 N	108.56 E
Hang Hau Town	271d	22.19 N	114.16 E
Hanging Gardens ♦	272c	18.58 N	72.48 E
Hanging Rock State Park ♦	192	36.25 N	80.15 W
Hangingstone Hill ⩲²	42	50.39 N	3.57 W
Hanging Woman Creek ≃	202	45.19 N	106.31 W
Hangklip, Kaap ⋗	158	34.26 S	18.48 E
Hangkou	100	29.03 N	114.27 E
Hangman Creek ≃	202	47.38 N	117.27 W
Hangö (Hanko)	26	59.50 N	22.57 E
Hangou	105	39.18 N	117.07 E
Hang-Tcheou			
— Hangzhou	106	30.15 N	120.10 E
Hangtou	106	31.01 N	121.35 E
Hangtchou			
— Hangzhou	106	30.15 N	120.10 E
Hangu, Päk.	123	33.32 N	71.04 E
Hangu, Zhg.	105	39.15 N	117.47 E
Hanguang	100	24.16 N	113.08 E
Hanguchang	105	29.32 N	106.21 E
Hangzhou (Hangchow)	106	30.15 N	120.10 E
Hangzhou Wan (Hangchow Bay) c	100	30.25 N	121.00 E
Hani	130	38.24 N	40.24 E
Hänigsen	52	52.29 N	10.05 E
Hanimadu I	122	6.45 N	73.09 E
Hani̇sh II	144	13.45 N	42.45 E
Hanish al-Kabīr, Jazīrat al- I	144	13.43 N	42.45 E
Hanita	132	33.05 N	35.10 E
Hanjalipan	102	2.15 S	112.47 E
Hanjiagou	104	40.42 N	120.47 E
Hanjiang	100	25.30 N	119.06 E
Hanjiapuzi	104	40.48 N	123.14 E
Hanjiang	105	31.16 N	119.18 E
Hanjiawan	106	31.16 N	119.18 E
Hanjiawan	222	29.51 N	94.38 W
Hankasalmi	26	62.23 N	26.26 E
Hanke	26	59.12 N	10.47 E
Hankendi	130	38.35 N	39.04 E
Hankensbüttel	54	52.44 N	10.36 E
Hankey	158	33.50 S	24.53 E
Hankinson	198	46.04 N	96.54 W
Hanko — Hangö	26	59.50 N	22.57 E
Hankow — Wuhan	100	30.36 N	114.17 E
Hanks Pond ⊜	276	41.05 N	74.26 W
Hanku — Hangu	105	39.15 N	117.47 E
Hänle	123	32.48 N	79.00 E
Hanley	184	51.37 N	106.26 W
Hanmer	192	46.39 N	80.56 W
Hanmer Springs	172	42.31 S	172.49 E
Hanna, Ab., Can.	182	51.38 N	111.54 W
Hanna, Ok., U.S.	196	35.12 N	95.53 W
Hanna City	192	40.41 N	89.47 W
Hannaford	198	47.19 N	98.11 W
Hannah Bay c	176	51.05 N	79.45 W
Hannastown	214	40.19 N	79.32 W
Hannibal, Mo., U.S.	219	39.42 N	91.21 W
Hannibal, N.Y., U.S.	210	43.19 N	76.34 W
Hanningfield Reservoir ⊜¹	260	51.39 N	0.31 E
Hannover	52	52.24 N	9.44 E
Hannover □⁸	52	52.22 N	9.48 E
Hannover, Flughafen ⇄	52	52.27 N	9.42 E
Hannover, Isla I	254	51.00 S	74.50 W
Hannover, On., Can.	212	44.09 N	81.02 W
Hannover — Hannover	52	52.24 N	9.44 E
Hanover, S. Afr.	158	31.04 S	24.29 E
Hanover, II., U.S.	204	42.15 N	84.33 W
Hanover, Ks., U.S.	198	39.54 N	96.53 W
Hanover, Ma., U.S.	207	42.08 N	70.49 W
Hanover, N.H., U.S.	188	43.42 N	72.17 W
Hanover, Pa., U.S.	208	39.48 N	76.59 W
Hanover, Va., U.S.	208	37.46 N	77.22 W
Hanover □⁶, Va., U.S.	208	37.46 N	77.22 W
Hanover Center	283	42.07 N	70.50 W
Hansard	182	54.05 N	121.52 W

Hanscom Air Force Base ■	207	42.28 N	71.17 W
Hans Creek ≃	210	43.06 N	74.08 W
Handina	124	24.36 N	87.05 E
Hansen Dam ⩲⁶	280	34.16 N	118.23 W
Hansen Flood Control Basin ⊜¹	228	34.16 N	118.23 W
Hanshan	100	31.44 N	118.08 E
Hansharo ⊥	94	35.02 N	138.56 E
Hansi, India	120	32.27 N	77.50 E
Hänsi, India	123	29.06 N	75.58 E
Hansika	272b	22.48 N	88.24 E
Hanska	198	44.09 N	94.29 W
Hänskhäli	126	23.21 N	88.37 E
Hans Lollik Island I	240m	18.24 N	64.55 W
Hanslope	42	52.06 N	0.49 W
Hans Meyer Range ⩲	164	4.20 S	152.55 E
Hanson	207	42.04 N	70.52 W
Hanson ≃	162	20.15 S	133.25 E
Hanson Lake ⩲	184	54.42 N	102.49 W
Hanstedt	54	51.02 N	3.00 E
Hanstholm	26	57.07 N	8.38 E
Han-sur-Lesse	56	50.08 N	5.11 E
Han-sur-Nied	56	48.59 N	6.26 E
Hansville	224	47.55 N	122.33 W
Hansweert	52	51.26 N	4.00 E
Hantaj	88	49.31 N	103.13 E
Häntälbunia	126	22.44 N	89.31 E
Hantamsberg ⩲	158	31.22 S	19.45 E
Hantan			
— Handan	98	36.37 N	114.29 E
Hantes ≃	50	50.19 N	4.11 E
Hant's Harbour	186	48.01 N	53.16 W
Hantsport	186	45.04 N	64.11 W
Hantu, Pulau I	271c	1.14 N	103.45 E
Hantu, Tanjong ⋗	116	4.01 N	100.37 E
Hanumangarh	124	29.35 N	74.19 E
Hanumän Nagar	123	29.35 N	74.19 E
Hanušovce nad Topl'ou	30	49.02 N	21.30 E
Hanušovice	16	55.16 N	0.23 W
Hanved	260	59.07 N	18.00 E
Hanven ⩲²	40	59.07 N	18.00 E
Hanwood	166	34.20 S	146.03 E
Hanworth ⩲⁸	260	51.26 N	0.23 W
Hanxinzhuang	105	40.16 N	116.44 E
Hanyang	100	29.44 N	103.44 E
Hanyangping	102	32.41 N	108.34 E
Hanyin	102	32.42 N	108.50 E
Hanyü	94	36.10 N	139.32 E
Hanyuan	100	29.22 N	102.38 E
HanyuangXi	102	32.11 N	108.30 E
Hanzan	98	34.16 N	133.51 E
Hanzhong	102	33.08 N	107.02 E
Hanzhuang	105	34.38 N	117.24 E
Hao I	14	18.15 S	140.54 W
Haohekou	100	28.27 N	119.56 E
Haojiadian	100	31.47 N	113.44 E
Haoli			
— Hegang	89	47.24 N	130.17 E
Haoluqi	106	30.38 N	119.34 E
HaOn	132	32.43 N	35.38 E
Häora	126	22.35 N	88.20 E
Häora Bridge ⩲⁵	272b	22.35 N	88.21 E
Häora Railway Station ⇄	272b	22.35 N	88.21 E
Haouach, Ouadi V	146	16.45 N	19.35 E
Haoxue	100	30.00 N	112.20 E
Haozhikou	102	29.36 N	105.02 E
Haparanda	26	65.50 N	24.10 E
Hapatoni, Baie c	174x	9.58 S	139.07 W
Hapert	52	51.23 N	5.15 E
Häpo'o-ri	98	40.40 N	127.49 E
Happ, Mount ⩲	196	34.45 N	101.52 W
Happy Camp	204	41.47 N	123.22 W
Happy Jack	200	34.45 N	111.11 W
Happy Valley-Goose Bay	176	53.20 N	60.25 W
Happy Valley Race Course ♦	271d	22.16 N	114.10 E
Hapsford	262	53.16 N	2.48 W
Hapsu	98	41.13 N	128.51 E
Hapton	262	53.47 N	2.19 W
Häpur	123	28.43 N	77.47 E
Haqira	144	14.13 S	72.11 W
Har, Laga ≃	154	1.40 N	39.36 E
Hara, Nihon	94	35.58 N	138.14 E
Harad, Ar. Su.	144	24.08 N	49.05 E
Härad, Sve.	40	59.23 N	16.55 E
Harad, Yaman	144	16.20 N	43.06 E
Härädok	76	55.26 N	29.59 E
Haradzec, Bela.	76	53.20 N	26.62 E
Haradzec, Bela.	76	53.19 N	26.32 E
Haradziszča	76	53.19 N	26.32 E
Haradok	76	55.30 N	30.00 E
Harajuku	98	40.50 N	140.33 E
Haraldsted	41	55.30 N	11.47 E
Haram	26	62.35 N	6.15 E
Haramachi	98	37.38 N	141.00 E
Haramosh Range ⩲	123	35.40 N	74.54 E
Harany	76	55.25 N	29.32 E
Harappa Road	123	30.36 N	72.55 E
Harar — Harer (Salisbury)	144	9.18 N	42.08 E
Harare (Salisbury)	154	17.50 S	31.03 E
Harasta, Bi'r al- ⊤¹	132	33.33 N	36.22 E
Harastah al-Basal	132	33.35 N	36.21 E
Harāt	272b	22.35 N	88.11 E
Haraz-Djombo	146	13.57 N	19.08 E
Haraze-Mangueigne	146	9.55 N	20.48 E
Harbatj	88	55.30 N	109.35 E
Harbavičy	76	53.49 N	30.41 E
Harbel	150	6.18 N	10.21 W
Harbin	88	45.45 N	126.41 E
Harbke	54	52.12 N	11.03 E
Harbiye	130	36.11 N	36.10 E
Harbo	40	60.11 N	17.33 E
Harboør	26	56.37 N	8.10 E
Harbor Beach	204	43.50 N	82.39 W
Harbor Bluffs	220	27.56 N	82.49 W
Harbor City ⩲⁸	280	33.48 N	118.17 W
Harborcreek	214	42.10 N	79.57 W
Harborside	207	44.20 N	68.48 W
Harbor Side	276	40.43 N	73.40 W
Harbor Isle	276	40.36 N	73.40 W
Harbor Springs	204	45.25 N	84.59 W
Harbor Tunnel ⩲⁵	284b	39.15 N	76.34 W
Harbour Breton	186	47.29 N	55.48 W
Harbour Deep	186	50.25 N	56.32 W
Harbour Grace	186	47.42 N	53.13 W
Harbours, Bay of c	254	52.25 S	59.25 W
Harbourville	186	45.09 N	64.44 W
Harburg	64	48.47 N	9.59 E
Harbury	42	52.14 N	1.27 W
Harcourt, Austl.	274d	37.00 S	144.15 E
Harcourt, Ia., U.S.	198	42.16 N	94.10 W
Harcuvar Mountains ⩲	200	34.00 N	113.30 W
Hard	64	47.29 N	9.41 E
Harda	124	22.20 N	77.06 E
Hardangerfjorden c²	26	60.10 N	6.00 E
Hardangerjøkulen ⌊	26	60.33 N	7.28 E
Hardangervidda ⩲¹	26	60.20 N	7.30 E

	Page	Lat.	Long.
Hardangervidda Nasjonalpark ♦	26	60.15 N	7.05 E
Hardap □⁴	156	24.30 S	17.00 E
Hardapdam @¹	156	24.28 S	17.48 E
Hardee □⁶	220	27.29 N	81.48 W
Hardeeville	192	32.17 N	81.04 W
Hardegarijp	52	53.13 N	5.56 E
Hardegsen	52	51.39 N	9.49 E
Hardelot-Plage	50	50.38 N	1.35 E
Hardenberg	52	52.34 N	6.37 E
Harderwijk	52	52.21 N	5.38 E
Hardesty	196	36.36 N 101.11 W	
Hardey ≃	162	22.45 S 116.07 E	
Hardgrave, Mount ∧²	171a	27.30 S 153.29 E	
Hardheim	56	49.36 N	9.28 E
Hardin, Il., U.S.	219	39.09 N	90.37 W
Hardin, Mt., U.S.	202	45.43 N 107.36 W	
Hardin, Tx., U.S.	222	30.09 N	94.44 W
Hardin □⁶, Oh., U.S.	216	40.39 N	83.36 W
Hardin □⁶, Tx., U.S.	222	30.30 N	94.35 W
Harding, S. Afr.	158	30.34 S	29.58 E
Harding, Il., U.S.	216	41.31 N	88.51 W
Harding, Ma., U.S.	283	42.12 N	71.27 W
Harding, Lake @¹	192	32.40 N	85.06 W
Harding Lake	184	56.13 N	98.23 W
Harding Lakes	208	39.27 N	74.45 W
Hardinsburg, In., U.S.	218	38.27 N	86.16 W
Hardinsburg, Ky., U.S.	194	37.46 N	86.27 W
Hardisty	182	52.40 N 111.18 W	
Hardisty Lake	176	64.30 N 117.45 W	
Hardoi	124	27.25 N	80.07 E
Hardoi Branch ≃	124	28.41 N	80.08 E
Hardricourt	261	49.01 N	1.54 E
Hardscrabble Wash V	200	34.39 N 109.28 W	
Hardt	263	51.07 N	6.58 E
Hardtner	198	37.00 N	98.38 W
Hardwick, Ga., U.S.	192	33.04 N	83.13 W
Hardwick, Ma., U.S.	207	42.21 N	72.12 W
Hardwood	194	30.49 N	91.23 W
Hardwood Ridge ∧	210	41.15 N	75.23 W
Hardy, Ar., U.S.	194	36.18 N	91.28 W
Hardy, Ne., U.S.	198	40.00 N	97.55 W
Hardy, Península ›¹	254	55.25 S	68.30 W
Hardy Bay C	176	75.02 N 115.16 W	
Hardy Creek ≃	214	42.52 N	81.52 W
Hardy Lake @	218	38.47 N	85.42 W
Hardy Lake State Recreation Area ♦	218	38.44 N	86.26 W
Hardys Pond ≃	283	42.25 N	71.15 W
Hare, Mount ∧	180	66.38 N 136.12 W	
Hare Bay	186	48.51 N	54.01 W
Hare Bay C	186	51.18 N	55.50 W
Harefield ♦⁸	260	51.36 N	0.29 W
Hareid	26	62.22 N	6.02 E
Hare Indien ≃	180	66.18 N 128.38 W	
Harelbeke	50	50.51 N	3.18 E
Haren, Dtsch.	52	52.47 N	7.14 E
Haren, Ned.	52	53.10 N	6.35 E
Hareøen I	176	70.25 N	54.50 W
Harer	148	9.19 N	42.07 E
Harerge □⁴	144	8.00 N	43.00 E
Hareskov	41	55.46 N	12.25 E
Hareto	144	9.20 N	37.06 E
Harewa	144	9.55 N	41.59 E
Harewood	172	43.29 S 172.35 E	
Harewood Park	284b	39.23 N	76.22 W
Harfleur	50	49.30 N	0.12 E
Harford, N.Y., U.S.	210	42.26 N	76.14 W
Harford, Pa., U.S.	210	41.47 N	75.42 W
Harford □⁶	208	39.32 N	76.21 W
Harford Heights	279b	40.22 N	79.46 W
Harford Mills	210	42.25 N	76.12 W
Harg, Sve.	40	59.49 N	18.57 E
Harg, Sve.	40	60.11 N	18.24 E
Hargele	144	5.20 N	42.05 E
Hargeville	261	48.53 N	1.45 E
Hargeysa	144	9.35 N	44.04 E
Harghita, Munţii ∧	38	46.35 N	25.30 E
Harghita, Munţii ∧	38	46.15 N	25.45 E
Hargrave	184	54.24 N	98.48 W
Hargrave Lake @	184	54.29 N	99.40 W
Hargshamn	40	60.10 N	18.28 E
Har Hu (Heihai) @	102	38.15 N	97.40 E
Hăriābhānga ≃¹	124	21.43 N	89.05 E
Hariāna	123	31.38 N	75.51 E
Hariarapitu	114	2.33 N	98.35 E
Harīb	144	14.57 N	45.30 E
Haribes	156	24.20 S	17.42 E
Haricha, Ḥamâda el ∼²	148	22.36 N	3.31 W
Haridwār	124	29.58 N	78.10 E
Harigabessho	270	34.37 N 135.58 E	
Harihar	122	14.31 N	75.48 E
Harihari	172	43.09 S 170.33 E	
Harihareṗēra	126	24.02 N	88.27 E
Harīke	123	31.10 N	74.57 E
Hārim	130	36.12 N	36.31 E
Harim, Jabal al- ∧	128	25.58 N	56.14 E
Harima	96	34.42 N 134.53 E	
Harima-nada ²²	92	34.30 N 134.33 E	
Harinagar	124	27.09 N	84.19 E
Harinākunda	126	23.39 N	89.03 E
Haringey □⁸	42	51.35 N	0.07 W
Hāringhāṭa ≃¹	126	21.54 N	89.57 E
Haringvliet V	52	51.47 N	4.10 E
Haringvlietbrug ♦⁵	52	51.45 N	4.20 E
Haringvlietdam ♦⁵	52	51.50 N	4.03 E
Haripāl	272b	22.49 N	88.07 E
Haripur, India	126	24.18 N	87.05 E
Haripur, India	272b	22.56 N	88.10 E
Harīpur, Pāk.	123	33.59 N	72.56 E
Harirāmpur	124	23.42 N	89.57 E
Harīrūd (Tedžen) ≃	128	37.24 N	60.38 E
Harischandra Range ∧			
Hārithān	129	19.15 N	74.05 E
Hariyo	130	36.16 N	37.05 E
Harjavalta	144	5.00 N	42.08 E
Härjedalen □⁹	26	61.19 N	22.08 E
Harkeberga	274b	38.00 S 145.21 E	
Härkeberga	40	59.42 N	17.11 E
Harkema-Opeinde	52	53.11 N	6.08 E
Harker Heights	222	31.06 N	97.40 W
Harkers Island	192	34.41 N	76.33 W
Harker Village	285	39.51 N	75.09 W
Harkness Memorial State Park ♦	207	41.18 N	72.07 W
Harkortsee @	263	51.24 N	7.25 E
Harlan, Ia., U.S.	216	41.11 N	84.55 W
Harlan, Ky., U.S.	192	36.50 N	83.19 W
Harlan County Lake @¹	198	40.04 N	99.16 W
Hårlau	38	47.26 N	26.54 E
Harlech	42	52.52 N	4.07 W
Harlem, Fl., U.S.	220	26.44 N	80.58 W
Harlem, Ga., U.S.	192	33.24 N	82.18 W
Harlem, Mt., U.S.	202	48.32 N 108.47 W	
Harlem	276	40.49 N	73.56 W
Harlem River ∨	284	40.48 N	73.54 W
Harlem Springs	214	40.31 N	81.02 W
Harlesien	260	51.32 N	0.14 W
Harleston	42	52.24 N	1.18 E
Harleton	222	32.40 N	94.34 W
Hårlev	41	55.21 N	12.15 E
Harleysville	208	40.16 N	75.17 W
Harlin	171a	26.59 S 152.22 E	
Harlingen, Ned.	52	53.10 N	5.25 E
Harlingen, Tx., U.S.	196	26.11 N	97.41 W
Harlingerode	54	51.54 N	10.31 E
Harlösa	41	55.43 N	13.32 E
Harlow	42	51.47 N	0.08 E
Harlow □⁸	260	51.43 N	0.07 E
Harlowton	202	46.26 N 109.50 W	

	Page	Lat.	Long.
Harlpur	272b	22.42 N	88.10 E
Harman	188	38.55 N	79.31 W
Harmancık	130	39.41 N	29.10 E
Harmånger	26	61.56 N	17.13 E
Harmanlı, Blg.	38	41.56 N	25.54 E
Harmanlı, Tür.	130	37.51 N	37.45 E
Harmanschlag	61	48.39 N	14.47 E
Harmar Heights	279b	40.33 N	79.49 W
Harmarville	279b	40.32 N	79.51 W
Hármashatár-hegy ∧	264c	47.33 N	19.00 E
Harmelen	52	52.05 N	4.58 E
Harmil I	144	16.31 N	40.09 E
Harmonsburg	214	41.40 N	80.19 W
Harmonville	285	40.06 N	75.17 W
Harmony, Ca., U.S.	226	35.35 N 121.01 W	
Harmony, In., U.S.	194	39.32 N	87.06 W
Harmony, Mn., U.S.	190	43.33 N	92.00 W
Harmony, N.J., U.S.	210	40.44 N	75.08 W
Harmony, Pa., U.S.	214	40.48 N	80.07 W
Harmony, R.I., U.S.	207	41.53 N	71.35 W
Harmony Brook ≃	276	40.48 N	74.34 W
Harmony Heights	220	27.29 N	80.21 W
Harmony Hills	285	39.42 N	75.41 W
Harmonyville	285	40.11 N	75.43 W
Harnai, India	122	17.48 N	73.06 E
Harnai, Pāk.	123	30.06 N	67.56 E
Harnäs	40	60.39 N	17.22 E
Harnätänr	124	27.19 N	84.01 E
Harndrup	41	55.28 N	10.02 E
Harney, Lake @	220	28.45 N	81.03 W
Harney, Lake @¹	220	28.45 N	81.03 W
Harney Basin ≃¹	200	43.14 N 119.00 W	
Harney Lake @	202	43.14 N 119.07 W	
Harney Peak ∧	198	43.51 N 103.31 W	
Harney Pond Canal ≃	220	27.00 N	81.04 W
Härnösand	26	62.38 N	17.56 E
Haro, Esp.	34	42.35 N	2.51 W
Haro, Ityo.	144	8.28 N	38.37 E
Haro, Cabo ›	232	27.52 N 110.54 W	
Harod ≃	132	32.31 N	35.33 E
Haroldo	272a	28.36 N	77.19 E
Harold Hill ♦⁸	260	51.36 N	0.13 E
Harold Parker State Forest ♦	283	42.37 N	71.05 W
Haroldswick	46a	60.41 N	0.50 W
Harold Wood ♦⁸	260	51.36 N	0.14 E
Haro Strait V	224	48.30 N 123.15 W	
Haroué	58	48.28 N	6.11 E
Harpālpur	124	25.17 N	79.20 E
Harpanahalli	122	14.48 N	75.59 E
Harpenden	42	51.49 N	0.22 W
Harper, Liber.	150	4.25 N	7.43 W
Harper, Ks., U.S.	198	37.17 N	98.01 W
Harper, Tx., U.S.	196	30.18 N	99.15 W
Harper, Wa., U.S.	224	47.31 N 122.31 W	
Harper, Mount ∧	180	64.14 N 143.50 W	
Harper Lake @	228	35.02 N 117.17 W	
Harpers Ferry National Historical Park ♦	188	39.13 N	77.45 W
Harpersfield	210	42.26 N	74.41 W
Harper Town	44	54.55 N	2.31 W
Harper Woods	214	42.25 N	82.55 W
Harpstedt	62	43.50 N	6.48 E
Harpster	214	40.44 N	83.15 W
Harpsund ♥	40	59.06 N	16.29 E
Harpur Hill	262	53.31 N	2.13 W
Harpur Hill	262	53.14 N	1.54 W
Harpursville	210	42.11 N	75.38 W
Harqahala Mountain ∧	200	33.49 N 113.21 W	
Harqahala Mountain ∧	200	33.49 N 113.21 W	
Harracksfield	210	42.26 N	74.41 W
Harrah, Jabal al- ∧	132	33.04 N	35.59 E
Harrai	124	22.37 N	79.13 E
Harran	130	36.51 N	39.00 E
Harrān al-'Awāmīd	132	33.27 N	36.34 E
Harray, Loch of @	46	59.01 N	3.13 W
Harrell	194	33.30 N	92.23 W
Harricana ≃	176	51.15 N	79.45 W
Harrietfield	46	56.25 N	3.39 W
Harriesham	42	51.15 N	0.41 E
Harriman, Tn., U.S.	192	35.56 N	84.33 W
Harriman State Park ♦	210	41.14 N	74.09 W
Harrington, Eng., U.K.	44	54.37 N	3.34 W
Harrington, De., U.S.	208	38.55 N	75.34 W
Harrington, Me., U.S.	188	44.37 N	67.48 W
Harrington, Wa., U.S.	202	47.28 N 118.15 W	
Harrington Creek ≃	282	37.19 N 122.18 W	
Harrington Drain ≃	281	42.36 N	82.54 W
Harrington Park	276	40.59 N	73.58 W
Harris, Sk., Can.	184	51.45 N 107.35 W	
Harris, Scot., U.K.	46	56.59 N	6.20 W
Harris, Mn., U.S.	190	45.35 N	92.58 W
Harris, N.Y., U.S.	210	41.43 N	74.44 W
Harris, R.I., U.S.	207	41.43 N	71.31 W
Harris □⁶	222	29.50 N	95.22 W
Harris ›¹	46	57.55 N	6.50 W
Harris, Lake @, Austl.	162	31.10 N 135.14 E	
Harris, Lake @, Fl., U.S.	220	28.46 N	81.49 W
Harris, Sound of V	46	57.45 N	7.10 W
Harris Bay C	182	45.23 N	77.50 W
Harris Brook ≃	283	42.44 N	71.13 W
Harrisburg, Il., U.S.	194	35.33 N	90.43 W
Harrisburg, Il., U.S.	194	37.44 N	88.32 W
Harrisburg, Mo., U.S.	218	39.41 N	85.11 W
Harrisburg, Oh., U.S.	214	39.37 N	83.06 W
Harrisburg, Or., U.S.	208	44.16 N 123.10 W	
Harrisburg, Pa., U.S.	208	40.16 N	76.53 W
Harrisdale	210	41.01 N	73.47 W
Harriseahes	56	34.26 N	86.56 W
Härtsfeld ♦¹	56	48.50 N	10.15 E
Harrisfield	274b	37.57 S 145.11 E	
Harris Hill	207	42.53 N	78.44 W
Harrislee	54	54.48 N	9.22 E
Harrison, Austl.	162	32.56 S 117.52 E	
Harrison, S. Afr.	158	28.43 S	23.45 E
Harrison, Ar., U.S.	194	36.13 N	93.06 W
Harrison, Id., U.S.	202	47.27 N 116.47 W	
Harrison, Il., U.S.	216	42.12 N	89.11 W
Harrison, Mi., U.S.	216	44.01 N	84.47 W
Harrison, N.J., U.S.	284	40.45 N	74.09 W
Harrison, N.Y., U.S.	208	40.16 N	76.53 W
Harrison, Oh., U.S.	216	39.15 N	84.47 W
Harrison, Ar., U.S.	194	38.13 N	93.06 W
Harrison, Cape ›	176	54.55 N	57.55 W
Harrison Bay C	180	70.30 N 151.30 W	
Harrisonburg, La., U.S.	194	31.46 N	91.49 W
Harrisonburg, Va., U.S.	188	38.26 N	78.52 W
Harrison City	279b	40.21 N	79.39 W
Harrison Hot Springs	224	49.18 N 121.47 W	
Harrison Islands II	176	69.13 N 90.30 W	
Harrison Lake @	182	49.33 N 121.50 W	
Harrison Mills	224	49.15 N 121.57 W	
Harrisons Brook ≃	276	40.38 N	74.34 W

	Page	Lat.	Long.
Harrison Tomb State Memorial ⊥	218	39.09 N	84.46 W
Harrison Valley	214	41.57 N	77.39 W
Harrisonville, Md., U.S.	284b	39.23 N	77.50 W
Harrisonville, Mo., U.S.	194	38.39 N	94.20 W
Harrisonville, N.J., U.S.	285	39.41 N	75.15 W
Harris Park	274a	33.49 S 151.01 E	
Harris Pond ≃	283	42.45 N	71.16 W
Harris Reservoir @¹	222	29.14 N	95.33 W
Harriston, On., Can.	212	43.54 N	80.53 W
Harriston, Ms., U.S.	194	31.43 N	91.01 W
Harristown	219	39.51 N	89.05 W
Harrisville, Austl.	171a	27.49 S 152.40 E	
Harrisville, Mi., U.S.	190	44.39 N	83.17 W
Harrisville, N.Y., U.S.	212	44.09 N	75.19 W
Harrisville, Oh., U.S.	214	40.11 N	80.53 W
Harrisville, Pa., U.S.	214	41.08 N	80.00 W
Harrisville, R.I., U.S.	207	41.57 N	71.40 W
Harrisville, W.V., U.S.	188	39.12 N	81.03 W
Harrod	216	40.42 N	83.55 W
Harrodsburg	194	37.45 N	84.50 W
Harrods Creek ≃	218	38.20 N	85.38 W
Harrogate	44	54.00 N	1.33 W
Harrold	44	53.20 N	0.12 W
Harrop Lake @	184	52.38 N	95.58 W
Harrow	214	42.02 N	82.55 W
Harrow △	42	51.35 N	0.21 W
Harrow on the Hill	260	51.34 N	0.20 W
Harrow School ♥²	260	51.34 N	0.20 W
Harrowsmith	212	44.24 N	76.40 W
Harry S. Truman Airport ✈	240m	18.21 N	64.59 W
Harry S. Truman Reservoir @¹	194	38.10 N	93.45 W
Har Sai Shan ∧	102	35.28 N	97.55 E
Harsefeld	52	53.27 N	9.30 E
Harsens Island	214	42.34 N	82.34 W
Harsens Island I	281	42.35 N	82.38 W
Harsewinkel	52	51.58 N	8.13 E
Harsīn	128	34.16 N	47.35 E
Harşīt ≃	130	41.01 N	38.52 E
Harskamp	52	52.07 N	5.45 E
Harsleben	54	51.52 N	11.05 E
Hårşova	38	44.41 N	27.57 E
Harstad	26	68.46 N	16.30 E
Harstena	26	58.16 N	17.01 E
Har Su	89	48.09 N 122.25 E	
Harsūd	124	22.06 N	76.44 E
Harsum	54	52.12 N	9.57 E
Hart, Mi., U.S.	216	43.41 N	86.21 W
Hart, Tx., U.S.	196	34.23 N 102.07 W	
Hart □⁶	192	34.20 N	82.56 W
Hart, Lake @, Austl.	162	31.08 S 136.24 E	
Hart, Lake @, Fl., U.S.	220	28.22 N	81.13 W
Hartå	132	32.42 N	35.51 E
Hartbees ≃	158	28.45 S	20.32 E
Hartbeesfontein	158	26.42 S	26.26 E
Hartbeespoort	158	25.44 S	27.52 E
Hartberg	61	47.17 N	15.59 E
Hartenholm	52	53.54 N	10.03 E
Hartenstein	54	50.39 N	12.40 E
Hart Fell ∧	44	55.25 N	3.25 W
Hartford, Eng., U.K.	262	53.15 N	2.33 W
Hartford, Al., U.S.	191	31.06 N	85.41 W
Hartford, Ar., U.S.	222	35.01 N	94.22 W
Hartford, Ct., U.S.	207	41.46 N	72.41 W
Hartford, Il., U.S.	219	38.50 N	90.05 W
Hartford, In., U.S.	218	38.59 N	84.57 W
Hartford, Ks., U.S.	198	38.18 N	95.57 W
Hartford, Ky., U.S.	194	37.27 N	86.54 W
Hartford, Mi., U.S.	216	42.12 N	86.10 W
Hartford, N.J., U.S.	285	39.58 N	74.53 W
Hartford, N.Y., U.S.	210	43.21 N	73.22 W
Hartford, Oh., U.S.	214	41.18 N	80.34 W
Hartford, S.D., U.S.	198	43.37 N	96.56 W
Hartford, Wi., U.S.	190	43.19 N	88.23 W
Hartford □⁶	207	41.46 N	72.41 W
Hartford City	216	40.27 N	85.22 W
Hartha	54	51.05 N	12.58 E
Hartmannsdorf	54	50.53 N	9.16 E
Hart-Miller Island I	284b	39.15 N	76.23 W
Hart Mountain ∧	184	52.29 N 101.25 W	
Hartney	184	49.28 N 100.30 W	
Hartola	26	61.35 N	26.01 E
Harts ≃	158	28.24 S	24.17 E
Hartsburg	219	38.41 N	92.18 W
Hartsdale	210	41.01 N	73.47 W
Hartselle	191	34.26 N	86.56 W
Hartshill	42	52.32 N	1.32 W
Hartshorne	196	34.50 N	95.33 W
Harts Range	162	23.00 S 134.55 E	
Hartstene Island I	224	47.14 N 122.53 W	
Hartstown	214	41.33 N	80.23 W
Hart Township	216	43.41 N	86.21 W
Hartville	198	37.15 N	92.30 W
Hartwell Lake @¹	192	34.30 N	82.52 W
Hartwick	210	42.42 N	74.54 W
Hartwick Pines State Park ♦	190	44.47 N	84.41 W
Hartz Mountains National Park ♦	166	43.15 S 146.50 E	
Harue	96	36.08 N 136.14 E	
Haruki	270	34.29 N 135.23 E	
Haruku, Pulau I	164	3.34 S 128.29 E	
Hărūn	128	31.20 N	25.42 E
Haruna	96	36.28 N 138.50 E	
Haruna-san ∧	96	36.28 N 138.50 E	
Haruniye	130	37.22 N	36.24 E
Haruno, Nihon	94	34.57 N 137.53 E	
Harūr	128	12.04 N	78.30 E
Harūt ≃	128	31.34 N	61.18 E
Harvard, Il., U.S.	216	42.25 N	88.36 W
Harvard, Ma., U.S.	207	42.30 N	71.35 W
Harvard, Mount ∧	204	38.55 N 106.19 W	
Harvard University ♦²	283	42.22 N	71.07 W
Harvel, Il., U.S.	219	39.21 N	89.32 W
Harvest, Al., U.S.	191	34.51 N	86.45 W
Harvey, Austl.	162	33.05 S 115.54 E	
Harvey, N.B., Can.	186	45.43 N	64.45 W
Harvey, Il., U.S.	216	41.36 N	87.38 W
Harvey, N.D., U.S.	198	47.46 N	99.55 W
Harvey Estuary C¹	168a	32.43 S 115.42 E	

	Page	Lat.	Long.
Harvey Mountain ∧	207	42.18 N	73.25 W
Harvey Reservoir @¹	168a	33.05 S 115.58 E	
Harveysburg	218	39.30 N	84.00 W
Harveys Lake	210	41.23 N	76.02 W
Harwell	42	51.37 N	1.18 W
Harwich, Eng., U.K.	42	51.57 N	1.17 E
Harwich, Ma., U.S.	207	41.41 N	70.04 W
Harwich Port	207	41.40 N	70.04 W
Harwick	279b	40.34 N	79.48 W
Harwinton	207	41.46 N	73.03 W
Harwood, Eng., U.K.	262	53.35 N	2.23 W
Harwood, Tx., U.S.	222	29.40 N	97.30 W
Harwood Heights	278	41.58 N	87.48 W
Harwood Mines	210	40.57 N	76.01 W
Harwood Park	284b	39.12 N	76.44 W
Haryāṇa □³	120	29.20 N	76.20 E
Haryn' (Horyn') ≃	78	52.08 N	27.17 E
Harz ∧	54	51.45 N	10.30 E
Harzgerode	54	51.38 N	11.08 E
Haṭeg	38	45.37 N	22.57 E
Haterumu-shima I	175d	24.03 N 123.47 E	
Hatfield, Austl.	166	33.52 S 143.45 E	
Hatfield, Eng., U.K.	42	51.46 N	0.13 W
Hatfield, Eng., U.K.	44	53.34 N	1.00 W
Hatfield, Ar., U.S.	194	34.29 N	94.22 W
Hatfield, Ma., U.S.	207	42.22 N	72.35 W
Hatfield Aerodrome ✈	260	51.46 N	0.16 W
Hatfield House ⊥	260	51.46 N	0.13 W
Hatfield Peverel	42	51.47 N	0.35 E
Hatfield Swamp ⌂	276	40.50 N	74.20 W
Hathā	123	32.03 N	70.34 E
Hathaway Pines	226	38.07 N 120.28 W	
Hatherleigh	42	50.49 N	4.04 W
Hathersage	44	53.19 N	1.38 W
Hāthras	124	27.36 N	78.03 E
Hātia I	124	22.30 N	91.15 E
Hātibah, Ra's ›	144	21.55 N	38.58 E
Ha Tien	110	10.23 N 104.29 E	
Hatillo	240m	18.29 N	66.49 W
Hatinoe — Hachinohe	92	40.30 N 141.29 E	
Hatioci — Hachiōji	94	35.39 N 139.20 E	
Hatip	130	37.46 N	32.25 E
Hātisāba	272b	22.33 N	88.32 E
Hato, Bocht van C	241s	12.13 N	68.58 W
Hatogaya	94	35.50 N 139.44 E	
Hato Mayor [del Rey]	238	18.46 N	69.15 W
Hato Rey	240m	18.26 N	66.03 W
Hatoyuga	76	53.17 N	7.18 E
Hatsugai	94	35.59 N 139.20 E	
Hatsukaichi	96	34.21 N 132.20 E	
Hatsu-shima I	95	35.02 N 139.10 E	
Hatsumoto	268	35.46 N 140.01 E	
Hatta	124	24.07 N	79.36 E
Hattah, Oued el ∨	36	35.33 N	9.32 E
Hattah-Kulkyne National Park ♦	166	34.40 S 142.30 E	
Hatten, Dtsch.	52	53.02 N	8.22 E
Hatten, Fr.	56	48.54 N	7.59 E
Hattenhofen	60	48.13 N	11.07 E
Hatteras, Cape ›	192	35.13 N	75.41 W
Hatteras Island I	192	35.25 N	75.30 W
Hattiesburg	194	31.19 N	89.17 W
Hatting	41	55.51 N	9.46 E
Hattingen	56	51.23 N	7.10 E
Hattingspruit	158	28.09 S	30.11 E
Hatton, Eng., U.K.	262	53.20 N	2.40 W
Hatton, Scot., U.K.	46	57.25 N	1.54 W
Hatton, Al., U.S.	191	34.33 N	87.24 W
Hatton, N.D., U.S.	198	47.38 N	97.27 W
Hatton □⁸	260	51.28 N	0.25 W
Hatton Fields	226	36.33 N 121.54 W	
Hattorf [am Harz]	52	51.39 N	10.14 E
Hattori, Nihon	270	34.46 N 135.27 E	
Hattori, Nihon	270	34.52 N 135.36 E	
Hattstatt	45	47.59 N	7.16 E
Hattstedt	41	54.31 N	9.01 E
Hatunsaray	130	37.35 N	32.21 E
Hatyzfeld	56	51.00 N	8.33 E
Hatzic	224	49.09 N 122.16 W	
Hatzic Lake @	224	49.10 N 122.16 W	
Häudullāpur	272b	22.25 N	88.23 E
Hauge	26	58.18 N	6.15 E
Haughton Green	262	53.27 N	2.06 W
Haugsdorf	61	48.42 N	16.05 E
Hau Hin ⌂	100	22.28 N 113.56 E	
Hauja	172	38.50 S 175.34 E	
Haukeligrend	26	59.45 N	7.31 E
Haukipudas	26	65.11 N	25.21 E
Haukivesi @	26	62.06 N	28.26 E
Haulatasaina	240m	18.03 N	67.11 W
Haultain ≃	184	55.51 N 106.46 W	
Haunan ≃	58	48.20 N	7.38 E
Haunersdorf	60	48.36 N	12.43 E
Haunstetten	60	48.20 N	10.54 E
Hauppauge	210	40.49 N	73.13 W
Hauraki Gulf C	172	36.30 S 175.00 E	
Hauroko, Lake @	172	46.00 S 167.20 E	
Hauru, Pointe ›	174s	17.29 S 149.55 W	
Haus	26	60.34 N	5.28 E
Hausach	273a	48.17 N	8.11 E
Hausham	60	47.45 N	11.50 E
Hausnack ≃	264a	52.38 N	13.35 E
Haussömmern	54	51.11 N	10.49 E
Haut, Isle au I	188	44.03 N	68.38 W
Haut Atlas ∧	148	31.30 N	6.00 W
Haut-Bocage □⁵	261	50.50 N	2.12 E
Haute Colme, Canal de ∨			
Hautecombe, Abbaye de ⊥	59	45.45 N	5.50 E
Haute-Corse □⁵	62	42.30 N	9.15 E
Haute-Garonne □⁵	48	43.25 N	1.15 E
Haut-Mbomou □⁴	154	6.00 N	26.00 E
Haute-Kotto □⁴	152	8.00 N	22.30 E
Hautelouce	59	45.41 N	6.33 E
Haute-Marne □⁵	48	48.12 N	5.10 E
Hauterive	186	49.12 N	68.16 W
Hautes-Alpes □⁵	48	44.40 N	6.25 E
Haute-Sangha □⁴	152	4.30 N	15.30 E
Haute-Savoie □⁵	48	46.00 N	6.20 E
Haute Seine, Canal de ∨			
Hautes Fagnes ✦	50	50.30 N	6.05 E
Hautes-Pyrénées □⁵	48	43.00 N	0.10 E
Haute Sûre, Lac de @¹	263	49.52 N	5.52 E
— Burkina Faso ¹	150	13.00 N	2.00 W
Haut-Koenigsbourg, Château du ⊥	45	48.15 N	7.20 E
Hautmont	50	50.15 N	3.56 E
Haut-Ogooué □⁴	152	1.30 S	13.30 E
Haut-Rhin □⁵	48	47.53 N	7.13 E
Haute-Saône □⁵	261	47.38 N	2.11 E
Hautvillers	58	49.05 N	3.57 E

	Page	Lat.	Long.
Hatay □⁴	130	36.30 N	36.15 E
Hatboro	208	40.10 N	75.06 W
Hatch, N.M., U.S.	200	32.39 N 107.09 W	
Hatch, Ut., U.S.	200	37.38 N 112.26 W	
Hat Chao Mai National Park ♦	110	7.40 N	99.35 E
Hatches Creek	162	20.56 S 135.12 E	
Hatchet Creek ≃	134	32.52 N	86.20 W
Hatchet Lake	186	44.35 N	63.40 W
Hatchie ≃	194	35.35 N	89.53 W
Hatchineha, Lake @	220	28.02 N	81.25 W
Hatchlands ⊥	260	51.15 N	0.28 W
Hatchville	207	41.37 N	70.33 W
Hatch Wash ∨	200	38.32 N 109.36 W	
Hat Creek ≃, U.S.	198	43.16 N 103.36 W	
Hat Creek ≃, Ca., U.S.	204	40.59 N 121.33 W	
Hatherleigh	42	50.49 N	4.04 W
Havana ³ — La Habana, Cuba	240p	23.08 N	82.22 W
Havana, Ar., U.S.	194	35.06 N	93.31 W
Havana, Il., U.S.	194	40.18 N	90.03 W
Havana, N.D., U.S.	198	45.57 N	97.37 W
Havane, La — La Habana	240p	23.08 N	82.22 W
Havannah, Canal de la ∨	175f	22.22 S 167.01 E	
Havant	42	50.51 N	0.59 W
Havasu, Lake @¹	200	34.30 N 114.20 W	
Havasu Creek ≃	200	36.19 N 112.46 W	
Havasupai Indian Reservation ♦⁴	200	36.10 N 112.40 W	
Havdrup	41	55.32 N	12.08 E
Havel ≃	54	52.53 N	11.58 E
Havelange	50	50.23 N	5.14 E
Havelberg	54	52.50 N	12.04 E
Havelberg ∧²	264a	52.28 N	13.12 E
Haveli	123	30.27 N	73.42 E
Havelián	123	34.03 N	73.10 E
Havel-Kanal ⌂	264a	52.36 N	13.12 E
Havelland ∼¹	54	52.25 N	12.45 E
Havelländischer Grosser Hauptkanal ⌂	264a	52.37 N	13.03 E
Havelländisches Luch ⌂			
Havelock, On., Can.	212	44.26 N	77.53 W
Havelock, N.Z.	172	41.17 S 173.46 E	
Havelock, N.C., U.S.	192	34.52 N	76.54 W
Havelock Island I	110	11.58 N	93.00 E
Havelock North	172	39.40 S 176.53 E	
Haven	198	37.53 N	97.46 W
Haverford	285	40.00 N	75.17 W
Haverford College ♥²	285	40.00 N	75.18 W
Haverfordwest	42	51.49 N	4.58 W
Haverhill, Eng., U.K.	42	52.05 N	0.26 E
Haverhill, Ma., U.S.	207	42.46 N	71.04 W
Haverhill Airport ✈	283	42.48 N	71.04 W
Haverhill-Riverside Airport ✈	283	42.46 N	71.02 W
Häveri	122	14.48 N	75.24 E
Haverigg	44	54.11 N	3.17 W
Havering ∼⁸	42	51.34 N	0.14 E
Havering-atte-Bower	260	51.37 N	0.11 E
Havering's Grove	260	51.38 N	0.23 E
Havern	26	62.17 N	15.07 E
Haverö	26	62.24 N	15.05 E
Haverstraw	210	41.11 N	73.57 W
Havertown	208	39.58 N	75.18 W
Haviland, S., U.S.	198	37.37 N	99.06 W
Haviland, Oh., U.S.	216	41.01 N	84.35 W
Haviland Brook ≃	276	41.07 N	73.33 W
Havlíq	128	38.10 N	48.54 E
Havixbeck	52	51.59 N	7.24 E
Hävla	40	58.55 N	15.52 E
Havlíčkův Brod	30	49.36 N	15.35 E
Havnbjerg	41	55.02 N	9.48 E
Havnsø	41	55.45 N	11.20 E
Havran	130	39.33 N	27.06 E
Havre, Bel.	50	50.28 N	4.02 E
— Le Havre, Fr.	50	49.30 N	0.08 E
Havre, Mt., U.S.	202	48.32 N 109.40 W	
Havre-Aubert	186	47.14 N	61.51 W
Havre-Aubert, Île de I	186	47.14 N	61.51 W
Havre aux Maisons, Île du I	186	47.25 N	61.47 W
Havre de Grace	208	39.32 N	76.05 W
Havre North	208	48.36 N 109.41 W	
Havre-Saint-Pierre	186	50.14 N	63.36 W
Havsa	130	41.33 N	26.49 E
Havza	130	40.58 N	35.41 E
Haw ≃	192	35.36 N	79.03 W
Hawaii ᴵᴵ²	235a	20.00 N 157.45 W	
Hawaii □³	174b	21.36 N 157.54 W	
Hawaii I	173	19.30 N 155.30 W	
Hawarden, N.Z.	172	42.56 S 172.38 E	
Hawarden, Ia., U.S.	198	42.59 N	96.29 W
Hawarden, Wales, U.K.	44	53.11 N	3.02 W
Hawashīyah, Wādī ∨	140	28.31 N	32.58 E
Hawea, Lake @	172	44.30 S 169.17 E	
Hawera	172	39.35 S 174.17 E	
Hawes	44	54.18 N	2.12 W
Haweswater Reservoir @¹	44	54.30 N	2.48 W
Hawi	173	20.14 N 155.50 W	
Hawick	44	55.25 N	2.47 W
Hawk Creek ≃	198	44.54 N	95.25 W
Hawkdun Range ∧	172	44.46 S 170.00 E	
Hawke, Cape ›	166	32.13 S 152.34 E	
Hawke Bay C	172	39.20 S 177.30 E	
Hawkes, Mount ∧	181	83.56 S 55.45 W	
Hawkesbury	212	45.37 N	74.37 W
Hawkesbury ≃	166	33.33 S 151.11 E	
Hawkesbury Island I	178	53.37 N 129.02 W	
Hawkesbury Pond ≃	283	42.15 N	71.57 W
Hawkeye	190	42.56 N	91.57 W
Hawkhurst	260	51.03 N	0.31 E
Hawkins, Tx., U.S.	222	32.35 N	95.12 W
Hawkins, Wi., U.S.	190	45.30 N	90.43 W
Hawkins Island I	180	60.34 N 146.00 W	
Hawks	190	45.17 N	83.53 W
Hawk Junction	184	48.05 N	84.38 W
Hawk Run	214	40.54 N	78.11 W
Hawk Point	219	38.58 N	91.07 W
Hawksbill Creek ≃	214	38.33 N	78.22 W
Hawks Nest Point ›	238	24.09 N	75.32 W
Hawkwell	260	51.36 N	0.40 E
Hawkwood	171a	25.45 S 150.50 E	
Hawkesville	207	43.22 N	80.34 W
Haworth, Eng., U.K.	44	53.50 N	1.57 W
Haworth, N.J., U.S.	276	40.58 N	73.59 W
Haw Par Villa ♥¹	271c	1.17 N 103.47 E	
Hawsker	44	54.27 N	0.34 W
Hawthorn, Austl.	274b	37.49 S 145.02 E	
Hawthorne, Ca., U.S.	228	33.54 N 118.21 W	
Hawthorne, Nv., U.S.	204	38.31 N 118.37 W	
Hawthorne, N.J., U.S.	210	40.56 N	74.09 W
Hawthorne Lake @	276	41.03 N	74.35 W

Hawt-Herk I · 71

ESPAÑOL — Nombre | Página | Lat.°′ | Long.°′ W = Oeste
FRANÇAIS — Nom | Page | Lat.°′ | Long.°′ W = Ouest
PORTUGUÊS — Nome | Página | Lat.°′ | Long.°′ W = Oeste

Nombre	Página	Lat.°′	Long.°′ W = Oeste
Hawthorne Municipal Airport ⊠	280	33.55 N	118.20 W
Hawthorne Race Course ♠	278	41.50 N	87.45 W
Hawthorn Woods	278	42.13 N	88.03 W
Ḥawwārah	132	32.32 N	35.54 E
Hawwārat ʿAdlān	142	29.12 N	30.58 E
Hawwārat al-Maqṭaʿ	142	29.15 N	30.54 E
Hawza	148	27.06 N	10.55 W
Hawzen	144	13.56 N	39.28 E
Haxby	44	54.01 N	1.04 W
Haxey	44	53.29 N	0.50 W
Haxtun	198	40.38 N	102.37 W
Hay	166	34.30 S	144.51 E
Hay ≃, Austl.	166	25.14 S	138.00 E
Hay ≃, Can.	176	60.52 N	115.44 W
Hay ≃, Wi., U.S.	190	44.59 N	91.51 W
Hay, Cape ≻	176	74.25 N	113.00 W
Hay, Mount ∧, Austl.	162	23.28 S	133.05 E
Hay, Mount ∧, Austl.	170	33.37 S	150.26 E
Hay, Mount ∧, N.A.	180	59.15 N	137.37 W
Hay, South Fork ≃	190	45.03 N	91.57 W
Haya	164	3.27 S	129.33 E
Haya ≃, Nihon	94	35.14 N	139.09 E
Haya ≃, Nihon	94	35.25 N	138.27 E
Hayachine-san ∧	92	39.34 N	141.29 E
Hayakawa	94	35.25 N	138.22 E
Hayama, Nihon	94	35.16 N	139.35 E
Hayama, Nihon	96	33.26 N	133.13 E
Hayang	98	35.55 N	128.47 E
Hayange	56	49.20 N	6.03 E
Hayashima	96	34.36 N	133.50 E
Hayastan → Armenia □[1]	22	40.00 N	45.00 E
Hayasui-seto ꭒ	96	33.18 N	131.59 E
Haybān	140	11.13 N	30.31 E
Haybān, Jabal ∧	140	11.15 N	30.31 E
Hay Bay ⊂	212	44.10 N	76.55 W
Haybes	56	50.00 N	4.43 E
Haychur ≃	78	47.57 N	36.11 E
Haydān, Wādī al- V	132	31.27 N	35.36 E
Haydarlı	130	38.16 N	30.23 E
Hayden, Az., U.S.	200	33.00 N	110.47 W
Hayden, Co., U.S.	200	40.29 N	107.15 W
Hayden, In., U.S.	218	38.58 N	85.44 W
Hayden Peak ∧	202	42.59 N	116.39 W
Haydenville, Ma., U.S.	207	42.22 N	72.42 W
Haydenville, Oh., U.S.	188	39.28 N	82.19 W
Haydock	44	53.28 N	2.39 W
Haydock Park Race Course ♠	262	53.29 N	2.37 W
Haydon Bridge	44	54.58 N	2.14 W
Haye, La → 's-Gravenhage	52	52.06 N	4.18 E
Hayes	194	30.06 N	92.55 W
Hayes ◆[8], Eng., U.K.	260	51.31 N	0.25 W
Hayes ◆[8], Eng., U.K.	260	51.23 N	0.01 E
Hayes ≃, Mb., Can.	184	57.03 N	92.09 W
Hayes ≃, N.T., Can.	176	67.18 N	95.02 W
Hayes, Mount ∧	180	63.37 N	146.43 W
Hayes Center	198	40.30 N	101.01 W
Hayes State Memorial ⊥	214	41.21 N	83.08 W
Hayesville, N.C., U.S.	192	35.02 N	83.49 W
Hayesville, Oh., U.S.	214	40.46 N	82.15 W
Hayesville, Or., U.S.	224	44.59 N	122.58 W
Hayfield, Eng., U.K.	262	53.23 N	1.57 W
Hayfield, Mn., U.S.	190	43.53 N	92.50 W
Hayford Peak ∧	204	36.40 N	115.11 W
Hayfork	204	40.33 N	123.10 W
Hayfork Bally ∧	204	40.39 N	123.13 W
Hayfork Creek ≃	204	40.37 N	123.26 W
Hayingen	58	48.17 N	9.29 E
Hay Island I	212	44.53 N	80.58 W
Hayk, Lake ⊜	144	11.21 N	39.43 E
Haykota	144	15.10 N	37.03 E
Hay Lake ⊜	212	45.23 N	78.11 W
Hay Lakes	182	53.13 N	113.03 W
Hayle	42	50.11 N	5.23 W
Haymakers Run ≃	279b	40.25 N	79.43 W
Haymana	130	39.27 N	32.30 E
Haynes	194	34.53 N	90.47 W
Haynes Creek ≃	285	39.53 N	74.50 W
Haynesville, La., U.S.	194	32.57 N	93.08 W
Haynesville, Va., U.S.	208	37.57 N	76.40 W
Hayneville	194	32.11 N	86.34 W
Haynin	144	15.50 N	48.19 E
Hay-on-Wye	42	52.04 N	3.07 W
Hay Point ≻	166	21.17 S	149.18 E
Hayrabolu	130	41.12 N	27.06 E
Hay River	176	60.51 N	115.40 W
Hays, Ab., Can.	182	50.06 N	111.48 W
Hays, Ks., U.S.	198	38.52 N	99.19 W
Hays, Mt., U.S.	202	47.59 N	108.41 W
Hays □[6]	222	30.02 N	97.45 W
Hays ◆[8]	279b	40.23 N	79.56 W
Hayshah, Sabkhat al- ⩶	146	31.45 N	15.20 E
Hays Mill Creek ≃	285	39.44 N	74.50 W
Hay Springs	198	42.41 N	102.41 W
Haystack Mountain ∧	204	41.39 N	115.38 W
Haysville, Ks., U.S.	198	37.33 N	97.21 W
Haysville, Pa., U.S.	279b	40.32 N	80.09 W
Haysyn	78	48.48 N	29.24 E
Hayti, Mo., U.S.	194	36.14 N	89.44 W
Hayti, Pa., U.S.	208	39.59 N	75.51 W
Hayti, S.D., U.S.	198	44.39 N	97.12 W
Hayvoron	78	48.22 N	29.52 E
Hayward, Ca., U.S.	226	37.40 N	122.04 W
Hayward, Wi., U.S.	190	46.00 N	91.29 W
Hayward Brook ≃	283	42.22 N	71.20 W
Hayward Municipal Airport ⊠	282	37.40 N	122.08 W
Haywards Heath	42	51.00 N	0.06 W
Haywood	184	49.40 N	98.12 W
Ḥayy, Jabal al- ∧	142	29.43 N	31.35 E
HaẔafon □[5]	132	32.50 N	35.20 E
Hazār, Kūh-e ∧	128	29.30 N	57.18 E
Hazard	192	37.14 N	83.11 W
Hazardville	207	41.59 N	72.32 W
Hazar Gölü ⊜	130	38.30 N	39.25 E
Hazārībāg	124	23.59 N	85.21 E
Hazārībāg Plateau ⋏[1]	124	24.00 N	85.10 E
Haze, Cape ≻	220	26.46 N	82.10 W
Hazebrouck	50	50.43 N	2.32 E
Hazel ≃	188	38.33 N	77.51 W
Hazelbrook	170	33.44 S	150.27 E
Hazel Crest	278	41.34 N	87.41 W
Hazel Dell	224	45.40 N	122.39 W
Hazel Green	190	42.31 N	90.26 W
Hazelgrove, Austl.	170	33.40 S	149.52 E
Hazel Grove, Eng., U.K.	44	53.23 N	2.08 W
Hazel Hurst	214	41.42 N	78.35 W
Hazel Kirk	279b	40.11 N	79.57 W
Hazel Park	216	42.27 N	83.06 W
Hazel Park Raceway ♠	281	42.29 N	83.05 W
Hazelton, B.C., Can.	182	55.15 N	127.40 W
Hazelton, Id., U.S.	202	42.35 N	114.08 W
Hazelton, N.D., U.S.	198	46.29 N	100.16 W
Hazelton Mountains ⋏	182	54.30 N	128.20 W
Hazelton Peak ∧	202	44.06 N	107.03 W
Hazelwood, Mo., U.S.	219	38.46 N	90.22 W
Hazelwood, N.C., U.S.	192	35.28 N	83.00 W
Hazelwood ◆[8]	279b	40.25 N	79.56 W
Hazen, Ar., U.S.	194	34.46 N	91.34 W
Hazen, Nv., U.S.	226	39.33 N	119.02 W
Hazen, N.D., U.S.	198	47.17 N	101.37 W
Hazen, Pa., U.S.	214	41.12 N	78.58 W
Hazen Bay ⊂	180	61.00 N	165.10 W
Ḥazerim	132	31.14 N	34.43 E
Hazlehurst, Ga., U.S.	192	31.52 N	82.35 W
Hazlehurst, Ms., U.S.	194	31.51 N	90.23 W
Hazlet, Sk., Can.	184	50.25 N	108.36 W
Hazlet, N.J., U.S.	208	40.26 N	74.13 W
Hazleton, Ia., U.S.	190	42.37 N	91.54 W
Hazleton, Pa., U.S.	210	40.57 N	75.58 W
Hazlett, Lake ⊜	162	21.30 S	128.48 E
Ḥazor HaGelilit	132	32.59 N	35.33 E
Hazro, Pāk.	123	33.54 N	72.29 E
Hazro, Tür.	130	38.15 N	40.47 E
Hazu	94	34.47 N	137.08 E
He ≃, Zhg.	100	27.05 N	114.59 E
He ≃, Zhg.	102	23.26 N	111.30 E
Heacham	42	52.55 N	0.30 E
Head ≃	212	44.44 N	79.15 W
Head Bay d'Espoir	186	47.56 N	55.45 W
Headcorn	42	51.11 N	0.37 E
Headford	48	53.28 N	9.05 W
Head Lake ⊜	212	44.45 N	78.55 W
Headland	194	31.21 N	85.20 W
Headlands	154	18.14 S	32.03 E
Headley, Eng., U.K.	42	51.07 N	0.50 W
Headley, Eng., U.K.	260	51.17 N	0.16 W
Headley, Mount ∧	202	47.44 N	115.15 W
Head of the Harbor	276	40.54 N	73.10 W
Heald Green	262	53.22 N	2.14 W
Heald Moor ◆[3]	262	53.44 N	2.10 W
Healdsburg	204	38.36 N	122.52 W
Healdton	196	34.13 N	97.29 W
Healesville	169	37.40 S	145.31 E
Healing	44	53.34 N	0.10 W
Healy, Ak., U.S.	180	63.52 N	148.58 W
Healy, Ks., U.S.	198	38.36 N	100.37 W
Healy, Mount ∧	180	63.46 N	149.01 W
Healy Lake ⊜	212	45.10 N	79.55 W
Heani, Mont ∧	174x	9.47 S	139.04 W
Heanna	174m	26.19 N	127.54 E
Heanor	44	53.01 N	1.22 W
Heany Junction	154	20.06 S	28.54 E
Heard Island I	6	53.06 S	73.30 E
Heard Pond ⊜	283	42.21 N	71.22 W
Hearne	222	30.52 N	96.35 W
Hearst	176	49.41 N	83.40 W
Hearst Island I	9	69.25 S	62.10 W
Hearst San Simeon State Historical Park ♠	226	35.42 N	121.10 W
Heart ≃, Ab., Can.	182	56.14 N	117.17 W
Heart ≃, N.D., U.S.	198	46.47 N	100.51 W
Heart Lake ⊜, Ab., Can.	182	55.02 N	111.30 W
Heart Lake ⊜, On., Can.	275b	43.44 N	79.48 W
Heart Lake Indian Reserve ◆[4]	182	55.02 N	111.30 W
Heart Pond ⊜	283	42.34 N	71.23 W
Heart's Content	186	47.53 N	53.22 W
Heath, Ma., U.S.	207	42.40 N	72.49 W
Heath, Oh., U.S.	214	40.02 N	82.28 W
Heath, Tx., U.S.	222	32.50 N	96.29 W
Heath ≃	248	12.31 S	68.38 W
Heath, Pointe ≻	186	49.05 N	61.42 W
Heathcote, Austl.	169	36.55 S	144.42 E
Heathcote, Austl.	274a	34.05 S	151.01 E
Heathcote Brook ≃	276	40.23 N	74.37 W
Heath End	42	51.22 N	1.09 W
Heatherton	274b	37.58 S	145.06 E
Heathfield	42	50.59 N	0.17 E
Heathmont	274b	37.49 S	145.15 E
Heath Springs	192	34.35 N	80.40 W
Heathsville	208	37.55 N	76.28 W
Heatley	262	53.24 N	2.27 W
Heaton Hall ⊥	262	53.32 N	2.15 W
Heaton Moor	262	53.25 N	2.11 W
Heaven, Temple of ʊ[1]	271a	39.53 N	116.25 E
Heavener	194	34.53 N	94.36 W
Heaverham	260	51.18 N	0.15 E
Heaviley	262	53.24 N	2.09 W
Hebaochang	107	29.33 N	105.32 E
Hebao Dao I	100	21.52 N	113.09 E
Hebbronville	196	27.18 N	98.40 W
Hebburn	44	54.59 N	1.30 W
Hebbville	284b	39.20 N	77.46 W
Hebden Bridge	44	53.45 N	2.00 W
Hebden Water ≃	262	53.44 N	2.00 W
Hebei, Zhg.	104	40.43 N	122.12 E
Hebei, Zhg.	104	41.01 N	123.51 E
Hebei (Hopeh) □[4]	98	38.00 N	116.00 E
Hebeitun	105	39.35 N	117.07 E
Hebel	166	28.59 S	147.48 E
Heber, Az., U.S.	200	34.25 N	110.35 W
Heber, Ca., U.S.	204	32.44 N	115.32 W
Heber City	200	40.30 N	111.24 W
Heber Springs	194	35.29 N	92.01 W
Hebertsfelden	60	48.24 N	12.49 E
Hebgen Lake ⊜[1]	202	44.47 N	111.14 W
Hebi	98	35.59 N	114.11 E
Hebian	107	30.29 N	105.08 E
Hebo, Or., U.S.	224	45.13 N	123.51 W
Hebo, Zhg.	102	31.29 N	98.58 E
Hebo, Mount ∧	224	45.12 N	123.45 W
Hébridas, Islas → Hebrides II	46	57.00 N	6.30 W
Hebrides II	22	57.00 N	6.30 W
Hebrides, Sea of the ⚲[2]	46	57.07 N	6.55 W
Hebron, Nf., Can.	176	58.12 N	62.38 W
Hebron, Ct., U.S.	207	41.39 N	72.21 W
Hebron, Il., U.S.	216	42.28 N	88.25 W
Hebron, In., U.S.	216	41.19 N	87.12 W
Hebron, Ky., U.S.	218	39.03 N	84.42 W
Hebron, Md., U.S.	208	38.25 N	75.41 W
Hebron, Ne., U.S.	198	40.09 N	97.35 W
Hebron, N.D., U.S.	198	46.54 N	102.02 W
Hebron, Pa., U.S.	208	40.21 N	76.24 W
Hebron, Tx., U.S.	222	33.01 N	96.52 W
Hebron, Wi., U.S.	216	42.56 N	88.42 W
Hebron → Al-Khalīl, W.B.	132	31.32 N	35.06 E
Hebu	100	27.50 N	115.22 E
Hebutu	104	42.19 N	122.20 E
Heby	40	59.56 N	16.53 E
Hecao	105	40.21 N	116.47 E
Hecate Strait ꭒ	182	53.00 N	131.00 W
Hecelchakán	232	20.10 N	90.08 W
Heceta Island I	180	55.45 N	133.35 W
Hechi	102	24.42 N	108.02 E
Hechiceros	196	28.33 N	103.38 W
Hechingen	58	48.21 N	8.58 E
Hechtel	56	51.08 N	5.21 E
Hechthausen	52	53.38 N	9.14 E
Hechuan	107	30.00 N	106.16 E
Heckelberg	54	52.44 N	13.50 E
Hecker	219	38.18 N	90.00 W
Heckington	42	52.59 N	0.18 W
Hecklingen	54	51.51 N	11.32 E
Heckscher State Park ♠	210	40.43 N	73.10 W
Hecla, Mb., Can.	184	51.08 N	96.40 W
Hecla, S.D., U.S.	198	45.52 N	98.09 W
Hecla Island I	184	51.08 N	96.45 W
Hecla Provincial Park ♠	184	51.12 N	96.35 W
Hectanooga	186	44.06 N	66.02 W
Hector, N.Z.	172	41.36 S	171.53 E
Hector, Mn., U.S.	198	44.44 N	94.42 W
Hector, Mount ∧	172	40.57 S	175.17 E
Heda	94	34.58 N	138.46 E
Hedal	26	60.37 N	9.42 E
Hedaru	154	4.30 S	37.54 E
Heddal ʊ[1]	26	59.35 N	9.11 E
Hedding	285	40.06 N	74.44 W
Hédé, Fr.	32	48.18 N	1.48 W
Hede, Sve.	26	62.25 N	13.30 E
Hedehusene	41	55.39 N	12.12 E
Hedel	52	51.45 N	5.15 E
Hedemora	40	60.17 N	15.59 E
Hedemünden	56	51.23 N	9.46 E
Hedensted	41	55.46 N	9.42 E
Hedersleben	54	51.51 N	11.15 E
Hedesunda	40	60.24 N	16.59 E
Hedesundafjärdarna ⊜	40	60.20 N	17.00 E
He Devil ∧	202	45.21 N	116.33 W
Hedge End	42	50.54 N	1.18 W
Hedgerley	260	51.35 N	0.36 W
Hedian	100	32.45 N	114.18 E
Hedley, B.C., Can.	182	49.21 N	120.04 W
Hedley, Tx., U.S.	196	34.52 N	100.39 W
Hedmark □[6]	26	61.30 N	11.45 E
Hednesford	42	52.43 N	2.00 W
Hedo	174m	26.51 N	128.16 E
Hedo-misaki ≻	174m	26.52 N	128.16 E
Hedon	44	53.44 N	0.12 W
Hedrick	190	41.10 N	92.18 W
Hedströmmen ≃	40	59.28 N	16.04 E
Hedutne	272c	19.10 N	73.06 E
Hedwig Village	222	29.47 N	95.27 W
Heek	52	52.07 N	7.06 E
Heel	52	51.11 N	5.53 E
Heel Point ≻	174a	19.19 N	166.37 E
Heemskerk	52	52.31 N	4.40 E
Heemstede	52	52.21 N	4.37 E
Heepen	52	52.01 N	8.35 E
Heer, Bel.	56	50.10 N	4.50 E
Heer, Ned.	56	50.50 N	5.44 E
Heerde	52	52.23 N	6.03 E
Heerdt ◆[8]	263	51.13 N	6.43 E
Heerenveen	52	52.57 N	5.55 E
Heeren-Werve	52	51.35 N	7.43 E
Heerhugowaard	52	52.40 N	4.50 E
Heerkan	107	29.32 N	103.56 E
Heerlen	56	50.54 N	5.59 E
Heesch	52	51.44 N	5.32 E
Heeslingen	52	53.19 N	9.20 E
Heessen	52	51.42 N	7.50 E
Heeze	52	51.24 N	5.35 E
Ḥefa (Haifa)	132	32.50 N	35.00 E
Ḥefa □[5]	132	32.35 N	35.00 E
Ḥefa, Mifraẕ ⊂	132	32.52 N	35.03 E
Ḥefa, Sede-Teʿufa ⊠	132	32.49 N	35.02 E
Hefei	100	31.51 N	117.17 E
Hefengchang	107	30.26 N	104.43 E
Heffron Park ♠	274a	33.57 S	151.15 E
Heflin	194	33.38 N	85.35 W
Hegang	89	47.24 N	130.22 E
Hegau ◆[1]	58	47.50 N	8.45 E
Hégenheim	58	47.34 N	7.32 E
Hegewisch ◆[8]	278	41.40 N	87.33 W
Hegins	208	40.39 N	76.29 W
Hegra	26	63.28 N	11.07 E
Hegura-jima I	92	37.51 N	136.55 E
Heguri	270	34.38 N	135.42 E
Hegyeshalom	61	47.55 N	17.10 E
Heha, Mont ∧	154	3.38 S	29.30 E
Hehlen	52	51.59 N	9.28 E
Heho	110	20.43 N	96.49 E
Hehou	100	28.40 N	114.28 E
Hei ≃, Zhg.	102	40.18 N	99.26 E
Hei ≃, Zhg.	105	40.44 N	116.27 E
Heicheng (Karakhoto) ⊥	102	41.47 N	101.03 E
Heichengzhen	102	36.16 N	106.06 E
Heichengzi	104	42.10 N	121.01 E
Heidayingzi	98	40.52 N	116.12 E
Heidberg ∧[2]	263	51.15 N	7.21 E
Heide	30	54.12 N	9.06 E
Heide ◆[8], Dtsch.	263	51.26 N	7.01 E
Heide ◆[8], Dtsch.	263	51.31 N	6.52 E
Heideck	60	49.08 N	11.07 E
Heidelberg, Austl.	169	37.45 S	145.04 E
Heidelberg, On., Can.	212	43.31 N	80.37 W
Heidelberg, Dtsch.	56	49.25 N	8.43 E
Heidelberg, S. Afr.	158	34.06 S	20.59 E
Heidelberg, S. Afr.	158	26.32 S	28.18 E
Heidelberg, Ms., U.S.	194	31.53 N	88.59 W
Heidelberg, Pa., U.S.	279b	40.23 N	80.05 W
Heidelberg □[5]	273d	26.19 S	28.16 E
Heidelberg, Schloss ⊥	56	49.24 N	8.42 E
Heidelsheim	56	49.06 N	8.38 E
Heiden, Dtsch.	52	51.50 N	6.56 E
Heiden, Dtsch.	52	51.59 N	8.50 E
Heiden, Schw.	58	47.27 N	9.33 E
Heiden, Port ⊂	180	56.55 N	158.45 W
Heidenau, Dtsch.	52	53.19 N	9.39 E
Heidenau, Dtsch.	54	50.59 N	13.52 E
Heidenheim	56	49.01 N	10.44 E
Heidenheim an der Brenz	56	48.40 N	10.08 E
Heidenheimer	222	31.01 N	97.18 W
Heidenoldendorf	52	51.57 N	8.50 E
Heidenreichstein	61	48.52 N	15.07 E
Heider Ditch ≊	279a	41.31 N	82.01 W
Heiderscheid	56	49.53 N	5.54 E
Heidhausen ◆[8]	263	51.23 N	7.01 E
Heidhof ◆[8]	263	51.11 N	7.11 E
Heidlersburg	208	39.57 N	77.09 W
Heidouwo	105	39.42 N	117.15 E
Heigenbrücken	56	50.02 N	9.23 E
Heigoutaicun	104	41.30 N	123.01 E
Heigun-tō I	96	33.47 N	132.14 E
Heihai → Har Hu ⊜	102	38.15 N	97.40 E
Heihe → Aihui	89	50.16 N	127.28 E
Heijō → P'yŏngyang	98	39.01 N	125.45 E
Heikega-dake ∧	96	34.19 N	131.54 E
Heikendorf	54	54.22 N	10.12 E
Heil	263	51.38 N	7.35 E
Heilangkou	105	39.37 N	117.24 E
Heilbad Heiligenstadt	56	51.23 N	10.09 E
Heilbron	158	27.21 S	27.58 E
Heilbronn	56	49.08 N	9.13 E
Heilenbecker-Stausee ⊜[1]	263	51.15 N	7.22 E
Heiligenberg	58	47.49 N	9.19 E
Heiligenblut	64	47.02 N	12.50 E
Heiligendamm	54	54.08 N	11.50 E
Heiligenhafen	54	54.22 N	10.58 E
Heiligenhaus	56	51.19 N	6.59 E
Heiligensee ◆[8]	264a	52.36 N	13.13 E
Heiligenstadt	60	49.51 N	11.10 E
Heilin	98	35.01 N	118.58 E
Hei Ling Chau I	271d	22.15 N	114.02 E
Heilong (Amur) ≃	89	52.56 N	141.10 E
Heilongguan	102	36.19 N	111.11 E
Heilongjiang □[4]	89	48.00 N	128.00 E
Heilongtan, Zhg.	105	40.44 N	116.31 E
Heilongtan, Zhg.	105	40.02 N	116.11 E
Heilongtan Shuiku ⊜[1]	107	30.03 N	104.02 E
Heiloo	52	52.36 N	4.43 E
Heilsbronn	56	49.20 N	10.47 E
Heiltz-le-Maurupt	56	48.48 N	4.49 E
Heilungkiang → Heilongjiang □[4]	89	48.00 N	128.00 E
Heilwood	214	40.37 N	78.54 W
Heimaey I	24a	63.26 N	20.17 W
Heimbach	56	50.38 N	6.28 E
Heimbuchenthal	56	49.53 N	9.17 E
Heimburg	54	51.49 N	10.54 E
Heimdal	26	63.21 N	10.22 E
Heimenkirch	58	47.37 N	9.53 E
Heimsheim	56	48.48 N	8.51 E
Heinävesi	26	62.26 N	28.36 E
Heinersdorf, Dtsch.	54	52.27 N	14.13 E
Heinersdorf, Dtsch.	264a	52.23 N	13.20 E
Heinersdorf ◆[8]	264a	52.34 N	13.27 E
Heiniuyingzi	98	41.07 N	120.19 E
Heino	52	52.26 N	6.14 E
Heinola	26	61.13 N	26.02 E
Heinsberg	56	51.03 N	6.05 E
Heiquan	102	39.32 N	99.42 E
Heirnkut	110	25.14 N	94.45 E
Heisfelde	52	53.15 N	7.26 E
Heishan	104	41.41 N	122.07 E
Heishanguan	98	38.33 N	113.41 E
Heishantou, Zhg.	89	50.13 N	119.28 E
Heishantou, Zhg.	98	42.28 N	125.33 E
Heishui	98	42.09 N	119.28 E
Heishuisi	102	36.08 N	108.42 E
Heisingen ◆[8]	263	51.25 N	7.04 E
Heisler	182	52.41 N	112.13 W
Heislerville	208	39.13 N	74.59 W
Heissen ◆[8]	263	51.26 N	6.56 E
Heist-aan-Zee	50	51.21 N	3.15 E
Heist-op-den-Berg	56	51.05 N	4.43 E
Heitang	102	26.29 N	105.09 E
Heitersheim	58	47.53 N	7.40 E
Heiwa	94	35.12 N	136.44 E
Heiyanghebao	105	39.07 N	118.15 E
Heiyantang	102	27.28 N	101.11 E
Heiyanzi	105	39.13 N	118.08 E
Hejaz → Al-Ḥijāz ◆[1]	118	24.30 N	38.30 E
Hejiachang	107	29.24 N	104.56 E
Hejian, Zhg.	98	38.26 N	116.05 E
Hejian, Zhg.	105	39.25 N	116.25 E
Hejiang	107	28.49 N	105.50 E
Hejiangzhen	107	29.16 N	104.16 E
Hejiaqiao	100	27.24 N	113.21 E
Hejiawopeng	104	41.32 N	122.07 E
Hejiaying	105	39.55 N	118.19 E
Hejiazhen	107	29.52 N	104.26 E
Hejin	102	35.39 N	110.40 E
Hejlsminde	41	55.22 N	9.37 E
Hejnsvig	41	55.41 N	8.59 E
Hekelgem	50	50.54 N	4.06 E
Hekili Point ≻	229a	20.48 N	156.37 W
Hekimhan	130	38.49 N	37.56 E
Hekinan	94	34.51 N	136.58 E
Hekla ∧[1]	24a	64.00 N	19.39 W
Hekou, Zhg.	100	31.22 N	114.26 E
Hekou, Zhg.	102	36.09 N	103.22 E
Hekou, Zhg.	102	28.22 N	108.14 E
Hekou, Zhg.	102	29.57 N	111.04 E
Hekou, Zhg.	102	22.38 N	103.56 E
Hekouchang	107	29.21 N	104.21 E
Hekouji	100	32.09 N	116.04 E
Hekoujie	102	26.31 N	100.39 E
Hekpoort	158	25.55 S	27.38 E
Hel	30	54.37 N	18.48 E
Helagsfjället ∧	26	62.55 N	12.27 E
Helaluo	102	33.56 N	102.10 E
Helangou	104	41.00 N	123.25 E
Helan Shan ⋏	102	38.40 N	105.57 E
Helbe ≃	54	51.13 N	11.06 E
Helbra	54	51.33 N	11.29 E
Helchteren	56	51.03 N	5.22 E
Heldburg	54	50.17 N	10.44 E
Helden	56	51.07 N	7.56 E
Heldra	56	51.07 N	10.11 E
Heldrungen	54	51.18 N	11.13 E
Helechos, Cañada de los ≃	286a	19.22 N	99.12 W
Helemano Stream ≃	229c	21.35 N	158.06 W
Helen, Mount ∧	166	21.34 S	141.13 E
Helena, Ar., U.S.	194	34.31 N	90.35 W
Helena, Mt., U.S.	202	46.35 N	112.02 W
Helena, N.Y., U.S.	206	44.55 N	74.44 W
Helena, Oh., U.S.	214	41.21 N	83.18 W
Helena, Ok., U.S.	196	36.32 N	98.16 W
Helena ≃	168a	31.54 S	116.00 E
Helena River Reservoir ⊜[1]	168a	31.59 S	116.13 E
Helendale	228	34.45 N	117.18 W
Helenenberg	56	49.51 N	6.32 E
Helenental V	264b	48.01 N	16.11 E
Helen Island I	108	2.58 N	131.49 E
Helensburgh, Austl.	170	34.11 S	150.59 E
Helensburgh, Scot., U.K.	46	56.01 N	4.44 W
Helen Springs	162	18.26 S	133.52 E
Helensville	172	36.40 S	174.28 E
Helenville	216	43.01 N	88.41 W
Helenwood	192	36.25 N	84.32 W
Ḥeleẕ	132	31.35 N	34.40 E
Helfenberg	61	48.32 N	14.08 E
Helfenstein	208	40.45 N	76.27 W
Helgaå ≃	26	55.53 N	14.08 E
Helgenæs ≻[1]	41	56.08 N	10.32 E
Helgoland I	30	54.12 N	7.53 E
Helgoländer Bucht ⊂	30	54.10 N	8.04 E
Heli	89	47.05 N	130.16 E
Helicoide ◆[9]	286c	10.29 N	66.55 W
Helidon	171a	27.33 S	152.08 E
Heliodora	256	22.04 S	45.32 W
Heliópolis	287a	22.45 S	43.25 W
Heliopolis → Miṣr al-Jadīdah ◆[8]	273c	30.06 N	31.20 E
Heliopolis ⊥	142	30.08 N	31.17 E
Heliopolis Aerodrome ⊠	273c	30.04 N	31.19 E
Heliopolis Racing Club ♠	273c	30.06 N	31.19 E
Heliuji	100	33.02 N	116.57 E
Helixi	106	30.40 N	118.59 E
Hell	26	63.26 N	10.54 E
Hellam	208	40.00 N	76.36 W
Hellbrunn, Schloss ⊥	64	47.46 N	13.04 E
Hellebæk	41	56.04 N	12.34 E
Helleh ≃	128	29.10 N	50.40 E
Hellen Blazes, Lake ⊜	220	28.01 N	80.47 W
Hellendoorn	52	52.24 N	6.26 E
Hellenthal	56	50.29 N	6.26 E
Hellern	52	52.15 N	7.58 E
Hellersen	263	51.12 N	7.39 E
Hellertown	208	40.34 N	75.20 W
Hellesylt	26	62.05 N	6.54 E
Hellevad	41	55.05 N	9.13 E
Hellevoetsluis	52	51.49 N	4.08 E
Hell Gate ꭒ	276	40.47 N	73.56 W
Hell Hole Reservoir ⊜[1]	226	39.04 N	120.22 W
Hellifield	44	54.01 N	2.12 W
Hellín	34	38.31 N	1.41 W
Helli Ness ≻	46a	60.02 N	1.10 W
Hellmonsödt	61	48.26 N	14.18 E
Hell Point ≻	186	44.16 N	64.15 W
Hells Canyon V	202	45.20 N	116.45 W
Hellsee ⊜	264a	52.45 N	13.35 E
Hells Gate V	182	49.47 N	121.27 W
Hell-Ville	157b	13.25 S	48.16 E
Hellweg ◆[1]	52	51.36 N	8.32 E
Helm	226	36.31 N	120.05 W
Helmand □[4]	128	31.00 N	64.00 E
Helmand ≃	128	31.12 N	61.34 E
Helmbrechts	54	50.14 N	11.43 E
Helmcken Falls ∟	182	51.57 N	120.11 W
Helme ≃	54	51.20 N	11.20 E
Helmeringhausen	156	25.54 S	16.57 E
Helmetta	276	40.22 N	74.25 W
Helmetta Pond ⊜	276	40.23 N	74.26 W
Helmond	52	51.29 N	5.40 E
Helmsburg	218	39.16 N	86.18 W
Helmsdale	46	58.07 N	3.40 W
Helmsdale ≃	46	58.07 N	3.40 W
Helmshore	262	53.41 N	2.20 W
Helmsley	44	54.14 N	1.04 W
Helmstedt	54	52.13 N	11.00 E
Hel'myaziv	78	49.49 N	31.49 E
Helnæs I	41	55.08 N	10.02 E
Helong	98	42.32 N	128.59 E
Helper	200	39.41 N	110.51 W
Helpmekaar	158	28.29 S	30.29 E
Helpter Berg ∧[2]	54	53.30 N	13.36 E
Helsby	44	53.16 N	2.46 W
Helsby Hill ∧[2]	262	53.16 N	2.46 W
Helsingborg	41	56.03 N	12.42 E
Helsinge	41	56.01 N	12.12 E
Helsingfors → Helsinki	26	60.10 N	24.58 E
Helsingør (Elsinore)	41	56.02 N	12.37 E
Helsinki (Helsingfors)	26	60.10 N	24.58 E
Helska, Mierzeja ≻[2]	30	54.45 N	18.39 E
Helston	42	50.05 N	5.16 W
Heltonville	218	38.55 N	86.22 W
Helvecia	252	31.06 S	60.05 W
Helvellyn ∧	44	54.31 N	3.01 W
Helvick Head ≻	48	52.03 N	7.33 W
Helvoirt	52	51.38 N	5.13 E
Hem ≃	50	50.51 N	2.06 E
Ḥemar, Naḥal V	132	31.08 N	35.22 E
Hemau	60	49.03 N	11.47 E
Hemāvati ≃	122	12.31 N	76.27 E
Hembe	152	1.54 N	22.42 E
Hemel Hempstead	42	51.46 N	0.28 W
Hemelingen ◆[8]	52	53.03 N	8.53 E
Hemeln	52	51.30 N	9.36 E
Hemer	56	51.23 N	7.46 E
Hemet	228	33.44 N	116.58 W
Hemfjärden ⊂	40	59.17 N	15.20 E
Hemford	186	44.30 N	64.47 W
Hemfurth-Edersee	56	51.10 N	9.02 E
Hemiksem	50	51.09 N	4.21 E
Héming	58	48.42 N	6.57 E
Hemingford	198	42.19 N	103.04 W
Hemingway	192	33.45 N	79.26 W
Hemlock, In., U.S.	216	40.25 N	86.03 W
Hemlock, N.Y., U.S.	210	42.47 N	77.36 W
Hemlock Lake ⊜	210	42.43 N	77.37 W
Hemmerde	52	51.33 N	7.48 E
Hemmerden	263	51.07 N	6.36 E
Hemmingen	52	52.19 N	9.45 E
Hemmoor	52	53.41 N	9.08 E
Hemphill	194	31.20 N	93.50 W
Hempnall	42	52.30 N	1.19 E
Hempstead, N.Y., U.S.	210	40.42 N	73.37 W
Hempstead, Tx., U.S.	222	30.05 N	96.04 W
Hempstead Harbor ⊂	276	40.50 N	73.39 W
Hempstead Lake ⊜	276	40.41 N	73.38 W
Hempstead Lake State Park ♠	276	40.41 N	73.38 W
Hemsbach	56	49.36 N	8.40 E
Hemsby	42	52.41 N	1.42 E
Hemse	26	57.14 N	18.22 E
Hemsedal	26	60.52 N	8.34 E
Hemslingen	52	53.05 N	9.36 E
Hemsön I	26	62.43 N	18.05 E
Hemstreet Park	210	42.54 N	73.41 W
Hemsworth	44	53.38 N	1.21 W
Hemujing	98	37.54 N	115.22 E
Henan	102	34.35 N	101.34 E
Henan (Honan) □[4]	90	34.00 N	114.00 E
Hen and Chickens II	172	35.55 S	174.45 E
Henares ≃	34	40.24 N	3.30 W
Henbury, Austl.	162	24.35 S	133.15 E
Henbury, Eng., U.K.	262	53.15 N	2.11 W
Hendek	130	40.48 N	30.45 E
Henderson, Arg.	252	36.18 S	61.43 W
Henderson, In., U.S.	218	39.40 N	85.31 W
Henderson, Ky., U.S.	194	37.50 N	87.35 W
Henderson, Mn., U.S.	190	44.31 N	93.54 W
Henderson, Ne., U.S.	198	40.46 N	97.48 W
Henderson, Nv., U.S.	204	36.02 N	114.58 W
Henderson, N.Y., U.S.	212	43.51 N	76.11 W
Henderson, N.C., U.S.	192	36.19 N	78.23 W
Henderson, Tn., U.S.	194	35.26 N	88.38 W
Henderson, Tx., U.S.	222	32.09 N	94.47 W
Henderson □[6]	222	32.13 N	95.50 W
Henderson Bay ⊂, N.Y., U.S.	212	43.54 N	76.10 W
Henderson Bay ⊂, Wa., U.S.	224	47.18 N	122.42 W
Henderson Creek ≃	190	40.52 N	91.02 W
Henderson Island I	6	24.22 S	128.19 W
Hendersonville, N.C., U.S.	192	35.19 N	82.27 W
Hendersonville, Pa., U.S.	214	40.18 N	80.09 W
Hendersonville, Tn., U.S.	194	36.18 N	86.37 W
Hendījān	128	30.14 N	49.43 E
Hendon ◆[8]	260	51.35 N	0.14 W
Hendorābī, Jazīreh-ye I	128	26.40 N	53.37 E
Hendricks, Mn., U.S.	198	44.30 N	96.25 W
Hendricks, W.V., U.S.	188	39.04 N	79.37 W
Hendricks □[6]	218	39.46 N	86.26 W
Hendrina	158	26.11 S	29.45 E
Hendry □[6]	220	26.36 N	81.13 W
Hendrysburg	214	40.04 N	81.10 W
Hendy	42	51.43 N	4.04 W
Henefer	200	41.01 N	111.29 W
Henfield	42	50.56 N	0.17 W
Heng ≃, Zhg.	102	28.40 N	104.25 E
Heng ≃, Zhg.	107	28.57 N	105.22 E
Hengām, Jazīreh-ye I	128	26.39 N	55.53 E
Henganofi	164	6.15 S	145.35 E
Hengchow → Hengyang	102	26.54 N	112.36 E
Hengdaochuan	98	41.15 N	125.31 E
Hengdaohe	104	42.02 N	123.51 E
Hengdaohezi	89	43.13 N	126.44 E
Hengdaozi	89	43.18 N	127.18 E
Hengdong	100	27.03 N	112.57 E
Hengelo	52	52.15 N	6.45 E
Hengersberg	60	48.47 N	13.03 E
Hengfan	106	30.20 N	119.45 E
Hengfeng	100	28.24 N	117.34 E
Henggang	100	29.32 N	115.27 E
Henggouzi	89	43.12 N	124.47 E
Henghutou	104	42.05 N	124.00 E
Hengjie	106	31.13 N	119.30 E
Hengjing	106	31.11 N	120.32 E
Hengjinghong	106	30.34 N	120.59 E
Hengli	100	23.12 N	114.37 E
Henglin	106	31.42 N	120.06 E
Henglu	98	41.26 N	126.04 E
Henglutou	106	30.19 N	119.19 E
Hengmian	106	31.09 N	121.38 E
Hengoed	42	51.39 N	3.10 W
Hengsen	263	51.29 N	7.38 E
Heng Sha I	106	31.20 N	121.50 E
Hengshan, Zhg.	100	27.15 N	112.51 E
Hengshan, Zhg.	102	37.56 N	108.53 E
Hengshan, Zhg.	106	31.01 N	120.32 E
Heng Shan ∧	100	27.16 N	112.35 E
Heng Shan ⋏	102	39.30 N	113.45 E
Hengshanchang	107	30.33 N	105.24 E
Hengshanqiao	106	31.46 N	120.07 E
Hengshanxia	106	30.18 N	118.44 E
Hengshi, Zhg.	100	26.05 N	114.38 E
Hengshi, Zhg.	100	23.52 N	113.15 E
Hengshi, Zhg.	100	29.32 N	114.41 E
Hengshui	98	37.43 N	115.40 E
Hengsteysee ⊜[1]	263	51.25 N	7.28 E
Hengtangshi	106	31.41 N	121.02 E
Hengtianchi	107	29.07 N	105.01 E
Hengtianxi	107	29.05 N	105.03 E
Hengxi, Zhg.	100	29.42 N	121.35 E
Hengxi, Zhg.	100	28.46 N	120.29 E
Hengxi, Zhg.	106	31.43 N	118.46 E
Hengxian	102	22.42 N	109.13 E
Hengxiang	106	32.12 N	120.15 E
Hengxikou	100	29.26 N	121.26 E
Hengyang	102	26.54 N	112.36 E
Heniches'k	78	46.11 N	34.48 E
Hénin-Beaumont	50	50.25 N	2.56 E
Henley Beach	168b	34.55 S	138.30 E
Henley-in-Arden	42	52.17 N	1.46 W
Henley-on-Thames	42	51.32 N	0.56 W
Henlopen, Cape ≻	208	38.48 N	75.05 W
Henlow	42	52.02 N	0.18 W
Hennan ⊜	26	62.06 N	15.46 E
Hennaya	34	34.58 N	1.22 W
Henneberg	54	50.29 N	10.21 E
Hennebont	32	47.48 N	3.17 W
Hennef	56	50.46 N	7.16 E
Hennen	56	51.27 N	7.39 E
Hennenman	158	27.59 S	27.01 E
Hennepin	190	41.15 N	89.21 W
Hennepin, Point ≻	281	42.12 N	83.09 W
Hennersdorf	264b	48.07 N	16.22 E
Hennessey	196	36.06 N	97.53 W
Hennessey, Lake ⊜[1]	226	38.29 N	122.22 W
Hennickendorf	54	52.30 N	13.51 E
Henniez	58	46.44 N	6.54 E
Hennigsdorf	54	52.38 N	13.12 E
Henniker	188	43.10 N	71.49 W
Henning, Il., U.S.	216	40.18 N	87.42 W
Henning, Mn., U.S.	198	46.19 N	95.26 W
Henning, Tn., U.S.	194	35.40 N	89.34 W
Henri ≃	206	46.30 N	71.47 W
Henri, Cap ≻	186	49.48 N	64.23 W
Henri-Chapelle	56	50.40 N	5.56 E
Henrichemont	50	47.18 N	2.32 E
Henrichenburg	263	51.35 N	7.19 E
Henrico □[6]	208	37.30 N	77.20 W
Henrietta, N.Y., U.S.	210	43.03 N	77.36 W
Henrietta, N.C., U.S.	192	35.15 N	81.47 W
Henrietta, Tx., U.S.	196	33.49 N	98.11 W
Henrietta Maria, Cape ≻	176	55.09 N	82.20 W
Henri Pittier, Parque Nacional ♠	246	10.25 N	67.43 W
Henry, Il., U.S.	190	41.06 N	89.21 W
Henry, S.D., U.S.	198	44.52 N	97.27 W
Henry □[6], In., U.S.	218	39.55 N	85.22 W
Henry □[6], Ky., U.S.	218	38.26 N	85.09 W
Henry □[6], Oh., U.S.	216	41.20 N	84.04 W
Henry ≃	162	22.40 S	115.40 E
Henry, Cape ≻	208	36.55 N	76.01 W
Henry, Mount ∧	202	48.53 N	115.31 W
Henry, Mount ∧[2]	274a	33.50 S	150.38 E
Henry, Point ≻	162	34.29 S	119.23 E
Henry Cowell Redwoods State Park ♠	226	37.02 N	122.03 W
Henryetta	196	35.26 N	95.58 W
Henry Hagg Lake ⊜[1]	224	45.29 N	123.13 E
Henry Island I	224	48.35 N	123.11 W
Henry Kater, Cape ≻	176	69.05 N	66.44 W
Henry Mountains ⋏	200	38.00 N	110.50 W
Henrys Bend	214	41.28 N	79.37 W
Henrys Fork ≃, U.S.	200	41.00 N	109.39 W
Henrys Fork ≃, Id., U.S.	202	43.45 N	111.56 W
Henryville, P.Q., Can.	206	45.08 N	73.11 W
Henryville, In., U.S.	218	38.32 N	85.46 W
Henry W. Coe State Park ♠	226	37.12 N	121.30 W
Hensall	190	43.26 N	81.30 W
Henshaw, Lake ⊜[1]	204	33.15 N	116.45 W
Hensley	194	34.30 N	92.12 W
Hensley Lake ⊜[1]	226	37.07 N	119.53 W
Henslow, Cape ≻	175e	9.56 S	160.38 E
Henson Creek ≃	284b	38.46 N	77.00 W
Hensonville	210	42.17 N	74.13 W
Henstedt-Ulzburg	52	53.47 N	9.58 E
Henstridge	42	50.59 N	2.24 W
Hentiesbaai	156	22.08 S	14.18 E
Henty	166	35.31 S	147.02 E
Henzada	110	17.38 N	95.28 E
Heorhiyivka	83	48.26 N	39.17 E
Hepburn	184	52.31 N	106.43 W
Hepburn Springs	169	37.19 S	144.09 E
Hephzibah	192	33.18 N	82.05 W
Heping, Zhg.	100	27.10 N	117.18 E
Heping, Zhg.	100	22.01 N	112.59 E
Heping, Zhg.	100	23.17 N	116.29 E
Heping, Zhg.	100	24.28 N	114.58 E
Heping, Zhg.	106	30.50 N	119.54 E
Heppenheim	56	49.39 N	8.38 E
Heppner	202	45.21 N	119.33 W
Heptonstall	262	53.45 N	2.01 W
Heptonstall Moor ≃	262	53.46 N	2.05 W
Hepu (Lianzhou)	102	21.39 N	109.11 E
Hepworth	212	44.37 N	81.09 W
Heqiao, Zhg.	100	32.55 N	118.22 E
Heqiao, Zhg.	106	31.30 N	119.53 E
Heqing	102	26.34 N	100.12 E
Hequ	102	39.26 N	111.08 E
Héraðsflói ⊂	24a	65.45 N	14.10 W
Hera Lacinia, Tempio di ⊥	68	39.01 N	17.13 E
Herāt	128	34.20 N	62.12 E
Herāt □[4]	128	34.30 N	62.00 E
Hérault □[5]	32	43.40 N	3.30 E
Hérault ≃	32	43.17 N	3.26 E
Herbasse ≃	62	45.02 N	4.57 E
Herbault	50	47.36 N	1.08 E
Herbede	56	51.25 N	7.16 E
Herbern	52	51.44 N	7.39 E
Herbert, Sk., Can.	184	50.26 N	107.12 W
Herbert, N.Z.	172	45.14 S	170.47 E
Herbert ≃	166	18.32 S	146.17 E
Herbert, Mount ∧	172	43.41 S	172.44 E
Herbertabad	110	11.43 N	92.37 E
Herbert Hoover National Historic Site ⊥	190	41.38 N	91.23 W
Herbertingen	58	48.04 N	9.26 E
Herbert Island I	180	52.45 N	170.10 W
Herberton	166	17.23 S	145.23 E
Herbertsdale	158	34.01 S	21.46 E
Herbeumont	56	49.47 N	5.14 E
Herbignac	32	47.27 N	2.19 W
Herb Lake	184	54.47 N	99.47 W
Herblay	50	49.00 N	2.10 E
Herblet Lake ⊜	184	54.56 N	99.54 W
Herbolzheim	58	48.13 N	7.47 E
Herborn	56	50.40 N	8.17 E
Herbrechtingen	56	48.37 N	10.10 E
Herbringhauser-Stausee ⊜[1]	263	51.14 N	7.16 E
Herbsleben	54	51.07 N	10.50 E
Herbstein	56	50.34 N	9.20 E
Herceg-Novi	38	42.27 N	18.32 E
Hercegovina □[9]	36	43.15 N	17.50 E
Herculaneum	219	38.16 N	90.22 W
Hércules, Méx.	232	28.02 N	103.48 W
Hercules, Ca., U.S.	282	38.01 N	122.17 W
Herdecke	56	51.24 N	7.26 E
Herdorf	56	50.46 N	7.56 E
Herdringen	52	51.25 N	7.58 E
Herðubreið ∧	24a	65.13 N	16.18 W
Herdwangen-Schönach	58	47.52 N	9.10 E
Heredia	236	10.00 N	84.07 W
Heredia □[4]	236	10.30 N	84.00 W
Hereford, Eng., U.K.	42	52.04 N	2.43 W
Hereford, Az., U.S.	200	31.26 N	110.05 W
Hereford, Md., U.S.	208	39.35 N	76.39 W
Hereford, Tx., U.S.	196	34.48 N	102.23 W
Hereford and Worcester □[6]	42	52.10 N	2.30 W
Hereford Cathedral ʊ[1]	42	52.04 N	2.43 W
Hereford Mountain ∧	206	45.05 N	71.36 W
Hereke	130	40.48 N	29.39 E
Herekino	172	35.15 S	173.13 E
Herencia	34	39.21 N	3.22 W
Herent	56	50.54 N	4.40 E
Herentals	56	51.11 N	4.50 E
Herfølge	41	55.25 N	12.10 E
Herford	52	52.06 N	8.40 E
Hergatz	58	47.39 N	9.50 E
Hergisdorf	54	51.32 N	11.28 E
Hergla	36	36.02 N	10.31 E
Herhahn	56	50.33 N	6.26 E
Héricourt	58	47.35 N	6.45 E
Hérimoncourt	58	47.26 N	6.53 E
Heringen, Dtsch.	54	51.27 N	10.52 E
Heringen, Dtsch.	56	50.53 N	10.00 E
Heringsdorf, Dtsch.	54	54.18 N	11.00 E
Heringsdorf, Dtsch.	54	53.56 N	14.08 E
Herington	198	38.40 N	96.56 W
Heriot	172	45.50 S	169.16 E
Herisau	58	47.23 N	9.17 E
Heritage Range ⋏	9	79.30 S	84.00 W
Herk ≃	56	50.58 N	5.07 E
Herk-de-Stad	56	50.56 N	5.10 E
Herkimer	210	43.01 N	74.59 W
Herkimer □[6]	210	43.02 N	74.59 W

≃ River	Fluß	Río	Rivière	Rio
≊ Canal	Kanal	Canal	Canal	Canal
∟ Waterfall, Rapids	Wasserfall, Stromschnellen	Cascada, Rápidos	Chute d'eau, Rapides	Cascata, Rápidos
ꭒ Strait	Meeresstraße	Estrecho	Détroit	Estreito
⊂ Bay, Gulf	Bucht, Golf	Bahía, Golfo	Baie, Golfe	Baía, Golfo
⊜ Lake, Lakes	See, Seen	Lago, Lagos	Lac, Lacs	Lago, Lagos
⩶ Swamp	Sumpf	Pantano	Marais	Pântano
⍓ Ice Features, Glacier	Eis- und Gletscherformen	Accidentes Glaciales	Formes glaciaires	Acidentes glaciares
⚲ Other Hydrographic Features	Andere Hydrographische Objekte	Otros Elementos Hidrográficos	Autres données hydrographiques	Outros acidentes hidrográficos
✢ Submarine Features	Untermeerische Objekte	Accidentes Submarinos	Formes de relief sous-marin	Acidentes submarinos
□ Political Unit	Politische Einheit	Unidad Politica	Entité politique	Unidade política
ʊ Cultural Institution	Kulturelle Institution	Institución Cultural	Institution culturelle	Instituição cultural
⊥ Historical Site	Historische Stätte	Sitio Histórico	Site historique	Sitio histórico
♠ Recreational Site	Erholungs- und Ferienort	Sitio de Recreo	Centre de loisirs	Area de Lazer
⊠ Airport	Flughafen	Aeropuerto	Aéroport	Aeroporto
■ Military Installation	Militäranlage	Instalación Militar	Installation militaire	Instalação militar
◆ Miscellaneous	Verschiedenes	Misceláneo	Divers	Diversos

Name	Page	Lat.°′	Long.°′
Herlen → Kerulen ≃	90	48.48 N	117.00 E
Herleshausen	56	51.00 N	10.09 E
Herlev	41	55.43 N	12.27 E
Herlong	204	40.09 N	120.08 W
Herlufmagle	41	55.19 N	11.46 E
Herlufsholm	41	55.15 N	11.46 E
Hermagor	64	46.37 N	13.22 E
Herman, Mn., U.S.	198	45.48 N	96.08 W
Herman, Ne., U.S.	198	41.40 N	96.12 W
Herman, Pa., U.S.	214	40.50 N	79.54 W
Herman, Lake ⊜	282	38.05 N	122.09 W
Hermana Mayor Island I	116	15.48 N	119.48 E
Hermanas	196	27.13 N	101.14 W
Hermanavičy	76	55.25 N	27.44 E
Herman Eksteen Park ♦	273d	26.10 S	28.02 E
Herma Ness ⟩	46a	60.50 N	0.55 W
Hermann	219	38.42 N	91.26 W
Hermannsburg, Austl.	162	23.57 S	132.45 E
Hermannsburg, Dtsch.	52	52.50 N	10.05 E
Hermannsburg Aboriginal Reserve ♦⁴	162	24.00 S	132.45 E
Hermanns-Denkmal ⊥	52	51.55 N	8.50 E
Hermannskogel ∧	264b	48.16 N	16.18 E
Hermannstadt → Sibiu	38	45.48 N	24.09 E
Hermano Peak ∧	200	37.13 N	108.48 W
Hermansverk	26	61.11 N	6.51 E
Hermansville	190	45.42 N	87.36 W
Hermanus	158	34.25 S	19.16 E
Hermanville	194	31.50 N	90.50 W
Hermeray	261	48.38 N	1.41 E
Hermes	50	49.22 N	2.15 E
Hermeskeil	56	49.39 N	6.56 E
Hermidale	166	31.33 S	146.43 E
Hermies	50	50.07 N	3.02 E
Hermie	214	40.15 N	79.43 W
Herminston	202	45.50 N	119.17 W
Hermitage, Nf., Can.	186	47.33 N	55.56 W
Hermitage, Eng., U.K.	42	51.27 N	1.16 W
Hermitage, Ar., U.S.	194	33.26 N	92.10 W
Hermitage, Mo., U.S.	194	37.55 N	93.18 W
Hermitage Bay c	186	47.35 N	56.05 W
Hermitage Park	284c	39.05 N	77.04 W
Hermit, Isla I	254	55.52 S	67.20 W
Hermit Islands II	164	1.30 S	145.05 E
Hermleigh	196	32.38 N	100.46 W
Hermon, S. Afr.	158	33.27 S	18.59 E
Hermon, N.Y., U.S.	212	44.28 N	75.13 W
Hermon, Mount — Shaykh, Jabal ash- ∧	92a	33.26 N	35.51 E
Hermosa Beach	280	33.51 N	118.23 W
Hermosillo, Méx.	200	32.30 N	114.59 W
Hermosillo, Méx.	232	29.04 N	110.58 W
Hermoso, Cerro ∧	246	1.10 S	78.12 W
Hermsdorf	54	52.37 N	11.52 E
Hermsdorf ♦⁸	54	52.37 N	13.18 E
Hermyingyi	110	14.15 N	98.21 E
Hernád ≃	30	47.56 N	21.08 E
Hernals ♦⁸	264b	48.13 N	16.20 E
Hernandarias	252	25.22 S	54.45 W
Hernández	232	23.01 N	102.01 W
Hernandez Reservoir ⊜¹	226	36.22 N	120.49 W
Hernando, Arg.	252	32.25 S	63.44 W
Hernando, Fl., U.S.	220	28.54 N	82.22 W
Hernando, Ms., U.S.	194	34.49 N	89.59 W
Hernando ◻⁶	220	28.34 N	82.22 W
Hernando de Magallanes, Parque Nacional ♦	254	54.15 S	72.00 W
Hernani	116	11.20 N	125.37 E
Herndon, Ca., U.S.	226	36.49 N	119.54 W
Herndon, Ks., U.S.	198	39.54 N	100.47 W
Herndon, Pa., U.S.	210	40.42 N	76.50 W
Herndon, Va., U.S.	208	38.58 N	77.23 W
Herndon Canal ≃	226	36.46 N	119.46 W
Herne	52	51.32 N	7.13 E
Herne Bay	42	51.23 N	1.08 E
Herne Hill	168a	31.50 S	116.01 E
Herning	41	56.08 N	8.59 E
Hernwood Heights	284b	39.22 N	77.50 W
Heroica Zitácuaro	219	19.24 N	100.22 W
Heroldsbach	60	49.42 N	11.00 E
Herongate	260	51.36 N	0.21 E
Herongen	56	51.24 N	6.15 E
Heron Island I	166	23.26 S	151.55 E
Heron Lake	198	43.47 N	95.19 W
Hérons, Île aux II	275a	45.25 N	73.35 W
Heronsgate	261	51.38 N	0.31 W
Hérouville	261	49.06 N	2.08 E
Hérouville-Saint-Clair	50	49.12 N	0.21 W
Herpf	52	50.34 N	10.20 E
Herradura	252	26.29 S	58.18 W
Herräng	40	60.08 N	18.39 E
Herreid	198	45.50 N	100.04 W
Herrenberg	56	48.35 N	8.52 E
Herrenchiemsee, Schloss ⊥	64	47.52 N	12.23 E
Herrera ∧	252	28.29 S	63.04 W
Herrera ◻⁴	236	7.54 N	80.38 W
Herrera del Duque	34	39.10 N	5.03 W
Herrera de Pisuerga	34	42.36 N	4.20 W
Herrick, Austl.	166	41.06 S	147.52 E
Herrick, Il., U.S.	219	39.13 N	88.58 W
Herrick Grove	194	36.04 N	121.30 W
Herrick Grove	212	44.04 N	76.12 W
Herricks	276	40.45 N	73.40 W
Herrieden	60	49.14 N	10.30 E
Herrin	194	37.48 N	89.01 W
Herring Bay c	208	38.46 N	76.33 W
Herring Brook ≃	283	42.10 N	70.44 W
Herring Cove, N.S., Can.	186	44.34 N	63.34 W
Herring Cove, Ak., U.S.	182	55.21 N	131.41 W
Herringen	208	39.43 N	77.01 W
Herring Run ≃	284b	39.18 N	76.31 W
Herring Run Park ♦	284b	39.19 N	76.33 W
Herrisleev	41	54.42 N	11.41 E
Herrljunga	40	58.05 N	13.02 E
Herrnburg	54	53.47 N	10.45 E
Herrnhut	54	51.01 N	14.44 E
Herrsching am Ammersee	60	48.00 N	11.10 E
Herrs Island I	279b	40.28 N	79.58 W
Herrskogen	40	52.58 N	16.15 E
Herry	50	47.13 N	2.57 E
Hersbruck	60	49.30 N	11.26 E
Herschbach	56	50.34 N	7.44 E
Herscheid	56	51.10 N	7.44 E
Herschel, Sk., Can.	184	51.38 N	108.21 W
Herschel, S. Afr.	158	30.37 S	27.12 E
Herschel Island I	180	69.35 S	139.05 W
Herscher	190	41.03 N	88.06 W
Herselt	56	51.03 N	4.53 E
Herserange	56	49.31 N	5.47 E
Hersham	261	51.22 N	0.24 W
Hershey, Ne., U.S.	198	41.09 N	101.00 W
Hershey, Pa., U.S.	208	40.17 N	76.39 W
Hersman	219	39.50 N	90.44 W
Herstal	56	50.40 N	5.38 E
Herstedberg	58	58.38 N	16.10 E
Herstal	56	50.40 N	5.38 E
Herstmonceux	42	50.53 N	0.20 E
Herten	56	51.36 N	7.08 E
Hertford, Eng., U.K.	42	51.48 N	0.05 W
Hertford, N.C., U.S.	192	36.11 N	76.27 W
Hertford ◻⁶	42	51.48 N	0.10 W
Hertfordshire ◻⁵	262	50.28 N	77.07 W
Hertingfordbury	260	51.48 N	0.07 W
Hertsa	78	48.09 N	26.16 E
Hertsmere ◻⁶	260	51.41 N	0.17 W
Hertzogville	158	28.08 S	25.33 E
Heruncun	100	40.58 N	123.47 E
Hervás	34	40.16 N	5.51 W
Herve	56	50.38 N	5.48 E
Hervest	263	51.40 N	7.01 E
Hervey Bay c	166	25.33 S	153.00 E
Herxheim	56	49.09 N	8.13 E
Héry, Fr.	50	47.54 N	3.38 E
Héry, Fr.	62	45.46 N	6.28 E
Herzberg, Dtsch.	54	52.54 N	12.58 E
Herzberg, Dtsch.	54	51.41 N	13.14 E
Herzberg am Harz	52	51.39 N	10.20 E
Herzebrock	52	51.53 N	8.14 E
Herzfelde	54	52.29 N	13.50 E
Herzhausen	56	51.11 N	8.53 E
Herzlake	52	52.41 N	7.36 E
Herzliyya	132	32.10 N	34.51 E
Herznach	58	47.28 N	8.03 E
Herzogenaurach	56	49.34 N	10.53 E
Herzogenbuchsee	58	47.12 N	7.41 E
Herzogenburg	61	48.17 N	15.42 E
Herzogenrath	56	50.52 N	6.06 E
Herzsprung	54	53.04 N	12.28 E
Hesãr, Kūh-e ∧	120	34.50 N	66.30 E
Hesdin	50	50.22 N	2.02 E
Hesel	52	53.18 N	7.35 E
Heshan	110	23.52 N	108.52 E
Heshangqiao	100	34.15 N	113.47 E
Heshengqiao	100	30.00 N	114.22 E
Heshi, Zhg.	100	25.04 N	118.37 E
Heshi, Zhg.	100	24.24 N	114.56 E
Heshui, Zhg.	102	22.48 N	112.29 E
Heshuijian	100	30.33 N	116.05 E
Heshun, Zhg.	100	27.30 N	117.24 E
Heshun, Zhg.	102	37.21 N	113.35 E
Hesketh Bank	262	53.42 N	2.51 W
Hesketh Out Marsh ⧉	262	53.44 N	2.55 W
Heskin Green	262	53.38 N	2.42 W
Hesler	218	38.28 N	84.47 W
Hesperange	56	49.34 N	6.09 E
Hesperia, Ca., U.S.	228	34.25 N	117.18 W
Hesperia, Mi., U.S.	190	43.34 N	86.02 W
Hesperus Mountain ∧	200	37.27 N	108.05 W
Hess ≃	180	63.34 N	133.57 W
Hesselager	41	55.10 N	10.45 E
Hesselberg ∧	56	49.04 N	10.32 E
Hesselte	41	56.12 N	7.22 E
Hessen	54	52.01 N	10.47 E
Hessen ◻³	30	50.30 N	9.15 E
Hessen Cassal	54	41.00 N	85.05 W
Hessental	56	49.05 N	9.17 E
Hessisch Lichtenau	56	51.12 N	9.43 E
Hessisch Oldendorf	52	52.10 N	9.15 E
Hessle	44	53.44 N	0.26 W
Hesso	166	32.08 S	137.27 E
Hess Tablemount �∵³	14	17.50 N	174.15 W
Hesston, Ks., U.S.	198	38.08 N	97.25 W
Hesston, Pa., U.S.	214	40.24 N	78.07 W
Heston ♦⁸	261	51.29 N	0.22 W
Heswall	44	53.20 N	3.06 W
Het ≃	110	20.49 N	104.01 E
Hetai	102	23.22 N	112.19 E
Hetang, Zhg.	100	24.40 N	119.09 E
Hetang, Zhg.	106	31.43 N	120.27 E
Hetauda	124	27.26 N	85.02 E
Hetch Hetchy Aqueduct ≃¹	226	37.29 N	122.19 W
Hetch Hetchy Reservoir ⊜¹	226	37.57 N	119.43 W
Hethersett	42	52.36 N	1.11 E
Hetian, Zhg.	100	25.14 N	115.44 E
Hetian, Zhg.	100	23.19 N	115.38 E
Het Loo, Paleis ⊥	52	52.14 N	5.56 E
Hetou	100	24.18 N	113.29 E
Hetoudian	98	37.02 N	120.35 E
Hettange-Grande	56	49.22 N	6.09 E
Hettenleidelheim	56	49.32 N	8.04 E
Hettick	219	39.11 N	90.02 W
Hettingen	56	48.13 N	9.14 E
Hettinger	198	46.00 N	102.38 W
Hetton-le-Hole	44	54.50 N	1.27 W
Hettstedt	54	51.38 N	11.30 E
Hetupu	100	30.50 N	116.03 E
Hetzendorf ♦⁸	264b	48.10 N	16.18 E
Hetzerath	56	49.52 N	6.49 E
Het Zoute	56	51.21 N	3.18 E
Heubach	56	48.48 N	9.56 E
Heuchin	50	50.28 N	2.16 E
Heudeber	54	51.54 N	10.50 E
Heule	56	50.49 N	3.15 E
Heuningspruit	158	27.26 S	27.28 E
Heure, Eau d' ≃	56	50.18 N	4.24 E
Heusden, Bel.	56	51.02 N	3.48 E
Heusden, Bel.	56	51.04 N	5.16 E
Heustreu	52	50.21 N	10.16 E
Heusweiler	56	49.20 N	6.55 E
Heuvelton	212	44.37 N	75.24 W
Hève, Cap de la ⟩	50	49.31 N	0.04 E
Heverlee	263	51.26 N	7.17 E
Heverlee	56	50.52 N	4.42 E
Heves	30	47.36 N	20.17 E
Heves ◻⁶	30	47.50 N	20.15 E
Hevlín	61	48.45 N	16.23 E
Hevron, Naḥal ≃	132	31.15 N	34.50 E
Hewanorra International Airport ⊠	241l	13.45 N	60.56 W
Hewitt, N.J., U.S.	210	41.08 N	74.16 W
Hewitt, Tx., U.S.	222	31.27 N	97.11 W
Hewittsville	219	39.32 N	89.19 W
Hewlett, N.Y., U.S.	276	40.38 N	73.41 W
Hewlett Bay Park	276	40.38 N	73.41 W
Hewlett Harbor	276	40.38 N	73.41 W
Hewlett Neck	276	40.37 N	73.42 W
Hewlett Point ⟩	276	40.50 N	73.45 W
Hewu	104	26.41 N	113.40 E
Hexenkopf ∧	58	47.01 N	10.28 E
Hexham	44	54.58 N	2.06 W
Hexi, Zhg.	100	24.52 N	117.15 E
Hexi, Zhg.	100	29.32 N	102.39 E
Hexian	100	31.43 N	118.22 E
Hexian (Caozhou)	102	24.54 N	115.14 E
Hexigten	105	39.38 N	116.58 E
Hex Rivierberge ∧	158	33.25 S	19.35 E
Hextable	260	51.25 N	0.11 E
Hexton	172	38.37 S	177.58 E
Heyan	104	40.40 N	74.53 W
Heyang, Zhg.	98	35.17 N	110.08 E
Heyang, Zhg.	102	31.18 N	118.33 E
Heyban	148	11.13 N	30.38 E
Heyburn	202	42.33 N	113.46 W
Heybridge, Eng., U.K.	260	51.44 N	0.41 E
Heybridge, Eng., U.K.	260	51.44 N	0.40 E
Heye ≃⁸	262	53.30 N	2.09 W
Heyerode	52	51.13 N	10.23 E
Heyersum	52	52.06 N	9.52 E
Heyin → Guide	96	36.02 N	101.25 E
Heyrieux	62	45.38 N	5.03 E
Heysham	44	54.03 N	2.54 W
Heytesbury	42	51.11 N	2.06 W
Heywood, Austl.	166	38.08 S	141.38 E
Heywood, Eng., U.K.	44	53.36 N	2.13 W
Heyworth	219	40.18 N	88.58 W
Heze (Caozhou)	102	35.14 N	115.26 E
Hezhang	102	27.08 N	104.43 E
Hezheng	96	35.25 N	103.21 E
Hezhou	100	24.23 N	111.33 E
Hezuo	96	35.00 N	102.54 E
Hezuozhen	100	34.56 N	120.29 E
Hiale	110	15.55 N	107.34 E
Hialeah	220	25.51 N	80.16 W
Hialeah Park Race Track ♦	220	25.51 N	80.17 W
Hiaohexi	100	31.21 N	114.02 E
Hiawassee	192	34.56 N	83.45 W
Hiawatha, Ks., U.S.	198	39.51 N	95.32 W
Hiawatha, Ut., U.S.	200	39.29 N	111.00 W
Hiba-Dōgo-Taishaku-kokutei-kōen ♦	96	35.07 N	133.08 E
Hibbard	44	53.31 N	0.32 W
Hibbing	190	47.25 N	92.56 W
Hibbs, Point ⟩	166	42.38 S	145.15 E
Hibernia	276	40.57 N	74.30 W
Hibernia Reef ⊹²	166	12.00 S	123.23 E
Hibiki-nada ⊏	96	34.00 N	130.30 E
Hiburi-shima I	96	33.10 N	132.17 E
Hibuson Island I	116	10.27 N	125.29 E
Hickam Air Force Base ♦	229c	21.20 N	157.57 W
Hickey, Mount ∧	169	37.22 S	145.19 E
Hickman, Ca., U.S.	226	37.37 N	120.45 W
Hickman, Ky., U.S.	194	36.34 N	89.11 W
Hickman, Ne., U.S.	198	40.37 N	96.37 W
Hickman, Pa., U.S.	214	40.23 N	80.09 W
Hickman's Harbour	186	48.06 N	53.44 W
Hickory, Ms., U.S.	194	32.19 N	89.01 W
Hickory, N.C., U.S.	192	35.43 N	81.20 W
Hickory, Pa., U.S.	214	40.18 N	80.18 W
Hickory Corners	216	42.26 N	85.22 W
Hickory Creek ≃, Il., U.S.	278	41.30 N	88.06 W
Hickory Creek ≃, Mi., U.S.	216	42.05 N	86.29 W
Hickory Creek ≃, Tx., U.S.	222	31.29 N	95.07 W
Hickory Flat	194	34.36 N	89.11 W
Hickory Hills	278	41.43 N	87.49 W
Hickory Run State Park ♦	210	41.02 N	75.41 W
Hickory Township	210	41.15 N	80.27 W
Hicks, Point ⟩	166	37.48 S	149.17 E
Hicks Bay	172	37.36 S	178.18 E
Hickson Lake ⊜	184	56.17 N	104.25 W
Hicksville, N.Y., U.S.	210	40.46 N	73.31 W
Hicksville, Oh., U.S.	216	41.17 N	84.45 W
Hico	220	26.50 N	81.10 W
Hida — Hita	96	33.19 N	130.56 E
Hidaka, Nihon	96	35.26 N	137.03 E
Hidaka, Nihon	96	35.54 N	139.21 E
Hidaka, Nihon	96	35.28 N	134.47 E
Hidaka ⦿	96	33.52 N	135.09 E
Hidaka-sammyaku ∧	92a	42.35 N	142.45 E
Hida-Kiso-gawa-kokutei-kōen ♦	96	35.37 N	137.15 E
Hida-kōchi ∧¹	96	36.16 N	137.05 E
Hidalgo, Méx.	232	27.47 N	99.52 W
Hidalgo, Méx.	232	25.59 N	100.27 W
Hidalgo, Méx.	232	24.15 N	99.26 W
Hidalgo, Tx., U.S.	230	26.06 N	98.15 W
Hidalgo ◻³	219	20.30 N	99.00 W
Hidalgo del Parral	232	26.56 N	105.40 W
Hidalgo-sammyaku ∧	96	36.25 N	137.40 E
Hiddenhausen	52	52.08 N	8.38 E
Hiddensee	54	54.33 N	13.05 E
Hiddensee I	54	54.33 N	13.07 E
Hidden Valley, Ca., U.S.	226	38.46 N	121.09 W
Hidden Valley, Tx., U.S.	222	29.54 N	95.25 W
Hiddenhausen	263	51.22 N	7.17 E
Hiddesen	52	51.55 N	8.50 E
Hidrobandi	130	38.47 N	39.00 E
Hidrolândia	255	16.58 S	49.14 W
Hidrolina	255	14.37 S	49.25 W
Hiefiau	61	47.36 N	14.44 E
Hienghène	175f	20.41 S	164.56 E
Hierapolis — Pamukkale ⊥	130	37.58 N	29.19 E
Hierges	56	50.06 N	4.44 E
Hierro (Ferro) I	148	27.45 N	18.00 W
Hiesfeld	263	51.33 N	6.46 E
Hietzing ♦⁸	264b	48.11 N	16.18 E
Higashi ∧	174m	26.38 N	128.09 E
Higashi ♦⁸	270	34.41 N	135.31 E
Higashibetsuin	270	34.56 N	135.34 E
Higashifuji-enshūjō ♠	96	35.17 N	138.51 E
Higashihiroshima	96	34.26 N	132.42 E
Higashichiki	92	31.40 N	130.20 E
Higashiizumi ♦⁸	268	35.45 N	139.36 E
Higashi-jima I	174f	24.47 N	141.23 E
Higashikurume	268	35.45 N	139.32 E
Higashimatsuyama	96	36.02 N	139.24 E
Higashimurayama	268	35.46 N	139.40 E
Higashinada ♦⁸	270	34.43 N	135.16 E
Higashinakano	268	35.38 N	139.25 E
Higashinari ♦⁸	270	34.40 N	135.33 E
Higashine	92	38.26 N	140.24 E
Higashinose	270	34.55 N	135.30 E
Higashiōsaka	96	34.39 N	135.35 E
Higashishirakawa	268	35.45 N	139.36 E
Higashisumiyoshi ♦⁸	270	34.37 N	135.32 E
Higashitokonoo-san ∧	96	35.25 N	134.55 E
Higashiura, Nihon	96	33.23 N	133.02 E
Higashiura, Nihon	96	34.59 N	136.58 E
Higashiyama ♦⁸	270	35.00 N	135.48 E
Higashiyamato	268	35.44 N	139.26 E
Higashiyodogawa ♦⁸	270	34.44 N	135.31 E
Higashiyoshino	96	34.24 N	135.58 E
Higbee	194	39.18 N	92.30 W
Higganum	207	41.29 N	72.33 W
Higgins	196	36.07 N	100.02 W
Higgins, Mount ∧	224	48.19 N	121.45 W
Higgins Lake ⊜	190	44.29 N	84.43 W
Higginsport	218	38.47 N	83.58 W
Higginsville	194	39.04 N	93.43 W
Higgins' Hope	194	29.19 S	23.16 E
High Atlas	144	31.30 N	6.00 W
High Bank Creek ≃	216	42.37 N	85.11 W
High Bar Indian Reserve ♦⁴	182	51.06 N	122.00 W
High Beach	260	51.39 N	0.02 E
High Bentham	44	54.08 N	2.30 W
High Bluff Island I	212	43.58 N	77.45 W
Highbridge, Eng., U.K.	42	51.13 N	2.49 W
High Bridge, N.J., U.S.	210	40.40 N	74.53 W
Highbury	164	16.25 S	143.09 E
Highcliff	42	50.43 N	1.34 W
Higher Ballam	262	53.46 N	2.59 W
Higher Broughton	262	53.30 N	2.15 W
Higher Hogshead	262	53.42 N	2.09 W
Higher Penwortham	262	53.45 N	2.44 W
Higher Walton, Eng., U.K.	262	53.19 N	2.35 W
Higher Walton, Eng., U.K.	44	53.44 N	2.39 W
Highet	262	53.32 N	2.35 W
High Falls	210	41.50 N	74.08 W
High Force ⊾	44	54.38 N	2.13 W
Highgate	214	41.59 N	82.28 W
Highgate Center	206	44.56 N	73.00 W
High Halstow	260	51.27 N	0.34 E
High Hill	219	38.52 N	91.23 W
High Hill ∧	276	40.49 N	73.25 W
High Hill ≃, Can.	184	56.45 N	110.30 W
High Hill ≃, Mb., Can.	184	55.52 N	94.42 W
High Hill Lake ⊜	184	55.34 N	95.40 W
High Island I, Zhg.	271d	22.22 N	114.21 E
High Island I, Mi., U.S.	190	45.42 N	85.40 W
High Island Creek ≃	190	44.35 N	93.54 W
High Island Reservoir ⊜¹	271d	22.23 N	114.21 W
Highland, Ca., U.S.	228	34.07 N	117.12 W
Highland, Il., U.S.	219	38.44 N	89.40 W
Highland, In., U.S.	216	41.33 N	87.27 W
Highland, Ks., U.S.	198	39.51 N	95.16 W
Highland, Md., U.S.	208	39.11 N	76.57 W
Highland, Mi., U.S.	281	42.38 N	83.37 W
Highland, N.Y., U.S.	210	41.43 N	73.57 W
Highland, Oh., U.S.	218	39.21 N	83.36 W
Highland, Wi., U.S.	279b	40.33 N	90.40 W
Highland ◻⁶	46	57.40 N	5.00 W
Highland ◻⁶	218	39.12 N	83.10 W
Highland Beach	220	26.25 N	80.04 W
Highland City	220	27.58 N	81.53 W
Highland Creek ≃, On., Can.	275b	43.46 N	79.08 W
Highland Creek ≃, Ca., U.S.	226	38.24 N	121.14 W
Highland Falls	210	41.22 N	73.58 W
Highland Heights, Ky., U.S.	218	39.04 N	84.27 W
Highland Heights, Oh., U.S.	279a	41.33 N	81.28 W
Highland Hills	278	41.52 N	88.01 W
Highland Home	194	31.57 N	86.18 W
Highland Lake, Il., U.S.	278	42.21 N	88.04 W
Highland Lake, Ma., U.S.	283	42.41 N	72.37 W
Highland Lake, N.Y., U.S.	210	41.32 N	74.51 W
Highland Lake ⊜, Ct., U.S.	207	41.54 N	73.06 W
Highland Lake ⊜, Il., U.S.	278	42.22 N	88.04 W
Highland Lakes	276	41.10 N	74.28 W
Highland-on-the-Lake	284a	42.42 N	79.59 W
Highland Park, Il., U.S.	216	42.10 N	87.48 W
Highland Park, Md., U.S.	284c	38.54 N	76.54 W
Highland Park, Mi., U.S.	281	42.24 N	83.05 W
Highland Park, N.J., U.S.	210	40.29 N	74.25 W
Highland Park, Pa., U.S.	210	40.38 N	77.33 W
Highland Park, Tx., U.S.	222	32.50 N	96.48 W
Highland Park ♦, Ma., U.S.	280	34.07 N	118.13 W
Highland Park ♦, Pa., U.S.	279b	40.29 N	79.55 W
Highland Peak ∧	226	38.33 N	119.45 W
Highland Point ⟩	220	25.30 N	81.12 W
Highlands, N.J., U.S.	208	40.24 N	73.59 W
Highlands, N.C., U.S.	192	35.03 N	83.11 W
Highlands, Tx., U.S.	222	29.49 N	95.03 W
Highlands, Tx., U.S.	220	27.20 N	81.16 W
Highlands Hammock State Park ♦	220	27.28 N	81.33 W
Highland Silver Lake ⊜¹	219	38.47 N	89.39 W
Highlands North ♦⁸	273d	26.09 S	28.05 E
Highland Springs	208	37.32 N	77.19 W
Highlands Reservoir ⊜¹	222	29.50 N	95.02 W
Highland State Recreation Area ♦	216	42.39 N	83.33 W
Highlandtown ♦⁸	284b	39.17 N	76.33 W
High Laver	260	51.44 N	0.13 E
High Legh	262	53.20 N	2.28 W
Highley	42	52.27 N	2.23 W
Highmore	198	44.31 N	99.26 W
High Ongar	260	51.43 N	0.16 E
High Park ∧	280	34.11 N	117.53 W
High Peak ∧, N.Y., U.S.	44	53.22 N	1.50 W
High Peak ∧	226	42.09 N	74.05 W
High Peak, Fl., U.S.	220	27.55 N	82.42 W
High Peak, N.C., U.S.	192	35.57 N	80.10 W
Highpoint, Oh., U.S.	218	39.14 N	84.24 W
High Point, N.J., U.S.	210	41.19 N	74.40 W
High Point ∧, Wy., U.S.	202	41.37 N	107.47 W
High Point State Park	210	41.18 N	74.41 W
High Prairie	182	55.26 N	116.29 W
High Ridge	219	38.27 N	90.32 W
High River	182	50.35 N	113.52 W
High Rock ∧	188	36.22 N	121.13 W
High Rock ∧	188	39.33 N	79.06 W
Highrock Indian Reserve ♦⁴	184	55.54 N	100.30 W
Highrock Lake ⊜, Mb., Can.	184	55.45 N	100.30 W
Highrock Lake ⊜, Sk., Can.	184	57.04 N	105.30 W
High Rock Lake ⊜¹	192	35.40 N	80.17 W
High Seat ∧	44	54.24 N	2.00 W
High Spire	210	40.12 N	76.47 W
High Springs	220	29.49 N	82.35 W
High Street ∧	44	54.29 N	2.52 W
Hightown	262	53.31 N	3.03 W
High View	210	41.33 N	74.27 W
Highwater	206	45.01 N	72.26 W
Highway City	226	36.49 N	119.54 W
High Willhays ∧	42	50.41 N	3.59 W
High Wood ∧	216	42.11 N	87.48 W
Highwood, Il., U.S.	278	42.12 N	87.48 W
Highwood, Mt., U.S.	202	47.32 N	110.46 W
Highwood Baldy ∧	202	47.04 N	110.40 W
Highwood Mountains ∧²	202	47.05 N	110.40 W
Hikawa	96	35.25 N	132.50 E
Hikawa Shrine ⊥¹	268	35.54 N	139.38 E
Hiketa	96	34.13 N	134.24 E
Hiki ≃	96	33.33 N	135.27 E
Hikigawa	96	33.34 N	135.27 E
Hikimi ≃	96	34.37 N	131.48 E
Hikiura	270	34.33 N	134.58 E
Hikone	94	35.15 N	136.15 E
Hiko-san ∧	96	35.15 N	136.14 E
Hikueru I¹	14	17.36 S	142.37 W
Hikurangi	172	35.36 S	174.18 E
Hikurangi ∧	172	37.55 S	178.04 E
Hikutaia	172	37.17 S	175.39 E
Hikutavake	174v	18.56 S	169.53 W
Hilāl, Jabal ∧	132	30.40 N	34.00 E
Hilāl, Ra's al- ⟩	146	32.57 N	22.10 E
Hilbersdorf	54	50.55 N	13.23 E
Hilbert	190	44.08 N	88.09 W
Hilbre Islands II	262	53.23 N	3.13 W
Hilbre Point ⟩	262	53.23 N	3.12 W
Hilchenbach	56	51.00 N	8.06 E
Hilda, Ab., Can.	184	50.25 N	10.44 E
Hildburghausen	54	50.25 N	10.44 E
Hilden	56	51.10 N	6.56 E
Hildenborough	260	51.13 N	0.15 E
Hilders	52	50.34 N	10.00 E
Hildesheim	52	52.09 N	9.57 E
Hildreth	198	40.20 N	99.02 W
Hilgen	263	51.06 N	7.09 E
Hilalawa	114	0.44 N	97.53 E
Hilgeo	114	1.22 N	97.10 E
Hiliotaluwa	114	0.44 N	97.53 E
Hill ◻⁶	222	32.02 N	97.10 W
Hill, Mount ∧	241g	13.12 N	59.35 W
Hill Air Force Base ♦	202	41.05 N	111.58 W
Hillandale, S. Afr.	158	33.06 S	20.36 E
Hillandale, Md., U.S.	284c	39.01 N	76.58 W
Hillandale Heights	284c	39.01 N	76.59 W
Hill Bank	232	17.35 N	88.42 W
Hillburn	276	41.08 N	74.10 W
Hill City, Ks., U.S.	198	39.21 N	99.50 W
Hill City, Mn., U.S.	190	46.59 N	93.35 W
Hill City, S.D., U.S.	198	43.56 N	103.34 W
Hill Creek ≃	200	39.55 N	109.40 W
Hillcrest, Il., U.S.	278	41.58 N	89.05 W
Hillcrest, N.Y., U.S.	210	41.07 N	74.02 W
Hillcrest Heights	284c	38.49 N	76.57 W
Hillcrest Mines	182	49.34 N	114.23 W
Hillcrest Orchard	282	41.51 N	83.29 W
Hillcrest Park	282	34.07 N	122.16 W
Hill Cumorah ⊥	210	43.01 N	77.15 W
Hille, Dtsch.	52	52.20 N	8.44 E
Hille, Sve.	40	60.44 N	17.11 E
Hillegom	52	52.18 N	4.35 E
Hillegossen	263	51.59 N	8.37 E
Hillerød	41	55.56 N	12.19 E
Hillers Creek ≃	219	38.38 N	91.54 W
Hillesheim	56	50.18 N	6.38 E
Hilliard, Fl., U.S.	220	30.41 N	81.55 W
Hilliard, Oh., U.S.	218	40.02 N	83.09 W
Hilliards	42	51.32 N	0.27 W
Hillingdon ♦⁸	42	51.32 N	0.27 W
Hillister	222	30.40 N	94.23 W
Hillman	190	45.03 N	83.54 W
Hillmersdorf	54	51.42 N	13.29 E
Hill of Fearn	46	57.45 N	3.56 W
Hills	198	43.31 N	96.21 W
Hills and Dales	214	39.42 N	84.13 W
Hillsboro, Il., U.S.	219	39.09 N	89.29 W
Hillsboro, Ks., U.S.	198	38.21 N	97.12 W
Hillsboro, Md., U.S.	208	38.55 N	75.56 W
Hillsboro, Mo., U.S.	219	38.13 N	90.33 W
Hillsboro, N.D., U.S.	198	47.24 N	97.03 W
Hillsboro, N.H., U.S.	206	43.06 N	71.53 W
Hillsboro, Oh., U.S.	218	39.12 N	83.36 W
Hillsboro, Or., U.S.	224	45.31 N	122.59 W
Hillsboro, Tx., U.S.	222	32.00 N	97.07 W
Hillsboro Beach	220	26.17 N	80.05 W
Hillsboro Canal ≃	220	26.19 N	80.05 W
Hillsborough, N.B., Can.	186	45.56 N	64.39 W
Hillsborough, N. Ire., U.K.	44	54.28 N	6.05 W
Hillsborough, N.C., U.S.	192	36.04 N	79.06 W
Hillsborough ◻⁶, Fl., U.S.	220	27.55 N	82.15 W
Hima	192	37.07 N	83.46 W
Himāchal Pradesh ◻³	120	32.00 N	77.00 E
Himalayas ∧	120	28.00 N	84.00 E
Himāl Chuli ∧	124	28.25 N	84.39 E
Himamaylan	116	10.06 N	122.52 E
Himanka	26	64.04 N	23.39 E
Himarë	38	40.07 N	19.44 E
Himatnagar	120	23.36 N	72.57 E
Himberg	61	48.05 N	16.26 E
Hime ≃	94	37.02 N	137.49 E
Himeji	94	34.49 N	134.42 E
Himeville	158	29.44 S	29.31 E
Himi	94	36.51 N	136.59 E
Himmelberget ∧²	41	56.06 N	9.42 E
Himmelgeist ♦⁸	263	51.10 N	6.49 E
Himmelpforten	52	53.36 N	9.18 E
Himmelsfjärden c²	40	58.34 N	17.43 E
Himmerland ◻⁹	26	56.50 N	9.45 E
Himmetdede	130	38.53 N	35.07 E
Himrod	210	42.35 N	76.57 W
Hims (Homs)	132	34.44 N	36.43 E
Hims ◻⁸	130	34.30 N	38.00 E
Hinabangan	116	11.42 N	125.04 E
Hinase	96	34.44 N	134.16 E
Hinatuan	116	8.23 N	126.20 E
Hinatuan Island I	116	9.47 N	125.43 E
Hinatuan Passage ⊔	116	9.47 N	125.47 E
Hinche	238	19.09 N	72.01 W
Hinckley, Eng., U.K.	42	52.33 N	1.21 W
Hinckley, Mn., U.S.	190	46.01 N	92.56 W
Hinckley, Oh., U.S.	214	41.14 N	81.45 W
Hinckley, Ut., U.S.	200	39.19 N	112.40 W
Hinckley Reservoir ⊜¹	210	43.20 N	75.05 W
Hindan ≃	272a	28.30 N	77.27 E
Hindaun	124	26.43 N	77.01 E
Hindaun	124	26.43 N	77.01 E
Hindelang	58	47.30 N	10.22 E
Hindeloopen	52	52.56 N	5.24 E
Hindenburg — Zabrze	30	50.18 N	18.46 E
Hindley	44	53.32 N	2.35 W
Hindley Green	262	53.31 N	2.32 W
Hindman	192	37.20 N	82.58 W
Hindmarsh, Lake ⊜	166	36.03 S	141.55 E
Hindmarsh Valley	168b	35.30 S	138.38 E
Hinds ◻⁶	194	32.16 N	90.26 W
Hinds Creek ≃	192	36.12 N	84.04 W
Hindsholm ⟩¹	41	55.37 N	10.40 E
Hinds Lake ⊜	186	48.57 N	57.00 W
Hindu Kush ∧	120	36.00 N	71.30 E
Hindubagh	123	30.56 N	67.50 E
Hindupur	122	13.49 N	77.29 E
Hi-Nella	285	39.50 N	75.01 W
Hines Creek	182	56.15 N	118.36 W
Hines Creek ≃	182	56.15 N	118.37 W
Hines Peak ∧	228	34.31 N	119.05 W
Hinesville	192	31.50 N	81.35 W
Hinganghāt	120	20.34 N	78.50 E
Hingham, Eng., U.K.	42	52.35 N	0.59 E
Hingham, Ma., U.S.	207	42.14 N	70.53 W
Hingham Harbor c	283	42.15 N	70.53 W
Hingol ≃	120	25.23 N	65.28 E
Hingoli	120	19.43 N	77.09 E
Hinis	130	39.22 N	41.42 E
Hinis ≃	130	10.17 N	122.51 E
Hinnøya I	26	68.30 N	16.00 E
Hinnerjoki	26	56.15 N	6.17 E
Hino, Nihon	96	35.06 N	133.29 E
Hino, Nihon	270	34.59 N	135.11 E
Hino, Nihon	268	35.27 N	133.23 E
Hino ≃	96	35.14 N	139.23 E
Hinoba-an	116	9.35 N	122.28 E
Hinode	268	35.44 N	139.16 E
Hinoemata	92	37.01 N	139.23 E
Hinohara	268	35.44 N	139.08 E
Hinojosa del Duque	34	38.30 N	5.09 W
Hinomi-saki ⟩, Nihon	96	35.26 N	132.38 E
Hinomi-saki ⟩, Nihon	96	34.16 N	135.05 E
Hino-shi	268	35.40 N	139.24 E
Hinsberg ∧	52	51.09 N	9.00 E
Hinsdale, Il., U.S.	278	41.48 N	87.56 W
Hinsdale, Ma., U.S.	207	42.26 N	73.07 W
Hinsdale, N.H., U.S.	207	42.47 N	72.29 W
Hinsdale, N.Y., U.S.	214	42.12 N	78.23 W
Hinterbichl	60	47.01 N	12.18 E
Hinterbrühl	61	48.05 N	16.15 E
Hinterrhein ≃	58	46.49 N	9.26 E
Hinterstoder	61	47.42 N	14.09 E
Hintertux	60	47.04 N	11.40 E
Hinterweidenthal	56	49.12 N	7.45 E
Hinterzarten	56	47.54 N	8.06 E
Hinton, Ab., Can.	182	53.25 N	117.34 W
Hinton, W.V., U.S.	208	37.40 N	80.53 W
Hinwil	58	47.18 N	8.51 E
Hio	34	42.15 N	8.51 W
Hipolito	232	25.41 N	101.26 W
Hipólito Yrigoyen	252	23.13 S	64.15 W
Hiponcon	116	9.06 N	125.44 E
Hippo, Club ⊠	286d	33.28 S	70.41 W
Hipswell	44	54.22 N	1.43 W
Hirado	96	33.22 N	129.33 E
Hirado-shima I	96	33.19 N	129.25 E
Hiraiwa-shima I	174f	24.14 N	141.18 E
Hiraizumi	92	38.59 N	141.07 E
Hirakata	94	34.48 N	135.38 E
Hirakawa	270	34.32 N	135.47 E
Hirano, Nihon	96	34.36 N	135.34 E
Hirano-dai ∧²	96	32.05 N	130.52 E
Hirano-gawa ≃	270	34.39 N	135.29 E
Hirao	96	33.56 N	132.04 E
Hirara	174l	24.48 N	125.17 E
Hirata, Nihon	92	37.13 N	140.33 E
Hirata, Nihon	96	35.26 N	132.49 E
Hiratsuka	94	35.19 N	139.21 E

Symbols in the index entries represent the broad categories identified in the key at the right. Symbols with superior numbers (∧¹) identify subcategories (see complete key on page I · 1).

Symbole im Register stellen die rechts im Schlüssel erklärten Kategorien dar. Symbole mit hochgestellten Ziffern (∧¹) bezeichnen Unterteilungen einer Kategorie (vgl. vollständiger Schlüssel auf Seite I · 1).

Los símbolos incluidos en el texto del índice representan las grandes categorías identificadas con la clave a la derecha. Los símbolos con numeros en su parte superior (∧¹) identifican las subcategorías (véase la clave completa en la página I · 1).

Os símbolos incluídos no texto do índice representam as grandes categorias identificadas com a chave à direita. Os símbolos com números em sua parte superior (∧¹) identificam as subcategorias (veja-se a chave completa à página I · 1).

Les symboles de l'index représentent les catégories indiquées dans la légende à droite. Les symboles suivis d'un indice (∧¹) représentent les sous-catégories (voir légende complète à la page I · 1).

∧	Mountain	Berg	Montaña	Montagne	Montanha
∧	Mountains	Gebirge	Montañas	Montagnes	Montanhas
⋊	Pass	Paß	Paso	Col	Passo
⛰	Valley, Canyon	Tal, Cañon	Valle, Cañón	Vallée, Canyon	Vale, Canhão
≃	Plain	Ebene	Llano	Plaine	Planície
⟩	Cape	Kap	Cabo	Cap	Cabo
I	Island	Insel	Isla	Île	Ilha
II	Islands	Inseln	Islas	Îles	Ilhas
⊥	Other Topographic Features	Andere Topographische Objekte	Otros Elementos Topográficos	Autres données topographiques	Outros acidentes topográficos

ESPAÑOL — Nombre, Página, Lat.°′, Long.°′ W = Oeste
FRANÇAIS — Nom, Page, Lat.°′, Long.°′ W = Ouest
PORTUGUÊS — Nome, Página, Lat.°′, Long.°′ W = Oeste

Nombre / Nom / Nome	Página / Page	Lat.°′	Long.°′
Hiraya	94	35.19 N	137.37 E
Hirfanlı Barajı ⊜[1]	130	39.10 N	33.35 E
Hirhafok	148	23.49 N	5.45 E
Hiriyūr	122	13.58 N	76.36 E
Hirjillah	132	33.22 N	36.18 E
Hirnyk, Ukr.	78	50.20 N	24.10 E
Hirnyk, Ukr.	83	48.04 N	37.24 E
Hirnyts'ke	78	47.42 N	34.08 E
Hirokawa, Nihon	96	33.15 N	130.32 E
Hirokawa, Nihon	96	34.01 N	135.11 E
Hirok Sāmi	128	26.02 N	63.25 E
Hiromi	96	33.15 N	132.41 E
Hiroo	92a	42.17 N	143.19 E
Hirooka	268	35.15 N	140.04 E
Hirosaki	92	40.35 N	140.28 E
Hiroschima → Hiroshima	96	34.24 N	132.27 E
Hirose	96	35.22 N	133.10 E
Hiroshima	96	34.24 N	132.27 E
Hiroshima □[5]	96	34.30 N	133.00 E
Hiro-shima I	96	34.22 N	133.43 E
Hiroshima-wan C	96	34.06 N	132.20 E
Hirosima → Hiroshima	96	34.24 N	132.27 E
Hirota	270	34.45 N	135.21 E
Hirsau	56	48.44 N	8.44 E
Hirschaid	56	49.49 N	10.59 E
Hirschau	60	49.33 N	11.57 E
Hirschbach	54	50.33 N	10.44 E
Hirschberg, Dtsch.	54	50.24 N	11.49 E
Hirschberg → Jelenia Góra, Pol.	30	50.55 N	15.46 E
Hirschfeld	54	51.23 N	13.37 E
Hirschfelde, Dtsch.	54	50.57 N	14.53 E
Hirschfelde, Dtsch.	264a	52.38 N	13.48 E
Hirschhorn	56	49.27 N	8.53 E
Hirschstetten ⊷[8]	264b	48.14 N	16.29 E
Hirshfeld Brook ≃	276	40.57 N	74.02 W
Hirsingue	58	47.35 N	7.15 E
Hirs'ke	83	48.46 N	38.30 E
Hirs'kyy Tikych ≃	78	48.47 N	30.53 E
Hirson	50	49.55 N	4.05 E
Hirsts Hill ∧	171a	27.13 S	152.06 E
Hirtshals	26	57.35 N	9.58 E
Hirtzfelden	58	47.55 N	7.27 E
Hirukawa	94	35.31 N	137.23 E
Hiru-zen ∧	96	35.19 N	133.40 E
Hirwaun	42	51.45 N	3.30 W
Hisābpur	272b	22.51 N	88.32 E
Hisai, Nihon	94	34.40 N	136.28 E
Hisai, Nihon	270	34.25 N	135.28 E
Hisār	123	29.10 N	75.43 E
Hisarönü	130	41.33 N	32.02 E
Ḥisbān	132	31.48 N	35.48 E
Hisiu	164	9.05 S	146.45 E
Hisn al-'Abr	144	16.05 N	47.22 E
Ḥiṣn al-Qarn	144	15.11 N	49.05 E
Hispaniola I	238	19.00 N	71.00 W
Hispar Glacier ⊓	123	36.05 N	75.20 E
Histon	42	52.15 N	0.06 E
Hisua	124	24.50 N	85.25 E
Ḥisyah	130	34.24 N	36.45 E
Hīt	128	33.38 N	42.49 E
Hita	96	33.19 N	130.56 E
Hitachi	94	36.36 N	140.39 E
Hitachi-ōta	94	36.32 N	140.31 E
Hitati → Hitachi	94	36.36 N	140.39 E
Hitchcock	222	29.20 N	95.00 W
Hitchin	42	51.57 N	0.17 W
Hitchins	218	38.16 N	82.55 W
Hither Green ⊷[8]	260	51.27 N	0.01 W
Hither Hills State Park ♦	207	41.01 N	72.01 W
Hitiaa	174s	17.36 S	149.18 W
Hitokura	270	34.55 N	135.25 E
Hitotsubashi University ʋ[2]	268	35.42 N	139.27 E
Hitoyoshi	92	32.13 N	130.45 E
Hitra I	26	63.33 N	8.45 E
Hittarp	41	56.06 N	12.38 E
Hittisau	58	47.27 N	9.57 E
Hitzacker	54	53.09 N	11.02 E
Hitze-Berge ∧[2]	264a	52.35 N	13.07 E
Hiu I	175f	13.10 S	166.35 E
Hiuchiga-take ∧	94	36.57 N	139.17 E
Hiuchi-nada ⊤[2]	96	34.05 N	133.20 E
Hiūnchuli Pātan ∧	124	28.50 N	82.37 E
Hiva Oa I	174x	9.45 S	139.00 W
Hi Vista	228	34.44 N	117.47 W
Hiwa	96	34.59 N	132.59 E
Hiwannee	194	31.48 N	88.41 W
Hiwasa	96	33.44 N	134.32 E
Hiwassee ≃	192	35.19 N	84.47 W
Hiwassee Lake ⊜[1]	192	35.10 N	84.05 W
Hixon	182	53.27 N	122.36 W
Hixson	192	35.09 N	85.14 W
Hiyoshi, Nihon	94	35.53 N	137.45 E
Hiyoshi, Nihon	96	33.20 N	132.48 E
Hiyoshi, Nihon	96	35.09 N	135.31 E
Hiyoshi ⊷[8]	268	35.33 N	139.39 E
Ḥiyyon, Naḥal V	132	30.12 N	35.07 E
Hizaonna	174m	26.24 N	127.50 E
Hjälmare kanal ≊	40	59.24 N	15.56 E
Hjälmaren ⊜	40	59.15 N	15.45 E
Hjälmaresund ʊ	40	59.15 N	16.06 E
Hjarnø I	41	55.50 N	10.05 E
Hjelm I	41	56.08 N	10.48 E
Hjelmelandsvågen	26	59.14 N	6.11 E
Hjeltefjorden C[2]	26	60.40 N	4.55 E
Hjembæk	41	55.42 N	11.25 E
Hjo	26	58.18 N	14.17 E
Hjøllund	41	56.05 N	9.25 E
Hjordkær	41	55.01 N	9.19 E
Hjørring	26	57.28 N	9.59 E
Hjortkvarn	40	58.53 N	15.25 E
Hjørundfjorden C[2]	26	62.21 N	6.23 E
Hkakabo Razi ∧	102	28.20 N	97.32 E
Hkok (Kok) ≃	110	20.14 N	100.09 E
Hlabisa	158	28.08 S	31.52 E
Hladkivka	78	46.23 N	32.36 E
Hlaingbwe	110	17.08 N	97.50 E
Hlatikulu	158	27.00 S	31.25 E
Hlegu	110	17.06 N	96.14 E
Hlinsko	30	49.45 N	15.55 E
Hlobane	158	27.42 S	31.00 E
Hlobyne	78	49.23 N	33.17 E
Hlohovec	30	48.25 N	17.47 E
Hluboká ⊥	61	49.05 N	14.25 E
Hluboká nad Vltavou	61	49.03 N	14.27 E
Hluboš	60	49.45 N	14.02 E
Hlučín	30	49.54 N	18.12 E
Hluhluwe	158	28.01 S	32.15 E
Hluhluwe Game Reserve ⊷[4]	158	28.05 S	32.04 E
Hlukhiv	78	51.41 N	33.53 E
Hluša	76	53.05 N	28.52 E
Hlusk	76	52.54 N	28.41 E
Hluškavičy	78	51.34 N	27.47 E
Hluti	158	27.13 S	31.35 E
Hlyboka	78	48.07 N	25.56 E
Hlybokae	76	55.08 N	27.41 E
Hlynyany	78	49.49 N	24.30 E
Hmawbi	110	17.06 N	96.02 E
H. Neely Henry Lake ⊜[1]	194	33.55 N	86.05 W
Hnivan'	78	49.06 N	28.20 E
Hnyla Lypa ≃	78	49.07 N	24.44 E
Hnylyy Tikych ≃	78	48.47 N	30.53 E
Hnylyy Yalanets' ≃	78	47.20 N	31.44 E
Ho	150	6.35 N	0.30 E
Hoa Binh	110	20.50 N	105.20 E
Hoa Da	110	11.11 N	108.33 E
Hoagland	216	40.56 N	84.59 W
Hoagland Ditch ≊	216	40.48 N	86.48 W
Hoanib ≃	156	19.27 S	12.46 E
Hoare Bay C	176	65.20 N	62.30 W
Hoarusib ≃	156	19.03 S	12.36 E
Hoa Thoi	269c	10.44 N	106.35 E
Hoback ≃	202	43.19 N	110.44 W
Hobart, Austl.	166	42.53 S	147.19 E
Hobart, In., U.S.	216	41.31 N	87.15 W
Hobart, N.Y., U.S.	210	42.22 N	74.40 W
Hobart, Ok., U.S.	196	35.01 N	99.05 W
Hobart, Wa., U.S.	224	47.25 N	121.58 W
Hobbs, In., U.S.	216	40.17 N	85.57 W
Hobbs, N.M., U.S.	196	32.42 N	103.08 W
Hobbs Coast ≚[2]	9	74.45 S	131.00 W
Hobe Sound	220	27.03 N	80.08 W
Hobgood	192	36.01 N	77.23 W
Hobhole Drain ≊	44	52.59 N	0.02 E
Hobhouse	158	29.31 S	27.08 E
Hobo	246	2.35 N	75.27 W
Hoboken, Bel.	50	51.10 N	4.21 E
Hoboken, N.J., U.S.	210	40.44 N	74.01 W
Hoboksar	86	46.47 N	85.43 E
Hobq Shamo ⊷[2]	102	40.30 N	107.55 E
Hobro	26	56.38 N	9.48 E
Hobson	202	47.00 N	109.52 W
Hobson Lake ⊜	182	52.30 N	120.20 W
Hobsons Bay C	274b	37.51 S	144.56 E
Hoburgen ›	26	56.55 N	18.07 E
Hobyo	144	5.21 N	48.32 E
Hocaköy	130	41.03 N	30.17 E
Hocalar	130	38.34 N	30.00 E
Hocalı	130	38.41 N	27.41 E
Hochalmspitze ∧	64	47.01 N	13.19 E
Hochandochtla Mountain ∧	180	65.32 N	154.50 W
Höchberg	56	49.49 N	9.51 E
Hochburg	60	48.07 N	12.52 E
Hochdahl	56	51.13 N	6.56 E
Hochdorf	58	47.10 N	8.17 E
Höchenschwand	58	47.44 N	8.10 E
Hochfeiler (Gran Pilastro) ∧	64	46.58 N	11.44 E
Hochfeld	156	21.28 S	17.58 E
Hochfeld ⊷[8]	263	51.25 N	6.46 E
Hochfelden	56	48.45 N	7.34 E
Hochfilzen	64	47.28 N	12.37 E
Hochfinstermünz	58	46.56 N	10.29 E
Hochgern ∧	64	47.45 N	12.30 E
Hochgolling ∧	64	47.16 N	13.45 E
Hochheide ⊷[8]	263	51.27 N	6.41 E
Hochheim, Dtsch.	56	50.01 N	8.20 E
Hochheim, Tx., U.S.	222	29.19 N	97.17 W
Ho Chi Minh City → Thanh Pho Ho Chi Minh	110	10.45 N	106.40 E
Hochiss ∧	64	47.27 N	11.46 E
Hochkirch	54	51.09 N	14.34 E
Hochkönig ∧	64	47.25 N	13.04 E
Hochkreuz ∧	64	46.49 N	13.04 E
Hochlantsch ∧	61	47.21 N	15.25 E
Hochlar	263	51.36 N	7.10 E
Hochneukirch	56	51.06 N	6.26 E
Hochobir ∧	61	46.30 N	14.29 E
Hochreichhart ∧	61	47.22 N	14.41 E
Hochries ∧	64	47.45 N	12.14 E
Hochschwab ∧	61	47.37 N	15.09 E
Hochschwab ⋏	61	47.36 N	15.05 E
Hochsimmer ∧	56	50.21 N	7.12 E
Hochspeyer	56	49.26 N	7.54 E
Höchst, Dtsch.	56	49.48 N	8.59 E
Höchst, Öst.	58	47.28 N	9.38 E
Höchstadt an der Aisch	56	49.42 N	10.44 E
Höchstädt an der Donau	56	48.36 N	10.34 E
Höchsten ⊷[8]	263	51.27 N	7.29 E
Höchstenbach	56	50.38 N	7.44 E
Hochstuhl (Veliki Stol) ∧	61	46.26 N	14.10 E
Hochtor)(	64	47.05 N	12.51 E
Hoch'uan → Hechuan	107	30.00 N	106.16 E
Ho Chung	271d	22.22 N	114.14 E
Hochvogel ∧	58	47.23 N	10.26 E
Hochwildstelle ∧	64	47.20 N	13.50 E
Hocimsk	76	53.26 N	32.35 E
Hockenheim	56	49.19 N	8.33 E
Hockeroda	54	50.35 N	11.26 E
Hockessin	285	39.47 N	75.41 W
Hocking ≃	188	39.12 N	81.45 W
Hocking Hills State Park ♦	188	39.30 N	82.32 W
Hockley, Eng., U.K.	42	51.37 N	0.40 E
Hockley, Tx., U.S.	222	30.02 N	95.51 W
Hockomock Swamp ≡	283	41.59 N	71.05 W
Hôḍ ⊷[1]	150	16.10 N	8.40 W
Hodal	124	27.54 N	77.22 E
Hodasy	76	53.56 N	31.29 E
Hōdatsu-zan ∧	94	36.47 N	136.49 E
Hodder ≃	44	53.50 N	2.25 W
Hoddesdon	42	51.46 N	0.01 W
Hoddlesden	262	53.42 N	2.26 W
Hodeida → Al-Ḥudaydah	144	14.48 N	42.57 E
Hodenhagen	52	52.46 N	9.35 E
Hodge	194	32.16 N	92.43 W
Hodgenville	194	37.34 N	85.44 W
Hodges, Lake ⊜[1]	228	33.03 N	117.05 W
Hodges Brook ≃	283	41.58 N	71.14 W
Hodges Hill ∧[2]	186	49.04 N	55.53 W
Hodgeville	184	50.08 N	106.58 W
Hodgkins	278	41.46 N	87.51 W
Hodgson	184	51.13 N	97.34 W
Hodgson ≃	164	14.48 S	134.35 E
Hodgson, Mount ∧[2]	162	22.26 S	121.10 E
Hod HaSharon	132	32.09 N	34.53 E
Hodh ech Chargui □[4]	150	18.10 N	7.15 W
Hodh el Gharbi □[4]	150	16.30 N	10.00 W
Hódmezővásárhely	30	46.25 N	20.20 E
Hodmo V	144	10.41 N	46.13 E
Hodna, Chott el ⊜	148	35.25 N	4.45 E
Hodna, Monts du ⋏	34	35.50 N	4.50 E
Hodna, Plaine du ≚	34	35.38 N	4.30 E
Hodnet	42	52.51 N	2.35 W
Hodogaya ⊷[8]	268	35.27 N	139.36 E
Hodogaya Baseball Ground ♦	268	35.27 N	139.35 E
Hodonín	30	48.51 N	17.08 E
Hodoš	61	46.50 N	16.20 E
Hodzana ≃	180	66.15 N	147.48 W
Hoed	41	56.19 N	10.49 E
Hoedekenskerke	52	51.25 N	3.55 E
Hoehne	198	37.16 N	104.22 W
Hoeksche Waard I	52	51.45 N	4.30 E
Hoek van Holland	52	51.59 N	4.09 E
Hoeningen	263	51.05 N	6.41 E
Hoensbroek	56	50.55 N	5.55 E
Hœrdt	58	48.42 N	7.47 E
Hoerstgen	263	51.30 N	6.27 E
Hoeryŏng	98	42.27 N	129.44 E
Hoeyang	98	38.43 N	127.36 E
Hof, Dtsch.	54	50.18 N	11.55 E
Hof, Ísland	24a	64.34 N	14.39 W
Hofbieber	56	50.35 N	9.50 E
Hofburg ʋ	264b	48.12 N	16.22 E
Höfđakaupstađur	24a	65.50 N	20.19 W
Hofei → Hefei	100	31.51 N	117.17 E
Höfen	56	50.32 N	6.15 E
Hoffman, Il., U.S.	219	38.32 N	89.16 W
Hoffman, Mn., U.S.	198	45.49 N	95.47 W
Hoffman Estates	216	42.02 N	88.04 W
Hoffman Island I	276	40.35 N	74.03 W
Hoffmans	210	42.54 N	74.05 W
Hoffman Station	284a	43.04 N	78.50 W
Hoffnung	263	51.07 N	7.13 E
Hofgeismar	52	51.30 N	9.22 E
Hofheim	56	50.07 N	8.26 E
Hofheim in Unterfranken	56	50.08 N	10.31 E
Hofkirchen	60	48.41 N	13.07 E
Hofkirchen an der Trattnach	60	48.13 N	13.44 E
Höflein an der Donau	264b	48.21 N	16.17 E
Hofmeyr	158	31.39 S	25.50 E
Höfn	24a	64.17 N	15.10 W
Hofors	40	60.33 N	16.17 E
Hofsjökull ⊓	24a	64.48 N	18.50 W
Hofstade	50	50.58 N	4.02 E
Hofstede ⊷[8]	263	51.30 N	7.12 E
Hofstra University ʋ[2]	276	40.43 N	73.36 W
Hōfu	96	34.03 N	131.34 E
Hofuf → Al-Hufūf	128	25.22 N	49.34 E
Hog, Tanjong ›	116	5.18 N	119.16 E
Hogalbāria	126	23.53 N	88.51 E
Höganäs	41	56.12 N	12.33 E
Hogan Lake ⊜	190	45.52 N	78.30 W
Hogansburg	206	44.58 N	74.39 W
Hogansville	192	33.10 N	84.54 W
Hogatza ≃	180	66.00 N	155.29 W
Hogback Mountain ∧, U.S.	207	42.43 N	72.25 W
Hogback Mountain ∧, Mt., U.S.	202	44.54 N	112.07 W
Hogback Mountain ∧, Ne., U.S.	198	41.40 N	103.44 W
Hogback Mountain ∧, S.C., U.S.	192	35.10 N	82.17 W
Högbo	40	60.40 N	16.48 E
Hog Canyon V	226	35.42 N	120.35 W
Hog Creek ≃	222	31.32 N	97.18 W
Hoge Veluwe, Nationale Park de ♦	52	52.02 N	5.55 E
Högfors	40	59.59 N	15.01 E
Hoggar → Ahaggar ⋏	148	23.00 N	6.30 E
Hoghton	262	53.44 N	2.35 W
Hoghton Tower ⊥	262	53.44 N	2.34 W
Hog Island I, Ma., U.S.	283	42.40 N	70.46 W
Hog Island I, Mi., U.S.	190	45.48 N	85.22 W
Hog Island I, Vt., U.S.	206	44.57 N	73.13 W
Hog Island I, Va., U.S.	208	37.25 N	75.41 W
Hog Island Bay C	208	37.27 N	75.46 W
Hogoro	154	5.57 S	36.27 E
Hog Point ›	208	37.12 N	76.41 W
Hogs Back ≚[4]	42	51.13 N	0.40 W
Högsby	26	57.10 N	16.02 E
Högsjö	40	59.02 N	15.41 E
Hoh ≃	224	47.45 N	124.29 W
Hoh, South Fork ≃	224	47.46 N	124.01 W
Hohberg	58	48.25 N	7.55 E
Hohe Acht ∧	56	50.23 N	7.00 E
Hohebach	56	49.22 N	9.44 E
Hohe Eifel ⋏	56	50.15 N	6.45 E
Hohegeiss	54	51.40 N	10.40 E
Hohenahr	56	50.41 N	8.32 E
Hohenau	252	27.05 S	55.45 W
Hohenau an der March	61	48.36 N	16.55 E
Höhenberg	61	48.46 N	14.53 E
Hohenbrunn	60	48.03 N	11.42 E
Hohenbucko	54	51.46 N	13.28 E
Hohenbudberg ⊷[8]	263	51.23 N	6.40 E
Hohenburg	60	49.18 N	11.48 E
Hohendorf	54	54.01 N	13.44 E
Hohenebra	54	51.18 N	10.49 E
Hohenems	58	47.22 N	9.41 E
Hohenfels	60	49.12 N	11.51 E
Hohenfurch	58	47.51 N	10.54 E
Hohengüstow	54	53.14 N	13.59 E
Hohenhameln	52	52.15 N	10.03 E
Hohenheide	263	51.29 N	7.47 E
Hohenkammer	60	48.25 N	11.32 E
Hohenkirchen, Dtsch.	52	53.39 N	7.55 E
Hohenkirchen, Dtsch.	54	50.51 N	10.41 E
Hohenkirchen, Dtsch.	54	53.51 N	11.17 E
Hohenkirchen, Dtsch.	56	51.23 N	9.29 E
Hohenleipisch	54	51.30 N	13.34 E
Hohenleuben	54	50.43 N	12.03 E
Hohenlimburg	56	51.21 N	7.35 E
Hohenlimburg, Schloss ⊥	263	51.21 N	7.34 E
Hohenlinden	60	48.09 N	12.00 E
Hohenlockstedt	52	53.58 N	9.38 E
Hohenmölsen	54	51.09 N	12.06 E
Hohen Neuendorf	54	52.40 N	13.16 E
Hohenpolding	60	48.23 N	12.08 E
Hohensalza → Inowrocław	30	52.48 N	18.15 E
Hohenschönhausen ⊷[8]	264a	52.33 N	13.30 E
Hohenseeden	54	52.19 N	12.01 E
Hohenseefeld	54	51.53 N	13.18 E
Hohenstaufen	56	48.44 N	9.43 E
Hohenstein-Ernstthal	54	50.48 N	12.42 E
Hohensyburg ⊥	56	51.25 N	7.29 E
Hohentauern	61	47.26 N	14.29 E
Hohentengen	58	48.02 N	9.23 E
Hohenthurm	54	51.31 N	12.05 E
Hohenthurn	64	46.33 N	13.40 E
Hohentwiel ∧	58	47.46 N	8.49 E
Hohenwald	194	35.32 N	87.33 W
Hohenwart	60	48.36 N	11.23 E
Hohenwarte-Stausee ⊜[1]	54	50.32 N	11.30 E
Hohenwarthe	54	52.13 N	11.42 E
Hohenwutzen	54	52.51 N	14.07 E
Hohenzethen	54	53.03 N	10.49 E
Hohenzollern, Burg ⊥	58	48.19 N	8.58 E
Hohenzollernkanal ≊	264a	52.32 N	13.20 E
Hoher Bogen ∧	60	49.15 N	12.55 E
Hoher Dachstein ∧	64	47.28 N	13.35 E
Hoher Freschen ∧	58	47.18 N	9.46 E
Hohe Rhön ⋏	56	50.30 N	10.00 E
Hoher Ifen ∧	58	47.21 N	10.05 E
Hoherlehme	264a	52.19 N	13.37 E
Hoher Mechtin ∧[2]	54	53.03 N	10.55 E
Hoher Riffler ∧	58	47.07 N	10.22 E
Hoher Sonnblick ∧	64	47.03 N	12.57 E
Hoher Zinken ∧	64	47.40 N	13.20 E
Hohe Tauern ⋏	64	47.10 N	12.45 E
Hohe Warte (Monte Coglians) ∧	64	46.37 N	12.53 E
Hoh Head ›	224	47.46 N	124.29 W
Hohhot	102	40.51 N	111.40 E
Höhn	56	50.37 N	8.00 E
Hohndorf	54	50.45 N	12.40 E
Hohne	52	52.35 N	10.22 E
Hohneck, Le ∧	58	48.02 N	7.01 E
Hohnstein	54	50.59 N	14.10 E
Hohoe	150	7.09 N	0.28 E
Hōhoku	96	34.17 N	130.57 E
Ho-Ho-Kus	276	40.59 N	74.06 W
Hohokus Brook ≃	276	40.57 N	74.06 W
Hoholeve	78	49.56 N	33.48 E
Hoholitna ≃	180	61.31 N	157.00 W
Hoh Sai Hu ⊜	120	35.43 N	92.45 E
Höhscheid ⊷[8]	263	51.09 N	7.04 E
Hohultslätt	26	56.58 N	15.39 E
Hohwacht	54	54.19 N	10.41 E
Hohwachter Bucht C	54	54.20 N	10.45 E
Hoh Xil Hu ⊜	120	35.35 N	91.06 E
Hoh Xil Shan ⋏	120	35.20 N	90.00 E
Hoi An	110	15.52 N	108.19 E
Hoihow → Haikou	102	20.03 N	110.19 E
Hoima	154	1.26 N	31.21 E
Hoisdorf	52	53.39 N	10.20 E
Hoisington	198	38.31 N	98.46 W
Hoisten	263	51.08 N	6.42 E
Hoi Xuan	110	20.22 N	105.07 E
Hojāi	120	26.00 N	92.51 E
Højby, Dan.	41	55.55 N	11.37 E
Højby, Dan.	41	55.20 N	10.27 E
Höje	40	59.54 N	13.33 E
Højer	26	54.58 N	8.43 E
Højerup	41	55.17 N	12.27 E
Hojniki	78	51.53 N	29.56 E
Hōjō, Nihon	96	34.54 N	134.56 E
Hōjō, Nihon	96	33.58 N	132.46 E
Hōjō → Kasai, Nihon	96	34.56 N	134.50 E
Hokah	190	43.45 N	91.20 W
Hokang → Hegang	89	47.24 N	130.17 E
Hökåsen	40	59.40 N	16.35 E
Hokendauqua	208	40.39 N	75.29 W
Hökensås ⋏[2]	26	58.11 N	14.08 E
Hokes Bluff	194	33.59 N	85.51 W
Hōki ≃	94	36.47 N	140.08 E
Hokianga Harbour C	172	35.32 S	173.22 E
Hokitika	172	42.43 S	170.58 E
Hokkaidō □[5]	92a	44.00 N	143.00 E
Hokkaidō I	92a	44.00 N	143.00 E
Hokksund	26	59.47 N	9.59 E
Hoko ≃	224	48.17 N	124.22 W
Hōkōji	270	34.52 N	135.07 E
Hököpinge	41	55.30 N	13.00 E
Hokota	94	36.09 N	140.31 E
Hok So Wan	271d	22.13 N	114.14 E
Hokubo	96	34.57 N	133.38 E
Hokudan	96	34.32 N	134.56 E
Hokura ≃	94	37.10 N	138.16 E
Hokuriku-tunnel ⊷[5]	94	35.42 N	136.10 E
Hokusei	94	35.09 N	136.31 E
Hola	154	1.29 S	40.02 E
Holalkere	122	14.02 N	76.11 E
Holanda → Netherlands □[1]	30	52.15 N	5.30 E
Hola Prystan'	78	46.31 N	32.31 E
Holbæk	41	55.43 N	11.43 E
Holbeach	42	52.49 N	0.01 E
Holbeach Marsh ≡	42	52.52 N	0.05 E
Holberg	182	50.39 N	128.00 W
Holborn ⊷[8]	260	51.31 N	0.07 W
Holbrook, Austl.	171b	35.44 S	147.19 E
Holbrook, Az., U.S.	200	34.54 N	110.09 W
Holbrook, Il., U.S.	278	41.32 N	87.38 W
Holbrook, Md., U.S.	284b	39.24 N	76.51 W
Holbrook, Ma., U.S.	207	42.09 N	71.00 W
Holbrook, Ne., U.S.	198	40.18 N	100.00 W
Holbrook, N.Y., U.S.	210	40.48 N	73.04 W
Holbrook, Lake ⊜[1]	222	32.42 N	95.33 W
Holbrook Mountain ∧[2]	212	44.25 N	77.51 W
Holckenhavn	41	55.17 N	10.47 E
Holcomb, Il., U.S.	216	42.04 N	89.06 W
Holcomb, N.Y., U.S.	210	42.54 N	77.25 W
Holcomb Creek ≃	228	34.17 N	117.08 W
Holden, Ab., Can.	182	53.14 N	112.14 W
Holden, Ma., U.S.	207	42.21 N	71.51 W
Holden, Mo., U.S.	194	38.42 N	93.59 W
Holden, Ut., U.S.	200	39.05 N	112.16 W
Holden, W.V., U.S.	188	37.49 N	82.03 W
Holden, Mount ∧[2]	216	41.40 N	87.03 W
Holdenstedt	52	52.55 N	10.31 E
Holden Village	224	48.12 N	120.47 W
Holdenville	196	35.04 N	96.23 W
Holder	220	28.58 N	82.25 W
Holderness ›[1]	44	53.47 N	0.10 W
Holdfast	184	50.58 N	105.25 W
Holdich	254	45.57 S	68.13 W
Holdingford	190	45.43 N	94.28 W
Holdorf	52	52.35 N	8.07 E
Holdrege	198	40.26 N	99.22 W
Holeby	41	54.43 N	11.28 E
Hole in the Mountain Peak ∧	204	40.55 N	115.05 W
Hole Narsipur	122	12.47 N	76.15 E
Holešov	30	49.20 N	17.35 E
Holetown	241g	13.11 N	59.39 W
Holgate, S. Afr.	158	33.59 S	22.21 E
Holgate, Oh., U.S.	216	41.14 N	84.07 W
Holguín	240p	20.53 N	76.15 W
Holguín □[4]	240p	20.55 N	75.50 W
Hol-Hol	144	11.19 N	42.57 E
Holíč	30	48.49 N	17.10 E
Holiday Beach Provincial Park ♦	214	42.02 N	83.05 W
Holiday Hills	216	42.18 N	88.13 W
Holiday Lake Amusement Park ♦	285	40.02 N	74.56 W
Holiday Shores	219	38.55 N	89.56 W
Holitna ≃	180	61.40 N	157.12 W
Höljes	26	60.54 N	12.36 E
Hollabrunn	61	48.34 N	16.05 E
Holladay	200	40.40 N	111.49 W
Holland, Mb., Can.	184	49.36 N	98.53 W
Holland, Mi., U.S.	216	42.47 N	86.06 W
Holland, N.Y., U.S.	210	42.38 N	78.32 W
Holland, Oh., U.S.	216	41.37 N	83.42 W
Holland, Pa., U.S.	285	40.10 N	74.59 W
Holland, Tx., U.S.	222	30.53 N	97.24 W
Holland, Va., U.S.	208	36.41 N	76.47 W
Holland □[9]	52	52.20 N	4.45 E
Holland → Netherlands □[1]	30	52.15 N	5.30 E
Holland ≃	212	44.12 N	79.31 W
Holland, Mount ∧[2]	162	32.12 S	119.44 E
Hollandale	194	33.10 N	90.51 W
Holland Creek ≃	169	36.43 S	146.06 E
Hollande, Étangs de ⊜	261	48.44 N	1.48 E
Holland Fen ≡	44	53.00 N	0.10 W
Hollandia → Jayapura	164	2.32 S	140.42 E
Holland Landing	212	44.06 N	79.29 W
Holland Park	171a	27.31 S	153.03 E
Holland Patent	210	43.14 N	75.15 W
Holland Point ›	208	38.43 N	76.32 W
Holland Pond State Park ♦	207	42.04 N	72.09 W
Hollandsbird Island I	156	24.45 S	14.34 E
Hollandsch Diep ʊ	52	51.42 N	4.30 E
Hollandstoun	46	59.21 N	2.26 W
Holland Straits ʊ	208	38.08 N	76.02 W
Holland Tunnel ⊷[5]	276	40.44 N	74.02 W
Hollansburg	218	39.59 N	84.47 W
Holle	52	52.05 N	10.10 E
Holleben	54	51.26 N	11.53 E
Hollenfels, Château ⊥	56	49.43 N	6.03 E
Höllengebirge ⋏	64	47.48 N	13.39 E
Hollenstedt	52	53.22 N	9.43 E
Hollenstein an der Ybbs	61	47.48 N	14.46 E
Höllensteinberg ∧	264b	48.06 N	16.11 E
Höllental V	61	47.45 N	15.47 E
Hollern	52	53.36 N	9.32 E
Holleton	162	31.57 S	119.02 E
Holley	210	43.13 N	78.01 W
Hollfeld	60	49.56 N	11.18 E
Hollick-Kenyon Plateau ⋏[1]	9	79.00 S	97.00 W
Holliday, Mo., U.S.	219	39.29 N	92.07 W
Holliday, Tx., U.S.	196	33.49 N	98.42 W
Holliday Creek ≃	196	33.55 N	98.28 W
Holliday Park ♦	281	42.21 N	83.24 W
Hollidaysburg	214	40.25 N	78.23 W
Hollingbourne	260	51.16 N	0.38 E
Hollingstedt	41	54.27 N	9.19 E
Hollingworth	262	53.28 N	1.59 W
Hollingworth Lake ⊜	262	53.38 N	2.06 W
Hollins, Eng., U.K.	262	53.34 N	2.17 W
Hollins, Va., U.S.	192	37.20 N	79.56 W
Hollins Green	262	53.25 N	2.27 W
Hollinswood	284c	38.55 N	77.13 W
Hollis, N.H., U.S.	207	42.44 N	71.35 W
Hollis, Ok., U.S.	196	34.41 N	99.54 W
Hollis ⊷[8]	276	40.43 N	73.46 W
Hollister	226	36.51 N	121.24 W
Hollister, Mount ∧[2]	162	22.08 S	114.01 E
Holliston	207	42.12 N	71.25 W
Hollman, Cape ›	164	4.59 S	150.06 E
Holloman Air Force Base ■	200	32.51 N	106.05 W
Holloway	214	40.10 N	81.08 W
Holloway Terrace	285	39.42 N	75.32 W
Hollow Rock	194	36.02 N	88.16 W
Hollowville	210	42.12 N	73.42 W
Hollsopple	214	40.13 N	78.56 W
Hollum	52	53.26 N	5.37 E
Höllviken C	41	55.26 N	12.54 E
Höllviksnäs	41	55.25 N	12.57 E
Holly, Co., U.S.	198	38.03 N	102.07 W
Holly, Mi., U.S.	216	42.47 N	83.37 W
Holly, Wa., U.S.	224	47.34 N	122.58 W
Holly, Mount ∧[2]	285	40.00 N	74.47 W
Holly Brook	285	39.59 N	74.48 W
Holly Grove	194	34.35 N	91.11 W
Holly Hill, Fl., U.S.	192	29.14 N	81.02 W
Holly Hill, S.C., U.S.	192	33.19 N	80.24 W
Holly Park, N.J., U.S.	208	39.53 N	74.10 W
Holly Park, Va., U.S.	284c	38.50 N	77.17 W
Holly Pond ⊜	276	41.03 N	73.30 W
Holly River State Park ♦	188	38.40 N	80.21 W
Holly Run ≃	285	39.47 N	75.03 W
Holly Springs	194	34.46 N	89.26 W
Holly State Recreation Area ♦	216	42.49 N	83.32 W
Hollywood, Ire.	48	53.06 N	6.35 W
Hollywood, Fl., U.S.	220	26.00 N	80.08 W
Hollywood, Md., U.S.	208	38.20 N	76.34 W
Hollywood, Pa., U.S.	285	40.05 N	75.06 W
Hollywood ⊷[8]	228	34.06 N	118.21 W
Hollywood, Mount ∧	280	34.08 N	118.18 W
Hollywood Bowl ♦	280	34.07 N	118.20 W
Hollywood-Burbank Airport ⊠	228	34.12 N	118.21 W
Hollywood Heights	219	38.39 N	89.59 W
Hollywood Indian Reservation ⊷[4]	220	26.02 N	80.13 W
Hollywood Park Race Track ♦	280	33.57 N	118.20 W
Hollywood Reservoir ⊜[1]	280	34.07 N	118.20 W
Holman	176	70.43 N	117.43 W
Hólmavík	24a	65.43 N	21.43 W
Holmdel	208	40.20 N	74.11 W
Holme, Dan.	41	56.07 N	10.11 E
Holme, Eng., U.K.	262	53.33 N	1.50 W
Holme ≃	44	53.41 N	1.43 W
Holme Chapel	262	53.45 N	2.11 W
Holmen, Nor.	26	60.40 N	10.22 E
Holmen, Wi., U.S.	190	43.57 N	91.15 W
Holme-on-Spaulding-Moor	44	53.50 N	0.46 W
Holmes, N.Y., U.S.	210	41.31 N	73.39 W
Holmes, Pa., U.S.	285	39.54 N	75.19 W
Holmes □[6]	214	40.33 N	81.55 W
Holmes, Mount ∧	202	44.49 N	110.51 W
Holmes Beach	220	27.31 N	82.43 W
Holmesburg ⊷[8]	285	40.02 N	75.03 W
Holmes Chapel	44	53.12 N	2.22 W
Holmes Creek ≃	194	30.30 N	85.47 W
Holmesglen	274b	37.53 S	145.06 E
Holmes Harbor C	224	48.04 N	122.32 W
Holmes Lake ⊜	184	57.05 N	96.45 W
Holmes Reef ⊹[2]	164	16.27 S	148.00 E
Holmes Run ≃	284c	38.48 N	77.07 W
Holmes Run Acres	284c	38.51 N	77.13 W
Holmestrand	26	59.29 N	10.18 E
Holmesville, N.Y., U.S.	210	42.31 N	75.24 W
Holmesville, Oh., U.S.	214	40.37 N	81.55 W
Holmeswood	262	53.39 N	2.52 W
Holmfirth	44	53.35 N	1.46 W
Holmia	246	4.58 N	59.35 W
Holmivs'kyy	83	48.25 N	38.05 E
Holmön I	26	63.47 N	20.53 E
Holmsbu	26	59.33 N	10.27 E
Holmsjön ⊜, Sve.	26	62.41 N	16.33 E
Holmsjön ⊜, Sve.	26	62.25 N	15.20 E
Holmsund	26	63.42 N	20.21 E
Hölö	40	59.01 N	17.35 E
Holoby	78	51.06 N	24.59 E
Holod	38	46.47 N	22.08 E
Holohory ⋏	78	49.45 N	24.35 E
Holoit, Punta ›	232	21.37 N	88.08 W
Ḥolon	132	32.01 N	34.46 E
Holoog	156	27.22 S	17.55 E
Holopaw	220	28.08 N	81.04 W
Holovanivs'k	78	48.23 N	30.28 E
Holovne	78	51.21 N	24.04 E
Holroyd	274a	33.50 S	150.58 E
Holroyd ≃	164	14.10 S	141.36 E
Holsloot	52	52.44 N	6.48 E
Holstebro	26	56.21 N	8.38 E
Holsted	41	55.30 N	8.55 E
Holstein	198	42.29 N	95.32 W
Holsteinborg ⊥	41	55.13 N	11.28 E
Holsteinische Schweiz ⊷[1]	54	54.11 N	10.36 E
Holsteinsborg (Sisimiut)	176	66.55 N	53.40 W
Holsterhausen	263	51.41 N	6.57 E
Holston ≃	192	35.57 N	83.51 W
Holston, North Fork ≃	192	36.33 N	82.36 W
Holston High Knob ∧	192	36.27 N	82.05 W
Holsworthy	42	50.49 N	4.21 W
Holt, Eng., U.K.	42	52.55 N	1.05 E
Holt, Wales, U.K.	44	53.05 N	2.53 W
Holt, Al., U.S.	194	33.14 N	87.29 W
Holt, Ca., U.S.	226	37.56 N	121.26 W
Holt, Fl., U.S.	194	30.42 N	86.44 W
Holt, Mi., U.S.	216	42.38 N	84.30 W
Holt Creek ≃	198	42.28 N	98.50 W
Holte	41	55.49 N	12.28 E
Holtemme ≃	54	51.57 N	11.10 E
Holten	52	52.17 N	6.25 E
Holten ⊷[8]	263	51.31 N	6.48 E
Holtenau ⊷[8]	54	54.22 N	10.08 E
Holter Lake ⊜[1]	202	46.55 N	111.57 W
Holthausen, Dtsch.	52	52.33 N	7.17 E
Holthausen, Dtsch.	263	51.23 N	7.13 E
Holthausen, Dtsch.	263	51.12 N	7.01 E
Holthausen ⊷[8]	263	51.34 N	7.26 E
Holthusen	52	53.08 N	7.18 E
Holton, In., U.S.	218	39.04 N	85.23 W
Holton, Ks., U.S.	198	39.27 N	95.44 W
Holtorf	52	52.40 N	9.13 E
Holts Summit	219	38.39 N	92.07 W
Holtsville	210	40.49 N	73.02 W
Holtug	41	55.21 N	12.25 E
Holtville	204	32.48 N	115.22 W
Holtwick	52	52.00 N	7.05 E
Holtwood	208	39.50 N	76.19 W
Holubivka	78	48.53 N	35.19 E
Holwerd	52	53.22 N	5.54 E
Holycross, Ire.	48	52.38 N	7.52 W
Holy Cross, Ak., U.S.	180	62.12 N	159.47 W
Holy Cross Mountain ∧	182	53.47 N	120.47 W
Holyhead	44	53.19 N	4.38 W
Holyhead Bay C	44	53.23 N	4.37 W
Holy Island I, Eng., U.K.	44	55.41 N	1.48 W
Holy Island I, Scot., U.K.	46	55.32 N	5.04 W
Holy Island I, Wales, U.K.	44	53.18 N	4.37 W
Holy Island I, Ma., U.S.	283	42.43 N	70.50 W
Holyoke, Co., U.S.	198	40.35 N	102.18 W
Holyoke, Ma., U.S.	207	42.12 N	72.37 W
Holyrood	198	38.35 N	98.24 W
Holyrood Palace ʋ	46	55.56 N	3.12 W
Holýšov	60	49.36 N	13.05 E
Holywell	44	53.17 N	3.13 W
Holywell Green	262	53.41 N	1.52 W
Holywood	48	54.38 N	5.50 W
Holzbüttgen	263	51.12 N	6.37 E
Holzdorf	54	51.46 N	13.08 E
Holzen	56	51.26 N	7.31 E
Holzgau	58	47.16 N	10.21 E
Holzgerlingen	56	48.38 N	9.00 E
Holzhausen, Dtsch.	52	52.17 N	8.32 E
Holzhausen, Dtsch.	52	52.13 N	8.01 E
Holzhausen, Dtsch.	52	52.01 N	8.44 E
Holzhausen, Dtsch.	54	51.18 N	12.28 E
Holzhausen an der Haide	56	50.13 N	7.55 E
Holzheim	56	51.09 N	6.39 E
Holzkirchen	64	47.52 N	11.42 E
Holzminden	52	51.50 N	9.27 E
Holzweissig	54	51.36 N	12.18 E
Holzwickede	52	51.30 N	7.36 E
Hom ≃	158	28.51 S	18.37 E
Homa Bay	154	0.31 S	34.27 E
Homalin	110	24.52 N	94.55 E
Homathko ≃	182	50.55 N	124.50 W
Homathko Icefield ⊓	182	51.05 N	124.30 W
Homberg, Dtsch.	56	50.43 N	8.59 E
Homberg, Dtsch.	56	51.02 N	9.24 E
Homberg, Dtsch.	56	51.28 N	6.43 E
Homberg, Dtsch.	263	51.18 N	6.56 E
Hombori	150	15.17 N	1.42 W
Hombori Tondo ∧	150	15.16 N	1.40 W
Hombourg-Haut	56	49.08 N	6.46 E
Hombre Muerto, Salar del ≚	252	25.23 S	67.06 W
Hombruch ⊷[8]	263	51.29 N	7.26 E
Homburg, Dtsch.	56	49.19 N	7.20 E
Homburg → Bad Homburg vor der Höhe, Dtsch.	56	50.13 N	8.37 E
Home, Pa., U.S.	214	40.44 N	79.06 W
Home, Wa., U.S.	224	47.17 N	122.46 W
Homeacre	214	40.51 N	79.55 W
Home Bay C, N.T., Can.	176	68.45 N	67.10 W
Home Bay C, Kiribati	174d	0.53 S	169.35 E
Homebush Bay C	274a	33.50 S	151.05 E
Home Corner	216	40.31 N	85.38 W
Homécourt	56	49.14 N	5.59 E
Home Creek ≃	196	31.29 N	99.14 W
Homedale, Id., U.S.	202	43.37 N	116.55 W
Homedale, Oh., U.S.	214	40.04 N	83.02 W
Home Gardens	228	33.52 N	117.31 W
Home Hill	166	19.40 S	147.25 E
Homel'	76	52.25 N	31.00 E
Homel' □[8]	76	52.30 N	30.00 E
Homeland, Ca., U.S.	228	33.44 N	117.07 W
Homeland, Fl., U.S.	220	27.49 N	81.49 W
Homeland Canal ≊	226	35.57 N	119.27 W
Homeland Park	192	34.27 N	82.41 W
Home Place	218	39.56 N	86.08 W
Homer, Ak., U.S.	180	59.39 N	151.33 W
Homer, Ga., U.S.	192	34.20 N	83.29 W
Homer, La., U.S.	194	32.47 N	93.03 W
Homer, Mi., U.S.	216	42.08 N	84.48 W
Homer, Ne., U.S.	198	42.19 N	96.29 W
Homer, N.Y., U.S.	210	42.38 N	76.10 W
Homer, Oh., U.S.	214	40.15 N	82.31 W
Homer, Tx., U.S.	222	31.18 N	94.36 W
Homer City	214	40.32 N	79.09 W
Homert ∧[2]	263	51.11 N	7.39 E
Homer Tunnel ⊷[5]	172	44.45 S	168.00 E
Homerville, Ga., U.S.	192	31.02 N	82.44 W
Homerville, Oh., U.S.	214	41.02 N	82.08 W
Homer Wash V	204	34.20 N	115.02 W
Homer Youngs Peak ∧	202	45.19 N	113.41 W
Home Seamount ⊹[3]	14	12.55 S	175.37 W
Homestead, Austl.	166	20.22 S	145.39 E
Homestead, Fl., U.S.	220	25.28 N	80.28 W
Homestead, Pa., U.S.	279b	40.24 N	79.54 W
Homestead Air Force Base ■	220	25.29 N	80.23 W
Homestead National Monument of America ♦	198	40.14 N	96.54 W
Homestead Valley	282	37.54 N	122.32 W
Hometown, Il., U.S.	278	41.44 N	87.43 W
Hometown, Pa., U.S.	210	40.49 N	75.59 W
Homewood, Al., U.S.	194	33.28 N	86.48 W
Homewood, Ca., U.S.	226	39.05 N	120.09 W
Homewood, Il., U.S.	216	41.33 N	87.39 W
Homewood, Oh., U.S.	218	39.23 N	84.33 W
Homewood ⊷[8]	279b	40.27 N	79.54 W
Homewood Acres	278	41.34 N	87.43 W
Homeworth	214	40.50 N	81.03 W
Hominy	196	36.24 N	96.23 W
Hominy Creek ≃	196	36.20 N	96.00 W
Hommersåk	26	58.58 N	5.42 E
Hommura	92	34.22 N	139.15 E
Homnābād	122	17.46 N	77.08 E
Homochitto ≃	194	31.09 N	91.31 W
Homoíne	156	23.52 S	35.09 E
Homonhon Island I	116	10.44 N	125.43 E
Homosassa	220	28.46 N	82.36 W
Homosassa Bay C	220	28.45 N	82.43 W
Homosassa Springs	220	28.48 N	82.35 W
Homs → Al-Khums, Lībiyā	146	32.39 N	14.16 E
Homs → Ḥimṣ, Sūrīy.	130	34.44 N	36.43 E
Honai	96	33.30 N	132.25 E
Honaker	192	37.00 N	81.58 W
Honami	96	33.36 N	130.42 E
Honan → Luoyang	102	34.41 N	112.28 E
Honan → Henan □[4]	90	34.00 N	114.00 E
Honāvar	122	14.17 N	74.27 E
Honaz	130	37.45 N	29.17 E
Honbetsu	92a	43.07 N	143.37 E
Hon Chong	110	10.10 N	104.37 E
Honda	246	5.12 N	74.45 W
Honda, Bahía C, Col.	246	12.21 N	71.47 W
Honda, Bahía C, Cuba	240p	22.57 N	83.10 W
Honda, Cañada ≃	258	33.57 S	59.21 W
Honda Bay C	116	9.53 N	118.49 E
Honddu ≃, U.K.	42	51.54 N	2.58 W
Honddu ≃, Wales, U.K.	42	51.57 N	3.23 W
Hondeklipbaai	156	30.20 S	17.18 E
Honderfontein	158	32.12 S	21.22 E
Hon Dien, Nui ∧	110	11.33 N	108.38 E
Hondo, Ab., Can.	182	55.04 N	114.02 W
Hondo, Nihon	92	32.27 N	130.12 E
Hondo, N.M., U.S.	200	33.23 N	105.16 W
Hondo, Tx., U.S.	196	29.20 N	99.08 W
Hondo ≃, Méx.	286a	19.26 N	99.15 W
Hondo ≃, N.A.	232	18.29 N	88.19 W
Hondo, Arroyo ≃	226	37.28 N	121.47 W
Hondo, Rio ≃, Ca., U.S.	280	33.55 N	118.10 W
Hondo, Rio ≃, N.M., U.S.	196	33.22 N	104.24 W
Hondo Creek ≃	196	28.45 N	99.11 W
Hondoji Temple ʋ[1]	268	35.51 N	139.56 E
Hondschoote	50	50.59 N	2.35 E
Hondsrug ⋏[2]	52	52.55 N	6.50 E
Honduras □[1], N.A.	230	15.00 N	86.30 W
Honduras □[1], N.A.	236	15.00 N	86.30 W
Honduras, Cabo de ›	236	16.01 N	86.02 W
Honduras, Gulf of C	230	16.10 N	87.50 W
Honduras, Port C	236	16.13 N	88.41 W
Honea Path	192	34.26 N	82.23 W
Hönebach	56	50.56 N	9.56 E
Hønefoss	26	60.10 N	10.18 E
Honeoye	210	42.47 N	77.31 W
Honeoye Creek ≃	210	42.58 N	77.43 W
Honeoye Falls	210	42.57 N	77.35 W
Honeoye Lake ⊜	210	42.45 N	77.31 W
Honesdale	210	41.34 N	75.15 W
Honey Brook	208	40.05 N	75.54 W
Honey Creek	216	42.44 N	88.18 W
Honey Creek ≃, Ia., U.S.	190	42.09 N	93.03 W

Symbol	English	Deutsch	Español	Français	Português
≃	River	Fluß	Río	Rivière	Rio
≊	Canal	Kanal	Canal	Canal	Canal
⌊	Waterfall, Rapids	Wasserfall, Stromschnellen	Cascada, Rápidos	Chute d'eau, Rapides	Cascata, Rápidos
ʊ	Strait	Meeresstraße	Estrecho	Détroit	Estreito
C	Bay, Gulf	Bucht, Golf	Bahía, Golfo	Baie, Golfe	Baía, Golfo
⊜	Lake, Lakes	See, Seen	Lago, Lagos	Lac, Lacs	Lago, Lagos
≡	Swamp	Sumpf	Pantano	Marais	Pântano
⊓	Ice Features, Glacier	Eis- und Gletscherformen	Accidentes Glaciales	Formes glaciaires	Acidentes glaciares
⊤	Other Hydrographic Features	Andere Hydrographische Objekte	Otros Elementos Hidrográficos	Autres données hydrographiques	Outros acidentes hidrográficos
⊹	Submarine Features	Untermeerische Objekte	Accidentes Submarinos	Formes de relief sous-marin	Acidentes submarinos
□	Political Unit	Politische Einheit	Unidad Politica	Entité politique	Unidade política
ʋ	Cultural Institution	Kulturelle Institution	Institución Cultural	Institution culturelle	Instituição cultural
⊥	Historical Site	Historische Stätte	Sitio Histórico	Site historique	Sitio histórico
♦	Recreational Site	Erholungs- und Ferienort	Sitio de Recreo	Centre de loisirs	Area de Lazer
⊠	Airport	Flughafen	Aeropuerto	Aéroport	Aeroporto
■	Military Installation	Militäranlage	Instalación Militar	Installation militaire	Instalação militar
⊷	Miscellaneous	Verschiedenes	Misceláneo	Divers	Diversos

I · 74 Hone-Huai

ENGLISH / DEUTSCH

Name (Name)	Page (Seite)	Lat.°′ (Breite°′)	Long.°′ (Länge°′ E = Ost)
Honey Creek ≃, Mo., U.S.	194	39.53 N	93.34 W
Honey Creek ≃, Oh., U.S.	214	41.05 N	83.12 W
Honey Creek ≃, Pa., U.S.	208	40.36 N	77.35 W
Honey Creek ≃, Wi., U.S.	216	42.41 N	88.17 W
Honeydew	273d	26.05 S	27.55 E
Honeygo Run ≃	284b	39.22 N	76.25 W
Honey Grove	196	33.35 N	95.54 W
Honey Lake ⊜	204	40.16 N	120.19 W
Honeymoon Bay	224	48.49 N	124.10 W
Honeyville	200	41.38 N	112.04 W
Honfleur	50	49.25 N	0.14 E
Høng	41	55.31 N	11.18 E
Hong → Red ≃, Asia	110	20.17 N	106.34 E
Hong ≃, Zhg.	100	32.25 N	115.35 E
Honga	152	15.09 S	15.12 E
Hon Gai	110	20.57 N	107.05 E
Hong'an	100	31.18 N	114.37 E
Honga River c	208	38.19 N	76.10 W
Hongawa	96	33.43 N	133.19 E
Hongchang	100	34.05 N	113.20 E
Hongch'ŏn	98	37.42 N	127.52 E
Hongchoudai	100	29.03 N	121.11 E
Hongcun, Zhg.	100	27.10 N	116.48 E
Hongcun, Zhg.	106	31.01 N	119.15 E
Höngen	56	51.02 N	5.56 E
Honggun	98	40.46 N	128.27 E
Honghai Wan c	100	22.40 N	115.10 E
Honghe	102	23.23 N	102.35 E
Honghu	100	29.48 N	113.27 E
Hong Hu ⊜	100	29.52 N	113.23 E
Honghuaerji	89	48.15 N	120.01 E
Honghuaji	100	33.52 N	114.26 E
Honghualiangzi	89	48.06 N	123.12 E
Honghuamu	89	48.33 N	125.39 E
Hongjiang, Zhg.	100	26.49 N	120.03 E
Hongjiang, Zhg.	102	27.07 N	109.56 E
Hong Kong → Xianggang	271d	22.17 N	114.09 E
Hong Kong → Xianggang □[4]	100	22.15 N	114.10 E
Hong Kong I	271d	22.15 N	114.11 E
Hong Kong, University of ᵿ[2]	271d	22.17 N	114.08 E
Hongkou Park ♦	269b	31.16 N	121.28 E
Honglai	100	25.08 N	118.32 E
Honglanbu	106	31.37 N	118.57 E
Honglinqiao	106	30.59 N	118.59 E
Hongliutai	85	39.48 N	77.26 E
Hongliuyuan	102	41.04 N	95.26 E
Honglongdian	106	30.30 N	119.00 E
Honglongtang	105	40.41 N	117.37 E
Honglu	100	25.44 N	119.20 E
Hongluan	100	28.31 N	117.01 E
Hongluo Shan ∧	104	40.56 N	120.42 E
Hongluoxian	104	41.01 N	120.53 E
Hongmeichang	105	39.50 N	115.51 E
Hongmendu	102	26.10 N	102.37 E
Hongmenkou	102	27.22 N	100.30 E
Hongmenpu	107	30.37 N	104.08 E
Hongmiaozi	107	28.47 N	104.02 E
Hong Ngu	110	10.48 N	105.21 E
Hongō, Nihon	96	34.24 N	132.59 E
Hongō, Nihon	96	34.17 N	132.02 E
Hongō •[8]	268	35.42 N	139.47 E
Hongpailou	107	30.38 N	104.01 E
Hongqi	89	44.23 N	126.32 E
Hongqiao, Zhg.	100	28.14 N	121.01 E
Hongqiao, Zhg.	105	39.50 N	117.44 E
Hongqiao, Zhg.	106	31.29 N	121.49 E
Hongqiao, Zhg.	269b	31.12 N	121.22 E
Hongqiao Ji Chang ⊠	106	31.12 N	121.20 E
Hongrie → Hungary □[1]	30	47.00 N	20.00 E
Hongshan, Zhg.	89	48.02 N	129.00 E
Hongshan, Zhg.	98	36.37 N	118.00 E
Hongshanzi	98	42.34 N	117.14 E
Hongshi, Zhg.	89	43.00 N	127.04 E
Hongshi, Zhg.	98	41.21 N	119.32 E
Hongshidou	104	41.52 N	122.11 E
Hongshili	98	40.41 N	125.03 E
Hongshui	102	37.24 N	104.00 E
Hongshui ≃	102	23.45 N	109.30 E
Hongshuichuan	105	40.06 N	117.55 E
Hongshuyangzi	105	40.36 N	116.36 E
Hongsŏng	98	36.36 N	126.39 E
Hongtang	100	26.06 N	119.14 E
Hongtian	100	25.52 N	117.15 E
Hongtong	102	36.19 N	111.39 E
Hongtuwan	98	41.03 N	113.39 E
Hongtu Zhang ∧	100	23.46 N	115.56 E
Honguedo, Détroit d' ʯ	186	49.15 N	64.00 W
Hongwŏn	98	40.02 N	127.57 E
Hongxin	100	32.43 N	117.47 E
Hongxing	105	39.48 N	116.27 E
Hongxingqiao	106	30.55 N	119.52 E
Hongyang, Zhg.	100	26.32 N	119.27 E
Hongyang, Zhg.	100	23.28 N	116.13 E
Hongyanzi	104	40.38 N	120.31 E
Hongyōtoku	268	35.41 N	139.55 E
Hongze	100	33.19 N	118.53 E
Hongze Hu ⊜	100	33.16 N	118.34 E
Honiara	175e	9.26 S	159.57 E
Honiton	42	50.48 N	3.13 W
Hon-jima I	96	34.23 N	133.47 E
Honjō, Nihon	92	39.23 N	140.03 E
Honjō, Nihon	94	36.24 N	138.01 E
Honjō, Nihon	94	36.14 N	139.11 E
Honkamäki ∧[2]	26	62.58 N	27.05 E
Hon-kawane	94	35.07 N	138.09 E
Honker Bay c	282	38.04 N	121.56 W
Hönne ≃	263	51.28 N	7.46 E
Honnecourt-sur-Escaut	50	50.02 N	3.12 E
Honningsvåg	24	70.59 N	25.59 E
Hönö	26	57.42 N	11.39 E
Honokaa	229d	20.04 N	155.28 W
Honokahua	229a	21.00 N	156.39 W
Honokawai	229a	20.57 N	156.41 W
Honolulu	229c	21.18 N	157.51 W
Honolulu □[6]	229c	21.19 N	157.52 W
Honolulu International Airport ⊠	229c	21.20 N	157.55 W
Honomu	229d	19.52 N	155.07 W
Honouliuli	229c	21.22 N	158.02 W
Hönow	54	52.32 N	13.38 E
Hon Quan	110	11.39 N	106.36 E
Honshū I	92	36.00 N	138.00 E
Hontoon Island State Park ♦	220	28.59 N	81.22 W
Höntrop •[8]	263	51.27 N	7.08 E
Honuapo Bay c	229d	19.05 N	155.33 W
Hoo	260	51.25 N	0.34 E
Hood	226	38.22 N	121.31 W
Hood □[6]	222	32.25 N	97.45 W
Hood ≃, N.T., Can.	176	67.26 N	108.53 W
Hood ≃, Or., U.S.	224	45.42 N	121.30 W
Hood, East Fork ≃	224	45.36 N	121.38 W
Hood, Mount ∧	224	45.23 N	121.41 W
Hood, West Fork ≃	224	45.36 N	121.38 W
Hood Canal c	224	47.35 N	123.00 W
Hood Canal Floating Bridge •[5]	224	47.52 N	122.38 W
Hoodoo Peak ∧	202	48.15 N	120.19 W
Hood Point ≻, Austl.	162	34.23 S	119.34 E
Hood Point ≻, Pap. N. Gui.	164	10.05 S	147.45 E
Hood Pond ⊜	283	42.40 N	70.57 W
Hood River	224	45.42 N	121.31 W
Hoodsport	224	47.24 N	123.08 W
Hoods Range ⋏	166	28.35 S	144.30 E
Hoof	56	51.17 N	9.20 E
Hoogerheide	52	51.25 N	4.20 E
Hoogeveen	52	52.43 N	6.29 E
Hoogeveense Vaart ≅	52	52.42 N	6.11 E
Hoogezand-Sappemeer	52	53.09 N	6.47 E
Hoogkerk	52	53.13 N	6.30 E
Hooglede	50	50.59 N	3.05 E
Hoogstede	52	52.34 N	6.56 E
Hoogstraten	56	51.24 N	4.46 E
Hoogte	158	27.28 S	28.03 E
Hoogvliet	52	51.52 N	4.21 E
Hook	42	51.17 N	0.58 W
Hook •[8]	260	51.22 N	0.18 W
Hooker	196	36.51 N	101.12 W
Hooker, Bi'r ⊤[4]	142	30.23 N	30.20 E
Hooker Creek	162	18.20 S	130.40 E
Hooker Creek Aboriginal Reserve •[4]	162	18.10 S	130.25 E
Hook Head ≻	48	52.07 N	6.55 W
Hookina	166	31.45 S	138.20 E
Hook Island I	166	20.08 S	148.55 E
Hook Mountain State Park ♦	276	41.09 N	73.55 W
Hook Norton	42	51.59 N	1.29 W
Hook Point ≻	166	25.48 S	153.05 E
Hooks	194	33.28 N	94.15 W
Hooksiel	52	53.38 N	8.01 E
Hoolehua	229a	21.10 N	157.04 W
Hoonah	180	58.07 N	135.26 W
Hoopa	204	41.03 N	123.40 W
Hoopa Valley Indian Reservation •[4]	204	41.08 N	123.40 W
Hooper	198	41.36 N	96.32 W
Hooper Bay	180	61.31 N	166.06 W
Hooper Islands II	208	38.20 N	76.13 W
Hooper Strait ʯ	208	38.12 N	76.03 W
Hoopersville	208	38.15 N	76.10 W
Hoopes Reservoir ⊜[1]	285	39.47 N	75.37 W
Hoopeston	216	40.28 N	87.40 W
Hooping Harbour	186	50.37 N	56.17 W
Hoople	198	48.32 N	97.38 W
Hoopstad	158	27.54 S	25.58 E
Hoopstick Brook ≃	276	40.39 N	74.41 W
Höör	41	55.56 N	13.32 E
Hoorn	52	52.38 N	5.04 E
Hoorn, Kap → Hornos, Cabo de ≻	254	55.59 S	67.16 W
Hoosac Range ⋏	207	42.45 N	73.02 W
Hoosac Tunnel •[5]	207	42.41 N	73.03 W
Hoosic ≃	210	42.54 N	73.39 W
Hoosick	210	42.52 N	73.20 W
Hoosick Falls	210	42.54 N	73.21 W
Hooton	262	53.18 N	2.57 W
Hoot Owl Estates	285	39.53 N	74.50 W
Hoover Dam •[6]	200	36.00 N	114.27 W
Hoover Reservoir ⊜[1]	214	40.08 N	82.53 W
Hooversville	214	40.08 N	78.54 W
Hopa	130	41.25 N	41.24 E
Hopatcong	210	40.55 N	74.39 W
Hopatcong, Lake ⊜	210	40.57 N	74.38 W
Hopatcong State Park ♦	276	40.55 N	74.40 W
Hop Bottom	210	41.42 N	75.46 W
Hop Brook ≃	276	40.19 N	74.08 W
Hope, B.C., Can.	182	49.23 N	121.26 W
Hope, Ak., U.S.	180	60.55 N	149.38 W
Hope, Ar., U.S.	194	33.40 N	93.35 W
Hope, In., U.S.	218	39.18 N	85.46 W
Hope, N.J., U.S.	210	40.54 N	74.58 W
Hope, N.D., U.S.	198	47.19 N	97.43 W
Hope, R.I., U.S.	207	41.44 N	71.33 W
Hope, Ben ∧	46	58.24 N	4.37 W
Hope, Loch ⊜	46	58.27 N	4.39 W
Hope, Point ≻	180	68.21 N	166.50 W
Hope Bay c	212	44.55 N	81.08 W
Hopedale, Nf., Can.	176	55.28 N	60.13 W
Hopedale, Il., U.S.	194	40.25 N	89.24 W
Hopedale, La., U.S.	194	29.49 N	89.39 W
Hopedale, Ma., U.S.	207	42.07 N	71.32 W
Hopedale, Oh., U.S.	214	40.19 N	80.54 W
Hope Farm	210	41.44 N	73.40 W
Hopefield	158	33.04 S	18.22 E
Hopeh → Hebei □[4]	98	38.00 N	116.00 E
Hope Island I, B.C., Can.	182	50.55 N	127.53 W
Hope Island I, On., Can.	212	44.55 N	80.12 W
Hopeland	208	40.14 N	76.16 W
Hopelawn	276	40.31 N	74.17 W
Hopelchén	232	19.46 N	89.51 W
Hopeman	46	57.42 N	3.25 W
Hope Mills	192	34.58 N	78.56 W
Hopes Advance, Cap ≻	176	61.04 N	69.34 W
Hopetoun, Austl.	162	33.57 S	120.07 E
Hopetoun, Austl.	166	35.44 S	142.22 E
Hopetown	158	29.34 S	24.03 E
Hope Vale Aboriginal Reserve •[4]	164	15.10 S	145.15 E
Hope Valley, Austl.	168b	34.50 S	138.44 E
Hope Valley, R.I., U.S.	207	41.30 N	71.43 W
Hopewell, N.J., U.S.	208	40.23 N	74.45 W
Hopewell, Pa., U.S.	214	40.08 N	78.16 W
Hopewell, Va., U.S.	208	37.18 N	77.17 W
Hopewell Islands II	176	58.25 N	78.00 W
Hopewell Junction	210	41.35 N	73.48 W
Hopewell Village National Historic Site ⊥	208	40.12 N	75.46 W
Hopfgarten	64	47.27 N	12.10 E
Hopfgarten in Defereggen	64	46.55 N	12.31 E
Hopi → Hebi	98	35.59 N	114.11 E
Hopi Buttes ∧	200	35.20 N	110.15 W
Hopi Indian Reservation •[4]	200	35.45 N	110.35 W
Hopkins, Mi., U.S.	216	42.37 N	85.45 W
Hopkins, Mo., U.S.	194	40.33 N	94.49 W
Hopkins □[6]	222	33.07 N	95.35 W
Hopkins ≃	166	38.24 S	142.31 E
Hopkins, Lake ⊜	162	24.15 S	128.50 E
Hopkins Creek ≃	284a	43.17 N	78.46 W
Hopkinsville	194	36.51 N	87.29 W
Hopkinton, Ia., U.S.	190	42.20 N	91.14 W
Hopkinton, Ma., U.S.	207	42.13 N	71.31 W
Hopkinton, R.I., U.S.	207	41.27 N	71.46 W
Hopland	204	38.58 N	123.06 W
Hopólito Bouchard	252	34.43 S	63.31 W
Hoppegarten	264a	52.31 N	13.40 E
Hoppenrade	264a	52.32 N	12.56 E
Hoppo → Hepu	102	21.39 N	109.11 E
Hopsten	52	52.23 N	7.36 E
Hoptrup	41	55.11 N	9.28 E
Ho Pui	271d	22.25 N	114.03 E
Hopwood, Mount ∧	166	21.49 S	144.26 E
Hoque	152	14.39 S	13.54 E
Hoquiam	224	46.58 N	123.53 W
Hoquiam, East Fork ≃	224	46.58 N	123.54 W
Hora Califo	144	8.49 N	43.07 E
Horace Mountain ∧	180	67.40 N	149.06 W
Horadiz	84	39.27 N	47.20 E
Horado	94	35.36 N	136.50 E
Hōrai	94	34.56 N	137.34 E
Horancia	144	6.31 N	38.44 E
Horasan	130	40.03 N	42.11 E
Horatio	194	33.56 N	94.21 W
Horatio Gardens	278	42.10 N	87.57 W
Horažd'ovice	60	49.20 N	13.43 E
Horbachevo-Mykhaylivka	83	47.50 N	38.00 E
Horb am Neckar	58	48.26 N	8.41 E
Horbelev	41	54.49 N	12.04 E
Horbourg	58	48.05 N	7.23 E
Hörby	41	55.51 N	13.39 E
Horconcitos	236	8.19 N	82.10 W
Hordaland □[6]	26	60.15 N	6.30 E
Hörde •[8]	263	51.29 N	7.30 E
Horden	44	54.46 N	1.18 W
Horden ≃	164	3.50 S	141.25 E
Horezu	38	45.08 N	23.59 E
Horgen	58	47.15 N	8.36 E
Horgenzell	58	47.48 N	9.30 E
Horhany ⋏	78	48.30 N	24.00 E
Hořice	30	50.22 N	15.38 E
Horicon	190	43.27 N	88.37 W
Horigane	268	35.50 N	139.27 E
Horine	219	38.16 N	90.25 W
Horinger	102	40.23 N	111.53 E
Horinouchi	94	37.14 N	138.56 E
Horinouchi •[8]	268	35.41 N	139.40 E
Horizon Tablemount ✦[3]	14	19.40 N	168.30 W
Horizontina	252	27.37 S	54.19 W
Horka	54	51.16 N	14.56 E
Hörken	40	60.02 N	14.56 E
Horki	76	54.17 N	30.59 E
Horley	42	51.11 N	0.11 W
Horlick Mountains ⋏	9	85.23 S	121.00 W
Horlivka	83	48.18 N	38.03 E
Horloff ≃	56	50.20 N	8.52 E
Hormigueros	240m	18.09 N	67.08 W
Hormoz, Jazīreh-ye I	128	27.04 N	56.28 E
Hormozgān □[4]	128	27.50 N	56.00 E
Hormuz, Strait of ʯ	128	26.34 N	56.15 E
Horn, Dtsch.	52	51.52 N	8.56 E
Horn, Öst.	61	48.40 N	15.40 E
Horn ≻	24a	66.28 N	22.28 W
Horn ≃, N.T., Can.	176	61.30 N	118.01 W
Horn ≃, Europe	56	49.15 N	7.20 E
Horn, Ben ∧[2]	46	58.01 N	4.02 W
Horn, Cape → Hornos, Cabo de ≻	254	55.59 S	67.16 W
Hornaday ≃	180	69.22 N	123.50 W
Hornafjörður c	24a	64.17 N	15.16 W
Hornavan ⊜	24	66.10 N	17.30 E
Hornbach	56	49.11 N	7.22 E
Hornbæk	41	56.05 N	12.28 E
Hornbeak	194	36.19 N	89.17 W
Hornbeck	194	31.19 N	93.23 W
Hornberg	58	48.13 N	8.13 E
Hornbrook	204	41.55 N	122.33 W
Hornburg	54	52.01 N	10.36 E
Hornby, On., Can.	275b	43.34 N	79.50 W
Hornby, N.Z.	172	43.33 S	172.32 E
Hornby Bay c	176	66.35 N	117.50 W
Horncastle	44	53.13 N	0.07 W
Hornchurch •[8]	260	51.34 N	0.12 E
Horndal	40	60.18 N	16.25 E
Horndean	42	50.55 N	1.00 W
Horndon on the Hill	260	51.31 N	0.25 E
Horne	41	55.06 N	10.11 E
Hornebach ≃	263	51.39 N	7.38 E
Horneburg, Dtsch.	52	53.30 N	9.34 E
Horneburg, Dtsch.	263	51.38 N	7.18 E
Hörnefors	26	63.38 N	19.54 E
Hornell	210	42.19 N	77.39 W
Hornepayne	176	49.13 N	84.47 W
Hornerstown	208	40.06 N	74.30 W
Hornhausen	54	52.02 N	11.10 E
Horn Head ≻	48	55.14 N	7.59 W
Horn Hill	260	51.37 N	0.32 W
Horní Jiřetín	54	50.35 N	13.32 E
Hornindal	26	61.58 N	6.31 E
Hornindalsvatnet ⊜	26	61.56 N	6.22 E
Hørning	41	56.05 N	10.03 E
Hörningsholm	40	59.03 N	17.40 E
Horní Počernice	54	50.06 N	14.38 E
Hornisgrinde ∧	56	48.36 N	8.12 E
Horn Island I, Austl.	164	10.37 S	142.17 E
Horn Island I, Ms., U.S.	194	30.13 N	88.38 W
Horní Slavkov	54	50.07 N	12.46 E
Horní Stropnice	61	48.46 N	14.44 E
Hornito, Cerro ∧	236	8.39 N	82.09 W
Hornitos	226	37.30 N	120.14 W
Horní Vltavice	60	48.57 N	13.46 E
Horn Lake	194	34.58 N	90.02 W
Horn Lake ⊜	212	45.24 N	79.36 W
Hornos, Cabo de (Cape Horn) ≻	254	55.59 S	67.16 W
Hornos, Isla I	254	55.57 S	67.17 W
Hornos, Islas de II	288	34.25 S	57.55 W
Hornostayivka	78	47.01 N	33.44 E
Hornow	54	51.38 N	14.31 E
Hornoy	50	49.51 N	1.54 E
Horn Plateau ⋏[1]	176	62.15 N	119.15 W
Horn Pond ⊜	283	42.28 N	71.09 W
Hornsby, Austl.	170	33.42 S	151.06 E
Hornsby, Il., U.S.	219	39.10 N	89.45 W
Hornsbyville	208	37.11 N	76.28 W
Hornsea	44	53.55 N	0.10 W
Hornsey •[8]	260	51.35 N	0.07 W
Hornslet	41	56.19 N	10.20 E
Hornstorf	54	53.54 N	11.32 E
Hornsyld	41	55.45 N	9.51 E
Horntown	208	37.58 N	75.28 W
Hornu	50	50.26 N	3.49 E
Horodenka, Ukr.	38	48.41 N	25.29 E
Horodenka, Ukr.	78	48.41 N	25.29 E
Horodets'	78	51.17 N	26.19 E
Horodkivka	78	48.23 N	28.42 E
Horodne	78	45.53 N	28.50 E
Horodnya	78	51.53 N	31.36 E
Horodnytsya	78	50.48 N	27.20 E
Horodok, Ukr.	78	49.10 N	26.34 E
Horodok, Ukr.	78	49.47 N	23.39 E
Horodyshche, Ukr.	78	49.17 N	31.27 E
Horodyshche, Ukr.	83	48.19 N	38.39 E
Horodyshche, Ukr.	83	49.03 N	39.38 E
Horokhiv	78	50.30 N	24.45 E
Horokhuvatka	83	49.21 N	37.31 E
Horoshiri-dake ∧	92a	42.43 N	142.41 E
Horotiu	172	37.43 S	175.12 E
Hořovice	60	49.50 N	13.54 E
Horqin Youyi Qianqi (Ulan Hot)	89	46.05 N	122.05 E
Horqin Youyi Zhongqi	89	45.09 N	121.24 E
Horqin Zuoyi Houqi	89	42.58 N	122.20 E
Horqin Zuoyi Zhongqi	89	44.07 N	123.18 E
Horqueta	252	23.24 S	56.53 W
Horrabridge	42	50.31 N	4.05 W
Horrelville	172	43.20 S	172.20 E
Horrem	263	51.06 N	6.48 E
Hörsching	61	48.14 N	14.11 E
Horse ≃	184	56.43 N	111.23 W
Horseback Knob ∧[2]	218	39.14 N	83.06 W
Horse Cave	194	37.10 N	85.54 W
Horse Creek	200	41.25 N	105.11 W
Horse Creek ≃, U.S.	198	41.57 N	103.58 W
Horse Creek ≃, Co., U.S.	198	38.05 N	103.19 W
Horse Creek ≃, Fl., U.S.	220	27.06 N	81.58 W
Horse Creek ≃, Il., U.S.	219	39.45 N	89.34 W
Horse Creek ≃, Mo., U.S.	194	37.46 N	93.53 W
Horsefly	182	52.20 N	121.24 W
Horsefly Lake ⊜	182	52.25 N	121.00 W
Horsehead Creek ≃	198	43.17 N	103.22 W
Horsehead Lake ⊜	198	47.02 N	99.47 W
Horseheads	210	42.10 N	76.49 W
Horse Islands II	186	50.13 N	55.45 W
Horsell	260	51.19 N	0.34 W
Horseneck Brook ≃	276	41.01 N	73.38 W
Horsens	41	55.52 N	9.52 E
Horsens Fjord c	41	55.50 N	10.05 E
Horseshoe Bend, Ar., U.S.	194	36.15 N	91.43 W
Horseshoe Bend, Id., U.S.	202	43.55 N	116.12 W
Horseshoe Bend National Military Park ♦	194	33.00 N	85.46 W
Horseshoe Cove c	276	40.27 N	74.00 W
Horseshoe Creek ≃	198	42.27 N	104.56 W
Horseshoe Falls ᒪ	284a	43.05 N	79.04 W
Horseshoe Lake ⊜, Mb., Can.	184	52.12 N	95.50 W
Horseshoe Lake ⊜, Mi., U.S.	281	42.24 N	83.45 W
Horseshoe Lake ⊜, N.J., U.S.	276	40.52 N	74.38 W
Horse Shoe Reef ✦[2]	240m	18.40 N	64.12 W
Horsfjärden c	40	59.04 N	18.09 E
Horsford	42	52.41 N	1.15 E
Horsforth	44	53.51 N	1.39 W
Horsham, Austl.	166	36.43 S	142.13 E
Horsham, Eng., U.K.	42	51.04 N	0.21 W
Horsham, Pa., U.S.	208	40.10 N	75.07 W
Hørsholm	41	55.53 N	12.30 E
Hörsingen	54	52.16 N	11.09 E
Horsley	274a	33.51 S	150.51 E
Horslunde	41	54.54 N	11.14 E
Horšovský Týn	60	49.32 N	12.56 E
Horst, Dtsch.	52	53.48 N	9.37 E
Horst, Dtsch.	54	53.22 N	10.37 E
Horst, Ned.	52	51.27 N	6.04 E
Horst •[8]	263	51.32 N	7.02 E
Horsted Keynes	42	51.02 N	0.01 W
Hörstel	52	52.18 N	7.35 E
Horstmar, Dtsch.	52	52.05 N	7.17 E
Horstmar, Dtsch.	263	51.36 N	7.33 E
Horsunlu	130	37.55 N	28.36 E
Horta	148a	38.32 N	28.38 W
Horta □[5]	148a	38.30 N	29.00 W
Horta •[8]	266d	41.26 N	2.00 E
Hortaleza •[8]	266a	40.28 N	3.39 W
Horten	26	59.25 N	10.30 E
Hortobágy •[1]	30	47.35 N	21.00 E
Hortobágyi Nemzeti Park ♦	30	47.30 N	21.10 E
Horton, Eng., U.K.	260	51.28 N	0.32 W
Horton, In., U.S.	218	40.05 N	86.09 W
Horton, Ks., U.S.	198	39.39 N	95.31 W
Horton, Mi., U.S.	216	42.09 N	84.31 W
Horton ≃	180	70.00 N	126.53 W
Horton in Ribblesdale	44	54.09 N	2.17 W
Horton Kirby	260	51.23 N	0.15 E
Horton Lake ⊜	180	67.29 N	122.31 W
Hortonville, N.Y., U.S.	210	41.46 N	75.02 W
Hortonville, Wi., U.S.	190	44.20 N	88.38 W
Horumersiel	52	53.41 N	8.00 E
Hørup	41	54.56 N	9.55 E
Hørve	41	55.45 N	11.28 E
Horw	58	47.01 N	8.18 E
Horwich	44	53.37 N	2.33 W
Horwood Lake ⊜	190	48.03 N	82.20 W
Hory	76	54.16 N	31.34 E
Hory Matky Boží	60	49.16 N	13.27 E
Horyn' (Haryn') ≃	78	52.08 N	27.17 E
Hōryūji Temple ᵿ[1]	270	34.36 N	135.44 E
Hosaina	144	7.38 N	37.52 E
Hösbach	56	50.00 N	9.12 E
Hosei University ᵿ[2]	268	35.42 N	139.44 E
Hösel	56	51.19 N	6.54 E
Hosena	54	51.27 N	14.01 E
Hoséré Vokré ∧	146	8.20 N	13.15 E
Ḥoseynābād	128	35.33 N	47.08 E
Ḥoseynīyeh-ye Khodā-Dād	128	32.42 N	48.14 E
Hosford	192	30.23 N	84.47 W
Hoshāb	128	26.01 N	63.56 E
Hoshangābād	124	22.45 N	77.43 E
Hoshangābād Plain ≚	124	22.35 N	77.25 E
Hoshcha	78	50.36 N	26.41 E
Hoshiārpur, India	123	31.32 N	75.54 E
Hoshiarpur, India	272a	28.35 N	77.22 E
Hoshigajō ∧	96	34.31 N	134.19 E
Hosingen	56	50.01 N	6.05 E
Hosjö	40	60.35 N	15.46 E
Hoskins	164	5.27 S	150.30 E
Hosmer, B.C., Can.	182	49.35 N	114.57 W
Hosmer, S.D., U.S.	198	45.34 N	99.28 W
Hosoe	94	34.49 N	137.39 E
Hospental	58	46.37 N	8.34 E
Hospers	198	43.04 N	95.54 W
Hospet	122	15.16 N	76.24 E
Hospital	48	52.29 N	8.25 W
Hospital de Orbigo	34	42.28 N	5.53 W
Hossegor	32	43.40 N	1.27 W
Hosston	194	32.53 N	93.52 W
Hosta Butte ∧	200	35.35 N	108.12 W
Hoste, Isla I	254	55.15 S	69.00 W
Hostěradice	61	48.57 N	16.15 E
Hostetter	214	40.16 N	79.24 W
Hostigrām	272b	22.26 N	88.31 E
Hostivař •[8]	54	50.01 N	14.32 E
Hostivice	54	50.04 N	14.15 E
Hošt'ka	54	50.30 N	14.20 E
Hostomice	54	50.35 N	13.46 E
Hostotipaquillo	234	21.04 N	104.04 W
Hostouň	60	49.34 N	12.46 E
Hosūr	122	12.43 N	77.49 E
Hot	110	18.06 N	98.36 E
Hota	268	35.08 N	139.51 E
Hotagen	26	63.59 N	14.15 E
Hotagen ⊜	26	63.53 N	14.29 E
Hotagsfjällen ∧	26	64.20 N	14.30 E
Hotaka	94	36.20 N	137.53 E
Hotaka-dake ∧	94	36.17 N	137.39 E
Hotamış	130	37.36 N	33.13 E
Hotan	120	37.08 N	79.54 E
Hotan ≃	90	40.30 N	80.45 E
Hotarele	38	44.10 N	26.22 E
Hotazel	158	27.15 S	23.00 E
Hotchkiss	200	38.47 N	107.43 W
Hotchkissville	207	41.34 N	73.13 W
Hot Creek Range ⋏	204	38.30 N	116.25 W
Hötensleben	54	52.08 N	11.01 E
Hotevilla	200	35.55 N	110.40 W
Hotham ≃	168a	32.58 S	116.22 E
Hotham Inlet c	180	66.45 N	162.00 W
Hotham Peak ∧	180	66.48 N	160.42 W
Hoting	26	64.07 N	16.10 E
Hot Springs, Mt., U.S.	202	47.36 N	114.40 W
Hot Springs → Truth or Consequences, N.M., U.S.	200	33.08 N	107.15 W
Hot Springs, N.C., U.S.	192	35.53 N	82.49 W
Hot Springs, S.D., U.S.	198	43.25 N	103.28 W
Hot Springs, Va., U.S.	192	37.59 N	79.49 W
Hot Springs National Park	194	34.30 N	93.04 W
Hot Springs Peak ∧, Ca., U.S.	204	40.22 N	120.07 W
Hot Springs Peak ∧, Nv., U.S.	204	41.22 N	117.26 W
Hot Springs State Park ♦	202	43.40 N	108.10 W
Hot Sulphur Springs	200	40.04 N	106.06 W
Hottah Lake ⊜	176	65.04 N	118.29 W
Hottentotbaai c	156	26.05 S	14.58 E
Hottentotskloof	158	33.15 S	19.40 E
Hotton	56	50.16 N	5.27 E
Hötzum	54	52.13 N	10.37 E
Houaïlou	175f	21.17 S	165.38 E
Houamuang	110	20.09 N	103.38 E
Houbaishu	106	31.49 N	119.10 E
Houbao	98	41.54 N	125.14 E
Houcheng	106	31.55 N	120.26 E
Houdahepao	104	41.49 N	123.01 E
Houdain	50	50.27 N	2.32 E
Houdan	50	48.47 N	1.36 E
Houdelaincourt	58	48.33 N	5.28 E
Houdeng-Aimeries	50	50.29 N	4.08 E
Houeillès	32	44.12 N	0.02 E
Houffalize	56	50.08 N	5.47 E
Hougang	271c	1.22 N	103.54 E
Hough Green	262	53.23 N	2.47 W
Houghton, Mi., U.S.	190	47.07 N	88.34 W
Houghton, N.Y., U.S.	210	42.25 N	78.09 W
Houghton, Wa., U.S.	224	47.40 N	122.12 W
Houghton Estates •[8]	273d	26.10 S	28.04 E
Houghton Green	262	53.25 N	2.34 W
Houghton Lake	190	44.18 N	84.45 W
Houghton Lake ⊜, Sk., Can.	184	52.23 N	105.08 W
Houghton Lake ⊜, Mi., U.S.	190	44.20 N	84.45 W
Houghton-le-Spring	44	54.51 N	1.28 W
Houghton Regis	42	51.55 N	0.31 W
Houguangzhengtai	104	41.13 N	122.07 E
Hougujiazi	104	42.21 N	123.22 E
Houhuangtukan	104	41.02 N	122.29 E
Houille ≃	56	50.08 N	4.49 E
Houillères de la Sarre, Canal des ≅	56	48.42 N	6.55 E
Houilles	261	48.56 N	2.11 E
Houjiangfushan	105	40.03 N	117.09 E
Houjiaping	107	30.02 N	104.38 E
Houjiaying	105	39.51 N	117.15 E
Houjie	100	22.58 N	113.39 E
Houjiumen	104	42.38 N	123.18 E
Houkou	98	37.34 N	115.09 E
Houliujia	104	40.47 N	122.19 E
Houlka	194	34.02 N	89.01 W
Houlton	188	46.07 N	67.50 W
Houluan	105	39.13 N	116.32 E
Houma, Tonga	174w	21.09 S	175.19 W
Houma, La., U.S.	194	29.35 N	90.43 W
Houma, Zhg.	102	35.36 N	111.21 E
Houmanzhoutun	104	42.29 N	123.14 E
Houmen	100	22.51 N	115.09 E
Houmet Essouq	148	33.59 N	10.51 E
Houmont Park	222	29.50 N	95.13 W
Hound Creek ≃	202	47.13 N	111.23 W
Houndé	150	11.30 N	3.31 W
Hounslow •[8]	42	51.29 N	0.22 W
Houplines	50	50.42 N	2.55 E
Houqianjiayu	104	40.50 N	120.41 E
Houqiao	105	40.04 N	116.39 E
Hourn, Loch c	46	57.08 N	5.36 W
Housatonic	207	42.15 N	73.22 W
Housatonic ≃	207	41.10 N	73.07 W
House	196	34.38 N	103.54 W
House ≃	184	56.13 N	112.31 W
House of Seven Gables ⊥	283	42.32 N	70.53 W
Houserville	214	40.50 N	77.50 W
House Springs	219	38.24 N	90.34 W
Houshan	106	31.03 N	120.21 E
Houston, B.C., Can.	182	54.24 N	126.38 W
Houston, De., U.S.	208	38.55 N	75.30 W
Houston, Mn., U.S.	190	43.45 N	91.34 W
Houston, Ms., U.S.	194	33.53 N	88.59 W
Houston, Mo., U.S.	194	37.19 N	91.57 W
Houston, Oh., U.S.	216	40.15 N	84.20 W
Houston, Pa., U.S.	214	40.14 N	80.12 W
Houston, Tx., U.S.	222	29.45 N	95.21 W
Houston □[6]	222	31.20 N	95.20 W
Houston ≃	194	30.16 N	93.13 W
Houston, Lake ⊜[1]	222	29.58 N	95.07 W
Houston County Lake ⊜[1]	222	31.25 N	95.35 W
Houston Creek ≃	218	38.13 N	84.15 W
Houston Intercontinental Airport ⊠	222	29.59 N	95.27 W
Houston Ship Channel ≅	222	29.21 N	94.47 W
Hout ≃	156	23.04 S	29.36 E
Houtbaai	158	34.03 S	18.21 E
Houthalen	56	51.02 N	5.22 E
Houthulst	50	50.59 N	2.57 E
Houtkop	158	26.36 S	27.52 E
Houtkraal	158	30.23 S	24.05 E
Houtman Abrolhos II	162	28.43 S	113.48 E
Houtskär I	26	60.12 N	21.22 E
Houtzdale	214	40.49 N	78.21 W
Houwuliangdian	104	41.31 N	121.55 E
Houwutaigou	104	41.46 N	121.42 E
Houx	261	48.34 N	1.37 E
Houxijie	100	28.46 N	118.49 E
Houxinlitun	104	41.05 N	122.33 E
Houxinqiu	104	42.34 N	122.43 E
Houyatai	104	41.26 N	121.49 E
Houying	105	39.42 N	118.18 E
Houyingzi	98	40.24 N	123.50 E
Houzhangcun	105	40.08 N	116.11 E
Houzhou	106	31.35 N	119.22 E
Houzitun	104	41.04 N	121.18 E
Hov	41	55.55 N	10.16 E
Hova	40	58.52 N	14.13 E
Hovborg	41	55.36 N	8.57 E
Høve, Dan.	41	55.50 N	11.30 E
Hove, Eng., U.K.	42	50.49 N	0.10 W
Hovedgård	41	55.57 N	9.58 E
Hövelhof	52	51.49 N	8.40 E
Hoven, Dan.	41	55.51 N	8.46 E
Hoven, S.D., U.S.	198	45.14 N	99.46 W
Hovenweep National Monument ♦	200	37.25 N	109.04 W
Hoverla, hora ∧	78	48.10 N	24.32 E
Hovmantorp	26	56.47 N	15.08 E
Hovran ⊜	40	60.16 N	16.03 E
Hovsta	40	59.21 N	15.13 E
Howa, Ouadi (Wādī Howar) V	140	17.30 N	27.08 E
Howakil I	144	15.10 N	40.16 E
Howar, Wādī (Ouadi Howa) V	140	17.30 N	27.08 E
Howard, Austl.	166	25.19 S	152.34 E
Howard, Ks., U.S.	198	37.28 N	96.15 W
Howard, Oh., U.S.	214	40.24 N	82.19 W
Howard, Pa., U.S.	214	41.00 N	77.39 W
Howard, S.D., U.S.	198	44.00 N	97.31 W
Howard, Wi., U.S.	190	44.32 N	88.05 W
Howard □[6], In., U.S.	216	40.29 N	86.08 W
Howard □[6], Md., U.S.	208	39.16 N	76.48 W
Howard Beach •[8]	276	40.40 N	73.51 W
Howard City	190	43.23 N	85.28 W
Howard Draw V	196	30.08 N	101.35 W
Howard Hanson Reservoir ⊜[1]	224	47.15 N	121.45 W
Howard Heights	284b	39.17 N	76.50 W
Howardian Hills ⋏[2]	44	54.07 N	1.00 W
Howard Island I	164	12.10 S	135.24 E
Howard Lake	190	45.03 N	94.04 W
Howard Prairie Lake ⊜[1]	202	42.15 N	122.20 W
Howard University ᵿ[2]	284c	38.55 N	77.01 W
Howden	44	53.45 N	0.52 W
Howe, In., U.S.	216	41.43 N	85.25 W
Howe, Tx., U.S.	196	33.30 N	96.37 W
Howe, Cape ≻	166	37.31 S	149.59 E
Howe Caverns ⊥[5]	210	42.42 N	74.25 W
Howe Green	260	51.42 N	0.32 E
Howe Island I	212	44.17 N	76.15 W
Howeke	150	4.50 N	7.45 W
Howell	216	42.36 N	83.55 W
Howell Airport ⊠	278	41.39 N	87.45 W
Howell Island I	219	38.40 N	90.42 W
Howells	198	41.43 N	97.00 W
Howells Pond ⊜	276	41.03 N	74.42 W
Howes Cave	210	42.41 N	74.23 W
Howe Sound ʯ	182	49.22 N	123.18 W
Howe's Range ⋏	170	33.08 S	150.47 E
Howes Valley	170	32.50 S	150.51 E
Howey In The Hills	220	28.43 N	81.47 W
Howick, P.Q., Can.	206	45.11 N	73.51 W
Howick, S. Afr.	158	29.28 S	30.14 E
Howitt, Mount ∧	166	37.10 S	146.40 E
Howland	188	45.14 N	68.39 W
Howland Island I	14	0.48 N	176.38 W
Howley	186	49.10 N	57.07 W
Howley, Mount ∧	186	48.17 N	58.26 W
Howmore	46	57.18 N	7.23 W
Howqua ≃	169	37.14 S	146.08 E
Howrah → Hāora	126	22.35 N	88.20 E
Howse Peak ∧	182	51.49 N	116.41 W
Howser	182	50.18 N	116.57 W
Howson Peak ∧	182	54.25 N	127.44 W
Howth	48	53.23 N	6.04 W
Howth Head ≻	48	53.22 N	6.03 W
Ho Xa	110	17.04 N	107.02 E
Hoxie, Ar., U.S.	194	36.03 N	90.58 W
Hoxie, Ks., U.S.	198	39.21 N	100.26 W
Höxter	52	51.46 N	9.23 E
Hoxtolgay	86	46.35 N	86.01 E
Hoxton Park	274a	33.55 S	150.51 E
Hoxton Park Aerodrome ⊠	274a	33.54 S	150.50 E
Hoy I	46	58.51 N	3.18 W
Hoya, Dtsch.	52	52.48 N	9.08 E
Hōya, Nihon	94	35.43 N	139.34 E
Høyanger	26	61.13 N	6.05 E
Hoyerswerda	54	51.26 N	14.14 E
Hoylake	44	53.23 N	3.11 W
Hoyleton, Austl.	168b	34.01 S	138.33 E
Hoyleton, Il., U.S.	219	38.27 N	89.16 W
Hoym	54	51.47 N	11.19 E
Hoyos	34	40.10 N	6.43 W
Hōyo-shotō II	96	33.52 N	132.18 E
Höytiäinen ⊜	26	62.48 N	29.39 E
Hoyt Lakes	190	47.31 N	92.08 W
Hoytville, Mi., U.S.	216	42.45 N	84.53 W
Hoytville, Oh., U.S.	216	41.11 N	83.47 W
Hozain ≃	50	48.16 N	4.06 E
Hozat	130	39.07 N	39.14 E
Hozumi	94	35.24 N	136.41 E
Hpru-so	110	19.25 N	97.08 E
Hracholusky, údolní nádrž ⊜[1]	60	49.47 N	13.07 E
Hradec Králové	30	50.12 N	15.50 E
Hrádek	61	48.46 N	16.16 E
Hrádek nad Nisou	54	50.48 N	14.51 E
Hradiště ∧	54	50.13 N	13.08 E
Hradyz'k	78	49.13 N	33.07 E
Hradzjanka	76	53.33 N	28.45 E
Hrandzičy	76	53.43 N	23.49 E
Hranice, Česká Rep.	30	49.33 N	17.44 E
Hranice, Česká Rep.	54	50.15 N	12.10 E
Hranitne	83	47.27 N	37.52 E
Hraniv	78	48.52 N	29.34 E
Hrdlovka	54	50.36 N	13.40 E
Hrebinka	78	50.07 N	32.25 E
Hrebinky	78	49.57 N	30.12 E
Hrechyshkyne	83	48.52 N	38.54 E
Hřensko	54	50.50 N	14.14 E
Hrèsk	76	53.10 N	27.29 E
Hriňová	30	48.36 N	19.31 E
Hrob	54	50.39 N	13.44 E
Hrodivka	83	48.15 N	37.23 E
Hrodna	76	53.41 N	23.50 E
Hrodna □[8]	76	53.30 N	25.00 E
Hromivka	78	46.19 N	34.06 E
Hromokliya ≃	78	47.21 N	32.14 E
Hron ≃	30	47.49 N	18.45 E
Hronov	30	50.29 N	16.12 E
Hrotovice	61	49.06 N	16.07 E
Hrubieszów	30	50.49 N	23.55 E
Hrubý Jeseník ⋏	30	50.00 N	17.20 E
Hrun'	78	50.16 N	34.36 E
Hrušovany	61	48.50 N	16.23 E
Hruzs'kyy Yalanchyk ≃	83	47.07 N	38.04 E
Hrvatska → Croatia □[1]	36	45.10 N	15.30 E
Hrybova Balka, lis ♦	83	48.09 N	38.37 E
Hryhorivka, Ukr.	78	46.17 N	33.44 E
Hryhorivka, Ukr.	78	51.03 N	32.51 E
Hryhorivka, Ukr.	78	50.05 N	30.39 E
Hrymayliv	78	49.20 N	26.01 E
Hrynyava	78	47.59 N	24.49 E
Hryshkivtsi	78	49.56 N	28.36 E
Hrytsiv	78	49.58 N	27.14 E
Hsenwi	110	23.18 N	97.58 E
Hsiakuan → Xiaguan	102	25.34 N	100.14 E
Hsiamen → Xiamen	100	24.28 N	118.07 E
Hsian → Xi'an	102	34.15 N	108.52 E
Hsiangt'an → Xiangtan	100	27.51 N	112.54 E
Hsiangyang → Xiangfan	102	32.03 N	112.01 E
Hsiaohungt'ou Yü I	100	21.57 N	121.36 E
Hsichih	269d	25.04 N	121.39 E
Hsichi Yü I	100	23.15 N	119.37 E
Hsich'üan Tao I	100	25.59 N	119.56 E
Hsientung	269d	25.09 N	121.44 E
Hsienyang → Xianyang	102	34.22 N	108.42 E
Hsi-hseng	110	20.09 N	97.15 E
Hsihu	100	23.58 N	120.28 E
Hsilo	100	23.48 N	120.27 E
Hsilo ≃	100	23.50 N	120.15 E
Hsim ≃	110	20.48 N	98.31 E
Hsinch'eng	100	24.08 N	121.39 E
Hsinchu	100	24.48 N	120.58 E
Hsinchuang	100	25.02 N	121.27 E
Hsinghua → Xinghua	100	32.57 N	119.50 E
Hsingt'ai → Xingtai	98	37.04 N	114.29 E
Hsinhailien → Lianyungang	98	34.39 N	119.16 E
Hsinhsiang → Xinxiang	98	35.20 N	113.51 E
Hsinhua	100	23.02 N	120.18 E
Hsining → Xining	102	36.38 N	101.55 E
Hsinking → Changchun	89	43.53 N	125.19 E
Hsinpeit'ou •[8]	269d	25.09 N	121.30 E
Hsinp'u → Lianyungang	98	34.39 N	119.16 E
Hsinshih	100	23.05 N	120.17 E
Hsintien	100	24.57 N	121.32 E
Hsintien ≃	269d	25.02 N	121.29 E
Hsinyang → Xinyang	100	32.08 N	114.04 E
Hsipaw	110	22.37 N	97.18 E
Hsiukuluan ≃	100	23.28 N	121.30 E
Hsiyü	100	23.36 N	119.30 E
Hsüanhua → Xuanhua	105	40.37 N	115.03 E
Hsüch'ang → Xuchang	100	34.03 N	113.49 E
Hsüchou → Xuzhou	98	34.16 N	117.11 E
Hsüehchia	100	23.14 N	120.10 E
Hsüeh Shan ∧	100	24.23 N	121.13 E
Hsuphāng	110	20.18 N	98.42 E
Hua'an	100	25.02 N	117.34 E
Huab ≃	156	20.52 S	13.25 E
Huabu	100	29.00 N	118.20 E
Huacaña	248	14.02 S	74.02 W
Huacao	269b	31.14 N	121.19 E
Huacaraje	248	13.33 S	63.45 W
Huachacalla	248	18.45 S	68.17 W
Huacheng	100	24.04 N	115.38 E
Huachi	102	36.43 N	107.52 E
Huachi, Laguna ⊜	248	14.11 S	63.30 W
Huachipa	286d	12.00 S	76.56 W
Huacho	248	11.07 S	77.37 W
Huachón	248	10.40 S	75.57 W
Huachos	248	13.12 S	75.31 W
Huachuca City	200	31.37 N	110.20 W
Huaco	252	30.09 S	68.31 W
Huacrachuco	248	8.39 S	77.05 W
Huade	98	41.46 N	114.16 E
Huadian	89	42.58 N	126.43 E
Huading Shan ∧	100	29.15 N	121.05 E
Huafeng	106	32.14 N	121.16 E
Huagutang	106	30.55 N	119.18 E
Hua Hin	110	12.34 N	99.58 E
Huai ≃, Zhg.	98	37.28 N	114.55 E
Huai ≃, Zhg.	100	32.58 N	118.17 E
Huaiá-Miçu ≃	250	10.52 S	53.15 W

Symbols in the index entries represent the broad categories identified in the key at the right. Symbols with superior numbers (⋏[1]) identify subcategories (see complete key on page I · 1).

Symbole im Register stellen die rechts im Schlüssel erklärten Kategorien dar. Symbole mit hochgestellten Ziffern (⋏[1]) bezeichnen Unterabteilungen einer Kategorie (vgl. vollständiger Schlüssel auf Seite I · 1).

Los símbolos incluídos en el texto del índice representan las grandes categorías identificadas con la clave a la derecha. Los símbolos con numeros en su parte superior (⋏[1]) identifican las subcategorías (véase la clave completa en la página I · 1).

Les symboles de l'index représentent les catégories indiquées dans la légende à droite. Les symboles suivis d'un indice (⋏[1]) représentent des sous-catégories (voir légende complète à la page I · 1).

Os símbolos incluídos no texto do índice representam as grandes categorias identificadas com a chave à direita. Os símbolos com números em sua parte superior (⋏[1]) identificam as subcategorias (veja-se a chave completa à página I · 1).

∧	Mountain	Berg	Montaña	Montagne	Montanha
⋏	Mountains	Gebirge	Montañas	Montagnes	Montanhas
)(	Pass	Paß	Paso	Col	Passo
V	Valley, Canyon	Tal, Cañon	Valle, Cañón	Vallée, Canyon	Vale, Canhão
≚	Plain	Ebene	Llano	Plaine	Planície
≻	Cape	Kap	Cabo	Cap	Cabo
I	Island	Insel	Isla	Île	Ilha
II	Islands	Inseln	Islas	Îles	Ilhas
⊥	Other Topographic Features	Andere Topographische Objekte	Otros Elementos Topográficos	Autres données topographiques	Outros acidentes topográficos

ESPAÑOL / FRANÇAIS / PORTUGUÊS

Nombre / Nom / Nome	Página / Page / Página	Lat.°′	Long.°′ W = Oeste / W = Ouest / W = Oeste
Huai'an (Chaigoubu), Zhg.	98	40.39 N	114.27 E
Huai'an, Zhg.	100	33.32 N	119.10 E
Huaibin	100	32.28 N	115.24 E
Huaide	89	43.32 N	124.50 E
Huaidezhen, Zhg.	89	43.54 N	124.47 E
Huaidezhen, Zhg.	107	28.59 N	105.15 E
Huaihuazhenshi	106	31.05 N	119.41 E
Huaiji	102	24.01 N	112.18 E
Huailai (Shacheng)	105	40.23 N	115.33 E
Huailin	100	31.26 N	117.36 E
Huaillati	248	14.05 S	72.31 W
Huainan	100	32.40 N	117.00 E
Huaining	100	30.25 N	116.38 E
Huairou	105	40.19 N	116.37 E
Huaite → Huaide	89	43.32 N	124.50 E
Huaitunas, Lagunas ⊜	248	13.06 S	66.00 W
Huaiyang	100	33.44 N	114.53 E
Huai Yot	110	7.45 N	99.37 E
Huaiyuan	100	32.57 N	117.12 E
Huaiyu Shan ⩘	100	28.50 N	117.50 E
Huaji	100	32.46 N	115.20 E
Huajiang	102	25.50 N	110.21 E
Huajianzi	104	40.48 N	122.12 E
Huajiapuzi	104	40.52 N	123.14 E
Huajiayingzi	104	42.20 N	121.00 E
Huajimic	234	21.42 N	104.20 W
Huajintepec	234	16.36 N	98.14 W
Huajuapan de León	234	17.48 N	97.46 W
Huakou	100	25.13 N	117.35 E
Hualahuises	232	24.53 N	99.41 W
Hualalai ∧ 1	229d	19.42 N	155.52 W
Hualañé	252	34.59 S	71.49 W
Hualapai Indian Reservation ◂ 4	200	35.38 N	113.30 W
Hualapai Mountains ⩘	200	34.50 N	113.55 W
Hualapai Peak ∧	200	35.04 N	113.54 W
Hualfín	252	27.14 S	66.50 W
Hualgayoc	248	6.46 S	78.37 W
Hualien	100	23.59 N	121.36 E
Hualien ≐	100	23.57 N	121.36 E
Hualingpuzi	104	41.31 N	123.54 E
Huallaga ≐	248	5.10 S	75.32 W
Huallamarca, Museo ⊍	286d	12.05 S	77.02 W
Huallanca, Perú	248	8.49 S	77.52 W
Huallanca, Perú	248	9.51 S	76.56 W
Huallayabamba ≐	248	7.04 S	77.10 W
Hualmay	248	11.06 S	77.38 W
Hualong	102	36.05 N	102.36 E
Huamanquiquia	248	13.44 S	74.15 W
Huamantla	234	19.19 N	97.56 W
Huambo (Nova Lisboa)	152	12.44 S	15.47 E
Huambo □ 5	152	12.30 S	15.40 E
Huambos	248	6.28 S	78.58 W
Huameiao	100	26.32 N	115.47 E
Huamei Shan ∧	100	25.28 N	113.58 E
Huamuxtitlán	234	17.49 N	98.34 W
Huan ≐	100	30.40 N	114.05 E
Huanan	89	46.13 N	130.32 E
Huancabamba, Perú	248	10.21 S	75.32 W
Huancabamba, Perú	248	5.14 S	79.28 W
Huancané	248	15.12 S	69.46 W
Huancapi	248	13.41 S	74.04 W
Huancarama	248	13.39 S	73.05 W
Huancarqui	248	16.06 S	72.29 W
Huancavelica	248	12.46 S	75.02 W
Huancavelica □ 5	248	13.00 S	75.00 W
Huancaybamba	248	9.05 S	76.50 W
Huancayo	248	12.04 S	75.14 W
Huanchaca	248	20.20 S	66.39 W
Huanchaca, Serranía de ⩘	248	14.30 S	60.39 W
Huandacareo	234	19.59 N	101.17 W
Huando	248	12.29 S	74.58 W
Huang ≐, Asia	110	17.49 N	101.33 E
Huang ≐, T'aiwan	269d	25.14 N	121.37 E
Huang (Yellow) ≐, Zhg.	90	37.32 N	118.19 E
Huang'aicun	106	31.43 N	118.40 E
Huang'an	98	35.28 N	115.42 E
Huang'anshi	100	29.06 N	113.34 E
Huangbai	98	41.17 N	126.21 E
Huangbaozi	102	39.54 N	99.26 E
Huangbeipu	104	42.21 N	123.25 E
Huangcaoping	100	25.42 N	113.27 E
Huangchong	100	22.18 N	113.03 E
Huangchuan	100	32.09 N	115.03 E
Huangcun	105	39.56 N	116.11 E
Huangdaizhen	106	31.26 N	120.33 E
Huangdan	107	29.10 N	103.44 E
Huangda Yang ⊔	100	30.03 N	122.26 E
Huangdi, Zhg.	98	40.14 N	120.15 E
Huangdi, Zhg.	105	40.57 N	118.24 E
Huangdu, Zhg.	106	30.47 N	118.51 E
Huangdu, Zhg.	106	31.16 N	121.13 E
Huangduqiao	100	29.18 N	120.55 E
Huanggai Hu ⊜	100	29.44 N	113.23 E
Huanggang	100	30.27 N	114.52 E
Huanggangji	98	34.39 N	116.03 E
Huanggangkou	100	28.32 N	114.33 E
Huanggang Shan ∧	100	27.50 N	117.45 E
Huanggangshi	100	33.09 N	115.55 E
Huangguayingzi	104	41.46 N	120.46 E
Huangguoshu	102	26.02 N	105.32 E
Huang Hai → Yellow Sea ⊤ 2	90	36.00 N	123.00 E
Huanghe Kou ≐ 1	98	37.54 N	118.48 E
Huangho → Huang ≐	90	37.32 N	118.19 E
Huanghu	106	30.27 N	119.48 E
Huanghua	98	38.22 N	117.21 E
Huanghuadianzi	104	41.44 N	122.48 E
Huanghuashi	100	28.14 N	113.14 E
Huangjialing	104	42.12 N	122.55 E
Huangjialu	106	31.00 N	121.45 E
Huangjiatun	104	41.11 N	122.54 E
Huangjiazhai	106	32.01 N	121.36 E
Huangjinbu	100	28.27 N	116.47 E
Huangjing	106	31.39 N	121.06 E
Huangjinggou	107	29.37 N	104.35 E
Huangjinjing	107	29.44 N	104.38 E
Huangjinzi	89	50.02 N	127.20 E
Huangjuezhen	107	29.50 N	106.27 E
Huangkan	105	40.22 N	116.28 E
Huangkeng	100	27.35 N	117.39 E
Huangkou	102	42.46 N	93.58 E
Huanglaomen	100	29.30 N	115.49 E
Huangli	106	31.39 N	119.42 E
Huanglian	107	29.17 N	106.18 E
Huangling	102	35.41 N	109.09 E
Huanglingji	100	30.25 N	114.03 E
Huanglong, Zhg.	100	31.58 N	112.28 E
Huanglong, Zhg.	102	35.45 N	109.42 E
Huanglongxi	107	30.19 N	103.58 E
Huangmao	100	28.07 N	114.04 E
Huangmapi	100	23.30 N	114.33 E
Huangmei	100	30.04 N	115.56 E
Huangnihe, Zhg.	89	43.32 N	127.59 E
Huangnihe, Zhg.	100	31.06 N	117.22 E
Huangpi, Zhg.	100	30.53 N	114.22 E
Huangpi, Zhg.	100	26.39 N	115.51 E
Huangpu ≐	106	31.24 N	121.31 E
Huangqi	100	26.21 N	119.54 E
Huangqiao	106	32.15 N	120.13 E
Huangqiao ≐	106	32.00 N	120.20 E
Huangshahe	102	26.03 N	110.58 E
Huangshajie	100	29.03 N	113.08 E
Huangshan	98	36.57 N	122.18 E
Huangshanguan	98	37.32 N	120.16 E
Huangshapu, Zhg.	100	26.50 N	113.26 E
Huangshapu, Zhg.	100	25.08 N	112.44 E
Huangshaqiao	100	28.56 N	114.40 E
Huangshatuo	104	41.12 N	122.31 E
Huangshi, Zhg.	100	25.23 N	119.04 E
Huangshi, Zhg.	100	30.13 N	115.05 E
Huangshi, Zhg.	102	29.00 N	111.02 E
Huangshidu	100	27.44 N	116.44 E
Huangshiguan	100	26.15 N	115.54 E
Huangshui	107	30.32 N	103.55 E
Huangtan, Zhg.	100	27.44 N	119.58 E
Huangtan, Zhg.	100	26.41 N	117.17 E
Huangtan ≐	100	24.48 N	116.31 E
Huangtang, Zhg.	100	23.44 N	114.58 E
Huangtang, Zhg.	106	31.47 N	119.40 E
Huangtang, Zhg.	106	31.46 N	120.21 E
Huangtang Hu ⊜	100	30.00 N	114.12 E
Huangtankou	100	28.50 N	118.53 E
Huangtantuan	100	30.53 N	113.33 E
Huangtian	100	23.52 N	114.58 E
Huangtianfan	100	29.10 N	120.08 E
Huangtu, Zhg.	100	27.36 N	118.00 E
Huangtu, Zhg.	106	31.52 N	120.03 E
Huangtuchang	107	30.41 N	104.18 E
Huangtugang	100	31.25 N	115.05 E
Huangtukan	104	41.21 N	122.45 E
Huangtuliangzi	98	41.14 N	118.39 E
Huangtuling	100	27.18 N	113.30 E
Huangtupo	105	39.47 N	116.16 E
Huanguelén	252	37.02 S	61.57 W
Huangwan	106	30.22 N	120.48 E
Huangxian	98	37.38 N	120.29 E
Huangxu	106	32.06 N	119.37 E
Huangyaguan	105	40.14 N	117.26 E
Huangyan	100	28.39 N	121.15 E
Huangyang Shan ⩘	105	40.20 N	115.00 E
Huangyanzhuang	105	40.01 N	118.21 E
Huangyuan	102	36.40 N	101.12 E
Huangyuzeng	104	42.05 N	124.11 E
Huangze	100	29.35 N	120.55 E
Huangze Yang ⊔	100	30.36 N	122.28 E
Huangzhai	100	29.27 N	120.00 E
Huangzhong	102	36.31 N	101.40 E
Huangzhu	110	19.29 N	110.24 E
Huangzhuang, Zhg.	100	34.05 N	112.15 E
Huangzhuang, Zhg.	105	39.29 N	117.31 E
Huangzhuang, Zhg.	105	39.53 N	117.05 E
Huangzhuang Wa ⊜	105	39.33 N	117.33 E
Huaning	102	24.14 N	102.56 E
Huaniugouzi	104	41.34 N	122.35 E
Huaniupuzi	104	41.23 N	123.31 E
Huanjiang	102	24.54 N	108.21 E
Huanren	98	41.14 N	125.21 E
Huanta	248	12.56 S	74.15 W
Huantai (Suozhen)	98	36.59 N	118.06 E
Huantan	100	31.49 N	113.04 E
Huántar	248	9.26 S	77.15 W
Huánuco	248	9.55 S	76.14 W
Huánuco □ 5	248	9.30 S	75.50 W
Huanuni	248	18.16 S	66.51 W
Huanxi	100	26.34 N	113.36 E
Huanxian	102	36.39 N	107.18 E
Huanxiang ≐	105	39.34 N	117.45 E
Huanxiling	104	41.17 N	123.54 E
Huanzo, Cordillera de ⩘	248	14.30 S	73.20 W
Huapango, Presa ⊜ 1	234	20.00 N	99.40 W
Huapí, Serranías ⩘	236	12.30 N	85.00 W
Huap'ing Yü I	100	25.26 N	121.56 E
Huaqiao, Zhg.	100	28.56 N	121.27 E
Huaqiao, Zhg.	100	29.32 N	117.11 E
Huaqiao, Zhg.	102	27.28 N	110.02 E
Huaqiao, Zhg.	107	30.28 N	103.52 E
Huaqiaozhen	107	30.47 N	106.41 E
Huaqiying	106	32.10 N	118.38 E
Huara	248	19.59 S	69.47 W
Huaral	248	11.30 S	77.12 W
Huaráz	248	9.32 S	77.32 W
Huari	248	9.20 S	77.14 W
Huariaca	248	10.27 S	76.07 W
Huaribamba	248	12.16 S	74.57 W
Huarina	248	16.12 S	68.38 W
Huarmey	248	10.04 S	78.10 W
Huarochirí	248	12.09 S	76.14 W
Huarocondo	248	13.25 S	72.13 W
Huarong	100	29.30 N	112.34 E
Huasaga ≐	246	3.42 S	76.26 W
Hua Sai	110	8.02 N	100.18 E
Huascarán, Nevado ∧	248	9.07 S	77.37 W
Huasco	252	28.28 S	71.14 W
Huasco ≐	252	28.27 S	71.13 W
Huashan	98	34.39 N	116.44 E
Huashaoying	98	40.12 N	114.36 E
Huashi	106	31.50 N	120.28 E
Huatabampo	232	26.50 N	109.38 W
Huatangpu	100	25.48 N	112.52 E
Huating	102	35.09 N	106.38 E
Huatong, Zhg.	98	40.03 N	121.56 E
Huatong, Zhg.	102	23.01 N	106.36 E
Huatusco	234	19.09 N	96.57 W
Huauchinango	234	20.11 N	98.03 W
Huaura	248	11.04 S	77.36 W
Huaura ≐	248	11.06 S	77.39 W
Huautla, Méx.	234	21.02 N	98.17 W
Huautla, Méx.	234	18.08 N	96.51 W
Huaxian (Daokou), Zhg.	98	35.37 N	114.32 E
Huaxian, Zhg.	100	23.22 N	113.12 E
Huaxian, Zhg.	102	34.30 N	109.40 E
Huayan	107	30.01 N	105.02 E
Huayang	107	30.32 N	104.04 E
Huayangzhen	102	33.25 N	107.44 E
Huaying Shan ∧	107	30.10 N	106.42 E
Huayingtai	104	40.43 N	122.19 E
Huayllay	248	11.01 S	76.21 W
Huayna Potosí, Nevado ∧	248	16.16 S	68.11 W
Huaytará	248	13.36 S	75.22 W
Hua Yü I	100	23.24 N	119.19 E
Huayuan, Zhg.	98	42.17 N	127.07 E
Huayuan, Zhg.	100	31.16 N	113.58 E
Huayuan, Zhg.	102	28.34 N	109.13 E
Huayuanzui	100	33.00 N	118.16 E
Huayunca, Nevado ∧	248	14.39 S	72.28 W
Huayuri, Pampa de ⊻	248	14.30 S	75.30 W
Huazhou	102	21.40 N	110.33 E
Huazi	104	41.25 N	123.29 E
Huazigou	104	41.50 N	121.01 E
Huazikou	106	32.13 N	118.57 E
Ḥubārah, Wādī V	142	27.21 N	31.39 E
Ḥubaytah, Bi'r ⊤ 4	142	30.27 N	32.27 E
Hubbard, Ia., U.S.	190	42.18 N	93.18 W
Hubbard, Oh., U.S.	214	41.09 N	80.34 W
Hubbard, Or., U.S.	224	45.10 N	122.48 W
Hubbard, Tx., U.S.	222	31.50 N	96.47 W
Hubbard Creek ≐	196	32.54 N	98.53 W
Hubbard Creek Reservoir ⊜ 1	196	32.45 N	99.00 W
Hubbard Lake ⊜	190	44.49 N	83.34 W
Hubbards	186	44.38 N	64.04 W
Hubbardston	207	42.28 N	72.00 W
Hubbell	190	47.10 N	88.25 W
Hubbell Trading Post National Historic Site ⊥	200	35.43 N	109.33 W
Hubbelrath ◂ 8	263	51.16 N	6.55 E
Hubei (Hupeh) □ 4	90	31.00 N	112.00 E
Huben, Öst.	64	47.03 N	10.58 E
Huben, Öst.	64	46.56 N	12.34 E
Huberdeau	206	45.58 N	74.38 W
Huber Heights	218	39.50 N	84.07 W
Hublersburg	210	40.58 N	77.37 W
Hubli-Dhārwār	122	15.21 N	75.10 E
Hubuleng	102	41.19 N	111.08 E
Hubynykha	78	48.48 N	35.15 E
Hucaogang	106	32.00 N	120.29 E
Hucclecote	42	51.51 N	2.11 W
Huch'ang	98	41.25 N	127.03 E
Hucheng	100	25.26 N	118.27 E
Huchi	100	31.08 N	117.40 E
Huchow → Huzhou	106	30.52 N	120.06 E
Huckarde ◂ 8	263	51.32 N	7.24 E
Hückelhoven	56	51.03 N	6.13 E
Hückeswagen	56	51.08 N	7.20 E
Hucking	260	51.18 N	0.39 E
Huckingen ◂ 8	263	51.22 N	6.43 E
Huckitta Creek ≐	162	22.38 S	135.30 E
Huckleberry Island I	276	40.53 N	73.45 W
Huckleberry Mountain ∧	202	43.51 N	122.19 W
Huckleberry Mountain ∧ 2	212	44.28 N	75.28 W
Hucknall	42	53.02 N	1.11 W
Hucqueliers	50	50.34 N	1.54 E
Hucun	105	39.02 N	115.56 E
Hudangtou	106	30.48 N	121.22 E
Huddart Park ♦	282	37.26 N	122.19 W
Hudderfield Narrow Canal ≡	262	53.29 N	2.06 W
Huddersfield	44	53.39 N	1.47 W
Huddinge	40	59.14 N	17.59 E
Huddle Park Municipal Golf Course ♦	273d	26.09 S	28.07 E
Huddunge	40	60.03 N	16.59 E
Hude	52	53.07 N	8.27 E
Huder	89	50.00 N	121.37 E
Hudgin Creek ≐	194	33.40 N	91.59 W
Hūdī	140	17.42 N	34.17 E
Hudiksvall	26	61.44 N	17.07 E
Hudong	100	22.51 N	115.56 E
Hudson, P.Q., Can.	206	45.27 N	74.09 W
Hudson, Il., U.S.	216	40.36 N	88.59 W
Hudson, In., U.S.	216	41.31 N	85.04 W
Hudson, Ia., U.S.	190	42.24 N	92.27 W
Hudson, Md., U.S.	208	38.35 N	76.15 W
Hudson, Ma., U.S.	207	42.23 N	71.34 W
Hudson, Mi., U.S.	216	41.51 N	84.21 W
Hudson, N.H., U.S.	207	42.45 N	71.26 W
Hudson, N.Y., U.S.	210	42.15 N	73.47 W
Hudson, N.C., U.S.	192	35.50 N	81.29 W
Hudson, Oh., U.S.	214	41.14 N	81.26 W
Hudson, S.D., U.S.	198	43.07 N	96.27 W
Hudson, Tx., U.S.	222	31.19 N	94.50 W
Hudson, Wi., U.S.	190	44.58 N	92.45 W
Hudson, Wy., U.S.	200	42.54 N	108.34 W
Hudson □ 6	276	40.44 N	74.02 W
Hudson ≐, U.S.	188	40.42 N	74.02 W
Hudson ≐, Ga., U.S.	192	34.14 N	83.10 W
Hudson, Cerro ∧	254	46.04 S	73.10 W
Hudson, Lake ⊜ 1	194	36.20 N	95.05 W
Hudson Bay	184	52.52 N	102.25 W
Hudson Bay ⊂	176	60.00 N	86.00 W
Hudson-Bayonet Point	220	28.21 N	82.41 W
Hudson Falls	210	43.18 N	73.35 W
Hudson Highlands State Park ♦	210	41.26 N	73.58 W
Hudson Hope	182	56.02 N	121.55 W
Hudson Lake	216	41.42 N	86.32 W
Hudson Mountains ⩘	9	74.32 S	99.20 W
Hudsons Peak ∧	171b	36.26 S	149.10 E
Hudson Strait ⊔	176	62.30 N	72.00 W
Hudsonville	216	42.52 N	85.51 W
Hudwin Lake ⊜	184	53.12 N	95.42 W
Hue	110	16.28 N	107.36 E
Huebra ≐	34	41.02 N	6.48 W
Huechucuicui, Punta ›	254	41.47 S	74.02 W
Huechulafquen, Lago ⊜	254	39.46 S	71.28 W
Huechuraba	286e	33.21 S	70.40 W
Huedin	38	46.52 N	23.02 E
Huehuetán	236	15.01 N	92.22 W
Huehuetenango	236	15.20 N	91.28 W
Huehuetenango □ 5	236	15.40 N	91.35 W
Huehuetlán El Chico	234	18.21 N	98.42 W
Huejúcar	234	22.21 N	103.13 W
Huejuquilla El Alto	234	22.36 N	103.52 W
Huejutla de Reyes	234	21.08 N	98.25 W
Huelgoat	32	48.22 N	3.45 W
Huelma	34	37.39 N	3.27 W
Huelva	34	37.16 N	6.57 W
Huelva □ 4	34	37.30 N	6.55 W
Huelva, Río de ≐	34	37.27 N	6.00 W
Huenque ≐	248	16.12 S	69.44 W
Huentelauquén	252	31.35 S	71.32 W
Huércal-Overa	34	37.23 N	1.57 W
Huerfano ≐	198	38.14 N	104.15 W
Huerfano Mountain ∧	200	36.26 N	107.51 W
Huerhuero Creek ≐	226	35.40 N	120.42 W
Huerlumada	120	32.45 N	90.00 E
Huerva ≐	34	41.39 N	0.52 W
Huesca	34	42.08 N	0.25 W
Huesca □ 4	34	42.05 N	0.10 W
Huéscar	34	37.49 N	2.32 W
Hueston Woods State Park ♦	218	39.34 N	84.44 W
Huetamo de Núñez	234	18.35 N	100.53 W
Huete	34	40.08 N	2.41 W
Huey	219	38.36 N	89.17 W
Hueyapan de Ocampo	234	18.07 N	95.09 W
Hueytown	194	33.27 N	86.59 W
Hufengzhen	107	29.43 N	106.07 E
Hüffenhardt	56	49.18 N	9.04 E
Huffman	222	30.01 N	95.05 W
Huffman Dam ◂ 6	218	39.48 N	84.05 W
Hüfingen	58	47.55 N	8.29 E
Ḥufrat an-Naḥās	140	9.45 N	24.19 E
Hufu	106	31.16 N	119.47 E
Hügel, Villa ⊍	263	51.25 N	7.01 E
Huggins, Mount ∧	9	78.17 S	162.28 E
Hugh ≐	162	25.01 S	134.01 E
Hugh Butler Lake ⊜ 1	198	40.22 N	100.42 W
Hughenden	166	20.51 S	144.12 E
Hughes, Austl.	162	30.42 S	129.31 E
Hughes, Ak., U.S.	180	66.03 N	154.16 W
Hughes, Ar., U.S.	194	34.56 N	90.28 W
Hughes ≐	184	56.46 N	100.01 W
Hughes, South Fork ≐	188	39.08 N	81.20 W
Hughes Airport ⊠	280	33.58 N	118.25 W
Hughes Creek ≐	169	36.53 S	145.08 E
Hughes Springs	222	33.05 N	94.38 W
Hughesville, Md., U.S.	208	38.31 N	76.47 W
Hughesville, Pa., U.S.	210	41.14 N	76.43 W
Hugh Keenleyside Dam ◂ 6	182	49.20 N	117.49 W
Hughson	226	37.36 N	120.52 W
Hughsonville	210	41.35 N	73.56 W
Hugh Town	42a	49.55 N	6.17 W
Hugli ≐	126	21.55 N	88.05 E
Hugli-Chinsurah	126	22.54 N	88.24 E
Hugo, Co., U.S.	198	39.08 N	103.28 W
Hugo, Ok., U.S.	196	34.00 N	95.30 W
Hugo Lake ⊜ 1	196	34.05 N	95.25 W
Hugoton	198	37.10 N	101.20 W
Hugou	100	33.23 N	117.08 E
Huguenot	210	41.25 N	74.38 W
Huguenot Lake ⊜	276	40.56 N	73.47 W
Huhehot → Hohhot	102	40.51 N	111.40 E
Huhsi	100	23.35 N	119.39 E
Hui'an, Zhg.	100	25.04 N	118.47 E
Huian, Zhg.	106	31.47 N	121.45 E
Huiarau Range ⩘	172	38.45 S	177.00 E
Huib-Hoch Plateau ⩘ 1	156	27.00 S	16.45 E
Huibie Yang ⊔	100	30.08 N	121.44 E
Huibu	100	28.18 N	115.15 E
Huichang, Zhg.	100	25.34 N	115.49 E
Huichang, Zhg.	105	39.04 N	115.04 E
Huichapan	234	20.23 N	99.39 W
Hŭich'ŏn	98	40.10 N	126.17 E
Huichou → Huizhou	100	23.05 N	114.24 E
Huichuan	102	35.11 N	104.02 E
Huicungo	248	7.17 S	76.48 W
Huidong	102	26.41 N	102.36 E
Huidui	105	39.04 N	117.16 E
Huihe, Zhg.	89	48.12 N	119.17 E
Huihe, Zhg.	106	31.45 N	121.43 E
Huiji ≐	100	33.53 N	115.36 E
Huíla	152	15.04 S	13.32 E
Huíla □ 5, Ang.	152	15.00 S	15.00 E
Huila □ 5, Col.	246	2.30 N	75.45 W
Huila, Nevado del ∧	246	3.00 N	76.00 W
Huilai	100	23.04 N	116.18 E
Huili	102	26.43 N	102.10 E
Huiliuji	100	32.50 N	115.58 E
Huillapima	252	28.44 S	65.59 W
Huilong, Zhg.	100	27.30 N	118.24 E
Huilong, Zhg.	100	25.22 N	116.24 E
Huilong, Zhg.	100	24.09 N	113.58 E
Huilong, Zhg.	107	30.28 N	105.26 E
Huilong, Zhg.	107	30.35 N	105.49 E
Huilongchang, Zhg.	107	29.41 N	104.17 E
Huilongchang, Zhg.	107	30.18 N	103.39 E
Huilongchang, Zhg.	107	30.41 N	106.34 E
Huilongchang, Zhg.	107	29.17 N	105.01 E
Huimanguillo	234	17.51 N	93.23 W
Huimin	98	37.29 N	117.29 E
Huinan (Chaoyang)	98	42.40 N	126.00 E
Huínaymarca, Lago ⊜	248	16.20 S	68.50 W
Huinca Renancó	252	34.50 S	64.23 W
Hüinghausen	263	51.11 N	7.48 E
Huining	102	35.41 N	105.08 E
Huisachal	196	26.47 N	101.07 W
Huisduinen	52	52.56 N	4.44 E
Huishan	106	31.35 N	120.16 E
Huishui	102	26.07 N	106.24 E
Huismes	50	47.14 N	0.15 E
Huisne ≐	50	47.59 N	0.11 E
Huissen	52	51.57 N	5.56 E
Huistepec	234	16.39 N	98.20 W
Huiten Nur ⊜	120	35.30 N	92.00 E
Huiting	98	34.05 N	116.04 E
Huitiupan	234	17.13 N	92.39 W
Huitong	102	26.54 N	109.31 E
Huitongqiao	102	24.43 N	98.56 E
Huittinen (Lauttakylä)	26	61.11 N	22.42 E
Huitzilán	234	19.58 N	97.41 W
Huitzo	234	17.15 N	96.52 W
Huitzuco de los Figueroa	234	18.18 N	99.21 W
Huixian	102	33.47 N	106.16 E
Huixtla	232	15.09 N	92.28 W
Huiyang → Huizhou	100	23.05 N	114.24 E
Huiyao	100	27.16 N	118.05 E
Huize	102	26.27 N	103.09 E
Huizen	52	52.17 N	5.14 E
Huizhou	100	23.05 N	114.24 E
Hujia, Zhg.	104	41.20 N	121.52 E
Hujia, Zhg.	106	31.25 N	121.37 E
Hujiadian	107	29.41 N	104.07 E
Hujiajie	104	41.06 N	122.10 E
Hujiasi	107	29.16 N	105.13 E
Hujiawopu	104	42.34 N	122.11 E
Hujiayu	105	39.28 N	115.27 E
Hujiazhuang, Zhg.	105	39.51 N	117.07 E
Hujiazhuang, Zhg.	269b	31.21 N	121.25 E
Hujie	102	24.56 N	100.32 E
Hukeng	100	27.29 N	114.18 E
Hukou	100	29.45 N	116.13 E
Hŭksan-chedo II	98	34.30 N	125.20 E
Hukui → Fukui	94	36.04 N	136.13 E
Ḥukūmah	140	13.52 N	36.07 E
Hukuntsi	156	24.02 S	21.48 E
Hukuoka → Fukuoka	96	33.35 N	130.24 E
Hukusima → Fukushima	92	37.45 N	140.28 E
Hukuyama → Fukuyama	96	34.29 N	133.22 E
Ḥula, 'Émeq ⊻ 1	132	33.08 N	35.37 E
Hulahula ≐	180	70.00 N	144.01 W
Hulan	89	46.00 N	126.38 E
Hulan ≐	89	45.55 N	126.41 E
Hulan Ergi	89	47.13 N	123.39 E
Hulbert, Mi., U.S.	190	46.21 N	85.09 W
Hulbert, Ok., U.S.	194	35.55 N	95.08 W
Hulberton	210	43.15 N	78.04 W
Ḥulda	132	31.50 N	34.53 E
Huldrefossen ∟	26	61.28 N	5.58 E
Hulei	100	24.50 N	116.48 E
Huleia Stream ≐	229b	21.57 N	159.22 W
Hulett	198	44.40 N	104.36 W
Hulín, Česká Rep.	30	49.19 N	17.28 E
Hulin, Zhg.	89	45.46 N	132.59 E
Hulin ≐, Zhg.	89	45.19 N	124.06 E
Hulin ≐, Zhg.	89	44.55 N	122.35 E
Huliu ≐	98	40.10 N	114.33 E
Hull, P.Q., Can.	212	45.26 N	75.43 W
Hull → Kingston upon Hull, Eng., U.K.	44	53.45 N	0.20 W
Hull, Il., U.S.	219	39.43 N	91.13 W
Hull, Ia., U.S.	198	43.11 N	96.08 W
Hull, Ma., U.S.	207	42.18 N	70.54 W
Hull, Tx., U.S.	222	30.09 N	94.39 W
Hull □ 6	212	45.40 N	75.35 W
Hull ≐	44	53.44 N	0.19 W
Hullavington	42	51.33 N	2.09 W
Hull Bay ⊂	283	42.18 N	70.53 W
Hullbridge	42	51.37 N	0.38 E
Hullo	76	59.00 N	23.14 E
Hulmeville	285	40.08 N	74.55 W
Hüls, Dtsch.	56	51.22 N	6.30 E
Hüls, Dtsch.	263	51.40 N	7.08 E
Hülscheid	56	51.16 N	7.34 E
Hülser Berg ◂ 8	263	51.24 N	6.31 E
Hülser Berg ∧ 2	263	51.23 N	6.33 E
Hulst	52	51.17 N	4.03 E
Hult	40	58.40 N	16.07 E
Hultsfred	26	57.29 N	15.50 E
Huludao	104	40.43 N	121.00 E
Hulufa	105	39.42 N	116.12 E
Hulun → Hailar	89	49.12 N	119.42 E
Hulun Nur ⊜	88	49.01 N	117.32 E
Huluyu	105	40.14 N	116.53 E
Ḥulwān	142	29.51 N	31.20 E
Ḥulwān Observatory ⊍ 3	142	29.52 N	31.21 E
Hulyaypole	78	47.38 N	36.16 E
Huma, Tonga	174w	21.19 S	174.57 E
Huma, Zhg.	89	51.43 N	126.38 E
Huma ≐	89	51.40 N	126.44 E
Humacao	240m	18.09 N	65.50 W
Humahuaca	252	23.12 S	65.21 W
Humaitá, Bra.	248	7.31 S	63.02 W
Humaitá, Para.	252	27.03 S	58.33 W
Humaitá ≐	248	8.16 S	72.44 W
Humansdorp	158	34.02 S	24.46 E
Humansville	194	37.47 N	93.34 W
Humara, Jabal al- ∧	140	16.16 N	30.59 E
Humarock	283	42.08 N	70.41 W
Ḥumaydah	140	14.22 N	22.31 E
Humayingzi	98	41.06 N	116.48 E
Humayun's Tomb ⊥	272a	28.36 N	77.15 E
Humbe	152	16.40 S	14.55 E
Humbe, Serra do ⩘	152	12.13 S	15.25 E
Humbeek	50	50.58 N	4.23 E
Humber ≐, On., Can.	212	43.38 N	79.28 W
Humber ≐, Eng., U.K.	44	53.40 N	0.10 W
Humber, Mouth of the ≐ 1	44	53.32 N	0.08 E
Humber Bay ⊂	275b	43.38 N	79.29 W
Humber Bridge ◂ 5	44	53.42 N	0.27 W
Humberside □ 6	44	53.55 N	0.40 W
Humberston	44	53.32 N	0.02 W
Humberto de Campos	250	2.37 S	43.27 W
Humber Valley Park ♦	275b	43.39 N	79.30 W
Humbird	190	44.31 N	90.53 W
Humble, Dan.	41	54.50 N	10.42 E
Humble, Tx., U.S.	222	29.59 N	95.15 W
Humboldt, Sk., Can.	184	52.12 N	105.07 W
Humboldt, Az., U.S.	200	34.30 N	112.14 W
Humboldt, Il., U.S.	194	39.36 N	88.19 W
Humboldt, Ia., U.S.	198	42.43 N	94.12 W
Humboldt, Ks., U.S.	198	37.48 N	95.26 W
Humboldt, Ne., U.S.	198	40.09 N	95.56 W
Humboldt, S.D., U.S.	198	43.38 N	97.04 W
Humboldt, Tn., U.S.	194	35.49 N	88.54 W
Humboldt ∧	175f	21.53 S	166.25 E
Humboldt ≐	204	40.02 N	118.31 W
Humboldt, North Fork ≐	204	40.56 N	115.32 W
Humboldt, Planetario ⊍	286c	10.30 N	66.50 W
Humboldt, South Fork ≐	204	40.47 N	115.53 W
Humboldt Bay ⊂	204	40.47 N	124.11 W
Humboldt Lake ⊜	204	39.58 N	118.38 W
Humboldt Mountains ⩘	9	71.45 S	11.30 E
Humboldt Park ♦	278	41.54 N	87.42 W
Humboldt Redwoods State Park ♦	204	40.19 N	124.00 W
Humboldt Salt Marsh ⁝	204	39.50 N	117.55 W
Hume, Ca., U.S.	204	36.47 N	118.55 W
Hume, N.Y., U.S.	210	42.29 N	78.08 W
Hume, Lake ⊜ 1	166	36.06 S	147.05 E
Hume and Hovell Lookout ♦	169	37.15 S	144.59 E
Humeburn	166	27.24 S	145.14 E
Hūmedān	128	25.24 N	59.39 E
Hu Men ⊂ 1	100	22.44 N	113.40 E
Humenné	30	48.56 N	21.55 E
Húmera	266a	40.26 N	3.47 W
Humeston	190	40.51 N	93.29 W
Humlā Karṇālī ≐	124	29.38 N	81.52 E
Humlebæk	41	55.58 N	12.33 E
Hummelo	52	52.00 N	6.14 E
Hummelstown	208	40.16 N	76.43 W
Hummels Wharf	210	40.49 N	76.50 W
Hümmling ⩘	52	52.52 N	7.31 E
Humos, Isla I	254	45.38 S	73.59 W
Humpata	152	15.02 S	13.24 E
Hümpfershausen	56	50.40 N	10.13 E
Humphrey, Ar., U.S.	194	34.25 N	91.42 W
Humphrey, Ne., U.S.	198	41.41 N	97.29 W
Humphreys, Mount ∧	204	37.17 N	118.40 W
Humphreys Peak ∧	200	35.20 N	111.40 W
Humpolec	30	49.32 N	15.22 E
Humppila	26	60.56 N	23.22 E
Humptulips	224	47.13 N	123.57 W
Humptulips ≐	224	47.03 N	124.03 W
Humptulips, East Fork ≐	224	47.15 N	123.54 W
Humptulips, West Fork ≐	224	47.15 N	123.54 W
Humptulips Ridge ∧	224	47.20 N	123.45 W
Humpty Doo	164	12.38 S	131.15 E
Humula	171b	35.29 S	147.45 E
Humuya ≐	236	15.01 N	87.44 W
Hūn	146	29.07 N	15.56 E
Hun ≐, Zhg.	98	41.01 N	122.27 E
Hun ≐, Zhg.	98	40.52 N	125.42 E
Hunabasi → Funabashi	94	35.42 N	139.59 E
Húnaflói ⊂	24a	65.50 N	20.50 W
Hunan □ 4	102	28.00 N	111.00 E
Ḥunayshāt, Ghurd al- • 8	142	30.07 N	29.47 E
Hunchun	98	42.54 N	130.22 E
Huncoat	262	53.46 N	2.20 W
Hundeluft	54	51.58 N	12.20 E
Hundested	41	55.58 N	11.52 E
Hundewāli	123	31.55 N	72.38 E
Hundorp	26	61.33 N	9.54 E
Hundred	188	39.41 N	80.27 W
Hundred End	262	53.42 N	2.53 W
Hundslund	41	55.55 N	10.04 E
Hundstein ∧	64	47.20 N	12.54 E
Hundwil	58	47.22 N	9.19 E
Hunedoara	38	45.45 N	22.54 E
Hunedoara □ 6	38	45.45 N	23.00 E
Hünfeld	56	50.40 N	9.46 E
Hungary (Magyarország) □ 1, Europe	22	47.00 N	20.00 E
Hungary (Magyarország) □ 1, Europe	30	47.00 N	20.00 E
Hungchiang → Hongjiang	102	27.07 N	109.56 E
Hungen	56	50.28 N	8.54 E
Hungerford, Austl.	166	29.00 S	144.25 E
Hungerford, Eng., U.K.	42	51.26 N	1.30 W
Hungerford, Tx., U.S.	222	29.24 N	96.05 W
Hŭngho-ri	98	37.14 N	127.44 E
Hŭngin-ni	98	39.03 N	126.26 E
Hung Long	269c	10.40 N	106.39 E
Hungmao	100	24.55 N	120.58 E
Hŭngnam	98	39.50 N	127.38 E
Hungría → Hungary □ 1	30	47.00 N	20.00 E
Hungry Hill ∧	48	51.41 N	9.48 W
Hungry Horse	202	48.23 N	114.03 W
Hungry Horse Dam ◂ 6	202	48.14 N	114.04 W
Hungry Horse Reservoir ⊜ 1	202	48.15 N	113.50 W
Hungry Lake ⊜	212	44.48 N	76.53 W
Hungry Law ∧ 2	44	55.21 N	2.24 W
Hung Yen	110	20.39 N	106.04 E
Hunhe	104	41.43 N	123.22 E
Huningue	58	47.36 N	7.35 E
Hunish, Rubha ›	46	57.41 N	6.21 W
Huni Valley	150	5.28 N	1.55 W
Hunjiang (Badaojiang)	98	41.56 N	126.29 E
Hunker	279b	40.12 N	79.38 W
Ḥunkurāb, Ra's ›	140	24.34 N	35.10 E
Hunlen Falls ∟	182	52.17 N	125.47 W
Hunmanby	44	54.10 N	0.19 W
Hunn ⊜	40	58.51 N	15.57 E
Hunneberg ∧ 2	26	58.20 N	12.27 E
Hunnebostrand	26	58.27 N	11.18 E
Hunnewell	219	39.40 N	91.51 W
Hunnewell Lake ⊜	219	39.42 N	91.52 W
Hunsberge ⩘	156	27.45 S	17.12 E
Hunseby	41	54.48 N	11.32 E
Hunspach	56	48.57 N	7.57 E
Hunsrück ⩘	56	49.50 N	6.40 E
Hunstanton	42	52.57 N	0.30 E
Hunstein Range ⩘	164	4.30 S	142.40 E
Hunsūr	122	12.18 N	76.17 E
Hunswinkel	263	51.05 N	7.48 E
Hunt □ 6	222	33.03 N	96.05 W
Hunte ≐	52	53.15 N	8.29 E
Hunter, N.Y., U.S.	210	42.13 N	74.13 W
Hunter, N.D., U.S.	198	47.11 N	97.13 W
Hunter ≐, Austl.	170	32.50 S	151.42 E
Hunter ≐, N.Z.	172	44.22 S	169.25 E
Hunter, Île I	14	22.24 S	172.03 E
Hunter, Mount ∧	180	62.57 N	151.05 W
Hunter, Port ⊂	170	32.55 S	151.48 E
Hunterdon □ 6	208	40.31 N	74.52 W
Hunter Island I, Austl.	166	40.32 S	144.45 E
Hunter Island I, B.C., Can.	182	51.55 N	128.05 W
Hunter Island I, N.Y., U.S.	276	40.53 N	73.47 W
Hunter Mountain ∧	210	42.10 N	74.14 W
Hunter Mountains ⩘	172	45.42 S	167.25 E
Hunter Range ⩘	170	32.50 S	150.50 E
Hunter Ridge ✣ 3	14	21.30 S	174.30 E
Hunter River	186	46.21 N	63.21 W
Hunters	182	48.07 N	118.12 W
Hunters Bay ⊂	110	19.57 N	93.19 E
Hunters Creek Village	222	29.46 N	95.24 W
Huntersfield Mountain ∧	210	42.21 N	74.21 W
Hunters Hill	274a	33.50 S	151.09 E
Hunters Point ›	282	37.43 N	122.22 W
Hunter's Quay	46	55.58 N	4.55 W
Hunters Road	154	19.09 S	29.48 E
Hunters Run	208	40.05 N	77.11 W
Huntersville	192	35.25 N	80.50 W
Huntertown	216	41.13 N	85.10 W
Hunterville	172	39.56 S	175.34 E
Hunter Wash V	200	36.17 N	108.34 W
Huntingburg	194	38.17 N	86.57 W
Huntingdon, B.C., Can.	224	49.00 N	122.16 W
Huntingdon, P.Q., Can.	206	45.05 N	74.10 W
Huntingdon, Eng., U.K.	42	52.20 N	0.12 W
Huntingdon, Pa., U.S.	214	40.29 N	78.00 W
Huntingdon, Tn., U.S.	194	36.00 N	88.25 W
Huntingdon □ 6, P.Q., Can.	206	45.05 N	74.00 W
Huntingdon □ 6, Pa., U.S.	214	40.29 N	78.01 W
Huntingdon Valley	285	40.07 N	75.03 W
Huntingdon Valley Creek ≐	285	40.07 N	75.04 W
Hunting Island State Park ♦	192	32.20 N	80.30 W
Hunting Ridge	284c	38.55 N	77.12 W
Huntington, Eng., U.K.	44	54.01 N	1.04 W
Huntington, In., U.S.	216	40.52 N	85.29 W
Huntington, Ma., U.S.	207	42.14 N	72.52 W
Huntington, N.Y., U.S.	210	40.51 N	73.25 W
Huntington, Or., U.S.	202	44.21 N	117.15 W
Huntington, Tx., U.S.	222	31.16 N	94.34 W
Huntington, Ut,. U.S.	200	39.19 N	110.57 W
Huntington, Va., U.S.	284c	38.48 N	77.15 W
Huntington, W.V., U.S.	188	38.25 N	82.26 W
Huntington □ 6	216	40.53 N	85.30 W
Huntington Bay	276	40.53 N	73.24 W
Huntington Bay ⊂	276	40.55 N	73.25 W
Huntington Beach, Ca., U.S.	228	33.39 N	117.59 W
Huntington Beach, N.Y., U.S.	276	40.54 N	73.23 W
Huntington Creek ≐, Nv., U.S.	204	40.37 N	115.43 W
Huntington Creek ≐, Pa., U.S.	210	41.06 N	76.22 W
Huntington Creek ≐, Ut,. U.S.	200	39.09 N	110.55 W
Huntington Harbor ⊂	276	40.54 N	73.26 W
Huntington Lake	226	37.15 N	119.14 W
Huntington Lake ⊜ 1, Ca., U.S.	226	37.14 N	119.12 W
Huntington Lake ⊜ 1, In., U.S.	216	40.50 N	85.25 W
Huntington Library ⊍ 3	280	34.08 N	118.07 W
Huntington Mills	210	41.11 N	76.14 W
Huntington Park	228	33.58 N	118.13 W
Huntington Park ♦	279a	41.29 N	81.56 W
Huntington Station	210	40.51 N	73.24 W
Huntington Woods	281	42.28 N	83.10 W
Huntingtown	208	38.36 N	76.36 W
Hunting Valley	279a	41.31 N	81.23 W
Huntingville	206	45.20 N	71.51 W
Huntland	194	35.03 N	86.16 W
Huntley, Il., U.S.	216	42.10 N	88.25 W
Huntley, Mt., U.S.	202	45.53 N	108.18 W
Huntly, N.Z.	172	37.33 S	175.10 E
Huntly, Scot., U.K.	46	57.27 N	2.47 W
Hunt Mountain ∧	202	44.44 N	107.45 W
Hunton	260	51.13 N	0.28 E
Huntsburg	214	41.32 N	81.03 W
Hunt's Cross ◂ 8	262	53.21 N	2.51 W
Hunts Point	224	47.39 N	122.14 W
Huntsville, On., Can.	212	45.20 N	79.13 W
Huntsville, Al., U.S.	194	34.43 N	86.35 W
Huntsville, Ar., U.S.	194	36.05 N	93.44 W
Huntsville, Il., U.S.	219	40.11 N	90.52 W
Huntsville, In., U.S.	218	40.00 N	85.43 W
Huntsville, Mo., U.S.	194	39.26 N	92.33 W
Huntsville, Oh., U.S.	216	40.26 N	83.49 W
Huntsville, Tn., U.S.	192	36.24 N	84.29 W
Huntsville, Tx., U.S.	222	30.43 N	95.33 W
Huntsville, Ut,. U.S.	200	41.15 N	111.46 W
Huntsville State Park ♦	222	30.37 N	95.32 W
Hunū, Kathīb al- • 8	142	30.37 N	32.49 E
Hunucmá	232	21.01 N	89.52 W
Hunut	130	40.39 N	41.09 E
Hünxe	52	51.38 N	6.46 E
Hünxerwald ♦	263	51.40 N	6.50 E
Hunyani ≐	154	15.37 S	30.39 E
Hunyuan	98	39.48 N	113.41 E
Hun-yung	98	42.53 N	130.12 E
Hunza □ 9	123	36.30 N	75.00 E
Hunza ≐	123	35.55 N	74.22 E
Huocheng	86	44.12 N	80.26 E
Huoergeluo	89	45.35 N	120.56 E
Huokou	100	26.28 N	119.16 E
Huolong	106	32.04 N	121.17 E
Huolongmen	89	49.48 N	125.47 E
Huolu	98	38.05 N	114.18 E
Huong Hoa	110	16.37 N	106.45 E
Huong Khe	110	18.13 N	105.41 E
Huong Thuy	110	16.25 N	107.40 E
Huon Gulf ⊂	164	7.10 S	147.25 E
Huon Peninsula › 1	164	6.25 S	147.25 E
Huonville	166	43.01 S	147.02 E
Huoqiu	100	32.20 N	116.16 E
Huorili	89	49.00 N	124.41 E
Huoshan	100	31.25 N	116.20 E
Huo Shan ∧	100	31.06 N	116.12 E
Huoshaoliao	100	25.00 N	121.45 E
Huotong	100	26.53 N	119.25 E
Huotong ≐	100	26.50 N	119.32 E
Huotuolaihuduke	102	40.19 N	104.18 E
Huoxian, Zhg.	102	36.37 N	111.40 E
Huoxian, Zhg.	105	39.46 N	116.46 E
Huoyan	100	33.42 N	113.40 E
Hupeh → Hubei □ 4	90	31.00 N	112.00 E
Huqiao	106	31.25 N	119.24 E
Hura	126	23.18 N	86.39 E
Hūrand	84	38.51 N	47.22 E
Hurāsāgar ≐	126	24.04 N	89.40 E
Ḥuraydīn, Wādī V	132	30.59 N	33.53 E
Ḥuraymilā	128	25.08 N	46.08 E
Hūrayn	142	30.39 N	31.08 E
Hurd, Cape ›	190	45.13 N	81.44 W
Hurdalssjøen ⊜	26	60.20 N	11.05 E
Hurdiyo	144	10.33 N	51.08 E
Hurdland	219	40.09 N	92.18 W
Hurdsfield	262	53.16 N	2.06 W
Hurepoix ◂ 1	261	48.37 N	2.07 E
Hure Qi	98	42.44 N	121.40 E
Hurffville	285	39.46 N	75.07 W
Huri ∧ 2	154	3.41 N	37.51 E
Huriel	32	46.23 N	2.29 E
Hurleg Hu ⊜	102	37.20 N	96.54 E
Hurley, Ms., U.S.	194	30.39 N	88.29 W
Hurley, N.M., U.S.	200	32.41 N	108.07 W
Hurley, N.Y., U.S.	210	41.55 N	74.03 W
Hurley, S.D., U.S.	198	43.16 N	97.05 W
Hurley, Wi., U.S.	190	46.26 N	90.11 W
Hurleyville	210	41.44 N	74.40 W
Hurlford	46	55.36 N	4.28 W
Hurliness	46	58.47 N	3.15 W
Hurlingham	258	34.36 S	58.38 W
Hurlock	208	38.37 N	75.51 W
Hurmāgai	128	28.18 N	64.26 E
Huron, Ca., U.S.	226	36.12 N	120.06 W
Huron, Oh., U.S.	214	41.22 N	82.33 W
Huron, S.D., U.S.	198	44.21 N	98.12 W
Huron □ 6, On., Can.	212	43.45 N	81.10 W
Huron □ 6, Oh., U.S.	214	41.15 N	82.37 W
Huron ≐, Mi., U.S.	216	42.03 N	83.14 W
Huron ≐, Oh., U.S.	214	41.23 N	82.33 W
Huron, East Branch ≐	214	41.17 N	82.38 W
Huron, Lake ⊜	190	44.30 N	82.15 W

	English	Deutsch	Español	Français	Português
≐	River	Fluß	Río	Rivière	Rio
≡	Canal	Kanal	Canal	Canal	Canal
∟	Waterfall, Rapids	Wasserfall, Stromschnellen	Cascada, Rápidos	Chute d'eau, Rapides	Cascata, Rápidos
⊔	Strait	Meeresstraße	Estrecho	Détroit	Estreito
⊂	Bay, Gulf	Bucht, Golf	Bahía, Golfo	Baie, Golfe	Baía, Golfo
⊜	Lake, Lakes	See, Seen	Lago, Lagos	Lac, Lacs	Lago, Lagos
⁝	Swamp	Sumpf	Pantano	Marais	Pântano
⊓	Ice Features, Glacier	Eis- und Gletscherformen	Accidentes Glaciales	Formes glaciaires	Acidentes glaciares
⊤	Other Hydrographic Features	Andere Hydrographische Objekte	Otros Elementos Hidrográficos	Autres données hydrographiques	Outros acidentes hidrográficos

	English	Deutsch	Español	Français	Português
✣	Submarine Features	Untermeerische Objekte	Accidentes Submarinos	Formes de relief sous-marin	Acidentes submarinos
□	Political Unit	Politische Einheit	Unidad Política	Entité politique	Unidade política
⊍	Cultural Institution	Kulturelle Institution	Institución Cultural	Institution culturelle	Instituição cultural
⊥	Historical Site	Historische Stätte	Sitio Histórico	Site historique	Sitio histórico
♦	Recreational Site	Erholungs- und Ferienort	Sitio de Recreo	Centre de loisirs	Area de Lazer
⊠	Airport	Flughafen	Aeropuerto	Aéroport	Aeroporto
■	Military Installation	Militäranlage	Instalación Militar	Installation militaire	Instalação militar
◂	Miscellaneous	Verschiedenes	Misceláneo	Divers	Diversos

Huron, Point ⊁	214	42.34 N	82.47 W
Huron, West Branch ≃	214	41.17 N	82.38 W
Huron Gardens	216	42.38 N	83.20 W
Huron Mountains ⊀²	190	46.50 N	87.55 W
Hurons, Rivière des ≃	206	45.28 N	73.16 W
Hurricane, Ak., U.S.	180	62.59 N	149.38 W
Hurricane, Ut., U.S.	200	37.10 N	113.17 W
Hurricane, W.V., U.S.	188	38.25 N	82.01 W
Hurricane Bayou ≃	222	31.21 N	95.35 W
Hurricane Cliffs ⊀⁴	200	37.20 N	113.10 W
Hurricane Creek ≃, Ar., U.S.	194	34.05 N	92.23 W
Hurricane Creek ≃, Ga., U.S.	192	31.23 N	82.19 W
Hurricane Creek ≃, Il., U.S.	219	38.53 N	89.13 W
Hurricane Lake ☒	198	48.25 N	99.30 W
Hurricane Wash ⣠	200	37.00 N	113.23 W
Hurshi	126	24.17 N	88.28 E
Hursley	42	51.02 N	1.24 W
Hurso	144	9.38 N	41.38 E
Hurst	222	32.49 N	97.10 W
Hurstbourne Tarrant	42	51.17 N	1.23 W
Hurstbridge	169	37.38 S	145.12 E
Hurst Green	260	51.15 N	0.01 E
Hurstpierpoint	42	50.56 N	0.11 W
Hurstville	170	33.58 S	151.06 E
Hurstwood Reservoir ☒¹	262	53.47 N	2.10 W
Hurt	192	37.05 N	79.17 W
Hurtado ≃	252	30.35 S	71.11 W
Hurtaut ≃	50	49.42 N	4.01 E
Hürth	56	50.52 N	6.51 E
Hurtsboro	194	32.14 N	85.24 W
Hurunui ≃	172	42.55 S	173.17 E
Hurup	26	56.45 N	8.25 E
Hurworth-on-Tees	44	54.29 N	1.31 W
Hurzuf	78	44.33 N	34.17 E
Husainābād	124	24.30 N	84.01 E
Husainīwāla	123	30.59 N	74.34 E
Husainpur	124	24.25 N	90.40 E
Husarka	78	47.23 N	36.31 E
Húsavík	24a	66.04 N	17.18 W
Husby-Långhundra	40	59.45 N	18.01 E
Huse → Higashiōsaka	96	34.39 N	135.35 E
Husen ⊕⁸	263	51.33 N	7.36 E
Hushan, Zhg.	89	45.35 N	130.35 E
Hushan, Zhg.	100	28.36 N	118.59 E
Hushan, Zhg.	100	22.09 N	113.10 E
Husheib	140	14.54 N	35.07 E
Hushi	107	28.57 N	105.22 E
Hushiha	98	40.52 N	116.59 E
Hushitai	104	41.57 N	123.30 E
Hushu, Zhg.	106	31.52 N	118.59 E
Hushu, Zhg.	106	30.18 N	120.08 E
Husi	38	46.40 N	28.04 E
Husinec	60	49.03 N	13.58 E
Huskisson	170	35.02 S	150.40 E
Huskvarna	26	57.48 N	14.16 E
Huslia	180	65.42 N	156.25 W
Hussar	182	51.03 N	112.41 W
Hussigny-Godbrange	54	49.29 N	5.52 E
Hustisford	190	43.21 N	88.36 W
Huston ≃	220	25.42 N	81.17 W
Hustontown	214	40.03 N	78.02 W
Hustopeče	61	48.57 N	16.44 E
Husum, Dtsch.	41	54.28 N	9.03 E
Husum, Sve.	26	63.20 N	19.10 E
Husum, Wa., U.S.	224	45.47 N	121.29 W
Husyatyn	78	49.05 N	26.11 E
Hutaimbaru	114	1.34 N	99.44 E
Hutangqiao	106	31.46 N	119.57 E
Hutan Melintang	114	3.53 N	100.56 E
Hutanopan	114	0.41 N	99.42 E
Hutaym, Ḥarrat ⧖⁹	128	26.15 N	40.20 E
Hutberg ⊼²	54	52.09 N	14.33 E
Hutchins	222	32.39 N	96.43 W
Hutchinson, S. Afr.	158	31.30 S	23.09 E
Hutchinson, Ks., U.S.	198	38.03 N	97.55 W
Hutchinson, Mn., U.S.	190	44.53 N	94.22 W
Hutchinson, Pa., U.S.	214	40.13 N	79.44 W
Hutchinson ≃	276	40.52 N	73.50 W
Hutchinson Island I	220	27.25 N	80.17 W
Hutt Mountain ⋀	200	34.47 N	117.22 W
Huti	78	50.08 N	35.21 E
Hutou, Zhg.	100	25.15 N	118.03 E
Hutou, Zhg.	100	26.04 N	118.46 E
Hutou, Zhg.	106	31.37 N	117.03 E
Hutou, Zhg.	106	32.14 N	120.17 E
Houuyqa	98	37.13 N	119.46 E
Hutsonville	194	39.06 N	87.39 W
Hüttau	64	47.25 N	13.18 E
Hütteldorf ⊕⁸	264b	48.12 N	16.16 E
Hüttener Berge ⊼²	41	54.26 N	9.40 E
Hüttenheim ⊕⁸	263	51.22 N	6.43 E
Hüttental	56	50.54 N	8.02 E
Hutte Sauvage, Lac de la ☒	176	56.15 N	64.45 W
Hutthurm	60	48.43 N	13.28 E
Huttig	194	33.02 N	92.10 W
Hütting	60	48.54 N	11.07 E
Hüttlingen	56	48.51 N	10.12 E
Hutton, Eng., U.K.	260	51.38 N	0.22 E
Hutton, Eng., U.K.	262	53.44 N	2.46 W
Hutton, Mount ⋀	166	25.51 S	148.20 E
Hutton Rudby	44	54.27 N	1.17 W
Huttonsville	212	43.38 N	79.48 W
Huttrop ⊕⁸	263	51.27 N	7.03 E
Hüttschlag	64	47.10 N	13.14 E
Huttwil	58	47.07 N	7.51 E
Hutuhi	86	44.08 N	86.38 E
Hutuo ≃	98	38.14 N	116.05 E
Hutwisch ⋀	61	47.28 N	16.13 E
Huu	115b	8.48 S	118.25 E
Huvalu Forest ⬥³	174v	19.03 S	169.51 W
Huveaune ≃	52	43.17 N	5.22 E
Huvudskär I	40	58.57 N	18.34 E
Huwait	100	31.41 N	114.53 E
Huwei	100	23.43 N	120.26 E
Huwun	144	4.23 N	40.08 E
Huwwārah	132	32.09 N	35.15 E
Huxford	194	31.13 N	87.28 W
Huxi	106	26.12 N	114.44 E
Huxian	102	34.09 N	108.32 E
Huxley	182	51.56 N	113.14 W
Huy	56	50.31 N	5.14 E
Huy ⋀	54	51.57 N	10.57 E
Huyangzhen	100	32.25 N	112.45 E
Huyton-with-Roby	262	53.25 N	2.52 W
Huyuesi	106	30.33 N	116.32 E
Hüyük	130	37.57 N	31.37 E
Huyutou	100	26.44 N	119.49 E
Hüzgän	128	31.27 N	48.04 E
Huzhen	100	28.50 N	120.15 E
Huzhou	106	30.52 N	120.06 E
Huzhu	102	36.54 N	101.58 E
Huzhuangtun	104	40.43 N	122.33 E
Huzi	106	29.47 N	112.33 E
Huzi → Fujisawa	94	35.21 N	139.29 E
Hvalsø	26	55.35 N	11.53 E
Hvannadalshnúkur ⋀	24a	64.01 N	16.41 W
Hvar	64	43.10 N	16.45 E
Hvar, Otok I	64	43.09 N	16.45 E
Hvardijs'ke, Ukr.	78	45.07 N	34.01 E
Hvardijs'ke, Ukr.	38	45.49 N	26.42 E
Hvarski Kanal ⬚	64	43.04 N	16.28 E
Hveragerði	24a	64.03 N	21.10 W
Hvide Sande	26	55.59 N	8.07 E
Hvidovre	26	55.39 N	12.29 E
Hvittingfoss	26	59.29 N	10.01 E
Hvizdec'	38	48.40 N	25.08 E
Hvolsvöllur	24a	63.45 N	20.10 W
Hwach'ŏn	98	38.06 N	127.41 E
Hwach'ŏn-chŏsuji ☒¹	98	38.07 N	127.52 E

Hwach'ŏn-ni	98	39.01 N	126.02 E
Hwainan → Huainan	100	32.40 N	117.00 E
Hwaining → Anqing	100	30.31 N	117.02 E
Hwange	154	18.22 S	26.29 E
Hwange National Park ⬥	154	19.00 S	26.35 E
Hwanggong-ni	98	40.03 N	129.27 E
Hwanghae Namdo ◻⁴	98	38.15 N	125.03 E
Hwanghae Pukdo ◻⁴	98	38.30 N	126.25 E
Hwang Ho → Huang ≃	90	37.32 N	118.19 E
Hwangju	98	38.42 N	125.46 E
Hwangshih → Huangshi	100	30.13 N	115.05 E
Hyak	224	47.23 N	121.23 W
Hyakuna	174m	26.08 N	127.48 E
Hyakuri-ga-dake ⋀	94	35.23 N	135.49 E
Hyakuri-kichi, Kōkū-jieitai- ⊹	94	36.11 N	140.25 E
Hyannis, Ma., U.S.	207	41.39 N	70.17 W
Hyannis, Ne., U.S.	198	42.00 N	101.45 W
Hyannis Port	207	41.38 N	70.18 W
Hyattsville	208	38.57 N	76.56 W
Hyattville	202	44.14 N	107.36 W
Hybla Valley	208	38.44 N	77.05 W
Hyco ≃	192	36.44 N	78.45 W
Hyco Lake ☒¹	192	36.30 N	79.05 W
Hydaburg	182	55.12 N	132.49 W
Hyde, N.Z.	172	45.18 S	170.15 E
Hyde, Eng., U.K.	44	53.27 N	2.04 W
Hyde, Pa., U.S.	214	41.00 N	78.28 W
Hyden, Austl.	162	32.27 S	118.53 E
Hyden, Ky., U.S.	192	37.10 N	83.22 W
Hyde Park, Guy.	246	6.30 N	58.16 W
Hyde Park, N.Y., U.S.	210	41.47 N	73.56 W
Hyde Park, Vt., U.S.	188	44.35 N	72.37 W
Hyde Park ⊕⁸, Il., U.S.	278	41.48 N	87.36 W
Hyde Park ⊕⁸, Ma., U.S.	283	42.15 N	71.08 W
Hyde Park ⊕, Austl.	274a	33.53 S	151.13 E
Hyde Park ⬥, Eng., U.K.	260	51.30 N	0.10 W
Hyde Park ⬥, N.Y., U.S.	284a	43.06 N	79.01 W
Hyder	182	55.55 N	130.01 W
Hyderābād, India	122	17.23 N	78.29 E
Hyderābād, Pāk.	120	25.22 N	68.22 E
Hydetown	214	41.40 N	79.44 W
Hydra → Idhra I	38	37.20 N	23.32 E
Hydraulic	182	52.36 N	121.42 W
Hydro	196	35.21 N	98.22 W
Hydrographers Passage ⨇	166	20.45 S	150.15 E
Hyen ⊕	40	60.36 N	16.12 E
Hyères	62	43.07 N	6.07 E
Hyères, Îles d' II	62	43.00 N	6.20 E
Hyères-Plage	62	43.06 N	6.10 E
Hyesan	98	41.23 N	128.12 E
Hyland ≃	182	59.50 N	128.10 W
Hylestad	26	59.05 N	7.32 E
Hyllekrog I	41	54.36 N	11.30 E
Hyllinge, Dan.	41	55.16 N	11.37 E
Hyllinge, Sve.	41	56.06 N	12.51 E
Hyllstofta	41	56.08 N	13.16 E
Hyltebruk	26	57.00 N	13.14 E
Hymaya ≃	232	24.31 N	107.41 W
Hymera	194	39.11 N	87.18 W
Hyndburn ⊕⁸	262	53.45 N	2.23 W
Hyndman	188	39.49 N	78.43 W
Hyndman Peak ⋀	202	43.45 N	114.08 W
Hynish Bay c	46	56.28 N	6.50 W
Hyōgo ◻⁵	96	35.00 N	135.00 E
Hyōgo ⊕⁸	270	34.39 N	135.10 E
Hyŏno-ni	98	37.57 N	128.20 E
Hyŏno-sen ⋀	96	35.21 N	134.31 E
Hyŏno-sen– Ushiroyama– Nagisan-kokutei-kōen ⬥	96	35.15 N	134.30 E
Hyōpch'ŏn	98	35.33 N	128.08 E
Hyrum	200	41.38 N	111.51 W
Hyrynsalmi	26	64.40 N	28.32 E
Hysham	202	46.17 N	107.14 W
Hythe, Ab., Can.	182	55.20 N	119.33 W
Hythe, Eng., U.K.	42	51.05 N	1.05 E
Hythe, Eng., U.K.	42	50.51 N	1.24 W
Hythe End	260	51.27 N	0.32 W
Hyūga	92	32.25 N	131.38 E
Hyūga-nada ⬚²	92	32.00 N	131.35 E
Hyvinge → Hyvinkää	26	60.38 N	24.52 E
Hyvinkää	26	60.38 N	24.52 E

I

Iacanga	255	21.54 S	49.01 W
Iaciara	255	14.09 S	46.40 W
Iaco (Yaco) ≃	248	9.03 S	68.34 W
Iaçu	255	12.45 S	40.13 W
Iaeger	192	37.27 N	81.48 W
Iago	222	29.17 N	95.02 E
Iakora	157b	23.06 S	46.40 E
Ialomiţa ◻⁶	38	44.40 N	27.20 E
Ialomiţa ≃	38	44.42 N	27.51 E
Ialomiţei, Balta ☒	38	44.30 N	28.00 E
Ialomiţei, Lunca ⬚	38	45.41 N	28.35 E
Ianaivo ≃	192	30.38 N	64.14 W
Ianakafy	157b	22.56 S	46.54 E
Iango	157b	23.21 S	45.28 E
Iango, Monte ⋀	146	9.07 N	18.11 E
Iapu	255	19.26 S	42.13 W
Iaşi	38	46.27 N	27.35 E
Iaşi ◻⁶	38	47.10 N	27.35 E
Iato ≃	70	37.58 N	13.02 E
Iatt, Lake ☒¹	246	31.35 N	92.40 W
Iauaretê	246	0.37 N	69.12 W
Ib ≃	120	21.36 N	83.48 E
Iba, Pil.	116	15.20 N	119.58 E
'Ibādah, Wādī V	144	3.05 S	37.38 E
Ibadan	150	7.17 N	3.30 E
Ibagué	246	4.27 N	75.14 W
Ibaiti	255	23.50 S	50.10 W
Ibajay	116	11.49 N	122.10 E
Ibaka	152	4.16 S	23.12 E
Ibambi	152	2.22 N	27.37 E
Ibanda	152	0.08 S	30.29 E
Ibănești	38	46.04 N	26.21 E
Ibanga, Laguna de c	116	15.53 N	84.52 E
Ibapah	200	39.49 N	113.55 W
Ibapah Peak ⋀	200	39.49 N	113.55 W
Ibar ≃	38	43.44 N	20.45 E
Ibaraki	96	34.49 N	135.34 E
Ibaraki ◻⁵	96	36.17 N	140.26 E
Ibaraki, Nihon	96	36.17 N	140.26 E
Ibaraki ◻⁵	94	36.15 N	140.26 E
Ibarra	246	0.21 N	78.07 W
Ibarreta	252	25.13 S	59.51 W
Ibba ≃	144	7.09 N	28.41 E
Ibbenbüren	52	52.16 N	7.43 E
Ibeke Gembo	152	1.24 S	18.51 E
Ibembo	152	2.38 S	23.37 E
Ibenga ≃	152	2.20 N	18.08 E
Iberá, Esteros del ⬚	252	28.05 S	57.05 W

Iberia, Mo., U.S.	194	38.05 N	92.17 W
Iberia, Oh., U.S.	214	40.40 N	82.51 W
Ibérica, Península ⊁¹	10	40.00 N	5.00 W
Ibérico, Sistema ⊀	34	41.00 N	2.30 W
Iberlioga	256	21.25 S	43.58 W
Iberville	206	45.18 N	73.14 W
Iberville ◻⁶	206	45.15 N	73.10 W
Ibi	150	8.12 N	9.45 E
Ibi ≃	94	35.03 N	136.42 E
Ibiá	255	19.29 S	46.32 W
Ibiapina	250	3.55 S	40.54 W
Ibicaraí	255	14.51 S	39.36 W
Ibicuí	255	14.51 S	39.59 W
Ibicuí ≃	256	29.25 S	56.47 W
Ibicuicito, Arroyo ≃	258	33.49 S	58.49 W
Ibicuy	258	33.44 S	59.10 W
Ibicuy ≃¹	258	33.48 S	59.10 W
Ibigawa	94	35.29 N	136.34 E
Ibipira	250	6.31 S	44.38 W
Ibiquera	255	12.38 S	40.57 W
Ibiraci	255	20.28 S	47.08 W
Ibiraçu	255	19.50 S	40.22 W
Ibirama	252	27.04 S	49.31 W
Ibirapuã	255	17.39 S	40.07 W
Ibirapuera ⊕⁸	287b	23.37 S	46.40 W
Ibirapuera, Parque ⬥	287b	23.35 S	46.39 W
Ibirapuitã ≃	252	29.22 S	55.57 W
Ibirataia	255	14.04 S	39.38 W
Ibiri	154	4.56 S	32.33 E
Ibirubá	255	28.38 S	53.06 W
Ibitiara	255	12.39 S	42.13 W
Ibitinga	255	21.45 S	48.49 W
Ibitiúra De Minas	256	22.04 S	46.26 W
Ibiúna	255	23.39 S	47.13 W
Ibiza → Eivissa I	34	39.00 N	1.25 E
Ibiei, Monti ⊀	70	37.10 N	14.50 E
Ibnahs	142	30.34 N	31.07 E
Ibn Hāni', Ra's ⊁	130	35.35 N	35.43 E
Ibn Sarrār, Bi'r ⧖⁴	144	19.30 N	42.41 E
Ibo	154	12.20 S	40.35 E
Ibo ≃	96	34.46 N	134.35 E
Iboko	154	2.38 S	32.40 E
Ibonma	164	3.28 S	133.28 E
Ibor ≃	34	39.49 N	5.10 W
Iboteirama	255	12.11 S	43.13 W
Iboundji, Mont ⋀	152	1.08 S	11.48 E
Ibrah, Wādī V	140	10.36 N	24.58 E
Ibrāhīmīyah, Qanāt al- ⬚	142	29.10 N	31.10 E
Ibresi	80	55.18 N	47.03 E
I'brï	128	23.14 N	56.30 E
Ibriktepe	130	41.00 N	26.30 E
Ibshān	142	31.10 N	31.10 E
Ibshawāy	142	29.22 N	30.41 E
Ibu	174m	26.45 N	128.19 E
Ibuki	94	35.24 N	136.23 E
Ibuki-jima I	96	34.08 N	133.32 E
Ibuki-sanchi ⊀	94	35.35 N	136.18 E
Ibuki-yama ⋀	94	35.25 N	136.24 E
Ibusuki	92	31.16 N	130.39 E
Ibwe Munyama	154	16.09 S	28.34 E
Ibychen, gora ⋀	88	51.36 N	109.45 E
Ica	248	14.04 S	75.42 W
Ica ≃⁵	214	14.20 S	75.30 W
Iça ≃, Lat.	76	56.52 N	26.59 E
Iça ≃, Perú	248	14.54 S	75.34 W
Iça ≃, Ross.	86	55.30 N	77.13 E
Içá (Putumayo) ≃, S.A.	246	3.07 S	67.58 W
Icabarú ≃	246	4.45 N	62.15 W
Icacos Point ⊁	241r	10.03 N	61.56 W
Icadambanauan I			
Icamaquã ≃	252	28.34 S	56.00 W
Icamole	196	25.55 N	100.43 W
Içana	246	0.21 N	67.19 W
Içana (Isana) ≃	246	0.26 N	67.19 W
Icaño, Arg.	252	28.55 S	65.19 W
Icaño, Arg.	252	28.41 S	62.54 W
Icatu	250	2.46 S	44.04 W
Iceberg Pass)(	200	40.25 N	105.45 W
Ice House Reservoir ☒¹	226	38.49 N	120.23 W
İçel (Mersin)	130	36.48 N	34.38 E
İçel ◻⁴	130	36.45 N	34.00 E
Iceland (Ísland) ◻¹	22	65.00 N	18.00 W
Iceland (Ísland) ◻¹, Europe	22	65.00 N	18.00 W
Iceland Basin ⊹¹	10	59.00 N	23.00 W
Icém	255	20.21 S	49.12 W
Ice Mountain ⋀	182	56.25 N	123.19 W
Icera	88	58.32 N	109.47 E
Ichaikaronji	122	16.42 N	74.28 E
Ichāmati ≃, Asia	126	22.35 N	88.57 E
Ichāmati ≃, Bngl.	126	24.00 N	89.15 E
Ichang → Yichang	100	30.42 N	111.17 E
Ichawaynochaway Creek ≃	192	31.10 N	84.28 W
Ich Bajan Ajrag uul ⋀	88	47.55 N	95.02 E
Ichbulag	96	45.21 N	113.10 E
Ich Buural uul ⋀	88	48.00 N	94.30 E
Ichchāpuram	122	19.07 N	84.42 E
Ichenberg ⬚	58	48.22 N	10.18 E
Ichenhausen	58	48.22 N	10.18 E
Ichenheim	58	48.26 N	7.49 E
Ichhāwar	124	22.50 N	88.24 E
Ichhri ≃	130	34.46 N	134.41 E
Ichi ≃	96	34.46 N	134.41 E
Ichijima	96	34.05 N	134.17 E
Ichikai	94	36.32 N	140.05 E
Ichikawa, Nihon	94	35.44 N	139.55 E
Ichikawa, Nihon	96	34.59 N	134.37 E
Ichikawa-daimon	94	35.34 N	138.30 E
Ichinohe	90	40.13 N	141.17 E
Ichinomiya, Nihon	94	35.18 N	136.48 E
Ichinomiya, Nihon	96	35.23 N	138.41 E
Ichinomiya, Nihon	94	35.39 N	138.41 E
Ichinoseki	90	38.55 N	141.08 E
Ichoa ≃	248	15.45 S	65.15 W
Ich'ŏn, C.M.I.K.	98	38.30 N	126.50 E
Ich'ŏn, Taehan	98	37.17 N	127.27 E
Ich Ovoo uul ⋀	90	44.30 N	95.00 E
Ichtegem	54	51.06 N	3.00 E
Ichtershausen	54	50.52 N	10.58 E
Ichu → Yichun	100	27.48 N	114.23 E
Ichun ≃	90	48.33 N	128.56 E

Icó	250	6.24 S	38.51 W
Icoca	152	6.11 S	16.19 E
Iconha	255	20.48 S	40.48 W
Icy Bay c	180	60.00 N	141.15 W
Icy Cape ⊁	180	70.20 N	161.52 W
Icy Strait ⧉	180	58.18 N	135.30 W
Ida	216	41.54 N	83.34 W
Ida, Mount ⋀, Austl.	162	29.14 S	120.25 E
Ida, Mount ⋀, Jam.	241q	17.58 N	77.43 W
Idabel	194	33.53 N	94.49 W
Idaga Hamus	144	14.12 N	39.48 E
Ida Grove	198	42.20 N	95.28 W
Idah	150	7.07 N	6.43 E
Idaho ◻³, U.S.	178	45.00 N	115.00 W
Idaho ◻³, U.S.	202	45.00 N	115.00 W
Idaho City	202	43.49 N	115.50 W
Idaho Falls	202	43.28 N	112.02 W
Idaho National Engineering Laboratory ⬥³	202	43.40 N	112.45 W
Idaho Springs	200	39.44 N	105.00 W
Idalou	196	33.39 N	101.40 W
Idanha-a-Nova	34	39.55 N	7.14 W
Idāppādi	122	11.35 N	77.51 E
Idar	120	23.50 N	73.00 E
Idar-Oberstein	56	49.42 N	7.19 E
Idarwald ⊕³	56	49.49 N	7.12 E
Idaville, In., U.S.	216	40.45 N	86.38 W
Idaville, Or., U.S.	224	45.30 N	123.51 W
Iddo ⊕⁸	273a	6.28 N	3.23 E
Ide	96	34.47 N	135.49 E
Idel'	24	64.08 N	34.14 E
Idelès	148	23.58 N	5.53 E
Idemba	152	2.38 S	11.38 E
Iden	54	52.46 N	11.55 E
Ider	88	48.13 N	97.23 E
Iderijn ≃	88	48.16 N	100.41 E
Idermeg	88	47.40 N	111.05 E
Idfīnā	142	31.18 N	30.31 E
Idfū	140	24.58 N	32.52 E
Idhi Óros ⋀	38	35.18 N	24.43 E
Idhra	38	37.20 N	23.29 E
Idhra (Hydra) I	38	37.20 N	23.32 E
Idice ≃	114	4.57 N	97.46 E
Idi-cut	114	4.59 N	97.42 E
Ididde	144	5.53 N	43.36 E
Idimu	273a	6.35 N	3.17 E
Idiofa	152	5.02 S	19.36 E
Iditarod ≃	180	62.02 N	158.58 W
Idjwi, Île I	154	2.09 S	29.04 E
Idlewild	192	37.05 N	83.16 W
Idku	142	31.18 N	30.18 E
Idkū, Buhayrat ☒	142	31.16 N	30.17 E
Idlib	130	35.55 N	36.38 E
Idlib ◻⁴	130	35.50 N	36.40 E
Idmön	142	29.20 N	30.41 E
Idnah	132	31.34 N	34.59 E
Idodi	154	7.47 S	35.11 E
Idomogu	273a	6.43 N	3.30 E
Idoukâl-n-Taghès ⋀	150	17.43 N	8.45 E
Idracowra	162	25.00 S	133.47 E
Idre	26	61.52 N	12.43 E
Idrica	76	56.20 N	28.07 E
Idrigill Point ⊁	46	57.20 N	6.35 W
Idrija	64	46.00 N	14.01 E
Idrijca ≃	64	46.09 N	13.45 E
Idrinskoje	84	54.21 N	92.07 E
Idro	64	45.44 N	10.29 E
Idro, Lago d' ☒	64	45.47 N	10.30 E
Idroscalo ⬥	266b	45.28 N	9.18 E
Idstein	56	50.13 N	8.16 E
Idutywa	158	32.02 S	28.16 E
Idylwild	204	33.45 N	116.43 W
Idylwood	284c	38.54 N	77.12 W
Idževan	84	40.53 N	45.07 E
Ie	174m	26.42 N	127.48 E
Iecava	76	56.36 N	24.12 E
Ielsi	66	41.30 N	14.48 E
Ienne	66	41.53 N	13.10 E
Iepê	255	22.40 S	51.05 W
Ieper (Ypres)	50	50.51 N	2.53 E
Ierápetra	38	35.00 N	25.45 E
Ieriki	76	57.16 N	25.04 E
Ierzu	71	39.47 N	9.31 E
Ieshima	96	34.40 N	134.32 E
Ie-shima I	174m	26.43 N	127.47 E
Iešjavri ☒	26	69.41 N	24.39 E
Iesolo	64	45.32 N	12.38 E
Ie-suidō ⧉	174m	26.42 N	127.51 E
If, Château d' ⌐	62	43.17 N	5.19 E
Ifakara	154	8.08 S	36.41 E
Ifa 'adane	273a	6.30 S	46.32 E
Ifalik I¹	157b	7.15 N	144.27 E
Ifanadiana	157b	21.17 S	47.38 E
Ife	150	7.30 N	4.30 E
Iferouâne	150	19.04 N	8.24 E
Iferten → Yverdon	58	46.47 N	6.39 E
Iffezheim	58	48.49 N	8.08 E
Ifni ◻⁴	148	29.15 N	10.00 W
Ifôghas, Adrar des ⊼	150	20.00 N	2.00 E
Ifon	150	6.48 N	5.45 E
Ifould Lake ☒	162	30.53 S	132.09 E
Ifrane	148	33.32 N	5.06 W
Ifrane	148	33.15 N	5.09 W
Ifta	156	51.04 N	10.11 E
Ifugao ◻⁴	116	17.00 N	121.15 E
Iga ≃	94	34.45 N	136.01 E
Igalula, Tan.	154	5.14 S	33.00 E
Igalula, Tan.	154	5.38 S	32.38 E
Igan ≃	112	2.49 N	111.43 E
Iganga	154	0.37 N	33.29 E
Iganmu ⊕⁸	273a	6.29 N	3.22 E
Iganna	150	8.00 N	3.11 E
Igara Paraná ≃	246	1.54 S	72.55 W
Igarapava	255	20.02 S	47.47 W
Igarapé	256	20.04 S	44.18 W
Igarapé Grande	250	4.38 S	44.51 W
Igarapé-Mirí	250	1.59 S	48.57 W
Igarapé-Açu	250	1.07 S	47.37 W
Igari ≃	154	9.36 S	32.24 E
Igarka	84	67.28 N	86.34 E
Igarra	150	7.17 N	6.08 E
Igatimi	252	24.05 S	55.30 W
Igatpuri	122	19.42 N	73.33 E
Igbetti	150	8.44 N	4.07 E
Igbo-Ora	150	7.26 N	3.17 E
Igboho	150	8.32 N	3.45 E
Igbor	150	7.26 N	8.59 E
Iğdır	130	39.55 N	44.02 E
Igdy	128	39.54 N	56.54 E
Igel Marina ⬥	66	44.08 N	12.29 E
Igelfors	40	58.51 N	15.32 E
Iggesund	26	61.39 N	17.05 E
Igersheim	58	49.34 N	9.46 E
Iggesund	60	48.44 N	13.08 E
Iggesund	181	61.38 N	131.04 W
Igharghar, Oued V, Afr.	148	20.25 N	6.10 E

Igharghar, Oued V, Alg.	148	28.03 N	6.15 E
Ightham	260	51.17 N	0.17 E
Ightham Mote ⊥	260	51.15 N	0.16 E
Igikpak, Mount ⋀	180	67.25 N	154.58 W
Igirma	88	56.59 N	103.37 E
Igiugig	180	59.20 N	155.55 W
Iglau → Jihlava	30	49.24 N	15.36 E
Iglesia	252	30.24 S	69.13 W
Iglesias	71	39.19 N	8.32 E
Iglesiente ⊕¹	71	39.18 N	8.40 E
Igli	148	30.25 N	2.12 W
Iglino	86	54.50 N	56.26 E
Igloolik	176	69.24 N	81.49 W
Igls	64	47.14 N	11.25 E
Ignacio, Ca., U.S.	226	38.05 N	122.32 W
Ignacio, Co., U.S.	200	37.06 N	107.37 W
Ignacio de la Llave	234	18.43 N	95.59 W
Ignacio Zaragoza, Méx.	232	29.35 N	107.30 W
Ignacio Zaragoza, Méx.	234	23.15 N	98.50 W
Ignacio Zaragoza, Méx.	234	23.15 N	98.50 W
Ignalina	76	55.21 N	26.10 E
Ignatei	38	47.41 N	28.40 E
Ignatjevcy	88	57.32 N	51.39 E
Ignatovka	80	53.57 N	47.38 E
Ignatovo	82	56.10 N	37.32 E
Igneada	130	41.52 N	27.58 E
Iğneada Burnu ⊁	130	41.54 N	28.03 E
Igney	58	48.17 N	6.24 E
Ignon ≃	58	47.31 N	5.10 E
Igny	261	48.45 N	2.14 E
Igodovo	80	58.01 N	42.21 E
Igombe ≃	154	4.38 S	31.40 E
Igoumenitsa	38	39.30 N	20.16 E
Igra	80	57.33 N	53.04 E
Iguaçu, Bra.	250	10.07 S	36.39 W
Iguaçu ≃, S.A.	256	25.36 S	54.36 W
Iguaçu, Cataratas do (Iguassu Falls) ↆ	252	25.41 S	54.26 W
Iguaçu, Parque Nacional do ⬥	252	25.30 S	53.50 W
Iguaí	255	14.45 S	40.04 W
Iguala	234	18.21 N	99.32 W
Igualada	34	41.35 N	1.38 E
Iguana ≃	246	7.54 N	65.46 W
Iguape	256	24.43 S	47.33 W
Iguará ≃	250	3.28 S	43.55 W
Iguassu Falls → Iguaçu, Cataratas 99do ↆ	252	25.41 S	54.26 W
Iguatemi ≃	255	23.40 S	54.34 W
Iguatemi ≃	255	23.55 S	54.10 W
Iguatu	250	6.22 S	39.18 W
Iguazú, Parque Nacional ⬥	252	25.35 S	54.20 W
Iguéla	152	1.55 S	9.19 E
Iguidi, 'Erg ⊕⁸	148	26.35 N	5.40 W
Iguig	116	17.45 N	121.44 E
Igumale	150	6.49 N	7.59 E
Igumnovo	82	55.37 N	38.18 E
Igvak, Cape ⊁	180	57.16 N	156.00 W
Iǧźej	88	53.59 N	103.10 E
Iħ → Sri Lanka ◻¹	122	7.00 N	81.00 E
Iĥam Bāzār	126	23.38 N	87.32 E
Ihiala	150	5.51 N	6.51 E
Ihirène, Oued V	148	20.25 N	4.35 E
Ihlane	100	24.43 N	121.49 E
Ihlenworth	56	53.44 N	8.55 E
Ihlow	52	53.34 N	7.27 E
Iharionove	78	46.42 N	33.09 E
Ihnāsiyat al-Madīnah	142	29.05 N	30.56 E
Ihorombe ⊕¹	157b	23.00 S	47.33 E
Ihosy	157b	22.24 S	46.08 E
Ihosy ≃	157b	21.44 S	45.53 E
Ihotry, Lac ☒	157b	21.56 S	43.41 E
Ihringen	58	48.02 N	7.39 E
Ihrlerstein	60	48.56 N	11.52 E
Ihsangazi	130	41.16 N	33.33 E
Ih Tal	88	43.13 N	122.15 E
Ihtiman	38	42.26 N	23.49 E
Ihu	164	7.55 S	145.25 E
Ihugh	150	7.02 N	9.00 E
Ihwah	142	29.03 N	31.10 E
Iida	94	35.31 N	137.50 E
Iijima	94	35.40 N	137.56 E
Ijoki ≃	26	65.20 N	25.17 E
Iiku, gora ⋀	88	49.51 N	87.47 E
Iinäshi ≃	94	34.27 N	136.24 E
Iioka	94	35.42 N	140.43 E
Iisalmi	26	63.34 N	27.11 E
Iisvesi	26	62.40 N	27.02 E
Iitaka	94	34.26 N	136.18 E
Iiyama	94	36.51 N	138.22 E
Iizuka	92	33.38 N	130.41 E
Ijåfene ⬚	148	20.30 N	8.00 W
Ijaiye	273a	6.40 N	3.13 E
Ijáyi	273a	6.40 N	3.13 E
Ilet' ≃	80	55.55 N	48.14 E
Ilevskij Pogost	80	55.56 N	43.34 E
Ijebu-Igbo	150	6.56 N	4.01 E
Ijebu-Ode	150	6.50 N	3.56 E
Ijesa-Tedo	273a	6.29 N	3.26 E
Ijevan	84	40.53 N	45.09 E
IJmuiden	50	52.27 N	4.35 E
Ijora ⊕⁸	273a	6.28 N	3.22 E
Ijsselmeer (Zuiderzee) ⧣²	50	52.45 N	5.25 E
IJsselmuiden	50	52.34 N	5.56 E
IJsselstein	50	52.01 N	5.02 E
Ijuí	252	28.23 S	53.55 W
Iju → Ju ≃	252	27.58 S	55.20 W
Iju Junction	273a	6.40 N	3.19 E
Iju Water Works ⬥	273a	6.40 N	3.19 E
IJzendijke	50	51.19 N	3.37 E
IJzer (Yser) ≃	50	51.09 N	2.44 E
Ika	248	21.25 S	46.49 W
Ikaalinen	26	61.46 N	23.04 E
Ikaba	150	7.47 N	8.28 E
Ikalamavony	157b	21.09 S	46.35 E
Ikali	154	3.29 S	25.51 E
Ikamatua	172	42.16 S	171.41 E
Ikamba	154	4.22 S	25.16 E
Ikang	150	4.58 N	8.20 E
Ikare	150	7.32 N	5.45 E
Ikari-dam ⬚⁶	94	36.50 N	139.42 E
Ikaria I	38	37.41 N	26.20 E
Ikast	26	56.08 N	9.10 E
Ikatskij chrebet ⊀	88	54.30 N	111.00 E
Ikawa	94	35.12 N	138.13 E
Ikawa-dam ⬚⁶	94	35.18 N	138.13 E
Ikazaki	96	33.36 N	132.34 E
Ikeda	96	34.01 N	135.23 E

Ikej	88	54.12 N	100.04 E
Ikeja	150	6.36 N	3.21 E
Ikela	152	1.11 S	23.16 E
Ikelemba ≃	152	1.14 N	16.31 E
Ikelemba ≃	152	0.07 N	18.17 E
Ikema-jima I	175d	24.56 N	125.16 E
Ikerre	150	7.31 N	5.14 E
Ikeuara	270	34.30 N	135.25 E
Iki I	92	33.47 N	129.43 E
Iki-Burul	84	45.49 N	44.39 E
Ikimba, Lake ☒	154	1.28 S	31.30 E
Ikinji Maryŭt	142	31.00 N	29.45 E
Ikire	150	7.23 N	4.12 E
Ikirun	150	7.55 N	4.41 E
Ikizce	130	39.36 N	32.40 E
Ikizdere	130	40.47 N	40.33 E
Ikko	152	0.35 S	16.01 E
Ikole	150	7.48 N	5.30 E
Ikom	150	5.58 N	8.42 E
Ikoma, Nihon	96	34.41 N	135.42 E
Ikoma, Tan.	154	2.04 S	34.37 E
Ikoma-sanchi ⊀	270	34.40 N	135.41 E
Ikoma-yama ⋀	270	34.40 N	135.41 E
Ikon-Chal'	84	44.18 N	41.45 E
Ikopa ≃	157b	17.01 S	46.43 E
Ikorec ≃	78	50.58 N	39.45 E
Ikorodu	150	6.37 N	3.31 E
Ikot Ekpene	150	5.12 N	7.40 E
Ikoyi ⊕⁸	152	0.53 S	10.36 E
Ikoyi Island I	273a	6.27 N	3.26 E
Ikoyi Prison ⌐	273a	6.25 N	3.25 E
Ikoži	154	2.32 S	27.37 E
Ikpikpuk ≃	180	70.50 N	154.25 W
Ikša	126	23.42 N	87.07 E
Ikša	82	56.10 N	37.31 E
Ikta, Cape ⊁	180	56.00 N	158.30 W
Ikuata	236a	6.25 N	3.22 E
Ikuchi-shima I	96	34.17 N	133.07 E
Ikuji-hana ⊁	94	36.54 N	137.25 E
Ikuktlitlig Mountain ⋀	180	59.16 N	161.27 W
Ikungu	154	1.34 S	33.40 E
Ikuno	96	35.10 N	134.48 E
Ikuno ⊕⁸	270	34.39 N	135.32 E
Ikurangi, Mount ⋀²	174k	21.13 S	159.45 W
Ikusaka	94	36.25 N	137.56 E
Ikusu ≃	273b	4.24 S	15.14 E
Ikuta	268	35.36 N	139.32 E
Ikva ≃, Magy.	61	47.42 N	16.58 E
Ikva ≃, Ukr.	78	50.33 N	25.24 E
Il, Nig.	150	8.01 N	4.55 E
Ila, R.D.C.	152	2.53 S	21.05 E
Ilabaya	248	17.25 S	70.31 W
Ilacaon Point ⊁	116	11.00 N	123.12 E
Ilagala	154	5.12 S	29.50 E
Ilagan	116	17.10 N	121.54 E
Ilaguh ≃	116	18.20 N	122.24 E
Ilaiyānkudi	122	9.38 N	78.38 E
Ilaka, Madag.	157b	19.33 S	48.52 E
Ilaka, Madag.	157b	20.20 S	47.09 E
Ilām, Īrān	128	33.38 N	46.26 E
Ilām, Nepāl	124	26.55 N	87.56 E
Ilam	46	53.03 N	1.48 W
Ilam ◻⁴	128	33.15 N	46.45 E
Ilamonde ≃	154	10.33 S	26.24 E
Ilan	88	46.19 N	129.33 E
Ilanz	58	46.47 N	9.12 E
Ilara	273a	6.42 N	3.27 E
Ilarionove	78	48.13 N	35.03 E
Ilaro	150	6.53 N	3.03 E
Ilasco	219	39.40 N	91.34 W
Ilave	248	16.06 S	69.41 W
Ilawa	30	53.37 N	19.33 E
Ilawe-Ekiti	150	7.37 N	5.06 E
Ilay	58	46.37 N	5.53 E
Ilbeşti	150	10.00 N	14.40 E
Ilberstedt	54	51.48 N	11.40 E
Il Catalano I	71	39.53 N	8.17 E
Ilchester, Eng., U.K.	42	51.01 N	2.41 W
Ilchester, Md., U.S.	284b	39.15 N	76.45 W
Ildefonso, Islas II	254	55.44 S	69.23 W
Île-à-la-Crosse	184	55.27 N	107.53 W
Île-à-la-Crosse, Lac ☒	184	55.40 N	108.00 W
Ilede (Port-Francqui)	152	4.19 S	20.35 E
Île-Cadieux	275a	45.25 N	74.01 W
Île-de-France ⬚⁹	50	49.00 N	2.20 E
Île-de-Montréal ◻⁶	206	45.33 N	73.40 W
Île-Jésus ◻⁶	275a	45.35 N	73.45 W
Ilek	84	51.31 N	53.21 E
Ilek ≃	84	51.30 N	53.22 E
Ilen ≃	48	51.33 N	9.18 W
Ilesa	150	7.38 N	4.45 E
Ilesha Baruba	150	9.04 N	3.25 E
Ilesha Loyauté ≃	175f	21.00 S	167.00 E
Ilet' ≃	80	55.56 N	48.14 E
Ilford, Austl.	160	40.13 S	148.15 E
Ilford, Mb., Can.	184	56.04 N	95.35 W
Ilford ⊕⁸	260	51.33 N	0.05 E
Ilfracombe, Austl.	166	23.30 S	144.30 E
Ilfracombe, Eng., U.K.	42	51.13 N	4.08 W
Il Fuorn	58	46.40 N	10.12 E
Ilgaz	130	41.02 N	33.27 E
Ilgaz Dağları ⊼	130	41.05 N	33.40 E
Ilgın	130	38.17 N	31.55 E
Ilha	255	15.28 S	39.55 E
Ilha das Flores	252	27.10 S	53.53 W
Ilha Grande, Baía da c	256	23.09 S	44.30 W
Ilha Solteira, Represa ☒¹	255	20.30 S	51.20 W
Ilhavo	34	40.36 N	8.40 W
Ilhéa Point ⊁	33	23.25 N	14.27 E
Ilhéos → Ilhéus	255	14.49 S	39.02 W
Ilhéus	255	14.49 S	39.02 W
Iliamna	180	59.45 N	154.55 W
Iliamna, Lake ☒	180	59.30 N	155.00 W
Iliamna Lake ☒	180	59.30 N	155.00 W
Iliamna Volcano ⋀¹	180	60.02 N	153.05 W
Ilianá ≃	234	16.58 N	94.30 W
Iliatenco	234	16.58 N	94.30 W
Il'ič, Azer.	130	39.54 N	45.00 E
Il'ič, Kaz.	130	42.52 N	71.22 E
Ilica, Tür.	130	39.58 N	29.07 E
Ilıca, Tür.	130	39.58 N	41.06 E
Iliç	130	39.27 N	38.34 E
Ilič	84	39.23 N	45.02 E
Iligan	116	8.14 N	124.14 E
Iligan Bay c	116	8.20 N	124.10 E
Il'inskij	86	57.58 N	56.13 E
Ilin Island I	116	12.14 N	121.05 E

		ENGLISH	DEUTSCH	ESPAÑOL	PORTUGUÊS	FRANÇAIS
⋀	Mountain	Berg	Montaña	Montanha	Montagne
⊼		Gebirge	Montaña	Montanha	Montagnes
)(	Pass		Paso	Passo	Col
V	Valley, Canyon	Tal, Cañon	Valle, Cañón	Vale, Canhão	Vallée, Canyon
⊕	Plain	Ebene	Llano	Planície	Plaine
⊁	Cape	Kap	Cabo	Cabo	Cap
I	Island	Insel	Isla	Ilha	Île
II	Islands	Inseln	Islas	Ilhas	Îles
⬥	Other Topographic Features	Andere Topographische Objekte	Otros Elementos Topográficos	Outros acidentes topográficos	Autres données topographiques

ESPAÑOL — Nombre | Página | Lat.°' | Long.°' W = Oeste
FRANÇAIS — Nom | Page | Lat.°' | Long.°' W = Ouest
PORTUGUÊS — Nome | Página | Lat.°' | Long.°' W = Oeste

Ilinka 82 54.04 N 38.12 E
Ilinza ∧ 246 0.40 S 78.42 W
Ilion 210 43.00 N 75.02 W
Ilio Point › 229a 21.13 N 157.15 W
Ilioúpolis 267c 37.56 N 23.45 E
Ilir 88 55.13 N 100.40 E
Ilirska Bistrica 36 45.34 N 14.15 E
Ilisós ≃ 267c 37.57 N 23.41 E
Ilizi 148 26.29 N 8.28 E
Il'ja 76 54.25 N 27.18 E
Iljak 86 60.11 N 77.59 E
Iljinka 80 48.32 N 41.05 E
Iljino 76 55.57 N 31.40 E
Iljinskij, Ross. 24 61.02 N 32.41 E
Iljinskij, Ross. 86 58.35 N 55.41 E
Iljinskij, Ross. 88 52.05 N 114.10 E
Iljinskij, Ross. 89 47.58 N 142.12 E
Iljinskij, Ross. 265b 55.37 N 38.06 E
Iljinskij Pogost 82 55.28 N 38.54 E
Iljinskoje, Ross. 76 56.58 N 37.11 E
Iljinskoje, Ross. 76 58.47 N 44.36 E
Iljinskoje, Ross. 76 53.14 N 35.26 E
Iljinskoje, Ross. 76 57.19 N 38.32 E
Iljinskoje, Ross. 80 56.29 N 52.49 E
Iljinskoje, Ross. 82 54.59 N 36.11 E
Iljinskoje, Ross. 82 56.34 N 35.57 E
Iljinskoje, Ross. 265b 55.46 N 37.15 E
Iljinskoje-Chovanskoje 80 56.58 N 39.46 E
Iljinsko-Podomskoje 24 61.08 N 47.56 E
Iljinsko-Zaborskoje 80 57.16 N 44.23 E
Iljiny gory ⋏[2] 76 56.34 N 34.12 E
Il'ka 88 51.43 N 108.32 E
Ilkal 122 15.58 N 76.08 E
Ilkeston 42 52.59 N 1.18 W
Il'kino 80 55.13 N 41.36 E
Ilkley 44 53.55 N 1.50 W
Ill ≃, Fr. 58 48.40 N 7.53 E
Ill ≃, Öst. 58 47.17 N 9.33 E
Illabot Creek ≃ 224 48.29 N 121.30 W
Illampu, Nevado ∧ 248 15.50 S 68.34 W
Illana Bay ⊂ 116 7.25 N 123.45 E
Illapel 252 31.38 S 71.10 W
Illasi 64 45.28 N 11.10 E
Illawarra, Lake ⊂ 170 34.32 S 150.50 E
Illbillee, Mount ∧ 162 27.02 S 132.30 E
Ille-et-Vilaine □[5] 32 48.10 N 1.30 W
Illéla 150 14.28 N 5.15 E
Iller ≃ 58 48.23 N 9.58 E
Illerkirchberg 58 48.20 N 10.00 E
Illertissen 58 48.13 N 10.06 E
Illescas, Esp. 34 40.07 N 3.50 W
Illescas, Méx. 234 23.13 N 102.07 W
Illfurth 58 47.40 N 7.16 E
Illhaeusern 58 48.11 N 7.26 E
Illi, Ba ≃ 146 10.44 N 15.21 E
Illichivs'k 78 46.18 N 30.39 E
Illiers 50 48.18 N 1.15 E
Illimani, Nevado ∧ 248 16.50 S 67.54 W
Illimo 248 6.28 S 79.51 W
Illingen, Dtsch. 56 48.57 N 8.55 E
Illingen, Dtsch. 56 49.23 N 7.03 E
Illingworth 262 53.45 N 1.54 W
Illinois □[3], U.S. 178 40.00 N 89.00 W
Illinois □[3], U.S. 194 40.00 N 89.00 W
Illinois ≃, U.S. 194 35.30 N 95.06 W
Illinois ≃, Co., U.S. 200 40.45 N 106.18 W
Illinois ≃, Il., U.S. 194 38.58 N 90.27 W
Illinois ≃, Or., U.S. 202 42.33 N 124.03 W
Illinois and Michigan Canal ≍ 278 41.32 N 88.05 W
Illinois at Chicago, University of ♁[2] 278 41.52 N 87.39 W
Illinois Beach State Park ♠ 216 42.26 N 87.48 W
Illinois Institute of Technology ♁[2] 278 41.50 N 87.38 W
Illinois Peak ∧ 202 47.02 N 115.04 W
Illintsi 78 49.07 N 29.12 E
Illiopolis 219 39.51 N 89.14 W
Illkirch-Graffenstaden 58 48.32 N 7.43 E
Illminster 42 50.56 N 2.55 W
Illo 150 11.33 N 3.42 E
Illovo, S. Afr. 158 30.05 S 30.50 E
Illovo, S. Afr. 273d 26.08 S 28.03 E
Illzach 58 47.47 N 7.20 E
Ilm ≃, Dtsch. 54 51.07 N 11.40 E
Ilm ≃, Dtsch. 60 48.49 N 11.45 E
Ilmajoki 26 62.44 N 22.34 E
Il'men', ozero ⊜ 76 58.17 N 31.20 E
Ilmenau 54 50.41 N 10.55 E
Ilmenau ≃ 54 53.23 N 10.10 E
Il'menskij zapovednik ♠ 86 55.16 N 60.17 E
Il'mino 80 53.47 N 45.40 E
Ilo 248 17.38 S 71.20 W
Ilobasco 236 13.51 N 88.51 W
Ilobu 150 7.51 N 4.30 E
Iloc Island I 116 11.18 N 119.41 E
Ilocos Norte □[4] 116 18.10 N 120.45 E
Ilocos Sur □[4] 116 17.05 N 120.35 E
Iloilo 116 10.42 N 122.34 E
Iloilo □[4] 116 11.00 N 122.35 E
Iloilo Strait ⊍ 116 10.43 N 122.36 E
Ilomantsi 24 62.40 N 30.55 E
Ilondola Mission 154 10.42 S 31.47 E
Ilongero 154 4.40 S 34.52 E
Ilop 164 2.54 S 141.13 E
Ilopango, Lago de ⊜ 236 13.40 N 89.03 W
Ilora 150 7.45 N 3.50 E
Ilorin 150 8.30 N 4.32 E
Ilovatka 80 50.31 N 45.55 E
Ilovays'k 83 47.56 N 38.13 E
Ilovka 78 50.43 N 38.38 E
Ilovl'a 80 49.18 N 43.59 E
Ilovl'a ≃ 80 49.14 N 43.54 E
Iłowa 30 51.30 N 15.12 E
Il Palone ∧ 64 46.02 N 11.04 E
Il'pyrskij 74 59.56 N 164.10 E
Ilsan-ni 271b 37.41 N 126.46 E
Ilse ≃ 54 52.06 N 10.35 E
Ilsenburg 54 51.52 N 10.41 E
Ilshofen 56 49.10 N 9.55 E
Il'skij 78 44.51 N 38.35 E
Ilskov 41 56.14 N 9.06 E
Il Telegrafo ∧ 66 42.22 N 11.10 E
Ilten 52 52.21 N 9.55 E
Ilu 152 4.12 N 23.02 E
Ilubabor □[4] 144 7.50 N 35.00 E
Iluhār 126 22.48 N 90.06 E
Ilūkste 76 55.58 N 26.18 E
Ilverich 263 51.17 N 6.42 E
Ilwaco 224 46.19 N 124.03 W
Ilwaki 112 7.56 S 126.26 E
Ilwŏl-san ∧ 98 36.50 N 129.06 E
İlyasbey 130 40.13 N 29.52 E
Ilz 61 47.05 N 15.55 E
Ilz ≃ 60 48.35 N 13.29 E
Iłża 30 51.11 N 21.14 E
Ima 88 55.13 N 115.55 E
Ima ≃ 96 33.45 N 131.01 E
Imabari 96 34.03 N 133.00 E
Imabu ≃ 250 0.44 S 57.22 W
Imadomi 268 35.28 N 140.06 E
Imaichi 94 36.43 N 139.41 E
Imajō 94 35.46 N 136.12 E
Imajuku 268 35.58 N 139.21 E
Imajuku ◆[8] 268 35.29 N 139.32 E
Imaki 270 34.24 N 135.46 E
Imaloto ≃ 157b 23.27 S 45.13 E
Imambara ♁[1] 272b 22.54 N 88.25 E
Imanbaj ⊥ 86 43.13 N 60.25 E
Imandan-Makit, gora ∧ 88 54.07 N 117.43 E
Imandra, ozero ⊜ 24 67.30 N 33.00 E
Imanombo 157b 24.26 S 45.49 E
Imantau 86 52.58 N 68.22 E
Imari 92 33.16 N 129.53 E
Imaruí 252 28.21 S 48.49 W
Imaruí, Lagoa do ⊂ 252 28.21 S 48.52 W
Imasa 140 18.01 N 36.12 E
Imatra 26 61.10 N 28.46 E
Imavere 76 58.44 N 25.48 E
Imazu 94 35.24 N 136.02 E
Imbābah ◆[8] 142 30.04 N 31.13 E
Imbabura □[4] 246 0.22 N 78.25 W
Imba-numa ⊜ 94 35.45 N 140.12 E
Imbariê 256 22.39 S 43.13 W
Imbituba 252 28.14 S 48.40 W
Imbituva 252 25.12 S 50.35 W
Imboaçu, Canal ≍ 287a 22.48 S 43.04 W
Imboden 194 36.12 N 91.10 W
Imbonga 152 0.43 S 19.46 E
Imbundi 152 5.44 S 16.16 E
Ime, Beinn ∧ 46 56.14 N 4.49 W
Imeni Babuškina 76 59.45 N 43.07 E
Imeni Čapajeva 85 43.28 N 76.50 E
Imeni C'urupy 82 55.30 N 38.39 E
Imeni Džambula, Kaz. 86 45.26 N 74.24 E
Imeni Džambula, Kaz. 86 47.43 N 74.09 E
Imeni Frunze 86 46.23 N 77.20 E
Imeni Il-Go Okt'abr'a 88 55.54 N 119.36 E
Imeni Kalinina, Kaz. 85 43.16 N 74.03 E
Imeni Kalinina, Kyrg. 85 41.28 N 76.22 E
Imeni Kalinina, Ross. 80 51.51 N 52.43 E
Imeni Kalinina, Uzb. 86 43.40 N 59.07 E
Imeni Karla Libknechta 78 51.37 N 35.27 E
Imeni Kirova, Kaz. 86 46.27 N 77.13 E
Imeni Kirova, Ross. 74 59.42 N 128.12 E
Imeni Leninskogo Komsomola 86 50.45 N 66.44 E
Imeni Marta 86 46.57 N 58.58 E
Imeni Michajla Ivanoviča Kalinina 80 57.59 N 45.07 E
Imeni Panfilova 85 43.23 N 77.07 E
Imeni Poliny Osipenko 89 52.25 N 136.28 E
Imeni Sardarova Karachana 85 38.26 N 68.46 E
Imeni Şeredy 83 46.52 N 40.03 E
Imeni Ševčenko 86 45.58 N 61.04 E
Imeni Stepana Razina 80 54.54 N 44.18 E
Imeni Tel'mana 89 48.36 N 134.59 E
Imeni Vladimira Il'iča Lenina 80 53.36 N 46.58 E
Imeni Vorovskogo, Ross. 80 55.43 N 41.06 E
Imeni Vorovskogo, Ross. 82 55.43 N 38.20 E
Imeni XXI Partsjezda 86 50.43 N 67.50 E
Imeni Žel'abova 76 58.57 N 36.36 E
Imera ⊥ 70 37.59 N 13.49 E
Imerimandroso 157b 17.23 S 48.38 E
Imese 152 2.07 N 18.06 E
Imgenbroich 56 50.34 N 6.16 E
Imi 144 6.28 N 42.18 E
Imías 240p 20.04 N 74.38 W
Imilac 252 24.14 S 68.53 W
Imilili ⊤[4] 148 23.18 N 15.54 W
Imi-n'Tanout 148 31.10 N 8.50 W
İmişli 84 39.52 N 48.04 E
Imittós 267c 37.57 N 23.45 E
Imittós Óros ⋏ 267c 37.55 N 23.47 E
Imja-do I 98 35.05 N 126.05 E
Imjin-gang ≃ 98 37.47 N 126.40 E
Imlay 204 40.39 N 118.08 W
Imlay City 190 43.01 N 83.04 W
Imlaystown 208 40.10 N 74.31 W
Imler 214 40.12 N 78.31 W
Immarna 162 30.30 S 132.09 E
Immendingen 58 47.56 N 8.44 E
Immenhausen 56 51.25 N 9.28 E
Immensen 52 52.23 N 10.04 E
Immenstaad 58 47.40 N 9.22 E
Immenstadt 58 47.33 N 10.13 E
Immigrath 263 51.06 N 6.57 E
Immingham 44 53.36 N 0.13 W
Immokalee 220 26.25 N 81.25 W
Imnaha ≃ 202 45.49 N 116.46 W
Imo ≃ 150 4.36 N 7.35 E
Imogiri 115a 7.55 S 110.23 E
Imokt'an 98 38.50 N 126.41 E
Imola 66 44.21 N 11.42 E
Imonda 164 3.20 S 141.10 E
Imore 273a 6.26 N 3.17 E
Imoro 273a 6.43 N 3.30 E
Im Ostholz ◆[8] 263 51.26 N 7.12 E
Imotski 36 43.27 N 17.13 E
Imp'a 98 35.59 N 126.49 E
Impasugong 116 8.19 N 125.00 E
Impe 152 2.44 S 15.17 E
Impendle 158 29.37 S 29.55 E
Imperatore, Campo ⊻ 66 42.25 N 13.40 E
Imperatriz 250 5.32 S 47.29 W
Imperia 62 43.53 N 8.03 E
Imperia □[4] 62 43.58 N 7.47 E
Imperial, Sk., Can. 184 51.22 N 105.27 W
Imperial, Perú 248 13.04 S 76.21 W
Imperial, Ca., U.S. 204 32.50 N 115.34 W
Imperial, Mo., U.S. 219 38.22 N 90.22 W
Imperial, Ne., U.S. 198 40.31 N 101.38 W
Imperial, Pa., U.S. 214 40.26 N 80.14 W
Imperial, Tx., U.S. 196 31.16 N 102.41 W
Imperial ≃ 254 38.48 S 73.24 W
Imperial Beach 228 32.35 N 117.06 W
Imperial Dam ◆[6] 204 32.55 N 114.30 W
Imperial de Aragón, Canal ≍ 34 42.02 N 1.33 W
Imperiale 68 40.07 N 16.35 E
Imperial Mills 182 55.00 N 111.44 W
Imperial Palace ♁ 268 35.41 N 139.45 E
Imperial Valley V 204 32.50 N 115.30 W
Impflingen 56 49.10 N 8.07 E
Impfondo 152 1.37 N 18.04 E
Imphāl 120 24.49 N 93.57 E
Impilachti 24 61.40 N 31.04 E
Impruneta 66 43.41 N 11.15 E
Impulo 152 13.53 S 13.39 E
İmralı Adası I 130 40.32 N 28.32 E
İmranlı 130 39.54 N 38.07 E
Imroz 130 40.11 N 25.55 E
Imsil 98 35.37 N 127.15 E
Imst 64 47.14 N 10.44 E
Imtān 132 32.24 N 36.49 E
Imuris 232 30.47 N 110.52 W
Imuruan Bay ⊂ 116 10.40 N 119.16 E
Imuruk Basin ⊜ 180 65.06 N 165.36 W
Imuruk Lake ⊜ 180 65.36 N 163.10 W
Imute 273a 6.42 N 3.29 E
Imwŏn-ni 98 37.15 N 129.20 E
Ina, Nihon 94 37.10 N 139.32 E
Ina, Nihon 94 35.59 N 140.03 E
Ina, Nihon 94 35.50 N 137.57 E
Ina, Nihon 268 35.59 N 139.38 E
In'a, Ross. 74 59.24 N 144.48 E
In'a, Ross. 86 53.31 N 82.40 E
In'a, Ross. 86 50.48 N 86.37 E
Ina, Il., U.S. 194 38.09 N 88.54 W
Ina ≃, Nihon 94 37.16 N 139.33 E
Ina ≃, Nihon 96 34.43 N 135.28 E
Ina ≃, Pol. 54 53.32 N 14.38 E
In'a ≃, Ross. 74 59.23 N 144.54 E
In'a ≃, Ross. 86 54.59 N 82.59 E
Inaba 270 34.26 N 135.27 E
Inabe 94 35.07 N 136.33 E
Ina-bonchi ⊻[1] 94 35.45 N 137.57 E
Inabu 94 35.13 N 137.30 E
Inaccessible Island I 10 37.17 S 12.45 W
Inada 270 34.54 N 135.08 E
Inagawa 96 34.53 N 135.22 E
Inagawan 116 9.33 N 118.39 E
Inage 268 35.38 N 140.05 E
Inagi 94 35.38 N 139.30 E
Inajá 250 8.54 S 37.49 W
Inajá ≃ 250 8.53 S 49.44 W
In'akino 80 54.26 N 41.07 E
Inakona 175e 9.49 S 160.02 E
Inala 171a 27.35 S 152.58 E
Inamangando ≃ 152 14.03 S 12.23 E
Inambari ≃ 248 12.41 S 69.44 W
In Amguel 148 23.40 N 5.10 E
Inami, Nihon 94 36.33 N 136.58 E
Inami, Nihon 96 34.45 N 134.54 E
Inami, Nihon 96 33.48 N 135.13 E
In Amnas 148 28.05 N 9.30 E
Inampulugan Island I 116 10.28 N 122.42 E
Inamuragasaki Point ⊥ 268 35.18 N 139.32 E
Inanda 273d 26.07 S 28.03 E
Inangahua Junction 172 41.51 S 171.57 E
Inanwatan 164 2.08 S 132.10 E
Iñapari 248 10.57 S 69.35 W
Inaporok 164 8.15 S 141.55 E
In'aptuk, gora ∧ 88 56.22 N 110.11 E
Inari 24 68.54 N 27.01 E
Inarigda 74 63.14 N 107.27 E
Inarijärvi ⊜ 24 69.00 N 28.00 E
Inas, Gunong ∧ 114 5.15 N 100.56 E
Inasa 94 34.50 N 137.40 E
Inatsuki 96 33.36 N 130.43 E
Inauini ≃ 248 8.30 S 67.24 W
Inawaia 164 8.40 S 146.35 E
Inawashiro-ko ⊜ 92 37.29 N 140.06 E
I-n-Azaoua ⊤[4] 148 20.49 N 7.30 E
Inazawa 94 35.15 N 136.47 E
Inba 94 35.46 N 140.14 E
Inba-numa ⊜ 94 35.46 N 140.12 E
In Belbel 148 27.54 N 1.10 E
Inca 34 39.43 N 2.54 E
Inca de Oro 252 26.45 S 69.54 W
Incaguasi 252 29.13 S 71.03 W
Incahuasi, Nevado de ∧ 252 27.02 S 68.18 W
Ince 262 53.17 N 2.49 W
Ince Blundell 262 53.31 N 3.02 W
İnce Burun › 130 42.06 N 34.56 E
Ince-in-Makerfield 262 53.32 N 2.37 W
İncekum Burnu › 130 36.13 N 33.58 E
İncesu 130 38.38 N 35.11 E
Inch 48 52.08 N 9.59 W
I-n-Chaouag ≃ 150 16.23 N 0.10 E
Inchard, Loch ⊂ 46 58.27 N 5.04 W
Inchas Military Base ■ 142 30.20 N 31.27 E
Inchbare 46 56.47 N 2.38 W
Inchcape I[2] 46 56.26 N 2.23 W
Inchelium 182 48.17 N 118.11 W
Inchiri □[4] 150 19.50 N 15.00 W
Inchmarnock I 46 55.47 N 5.09 W
Inchnadamph 46 58.09 N 4.59 W
Inch'ŏn 98 37.28 N 126.38 E
Inch'ŏn □[4] 98 37.28 N 126.38 E
Inchture 46 56.26 N 3.10 W
Inchwagh Lake ⊜ 281 42.27 N 83.41 W
İncirliova 130 37.50 N 27.43 E
Incisa in Val d'Arno 66 43.40 N 11.27 E
Incline Village 226 39.16 N 119.56 W
Incomáti (Komati) ≃ 156 25.46 S 32.43 E
Inconfidência 256 22.16 S 43.13 W
Inconfidentes 256 22.20 S 46.20 W
Inčoun 180 66.18 N 170.17 W
Incudine 64 46.14 N 10.22 E
Incudine, Monte ∧ 36 41.51 N 9.12 E
Incy 24 65.48 N 40.26 E
Indaal, Loch ⊂ 46 55.45 N 6.21 W
Indaiá ≃ 255 18.27 S 45.22 W
Indaiatuba 256 23.05 S 47.14 W
Indalsälven ≃ 26 62.31 N 17.27 E
Indanan 116 5.58 N 120.59 E
Indaparapeo 234 19.47 N 100.58 W
Inda Silase 144 14.05 N 38.20 E
Indaw 110 23.40 N 94.46 E
Indawgyi Lake ⊜ 110 25.10 N 96.19 E
Indé 232 25.54 N 105.13 W
Inde → India □[1] 118 20.00 N 77.00 E
Inde ≃ 56 50.54 N 6.21 E
Indemini 58 46.06 N 8.50 E
Inden 56 50.52 N 6.21 E
Independence, Ca., U.S. 204 36.48 N 118.11 W
Independence, In., U.S. 216 40.20 N 87.10 W
Independence, Ia., U.S. 190 42.28 N 91.53 W
Independence, Ks., U.S. 198 37.13 N 95.42 W
Independence, Ky., U.S. 218 38.56 N 84.32 W
Independence, La., U.S. 194 30.38 N 90.30 W
Independence, Mo., U.S. 194 39.05 N 94.24 W
Independence, Oh., U.S. 279a 41.23 N 81.38 W
Independence, Or., U.S. 202 44.51 N 123.11 W
Independence, Pa., U.S. 214 40.15 N 80.31 W
Independence, Tx., U.S. 222 30.19 N 96.21 W
Independence, Va., U.S. 192 36.37 N 81.09 W
Independence, Wi., U.S. 190 44.21 N 91.25 W
Independence ≃ 188 43.45 N 75.20 W
Independence Creek ≃ 196 30.27 N 101.44 W
Independence Hall ⊥ 285 39.57 N 75.09 W
Independence Lake ⊜[1] 226 39.26 N 120.18 W
Independence Mountains ⋏ 204 41.15 N 115.55 W
Independencia, Bol. 248 17.07 S 66.53 W
Independência, Bra. 250 5.23 S 40.19 W
Independencia, Chile 286e 33.23 S 70.40 W
Independencia, Perú 286d 11.59 S 77.02 W
Independencia, Isla I 248 14.15 S 76.12 W
Independenţa 38 43.58 N 28.05 E
Inder, ozero ⊜ 80 48.27 N 51.54 E
Inderborskij 80 48.33 N 51.44 E
In der Bredde 263 51.20 N 7.23 E
İnderesi 130 37.50 N 35.40 E
Index 224 47.49 N 121.33 W
Index, Mount ∧ 224 47.46 N 121.35 W
Indi 122 17.10 N 75.58 E
India (Bhārat) □[1] 118 20.00 N 77.00 E
India Brook ≃ 276 40.47 N 74.37 W
India Gate ⊥ 272a 28.37 N 77.18 E
Indialantic 220 28.05 N 80.34 W
Indian ≃, On., Can. 212 45.16 N 76.14 W
Indian ≃, On., Can. 212 44.13 N 78.08 W
Indian ≃, De., U.S. 208 38.36 N 75.10 W
Indian ≃, Ma., U.S. 283 42.47 N 70.58 W
Indian ≃, Mi., U.S. 190 45.59 N 86.15 W
Indian ≃, N.Y., U.S. 212 44.24 N 75.39 W
Indiana 214 40.37 N 79.09 W
Indiana □[6] 214 40.37 N 79.09 W
Indiana □[3], U.S. 178 40.00 N 86.15 W
Indiana □[3], U.S. 194 40.00 N 86.15 W
Indiana Dunes National Lakeshore ♠ 216 41.40 N 87.00 W
Indiana Dunes State Park ♠ 216 41.40 N 87.02 W
Indian Agricultural Research Institute ♁[3] 272a 28.38 N 77.10 E
Indiana Harbor ⊂ 278 41.40 N 87.27 W
Indiana Harbor Canal ≍ 278 41.40 N 87.27 W
Indianapolis 218 39.46 N 86.09 W
Indianapolis International Airport ⊠ 218 39.43 N 86.16 W
Indianapolis Motor Speedway ♠ 218 39.48 N 86.14 W
Indian Bayou ≃ 194 34.14 N 91.52 W
Indian Brook 186 46.23 N 60.32 W
Indian Caverns ±[5] 214 40.38 N 78.05 W
Indian Church 232 17.45 N 88.40 W
Indian Creek 278 42.14 N 87.59 W
Indian Creek ≃, U.S. 218 39.19 N 84.38 W
Indian Creek ≃, Ca., U.S. 228 35.18 N 118.26 W
Indian Creek ≃, Il., U.S. 216 41.26 N 88.46 W
Indian Creek ≃, Il., U.S. 219 39.56 N 90.32 W
Indian Creek ≃, Il., U.S. 278 42.11 N 87.55 W
Indian Creek ≃, In., U.S. 216 40.55 N 86.42 W
Indian Creek ≃, In., U.S. 218 39.23 N 86.29 W
Indian Creek ≃, In., U.S. 218 38.10 N 86.14 W
Indian Creek ≃, In., U.S. 218 38.43 N 85.06 W
Indian Creek ≃, Md., U.S. 284c 38.59 N 76.55 W
Indian Creek ≃, Mo., U.S. 194 36.33 N 94.29 W
Indian Creek ≃, Mo., U.S. 219 39.10 N 91.11 W
Indian Creek ≃, N.M., U.S. 200 36.11 N 108.23 W
Indian Creek ≃, N.Y., U.S. 276 40.43 N 73.06 W
Indian Creek ≃, Oh., U.S. 218 39.19 N 84.38 W
Indian Creek ≃, Oh., U.S. 279a 41.17 N 81.31 W
Indian Creek ≃, S.D., U.S. 198 44.39 N 103.19 W
Indian Creek ≃, Tn., U.S. 194 35.13 N 88.08 W
Indian Creek Lake ⊜[1] 222 31.44 N 95.58 W
Indianford 216 42.49 N 88.35 W
Indian Grave Mountain ∧[2] 192 32.59 N 84.21 W
Indian Harbor Beach 220 28.08 N 80.35 W
Indian Head, Sk., Can. 184 50.32 N 103.40 W
Indian Head, Md., U.S. 208 38.36 N 77.09 W
Indian Head ≃ 283 42.04 N 70.52 W
Indian Head Park 278 41.47 N 87.54 W
Indian Head Pond ⊜ 283 42.03 N 70.51 W
Indian Heights 216 40.25 N 86.07 W
Indian Island I 224 48.04 N 122.43 W
Indian Kentuck Creek ≃ 218 38.43 N 85.16 W
Indian Lake, Mi., U.S. 216 41.59 N 86.12 W
Indian Lake, N.Y., U.S. 188 43.46 N 74.16 W
Indian Lake ⊜, On., Can. 190 47.08 N 82.08 W
Indian Lake ⊜, Mi., U.S. 190 45.59 N 86.20 W
Indian Lake ⊜, Mi., U.S. 216 42.09 N 85.29 W
Indian Lake ⊜, Mi., U.S. 216 42.00 N 86.13 W
Indian Lake ⊜, N.J., U.S. 276 40.53 N 74.29 W
Indian Lake ⊜, Oh., U.S. 216 40.29 N 83.53 W
Indian Lake Estates 220 27.48 N 81.19 W
Indian Lakes ⊜ 216 41.33 N 85.25 W
Indian Lake State Park ♠ 216 40.29 N 83.52 W
Indian Mills Brook ≃ 285 39.47 N 74.44 W
Indian Mills Lake ⊜ 285 39.48 N 74.44 W
Indian Neck 207 41.15 N 72.48 W
Indian Ocean ⊤[1] 4 10.00 S 70.00 E
Indian Ocean ⊤[1] 6 10.00 S 70.00 E
Indianola, Ia., U.S. 190 41.21 N 93.33 W
Indianola, Ms., U.S. 194 33.27 N 90.39 W
Indianola, Ne., U.S. 198 40.14 N 100.25 W
Indianola, Pa., U.S. 279b 40.34 N 79.51 W
Indianola, Wa., U.S. 224 47.45 N 122.31 W
Indianópolis 255 19.02 S 47.55 W
Indianópolis ◆[8] 287b 23.36 S 46.38 W
Indian Peak ∧, Ut., U.S. 200 38.16 N 113.53 W
Indian Peak ∧, Wy., U.S. 202 44.47 N 109.51 W
Indian Point › 212 44.37 N 78.49 W
Indian Prairie Canal ≍ 220 27.02 N 80.57 W
Indian Queen Estates 284c 38.46 N 77.02 W
Indian River 190 45.24 N 84.36 W
Indian River □[6] 220 27.43 N 80.36 W
Indian River ⊂ 220 28.00 N 80.30 W
Indian River Bay ⊂ 208 38.36 N 75.05 W
Indian River Inlet ⊂ 208 38.37 N 75.03 W
Indian Rock ∧ 224 45.59 N 120.49 W
Indian Rock Dam ◆[6] 208 39.57 N 76.45 W
Indian Rock Paintings ⊥ 224 46.38 N 120.31 W
Indian Rocks Beach 220 27.52 N 82.51 W
Indian Springs, Nv., U.S. 204 36.34 N 115.40 W
Indian Springs, Va., U.S. 284c 38.49 N 77.10 W
Indian Stream ≃ 206 45.03 N 71.26 W
Indiantown 220 27.01 N 80.29 W
Indian Town Point › 240c 17.06 N 61.40 W
Indian Valley Reservoir ⊜[1] 226 39.07 N 122.32 W
Indian Village, In., U.S. 218 40.10 N 85.22 W
Indian Village, N.Y., U.S. 210 42.57 N 76.10 W
Indiaporã 255 19.57 S 50.17 W
Indiaroba 250 11.32 S 37.31 W
Indibir 144 8.05 N 37.58 E
Indico, Océano → Indian Ocean ⊤[1] 6 10.00 S 70.00 E
Indien → India □[1] 118 20.00 N 77.00 E
Indien, Océan → Indian Ocean ⊤[1] 6 10.00 S 70.00 E
Indien, territoires britanniques de l'Ocean → British Indian Ocean Territory □[2] 12 7.00 S 72.00 E
Indiera Alta 240m 18.09 N 66.53 W
Indiga 24 67.41 N 49.00 E
Indigirka ≃ 74 70.48 N 148.54 E
Inđija 38 45.03 N 20.05 E
Indin 120 20.16 N 92.57 E
Indio 204 33.43 N 116.12 W
Indio ≃, Nic. 236 10.57 N 83.44 W
Indio ≃, Pan. 236 9.12 N 80.11 W
Indio, Punta › 258 35.16 S 57.13 W
Indios, Canal de los ⊍ 240p 21.56 N 83.16 W
Indira Gandhi Canal ≍ 120 31.10 N 75.00 E
Indira Gandhi International Airport ⊠ 272a 28.35 N 77.07 E
Indischer Ozean → Indian Ocean ⊤[1] 6 10.00 S 70.00 E
Indispensable Reefs ✦[2] 160 12.40 S 160.25 E
Indispensable Strait ⊍ 175e 9.00 S 160.30 E
Indo → Indus ≃ 120 24.20 N 67.47 E
Indochina ◆[1] 108 16.00 N 107.00 E
Indom 24 64.36 N 55.22 E
Indonesia □[1] 108 5.00 S 120.00 E
Indonesia, University of ♁[2] 269e 6.12 S 106.51 E
Indonesia in Miniature ♠ 269e 6.08 S 106.49 E
Indonesian Culture, Museum of ♁[3] 269e 6.09 N 106.49 E
Indonésie → Indonesia □[1] 108 5.00 S 120.00 E
Indonesien → Indonesia □[1] 108 5.00 S 120.00 E
Indooroopilly 171a 27.30 S 152.58 E
Indore 120 22.43 N 75.50 E
Indpur 126 23.10 N 86.56 E
Indragiri ≃ 112 0.22 S 103.26 E
Indramayu 115a 6.20 S 108.19 E
Indramayu, Ujung › 115a 6.14 S 108.17 E
Indrapuri 114 5.26 N 95.27 E
Indrāvati ≃ 122 18.44 N 80.16 E
Indre □[5] 32 46.45 N 1.30 E
Indre ≃ 32 47.16 N 0.19 E
Indre-et-Loire □[5] 32 47.15 N 0.45 E
Indrois ≃ 50 47.13 N 0.56 E
Indungo 152 14.48 S 16.17 E
Induno Olona 62 45.52 N 8.51 E
Indur → Indore 120 22.43 N 75.50 E
Indura 76 53.27 N 23.53 E
Indus ≃ 120 24.20 N 67.47 E
Industry, Il., U.S. 194 40.20 N 90.36 W
Industry, Pa., U.S. 214 40.39 N 80.25 W
Industry, Tx., U.S. 222 29.58 N 96.30 W
Indwe 158 31.27 S 27.23 E
Indwe ≃ 158 32.01 S 27.21 E
Ine 96 35.39 N 135.17 E
İnebolu 130 41.58 N 33.46 E
İnece 130 41.41 N 27.04 E
İnecik 130 40.56 N 27.16 E
In Ecker 148 24.09 N 5.03 E
İnegöl 130 40.05 N 29.31 E
Inerie, Gunung ∧ 115b 8.52 S 120.56 E
Inés, Monte ∧ 254 48.29 S 69.40 W
Ineu 38 46.26 N 21.49 E
Inez, Ky., U.S. 192 37.51 N 82.32 W
Inez, Tx., U.S. 222 28.54 N 96.47 W
Inez, Lake ⊜ 276 41.01 N 74.17 W
Infanta, Pil. 116 15.50 N 119.55 E
Infanta, Pil. 116 14.45 N 121.39 E
Infante, Kaap › 158 34.29 S 20.51 E
Inferior, Laguna ⊂ 234 16.20 N 94.40 W
Inferno, Cachoeira do ∟ 250 1.00 S 56.04 W
Infiernillo, Presa del ⊜[1] 234 18.35 N 101.45 W
Infiesto 34 43.21 N 5.22 W
Infreschi, Ponta degli › 68 39.59 N 15.25 E
Ing ≃ 110 20.13 N 100.27 E
Ingá 250 7.17 S 35.36 W
Ingabu 110 17.49 N 95.16 E
Ingaí 256 21.24 S 44.55 W
Ingaí ≃ 256 21.23 S 44.52 W
Ingal 150 16.47 N 6.56 E
Ingalls 218 39.57 N 85.48 W
Ingalls Creek ≃ 224 47.28 N 120.39 W
Ingalls Park 216 41.32 N 88.03 W
Inganda 152 0.05 S 20.57 E
Inganno ≃ 70 38.04 N 14.37 E
Ingarö I 40 59.16 N 18.28 E
Ingatestone 42 51.41 N 0.22 E
Ingatestone Hall ⊥ 260 51.39 N 0.23 E
Ingelfingen 56 49.18 N 9.39 E
Ingelheim 56 49.59 N 8.05 E
Ingelmunster 50 50.55 N 3.15 E
Ingelstad 26 56.45 N 14.55 E
Ingende 152 0.15 S 18.57 E
Ingeniería, Universidad Nacional de ♁[2] 286d 12.02 S 77.02 W
Ingeniero Budge ◆[8] 288 34.43 S 58.28 W
Ingeniero Jacobacci 254 41.18 S 69.35 W
Ingeniero Juan Allan 258 34.53 S 58.11 W
Ingeniero Luiggi 252 35.25 S 64.29 W
Ingeniero Luis A. Huergo 252 39.05 S 67.14 W
Ingeniero Maschwitz 258 34.23 S 58.44 W
Ingeniero Romulo Otamendi 258 34.13 S 58.54 W
Ingeniero White 252 38.47 S 62.16 W
Ingeniero Williams 258 34.54 S 59.22 W
Ingenio La Esperanza 252 24.13 S 64.51 W
Ingenio Santa Ana 252 27.28 S 65.41 W
Ingeringbach ≃ 61 47.12 N 14.49 E
Ingersheim 58 48.06 N 7.18 E
Ingersoll 212 43.02 N 80.53 W
Ingham 166 18.39 S 146.10 E
Ingham □[6] 216 42.37 N 84.22 W
Ingička 85 39.52 N 67.20 E
Ingleborough ∧ 44 54.11 N 2.23 W
Ingleburn 170 34.00 S 150.52 E
Inglesa, Costa → English Coast ±[2] 9 73.45 S 73.00 W
Ingleside, Austl. 274a 33.41 S 151.13 E
Ingleside, On., Can. 206 45.00 N 75.00 W
Ingleside, Il., U.S. 216 42.23 N 88.09 W
Ingleside, Tx., U.S. 196 27.52 N 97.12 W
Ingleside ◆[8] 282 37.43 N 122.28 W
Ingleton 44 54.10 N 2.27 W
Inglewood, Austl. 166 28.25 S 151.05 E
Inglewood, Austl. 166 36.34 S 143.52 E
Inglewood, On., Can. 212 43.47 N 79.56 W
Inglewood, N.Z. 172 39.09 S 174.12 E
Inglewood, Ca., U.S. 228 33.57 N 118.21 W
Inglewood, Wa., U.S. 224 47.44 N 122.15 W
Inglewood Forest ◆[3] 44 54.45 N 2.50 W
Inglis, Mb., Can. 184 50.57 N 101.15 W
Inglis, Fl., U.S. 220 29.02 N 82.40 W
Inglis Lock ◆[5] 220 29.02 N 82.37 W
Ingoda ≃ 88 51.42 N 115.48 E
Ingogo 158 27.32 S 29.56 E
Ingoldmells 44 53.11 N 0.20 E
Ingolstadt 60 48.46 N 11.27 E
Ingomar 279b 40.35 N 80.05 W
Ingonish 186 46.42 N 60.22 W
Ingornachoix Bay ⊂ 186 50.38 N 57.20 W
Ingraham, Lake ⊜ 220 25.09 N 81.08 W
Ingrāj Bāzār 124 25.00 N 88.09 E
Ingram, Pa., U.S. 279b 40.26 N 80.04 W
Ingram, Tx., U.S. 196 30.04 N 99.14 W
Ingram Bay ⊂ 208 37.48 N 76.17 W
Ingrave 260 51.36 N 0.21 E
Ingrid Christensen Coast ±[2] 9 69.30 S 76.00 E
In Guezzam 150 19.32 N 5.42 E
Inguri ≃ 84 42.24 N 41.33 E
Ingushetia → Čečnja-Ingušetija □[3] 84 43.15 N 45.40 E
Inguzet 86 58.50 N 83.52 E
Ingvallsbenning 40 60.15 N 15.53 E
Ingwavuma 158 27.09 S 32.00 E
Ingwe 154 13.02 S 26.25 E
Ingwiller 56 48.52 N 7.29 E
Inhaca, Ilha da I 158 26.03 S 32.57 E
Inhafenga 156 20.35 S 33.53 E
Inhambane 156 23.51 S 35.29 E
Inhambane □[5] 156 23.00 S 34.30 E
Inhambane, Baía de ⊂ 156 23.58 S 35.51 E
Inhambupe 255 11.47 S 38.21 W
Inhaminga 156 18.24 S 35.00 E
Inhanduí ≃ 255 21.37 S 52.59 W
Inhapim 255 19.33 S 42.07 W
Inharrime 156 24.29 S 35.01 E
Inharrime ≃ 156 24.29 S 35.01 E
Inhassoro 156 21.33 S 35.11 E
Inhaúma 255 19.29 S 44.22 W
Inhaúma ◆[8] 287a 22.52 S 43.17 W
İnhisar 130 40.03 N 30.23 E
Inhoaíba ◆[8] 256 22.54 S 43.36 W
Inhomirim 256 22.35 S 43.10 W
Inhomirim ≃ 287a 22.41 S 43.13 W
Inhul ≃ 78 47.00 N 31.59 E
Inhulets' 78 47.43 N 33.14 E
Inhulets' ≃ 78 46.41 N 32.48 E
Inhulo-Kam'yanka 78 48.17 N 32.30 E
Inhuma 250 6.40 S 41.42 W
Inhumas 255 16.22 S 49.30 W
Ini ≃ 146 9.30 N 12.20 E
Iniesta 34 39.26 N 1.45 W
Inimutaba 255 18.45 S 44.22 W
Ining → Yining 86 43.54 N 81.21 E
Inírida ≃ 246 3.55 N 67.52 W
Inisa 150 7.52 N 4.20 E
Inishbofin I, Ire. 48 53.37 N 10.15 W
Inishbofin I, Ire. 48 55.09 N 8.11 W
Inishcrone 48 54.12 N 9.06 W
Inisheer I 48 53.02 N 9.26 W
Inishkea North I 48 54.08 N 10.12 W
Inishkea South I 48 54.07 N 10.13 W
Inishmaan I 48 53.05 N 9.32 W
Inishmore I 48 53.07 N 9.45 W
Inishmurray I 48 54.26 N 8.40 W
Inishowen ›[1] 48 55.12 N 7.20 W
Inishowen Head › 48 55.14 N 6.56 W
Inishshark I 48 53.37 N 10.18 W
Inishtrahull I 48 55.26 N 7.14 W
Inishturk I 48 53.43 N 10.08 W
Inistioge 48 52.29 N 7.04 W
Initao 116 8.30 N 124.18 E
Inje 98 38.05 N 128.09 E
Injibara 144 11.00 N 36.59 E
Injune 166 25.51 S 148.34 E
Inkeroinen 26 60.42 N 26.51 E
Inketete 152 2.37 S 21.53 E
Inkisi (Zadi) ≃ 152 4.46 S 14.52 E
Inkom 202 42.47 N 112.15 W
Inkster, Mi., U.S. 216 42.17 N 83.18 W
Inkster, N.D., U.S. 198 48.09 N 97.38 W
Inland Kaikoura Range ⋏ 172 42.00 S 173.40 E
Inland Lake ⊜, Mb., Can. 184 52.17 N 99.42 W
Inland Lake ⊜, Ak., U.S. 180 66.27 N 159.47 W
Inland Sea → Seto-naikai ⊤[2] 96 34.20 N 133.30 E
Inle Lake ⊜ 110 20.32 N 96.55 E
Inman, Ks., U.S. 198 38.13 N 97.46 W
Inman, S.C., U.S. 192 35.02 N 82.05 W
Inman Mills 192 35.02 N 82.06 W
Inman Valley 168b 35.30 S 138.28 E
Inn (En) ≃ 32 48.35 N 13.28 E
Innamincka 166 27.45 S 140.44 E
Innbach ≃ 61 48.18 N 14.07 E
Innellan 46 55.54 N 4.57 W
Inner Bay ⊂ 214 42.37 N 80.24 W
Innerbraz 58 47.09 N 9.55 E
Inner Channel ⊍ 232 16.35 N 88.17 W
Innerferrera 58 46.31 N 9.28 E
Innerfragant 64 46.58 N 13.04 E
Inner Harbor ⊂ 276 40.52 N 73.28 W
Inner Hebrides II 46 56.30 N 6.00 W
Innerkip 212 43.13 N 80.42 W
Innerleithen 46 55.38 N 3.05 W
Inner Mongolia → Nei Monggol Zizhiqu □[4] 90 43.00 N 115.00 E
Inner Sister Island I 166 39.42 S 147.55 E
Inner Sound ⊍ 46 57.25 N 5.56 W
Innerste ≃ 52 52.15 N 9.50 E
Innerstetalsperre ◆[6] 52 51.55 N 10.17 E
Innerthal 58 47.06 N 8.56 E
Innertkirchen 58 46.42 N 8.14 E
Innervillgraten 64 46.48 N 12.23 E
Innichen → San Candido 64 46.44 N 12.17 E
Inning 60 48.05 N 11.09 E
Innisfail, Austl. 166 17.32 S 146.02 E
Innisfail, Ab., Can. 182 52.02 N 113.57 W
Innisfil Creek ≃ 212 44.08 N 79.49 W
Innisfree 182 53.22 N 111.32 W
Innisplain 171a 28.10 S 152.55 E
Innokentjevka 89 49.42 N 136.57 E
Innokentjevskij 89 48.37 N 140.10 E
Innoko ≃ 180 62.14 N 159.45 W
Innolovo 265a 59.47 N 29.59 E
Innoshima 96 34.17 N 133.11 E
Inno-shima I 96 34.19 N 133.10 E
Innsbruck 64 47.16 N 11.24 E
Innviertel ◆[1] 60 48.10 N 13.15 E
Inny ≃, Ire. 48 53.33 N 7.48 W
Inny ≃, Eng., U.K. 42 50.35 N 4.17 W
Ino, Nihon 96 33.33 N 133.26 E
Ino, Va., U.S. 208 37.46 N 76.48 W
Inoã 256 22.55 S 42.57 W
Inobonto 112 0.52 N 123.57 E
Inocência 255 19.47 S 51.48 W
Inokashira Park ♠ 268 35.42 N 139.34 E
Inokovka 80 52.33 N 42.34 E
Inola 196 36.09 N 95.30 W
Ino-misaki › 96 33.01 N 133.06 E
Inongo 152 1.57 S 18.16 E
Inoni 152 3.04 S 15.39 E
İnönü 130 39.48 N 30.09 E
Inoue 270 34.48 N 135.03 E
Inowrocław 30 52.48 N 18.15 E
Inozemcevo 84 44.06 N 43.06 E
Inp'ung-dong 98 41.25 N 126.34 E
Inrath ◆[8] 263 51.21 N 6.32 E
In Rhar 148 27.10 N 1.59 E
Ins 58 47.00 N 7.06 E
In Salah 148 27.12 N 2.28 E
Insan-ni 98 41.01 N 127.21 E
Insar 80 53.52 N 44.21 E
Insar ≃ 80 54.43 N 45.18 E
Insch 46 57.21 N 2.37 W
Inscription, Cape › 162 25.29 S 112.59 E
Inscription Point › 274a 34.00 S 151.13 E
Insel Man → Isle of Man □[2] 44 54.15 N 4.30 W
Inshar 150 8.49 N 9.40 E
Inshāș ar-Raml 142 30.23 N 31.27 E
Insjön 26 60.41 N 15.05 E
Ińsko 30 53.27 N 15.33 E
In Sokki, Oued V 148 29.37 N 4.13 E
Inspiration 200 33.24 N 110.52 W
Insterburg → Čern'achovsk 76 54.38 N 21.49 E
Instow 184 49.44 N 108.16 W
Insurgente José María Morelos, Parque Nacional ♠ 234 19.35 N 100.55 W
Inta 24 66.02 N 60.08 E
Intendente Alvear 252 35.14 S 63.35 W
İntepe 130 40.00 N 26.20 E
Intercession City 220 28.15 N 81.30 W
Intercourse 208 40.02 N 76.06 W
Interlagos ◆[8] 287b 23.42 S 46.42 W
Interlaken, Schw. 58 46.41 N 7.51 E
Interlaken, Ma., U.S. 210 42.18 N 73.19 W
Interlaken, N.J., U.S. 208 40.14 N 74.01 W
Interlaken, N.Y., U.S. 210 42.37 N 76.43 W
Interlândia 255 16.12 S 49.02 W
Internacional (Guarulhos), Aeroporto ⊠ 287b 23.29 S 46.28 W
International Falls 190 48.36 N 93.24 W
International Peace Garden ♠ 198 49.00 N 100.04 W
International Trade Fair ♠ 267d 35.47 N 51.24 E
Interstate State Park ♠ 190 45.23 N 92.40 W
Inthanon, Doi ∧ 110 18.35 N 98.29 E
Intibucá 236 14.16 N 88.10 W
Intibucá □[5] 236 14.20 N 88.15 W
Intipucá 236 13.12 N 88.04 W
Intiyaco 252 28.39 S 60.05 W
Intracoastal Waterway ≍, U.S. 192 24.33 N 81.46 W

≃ River	Fluß	Río	Rivière	Rio
≍ Canal	Kanal	Canal	Canal	Canal
∟ Waterfall, Rapids	Wasserfall, Stromschnellen	Cascada, Rápidos	Chute d'eau, Rapides	Cascata, Rápidos
⊍ Strait	Meeresstraße	Estrecho	Détroit	Estreito
⊂ Bay, Gulf	Bucht, Golf	Bahía, Golfo	Baie, Golfe	Baía, Golfo
⊜ Lake, Lakes	See, Seen	Lago, Lagos	Lac, Lacs	Lago, Lagos
≋ Swamp	Sumpf	Pantano	Marais	Pântano
⊓ Ice Features, Glacier	Eis- und Gletscherformen	Accidentes Glaciales	Formes glaciaires	Acidentes glaciares
⊤ Other Hydrographic Features	Andere Hydrographische Objekte	Otros Elementos Hidrográficos	Autres données hydrographiques	Outros acidentes hidrográficos
✦ Submarine Features	Untermeerische Objekte	Accidentes Submarinos	Formes de relief sous-marin	Acidentes submarinos
□ Political Unit	Politische Einheit	Unidad Politica	Entité politique	Unidade política
♁ Cultural Institution	Kulturelle Institution	Institución Cultural	Institution culturelle	Institução cultural
⊥ Historical Site	Historische Stätte	Sitio Histórico	Site historique	Sitio histórico
♠ Recreational Site	Erholungs- und Ferienort	Sitio de Recreo	Centre de loisirs	Area de Lazer
⊠ Airport	Flughafen	Aeropuerto	Aéroport	Aeroporto
■ Military Installation	Militäranlage	Instalación Militar	Installation militaire	Instalação militar
◆ Miscellaneous	Verschiedenes	Misceláneo	Divers	Diversos

ENGLISH — Name | Page | Lat.°′ | Long.°′
DEUTSCH — Name | Seite | Breite°′ | Länge°′ E = Ost

Intracoastal Waterway ≊, U.S. 196 26.04 N 97.12 W
Intragna 58 46.10 N 8.42 E
Intrånget 40 60.20 N 16.09 E
Introbio 58 45.57 N 9.27 E
Introdacqua 66 42.00 N 13.54 E
Intschön → Inch'ŏn 98 37.28 N 126.38 E
Intu 112 0.15 S 115.21 E
Intuto 246 3.39 S 74.44 W
Inubō-saki › 94 35.42 N 140.53 E
Inukai 96 33.04 N 131.38 E
Inukjuak 176 58.27 N 78.06 W
Inútil, Bahía c 254 53.30 S 69.50 W
Inuvik 180 68.25 N 133.30 W
Inuya ≃ 248 10.41 S 73.30 W
Inuyama 94 35.23 N 136.56 E
In'va ≃ 86 58.59 N 55.40 E
Inver 46 57.49 N 3.55 W
Inverallochy 46 57.40 N 1.55 W
Inveralochy 170 34.57 S 149.39 E
Inveraray 46 56.13 N 5.05 W
Inverarish 46 57.21 N 6.04 W
Inverarity 46 56.35 N 2.53 W
Inverbervie 46 56.51 N 2.17 W
Invercargill 172 46.24 S 168.21 E
Inverdruie 46 57.10 N 3.48 W
Inverell 166 29.47 S 151.07 E
Invergarry 46 57.02 N 4.47 W
Invergordon 46 57.42 N 4.10 W
Inverkeilor 46 56.38 N 2.32 W
Inverkeithing 46 56.02 N 3.25 W
Inverkeithny 46 57.30 N 2.37 W
Inverleigh 169 38.06 S 144.03 E
Inverloch 169 38.38 S 145.43 E
Invermay 184 51.48 N 103.09 W
Invermere 182 50.30 N 116.02 W
Invermoriston 46 57.13 N 4.38 W
Inverness, N.S., Can. 186 46.14 N 61.18 W
Inverness, P.Q., Can. 206 46.15 N 71.31 W
Inverness, Scot., U.K. 46 57.27 N 4.15 W
Inverness, Ca., U.S. 204 38.06 N 122.51 W
Inverness, Fl., U.S. 220 28.50 N 82.19 W
Inverness, Il., U.S. 216 42.07 N 88.05 W
Inverness, Ms., U.S. 194 33.21 N 90.35 W
Inveruglas 46 56.15 N 4.43 W
Inveruno 62 45.31 N 8.51 E
Inverurie 46 57.17 N 2.23 W
Inverway 162 17.50 S 129.38 E
Investigator Group II 162 33.45 S 134.30 E
Investigator Shoal ⊹[2] 108 8.09 N 114.44 E
Investigator Strait ⊔ 166 35.25 S 137.10 E
Inwood, Mb., Can. 184 50.30 N 97.30 W
Inwood, On., Can. 214 42.49 N 81.59 W
Inwood, Fl., U.S. 220 28.02 N 81.45 W
Inwood, In., U.S. 216 41.19 N 86.12 W
Inwood, Ia., U.S. 198 43.18 N 96.25 W
Inwood, N.Y., U.S. 276 40.37 N 73.44 W
Inwood Hill Park ♠ 276 40.52 N 73.56 W
Inyanga 154 18.13 S 32.46 E
Inyanga Mountains ⋏ 154 18.00 S 33.00 E
Inyangani ∧ 154 18.20 S 32.50 E
Inyan Kara Mountain ∧ 198 44.13 N 104.21 W
Inyantue 154 18.32 S 26.41 E
Inyati 154 19.39 S 28.54 E
Inyo, Mount ∧ 204 36.44 N 117.59 W
Inyokern 204 35.38 N 117.48 W
Inyo Mountains ⋏ 204 36.40 N 118.10 W
Inyonga 154 6.43 S 32.04 E
Inywa 110 23.56 N 96.17 E
Inza 80 53.51 N 46.21 E
Inza ≃ 80 53.54 N 45.44 E
Inzago 62 45.32 N 9.29 E
Inzai 94 35.50 N 140.09 E
Inzana Lake ⊜ 182 54.58 N 124.40 W
Inžavino 80 52.19 N 42.30 E
Inzell 64 47.46 N 12.44 E
Inzer 86 54.14 N 57.34 E
Inzer ≃ 86 54.30 N 56.28 E
Inzersdorf ⊸[8] 264b 48.09 N 16.21 E
Inzia ≃ 152 3.45 S 17.57 E
Ioanna, gora ∧ 180 64.50 N 178.08 E
Ioánnina 38 39.40 N 20.50 E
Ioco 224 49.18 N 122.52 W
Iō-jima (Iwo Jima) I 174f 24.47 N 141.20 E
Iokanga ≃ 24 68.00 N 39.43 E
Iola, Ks., U.S. 198 37.55 N 95.23 W
Iola, Pa., U.S. 210 45.08 N 76.32 W
Iola, Tx., U.S. 222 30.46 N 96.05 W
Iola, Wi., U.S. 190 44.30 N 89.07 W
Iolgo, chrebet ⋏ 86 51.30 N 86.25 E
Iolotan' 72 37.18 N 62.21 E
Ioma 164 8.20 S 147.50 E
Iôna, Ang. 152 16.50 S 12.20 E
Iona, N.S., Can. 186 45.58 N 60.48 W
Iona, Id., U.S. 202 43.31 N 111.55 W
Iona I 46 56.19 N 6.25 W
Iôna, Parque Nacional do ♠ 152 16.30 S 12.00 E
Iona, Sound of ⊔ 46 56.19 N 6.24 W
Iona College ʋ[2] 276 40.56 N 73.47 W
Ione, Ca., U.S. 226 38.21 N 120.55 W
Ione, Or., U.S. 202 45.30 N 119.50 W
Ione, Wa., U.S. 202 48.44 N 117.24 W
Ionia, Mi., U.S. 216 42.59 N 85.04 W
Ionia, N.Y., U.S. 210 42.56 N 77.30 W
Ionia □[6] 216 42.56 N 85.04 W
Ionian Islands → Iónioi Nísoi II 38 38.30 N 20.30 E
Ionian Sea ⊽[2] 22 39.00 N 19.00 E
Ionia State Recreation Area ♠ 216 42.58 N 85.36 W
Ionico, Mare → Ionian Sea ⊽[2] 22 39.00 N 19.00 E
Ionienne, Mer → Ionian Sea ⊽[2] 22 39.00 N 19.00 E
Iónioi Nísoi □[4] 38 38.15 N 20.30 E
Iónioi Nísoi II 38 38.30 N 20.30 E
Ionische Inseln → Iónioi Nísoi II 38 38.30 N 20.30 E
Ionisches Meer → Ionian Sea ⊽[2] 22 39.00 N 19.00 E
Ionivejem ≃ 180 66.12 N 174.00 W
Iony, ostrov I 74 56.26 N 143.25 E
Ioppolo 68 38.35 N 15.53 E
Ioppolo Giancaxio 70 37.23 N 13.33 E
Iordan 85 39.58 N 71.46 E
Iori (Qabırrı) ≃ 84 41.03 N 46.17 E
Iorskoje ploskogorje ⋏[1] 84 41.20 N 46.00 E
Iory 85 39.30 N 67.53 E
Íos 38 36.44 N 25.17 E
Íos I 38 36.42 N 25.24 E
Ioscoe, Lake ⊜ 276 41.02 N 74.19 W
Iosegun ≃ 182 54.44 N 117.11 W
Iosegun Lake 182 54.29 N 116.50 W
Iō-shima I 93b 30.48 N 130.18 E
Iota 194 30.19 N 92.29 W
Iovlevo 82 56.10 N 38.20 E
Iowa 194 30.14 N 93.00 W
Iowa □[3] 178 42.15 N 93.15 W
Iowa ≃ 190 41.10 N 91.02 W
Iowa, South Fork ≃ 190 42.18 N 93.04 W
Iowa City 190 41.39 N 91.31 W
Iowa Falls 190 42.31 N 93.15 W
Iowa Park 196 33.57 N 98.40 W
Iō-zen ∧ 94 36.31 N 136.48 E
Ipa ≃ 76 52.13 N 29.08 E
Ipala 154 4.30 S 32.53 E
Ipameri 255 17.43 S 48.09 W
Ipanema ⊸[8] 256 22.59 S 43.12 W
Ipanema ≃ 250 9.53 S 37.15 W
Ipanguaçu 250 5.30 S 36.52 W
Ipat 24 66.13 N 56.33 E
Ipatinga 255 19.30 S 42.32 W
Ipatovo 80 45.43 N 42.53 E
Ipaumirim 250 6.47 S 38.43 W
Ipava 194 40.21 N 90.19 W
Ípeiros □[9] 38 39.40 N 20.50 E
Ipel' (Ipoly) ≃ 30 47.49 N 18.52 E
Iperu 150 6.52 N 3.38 E
Iphigenia Bay c 180 55.40 N 133.55 W
Iphofen 56 49.42 N 10.15 E
Ipiabas 256 22.23 S 43.53 W
Ipiales 246 0.50 N 77.37 W
Ipiaú 255 14.08 S 39.44 W
Ipiíba 256 22.52 S 42.57 W
Ipil 116 7.47 N 122.35 E
Ipin → Yibin 107 28.47 N 104.38 E
Ipirá 255 12.10 S 39.44 W
Ipiranga, Bra. 252 25.01 S 50.35 W
Ipiranga, Bra. 287a 22.43 S 43.12 W
Ipiranga ⊸[8] 287b 23.36 S 46.35 W
Ipiranga ≃, Bra. 256 23.21 S 45.10 W
Ipiranga ≃, Bra. 287a 22.48 S 43.37 W
Ipiranga, Canal ≊ 287a 22.46 S 43.37 W
Ipiranga, Museu do ʋ 287b 23.35 S 46.36 W
Ípiros □[4] 38 39.30 N 20.30 E
Ipis I 175c 6.59 N 151.59 E
Ipita 248 19.20 S 63.32 W
Ipitinga ≃ 250 0.02 N 53.01 W
Ipixuna 250 4.22 S 44.34 W
Ipixuna ≃, Bra. 248 7.11 S 71.51 W
Ipixuna ≃, Bra. 248 5.45 S 63.02 W
Ipixuna ≃, Bra. 248 6.16 S 61.52 W
Ipixuna, Igarapé ≃ 250 4.32 S 52.40 W
Ipoh 114 4.35 N 101.05 E
Ipojuca ≃ 250 8.25 S 34.58 W
Ipokera 154 8.03 S 35.41 E
Ipole 154 5.47 S 32.44 E
Ipoly (Ipel') ≃ 30 47.49 N 18.52 E
Iporá, Bra. 255 16.28 S 51.07 W
Iporã, Bra. 255 23.59 S 53.37 W
Ipota 175f 18.48 S 169.16 E
Ippari ≃ 70 36.52 N 14.26 E
Ippinghausen 56 51.17 N 9.08 E
Ipplepen 42 50.29 N 3.38 W
Ippy 152 6.15 N 21.12 E
İpsala 130 40.55 N 26.23 E
Ipswich, Austl. 171a 27.36 S 152.46 E
Ipswich, Eng., U.K. 42 52.04 N 1.10 E
Ipswich, Ma., U.S. 207 42.40 N 70.50 W
Ipswich, S.D., U.S. 198 45.26 N 99.01 W
Ipswich ≃ 207 42.42 N 70.48 W
Ipswich Bay c 207 42.41 N 70.42 W
Ipu 250 4.20 S 40.42 W
Ipubi 250 7.39 S 40.07 W
Ipueiras 250 4.33 S 40.43 W
Ipuh 112 3.00 S 101.30 E
Ipuiúna 256 22.06 S 46.11 W
Ipun, Isla I 254 44.37 S 74.46 W
Ipupiara 255 11.49 S 42.37 W
Iput' ≃ 76 52.26 N 31.02 E
Iqaluit 176 63.44 N 68.28 W
Iqe ≃ 102 38.14 N 94.18 E
Iqfahs 142 28.47 N 30.49 E
Iquique 248 20.13 S 70.10 W
Iquitos 246 3.46 S 73.15 W
Ira 196 32.35 N 101.00 W
Iraan, Pil. 116 9.04 N 117.42 E
Iraan, Tx., U.S. 196 30.54 N 101.53 W
Ira Banda 152 5.57 N 22.04 E
Irabu 175d 24.50 N 125.09 E
Irabu-jima I 175d 24.50 N 125.10 E
Iracajá, Cachoeira do ∟ 248 10.29 S 64.05 W
Iracema 250 5.48 S 38.18 W
Iracoubo 250 5.29 N 53.13 W
Irago-misaki › 94 34.35 N 137.01 E
Irago-suidō ⊔ 94 34.35 N 137.00 E
Iraí 252 27.11 S 53.15 W
Irajá ⊸[8] 287a 22.51 S 43.19 W
Irajá ≃ 287a 22.49 S 43.17 W
Irajol' 24 64.27 N 55.08 E
Irak → Iraq □[1] 128 33.00 N 44.00 E
Iráklia I 38 36.50 N 25.26 E
Iráklion, Ellás 38 35.20 N 25.09 E
Iráklion, Ellás 267c 38.04 N 23.46 E
Iran (Īrān) □[1], Asia 118 32.00 N 53.00 E
Iran (Īrān) □[1], Asia 128 32.00 N 53.00 E
Iran, Pegunungan ⋏ 112 2.05 N 114.55 E
Iran National Arts Museum ʋ 267d 35.41 N 51.27 E
Īrānshahr 128 27.13 N 60.41 E
Irapa 246 10.34 N 62.35 W
Irapuato 234 20.41 N 101.21 W
Iraq (Al-ʿIrāq) □[1], Asia 118 33.00 N 44.00 E
Iraq (Al-ʿIrāq) □[1], Asia 128 33.00 N 44.00 E
Irará 255 12.02 S 38.46 W
Iratapuru ≃ 250 0.36 S 52.35 W
Irati 252 25.27 S 50.39 W
Irati ≃ 34 42.35 N 1.16 W
Irauçuba 250 3.45 S 39.47 W
Irazú, Volcán ∧[1] 236 9.58 N 83.53 W
Irba 88 58.07 N 99.00 E
Irbejskoje 88 55.39 N 95.28 E
Irbeni väin (Irbes jūras šaurums) ⊔ 76 57.48 N 22.05 E
Irbes jūras šaurums (Irbeni väin) ⊔ 76 57.48 N 22.05 E
Irbid 132 32.33 N 35.51 E
Irbid □[8] 132 32.30 N 35.45 E
Irbīl 128 36.11 N 44.01 E
Irbīl □[4] 128 36.10 N 44.00 E
Irbit 86 57.41 N 63.03 E
Irby 262 53.21 N 3.07 W
Irchester 42 52.16 N 0.38 W
Irdning 61 47.33 N 14.01 E
Irdyn' 78 49.23 N 31.44 E
Ire, Mount ∧ 175e 9.10 S 161.05 E
Irebu 152 0.37 S 17.45 E
Irecê 250 11.18 S 41.52 W
Iregua ≃ 34 42.27 N 2.24 W
Ireland (Éire) □[1], Europe 22 53.00 N 8.00 W
Ireland (Éire) □[1], Europe 48 53.00 N 8.00 W
Ireland Brook ≃ 276 40.25 N 74.29 W
Iren' ≃ 86 57.27 N 56.56 E
Irene, S. Afr. 158 25.53 S 28.13 E
Irene, S.D., U.S. 198 43.05 N 97.10 W
Irene, Tx., U.S. 222 31.59 N 96.52 W
Irene, Mount ∧ 172 45.10 S 167.22 E
Ireng (Maú) ≃ 246 3.33 N 59.51 W
Iresick Brook ≃ 276 40.24 N 74.22 W
Ireton 198 42.58 N 96.19 W
Irfon ≃ 42 52.09 N 3.24 W
Irgakly 84 44.22 N 44.45 E
Irgiz 86 48.37 N 61.16 E
Irgiz ≃ 86 48.13 N 62.08 E
Iri 98 35.56 N 126.57 E
Irian Jaya □[4] 164 5.00 S 138.00 E
Iriba 146 15.07 N 22.15 E
Irié 150 8.17 N 9.11 W
Iriga 116 13.25 N 123.25 E
Irigny 62 45.40 N 4.49 E
Irîgui ⊸[1] 150 16.43 N 5.30 W
Iriklinskij 86 51.39 N 58.38 E
Iringa 154 7.46 S 35.42 E
Iringa □[4] 154 9.00 S 35.00 E
Irinjālakuda 122 10.20 N 76.14 E
Iriomote-jima I 175d 24.20 N 123.50 E
Iriona 236 15.57 N 85.11 W
Iriri ≃, Bra. 250 3.52 S 52.37 W
Iriri ≃, Bra. 287a 22.41 S 43.05 W
Iriri Novo ≃ 250 8.46 S 53.22 W
Irische See → Irish Sea ⊽[2] 28 53.30 N 5.20 W
Irish, Mount ∧ 204 37.38 N 115.24 W
Irish Sea ⊽[2] 28 53.30 N 5.20 W
Irishtown 166 40.55 S 145.08 E
Irituia 250 1.46 S 47.26 W
Iriyamazu 268 35.16 N 139.39 E
Irkās, Wādī V 142 28.57 N 32.00 E
Irkeštam 85 39.41 N 73.55 E
Irkinejeva ≃ 88 58.30 N 96.48 E
Irkinejevo 88 58.30 N 96.49 E
Irklijevskaja 78 45.51 N 39.39 E
Irkliyiv 78 49.32 N 32.18 E
Irkoutsk → Irkutsk 88 52.16 N 104.20 E
Irkut ≃ 88 52.18 N 104.15 E
Irkutsk 88 52.16 N 104.20 E
Irkutsk Oblast' □[4] 88 56.00 N 106.00 E
Irlam 44 53.28 N 2.25 W
Irland → Ireland □[1] 48 53.00 N 8.00 W
Irlanda, Mar de → Irish Sea ⊽[2] 28 53.30 N 5.20 W
Irlande → Ireland □[1] 48 53.00 N 8.00 W
Irlande, Mer d' → Irish Sea ⊽[2] 28 53.30 N 5.20 W
Irma 182 52.55 N 111.14 W
Irmauw 164 7.25 S 131.42 E
Irminger Basin ⊹[1] 10 61.00 N 35.00 W
Irminio ≃ 70 36.46 N 14.36 E
Irnijärvi ⊜ 26 65.36 N 29.05 E
Irnsum 52 53.05 N 5.47 E
Iro, Lac ⊜ 146 10.06 N 19.25 E
Iroise c 32 48.15 N 4.55 W
Iron Baron 166 32.59 S 137.09 E
Iron Belt 190 46.24 N 90.19 W
Iron Bottom Sound ⊔ 175e 9.15 S 160.00 E
Iron Bridge, On., Can. 190 46.17 N 83.14 W
Iron Bridge, Eng., U.K. 42 52.38 N 2.29 W
Iron Bridge Dam ⊸[6] 222 32.50 N 95.54 W
Iron City 194 35.01 N 87.34 W
Iron Cove c 274a 33.52 S 151.10 E
Iron Creek ≃ 182 52.43 N 111.14 W
Irondale, Al., U.S. 194 33.32 N 86.42 W
Irondale, Mo., U.S. 194 37.49 N 90.40 W
Irondale, Oh., U.S. 214 40.34 N 80.43 W
Irondale ≃ 212 44.49 N 78.37 W
Irondequoit 210 43.12 N 77.36 W
Irondequoit Bay c 210 43.12 N 77.32 W
Iron Gate V 38 44.41 N 22.31 E
Iron Gate Reservoir ⊜[1] 38 44.30 N 22.00 E
Ironia 276 40.49 N 74.37 W
Iron Knob 166 32.44 S 137.08 E
Iron Mountain 190 45.49 N 88.03 W
Iron Mountain ∧, Az., U.S. 200 33.27 N 111.10 W
Iron Mountain ∧, Ca., U.S. 280 34.17 N 117.43 W
Iron Mountains ⋏ 192 36.30 N 81.50 W
Iron Range 164 12.42 S 143.18 E
Iron Range National Park ♠ 164 12.44 S 143.16 E
Iron River, Mi., U.S. 190 46.05 N 88.38 W
Iron River, Wi., U.S. 190 46.33 N 91.24 W
Iron Springs 208 39.46 N 77.25 W
Ironton, Mn., U.S. 190 46.28 N 93.58 W
Ironton, Mo., U.S. 194 37.35 N 90.37 W
Ironton, Oh., U.S. 188 38.32 N 82.40 W
Ironwood 190 46.27 N 90.10 W
Ironworks Creek ≃ 285 40.10 N 74.59 W
Iroquois, On., Can. 212 44.51 N 75.19 W
Iroquois, Il., U.S. 216 40.50 N 87.35 W
Iroquois, S.D., U.S. 198 44.22 N 97.51 W
Iroquois □[6] 216 40.47 N 87.44 W
Iroquois ≃ 216 41.05 N 87.49 W
Iroquois Falls 190 48.46 N 80.41 W
Iroquois Lock and Dam ⊸[5] 212 44.45 N 75.23 W
Irosin 116 12.42 N 124.02 E
Írottkő (Geschriebenstein) ∧ 61 47.21 N 16.26 E
Irō-zaki › 94 34.36 N 138.51 E
Irpin' 78 50.31 N 30.15 E
Irpin' ≃ 78 50.34 N 30.16 E
Irrawaddy → Ayeyarwady ≃ 110 20.32 N 96.55 E
Irrawaddy, Mouths of the ≃[1] 110 15.45 N 94.50 E
Irregully Creek ≃ 162 23.06 S 116.21 E
Irrel 56 49.51 N 6.28 E
Irricana 182 51.19 N 113.37 W
Irrigon 202 45.53 N 119.29 W
Irschenberg 64 47.50 N 11.55 E
Irsee 58 47.54 N 10.34 E
Irsha ≃ 78 50.45 N 29.30 E
Irshava 78 48.20 N 23.03 E
Irsina 68 40.45 N 16.15 E
Irt ≃ 44 54.22 N 3.26 W
Irtek ≃ 80 51.28 N 52.39 E
Irthing ≃ 44 54.55 N 2.50 W
Irthlingborough 42 52.20 N 0.37 W
Irtyš 86 54.29 N 74.22 E
Irtysh (Irtyš) (Ertix) ≃ 74 61.04 N 68.52 E
Irtyšsk 86 53.21 N 75.27 E
Irubaj 80 50.11 N 51.21 E
Iruma 94 35.50 N 139.24 E
Iruma ≃ 94 35.57 N 139.30 E
Iruma Air Base ■ 268 35.50 N 139.24 E
Iruma-kichi, Kaijō-jieitai- ■ 94 35.50 N 139.24 E
Irumu 154 1.27 N 29.52 E
Irún 34 43.21 N 1.47 W
Irupana 248 16.28 S 67.28 W
Irurzun 34 42.55 N 1.50 W
Irú Tepuy ∧ 246 5.25 N 61.02 W
Irvine, Ab., Can. 184 49.57 N 110.16 W
Irvine, Scot., U.K. 46 55.37 N 4.40 W
Irvine, Ca., U.S. 228 33.40 N 117.49 W
Irvine, Ky., U.S. 192 37.42 N 83.58 W
Irvine, Pa., U.S. 214 41.50 N 79.17 W
Irvine ≃ 46 55.37 N 4.41 W
Irvine, Mount ∧ 210 42.03 N 78.40 W
Irvine Creek ≃ 212 43.41 N 80.25 W
Irvine Park ♠ 280 33.48 N 117.45 W
Irvines Landing 182 49.38 N 124.03 W
Irvinestown 48 54.28 N 7.38 W
Irving, Il., U.S. 219 39.12 N 89.24 W
Irving, N.Y., U.S. 214 42.34 N 79.07 W
Irving, Tx., U.S. 222 32.48 N 96.56 W
Irving Park ⊸[8] 278 41.57 N 87.43 W
Irvington, Il., U.S. 219 38.26 N 89.10 W
Irvington, Ky., U.S. 194 37.52 N 86.17 W
Irvington, N.J., U.S. 210 40.43 N 74.13 W
Irvington, N.Y., U.S. 210 41.02 N 73.51 W
Irvington, Oh., U.S. 218 39.51 N 84.15 W
Irvington, Va., U.S. 208 37.39 N 76.25 W
Irvington ⊸[8] 284b 39.17 N 76.41 W
Irvona 214 40.46 N 78.33 W
Irwell ≃ 44 53.27 N 2.17 W
Irwin, Austl. 162 29.12 S 115.04 E
Irwin, Oh., U.S. 218 40.07 N 83.29 W
Irwin, Pa., U.S. 279b 40.19 N 79.42 W
Irwin ≃ 162 29.15 S 114.56 E
Irwin, Point › 162 35.04 S 116.56 E
Irwindale 280 34.06 N 117.56 W
Irwinton 192 32.48 N 83.10 W
Is 86 58.48 N 59.43 E
Is, Jabal ∧ 140 21.49 N 35.39 E
Isa 150 13.14 N 6.24 E
ʿĪsā, Ra's › 144 15.11 N 42.39 E
Isaac ≃ 166 22.52 S 149.20 E
Isaac Lake ⊜, B.C., Can. 182 53.10 N 120.50 W
Isaac Lake ⊜, On., Can. 212 44.47 N 81.14 W
Isaba 34 42.52 N 0.55 W
Isabel, Pil. 116 10.56 N 124.26 E
Isabel, S.D., U.S. 198 45.23 N 101.25 W
Isabel □[4] 175e 7.55 S 159.10 E
Isabela, Pil. 116 10.12 N 122.59 E
Isabela (Basilan), Pil. 116 6.42 N 121.58 E
Isabela, P.R. 240m 18.30 N 67.01 W
Isabela □[4] 116 17.00 N 122.00 E
Isabela, Cabo › 238 19.56 N 71.01 W
Isabela, Canal ⊔ 246a 0.20 S 90.55 W
Isabela, Isla I, Ec. 246a 0.30 S 91.06 W
Isabela, Isla I, Méx. 234 21.51 N 105.55 W
Isabela de Sagua 240p 22.57 N 80.01 W
Isabelia, Cordillera ⋏ 236 13.45 N 85.15 W
Isabella Indian Reservation ⊸[4] 190 43.41 N 84.48 W
Isabella Lake ⊜ 212 45.24 N 79.49 W
Isabella Lake ⊜[1] 204 35.40 N 118.26 W
Isabelle ≃ 190 47.50 N 91.41 W
Isábena ≃ 34 42.11 N 0.21 E
Isaccea 38 45.16 N 28.28 E
Ísafjarðardjúp c[2] 24a 66.10 N 23.00 W
Ísafjörður 24a 66.08 N 23.13 W
Isāgarh 124 24.50 N 77.53 E
Isagatedo 273a 6.32 N 3.20 E
Isahaya 92 32.50 N 130.03 E
Isak 114 4.28 N 96.55 E
Isaka, Tan. 154 3.54 S 32.56 E
Isaka, R.D.C. 152 2.35 S 18.48 E
Isaka-Buku 152 3.55 S 22.03 E
Īsa Khel 123 32.41 N 71.17 E
Isakly 80 54.08 N 51.32 E
Isakovka 86 55.45 N 74.24 E
Isakovo, Ross. 76 55.11 N 34.40 E
Isakovo, Ross. 76 60.30 N 41.13 E
Isakovo, Ross. 82 54.36 N 37.02 E
Isakovo, Ross. 265b 55.59 N 37.23 E
Isalnița 38 44.24 N 23.44 E
Isalo, Massif de l' ⋏ 157b 22.45 S 45.15 E
Isalo, Parc National de l' ♠ 157b 22.45 S 45.15 E
Isana (Içana) ≃ 246 0.26 N 67.19 W
Īsānagar 124 27.54 N 81.13 E
Isandhlwana ⊥ 158 28.21 S 30.39 E
Isandja Etat 152 2.59 S 22.00 E
Isando 273d 26.09 S 28.12 E
Isanga 152 1.26 S 22.18 E
Isangano National Park ♠ 154 11.10 S 30.40 E
Isangel 175f 19.32 S 169.16 E
Isangi 152 0.46 N 24.15 E
Is'angulovo 86 52.12 N 56.36 E
Isanlu Makutu 150 8.17 N 5.46 E
Isan-ni 98 40.46 N 128.55 E
Isanti 190 45.29 N 93.14 W
Isar ≃ 60 48.49 N 12.58 E
Isara 150 6.59 N 3.41 E
Isarco (Eisack) ≃ 64 46.27 N 11.18 E
Isarco, Valle V 64 46.45 N 11.37 E
Isarog, Mount ∧ 116 13.39 N 123.23 E
Isasi 273a 6.40 N 3.23 E
Isawa 94 35.39 N 138.38 E
Isbergues 50 50.37 N 2.27 E
Isbister 46a 60.36 N 1.19 W
İscehisar 130 38.51 N 30.45 E
Iščeino 76 52.57 N 38.50 E
Iščerskaja 84 43.43 N 45.08 E
Ischgl 58 47.01 N 10.17 E
Ischia 68 40.44 N 13.57 E
Ischia, Isola d' I 68 40.43 N 13.54 E
Ischia di Castro 66 42.33 N 11.45 E
Ischim → Išim ≃ 86 57.45 N 71.12 E
Ischitella 68 41.54 N 15.54 E
Ischma → Ižma ≃ 24 65.19 N 52.54 E
Ischodnaja, gora ∧ 180 64.50 N 173.26 W
Ischua 210 42.15 N 78.24 W
Ischua Creek ≃ 210 42.10 N 78.23 W
Iscuandé ≃ 246 2.38 N 78.04 W
Isdell ≃ 162 16.27 S 124.51 E
Isdes 50 47.40 N 2.15 E
Ise (Uji-yamada) 94 34.29 N 136.42 E
Ise ≃ 54 52.30 N 10.33 E
Isefjord c 41 55.52 N 11.49 E
Isehara 94 35.24 N 139.18 E
Išejevka 80 54.25 N 48.16 E
Iseke 154 6.25 S 35.01 E
Isel ≃ 64 46.50 N 12.47 E
Iselin, N.J., U.S. 210 40.34 N 74.19 W
Iselin, Pa., U.S. 214 40.33 N 79.23 W
Iselle 58 46.12 N 8.12 E
Iseltwald 58 46.43 N 7.58 E
Isen 60 48.13 N 12.04 E
Isen ≃ 60 48.15 N 12.40 E
Isenbajevo 80 56.03 N 53.25 E
Isenbüttel 52 52.26 N 10.34 E
Isenyela 154 8.36 S 33.30 E
Iseo 64 45.39 N 10.03 E
Iseo, Lago d' ⊜ 64 45.43 N 10.04 E
Iseramagazi 154 4.40 S 32.09 E
Iseran, Col de l')(62 45.25 N 7.02 E
Isère □[5] 62 45.10 N 5.50 E
Isère ≃ 62 44.59 N 4.51 E
Iseri 273a 6.39 N 3.23 E
Iseri-Oke 273a 6.38 N 3.23 E
Iseri-Osun 273a 6.31 N 3.17 E
Iserlohn 56 51.22 N 7.41 E
Isernhagen 52 52.26 N 9.51 E
Isernia 66 41.36 N 14.14 E
Isernia □[4] 66 41.40 N 14.15 E
Isesaki 94 36.19 N 139.12 E
Ise-Shima-kokuritsu-kōen ♠ 92 34.23 N 136.48 E
Iset' ≃ 86 56.36 N 66.24 E
Isetskoje 86 56.29 N 65.21 E
Ise-wan c 94 34.43 N 136.43 E
Iseyin 150 7.58 N 3.36 E
Isezaki → Isesaki 92 36.19 N 139.12 E
Isfahan → Eşfahān 128 32.40 N 51.38 E
Isfana 85 39.50 N 69.31 E
Isfana ≃ 85 40.13 N 69.26 E
Isfara 85 40.07 N 70.38 E
ʿIsfiyā 132 32.43 N 35.04 E
Ishenga Oswe 152 3.46 S 22.34 E
Isheri-Olofin 273a 6.35 N 3.17 E
Isherton 246 2.19 N 59.22 W
Ishi ≃ 270 34.35 N 135.38 E
Ishibashi 94 36.26 N 139.52 E
Ishibe 94 35.00 N 136.04 E
Ishigaki 175d 24.20 N 124.09 E
Ishigaki-shima I 175d 24.24 N 124.12 E
Ishige 94 36.07 N 139.58 E
Ishii 96 34.04 N 134.26 E
Ishikari ≃ 92a 43.15 N 141.23 E
Ishikari-dake ∧ 92a 43.33 N 143.02 E
Ishikari-heiya ≚ 92a 43.15 N 141.23 E
Ishikari-sanchi ⋏ 92a 43.35 N 143.00 E
Ishikari-wan c 92a 43.25 N 141.01 E
Ishikawa, Nihon 94 37.09 N 140.27 E
Ishikawa, Nihon 174m 26.25 N 127.50 E
Ishikawa □[5] 94 36.45 N 136.45 E
Ishiki 94 34.48 N 137.01 E
Ishikiri 270 34.41 N 135.39 E
I-shima I 96 33.51 N 134.49 E
Ishinomaki 92 38.25 N 141.18 E
Ishinomaki-wan c 92 38.18 N 141.18 E
Ishioka 94 36.11 N 140.16 E
Ishiyama 270 34.58 N 135.55 E
Ishizuchi-san ∧ 96 33.46 N 133.07 E
Ishkumān 123 36.32 N 73.49 E
Ishmant 142 29.12 N 31.11 E
Ishpeming 190 46.29 N 87.40 W
Ishuizu ≃ 270 34.33 N 135.27 E
Ishurdi 124 24.08 N 89.05 E
Isidro Casanova 288 34.42 S 58.35 W
Isigny 32 49.19 N 1.06 W
Işık Dağı ∧ 130 38.21 N 36.32 E
Işıklı 130 38.19 N 29.51 E
Işıkli Burnu › 267b 41.14 N 29.15 E
Isili 71 39.44 N 9.06 E
Isil'kul' 86 54.55 N 71.16 E
Išim 86 56.09 N 69.27 E
Išim ≃ 86 57.45 N 71.12 E
Išimbaj 86 53.28 N 56.02 E
Išimskaja step' ≚ 86 55.00 N 70.00 E
Išimskoje 86 51.24 N 67.08 E
Isimu 112 0.40 N 122.51 E
Isinga 88 52.55 N 112.00 E
Isiolo 154 0.21 N 37.35 E
Isiolo Game Reserve ⊸[4] 154 0.32 N 37.34 E
Isipingo 158 29.59 S 30.56 E
Isipingo Beach 158 29.59 S 30.57 E
Isiro (Paulis) 154 2.47 N 27.37 E
Isis 166 25.12 S 152.13 E
Isisford 166 24.16 S 144.26 E
Iskandar 85 41.36 N 69.43 E
Iskăr ≃ 38 43.44 N 24.27 E
Iskăr, Jazovir ⊜[1] 38 42.28 N 23.35 E
Iškašim 123 36.44 N 71.37 E
Iskaten', chrebet ⋏ 180 66.30 N 179.00 W
Iškejevo 80 55.51 N 50.56 E
İskele 130 35.17 N 33.52 E
İskenderun 130 36.37 N 36.07 E
İskenderun Körfezi (Gulf of Alexandretta) c 130 36.30 N 35.40 E
Iske-R'az'ap 80 54.36 N 49.42 E
İskilip 130 40.45 N 34.29 E
Iski-Naukat 85 40.16 N 72.36 E
Iskininskij 80 47.13 N 52.41 E
Iskitim 86 54.38 N 83.18 E
Iskona ≃ 82 55.34 N 36.05 E
Iskushuban 144 10.17 N 50.14 E
Iskut ≃ 180 56.42 N 131.45 W
Isla 234 18.01 N 95.30 W
Isla ≃ 46 57.30 N 2.47 W
Isla, Salar de la ≚ 252 25.49 S 68.53 W
Islač ≃ 76 53.55 N 26.13 E
Isla Cristina 34 37.12 N 7.19 W
Isla de Maipo 252 33.45 S 70.54 W
İslâhiye 130 37.03 N 36.36 E
Islāmābād → Anantnāg, India 123 33.44 N 75.09 E
Islāmābād, Pāk. 123 33.42 N 73.10 E
Isla Mala 258 34.12 S 56.21 W
Islāmkot 120 24.42 N 70.11 E
Islamorada 220 24.55 N 80.37 W
Islāmpur, India 122 17.03 N 74.16 E
Islāmpur, India 124 25.09 N 85.12 E
Islāmpur, India 124 26.16 N 88.12 E
Islāmpur, India 126 24.09 N 88.28 E
Islāmpur, India 126 21.43 N 87.39 E
Isla Mujeres 232 21.12 N 86.43 W
Island 194 37.26 N 87.08 W
Island □[6] 224 48.07 N 122.36 W
Island → Iceland □[1] 24a 65.00 N 18.00 W
Island ≃ 262 53.44 N 2.51 W
Island Bay c 116 9.06 N 118.10 E
Island Beach State Park ♠ 208 39.50 N 74.06 W
Island Bend 171b 36.19 S 148.29 E
Island Creek 283 42.00 N 70.43 W
Island Falls, Sk., Can. 184 55.32 N 102.21 W
Island Falls, Me., U.S. 188 46.00 N 68.16 W
Island Heights 208 39.56 N 74.09 W
Islandia → Iceland □[1] 24a 65.00 N 18.00 W
Island Lagoon ⊜ 166 31.30 S 136.40 E
Island Lake, Mb., Can. 184 53.58 N 94.47 W
Island Lake, Il., U.S. 216 42.17 N 88.12 W
Island Lake, Mi., U.S. 281 42.31 N 83.44 W
Island Lake ⊜ 184 53.47 N 94.25 W
Island Lake State Recreation Area ♠ 216 42.30 N 83.43 W
Island Park, Id., U.S. 202 44.24 N 111.19 W
Island Park, N.Y., U.S. 276 40.36 N 73.39 W
Island Park, R.I., U.S. 207 41.37 N 71.13 W
Island Park Reservoir ⊜[1] 202 44.25 N 111.29 W
Island Point › 162 30.20 S 115.02 E
Island Pond 188 44.48 N 71.52 W
Island Pond ⊜ 186 48.25 N 56.23 W
Islands, Bay of c, Nf., Can. 186 49.10 N 58.15 W
Islands, Bay of c, N.Z. 172 35.12 S 174.10 E
Island View 216 40.31 N 83.53 W
Isla Patrulla 252 32.59 S 54.35 W
Islas de la Bahía □[5] 236 16.20 N 86.30 W
Islas Malvinas → Falkland Islands □[2] 254 51.45 S 59.00 W
Isla Verde 252 33.14 S 62.24 W
Isla Vista 204 34.25 N 119.50 W
Islay I 46 55.46 N 6.10 W
Islay, Punta › 248 17.01 S 72.07 W
Islay, Rhinns of ›[1] 46 55.45 N 6.25 W
Islay, Sound of ⊔ 46 55.50 N 6.06 W
Isle 190 46.08 N 93.28 W
Isle ≃, Fr. 32 44.55 N 0.15 W
Isle ≃, Eng., U.K. 42 50.59 N 2.53 W
Isle-Adam, Forêt de l' ♠ 261 49.05 N 2.15 E
Isle-aux-Morts 186 47.35 N 58.59 W
Isle of Hope 192 31.58 N 81.05 W
Isle of Man □[2], Europe 22 54.15 N 4.30 W
Isle of Man □[2], Europe 44 54.15 N 4.30 W
Isle of Man (Ronaldsway) Airport ⊠ 44 54.06 N 4.36 W
Isle of Palms 192 32.47 N 79.48 W
Isle of Wight 208 36.54 N 76.42 W
Isle of Wight □[6], Eng., U.K. 42 50.40 N 1.20 W
Isle of Wight □[6], Va., U.S. 208 36.50 N 76.42 W
Isle of Wight Bay c 208 38.22 N 75.06 W
Isle Royale National Park ♠ 190 48.00 N 89.00 W
Isles, Lake of the ⊜ 212 44.19 N 75.59 W
Isle Saint George 214 41.43 N 82.49 W
Islesboro Island I 188 44.20 N 68.53 W
Isleta 200 34.54 N 106.41 W
Isleta Indian Reservation ⊸[4] 200 34.55 N 106.45 W
Isleton 226 38.09 N 121.36 W
Islets-Caribou 186 49.30 N 67.14 W
Isleworth ⊸[8] 260 51.28 N 0.20 W
Islington 207 42.13 N 71.11 W
Islington ⊸[8], On., Can. 275b 43.39 N 79.32 W
Islington ⊸[8], Eng., U.K. 42 51.34 N 0.06 W
Islip, Eng., U.K. 42 51.50 N 1.14 W
Islip, N.Y., U.S. 276 40.43 N 73.12 W
Islip Terrace 276 40.44 N 73.11 W
Islivig 46 58.05 N 7.11 W
Islón 252 29.54 S 71.12 W
Isluga, Volcán ∧[1] 248 19.10 S 68.51 W
Ismael Cortinas (Arroyo Grande) 258 33.58 S 57.06 W
Ismailia → Al-Ismāʿīlīyah 142 30.35 N 32.16 E
Ismāʿīlīyah ⊸[8] 273c 30.03 N 31.14 E
Ismāʿīlīyah, Turʿat al- ≊ 142 30.04 N 31.16 E
İsmailli 130 38.56 N 27.13 E
Ismailovo 80 55.34 N 54.39 E
Ismaning 60 48.14 N 11.41 E
İsmayıllı 84 40.47 N 48.09 E
Isnā 140 25.18 N 32.33 E
Isny 58 47.41 N 10.02 E
Isoanala 157b 23.50 S 45.44 E
Isobe 94 34.22 N 136.49 E
Isogo ⊸[8] 268 35.23 N 139.37 E
Isojoki 26 62.07 N 21.58 E
Isoka 154 10.10 S 32.35 E
Isokyrö 26 63.00 N 22.19 E
Isola, Fr. 62 44.11 N 7.03 E
Isola, Ms., U.S. 194 33.15 N 90.35 W
Isola, Monte ∧ 64 45.42 N 10.05 E
Isola d'Asti 62 44.50 N 8.11 E
Isola del Cantone 62 44.39 N 8.57 E
Isola del Gran Sasso d'Italia 66 42.30 N 13.40 E
Isola della Scala 64 45.16 N 11.00 E
Isola del Liri 66 41.41 N 13.34 E
Isola di Capo Rizzuto 68 38.58 N 17.06 E
Isola Dovarese 64 45.10 N 10.18 E
Isola Farnese ⊸[8] 66 42.01 N 12.23 E
Isola Vicentina 64 45.38 N 11.25 E
Isoletta 66 41.30 N 13.34 E
Isolillock Peak ∧ 224 49.18 N 121.27 W
Isolo 273a 6.32 N 3.19 E
Isone 58 46.08 N 8.59 E
Isonzo (Soča) ≃ 64 45.47 N 13.32 E
Isorella 64 45.18 N 10.19 E
Iso-Syöte ∧[2] 26 65.37 N 27.35 E
Iso-zaki › 94 36.23 N 140.38 E
Ispani 68 40.08 N 15.34 E
Isparta 130 37.46 N 30.33 E
Isparta □[4] 130 38.00 N 31.00 E
Isperih 38 43.43 N 26.50 E
Ispica 70 36.47 N 14.55 E
Ispica, Cava d' ±[5] 70 36.51 N 14.51 E
Ispikān 128 26.14 N 62.12 E
İspir 130 40.29 N 41.00 E
Ispra 62 45.49 N 8.37 E
Ispringen 56 48.55 N 8.40 E
Israel (Yisra'el) □[1], Asia 118 31.30 N 35.00 E
Israel (Yisra'el) □[1], Asia 132 31.30 N 35.00 E
Israel ≃ 188 44.29 N 71.35 W
Issa 80 53.52 N 44.51 E
Issa ≃ 76 56.58 N 28.47 E
Issano 246 5.49 N 59.25 W
Issaquah 224 47.31 N 122.01 W
Issaran, Ra's › 142 28.48 N 32.47 E
Issel (Oude IJssel) ≃ 52 52.00 N 6.10 E
Isselburg 52 51.51 N 6.28 E
Isselhorst 52 51.57 N 8.24 E
Isser, Oued ≃, Alg. 34 36.52 N 3.48 E
Isser, Oued ≃, Alg. 34 35.08 N 1.28 W
Issia 150 6.29 N 6.35 W
Issigeac 32 44.44 N 0.36 E
Issime 62 45.41 N 7.51 E
Issogne 62 45.39 N 7.41 E
Issoire 32 45.33 N 3.15 E
Issole ≃ 62 43.27 N 6.12 E
Issou 261 48.59 N 1.48 E
Issoudun 32 46.57 N 2.00 E
Issum 52 51.32 N 6.25 E
Issuna 154 5.23 S 34.46 E
Is-sur-Tille 58 47.31 N 5.06 E
Issy 50 48.49 N 2.17 E
Issyk-Kul' (Rybačje) 85 42.26 N 76.12 E
Issyk-Kul' □[4] 85 42.15 N 77.15 E
Issyk-Kul', ozero ⊜ 85 42.25 N 77.15 E
Īstādeh-ye Moqor, Āb-e ⊜ 120 32.32 N 67.57 E
Istana Presidential Palace ʋ 269e 6.10 S 106.49 E
İstanbul, Tür. 130 41.01 N 28.58 E
İstanbul, Tür. 267b 41.01 N 28.58 E
İstanbul □[4] 130 41.10 N 28.45 E
Istanbul (Yeşilköy) International Airport ⊠ 267b 40.58 N 28.49 E
İstanbul Boğazı (Bosporus) ⊔ 130 41.06 N 29.04 E
Istanbul University ʋ[2] 267b 41.00 N 28.58 E
Istanhā 142 30.28 N 31.07 E
Istead Rise 260 51.24 N 0.22 E
Isteren ⊜ 26 61.58 N 11.48 E
Isthmus Bay c 212 45.00 N 81.15 W
Istiaía 38 38.57 N 23.09 E
İstinye ⊸[8] 267b 41.06 N 29.03 E
İstisu 84 39.57 N 45.59 E
Istmina 246 5.10 N 76.39 W
Isto, Mount ∧ 180 69.12 N 143.48 W
Istobensk 80 58.25 N 48.48 E
Istobnoje, Ross. 78 51.08 N 37.21 E
Istobnoje, Ross. 78 51.16 N 38.39 E
Istok 38 42.47 N 20.29 E
Istokpoga, Lake ⊜ 220 27.22 N 81.17 W
Istra 82 55.55 N 36.52 E
Istra ›[1] 36 45.15 N 14.00 E
Istra ≃ 82 55.44 N 37.08 E
Istrana 64 45.41 N 12.07 E
Istres 62 43.31 N 4.59 E
Istria → Istra ›[1] 36 45.15 N 14.00 E
Istrinskoje vodochranilišče ⊜[1] 82 56.04 N 36.49 E
Isulan 116 6.34 N 124.37 E
Isumi 94 35.17 N 140.19 E
Isumi ≃ 94 35.18 N 140.25 E
Isumrud Strait ⊔ 164 4.45 S 145.50 E
Isunba 273a 6.27 N 3.17 E
Iswarīpur 126 22.19 N 89.07 E
Iswepe 158 26.50 S 30.31 E
Itá 252 25.29 S 57.21 W
Itabaiana, Bra. 250 7.20 S 35.20 W
Itabaiana, Bra. 250 10.41 S 37.26 W
Itabaiana, Bra. 250 11.16 S 37.47 W
Itabapoana 255 21.18 S 40.58 W
Itabashi ⊸[8] 268 35.45 N 139.43 E
Itaberá 255 23.51 S 49.09 W
Itaberaba 255 12.32 S 40.18 W
Itaberaí 255 16.02 S 49.48 W
Itabi 250 10.08 S 37.06 W
Itabira 255 19.37 S 43.13 W
Itaboca 256 22.03 S 44.05 W
Itaboraí 256 22.45 S 42.52 W
Itaboraí □[7] 287a 22.43 S 43.00 W
Itabuna 255 14.48 S 39.16 W
Itacaiuna ≃ 250 5.21 S 49.08 W
Itacajá 250 8.19 S 47.46 W
Itacambiruçu ≃ 255 16.44 S 42.45 W
Itacaré 255 14.18 S 39.00 W
Itacoatiara 250 3.08 S 58.25 W
Itacoatiara, Ponta de › 287a 22.59 S 43.02 W
Itacurubí del Rosario 252 24.29 S 56.41 W
Itacurussá 256 22.55 S 43.55 W
Itacurussá, Ilha de I 256 22.56 S 43.53 W
Itaeté 255 12.59 S 40.58 W
Itagacaba ≃ 256 22.34 S 44.56 W
Itagi 255 14.10 S 40.01 W
Itaguaçu 255 19.48 S 40.51 W
Itaguaí 256 22.52 S 43.47 W
Itaguajé 255 22.37 S 51.59 W
Itaguara 255 20.23 S 44.29 W
Itaguaré, Pico do ∧ 256 22.30 S 45.10 W
Itaguari ≃ 255 14.11 S 44.40 W
Itaguaru 255 15.44 S 49.37 W
Itaguatins 250 5.47 S 47.29 W
Itagüí 246 6.10 N 75.36 W
Itaí 255 23.24 S 49.06 W
Itá-Ibaté 252 27.26 S 57.20 W
Itaiçaba 250 4.40 S 37.51 W
Itaim 256 22.24 S 45.53 W
Itaim ≃, Bra. 250 7.02 S 42.02 W
Itaim ≃, Bra. 256 23.07 S 45.08 W
Itaim ≃, Bra. 256 22.19 S 45.51 W
Itainópolis 250 7.24 S 41.31 W
Itaiópolis 252 26.20 S 49.56 W
Itaipava 256 22.23 S 43.08 W
Itaipu, Bra. 256 22.58 S 43.02 W
Itaipu, Bra. 287a 22.44 S 43.26 W
Itaipu, Lagoa de c 287a 22.58 S 43.02 W
Itaipu, Ponta de › 287a 22.59 S 43.03 W
Itaipu, Represa de ⊜[1] 252 25.00 S 54.30 W
Itäisen Suomenlahden kansallispuisto ♠ 26 60.15 N 27.00 E
Itaituba 250 4.17 S 55.59 W
Itajá 255 19.07 S 51.37 W
Itajaí 252 26.53 S 48.39 W
Itajaí do Sul ≃ 252 27.12 S 49.39 W
Itajipora 256 22.19 S 46.28 W
Itajubá 256 22.26 S 45.27 W

Symbols in the index entries represent the broad categories identified in the key at the right. Symbols with superior numbers (⋏[1]) identify subcategories (see complete key on page *I · 1).*

Symbole im Register stellen die rechts im Schlüssel erklärten Kategorien dar. Symbole mit hochgestellten Ziffern (⋏[1]) bezeichnen Unterabteilungen einer Kategorie (vgl. vollständiger Schlüssel auf Seite *I · 1).*

Los símbolos incluídos en el texto del índice representan las grandes categorías identificadas con la clave a la derecha. Los símbolos con numeros en su parte superior (⋏[1]) identifican las subcategorías (véase la clave completa en la página *I · 1).*

Les symboles de l'index représentent les catégories indiquées dans la légende à droite. Les symboles suivis d'un indice (⋏[1]) représentent des sous-catégories (voir légende complète à la page *I · 1).*

Os símbolos incluídos no texto do índice representam as grandes categorias identificadas com a chave à direita. Os símbolos com números em sua parte superior (⋏[1]) identificam as subcategorias (veja-se a chave completa à página *I · 1).*

∧	Mountain	Berg	Montaña	Montagne	Montanha
⋏	Mountains	Gebirge	Montañas	Montagnes	Montanhas
)(	Pass	Paß	Paso	Col	Passo
V	Valley, Canyon	Tal, Cañon	Valle, Cañón	Vallée, Canyon	Vale, Canhão
≚	Plain	Ebene	Llano	Plaine	Planície
›	Cape	Kap	Cabo	Cap	Cabo
I	Island	Insel	Isla	Île	Ilha
II	Islands	Inseln	Islas	Îles	Ilhas
±	Other Topographic Features	Andere Topographische Objekte	Otros Elementos Topográficos	Autres données topographiques	Outros acidentes topográficos

ESPAÑOL — Nombre | Página | Lat.°′ | Long.°′ W = Oeste
FRANÇAIS — Nom | Page | Lat.°′ | Long.°′ W = Ouest
PORTUGUÊS — Nome | Página | Lat.°′ | Long.°′ W = Oeste

Nombre	Página	Lat.°′	Long.°′
Itaju do Colônia	255	15.09 S	39.44 W
Itajuípe	255	14.41 S	39.22 W
Itaka, Ross.	88	53.53 N	118.42 E
Itaka, Tan.	154	8.52 S	32.47 E
Itaki	273a	6.43 N	3.17 E
Itako	94	35.56 N	140.33 E
Itakura, Nihon	94	36.13 N	139.36 E
Itakura, Nihon	94	37.03 N	138.18 E
Itala Game Reserve ◆[4]	158	27.31 S	31.19 E
Italia → Italy □[1]	36	42.50 N	12.50 E
Itálica ⊥	34	37.30 N	6.05 W
Italie → Italy □[1]	36	42.50 N	12.50 E
Italien → Italy □[1]	36	42.50 N	12.50 E
Italy	222	32.11 N	96.53 W
Italy (Italia) □[1], Europe	22	42.50 N	12.50 E
Italy (Italia) □[1], Europe	36	42.50 N	12.50 E
Itamaraju	255	17.05 S	39.31 W
Itamarandiba	255	17.51 S	42.51 W
Itamarandiba ≃	255	17.18 S	42.48 W
Itamarati de Minas	256	21.25 S	42.49 W
Itamari	255	13.47 S	39.37 W
Itamataré	250	2.16 S	46.24 W
Itambacuri	255	18.01 S	41.42 W
Itambé	255	15.15 S	40.37 W
Itambi	256	22.44 S	42.58 W
Itami	96	34.46 N	135.25 E
Itami, Camp ■	270	34.47 N	135.24 E
Itamonte	256	22.17 S	44.53 W
Itampolo	157b	24.41 S	43.57 E
Itānagar	120	27.09 N	93.33 E
Itandéua, Lago ⊜	250	2.01 S	55.10 W
Itandrano	157b	21.47 S	45.17 E
Itanhaém	255	24.11 S	46.47 W
Itanhandu	256	22.18 S	44.57 W
Itanhauã ≃	248	4.45 S	63.48 W
Itanhém	255	17.09 S	40.20 W
Itanhomi	255	19.10 S	41.52 W
Itano	96	34.07 N	134.28 E
Itaobim	255	16.34 S	41.30 W
Itaocaia	287a	22.58 S	43.01 W
Itapaci	255	14.57 S	49.34 W
Itapagipe	255	19.54 S	49.22 W
Itapajé	250	3.41 S	39.34 W
Itapanhaú ≃	256	23.51 S	46.10 W
Itaparaná ≃	248	5.47 S	63.03 W
Itaparica, Ilha de I	255	13.00 S	38.42 W
Itaparica, Represa de ⊜[1]	250	8.50 S	38.40 W
Itapaya	248	17.34 S	66.21 W
Itapé	255	14.54 S	39.26 W
Itapebi	255	15.56 S	39.32 W
Itapecerica	255	20.28 S	45.07 W
Itapecerica da Serra	256	23.43 S	46.50 W
Itapecerica da Serra □[7]	287b	23.44 S	46.52 W
Itapecuru-Mirim	250	3.24 S	44.20 W
Itapemirim	255	21.01 S	40.50 W
Itapera	250	2.32 S	43.47 W
Itaperina, Pointe ›	157b	24.59 S	47.06 E
Itaperuna	255	21.12 S	41.54 W
Itapetim	250	7.22 S	37.11 W
Itapetinga	255	15.15 S	40.15 W
Itapetininga	255	23.36 S	48.03 W
Itapetininga ≃	255	23.35 S	48.27 W
Itapeva, Bra.	255	23.58 S	48.52 W
Itapeva, Bra.	256	22.46 S	46.13 W
Itapevi	256	23.33 S	46.56 W
Itapevi □[7]	287b	23.31 S	46.55 W
Itapicuru	250	11.19 S	38.15 W
Itapicuru ≃, Bra.	250	2.52 S	44.12 W
Itapicuru ≃, Bra.	250	11.47 S	37.32 W
Itapipoca	250	3.30 S	39.35 W
Itapira	256	22.26 S	46.50 W
Itapiranga, Bra.	250	2.45 S	58.01 W
Itapiranga, Bra.	252	27.08 S	53.43 W
Itapirapuã	255	15.52 S	50.36 W
Itapitanga	255	14.26 S	39.34 W
Itapiúna	250	4.33 S	38.57 W
Itápolis	255	21.35 S	48.46 W
Itaporã	255	22.01 S	54.54 W
Itaporã de Goiás	250	8.02 S	48.39 W
Itaporanga, Bra.	250	7.18 S	38.10 W
Itaporanga, Bra.	255	23.42 S	49.29 W
Itaporanga d'Ajuda	250	10.59 S	37.18 W
Itapúa □[5]	252	26.50 S	55.50 W
Itapuranga	255	15.35 S	49.59 W
Itaquaí ≃	246	4.20 S	70.12 W
Itaquaquecetuba	256	23.29 S	46.21 W
Itaquaquecetuba □[7]	287b	23.28 S	46.20 W
Itaquara	255	13.27 S	39.57 W
Itaquari	255	20.20 S	40.22 W
Itaquaxiara	287b	23.47 S	46.51 W
Itaquaxiara, Ribeirão ≃	287b	23.44 S	46.47 W
Itaquera ◆[8]	256	23.32 S	46.27 W
Itaquera, Ribeirão ≃	287b	23.28 S	46.26 W
Itaqui	252	29.08 S	56.33 W
Itaquyry	252	24.56 S	55.13 W
Itarantim	255	15.39 S	40.03 W
Itararé	255	24.07 S	49.20 W
Itārsi	124	22.37 N	77.45 E
Itarumã	255	18.42 S	51.25 W
Itasca, Il., U.S.	278	41.58 N	88.00 W
Itasca, Tx., U.S.	222	32.09 N	97.08 W
Itasca, Lake ⊜	198	47.11 N	95.12 W
Itasca State Park ♠	198	47.18 N	95.18 W
Itata ≃	252	36.23 S	72.52 W
Itatí	252	27.16 S	58.15 W
Itatiaia	256	22.30 S	44.34 W
Itatiaia, Parque Nacional do ♠	256	22.28 S	44.37 W
Itatiba	256	23.00 S	46.51 W
Itatinga	255	23.07 S	48.36 W
Itatira	250	4.30 S	39.37 W
Itatka	86	56.49 N	85.37 E
Itatolo	273b	4.09 S	15.15 E
Itatskij	86	56.04 N	89.05 E
Itatupã	250	0.37 S	51.12 W
Itaú	250	5.50 S	37.59 W
Itaueira	250	7.36 S	43.02 W
Itaueira ≃	250	6.41 S	42.55 W
Itaúna	255	20.04 S	44.34 W
Itaúna, Morro do ∧[2]	287a	22.46 S	43.02 W
Itāwa	124	25.32 N	76.22 E
Itazuke-kūkō ⊠	96	33.35 N	130.28 E
Itbayat Island I	108	20.46 N	121.50 E
Itéa	38	38.26 N	22.24 E
Itenes (Guaporé) ≃	248	11.54 S	65.01 W
Ith ∧	52	52.05 N	9.35 E
Ithaca, Mi., U.S.	190	43.17 N	84.36 W
Ithaca, N.Y., U.S.	210	42.26 N	76.29 W
Itháki	38	38.23 N	20.42 E
Itháki I	38	38.24 N	20.42 E
Ithan Creek ≃	285	40.00 N	75.21 W
Ithnayn	142	30.41 N	32.21 E
Ithon ≃	42	52.12 N	3.27 W
Itigi	154	5.42 S	34.29 E
Itikawa → Ichikawa	94	35.44 N	139.55 E
Itimādpur	124	27.15 N	78.12 E
Itimbiri ≃	152	2.02 N	22.44 E
Itinga	255	16.36 S	41.47 W
Itinga ≃	255	16.35 S	41.45 W
Itinomiya → Ichinomiya	94	35.18 N	136.48 E
Itipo	152	0.50 S	18.35 E
Itiquira	255	17.12 S	54.07 W
Itiquira ≃	248	17.21 S	55.37 W
Itirapina	255	22.15 S	47.49 W
Itire	273a	6.31 N	3.21 E
Itiruçu	255	13.31 S	40.09 W
Itiúba	250	10.43 S	39.51 W
Itkillik ≃	180	70.08 N	150.57 W
Itlar'	82	56.51 N	39.17 E
Itlīdim	142	27.52 N	30.48 E
Itmīdah	142	30.46 N	31.20 E
Itmuryn, ozero ⊜	80	49.30 N	52.22 E
Itō	94	34.58 N	139.05 E
Itobi	256	21.44 S	46.58 W
Itobo	154	4.10 S	33.01 E
Itoculo	154	14.42 S	40.18 E
Itoigawa	94	37.02 N	137.51 E
Itoko	152	1.00 S	21.45 E
Itomamo, Lac ⊜	186	49.11 N	70.28 W
Itoman	174m	26.08 N	127.40 E
Iton ≃	50	49.09 N	1.12 E
Itonamas ≃	248	12.28 S	64.24 W
Itororó	255	15.07 S	40.06 W
Itri	66	41.17 N	13.32 E
Itsā	142	29.15 N	30.48 E
Itsukaichi, Nihon	94	35.44 N	139.13 E
Itsukaichi, Nihon	96	34.24 N	132.22 E
Itsuki	92	32.24 N	130.50 E
Itsuku-shima I	96	34.16 N	132.19 E
Itsuwa	92	32.30 N	130.10 E
Itta Bena	194	33.29 N	90.19 W
Ittel, Oued V	148	34.19 N	6.01 E
Itter ≃	263	51.09 N	6.52 E
Ittersum	52	52.28 N	6.07 E
Itteville	261	48.31 N	2.21 E
Ittiri	71	40.36 N	8.34 E
Itú	255	23.16 S	47.19 W
Itu ≃	252	29.25 S	55.51 W
Ituaçu	255	13.49 S	41.18 W
Ituango	246	7.04 N	75.45 W
Ituberá	255	13.44 S	39.09 W
Itucumã ≃	248	6.59 S	69.48 W
Itueta	255	19.23 S	41.11 W
Ituí	256	21.32 S	42.55 W
Ituí ≃	246	4.38 S	70.19 W
Ituim ≃	252	28.35 S	51.20 W
Ituiutaba	255	18.58 S	49.28 W
Itula	154	3.29 S	27.52 E
Itumbiara	255	18.25 S	49.13 W
Itumirim	256	21.19 S	44.53 W
Itum-Kale	84	42.43 N	45.35 E
Ituna	184	51.10 N	103.30 W
Itungi Port	154	9.35 S	33.56 E
Ituni	246	5.30 N	58.14 W
Itupararanga, Represa de ⊜[1]	256	23.37 S	47.16 W
Itupeva	256	23.09 S	47.04 W
Itupeva, Rio da ≃	256	22.03 S	47.15 W
Itupiranga	250	5.09 S	49.20 W
Ituporanga	252	27.25 S	49.36 W
Iturama	255	19.44 S	50.11 W
Iturbe	252	26.01 S	56.30 W
Iturbide	232	19.40 N	89.37 W
Ituri ≃	154	1.40 N	27.01 E
Iturup, ostrov (Etorofu-tō) I	92a	44.35 N	147.10 E
Itutinga	256	21.18 S	44.40 W
Ituverava	255	20.20 S	47.47 W
Ituxi ≃	248	7.18 S	64.51 W
Ituzaingó, Arg.	252	27.36 S	56.41 W
Ituzaingó, Arg.	258	34.40 S	58.40 W
Ituzaingó, Ur.	258	34.25 S	56.26 W
Itwa	124	27.20 N	82.42 E
Ityāy al-Bārūd	142	30.53 N	30.40 E
Ityopiya → Ethiopia □[1]	144	9.00 N	39.00 E
Itz ≃	56	49.58 N	10.52 E
Itzehoe	52	53.55 N	9.31 E
Iubundha ≃	126	24.06 N	90.20 E
Iue	76	53.56 N	25.46 E
Iuka, Il., U.S.	219	38.37 N	88.47 W
Iuka, Ms., U.S.	194	34.48 N	88.11 W
Iul'tin	180	67.50 N	178.48 W
Iul'tin, gora ∧	180	67.50 N	178.25 W
Iúna	255	20.21 S	41.32 W
Iupeba	256	23.41 S	46.22 W
Iva	192	34.18 N	82.39 W
Ivacèvičy	76	52.43 N	25.21 E
Ivačovo	76	60.32 N	36.22 E
Ivahona	157b	23.27 S	46.10 E
Ivaí ≃	255	23.18 S	53.42 W
Ivaiporã	252	24.15 S	51.45 W
Ivajlovgrad	38	41.32 N	26.08 E
Ivakoany, Massif de l' ⩘	157b	23.50 S	46.25 E
Ivalo	24	68.42 N	27.30 E
Ivalojoki ≃	24	68.43 N	27.36 E
Ivanava	76	52.09 N	25.32 E
Ivancevo	82	55.58 N	36.07 E
Ivančice	61	49.06 N	16.23 E
Ivancovo	82	56.39 N	35.50 E
Ivanec	36	46.13 N	16.08 E
Ivane-Puste	78	48.39 N	26.11 E
Ivangorod	76	59.24 N	28.10 E
Ivangrad	38	42.50 N	19.52 E
Ivanhoe, Austl.	166	32.54 S	144.18 E
Ivanhoe, Austl.	274b	37.46 S	145.03 E
Ivanhoe, Ca., U.S.	226	36.23 N	119.13 W
Ivanhoe, Il., U.S.	278	42.17 N	88.02 W
Ivanhoe, Mn., U.S.	198	44.27 N	96.14 W
Ivanhoe, Va., U.S.	192	36.50 N	80.58 W
Ivanhoe ≃	190	48.40 N	82.11 W
Ivanhoe Lake ⊜	190	48.05 N	82.38 W
Ivanić Grad	36	45.42 N	16.24 E
Ivanišči, Ross.	76	56.36 N	35.13 E
Ivanišči, Ross.	80	55.46 N	40.26 E
Ivaniv	78	49.28 N	28.21 E
Ivanivka, Ukr.	78	46.58 N	30.28 E
Ivanivka, Ukr.	78	46.43 N	34.33 E
Ivanivka, Ukr.	83	48.14 N	38.58 E
Ivanivka, Ukr.	83	47.35 N	37.19 E
Ivanjci	61	46.38 N	15.54 E
Ivanjica	38	43.35 N	20.14 E
Ivankov	78	50.56 N	29.54 E
Ivankovcy	89	49.06 N	134.28 E
Ivan'kovo	82	54.44 N	37.57 E
Ivan'kovskij	80	56.39 N	40.05 E
Ivan'kovskoje vodochranilišče ⊜[1]	82	56.37 N	36.32 E
Ivanof Bay	180	55.54 N	159.29 W
Ivano-Frankivs'k	78	48.55 N	24.43 E
Ivano-Frankivs'k □[4]	78	48.45 N	24.30 E
Ivano-Frankove	78	49.55 N	23.43 E
Ivanopil'	78	49.52 N	28.12 E
Ivano-Šamševo	83	46.52 N	39.54 E
Ivanovka, Kyrg.	85	42.54 N	75.05 E
Ivanovka, Ross.	80	52.51 N	53.48 E
Ivanovka, Ross.	80	51.54 N	43.46 E
Ivanovka, Ross.	80	52.15 N	41.35 E
Ivanovka, Ross.	89	50.22 N	128.02 E
Ivanovka, Ross.	89	43.58 N	132.30 E
Ivanovo	80	57.00 N	40.59 E
Ivanovo Oblast' □[4]	76	57.00 N	41.00 E
Ivanovo-Voznesensk → Ivanovo	80	57.00 N	40.59 E
Ivanovskaja, Ross.	24	60.48 N	55.52 E
Ivanovskaja, Ross.	78	45.17 N	38.29 E
Ivanovskoje, Ross.	76	59.17 N	28.49 E
Ivanovskoje, Ross.	78	51.37 N	34.57 E
Ivanovskoje, Ross.	82	55.05 N	37.50 E
Ivanovskoje, Ross.	82	54.55 N	36.50 E
Ivanovskoje, Ross.	82	55.52 N	36.55 E
Ivanovskoje, Ross.	82	56.23 N	37.07 E
Ivanovskoje, Ross.	265a	59.46 N	30.47 E
Ivan-Ozero	82	54.04 N	38.20 E
Ivan-Ozero, ozero ⊜	82	54.07 N	38.17 E
Ivanpah Lake ⊜	204	35.35 N	115.25 W
Ivantejevka, Ross.	80	52.16 N	49.07 E
Ivantejevka, Ross.	82	55.58 N	37.55 E
Ivantejevo	76	57.48 N	33.09 E
Ivanychi	78	50.39 N	24.20 E
Ivanytsya	78	50.47 N	32.36 E
Ivato	157b	20.37 S	47.12 E
Ivatuba	255	23.37 S	52.13 W
Ivdel'	72	60.42 N	60.24 E
Ivel ≃	42	52.10 N	0.18 W
Iver	260	51.31 N	0.30 W
Iver Heath	260	51.32 N	0.31 W
Iverny	261	49.00 N	2.47 E
Ivigtut	176	61.12 N	48.10 W
Ivindo ≃	152	0.09 S	12.09 E
Ivinghoe	42	51.50 N	0.37 W
Ivinheima ≃	255	23.14 S	53.42 W
Ivjanec	76	53.53 N	26.45 E
Ivn'a	78	51.04 N	36.08 E
Ivnytsya	78	50.09 N	29.03 E
Ivohibe	157b	22.29 S	46.52 E
Ivolginsk	88	51.45 N	107.14 E
Ivón ≃	248	11.06 S	66.08 W
Ivondro	157b	24.47 S	46.52 E
Ivor	208	36.54 N	76.54 W
Ivorogbo	150	5.30 N	6.21 E
Ivory Coast → Cote d'Ivoire □[1]	150	8.00 N	5.00 W
Ivory Coast ⩘[2]	150	5.10 N	5.00 W
Ivoryton	207	41.20 N	72.26 W
Ivösjön ⊜	26	56.06 N	14.27 E
Ivot, Ross.	76	53.42 N	34.12 E
Ivot, Ukr.	78	51.58 N	33.28 E
Ivotka ≃	78	51.57 N	33.22 E
Ivrea	62	45.28 N	7.52 E
İvrindi	130	39.34 N	27.29 E
Ivry-la-Bataille	50	48.53 N	1.28 E
Ivry [-sur-Seine]	50	48.49 N	2.23 E
Ivujivik	176	62.24 N	77.55 W
Ivybridge	42	50.23 N	3.56 W
Ivy Hatch	260	51.16 N	0.16 E
Ivyland	285	40.12 N	75.04 W
Iwade	96	34.15 N	135.19 E
Iwafune, Nihon	94	36.19 N	139.40 E
Iwafune, Nihon	270	34.44 N	135.54 E
Iwagi	96	34.15 N	133.09 E
Iwai	94	36.03 N	139.54 E
Iwai-shima I	96	33.47 N	131.58 E
Iwaizumi	92	39.50 N	141.48 E
Iwaki (Taira)	94	37.03 N	140.55 E
Iwaki ≃	92	41.01 N	140.22 E
Iwaki-san ∧	92	40.39 N	140.18 E
Iwakuni	96	34.09 N	132.11 E
Iwakuni Marine Corps Air Station ■	96	34.08 N	132.14 E
Iwakura	94	35.17 N	136.52 E
Iwama	94	36.18 N	140.16 E
Iwami, Nihon	96	34.53 N	132.26 E
Iwami, Nihon	96	35.35 N	134.20 E
Iwami-kōgen ⩘[1]	96	35.00 N	132.30 E
Iwami-kokubun-ji ʋ[1]	96	34.56 N	132.08 E
Iwamizawa	92a	43.12 N	141.46 E
Iwamura	94	35.22 N	137.26 E
Iwanai	92a	42.58 N	140.30 E
Iwanowo → Ivanovo	80	57.00 N	40.59 E
Iwanuma	92	38.06 N	140.52 E
Iwaoka ◆[8]	270	34.44 N	134.58 E
Iwase, Nihon	94	36.21 N	140.06 E
Iwase, Nihon	268	35.17 N	139.52 E
Iwata	94	34.42 N	137.48 E
Iwataki	96	35.34 N	135.09 E
Iwate □[5]	92	39.37 N	141.22 E
Iwate-san ∧	92	39.51 N	141.00 E
Iwatsuki	94	35.57 N	139.42 E
Iwaya → Awaji, Nihon	96	34.35 N	135.01 E
Iwaya, Nihon	270	34.35 N	135.02 E
Iwayama	270	34.52 N	135.52 E
Iwazono	270	34.45 N	135.19 E
Iwo	150	7.38 N	4.11 E
Iwo Jima → Iō-jima I	174f	24.47 N	141.20 E
Iwŏn	98	40.19 N	128.39 E
Iwuy	50	50.14 N	3.19 E
Ixcán ≃	236	16.07 N	91.05 W
Ixchiguán	236	15.12 N	91.53 W
Ixelles	56	50.50 N	4.22 E
Ixhuatlán	234	19.04 N	96.59 W
Ixiamas	248	13.45 S	68.09 W
Iximché ⊥	236	14.44 N	90.59 W
Ixmiquilpan	234	20.29 N	99.14 W
Ixonia	216	43.09 N	88.36 W
Ixopo	158	30.08 S	30.00 E
Ixtahuacán	236	15.25 N	91.46 W
Ixtapa	234	17.39 N	101.36 W
Ixtapa, Punta ›	234	17.39 N	101.40 W
Ixtapan de la Sal	234	18.50 N	99.41 W
Ixtepec	234	16.34 N	95.06 W
Ixtlahuacán del Río	234	20.52 N	103.15 W
Ixtlán	234	20.11 N	102.24 W
Ixtlán de Juárez	234	17.20 N	96.29 W
Ixtlán del Río	234	21.02 N	104.22 W
Ixworth	42	52.18 N	0.50 E
Iya ≃	96	33.58 N	133.47 E
ʻIyādh	144	14.59 N	46.51 E
ʻIyāl Bakhīt	140	13.25 N	28.41 E
Iyang, Taehan	98	34.53 N	127.01 E
Iyang → Yiyang, Zhg.	102	28.36 N	112.20 E
Iyang, Gili I	115a	6.59 S	114.10 E
Iyo	96	33.46 N	132.42 E
Iyo-mishima	96	33.58 N	133.33 E
Iyo-nada ╤[2]	96	33.40 N	132.20 E
Iž ≃	80	55.58 N	52.38 E
Izabal	236	15.24 N	89.08 W
Izabal □[5]	236	15.30 N	89.00 W
Izabal, Lago de ⊜	236	15.30 N	89.10 W
ʻIzab al-Baṣāriṭah	142	31.23 N	31.47 E
Īzad Khvāst	128	31.31 N	52.07 E
Izalco	236	13.45 N	89.40 W
ʻIzam, Jabal al- ∧	132	30.51 N	35.46 E
Izamal	232	20.56 N	89.01 W
Izapa ⊥	232	14.55 N	92.10 W
ʻIzbat Abū Ṣuql	132	31.09 N	33.49 E
Izberbaš	84	42.33 N	47.52 E
Izbica, Pol.	30	54.42 N	17.26 E
Izbica, Pol.	30	50.54 N	23.09 E
Izd'oškovo	76	55.08 N	33.37 E
Izegem	50	50.55 N	3.12 E
Īzeh	128	31.50 N	49.50 E
Izena-shima I	174m	26.56 N	127.56 E
Izency	86	45.48 N	59.28 E
Izernore	58	46.13 N	5.33 E
Iževsk	80	56.51 N	53.14 E
Iževskoje	80	54.34 N	40.53 E
Izkī	128	22.56 N	57.46 E
Ižma	24	65.02 N	53.55 E
Ižma ≃	24	65.19 N	52.54 E
Izmajlovo	80	53.43 N	47.14 E
Izmajlovo ◆[8]	265b	55.48 N	37.46 E
Izmajlovo Park ♠	265b	55.46 N	37.47 E
Izmalkovo	76	52.41 N	37.58 E
Izmayil	78	45.21 N	28.50 E
İzmir	130	38.25 N	27.09 E
İzmir □[4]	130	38.30 N	27.15 E
İzmir Körfezi ⊂	130	38.30 N	26.50 E
İzmit (Kocaeli)	130	40.46 N	29.55 E
İzmit Körfezi ⊂	130	40.45 N	29.35 E
Ižmorskij	86	56.11 N	86.38 E
Iznájar, Embalse de ⊜[1]	34	37.15 N	4.30 W
Iznalloz	34	37.23 N	3.31 W
İznik	130	40.26 N	29.43 E
İznik Gölü ⊜	130	40.26 N	29.30 E
Iznoski	76	54.59 N	35.19 E
Izola	64	45.32 N	13.40 E
Izoplit	82	56.38 N	36.12 E
Izopo, Punta ›	236	15.48 N	87.23 W
Ižora ≃	265a	59.48 N	30.36 E
Izozog, Bañados del ☷	248	18.48 S	62.10 W
Izraʻ	132	32.51 N	36.15 E
Izsák	30	46.48 N	19.22 E
Iztacalco ◆[8]	286a	19.23 N	99.07 W
Iztaccíhuatl, Volcán ∧[1]	234	19.11 N	98.39 W
Iztaccíhuatl y Popocatéptl, Parques Nacionales ♠	234	19.10 N	98.38 W
Iztapa	236	13.56 N	90.43 W
Iztapalapa ◆[8]	286a	19.21 N	99.06 W
Izucar de Matamoros	234	18.36 N	98.28 W
Izu-hantō ›[1]	94	34.45 N	139.00 E
Izuhara	92	34.12 N	129.17 E
Izumi, Nihon	92	32.05 N	130.22 E
Izumi, Nihon	92	38.20 N	140.53 E
Izumi, Nihon	94	35.54 N	136.40 E
Izumi, Nihon	96	34.55 N	134.55 E
Izumi, Nihon	96	34.29 N	135.26 E
Izumi ◆[8]	268	35.25 N	139.30 E
Izumi-ōtsu	96	34.30 N	135.24 E
Izumi-sano	96	34.25 N	135.19 E
Izumizaki	94	37.09 N	140.17 E
Izumo	96	35.22 N	132.46 E
Izumo ≃	94	34.38 N	136.33 E
Izumo-kokubun-ji ʋ[1]	96	35.26 N	133.06 E
Izumrud	86	57.05 N	61.23 E
Izu-nagaoka	94	35.02 N	138.56 E
Izushi	96	35.28 N	134.52 E
Izu-shotō II	6	32.00 N	140.00 E
Izu Trench ✢[1]	6	31.00 N	142.00 E
Izuwara	270	34.53 N	135.32 E
Izvaryne	83	48.17 N	39.52 E
Izvestij CIK, ostrova II	74	75.55 N	82.30 E
Izvestkovyj	89	48.59 N	131.33 E
Izvorul Muntelui, Lacul ⊜[1]	38	47.00 N	26.00 E
Izyaslav	78	50.07 N	26.51 E
Izynžul'	86	52.24 N	90.13 E
Izyum	83	49.12 N	37.19 E
J			
Jaʻār, Birkat al- ⊜	142	30.28 N	30.10 E
Jääsjärvi ⊜	26	61.36 N	26.07 E
Jaba, Ityo.	144	6.17 N	35.12 E
Jaba, Pap. N. Gui.	175e	6.32 S	155.12 E
Jabā, Sūrīy.	132	33.10 N	35.56 E
Jabal, Bahr al- → Mountain Nile ≃	136	9.30 N	30.30 E
Jabal Abyad Plateau ⩘[1]	140	19.00 N	29.00 E
Jabal al-Awliyā'	140	15.14 N	32.30 E
Jabal al-Awliyā', Khazzān (White Nile Dam) ◆[6]	140	15.14 N	32.29 E
Jabalambre ∧	34	40.06 N	1.03 W
Jabal an-Nūr	142	28.57 N	31.02 E
Jabal Aṭ-Ṭayr	142	28.14 N	30.45 E
Jabal Dūd	140	13.25 N	33.09 E
Jabal Lubnān □[4]	132	33.50 N	35.40 E
Jabalón ≃	34	38.53 N	4.05 W
Jabal os Sarāj	120	35.07 N	69.14 E
Jabalpur	124	23.10 N	79.57 E
Jabal Qerri	140	16.15 N	32.48 E
Jabal ʻUwaybid	142	30.09 N	32.12 E
Jabālyah	132	31.32 N	34.29 E
Jabal Zuqar, Jazīrat I	144	14.00 N	42.45 E
Jabbān, Arḍ al- ◆[1]	132	32.08 N	36.35 E
Jabbeke	50	51.11 N	3.05 E
Jabbi	123	32.24 N	72.06 E
Jabbū, Qāʻ ☷	132	29.35 N	36.13 E
Jabbūl, Sabkhat al- ⊜	130	36.03 N	37.39 E
Jabel	54	53.32 N	12.32 E
Jabi	114	2.32 N	102.48 E
Jabiru	164	12.40 S	132.53 E
Jabjabah, Wādī V	140	22.37 N	33.17 E
Jablah	130	35.21 N	35.55 E
Jablanac	36	44.42 N	14.54 E
Jablanica	36	43.39 N	17.45 E
Jablanica ≃	38	43.07 N	21.57 E
Jablaničko Jezero ⊜[1]	36	43.40 N	17.50 E
Jablines	261	48.55 N	2.46 E
Jabločnyj	89	47.10 N	142.04 E
Jablonec nad Nisou	30	50.44 N	15.10 E
Jablonica	30	48.37 N	17.25 E
Jabłonka	30	49.29 N	19.41 E
Jablonné v Podještědí	54	50.48 N	14.47 E
Jablonoj → Jablonovyj chrebet ⩘	88	53.30 N	115.00 E
Jablonovo	88	51.51 N	112.49 E
Jablonovyj chrebet ⩘	88	53.30 N	115.00 E
Jabłonowo	30	53.24 N	19.09 E
Jablonowy-Gebirge → Jablonovyj chrebet ⩘	88	53.30 N	115.00 E
Jablunkov	30	49.35 N	18.47 E
Jaboatão	250	8.07 S	35.01 W
Jaboncillos Creek ≃	196	27.23 N	97.45 W
Jabonga	116	9.20 N	125.32 E
Jaborandi	255	20.40 S	48.25 W
Jaboticabal	255	21.16 S	48.19 W
Jabrat Saʻīd ╤[4]	140	16.06 N	31.50 E
Jabron ≃	62	44.33 N	4.45 E
Jabron, Torrent le ≃	62	44.09 N	5.57 E
Jabung	115a	5.29 S	105.40 E
Jabung, Tanjung ›	112	1.01 S	104.22 E
Jaca	34	42.34 N	0.33 W
Jacala	234	21.01 N	99.11 W
Jacaleapa	236	14.00 N	86.40 W
Jacaltenango	236	15.40 N	91.44 W
Jacana	274b	37.42 S	144.55 E
Jacaraci	255	14.51 S	42.26 W
Jacaré ≃, Bra.	248	5.49 S	63.35 W
Jacaré ≃, Bra.	250	10.10 S	41.58 W
Jacaré ≃, Bra.	255	13.50 S	40.42 W
Jacareí	256	23.19 S	45.58 W
Jacarepaguá ◆[8]	256	22.56 S	43.20 W
Jacarepaguá, Lagoa de ⊂	256	22.59 S	43.24 W
Jacarezinho	255	23.09 S	49.59 W
Jaceel V	144	10.25 N	51.01 E
Jaceruba	256	22.35 S	43.34 W
Jáchal ≃	252	30.44 S	68.08 W
Jachenau	64	47.36 N	11.25 E
Jachroma	82	56.17 N	37.30 E
Jachroma ≃	82	56.31 N	37.07 E
Jáchymov	54	50.20 N	12.55 E
Jaciara	255	15.59 S	54.57 W
Jacinto	255	16.10 S	40.17 W
Jacinto Aráuz	252	38.04 S	63.26 W
Jacinto City	222	29.46 N	95.14 W
Jacinto Machado	252	29.00 S	49.46 W
Jaciparaná	248	9.15 S	64.23 W
Jaciparaná ≃	248	9.22 S	64.22 W
Jackass Creek ≃	226	37.22 N	119.23 W
Jack Creek ≃	202	42.59 N	121.32 W
Jackfish Lake ⊜	184	53.05 N	108.25 W
Jackhead Harbour	184	51.52 N	97.16 W
Jack Lake ⊜	212	44.42 N	78.03 W
Jack London State Historical Park ♠	226	38.21 N	122.32 W
Jackman	188	45.38 N	70.15 W
Jackman Creek ≃	224	48.30 N	121.43 W
Jack Mountain ∧, Mt., U.S.	202	46.21 N	112.18 W
Jack Mountain ∧, Wa., U.S.	224	48.47 N	120.57 W
Jackpot	204	41.59 N	114.40 W
Jacksboro, Tn., U.S.	192	36.19 N	84.11 W
Jacksboro, Tx., U.S.	196	33.13 N	98.09 W
Jacks Creek ≃	208	40.35 N	77.33 W
Jacks Fork ≃	194	37.12 N	91.17 W
Jacks Island I	279b	40.37 N	79.43 W
Jacks Mountain ∧	210	40.45 N	77.30 W
Jackson, Al., U.S.	194	31.30 N	87.53 W
Jackson, Ca., U.S.	226	38.20 N	120.46 W
Jackson, Ga., U.S.	192	33.17 N	83.57 W
Jackson, Ky., U.S.	192	37.33 N	83.23 W
Jackson, La., U.S.	194	30.50 N	91.13 W
Jackson, Mi., U.S.	216	42.14 N	84.24 W
Jackson, Mn., U.S.	198	43.37 N	94.59 W
Jackson, Ms., U.S.	194	32.17 N	90.11 W
Jackson, Mo., U.S.	194	37.22 N	89.39 W
Jackson, N.J., U.S.	208	40.08 N	74.19 W
Jackson, N.C., U.S.	192	36.23 N	77.25 W
Jackson, Oh., U.S.	188	39.03 N	82.38 W
Jackson, Pa., U.S.	210	41.50 N	75.36 W
Jackson, S.C., U.S.	192	33.19 N	81.47 W
Jackson, Tn., U.S.	194	35.36 N	88.48 W
Jackson, Wy., U.S.	200	43.28 N	110.45 W
Jackson □[6], In., U.S.	218	38.53 N	86.03 W
Jackson □[6], Mi., U.S.	216	42.15 N	84.24 W
Jackson □[6], Tx., U.S.	222	29.00 N	96.35 W
Jackson ≃	188	37.47 N	79.46 W
Jackson, Cape ›	172	41.00 S	174.18 E
Jackson, Lake ⊜, Fl., U.S.	192	30.30 N	84.17 W
Jackson, Lake ⊜, Fl., U.S.	220	27.55 N	81.10 W
Jackson, Lake ⊜, Fl., U.S.	220	27.29 N	81.28 W
Jackson, Mount ∧, Ant.	9	71.23 S	63.22 W
Jackson, Mount ∧, Austl.	162	30.15 S	119.16 E
Jackson, Port ⊂	170	33.50 S	151.16 E
Jackson Bay ⊂	172	43.58 S	168.42 E
Jackson Brook ≃	276	40.53 N	74.34 W
Jackson Butte ∧	226	38.20 N	120.43 W
Jackson Center, Oh., U.S.	216	40.27 N	84.02 W
Jackson Center, Pa., U.S.	214	41.16 N	80.09 W
Jackson Creek ≃, Can.	184	49.18 N	100.50 W
Jackson Creek ≃, Ca., U.S.	226	38.18 N	121.01 W
Jackson Creek ≃, Il., U.S.	216	41.26 N	88.10 W
Jackson Head ›	172	43.58 S	168.37 E
Jackson Heights ◆[8]	276	40.45 N	73.53 W
Jackson Lake ⊜	202	43.55 N	110.40 W
Jackson Lake ⊜[1]	192	33.22 N	83.52 W
Jackson Meadows Reservoir ⊜[1]	226	39.29 N	120.32 W
Jackson Mountain ∧	188	44.46 N	70.32 W
Jackson Park ♠, On., Can.	281	42.17 N	83.01 W
Jackson Park ♠, Il., U.S.	278	41.47 N	87.35 W
Jackson's Arm	186	49.52 N	56.47 W
Jacksons Creek ≃	169	37.40 S	144.48 E
Jacksonville, Al., U.S.	194	33.48 N	85.45 W
Jacksonville, Ar., U.S.	194	34.51 N	92.06 W
Jacksonville, Fl., U.S.	192	30.19 N	81.39 W
Jacksonville, Il., U.S.	219	39.44 N	90.13 W
Jacksonville, N.J., U.S.	285	40.03 N	74.46 W
Jacksonville, N.Y., U.S.	210	42.31 N	76.37 W
Jacksonville, N.C., U.S.	192	34.45 N	77.25 W
Jacksonville, Or., U.S.	202	42.18 N	122.57 W
Jacksonville, Tx., U.S.	222	31.57 N	95.16 W
Jacksonville, Vt., U.S.	207	42.47 N	72.49 W
Jacksonville, Lake ⊜[1]	222	31.55 N	95.17 W
Jacksonville Beach	192	30.17 N	81.23 W
Jacksonville Naval Air Station ■	192	30.14 N	81.41 W
Jacks Reef	210	43.06 N	76.25 W
Jacks Run ≃	279b	40.13 N	79.35 W
Jacktown Acres	279b	40.19 N	79.45 W
Jacmel	238	18.14 N	72.32 W
Jaco	232	27.50 N	104.00 W
Jacob, Morne ∧	240e	14.46 N	61.06 W
Jacobābād	120	28.17 N	68.26 E
Jacobina	250	11.11 S	40.31 W
Jacob Island I	212	44.28 N	78.28 W
Jacob Riis Park ♠	276	40.34 N	73.52 W
Jacobs Creek ≃	214	40.07 N	79.44 W
Jacobsdal	158	29.13 S	24.41 E
Jacobus	208	39.53 N	76.43 W
Jacona de Plancarte	234	19.57 N	102.16 W
Jacques, Lac à ⊜	180	66.10 N	127.25 W
Jacques-Cartier	275a	45.31 N	73.29 W
Jacques-Cartier ≃	206	46.40 N	71.45 W
Jacques-Cartier, Détroit de Ʉ	186	50.00 N	63.30 W
Jacques-Cartier, Mont ∧	186	48.59 N	65.57 W
Jacques-Cartier, Pont ◆[5]	275a	45.31 N	73.32 W
Jacquet River	186	47.55 N	66.00 W
Jacqueville	150	5.12 N	4.25 W
Jacquinot Bay ⊂	164	5.35 S	151.30 E
Jacu ≃, Bra.	250	6.13 S	35.09 W
Jacú ≃, Bra.	256	23.05 S	45.08 W
Jacu, Rio do ≃	287b	23.29 S	46.27 W
Jacuba ≃	255	18.25 S	52.28 W
Jacuecanga	256	23.01 S	44.13 W
Jacuí ≃	252	30.02 S	51.15 W
Jacuípe ≃	255	12.30 S	39.05 W
Jacumba	204	32.37 N	116.11 W
Jacundá	250	4.33 S	49.28 W
Jacundá ≃	250	1.57 S	50.26 W
Jacupiranga	252	24.42 S	48.00 W
Jacuriaí ≃	250	10.57 S	39.35 W
Jacutinga	256	22.17 S	46.37 W
Jada	146	8.46 N	12.09 E
Jadaʻah, Jabal ∧[2]	142	29.58 N	30.40 E
Jādabpur	126	22.29 N	88.23 E
Jaddi, Rās ›	128	25.14 N	63.31 E
Jade	52	53.20 N	8.14 E
Jade Buddha, Temple of the ʋ[1]	269b	31.14 N	121.26 E
Jadebusen ⊂	52	53.30 N	8.10 E
Jäder	40	59.25 N	16.41 E
Jäderfors	40	60.41 N	16.40 E
Jade Run ≃	285	39.56 N	74.45 W
Jadīdah	128	34.01 N	42.28 E
Jadito Wash V	200	35.22 N	110.50 W
J.A.D. Jensens Nunatakker ∧	176	62.45 N	48.00 W
Jadotville → Likasi	154	10.59 S	26.44 E
Jadraque	34	40.55 N	2.55 W
Jadrin	80	55.56 N	46.12 E
Jadromino	82	55.57 N	36.36 E
Jādū	146	31.57 N	12.01 E
Jægerspris	41	55.51 N	11.59 E
Jaeger Summit ∧	154	2.52 S	35.47 E
Jaén, Esp.	34	37.46 N	3.47 W
Jaén, Perú	248	5.42 S	78.47 W
Jaén □[4]	34	38.00 N	3.30 W
Jæren ◆[1]	26	58.45 N	5.45 E
Jāfarābād, India	120	20.52 N	71.22 E
Jaʻfarābād, Īrān	128	35.43 N	50.43 E
Jāfarpur	126	22.29 N	89.06 E
Jāfarpur ◆[8]	272a	28.40 N	77.01 E
Jaffa, Cape ›	166	36.58 S	139.40 E
Jaffa, Tel Aviv- → Tel Aviv-Yafo	132	32.04 N	34.46 E
Jaffna	122	9.40 N	80.00 E
Jaffna Lagoon ⊂	122	9.35 N	80.15 E
Jaffrey	207	42.48 N	72.01 W
Jafr, Qāʻ al- ⩘[7]	132	30.17 N	36.20 E
Jagādhri	124	30.10 N	77.18 E
Jägala ≃	76	59.29 N	25.09 E
Jagalūr	122	14.32 N	76.21 E
Jāgan	120	28.05 N	68.30 E
Jagannāthganj Ghāt	124	24.45 N	89.49 E
Jagannāthpūr	272b	22.43 N	88.19 E
Jagati	126	23.54 N	89.06 E
Jagatnagar	272b	22.47 N	88.13 E
Jagatpur ◆[8]	272a	28.44 N	77.14 E
Jagatsingpur	120	20.16 N	86.10 E
Jagdalpur	122	19.04 N	82.02 E
Jagdīspur	124	25.29 N	84.25 E
Jagel	41	54.27 N	9.32 E
Jagel'urta, gora ∧[2]	24	67.33 N	38.02 E
Jagenbach	61	48.38 N	15.02 E
Jägerndorf → Krnov	30	50.05 N	17.41 E
Jagersfontein	158	29.44 S	25.29 E
Jaggayyapeta	122	16.54 N	80.06 E
Jagged Mountain ∧	180	58.38 N	162.02 W
Jagīn ≃	128	25.35 N	58.18 E
Jagnob ≃	85	39.15 N	68.35 E
Jagny-sous-Bois	261	49.05 N	2.27 E
Jagodnoje, Ross.	74	62.33 N	149.40 E
Jagodnoje, Ross.	80	53.36 N	49.04 E
Jagodnyj	86	59.44 N	65.04 E
Jagraon	123	30.47 N	75.29 E
Jagst ≃	56	49.14 N	9.11 E
Jagstzell	56	49.02 N	10.05 E
Jagtiāl	122	18.48 N	78.56 E
Jaguaquara	255	13.32 S	39.58 W
Jaguarão	252	32.34 S	53.23 W
Jaguarão (Yaguarón) ≃	252	32.39 S	53.12 W
Jaguarari	250	10.16 S	40.12 W
Jaguaretama	250	5.37 S	38.46 W
Jaguari	252	29.30 S	54.41 W
Jaguari ≃, Bra.	256	22.41 S	47.17 W
Jaguari ≃, Bra.	256	23.10 S	45.55 W
Jaguariaíva	252	24.15 S	49.42 W
Jaguaribara	250	5.40 S	38.37 W
Jaguaribe	250	5.53 S	38.37 W
Jaguaribe ≃	250	4.25 S	37.45 W
Jaguari-Mirim ≃	256	21.59 S	47.17 W
Jaguaripe	255	13.06 S	38.53 W
Jaguariúna	256	22.41 S	46.59 W
Jaguaruna	252	28.36 S	49.02 W
Jagüé	252	28.38 S	68.24 W
Jagüey Grande	240p	22.32 N	81.08 W
Jāguli	126	22.56 N	88.32 E
Jāgulia	272b	22.44 N	88.32 E
Jagungal, Mount ∧	171b	36.09 S	148.23 E
Jagunovskij	86	55.17 N	85.59 E
Jahānābād, India	124	25.13 N	84.59 E
Jahānābād, Pāk.	123	32.11 N	72.29 E
Jahāngīra	123	33.58 N	72.13 E
Jahāngīrābād	124	28.25 N	78.06 E
Jahangirpur ◆[8]	272a	28.44 N	77.13 E
Jahānia	123	30.02 N	71.49 E
Jahannam, Qārat ∧[2]	142	29.19 N	30.09 E
Jahdānīyah, Wādī al- V	132	30.12 N	36.22 E
Jahnsdorf	54	50.44 N	12.51 E
Jahrom	128	28.31 N	53.33 E
Jahú → Jaú	255	22.18 S	48.33 W
Jaicós	250	7.21 S	41.08 W
Jaidak	120	31.58 N	66.43 E
Jaihti ≃	126	24.08 N	86.48 E
Jaijon	123	31.21 N	76.09 E
Jailolo	108	1.05 N	127.30 E
Jaimanitas ≃	286b	23.05 N	82.29 W
Jainca	102	35.59 N	102.02 E
Jainti	124	26.42 N	89.36 E
Jaintiāpur	120	25.08 N	92.07 E
Jaipur	120	26.55 N	75.49 E
Jaipur Hāt	124	25.06 N	89.01 E
Jais	124	26.15 N	81.32 E
Jaisalmer	120	26.55 N	70.54 E
Jaito	123	30.28 N	74.53 E
Jaja	86	56.12 N	86.26 E
Jaja ≃	86	56.58 N	86.23 E
Jājapur	120	20.51 N	86.20 E
Jājarkoṭ	124	28.42 N	82.12 E
Jājarm	128	36.58 N	56.27 E
Jajce	36	44.21 N	17.16 E
Jajichi	174m	26.47 N	128.13 E
Jajjha	123	28.45 N	70.34 E
Jajl'u	86	51.48 N	87.36 E
Jajpan	85	40.23 N	70.48 E
Jajsan	86	50.51 N	56.14 E
Jajva	86	59.20 N	57.15 E
Jajva ≃	86	59.13 N	56.40 E
Ják	61	47.08 N	16.35 E
Jakarta, Indon.	115a	6.10 S	106.48 E
Jakarta, Indon.	269e	6.10 S	106.48 E
Jakarta, Teluk ⊂	115a	6.05 S	106.48 E
Jakarta Kota Station ◆[5]	269e	6.08 S	106.49 E
Jakarta Raya □[4]	115a	6.10 S	106.45 E
Jakaulevičy	76	54.20 N	30.31 E
Jakdūl ⊜	140	17.39 N	32.59 E
Jake Creek Mountain ∧	204	41.13 N	116.54 W
Jakenan	115a	6.45 S	111.11 E
Jākhal	123	29.48 N	75.50 E
Jakhāu	120	23.13 N	68.43 E
Jakkonen	24	66.33 N	29.52 E
Jakobsberg	40	59.26 N	17.50 E
Jakobsdalsberget ∧[2]	40	58.41 N	16.07 E
Jakobshavn (Ilulissat)	176	69.13 N	51.06 W
Jakobstad (Pietarsaari)	26	63.40 N	22.42 E
Jakovlevka	89	44.26 N	133.28 E
Jakovlevo, Ross.	78	50.51 N	36.27 E
Jakovlevo, Ross.	82	54.48 N	37.26 E
Jakša	24	61.48 N	56.49 E
Jakšanga	80	58.23 N	45.56 E
Jakšur-Bodja	80	57.11 N	53.09 E
Jakupica ⩘	38	41.43 N	21.26 E
Jakutija □[3]	74	67.00 N	125.00 E
Jakutsk	74	62.00 N	129.40 E
Jal	196	32.06 N	103.11 W
Jalacingo	234	19.48 N	97.18 W
Jalaid Qi	89	46.40 N	122.55 E
Jalājil	128	25.41 N	45.28 E
Jalālābād, Afg.	120	34.26 N	70.28 E
Jalālābād, India	123	30.37 N	74.15 E
Jalālābād, India	124	27.43 N	79.40 E
Jalālah al-Baḥrīyah, Jabal ⩘[1]	142	29.20 N	32.00 E
Jalālat al-Qiblīyah, Jabal al- ⩘	142	28.42 N	32.22 E
Jalālpur, India	124	26.19 N	82.44 E
Jalālpur, Pāk.	123	32.38 N	74.12 E
Jalālpur Pīrwāla	123	29.30 N	71.13 E
Jalan'	86	58.21 N	91.53 E
Jalán ≃	236	14.39 N	86.12 W
Jalan Besar Stadium ♠	271c	1.18 N	103.52 E
Jalandhar	123	31.19 N	75.34 E
Jalangi	126	24.08 N	88.42 E
Jalangi ≃	126	23.25 N	88.22 E
Jalan Kayu	271c	1.24 N	103.52 E
Jalapa, Guat.	236	14.38 N	89.59 W
Jalapa, Méx.	234	17.43 N	92.49 W
Jalapa, Nic.	236	13.55 N	86.08 W
Jalapa □[5]	236	14.35 N	89.55 W
Jalasjärvi	26	62.30 N	22.45 E
Jalaud ≃	116	10.45 N	122.40 E
Jālaun	124	26.09 N	79.21 E
Jal'čiki	80	55.09 N	48.01 E
Jalcocotán	234	21.28 N	105.07 W
Jalda	126	21.56 N	87.30 E
Jaleaca de Catalán	234	17.26 N	99.51 W
Jalesar	124	27.29 N	78.19 E
Jaleshwar	126	21.49 N	87.13 E
Jaleśwar	124	26.38 N	85.48 E
Jālgaon, India	122	21.01 N	75.34 E
Jālgaon, India	122	21.03 N	76.32 E
Jal'gelevo	265a	59.44 N	29.57 E
Jalhay	56	50.34 N	5.58 E
Jalingo	146	8.53 N	11.22 E
Jalirpār	126	23.13 N	89.58 E
Jalisco □[3]	234	20.20 N	103.40 W
Jalizava	76	53.24 N	29.01 E
Jālna	122	19.50 N	75.53 E
Jalón ≃	34	41.47 N	1.04 W
Jālor	120	25.21 N	72.37 E
Jalostotitlán	234	21.12 N	102.28 W
Jalpa	234	21.38 N	102.58 W
Jalpa de Méndez	234	18.08 N	93.05 W
Jalpāiguri	124	26.31 N	88.44 E
Jalpan de Serra	234	21.14 N	99.29 W
Jaltepec ≃	234	17.26 N	94.59 W

≃ River	Fluß	Río	Rivière	Rio
≋ Canal	Kanal	Canal	Canal	Canal
⌞ Waterfall, Rapids	Wasserfall, Stromschnellen	Cascada, Rápidos	Chute d'eau, Rapides	Cascata, Rápidos
Ʉ Strait	Meeresstraße	Estrecho	Détroit	Estreito
⊂ Bay, Gulf	Bucht, Golf	Bahía, Golfo	Baie, Golfe	Baía, Golfo
⊜ Lake, Lakes	See, Seen	Lago, Lagos	Lac, Lacs	Lago, Lagos
☷ Swamp	Sumpf	Pantano	Marais	Pântano
⍓ Ice Features, Glacier	Eis- und Gletscherformen	Accidentes Glaciales	Formes glaciaires	Acidentes glaciares
╤ Other Hydrographic Features	Andere Hydrographische Objekte	Otros Elementos Hidrográficos	Autres données hydrographiques	Outros acidentes hidrográficos

✢ Submarine Features	Untermeerische Objekte	Accidentes Submarinos	Formes de relief sous-marin	Acidentes submarinos
□ Political Unit	Politische Einheit	Unidad Política	Entité politique	Unidade política
ʋ Cultural Institution	Kulturelle Institution	Institución Cultural	Institution culturelle	Instituição cultural
⊥ Historical Site	Historische Stätte	Sitio Histórico	Site historique	Sitio histórico
♠ Recreational Site	Erholungs- und Ferienort	Sitio de Recreo	Centre de loisirs	Area de Lazer
⊠ Airport	Flughafen	Aeropuerto	Aéroport	Aeroporto
■ Military Installation	Militäranlage	Instalación Militar	Installation militaire	Instalação militar
◆ Miscellaneous	Verschiedenes	Misceláneo	Divers	Diversos

Name	Page	Lat.°′	Long.°′
Jáltipan de Morelos	234	17.58 N	94.42 W
Jaluit I[1]	14	6.00 N	169.35 E
Jalūlā'	128	34.16 N	45.10 E
Jalutorovsk	86	56.40 N	66.18 E
Jam, Ross.	82	55.29 N	37.45 E
Jam, Uzb.	85	40.07 N	68.11 E
Jām ≃	128	35.10 N	61.06 E
Jamaame (Margherita)	144	0.04 N	42.45 E
Jamaare ≃	146	12.06 N	10.14 E
Jāmāibāti	272b	22.51 N	88.08 E
Jamaica	240p	20.12 N	75.09 W
Jamaica •[8]	276	40.42 N	73.47 W
Jamaica □[1], N.A.	230	18.15 N	77.30 W
Jamaica □[1], N.A.	241q	18.15 N	77.30 W
Jamaica Bay c	210	40.36 N	73.51 W
Jamaica Channel ⊔	238	18.00 N	75.30 W
Jamaica Plain •[8]	283	42.19 N	71.06 W
Jamaica Pond ⊜	283	42.19 N	71.07 W
Jamaika → Jamaica □[1]	241q	18.15 N	77.30 W
Jamaïque → Jamaica □[1]	241q	18.15 N	77.30 W
Jamal, poluostrov >[1]	74	70.00 N	70.00 E
Jam-Alin', chrebet ⋏	89	53.00 N	134.36 E
Jamālīyah •[8]	273c	30.03 N	31.16 E
Jamālpur, Bngl.	124	24.55 N	89.56 E
Jamālpur, India	124	25.18 N	86.30 E
Jamālpurganj	126	23.04 N	87.59 E
Jamanchalinka	80	47.40 N	51.35 E
Jamanota ∧[2]	241s	12.29 N	69.57 W
Jamantau, gora ∧	86	54.15 N	58.06 E
Jamanxim ≃	250	4.43 S	56.18 W
Jamapará	256	21.55 S	42.43 W
Jamari ≃	248	8.27 S	63.30 W
Jamarovka	88	50.38 N	110.16 E
Jamašurma	80	55.58 N	49.36 E
Jamay	234	20.18 N	102.43 W
Jamba	152	13.50 S	15.30 E
Jāmbād	126	22.42 N	86.35 E
Jambeiro	256	23.16 S	45.41 W
Jambeiro, Serra do ⋏[2]	256	23.13 S	45.38 W
Jambelí, Canal de ⊔	246	3.00 S	80.00 W
Jamberoo	170	34.39 S	150.47 E
Jambes	56	50.28 N	4.52 E
Jambi	112	1.36 S	103.37 E
Jambi □[4]	112	1.30 S	103.00 E
Jambin	166	24.12 S	150.22 E
Jamboaye ≃	114	5.16 N	97.29 E
Jambol	38	42.29 N	26.30 E
Jambongan, Pulau I	116	6.40 N	117.27 E
Jambuair, Tanjung >	114	5.16 N	97.30 E
Jambusar	120	22.03 N	72.48 E
James ≃, Austl.	166	20.36 S	137.41 E
James ≃, Ab., Can.	182	51.55 N	114.34 W
James ≃, U.S.	198	42.52 N	97.18 W
James ≃, Mo., U.S.	194	36.45 N	93.30 W
James ≃, Va., U.S.	192	36.57 N	76.26 W
James, Isla I	254	44.57 S	74.07 W
James, Lake ⊜	216	41.42 N	85.02 W
James, Lake ⊜[1]	192	35.45 N	81.55 W
James Bay c	176	53.30 N	80.30 W
Jamesburg	208	40.21 N	74.26 W
James Bypass ≊	226	36.41 N	120.16 W
James City, N.C., U.S.	192	35.05 N	77.02 W
James City, Pa., U.S.	214	41.37 N	78.50 W
James City □[6]	208	37.17 N	76.48 W
James Craik	252	32.09 S	63.28 W
James Creek	214	40.23 N	78.10 W
James Gardens ♠	275b	43.40 N	79.31 W
James Island, B.C., Can.	224	48.37 N	123.22 W
James Island, S.C., U.S.	192	32.44 N	79.57 W
James Island I	208	38.31 N	76.20 W
Jameson Raid Memorial ⊥	273d	26.11 S	27.49 E
James Point >	192	25.21 N	76.24 W
Jamesport	194	39.58 N	93.48 W
James Price Point >	162	17.30 S	122.08 E
James Ranges ⋏	162	24.06 S	132.30 E
James River Bridge •[5]	208	37.00 N	76.30 W
James Ross, Cape >	176	74.40 N	114.25 W
James Ross Island I	9	64.15 S	57.45 W
James Ross Strait ⊔	176	69.40 N	95.30 W
James Smith Indian Reserve •[4]	184	53.08 N	104.52 W
Jamestown, Austl.	166	33.12 S	138.36 E
Jamestown, Ire.	48	53.55 N	8.02 W
Jamestown, S. Afr.	158	31.06 S	26.45 E
Jamestown, Ca., U.S.	226	37.57 N	120.25 W
Jamestown, Ks., U.S.	198	39.35 N	97.51 W
Jamestown, Ky., U.S.	194	36.59 N	85.03 W
Jamestown, Mi., U.S.	216	42.50 N	85.51 W
Jamestown, N.Y., U.S.	214	42.05 N	79.14 W
Jamestown, N.C., U.S.	192	35.59 N	79.56 W
Jamestown, N.D., U.S.	198	46.54 N	98.42 W
Jamestown, Oh., U.S.	218	39.39 N	83.44 W
Jamestown, Pa., U.S.	214	41.29 N	80.26 W
Jamestown, R.I., U.S.	207	41.29 N	71.22 W
Jamestown, Tn., U.S.	194	36.25 N	84.55 W
Jamestown ⊥	208	37.12 N	76.46 W
Jamestown Festival Park ♠	208	37.14 N	76.48 W
Jamestown Island I	208	37.12 N	76.46 W
Jamestown Reservoir ⊜[1]	198	47.15 N	98.40 W
Jamesville, N.Y., U.S.	210	42.59 N	76.04 W
Jamesville, Va., U.S.	208	37.30 N	75.55 W
Jamet, Lac ⊜	206	46.34 N	74.30 W
Jametz	56	49.26 N	5.23 E
Jamieson ≃	169	37.18 S	146.08 E
Jaminauá ≃	248	9.20 S	70.59 W
Jaminskij	80	50.21 N	42.14 E
Jāmira ≃	126	21.45 N	87.02 E
Jamira ≃[1]	126	21.35 N	88.28 E
Jamison	208	40.16 N	75.05 W
Jamison City	210	41.18 N	76.22 W
Jamison Town	274a	33.46 S	150.41 E
Jam-Ižora	265a	59.42 N	30.36 E
Jām Jodhpur	120	21.54 N	70.01 E
Jamkhandi	122	16.31 N	75.18 E
Jamki	86	59.33 N	66.47 E
Jamkino	82	55.55 N	38.24 E
Jamm	76	58.26 N	28.03 E
Jammalamadugu	122	14.50 N	78.24 E
Jammerbugten c	26	57.20 N	9.30 E
Jammerland Bugt c	41	55.35 N	11.05 E
Jammu	123	32.42 N	74.52 E
Jammu Airport ⊠	123	32.42 N	74.51 E
Jammu and Kashmīr □[2]	120	34.00 N	76.00 E
Jamnagar	120	22.28 N	70.04 E
Jamoigne	56	49.42 N	5.25 E
Jamor ≃	266c	38.42 N	9.15 W
Jampang-kulon	115a	7.16 S	106.37 E
Jāmpur, India	272b	22.56 N	88.12 E
Jāmpur, Pāk.	123	29.39 N	70.36 E
Jämsä	26	61.52 N	25.12 E
Jamsah	140	27.38 N	33.35 E
Jämsänkoski	26	61.55 N	25.11 E
Jamshedpur	126	22.48 N	86.11 E
Jamsk	74	59.35 N	154.10 E
Jamskaja Sloboda	82	55.29 N	36.01 E
Jāmtāra	126	23.57 N	86.48 E
Jämtland □[9]	26	63.30 N	14.00 E
Jämtlands Län □[6]	24	63.00 N	14.40 E
Jamuāni	126	21.57 N	86.14 E
Jamuga	82	56.24 N	36.40 E
Jamūi	124	24.55 N	86.13 E
Jamuna ≃, Bngl.	124	23.51 N	89.45 E
Jamuna ≃, India	272b	22.57 N	88.35 E
Jamundí	246	3.15 N	76.32 W
Jāmuria	126	23.44 N	87.02 E
Jāmurki	126	24.09 N	90.02 E
Jana ≃	74	71.31 N	136.32 E
Janāi	272b	22.43 N	88.16 E
Janāj	142	31.00 N	30.46 E
Janajkino	80	50.43 N	51.06 E
Janakpur	124	26.39 N	85.55 E
Janakpur □[8]	124	27.15 N	86.00 E
Janas	266c	38.49 N	9.26 W
Janauacá, Lago ⊜	246	3.28 S	60.17 W
Janaúba	255	15.48 S	43.19 W
Janaucu, Ilha I	250	0.30 N	50.10 W
Janaul	86	56.16 N	54.56 E
Janavičy	76	55.17 N	30.42 E
Jand	123	33.26 N	72.01 E
Jandaia	255	17.06 S	50.07 W
Jandaia do Sul	255	23.36 S	51.39 W
Jandaíra	250	11.34 S	37.47 W
Jandalī, Wādī al- V	142	30.05 N	31.52 E
Jandaq	128	34.02 N	54.26 E
Jandelsbrunn	60	48.44 N	13.42 E
Jandiāla	123	31.36 N	75.03 E
Jandiatuba ≃	246	3.28 S	68.42 W
Jandira	256	23.31 S	46.54 W
Jandira □[7]	287b	23.32 S	46.54 W
Jandowae	166	26.47 S	151.06 E
Jandrakinot	180	64.54 N	172.32 W
Jándula ≃	34	38.03 N	4.06 W
Jándula, Embalse de ⊜[1]	34	38.30 N	4.00 W
Janeiro, Rio de ≃	250	11.51 S	45.09 W
Jane Peak ∧	172	45.20 S	168.19 E
Janes Island I	208	38.00 N	75.52 W
Janes Island State Park ♠	208	38.00 N	75.52 W
Janesville, Ca., U.S.	204	40.17 N	120.31 W
Janesville, Mn., U.S.	190	44.06 N	93.42 W
Janesville, Wi., U.S.	216	42.40 N	89.01 W
Jangal Bādhāl	126	23.07 N	89.21 E
Jangamo	156	24.06 S	35.21 E
Jangany	157b	23.14 S	45.27 E
Jangarej	24	68.46 N	61.25 E
Jangel'skij	86	53.08 N	58.59 E
Jangeru	112	2.20 S	116.29 E
Jangiabad	85	41.08 N	70.05 E
Jangi-Bazar	85	41.40 N	70.53 E
Jangijer	85	40.17 N	68.50 E
Jangijul'	85	41.07 N	69.03 E
Jangikišlak	85	40.25 N	67.10 E
Jangikurgan, Uzb.	85	40.34 N	71.09 E
Jangikurgan, Uzb.	85	41.12 N	71.44 E
Jangipāra	126	22.45 N	88.04 E
Jangīpur	124	24.28 N	88.04 E
Jangong	114	4.23 N	96.48 E
Jangoon	122	17.43 N	79.11 E
Jangulovo	80	56.26 N	50.25 E
Janikowo	30	52.45 N	18.07 E
Janīn	132	32.28 N	35.18 E
Janina → Ioánnina	38	39.40 N	20.50 E
Janino	265a	59.56 N	30.36 E
Janisjarvi, ozero ⊜	24	61.59 N	30.57 E
Janiuay	116	10.58 N	122.30 E
Janja	38	44.40 N	19.15 E
Janjina, Hrv.	36	42.56 N	17.26 E
Janjina, Madag.	157b	20.30 S	45.50 E
Janka	126	21.52 N	87.56 E
Jankan, chrebet ⋏	88	55.45 N	118.00 E
Jankāpur	126	21.54 N	87.23 E
Jan Kempdorp (Andalusia)	158	27.55 S	24.51 E
Jan Lake ⊜	184	54.55 N	102.55 W
Janlohong	112	2.15 N	117.03 E
Jan Mayen I, Nor.	10	71.00 N	8.20 W
Jan Mayen I, Nor.	12	71.00 N	8.20 W
Jan Mayen Ridge ✦[3]	10	69.00 N	8.00 W
Jannaale	144	1.48 N	44.42 E
Jannali	274a	34.01 S	151.04 E
Jannali Park ♠	274a	34.01 S	151.03 E
Janos	232	30.54 N	108.10 W
Jánoshalma	30	46.18 N	19.20 E
Jánosháza	30	47.08 N	17.10 E
János-hegy ∧	264c	47.31 N	18.58 E
Jánossomorja	61	47.47 N	17.08 E
Janowiec Wielkopolski	30	52.46 N	17.31 E
Janów Lubelski	30	50.43 N	22.24 E
Jānsath	124	29.20 N	77.51 E
Jänschwalde	54	51.48 N	14.31 E
Jansen	184	51.47 N	104.43 W
Jansenville	158	32.56 S	24.40 E
Janskij	74	68.28 N	134.48 E
Janskij zaliv c	74	71.50 N	136.00 E
Jantarnyj	76	54.52 N	19.57 E
Jantetelco	234	18.42 N	98.46 W
Jantikovo	80	55.32 N	47.48 E
Jantra ≃	38	43.38 N	25.34 E
Januária	255	15.29 S	44.22 W
Januário Cicco	250	6.09 S	35.35 W
Jan Van Riebeeck Park ♠	273d	26.10 S	27.59 E
Janvarcevo	80	51.26 N	52.15 E
Janville	50	48.12 N	1.53 E
Janville-sur-Juine	261	48.31 N	2.16 E
Janvry	261	48.39 N	2.09 E
Janzé	32	47.58 N	1.30 W
Janzūr	142	30.41 N	31.02 E
Jaora	120	23.38 N	75.08 E
Japan (Nihon) □[1], Asia	90	36.00 N	138.00 E
Japan (Nihon) □[1], Asia	92	36.00 N	138.00 E
Japan, Sea of ▽[2]	90	40.00 N	135.00 E
Japan Basin ✦[1]	12	40.00 N	135.00 E
Japanisches Meer → Japan, Sea of ▽[2]	90	40.00 N	135.00 E
Japan Trench ✦[1]	6	37.00 N	143.00 E
Japaratinga	250	9.05 S	35.15 W
Japaratuba	250	10.35 S	36.57 W
Japeri	256	22.39 S	43.40 W
Japi	250	6.27 S	35.56 W
Japim	248	7.37 S	72.54 W
Japla	124	24.33 N	84.01 E
Japoatã	250	10.20 S	36.48 W
Japon → Japan □[1]	92	36.00 N	138.00 E
Japón, Mar del → Japan, Sea of ▽[2]	90	40.00 N	135.00 E
Japtiksal'a	74	69.21 N	72.32 E
Japuíba	256	22.35 S	42.42 W
Japurá	246	1.48 S	66.30 W
Japurá (Caquetá) ≃	246	3.08 S	64.46 W
Jaqué	246	7.31 N	78.10 W
Jaqueri-mirim ≃	287b	23.31 S	46.51 W
Jaquí	248	15.30 S	74.26 W
Jar	80	58.15 N	52.06 E
Jār, Jabal ∧	128	24.34 N	38.18 E
Jarābulus	130	36.49 N	38.01 E
Jarad	144	18.59 N	41.24 E
Jaradū	142	29.18 N	30.42 E
Jaraguá	255	15.45 S	49.20 W
Jaraguá •[8]	287b	23.27 S	46.44 W
Jaraguá, Pico do ∧	287b	23.26 S	46.46 W
Jaraguá do Sul	252	26.29 S	49.04 W
Jaraicejo	34	39.40 N	5.49 W
Jaraíz de la Vera	34	40.04 N	5.45 W
Jaral del Progreso	234	20.22 N	101.04 W
Jarales	200	34.36 N	106.45 W
Jarama ≃	34	40.02 N	3.39 W
Jarama, Canal del ≊	266a	40.18 N	3.32 W
Jaramānah	132	33.29 N	36.21 E
Jaramillo	254	47.11 S	67.09 W
Jaramor	80	56.07 N	48.44 E
Jaran' ≃	80	57.35 N	48.14 E
Jarandilla	34	40.08 N	5.39 W
Jaraniyo	144	10.42 N	39.55 E
Jaransk	80	57.19 N	47.54 E
Jarānwāla	123	31.20 N	73.26 E
Jarash	132	32.17 N	35.54 E
Jaraucu ≃	250	1.48 S	52.22 W
Jarawī, Wādī V	142	29.47 N	31.19 E
Jarbah, Jabal al- ∧	142	30.16 N	32.03 E
Jarbah, Wāḥat ▽[4]	140	29.21 N	25.20 E
Jarbidge ≃	202	42.19 N	115.39 W
Järbo	40	60.43 N	16.36 E
Jarcevo	76	55.04 N	32.41 E
Jardas al-'Abīd	146	32.19 N	20.56 E
Jardim, Bra.	248	21.28 S	56.09 W
Jardim, Bra.	250	7.35 S	39.16 W
Jardim América •[8]	287b	23.34 S	46.41 W
Jardim de Piranhas	250	6.22 S	37.20 W
Jardim do Seridó	250	6.35 S	36.46 W
Jardim Paraiso	256	22.48 S	43.35 W
Jardim Paulista •[8]	287b	23.35 S	46.40 W
Jardín América	252	27.03 S	55.14 W
Jardine ≃	164	10.55 S	142.13 E
Jardine River National Park ♠	164	11.20 S	142.40 E
Jardines de la Reina, Archipiélago de los II	240p	20.50 N	78.55 W
Jardinópolis	255	21.02 S	47.46 W
Jaredi	150	12.46 N	5.05 E
Jaren'ga, Ross.	24	63.27 N	53.26 E
Jarenga, Ross.	24	62.43 N	49.30 E
Jarensk	24	62.11 N	49.02 E
Järfälla	40	59.24 N	17.50 E
Jargalang	89	43.06 N	122.54 E
Jargeau	50	47.52 N	2.07 E
Jari ≃, Bra.	248	5.07 S	62.21 W
Jari ≃, Bra.	250	1.09 S	51.54 W
Jari, Lago ⊜	246	5.00 S	62.19 W
Jāria Jhānjail	124	25.02 N	90.39 E
Jaridih	124	23.38 N	86.04 E
Jarinu	256	23.06 S	46.44 W
Jarīr, Wādī al- V	128	25.38 N	42.30 E
Jarkino	88	59.08 N	99.23 E
Jarkovo	86	57.24 N	67.05 E
Jarkul'-Mat'uškino	86	55.51 N	76.06 E
Järlåsa	40	59.53 N	17.12 E
Jarmen	54	53.55 N	13.20 E
Järna	40	59.06 N	17.34 E
Jarnac	32	45.41 N	0.10 W
Jarny	56	49.09 N	5.53 E
Jaro	116	11.11 N	124.47 E
Jarochta	88	58.58 N	98.58 E
Jarocin	30	51.59 N	17.31 E
Jaroměř	30	50.21 N	15.55 E
Jaroměřice	61	49.05 N	15.53 E
Jaropolec	82	56.08 N	35.49 E
Jaroslavl'	80	57.37 N	39.52 E
Jaroslavl' Oblast' □[4]	76	57.45 N	39.00 E
Jaroslavl' Station •[5]	265b	55.47 N	37.39 E
Jaroslavskaja	84	44.36 N	40.27 E
Jaroslavskij	89	44.10 N	132.13 E
Jarosław	30	50.02 N	22.42 E
Järpen	26	63.21 N	13.29 E
Jarrahdale	168a	32.21 S	116.04 E
Jarratt	208	36.48 N	77.28 W
Jarreau	194	30.39 N	91.29 W
Jarrell	222	30.49 N	97.36 W
Jarrettsville	208	39.36 N	76.28 W
Jarrīs	142	27.55 N	30.46 E
Jarrow	44	54.59 N	1.29 W
Jarry, Parc ♠	275a	45.32 N	73.38 W
Jar-Sale	74	66.50 N	70.50 E
Jarsomovy	86	60.15 N	73.38 E
Jartai Yanchi ⊜	102	39.43 N	105.41 E
Jaru	248	10.26 S	62.27 W
Jaru ≃	248	10.05 S	61.59 W
Jarud Qi	89	44.37 N	120.58 E
Jaruu	88	48.08 N	96.45 E
Järva-Jaani	76	59.02 N	25.53 E
Järvakandi	76	58.47 N	24.49 E
Järvelä	26	60.52 N	25.17 E
Järvenpää	26	60.28 N	25.06 E
Jarvie	182	54.27 N	113.59 W
Jarville-la-Malgrange	58	48.40 N	6.13 E
Jarvis	212	42.53 N	80.06 W
Jarvisburg	192	36.12 N	75.52 W
Jarvis Island I	14	0.23 S	160.02 W
Järvsö	26	61.43 N	16.10 E
Jarwa	124	27.39 N	82.31 E
Jasaan	116	8.39 N	124.45 E
Jasai	272c	18.56 N	73.01 E
Jašalta	80	46.20 N	42.17 E
Jasašnaja Tašla	80	53.55 N	48.16 E
Jaša Tomić	38	45.27 N	20.51 E
Jasdan	120	22.02 N	71.12 E
Jasel'da ≃	76	52.07 N	26.28 E
Jasenevo •[8]	265b	55.36 N	37.33 E
Jasenki	78	51.32 N	38.12 E
Jasenovoje	82	54.10 N	36.47 E
Jasenskaja	78	46.22 N	38.16 E
Jashpurnagar	124	22.54 N	84.09 E
Jāshpur Pāts •[1]	124	22.55 N	84.00 E
Jasidih	124	24.31 N	86.39 E
Jasień	30	51.46 N	15.01 E
Jasienica	54	53.37 N	14.32 E
Jasikan	150	7.24 N	0.28 E
Jašil'kul', ozero ⊜	120	37.45 N	72.55 E
Jasin	114	2.19 N	102.26 E
Jasinga	115a	6.29 S	106.27 E
Jāsk	128	25.38 N	57.46 E
Jaskhar	272c	18.54 N	72.59 E
Jaškino, Ross.	80	52.41 N	53.26 E
Jaškino, Ross.	86	55.54 N	85.26 E
Jaskino, Ross.	265b	55.40 N	37.16 E
Jaškul'	80	46.11 N	45.21 E
Jaškul' ≃	80	46.15 N	45.05 E
Jasło	30	49.45 N	21.29 E
Jasmine Estates	220	28.17 N	82.42 W
Jasmund >[1]	54	54.32 N	13.35 E
Jasnaja Pol'ana ⊥	82	54.05 N	37.32 E
Jasnogorsk	82	54.29 N	37.42 E
Jasnomorskij	89	46.45 N	141.54 E
Jasnyj, Ross.	86	51.04 N	59.58 E
Jasnyj, Ross.	89	53.17 N	127.59 E
Jason Islands II	254	51.05 S	61.00 W
Jason Peninsula >[1]	9	66.10 S	61.00 W
Jasonville	194	39.09 N	87.11 W
Jasper, Ab., Can.	182	52.53 N	118.05 W
Jasper, Al., U.S.	194	33.49 N	87.16 W
Jasper, Ar., U.S.	194	36.00 N	93.11 W
Jasper, Fl., U.S.	192	30.31 N	82.56 W
Jasper, Ga., U.S.	192	34.28 N	84.25 W
Jasper, In., U.S.	194	38.23 N	86.55 W
Jasper, Mi., U.S.	216	41.48 N	84.02 W
Jasper, Mn., U.S.	198	43.51 N	96.23 W
Jasper, Mo., U.S.	194	37.20 N	94.18 W
Jasper, N.Y., U.S.	210	42.07 N	77.30 W
Jasper, Tn., U.S.	194	35.04 N	85.37 W
Jasper, Tx., U.S.	194	30.55 N	93.59 W
Jasper □[6]	216	40.57 N	87.09 W
Jasper Lake ⊜	182	53.07 N	118.00 W
Jasper National Park ♠	182	52.53 N	118.03 W
Jaspur	124	29.17 N	78.49 E
Jasra	124	25.17 N	81.48 E
Jassans-Riottier	58	45.59 N	4.45 E
Jassar	123	32.06 N	74.57 E
Jassy → Iași	38	47.10 N	27.35 E
Jassy ≃	85	40.46 N	73.05 E
Jastarnia	30	54.43 N	18.40 E
Jastrebarsko	36	45.40 N	15.39 E
Jastrebovka, Ross.	78	51.27 N	37.32 E
Jastrebovka, Ross.	82	54.36 N	36.24 E
Jastrowie	30	53.26 N	16.49 E
Jaswantnagar	124	26.53 N	78.55 E
Jászapáti	30	47.31 N	20.09 E
Jászberény	30	47.30 N	19.55 E
Jász-Nagykun-Szolnok □[6]	30	47.12 N	20.11 E
Jataí	255	17.53 S	51.43 W
Jatapu ≃	246	2.13 S	58.17 W
Jataté ≃	232	16.15 N	91.17 W
Jati, Bra.	250	7.41 S	39.01 W
Jāti, Pāk.	120	24.21 N	68.16 E
Jatibarang	115a	6.28 S	108.17 E
Jatibonico	240p	21.56 N	79.10 W
Jatibonico del Sur ≃	240p	21.33 N	79.09 W
Jatilawang	115a	7.32 S	109.06 E
Jatiluhur, Waduk ⊜[1]	115a	6.35 S	107.20 E
Jatinegara •[8]	269e	6.13 S	106.52 E
Jatiroto	115a	8.07 S	113.21 E
Jatisrono	115a	7.49 S	111.07 E
Jatiwangi	115a	6.44 S	108.15 E
Jatni	120	20.10 N	85.42 E
Jatniel	273d	26.07 S	28.19 E
Jatobá ≃	255	12.23 S	54.07 W
Jatobá, Ribeirão ≃	256	21.28 S	42.49 W
Jatoi Janūbi	123	29.31 N	70.51 E
Jātrāpur	126	22.44 N	89.45 E
Jatt (Tel Gat)	132	32.24 N	35.02 E
Jatznick	54	53.35 N	13.56 E
Jáu, Ang.	152	15.12 S	13.31 E
Jaú, Bra.	255	22.18 S	48.33 W
Jaú ≃	246	1.54 S	61.26 W
Jaú, Parque Nacional do ♠	246	2.30 S	63.00 W
Jauaperi ≃	246	1.26 S	61.35 W
Jauerling ∧	61	48.20 N	15.20 E
Jaugrām	126	23.06 N	88.05 E
Jauja	248	11.48 S	75.30 W
Jauli	272a	28.44 N	77.21 E
Jaumave	234	23.25 N	99.23 W
Jaunde → Yaoundé	152	3.52 N	11.31 E
Jaune, Mer → Yellow Sea ▽[2]	90	36.00 N	123.00 E
Jaungulbene	76	57.04 N	26.36 E
Jaunjelgava	76	56.37 N	25.05 E
Jaunpass)(	58	46.36 N	7.20 E
Jaunpiebalga	76	57.11 N	26.03 E
Jaunpils	76	56.44 N	23.01 E
Jaunpur	124	25.44 N	82.41 E
Jaupaci	255	16.18 S	50.54 W
Jauquara ≃	248	15.06 S	57.06 W
Jáuregui	258	34.36 S	59.10 W
Jauru	250	11.06 S	57.30 W
Jauru ≃, Bra.	248	16.22 S	57.46 W
Jauru ≃, Bra.	255	18.40 S	54.36 W
Jausiers	62	44.25 N	6.44 E
Jauza ≃, Ross.	82	56.25 N	36.05 E
Jauza ≃, Ross.	265b	55.45 N	37.38 E
Java	198	45.30 N	99.53 W
Java → Jawa I	115a	7.30 S	110.00 E
Java Center	210	42.39 N	78.23 W
Javādi Hills ⋏[2]	122	12.35 N	78.50 E
Javan	85	38.19 N	69.02 E
Javari (Yavarí) ≃	242	4.21 S	70.02 W
Javas	80	54.26 N	42.51 E
Java Sea → Jawa, Laut ▽[2]	112	5.00 S	110.00 E
Java Trench ✦[1]	12	10.30 S	110.00 E
Java Village	210	42.40 N	78.26 W
Jävenitz	54	52.31 N	11.30 E
Javier, Isla I	254	47.06 S	74.24 W
Javlenka	86	54.21 N	68.27 E
Javor ⋏	38	44.05 N	18.55 E
Javořice ∧	61	49.14 N	15.20 E
Javorie ∧	30	48.27 N	19.18 E
Javorná	60	49.13 N	13.18 E
Javorník	30	50.23 N	17.00 E
Javorová skála ∧	30	49.31 N	14.30 E
Javr ≃	24	68.09 N	30.06 E
Jävre	26	65.09 N	21.59 E
Jawa (Java) I	115a	7.30 S	110.00 E
Jawa, Laut (Java Sea) ▽[2]	112	5.00 S	110.00 E
Jawa Barat □[4]	115a	7.00 S	107.00 E
Jaw'āīyāt, Jabal al- ∧	132	31.26 N	36.26 E
Jawāla Mukhi	123	31.53 N	76.19 E
Jawa Tengah □[4]	115a	7.30 S	110.00 E
Jawa Timur □[4]	115a	8.00 S	113.00 E
Jawbar	132	33.31 N	36.19 E
Jawf, Wādī V	144	15.50 N	45.30 E
Jawi	112	0.48 S	109.16 E
Jawor	30	51.03 N	16.11 E
Jaworzno	30	50.13 N	19.15 E
Jay, Fl., U.S.	194	30.57 N	87.09 W
Jay, Ok., U.S.	196	36.25 N	94.47 W
Jay □[6]	216	40.26 N	84.59 W
Jaya, Puncak ∧	164	4.05 S	137.11 E
Jayanca	248	6.24 S	79.50 W
Jayapura (Sukarnapura)	164	2.32 S	140.42 E
Jayb, Wādī al- (Ha'Arava) V	132	30.58 N	35.24 E
Jay Cooke State Park ♠	190	46.41 N	92.23 W
Jay Creek Aboriginal Reserve •[4]	162	23.45 S	133.35 E
Jaydebpur	124	24.00 N	90.26 E
Jaynagar	126	22.36 N	90.42 E
Jaynagar Majilpur	126	22.11 N	88.25 E
Jaynes	200	32.16 N	111.01 W
Jay Peak ∧	188	44.55 N	72.32 W
Jaypur, India	122	18.51 N	82.35 E
Jaypur, India	126	23.03 N	87.27 E
Jayrūd	130	33.49 N	36.44 E
Jayton	196	33.15 N	100.34 W
Jayuya	240m	18.13 N	66.36 W
Jaywick	42	51.47 N	1.08 E
Jaz	80	54.54 N	45.13 E
Jaželbicy	76	58.02 N	32.58 E
Jazevec	24	65.43 N	46.30 E
Jazgulem ≃	85	38.12 N	71.21 E
Jazīrat Muḥammad	273c	30.07 N	31.12 E
Jazjavan	85	40.39 N	71.44 E
Jažma	24	66.56 N	44.29 E
Jaz Mūrīān, Hāmūn-e ⊜	128	27.20 N	58.55 E
Jazovaja	86	49.27 N	85.20 E
Jazykovo	80	54.18 N	47.24 E
Jazzīn	132	33.32 N	35.34 E
Jbā'	132	33.29 N	35.31 E
J.B. Thomas, Lake ⊜[1]	196	32.35 N	101.10 W
J. C. Murphey Lake ⊜	216	40.58 N	87.30 W
Jdiouia	34	35.57 N	0.50 E
Jeanerette	194	29.54 N	91.39 W
Jeanesville	210	40.56 N	75.58 W
Jeannette	214	40.19 N	79.36 W
Jebba	150	9.08 N	4.50 E
Jebel	38	45.33 N	21.14 E
Jebeniana	148	35.02 N	10.55 E
Jeber-Bergfrieden	54	51.59 N	12.20 E
Jeberos	248	5.17 S	76.13 W
Jebri	120	27.18 N	65.44 E
Jebus	112	1.44 S	105.29 E
Jechegnadzor	84	39.46 N	45.21 E
Jéci, Serra ∧	154	12.48 S	35.12 E
Jedane, Oued ti-n- V	148	24.55 N	6.30 E
Jedarma	88	58.44 N	102.36 E
Jedburgh	44	55.29 N	2.34 W
Jedburgh Abbey ʊ[1]	44	55.27 N	2.34 W
Jeddah → Jiddah	144	21.30 N	39.12 E
Jeddore Lake ⊜[1]	186	48.03 N	55.55 W
Jedelevo	80	53.24 N	47.45 E
Jedepo	150	5.16 N	8.20 W
Jedisa	84	42.31 N	44.16 E
Jedlesee •[8]	264b	48.16 N	16.23 E
Jednevo	82	56.06 N	36.14 E
Jedogon	88	54.15 N	100.15 E
Jedrovo	76	57.55 N	33.38 E
Jędrzejów	30	50.39 N	20.18 E
Jedwabne	30	53.17 N	22.19 E
Jed Water ≃	46	55.32 N	2.33 W
Jeetzel (Jeetze) ≃	54	53.09 N	11.04 E
Jefawa	140	10.57 N	23.48 E
Jeffara (Al-Jifārah) ≚	146	32.30 N	11.45 E
Jeffers	198	44.03 N	95.11 W
Jefferson, Ga., U.S.	192	34.07 N	83.34 W
Jefferson, In., U.S.	216	40.17 N	86.36 W
Jefferson, Ia., U.S.	198	42.00 N	94.22 W
Jefferson, Md., U.S.	208	39.21 N	77.31 W
Jefferson, Ma., U.S.	207	42.21 N	71.52 W
Jefferson, N.J., U.S.	285	39.45 N	75.13 W
Jefferson, N.Y., U.S.	210	42.14 N	73.54 W
Jefferson, N.Y., U.S.	210	42.29 N	74.37 W
Jefferson, N.C., U.S.	192	36.25 N	81.28 W
Jefferson, Oh., U.S.	214	41.44 N	80.46 W
Jefferson, Or., U.S.	202	44.43 N	123.00 W
Jefferson, Pa., U.S.	279b	40.18 N	80.03 W
Jefferson, S.C., U.S.	192	34.39 N	80.23 W
Jefferson, S.D., U.S.	198	42.36 N	96.33 W
Jefferson, Tx., U.S.	194	32.45 N	94.20 W
Jefferson, Wi., U.S.	216	43.00 N	88.48 W
Jefferson □[6], Il., U.S.	219	38.19 N	88.55 W
Jefferson □[6], In., U.S.	218	38.44 N	85.23 W
Jefferson □[6], Ky., U.S.	218	38.14 N	85.10 W
Jefferson □[6], Mo., U.S.	219	38.20 N	90.34 W
Jefferson □[6], N.Y., U.S.	212	43.59 N	75.55 W
Jefferson □[6], Oh., U.S.	214	40.22 N	80.37 W
Jefferson □[6], Pa., U.S.	214	41.09 N	79.05 W
Jefferson □[6], Wa., U.S.	224	47.50 N	122.36 W
Jefferson □[6], Wi., U.S.	216	43.02 N	88.46 W
Jefferson ≃	202	45.56 N	111.30 W
Jefferson, Mount ∧, U.S.	202	44.34 N	111.30 W
Jefferson, Mount ∧, Nv., U.S.	204	38.46 N	116.55 W
Jefferson, Mount ∧, Or., U.S.	202	44.40 N	121.47 W
Jefferson City, Mo., U.S.	219	38.34 N	92.10 W
Jefferson City, Tn., U.S.	192	36.07 N	83.29 W
Jefferson Farms	285	39.40 N	75.34 W
Jefferson Manor	284c	38.47 N	77.04 W
Jefferson Park •[8]	278	41.59 N	87.46 W
Jefferson Proving Ground ■	218	38.50 N	85.25 W
Jeffersonton	188	38.38 N	77.55 W
Jeffersontown	218	38.11 N	85.33 W
Jefferson Village	284c	38.52 N	77.10 W
Jeffersonville, Ga., U.S.	192	32.41 N	83.20 W
Jeffersonville, In., U.S.	218	38.16 N	85.44 W
Jeffersonville, N.Y., U.S.	210	41.46 N	74.56 W
Jeffersonville, Oh., U.S.	218	39.39 N	83.33 W
Jeffrey City	200	42.29 N	107.49 W
Jeffreys Bay	158	34.02 S	24.54 E
Jeffries Creek ≃	192	34.05 N	79.32 W
Jefimovka	80	52.13 N	52.03 E
Jefimovskij	76	59.30 N	34.40 E
Jefremov	76	53.09 N	38.07 E
Jefremova	82	56.13 N	38.59 E
Jefremovka	83	47.19 N	38.29 E
Jefremovo-Stepanovka	78	48.43 N	40.50 E
Jefremovskaja	82	55.25 N	38.59 E
Jega	150	12.15 N	4.23 E
Jegenstorf	58	47.03 N	7.30 E
Jegindybulak, Kaz.	86	49.45 N	76.23 E
Jegindybulak, Kaz.	86	48.42 N	81.48 E
Jegizkara, gora ∧	86	46.24 N	64.09 E
Jegorjevka	89	50.42 N	127.42 E
Jegorjevsk	82	55.23 N	39.02 E
Jegorlyk ≃	80	46.33 N	41.52 E
Jehol → Chengde	105	40.58 N	117.53 E
Jeja ≃	78	46.41 N	38.36 E
Jejsk	78	46.42 N	38.16 E
Jejskij liman c	78	46.42 N	38.25 E
Jeju → Cheju	90	33.31 N	126.32 E
Jejur	272b	22.53 N	88.08 E
Jēkabpils	76	56.29 N	25.51 E
Jekaterinburg (Sverdlovsk)	86	56.51 N	60.36 E
Jekaterinburg Oblast' □[4]	86	58.00 N	62.00 E
Jekaterinino	76	55.49 N	33.58 E
Jekaterininskoje	86	56.53 N	74.34 E
Jekaterinoslav → Dnipropetrovs'k	78	48.27 N	34.59 E
Jekaterinoslavka	89	50.23 N	129.08 E
Jekaterinovka, Kaz.	86	54.36 N	70.58 E
Jekaterinovka, Ross.	78	46.42 N	38.46 E
Jekaterinovka, Ross.	80	53.04 N	49.28 E
Jekaterinovka, Ross.	80	46.32 N	41.42 E
Jekaterinovka, Ross.	80	52.03 N	44.21 E
Jekaterinovka, Ross.	83	47.33 N	38.23 E
Jekaterinovka •[8]	265b	55.46 N	37.23 E
Jekaterinovskaja	78	46.20 N	39.58 E
Jekateriny, proliv ⊔, Ross.	74	44.30 N	146.45 E
Jekateriny, proliv ⊔, Ross.	92a	44.25 N	146.40 E
Jekimoviči	76	54.07 N	33.18 E
Jekpindykurylys	80	47.49 N	47.17 E
Jekyll Island I	192	31.04 N	81.25 W
Jekyll Island State Park ♠	192	31.02 N	81.25 W
Jelabuga	80	55.47 N	52.04 E
Jelai ≃, Indon.	112	2.59 S	110.45 E
Jelai ≃, Malay.	114	4.04 N	102.20 E
Jelan', Ross.	80	52.13 N	44.11 E
Jelan', Ross.	80	50.57 N	43.44 E
Jelan', Ross.	83	48.41 N	39.47 E
Jelan', Ross.	86	57.39 N	63.42 E
Jelan' ≃, Ross.	78	51.07 N	41.25 E
Jelan' ≃, Ross.	80	50.57 N	43.44 E
Jelan' ≃, Ross.	80	51.07 N	41.26 E
Jelancy	88	52.49 N	106.25 E
Jelanka	86	55.37 N	75.18 E
Jelan'-Koleno	78	51.09 N	41.14 E
Jelan'-Kolenovskij	78	51.10 N	41.10 E
Jelat'ma	80	54.58 N	41.45 E
Jelaur, Ross.	80	54.34 N	50.21 E
Jelaur, Ross.	80	53.50 N	48.48 E
Jelchovka	80	53.51 N	50.18 E
Jel'covka	86	53.15 N	86.15 E
Jel'cy, Ross.	76	56.40 N	33.51 E
Jel'cy, Ross.	82	56.11 N	38.46 E
Jelec	76	52.37 N	38.30 E
Jeleckij	24	67.03 N	64.10 E
Jelenia Góra (Hirschberg)	30	50.55 N	15.46 E
Jelenia Góra □[4]	30	51.10 N	15.30 E
Jelenskij	76	53.29 N	35.23 E
Jelep La Pass)(	124	27.23 N	88.51 E
Jelgava	76	56.39 N	23.42 E
Jelgavkrasti	76	57.28 N	24.26 E
Jelizarovo	80	58.33 N	44.50 E
Jelizavetinka	86	51.28 N	71.12 E
Jelizavetopol'skoje	86	52.51 N	60.36 E
Jelizavetovka	78	46.39 N	38.53 E
Jelizavety, mys >	89	54.26 N	142.42 E
Jelli	154	5.22 N	31.48 E
Jellico	192	36.35 N	84.07 W
Jelling	41	55.45 N	9.26 E
Jelloway	214	40.33 N	82.18 W
Jelm Mountain ∧	200	41.06 N	105.58 W
Jel'n'a	76	54.35 N	33.11 E
Jelnat'	80	57.20 N	42.49 E
Jel'niki	80	54.37 N	43.53 E
Jeloguj ≃	74	63.13 N	87.45 E
Jelošnoje	86	55.27 N	66.44 E
Jelovo	80	57.03 N	54.54 E
Jels	41	55.21 N	9.12 E
Jelšanka, Ross.	80	51.49 N	46.23 E
Jelšanka, Ross.	80	52.35 N	47.59 E

Name	Seite	Breite°′	Länge°′ E = Ost
Jelšanka Pervaja	80	52.53 N	52.02 E
Jelšava	30	48.39 N	20.14 E
Jema ≃	144	10.09 N	38.20 E
Jemaa	150	9.27 N	8.23 E
Jemaja, Pulau I	112	2.55 N	105.45 E
Jemaluang	114	2.17 N	103.52 E
Jemantajevo	80	53.34 N	53.50 E
Jemanželinsk	86	54.45 N	61.20 E
Jember	115a	8.10 S	113.42 E
Jemca	24	63.04 N	40.20 E
Jemca ≃	24	63.15 N	41.20 E
Jemeljanovo	86	56.11 N	92.40 E
Jemel'stan	24	61.13 N	52.29 E
Jemen → Yemen □[1]	144	15.00 N	47.00 E
Jemen, Volksrepublik → Yemen □[1]	144	15.00 N	47.00 E
Jemez ≃	200	35.22 N	106.31 W
Jemez Canyon Reservoir ⊜[1]	200	35.28 N	106.39 W
Jemez Indian Reservation •[4]	200	35.35 N	106.45 W
Jemez Springs	200	35.46 N	106.41 W
Jemgum	52	53.16 N	7.23 E
Jeminary	86	47.32 N	85.38 E
Jemmal	148	35.38 N	10.46 E
Jemnice	61	49.01 N	15.35 E
Jempang, Kenohan ⊜	112	0.26 S	116.12 E
Jena, Dtsch.	54	50.56 N	11.35 E
Jena, La., U.S.	194	31.40 N	92.08 W
Jenašimskij Polkan, gora ∧	74	59.50 N	92.52 E
Jenaz	58	46.55 N	9.45 E
Jenbach	64	47.24 N	11.47 E
Jenbek	86	48.53 N	77.12 E
Jendarata	114	3.55 N	100.57 E
Jendongin	88	53.27 N	113.01 E
Jendouba (Souk el Arba)	148	36.30 N	8.47 E
Jeneponto	112	5.41 S	119.42 E
Jenera	216	40.54 N	83.44 W
Jeniang	114	5.49 N	100.38 E
Jenisej (Yenisey) ≃	72	71.50 N	82.40 E
Jenisejsk	86	58.27 N	92.10 E
Jenisejskij kr'až ⋏	74	59.00 N	93.00 E
Jenisejskij zaliv c	74	72.30 N	80.00 E
Jenison	216	42.54 N	85.47 W
Jenkins, Ky., U.S.	192	37.10 N	82.37 W
Jenkins, Tx., U.S.	222	32.59 N	94.44 W
Jenkins, Mount ∧	162	25.36 S	129.41 E
Jenkinson Lake ⊜[1]	226	38.44 N	120.33 W
Jenkinsville	192	34.16 N	81.17 W
Jenkintown	208	40.05 N	75.07 W
Jenks	196	36.01 N	95.58 W
Jenli	100	23.15 N	120.08 E
Jenners	214	40.08 N	79.02 W
Jennersdorf	61	46.57 N	16.08 E
Jennerstown	214	40.10 N	79.04 W
Jennifer Branch ≃	284b	39.25 N	76.30 W
Jennings, Fl., U.S.	192	30.36 N	83.05 W
Jennings, La., U.S.	194	30.13 N	92.39 W
Jennings, Mo., U.S.	219	38.43 N	90.15 W
Jennings □[6]	218	38.59 N	85.36 W
Jennings Creek ≃	216	40.53 N	84.17 W
Jennings Lodge	224	45.23 N	122.36 W
Jenotajevka	80	47.15 N	47.03 E
Jenpeg Dam •[6]	184	54.33 N	98.02 W
Jensen	200	40.22 N	109.20 W
Jensen Beach	220	27.15 N	80.13 W
Jens Munk Island I	176	69.42 N	79.30 W
Jens Munks Ø I	176	64.40 N	40.30 W
Jenu	112	0.36 S	109.52 E
Jen'uka	88	57.58 N	121.42 E
Jeonju → Chŏnju	98	35.49 N	127.08 E
Jepač	24	66.58 N	61.22 E
Jepara	115a	6.35 S	110.39 E
Jeparit	166	36.09 S	141.59 E
Jepelacio	248	6.07 S	76.57 W
Jepichin	80	48.16 N	45.14 E
Jepifan'	76	53.49 N	38.33 E
Jeppener	258	35.17 S	58.12 W
Jeptha Knob ∧[2]	218	38.11 N	85.07 W
Jepua (Jeppo)	26	63.24 N	22.37 E
Jequeri	255	20.27 S	42.40 W
Jequetepeque ≃	248	7.21 S	79.36 W
Jequié	255	13.51 S	40.05 W
Jequitaí	255	17.15 S	44.28 W
Jequitinhonha	255	16.26 S	41.00 W
Jequitinhonha ≃	255	15.51 S	38.53 W
Jerachtur	80	54.43 N	41.09 E
Jerada	148	34.17 N	2.13 W
Jeradou	36	36.15 N	10.23 E
Jerangle	171b	35.52 S	149.22 E
Jeransang	114	3.52 N	102.22 E
Jerantut	114	3.56 N	102.22 E
Jerba, Île de I	148	33.48 N	10.54 E
Jerbar	140	5.39 N	31.05 E
Jerbent	128	39.19 N	58.36 E
Jerbogačon	74	61.16 N	108.00 E
Jercevo	24	60.48 N	40.05 E
Jerdenevo	82	54.55 N	36.27 E
Jerécuaro	234	20.09 N	100.31 W
Jeremejevka	83	46.58 N	39.33 E
Jeremejevo	82	55.57 N	37.01 E
Jérémie	238	18.39 N	74.07 W
Jeremino	82	56.27 N	37.58 E
Jeremoabo	250	10.04 S	38.21 W
Jeremy Hill ∧[2]	207	42.45 N	71.21 W
Jeremy Point >	207	41.53 N	70.04 W
Jerevan	84	40.11 N	44.30 E
Jerez ≃	234	22.15 N	103.11 W
Jerez de García Salinas	234	22.39 N	103.00 W
Jerez de la Frontera	34	36.41 N	6.08 W
Jerez de los Caballeros	34	38.19 N	6.46 W
Jergač	86	57.28 N	56.39 E
Jergeni ⋏[2]	80	47.00 N	44.00 E
Jergeninskij	80	47.07 N	44.28 E
Jericho → Arīḥā, Ariha	132	31.52 N	35.27 E
Jericho, Austl.	166	23.36 S	146.08 E
Jericho, N.J., U.S.	285	39.48 N	75.09 W
Jericho, N.Y., U.S.	210	40.47 N	73.32 W
Jericho Area □[8]	132	31.50 N	35.25 E
Jericho Dam ⊜[1]	158	26.39 S	30.28 E
Jerichow	54	52.30 N	12.01 E
Jericó, Bra.	250	6.33 S	37.48 W
Jericó, Col.	246	5.47 N	75.47 W
Jericoacoara, Ponta de >	250	2.48 S	40.29 W
Jerid, Chott ≡	148	33.42 N	8.26 E
Jerilderie	166	35.22 S	145.44 E
Jerimoth Hill ∧[2]	207	41.52 N	71.47 W
Jermak	86	52.02 N	76.55 E
Jermakovo	80	53.11 N	49.38 E
Jermakovskaja	80	48.03 N	41.17 E
Jermakovskoje	86	53.16 N	92.24 E
Jermekejevo	80	54.05 N	53.40 E
Jermentau	86	51.38 N	73.10 E
Jermentau ⋏	86	51.10 N	73.10 E
Jermica	24	66.56 N	52.15 E
Jermilovka	86	57.40 N	72.55 E
Jermiš'	80	54.46 N	42.16 E
Jermolajevo, Ross.	86	55.13 N	92.10 E
Jermolajevo, Ross.	86	52.46 N	55.47 E
Jermolino, Ross.	82	55.12 N	36.36 E
Jermolino, Ross.	82	55.57 N	36.54 E
Jermolino, Ross.	82	56.48 N	37.49 E
Jermolino, Ross.	86	57.20 N	64.43 E
Jermyn	210	41.31 N	75.32 W
Jernhatten ∧[2]	41	56.15 N	10.48 E
Jernih	114	4.25 N	97.43 E
Jeroaquara	255	15.23 S	50.25 W
Jerofej Pavlovič	89	53.58 N	122.01 E
Jerome, Az., U.S.	200	34.44 N	112.06 W
Jerome, Id., U.S.	202	42.43 N	114.31 W
Jerome, Il., U.S.	219	39.46 N	89.41 W
Jerome, Mi., U.S.	216	42.01 N	84.28 W
Jerome, Pa., U.S.	214	40.12 N	78.59 W

Symbols in the index entries represent the broad categories identified in the key at the right. Symbols with superior numbers (⋏[1]) identify subcategories (see complete key on page *I · 1).*

Symbole im Register stellen die rechts im Schlüssel erklärten Kategorien dar. Symbole mit hochgestellten Ziffern (⋏[1]) bezeichnen Unterabteilungen einer Kategorie (vgl. vollständiger Schlüssel auf Seite *I · 1).*

Los símbolos incluídos en el texto del índice representan las grandes categorías identificadas con la clave a la derecha. Los símbolos con numeros en su parte superior (⋏[1]) identifican las subcategorías (véase la clave completa en la página *I · 1).*

Les symboles de l'index représentent les catégories indiquées dans la légende à droite. Les symboles suivis d'un indice (⋏[1]) représentent des sous-catégories (voir légende complète à la page *I · 1).*

Os símbolos incluídos no texto do índice representam as grandes categorias identificadas com a chave à direita. Os símbolos com números em sua parte superior (⋏[1]) identificam as subcategorias (veja-se a chave completa à página *I · 1).*

∧ Mountain	Berg	Montaña	Montagne	Montanha
⋏ Mountains	Gebirge	Montañas	Montagnes	Montanhas
)(Pass	Paß	Paso	Col	Passo
V Valley, Canyon	Tal, Cañon	Valle, Cañón	Vallée, Canyon	Vale, Canhão
≚ Plain	Ebene	Llano	Plaine	Planície
> Cape	Kap	Cabo	Cap	Cabo
I Island	Insel	Isla	Île	Ilha
II Islands	Inseln	Islas	Îles	Ilhas
⊥ Other Topographic Features	Andere Topographische Objekte	Otros Elementos Topográficos	Autres données topographiques	Outros acidentes topográficos

ESPAÑOL — Nombre | Página | Lat.°′ | Long.°′ W = Oeste
FRANÇAIS — Nom | Page | Lat.°′ | Long.°′ W = Ouest
PORTUGUÊS — Nome | Página | Lat.°′ | Long.°′ W = Oeste

Jeromesville	214	40.48 N	82.11 W
Jer'omino	86	58.35 N	79.25 E
Jerónimos, Mosteiro dos ⊍[1]	266c	38.42 N	9.12 W
Jeröö	88	49.45 N	106.40 E
Jeröö ≃	88	49.54 N	106.08 E
Jeropol	74	65.15 N	168.40 E
Jerpoint Abbey ⊥	48	52.29 N	7.08 W
Jerry City	216	41.15 N	83.36 W
Jerry Slough ≃	226	35.33 N	119.31 W
Jersey	214	40.03 N	82.46 W
Jersey □[6]	219	39.07 N	90.20 W
Jersey □[2], Europe	22	49.15 N	2.10 W
Jersey □[2], Europe	43b	49.15 N	2.10 W
Jersey City	210	40.43 N	74.04 W
Jersey City State College ⊍[2]	276	40.43 N	74.05 W
Jersey Mountain ∧	202	45.29 N	115.34 W
Jersey Shore	210	41.12 N	77.16 W
Jersey Village	222	29.52 N	95.35 W
Jerseyville	219	39.07 N	90.19 W
Jerši	76	54.24 N	34.12 E
Jeršiči	76	53.40 N	32.44 E
Jeršov	80	51.20 N	48.17 E
Jeršovka	86	54.07 N	64.59 E
Jeršovo	82	55.46 N	36.52 E
Jeršovskij	86	52.29 N	59.08 E
Jertarskij	86	56.47 N	64.18 E
Jerte ≃	34	39.58 N	6.17 W
Jerteh	114	5.45 N	102.30 E
Jertoma	24	63.32 N	47.48 E
Jerumenha	250	7.05 S	43.30 W
Jerusalem → Yerushalayim	132	31.46 N	35.14 E
Jerusalem Airport ⊠	132	31.52 N	35.12 E
Jerusalim (Talusan)	116	7.26 N	122.49 E
Jeruslan ≃	80	50.15 N	45.42 E
Jervaulx Abbey ⊍[1]	44	54.16 N	1.43 W
Jervis, Cape ›	168b	35.38 S	138.06 E
Jervis Bay	170	35.08 S	150.42 E
Jervis Bay ᴄ	170	35.05 S	150.44 E
Jervis Bay Territory □[8]	170	35.05 S	150.44 E
Jervis Inlet ᴄ	182	49.46 N	124.10 W
Jervois Range ⋀	162	22.38 S	136.05 E
Jerxheim	54	52.05 N	10.54 E
Jerykly	80	55.11 N	51.26 E
Jerzens	58	47.10 N	10.45 E
Jesenankaty ≃	80	50.32 N	51.47 E
Jesenice, Česká Rep.	54	50.04 N	13.29 E
Jesenice, Slvn.	61	46.27 N	14.04 E
Jesenice, údolní nádrž ⊜[1]	60	50.04 N	12.27 E
Jeseník	30	50.14 N	17.13 E
Jesenoviči	76	57.17 N	34.14 E
Jesensaj	80	49.54 N	51.28 E
Ješera	84	43.04 N	40.55 E
Jeserig bei Wiesenburg	54	52.05 N	12.27 E
Jesi	66	43.31 N	13.14 E
Jesik	85	43.22 N	77.28 E
Jesil'	86	51.58 N	66.24 E
Jes'ki	76	57.56 N	36.23 E
Jesönbulag → Altaj	90	46.20 N	96.18 E
Jessej	74	68.29 N	102.10 E
Jesselton → Kota Kinabalu	112	5.59 N	116.04 E
Jessen	54	51.47 N	12.58 E
Jessentuki	84	44.03 N	42.51 E
Jesser Point ›	158	27.32 S	32.40 E
Jessheim	26	60.09 N	11.11 E
Jessnitz	54	51.41 N	12.17 E
Jessore	124	23.10 N	89.13 E
Jessup, Md., U.S.	208	39.08 N	76.46 W
Jessup, Pa., U.S.	210	41.28 N	75.33 W
Jessup Park ♠	280	34.15 N	118.24 W
Jestetten	58	47.39 N	8.34 E
Jestřebí	54	50.38 N	14.36 E
Jésuite, Lac du ⊜	206	46.53 N	72.36 W
Jesup, Ga., U.S.	192	31.36 N	81.53 W
Jesup, Ia., U.S.	190	42.28 N	92.03 W
Jesup, Lake ⊜	220	28.43 N	81.14 W
Jesús	252	27.03 S	55.47 W
Jésus, Île I	206	45.35 N	73.45 W
Jesús Carranza	234	17.26 N	95.02 W
Jesús de Otoro	236	14.26 N	87.59 W
Jesús María, Arg.	252	30.59 S	64.06 W
Jesús María, Méx.	232	25.06 N	107.28 W
Jesús María, Méx.	234	21.58 N	102.21 W
Jesús María, Perú	286d	12.04 S	77.04 W
Jesús María ≃	234	21.51 N	104.42 W
Jesús María, Punta ›	258	34.39 S	56.55 W
Jesús Menéndez	240p	21.10 N	76.29 W
Jet	196	36.39 N	98.10 W
Jeta, Ilha de I	150	11.53 N	16.15 W
Jetafe	116	10.09 N	124.09 E
Jetmore	198	38.05 N	99.53 W
Jet Propulsion Laboratory ⊍[3]	280	34.12 N	118.11 W
Jetpur	120	21.44 N	70.37 E
Jetřichovice	54	50.49 N	14.25 E
Jett	218	38.11 N	84.49 W
Jette	50	50.52 N	4.20 E
Jettingen, Dtsch.	58	48.35 N	8.46 E
Jettingen, Dtsch.	58	48.23 N	10.26 E
Jeumont	50	50.18 N	4.06 E
Jeune Landing	182	50.27 N	127.30 W
Jeunieb	114	5.10 N	96.29 E
Jeuram	114	4.14 N	96.18 E
Jever	52	53.34 N	7.54 E
Jeverland ◆[1]	52	53.35 N	8.00 E
Jevgaščino	86	56.26 N	74.41 E
Jevgenjevka	85	43.31 N	77.40 E
Jevíčko	30	49.38 N	16.43 E
Jevišovice	61	48.59 N	16.00 E
Jevišovka ≃	61	48.49 N	16.28 E
Jevlaš'ovo	80	53.07 N	46.51 E
Jevnaker	26	60.15 N	10.28 E
Jevra	86	59.56 N	64.27 E
Jevrej □[3]	89	48.30 N	132.00 E
Jewel Cave National Monument ♠	198	43.42 N	103.50 W
Jewell, Ia., U.S.	190	42.18 N	93.38 W
Jewell, Ks., U.S.	198	39.40 N	98.09 W
Jewell, N.Y., U.S.	210	43.13 N	75.48 W
Jewell, Oh., U.S.	216	41.20 N	84.17 W
Jewell, Or., U.S.	224	45.56 N	123.30 W
Jewell Ridge	192	37.11 N	81.47 W
Jewell Village	218	39.10 N	85.51 W
Jewett, Il., U.S.	194	39.13 N	88.15 W
Jewett, Oh., U.S.	214	40.22 N	81.00 W
Jewett, Tx., U.S.	222	31.22 N	96.09 W
Jewett City	207	41.36 N	71.58 W
Jewett Creek ≃	212	44.22 N	75.45 W
Jewett Lake ⊜	184	56.09 N	104.40 W
Jewettville	284a	42.43 N	78.52 W
Jey ◆[8]	267d	35.41 N	51.21 E
Jeyretān	120	37.10 N	67.20 E
Jezerce ∧	38	42.26 N	19.49 E
Jezerní hora ∧	60	49.10 N	13.11 E
Ježicha	80	58.06 N	47.40 E
Jeziorany	30	53.58 N	20.46 E
Ježovo	80	58.02 N	52.14 E
Jezreel, Valley of → Yizre'el, 'Émeq ⊻	132	32.36 N	35.14 E
J. G. Strijdomdam ⊜[1]	158	27.25 S	32.05 E
Jhābua	120	22.46 N	74.36 E
Jhāhtipahāri	126	23.22 N	86.54 E
Jha Jha	124	24.46 N	86.22 E
Jhajjar	124	28.37 N	76.39 E
Jhal	120	28.17 N	67.27 E
Jhālakāti	124	22.39 N	90.12 E
Jhālārāpātan	124	24.33 N	76.10 E
Jhālāwār	124	24.36 N	76.09 E
Jhalida	124	23.22 N	85.58 E
Jhal Jhao	120	26.18 N	65.35 E
Jhālod	120	23.06 N	74.09 E
Jhang Sadar	123	31.16 N	72.19 E
Jhānsi	124	25.26 N	78.35 E
Jhānsi Post	123	33.52 N	71.24 E
Jhāpā	124	26.29 N	87.51 E
Jhārgrām	126	22.27 N	86.59 E
Jharia	126	23.45 N	86.24 E
Jhārpokhariā	126	22.10 N	86.38 E
Jhārsuguda	120	21.51 N	84.02 E
Jhawāriān	123	32.22 N	72.38 E
Jhelum	123	32.56 N	73.44 E
Jhelum ≃	123	31.12 N	72.08 E
Jhenida	124	23.33 N	89.10 E
Jhenkāri	272b	22.46 N	88.18 E
Jhikergacha	126	23.07 N	89.07 E
Jhikra	126	22.37 N	87.55 E
Jhilimili	126	22.49 N	86.37 E
Jhil Kuranga ◆[8]	272a	28.40 N	77.17 E
Jhilla ≃[1]	126	21.58 N	88.56 E
Jhinkpāni	124	22.25 N	85.47 E
Jhok Rind	120	31.27 N	70.26 E
Jhumra	123	31.34 N	73.11 E
Jhunjhunūn	120	28.08 N	75.24 E
Jiaban, Zhg.	102	25.10 N	107.03 E
Jiaban, Zhg.	102	25.38 N	107.07 E
Jiabong	116	11.46 N	124.57 E
Jiacha	120	29.11 N	92.44 E
Jiading	106	31.23 N	121.15 E
Jiāganj	126	24.14 N	88.16 E
Jiagedan	89	51.35 N	120.55 E
Jiahashitai	89	46.25 N	122.17 E
Jiahe	102	25.43 N	112.05 E
Jiajiachang, Zhg.	107	29.44 N	105.06 E
Jiajiachang, Zhg.	107	30.26 N	104.21 E
Jiajiagou, Zhg.	104	41.44 N	120.58 E
Jiajiagou, Zhg.	104	42.20 N	121.46 E
Jiajiang	107	29.45 N	103.34 E
Jiajiayuan	106	32.18 N	120.55 E
Jiakou	100	30.10 N	119.03 E
Jiakou Wa ≡	105	38.58 N	116.50 E
Jiali	120	30.47 N	93.24 E
Jialing ≃	102	29.34 N	106.35 E
Jialou	100	32.54 N	113.26 E
Jialu	106	30.26 N	118.50 E
Jialu ≃	100	33.38 N	114.36 E
Jiamingzhen	107	29.16 N	105.20 E
Jiamusi (Kiamusze)	89	46.50 N	130.21 E
Jiamuyingzi	104	41.56 N	121.43 E
Ji'an, Zhg.	98	41.06 N	126.08 E
Ji'an, Zhg.	100	27.07 N	114.58 E
Jian ≃, Zhg.	100	26.38 N	118.12 E
Jian ≃, Zhg.	104	40.59 N	121.51 E
Jian'an	89	43.04 N	125.03 E
Jianba	106	31.59 N	120.35 E
Jianbi	106	32.11 N	119.35 E
Jianchang, Zhg.	98	40.51 N	119.46 E
Jianchang, Zhg.	98	39.58 N	122.35 E
Jianchang, Zhg.	98	41.16 N	124.29 E
Ji'anchang, Zhg.	107	30.31 N	106.02 E
Jianchangying	98	40.06 N	118.49 E
Jianchapu	105	39.06 N	116.31 E
Jianchaxi, Zhg.	102	28.08 N	108.04 E
Jianchaxi, Zhg.	107	30.22 N	104.03 E
Jianchuan	102	26.34 N	99.53 E
Jiande	100	29.29 N	119.16 E
Jiang'an	107	28.44 N	105.05 E
Jiangba	100	33.08 N	118.45 E
Jiangbei (Lianglukou)	107	29.44 N	106.38 E
Jiangbeixu	100	26.20 N	115.26 E
Jiangbian	102	24.03 N	103.37 E
Jiangbianzhai	102	23.49 N	100.11 E
Jiangcheng, Zhg.	102	22.40 N	101.48 E
Jiangcheng, Zhg.	105	38.52 N	115.22 E
Jiangcun	100	28.17 N	117.49 E
Jiangdi	102	25.08 N	104.45 E
Jiangdihe	102	25.55 N	101.31 E
Jiangdu	100	32.26 N	119.34 E
Jiangduo	100	32.22 N	120.15 E
Jiange	102	32.06 N	105.29 E
Jianggezhuang	98	39.27 N	119.09 E
Jianghua (Shuikou)	102	24.58 N	111.38 E
Jianghuaqiao	106	32.05 N	120.00 E
Jiangji	100	32.19 N	115.44 E
Jiangjia, Zhg.	106	31.40 N	121.09 E
Jiangjia, Zhg.	106	31.58 N	121.28 E
Jiangjiadian	104	41.41 N	121.03 E
Jiangjiagou	104	41.44 N	121.44 E
Jiangjiaji	100	31.59 N	115.16 E
Jiangjiatun, Zhg.	104	41.42 N	122.02 E
Jiangjiatun, Zhg.	104	41.42 N	122.25 E
Jiangjin	107	29.17 N	106.15 E
Jiangjing	100	25.34 N	119.25 E
Jiangjunmiao	86	44.43 N	90.05 E
Jiangjunqiao	102	31.18 N	100.55 E
Jiangkou, Zhg.	100	29.43 N	121.25 E
Jiangkou, Zhg.	100	27.27 N	118.03 E
Jiangkou, Zhg.	100	25.29 N	119.12 E
Jiangkou, Zhg.	100	27.21 N	115.31 E
Jiangkou, Zhg.	100	27.44 N	114.49 E
Jiangkou, Zhg.	102	23.31 N	110.17 E
Jiangkou, Zhg.	102	27.37 N	108.48 E
Jiangkou, Zhg.	102	30.26 N	111.42 E
Jiangkou, Zhg.	102	33.39 N	107.12 E
Jiangkou, Zhg.	102	29.38 N	110.20 E
Jiangkou, Zhg.	107	30.14 N	103.55 E
Jiangkouji	100	32.50 N	116.16 E
Jiangkoutang	100	27.30 N	112.44 E
Jiangle	100	26.42 N	117.25 E
Jiangliadian	98	42.33 N	117.27 E
Jiangling	102	30.20 N	112.06 E
Jianglingxi	102	31.28 N	107.13 E
Jiangmen	100	22.35 N	113.05 E
Jiangmifeng	89	43.58 N	126.45 E
Jiangning	106	31.58 N	118.50 E
Jiangpu	100	32.04 N	118.37 E
Jiangqiao	89	46.48 N	123.45 E
Jiangqiaotou	106	30.37 N	120.38 E
Jiangshan	100	28.45 N	118.37 E
Jiangshan ≃	100	28.57 N	118.50 E
Jiangshe	106	31.34 N	120.08 E
Jiangshui	98	37.13 N	113.59 E
Jiangsu (Kiangsu) □[4]	90	33.00 N	120.00 E
Jiangtian	100	25.52 N	119.34 E
Jiangtun, Zhg.	102	23.41 N	112.37 E
Jiangtun, Zhg.	104	41.37 N	122.22 E
Jiangwakou	105	39.31 N	117.42 E
Jiangwan, Zhg.	100	29.25 N	118.02 E
Jiangwan, Zhg.	106	31.18 N	121.29 E
Jiangwan Airport ⊠	269b	31.20 N	121.30 E
Jiangxi	102	22.51 N	101.50 E
Jiangxi (Kiangsi) □[4]	100	28.00 N	116.00 E
Jiangxiacun	106	31.44 N	121.50 E
Jiangxiang	100	32.16 N	117.37 E
Jiangxikou	100	27.36 N	118.23 E
Jiangya	102	29.17 N	110.39 E
Jiangyi	100	29.12 N	115.46 E
Jiangyin	106	31.55 N	120.16 E
Jiangyou	102	31.47 N	104.45 E
Jiangyu, Zhg.	98	36.16 N	118.40 E
Jiangyu, Zhg.	100	27.50 N	112.46 E
Jiangyuanzhen	107	30.35 N	103.48 E
Jiangzaogang	106	32.01 N	121.03 E
Jiangzhasiji	120	30.28 N	88.55 E
Jiangzhong	120	29.10 N	93.32 E
Jianhe, Zhg.	102	26.27 N	108.33 E
Jianhe, Zhg.	105	39.14 N	118.03 E
Jianhu	100	33.28 N	119.50 E
Jianli	100	29.49 N	112.53 E
Jianling	100	32.45 N	113.12 E
Jianning	100	26.50 N	116.49 E
Jian'ou	100	27.03 N	118.19 E
Jianping (Yebaishou)	98	41.24 N	119.37 E
Jianqiao	106	30.20 N	120.12 E
Jianqigou	104	40.54 N	123.17 E
Jianshan, Zhg.	100	29.14 N	120.44 E
Jianshan, Zhg.	100	29.58 N	120.16 E
Jian Shan ∧	104	41.49 N	121.44 E
Jianshi	102	30.36 N	109.38 E
Jianshui	102	23.38 N	102.49 E
Jiantiao	100	29.04 N	121.36 E
Jiantou	105	39.26 N	115.41 E
Jiantouji	98	34.35 N	117.34 E
Jianyang, Zhg.	100	27.22 N	118.04 E
Jianyang, Zhg.	100	33.27 N	119.40 E
Jianyang, Zhg.	107	30.24 N	104.32 E
Jiao ≃	100	26.48 N	119.42 E
Jiaocheng	102	37.33 N	112.02 E
Jiaodao	105	39.39 N	116.06 E
Jiaodianzi	104	41.32 N	121.49 E
Jiaodonggou	104	40.50 N	123.58 E
Jiaohe, Zhg.	89	43.42 N	127.19 E
Jiaohe, Zhg.	98	38.01 N	116.17 E
Jiaojiapuzi	104	40.47 N	123.48 E
Jiaolai ≃, Zhg.	89	43.43 N	123.05 E
Jiaolai ≃, Zhg.	98	42.47 N	120.44 E
Jiaolai ≃, Zhg.	98	37.07 N	119.35 E
Jiaoling	100	24.41 N	116.10 E
Jiaomei	100	24.32 N	117.54 E
Jiaonan (Wanggezhuang)	98	35.51 N	119.59 E
Jiao Shan I	106	31.21 N	120.06 E
Jiaoshanhe	100	29.38 N	112.33 E
Jiaoxi	106	31.49 N	120.10 E
Jiaoxian	98	36.18 N	119.58 E
Jiaoyang	100	27.56 N	119.16 E
Jiaozhou Wan ᴄ	98	36.10 N	120.15 E
Jiaozhuang	100	33.14 N	114.02 E
Jiaozuo	102	35.15 N	113.13 E
Jiapu	106	31.06 N	119.56 E
Jiashan, Zhg.	100	32.47 N	118.00 E
Jiashan, Zhg.	106	30.51 N	120.54 E
Jiashi	85	39.28 N	76.45 E
Jiashun Hu ⊜	120	34.35 N	86.05 E
Jiasi	107	29.06 N	106.24 E
Jiatan	107	30.12 N	106.29 E
Jiatanchang	107	29.09 N	106.16 E
Jiawang	98	34.27 N	117.27 E
Jiaxian, Zhg.	100	33.58 N	113.13 E
Jiaxian, Zhg.	102	38.01 N	110.31 E
Jiaxiang	98	35.25 N	116.21 E
Jiaxing	106	30.46 N	120.45 E
Jiayin	89	48.53 N	130.24 E
Jiayu	100	29.58 N	113.55 E
Jiayun Hu ⊜	120	35.02 N	85.40 E
Jiaze	106	31.42 N	119.47 E
Jiazhai	98	34.33 N	115.48 E
Jiazhuang	105	39.19 N	117.22 E
Jiazi	100	22.55 N	116.04 E
Jiazier	85	38.40 N	76.33 E
Jibacoa ≃	240p	20.15 N	77.12 W
Jibagalle	144	8.04 N	48.39 E
Jibalei	144	10.09 N	50.53 E
Jibannagar	126	23.25 N	88.50 E
Jíbaro ≃	286b	23.03 N	82.23 W
Jibat ∧	144	8.45 N	37.29 E
Jibiya	150	13.05 N	7.12 E
Jiboa ≃	236	13.22 N	89.04 W
Jibóia, Ilha da I	256	23.03 S	44.22 W
Jibuti → Djibouti	144	11.36 N	43.09 E
Jicamarca, Quebrada ∨	286d	12.02 S	76.57 W
Jicarilla Apache Indian Reservation ◆[4]	200	36.40 N	107.00 W
Jicarón, Isla I	246	7.16 N	81.47 W
Jicatuyo ≃	236	14.59 N	88.16 W
Jicheng	105	39.23 N	116.17 E
Jičín	30	50.26 N	15.21 E
Jicotea ≃	286b	23.01 N	82.14 W
Jidād	140	11.05 N	24.44 E
Jiddah (Jeddah)	144	21.30 N	39.12 E
Jidingxilin	120	32.52 N	92.21 E
Jidy, Wādī al- ∨	142	30.13 N	32.46 E
Jiebu	100	28.15 N	115.02 E
Jiedong	100	26.02 N	113.00 E
Jiegou	100	33.21 N	117.55 E
Jiehe	98	35.16 N	117.04 E
Jieji	100	33.33 N	118.24 E
Jiejiang	106	31.58 N	120.43 E
Jiejinkou	89	47.57 N	132.50 E
Jielingkou	98	40.09 N	119.15 E
Jielongchang	107	29.13 N	106.32 E
Jiemian	100	25.56 N	118.02 E
Jiepai, Zhg.	100	26.41 N	112.46 E
Jiepai, Zhg.	100	29.34 N	115.06 E
Jiepai, Zhg.	106	30.55 N	119.32 E
Jiepai, Zhg.	107	29.28 N	104.43 E
Jiepaiji	100	32.15 N	117.50 E
Jiesheng	100	22.45 N	115.25 E
Jieshi, Zhg.	100	22.51 N	115.49 E
Jieshi, Zhg.	107	29.27 N	105.17 E
Jieshi Wan ᴄ	100	22.46 N	115.40 E
Jieshou, Zhg.	100	33.18 N	115.20 E
Jieshou, Zhg.	100	27.22 N	117.40 E
Jieshou, Zhg.	100	33.00 N	119.27 E
Jiexi	100	23.28 N	115.56 E
Jiexiu	102	37.05 N	111.51 E
Jieyang	100	23.35 N	116.21 E
Jiezhongdian	100	32.41 N	112.29 E
Jieznas	76	54.36 N	24.10 E
Jifjāfah, Bi'r ⫪[4]	140	30.27 N	33.11 E
Jiftūn, Jazā'ir II	140	27.13 N	33.56 E
Jiggalong	162	23.25 S	120.47 E
Jiggalong Creek ≃	162	22.53 S	120.14 E
Jigongying	102	26.18 N	104.48 E
Jigongzhen	98	34.02 N	115.32 E
Jiguaní	240p	20.22 N	76.26 W
Jiguanshan, Zhg.	98	40.32 N	123.55 E
Jiguanshan, Zhg.	104	41.18 N	123.36 E
Jiguanshan, Zhg.	104	42.08 N	124.15 E
Jigüey, Bahía de ᴄ	240p	22.08 N	78.05 W
Jigzhi	102	33.28 N	101.29 E
Jihe	100	32.15 N	112.48 E
Jiheier	85	38.11 N	75.46 E
Jihlava	30	49.24 N	15.36 E
Jihlava ≃	61	48.55 N	16.37 E
Jihočeský Kraj □[4]	30	49.05 N	14.30 E
Jihomoravský Kraj □[4]	30	49.10 N	16.40 E
Jiiqley	144	4.25 N	45.22 E
Jijel	148	36.48 N	5.46 E
Jijia ≃	38	46.54 N	28.05 E
Jijiadianzi	98	35.31 N	118.59 E
Jijiamiao	107	29.18 N	104.06 E
Jijiapuzi	104	41.16 N	124.12 E
Jijiashi	106	32.08 N	120.18 E
Jijiaying	105	40.20 N	115.24 E
Jijiga	144	9.22 N	42.47 E
Jikawo	144	8.22 N	33.46 E
Jikawo ≃	144	8.22 N	33.47 E
Jike	102	31.00 N	99.41 E
Jilalin	89	51.19 N	119.55 E
Jilantai	102	39.47 N	105.45 E
Jilbānah, Bi'r al- ⫪[4]	142	30.55 N	32.29 E
Jilemutu	89	52.14 N	120.47 E
Jilib	144	0.29 N	42.46 E
Jilibulake	120	33.05 N	93.10 E
Jili Hu ⊜	86	46.57 N	87.27 E
Jilin (Kirin)	89	43.51 N	126.33 E
Jilin (Kirin) □[4]	90	44.00 N	126.00 E
Jiliu ≃	89	52.04 N	120.48 E
Jill, Kediet ej ∧	148	22.38 N	12.33 W
Jill, Sebkhet ej ⊜	148	22.47 N	12.53 W
Jiloca ≃	34	41.21 N	1.39 W
Jilotepec de Abasolo	234	19.58 N	99.32 W
Jilotlán de los Dolores	234	19.14 N	102.59 W
Jílové	54	50.46 N	14.07 E
Jima	144	7.36 N	36.50 E
Jimbaran	115b	8.46 S	115.11 E
Jimbolia	38	45.47 N	20.43 E
Jimboomba	171a	27.50 S	153.02 E
Jimei	100	24.37 N	118.07 E
Jimena de la Frontera	34	36.26 N	5.27 W
Jiménez, Méx.	232	29.02 N	100.41 W
Jiménez, Méx.	232	27.08 N	104.55 W
Jimenez, Pil.	116	8.20 N	123.50 E
Jiménez, Arroyo ≃	288	34.44 S	58.13 W
Jiménez, Laguna de ⊜	258	35.26 S	59.01 W
Jiménez del Téul	234	23.10 N	104.05 W
Jimeta	146	9.16 N	12.27 E
Jimi ≃	164	5.20 S	144.20 E
Jimingcun	105	39.19 N	116.09 E
Jiminghe	100	30.36 N	115.32 E
Jim Ned Creek ≃	196	31.50 N	99.07 W
Jimo	98	36.23 N	120.27 E
Jimsar	86	44.00 N	89.04 E
Jim Thorpe	210	40.52 N	75.43 W
Jimuganayaji	85	38.36 N	75.39 E
Jin (Gam) ≃, Asia	110	21.55 N	105.12 E
Jin ≃, Zhg.	100	24.54 N	118.35 E
Jin ≃, Zhg.	100	28.24 N	115.49 E
Jin ≃, Zhg.	100	26.51 N	117.46 E
Jināḥ	140	25.20 N	30.31 E
Jinan (Tsinan), Zhg.	98	36.40 N	116.57 E
Jin'an, Zhg.	100	28.38 N	119.18 E
Jinbang	100	25.01 N	118.01 E
Jinbo ≃	107	28.54 N	103.40 E
Jincang	89	43.20 N	130.30 E
Jince	60	49.47 N	13.59 E
Jinchanggouliang	98	41.56 N	120.19 E
Jincheng, Zhg.	102	35.30 N	112.50 E
Jincheng, Zhg.	104	41.12 N	121.25 E
Jinchengshai	102	26.43 N	111.00 E
Jincheng Shan ∧	107	30.47 N	106.32 E
Jinchuan	102	31.25 N	102.08 E
Jinchuanqiao	102	27.18 N	101.48 E
Jincun	106	31.08 N	119.49 E
Jīnd	123	29.19 N	76.19 E
Jindabyne	171b	36.25 S	148.38 E
Jindabyne, Lake ⊜[1]	171b	36.22 S	148.37 E
Jindaichang	107	29.43 N	104.49 E
Jindālī, Bi'r ⫪[4]	142	29.55 N	31.40 E
Jindřichovice	54	50.15 N	12.37 E
Jindřichův Hradec	30	49.09 N	15.00 E
Jinfeng	100	26.01 N	119.36 E
Jinfosi	102	39.29 N	99.00 E
Jing ≃, Zhg.	86	44.52 N	82.50 E
Jing ≃, Zhg.	102	34.28 N	109.00 E
Jing'an	100	28.52 N	115.20 E
Jin'gangpo	107	29.38 N	106.25 E
Jingangtou	100	27.54 N	113.40 E
Jingangtuo	107	29.10 N	106.07 E
Jing'anji	98	34.30 N	116.55 E
Jingbian	102	37.25 N	108.21 E
Jingbohu ⊜	89	43.54 N	128.54 E
Jingcheng	100	24.36 N	117.30 E
Jingde	100	30.19 N	118.31 E
Jingdezhen (Kingtechen)	100	29.16 N	117.11 E
Jingdong	102	24.28 N	100.52 E
Jingellic	171b	35.56 S	147.42 E
Jingeryu	105	39.43 N	115.36 E
Jinggang	100	28.28 N	112.46 E
Jinggangshan (Ciping)	100	26.36 N	114.05 E
Jinggongqiao	100	29.45 N	117.11 E
Jinggu	102	23.32 N	100.41 E
Jingguanzhen	107	29.55 N	106.33 E
Jinghai, Zhg.	100	23.03 N	116.31 E
Jinghai, Zhg.	105	38.56 N	116.55 E
Jinghaiwei	98	36.52 N	122.13 E
Jinghe	86	44.39 N	82.50 E
Jinghong	102	22.01 N	100.49 E
Jinghuiling	105	40.22 N	117.27 E
Jingjiang, Zhg.	102	26.19 N	100.33 E
Jingjiang, Zhg.	106	32.01 N	120.15 E
Jingjiayu	104	41.40 N	123.51 E
Jingle	102	38.24 N	111.54 E
Jinglou	100	32.39 N	112.56 E
Jingmen	102	31.00 N	112.09 E
Jingning, Zhg.	100	27.59 N	119.38 E
Jingning, Zhg.	102	35.25 N	105.56 E
Jingou	104	41.38 N	120.35 E
Jingoutun	98	41.03 N	117.27 E
Jingshan	100	31.02 N	113.05 E
Jingtai	102	37.17 N	104.09 E
Jingu	100	25.13 N	118.07 E
Jingxi	102	23.08 N	106.29 E
Jingxian, Zhg.	98	37.42 N	116.16 E
Jingxian, Zhg.	100	30.42 N	118.24 E
Jingxian, Zhg.	102	26.40 N	109.25 E
Jingxin	100	24.14 N	115.56 E
Jingxing, Zhg.	89	47.04 N	123.01 E
Jingxing, Zhg.	98	38.02 N	114.08 E
Jingyan	107	29.40 N	104.04 E
Jingyu	98	42.22 N	126.50 E
Jingyuan, Zhg.	102	36.38 N	104.37 E
Jingyuan, Zhg.	102	35.30 N	106.48 E
Jingzhi	98	36.19 N	119.23 E
Jingzichang	107	29.00 N	104.41 E
Jinhae → Chinhae	98	35.09 N	128.40 E
Jinhu	100	33.00 N	119.02 E
Jinhua	100	29.07 N	119.39 E
Jinhua ≃	100	29.06 N	119.39 E
Jinhui	106	30.59 N	121.29 E
Jining, Zhg.	98	35.25 N	116.36 E
Jining, Zhg.	102	40.57 N	113.02 E
Jinja	154	0.26 N	33.12 E
Jinjiadian	98	41.39 N	118.18 E
Jinjiang, Zhg.	100	24.50 N	118.35 E
Jinjiang, Zhg.	110	26.19 N	100.33 E
Jinjiawopeng	104	41.38 N	122.16 E
Jinjiawopu	104	42.32 N	122.10 E
Jinjiazhen	89	42.49 N	123.40 E
Jinjing, Zhg.	100	24.37 N	118.36 E
Jinjing, Zhg.	100	28.31 N	113.25 E
Jinjini	150	7.26 N	2.39 W
Jinju → Chinju	98	35.11 N	128.05 E
Jinkeng	100	27.15 N	117.14 E
Jinkichi-mori ∧	96	33.41 N	134.07 E
Jinkou, Zhg.	98	36.35 N	120.46 E
Jinkou, Zhg.	100	30.22 N	114.10 E
Jinkou, Zhg.	100	29.18 N	115.15 E
Jinkuang	102	28.20 N	101.54 E
Jinlijing	107	29.48 N	104.45 E
Jinlingsi	104	41.42 N	120.49 E
Jinlingyu	105	40.06 N	117.32 E
Jinlingzhen	98	36.49 N	118.11 E
Jinlonggou	89	51.45 N	125.51 E
Jinmachi-chūtonchi, Rikujō-jieitai- ■	92	38.25 N	140.27 E
Jinmu Jiao ›	110	18.09 N	109.34 E
Jinnah Barrage ◆[6]	123	32.57 N	71.30 E
Jinning	102	24.41 N	102.35 E
Jinniu, Zhg.	100	31.24 N	117.12 E
Jinniu, Zhg.	100	29.59 N	114.38 E
Jinotega	236	13.06 N	86.00 W
Jinotega □[5]	236	14.00 N	85.25 W
Jinotepe	236	11.51 N	86.12 W
Jinping, Zhg.	102	26.38 N	109.03 E
Jinping, Zhg.	102	22.50 N	103.10 E
Jinpingchang	107	28.54 N	104.43 E
Jinpo	105	39.18 N	115.15 E
Jinqian ≃	102	32.52 N	110.01 E
Jinqiao	100	31.46 N	116.50 E
Jinrui	100	27.57 N	114.12 E
Jinseki	96	34.48 N	133.11 E
Jinsen → Inch'ŏn	98	37.28 N	126.38 E
Jinsha, Zhg.	100	26.12 N	118.39 E
Jinsha, Zhg.	102	27.18 N	106.10 E
Jinsha, Zhg.	106	32.06 N	121.05 E
Jinsha (Yangtze) ≃	102	28.50 N	104.36 E
Jinshan, Zhg.	89	51.51 N	126.30 E
Jinshan, Zhg.	106	30.54 N	121.09 E
Jinshanwei	106	30.44 N	121.19 E
Jinshanxiang	107	30.35 N	104.52 E
Jinshanzui	106	30.44 N	121.22 E
Jinshi	102	29.39 N	111.52 E
Jinshijing	107	29.23 N	104.08 E
Jinshuzhen	106	31.23 N	120.24 E
Jinsiniangqiao	106	30.43 N	121.15 E
Jinta	102	40.03 N	98.53 E
Jintan	106	31.45 N	119.34 E
Jintang, Zhg.	102	30.54 N	104.19 E
Jintang, Zhg.	102	30.19 N	102.19 E
Jintian	100	27.10 N	114.27 E
Jintotolo Channel ꭒ	116	11.48 N	123.05 E
Jintotolo Island I	116	11.51 N	123.08 E
Jinxi, Zhg.	100	27.54 N	116.43 E
Jinxi, Zhg.	104	40.45 N	120.50 E
Jinxian, Zhg.	98	38.02 N	115.02 E
Jinxian, Zhg.	98	39.04 N	121.40 E
Jinxian, Zhg.	100	28.22 N	116.14 E
Jinxian (Dalinghe), Zhg.	104	41.11 N	121.22 E
Jinxiang, Zhg.	98	35.05 N	116.18 E
Jinxiang, Zhg.	100	27.26 N	120.35 E
Jin-ya ⊥	94	36.06 N	137.15 E
Jinyun	100	28.40 N	120.03 E
Jinz, Qā' al- ⊻	132	30.45 N	36.04 E
Jinze	106	31.02 N	120.56 E
Jinzhai	100	31.44 N	115.54 E
Jinzhaizhen	100	31.32 N	115.46 E
Jinzhen	100	33.39 N	118.17 E
Jinzhong ≃	105	39.08 N	117.42 E
Jinzhou (Chinchou)	104	41.07 N	121.08 E
Jinzisi	107	29.09 N	106.22 E
Jinzū ≃	94	36.46 N	137.13 E
Jiō	270	34.58 N	135.28 E
Ji-Paraná	248	10.52 S	61.57 W
Jipijapa	246	1.20 S	80.35 W
Jipioca, Ilha I	250	1.53 N	50.12 W
Jiquí ≃	240p	21.22 N	78.32 W
Jiquilisco	236	13.19 N	88.35 W
Jiquilisco, Bahía de ᴄ	236	13.10 N	88.28 W
Jiquilpan de Juárez	234	19.59 N	102.43 W
Jiquipilas	234	16.40 N	93.39 W
Jiquipilco	234	19.32 N	99.36 W
Jiquiriçá ≃	255	13.12 S	38.57 W
Jirāfī, Wādī al- (Naḥal Paran) ∨	132	30.24 N	35.10 E
Jirbān	140	11.03 N	30.36 E
Jiřetín	54	50.50 N	14.35 E
Jiri ≃	120	24.42 N	93.06 E
Jiřikov	54	50.59 N	14.35 E
Jirjā	140	26.20 N	31.53 E
Jirkov	54	50.30 N	13.27 E
Jīroft	128	28.40 N	57.46 E
Jīsh (Gush Ḥalav)	132	33.02 N	35.27 E
Jishou	102	28.17 N	109.29 E
Jishui, Zhg.	100	27.14 N	115.06 E
Jishui, Zhg.	100	33.46 N	115.24 E
Jisr ash-Shughūr	130	35.48 N	36.19 E
Jitan	100	24.56 N	115.43 E
Jitarning	162	32.48 S	117.59 E
Jitaúna	255	14.01 S	39.57 W
Jitianzhen	107	30.19 N	104.01 E
Jitotol	234	17.02 N	92.52 W
Jitra	114	6.16 N	100.25 E
Jituo	120	34.15 N	82.05 E
Jiu ≃	38	43.47 N	23.48 E
Jiubao	100	25.57 N	115.48 E
Jiubingtai	104	41.39 N	124.07 E
Jiucheng, Zhg.	98	38.12 N	117.18 E
Jiucheng, Zhg.	105	39.23 N	116.44 E
Jiuchuchang	107	29.55 N	104.38 E
Jiudaoliang	102	31.35 N	110.12 E
Jiudhara	126	22.24 N	89.44 E
Jiudian	106	32.10 N	120.57 E
Jiudongle	102	38.49 N	101.05 E
Jiudu	106	30.31 N	119.53 E
Jiufanxian	98	35.51 N	115.41 E
Jiufeng, Zhg.	100	24.20 N	117.02 E
Jiufeng, Zhg.	100	25.33 N	119.08 E
Jiugang	105	39.03 N	116.12 E
Jiugongan	102	29.52 N	112.00 E
Jiugongkou	105	39.50 N	114.43 E
Jiugong Shan ∧	100	29.26 N	114.42 E
Jiuguan, Zhg.	98	37.26 N	121.53 E
Jiuguan, Zhg.	106	30.51 N	120.16 E
Jiuguantao	98	36.40 N	115.25 E
Jiuhe	100	23.32 N	115.04 E
Jiuhongshui	102	37.14 N	103.57 E
Jiuhu	98	37.03 N	117.36 E
Jiuhuai'an	98	40.24 N	114.31 E
Jiuhuajie	100	30.25 N	117.51 E
Jiuhuaxian	100	23.30 N	113.16 E
Jiuhuinan	98	42.37 N	126.14 E
Jiujiang, Zhg.	100	29.44 N	115.59 E
Jiujiang, Zhg.	100	22.51 N	113.02 E
Jiujiang, Zhg.	100	29.36 N	115.52 E
Jiujiawopeng	104	40.59 N	121.22 E
Jiujiji	98	35.09 N	114.48 E
Jiujing	107	29.05 N	103.54 E
Jiukou	100	30.52 N	112.38 E
Jiuli	107	29.32 N	103.32 E
Jiulian Shan ⋀	100	24.40 N	114.46 E
Jiuliguan	100	31.50 N	114.14 E
Jiuling Shan ⋀	100	28.46 N	114.45 E
Jiulong, Zhg.	100	24.08 N	112.55 E
Jiulong, Zhg.	102	29.00 N	101.50 E
Jiulong (Kowloon), Zhg.	271d	22.18 N	114.10 E
Jiulong ≃, Zhg.	100	24.28 N	117.48 E
Jiulong ≃, Zhg.	100	25.59 N	117.18 E
Jiulongchang	107	29.32 N	106.05 E
Jiulonggang	100	32.38 N	117.03 E
Jiulongpo	107	29.29 N	106.32 E
Jiulongzhen	106	31.54 N	121.34 E
Jiumen	98	40.42 N	120.27 E
Jiumianyang	100	30.16 N	113.13 E
Jiumiao	104	42.24 N	121.36 E
Jiumu	100	28.11 N	118.27 E
Jiuninghe	105	39.28 N	117.46 E
Jiuningyang	100	25.38 N	117.21 E
Jiupu, Zhg.	100	32.50 N	118.45 E
Jiupu, Zhg.	105	40.21 N	115.18 E
Jiuquan (Suzhou)	102	39.45 N	98.34 E
Jiurongcheng	98	37.21 N	122.32 E
Jiushangshui	100	33.32 N	114.32 E
Jiushan Liedao II	100	29.26 N	122.12 E
Jiushenqiu	100	33.11 N	115.08 E
Jiusiyang	100	33.41 N	118.39 E
Jiusongyu	105	40.27 N	116.58 E
Jiutai	89	44.08 N	125.50 E
Jiuwuqing	105	39.31 N	116.52 E
Jiuxian, Zhg.	98	37.53 N	117.06 E
Jiuxian, Zhg.	100	31.11 N	118.04 E
Jiuxian, Zhg.	100	33.15 N	115.35 E
Jiuxian, Zhg.	100	25.14 N	116.31 E
Jiuxian, Zhg.	100	33.32 N	113.17 E
Jiuxian, Zhg.	100	25.54 N	113.22 E
Jiuxian, Zhg.	107	30.27 N	103.51 E
Jiuxian, Zhg.	107	29.51 N	106.13 E
Jiuxian ≃	100	25.07 N	116.24 E
Jiuxiangcheng	100	33.13 N	114.49 E
Jiuyingkou	105	39.42 N	114.44 E
Jiuyingzi	104	42.03 N	121.38 E
Jiuyuanqu	102	35.09 N	111.51 E
Jiuyuhang	106	30.17 N	119.56 E
Jiuyunjie	86	44.12 N	88.05 E
Jiuzhan	89	43.57 N	126.29 E
Jiuzhen	100	24.05 N	117.42 E
Jiuzhou	105	39.30 N	116.33 E
Jiuzhuangwo	105	40.11 N	115.36 E
Jiwangmiao	269b	31.14 N	121.17 E
Jiwangtun	104	41.02 N	122.58 E
Jīwani	128	25.03 N	61.45 E
Jiwen	89	50.32 N	123.15 E
Jixi, Zhg.	89	45.17 N	130.59 E
Jixi, Zhg.	100	30.06 N	118.35 E
Jixian, Zhg.	98	35.26 N	114.05 E
Jixian, Zhg.	98	37.36 N	115.31 E
Jixian, Zhg.	105	40.03 N	117.24 E
Jixiangsi	107	30.39 N	105.32 E
Jixiashi	100	28.22 N	118.44 E
Jixingji	100	32.55 N	116.46 E
Jiyang, Zhg.	98	36.59 N	117.11 E
Jiyang, Zhg.	100	27.10 N	118.07 E
Jiyang, Zhg.	105	39.38 N	115.59 E
Jiyi	102	35.50 N	110.23 E
Jiyuan	102	35.08 N	112.35 E
Jiyun ≃	105	39.07 N	117.43 E
Jiz', Wādī al- ∨	144	16.19 N	52.00 E
Jīzah, Ahrāmāt al- (Pyramids of Giza) ⊥	142	29.59 N	31.08 E
Jīzah, Tur'at al- ≅	273c	29.50 N	31.16 E
Jīzān	144	16.54 N	42.29 E
Jizayy	142	30.28 N	30.51 E
Jize	98	36.54 N	114.52 E
Jizera ≃	54	50.10 N	14.43 E
Jizl, Wādī al- ∨	128	25.38 N	38.21 E
Jizō-dake ∧	94	36.36 N	139.28 E
Jizō-zaki ›	96	35.34 N	133.20 E
Joaçaba	252	27.10 S	51.30 W
Joachimsthal → Jáchymov, Česká Rep.	54	50.20 N	12.55 E
Joachimsthal, Dtsch.	54	52.58 N	13.44 E
Joaíma	255	16.39 S	41.02 W
Joal Fadiout	150	14.10 N	16.51 W
Joana Coeli	250	1.58 S	49.23 W
Joana Peres	250	3.18 S	49.42 W
Joanes	250	0.51 S	48.31 W
Joanicó	258	34.36 S	56.15 W
Joanna	192	34.24 N	81.48 W
Joanópolis	256	22.56 S	46.17 W
João Câmara	250	5.32 S	35.48 W
João Mendes ≃	287a	22.57 S	43.03 W
João Neiva	255	19.45 S	40.24 W
João Pessoa	250	7.07 S	34.52 W
João Pinheiro	255	17.45 S	46.10 W
Joaquim Egídio	256	22.53 S	46.59 W
Joaquim Távora	255	23.30 S	49.58 W
Joaquin	194	31.58 N	94.03 W
Joaquin Miller Park ♠	282	37.49 N	122.11 W
Joaquín Suárez	258	34.44 S	56.02 W
Joaquín V. González	252	25.05 S	64.11 W
Job	62	45.37 N	3.45 E
Jobabo	240p	20.54 N	77.17 W
Jobat	120	22.25 N	74.34 E
Jobo Point ›	116	8.42 N	126.15 E
Jobos	240m	17.58 N	66.10 W
Jobos, Bahía de ᴄ	240m	17.56 N	66.13 W
Job Peak ∧	204	39.35 N	118.14 W
Jobstown	285	40.02 N	74.41 W
Jochberg	64	47.23 N	12.24 E
Jock ≃	212	45.16 N	75.43 W
Jocketa	54	50.33 N	12.10 E
Jockgrim	56	49.06 N	8.17 E
Jocko ≃	202	47.20 N	114.17 W
Jocolí	252	32.35 S	68.41 W
Jo Co Marsh ≡	276	40.37 N	73.47 W
Jocón	236	15.17 N	86.58 W
Jocoro	236	13.37 N	88.01 W
Jocotán	236	14.49 N	89.23 W
Jocotepec	234	20.18 N	103.26 W
Jocotitlán	234	19.42 N	99.48 W
Jódar	34	37.50 N	3.21 W
Jodhpur	120	26.17 N	73.02 E
Jodiya	120	22.42 N	70.18 E
Jodoigne	56	50.43 N	4.52 E
Jodrell Bank Radio Telescope ⊍[3]	262	53.14 N	2.18 W
Joe ≃	220	25.17 N	81.05 W
Joe Batt's Arm	186	49.44 N	54.10 W
Joel	158	28.42 S	28.21 E
Joensuu	26	62.36 N	29.46 E
Joe Pool Lake ⊜[1]	222	32.36 N	97.01 W
Joetsu	94	37.06 N	138.15 E
Jœuf	56	49.14 N	6.01 E
Jofane	156	21.17 S	34.16 E
Joffre, Mount ∧	182	50.32 N	115.13 W
Jōganzi ≃	94	36.46 N	137.18 E
Jōga-shima I	94	35.08 N	139.37 E
Jōgawara	268	35.42 N	139.22 E
Jōge	96	34.42 N	133.07 E
Jogeshvari ◆[8]	272c	19.08 N	72.51 E
Jogeshvari Cave ⊥[5]	272c	19.08 N	72.51 E
Jõgeva	76	58.45 N	26.24 E
Jog Falls ʟ	122	14.13 N	74.45 E
Joggins	186	45.42 N	64.27 W
Joghatāy	128	36.36 N	57.01 E
Jogindarnagar	123	31.59 N	76.46 E
Jogjakarta → Yogyakarta	115a	7.48 S	110.22 E
Jogui ≃	255	23.45 S	54.40 W
Jōhana	94	36.31 N	136.54 E
Johannesburg, S. Afr.	158	26.12 S	28.05 E
Johannesburg, S. Afr.	273d	26.12 S	28.05 E
Johannesburg, Ca., U.S.	228	35.22 N	117.38 W
Johannesburg □[5]	273d	26.13 S	28.02 E
Johannesburg (Jan Smuts) Airport ⊠	273d	26.08 S	28.14 E
Johanngeorgenstadt	54	50.26 N	12.43 E
Johanniskreuz	56	49.20 N	7.49 E
Johannisthal ◆[8]	264a	52.26 N	13.30 E
Jōhen	92	32.57 N	132.35 E
Johi	120	26.41 N	67.37 E
Johilla ≃	124	23.37 N	81.14 E
John ≃	180	66.55 N	151.35 W
John Boyd Thacher State Park ♠	210	42.38 N	74.01 W
John Carroll University ⊍[2]	279a	41.29 N	81.32 W
John Day	202	44.24 N	118.57 W
John Day ≃	202	45.44 N	120.39 W
John Day, Middle Fork ≃	202	44.55 N	119.18 W
John Day, North Fork ≃	202	44.45 N	119.38 W
John Day, South Fork ≃	202	44.28 N	119.31 W
John Day Dam ◆[6]	224	45.43 N	120.41 W
John Day Fossil Beds National Monument ♠	202	44.34 N	119.39 W
John F. Kennedy International Airport ⊠	210	40.38 N	73.47 W
John F. Kennedy National Historic Site ⊥	283	42.21 N	71.08 W
John F. Kennedy Space Center ⊍[3]	220	28.40 N	80.40 W
John Forrest National Park ♠	168a	31.53 S	116.06 E
John Hancock Center ⊍	278	41.55 N	87.37 W
John H. Kerr Reservoir ⊜[1]	192	36.35 N	78.35 W
John J. Duffy Preserve ♠	278	41.39 N	87.55 W
John Martin Reservoir ⊜[1]	198	38.05 N	103.02 W
John McLaren Park ♠	282	37.43 N	122.25 W
John Muir National Historic Site ⊥	282	37.59 N	122.08 W
Johnny Run ≃	216	41.17 N	88.21 W
John o' Groats	46	58.38 N	3.05 W
John Pennekamp Coral Reef State Park ♠	220	25.11 N	80.15 W
John Redmond Reservoir ⊜[1]	198	38.18 N	95.55 W
Johns ≃	224	46.54 N	124.01 W
Johns Creek ≃	192	37.30 N	80.06 W
Johnshaven	46	56.47 N	2.20 W
Johns Hopkins University ⊍[2]	284b	39.20 N	76.37 W
Johns Island I	192	32.40 N	80.05 W
Johnson, Ar., U.S.	194	36.07 N	94.09 W
Johnson, Ks., U.S.	198	37.34 N	101.45 W
Johnson, Ne., U.S.	198	40.24 N	95.59 W
Johnson, N.Y., U.S.	210	41.22 N	74.30 W
Johnson, Vt., U.S.	188	44.38 N	72.40 W
Johnson □[6], In., U.S.	218	39.29 N	86.03 W
Johnson □[6], Tx., U.S.	222	32.20 N	97.20 W
Johnson, Mount ∧	226	36.37 N	121.19 W
Johnson Bay ᴄ	208	38.03 N	75.20 W
Johnsonburg, N.J., U.S.	210	40.58 N	74.53 W

≃	River	Fluß	Río	Rivière	Rio
≅	Canal	Kanal	Canal	Canal	Canal
ʟ	Waterfall, Rapids	Wasserfall, Stromschnellen	Cascada, Rápidos	Chute d'eau, Rapides	Cascata, Rápidos
ꭒ	Strait	Meeresstraße	Estrecho	Détroit	Estreito
ᴄ	Bay, Gulf	Bucht, Golf	Bahía, Golfo	Baie, Golfe	Baía, Golfo
⊜	Lake, Lakes	See, Seen	Lago, Lagos	Lac, Lacs	Lago, Lagos
≡	Swamp	Sumpf	Pantano	Marais	Pântano
⊓	Ice Features, Glacier	Eis- und Gletscherformen	Accidentes Glaciales	Formes glaciaires	Acidentes glaciares
⫪	Other Hydrographic Features	Andere Hydrographische Objekte	Otros Elementos Hidrográficos	Autres données hydrographiques	Outros acidentes hidrográficos
✥	Submarine Features	Untermeerische Objekte	Accidentes Submarinos	Formes de relief sous-marin	Acidentes submarinos
□	Political Unit	Politische Einheit	Unidad Politica	Entité politique	Unidade política
⊍	Cultural Institution	Kulturelle Institution	Institución Cultural	Institution culturelle	Instituição cultural
⊥	Historical Site	Historische Stätte	Sitio Histórico	Site historique	Sitio histórico
♠	Recreational Site	Erholungs- und Ferienort	Sitio de Recreo	Centre de loisirs	Area de Lazer
⊠	Airport	Flughafen	Aeropuerto	Aéroport	Aeroporto
■	Military Installation	Militäranlage	Instalación Militar	Installation militaire	Instalação militar
◆	Miscellaneous	Verschiedenes	Misceláneo	Divers	Diversos

Johnsonburg, N.Y., U.S. 210 42.44 N 78.18 W
Johnsonburg, Pa., U.S. 214 41.29 N 78.40 W
Johnson City, N.Y., U.S. 210 42.06 N 75.57 W
Johnson City, Tn., U.S. 192 36.18 N 82.21 W
Johnson City, Tx., U.S. 196 30.16 N 98.24 W
Johnson Creek, N.Y., U.S. 210 43.15 N 78.31 W
Johnson Creek, Wi., U.S. 216 43.04 N 88.46 W
Johnson Creek ≃, Id., U.S. 202 44.58 N 115.30 W
Johnson Creek ≃, Ky., U.S. 218 38.27 N 84.04 W
Johnson Creek ≃, N.Y., U.S. 210 43.22 N 78.16 W
Johnson Creek ≃, Tx., U.S. 222 32.02 N 94.59 W
Johnson Creek ≃, Wa., U.S. 224 46.35 N 121.42 W
Johnsondale 204 35.58 N 118.32 W
Johnson Drain ≊ 281 42.26 N 83.28 W
Johnson Draw V, Tx., U.S. 196 31.58 N 101.41 W
Johnson Draw V, Tx., U.S. 196 30.08 N 101.07 W
Johnson Hall State Historic Site ⊥ 210 43.01 N 74.23 W
Johnson Park ♠ 276 40.30 N 74.27 W
Johnson Point › 241h 13.07 N 61.12 W
Johnsons Crossing 180 60.29 N 133.16 W
Johnsons Point › 240c 17.02 N 61.53 W
Johnsons Pond ⊜ 283 42.44 N 71.03 W
Johnsons Station 222 32.42 N 97.08 W
Johnsonville, N.Z. 172 41.14 S 174.47 E
Johnsonville, N.Y., U.S. 210 42.55 N 73.31 W
Johnsonville, S.C., U.S. 192 33.49 N 79.26 W
Johnston, Wales, U.K. 42 51.46 N 5.00 W
Johnston, Ia., U.S. 190 41.40 N 93.41 W
Johnston, R.I., U.S. 207 41.46 N 71.21 W
Johnston, S.C., U.S. 192 33.49 N 81.48 W
Johnston, Lake ⊜ 162 32.25 S 120.30 E
Johnston Atoll I[1] 14 16.45 N 169.32 W
Johnston City 194 37.49 N 88.55 W
Johnstone 46 55.50 N 4.31 W
Johnstone Peak ∧ 280 34.10 N 117.48 W
Johnstone Strait ʊ 182 50.25 N 126.00 W
Johnston Falls ⊾ 154 10.35 S 28.40 E
Johnstown, Co., U.S. 200 40.20 N 104.54 W
Johnstown, N.Y., U.S. 210 43.00 N 74.22 W
Johnstown, Oh., U.S. 214 40.09 N 82.41 W
Johnstown, Pa., U.S. 214 40.19 N 78.55 W
Johnstown Center 216 42.42 N 88.50 W
Johnstown Flood National Memorial ⊥ 214 40.21 N 78.47 W
John Tyler Arboretum ♠ 285 39.56 N 75.26 W
Jōhoku 94 36.28 N 140.22 E
Johol 114 2.36 N 102.16 E
Johor □[3] 114 2.00 N 103.30 E
Johor ≃ 114 1.27 N 104.02 E
Johor, Selat ʊ 271c 1.28 N 103.48 E
Johor Baharu 114 1.28 N 103.45 E
Jöhstadt 54 50.30 N 13.05 E
Joice Island I 282 38.08 N 122.02 W
Joigny 50 47.59 N 3.24 E
Joiner 194 35.30 N 90.08 W
Joinerville 222 32.11 N 94.55 W
Joinvile 252 26.18 S 48.50 W
Joinville 58 48.27 N 5.08 E
Joinville, Lac ⊜ 206 46.18 N 75.12 W
Joinville Island I 9 63.15 S 55.45 W
Joinville-le-Pont 261 48.49 N 2.28 E
Jōjima 96 33.15 N 130.26 E
Jojogan 115a 6.58 S 111.46 E
Jojutla 234 18.37 N 99.11 W
Joka 272b 22.27 N 88.18 E
Jokau 140 8.24 N 33.49 E
Jokioinen 26 60.49 N 23.28 E
Jokkmokk 24 66.37 N 19.50 E
Jökulsá á Brú ≃ 24a 65.41 N 14.13 W
Jökulsárgljúfur National Park ♠ 24a 66.00 N 16.20 W
Jolārpettai 122 12.34 N 78.35 E
Jolfā 128 38.57 N 45.38 E
Joliet, Il., U.S. 216 41.31 N 88.04 W
Joliet, Mt., U.S. 202 45.29 N 108.58 W
Joliet Correctional Center ◆ 278 41.33 N 88.04 W
Joliett 208 40.37 N 76.27 W
Joliette 206 46.01 N 73.27 W
Joliette □[6] 206 46.25 N 74.00 W
Jolietville 218 40.03 N 86.15 W
Jollyville 222 30.27 N 97.47 W
Jolo 116 6.03 N 121.00 E
Jolo Group II 116 6.00 N 121.09 E
Jolo Island I 116 5.58 N 121.06 E
Jølstravatnet ⊜ 26 61.32 N 6.13 E
Jomalig Island I 116 14.42 N 122.22 E
Jomba 102 31.27 N 98.15 E
Jombang 115a 7.33 S 112.14 E
Jombo ≃ 152 10.36 S 17.32 E
Jona 58 47.14 N 8.52 E
Jonacatepec 234 18.41 N 98.48 W
Jonah 222 30.38 N 97.32 W
Jönåker 40 58.44 N 16.40 E
Jonathan Dickinson State Park ♠ 220 27.01 N 80.08 W
Jonava 76 55.05 N 24.17 E
Jones, Pil. 116 16.33 N 121.42 E
Jones, Mi., U.S. 216 41.54 N 85.48 W
Jones, Ok., U.S. 196 35.33 N 97.17 W
Jones ≃ 283 42.00 N 70.42 W
Jones and Laughlin Steel Corporation ◆[3], Pa., U.S. 279b 40.26 N 79.58 W
Jones and Laughlin Steel Corporation ◆[3], Pa., U.S. 279b 40.37 N 80.14 W
Jones Beach State Park ♠ 210 40.35 N 73.31 W
Jonesboro, Ar., U.S. 194 35.50 N 90.42 W
Jonesboro, Ga., U.S. 192 33.31 N 84.21 W
Jonesboro, Il., U.S. 194 37.27 N 89.16 W
Jonesboro, In., U.S. 216 40.28 N 85.37 W
Jonesboro, La., U.S. 194 32.14 N 92.42 W
Jonesboro, Tn., U.S. 192 36.17 N 82.28 W
Jonesburg 219 38.51 N 91.18 W
Jones Creek 222 28.58 N 95.27 W
Jones Creek ≃, On., Can. 212 44.30 N 75.49 W
Jones Creek ≃, Tx., U.S. 222 29.08 N 96.03 W
Jones Falls ≃ 284b 39.18 N 76.37 W
Jones Falls, North Branch ≃ 284b 39.25 N 76.42 W
Jones Inlet ᑕ 210 40.35 N 73.34 W
Jones Mill 194 34.27 N 92.50 W
Jones Mountains ⋏ 9 73.32 S 94.00 W
Jonesport 188 44.31 N 67.35 W
Jones Sound ʊ 176 76.00 N 85.00 W
Jonestown 194 34.19 N 90.27 W
Jonesville, In., U.S. 218 39.04 N 85.53 W
Jonesville, La., U.S. 194 31.37 N 91.49 W
Jonesville, Mi., U.S. 216 41.59 N 84.40 W
Jonesville, N.Y., U.S. 210 42.55 N 73.49 W
Jonesville, N.C., U.S. 192 36.14 N 80.50 W
Jonesville, S.C., U.S. 192 34.50 N 81.40 W
Jonesville, Va., U.S. 192 36.41 N 83.06 W
Jong ≃ 150 7.32 N 12.23 W
Jonglei Canal ≊ 136 9.21 N 31.32 E
Jongunjärvi ⊜ 26 65.17 N 27.15 E
Jónico, Mar → Ionian Sea ⫧[2] 22 39.00 N 19.00 E
Joniškėlis 76 56.02 N 24.10 E
Joniškis 76 56.14 N 23.37 E
Jonkersberg 158 33.55 S 22.15 E
Jönköping 26 57.47 N 14.11 E
Jönköpings Län □[6] 26 57.30 N 14.30 E
Jonquière 186 48.24 N 71.15 W
Jonquières 62 44.07 N 4.54 E
Jonsdorf 54 50.51 N 14.43 E
Jonstorp 41 56.14 N 12.40 E
Jonuta 232 18.05 N 92.08 W
Jonvilliers 261 48.34 N 1.42 E
Jonzac 32 45.27 N 0.26 W
Joondalup, Lake ⊜ 168a 31.45 S 115.47 E
Joplin, Mo., U.S. 194 37.05 N 94.30 W
Joplin, Mt., U.S. 202 48.33 N 110.46 W
Joppa, Il., U.S. 194 37.12 N 88.50 W
Joppa, Md., U.S. 208 39.26 N 76.21 W
Jóquei Clube ♠ 287b 23.35 S 46.41 W
Joquicingo 234 19.03 N 99.33 W
Jora 124 26.20 N 77.49 E
Jordan, Pil. 116 10.40 N 122.35 E
Jordan, Mn., U.S. 190 44.40 N 93.37 W
Jordan, Mt., U.S. 202 47.19 N 106.54 W
Jordan, N.Y., U.S. 210 43.03 N 76.28 W
Jordan (Al-Urdun) □[1], Asia 118 31.00 N 36.00 E
Jordan (Al-Urdun) □[1], Asia 128 31.00 N 36.00 E
Jordan (Nahr al-Urdun) (HaYarden) ≃, Asia 132 31.46 N 35.33 E
Jordan ≃, B.C., Can. 224 48.26 N 124.08 W
Jordan ≃, Ut,. U.S. 200 40.49 N 112.08 W
Jordan Creek ≃ 202 42.52 N 117.38 W
Jordânia 255 15.54 S 40.11 W
Jordania → Jordan □[1] 128 31.00 N 36.00 E
Jordanie → Jordan □[1] 128 31.00 N 36.00 E
Jordanien → Jordan □[1] 128 31.00 N 36.00 E
Jordan Lake ⊜ 216 42.46 N 85.09 W
Jordanów 30 49.40 N 19.50 E
Jordans 260 51.37 N 0.36 W
Jordan Valley 202 42.58 N 117.03 W
Jordanville 210 42.55 N 74.57 W
Jordão ≃ 252 25.46 S 52.07 W
Jordbro 40 59.09 N 18.07 E
Jördenstorf 54 53.52 N 12.37 E
Jordet 26 61.25 N 12.09 E
Jorge Chávez, Aeropuerto Internacional ⊠ 286d 12.02 S 77.07 W
Jorge Grego, Ilha I 256 23.13 S 44.09 W
Jorge Montt, Isla I 254 51.20 S 74.45 W
Jorge V, Costade → George V Coast ⊥[2] 9 68.30 S 147.30 E
Jorge VI, Estrecho de → George VI Sound ʊ 9 71.00 S 68.00 W
Jorhāt 120 26.46 N 94.13 E
Jork 52 53.32 N 9.41 E
Jorm 120 36.52 N 70.51 E
Jörn 26 65.04 N 20.02 E
Jornado del Muerto ◆[2] 200 33.20 N 106.50 W
Joroinen 26 62.11 N 27.50 E
Jorong 112 3.58 S 114.56 E
Jørpeland 26 59.01 N 6.03 E
J'orzovka 80 48.56 N 44.38 E
Jos 150 9.55 N 8.53 E
Jose Abad Santos 116 5.38 N 125.27 E
José Batlle y Ordóñez 252 33.28 S 55.07 W
José Bonifácio 255 21.03 S 49.41 W
José Cardel 234 19.22 N 96.22 W
José C. Paz 258 34.30 S 58.45 W
José de Freitas 250 4.45 S 42.35 W
José de San Martín 254 44.02 S 70.29 W
José Enrique Rodó (Drabble) 258 33.41 S 57.34 W
José Francisco Vergara 252 22.28 S 69.38 W
Joselândia 248 16.32 S 56.12 W
José Martí, Aeropuerto Internacional ⊠ 286b 23.00 N 82.24 W
Jose Panganiban 116 14.17 N 122.41 E
José Pedro Varela 252 33.27 S 54.32 W
Joseph 202 45.21 N 117.13 W
Joseph, Lac ⊜ 176 52.45 N 65.15 W
Joseph, Lake ⊜ 212 45.10 N 79.44 W
Joseph Bonaparte Gulf ᑕ 164 14.15 S 128.30 E
Joseph City 200 34.57 N 110.20 W
Joseph Creek ≃ 202 46.03 N 117.01 W
Joseph Davis State Park ♠ 284a 43.13 N 79.03 W
Josephine, Pa., U.S. 214 40.29 N 79.11 W
Josephine, Tx., U.S. 222 33.04 N 96.19 W
Josephine, Lake ⊜ 220 27.24 N 81.26 W
Josephine Peak ∧ 280 34.17 N 118.09 W
Josephstaal 164 4.44 S 145.01 E
José Santos Arévalo 258 35.10 S 59.14 W
Joshīmath 120 30.34 N 79.34 E
Jōshin-Etsu-kōgen-kokuritsu-kōen ♠ 94 36.46 N 138.40 E
Joshua 222 32.28 N 97.23 W
Joshuas Creek ≃ 275b 43.29 N 79.37 W
Joshua Tree 204 34.08 N 116.18 W
Joshua Tree National Park ♠ 204 33.55 N 116.00 W
Joshua Trees State Park ♠ 228 34.41 N 117.47 W
Joškar-Ola 80 56.38 N 47.52 E
Jos Plateau ⋏[1] 150 9.30 N 9.00 E
Jossa 56 50.14 N 9.35 E
Josselin 32 47.57 N 2.33 W
Jossigny 50 48.50 N 2.45 E
Jostedalsbreen ⊓ 26 61.40 N 7.00 E
Jost Van Dyke I 240m 18.28 N 64.45 W
Jōtō ◆[8] 270 34.42 N 135.34 E
Jotunheimen ⋏ 26 61.38 N 8.18 E
Jotunheimen Nasjonalpark ♠ 26 61.35 N 8.30 E
Jouarre 50 48.56 N 3.08 E
Jouars-Pontchartrain 261 48.47 N 1.54 E
Joubertina 158 33.50 S 23.51 E
Joué-lès-Tours 50 47.21 N 0.40 E
Jougne 58 46.46 N 6.24 E
Jouques 62 43.38 N 5.38 E
Jourdanton 196 28.55 N 98.32 W
Joure 52 52.57 N 5.47 E
Joutsa 26 61.44 N 26.07 E
Joutseno 26 61.06 N 28.30 E
Joutsijärvi 24 66.40 N 28.00 E
Joux, Lac de ⊜ 58 46.38 N 6.18 E
Joux, Vallée de V 58 46.35 N 6.15 E
Jouy 50 48.31 N 1.33 E
Jouy-en-Josas 261 48.46 N 2.10 E
Jouy-le-Moutier 261 49.01 N 2.03 E
Jouy-le-Potier 50 47.45 N 1.49 E
Jovellanos 240p 22.48 N 81.12 W
Jovellar 116 13.04 N 123.36 E
Jovet, Mont ∧ 62 45.30 N 6.39 E
Joveyn ≃ 128 36.48 N 56.28 E
Joviânia 255 17.49 S 49.30 W
Jowai 120 25.27 N 92.12 E
Jowhar 144 2.46 N 45.31 E
Jowlaenga, Mount ∧ 162 17.21 S 122.56 E
Jowzjān □[4] 120 36.30 N 66.00 E
Joy 190 41.12 N 90.55 W
Joy, Mount ∧ 180 63.46 N 132.55 W
Joyce 194 31.56 N 92.35 W
Joyeuse 62 44.29 N 4.14 E
Jōyō 96 34.51 N 135.47 E
Joyous Pavilion Park ♠ 271a 39.52 N 116.22 E
Joyuda 240m 18.07 N 67.11 W
Józefów 30 52.09 N 21.12 E
J. Percy Priest Lake ⊜[1] 194 36.05 N 86.30 W
Ju ≃, Zhg. 100 30.38 N 114.51 E
Ju ≃, Zhg. 105 39.45 N 117.35 E
Juaba 250 2.23 S 49.33 W
Juagdan 116 10.00 N 124.35 E
Juami ≃ 246 1.45 S 67.30 W
Juanacatlán 234 20.31 N 103.10 W
Juana Díaz 240m 18.03 N 66.31 W
Juan Aldama 232 24.19 N 103.21 W
Juan Anchorena ◆[8] 288 34.29 S 58.30 W
Juan Atucha 258 35.32 S 59.21 W
Juan B. Arruabarrena 252 30.20 S 58.19 W
Juan Bautista Alberdi 252 27.35 S 65.37 W
Juan Blanco, Arroyo ≃ 258 35.05 S 57.26 W
Juancheng 98 35.35 N 115.29 E
Juan de Fuca, Strait of ʊ 224 48.18 N 124.00 W
Juan de Garay 254 38.52 S 64.34 W
Juan de Mena 252 24.55 S 56.44 W
Juan de Nova, Île I 138 17.03 S 42.45 E
Juan Díaz Covarrubias 234 18.07 N 95.09 W
Juan E. Barra 252 37.48 S 60.29 W
Juan Eugenio 232 25.10 N 103.20 W
Juan Fernández, Archipiélago II 244 33.00 S 80.00 W
Juan González Grande, Arroyo ≃ 258 34.00 S 58.14 W
Juan González Romero ◆[8] 286a 19.30 N 99.04 W
Juangriego 246 11.05 N 63.57 W
Juan Gualberto Gómez 240p 22.52 N 81.33 W
Juan Guerra 248 6.35 S 76.21 W
Juan Jorba 252 33.37 S 65.16 W
Juan José Castelli 252 25.57 S 60.37 W
Juán José Perez 248 15.14 S 68.58 W
Juanjuí 248 7.11 S 76.45 W
Juankoski 26 63.04 N 28.21 E
Juan-les-Pins 62 43.34 N 7.06 E
Juan L. Lacaze 258 34.26 S 57.27 W
Juan N. Fernández 252 38.00 S 59.16 W
Juan Perez Sound ʊ 182 52.30 N 131.18 W
Juan Ramírez, Isla I 234 21.50 N 97.40 W
Juan Rodríguez Clara 234 18.00 N 95.25 W
Juan Tronconi 258 35.30 S 59.15 W
Juan Viñas 236 9.54 N 83.45 W
Juárez, Méx. 232 27.37 N 100.44 W
Juárez, Méx. 232 30.19 N 108.05 W
Juárez → Ciudad Juárez, Méx. 232 31.44 N 106.29 W
Juárez, Méx. 234 17.39 N 93.10 W
Juárez, Cerro ∧ 234 20.37 N 99.17 W
Juárez, Sierra ⋏ 234 17.30 N 96.30 W
Juárez, Sierra de ⋏ 232 32.00 N 115.50 W
Juarzon 150 5.20 N 8.52 W
Juatinga, Ponta de › 256 23.17 S 44.30 W
Juazeirinho 250 7.04 S 36.35 W
Juàzeiro 250 9.25 S 40.30 W
Juazeiro do Norte 250 7.12 S 39.20 W
Jūbā 154 4.51 N 31.37 E
Juba ≃ 248 14.59 S 57.44 W
Jubachstausee ⊜[1] 263 51.10 N 7.37 E
Jūbāl, Maḍīq ʊ 140 27.40 N 33.55 E
Jubal, Strait of → Jūbāl, Maḍīq ʊ 140 27.40 N 33.55 E
Jubayl (Byblos) 130 34.07 N 35.39 E
Jubaysho 144 5.48 N 37.22 E
Jubayt 140 18.57 N 36.50 E
Jubba (Genale) ≃ 144 0.15 S 42.38 E
Jubbada Dhexe □[4] 144 1.00 N 43.00 E
Jubbada Hoose □[4] 144 0.00 42.00 E
Jubbah 128 28.02 N 40.56 E
Jubb al-Jarrāḥ 130 34.49 N 37.19 E
Jubbātā al-Khashab 132 33.13 N 35.49 E
Jubb Jannīn 132 33.37 N 35.47 E
Jubbulpore → Jabalpur 124 23.10 N 79.57 E
Jubilee Downs 162 18.22 S 125.17 E
Jubilee Lake ⊜, Austl. 162 29.12 S 126.38 E
Jubilee Lake ⊜, Nf., Can. 186 48.04 N 55.11 W
Jubones ≃ 246 3.13 S 79.57 W
Jūbu-san ∧ 270 34.50 N 135.55 E
Juby, Cap › 148 27.58 N 12.55 W
Júcar (Xúquer) ≃ 34 39.09 N 0.14 W
Juçara 255 15.53 S 50.51 W
Júcaro 240p 21.37 N 78.51 W
Jucás 250 6.32 S 39.32 W
Jüchen 56 51.06 N 6.30 E
Juchipila 234 21.25 N 103.07 W
Juchipila ≃ 234 21.03 N 103.25 W
Juchitán de Zaragoza 234 16.26 N 95.01 W
Juchitepec 234 19.06 N 98.53 W
Juchitlán 234 20.05 N 104.07 W
Juchnov 76 54.45 N 35.14 E
Jüchsen 54 50.29 N 10.29 E
Jucuapa 236 13.31 N 88.24 W
Jucurucu ≃ 255 17.21 S 39.13 W
Jucurutu 250 6.02 S 37.01 W
Judaea □[9] 132 31.35 N 35.00 E
Judas, Punta › 236 9.31 N 84.32 W
Judaydat al-Khās 132 33.24 N 36.33 E
Judaydat ʿArṭūz 132 33.26 N 36.10 E
Juddah → Jiddah 144 21.30 N 39.12 E
Jude Island I 186 47.15 N 54.49 W
Judenau 61 48.17 N 16.00 E
Judenburg 61 47.10 N 14.40 E
Judges Hill ∧[2] 283 42.12 N 70.49 W
Judian 102 27.20 N 99.36 E
Judinki, Ross. 82 54.37 N 37.17 E
Judinki, Ross. 82 55.27 N 35.48 E
Judino, Ross. 76 58.43 N 39.17 E
Judino, Ross. 80 55.51 N 48.55 E
Judino, Ross. 82 54.09 N 38.19 E
Judino, Ross. 265b 55.40 N 37.12 E
Judío, Rambla del ≃ 34 38.15 N 1.27 W
Judique 186 45.52 N 61.30 W
Judith ≃ 202 47.44 N 109.38 W
Judith, Point › 207 41.22 N 71.29 W
Judith Gap 202 46.40 N 109.45 W
Judith Mountains ⋏ 202 47.12 N 109.15 W
Judith Peak ∧ 202 47.13 N 109.13 W
Judoma ≃ 74 59.08 N 135.06 E
Judson, S.C., U.S. 192 34.50 N 82.27 W
Judson, Tx., U.S. 222 32.35 N 94.45 W
Judsonia 194 35.16 N 91.38 W
Jue ≃ 100 31.42 N 113.20 E
Juehedian 105 39.26 N 117.06 E
Juelsminde 41 55.43 N 10.01 E
Juexi 100 29.27 N 121.57 E
Juexizhen 107 28.55 N 104.16 E
Jufari ≃ 246 1.13 S 62.00 W
Jufayr, Bi'r al- ⫧[4] 142 30.49 N 32.40 E
Jufrah, Wādī al- V 142 30.24 N 31.35 E
Jug 86 57.43 N 56.10 E
Jug ≃ 24 60.45 N 46.20 E
Jughna 140 12.24 N 25.06 E
Jugo-Kamskij 86 57.42 N 55.35 E
Jugon 32 48.25 N 2.20 W
Jugo-Osetija (South Ossetia) □[9] 84 42.20 N 44.00 E
Jugoslavija → Yugoslavia □[1] 22 44.00 N 21.00 E
Jugoslawien → Yugoslavia □[1] 22 44.00 N 21.00 E
Jugo-Zapad ◆[8] 265b 55.40 N 37.32 E
Juḥā 144 16.41 N 42.54 E
Juḥavičy 76 56.02 N 28.39 E
Jühnsdorf 264a 52.18 N 13.23 E
Jühnsdorfer Heide ◆[3] 264a 52.19 N 13.24 E
Juhu ◆[8] 272c 19.07 N 72.49 E
Juhua Dao I 98 40.29 N 120.47 E
Juhu Airport ⊠ 272c 19.06 N 72.50 E
Jui 272c 19.01 N 73.05 E
Juidongshan 100 23.46 N 117.31 E
Juigalpa 236 12.05 N 85.24 W
Juillac 32 45.19 N 1.19 E
Juilly 261 49.01 N 2.42 E
Juína ≃ 248 12.36 S 58.57 W
Juine ≃ 50 48.32 N 2.23 E
Juist 52 53.40 N 6.59 E
Juist I 52 53.40 N 7.00 E
Juisui 100 23.30 N 121.21 E
Juiz de Fora 256 21.45 S 43.20 W
Jūjō Base ■ 268 35.45 N 139.43 E
Jujurieux 58 46.02 N 5.25 E
Jujuy → San Salvador de Jujuy 252 24.11 S 65.18 W
Jujuy □[4] 252 23.00 S 66.00 W
Jukagirskoje ploskogorje ⋏[1] 74 66.00 N 155.00 E
Jukamenskoje 80 57.53 N 52.15 E
Jukonda ≃ 86 59.38 N 67.26 E
Juksa 86 56.55 N 85.10 E
Juksejevo 24 59.52 N 54.19 E
Jukskei ≃ 273d 26.06 S 28.06 E
Jukta 74 63.23 N 105.41 E
Jula ≃ 24 63.49 N 44.44 E
Julāna 124 29.08 N 76.25 E
Julayfah, Bi'r al- ⫧[4] 142 30.43 N 29.35 E
Julbach 60 48.40 N 13.52 E
Juldybajevo 86 52.20 N 57.52 E
Julebu 98 40.09 N 113.36 E
Julesburg 198 40.59 N 102.15 W
Juli 248 16.13 S 69.27 W
Juliaca 248 15.30 S 70.08 W
Julia Creek 166 20.39 S 141.45 E
Julia Creek ≃ 166 20.00 S 141.11 E
Julian 214 40.52 N 77.56 W
Juliana, Lake ⊜ 220 28.07 N 81.48 W
Julianakanaal ≊ 56 51.05 N 5.50 E
Julian Alps ⋏ 36 46.00 N 14.00 E
Juliana Top ∧ 250 3.41 N 56.32 W
Julianehåb (Qaqortoq) 176 60.43 N 46.01 W
Julia Pfeiffer Burns State Park ♠ 226 36.10 N 120.40 W
Jülich 56 50.55 N 6.21 E
Juliénas 58 46.14 N 4.43 E
Juliette, Lake ⊜[1] 192 33.05 N 83.50 W
Julijske Alpe → Julian Alps ⋏ 36 46.00 N 14.00 E
Julimes 232 28.25 N 105.27 W
Júlio de Castilhos 252 29.14 S 53.41 W
Julio Prestes, Estação ◆[5] 287b 23.32 S 46.38 W
Julita ◆ 40 59.09 N 16.02 E
Juliuhe 104 42.03 N 122.55 E
Juliustown 285 40.00 N 74.40 W
Julu 98 37.13 N 115.01 E
Juma 24 65.07 N 33.16 E
Juma ≃ 98 39.34 N 115.42 E
Jumaguzino 86 52.54 N 56.23 E
Jumapolo 115a 7.42 S 111.00 E
Jumaševo 80 54.59 N 54.25 E
Jumay, Volcán ∧[1] 236 14.41 N 89.59 W
Jumbilla 248 5.54 S 77.45 W
Jumbo 154 17.28 S 30.55 E
Jumbo, Raas › 144 1.39 S 41.36 E
Jumboo 144 0.15 S 42.38 E
Jumbo Peak ∧ 204 36.12 N 114.11 W
Jumeauville 261 48.55 N 1.47 E
Jumentos Cays II 238 22.42 N 75.55 W
Jumet 50 50.26 N 4.25 E
Jumièges 50 49.26 N 0.49 E
Jumilla 34 38.29 N 1.17 W
Jumlā 124 29.17 N 82.10 E
Jummayzat Banī ʿAmr 142 30.48 N 31.32 E
Jump ≃ 190 45.17 N 91.05 W
Jump, North Fork ≃ 190 45.25 N 90.40 W
Jump, South Fork ≃ 190 45.25 N 90.40 W
Jumt uul ∧ 102 44.29 N 97.10 E
Jūn 132 33.35 N 35.27 E
Jun ≃ 100 25.57 N 118.03 E
Jūnāgadh 120 21.31 N 70.28 E
Junan (Shizilu) 98 35.11 N 118.51 E
Junayfah 142 30.12 N 32.25 E
Junaynah, Ra's al- ∧ 140 29.01 N 33.58 E
Juncal, Isla I 258 33.58 S 58.24 W
Juncal do Norte ⩸ 266c 38.52 N 8.59 W
Juncal do Sul ⩸ 266c 38.51 N 8.58 W
Juncheng 98 38.57 N 114.41 E
Juncos 240m 18.14 N 65.55 W
Junction, Tx., U.S. 196 30.29 N 99.46 W
Junction, Ut,. U.S. 200 38.14 N 112.13 W
Junction City, Ar., U.S. 194 33.00 N 92.43 W
Junction City, Il., U.S. 219 38.34 N 89.07 W
Junction City, Ks., U.S. 198 39.01 N 96.49 W
Junction City, Ky., U.S. 194 37.35 N 84.47 W
Junction City, Or., U.S. 202 44.13 N 123.12 W
Junction City, Wa., U.S. 224 46.58 N 123.46 W
Jundah 166 24.50 S 143.04 E
Jundiaí 256 23.11 S 46.52 W
Jundiaí ≃, Bra. 256 23.32 S 46.15 W
Jundiaí ≃, Bra. 256 23.11 S 47.16 W
Jundiaí do Sul 255 23.27 S 50.17 W
Jundiaí-mirim ≃ 256 23.10 S 46.56 W
Jundiapeba 256 23.33 S 46.15 W
Jundu Shan ⋏ 105 40.30 N 116.05 E
Juneau, Ak., U.S. 180 58.20 N 134.27 W
Juneau, Wi., U.S. 190 43.24 N 88.42 W
Junee 166 34.52 S 147.35 E
June in Winter, Lake ⊜ 220 27.18 N 81.24 W
June Lake 226 37.46 N 119.04 W
June Park 220 28.04 N 80.41 W
Jungapeo de Juárez 234 19.27 N 100.29 W
Jungar Qi 102 39.49 N 111.10 E
Jungbluth Ditch ≊ 279a 41.27 N 82.07 W
Jungfernheide ◆[3] 264a 52.34 N 13.17 E
Jungfernheide, Volkspark ♠ 264a 52.33 N 13.16 E
Jungfern-Inseln → Virgin Islands □[2] 240m 18.20 N 64.50 W
Jungfern-See ⊜ 264a 52.25 N 13.05 E
Jungfrau ∧ 58 46.32 N 7.58 E
Jungfraujoch ◆ 58 46.33 N 7.58 E
Junggar Pendi (Dzungarian Basin) ≚[1] 86 45.00 N 88.00 E
Jungle Habitat ♠ 276 41.08 N 74.21 W
Junglinster 56 49.43 N 6.15 E
Jungshāhi 120 24.51 N 67.46 E
Juniata 198 40.35 N 98.30 W
Juniata □[6] 208 40.34 N 77.24 W
Juniata ◆[8] 285 40.01 N 75.07 W
Juniata ≃ 188 40.24 N 77.01 W
Juniata, Frankstown Branch ≃ 214 40.34 N 78.03 W
Juniata, Raystown Branch ≃ 214 40.25 N 77.58 W
Juniata Gap 214 40.33 N 78.26 W
Juniata Terrace 208 40.35 N 77.34 W
Junín, Arg. 252 34.35 S 60.57 W
Junín, Ec. 246 0.56 S 80.13 W
Junín, Perú 248 11.10 S 76.00 W
Junín □[5] 248 11.30 S 75.00 W
Junín, Lago de ⊜ 248 11.02 S 76.06 W
Junín de los Andes 254 39.56 S 71.05 W
Junior 188 38.59 N 79.57 W
Juniper 186 46.33 N 67.13 W
Junipero Serra Peak ∧ 226 36.08 N 121.25 W
Juniville 50 49.24 N 4.23 E

ENGLISH Name	Page	Lat.°′	Long.°′

Jūniyah 130 33.59 N 35.38 E
Junk Bay ᑕ 271d 22.17 N 114.15 E
Jun Kharchanai 123 36.52 N 75.01 E
Junk Island I 271d 22.17 N 114.16 E
Junkou 100 26.42 N 116.49 E
Junlian 102 28.08 N 104.35 E
Junliangcheng 105 39.04 N 117.27 E
Junling 100 28.17 N 116.28 E
Junnar 122 19.12 N 73.53 E
Juno Beach 220 26.52 N 80.04 W
Junqalī □[4] 140 7.30 N 32.20 E
Junqueiro 250 9.56 S 36.29 W
Junqueirópolis 255 21.32 S 51.26 W
Junsele 26 63.41 N 16.54 E
Juntas 236 10.16 N 85.00 W
Jun Ul Shan ⋏ 102 37.30 N 97.00 E
Junxian 102 32.31 N 111.30 E
Jūō 94 36.40 N 140.41 E
Juodkrantė 76 55.33 N 21.08 E
Juodupė 76 56.05 N 25.37 E
Juojärvi ⊜ 26 62.43 N 28.33 E
Juozapinės kalnas ∧[2] 76 54.32 N 25.37 E
Juparanã, Lagoa ⊜ 255 19.35 S 40.18 W
Jupilingo ≃ 236 14.48 N 89.14 W
Jupille 56 50.39 N 5.38 E
Jupiter 220 26.56 N 80.05 W
Jupiter ≃ 186 49.29 N 63.37 W
Jupiter Inlet ᑕ 220 26.57 N 80.04 W
Jupiter Island I 220 27.04 N 80.07 W
Juqueri ≃ 256 23.24 S 46.52 W
Juqueri, Reservatório do ⊜[1] 256 23.20 S 46.38 W
Juqueriquerê, Serra do ⋏ 256 23.43 S 45.37 W
Juquiá 252 24.19 S 47.38 W
Juquiá ≃ 256 23.56 S 47.09 W
Juquiá, Ponta do › 252 24.25 S 47.00 W
Juquiá-guaçu ≃ 256 24.00 S 47.16 W
Juquitiba 256 23.57 S 47.03 W
Jur 74 59.52 N 137.39 E
Jur ≃ 140 8.39 N 29.18 E
Jura 38 47.31 N 29.04 E
Jura □[3] 58 47.20 N 7.15 E
Jura □[5] 58 46.50 N 5.50 E
Jura ⋏ 58 46.45 N 6.30 E
Jura I 46 56.00 N 5.50 W
Jūra ≃ 76 55.03 N 22.09 E
Jura, Sound of ʊ 46 55.57 N 5.48 W
Juraciški 76 54.02 N 25.54 E
Juramento 255 16.50 S 43.35 W
Jurayrah, Jabal al- ∧ 128 24.06 N 39.16 E
Jurays wa ʿIzbatuhā 142 30.19 N 30.55 E
Jurbarkas 76 55.05 N 22.48 E
Jurcevo 76 60.02 N 32.36 E
Juréia 256 21.17 S 46.22 W
Jurenino 76 59.24 N 42.47 E
Jurf ad-Darāwīsh 132 30.42 N 35.52 E
Jurga 86 55.42 N 84.51 E
Jurgamyš 86 55.21 N 64.28 E
Jurgenson Woods ♠ 278 41.34 N 87.36 W
Jurien 162 30.19 S 115.02 E
Juriesfontein 158 31.40 S 22.08 E
Juring 164 6.26 S 134.20 E
Jurino 80 56.18 N 46.18 E
Jurja 24 59.03 N 49.14 E
Jurjev → Tartu 76 58.23 N 26.43 E
Jurjevec 80 57.18 N 43.06 E
Jurjev-Pol'skij 80 56.30 N 39.41 E
Jurjevskoje 82 55.05 N 36.13 E
Jurla 86 59.17 N 54.19 E
Jurlovo, Ross. 82 55.54 N 37.16 E
Jurlovo, Ross. 82 55.19 N 35.52 E
Jūrmala 76 56.58 N 23.42 E
Jurong, Sing. 271c 1.19 N 103.43 E
Jurong, Zhg. 106 31.57 N 119.10 E
Jurong ≃ 271c 1.18 N 103.44 E
Jurong, Selat ʊ 271c 1.18 N 103.42 E
Jurovo, Ross. 80 57.30 N 43.50 E
Jurovo, Ross. 82 55.30 N 38.22 E
Jurovskoje 86 59.29 N 69.02 E
Jursla 40 58.40 N 16.11 E
Jurty 88 56.03 N 97.37 E
Juruá 246 3.27 S 66.03 W
Juruá ≃ 242 2.37 S 65.44 W
Juruaia 256 21.15 S 46.35 W
Juruá-mirim ≃ 248 8.08 S 72.48 W
Juruena ≃ 248 7.20 S 58.03 W
Jurujuba, Enseada de ᑕ 287a 22.56 S 43.07 W
Jurumirim, Represa ⊜[1] 255 23.20 S 49.15 W
Jurumkuvejem ≃ 180 66.14 N 173.35 E
Jurupari ≃ 248 7.45 S 70.10 W
Jurupari, Arquipélago II 250 0.07 N 50.30 W
Jurupari, Ilha de I 250 0.20 N 50.07 W
Juruti 250 2.09 S 56.04 W
Jur'uzan' 86 54.52 N 58.26 E
Jur'uzan' ≃ 86 55.42 N 57.00 E
Jurva 26 62.41 N 21.59 E
Jušala 86 57.04 N 64.17 E
Juscelândia 255 15.20 S 51.19 W
Jusepín 246 9.45 N 63.31 W
Jushiguan 102 24.47 N 97.38 E
Jūshiyama 94 35.06 N 136.46 E
Juskatla 182 53.37 N 132.18 W
Jus'ki 80 56.39 N 53.05 E
Juškovo 76 59.46 N 45.11 E
Juškozero 24 64.44 N 32.06 E
Jūsō ◆[8] 270 34.43 N 135.28 E
Jussey 58 47.49 N 5.54 E
Justa 80 47.07 N 46.18 E
Justice 278 41.44 N 87.50 W
Justin 222 33.05 N 97.18 W
Justineberg ∧[2] 40 58.43 N 15.04 E
Justiniano Posse 252 32.53 S 62.40 W
Justo Daract 252 33.52 S 65.11 W
Justus 214 40.42 N 81.35 W
Jušut ≃ 80 56.12 N 48.23 E
Jus'va 24 58.56 N 54.57 E
Jutaí 248 5.11 S 68.54 W
Jutaí ≃ 242 2.43 S 66.57 W
Jutaza 80 54.35 N 53.16 E
Jütchendorf 264a 52.16 N 13.10 E
Jüterbog 54 51.59 N 13.04 E
Juththah, Jabal al- ∧ 132 30.12 N 35.36 E
Juti 255 22.52 S 54.37 W
Jutiapa 236 14.17 N 89.54 W
Jutiapa □[5] 236 14.10 N 89.50 W
Juticalpa 236 14.42 N 86.15 W
Jutiquile 236 14.45 N 86.08 W
Jutland → Jylland ◆[1] 26 56.00 N 9.15 E
Jutogh 123 31.06 N 77.07 E
Jutrosin 30 51.40 N 17.10 E
Juupajoki 26 61.47 N 24.27 E
Juuru 76 59.04 N 24.59 E
Juva 26 61.54 N 27.51 E
Juventud, Isla de la (Isla de Pinos) I 240p 21.40 N 82.50 W
Juvisy-sur-Orge 50 48.41 N 2.23 E
Juvuln ⊜ 26 63.43 N 13.09 E
Juwana 115a 6.42 S 111.09 E
Juwangi 115a 7.10 S 110.45 E
Juxi 100 27.30 N 119.08 E
Juxian 98 35.37 N 118.54 E
Juxing 106 31.56 N 121.33 E
Juyanhai → Gaxun Nur ⊜ 102 42.22 N 100.34 E
Juye 98 35.23 N 116.06 E
Jūyom 128 28.34 N 53.56 E
Juyongguan 105 40.18 N 116.04 E
Juža 80 56.35 N 42.01 E
Juzennecourt 58 48.11 N 4.59 E
Juzi ≃ 98 40.18 N 123.35 E
Juziers 261 49.00 N 1.51 E
Južna Morava ≃ 38 43.41 N 21.24 E
Južno-Aleksandrovka 88 55.51 N 96.10 E
Južno-Aličurskij chrebet ⋏ 120 37.30 N 73.20 E

DEUTSCH Name	Seite	Breite°′	Länge°′ E = Ost

Južno-Golodnostepskij kanal ≊ 85 40.15 N 69.08 E
Južno-Jenisejskij 86 58.48 N 94.39 E
Južno-Kazachstan □[4] 85 42.30 N 68.30 E
Južno-Mujskij chrebet ⋏ 88 55.40 N 114.00 E
Južno-Sachalinsk 89 46.58 N 142.42 E
Južno-Suchokumsk 84 44.37 N 45.34 E
Južno-Ural'sk 86 54.26 N 61.15 E
Južnyj, Kaz. 86 49.21 N 73.01 E
Južnyj, Ross. 80 56.08 N 44.09 E
Južnyj, Ross. 80 47.20 N 41.51 E
Južnyj, Ross. 86 53.14 N 83.42 E
Južnyj, Ross. 86 53.33 N 60.02 E
Južnyj, mys › 74 57.45 N 156.45 E
Južnyj-Alamyšik 85 40.46 N 72.38 E
Južnyj Prijut 84 43.12 N 41.55 E
Južnyj Ural ⋏ 86 54.00 N 58.30 E
Juzovka → Donets'k 83 48.00 N 37.48 E
Jwālahari ◆[8] 272a 28.40 N 77.06 E
Jwayyā 132 33.14 N 35.19 E
Jyderup 41 55.40 N 11.26 E
Jylland (Jutland) ◆[1] 26 56.00 N 9.15 E
Jyllinge 41 55.45 N 12.07 E
Jyväskylä 26 62.14 N 25.44 E

K

K2 (Qogir Feng) ∧ 123 35.53 N 76.30 E
Ka ≃ 150 11.40 N 4.10 E
Kaaawa 229c 21.33 N 157.51 W
Kaabong 154 3.31 N 34.08 E
Kaachka 128 37.21 N 59.36 E
Kaala ∧ 229c 21.31 N 158.09 W
Kaalaea 229c 21.28 N 157.51 W
Kaala-Gomén 175f 20.40 S 164.25 E
Kaalspruit 158 29.15 S 26.10 E
Kaapahu Bay ᑕ 229a 20.39 N 156.05 W
Kaapmuiden 156 25.33 S 31.20 E
Kaappunt › 158 34.21 S 18.30 E
Kaapstad → Cape Town 158 33.55 S 18.22 E
Kaarli 76 59.24 N 26.27 E
Kaarssen 54 53.12 N 11.02 E
Kaarst 56 51.14 N 6.37 E
Kaaterskill Creek ≃ 210 42.13 N 73.53 W
Kaatoan, Mount ∧ 116 8.07 N 124.55 E
Kaatsheuvel 52 51.40 N 5.02 E
Kaavi 26 62.59 N 28.30 E
Kaba 150 10.09 N 11.40 W
Kaba ≃ 86 47.53 N 86.12 E
Kaba, Goulbin V 150 13.42 N 6.19 E
Kabacan 116 7.08 N 124.49 E
Kabacan ≃ 116 7.08 N 124.50 E
Kabadak 126 22.13 N 89.19 E
Kabadak ≃[1] 126 22.13 N 89.18 E
Kabadüz 130 40.53 N 37.56 E
Kabaena, Pulau I 112 5.15 S 121.55 E
Kabaena, Selat ʊ 112 5.00 S 122.00 E
Kabah ⊥ 232 20.07 N 89.29 W
Kabala 150 9.35 N 11.33 W
Kabale 154 1.15 S 29.59 E
Kabalebo ≃ 250 5.02 N 57.21 W
Kabalega Falls ⊾ 154 2.17 N 31.41 E
Kabalega Falls National Park ♠ 154 2.15 N 31.50 E
Kabali, Indon. 112 1.42 S 121.54 E
Kabalı, Tür. 130 41.52 N 35.05 E
Kabalo 154 6.03 S 26.55 E
Kabambare 154 4.42 S 27.43 E
Kaban' 86 54.39 N 66.28 E
Kabanbaj 86 45.50 N 80.35 E
Kabangu Kuta 154 14.00 S 24.03 E
Kabanjahe 114 3.06 N 98.30 E
Kabankalan 116 9.59 N 122.49 E
Kabanovka 80 53.39 N 51.18 E
Kabanovo 86 55.20 N 70.52 E
Kabansk 88 52.03 N 106.39 E
Kabardinka 78 44.39 N 37.57 E
Kabardino-Balkarija □[3], Ross. 72 43.30 N 43.30 E
Kabardino-Balkarija □[3], Ross. 84 43.30 N 43.30 E
Kabasalan 116 7.48 N 122.45 E
Kabayan 116 16.37 N 120.51 E
Kabba 150 7.50 N 6.03 E
Kabbani ≃ 122 12.13 N 76.54 E
Kåbdalis 24 66.10 N 20.00 E
Kabd aṣ-Ṣārim ◆[1] 130 34.34 N 39.33 E
Kabd Warqah ◆[1] 130 34.20 N 39.37 E
Kabel ◆[8] 263 51.24 N 7.29 E
Kabenung Lake ⊜ 190 48.16 N 85.00 W
Kabetogama Lake ⊜ 190 48.28 N 92.59 W
Kabeya 154 5.40 S 27.58 E
Kab-hegy ∧ 30 47.03 N 17.39 E
Kabia ≃ 146 9.54 N 15.10 E
Kabid, Wādī V 132 30.08 N 36.31 E
Kabinakagami Lake ⊜ 190 48.54 N 84.25 W
Kabin Buri 110 13.59 N 101.43 E
Kabinda 152 6.08 S 24.29 E
Kabinu 112 4.00 N 116.05 E
Kabir 112 8.17 S 124.13 E
Kabira 175d 24.27 N 124.08 E
Kabīr Kili 123 33.11 N 71.19 E
Kabīr Kūh ⋏ 128 33.25 N 46.45 E
Kabīrwāla 123 30.24 N 71.52 E
Kabkābīyah 140 13.39 N 24.05 E
Kablow 264a 52.18 N 13.44 E
Kablower Ziegelei 264a 52.19 N 13.43 E
Kablukovo, Ross. 82 56.50 N 36.12 E
Kablukovo, Ross. 82 56.02 N 38.10 E
Kablumgu, Cape › 164 6.20 S 150.00 E
Kabna 140 19.10 N 32.41 E
Kabo 152 7.39 N 18.37 E
Kabobo 154 5.07 S 29.03 E
Kaboe ≃ 158 28.55 S 19.17 E
Kābol 120 34.31 N 69.12 E
Kābol □[4] 120 34.30 N 69.15 E
Kābol ≃ 120 33.55 N 72.14 E
Kabompo 154 13.36 S 24.12 E
Kabompo ≃ 138 14.10 S 23.11 E
Kabondo-Dianda 154 8.53 S 25.40 E
Kabongo, R.D.C. 154 7.19 S 25.35 E
Kabongo, R.D.C. 154 8.43 S 28.11 E
Kabongo-Lunda, Chutes ⊾ 152 7.34 S 17.17 E
Kaboro 152 6.59 N 17.33 E
Kabot 150 10.48 N 14.57 W
Kabotshome 154 3.46 S 26.54 E
Kabou, Centraf. 152 5.20 N 21.43 E
Kabou, Togo 150 9.27 N 0.49 E
Kaboudia, Rass › 148 35.14 N 11.10 E
Kaboul → Kābol 120 34.31 N 69.12 E
Kabr 140 10.54 N 26.50 E
Kabri 132 33.01 N 35.09 E
Kabūdarāhang 128 35.12 N 48.44 E
Kabūd Gonbad 128 37.00 N 59.45 E
Kābul → Kābol 120 34.30 N 69.11 E
Kabunda 154 12.25 S 29.22 E
Kabunga 154 1.42 S 28.08 E
Kabura ≃ 94 36.17 N 139.04 E
Kaburuang, Pulau I 108 3.48 N 126.48 E
Kabūshīyah 140 16.53 N 33.42 E
Kabwanga 152 7.01 S 22.37 E
Kabwe (Broken Hill) 154 14.27 S 28.27 E
Kabwe-Katanda 152 7.59 S 24.29 E
Kabychivka 83 49.28 N 39.45 E
Kabylie ◆[1] 34 36.30 N 4.30 E
Kačalinskaja 80 49.07 N 44.03 E
Kačanik 38 42.13 N 21.14 E
Kačanovo 76 57.28 N 27.46 E
Kacbachskij 86 52.58 N 59.40 E
Kačerginė 76 54.56 N 23.44 E
Kacha 78 44.47 N 33.32 E

Symbols in the index entries represent the broad categories identified in the key at the right. Symbols with superior numbers (⋏[1]) identify subcategories (see complete key on page *I · 1*).

Symbole im Register stellen die rechts im Schlüssel erklärten Kategorien dar. Symbole mit hochgestellten Ziffern (⋏[1]) bezeichnen Unterabteilungen einer Kategorie (vgl. vollständiger Schlüssel auf Seite *I · 1*).

Los símbolos incluídos en el texto del índice representan las grandes categorías identificadas con la clave a la derecha. Los símbolos con numeros en su parte superior (⋏[1]) identifican las subcategorías (véase la clave completa en la página *I · 1*).

Les symboles de l'index représentent les catégories indiquées dans la légende à droite. Les symboles suivis d'un indice (⋏[1]) représentent des sous-catégories (voir légende complète à la page *I · 1*).

Os símbolos incluídos no texto do índice representam as grandes categorias identificadas com a chave à direita. Os símbolos com números em sua parte superior (⋏[1]) identificam as subcategorias (veja-se a chave completa à página *I · 1*).

∧ Mountain	Berg	Montaña	Montagne	Montanha
⋏ Mountains	Gebirge	Montañas	Montagnes	Montanhas
)(Pass	Paß	Paso	Col	Passo
V Valley, Canyon	Tal, Cañon	Valle, Cañón	Vallée, Canyon	Vale, Canhão
≚ Plain	Ebene	Llano	Plaine	Planície
› Cape	Kap	Cabo	Cap	Cabo
I Island	Insel	Isla	Île	Ilha
II Islands	Inseln	Islas	Îles	Ilhas
⊥ Other Topographic Features	Andere Topographische Objekte	Otros Elementos Topográficos	Autres données topographiques	Outros acidentes topográficos

ESPAÑOL / FRANÇAIS / PORTUGUÊS

Nombre / Nom / Nome	Página / Page / Página	Lat.°′	Long.°′ W = Oeste / W = Ouest / W = Oeste
Kacha ≃ [1]	126	22.23 N	89.54 E
Kachagalau ∧	154	2.19 N	35.03 E
Kach'ang-ni	98	38.24 N	126.11 E
Kachati	84	42.30 N	41.46 E
Kachchh, Gulf of c	120	22.36 N	69.30 E
Kachemak Bay c	180	59.35 N	151.30 W
Kachess Lake ⊜ [1]	224	47.20 N	121.14 W
Kachhwa	124	25.13 N	82.43 E
Kachia	150	9.53 N	7.58 E
Kachib	84	42.25 N	46.36 E
Kachin □ [3]	102	26.00 N	97.30 E
Kach'i-ri	98	34.27 N	126.08 E
Kachisi	144	9.39 N	37.50 E
Kachkarivka	78	47.06 N	33.44 E
Kachowka-Stausee → Kakhovs'ke vodoskhovyshche ⊜ [1]	78	47.25 N	34.10 E
K'achta	88	50.26 N	106.25 E
Kachua, Bngl.	126	22.39 N	89.53 E
Kachua, Bngl.	126	23.21 N	90.54 E
Kačiry	86	53.05 N	76.07 E
Kačkanar	86	58.42 N	59.38 E
Kačkanar, gora ∧	86	58.47 N	59.23 E
Kaçkar Dağı ∧	130	40.50 N	41.10 E
Kačug	88	53.58 N	105.52 E
Kada ≃	88	55.03 N	102.04 E
Kadada ≃	80	53.09 N	46.01 E
Kadaingti	110	17.37 N	97.32 E
Kadaiyanallūr	122	9.05 N	77.21 E
Kadamatt Island I	122	11.14 N	72.47 E
Kadaň	54	50.20 N	13.15 E
Kadanai (Kadaney) ≃	120	31.02 N	66.09 E
Kadaney (Kadanai) ≃	120	31.02 N	66.09 E
Kadan Kyun I	110	12.30 N	98.22 E
Kadapongan, Pulau I	112	4.43 S	115.44 E
Kadassa ≃	115b	9.24 S	120.02 E
Kaddam ⊜ [1]	122	19.07 N	78.46 E
Kade	150	6.05 N	0.50 W
Kadéï ≃	152	3.31 N	16.05 E
Kadena	174m	26.22 N	127.45 E
Kadena Airfield ⊠	174m	26.22 N	127.45 E
Kadeshiki	80	58.08 N	49.11 E
Kadetrenden (Kadet Rinne) ʊ	41	54.30 N	12.15 E
Kadet Rinne (Kadetrenden) ʊ	41	54.30 N	12.15 E
Kadgo, Lake ⊜	162	26.42 S	127.18 E
Kadi	120	23.18 N	72.20 E
Kadiana	150	10.45 N	6.30 W
Kadıköy	130	40.46 N	26.46 E
Kadina	168b	33.58 S	137.43 E
Kading ≃	110	18.19 N	104.00 E
Kadınhanı	130	38.15 N	32.14 E
Kadiolo	150	10.33 N	5.46 W
Kadipaten	115a	6.46 S	108.10 E
Kādīpur	124	26.10 N	82.23 E
Kadiri	122	14.07 N	78.10 E
Kadirli	130	37.23 N	36.05 E
Kadışehri	130	40.00 N	35.49 E
Kadiyevka → Stakhanov	83	48.34 N	38.40 E
Kadja, Ouadi (Wādī Kaja) V	146	12.02 N	22.28 E
Kadkan	128	35.35 N	58.50 E
Kadnikov	76	59.30 N	40.20 E
Kadnikovskij	76	60.19 N	40.15 E
Kado	150	7.39 N	9.44 E
Ka-do I	98	39.33 N	124.40 E
Kadodo	140	11.04 N	29.31 E
Kadogawa	92	32.28 N	131.39 E
Kadoka	198	43.50 N	101.30 W
Kadom	80	54.34 N	42.30 E
Kadoma, Nihon	270	34.44 N	135.35 E
Kadoma, Zimb.	154	18.21 S	29.55 E
Kadoškino	80	54.01 N	44.25 E
Kadov	60	49.24 N	13.47 E
Kaduj	76	59.12 N	37.09 E
Kadumbul ≃	115b	9.42 S	120.32 E
Kaduna	150	10.33 N	7.27 E
Kaduna ≃	150	8.45 N	5.45 E
Kāduqlī	140	11.01 N	29.43 E
Kadūr	122	13.34 N	76.01 E
Kadyj	80	57.47 N	43.11 E
Kadykčan	74	63.02 N	146.50 E
Kadyšovo	80	54.20 N	46.45 E
Kadžerom	24	64.41 N	55.54 E
Kadži-Saj	85	42.08 N	77.10 E
Kaech'ŏn	98	39.42 N	125.53 E
Kaédi	150	16.09 N	13.30 W
Kaedo-ri	98	34.35 N	127.39 E
Kaegudeck Lake ⊜	186	48.07 N	55.11 W
Kaélé	146	10.07 N	14.27 E
Kaena Point ›	229c	21.35 N	158.17 W
Kaeo	172	35.06 S	173.47 E
Kaesŏng	98	37.59 N	126.33 E
Kāf	128	31.24 N	37.24 E
Kafakumba	152	9.41 S	23.44 E
Kafan	84	39.13 N	46.24 E
Kafanchan	150	9.36 N	8.17 E
Kaffraria □ [9]	158	31.30 S	28.30 E
Kaffrine	150	14.06 N	15.33 W
Kafia Kingi	140	9.16 N	24.25 E
Kafin	150	9.30 N	7.04 E
Kafinda	154	12.39 S	30.20 E
Kafin Madaki	150	10.41 N	9.46 E
Kafirévs, Ákra ›	38	38.09 N	24.36 E
Kafirnigan ≃	120	36.58 N	68.02 E
Kafo ≃	154	1.08 N	31.05 E
Kafr ad-Dawwār	142	31.08 N	30.07 E
Kafr ad-Difrāwī	142	31.03 N	30.40 E
Kafr al-ʿĀ'id	142	30.27 N	31.35 E
Kafr al-Baṭṭīkh	142	31.24 N	31.44 E
Kafr al-Jarā'idah	142	31.13 N	31.16 E
Kafr ash-Shaykh	142	31.07 N	30.56 E
Kafr ash-Shaykh □ [4]	142	31.15 N	30.50 E
Kafrat Ṭā'il Mūsā	142	30.53 N	29.44 E
Kafr at-Tamīmī	142	30.37 N	31.21 E
Kafr az-Zayyāt	142	30.49 N	30.49 E
Kafr Diyamā	142	30.48 N	30.52 E
Kafr el-Zaiyat → Kafr az-Zayyāt	142	30.49 N	30.49 E
Kafr Ḥakīm	273c	30.05 N	31.07 E
Kafr Ḥūnah	132	33.29 N	35.35 E
Kafr Kanna	132	32.45 N	35.20 E
Kafr Kilā al-Bāb	142	30.41 N	31.09 E
Kafr Nabrakh	132	33.42 N	35.38 E
Kafr Naffākh	132	33.04 N	35.44 E
Kafr Nāsij	132	33.09 N	36.03 E
Kafr Rabīʿ	142	30.42 N	30.50 E
Kafr Saʿd	142	31.19 N	31.39 E
Kafr Salīm	142	31.09 N	30.06 E
Kafr Ṣaqr	142	30.48 N	31.37 E
Kafr Shanawān	142	30.30 N	31.01 E
Kafr Shibīn	142	30.18 N	31.18 E
Kafr Shīmā	132	33.49 N	35.32 E
Kafr Shukr	142	30.33 N	31.16 E
Kafr Sūsah	132	33.29 N	36.16 E
Kafr Takhārīm	130	36.07 N	36.31 E
Kafr Ṭarkhān al-Gharbī	142	29.29 N	31.13 E
Kafr Yasif	132	32.57 N	35.10 E
Kafue	154	15.47 S	28.11 E
Kafue ≃	154	15.56 S	28.55 E
Kafue Flats ≡	154	15.40 S	27.25 E
Kafue Gorge V	154	15.54 S	28.34 E
Kafue National Park ♠	154	15.00 S	25.45 E
Kafulwe Mission	154	9.00 S	29.02 E
Kafumba	152	5.23 S	18.55 E
Kafwira	154	12.10 S	27.33 E
Kaga	94	36.18 N	136.18 E
Kaga Bandoro	152	6.59 N	19.11 E
Kagalaska Island I	180	51.47 N	176.23 W
Kagal'nickaja	83	46.53 N	40.09 E
Kagal'nik	83	47.05 N	39.19 E
Kagal'nik ≃	83	47.04 N	39.18 E
Kagami	96	33.37 N	133.26 E
Kagamigahara	94	35.24 N	136.54 E
Kagamil Island I	180	53.00 N	169.43 W
Kagamino	96	35.05 N	133.56 E
Kāgān, Pāk.	123	34.47 N	73.32 E
Kagan, Uzb.	128	39.43 N	64.33 E
Kagan Valley V	123	34.25 N	73.17 E
Kagarko	150	9.29 N	7.41 E
Kagawa	96	34.15 N	134.02 E
Kagawa □ [5]	96	34.15 N	134.00 E
Kagawong, Lake ⊜	190	45.49 N	82.18 W
Kagaznagar	122	19.18 N	79.50 E
Kåge	26	64.50 N	20.59 E
Kagelike	120	37.20 N	87.02 E
Kagera (Akagera) ≃	154	0.57 S	31.47 E
Kågeröd	41	56.01 N	13.06 E
Kâgheṭ ◆ [1]	148	24.00 N	7.30 W
Kâğıthane ◆ [8]	267b	41.04 N	28.58 E
Kagitumba	154	1.04 S	30.27 E
Kağızman	84	40.09 N	43.08 E
Käglan ⋏ [2]	40	59.23 N	15.31 E
Kagmar	140	14.24 N	30.25 E
Kagopal	146	8.17 N	16.27 E
Kagoshima	92	31.36 N	130.33 E
Kagoshima □ [5]	93b	29.00 N	129.30 E
Kagoshima-wan c	92	31.25 N	130.38 E
Kagran ◆ [8]	264b	48.15 N	16.27 E
Kagulu	154	1.15 N	33.18 E
Kagyo-ri	98	34.25 N	126.48 E
Kahalīya, Jabal ∧	142	29.55 N	32.09 E
Kahaluu	229c	21.27 N	157.50 W
Kahama	154	3.50 S	32.36 E
Kahana Bay c	229c	21.34 N	157.52 W
Kahanavičy	76	55.52 N	28.08 E
Kaharlyk	78	49.51 N	30.50 E
Kahayan ≃	112	3.20 S	114.04 E
Kahe	154	3.30 S	37.26 E
Kahemba	152	7.17 S	19.00 E
Kahia	154	6.21 S	28.24 E
Kahiu Point ›	229a	21.13 N	156.58 W
Kaḥk	142	29.25 N	30.38 E
Kahl ≃	56	50.04 N	9.00 E
Kahla	54	50.48 N	11.35 E
Kahl am Main	56	50.04 N	9.00 E
Kahlenberg ∧ [2]	264b	48.16 N	16.21 E
Kahler Asten ∧	56	51.11 N	8.29 E
Kahlersberg ∧	64	47.32 N	13.02 E
Kāhna	123	31.22 N	74.22 E
Kahnūj	128	27.58 N	57.45 E
Kahoka	194	40.25 N	91.43 W
Kahoku, Nihon	96	33.39 N	133.47 E
Kahoku, Nihon	96	33.06 N	130.41 E
Kahoku-gata ⊜	94	36.40 N	136.41 E
Kahoolawe I	229a	20.33 N	156.37 W
Kahouanne, Îlet à I	241o	16.22 N	61.47 W
Kahoué, Mont ∧	150	7.06 N	7.15 W
Kahramanmaraş	130	37.36 N	36.55 E
Kahraman Maraş □ [4]	130	38.00 N	37.05 E
Kahror Pakka	123	29.37 N	71.55 E
Kahshe Lake ⊜	212	44.52 N	79.16 W
Kâhta	130	37.46 N	38.36 E
Kahuku	229c	21.40 N	157.57 W
Kahuku Point ›	229c	21.43 N	157.59 W
Kahului	229a	20.54 N	156.28 W
Kahului Airport ⊠	229a	20.54 N	156.26 W
Kahului Bay c	229a	20.54 N	156.28 W
Kahurangi Point ›	172	40.47 S	172.13 E
Kahūta	123	33.35 N	73.23 E
Kahuzi-Biega, Parc National de ♠	154	1.50 N	28.40 E
Kahyŏn-bong ∧	271b	37.38 N	126.39 E
Kahyŏn-ni	271b	37.32 N	126.44 E
Kai	164	2.15 S	136.32 E
Kai, Kepulauan II	164	5.35 S	132.45 E
Kai, Tanjung ›	112	2.52 S	118.45 E
Kaia, Wādī V	140	11.31 N	24.15 E
Kaiai, Jabal ∧	140	19.54 N	36.48 E
Kaiama	150	9.37 N	3.58 E
Kaiapit	164	6.15 S	146.15 E
Kaiapoi	172	43.23 S	172.40 E
Kaibab Indian Reservation ◆ [4]	200	36.55 N	112.40 W
Kaibab Plateau ⋏ [1]	200	36.30 N	112.15 W
Kaibara	96	35.08 N	135.05 E
Kai Beab	164	7.29 S	139.40 E
Kaibing	61	47.12 N	15.50 E
Kaibito Plateau ⋏ [1]	200	36.40 N	111.20 W
Kaichengqiao	100	31.18 N	117.44 E
Kaida	94	35.56 N	137.36 E
Kaidori	268	35.37 N	139.27 E
Kaidu ≃	90	41.55 N	86.38 E
Kaiedin	140	9.45 N	32.11 E
Kaieteur Fall ∟	246	5.10 N	59.28 W
Kaieteur National Park ♠	246	5.10 N	59.45 W
Kaifeng	98	34.51 N	114.21 E
Kaifu	96	33.35 N	134.21 E
Kaifu ≃	96	33.35 N	134.22 E
Kaihe	98	35.42 N	116.20 E
Kaihu	172	35.46 S	173.42 E
Kaihua	100	29.09 N	118.23 E
Kai Iwi	172	39.51 S	174.56 E
Kaijian	102	23.42 N	111.48 E
Kaijiang	102	31.05 N	107.55 E
Kaijo → Kaesŏng	98	37.59 N	126.33 E
Kai Kecil I	164	5.45 S	132.40 E
Kaikohe	172	35.25 S	173.48 E
Kaikoura	172	42.25 S	173.41 E
Kaikoura Peninsula › [1]	172	42.26 S	173.42 E
Kaikukang	89	53.07 N	124.46 E
Kailahun	150	8.17 N	10.34 W
Kailas → Kangrinboqê Feng ∧	120	31.04 N	81.18 E
Kailāshahar	120	24.20 N	92.01 E
Kaili	102	26.35 N	107.55 E
Kailu	89	43.36 N	121.14 E
Kailua	229c	21.24 N	157.44 W
Kailua Bay c	229c	21.25 N	157.44 W
Kailua Kona	229d	19.22 N	155.59 W
Kaim ≃	164	6.40 S	141.45 E
Kaimai Range ⋏	172	37.45 S	175.55 E
Kaïmaktsalán ∧	38	40.58 N	21.48 E
Kaimana	164	3.39 S	133.45 E
Kaimanawa Mountains ⋏	172	39.15 S	175.54 E
Kaiman-Inseln → Cayman Islands □ [2]	238	19.30 N	80.40 W
Kaimenshan	104	41.03 N	123.08 E
Kaimganj	124	27.34 N	79.21 E
Kaimon-dake ∧	92	31.11 N	130.32 E
Kain	50	50.38 N	3.22 E
Käina	76	58.50 N	22.45 E
Kainab ≃	158	28.31 S	19.35 E
Kainach ≃	61	46.54 N	15.31 E
Kainan, Nihon	96	33.36 N	134.22 E
Kainan, Nihon	96	34.09 N	135.12 E
Kainantu	164	6.15 S	145.55 E
Kainda	85	42.50 N	73.41 E
Kai-Ndunda	152	5.42 S	12.42 E
Kaingan ≃	115a	7.44 S	107.54 E
Kainji Lake ⊜ [1]	150	10.30 N	4.35 E
Kaioba	112	5.20 S	122.37 E
Kaipara Harbour c	172	36.25 S	174.13 E
Kaiparowits Plateau ⋏ [1]	200	37.20 N	111.15 W
Kaiping, Zhg.	102	22.23 N	112.35 E
Kaiping, Zhg.	105	39.41 N	118.16 E
Kaipuri, Pulau I	164	1.51 S	137.01 E
Kairābani	126	24.08 N	87.02 E
Kairaku-en ♠	94	36.22 N	140.27 E
Kairāna	124	29.24 N	77.12 E
Kairatu	164	3.21 S	128.22 E
Kairiru Island I	164	3.20 S	143.35 E
Kairo → Al-Qāhirah	142	30.03 N	31.15 E
Kairouan	148	35.41 N	10.07 E
Kairuku	164	8.50 S	146.35 E
Kaisarganj	124	27.15 N	81.33 E
Kaisariani	267c	37.58 N	23.47 E
Kaisariani Monastery ʋ [1]	267c	37.58 N	23.47 E
Kaisergebirge ⋏	64	47.36 N	12.20 E
Kaisermühlen ◆ [8]	264b	48.14 N	16.26 E
Kaiser Pass)(	226	37.17 N	119.06 W
Kaisersesch	56	50.14 N	7.08 E
Kaiserslautern	56	49.26 N	7.46 E
Kaiserstuhl ⋏ [2]	58	48.06 N	7.40 E
Kaiserswerth ◆ [8]	263	51.18 N	6.44 E
Kaiser-Wilhelm-Museum ʋ	263	51.20 N	6.34 E
Kaishantun	98	42.43 N	129.43 E
Kaisheim	56	48.46 N	10.48 E
Kaišiadorys	76	54.52 N	24.27 E
Kait, Tanjung ›	112	3.14 S	106.05 E
Kaita	96	34.20 N	132.32 E
Kaitaia	172	35.07 S	173.16 E
Kaitaichi-chūtonchi, Rikujō-jieitai- ■	96	34.21 N	132.32 E
Kai Tak Airport ⊠	271d	22.20 N	114.12 E
Kaitangata	172	46.18 S	169.51 E
Kaitersberg ⋏	60	49.11 N	12.57 E
Kaithal	124	29.48 N	76.23 E
Kaituma ≃	246	8.11 N	59.41 W
Kaiwaka	172	36.10 S	174.27 E
Kaiwatu	164	8.07 S	127.49 E
Kaiwi Channel ʊ	229b	21.15 N	157.30 W
Kaixian	102	31.13 N	108.25 E
Kaiyang	102	26.58 N	106.40 E
Kaiyuan, Zhg.	102	23.44 N	103.11 E
Kaiyuan, Zhg.	104	42.32 N	124.01 E
Kaiyuancheng	98	42.37 N	124.04 E
Kaiyuh Mountains ⋏	180	64.00 N	158.00 W
Kaizhou	104	41.22 N	121.19 E
Kaizu	94	35.13 N	136.38 E
Kaizuka	96	34.27 N	135.21 E
Kaja, Wādī (Ouadi Kadja) V	146	12.02 N	22.28 E
Kajaani	26	64.14 N	27.41 E
Kajabbi	166	20.02 S	140.02 E
Kajakī, Band-e ⊜ [1]	128	32.22 N	65.16 E
Kajang, Indon.	112	5.20 S	120.21 E
Kajang, Malay.	114	2.59 N	101.47 E
Kajang, Gunong ∧	114	2.46 N	104.09 E
Kajasan	86	55.12 N	62.16 E
Kajasula	84	44.19 N	44.59 E
Kajen	115a	7.02 S	109.34 E
Kajga	86	50.55 N	64.43 E
Kajiado	154	1.51 S	36.47 E
Kajikazawa	94	35.33 N	138.27 E
Kajiki	92	31.44 N	130.40 E
Kājiāgarh	126	22.02 N	87.47 E
Kajmanačicha	86	53.32 N	75.11 E
Kajmonovo	88	56.50 N	104.54 E
Kajmysovy	86	59.48 N	76.31 E
Kajnar	86	49.12 N	77.25 E
Kajo Kaji	154	3.53 N	31.40 E
Kajrakkum	85	40.16 N	69.49 E
Kajrakkumskoje vodochranilišče ⊜ [1]	85	40.20 N	70.10 E
Kajrakty	86	48.31 N	73.14 E
Kajsackoje	80	49.44 N	46.51 E
Kājū ≃	128	25.34 N	61.13 E
Kājulia	126	23.01 N	89.57 E
Kajuru	150	10.21 N	7.40 E
Kaka, Centraf.	140	6.01 N	26.30 E
Kākā, Sūd.	140	10.36 N	32.11 E
Kaka, Lae o ›	229a	20.31 N	156.33 W
Kakabeka Falls ∟	190	48.24 N	89.37 W
Kakabia, Pulau I	112	6.54 S	122.13 E
Kakadu National Park ♠	164	13.00 S	132.45 E
Kakagi Lake ⊜	184	49.13 N	93.52 W
Kakamas	158	28.45 S	20.33 E
Kakamega	154	0.17 N	34.45 E
Kakamigahara	94	35.24 N	136.54 E
Kakana	110	9.07 N	92.49 E
Kakanui Mountains ⋏	172	45.09 S	170.26 E
Kaka Point	172	46.23 S	169.47 E
Kakaramea	172	39.43 S	174.27 E
Kakasa	164	9.20 S	148.45 E
Kakata	150	6.35 N	10.19 W
Kakatahi	172	39.41 S	175.20 E
Kākdwīp	126	21.53 N	88.11 E
Kake, Nihon	96	34.36 N	132.19 E
Kake, Ak., U.S.	180	56.58 N	133.56 W
Kakegawa	94	34.46 N	138.01 E
Kakehashi ≃	94	36.25 N	136.25 E
Kakelwe	154	4.49 S	29.00 E
Kakenge	152	4.51 S	21.55 E
Kakerbeck	54	52.40 N	11.17 E
Kakeya	96	35.11 N	132.49 E
Kakhonak	180	59.26 N	154.51 W
Kakhovka	78	46.47 N	33.30 E
Kakhovs'ke vodoskhovyshche ⊜ [1]	78	47.25 N	34.10 E
Kakhra	126	21.38 N	87.27 E
Kākī	128	28.19 N	51.34 E
Kākināda	122	16.56 N	82.13 E
Kakino	80	55.12 N	44.53 E
Kakinoki	96	34.26 N	131.52 E
Kakisa Lake ⊜	176	60.55 N	117.40 W
Kakizaki	92	37.15 N	138.25 E
Kako ≃, Guy.	246	5.46 N	60.35 W
Kako ≃, Nihon	96	34.44 N	134.49 E
Kakoaka	156	18.40 S	24.22 E
Kakogawa	96	34.46 N	134.51 E
Kakrāla	272a	28.33 N	77.25 E
Kāksa	126	23.28 N	87.28 E
Kaktovik	180	70.08 N	143.37 W
Kakuda	92	37.58 N	140.47 E
Kakui-shima I	96	34.43 N	134.19 E
Kakuma	154	3.43 N	34.52 E
Kakunodate	92	39.35 N	140.34 E
Kakus ≃	112	2.46 N	113.01 E
Kakwa ≃	182	54.36 N	118.28 W
Kala	146	12.05 N	14.27 E
Kala ≃	122	8.18 N	79.50 E
Kalaa Kebira	148	35.52 N	10.32 E
Kalaallit Nunaat → Greenland □ [2]	16	70.00 N	40.00 W
Kalaa Sghira	36	35.49 N	10.33 E
Kālābāgh	123	32.58 N	71.34 E
Kalabahi	112	8.13 S	124.31 E
Kalabáka	38	39.42 N	21.43 E
Kalabakan	112	4.25 N	117.29 E
Kalabo	152	14.57 S	22.40 E
Kalabula	86	43.24 N	83.06 E
Kalač	78	50.25 N	41.01 E
Kalačinsk	86	55.03 N	74.34 E
Kalač-Kurtlak	80	49.00 N	42.26 E
Kalač-na-Donu	80	48.43 N	43.31 E
Kalačskaja vozvyšennost' ⋏ [1]	80	50.30 N	41.30 E
Kaladan ≃	110	20.09 N	92.57 E
Kaladar	212	44.39 N	77.07 W
Kalae	229a	21.10 N	157.00 W
Ka Lae ›	229d	18.55 N	155.41 W
Kalaena ≃	112	2.40 S	120.53 E
Kalagan	89	50.30 N	119.55 E
Kalagwe	110	22.31 N	96.31 E
Kalahari Desert ◆ [2]	156	24.00 S	21.30 E
Kalahari Gemsbok National Park ♠	156	25.30 S	20.30 E
Kalaheo	229b	21.55 N	159.31 W
Kālaia	126	22.23 N	90.36 E
Kalai-Chumb	85	38.28 N	70.46 E
Kalai-Mor	128	35.39 N	62.33 E
Kalais	80	52.38 N	42.38 E
Kalaiyā	124	27.02 N	85.00 E
Kalajka	88	58.28 N	111.46 E
Kalajoki	26	64.15 N	23.57 E
Kalajoki ≃	26	64.17 N	23.55 E
Kalakamate	156	20.39 S	27.21 E
Kalakan	88	55.08 N	116.45 E
Kalakan ≃	88	55.07 N	116.46 E
Kalakepen	114	2.45 N	97.50 E
Kalām	123	35.32 N	72.35 E
Kalama, Wa., U.S.	224	46.00 N	122.50 W
Kalama, R.D.C.	154	2.55 S	28.33 E
Kalama ≃	224	46.02 N	122.52 W
Kalama, Pulau I	112	3.15 N	125.28 E
Kalámai	38	37.04 N	22.07 E
Kalamákion	267c	37.55 N	23.43 E
Kalamalka Lake ⊜	182	50.09 N	119.22 W
Kalamazoo	216	42.17 N	85.35 W
Kalamazoo □ [6]	216	42.14 N	85.32 W
Kalamazoo ≃	216	42.40 N	86.10 W
Kalamazoo, North Branch ≃	216	42.14 N	84.44 W
Kalamazoo, South Branch ≃	216	42.14 N	84.44 W
Kalamazoo Lake c	216	42.39 N	86.13 W
Kalamb	122	19.03 N	73.57 E
Kalamba	152	0.26 S	18.17 E
Kalambau, Pulau I	112	4.55 S	115.39 E
Kalambo Falls ∟	154	8.36 S	31.14 E
Kalamboli	272c	19.01 N	73.06 E
Kalamits'ka zatoka c	78	45.05 N	33.23 E
Kalamo	216	42.32 N	85.01 W
Kalampising	112	3.44 N	116.42 E
Kalamunda	168a	31.57 S	116.03 E
Kalamunda National Park ♠	168a	31.59 S	116.04 E
Kalana	150	10.47 N	8.12 W
Kalanchak	78	46.16 N	33.17 E
Kalandula	152	9.06 S	15.57 E
Kalange-Bushimaie ≃	152	7.55 S	23.11 E
Kalanguj	88	51.01 N	116.31 E
Kalankalan	150	10.07 N	8.54 W
Kalannie	162	30.21 S	117.04 E
Kalanshiyū ar-Ramlī al-Kabīr, Sarīr ≛ [8]	146	28.00 N	23.00 E
Kālānwāli	123	29.51 N	74.57 E
Kalao, Pulau I	112	7.18 S	120.58 E
Kalaong	116	6.04 N	124.28 E
Kalaotoa, Pulau I	112	7.22 S	121.47 E
Kalapana	229d	19.21 N	154.58 W
Kalāpāra	126	21.59 N	90.14 E
Kalar ≃	88	55.23 N	116.18 E
Kalār, Kūh-e ∧	128	31.50 N	50.53 E
Kälarne	26	62.59 N	16.05 E
Kālāroa	126	22.52 N	89.02 E
Kalasarv	84	39.11 N	48.03 E
Kalasi	86	48.43 N	86.59 E
Kalasin, Indon.	112	0.12 N	114.16 E
Kalasin, Thai	110	16.29 N	103.30 E
Kalašnikovo	76	57.17 N	35.13 E
Kalāt	120	29.02 N	66.35 E
Kalatungan Mountain ∧	116	7.58 N	124.47 E
Kalaupapa	229a	21.11 N	156.59 W
Kalaupapa National Historical Park ♠	229a	21.12 N	156.58 W
Kalaupapa Peninsula › [1]	229a	21.13 N	156.58 W
Kalauri	84	41.49 N	45.42 E
Kalaus ≃	80	45.43 N	44.07 E
Kalavárdha	38	36.20 N	27.57 E
Kalávrita	38	38.01 N	22.06 E
Kalaw	110	20.38 N	96.34 E
Kalawao □ [6]	229a	21.12 N	156.58 W
Kal'azin	76	57.15 N	37.52 E
Kalb, Nahr al- ≃	132	33.57 N	35.35 E
Kalb, Ra's al- ›	144	14.02 N	48.41 E
Kalbā'	128	25.03 N	56.21 E
Kälbäcär	84	40.07 N	46.02 E
Kalbar	171a	27.56 S	152.37 E
Kalbarri	162	27.42 S	114.09 E
Kalbarri National Park ♠	162	27.45 S	114.25 E
Kalbe	54	52.40 N	11.25 E
Kalbinskij chrebet ⋏	86	49.10 N	83.00 E
Kalchās	120	29.21 N	69.42 E
Kal'chyk ≃	83	47.07 N	37.36 E
Kaldırım ≃	267b	41.10 N	29.12 E
Kaldygajty ≃	80	49.20 N	52.38 E
Kale, Tür.	130	40.23 N	39.39 E
Kale, Tür.	130	37.26 N	28.51 E
Kale, Tür.	130	36.14 N	29.59 E
Kalecik, Tür.	130	40.06 N	33.25 E
Kalecik, Tür.	130	37.17 N	39.02 E
Kaleden	182	49.23 N	119.35 W
Kaledupa, Pulau I	112	5.32 S	123.47 E
Kalefeld	52	51.48 N	10.02 E
Kalegauk Island I	110	15.32 N	97.40 E
Kalehe	154	2.06 S	28.55 E
Kaleindaung ≃	110	18.50 N	94.00 E
Kalema, Tan.	154	1.12 S	31.50 E
Kalema, R.D.C.	152	4.08 S	24.15 E
Kalemie (Albertville)	154	5.56 S	29.12 E
Kalemyo	120	23.12 N	94.10 E
Kalene Hill	152	11.11 S	24.10 E
Kaleščatovka	83	49.35 N	39.55 E
Kaletwa	110	21.45 N	92.48 E
Kalety	30	50.34 N	18.54 E
Kalevala	24	65.13 N	31.08 E
Kalewa	110	23.12 N	94.17 E
Kale Water ≃	46	55.32 N	2.28 W
Kaleybar	128	38.47 N	47.02 E
Kálfafell	24a	63.58 N	17.40 W
Kalga	88	50.57 N	118.48 E
Kalgačicha	24	63.20 N	36.44 E
Kalgan, Austl.	162	34.53 S	118.01 E
Kalgan → Zhangjiakou, Zhg.	105	40.50 N	114.53 E
Kalgin Island I	180	60.28 N	151.55 W
Kalgoorlie-Boulder	162	30.45 S	121.28 E
Kalhe	272c	18.52 N	73.06 E
Kali	150	12.10 N	11.29 W
Kāli ≃ [1]	126	23.40 N	89.12 E
Kālia	126	23.03 N	89.38 E
Kāliāganj	124	25.38 N	88.19 E
Kāliāghaj ≃	126	22.10 N	87.50 E
Kāliākair	126	24.05 N	90.14 E
Kaliakra, nos ›	38	43.21 N	28.27 E
Kalianda	115a	5.45 S	105.38 E
Kalianget	115a	7.03 S	113.56 E
Kalibek, ozero ⊜	86	53.52 N	70.40 E
Kālībhīt Hills ⋏ [2]	124	22.10 N	77.30 E
Kalibo	116	11.43 N	122.22 E
Kalida	216	40.59 N	84.12 W
Kalifornien, Golf von → California, Golfo de c	232	28.00 N	112.00 W
Kālī Gaṇḍakī ≃	124	27.42 N	84.25 E
Kāliganga ≃	126	23.43 N	90.15 E
Kālīganj, Bngl.	126	23.55 N	90.34 E
Kālīganj, Bngl.	126	23.25 N	89.08 E
Kālīganj, Bngl.	126	22.28 N	89.02 E
Kāliganj, India	126	23.44 N	88.14 E
Kalihiwai ≃	229b	22.13 N	159.26 W
Kalijati	115a	6.32 S	107.40 E
Kālikāpur, Bngl.	126	22.43 N	89.26 E
Kālikāpur, Bngl.	126	23.46 N	89.55 E
Kālikāpur, India	126	22.37 N	86.17 E
Kālikāpur, India	272b	22.29 N	88.32 E
Kalikino, Ross.	76	52.57 N	39.50 E
Kalikino, Ross.	80	52.55 N	54.05 E
Kalima, R.D.C.	154	2.34 S	26.37 E
Kalima, Zhg.	104	41.32 N	122.40 E
Kalimantan → Borneo I	112	0.30 N	114.00 E
Kalimantan Barat □ [4]	112	0.30 N	110.00 E
Kalimantan Selatan □ [4]	112	2.30 S	115.30 E
Kalimantan Tengah □ [4]	112	2.00 S	113.30 E
Kalimantan Timur □ [4]	112	1.30 N	116.30 E
Kálimnos	38	36.57 N	26.59 E
Kálimnos I	38	37.00 N	27.00 E
Kālimpang	124	27.04 N	88.29 E
Kalina, Pointe de ›	273b	4.18 S	15.16 E
Kālīnadi ≃	122	14.50 N	74.08 E
Kālinagar	126	22.26 N	88.51 E
Kalinga-Apayao □ [4]	116	17.50 N	121.10 E
Kalinga Bil ⊜	272b	22.33 N	88.33 E
Kalinin, Ross.	80	47.11 N	42.10 E
Kalinin → Tver', Ross.	82	56.52 N	35.55 E
Kalininabad	85	39.45 N	69.08 E
Kaliningrad (Königsberg), Ross.	76	54.43 N	20.30 E
Kaliningrad, Ross.	82	55.55 N	37.49 E
Kaliningrad Oblast' □ [4]	76	54.45 N	21.15 E
Kalinino, Ross.	78	45.07 N	39.00 E
Kalinino, Ross.	80	46.21 N	48.53 E
Kalinino, Ross.	86	57.20 N	56.20 E
Kalinino, Ross.	89	49.24 N	129.20 E
Kalininsk, Kyrg.	85	42.29 N	72.06 E
Kalininsk, Ross.	80	51.30 N	44.28 E
Kalininskaja, Ross.	78	45.29 N	38.40 E
Kalininskaja, Ross.	80	47.52 N	42.15 E
Kalinins'ke	78	47.07 N	32.59 E
Kalininskoje	85	42.50 N	73.49 E
Kalinkavičy	76	52.08 N	29.21 E
Kalinku	154	11.12 S	33.12 E
Kalinovik	38	43.31 N	18.26 E
Kalinovka, Kaz.	86	49.58 N	55.22 E
Kalinovka, Ross.	78	51.54 N	34.28 E
Kalinovo	82	54.54 N	37.17 E
Kālipur	272b	22.41 N	88.17 E
Kaliro	154	0.54 N	33.30 E
Kalis	144	8.23 N	49.05 E
Kalisat	115a	8.08 S	113.48 E
Kalisch → Kalisz	30	51.46 N	18.06 E
Kāli Sindh ≃	124	25.32 N	76.17 E
Kalispell	202	48.11 N	114.18 W
Kalistraticha	86	52.59 N	83.35 E
Kalisz	30	51.46 N	18.06 E
Kalisz □ [4]	30	51.40 N	17.45 E
Kalisz Pomorski	30	53.19 N	15.54 E
Kalitva ≃	78	48.10 N	40.46 E
Kaliua	154	5.04 S	31.48 E
Kaliveli Tank ⊜ [1]	122	12.05 N	79.50 E
Kaliwiro	115a	7.27 S	109.51 E
Kaliwungu	115a	6.57 S	110.14 E
Kalix	26	65.51 N	23.08 E
Kalixälven ≃	24	65.50 N	23.11 E
Kälka	123	30.50 N	76.56 E
Kālkāji ◆ [8]	272a	28.33 N	77.16 E
Kalkaman	86	51.58 N	76.02 E
Kalkan	130	36.15 N	29.24 E
Kalkar	52	51.44 N	6.18 E
Kalkaska	190	44.44 N	85.10 W
Kalkfeld	156	20.53 S	16.11 E
Kalkfontein	156	22.08 S	20.53 E
Kalkfonteindam ⊜ [1]	158	29.30 S	25.15 E
Kalkhorst	54	53.58 N	11.02 E
Kalkım	130	39.48 N	27.13 E
Kālkini	126	23.06 N	90.16 E
Kalkmond	158	28.40 S	20.26 E
Kalkrand	156	24.03 S	17.33 E
Kalksburg ◆ [8]	264b	48.08 N	16.15 E
Kalk-See ⊜	264a	52.26 N	13.46 E
Kalkstasie	158	30.00 S	18.55 E
Kalkum ◆ [8]	263	51.18 N	6.46 E
Kalkutta → Calcutta	126	22.32 N	88.22 E
Kalkwerf	158	28.39 S	21.43 E
Kall	56	50.32 N	6.32 E
Kallakkurichchi	122	11.44 N	78.58 E
Kallakoopah Creek ≃	166	27.29 S	138.15 E
Kållandsö I	26	58.40 N	13.09 E
Kallang ≃	271c	1.19 N	103.52 E
Kallar Kahār	123	32.47 N	72.42 E
Kallaste	76	58.39 N	27.09 E
Kallavesi ⊜	26	62.50 N	27.45 E
Kalletal	52	52.06 N	8.56 E
Källfallet	40	59.50 N	15.31 E
Kallhäll	40	59.27 N	17.48 E
Kalliecahoolie Lake ⊜	184	54.14 N	95.29 W
Kallinge	26	56.14 N	15.17 E
Kallista	274b	37.53 S	145.22 E
Kallithéa	267c	37.57 N	23.42 E
Kallmünz	60	49.09 N	11.58 E
Kallnach	58	47.01 N	7.14 E
Kallsjön ⊜	26	63.37 N	13.00 E
Kalmakkora	86	44.03 N	78.44 E
Kalmakkyrgan ≃	86	46.58 N	64.30 E
Kalmar	26	56.40 N	16.22 E
Kalmar Län □ [6]	26	57.20 N	16.00 E
Kalmarsund ʊ	26	56.40 N	16.25 E
Kalmit ∧	56	49.19 N	8.05 E
Kal'mius ≃	83	47.05 N	37.34 E
Kalmthout	50	51.23 N	4.28 E
Kalmyckije Mysy	86	51.53 N	82.16 E
Kalmykia → Kalmykija □ [3]	72	46.30 N	45.30 E
Kalmykija □ [3]	72	46.30 N	45.30 E
Kalmykivka, Ukr.	83	49.17 N	38.39 E
Kalmykivka, Ukr.	83	49.17 N	39.52 E
Kalmykov	80	49.01 N	42.49 E
Kalmykovo	80	49.03 N	51.47 E
Kālna	126	23.13 N	88.22 E
Kalnciems	76	56.50 N	23.37 E
Kalnibolotskaja	78	46.01 N	40.28 E
Kalničko Gorje ⋏	36	46.10 N	16.30 E
Kal'nyboloto	78	48.44 N	31.00 E
Kalo	164	10.00 S	147.45 E
Kálócfa	61	46.45 N	16.34 E
Kalocsa	30	46.32 N	18.59 E
Kalofer	38	42.37 N	24.59 E
Kalohi Channel ʊ	229a	21.00 N	156.56 W
Kaloko	154	6.47 S	25.48 E
Kalol, India	120	22.36 N	73.27 E
Kālol, India	120	23.15 N	72.29 E
Kalole	154	3.42 S	27.22 E
Kalolio	112	0.11 S	121.38 E
Kaloli Point ›	229d	19.38 N	154.57 W
Kalomo	154	17.02 S	26.30 E
Kalomo ≃	154	17.57 S	26.24 E
Kalona	190	41.28 N	91.42 W
Kalonda	152	4.48 S	17.33 E
Kalone Peak ∧	182	52.38 N	126.37 W
Kalonga	154	9.10 S	27.25 E
Kalorama	274b	37.49 S	145.22 E
Kaloran	115a	7.15 S	110.15 E
Kalø Vig c	41	56.15 N	10.25 E
Kalpáki	38	39.53 N	20.38 E
Kalpeni Island I	122	10.05 N	73.38 E
Kālpi	124	26.07 N	79.44 E
Kāl Qalʿeh	128	32.38 N	62.32 E
Kalri	123	31.39 N	72.33 E
Kalsdorf bei Graz	61	46.57 N	15.28 E
Kalskag	180	61.30 N	160.23 W
Kalsūbai ∧	122	19.36 N	73.43 E
Kaltag	180	64.20 N	158.44 W
Kaltan	86	53.30 N	87.17 E
Kaltbrunn	58	47.12 N	9.02 E
Kalte Herberge ∧	56	50.03 N	7.59 E
Kalteneber	56	51.19 N	10.08 E
Kaltenhouse	56	48.48 N	7.50 E
Kaltenkirchen	52	53.50 N	9.58 E
Kaltenleutgeben	264b	48.07 N	16.12 E
Kaltennordheim	56	50.38 N	10.10 E
Kaltensundheim	56	50.36 N	10.10 E
Kalter Gang ≃	264b	48.02 N	16.25 E
Kalthof	263	51.26 N	7.40 E
Kal'tino	265a	59.58 N	30.40 E
Kaltungo	146	9.50 N	11.19 E
Kaluga	82	54.31 N	36.16 E
Kaluga Oblast' □ [4]	76	54.30 N	35.30 E
Kalugino	82	54.59 N	37.11 E
Kalukalukuang, Pulau I	112	5.14 S	117.38 E
Kālu Khuhar	120	25.08 N	67.46 E
Kalulushi	154	12.50 S	28.03 E
Kalumba, Mount ∧	166	31.49 S	146.22 E
Kalumburu	164	14.18 S	126.39 E
Kalumburu Aboriginal Reserve ◆ [4]	164	14.15 S	126.50 E
Kalundborg	41	55.41 N	11.06 E
Kalundborg Fjord c	41	55.41 N	11.00 E
Kālundri	272c	18.59 N	73.08 E
Kalundu, R.D.C.	154	3.26 S	29.08 E
Kalundu, Zam.	154	10.16 S	29.24 E
Kalungwishi ≃	154	9.01 S	28.57 E
Kalūr Kot	123	32.09 N	71.16 E
Kalush	78	49.03 N	24.23 E
Kałuszyn	30	52.13 N	21.49 E
Kalutara	122	6.35 N	79.58 E
Kalvåg	26	61.46 N	4.53 E
Kalvarija	76	54.21 N	23.14 E
Kälväz	84	38.39 N	48.18 E
Kalvehave	41	55.00 N	12.10 E
Kälviä	26	63.52 N	23.26 E
Kalwa	272c	19.12 N	72.59 E
Kalwang	61	47.26 N	14.46 E
Kalwaria Zebrzydowska	30	49.52 N	19.41 E
Kalyān	122	19.15 N	73.09 E
Kalyāndurg	122	14.33 N	77.06 E
Kalynivka, Ukr.	78	50.14 N	30.14 E
Kalynivka, Ukr.	78	49.27 N	28.32 E
Kalynove	83	48.34 N	38.31 E
Kam ≃	146	8.15 N	11.00 E
Kama, Mya.	110	19.02 N	95.06 E
Kama, Ross.	80	56.19 N	54.06 E
Kama, Ross.	86	60.08 N	62.10 E
Kama, R.D.C.	154	3.32 S	27.07 E
Kama ≃, Ross.	72	55.45 N	52.00 E
Kama ≃, Ross.	86	55.35 N	76.54 E
Kamachumu	154	1.35 S	31.37 E
Kamado-zaki ›	96	33.04 N	132.02 E
Kamae	92	32.48 N	131.56 E
Kamagaya	94	35.45 N	140.01 E
Kamaiki Point ›	229a	20.46 N	156.50 W
Kamaishi	92	39.16 N	141.53 E
Kama-iwa I	174f	24.47 N	141.17 E
Kamajai	76	55.49 N	25.30 E
Kamakou ∧	229a	21.07 N	156.52 W
Kamakura	94	35.19 N	139.33 E
Kamakwie	150	9.30 N	12.14 W
Kamal	115a	7.10 S	112.42 E
Kamālia	123	30.44 N	72.39 E
Kamamaung	110	17.21 N	97.40 E
Kāman, India	124	27.39 N	77.16 E
Kaman, Tür.	130	39.22 N	33.44 E
Kaman ≃	110	14.48 N	106.51 E
Kamana	154	5.59 S	24.56 E
Kamanashi ≃	94	35.33 N	138.28 E
Kamango	154	0.39 N	29.53 E
Kamaniskeg Lake ⊜	212	45.25 N	77.42 W
Kamanjab	156	19.35 S	14.51 E
Kamapanda	152	12.00 S	24.10 E
Kamara Forest ♠	264c	47.26 N	19.00 E
Kamarān I	144	15.21 N	42.35 E
Kamaran, Hadjer ∧	146	12.41 N	21.46 E
Kamarang ≃	246	5.53 N	60.35 W
Kāmāreddi	122	18.19 N	78.21 E
Kāmārhāti	272b	22.40 N	88.22 E
Kamarik	130	39.37 N	39.18 E
Kāmārkhāli Ghāt	126	23.32 N	89.33 E
Kāmārkunda	272b	22.49 N	88.13 E
Kamaryn	78	51.26 N	30.31 E
Kamas	200	40.38 N	111.16 W
Kamata ◆ [8]	268	35.33 N	139.43 E
Kamatsi Lake ⊜	184	56.10 N	102.15 W
Kamay	196	33.51 N	98.48 W
Kamba	150	11.53 N	3.36 E
Kamba Kota	152	7.10 N	17.54 E
Kambalda	162	31.12 S	121.40 E
Kambam	122	9.44 N	77.18 E
Kambang	112	1.42 S	100.42 E
Kambanga	152	13.23 S	23.03 E
Kambar	120	27.36 N	68.00 E
Kambara	94	35.07 N	138.36 E
Kambara Island I	175g	18.57 S	178.57 W
Kambara-tunnel ◆ [5]	94	35.02 N	138.31 E
Kambarka	80	56.17 N	54.12 E
Kambia	150	9.07 N	12.55 W
Kambja	76	58.14 N	26.42 E
Kambolé	150	8.45 N	1.36 E
Kambole Mission	154	8.46 S	30.46 E
Kambove	154	10.52 S	26.38 E
Kambu	115b	8.23 S	118.20 E
Kambuye	152	7.18 S	22.50 E
Kamčatka ≃	74	56.15 N	162.30 E
Kamčatka, poluostrov (Kamchatka) › [1]	74	56.00 N	160.00 E
Kamčatskij poluostrov › [1]	74	56.15 N	163.00 E
Kamčatskij zaliv c	74	55.35 N	162.21 E
Kamchatka → Kamčatka, poluostrov › [1]	74	56.00 N	160.00 E
Kâmchay Méa	110	11.35 N	105.40 E
Kamčija ≃	38	43.02 N	27.53 E
Kāmdebpur, India	272b	22.47 N	88.30 E
Kāmdebpur, India	272b	22.54 N	88.20 E
Kāmdeysh	123	35.24 N	71.20 E
Kameari ◆ [8]	268	35.46 N	139.51 E
Kameda	92	37.52 N	139.07 E
Kameel	158	26.38 S	24.58 E
Kamegamori ∧	96	33.47 N	133.12 E
Kameido ◆ [8]	268	35.42 N	139.50 E
Kamelik ≃	80	52.06 N	49.30 E
Kamen', Bela.	76	55.01 N	28.53 E
Kamen, Dtsch.	52	51.35 N	7.40 E
Kamen', gora ∧	74	69.06 N	94.48 E
Kamenda	154	6.28 S	24.33 E
Kameng ≃	120	26.38 N	92.54 E
Kamenický Šenov	54	50.45 N	14.29 E
Kamenjak, Rt ›	36	44.46 N	13.55 E
Kamenka, Kaz.	80	51.07 N	50.19 E
Kamenka, Kaz.	85	42.55 N	72.50 E
Kamenka, Kaz.	86	52.22 N	69.04 E
Kamenka, Ross.	24	65.54 N	44.05 E
Kamenka, Ross.	78	50.43 N	39.25 E
Kamenka, Ross.	80	56.11 N	45.35 E
Kamenka, Ross.	80	57.23 N	41.49 E
Kamenka, Ross.	80	53.13 N	44.03 E
Kamenka, Ross.	80	52.04 N	41.49 E
Kamenka, Ross.	82	54.43 N	38.19 E
Kamenka, Ross.	82	56.11 N	37.18 E
Kamenka, Ross.	82	55.13 N	36.59 E
Kamenka, Ross.	86	58.33 N	95.51 E
Kamenka, Ross.	89	44.28 N	136.01 E
Kamenka, Ross.	265a	59.59 N	30.53 E
Kamenka ◆ [8]	265a	60.03 N	30.11 E
Kamenka ≃, Ross.	83	47.30 N	38.54 E
Kamenka ≃, Ross.	88	58.33 N	95.51 E
Kamenka ≃, Ross.	265a	60.01 N	30.12 E
Kamen'-na-Obi	86	53.47 N	81.20 E
Kamennogorsk	24	60.58 N	29.07 E
Kamennomostskij	84	44.18 N	40.12 E
Kamennyj Brod	83	47.26 N	39.51 E
Kamennyj Jar	80	48.27 N	45.34 E
Kamenolomni	83	47.40 N	40.13 E
Kamen'-Rybolov	89	44.46 N	132.02 E
Kamensk	88	51.58 N	106.36 E
Kamenskij	80	50.53 N	45.29 E
Kamenskoje, Ross.	74	62.30 N	166.12 E
Kamenskoje, Ross.	82	55.16 N	36.50 E
Kamensk-Šachtinskij	83	48.21 N	40.19 E
Kamensk-Ural'skij	86	56.28 N	61.54 E
Kamenz	54	51.16 N	14.06 E
Kameoka	96	35.00 N	135.35 E
Kamerik	52	52.06 N	4.54 E
Kamern	54	52.45 N	12.07 E
Kamerun → Cameroon □ [1]	134	6.00 N	12.00 E
Kamerunberg → Cameroon Mountain ∧	152	4.12 N	9.11 E
Kames	46	55.54 N	5.15 W
Kameškovo	80	56.21 N	41.00 E
Kāmet ∧	120	30.54 N	79.37 E
Kameur, Bahr ≃	146	9.26 N	20.50 E
Kameyama	94	34.51 N	136.27 E
Kami, Nihon	94	34.41 N	137.42 E
Kami, Nihon	96	35.05 N	134.53 E
Kamiah	202	46.13 N	116.01 W
Kamiak Butte ∧	202	46.52 N	117.10 W
Kamiakotani	270	34.56 N	135.23 E

Symbol	English	Deutsch	Español	Français	Português
≃	River	Fluß	Río	Rivière	Rio
≅	Canal	Kanal	Canal	Canal	Canal
∟	Waterfall, Rapids	Wasserfall, Stromschnellen	Cascada, Rápidos	Chute d'eau, Rapides	Cascata, Rápidos
ʊ	Strait	Meeresstraße	Estrecho	Détroit	Estreito
c	Bay, Gulf	Bucht, Golf	Bahía, Golfo	Baie, Golfe	Baía, Golfo
⊜	Lake, Lakes	See, Seen	Lago, Lagos	Lac, Lacs	Lago, Lagos
≡	Swamp	Sumpf	Pantano	Marais	Pântano
⊓	Ice Features, Glacier	Eis- und Gletscherformen	Accidentes Glaciales	Formes glaciaires	Acidentes glaciares
⊤	Other Hydrographic Features	Andere Hydrographische Objekte	Otros Elementos Hidrográficos	Autres données hydrographiques	Outros acidentes hidrográficos

Symbol	English	Deutsch	Español	Français	Português
✦	Submarine Features	Untermeerische Objekte	Accidentes Submarinos	Formes de relief sous-marin	Acidentes submarinos
□	Political Unit	Politische Einheit	Unidad Politica	Entité politique	Unidade política
ʋ	Cultural Institution	Kulturelle Institution	Institución Cultural	Institution culturelle	Instituição cultural
⊥	Historical Site	Historische Stätte	Sitio Histórico	Site historique	Sitio histórico
♠	Recreational Site	Erholungs- und Ferienort	Sitio de Recreo	Centre de loisirs	Area de Lazer
⊠	Airport	Flughafen	Aeropuerto	Aéroport	Aeroporto
■	Military Installation	Militäranlage	Instalación Militar	Installation militaire	Instalação militar
◆	Miscellaneous	Verschiedenes	Misceláneo	Divers	Diversos

Name	Page	Lat.°'	Long.°'	Name	Seite	Breite°'	Länge°' E = Ost

Symbols in the index entries represent the broad categories identified in the key at the right. Symbols with superior numbers (⋀¹) identify subcategories (see complete key on page *I · 1*).

Symbole im Register stellen die rechts im Schlüssel erklärten Kategorien dar. Symbole mit hochgestellten Ziffern (⋀¹) bezeichnen Unterteilungen einer Kategorie (vgl. vollständiger Schlüssel auf Seite *I · 1*).

Los símbolos incluidos en el texto del índice representan las grandes categorías identificadas con la clave a la derecha. Los símbolos con números en su parte superior (⋀¹) identifican las subcategorías (véase la clave completa en la página *I · 1*).

Les symboles de l'index représentent les grandes catégories indiquées dans la légende à droite. Les symboles suivis d'un indice (⋀¹) représentent des sous-catégories (voir légende complète à la page *I · 1*).

Os símbolos incluídos no texto do índice representam as grandes categorias identificadas com a chave à direita. Os símbolos com números em sua parte superior (⋀¹) identificam as subcategorias (veja-se a chave completa na página *I · 1*).

	English	Deutsch	Español	Français	Português
⋀	Mountain	Berg	Montaña	Montagne	Montanha
⋀	Mountains	Gebirge	Montañas	Montagnes	Montanhas
⨯	Pass	Paß	Paso	Col	Passo
V	Valley, Canyon	Tal, Cañon	Valle, Cañón	Vallée, Canyon	Vale, Canhão
⇌	Plain	Ebene	Llano	Plaine	Planície
⊁	Cape	Kap	Cabo	Cap	Cabo
I	Island	Insel	Isla	Île	Ilha
II	Islands	Inseln	Islas	Îles	Ilhas
⋀	Other Topographic Features	Andere Topographische Objekte	Otros Elementos Topográficos	Autres données topographiques	Outros acidentes topográficos

ESPAÑOL

Nombre	Página	Lat.°′	Long.°′ W = Oeste
Karaunk'ur ≃	85	40.54 N	72.20 E
Karaurğan	130	40.15 N	42.17 E
Karauzak	86	42.59 N	60.02 E
Karauzek	80	47.15 N	48.25 E
Karavan	85	41.30 N	71.45 E
Karavannoje, Ross.	80	45.59 N	47.08 E
Karavannoje, Ross.	80	57.47 N	47.41 E
Karave	272c	19.01 N	73.01 E
Karawa	152	3.20 N	20.18 E
Karawang	115a	6.19 S	107.17 E
Karawang, Tanjung ›	115a	5.56 S	107.00 E
Karawanken ⋏	36	46.30 N	14.25 E
Karayaka	130	40.45 N	36.37 E
Karayashnyk	83	49.22 N	39.10 E
Karayazı	130	39.41 N	42.08 E
Karaye	150	11.48 N	8.02 E
Karayün	130	39.41 N	37.19 E
Karažal	86	48.02 N	70.49 E
Karbalā'	128	32.36 N	44.02 E
Karbalā' □[4]	128	32.00 N	42.15 E
Karbenning	40	60.02 N	16.04 E
Kårberg	40	58.58 N	14.57 E
Karbeyaz	130	36.02 N	36.12 E
Kårböle	26	61.59 N	15.19 E
Karby	40	59.34 N	18.13 E
Karcag	30	47.19 N	20.56 E
Karczew	30	52.06 N	21.15 E
Kardail ≃	80	50.43 N	42.54 E
Kardašova Řečice	61	49.11 N	14.53 E
Kardeljevo	36	43.04 N	17.26 E
Kardhámaina	38	36.47 N	27.09 E
Kardhámila	38	38.32 N	26.05 E
Kardhítsa	38	39.21 N	21.55 E
Kärdla	76	59.00 N	22.45 E
Kardymovo	76	54.54 N	32.26 E
Kărdžali	38	41.39 N	25.22 E
Kardžin	84	43.16 N	44.16 E
Karea	272b	22.42 N	88.33 E
Kareeberge ⋏	158	30.53 S	21.57 E
Kareedouw	158	33.57 S	24.18 E
Kareli	84	42.01 N	43.54 E
Karelia → Karelija □[3]	24	64.00 N	32.30 E
Karelia □[9]	24	63.00 N	32.00 E
Karèličy	76	53.34 N	26.08 E
Karelija □[3], Ross.	24	64.00 N	32.30 E
Karelija □[3], Ross.	72	64.00 N	32.30 E
Karel'skij Gorodok	76	58.04 N	36.30 E
Karema, Pap. N. Gui.	164	9.12 S	147.14 E
Karema, Tan.	154	6.49 S	30.26 E
Karen	110	12.51 N	92.53 E
Karenga ≃	88	54.28 N	116.32 E
Karepino	24	61.02 N	57.02 E
Karera	272a	28.41 N	77.23 E
Karesuando	24	68.25 N	22.30 E
Kärevere	76	58.26 N	26.29 E
Kāreyz-e Elyās	128	35.25 N	61.20 E
Kargali	80	55.12 N	50.54 E
Kargalinskaja	84	43.44 N	46.30 E
Karganaj	180	65.21 N	175.25 E
Kargapazarı Dağları ⋏	130	40.07 N	41.35 E
Kargapolje	86	55.57 N	64.27 E
Kargasok	86	59.07 N	80.53 E
Kargat	86	55.10 N	80.17 E
Kargat ≃	86	54.37 N	78.12 E
Kargı	130	41.08 N	34.30 E
Kargil	123	34.34 N	76.06 E
Karginskaja	80	49.21 N	41.38 E
Karginskij ≃	265a	59.50 N	30.01 E
Kargopol'	24	61.30 N	38.58 E
Karguéri	146	13.27 N	10.25 E
Karhal	124	27.01 N	78.57 E
Karhijärvi ⊜	26	61.35 N	22.30 E
Karhula	26	60.31 N	26.57 E
Kari	146	11.14 N	10.34 E
Karia-ba-Mohammed	148	34.19 N	5.10 W
Kariaí	38	40.16 N	24.15 E
Karianga	157b	22.22 S	47.26 E
Kariba	154	16.30 S	28.45 E
Kariba, Lake ⊜[1]	154	17.00 S	28.00 E
Karibib	156	21.58 S	15.51 E
Karibisches Meer → Caribbean Sea ⊤[2]	230	15.00 N	73.00 W
Karibumba	154	0.22 N	29.22 E
Kariega ≃	158	33.03 S	23.28 E
Karigasniemi	24	69.24 N	25.50 E
Karikari, Cape ›	172	34.47 S	173.24 E
Karimata	175d	24.54 N	125.17 E
Karimata, Kepulauan II	112	1.25 S	109.05 E
Karimata, Pulau I	112	1.36 S	108.55 E
Karimata, Selat (Karimata Strait) ɰ	112	2.05 S	108.40 E
Karīmganj	120	24.52 N	92.21 E
Karīmnagar	122	18.26 N	79.09 E
Karīmpur	126	23.58 N	88.37 E
Karimun, Pulau I	114	1.03 N	103.22 E
Karimunjawa, Kepulauan II	115a	5.50 S	110.25 E
Karimunjawa, Pulau I	115a	5.51 S	110.27 E
Karin, Som.	144	10.59 N	49.13 E
Karin, Som.	144	10.51 N	45.47 E
Karino	82	54.42 N	38.56 E
Karin Seamount ✢[3]	14	17.55 N	168.58 W
Karinskoje	82	55.42 N	36.41 E
Karintorf	80	58.33 N	50.11 E
Karis (Karjaa)	26	60.05 N	23.40 E
Karise	41	55.18 N	12.13 E
Karisimbi, Volcan ∧[1]	154	1.30 S	29.27 E
Káristos	38	38.00 N	24.24 E
Kariya	94	34.59 N	136.59 E
Kariye Museum ʊ[1]	267b	41.01 N	28.55 E
Kārīz	128	34.49 N	60.47 E
Karjaa → Karis	26	60.05 N	23.40 E
Karjepolje	24	65.34 N	43.40 E
Kārkal	122	13.12 N	74.59 E
Karkalaj	80	57.00 N	52.24 E
Karkaralinsk	86	49.23 N	75.21 E
Karkar Dūmān ⬥[8]	272a	28.39 N	77.18 E
Karkar Island I	164	4.40 S	146.00 E
Karkas, Kūh-e ∧	128	33.29 N	51.50 E
Karkheh ≃	128	31.46 N	47.55 E
Karkīndar	128	25.47 N	59.15 E
Karkinits'ka zatoka ⊂	78	45.55 N	33.00 E
Karkkila	26	60.32 N	24.11 E
Karkku	26	61.25 N	23.01 E
Karkom, Har ∧	132	30.17 N	34.44 E
Karkonoski Park Narodowy ♦	30	50.45 N	15.35 E
Kärla	76	58.20 N	22.15 E
Karlholmsbruk	40	60.31 N	17.35 E
Karlik Shan ∧	102	43.08 N	94.20 E
Karlino	30	54.03 N	15.51 E
Karlıova	130	39.18 N	41.01 E
Karlivka	78	49.27 N	35.08 E
Karl-Marx-Stadt → Chemnitz	54	50.50 N	12.55 E
Karlobag	36	44.32 N	15.05 E
Karlo-Marksove	83	48.16 N	38.09 E
Karloske ≃	184	55.41 N	93.56 W
Karlovac	36	45.29 N	15.34 E
Karlovo	38	42.38 N	24.48 E
Karlovy Vary (Carlsbad)	54	50.11 N	12.52 E
Karlsbad → Karlovy Vary, Česká Rep.	54	50.11 N	12.52 E
Karlsbad, Dtsch.	56	48.55 N	8.30 E
Karlsborg, Sve.	26	58.32 N	14.31 E
Karlsborg, Sve.	26	65.48 N	23.17 E
Karlsburg, Dtsch.	54	53.58 N	13.37 E
Karlsburg → Alba Iulia, Rom.	38	46.04 N	23.35 E
Karlsby	40	58.38 N	15.08 E
Karlsfeld	60	48.13 N	11.28 E
Karlshagen	54	54.07 N	13.50 E
Karlshamn	26	56.10 N	14.51 E
Karlshorst ⬥[8]	264a	52.29 N	13.32 E

FRANÇAIS

Nom	Page	Lat.°′	Long.°′ W = Ouest
Karlshorst, Trabrennbahn ♦	264a	52.29 N	13.31 E
Karlshuld	60	48.41 N	11.18 E
Karlskoga	40	59.20 N	14.31 E
Karlskron	60	48.41 N	11.25 E
Karlskrona	26	56.10 N	15.35 E
Karlslunde Strand	41	55.34 N	12.14 E
Karlsöarna II	26	57.17 N	17.58 E
Karlsruhe	56	49.03 N	8.24 E
Karlsruhe □[5], Dtsch.	56	49.20 N	8.45 E
Karlsruhe □[5], Dtsch.	58	48.30 N	8.30 E
Karlstad, Sve.	40	59.22 N	13.30 E
Karlstad, Mn., U.S.	198	48.34 N	96.31 W
Karlstadt	56	49.57 N	9.45 E
Karlstift	61	48.35 N	14.45 E
Karluk, Ross.	88	53.27 N	105.58 E
Karluk, Ak., U.S.	180	57.34 N	154.28 W
Karl'uk, Uzb.	85	38.12 N	67.42 E
Karma, Bela.	76	53.08 N	30.48 E
Karma, Bela.	76	52.21 N	31.31 E
Karma, Niger	150	13.40 N	1.49 E
Karma, Ouadi V	146	15.38 N	20.01 E
Karmah	140	19.38 N	30.25 E
Karmāla	122	18.25 N	75.12 E
Karmanovka	80	49.24 N	50.22 E
Karmanovo	76	55.52 N	34.52 E
Karmansbo	40	59.42 N	15.44 E
Karmatānr	126	24.05 N	86.42 E
Karmel, Har (Mount Carmel) ∧	132	32.44 N	35.02 E
Karmi'el	132	32.55 N	35.18 E
Karmiyya	132	31.36 N	34.33 E
Karmøy I	26	59.15 N	5.15 E
Karnack	194	32.40 N	94.10 W
Karnak → Al-Karnak, Miṣr	140	25.43 N	32.39 E
Karnak, Il., U.S.	194	37.17 N	88.58 W
Karnāl	124	29.41 N	76.59 E
Karnāla Fort ⊥	272c	18.53 N	73.07 E
Karṇālī □[8]	124	29.30 N	82.30 E
Karṇālī ≃	124	28.15 N	81.05 E
Karnap ⬥[8]	263	51.31 N	7.01 E
Karnaphuli Reservoir ⊜[1]	120	22.42 N	92.12 E
Karnātaka □[3]	122	14.00 N	76.00 E
Karnaukhivka	78	48.28 N	34.44 E
Karnes □[6]	222	29.00 N	97.47 W
Karnes City	196	28.53 N	97.54 W
Karni	150	10.40 N	2.37 W
Karniki	82	54.12 N	38.05 E
Karnische Alpen (Alpi Carniche) ⋏	64	46.40 N	13.00 E
Karnobat	38	42.39 N	26.59 E
Karns City	214	41.00 N	79.44 W
Kärnten □[3]	30	46.50 N	13.50 E
Karnzow	54	52.59 N	12.26 E
Karoi	154	16.50 S	29.40 E
Karokh	128	34.28 N	62.35 E
Karoli	124	22.55 N	79.04 E
Karolinenhof ⬥[8]	264a	52.23 N	13.38 E
Karomatan	116	7.46 N	123.44 E
Karompa Lompo, Pulau I	112	7.15 S	121.45 E
Karon	126	24.07 N	86.44 E
Karonga	154	9.56 S	33.56 E
Karonie	162	30.58 S	122.32 E
Karoonda	166	35.06 S	139.54 E
Karor	123	31.13 N	70.57 E
Karora	140	17.42 N	38.22 E
Karos	158	28.24 S	21.35 E
Káros I	38	36.53 N	25.39 E
Karosa	112	1.48 S	119.20 E
Karoso, Tanjung ›	115b	9.33 S	118.50 E
Karotho Post	154	5.11 N	35.50 E
Karou	150	15.07 N	0.39 E
Karow, Dtsch.	54	52.20 N	12.15 E
Karow, Dtsch.	54	53.32 N	12.15 E
Karow ⬥[8]	264a	52.37 N	13.29 E
Karpathen → Carpathian Mountains ⋏	22	48.00 N	24.00 E
Kárpathos, Ellás	38	35.30 N	27.14 E
Kárpathos, Ellás	130	35.31 N	27.12 E
Kárpathos I	38	35.40 N	27.10 E
Karpats'kyy Pryrodnyy Natsional'nyy Park ♦	78	48.25 N	24.30 E
Karpenísion	38	38.55 N	21.40 E
Karpinsk	86	59.45 N	60.01 E
Karpivka	83	49.10 N	37.43 E
Karpogory	24	64.00 N	44.24 E
Karpovo, Ross.	76	60.02 N	36.43 E
Karpovo, Ross.	82	55.35 N	38.34 E
Karpunicha	80	57.42 N	45.20 E
Karpuninskij	86	58.43 N	61.50 E
Karpuzlu	130	37.33 N	27.50 E
Karratha	162	20.44 S	116.51 E
Karrats Fjord ⊂[2]	176	71.20 N	54.00 W
Karrebæksminde	41	55.11 N	11.40 E
Karres	58	47.13 N	10.47 E
Kärrgruvan	40	60.05 N	15.56 E
Karridale	162	34.13 S	115.05 E
Kars	84	40.36 N	43.05 E
Kars □[4]	84	40.35 N	43.00 E
Kars ≃	84	40.37 N	43.41 E
Karša	80	49.48 N	51.27 E
Karsakpaj	86	47.49 N	66.41 E
Karsakuwigamak Lake ⊜	184	56.22 N	99.30 W
Kärsämäki	26	63.58 N	25.46 E
Karsantı	130	37.33 N	35.24 E
Kārsava	76	56.47 N	27.40 E
Karsdorf	54	51.17 N	11.39 E
Karši	128	38.53 N	65.48 E
Karsin	30	53.54 N	17.56 E
Karšinskaja step' ≚	128	39.10 N	65.00 E
Karskije Vorota, proliv ɰ	72	70.30 N	58.00 E
Karskoje more (Kara Sea) ⊤[2]	72	76.00 N	80.00 E
Karsovaj	80	58.14 N	53.11 E
Karst → Kras ⋏[1]	64	45.48 N	14.00 E
Kårsta, Sve.	40	59.39 N	18.14 E
Kärsta, Sve.	40	59.40 N	16.49 E
Karstädt	54	53.09 N	11.44 E
Karstula	26	62.52 N	24.47 E
Karsun	80	54.11 N	46.59 E
Kartajol'	24	64.32 N	53.14 E
Kartala ∧	157a	11.45 S	43.22 E
Kartaly	86	53.03 N	60.40 E
Kartārpur	123	31.27 N	75.30 E
Karthaus	214	41.07 N	78.07 W
Kartlijskij chrebet ⋏	84	42.10 N	44.55 E
Kartosuro	115a	7.33 S	110.44 E
Karttula	26	62.53 N	26.58 E
Kartuzy	30	54.20 N	18.12 E
Kartzow	54	52.29 N	12.58 E
Käru	76	58.50 N	25.11 E
Karuah ≃	170	32.39 S	151.58 E
Karufa	164	3.50 S	133.27 E
Karuizawa	94	36.21 N	138.38 E
Karukuwisa	156	18.56 S	19.40 E
Karumai	92	40.19 N	141.28 E
Karumba	166	17.29 S	140.50 E
Kārūn ≃	128	30.26 N	48.10 E
Karungi	26	66.03 N	23.57 E
Karungu	154	0.51 S	34.09 E
Karuni	115b	9.26 S	119.19 E
Karunjie	164	16.18 S	127.12 E
Karunki	26	66.02 N	24.01 E
Karup	41	56.18 N	9.10 E
Karup ≃	41	56.18 N	9.10 E
Karūr	122	10.57 N	78.05 E
Karuscia, Punta ›	70	36.49 N	11.59 E
Karvala	265a	59.41 N	30.09 E
Karviná	30	49.50 N	18.30 E
Kārwār	122	14.48 N	74.08 E
Karwendel ⋏	64	47.27 N	11.20 E

PORTUGUÊS

Nome	Página	Lat.°′	Long.°′ W = Oeste
Karwi	124	25.12 N	80.54 E
Karym	86	60.07 N	66.41 E
Karymskoje, Ross.	88	51.37 N	114.21 E
Karymskoje, Ross.	88	54.07 N	101.49 E
Karza	86	58.35 N	80.50 E
Karzachi	84	41.15 N	43.16 E
Kas, Sūd.	140	12.30 N	24.17 E
Kaş, Tür.	130	36.12 N	29.38 E
Kas ≃	86	59.40 N	90.00 E
Kasaan	182	55.32 N	132.24 W
Kasabi	152	14.48 S	23.42 E
Kasach ≃	84	40.03 N	43.52 E
Kasadi ≃	272c	19.01 N	73.03 E
Kasa-do I	98	34.28 N	126.03 E
Kasado-shima I	96	33.57 N	131.51 E
Kasagi	94	34.45 N	135.56 E
Kasagi-sanchi ⋏	270	34.37 N	135.56 E
Kasagi-yama ∧	94	35.31 N	137.21 E
Kasahara	94	35.17 N	137.09 E
Kasahata	268	35.54 N	139.25 E
Kasai	96	34.56 N	134.50 E
Kasai ⬥[3]	268	35.39 N	139.53 E
Kasai (Cassai) ≃, Afr.	152	3.02 S	16.57 E
Kāsai ≃, India	124	22.09 N	87.50 E
Kasai-Occidental □[4]	152	5.30 S	21.40 E
Kasai-Oriental □[4]	152	4.00 S	23.30 E
Kasaji	152	10.22 S	23.27 E
Kasakake	94	36.23 N	139.17 E
Kasama, Nihon	94	36.23 N	140.16 E
Kasama, Zam.	154	10.13 S	31.12 E
Kasamatsu	94	35.22 N	136.46 E
Kasan → Kazan', Ross.	80	55.49 N	49.08 E
Kasan, Uzb.	128	39.02 N	65.35 E
Kasan-dong	98	41.18 N	126.55 E
Kasane	156	17.50 S	25.05 E
Kasanga	154	8.28 S	31.09 E
Kasangale	152	6.20 S	22.42 E
Kasangeshi ≃	152	8.24 S	21.56 E
Kasangulu	152	4.36 S	15.10 E
Kasanka National Park ♦	154	12.35 S	30.12 E
Kasano-misaki ›	94	36.21 N	136.18 E
Kasansaj	85	41.15 N	71.32 E
Kasansaj ≃	85	40.57 N	71.30 E
Kasaoka	96	34.30 N	133.30 E
Kāsaragod	122	12.30 N	75.00 E
Kasari ≃	76	58.45 N	23.49 E
Kašary	78	49.03 N	41.00 E
Kasatori-yama ∧, Nihon	94	34.44 N	136.18 E
Kasatori-yama ∧, Nihon	96	33.33 N	132.55 E
Kasauli	123	30.55 N	76.57 E
Kasba	124	25.51 N	87.33 E
Kasbagoas	126	24.11 N	88.30 E
Kasba Kamarda	126	21.46 N	87.21 E
Kasba Lake ⊜	176	60.18 N	102.07 W
Kasba Mirgoda	126	21.42 N	87.28 E
Kasba Nārāyangarh	126	22.10 N	87.23 E
Kasba Patāspur	126	22.02 N	87.32 E
Kasba-Tadla	148	32.34 N	6.18 W
Kaschau → Košice	30	48.43 N	21.15 E
Kascjukouka	76	52.32 N	30.56 E
Kascjukovičy	76	53.20 N	32.03 E
Kåseberga	26	55.23 N	14.04 E
Kaseda	92	31.25 N	130.19 E
Kasempa	154	13.27 S	25.50 E
Kasenga	154	10.22 S	28.38 E
Kasenyi	154	1.24 N	30.26 E
Kasese, Ug.	154	0.10 N	30.05 E
Kasese, R.D.C.	154	1.38 S	27.07 E
Kaset Sombun	110	16.17 N	101.57 E
Kasfareet Military Base ■	142	30.15 N	32.24 E
Kāsganj	124	27.49 N	78.39 E
Kashabowie Lake ⊜	190	48.42 N	90.25 W
Kashaf ≃	128	35.58 N	61.07 E
Kashagawigamog Lake ⊜	212	44.59 N	78.37 W
Kāshān	128	33.59 N	51.29 E
Kashasha	154	1.44 S	31.37 E
Kashegelok	180	60.50 N	157.50 W
Kashgar → Kashi	85	39.29 N	75.59 E
Kashi	85	39.29 N	75.59 E
Kashiba	96	34.33 N	135.42 E
Kashihara	96	34.30 N	135.46 E
Kashiji Plain ≚	152	13.20 S	22.30 E
Kashileshi ≃	152	9.46 S	23.05 E
Kashima, Nihon	92	33.07 N	130.06 E
Kashima, Nihon	94	35.58 N	140.38 E
Kashima, Nihon	94	36.58 N	136.55 E
Kashima, Nihon	96	35.30 N	133.01 E
Kashima-jingū ʊ[1]	94	35.59 N	140.40 E
Kashima-nada ⊤[2]	94	36.15 N	140.45 E
Kashima-Yariga-take ∧	94	36.37 N	137.45 E
Kashimo	94	35.43 N	137.23 E
Kāshināthpur	126	23.58 N	89.37 E
Kashing → Jiaxing	106	30.46 N	120.45 E
Kashio ⬥[8]	268	35.25 N	139.33 E
Kāshīpur, India	124	29.13 N	78.57 E
Kāshipur, India	126	23.26 N	86.40 E
Kashitu	154	13.42 S	28.40 E
Kashiwa	94	35.52 N	139.59 E
Kashiwara	96	34.35 N	135.37 E
Kashiwazaki, Nihon	92	37.22 N	138.33 E
Kashiwazaki, Nihon	268	35.56 N	139.42 E
Kashlahach ≃	83	47.45 N	37.16 E
Kāshmar	128	35.12 N	58.27 E
Kashmir → Jammu and Kashmīr □[2]	120	34.00 N	76.00 E
Kashmir, Vale of V	123	34.00 N	75.00 E
Kashmor	120	28.26 N	69.35 E
Kashmūnd Ghar ⋏	123	34.42 N	70.31 E
Kashperivka	78	49.26 N	29.41 E
Kashunuk ≃	180	61.18 N	165.36 W
Kashwakamak Lake ⊜	212	44.50 N	77.04 W
Kasia	124	26.45 N	83.55 E
Kāsiāni	126	23.14 N	89.45 E
Kāsiāri	126	22.08 N	87.14 E
Kasidiji ≃	152	7.57 S	23.12 E
Kasigau ∧	154	3.50 S	38.40 E
Kasigluk	180	60.52 N	162.32 W
Kasilof	180	60.24 N	151.18 W
Kasilovo	78	50.38 N	35.37 E
Kasimbar	112	0.09 S	120.00 E
Kasimov	80	54.56 N	41.24 E
Kāsimpur, Bngl.	126	23.59 N	90.19 E
Kāsimpur, India	272b	22.46 N	88.31 E
Kašin	76	57.21 N	37.37 E
Kāsināthpur	272b	22.35 N	88.31 E
Kasinge	154	6.20 S	26.59 E
Kasinka	156	18.13 S	24.22 E
Kāsipur	272b	22.25 N	88.10 E
Kašira	82	54.51 N	38.10 E
Kaširka ≃	82	54.52 N	38.13 E
Kasiruta, Pulau I	108	0.25 S	127.12 E
Kasiui, Pulau I	164	4.30 S	131.40 E
Kasiwa → Kashiwa	94	35.52 N	139.59 E
Kaskabulak	86	49.34 N	79.52 E
Kaškadarja □[8]	128	39.00 N	66.00 E
Kaskaden-Kette → Cascade Range ⋏	202	45.00 N	121.30 W
Kaskana	85	40.45 N	69.36 E
Kaskaskia ≃	194	37.59 N	89.56 W
Kaskaskia, East Fork ≃	219	38.43 N	89.09 W
Kaskaskia, North Fork ≃	219	38.46 N	89.09 W
Kaskattama ≃	176	57.03 N	90.07 W
Kaskelen	85	43.12 N	76.37 E
Kaskelen ≃	85	43.53 N	77.08 E

Kaskinen → Kaskö	26	62.23 N	21.13 E
Kaskö (Kaskinen)	26	62.23 N	21.13 E
Kaslātu ∧	124	23.58 N	84.54 E
Kasli	86	55.53 N	60.46 E
Kaslo	182	49.55 N	116.55 W
Kasn'a	76	55.24 N	34.20 E
Kasn'a ≃	76	55.51 N	34.25 E
Kaso ≃	115a	7.25 S	106.40 E
Kasongo	154	4.27 S	26.40 E
Kasongo-Lunda	152	6.28 S	16.49 E
Kásos I	38	35.22 N	26.56 E
Kasota	190	44.18 N	93.57 W
Kaspi	84	41.57 N	44.25 E
Kaspijsk	84	42.52 N	47.38 E
Kaspijskij	22	45.22 N	47.24 E
Kaspijskoje more → Caspian Sea ⊤[2]	72	42.00 N	50.30 E
Kaspische Senke → Prikaspijskaja nizmennost' ≚	80	48.00 N	52.00 E
Kaspisches Meer → Caspian Sea ⊤[2]	72	42.00 N	50.30 E
Kaspl'a	76	55.00 N	31.38 E
Kaspl'a ≃	76	55.24 N	30.43 E
Kasr, Ra's ›	140	18.02 N	38.35 E
Kasrik	130	38.13 N	41.54 E
Kassa → Košice	30	48.43 N	21.15 E
Kassab	130	35.56 N	35.59 E
Kassai → Cassai (Kasai) ≃	152	3.02 S	16.57 E
Kassalā	140	15.28 N	36.24 E
Kassalā □[4]	140	15.00 N	35.00 E
Kassándra ›[1]	38	40.06 N	23.22 E
Kassándras, Kólpos ⊂	38	40.06 N	23.30 E
Kassel	56	51.19 N	9.29 E
Kassel □[5]	56	51.10 N	9.20 E
Kasserine	148	35.11 N	8.48 E
Kasshabog Lake ⊜	212	44.38 N	77.58 W
Kassikaityu ≃	246	1.49 N	58.32 W
Kassinger	140	18.45 N	31.54 E
Kassîr, Sabkhat al- ⊜	130	35.03 N	41.07 E
Kasslerfeld ⬥[8]	263	51.26 N	6.45 E
Kasson	190	44.01 N	92.45 W
Kassou	150	11.35 N	2.03 W
Kassoum	150	13.05 N	3.18 W
Kastamonu	130	41.22 N	33.47 E
Kastamonu □[4]	130	41.40 N	33.45 E
Kastanéai	38	41.38 N	26.28 E
Kastelholm	26	60.14 N	20.04 E
Kastellaun	56	50.04 N	7.26 E
Kasterlee	56	51.15 N	4.57 E
Kastiyu, Puntan ›	174n	14.57 N	145.40 E
Kastl, Dtsch.	60	49.50 N	11.54 E
Kastl, Dtsch.	60	49.22 N	11.42 E
Kastorf	52	53.44 N	10.34 E
Kastoría	38	40.31 N	21.15 E
Kastorías, Límni ⊜	38	40.30 N	21.17 E
Kastornoje	78	51.50 N	38.06 E
Kastrávion, Tekhnití Límni ⊜[1]	38	38.50 N	21.20 E
Kastrup Lufthavn ⊠	41	55.38 N	12.39 E
Kasuga, Nihon	94	35.28 N	136.29 E
Kasuga, Nihon	96	33.32 N	130.27 E
Kasuga, Nihon	96	35.10 N	135.06 E
Kasugai, Nihon	94	35.14 N	136.58 E
Kasugai, Nihon	94	35.39 N	138.39 E
Kasuga-kōkūkichi, Kaijō-jieitai- ■	96	33.31 N	130.28 E
Kasuga Shrine ʊ[1]	270	34.41 N	135.51 E
Kasuka	158	33.40 S	26.41 E
Kasukabe	94	35.58 N	139.45 E
Kasukawa	94	36.24 N	139.13 E
Kasulu	154	4.34 S	30.06 E
Kasumi	96	35.38 N	134.38 E
Kasumiga-ura ⊜	94	36.00 N	140.25 E
Kasumkent	84	41.41 N	48.07 E
Kasungan	112	1.58 S	113.24 E
Kasungu	154	13.01 S	33.30 E
Kasungu National Park ♦	154	12.55 S	33.15 E
Kasupe	154	15.10 S	35.15 E
Kasūr	123	31.07 N	74.27 E
Kaszuby ⬥[1]	30	54.10 N	18.15 E
Kata	88	58.46 N	102.40 E
Kataba	154	16.05 S	25.10 E
Kataeregi	150	9.22 N	6.17 E
Katagum	146	12.17 N	10.21 E
Katahdin, Mount ∧	188	45.55 N	68.55 W
Katai	272c	19.10 N	73.05 E
Katajevo	88	50.57 N	108.41 E
Katajsk	86	56.18 N	62.35 E
Katako-Kombe	152	3.24 S	24.25 E
Katakura	270	34.29 N	135.31 E
Katakwi	154	1.55 N	33.57 E
Katale	154	4.59 S	31.03 E
Katalla	180	60.12 N	144.31 W
Katanda	154	0.50 S	29.22 E
Katanga □[9]	138	10.00 S	26.00 E
Katanga ≃	74	60.08 N	102.13 E
Katangi	124	23.27 N	79.47 E
Katanglad Mountains ⋏	116	8.06 N	124.54 E
Katangli	89	51.42 N	143.14 E
Katanimara	126	22.17 N	87.11 E
Katanning	162	33.42 S	117.33 E
Katano	270	34.47 N	135.40 E
Katano-hana ›	174f	24.49 N	141.20 E
Katanti	154	2.18 S	27.08 E
Kataoka	270	35.03 N	135.58 E
Katapakishi	152	8.15 S	22.49 E
Katar → Qatar □[1]	128	25.00 N	51.10 E
Katara, Depresión de → Qaṭṭārah, Munkhafaḍ al- ⍊[7]	140	30.00 N	27.30 E
Katârniān Ghāt	124	28.20 N	81.09 E
Katase	268	35.19 N	139.29 E
Katashina	94	36.46 N	139.14 E
Katašin	76	52.36 N	32.10 E
Katav-Ivanovsk	86	54.45 N	58.12 E
Katayama	268	35.46 N	139.34 E
Katchall Island I	110	7.57 N	93.22 E
Katchewanooka Lake ⊜	212	44.27 N	78.16 W
Katchin-wan ⊂	174m	26.18 N	127.53 E
Katchirga	150	14.03 N	0.06 E
Katchiungo	152	12.35 S	16.13 E
Kateel ≃	180	65.28 N	157.35 W
Katélé	150	10.38 N	5.37 W
Katena-wan ⊂	174m	26.50 N	128.05 E
Katepwa Beach	184	50.42 N	103.38 W
Katerbow	54	52.59 N	12.39 E
Kateríni	38	40.16 N	22.30 E
Katerloch ⍊[5]	61	47.16 N	15.32 E
Katernberg ⬥[8], Dtsch.	263	51.16 N	7.06 E
Katernberg ⬥[8], Dtsch.	263	51.29 N	7.04 E
Katerynopil'	78	48.56 N	30.59 E
Katesbridge	48	54.18 N	6.08 W
Kates Needle ∧	180	57.03 N	132.03 W
Katešovo	82	54.08 N	37.00 E
Katete, Malaŵi	154	12.17 S	33.39 E
Katete, Zam.	154	14.05 S	32.07 E
Katex	84	41.39 N	46.34 E
Katghora	124	22.30 N	82.33 E
Katha	110	24.11 N	96.21 E
Kathangor, Jabal ∧	140	5.45 N	33.59 E
Katherine	164	14.28 S	132.16 E
Katherine ≃	164	14.39 S	131.42 E
Katherine Creek ≃	166	23.48 S	143.42 E
Katherine Gorge National Park ♦	164	14.10 S	132.30 E
Kāthgodām	124	29.16 N	79.32 E
Kāthiāwār Peninsula ›[1]	120	22.00 N	71.00 E
Kathīb, Ra's ›	144	14.55 N	42.53 E
Kathla	123	31.59 N	76.47 E
Kathleen	220	28.07 N	82.01 W
Kathleen Valley	162	27.23 S	120.38 E
Kathlow	54	51.43 N	14.29 E
Kāṭhmāṇḍau	124	27.43 N	85.19 E
Kathmandu → Kāṭhmāṇḍau	124	27.43 N	85.19 E
Kathor	120	21.18 N	72.56 E
Kathrabbā	132	31.08 N	35.37 E
Kathua	123	32.22 N	75.31 E
Kāthuli	126	23.52 N	88.40 E
Kati	150	12.44 N	8.04 W
Kātiādi	126	24.15 N	90.48 E
Katibas ≃	112	2.01 N	112.33 E
Katihār	124	25.32 N	87.35 E
Katikati	172	37.33 S	175.55 E
Katima Mulilo	152	17.30 S	24.16 E
Katimik Lake ⊜	184	52.54 N	99.22 W
Katiola	150	8.08 N	5.06 W
Katipunan	116	8.31 N	123.17 E
Katiti Aboriginal Land Reserve ⬥[4]	162	25.10 S	131.15 E
Kātlang	123	34.22 N	72.05 E
Katlehong	273d	26.19 S	28.09 E
Katlenburg-Duhm	52	51.41 N	10.06 E
Katmai, Mount ∧	180	58.17 N	154.56 W
Katmai National Park ♦	180	58.30 N	155.00 W
Katmandu → Kāṭhmāṇḍau	124	27.43 N	85.19 E
Katni → Murwāra, India	124	23.51 N	80.24 E
Katni, Ross.	80	57.59 N	47.46 E
Káto Akhaïa	38	38.09 N	21.32 E
Kātol	120	21.16 N	78.35 E
Katompi	154	6.11 S	26.20 E
Katonah	210	41.16 N	73.41 W
Katonga ≃	154	0.34 N	31.50 E
Katon-Karagaj	86	49.11 N	85.37 E
Katoomba	170	33.42 S	150.18 E
Katopa	154	2.45 S	25.06 E
Katori-jingū ʊ[1]	94	35.52 N	140.30 E
Katoúna	38	38.47 N	21.07 E
Katovice	60	49.16 N	13.49 E
Katowice	30	50.16 N	19.00 E
Katowice □[4]	30	50.15 N	19.00 E
Katra	123	32.59 N	74.57 E
Kātrās	126	23.48 N	86.17 E
Katričev	80	49.23 N	45.33 E
Kātrīnā, Jabal ∧	140	28.31 N	33.57 E
Katrine, Loch ⊜	46	56.15 N	4.31 W
Katrineholm	40	59.00 N	16.12 E
Katsch, Golf von → Kachchh, Gulf of ⊂	120	22.36 N	69.30 E
Katschbach ≃	61	47.08 N	14.17 E
Katschberg)(	64	47.03 N	13.37 E
Katsepe	157b	15.45 S	46.15 E
Katshungu	154	2.27 S	27.23 E
Katsina	150	13.00 N	7.32 E
Katsina Ala	150	7.10 N	9.17 E
Katsina Ala ≃	152	7.48 N	8.52 E
Katsunuma	94	35.39 N	138.44 E
Katsura ⬥[8]	270	34.59 N	135.42 E
Katsura ≃, Nihon	94	35.36 N	139.15 E
Katsura ≃, Nihon	94	34.53 N	135.42 E
Katsura ≃, Nihon	96	34.02 N	134.35 E
Katsura ≃, Nihon	270	34.53 N	135.42 E
Katsuragi	96	34.15 N	135.30 E
Katsuragi-san ∧	96	34.20 N	135.27 E
Katsushika ⬥[8]	268	35.43 N	139.51 E
Katsuta, Nihon	94	36.24 N	140.30 E
Katsuta, Nihon	96	35.04 N	134.11 E
Katsuura, Nihon	94	35.08 N	140.18 E
Katsuura, Nihon	96	33.56 N	134.30 E
Katsuyama, Nihon	94	36.03 N	136.30 E
Katsuyama, Nihon	96	35.05 N	133.41 E
Kattakurgan	72	39.55 N	66.15 E
Kattara-Senke → Qaṭṭārah, Munkhafaḍ al- ⍊[7]	140	30.00 N	27.30 E
Kattarp	41	56.09 N	12.46 E
Katta-Taldyk	85	40.19 N	73.12 E
Kattaviá	38	35.57 N	27.46 E
Kattegat ɰ	26	57.00 N	11.00 E
Katternberg ⬥[8]	263	51.09 N	7.02 E
Katthammarsvik	26	57.26 N	18.50 E
Kattowitz → Katowice	30	50.16 N	19.00 E
Kattrup	41	55.57 N	9.56 E
Kāttuputtūr	122	10.59 N	78.14 E
Katul, Jabal ∧	140	14.16 N	29.23 E
Katuma	154	6.10 S	30.34 E
Katumba	154	7.45 S	25.18 E
Katun' ≃	86	52.25 N	85.05 E
Katunino	80	58.01 N	45.39 E
Katunki	80	56.50 N	43.14 E
Kātūria	124	24.44 N	86.43 E
Katu Shan ∧	86	45.40 N	82.55 E
Katusice	54	50.26 N	14.50 E
Kātwa	126	23.39 N	88.08 E
Katwijk aan de Rijn	52	52.11 N	4.26 E
Katwijk aan Zee	52	52.13 N	4.24 E
Katy	222	29.47 N	95.49 W
Katyn	76	54.47 N	31.44 E
Kąty Wrocławskie	30	51.02 N	16.46 E
Katzenbuckel ∧	56	49.28 N	9.02 E
Katzenelnbogen	56	50.17 N	7.59 E
Katzhütte	54	50.33 N	11.03 E
Kaua ≃	156	19.24 S	22.03 E
Kauai □[6]	229b	21.59 N	159.22 W
Kauai I	229b	22.00 N	159.30 W
Kauai Channel ɰ	229b	21.45 N	158.50 W
Kaub	56	50.05 N	7.46 E
Kau Desert ⬥[2]	229d	19.21 N	155.19 W
Kaufbeuren	58	47.53 N	10.37 E
Kaufering	58	48.05 N	10.52 E
Kaufman	222	32.35 N	96.18 W
Kaufman □[6]	222	32.38 N	96.18 W
Kaufungen	56	51.17 N	9.38 E
Kaugama	150	12.28 N	9.44 E
Kauhajoki	26	62.26 N	22.11 E
Kauhanevan-Pohjankankaan kansallispuisto ♦	26	62.08 N	22.25 E
Kauhava	26	63.06 N	23.05 E
Kauiki Head ›	229a	20.45 N	155.59 W
Kaukapakapa	172	36.37 S	174.30 E
Kaukasus → Caucasus ⋏	84	42.30 N	45.00 E
Kaukauna	190	44.16 N	88.16 W
Kaukau Veld ⋏[1]	156	19.30 S	20.30 E
Kaukhāli	126	22.38 N	90.04 E
Kaukura I[1]	14	15.45 S	146.42 W
Kaula I	229d	21.45 N	160.30 W
Kaulakahi Channel ɰ	229b	22.00 N	159.53 W
Kaulille	56	51.11 N	5.31 E
Kauliranta	24	66.27 N	23.41 E
Kaŭl-li	98	37.58 N	124.37 E
Kaulsdorf	54	50.37 N	11.26 E
Kaulsdorf ⬥[8]	264a	52.31 N	13.33 E
Kaulsdorf-Süd ⬥[8]	264a	52.29 N	13.34 E
Kaumakani	229b	21.55 N	159.37 W
Kaumalapau	229a	20.47 N	156.59 W
Kaunakakai	229a	21.05 N	157.01 W
Kaunas	76	54.54 N	23.54 E
Kauneonga Lake	210	41.41 N	74.50 W
Kauner Tal V	64	47.01 N	10.44 E
Kaunghein	110	25.40 N	95.26 E
Kauniainen → Grankulla	26	60.13 N	24.45 E
Kaununui ›	229b	21.56 N	160.10 W
Kaup	164	3.50 S	144.00 E
Kaupanger	26	61.11 N	7.14 E
Kaura Namoda	150	12.35 N	6.35 E
Kauriyāla Ghāt	124	28.23 N	81.02 E
Kauru	150	10.33 N	8.12 E
Kausa	272c	19.10 N	73.02 E
Kau Sai Chau I	271d	22.22 N	114.18 E
Kausala	26	60.54 N	26.22 E
Kaustinen	26	63.32 N	23.42 E
Kauswagan	116	8.11 N	124.05 E
Kautokeino	24	69.00 N	23.02 E
Kauttua	26	61.06 N	22.10 E
Kau-ye Kyun I	110	11.01 N	98.32 E
Kavača	74	60.16 N	169.51 E
Kavacık	130	39.40 N	28.30 E
Kavadarci	38	41.26 N	22.00 E
Kavajë	38	41.11 N	19.33 E
Kavak, Tür.	130	38.24 N	39.26 E
Kavak, Tür.	130	41.05 N	36.03 E
Kavak, Tür.	130	39.18 N	37.30 E
Kavakbaşı	130	38.29 N	41.49 E
Kavaklıdere	130	37.26 N	28.22 E
Kavála	38	40.56 N	24.25 E
Kavalerovo	89	44.15 N	135.04 E
Kāvali	122	14.55 N	79.59 E
Kavaratti	122	10.34 N	72.39 E
Kavaratti Island I	122	10.33 N	72.38 E
Kavarna	38	43.25 N	28.20 E
Kavendou, Mont ∧	150	10.41 N	12.12 W
Kāveri ≃	122	11.09 N	79.52 E
Kāveri Falls ∟	122	12.18 N	77.17 E
Kaverino, Ross.	80	54.10 N	41.47 E
Kaverino, Ross.	82	56.11 N	36.15 E
Kavieng	164	2.35 S	150.50 E
Kavimba	156	18.02 S	24.33 E
Kavīr, Dasht-e ⬥[2]	128	34.40 N	54.30 E
Kavkazskij zapovednik ♦	84	43.55 N	40.30 E
Kävlinge	41	55.48 N	13.06 E
Kävlingeån ≃	41	55.47 N	13.06 E
Kavungo	152	11.31 S	23.03 E
Kavuu ≃	154	7.40 S	31.46 E
Kavykuči-Gazimurskije	88	51.22 N	118.10 E
Kaw, Guy. fr.	250	4.29 N	52.02 W
Kaw, Ok., U.S.	196	36.46 N	96.50 W
Kawa	110	17.05 N	96.28 E
Kawaba	94	36.41 N	139.07 E
Kawabe, Nihon	94	35.29 N	137.04 E
Kawabe, Nihon	96	33.55 N	135.11 E
Kawachi, Nihon	94	35.53 N	140.15 E
Kawachi, Nihon	94	36.24 N	136.38 E
Kawachi, Nihon	94	36.37 N	139.56 E
Kawachi-nagano	96	34.27 N	135.34 E
Kawagama Lake ⊜	212	45.18 N	78.45 W
Kawage	94	34.47 N	136.33 E
Kawagoe	94	35.55 N	139.29 E
Kawaguchi	94	35.48 N	139.43 E
Kawaguchiko	94	35.30 N	138.46 E
Kawaguchi-ko ⊜	94	35.31 N	138.45 E
Kawahara	96	35.24 N	134.12 E
Kawai, Nihon	94	36.18 N	137.07 E
Kawai, Nihon	270	34.35 N	135.45 E
Kawaihae Bay ⊂	229d	20.02 N	155.50 W
Kawaihoa ›	229b	21.47 N	160.12 W
Kawaikini ∧	229b	22.05 N	159.29 W
Kawailoa	229c	21.36 N	158.05 W
Kawailoa Beach	229c	21.37 N	158.04 W
Kawajiri	96	34.14 N	132.42 E
Kawakami, Nihon	94	35.58 N	138.35 E
Kawakami, Nihon	96	34.44 N	133.29 E
Kawakami, Nihon	96	35.17 N	133.39 E
Kawakawa	172	35.23 S	174.04 E
Kawakubo	270	34.54 N	135.38 E
Kawali	115a	7.11 S	108.22 E
Kawama Mission	154	10.04 S	28.37 E
Kawamata	92	37.39 N	140.36 E
Kawambwa	154	9.47 S	29.05 E
Kawamoto, Nihon	94	36.09 N	139.17 E
Kawamoto, Nihon	96	34.59 N	132.30 E
Kawane	94	34.57 N	138.05 E
Kawanishi, Nihon	94	37.09 N	138.45 E
Kawanishi, Nihon	96	34.49 N	135.24 E
Kawanishi, Nihon	270	34.35 N	135.47 E
Kawanoe	96	34.01 N	133.34 E
Kawara, Nihon	96	33.40 N	130.51 E
Kawara, Nihon	270	34.59 N	135.18 E
Kawara Débé	150	12.20 N	3.26 E
Kawarai	268	35.25 N	140.05 E
Kawardha	124	22.01 N	81.15 E
Kawartha Park	212	44.32 N	78.12 W
Kawasaki, Nihon	94	35.32 N	139.43 E
Kawasaki, Nihon	96	33.35 N	130.49 E
Kawasaki-kō ⊂	268	35.30 N	139.47 E
Kawasaki Stadium ♦	268	35.32 N	139.43 E
Kawashima, Nihon	94	35.21 N	136.50 E
Kawashima, Nihon	94	35.59 N	139.30 E
Kawashima, Nihon	96	34.04 N	134.19 E
Kawashima ⬥[8]	268	35.28 N	139.35 E
Kawashiri-misaki ›	96	34.26 N	130.58 E
Kawatana	92	33.04 N	129.52 E
Kawauchi	96	33.48 N	132.55 E
Kawau Island I	172	36.25 S	174.51 E
Kawawa ⬥[8]	268	35.31 N	139.33 E
Kawayan	116	11.41 N	124.21 E
Kawazu	94	34.44 N	138.59 E
Kawbein	110	16.33 N	97.52 E
Kawdut	110	15.31 N	97.47 E
Kawe	164	7.50 S	138.14 E
Kawe, Pulau I	164	0.03 S	130.07 E
Kaweenakumik Lake ⊜	184	52.52 N	99.30 W
Kaweka ∧	172	39.17 S	176.23 E
Kaweka Range ⋏	172	39.15 S	176.20 E
Kawerau	172	38.03 S	176.43 E
Kawhia	172	38.04 S	174.49 E
Kawhia Harbour ⊂	172	38.05 S	174.50 E
Kawich Peak ∧	204	37.58 N	116.27 W
Kawich Range ⋏	204	37.40 N	116.30 W
Kawin	164	2.45 S	150.45 E
Kawinda	115b	8.07 S	118.04 E
Kawit	269f	14.27 N	120.54 E
Kawkabān	144	15.40 N	43.52 E
Kawkareik	110	16.33 N	98.14 E
Kaw Lake ⊜[1]	196	36.55 N	96.57 W
Kawludo	110	18.29 N	97.19 E
Kawm	140	13.31 N	22.50 E
Kawm al-Farā'in (Buto) ⊥	142	31.11 N	30.45 E
Kawm ar-Rāhib	142	28.20 N	30.37 E
Kawm Birah	273c	30.05 N	31.08 E
Kawm Dafanah (Daphnæ) ⊥	142	30.52 N	32.11 E
Kawm Ḥamādah	142	30.46 N	30.42 E
Kawm Ishfīn	273c	30.11 N	31.15 E
Kawm Ishū	142	31.07 N	30.00 E
Kawm Ju'ayf (Naucratis) ⊥	142	30.54 N	30.36 E
Kawm Umbū	140	24.28 N	32.57 E
Kawnglanghpu	102	27.04 N	98.21 E
Kawnipi Lake ⊜	190	48.24 N	91.14 W
Kawthaung	110	9.59 N	98.33 E
Kax ≃	86	43.40 N	81.45 E
Kaxgar ≃	85	39.40 N	78.00 E
Kaya, Burkina	150	13.05 N	1.05 W
Kaya, Nihon	96	35.30 N	135.06 E
Kayaapu	112	5.26 S	102.24 E
Kayadibi, Tür.	130	39.29 N	36.43 E
Kayadibi, Tür.	130	39.55 N	34.15 E
Kayah □[3]	110	19.15 N	97.30 E
Kayak Island I	180	59.52 N	144.30 W
Kāyalpattinam	122	8.34 N	78.07 E
Kāyamba	272b	22.41 N	88.32 E
Kayambi	154	9.27 S	31.58 E
Kayan	110	16.54 N	96.34 E
Kayan ≃	112	2.55 N	117.35 E
Kayangel Islands II	108	8.04 N	134.43 E
Kayang-san ∧[2]	271b	37.33 N	126.43 E
Kāyankulam	122	9.11 N	76.30 E
Kayapa	116	16.22 N	120.53 E
Kayapınar	130	37.34 N	41.10 E
Kayaş	130	39.56 N	32.58 E
Kaya-san ∧	98	35.49 N	128.07 E
Kaya-san Kukrip Kongwŏn ♦	98	35.47 N	128.06 E
Kaycee	200	43.42 N	106.38 W
Kayeli	164	3.23 S	127.06 E

≃	River	Fluß	Río	Rivière	Rio
≍	Canal	Kanal	Canal	Canal	Canal
∟	Waterfall, Rapids	Wasserfall, Stromschnellen	Cascada, Rápidos	Chute d'eau, Rapides	Cascata, Rápidos
ɰ	Strait	Meeresstraße	Estrecho	Détroit	Estreito
⊂	Bay, Gulf	Bucht, Golf	Bahía, Golfo	Baie, Golfe	Baía, Golfo
⊜	Lake, Lakes	See, Seen	Lago, Lagos	Lac, Lacs	Lago, Lagos
≚	Swamp	Sumpf	Pantano	Marais	Pântano
⩩	Ice Features, Glacier	Eis- und Gletscherformen	Accidentes Glaciales	Formes glaciaires	Acidentes glaciares
⊤	Other Hydrographic Features	Andere Hydrographische Objekte	Otros Elementos Hicrográficos	Autres données hydrographiques	Outros acidentes hidrográficos

✢	Submarine Features	Untermeerische Objekte	Accidentes Submarinos	Formes de relief sous-marin	Acidentes submarinos
□	Political Unit	Politische Einheit	Unidad Politica	Entité politique	Unidade política
ʊ	Cultural Institution	Kulturelle Institution	Institución Cultural	Institution culturelle	Instituição cultural
⊥	Historical Site	Historische Stätte	Sitio Histórico	Site historique	Sitio histórico
♦	Recreational Site	Erholungs- und Ferienort	Sitio de Recreo	Centre de loisirs	Area de Lazer
⊠	Airport	Flughafen	Aeropuerto	Aéroport	Aeroporto
■	Military Installation	Militäranlage	Instalación Militar	Installation militaire	Instalação militar
⬥	Miscellaneous	Verschiedenes	Misceláneo	Divers	Diversos

Symbols in the index entries represent the broad categories identified in the key at the right. Symbols with superior numbers (⋏¹) identify subcategories (see complete key on page *I · 1*).

Symbole im Register stellen die rechts im Schlüssel erklärten Kategorien dar. Symbole mit hochgestellten Ziffern (⋏¹) bezeichnen Unterabteilungen einer Kategorie (vgl. vollständiger Schlüssel auf Seite *I · 1*).

Los símbolos incluídos en el texto del índice representan las grandes categorías identificadas con la clave a la derecha. Los símbolos con numeros en su parte superior (⋏¹) identifican las subcategorías (véase la clave completa en la página *I · 1*).

Les symboles de l'index représentent les catégories indiquées dans la légende à droite. Les symboles suivis d'un indice (⋏¹) représentent des sous-catégories (voir légende complète à la page *I · 1*).

Os símbolos incluídos no texto do índice representam as grandes categorias identificadas com a chave à direita. Os símbolos com números em sua parte superior (⋏¹) identificam as subcategorias (veja-se a chave completa à página *I · 1*).

⋏ Mountain	Berg	Montaña	Montagne	Montanha
⋏ Mountains	Gebirge	Montañas	Montagnes	Montanhas
⋊ Pass	Paß	Paso	Col	Passo
ᴸ Valley, Canyon	Tal, Cañon	Valle, Cañón	Vallée, Canyon	Vale, Canhão
⌓ Plain	Ebene	Llano	Plaine	Planície
› Cape	Kap	Cabo	Cap	Cabo
I Island	Insel	Isla	Île	Ilha
II Islands	Inseln	Islas	Îles	Ilhas
⋨ Other Topographic Features	Andere Topographische Objekte	Otros Elementos Topográficos	Autres données topographiques	Outros acidentes topográficos

ESPAÑOL				FRANÇAIS				PORTUGUÊS			
Nombre	Página	Lat.°′	Long.°′ W=Oeste	Nom	Page	Lat.°′	Long.°′ W=Ouest	Nome	Página	Lat.°′	Long.°′ W=Oeste

ESPAÑOL			
Keszthely	30	46.46 N	17.15 E
Ket' ≃	86	58.55 N	81.32 E
Keta	150	5.55 N	1.00 E
Keta ≃	94	34.56 N	137.50 E
Keta, ozero ⊜	74	68.44 N	90.00 E
Ketaka	96	35.30 N	134.03 E
Keta Lagoon ⊂	150	5.54 N	0.56 E
Ketam, Pulau I	271c	1.24 N	103.57 E
Ketama	34	34.40 N	4.37 W
Ketang	100	22.58 N	115.28 E
Ketapang, Indon.	112	1.52 S	109.59 E
Ketapang, Indon.	115a	6.54 S	113.17 E
Ketapang, Indon.	115a	5.44 S	105.48 E
Ketaun	112	3.23 S	101.49 E
Ketčenery	80	47.18 N	44.31 E
Ketchikan	182	55.21 N	131.35 W
Ketchum	202	43.40 N	114.21 W
Kete Krachi	150	7.46 N	0.03 W
Ketelmeer ⊜	52	52.35 N	5.45 E
Keti Bandar	120	24.08 N	67.27 E
Ketingwan ⋏	154	0.40 N	35.50 E
Ketoj, ostrov I	74	47.20 N	152.28 E
Ketovo	86	55.21 N	65.18 E
Ketrzyn (Rastenburg)	30	54.06 N	21.23 E
Ketsch	56	49.22 N	8.31 E
Ketta	152	1.28 N	15.56 E
Kettering, Eng., U.K.	42	52.24 N	0.44 W
Kettering, Md., U.S.	284c	38.53 N	76.49 W
Kettering, Oh., U.S.	218	39.41 N	84.10 W
Kettinge	41	54.42 N	11.45 E
Kettle ≃, Mb., Can.	184	56.23 N	94.34 W
Kettle ≃, N.A.	182	48.42 N	118.07 W
Kettle ≃, Wn., U.S.	190	45.52 N	92.45 W
Kettle Creek ≃, On., Can.	212	42.40 N	81.13 W
Kettle Creek ≃, Pa., U.S.	210	41.18 N	77.51 W
Kettle Creek State Park ♦	214	41.23 N	77.56 W
Kettle Falls	202	48.36 N	118.03 W
Kettleman City	226	36.00 N	119.57 W
Kettleman Hills ⋏²	226	36.00 N	120.00 W
Kettle Rapids Dam ⌷⁶	184	56.23 N	94.38 W
Kettlesville	216	40.22 N	84.16 W
Kettleshulme	262	53.19 N	2.01 W
Kettlewell	44	54.09 N	2.02 W
Kettwig	56	51.22 N	6.56 E
Kęty	30	49.53 N	19.13 E
Ketzin	54	52.28 N	12.50 E
Keudemane	114	5.15 N	96.55 E
Keudepasi	114	4.18 N	95.56 E
Keudeteunom	114	4.27 N	95.48 E
Keudeunga	114	5.01 N	95.22 E
Keuka Lake ⊜	210	42.27 N	77.10 W
Keuka Lake, West Branch ⊂	210	42.33 N	77.09 W
Keuka Park	210	42.37 N	77.06 W
Keukenhof ♦	52	52.16 N	4.33 E
Keul' ≃	88	58.25 N	102.49 E
Keula	54	51.20 N	10.31 E
Keum ≃	86	59.32 N	70.35 E
Keurboomsrivier	158	34.00 S	23.24 E
Keurusselkä ⊜	26	62.16 N	24.40 E
Keuruu	26	62.16 N	24.42 E
Kevdo-Mel'sitovo	80	53.09 N	43.54 E
Kevelaer	52	51.35 N	6.15 E
Kevin	202	48.44 N	111.57 W
Kevsala	80	45.48 N	42.41 E
Kew, Austl.	169	37.49 S	145.02 E
Kew, T./C. Is.	238	21.54 N	72.02 W
Kewanee	190	41.14 N	89.55 W
Kewanna	216	41.01 N	86.25 W
Kewaunee	190	44.27 N	87.30 W
Keweenaw Bay ⊂	190	46.56 N	88.23 W
Keweenaw Peninsula ⋏¹	190	47.12 N	88.25 W
Keweenaw Point ⊁	190	47.30 N	87.50 W
Kew Gardens ♦, Can.	275b	43.40 N	79.18 W
Kew Gardens ♦, Eng., U.K.	260	51.28 N	0.18 W
Key, Lough ⊜	48	54.00 N	8.15 W
Keyala	154	4.27 N	32.52 E
Keyangkeer Shan ⋏	124	31.20 N	87.13 E
Keya Paha ≃	198	42.54 N	99.00 W
Key Biscayne	226	37.33 N	120.54 W
Keyes, Ca., U.S.	226	37.33 N	120.54 W
Keyes, Ok., U.S.	196	36.48 N	102.15 W
Keyesport	219	38.44 N	89.17 W
Keyhole Reservoir ⊜¹	198	44.29 N	104.48 W
Keyhole State Park ♦	198	44.19 N	104.48 W
Keyihe	89	50.40 N	122.27 E
Keyingham	44	53.42 N	0.07 W
Key Largo	220	25.04 N	80.29 W
Key Largo I	220	25.16 N	80.19 W
Keymer	42	50.55 N	0.08 W
Keynes Hill ⋏²	168b	34.37 S	139.06 E
Keyneton	168b	34.34 S	139.08 E
Keynsham	42	51.26 N	2.30 W
Keynshamburg	154	19.15 S	29.39 E
Keyport, N.J., U.S.	276	40.25 N	74.12 W
Keyport, Wa., U.S.	224	47.42 N	122.38 W
Keyport Harbor ⊂	276	40.26 N	74.12 W
Keysborough	169	38.00 S	145.10 E
Keysbrook	168a	32.26 S	115.59 E
Keyser	188	39.26 N	78.58 W
Keystone, In., U.S.	216	40.36 N	85.16 W
Keystone, Ia., U.S.	190	41.59 N	92.11 W
Keystone, S.D., U.S.	198	43.53 N	103.25 W
Keystone, W.V., U.S.	192	37.24 N	81.27 W
Keystone Lake ⊜¹, Ok., U.S.	196	36.15 N	96.25 W
Keystone Lake ⊜¹, Pa., U.S.	214	40.44 N	79.15 W
Keystone Peak ⋏	200	31.53 N	111.13 W
Keystone State Park ♦	214	40.23 N	79.24 W
Keysville, Fl., U.S.	220	27.52 N	82.06 W
Keysville, Va., U.S.	192	37.02 N	78.29 W
Keytesville	194	39.26 N	92.56 W
Key West	220	24.33 N	81.46 W
Key West Island I	220	24.33 N	81.46 W
Key West Naval Air Station ⋇	220	24.34 N	81.41 W
Keyworth	42	52.52 N	1.05 W
Kez	80	57.53 N	53.43 E
Kezi	154	20.58 S	28.32 E
Kezilesu Zizhizhou ⌷⁸	100	40.00 N	75.30 E
Kežma	88	58.59 N	101.09 E
Kežmarok	30	49.08 N	20.25 E
Kgalagadi ⌷⁵	156	25.00 S	22.00 E
Kgatleng ⌷⁵	156	24.28 S	26.05 E
Kgokgole ≃	158	26.44 S	22.28 E
Kgun Lake ⊜	180	61.32 N	163.45 W
Khaanzir, Ras ⊁	132	33.00 N	36.16 E
Khabab	132	33.00 N	36.16 E
Khabb, Kūh-e ⋏	128	28.48 N	56.26 E
Khābūr, Nahr al- (Habur) ≃	130	35.08 N	40.26 E
Khādar	272a	28.33 N	77.22 E
Khadari, Wādī al- ∨	140	10.29 N	26.15 E
Khadaungnge Taung ⋏	110	18.57 N	94.37 E
Khadki (Kirkee)	122	18.34 N	73.52 E
Khadra	34	36.15 N	0.35 E
Khadzhybeys'ky lyman ⊂	78	46.39 N	30.33 E
Khafūrī, Wādī ∨	124	30.50 N	86.29 E
Khagaria	124	25.30 N	86.29 E
Khagdon ≃	126	22.09 N	90.05 E
Khagrāmuri	126	22.19 N	90.10 E
Khaidhárion	267c	38.01 N	23.38 E
Khairābād	124	27.57 N	77.50 E
Khairagarh	124	27.32 N	80.45 E
Khairbani	126	22.14 N	87.05 E
Khairna	272c	19.06 N	73.01 E
Khairpur, Pāk.	120	27.32 N	68.46 E

FRANÇAIS			
Khairpur, Pāk.	123	29.35 N	72.14 E
Khairwāra	120	23.59 N	73.35 E
Khajrāho	120	24.50 N	79.58 E
Khajuri	126	21.52 N	87.58 E
Khajuri ⊶⁸	272a	28.43 N	77.16 E
Khakassia — Chakasija ⌷³	86	53.00 N	90.00 E
Kha Khaeng ≃	110	14.55 N	99.07 E
Khakhea	156	24.51 S	23.20 E
Khalándrion	267c	38.01 N	23.48 E
Khalatse	123	34.20 N	76.49 E
Khālidī, Khirbat al- ⋏	132	29.39 N	35.14 E
Khalkhāl	128	37.37 N	48.32 E
Khalkhalah	132	33.04 N	36.32 E
Khálki I	38	36.17 N	27.35 E
Khalkidhikí ⌷⁹	38	40.25 N	23.27 E
Khalkís	38	38.28 N	23.36 E
Khālsar	120	34.31 N	77.41 E
Khalturyne	78	49.31 N	35.17 E
Khambhāliya	120	22.12 N	69.39 E
Khambhāt	120	22.18 N	72.37 E
Khambhāt, Gulf of ⊂	120	21.00 N	72.30 E
Khāmgaon	122	20.41 N	76.34 E
Khamir	144	16.05 N	43.55 E
Khāmis, Ash-Shailāl al- (Fifth Cataract) ⊾	144	18.23 N	33.47 E
Khamīs Mushayt	144	18.18 N	42.44 E
Khamkeut	110	18.15 N	104.43 E
Khamma	70	36.47 N	12.02 E
Khammam	122	17.15 N	80.09 E
Khamsah	142	30.25 N	32.23 E
Khan ≃, Lao	110	19.54 N	102.09 E
Khan ≃, Namibia	156	22.37 S	14.56 E
Khāna	126	23.20 N	87.44 E
Khānābād	120	36.41 N	69.07 E
Khān Abū Shāmāt	132	33.40 N	36.54 E
Khānakul	126	22.43 N	87.51 E
Khān al-Baghdādī	128	33.51 N	42.33 E
Khānaqin	128	34.21 N	45.22 E
Khān Arnabah	132	33.11 N	35.53 E
Khancoban	171b	36.12 S	148.05 E
Khandaghosh	126	23.13 N	87.41 E
Khandela	120	27.36 N	75.30 E
Khandwa	124	21.50 N	76.20 E
Khāne-e Chahār Bāgh, Afg.	120	35.58 N	69.38 E
Khān-e Chahār Bāgh, Afg.	128	37.00 N	65.14 E
Khānewāl	123	30.18 N	71.56 E
Khāngāh Dogrān	123	31.50 N	73.37 E
Khāngarh, Pāk.	120	28.22 N	71.43 E
Khāngarh, Pāk.	123	29.55 N	71.10 E
Khangkhai	110	19.28 N	103.15 E
Khania	38	35.31 N	24.02 E
Khanion, Kólpos ⊂	38	35.34 N	23.48 E
Khanka	126	22.00 N	87.25 E
Khanna, Qā' ≃	132	32.04 N	36.26 E
Khanozai	120	30.37 N	67.19 E
Khānpur, India	272b	22.40 N	88.16 E
Khānpur, Pāk.	123	28.39 N	70.39 E
Khānpur ⊶⁸, India	272a	28.34 N	77.01 E
Khānpur ⊶⁸, India	272a	28.31 N	77.14 E
Khān Shaykhūn	130	35.26 N	36.39 E
Khanty-Mansiysk — Chanty-Mansijsk	74	61.00 N	69.06 E
Khān Yūnus	132	31.21 N	34.19 E
Khao Laem Reservoir ⊜¹	110	14.50 N	98.30 E
Khao Saming	110	12.21 N	102.27 E
Khao Sok National Park ♦	110	8.55 N	98.35 E
Khao Yoi	110	13.14 N	99.50 E
Khapalu	123	35.10 N	76.20 E
Kharab, Ghoubet al ⊂	144	11.30 N	42.35 E
Kharabā	132	32.45 N	36.23 E
Kharagdiha	124	24.25 N	86.10 E
Kharagpur, India	124	25.07 N	86.33 E
Kharagpur, India	126	22.20 N	87.20 E
Kharak	123	33.07 N	71.06 E
Khārān	120	28.35 N	65.25 E
Kharānoq	128	32.54 N	54.39 E
Kharar, India	123	30.45 N	76.39 E
Kharar, India	126	22.42 N	87.41 E
Kharāvli ⋏²	272c	18.54 N	72.55 E
Kharbyij, Sabkhat al- ≃	130	35.40 N	37.20 E
Kharaz, Jabal ⋏	144	12.44 N	44.09 E
Kharbatā	132	31.57 N	35.04 E
Kharbine — Harbin	89	45.45 N	126.41 E
Khardah	126	22.44 N	88.22 E
Kharghar	272c	19.03 N	73.04 E
Kharg Island — Khārk, Jazīreh-ye I	128	29.15 N	50.20 E
Khargon	120	21.49 N	75.36 E
Khārān Cantonment	123	32.49 N	73.52 E
Khariar Road	122	20.54 N	82.31 E
Khārijah, Al-Wāhāt al- ⋏⁴	140	25.20 N	30.35 E
Khārīm, Jabal ⋏	132	30.17 N	33.58 E
Khāravli ⋏²	144	24.26 N	33.03 E
Khārk, Jazīreh-ye (Kharg Island) I	128	29.15 N	50.20 E
Khārki (Kharkov)	78	50.00 N	36.15 E
Khárkov — Kharkiv	78	49.30 N	36.30 E
Kharmān, Kūh-e ⋏	78	50.00 N	36.15 E
Kharri	272b	22.55 N	88.14 E
Kharsāwān	124	22.48 N	85.50 E
Kharta	124	21.58 N	83.07 E
Khartoum — Al-Khartūm	140	15.36 N	32.32 E
Khartoum North — Al-Khartūm Bahrī	140	15.38 N	32.33 E
Khartsyz'k	83	48.02 N	38.09 E
Khartum — Al-Khartūm	140	15.36 N	32.32 E
Kharumawa	154	3.12 S	32.39 E
Khasbāti	272b	22.55 N	88.25 E
Khasebake	156	20.41 S	24.29 E
Khāsh, Afg.	128	31.31 N	62.52 E
Khāsh, Īrān	128	28.13 N	61.14 E
Khāsh ≃	128	31.11 N	62.05 E
Khāsh, Dasht-e ⋏²	128	31.50 N	62.30 E
Khashab, Jabal al- ⋏²	142	29.56 N	31.01 E
Khashm al-Qirbah	140	14.58 N	35.55 E
Khashm al-Qirbah, Khazzān ⌷¹	140	14.40 N	35.55 E
Khashshab, Tur'at al- ≃	273c	29.53 N	31.17 E
Khashum	140	12.27 N	28.02 E
Khāş Konar	120	34.39 N	70.54 E
Khaskovo	38	41.56 N	25.33 E
Khataulī — Haskovo	124	29.17 N	77.43 E
Khātegaon	124	22.36 N	76.55 E
Khātra	126	22.59 N	86.51 E
Khatt, Oued al ∨	148	26.45 N	13.03 W
Khāvda	123	33.51 N	69.43 E
Khawrah	144	14.00 N	48.29 E
Khawsa	110	15.40 N	97.50 E
Khayāla ⋏⁸	272a	28.40 N	77.06 E
Khaybar, Harrat ⋏⁸	144	25.30 N	39.45 E
Khayerpur	272b	22.35 N	88.33 E
Khayrli, Kūh-e al- ⋏¹	142	30.33 N	32.28 E
Khayra Bil ⋏²	272b	22.52 N	88.29 E
Khayrasole	126	23.48 N	87.16 E
Kheardaha	272b	22.42 N	88.22 E
Khe Bo	110	19.08 N	104.41 E

PORTUGUÊS			
Khed	122	17.43 N	73.23 E
Khefapur	272a	28.30 N	77.05 E
Khejurdaha	272b	22.59 N	88.10 E
Khemis	148	36.16 N	2.13 E
Khemis el Khechna	34	36.39 N	3.20 E
Khemisset	148	33.50 N	6.03 W
Khemisset ⌷⁴	148	33.50 N	6.05 W
Khem Karan	123	31.09 N	74.34 E
Khemmarat	110	16.03 N	105.13 E
Khenchla	148	35.28 N	7.11 E
Khenifra	148	33.00 N	5.40 W
Khenifra ⌷⁴	148	32.35 N	5.10 W
Khenjān	120	35.36 N	70.59 E
Khenyen	272b	22.59 N	88.19 E
Khera ⊶⁸	272a	28.46 N	77.08 E
Kheri	124	27.54 N	80.48 E
Kheri Branch ≃	124	28.11 N	80.25 E
Kherli	124	27.12 N	77.02 E
Kherratā	148	36.31 N	5.26 E
Khersān ≃	128	31.33 N	50.22 E
Kherson	78	46.45 N	33.30 E
Khersónes, mys ⊁	78	44.35 N	33.23 E
Khetia	120	21.40 N	74.35 E
Khevāj	120	38.13 N	71.02 E
Khewāri	120	26.36 N	68.52 E
Khewra	123	32.39 N	73.01 E
Kheyr Khāneh	128	34.57 N	63.37 E
Khichliwāra Plateau ⋏¹	124	24.25 N	77.30 E
Khichripur ⊶⁸	272a	28.37 N	77.19 E
Khilchipur	124	24.02 N	76.34 E
Khilkāpur	272b	22.46 N	88.29 E
Khimki — Chimki	82	55.54 N	37.26 E
Khios	38	38.22 N	26.08 E
Khios (Chios) I	38	38.22 N	26.00 E
Khpro	120	25.50 N	69.22 E
Khrbat al-Ghazālah	132	32.44 N	36.12 E
Khrbat ʿAwwād	132	32.19 N	36.43 E
Khrbat Qanāfar	132	33.38 N	35.43 E
Khrbat Umm as-Surab	132	32.26 N	36.19 E
Khri Mat	110	16.50 N	99.48 E
Khrpai	126	22.42 N	87.37 E
Khrr, Wādī al- ∨	128	31.51 N	44.29 E
Khsfīn	132	32.51 N	35.49 E
Khuri Khala ⋏	124	29.58 N	81.18 E
Khva — Chiva	72	41.24 N	60.22 E
Khibodarivka	83	47.29 N	37.23 E
Khong Khlung	110	16.12 N	99.43 E
Khong Thom	110	7.56 N	99.09 E
Khong Yai	110	11.46 N	102.54 E
Kh'ung	110	12.27 N	102.14 E
Khm'el'nyts'kyy	78	49.25 N	27.00 E
Khm'el'nyts'kyy ⌷⁴	78	49.30 N	27.00 E
Khm'el'nyk	78	48.34 N	31.24 E
Khm'il'nyk	78	49.33 N	27.57 E
Khoai, Hon I	110	8.26 N	104.50 E
Khodoriv	78	49.24 N	24.17 E
Khogali	140	6.08 N	27.47 E
Khojāng ⋏	124	28.41 N	85.09 E
Khok Kloi	110	8.17 N	98.19 E
Khok Pho	110	6.43 N	101.06 E
Khoksa	126	23.48 N	89.17 E
Khok Samrong	110	15.04 N	100.44 E
Kholargós	267c	38.00 N	23.48 E
Kholm	120	36.42 N	67.41 E
Kholmy	78	51.52 N	32.36 E
Kholombidzo Falls ∟	154	15.54 S	34.44 E
Khomas ⌷⁴	156	23.00 S	17.00 E
Khomas Hochland ⋏¹	156	22.30 S	16.30 E
Khomeyn	128	33.38 N	50.04 E
Khomeynīshahr	128	32.41 N	51.31 E
Khomocomo	156	24.46 S	23.52 E
Khomutets'	78	50.06 N	33.44 E
Khondmāl Hills ⋏²	122	20.20 N	84.00 E
Khong — Mekong ≃	12	10.33 N	105.24 E
Khoni	272c	19.10 N	73.07 E
Khon Kaen	110	16.26 N	102.50 E
Khóra	38	37.04 N	21.43 E
Khorāsān ⌷⁴	128	35.00 N	58.00 E
Khóra Sfakíon	38	35.12 N	24.08 E
Khordha	122	20.11 N	85.37 E
Khorel	272b	22.42 N	88.19 E
Khorol	78	49.47 N	33.17 E
Khorol ≃	78	49.28 N	33.47 E
Khorostkiv	78	49.13 N	25.55 E
Khorramābād	128	33.30 N	48.20 E
Khorram Daraq	128	35.28 N	48.11 E
Khorramshahr	128	30.25 N	48.11 E
Khoru	272b	22.51 N	88.31 E
Khoryna ≃	83	49.23 N	38.13 E
Khossanto	150	13.08 N	11.58 W
Khoteshiv	78	51.43 N	24.47 E
Khotin'	78	51.07 N	34.46 E
Khotyn	78	48.29 N	26.30 E
Khouribga	148	32.54 N	6.57 W
Khouribga ⌷⁴	148	32.50 N	6.30 W
Khowai	124	24.06 N	91.38 E
Khowāng	124	27.16 N	94.53 E
Khowst	120	33.22 N	69.57 E
Khrestyshche	83	48.55 N	37.30 E
Khrisokhoús, Kólpos ⊂	130	35.06 N	32.25 E
Khrisoúpolis	38	40.58 N	24.42 E
Khrysto'orivka	78	49.49 N	33.05 E
Khrystynivka	78	48.49 N	29.58 E
Khudián	123	30.59 N	74.17 E
Khuff	144	24.57 N	44.42 E
Khugaung	110	26.07 N	96.18 E
Khugiānī Sānī	120	31.35 N	66.12 E
Khujaly	120	31.16 N	70.30 E
Khu Khan	110	14.42 N	104.12 E
Khukhra	78	50.13 N	34.49 E
Khulna	126	22.48 N	89.33 E
Khulna ⌷⁴	126	22.45 N	89.30 E
Khuma	158	27.55 S	26.37 E
Khumbu Khōlē Ghar ≃	124	27.40 N	86.44 E
Khungdugang ⋏	124	27.31 N	89.02 E
Khūnjerāb Pass ⋋	123	36.52 N	75.27 E
Khun Tan, Doi ⋏	110	18.30 N	99.20 E
Khunti	124	23.05 N	85.17 E
Khurai	124	24.03 N	78.19 E
Khuralji Khās ⊶⁸	272a	28.39 N	77.17 E
Khuria Tank ⊜¹	124	22.25 N	81.36 E
Khurigāchi	272b	22.49 N	88.20 E
Khurīyā Murīyā, Jazā'ir II	118	17.30 N	56.00 E
Khurja	120	28.15 N	77.51 E
Khurli	126	22.55 N	89.52 E
Khurramshahr — Khorramshahr	128	30.25 N	48.11 E
Khūsf	128	32.46 N	58.53 E
Khushāb	123	32.18 N	72.21 E
Khushālgarh	123	33.03 N	71.54 E
Khushk Khurd ⊶⁸	272a	28.49 N	77.02 E
Khust	78	48.10 N	23.18 E
Khutubi	86	44.11 N	86.25 E
Khuwayy	140	13.05 N	29.14 E
Khūzestān ⌷⁴	128	31.00 N	49.00 E
Khvājeh Mohammad, Kūh-e ⋏	120	36.22 N	70.17 E
Khvājeh Ra'ūf	128	33.47 N	55.03 E
Khvor	128	33.47 N	55.03 E
Khvormūj	128	28.39 N	51.23 E
Khvoy	128	38.33 N	44.58 E
Khvrive Noi ≃	110	19.08 N	104.42 E
Khyber Pass ⋋	123	34.05 N	71.10 E
Khvriv	78	49.33 N	22.49 E
Kia	175e	7.33 S	158.26 E

Kialwe	154	9.22 S	27.08 E
Kiama, Austl.	170	34.41 S	150.51 E
Kiama, R.D.C.	152	7.15 S	17.44 E
Kiamba	116	5.59 N	124.37 E
Kiambi	154	7.20 S	28.01 E
Kiamboni, Kap — Jumbo, Raas ⊁	144	1.39 S	41.36 E
Kiambu	154	1.10 S	36.50 E
Kiamesha Lake	210	41.41 N	74.40 W
Kiamichi ≃	194	33.57 N	95.14 W
Kiamika ⌷⁴	188	46.38 N	75.15 W
Kiamika, Barrage ⌷⁶	206	46.37 N	75.08 W
Kiamika, Réservoir ⊜¹	206	46.40 N	75.05 W
Kiamusze — Jiamusi	89	46.50 N	130.21 E
Kian — Ji'an	100	25.08 N	121.44 E
Kiandra	171b	35.53 S	148.30 E
Kiangara	157b	17.58 S	47.02 E
Kiangarow, Mount ⋏	166	26.49 S	151.33 E
Kiangsi — Jiangxi ⌷⁴	100	28.00 N	116.00 E
Kiangsu — Jiangsu ⌷⁴	90	33.00 N	120.00 E
Kiantajärvi ⊜	26	65.03 N	29.07 E
Kiaohsien — Jiaoxian	86	36.18 N	119.58 E
Kipaek	41	56.02 N	8.51 E
Kibaha	154	6.46 S	38.55 E
Kibali-Sturi Game Reserve ♦⁴	152	3.37 N	28.34 E
Kibamba	154	2.45 N	29.33 E
Kibanga Port	154	4.53 S	26.33 E
Kibangou	152	3.27 S	12.21 E
Kibanseke	273b	4.26 S	15.23 E
Kibar	120	32.20 N	78.01 E
Kibara	154	2.09 S	33.27 E
Kibāsī	154	2.04 S	36.48 E
Kibau Iyayi	154	8.52 S	34.32 E
Kibawe	116	7.34 N	125.00 E
Kibaya	154	5.18 S	36.34 E
Kibenga	152	7.55 S	17.35 E
Kibeni	164	7.25 S	143.48 E
Kiberashi	154	5.23 S	37.26 E
Kibre Mengist	144	5.52 N	39.00 E
Kibi	150	6.10 N	0.33 W
Kibi-kōgen ⋏¹	96	34.45 N	133.15 E
Kibili	154	8.14 S	26.23 E
Kibiti	154	7.44 S	38.57 E
Kibler Park	273d	26.18 S	28.00 E
Kiboga	154	1.02 N	30.58 E
Kibombo	154	3.54 S	25.55 E
Kibondo	154	3.35 S	30.42 E
Kibouende, Congo	273b	4.19 S	15.11 E
Kibouende, Congo	273b	4.17 S	15.09 E
Kibouendé II	273b	4.12 S	15.09 E
Kibre Mengist	144	5.52 N	39.00 E
Kibns			
— Cyprus ⌷¹	130	35.00 N	33.00 E
Kibrisçik	130	40.25 N	31.51 E
Kibuye, Bdi.	154	3.32 S	29.45 E
Kibungo	154	2.10 S	30.32 E
Kibuye, Rw.	154	2.03 S	29.21 E
Kibwesa	154	6.28 S	29.57 E
Kibwezi	154	2.25 S	37.58 E
Kibworth Harcourt	42	52.32 N	0.59 W
Kičevo	38	41.31 N	20.57 E
Kichčik	74	53.24 N	156.03 E
Kichijōji	268	35.42 N	139.35 E
Kickapoo ≃	190	43.05 N	90.53 W
Kickapoo Creek ≃, Il., U.S.	194	40.08 N	89.27 W
Kickapoo Creek ≃, Il., U.S.	219	40.08 N	89.27 W
Kickapoo Creek ≃, Tx., U.S.	196	31.31 N	99.58 W
Kickapoo Creek ≃, Tx., U.S.	222	30.47 N	95.08 W
Kickapoo Creek ≃, Tx., U.S.	222	32.16 N	98.19 W
Kicking Horse Pass ⋋	182	51.27 N	116.18 W
Kičkino	80	49.45 N	44.02 E
Kičma	80	57.12 N	48.55 E
Kičmengskij Gorodok	74	59.59 N	45.48 E
Kičuj ≃	80	55.13 N	51.16 E
Kidal	150	18.26 N	1.24 E
Kidapawan	116	7.01 N	125.03 E
Kidatu	154	7.42 S	36.57 E
Kidbrooke ⊶⁸	260	51.28 N	0.02 E
Kidderminster	42	52.23 N	2.14 W
Kidderpore ⊶⁸	272b	22.31 N	88.19 E
Kidd's Beach	158	33.09 S	27.42 E
Kidepo National Park ♦			
Kidete, Tan.	154	6.25 S	37.16 E
Kidete, Tan.	154	6.39 S	36.42 E
Kidira	150	14.28 N	12.13 W
Kidlington	42	51.50 N	1.17 W
Kidnappers, Cape ⊁	172	39.39 S	177.07 E
Kido	91	34.15 N	146.55 E
Kidričevo	61	46.24 N	15.47 E
Kidron	214	40.44 N	81.45 W
Kidsgrove	44	53.05 N	2.15 W
Kidston	166	18.53 S	144.10 E
Kidugallo	154	6.49 S	38.11 E
Kidul, Pegunungan ⋏	115a	8.13 S	111.30 E
Kidwelly	42	51.45 N	4.18 W
Kiefersfelden	64	47.37 N	12.11 E
Kiekiebusch	264	52.21 S	13.30 E
Kiekka	154	6.36 S	26.33 E
Kiel, Wi., U.S.	190	43.54 N	88.02 W
Kiel Canal — Nord-Ostsee-Kanal ≃	30	53.53 N	9.08 E
Kielce	30	50.52 N	20.37 E
Kielce ⌷⁴	30	50.30 N	20.30 E
Kielder	44	55.14 N	2.35 W
Kielder Reservoir ⊜¹	44	55.11 N	2.30 W
Kieler Bucht (Kiel Bay) ⊂	30	54.35 N	10.35 E
Kieler Förde ⊂	41	54.24 N	10.12 E
Kiembara	150	13.15 N	2.44 W
Kiemberg	264a	52.40 N	12.54 E
Kienge	152	10.33 S	27.29 E
Kienitz	54	52.40 N	14.26 E
Kiens — Chienes	64	46.48 N	11.50 E
Kiental	58	46.35 N	7.43 E
Kienrbtal	264b	48.19 N	16.17 E
Kierspe	263	51.08 N	7.35 E
Kierspe-Bahnhof	263	51.08 N	7.33 E
Kieta	175e	6.13 S	155.38 E
Kietrz	30	50.05 N	18.01 E
Kieu	154	3.21 S	14.36 E
— Kyyiv	78	50.26 N	30.31 E
Kiev Station ⊶⁵	265b	50.03 N	30.16 E
Kiew	78	50.26 N	30.31 E
Kifaya	150	12.24 N	9.36 W
Kiffa	150	16.37 N	11.24 W
Kifisós ≃, Ellás	38	38.26 N	23.15 E
Kifisós ≃, Ellás	267c	37.59 N	23.40 E
Kifrī	128	34.42 N	44.58 E
Kifri, Jabal ⋏	132	32.50 N	36.01 E
Kigač ≃	80	46.50 N	49.04 E
Kigali	154	1.57 S	30.04 E
Kigilyah	76	73.20 N	139.50 E
Kigille	140	8.40 N	34.02 E
Kigoma	154	4.52 S	29.38 E

Kigoma ⌷⁴	154	4.30 S	30.30 E
Kigun, Cape ⊁	180	52.00 N	175.21 W
Kiga	154	5.10 S	33.08 E
Kihei	229a	20.47 N	156.27 W
Kihikihi	172	38.02 S	175.21 E
Kihnu I	26	62.12 N	23.11 E
Kihnu I	76	58.08 N	24.00 E
Kiholo Bay ⊂	229d	19.52 N	155.56 W
Kihundo	154	9.25 S	38.59 E
Kihurio	154	4.28 S	38.04 E
Kii-hantō ⋏¹	92	34.00 N	135.45 E
Kiik	86	47.31 N	72.55 E
Kiikkaškan	86	49.28 N	77.04 E
Kiiminginjoki ≃	26	65.12 N	25.18 E
Kii-nagashima	92	34.12 N	136.20 E
Kiirun	190	46.05 N	81.30 W
— Chilung	100	25.08 N	121.44 E
Killashandra	48	54.00 N	7.32 W
Killavally	48	53.45 N	9.23 W
Killawog	210	42.24 N	76.01 W
Kilbear Provincial Park ♦	212	45.21 N	80.12 W
Kilbeggan	48	53.22 N	7.30 W
Kilbirnie	154	5.46 S	36.34 E
Kilbride	46	56.00 N	4.41 W
Kilbuck Mountains ⋏	180	60.50 N	160.00 W
Kilbuck Run ≃	279b	40.31 N	80.05 W
Kilby	46	54.08 N	2.56 W
Kilchattan	46	55.44 N	5.01 W
Kilchberg	58	47.19 N	8.33 E
Kilchis ≃	224	45.30 N	123.52 W
Kilchoman	46	55.47 N	6.27 W
Kilchrenan	46	56.20 N	5.11 W
Kilchrist ⊶⁸	260	51.34 N	0.06 E
Kilcock	48	53.24 N	6.40 W
Kilcolgan	48	53.13 N	8.52 W
Kilconnell	48	53.20 N	8.25 W
Kilcormac	48	53.10 N	7.44 W
Kilcoole	48	53.06 N	6.03 W
Kilcoy	171a	26.57 S	152.33 E
Kilcullen	48	53.08 N	6.45 W
Kildare, Saint-Ambroise-de-Kildare), P.Q., Can.	206	46.05 N	73.32 W
Kildare, Ire.	48	53.10 N	6.55 W
Kildare ⌷⁶	48	53.15 N	6.45 W
Kildare, Cape ⊁	206	46.52 N	63.58 W
Kildeer	278	42.10 N	88.03 W
Kil'din, ostrov I	26	69.20 N	34.04 E
Kil'dinstroy	26	68.48 N	33.06 E
Kildonan, Scot., U.K.	46	58.10 N	3.51 W
Kildonan, Zimb.	154	17.21 S	30.37 E
Kildonan, Strath of ∨	46	58.09 N	3.51 W
Kildorrery	48	52.14 N	8.25 W
Kildrummy Castle ⊥	46	57.14 N	2.54 W
Kildurk	164	16.26 S	129.37 E
Kilfenora	48	52.59 N	9.13 W
Kilfinane	48	52.21 N	8.28 W
Kilgarvan	48	51.54 N	9.27 W
Kilgore, Oh., U.S.	214	40.06 N	80.59 W
Kilgore, Tx., U.S.	222	32.23 N	94.52 W
Kilham	44	54.04 N	0.23 W
Kilian Island I	176	73.35 N	107.53 W
Kiliba	154	3.14 S	29.18 E
Kiliç	128	41.09 N	38.29 E
Kilifi	154	3.38 S	39.51 E
Kiliköllür	122	9.30 N	78.22 E
Kilima	154	4.29 S	12.54 E
Kilimanjaro ⋏	154	3.04 S	37.22 E
Kilimanjaro Game Reserve ♦⁴		3.05 S	37.20 E
Kilimatinde	154	5.51 S	34.57 E
Kilimavony	157b	23.48 S	43.41 E
Kilimi	150	9.55 N	11.33 W
Kilindoni	154	7.55 S	39.40 E
Kilingi-Nõmme	76	58.09 N	24.58 E
Kilini ⋏	38	37.57 N	22.23 E
Kiliniq Island I	176	60.24 N	64.40 W
Kilinkoski	26	62.24 N	23.52 E
Kilirorglin	48	52.06 N	9.47 W
Killough	48	54.16 N	5.39 W
Killpecker Creek ≃	202	41.55 N	109.14 W
Kilucan	48	53.31 N	7.07 W
Kil Van Kull ≃	276	40.39 N	74.05 W
Killybegs	48	54.38 N	8.27 W
Killyleagh	48	54.24 N	5.39 W
Killua ≃	154	6.03 S	35.56 E
Kilmacthomas	48	52.12 N	7.25 W
Kilmaine	48	53.34 N	9.09 W
Kilmallock	48	52.23 N	8.34 W
Kilmaluag	46	57.41 N	6.17 W
Kilmarnock, Scot., U.K.	46	55.36 N	4.30 W
Kilmarnock, Va., U.S.	208	37.42 N	76.22 W
Kilmartin	46	56.07 N	5.29 W
Kilmar Tor ⋏²	42	50.33 N	4.32 W
Kilmaurs	46	55.38 N	4.32 W
Kilmelford	46	56.16 N	5.29 W
Kil'mez', Ross.	80	57.04 N	51.04 E
Kil'mez', Ross.	80	57.04 N	51.21 E
Kil'mez' ≃	80	56.58 N	50.28 E
Kilmichael	48	51.54 N	8.56 W
Kilmichael Point ⊁	48	52.44 N	6.10 W
Kilmore	169	37.18 S	144.57 E
Kilmore Creek ≃	216	40.20 N	80.18 W
Kilmory	46	55.43 N	6.22 W
Kilnaleck	48	53.52 N	7.19 W
Kilninver	46	56.20 N	5.31 W
Kilo	115b	8.21 S	118.24 E
Kilokri ⊶⁸	272a	28.35 N	77.16 E
Kilombero ≃	154	8.35 S	37.22 E
Kilombo ≃	154	4.30 S	30.14 E
Kilondo	154	9.46 S	34.21 E
Kilosa	154	6.50 S	36.59 E
Kilpisjärvi	24	69.03 N	20.48 E
Kilrea	48	54.57 N	6.35 W
Kilrenny	46	56.14 N	2.41 W
Kilrush	48	52.39 N	9.30 W
Kilsbergen ⋏²	30	59.22 N	14.47 E
Kilsmo	30	59.04 N	15.31 E
Kilsyth, Austl.	274b	37.48 S	145.19 E
Kilsyth, Scot., U.K.	46	55.59 N	4.04 W
Kiltamagh	48	53.52 N	8.59 W
Kiltimagh	48	53.51 N	9.00 W
Kilttan Island I	122	11.29 N	73.00 E
Kiltu-ri	94	34.35 N	127.20 E
Kilwa	154	9.18 S	28.25 E
Kilwa Island I	154	8.58 S	39.32 E
Kilwa Kivinje	154	8.45 S	39.24 E
Kilwa Masoko	154	8.55 S	39.31 E
Kilwinning	46	55.40 N	4.42 W
Kim	198	37.14 N	103.21 W
Kim ≃	152	5.26 N	11.07 E
Kima ≃	152	1.26 S	26.43 E
Kimaam	164	7.58 S	138.53 E
Kimamba	154	6.47 S	37.08 E
Kimande	154	7.22 S	35.30 E

⇋ River	Fluß	Río	Rivière	Rio	✛ Submarine Features	Untermeerische Objekte	Accidentes Submarinos	Formes de relief sous-marin	Acidentes submarinos
≃ Canal	Kanal	Canal	Canal	Canal	⌷ Political Unit	Politische Einheit	Unidad Política	Entité politique	Unidade política
∟ Waterfall, Rapids	Wasserfall, Stromschnellen	Cascada, Rápidos	Cascade, Rápides	Cascata, Rápidos	⌷ Cultural Institution	Kulturelle Institution	Institución Cultural	Institution culturelle	Instituição cultural
✕ Strait	Meeresstraße	Estrecho	Détroit	Estreito	⌖ Historical Site	Historische Stätte	Sitio Histórico	Site historique	Sítio histórico
⊂ Bay, Gulf	Bucht, Golf	Bahía, Golfo	Baie, Golfe	Baía, Golfo	♦ Recreational Site	Erholungs- und Ferienort	Sitio de Recreo	Centre de loisirs	Área de Lazer
⊜ Lake, Lakes	See, Seen	Lago, Lagos	Lac, Lacs	Lago, Lagos	⋇ Airport	Flughafen	Aeropuerto	Aéroport	Aeroporto
✷ Swamp	Sumpf	Pantano	Marais	Pântano	⋇ Military Installation	Militäranlage	Instalación Militar	Installation militaire	Instalação militar
⌀ Ice Features, Glacier	Eis- und Gletscherformen	Accidentes Glaciales	Formes glaciaires	Acidentes glaciares	⌷ Miscellaneous	Verschiedenes	Misceláneo	Divers	Diversos
⟂ Other Hydrographic Features	Andere Hydrographische Objekte	Otros Elementos Hidrográficos	Autres données hydrographiques	Outros acidentes hidrográficos					

ENGLISH / DEUTSCH

Name	Page / Seite	Lat.°′ / Breite°′	Long.°′ / Länge°′ E = Ost
Kimsquit	182	52.49 N	126.58 W
Kimstad	40	58.32 N	15.58 E
Kimu ≃	268	35.56 N	139.57 E
Kimuenza	273b	4.27 S	15.17 E
Kimvula	152	5.44 S	15.58 E
Kimwanga	154	7.08 S	28.42 E
Kin	174m	26.26 N	127.55 E
Kinabalian, Mount ∧	116	8.14 N	125.25 E
Kinabalu, Gunong ∧	112	6.05 N	116.33 E
Kinabalu National Park ♦	112	6.05 N	116.33 E
Kinabatangan ≃	112	5.42 N	118.23 E
Kınalı ◀[8]	267b	40.55 N	29.03 E
Kınalı Ada I	267b	40.55 N	29.03 E
Kinangaly ∧	157b	19.12 S	45.40 E
Kinango	154	4.08 S	39.19 E
Kinapusan Island I	116	5.13 N	120.40 E
Kinara	164	2.16 S	132.44 E
Kinasa	94	36.42 N	138.01 E
Kinaūni	272a	28.39 N	77.23 E
Kinbasket Lake ⊜[1]	182	51.58 N	118.03 W
Kinbrace	46	58.15 N	3.56 W
Kinbuck	46	56.13 N	3.57 W
Kincaid, Sk., Can.	184	49.39 N	107.00 W
Kincaid, Il., U.S.	219	39.35 N	89.24 W
Kincardine, On., Can.	190	44.11 N	81.38 W
Kincardine, Scot., U.K.	46	56.04 N	3.44 W
Kinchafoonee Creek ≃	192	31.38 N	84.10 W
Kinchang	110	26.32 N	98.02 E
Kinchara	272b	22.53 N	88.32 E
Kinchega National Park ♦	166	32.30 S	142.20 E
Kincheloe Air Force Base ■	190	46.15 N	84.28 W
Kincolith	182	55.00 N	129.57 W
Kincraig	46	57.08 N	3.55 W
Kinda, R.D.C.	152	4.47 S	21.48 E
Kinda, R.D.C.	154	9.18 S	25.04 E
Kindadal	112	1.35 S	123.11 E
Kindanba	152	3.44 S	14.31 E
Kindarun Mountain ∧	170	32.49 S	150.41 E
Kindberg	61	47.31 N	15.27 E
Kinde	190	43.56 N	82.59 W
Kindeje	152	7.07 S	13.44 E
Kindel'a	80	51.36 N	52.58 E
Kindel'a ≃	80	51.30 N	52.45 E
Kindelbrück	54	51.16 N	11.05 E
Kindele	152	8.39 S	24.11 E
Kinder	194	30.29 N	92.51 W
Kinderhook, Il., U.S.	219	39.42 N	91.09 W
Kinderhook, Mi., U.S.	216	41.48 N	85.00 W
Kinderhook, N.Y., U.S.	210	42.23 N	73.41 W
Kinderhook Creek ≃	210	42.19 N	73.45 W
Kinder Reservoir ⊜[1]	262	53.23 N	1.55 W
Kinder Scout ∧	44	53.23 N	1.52 W
Kindersley	184	51.27 N	109.10 W
Kindia	150	10.04 N	12.51 W
Kindikan	88	56.02 N	115.15 E
Kinding	60	49.00 N	11.23 E
Kindley Field ⊠	240a	32.22 N	64.40 W
Kindred	198	46.38 N	97.01 W
Kindu	154	2.57 S	25.56 E
Kindykty, ozero ⊜	86	51.15 N	62.14 E
Kinel'	80	53.14 N	50.39 E
Kinel'-Čerkasy	80	53.29 N	51.29 E
Kinel'skije jary ⋏[1]	80	53.42 N	52.00 E
Kineo, Mount ∧	188	45.42 N	69.44 W
Kinesi	154	1.28 S	33.52 E
Kinešma	80	57.26 N	42.09 E
Kineton	42	52.10 N	1.30 W
Kinfauns	46	56.22 N	3.21 W
King	192	36.16 N	80.21 W
King □[6]	224	47.26 N	121.48 W
King ≃, Austl.	164	14.41 S	131.59 E
King ≃, Austl.	169	36.41 S	146.25 E
King, Lake ⊜	162	25.38 S	120.06 E
King, Mont ∧	212	45.29 N	75.52 W
King, Mount ∧	166	25.10 S	147.31 E
Kingabwa ◀[8]	273b	4.19 S	15.20 E
King and Queen □[6]	208	37.42 N	76.50 W
King and Queen Court House	208	37.40 N	76.52 W
Kingaroy	166	26.33 S	151.50 E
Kingarth	46	55.46 N	5.03 W
King City, On., Can.	212	43.56 N	79.32 W
King City, Ca., U.S.	226	36.12 N	121.07 W
King City, Mo., U.S.	194	40.03 N	94.31 W
King Cove	180	55.04 N	162.19 W
Kingdom City	219	38.58 N	91.56 W
King Edward ≃	164	14.14 S	126.35 E
Kingersheim	58	47.48 N	7.20 E
King Ferry	210	42.39 N	76.37 W
Kingfield	188	44.57 N	70.09 W
Kingfisher	196	35.51 N	97.55 W
King George	208	38.16 N	77.11 W
King George □[6]	208	38.15 N	77.10 W
King George, Mount ∧	182	50.35 N	115.24 W
King George Bay c	254	51.33 S	60.37 W
King George Island I	9	62.00 S	58.15 W
King George Islands II	176	57.20 N	78.25 W
King George's Dock ◀[5]	272b	22.32 N	88.18 E
King George Sound ʊ	162	35.03 S	117.57 E
King George's Reservoir ⊜[1]	260	51.39 N	0.01 W
King George VI Reservoir ⊜[1]	260	51.27 N	0.32 W
King Hill	202	43.00 N	115.12 W
Kinghorn	46	56.04 N	3.10 W
Kingie ≃	46	57.04 N	5.08 W
Kingisepp	76	59.22 N	28.36 E
King Island I, Austl.	166	39.50 S	144.00 E
King Island I, B.C., Can.	182	52.12 N	127.42 W
King Island I, Ak., U.S.	180	64.58 N	168.05 W
Kinglake National Park ♦	169	37.35 S	145.25 E
King Lear Peak ∧	204	41.12 N	118.34 W
King Leopold Ranges ⋏	160	17.30 S	125.45 E
Kingman, Az., U.S.	200	35.11 N	114.03 W
Kingman, Ks., U.S.	198	37.38 N	98.06 W
Kingman Reef ✢[2]	14	6.24 N	162.22 W
King Mountain ∧, B.C., Can.	180	58.17 N	128.54 W
King Mountain ∧, Ok., U.S.	196	34.52 N	99.17 W
King Mountain ∧, Or., U.S.	202	42.42 N	123.14 W
King Mountain ∧, Or., U.S.	202	43.49 N	118.52 W
King of Prussia	208	40.05 N	75.23 W
King of Prussia Plaza ◀[9]	285	40.05 N	75.25 W
Kingoma	152	5.11 S	13.34 E
Kingoma-Ngoma	152	5.50 S	16.49 E
Kingombe, R.D.C.	154	3.56 S	26.35 E
Kingombe, R.D.C.	154	7.24 S	26.11 E
Kingoonya	162	30.54 S	135.18 E
Kingoué	152	3.43 S	14.09 E
King Peak ∧	204	40.10 N	124.08 W
King Peninsula ≻[1]	9	73.12 S	101.00 W
Kingri	120	30.27 N	69.49 E
Kings, Il., U.S.	216	42.00 N	89.06 W
Kings, Ms., U.S.	194	32.23 N	90.51 W
Kings □[6], Ca., U.S.	226	36.20 N	119.39 W
Kings □[6], N.Y., U.S.	210	40.42 N	74.00 W
Kings ≃, Ar., U.S.	194	36.29 N	93.35 W
Kings ≃, Ca., U.S.	226	36.03 N	119.49 W
Kings ≃, Nv., U.S.	204	41.31 N	118.08 W
Kings, Middle Fork ≃	204	36.50 N	118.52 W
Kings, North Fork ≃, Ca., U.S.	204	36.52 N	119.08 W
Kings, North Fork ≃, Ca., U.S.	226	36.18 N	119.52 W
Kings, South Fork ≃	226	36.18 N	119.52 W
King Salmon	180	58.41 N	156.39 W
King Salmon ≃	180	58.15 N	157.30 W
Kingsbarns	46	56.18 N	2.39 W
Kings Beach	226	39.14 N	120.01 W
Kingsbridge	42	50.17 N	3.46 W
Kingsburg	226	36.30 N	119.33 W
Kingsbury, Eng., U.K.	42	52.35 N	1.40 W
Kingsbury, In., U.S.	216	41.31 N	86.42 W
Kingsbury ◀[8]	260	51.35 N	0.17 W
Kings Canyon National Park ♦	204	36.48 N	118.30 W
Kingsclere	42	51.20 N	1.14 W
Kingscote	168b	35.40 S	137.38 E
Kingscourt	48	53.53 N	6.48 W
Kings Creek	218	40.10 N	83.44 W
Kings Creek ≃, Austl.	171a	27.57 S	151.42 E
Kings Creek ≃, Tx., U.S.	222	32.25 N	96.15 W
King's Cross Station ◀[5]	260	51.32 N	0.07 W
Kings Dominion ♦	208	37.51 N	77.27 W
Kingsdown, Eng., U.K.	42	51.11 N	1.25 E
Kingsdown, Eng., U.K.	260	51.21 N	0.17 E
Kings Falls ∟	212	43.55 N	75.38 W
Kingsford, Austl.	274a	33.56 S	151.14 E
Kingsford, Mi., U.S.	190	45.47 N	88.04 W
Kingsford Heights	216	41.29 N	86.42 W
Kingsford Smith Airport ⊠	170	33.57 S	151.11 E
Kingsgate	182	49.00 N	116.11 W
Kingsgrove	274a	33.57 S	151.06 E
Kingshill	241n	17.44 N	64.48 W
Kingshouse	46	56.21 N	4.19 W
Kings Island ♦	218	39.21 N	84.16 W
Kingskerswell	42	50.30 N	3.33 W
Kingsland, Eng., U.K.	42	52.15 N	2.47 W
Kingsland, Ar., U.S.	194	33.51 N	92.17 W
Kingsland, Ga., U.S.	192	30.47 N	81.41 W
Kingsland, Tx., U.S.	196	30.40 N	98.26 W
Kingsland, Va., U.S.	208	37.24 N	77.26 W
Kings Langley	42	51.43 N	0.28 W
Kingsley, S. Afr.	158	27.55 S	30.33 E
Kingsley, Eng., U.K.	42	53.01 N	1.59 W
Kingsley, Eng., U.K.	262	53.16 N	2.40 W
Kingsley, Ia., U.S.	198	42.35 N	95.58 W
Kingsley, Mi., U.S.	190	44.35 N	85.32 W
Kingsley, Pa., U.S.	210	41.46 N	75.45 W
Kingsley Dam ◀[6]	198	41.11 N	101.39 W
King's Lynn	42	52.45 N	0.24 E
Kings Manor	285	40.05 N	75.21 W
Kingsmere Lake ⊜	184	54.06 N	106.27 W
Kings Mills	218	39.21 N	84.14 W
Kings Mountain	192	35.14 N	81.20 W
Kings Mountain National Military Park ♦	192	35.07 N	81.33 W
King Solomon's Mines → Mikhrot Shelomo Hamelekh ⊥	132	29.45 N	34.56 E
King Sound ʊ	162	17.00 S	123.30 E
Kings Park, N.Y., U.S.	210	40.53 N	73.16 W
Kings Park, Va., U.S.	284c	38.48 N	77.14 W
Kings Park ♦	168a	31.57 S	115.49 E
Kings Peak ∧	200	40.46 N	110.22 W
Kings Plaza ◀[9]	276	40.37 N	73.55 W
King's Point, Nf., Can.	186	49.35 N	56.11 W
Kings Point, N.Y., U.S.	210	40.49 N	73.44 W
Kingsport	192	36.32 N	82.33 W
King's Sutton	42	52.01 N	1.16 W
Kingsteignton	42	50.33 N	3.35 W
King Sterndale	262	53.15 N	1.52 W
Kingsthorpe	171a	27.29 S	151.49 E
Kingston, Austl.	171a	27.40 S	153.07 E
Kingston, N.S., Can.	186	44.59 N	64.57 W
Kingston, On., Can.	212	44.14 N	76.30 W
Kingston, Jam.	241q	18.00 N	76.48 W
Kingston, N.Z.	172	45.20 S	168.42 E
Kingston, Norf. I.	174c	29.03 S	167.58 E
Kingston, Ga., U.S.	192	34.14 N	84.56 W
Kingston, Il., U.S.	216	42.06 N	88.46 W
Kingston, Ma., U.S.	207	41.59 N	70.43 W
Kingston, Mo., U.S.	194	39.38 N	94.02 W
Kingston, N.J., U.S.	276	40.22 N	74.36 W
Kingston, N.Y., U.S.	210	41.55 N	73.59 W
Kingston, Oh., U.S.	218	39.28 N	82.54 W
Kingston, Ok., U.S.	196	33.59 N	96.43 W
Kingston, Pa., U.S.	210	41.15 N	75.53 W
Kingston, R.I., U.S.	207	41.29 N	71.31 W
Kingston, Tn., U.S.	192	35.52 N	84.30 W
Kingston, Wa., U.S.	224	47.48 N	122.30 W
Kingston Bay c	283	42.00 N	70.42 W
Kingston Mills	212	44.17 N	76.27 W
Kingston Southeast	166	36.50 S	139.51 E
Kingston upon Hull	44	53.45 N	0.20 W
Kingston [upon Thames]	28	51.25 N	0.19 W
Kingston [upon Thames] ◀[8]	42	51.25 N	0.19 W
Kingstown → Dún Laoghaire, Ire.	48	53.17 N	6.08 W
Kingstown, St. Vin.	241h	13.09 N	61.14 W
Kingstree	192	33.40 N	79.49 W
Kingsville, Austl.	274b	37.49 S	144.52 E
Kingsville, On., Can.	214	42.02 N	82.45 W
Kingsville, Md., U.S.	284b	39.26 N	76.25 W
Kingsville, Oh., U.S.	214	41.53 N	80.41 W
Kingsville, Tx., U.S.	196	27.30 N	97.51 W
Kingsville Naval Air Station ■	196	27.31 N	97.47 W
Kingswear	42	50.21 N	3.34 W
Kingswinford	42	52.29 N	2.10 W
Kingswood, Austl.	274a	33.46 S	150.43 E
Kingswood, S. Afr.	158	27.29 S	25.46 E
Kingswood, Eng., U.K.	42	51.27 N	2.22 W
Kingswood, Eng., U.K.	260	51.17 N	0.13 W
Kingswood Park	285	40.07 N	74.51 W
King's Worthy	42	51.06 N	1.18 W
Kingtechen → Jingdezhen	100	29.16 N	117.11 E
Kington	42	52.12 N	3.01 W
Kingunda	152	6.34 S	16.58 E
Kingungi	152	5.24 S	17.56 E
Kingussie	46	57.05 N	4.03 W
King William	208	37.41 N	77.00 W
King William □[6]	208	37.42 N	77.05 W
King William Island I	176	69.00 N	97.30 W
King William's Town	158	32.51 S	27.22 E
Kingwood, Tx., U.S.	222	29.54 N	95.18 W
Kingwood, W.V., U.S.	188	39.28 N	79.41 W
Kinh Duc	110	11.49 N	107.58 E
Kinhwa → Jinhua	100	29.07 N	119.39 E
Kınık	130	39.05 N	27.23 E
Kinira ≃	158	31.12 S	29.17 E
Kinistino	184	52.57 N	105.00 W
Kinjar Khās	123	29.55 N	70.58 E
Kinkala	152	4.22 S	14.46 E
Kinker Creek ≃	282	38.02 N	121.52 W
Kinkony, Lac ⊜	157b	16.08 S	45.50 E
Kinkora	285	40.07 N	74.45 W
Kinleith	172	38.16 S	175.54 E
Kinloch	46	57.01 N	6.17 W
Kinlochbervie	46	58.28 N	5.03 W
Kinlocheil	46	56.51 N	5.20 W
Kinlochewe	46	57.36 N	5.20 W
Kinloch Hourn	46	57.06 N	5.22 W
Kinlochleven	46	56.42 N	4.58 W
Kinloch Rannoch	46	56.42 N	4.11 W
Kinloss	46	57.37 N	3.34 W
Kinmount	212	44.47 N	78.39 W
Kinmundy	219	38.46 N	88.50 W
Kinn	26	61.36 N	4.45 E
Kinna	26	57.30 N	12.41 E
Kinnaird	182	49.17 N	117.39 W
Kinnaird Head ≻	46	57.42 N	2.00 W
Kinnegad	48	53.26 N	7.05 W
Kinnekulle ∧[2]	26	58.35 N	13.23 E
Kinnelon	210	40.59 N	74.23 W
Kinnel Water ≃	44	55.08 N	3.25 W
Kinneret	132	32.43 N	35.33 E
Kinneret, Yam (Sea of Galilee) ⊜	132	32.48 N	35.35 E
Kinneret-Negev Conduit ≋[1]	132	32.52 N	35.32 E
Kinnerley	42	52.47 N	2.59 W
Kinniconick Creek ≃	218	38.37 N	83.09 W
Kinnula	26	63.22 N	24.58 E
Kino ≃	96	34.13 N	135.09 E
Kinoe	96	34.14 N	132.55 E
Kinogitan	116	9.00 N	124.48 E
Kinojévis ≃	190	48.23 N	78.21 W
Kinomoto	94	35.30 N	136.13 E
Kinonge ≃	206	45.39 N	74.55 W
Kinoni	154	0.39 S	30.27 E
Kinosaki	96	35.37 N	134.49 E
Kinpoku-san ∧	92	38.05 N	138.22 E
Kinrola	166	23.46 S	148.45 E
Kinross, S. Afr.	158	26.22 S	29.03 E
Kinross, Scot., U.K.	46	56.13 N	3.27 W
Kin-saki ≻	174m	26.26 N	127.57 E
Kinsale, Ire.	48	51.42 N	8.32 W
Kinsale, Va., U.S.	208	38.01 N	76.34 W
Kinsale, Old Head of ≻	48	51.36 N	8.32 W
Kinsale Harbour c	48	51.41 N	8.30 W
Kinsarvik	26	60.23 N	6.43 E
Kinschasa → Kinshasa	152	4.18 S	15.18 E
Kinshasa (Léopoldville), R.D.C.	152	4.18 S	15.18 E
Kinshasa (Léopoldville), R.D.C.	273b	4.18 S	15.18 E
Kinshasa □[4]	152	4.18 S	15.18 E
Kinshasa (Ndjili) Airport ⊠, R.D.C.	273b	4.23 S	15.27 E
Kinshasa (Ndolo) Airport ⊠, R.D.C.	273b	4.20 S	15.19 E
Kinshasa-Est ◀[8]	273b	4.18 S	15.18 E
Kinshasa-Ouest ◀[8]	273b	4.20 S	15.15 E
Kins'ka ≃	78	47.40 N	35.22 E
Kinsley	198	37.55 N	99.24 W
Kinsman, Il., U.S.	216	41.11 N	88.34 W
Kinsman, Oh., U.S.	214	41.27 N	80.36 W
Kinston, Al., U.S.	194	31.12 N	86.10 W
Kinston, N.C., U.S.	192	35.15 N	77.34 W
Kintamani	115b	8.14 S	115.19 E
Kintamo, Rapides de ∟	273b	4.19 S	15.15 E
Kintampo	150	8.03 N	1.43 W
Kintap	112	3.51 S	115.13 E
Kintari, Mont ∧[2]	273b	4.08 S	15.23 E
Kintélé	273b	4.09 S	15.21 E
Kintinian	150	11.36 N	9.23 W
Kintinku	154	5.53 S	35.14 E
Kintobongo-Bunge	154	8.54 S	26.23 E
Kintore	46	57.13 N	2.21 W
Kintore, Mount ∧	162	26.34 S	130.30 E
Kintore Range ⋏	162	23.25 S	129.20 E
Kintsana	273b	4.19 S	15.10 E
Kintus	86	60.09 N	71.25 E
Kintyre ≻[1]	46	55.32 N	5.35 W
Kintyre, Mull of ≻	46	55.17 N	5.55 W
Kinu ≃	94	35.56 N	139.57 E
Kinuseo Falls ∟	182	54.47 N	121.12 W
Kinuso	182	55.20 N	115.25 W
Kinvarra	48	53.08 N	8.55 W
Kinver	42	52.27 N	2.14 W
Kin-wan c	174m	26.25 N	127.54 E
Kinyangiri	154	4.27 S	34.37 E
Kinyeti ∧	154	3.57 N	32.54 E
Kinzia	152	3.36 S	18.26 E
Kinzig ≃, Dtsch.	56	50.08 N	8.54 E
Kinzig ≃, Dtsch.	58	48.37 N	7.49 E
Kinzua	202	44.59 N	120.03 W
Kinzua Creek ≃	214	41.47 N	78.50 W
Kinzua Dam ◀[6]	214	41.50 N	79.01 W
Kioga-See → Kyoga, Lake ⊜	154	1.30 N	33.00 E
Kioshkokwi Lake ⊜	190	46.05 N	78.52 W
Kioto → Kyōto	94	35.00 N	135.45 E
Kiowa, Co., U.S.	198	39.20 N	104.27 W
Kiowa, Ks., U.S.	198	37.01 N	98.29 W
Kiowa, Ok., U.S.	196	34.43 N	95.53 W
Kiowa Creek ≃, U.S.	196	36.46 N	99.55 W
Kiowa Creek ≃, Co., U.S.	198	40.20 N	104.05 W
Kipahigan Lake ⊜	184	55.20 N	101.55 W
Kipandi	152	5.19 S	16.46 E
Kipanga	154	6.14 S	35.21 E
Kiparissía	38	37.14 N	21.40 E
Kiparissiakós Kólpos c	38	37.37 N	21.24 E
Kipatimu	154	8.29 S	38.56 E
Kipawa ≃	190	47.03 N	79.23 W
Kipawa, Lac ⊜	190	46.55 N	79.00 W
Kipawa, Réserve ♦	190	47.15 N	78.15 W
Kipembawe	154	7.39 S	33.24 E
Kipengere Range ⋏	154	9.10 S	34.15 E
Kipfenberg	60	48.57 N	11.24 E
Kipijevo	24	65.40 N	54.30 E
Kipili	154	7.26 S	30.36 E
Kipini	154	2.32 S	40.31 E
Kipling	184	50.10 N	102.38 W
Kipnuk	180	59.56 N	164.03 W
Kippax	44	53.46 N	1.22 W
Kippen	46	56.08 N	4.11 W
Kippenheim	58	48.17 N	7.49 E
Kippure ∧	48	53.10 N	6.20 W
Kípros → Cyprus □[1]	130	35.00 N	33.00 E
Kipsdorf	54	50.47 N	13.32 E
Kipton	214	41.16 N	82.18 W
Kipushi	154	11.46 S	27.14 E
Kipushia, R.D.C.	154	6.10 S	25.12 E
Kipushia, R.D.C.	154	12.58 S	29.30 E
Kira, Nihon	94	34.49 N	137.05 E
Kir'a, Ross.	80	55.04 N	46.53 E
Kirakira	175e	10.27 S	161.55 E
Kirandul	122	18.40 N	81.16 E
Kirane	150	15.25 N	10.14 W
Kiranlık	130	39.07 N	41.41 E
Kiranomena	157b	18.17 S	46.03 E
Kīratpur	124	29.31 N	78.12 E
Kirau̯	78	51.29 N	29.24 E
Kirau̯sk	76	53.16 N	29.29 E
Kiraz	130	38.13 N	28.13 E
Kirazlı	130	40.02 N	26.41 E
Kırbaçbayırı ∧	267b	40.56 N	29.10 E
Kırbaşı	130	40.01 N	31.50 E
Kirbla	76	58.44 N	23.57 E
Kirby Muxloe	42	52.38 N	1.13 W
Kirbys Creek ≃	208	36.28 N	77.06 W
Kirbyville	194	30.39 N	93.53 W
Kırçal	130	41.39 N	35.16 E
Kırcasalih	130	41.23 N	26.48 E
Kirchanschöring	64	47.57 N	12.50 E
Kirchardt	56	49.12 N	8.59 E
Kirchbach in Steiermark	61	46.54 N	15.44 E
Kirchberg, Dtsch.	54	50.37 N	12.32 E
Kirchberg, Dtsch.	56	49.12 N	9.58 E
Kirchberg, Dtsch.	56	49.56 N	7.24 E
Kirchberg, Dtsch.	60	48.54 N	13.11 E
Kirchberg, Schw.	58	47.25 N	9.03 E
Kirchberg, Schw.	58	47.05 N	7.35 E
Kirch-Berg ∧[2]	264a	52.27 N	13.02 E
Kirchberg am Wagram	61	48.26 N	15.53 E
Kirchberg an der Pielach	61	48.02 N	15.26 E
Kirchberg in Tirol	64	47.27 N	12.19 E
Kirchbichl	64	47.31 N	12.05 E
Kirchderne ◀[8]	263	51.33 N	7.30 E
Kirchdorf, Dtsch.	52	52.36 N	8.49 E
Kirchdorf, Dtsch.	54	54.00 N	11.26 E
Kirchdorf an der Krems	61	47.56 N	14.07 E
Kirchdorf im Wald	60	48.55 N	13.16 E
Kirchen	56	50.48 N	7.53 E
Kirchende	263	51.25 N	7.26 E
Kirchenlamitz	54	50.09 N	11.56 E
Kirchenthumbach	60	49.45 N	11.43 E
Kirchhain	56	50.49 N	8.55 E
Kirchheilingen	54	51.11 N	10.42 E
Kirchheim, Dtsch.	56	50.50 N	9.35 E
Kirchheim, Dtsch.	64	48.11 N	11.45 E
Kirchheimbolanden	56	49.40 N	8.00 E
Kirchheim in Schwaben	58	48.10 N	10.30 E
Kirchheim unter Teck	56	48.39 N	9.27 E
Kirchhellen	52	51.36 N	6.55 E
Kirchhellen Heide ◀[3]	263	51.36 N	6.53 E
Kirchhofen	264a	52.22 N	13.53 E
Kirchhörde ◀[8]	263	51.27 N	7.27 E
Kirchhundem	56	51.05 N	8.05 E
Kirchlengern	52	52.12 N	8.35 E
Kirchlinde ◀[8]	263	51.32 N	7.22 E
Kirchlinteln	52	52.56 N	9.19 E
Kirchmöser	54	52.22 N	12.25 E
Kirchroth	60	48.57 N	12.33 E
Kirchschlag in der Buckligen Welt	61	47.31 N	16.18 E
Kirchseeon	64	48.04 N	11.53 E
Kirchveischede	56	51.05 N	7.59 E
Kirchwalsede	52	53.01 N	9.23 E
Kirchwerder ◀[8]	52	53.25 N	10.11 E
Kirchzarten	58	47.58 N	7.56 E
Kircubbin	48	54.29 N	5.32 W
Kirda	85	41.06 N	69.00 E
Kirdāsah	142	30.02 N	31.07 E
Kireç	130	39.33 N	28.22 E
Kirej ≃	88	54.12 N	100.40 E
Kirejevo	80	50.01 N	44.29 E
Kirejevsk	76	53.56 N	37.56 E
Kirejkovo	76	53.38 N	35.49 E
Kirenga ≃	88	57.47 N	108.07 E
Kirensk	88	57.46 N	108.08 E
Kirghizia → Kyrgyzstan □[1]	72	41.30 N	75.00 E
Kirgili	85	40.24 N	71.43 E
Kirgizija → Kyrgyzstan □[1]	72	41.30 N	75.00 E
Kirgiziya → Kyrgyzstan □[1]	72	41.30 N	75.00 E
Kirgiz-Mijaki	86	53.38 N	54.47 E
Kirgizskij chrebet ⋏	85	42.30 N	74.00 E
Kiri	152	1.27 S	19.00 E
Kiribati □[1]	14	5.00 S	170.00 W
Kiribati II	14	0.30 S	174.00 E
Kiries West	158	26.34 S	19.00 E
Kiriga-mine ∧	94	36.06 N	138.12 E
Kırıkhan, Tür.	130	39.32 N	41.20 E
Kırıkhan, Tür.	130	36.32 N	36.19 E
Kirikiri Prisons ʋ	273a	6.27 N	3.19 E
Kırıkkale	130	39.50 N	33.31 E
Kırıkkale □[4]	130	40.00 N	33.45 E
Kirillov	76	59.52 N	38.23 E
Kirillovka	265b	55.57 N	37.20 E
Kirillovo, Ross.	80	57.07 N	45.27 E
Kirillovo, Ross.	80	53.47 N	42.40 E
Kirillovskoje	76	60.28 N	29.17 E
Kirin → Jilin	89	43.51 N	126.33 E
Kirin → Jilin □[4]	90	44.00 N	126.00 E
Kirinyaga (Mount Kenya) ∧	154	0.10 S	37.20 E
Kirishima-Yaku-kokuritsu-kōen ♦	92	31.55 N	130.51 E
Kirishima-yama ∧	92	31.56 N	130.52 E
Kiriši	76	59.27 N	32.02 E
Kiritimati (Christmas Island) I[1]	174o	1.52 N	157.20 W
Kiriwina Island I	164	8.35 S	151.05 E
Kiriwina Islands II	164	8.35 S	151.05 E
Kirizume-tōge ∧[2]	270	34.56 N	135.16 E
Kirjanovskaja Kontora	88	58.18 N	104.13 E
Kirka	130	39.17 N	30.33 E
Kirkabister	46a	60.07 N	1.08 W
Kırkağaç	130	39.06 N	27.40 E
Kirkbride	44	54.54 N	3.12 W
Kirkburton	44	53.37 N	1.42 W
Kirkby	44	53.29 N	2.54 W
Kirkby in Ashfield	44	53.06 N	1.15 W
Kirkby Lonsdale	44	54.13 N	2.36 W
Kirkby Malzeard	44	54.11 N	1.38 W
Kirkbymoorside	44	54.16 N	0.55 W
Kirkby Stephen	44	54.28 N	2.20 W
Kirkcaldy	46	56.07 N	3.10 W
Kirkcolm	44	54.58 N	5.05 W
Kirkconnel	44	55.23 N	4.00 W
Kirkcudbright	44	54.50 N	4.03 W
Kirkcudbright Bay c	44	54.48 N	4.04 W
Kirkdale ◀[8]	262	53.26 N	2.59 W
Kirkeby	41	56.09 N	9.27 E
Kirkee → Khadki	122	18.34 N	73.52 E
Kirkel	56	49.17 N	7.13 E
Kirkenær	26	60.28 N	12.03 E
Kirkenes	24	69.40 N	30.03 E
Kirke Stillinge	41	55.26 N	11.15 E
Kirkham	44	53.47 N	2.53 W
Kirkhill	46	57.28 N	4.26 W
Kirkintilloch	46	55.57 N	4.10 W
Kirkjubæjarklaustur	24a	63.47 N	18.04 W
Kirkkonummi → Kyrkslätt	26	60.07 N	24.26 E
Kirkland, P.Q., Can.	275a	45.27 N	73.52 W
Kirkland, Il., U.S.	216	42.05 N	88.51 W
Kirkland, Tx., U.S.	196	34.23 N	100.04 W
Kirkland, Wa., U.S.	224	47.40 N	122.12 W
Kirkland Creek ≃	200	34.32 N	113.00 W
Kirkland Lake	190	48.09 N	80.02 W
Kırklar Dağı ∧	130	40.32 N	40.35 E
Kırklareli	130	41.44 N	27.12 E
Kırklareli □[4]	130	41.40 N	27.30 E
Kirklees □[8]	262	53.36 N	1.52 W
Kirkleyditch	262	53.18 N	2.12 W
Kirklin	194	40.11 N	86.21 W
Kirkliston	46	55.58 N	3.25 W
Kirk Michael, I. of Man	44	54.17 N	4.35 W
Kirkmichael, Scot., U.K.	46	56.43 N	3.29 W
Kirkmuirhill	46	55.40 N	3.55 W
Kirkness Lake ⊜	184	51.32 N	93.56 W
Kirkpatrick, Mount ∧	9	84.20 S	166.19 E
Kirkpatrick Lake ⊜	182	51.52 N	111.18 W
Kirk Sandall	44	53.33 N	1.04 W
Kirksville, Il., U.S.	219	39.34 N	88.40 W
Kirksville, Mo., U.S.	194	40.11 N	92.34 W
Kirkton	46	56.13 N	2.55 W
Kirkton of Culsalmond	46	57.23 N	2.34 W
Kirkton of Glenisla	46	56.44 N	3.17 W
Kirktown of Auchterless	46	57.27 N	2.28 W
Kirkūk	128	35.28 N	44.28 E
Kirkville	210	43.05 N	75.57 W
Kirkwall	46	58.59 N	2.58 W
Kirkwood, S. Afr.	158	33.24 S	25.26 E
Kirkwood, De., U.S.	208	39.34 N	75.41 W
Kirkwood, Il., U.S.	190	40.51 N	90.44 W
Kirkwood, Mo., U.S.	219	38.35 N	90.24 W
Kirkwood, N.J., U.S.	285	39.50 N	75.01 W
Kirkwood, N.Y., U.S.	210	42.02 N	75.48 W
Kirmir ≃	130	40.07 N	31.43 E
Kirn	56	49.47 N	7.28 E
Kirnāhar	126	23.45 N	87.52 E
Kirotshe	154	1.37 S	29.02 E
Kirov, Ross.	76	54.05 N	34.20 E
Kirov, Ross.	80	58.38 N	49.42 E
Kirovabad → Gäncä	84	40.40 N	46.22 E
Kirovakan	84	40.48 N	44.30 E
Kirove, Ukr.	78	47.41 N	35.46 E
Kirove, Ukr.	83	48.23 N	37.55 E
Kirovgrad	86	57.26 N	60.04 E
Kirovka	86	47.07 N	82.00 E
Kirovo, Ross.	86	55.33 N	63.46 E
Kirovo, Uzb.	85	40.26 N	70.34 E
Kirov Oblast' □[4]	24	59.00 N	50.00 E
Kirovo-Čepeck	80	58.33 N	50.01 E
Kirovohrad	78	48.30 N	32.18 E
Kirovohrad □[4]	78	48.30 N	32.00 E
Kirovsk, Ross.	24	67.37 N	33.35 E
Kirovsk, Ross.	265a	59.52 N	31.00 E
Kirovsk, Turk.	128	37.42 N	60.23 E
Kirovs'k, Ukr.	83	49.01 N	37.56 E
Kirovs'k, Ukr.	83	48.38 N	38.39 E
Kirovs'ke, Ukr.	78	48.33 N	34.53 E
Kirovs'ke, Ukr.	78	45.14 N	35.13 E
Kirovs'ke, Ukr.	83	48.09 N	38.21 E
Kirovskij, Kaz.	86	44.52 N	78.12 E
Kirovskij, Ross.	74	54.18 N	155.47 E
Kirovskij, Ross.	80	45.51 N	48.07 E
Kirovskij, Ross.	89	54.26 N	126.55 E
Kirovskij, Ross.	89	45.07 N	133.30 E
Kirovskije ostrova II	265a	59.58 N	30.15 E
Kirovskoje	85	42.39 N	71.35 E
Kirov Stadium ♦	265a	59.58 N	30.14 E
Kirov Theatre ʋ	265a	59.55 N	30.18 E
Kirpičnyj Zavod	265a	60.01 N	30.48 E
Kirpil'skaja	78	45.23 N	39.43 E
Kirriemuir	46	56.41 N	3.01 W
Kirs	86	59.21 N	52.14 E
Kirsanov	80	52.38 N	42.43 E
Kirsanovka	80	52.30 N	52.53 E
Kirschau	54	51.04 N	14.27 E
Kırşehir	130	39.09 N	34.10 E
Kırşehir □[4]	130	39.20 N	34.10 E
Kīrthar National Park ♦	120	25.50 N	67.40 E
Kīrthar Range ⋏	120	27.00 N	67.10 E
Kirtland, N.M., U.S.	200	36.44 N	108.21 W
Kirtland, Oh., U.S.	214	41.37 N	81.21 W
Kirtland Air Force Base ■	200	35.02 N	106.37 W
Kirtland Hills	214	41.37 N	81.24 W
Kirtle Water ≃	44	54.58 N	3.05 W
Kirton	42	52.56 N	0.04 W
Kirton in Lindsey	44	53.28 N	0.36 W
Kirtorf	56	50.46 N	9.06 E
Kiruna	24	67.51 N	20.16 E
Kirundu	154	0.44 S	25.32 E
Kirurumo	154	5.53 S	34.11 E
Kirvin	222	31.46 N	96.20 W
Kirwan Heights	279b	40.22 N	80.06 W
Kirwee	172	43.30 S	172.13 E
Kirwin	198	39.40 N	99.07 W
Kirwin Reservoir ⊜[1]	198	39.39 N	99.10 W
Kiryandongo	154	1.53 N	32.03 E
Kiryū	94	36.24 N	139.20 E
Kirza	86	54.14 N	81.40 E
Kiržač	82	56.09 N	38.52 E
Kiržač ≃	82	55.52 N	39.04 E
Kisa, Nihon	96	34.43 N	132.59 E
Kisa, Sve.	26	57.59 N	15.37 E
Kisai	94	36.06 N	139.35 E
Kisaichi	270	34.46 N	135.42 E
Kisakata	92	39.13 N	139.54 E
Kisaki	154	7.28 S	37.36 E
Kis Alföld ≚	61	47.35 N	17.00 E
Kišaly	76	54.23 N	43.12 E
Kisambo	152	6.25 S	18.14 E
Kisanga	154	2.29 N	26.35 E
Kisangani (Stanleyville)	154	0.30 N	25.12 E
Kisantu	152	5.07 S	15.05 E
Kisar, Pulau I	112	8.05 S	127.10 E
Kisaralik ≃	180	60.51 N	161.16 W
Kisaran	114	2.59 N	99.37 E
Kisarawe	154	6.54 S	39.04 E
Kisarazu	94	35.23 N	139.55 E
Kisarazu-Kichi, Kōkū-jieitai ■	94	35.24 N	139.55 E
Kisawa	96	33.49 N	134.18 E
K.I. Sawyer Air Force Base ■	190	46.21 N	87.25 W
Kisbér	30	47.30 N	18.02 E
Kisbey	184	49.38 N	102.41 W
Kise ≃	94	35.06 N	138.53 E
Kiselevsk → Kisel'ovsk	86	54.00 N	86.39 E
Kisel'ovka	80	47.18 N	44.07 E
Kisel'ovsk	86	54.00 N	86.39 E
Kisengwa	154	6.00 S	25.50 E
Kisen-yama ∧[2]	270	34.54 N	135.51 E
Kiser Lake ⊜	218	40.11 N	83.58 W
Kīsh, Jazīreh-ye I	128	26.32 N	53.56 E
Kishanda	154	1.42 S	31.34 E
Kishanganga ≃	123	34.22 N	73.30 E
Kishanganj	124	26.07 N	87.56 E
Kishangarh	120	27.52 N	70.34 E
Kishangarh ◀[8]	272a	28.31 N	77.08 E
Kishangarh Bās	120	26.34 N	74.52 E
Kishb, Ḥarrat al- ⍊[9]	144	23.00 N	41.25 E
Kishi, Nig.	150	9.05 N	3.52 E
Kishi, R.D.C.	154	10.04 S	26.26 E
Kishida ≃	96	35.38 N	134.27 E
Kishigawa	96	34.13 N	135.20 E
Kishikas ≃	184	52.45 N	91.43 W
Kishimoto	96	35.23 N	133.25 E
Kishinev → Chişinău	38	47.00 N	28.50 E
Kishiwada	96	34.28 N	135.22 E
Kishorganj	124	24.26 N	90.46 E
Kishorn, Loch c	46	57.21 N	5.41 W
Kishtwār	123	33.19 N	75.46 E
Kishwaukee ≃	216	42.11 N	89.08 W
Kishwaukee, South Branch ≃	216	42.12 N	88.59 W
Kisia	152	4.35 S	18.22 E
Kisigo ≃	154	7.03 S	35.50 E
Kisii	154	0.41 S	34.46 E
Kisiju	154	7.24 S	39.20 E
Kiši-Karoj, ozero ⊜	86	54.03 N	71.20 E
Kisika-zaki ≻	93b	30.50 N	131.04 E
Kısıklı ◀[8]	267b	41.01 N	29.03 E
Kısır Dağı ∧	84	40.58 N	43.04 E
Kısırkaya ◀[8]	267b	41.14 N	28.58 E
Kısırmandıra ◀[8]	267b	41.14 N	28.49 E
Kisiwada → Kishiwada	96	34.28 N	135.22 E
Kisiwani	154	4.08 S	37.57 E
Kisizi	154	1.00 S	29.56 E
Kiska Island I	181a	52.00 N	177.30 E
Kiskatinaw ≃	182	56.06 N	120.08 W
Kiska Volcano ∧[1]	181a	52.07 N	177.36 E
Kis-Kevély ∧[2]	264c	47.38 N	18.59 E
Kiski Lake ⊜	184	54.46 N	98.55 W
Kiskimere	279b	40.37 N	79.35 W
Kiskiminetas ≃	214	40.41 N	79.40 W
Kiskittogisu Lake ⊜	184	54.13 N	98.20 W
Kiskitto Lake ⊜	184	54.16 N	98.34 W
Kiskörei-víztároló ⊜[1]	30	47.35 N	20.40 E
Kiskőrös	30	46.38 N	19.17 E
Kiskunfélegyháza	30	46.43 N	19.52 E
Kiskunhalas	30	46.26 N	19.30 E
Kiskunmajsa	30	46.30 N	19.45 E
Kiskunsági Nemzeti Park ♦	30	46.40 N	19.25 E
Kisl'akovskaja	78	46.27 N	39.40 E
Kislovo	80	49.54 N	45.25 E
Kislovodsk	84	43.55 N	42.44 E
Kismaayo	144	0.22 S	42.32 E
Kismet	276	40.38 N	73.12 W
Kisnema	76	60.20 N	37.39 E
Kiso, Nihon	94	35.56 N	137.47 E
Kiso, Nihon	268	35.34 N	139.26 E
Kiso ≃	94	35.02 N	136.45 E
Kisofukushima	94	35.51 N	137.42 E
Kisogawa	94	35.20 N	136.47 E
Kisoripur	126	22.05 N	88.34 E
Kisoro	154	1.17 S	29.41 E
Kiso-sammyaku ⋏	94	35.43 N	137.50 E
Kisozaki	94	35.04 N	136.44 E
Kispest ◀[8]	264c	47.27 N	19.08 E
Kispiox	182	55.21 N	127.41 W
Kispiox ≃	182	55.16 N	127.41 W
Kispiox Mountain ∧	182	55.25 N	127.57 W
Kissamos	38	35.30 N	23.38 E
Kissena Park ♦	276	40.45 N	73.49 W
Kisseynew Lake ⊜	184	54.58 N	101.35 W
Kissidougou	150	9.11 N	10.06 W
Kissimmee	220	28.17 N	81.24 W
Kissimmee ≃	220	27.10 N	80.53 W
Kissimmee, Lake ⊜	220	27.55 N	81.16 W
Kissing	60	48.18 N	10.59 E
Kississing	184	55.07 N	101.07 W
Kississing Lake ⊜	184	55.10 N	101.20 W
Kisslegg	58	47.47 N	9.53 E
Kissū, Jabal ∧	140	21.35 N	25.09 E
Kista	80	46.05 N	43.06 E
Kistanje	36	43.59 N	15.58 E
Kistarcsa	264c	47.33 N	19.16 E
Kistendej	80	52.08 N	43.39 E
Kistigan Lake ⊜	184	54.38 N	92.37 W
Kistler	214	40.22 N	77.51 W
Kisújszállás	30	47.13 N	20.46 E
Kisuki	96	35.17 N	132.54 E
Kisumu	154	0.06 S	34.45 E
Kisvárda	30	48.13 N	22.05 E
Kiswere	154	9.26 S	39.33 E
Kita	150	13.03 N	9.29 W
Kita ◀[8], Nihon	268	35.45 N	139.44 E
Kita ◀[8], Nihon	270	34.45 N	135.08 E
Kita ◀[8], Nihon	270	34.42 N	135.30 E
Kita ◀[8], Nihon	270	35.03 N	135.45 E
Kitaaiki	94	36.04 N	138.34 E
Kita-Daitō-jima I	90	25.57 N	131.18 E
Kitafuji-enshūjō ■	94	35.25 N	138.48 E
Kitagata	94	35.26 N	136.41 E
Kitagawa	96	33.27 N	134.03 E
Kitagi-shima I	96	34.23 N	133.32 E
Kitaibaraki	94	36.48 N	140.45 E
Kitain Temple ʋ[1]	268	35.54 N	139.30 E
Kita-Iō-jima I	14	25.26 N	141.17 E
Kitairiso	268	35.50 N	139.26 E
Kitajima	96	34.05 N	134.35 E
Kitakami	92	39.18 N	141.07 E
Kitakami ≃	92	38.25 N	141.19 E
Kitakami-kōchi ⋏	92	39.30 N	141.30 E
Kitakata	92	37.39 N	139.52 E
Kitakyuschu → Kitakyūshū	96	33.53 N	130.50 E
Kitakyūshū	96	33.53 N	130.50 E
Kitakyushu-kokutei-kōen ♦	96	33.45 N	130.50 E
Kitale	154	1.01 N	35.00 E
Kitamachi ◀[8]	268	35.46 N	139.39 E
Kitamba ◀[8]	273b	4.19 S	15.14 E
Kitami	92a	43.48 N	143.54 E
Kitami-sanchi ⋏	92a	44.22 N	142.43 E
Kitamoto	94	36.02 N	139.32 E
Kita-Nagato-kaigan-kokutei-kōen ♦	96	34.24 N	131.16 E
Kitanakagusuku	174m	26.21 N	127.51 E
Kitanda, R.D.C.	154	6.36 S	26.27 E
Kitanda, R.D.C.	154	9.59 S	27.28 E
Kitangari	154	10.39 S	39.20 E
Kitangiri, Lake ⊜	154	4.05 S	34.19 E
Kitangua	152	6.17 S	20.22 E
Kitano, Nihon	96	33.20 N	130.35 E
Kitano, Nihon	268	35.47 N	139.26 E
Kitanoshinden	268	35.48 N	139.26 E
Kitatachibana	94	36.29 N	139.03 E
Kitatajima	268	35.56 N	139.30 E
Kitatawara	270	34.44 N	135.42 E
Kitaura	94	36.04 N	140.32 E
Kita-ura ⊜	94	36.00 N	140.34 E
Kitava Island I	164	8.40 S	151.20 E
Kitaya	154	10.39 S	40.10 E
Kit Carson, Ca., U.S.	226	38.41 N	120.07 W
Kit Carson, Co., U.S.	198	38.45 N	102.47 W
Kitchener, Austl.	162	31.02 S	124.11 E
Kitchener, On., Can.	212	43.27 N	80.29 W
Kitee	26	62.06 N	30.09 E
Kitega → Gitega	154	3.26 S	29.56 E
Kiteiyab	140	17.12 N	33.43 E
Kitenda	152	6.53 S	17.21 E
Kitenevo	82	56.21 N	36.13 E
Kitengo	152	7.26 S	24.08 E
Kitéssa	154	5.20 N	25.20 E
Kitgum	154	3.18 N	32.53 E
Kíthira	38	36.09 N	23.00 E
Kíthira I	38	36.20 N	22.58 E
Kíthnos	38	37.26 N	24.26 E
Kíthnos I	38	37.25 N	24.28 E
Kitimat	182	54.03 N	128.33 W
Kitimat ≃	182	54.06 N	128.38 W
Kitimat Ranges ⋏	182	53.30 N	128.50 W
Kitinen ≃	24	67.08 N	27.29 E
Kitíou, Akrotírion ≻	130	34.48 N	33.36 E
Kitlope ≃	182	53.10 N	127.45 W
Kitlope Lake ⊜	182	53.07 N	127.47 W
Kitō, Nihon	94	34.42 N	138.03 E
Kitō, Nihon	96	33.46 N	134.12 E
Kitoj ≃	88	52.39 N	103.56 E
Kitridge Point ≻	241g	13.09 N	59.25 W
Kitsap □[6]	224	47.41 N	122.44 W
Kitscoty	184	53.20 N	110.20 W
Kit's Coty House ʋ	260	51.19 N	0.30 E
Kitshua-Nseke	152	4.26 S	19.36 E
Kitsman'	78	48.27 N	25.44 E
Kitsuki	92	33.25 N	131.37 E
Kitsuregawa	94	36.43 N	140.01 E
Kittanning	214	40.48 N	79.31 W
Kittatinny Mountain ∧	210	41.10 N	74.55 W
Kittatinny Tunnel ◀[5]	214	40.09 N	77.41 W
Kittendorf	54	53.37 N	12.54 E
Kittery	188	43.05 N	70.44 W
Kitt Green	262	53.33 N	2.41 W
Kittilä	24	67.40 N	24.54 E
Kittitas	202	46.59 N	120.24 W
Kittitas □[6]	224	47.13 N	121.01 W
Kitt Peak National Observatory ʋ[3]	200	31.58 N	111.36 W
Kittsee	61	48.05 N	17.04 E
Kitu	154	7.38 S	27.42 E
Kitui	154	1.22 S	38.01 E
Kitumbeine ∧[1]	154	2.44 S	36.16 E
Kitunda	154	6.48 S	33.13 E
Kitutu	154	3.17 S	28.05 E
Kitwanga	182	55.06 N	128.03 W
Kitwangar Indian Reserve ◀[4]	182	55.06 N	128.04 W
Kitwe	154	12.49 S	28.13 E
Kitwitwi	156	17.25 S	18.25 E
Kityang → Jieyang	100	23.35 N	116.21 E
Kitzbühel	64	47.27 N	12.23 E
Kitzbüheler Alpen ⋏	64	47.20 N	12.20 E
Kitzingen	56	49.44 N	10.09 E
Kitzscher	54	51.09 N	12.33 E
Kiukiang → Jiujiang	100	29.44 N	115.59 E
Kiukiu, Pointe ≻	174x	9.47 S	139.09 W
Kiul	124	25.09 N	86.06 E
Kiunga, Kenya	154	1.45 S	41.29 E
Kiunga, Pap. N. Gui.	164	6.10 S	141.15 E
Kiuruvesi	26	63.39 N	26.37 E
Kiuschu → Kyūshū I	92	33.00 N	131.00 E
Kivak	180	64.16 N	172.57 W
Kivalina	180	67.44 N	164.33 W
Kiveriči	76	57.22 N	36.36 E

Symbols in the index entries represent the broad categories identified in the key at the right. Symbols with superior numbers (⋏[1]) identify subcategories (see complete key on page *I · 1).*

Symbole im Register stellen die rechts im Schlüssel erklärten Kategorien dar. Symbole mit hochgestellten Ziffern (⋏[1]) bezeichnen Unterabteilungen einer Kategorie (vgl. vollständiger Schlüssel auf Seite *I · 1).*

Los símbolos incluídos en el texto del índice representan las grandes categorías identificadas con la clave a la derecha. Los símbolos con numeros en su parte superior (⋏[1]) identifican las subcategorías (véase la clave completa en la página *I · 1).*

Les symboles de l'index représentent les catégories indiquées dans la légende à droite. Les symboles suivis d'un indice (⋏[1]) représentent des sous-catégories (voir légende complète à la page *I · 1).*

Os símbolos incluídos no texto do índice representam as grandes categorias identificadas com a chave à direita. Os símbolos com números em sua parte superior (⋏[1]) identificam as subcategorias (veja-se a chave completa à página *I · 1).*

	English	Deutsch	Español	Français	Português
∧	Mountain	Berg	Montaña	Montagne	Montanha
⋏	Mountains	Gebirge	Montañas	Montagnes	Montanhas
)(	Pass	Paß	Paso	Col	Passo
V	Valley, Canyon	Tal, Cañon	Valle, Cañón	Vallée, Canyon	Vale, Canhão
≚	Plain	Ebene	Llano	Plaine	Planície
≻	Cape	Kap	Cabo	Cap	Cabo
I	Island	Insel	Isla	Île	Ilha
II	Islands	Inseln	Islas	Îles	Ilhas
⍊	Other Topographic Features	Andere Topographische Objekte	Otros Elementos Topográficos	Autres données topographiques	Outros acidentes topográficos

ESPAÑOL Nombre	Página	Lat.°'	Long.°' W = Oeste
Kivertsi	78	50.50 N	25.27 E
Kivijärvi	26	63.04 N	25.03 E
Kivijärvi ⌀	26	63.10 N	25.09 E
Kivik	26	55.41 N	14.15 E
Kiviöli	76	59.21 N	26.57 E
Kivshyvata	78	49.29 N	30.38 E
Kivu, Lac ⌀	154	2.00 S	29.10 E
Kiwaba N'zogi	152	8.57 S	16.32 E
Kiwai Island ▮	164	8.30 S	143.25 E
Kiwalik	180	66.02 N	161.50 W
Kiwanis Lake	214	41.28 N	81.09 W
Kiyama	96	33.25 N	130.32 E
Kly'makī Dāgh ⌃	84	38.47 N	45.51 E
Kiyan	174m	26.05 N	127.47 E
Kiyan-zaki ⟩	174m	26.05 N	127.39 E
Kiyikōy	130	41.38 N	28.05 E
Kiyiu Lake ⌀	184	51.38 N	108.55 W
Kiyl ⌃	86	49.25 N	54.50 E
Kiyomi	94	35.29 N	139.17 E
Kiyomi	94	36.07 N	137.11 E
Kiyosawa	94	35.03 N	138.15 E
Kiyose	94	35.47 N	139.32 E
Kiyosu	94	35.12 N	136.50 E
Kiyosumi-yama ⌃	94	35.09 N	140.09 E
Kiyotani	270	34.52 N	134.59 E
Kiyotsu ≃	94	37.03 N	138.41 E
Kizel	86	59.03 N	57.40 E
Kizevatovo	80	53.13 N	45.18 E
Kizil ⌃	130	41.44 N	35.58 E
Kizil Adalar ▯▯	130	40.52 N	29.05 E
Kizilcabölük	130	37.37 N	29.01 E
Kizilcadağ	130	37.01 N	29.58 E
Kizilcahamam	130	40.28 N	32.39 E
Kizilçakçak	84	40.46 N	43.37 E
Kizildağ Milli Parkı ♦	130	37.58 N	31.28 E
Kizildikme	130	39.05 N	37.01 E
Kizilhisar	130	37.33 N	29.18 E
Kizilirmak	130	40.21 N	33.59 E
Kizilören	130	37.52 N	32.07 E
Kizil'skoje	86	52.44 N	58.54 E
Kizilsu	130	37.28 N	42.13 E
Kiziltaškskij liman ⊂	78	45.07 N	37.05 E
Kizitepe	130	37.12 N	40.36 E
Kiziltoprak ⌃	267b	40.58 N	29.03 E
Kizil'urt	84	43.12 N	46.53 E
Kizilyaka	130	37.09 N	32.54 E
Kižimiz, gora ⌃	24	63.12 N	58.48 E
Kizimkazi	154	6.27 S	39.28 E
Kižinga	88	51.34 N	109.55 E
Kizir ≃	88	53.51 N	93.06 E
Kizkalesi ▮	130	36.28 N	34.04 E
Kizkulesi ◆⁵	267b	41.01 N	29.00 E
Kizl'ar	84	43.50 N	46.40 E
Kizl'arskij zaliv ⊂	84	44.33 N	46.55 E
Kizner	80	56.17 N	51.31 E
Kiz'oma	24	61.08 N	44.50 E
Kizu	96	34.53 N	135.49 E
Kizu ≃	94	34.53 N	135.42 E
Kizuki	268	35.34 N	139.40 E
Kizuri	270	34.39 N	135.34 E
Kizyl-Ajak	128	37.40 N	65.23 E
Kizyl-Arvat	128	38.58 N	56.15 E
Kizyl-Atrek	128	37.36 N	54.46 E
Kizyl-Su	128	39.48 N	53.15 E
Kjellerup	41	56.17 N	9.26 E
København			
— København	41	55.40 N	12.35 E
Kjustendil	38	42.17 N	22.41 E
Klaarstrom	158	33.20 S	22.32 E
Klaaswaal	52	51.46 N	4.26 E
Klabat, Gunung ⌃	112	1.28 N	125.02 E
Kladanj	38	44.13 N	18.41 E
Kladbišči	85	55.32 N	45.33 E
Kläden	54	52.38 N	11.39 E
Kladkovo	82	55.34 N	38.51 E
Kladno	54	50.08 N	14.05 E
Kladovo	38	44.37 N	22.37 E
Kladow ◆⁸	54	52.27 N	13.09 E
Kladruby	60	49.43 N	12.59 E
Klagan	110	12.47 N	101.39 E
Klagenfurt	61	46.37 N	14.18 E
Klâgerup	41	55.36 N	13.15 E
Klagshamn	41	55.32 N	12.55 E
Klagstorp	41	55.24 N	13.22 E
Klahoose Indian			
Reserve ◆	182	50.31 N	124.19 W
Klaipeda (Memel)	76	55.43 N	21.07 E
Klakah	115a	7.59 S	113.15 E
Klamath	204	41.31 N	124.02 W
Klamath Falls	204	42.13 N	121.46 W
Klamath Marsh ☰	202	42.54 N	121.44 W
Klamath Mountains ⌃	204	41.40 N	123.20 W
K. Lamido	146	9.21 N	11.12 E
Klämmingen ⌀	40	59.07 N	17.15 E
Klammpass ⋈	64	47.17 N	13.05 E
Klamono	164	1.08 S	131.30 E
Klang			
— Kelang	114	3.02 N	101.27 E
Klangenan	115a	6.42 S	108.28 E
Klangpi	110	22.59 N	93.20 E
Klarälven (Trysilelva)			
≃	26	59.23 N	13.32 E
Kl'as'ma ≃	265b	55.59 N	37.50 E
Klåšterec	54	50.13 N	13.10 E
Klaten	115a	7.42 S	110.35 E
Klatovy	60	49.24 N	13.18 E
Klausdorf, Dtsch.	54	54.18 N	10.15 E
Klausdorf, Dtsch.	54	52.18 N	13.18 E
Klausenburg			
— Cluj-Napoca	38	46.47 N	23.36 E
Klausenpass ⋈	58	46.52 N	8.51 E
Klawer	158	31.44 S	18.36 E
Klawock	182	55.33 N	133.06 W
Klazienaveen	52	52.44 N	7.00 E
Kl'az'ma ≃	80	56.10 N	42.58 E
Kl'az'minskoje			
vodochranilišče ⌀	265b	55.59 N	37.35 E
Klecko	60	52.38 N	17.26 E
Kleczew	60	52.23 N	18.10 E
Kledering ◆⁸	264a	48.08 N	16.26 E
Kleef	263	51.11 N	6.56 E
Kleena Kleene	182	51.58 N	124.50 W
Kleinasien			
— Asia Minor ▯⁹	22	39.00 N	32.00 E
Kleinbegin	158	28.50 S	21.46 E
Klein-Blesbokspruit ≃	273d	26.16 S	28.29 E
Kleinbodungen	54	51.33 N	10.38 E
Klein Bonaire ▮	241s	12.10 N	68.18 W
Klein Bünzow	54	53.53 N	13.48 E
Kleinburg	275b	43.50 N	79.38 W
Klein Curaçao ▮	241s	12.00 N	68.41 W
Kleine Elster ≃	54	51.32 N	13.23 E
Kleine Emme ≃	58	47.04 N	8.17 E
Kleine Emscher ≃	263	51.31 N	6.43 E
Kleine Erlauf ≃	64	48.11 N	15.08 E
Kleineichen	263	51.08 N	7.21 E
Kleine Laber ≃	60	48.50 N	12.12 E
Kleinenbroich	263	51.12 N	6.35 E
Kleiner Jasmunder			
Bodden ⊂	54	54.28 N	13.32 E
Kleiner Ravens-Berg			
⌃ ²	264a	52.22 N	13.04 E
Kleiner Wannsee ⌀	264a	52.25 N	13.11 E
Kleine Zern-See ⌀	264a	52.26 N	12.55 E
Kleine Spree ≃	54	51.31 N	14.25 E
Kleines Walsertal ⌄	64	47.23 N	10.12 E
Kleinfeltersville	208	40.31 N	76.25 W
Kleinglödnitz	64	46.51 N	14.08 E
Kleinhammer	263	51.12 N	7.46 E
Klein-Jukskei ≃	273d	26.08 S	27.56 E
Klein Karoo			
— Little Karroo ⌄¹	158	33.45 S	21.30 E
Klein Kienitz	264a	52.18 N	13.29 E

FRANÇAIS Nom	Page	Lat.°'	Long.°' W = Ouest
Kleinlützel	58	47.26 N	7.25 E
Kleinmachnow	54	52.24 N	13.15 E
Klein Marzehns	54	52.01 N	12.37 E
Kleinmond	158	34.21 S	19.03 E
Klein-Olifants ≃	158	25.41 S	29.19 E
Kleinschönebeck	264a	52.29 N	13.43 E
Klein-Soutpan	158	30.26 S	22.26 E
Klein-Vis ≃	158	33.05 S	26.00 E
Klein Wanzleben	54	52.04 N	11.21 E
Klein Ziethen	264a	52.23 N	13.27 E
Klein Ziethener-Berge			
⌃²	264a	52.22 N	13.26 E
Klekovača ⌃	36	44.26 N	16.31 E
Klementjevka	86	50.16 N	80.56 E
Klemme	190	43.00 N	93.36 W
Klemtu	182	52.36 N	128.31 W
Klenovka	80	57.45 N	54.19 E
Klenovo	82	55.19 N	37.21 E
Klenoxdorp	158	26.58 S	26.39 E
Klerksdraal	158	26.15 S	27.10 E
Klesiv	78	51.19 N	26.54 E
Klésso	150	10.57 N	3.59 W
Klet' ⌃	61	48.52 N	14.17 E
Kletn'a	76	53.23 N	33.12 E
Kletskij	80	49.19 N	43.04 E
Kletsko-Počtovskij	80	49.36 N	43.03 E
Klettgau ◆¹	58	47.40 N	8.25 E
Klettwitz	54	51.32 N	13.53 E
Klevan'	78	50.44 N	26.02 E
Kleve	52	51.48 N	6.09 E
Klevenka	80	52.07 N	49.33 E
Kley ◆⁸	263	51.30 N	7.22 E
Kilbreck, Ben ⌃	46	58.14 N	4.22 W
Kličag ≃	76	53.29 N	29.21 E
Klickitat	204	45.49 N	121.09 W
Klickitat ◆⁶	224	45.50 N	121.07 W
Klickitat ≃	204	45.42 N	121.17 W
Kliedbruch ◆¹	263	51.22 N	6.33 E
Klieken	54	51.53 N	12.22 E
Klietz	54	52.40 N	12.04 E
Klimavičy	76	53.37 N	31.58 E
Klimino	88	58.39 N	88.42 E
Klimino, Ross.	88	56.23 N	32.11 E
Klimovo	82	55.22 N	38.52 E
Klimovskoje	82	54.42 N	37.48 E
Klimov Zavod	76	54.50 N	34.55 E
Klimpfjäll	26	65.04 N	14.52 E
Klin, Ross.	82	56.20 N	36.44 E
Klin, Ross.	82	55.19 N	36.20 E
Klinaklini ≃	182	51.05 N	125.36 W
Klin-Bel'din	82	54.45 N	39.13 E
Klincy	76	52.47 N	32.14 E
Kline Ditch ≃	279a	41.28 N	82.04 W
Kling	116	5.58 N	124.42 E
Klingbach ≃	56	49.10 N	8.20 E
Klingenberg am Main	56	49.47 N	9.11 E
Klingenmünster	56	49.08 N	8.01 E
Klingenthal	54	50.21 N	12.28 E
Klinger Lake ⌀	216	41.47 N	85.33 W
Klingnau	58	47.35 N	8.15 E
Klinhartberge ⌃	158	27.18 S	15.48 E
Klingnau	58	47.35 N	8.15 E
Klinovec ⌃	54	50.24 N	12.58 E
Klintehamn	26	57.24 N	18.12 E
Klintsy			
— Klincy	76	52.47 N	32.14 E
Klip ≃, S. Afr.	158	27.03 S	29.03 E
Klip ≃, S. Afr.	273d	26.19 S	27.53 E
Klipbakken ≃	158	28.50 S	21.21 E
Klipdale	158	34.19 S	19.57 E
Klipdam	158	27.35 S	19.56 E
Klipliev	158	31.54 S	24.21 E
Klippan	41	56.08 N	13.06 E
Klippiaat	158	33.02 S	24.21 E
Klippoortjie	273d	26.13 S	28.10 E
Kliprviersberg ≃	273d	26.17 S	28.02 E
Klipstoel	273d	26.17 S	27.53 E
Klipwerf	158	31.09 S	19.52 E
Klishkivtsi	78	48.26 N	26.15 E
Klisura	38	42.42 N	24.27 E
Klitmøller	41	57.02 N	8.31 E
Klitsa ≃	80	59.55 N	48.30 E
Ključ	36	44.32 N	16.47 E
Klobbicke	54	52.52 N	13.48 E
Klobouky	61	49.00 N	16.52 E
Klobuticy	84	58.51 N	29.35 E
Kłodawa	60	52.15 N	18.55 E
Kłodzko	60	50.28 N	16.39 E
Kløfta	26	60.04 N	11.09 E
Klomnice	60	50.56 N	19.21 E
Klondike ◆⁹	216	40.28 N	86.57 W
Klondike ≃	180	64.05 N	139.20 W
Klooga	76	59.19 N	24.16 E
Kloosterveen	52	52.59 N	6.33 E
Kloosterzande	52	51.22 N	4.02 E
Kloster	54	54.35 N	13.06 E
Klosterfelde	54	52.48 N	13.29 E
Klosterhardt ◆⁸	263	51.31 N	6.53 E
Klösterle	54	47.08 N	10.05 E
Klostermansfeld	54	51.36 N	11.29 E
Kloster Oesede	52	52.12 N	8.07 E
Klosterneuburg	61	48.18 N	16.20 E
Kloster Zinna	54	52.00 N	13.07 E
Kloten, Schw.	58	47.27 N	8.35 E
Kloten, Sve.	40	59.54 N	15.17 E
Klotz, Lac ⌀	176	60.32 N	73.40 W
Klötze	54	52.38 N	11.10 E
Kloulklubed	175b	7.02 N	134.15 E
Klouto	150	6.57 N	0.34 E
Kl'ukvenka ≃	88	57.30 N	85.30 E
Klukwan	182	59.24 N	135.54 W
Kluess ≃	54	53.46 N	12.04 E
Klukung	115b	8.32 S	115.24 E
Klüterthöhle ◆⁵	56	51.18 N	7.21 E
Kluane Lake ⌀	180	61.15 N	138.40 W
Kandidie gruver	180	61.30 N	139.00 W
Klynkyne	83	51.18 N	38.15 E
Knaddah	130	36.12 E
Kn'aginino	80	55.48 N	45.01 E
Knaik ≃	52	50.14 N	3.27 E
Knapdale ◆¹	46	55.55 N	5.30 W
Knaphill	260	51.19 N	0.37 W
Knapp	190	44.57 N	92.04 W

PORTUGUÊS Nome	Página	Lat.°'	Long.°' W = Oeste
Knapp Creek ≃	210	42.00 N	78.30 W
Knapperiberg	61	46.56 N	14.35 E
Knärad	26	56.32 N	13.19 E
Knaresborough	44	54.00 N	1.27 W
Knargram	126	24.01 N	87.59 E
Knauertown	285	40.10 N	75.44 W
Kn'ažaja Bajgora	76	52.23 N	40.02 E
Kn'azevka	86	57.35 N	74.10 E
Kn'ažji Gory	76	56.05 N	35.14 E
Kn'ažovo	76	59.40 N	43.54 E
Knebel	41	56.13 N	10.30 E
Knebworth	42	51.52 N	0.12 W
Kneehills Creek ≃	182	51.30 N	112.50 W
Knee Lake ⌀, Mb., Can.	184	55.03 N	94.40 W
Knee Lake ⌀, Sk., Can.	184	55.51 N	107.00 W
Knesebeck	54	52.41 N	10.42 E
Knesselare	50	51.08 N	3.25 E
Knetzgau	56	50.00 N	10.33 E
Knevicy	76	57.56 N	32.14 E
Kneža	38	43.30 N	24.05 E
Kniažja	38	43.55 N	20.43 E
Knickerbocker	196	31.16 N	100.38 W
Kniebis	56	48.28 N	8.17 E
Knife ≃	198	47.20 N	101.23 W
Knife Lake ⌀	184	53.47 N	91.20 W
Knife River Indian			
Villages National			
Historic Site ⊥	198	47.21 N	101.23 W
Knight Inlet ⊂	182	50.41 N	125.40 W
Knight Island ▮	180	60.20 N	147.45 W
Knighton	42	52.21 N	3.03 W
Knightsen	228	37.58 N	121.40 W
Knights Landing	226	38.47 N	121.43 W
Knightstown	218	39.47 N	85.31 W
Knightville Dam ◆⁶	207	42.17 N	72.52 W
Knik ≃	180	61.25 N	149.45 W
Knin	36	44.02 N	16.12 E
Knippa	196	29.18 N	99.38 W
Knislinge	26	56.11 N	14.05 E
Knittlingen	56	49.01 N	8.45 E
Knivsbjerg ⌃²	41	55.08 N	9.27 E
Knivsta	40	59.43 N	17.48 E
Knjaževac	38	43.34 N	22.16 E
Knob, Cape ⟩	162	34.32 S	119.16 E
Knobby Head ⟩	162	29.40 S	114.58 E
Knob Noster	194	38.45 N	93.33 W
Knob Peak ⌃	116	12.28 N	121.21 E
Knočon'ovo	86	55.02 N	82.12 E
Knock ⟩	48	52.38 N	9.20 W
Knock ≃	48	57.33 N	2.45 W
Knockholt	260	51.18 N	0.06 E
Knockholt Pound	260	51.19 N	0.08 E
Knocklayd ⌃	48	55.09 N	6.15 W
Knockmealdown	48	52.26 N	8.24 W
Knockmealdown			
Mountains ⌃	48	52.10 N	8.00 W
Knoke	50	51.21 N	3.17 E
Knoke ⊥	260	51.16 N	0.12 E
Knolls Green	262	53.19 N	2.18 W
Knowlood, Ct., U.S.	207	41.16 N	72.23 W
Knowlood, Il., U.S.	216	42.17 N	87.53 W
Knowlood, Md., U.S.	284c	39.02 N	76.58 W
Knolwood Park	285	40.14 N	84.22 W
Knoxe ◆⁹	38	40.30 N	25.10 E
Knossós ▯	38	35.20 N	25.10 E
Knottingley	44	53.43 N	1.14 W
Knott's Berry Farm ♦	280	33.50 N	118.00 W
Knotts Island	208	36.31 N	75.56 W
Knotty Ash ◆⁸	262	53.25 N	2.54 W
Knotty Green	260	51.37 N	0.39 W
Knowland State			
Arboretum and			
Park ♦	282	37.45 N	122.09 W
Knowle	42	52.23 N	1.43 W
Knowlesville	210	43.14 N	78.19 W
Knowlton Lake ⌀	212	44.28 N	76.41 W
Knowltonwood	285	39.53 N	75.24 W
Knowsley	262	53.27 N	2.50 W
Knowsley ◆⁸	262	53.26 N	2.50 W
Knowsley Hall ⊽	262	53.26 N	2.50 W
Knowsley Park ♦	262	53.27 N	2.49 W
Knox, In., U.S.	216	41.17 N	86.37 W
Knox, N.Y., U.S.	210	42.40 N	74.07 W
Knox, Pa., U.S.	214	41.14 N	79.32 W
Knox ◆⁵, Mo., U.S.	219	40.08 N	92.09 W
Knox ◆⁶, Oh., U.S.	214	40.23 N	82.26 W
Knox, Cape ⟩	182	54.11 N	133.04 W
Knoxboro	210	42.58 N	75.36 W
Knox City, Mo., U.S.	219	40.08 N	92.00 W
Knox City, Tx., U.S.	196	33.25 N	99.49 W
Knox Coast ⌃²	6	66.30 S	105.00 E
Knoxdale	214	41.05 N	79.02 W
Knoxfield	274b	37.53 S	145.15 E
Knox Lake ⌀¹	214	40.25 N	82.25 W
Knoxville, Ga., U.S.	192	32.43 N	83.59 W
Knoxville, Il., U.S.	190	40.54 N	90.16 W
Knoxville, Ia., U.S.	190	41.19 N	93.06 W
Knoxville, Tn., U.S.	192	35.57 N	83.55 W
Knucklaws ⌃²	122	7.24 N	80.48 E
Knudshoved Odde ⟩¹	41	55.03 N	11.45 E
Knüll ⌃	56	50.55 N	9.24 E
Knutby	40	59.55 N	18.15 E
Knuthenborg ♦	41	54.51 N	11.30 E
Knutsford	44	53.18 N	2.22 W
Knysna	158	34.02 S	23.02 E
Knyszyn	60	53.19 N	22.55 E
Koala Sanctuary ♦⁴	274a	33.40 S	151.10 E
Koani ⟩	154	6.08 S	39.17 E
Kob'	88	58.25 N	101.24 E
Kob'ágya ◆⁸	74	63.34 N	126.30 E
Kobarid	36	46.15 N	13.35 E
Kobbér Sink ≃⁷	144	13.35 N	40.50 E
Kobayashi	92	31.59 N	130.59 E
Kobe, Nihon	96	34.41 N	135.10 E
Kobe, Nihon	96	34.41 N	135.10 E
Kobe-kō ⊂	270	34.40 N	135.12 E
Kobelyaky	78	49.09 N	34.12 E
København			
(Copenhagen)	41	55.40 N	12.35 E
København ⊐	41	55.45 N	12.25 E
København University ▼²	270	34.43 N	135.14 W
Kobi	154	6.08 N	9.30 E
Koblenz, Dtsch.	56	50.21 N	7.35 E
Koblenz, Schw.	58	47.37 N	8.14 E
Koblenz ▯⁵	56	50.10 N	7.30 E
Kobo, Ityo.	144	12.11 N	39.33 E
Kobo, R.D.C.	152	4.54 S	17.09 E
Ko-boke ◆⁵	96	33.54 N	133.58 E
Koboldo	74	53.10 N	134.52 E
Kobona	80	59.57 N	31.40 E
Koboža ≃	76	58.52 N	36.17 E
Kobra	80	60.03 N	50.44 E
Kobrinskoje	84	59.28 N	30.07 E
Kobroor, Pulau ▮	164	6.12 S	134.32 E
Kobu ≃	88	58.50 N	94.10 E
Kobuchizawa	94	35.52 N	138.21 E
Kobuga-hara ≃	94	36.46 N	139.30 E
Kobuk	180	66.54 N	156.52 W
Kobuk Valley			
National Park ♦	180	67.20 N	159.00 W
Kobuleti	84	41.50 N	41.47 E
Kobushiga-take ⌃	94	35.54 N	138.44 E
Kobylin	60	51.43 N	17.13 E
Kobyzhcha	78	50.49 N	31.35 E
Kočaali	130	41.04 N	30.50 E
Kočaalier	130	39.41 N	31.47 E
Kocaeli	130	40.45 N	29.57 E
Kocaeli ◆⁴	130	40.55 N	29.55 E

Nome	Página	Lat.°'	Long.°' W = Oeste
Kocaeli ▯⁴	130	40.55 N	29.55 E
Kocali	130	37.55 N	38.15 E
Kočani	38	41.55 N	22.25 E
Kočarli	130	37.45 N	27.42 E
Kocasinan ◆⁸	267b	41.01 N	28.50 E
Kocaşı Tepe ⌃	84	39.25 N	43.21 E
Kočečum ≃	74	64.17 N	101.10 E
Kočelajevo	80	54.01 N	44.02 E
Kočemary	80	54.50 N	40.58 E
Kočen'ajevka	80	53.52 N	46.59 E
Kočen'ga, Ross.	76	60.09 N	43.33 E
Kočenga, Ross.	88	55.55 N	104.06 E
Kočevalat	88	55.55 N	104.06 E
Kočerdyk	86	54.35 N	62.58 E
Kočerga	88	55.15 N	103.46 E
Kočetovka, Ross.	80	55.16 N	46.07 E
Kočetovka, Ross.	80	52.58 N	40.29 E
Kočevar	76	60.26 N	42.11 E
Kočevje	36	45.38 N	14.52 E
Kočevo	86	59.36 N	54.18 E
Koch'ang, Taehan	98	35.26 N	126.42 E
Koch'ang, Taehan	98	35.41 N	127.55 E
Koch Bihār	124	26.19 N	89.26 E
Kochel	64	47.39 N	11.22 E
Kochelsee ⌀	64	47.38 N	11.20 E
Kochena	158	22.00 S	18.50 E
Kocher ≃	56	49.14 N	9.12 E
Kochi, India	122	9.58 N	76.14 E
Kōchi, Nihon	96	33.33 N	133.33 E
Kōchi, Nihon	96	34.28 N	132.53 E
Kōchi □⁵	96	33.40 N	133.30 E
Kōchi-dani ◆	94	34.34 N	136.10 E
Kochinda	174m	26.08 N	127.43 E
Koch Island ▮	176	69.38 N	78.15 W
Kochki	88	54.20 N	80.49 E
Kochma	80	56.56 N	41.06 E
Koch Peak ⌃	202	45.02 N	111.28 W
Kochugan	124	26.34 N	90.04 E
Kock	60	51.39 N	22.27 E
Kočki, Ross.	86	52.24 N	80.40 E
Kočki, Ross.	86	52.20 N	80.29 E
Kočkor-Ata	85	41.04 N	72.29 E
Kočkorka	85	42.14 N	75.45 E
Kočkurovo	80	54.02 N	45.26 E
Kočkurovo	85	66.12 N	60.44 E
Koçn'ovo	86	55.02 N	82.12 E
Kočo ◆⁹	88	49.49 N	12.44 E
Kočubej	84	44.24 N	46.33 E
Kočubejevskoje	84	44.41 N	41.41 E
Kočubejevo	84	44.41 N	41.41 E
Kočubeypozo	150	5.08 N	6.46 E
Kōda, Nihon	94	34.52 N	137.10 E
Kōda, Nihon	96	34.42 N	132.45 E
Kodačikost	82	63.11 N	55.49 E
Kodaikānal	122	10.14 N	77.29 E
Kodaira	94	35.43 N	139.29 E
Kodak	180	57.48 N	152.23 W
Kodiak	180	57.30 N	153.30 W
Kodiak Island ▮	180	57.50 N	153.00 W
Kodiang	114	6.24 N	100.18 E
Kodinar	120	20.47 N	70.42 E
Kodino	24	63.43 N	39.41 E
Kodkod	202	40.08 N	100.00 W
Kodo, Jabal ⌃	140	12.26 N	23.38 E
Kodok	144	9.53 N	32.07 E
Kodori ≃	84	42.47 N	41.10 E
Kodorskij chrebet ⌃	84	43.00 N	42.00 E
Kodra	78	50.36 N	29.34 E
Kodyma	78	48.07 N	29.07 E
Kodyma ≃	78	48.01 N	30.48 E
Kodžori	84	41.40 N	44.41 E
Koehn Lake ⌀	228	35.18 N	117.53 W
Koekenaap	158	31.30 S	18.18 E
Koekelare	50	51.05 N	2.58 E
Koeltztown	219	38.20 N	92.11 W
Koenigsmacker	56	49.24 N	6.17 E
Koersel	50	51.04 N	5.16 E
Kofa Mountains ⌃	200	33.20 N	114.00 W
Kofaz	84	41.58 N	27.12 E
Köfering	60	48.54 N	12.12 E
Koffiefontein	158	29.30 S	25.00 E
Koflach	61	47.04 N	15.05 E
Kōfu, Nihon	94	35.39 N	138.35 E
Kōfu, Nihon	96	34.53 N	133.14 E
Koga, Nihon	94	36.11 N	139.43 E
Koga, Nihon	98	33.44 N	130.28 E
Koga, Tan.	154	5.38 S	33.25 E
Kogaluc ≃	176	59.40 N	77.30 W
Kogaluc, Baie ⊂	176	59.30 N	77.45 W
Kogaluk ≃	176	56.12 N	61.45 W
Koganei	94	35.42 N	139.30 E
Kogarah	274a	33.58 S	151.08 E
Kogarah Bay ⊂	274a	33.59 S	151.07 E
Køge	41	55.27 N	12.11 E
Køge Bugt ⊂, Dan.	41	55.30 N	12.25 E
Køge Bugt ⊂, Kal.			
Nun.	176	65.00 N	40.30 W
Kogin Baba	146	7.55 N	11.30 E
Koghol	85	47.10 N	75.40 E
Kogon ≃	150	11.09 N	14.42 W
Kogum-do ▮	98	34.30 N	127.10 E
Koha	144	14.34 N	36.56 E
Kohala Mountains ⌃	229d	20.05 N	155.45 W
Kohama-shima ▮	175d	24.19 N	123.59 E
Kohanava	76	54.27 N	30.01 E
Kohat	120	33.35 N	71.26 E
Kohatk Wash ⋁	200	32.50 N	111.52 W
Kohila	76	59.10 N	24.45 E
Kohlberg ⌃	54	49.35 N	11.14 E
Kohistan ▯⁹	120	36.30 N	73.30 E
Kōhoku	96	35.26 N	136.15 E
Kōhoku ◆⁵	268	35.30 N	139.38 E
Kohren-Sahlis	54	51.00 N	12.36 E
Kohtla-Järve	76	59.24 N	27.15 E
Kohukohu	172	35.21 S	173.32 E
Kohunlich ▯	232	18.25 N	88.46 W
Kohyl'nyk (Cogălnic)			
≃	78	46.14 N	30.00 E

Nombre	Página	Lat.°'	Long.°' W = Oeste
Koidern	180	61.58 N	140.25 W
Koidu	150	8.38 N	11.00 W
Koigi	76	58.52 N	25.45 E
Koihoa	110	8.18 N	93.05 E
Koija ≃	152	2.35 S	23.02 E
Koil-Aligarh	124	27.53 N	78.05 E
Koimala	122	4.50 N	73.23 E
Koimbani	157	11.37 S	43.14 E
Koinö	88	56.13 N	95.59 E
Koito ≃	94	35.19 N	139.56 E
Koitere ⌀	26	63.00 N	30.48 E
Koivu	26	66.19 N	25.01 E
Kōj ≃	96	33.27 N	135.46 E
Kojama	154	4.36 S	36.30 E
Kojanup	162	33.50 S	117.09 E
Kojsug	83	47.07 N	39.41 E
Kojtas, Kaz.	86	51.32 N	76.15 E
Kojtaš, Uzb.	85	40.11 N	67.19 E
Kok (Hkok) ≃	110	20.14 N	100.09 E
Kōka	94	34.54 N	136.13 E
Koka, Lake ⌀¹	144	8.23 N	39.05 E
Kokai ≃	94	35.52 N	140.08 E
K'okajgyr	85	40.43 N	75.37 E
Kokalaat	86	55.55 N	104.06 E
Kokand	85	40.33 N	70.57 E
Kokanee Glacier			
Provincial Park ♦	182	49.47 N	117.10 W
Kokanikšlak	85	40.56 N	72.30 E
Kökar ▮	26	59.56 N	20.55 E
Kokas	164	2.42 S	132.26 E
Kokašice	60	49.53 N	12.57 E
Kokava nad			
Rimavicou	60	48.34 N	19.50 E
Kokawa	96	34.16 N	135.24 E
K'okbel'	85	40.17 N	72.55 E
Kokčetav	86	53.17 N	69.25 E
Kokčetav ▯⁸	86	53.30 N	70.00 E
Kokčetavskaja			
vozvyšennost' ≃¹	86	52.50 N	69.00 E
Kokemäenjoki ≃	26	61.33 N	21.42 E
Kokemäki	26	61.15 N	22.21 E
Kokenau	164	4.43 S	136.26 E
Ko Kha	110	18.11 N	99.24 E
Kokhav HaYarden			
(Belvoir) ⊥	132	32.36 N	35.31 E
Kōki, Äkra ⟩	267c	37.53 N	23.27 E
Koki	150	15.30 N	15.59 W
Kokiu	88	35.59 N	139.59 E
— Gejiu	90	23.22 N	103.06 E
Kokiu	80	56.56 N	41.06 E
— Gejiu	102	23.22 N	103.06 E
Kok-Jangak	85	41.02 N	73.12 E
Kokkala Lagoon ⊂	122	9.00 N	80.56 E
Kokkola (Karleby)	26	63.50 N	23.07 E
Koku	98	40.22 N	128.44 E
Koknese	76	56.39 N	25.29 E
Koko	150	11.26 N	4.32 E
— Qinghai Hu ⌀	102	36.50 N	100.20 E
Kokopo	164	4.20 S	152.15 E
Kokorevka	76	52.35 N	34.16 E
Kokosing ≃	214	40.22 N	82.12 W
Kokos-Inseln			
— Cocos (Keeling)			
Islands □²	14	12.10 S	96.55 E
Kokoškino	82	55.38 N	37.11 E
Kokpara			
Narsinghgarh	126	22.31 N	86.33 E
Kokpekti	86	48.45 N	82.24 E
Kokrajhār	124	26.24 N	90.16 E
Kokrines	180	64.58 N	154.40 W
Kokrines Hills ⌃²	180	65.15 N	154.00 W
Kokša ≃	86	50.16 N	85.36 E
Kokšaalatau, chrebet			
⌃	72	41.00 N	78.00 E
Koksan	98	38.46 N	126.40 E
Kökšekol', ozero ⌀	86	46.05 N	62.00 E
Kokšijde	50	51.07 N	2.38 E
Koksilah ≃	224	48.40 N	123.38 W
Koksilah ≃	224	48.45 N	123.39 W
Koksoak ≃	176	58.30 N	68.10 W
Kokstad	158	30.33 S	29.25 E
Koksu ≃	85	42.27 N	78.31 E
Koksu, Kaz.	85	44.27 N	69.01 E
Koksu, Kaz.	86	45.58 N	80.13 E
Koktal	86	44.09 N	79.48 E
Koktas ≃	86	48.00 N	70.55 E
Koktas, Kaz.	86	48.37 N	70.25 E
Kok-Taš, Kyrg.	85	40.37 N	73.00 E
Kokubu	92	31.44 N	130.46 E
Kokubunji ▮	96	34.18 N	134.03 E
Kokubunji, Nihon	94	35.42 N	139.29 E
Kokubunji, Nihon	96	34.18 N	134.08 E
Kokubunji Temple ▼¹	268	35.42 N	139.28 E
Kokufu	96	35.34 N	134.12 E
Kokura	96	33.53 N	130.52 E
Kok'učinskaja guba ⊂	88	70.56 N	174.30 E
Koluel Kayke	254	46.43 S	68.14 W
Kolumbien			
— Colombia □¹	246	4.00 N	72.00 W
Kolpino	76	59.45 N	30.36 E
Kolpny	76	52.14 N	37.05 E
Kolpos Kassandras ⊂	267b	40.05 N	23.25 E
Kolsva	40	59.36 N	15.50 E
Kolonia Stolp	264a	52.28 N	13.46 E
Kolín	54	50.01 N	15.13 E
Kolisne	78	46.02 N	29.56 E
Kolitzheim	56	49.55 N	10.14 E
Kolka	76	57.45 N	22.35 E
Kolkar	41	56.04 N	9.06 E
Kolkasrags ⟩	76	57.47 N	22.36 E
Kolkwitz	54	51.37 N	14.15 E
Kolky, Ukr.	78	51.07 N	25.41 E
Kolky, Ukr.	78	51.37 N	26.37 E
Kollbach ≃	60	48.36 N	12.58 E
Kölleda	54	51.11 N	11.15 E
Kollegāl	122	12.09 N	77.07 E
Kolleru Lake ⌀	122	16.39 N	81.13 E
Kollum	52	53.16 N	6.09 E
Kollund	41	54.51 N	9.27 E
Kolmanskop	158	26.40 S	15.12 E
Kolmården	40	58.40 N	16.23 E
Kolmården ▼²	41	58.40 N	16.35 E
Kolmårdens Djurpark			
♦	40	58.40 N	16.29 E
Kolmogorovo	86	59.15 N	91.20 E
Köln (Cologne)	56	50.56 N	6.59 E
Kolki	50	50.55 N	6.40 E
Köln-Bonn, Flughafen			
◆	56	50.50 N	7.10 E
Kolno	60	53.25 N	21.56 E
Kolo, Niger	150	13.19 N	2.20 E
Kolo, Pol.	60	52.12 N	18.38 E
Kolo, Tan.	154	4.44 S	35.50 E
Koloa	229b	21.54 N	159.28 W
Kolobovo	80	56.42 N	41.21 E
Kolobrzeg	30	54.12 N	15.33 E
Koloč	54	55.34 N	35.52 E
Kolochau	54	51.44 N	13.16 E
Kolok	60	54.33 N	23.26 E
Kologriv	76	58.51 N	44.17 E
Kologrivovka	80	52.04 N	45.20 E
Kolojar	80	52.34 N	46.58 E
Kolok (Golok) ≃	114	6.15 N	102.05 E
Kolokani	150	13.35 N	8.02 W
Koloko	150	11.05 N	5.19 W
Kolokol'covka, Ross.	80	59.39 N	49.48 E
Kolomak	78	49.50 N	35.18 E
Kolombangara Island			
▮	175e	8.00 S	157.05 E
Kolomea			
— Kolomyya	78	48.32 N	25.04 E
Kolomenka ≃	82	55.06 N	38.46 E
Kolomenskoje			
Sloboda	82	54.22 N	38.15 E
Kolomenskoje ◆⁸	265b	55.40 N	37.41 E
Kolomna	82	55.05 N	38.49 E
Kolomyja	78	48.32 N	25.04 E
Kolonderk	164	5.26 S	134.29 E
Kolondiéba	150	11.05 N	6.54 W
Kolonga	174w	21.08 S	175.04 W
Kolonia	164	6.58 N	158.13 E
Kolonodale	112	2.00 S	121.19 E
Kolosovka	86	56.28 N	73.36 E
Kolovertnoje	80	50.36 N	51.06 E
Kolowana Watobo,			
Teluk ⊂	112	5.00 S	123.06 E
Kołozsvár			
— Cluj-Napoca	38	46.47 N	23.36 E
Kolp ≃	76	59.22 N	36.49 E
Kolpaševo	88	58.20 N	82.50 E
Kolpino	76	59.45 N	30.36 E

Nombre	Página	Lat.°'	Long.°' W = Oeste
Kolenté	150	10.06 N	12.37 W
Kolenté (Great			
Scarcies) ≃	150	8.55 N	13.08 W
Kolga	76	59.32 N	25.42 E
Kolguev, ostrov ▮	24	69.05 N	49.15 E
Kolhāpur, India	122	16.06 N	78.16 E
Kolhāpur, India	122	16.42 N	74.13 E
Kolho	26	62.08 N	24.31 E
Koli	76	59.30 N	34.30 E
Koli ▯²	26	63.06 N	29.48 E
Koli, Jabal ⌃	140	14.05 N	25.31 E
Kolia	150	9.46 N	6.28 W
Koliba (Corubal) ≃	150	11.57 N	15.06 W
Koliganek	180	59.48 N	157.25 W
Kolima	26	63.16 N	25.50 E
Kolimbine ≃	150	14.26 N	11.23 W
Kolín	30	50.01 N	15.13 E
Kolisne	78	46.02 N	29.56 E
Kolitzheim	56	49.55 N	10.14 E
Kolka	76	57.45 N	22.35 E
Kolkar	41	56.04 N	9.06 E
Kolkasrags ⟩	76	57.47 N	22.36 E
Kolkwitz	54	51.37 N	14.15 E
Kolky, Ukr.	78	51.07 N	25.41 E
Kolky, Ukr.	78	51.37 N	26.37 E
Kollbach ≃	60	48.36 N	12.58 E
Kölleda	54	51.11 N	11.15 E
Kollegāl	122	12.09 N	77.07 E
Kolochau	54	51.44 N	13.16 E
Kolok	60	54.33 N	23.26 E
Kolomyya	78	48.32 N	25.04 E
Kol'cug-Komsomol'sk			
Nihon	92a	32.04 N	140.41 E
Koltczewo	54	55.45 N	138.14 E
Koma	76	52.54 N	49.48 E
Kom ⌃	38	43.09 N	23.03 E
Koma, Ityo.	144	8.23 N	36.47 E
Komádi	61	47.21 N	21.30 E
Komadougou Yobé			
(Komadugu Yobe)			
≃	146	13.43 N	13.23 E
Komadugu Gana ≃	146	12.24 N	13.09 E
Komagane	94	35.43 N	137.56 E
Komaga-take ⌃	94	35.47 N	137.48 E
Komandirščina	80	53.32 N	42.03 E
Komandorskije			
ostrova ▮▮	74	55.00 N	167.00 E
Komандор Village	282	37.45 N	122.27 W
Komarno, Slvk.	61	47.45 N	18.09 E
Komarno, Ukr.	78	49.38 N	23.42 E

ENGLISH				DEUTSCH			
Name	Page	Lat.°′	Long.°′	Name	Seite	Breite°′	Länge°′ E = Ost

Komarnyky 78 49.00 N 23.04 E
Komárom 30 47.44 N 18.08 E
Komárom-Esztergom □6 30 47.40 N 18.15 E
Komarovo 76 58.39 N 33.26 E
Komarovy 86 60.26 N 75.50 E
Komati (Incomáti) ≐ 156 25.46 S 32.43 E
Komatipoort 156 25.25 S 31.55 E
Komatsu, Nihon 94 36.24 N 136.27 E
Komatsu, Nihon 96 33.53 N 133.07 E
Komatsu-kūkō ⊠ 94 36.24 N 136.26 E
Komatsushima 96 34.00 N 134.35 E
Kombissiri 150 12.04 N 1.20 W
Kombone 152 4.37 N 9.19 E
Komdhārā 272b 22.53 N 88.14 E
Kome Island I 154 0.06 S 32.45 E
Komen 64 45.49 N 13.44 E
Komenda 150 5.03 N 1.29 W
Komenoi 268 35.55 N 140.01 E
Komering ≐ 112 2.59 S 104.50 E
Komeshia 154 8.01 S 27.07 E
Komfane 164 5.39 S 134.44 E
Komga 158 32.35 S 27.55 E
Komi □3 72 64.00 N 54.00 E
Kominato
— Amatsu-kominato 94 35.07 N 140.10 E
Kominternivs'ke 78 46.49 N 30.56 E
Komin Yanga 150 11.42 N 0.08 E
Komi-Perm'ackij Avtonomnyj Okrug □8 24 60.00 N 54.30 E
Komissarovka 83 48.07 N 40.09 E
Komissarovo 89 44.59 N 131.46 E
Komissarovskij 80 47.29 N 42.59 E
Komkans 158 31.16 S 18.09 E
Komló 30 46.12 N 18.16 E
Kommadagga 158 33.09 S 25.55 E
Kommandodrif 158 27.30 S 26.14 E
Kommandokraal 158 33.06 S 22.51 E
Kommetjie 158 34.08 S 18.21 E
Kommunal'naja 88 52.03 N 115.06 E
Kommunar, Ross. 80 58.10 N 43.33 E
Kommunar, Ross. 86 54.20 N 89.18 E
Kommunarka 265b 55.34 N 37.29 E
Kommunary 26 60.54 N 29.47 E
Kommunizma, pik ⋀ 85 38.57 N 72.01 E
Komo ≐ 152 0.09 N 9.50 E
Komodo 115b 8.35 S 119.30 E
Komodo, Pulau I 115b 8.36 S 119.30 E
Komoé ≐ 150 5.12 N 3.44 W
Komoé, Parc National de la ♦ 150 9.00 N 3.30 W
Komoka 214 42.57 N 81.26 W
Komono, Congo 152 3.15 S 13.14 E
Komono, Nihon 94 35.00 N 136.31 E
Komoran, Pulau I 164 8.18 S 138.45 E
Komoren
— Comoros □1 157a 12.10 S 44.10 E
Komorin, Kap
— Comorin, Cape › 122 8.04 N 77.34 E
Komorn
— Komárno 30 47.45 N 18.09 E
Komoro 94 36.19 N 138.26 E
Komotau
— Chomutov 54 50.28 N 13.26 E
Komotiní 38 41.08 N 25.25 E
Kompaniyivka 78 48.15 N 32.12 E
Kompasberg ⋀ 158 31.45 S 24.32 E
Kompiam 164 5.20 S 143.55 E
Kompot 112 0.24 N 124.10 E
Komsomolabad 85 38.52 N 69.57 E
Komsomolec 86 53.45 N 62.02 E
Komsomolec, ostrov I 74 80.30 N 95.00 E
Komsomolec, zaliv c 72 45.30 N 52.45 E
Komsomol'sk, Ross. 80 57.02 N 40.21 E
Komsomol'sk, Ross. 86 55.38 N 88.11 E
Komsomol'sk, Ross. 86 57.27 N 86.02 E
Komsomol'sk, Turk. 128 39.02 N 63.36 E
Komsomol's'ke, Ukr. 78 49.35 N 36.30 E
Komsomol's'ke, Ukr. 78 49.43 N 28.40 E
Komsomol's'ke, Ukr. 83 47.40 N 38.05 E
Komsomol'skij, Kaz. 86 51.40 N 66.39 E
Komsomol'skij, Kaz. 86 47.20 N 53.42 E
Komsomol'skij, Ross. 80 54.27 N 45.49 E
Komsomol'skij, Ross. 89 50.22 N 142.10 E
Komsomol'sk-na-Amure 89 50.35 N 137.02 E
Komsomol'sk-na-Ust'urte 86 44.03 N 58.20 E
Komsomol'skoje, Ross. 80 55.16 N 47.33 E
Komsomol'skoje, Ross. 80 50.46 N 47.03 E
Komsomol'skoje, Ross. 88 52.29 N 111.06 E
Komsomol'skoj Pravdy, ostrova II 74 77.20 N 107.40 E
Komsomol's'kyy 83 47.40 N 37.26 E
Kŏmun-do I 98 34.02 N 127.19 E
Kömürcüpınar ◆8 267b 41.15 N 28.51 E
Komusan 98 42.08 N 129.41 E
Komyshnya 78 50.12 N 33.41 E
Komyshuvakha, Ukr. 78 47.43 N 35.32 E
Komyshuvakha, Ukr. 83 48.42 N 38.23 E
Kona, India 272b 22.37 N 88.18 E
Kona, Mali 150 14.57 N 3.53 W
Kona Coast ±2 229d 19.25 N 155.55 W
Konakovo 82 56.42 N 36.46 E
Konakpınar, Tür. 130 38.53 N 37.22 E
Konakpınar, Tür. 130 39.26 N 27.53 E
Konan
— Hŭngnam, C.M.I.K. 98 39.50 N 127.38 E
Konan, C. Iv. 150 8.21 N 8.00 W
Kōnan, Nihon 94 35.20 N 136.53 E
Kōnan, Nihon 94 34.56 N 136.11 E
Kōnan ◆8 268 35.22 N 139.35 E
Konar (Kunar) ≐ 123 34.25 N 70.32 E
Konārak 120 19.54 N 86.07 E
Konār Dam ◆6 124 23.58 N 85.45 E
Konarhā □4 120 35.15 N 71.00 E
Konawa 196 34.57 N 96.45 W
Končanskoje-Suvorovskoje 76 58.39 N 34.04 E
Konch 124 25.59 N 79.09 E
Konda 74 61.20 N 63.58 E
Konda ≐, Ross. 86 60.40 N 69.46 E
Konda ≐, Ross. 88 53.30 N 113.32 E
Kondagaon 122 19.36 N 81.40 E
Konde 154 4.57 S 39.45 E
Kondega 76 60.14 N 33.30 E
Kondiaronk, Lac ⊜ 190 46.56 N 76.45 W
Kondinin 162 32.30 S 118.16 E
Kondinskoje 86 59.40 N 67.22 E
Kondli ◆8 272a 28.37 N 77.19 E
Kondoa 154 4.54 S 35.47 E
Kondol' 80 52.49 N 45.03 E
Kondolole 154 1.20 N 25.58 E
Kondopoga 24 62.12 N 34.17 E
Kondorfa 61 46.54 N 16.24 E
Kondratjevo, Ross. 76 60.38 N 28.08 E
Kondratjevo, Ross. 88 57.21 N 98.11 E
Kondrovka 80 54.36 N 43.17 E
Kondrovo 82 54.48 N 35.56 E
Kondr'učja ≐ 80 47.43 N 40.55 E
Konduga 146 11.39 N 13.24 E
Kondukūr 122 15.13 N 79.55 E
Kondurča ≐ 80 53.31 N 50.24 E
Kondūz 120 37.45 N 68.51 E
Kondūz □4 120 36.45 N 68.30 E
Koné 175f 21.04 S 164.52 E
Konecbor 24 64.52 N 57.44 E
Konergino 180 65.54 N 178.50 W
Konfara 150 11.55 N 8.50 W
Kong, C. Iv. 150 9.09 N 4.37 W
Kong, Dan. 41 55.07 N 11.50 E
Kông ≐ 110 13.32 N 105.58 E
Kŏng, Kaôh I 110 11.20 N 103.00 E
Kongakut ≐ 180 69.48 N 141.50 W
Kongbo 152 4.44 N 21.23 E
Kongcheng 100 31.02 N 117.05 E
Kongeå ≐ 41 55.23 N 8.40 E
Kongens Lyngby 41 55.46 N 12.31 E
Kongfang 100 27.58 N 116.53 E
Kongiganak 180 59.58 N 162.45 W
Konginkangas 26 62.46 N 25.48 E
Kongjiamatou 105 39.07 N 116.10 E
Kongjiatun 104 40.42 N 124.04 E
Kongjiawopeng 89 43.58 N 122.41 E
Kongjiazhuang 105 40.47 N 114.48 E
Kongju 98 36.27 N 127.07 E
Konglong 100 29.56 N 115.54 E
Konglongshan 105 40.33 N 117.17 E
Konglu 102 27.16 N 97.56 E
Kongmoon
— Jiangmen 100 22.35 N 113.05 E
Kongo
— Congo ≐ 138 6.04 S 12.24 E
Kongo, Republik
— Zaire □1 138 4.00 S 25.00 E
Kongō-Ikoma-kokutei-kōen ♦ 96 34.28 N 135.40 E
Kongolo, R.D.C. 154 5.26 S 24.49 E
Kongolo, R.D.C. 154 5.23 S 27.00 E
Kongor 140 7.10 N 31.21 E
Kongō-sanchi ⋏ 270 34.27 N 135.41 E
Kongoussi 150 13.19 N 1.32 W
Kongō-zan ⋀ 96 34.25 N 135.41 E
Kongsberg 26 59.39 N 9.39 E
Kongsvinger 26 60.12 N 12.00 E
Kongsvoll 26 62.18 N 9.37 E
Kongtan 107 29.10 N 104.42 E
Kongur Shan ⋀ 85 38.37 N 75.20 E
Kongwa 154 6.12 S 36.25 E
Kongyangcun 106 31.23 N 118.54 E
Kongzhen 106 31.29 N 119.00 E
Koni 154 10.42 S 27.15 E
Koni ≐ 150 13.05 N 5.37 W
Koniakari 150 14.34 N 10.54 W
Konice 30 49.35 N 16.53 E
Koniecpol 30 50.48 N 19.41 E
Königgrätz
— Hradec Králové 30 50.12 N 15.50 E
Königheim 56 49.37 N 9.35 E
Königin Alexandra-Kette
— Queen Alexandra Range ⋏ 9 84.00 S 168.00 E
Königin Fabiola-Gebirge
— Queen Fabiola Mountains ⋏ 9 71.30 S 35.40 E
Königin Mary-Küste
— Queen Mary Coast ±2 9 67.00 S 96.00 E
Königin Maud-Land
— Queen Maud Land ◆1 9 72.30 S 12.00 E
König-Otto-Höhe ±5 60 49.15 N 11.42 E
Königsbach 56 48.58 N 8.36 E
Königsberg, Dtsch. 56 50.05 N 10.34 E
Königsberg
— Kaliningrad, Ross. 76 54.43 N 20.30 E
Königsborn 263 51.33 N 7.41 E
Königsbrück 54 51.16 N 13.54 E
Königsbrunn, Dtsch. 58 48.16 N 10.53 E
Königsbrunn, Öst. 264b 48.21 N 16.25 E
Königsdorf 64 47.49 N 11.28 E
Königsee 54 50.39 N 11.05 E
Königsfelden ʋ1 58 47.29 N 8.14 E
Königsfeld im Schwarzwald 58 48.08 N 8.25 E
Königshain 54 51.11 N 14.52 E
Königshardt ◆8 263 51.33 N 6.51 E
Königsheim 58 48.06 N 8.51 E
Königslutter 54 52.15 N 10.49 E
Königsmoor ◆3 52 53.15 N 9.40 E
Königssee 64 47.33 N 12.58 E
Königssee ⊜ 64 47.36 N 12.59 E
Königsstuhl ±4 54 54.34 N 13.40 E
Königstein, Dtsch. 54 50.55 N 14.04 E
Königstein, Dtsch. 56 50.11 N 8.29 E
Königstein, Dtsch. 60 49.37 N 11.38 E
Königstetten 264b 48.18 N 16.09 E
Königswalde 54 50.33 N 13.02 E
Königswartha 54 51.18 N 14.20 E
Königswiesen 61 48.24 N 14.50 E
Königswinter 56 50.40 N 7.11 E
Königs Wusterhausen 54 52.18 N 13.37 E
Konin 30 52.13 N 18.16 E
Konin □4 30 52.20 N 18.20 E
Konispol 38 39.39 N 20.10 E
Kónitsa 38 40.02 N 20.45 E
Köniz 58 46.56 N 7.25 E
Konjic 38 43.39 N 17.57 E
Könkämäälven ≐ 24 68.29 N 22.17 E
Konkapot ≐ 210 42.03 N 73.20 W
Konkiep ≐ 156 28.03 S 17.21 E
Konkō 96 34.32 N 133.37 E
Kon'-Kolodez' 76 52.08 N 39.11 E
Konkouré ≐ 150 9.58 N 13.42 W
Kon'kove 83 47.20 N 38.10 E
Konkudera 88 57.33 N 112.30 E
Konkug University ʋ2 271b 37.32 N 127.05 E
Konnagar 126 22.42 N 88.22 E
Könnern 54 51.40 N 11.46 E
Konnevesi ⊜ 26 62.40 N 26.35 E
Konnur 122 16.12 N 74.45 E
Kōno 94 35.49 N 136.04 E
Konobejevo 82 55.24 N 38.40 E
Konohana ◆8 270 34.41 N 135.26 E
Kōnoike 270 34.42 N 135.37 E
Konolfingen 58 46.53 N 7.38 E
Konongo 150 6.37 N 1.11 W
Konoša 24 60.58 N 40.15 E
Kōno-shima I 96 34.28 N 133.31 E
Kōnosu 94 36.03 N 139.31 E
Konotop 78 51.14 N 33.12 E
Konovalovka 80 53.06 N 51.34 E
Kon'ovo, Ross. 24 62.08 N 39.16 E
Kon'ovo, Ross. 86 56.18 N 70.43 E
Konqi ≐ 90 40.40 N 90.10 E
Konradshöhe ◆8 264a 52.35 N 13.14 E
Konradsreuth 54 50.16 N 11.50 E
Konsankoro 150 9.02 N 9.00 W
Konsen-daichi ⋏1 92a 43.25 N 144.52 E
Końskie 30 51.12 N 20.26 E
Konsomol's'kyy 83 48.07 N 39.39 E
Konstabel 158 33.16 S 20.17 E
Konstantinopel
— İstanbul 130 41.01 N 28.58 E
Konstantinovka, Ross. 80 56.41 N 50.53 E
Konstantinovka, Ross. 265a 59.47 N 30.08 E
Konstantinovka, Ukr. 83 47.52 N 37.24 E
Konstantinovo 82 56.33 N 38.02 E
Konstantinovsk 80 47.35 N 41.06 E
Konstantinovskij 76 57.50 N 39.36 E
Konstantinovskije Porogi 76 60.34 N 37.04 E
Konstantynów Łódzki 30 51.45 N 19.20 E
Konstanz 58 47.40 N 9.10 E
Kontagora 150 10.24 N 5.28 E
Kontcha 152 7.58 N 12.14 E
Kontejevo 80 58.26 N 41.21 E
Kontha 110 19.30 N 96.03 E
Kontich 50 51.08 N 4.27 E
Kontiolahti 26 62.46 N 29.51 E
Kontiomäki 26 64.21 N 28.09 E
Kontseba 78 48.07 N 29.56 E
Kon Tum 110 14.21 N 108.00 E
Kontum, Plateau du ⋏1 110 13.55 N 108.05 E
Kōnu 96 34.42 N 133.05 E
Kon'uchovo 86 55.08 N 70.38 E
Konus, gora ⋀ 180 67.34 N 178.10 E
Konya 130 37.52 N 32.31 E
Konya □4 130 38.00 N 33.00 E
Konyr 80 50.25 N 53.25 E
Konyrat 80 49.36 N 47.01 E
Konyrolen 86 44.16 N 79.19 E
Konyševka 78 51.51 N 35.18 E
Konystanu 80 48.51 N 53.20 E
Konz 56 49.42 N 6.34 E
Konza 154 1.45 S 37.07 E
Konžakovskij Kamen', gora ⋀ 86 59.38 N 59.08 E
Konzell 60 49.04 N 12.43 E
Koocanusa, Lake ⊜1 202 49.00 N 115.10 W
Koog [aan de Zaan] 52 52.27 N 4.49 E
Kookynie 162 29.20 S 121.29 E
Koolamarra 166 20.12 S 140.14 E
Koolatah 164 15.53 S 142.27 E
Koolau Range ⋏ 229c 21.35 N 158.00 W
Kooloonong 166 34.53 S 143.09 E
Koolskamp 50 51.00 N 3.12 E
Koolyanobbing 162 30.50 S 119.35 E
Koolywurtie 168b 34.38 S 137.37 E
Koombana Bay c 168a 33.18 S 115.36 E
Koonap ≐ 158 33.03 S 26.39 E
Koondrook 166 35.39 S 144.08 E
Koonga 76 58.35 N 24.12 E
Koonibba 162 31.58 S 133.27 E
Koontz Lake 216 41.25 N 86.29 W
Koontz Lake ⊜ 216 41.25 N 86.28 W
Koopan-Noord 158 26.53 S 20.41 E
Koopan-Suid 158 27.15 S 20.22 E
Koopmansfontein 158 28.14 S 24.01 E
Koorawatha 166 34.02 S 148.33 E
Koorda 162 30.50 S 117.29 E
Koosa 76 58.33 N 27.07 E
Koosfontein 158 27.22 S 25.27 E
Koosharem 200 38.30 N 111.52 W
Kooskia 202 46.08 N 115.58 W
Koossa 150 9.32 N 8.32 W
Kootenai (Kootenay) ≐ 182 49.15 N 117.39 W
Kootenay (Kootenai) ≐ 182 49.15 N 117.39 W
Kootenay Indian Reserve ◆4 182 49.37 N 115.45 W
Kootenay Lake ⊜ 182 49.35 N 116.50 W
Kootenay National Park ♦ 182 51.00 N 116.00 W
Kootjieskolk 158 31.15 S 20.21 E
Kootwijk 52 52.12 N 5.45 E
Koo-wee-rup 169 38.12 S 145.30 E
Kopa 85 43.32 N 75.50 E
Kopa ≐ 85 43.40 N 76.15 E
Kopāganj 124 26.01 N 83.34 E
Kopāi ≐ 126 23.48 N 87.47 E
Kopanbulak 86 48.56 N 80.52 E
Kopang 115b 8.39 S 116.21 E
Kopanovka 80 47.27 N 46.48 E
Kopanskaja 78 46.17 N 38.29 E
Kopapan 80 50.20 N 50.26 E
Kopargaon 122 19.53 N 74.29 E
Koparkhairna 272c 19.06 N 72.59 E
Koparpāda 272c 19.02 N 73.04 E
Kópasker 24a 66.20 N 16.24 W
Kópavogur 24a 64.06 N 21.50 W
Kopayhorod 78 48.51 N 27.48 E
Kopé, Mont ⋀2 150 4.59 N 7.27 W
Kopejsk 86 55.07 N 61.37 E
Kopenhagen
— København 41 55.40 N 12.35 E
Köpenick ◆8 54 52.27 N 13.34 E
Köpenick, Schloss ʋ 264a 52.27 N 13.34 E
Koper 36 45.33 N 13.44 E
Köpernitz 54 53.04 N 12.56 E
Kopervik 26 59.17 N 5.18 E
Kopetdag, chrebet ⋏ 128 37.50 N 58.00 E
Kopeysk
— Kopejsk 86 55.07 N 61.37 E
Kop Geçidi)(130 40.03 N 40.33 E
Kopice 54 53.44 N 14.32 E
Köping 40 59.31 N 16.00 E
Kopisty 54 50.34 N 13.35 E
Kopjevo 86 55.03 N 89.50 E
Koplik 38 42.13 N 19.26 E
Köpmanholmen 26 63.10 N 18.34 E
Kopnino 82 56.53 N 38.29 E
Kopondei, Tanjung › 115b 8.04 S 122.52 E
Koporje 76 59.44 N 29.01 E
Koporskaja guba c 76 59.52 N 28.55 E
Koppal 122 15.21 N 76.09 E
Koppang 26 61.34 N 11.04 E
Koppány ≐ 30 46.35 N 18.26 E
Kopparberg 40 59.52 N 14.59 E
Kopparbergs Län □6 26 61.00 N 14.30 E
Koppel 214 40.50 N 80.19 W
Kopperå 26 63.24 N 11.51 E
Kopperby 41 54.38 N 9.56 E
Kopperl 222 32.04 N 97.30 W
Koppi 89 48.32 N 140.07 E
Koppi ≐ 89 48.33 N 140.08 E
Koppies 158 27.20 S 27.30 E
Koppom 26 59.43 N 12.09 E
Kopri 272c 19.11 N 72.58 E
Koprivnica 36 46.10 N 16.50 E
Köprü ≐ 130 36.50 N 31.10 E
Köprülü Kanyon Milli Parkı ♦ 130 37.20 N 31.18 E
Köprüören 130 39.30 N 29.47 E
Kopt'ovo 80 56.43 N 40.31 E
Kopychyntsi 78 49.06 N 25.55 E
Kopylovka 86 58.40 N 82.22 E
Kopylovo, Ross. 24 60.35 N 45.02 E
Kopylovo, Ross. 82 56.26 N 36.25 E
Kopys' 76 54.19 N 30.18 E
Kor ≐ 128 29.36 N 53.18 E
Kōra 94 35.12 N 136.15 E
Koraa Shiir 144 3.18 N 46.16 E
Korab (Maja e Korabit) ⋀ 38 41.47 N 20.34 E
Kor Aban 144 3.58 N 42.44 E
Korabit, Maja e (Korab) ⋀ 38 41.47 N 20.34 E
Korablino 80 53.55 N 40.01 E
Korahe 144 6.35 N 44.23 E
Kor'akovka 86 52.24 N 77.08 E
Kor'akskaja Sopka, vulkan ⋀1 74 53.20 N 158.43 E
Kor'akskoje nagorje ⋏ 74 62.30 N 172.00 E
Kōrakuen ♦ 96 34.38 N 133.53 E
Korakuen Stadium ♦ 268 35.43 N 139.45 E
Korallenmeer
— Coral Sea ▿2 14 20.00 S 158.00 E
Koralpe ⋏ 61 46.50 N 14.58 E
Korannaberg ⋏ 158 27.25 S 22.32 E
Korapun 164 5.25 S 152.00 E
Korāput 122 18.49 N 82.43 E
Korarou, Lac ⊜ 150 15.15 N 3.16 W
Korat
— Nakhon Ratchasima 110 14.58 N 102.07 E
Koratla 122 18.49 N 78.43 E
Kor'ažma 24 61.18 N 47.06 E
Korba, India 124 22.21 N 82.41 E
Korba, Tun. 36 36.35 N 10.52 E
Korbach 56 51.16 N 8.52 E
Korbeta 144 13.03 N 39.43 E
Korbol 146 10.01 N 17.43 E
Korbous 36 36.49 N 10.35 E
Korbu, Gunong ⋀ 114 4.43 N 101.17 E
Korçë 38 40.37 N 20.46 E
Korcovo 76 58.52 N 42.13 E
Korčula 36 42.58 N 17.08 E
Korčula, Otok I 36 42.57 N 16.50 E
Korčulanski Kanal Ꮜ 36 43.03 N 16.40 E
Kordestān □4 128 35.30 N 47.00 E
Kord Kūy 128 36.48 N 54.07 E
Kordovo 86 54.06 N 93.17 E
Korea, North □1, Asia 90 40.00 N 127.00 E
Korea, North □1, Asia 98 40.00 N 127.00 E
Korea, South □1, Asia 90 36.30 N 128.00 E
Korea, South □1, Asia 98 36.30 N 128.00 E
Korea Bay c 98 39.00 N 124.00 E
Korea Strait Ꮜ 90 34.00 N 129.00 E
Korea University ʋ2 271b 37.36 N 127.02 E
Korekozevo 82 54.20 N 36.11 E
Korelakša 24 65.33 N 32.22 E
Korem 144 12.30 N 39.30 E
Koré Mayroua 150 13.18 N 3.55 E
Koren (Die Wurzen))(64 46.31 N 13.45 E
Korenkovo 78 45.07 N 36.24 E
Koren'ovo, Ross. 78 51.25 N 34.55 E
Koren'ovo, Ross. 265b 55.40 N 38.00 E
Korenovsk 78 45.29 N 39.28 E
Korets', Ukr. 78 50.37 N 27.09 E
Korets', Ukr. 78 50.35 N 27.01 E
Korf 74 60.19 N 165.50 E
Korfovskij 89 48.13 N 135.03 E
Korga 158 30.12 S 20.28 E
Korgan 130 40.44 N 37.13 E
Korgašino 82 54.45 N 37.41 E
Korgasyn 86 49.15 N 66.43 E
Kõrgessaare 76 58.59 N 22.28 E
Korgonskij chrebet ⋏ 86 50.45 N 84.30 E
Korgöz 84 40.18 N 49.38 E
Korgus 140 19.13 N 33.29 E
Korhogo 150 9.27 N 5.38 W
Kōri 270 34.47 N 135.39 E
Koridhallós 267c 37.59 N 23.39 E
Korido 164 0.50 S 135.35 E
Koriella 169 37.10 S 145.39 E
Korienzé 150 15.24 N 3.47 W
Korim 164 0.54 S 136.02 E
Korima, Oued el V 148 33.51 N 0.23 W
Koringberg 158 33.01 S 18.40 E
Koringplaas 158 32.48 S 20.58 E
Korinth 41 55.08 N 10.21 E
Korinthiakós Kólpos (Gulf of Corinth) c 38 38.19 N 22.04 E
Kórinthos (Corinth) 38 37.56 N 22.56 E
Korínthou, Dhiórix ≚ 38 37.57 N 22.56 E
Kőris-hegy ⋀ 30 47.18 N 17.45 E
Koritsa
— Korçë 38 40.37 N 20.46 E
Köritz 54 52.51 N 12.27 E
Kōriyama, Nihon 92 37.24 N 140.23 E
Kōriyama
— Yamato-kōriyama, Nihon 96 34.38 N 135.47 E
Korizo, Passe de)(146 22.28 N 15.27 E
Korkino, Ross. 86 54.54 N 61.23 E
Korkino, Ross. 88 54.23 N 105.14 E
Korkinskoje, ozero ⊜ 265a 59.55 N 30.44 E
Korkuteli 130 37.04 N 30.13 E
Korla 90 41.44 N 86.09 E
Korl'aki 80 57.06 N 46.57 E
Korliki 74 61.31 N 82.22 E
Körmend 30 47.01 N 16.37 E
Kormilovka 86 55.00 N 74.06 E
Kormovoje 80 46.17 N 43.30 E
Kornat, Otok I 36 43.50 N 15.16 E
Körnebach ≐ 263 51.35 N 7.38 E
Kornejevka, Kaz. 86 54.01 N 68.27 E
Kornejevka, Kaz. 86 50.12 N 74.19 E
Kornejevka, Ross. 80 51.45 N 48.46 E
Kornelimünster 56 50.43 N 6.11 E
Körner, Dtsch. 54 51.13 N 10.35 E
Korner, Mt., U.S. 182 48.59 N 112.15 W
Korneuburg 61 48.21 N 16.20 E
Kórnik 30 52.17 N 17.04 E
Kornilovo 86 53.32 N 81.05 E
Kornouchovo 80 55.33 N 49.53 E
Korn'ovo 265a 60.03 N 30.45 E
Kornsjø 26 58.57 N 11.39 E
Korntal-Münchingen 56 48.50 N 9.07 E
Kornwestheim 56 48.52 N 9.11 E
Kornyn 78 50.06 N 29.32 E
Koro, C. Iv. 150 8.34 N 7.28 W
Koro, Mali 150 14.04 N 3.05 W
Koro I 175g 17.19 S 179.23 E
Koroba 164 5.40 S 142.45 E
Koroča 78 50.48 N 37.11 E
Korodougou Markala 150 12.26 N 6.17 W
Köroğlu Tepesi ⋀ 130 40.31 N 31.53 E
Korogwe 154 5.09 S 38.29 E
Koroit 166 38.17 S 142.22 E
Korolenko, gora ⋀ 88 58.15 N 115.01 E
Koroleve 78 48.09 N 23.08 E
Korolevskij Belok, gora ⋀ 86 51.00 N 83.43 E
Korol'ovščina 76 55.49 N 31.45 E
Korom, Bahr ≐ 146 10.35 N 19.45 E
Koromba ⋀ 175g 17.53 S 177.34 E
Koromiri I 174k 21.15 S 159.43 W
Koromo
— Toyota 94 35.05 N 137.09 E
Koronadal 116 6.30 N 124.51 E
Koróni 38 36.48 N 21.56 E
Korónia, Límni ⊜ 38 40.41 N 23.05 E
Koronowo 30 53.19 N 17.57 E
Korop 78 51.34 N 32.56 E
Koropélé 152 4.44 N 17.11 E
Koropíon 38 37.54 N 23.53 E
Koror 175b 7.20 N 134.29 E
Koror I 175b 7.20 N 134.30 E
Kororoit Creek ≐ 274b 37.52 S 144.52 E
Körös ≐ 30 46.43 N 20.12 E
Koro Sea ▿2 175g 18.00 S 179.50 E
Korosten' 78 50.57 N 28.39 E
Korostyshiv 78 50.19 N 29.03 E
Korotkova 88 56.43 N 107.55 E
Korotojak 78 50.59 N 39.10 E
Koro Toro 146 16.05 N 18.30 E
Korotovo 76 58.57 N 37.28 E
Korotyš 76 52.22 N 37.27 E
Korovin Island I 180 55.25 N 160.15 W
Korovino, Ross. 78 51.25 N 36.45 E
Korovino, Ross. 80 53.49 N 53.03 E
Korovin Volcano ⋀1 180 52.22 N 174.10 W
Korovou 175g 17.57 S 178.21 E
Korovyntsi 78 50.48 N 33.45 E
Koroyanitu ⋀ 175g 17.40 S 177.35 E
Korožečna ≐ 76 57.32 N 38.18 E
Korpilahti 26 62.01 N 25.33 E
Korpo (Korppoo) 26 60.10 N 21.34 E
Korså 40 60.38 N 16.08 E
Korsakov 89 46.38 N 142.46 E
Korsakovo 76 53.16 N 37.21 E
Korschenbroich 56 51.11 N 6.31 E
Korselbränna 26 64.27 N 15.35 E
Korševo 78 51.11 N 40.07 E
Korsika
— Corse I 36 42.00 N 9.00 E
Korsnäs, Suomi 26 62.47 N 21.12 E
Korsnäs, Sve. 40 60.35 N 15.43 E
Korsør 41 55.20 N 11.09 E
Korsør Nor c 41 55.20 N 11.11 E
Koršunovo 88 58.37 N 110.10 E
Korsun'-Shevchenkivs'kyy 78 49.26 N 31.16 E
Korsze 30 54.10 N 21.09 E
Kortelisy 78 51.51 N 24.25 E
Kortgene 52 51.34 N 3.48 E
Kortkeros 24 61.49 N 51.28 E
Kortrijk (Courtrai) 50 50.50 N 3.16 E
Kortuz, gora ⋀ 86 54.33 N 91.56 E
Koruçam Burnu › 130 35.24 N 32.56 E
Korucu 130 39.28 N 27.22 E
Korumburra 169 38.26 S 145.49 E
Korwai 124 24.08 N 78.03 E
Kōryō 96 34.33 N 135.45 E
Koryŏng 98 35.44 N 128.15 E
Koryta 60 49.24 N 13.13 E
Koryukivka 78 51.46 N 32.14 E
Korženevskoj, pik ⋀ 85 39.04 N 72.00 E
Korževka 80 54.12 N 46.22 E
Kos 38 36.53 N 27.18 E
Kos (Cos) I 38 36.50 N 27.10 E
Kosa, Ityo. 144 7.51 N 36.51 E
Kosa, Ross. 24 59.56 N 54.55 E
Kosa, Ross. 88 54.47 N 108.52 E
Kosa ≐, Ross. 24 60.11 N 55.10 E
Kosa ≐, Ross. 80 58.26 N 51.15 E
Kosa ⊥ 150 15.50 N 7.00 W
Kosa Arabats'ka strilka ›2 78 45.40 N 35.00 E
Koš-Agač 86 50.00 N 88.40 E
Kosai 94 34.43 N 137.33 E
Kosaja, šivera ∟ 88 58.24 N 97.48 E
Kosaja Gora 82 54.07 N 37.33 E
Kosaka 92 40.19 N 140.44 E
Kosan 98 38.52 N 127.24 E
Košankol' 80 49.56 N 48.11 E
Kosava 76 52.45 N 25.09 E
Koscagyl 86 46.51 N 53.48 E
Kösching 60 48.49 N 11.30 E
Kościan 30 52.06 N 16.38 E
Kościerzyna 30 54.08 N 18.00 E
Kosciusko 194 33.03 N 89.35 W
Kosciusko □6 216 41.14 N 85.51 W
Kosciusko, Mount ⋀ 171b 36.27 S 148.16 E
Kosciusko National Park ♦ 166 36.10 S 148.15 E
Kös Dağı ⋀ 130 40.59 N 34.25 E
Kosdaulet, peski ◆2 80 47.45 N 49.30 E
Kose, Eesti 76 59.11 N 25.10 E
Kose, Nihon 270 34.25 N 135.46 E
Köse, Tür. 130 40.13 N 39.39 E
Kösedağı ⋀ 130 39.54 N 42.39 E
Kösefakılı 130 39.36 N 34.09 E
Koševelka 82 55.09 N 38.05 E
Koševlicha 80 55.02 N 43.33 E
Koševrovo 82 55.38 N 38.22 E
Koserow 54 54.03 N 13.59 E
Kosha 140 20.49 N 30.32 E
Koshien Stadium ♦ 270 34.42 N 135.22 E
Koshigaya 94 35.54 N 139.48 E
Koshigoe 268 35.18 N 139.30 E
Koshikijima-rettō II 92 31.45 N 129.49 E
Koshino 94 36.02 N 136.01 E
Koshk-e Kohneh 128 34.52 N 62.31 E
Koshkonong 194 36.35 N 91.38 W
Koshkonong, Lake ⊜ 216 42.52 N 88.58 W
Koshkonong Creek ≐ 216 42.53 N 88.59 W
Koshlong Lake ⊜ 212 44.58 N 78.29 W
Kōshoku 94 36.32 N 138.06 E
Koshu
— Kwangju 98 35.09 N 126.54 E
Kosī □8 124 27.15 N 87.15 E
Kosi ≐ 124 25.26 N 87.22 E
Košice 30 48.43 N 21.15 E
Kosigi 122 15.51 N 77.16 E
Kosi Kalan 124 27.48 N 77.26 E
Kosikovo 76 59.52 N 43.23 E
Kosimeer ⊜ 158 26.55 S 32.52 E
Kosino, Ross. 80 58.23 N 51.17 E
Kosino, Ross. 82 55.43 N 37.52 E
Kosiv 78 48.19 N 25.05 E
Kosju 24 65.38 N 59.03 E
Kosju ≐ 24 66.18 N 59.53 E
Kosjuvom 24 66.17 N 59.50 E
Köşk 130 37.51 N 28.03 E
Koskaecodde Lake ⊜ 186 48.00 N 55.20 W
Koškar 80 47.27 N 53.29 E
Koški, Ross. 80 54.12 N 50.28 E
Koski, Suomi 26 60.39 N 23.09 E
Koškino 80 56.20 N 50.49 E
Koskol' 86 49.31 N 67.05 E
Koskuduk 86 44.06 N 77.22 E
Koskullskulle 24 67.12 N 20.50 E
Koslan 24 63.28 N 48.52 E
Köslin
— Koszalin 30 54.12 N 16.09 E
Kosmonosy 54 50.26 N 15.00 E
Kosmynino 80 57.35 N 40.46 E
Kosoba, gora ⋀ 86 48.15 N 79.40 E
Kosogor 80 57.07 N 47.34 E
Kosoj, porog ∟, Ross. 86 57.30 N 95.30 E
Kosoj, porog ∟, Ross. 88 57.44 N 96.20 E
Kosolapovo 80 56.57 N 49.37 E
Kosŏng, C.M.I.K. 98 38.40 N 128.19 E
Kosŏng, Taehan 98 34.58 N 128.18 E
Kosovo-Metohija □4 38 42.35 N 21.00 E
Kosovska Mitrovica 38 42.53 N 20.52 E
Kosový potok ≐ 60 49.46 N 12.48 E
Kosrae I 14 5.19 N 162.59 E
Kösreli 130 37.11 N 35.59 E
Kossdorf 54 51.29 N 13.14 E
Kosse 222 31.18 N 96.38 W
Kössen 64 47.40 N 12.24 E
Kossindi 152 3.51 N 16.19 E
Kösslarn 60 48.22 N 13.07 E
Kossou, Lac de ⊜1 150 7.25 N 5.45 W
Kossuth 214 41.17 N 79.35 W
Kosta 26 56.51 N 15.23 E
Kostajnica 36 45.14 N 16.33 E
Košt'any 54 50.39 N 13.45 E
Koš-Tegirmen 85 42.47 N 73.53 E
Kostelec nad Labem 54 50.11 N 14.35 E
Kostenec 38 42.16 N 23.49 E
Koster 158 25.57 S 26.42 E
Kosterevo 80 55.56 N 39.37 E
Kosteröarna I 26 58.54 N 11.02 E
Koštice 54 50.24 N 13.55 E
Kostino, Ross. 80 52.11 N 51.20 E
Kostino, Ross. 80 52.24 N 51.39 E
Kostino, Ross. 82 56.18 N 37.43 E
Kostino, Ross. 265b 55.55 N 37.51 E
Kostino-Otdelec 78 51.33 N 41.26 E
Kost'kovo 76 60.02 N 33.14 E
Košt'ob'o 85 41.06 N 74.15 E
Kostomukša 24 64.41 N 30.49 E
Kostonjärvi ⊜ 26 65.47 N 28.27 E
Kostopil' 78 50.53 N 26.26 E
Kostroma 76 57.46 N 40.55 E
Kostroma ≐ 24 57.47 N 40.55 E
Kostroma Oblast' □4 24 58.30 N 44.00 E
Kostrovo 82 55.53 N 36.42 E
Kostryzhivka 78 48.38 N 25.41 E
Kostrzyn 30 52.37 N 14.39 E
Kostyantynivka, Ukr. 78 49.57 N 35.07 E
Kostyantynivka, Ukr. 78 47.51 N 31.09 E
Kostyantynivka, Ukr. 83 48.32 N 37.43 E
Kosugaya ◆8 268 35.22 N 139.33 E
Kosuge 94 35.45 N 138.57 E
Kosugi 94 36.43 N 137.06 E
Kosum Phisai 110 16.13 N 103.01 E
Koszalin (Köslin) 30 54.12 N 16.09 E
Koszalin □4 30 54.00 N 16.00 E
Kőszeg 30 47.23 N 16.33 E
Koszyce 30 50.11 N 20.35 E
Kota, India 120 25.11 N 75.50 E
Kota, India 124 22.18 N 82.02 E
Kota, Malay. 114 2.31 N 102.10 E
Kota, Malay. 114 5.35 N 100.23 E
Kotaagung 112 5.30 S 104.38 E
Kotabaharu, Indon. 112 0.48 S 111.33 E
Kota Baharu, Malay. 114 6.08 N 102.15 E
Kotabangun 112 0.16 S 116.35 E
Kotabaru, Indon. 112 3.14 S 116.13 E
Kotabaru, Indon. 112 1.08 S 101.43 E
Kotabaru
— Jayapura, Indon. 164 2.32 S 140.42 E
Kota Belud 112 6.25 N 116.31 E
Kotabumi 112 4.50 S 104.54 E
Kotabunan 112 0.49 N 124.38 E
Kotadabok 112 0.30 S 104.33 E
Kot Addu 123 30.28 N 70.58 E
Kotagiri 122 11.26 N 76.53 E
Kot'ajevka 80 46.33 N 48.46 E
Kotake 96 33.41 N 130.43 E
Kota Kinabalu (Jesselton) 112 5.59 N 116.04 E
Kota Kota
— Nkhotakota 154 12.57 S 34.17 E
Kotālpur 126 23.02 N 87.36 E
Kotamobagu 112 0.46 N 124.19 E
Kotanemel', gora ⋀ 86 47.43 N 77.18 E
Kotapinang 114 1.53 N 100.05 E
Kotari ⋏ 36 44.05 N 15.30 E
Kotaringin 114 0.53 N 102.03 E
Kota Sarang Semut 114 5.59 N 100.24 E
Kotatengah 114 1.05 N 100.33 E
Kota Tinggi 114 1.44 N 103.54 E
Kotawaringin 112 2.29 S 111.25 E
Kotchāndpur 124 23.24 N 89.01 E
Kotcho Lake ⊜ 176 59.05 N 121.10 W
Kot Chutta 123 29.53 N 70.39 E
Kotdwāra 124 29.45 N 78.32 E
Kotel 38 42.53 N 26.27 E
Kotel'nič 80 58.18 N 48.20 E
Kotel'niki 82 55.39 N 37.52 E
Kotel'nikovo 80 47.38 N 43.09 E
Kotel'nyj, ostrov I 74 75.45 N 138.44 E
Kotel'va 78 50.05 N 34.45 E
Kot Fateh 123 30.07 N 75.05 E
Köthen 54 51.45 N 11.58 E
Koti
— Kōchi 96 33.33 N 133.33 E
Kotido 154 3.00 N 34.06 E
Kotikovo 89 49.08 N 144.13 E
Kotivka 78 49.08 N 34.57 E
Kotka 26 60.28 N 26.55 E
Kot Kapūra 123 30.35 N 74.54 E
Kotkino 24 67.02 N 51.03 E
Kotla 123 32.15 N 76.02 E
Kotl'akovo 82 56.17 N 35.49 E
Kotlas 24 61.16 N 46.35 E
Kotli 123 33.31 N 73.55 E
Kotlik 180 63.02 N 163.33 W
Kotlin, ostrov I 76 60.00 N 29.46 E
Kotly 76 59.36 N 28.45 E
Kot Mūmin 123 32.11 N 73.02 E
Kotō 94 35.08 N 136.14 E
Kōtō ◆8 268 35.41 N 139.48 E
Koto ≐, Nihon 96 33.58 N 131.13 E
Kotō ≐, Nihon 96 34.21 N 134.02 E
Kotobiki-san ⋀ 96 35.03 N 132.47 E
Kotohira 96 34.11 N 133.49 E
Kotohira-gu ʋ1 96 34.11 N 133.49 E
Kotohira-yama ⋀ 96 34.11 N 133.48 E
Kôtomo, Île I 175f 22.40 S 167.33 E
Kotonami 96 34.10 N 133.56 E
Koton-Karifi 150 8.08 N 6.48 E
Kotonkoro 150 11.02 N 5.58 E
Kotor 38 42.25 N 18.46 E
Kotoriba 36 46.21 N 16.49 E
Kotorovo 80 54.54 N 41.35 E
Kotor Varoš 36 44.37 N 17.23 E
Kotouba 150 8.41 N 3.12 W
Kotovo 80 50.18 N 44.50 E
Kotovsk, Ross. 80 52.36 N 41.32 E
Kotovs'k, Ukr. 78 47.45 N 29.33 E
Kot Pūtli 124 27.43 N 76.12 E
Kotra, India 120 24.22 N 73.10 E
Kotra, India 272b 22.46 N 88.34 E
Kot Rādha Kishan 123 31.10 N 74.06 E
Kotri 120 25.22 N 68.18 E
Kotri Allāhrakhio 120 24.24 N 67.50 E
Kotrung
— Uttarpara-Kotrung 272b 22.40 N 88.21 E
Kötschach [-Mauthen] 64 46.40 N 13.00 E
Kot Sultān 123 30.46 N 70.56 E
Kōtsu-zan ⋀ 96 34.01 N 134.12 E
Kottagūdem 122 17.33 N 80.38 E
Kottas Mountains ⋏ 9 74.20 S 12.00 W
Kottayam 122 9.35 N 76.31 E
Kotte
— Sri Jayawardenepura 122 6.54 N 79.54 E
Kottingbrunn 61 47.57 N 16.14 E
Kotto ≐ 136 4.14 N 22.02 E
Kotton 144 9.35 N 50.28 E
Kottūru 122 14.49 N 76.13 E
Kotuj ≐ 74 71.55 N 102.05 E
Kotwālīpāra 126 22.59 N 89.59 E
Kötz 58 48.25 N 10.17 E
Kotzebue 180 66.53 N 162.39 W
Kotzebue Sound Ꮜ 180 66.20 N 163.00 W
Kötzting 60 49.11 N 12.52 E
Koualé 150 11.24 N 7.01 W
Kou'an 106 32.19 N 119.52 E
Kouandé 150 10.20 N 1.42 E
Kouango 152 4.58 N 19.59 E
Kouassi-Datékro 150 7.49 N 3.31 W
Koubansaki 273b 4.22 S 15.09 E
Koubča 76 53.39 N 29.14 E
Koubia 150 11.35 N 11.54 W
Kouchibouguac National Park ♦ 186 46.50 N 65.00 W
Koudougou 150 12.15 N 2.22 W
Kouéré 150 10.27 N 3.59 W
Kouffo ≐ 150 6.35 N 1.59 E
Kouga 146 9.56 N 21.03 E
Kouga ≐ 158 33.37 S 22.14 E
Kougaberge ⋏ 158 33.40 S 23.50 E
Kougarok Mountain ⋀ 180 65.41 N 165.13 W
K'ouhu 100 23.35 N 120.11 E
Kouilou □5 152 4.30 S 12.00 E
Kouilou ≐ 152 4.28 S 11.41 E
Koukdjuak ≐ 176 66.45 N 73.09 W
Kouki 152 7.10 N 17.18 E
Koúklia 130 34.42 N 32.34 E
Koukourou ≐ 152 7.32 N 19.42 E
Koukourou-Bamingui, Réserve de Faune du ◆4 152 7.20 N 20.00 E
Koula ≐ 229b 21.54 N 159.36 W
Koulamoutou 152 1.08 S 12.29 E
Koulikoro 150 12.53 N 7.33 W
Koulikoro □4 150 13.00 N 8.00 W
Koulouguidi 150 13.27 N 11.03 W
Koulountou ≐ 150 13.15 N 13.37 W
Koumac 175f 20.33 S 164.17 E
Koumac, Grand Récif de ✢2 175f 20.32 S 164.04 E
Koumala 166 21.37 S 149.15 E
Koumaméyong 152 0.11 N 11.51 E
Koumankou 150 12.06 N 6.08 W
Koumbakara 150 12.42 N 14.29 W
Koumbal 146 9.26 N 22.39 E
Koumbala ≐ 146 9.14 N 20.42 E
Koumbia, Burkina 150 11.14 N 3.42 W
Koumbia, Guinée 150 11.48 N 13.30 W
Koumbisaleh ⊥ 150 15.46 N 7.59 W
Koumbouma 150 10.24 N 12.56 W
Koumi 94 36.05 N 138.29 E
Koumpentoum 150 13.59 N 14.34 W
Koumra 146 8.55 N 17.33 E
Koundara 150 12.29 N 13.18 W
Koundé 152 6.07 N 14.38 E
Koundian ⊥ 150 13.10 N 10.41 W
Koundougou 150 11.44 N 4.31 W
Koun-Fao 150 7.29 N 3.15 W
Koungheul 150 13.59 N 14.48 W
Koungoulou 152 3.32 S 13.20 E
Kouniohou 150 7.40 N 0.48 E
Kounradskij 86 46.59 N 75.00 E
Kountze 194 30.22 N 94.18 W
Koupé, Mont ⋀ 152 4.47 N 9.43 E
Koupéla 150 12.11 N 0.21 W
Kouragué 150 12.18 N 10.02 W
Kourak 86 54.50 N 84.40 E
Kouriles, Détroit des
— Pervyj Kuril'skij proliv Ꮜ 74 50.50 N 156.36 E
Kouri-shima I 174m 26.42 N 128.01 E
Kourou 250 5.09 N 52.39 W
Kouroukoto 150 12.35 N 10.05 W
Kourouma 150 11.37 N 4.48 W
Kourouninkoto 150 13.52 N 9.35 W
Kouroussa 150 10.39 N 9.53 W
Koury 150 12.11 N 4.48 W
Koussanar 150 13.52 N 14.05 W
Koussané, Mali 150 14.53 N 11.14 W
Koussane, Sén. 150 14.08 N 12.26 W
Kousser, Massif de ⋀ 148 32.02 N 5.59 W
Koussi, Emi ⋀ 146 19.50 N 18.30 E

Symbols in the index entries represent the broad categories identified in the key at the right. Symbols with superior numbers (⋏1) identify subcategories (see complete key on page *I · 1)*.

Symbole im Register stellen die rechts im Schlüssel erklärten Kategorien dar. Symbole mit hochgestellten Ziffern (⋏1) bezeichnen Unterabteilungen einer Kategorie (vgl. vollständiger Schlüssel auf Seite *I · 1)*.

Los símbolos incluídos en el texto del índice representan las grandes categorías identificadas con la clave a la derecha. Los símbolos con numeros en su parte superior (⋏1) identifican las subcategorías (véase la clave completa en la página *I · 1)*.

Les symboles de l'index représentent les catégories indiquées dans la légende à droite. Les symboles suivis d'un indice (⋏1) représentent des sous-catégories (voir légende complète à la page *I · 1)*.

Os símbolos incluídos no texto do índice representam as grandes categorias identificadas com a chave à direita. Os símbolos com números em sua parte superior (⋏1) identificam as subcategorias (veja-se a chave completa à página *I · 1)*.

⋀	Mountain	Berg	Montaña	Montagne	Montanha
⋏	Mountains	Gebirge	Montañas	Montagnes	Montanhas
)(	Pass	Paß	Paso	Col	Passo
V	Valley, Canyon	Tal, Cañon	Valle, Cañón	Vallée, Canyon	Vale, Canhão
≚	Plain	Ebene	Llano	Plaine	Planície
›	Cape	Kap	Cabo	Cap	Cabo
I	Island	Insel	Isla	Île	Ilha
II	Islands	Inseln	Islas	Îles	Ilhas
±	Other Topographic Features	Andere Topographische Objekte	Otros Elementos Topográficos	Autres données topographiques	Outros acidentes topográficos

ESPAÑOL Nombre	Página	Lat.°'	Long.°' W=Oeste
Koussili	150	13.30 N	11.38 W
Koutia Ba	150	14.11 N	14.28 W
Koutiala	150	12.23 N	5.28 W
Kouto	150	9.53 N	6.25 W
Koutou	98	38.35 N	114.24 E
Kouts	216	41.19 N	87.01 W
Kouvola	26	60.52 N	26.42 E
Kouya ≏	150	10.09 N	9.45 W
Kouyou ≏	152	0.45 S	16.38 E
Kova	88	58.18 N	100.21 E
Kova ≏	88	58.18 N	100.58 E
Kovada Milli Parkı ♦	130	37.32 N	30.53 E
Kovaksa	88	55.31 N	43.30 E
Kovalivka	78	47.16 N	31.43 E
Kovarskas	76	55.26 N	24.55 E
Kovarzino	76	60.09 N	38.33 E
Kovdor	24	67.34 N	30.22 E
Kovdozero, ozero @	24	66.47 N	32.00 E
Kovel'	78	51.14 N	24.41 E
Kovernino	78	57.07 N	43.49 E
Kovilpatti	122	9.10 N	77.52 E
Kovin	38	44.45 N	20.59 E
Kovno — Kaunas	76	54.54 N	23.54 E
Kovrina Vtoraja	80	47.01 N	41.44 E
Kovrov	80	56.22 N	41.18 E
Kovsuh ≏	48	48.48 N	39.17 E
Kovŭr	122	14.29 N	79.59 E
Kovvur	122	17.01 N	81.44 E
Kovylkin	80	48.16 N	41.28 E
Kovylkino	80	54.02 N	43.56 E
Kovža ≏	64	61.09 N	38.58 E
Kovžinskij Zavod	76	60.24 N	37.04 E
Kowal	30	52.32 N	19.09 E
Kowalewo Pomorskie	30	53.10 N	18.53 E
Kowangge	115b	8.16 S	118.32 E
Kowanyama	164	15.28 S	141.44 E
Kowanyama Aboriginal Reserve ⚬⁴	164	15.15 S	141.45 E
Kowår	126	24.13 N	86.11 E
Koweït — Kuwait ⚬¹	128	29.30 N	47.45 E
Kowel — Kovel'	78	51.14 N	24.41 E
Kowghån ⚏	128	34.15 N	62.57 E
Kowhitirangi	172	42.52 S	171.01 E
Kowie — Port Alfred	158	33.36 S	26.55 E
Kowkcheh ≏	120	37.10 N	69.23 E
Kowloon — Jiulong, Zhg.	271d	22.18 N	114.10 E
Kowloon City	271d	22.19 N	114.11 E
Kowloon Peak ⋀	271d	22.21 N	114.13 E
Kowmung ≏	170	33.52 S	150.16 E
Kowön	98	39.26 N	127.14 E
Kowt-e 'Ashrow	120	34.27 N	68.48 E
Koxtag	120	37.23 N	78.05 E
Kōya	96	34.12 N	135.35 E
Koyadaira	96	33.56 N	134.13 E
Kōyaguchi	96	34.18 N	135.33 E
Koyama ⚫⁸	268	35.37 N	139.43 E
Kōyama-ike @	96	35.30 N	134.09 E
Kōyama-misaki ➤	96	34.10 N	131.36 E
Koyambattur — Coimbatore	122	11.00 N	76.58 E
Koyang-ni	98	37.42 N	126.56 E
Koya-Ryūjin-kokutei-köen ♦	96	34.10 N	135.35 E
Köyceğiz	130	36.57 N	28.41 E
Köyceğiz Gölü @	130	36.55 N	28.40 E
Koyna Reservoir @¹	122	17.25 N	73.45 E
Koyra ≏¹	126	22.07 N	89.16 E
Koyuk	180	64.56 N	161.08 W
Koyuk ≏	180	64.55 N	161.12 W
Koyukuk	180	64.53 N	157.43 W
Koyukuk ≏	180	64.55 N	157.30 W
Koyukuk, Middle Fork ≏	180	67.03 N	151.04 W
Koyukuk, North Fork ≏	180	67.03 N	151.04 W
Koyukuk, South Fork ≏	180	66.35 N	151.57 W
Koyulhisar	130	40.18 N	37.51 E
Koža	78	57.47 N	48.57 E
Kozacha Lopan'	78	50.21 N	36.11 E
Kozachi Laheri	78	46.42 N	32.59 E
Kozakai	94	34.48 N	137.22 E
Kōzaki	94	35.54 N	140.24 E
Kō-zaki ➤	92	34.05 N	129.13 E
Kozakli	130	39.14 N	34.49 E
Kožan, Nihon	96	34.35 N	133.03 E
Kozan, Tür.	130	37.27 N	35.49 E
Kozáni	38	40.18 N	21.47 E
Kozara ⚏	36	45.00 N	16.50 E
Kozarac	36	44.58 N	16.51 E
Kozats'ke	78	51.38 N	33.29 E
Kozdinga	24	63.43 N	47.32 E
Kozelets'	78	50.55 N	31.08 E
Kozel'shchyna	78	49.13 N	33.51 E
Kozel'sk	82	54.02 N	35.48 E
Koževnikovo	78	56.19 N	29.46 E
Kozhanka	78	49.58 N	29.46 E
Kozhikode	122	11.15 N	75.46 E
Kozieglowy	30	50.36 N	19.09 E
Kozienice	30	51.35 N	21.33 E
Kožim	24	65.44 N	59.28 E
Kozino	265b	55.54 N	37.11 E
Kozjak (Possruck) ⚏	61	46.37 N	15.28 E
Kozlov Bereg	78	49.33 N	25.20 E
Kozlovka, Ross.	78	51.39 N	41.16 E
Kozlovka, Ross.	80	50.52 N	40.27 E
Kozlovka, Ross.	80	52.33 N	48.14 E
Kozlovka, Ross.	80	55.35 N	39.29 E
Kozlovo, Ross.	82	56.31 N	36.16 E
Kozlu, Tür.	130	41.26 N	31.46 E
Kozluk, Tür.	130	40.37 N	36.30 E
Kozluk	130	38.11 N	41.29 E
Kozmin	30	51.50 N	17.28 E
Koz'modemjansk	24	56.20 N	46.36 E
Koz'mogorodskoje	24	65.32 N	44.55 E
Kozopos'olok	24	63.10 N	38.06 E
Kožuchovo	265b	55.43 N	37.54 E
Kožučkovo	78	56.11 N	35.35 E
Kozuka	268	35.09 N	139.57 E
Kōzuki	96	34.59 N	134.20 E
Kozukue ⚫⁸	268	35.29 N	139.37 E
Koźla	66	56.10 N	91.24 E
Kožurla	80	55.21 N	79.02 E
Kozu-shima I	92	34.13 N	139.10 E
Kozuya	270	34.52 N	135.45 E
Kozyn	78	50.14 N	30.39 E
Kozyatyn	78	49.43 N	28.50 E
Kpandae	150	9.30 N	0.01 W
Kpandu	150	6.59 N	0.17 E
Kpong	150	6.09 N	0.04 E
Kpo Range ⚏	150	7.15 N	10.15 W
Kra, Isthmus of ⸗³	116	10.20 N	99.00 E
Kraai ≏	158	30.40 S	26.45 E
Kraaifontein	158	33.51 S	18.42 E
Kraal	158	26.34 S	28.26 E
Krankuil	158	29.52 S	24.07 E
Krabbendijke	52	51.26 N	4.07 E
Krabi	116	8.04 N	98.55 E
Kråchéh	116	12.29 N	106.01 E
Krackow	54	53.20 N	14.10 E
Kraftsdorf	54	50.52 N	11.53 E
Kragan	115a	6.42 S	111.37 E
Kragenæs	41	54.55 N	11.22 E
Kragerø	26	58.52 N	9.25 E
Kragujevac	38	44.01 N	20.55 E
Krahenhöhe ⚫⁸	263	51.10 N	7.06 E
Kraiburg	61	48.10 N	12.26 E
Kraichgau ⸗¹	56	49.10 N	8.50 E

FRANÇAIS Nom	Page	Lat.°'	Long.°' W=Ouest
Krailling	64	48.06 N	11.25 E
Krainburg — Kranj	36	46.15 N	14.21 E
Krainka	82	54.07 N	36.21 E
Krai-Russkije	80	57.23 N	46.50 E
Krajčíkovo	86	56.16 N	73.20 E
Krajenka	30	53.19 N	17.00 E
Krajeva	89	44.54 N	131.08 E
Krajina ⚬⁹	36	45.00 N	15.40 E
Krajneje	80	47.29 N	46.01 E
Krajnik Dolny	54	53.05 N	14.25 E
Krajnovka	84	43.57 N	47.24 E
Krakatau ⋀¹	115a	6.07 S	105.24 E
Krakau — Krakatau ⋀¹	115a	6.07 S	105.24 E
Krakau			
— Kraków	30	50.03 N	19.58 E
Kråkôr	110	12.32 N	104.12 E
Krakovets'	78	49.57 N	23.07 E
Krakovo	80	53.36 N	50.51 E
Kraków, Dtsch.	54	53.39 N	12.16 E
Kraków, Pol.	30	50.03 N	19.58 E
Kraków ⚬⁴	80	49.50 N	20.00 E
Krakower See @	54	53.37 N	12.17 E
Krakatau — Krakatau ⋀¹	115a	7.46 S	113.25 E
Krakraan — Kraków	30	50.03 N	19.58 E
Kråkôr	110	12.32 N	104.12 E
Kraksaal	54	54.18 N	11.04 E
Krålendijk	241s	12.10 N	68.17 W
Kralice	61	49.11 N	16.12 E
Kraljevica	36	45.16 N	14.34 E
Kraljevo	38	43.43 N	20.41 E
Kraljovice	60	49.59 N	13.29 E
Králové Vinohrady ➤⁸	54	50.01 N	14.29 E
Kralupy nad Vltavou	54	50.11 N	14.18 E
Kralupy u Chomutova	54	50.25 N	13.20 E
Králův Dvůr	60	49.56 N	14.02 E
Kramators'k	83	48.43 N	37.32 E
Kramer	216	40.20 N	87.17 W
Kramfors	26	62.56 N	17.47 E
Krammer ≏	52	51.38 N	4.15 E
Krampen	61	47.40 N	15.32 E
Krampnitz ⚫⁸	264a	52.28 N	13.04 E
Krampnitzsee @	264a	52.27 N	13.03 E
Kramsach	64	47.27 N	11.52 E
Kranebitten, Flughafen ⚑	64	47.16 N	11.20 E
Kranenburg	52	51.47 N	6.03 E
Krångede	26	63.09 N	16.05 E
Kranichfeld	54	50.51 N	11.12 E
Kranidhion	38	37.22 N	23.10 E
Kranj	36	46.15 N	14.21 E
Kranj, Sing.	271c	1.26 N	103.46 E
Kranji, Sing.	271c	1.26 N	103.45 E
Kranji ≏	271c	1.26 N	103.45 E
Kranji Reservoir @¹	271c	1.26 N	103.45 E
Kranji War Memorial ⚑	271c	1.26 N	103.45 E
Kranjska Gora	36	46.29 N	13.47 E
Kransaja Pol'ana	84	43.41 N	40.13 E
Kranskop	158	27.43 S	30.47 E
Kranzberg, Dtsch.	60	48.24 N	11.37 E
Kranzberg, Namíbia	156	21.55 S	15.43 E
Krapina	36	46.10 N	15.52 E
Krapivinskij	86	54.10 N	86.49 E
Krapivna	82	53.58 N	37.11 E
Krapkowice	30	50.29 N	17.56 E
Krapp	41	3.39 N	98.10 E
Kras (Karst) ⚏¹	64	45.48 N	14.00 E
Krasavino	24	60.58 N	46.26 E
Krasino	72	70.45 N	54.27 E
Krasivaja Meča ≏	80	52.59 N	39.03 E
Krasivka	80	52.16 N	42.31 E
Krasivoje	86	51.54 N	66.46 E
Kraskino	89	42.44 N	130.48 E
Krasková	265b	55.39 N	37.59 E
Kråslava	76	55.54 N	27.10 E
Kraslice	54	50.18 N	12.31 E
Krasna ⚬¹	78	49.01 N	38.10 E
Krasnae	76	54.14 N	27.05 E
Krasnaja Gora, Ross.	76	53.01 N	31.37 E
Krasnaja Gorbatka	80	55.52 N	41.46 E
Krasnaja Jaranga	86	65.40 N	172.50 W
Krasnaja Jaruga	78	50.48 N	35.39 E
Krasnaja Pachra	82	55.27 N	37.17 E
Krasnaja Pol'ana, Ross.	86	56.15 N	51.09 E
Krasnaja Pol'ana, Ross.	82	52.13 N	53.38 E
Krasnaja Pol'ana, Ross.	80	46.06 N	41.34 E
Krasnaja Slabada	76	52.51 N	27.10 E
Krasnaja Sloboda	84	51.24 N	48.31 E
Krasnaja Zar'a	82	52.57 N	37.53 E
Krásná Lípa	54	50.54 N	14.31 E
Krasnaluki	76	54.37 N	28.50 E
Krasnapolle	76	53.20 N	31.24 E
Krasna Polyana	78	53.20 N	31.24 E
Krasne	80	50.07 N	44.46 E
Krasnenkij	80	50.56 N	42.13 E
Krasnik	30	50.56 N	22.13 E
Krasni Okny	78	47.32 N	29.27 E
Krasno ⚬¹	80	50.57 N	46.58 E
Krasnoarmejsk, Kaz.	86	53.50 N	69.42 E
Krasnoarmejsk, Ross.	80	51.02 N	45.42 E
Krasnoarmejsk, Ross.	82	56.08 N	38.08 E
Krasnoarmejskaja	78	45.23 N	38.12 E
Krasnoarmejskij, Ross.	74	69.35 N	172.00 E
Krasnoarmejskij, Ross.	80	48.17 N	44.33 E
Krasnoarmejsk, Ross.	82	47.01 N	42.13 E
Krasnoarmejskoje, Ross.	80	55.46 N	47.11 E
Krasnoarmiys'k	83	48.17 N	37.11 E
Krasnoarmiys'ke	83	48.18 N	37.10 E
Krasnobrod	30	50.33 N	23.13 E
Krasnoborsk, Ross.	80	53.46 N	45.04 E
Krasnoborsk, Ross.	24	61.33 N	45.59 E
Krasnobrodskij	86	54.10 N	86.30 E
Krasnodar	80	45.02 N	39.00 E
Krasnodar Kraj ⚬³	80	45.00 N	39.00 E
Krasnodarskoje vodochranilišče @¹	80	45.06 N	39.31 E
Krasnodon, Tür.	83	48.18 N	39.37 E
Krasnodon, Ukr.	83	48.17 N	39.44 E
Krasnofarfornyj	82	59.08 N	31.14 E
Krasnoflotskoje	80	55.09 N	40.14 E
Krasnogorodskoje	76	56.50 N	28.17 E
Krasnogorskij, Ross.	78	50.39 N	38.24 E
Krasnogorskij, Ross.	80	50.39 N	38.24 E
Krasnogorsk, Ross.	80	57.42 N	46.58 E
Krasnogvardejsk ⸗ Kaz.	86	51.24 N	69.28 E
Krasnogvardejskoje	78	45.50 N	38.24 E
Krasnogvardejskoje, Ross.	78	50.39 N	38.24 E
Krasnogvardejskoje @¹	86	51.24 N	69.28 E
Krasnohorivka	83	48.01 N	37.31 E
Krasnohvardijs'ke	78	45.29 N	34.17 E

PORTUGUÊS Nome	Página	Lat.°'	Long.°' W=Oeste
Krasnojar	80	48.54 N	51.46 E
Krasnojarka, Ross.	86	55.20 N	73.04 E
Krasnojarka, Ross.	86	59.26 N	60.30 E
Krasnoj Armii, proliv ⸜	74	80.00 N	94.35 E
Krasnojarovo	89	51.27 N	128.28 E
Krasnojarsk	86	56.01 N	92.50 E
Krasnojarskij	86	51.58 N	59.55 E
Krasnojarskij Kraj ⚬⁸	86	56.00 N	92.22 E
Krasnojarskoje vodochranilišče @¹	86	55.00 N	92.00 E
Krasnoje, Ross.	24	59.12 N	47.49 E
Krasnoje, Ross.	76	53.06 N	33.55 E
Krasnoje, Ross.	76	52.51 N	38.47 E
Krasnoje, Ross.	78	50.56 N	38.41 E
Krasnoje, Ross.	78	50.21 N	38.50 E
Krasnoje, Ross.	78	46.44 N	39.34 E
Krasnoje, Ross.	82	54.26 N	38.38 E
Krasnoje, Ross.	86	54.37 N	85.23 E
Krasnoje, ozero @	74	64.30 N	174.24 E
Krasnoje Echo	78	55.48 N	40.42 E
Krasnoje Gorodišče	82	54.04 N	38.44 E
Krasnoje-na-Volge	82	57.31 N	41.14 E
Krasnoje Selo, Ross.	80	48.02 N	45.13 E
Krasnoje Selo, Ross.	80	48.46 N	42.20 E
Krasnoje Selo, Ross.	265a	59.44 N	30.05 E
Krasnoje Znam'a, Ross.	76	57.26 N	35.13 E
Krasnoje Znam'a, Turk.	128	36.58 N	62.30 E
Krasnokamsk	86	58.04 N	55.48 E
Krasnokutsk, Kaz.	86	53.01 N	79.59 E
Krasnokuts'k, Ukr.	78	50.06 N	35.09 E
Krasnolesje	76	54.24 N	22.23 E
Krasnolesnyj	81	51.53 N	39.35 E
Krasnomajskij	76	57.37 N	34.22 E
Krasnoökt'abr'skij, Kyrg.	85	42.50 N	74.18 E
Krasnoökt'abr'skij, Ross.	80	56.40 N	47.45 E
Krasnoökt'abr'skij, Ross.	80	48.53 N	44.45 E
Krasnoostrovskij	76	60.18 N	28.40 E
Krasnopavlivka	78	49.08 N	36.19 E
Krasnoperekops'k	78	45.57 N	33.47 E
Krasnopil'a	78	50.46 N	35.16 E
Krasnorečenskij	89	44.41 N	135.14 E
Krasnorichens'ke	83	49.11 N	38.24 E
Krasnošče	24	67.21 N	37.02 E
Krasnoščokovo	86	51.40 N	82.45 E
Krasnose'kup	74	65.41 N	82.28 E
Krasnosielc	30	53.03 N	21.10 E
Krasnosil's'ke	78	45.25 N	32.42 E
Krasnoslobodsk, Ross.	80	54.26 N	43.48 E
Krasnoslobodsk, Ross.	80	48.42 N	44.34 E
Krasnotorka	80	48.41 N	37.31 E
Krasnoturansk	86	54.16 N	91.29 E
Krasnoturjinsk	86	59.46 N	60.13 E
Krasnoufimsk	86	56.37 N	57.46 E
Krasnoural'sk	86	58.21 N	60.03 E
Krasnousol'skij	86	53.54 N	56.27 E
Krasnoviŝarsk	24	60.23 N	56.59 E
Krasnovka	83	48.47 N	40.07 E
Krasnovodsk	128	40.00 N	53.00 E
Krasnovodskij zaliv ⸜	128	39.55 N	53.15 E
Krasnoyarsk — Krasnojarsk	86	56.01 N	92.50 E
Krasnoyil's'k	78	48.01 N	25.34 E
Krasnozatonskij	24	61.41 N	50.58 E
Krasnozavodsk	82	56.27 N	38.13 E
Krasnoznamensk	78	54.57 N	22.30 E
Krasnoznamenskoje	86	51.03 N	69.30 E
Krasnoz'or'skoje	86	53.59 N	79.14 E
Krásný Dvůr	54	50.10 N	13.24 E
Krasnyj, Ross.	76	54.35 N	31.27 E
Krasnyj, Ross.	92a	46.15 N	141.15 E
Krasnyj Aul	86	51.03 N	81.02 E
Krasnyj Bogatyr'	80	55.17 N	43.59 E
Krasnyj Bor, Ross.	76	60.16 N	35.42 E
Krasnyj Bor, Ross.	265a	59.41 N	30.41 E
Krasnyj Cholm, Ross.	76	58.03 N	37.07 E
Krasnyj Cholm, Ross.	84	54.11 N	40.42 E
Krasnyj Cholm, Ross.	86	51.35 N	54.09 E
Krasnyj Čuuluk	80	46.18 N	46.56 E
Krasnyj Čikoj	87	50.22 N	108.15 E
Krasnyj Jar	80	57.08 N	45.10 E
Krasnyje Barrikady	80	46.14 N	47.53 E
Krasnyje Gory	80	58.57 N	29.45 E
Krasnyje Tkači	80	57.30 N	39.45 E
Krasnyj Gorodok	80	57.11 N	30.44 E
Krasnyj Gul'aj	80	54.00 N	48.21 E
Krasnyj Jar, Kaz.	86	53.20 N	69.14 E
Krasnyj Liman	78	53.50 N	69.42 E
Krasnyj Log	78	51.23 N	39.46 E
Krasnyj Luč	78	48.08 N	38.56 E
Krasnyj Majak	86	56.03 N	41.23 E
Krasnyj Manyč, Ross.	80	46.33 N	42.10 E
Krasnyj Manyč, Ross.	80	46.33 N	42.10 E
Krasnyj Melïorator	80	50.02 N	46.06 E
Krasnyj Okt'abr'	80	55.46 N	47.11 E
Krasnyj Okt'abr', Kaz.	86	—	75.59 E
Krasnyj Okt'abr', Ross.	80	52.44 N	50.02 E
Krasnyj Okt'abr', Ross.	83	48.17 N	37.11 E
Krasnyj Partizan	80	55.57 N	64.48 E
Krasnyj Perfintern	80	58.02 N	43.10 E
Krasnyj Rog	76	52.58 N	33.45 E
Krasnyj Steklovar	80	56.06 N	48.23 E
Krasnyj Stroitel' ⚫⁸	265b	55.35 N	37.37 E
Krasnyj — Kryvyy Rih	78	47.55 N	33.21 E
Kriwoi-Rog	78	47.55 N	33.21 E
Krasnyj TkačDa	78	53.41 N	33.25 E
Krasnystaw	30	50.59 N	23.11 E
Krasnyj Kut	80	50.57 N	46.58 E
Krasnyj Lyman	83	49.00 N	37.49 E
Krasnyj Perekop	80	57.23 N	33.12 E
Krasnyj'ukovskaja	80	51.47 N	41.58 E
Krasyliv	78	49.39 N	26.59 E
Krasnra (Crasna) ≏¹	38	48.09 N	22.20 E
Kratovo	265b	55.22 N	37.56 E
Krauchenwies	58	48.01 N	9.15 E
Kraul Mountains ⚏	9	73.10 S	14.10 W
Krauthein, Ross.	86	51.31 N	14.41 E
Krauthára, Česká Rep.	86	56.16 N	73.01 E
Kravaře, Česká Rep.	60	49.34 N	17.03 E
Kray ⚫⁸	263	51.26 N	7.05 E
Kražiai	76	55.36 N	22.40 E
Krbava ⚏¹	36	44.40 N	15.35 E
Kreamer Island I	220	26.46 N	80.44 W

(continuación)		Lat.°'	Long.°'
Kreba-Neudorf	54	51.20 N	14.40 E
Krebs	196	34.55 N	95.42 W
Krečetovo	24	60.56 N	38.30 E
Krečevicy	76	58.37 N	31.21 E
Krefeld	56	51.20 N	6.34 E
Kregme	41	55.57 N	12.04 E
Kreiensen	52	51.51 N	9.58 E
Kreischa	54	50.56 N	13.45 E
Kremastón, Tekhnití Límni @¹	38	38.55 N	21.30 E
Kremenchuk	78	49.04 N	33.25 E
Kremenchuts'ke vodoskhovyshche @¹	78	49.20 N	32.30 E
Kremenets'	78	50.07 N	25.45 E
Kremenivka	83	47.20 N	37.29 E
Kremenskoj	80	47.49 N	41.08 E
Kremenskoje	82	55.06 N	35.57 E
Kreminna	83	49.03 N	38.14 E
Kreml' ⚫	265b	55.45 N	37.37 E
Kremmen	54	52.45 N	13.01 E
Kremmling	200	40.03 N	106.23 W
Kremnica	30	48.43 N	18.54 E
Krempe	52	53.50 N	9.29 E
Krems ≏, Öst.	61	48.14 N	14.19 E
Krems ≏, Öst.	61	48.25 N	15.36 E
Krems an der Donau	61	48.25 N	15.36 E
Kremsbrücke	61	46.57 N	13.37 E
Kremsmünster	61	48.03 N	14.08 E
Krenitzin Islands II	180	54.08 N	166.00 W
Krenstj	76	51.29 N	122.17 E
Krepkaja ≏	83	47.35 N	39.23 E
Krepoljin	38	44.16 N	21.37 E
Kreschonka	86	55.52 N	80.06 E
Kresgeville	210	40.54 N	75.30 W
Kress	196	34.22 N	101.45 W
Kressbronn	57	47.35 N	9.36 E
Kresta, zaliv ⸜	180	66.00 N	179.15 W
Krestcy, Ross.	76	58.15 N	32.31 E
Krestcy, Ross.	76	58.23 N	39.00 E
Krestjanskij	85	40.32 N	69.02 E
Krestjanskoje	80	45.34 N	42.56 E
Krest-Major	74	67.37 N	144.45 E
Krestovaja Guba	72	74.07 N	55.33 E
Krestovo-Gorodišče	82	54.06 N	48.36 E
Krestovyj, pereval)(	84	42.32 N	44.28 E
Kresty	82	55.16 N	37.06 E
Kreta — Kríti I	38	35.15 N	25.00 E
Kretek	115a	7.59 S	110.19 E
Kretinga	76	55.53 N	21.13 E
Kreuth	64	47.38 N	11.45 E
Kreuzau	56	50.45 N	6.29 E
Kreuzberg	263	51.09 N	7.27 E
Kreuzberg ➤⁸	264a	52.30 N	13.23 E
Kreuzberg ⋀	56	50.22 N	9.58 E
Kreuzeck-Gruppe ⚏	64	46.51 N	13.06 E
Kreuzen	64	46.40 N	13.35 E
Kreuzlingen	57	47.39 N	9.11 E
Kreuznach — Bad Kreuznach	56	49.52 N	7.51 E
Kreuztal	56	50.58 N	7.59 E
Kreuzwertheim	56	49.46 N	9.31 E
Kréva	76	54.19 N	26.17 E
Kreyenhagen	54	52.55 N	10.52 E
Krian	115a	7.24 S	112.35 E
Kria Vrísi	38	40.47 N	22.18 E
Kriebstein, Burg ⼯	54	51.02 N	13.00 E
Krieglach	61	47.33 N	15.34 E
Kriel	158	26.16 S	29.14 E
Kriens	58	47.03 N	8.17 E
Kriguigun, mys ➤	180	65.30 N	171.05 W
Kriljon, mys ➤	89	45.53 N	142.05 E
Krishna — Kryms'kyy pivostriv ➤¹	78	45.00 N	34.00 E
Krishna ≏	122	15.57 N	80.59 E
Krishna, Mouths of the ≏¹	122	15.43 N	80.55 E
Krishnachaadrapur	126	21.50 N	86.49 E
Krishnagiri	122	12.31 N	78.14 E
Krishnanagar, India	126	23.24 N	88.30 E
Krishnanagar, India	126	23.13 N	87.33 E
Krishnapur, India	272b	22.40 N	88.32 E
Krishna Sãgara @¹	122	12.30 N	76.26 E
Krishnaräjpet	122	12.39 N	76.30 E
Krishnarämpur	126	22.43 N	88.14 E
Kristdala	26	57.24 N	16.11 E
Kristiania — Oslo	26	59.55 N	10.45 E
Kristiancpel	86	56.15 N	16.02 E
Kristiansand	26	58.10 N	8.00 E
Kristiansand Län ⚬⁶	26	58.20 N	7.45 E
Kristianstad	26	56.02 N	14.08 E
Kristianstads Län ⚬⁶	26	56.15 N	14.00 E
Kristiinankaupunki (Kristinestad)	63	62.17 N	21.23 E
Kristinehamn	26	59.20 N	14.07 E
Kristinestad (Kristiinankaupunki)	26	62.17 N	21.23 E
Kríti I (Crete) I	38	35.15 N	25.00 E
Kritikón Pélagos (Sea of Crete) ⸜²	38	35.46 N	23.54 E
Kritzendorf	264b	48.20 N	16.18 E
Kritzmow	54	54.04 N	12.03 E
Kriva ≏	38	42.04 N	22.07 E
Krivača	76	56.06 N	41.23 E
Kriva'anskaja	80	47.15 N	42.04 E
Kriva Palanka	38	42.12 N	22.20 E
Krivcy	82	55.28 N	38.12 E
Krivinka	76	53.55 N	28.10 E
Krivodol	38	43.22 N	23.30 E
Krivoj Rog — Kryvyy Rih	78	47.55 N	33.21 E
Kriwoi-Rog	78	47.55 N	33.21 E
Křižanov	60	49.23 N	16.06 E
Križevci	36	46.02 N	16.32 E
Krk	36	45.02 N	14.36 E
Krk I	36	45.05 N	14.35 E
Krka ≏	36	43.55 N	15.57 E
Krkonoše ⚏	54	50.45 N	15.35 E
Krkonošský národní park ♦	54	50.45 N	15.35 E
Krma ≏¹	38	42.41 N	24.34 E
Krn ⋀	36	46.16 N	13.40 E
Krnov	30	50.05 N	17.41 E
Krobia	30	51.47 N	16.58 E
Krokek	26	58.40 N	16.24 E
Krokodil ≏, S. Afr.	156	25.26 S	32.58 E
Krokodil ≏, S. Afr.	158	24.12 S	26.52 E
Krokom	26	63.20 N	14.30 E
Krokowa	30	54.47 N	18.01 E
Krokowá, Česká Rep.	60	49.38 N	14.03 E
Kroken	26	65.23 N	14.15 E
Kružmeca	36	42.54 N	21.32 E

(continuación)		Lat.°'	Long.°'
Krombi Pits	156	19.30 S	25.02 E
Kroměříž	30	49.18 N	17.24 E
Krommenie	52	52.29 N	4.45 E
Krompachy	30	48.56 N	20.52 E
Kromy	76	52.43 N	35.46 E
Kronach	56	50.14 N	11.20 E
Kronberg	56	50.10 N	8.30 E
Kronborg ⼯	41	56.02 N	12.38 E
Krone	263	51.27 N	7.20 E
Krong Ana @¹	110	12.30 N	108.00 E
Krong Kaôh Kông	110	11.37 N	102.59 E
Krŏng Kêb	110	10.29 N	104.19 E
Kronobergs Län ⚬⁶	26	56.40 N	14.40 E
Kronoby (Kruunupyy)	26	63.43 N	23.02 E
Kronockaja Sopka, vulkan ⋀¹	74	54.44 N	160.31 E
Kronockij zaliv ⸜	74	54.12 N	160.36 E
Kronoki	74	54.36 N	161.10 E
Kronshagen	41	54.20 N	10.05 E
Kronstadt — Brașov, Rom.	38	45.39 N	25.37 E
Kronštadt, Ross.	76	59.59 N	29.45 E
Kronwa	110	15.25 N	98.26 E
Kroondal	158	25.45 S	27.19 E
Kroonstad	158	27.45 S	27.12 E
Kröpelin	54	54.04 N	11.48 E
Kropotkin, Ross.	72	45.26 N	40.34 E
Kropotkin, Ross.	88	58.30 N	115.17 E
Kropotkina, gora ⋀	87	58.43 N	117.32 E
Kropp	41	54.24 N	9.31 E
Kroppefjäll ⚏²	26	58.40 N	12.13 E
Kroppenstedt	54	51.56 N	11.18 E
Kropstädt	54	51.58 N	12.44 E
Kropufino	76	60.23 N	39.10 E
Krościenko	30	49.27 N	20.26 E
Kroshna	78	50.18 N	28.39 E
Kröslin	54	54.07 N	13.45 E
Krośniewice	30	52.16 N	19.10 E
Krosno	30	49.42 N	21.46 E
Krosno ⚬⁴	30	49.30 N	22.00 E
Krosno Odrzańskie	30	52.04 N	15.05 E
Krossen, Dtsch.	54	50.58 N	11.59 E
Krossen, Dtsch.	54	50.58 N	11.59 E
Krostitz	54	51.28 N	12.27 E
Krotoszyn	30	51.42 N	17.26 E
Krotovka	80	53.18 N	51.12 E
Krotovo	86	56.57 N	69.20 E
Krotz Springs	194	30.32 N	91.45 W
Kroya	115a	7.38 S	109.14 E
Krško	36	45.58 N	15.29 E
Krsy	60	49.54 N	13.03 E
Kr'učkov	84	48.01 N	45.40 E
Kr'učkovo	76	57.03 N	35.34 E
Kruckow	54	53.54 N	13.14 E
Krudenburg	263	51.39 N	6.45 E
Kruenggeukueh	114	5.19 N	97.02 E
Kruengluak	114	2.50 N	97.45 E
Kruft	56	50.23 N	7.20 E
Kruger National Park ♦	156	24.00 S	31.40 E
Krugersdorp	158	26.05 S	27.35 E
Krugersdorp ⚬⁵	273d	26.05 S	27.35 E
Krugersdorp Race Course ➤	273d	26.08 S	27.45 E
Krugersdorp West	273d	26.06 S	27.45 E
Krugloje	83	47.01 N	39.15 E
Krugloz'ornoje, Kaz.	80	51.06 N	51.17 E
Krugloz'ornoje, Ross.	86	55.13 N	79.01 E
Kruglyži	80	58.31 N	47.42 E
Krugzell	58	47.47 N	10.16 E
Kruhlae	76	54.15 N	29.48 E
Kruibeke	52	51.11 N	4.18 E
Kruidfontein	158	32.51 S	21.57 E
Kruiningen	52	51.27 N	4.02 E
Kruisfontein	158	34.00 S	24.43 E
Kruishoutem	52	50.54 N	3.31 E
Kruisland	52	51.34 N	4.24 E
Kruisvallei	158	33.26 S	25.55 E
Krujë	83	41.30 N	19.48 E
Krukira, Laguna de c	236	13.36 N	83.30 W
Kr'ukov	80	47.24 N	42.28 E
Kr'ukovo, Ross.	74	66.30 N	159.31 E
Kr'ukovo, Ross.	82	55.59 N	37.10 E
Krumau — Český Krumlov	60	48.49 N	14.19 E
Krumbach, Bngl.	126	24.00 N	91.00 E
Krumbach, Dtsch.	58	48.14 N	10.22 E
Krumme Lanke @	264a	52.27 N	13.14 E
Krummendeich	54	53.50 N	9.09 E
Krummennaab	58	49.48 N	12.08 E
Krummer See @	264b	52.28 N	13.39 E
Krummhörn	52	53.22 N	7.10 E
Krummhörn ⚫¹	52	53.25 N	7.10 E
Krumovgrad	38	41.28 N	25.39 E
Krün	58	47.29 N	11.16 E
Krung Thep (Bangkok), Thai	116	13.45 N	100.31 E
Krung Thep (Bangkok), Thai	269a	13.45 N	100.31 E
Krung Thep Mahanakhon ⚬¹	269a	13.47 N	100.43 E
Krung Thon Bridge ⼯	269a	13.45 N	100.30 E
Krupá	54	50.08 N	13.41 E
Krupac	38	43.13 N	22.34 E
Krupec	76	51.11 N	34.21 E
Krupina	30	48.21 N	19.05 E
Krupinská vrchovina ⚏	30	48.20 N	19.10 E
Krupka	54	50.41 N	13.52 E
Krupki	76	54.19 N	29.08 E
Kruså	41	54.50 N	9.24 E
Kruščica ⚏	36	44.39 N	16.37 E
Kruševac	38	43.35 N	21.20 E
Kruševo	38	41.22 N	21.14 E
Krušné hory (Erzgebirge) ⚏	54	50.30 N	13.10 E
Kruszwica	30	52.41 N	18.19 E
Krutaja, Ross.	86	63.02 N	54.38 E
Krutaja Gorka	76	53.51 N	30.03 E
Kruté	80	56.29 N	43.17 E
Krutec, Ross.	82	58.42 N	36.36 E
Krutec, Ross.	82	56.25 N	36.03 E
Kruticha	86	53.35 N	81.19 E
Krutinka	86	56.19 N	71.31 E
Krutoj Log	80	51.30 N	44.36 E
Krutaja ≏	82	54.31 N	36.54 E
Krutoje ≏¹	80	52.24 N	44.24 E
Kruunupyy (Kronoby)	26	63.43 N	23.02 E
Kruzof Island I	180	57.10 N	135.40 W
Kryčav	76	53.42 N	31.43 E
Krydor	184	52.47 N	107.03 W
Krylbo	26	60.07 N	16.13 E
Krylovskaja	80	46.22 N	39.59 E
Krym, Respublika ⚬³	78	45.00 N	34.00 E
Krymsk	84	44.56 N	37.59 E
Krym's'ke	83	48.49 N	38.31 E
Krym's'kyy hory ⚏	78	44.45 N	34.15 E
Krymskij	78	45.20 N	37.41 E

(continuación)		Lat.°'	Long.°'
Kryms'kyy pivostriv (Crimean Peninsula) ➤¹	78	45.00 N	34.00 E
Krynica	30	49.25 N	20.56 E
Krynka ≏	83	47.36 N	38.47 E
Krynychky	78	48.22 N	34.27 E
Krynychne	78	45.32 N	28.40 E
Kryva kosa ➤²	83	47.02 N	38.06 E
Kryva Ruda	78	49.31 N	32.59 E
Kryve Ozero	78	47.56 N	30.21 E
Kryvichy	76	54.43 N	27.17 E
Kryvošyn	76	52.52 N	26.08 E
Kryvyy Rih	78	47.55 N	33.21 E
Kryvyy Torets' ≏	83	48.39 N	37.32 E
Kryzhopil'	78	48.23 N	28.52 E
Kryžina, chrebet ⚏	88	54.00 N	95.00 E
Kryzs'ke	83	49.28 N	39.38 E
Krzepice	30	50.58 N	18.44 E
Krzeszowice	30	50.09 N	19.39 E
Krzeszyce	54	52.36 N	15.01 E
Krzna ≏	30	52.08 N	23.31 E
Krzywiń	30	51.58 N	16.49 E
Krzyż	30	52.53 N	16.00 E
Ksar Chellala	148	35.13 N	2.18 E
Ksar el-Kebir	150	35.01 N	5.54 W
Ksar-el-Seghir	34	35.50 N	5.32 W
Ksar Hellal	36	35.39 N	10.54 E
Ksaverivka	78	50.03 N	30.12 E
Ksel, Djebel ⋀	148	33.44 N	1.10 E
Kšen' ≏	76	52.23 N	37.44 E
Ksenjevka	88	53.34 N	118.44 E
Ksenofontova	24	60.58 N	56.12 E
Kšenskij	76	51.52 N	37.43 E
Ksiąž Wielkopolski	30	52.05 N	17.14 E
Ksob, Oued ≏	148	34.46 N	0.58 E
Ksour, Monts des ⚏	148	32.45 N	0.30 W
Ksour Essaf	148	35.25 N	11.00 E
Kstovo	80	56.09 N	44.11 E
Kū', Wâdî al- ≏	140	13.37 N	25.15 E
Kuah	114	6.19 N	99.51 E
Kuai ≏	100	33.09 N	117.32 E
Kuala, Indon.	112	2.55 N	105.48 E
Kuala, Indon.	114	3.32 N	98.24 E
Kualabee	114	4.24 N	96.03 E
Kuala Berang	114	5.04 N	103.01 E
Kualacenako	112	0.28 S	102.40 E
Kuala Kangsar	114	4.46 N	100.56 E
Kualakapuas	112	3.01 S	114.21 E
Kuala Kedah	114	6.06 N	100.18 E
Kuala Kelawang	114	2.56 N	102.05 E
Kuala Kerai	114	5.32 N	102.12 E
Kuala Kerau	114	3.43 N	102.22 E
Kuala Kubu Baharu	114	3.34 N	101.39 E
Kualakurun	112	1.07 S	113.53 E
Kualalangsa	114	4.32 N	98.01 E
Kuala Lipis	114	4.11 N	102.03 E
Kuala Lumpur	114	3.10 N	101.42 E
Kuala Lumpur ⚬³	114	3.10 N	101.42 E
Kuala Manjung	114	1.25 S	112.00 E
Kuala Nerang	114	6.15 N	100.37 E
Kualapapuan	229a	21.09 N	157.02 W
Kuala Penyu	115b	5.38 N	115.35 E
Kuala Pilah	114	2.44 N	102.15 E
Kualapuu	229a	21.09 N	157.02 W
Kuala Selangor	114	3.21 N	101.15 E
Kuala Terengganu	114	5.20 N	103.08 E
Kualu ≏	114	2.45 N	100.00 E
Kuamut	114	5.13 N	117.30 E
Kuamut ≏	114	5.13 N	117.32 E
Kuanbang	98	40.29 N	124.04 E
Kuancheng, Zhg.	98	40.37 N	118.31 E
Kuancheng, Zhg.	98	40.37 N	118.31 E
Kuandang	105	40.38 N	117.22 E
Kuandang	112	0.52 N	122.55 E
Kuandian	98	40.43 N	124.44 E
Kuando — Cuando ≏	152	18.27 S	23.32 E
Kuanhsi	100	24.48 N	121.10 E
Kuanshan	100	22.58 N	120.19 E
Kuan Shan ⋀	100	23.14 N	120.54 E
Kuantan	114	3.48 N	103.20 E
Kuantan ≏	114	3.50 N	103.17 E
Kuanyin	100	25.01 N	121.04 E
Kuanyün — Guanyun	98	34.20 N	119.17 E
Kuanza — Cuanza ≏	152	9.19 S	13.08 E
Kuba — Cuba ⚬¹	240f	21.30 N	80.00 W
Kuban' ≏	72	45.20 N	37.30 E
Kubbi	140	11.08 N	25.14 E
Kubbum	140	11.47 N	23.47 E
Kubena ≏	24	59.36 N	39.39 E
Kubenskoje, ozero @	24	59.40 N	39.25 E
Kubinka	82	55.35 N	36.43 E
Kubitzer Bodden c	54	54.24 N	13.12 E
Kublis	58	46.55 N	9.47 E
Kubokawa	96	33.12 N	133.08 E
Kubor, Mount ⋀	166	6.05 S	144.45 E
Kubrat	38	43.48 N	26.29 E
Kubsas' ≏	86	62.33 N	66.27 E
Kučevo	38	44.28 N	21.40 E
Kuchaman	124	27.09 N	74.52 E
Kuchar ≏	96	43.12 N	144.29 E
Kuchchamli	114	4.52 N	100.38 E
Kuchelmiß	54	53.43 N	12.18 E
Kuchinoerabu-jima I	93b	30.28 N	130.11 E
Kuchino-shima I	93b	29.58 N	129.57 E
Kuchl	61	47.37 N	13.09 E
Kuchnay Darweyshãn	128	31.02 N	64.10 E
Kuchurhan ≏	78	46.32 N	30.02 E
Kučicy ≏	76	56.00 N	35.59 E
Kučma	36	42.54 N	21.32 E
Kucova	265b	55.55 N	37.58 E
Kucukbakkal ⚫⁸	267b	40.58 N	29.05 E
Küçük Ağrı Dağı ⋀	130	39.42 N	44.18 E
Kücükçekmece	130	41.00 N	28.46 E
Kücükçekmece Gölü c	267b	41.00 N	28.46 E
Kud ≏	124	32.55 N	75.17 E
Kuda-jima I	174	26.09 N	127.54 E
Kudangou	84	41.06 N	124.04 E
Kudara-Somon	88	51.13 N	106.39 E
Kudat	114	6.53 N	116.50 E
Kudever'	76	56.47 N	29.23 E

Symbol	Deutsch	Español	English	Français	Português
≏ River	Fluß	Río	River	Rivière	Rio
≍ Canal	Kanal	Canal	Canal	Canal	Canal
ʟ Waterfall, Rapids	Wasserfall, Stromschnellen	Cascada, Rápidos	Waterfall, Rapids	Chute d'eau, Rapides	Cascata, Rápidos
)(Strait	Meeresstraße	Estrecho	Strait	Détroit	Estreito
⸜ Bay, Gulf	Bucht, Golf	Bahía, Golfo	Bay, Gulf	Baie, Golfe	Baía, Golfo
@ Lake, Lakes	See, Seen	Lago, Lagos	Lake, Lakes	Lac, Lacs	Lago, Lagos
≋ Swamp	Sumpf	Pantano	Swamp	Marais	Pântano
⊼ Ice Features, Glacier	Eis- und Gletscherformen	Accidentes Glaciares	Ice Features, Glacier	Formes glaciaires	Formas glaciares
▽ Other Hydrographic Features	Andere Hydrographische Objekte	Otros Elementos Hidrográficos	Other Hydrographic Features	Autres données hydrographiques	Outros acidentes hidrográficos
➤ Submarine Features	Untermeerische Objekte	Accidentes Submarinos	Submarine Features	Formes de relief sous-marin	Acidentes submarinos
⚬ Political Unit	Politische Einheit	Unidad Política	Political Unit	Entité politique	Unidade política
⚏ Cultural Institution	Kulturelle Institution	Institución Cultural	Cultural Institution	Institution culturelle	Instituição cultural
⼯ Historical Site	Historische Stätte	Sitio Histórico	Historical Site	Site historique	Sítio histórico
➤ Recreational Site	Erholungs- und Ferienort	Sitio de Recreo	Recreational Site	Centre de loisirs	Area de Lazer
⚑ Airport	Flughafen	Aeropuerto	Airport	Aéroport	Aeroporto
⚒ Military Installation	Militäranlage	Instalación Militar	Military Installation	Installation militaire	Instalação militar
⚫ Miscellaneous	Verschiedenes	Misceláneo	Miscellaneous	Divers	Diversos

Kudinovo 82 55.45 N 38.12 E
Kudirkos Naumiestis 76 54.46 N 22.53 E
Kudongho 98 35.31 N 126.29 E
Kudoyama 96 34.17 N 135.34 E
Kudremukh ∧ 122 13.08 N 75.16 E
Kudrovo 265a 59.54 N 30.31 E
Kudus 115a 6.48 S 110.50 E
Kudyat al-Islām 142 27.32 N 30.45 E
Kudymkar 86 59.01 N 54.37 E
Kuee Ruins ⊥ 229d 19.21 N 155.23 W
Kueishan Tao I 100 24.51 N 121.57 E
Kueisui → Hohhot 102 40.51 N 111.40 E
Kueiyang → Guiyang 102 26.35 N 106.43 E
Kuekvun' ≃ 180 69.14 N 179.25 E
Kuënlun → Kunlun Shan ⋏ 120 36.30 N 88.00 E
Kuerbin 89 49.25 N 128.59 E
K'uerhlo → Korla 90 41.44 N 86.09 E
Kufayr az-Zayt 132 33.26 N 35.44 E
Kufayr Yābūs 132 33.42 N 36.01 E
Kufrinjah 132 32.18 N 35.42 E
Kufstein 64 47.35 N 12.10 E
Kufūr Bilshāy 142 30.51 N 30.48 E
Kufūr Najm 142 30.44 N 31.35 E
Kuga, Nihon 96 34.05 N 132.05 E
Kuga, Nihon 96 33.56 N 132.16 E
Kugaluk ≃ 180 69.10 N 131.00 W
Kugaly 86 44.29 N 78.40 E
Kugarčino 80 55.33 N 50.29 E
Kugart ≃ 85 40.52 N 72.53 E
Kugas 85 38.21 N 70.48 E
Kugej 83 46.53 N 39.19 E
Kugesi 80 56.02 N 47.18 E
Kugmallit Bay c 180 69.33 N 133.25 W
Kugojeja ≃ 78 46.34 N 39.38 E
Kuguno 94 36.03 N 137.16 E
Kuḩaylī 140 19.25 N 32.50 E
Kühbach 60 48.29 N 11.11 E
Kūhdasht 128 33.32 N 47.36 E
Kūh Lab, Ra's-e > 128 25.17 N 60.28 E
Kuḩlīyah, Wādī V 142 30.05 N 31.58 E
Kühlungsborn 54 54.09 N 11.43 E
Kuhmo 26 64.08 N 29.31 E
Kuhmoinen 26 61.34 N 25.11 E
Kühnhausen 54 51.02 N 10.58 E
Kühnsdorf 61 46.37 N 14.37 E
Kūhpāyeh 128 32.43 N 52.26 E
Kühren 54 51.20 N 12.50 E
Kuhstedt 52 53.23 N 8.58 E
Kui 164 7.30 S 147.15 E
Kuibyschew → Samara 80 53.12 N 50.09 E
Kuidesu 98 41.46 N 119.29 E
Kuidou 100 25.10 N 118.11 E
Kuikkol', ozero ⊜ 86 50.57 N 64.30 E
Kuikui, Lae o > 229a 20.36 N 156.35 W
Kuilāpāl 126 22.50 N 86.38 E
Kuinre 52 52.47 N 5.50 E
Kuiseb ≃ 156 22.59 S 14.31 E
Kuishi-yama ∧, Nihon 96 33.51 N 133.35 E
Kuishi-yama ∧, Nihon 96 33.40 N 133.31 E
Kuitan 100 23.05 N 115.58 E
Kuito 152 12.22 S 16.56 E
Kuiu Island I 180 56.45 N 134.10 W
Kuivaniemi 26 65.35 N 25.11 E
Kuivastu 76 58.35 N 23.22 E
Kuja, Ross. 24 67.46 N 53.10 E
Kuja, Ross. 24 65.05 N 40.06 E
Kujang 98 39.52 N 126.01 E
Kujani Game Reserve ◆[4] 150 7.10 N 0.50 W
Kujawy ◆[1] 30 52.45 N 18.30 E
Kujbyšev → Samara, Ross. 80 53.12 N 50.09 E
Kujbyšev, Ross. 86 55.27 N 78.19 E
Kujbyševo, Ross. 83 47.49 N 38.55 E
Kujbyševo, Uzb. 85 40.22 N 71.17 E
Kujbyševskij, Kaz. 86 53.15 N 66.51 E
Kujbyševskij, Uzb. 72 37.52 N 68.44 E
Kujbyševskij Zaton 80 55.09 N 49.12 E
Kujbyševskoje vodochranilišče ⊜[1] 80 54.30 N 48.30 E
Kujeda 86 56.26 N 55.35 E
Kujgan 86 45.25 N 74.10 E
Kujgenkol' 80 49.17 N 47.59 E
Kuji 92 40.11 N 141.46 E
Kuji ≃ 94 36.29 N 140.37 E
Kujirai 268 35.56 N 139.27 E
Kujl'uk 85 41.15 N 69.20 E
Kujman' 76 52.52 N 39.16 E
Kujŏng-ni 98 37.53 N 125.54 E
Kujten-Uul ∧ 86 49.08 N 87.49 E
Kujtun 88 54.21 N 101.29 E
Kujū 96 33.01 N 131.18 E
Kujūkuri 94 35.32 N 140.25 E
Kujūkuri-hama ±[2] 94 35.35 N 140.30 E
Kujū-san ∧ 96 33.05 N 131.15 E
Kuk ∧ 64 46.16 N 13.45 E
Kuk ≃ 180 70.36 N 160.00 W
Kukaklek Lake ⊜ 180 59.09 N 155.20 W
Kukalaya ≃ 236 13.39 N 83.37 W
Kukan 89 49.12 N 133.28 E
Kukarinc 82 55.31 N 35.59 E
Kukawa 146 12.56 N 13.35 E
Kukerin 162 33.11 S 118.05 E
Kukës 38 42.05 N 20.24 E
Kuke Shan ⋏ 85 40.00 N 75.00 E
Kuki 94 36.04 N 139.40 E
Kukipi 164 8.10 S 146.05 E
Kukkola 26 65.59 N 24.04 E
Kukmirn 61 47.04 N 16.13 E
Kukmor 80 56.13 N 50.54 E
Kukoboj 76 58.42 N 39.54 E
Kukol' 76 59.52 N 32.35 E
Kükong → Shaoguan 100 24.50 N 113.37 E
Kukpowruk ≃ 180 69.35 N 163.00 W
Kukpuk ≃ 180 68.23 N 166.20 W
Kukshi 120 22.12 N 74.45 E
Kukuj 76 59.21 N 32.33 E
Kuku-Nor → Qinghai Hu ⊜ 102 36.50 N 100.20 E
Kukup 114 1.19 N 103.27 E
Kuku Point > 174a 19.18 N 166.34 E
Kukuri Mukuri Char I 126 21.56 N 90.39 E
Kukuštan 86 57.38 N 56.30 E
Kula, Blg. 38 43.53 N 22.31 E
Kula, Jugo. 38 45.36 N 19.32 E
Kula, Tür. 130 38.32 N 28.40 E
Kula, Hi., U.S. 229a 20.52 N 156.40 W
Kul'ab 120 37.55 N 69.46 E
Kul'ab □[4] 85 38.15 N 69.45 E
Kulāchi 123 31.56 N 70.27 E
Kulagi 76 52.56 N 32.24 E
Kulagino 80 48.22 N 51.33 E
Kula Gulf ʊ 175e 8.05 S 157.18 E
Kulai 114 1.40 N 103.36 E
Kulaj 86 57.42 N 75.15 E
Kula Kangri ∧ 124 28.03 N 90.27 E
Kulākh 144 21.18 N 40.41 E
Kulakovo, Ross. 82 55.06 N 37.28 E
Kulakovo, Ross. 86 58.06 N 93.57 E
Kulakši 86 47.12 N 55.24 E
Kulal, Mount ∧ 154 2.43 N 36.56 E
Kulanak 85 41.22 N 75.31 E
Kulandy 86 46.08 N 59.31 E
Kulanotpes ≃ 86 50.21 N 69.08 E
Kular 74 70.41 N 134.22 E
Kulassein Island I 116 6.25 N 120.41 E
Kulaura 120 24.32 N 92.03 E
Kulautuva 76 54.58 N 23.38 E
Kulaykilī 140 11.21 N 25.36 E
Kul'či 89 53.33 N 139.36 E
Kuldīga 76 56.58 N 21.59 E
Kuldja → Yining 86 43.54 N 81.21 E
Kul'dur 89 49.13 N 131.38 E
Kule 156 23.05 S 20.05 E
Kulebaki 80 55.24 N 42.32 E
Kulejevo 86 59.40 N 80.59 E
Kulen Vakuf 36 44.34 N 16.06 E
Kulešovka 83 47.05 N 39.33 E
Kulevčinskij 86 53.12 N 61.26 E
Kulgām 123 33.39 N 75.01 E
Kulgera 162 25.50 S 133.18 E
Kulgunino 86 53.35 N 56.56 E
Kuligi 80 58.11 N 53.46 E
Kulikovka 80 52.14 N 47.36 E
Kulikovo 76 52.14 N 39.35 E
Kulikovskij 80 50.51 N 42.34 E
Kulim 114 5.22 N 100.34 E
Kulin 162 32.40 S 118.10 E
Kuliushucun 105 40.07 N 116.34 E
Kulju 26 61.23 N 23.46 E
Kulkyne Creek ≃ 166 30.16 S 144.12 E
Kullaberg ⋏[2] 41 56.18 N 12.30 E
Kullamaa 76 58.53 N 24.05 E
Küllenhahn ◆[8] 263 51.14 N 7.08 E
Küllstedt 56 51.16 N 10.17 E
Kullu 123 31.58 N 77.06 E
Kulm 198 46.18 N 98.57 W
Kulmbach 54 50.06 N 11.27 E
Kulnura 170 33.14 S 151.13 E
Kuloj, Ross. 24 64.58 N 43.28 E
Kuloj, Ross. 24 61.02 N 42.29 E
Kuloj ≃, Ross. 24 66.03 N 43.22 E
Kuloj ≃, Ross. 76 60.25 N 42.30 E
Kuloli 85 39.22 N 68.03 E
Kulongshan 98 41.43 N 116.54 E
Kulongshanpuzi 104 41.16 N 123.59 E
Kulotino 76 58.27 N 33.21 E
Kulp 130 38.30 N 41.02 E
Kulpahar 124 25.19 N 79.39 E
Kulpara 168b 34.04 S 138.02 E
Kulpawn ≃ 150 10.21 N 1.05 W
Kulpi 126 22.06 N 88.15 E
Kul'pino 82 56.18 N 37.09 E
Kulpmont 208 40.47 N 76.28 W
Kulpsville 285 40.15 N 75.20 W
Kul'sary 86 46.59 N 54.01 E
Kulsbjerge ⋏[2] 41 55.01 N 12.01 E
Külsheim 56 49.40 N 9.31 E
Kültepe ⊥ 130 38.44 N 35.34 E
Kulti 126 23.44 N 86.51 E
Kultikri 126 22.10 N 87.09 E
Kultuk 88 51.44 N 103.42 E
Kulu 130 39.06 N 33.05 E
Kuluha, Jabal ∧ 140 15.31 N 23.25 E
Kulumadau 164 9.03 S 152.43 E
Kulunda 86 52.35 N 78.57 E
Kulunda ≃ 86 52.59 N 79.48 E
Kulundinskaja step' ≚ 86 53.00 N 79.00 E
Kulundinskoje, ozero ⊜ 86 53.00 N 79.36 E
Kuluqi 89 50.23 N 124.13 E
Kulwin 166 35.02 S 142.33 E
Kulykiv 78 49.58 N 24.04 E
Kulykivka 78 51.23 N 31.37 E
Kum ≃ 130 38.38 N 27.32 E
Kuma 96 33.39 N 132.54 E
Kuma ≃, Nihon 92 32.30 N 130.34 E
Kuma ≃, Ross. 72 44.56 N 47.00 E
Kuma ≃, Ross. 86 59.32 N 66.45 E
Kumagaya 94 36.08 N 139.23 E
Kumai, Indon. 112 3.23 S 112.33 E
Kumai, Indon. 112 2.44 S 111.43 E
Kumai, Teluk c 112 3.00 S 111.43 E
Kumaishi 92a 42.08 N 139.59 E
Kumajri 84 40.48 N 43.50 E
Kumakanda 88 52.44 N 116.55 E
Kumalarang 116 7.44 N 123.08 E
Kumamba, Kepulauan II 164 1.36 S 138.45 E
Kumamoto 92 32.48 N 130.43 E
Kumamoto □[5] 96 32.58 N 130.55 E
Kumano, Nihon 92 33.54 N 136.05 E
Kumano, Nihon 96 34.20 N 132.34 E
Kumano ≃ 92 33.44 N 136.01 E
Kumano-nada ⊤[2] 92 33.47 N 136.20 E
Kumanovo 38 42.08 N 21.43 E
Kumār ≃[1], Bngl. 126 23.11 N 90.10 E
Kumār ≃[1], Bngl. 126 23.31 N 89.28 E
Kumara, N.Z. 172 42.38 S 171.11 E
Kumara, Ross. 89 51.37 N 126.47 E
Kumārapālaiyam 122 11.28 N 77.43 E
Kumardhubi 126 23.48 N 86.43 E
Kumarganj 126 22.59 N 87.44 E
Kumārghāt 120 24.04 N 92.04 E
Kumārgrām 124 26.37 N 89.50 E
Kumāri ≃ 126 22.57 N 86.48 E
Kumārkhāli 124 23.51 N 89.15 E
Kumarl 162 32.47 S 121.33 E
Kumasi 150 6.41 N 1.35 W
Kumatori 270 34.24 N 135.22 E
Kumawa, Pegunungan ⋏ 164 3.50 S 132.50 E
Kumba 152 4.38 N 9.25 E
Kumbakonam 122 10.58 N 79.23 E
Kumba Pits 156 18.45 S 24.45 E
Kumbar 140 12.03 N 30.16 E
Kumbarilla 166 27.19 S 150.53 E
Kumbe 164 8.21 S 140.13 E
Kumbel' 85 42.30 N 73.11 E
Kŭmch'ŏn 98 38.10 N 126.29 E
Kum-Dag 128 39.16 N 54.35 E
Kumdah ⊤[4] 144 20.23 N 45.05 E
Kumdan ∧ 123 35.09 N 77.35 E
Kumdanlı 130 38.19 N 30.59 E
Kume 96 35.03 N 133.54 E
Kume-jima I 93b 26.20 N 126.47 E
Kumenan 96 34.56 N 133.58 E
Kumeny 80 58.07 N 49.56 E
Kŭm-gang ≃ 98 36.00 N 126.40 E
Kŭmgang-san ∧ 98 38.35 N 128.10 E
Kumhausen 60 48.30 N 12.10 E
Kŭmhwa 98 38.17 N 127.28 E
Kumi 154 1.29 N 33.56 E
Kumihama 96 35.36 N 134.55 E
Kuminovskoje 86 57.48 N 64.07 E
Kuminskij 86 58.40 N 66.04 E
Kumiyama 270 34.53 N 135.45 E
Kumizawa ◆[8] 268 35.23 N 139.31 E
Kumköy ◆[8] 267b 41.15 N 29.02 E
Kumla 40 59.08 N 15.08 E
Kumli 84 43.58 N 46.04 E
Kumlinge I 26 60.16 N 20.47 E
Kumluca, Tür. 130 36.22 N 30.18 E
Kumluca, Tür. 130 41.27 N 32.28 E
Kummelnäs 40 59.21 N 18.17 E
Kummerow 54 54.17 N 12.53 E
Kummerower See ⊜ 54 53.49 N 12.52 E
Kümmersbruck 60 49.25 N 11.53 E
Kumo 146 10.03 N 11.13 E
Kŭmŏ-do I 98 34.31 N 127.45 E
Kumon Range ⋏ 102 26.30 N 97.15 E
Kumora 88 55.53 N 111.13 E
Kumosō-yama ∧ 96 33.54 N 134.18 E
Kumotori-yama ∧ 94 35.51 N 138.57 E
Kumphawapi 110 17.07 N 103.01 E
Kumrābād 126 24.10 N 87.16 E
Kumru 130 40.53 N 37.17 E
Kŭmsan 98 36.07 N 127.30 E
Kŭmsan-ni 98 37.55 N 125.41 E
Kumsenga 154 3.47 S 30.25 E
Kumta 122 14.25 N 74.24 E
Kumu 154 3.04 N 25.09 E
Kumu ≃ 114 1.24 N 100.43 E
Kumuch 84 42.11 N 47.07 E
Kumukahi, Cape > 229d 19.31 N 154.49 W
Kumukuli 120 37.33 N 88.50 E
Kumusi ≃ 164 8.35 S 148.00 E
Kümüx 86 42.14 N 88.11 E
Kumzār 128 26.20 N 56.25 E
Kuna 202 43.29 N 116.25 W
Kunar (Konar) ≃ 123 34.25 N 70.32 E
Kunašak 86 55.43 N 61.36 E
Kunashiri-tō → Kunašir, ostrov I 92a 44.10 N 146.00 E
Kunašir, ostrov (Kunashiri-tō) I 92a 44.10 N 146.00 E
Kun'batar 84 44.17 N 45.34 E
Kuncheng Hu ⊜ 106 31.35 N 120.45 E
Kunchhā 124 28.08 N 84.20 E
Kunc'ovo ◆[8] 265b 55.44 N 37.26 E
Kunda, Eesti 76 59.29 N 26.32 E
Kunda, R.D.C. 154 3.57 S 26.35 E
Kunda Hills ⋏[2] 122 11.10 N 76.30 E
Kundahit 126 23.58 N 87.10 E
Kundam 124 23.13 N 80.21 E
Kundāpura 122 13.38 N 74.42 E
Kundar ≃ 120 31.56 N 69.19 E
Kundat 86 55.14 N 87.51 E
Kundelungu, Parc National de ♠ 154 10.30 S 27.45 E
Kunderu ≃ 122 14.38 N 78.42 E
Kundi 154 1.08 S 40.41 E
Kundiān 123 32.27 N 71.28 E
Kundiawa 164 6.00 S 145.00 E
Kundima 164 4.14 S 143.52 E
Kundl 64 47.28 N 11.59 E
Kundla 120 21.20 N 71.18 E
Kundr'učje ≃ 83 47.52 N 40.15 E
Kundur, Pulau I 112 0.45 N 103.26 E
Kunene □[4] 156 19.00 S 14.00 E
Kunene (Cunene) ≃ 152 17.20 S 11.50 E
Kunersdorf, Forst ◆[3] 264a 52.17 N 12.59 E
Kunes 24 70.21 N 26.31 E
Künes ≃ 86 43.55 N 80.55 E
Kunga ≃[1] 126 21.45 N 89.30 E
Kungälv 26 57.52 N 11.58 E
Kungana 146 7.50 N 10.42 E
Kungchuling → Huaide 89 43.32 N 124.50 E
K'ungej-Ala-Too, chrebet ⋏ 85 42.50 N 77.00 E
Kunggyü Yumco ⊜ 124 30.35 N 82.09 E
Kunghit Island I 182 52.06 N 131.04 W
Kunghsi 100 24.37 N 121.16 E
Kung-pei-tien 269d 25.06 N 121.38 E
Kungrad 86 43.06 N 58.54 E
Kungsängen 40 59.29 N 17.45 E
Kungsängen flygplats ⊠ 40 58.36 N 16.15 E
Kungsbacka 26 57.29 N 12.04 E
Kungsgården 40 60.36 N 16.37 E
Kungshamn 26 58.22 N 11.15 E
Kungsör 40 59.25 N 16.05 E
Kungu 152 2.47 N 19.12 E
Kungur 86 57.25 N 56.57 E
Kunhār ≃ 123 34.17 N 73.29 E
Kunhegyes 30 47.22 N 20.38 E
Kunhing 110 21.18 N 98.26 E
Kuni 94 36.35 N 138.38 E
Kunia 229c 21.29 N 158.07 W
Kunigami 174m 26.45 N 128.10 E
Kunimi 96 33.41 N 131.36 E
Kuningan 115a 6.59 S 108.29 E
Kunisaki 96 33.33 N 131.45 E
Kunisaki-hantō >[1] 96 33.30 N 131.40 E
Kunitachi 268 35.41 N 139.26 E
Kuni Vyselki 82 54.18 N 38.41 E
Kunja 76 56.18 N 30.59 E
Kunja ≃, Ross. 76 57.09 N 31.10 E
Kunja ≃, Ross. 82 56.31 N 38.12 E
Kunjāh 123 32.32 N 73.59 E
Kunkle 216 41.38 N 84.30 W
Kunkletown 210 40.51 N 75.27 W
Kunkuri 124 22.45 N 83.57 E
Kunlong 110 23.25 N 98.39 E
Kunlun Shan ⋏ 120 36.30 N 88.00 E
Kunming 102 25.05 N 102.40 E
Kunming Hu ⊜ 271a 39.59 N 116.15 E
Kunmunya Aboriginal Reserve ◆[4] 164 15.45 S 124.45 E
Kunnamkulam 122 10.39 N 76.05 E
Kunost' 76 60.01 N 37.38 E
Kunovice 30 49.03 N 17.29 E
Kunow 54 53.00 N 12.07 E
Kunowice 54 52.20 N 14.50 E
Kunrau 54 52.35 N 11.01 E
Kunsan 98 35.58 N 126.41 E
Kunshan 106 31.23 N 120.57 E
Kunszentmárton 30 46.51 N 20.18 E
Kuntair 150 13.32 N 16.13 W
Kuntaur 150 13.40 N 14.48 W
Kuntiki 86 58.29 N 76.24 E
Kunting 100 29.48 N 121.56 E
Kuntshankoie 152 3.20 S 23.34 E
Kuntuolun 102 45.13 N 115.21 E
Kununurra 164 15.47 S 128.44 E
Kunwi 98 36.15 N 128.34 E
Kunya 150 12.14 N 8.34 E
Kun'ye 83 49.23 N 37.15 E
Kunyo 144 6.17 N 42.33 E
Kunžak 61 49.07 N 15.11 E
Künzell 56 50.33 N 9.42 E
Künzelsau 56 49.16 N 9.41 E
Künzing 60 48.40 N 13.05 E
Kunzulu 152 3.29 S 16.09 E
Kuocang Shan ⋏ 100 28.36 N 120.30 E
Kuohsing 100 24.02 N 120.51 E
Kuokegan 120 37.30 N 89.55 E
Kuolajarvi 24 66.58 N 29.12 E
Kuopio 26 62.54 N 27.41 E
Kuopion lääni □[4] 26 63.00 N 27.30 E
Kuortane 26 62.48 N 23.30 E
Kupa ≃ 36 45.28 N 16.24 E
Kup'abal 271b 37.37 N 126.54 E
Kupang 112 10.10 S 123.35 E
Kupang, Teluk c 112 10.04 S 123.40 E
Kupanskoje 82 56.51 N 38.43 E
Kuparuk ≃ 180 70.25 N 148.55 W
Kupava 80 51.07 N 42.57 E
Kupavna 265b 55.45 N 38.08 E
Kuper Island I 224 48.58 N 123.39 W
Kupferberg 263 51.09 N 7.27 E
Kupferdreh ◆[8] 263 51.23 N 7.05 E
Kupfermühle 41 54.50 N 9.24 E
Kupferzell 56 49.14 N 9.41 E
Kupiano 164 10.05 S 148.11 E
Kupino 86 54.22 N 77.18 E
Kupiškis 76 55.50 N 24.58 E
Küplü, Tür. 130 41.07 N 26.21 E
Küplü, Tür. 130 40.06 N 30.00 E
Kupol, gora ∧ 180 68.38 N 174.45 E
Kuppenheim 56 48.49 N 8.15 E
Kupper Airport ⊠ 276 40.31 N 74.36 W
Kupreanof 180 56.49 N 132.57 W
Kupreanof Island I 180 56.50 N 133.30 W
Kupreanof Point > 180 55.34 N 159.35 W
Kupres 36 44.00 N 17.17 E
Küps 54 50.11 N 11.16 E
Kupuri 89 54.44 N 130.30 E
Kup'yans'k 83 49.42 N 37.38 E
Kup'yans'k-Vuzlovyy 83 49.39 N 37.39 E
Kupychiv 78 51.00 N 24.44 E
Kuqa 90 41.43 N 82.54 E
Kür (Kura) ≃, Asia 84 39.24 N 49.19 E
Kur ≃, Ross. 89 48.44 N 134.14 E
Kur, Pulau I 164 5.20 S 132.00 E
Kura (Kür) ≃, Asia 84 39.24 N 49.19 E
Kura ≃, Ross. 84 44.06 N 44.57 E
Kurabuchi 94 36.25 N 138.48 E
Kurach 84 41.36 N 47.46 E
Kurach ≃ 84 41.40 N 48.11 E
Kuragaty 85 43.06 N 72.59 E
Kuragaty ≃ 85 43.57 N 73.34 E
Kuragino 86 53.53 N 92.40 E
Kurahashi 96 34.06 N 132.30 E
Kurahashi-jima I 96 34.08 N 132.31 E
Kuraj 86 56.42 N 95.29 E
Kurajlysaj 80 50.07 N 51.51 E
Kurakaki 270 34.59 N 135.28 E
Kurakhivka 83 48.02 N 37.23 E
Kurakhove 83 47.59 N 37.16 E
Kurakino, Ross. 80 52.33 N 44.03 E
Kurakino, Ross. 82 54.30 N 35.48 E
Kurakovo 82 54.05 N 37.14 E
Kūrāli 123 30.50 N 76.35 E
Kuram 85 43.33 N 78.08 E
Kuramā', Ḩarrat ±[9] 128 24.30 N 40.15 E
Kurama-yama ∧ 96 35.07 N 135.46 E
Kuraminskij chrebet ⋏ 85 40.45 N 70.10 E
Kuramo Waters c 273a 6.26 N 3.26 E
Kuranami 268 35.27 N 140.00 E
Kuranec 76 54.33 N 26.57 E
Kuraon 124 24.59 N 82.05 E
Kurar ◆[8] 272c 19.11 N 72.52 E
Kurašasaj 86 50.18 N 56.55 E
Kurashiki 96 34.35 N 133.46 E
Kurasiki → Kurashiki 96 34.35 N 133.46 E
Kurate 96 33.47 N 130.41 E
Kurauli 124 27.24 N 78.59 E
Kuraymah 140 18.33 N 31.51 E
Kurayoshi 96 35.26 N 133.49 E
Kurayyimah 132 32.16 N 35.36 E
Kurba 80 57.34 N 39.32 E
Kurba ≃ 88 52.02 N 108.30 E
Kurbağa Gölü ⊜ 130 38.21 N 35.17 E
Kurbağalı ≃ 267b 40.59 N 29.02 E
Kurbatovo 86 55.34 N 91.10 E
Kurbulik 88 53.45 N 108.57 E
Kurčaloj 84 43.12 N 46.05 E
Kurchatov 78 51.39 N 35.36 E
Kurčum 86 48.37 N 83.40 E
Kurdaj 85 43.21 N 74.59 E
Kürdämir 84 40.21 N 48.08 E
Kurdgelauri 84 41.58 N 45.32 E
Kür dili >[2] 84 39.03 N 49.13 E
Kurdistan □[9] 128 37.00 N 45.00 E
Kurdufān al-Janūbīyah □[4] 140 11.00 N 30.00 E
Kurdufān ash-Shamālīyah □[4] 140 14.00 N 29.45 E
Kurduvādi 122 18.05 N 75.26 E
Kurdyumivka 83 48.28 N 37.59 E
Kure, Austl. 164 15.27 S 124.33 E
Kure, Nihon 96 34.14 N 132.34 E
Küre, Tür. 130 41.48 N 33.43 E
Kure Atoll I[1] 14 28.25 N 178.25 W
Küre Dağları ⋏ 130 41.45 N 34.00 E
Kurejka ≃ 74 66.30 N 87.12 E
Kurejskaja 88 58.56 N 111.20 E
Kurenalus 26 65.21 N 26.59 E
Kuresaare 76 58.15 N 22.28 E
Kurgal'džinskij 86 50.36 N 70.01 E
Kurgan 86 55.26 N 65.18 E
Kurgan Oblast' □[4] 86 55.30 N 64.30 E
Kurgan-T'ube 120 37.50 N 68.48 E
Kurgan T'ube □[4] 85 38.15 N 68.50 E
Kurgatej 88 54.23 N 99.27 E
Kurgolovo 76 59.46 N 28.06 E
Kurhan-Mechetnyy, hora ∧[2] 83 48.06 N 39.21 E
Kuria I 14 0.14 N 173.25 E
Kuria Muria Islands → Khurīyā Murīyā, Jazā'ir II 118 17.30 N 56.00 E
Kuriasol 126 22.06 N 86.39 E
Kuridala 166 21.17 S 140.30 E
Kurīgrām 124 25.49 N 89.39 E
Kurihama 268 35.13 N 139.43 E
Kurihashi 94 36.08 N 139.42 E
Kurikka 26 62.37 N 22.25 E
Kurilen → Kuril'skije ostrova II 74 46.10 N 152.00 E
Kurilen-Strasse → Pervyj Kuril'skij proliv ʊ 74 50.50 N 156.36 E
Kuriles, Islas → Kuril'skije ostrova II 74 46.10 N 152.00 E
Kuril Islands → Kuril'skije ostrova II 74 46.10 N 152.00 E
Kurilovka 80 50.44 N 48.02 E
Kuril'sk 74 45.14 N 147.53 E
Kuril'skije ostrova (Kuril Islands) II 74 46.10 N 152.00 E
Kuril Strait → Pervyj Kuril'skij proliv ʊ 74 50.50 N 156.36 E
Kuril Trench ⊹[1] 6 47.00 N 155.00 E
Kuřim 30 49.18 N 16.32 E
Kurimoto 94 35.49 N 140.30 E
Kurin' 78 51.09 N 32.44 E
Ku-Ring-Gai Chase National Park ♠ 170 33.38 S 151.15 E
Kurinjippadi 122 11.34 N 79.36 E
Kurinwás ≃ 236 12.49 N 83.41 W
Kuripapango 172 39.23 S 176.21 E
Kuriyama, Nihon 92a 43.03 N 141.47 E
Kuriyama, Nihon 94 36.52 N 139.37 E
Kurja, Ross. 24 61.42 N 57.09 E
Kurja, Ross. 86 51.36 N 82.19 E
Kurjanovskaja 76 60.19 N 41.33 E
Kurkijoki 26 61.18 N 29.54 E
Kurkino, Ross. 76 53.26 N 38.40 E
Kurkino, Ross. 265b 55.53 N 37.23 E
Kurkliai 76 55.25 N 25.03 E
Kurl ◆[8] 263 51.35 N 7.35 E
Kurla ◆[8] 272c 19.05 N 72.53 E
Kurlackoje 83 47.21 N 39.03 E
Kurleja 88 52.11 N 119.11 E
Kurlin 80 51.48 N 51.00 E
Kurlovskij 80 55.27 N 40.36 E
Kurmanajevka 80 52.31 N 52.06 E
Kurmani 126 22.47 N 89.53 E
Kurmankol' 80 49.09 N 48.27 E
Kurmenty 85 42.48 N 78.15 E
Kurmuk 140 10.33 N 34.17 E
Kurnell 274a 34.01 S 151.13 E
Kurnell Peninsula >[1] 274a 34.02 S 15.11 E
Kurnool 122 15.50 N 78.03 E
Kurobane 94 36.51 N 140.07 E
Kurobe 94 36.51 N 137.26 E
Kurobe ≃ 94 36.55 N 137.25 E
Kurobe-dam ◆[6] 94 36.36 N 137.38 E
Kurodashō 96 35.01 N 135.00 E
Kurogi 96 33.12 N 130.40 E
Kurohone 94 36.30 N 139.17 E
Kuroishi 92 40.38 N 140.36 E
Kuroiso 94 36.58 N 140.03 E
Kuroo-tōge)(96 35.11 N 134.12 E
Kuropatkino, Ross. 80 46.32 N 45.20 E
Kuropatkino, Uzb. 85 39.57 N 67.27 E
Kurort-Darasun 88 51.12 N 113.44 E
Kurort Hartha 54 50.59 N 13.33 E
Kurort Schmalkalden 54 50.43 N 10.26 E
Kurort Steinbach-Hallenberg 54 50.42 N 10.34 E
Kurort Stolberg 54 51.34 N 10.57 E
Kurort Wippra 54 51.34 N 11.16 E
Kurose 96 34.19 N 132.40 E
Kurose ≃ 96 34.13 N 132.36 E
Kuro-shima I, Nihon 93b 30.50 N 129.57 E
Kuro-shima I, Nihon 175d 24.19 N 124.05 E
Kurosu 268 35.51 N 139.23 E
Kurovo 82 55.49 N 36.00 E
Kurovskoje 82 55.34 N 38.55 E
Kurow 172 44.44 S 170.28 E
Kuroya 268 35.55 N 139.44 E
Kurrajong 170 33.33 S 150.40 E
Kurram 120 30.06 N 66.31 E
Kurram ≃ 123 32.36 N 71.20 E
Kurri Kurri 170 32.49 S 151.29 E
Kuršab ≃ 85 40.46 N 73.06 E
Kursavka 84 44.28 N 42.31 E
Kursela 124 25.27 N 87.15 E
Kuršėnai 76 56.00 N 22.56 E
Kurseong 120 26.53 N 88.17 E
Kuršių marios (Kurššskij zaliv) c 76 55.00 N 21.00 E
Kursk 78 51.42 N 36.12 E
Kurskaja 84 44.03 N 44.27 E
Kursk Oblast' □[4] 78 51.40 N 36.00 E
Kursk Station ◆[5] 265b 55.46 N 37.40 E
Kurššskaja kosa >[2] 76 55.18 N 21.00 E

ENGLISH Name	Page	Lat.°′	Long.°′

Kurššskij zaliv (Kuršių marios) c 76 55.00 N 21.00 E
Kuršumlija 38 43.08 N 21.17 E
Kurşunlu, Tür. 130 40.51 N 33.16 E
Kurşunlu, Tür. 130 38.40 N 37.51 E
Kurtalan 130 37.57 N 41.42 E
Kurtamyš 86 54.55 N 64.27 E
Kurtatsch → Cortaccia 64 46.19 N 11.13 E
Kürten, Dtsch. 56 51.03 N 7.16 E
Kurten, Tx., U.S. 222 30.47 N 96.16 W
Kurthasanlı 130 38.20 N 32.11 E
Kurth Lake ⊜ 222 31.26 N 94.42 W
Kūrtī 140 18.07 N 31.33 E
Kurtino 82 54.59 N 38.17 E
Kurtistown 229d 19.36 N 155.03 W
Kurtoğlu Burnu > 130 36.35 N 28.50 E
Kurttinskoje vodochranilišče ⊜[1] 85 43.50 N 76.20 E
Kurtty ≃ 85 44.05 N 76.20 E
Kurtušibinskij chrebet ⋏ 88 52.10 N 93.30 E
Kurtz 218 38.58 N 86.12 W
Kuru, Sūd. 140 7.43 N 26.31 E
Kuru, Suomi 26 61.52 N 23.44 E
Kuru ≃ 140 9.08 N 26.57 E
Kurucaşile 130 41.50 N 32.43 E
Kuruçay 130 39.39 N 38.29 E
Kuruçeşme ◆[8] 267b 41.03 N 29.02 E
Kuruktag ⋏ 90 41.30 N 90.00 E
Kurum 164 4.45 S 145.55 E
Kuruman 158 27.28 S 23.28 E
Kuruman ≃ 158 26.56 S 20.39 E
Kurumanheuwels ⋏[2] 158 27.40 S 23.25 E
Kurumdy, gora ∧ 85 39.28 N 73.32 E
Kurume 96 33.19 N 130.31 E
Kurumkan 88 54.18 N 110.18 E
Kurun ≃ 144 5.30 N 34.17 E
Kurunegala 122 7.29 N 80.22 E
Kurungbaja, Tanjung > 115b 8.15 S 120.35 E
Kurung Tank ⊜[1] 124 22.19 N 82.14 E
Kurunzulaj 88 51.00 N 117.10 E
Kuruqi 89 48.58 N 123.50 E
Kurur, Jabal ∧ 140 20.31 N 31.32 E
Kurusaj 85 40.35 N 69.24 E
Kurushima-kaikyo ʊ 96 34.07 N 133.00 E
Kuruson-zan ∧ 96 34.12 N 130.58 E
Kuryachivka, Ukr. 83 49.39 N 38.42 E
Kuryachivka, Ukr. 83 49.22 N 39.36 E
Kurylys 86 48.38 N 60.47 E
Kuryongp'o 98 35.59 N 129.32 E
Kurzeme □[9] 76 56.50 N 22.30 E
Kusa 86 55.20 N 59.29 E
Kusabe 270 34.31 N 135.29 E
Kuşadası 130 37.51 N 27.15 E
Kuşadası Körfezi c 130 37.50 N 27.08 E
Kusak ≃ 86 47.50 N 75.45 E
Kušalino 76 57.07 N 36.05 E
Kusan-ni, Taehan 98 37.43 N 128.49 E
Kusan-ni, Taehan 271b 37.29 N 126.45 E
Kusatsu, Nihon 94 36.37 N 138.36 E
Kusatsu, Nihon 94 35.00 N 135.57 E
Kusawa Lake ⊜ 180 60.20 N 136.15 W
Kusaybah, Bi'r ⊤[4] 140 22.41 N 29.55 E
Kuščovskaja 78 46.33 N 39.37 E
Kuse 96 35.04 N 133.45 E
Kusel 56 49.32 N 7.24 E
Kusey 54 52.36 N 11.05 E
Kuş Gölü ⊜ 130 40.10 N 27.57 E
Kuş Gölü Milli Parkı ♠ 130 40.15 N 27.55 E
Kushaka 150 10.32 N 6.48 E
Kushālgarh 120 23.10 N 74.27 E
Kusheriki 150 10.33 N 6.28 E
Kushi 174m 26.33 N 128.06 E
Kushida ≃ 94 34.36 N 136.34 E
Kushigata 94 35.36 N 138.28 E
Kushihiki 268 35.55 N 139.36 E
Kushikino 92 31.44 N 130.16 E
Kushima 92 31.29 N 131.14 E
Kushimoto 92 33.28 N 135.47 E
Kushira 270 34.28 N 135.43 E
Kushiro 92a 42.58 N 144.23 E
Kushnytsya 78 48.27 N 23.14 E
Kushog Lake ⊜ 212 45.05 N 78.48 W
Kushtia 124 23.55 N 89.07 E
Kushuhum 78 47.42 N 35.14 E
Kushui 102 42.11 N 94.25 E
Kusiro → Kushiro 92a 42.58 N 144.23 E
Kusiyāra ≃ 120 24.36 N 91.44 E
Kuška 128 35.16 N 62.20 E
Kuška ≃ 128 36.00 N 62.40 E
Kuskokwim ≃ 180 60.17 N 162.27 W
Kuskokwim, North Fork ≃ 180 63.06 N 154.37 W
Kuskokwim, South Fork ≃ 180 63.06 N 154.37 W
Kuskokwim Bay c 180 59.45 N 162.25 W
Kuskokwim Mountains ⋏ 180 62.30 N 156.00 W
Kuskovo ◆[8] 265b 55.44 N 37.49 E
Kuškušara 24 64.58 N 40.21 E
Kuśmā 124 28.14 N 83.41 E
Kušmurun 86 52.27 N 64.36 E
Kušmurun, ozero ⊜ 86 52.40 N 64.48 E
Küsnacht 58 47.19 N 8.35 E
Kušnarenkovo 86 55.06 N 55.22 E
Kusŏng 98 39.59 N 125.15 E
Kusria 272b 22.58 N 88.14 E
Kussharo-ko ⊜ 92a 43.38 N 144.21 E
Küssnacht am Rigi 58 47.05 N 8.27 E
Kustanaj 86 53.10 N 63.35 E
Kustanaj □[8] 86 53.00 N 63.00 E
Kustar'ovka 80 54.16 N 42.16 E
Küsten-Gebirge → Coast Mountains ⋏ 176 55.00 N 129.00 W
Küstenkanal ≅ 52 52.57 N 7.18 E
Küsten-Ketten → Coast Ranges ⋏ 178 41.00 N 123.30 W
Kusthalia 126 23.29 N 87.03 E
Kūstī 140 13.10 N 32.40 E
Kusu, Nihon 94 34.55 N 136.38 E
Kusu, Nihon 96 33.16 N 131.09 E
Kušum ≃ 80 48.54 N 50.32 E
Kusumba 272b 22.27 N 88.24 E
Kusumbāni ∧ 126 21.57 N 86.26 E
Kušumskij 80 51.38 N 48.21 E
Kusung 98 36.18 N 128.55 E
Kusunoki 96 34.03 N 131.15 E
K'us'ur 74 70.39 N 127.15 E
Kušva 86 58.18 N 59.45 E
Kut, Ko I 110 11.40 N 102.35 E
Kuta 150 9.52 N 6.43 E
Kuta ≃ 88 56.46 N 105.40 E
Kutabaru 112 0.44 S 102.56 E
Kutabuloh 114 3.28 N 97.04 E
Kutacane 114 3.30 N 97.48 E
Kütahya 130 39.25 N 29.59 E
Kütahya □[4] 130 39.20 N 29.30 E
Kutais 78 44.32 N 39.18 E
Kutaisi 84 42.15 N 42.40 E
Kutāmat al-Ghābah 142 30.55 N 30.54 E
Kutanibong 114 3.53 N 96.22 E
Kutaradja → Banda Aceh 114 5.34 N 95.20 E
Kutarere 172 38.03 S 177.09 E
Kutasawang 114 5.08 N 96.54 E
Kutch, Rann of (Rann of Kachchh) ◆[1] 120 24.05 N 70.10 E
Kutchan 92a 42.54 N 140.45 E
Kutcharo-ko ⊜ 92a 45.09 N 142.19 E
Kutejnikovo 83 47.34 N 39.46 E
Kutenholz 52 53.29 N 9.19 E
Kuteynykove 83 47.49 N 38.18 E
Kutima 88 57.10 N 108.16 E
Kutima ≃ 88 57.08 N 108.14 E
Kutina 36 45.29 N 16.46 E
Kutiyāna 120 21.38 N 69.59 E
Kutkai 110 23.27 N 97.56 E

DEUTSCH Name	Seite	Breite°′	Länge°′ E = Ost

Kutluškino 80 55.14 N 50.24 E
Kutná Hora 30 49.57 N 15.16 E
Kutno 30 52.15 N 19.23 E
Kutoarjo 115a 7.43 S 109.54 E
Kutomara 88 51.06 N 118.49 E
Kutse Game Reserve ◆[4] 156 23.30 S 24.05 E
Kutsuki 94 35.21 N 135.55 E
Küttigen 58 47.25 N 8.03 E
Kuttura 24 68.24 N 26.28 E
Kuttusoja 24 67.46 N 28.50 E
Kuttuzi 265a 59.45 N 30.04 E
Kutu 152 2.44 S 18.09 E
Kutubdia Island I 120 21.50 N 91.52 E
Kutubu, Lake ⊜ 164 6.23 S 143.18 E
Kutukovo 80 54.26 N 40.31 E
Kutulik 88 53.21 N 102.48 E
Kutulo, Lagh ≃ 154 2.08 N 40.56 E
Kutuluk ≃ 80 53.19 N 51.09 E
Kutum 140 14.12 N 24.40 E
Kutu-Moke 152 3.12 S 17.21 E
Kúty, Slvk. 30 48.40 N 17.03 E
Kuty, Ukr. 78 48.16 N 25.10 E
Kutztown 210 40.31 N 75.46 W
Kuujjuaq 176 58.06 N 68.25 W
Kuuli-Majak 128 40.14 N 52.42 E
Kuurne 50 50.51 N 3.17 E
Kuusamo 26 65.58 N 29.11 E
Kuusankoski 26 60.54 N 26.38 E
Kuva 85 40.32 N 72.05 E
Kuvak-Nikol'skoje 80 53.37 N 43.30 E
Kuvandyk 86 51.28 N 57.21 E
Kuvango 152 14.28 S 16.20 E
Kuvasaj 85 40.18 N 71.58 E
Kuvet ≃ 180 69.14 N 175.00 E
Kuvšinovo 76 57.02 N 34.10 E
Kuwabara 270 34.53 N 135.15 E
Kuwait → Al-Kuwayt 128 29.20 N 47.59 E
Kuwait (Al-Kuwayt) □[1], Asia 118 29.30 N 47.45 E
Kuwait (Al-Kuwayt) □[1], Asia 128 29.30 N 47.45 E
Kuwait Bay → Kuwayt, Jūn al- c 128 29.30 N 48.00 E
Kuwana 94 35.04 N 136.42 E
Kuwayt, Jūn al- (Kuwait Bay) c 128 29.30 N 48.00 E
Kuyāli 126 22.31 N 86.11 E
Kuyal'nyts'kyy lyman ⊜ 78 46.40 N 30.42 E
Kuybyshev → Samara 80 53.12 N 50.09 E
Kuybysheve, Ukr. 78 44.38 N 33.52 E
Kuybysheve, Ukr. 78 47.22 N 36.39 E
Kuybyshevka 78 47.37 N 31.42 E
Kuye ≃ 102 38.30 N 110.44 E
Kūysanjaq 128 36.05 N 44.38 E
Kuyucak, Tür. 130 37.51 N 38.21 E
Kuyucak, Tür. 130 37.55 N 28.28 E
Kuyuwini ≃ 246 2.16 N 58.16 W
Kuyuyukak, Cape > 180 56.54 N 156.50 W
Kuzaranda 24 62.22 N 35.37 E
Kuze 94 35.33 N 136.30 E
Kuze ◆[8] 270 34.57 N 135.43 E
Kuzedejevo 86 53.20 N 87.10 E
Kuzemivka 83 49.31 N 37.59 E
Kuzemyn 78 50.09 N 34.39 E
Kužener 80 56.48 N 48.56 E
Kuženkino 76 57.44 N 33.59 E
Kuzitrin ≃ 180 65.10 N 165.28 W
Kuzkejevo 80 55.46 N 52.48 E
Kuz'miniči 76 54.16 N 33.42 E
Kuz'minka ≃ 265a 59.48 N 30.31 E
Kuz'minki ◆[8] 265b 55.42 N 37.48 E
Kuz'mino, Ross. 82 55.09 N 37.53 E
Kuz'mino, Ross. 82 56.36 N 37.55 E
Kuzmiščevo 82 54.46 N 37.12 E
Kuz'movka 74 62.19 N 92.02 E
Kuznečicha 80 54.43 N 49.38 E
Kuznečikovo 82 56.13 N 36.35 E
Kuzneck, Ross. 80 53.07 N 46.36 E
Kuzneck → Novokuzneck, Ross. 86 53.45 N 87.06 E
Kuzneckij Alatau ⋏ 86 54.45 N 88.00 E
Kuznečnoje 26 61.09 N 29.52 E
Kuznecova 89 46.16 N 138.03 E
Kuznecovka 76 56.18 N 28.33 E
Kuznecovo, Ross. 82 55.30 N 38.21 E
Kuznecovo, Ross. 82 55.27 N 36.57 E
Kuznecovo, Ross. 86 59.15 N 63.28 E
Kuznecovskij 80 47.25 N 40.57 E
Kuznecy 82 55.51 N 38.40 E
Kuznetsk → Kuzneck 80 53.07 N 46.36 E
Kuznetsovo-Mykhaylivka 83 47.27 N 38.13 E
Kuznetsovs'k 78 51.22 N 25.53 E
Kuzomen', Ross. 24 64.17 N 42.53 E
Kuzomen', Ross. 24 66.17 N 36.54 E
Kuzovatovo 80 53.33 N 47.41 E
Kuzucubelen 130 36.51 N 34.27 E
Kuzuha 270 34.52 N 135.41 E
Kuzuryū ≃ 94 36.13 N 136.08 E
Kuzuu 94 36.24 N 139.37 E
Kuzyaka 130 41.14 N 33.44 E
Kvænangen c[2] 24 70.05 N 21.13 E
Kværndrup 41 55.10 N 10.32 E
Kvaisi 84 42.31 N 43.40 E
Kvaløy I 24 69.40 N 18.30 E
Kvaløya I 24 70.37 N 23.52 E
Kvam 26 61.40 N 9.42 E
Kvanløse 41 55.39 N 11.41 E
Kvanndal 26 60.29 N 6.36 E
Kvareli 84 41.56 N 45.54 E
Kvarner c 36 44.45 N 14.15 E
Kvarnerić ʊ 36 44.45 N 14.35 E
Kvarnsveden 40 60.31 N 15.24 E
Kvarntorp 40 59.08 N 15.15 E
Kvarsa 80 56.58 N 53.57 E
Kvarsebo 40 58.39 N 16.39 E
Kvašenki 82 56.48 N 37.33 E
Kvenna ≃ 26 60.01 N 7.56 E
Kverkfjöll ∧ 24a 64.43 N 16.38 W
Kvichak Bay c 180 58.48 N 157.30 W
Kvicksund 40 59.27 N 16.19 E
Kvidinge 41 56.08 N 13.04 E
Kvien ⊜ 40 60.24 N 13.48 E
Kvikkjokk 24 66.55 N 17.50 E
Kvilda 60 49.01 N 13.35 E
Kvina ≃ 26 58.17 N 6.56 E
Kvismare kanal ≅ 40 59.12 N 15.11 E
Kvissleby 26 62.17 N 17.21 E
Kvistbro 40 59.09 N 14.49 E
Kvistgård 41 55.59 N 12.30 E
Kvitok 88 56.03 N 98.30 E
Kwa ≃ 152 3.10 S 16.11 E
Kwachaga 154 5.38 S 38.08 E
Kwada 164 6.09 S 141.53 E
Kwahae-ri ◆[8] 271b 37.33 N 126.50 E
Kwahu Plateau ⋏[1] 150 6.30 N 0.30 W
Kwai → Khwae Noi ≃ 110 14.00 N 99.33 E
Kwajalein I[1] 14 9.05 N 167.20 E
Kwajok 140 8.19 N 28.00 E
Kwakoegron 250 5.15 N 55.20 W
Kwale, Kenya 154 4.11 S 39.27 E
Kwale, Nig. 150 5.46 N 6.26 E
Kwambilo ≃ 273b 4.26 S 15.20 E
Kwa-Mbonambi 158 28.36 S 32.05 E
Kwamisa ∧ 150 7.08 N 1.53 W
Kwamouth 152 3.10 S 16.12 E
Kwa Mtoro 154 5.14 S 35.26 E
Kwanak-san ∧ 271b 37.27 N 126.58 E
Kwando (Cuando) ≃ 152 18.27 S 23.32 E
Kwangchow → Guangzhou 100 23.06 N 113.16 E
Kwangju 98 35.09 N 126.54 E
Kwangju □[4] 98 35.09 N 126.55 E

Symbols in the index entries represent the broad categories identified in the key at the right. Symbols with superior numbers (⋏[1]) identify subcategories (see complete key on page *I · 1).*

Symbole im Register stellen die rechts im Schlüssel erklärten Kategorien dar. Symbole mit hochgestellten Ziffern (⋏[1]) bezeichnen Unterabteilungen einer Kategorie (vgl. vollständiger Schlüssel auf Seite *I · 1).*

Los símbolos incluídos en el texto del índice representan las grandes categorías identificadas con la clave a la derecha. Los símbolos con numeros en su parte superior (⋏[1]) identifican las subcategorías (véase la clave completa en la página *I · 1).*

Les symboles de l'index représentent les catégories indiquées dans la légende à droite. Les symboles suivis d'un indice (⋏[1]) représentent des sous-catégories (voir légende complète à la page *I · 1).*

Os símbolos incluídos no texto do índice representam as grandes categorias identificadas com a chave à direita. Os símbolos com números em sua parte superior (⋏[1]) identificam as subcategorias (veja-se a chave completa à página *I · 1).*

Symbol	English	Deutsch	Español	Français	Português
∧	Mountain	Berg	Montaña	Montagne	Montanha
⋏	Mountains	Gebirge	Montañas	Montagnes	Montanhas
)(	Pass	Paß	Paso	Col	Passo
V	Valley, Canyon	Tal, Cañon	Valle, Cañón	Vallée, Canyon	Vale, Canhão
≚	Plain	Ebene	Llano	Plaine	Planície
>	Cape	Kap	Cabo	Cap	Cabo
I	Island	Insel	Isla	Île	Ilha
II	Islands	Inseln	Islas	Îles	Ilhas
±	Other Topographic Features	Andere Topographische Objekte	Otros Elementos Topográficos	Autres données topographiques	Outros acidentes topográficos

ESPAÑOL — Nombre | Página | Lat.°′ | Long.°′ W = Oeste
FRANÇAIS — Nom | Page | Lat.°′ | Long.°′ W = Ouest
PORTUGUÊS — Nome | Página | Lat.°′ | Long.°′ W = Oeste

Kwango (Cuango) ≃ 152 3.14 S 17.23 E
Kwangsi Chuang Autonomous Region → Guangxi Zhuangzu Zizhiqu □4 102 24.00 N 109.00 E
Kwangtung → Guangdong □4 90 23.00 N 113.00 E
Kwangwazi 154 7.47 S 38.15 E
Kwangyang 98 34.59 N 127.34 E
Kwania, Lake ◎ 154 1.45 N 32.45 E
Kwanmo-bong ∧ 98 41.42 N 129.13 E
Kwansan-ni 271b 37.43 N 126.51 E
Kwanto Plain → Kantō-heiya ≚ 94 36.00 N 139.30 E
Kware 150 13.12 N 5.14 E
Kwa-Thema 273d 26.18 S 28.23 E
Kwatisore 164 3.15 S 134.57 E
Kwazulu → KwaZulu-Natal □4 158 28.40 S 30.40 E
KwaZulu-Natal □4 158 28.40 S 30.40 E
Kweichow → Guizhou □4 102 27.00 N 107.00 E
Kweihwa → Hohhot 102 40.51 N 111.40 E
Kweijang → Guiyang 102 26.35 N 106.43 E
Kweilin → Guilin 102 25.17 N 110.17 E
Kweisui → Hohhot 102 40.51 N 111.40 E
Kweiyang → Guiyang 102 26.35 N 106.43 E
Kwekwe 156 18.55 S 29.49 E
Kweneng □5 156 24.00 S 24.00 E
Kwenge (Caengo) ≃ 152 4.50 S 18.42 E
Kwesimintim 150 4.54 N 1.47 W
Kwethluk 180 60.49 N 161.27 W
Kwethluk ≃ 180 60.46 N 161.26 W
Kwidzyn 30 53.45 N 18.56 E
Kwigillingok 180 59.51 N 163.08 W
Kwiguk 180 62.45 N 164.28 W
Kwiha 144 13.31 N 39.32 E
Kwikila 164 9.48 S 147.41 E
Kwilu (Cuilo) ≃ 152 3.22 S 17.22 E
Kwinana 168a 32.15 S 115.48 E
Kwitaro ≃ 246 3.19 N 58.47 W
Kwobrup 162 33.37 S 117.46 E
Kwoka, Gunung ∧ 164 0.31 S 132.27 E
Kwolla 150 9.00 N 9.15 E
Kwun Tong 271d 22.19 N 114.12 E
Kyabé 146 9.27 N 18.57 E
Kyabra 166 26.18 S 143.10 E
Kyabra Creek ≃ 166 25.36 S 142.55 E
Kyabram 166 36.19 S 145.03 E
Kyaikkami 110 16.04 N 97.34 E
Kyaiklat 110 16.26 N 95.44 E
Kyaikto 110 17.18 N 97.01 E
Kya-in 110 16.02 N 98.08 E
Kyaka 154 1.16 S 31.25 E
Kyalite 166 34.57 S 143.29 E
Kyancutta 166 33.08 S 135.34 E
Ky Anh 110 18.05 N 106.18 E
Kyat-aw 110 12.29 N 98.19 E
Kyaukhnyat 110 18.15 N 97.31 E
Kyaukkyi 110 18.19 N 96.46 E
Kyaukme 110 22.32 N 97.02 E
Kyaukpa 110 13.05 N 98.59 E
Kyaukpyu 110 19.05 N 93.52 E
Kyaukpyu, Mya. 110 19.26 N 93.33 E
Kyaukse 110 21.36 N 96.08 E
Kyauktaw 110 20.51 N 92.59 E
Kyaunggon 110 17.06 N 95.11 E
Kybartai 76 54.39 N 22.45 E
Kybean 171b 36.22 S 149.25 E
Kybeyan Range ∧ 171b 36.10 S 149.30 E
Kyburz 226 38.47 N 120.18 W
Kydra 171b 36.27 S 149.23 E
Kyeamba 171b 35.26 S 147.37 E
Kyeamba Creek ≃ 171b 35.06 S 147.29 E
Kyebang-san ∧ 98 37.43 N 128.29 E
Kyegegwa 154 0.29 N 31.03 E
Kyeikdon 110 16.00 N 98.24 E
Kyeintali 110 18.00 N 94.29 E
Kyenjojo 154 0.37 N 30.38 E
Kyeryong-san Kukrip Kongwŏn ♦ 98 36.21 N 127.13 E
Kyes Peak ∧ 224 47.57 N 121.19 W
Kyffhäuser ∧ 54 51.23 N 11.05 E
Kyffhäuser-Denkmal ⊥ 54 51.23 N 11.06 E
Kyidaunggan 110 19.53 N 96.12 E
Kyindwe 110 20.58 N 93.51 E
Kyje ✦8 54 50.04 N 14.32 E
Kyjov 30 49.01 N 17.08 E
Kykladen → Kikládhes II 38 37.30 N 25.00 E
Kykotsmovi Village 200 35.52 N 110.37 W
Kylva 80 57.22 N 53.50 E
Kylās ∧ 124 25.18 N 90.45 E
Kyle, Sk., Can. 184 50.50 N 108.02 W
Kyle, S.D., U.S. 198 43.25 N 102.10 W
Kyle, Tx., U.S. 196 29.59 N 97.52 W
Kyle □9 46 55.29 N 4.24 W
Kyle, Lake ◎1 154 20.14 S 31.00 E
Kyleakin 46 57.16 N 5.44 W
Kyle of Lochalsh 46 57.17 N 5.43 W
Kylerhea 46 57.14 N 5.41 W
Kylertown 214 41.00 N 78.10 W
Kylestrome 46 58.16 N 5.02 W
Kyll ≃ 56 49.48 N 6.42 E
Kyllburg 56 50.02 N 6.35 E
Kym ≃ 42 52.14 N 0.17 W
Kymen lääni □4 26 61.00 N 28.00 E
Kymijoki ≃ 26 60.30 N 26.52 E
Kyn 86 57.52 N 58.38 E
Kyndby 41 55.48 N 11.56 E
Kyneton 169 37.15 S 144.27 E
Kynnefjäll ∧2 26 58.42 N 11.41 E
Kynšperk nad Ohří 54 50.04 N 12.32 E
Kynuna 166 21.35 S 141.55 E
Kyodong-do I 98 37.45 N 126.16 E
Kyoga, Lake ◎ 154 1.30 N 33.00 E
Kyōga-misaki ≻ 96 35.46 N 135.13 E
Kyogle 166 28.37 S 153.00 E
Kyŏha-ri 271b 37.46 N 126.46 E
Kyohyŏn-ni 271b 37.43 N 126.58 E
Kyom ≃ 140 8.58 N 28.13 E
Kyŏmip'o → Songnim 98 38.44 N 125.38 E
Kyonan 94 35.07 N 139.50 E
Kyondo 110 16.35 N 98.03 E
Kyŏnggi Do □4 98 37.30 N 127.30 E
Kyŏnggi-man ᑕ 98 37.25 N 126.00 E
Kyŏngju 98 35.51 N 129.14 E
Kyŏngju Kukrip Kongwŏn ♦ 98 35.47 N 129.15 E
Kyŏngsan 98 35.48 N 128.43 E
Kyŏngsang Namdo □4 98 35.15 N 128.30 E
Kyŏngsang Pukdo □4 98 36.15 N 128.45 E
Kyŏngsŏng, C.M.I.K. 98 41.35 N 129.36 E
Kyŏngsŏng → Sŏul, Taehan 98 37.33 N 126.58 E
Kyŏngwŏn 98 42.48 N 130.09 E
Kyŏnkadun 110 16.04 N 95.38 E
Kyonmange 110 18.50 N 95.50 E
Kyonpyaw 110 17.18 N 95.12 E
Kyotera 154 0.33 S 31.19 E
Kyōto, Nihon 94 35.00 N 135.45 E
Kyōto, Nihon 270 35.00 N 135.45 E
Kyōto □5 94 35.05 N 135.45 E
Kyōto-bonchi ≚ 270 35.03 N 135.45 E
Kyōto Race Track ♦ 270 34.54 N 135.43 E
Kyōto University ⊥2 270 35.02 N 135.46 E
Kyōwa 94 36.19 N 140.03 E
Kyōyomi-dake ∧ 92 33.31 N 131.02 E
Kypšak, ozero ◎ 86 50.09 N 68.28 E
Kyra 88 49.36 N 111.58 E
Kyra ≃ 88 49.24 N 112.19 E
Kyrčany 80 57.37 N 50.10 E
Kyren 88 51.41 N 102.08 E
Kyrenia → Girne 130 35.20 N 33.19 E
Kyrgyzstan □1, Asia 72 41.30 N 75.00 E
Kyrgyzstan □1, Asia 85 41.30 N 75.00 E
Kyritz 54 52.56 N 12.23 E
Kyrkheden 40 60.10 N 13.29 E
Kyrkkazyk 85 42.30 N 72.20 E
Kyrksæterøra 26 63.17 N 9.06 E
Kyrkslätt (Kirkkonummi) 26 60.07 N 24.26 E
Kyrö 26 60.42 N 22.45 E
Kyrönjoki ≃ 26 63.14 N 21.45 E
Kyrösjärvi ◎ 26 61.45 N 23.10 E
Kyröskoski 26 61.40 N 23.11 E
Kyrta 24 64.04 N 57.42 E
Kyrykhiva 78 50.22 N 35.07 E
Kyrykkuduk 80 49.51 N 51.54 E
Kyshen'ky 78 48.53 N 34.08 E
Kyshyn 78 51.08 N 27.41 E
Kyslivka 83 49.38 N 37.53 E
Kyslyakivka 78 46.44 N 31.59 E
Ky Son 110 19.24 N 104.08 E
Kyštovka 86 56.33 N 76.38 E
Kyštym 86 55.42 N 60.34 E
Kysykkamys 80 49.14 N 50.19 E
Kyte ≃ 190 42.00 N 89.19 W
Kytlym 86 59.30 N 59.12 E
Kytmanovo 86 53.28 N 85.28 E
Kyūhōji 270 34.38 N 135.35 E
Kyunchaung 110 15.33 N 98.15 E
Kyundon 110 20.31 N 95.44 E
Kyungyi I 110 15.04 N 97.44 E
Kyunhla 110 23.21 N 95.18 E
Kyuquot 182 50.02 N 127.23 W
Kyuquot Sound ⊻ 182 50.05 N 127.15 W
Kyūroku-jima I 92 40.32 N 139.29 E
Kyū-shizudani-gakkō ⊥ 96 34.45 N 134.13 E
Kyūshū I 92 33.00 N 131.00 E
Kyushu-Palau Ridge ✦3 14 20.00 N 136.00 E
Kyūshū-sanchi ∧ 92 32.35 N 131.17 E
Kywebwe 110 18.42 N 96.25 E
Kywong 166 34.59 S 146.44 E
Kyyiv (Kiev) 78 50.26 N 30.31 E
Kyyiv □4 78 50.15 N 30.30 E
Kyyivs'ke vodoskhovyshche ◎1 78 51.00 N 30.25 E
Kyyjärvi 26 63.02 N 24.34 E
Kyyvesi ◎ 26 61.58 N 27.07 E
Kyzas 86 52.20 N 89.20 E
Kyzyl 88 51.42 N 94.27 E
Kyzylagaš 86 45.54 N 81.37 E
Kyzylaryk 85 43.57 N 70.42 E
Kyzylbejit 85 41.30 N 72.24 E
Kyzyl-Chaja 86 50.03 N 89.54 E
Kyzyl-Chem (Šišchid) ≃ 88 51.21 N 96.58 E
Kyzyl-Džar 85 41.17 N 72.02 E
Kyzylemgek 85 41.57 N 74.56 E
Kyzylespe 86 47.27 N 73.53 E
Kyzylkak, ozero ◎ 86 53.25 N 73.48 E
Kyzyl-Kija 85 40.16 N 72.08 E
Kyzyl-Kommuna 86 48.44 N 67.32 E
Kyzylkum ✦2 72 42.00 N 64.00 E
Kyzylkup 128 40.38 N 53.58 E
Kyzyl-Mažalyk 86 51.10 N 90.32 E
Kyzylmazar 85 39.39 N 68.25 E
Kyzyloba 80 49.37 N 50.38 E
Kyzylsu ≃ 85 39.17 N 71.23 E
Kyzyltas, gory ∧ 86 48.12 N 73.00 E
Kyzyltau 86 47.53 N 72.05 E
Kyzylt'ob'o 85 42.13 N 75.16 E
Kyzyltu, Kaz. 86 47.46 N 59.08 E
Kyzyltu, Kaz. 86 47.43 N 75.42 E
Kyzyltu, Kyrg. 85 42.11 N 76.40 E
Kyzyluj 86 48.07 N 65.28 E
Kyzylžar 86 48.17 N 69.39 E
Kzyl-Kuga 80 48.28 N 53.01 E
Kzyl-Orda 86 44.48 N 65.28 E
Kzyl-Orda □8 86 45.00 N 64.00 E
Kzyltu 86 53.38 N 72.20 E

L

La'a ⊥ 102 29.44 N 101.26 E
Laa an der Thaya 61 48.43 N 16.23 E
Laaben 61 48.06 N 15.52 E
Laaber 60 49.04 N 11.53 E
Laab im Walde 264b 48.09 N 16.11 E
Laacher See ◎ 56 50.25 N 7.16 E
Laaerberg ∧2 264b 48.09 N 16.24 E
Laage 54 53.56 N 12.20 E
La Aguja, Cabo de ≻ 244 11.18 N 74.12 W
Laakajärvi ◎ 26 63.50 N 27.55 E
Laakirchen 64 47.58 N 13.49 E
La Albuera 34 38.43 N 6.49 W
La Alcarria ✦1 34 40.45 N 2.45 W
La Aldea 234 20.54 N 101.29 W
La Aldehuela 266a 40.18 N 3.36 W
La Algaba 34 37.28 N 6.01 W
La Almarcha 34 39.41 N 2.22 W
La Almunia de Doña Godina 34 41.29 N 1.22 W
Laanecoorie Reservoir ◎1 169 36.52 S 143.53 E
La Antigua, Salina ≚ 252 30.00 S 66.06 W
La Antorcha, Cerro ∧ 234 21.43 N 102.45 W
Laar 52 52.37 N 6.44 E
Laar ✦8 263 51.28 N 6.43 E
La Araucania □4 252 38.45 S 72.30 W
La Arena, Pan. 236 7.58 N 80.28 W
La Arena, Perú 248 5.20 S 80.44 W
Laas → Lasa 64 46.37 N 10.42 E
Laas Caanood 144 8.28 N 47.21 E
La Ascención 232 24.20 N 99.55 W
Laas Dawaco 144 10.28 N 49.05 E
Laas Dhaareed 144 10.10 N 45.59 E
Laase 54 53.04 N 11.18 E
Laas Qoray 144 11.10 N 48.13 E
La Asunción 246 11.02 N 63.53 W
La Atravesada, Loma ∧2 232 29.57 N 112.12 W
Laatzen 52 52.19 N 9.47 E
Laau Point ≻ 229a 21.06 N 157.19 W
La Aurora 286e 33.36 S 70.38 W
La Azufrosa 196 28.14 N 100.50 W
Laba ≃ 78 45.11 N 39.42 E
La Babia 232 28.34 N 102.04 W
Labadie 219 38.31 N 90.51 W
Labadieville 194 29.50 N 90.57 W
La Baie 186 48.19 N 70.53 W
La Balme-de-Sillingy 58 45.58 N 6.02 E
La Balme-les-Grottes 62 45.51 N 5.20 E
Laban 208 37.24 N 76.17 W
La Banda 252 27.44 S 64.15 W
La Bandera, Cerro ∧ 232 24.35 N 105.07 W
La Bañeza 34 42.18 N 5.54 W
La Barca 234 20.17 N 102.34 W
La Barceloneta ✦8 266d 41.22 N 2.11 E
La Barge 200 42.15 N 110.11 W
La Barge Creek ≃ 200 42.14 N 110.12 W
La Barra 236 12.54 N 83.32 W
La Barre-en-Ouche 50 48.57 N 0.40 E
La Barrita 236 14.05 N 91.03 W
La Barr Meadows 226 39.11 N 121.02 W
Labason 116 8.04 N 122.31 E
La Bassée 50 50.32 N 2.48 E
Labastide-Murat 32 44.39 N 1.34 E
La Bastide-Puylaurent 62 44.36 N 3.54 E
La Bâte 261 48.35 N 2.01 E
La Baule-Escoublac 32 47.17 N 2.24 W
La Bazoche-Gouet 50 48.08 N 0.59 E
L'Abbé 261 48.34 N 1.50 E
Labdah (Leptis Magna) ⊥ 146 32.38 N 14.18 E
Labé 150 11.19 N 12.17 W
Labe (Elbe) ≃ 30 53.50 N 9.00 E
Labégude 62 44.39 N 4.22 E
La Bégude-Blanche 62 43.55 N 6.08 E
La Bégude-de-Mazenc 62 44.32 N 4.56 E
Labelle, P.Q., Can. 206 46.16 N 74.44 W
La Belle, Fl., U.S. 220 26.45 N 81.26 W
La Belle, Mo., U.S. 219 40.07 N 91.54 W
Labelle □6 206 46.20 N 75.00 W
Labelle, Lac ◎, P.Q., Can. 206 46.13 N 74.52 W
La Belle, Lac ◎, Wi., U.S. 216 43.08 N 88.31 W
Labengke, Pulau I 112 3.27 S 122.25 E
La Bérarde 62 44.56 N 6.18 E
Laberge, Lake ◎ 180 61.11 N 135.12 W
La Berra ∧ 58 46.41 N 7.11 E
Laberweinting 60 48.48 N 12.19 E
La Besace 56 49.34 N 4.58 E
Labette Creek ≃ 198 37.03 N 95.05 W
Labi 112 4.25 N 114.22 E
La Biche ≃ 182 55.01 N 112.44 W
Labico 66 41.47 N 12.53 E
Labin 36 45.05 N 14.07 E
Labinsk 84 44.38 N 40.44 E
Labis 114 2.23 N 103.02 E
La Bisbal 34 41.57 N 3.03 E
Łabiszyn 30 52.57 N 17.55 E
Labkoviči 76 53.50 N 31.45 E
Labābah, Wādī al- ∨ 273c 30.02 N 31.19 E
La Blanca 286e 33.31 S 70.41 W
La Blanca Grande, Laguna ◎ 252 38.26 S 63.55 W
Labnā ⊥ 232 20.11 N 89.34 W
Labo 116 14.09 N 122.51 E
Labo ≃ 116 14.11 N 122.56 E
Labo, Mount ∧ 116 14.01 N 122.48 E
Laboe 54 54.24 N 10.15 E
La Boissière 261 48.46 N 1.59 E
La Boissière-Ecole 261 48.41 N 1.39 E
La Bollène-Vésubie 62 43.59 N 7.20 E
La Bonneville-sur-Iton 50 49.00 N 1.02 E
Laboratory 214 40.09 N 80.13 W
Laborde, Arg. 252 33.09 S 62.51 W
La Borde, Fr. 261 48.32 N 2.50 E
Laborec ≃ 30 48.36 N 22.00 E
Laborie 241f 13.45 N 61.00 W
Labouchere, Mount ∧ 162 25.12 S 118.18 E
Labouheyre 32 44.13 N 0.55 W
Laboulaye 252 34.07 S 63.24 W
La Bouverie 50 50.24 N 3.52 E
La Boyera, Ven. 286c 10.23 N 66.57 W
La Boyera, Ven. 286c 10.25 N 66.50 W
Lābpur 126 23.50 N 87.49 E
Labrador ✦1 176 54.00 N 62.00 W
Labrador Basin ✦1 16 53.00 N 48.00 W
Labrador City 176 52.57 N 66.55 W
Labrador Sea ≂2 176 57.00 N 53.00 W
Lábrea, Bra. 248 7.16 S 64.47 W
La Brea, Trin. 241r 10.15 N 61.37 W
Labrède 32 44.41 N 0.31 W
La Bresse 58 48.00 N 6.53 E
La Brévine 58 46.59 N 6.36 E
Labrieville, Réserve ♦ 186 49.20 N 69.40 W
La Brigue 62 44.04 N 7.37 E
La Brillanne 62 43.55 N 5.53 E
Labrit 32 44.07 N 0.33 W
La Broquerie 184 49.28 N 96.27 W
Labroye 50 50.17 N 1.59 E
Labry 56 49.10 N 5.52 E
Labuan, Pulau I 112 5.21 N 115.13 E
Labuha 164 0.37 S 127.29 E
Labunan 115a 6.22 N 125.50 E
Labuhanbajo 115b 8.29 S 119.54 E
Labuhanbatu 114 2.12 N 100.12 E
Labuhanbilik 114 2.31 N 100.10 E
Labuhandeli 114 3.45 N 98.41 E
Labuhanhaji, Indon. 114 3.33 N 97.00 E
Labuhanhaji, Indon. 115b 8.42 S 116.34 E
Labuhanmarege 112 7.06 S 120.40 E
Labuhanmaringgai 115a 5.21 S 105.48 E
Labuhanruku 114 3.13 N 99.35 E
Labuk ≃ 112 5.54 N 117.30 E
Labuk, Telukan ᑕ 116 6.07 N 117.46 E
Labu Kananga 115b 8.08 S 117.47 E
Labutta 110 16.09 N 94.46 E
Labytnangi 72 66.39 N 66.21 E
Lač, Ross. 24 63.18 N 54.28 E
Laç, Shq. 38 41.38 N 19.43 E
Lac □5 146 13.30 N 14.15 E
Lača, ozero ◎ 24 61.20 N 38.48 E
La Cadena 196 25.53 N 104.12 W
L'Acadie 275a 45.19 N 73.21 W
L'Acadie ≃ 206 45.29 N 73.16 W
La Cadière-d'Azur 62 43.12 N 5.46 E
Lacadivas, Islas → Lakshadweep II 122 10.00 N 73.00 E
Laca Jahuira ≃ 248 19.21 S 67.54 W
La Cal ≃ 248 17.27 S 58.15 W
Lac-à-la-Tortue 206 46.37 N 72.38 W
La Calera, Chile 252 32.47 S 71.12 W
La Calera, Perú 248 15.52 S 71.24 W
Lac-Allard 186 50.33 N 63.25 W
Lacamas Creek ≃ 224 46.20 N 122.16 W
Lacamas Lake ◎ 224 45.37 N 122.26 W
La Campana, Esp. 34 37.34 N 5.26 W
La Campana, Méx. 234 22.45 N 105.35 W
La Cañada 234 20.37 N 100.19 W
La Cañada, Cerro ∧ 234 21.24 N 99.13 W
La Canada Flintridge 228 34.12 N 118.12 W
La Canada Verde Creek ≃ 280 33.52 N 118.02 W
Lacanau 32 44.59 N 1.05 W
Lacanau, Lac de ᑕ 32 44.58 N 1.07 W
La Candelaria, Arg. 252 26.06 S 65.06 W
La Candelaria, Méx. 200 31.07 N 106.29 W
La Canourgue 32 44.26 N 3.13 E
Lacantún ≃ 232 16.36 N 90.39 W
La Capelle-en-Thiérache 50 49.58 N 3.55 E
La Capelle-lès-Boulogne 50 50.44 N 1.42 E
La Carlota, Arg. 252 33.26 S 63.18 W
La Carlota, Pil. 116 10.25 N 122.55 E
Lacarne 214 41.31 N 83.03 W
La Carolina 34 38.15 N 3.37 W
La Casita 234 23.43 N 104.46 W
La Castellana 116 10.20 N 123.03 E
Lacaune 32 43.42 N 2.42 E
Lac-Bellemare 206 46.34 N 72.55 W
Lac-Brome 206 45.13 N 72.31 W
Laccadive, Minicoy, and Amindivi → Lakshadweep □3 122 10.00 N 73.00 E
Laccadive Islands → Lakshadweep II 122 10.00 N 73.00 E
Lacchiarella 62 45.19 N 9.08 E
Lacco Ameno 68 40.45 N 13.54 E
Lac Courte Oreilles Indian Reservation ✦4 190 45.55 N 91.19 W
Lac du Flambeau 190 45.58 N 89.51 W
Lac du Flambeau Indian Reservation ✦4 190 45.59 N 89.53 W
Laceby 44 53.32 N 0.10 W
Lacedonia 68 41.03 N 15.25 E
La Ceiba, Hond. 236 15.47 N 86.50 W
La Ceiba, Ven. 246 9.28 N 71.04 W
La Celle-les-Bordes 261 48.38 N 1.57 E
La Celle-Saint-Cloud 261 48.51 N 2.08 E
La Celle-Saint-Cyr 50 47.58 N 3.18 E
La Center, Ky., U.S. 194 37.04 N 88.58 W
La Center, Wa., U.S. 224 45.52 N 122.40 W
Lacepede Bay ᑕ 166 36.47 S 139.45 E
Lacerdónia 156 18.01 S 35.30 E
Laces (Latsch) 64 46.37 N 10.52 E
Lac-Etchemin 186 46.24 N 70.30 W
Lacey 224 47.02 N 122.49 W
Lacey Creek ≃ 278 41.50 N 88.03 W
Laceyville 210 41.39 N 76.10 W
Lac-Frontière 186 46.42 N 70.00 W
La Chaise-Dieu 62 45.19 N 3.42 E
La Chambre 62 45.22 N 6.18 E
La Chapelle-d'Angillon 50 47.22 N 2.26 E
La Chapelle-en-Vercors 62 44.58 N 5.25 E
La Chapelle-Gauthier 261 48.33 N 2.54 E
La Chapelle-la-Reine 50 48.19 N 2.35 E
La Chapelle-Saint-Luc 50 48.20 N 4.03 E
La Chapelle-Vendômoise 50 47.40 N 1.15 E
La Charité-sur-Loire 50 47.11 N 3.01 E
La Chartre-sur-le-Loir 50 47.44 N 0.35 E
La Châtaigneraie 32 46.39 N 0.44 W
La Châtre 32 46.35 N 1.59 E
Lachaussée, Étang de ◎ 56 49.02 N 5.48 E
La Chaux-de-Fonds 58 47.06 N 6.50 E
Lachay, Punta ≻ 248 11.18 S 77.39 W
Lach Dennis 262 53.15 N 2.26 W
Lachdenpochja 24 61.31 N 30.08 E
Lachen 58 47.12 N 8.51 E
Lachenaie 275a 45.42 N 73.34 W
Lachendorf 52 52.37 N 10.14 E
Lachhmangarh Sīkar 120 27.49 N 75.02 E
L'achi 80 55.20 N 41.56 E
Lachine 206 45.26 N 73.40 W
Lachine, Canal de ≂ 275a 45.26 N 73.40 W
Lachine, Rapides de ⊔ 275a 45.25 N 73.36 W
La Chira, Punta ≻ 286d 12.13 S 77.03 W
La Chivera 286c 10.37 N 66.54 W
Lachkaltsap Indian Reserve ✦4 182 55.03 N 129.34 W
Lachlan ≃ 166 34.21 S 143.57 E
La Chorrera, Col. 246 0.44 S 73.01 W
La Chorrera, Pan. 236 8.53 N 79.47 W
L'achovskije ostrova II 74 73.30 N 141.00 E
La Choza 258 34.47 S 59.07 W
La Choza, Arroyo ≃ 258 34.40 S 58.58 W
Lachta ✦8 265a 60.00 N 30.09 E
Lachtinskij Razliv, ozero ◎ 265a 60.00 N 30.11 E
Lachute 206 45.38 N 74.20 W
La Ciénaga 252 27.30 S 66.57 W
La Ciénega 234 16.54 N 96.46 W
Lâçin 130 40.47 N 34.54 E
La Cinta Creek ≃ 196 35.24 N 104.06 W
La Ciotat 62 43.10 N 5.36 E
La Cisterna 286e 33.33 S 70.41 W
La Citadelle ⊥ 238 19.35 N 72.14 W
La Ciudad 234 23.44 N 105.42 W
Lack 48 54.33 N 7.35 W
Lackawanna 210 42.49 N 78.49 W
Lackawanna □6 210 41.24 N 75.40 W
Lackawanna ≃ 210 41.21 N 75.47 W
Lackawanna, Lake ◎ 276 40.57 N 74.42 W
Lackawanna State Park ♦ 210 41.33 N 75.44 W
Lackawaxen 210 41.29 N 74.59 W
Lackawaxen ≃ 210 41.29 N 74.59 W
Lackey 208 37.14 N 76.33 W
Lackland Air Force Base ■ 196 29.27 N 98.37 W
Läckö 26 58.41 N 13.13 E
Lackoje 76 58.05 N 38.08 E
Lac La Belle 216 43.09 N 88.32 W
Lac la Biche 182 54.46 N 111.58 W
Lac la Hache 182 51.49 N 121.28 W
Lac la Ronge Provincial Park ♦ 184 55.15 N 104.55 W
La Clayette 32 46.18 N 4.19 E
Laclede, Id., U.S. 182 48.10 N 116.45 W
La Clede, Il., U.S. 219 38.53 N 88.43 W
Laclede, Mo., U.S. 194 39.47 N 93.09 W
La Clotilde 252 27.08 S 60.40 W
La Clusaz 58 45.54 N 6.25 E
La Cluse 58 46.10 N 5.34 E
La Cluse-et-Mijoux 58 46.53 N 6.23 E
Lacmalac 171b 35.19 S 148.19 E
Lac-Masson 206 46.02 N 74.04 W
Lac-Mégantic 188 45.36 N 70.53 W
Lacob ti-duyong, Mount ∧ 116 17.35 N 121.09 E
La Cocha 252 27.47 S 65.34 W
Lacolle 206 45.05 N 73.22 W
Lacolle ≃ 206 45.04 N 73.20 W
La Colle-sur-Loup 62 43.41 N 7.06 E
La Colmena 286a 19.36 N 99.18 W
La Colorada 232 28.41 N 110.25 W
La Columna → Bolívar, Pico ∧ 246 8.30 N 71.02 W
La Coma 232 24.28 N 98.19 W
Lacombe, Ab., Can. 182 52.28 N 113.44 W
Lacombe, La., U.S. 194 30.18 N 89.56 W
Lacon 190 41.01 N 89.24 W
Lacona, Ia., U.S. 190 41.11 N 93.22 W
Lacona, N.Y., U.S. 212 43.38 N 76.04 W
La Concepción, Pan. 236 8.31 N 82.37 W
La Concepción, Ven. 246 10.38 N 71.50 W
La Condamine-Châtelard 62 44.27 N 6.45 E
Laconi 71 39.51 N 9.03 E
Laconia 188 43.31 N 71.28 W
La Conner 224 48.23 N 122.29 W
La Consulta 252 33.44 S 69.07 W
Lacoochee 220 28.27 N 82.10 W
La Coruña □4 34 43.00 N 8.35 W
Lacoste, Fr. 62 43.50 N 5.16 E
La Coste, Tx., U.S. 196 29.19 N 98.49 W
La Côte-Saint-André 62 45.23 N 5.15 E
La Courneuve 261 48.56 N 2.23 E
La Couronne 62 43.20 N 5.03 E
La Courtine 32 45.42 N 2.16 E
Lac qui Parle ≃ 198 45.01 N 95.53 W
Lac qui Parle, West Branch ≃ 198 44.55 N 96.02 W
La Crau 62 43.09 N 6.04 E
Lacre Punt ≻ 241s 12.02 N 68.15 W
La Crescent 190 43.49 N 91.18 W
La Crescenta 228 34.13 N 118.14 W
La Croft 214 40.39 N 80.35 W
Lacroix-Saint-Ouen 50 49.21 N 2.47 E
La Crosse, In., U.S. 216 41.19 N 86.53 W
La Crosse, Ks., U.S. 198 38.31 N 99.18 W
La Crosse, Va., U.S. 192 36.41 N 78.05 W
Lacrosse, Wa., U.S. 202 46.49 N 117.53 W
La Crosse, Wi., U.S. 190 43.48 N 91.14 W
La Crosse ≃ 190 43.49 N 91.15 W
La Cruz, Arg. 252 29.10 S 56.38 W
La Cruz, Col. 246 1.35 N 76.58 W
La Cruz, C.R. 236 11.04 N 85.39 W
La Cruz, Méx. 196 28.33 N 100.48 W
La Cruz, Ur. 258 33.56 S 56.15 W
La Cruz, Cerro ∧ 234 17.55 N 101.31 W
La Cruz de Río Grande 236 13.06 N 84.10 W
Lac-Saguay 206 46.30 N 75.09 W
Lac Seul 184 50.20 N 92.16 W
Lac Seul Indian Reserve ✦4 184 50.15 N 92.10 W
La Cuchilla 234 18.54 N 103.19 W
La Cuesta, C.R. 236 8.30 N 82.50 W
La Cuesta, Méx. 234 20.10 N 104.51 W
La Cuesta, P.R. 240m 18.25 N 66.49 W
La Cumbre, Arg. 252 30.58 S 64.30 W
La Cumbre, Ven. 286c 10.32 N 66.57 W
La Cumbre, Volcán ∧1 246a 0.20 S 91.30 W
La Cure 58 46.28 N 6.05 E
Lacy Fork ≃ 222 32.24 N 96.08 W
La Cygne 198 38.21 N 94.45 W
Lacy-Lakeview 222 31.37 N 97.06 W
Lada, Teluk ᑕ 115a 6.29 S 105.44 E
Ladainha 255 17.39 S 41.44 W
Ladākh □9 120 35.10 N 76.10 E
Ladākh Range ∧ 120 34.00 N 78.00 E
Ladan 78 50.31 N 32.35 E
La Dang, Ko I 114 6.33 N 99.18 E
Ladang Jagor 114 4.42 N 101.35 E
Ladara 114 1.28 N 97.28 E
Ladário 248 19.01 S 57.35 W
Ladbergen 52 52.08 N 7.44 E
Ladby 41 55.26 N 10.38 E
Ladd 190 41.22 N 89.13 W
Låddenhøj ∧2 41 56.13 N 9.48 E
Ladder Creek ≃ 198 38.48 N 100.52 W
Laddingford 260 51.12 N 0.25 E
Laddonia 219 39.14 N 91.38 W
Ladeburg 264a 52.42 N 13.35 E
La Défense ⊕ 261 48.53 N 2.15 E
La Dehesa 286e 33.22 S 70.33 W
Ladenburg 56 49.28 N 8.37 E
La Dent d'Oche ∧ 58 46.21 N 6.44 E
Ladera Heights 280 33.59 N 118.22 W
La Désirade I 241o 16.19 N 61.03 W
Ládhi 38 41.27 N 26.17 E
Ladhurka 126 23.22 N 86.32 E
La Digue I 138 4.21 S 55.50 E
Lâdik 130 40.55 N 35.55 E
Ladinger Spitze ∧ 61 46.51 N 14.39 E
L'adiny 24 61.33 N 38.20 E
Ladismith 158 33.30 S 21.16 E
Ladispoli 66 41.56 N 12.05 E
Lādīz 128 28.56 N 61.19 E
Ladner 224 49.05 N 123.05 W
Lādnūn 120 27.39 N 74.23 E
Ladoga 194 39.54 N 86.48 W
Ladoga, Lake → Ladožskoje ozero ◎ 24 61.00 N 31.30 E
La Dolorita 286c 10.29 N 66.47 W
Ladon 50 48.00 N 2.32 E
Ladonia 196 33.25 N 95.56 W
La Dorada 246 5.27 N 74.40 W
La Dormida 252 33.21 S 67.55 W
Lado Sarāi ✦8 272a 28.32 N 77.12 E
Ladovskaja Balka 80 45.38 N 41.25 E
Ladožskaja 78 45.19 N 39.54 E
Ladožskoje Ozero 76 60.08 N 31.04 E
Ladožskoje ozero (Lake Ladoga) ◎ 24 61.00 N 31.30 E
Lādpur ✦8 272a 28.44 N 76.59 E
Ladrillero, Golfo ᑕ 254 49.20 S 75.37 W
Ladson 192 32.59 N 80.06 W
Ladue 219 38.38 N 90.23 W
Ladue ≃ 180 63.09 N 140.25 W
Laduozang 102 31.27 N 97.19 E
Ladušhkin 76 54.36 N 20.11 E
Ladva 24 61.21 N 34.34 E
Ladva-Vetka 24 61.21 N 34.27 E
Lādwa 124 29.59 N 77.03 E
Lady, Fr. 261 48.35 N 2.54 E
L'ady, Ross. 76 58.38 N 28.47 E
Lady Ann Strait ⊻ 176 75.40 N 79.50 W
Ladybank 46 56.16 N 3.08 W
Lady Barron 166 40.12 S 148.14 E
Ladybower Reservoir ◎1 44 53.20 N 1.45 W
Ladybrand 158 29.19 S 27.25 E
Lady Elliot Island I 166 24.07 S 152.42 E
Lady Evelyn Lake ◎ 190 47.20 N 80.10 W
Lady Frere 158 31.44 S 27.16 E
Lady Grey 158 30.45 S 27.13 E
Lady Lake 220 28.55 N 81.55 W
Ladysmith, Austl. 171b 35.12 S 147.31 E
Ladysmith, B.C., Can. 182 48.58 N 123.49 W
Ladysmith, S. Afr. 158 28.34 S 29.45 E
Ladysmith, Wi., U.S. 190 45.27 N 91.06 W
Ladyženka 86 51.00 N 68.42 E
Ladyzhyn 78 48.41 N 29.15 E
Ladžanurges 84 42.37 N 42.50 E
Lae 164 6.45 S 147.00 E
Lae I1 14 8.56 N 166.14 E
Laem, Khao ∧ 110 14.27 N 101.30 E
Laem Ngop 110 12.10 N 102.26 E
La Encantada 232 25.17 N 101.04 W
La Encarnacion 234 23.23 N 98.01 W
Laer 52 52.03 N 7.21 E
Laer ✦8 263 51.28 N 7.16 E
Lærdalsøyri 26 61.06 N 7.29 E
La Escondida 196 26.17 N 99.46 W
La Esmeralda, Méx. 232 27.17 N 103.39 W
La Esmeralda, Para. 252 22.13 S 62.38 W
La Esmeralda, Ven. 246 3.10 N 65.33 W
Læsø I 26 57.16 N 11.01 E
La Esperanza, Cuba 240p 22.46 N 83.44 W
La Esperanza, Hond. 236 14.20 N 88.10 W
La Esperanza, Méx. 196 26.46 N 104.00 W
La Esperanza, Méx. 200 32.06 N 114.47 W
La Esperanza, Perú 248 8.05 S 79.04 W
La Esperanza, P.R. 240m 18.22 N 66.07 W
La Estación ✦8 266a 40.27 N 3.48 W
La Estrella, Bol. 248 16.30 S 63.45 W
La Estrella, Ven. 286c 10.25 N 66.48 W
La Estrella, Cerro ∧ 286a 19.20 N 99.05 W
Lafa 89 43.50 N 127.19 E
La Falda 252 31.05 S 64.30 W
La Farge 190 43.34 N 90.38 W
LaFargeville 212 44.11 N 75.57 W
Lafayette, Fr. 62 45.35 N 5.04 E
Lafayette, Al., U.S. 194 32.53 N 85.24 W
Lafayette, Ca., U.S. 226 37.53 N 122.07 W
Lafayette, Co., U.S. 198 39.59 N 105.05 W
Lafayette, Ga., U.S. 192 34.42 N 85.16 W
Lafayette, In., U.S. 216 40.25 N 86.52 W
Lafayette, La., U.S. 194 30.13 N 92.01 W
Lafayette, Mn., U.S. 190 44.26 N 94.23 W
Lafayette, N.J., U.S. 210 41.05 N 74.41 W
La Fayette, N.Y., U.S. 210 42.54 N 76.06 W
Lafayette, Oh., U.S. 216 40.46 N 83.57 W
Lafayette, Or., U.S. 224 45.14 N 123.06 W
La Fayette, R.I., U.S. 207 41.34 N 71.28 W
Lafayette, Tn., U.S. 194 36.31 N 86.01 W
La Fayette, Tx., U.S. 222 32.54 N 94.51 W
Lafayette, Mount ∧ 188 44.10 N 71.38 W
Lafayette Hill 285 40.05 N 75.15 W
Lafayette Reservoir ◎1 282 37.53 N 122.08 W
Lafayette Water Tunnel ✦5 282 37.54 N 122.12 W
La Fé 240p 21.45 N 82.45 W
La Fère 50 49.40 N 3.22 E
La Feria 196 26.09 N 97.49 W
Laferrere 288 34.45 S 58.35 W
La Ferrière-sur-Risle 50 48.59 N 0.48 E
La Ferté-Alais 50 48.29 N 2.21 E
La Ferté-Bernard 50 48.11 N 0.40 E
La Ferté-Frênel 50 48.50 N 0.30 E
La Ferté-Gaucher 50 48.47 N 3.18 E
La Ferté-Imbault 50 47.23 N 1.58 E
La Ferté-Macé 32 48.36 N 0.22 W
La Ferté-Milon 50 49.10 N 3.07 E
La Ferté-Saint-Aubin 50 47.43 N 1.56 E
La Ferté-sous-Jouarre 50 48.57 N 3.08 E
Laferté-sur-Amance 58 47.50 N 5.42 E
La Ferté-Vidame 50 48.37 N 0.55 E
La Ferté-Villeneuil 50 47.59 N 1.21 E
Lafferty 214 40.06 N 81.01 W
Laffrey 62 45.02 N 5.46 E
Lafia 150 8.30 N 8.30 E
Lafiagi 150 8.52 N 5.25 E
Laflamme ≃ 190 48.56 N 77.18 W
Laflèche, P.Q., Can. 275a 45.30 N 73.28 W
Lafleche, Sk., Can. 184 49.43 N 106.35 W
La Flèche, Fr. 32 47.42 N 0.05 W
La Floresta 266d 41.27 N 2.04 E
La Florida, Chile 286e 33.33 S 70.34 W
La Florida, Esp. 266d 41.31 N 2.12 E
La Florida, Guat. 232 16.33 N 90.27 W
Lafnitz ≃ 61 46.57 N 16.16 E
La Foa 175f 21.43 S 165.50 E
La Foce 62 44.08 N 9.47 E
La Follette 192 36.22 N 84.07 W
Lafon 154 5.02 N 32.27 E
Lafontaine, P.Q., Can. 206 45.48 N 74.01 W
La Fontaine, In., U.S. 216 40.40 N 85.43 W
Lafontaine, Parc ♦ 275a 45.32 N 73.34 W
Lafourche, Bayou ≃ 194 29.05 N 90.14 W
La Foux, Fr. 62 43.16 N 6.35 E
La Foux, Fr. 62 44.17 N 6.34 E
La Fragua 252 26.05 S 64.20 W
La Francia 252 31.24 S 62.38 W
La Fregeneda 34 40.59 N 6.52 W
La Frette-sur-Seine 261 48.58 N 2.11 E
La Fría 246 8.13 N 72.15 W
Lafrimbolle 58 48.36 N 7.01 E
La Fuente de San Esteban 34 40.48 N 6.15 W
Laga, Monti della ∧ 66 42.37 N 13.24 E
La Gacilly 28 47.46 N 2.09 W
Lagaip ≃ 164 5.05 S 142.40 E
La Galite I 36 37.32 N 8.56 E
La Gallareta 252 29.34 S 60.23 W
La Gallega 34 41.54 N 3.16 W
Lagan 26 56.55 N 13.59 E
Lagan ≃, Sve. 26 56.33 N 12.56 E
Lagan ≃, N. Ire., U.K. 48 54.37 N 5.53 W
Lagangzong 120 28.05 N 91.04 E
Lagantu 102 42.20 N 108.22 E
La Garde 62 43.07 N 6.01 E
La Garde-Freinet 62 43.19 N 6.28 E
La Garenne-Colombes 261 48.55 N 2.15 E
Lagarina, Val ∨ 64 45.45 N 11.00 E
Lagarto, Bra. 250 10.54 S 37.41 W
Lagarto, C.R. 236 10.07 N 84.56 W
Lagarto Creek ≃ 196 28.08 N 97.56 W
Lagawe 116 16.49 N 121.06 E
Lagay 116 14.06 N 122.12 E
Lagayan 116 17.43 N 120.42 E
Lage, Dtsch. 52 51.59 N 8.48 E
Lage, Zhg. 120 29.26 N 85.51 E
Lagedu 102 26.24 N 101.11 E
Lågen ≃, Nor. 26 59.03 N 10.05 E
Lågen ≃, Nor. 26 61.08 N 10.25 E
Lägerdorf 52 53.53 N 9.34 E
Lages 252 27.48 S 50.19 W
Lageuen 114 4.44 N 95.31 E
Lage Zwaluwe 52 51.43 N 4.41 E
Laggan 46 57.02 N 4.16 W
Laggan, Loch ◎1 46 56.57 N 4.28 W
Laggan Bay ᑕ 46 55.41 N 6.19 W
Lagginhorn ∧ 58 46.11 N 8.01 E
Laghmān □4 120 35.00 N 70.15 E
Laghouat 148 33.50 N 2.59 E
Laghy 48 54.37 N 8.05 W
La Giettaz 62 45.52 N 6.30 E
La Giganta, Cerro ∧ 234 21.08 N 101.19 W
La Giustiniana ✦8 267a 41.59 N 12.24 E
La Gleize 56 50.25 N 5.51 E
La Gloria 246 8.37 N 73.48 W
Lagnieu 58 45.54 N 5.21 E
Lagny 50 48.52 N 2.43 E
Lagny-le-Sac 261 49.05 N 2.45 E
Lago 68 39.10 N 16.09 E
Lago, Mount ∧ 224 48.51 N 120.32 W
Lagoa Branca 256 21.54 S 47.02 W
Lagoa da Prata 255 20.01 S 45.33 W
Lagoa Formosa 255 18.47 S 46.24 W
Lago Argentino → Calafate 254 50.20 S 72.18 W
Lagoa Santa 255 19.38 S 43.53 W
Lagoa Vermelha 252 28.13 S 51.32 W
Lago Blanco 254 45.55 S 71.15 W
Lago da Pedra 250 4.20 S 45.10 W
Lagodechi 84 41.49 N 46.18 E
Lagodechskij zapovednik ♦ 84 41.53 N 46.22 E
Lagoinha 256 23.06 S 45.11 W
Lagolândia 255 15.37 S 49.02 W
Lagolovo 265a 59.42 N 30.00 E
Lagonegro 68 40.07 N 15.46 E
Lagonglong 116 8.48 N 124.47 E
Lagonoy 116 13.44 N 123.31 E
Lagonoy Gulf ᑕ 116 13.35 N 123.45 E
Lagopesole, Castel di ⊥ 68 40.48 N 15.45 E
Lago Posadas 254 47.32 S 71.45 W
Lagorai, Catena del ∧ 64 46.18 N 11.35 E
Lago Ranco 254 40.20 S 72.38 W
La Gorgue 50 50.38 N 2.42 E
Lagos, Ang. 152 16.04 S 17.03 E
Lagos, Nig. 150 6.27 N 3.24 E
Lagos, Nig. 273a 6.27 N 3.24 E
Lagos, Port. 34 37.06 N 8.40 W
Lagos (Ikeja) Airport ⊗ 273a 6.35 N 3.20 E
Lagos, University of ⊥2 273a 6.32 N 3.24 E
Lagosanto 66 44.46 N 12.08 E
Lagos de Moreno 234 21.21 N 101.55 W
Lagos Harbour ᑕ 273a 6.26 N 3.24 E
Lagos Island I 273a 6.27 N 3.26 E
Lagos Lagoon ᑕ 273a 6.30 N 3.26 E
Lagos Terminus ✦5 273a 6.28 N 3.23 E
La Gouèra 148 20.48 N 17.08 W
La Goulette 148 36.49 N 10.18 E
Lago Viedma 254 49.48 S 72.07 W
La Granadella 34 41.21 N 0.40 E
La Grand'Combe 62 44.13 N 4.02 E
La Grande 202 45.19 N 118.05 W
La Grande Deux, Réservoir ◎1 176 53.40 N 76.55 W
La Grande Moucherolle ∧ 62 45.00 N 5.34 E
La Grande Quatre, Réservoir ◎1 176 54.00 N 73.15 W
La Grange, Austl. 162 18.41 S 121.45 E
LaGrange, Ca., U.S. 226 37.40 N 120.28 W
La Grange, Ga., U.S. 192 33.02 N 85.01 W
La Grange, Il., U.S. 216 41.48 N 87.52 W
Lagrange, In., U.S. 216 41.39 N 85.25 W
La Grange, Ky., U.S. 218 38.24 N 85.22 W
La Grange, Mo., U.S. 219 40.02 N 91.29 W
La Grange, N.C., U.S. 192 35.18 N 77.47 W
Lagrange, Oh., U.S. 214 41.14 N 82.07 W
La Grange, Tx., U.S. 222 29.54 N 96.52 W
Lagrange, Wy., U.S. 198 41.38 N 104.10 W
Lagrange □6 216 41.39 N 85.25 W
Lagrange Bay ᑕ 162 18.38 S 121.42 E
La Grange Highlands 278 41.50 N 87.51 W
La Grange Lock and Dam ✦5 219 39.57 N 90.32 W
La Grange Park 278 41.50 N 87.51 W
Lagrangeville 210 41.39 N 73.46 W
La Granja 286e 33.32 S 70.39 W
La Gran Piedra ∧ 240p 20.01 N 75.38 W
La Gran Sabana ≚ 246 5.30 N 61.30 W
La Grave 62 45.03 N 6.18 E
La Grita 246 8.08 N 71.59 W
Lagro 216 40.50 N 85.43 W
La Groise 50 50.05 N 3.41 E
La Grue Bayou ≃ 194 34.05 N 91.10 W
Lagu 102 26.26 N 101.30 E
La Guadeloupe (Saint-Évariste) 188 45.57 N 70.56 W
La Guajira □5 246 11.30 N 72.30 W
La Guajira, Península de ≻ 246 12.00 N 71.40 W
La Guardia, Arg. 252 29.33 S 65.27 W

≃ River — Fluß — Río — Rivière — Rio
≂ Canal — Kanal — Canal — Canal — Canal
⊔ Waterfall, Rapids — Wasserfall, Stromschnellen — Cascada, Rápidos — Chute d'eau, Rapides — Cascata, Rápidos
⊻ Strait — Meeresstraße — Estrecho — Détroit — Estreito
ᑕ Bay, Gulf — Bucht, Golf — Bahía, Golfo — Baie, Golfe — Baía, Golfo
◎ Lake, Lakes — See, Seen — Lago, Lagos — Lac, Lacs — Lago, Lagos
≚ Swamp — Sumpf — Pantano — Marais — Pântano
Ice Features, Glacier — Eis- und Gletscherformen — Accidentes Glaciales — Formes glaciaires — Acidentes glaciares
Other Hydrographic Features — Andere Hydrographische Objekte — Otros Elementos Hidrográficos — Autres données hydrographiques — Outros acidentes hidrográficos

✦ Submarine Features — Untermeerische Objekte — Accidentes Submarinos — Formes de relief sous-marin — Acidentes submarinos
□ Political Unit — Politische Einheit — Unidad Politica — Entité politique — Unidade política
⊥ Cultural Institution — Kulturelle Institution — Institución Cultural — Institution culturelle — Instituição cultural
⊥ Historical Site — Historische Stätte — Sitio Histórico — Site historique — Sitio histórico
♦ Recreational Site — Erholungs- und Ferienort — Sitio de Recreo — Centre de loisirs — Área de Lazer
⊗ Airport — Flughafen — Aeropuerto — Aéroport — Aeroporto
■ Military Installation — Militäranlage — Instalación Militar — Installation militaire — Instalação militar
✦ Miscellaneous — Verschiedenes — Misceláneo — Divers — Diversos

Symbols in the index entries represent the broad categories identified in the key at the right. Symbols with superior numbers (⊶¹) identify subcategories (see complete key on page *I · 1*).

Los símbolos incluídos en el texto del índice representan las grandes categorías identificadas con la clave a la derecha. Los símbolos con números en la parte superior (⊶¹) identifican las subcategorías (véase la clave completa en la página *I · 1*).

Os símbolos incluídos no texto do índice representam as grandes categorias identificadas com a chave à direita. Os símbolos com números na parte superior (⊶¹) identificam as subcategorias (veja-se a chave completa à página *I · 1*).

Symbole im Register stellen die im Schlüssel erklärten Kategorien dar. Symbole mit hochgestellten Ziffern (⊶¹) bezeichnen Unterabteilungen einer Kategorie (vgl. vollständiger Schlüssel auf Seite *I · 1*).

Symbol				
⋀ Mountain	Berg	Montaña	Montagne	Montanha
⋌ Mountains	Gebirge	Montañas	Montagnes	Montanhas
⋋ Pass	Paß	Paso	Col	Passo
⋁ Valley, Canyon	Tal, Cañon	Valle, Cañón	Vallée, Canyon	Vale, Canhão
⊳ Plain	Ebene	Llano	Plaine	Planicie
⊁ Cape	Kap	Cabo	Cap	Cabo
I Island	Insel	Isla	Île	Ilha
II Islands	Inseln	Islas	Îles	Ilhas
⋲ Other Topographic Features	Andere Topographische Objekte	Otros Elementos Topográficos	Autres données topographiques	Outros acidentes topográficos

ESPAÑOL Nombre	Página	Lat.°'	Long.°' W=Oeste
Lancang → Mekong ≃	12	10.33 N	105.24 E
Lancashire	285	39.49 N	75.29 W
Lancashire □⁶	44	53.45 S	2.40 W
Lancashire Plain ≃	44	53.40 N	2.45 W
Lancaster, On., Can.	206	45.08 N	74.30 W
Lancaster, Eng., U.K.	44	54.03 N	2.48 W
Lancaster, Ca., U.S.	228	34.41 N	118.08 W
Lancaster, Ky., U.S.	192	37.37 N	84.34 W
Lancaster, Ma., U.S.	207	42.27 N	71.40 W
Lancaster, Mn., U.S.	188	48.51 N	96.48 W
Lancaster, Mo., U.S.	194	40.31 N	92.31 W
Lancaster, N.H., U.S.	188	44.29 N	71.34 W
Lancaster, N.Y., U.S.	210	42.54 N	78.40 W
Lancaster, Oh., U.S.	188	39.43 N	82.36 W
Lancaster, Pa., U.S.	208	40.02 N	76.18 W
Lancaster, S.C., U.S.	192	34.43 N	80.46 W
Lancaster, Tx., U.S.	222	32.36 N	96.47 W
Lancaster, Va., U.S.	208	37.46 N	76.28 W
Lancaster, Wi., U.S.	190	42.50 N	90.42 W
Lancaster □⁶, Pa., U.S.	208	40.02 N	76.19 W
Lancaster □⁶, Va., U.S.	208	37.45 N	76.30 W
Lancaster Canal ☰	262	53.46 N	2.43 W
Lancaster Sound ☵	176	74.13 N	84.00 W
Lancaster Village	285	39.45 N	75.35 W
Lančhuti	84	42.06 N	42.01 E
Lance Creek	200	43.01 N	104.38 W
Lance Creek ≃	200	43.02 N	104.16 W
Lancefield	169	37.17 S	144.44 E
Lancelin	163	31.02 S	115.20 E
Lancelot, Mount ⋀	162	26.13 S	123.12 E
Lancey	62	45.14 N	5.53 E
Lanchang	114	3.30 N	102.11 E
Lanchester	54	54.49 N	1.44 W
Lanchow → Lanzhou	102	36.03 N	103.41 E
Lanchyn	78	48.34 N	24.45 E
Lanciano	66	42.14 N	14.23 E
Lancin	62	45.43 N	5.24 E
Lancing	42	50.50 N	0.19 W
Lanco	254	39.24 S	72.46 W
Lancones	246	4.35 S	80.30 W
Lancun	98	36.24 N	120.10 E
Lańcut	50	50.05 N	22.13 E
Lancy	58	46.11 N	6.07 E
Lândana	152	5.13 S	12.08 E
Landang Gua	116	6.58 N	122.15 E
Landau	56	49.12 N	8.07 E
Landau an der Isar	60	48.40 N	12.43 E
Landay	128	30.31 N	63.47 E
Land Between the Lakes ⋀	194	36.55 N	88.05 W
Landeck	58	47.08 N	10.34 E
Landen	56	50.45 N	5.05 E
Landenberg	208	39.47 N	75.46 W
Landenhausen	56	50.36 N	9.28 E
Lander	200	42.49 N	108.43 W
Lander ≃	162	20.25 S	132.00 E
Landerneau	32	48.27 N	4.15 W
Landes □⁵	32	44.00 N	1.00 W
Landes ←¹	32	44.15 N	1.00 W
Landesbergen	52	52.33 N	9.07 E
Landeskrone ⋀²	54	51.08 N	14.56 E
Landess	216	40.37 N	85.34 W
Landete	34	39.54 N	1.22 W
Landham Brook ≃	283	42.22 N	71.25 W
Landhausen	263	51.24 N	7.45 E
Landi	98	36.35 N	119.59 E
Landi Kotal	123	34.06 N	71.09 E
Landina	86	59.12 N	67.02 E
Landing	284	40.54 N	74.40 W
Landing Lake ◎	184	55.17 N	97.26 W
Landis, Sk., Can.	184	52.12 N	108.28 W
Landis, N.C., U.S.	192	35.32 N	80.36 W
Landisburg	208	40.20 N	77.18 W
Landisville	208	40.06 N	76.25 W
Landivisiau	32	48.31 N	4.04 W
Landkey	42	51.04 N	4.00 W
Landkirchen	54	54.27 N	11.08 E
Lando	34	34.46 N	81.00 W
Land O'Lakes, Fl., U.S.	220	28.11 N	82.34 W
Land O'Lakes, Wi., U.S.	190	46.10 N	89.13 W
Landor	162	25.09 S	116.54 E
Landos	62	44.51 N	3.50 E
Landösjön ◎	26	63.35 N	14.04 E
Landover Estates	284c	38.56 N	76.54 W
Landover Hills	284c	38.57 N	76.53 W
Landover Mall ⋀⁹	284c	38.55 N	76.51 W
Landquart	58	46.58 N	9.33 E
Landquart ≃	58	46.58 N	9.32 E
Landrecies	50	50.08 N	3.42 E
Landres	56	49.19 N	5.48 E
Landreth Draw ≃	196	31.14 N	102.29 W
Landriano	62	45.19 N	9.15 E
Landri Sales	250	7.16 S	43.55 W
Landro (Höhlenstein)	64	46.39 N	12.14 E
Landrum	192	35.10 N	82.11 W
Landry	62	44.16 N	6.45 E
Landsberg	54	51.31 N	12.10 E
Landsberg am Lech	58	48.03 N	10.55 E
Landsberg an der Warthe → Gorzów Wielkopolski	30	52.44 N	15.15 E
Landsborough	166	26.49 S	152.58 E
Landsborough Creek ≃	166	22.30 S	144.33 E
Landsbro	26	57.22 N	14.54 E
Land's End ⤙, Eng., U.K.	42	50.03 N	5.44 W
Lands End ⤙, Ca., U.S.	228	33.28 N	118.36 W
Lands End ⤙, R.I., U.S.	207	41.27 N	71.19 W
Landshut	60	48.33 N	12.09 E
Landskrona	26	55.52 N	12.50 E
Landsman Creek ≃	198	39.35 N	102.19 W
Landsmeer	52	52.26 N	4.52 E
Landštejn	61	49.00 N	15.13 E
Landstuhl	56	49.25 N	7.34 E
Landvetter	263	57.29 N	7.37 E
Landwehrbach ≃	263	51.26 N	6.26 E
Lane	219	40.07 N	88.51 W
Lane City	50	41.50 N	0.05 E
Lane Cove	274a	33.49 S	151.10 E
Lane Cove ≃	274a	33.48 S	151.09 E
Lane Cove River Park ⋀	274a	33.47 S	151.09 E
La Negra	252	23.45 S	70.19 W
Lane Mountain ⋀	228	35.05 N	116.56 W
Lanersbach	64	47.09 N	11.44 E
Lanesboro, Ma., U.S.	207	42.33 N	73.14 W
Lanesboro, Mn., U.S.	190	43.43 N	91.58 W
Lanesboro, Pa., U.S.	210	41.57 N	75.35 W
Lanester	32	47.46 N	3.21 W
Lanesville, In., U.S.	218	38.14 N	85.59 W
Lanesville, N.Y., U.S.	210	42.08 N	74.16 W
Lanett	194	32.52 N	85.11 W
La Neuveville	58	47.04 N	7.06 E
Laneville	222	31.58 N	94.49 W
Lanexa	208	37.24 N	76.55 W
Lanezi Lake ◎	182	53.03 N	120.56 W
Lang	184	49.56 N	104.23 W
La'nga Co ◎	124	30.42 N	81.16 E
Langádhia	38	40.40 N	21.01 E
Langadás	38	40.45 N	23.04 E
Langangen	40	59.43 N	9.41 E
Langa-Langa	144	7.35 N	38.48 E
Langao	102	32.13 N	109.02 E
Langar, Afg.	122	37.02 N	73.47 E
Langar, Kyrg.	85	40.03 N	71.03 E
L'angar, Taj.	123	37.02 N	72.42 E
Langara	112	4.02 S	123.00 E

FRANÇAIS Nom	Page	Lat.°'	Long.°' W=Ouest
Langara Island I	182	54.14 N	133.00 W
Langarud	128	37.11 N	50.10 E
L'angasovo	80	58.32 N	49.30 E
Langue ≃	236	13.37 N	87.39 W
Languedoc □⁹	32	44.00 N	4.00 E
Langau	61	48.49 N	15.42 E
Langavat, Loch ◎	46	58.04 N	6.48 W
Langdai	40	59.51 N	14.15 E
Langbank	184	50.05 N	102.20 W
Lang Bay	182	49.47 N	124.21 W
Langberg	158	28.20 S	22.35 E
Langburkersdorf	54	51.02 N	14.14 E
Langda	102	31.12 N	96.59 E
Langdai	102	26.06 N	105.20 E
Langdon	198	48.45 N	98.22 W
Langdondale	214	40.08 N	78.15 W
Langdon Hills	260	51.34 N	0.25 E
Langeac	32	45.06 N	3.30 E
Langeais	50	47.20 N	0.24 E
Langebaan	158	33.06 S	18.02 E
Langeberg ⋀	158	33.55 S	20.30 E
Lange Berge ⋀²	56	50.20 N	10.55 E
Langebrück	54	51.07 N	13.50 E
Langeland I	41	55.00 N	10.50 E
Langelandsbaelt ☵	41	54.50 N	10.55 E
Langelmävesi ◎	26	61.32 N	24.22 E
Langeloth	214	40.21 N	80.24 W
Langelsheim	52	51.56 N	10.19 E
Langemark	50	50.55 N	2.55 E
Langen, Dtsch.	52	53.36 N	8.35 E
Langen, Dtsch.	56	49.59 N	8.41 E
Langenargen	58	47.35 N	9.32 E
Langenau, Dtsch.	54	50.50 N	13.18 E
Langenau, Dtsch.	58	48.30 N	10.07 E
Langenberg, Dtsch.	52	51.46 N	8.19 E
Langenberg, Dtsch.	56	51.21 N	7.09 E
Langenbernsdorf	54	50.45 N	12.13 E
Langenbielau → Bielawa	30	50.41 N	16.38 E
Langenbochum	263	51.37 N	7.07 E
Langenbruck	58	47.21 N	7.43 E
Langenburg, Sk., Can.	184	50.50 N	101.43 W
Langendorf	54	49.15 N	9.53 E
Langendorf	54	51.11 N	11.53 E
Langendreer ←⁸	263	51.28 N	7.19 E
Langeneichstädt	54	51.20 N	11.41 E
Langenfeld, Dtsch.	56	51.07 N	6.53 E
Langenfeld, Öst.	58	47.04 N	10.53 E
Langenhagen	52	52.27 N	9.44 E
Langenhessen	54	50.45 N	12.22 E
Langenhorn	41	54.41 N	8.53 E
Langenhorst	263	51.22 N	7.02 E
Langenlois	61	48.28 N	15.40 E
Langennaundorf	54	51.36 N	13.20 E
Langenneufnach	58	48.16 N	10.36 E
Langenselbold	56	50.10 N	9.02 E
Langensteinach	56	49.30 N	10.10 E
Langenthal	58	47.13 N	7.47 E
Langenwang	61	47.34 N	15.37 E
Langenwetzendorf	54	50.41 N	12.05 E
Langenzersdorf	61	48.18 N	16.22 E
Langeoog	52	53.45 N	7.29 E
Langeoog I	52	53.46 N	7.32 E
Langerfeld ←⁸	263	51.16 N	7.15 E
Langer See ◎	264a	52.25 N	13.38 E
Langeskov	41	55.22 N	10.36 E
Langesund	26	59.00 N	9.45 E
Langevåg	26	62.27 N	6.12 E
Langewiesen	54	50.40 N	10.58 E
Langfang → Anci	100	39.31 N	116.41 E
Langford □²	26	62.43 N	7.30 E
Langford, Eng., U.K.	260	51.45 N	0.40 E
Langford, N.Y., U.S.	210	42.35 N	78.51 W
Langford, S.D., U.S.	198	45.36 N	97.49 W
Langförden	52	52.47 N	8.14 E
Langgam	112	0.15 N	101.43 E
Langgapayung	114	1.43 N	99.59 E
Langgöns	56	50.30 N	8.40 E
Langhalsen	40	58.56 N	6.41 E
Langji Shan \	100	28.32 N	121.36 E
Langjökull ⋀	24a	64.42 N	20.12 W
Langkampfen	58	47.35 N	12.05 E
Lang Ka, Doi ⋀	110	19.09 N	99.20 E
Langkawi, Pulau I	114	6.22 N	99.50 E
Langklip	158	28.12 S	20.20 E
Langkrans	158	27.47 S	31.03 E
Langlade I	186	46.50 N	56.20 W
Lang Lang ≃	169	38.17 S	145.31 E
Langley, B.C., Can.	294	49.06 N	122.39 W
Langley, Eng., U.K.	260	51.30 N	0.33 W
Langley, Eng., U.K.	262	51.14 N	0.35 E
Langley, Eng., U.K.	262	53.15 N	2.05 W
Langley, Ok., U.S.	196	36.27 N	95.02 W
Langley, S.C., U.S.	192	33.31 N	81.50 W
Langley, Wa., U.S.	294	48.02 N	122.25 W
Langley Air Force Base ⋀	208	37.05 N	76.21 W
Langley Forest	284c	38.57 N	77.10 W
Langley Hill ⋀²	282	37.20 N	122.14 W
Langley Park	284c	38.59 N	76.58 W
Langleyville	219	39.34 N	89.21 W
Langlo ≃	166	26.26 S	146.05 E
Langlois	202	42.55 N	124.26 W
Langmazong	120	30.52 N	89.58 E
Lang Mo	110	17.14 N	106.27 E
Lângnäs ⤙	26	60.06 N	20.17 E
Langnau	58	46.56 N	7.47 E
Langogne	32	44.43 N	3.50 E
Langon	32	44.33 N	0.15 W
Langøya I	24	68.44 N	14.50 E
Langping	102	30.38 N	110.21 E
Langquaid	60	48.49 N	12.03 E
Langreo → Sama [de Langreo], Esp.	34	43.18 N	5.41 W
Langres, Esp.	34	43.58 N	5.41 W
Langres	32	47.52 N	5.20 E
Langres, Plateau de ⋀¹	58	47.41 N	5.03 E
Lang Son	110	21.50 N	106.44 E
Langstaff	275b	43.50 N	79.25 W
Langsur	56	49.45 N	6.33 E
Lângsvan	110	9.57 N	99.04 E
Langtang National Park ⋀	124	28.10 N	85.30 E
Langtjan	120	25.11 N	113.28 E
Langtoft	262	53.18 N	0.22 W
Langtou	100	40.10 N	124.19 E

PORTUGUÊS Nome	Página	Lat.°'	Long.°' W=Oeste
Largtuozi	104	41.01 N	121.43 E
Largu	90	27.56 N	118.11 E
Langue ≃	236	13.37 N	87.39 W
Languedoc □⁹	32	44.00 N	4.00 E
Langui Layo, Laguna de ◎	248	14.29 S	71.13 W
L'Anguille ≃	194	34.44 N	90.40 W
Langula	54	51.09 N	10.25 E
Langundu, Tanjung ⤙	115b	8.49 S	118.58 E
Langwarden	52	53.36 N	8.19 E
Langwecel	52	52.59 N	9.12 E
Langweer	52	52.57 N	5.43 E
Langweid	58	48.29 N	10.51 E
Langweiler	56	49.40 N	7.31 E
Langwies	58	46.49 N	9.43 E
Langwo	104	41.13 N	121.44 E
Langwozhuang	105	39.05 N	115.37 E
Langxi	106	31.08 N	119.10 E
Langxi ≃	106	31.10 N	118.59 E
Langzhong	102	31.35 N	105.59 E
Langzishan	104	41.02 N	123.23 E
Lanham	284c	38.58 N	76.51 W
Lanhill Island ⤙	116	6.46 N	122.22 E
Lanibga, Mount ⋀	116	10.27 N	123.56 E
Langan	184	51.52 N	105.02 W
Lan'gan Creek ≃	184	51.23 N	105.13 W
Lann, Parque Nacional ⊹	254	39.36 S	71.24 W
Lanin, Volcán ⋀¹	254	39.38 S	71.30 W
Lan'vtsi	78	49.52 N	26.05 E
Lanjang	107	30.24 N	105.11 E
Lanjao (Lanfeng)	98	34.50 N	114.49 E
Länkäran	84	38.45 N	48.50 E
Lanker See ◎	54	54.12 N	10.17 E
Lankeys Creek	171b	35.49 S	147.39 E
Länkipoh.a	26	61.44 N	24.48 E
Lanklaar	56	51.01 N	5.44 E
Lanh-Latum	263	51.18 N	6.41 E
Lankou	100	23.59 N	115.05 E
Lankoviri	146	9.00 N	11.25 E
Lankwitz ←⁸	264a	52.26 N	13.21 E
Lanling	89	45.15 N	126.12 E
Lannabruk	40	59.21 N	15.16 E
Lannach	61	46.56 N	15.19 E
Lannhælm	40	59.53 N	17.57 E
Lannemezan	32	43.08 N	0.23 E
Lannilis	32	48.34 N	4.31 W
Lannion	32	48.44 N	3.28 W
Lannoy	263	43.08 N	80.09 W
Lanoka Harbor	208	39.52 N	74.10 W
La Noria	258	35.10 S	58.48 W
Lanping	102	26.29 N	99.23 E
Langibao	104	40.56 N	122.26 E
Lanqikoucun	104	40.52 N	122.26 E
Lanqipuzi	104	42.12 N	123.15 E
Lanquín	232	15.34 N	89.58 W
Lans, Montagnes de ⋀¹	62	44.52 N	5.29 E
Lansdale	208	40.14 N	75.17 W
Lansdowne, Austl.	162	17.53 S	126.39 E
Lansdowne, Austl.	274a	33.54 S	150.59 E
Lansdowne, On., Can.	212	44.24 N	76.01 W
Lansdowne, India	124	29.50 N	78.41 E
Lansdowne, Md., U.S.	284b	39.14 N	76.39 W
Lansdowne, Pa., U.S.	285	39.56 N	75.16 W
L'Anse, Mi., U.S.	190	46.45 N	88.27 W
Lanse, Pa., U.S.	214	40.59 N	78.08 W
L'Anse-aux-Meadows National Historic Park ⋀	186	51.36 N	55.32 W
L'anse Crause Bay c	214	42.34 N	82.49 W
L'Anse Indian Reservation ⋀⁴	190	46.48 N	88.22 W
Lans-en-Vercors	62	45.07 N	5.35 E
Lansford, N.D., U.S.	198	48.37 N	101.22 W
Lansford, Pa., U.S.	210	40.49 N	75.52 W
Lans Paz □⁵, Bol.	248	15.30 S	68.00 W
Lanshantou	98	35.07 N	119.21 E
Lansing, Il., U.S.	216	41.33 N	87.32 W
Lansing, Ia., U.S.	190	43.21 N	91.12 W
Lansing, Ks., U.S.	198	39.14 N	94.54 W
Lansing, Mi., U.S.	216	42.43 N	84.33 W
Lansing, N.Y., U.S.	210	42.32 N	76.30 W
Lansing, Oh., U.S.	214	40.04 N	80.47 W
Lansing ≃	216	42.46 N	84.25 W
Lansing Municipal Airport ⋀	278	41.32 N	87.32 W
Lańskroun	30	49.55 N	16.37 E
Lansvall'edd	82	51.15 N	7.34 E
Lantana	220	26.35 N	80.03 W
Lantana	100	23.25 N	114.56 E
Lantau Island → Dahao Dao I	100	22.17 N	113.59 E
Lanta Yai, Ko I	110	7.35 N	99.05 E
Lanterne ≃	58	47.44 N	6.03 E
Lantewa	146	12.16 N	11.44 E
Lantian	102	34.10 N	109.12 E
Lantianbcheng	271a	39.58 N	116.17 E
Lantschou → Lanzhou	102	36.03 N	103.41 E
Lantzville	224	49.15 N	124.05 W
La Nurra ⋀¹	71	40.45 N	8.15 E
Lanús	258	34.43 S	58.24 W
Lanús □⁵	288	34.42 S	58.28 W
Lanuvio	71	41.40 N	12.42 E
Lanuza Bay c	116	9.17 N	126.04 E
Lanxi, Zhg.	98	45.15 N	126.14 E
Lanxi, Zhg.	100	29.12 N	119.28 E
Lanxian	102	38.22 N	111.46 E
Lány	54	50.06 N	13.58 E
Lan Yü I	100	22.03 N	121.32 E
Lanzarote I	148	29.00 N	13.40 W
Lanzendorf²	264b	48.06 N	16.26 E
Lanzhou (Lanchow)	102	36.03 N	103.41 E
Lanzo Torinese	62	45.16 N	7.28 E
Lao → Laos □¹	110	18.00 N	105.00 E
Lao ≃, Thai.	110	19.55 N	99.54 E
Lao ≃, Zhg.	100	29.11 N	116.00 E
Laoag	116	18.12 N	120.36 E
Laoang	116	12.34 N	125.00 E
Laoangli	104	40.53 N	120.31 E
Laoang Island I	116	12.35 N	125.01 E
Lao Bao	110	16.37 N	106.36 E
Laobian, Zhg.	104	40.42 N	122.21 E
Laobian, Zhg.	104	41.58 N	123.10 E
Lao Cai	110	22.30 N	103.57 E
Laochang, Zhg.	102	24.34 N	104.11 E
Laochang, Zhg.	102	29.30 N	106.36 E
Laodeodian	89	45.08 N	125.00 E
Laofengkou	86	46.11 N	83.38 E
Laofu	98	42.13 N	118.17 E
Laoge	100	31.01 N	121.49 E
Laoguan	102	33.30 N	111.52 E
Laoganpu	104	40.53 N	120.51 E
Laoha ≃	98	43.24 N	120.39 E
Laoheba	107	30.21 N	103.49 E
Laoheshangtai	104	40.43 N	120.49 E
Laohokow → Guanghua	102	32.25 N	111.36 E

PORTUGUÊS Nome	Página	Lat.°'	Long.°' W=Oeste
Laohuk'ou	100	24.53 N	121.03 E
Laohumiao	271a	39.58 N	116.20 E
Laohutuozi	104	42.25 N	122.34 E
Laois □⁶	48	53.00 N	7.24 W
Laojunguan	105	40.22 N	114.47 E
Laojunmiao → Yumen	102	39.56 N	97.51 E
Laoka	89	52.47 N	125.52 E
Laolao, Bahía c	174n	15.08 N	145.46 E
Lao Ling ⋀	89	43.27 N	130.11 E
Laolong ≃	106	32.11 N	120.00 E
Laolongtan	107	30.01 N	104.48 E
Laomocun	106	30.51 N	119.11 E
Laon	50	49.34 N	3.40 E
Laona, N.Y., U.S.	214	42.25 N	79.19 W
Laona, Wi., U.S.	190	45.33 N	88.40 W
La Orchila, Isla I	246	11.48 N	66.09 W
La Orotava	148	28.23 N	16.31 W
La Oroya	248	11.32 S	75.54 W
Laos □¹, Asia	108	18.00 N	105.00 E
Laos (Lao) □¹, Asia	110	18.00 N	105.00 E
Laoshan (Licun)	98	36.10 N	120.25 E
Laoshan Wan c	98	36.24 N	120.45 E
Laosolu	114	3.11 N	98.02 E
Laotto	216	41.17 N	85.12 W
Laou, Oued ≃	34	35.29 N	5.04 W
Laowushi	100	31.43 N	121.00 E
Laoxinkou	100	30.12 N	112.50 E
Laoyemiao	98	41.03 N	119.53 E
Laoyezhuang	106	32.16 N	120.04 E
Laoyingpan	100	36.34 N	115.01 E
Laozha	106	31.35 N	121.07 E
Laozhen	100	31.34 N	118.19 E
Laozhong	98	33.56 N	114.51 E
Laozhuangzi	105	39.44 N	118.05 E
Laozishan	100	33.11 N	118.36 E
Lapa	252	25.45 S	49.42 W
Lapa ←⁸, Bra.	287a	22.55 S	43.11 W
Lapa ←⁸, Bra.	286d	23.32 S	46.42 W
Lapacity	76	53.34 N	30.53 E
Lapac Island I	116	5.32 N	120.47 E
Lapai	150	9.06 N	6.45 E
Lapaich, Sgurr na ⋀	46	57.21 N	5.04 W
Lapalisse	32	46.15 N	3.38 E
La Palma, Col.	246	5.22 N	74.24 W
La Palma, Cuba	240p	22.45 N	83.33 W
La Palma, El Sal.	236	14.19 N	89.11 W
La Palma, Méx.	234	17.05 N	99.29 W
La Palma, Méx.	234	20.09 N	102.46 W
La Palma, Pan.	246	8.25 N	78.09 W
La Palma, Ca., U.S.	228	33.50 N	118.02 W
La Palma I	148	28.40 N	17.52 W
La Palma de Cervelló	266d	41.25 N	1.58 E
La Palma del Condado	34	37.23 N	6.33 W
La Palmita	196	25.57 N	99.18 W
La Paloma	252	34.40 S	54.10 W
La Palud	62	43.47 N	6.20 E
La Pampa □⁴	258	38.00 S	66.00 W
La Panza Range ⋀	226	35.18 N	120.18 W
Lapão	250	11.24 S	41.50 W
La Paragua	246	6.50 N	63.20 W
Laparota	234	18.20 N	101.08 W
La Pasión, Laguna ◎	234	15.59 N	97.40 W
La Pasión, Río de ≃	232	16.31 N	90.10 W
La Patrie	206	45.24 N	71.15 W
La Paz, Arg.	252	30.45 S	59.39 W
La Paz, Arg.	252	33.28 S	67.33 W
La Paz, Bol.	248	16.30 S	68.09 W
La Paz, Hond.	236	14.16 N	87.40 W
La Paz, Méx.	234	23.41 N	100.43 W
La Paz, Pil.	116	8.19 N	125.43 E
Lapaz, In., U.S.	216	41.28 N	86.18 W
La Paz, Ur.	258	34.21 S	57.18 W
La Paz □⁵, Bol.	248	15.30 S	68.00 W
La Paz □⁵, Hond.	236	14.15 N	87.50 W
La Paz, Bahía c	234	24.15 N	110.40 W
La Paz, Río de ≃	246	16.27 S	67.19 W
La Paz Centro	236	12.20 N	86.41 W
Lapedra	115b	8.39 S	117.37 E
La Pedrera	246	1.18 S	69.43 W
Lapeer	216	43.03 N	83.19 W
La Perla, Méx.	196	28.18 N	104.33 W
La Perla, Méx.	196	30.46 N	104.42 W
La Perla, Perú	286d	12.05 S	77.08 W
La Perouse	274a	33.59 S	151.14 E
La Perouse, Bahía c	174z	27.04 S	109.18 W
La Perouse Bay c	229a	20.35 N	156.25 W
La Perouse Strait ☵	89	45.45 N	142.00 E
La Pesca	234	23.46 N	97.47 W
La Pesse	58	46.18 N	5.51 E
La Petite-Pierre	56	48.52 N	7.19 E
La Piedad de Cabadas	234	20.21 N	102.00 W
La Pimienta	234	21.28 N	99.01 W
La Pine	202	43.40 N	121.30 W
Lapinig	116	12.34 N	125.21 E
Lapinjärvi (Lappträsk)	26	60.38 N	26.13 E
Lapinlahti	26	63.22 N	27.24 E
Lapino	82	54.57 N	37.49 E
La Pintada	246	8.36 N	80.28 W
La Pintana	286e	33.38 S	70.38 W
La Pizzuta ⋀	71	38.00 N	13.18 E
La Place, Il., U.S.	219	39.48 N	88.43 W
La Place, La., U.S.	194	30.03 N	90.28 W
Lap Lae	110	17.40 N	100.03 E
La Plaine	240d	15.20 N	61.15 W
La Plant	198	45.09 N	100.39 W
La Plata, Arg.	252	34.55 S	57.57 W
La Plata, Col.	246	2.23 N	75.53 W
La Plata, Md., U.S.	208	38.31 N	76.58 W
La Plata, Mo., U.S.	194	40.01 N	92.29 W
La Plata ≃	240m	18.25 N	66.14 W
La Plata, Lago ◎	254	44.53 S	71.50 W
La Plata, Universidad Nacional de ⊡²	288	35.55 S	57.57 W
La Plata Peak ⋀	200	39.02 N	106.28 W
La Playa ≃	286b	23.06 N	82.27 W
La Ponge Indian Reserve ⋀⁴	184	55.15 N	107.36 W
La Pobla de Segur	34	42.14 N	0.59 E
La Pocatière	186	47.22 N	70.02 W
La Poile Bay c	186	47.38 N	58.20 W
Lapominka	24	64.53 N	40.28 E
Laponie → Lapland □⁹	24	68.00 N	25.00 E
Laporte, Co., U.S.	200	40.38 N	105.08 W
La Porte, In., U.S.	216	41.36 N	86.43 W
La Porte, Pa., U.S.	210	41.25 N	76.30 W
La Porte, Tx., U.S.	216	29.39 N	95.01 W
La Porte City	190	42.19 N	92.11 W
Laposo, Bulu ⋀	112	4.29 S	119.47 E
La Poste	240m	16.34 N	61.49 W
Lapoutroie	58	48.09 N	7.10 E

PORTUGUÊS Nome	Página	Lat.°'	Long.°' W=Oeste
La Poveda	266a	40.19 N	3.29 W
La Poza Grande	232	25.50 N	112.05 W
Lappago (Lappach)	64	46.55 N	11.48 E
Lappajärvi	26	63.12 N	23.38 E
Lappajärvi ◎	26	63.08 N	23.40 E
Lappeenranta	26	61.04 N	28.11 E
Lappersdorf	60	49.03 N	12.05 E
Lappfjärd (Lapväärtti)	26	62.15 N	21.32 E
Lappi	26	61.06 N	21.50 E
Lappland → Lapland □⁹	24	68.00 N	25.00 E
Lappträsk → Lapinjärvi	26	60.38 N	26.13 E
La Prairie	206	45.25 N	73.30 W
Laprairie □⁶	206	45.22 N	73.30 W
La Prele Creek ≃	198	42.50 N	105.30 W
La Presa	232	24.25 N	111.34 W
Laprida, Arg.	252	37.33 S	60.49 W
Laprida, Arg.	252	28.23 S	64.33 W
La Pryor	196	28.57 N	99.51 W
Lapšanga	80	57.27 N	45.03 E
Lâpseki	130	40.20 N	26.41 E
Lapta	130	35.20 N	33.10 E
Laptev Sea → Laptevych, more ▽²	74	76.00 N	126.00 E
Laptevych, more (Laptev Sea) ▽²	74	76.00 N	126.00 E
Lapua	26	62.57 N	23.00 E
Lapuanjoki ≃	26	63.34 N	22.30 E
La Puebla de Cazalla	34	37.14 N	5.19 W
La Puebla de Montalbán	34	39.52 N	4.21 W
La Puente	228	34.01 N	117.56 W
La Puerta	252	28.10 S	65.48 W
Lapu-Lapu (Opon)	116	10.19 N	123.57 E
La Punt	58	46.35 N	9.55 E
La Punta	286d	12.05 S	77.11 W
La Purísima, Chile	286e	33.34 S	70.39 W
La Purísima, Méx.	232	26.10 N	112.04 W
Lapush	38	47.30 N	24.01 E
La Push	224	47.54 N	124.38 W
Lapuyan	116	7.36 N	123.12 E
Lapväärtti → Lappfjärd	26	62.15 N	21.32 E
Lapwai	202	46.24 N	116.48 W
Łapy	30	53.00 N	22.53 E
La Queue-en-Brie	261	48.47 N	2.35 E
La Queue-lès-Yvelines	261	48.48 N	1.46 E
La Quiaca	252	22.06 S	65.37 W
L'Aquila	66	42.22 N	13.22 E
L'Aquila □⁴	66	42.05 N	13.40 E
Lär	128	27.41 N	54.17 E
Lara	169	38.01 S	144.24 E
Lara □³	246	10.10 N	69.50 W
Larabanga	150	9.13 N	1.51 W
Laracha	34	43.15 N	8.35 W
Larache	148	35.12 N	6.10 W
Laragne-Montéglin	62	44.19 N	5.49 E
Lärak, Jazïreh-ye I	128	26.52 N	56.22 E
Laramate	248	14.15 S	74.52 W
La Rambla	34	37.36 N	4.44 W
Laramie	200	41.18 N	105.35 W
Laramie ≃	200	42.12 N	104.32 W
Laramie Mountains ⋀	200	42.00 N	105.40 W
Laramie Peak ⋀	200	42.17 N	105.27 W
Laranjal	255	23.12 S	53.45 W
Laranjal ≃	251	21.22 S	42.28 W
Laranjeiras	250	10.48 S	37.10 W
Laranjeiras ←⁸	287a	22.56 S	43.11 W
Laranjeiras do Sul	252	25.25 S	52.25 W
Larantuka	115b	8.21 S	122.59 E
Larap	116	14.17 N	122.39 E
Laras	116	14.19 N	122.39 E
Larat	164	7.09 S	131.45 E
Larat, Pulau I	164	7.10 S	131.50 E
Laravale	171a	28.05 S	152.56 E
La Raya, Abra ⤙	248	14.35 S	70.59 W
La Réole	32	44.35 N	0.02 W
Lares, Perú	248	13.04 S	72.05 W
Lares, P.R.	240m	18.18 N	66.53 W
Large, Laguna ◎	234	17.30 N	97.25 W
Large Island I	240k	12.05 N	61.40 W
Lárgio Itálni □⁴	82	57.00 N	27.00 E
Largo	220	27.54 N	82.47 W
Largoward	46	56.16 N	2.55 W
Largs	46	55.48 N	4.52 W
Largue ≃	62	43.51 N	5.22 E
Lari, It.	66	43.34 N	10.36 E
Lari, Perú	248	15.37 S	71.46 W
Laria	112	1.26 S	119.17 E
Lariang	112	1.26 S	119.17 E
La Ricamarie	214	40.21 N	79.44 W
Larimore	198	47.54 N	97.37 W
La Rioja, Arg.	252	29.26 S	66.51 W
La Rioja □⁴, Arg.	252	29.30 S	67.30 W
La Rioja □³, Esp.	34	42.15 N	2.20 W
Lárisa	38	39.38 N	22.25 E
Larisa Station ⤙⁵	267c	37.59 S	23.43 E
Larjak	74	61.16 N	80.15 E
Larkana	123	27.33 N	68.13 E
Larkhall	46	55.45 N	3.59 W
Lark Harbour	186	49.06 N	58.23 W
Larkspur	282	37.56 N	122.32 W
Larnaca → Lárnakos, Kólpos c	130	34.53 N	33.38 E
Lárnax (Larnaca)	130	34.55 N	33.38 E
Larne	48	54.51 N	5.49 W
La Robe Noire, Lac ◎	186	50.23 N	66.37 W
La Robla	34	42.48 N	5.37 W
La Roca de la Sierra	34	39.06 N	6.41 W
La Roche-Bernard	32	47.31 N	2.18 W
La Roche-Chalais	32	45.09 N	0.00
La Roche-Derrien	32	48.45 N	3.16 W

PORTUGUÊS Nome	Página	Lat.°'	Long.°' W=Oeste
La Roche-des-Arnauds	62	44.34 N	5.57 E
La Roche-en-Ardenne	56	50.11 N	5.35 E
La Roche-en-Brenil	50	47.22 N	4.10 E
La Rochefoucauld	32	45.45 N	0.23 E
La Roche-Guyon	50	49.05 N	1.38 E
La Rochelle	32	46.10 N	1.10 W
Laroche-Saint-Cydroine	50	47.58 N	3.31 E
La Roche-sur-Foron	58	46.04 N	6.19 E
La Roche-sur-Yon	32	46.40 N	1.26 W
La Rochette, Fr.	62	45.28 N	6.07 E
La Rochette, Fr.	261	48.30 N	2.40 E
Larochette, Lux.	56	49.47 N	6.15 E
La Roda	34	39.13 N	2.09 W
La Romaine	186	50.13 N	60.40 W
La Romana	238	18.25 N	68.58 W
Larona	112	2.45 S	121.20 E
La Ronge	184	55.06 N	105.17 W
Laroquebrou	32	44.58 N	2.11 E
La Roquebrussanne	62	43.20 N	5.59 E
Larose	194	29.34 N	90.22 W
La Rosita	236	13.53 N	84.24 W
La Route	261	48.48 N	2.47 E
Larrabee State Park ⋀	224	48.41 N	122.29 W
Larreynaga	236	12.40 N	86.34 W
Larrey Point ⤙	162	19.58 S	119.07 E
Larrimah	164	15.35 S	133.12 E
Larringes	58	46.22 N	6.35 E
Larrison Creek ≃	222	31.27 N	95.03 W
Larroque	252	33.02 S	59.01 W
Larrys Creek ≃	210	41.13 N	77.13 W
Larrys River	186	45.13 N	61.23 W
Larsen Air Park ⤙	224	47.11 N	119.19 W
Larsen Bay	180	57.33 N	154.00 W
Larsen Ice Shelf ⸬	9	68.30 S	62.30 W
Lartèh Aheneasi	150	5.56 N	0.04 E
La Rubia	252	30.06 S	61.48 W
La Rue, Oh., U.S.	214	40.35 N	83.23 W
Larue, Tx., U.S.	222	32.07 N	95.41 W
La Rumorosa	228	32.34 N	116.06 W
Laruns	32	42.59 N	0.25 W
Larus Lake ◎	184	51.17 N	94.40 W
Larvik	26	59.04 N	10.00 E
Larwill	216	41.10 N	85.37 W
Laryne	83	47.53 N	37.56 E
Larzac, Causse du ⋀¹	32	43.50 N	3.25 E
Lasa (Laas)	64	46.37 N	10.42 E
La Sabana	252	27.52 S	59.57 W
Las Adjuntas	286e	10.26 N	67.01 W
La Sagne	58	47.03 N	6.48 E
La Sal	200	38.18 N	109.14 W
La Salette-Fallavaux	244	44.51 S	5.59 E
La Salle, On., Can.	214	42.14 N	83.06 W
La Salle, P.Q., Can.	206	45.26 N	73.38 W
Lasalle, Fr.	62	44.03 N	3.51 E
La Salle, Il., U.S.	216	41.20 N	89.06 W
La Salle, II., U.S.	216	41.21 N	88.51 W
La Salle ≃	214	39.45 N	97.08 W
Lasalle, Parc ⋀	275a	45.26 N	73.40 W
La Salle College ⊡²	285	40.02 N	75.09 W
La Salle Gardens	216	42.24 N	83.06 W
Las Almejas, Bahía c	232	24.29 N	111.44 W
La Sal Mountains ⋀	200	38.30 N	109.10 W
Lasan	112	1.14 N	115.13 E
Lasanga Island I	166	7.25 S	147.16 E
Las Animas	198	38.04 N	103.13 W
La Santa, Cerro ⋀	240m	18.07 N	66.03 W
Las Arenas	240m	18.02 N	67.09 W
La Sarraz	58	46.40 N	6.31 E
La Sarre	186	48.48 N	79.12 W
La Sarre ≃	190	48.43 N	79.16 W
Las Arrias	252	30.21 S	63.35 W
La Sauceda	196	28.26 N	100.38 W
La Saulce	62	44.25 N	6.01 E
Las Aves, Isla I	238	15.42 N	63.38 W
Las Ballenas, Canal ☵	232	29.10 N	113.29 W
Lasberg	61	48.28 N	14.32 E
Las Blancas	196	25.42 N	97.35 W
Las Bonitas	246	7.52 N	65.40 W
Las Breñas	252	27.05 S	61.05 W
Lasby	41	56.09 N	9.49 E
Las Cabezas de San Juan	34	36.59 N	5.56 W
Las Cabras	252	34.18 S	71.19 W
Las Cañas ≃	234	20.09 N	105.36 W
Lascano	252	33.40 S	54.12 W
Lascar, Volcán ⋀¹	252	23.22 S	67.45 W
Lascari	70	38.00 N	13.54 E
Las Casas → San Cristóbal de las Casas	234	16.45 N	92.38 W
Las Catitas	252	33.18 S	68.03 W
Las Catonas, Arroyo ≃	288	34.37 S	58.43 W
Lascaux, Grotte de ⌂	32	45.01 N	1.08 E
Las Cejas	252	26.53 S	64.44 W
L'Ascension	206	46.33 N	74.50 W
Las Chacras	252	30.51 S	65.49 W
La Scie	186	49.57 N	55.36 W
Las Coloradas	234	21.36 N	88.08 W
Las Cruces	234	16.37 N	93.54 W
Las Cuevas	252	29.38 N	
La Selle, Morne ⋀	238	18.22 N	71.59 W
Las Flores, Arg.	252	36.03 S	59.07 W
Las Flores, Arg.	252	24.04 S	64.56 W
Las Flores, P.R.	240m	18.01 N	66.22 W
Las Flores ≃	228	33.17 N	117.27 W
Las Flores, Arroyo ≃	252	36.21 S	59.10 W
Las Flores, Cerro ⋀	280	34.03 S	69.38 W
Las Flores Canyon ✦	282	34.03 N	
La Serena	252	29.54 S	71.16 W
La Serena ⋀¹	34	38.45 N	5.30 W
La Seyne-sur-Mer	32	43.06 N	5.53 E
Las Flores Grande, Arroyo ≃	288	35.30 S	59.01 W
La Sierra	266c	39.30 N	
Las Galeras	238	19.18 N	69.10 W
Las Garcitas	252	26.10 S	59.48 W
Las Guacamatas	232	30.02 N	112.54 W
Las Guayabas	234	24.00 N	97.45 W
Lasham	42	51.11 N	1.03 W
Lashburn	184	53.08 N	109.36 W
Lâsh-e Joveyn	128	31.43 N	61.37 E
Las Heras, Arg.	252	46.33 S	68.49 W
Las Heras, Arg.	252	32.51 S	68.49 W
Lashio	110	22.56 N	97.45 E
La Sierra, Montaña ⋀	114	2.10 N	96.39 E
La Sila ⋀¹	70	39.15 N	16.30 E
La Silla de Caracas ⋀	286c	10.33 N	66.51 W
Lašino	30	53.30 N	19.49 E
Lashkar → Gwalior	124	26.13 N	78.10 E
Lashkar Gāh	123	31.35 N	64.21 E

Name	Page	Lat.	Long.	Name	Page	Lat.	Long.
Läsjerd	128	35.24 N	53.04 E	Latimer, Eng., U.K.	260	51.41 N	0.33 W
Łask	30	51.36 N	19.07 E	Latimer, Ia., U.S.	190	42.45 N	93.22 W
Łaskarzew	30	51.48 N	21.35 E	Latina	66	41.28 N	12.52 E
L'askel'a	24	61.45 N	30.59 E	Latina □⁴	66	41.27 N	13.06 E
Laško	36	46.09 N	15.14 E	Latiri	140	9.10 N	25.43 E
Las Lajas, Arg.	252	38.31 S	70.22 W	Latisana	64	45.47 N	13.00 E
Las Lajas, Pan.	236	8.15 N	81.52 W	Latuga	24	64.16 N	48.46 E
Las Lajitas	252	24.43 S	64.15 W	Latnaja	78	54.33 N	38.55 E
Las Lomas	246	4.40 S	80.15 W	La Toma	252	33.03 S	65.37 W
Las Lomitas	252	24.42 S	60.36 W	Laton	226	36.26 N	119.41 W
Lašma	80	54.56 N	41.09 E	Latonovo	83	47.29 N	38.38 E
Las Malvinas	252	34.50 S	68.15 W	Latornell ≃	182	54.58 N	118.00 W
Lašmanka	80	54.44 N	51.28 E	La Torrecilla ʌ	240m	18.12 N	66.20 W
Las Mareas	240m	17.56 N	66.09 W	La Tortuga, Isla I	246	10.56 N	65.20 W
Las Margaritas	232	16.19 N	91.59 W	Latorytsyá ≃	30	48.28 N	21.50 E
Las Margaritas, Laguna ⊜	258	35.28 S	57.56 W	Latouche Island I	180	60.00 N	147.55 W
Las Marianas	258	35.01 S	58.44 W	Latouche Treville, Cape ›	162	18.27 S	121.49 E
Las Marías	240m	18.15 N	67.00 W	La Tour	62	43.57 N	7.11 E
Las Mayas	236	10.26 N	66.56 W	La Tour-d'Aigues	62	43.44 N	5.33 E
Las Mercedes	246	9.07 N	66.24 W	La Tour-d'Auvergne	62	45.32 N	2.41 E
Las Mesas de San Isidro	234	21.55 N	100.15 W	La Tour-de-Peilz	58	46.27 N	6.52 E
Las Minas	286c	10.27 N	66.52 W	La Tour-du-Pin	62	45.34 N	5.27 E
Las Minas, Cerro ʌ	236	14.33 N	88.39 W	La Tourette Park ◆	276	40.35 N	74.08 W
Las Minillas, Cerro ʌ	286e	33.31 S	70.29 W	Latowicz	30	52.02 N	21.48 E
Las Moras Creek ≃	196	29.00 N	100.39 W	Lat Phrao, Khlong ≃	269a	13.48 N	100.35 E
Las Mulas, Laguna ⊜	258	35.32 S	57.54 W	La Tremblade	32	45.46 N	1.08 W
Las Navas	116	12.21 N	125.02 E	La Trimouille	32	46.28 N	1.02 E
Las Nieves	232	26.24 N	105.22 W	La Trinidad, Arg.	252	27.24 S	65.31 W
Las Nopaleras, Cerro ʌ	232	25.08 N	103.14 W	La Trinidad, Nic.	236	12.58 N	86.14 W
La Solana	34	38.56 N	3.14 W	La Trinidad, Pil.	116	16.28 N	120.35 E
La Soledad, Cerro ʌ	232	26.32 N	107.17 W	La Trinidad, Ven.	286c	10.27 N	66.52 W
Lasolo	112	3.29 S	122.04 E	La Trinidad de Orichuna	246	7.07 N	69.45 W
Lasolo ≃	112	3.28 S	122.06 E	La Trinitaria	232	16.07 N	92.03 W
Las Ortegas, Arroyo ≃	288	34.45 S	58.32 W	La Trinité	240e	14.44 N	60.58 W
Las Ovejas	252	37.01 S	70.45 W	La Trobe ≃	169	38.10 S	146.32 E
Las Palmas, Arg.	252	27.04 S	58.42 W	La Trobe University ʋ²	274b	37.43 S	145.03 E
Las Palmas, Arg.	258	34.05 S	59.10 W	La Tronche	62	45.12 N	5.44 E
Las Palmas, Pan.	236	8.08 N	81.27 W	Latronico	66	40.05 N	16.01 E
Las Palmas, P.R.	240m	17.59 N	66.02 W	Latsch			
Las Palmas ʌ	148	28.25 N	14.15 W	— Laces	64	46.37 N	10.52 E
Las Palmas de Gran Canaria	148	28.06 N	15.24 W	Latta	192	34.20 N	79.25 W
Las Palomas	200	31.44 N	107.37 W	Lattarico	66	39.28 N	16.08 E
Las Perdices, Canal ≊	286e	33.31 S	70.33 W	Lattasburg	214	40.53 N	82.06 W
La Spezia	62	44.07 N	9.50 E	Latterbach	58	46.40 N	7.35 E
La Spezia □⁴	62	44.05 N	9.42 E	Lattingtown	276	40.54 N	73.36 W
Las Piedras, P.R.	240m	18.11 N	65.52 W	Latty	216	41.05 N	84.35 W
Las Piedras, Ur.	258	34.44 S	56.13 W	La Tuilerie	161	48.34 N	2.08 E
Las Piedras, Río de ≃	248	12.30 S	69.14 W	La Tuilière	62	44.11 N	5.32 E
Las Piñas, Pil.	269f	14.29 N	120.59 E	Laturra	112	8.23 S	124.06 E
Las Piñas, P.R.	240m	18.15 N	65.55 W	La Tuque	176	47.26 N	72.47 W
Las Plumas	252	43.43 S	67.15 W	Lätür	122	18.24 N	76.35 E
Lasqueti Island I	182	49.29 N	124.17 W	La Turbie	62	43.45 N	7.24 E
Las Raíces Creek ≃	196	28.09 N	99.02 W	Latvia (Latvija) □¹, Europe	22	57.00 N	25.00 E
Las Ratas, Cerro ʌ	234	18.37 N	103.37 W	Latvia (Latvija) □¹, Europe	22	57.00 N	25.00 E
Las Rejas	286e	33.28 S	70.44 W	Lau, Nig.	146	9.13 N	11.17 E
Las Rosas, Arg.	252	32.28 S	61.34 W	Lau, Pap. N. Gui.	164	5.50 S	151.20 E
Las Rosas, Chile	286e	33.35 S	70.37 W	Laubach	56	50.33 N	8.59 E
Las Rosas, Méx.	232	16.24 N	92.23 W	Lau Basin ʌ¹	14	20.00 S	177.00 W
Las Rozas de Madrid	286a	40.29 N	3.52 W	Laubusch	56	51.28 N	14.10 E
Las Sales, Canal ≃	286e	19.26 N	99.03 W	Laubuseschbach	56	50.26 N	8.20 E
Lassan	54	53.57 N	13.50 E	Lauca ʌ	248	19.10 S	68.10 W
Lassance	255	17.54 S	44.34 W	Lauca, Parque Nacional ♦	248	18.20 S	69.15 W
Lassay	32	48.26 N	0.30 W	Laucha	54	51.13 N	11.41 E
Lassee	61	48.13 N	16.49 E	Lauchhammer	54	51.30 N	13.47 E
Lasselsville	210	43.03 N	74.36 W	Lauchheim	56	48.52 N	10.14 E
Lassen Peak ʌ¹	204	40.29 N	121.31 W	Lauchröden	56	51.01 N	10.14 E
Lassen Volcanic National Park ♦	204	40.30 N	121.19 W	Lauda-Königshofen	56	49.34 N	9.41 E
Lassigny	50	49.35 N	2.51 E	Lauder	46	55.43 N	2.45 W
Lassnitz ≃	61	46.46 N	15.32 E	Lauderdale	194	32.31 N	88.30 W
Lassnitzhöhe	61	47.05 N	15.35 E	Lauderdale V	46	55.43 N	2.42 W
L'Assomption	174n	15.02 N	145.38 E	Lauderdale-by-the-Sea	220	26.12 N	80.07 W
L'Assomption	206	45.50 N	73.25 W	Lauderdale Lakes	220	26.09 N	80.12 W
L'Assomption □⁶	206	45.43 N	73.35 W	Lauderhill	220	26.09 N	80.12 W
L'Assomption ≃	206	45.43 N	73.29 W	Laudun	62	44.06 N	4.40 E
Lasswade	46	55.53 N	3.08 W	Lauenbrück	52	53.12 N	9.33 E
Lassy	261	49.06 N	2.27 E	Lauenburg ≃	52	53.22 N	10.33 E
Las Tablas	246	7.46 N	80.17 W	— Lębork, Pol.	30	54.33 N	17.44 E
Lastarrio, Parque Nacional ♦	254	44.50 S	72.05 W	Lauenförde	52	51.39 N	9.23 E
Las Tinajas	252	27.27 S	62.55 W	Lauenstein, Dtsch.	54	52.04 N	9.33 E
Last Mountain ʌ	184	51.07 N	104.54 W	Lauenstein, Dtsch.	54	50.47 N	13.49 E
Last Mountain Lake ⊜	184	51.05 N	105.10 W	Lauenstein, Dtsch.	54	50.31 N	11.20 E
Las Toscas	252	28.21 S	59.17 W	Lauer ≃	56	50.18 N	10.10 E
Lastoursville	152	0.49 S	12.42 E	Lauerzer See ⊜	58	47.02 N	8.36 E
Lastovo, Otok I	36	42.45 N	16.53 E	Lauf an der Pegnitz	56	49.30 N	11.17 E
Lastovski Kanal ☈	36	42.50 N	16.59 E	Laufelfingen	58	47.24 N	7.51 E
Lastra a Signa	66	43.46 N	11.06 E	Laufen, Dtsch.	56	47.57 N	12.56 E
Las Trampas Creek ≃	282	37.53 N	122.03 W	Laufen, Schw.	58	47.25 N	7.30 E
Las Trampas Peak ʌ	282	37.50 N	122.03 W	Laufenburg (Baden), Dtsch.	58	47.33 N	8.04 E
Las Trampas Regional Park ♦	282	37.50 N	122.03 W	Laufenburg (Baden), Schw.	58	47.33 N	8.04 E
Las Trampas Ridge ʌ	282	37.49 N	122.02 W	Laufersfort, Schloss ⊡	263	51.25 N	6.37 E
Lästringe	40	58.54 N	17.18 E	Laugharne	50	51.47 N	4.28 W
Las Truchas	234	17.55 N	102.12 W	Laughery Creek ≃	218	39.02 N	84.53 W
Lastrup	52	52.48 N	7.52 E	Laughlen, Mount ʌ	162	23.23 S	134.23 E
Las Tunas	240p	21.00 N	76.57 W	Laughlin Air Force Base ■	196	29.22 N	100.47 W
Las Tunas □⁴	240p	21.00 N	77.00 W	Laughlin Peak ʌ	196	36.38 N	104.12 W
Las Tunas, Arroyo ≃	288	34.27 S	58.41 W	Laughlintown	214	40.13 N	79.12 W
Las Tunas, Punta ›	240m	18.30 N	66.38 W	Lau Group II	175g	18.20 S	178.30 W
Las Tunas Grandes, Laguna ⊜	252	35.58 S	62.25 W	Lauingen	56	48.34 N	10.25 E
La Suze	32	47.54 N	0.02 E	Lais — Lugano	58	46.01 N	8.58 E
Las Varas, Méx.	232	29.29 N	108.01 W	Laukaa	26	62.25 N	25.57 E
Las Varas, Méx.	234	21.10 N	105.10 W	Laukuva	16	55.37 N	22.14 E
Las Varillas	252	31.52 S	62.43 W	Laul'u	89	45.30 N	135.16 E
Las Vegas, P.R.	240m	18.11 N	67.02 W	Launceston, Austl.	166	41.26 S	147.08 E
Las Vegas, Nv., U.S.	204	36.10 N	115.08 W	Launceston, Eng., U.K.	50	50.38 N	4.21 W
Las Vegas, N.M., U.S.	200	35.36 N	105.13 W	Laundi, Tanjung ›	115b	9.28 S	120.12 E
Las Vegas, Ven.	286c	10.26 N	68.37 W	Laundi ≃	48	52.07 N	9.48 W
Las Vigías de Ramírez	234	19.38 N	97.05 W	Langlon	110	13.58 N	98.07 E
La Tabatière	186	50.50 N	58.58 W	Laungowāl	120	30.13 N	75.41 E
Latacunga	246	0.56 S	78.37 W	La Unión, Chile	254	40.17 S	73.05 W
Latady Island I	9	70.45 S	74.35 W	La Unión, El Sal.	236	13.20 N	87.51 W
La Tagua	246	0.03 S	74.40 W	La Unión, Esp.	34	37.37 N	0.52 W
Latakia — Al-Lādhiqīyah	128	35.31 N	35.47 E	La Unión, Méx.	234	17.58 N	101.49 W
Latakia □³	130	35.30 N	36.00 E	La Unión, Perú	248	9.46 S	76.48 W
Latamber	120	33.07 N	70.52 E	La Unión, Perú	248	5.24 S	80.45 W
Lata Mountain ʌ	174y	14.14 S	169.29 W	La Unión, Pil.	116	6.42 N	126.05 E
La Tapona	234	22.48 N	100.38 W	La Unión, N.M., U.S.	200	31.57 N	106.39 W
Latacunga ≃	26	59.57 N	6.37 E	La Unión, Ven.	246	8.13 N	67.46 W
Latefar	124	23.45 N	84.30 E	La Unión ≃	286c	10.05 N	68.16 W
Latehar	262	53.29 N	2.30 W	La Unión ʌ	116	16.33 N	120.25 E
Latera	66	42.38 N	11.50 E	Launois-sur-Vence	61	49.34 N	4.32 E
Laterina	66	43.31 N	11.43 E	Launsdorf	61	46.46 N	14.27 E
Laterns	58	47.16 N	9.43 E	Laupen	58	46.54 N	7.14 E
Laterrière	186	48.18 N	71.06 W	Laupenmühle ◦	263	51.21 N	6.56 E
Laterza	66	40.37 N	16.48 E	Laupheim	56	48.14 N	9.52 E
La Teste-de-Buch	32	44.38 N	1.09 W	Laura, Austl.	116	15.35 N	124.28 E
La Tetilla, Cerro ʌ	234	21.24 N	95.29 W	Laura, Oh., U.S.	218	39.59 N	84.24 W
Latexo	222	31.24 N	95.29 W	La Urbana	246	7.08 N	66.56 W
Latgale □⁹	16	56.20 N	27.10 E	Laureana di Borrello	66	38.30 N	16.05 E
Latham, Austl.	162	29.45 S	116.26 E	Laurel, De., U.S.	204	38.33 N	75.34 W
Latham, Il., U.S.	216	39.59 N	89.10 W	Laurel, Fl., U.S.	220	27.07 N	82.27 W
Latham, N.Y., U.S.	210	42.44 N	73.45 W	Laurel, In., U.S.	218	39.30 N	85.11 W
Latham, N.Y., U.S.	218	39.06 N	83.15 W	Laurel, Md., U.S.	210	39.05 N	76.51 W
Lathen	52	52.52 N	7.19 E	Laurel, Mt., U.S.	198	45.40 N	108.46 W
Latheron	46	58.17 N	3.23 W	Laurel, Ne., U.S.	190	42.25 N	97.05 W
Läthi	120	21.43 N	71.23 E	Laurel, Va., U.S.	198	37.38 N	77.32 W
Lathrop, Ca., U.S.	226	37.49 N	121.16 W	Laurel ≃	192	37.38 N	77.30 W
Lathrop, Mo., U.S.	194	39.32 N	94.19 W	Laurel, Mount ʌ	283	40.09 N	74.44 W
Lathrop Village	281	42.29 N	83.14 W	Laurel Bay	192	32.26 N	80.47 W
La Thuile	64	45.42 N	6.57 E	Laureldale, N.J., U.S.	283	40.29 N	74.41 W
La Tiarra	286c	10.26 N	66.46 W	Laureldale, Pa., U.S.	208	40.23 N	75.55 W
Latian, Mount ʌ	116	6.13 N	125.30 E				
Latiano	68	40.33 N	17.43 E				

Name	Page	Lat.	Long.	Name	Page	Lat.	Long.
Laureles	252	31.22 S	55.51 W	Laverton, Austl.	162	28.38 S	122.25 E
Laureles, Isla de los I	258	33.45 S	59.23 W	Laverton, Austl.	169	37.52 S	144.45 E
Laurel Gardens	279b	40.31 N	80.01 W	Laverton Royal Australian Air Force Base ■	169	37.52 S	144.43 E
Laurel Hill, Austl.	171b	35.37 S	148.05 E	La Veta	200	37.30 N	105.00 W
Laurel Hill, N.C., U.S.	192	34.48 N	79.32 W	Levezares	116	12.32 N	124.00 E
Laurel Hill ʌ	214	40.15 N	79.05 W	Levezzi, Îles II	71	41.20 N	9.15 E
Laurel Hollow	276	40.52 N	73.28 W	Lavezzola	66	44.34 N	11.52 E
Laurel Reservoir ⊜¹	276	41.10 N	73.33 W	Lavia	26	61.36 N	22.36 E
Laurel Ridge State Park ♦	188	39.58 N	79.23 W	Laviano	68	40.47 N	15.18 E
Laurel River Lake ⊜¹	192	36.55 N	84.15 W	Lavic Lake ⊜	204	34.40 N	116.21 W
Laurel Run	210	41.13 N	75.51 W	La Victoria, Perú	286d	12.04 S	77.02 W
Laurel Run ≃	208	40.20 N	77.20 W	La Victoria, Ven.	246	10.14 N	67.20 W
Laurel Springs	285	39.49 N	75.00 W	Lavieille, Lake ⊜	190	45.51 N	78.14 W
Laurelton	210	40.52 N	77.11 W	Lavik	26	61.06 N	5.30 E
Laurelville, Oh., U.S.	188	39.28 N	82.44 W	La Vila Joiosa	34	38.30 N	0.14 W
Laurelville, Pa., U.S.	214	40.09 N	79.29 W	La Villa	64	46.36 N	11.54 E
Laurenburg	56	50.20 N	7.54 E	La Villa	236	7.59 N	80.23 W
Laurence Harbor	276	40.27 N	74.14 W	La Villeneuve-Saint-Martin	261	49.04 N	1.58 E
Laurencekirk	46	56.50 N	2.29 W	La Viña, Arg.	252	25.27 S	65.35 W
Laurens, Ia., U.S.	190	42.32 N	75.06 W	Lavin	58	46.46 N	10.06 E
Laurens, N.Y., U.S.	210	42.32 N	75.06 W	Lavina, Mt., U.S.	198	46.17 N	108.56 W
Laurens, S.C., U.S.	192	34.29 N	82.00 W	Lavinio Lido di Enea	66	41.30 N	12.05 E
Laurentides	206	45.51 N	73.46 W	Laviolette, Lac ⊜	206	46.51 N	73.58 W
Laurentides, Les ʌ¹	176	48.00 N	71.00 W	La Virginia	246	4.54 N	75.53 W
Laurentides, Parc Provincial des ♦	32	45.46 N	1.08 W	Lavis	64	46.08 N	11.07 E
Laurenzana	124	26.59 N	84.24 E	La Vista	198	41.11 N	96.01 W
Lauria	68	40.03 N	15.50 E	Lavon	222	33.02 N	96.26 W
Lau Ridge ←³	14	21.00 S	178.30 W	Lavon ⊜¹	222	33.05 N	96.28 W
Laurie Island I	9	60.45 S	44.35 W	Lavon Lake ⊜¹	222	33.05 N	96.28 W
Laurie Lake ⊜	184	56.34 N	101.54 W	Lavougba	152	5.46 N	23.21 E
Laurier, Mb., Can.	184	50.54 N	99.33 W	La Voulte-sur-Rhône	62	44.48 N	4.47 E
Laurier, P.Q., Can.	206	46.32 N	71.38 W	Lavoute-sur-Loire	62	45.07 N	3.54 E
Laurière	32	46.05 N	1.28 E	Lavoutte, Anse ☌	241l	14.06 N	60.56 W
Laurinburg	192	34.46 N	79.27 W	Lavradia	266c	38.40 N	9.03 W
Laurino	68	40.20 N	15.20 E	Lavras	255	21.14 S	45.00 W
Laurito	68	40.10 N	15.24 E	Lavras da Mangabeira	250	6.45 S	38.57 W
Lauritsana	26	61.04 N	28.16 E	Lavras do Sul	252	30.49 S	53.55 W
Lauritzen Bay ☌	9	69.05 S	156.50 E	Lavrentija, zaliv ☌	180	65.35 N	171.00 W
Laurium	190	47.14 N	88.26 W	Lavrinhas	256	22.35 S	44.54 W
Lauriya Nandangarh	124	26.59 N	84.24 E	Lávrion	38	37.44 N	24.04 E
Lauro, Monte ʌ	70	37.07 N	14.49 E	Lavumisa	158	27.19 S	31.54 E
Laurys Station	208	40.43 N	75.32 W	Lavushi Manda National Park ♦	154	12.20 S	30.50 E
Lausanne	58	46.31 N	6.38 E	Lawa	116	6.12 N	125.41 E
Lauscha	54	50.28 N	11.10 E	Lawai	229b	21.55 N	159.30 W
Laussig, Dtsch.	54	51.33 N	12.38 E	Lawang	115a	7.49 S	112.42 E
Laussig, Dtsch.	54	51.33 N	12.38 E	La Wantzenau	58	48.40 N	7.50 E
Laut	86	59.18 N	66.02 E	La Ward	222	28.51 N	96.28 W
Laut, Pulau I, Indon.	112	3.40 S	116.10 E	Lawas	112	4.51 N	115.24 E
Laut, Pulau I, Indon.	112	4.43 N	107.59 E	Lawatu	112	4.51 N	122.46 E
Laut, Selat ☈	112	3.25 S	116.03 E	Lawdar	144	13.53 N	45.52 E
Lauta	54	51.27 N	14.04 E	Lawele	112	5.13 S	122.57 E
Lautaro	252	38.31 S	72.27 W	Lawers, Ben ʌ	46	56.34 N	4.13 W
Lautaro, Volcán ʌ¹	254	49.00 S	73.32 W	Lawford Lake ⊜	184	54.30 N	96.43 W
Lautem	112	8.22 S	126.54 E	Lawgi	166	24.34 S	150.39 E
Lautenbach	58	48.23 N	7.18 E	Lawin, Pulau I	116	5.25 N	102.35 E
Lautenthal	52	51.52 N	10.17 E	Lawit, Gunung ʌ	114	5.25 N	102.35 E
Lauter ≃, Dtsch.	56	49.39 N	7.35 E	Lawksawk	110	21.15 N	96.52 E
Lauter ≃, Europe	56	48.58 N	8.11 E	Lawler	190	43.04 N	92.09 W
Lauterach	58	47.29 N	9.44 E	Lawlor, Mount ʌ	204	34.16 N	118.06 W
Lauterbach, Dtsch.	56	50.38 N	9.24 E	Lawn, Nf., Can.	186	46.57 N	55.32 W
Lauterbach, Dtsch.	58	48.14 N	8.20 E	Lawn, Pa., U.S.	208	40.13 N	76.32 W
Lauterbrunnen	58	46.36 N	7.55 E	Lawn, Tx., U.S.	196	32.08 N	99.45 W
Lauterecken	56	49.39 N	7.35 E	Lawn Bay ☌	186	46.55 N	55.18 W
Lauterhofen	60	49.22 N	11.37 E	Lawndale, Ca., U.S.	228	33.53 N	118.21 W
Lauter [Sachsen]	54	50.33 N	12.44 E	Lawndale, Il., U.S.	219	40.13 N	89.17 W
Lauterstein	58	48.42 N	9.53 E	Lawndale, N.C., U.S.	192	35.24 N	81.33 W
Laut Kecil, Kepulauan II	112	4.50 S	115.45 E	Lawndale ◆, Il., U.S.	278	41.51 N	87.43 W
Lautoka	175g	17.37 S	177.27 E	Lawnes Creek ≃	285	37.08 N	76.40 W
Lauttakylä — Huittinen	26	61.11 N	22.42 E	Lawn Hill	166	18.35 S	138.35 E
Laut Tawar, Danau ⊜	114	4.38 N	96.54 E	Lawn Hill Creek ≃	166	18.03 S	139.09 E
Lauwe	50	50.48 N	3.11 E	Lawn Hill National Park ♦	166	18.45 S	138.27 E
Lauwerszee ☈	52	53.20 N	6.12 E	Lawrence, N.Z.	218	45.55 S	169.41 E
Lauzerte	32	44.15 N	1.08 E	Lawrence, In., U.S.	218	39.50 N	86.01 W
Lauzon	206	46.50 N	71.10 W	Lawrence, Ks., U.S.	194	38.58 N	95.14 W
Lauzun	32	44.38 N	0.28 E	Lawrence, Ma., U.S.	208	42.42 N	71.09 W
Lava, Nosy I	157b	14.33 S	47.36 E	Lawrence, Mi., U.S.	216	42.13 N	86.03 W
Lava Beds National Monument ♦	204	41.42 N	121.30 W	Lawrence, Ne., U.S.	190	40.17 N	98.15 W
Lavaca □⁶	222	29.22 N	96.55 W	Lawrence, N.Y., U.S.	276	40.36 N	73.43 W
Lavaca ≃	222	28.42 N	96.38 W	Lawrence, Tx., U.S.	222	32.45 N	96.21 W
Lavaca Bay ☌	196	28.36 N	96.35 W	Lawrence Fork ≃	194	40.17 N	99.34 W
La Vacherie	62	44.53 N	5.11 E	Lawrence Institute of Technology ʋ²	281	42.28 N	83.15 W
Lavagh More ʌ	48	54.45 N	8.05 W	Lawrence Park	214	42.10 N	79.59 W
Lavagna	64	44.18 N	9.20 E	Lawrence Brook ≃	276	40.29 N	74.24 W
Lavagna ≃	62	44.21 N	9.20 E	Lawrence Municipal Airport ■	283	42.43 N	71.07 W
La Vega, Hot Springs	252	42.37 N	112.00 W	Lawrenceburg, Ky., U.S.	218	38.02 N	84.54 W
La Vega, Rep. Dom.	240	19.13 N	70.31 W	Lawrenceburg, Tn., U.S.	194	35.14 N	87.20 W
La Vega ʌ²	286c	10.20 N	66.52 W	Lawrence Fork ≃	194	41.36 N	103.04 W
La Vela, Cabo de ›	246	12.15 N	72.11 W	Lawrenceville, Ga., U.S.	192	33.57 N	83.59 W
La Vela de Coro	246	11.27 N	69.34 W	Lawrenceville, Il., U.S.	216	38.43 N	87.40 W
Lavalanet	32	42.56 N	1.51 E	Lawrenceville, N.J., U.S.	283	40.17 N	74.43 W
Lavelle	208	40.35 N	76.22 W	Lawrenceville, Pa., U.S.	210	41.59 N	77.08 W
Lavello	68	41.03 N	15.48 E	Lawrenceville, Va., U.S.	192	36.45 N	77.50 W
Laven	41	56.07 N	9.43 E	Lawson, Austl.	170	33.43 S	150.26 E
La Venada	234	22.52 N	97.30 W	Lawson, Mo., U.S.	194	39.26 N	94.12 W
Lavenham	262	52.06 N	0.48 E	Lawson Creek ≃	182	54.51 N	123.38 W
La Venta	234	18.08 N	94.03 W	Lawton, Ky., U.S.	192	38.06 N	83.13 W
La Ventura	234	24.38 N	100.54 W	Lawton, Mi., U.S.	216	42.16 N	85.51 W
Lawu, Gunung ʌ	115a	7.38 S	111.11 E	Lawton, N.D., U.S.	198	48.17 N	98.22 W
Lawz, Jabal al- ʌ	128	28.40 N	35.18 E	Lawyer Creek ≃	202	46.14 N	116.01 W
Laxax	60	48.02 N	16.11 E	Lawyersville	210	42.40 N	74.30 W
Laxe	34	58.10 N	8.28 W	Lawz, Jabal al- ʌ	128	28.40 N	35.18 E
Laxenburg Park ◆	264b	48.04 N	16.22 E	Laxax	60	48.02 N	16.11 E
Laxford, Loch c	46	58.25 N	5.05 W	Lax Kw'alaams	182	54.34 N	130.27 W
Laxou	161	48.41 N	6.08 E	Laxou	161	48.41 N	6.08 E

ʌ Mountain	Berg	Montaña	Montagne	Montanha
ʌ Mountains	Gebirge	Montañas	Montagnes	Montanhas
⋊ Pass	Paß	Paso	Col	Passo
Ⅴ Valley, Cañyon	Tal, Cañon	Valle, Cañón	Vallée, Canyon	Vale, Canhão
≃ Plain	Ebene	Llano	Plaine	Planície
› Cape	Kap	Cabo	Cap	Cabo
I Island	Insel	Isla	Île	Ilha
II Islands	Inseln	Islas	Îles	Ilhas
♦ Other Topographic Features	Andere Topographische Objekte	Otros Elementos Topográficos	Autres données topographiques	Outros accidentes topográficos

ESPAÑOL — Nombre / Página / Lat.°′ / Long.°′ W = Oeste
FRANÇAIS — Nom / Page / Lat.°′ / Long.°′ W = Ouest
PORTUGUÊS — Nome / Página / Lat.°′ / Long.°′ W = Oeste

Leek, Ned. 52 53.09 N 6.24 E
Leek, Eng., U.K. 44 53.06 N 2.01 W
Leelanau, Lake ⊜ 190 44.55 N 85.43 W
Leelanau Peninsula ≻[1] 190 45.10 N 85.35 W
Leeming 44 54.17 N 1.32 W
Leenaun 48 53.36 N 9.45 W
Leende 52 51.21 N 5.33 E
Lee-on-the-Solent 42 50.47 N 1.12 W
Lee Park 210 41.14 N 75.55 W
Leeper 214 41.22 N 79.18 W
Leer 52 53.14 N 7.26 E
Leerdam 52 51.54 N 5.05 E
Leerhafe 52 53.32 N 7.47 E
Leersum 52 52.01 N 5.26 E
Lees 262 53.32 N 2.04 W
Leesburg, Fl., U.S. 220 28.48 N 81.52 W
Leesburg, Ga., U.S. 192 31.43 N 84.10 W
Leesburg, In., U.S. 216 41.19 N 85.51 W
Leesburg, N.J., U.S. 208 39.15 N 74.59 W
Leesburg, Oh., U.S. 218 39.20 N 83.33 W
Leesburg, Tx., U.S. 222 32.59 N 95.05 W
Leesburg, Va., U.S. 208 39.06 N 77.33 W
Lees Creek ≃ 218 39.21 N 83.29 W
Leese 52 52.30 N 9.06 E
Leesport 208 40.27 N 75.58 W
Lees Summit 194 38.55 N 94.23 W
Leeste 52 52.59 N 8.49 E
Leeston 172 43.46 S 172.18 E
Leesville, Il., U.S. 216 41.01 N 87.33 W
Leesville, In., U.S. 218 38.51 N 86.18 W
Leesville, La., U.S. 194 31.08 N 93.15 W
Leesville, Oh., U.S. 214 40.27 N 81.13 W
Leesville, S.C., U.S. 192 33.54 N 81.30 W
Leesville, Tx., U.S. 222 29.24 N 97.45 W
Leesville Lake ⊜[1], Oh., U.S. 214 40.30 N 81.10 W
Leesville Lake ⊜[1], Va., U.S. 192 37.05 N 79.25 W
Leeton 166 34.33 S 146.24 E
Leetonia 214 40.52 N 80.45 W
Leetsdale 214 40.33 N 80.12 W
Leeudoringstad 158 27.15 S 26.10 E
Leeu-Gamka 158 32.47 S 21.59 E
Leeupan ≡ 273d 26.14 S 28.19 E
Leeuwarden 52 53.12 N 5.46 E
Leeuwin, Cape ≻ 162 34.22 S 115.08 E
Lee Vining 226 37.57 N 119.07 W
Leeward Islands II 238 17.00 N 63.00 W
Le Faouët 28 48.02 N 3.29 W
Le Fayet 58 45.55 N 6.42 E
Lefèvre, Pointe ≻ 175f 20.54 S 167.01 E
Leffe 62 45.48 N 9.53 E
Lefferts, Lake ⊜ 276 40.25 N 74.14 W
Léfini ≃ 152 2.57 S 16.10 E
Léfini, Réserve de Chasse de la ⬥[4] 152 2.58 S 15.25 E
Lefke 130 35.07 N 32.51 E
Le Focette 64 43.55 N 10.13 E
Leforest 50 50.26 N 3.04 E
Lefors 196 35.26 N 100.48 W
Le François 240e 14.37 N 60.54 W
Le Freney-d'Oisans 62 45.02 N 6.07 E
Lefroy 212 44.16 N 79.34 W
Lefroy, Lake ⊜ 162 31.15 S 121.40 E
Leftrook Lake ⊜ 184 56.05 N 98.36 W
Lega Hida 144 7.56 N 41.04 E
Legal 182 53.57 N 113.35 W
Leganés 34 40.19 N 3.45 W
Le Gardeur 206 45.45 N 73.28 W
Legaspi 116 13.08 N 123.44 E
Legau 58 47.51 N 10.07 E
Legden 52 52.02 N 7.07 E
Legendre ≃ 206 45.44 N 71.08 W
Legendre Island I 162 20.23 S 116.54 E
Leggett, Ca., U.S. 204 39.51 N 123.42 W
Leggett, Tx., U.S. 222 30.49 N 94.52 W
Leghorn → Livorno 66 43.33 N 10.19 E
Legion Mine 154 21.23 S 28.33 E
Legion of Honor, Palace of the ʋ 282 37.47 N 122.30 W
Legionowo 30 52.25 N 20.56 E
Legnago 64 45.11 N 11.18 E
Legnano 62 45.36 N 8.54 E
Legnica (Liegnitz) 30 51.13 N 16.09 E
Legnica □[4] 30 51.25 N 16.10 E
Le Gosier 241o 16.12 N 61.30 W
Le Grand 226 37.13 N 120.14 W
LeGrand, Cape ≻ 162 34.01 S 122.06 E
Le Grand-Lucé 50 47.52 N 0.28 E
Le Grand-Quevilly 50 49.25 N 1.02 E
Le Grand-Serre 62 45.16 N 5.06 E
Le Grand Wintersberg ∧[2] 56 48.59 N 7.37 E
Le Grau-du-Roi 62 43.32 N 4.08 E
Le Gua 62 45.01 N 5.37 E
Le Guelta 34 36.22 N 0.50 E
Leguga 154 3.23 N 25.02 E
Legume 166 28.25 S 152.19 E
Legundi, Pulau I 115a 5.50 S 105.16 E
Leh 123 34.10 N 77.35 E
Le Havre 50 49.30 N 0.08 E
Lehčevo 38 43.32 N 23.32 E
Le Hérie-la-Viéville 50 49.49 N 3.38 E
Lehesten 54 50.29 N 11.28 E
Lehi 200 40.23 N 111.50 W
Lehigh, Ia., U.S. 190 42.21 N 94.03 W
Lehigh, Ok., U.S. 196 34.28 N 96.12 W
Lehigh □[6] 208 40.36 N 75.29 W
Lehigh ≃ 210 40.41 N 75.12 W
Lehigh Acres 220 26.37 N 81.37 W
Lehighton 210 40.50 N 75.42 W
Lehinch 48 52.56 N 9.21 W
Lehnin 54 52.19 N 12.44 E
Lehnitz 54 52.44 N 13.15 E
Lehnitz See ⊜ 264a 52.45 N 13.16 E
Leho 140 7.07 N 33.52 E
Le Hohwald 58 48.24 N 7.20 E
Le Houlme 50 49.31 N 1.02 E
Lehr 198 45.59 N 99.32 W
Lehra Gāga 123 29.55 N 75.49 E
Lehrbach 56 50.47 N 9.04 E
Lehrberg 56 49.21 N 10.30 E
Lehre 54 52.19 N 10.40 E
Lehrte 52 52.22 N 9.59 E
Lehtimäki 26 62.47 N 23.55 E
Lehtrār Bāla 123 33.42 N 73.26 E
Lehtse 76 59.15 N 25.50 E
Lehua I 229b 22.01 N 160.06 W
Lehututu 156 23.58 S 21.51 E
Lei ≃ 100 26.54 N 112.39 E
Leiah 123 30.58 N 70.56 E
Leião 266c 38.44 N 9.18 W
Leibnitz 61 46.47 N 15.32 E
Leibo 102 28.19 N 103.21 E
Leicester, Eng., U.K. 42 52.38 N 1.05 W
Leicester, Ma., U.S. 207 42.14 N 71.54 W
Leicester, N.Y., U.S. 210 42.46 N 77.53 W
Leicestershire □[6] 42 52.40 N 1.10 W
Leichhardt 274a 33.53 S 151.07 E
Leichhardt ≃ 166 17.35 S 139.48 E
Leichhardt Falls ⌊ 166 18.14 S 139.53 E
Leichhardt Range ⋏ 166 20.40 S 147.25 E
Leichlingen 56 51.06 N 7.01 E
Leiden 52 52.09 N 4.30 E
Leiderdorp 52 52.09 N 4.32 E
Leidschendam 52 52.05 N 4.24 E
Leie (Lys) ≃ 50 51.03 N 3.43 E
Leiferde 52 52.26 N 10.26 E
Leigh, N.Z. 172 36.17 S 174.49 E
Leigh, Eng., U.K. 44 53.30 N 2.33 W
Leigh, Eng., U.K. 260 51.12 N 0.13 E
Leigh ≃ 169 38.06 S 144.03 E
Leigh Canal ≊ 262 53.28 N 2.21 W
Leigh Creek 166 30.28 S 138.25 E
Leighlinbridge 48 52.44 N 6.59 W
Leigh-on-Sea 42 51.33 N 0.38 E
Leighton 194 34.42 N 87.31 W
Leighton Buzzard 42 51.55 N 0.40 W
Leikanger 26 61.10 N 6.52 E
Leiktho 110 19.13 N 96.35 E
Leimen 56 49.21 N 8.41 E
Leimstruth 56 50.59 N 8.19 E
Lein ≃ 56 48.54 N 10.01 E
Leinan 184 50.30 N 107.46 W
Leinburg 60 49.27 N 11.19 E
Leine ≃ 52 52.43 N 9.36 E
Leinefelde, Dtsch. 52 51.23 N 10.20 E
Leinefelde, Dtsch. 54 51.23 N 10.20 E
Leinfelden-Echterdingen 56 48.41 N 9.08 E
Leingarten 56 49.09 N 9.07 E
Leinster 162 27.51 S 120.36 E
Leinster □[9] 48 53.05 N 7.00 W
Leinster, Mount ∧ 48 52.37 N 6.44 W
Leintwardine 42 52.23 N 2.51 W
Leipalingis 76 54.05 N 23.51 E
Leipheim 58 48.27 N 10.13 E
Leipoldtville 158 32.14 S 18.30 E
Leipsic, De., U.S. 208 39.14 N 75.31 W
Leipsic, In., U.S. 218 38.40 N 86.22 W
Leipsic, Oh., U.S. 216 41.05 N 83.59 W
Leipsic ≃ 208 39.15 N 75.24 W
Leipzig 54 51.19 N 12.20 E
Leiria 34 39.45 N 8.48 W
Leirvik 26 59.45 N 5.30 E
Leisach 64 46.48 N 12.45 E
Leishendian 107 28.58 N 106.40 E
Leisi 76 58.34 N 22.39 E
Leisler, Mount ∧ 162 23.28 S 129.17 E
Leisnig 54 51.09 N 12.56 E
Leiston 42 52.12 N 1.34 E
Leisure City 220 25.29 N 80.25 W
Leitariegos, Puerto de)(34 43.00 N 6.25 W
Leitchfield 194 37.28 N 86.17 W
Leiters Ford 216 41.07 N 86.23 W
Leith 46 55.59 N 3.10 W
Leith, Water of ≃ 46 55.59 N 3.11 W
Leitha (Lajta) ≃ 61 47.54 N 17.17 E
Leithagebirge ⋏ 61 47.52 N 16.35 E
Leithe ⬥[8] 263 51.29 N 7.06 E
Leith Hill ∧[2] 42 51.11 N 0.23 W
Leitre 164 2.50 S 141.40 E
Leitrim 48 54.00 N 8.04 W
Leitrim □[6] 48 54.20 N 8.20 W
Leitzkau 54 52.03 N 11.57 E
Leixi 100 27.10 N 112.52 E
Leixlip 48 53.22 N 6.29 W
Leiyang 100 26.24 N 112.51 E
Lei Yue Mun ꙋ 271d 22.16 N 114.14 E
Leizhou Bandao ≻[1] 102 21.15 N 110.09 E
Leizhuang 98 39.47 N 118.34 E
Lejasciems 76 57.17 N 26.35 E
Lek ≃ 52 51.55 N 4.34 E
Lékana 152 2.19 S 14.36 E
Le Kef → El Kef 148 36.11 N 8.43 E
Lékéti ≃ 152 1.36 S 14.57 E
Lekhainá 38 37.56 N 21.17 E
Lekir 114 4.07 N 100.44 E
Lekitobi 112 1.58 S 124.33 E
Lekkeroog 158 30.43 S 20.00 E
Lekkerwater 156 23.38 S 17.14 E
Lekma ≃ 80 58.18 N 52.04 E
Łeknice 54 51.35 N 14.45 E
Lékoni ≃ 152 1.11 S 13.16 E
Lekotero 152 0.46 S 23.51 E
Lékoumou □[5] 152 3.00 S 13.30 E
Le Kreïder 148 34.06 N 0.02 E
Le Kremlin-Bicêtre 261 48.49 N 2.21 E
Leksand 26 60.44 N 14.59 E
Leksberg 40 58.41 N 13.49 E
Leksozero, ozero ⊜ 24 63.46 N 30.58 E
Leksvik 26 63.40 N 10.37 E
Lela 152 5.03 S 12.29 E
Le Lac-d'Issarlès 62 44.49 N 4.04 E
Le Lamentin 240e 14.37 N 61.01 W
Leland, Il., U.S. 216 41.37 N 88.48 W
Leland, Mi., U.S. 190 45.01 N 85.45 W
Leland, Ms., U.S. 194 33.24 N 90.53 W
Leland Grove 219 39.47 N 89.41 W
Leland Lake ⊜ 224 47.53 N 122.53 W
Lelång ⊜ 26 59.08 N 12.10 E
Lelant 42 50.11 N 5.26 W
Le Laus 62 44.31 N 6.09 E
Le Lauzet-Ubaye 62 44.26 N 6.26 E
Le Lavandou 62 43.08 N 6.22 E
Lel'čycy 78 51.47 N 28.19 E
Leleiwi Point ≻ 229d 19.44 N 155.00 W
Leleque 254 42.23 S 71.03 W
Leles 115a 7.07 S 107.53 E
Lelewau 112 3.02 S 121.05 E
Lélex 58 46.18 N 5.57 E
Le Liège 50 47.13 N 1.06 E
Le Limbé 238 19.42 N 72.24 W
Leling 98 37.45 N 117.12 E
Lelingluang 164 7.09 S 131.43 E
Lelintah 164 2.03 S 130.16 E
Le Lion-d'Angers 32 47.38 N 0.43 W
Leli Shan ∧ 120 33.26 N 81.42 E
Le Locle 58 47.03 N 6.45 E
Lelogama 112 9.44 S 123.57 E
Le Lorrain 240e 14.50 N 61.04 W
Le Luc 62 43.23 N 6.19 E
Le Lude 50 47.39 N 0.09 E
Lelydorp 250 5.42 N 55.16 W
Lelystad 52 52.31 N 5.27 E
Lema 150 12.57 N 4.14 E
Lemahabang 115a 6.17 S 107.27 E
Le Maire, Estrecho de ꙋ 254 54.50 S 65.00 W
Léman, Lac → Geneva, Lake ⊜ 58 46.25 N 6.30 E
Lemankoa 175e 5.02 S 154.35 E
Le Mans 50 48.00 N 0.12 E
Le Marin 240e 14.28 N 60.53 W
Le Markstein 58 47.56 N 7.02 E
Le Mars 198 42.47 N 96.09 W
Lema Shilindi 144 4.55 N 42.02 E
Lemay 219 38.32 N 90.17 W
Lemay, Lac ⊜ 186 50.35 N 68.25 W
Lembach 56 49.00 N 7.48 E
Lembach im Mühlkreis 60 48.29 N 13.53 E
Lemba-Gaba 273b 4.27 S 15.18 E
Lembak 112 0.52 N 117.32 E
Lembang 115a 6.49 S 107.36 E
Lembeck 52 51.45 N 7.00 E
Lembeek 50 50.43 N 4.13 E
Lembeh, Pulau I 112 1.26 N 125.13 E
Lembeni 154 3.47 S 37.37 E
Lemberg, Sk., Can. 184 50.44 N 103.13 W
Lemberg, Dtsch. 56 49.10 N 7.39 E
Lemberg, Fr. 56 49.00 N 7.23 E
Lemberg → L'viv, Ukr. 78 49.50 N 24.00 E
Lemberg ∧ 58 48.09 N 8.45 E
Lembruch 52 52.31 N 8.22 E
Lembu, Gunung ∧ 114 4.12 N 97.24 E
Lemdiyya 148 36.12 N 2.50 E
Leme 255 22.12 S 47.24 W
Leme, Morro do ∧[2] 287a 22.58 S 43.10 W
Le Mée-sur-Seine 261 48.32 N 2.38 E
Lemei Rock ∧ 224 46.01 N 121.46 W
Lemele 52 52.27 N 6.25 E
Le Mêle-sur-Sarthe 50 48.31 N 0.21 E
Lemene ≃ 64 45.37 N 12.53 E
Lemeris, Cape ≻ 164 3.15 S 152.03 E
Le Merlerault 50 48.42 N 0.18 E
Lemery 116 13.53 N 120.55 E
Lemeškino 80 51.01 N 44.27 E
Le Mesle 261 48.43 N 1.41 E
Le Mesnil-Amelot 261 49.01 N 2.36 E
Le Mesnil-Aubry 261 49.03 N 2.24 E
Le Mesnil-le-Roi 261 48.56 N 2.08 E
Le Mesnil-Saint-Denis 261 48.45 N 1.58 E
Le Mesnil-sur-Oger 50 48.57 N 4.01 E
Lemesós (Limassol) 130 34.40 N 33.02 E
Lemeta 180 64.52 N 147.44 W
Lemförde 52 52.28 N 8.22 E
Lemfu 152 5.18 S 15.13 E
Lemgo 52 52.02 N 8.54 E
Lemhi ≃ 202 45.12 N 113.53 W
Lemhi Pass)(202 44.58 N 113.27 W
Lemhi Range ⋏ 202 44.30 N 113.25 W
Lemie 62 45.14 N 7.17 E
Lemierzyce 54 52.35 N 14.56 E
Lemieux Islands II 176 64.30 N 64.40 W
Lemin 102 21.11 N 109.42 E
Leming 196 29.04 N 98.29 W
Lemitar 200 34.09 N 106.54 W
Lemland I 26 60.03 N 20.09 E
Lemmatsi 76 58.20 N 26.37 E
Lemmenjoen kansallispuisto ♠ 24 68.40 N 26.00 E
Lemmer 52 52.50 N 5.42 E
Lemmon 198 45.56 N 102.09 W
Lemmon, Mount ∧ 200 32.26 N 110.47 W
Lemnos → Límnos I 38 39.54 N 25.21 E
Lemoenshoek 158 33.51 S 20.51 E
Lemoine, Lac ⊜ 190 48.00 N 78.00 W
Lemon, Lake ⊜ 218 39.16 N 86.25 W
Le Monastier 62 44.56 N 4.00 E
Lemoncove 204 36.23 N 119.01 W
Lemon Creek ≃ 276 40.31 N 74.12 W
Le Monêtier-les-Bains 62 44.59 N 6.31 E
Lemon Grove 228 32.44 N 117.01 W
Lemon Heights 280 33.46 N 117.48 W
Lemont, Il., U.S. 216 41.40 N 88.00 W
Lemont, Pa., U.S. 214 40.49 N 77.49 W
Le Montet 32 46.25 N 3.03 E
Le Mont-Saint-Michel ʋ[1] 32 48.38 N 1.32 W
Lemoore 226 36.18 N 119.46 W
Lemoore Naval Air Station ■ 226 36.15 N 119.57 W
Lemoro 112 1.25 S 121.05 E
Le Moule 241o 16.20 N 61.21 W
Le Moutier 261 48.50 N 1.42 E
LeMoyne, P.Q., Can. 275a 45.31 N 73.29 W
Lemoyne, Oh., U.S. 214 41.30 N 83.28 W
Lemoyne, Pa., U.S. 208 40.15 N 76.54 W
Lempa ≃ 236 13.14 N 88.49 W
Lempäälä 26 61.19 N 23.45 E
Lempe 112 1.40 S 120.14 E
Lempira □[5] 236 14.20 N 88.40 W
Lemro ≃ 110 20.25 N 93.20 E
Lemsid 148 26.32 N 13.49 W
Lemukutan, Pulau I 112 0.45 N 108.43 E
Le Murge ⋏[1] 68 40.52 N 16.42 E
Lemutan 112 3.03 N 115.49 E
Le Muy 62 43.28 N 6.33 E
Lemva ≃ 24 66.30 N 61.48 E
Lemvig 26 56.32 N 8.18 E
Lemwerder 52 53.10 N 8.37 E
Lemyethna 110 17.36 N 95.09 E
Len ≃ 260 51.16 N 0.31 E
Lena, Il., U.S. 190 42.22 N 89.49 W
Lena, Wi., U.S. 190 44.57 N 88.02 W
Lena ≃ 74 72.25 N 126.40 E
Lenangguar 115b 8.44 S 117.24 E
Lenape 285 39.55 N 75.38 W
Lenart 36 46.35 N 15.50 E
Lenasia 273d 26.17 S 27.50 E
Lenawee □[6] 216 41.53 N 84.04 W
Lencloître 32 46.49 N 0.20 E
Lençóis 255 12.34 S 41.23 W
Lençois Maranhenses, Parque Nacional dos ♠ 250 2.25 S 43.15 W
Lend 64 47.18 N 13.04 E
Lenda ≃ 154 1.20 N 28.01 E
Lendava 61 46.34 N 16.27 E
Lendelede 50 50.53 N 3.14 E
Lendery 24 63.26 N 31.03 E
Lendinara 64 45.05 N 11.36 E
Lendorf 64 46.50 N 13.26 E
Lendringsen 56 51.24 N 7.49 E
Le Neubourg 50 49.09 N 0.55 E
Lenga 114 2.17 N 102.49 E
Lengduqiao 106 30.27 N 119.15 E
Lengede 52 52.12 N 10.18 E
Lengefeld, Dtsch. 54 50.43 N 13.11 E
Lengefeld, Dtsch. 54 50.50 N 11.20 E
Lengelscheid 263 51.08 N 7.40 E
Lengenfeld, Dtsch. 54 50.34 N 12.22 E
Lengenfeld, Dtsch. 56 51.13 N 10.13 E
Lenger 85 42.12 N 69.54 E
Lengerich, Dtsch. 52 52.11 N 7.50 E
Lengerich, Dtsch. 52 52.33 N 7.32 E
Lenggor ≃ 114 2.25 N 103.37 E
Lenggries 64 47.41 N 11.34 E
Lenghu 90 38.30 N 93.15 E
Lengjiagou 104 41.40 N 121.37 E
Lengkong 115a 7.32 S 112.04 E
Lenglingen ⊜ 26 64.14 N 13.45 E
Lengnau 58 47.11 N 7.22 E
Lengoué 152 1.13 N 15.43 E
Lengoué ≃ 152 0.49 N 15.47 E
Lengshuichang 107 29.27 N 106.26 E
Lengshuikeng 100 27.55 N 117.08 E
Lengshuitan 102 26.27 N 111.35 E
Lengua de Vaca, Punta ≻ 252 30.14 S 71.38 W
Lengulu 154 3.15 N 26.30 E
Lengwe National Park ♠ 154 16.15 S 34.45 E
Lengzipu 104 41.42 N 122.47 E
Lenham 42 51.14 N 0.43 E
Lenhartsville 208 40.34 N 75.53 W
Lenhovda 26 57.00 N 15.17 E
Lenina, gora ∧[2] 265b 55.42 N 37.31 E
Lenina, ozero ⊜ 78 48.33 N 35.12 E
Lenina, pik ∧ 85 39.20 N 72.55 E
Leninabad → Chudžand 85 40.17 N 69.37 E
Leninakan → Kumajri 84 40.48 N 43.50 E
Lenin Central Stadium ♠ 265b 55.43 N 37.33 E
Lenin-Džol 85 41.03 N 72.38 E
Lenine 78 45.18 N 35.47 E
Leningori 84 42.07 N 44.29 E
Leningrad → Sankt-Peterburg 76 59.55 N 30.15 E
Leningrado → Sankt-Peterburg 76 59.55 N 30.15 E
Leningrad Oblast' □[4] 24 60.00 N 32.00 E
Leningradskaja 78 46.19 N 39.24 E
Leningradskij 85 38.06 N 70.01 E
Leningradskoje 86 53.33 N 71.35 E
Lenino ⬥[8] 265b 55.37 N 37.41 E
Leninogorsk, Kaz. 86 50.27 N 83.32 E
Leninogorsk, Ross. 80 54.36 N 52.30 E
Leninpol' 85 42.29 N 71.55 E
Leninsk, Kaz. 86 45.40 N 63.20 E
Leninsk, Ross. 80 46.08 N 43.46 E
Leninsk, Ross. 80 48.42 N 45.11 E
Leninsk, Ross. 86 54.55 N 59.54 E
Leninsk, Uzb. 85 40.38 N 72.15 E
Leninskaja Sloboda 80 56.05 N 44.28 E
Lenins'ke, Ukr. 78 45.16 N 35.54 E
Lenins'ke, Ukr. 78 51.27 N 33.18 E
Lenins'ke, Ukr. 83 48.05 N 39.31 E
Leninskij, Kaz. 86 52.13 N 76.47 E
Leninskij, Ross. 80 46.31 N 44.28 E
Leninskij, Ross. 80 56.34 N 45.56 E
Leninskij, Ross. 82 54.18 N 37.28 E
Leninsk-Kuzneckij 86 54.38 N 86.10 E
Leninskoje, Kaz. 80 49.03 N 49.56 E
Leninskoje, Kaz. 85 41.45 N 69.23 E
Leninskoje, Kaz. 86 54.04 N 65.22 E
Leninskoje, Kaz. 86 50.44 N 57.53 E
Leninskoje, Kyrg. 85 40.42 N 73.11 E
Leninskoje, Ross. 80 58.19 N 47.06 E
Leninskoje, Ross. 89 47.56 N 132.38 E
Lenin-Stausee → Kujbyševskoje vodochranilišče ⊜[1] 80 54.30 N 48.30 E
Leninžol 80 49.20 N 47.05 E
Lenk 58 46.28 N 7.27 E
Lenkerville 208 40.32 N 76.58 W
Len'ki 86 52.57 N 80.26 E
Lenmalu 164 1.44 S 130.13 E
Lennard, Mount ∧[2] 168a 33.21 S 115.53 E
Lenne ≃ 56 51.25 N 7.30 E
Lennegebirge ⋏ 52 51.15 N 8.00 E
Lennep 56 51.12 N 7.16 E
Lennep ⬥[8] 52 51.12 N 7.16 E
Lennestadt 56 51.08 N 8.01 E
Lenni 285 39.54 N 75.27 W
Lenningen 58 48.33 N 9.28 E
Lennon 216 42.59 N 83.56 W
Lennonville 162 27.58 S 117.50 E
Lennox, Ca., U.S. 228 33.56 N 118.21 W
Lennox, S.D., U.S. 198 43.21 N 96.53 W
Lennox □[9] 46 56.02 N 4.15 W
Lennox, Isla I 254 55.18 S 66.50 W
Lennox and Addington □[6] 212 44.30 N 77.00 W
Lennoxtown 46 55.59 N 4.12 W
Lennoxville 206 45.22 N 71.51 W
Leno 64 45.22 N 10.13 E
Lenoir 192 35.54 N 81.32 W
Lenoir City 192 35.47 N 84.15 W
Le Noirmont 58 47.13 N 6.58 E
Lenola 66 41.24 N 13.28 E
Lenora 60 48.56 N 13.48 E
Lenore Lake ⊜ 184 52.30 N 105.00 W
Le Nouvion-en-Thiérache 50 50.01 N 3.47 E
Lenox, Ga., U.S. 192 31.16 N 83.27 W
Lenox, Ia., U.S. 198 40.52 N 94.33 W
Lenox, Ma., U.S. 207 42.22 N 73.17 W
Lenox, Tn., U.S. 194 36.05 N 89.29 W
Lenox Dale 207 42.20 N 73.14 W
Lens 50 50.26 N 2.50 E
Lensahn 54 54.13 N 10.52 E
Lensk 74 61.00 N 114.50 E
Lenskoje 86 58.09 N 63.11 E
Lenswood 168b 34.55 S 138.49 E
Lentate sul Seveso 266b 45.41 N 9.07 E
Lentechi 84 42.48 N 42.44 E
Lenti 30 46.37 N 16.33 E
Lenting 60 48.48 N 11.28 E
Lentini 70 37.17 N 15.00 E
Lentner 219 39.43 N 92.09 W
Lentua ⊜ 26 64.14 N 29.36 E
Lentvaris 76 54.39 N 25.03 E
Lenwood 228 34.53 N 117.07 W
Lenya 110 11.28 N 99.00 E
Lenya ≃ 110 11.40 N 98.43 E
Lenz 273d 26.19 S 27.49 E
Lenzburg 58 47.23 N 8.11 E
Lenzen 54 53.05 N 11.28 E
Lenzerheide (Lai) 58 46.44 N 9.33 E
Lenzkirch 58 47.52 N 8.12 E
Léo, Burkina 150 11.06 N 2.06 W
Leo, In., U.S. 216 41.13 N 85.00 W
Leoben 61 47.23 N 15.06 E
Leo Carrillo State Beach ♠ 228 34.03 N 118.56 W
Léogâne 238 18.31 N 72.38 W
Leogang 64 47.26 N 12.45 E
Leola, Ar., U.S. 194 34.10 N 92.35 W
Leola, Pa., U.S. 208 40.05 N 76.11 W
Leola, S.D., U.S. 198 45.43 N 98.56 W
Leominster, Eng., U.K. 42 52.14 N 2.45 W
Leominster, Ma., U.S. 207 42.31 N 71.45 W
León, Esp. 34 42.36 N 5.34 W
Léon, Fr. 32 43.53 N 1.18 W
León, Nic. 236 12.26 N 86.53 W
Leon, Pil. 116 10.47 N 122.23 E
Leon, Ia., U.S. 190 40.44 N 93.44 W
Leon, Ks., U.S. 198 37.41 N 96.46 W
Leon, N.Y., U.S. 210 42.18 N 79.01 W
León □[4] 34 42.35 N 6.00 W
León □[5] 236 12.35 N 86.35 W
Leon □[6] 222 31.18 N 95.55 W
León □[9] 34 42.00 N 6.00 W
Leon ≃ 196 30.59 N 97.24 W
Leon, Arroyo ≃ 282 37.28 N 122.25 W
León, Montes de ⋏ 34 42.30 N 6.18 W
Leona 222 31.09 N 95.58 W
Leona ≃ 196 28.45 N 99.11 W
Leona, Punta ≻ 236 9.41 N 84.41 W
Leonard, Mi., U.S. 214 42.51 N 83.08 W
Leonard, Mo., U.S. 219 39.53 N 92.10 W
Leonard, N.D., U.S. 198 46.39 N 97.14 W
Leonard, Tx., U.S. 196 33.22 N 96.14 W
Leonardo 276 40.25 N 74.03 W
Leonardo da Vinci, Aeroporto Intercontinentale ⊠ 66 41.48 N 12.13 E
Leonardsburg 214 40.21 N 82.59 W
Leonardsville 210 42.48 N 75.15 W
Leonardtown 208 38.17 N 76.38 W
Leonardville, Namibia 156 23.29 S 18.49 E
Leonardville, Ks., U.S. 198 39.21 N 96.51 W
Leona Vicario 200 32.10 N 115.10 W
Leonberg 56 48.48 N 9.01 E
Leondale 273d 26.18 S 28.12 E
Leondárion 267c 37.59 N 23.51 E
León [de los Aldamas] 234 21.07 N 101.40 W
Leonding 61 48.16 N 14.15 E
Leone 174u 14.20 S 170.47 W
Leone, Golfo del → Lion, Golfe du ⊂ 32 43.00 N 4.00 E
Leone, Monte ∧ 58 46.15 N 8.06 E
Leones 252 32.39 S 62.18 W
Leonessa 66 42.34 N 12.58 E
Leonforte 70 37.38 N 14.23 E
Leongatha 169 38.29 S 145.57 E
León Guzmán 196 25.31 N 103.34 W
Leonia 276 40.51 N 73.59 W
Leonicha 76 59.37 N 38.51 E
Leonidas 216 42.01 N 85.21 W
Leonídhion 38 37.10 N 22.52 E
Leonidovo 89 49.17 N 142.50 E
Leon Junction 222 31.20 N 97.36 W
Leonora 162 28.53 S 121.20 E
Leonovo 82 55.26 N 38.42 E
Leontjevka 85 43.03 N 69.50 E
Leontjevo 76 58.58 N 36.37 E
Leonville 194 30.28 N 91.58 W
Leopard 285 40.01 N 75.27 W
Leopold 169 38.11 S 144.28 E
Leopold and Astrid Coast ⊥[2] 9 67.10 S 84.10 E
Leopoldau ⬥[8] 264b 48.16 N 16.27 E
Leopold Downs 162 17.52 S 125.25 E
Léopold II, Lac → Mai-Ndombe, Lac ⊜ 152 2.00 S 18.20 E
Leopoldina 256 21.32 S 42.38 W
Leopoldkanaal ≊ 50 51.14 N 3.46 E
Leopoldo de Bulhões 255 16.37 S 48.46 W
Leopoldo y Astrid, Costa → Leopold and Astrid Coast ⊥[2] 9 67.10 S 84.10 E
Leopoldsburg 56 51.07 N 5.15 E
Leopoldsdorf 264b 48.06 N 16.24 E
Leopoldshagen 54 53.46 N 13.53 E
Leopoldstadt ⬥[8] 264b 48.13 N 16.23 E
Léopoldville → Kinshasa 152 4.18 S 15.18 E
Leoti 198 38.28 N 101.21 W
Leova 38 46.29 N 28.15 E
Leoville 184 53.37 N 107.35 W
Le Pailly 58 47.48 N 5.25 E
Le Palais 32 47.21 N 3.09 W
Lepanto, C.R. 236 9.57 N 85.02 W
Lepanto → Návpaktos, Ellás 38 38.23 N 21.50 E
Lepanto, Ar., U.S. 194 35.36 N 90.19 W
Lepar, Pulau I 112 2.57 S 106.50 E
Le Parcq 50 50.23 N 2.06 E
Le Pâté 261 48.32 N 2.18 E
Lepe 34 37.15 N 7.12 W
Le Péage-de-Roussillon 62 45.22 N 4.48 E
Le Pecq 261 48.54 N 2.07 E
Lepel' 76 54.53 N 28.42 E
Le Pellerin 32 47.12 N 1.45 W
Lepembusu, Keli ∧ 115b 8.40 S 121.49 E
Le Perray-en-Yuelines 261 48.42 N 1.51 E
Le Perreux-sur-Marne 261 48.51 N 2.30 E
Lepeški 82 56.05 N 38.07 E
Le Petit-Clamart ʋ 261 48.47 N 2.14 E
Le Petit-Couronne 50 49.23 N 1.01 E
Le Petit-Quevilly 50 49.26 N 1.02 E
Lephepe 156 23.20 S 25.50 E
Lépi 152 12.52 S 15.26 E
Le Piastre 66 44.00 N 10.50 E
Lepihué 254 41.37 S 73.36 W
Le Pin 261 48.55 N 2.38 E
Le Pin-au-Haras 50 48.44 N 0.09 E
L'Épine, Fr. 56 48.58 N 4.28 E
L'Épine, Fr. 261 48.32 N 2.21 E
Leping 100 28.57 N 117.05 E
Lepini, Monti ⋏ 66 41.35 N 13.00 E
Lépin-le-Lac 62 45.32 N 5.47 E
L'Épiphanie 206 45.51 N 73.30 W
Le Plessis-aux-Bois 261 49.00 N 2.46 E
Le Plessis-Belleville 50 49.06 N 2.46 E
Le Plessis-Bouchard 261 49.00 N 2.14 E
Le Plessis-Pâté 261 48.37 N 2.20 E
Le Plessis-Trévise 261 48.49 N 2.34 E
Leplyavo 78 49.48 N 31.32 E
Lépo, Lagoa de ⊜ 152 17.08 S 19.00 E
Le Poët 62 44.17 N 5.53 E
Le Pont 58 46.40 N 6.20 E
Le Pont-de-Beauvoisin 62 45.32 N 5.40 E
Le Pont-de-Montvert 62 44.22 N 3.45 E
Le Pontel 261 48.49 N 1.53 E
Lepontine, Alpi ⋏ 58 46.25 N 8.40 E
Leporano 68 40.23 N 17.20 E
Le Port 157c 20.55 S 55.18 E
Le Portel 50 50.42 N 1.34 E
Le Port-Marly 261 48.53 N 2.06 E
Le Pouzin 62 44.45 N 4.45 E
Leppävirta 26 62.29 N 27.47 E
Lepperton 172 39.04 S 174.13 E
Leppin 54 52.53 N 11.34 E
Leppington 274a 33.58 S 150.49 E
Le Pradet 62 43.06 N 6.01 E
Lepreau, Point ≻ 186 45.04 N 66.27 W
Le Prêcheur 240e 14.48 N 61.14 W
Le Pré-Saint-Gervais 261 48.53 N 2.25 E
Le Prese 58 46.18 N 10.04 E
Lepsinsk 86 45.32 N 80.37 E
Lepsy, Kaz. 86 46.18 N 78.20 E
Lepsy, Kaz. 86 46.15 N 78.55 E
Le Puy 62 45.02 N 3.53 E
Le Quesnoy 50 50.15 N 3.38 E
Léraba ≃ 150 9.42 N 4.35 W
Le Raincy 261 48.54 N 2.31 E
Le Rayol-Canadel-sur-Mer 62 43.10 N 6.28 E
Le Raysville 210 41.51 N 76.11 W
Lerberget 41 56.11 N 12.33 E
Lercara Friddi 70 37.45 N 13.36 E
Lerche ⬥[8] 263 51.37 N 7.43 E
Lerderderg ≃ 169 37.42 S 144.30 E
Lerdo → Ciudad Lerdo 196 25.32 N 103.32 W
Léré, Fr. 50 47.28 N 2.52 E
Léré, Mali 150 15.43 N 4.55 W
Lere, Nig. 150 9.43 N 9.21 E
Léré, Tchad 146 9.39 N 14.13 E
Lereh 164 3.08 S 139.54 E
Lerek ∧ 114 3.47 N 102.47 E
Le Reposoir 58 46.00 N 6.33 E
Leri ≃ 42 52.32 N 4.02 W
Leribe 158 28.58 S 28.00 E
Lerici 64 44.04 N 9.55 E
Lérida, Col. 246 0.10 N 70.42 W
Lérida → Lleida, Esp. 34 41.37 N 0.37 E
Lerik 84 38.46 N 48.25 E
Lérins, Îles de II 62 43.31 N 7.03 E
Lerma 34 42.02 N 3.45 W
Lerma ≃ 234 20.13 N 102.46 W
Lermontovka 89 47.10 N 134.20 E
Lermoos 64 47.24 N 10.53 E
Lerno, Monte ∧ 71 40.37 N 9.10 E
Le Robert 240e 14.41 N 60.57 W
Léros I, Ellás 38 37.08 N 26.52 E
Léros I, Ellás 267c 37.59 N 23.32 E
Lérouville 56 48.47 N 5.33 E
Leroux Wash V 200 34.54 N 110.12 W
Le Roy, Il., U.S. 216 40.21 N 88.45 W
Leroy, In., U.S. 216 41.22 N 87.16 W
Le Roy, Ks., U.S. 198 38.05 N 95.38 W
Le Roy, Mn., U.S. 190 43.30 N 92.30 W
Le Roy, N.Y., U.S. 210 42.58 N 77.59 W
Le Roy, Pa., U.S. 210 41.41 N 76.43 W
Leroy, Tx., U.S. 222 31.44 N 97.01 W
Lerum 26 57.46 N 12.16 E
Le Russey 58 47.10 N 6.44 E
Lerwick 46a 60.09 N 1.09 W
Léry 206 45.21 N 73.48 W
Lesa 62 45.50 N 8.34 E
Les Abrets 62 45.32 N 5.35 E
Les Abymes 241o 16.16 N 61.31 W
Lesage, Lac ⊜ 206 46.19 N 75.03 W
Le Saint-Esprit 240e 14.34 N 60.57 W
Les Aix-d'Angillon 50 47.12 N 2.34 E
Les Allues 62 45.26 N 6.33 E
Les Alluets-le-Roi 261 48.55 N 1.55 E
Les Andelys 50 49.15 N 1.25 E
Les Anses-d'Arlets 240e 14.29 N 61.05 W
Le Sappy-en-Chartreuse 62 45.16 N 5.47 E
Les Arcs 62 43.27 N 6.29 E
Lesatima, Oldoinyo ∧ 154 0.19 S 36.37 E
Le Sauze 62 44.22 N 6.41 E
Les Baux-en-Provence 62 43.45 N 4.48 E
Les Bézards 50 47.48 N 2.44 E
Les Bordes 261 48.39 N 1.58 E
Les Borges Blanques 34 41.31 N 0.52 E
Lesbos → Lésvos I 38 39.10 N 26.20 E
Les Bouchoux 58 46.18 N 5.49 E
Les Bréviaires 261 48.42 N 1.49 E
Lesbury 44 55.24 N 1.36 W
L'Escarène 62 43.50 N 7.21 E
Les Cayes 238 18.12 N 73.45 W
Les Chaises 261 48.39 N 1.42 E
Les Chapieux 62 45.42 N 6.44 E
Leschenault, Cape ≻ 162 31.18 S 115.27 E
Leschenault Estuary ⊂[1] 168a 33.15 S 115.42 E
Lesches 261 48.54 N 2.47 E
Les Clayes-sous-Bois 261 48.49 N 1.59 E
Les Contamines-Montjoie 62 45.50 N 6.44 E
Les Diablerets 58 46.21 N 7.10 E
Les Diablerets ∧ 58 46.19 N 7.12 E
Lesdiboderi 146 8.28 N 12.35 E
Les Echarmeaux 58 46.10 N 4.27 E
Les Échelles 62 45.26 N 5.45 E
Les Écureuils 206 46.39 N 71.43 W
Le Semnoz ∧ 62 45.48 N 6.07 E
Leseru 154 0.35 N 35.10 E
Les Essarts 32 46.46 N 1.14 W
Les Essarts-le-Roi 261 48.43 N 1.54 E
Les Estables 62 44.54 N 4.10 E
Les Étangs 56 49.09 N 6.23 E
Les Fonts 266d 41.32 N 2.02 E
Les Fourgs 58 46.50 N 6.25 E
Les Galleries d'Anjou ⬥[9] 275a 45.35 N 73.34 W
Les Gâtines 261 48.48 N 1.58 E
Les Gets 58 46.09 N 6.40 E
Les Granges-le-Roi 261 48.30 N 2.01 E
Les Grésillons 261 48.56 N 2.01 E
Les Halles 62 45.43 N 4.26 E
Leshan 107 29.34 N 103.45 E
Les Haudères 58 46.05 N 7.31 E
Les Hautes-Rivières 56 49.53 N 4.50 E
Les Herbiers 32 46.52 N 1.01 W
Les Houches 62 45.53 N 6.48 E
Lesignano de'Bagni 64 44.39 N 10.18 E
Lésigny 261 48.45 N 2.37 E
Lesima, Monte ∧ 62 44.41 N 9.15 E
Lesina 68 41.52 N 15.21 E
Lesina, Lago di ⊂ 68 41.53 N 15.26 E
Les Islettes 56 49.06 N 5.00 E
Lesjaskog 26 62.15 N 8.22 E
Lesjöfors 40 59.59 N 14.11 E
Lesken 84 43.16 N 43.48 E
Lesko 30 49.29 N 22.21 E
Leskovac 38 42.59 N 21.57 E
Leskov Island I 18 56.40 S 28.10 W
Les'ky 78 49.19 N 32.13 E
Les Laumes 58 47.32 N 4.27 E
Les Lecques 62 43.11 N 5.40 E
Leslie, S. Afr. 158 26.27 S 28.55 E
Leslie, Scot., U.K. 46 56.12 N 3.13 W
Leslie, Ar., U.S. 194 35.49 N 92.33 W
Leslie, Ga., U.S. 192 31.57 N 84.05 W
Leslie, Mi., U.S. 216 42.27 N 84.25 W
Leslie, W.V., U.S. 188 38.02 N 80.43 W
Les Lilas 261 48.53 N 2.25 E
Les Loges 261 48.34 N 2.03 E
Les Loges-en-Josas 261 48.46 N 2.09 E
Lesmahagow 46 55.39 N 3.55 W
Les Marécottes 58 46.07 N 7.00 E
Les Mées 62 44.02 N 5.59 E
Les Mesnuls 50 48.45 N 1.50 E
Lesmo 266b 45.39 N 9.18 E
Les Molières 261 48.40 N 2.04 E
Les Monges ∧ 62 44.16 N 6.12 E
Lesmont 50 48.26 N 4.25 E
Les Mosses 58 46.24 N 7.07 E
Lesmurdie Falls National Park ♠ 168a 32.01 S 116.04 E
Les Mureaux 261 49.00 N 1.55 E
Leśna 30 51.02 N 15.16 E
Lesneven 32 48.34 N 4.19 W
Les Neyrolles 58 46.08 N 5.38 E
Lešnica 38 44.39 N 19.19 E
Lesnoj, Ross. 24 59.48 N 52.08 E
Lesnoj, Ross. 80 54.11 N 40.27 E
Lesnoj, Ross. 86 56.57 N 67.15 E
Lesnoj ⬥[8] 265a 60.00 N 30.19 E
Lesnoje 76 58.17 N 35.32 E
Lesnoje Konobejevo 80 54.02 N 41.55 E
Lesnoje Mat'unino 80 53.27 N 47.26 E
Lesnoj Gorodok 265b 55.39 N 37.13 E
Lesnoj park ♠ 265a 59.59 N 30.21 E
Lesnyje Pol'any, Ross. 24 58.58 N 52.26 E
Lesnyje Pol'any, Ross. 265b 55.57 N 37.53 E
Lesogorsk, Ross. 80 55.06 N 43.56 E
Lesogorsk, Ross. 88 56.03 N 99.33 E
Lesogorsk, Ross. 89 49.27 N 142.08 E
Lesogorskij 24 61.02 N 28.53 E
Lesong, Gunung ∧ 114 2.44 N 103.17 E
Lesopil'noje 89 46.44 N 134.20 E
Lesosibirsk 86 58.16 N 92.29 E
Lesotho □[1], Afr. 138 29.30 S 28.30 E
Lesotho □[1], Afr. 158 29.30 S 28.30 E
Lesozavodsk 89 45.28 N 133.27 E
Lesozavodskij 24 66.44 N 32.49 E
Les Pavillons-sous-Bois 261 48.55 N 2.30 E
Les Pieux 32 49.31 N 1.48 W
Les Planches-en-Montagne 58 46.40 N 6.01 E
Les Ponts-de-Martel 58 46.54 N 6.41 E
Les Posets ∧ 34 42.39 N 0.25 E
Les Praz-de-Chamonix 58 45.56 N 6.52 E
Lesquin 50 50.35 N 3.07 E
Les Riceys 50 47.59 N 4.22 E
Les Roches-l'Evêque 50 47.47 N 0.53 E
Les Rousses 58 46.29 N 6.04 E
Les Ruelles 261 48.40 N 1.37 E
Les Sables-d'Olonne 32 46.30 N 1.47 W
Lessach 64 47.11 N 13.49 E
Les Saintes II 241o 15.52 N 61.37 W
Les Salles-sur-Verdon 62 43.46 N 6.12 E
Lessay 32 49.13 N 1.32 W
Les Scaffarels 62 43.57 N 6.41 E
Lesse ≃ 56 50.14 N 4.54 E
Lessebo 26 56.45 N 15.16 E
Lessen → Lessines 50 50.43 N 3.50 E
Lesser Antilles II 238 15.00 N 61.00 W
Lesser Caucasus ⋏ 84 41.00 N 44.35 E
Lesser Khingan Range → Xiao Hinggan Ling ⋏ 89 48.45 N 127.00 E
Lesser Slave ≃ 182 55.10 N 114.03 W
Lesser Slave Lake ⊜ 182 55.25 N 115.30 W
Lesser Sunda Islands → Tenggara, Nusa II 108 9.00 S 120.00 E
Lessines (Lessen) 50 50.43 N 3.50 E
Lessini, Monti ⋏ 64 45.41 N 11.13 E
L'Estaque 62 43.22 N 5.20 E
Leste ≃ 250 6.20 S 57.46 W
Lester, Pa., U.S. 285 39.52 N 75.17 W
Lester, Wa., U.S. 224 47.12 N 121.29 W
Lester B. Pearson International Airport ⊠ 212 43.41 N 79.38 W
Les Tessiers 62 44.24 N 4.16 E
Les Thilliers-en-Vexin 50 49.14 N 1.36 E
Lestijärvi 26 63.32 N 24.39 E
Lestijoki ≃ 26 64.04 N 23.38 E
Lestkov 60 49.54 N 12.52 E
Lestock 184 51.18 N 104.00 W
L'Estréchure 62 44.06 N 3.47 E
Les Trois-Îlets 240e 14.32 N 61.02 W
Les Trois Lacs ⊜ 206 45.48 N 71.54 W
Le Sueur 190 44.30 N 93.52 W
Le Sueur ≃ 190 44.07 N 94.03 W
Lesueur, Mount ∧[2] 162 30.10 S 115.11 E
Lešukonskoje 24 64.54 N 45.40 E
Les Ulis 261 48.41 N 2.11 E
Lesung, Tanjung ≻ 115a 6.28 S 105.40 E
Lesunovo 80 55.40 N 43.07 E
Les Vans 62 44.24 N 4.08 E
Les Verrières 58 46.54 N 6.30 E
Lésvos (Lesbos) I 38 39.10 N 26.20 E
Leszno 30 51.51 N 16.35 E
Leszno □[4] 30 51.45 N 16.45 E
Letälven ≃ 40 59.05 N 14.20 E
L'Étang-la-Ville 261 48.52 N 2.05 E
Letcher 198 43.53 N 98.08 W
Letchmore Heath 260 51.40 N 0.20 W
Letchworth 42 51.58 N 0.14 W
Letchworth State Park ♠ 210 42.42 N 77.56 W
Letea, Ostrovul I 38 45.20 N 29.20 E
Le Teil 62 44.33 N 4.41 E
Le Temple 261 49.00 N 1.58 E
Letenye 30 46.26 N 16.43 E
Le Tertre-Saint-Denis 261 48.56 N 1.36 E
Lethbridge, Austl. 274a 33.44 S 150.48 E
Lethbridge, Ab., Can. 182 49.42 N 112.50 W
Lethbridge, Nf., Can. 186 48.21 N 53.52 W

≃ River	Fluß	Río	Rivière	Rio	✦ Submarine Features	Untermeerische Objekte	Accidentes Submarinos	Formes de relief sous-marin	Acidentes submarinos
≊ Canal	Kanal	Canal	Canal	Canal	□ Political Unit	Politische Einheit	Unidad Politica	Entité politique	Unidade política
⌊ Waterfall, Rapids	Wasserfall, Stromschnellen	Cascada, Rápidos	Chute d'eau, Rapides	Cascata, Rápidos	ʋ Cultural Institution	Kulturelle Institution	Institución Cultural	Institution culturelle	Institução cultural
ꙋ Strait	Meeresstraße	Estrecho	Détroit	Estreito	⊥ Historical Site	Historische Stätte	Sitio Histórico	Site historique	Sitio histórico
⊂ Bay, Gulf	Bucht, Golf	Bahía, Golfo	Baie, Golfe	Baía, Golfo	♠ Recreational Site	Erholungs- und Ferienort	Sitio de Recreo	Centre de loisirs	Area de Lazer
⊜ Lake, Lakes	See, Seen	Lago, Lagos	Lac, Lacs	Lago, Lagos	⊠ Airport	Flughafen	Aeropuerto	Aéroport	Aeroporto
≡ Swamp	Sumpf	Pantano	Marais	Pântano	■ Military Installation	Militäranlage	Instalación Militar	Installation militaire	Instalação militar
⍂ Ice Features, Glacier	Eis- und Gletscherformen	Accidentes Glaciales	Formes glaciaires	Acidentes glaciares	⬥ Miscellaneous	Verschiedenes	Misceláneo	Divers	Diversos
⍑ Other Hydrographic Features	Andere Hydrographische Objekte	Otros Elementos Hidrográficos	Autres données hydrographiques	Outros acidentes hidrográficos					

Name	Page	Lat.°′	Long.°′
Le Theil-sur-Huisne	50	48.16 N	0.42 E
Lethem	246	3.23 N	59.48 W
Le Thillay	261	49.00 N	2.28 E
Le Thillot	58	47.53 N	6.46 E
Le Tholy	58	48.05 N	6.45 E
Le Thor	62	43.56 N	5.00 E
Le Thoronet	62	43.27 N	6.18 E
Leti, Kepulauan II	164	8.13 S	127.50 E
Leti, Pulau I	112	8.12 S	127.41 E
Leticia	246	4.09 S	69.57 W
Leting	98	39.27 N	118.53 E
Letino	68	41.26 N	14.17 E
Letjiesbos	158	32.34 S	22.16 E
Letka	24	59.36 N	49.22 E
Letlhakane	156	21.27 S	25.30 E
Letlhakeng	156	24.08 S	25.02 E
Letmathe	56	51.22 N	7.37 E
Letn'aja Zolotica	24	64.57 N	36.50 E
Letnerečenskij	24	64.17 N	34.23 E
Le Touquet-Paris-Plage	50	50.31 N	1.35 E
Le Touvet	62	45.21 N	5.57 E
Letovo	265b	55.34 N	37.24 E
Letpadan	110	17.47 N	95.45 E
Le Trait	50	49.28 N	0.49 E
Le Trayas	62	43.28 N	6.55 E
Le Tremblay-sur-Mauldre	261	48.47 N	1.53 E
Le Tréport	50	50.04 N	1.22 E
Letschin	54	52.39 N	14.21 E
Letsôk-aw Kyun I	110	11.37 N	98.15 E
Letter	52	52.24 N	9.38 E
Letterfrack	48	53.33 N	10.00 W
Letterkenny	48	54.57 N	7.44 W
Lettermullan	48	53.13 N	9.42 W
Letterston	42	51.56 N	5.00 W
Lettonie → Latvia □[1]	72	57.00 N	25.00 E
Letts	218	39.14 N	85.35 W
Letung	112	2.58 N	105.42 E
Letychiv	78	49.23 N	27.37 E
Letzlingen	54	52.26 N	11.29 E
Leu	38	44.11 N	24.00 E
Léua	152	11.34 S	20.32 E
Leuben	54	51.10 N	13.18 E
Leubnitz	54	50.43 N	12.21 E
Leubsdorf	54	50.48 N	13.08 E
Leuca	68	39.48 N	18.21 E
Leucate, Étang de C	32	42.51 N	3.00 E
Leuchars	46	56.23 N	2.53 W
Leuchtenberg	60	49.36 N	12.15 E
Leudeville	261	48.34 N	2.20 E
Leuenberger Forst •[3]	264a	52.40 N	13.53 E
Leuglay	58	47.49 N	4.48 E
Leuk	58	46.19 N	7.38 E
Leukerbad	58	46.23 N	7.38 E
Leulumoega	175a	13.49 S	171.55 W
Leumeah	274a	34.03 S	150.50 E
Leun	56	50.33 N	8.21 E
Leuna	54	51.19 N	12.01 E
Leupoldsgrün	54	50.17 N	11.47 E
Leura	170	33.43 S	150.20 E
Leura, Mount ∧[2]	169	38.15 S	143.09 E
Leuser, Gunung ∧	114	3.45 N	97.11 E
Leušinskij Tuman, ozero ⊜	86	59.42 N	65.35 E
Leutenberg	54	50.34 N	11.28 E
Leutersdorf	54	50.57 N	14.40 E
Leutershausen	56	49.18 N	10.24 E
Leutesdorf	56	50.27 N	7.23 E
Leutkirch	58	47.49 N	10.01 E
Leuven (Louvain)	56	50.53 N	4.42 E
Leuville-sur-Orge	261	48.37 N	2.16 E
Leuwiliang	115a	6.34 S	106.37 E
Leuze, Bel.	50	50.36 N	3.36 E
Leuze, Bel.	56	50.34 N	4.54 E
Levack	190	46.38 N	81.23 W
Levádhia	38	38.25 N	22.54 E
Levaja Mama ≃	88	57.10 N	111.54 E
Le Val-d'Ajol	58	47.55 N	6.29 E
Le Val-d'Albian	261	48.45 N	2.11 E
Levallois-Perret	261	48.54 N	2.18 E
Le Val-Saint-Germain	261	48.34 N	2.04 E
Levan	200	39.33 N	111.51 W
Levanger	26	63.45 N	11.18 E
Levanna, Monte ∧	62	45.24 N	7.12 E
Levant, Île du I	62	43.03 N	6.28 E
Levante, Riviera di ±[2]	62	44.15 N	9.30 E
Levanto	62	44.10 N	9.38 E
Levanzo	70	37.59 N	12.20 E
Levanzo, Isola di I	70	38.00 N	12.20 E
Levaši	84	42.27 N	47.20 E
Le Vauclin	240e	14.33 N	60.51 W
Levdym	86	60.29 N	66.19 E
Leveaux Mountain ∧[2]	190	47.37 N	90.47 W
Levél	61	47.54 N	17.12 E
Level, Isla I	254	44.29 S	74.23 W
Level Green	279b	40.24 N	79.43 W
Levelland	196	33.35 N	102.22 W
Levelock	180	59.07 N	156.52 W
Level Park	216	42.22 N	85.18 W
Leven, Eng., U.K.	44	53.53 N	0.19 W
Leven, Scot., U.K.	46	56.12 N	3.00 W
Leven ≃, Eng., U.K.	44	54.14 N	3.01 W
Leven ≃, Eng., U.K.	44	54.31 N	1.21 W
Leven, Loch ⊜, Scot., U.K.	46	56.41 N	5.07 W
Leven, Loch ⊜, Scot., U.K.	46	56.12 N	3.22 W
Leven Point ›	158	27.55 S	32.35 E
Levens	62	43.52 N	7.13 E
Levenshulme •[8]	262	53.27 N	2.10 W
Levent	130	38.27 N	37.52 E
Leventina, Valle V	58	46.25 N	8.52 E
Leveque, Cape ›	162	16.24 S	122.56 E
Leverano	68	40.17 N	18.00 E
Leverburgh	46	57.45 N	7.00 W
Leveretts Chapel	222	32.19 N	94.55 W
Levering	190	45.38 N	84.47 W
Leverkusen	56	51.03 N	6.59 E
Levern	52	52.22 N	8.26 E
Lever Park ♦	262	53.37 N	2.34 W
Le Vésinet	261	48.54 N	2.08 E
Le Vésuve → Vesuvio ∧[1]	68	40.49 N	14.26 E
Leviathan Peak ∧	226	38.41 N	119.37 W
Levice	30	48.13 N	18.37 E
Levicha	86	57.36 N	59.55 E
Levick, Mount ∧	9	74.08 S	163.12 E
Levico	64	46.01 N	11.18 E
Levie	36	41.42 N	9.07 E
Levier	58	46.57 N	6.08 E
Le Vigan	32	43.59 N	3.35 E
Levin	172	40.37 S	175.17 E
Levino	76	60.29 N	37.30 E
Lévis	206	46.48 N	71.11 W
Lévis □[6]	206	46.40 N	71.15 W
Levisa Fork ≃	192	38.06 N	82.36 W
Lévis-Saint Nom	261	48.43 N	1.58 E
Levítha I	38	37.00 N	26.28 E
Levittown, P.R.	240m	18.27 N	66.14 W
Levittown → Willingboro, N.J., U.S.	208	40.03 N	74.53 W
Levittown, N.Y., U.S.	210	40.43 N	73.30 W
Levittown, Pa., U.S.	208	40.09 N	74.49 W
Levittown Discount World •[9]	285	40.09 N	74.49 W
Lévka Óri ∧	38	35.18 N	24.01 E
Levkás	38	38.50 N	20.41 E
Levkás I	38	38.39 N	20.27 E
Levkímmi	38	39.25 N	20.04 E
Levoča	30	49.02 N	20.36 E
Levokumskoje	84	44.48 N	44.39 E
Levroux	32	46.59 N	1.37 E
Levski	38	43.22 N	25.08 E
Lev Tolstoj	76	53.13 N	39.27 E
Levuka	175g	17.41 S	178.50 E
Lėvuo ≃	76	56.04 N	24.23 E
Levyj Tuzlov ≃	83	47.35 N	39.23 E
Lewapaku	115b	9.43 S	119.55 E
Lewbeach	210	42.00 N	74.47 W
Lewe	110	19.38 N	96.07 E
Lewedorp	52	51.30 N	3.45 E
Lewellen	198	41.19 N	102.08 W
Lewer ≃	156	25.30 S	17.45 E
Lewes, Eng., U.K.	42	50.52 N	0.01 E
Lewes, De., U.S.	208	38.46 N	75.08 W
Lewin Brzeski	30	50.46 N	17.37 E
Lewis, Ia., U.S.	198	41.18 N	95.04 W
Lewis, Ks., U.S.	198	37.56 N	99.15 W
Lewis □[6], Ky., U.S.	218	38.32 N	83.21 W
Lewis □[6], Mo., U.S.	219	40.08 N	91.45 W
Lewis □[6], N.Y., U.S.	212	43.47 N	75.29 W
Lewis □[6], Wa., U.S.	224	46.35 N	122.22 W
Lewis ≃	224	45.51 N	122.48 W
Lewis, Butt of ›	46	58.31 N	6.16 W
Lewis, East Fork ≃	224	45.52 N	122.43 W
Lewis, Isle of I	46	58.10 N	6.40 W
Lewis, Mount ∧	204	40.24 N	116.51 W
Lewis and Clark ≃	224	46.10 N	123.52 W
Lewis and Clark Cavern State Park ♦	202	45.49 N	111.13 W
Lewis and Clark Lake ⊜[1]	198	42.50 N	97.45 W
Lewis and Clark Range ⋀	202	47.30 N	113.00 W
Lewisberry	208	40.08 N	76.52 W
Lewisburg, Ky., U.S.	194	36.59 N	86.56 W
Lewisburg, Oh., U.S.	218	39.50 N	84.32 W
Lewisburg, Pa., U.S.	210	40.57 N	76.53 W
Lewisburg, Tn., U.S.	194	35.26 N	86.47 W
Lewisburg, W.V., U.S.	188	37.48 N	80.26 W
Lewis Center	214	40.12 N	83.01 W
Lewis Creek ≃, Ca., U.S.	226	35.17 N	120.58 W
Lewis Creek ≃, In., U.S.	218	39.22 N	85.51 W
Lewis Creek Reservoir ⊜[1]	222	30.26 N	95.32 W
Lewisdale	284c	38.58 N	76.58 W
Lewisetta	208	38.01 N	76.28 W
Lewis Gut C	276	41.09 N	73.09 W
Lewisham	273d	26.07 S	27.49 E
Lewisham •[8]	42	51.27 N	0.01 E
Lewisham Location	273d	26.10 S	27.47 E
Lewis-Lockport Airport ⊠	278	41.36 N	88.05 W
Lewis Pass)(	172	42.23 S	172.24 E
Lewisport	194	37.56 N	86.54 W
Lewisporte	186	49.15 N	55.03 W
Lewis Range ⋀, Austl.	162	20.20 S	128.40 E
Lewis Range ⋀, Mt., U.S.	202	48.35 N	113.40 W
Lewis Run	214	41.52 N	78.39 W
Lewis Run ≃	279b	40.17 N	79.55 W
Lewis Smith Lake ⊜[1]	194	34.05 N	87.07 W
Lewiston, Ca., U.S.	204	40.43 N	122.48 W
Lewiston, Id., U.S.	202	46.25 N	117.01 W
Lewiston, Me., U.S.	188	44.06 N	70.12 W
Lewiston, Mi., U.S.	190	44.53 N	84.18 W
Lewiston, Mn., U.S.	190	43.59 N	91.52 W
Lewiston, N.Y., U.S.	210	43.10 N	79.02 W
Lewiston, Ut,. U.S.	200	41.58 N	111.51 W
Lewiston Orchards	202	46.23 N	116.59 W
Lewistown, Il., U.S.	194	40.23 N	90.09 W
Lewistown, Md., U.S.	208	39.32 N	77.24 W
Lewistown, Mo., U.S.	219	40.05 N	91.48 W
Lewistown, Mt., U.S.	202	47.03 N	109.25 W
Lewistown, Oh., U.S.	216	40.25 N	83.53 W
Lewistown, Pa., U.S.	208	40.35 N	77.34 W
Lewisville, N.B., Can.	186	46.06 N	64.46 W
Lewisville, Ar., U.S.	194	33.21 N	93.34 W
Lewisville, In., U.S.	218	39.48 N	85.21 W
Lewisville, Pa., U.S.	208	39.43 N	75.53 W
Lewisville, Tx., U.S.	222	33.02 N	96.59 W
Lewisville Dam •[6]	222	33.05 N	96.55 W
Lewisville Lake ⊜[1]	196	33.08 N	97.00 W
Lewoleba	112	8.23 S	123.24 E
Lewotobi-lakilaki, Ili ∧	115b	8.32 S	122.46 E
Lewvan	184	50.00 N	104.06 W
Lexa	194	34.35 N	90.44 W
Lexington, Ga., U.S.	192	33.52 N	83.06 W
Lexington, Il., U.S.	216	40.38 N	88.47 W
Lexington, In., U.S.	218	38.39 N	85.37 W
Lexington, Ky., U.S.	218	38.02 N	84.30 W
Lexington, Ma., U.S.	207	42.26 N	71.13 W
Lexington, Mi., U.S.	190	43.16 N	82.31 W
Lexington, Ms., U.S.	194	33.06 N	90.03 W
Lexington, Mo., U.S.	194	39.11 N	93.52 W
Lexington, Ne., U.S.	198	40.46 N	99.44 W
Lexington, N.Y., U.S.	210	42.15 N	74.22 W
Lexington, N.C., U.S.	192	35.49 N	80.15 W
Lexington, Oh., U.S.	214	40.40 N	82.34 W
Lexington, Ok., U.S.	196	35.00 N	97.20 W
Lexington, Or., U.S.	202	45.26 N	119.41 W
Lexington, S.C., U.S.	192	33.58 N	81.14 W
Lexington, Tn., U.S.	194	35.39 N	88.23 W
Lexington, Tx., U.S.	222	30.25 N	97.01 W
Lexington, Va., U.S.	192	37.47 N	79.26 W
Lexington Park	208	38.16 N	76.27 W
Lexington Reservoir ⊜[1]	226	37.12 N	121.59 W
Lexton	169	37.17 S	143.31 E
Leybourne	260	51.18 N	0.25 E
Leyburn	44	54.19 N	1.49 W
Leyden → Leiden	52	52.09 N	4.30 E
Leye	102	24.48 N	106.34 E
Leyland	44	53.42 N	2.42 W
Leyond ≃	184	51.40 N	96.32 W
Léyou ≃	152	1.07 S	13.08 E
Leyre ≃	32	44.39 N	1.01 W
Leysdown-on-Sea	42	51.24 N	0.55 E
Leysin	58	46.21 N	7.01 E
Leyte	116	11.23 N	124.29 E
Leyte □[4]	116	10.50 N	124.55 E
Leyte I	116	10.50 N	124.50 E
Leyte Gulf C	116	10.50 N	125.25 E
Leyton •[8]	260	51.33 N	0.01 W
Leyu	106	31.55 N	120.43 E
Lèz ≚	62	43.31 N	3.55 E
Leža	76	58.56 N	40.45 E
Leža ≃	76	59.15 N	40.10 E
Leżajsk	30	50.16 N	22.24 E
Lezama	246	9.43 N	66.24 W
Lézarde ≃	240e	14.36 N	61.01 W
Lézat	58	46.30 N	5.56 E
Lèze ≃	62	43.40 N	5.28 E
Lezhë	38	41.47 N	19.39 E
Lezhi	107	30.17 N	105.02 E
Lëzna	76	55.02 N	30.48 E
Ležn'ovo	80	56.46 N	40.53 E
Lezzeno	58	45.56 N	9.11 E
L'gov	78	51.43 N	35.17 E
Lhasa	120	29.40 N	91.09 E
Lhasa ≃	120	29.21 N	90.45 E
L'Hautil	261	49.00 N	2.01 E
Lhazê	120	29.10 N	87.42 E
L'Hillil	34	35.41 N	0.19 E
Lhokkruet	114	4.52 N	95.24 E
Lhoknga	114	5.29 N	95.15 E
Lhokseumawe	114	5.10 N	97.08 E
Lhoksukon	114	5.03 N	97.19 E
L'Hôpital-sous-Rochefort	62	45.46 N	3.56 E
Lhorong	102	30.45 N	96.09 E
L'Hospitalet de Llobregat	34	41.22 N	2.08 E
Lhotse ∧	124	27.57 N	86.56 E
Lhozhag	120	28.24 N	90.49 E
Lhuis	62	45.45 N	5.32 E
Lhuntsi Dzong	120	27.39 N	91.09 E
Lhünzê	120	28.25 N	92.31 E
Li	110	17.48 N	98.57 E
Li ≃, Thai	110	18.26 N	98.42 E
Li ≃, Zhg.	100	33.11 N	115.07 E
Li ≃, Zhg.	102	29.24 N	112.01 E
Lian ≃, Zhg.	100	25.46 N	115.38 E
Lian ≃, Zhg.	100	24.02 N	113.18 E
Lian ≃, Zhg.	102	24.02 N	113.18 E
Lian ≃, Zhg.	102	27.48 N	112.52 E
Liancheng	100	25.44 N	116.46 E
Liancourt	50	49.20 N	2.28 E
Liane ≃	50	50.43 N	1.36 E
Liang	164	3.30 S	128.19 E
Lianga	116	8.38 N	126.06 E
Lianga Bay C	116	8.37 N	126.12 E
Liang'anchang	107	30.30 N	104.56 E
Liangbao	102	34.37 N	110.45 E
Liangbingbao	89	45.48 N	128.19 E
Liangbingtai	89	43.12 N	128.47 E
Liangbuaya	112	0.05 N	116.46 E
Liangchahe	107	29.03 N	106.18 E
Liangcheng	98	35.35 N	119.35 E
Liangcun	100	26.36 N	115.34 E
Liangdang	102	33.56 N	106.12 E
Liangdawa	105	40.39 N	117.37 E
Liangfengwu	107	30.11 N	105.22 E
Lianggezhuang	105	39.21 N	115.22 E
Lianghe, Zhg.	89	45.09 N	128.45 E
Lianghe, Zhg.	102	24.51 N	98.25 E
Liangheguan	102	32.52 N	109.19 E
Lianghekou, Zhg.	102	33.42 N	104.25 E
Lianghekou, Zhg.	102	29.14 N	108.40 E
Lianghekou, Zhg.	102	31.27 N	102.13 E
Lianghekou, Zhg.	107	28.55 N	106.03 E
Liangiu	98	35.12 N	117.47 E
Liangjia	107	29.29 N	105.33 E
Liangjiadian	98	39.10 N	121.54 E
Liangjiafang	98	41.04 N	117.18 E
Liangjianfang	105	40.45 N	117.20 E
Liangjiang	102	23.23 N	108.22 E
Liangjiangkou	98	42.38 N	128.05 E
Liangjiawazi	104	40.40 N	120.42 E
Liangjiazi	104	42.13 N	122.31 E
Liangkou	100	23.43 N	113.43 E
Lianglukou	107	29.18 N	106.15 E
Liangmen	98	35.34 N	114.54 E
Liangmentou	100	28.58 N	121.12 E
Liangmushi	106	30.46 N	119.35 E
Liangpa	102	24.10 N	106.13 E
Liangpeng	106	30.47 N	119.38 E
Liangping	102	30.41 N	107.49 E
Liang Shan ∧	102	23.45 N	99.45 E
Liangshui ≃	271a	39.49 N	116.40 E
Liangtian	100	25.37 N	113.00 E
Liangtinghe	100	30.20 N	116.12 E
Liangtoumen	100	29.31 N	120.45 E
Liangtun	98	40.14 N	122.34 E
Liangwangzhuang	105	39.01 N	116.58 E
Liangxiangzhen	105	39.44 N	116.08 E
Liangying	100	23.14 N	116.21 E
Liangyuan	100	32.00 N	117.34 E
Liangzhu	106	30.23 N	120.03 E
Liangzi Hu ⊜	100	30.16 N	114.34 E
Lianhe	98	42.36 N	125.37 E
Lian Hu ⊜	106	32.02 N	119.32 E
Lianhua	100	27.07 N	113.57 E
Lianhuachi	105	40.28 N	116.33 E
Lianhuapao	89	45.32 N	129.50 E
Lianhua Shan ⋀	100	23.40 N	116.00 E
Lianjiang, Zhg.	100	26.12 N	119.31 E
Lianjiang, Zhg.	102	21.38 N	110.15 E
Lianjiechang	107	29.41 N	104.30 E
Liannan (Sanjiang)	102	24.38 N	112.10 E
Lianozovo •[8]	265b	55.54 N	37.35 E
Lianping	100	24.22 N	114.31 E
Lianpu	100	26.02 N	118.38 E
Lianshanguan	104	40.58 N	123.46 E
Lianshi	106	30.42 N	120.26 E
Lianshui	100	33.47 N	119.16 E
Liansiji	98	33.58 N	114.24 E
Liantang	106	31.37 N	120.38 E
Lianxian	102	24.48 N	112.25 E
Lianyin	89	53.28 N	123.51 E
Lianyuan (Lantian)	102	27.42 N	111.19 E
Lianyungang, Zhg.	98	34.44 N	119.30 E
Lianyungang (Xinpu), Zhg.	98	34.39 N	119.16 E
Lianyun Shan ∧	100	28.32 N	113.50 E
Lianzhou → Hepu	102	21.39 N	109.11 E
Liao ≃	90	40.50 N	121.48 E
Liaobinta	104	42.08 N	123.04 E
Liaocheng	98	36.30 N	115.59 E
Liaodong Bandao (Liaotung Peninsula) ›[1]	98	40.00 N	122.20 E
Liaodong Wan (Gulf of Liaotung) C	98	40.30 N	121.30 E
Liaohe Kou C[1]	104	40.42 N	122.05 E
Liaojiangshi	100	26.05 N	113.17 E
Liaoning □[4]	90	41.00 N	123.00 E
Liaotung, Gulf of → Liaodong Wan C	98	40.30 N	121.30 E
Liaotung Peninsula → Liaodong Bandao ›[1]	98	40.00 N	122.20 E
Liaoyang	104	41.17 N	123.11 E
Liaoyangwopu	89	43.00 N	123.28 E
Liaoyuan	89	42.54 N	125.07 E
Liaozhong	104	41.31 N	122.44 E
Liapádhes	38	39.40 N	19.44 E
Liāquatpur	123	28.56 N	70.57 E
Liard ≃	176	61.52 N	121.18 W
Liāri	120	25.41 N	66.29 E
Liart	50	49.46 N	4.20 E
Liat, Pulau I	112	2.53 S	107.05 E
Liathach ∧	46	57.35 N	5.29 W
Lib I	14	8.19 N	167.25 E
Libagon	116	10.18 N	125.03 E
Liban → Lebanon □[1]	128	34.00 N	36.00 E
Libanga	152	0.19 N	18.41 E
Líbano	246	4.55 N	75.04 W
Libano → Lebanon □[1]	128	34.00 N	36.00 E
Libanon → Lebanon □[1]	128	34.00 N	36.00 E
Libau → Liepāja	76	56.31 N	21.01 E
Libby	202	48.23 N	115.33 W
Libby Dam •[6]	202	48.24 N	115.20 W
Libčeves	54	50.26 N	13.50 E
Libčice nad Vltavou	54	50.10 N	14.20 E
Liběchov	54	50.20 N	14.28 E
Libenge	152	3.39 N	18.38 E
Liberal, Ks., U.S.	198	37.02 N	100.55 W
Liberal, Mo., U.S.	194	37.33 N	94.31 W
Liberdade	256	22.01 S	44.19 W
Liberdade •[8]	287b	23.35 S	46.37 W
Liberdade ≃, Bra.	248	7.10 S	71.51 W
Liberdade ≃, Bra.	250	9.40 S	52.17 W
Liberec	30	50.46 N	15.03 E
Liberia	236	10.38 N	85.27 W
Liberia □[1], Afr.	134	6.30 N	9.30 W
Liberia □[1], Afr.	150	6.30 N	9.30 W
Liberta	240c	17.02 N	61.47 W
Libertad, Arg.	258	34.42 S	58.41 W
Libertad, Ur.	258	34.38 S	56.39 W
Libertad, Ven.	246	8.20 N	69.37 W
Libertad, Ven.	246	9.23 N	68.44 W
Libertador □[5]	286c	10.27 N	66.57 W
Libertador General Bernardo O'Higgins □[4]	252	34.30 S	71.00 W
Libertador General San Martín	252	23.48 S	64.48 W
Liberty, Il., U.S.	219	39.53 N	91.06 W
Liberty, In., U.S.	218	39.38 N	84.55 W
Liberty, Ky., U.S.	194	37.19 N	84.56 W
Liberty, Ms., U.S.	194	31.09 N	90.48 W
Liberty, Mo., U.S.	194	39.14 N	94.25 W
Liberty, Ne., U.S.	198	40.05 N	96.28 W
Liberty, N.Y., U.S.	210	41.48 N	74.44 W
Liberty, N.C., U.S.	192	35.51 N	79.34 W
Liberty, Pa., U.S.	210	41.34 N	77.06 W
Liberty, Pa., U.S.	279b	40.20 N	79.51 W
Liberty, S.C., U.S.	192	34.47 N	82.41 W
Liberty, Tx., U.S.	222	30.03 N	94.47 W
Liberty □[6]	222	30.12 N	94.50 W
Liberty Acres	280	34.04 N	118.12 W
Liberty Center, In., U.S.	216	40.41 N	85.16 W
Liberty Center, Oh., U.S.	216	41.26 N	84.00 W
Liberty City	222	32.27 N	94.57 W
Liberty Corner	276	40.39 N	74.34 W
Liberty Ditch ≚	226	36.31 N	120.02 W
Liberty Farms	226	38.19 N	121.42 W
Liberty Hill	196	30.40 N	97.55 W
Liberty Island I	276	40.41 N	74.03 W
Liberty Lake ⊜[1]	208	39.25 N	76.53 W
Liberty Manor	284b	39.21 N	76.47 W
Liberty Mills	216	41.02 N	85.44 W
Liberty Park	216	41.26 N	87.22 W
Libertytown	208	39.29 N	77.14 W
Liberty Tree Mall •[9]	283	42.33 N	70.57 W
Liberty Tunnel •[5]	279b	40.26 N	80.01 W
Libertyville	216	42.16 N	87.57 W
Líbeznice	54	50.10 N	14.30 E
Libia → Libya □[1]	146	27.00 N	17.00 E
Libibi	152	14.42 S	17.44 E
Libishan	106	30.45 N	119.20 E
Lībiyā → Libya □[1]	146	27.00 N	17.00 E
Lībīyah, Aṣ-Ṣaḥrā' al- (Libyan Desert) •[2]	136	24.00 N	25.00 E
Liblín	60	49.55 N	13.32 E
Libni, Jabal ∧[2]	132	30.44 N	33.50 E
Libo	102	25.28 N	107.53 E
Libobo, Tanjung ›	164	0.54 S	128.28 E
Liboc ≃	54	50.10 N	13.31 E
Libochovice	54	50.22 N	14.03 E
Libode	158	31.33 S	29.02 E
Liboi	154	0.24 N	40.57 E
Liboko	152	2.43 N	21.28 E
Libomyšl	60	49.52 N	14.00 E
Libona	116	8.20 N	124.44 E
Liboumba ≃	152	0.38 N	12.54 E
Libourne	32	44.55 N	0.14 W
Libramont	56	49.55 N	5.23 E
Library	214	40.18 N	80.02 W
Librazhd	38	41.11 N	20.19 E
Libres	234	19.28 N	97.41 W
Libreville	152	0.23 N	9.27 E
Librizzi	70	38.06 N	14.57 E
Libro Point ›	116	11.26 N	119.29 E
Libu	102	23.41 N	111.30 E
Libucan Island I	116	11.54 N	124.39 E
Libuganon ≃	116	7.27 N	125.47 E
Libunga	154	1.49 N	26.35 E
Liburung	112	3.55 S	120.09 E
Libušín	54	50.09 N	14.04 E
Libya (Lībiyā) □[1], Afr.	136	27.00 N	17.00 E
Libya (Lībiyā) □[1], Afr.	146	27.00 N	17.00 E
Libyan Desert → Lībīyah, Aṣ-Ṣaḥrā' al- •[2]	136	24.00 N	25.00 E
Libyan Plateau → Aḍ-Diffah ⋀[1]	140	30.30 N	25.30 E
Libye → Libya □[1]	146	27.00 N	17.00 E
Libyen → Libya □[1]	146	27.00 N	17.00 E
Libysche Wüste → Lībīyah, Aṣ-Ṣaḥrā' al- •[2]	136	24.00 N	25.00 E
Licancábur, Volcán ∧[1]	248	22.50 S	67.50 W
Licantén	252	34.59 S	72.00 W
Licata	70	37.06 N	13.56 E
Licciana Nardi	64	44.16 N	10.02 E
Lice	130	38.28 N	40.39 E
Lich	56	50.33 N	8.50 E
Lichačova, mys ›	89	42.44 N	132.51 E
Lichaja ≃	83	48.08 N	40.15 E
Lichang	107	28.53 N	104.26 E
Licheng	102	36.30 N	113.21 E
Lichères-Près-Aigremont	50	47.43 N	3.51 E
Lichfield	42	52.42 N	1.48 W
Lichinga	154	13.18 S	35.14 E
Lichitișeni	38	46.23 N	27.17 E
Lichoborka ≃	265b	55.50 N	37.38 E
Lichoslavl'	76	57.07 N	35.28 E
Lichovskoj	83	48.07 N	40.12 E
Lichtaart	56	51.14 N	4.54 E
Lichte	54	50.31 N	11.10 E
Lichtenau, Dtsch.	56	49.17 N	10.41 E
Lichtenau, Dtsch.	56	48.43 N	8.01 E
Lichtenberg, Dtsch.	54	50.23 N	11.40 E
Lichtenberg, Fr.	56	48.55 N	7.29 E
Lichtenberg •[8]	264a	52.31 N	13.29 E
Lichtenburg	158	26.08 S	26.08 E
Lichtendorf	263	51.28 N	7.37 E
Lichtenfels, Dtsch.	56	50.09 N	11.04 E
Lichtenfels, Dtsch.	56	51.14 N	8.49 E
Lichtenplatz •[8]	263	51.15 N	7.12 E
Lichtenrade •[8]	264a	52.23 N	13.25 E
Lichtensee	54	51.23 N	13.22 E
Lichtensteig	58	47.19 N	9.05 E
Lichtenstein	54	50.45 N	12.37 E
Lichtenstein, Schloss ᵾ	58	48.24 N	9.15 E
Lichtentanne	54	50.42 N	12.25 E
Lichtenvoorde	52	51.59 N	6.34 E
Lichterfelde •[8]	264a	52.26 N	13.19 E
Lichtervelde	50	51.02 N	3.09 E
Lichuan, Zhg.	100	27.18 N	116.53 E
Lichuan, Zhg.	102	30.18 N	108.51 E
Lick Creek ≃, Il., U.S.	219	39.42 N	89.41 W
Lick Creek ≃, In., U.S.	218	38.33 N	86.31 W
Lick Creek ≃, Mo., U.S.	219	39.31 N	91.39 W
Lick Creek ≃, Oh., U.S.	216	41.21 N	84.25 W
Lick Creek ≃, Tn., U.S.	192	36.11 N	83.10 W
Lickershamn	26	57.50 N	18.31 E
Licking	194	37.29 N	91.51 W
Licking □[6]	214	40.10 N	82.30 W
Licking ≃, Ky., U.S.	188	39.06 N	84.30 W
Licking ≃, Oh., U.S.	214	40.03 N	82.20 W
Licking, North Fork ≃, Ky., U.S.	218	38.35 N	84.13 W
Licking, North Fork ≃, Oh., U.S.	214	40.03 N	82.23 W
Licking, South Fork ≃	218	38.41 N	84.20 W
Lickingville	214	41.23 N	79.22 W
Lick Observatory ᵾ[3]	226	37.22 N	121.37 W
Ličko Polje ≚	36	44.35 N	15.25 E
Lick Run ≃, Pa., U.S.	210	41.12 N	77.32 W
Lick Run ≃, Pa., U.S.	279b	40.17 N	79.57 W
Licodia Eubea	70	37.09 N	14.42 E
Licosa, Punta ›	68	40.15 N	14.54 E
Licun	98	38.32 N	117.08 E
Licungo ≃	154	17.40 S	37.15 E
Lid'	76	59.39 N	35.05 E
Lida	76	53.53 N	25.18 E
Lidan ≃	26	58.31 N	13.09 E
Lidao	98	37.15 N	122.32 E
Lidarentuncun	104	41.32 N	123.12 E
Lidcombe	274a	33.52 S	151.03 E
Liddel Water ≃	44	55.04 N	2.57 W
Liddesdale V	44	55.12 N	2.46 W
Liddon Gulf C	176	75.03 N	113.00 W
Liden	26	62.42 N	16.48 E
Lidesi	100	33.33 N	115.53 E
Lidgerwood	198	46.04 N	97.09 W
Lidgetton	158	29.25 S	30.05 E
Lidian	107	28.57 N	103.44 E
Lídice, Bra.	256	22.51 S	44.12 W
Lídice, Pan.	236	8.45 N	79.54 W
Lidice ⊥	54	50.03 N	14.08 E
Lidingö	40	59.22 N	18.08 E
Lidköping	26	58.30 N	13.10 E
Lido	64	45.25 N	12.22 E
Lido, Litorale di ±[2]	64	45.23 N	12.21 E
Lido, Porto di C	64	45.26 N	12.25 E
Lido Beach	276	40.35 N	73.38 W
Lido di Camaiore	64	43.54 N	10.13 E
Lido di Castel Fusano •[8]	66	41.43 N	12.20 E
Lido di Iesolo	64	45.30 N	12.39 E
Lido di Metaponto	68	40.22 N	16.50 E
Lido di Ostia •[8]	66	41.44 N	12.14 E
Lido di Pomposa	66	44.45 N	12.14 E
Lido di Siponto	68	41.37 N	15.55 E
Lido Key I	220	27.19 N	82.35 W
Lidsjön ⊜	40	58.55 N	16.51 E
Lidu	107	30.35 N	106.04 E
Lidzbark	30	53.17 N	19.49 E
Lidzbark Warmiński	30	54.09 N	20.35 E
Liebenau, Dtsch.	52	52.36 N	9.05 E
Liebenau, Dtsch.	52	51.30 N	9.17 E
Liebenau, Öst.	61	48.32 N	14.49 E
Liebenbergsvlei ≃	158	27.20 S	28.31 E
Liebenburg	52	52.01 N	10.26 E
Liebenwalde	54	52.52 N	13.23 E
Lieberhausen	56	51.03 N	7.40 E
Lieberose	54	51.59 N	14.17 E
Liebertwolkwitz	54	51.17 N	12.28 E
Liebig, Mount ∧	162	23.18 S	131.22 E
Liebstadt	54	50.52 N	13.51 E
Liechtenstein □[1], Europe	22	47.09 N	9.35 E
Liechtenstein □[1], Europe	58	47.09 N	9.35 E
Liechtensteinklamm V	64	47.18 N	13.12 E
Liedberg	263	51.10 N	6.32 E
Liedekerke	50	50.52 N	4.05 E
Liège (Luik)	56	50.38 N	5.34 E
Liège □[4]	56	50.30 N	5.30 E
Liège, Aéroport ⊠	56	50.39 N	5.30 E
Liegnitz → Legnica	30	51.13 N	16.09 E
Lieja → Liège	56	50.38 N	5.34 E
Lieksa	26	63.19 N	30.01 E
Lielais Liepu kalns ∧[2]	76	56.25 N	27.50 E
Lielupe ≃	76	57.01 N	23.56 E
Lielvārde	76	56.43 N	24.51 E
Liemienzhen	107	30.29 N	106.05 E
Lienart	154	3.04 N	25.31 E
Lienchou → Hepu	102	21.39 N	109.11 E
Lienen	52	52.09 N	7.58 E
Lienz	64	46.50 N	12.47 E
Liepāja	76	56.31 N	21.01 E
Liepājas ezers ⊜	76	56.27 N	21.03 E
Liepe	54	53.58 N	13.56 E
Liepna	76	57.25 N	27.25 E
Liepnitzsee ⊜	264a	52.45 N	13.30 E
Lièpvre	58	48.16 N	7.17 E
Lier (Lierre)	50	51.08 N	4.34 E
Lierenfeld •[8]	263	51.13 N	6.51 E
Lierna	58	45.57 N	9.18 E
Liernais	50	47.12 N	4.17 E
Lierneux	56	50.18 N	5.48 E
Liershizhai	104	41.49 N	123.43 E
Liesborn	52	51.43 N	8.15 E
Lieser ≃, Dtsch.	56	49.55 N	7.01 E
Lieser ≃, Öst.	64	46.47 N	13.39 E
Lieshout	52	51.32 N	5.35 E
Liesing •[8]	264b	48.08 N	16.17 E
Liesing ≃, Öst.	61	47.20 N	15.02 E
Liesing ≃, Öst.	264b	48.08 N	16.28 E
Liesjärven kansallispuisto ♦	26	60.40 N	23.54 E
Lieskau	54	51.37 N	13.48 E
Liesse	50	49.37 N	3.48 E
Liessies	50	50.07 N	4.05 E
Liestal	58	47.29 N	7.44 E
Liești	38	45.38 N	27.32 E
Lietuva → Lithuania □[1]	72	56.00 N	24.00 E
Lietzow	54	54.29 N	13.30 E
Lieurey	50	49.14 N	0.29 E
Lieusaint	261	48.38 N	2.33 E
Lieutel ≃	261	48.49 N	1.52 E
Lieutenant Robert J. Palenscar Memorial Airport ⊠	285	39.51 N	75.03 W
Liévin	50	50.25 N	2.46 E
Lièvre, Rivière du ≃	176	45.31 N	75.26 W
Lièvres, Île aux I	186	47.51 N	69.44 W
Liezen	61	47.35 N	14.15 E
Lifanga	152	0.19 N	21.57 E
Liffey ≃	48	53.21 N	6.16 W
Liffol-le-Grand	58	48.19 N	5.35 E
Lifford	48	54.50 N	7.29 W
Liffré	32	48.13 N	1.30 W
Lifjell ∧	26	59.30 N	8.52 E
Lifoku	152	0.04 S	21.18 E
Lifou I	175f	20.53 S	167.13 E
Lifoula	273b	4.06 S	15.25 E
Lifton	42	50.39 N	4.17 W
Liftwood	285	39.47 N	75.31 W
Lifune ≃	152	8.21 S	13.22 E
Ligačovo	265b	55.56 N	37.15 E
Ligang	100	30.04 N	121.52 E
Ligao, Pil.	116	13.14 N	123.32 E
Ligao, Pil.	116	6.17 N	124.09 E
Ligasa	152	0.42 N	23.45 E
Ligezhuang, Zhg.	105	39.49 N	115.56 E
Ligezhuang, Zhg.	105	39.42 N	118.12 E
Light ≃	168b	34.35 S	138.22 E
Lightfoot	208	37.20 N	76.45 W
Lighthouse Beach ±[2]	273a	6.24 N	3.22 E
Lighthouse Point	220	26.16 N	80.05 W
Lighthouse Point ›, On., Can.	214	41.50 N	82.38 W
Lighthouse Point ›, Fl., U.S.	192	29.54 N	84.21 W
Lighthouse Point ›, Mi., U.S.	190	45.13 N	85.32 W
Lighthouse Reef ✦[2]	232	17.20 N	87.32 W
Lightning Creek ≃, Sk., Can.	184	49.12 N	101.43 W
Lightning Creek ≃, N.A.	224	48.50 N	121.03 W
Lightning Creek ≃, Wy., U.S.	198	43.11 N	104.44 W
Lightning Ridge	166	29.26 S	147.59 E
Lightstreet	210	41.02 N	76.25 W
Lightsville	216	40.18 N	84.42 W
Ligist	61	46.59 N	15.12 E
Lignano Pineta	64	45.40 N	13.07 E
Lignano Sabbiadoro	64	45.42 N	13.09 E
Lignières	32	46.45 N	2.11 E
Lignite	198	48.52 N	102.33 W
Lignon ≃	62	45.44 N	4.08 E
Lignumvitae Key I	220	24.55 N	80.42 W
Ligny-en-Barrois	58	48.41 N	5.20 E
Ligny-en-Cambrésis	50	50.06 N	3.22 E
Ligny-le-Châtel	50	47.54 N	3.45 E
Ligny-le-Ribault	50	47.41 N	1.47 E
Ligonha ≃	154	16.54 S	39.09 E
Ligonier, In., U.S.	216	41.27 N	85.35 W
Ligonier, Pa., U.S.	214	40.14 N	79.14 W
Ligovo	76	60.13 N	31.48 E
Ligovo •[8]	265a	59.50 N	30.12 E
Ligovskij kanal ≚	265a	59.47 N	30.10 E
Liguantu	105	40.24 N	115.45 E
Ligueil	32	47.03 N	0.49 E
Ligui	232	25.43 N	111.16 W
Ligure, Mar → Ligurian Sea ⍑[2]	36	43.30 N	9.00 E
Liguria □[4]	36	44.30 N	8.50 E
Liguria, Mar de → Ligurian Sea ⍑[2]	36	43.30 N	9.00 E
Ligurian Sea ⍑[2]	36	43.30 N	9.00 E
Ligurisches Meer → Ligurian Sea ⍑[2]	36	43.30 N	9.00 E
Lihir Group II	164	3.05 S	152.40 E
Lihir Island I	164	3.05 S	152.35 E
Lihoi Seamount ✦[3]	14	18.56 N	155.16 W
Lihou Reef and Cays ✦[2]	166	17.25 S	151.40 E
Lihu	100	23.23 N	116.03 E
Lihue	229b	21.58 N	159.22 W
Lihue Airport ⊠	229b	21.59 N	159.21 W
Lihuel Calel, Parque Nacional ♦, Arg.	252	37.58 S	65.32 W
Lihuel Calel, Parque Nacional ♦, Arg.	254	37.58 S	65.32 W
Lihula	76	58.41 N	23.50 E
Liji, Zhg.	100	31.59 N	115.51 E
Liji, Zhg.	100	33.48 N	117.48 E
Lijia, Zhg.	98	37.49 N	118.01 E
Lijia, Zhg.	104	41.43 N	122.20 E
Lijiaba	107	29.37 N	105.33 E
Lijiadian	104	42.07 N	121.14 E
Lijiajie	107	29.49 N	105.30 E
Lijiakou	105	39.12 N	116.29 E
Lijiang	102	26.57 N	100.15 E
Lijiapuzi	104	40.59 N	123.38 E
Lijiaqiao, Zhg.	105	40.03 N	116.40 E
Lijiaqiao, Zhg.	105	39.47 N	117.47 E
Lijiaqiao, Zhg.	106	31.38 N	120.00 E
Lijiatun	104	41.19 N	121.23 E
Lijiatuo	107	29.28 N	106.33 E
Lijiawobao	104	41.00 N	122.26 E
Lijiaxiang	106	30.57 N	119.59 E
Lijiazao	105	39.17 N	118.19 E
Lijin, Zhg.	98	37.29 N	118.16 E
Lijin, Zhg.	104	41.40 N	121.20 E
Lik ≃	110	18.31 N	102.31 E
Likako	152	0.15 N	21.00 E
Likang	100	22.47 N	120.29 E
Likasi (Jadotville)	154	10.59 S	26.44 E
Likati	152	3.21 N	23.53 E
Likati ≃	152	2.53 N	24.03 E
Likely	182	52.37 N	121.34 W
Likėnai	76	56.12 N	24.37 E
Likete	152	0.43 S	21.25 E
Likhu ≃	124	27.15 N	86.12 E
Liki	112	1.36 S	101.11 E
Likimi	152	2.50 N	20.45 E
Likino	82	55.38 N	37.08 E
Likino-Dulevo	82	55.43 N	38.58 E
Liknes	26	58.19 N	6.59 E
Likoma Island I	154	12.05 S	34.45 E
Likou, Zhg.	100	29.53 N	117.28 E
Likou, Zhg.	100	33.51 N	113.20 E
Likou, Zhg.	106	31.24 N	120.37 E
Likouala □[5]	152	2.00 N	17.30 E
Likouala ≃	152	1.13 S	16.48 E
Likouala aux Herbes ≃	152	0.50 S	17.11 E
Likova ≃	265b	55.34 N	37.21 E
Likstammen ⊜	40	58.58 N	17.12 E
Liku	174v	19.02 S	169.47 W
Likupang	112	1.41 N	125.04 E
Likus ≃	236	14.14 N	83.35 W
Likuyu	154	10.20 S	36.14 E
Lilanchengzhen	105	39.12 N	116.43 E
Lilanga	152	0.34 S	23.55 E
Lilasi	124	29.22 N	84.30 E
Lilbert	222	31.44 N	94.54 W
Lilbourn	194	36.35 N	89.36 W
L'Île-Bouchard	32	47.07 N	0.25 E
Lilenga	152	0.54 N	22.06 E
L'Île-Rousse	36	42.38 N	8.56 E
Lili	106	31.00 N	120.42 E
Lilian Point ›	174d	0.53 S	169.35 E
Lilienfeld	61	48.03 N	15.36 E
Lilienthal	52	53.08 N	8.55 E
Liling	100	27.40 N	113.30 E
Lilio	116	14.08 N	121.26 E
Liljendal	40	60.08 N	14.04 E
Lilla Bharwana	123	32.34 N	72.45 E
Lilla Edet	26	58.08 N	12.08 E
Lillån	40	59.19 N	15.13 E
Lillby	26	63.28 N	23.00 E
Lille	50	50.38 N	3.04 E
Lillebælt Ա	41	55.20 N	9.45 E
Lillebonne	50	49.31 N	0.33 E
Lillehammer	26	61.08 N	10.30 E
Lille-Lesquin, Aéroport ⊠	50	50.35 N	3.07 E
Lillerød	41	55.52 N	12.22 E
Lillers	50	50.34 N	2.29 E
Lillesand	26	58.15 N	8.24 E
Lilleshall	42	52.44 N	2.21 W
Lillestrøm	26	59.57 N	11.05 E
Lille Værløse	41	55.47 N	12.23 E
Lillhärdal	26	61.51 N	14.04 E
Lillian	222	32.30 N	97.11 W
Lillington	192	35.23 N	78.48 W
Lillinonah Lake ⊜[1]	207	41.28 N	73.21 W
Lilli Pilli	274a	34.04 S	151.07 E
Lillo	34	39.43 N	3.18 W
Lillooet	182	50.42 N	121.56 W
Lillooet ≃	182	49.45 N	122.08 W
Lillooet Lake ⊜	182	50.13 N	122.29 W
Lilly	214	40.25 N	78.37 W
Lilly Creek ≃	222	32.47 N	94.56 W
Liloan	116	10.09 N	125.07 E
Lilongwe	154	13.59 S	33.44 E
Lilo Viejo	252	26.56 S	62.58 W
Liloy	116	8.08 N	122.40 E
Liluāh	272b	22.35 N	88.23 E
Lily	192	37.01 N	84.04 W
Lily Cache Creek ≃	278	41.41 N	88.07 W
Lilydale, Austl.	166	41.15 S	147.13 E
Lilydale, Austl.	169	37.45 S	145.21 E
Lily Dale, N.Y., U.S.	214	42.21 N	79.19 W
Lilyfield	274a	33.52 S	151.10 E
Lilyvale	273d	26.06 S	28.25 E
Lim ≃, Afr.	152	7.54 N	15.46 E
Lim ≃, Europe	38	43.45 N	19.13 E
Lima, Arg.	258	34.03 S	59.12 W
Lima, Para.	252	23.54 S	56.20 W
Lima, Perú	248	12.03 S	77.03 W
Lima, Perú	286d	12.03 S	77.03 W
Lima, Sve.	26	60.56 N	13.26 E
Lima, Il., U.S.	219	40.11 N	91.23 W
Lima, Mt., U.S.	202	44.38 N	112.35 W
Lima, N.Y., U.S.	210	42.54 N	77.36 W
Lima, Oh., U.S.	216	40.44 N	84.06 W
Lima, Pa., U.S.	285	39.55 N	75.26 W
Lima □[5]	248	12.00 S	76.35 W
Lima (Limia) ≃, Europe	34	41.41 N	8.50 W
Lima ≃, It.	64	44.00 N	10.35 E
Lima, Punta ›	240m	18.11 N	65.41 W
Lima Center	216	42.47 N	88.49 W
Limache	252	33.01 S	71.16 W
Lima Duarte	256	21.51 S	43.48 W
Liman, Ross.	80	45.47 N	47.14 E
Liman, Yis.	132	33.03 N	35.06 E
Liman ≃	115a	6.29 S	105.48 E
Limanowa	30	49.43 N	20.26 E
Limão •[8]	287b	23.30 S	46.40 W
Limapuluh	114	3.10 N	99.26 E
Lima Reservoir ⊜[1]	202	44.38 N	112.17 W
Limarí ≃	252	30.44 S	71.43 W
Limas	112	0.14 N	104.31 E
Limasawa Island I	116	9.56 N	125.05 E
Limassa	152	4.14 N	22.02 E
Limassol → Lemesós	130	34.40 N	33.02 E
Limavady	48	55.03 N	6.57 W
Limaville	214	40.59 N	81.09 W
Limay, Fr.	50	49.00 N	1.44 E
Limay, Pil.	116	14.34 N	120.36 E
Limay ≃	254	38.59 S	68.00 W
Limay Mahuida	252	37.12 S	66.42 W
Limbach-Oberfrohna	54	50.51 N	12.45 E
Limbadi	68	38.33 N	15.58 E
Limbang	112	4.45 N	115.00 E

Symbols in the index entries represent the broad categories identified in the key at the right. Symbols with superior numbers (⋀[1]) identify subcategories (see complete key on page *I · 1).*

Symbole im Register stellen die rechts im Schlüssel erklärten Kategorien dar. Symbole mit hochgestellten Ziffern (⋀[1]) bezeichnen Unterabteilungen einer Kategorie (vgl. vollständiger Schlüssel auf Seite *I · 1).*

Los símbolos incluídos en el texto del índice representan las grandes categorías identificadas con la clave a la derecha. Los símbolos con numeros en su parte superior (⋀[1]) identifican las subcategorías (véase la clave completa en la página *I · 1).*

Les symboles de l'index représentent les catégories indiquées dans la légende à droite. Les symboles suivis d'un indice (⋀[1]) représentent des sous-catégories (voir légende complète à la page *I · 1).*

Os símbolos incluídos no texto do índice representam as grandes categorias identificadas com a chave à direita. Os símbolos com números em sua parte superior (⋀[1]) identificam as subcategorias (veja-se a chave completa à página *I · 1).*

∧ Mountain	Berg	Montaña	Montagne	Montanha
⋀ Mountains	Gebirge	Montañas	Montagnes	Montanhas
)(Pass	Paß	Paso	Col	Passo
V Valley, Canyon	Tal, Cañon	Valle, Cañón	Vallée, Canyon	Vale, Canhão
≚ Plain	Ebene	Llano	Plaine	Planície
› Cape	Kap	Cabo	Cap	Cabo
I Island	Insel	Isla	Île	Ilha
II Islands	Inseln	Islas	Îles	Ilhas
± Other Topographic Features	Andere Topographische Objekte	Otros Elementos Topográficos	Autres données topographiques	Outros acidentes topográficos

ESPAÑOL Nombre	Página	Lat.°'	Long.°' W=Oeste
Limbang ≃	112	4.50 N	115.01 E
Limbani	248	14.08 S	69.42 W
Limbara, Monte ▲	71	40.51 N	9.10 E
Limbaži	76	57.31 N	24.42 E
Limbdi	120	22.34 N	71.48 E
Limbe, Cam.	152	4.01 N	9.12 E
Limbe, Malaŵi	154	15.49 S	35.03 E
Limbiate	62	45.36 N	9.07 E
Limboto	112	0.37 N	122.57 E
Limbourg	56	50.37 N	5.56 E
Limbrick	262	53.38 N	2.36 W
Limbuela	152	12.30 S	18.42 E
Limbunya	164	17.14 S	129.50 E
Limburg □⁴, Bel.	56	51.00 N	5.30 E
Limburg □⁴, Ned.	56	51.14 N	5.50 E
Limburg an der Lahn	56	50.23 N	8.04 E
Limburgerhof	56	49.25 N	8.24 E
Lim Chu Kang	271c	1.26 N	103.43 E
Limecrest	218	39.54 N	83.48 W
Limefield	262	53.37 N	2.18 W
Limeira	255	22.34 S	47.24 W
Limekiln Canyon V	280	34.18 N	118.33 W
Lime Lake	210	42.26 N	78.29 W
Limen	100	27.07 N	119.19 E
Limena	64	45.29 N	11.50 E
Limentra ≃	64	44.14 N	11.03 E
Limerick, Sk., Can.	184	49.40 N	106.15 W
Limerick (Luimneach), Ire.	48	52.40 N	8.38 W
Limerick, Pa., U.S.	285	40.14 N	75.32 W
Limerick □⁶	48	52.30 N	8.45 W
Limerick Lake ⊜	212	44.54 N	77.37 W
Limerock	207	41.55 N	71.28 W
Lime Springs	190	43.27 N	92.17 W
Limestone, Austl.	162	21.11 S	119.50 E
Limestone, Fl., U.S.	220	27.21 N	81.53 W
Limestone, Me., U.S.	186	46.54 N	67.49 W
Limestone, N.Y., U.S.	210	42.01 N	78.37 W
Limestone ≃, U.S.	214	41.08 N	79.20 W
Limestone □⁶	222	31.35 N	96.35 W
Limestone ≃	184	56.31 N	94.07 W
Limestone, Lake ⊜¹	222	31.25 N	96.20 W
Limestone Bay c	184	53.50 N	98.50 W
Limestone Lake V	280	33.45 N	117.41 W
Limestone Creek ≃	210	43.06 N	75.58 W
Limestone Lake ⊜, Mb., Can.	184	56.35 N	96.00 W
Limestone Lake ⊜, Sk., Can.	184	54.36 N	103.18 W
Limestone Point Lake ⊜	184	55.07 N	100.32 W
Lime Street Station ⊷⁵	262	53.25 N	2.59 W
Lime Village	180	61.21 N	155.28 W
Limfjorden ⊜	26	56.55 N	9.10 E
Limhamn ⊷⁸	41	55.35 N	12.54 E
Limia (Lima) ≃	34	41.41 N	8.50 W
Limina	70	37.56 N	15.17 E
Liminka	26	64.49 N	25.24 E
Liminzhen	98	34.31 N	115.56 E
Limt Brook ≃	283	42.42 N	71.25 W
Limmared	26	57.32 N	13.21 E
Limmaren ⊜	40	59.44 N	18.43 E
Limmen	52	52.34 N	4.41 E
Limmen Bight c³	164	14.45 S	135.40 E
Limmen Bight ≃	164	15.07 S	135.44 E
Limnos I	38	39.54 N	25.21 E
Limoeiro	250	7.52 S	35.27 W
Limoeiro do Norte	250	5.08 S	38.05 W
Limoges, On., Can.	212	45.20 N	75.15 W
Limoges, Fr.	32	45.50 N	1.16 E
Limoges-Fourches	261	48.38 N	2.40 E
Limogne	32	44.24 N	1.46 E
Limón, Hond.	236	15.52 N	85.33 W
Limon, Co., U.S.	198	39.15 N	103.41 W
Limón □⁴	236	10.00 N	83.15 W
Limonar	240p	22.57 N	81.24 W
Limone Piemonte	62	44.12 N	7.34 E
Limone sul Garda	62	45.49 N	10.47 E
Limours	50	48.39 N	2.05 E
Limousin, Plateaux du ⚹¹	32	45.50 N	1.15 E
Limoux	32	43.04 N	2.14 E
Limpopo ≃	156	25.15 S	33.30 E
Limpsfield	262	51.16 N	0.01 E
Limski kanal c	64	45.07 N	13.38 E
Limu	102	25.02 N	110.51 E
Limuru	154	1.06 S	36.39 E
Linachamari	24	60.30 N	31.20 E
Lĩnan	128	28.42 N	43.48 E
Lin'an	106	30.14 N	119.43 E
Lĩnanäs	26	59.38 N	18.31 E
Linao Bay c	116	6.45 N	124.00 E
Linapacan Island I	116	11.27 N	119.49 E
Linapacan Strait ⊔	116	11.37 N	119.56 E
Linares, Chile	252	35.51 S	71.36 W
Linares, Col.	246	1.23 N	77.31 W
Linares, Esp.	34	38.05 N	3.38 W
Linares, Méx.	232	24.52 N	99.34 W
Linariá	38	38.50 N	24.32 E
Linaro, Capo ⊁	66	42.02 N	11.50 E
Linas	261	48.38 N	2.16 E
Linas, Monte ▲	71	39.27 N	8.37 E
Linas-Montlhéry, Domaine Militaire de ⊗	261	48.37 N	2.13 E
Linate, Aeroporto di ⊠	62	45.27 N	9.16 E
Lincai	100	33.50 N	114.56 E
Lincang	102	23.45 N	102.20 E
Lince	286d	12.06 S	77.03 W
Linch	200	43.36 N	106.11 W
Lincheng, Zhg.	98	37.27 N	114.29 E
Lincheng, Zhg.	106	30.55 N	119.47 E
Linch'ing — Linqing	98	36.53 N	115.41 E
Lincoln, Arg.	252	34.52 S	61.32 W
Lincoln, On., Can.	212	43.10 N	79.29 W
Lincoln, N.Z.	172	43.39 S	172.29 E
Lincoln, Eng., U.K.	44	53.14 N	0.33 W
Lincoln, Al., U.S.	194	33.56 N	94.25 W
Lincoln, Ca., U.S.	226	38.53 N	121.17 W
Lincoln, De., U.S.	208	38.52 N	75.25 W
Lincoln, Il., U.S.	219	40.08 N	89.21 W
Lincoln, Ks., U.S.	198	39.02 N	98.08 W
Lincoln, Me., U.S.	188	45.21 N	68.30 W
Lincoln, Ma., U.S.	207	42.25 N	71.18 W
Lincoln, Mi., U.S.	190	44.41 N	83.24 W
Lincoln, Mt., U.S.	202	46.57 N	112.40 W
Lincoln, Ne., U.S.	198	40.48 N	96.40 W
Lincoln, N.H., U.S.	188	44.02 N	71.40 W
Lincoln, Pa., U.S.	228	40.12 N	76.12 W
Lincoln, R.I., U.S.	207	41.54 N	71.25 W
Lincoln, Tx., U.S.	222	30.17 N	96.52 W
Lincoln □⁵, Mo., U.S.	219	39.05 N	90.57 W
Lincoln □⁶, U.K.	224	44.59 N	123.52 W
Lincoln, Mount ▲	200	39.21 N	106.07 W
Lincoln Acres	228	32.40 N	117.04 W
Lincoln Boyhood National Memorial ⊥	194	38.10 N	86.58 W
Lincoln Cathedral ⊥¹	44	53.14 N	0.33 W
Lincoln Center ⊥¹	276	40.46 N	73.59 W
Lincoln City	224	44.57 N	124.00 W
Lincoln Creek ≃, Ne., U.S.	198	40.54 N	97.06 W
Lincoln Creek ≃, Wa., U.S.	224	46.45 N	123.02 W
Lincolndale	210	41.18 N	73.43 W
Lincoln Estates	278	41.31 N	87.49 W
Lincoln Heights, Oh., U.S.	218	39.15 N	84.28 W
Lincoln Heights, Pa., U.S.	279b	40.19 N	79.37 W

FRANÇAIS Nom	Page	Lat.°'	Lcng.°' W=Ouest
Lincoln Home National Historic Site ⊥	219	39.47 N	89.38 W
Lincolnia Heights	284c	38.50 N	77.09 W
Lincoln Memorial ⊥	284c	38.53 N	77.03 W
Lincoln Park, Co., U.S.	200	38.25 N	105.13 W
Lincoln Park, Ga., U.S.	192	32.52 N	84.19 W
Lincoln Park, Mi., U.S.	216	42.15 N	83.10 W
Lincoln Park, N.J., U.S.	276	40.55 N	74.18 W
Lincoln Park, N.Y., U.S.	210	41.57 N	74.30 W
Lincoln Park ⬧, Ca., U.S.	282	37.46 N	122.30 W
Lincoln Park ⬧, Il., U.S.	278	41.56 N	87.38 W
Lincoln Park Airport ⊠	276	40.57 N	74.19 W
Lincoln Place ⬧	279b	40.22 N	79.55 W
Lincoln Sea ⊤²	16	83.00 N	56.30 W
Lincolnshire	216	42.11 N	87.54 W
Lincolnshire □⁶	28	52.55 N	0.22 W
Lincoln's New Salem State Park ⬧	219	39.58 N	89.52 W
Lincoln Tomb State Memorial ⊥	219	39.50 N	89.39 W
Lincolnton, Ga., U.S.	192	33.47 N	82.28 W
Lincolnton, N.C., U.S.	192	35.28 N	81.15 W
Lincoln Tunnel ⊷⁵	276	40.46 N	74.31 W
Lincoln University	208	39.48 N	75.55 W
Lincoln Village, Ca., U.S.	226	38.00 N	121.19 W
Lincoln Village, Oh., U.S.	218	39.57 N	83.38 W
Lincolnville	214	41.47 N	79.51 W
Lincolnwood	278	42.00 N	87.43 W
Lincolnwood Hills	278	41.31 N	87.54 W
Linconia	285	40.08 N	74.59 W
Lincroft	208	40.19 N	74.07 W
Lind, Ross.	80	56.37 N	44.37 E
Linda, Ca., U.S.	226	39.08 N	121.32 W
Linda-a-Velha	266c	38.43 N	9.14 W
Lindale, Ga., U.S.	192	34.11 N	85.10 W
Lindale, Tx., U.S.	222	32.30 N	95.24 W
Lindau, Dtsch.	41	54.36 N	9.47 E
Lindau, Dtsch.	52	51.39 N	10.37 E
Lindau, Dtsch.	54	52.02 N	12.26 E
Lindau, Dtsch.	58	47.33 N	9.41 E
Lindbergh	219	39.02 N	92.38 W
Lindbergh Field ⊠	228	32.44 N	117.11 W
Lind Coulee V	202	47.00 N	119.10 W
Linde ≃	78	64.57 N	124.36 E
Lindeln, Dtsch.	58	50.31 N	8.39 E
Linden, Guy.	246	6.00 N	58.18 W
Linden, Al., U.S.	194	32.18 N	87.47 W
Linden, Ca., U.S.	226	38.01 N	121.05 W
Linden, In., U.S.	194	40.11 N	86.54 W
Linden, Mi., U.S.	216	42.48 N	83.46 W
Linden, N.J., U.S.	210	40.37 N	74.14 W
Linden, Pa., U.S.	210	41.14 N	77.08 W
Linden, Tn., U.S.	194	35.37 N	87.50 W
Linden, Tx., U.S.	194	33.00 N	94.21 W
Linden Airport ⊠	276	40.37 N	74.14 W
Lindenberg, Dtsch.	54	53.02 N	12.37 E
Lindenberg, Dtsch.	54	52.36 N	13.31 E
Lindenberg im Allgäu	58	47.36 N	9.53 E
Linden-Dahlhausen	263	51.26 N	7.09 E
Lindenfels	58	49.41 N	8.47 E
Lindenhorst ⊷⁸	263	51.33 N	7.27 E
Lindenhurst, Il., U.S.	216	42.24 N	88.01 W
Lindenhurst, N.Y., U.S.	210	40.41 N	73.22 W
Lindenthal, Pa., U.S.	285	40.14 N	74.54 W
Linden Park	216	40.13 N	85.23 W
Lindenthal	54	51.24 N	12.20 E
Lindenwold	208	39.49 N	74.59 W
Lindenwood, Il., U.S.	218	42.03 N	89.32 W
Linderhausen	263	51.18 N	7.17 E
Linderhof, Schloss ⊥	64	47.34 N	10.57 E
Lindesberg	40	59.35 N	15.14 E
Lindesnes ⊁	40	58.00 N	7.02 E
Lindesnes ⊁¹	26	58.00 N	7.02 E
Lindfield, Austl.	274a	33.47 S	151.10 E
Lindfield, Eng., U.K.	42	51.01 N	0.05 W
Lindfors	40	59.36 N	13.49 E
Lindholmen	40	59.35 N	18.06 E
Lindhorst	52	52.21 N	9.17 E
Lindi, Tan.	154	10.00 S	39.43 E
Lindi ≃, R.D.C.	154	9.15 S	38.45 E
Lindi ≃	154	0.33 N	25.05 E
Lindis Pass ⋈	172	44.35 S	169.40 E
Lindley, Afr. S.	157b	27.50 S	27.55 E
Lindley, N.Y., U.S.	210	42.02 N	77.08 W
Lindley, S. Afr.	158	28.00 S	27.37 E
Lindóia	256	58.37 N	16.15 E
Lindome	26	57.34 N	12.05 E
Lindong, Zhg.	100	39.44 N	103.04 E
Lindong, Zhg.	100	39.51 N	117.41 E
Lindsborg	198	38.35 N	97.40 W
Lindsay, Mount ▲²	162	34.49 S	117.18 E
Lindenäs	40	65.19 N	15.15 E
Lindsnäs	40	60.00 N	15.15 E
Lindsnes ⊁	26	58.00 N	7.02 E
Lindfield, Austl.	274a	33.47 S	151.10 E
Lindsay, Ca., U.S.	226	36.12 N	119.05 W
Lindsay, On., Can.	204	36.12 N	119.05 W
Lindsay, Ne., U.S.	198	41.42 N	97.41 W
Lindsay, Ok., U.S.	196	34.50 N	97.36 W
Lindsborg	198	38.35 N	97.40 W
Lindsey Lake ⊜	276	45.07 N	9.35 E
Lindved	41	55.47 N	9.35 E
LindØ	41	55.28 N	10.37 E
Line Creek ≃	194	33.34 N	88.42 W
Line Islands II	14	0.05 N	157.00 W
Line Lexington	208	40.17 N	75.16 W
Line Mountain ▲	208	40.45 N	76.37 W
Linesville	214	41.39 N	80.25 W
Lineville, Al., U.S.	194	33.18 N	85.45 W
Lineville, Ia., U.S.	190	40.34 N	93.31 W
Lĩnevo	86	54.05 N	83.24 E
Linfen	102	36.05 N	111.32 E
Linford	262	51.29 N	0.29 E
Lĩng'an	98	57.19 N	5.27 W
Lingamaki Reservoir ⊜¹	122	14.04 N	74.49 E
Lingayen	116	16.01 N	120.14 E
Lingayen Gulf c	116	16.15 N	120.14 E
Lingbi	100	33.33 N	117.33 E
Lingchuan, Zhg.	102	25.26 N	110.15 E
Lingchuan, Zhg.	102	35.46 N	113.26 E
Lingdale	44	54.34 N	0.57 W
Lingdianzheñ	106	30.51 N	121.00 E
Lingdou	100	26.22 N	118.56 E
Lingen	52	52.31 N	7.19 E
Lingesetausee ⊜¹	263	51.06 N	7.20 E
Lingfen ⊷	100	24.44 N	115.35 E

PORTUGUÊS Nome	Página	Lat.°'	Long.°' W=Oeste
Lingfield	42	51.11 N	0.01 W
Lingga, Kepulauan II	112	0.05 S	104.35 E
Lingga, Pulau I	112	0.12 S	104.35 E
Lingham' Lake ⊜	212	44.46 N	77.25 W
Linghe ≃	98	36.23 N	119.03 E
Linghu	106	30.44 N	120.10 E
Lingig	116	8.02 N	126.24 E
Lingjiachang	107	29.28 N	104.54 E
Lingjiaqiao	98	30.09 N	120.04 E
Lingkar Dzong	124	28.45 N	90.36 E
Lingkou, Zhg.	106	29.16 N	120.38 E
Lingkou, Zhg.	106	31.57 N	119.38 E
Lingle	200	42.08 N	104.20 W
Linglestown	208	40.21 N	76.48 W
Lingling	102	26.13 N	111.37 E
Lingonçta	98	40.54 N	119.59 E
Lingma	102	23.22 N	107.53 E
Lingolsheim	58	48.34 N	7.41 E
Lingomo	152	0.38 N	21.59 E
Lingqiu	98	39.24 N	114.13 E
Lingshan, Zhg.	98	36.33 N	120.27 E
Lingshan, Zhg.	102	22.28 N	109.17 E
Lingshanwei	98	35.58 N	120.13 E
Lingshi	102	36.54 N	111.43 E
Lingshou	98	38.18 N	114.24 E
Lingshui	110	18.31 N	110.01 E
Lingtangqiao	102	32.43 N	119.14 E
Linguaglossa	70	37.50 N	15.08 E
Linguère	150	15.24 N	15.07 W
Lingwala	273b	4.22 S	15.17 E
Lingwood	42	52.37 N	1.29 E
Lingwu	102	38.06 N	106.21 E
Lingxian, Zhg.	98	37.21 N	116.34 E
Lingxian, Zhg.	100	26.30 N	113.46 E
Lingxiazhu	100	29.03 N	119.46 E
Lingyang	98	41.15 N	119.16 E
Lingyuan	98	39.04 N	117.09 E
Lingzinan	105	39.29 N	115.15 E
Linh, Ngoc ▲	110	15.04 N	107.59 E
Linhai	98	28.51 N	121.07 E
Linhares	255	19.25 S	40.04 W
Linh Cam	110	18.31 N	105.34 E
Linhe	102	40.51 N	107.30 E
Linhezhuang	105	40.04 N	117.33 E
Linhigh	286c	39.21 N	76.31 W
Linhó	266c	38.46 N	9.23 W
Linhsia — Linxia	102	35.35 N	103.13 E
Linhuaiguan	100	32.56 N	117.38 E
Linhuanji	100	33.42 N	116.33 E
Linhsi — Linyi	98	35.04 N	118.22 E
Linjiang, Zhg.	102	31.44 N	126.55 E
Linjiang, Zhg.	100	27.50 N	118.26 E
Linjiang, Zhg.	100	28.04 N	115.21 E
Linjiangchang	100	28.41 N	105.01 E
Linjiangsi	107	30.15 N	104.37 E
Linjiatai	104	40.43 N	123.57 E
Linkenheim-Hochstetten	56	49.07 N	8.24 E
Linköping	26	58.25 N	15.37 E
Linkou	89	45.15 N	130.16 E
Linksfield ⊷⁸	273d	26.10 S	28.06 E
Linksmakalnis	26	54.45 N	23.55 E
Linksness	46	58.56 N	3.19 W
Linkuva	76	56.05 N	23.59 E
Linkwocd	58	58.32 N	75.57 W
Linli	102	29.18 N	111.30 E
Linlithgow	46	55.59 N	3.37 W
Linmeyer	273d	26.16 S	28.04 E
Linn, Ks., U.S.	198	39.40 N	97.05 W
Linn, Mo., U.S.	219	38.29 N	91.51 W
Linn □⁶	263	51.20 N	6.38 E
Linnancang	105	39.50 N	117.37 E
Linnansaaren kansallispuisto ⬧	26	62.07 N	28.31 E
Linnell	226	36.21 N	119.11 W
Linnés Hammarby ⊥	40	59.49 N	17.46 E
Linn Grove	226	40.38 N	85.01 W
Linnhe, Loch c	46	56.39 N	5.21 W
Linnich	58	50.59 N	6.16 E
Linntown	210	40.57 N	95.42 W
Linolne Bayou ≃	222	32.06 N	95.42 W
Linosa, sola di I	70a	35.51 N	12.52 E
Lin'ovo	80	50.53 N	44.51 E
Linow	54	53.06 N	12.49 E
Linping — Yuñang	106	30.25 N	120.18 E
Linqi	100	30.03 N	120.15 E
Linqi, Zhg.	105	35.48 N	113.53 E
Linqing	98	29.51 N	119.06 E
Linqing	98	36.53 N	115.41 E
Linquan	100	33.06 N	115.13 E
Linru	100	34.11 N	112.49 E
Linruzhen	100	34.17 N	112.35 E
Lins	255	21.40 S	49.45 W
Linshan	102	30.09 N	120.59 E
Linshanpu	104	41.34 N	123.20 E
Linshui	102	30.21 N	106.59 E
Linslade	42	51.55 N	0.41 W
Linstead	241d	18.08 N	77.02 W
Lintan	100	34.40 N	103.40 E
Lintao	100	35.27 N	103.46 E
Linté	152	5.24 N	11.42 E
Linthal, Fr.	58	47.07 N	9.07 E
Linthal, Schw.	58	46.55 N	9.00 E
Linthicum Heights	284b	39.12 N	76.39 W
Linthwaite	262	53.37 N	1.51 W
Lintingkou	105	39.39 N	117.30 E
Linton, Austl.	169	37.41 S	143.34 E
Linton, N.Z.	172	40.26 S	175.33 E
Linton, Eng., U.K.	42	52.06 N	0.17 E
Linton, In., U.S.	194	39.02 N	87.10 W
Linton, N.D., U.S.	198	46.16 N	100.13 W
Linton Park ⬧	260	51.13 N	0.31 E
Lintorf	58	51.20 N	6.49 E
Linville, Austl.	171a	26.53 S	152.16 E
Linwood, Austl.	168b	34.21 S	138.46 E
Linwood, N.J., U.S.	208	39.20 N	74.34 W
Linwood, Ne., U.S.	198	41.25 N	96.58 W
Linwood, Pa., U.S.	208	39.49 N	75.24 W
Linworth	218	40.06 N	83.04 W
Linxi	105	41.06 N	122.15 E
Linxi, Zhg.	100	39.48 N	118.24 E
Linxi, Zhg.	100	43.30 N	118.02 E
Linxia	102	35.35 N	103.13 E
Linxian, Zhg.	98	37.58 N	110.58 E
Linxian, Zhg.	100	36.01 N	120.30 E
Linyanti	156	18.04 S	24.01 E
Linyi, Zhg.	98	37.13 N	116.51 E
Linyi, Zhg.	98	35.15 N	118.21 E
Linyi — Shanhaiguan	98	40.01 N	119.44 E
Linyu	100	22.30 N	120.23 E
Linz, Dtsch.	58	50.34 N	7.17 E
Linz, Öst.	61	48.18 N	14.18 E
Linze, Zhg.	102	33.03 N	119.38 E
Linze, Zhg.	100	39.09 N	100.17 E
Linzgau ⚹¹	58	47.45 N	9.10 E
Linzhai	100	24.44 N	115.35 E

Nom	Page	Lat.°'	Long.°'
Linzhang	98	36.21 N	114.36 E
Linzhi	100	29.25 N	94.22 E
Linzikou	100	28.42 N	112.46 E
Linzolo	152	4.25 S	15.07 E
Lioko, R.D.C.	152	0.02 N	22.04 E
Lioko, R.D.C.	152	1.25 N	23.07 E
Lio Matoh	112	3.10 N	115.14 E
Liomer	50	49.51 N	1.49 E
Lion, Golfe du c	32	43.00 N	4.00 E
Lionel Town	241q	17.48 N	77.14 W
Lioni	68	40.52 N	15.11 E
Lion Rock ▲²	271d	22.22 N	114.11 E
Lion Rock Tunnel ⊷⁵	271d	22.21 N	114.09 E
Lions Den	154	17.16 S	30.02 E
Lion's Head	212	44.59 N	81.15 W
Lionville	208	40.03 N	75.39 W
Lioppa	112	7.40 S	126.00 E
Liouesso	152	1.02 N	15.43 E
Lipa	116	13.57 N	121.10 E
Lipan	196	32.31 N	98.03 W
Lipany	30	49.10 N	20.58 E
Lipari	70	38.28 N	14.57 E
Lipari, Isola I	70	38.29 N	14.56 E
Lipatkain	112	0.01 S	101.13 E
Lipayan	104	42.13 N	123.23 E
Lipeck	76	52.37 N	39.35 E
Lipeck Oblast' □⁴	76	52.30 N	39.00 E
Lipetsk	26	62.32 N	29.22 E
— Lipeck	76	52.37 N	39.35 E
Lipez, Cerro ▲	248	21.53 S	66.52 W
Liphook	42	51.05 N	0.49 W
Lipiany	30	53.00 N	14.59 E
Lipicy	76	53.22 N	37.17 E
Lipin Bor	76	60.16 N	37.57 E
Liping	102	26.17 N	109.00 E
Lipiyu	104	40.29 N	123.36 E
Lipka ≃	76	53.58 N	37.42 E
Lipki	76	53.58 N	37.42 E
Lipník nad Bečvou	30	49.31 N	17.35 E
Lipniški	76	54.00 N	25.37 E
Lipno	30	52.51 N	19.10 E
Lipno, údolní Nádrž ⊜¹	61	48.43 N	14.04 E
Lipno nad Vltavou	61	48.38 N	14.14 E
Lipoa Point ⊁	229a	21.02 N	156.38 W
Lipova	38	46.05 N	21.40 E
Lipovcy	89	44.11 N	131.44 E
Lipovka, Ross.	78	50.52 N	40.21 E
Lipovka, Ross.	80	52.26 N	46.11 E
Lipovka, Ross.	80	49.45 N	44.56 E
Lippborg	52	51.40 N	8.02 E
Lippe ≃	52	51.39 N	6.38 E
Lipperode	52	51.41 N	8.22 E
Lippetal	52	51.40 N	8.06 E
Lippoldsberg	52	51.37 N	9.34 E
Lippstadt	52	51.40 N	8.19 E
Lipscomb	196	36.14 N	100.16 W
Lipsko	30	51.09 N	21.39 E
Lipsói I, Ellás	38	37.20 N	26.45 E
Lipsói I, Ellás	130	37.20 N	26.45 E
Lipton	184	50.54 N	103.50 W
Liptovská Teplička	30	48.59 N	20.06 E
Liptovský Mikuláš	30	49.05 N	19.37 E
Liptrap, Cape ⊁	168	38.54 S	145.55 E
Lipu	102	24.25 N	110.29 E
Lipu La ⋈	124	30.21 N	81.05 E
Liqiao	100	29.03 N	104.48 E
Lira, Ug.	154	2.15 N	32.54 E
Lira, Ven.	286c	10.26 N	66.46 W
Lirangdan	102	31.49 N	116.14 E
Lircay	248	12.56 S	74.43 W
Liren	100	33.55 N	118.47 E
Lirentuncun	98	41.24 N	122.59 E
Liri ≃	66	41.25 N	13.52 E
Liro ≃	175t	16.27 S	168.13 E
Lisakovsk	82	52.33 N	62.36 E
Lisala	152	2.09 N	21.31 E
Lisavy	92	50.47 N	28.35 E
Lisboa (Lisbon), Port.	34	38.43 N	9.08 W
Lisboa □⁴, Port.	266c	38.43 N	9.08 W
Lisboa □⁵	266c	38.48 N	9.16 W
Lisbon — Lisboa, Port.	34	38.43 N	9.08 W
Lisbon, Md., U.S.	216	41.29 N	80.46 W
Lisbon, Md., U.S.	208	39.20 N	77.04 W
Lisbon, N.H., U.S.	188	44.12 N	71.54 W
Lisbon, Oh., U.S.	214	40.46 N	80.46 W
Lisbon Falls	188	44.00 N	70.03 W
Lisbon — Lisboa	34	38.43 N	9.08 W
Lisburn	48	54.31 N	6.03 W
Lisburne, Cape ⊁	180	68.52 N	166.14 W
Lisburne Peninsula ⊁¹	180	68.30 N	165.15 W
Liscannor Bay c	48	52.55 N	9.25 W
Liscarney	48	53.43 N	9.35 W
Liscia ≃	71	41.11 N	9.18 E
Liscia, Lago di ⊜	71	41.00 N	9.11 E
Lisdoonvarna	48	53.02 N	9.17 W
Liselеje	41	56.01 N	11.59 E
Lishan, Zhg.	104	31.50 N	113.16 E
Lishangzhuang	105	40.10 N	120.00 E
Lishčynivka	105	40.11 N	119.53 E
Lishe ≃	106	29.48 N	121.28 E
Lishi	102	37.32 N	111.09 E
Lishi, Zhg.	100	31.14 N	120.37 E
Lishui, Zhg.	106	28.27 N	119.54 E
Lishui, Zhg.	106	31.39 N	119.01 E
Lisianski Island I	14	25.02 N	174.00 W
Lisicy	82	56.47 N	36.21 E
Lisičansk	92	48.55 N	38.26 E
Lisichov — Lysychan'sk	83	48.55 N	38.26 E
Lisieux, Sk., Can.	184	49.17 N	105.59 W
Lisieux, Fr.	50	49.09 N	0.14 E
Lisi Nos	265a	60.01 N	29.59 E
Lisišvhchyna	105	50.47 N	28.35 E
Lisizhuang	105	38.56 N	115.07 E
Lisja	85	57.15 N	54.22 E
Lisje	65	50.58 N	39.50 E
Liskeard	42	50.28 N	4.28 W
Liski, Ross.	80	50.58 N	39.30 E
Liski, Ross.	92	51.04 N	39.30 E
L'Isle, Schw.	58	46.26 N	143.49 W
L'Isle, Il., U.S.	216	41.48 N	88.04 W
L'Isle-Adam	50	49.06 N	2.14 E
L'Isle-Jourdain	32	43.37 N	1.05 E
L'Isle-sur-la-Sorgue	32	43.55 N	5.03 E
L'Isle-sur-le-Doubs	58	47.27 N	6.35 E
L'Isle-sur-Serein	50	47.35 N	4.01 E
Lisman	194	32.10 N	88.16 W
Lismore, Austl.	168	37.58 S	143.22 E
Lismore, N.S., Can.	186	45.42 N	62.11 W
Lismore	48	52.08 N	7.55 W
Lismore Castle ⊥	48	52.08 N	7.52 W
Lismore Island I	46	56.29 N	5.33 W
Lišov	61	49.01 N	14.37 E
Lisoá	42	51.03 N	0.55 W
Lisovka, Ross.	84	59.27 N	63.22 E
Lisková	30	49.07 N	19.24 E
L'Isle, Il., U.S.	216	41.48 N	88.04 W
Lissabon — Lisboa	34	38.43 N	9.08 W

Nom	Page	Lat.°'	Long.°'
Lissberg	56	50.22 N	9.05 E
Lisse	52	52.15 N	4.33 E
Lisses	261	48.36 N	2.26 E
Lissewege	50	51.18 N	3.11 E
Lissie	222	29.33 N	96.13 W
Lissingen	56	50.14 N	6.38 E
Lissone	62	45.37 N	9.14 E
Lissy	261	48.38 N	2.42 E
Lista	80	47.44 N	45.54 E
Lista ⊁¹	26	58.07 N	6.40 E
Lister ≃	263	51.05 N	7.45 E
Listiċa	36	43.23 N	17.36 E
Listowel, On., Can.	212	43.44 N	80.57 W
Listowel, Ire.	48	52.27 N	9.29 W
Listv'anka	88	51.52 N	104.51 E
Listv'anskij	86	54.27 N	83.29 E
Lisui	105	40.05 N	116.44 E
Lit	26	63.19 N	14.49 E
Lita	100	37.22 N	116.34 E
Litang, Malay.	112	5.20 N	118.31 E
Litang, Zhg.	102	23.11 N	109.05 E
Litang, Zhg.	102	30.00 N	100.16 E
Litang ≃	102	28.04 N	101.30 E
Litani ≃	250	3.40 N	54.00 W
Lĩtāni, Nahr al- ≃	132	33.20 N	35.14 E
Litava ≃	61	49.02 N	16.36 E
Litcham	42	52.44 N	0.47 E
Litchfield, Ct., U.S.	207	41.44 N	73.11 W
Litchfield, Il., U.S.	219	39.10 N	89.39 W
Litchfield, Mi., U.S.	216	42.02 N	84.45 W
Litchfield, Ne., U.S.	198	41.09 N	99.09 W
Litchfield, Oh., U.S.	214	41.10 N	82.02 W
Litchfield □⁶	207	41.45 N	73.11 W
Litchfield Park	200	33.29 N	112.21 W
Litchville	198	46.39 N	98.11 W
Literberry	219	39.51 N	90.12 W
Lith, Wādĩ al- V	144	20.40 N	40.06 E
Litherlard	44	53.28 N	2.59 W
Lithgow	170	33.29 S	150.09 E
Lithia	220	27.51 N	82.10 W
Líthinon, Ákra ⊁	38	34.55 N	24.44 E
Lithonia	192	33.42 N	84.06 W
Lithuania (Lietuva) □¹, Europe	22	56.00 N	24.00 E
Lithuania (Lietuva) □¹, Europe	76	56.00 N	24.00 E
Litian	100	26.58 N	114.10 E
Litija	36	46.03 N	14.50 E
Litipāra	124	24.42 N	87.37 E
Lititz	208	40.09 N	76.18 W
Litke	89	53.57 N	140.15 E
Litókhoron	38	40.06 N	22.30 E
Litoa	154	1.13 S	24.47 E
Litoměřice	54	50.35 N	14.09 E
Litomyšl	30	49.52 N	16.19 E
Litoo	154	9.54 S	38.24 E
Litouqiao	106	31.15 N	118.54 E
Litovel	30	49.42 N	17.05 E
Litovko	89	49.15 N	135.11 E
Litschau	61	48.57 N	15.03 E
Littau	58	47.03 N	8.16 E
Little ≃, Austl.	169	38.01 S	144.35 E
Little ≃, On., Can.	281	42.20 N	82.56 W
Little ≃, U.S.	194	33.37 N	93.52 W
Little ≃, U.S.	194	35.32 N	90.25 W
Little ≃, U.S.	194	31.18 N	87.46 W
Little ≃, Al., U.S.	194	34.16 N	85.40 W
Little ≃, Al., U.S.	207	41.36 N	72.03 W
Little ≃, Ga., U.S.	192	30.55 N	83.21 W
Little ≃, Ga., U.S.	192	33.39 N	82.22 W
Little ≃, Ga., U.S.	194	33.34 N	83.24 W
Little ≃, In., U.S.	216	40.53 N	85.32 W
Little ≃, Ky., U.S.	194	31.38 N	91.49 W
Little ≃, Ma., U.S.	283	42.37 N	70.42 W
Little ≃, Ma., U.S.	283	42.46 N	70.51 W
Little ≃, N.Y., U.S.	210	43.16 N	75.20 W
Little ≃, S.C., U.S.	192	35.03 N	78.02 W
Little ≃, S.C., U.S.	192	35.15 N	78.42 W
Little ≃, Ok., U.S.	196	34.06 N	96.25 W
Little ≃, S.C., U.S.	192	34.11 N	81.45 W
Little ≃, Tn., U.S.	222	30.56 N	96.41 W
Little ≃, Va., U.S.	192	37.04 N	80.32 W
Little ≃, Va., U.S.	208	39.20 N	77.04 W
Little Abaco I	238	26.53 N	77.43 W
Little Alföld — Kis Alföld ⚹	61	47.30 N	17.00 E
Little Andaman I	110	10.45 N	92.30 E
Little Arkansas ≃	198	37.43 N	97.22 W
Little Auglaize ≃	216	41.07 N	84.25 W
Little Averill Lake ⊜	206	44.57 N	71.44 W
Little Baddow	260	51.44 N	0.35 E
Little Barrier Island I	172	36.12 S	175.05 E
Little Bay	241a	16.45 N	62.11 W
Little Bay Islands	186	49.37 N	55.47 W
Little Bear ≃	200	41.46 N	112.11 W
Little Bear Creek ≃	196	34.23 N	88.03 W
Little Beaver Creek ≃, U.S.	198	40.11 N	103.23 W
Little Beaver Creek ≃, U.S.	214	40.39 N	80.33 W
Little Beaver Creek ≃	214	40.43 N	80.37 W
Little Belt — Lille Bælt ⊔	41	55.20 N	9.45 E
Little Belt Mountains ⚹	202	46.45 N	110.35 W
Little Berkhamsted	260	51.45 N	0.08 W
Little Bighorn ≃	200	45.44 N	107.34 W
Little Bighorn Battlefield National Monument ⬧	202	45.32 N	107.20 W
Little Billabong ≃	171b	35.35 S	147.32 E
Little Bitter Lake — Murrah as-Sughrã, Al-Buhayrah al- ⊜	146	30.10 N	32.33 E
Little Black ≃, Ak., U.S.	180	66.26 N	143.49 W
Little Black Bear Indian Reserve ⬧	184	50.51 N	103.23 W
Little Blackfoot ≃	202	46.31 N	112.43 W
Little Blue ≃, In., U.S.	216	38.12 N	103.36 W

Nom	Page	Lat.°'	Long.°'
Little Chartiers Creek ≃	279b	40.17 N	80.08 W
Little Choptank River c	208	38.32 N	76.13 W
Little Churchill ≃	184	57.15 N	95.21 W
Little Chute	190	44.16 N	88.19 W
Little Coco Island I	110	14.00 N	93.13 E
Little Colorado ≃	200	36.11 N	111.48 W
Little Compton	207	41.30 N	71.10 W
Little Cooley	214	41.44 N	79.53 W
Little Cottonwood ≃	198	44.15 N	94.20 W
Little Creek	208	39.10 N	75.26 W
Little Creek ≃	285	39.56 N	74.48 W
Little Creek Naval Amphibious Base ⊗	208	36.55 N	76.10 W
Little Creek Reservoir ⊜¹	208	37.20 N	76.50 W
Little Cumbrae Island I	46	55.43 N	4.57 W
Little Current	190	45.58 N	81.56 W
Little Current ≃	176	50.57 N	84.36 W
Little Cypress Bayou ≃	194	32.41 N	94.15 W
Little Cypress Creek ≃	194	32.39 N	94.42 W
Little Darby Creek ≃	218	39.53 N	83.13 W
Little Dart ≃	42	50.54 N	3.51 W
Little Deep Creek ≃	198	43.36 N	100.52 W
Little Deer Creek ≃, In., U.S.	216	40.36 N	86.28 W
Little Deer Creek ≃, Pa., U.S.	279b	40.33 N	79.50 W
Little Deschutes ≃	202	43.51 N	121.44 W
Little Desert ⊷²	166	36.35 S	141.20 E
Little Desert National Park ⬧	166	36.25 S	141.25 E
Little Diomede Island I	180	65.45 N	168.57 W
Little Don ≃	275b	43.42 N	79.20 W
Little Dry Creek ≃, Ca., U.S.	226	39.22 N	121.52 W
Little Dry Creek ≃, Mt., U.S.	202	47.21 N	106.22 W
Little Ease Run ≃	285	39.39 N	75.04 W
Little Eau Pleine ≃	190	44.40 N	89.41 W
Little Egg Harbor c	208	39.35 N	74.18 W
Little Elkhart ≃	216	41.43 N	85.49 W
Little End	260	51.41 N	0.14 E
Little Etobicoke Creek ≃	275b	43.37 N	79.34 W
Little Exuma I	238	23.27 N	75.37 W
Little Fabius ≃	219	39.59 N	91.59 W
Little Falls, Mn., U.S.	190	45.58 N	94.21 W
Little Falls, N.J., U.S.	276	40.52 N	74.12 W
Little Falls, N.Y., U.S.	210	43.02 N	74.51 W
Little Falls Dam ⊷⁶	284c	38.57 N	77.08 W
Little Farms	284	30.06 N	90.13 W
Little Ferry	276	40.51 N	74.02 W
Littlefield	196	33.55 N	102.19 W
Little Flatrock ≃	218	39.26 N	85.33 W
Littlefork	190	48.23 N	93.33 W
Little Fork ≃	190	48.31 N	93.35 W
Little Fort	182	51.25 N	120.12 W
Little Genesee	210	42.00 N	78.13 W
Little Gold ≃	162	18.01 S	126.29 E
Little Gunpowder Falls ≃	208	39.25 N	76.22 W
Littlehampton	42	50.48 N	0.33 W
Little Harbour Deep	186	50.15 N	56.33 W
Little Haw Creek ≃	192	29.21 N	81.24 W
Little Hawk Lake ⊜	212	45.10 N	78.42 W
Little Hoosic ≃	210	42.49 N	73.20 W
Little Hope ≃	214	42.06 N	79.49 W
Little Hulton	262	53.32 N	2.25 W
Little Humboldt ≃	204	41.00 N	117.43 W
Little Humboldt, North Fork ≃	204	41.27 N	117.09 W
Little Humboldt, South Fork ≃	204	41.26 N	117.07 W
Little Hurricane Creek ≃	194	32.13 N	82.19 W
Little Inagua I	238	21.30 N	73.00 W
Little Indian Creek ≃, Il., U.S.	216	41.31 N	88.46 W
Little Island ≃	218	36.50 N	86.08 W
Little Island Pond ⊜	283	42.43 N	71.17 W
Little Juniata ≃	208	37.52 N	121.14 W
Little Juniata Creek ≃	214	40.34 N	78.03 W
Little Kanawha ≃	208	40.23 N	77.02 W
Little Kanawha, West Fork ≃	188	39.16 N	81.34 W
Little Karroo (Klein Karroo) ⚹¹	158	33.45 S	21.30 E
Little Kentucky ≃	218	38.35 N	85.12 W
Little Klickitat ≃	224	45.51 N	121.04 W
Little Koniuji Island I	180	55.01 N	159.26 W
Little Lake ⊜, Ca., U.S.	212	44.26 N	79.40 W
Little Lake ⊜, La., U.S.	194	29.30 N	90.10 W
Little Laramie ≃	200	41.20 N	105.44 W
Little Laver	260	51.46 N	0.14 E
Little Leigh	262	53.17 N	2.35 W
Little Lever	262	53.34 N	2.22 W
Little Limestone Lake ⊜	184	54.06 N	99.18 W
Little London	241q	18.15 N	78.13 W
Little Lost ≃	200	43.49 N	103.23 W
Little Lun	116	6.02 N	125.17 E
Little Mahoning Creek ≃	214	40.49 N	79.00 W
Little Maitland ≃	210	43.58 N	81.18 W
Little Manatee ≃	220	27.42 N	82.28 W
Little Manatee, South Fork ≃	220	27.39 N	82.18 W
Little Manistee ≃	190	44.15 N	86.19 W
Little Manitou Lake ⊜	184	51.43 N	105.30 W
Little Marco Pass ⊔	220	26.01 N	81.46 W
Little Meadows	210	41.59 N	76.08 W
Little Mecatina ≃	176	50.28 N	59.35 W
Little Medicine Bow ≃	200	41.58 N	106.18 W
Little Mexico	196	30.57 N	102.52 W
Little Miami ≃	218	39.05 N	84.26 W
Little Miami, East Fork ≃	218	39.09 N	84.18 W
Little Miami, North Fork ≃	218	39.48 N	83.47 W
Little Mississippi ≃	212	44.52 N	78.13 W
Little Missouri ≃, U.S.	194	33.43 N	93.28 W
Little Missouri ≃, U.S.	198	47.30 N	102.25 W
Little Missouri ≃, Ar., U.S.	194	33.49 N	92.54 W
Little Mountain ▲	208	40.47 N	76.40 W
Little Muddy ≃, Il., U.S.	219	38.10 N	89.11 W
Little Muddy ≃, N.D., U.S.	198	48.12 N	103.36 W
Little Mulberry Creek ≃	194	32.26 N	86.51 W
Little Naches ≃	224	46.59 N	121.06 W
Little Nahant ⊁¹	283	42.26 N	70.56 W
Little Namaquaknd ⚹¹	158	29.00 S	18.00 E
Little Neck	285	29.00 S	17.00 E
Little Neck ⊁	276	40.46 N	73.44 W
Little Neck Bay c	276	40.47 N	73.46 W
Little Neshaminy Creek ≃	285	40.15 N	75.02 W
Little Niangua ≃	219	38.04 N	92.54 W
Little Nicobar I	110	7.20 N	93.40 E
Little Ohoopee ≃	192	32.27 N	82.24 W
Little Osage ≃	198	38.02 N	94.14 W

Legend

Symbol	English	Deutsch	Español	Français	Português
≃	River	Fluß	Río	Rivière	Rio
▨	Canal	Kanal	Canal	Canal	Canal
L	Waterfall, Rapids	Wasserfall, Stromschnellen	Cascada, Rápidos	Chute d'eau, Rapides	Cascata, Rápidos
⊔	Strait	Meeresstraße	Estrecho	Détroit	Estreito
c	Bay, Gulf	Bucht, Golf	Bahía, Golfo	Baie, Golfe	Baía, Golfo
⊜	Lake, Lakes	See, Seen	Lago, Lagos	Lac, Lacs	Lago, Lagos
⧫	Swamp	Sumpf	Pantano	Marais	Pântano
▨	Ice Features, Glacier	Eis- und Gletscherformen	Accidentes Glaciares	Formes glaciaires	Acidentes glaciares
⊤	Other Hydrographic Features	Andere Hydrographische Objekte	Otros Elementos Hidrográficos	Autres données hydrographiques	Outros acidentes hidrográficos
⊷	Submarine Features	Untermeerische Objekte	Accidentes Submarinos	Formes de relief sous-marin	Acidentes submarinos
□	Political Unit	Politische Einheit	Unidad Política	Entité politique	Unidade política
⊥	Cultural Institution	Kulturelle Institution	Institución Cultural	Institution culturelle	Instituição cultural
⊥	Historical Site	Historische Stätte	Sitio Histórico	Site historique	Sítio histórico
⬧	Recreational Site	Erholungs- und Ferienort	Sitio de Recreo	Centre de loisirs	Area de Lazer
⊠	Airport	Flughafen	Aeropuerto	Aéroport	Aeroporto
⊗	Military Installation	Militäranlagen	Instalación Militar	Installation militaire	Instalação militar
⊷	Miscellaneous	Verschiedenes	Misceláneo	Divers	Diversos

ENGLISH / DEUTSCH

Name	Page	Lat.°′	Long.°′
Little Otter Creek ≃	212	42.44 N	80.51 W
Little Ouse ≃	42	52.30 N	0.22 E
Little Panoche Creek ≃	226	36.50 N	120.42 W
Little Patuxent ≃	284b	39.11 N	76.52 W
Little Paxton	42	52.15 N	0.15 W
Little Peconic Bay c	207	40.59 N	72.24 W
Little Pee Dee ≃	192	33.42 N	79.11 W
Little Pic ≃	190	48.48 N	86.37 W
Little Pine and Lucky Man Indian Reserve ◆[4]	184	52.56 N	109.05 W
Little Pine Creek ≃, Pa., U.S.	210	41.18 N	77.22 W
Little Pine Creek ≃, Pa., U.S.	279b	40.31 N	79.57 W
Little Pine Island I	220	26.36 N	82.05 W
Little Pine Key I	220	24.44 N	81.19 W
Little Pine State Park ♠	210	41.22 N	77.20 W
Little Pipe Creek ≃	208	39.36 N	77.16 W
Little Platte ≃	194	39.24 N	94.41 W
Little Plum Creek ≃	279b	40.30 N	79.51 W
Little Popo Aggie ≃	202	42.54 N	108.35 W
Little Porcupine Creek ≃, Mt., U.S.	202	46.18 N	106.34 W
Little Porcupine Creek ≃, Mt., U.S.	202	48.02 N	106.04 W
Littleport	42	52.28 N	0.19 E
Little Portage Creek ≃	216	42.00 N	85.27 W
Little Powder ≃	198	45.28 N	105.20 W
Little Pucketa Creek ≃	279b	40.33 N	79.45 W
Little Quill Lake ⊜	184	51.55 N	104.05 W
Little Rann of Kachchh ≚	120	23.25 N	71.15 E
Little Red ≃	194	35.11 N	91.27 W
Little Red, Middle Fork ≃	194	35.37 N	92.11 W
Little Red Deer ≃	182	52.04 N	114.09 W
Little Red River Indian Reserve ◆[4]	184	53.30 N	105.58 W
Little Redstone Lake ⊜	212	45.13 N	78.34 W
Little River, Austl.	169	37.58 S	144.30 E
Little River, N.Z.	172	43.46 S	172.47 E
Little River, Ks., U.S.	198	38.23 N	98.00 W
Little River, Tx., U.S.	222	30.59 N	97.22 W
Little Rock, Ar., U.S.	194	34.44 N	92.17 W
Littlerock, Ca., U.S.	228	34.31 N	117.59 W
Little Rock, Il., U.S.	216	41.43 N	88.34 W
Little Rock, Ia., U.S.	198	43.26 N	95.52 W
Littlerock, Wa., U.S.	224	46.54 N	123.01 W
Little Rock ≃	198	43.16 N	96.15 W
Little Rock Air Force Base ■	194	34.55 N	92.10 W
Little Rock Creek ≃	228	34.28 N	118.01 W
Little Rock Wash V	228	34.42 N	118.02 W
Little Rocky Mountains ⋏	202	47.50 N	108.10 W
Little Rouge Creek ≃	212	43.48 N	79.08 W
Little Ruaha ≃	154	7.17 S	35.28 E
Little Sable Point ›	190	43.38 N	86.32 W
Little Sac ≃	194	37.39 N	93.46 W
Little Sachigo Lake ⊜	184	54.09 N	92.11 W
Little Saint Bernard Pass → Petit-Saint-Bernard, Col du)(	62	45.41 N	6.53 E
Little Salkehatchie ≃	192	32.37 N	80.53 W
Little Salmon ≃, Id., U.S.	202	45.25 N	116.19 W
Little Salmon ≃, N.Y., U.S.	212	43.32 N	76.16 W
Little Salmon, North Branch ≃	212	43.24 N	76.09 W
Little Salmon, South Branch ≃	212	43.24 N	76.09 W
Little Salmon Lake ⊜	180	62.12 N	134.45 W
Little Salt Lake ⊜	200	37.55 N	112.53 W
Little Sandy ≃	188	38.35 N	82.51 W
Little Sandy, East Fork ≃	188	38.30 N	82.50 W
Little Sandy Creek ≃	200	42.06 N	109.27 W
Little Sandy Desert ◆[2]	162	24.20 S	120.50 E
Little Saskatchewan ≃	184	49.52 N	100.07 W
Little Scarcies ≃	150	8.51 N	13.09 W
Little Scioto ≃, Oh., U.S.	214	40.31 N	83.12 W
Little Scioto ≃, Oh., U.S.	218	38.46 N	82.53 W
Little Sewickley Creek ≃, Pa., U.S.	279b	40.15 N	79.45 W
Little Sewickley Creek ≃, Pa., U.S.	279b	40.33 N	80.12 W
Little Silver	276	40.20 N	74.02 W
Little Sioux ≃	198	41.49 N	96.04 W
Little Sioux, West Fork ≃	198	42.04 N	96.00 W
Little Sitkin Island I	181a	51.55 N	178.30 E
Little Smoky ≃	182	55.42 N	117.38 W
Little Snake ≃	200	40.27 N	108.26 W
Little Sodus Bay c	210	43.20 N	76.43 W
Little Southwest Miramichi ≃	186	46.57 N	65.50 W
Little Stanney	262	53.15 N	2.53 W
Little Stony Creek ≃	226	39.20 N	122.31 W
Little Stour ≃	42	51.19 N	1.15 E
Littlestown	208	39.44 N	77.05 W
Little Stukeley	42	52.21 N	0.13 W
Little Sugarloaf ∧[2]	274b	37.41 S	145.19 E
Little Sur ≃	226	36.20 N	121.54 W
Little Sutton	262	53.17 N	2.57 W
Little Swatara Creek ≃	208	40.24 N	76.29 W
Little Tallapoosa ≃	192	33.18 N	85.34 W
Little Tanaga Island I	180	51.48 N	176.10 W
Little Tennessee ≃	192	35.47 N	84.15 W
Little Thurrock	260	51.28 N	0.21 E
Little Timber Creek ≃	285	39.53 N	75.08 W
Little Tinicum Island I	285	39.51 N	75.17 W
Little Tobago I, Br. Vir. Is.	240m	18.26 N	64.51 W
Little Tobago I, Trin.	241r	11.18 N	60.30 W
Little Toby Creek ≃	214	41.22 N	78.49 W
Littleton, Eng., U.K.	260	51.24 N	0.28 W
Littleton, Co., U.S.	200	39.36 N	105.00 W
Littleton, Ma., U.S.	207	42.32 N	71.30 W
Littleton, N.H., U.S.	188	44.18 N	71.46 W
Littleton, N.C., U.S.	192	36.26 N	77.54 W
Littleton, W.V., U.S.	188	39.41 N	80.31 W
Little Traverse Bay c	190	45.24 N	85.03 W
Little Truckee ≃	226	39.25 N	120.05 W
Little Turtle ≃	184	48.46 N	92.36 W
Little Turtle State Recreation Area ♠	216	40.50 N	85.26 W
Little Valley	210	42.15 N	78.48 W
Little Vermilion ≃	216	41.20 N	89.05 W
Little Vermilion Lake ⊜	184	51.16 N	93.50 W
Little Vienna Estates	284c	38.54 N	77.18 W
Little Wabash ≃	194	37.54 N	88.05 W
Little Walsingham	42	52.54 N	0.51 E
Little Waltham	260	51.47 N	0.29 E
Little Warley	260	51.35 N	0.19 E
Little Washita ≃	196	34.58 N	97.51 W
Little Wellington, Isla I	254	48.30 S	74.45 W
Little White ≃	198	43.44 N	100.40 W
Little White Mountain ∧	182	49.42 N	119.20 W
Little White Salmon ≃	224	45.43 N	121.38 W
Little Wichita ≃	196	33.54 N	97.59 W
Little Wichita, East Fork ≃	196	33.52 N	98.07 W
Little Wind ≃	202	42.57 N	108.29 W
Little Wind, North Fork ≃	202	43.01 N	108.53 W
Little Wind, South Fork ≃	202	43.01 N	108.53 W
Little Wolf ≃	190	44.23 N	88.48 W
Little Wood ≃	202	42.57 N	114.21 W
Little York, In., U.S.	218	38.42 N	85.54 W
Little York, N.Y., U.S.	210	42.42 N	76.10 W
Little Zab (Zāb-e Kūchek) (Az-Zāb aṣ-Ṣaghīr) ≃	128	35.12 N	43.25 E
Littoral □[4]	152	4.13 N	10.25 E
Litunga	152	13.17 S	16.43 E
Litvínov	54	50.37 N	13.36 E
Litvinovo	76	59.34 N	38.01 E
Litvinskoje	86	50.42 N	72.42 E
Lityn	78	49.20 N	28.05 E
Litzmannstadt → Łódź	30	51.46 N	19.30 E
Liu ≃, Zhg.	98	41.48 N	122.43 E
Liu ≃, Zhg.	98	42.45 N	126.04 E
Liu ≃, Zhg.	98	40.38 N	118.09 E
Liu ≃, Zhg.	102	23.52 N	109.45 E
Liu ≃, Zhg.	105	40.38 N	118.09 E
Liu ≃, Zhg.	106	31.31 N	121.18 E
Liuanzhuang	105	39.14 N	117.11 E
Liuba	102	33.32 N	107.07 E
Liubotong	100	31.26 N	116.00 E
Liucao	106	31.07 N	121.41 E
Liuchen	102	23.09 N	110.29 E
Liucheng, Zhg.	100	24.03 N	115.08 E
Liucheng, Zhg.	100	28.36 N	119.34 E
Liucheng, Zhg.	102	24.32 N	109.21 E
Liuchengba	102	27.27 N	102.53 E
Liuch'iu Hsü I	100	22.21 N	120.22 E
Liuchow → Liuzhou	102	24.19 N	109.24 E
Liucun	106	30.44 N	119.23 E
Liucura	252	38.39 S	71.05 W
Liudaogou	98	41.34 N	127.12 E
Liudaohe	105	40.39 N	116.12 E
Liudongqiao	106	31.03 N	119.32 E
Liudu	100	26.44 N	119.33 E
Liuduo	100	34.01 N	120.17 E
Liuduzhuang	105	39.27 N	117.50 E
Liuerbao	104	41.13 N	122.55 E
Liufang	100	27.56 N	116.22 E
Liufangling	100	30.27 N	114.27 E
Liufentzu	269d	24.57 N	121.35 E
Liugezhuang, Zhg.	98	38.33 N	116.30 E
Liugezhuang, Zhg.	105	40.03 N	118.16 E
Liugou	105	40.57 N	118.18 E
Liugu ≃	98	40.22 N	120.26 E
Liuguan	100	29.56 N	113.08 E
Liuguantun	104	41.20 N	121.21 E
Liuhang	106	31.21 N	121.22 E
Liuhe, Zhg.	98	42.15 N	125.43 E
Liuhe, Zhg.	100	33.20 N	112.48 E
Liuhe, Zhg.	100	30.46 N	113.12 E
Liuhe, Zhg.	100	32.22 N	118.49 E
Liuhe, Zhg.	100	30.20 N	115.36 E
Liuhe, Zhg.	105	39.31 N	118.17 E
Liuhe, Zhg.	106	31.30 N	121.15 E
Liuhegou	104	41.56 N	122.44 E
Liuheita	104	42.09 N	123.56 E
Liuhejie	102	24.26 N	101.35 E
Liuhekou	105	40.39 N	118.09 E
Liuheng Dao I	100	29.43 N	122.08 E
Liuhuang	100	23.58 N	116.28 E
Liuhudang	104	42.31 N	122.22 E
Liujia	102	24.54 N	107.49 E
Liujiachang	107	29.46 N	103.49 E
Liujiachuan	105	40.07 N	114.47 E
Liujiadai	106	31.57 N	120.23 E
Liujiadian	89	50.07 N	124.17 E
Liujiadu	106	32.15 N	120.33 E
Liujiafen	105	39.58 N	115.47 E
Liujiagangzi	104	41.28 N	122.33 E
Liujiagou	98	37.47 N	120.53 E
Liujiahe, Zhg.	100	32.06 N	113.21 E
Liujiahe, Zhg.	104	40.40 N	123.58 E
Liujiang	98	40.04 N	119.34 E
Liujiashan	105	40.14 N	114.49 E
Liujiatun, Zhg.	104	41.52 N	122.44 E
Liujiatun, Zhg.	104	41.51 N	122.05 E
Liujiatun, Zhg.	104	42.08 N	122.44 E
Liujiawopeng	104	42.16 N	123.01 E
Liujiazhai	269b	31.21 N	121.27 E
Liujiazhen	106	32.04 N	121.30 E
Liujiazi, Zhg.	98	41.00 N	120.13 E
Liujiazi, Zhg.	104	42.36 N	122.15 E
Liujiazi, Zhg.	104	41.48 N	123.47 E
Liujingcun	105	39.27 N	115.26 E
Liujisu	105	40.01 N	117.13 E
Liukeshu	86	44.59 N	90.12 E
Liuku	102	25.48 N	98.52 E
Liuli	154	11.05 S	34.38 E
Liulicun	271a	39.56 N	116.28 E
Liulidian	106	31.31 N	119.17 E
Liuligou	104	41.24 N	121.29 E
Liulihezhen	105	39.36 N	116.01 E
Liulin	100	31.34 N	113.14 E
Liuliwei	100	24.20 N	114.03 E
Liulongtai	104	41.32 N	120.56 E
Liumachang	107	29.51 N	104.54 E
Liumaogou	89	48.12 N	127.13 E
Liupangtun	104	41.36 N	123.28 E
Liupan Shan ⋏	102	35.40 N	106.40 E
Liuqianhutun	104	42.01 N	123.41 E
Liuqiao	106	32.11 N	120.51 E
Liuquan, Zhg.	98	34.27 N	117.20 E
Liuquan, Zhg.	105	39.22 N	116.18 E
Liurenba	100	29.57 N	114.49 E
Liushi, Zhg.	98	38.33 N	115.44 E
Liushi, Zhg.	100	28.03 N	120.51 E
Liushilipu	100	32.45 N	115.58 E
Liushi Shan ∧	120	36.15 N	82.05 E
Liushouying	98	39.48 N	119.19 E
Liushudian	98	35.54 N	119.30 E
Liushudixia	104	42.26 N	121.14 E
Liushui	89	44.17 N	124.15 E
Liushuigou	100	31.34 N	112.27 E
Liushuquan	105	39.21 N	118.06 E
Liusiqiao	100	29.47 N	116.21 E
Liusong	105	39.40 N	117.08 E
Liuta	98	35.52 N	115.18 E
Liutai	98	41.20 N	113.43 E
Liutaizi	104	41.46 N	122.39 E
Liutang	102	24.58 N	110.21 E
Liutiaozhaicun	104	41.29 N	123.12 E
Liutuan	98	36.56 N	119.22 E
Liutuhutun	104	40.44 N	120.32 E
Liuwanglou	98	34.48 N	116.28 E
Liuwa Plain ≚	152	14.30 S	22.40 E
Liuwa Plain National Park ♠	152	14.30 S	22.40 E
Liuwei	106	32.16 N	119.28 E
Liuwudian	100	24.36 N	118.13 E
Liuxi ≃	100	23.22 N	112.54 E
Liuxia	106	30.15 N	120.03 E
Liuyang	100	28.09 N	113.38 E
Liuyang ≃	100	28.13 N	112.58 E
Liuyuan	98	36.10 N	114.34 E
Liuyuankou	98	34.54 N	114.20 E
Liuzhai	102	25.15 N	107.20 E
Liuzhou	102	24.19 N	109.24 E
Liuzhuang	100	33.10 N	120.19 E
Livada	38	47.52 N	23.07 E
Livadija	89	42.50 N	132.39 E
Livanátai	38	38.42 N	23.03 E
Līvāni	76	56.22 N	26.11 E
Livanjsko Polje ≚	36	43.55 N	16.45 E
Livanovka	86	52.06 N	61.59 E
Livarot	50	49.01 N	0.09 E
Lively, On., Can.	190	46.26 N	81.09 W
Lively, Va., U.S.	208	37.47 N	76.31 W
Lively Island I	254	52.02 S	58.30 W
Livengood	180	65.32 N	148.33 W
Livenka, Ross.	78	50.26 N	38.18 E
Livenka, Ross.	78	50.44 N	40.14 E
Livenza ≃	64	45.35 N	12.51 E
Live Oak, Ca., U.S.	226	39.16 N	121.39 W
Live Oak, Fl., U.S.	192	30.17 N	82.59 W
Live Oak Creek ≃	196	30.39 N	101.42 W
Liverdun	56	48.45 N	6.03 E
Liverdy-en-Brie	261	48.42 N	2.47 E
Livergnano	66	44.19 N	11.21 E
Liveringa	162	18.03 S	124.10 E
Livermore, Ca., U.S.	226	37.40 N	121.46 W
Livermore, Ia., U.S.	190	42.52 N	94.11 W
Livermore, Ky., U.S.	194	37.29 N	87.07 W
Livermore, Mount ∧	196	30.38 N	104.10 W
Livermore Falls	188	44.28 N	70.11 W
Liverpool, Austl.	170	33.54 S	150.56 E
Liverpool, N.S., Can.	186	44.02 N	64.43 W
Liverpool, Eng., U.K.	44	53.25 N	2.55 W
Liverpool, Eng., U.K.	262	53.25 N	2.55 W
Liverpool, In., U.S.	216	41.34 N	87.18 W
Liverpool, N.Y., U.S.	210	43.06 N	76.13 W
Liverpool, Pa., U.S.	208	40.34 N	76.59 W
Liverpool, Tx., U.S.	222	29.18 N	95.17 W
Liverpool □[8]	262	53.25 N	2.55 W
Liverpool ≃	164	12.02 S	134.13 E
Liverpool (Speke) Airport ⊠	44	53.21 N	2.52 W
Liverpool, Cape ›	176	73.38 N	78.06 W
Liverpool, University of ⊍[2]	262	53.24 N	2.58 W
Liverpool Bay c, N.T., Can.	180	69.45 N	130.00 W
Liverpool Bay c, N.S., Can.	186	44.02 N	64.41 W
Liverpool Bay c, Eng., U.K.	44	53.30 N	3.16 W
Liverpool Football Ground ♠	262	53.26 N	2.57 W
Liverpool Heights	210	43.07 N	76.13 W
Liverpool Range ⋏	166	31.40 S	150.30 E
Livet-et-Gavet	62	45.06 N	5.56 E
Livigno	64	46.32 N	10.04 E
Livigno, Lago di ⊜[1], It.	58	46.37 N	10.10 E
Livigno, Lago di ⊜[1], It.	64	46.37 N	10.10 E
Livilliers	261	49.06 N	2.06 E
Lívingston, Guat.	236	15.50 N	88.45 W
Livingston, Scot., U.K.	46	55.53 N	3.32 W
Livingston, Al., U.S.	194	32.35 N	88.11 W
Livingston, Ca., U.S.	226	37.23 N	120.43 W
Livingston, Il., U.S.	194	38.58 N	89.45 W
Livingston, Ky., U.S.	192	37.17 N	84.12 W
Livingston, La., U.S.	194	30.30 N	90.44 W
Livingston, Mt., U.S.	202	45.39 N	110.33 W
Livingston, N.J., U.S.	210	40.47 N	74.18 W
Livingston, N.Y., U.S.	210	42.09 N	73.47 W
Livingston, Tn., U.S.	194	36.23 N	85.19 W
Livingston, Tx., U.S.	222	30.42 N	94.55 W
Livingston, Wi., U.S.	190	42.54 N	90.25 W
Livingston □[6], Il., U.S.	216	40.53 N	88.38 W
Livingston □[6], Mi., U.S.	216	42.38 N	83.50 W
Livingston □[6], N.Y., U.S.	210	42.48 N	77.49 W
Livingstone	154	17.50 S	25.53 E
Livingstone, Chutes de (Livingstone Falls) ∟	152	4.50 S	14.30 E
Livingstone, Lake ⊜[1]	222	30.50 N	95.30 W
Livingstone Falls → Livingstone, Chutes de ∟	152	4.50 S	14.30 E
Livingstone Lake ⊜	212	45.22 N	78.43 W
Livingstonia	154	10.36 S	34.07 E
Livingston Island I	9	62.35 S	60.30 W
Livingston Mall ◆[9]	276	40.47 N	74.21 W
Livingston Manor	210	41.54 N	74.49 W
Livno	36	43.50 N	17.01 E
Livny	76	52.25 N	37.37 E
Livojoki ≃	26	65.24 N	26.48 E
Livonia, In., U.S.	218	38.34 N	86.17 W
Livonia, La., U.S.	194	30.33 N	91.33 W
Livonia, Mi., U.S.	216	42.22 N	83.21 W
Livonia, N.Y., U.S.	210	42.49 N	77.40 W
Livonia Center	210	42.49 N	77.38 W
Livonia Mall ◆[9]	281	42.26 N	83.20 W
Livorno (Leghorn)	66	43.33 N	10.19 E
Livorno □[4]	66	43.14 N	10.35 E
Livorno Ferraris	62	45.17 N	8.05 E
Livourne → Livorno	66	43.33 N	10.19 E
Livramento → Santana do Livramento	252	30.53 S	55.31 W
Livramento do Brumado	255	13.39 S	41.50 W
Livron-sur-Drôme	62	44.46 N	4.51 E
Livry-Gargan	261	48.56 N	2.33 E
Livry-sur-Seine	261	48.31 N	2.41 E
Liwa	112	5.04 S	104.06 E
Liwale	154	9.46 S	37.56 E
Liwale Chini	154	9.41 S	38.01 E
Liwan	154	4.54 N	35.40 E
Liwonde	154	14.52 S	35.28 E
Liwonde National Park ♠	154	14.50 S	35.20 E
Liwung ≃	115a	6.08 S	106.49 E
Lixi, Zhg.	100	29.15 N	114.46 E
Lixi, Zhg.	100	27.39 N	116.19 E
Lixian, Zhg.	98	38.29 N	115.34 E
Lixian, Zhg.	102	34.11 N	105.02 E
Lixian, Zhg.	102	29.30 N	111.37 E
Lixian, Zhg.	105	39.33 N	116.26 E
Lixian → Black ≃	110	21.15 N	105.20 E
Lixin, Zhg.	100	26.52 N	116.42 E
Lixin, Zhg.	100	33.06 N	116.08 E
Lixing	100	33.28 N	115.28 E
Lixingzhuang	105	39.25 N	117.56 E
Lixoúrion	38	38.12 N	20.26 E
Lixus ⊥	34	35.16 N	6.13 W
Liyang, Zhg.	98	37.28 N	113.37 E
Liyang, Zhg.	106	31.26 N	119.29 E
Liyuanbao	100	25.16 N	112.55 E
Liyujiang	100	25.57 N	113.15 E
Lizard	42	49.58 N	5.12 W
Lizarda	250	9.36 S	46.41 W
Lizard Head Peak ∧	200	42.47 N	109.11 W
Lizard Island I	164	14.40 S	145.28 E
Lizard Point ›	42	49.56 N	5.13 W
Lizard Point Indian Reserve ◆[4]	184	50.40 N	100.57 W
Lize	107	30.08 N	106.11 E
Lizhai	106	31.34 N	121.45 E
Lizhou	102	28.08 N	102.10 E
Lizhu	100	29.56 N	120.30 E
Lizhuang, Zhg.	100	34.24 N	116.30 E
Lizhuang, Zhg.	107	28.47 N	104.46 E
Lizhuangqiao	106	31.48 N	119.37 E
Lizinovka	78	50.08 N	39.28 E
Liziwei	107	30.19 N	106.39 E
Lizy-sur-Ourcq	50	49.01 N	3.02 E
Lizzana	64	45.51 N	11.03 E
Lizzanello	68	40.18 N	18.13 E
Lizzano	68	40.23 N	17.27 E
Lizzano in Belvedere	64	44.10 N	10.53 E
Ljady	76	54.36 N	31.10 E
Ljahavičy	76	53.02 N	26.16 E
Ljalovo	82	56.03 N	37.14 E
Ljan	26	59.51 N	10.48 E
Ljaskavičy	78	52.07 N	28.09 E
Ljasnaja	76	52.59 N	25.46 E
Ljasnaja ≃	76	52.10 N	23.33 E
Ljuban', Bela.	76	52.37 N	29.08 E
Ljuban', Bela.	76	52.48 N	27.59 E
Ljubča	76	53.45 N	26.03 E
Ljubelj (Loiblpass))(	61	46.26 N	14.16 E
Ljubija	36	44.56 N	16.37 E
Ljubimec	38	41.50 N	26.05 E
Ljubinje	38	42.57 N	18.05 E
Ljubljana	36	46.03 N	14.31 E
Ljubovija	38	44.11 N	19.22 E
Ljubuški	36	43.12 N	17.33 E
Ljugarn	26	57.19 N	18.42 E
Ljunga	40	58.31 N	16.21 E
Ljungan ≃	26	62.19 N	17.23 E
Ljungaverk	26	62.29 N	16.03 E
Ljungby	26	56.50 N	13.56 E
Ljungbyhed	41	56.04 N	13.12 E
Ljungbyholm	26	56.38 N	16.10 E
Ljungdalen	26	62.51 N	12.47 E
Ljungsbro	26	58.31 N	15.30 E
Ljungskile	26	58.14 N	11.55 E
Ljusdal	26	61.50 N	16.05 E
Ljusfallshammar	40	58.47 N	15.29 E
Ljusina	76	52.38 N	26.31 E
Ljusnan ≃	26	61.12 N	17.08 E
Ljusnaren ⊜	40	59.51 N	14.56 E
Ljusne	26	61.13 N	17.08 E
Ljusterö I	40	59.31 N	18.37 E
Ljutomer	36	46.31 N	16.12 E
Llagas Creek ≃	226	36.58 N	121.31 W
Llaima, Volcán ∧[1]	252	38.43 S	71.43 W
Llamara, Salar de ≚	248	21.13 S	69.40 W
Llanaber	42	52.45 N	4.05 W
Llanaelhaearn	42	52.59 N	4.24 W
Llanarth	42	52.12 N	4.18 W
Llanarthney	42	51.52 N	4.09 W
Llanbedrog	42	52.52 N	4.29 W
Llanberis, Pass of V	44	53.06 N	4.04 W
Llanbister	42	52.21 N	3.18 W
Llanboidy	42	51.54 N	4.36 W
Llanbryde	46	57.37 N	3.13 W
Llanbrynmair	42	52.37 N	3.57 W
Llançà	34	42.22 N	3.09 E
Llancanelo, Laguna ⊜	252	35.35 S	69.09 W
Llandaff	42	51.30 N	3.14 W
Llandaff Cathedral ⊍[1]	42	51.29 N	3.15 W
Llanddewi Brefi	42	52.10 N	3.57 W
Llandeilo	42	51.52 N	3.59 W
Llandilo	274a	33.43 S	150.45 E
Llandinam	42	52.29 N	3.26 W
Llandissilio	42	51.53 N	4.44 W
Llandovery	42	51.59 N	3.48 W
Llandrindod Wells	42	52.15 N	3.23 W
Llandudno	44	53.19 N	3.49 W
Llandybie	42	51.50 N	4.00 W
Llandysul	42	52.02 N	4.19 W
Llanelli	42	51.42 N	4.10 W
Llanelltyd	42	52.45 N	3.54 W
Llanelly	169	36.44 S	143.51 E
Llanenddwyn	42	52.49 N	4.06 W
Llanerchymedd	44	53.20 N	4.22 W
Llanes	34	43.25 N	4.45 W
Llanfaethlu	44	53.21 N	4.32 W
Llanfair-Caereinion	42	52.39 N	3.20 W
Llanfairfechan	44	53.15 N	3.58 W
Llanfairpwllgwyngyll	44	53.13 N	4.12 W
Llanfrynach	42	51.56 N	3.21 W
Llanfyllin	42	52.46 N	3.17 W
Llanfynydd	42	51.56 N	4.06 W
Llanfyrnach	42	51.57 N	4.35 W
Llangadog	42	51.56 N	3.53 W
Llangefni	44	53.16 N	4.18 W
Llangennech	42	51.41 N	4.04 W
Llangollen	42	52.58 N	3.10 W
Llangollen Estates	208	39.39 N	75.37 W
Llangranog	42	52.09 N	4.29 W
Llangurig	42	52.25 N	3.36 W
Llangwyryfon	42	52.19 N	4.03 W
Llangynog	42	52.50 N	3.25 W
Llanharan	42	51.33 N	3.25 W
Llanidloes	42	52.27 N	3.32 W
Llanilar	42	52.21 N	4.01 W
Llanllyfni	44	53.03 N	4.17 W
Llano	196	30.45 N	98.40 W
Llano ≃	196	30.35 N	98.25 W
Llano Colorado	204	31.38 N	115.55 W
Llanon	42	52.17 N	4.10 W
Llanos ≚	246	5.00 N	70.00 W
Llanpumsaint	42	51.56 N	4.18 W
Llanquihue	254	41.15 S	73.01 W
Llanquihue, Lago ⊜	254	41.08 S	72.48 W
Llanrhaeadr-ym-Mochnant	42	52.51 N	3.17 W
Llanrhidian	42	51.37 N	4.11 W
Llanrhystud	42	52.18 N	4.09 W
Llanrwst	44	53.08 N	3.48 W
Llansantffraid-ym-Mechain	42	52.47 N	3.08 W
Llansawel	42	52.01 N	4.00 W
Llantrisant	42	51.33 N	3.23 W
Llantwit Major	42	51.25 N	3.30 W
Llanuwchllyn	42	52.52 N	3.41 W
Llanwenog	42	52.06 N	4.12 W
Llanwrda	42	51.58 N	3.53 W
Llanwrtyd Wells	42	52.07 N	3.38 W
Llanybydder	42	52.04 N	4.09 W
Llata	248	9.25 S	76.47 W
Llavallol ◆[8]	288	34.48 S	58.28 W
Llay	44	53.06 N	2.59 W
Lleida	34	41.37 N	0.37 E
Lleida □[4]	34	42.00 N	1.10 E
Llentrisca, Cap ›	34	38.51 N	1.14 E
Llera de Canales	234	23.19 N	99.01 W
Llerena	34	38.14 N	6.01 W
Lleulleu, Lago ⊜	252	38.09 S	73.20 W
Lleyn Peninsula ›[1]	42	52.54 N	4.30 W
Llica	248	19.52 S	68.16 W
Llico	252	34.46 S	72.05 W
Lliria	34	39.38 N	0.36 W
Llivia	32	42.28 N	1.59 E
Llobregat ≃	34	41.19 N	2.09 E
Llobregat, Delta del ≚[2]	266d	41.17 N	2.08 E
Llorente	116	11.25 N	125.33 E
Llorente ≃	116	11.25 N	125.33 E
Llorona, Punta ›	236	8.39 N	83.45 W
Lloyd	218	38.37 N	82.51 W
Lloyd Harbor	210	40.54 N	73.27 W
Lloyd Harbor c	276	40.55 N	73.27 W
Lloydminster	184	53.17 N	110.00 W
Lloyd Neck ›[1]	276	40.56 N	73.28 W
Lloyd Point ›	210	40.57 N	73.29 W
Lloyds ≃	186	48.33 N	57.13 W
Llucena	34	40.08 N	0.17 W
Llucmajor	34	39.29 N	2.54 E
Llullaillaco, Volcán ∧[1]	252	24.43 S	68.33 W
Llusco	248	14.21 S	72.07 W
Lluta ≃	248	18.24 S	70.19 W
Llyn Brianne Reservoir ⊜[1]	42	52.08 N	3.45 W
Llyswen	42	52.02 N	3.17 W
Llys-y-frân Reservoir ⊜[1]	42	51.53 N	4.51 W
Lnáře	60	49.28 N	13.47 E
Lo (Panlong) ≃	110	21.18 N	105.25 E
Loa	200	38.24 N	111.38 W
Loa ≃, Chile	244	21.26 S	70.04 W
Loa ≃, Congo	273b	4.20 S	15.11 E
Loami	194	39.40 N	89.51 W
Loanda → Luanda, Ang.	152	8.48 S	13.14 E
Loanda, Bra.	255	22.54 S	53.10 W
Loanda, Gabon	152	0.55 S	9.00 E
Loande ≃	152	8.41 S	17.56 E
Loange (Luangue) ≃	152	4.17 S	20.02 E
Loango Buele	152	5.10 S	12.59 E
Loanhead	46	55.53 N	3.09 W
Loanja ≃	154	17.22 S	24.48 E
Loano	62	44.08 N	8.15 E
Loantaka Brook ≃	276	40.43 N	74.28 W
Lo Aranguiz	286e	33.23 S	70.40 W
Loay	116	9.36 N	124.01 E
Lob' ≃	82	56.29 N	35.51 E
Lobamba	158	26.27 S	31.12 E
Loban	24	65.44 N	45.25 E
Loban' ≃	80	56.58 N	51.12 E
Lobanovo	76	53.04 N	38.14 E
Lobanovskije Vyselki	82	54.18 N	38.58 E
Lo Barnechea	286e	33.21 S	70.31 W
Lobaski	80	54.38 N	45.09 E
Lobatos	234	22.49 N	103.24 W
Lobatse	156	25.11 S	25.40 E
Löbau	54	51.05 N	14.40 E
Lobau ≚	264b	48.10 N	16.32 E
Lobaye □[5]	152	4.00 N	18.30 E
Lobaye ≃	152	3.41 N	18.35 E
Lobbes	50	50.21 N	4.15 E
Lobbs Run ≃	279b	40.15 N	79.55 W
Lobdell Lake ⊜	216	42.48 N	83.48 W
Löbejün	54	51.38 N	11.53 E
Lobelville	194	35.46 N	87.47 W
Lo Benitez	286e	33.34 S	70.42 W
Lobería	252	38.09 S	58.47 W
Lo Bernales	286e	33.34 S	70.34 W
Löberöd	41	55.47 N	13.30 E
Lobethal	168b	34.54 S	138.52 E
Łobez	30	53.39 N	15.36 E
Lobito	152	12.20 S	13.34 E
Lobitos	246	4.26 S	81.17 W
Lobitos Creek ≃	282	37.22 N	122.24 W
Lobn'a	82	56.01 N	37.30 E
Löbnitz, Dtsch.	54	51.35 N	12.28 E
Löbnitz, Dtsch.	54	54.17 N	12.43 E
Lobo, Indon.	164	3.45 S	134.05 E
Lobo, Pil.	116	13.39 N	121.13 E
Lobo ≃	150	6.02 N	6.47 W
Loboko	152	0.45 S	16.38 E
Lobos	258	35.11 S	59.06 W
Lobos, Cay I	238	22.24 N	77.32 W
Lobos, Isla I	232	27.20 N	110.36 W
Lobos, Isla de I, Esp.	148	28.45 N	13.49 W
Lobos, Isla de I, Méx.	234	21.27 N	97.13 W
Lobos, Laguna de ⊜	258	35.17 S	59.07 W
Lobos, Point ›	226	37.47 N	122.31 W
Lobos, Punta ›	248	21.01 S	70.11 W
Lobos de Afuera, Islas II	248	6.57 S	80.42 W
Lobos de Tierra, Isla I	248	6.27 S	80.52 W
Lo Boza	286e	33.23 S	70.46 W
Lobskoje	24	62.45 N	35.16 E
Lobstädt	54	51.08 N	12.29 E
Loburg	54	52.07 N	12.05 E
Lobva	86	59.12 N	60.30 E
Łobżenica	30	53.16 N	17.15 E
Locana	62	45.25 N	7.27 E
Locana, Val di V	62	45.25 N	7.27 E
Locarno	58	46.10 N	8.48 E
Lo Castillo, Aeropuerto ⊠	286e	33.23 S	70.36 W
Locate Triulzi	62	45.21 N	9.13 E
Loccum	52	52.27 N	9.08 E
Loceri	71	39.51 N	9.35 E
Loch	169	38.22 S	145.43 E
Lochaber ◆[1]	46	56.57 N	5.06 W
Lochailort	46	56.53 N	5.40 W
Lochaline	46	56.32 N	5.47 W
Locharbriggs	44	55.06 N	3.35 W
Lochar Water ≃	44	54.59 N	3.27 W
Lochboisdale	46	57.09 N	7.19 W
Lochcarron	46	57.24 N	5.30 W
Lochdon	46	56.26 N	5.41 W
Lochearn	284b	39.21 N	76.43 W
Lochearnhead	46	56.23 N	4.17 W
Lochem	52	52.09 N	6.25 E
Loches	50	47.08 N	1.00 E
Lochgair	46	56.03 N	5.20 W
Loch Garman → Wexford	48	52.20 N	6.27 W
Lochgelly	46	56.08 N	3.19 W
Lochgilphead	46	56.03 N	5.26 W
Lochgoilhead	46	56.10 N	4.54 W
Lochiel	168b	33.56 S	138.10 E
Lochindorb ⊜	46	57.24 N	3.43 W
Lochino	265b	55.42 N	37.19 E
Lochinvar National Park ♠	154	15.55 S	27.15 E
Lochinver	46	58.09 N	5.15 W
Lochmaben	44	55.08 N	3.27 W
Lochmaddy	46	57.36 N	7.11 W
Lochnagar ∧	46	56.57 N	3.16 W
Lochovice	60	49.51 N	13.59 E
Lochranza	46	55.42 N	5.18 W
Loch Raven Dam ◆[6]	284b	39.26 N	76.33 W
Loch Raven Reservoir ⊜[1]	208	39.27 N	76.34 W
Lochristi	50	51.06 N	3.50 E
Lochsa ≃	202	46.08 N	115.36 W
Loch Sheldrake	210	41.46 N	74.39 W
Loch Sport	166	38.03 S	147.36 E
Lochwinnoch	46	55.48 N	4.39 W
Lochy, Loch ⊜	46	56.57 N	4.53 W
Lock	166	33.34 S	135.46 E
Lock and Dam No. 20 ◆[6], U.S.	219	40.09 N	91.30 W
Lock and Dam No. 21 ◆[6], U.S.	219	39.54 N	91.26 W
Lock and Dam No. 24 ◆[6], U.S.	219	39.22 N	90.55 W
Lock and Dam No. 25 ◆[6], U.S.	219	39.01 N	90.41 W
Lock and Dam No. 22 ◆[6], U.S.	219	39.39 N	91.16 W
Locke, Ca., U.S.	226	38.15 N	121.31 W
Locke, In., U.S.	216	41.28 N	86.00 W
Locke, N.Y., U.S.	210	42.39 N	76.25 W
Lockeford	226	38.10 N	121.09 W
Lockenhaus	61	47.24 N	16.25 E
Lockeport	186	43.42 N	65.07 W
Lockerbie	44	55.07 N	3.22 W
Lockesburg	194	33.58 N	94.10 W
Lockhart, Austl.	166	35.14 S	146.43 E
Lockhart, Fl., U.S.	220	28.37 N	81.26 W
Lockhart, Tx., U.S.	222	29.53 N	97.40 W
Lockhart River Aboriginal Reserve ◆[4]	164	13.00 S	143.15 E
Lock Haven	210	41.08 N	77.26 W
Lockheed Aircraft Corporation ⊍[3], Ca., U.S.	280	34.12 N	118.22 W
Lockheed Aircraft Corporation ⊍[3], Ca., U.S.	282	37.25 N	122.02 W
Lockington	216	40.12 N	84.13 W
Lockington Dam ◆[6]	216	40.17 N	84.15 W
Lock Mountain ∧	214	40.25 N	78.18 W
Lockney	196	34.07 N	101.26 W
Löcknitz	54	53.27 N	14.12 E
Löcknitz ≃, Dtsch.	54	53.07 N	11.16 E
Löcknitz ≃, Dtsch.	264a	52.25 N	13.49 E
Lockport, Mb., Can.	184	50.05 N	96.56 W
Lockport, Il., U.S.	216	41.35 N	88.03 W
Lockport, La., U.S.	194	29.39 N	90.32 W
Lockport, N.Y., U.S.	210	43.10 N	78.41 W
Lockport Lock ◆[5]	278	41.35 N	88.04 W
Locks Heath	42	50.52 N	1.15 W
Locksley Park	210	42.45 N	78.52 W
Lockvattnet ⊜	40	59.03 N	17.05 E
Lockview	279b	40.10 N	79.55 W
Lockwood, Ca., U.S.	226	35.56 N	121.05 W
Lockwood, Mo., U.S.	194	37.23 N	93.57 W
Lockwood Corners	214	41.00 N	81.34 W
Lockyer Creek ≃	171a	27.25 S	152.36 E
Locminé	28	47.53 N	2.50 W
Loc Ninh	110	11.51 N	106.36 E
Loco, Bayou ≃	222	31.28 N	94.44 W
Locon	50	50.34 N	2.40 E
Locorotondo	68	40.45 N	17.20 E
Locri	68	38.14 N	16.16 E
Locri Epizefiri ⊥	68	38.12 N	16.13 E
Locroja	248	12.41 S	74.26 W
Locsin	116	13.09 N	123.43 E
Locumba	248	17.36 S	70.46 W
Locumba ≃	248	17.54 S	70.57 W
Locust	208	40.18 N	73.59 W
Locust Creek ≃	194	39.40 N	93.17 W
Locust Fork ≃	194	33.33 N	87.11 W
Locust Grove, N.Y., U.S.	276	40.48 N	73.30 W
Locust Grove, Ok., U.S.	196	36.12 N	95.10 W
Locust Lake State Park ♠	208	40.46 N	76.08 W
Locust Point ›	276	40.49 N	73.48 W
Locust Valley	210	40.53 N	73.36 W
Lod (Lydda)	132	31.58 N	34.54 E
Lod, Nemel-Te'ufa (Ben Gurion Airport) ⊠	132	31.59 N	34.53 E
Loda	216	40.31 N	88.04 W
Lodal Creek ≃	285	40.14 N	75.27 W
Löddeköpinge	41	55.46 N	13.01 E
Loddon	42	52.32 N	1.29 E
Loddon ≃, Austl.	166	35.32 S	143.52 E
Loddon ≃, Eng., U.K.	42	51.30 N	0.53 W
Lodè	71	40.35 N	9.32 E
Lodejnoje Pole	76	60.44 N	33.30 E
Lodenau	54	51.24 N	14.57 E
Löderburg	54	51.52 N	11.32 E
Lodève	32	43.43 N	3.19 E
Lodge Creek ≃	202	48.35 N	109.10 W
Lodge Grass	202	45.18 N	107.21 W
Lodgepole, Ab., Can.	182	53.06 N	115.19 W
Lodgepole, Ne., U.S.	198	41.08 N	102.38 W
Lodgepole Creek ≃	198	40.57 N	102.22 W
Lodhāsuli	126	22.19 N	87.03 E
Lodhrān	123	29.32 N	71.38 E
Lodi, It.	62	45.19 N	9.30 E
Lodi, Ca., U.S.	226	38.07 N	121.16 W
Lodi, N.J., U.S.	210	40.52 N	74.05 W
Lodi, N.Y., U.S.	210	42.36 N	76.49 W
Lodi, Oh., U.S.	214	41.02 N	82.00 W
Lodi, Wi., U.S.	190	43.18 N	89.31 W
Lodi □[4]	62	45.15 N	9.35 E
Lodi Park ♠	272a	28.36 N	77.13 E
Lodi Vecchio	62	45.18 N	9.24 E
Lodja	152	3.29 S	23.26 E
Lodosa	34	42.25 N	2.05 W
Lodoyo	115a	8.10 S	112.13 E
Lodrone	64	45.50 N	10.32 E
Lods	58	47.03 N	6.15 E
Lodsch → Łódź	30	51.46 N	19.30 E
Lodwar	154	3.07 N	35.36 E
Łódź	30	51.46 N	19.30 E
Łódź □[4]	30	51.50 N	19.25 E
Loe Āgra	123	34.35 N	71.43 E
Loei	110	17.29 N	101.35 E
Loei ≃	110	17.51 N	101.37 E
Loen	26	61.52 N	6.52 E
Loenen	52	52.07 N	6.01 E
Loengo	154	4.45 S	26.27 E
Loeriesfontein	158	30.56 S	19.26 E
Lo Espejo	286e	33.32 S	70.43 W
Lo Espejo, Canal ≍	286e	33.32 S	70.43 W
Loeu	78	51.56 N	30.46 E
Lofa ≃	150	6.36 N	11.08 W
Lofer	64	47.35 N	12.41 E
Löffingen	58	47.53 N	8.20 E
Lofoten II	24	68.30 N	15.00 E
Lofoten Basin ✢[1]	10	70.00 N	4.00 E
Lofthouse	44	53.44 N	1.29 W
Lofthus	26	60.20 N	6.40 E
Loftus, Austl.	274a	34.03 S	151.03 E
Loftus, Eng., U.K.	44	54.33 N	0.53 W
Lofty, Mount ∧, Austl.	168b	34.59 S	138.42 E
Lofty, Mount ∧, Austl.	274b	37.43 S	145.17 E
Log	80	49.29 N	43.52 E
Loga, Dtsch.	52	53.14 N	7.29 E
Loga, Niger	150	13.37 N	3.14 E
Logačovka	80	52.23 N	52.21 E
Logan, Ia., U.S.	198	41.38 N	95.47 W
Logan, Ks., U.S.	198	39.39 N	99.34 W
Logan, N.M., U.S.	196	35.22 N	103.25 W
Logan, Oh., U.S.	188	39.32 N	82.24 W
Logan, Ut,. U.S.	200	41.44 N	111.50 W
Logan, W.V., U.S.	188	37.50 N	81.59 W
Logan □[6], Il., U.S.	219	40.09 N	89.22 W
Logan □[6], Oh., U.S.	216	40.22 N	83.46 W
Logan ◆[8]	285	40.02 N	75.09 W
Logan ≃, Austl.	171a	27.43 S	153.18 E
Logan ≃, Ab., Can.	182	55.09 N	111.42 W
Logan ≃, Ut,. U.S.	200	41.44 N	111.57 W
Logan, Mount ∧, Yk., Can.	180	60.34 N	140.24 W
Logan, Mount ∧, Wa., U.S.	224	48.32 N	120.57 W
Logan Creek ≃, Ca., U.S.	226	39.22 N	122.06 W
Logan Creek ≃, Mo., U.S.	194	37.11 N	90.49 W
Logan Creek ≃, Ne., U.S.	198	41.37 N	96.29 W
Logandale	204	36.35 N	114.29 W
Logan International Airport ⊠	283	42.22 N	71.00 W
Logan Lake ⊜	212	44.52 N	78.59 W
Logan Martin Lake ⊜[1]	194	33.40 N	86.15 W
Logan Mountains ⋏	180	61.45 N	128.38 W
Logan Pass)(	202	48.42 N	113.43 W
Logansport, In., U.S.	216	40.45 N	86.21 W
Logansport, La., U.S.	194	31.58 N	93.59 W
Logan Square ◆[8]	278	41.56 N	87.42 W
Loganton	210	41.02 N	77.18 W
Loganville, Ga., U.S.	192	33.50 N	83.54 W
Loganville, Pa., U.S.	208	39.52 N	76.42 W
Logärden ⊜	40	60.37 N	16.00 E
Lögdeälven ≃	26	63.33 N	19.25 E
Logduz	76	60.00 N	44.41 E
Loge ≃, Ang.	152	10.12 S	17.00 E
Loge ≃, Ang.	152	7.49 S	13.06 E
Logia	164	2.55 S	151.27 E
Loginovo	82	55.42 N	38.44 E
Logirim	154	4.43 N	33.14 E
Lognes	261	48.50 N	2.38 E
Lognes-Émerainville, Aérodrome de ⊠	261	48.49 N	2.37 E
Logo	154	5.20 N	30.18 E
Logone ≃	146	12.06 N	15.02 E
Logone Birni	146	11.47 N	15.06 E
Logone Gana	146	11.33 N	15.09 E
Logone-Occidental □[5]	146	8.50 N	16.00 E
Logone Occidental ≃	146	9.07 N	16.26 E
Logone-Oriental □[5]	146	8.15 N	16.20 E
Logone Oriental ≃	146	9.07 N	16.26 E
Logoualé	150	7.07 N	7.33 W
Logovskij	80	48.26 N	43.23 E
Log pod Mangartom	64	46.24 N	13.36 E
Logroño	34	42.28 N	2.27 W
Logrosán	34	39.20 N	5.29 W
Løgstør	26	56.58 N	9.15 E
Logtāk Lake ⊜	120	24.33 N	93.50 E
Løgten	41	56.17 N	10.19 E
Logudoro ◆[1]	71	40.35 N	8.40 E
Logue Brook Dam ◆[6]	168a	33.00 S	115.57 E
Løgumgårde	41	55.05 N	8.57 E
Løgumkloster	41	55.03 N	8.57 E
Logumukum	154	0.27 N	36.05 E
Logy Creek ≃	224	46.11 N	120.35 W
Loh I	175f	13.21 S	166.38 E
Lohāgara	126	23.11 N	89.39 E
Lohals	41	55.08 N	10.55 E
Lohārdaga	124	23.26 N	84.41 E
Lohāru	120	28.27 N	75.49 E
Lohatlha	158	28.02 S	23.04 E
Lohausen ◆[8]	263	51.16 N	6.44 E
Lohauserholz ◆[8]	263	51.39 N	7.48 E
Lohberg	263	51.35 N	6.46 E
Löhdorf ◆[8]	263	51.09 N	7.01 E
Lo Hermida	286e	33.29 S	70.33 W
Lohfelden	56	51.16 N	9.32 E
Lohheide ◆[8]	263	51.30 N	6.40 E
Lohiān	123	31.10 N	75.11 E
Lohiniva	24	67.10 N	24.58 E
Lohit ≃	120	27.48 N	95.28 E
Lohja	26	60.15 N	24.05 E

Symbols in the index entries represent the broad categories identified in the key at the right. Symbols with superior numbers (⋏[1]) identify subcategories (see complete key on page *I · 1).*

Symbole im Register stellen die rechts im Schlüssel erklärten Kategorien dar. Symbole mit hochgestellten Ziffern (⋏[1]) bezeichnen Unterabteilungen einer Kategorie (vgl. vollständiger Schlüssel auf Seite *I · 1).*

Los símbolos incluídos en el texto del índice representan las grandes categorías identificadas con la clave a la derecha. Los símbolos con numeros en su parte superior (⋏[1]) identifican las subcategorías (véase la clave completa en la página *I · 1).*

Les symboles de l'index représentent les catégories indiquées dans la légende à droite. Les symboles suivis d'un indice (⋏[1]) représentent des sous-catégories (voir légende complète à la page *I · 1).*

Os símbolos incluídos no texto do índice representam as grandes categorias identificadas com a chave à direita. Os símbolos com números em sua parte superior (⋏[1]) identificam as subcategorias (veja-se a chave completa à página *I · 1).*

	English	Deutsch	Español	Français	Português
∧	Mountain	Berg	Montaña	Montagne	Montanha
⋏	Mountains	Gebirge	Montañas	Montagnes	Montanhas
)(	Pass	Paß	Paso	Col	Passo
V	Valley, Canyon	Tal, Cañon	Valle, Cañón	Vallée, Canyon	Vale, Canhão
≚	Plain	Ebene	Llano	Plaine	Planície
›	Cape	Kap	Cabo	Cap	Cabo
I	Island	Insel	Isla	Île	Ilha
II	Islands	Inseln	Islas	Îles	Ilhas
⊥	Other Topographic Features	Andere Topographische Objekte	Otros Elementos Topográficos	Autres données topographiques	Outros acidentes topográficos

ESPAÑOL · FRANÇAIS · PORTUGUÊS

Nombre / Nom / Nome	Página / Page / Página	Lat.°′	Long.°′ W = Oeste / W = Ouest / W = Oeste
Lohjanharju ∧	26	60.15 N	24.30 E
Lohjanjärvi ⊚	26	60.15 N	23.55 E
Löhlbach	56	51.04 N	8.58 E
Lohmar	56	50.50 N	7.13 E
Lohme, Dtsch.	54	54.35 N	13.37 E
Löhme, Dtsch.	264a	52.37 N	13.40 E
Lohmen, Dtsch.	54	50.59 N	13.59 E
Lohmen, Dtsch.	54	53.41 N	12.05 E
Lohmühle	263	51.31 N	6.40 E
Löhnberg	56	50.31 N	8.17 E
Lohne, Dtsch.	52	52.42 N	8.12 E
Löhne, Dtsch.	52	52.11 N	8.41 E
Löhnen	263	51.36 N	6.39 E
Lohnsburg	60	48.09 N	13.24 E
Loho → Luohe	100	33.35 N	114.01 E
Lohr am Main	56	50.00 N	9.34 E
Lohrville	198	42.16 N	94.32 W
Lohsa	54	51.23 N	14.24 E
Loi ≃	110	21.19 N	100.44 E
Loi, Phou ∧	110	20.16 N	103.12 E
Loiano	66	44.16 N	11.19 E
Loiblpass (Ljubelj))(	61	46.26 N	14.16 E
Loiborsoit	154	3.52 S	36.26 E
Loi-kaw	110	19.41 N	97.13 E
Loile ≃	152	0.52 S	20.12 E
Loimaa	26	60.51 N	23.03 E
Loimijoki ≃	26	61.13 N	22.38 E
Loi Mwe	110	21.11 N	99.46 E
Loing ≃	50	48.23 N	2.48 E
Loing, Canal du ≚	50	48.22 N	2.50 E
Loir ≃	32	47.33 N	0.32 W
Loira → Loire ≃	32	47.16 N	2.11 W
Loire	62	45.33 N	4.48 E
Loire □ [5]	32	45.30 N	4.00 E
Loire ≃	32	47.16 N	2.11 W
Loire, Canal latéral à la ≚	50	47.37 N	2.44 E
Loire-Atlantique □ [5]	32	47.20 N	1.35 W
Loiret □ [5]	50	47.55 N	2.20 E
Loiret ≃	50	47.52 N	1.48 E
Loir-et-Cher □ [5]	50	47.30 N	1.30 E
Loïs, Lac ⊚	190	48.34 N	78.44 W
Loisach ≃	64	47.56 N	11.27 E
Loisdale	284c	38.46 N	77.11 W
Loisia	58	46.29 N	5.27 E
Loison ≃	56	49.30 N	5.17 E
Loitz	54	53.58 N	13.07 E
Loíza, Lago ⊚ [1]	240m	18.17 N	66.00 W
Loíza Aldea	240m	18.26 N	65.53 W
Loja, Ec.	246	4.00 S	79.13 W
Loja, Esp.	34	37.10 N	4.09 W
Loja □ [4]	246	4.10 S	79.30 W
Lojang → Luoyang	102	34.41 N	112.28 E
Lojga	24	61.05 N	44.37 E
Lojno	24	59.44 N	52.39 E
Løjt Kirkeby	41	55.05 N	9.28 E
Loka, Sūd.	154	4.16 N	31.01 E
Loka, R.D.C.	152	0.20 N	17.57 E
Loka brunn	40	59.36 N	14.28 E
Lokachi	78	50.44 N	24.39 E
Lokako	152	2.14 S	21.45 E
Lokalema	152	1.59 N	22.17 E
Lokan ≃	116	5.25 N	117.44 E
Lokandu	154	2.31 S	25.47 E
Lokan tekojärvi ⊚ [1]	24	67.55 N	27.40 E
Lökbatan	84	40.20 N	49.43 E
Løken	26	59.48 N	11.29 E
Lokeren	50	51.06 N	4.00 E
Loket	54	50.09 N	12.43 E
Lokhvytsya	78	50.22 N	33.16 E
Lokichar	154	2.23 N	35.39 E
Lokichokio	154	4.12 N	34.21 E
Lokitaung	154	4.16 N	35.45 E
Lokka	24	67.49 N	27.44 E
Løkken	26	57.22 N	9.43 E
Løkken verk	26	63.08 N	9.42 E
Lokn'a	76	56.50 N	30.09 E
Loknaš ≃	82	56.11 N	36.04 E
Loko	150	8.02 N	7.49 E
Lokofa-Bokolongo	152	0.12 N	19.22 E
Lokoja	150	7.47 N	6.45 E
Lokolama	152	2.34 S	19.53 E
Lokolenge	152	1.11 N	22.40 E
Lokolo ≃	152	0.43 S	19.40 E
Lokomo	152	2.41 N	15.19 E
Lokoro ≃	152	1.43 S	18.23 E
Lokossa	150	6.38 N	1.43 E
Lokosso	150	10.19 N	3.40 W
Lokot', Ross.	76	52.34 N	34.34 E
Lokot', Ross.	86	51.11 N	81.11 E
Lokoua ≃	273b	4.06 S	15.16 E
Loksa	76	59.35 N	25.45 E
Loks Land I	176	62.26 N	64.38 W
Lokve	64	46.01 N	13.49 E
Loky	157b	12.47 S	49.39 E
Lol	140	6.26 N	29.37 E
Lol ≃	140	9.13 N	28.59 E
Lóla, Ang.	152	14.22 S	13.42 E
Lola, Guinée	150	7.48 N	8.32 W
Lola, Mount ∧	226	39.26 N	120.22 W
Lolengi	152	0.07 N	20.59 E
Loleta	204	40.38 N	124.13 W
Lolingo	152	0.55 N	22.38 E
Loliondo	154	2.03 S	35.37 E
Lolita	222	28.50 N	96.32 W
Lolland I	41	54.46 N	11.30 E
Lollar	56	50.39 N	8.42 E
Lolo, Mt., U.S.	202	46.45 N	114.04 W
Lolo, R.D.C.	152	2.13 N	23.00 E
Lolo ≃	152	1.07 S	12.28 E
Lolobau Island I	164	4.55 S	151.10 E
Lolo Creek ≃, Id., U.S.	202	46.26 N	116.10 W
Lolo Creek ≃, Mt., U.S.	202	46.45 N	114.03 W
Lolodorf	152	3.14 N	10.44 E
Lolo Pass)(	202	46.38 N	114.35 W
Lolotique	236	13.33 N	88.21 W
Lolowai	175f	15.18 S	168.00 E
Loltong	175f	15.33 S	168.08 E
Lolvavana, Passage ʊ	175f	15.26 S	168.12 E
Lolwa	154	1.22 N	29.31 E
Lolworth Range ⩕	166	20.20 S	145.15 E
Lom, Blg.	38	43.49 N	23.14 E
Lom, Česká Rep.	54	50.37 N	13.40 E
Lom, Nor.	26	61.50 N	8.33 E
Lom, Ross.	80	57.54 N	39.12 E
Lom ∧	60	49.54 N	13.12 E
Lom ≃, Afr.	152	5.20 N	13.24 E
Lom ≃, Blg.	38	43.50 N	23.15 E
Loma	144	6.55 N	37.34 E
Loma, Point ›	228	32.41 N	117.14 W
Loma Blanca, Chile	286e	33.30 S	70.47 W
Loma Blanca, Méx.	200	31.35 N	106.17 W
Loma Bonita	234	18.07 N	95.53 W
Loma Echegareña	234	22.53 N	105.51 W
Lomakino	85	40.05 N	68.10 E
Lomako ≃	152	0.50 N	20.50 E
Loma Linda	228	34.02 N	117.15 W
Lomaloma	175g	17.17 S	178.59 W
Lomami ≃	138	0.46 N	24.16 E
Loma Mountains ⩕	150	9.10 N	11.07 W
Loma Ridge ∧	280	33.45 N	117.43 W
Lomas, Bahía ⊂	254	52.35 S	69.05 W
Lomas Alegres	234	17.38 N	92.36 W
Lomas Chapultepec ◆ [8]	286a	19.26 N	99.13 W
Lomas del Real	234	22.30 N	97.54 W
Lomas de Monreal	200	31.17 N	110.56 W
Lomas de Zamora	258	34.46 S	58.24 W
Lomas de Zamora □ [5]	288	34.45 S	58.24 W
Loma Verde	258	35.16 S	58.24 W
Lomax, Il., U.S.	190	40.41 N	91.04 W
Lomax, Tx., U.S.	222	29.41 N	95.04 W
Łomazy	30	51.55 N	23.10 E
Lomazzo	62	45.42 N	9.02 E
Lomba ≃	152	15.36 S	21.32 E
Lombagin	112	0.55 N	124.04 E
Lombard	216	41.52 N	88.00 W
Lombardia □ [4]	36	45.40 N	9.30 E
Lombardy East	273d	26.07 S	28.08 E
Lombe	152	9.27 S	16.13 E
Lomblen, Pulau I	112	8.25 S	123.30 E
Lombo do Tejo, Mouchão do I	266c	38.52 N	9.00 W
Lombok	115b	8.30 S	116.40 E
Lombok I	115b	8.45 S	116.30 E
Lombok, Selat ʊ	115b	8.30 S	115.50 E
Lombong	114	1.48 N	103.51 E
Lomé	150	6.08 N	1.13 E
Lomela	152	2.18 S	23.17 E
Lomela ≃	152	0.14 S	20.42 E
Lomellina □ [9]	62	45.15 N	8.45 E
Lometa	196	31.13 N	98.23 W
Lomi	24	67.05 N	16.09 E
Lomié	152	3.10 N	13.37 E
Lomira	190	43.35 N	88.26 W
Lo Miranda	252	34.11 S	70.54 W
Lomita	228	33.47 N	118.18 W
Lom Kao	110	16.53 N	101.14 E
Lomma	41	55.41 N	13.05 E
Lommabukten ⊂	41	55.40 N	12.58 E
Lommatzsch	54	51.12 N	13.18 E
Lomme	50	50.39 N	2.59 E
Lomme ≃	56	50.08 N	5.10 E
Lommel	56	51.14 N	5.18 E
Lomnice ≃	60	49.26 N	14.04 E
Lomnice nad Popelkou	30	50.32 N	15.22 E
Lomond	182	50.21 N	112.39 W
Lomond, Loch ⊚, N.S., Can.	186	45.46 N	60.35 W
Lomond, Loch ⊚, On., Can.	190	48.15 N	89.20 W
Lomond, Loch ⊚, Scot., U.K.	46	56.08 N	4.38 W
Lomond, Loch ⊚, Il., U.S.	278	42.17 N	88.01 W
Lomonosov	265a	59.55 N	29.46 E
Lomonosovka	86	52.50 N	66.28 E
Lomonosov Moscow State University ⊎ [2]	265b	55.43 N	37.32 E
Lomovoje	24	64.01 N	40.40 E
Lompobatang, Gunung ∧	112	5.20 S	119.55 E
Lompoc	204	34.38 N	120.27 W
Lom Sak	110	16.47 N	101.15 E
Lomuvatka	83	48.27 N	38.34 E
Lomy	88	52.17 N	117.59 E
Łomża	30	53.11 N	22.05 E
Łomża □ [4]	30	53.00 N	22.15 E
Lonaconing	188	39.33 N	78.58 W
Lonate Pozzolo	62	45.36 N	8.45 E
Lonato	64	45.27 N	10.29 E
Lonāvale	122	18.45 N	73.25 E
Lončakovo	89	47.05 N	134.10 E
Loncoche	254	39.22 S	72.38 W
Loncon ≃	64	45.42 N	12.47 E
Loncopué	252	38.04 S	70.37 W
Londela-Kaye	152	4.51 S	13.24 E
Londerzeel	50	51.00 N	4.18 E
Londinières	50	49.50 N	1.24 E
Londo	154	2.03 N	25.43 E
Londoko	89	49.02 N	131.59 E
London, On., Can.	212	42.59 N	81.14 W
London, Kiribati	174o	1.58 N	157.28 W
London, Eng., U.K.	42	51.30 N	0.10 W
London, Eng., U.K.	260	51.30 N	0.10 W
London, Ar., U.S.	194	35.19 N	93.15 W
London, Ca., U.S.	226	36.30 N	119.25 W
London, Ky., U.S.	192	37.07 N	84.05 W
London, Oh., U.S.	218	39.53 N	83.26 W
London, Tx., U.S.	196	30.41 N	99.35 W
London, Wi., U.S.	216	43.03 N	89.01 W
London (Gatwick) Airport ⊠, Eng., U.K.	42	51.09 N	0.21 W
London (Heathrow) Airport ⊠, Eng., U.K.	42	51.27 N	0.28 W
London Colney	260	51.43 N	0.18 W
Londonderry, N.S., Can.	186	45.29 N	63.36 W
Londonderry (Derry), N. Ire., U.K.	48	54.59 N	7.20 W
Londonderry, N.H., U.S.	207	42.51 N	71.22 W
Londonderry, Oh., U.S.	214	39.16 N	82.47 W
Londonderry, Cape ›	164	13.45 S	126.55 E
Londonderry, Isla I	254	55.03 S	70.35 W
Londontowne	208	38.59 N	76.32 W
London Zoo ♦	260	51.32 N	0.09 W
Londres, Arg.	252	27.43 S	67.07 W
Londres → London, Eng., U.K.	42	51.30 N	0.10 W
Londrina	255	23.18 S	51.09 W
Lonedell	219	38.18 N	90.50 W
Lone Grove	196	34.10 N	97.15 W
Lonely Lake ⊚	184	51.09 N	99.05 W
Lonelyville	276	40.39 N	73.11 W
Lone Mountain ∧	204	38.02 N	117.29 W
Lone Oak, Ky., U.S.	194	37.02 N	88.39 W
Lone Oak, Tx., U.S.	222	33.01 N	95.57 W
Lone Pine	204	36.36 N	118.03 W
Lone Pine Koala Sanctuary ♦	171a	27.32 S	152.57 E
Lone Rock	190	43.11 N	90.11 W
Lone Star	222	32.56 N	94.43 W
Lone Tree	190	41.29 N	91.25 W
Lone Tree Creek ≃, U.S.	200	40.25 N	104.35 W
Lone Tree Creek ≃, Ca., U.S.	226	37.53 N	121.14 W
Lone Wolf	196	34.59 N	99.14 W
Long	110	18.05 N	99.50 E
Long ≃, Fr.	50	47.41 N	0.28 E
Long ≃, Zhg.	100	23.26 N	114.38 E
Long ≃, Zhg.	102	24.32 N	109.15 E
Long ≃, Zhg.	105	39.23 N	116.49 E
Longa	152	14.42 S	18.32 E
Longa ≃, Ang.	152	16.25 N	19.04 E
Longa ≃, Ang.	152	10.15 S	13.30 E
Longá ≃, Bra.	250	3.09 S	41.56 W
Longa, proliv ʊ	74	70.20 N	178.00 E
Longairo	154	4.30 N	32.17 E
Long Akah	112	3.19 N	114.47 E
Long'an	102	25.03 N	109.00 E
Longana	175f	15.20 S	167.55 E
Long'anqiao	89	47.31 N	124.27 E
Longare	64	45.29 N	11.36 E
Longarone	64	46.16 N	12.18 E
Long Arroyo V	196	33.04 N	104.17 W
Longasy	24	61.58 N	35.09 E
Longaví	252	35.58 S	71.41 W
Longbangun	112	0.36 N	115.11 E
Long Bar Harbor	208	39.27 N	76.15 W
Long Barn	226	38.05 N	120.08 W
Long Bay ⊂, Austl.	274a	33.58 S	151.16 E
Long Bay ⊂, U.S.	192	33.35 N	78.45 W
Long Beach, Ca., U.S.	228	33.46 N	118.11 W
Long Beach, In., U.S.	216	41.44 N	86.51 W
Long Beach, Ms., U.S.	194	30.21 N	89.09 W
Long Beach, N.Y., U.S.	210	40.35 N	73.39 W
Long Beach, Wa., U.S.	224	46.21 N	124.03 W
Long Beach ⊥ [2]	208	39.39 N	74.11 W
Long Beach Breakwater ◆ [5]	280	33.43 N	118.09 W
Long Beach Middle Harbor ⊂	280	33.45 N	118.13 W
Long Beach Municipal Airport ⊠	280	33.49 N	118.09 W
Long Beach Naval Station ■	280	33.45 N	118.14 W
Longbeleh	112	0.16 N	116.11 E
Long Belepai	112	2.45 N	114.04 E
Longbenton	44	55.02 N	1.35 W
Longboat Key	220	27.24 N	82.39 W
Longboat Key I	220	27.23 N	82.39 W
Long Branch, N.J., U.S.	208	40.18 N	73.59 W
Longbranch, Wa., U.S.	224	47.12 N	122.45 W
Long Branch □ [8]	275b	43.35 N	79.32 W
Long Branch ≃	219	39.23 N	91.49 W
Long Branch Lake ⊚ [1]	194	39.49 N	92.31 W
Longbu	100	25.32 N	115.24 E
Long Buckby	42	52.19 N	1.04 W
Long Cane Creek ≃	192	33.57 N	82.24 W
Long Canyon V	226	38.59 N	120.41 W
Long Cay I	238	22.37 N	74.20 W
Longchamp, Hippodrome de ♦	261	48.51 N	2.14 E
Longchamps, Arg.	258	34.52 S	58.23 W
Longchamps, Bel.	56	50.03 N	5.42 E
Longchang, Zhg.	104	40.53 N	123.08 E
Longchang, Zhg.	107	29.21 N	105.17 E
Longchaumois	58	46.27 N	5.56 E
Longchêne	261	48.38 N	2.00 E
Longchuan, Zhg.	100	24.07 N	115.17 E
Longchuan, Zhg.	102	24.14 N	97.45 E
Longchuan (Shweli) ≃	102	23.56 N	96.17 E
Long Creek, Il., U.S.	219	39.48 N	88.50 W
Long Creek, Or., U.S.	202	44.42 N	119.06 W
Long Creek ≃	184	49.07 N	103.00 W
Long Crendon	42	51.47 N	1.01 W
Longcun	100	23.34 N	115.33 E
Longde	102	35.28 N	106.22 E
Longdendale V	262	53.29 N	1.56 W
Long Ditton	260	51.23 N	0.20 W
Longdongtuo	107	29.59 N	106.21 E
Longdor, gora ∧	88	58.24 N	116.47 E
Longdou	100	27.25 N	117.24 E
Longdu	106	31.51 N	118.56 E
Long Eaton	42	52.54 N	1.15 W
Longeau	58	47.46 N	5.18 E
Long Eddy	210	41.51 N	75.08 W
Longfellow National Historic Site ⊥	283	42.23 N	71.08 W
Longfengchang	107	30.26 N	105.38 E
Longfengkan	104	41.51 N	124.01 E
Longfengyutun	104	40.39 N	122.57 E
Longfield	260	51.24 N	0.18 E
Longford, Austl.	166	38.10 S	147.05 E
Longford, Ire.	48	53.44 N	7.47 W
Longford, Md., U.S.	284b	39.25 N	76.39 W
Longford □ [6]	48	53.40 N	7.40 W
Longford Park ♦	262	53.27 N	2.17 W
Longframlington	44	55.18 N	1.47 W
Longgang, Zhg.	100	29.38 N	114.57 E
Longgang, Zhg.	100	33.22 N	120.04 E
Longgang, Zhg.	102	24.41 N	101.09 E
Longgangzi	104	42.09 N	123.26 E
Long Green	208	39.28 N	76.31 W
Long Grove	216	42.11 N	88.00 W
Longguan	105	40.47 N	115.34 E
Longgudu	100	27.45 N	116.14 E
Longguntur	112	0.13 N	112.12 E
Long Harbour	186	47.26 N	53.48 W
Long Harbour ⊂, Nf., Can.	186	47.44 N	55.01 W
Long Harbour ⊂, Zhg.	271d	22.27 N	114.20 E
Longhorn Cavern State Park ♦	196	30.20 N	98.30 W
Longhorsley	44	55.15 N	1.46 W
Longhoughton	44	55.26 N	1.36 W
Long Hu ⊚	100	29.58 N	116.10 E
Longhua, Zhg.	98	41.17 N	117.37 E
Longhua, Zhg.	100	22.42 N	113.59 E
Longhua, Zhg.	100	23.37 N	114.14 E
Longhua, Zhg.	106	31.09 N	121.26 E
Longhua Airport ⊠	269b	31.10 N	121.26 E
Longhua Pagoda ⊎ [1]	269b	31.11 N	121.26 E
Longhui, Zhg.	100	25.32 N	114.47 E
Longhui (Taohuaping), Zhg.	102	27.00 N	110.59 E
Longhui, Zhg.	107	29.32 N	104.48 E
Longhutang	106	31.52 N	119.59 E
Longi	70	38.01 N	14.45 E
Longido	154	2.44 S	36.41 E
Longiram	112	0.02 S	115.38 E
Long Island I, Antig.	240c	17.08 N	61.45 W
Long Island I, Austl.	166	22.09 S	149.54 E
Long Island I, Ba.	238	23.15 N	75.07 W
Long Island I, Nf., Can.	186	47.35 N	54.05 W
Long Island I, N.T., Can.	176	54.50 N	79.20 W
Long Island I, N.S., Can.	186	44.20 N	66.15 W
Long Island I, Ak., U.S.	182	54.54 N	132.45 W
Long Island I, Ma., U.S.	283	42.19 N	70.58 W
Long Island I, N.Y., U.S.	188	40.50 N	73.00 W
Long Island I, Wa., U.S.	224	46.27 N	123.58 W
Long Island City ◆ [8]	276	40.45 N	73.56 W
Long Island MacArthur Airport ⊠	210	40.48 N	73.06 W
Long Island Sound ʊ	188	41.05 N	72.58 W
Long Island University ⊎ [2], N.Y., U.S.	276	40.41 N	73.59 W
Long Island University (C.W. Post Center) ⊎ [2], N.Y., U.S.	276	40.49 N	73.36 W
Longitudinal, Valle V	252	36.00 S	72.00 W
Long Jetty	170	33.22 S	151.29 E
Longji	107	29.23 N	106.04 E
Longjiadian	104	42.10 N	120.47 E
Longjiang, Zhg.	89	47.19 N	123.12 E
Longjiang, Zhg.	100	22.53 N	113.04 E
Longjiang, Zhg.	100	22.59 N	116.13 E
Longjiang, Zhg.	107	29.48 N	105.03 E
Longjie	107	29.53 N	104.32 E
Longjin	100	28.37 N	116.37 E
Longjing	100	23.53 N	112.52 E
Longjohn Slough ≃	278	41.43 N	87.53 W
Longjumeau	50	48.42 N	2.18 E
Longka	120	33.12 N	79.47 E
Longkamp	56	49.53 N	7.07 E
Longkangji	100	33.09 N	116.54 E
Long Ke	271d	22.23 N	114.22 E
Long Key I, Fl., U.S.	220	24.49 N	80.49 W
Long Key I, Fl., U.S.	220	27.44 N	82.45 W
Long King Creek ≃	222	30.34 N	94.58 W
Longkou, Zhg.	98	37.38 N	120.18 E
Longkou, Zhg.	100	32.56 N	114.57 E
Longkou, Zhg.	100	29.57 N	113.47 E
Longkou, Zhg.	100	26.11 N	115.15 E
Longkouqiao	85	39.40 N	77.09 E
Long Lake, Il., U.S.	216	42.22 N	88.08 W
Long Lake, N.Y., U.S.	188	43.58 N	74.25 W
Long Lake, Tx., U.S.	222	31.39 N	95.47 W
Long Lake ⊚, On., Can.	212	44.41 N	76.45 W
Long Lake ⊚, Mi., U.S.	190	45.12 N	83.30 W
Long Lake ⊚, Mi., U.S.	281	42.37 N	83.44 W
Long Lake ⊚, Mi., U.S.	281	42.36 N	83.28 W
Long Lake ⊚, N.Y., U.S.	188	44.04 N	74.20 W
Long Lake ⊚, N.D., U.S.	198	46.43 N	100.07 W
Long Lake ⊚, Wa., U.S.	224	47.03 N	122.47 W
Long Lake ⊚ [1]	202	47.50 N	117.40 W
Long Lake Creek ≃	198	46.40 N	100.13 W
Long Lake Shores	281	42.35 N	83.19 W
Long Lama	112	3.46 N	114.24 E
Longlaville	56	49.32 N	5.47 E
Longleaf	194	31.00 N	92.34 W
Long Leaf Park	192	34.12 N	77.56 W
Longleat ⊎	42	51.12 N	2.17 W
Longlegged Lake ⊚	184	50.46 N	94.08 W
Longli	102	26.26 N	106.58 E
Longlin	102	24.49 N	105.31 E
Longling	102	24.39 N	98.40 E
Longmeadow	207	42.03 N	72.35 W
Long Melford	42	52.05 N	0.43 E
Longmen, Zhg.	89	48.55 N	126.54 E
Longmen, Zhg.	100	29.53 N	119.57 E
Longmen, Zhg.	100	24.56 N	118.04 E
Longmen, Zhg.	100	25.06 N	116.58 E
Longmen, Zhg.	100	23.44 N	114.15 E
Longmen, Zhg.	107	29.27 N	104.59 E
Longmen, Zhg.	107	29.12 N	106.13 E
Longmenchang	107	30.53 N	106.10 E
Longmensuo	98	40.56 N	115.54 E
Longmenzhang	107	28.59 N	106.13 E
Longming	102	22.59 N	107.11 E
Longmire	224	46.45 N	121.49 W
Long Moc	110	18.51 N	105.01 E
Longmont	200	40.10 N	105.06 W
Longmorn	46	57.36 N	3.17 W
Long Mountain ∧	194	36.41 N	92.26 W
Long Mountain ∧ [2]	42	52.39 N	3.09 W
Longmu	100	24.16 N	115.28 E
Longnan	100	24.54 N	114.48 E
Longnawan	112	1.54 N	114.53 E
Long Neck › [1]	276	41.03 N	73.29 W
Long Neck Point ›	276	41.02 N	73.29 W
Longniddry	46	55.58 N	2.53 W
Longnüsi	107	30.23 N	106.11 E
Longny-au-Perche	50	48.32 N	0.45 E
Longobucco	68	39.27 N	16.37 E
Longperrier	261	49.03 N	2.40 E
Long Pine	198	42.32 N	99.42 W
Longping	100	29.53 N	115.41 E
Long Plains	168b	34.21 S	138.22 E
Long Point, Austl.	274a	34.01 S	150.54 E
Long Point, Il., U.S.	216	41.00 N	88.54 W
Long Point ›, Ba.	240b	25.01 N	77.20 W
Long Point ›, Nf., Can.	186	48.48 N	58.46 W
Long Point ›, N.S., Can.	186	46.51 N	60.18 W
Long Point ›, On., Can.	212	44.06 N	76.29 W
Long Point ›, On., Can.	212	44.32 N	80.18 W
Long Point ›, Pil.	116	9.39 N	118.20 E
Long Point ›, Ca., U.S.	280	33.44 N	118.23 W
Long Point ›, Vir. Is., U.S.	240m	18.18 N	64.53 W
Long Point › [1], Mb., Can.	184	53.02 N	98.40 W
Long Point › [1], On., Can.	214	42.34 N	80.15 W
Long Point Bay ⊂	212	42.40 N	80.14 W
Long Point Creek ≃	216	41.02 N	88.48 W
Long Point Provincial Park ♦	214	42.35 N	80.35 W
Long Pond ⊚, U.S.	283	42.41 N	71.21 W
Long Pond ⊚, Ma., U.S.	207	41.48 N	70.57 W
Long Pond ⊚, Ma., U.S.	207	41.43 N	70.04 W
Longpont, Fr.	50	49.16 N	3.13 E
Longpont, Fr.	261	48.38 N	2.17 E
Longport	208	39.18 N	74.31 W
Long Prairie	198	45.58 N	94.51 W
Long Prairie ≃	198	46.20 N	94.36 W
Longpré-les-Corps-Saints	50	50.01 N	1.59 E
Long Preston	44	54.02 N	2.15 W
Longqiantai	104	41.23 N	120.52 E
Longqu, Zhg.	98	34.16 N	114.49 E
Longqu, Zhg.	98	34.54 N	116.47 E
Longquan	100	28.04 N	119.07 E
Longquan ≃	100	28.17 N	119.44 E
Longquanguan	98	38.55 N	113.51 E
Longquan Shan ⩕	107	30.25 N	104.15 E
Longquanyi	107	30.34 N	104.16 E
Longquanzhen	107	30.21 N	104.39 E
Long Range Mountains ⩕	186	49.20 N	57.30 W
Longreach	166	23.26 S	144.15 E
Long Reach ⊂	186	45.26 N	66.09 W
Long Reach ʊ	212	44.07 N	77.04 W
Long Reef ✣ [2]	164	11.11 S	151.40 E
Long Reef Point ›	274a	33.45 S	151.19 E
Longridge	44	53.51 N	2.36 W
Long Run ≃, Il., U.S.	278	41.37 N	88.03 W
Long Run ≃, Pa., U.S.	279b	40.20 N	79.48 W
Long-Sault	206	45.02 N	74.53 W
Long Sault Dam ◆ [6]	206	45.00 N	74.45 W
Long Sault Islands II	206	45.00 N	74.55 W
Longsegah	112	2.15 N	116.42 E
Longshan, Zhg.	100	33.36 N	116.18 E
Longshan, Zhg.	102	29.28 N	109.20 E
Longshansuo	100	30.05 N	121.33 E
Longsheng, Zhg.	102	25.48 N	110.00 E
Longsheng, Zhg.	107	30.36 N	105.21 E
Longshizhen, Zhg.	107	30.12 N	106.26 E
Longshizhen, Zhg.	107	29.23 N	105.10 E
Longshu	107	29.33 N	105.45 E
Longs Peak ∧	200	40.15 N	105.37 W
Long Stratton	42	52.29 N	1.14 E
Long Sutton	42	52.47 N	0.08 E
Longtaichang	107	30.04 N	105.34 E
Longtan, Zhg.	100	23.40 N	113.24 E
Longtan, Zhg.	102	28.20 N	108.52 E
Longtan, Zhg.	106	32.11 N	119.04 E
Longtan, Zhg.	106	31.20 N	118.45 E
Longtansi	107	30.42 N	104.10 E
Longtanzhen	107	29.19 N	104.35 E
Long Teru	112	3.52 N	114.15 E
Long Thanh	110	10.47 N	106.57 E
Longtian	100	25.38 N	119.28 E
Longtian'an	106	31.10 N	120.49 E
Long Tom ≃	202	44.23 N	123.15 W
Longton, Eng., U.K.	44	53.43 N	2.48 W
Longton, Eng., U.K.	262	53.43 N	2.48 W
Longton, Ks., U.S.	198	37.22 N	96.04 W
Longtou	98	38.51 N	121.18 E
Longtoupu	100	27.54 N	113.12 E
Longtouwei	100	25.14 N	115.24 E
Longtown	44	55.01 N	2.58 W
Long Truong	269c	10.49 N	106.49 E
Longué	32	47.23 N	0.06 W
Longueau	50	49.52 N	2.21 E
Longuenesse	50	50.44 N	1.24 E
Longuesse	261	49.04 N	1.56 E
Longueuil	206	45.32 N	73.30 W
Longueville, Austl.	274a	33.50 S	151.10 E
Longueville, Fr.	50	48.31 N	3.15 E
Longueville-sur-Scie	50	49.48 N	1.06 E
Longuyon	56	49.26 N	5.36 E
Long Valley	210	40.47 N	74.46 W
Long Valley Creek ≃, Ca., U.S.	226	39.03 N	122.34 W
Long Valley Creek ≃, Nv., U.S.	226	39.31 N	119.39 W
Longvic	58	47.17 N	5.04 E
Longview, Ab., Can.	182	50.32 N	114.14 W
Longview, N.C., U.S.	192	35.43 N	81.23 W
Longview, Tx., U.S.	222	32.30 N	94.44 W
Longview, Wa., U.S.	224	46.08 N	122.56 W
Longview Heights	222	32.30 N	94.41 W
Longvilliers	261	48.35 N	2.00 E
Longvilly	56	50.01 N	5.50 E
Longwai	112	0.42 N	116.39 E
Longwan	105	38.57 N	116.10 E
Longwangmiao, Zhg.	98	36.12 N	115.13 E
Longwangmiao, Zhg.	102	40.36 N	95.52 E
Longwangmiao, Zhg.	104	41.38 N	121.04 E
Longwangmiao, Zhg.	104	42.35 N	123.42 E
Longwarry	169	38.07 S	145.46 E
Longwen	100	24.36 N	116.21 E
Longwo	100	23.28 N	115.17 E
Longwokou	106	32.18 N	119.52 E
Longwood	220	28.42 N	81.20 W
Longwood Gardens ♦	285	39.52 N	75.40 W
Longwood Lake	276	40.59 N	74.52 W
Longwood Park	192	34.55 N	79.42 W
Longworth	182	53.55 N	121.28 W
Longwy	56	49.31 N	5.46 E
Longxi → Zhangzhou, Zhg.	100	24.33 N	117.39 E
Longxi, Zhg.	102	34.56 N	104.47 E
Longxi, Zhg.	107	29.59 N	106.09 E
Longxian, Zhg.	102	34.51 N	106.59 E
Longxian, Zhg.	107	29.09 N	105.50 E
Long Xuyen	110	10.23 N	105.25 E
Longyan	100	25.08 N	117.02 E
Longyao	98	37.23 N	114.41 E
Longyou	100	29.02 N	119.10 E
Longyou ≃	106	32.08 N	120.38 E
Longyuanba	100	24.56 N	114.27 E
Longzhaogou	98	40.49 N	124.36 E
Longzhen	89	48.41 N	126.42 E
Longzhou	102	22.22 N	106.52 E
Loni	272a	28.45 N	77.17 E
Lonigo	64	45.23 N	11.23 E
Löningen	52	52.44 N	7.46 E
Lonja ≃	36	45.27 N	16.41 E
Lonkala	152	4.37 S	23.14 E
Lönnewitz	54	51.34 N	13.11 E
Lonny	56	49.49 N	4.35 E
Lonoke	194	34.47 N	91.53 W
Lonquimay, Volcán ∧ [1]	252	38.22 S	71.34 W
Lönsboda	26	56.24 N	14.19 E
Lønsdal	24	66.44 N	15.28 E
Lonsdale	190	44.28 N	93.25 W
Lonsdale, Point ›	169	38.17 S	144.37 E
Lonsee	58	48.33 N	9.55 E
Lons-le-Saunier	58	46.40 N	5.33 E
Lonton	110	25.06 N	96.17 E
Lontra ≃	250	6.37 S	48.39 W
Lontra, Ribeirão da ≃	255	21.28 S	53.37 W
Lonua ≃	152	1.16 N	22.38 E
Lonzhen	107	30.00 N	103.59 E
Loo	84	43.43 N	39.36 E
Looc	116	12.16 N	121.59 E
Looe	42	50.21 N	4.28 W
Loogootee	194	38.40 N	86.54 W
Looking Glass ≃	216	42.52 N	84.54 W
Lookout	210	41.47 N	75.11 W
Lookout, Cape ›, N.C., U.S.	192	34.35 N	76.32 W
Lookout, Cape ›, Or., U.S.	224	45.20 N	124.00 W
Lookout, Point ›, Austl.	171a	27.26 S	153.33 E
Lookout, Point ›, Md., U.S.	208	38.02 N	76.19 W
Lookout Mountain ∧, U.S.	194	34.25 N	85.40 W
Lookout Mountain ∧, Or., U.S.	202	44.20 N	120.22 W
Lookout Mountain ∧, Or., U.S.	224	45.21 N	121.31 W
Lookout Mountain ∧, Wa., U.S.	224	48.40 N	122.22 W
Lookout Pass)(	202	47.27 N	115.42 W
Lookout Point Lake ⊚ [1]	202	43.52 N	122.40 W
Lookout Ridge ⩕	180	69.07 N	158.36 W
Loolmalassin ∧ [1]	154	3.03 S	35.49 E
Loomis, Ca., U.S.	226	38.49 N	121.12 W
Loomis, Ne., U.S.	198	40.28 N	99.30 W
Loomis, Wa., U.S.	182	48.49 N	119.37 W
Loon	116	9.48 N	123.47 E
Loon ≃	184	55.50 N	101.59 W
Loon Creek ≃	202	44.49 N	114.49 W
Loongana	162	30.57 S	127.02 E
Loon Lake ⊚, Can.	184	55.51 N	102.00 W
Loon Lake ⊚, Mi., U.S.	281	42.41 N	83.22 W
Loon Lake ⊚ [1]	226	39.00 N	120.18 W
Loon op Zand	52	51.38 N	5.04 E
Loop	196	32.55 N	102.25 W
Loop ◆ [8]	278	41.53 N	87.38 W
Loop Head ›	48	52.34 N	9.56 W
Loosdorf	61	48.12 N	15.24 E
Loosduinen ◆ [8]	52	52.04 N	4.13 E
Loose, Dtsch.	41	54.31 N	9.53 E
Loose, Eng., U.K.	260	51.14 N	0.31 E
Loose Creek	219	38.30 N	91.57 W
Lop	120	37.02 N	80.15 E
Lop ≃	110	13.18 N	107.37 E
Lopandino	76	52.28 N	34.49 E
Lopanka	80	46.24 N	40.59 E
Lopar'ovo	80	58.20 N	42.41 E
Lopasn'a ≃	82	54.51 N	37.52 E
Lopatin	84	43.53 N	47.41 E
Lopatina, gora ∧	89	50.52 N	143.10 E
Lopatino, Ross.	80	52.37 N	45.47 E
Lopatino, Ross.	82	54.45 N	37.00 E
Lopatino, Ross.	89	48.24 N	142.15 E
Lopatinskij	82	55.21 N	38.34 E
Lopatka, mys ›	74	50.52 N	156.40 E
Lopatovo	76	56.08 N	29.12 E
Lopatyn	78	50.13 N	24.50 E
Lop Buri	110	14.48 N	100.37 E
Lopé-Okanda, Réserve de Chasse de ◆ [4]	152	0.30 S	11.40 E
Lopévi I	175f	16.30 S	168.21 E
López, Méx.	232	27.00 N	105.02 W
Lopez, Pa., U.S.	210	41.27 N	76.20 W
Lopez, Wa., U.S.	224	48.31 N	122.54 W
López, Arroyo de ≃	258	35.26 S	57.35 W
Lopez, Cap ›	152	0.37 S	8.43 E
Lopez Bay ⊂	116	13.56 N	122.12 E
Lopez Island I	224	48.30 N	122.54 W
Lopez Lake ⊚ [1]	226	35.12 N	120.28 W
Lopez Point ›	226	36.01 N	121.34 W
Lopik	52	51.58 N	4.56 E
Lop Nor → Lop Nur ⊚	90	40.20 N	90.15 E
Lop Nur (Lop Nor) ⊚	90	40.20 N	90.15 E
Lopori ≃	152	1.14 N	19.49 E
Lopotovo	82	56.04 N	36.49 E
Loppersum	52	53.19 N	6.45 E
Loppi	26	60.43 N	24.27 E
Lo Prado	286e	33.26 S	70.45 W
Lopšen'ga	24	64.58 N	37.41 E
Lopt'uga	24	63.16 N	47.56 E
Lopuchovka, Ross.	80	51.59 N	44.42 E
Lopuchovka, Ross.	80	50.37 N	44.29 E
Łopuszno	30	50.57 N	20.15 E
Lora	123	33.53 N	73.17 E
Lora ≃	246	9.25 N	72.25 W
Lora, Hāmūn-i- ⊚	128	29.20 N	64.50 E
Lora Creek ≃	162	28.10 S	135.22 E
Lora del Río	34	37.39 N	5.32 W
Lorain	214	41.27 N	82.10 W
Lorain □ [6]	214	41.22 N	82.06 W
Lorain County Regional Airport ⊠	279a	41.20 N	82.11 W
Loraine, Ca., U.S.	228	35.19 N	118.25 W
Loraine, Il., U.S.	219	40.09 N	91.13 W
Loraine, Tx., U.S.	196	32.24 N	100.42 W
Loralai	120	30.22 N	68.36 E
Loramie, Lake ⊚ [1]	216	40.23 N	84.18 W
Loramie Creek ≃	216	40.11 N	84.14 W
Lorca	34	37.40 N	1.42 W
Lorch, Dtsch.	56	48.49 N	9.40 E
Lorch, Dtsch.	56	50.02 N	7.48 E
Lorchhausen	56	50.03 N	7.47 E
Lord Howe Island I	160	31.33 S	159.05 E
Lord Howe Rise ✣ [3]	14	32.00 S	162.00 E
Lord Howe Seamounts ✣ [3]	14	28.00 S	159.00 E
Lord Mayor Bay ⊂	176	69.44 N	92.00 W
Lordsburg	200	32.21 N	108.42 W
Lord's Cricket Ground ♦	260	51.32 N	0.10 W
Lordstown	214	41.09 N	80.53 W
Lords Valley	210	41.23 N	75.04 W
Loreauville	194	30.03 N	91.44 W
Loreley ♦	56	50.08 N	7.44 E
Lorena, Bra.	256	22.44 S	45.08 W
Lorena, Tx., U.S.	222	31.23 N	97.13 W
Lorengau	164	2.00 S	147.15 E
Lorentz ≃	164	5.23 S	138.04 E
Lorentzen	56	48.57 N	7.10 E
Lorenzago di Cadore	64	46.29 N	12.28 E
Lorenzo	196	33.40 N	101.32 W
Lorenzo Geyres (Queguay)	252	32.05 S	57.55 W
Loreo	64	45.04 N	12.11 E
Lorestān □ [4]	128	33.30 N	48.30 E
Loreto, Arg.	252	27.46 S	57.17 W
Loreto, Bol.	248	15.13 S	64.40 W
Loreto, Bra.	250	7.05 S	45.09 W
Loreto, It.	66	43.26 N	13.36 E
Loreto, Méx.	232	26.01 N	111.21 W
Loreto, Méx.	234	22.16 N	101.58 W
Loreto, Para.	252	23.16 S	57.11 W
Loreto, Pil.	116	8.12 N	125.45 E
Loreto, Pil.	116	10.21 N	125.34 E
Loreto □ [5]	246	3.00 S	75.00 W
Loreto Aprutino	66	42.26 N	13.59 E
Loreto Mocagua	246	3.48 S	70.15 W
Lorette, Mb., Can.	184	49.44 N	96.52 W
Lorette, Fr.	62	45.31 N	4.35 E
Loretteville	206	46.51 N	71.21 W
Loretto → Loreto, It.	66	43.26 N	13.36 E
Loretto, Ky., U.S.	194	37.38 N	85.24 W
Loretto, Pa., U.S.	214	40.30 N	78.37 W
Loretto, Tn., U.S.	194	35.04 N	87.26 W
Lorgues	62	43.29 N	6.22 E
Lorian Swamp ⠿	154	0.40 N	39.35 E
Lorica	246	9.14 N	75.49 W
Lorida	220	27.26 N	81.15 W
Lorient	32	47.45 N	3.22 W
L'Orignal	206	45.37 N	74.42 W
Lorimer Park ♦	285	40.06 N	75.05 W
Lorimor	194	41.07 N	94.03 W
Loring, Aeródromo de ⊠	266a	40.22 N	3.47 W
Loring Air Force Base ■	186	46.57 N	67.54 W
Lorino	180	65.30 N	171.43 W
Loriol-sur-Drôme	62	44.45 N	4.49 E
Loris	192	34.03 N	78.53 W
Lorman	194	31.49 N	91.03 W
L'Orme	261	48.39 N	1.41 E
Lormes	50	47.17 N	3.49 E
Lorn, Firth of ⊂ [1]	46	56.20 N	5.45 W
Lorna Glen	162	26.14 S	121.33 E
Lorne, Austl.	169	38.33 S	143.59 E
Lorne, N.B., Can.	186	47.53 N	66.08 W
Loro Ciuffenna	66	43.35 N	11.38 E
Loronyo	154	4.39 N	32.38 E
Lorquin	58	48.40 N	7.00 E
Lörrach	58	47.37 N	7.40 E
Lorraine □ [9]	32	49.00 N	6.00 E
Lorrez-le-Bocage	50	48.14 N	2.54 E
Lorris	50	47.53 N	2.31 E
Lorsch	56	49.39 N	8.34 E
Lorsica	62	44.26 N	9.16 E
Lorup	52	52.55 N	7.38 E
Lorze ≃	58	47.15 N	8.25 E
Los	26	61.44 N	15.10 E
Los, Îles de II	150	9.30 N	13.48 W
Losa, Nuraghe ⊥	71	40.07 N	8.46 E
Losada ≃	246	2.12 N	73.55 W
Los Aguacates	286c	10.35 N	66.48 W
Los Alamitos	280	33.48 N	118.04 W
Los Alamitos Armed Forces Reserve Center ■	280	33.47 N	118.03 W
Los Alamitos Race Course ♦	280	33.48 N	118.03 W
Los Alamos, Ca., U.S.	204	34.44 N	120.16 W
Los Alamos, N.M., U.S.	200	35.53 N	106.19 W
Los Aldamas	232	26.03 N	99.11 W
Los Alerces, Parque Nacional ♦	254	42.50 S	71.52 W
Los Altos, Méx.	196	26.14 N	98.28 W
Los Altos, Ca., U.S.	226	37.23 N	122.06 W
Los Altos Hills	226	37.22 N	122.08 W
Los Amates, Guat.	236	15.16 N	89.06 W
Los Amates, Méx.	234	18.08 N	102.15 W
Los Americanos, Barra I	232	24.50 N	97.35 W
Los Andes	252	32.50 S	70.37 W
Los Ángeles, Chile	252	37.28 S	72.21 W
Los Angeles, Ca., U.S.	228	34.03 N	118.14 W
Los Angeles, Ca., U.S.	280	34.03 N	118.14 W
Los Angeles □ [6]	228	34.20 N	118.10 W
Los Angeles ≃	228	33.46 N	118.12 W
Los Angeles Aqueduct ≚ [1]	204	35.22 N	118.05 W
Los Angeles Coliseum and Sports Arena ♦	280	34.01 N	118.17 W
Los Angeles Convention Center ⊎	280	34.03 N	118.17 W
Los Angeles County Fairgrounds ♦	280	34.05 N	117.46 W
Los Angeles County Museum of Art ⊎	280	34.05 N	118.22 W
Los Angeles Harbor ⊂	280	33.42 N	118.16 W
Los Angeles International Airport ⊠	228	33.56 N	118.24 W
Los Antiguos	254	46.33 S	71.37 W
Losantville	218	40.01 N	85.10 W
Losap I [1]	14	6.54 N	152.44 E
Los Arabos	240p	22.44 N	80.43 W
Losarang	115a	6.24 S	108.10 E
Los Aros	234	22.46 N	102.57 W
Los Banos	226	37.03 N	120.50 W
Los Banos Creek ≃	226	37.20 N	120.57 W
Los Banos Creek, North Fork ≃	226	36.57 N	121.07 W
Los Banos Creek, South Fork ≃	226	36.57 N	121.07 W
Los Banos Reservoir ⊚ [1]	226	36.59 N	120.57 W
Los Berros	252	31.57 S	68.39 W
Los Blancos	252	23.36 S	62.36 W
Los Bolones, Cerro ∧, Méx.	232	16.50 N	92.38 W
Los Bolones, Cerro ∧, Méx.	234	16.39 N	92.34 W
Los Cardales	258	34.20 S	58.59 W
Los Cerrillos, Arg.	252	31.57 S	65.28 W
Los Cerrillos, Ur.	258	34.37 S	56.22 W
Los Cerrillos, Aeropuerto ⊠	286e	33.30 S	70.43 W

Symbol	English	Deutsch	Español	Français	Português
≃	River	Fluß	Río	Rivière	Rio
≚	Canal	Kanal	Canal	Canal	Canal
˪	Waterfall, Rapids	Wasserfall, Stromschnellen	Cascada, Rápidos	Chute d'eau, Rapides	Cascata, Rápidos
ʊ	Strait	Meeresstraße	Estrecho	Détroit	Estreito
⊂	Bay, Gulf	Bucht, Golf	Bahía, Golfo	Baie, Golfe	Baía, Golfo
⊚	Lake, Lakes	See, Seen	Lago, Lagos	Lac, Lacs	Lago, Lagos
⠿	Swamp	Sumpf	Pantano	Marais	Pântano
⍓	Ice Features, Glacier	Eis- und Gletscherformen	Accidentes Glaciales	Formes glaciaires	Acidentes glaciares
⊤	Other Hydrographic Features	Andere Hydrographische Objekte	Otros Elementos Hidrográficos	Autres données hydrographiques	Outros acidentes hidrográficos
✣	Submarine Features	Untermeerische Objekte	Accidentes Submarinos	Formes de relief sous-marin	Acidentes submarinos
□	Political Unit	Politische Einheit	Unidad Politica	Entité politique	Unidade política
⊎	Cultural Institution	Kulturelle Institution	Institución Cultural	Institution culturelle	Institução cultural
⊥	Historical Site	Historische Stätte	Sitio Histórico	Site historique	Sitio histórico
♦	Recreational Site	Erholungs- und Ferienort	Sitio de Recreo	Centre de loisirs	Area de Lazer
⊠	Airport	Flughafen	Aeropuerto	Aéroport	Aeroporto
■	Military Installation	Militäranlage	Instalación Militar	Installation militaire	Instalação militar
◆	Miscellaneous	Verschiedenes	Misceláneo	Divers	Diversos

Name (Name)	Page (Seite)	Lat.°′ (Breite°′)	Long.°′ (Länge°′ E = Ost)
Los Cerritos Center ◆[9]	280	33.52 N	118.05 W
Los Chacos	248	14.33 S	62.11 W
Los Chiles	236	11.02 N	84.43 W
Los Conquistadores	252	30.36 S	58.28 W
Los Coronados, Islas II	204	32.25 N	117.15 W
Los Coyotes Indian Reservation ◆[4]	204	33.20 N	116.35 W
Los Cuatro Álamos	286e	33.32 S	70.44 W
Los Dos Caminos	286c	10.31 N	66.50 W
Los Ebanos	196	26.14 N	98.34 W
Loseley House ⊥	260	51.13 N	0.36 W
Los Esclavos ≃	236	13.50 N	90.20 W
Losevo	78	50.40 N	40.02 E
Los Flamencos, Laguna ⊜	258	35.36 S	58.42 W
Los Frailes, Picacho ∧	234	23.53 N	106.03 W
Los Frentones	252	26.25 S	61.25 W
Los Fresnos	196	26.04 N	97.29 W
Los Garzas	196	26.23 N	99.46 W
Los Gatos	226	37.13 N	121.58 W
Los Gatos Creek ≃, Ca., U.S.	226	36.13 N	120.08 W
Los Gatos Creek ≃, Ca., U.S.	226	37.20 N	121.54 W
Los Glaciares, Parque Nacional ♠	254	49.52 S	73.05 W
Los Guerras	196	26.25 N	99.05 W
Loshan → Leshan	107	29.34 N	103.45 E
Losheim	56	49.30 N	6.44 E
Los Hermanos, Islas II	246	11.45 N	64.25 W
Los Herreras	196	25.55 N	99.24 W
Loshkarivka	78	47.57 N	34.12 E
Los Huacales, Cerro ∧	234	22.19 N	101.34 W
Losi	273a	6.40 N	3.31 E
Łosice	30	52.14 N	22.43 E
Los Idolos, Parque Arquelógico de ⊥	246	1.55 N	76.10 W
Lošinj, Otok I	36	44.36 N	14.24 E
Losinoborskaja	86	58.27 N	89.28 E
Losino-Petrovskij	82	55.52 N	38.12 E
Los Jazmines, Presa ⊜[1]	286a	19.25 N	99.16 W
Los Juríes	252	28.28 S	62.06 W
Loskopdam ⊜[1]	156	25.23 S	29.20 E
Loskop Dam Game Reserve ◆[4]	156	25.23 S	29.20 E
Los Lagos	254	39.51 S	72.50 W
Los Lagos □[4]	254	41.45 S	73.00 W
Los Llanos	240m	18.03 N	66.24 W
Los Llanos [de Aridane]	148	28.39 N	17.54 W
Los López	196	26.15 N	99.05 W
Los Lunas	200	34.48 N	106.43 W
Los Manglares de Tumbes, Santuario Nacional ♠	246	2.25 S	80.20 W
Los Maribios, Cordillera ⋏	236	12.35 N	86.50 W
Los Médanos, Istmo de ⊥[3]	241s	11.35 N	69.45 W
Los Menucos	254	40.50 S	68.08 W
Los Micos, Laguna de c	236	15.45 N	87.36 W
Los'mino	76	55.04 N	34.24 E
Los Mochis	232	25.45 N	108.57 W
Los Molinos	204	40.01 N	122.05 W
Los Muermos	254	41.24 S	73.29 W
Los Naranjos	286c	10.27 N	66.48 W
Los Navalmorales	34	39.43 N	4.38 W
Lošnica	76	54.17 N	28.46 E
Los Nietos	280	33.58 N	118.04 W
Løsning	41	55.48 N	9.42 E
Los Nogales	196	26.16 N	99.43 W
Losolava	175f	14.11 S	167.34 E
Los Olmos Creek ≃, Tx., U.S.	196	27.20 N	97.40 W
Los Olmos Creek ≃, Tx., U.S.	196	26.21 N	98.48 W
Los Osos	226	35.19 N	120.50 W
Los Oyameles	234	19.43 N	97.32 W
Los Padillas	200	34.58 N	106.41 W
Los Palacios, Arg.	252	29.22 S	68.11 W
Los Palacios, Cuba	240p	22.35 N	83.15 W
Los Palacios y Villafranca	34	37.10 N	5.56 W
Los Perros, Arroyo ≃	288	34.37 S	58.46 W
Los Pinos ◆[8]	286b	23.04 N	82.23 W
Los Pinos ≃	200	36.56 N	107.36 W
Los Placeres del Oro	234	18.13 N	100.54 W
Los Polvorines	288	34.30 S	58.41 W
Los Quillayes	286e	33.34 S	70.37 W
Los Quirquinchos	252	33.22 S	61.43 W
Los Rábanos	240m	18.11 N	66.50 W
Los Ramones	196	25.42 N	99.37 W
Los Remedios ≃	286a	19.31 N	99.05 W
Los Reyes de Salgado	234	19.35 N	102.29 W
Los Reyes la Paz	286a	19.21 N	98.58 W
Los Ríos □[4]	246	1.30 S	79.25 W
Los Rodríguez	232	27.11 N	101.21 W
Los Roques, Islas II	246	11.50 N	66.45 W
Lossa ≃	54	51.18 N	11.10 E
Los Santos □[4]	236	7.55 N	80.25 W
Los Santos de Maimona	34	38.27 N	6.23 W
Los Sauces	252	37.58 S	72.50 W
Lossburg	58	48.25 N	8.27 E
Lössel	263	51.21 N	7.39 E
Losser	52	52.15 N	7.00 E
Los Serranos	228	33.59 N	117.42 W
Lossie ≃	46	57.43 N	3.16 W
Lossiemouth	46	57.43 N	3.18 W
Lössnitz	54	50.37 N	12.43 E
Lost ≃, U.S.	202	41.56 N	121.30 W
Lost ≃, In., U.S.	194	38.33 N	86.49 W
Lost ≃, Mn., U.S.	198	47.51 N	96.02 W
Lost ≃, W.V., U.S.	188	39.05 N	78.36 W
Lostant	216	41.09 N	89.04 W
Los Taques	246	11.50 N	70.16 W
Lost Bridge State Recreation Area ♠	216	40.45 N	85.37 W
Lost Creek ≃, Al., U.S.	194	33.38 N	87.14 W
Lost Creek ≃, Ar., U.S.	194	34.10 N	92.31 W
Lost Creek ≃, Oh., U.S.	218	39.58 N	84.09 W
Lost Creek ≃, Ut., U.S.	200	41.04 N	111.32 W
Lost Creek ≃, Wy., U.S.	200	42.01 N	108.11 W
Lost Draw V	196	32.58 N	102.02 W
Los Telares	252	28.59 S	63.26 W
Los Teques	246	10.21 N	67.02 W
Los Testigos, Islas II	246	11.22 N	63.06 W
Lost Hills	226	35.36 N	119.41 W
Lostine ≃	202	45.33 N	117.29 W
Lost Lake ∈, Or., U.S.	224	45.29 N	121.49 W
Lost Lake ∈, Wa., U.S.	224	47.20 N	121.24 W
Lost Nation	190	41.57 N	90.49 W
Lostock ≃	262	53.40 N	2.48 W
Lostock Gralam	262	53.16 N	2.28 W
Los Trancos Creek ≃	282	37.25 N	122.12 W
Los Trancos Woods	282	37.21 N	122.12 W
Lost River Range ⋏	202	44.10 N	113.35 W
Lost Trail Pass)(	202	45.41 N	113.57 W
Lostwithiel	42	50.25 N	4.40 W
Losuia	164	8.32 S	151.04 E
Los Vidrios	232	31.59 N	113.28 W
Los Vilos	252	31.55 S	71.31 W
Los Yébenes	34	39.34 N	3.53 W
Losynivka	78	50.51 N	31.54 E
Lot □[5]	32	44.35 N	1.40 E
Lot ≃	32	44.18 N	0.20 E
Lota	252	37.05 S	73.10 W
Lotagipi Swamp (Lotikipi Plain) ≚	144	4.36 N	34.55 E
Lotak	112	0.11 S	115.54 E
Lotbinière □[6]	206	46.30 N	71.40 W
Lotela, Lake ⊜	220	27.34 N	81.29 W
Løten	26	60.49 N	11.19 E
Lot-et-Garonne □[5]	32	44.20 N	0.20 E
Lotfābād	128	37.32 N	59.20 E
Lothair, S. Afr.	158	26.26 S	30.27 E
Lothair, Ky., U.S.	192	37.14 N	83.10 W
Lothian □[4]	46	55.55 N	3.05 W
Lothringen → Lorraine □[9]	32	49.00 N	6.00 E
Lotikipi Plain (Lotagipi Swamp) ≚	144	4.36 N	34.55 E
Loto	152	2.49 S	22.29 E
Loto ≃	152	1.55 S	22.09 E
Lotofaga	175a	13.59 S	171.50 W
Lotoi ≃	152	1.35 S	18.30 E
Lotorp	40	58.44 N	15.50 E
Lotošino	76	56.14 N	35.38 E
Lotrului, Munții ⋏	38	45.30 N	23.52 E
Lotsane ≃	156	22.41 S	28.11 E
Lötschberg Tunnel ◆[5]	58	46.25 N	7.45 E
Lötschental V	58	46.25 N	7.50 E
Lotseninsel I	41	54.40 N	10.01 E
Lott	222	31.12 N	97.02 W
Lotta ≃	24	68.36 N	31.06 E
Lotte	52	52.17 N	7.55 E
Lottivue	214	42.40 N	82.46 W
Löttringhausen ◆[8]	263	51.27 N	7.27 E
Lottsburg	208	37.57 N	76.31 W
Lotts Creek ≃	192	32.09 N	81.47 W
Lottsford Branch ≃	284c	38.55 N	76.49 W
Lottstetten	58	47.38 N	8.34 E
Lotuke, Jabal ∧	154	4.07 N	33.48 E
Lotung	100	24.41 N	121.46 E
Lotzorai	71	39.58 N	9.39 E
Louang Namtha	110	20.57 N	101.25 E
Louangphrabang	110	19.52 N	102.08 E
L'Ouarsenis, Massif de ⋏	34	35.40 N	1.50 E
Loubaresse	62	44.36 N	4.03 E
Loube, Montagne de la ∧	62	43.22 N	5.59 E
Loubetsi	152	3.12 S	12.10 E
Louchi	24	66.04 N	33.00 E
Loučim	60	49.22 N	13.07 E
Loučná ∧	54	50.39 N	13.37 E
Loude	98	35.54 N	117.18 E
Loudéac	32	48.10 N	2.45 W
Louden Cove c	276	41.05 N	73.43 W
Loudes	62	45.05 N	3.45 E
Loudima Poste	152	4.07 S	13.04 E
Loudon	192	35.43 N	84.20 W
Loudonville, N.Y., U.S.	210	42.42 N	73.45 W
Loudonville, Oh., U.S.	214	40.38 N	82.14 W
Loudoun □[6]	208	39.05 N	77.30 W
Loudun	32	47.01 N	0.05 E
Loué	32	48.00 N	0.09 W
Loue ≃	58	47.01 N	5.27 E
Louga	150	15.37 N	16.13 W
Louga □[4]	150	15.25 N	15.30 W
Louge	252	36.57 S	61.40 W
Louge ≃	32	43.27 N	1.20 E
Lougguéré ≃	150	15.35 N	14.47 W
Loughborough	42	52.47 N	1.11 W
Loughborough Lake ⊜	212	44.23 N	76.30 W
Loughermore ∧[2]	48	54.59 N	7.05 W
Loughman	220	28.14 N	81.34 W
Loughor	42	51.40 N	4.04 W
Loughor ≃	42	51.40 N	4.04 W
Loughrea	48	53.12 N	8.34 W
Loughros More Bay c	48	54.47 N	8.35 W
Loughton	260	51.39 N	0.03 E
Louhans	58	46.38 N	5.13 E
Louin	194	32.04 N	89.15 W
Louisa, Ky., U.S.	192	38.06 N	82.36 W
Louisa, Va., U.S.	192	38.01 N	78.00 W
Louisa, Lake ⊜, On., Can.	212	45.28 N	78.30 W
Louisa, Lake ⊜, Fl., U.S.	220	28.29 N	81.44 W
Louisbourg	186	45.55 N	59.58 W
Louis Bull Indian Reserve ◆[4]	182	52.53 N	113.31 W
Louisburg, Ks., U.S.	198	38.37 N	94.40 W
Louisburg, N.C., U.S.	192	36.05 N	78.18 W
Louisburgh	48	53.46 N	9.51 W
Louisdale	186	45.36 N	61.04 W
Louise, Ms., U.S.	194	32.58 N	90.35 W
Louise, Tx., U.S.	222	29.06 N	96.25 W
Louise, Lac ⊜, P.Q., Can.	206	45.46 N	74.25 W
Louise, Lac ⊜, P.Q., Can.	206	45.43 N	71.25 W
Louise, Lake ⊜	180	62.20 N	146.30 W
Louise Island I	182	52.58 N	131.50 W
Louiseville	206	46.15 N	72.57 W
Louis Gentil → Youssoufia	148	32.16 N	8.33 W
Louisiade Archipelago II	160	11.00 S	153.00 E
Louisiana	219	39.26 N	91.03 W
Louisiana □[3], U.S.	178	31.15 N	92.15 W
Louisiana □[3], U.S.	194	31.15 N	92.15 W
Louisiana ♥	41	55.58 N	12.33 E
Lou Island I	164	2.25 S	147.20 E
Louis Trichardt	156	23.01 S	29.43 E
Louisvale	158	28.33 S	21.12 E
Louisville, On., Can.	214	42.28 N	82.07 W
Louisville, Al., U.S.	194	31.47 N	85.33 W
Louisville, Ga., U.S.	192	33.00 N	82.24 W
Louisville, Il., U.S.	194	38.46 N	88.30 W
Louisville, Ky., U.S.	218	38.15 N	85.45 W
Louisville, Ms., U.S.	194	33.07 N	89.03 W
Louisville, Ne., U.S.	198	40.59 N	96.09 W
Louisville, Oh., U.S.	214	40.50 N	81.15 W
Louisville Ridge ✣[3]	14	31.00 S	172.30 W
Louisville Seamount ✣[3]	14	31.15 S	172.15 W
Louis-XIV, Pointe >	176	54.37 N	79.45 W
Loujiaying	98	42.04 N	116.04 E
Loukanga	273b	4.20 S	15.09 E
Loukkos, Oued ≃	34	35.12 N	6.09 W
Loukoua ≃	273b	4.09 S	15.08 E
Loulé	34	37.08 N	8.02 W
Loum	152	4.43 N	9.44 E
Loumou	273b	4.08 S	15.09 E
Lount Lake ⊜	184	50.10 N	94.20 W
Louny	54	50.19 N	13.46 E
Loup ≃, Fr.	62	43.38 N	7.09 E
Loup ≃, Ne., U.S.	198	41.24 N	97.19 W
Loup, Gorge du V	56	49.47 N	6.23 E
Loup, Rivière du ≃	206	46.13 N	72.55 W
Loup City	198	41.16 N	98.57 W
Loups Marins, Lacs des ⊜	176	56.30 N	73.45 W
Lourches	50	50.19 N	3.21 E
Lourdes, Nf., Can.	186	48.39 N	59.00 W
Lourdes, Fr.	32	43.06 N	0.03 W
Lourel de Baixo	266c	38.49 N	9.22 W
Lourenço	250	2.30 N	51.40 W
Lourenço Marques → Maputo	156	25.58 S	32.35 E
Lourenço Velho	256	22.22 S	45.19 W
Lourenço Velho ≃, Bra.	256	23.26 S	45.35 W
Lourenço Velho ≃, Bra.	256	22.22 S	45.31 W
Loures	34	38.50 N	9.10 W
Loures ≃	266c	38.50 N	9.08 W
Lourinhã	34	39.14 N	9.19 W
Lourmarin	62	43.46 N	5.22 E
Lourosa	34	40.19 N	7.56 W
Loury	50	48.00 N	2.05 E
Lousã, Port.	34	40.07 N	8.15 W
Lousa, Port.	266c	38.53 N	9.12 W
Louse Creek ≃	198	46.22 N	100.57 W
Lou Shan ∧	89	45.15 N	128.58 E
Louta	150	13.30 N	3.10 W
Loutang	106	31.26 N	121.12 E
Loutézou, Île de I	273b	4.22 S	15.10 E
Louth, Austl.	166	30.32 S	145.07 E
Louth, Ire.	44	53.57 N	6.33 W
Louth, Ire.	48	53.57 N	6.33 W
Louth, Eng., U.K.	44	53.22 N	0.01 W
Louth □[6]	48	53.55 N	6.30 W
Louth Bay c	166	34.34 S	136.02 E
Louti, Mayo ≃	146	9.38 N	13.56 E
Loutit Bay c	169	38.33 S	144.00 E
Loutrá Aidhipsoú	38	38.51 N	23.02 E
Loutre ≃	219	38.42 N	91.25 W
Loutre, Bayou de ≃	194	32.41 N	92.08 W
Loutrópirgos	267c	38.02 N	23.28 E
Louvain → Leuven	56	50.53 N	4.42 E
Louveciennes	261	48.52 N	2.07 E
Louveigné	56	50.32 N	5.42 E
Louveira	256	23.04 S	46.58 W
Louviers, Fr.	50	49.13 N	1.10 E
Louviers, Co., U.S.	200	39.28 N	105.00 W
Louvre ♥	261	48.52 N	2.20 E
Louvres	50	49.02 N	2.30 E
Louvroil	50	50.16 N	3.58 E
Louwsburg	158	27.37 S	31.07 E
Lou Yaeger, Lake ⊜[1]	219	39.10 N	89.37 W
Lövånger	26	64.22 N	21.18 E
Lovászi	61	46.33 N	16.34 E
Lovat' ≃	76	58.14 N	31.28 E
Lovcy	82	55.00 N	39.15 E
Love	184	53.29 N	104.09 W
Loveč	38	43.08 N	24.43 E
Loveč □[4]	38	43.11 N	25.10 E
Love Clough	262	53.44 N	2.17 W
Lovedale	279b	40.17 N	79.52 W
Lovejoy	219	38.39 N	90.10 W
Lovelady	222	31.08 N	95.27 W
Loveland, Co., U.S.	200	40.23 N	105.04 W
Loveland, Oh., U.S.	218	39.16 N	84.16 W
Lovell	202	44.50 N	108.23 W
Lovell Island I	283	42.20 N	70.56 W
Lovelock	204	40.10 N	118.28 W
Lovely	192	37.49 N	82.24 W
Love Point >	208	39.02 N	76.18 W
Lovere	64	45.49 N	10.04 E
Lovering, Lac ⊜	206	45.10 N	72.09 W
Lovero	64	46.14 N	10.14 E
Loves Green	260	51.43 N	0.24 E
Loves Park	216	42.19 N	89.03 W
Loviisa → Lovisa	26	60.27 N	26.14 E
Lovilia	190	41.08 N	92.54 W
Loving, N.M., U.S.	196	32.17 N	104.05 W
Loving, Tx., U.S.	196	33.16 N	98.31 W
Lovingston	192	37.45 N	78.52 W
Lovington, Il., U.S.	219	39.42 N	88.37 W
Lovington, N.M., U.S.	196	32.56 N	103.20 W
Lovisa (Loviisa)	26	60.27 N	26.14 E
Lövő	61	47.30 N	16.47 E
Lovö I	40	59.20 N	17.50 E
Lovoi ≃	154	8.14 S	26.39 E
Lovosice	54	50.31 N	14.03 E
Lovozero, Ross.	24	68.00 N	35.00 E
Lovozero, Ross.	24	65.00 N	29.50 E
Lovozero, ozero ⊜	24	67.54 N	35.12 E
Lovrenc	61	46.32 N	15.23 E
Lövstabruk	40	60.24 N	17.53 E
Lövstabukten c	40	60.35 N	17.45 E
Lövstad slott ⊥	40	58.33 N	16.02 E
Lóvua, Ang.	152	11.36 S	23.53 E
Lóvua, Ang.	152	7.20 S	20.16 E
Lovua (Lóvua) ≃	152	6.07 S	20.35 E
Low	188	45.48 N	75.57 W
Low, Cape >	176	63.07 N	85.18 W
Lowa	154	1.24 S	25.51 E
Lowa ≃	154	1.24 S	25.51 E
Lowāda	126	22.27 N	87.37 E
Lowat → Lovat' ≃	76	58.14 N	31.28 E
Lowber	279b	40.15 N	79.46 W
Lowden	190	41.51 N	90.55 W
Lowder Brook ≃	283	43.14 N	71.11 W
Lowell, Ar., U.S.	194	36.15 N	94.07 W
Lowell, In., U.S.	216	41.17 N	87.25 W
Lowell, Ma., U.S.	207	42.38 N	71.19 W
Lowell, Mi., U.S.	216	42.56 N	85.20 W
Lowell, Or., U.S.	202	43.55 N	122.46 W
Lowell, Lake ⊜[1]	202	43.33 N	116.40 W
Lowell, University of ♥[2]	283	42.39 N	71.20 W
Lowell-Dracut State Forest ♠	283	42.40 N	71.22 W
Lowelli	140	5.59 N	33.45 E
Lowellville	214	41.02 N	80.32 W
Löwen → Leuven	56	50.53 N	4.42 E
Löwen ≃	158	26.51 S	18.17 E
Löwenberg	54	52.54 N	13.08 E
Löwenbruch	264a	52.18 N	13.19 E
Löwenstein	56	49.06 N	9.22 E
Lowe Pond ⊜	283	42.41 N	70.59 W
Lower Aetna Lake ⊜	285	39.51 N	74.48 W
Lower Arrow Lake ⊜	182	49.40 N	118.08 W
Lower Bay c	208	40.33 N	74.02 W
Lower Bear River Reservoir ⊜[1]	226	38.33 N	120.14 W
Lower Bershire Valley	276	40.54 N	74.37 W
Lower Beverley Lake ⊜	212	44.36 N	76.09 W
Lower Broughton ◆[8]	262	53.29 N	2.15 W
Lower Brule Indian Reservation ◆[4]	198	44.05 N	99.44 W
Lower Buckhorn Lake ⊜	212	44.33 N	78.17 W
Lower Burrell	214	40.33 N	79.45 W
Lower California → Baja California >[1]	232	28.00 N	113.30 W
Lower Chittering	168a	31.34 S	116.06 E
Lower Crystal Springs Reservoir ⊜[1]	226	37.32 N	122.22 W
Lower Darwen	262	53.43 N	2.28 W
Lower Egypt → Mişr Baḩrī □[9]	140	31.00 N	31.00 E
Lower Eltham Park ♠	274b	37.45 S	145.09 E
Lower Elwha Indian Reservation ◆[4]	224	48.09 N	123.33 W
Lower Fort Garry National Historic Park ♠	184	50.07 N	96.55 W
Lower Ganga Canal ≖	124	26.27 N	80.17 E
Lower Gap c	212	44.10 N	76.35 W
Lower Halstow	260	51.22 N	0.40 E
Lower Hay Lake ⊜	212	45.25 N	78.13 W
Lower Higham	260	51.26 N	0.28 E
Lower Huron Metropolitan Park ♠	281	42.12 N	83.25 W
Lower Hutt	172	41.13 S	174.55 E
Lower Kalskag	180	61.31 N	160.22 W
Lower Keechi Creek ≃	222	31.08 N	95.46 W
Lower Klamath Lake ⊜	204	41.55 N	121.42 W
Lower Lake	226	38.55 N	122.36 W
Lower Lake ⊜	204	41.15 N	120.02 W
Lower Loteni	158	29.32 S	29.36 E
Lower Manitou Lake ⊜	184	49.15 N	93.00 W
Lower Matecumbe Key I	220	24.51 N	80.43 W
Lower Montville	276	40.54 N	74.22 W
Lower Mystic Lake ⊜	283	42.26 N	71.09 W
Lower Nazeing	260	51.44 N	0.01 E
Lower Otay Lake ⊜[1]	228	32.37 N	116.55 W
Lower Paia	229a	20.55 N	156.23 W
Lower Paudash Lake ⊜	212	44.58 N	78.01 W
Lower Peirce Reservoir ⊜[1]	271c	1.22 N	103.49 E
Lower Peover	262	53.16 N	2.23 W
Lower Place	262	53.36 N	2.09 W
Lower Plenty	274b	37.44 S	145.06 E
Lower Portland	170	33.27 S	150.53 E
Lower Post	176	59.55 N	128.30 W
Lower Red Lake ⊜	198	48.00 N	94.50 W
Lower River Rouge ≃	281	42.18 N	83.14 W
Lower Rouge Parkway ♠	281	42.18 N	83.20 W
Lower Saxony → Niedersachsen □[3]	30	52.40 N	9.00 E
Lower Stoke	260	51.27 N	0.38 E
Lower Trajan's Wall ⊥	38	45.40 N	28.30 E
Lower Ugashik Lake ⊜	180	57.30 N	156.56 W
Lower Van Norman Lake ⊜[1]	280	34.17 N	118.29 W
Lower West Pubnico	186	43.38 N	65.48 W
Lower Whitley	262	53.18 N	2.35 W
Lower Wood's Harbour	186	43.31 N	65.44 W
Lowery, Lake ⊜	220	28.07 N	81.41 W
Lower Zambezi International Game Park ◆[4]	154	15.30 S	29.35 E
Lowestoft	42	52.29 N	1.45 E
Lowgar □[4]	120	33.50 N	69.00 E
Lowick	44	55.38 N	2.00 W
Łowicz	30	52.07 N	19.56 E
Lowman	210	42.02 N	76.44 W
Lowmoor	192	37.47 N	79.53 W
Lowood	171a	27.28 S	152.35 E
Lowrah (Pishīn Lora) ≃	120	29.09 N	64.55 E
Lowries Run ≃	279b	40.30 N	80.05 W
Low Rocky Point >	166	43.00 S	145.30 E
Lowry Air Force Base ■	198	39.43 N	104.53 W
Lowry City	194	38.08 N	93.43 W
Lowther ≃	44	54.39 N	2.44 W
Lowther Hills ⋏[2]	44	55.19 N	3.38 W
Lowton	262	53.28 N	2.35 W
Lowton Common	262	53.29 N	2.33 W
Lowville, N.Y., U.S.	212	43.47 N	75.29 W
Lowville, Pa., U.S.	214	42.01 N	79.49 W
Loxahatchee	220	26.49 N	80.13 W
Loxley	194	30.37 N	87.45 W
Loxstedt	52	53.28 N	8.38 E
Loxten	52	52.03 N	8.08 E
Loxton, Austl.	166	34.27 S	140.35 E
Loxton, S. Afr.	158	31.30 S	22.22 E
Loyal	190	44.44 N	90.29 W
Loyal, Loch ⊜	46	58.23 N	4.22 W
Loyalhanna	214	40.19 N	79.21 W
Loyalhanna Creek ≃	214	40.28 N	79.27 W
Loyalhanna Lake ⊜[1]	214	40.25 N	79.28 W
Loyalsock Creek ≃	210	41.14 N	76.56 W
Loyalton	204	39.40 N	120.14 W
Loyalty Islands → Loyauté, Îles II	175f	21.00 S	167.00 E
Loyang, Sing.	271c	1.22 N	103.58 E
Loyang → Luoyang, Zhg.	102	34.41 N	112.28 E
Loyauté, Îles (Loyalty Islands) II	175f	21.00 S	167.00 E
Loyne, Loch ⊜	46	57.06 N	5.00 W
Loyola College ♥[2]	284b	39.21 N	76.37 W
Loyola Marymount University ♥[2]	280	33.58 N	118.25 W
Loyola University ♥[2]	278	42.00 N	87.39 W
Loyoro	154	3.21 N	34.16 E
Loysburg	214	40.10 N	78.23 W
Loysville	208	40.22 N	77.21 W
Lozano	258	34.51 S	59.03 W
Lozère □[5]	32	44.30 N	3.30 E
Lozère, Mont ⋏	62	44.25 N	3.46 E
Loznica	38	44.32 N	19.13 E
Ložnikovo, Ross.	86	56.54 N	73.56 E
Ložnikovo, Ross.	88	51.22 N	117.03 E
Loznoje	80	49.17 N	44.26 E
Lozno-Oleksandrivka	78	49.50 N	38.44 E
L'Ozone ◆[8]	273b	4.21 S	15.14 E
Lozova	78	48.54 N	36.20 E
Lozove, Ukr.	78	49.18 N	27.18 E
Lozove, Ukr.	83	49.28 N	37.54 E
Lozove, Ukr.	83	49.13 N	37.36 E
Lozovoje	86	53.17 N	77.45 E
Lozoyuela	34	40.55 N	3.37 W
Loz'va ≃	86	59.36 N	62.20 E
Lozzo di Cadore	64	46.29 N	12.27 E
Lu	62	45.00 N	8.29 E
Lu ≃	100	27.04 N	115.00 E
Lua ≃	152	2.46 N	18.26 E
Luabo	156	18.30 S	36.10 E
Luabu ≃	152	2.46 S	18.19 E
Luachimo ≃	152	6.33 S	20.59 E
Luaha-sibuha	110	0.31 S	98.28 E
Luala ≃	154	17.57 S	36.30 E
Lualaba ≃	154	0.26 N	25.20 E
Luali	152	5.06 S	12.29 E
Lualoje ≃	152	12.18 S	21.38 E
Luama ≃	154	4.46 S	26.53 E
Luambe National Park ♠	154	12.25 S	32.15 E
Luambimba ≃	152	15.00 S	22.48 E
Luampa	154	15.03 S	24.28 E
Luampa ≃	154	14.33 S	24.10 E
Lu'an	100	31.44 N	116.31 E
Luan ≃	98	39.20 N	119.10 E
Luana ≃	152	7.56 S	21.06 E
Luan Balu	114	2.38 N	96.13 E
Luancheng, Zhg.	98	37.53 N	114.39 E
Luancheng, Zhg.	102	22.45 N	108.51 E
Luanchuan	102	33.51 N	111.36 E
Luancundo ≃	152	16.25 S	21.27 E
Luanda	152	8.48 S	13.14 E
Luanda □[5]	152	9.00 S	13.15 E
Luando ≃	152	10.19 S	16.40 E
Luando, Réserva do ◆[4]	152	11.10 S	17.30 E
Luang, Khao ∧	110	8.31 N	99.47 E
Luang, Thale c	110	7.30 N	100.15 E
Luang Chiang Dao, Doi ∧	110	19.23 N	98.54 E
Luanginga (Luanguinga) ≃	152	15.11 S	22.56 E
Luang Prabang → Louangphrabang	110	19.52 N	102.08 E
Luang Prabang Range ⋏	110	18.30 N	101.15 E
Luangue	152	7.19 S	19.38 E
Luangue (Loange) ≃	152	4.17 S	20.02 E
Luanguinga (Luanginga) ≃	152	15.11 S	22.56 E
Luangwa (Aruângua) ≃	154	15.36 S	30.25 E
Luanhaizi	120	34.27 N	93.12 E
Luanhe	105	40.57 N	117.44 E
Luannan (Bencheng)	98	39.32 N	118.39 E
Luanping (Anjiangying)	98	40.57 N	117.20 E
Luanshishan	104	42.10 N	123.41 E
Luanshya	154	13.08 S	28.24 E
Luán Toro	252	36.12 S	65.06 W
Luanxian	98	39.45 N	118.44 E
Luanza	154	8.42 S	28.42 E
Luapula □[4]	154	10.55 S	29.00 E
Luapula ≃	154	9.26 S	28.33 E
Luar, Danau ⊜	112	0.55 N	112.15 E
Luarca	34	43.32 N	6.32 W
Luashi	152	10.56 S	23.37 E
Luashi ≃	152	10.41 S	22.55 E
Luassinga ≃	152	15.47 S	18.50 E
Luati	152	14.35 S	21.13 E
Luatira	152	12.52 S	17.14 E
Luau	152	10.42 S	22.12 E
Lua-Vindu ≃	152	3.38 N	19.16 E
Luba	152	3.27 N	8.33 E
Lubaantun ⊥	232	16.17 N	88.58 W
Lubaczów	30	50.10 N	23.07 E
Lubalo	152	9.12 S	19.16 E
Lubalo ≃	152	7.22 S	19.20 E
Lubamiti	152	2.29 S	17.47 E
Lubań, Pol.	30	51.08 N	15.18 E
L'uban', Ross.	76	59.21 N	31.13 E
Lubāna	76	56.54 N	26.43 E
Lubang	116	13.52 N	120.07 E
Lubang Island I	116	13.46 N	120.11 E
Lubang Islands II	116	13.46 N	120.15 E
Lubango	152	14.55 S	13.30 E
Lubanowo	54	53.09 N	14.36 E
Lubāns ⊜	76	56.46 N	26.53 E
Lubansenshi ≃	154	11.21 S	30.35 E
Lub'any	80	56.02 N	51.24 E
Lubao	100	23.22 N	112.55 E
Lübars	54	52.39 N	12.02 E
Lübars ◆[8]	264a	52.37 N	13.22 E
Lubartów	30	51.28 N	22.38 E
Lubawa	30	53.30 N	19.45 E
Lubaynī, Baḩr al- ≖	273c	29.56 N	31.11 E
Lübbecke	52	52.18 N	8.36 E
Lübben	54	51.56 N	13.53 E
Lübbenau	54	51.52 N	13.57 E
Lubber Brook ≃	283	42.33 N	71.09 W
Lubbers Run ≃	276	40.56 N	74.43 W
Lübbesee ⊜	54	53.05 N	13.34 E
Lubbock	196	33.34 N	101.51 W
Lübbow	54	52.54 N	11.10 E
Lubbub Creek ≃	194	33.04 N	88.10 W
Lubec	188	44.51 N	66.59 W
Lübeck	54	53.52 N	10.40 E
Lübecker Bucht c	54	54.00 N	10.55 E
Lubefu	152	4.43 S	24.25 E
Lubefu ≃	152	4.10 S	23.00 E
Lubelska, Wyżyna ⋏[2]	30	51.00 N	23.00 E
Lubembe (Luembe) ≃	152	6.37 S	21.05 E
Lüben → Lubin	30	51.24 N	16.13 E
Lubenec	54	50.06 N	13.20 E
L'ubercy	82	55.41 N	37.53 E
Lubéron, Montagne du ⋏	62	43.48 N	5.22 E
Lubersac	32	45.27 N	1.24 E
Lübesse	54	53.29 N	11.28 E
Lubi ≃	152	4.58 S	23.26 E
Lubiana → Ljubljana	36	46.03 N	14.31 E
Lubic Island I	116	10.58 N	120.44 E
L'ubickoje	80	51.46 N	49.19 E
Lubień Kujawski	30	52.25 N	19.10 E
Lubilash ≃	152	6.02 S	23.45 E
Lubile	154	2.55 S	26.45 E
L'ubim	80	58.22 N	40.41 E
L'ubimovka, Kaz.	86	52.15 N	66.45 E
L'ubimovka, Ross.	78	51.31 N	35.37 E
Lubin, Pol.	30	51.24 N	16.13 E
Lubin, Pol.	54	53.50 N	14.25 E
L'ubino	86	57.30 N	88.47 E
L'ubinskij	86	55.09 N	72.42 E
Lubishi ≃	152	6.54 S	24.09 E
Lubja ≃	265a	59.58 N	30.30 E
Lublin	30	51.15 N	22.35 E
Lublin □[4]	30	51.30 N	22.30 E
Lubliniec	30	50.40 N	18.41 E
L'ublino ◆[8]	265b	55.41 N	37.44 E
Lubmin	54	54.08 N	13.37 E
Lubnān → Lebanon □[1]	128	34.00 N	36.00 E
Lubnān, Jabal (Lebanon Mountains) ⋏	132	34.00 N	36.00 E
L'ubnica	76	57.58 N	32.42 E
Lubny	78	50.01 N	33.00 E
L'ubochna	76	53.31 N	34.23 E
Lubok China	114	2.27 N	102.04 E
Lubomierz	30	51.01 N	15.30 E
Luboń	30	52.23 N	16.54 E
Lubondai	152	6.34 S	22.39 E
Lubondoi	154	8.02 S	26.31 E
L'ubostan'	78	51.19 N	35.44 E
Lubraniec	30	52.33 N	18.50 E
Lubsko	30	51.46 N	14.59 E
Lubsza ≃	54	51.56 N	14.43 E
Lübtheen	54	53.18 N	11.04 E
Lubu, Indon.	112	0.46 S	122.30 E
Lubu, Zhg.	102	23.09 N	112.13 E
Lubuagan	116	17.21 N	121.10 E
L'ubučany	82	55.15 N	37.33 E
Lubudi, R.D.C.	152	6.51 S	21.18 E
Lubudi, R.D.C.	154	9.57 S	25.58 E
Lubudi ≃, R.D.C.	152	4.03 S	21.23 E
Lubudi ≃, R.D.C.	154	9.13 S	25.38 E
Lubue	152	4.09 S	19.52 E
Lubue ≃	152	4.10 S	19.53 E
Lubukambacang	112	0.37 S	101.25 E
Lubukbatang	112	4.03 S	104.12 E
Lubukbertubung	112	0.02 N	102.08 E
Lubuklinggau	112	3.18 S	102.52 E
Lubukpakam	114	3.33 N	98.52 E
Lubukraya, Dolok ∧	114	1.29 N	99.13 E
Lubuksikaping	112	0.08 N	100.10 E
Lubumbaschi → Lubumbashi	154	11.40 S	27.28 E
Lubumbashi (Élisabethville)	154	11.40 S	27.28 E
Lubunda	154	5.10 S	26.40 E
Lubutu	154	0.44 S	26.35 E
Luby	54	50.12 N	12.25 E
L'ubytino	76	58.49 N	33.23 E
Lübz	54	53.27 N	12.01 E
Lučak	85	38.23 N	67.25 E
Lucala	152	9.16 S	15.15 E
Lucala ≃, Ang.	152	6.38 S	12.34 E
Lucala ≃, Ang.	152	9.37 S	14.14 E
Lucan, On., Can.	190	43.11 N	81.24 W
Lucan, Ire.	48	53.22 N	6.27 W
Lucanas	248	14.36 S	74.15 W
Lucania □[9]	68	40.30 N	16.00 E
Lucania, Mount ∧	180	61.01 N	140.28 W
Lucano	152	11.16 S	21.38 E
Lucaogou	102	42.26 N	96.55 E
Lucapa	152	8.36 S	20.54 E
Lucas, Ia., U.S.	190	41.01 N	93.27 W
Lucas, Ks., U.S.	198	39.03 N	98.32 W
Lucas, Oh., U.S.	214	40.45 N	82.30 W
Lucas, Tx., U.S.	222	33.05 N	96.35 W
Lucas □[6]	214	41.39 N	83.32 W
Lucas González	252	32.24 S	59.33 W
Lucas Heights	274a	34.02 S	150.58 E
Lucas Valley	282	38.03 N	122.35 W
Lucasville	218	38.52 N	82.59 W
Lucban	116	14.06 N	121.33 E
Lucca	66	43.50 N	10.29 E
Lucca □[4]	64	44.02 N	10.27 E
Lucca Sicula	70	37.35 N	13.18 E
Lucé	50	48.26 N	1.28 E
Luce, Water of ≃	44	54.52 N	4.48 W
Lucea	241q	18.27 N	78.10 W
Luce Bay c	44	54.47 N	4.50 W
Luce Bayou ≃	222	30.03 N	95.07 W
Lucedale	194	30.55 N	88.35 W
Lucena, Esp.	34	37.24 N	4.29 W
Lucena, Pil.	116	13.56 N	121.37 E
Lucenay-l'Évêque	32	47.05 N	4.15 E
Luc-en-Diois	62	44.37 N	5.27 E
Lučenec	30	48.20 N	19.40 E
Lucens	58	46.42 N	6.50 E
Luceque	152	14.41 S	15.04 E
Lucera	68	41.30 N	15.20 E
Lucéram	62	43.53 N	7.22 E
Lucerne → Luzern, Schw.	58	47.03 N	8.18 E
Lucerne, Ca., U.S.	204	39.05 N	122.47 W
Lucerne, In., U.S.	216	40.52 N	86.24 W
Lucerne, Lake → Vierwaldstätter See ⊜	58	47.00 N	8.28 E
Lucerne Lake ⊜	228	34.31 N	116.57 W
Lucernemines	214	40.33 N	79.09 W
Lucerne Valley	228	34.26 N	116.58 W
Lucero	200	30.49 N	106.30 W
Lucero, Lake ⊜	200	32.42 N	106.25 W
Luch	80	57.01 N	42.15 E
Luch ≃	80	56.14 N	42.25 E
Luchang	102	26.23 N	102.18 E
Lucheng, Zhg.	102	24.21 N	106.00 E
Lücheng, Zhg.	106	31.55 N	119.44 E
Lucheng, Zhg.	106	31.47 N	120.02 E
Luché-Pringé	50	47.42 N	0.05 E
Lucheringo ≃	154	11.43 S	36.17 E
Luchibe ≃	152	12.07 S	21.13 E
Luchico (Lushiko) ≃	152	6.13 S	19.40 E
Luchou	269d	25.05 N	121.28 E
Luchovicy	82	54.59 N	39.03 E
Lüchow, Dtsch.	54	52.58 N	11.10 E
Luchow → Luzhou, Zhg.	107	28.54 N	105.27 E
Lüchtringen	52	51.47 N	9.25 E
Luchuan	102	22.19 N	110.11 E
Luci	100	29.52 N	119.47 E
Luciara	250	10.27 S	50.32 W
Lucie ≃	250	3.35 N	57.38 W
Lucikou	100	28.56 N	116.04 E
Lucinda, Austl.	166	18.32 S	146.20 E
Lucinda, Pa., U.S.	214	41.19 N	79.22 W
Lucindale	166	36.59 S	140.22 E
Lucio Vázquez	234	22.47 N	99.46 W
Lucipara, Kepulauan II	164	5.30 S	127.33 E
Lucira	152	13.51 S	12.31 E
Lucito	66	41.44 N	14.41 E
Luci Yu I	100	25.07 N	119.22 E
Luck	190	45.34 N	92.28 W
Luck, Mount ∧[2]	162	28.47 S	123.33 E
Lucka	54	51.06 N	12.20 E
Luckau	54	51.51 N	13.43 E
Luckeesarai	124	25.11 N	86.05 E
Luckenwalde	54	52.05 N	13.10 E
Luckey	214	41.27 N	83.29 W
Luckhoff	158	29.44 S	24.43 E
Luckiamute ≃	202	44.45 N	123.09 W
Luck Lake ⊜	184	51.05 N	107.07 W
Lucknow, On., Can.	190	43.57 N	81.31 W
Lucknow, India	124	26.51 N	80.55 E
Lucknow, Pa., U.S.	208	40.20 N	76.54 W
Lucknow Branch ≖	124	27.57 N	80.03 E
Lückstedt	54	52.49 N	11.35 E
Lucky Lake	184	51.00 N	107.10 W
Lucky Peak Lake ⊜[1]	202	43.33 N	116.00 W
Luco dei Marsi	66	41.58 N	13.28 E
Lucomagno, Passo del)(	58	46.33 N	8.49 E
Luçon, Fr.	32	46.27 N	1.10 W
Lucon, Pa., U.S.	285	40.14 N	75.25 W
Luconha ≃	152	12.54 S	21.15 E
Lučosa ≃	76	55.10 N	30.11 E
Lucun, Zhg.	98	36.12 N	118.01 E
Lucun, Zhg.	106	30.49 N	119.26 E
Lucunga ≃	152	6.57 S	12.48 E
Lucungu ≃	152	6.41 S	14.26 E
Lucusse	152	12.32 S	20.48 E
Lucy Creek	166	22.25 S	136.20 E
Lučyn	76	53.01 N	30.01 E
Lüda → Dalian	98	38.53 N	121.35 E
Luda Kamčija ≃	38	43.03 N	27.29 E
Ludao	89	43.51 N	129.19 E
Ludbreg	36	46.15 N	16.37 E
Luddan	123	29.54 N	72.34 E
Luddenden	262	53.44 N	1.56 W
Luddenham	274a	33.53 S	150.41 E
Luddesdown	260	51.22 N	0.24 E
Lüdenscheid	56	51.13 N	7.38 E
Lüder ≃	56	50.31 N	9.27 E
Lüderitz, Dtsch.	54	52.30 N	11.44 E
Lüderitz, Namibia	156	26.38 S	15.10 E
Lüdersdorf	54	53.47 N	10.46 E
Ludgershall	42	51.16 N	1.37 W
Ludgo	40	58.55 N	17.08 E
Ludhiāna	123	30.54 N	75.51 E
Ludian	102	27.11 N	103.33 E
Luding	102	29.55 N	102.15 E
Lüdinghausen	52	51.46 N	7.26 E
Ludington	190	43.57 N	86.27 W
Ludingtonville	210	41.29 N	73.39 W
L'udinovo	76	53.52 N	34.27 E
L'udkovo	76	54.36 N	34.43 E
Ludlam Bay c	208	39.10 N	74.42 W
Ludlow, Eng., U.K.	42	52.22 N	2.43 W
Ludlow, Il., U.S.	216	40.23 N	88.08 W
Ludlow, Ky., U.S.	218	39.05 N	84.32 W
Ludlow, Ma., U.S.	207	42.09 N	72.28 W
Ludlow, Pa., U.S.	214	41.43 N	78.56 W
Ludlow, Vt., U.S.	188	43.23 N	72.42 W
Ludlow Falls	218	40.00 N	84.20 W
Ludlowville	210	42.33 N	76.32 W
Ludogorie ◆[1]	38	43.46 N	26.56 E
Ludonghe	102	25.53 N	103.33 E
Ludoni	76	58.12 N	29.21 E
Ludowici	192	31.42 N	81.44 W
Luduș	38	46.29 N	24.05 E
Ludvika	40	60.09 N	15.11 E
Ludwigkanal ≖	60	49.05 N	11.27 E
Ludwigsburg	56	48.53 N	9.11 E
Ludwigsfelde	54	52.17 N	13.16 E
Ludwigsfelder-Heide ◆[3]	264a	52.18 N	13.14 E
Ludwigshafen, Dtsch.	56	49.29 N	8.26 E
Ludwigshafen, Dtsch.	58	47.49 N	9.03 E
Ludwigslust	54	53.19 N	11.30 E
Ludwigsort → Laduškin	76	54.36 N	20.11 E
Ludwigsstadt	54	50.30 N	11.23 E
Ludwigstein, Burg ⊥	56	51.20 N	9.55 E
Ludza	76	56.33 N	27.43 E
Lue	170	32.39 S	149.51 E
Luebo	152	5.21 S	21.25 E
Lueders	196	32.48 N	99.37 W
Lueg, Pass)(	64	47.34 N	13.12 E
Lueki	154	3.22 S	25.51 E
Luele ≃	152	7.55 S	20.09 E
Luemba	154	3.42 S	28.40 E
Luembe (Lubembe) ≃, Afr.	152	6.37 S	21.05 E
Luembé ≃, R.D.C.	154	6.43 S	24.11 E
Luena, Ang.	152	11.47 S	19.52 E
Luena, R.D.C.	154	9.27 S	25.47 E
Luena ≃, Ang.	152	12.31 S	22.34 E
Luena ≃, Zam.	152	14.45 S	23.25 E
Luena Flats ≡	152	14.50 S	23.20 E
Luengué ≃	152	16.54 S	21.52 E
Luenha (Ruenya) ≃	154	16.24 S	33.48 E
Lueo ≃	152	9.06 S	23.51 E
Luepa	246	5.43 N	61.31 W
Lueta	152	7.19 S	22.06 E
Lueta ≃	152	7.04 S	21.40 E
Lueyang	102	33.20 N	106.10 E
Lüfangsicun	104	41.25 N	123.22 E
Lufeng, Zhg.	100	22.57 N	115.38 E
Lufeng, Zhg.	102	25.07 N	102.07 E
Lufico	152	6.24 S	13.23 E
Lufira ≃	154	8.16 S	26.27 E
Lufkin	222	31.20 N	94.43 W
Luftekopf ∧[2]	56	50.05 N	7.37 E
Lufubu ≃	154	8.36 S	30.47 E
Lufuidje ≃	152	12.52 S	22.47 E
Lufupa	154	10.37 S	24.56 E
Lufupa ≃	154	14.37 S	26.12 E
Luga	76	58.44 N	29.52 E
Luga ≃	76	59.40 N	28.18 E

Symbols in the index entries represent the broad categories identified in the key at the right. Symbols with superior numbers (⋏[1]) identify subcategories (see complete key on page *I · 1*).

Symbole im Register stellen die rechts im Schlüssel erklärten Kategorien dar. Symbole mit hochgestellten Ziffern (⋏[1]) bezeichnen Unterabteilungen einer Kategorie (vgl. vollständiger Schlüssel auf Seite *I · 1*).

Los símbolos incluídos en el texto del índice representan las grandes categorías identificadas con la clave a la derecha. Los símbolos con numeros en su parte superior (⋏[1]) identifican las subcategorías (véase la clave completa en la página *I · 1*).

Les symboles de l'index représentent les catégories indiquées dans la légende à droite. Les symboles suivis d'un indice (⋏[1]) représentent des sous-catégories (voir légende complète à la page *I · 1*).

Os símbolos incluídos no texto do índice representam as grandes categorias identificadas com a chave à direita. Os símbolos com números em sua parte superior (⋏[1]) identificam as subcategorias (veja-se a chave completa à página *I · 1*).

Symbol	English	Deutsch	Español	Français	Português
∧	Mountain	Berg	Montaña	Montagne	Montanha
⋏	Mountains	Gebirge	Montañas	Montagnes	Montanhas
)(	Pass	Paß	Paso	Col	Passo
V	Valley, Canyon	Tal, Cañon	Valle, Cañón	Vallée, Canyon	Vale, Canhão
≚	Plain	Ebene	Llano	Plaine	Planície
>	Cape	Kap	Cabo	Cap	Cabo
I	Island	Insel	Isla	Île	Ilha
II	Islands	Inseln	Islas	Îles	Ilhas
⊥	Other Topographic Features	Andere Topographische Objekte	Otros Elementos Topográficos	Autres données topographiques	Outros acidentes topográficos

ESPAÑOL — Nombre | Página | Lat.°′ | Long.°′ W = Oeste

FRANÇAIS — Nom | Page | Lat.°′ | Long.°′ W = Ouest

PORTUGUÊS — Nome | Página | Lat.°′ | Long.°′ W = Oeste

Lugagnano Val d'Arda	62	44.49 N	9.50 E
Lugang, Zhg.	100	31.17 N	118.22 E
Lugang, Zhg.	100	27.23 N	115.36 E
Luganga	154	7.31 S	35.32 E
Lugano	58	46.01 N	8.58 E
Lugano, Lago di ⊜	58	46.00 N	9.00 E
Lugansk → Luhans'k	83	48.34 N	39.20 E
Luganville	175f	15.32 S	167.10 E
Lugards Falls ʟ	154	3.03 S	38.42 E
Lugareño	240p	21.33 N	77.28 W
Lugarno	274a	33.59 S	151.03 E
Lugau	54	50.44 N	12.44 E
Lügde	52	51.57 N	9.15 E
Lugela	154	16.25 S	36.43 E
Lugenda	154	12.30 S	37.43 E
Lugenda ≃	154	11.25 S	38.33 E
Lugg ≃	42	52.02 N	2.38 W
Luggarus → Locarno	58	46.10 N	8.48 E
Luginino	76	57.43 N	35.17 E
Lugnano in Teverina	66	42.34 N	12.20 E
Lugnaquillia Mountain ∧	48	52.58 N	6.27 W
Lugnås	40	58.39 N	13.42 E
Lugny	58	46.28 N	4.49 E
Lugo, Esp.	34	43.00 N	7.34 W
Lugo, It.	66	44.25 N	11.54 E
Lugo □[4]	34	43.00 N	7.25 W
Lugoj	38	45.41 N	21.54 E
Lugongshi	106	31.38 N	121.12 E
Lugos → Lugoj	38	45.41 N	21.54 E
Lugouqiao	105	39.51 N	116.13 E
Lugovaja Subbota	86	59.52 N	69.45 E
Lugovoj, Kaz.	85	42.56 N	72.45 E
Lugovoj, Ross.	86	59.44 N	65.55 E
Lugovoje	85	42.55 N	72.43 E
Lugovskij	88	58.02 N	112.54 E
Lugovskoje	80	50.38 N	46.28 E
Lugu	102	28.21 N	102.09 E
Lugulu ≃	154	2.17 S	26.32 E
Lugunga ∧	154	6.47 S	36.19 E
Luguru	154	2.55 S	33.58 E
Lugus Island I	116	5.41 N	120.50 E
Luhan' ≃	83	48.37 N	39.27 E
Luhanchyk ≃	83	48.35 N	39.32 E
Luhanka	26	61.47 N	25.42 E
Luhans'k	83	48.34 N	39.20 E
Luhans'k □[4]	78	49.00 N	39.00 E
Luhans'ke	83	48.26 N	38.15 E
Luhe ≃	52	53.18 N	10.11 E
Lühedian	100	32.33 N	114.28 E
Luhe-Wildenau	60	49.35 N	12.09 E
Lühmannsdorf	54	54.00 N	13.38 E
Luhombero ≃	154	8.24 S	37.12 E
Luhsien → Luzhou	107	28.54 N	105.27 E
Luhuo	102	31.26 N	100.48 E
Luhyny	78	51.04 N	28.24 E
Lui ≃, Ang.	152	8.41 S	17.56 E
Lui ≃, Zam.	152	16.21 S	23.18 E
Lui, Beinn ∧	46	56.24 N	4.49 W
Luia	152	8.26 S	21.45 E
Luia (Ruya) ≃, Afr.	154	16.34 S	33.12 E
Luia ≃, Ang.	152	8.24 S	21.42 E
Lúia ≃, Moç.	154	15.34 S	32.58 E
Luiana	152	17.23 S	23.03 E
Luiana ≃	152	17.27 S	23.14 E
Luichart, Loch ⊜	46	57.37 N	4.46 W
Luido	156	21.31 S	34.41 E
Luie ≃	152	4.33 S	17.41 E
Luik → Liège	56	50.38 N	5.34 E
Luilaka ≃	152	0.52 S	20.12 E
Luilu ≃	152	6.22 S	23.50 E
Luimbale	152	12.15 S	15.19 E
Luimneach → Limerick	48	52.40 N	8.38 W
Luing I	46	56.13 N	5.40 W
Luino	58	46.00 N	8.44 E
Luio ≃	152	13.15 S	21.39 E
Luipaardsvlei	273d	26.16 S	27.42 E
Luiro ≃	24	67.08 N	27.29 E
Luisant	50	48.25 N	1.29 E
Luís Correia	250	2.53 S	41.40 W
Luisen-Berg ∧[2]	264a	52.27 N	13.07 E
Luisenthal	54	50.47 N	10.43 E
Luís Gomes	250	6.25 S	38.23 W
Luis Guillón	288	34.48 S	58.27 W
Luishia	154	11.10 S	27.02 E
Luis Moya, Méx.	234	22.25 N	102.15 W
Luis Moya, Méx.	234	23.05 N	103.56 W
Luis Muñoz Marin, Aeropuerto Internacional ⊠	240m	18.27 N	66.00 W
Luis Peña, Cayo de I	240m	18.18 N	65.20 W
Luis Pereira, Arroyo ≃	258	34.33 S	57.02 W
Luita	152	8.04 S	19.25 E
Luitpold Coast ⊞[2]	9	78.30 S	32.00 W
Luiza	152	7.12 S	22.25 E
Luiza ≃	152	7.35 S	22.40 E
Luizavo ≃	152	11.42 S	23.12 E
Luizi	154	6.03 S	27.28 E
Luiziânia	255	21.41 S	50.17 W
Luján, Arg.	252	33.03 S	68.52 W
Luján, Arg.	252	32.22 S	65.57 W
Luján, Arg.	258	34.34 S	59.07 W
Luján ≃	288	34.26 S	58.32 W
Lujia, Zhg.	106	31.15 N	121.37 E
Lujia, Zhg.	106	31.19 N	121.03 E
Lujia, Zhg.	269b	31.22 N	121.18 E
Lujiabang	106	31.20 N	121.01 E
Lujiachang	107	30.14 N	105.34 E
Lujiagangzi	104	42.05 N	122.59 E
Lujiang	100	31.14 N	117.17 E
Lujiao	100	29.10 N	112.52 E
Lujiaoxi	107	28.55 N	105.48 E
Lujiaqiao, Zhg.	106	31.47 N	120.27 E
Lujiaqiao, Zhg.	107	28.50 N	106.21 E
Lujiatun, Zhg.	98	40.14 N	122.11 E
Lujiatun, Zhg.	104	41.58 N	122.38 E
Lujiatun, Zhg.	104	42.18 N	124.15 E
Lujiatun, Zhg.	104	41.10 N	121.56 E
Lujiazhou	100	28.16 N	114.35 E
L'uk	80	56.55 N	52.48 E
Lukachukai Wash ∨	200	36.39 N	109.36 W
Lukačok	89	53.03 N	132.16 E
Lukala	152	5.31 S	14.32 E
Lukang	100	24.03 N	120.25 E
Lukanga, R.D.C.	152	1.00 S	18.08 E
Lukanga, R.D.C.	152	1.41 S	18.09 E
Lukanga Swamp ≡	154	14.25 S	27.45 E
Luk'anovo	82	54.52 N	37.25 E
Lukašin	84	40.12 N	44.01 E
Lukaškin Jar	86	60.20 N	78.24 E
Luke, Mount ∧	162	27.13 S	116.48 E
Luke Air Force Base ■	200	33.32 N	112.22 W
Lukenie ≃	152	2.44 S	18.09 E
Lukens, Mount ∧	280	34.16 N	118.14 W
Lukeville	200	31.52 N	112.48 W
Luki	76	53.29 N	26.15 E
Lukino, Ross.	82	55.26 N	37.04 E
Lukino, Ross.	82	55.50 N	36.49 E
Lukiv	78	51.13 N	24.19 E
Lukka	140	14.33 N	23.42 E
Luknovo	80	56.12 N	42.03 E
Lukojanov	80	55.02 N	44.30 E
Lukolela, R.D.C.	152	5.23 S	24.32 E
Lukolela, R.D.C.	152	1.03 S	17.12 E
Lukong	107	29.31 N	105.39 E
Lukoshi ≃	152	10.05 S	22.59 E
Lukosi	154	18.30 S	26.30 E
Lukoškino	82	55.19 N	37.16 E
Lukou, Zhg.	100	27.14 N	114.04 E
Lukou, Zhg.	106	31.48 N	118.52 E
Lukoupu	100	29.30 N	113.26 E
Lukouyu	100	28.24 N	113.18 E
Lukovit	38	43.12 N	24.10 E
Lukovskaja	80	50.35 N	41.52 E
Łuków	30	51.56 N	22.23 E
Lükqün	86	42.44 N	89.42 E
Lukuga ≃	154	5.40 S	26.55 E
Lukula	152	5.23 S	12.57 E
Lukula ≃, Afr.	152	5.08 S	12.28 E
Lukula ≃, R.D.C.	152	4.13 S	17.58 E
Lukuledi ≃	154	10.05 S	39.42 E
Lukulu	152	14.25 S	23.12 E
Lukulu ≃	154	10.56 S	31.05 E
Lukumburu	154	9.45 S	35.09 E
Lukunga ≃	273b	4.25 S	15.14 E
Lukuni	152	5.52 S	17.11 E
Lukusashi ≃	154	14.38 S	30.00 E
Lukusuzi National Park ♠	154	12.50 S	32.35 E
Lula, It.	71	40.28 N	9.29 E
Lula, Ms., U.S.	194	34.27 N	90.28 W
Lula, R.D.C.	152	5.22 S	16.02 E
Luleå	26	65.34 N	22.10 E
Luleälven ≃	24	65.35 N	22.03 E
Lüleburgaz	130	41.24 N	27.21 E
Lules	252	26.56 S	65.21 W
Luliang	102	25.05 N	103.36 E
Lüliang Shan ⛰	102	37.25 N	111.20 E
Luliāni	123	31.15 N	74.25 E
Luliao	269d	25.07 N	121.39 E
Luling	222	29.40 N	97.38 W
Lullingstone Castle ⊥	260	51.21 N	0.12 E
Lulo ≃	152	9.25 S	18.14 E
Lulong	98	39.54 N	118.50 E
Lulonga	152	0.37 N	18.23 E
Lulonga ≃	152	0.43 N	18.23 E
Lulu ≃	152	1.18 N	23.42 E
Lulua ≃	152	5.02 S	21.07 E
Luluabourg → Kananga	152	5.54 S	22.25 E
Lulu Island I, B.C., Can.	224	49.09 N	123.05 W
Lulu Island I, Ak., U.S.	182	55.28 N	133.30 W
Luluo	98	37.06 N	113.58 E
Lulworth, Mount ∧	162	26.53 S	117.42 E
Lumai	152	13.31 S	21.21 E
Lumajang	115a	8.08 S	113.13 E
Lumajangdong Co ⊜	120	34.00 N	81.45 E
Lumaku, Gunong ∧	112	4.52 N	115.38 E
Lumaling	120	29.53 N	92.37 E
Lumb	262	53.42 N	1.58 W
Lumbala ≃	152	12.38 S	22.34 E
Lumbala Kaquengue	152	12.39 S	22.34 E
Lumbala N'guimbo	152	14.08 S	21.25 E
Lumbangaraga	114	1.53 N	99.04 E
Lumbanlobu	114	2.31 N	99.08 E
Lumbe ≃	152	16.42 S	23.42 E
Lumber ≃	192	34.12 N	79.10 W
Lumber City	192	31.55 N	82.40 W
Lumberport	188	39.22 N	80.20 W
Lumberton, Ms., U.S.	194	31.00 N	89.27 W
Lumberton, N.J., U.S.	285	39.57 N	74.48 W
Lumberton, N.C., U.S.	192	34.37 N	79.00 W
Lumberton, Tx., U.S.	194	30.16 N	94.10 W
Lumbinī □[8]	124	27.45 N	83.30 E
Lumbis	112	4.18 N	116.15 E
Lumbo	154	15.00 S	40.44 E
Lumbovka	24	67.44 N	40.30 E
Lumbrales	34	40.56 N	6.43 W
Lumbrein	58	46.41 N	9.08 E
Lumbres	50	50.42 N	2.08 E
Lumbwa	154	0.12 S	35.28 E
Lumby	182	50.15 N	118.58 W
Lumding	120	25.45 N	93.10 E
Lumege ≃	152	11.55 S	20.58 E
Lumerau ≃	116	5.21 N	118.53 E
Lumi	164	3.29 S	142.02 E
Lumiei ≃	64	46.24 N	12.51 E
Luminárias	256	21.30 S	44.54 W
Luminosa	256	22.35 S	45.38 W
Lumintao ≃	116	12.43 N	120.55 E
Lummen	56	50.59 N	5.12 E
Lummi Bay ⊂	224	48.46 N	122.41 W
Lummi Indian Reservation ◆[4]	224	48.48 N	122.38 W
Lummi Island	224	48.42 N	122.40 W
Lummi Island I	224	48.42 N	122.40 W
Lumphanan	46	57.07 N	2.41 W
Lumphăt	110	13.30 N	106.59 E
Lumphini Park ♠	269a	13.44 N	100.33 E
Lumpkin	192	32.03 N	84.47 W
Lumpun ≃	80	57.01 N	51.22 E
Lumsån ≃	40	59.59 N	15.26 E
Lumsås	41	55.57 N	11.31 E
Lumsden, Nf., Can.	186	49.19 N	53.37 W
Lumsden, Sk., Can.	184	50.34 N	104.53 W
Lumsden, N.Z.	172	45.44 S	168.27 E
Lumsden, Scot., U.K.	46	57.15 N	2.52 W
Lumsheden	40	60.43 N	16.15 E
Lums Pond State Park ♠	208	39.34 N	75.43 W
Lumu, Indon.	112	2.11 S	119.09 E
Lumu, Zhg.	106	31.22 N	120.37 E
Lumuna	154	3.46 S	26.24 E
Lumuna ≃	152	16.59 S	21.25 E
Lumut, Indon.	114	1.33 N	98.56 E
Lumut, Malay.	114	4.14 N	100.38 E
Lumut, Tanjung ›	112	3.50 S	105.57 E
Lumwana	154	11.50 S	25.10 E
Lün, Mong.	88	47.24 N	102.52 E
Lün, Mong.	88	47.52 N	105.15 E
Luna, Pil.	116	16.51 N	120.23 E
Luna, Pil.	116	18.18 N	121.21 E
Luna ≃	246	4.32 S	60.41 W
Lunada Bay ⊂	280	33.46 N	118.25 W
Lunain ≃	50	48.20 N	2.47 E
Lunamatrona	71	39.39 N	8.54 E
Lunan	102	24.49 N	103.16 E
Lunan Bay ⊂	46	56.39 N	2.28 W
Lunano	66	43.44 N	12.26 E
Luna Pier	216	41.48 N	83.26 W
Lūnāvāda	120	23.08 N	73.37 E
Luncarty	46	56.27 N	3.28 W
Lund, B.C., Can.	182	49.58 N	124.44 W
Lund, Sve.	41	55.42 N	13.11 E
Lund, Nv., U.S.	204	38.51 N	115.00 W
Lunda ≃, Ang.	152	6.07 S	13.52 E
L'unda ≃, Ross.	80	56.32 N	46.03 E
Lundåkrabukten ⊂	41	55.48 N	12.53 E
Lundale	188	37.48 N	81.44 W
Lunda Norte □[5]	152	8.45 S	19.45 E
Lundar	184	50.42 N	98.02 W
Lunda Sul □[5]	152	10.00 S	20.30 E
Lundazi	154	12.19 S	33.13 E
Lundby	41	55.07 N	11.53 E
Lunde	41	55.29 N	10.21 E
Lundeborg	41	55.08 N	10.47 E
Lunden	41	54.20 N	9.01 E
Lunderskov	41	55.29 N	9.18 E
Lundevatn ⊜	26	58.22 N	6.36 E
Lundi ≃	154	21.43 S	32.34 E
Lundsberg	40	59.30 N	14.10 E
Lundsfjärden ⊜	40	59.38 N	14.41 E
Lundy I	42	51.10 N	4.40 W
Lundys Lane	214	41.53 N	80.21 W
Lune ≃	44	54.02 N	2.50 W
Lüneburg	52	53.15 N	10.23 E
Lüneburg □[5]	52	53.15 N	10.00 E
Lüneburger Heide ◆[1]	52	53.10 N	10.20 E
Lunel	62	43.41 N	4.08 E
Lünen	52	51.36 N	7.32 E
Lunenburg, N.S., Can.	186	44.23 N	64.19 W
Lunenburg, Ma., U.S.	207	42.35 N	71.43 W
Lunenburg, Va., U.S.	192	36.57 N	78.15 W
Luneray	50	49.50 N	0.55 E
Lünern	263	51.33 N	7.46 E
Lunéville	56	48.36 N	6.30 E
Lunga I	46	56.13 N	5.42 W
Lunga ≃, Ang.	152	5.59 S	16.20 E
Lunga ≃, Zam.	154	14.34 S	26.25 E
Lungälven ≃	40	59.34 N	14.10 E
Lunga Reservoir ⊜[1]	208	38.32 N	77.28 W
Lungau ◆[1]	64	47.07 N	13.39 E
Lungavilla	62	45.02 N	9.04 E
Lungch'i → Zhangzhou	100	24.33 N	117.39 E
Lunge	152	12.12 S	16.05 E
Lunge'nake	120	31.45 N	85.55 E
Lungern	58	46.47 N	8.10 E
Lunggar	120	31.10 N	84.00 E
Lunghezza ◆[8]	267a	41.55 N	12.40 E
Lungi	150	8.38 N	13.13 W
Lunglei	120	22.53 N	92.44 E
Lungro	68	39.44 N	16.07 E
Lungsang	124	29.51 N	88.41 E
Lungt'an	100	24.52 N	121.12 E
Lungué-Bungo (Lungwebungu) ≃	152	14.19 S	23.14 E
Lunguya	154	3.23 S	32.24 E
Lungwebungu (Lungué-Bungo) ≃	152	14.19 S	23.14 E
Lūni	120	26.00 N	73.00 E
Lūni ≃	120	24.41 N	71.15 E
Luni ⊥	64	44.04 N	10.01 E
Lunia-Bubi	154	7.30 S	24.49 E
Lunigiana ◆[1]	64	44.15 N	9.50 E
Lunin	76	52.18 N	26.38 E
Luninec	76	52.15 N	26.48 E
Lunino, Ross.	80	53.35 N	45.14 E
Lunino, Ross.	82	54.09 N	38.29 E
Lunjiao	100	22.53 N	113.13 E
Lūnkaransar	120	28.29 N	73.44 E
Lunna	76	53.27 N	24.16 E
Lunnaja, gora ∧	180	68.14 N	174.20 E
Lunndörrsfjällen ∧	26	63.00 N	13.00 E
Lunongzha	106	31.59 N	120.55 E
Lunsar	150	8.41 N	12.32 W
Lunsemfwa ≃	154	14.54 S	30.12 E
Lunt	262	53.31 N	2.59 W
Lunteren	52	52.05 N	5.37 E
Lunyuk	115b	8.57 S	117.14 E
Lunz am See	61	47.51 N	15.03 E
Lunzenau	54	50.58 N	12.45 E
Lunzhen	98	36.47 N	116.34 E
Luo ≃, Zhg.	102	34.42 N	110.15 E
Luo ≃, Zhg.	102	34.48 N	113.04 E
Luoba, Zhg.	100	24.51 N	114.13 E
Luoba, Zhg.	107	29.08 N	106.11 E
Luobei (Fengxiang)	89	47.34 N	130.50 E
Luobo	102	28.22 N	101.38 E
Luobu	102	24.30 N	109.40 E
Luobumiao	102	40.19 N	107.30 E
Luochanghe	100	31.01 N	117.18 E
Luocheng, Zhg.	102	24.51 N	108.59 E
Luocheng, Zhg.	107	29.23 N	104.01 E
Luochuan	102	35.55 N	109.26 E
Luoci	102	25.19 N	102.18 E
Luodian	106	31.25 N	121.20 E
Luoding	102	22.47 N	111.31 E
Luoduzhen	107	30.22 N	106.35 E
Luofa	105	39.25 N	116.50 E
Luofang, Zhg.	100	28.40 N	115.04 E
Luofang, Zhg.	100	27.52 N	115.06 E
Luofu, R.D.C.	154	0.10 S	29.14 E
Luofu, Zhg.	100	24.32 N	115.35 E
Luogang, Zhg.	100	23.11 N	113.30 E
Luogang, Zhg.	100	24.25 N	115.38 E
Luogosanto	71	41.03 N	9.13 E
Luoguhe	89	53.18 N	121.30 E
Luohan Shan ∧	100	25.51 N	119.13 E
Luohe	100	33.35 N	114.01 E
Luoheya	98	35.46 N	118.54 E
Luohua	100	26.35 N	118.43 E
Luoji	100	32.06 N	117.16 E
Luojiachang	107	30.49 N	106.32 E
Luojiang	102	31.21 N	104.28 E
Luojiatang	106	30.18 N	120.13 E
Luojiatun, Zhg.	98	40.11 N	118.34 E
Luojiatun, Zhg.	104	42.06 N	122.44 E
Luojiatun, Zhg.	104	40.55 N	122.04 E
Luojiawei	100	26.55 N	115.02 E
Luoke	100	24.07 N	114.28 E
Luokeng	100	24.32 N	113.23 E
Luokou, Zhg.	100	28.54 N	117.24 E
Luokou, Zhg.	100	25.46 N	115.39 E
Luolong	107	28.49 N	104.46 E
L'Uomo di Cagna ∧	71	41.33 N	9.04 E
Luonan	102	34.05 N	110.04 E
Luoning	102	34.25 N	111.42 E
Luoping	102	24.59 N	104.21 E
Luoqi	102	29.48 N	106.56 E
Luoqiao	100	26.28 N	119.01 E
Luoquanzhen	107	29.50 N	104.31 E
Luoshan, Zhg.	100	32.13 N	114.32 E
Luoshan, Zhg.	100	29.41 N	113.18 E
Luoshan, Zhg.	105	39.55 N	117.33 E
Luoshe, Zhg.	106	31.39 N	120.11 E
Luoshe, Zhg.	106	30.41 N	120.04 E
Luoshuihe	98	39.27 N	114.19 E
Luossa ≃	152	8.24 S	17.03 E
Luotian	100	30.48 N	115.22 E
Luotuodian	100	32.13 N	113.49 E
Luotuoqiao	100	29.56 N	121.32 E
Luotuo Shan ∧	104	42.14 N	121.42 E
Luowenba	102	31.48 N	107.48 E
Luowenyu	105	40.16 N	117.57 E
Luoxi	100	29.05 N	114.58 E
Luoxiao Shan ⛰	100	26.00 N	114.00 E
Luoyang (Loyang), Zhg.	102	34.41 N	112.28 E
Luoyang, Zhg.	106	31.39 N	120.05 E
Luoyuan	100	26.31 N	119.32 E
Luoyuan Wan ⊂	100	26.25 N	119.43 E
Luoyukou	102	38.23 N	110.43 E
Luozhexi	107	29.02 N	103.54 E
Luozi	152	4.57 S	14.08 E
Lupala	156	17.50 S	19.06 E
Lupani	154	18.54 S	27.44 E
Lupao	116	15.53 N	120.54 E
Lupar ≃	112	1.30 N	111.00 E
Łupawa	30	54.26 N	17.24 E
Lupberg	60	49.09 N	11.45 E
Lupembe	154	9.15 S	35.15 E
Lupeni	38	45.22 N	23.13 E
Lupire	152	14.36 S	19.29 E
Lupiro	154	8.23 S	36.40 E
Lupon	116	6.54 N	126.00 E
Luppa	54	51.20 N	12.57 E
Luputa	152	7.10 S	23.42 E
Luqiao, Zhg.	100	32.34 N	117.14 E
Luqiao, Zhg.	100	28.35 N	121.22 E
Luqu	102	34.41 N	102.22 E
Luque	34	37.33 N	4.16 W
Luquillo	240m	18.22 N	65.43 W
Luquillo, Sierra de ⛰	240m	18.17 N	65.47 W
Lūrah ≃	120	31.33 N	66.33 E
Luray	188	38.39 N	78.27 W
Lure	58	47.41 N	6.30 E
Lure, Montagne de ⛰	62	44.07 N	5.47 E
Lureco ≃	154	12.28 S	37.40 E
Luremo	152	8.31 S	17.50 E
Lurgan	48	54.28 N	6.20 W
Luribay	248	17.06 S	67.39 W
Lurigancho	286d	12.02 S	77.01 W
Lurín	248	12.17 S	76.52 W
Lúrio	154	13.35 S	40.30 E
Lúrio ≃	154	13.35 S	40.32 E
Lurisia	62	44.18 N	7.42 E
Lurnea	274a	33.56 S	150.54 E
Lurö I	26	58.48 N	13.14 E
Lürrip ◆[8]	263	51.12 N	6.28 E
Lusahunga	154	2.52 S	31.15 E
Lusaka, R.D.C.	154	7.10 S	29.27 E
Lusaka, Zam.	154	15.25 S	28.17 E
Lusaka □[4]	154	15.25 S	29.00 E
Lusakert	84	40.23 N	44.36 E
Lusambo	152	4.58 S	23.27 E
Lusancay Islands and Reefs II	164	8.25 S	150.20 E
Lusanga	152	4.50 S	18.44 E
Lusangaye	154	4.54 S	26.00 E
Lusangi	154	4.37 S	27.08 E
Luscar	182	53.04 N	117.24 W
Luseke	152	2.51 S	23.08 E
Luseland	184	52.05 N	109.24 W
Lusen ∧	60	48.56 N	13.31 E
Lusenga Plain National Park ♠	154	9.30 S	29.10 E
Lusengo	152	1.46 N	19.29 E
Luserna San Giovanni	62	44.48 N	7.15 E
Lush, Mount ∧	164	17.02 S	127.30 E
Lushan, Zhg.	100	33.45 N	112.53 E
Lushan, Zhg.	102	30.15 N	102.58 E
Lu Shan ∧	100	29.31 N	115.58 E
Lu Shan ⛰	98	36.05 N	118.05 E
Lushanguanliju	100	29.33 N	115.58 E
Lushi	102	34.05 N	111.01 E
Lushiko (Luchico) ≃	152	6.13 S	19.40 E
Lüshikou	100	29.16 N	120.17 E
Lushnje	38	40.56 N	19.42 E
Lushoto	154	4.47 S	38.17 E
Lushui	102	26.00 N	98.51 E
Lüshun (Port Arthur)	98	38.48 N	121.16 E
Lüsi	106	32.03 N	121.36 E
Lusi ≃	115a	7.05 S	110.55 E
Lusiana	64	45.47 N	11.34 E
Lusignan	32	46.26 N	0.07 E
Lusignan, Lac ⊜	206	46.40 N	74.09 W
Lusigny-sur-Barse	50	48.15 N	4.16 E
Lusikisiki	158	31.25 S	29.30 E
Lusk, Ire.	48	53.32 N	6.10 W
Lusk, Wy., U.S.	200	42.45 N	104.27 W
Lus-la-Croix-Haute	62	44.40 N	5.42 E
Lusongwa	152	12.58 S	24.16 E
Luspebryggan	24	67.01 N	19.51 E
Lussac-les-Châteaux	32	46.24 N	0.44 E
Lussan	62	44.09 N	4.22 E
Luṣṣān, Wādī ∨	132	30.30 N	34.18 E
Lüssow	54	53.50 N	12.09 E
Lustenau	58	47.26 N	9.39 E
Luster	26	61.26 N	7.24 E
Lustin	56	50.23 N	4.53 E
Lustrafjorden ⊂[2]	26	61.20 N	7.22 E
Lüstringen	52	52.16 N	8.08 E
Lusutfu (Maputo) (Great Usutu) ≃	158	26.11 S	32.42 E
Luswishi ≃	154	13.55 S	27.24 E
Lūt, Dasht-e ◆[2]	128	32.00 N	58.00 E
Lü-ta → Dalian	98	38.53 N	121.35 E
L'uta ≃	76	58.37 N	28.40 E
Lutago (Luttach)	64	46.57 N	11.55 E
Lutai	100	33.32 N	115.03 E
Lütan, Zhg.	98	34.07 N	114.27 E
Lütan, Zhg.	100	28.57 N	119.46 E
Lutang	100	25.39 N	112.46 E
Lutao	116	10.00 N	124.04 E
Lü Tao I	100	22.40 N	121.29 E
Lutcher	194	30.02 N	90.41 W
Lute	284c	39.04 N	77.03 W
Lutembo	152	13.26 S	21.16 E
Lutembo ≃	152	12.03 S	22.15 E
Lutesville	194	37.18 N	89.58 W
Lutéte ≃	152	9.21 S	15.14 E
Lutexu ≃	273b	4.24 S	15.12 E
Lütgendortmund ◆[8]	263	51.30 N	7.21 E
Luthe	52	52.26 N	9.28 E
Luther, Mi., U.S.	190	44.02 N	85.40 W
Luther, Ok., U.S.	196	35.39 N	97.11 W
Luther Lake ⊜	212	43.55 N	80.26 W
Luthersburg	214	41.03 N	78.43 W
Lutherstadt Eisleben	54	51.31 N	11.32 E
Lutherstadt Wittenberg	54	51.52 N	12.39 E
Lutherville-Timonium	284b	39.25 N	76.37 W
Luthrie	46	56.21 N	3.05 W
Luti	175e	7.14 S	156.59 E
Lutian, Zhg.	100	26.33 N	114.38 E
Lütian, Zhg.	100	23.48 N	113.56 E
Lütjenburg	54	54.17 N	10.35 E
Lütjensee	52	53.39 N	10.22 E
Luton, Eng., U.K.	42	51.53 N	0.25 W
Luton, Eng., U.K.	260	51.22 N	0.32 E
Lutong	112	4.28 N	114.00 E
Lutosn'a ≃	82	56.26 N	36.52 E
Lutou	100	32.16 N	112.53 E
Lutry	58	46.30 N	6.41 E
Lutshi	154	4.09 S	26.30 E
Lutshima ≃	152	5.22 S	18.59 E
Luts'k	78	50.44 N	25.20 E
Luttach → Lutago	64	46.57 N	11.55 E
Lutter	52	51.59 N	10.16 E
Lutterbach	58	47.46 N	7.17 E
Lutterworth	42	52.28 N	1.10 W
Lüttich → Liège	56	50.38 N	5.34 E
Luttrell	192	36.11 N	83.44 W
Lüttringhausen ◆[8]	263	51.13 N	7.14 E
Lutuai ≃	152	12.33 S	20.16 E
Lutuhyne	83	48.24 N	39.13 E
Lutz	220	28.09 N	82.27 W
Lützel	56	50.58 N	8.10 E
Lutzelbourg	56	48.44 N	7.15 E
Lützelflüh	58	47.00 N	7.41 E
Lützen	54	51.15 N	12.08 E
Lutzerath	56	50.07 N	7.00 E
Lutz Hill	284b	39.20 N	76.32 W
Lützow	54	53.40 N	11.11 E
Lützow-Holm Bay ⊂	9	69.10 S	37.30 E
Lutzputs	158	28.03 S	20.40 E
Lützschena	54	51.23 N	12.16 E
Lutzville	158	31.33 S	18.22 E
Luud, Waadi ∨	144	10.17 N	50.14 E
Luuq	144	3.48 N	42.33 E
Luus	102	45.30 N	105.45 E
Luverne, Al., U.S.	194	31.42 N	86.15 W
Lu Verne, Ia., U.S.	190	42.54 N	94.04 W
Luverne, Mn., U.S.	198	43.39 N	96.12 W
Luvo	152	5.51 S	14.05 E
Luvo ≃	152	10.18 S	17.08 E
Luvua	154	8.48 S	25.19 E
Lúvua ≃, Ang.	152	11.57 S	22.30 E
Luvua ≃, R.D.C.	154	6.46 S	26.58 E
Luvuvhu ≃	156	22.40 S	30.55 E
Luwegu ≃	154	8.31 S	37.23 E
Luwingu	154	10.15 S	29.55 E
Luwuk, Indon.	112	0.56 S	122.47 E
Luwuk → Banggai, Indon.	112	1.34 S	123.30 E
Luxana Bay ⊂	182	52.03 N	131.00 W
Luxapallila Creek ≃	194	33.28 N	88.26 W
Luxembourg	56	49.36 N	6.09 E
Luxembourg □[4]	56	50.00 N	5.30 E
Luxembourg □[1], Europe	22	49.45 N	6.05 E
Luxembourg □[1], Europe	56	49.45 N	6.05 E
Luxembourg, Aéroport de ⊠	56	49.37 N	6.10 E
Luxembourg, Jardin du ♠	261	48.51 N	2.19 E
Luxemburg	190	44.32 N	87.42 W
Luxemburg → Luxembourg □[1]	56	49.45 N	6.05 E
Luxemburgo → Luxembourg □[1]	56	49.45 N	6.05 E
Luxeuil-les-Bains	58	47.49 N	6.23 E
Luxi, Zhg.	102	24.32 N	103.41 E
Luxi (Mangshi), Zhg.	102	24.20 N	98.25 E
Lüxia	100	26.41 N	120.06 E
Luxian	107	28.55 N	105.29 E
Luxiang, Zhg.	106	31.32 N	120.45 E
Lüxiang, Zhg.	106	30.50 N	121.10 E
Luxi Dao I	100	27.59 N	121.11 E
Luxikou	100	29.54 N	113.42 E
Luxmanor	284c	39.02 N	77.07 W
Luxor → Al-Uqṣur	140	25.41 N	32.39 E
Luxora	194	35.45 N	89.55 W
Luxu	106	31.01 N	120.50 E
Lu Xun Museum ☗	269b	31.16 N	121.28 E
Lüxuqiao	106	31.50 N	119.31 E
Luy ≃	32	43.39 N	1.08 W
Luyan	106	30.25 N	120.53 E
Lüyang	104	41.23 N	121.40 E
Luyanó ≃	286b	23.07 N	82.21 W
Luyeh	100	22.55 N	121.08 E
Luyi	100	33.53 N	115.28 E
Luynes	50	47.23 N	0.33 E
Luyu	106	31.34 N	121.41 E
Luyuan, Zhg.	106	31.51 N	120.38 E
Luyuan, Zhg.	271a	39.54 N	116.27 E
Luz, Bra.	255	19.48 S	45.40 W
Luz, Bra.	287a	22.48 S	43.05 W
Luz ◆[8]	266c	38.46 N	9.10 W
Luz, Estação da ◆[5]	287b	23.32 S	46.38 W
Luz, Isla I	254	45.30 S	73.59 W
Luz, Ponta da ›	287a	22.47 S	43.05 W
Luza, Ross.	24	62.42 N	37.06 E
Luza, Ross.	24	60.39 N	47.10 E
Luža, Ross.	76	59.58 N	31.56 E
Luža ≃	82	55.03 N	36.35 E
Luzarches	50	49.07 N	2.25 E
Luzern	58	47.03 N	8.18 E
Luzern □[3]	58	47.05 N	8.05 E
Luzerne	210	41.17 N	75.54 W
Luzerne □[6]	210	41.14 N	75.53 W
Luzhai, Zhg.	102	24.31 N	109.50 E
Luzhai, Zhg.	269b	31.20 N	121.22 E
Luzhi	106	31.16 N	120.52 E
Luzhou	107	28.54 N	105.27 E
Luziânia	255	16.15 S	47.56 W
Lužické hory ⛰	54	50.48 N	14.40 E
Luzilândia	250	3.28 S	42.22 W
Lužki, Bela.	76	55.21 N	27.52 E
Lužki, Ross.	82	54.51 N	37.36 E
Lužná	54	50.06 N	13.45 E
Lužnice ≃	30	49.14 N	14.23 E
Lužniki ◆[8]	265b	55.43 N	37.33 E
Luzon I	116	16.00 N	121.00 E
Luzon Strait ⋃	108	20.30 N	121.00 E
Lužskaja guba ⊂	76	59.45 N	28.20 E
Luzy	32	46.48 N	3.58 E
Luzzara	64	44.58 N	10.41 E
Luzzi	68	39.27 N	16.17 E
L'va ≃	78	52.00 N	27.36 E
L'va Tolstogo	82	54.37 N	36.03 E
L'viv	78	49.50 N	24.00 E
L'viv □[4]	78	49.30 N	24.00 E
Lvov → L'viv	78	49.50 N	24.00 E
L'vovskij	82	55.19 N	37.31 E
Lwów → L'viv	78	49.50 N	24.00 E
Lwówek	30	52.28 N	16.10 E
Lwówek Śląski	30	51.07 N	15.35 E
Lyadova ≃	78	48.28 N	27.37 E
Lyall, Mount ∧	172	45.17 S	167.34 E
Lyallpur → Faisalabad	123	31.25 N	73.05 E
Lyantonde	154	0.24 S	31.09 E
Lyashchivka	78	49.33 N	32.41 E
Lybster	46	58.18 N	3.18 W
Lycaonia □[9]	130	37.50 N	33.15 E
Lychen	54	53.12 N	13.19 E
Lychkove	78	49.06 N	35.12 E
Lycia □[9]	130	36.20 N	30.00 E
Lyck → Ełk	30	53.50 N	22.22 E
Lyckeby	26	56.12 N	15.39 E
Lyčkovo	76	57.55 N	32.24 E
Lycksele	26	64.36 N	18.40 E
Lycoming □[6]	210	41.14 N	77.00 W
Lycoming Creek ≃	210	41.13 N	77.02 W
Lydd	42	50.57 N	0.55 E
Lydda → Lod	132	31.58 N	34.54 E
Lydden ≃	42	50.56 N	2.22 W
Lydenburg	156	25.10 S	30.29 E
Lydenburgh County Park ♠	276	40.50 N	73.14 W
Lydford	42	50.39 N	4.06 W
Lydgate	262	53.44 N	2.07 W
Lydham	42	52.31 N	2.58 W
Lydia □[9]	130	38.40 N	27.30 E
Lydia Mills	192	34.28 N	81.55 W
Lydiate	262	53.32 N	2.57 W
Lydick	216	41.42 N	86.22 W
Lydney	42	51.44 N	2.32 W
Lye Green	260	51.43 N	0.35 W
Lyell, Mount ∧, Can.	182	51.57 N	117.06 W
Lyell, Mount ∧, Ca., U.S.	226	37.44 N	119.16 W
Lyell Brown, Mount ∧	162	23.21 S	130.24 E
Lyell Island I	182	52.40 N	131.30 W
Lyerly	192	34.24 N	85.24 W
Lyford	196	26.24 N	97.47 W
Lygnern ⊜	26	57.29 N	12.20 E
Lyhivka	78	49.08 N	36.03 E
Lykens	208	40.34 N	76.42 W
Lykhivka	78	48.41 N	33.55 E
Lykošino	76	58.07 N	33.43 E
Lyle, Mn., U.S.	190	43.30 N	92.56 W
Lyle, Wa., U.S.	224	45.41 N	121.17 W
Lyles	194	35.55 N	87.20 W
Lyman, Ukr.	78	49.36 N	36.27 E
Lyman, Ukr.	78	45.41 N	29.45 E
Lyman, Ukr.	83	49.21 N	38.57 E
Lyman, Ne., U.S.	198	41.55 N	104.02 W
Lyman, S.C., U.S.	192	34.56 N	82.07 W
Lyman, Wa., U.S.	224	48.31 N	122.03 W
Lyman, Wy., U.S.	200	41.19 N	110.17 W
Lymans'ke	78	46.38 N	30.00 E
Lymbel'karamo	86	60.15 N	83.32 E
Lyme	207	41.18 N	72.19 W
Lyme Bay ⊂	42	50.38 N	3.00 W
Lyme Hall ⊥	262	53.20 N	2.03 W
Lyme Park ♠	262	53.21 N	2.04 W
Lyme Regis	42	50.44 N	2.57 W
Lyminge	42	51.08 N	1.05 E
Lymington	42	50.46 N	1.33 W
Lymkoj	86	59.31 N	70.22 E
Lymm	262	53.23 N	2.29 W
Lympne	42	51.05 N	1.02 E
Lympstone	42	50.39 N	3.25 W
Lymyshivka	78	52.04 N	31.38 E
Lyn	212	44.35 N	75.47 W
Łyna (Lava) ≃	76	54.37 N	21.14 E
Lynæs	41	55.57 N	11.52 E
Lynbrook	276	40.39 N	73.41 W
Lynch, Ky., U.S.	192	36.57 N	82.55 W
Lynch, Ne., U.S.	198	42.49 N	98.27 W
Lynch, Arg. ◆[8]	288	34.36 S	58.31 W
Lynch, Lac ⊜	190	46.25 N	77.05 W
Lynchburg, Oh., U.S.	218	39.14 N	83.47 W
Lynchburg, S.C., U.S.	192	34.03 N	80.04 W
Lynchburg, Tn., U.S.	194	35.16 N	86.22 W
Lynchburg, Va., U.S.	192	37.24 N	79.08 W
Lynches ≃	192	33.50 N	79.22 W
Lynchville	214	41.26 N	78.34 W
Lynd ≃	164	16.28 S	143.18 E
Lynde Creek ≃	212	43.51 N	78.57 W
Lynden, On., Can.	212	43.14 N	80.09 W
Lynden, Wa., U.S.	224	48.56 N	122.27 W
Lyndhurst, Austl.	166	19.12 S	144.23 E
Lyndhurst, Austl.	166	30.17 S	138.21 E
Lyndhurst, Austl.	274b	38.03 S	145.15 E
Lyndhurst, Eng., U.K.	42	50.52 N	1.34 W
Lyndhurst, N.J., U.S.	276	40.48 N	74.07 W
Lyndhurst, Oh., U.S.	214	41.31 N	81.29 W
Lyndoch	168b	34.37 S	138.53 E
Lyndon, Austl.	162	23.37 S	115.15 E
Lyndon, Ks., U.S.	198	38.38 N	95.41 W
Lyndon, Ky., U.S.	218	38.15 N	85.36 W
Lyndon ≃	162	23.29 S	114.06 E
Lyndon B. Johnson, Lake ⊜[1]	196	30.35 N	98.25 W
Lyndon B. Johnson Historical Park ♠	196	30.15 N	98.38 W
Lyndon B. Johnson Space Center ☗[3]	222	29.34 N	95.05 W
Lyndonville, N.Y., U.S.	210	43.19 N	78.23 W
Lyndonville, Vt., U.S.	188	44.32 N	72.00 W
Lyndora	214	40.51 N	79.55 W
Lyne	260	51.23 N	0.33 W
Lyne ≃, Eng., U.K.	44	54.58 N	3.01 W
Lyne ≃, Eng., U.K.	44	55.12 N	1.31 W
Lyneham	42	51.31 N	1.58 W
Lynemouth	44	55.12 N	1.31 W
Lyne Water ≃	46	55.39 N	3.16 W
Lynga	80	57.17 N	53.04 E
Lyngdal	26	58.08 N	7.05 E
Lynge	41	55.51 N	12.17 E
Lyngen	24	69.34 N	20.10 E
Lyngen ⊂[2]	24	69.58 N	20.30 E
Lyngør	26	58.38 N	9.10 E
Lynher ≃	42	50.28 N	4.12 W
Lynmouth	42	51.15 N	3.50 W
Lynn, Al., U.S.	194	34.02 N	87.32 W
Lynn, In., U.S.	218	40.02 N	84.56 W
Lynn, Ma., U.S.	207	42.28 N	70.57 W
Lynn ≃	212	42.47 N	80.12 W
Lynn Canal ⊂	180	58.50 N	135.15 W
Lynndyl	200	39.31 N	112.22 W
Lynne Acres	284b	39.21 N	76.45 W
Lynnfield	207	42.32 N	71.02 W
Lynn Garden	192	36.34 N	82.34 W
Lynn Harbor ⊂	283	42.27 N	70.57 W
Lynn Haven	194	30.14 N	85.38 W
Lynn Lake	184	56.51 N	101.03 W
Lynnville	190	41.34 N	92.47 W
Lynnwood, Pa., U.S.	210	41.14 N	75.56 W
Lynnwood, Pa., U.S.	214	40.07 N	79.51 W
Lynnwood, Wa., U.S.	224	47.49 N	122.18 W
Lynn Woods ♠	283	42.29 N	70.59 W
Lynovytsya	78	50.28 N	32.22 E
Lynton	42	51.15 N	3.50 W
Lyntupy	76	55.03 N	26.19 E
Lynwood, Ca., U.S.	228	33.55 N	118.12 W
Lynwood, Il., U.S.	278	41.32 N	87.32 W
Lynx Lake ⊜	176	62.25 N	106.15 W
Lyø I	41	55.02 N	10.10 E
Lyon	62	45.45 N	4.51 E
Lyon □[6]	226	39.00 N	119.15 W
Lyon ≃	46	56.37 N	4.01 W
Lyon, Gare ◆[5]	261	48.51 N	2.23 E
Lyon, Glen ∨	46	56.35 N	4.20 W
Lyon, Loch ⊜	46	56.32 N	4.36 W
Lyon Inlet ⊂	176	66.32 N	83.53 W
Lyon Mountain	188	44.43 N	73.54 W
Lyon Mountain ∧	188	44.41 N	73.53 W
Lyonnais □[9]	62	45.45 N	4.30 E
Lyonnais, Monts du ⛰	62	45.40 N	4.30 E
Lyons, Co., U.S.	200	40.13 N	105.16 W
Lyons, Ga., U.S.	192	32.12 N	82.19 W
Lyons, Il., U.S.	216	41.48 N	87.49 W
Lyons, In., U.S.	194	38.59 N	87.04 W
Lyons, Ks., U.S.	198	38.20 N	98.12 W
Lyons, Mi., U.S.	216	42.58 N	84.56 W
Lyons, Ne., U.S.	198	41.56 N	96.28 W
Lyons, N.Y., U.S.	210	43.03 N	76.59 W
Lyons, Oh., U.S.	216	41.41 N	84.04 W
Lyons, Tx., U.S.	222	30.23 N	96.34 W
Lyons, Wi., U.S.	216	42.39 N	88.21 W
Lyons ≃	162	25.02 S	115.09 E
Lyon-Satolas, Aéroport de ⊠	62	45.43 N	5.04 E
Lyons Creek ≃	284a	43.03 N	79.04 W
Lyons Falls	212	43.37 N	75.22 W
Lyons-la-Forêt	50	49.24 N	1.28 E
Lyons Plains	207	41.13 N	73.21 W
Lyons Run ≃	279b	40.25 N	79.43 W
Lyon Station	208	40.28 N	75.45 W
Lyonsville	276	40.57 N	74.25 W
Lypets'ke Druhe	78	47.46 N	29.41 E
Lypova Dolyna	78	50.35 N	33.48 E
Lypovets'	78	49.14 N	29.03 E
Lyptsi	78	50.13 N	36.25 E
Lyracrumpane	48	52.20 N	9.30 W
Lyrestad	40	58.48 N	14.04 E
Lys (Leie) ≃, Europe	50	51.03 N	3.43 E
Lys ≃, It.	62	45.36 N	7.47 E
Lysá ∧	60	49.29 N	12.42 E
Lysa Hora	78	48.11 N	31.06 E
Lysaker	26	59.54 N	10.36 E
Lysá pod Makytou	30	49.12 N	18.13 E
Lysefjorden ⊂[2]	26	59.00 N	6.14 E
Lysekil	26	58.16 N	11.26 E
Lysets'	78	48.52 N	24.36 E
Lyshnivka	78	51.28 N	25.25 E
Łysica ∧	30	50.54 N	20.55 E
Lysina ∧	60	50.02 N	12.37 E
Lysjön ⊜	40	60.07 N	14.18 E
Lyskovo	80	56.04 N	45.02 E
Lysogorka	83	47.42 N	39.12 E
Lyss	58	47.04 N	7.18 E
Lysterfield	274b	37.56 S	145.18 E
Lysterfield ∧[2]	274b	37.56 S	145.16 E
Lysterfield Reservoir ⊜[1]	274b	37.58 S	145.18 E
Lyster Station	206	46.22 N	71.37 W
Lys'va	86	58.07 N	57.47 E
Lys'va ≃	80	58.15 N	54.47 E
Lysyanka	78	49.16 N	30.50 E
Lysychans'k	83	48.55 N	38.26 E
Lysyje Gory	80	51.32 N	44.46 E
Lytham Saint Anne's	44	53.45 N	2.57 W
Lytkarino	82	55.35 N	37.54 E
Lytle	196	29.13 N	98.47 W
Lytle Creek ≃	228	34.09 N	117.23 W
Lyttelton, N.Z.	172	43.35 S	172.42 E
Lyttelton, S. Afr.	158	25.50 S	28.11 E
Lytton	182	50.14 N	121.34 W
Lytton Springs	222	30.00 N	97.37 W
Lytvynivka	83	49.18 N	39.27 E
Lyubar	78	49.55 N	27.44 E
Lyubashivka	78	47.51 N	30.15 E
Lyubech	78	51.42 N	30.39 E
Lyubertsy → L'ubercy	82	55.41 N	37.53 E
Lyubeshiv	78	51.46 N	25.31 E
Lyuboml'	78	51.14 N	24.01 E
Lyubotyn	78	49.57 N	35.57 E
Lyubymivka	78	46.47 N	33.34 E
Lyuten'ka	78	50.13 N	34.02 E
Lyzyne	83	49.33 N	38.51 E
M			
Ma ≃	110	19.47 N	105.56 E
Ma, Oued el ∨, Alg.	148	27.45 N	7.45 W
Ma, Oued el ∨, Maur.	148	24.03 N	9.10 W
Maadid, Djebel ∧	34	35.52 N	4.46 E
Maalaea Bay ⊂	229a	20.47 N	156.29 W
Ma'alot-Tarshiḥa	132	33.01 N	35.17 E
Maam Cross	48	53.27 N	9.31 W
Ma'ān	132	30.12 N	35.44 E
Ma'ān □[8]	132	30.20 N	36.30 E
Maaninka	26	63.09 N	27.18 E
Ma'anshan, Zhg.	100	31.42 N	118.30 E
Maanshan, Zhg.	107	29.52 N	104.59 E
Ma-ao	116	10.29 N	122.59 E
Maap I	174q	9.35 N	138.11 E
Maar	140	6.54 N	31.33 E
Maardu	76	59.28 N	25.02 E
Maarianhamina → Mariehamn	26	60.06 N	19.57 E
Ma'ārik, Qārat al- ∧[2]	142	29.59 N	30.52 E
Ma'arrat an-Nu'mān	130	35.38 N	36.40 E
Ma'arrat Miṣrīn	130	36.01 N	36.40 E

≃	River	Fluß	Río	Rivière	Rio
≍	Canal	Kanal	Canal	Canal	Canal
ʟ	Waterfall, Rapids	Wasserfall, Stromschnellen	Cascada, Rápidos	Chute d'eau, Rapides	Cascata, Rápidos
⋃	Strait	Meeresstraße	Estrecho	Détroit	Estreito
⊂	Bay, Gulf	Bucht, Golf	Bahía, Golfo	Baie, Golfe	Baía, Golfo
⊜	Lake, Lakes	See, Seen	Lago, Lagos	Lac, Lacs	Lago, Lagos
≡	Swamp	Sumpf	Pantano	Marais	Pântano
⊞	Ice Features, Glacier	Eis- und Gletscherformen	Accidentes Glaciales	Formes glaciaires	Acidentes glaciares
≑	Other Hydrographic Features	Andere Hydrographische Objekte	Otros Elementos Hidrográficos	Autres données hydrographiques	Outros acidentes hidrográficos

✣	Submarine Features	Untermeerische Objekte	Accidentes Submarinos	Formes de relief sous-marin	Acidentes submarinos
□	Political Unit	Politische Einheit	Unidad Politica	Entité politique	Unidade política
☗	Cultural Institution	Kulturelle Institution	Institución Cultural	Institution culturelle	Instituição cultural
⊥	Historical Site	Historische Stätte	Sitio Histórico	Site historique	Sitio histórico
♠	Recreational Site	Erholungs- und Ferienort	Sitio de Recreo	Centre de loisirs	Area de Lazer
⊠	Airport	Flughafen	Aeropuerto	Aéroport	Aeroporto
■	Military Installation	Militäranlage	Instalación Militar	Installation militaire	Instalação militar
◆	Miscellaneous	Verschiedenes	Misceláneo	Divers	Diversos

ENGLISH | DEUTSCH

Name	Page	Lat.°′	Long.°′
Ma'arrat Şaydnāyā	132	33.41 N	36.23 E
Maarssen	52	52.08 N	5.08 E
Maas	48	54.50 N	8.22 W
Maas (Meuse) ≃	30	51.49 N	5.01 E
Maasbracht	52	51.08 N	5.53 E
Maasdam	52	51.47 N	4.32 E
Maaseik	56	51.06 N	5.48 E
Maasholm	41	54.41 N	9.59 E
Maasin	116	10.08 N	124.50 E
Maasmechelen	56	50.58 N	5.42 E
Maasniel	52	51.13 N	6.01 E
Maassluis	52	51.55 N	4.15 E
Maastricht	56	50.52 N	5.43 E
Maave	156	21.03 S	34.47 E
Ma-ayon ≃	116	11.25 N	122.46 E
Maba	100	32.59 N	118.48 E
Maba, Ouadi ∨	146	15.10 N	21.00 E
Mababe Depression ⊻[7]	156	18.50 S	24.15 E
Mabaduan	164	9.16 S	142.44 E
Mabaho, Mount ∧	116	9.15 N	125.42 E
Mabaia	152	7.13 S	14.03 E
Mabalacat	116	15.14 N	120.34 E
Mabalane	156	23.37 S	32.31 E
Mabana	224	48.05 N	122.24 W
Mabanga	152	1.30 N	19.06 E
Mabank	222	32.21 N	96.06 W
Mabaoquan	105	40.09 N	115.53 E
Ma'barot	132	32.22 N	34.54 E
Mabaruma	246	8.12 N	59.47 W
Mabashi	268	35.49 N	139.55 E
Mabau	112	2.14 S	111.54 E
Mabay	240p	20.16 N	76.40 W
Mabber, Ras >	144	9.28 N	50.50 E
Mabel Creek	162	29.01 S	134.17 E
Mabeleapodi	156	20.58 S	22.36 E
Mabel Lake ⊜	182	50.35 N	118.44 W
Maben	194	33.33 N	89.05 W
Mabenga-Cité	152	3.39 S	18.40 E
Mabenge	152	4.14 N	24.09 E
Maberry, Loch ⊜	44	55.02 N	4.41 W
Mabeti ≃	92	40.31 N	141.31 E
Mabeul	36	36.27 N	10.46 E
Mabi, Nihon	96	34.38 N	133.41 E
Mabi, Zhg.	100	26.21 N	119.36 E
Mabi, Zhg.	102	35.59 N	112.15 E
Mabian	107	28.48 N	103.41 E
Mabian ≃	107	29.08 N	103.58 E
Mablethorpe	44	53.21 N	0.15 E
Mableton	192	33.49 N	84.34 W
Mabole ≃	150	9.01 N	12.44 W
Maboma	154	2.32 N	28.13 E
Mabonto	150	8.52 N	11.49 W
Mabote	156	22.03 S	34.09 E
Mabou	186	46.05 N	61.22 W
Mabrak, Jabal ∧	132	30.13 N	35.29 E
Mabrous ▼[4]	146	21.13 N	13.38 E
Mabrūk, Lībiyā	146	29.50 N	17.10 E
Mabrūk, Sūd.	140	8.07 N	29.25 E
Mabton	202	46.12 N	119.59 W
Mabuasehube Game Reserve ◈[4]	156	25.10 S	22.10 E
Mabuguai	100	29.49 N	112.42 E
Mabuki	154	2.59 S	33.11 E
Mabuni	174m	26.05 N	127.43 E
Mabwe	154	8.39 S	26.31 E
Mača, Ross.	74	59.54 N	117.35 E
Maca, Ven.	286c	10.28 N	66.48 W
Maca, Cerro ∧	254	45.06 S	73.12 W
Macachín	252	37.09 S	63.39 W
Macaco, Morro do ∧[2]	287a	22.56 S	43.07 W
Macacos, Ilha dos I	250	1.20 S	50.35 W
Macacu ≃	256	22.42 S	43.02 W
Macaé	255	22.23 S	41.47 W
Macaíba	250	5.51 S	35.21 W
Macajalar Bay ⊂	116	8.37 N	124.38 E
Macajuba	255	12.09 S	40.22 W
Macalaya	116	12.53 N	123.46 E
Macalelon	116	13.45 N	122.08 E
Macalister	182	52.27 N	122.24 W
Macalister ≃	166	38.02 S	146.59 E
Macalister, Mount ∧	170	34.27 S	149.45 E
Macallum Lake ⊜	184	55.02 N	108.25 W
Macaloge	154	12.25 S	35.25 E
MacAlpine Lake ⊜	176	66.40 N	103.15 W
Macamic, Lac ⊜	190	48.48 N	78.59 W
Macan, Kepulauan II	112	7.00 S	121.00 E
Macao → Macau, Macau	100	22.14 N	113.35 E
Macão, Port.	34	39.33 N	8.00 W
Macao → Macau □[2]	100	22.10 N	113.33 E
Macapá	250	0.02 N	51.03 W
Macará	246	4.23 S	79.57 W
Macarani	255	15.33 S	40.24 W
Macarao	286c	10.26 N	67.02 W
Macarao ≃	286c	10.26 N	67.01 W
Macareo, Caño ≃[1]	246	9.47 N	61.37 W
Macari ≃	250	1.52 N	50.31 W
MacArthur, Pil.	116	10.50 N	125.00 E
MacArthur, Il., U.S.	278	41.39 N	87.44 W
Macas	246	2.19 S	78.07 W
Macatawa ≃	216	42.48 N	86.05 W
Macatawa, Lake ⊂	216	42.47 N	86.10 W
Macaterick, Loch ⊜	44	55.12 N	4.26 W
Macau, Bra.	250	5.07 S	36.38 W
Macau (Aomen), Macau	100	22.14 N	113.35 E
Macau □[2], Asia	90	22.10 N	113.33 E
Macau □[2], Asia	100	22.10 N	113.33 E
Macau, Ilha I	156	20.55 S	35.05 E
Macauã ≃	248	9.13 S	68.44 W
Macaúbas	255	13.02 S	42.42 W
Macaya, Pic ∧	238	18.25 N	74.00 W
Macaza ≃	206	46.21 N	74.47 W
Maccarese ◈[8]	267a	41.53 N	12.13 E
Maccarese, Bonifica di ◈[1]	267a	41.51 N	12.13 E
Macchiagodena	66	41.33 N	14.24 E
MacClenny	192	30.16 N	82.07 W
Macclesfield, Austl.	168b	35.10 S	138.50 E
Macclesfield, Eng., U.K.	44	53.16 N	2.07 W
Macclesfield □[8]	262	53.17 N	2.15 W
Macclesfield Canal ≡	262	53.24 N	2.03 W
Macclesfield Forest ◈[3]	262	53.15 N	2.03 W
Macdhui, Ben ∧	158	30.39 S	27.58 E
MacDill Air Force Base ■	220	27.51 N	82.29 W
Macdonald ≃	170	33.23 S	150.59 E
Macdonald, Lake ⊜	162	23.30 S	129.00 E
MacDonald Downs	162	22.27 S	135.13 E
Macdonald Lake ⊜	212	45.14 N	78.34 W
MacDonald Pass)(	202	46.34 N	112.18 W
Macdonald Range ⋏	182	49.12 N	114.46 W
MacDonnell Ranges ⋏	162	23.45 S	133.20 E
Macdonnel Peninsula >[1]	168b	35.47 S	138.00 E
MacDowell Lake ⊜	184	52.15 N	92.45 W
Macduff	46	57.40 N	2.29 W
Macdui, Ben ∧	46	57.05 N	3.38 W
Mačecha	80	50.48 N	43.17 E
Maceday Lake ⊜	281	42.42 N	83.26 W
Macedo de Cavaleiros	34	41.32 N	6.58 W
Macedon, Austl.	169	37.25 S	144.34 E
Macedon, N.Y., U.S.	210	43.04 N	77.17 W
Macedonia, Ct., U.S.	207	41.47 N	73.30 W
Macedonia, Oh., U.S.	214	41.18 N	81.30 W
Macedonia □[9]	38	41.00 N	23.00 E
Macedonia □[1], Europe	22	41.50 N	22.00 E
Macedonia (Makedonija) □[1], Europe	38	41.50 N	22.00 E
Macedonia Brook State Park ♦	207	41.47 N	73.29 W
Maceió	250	9.40 S	35.43 W
Maceira	266c	38.52 N	9.19 W
Macenta	150	8.33 N	9.28 W
Maceo	246	6.33 N	74.47 W
Macerata	66	43.18 N	13.27 E
Macerata □[4]	66	43.12 N	13.10 E
Macerata Feltria	66	43.48 N	12.26 E
MacFarlane ≃	176	59.12 N	107.58 W
Macfarlane, Lake ⊜	166	31.55 S	136.42 E
Macfarlane, Mount ∧	172	43.56 S	169.23 E
Macgillycuddy's Reeks ⋏	48	51.55 N	9.45 W
MacGregor	184	49.57 N	98.49 W
Machacamarca	248	18.10 S	67.02 W
Machache ∧	158	29.21 S	27.55 E
Machachi	246	0.30 S	78.34 W
Machačkala	84	42.58 N	47.30 E
Machada, Mata Nacional da ♦	266c	38.36 N	9.02 W
Machadinho ≃	248	9.00 S	61.52 W
Machado	256	21.41 S	45.56 W
Machado ≃, Bra.	248	8.03 S	62.52 W
Machado ≃, Bra.	256	21.38 S	45.52 W
Machadodorp	156	25.40 S	30.14 E
Machagai	252	26.56 S	60.03 W
Machaila	156	22.15 S	32.55 E
Machakos	154	1.31 S	37.16 E
Machala	246	3.16 S	79.58 W
Machalí	252	34.11 S	70.40 W
Machalilla, Parque Nacional ♦	246	1.30 S	80.45 W
Machalino	80	53.05 N	46.14 E
Māchalpur	124	24.08 N	76.18 E
Machaneng	156	23.10 S	27.26 E
Machang, Malay.	114	5.46 N	102.13 E
Machang, Zhg.	98	34.06 N	119.02 E
Machang, Zhg.	98	42.05 N	119.42 E
Machanga	156	20.58 S	34.59 E
Machangcun	105	38.54 N	115.26 E
Machangfu	102	25.14 N	103.45 E
Machang Jianhe ≃	105	39.00 N	117.40 E
Machaquilá ≃	236	16.13 N	90.01 W
Machattie, Lake ⊜	166	24.50 S	139.48 E
Machault	50	49.21 N	4.30 E
Machava	156	25.54 S	32.29 E
Machaze	156	20.51 S	33.26 E
Machecoul	32	47.00 N	1.50 W
Macheke	154	18.05 S	31.51 E
Machekhy	78	49.31 N	34.26 E
Machelen	50	50.55 N	4.26 E
Macheng	100	31.13 N	115.00 E
Macherio	266b	45.38 N	9.16 E
Mācherla	122	16.29 N	79.26 E
Machern	54	51.21 N	12.37 E
Machery	261	48.36 N	2.05 E
Machesna Mountain ∧	226	35.17 N	120.14 W
Machesney Park	216	42.20 N	89.03 W
Māchhīwāra	123	30.55 N	76.12 E
Machhlīshahr	124	25.41 N	82.25 E
Machias, Me., U.S.	188	44.42 N	67.27 W
Machias, N.Y., U.S.	210	42.25 N	78.30 W
Machias ≃	188	44.43 N	67.22 W
Machias Bay ⊂	188	44.40 N	67.20 W
Machichi ≃	184	57.03 N	92.06 W
Machico	148	32.42 N	16.46 W
Machida	94	35.32 N	139.27 E
Machile ≃	154	17.26 S	25.02 E
Machilīpatnam (Bandar)	122	16.10 N	81.08 E
Machindžauri	84	41.40 N	41.43 E
Machiques	246	10.04 N	72.34 W
Machiya ≃	94	35.01 N	136.42 E
Machkund ⊜[1]	122	18.26 N	82.35 E
Machmud-Mekteb	84	44.26 N	45.13 E
Machn'ovo	86	58.27 N	61.42 E
Macho, Arroyo del ∨	196	33.36 N	104.28 W
Machočen, porog ∟	88	57.23 N	121.29 E
Machona, Laguna ⊂	234	18.20 N	93.40 W
Machrihanish	46	55.26 N	5.45 W
Machtaly	85	41.22 N	68.02 E
Machupicchu	248	13.07 S	72.34 W
Machupicchu ⊥	248	13.07 S	72.34 W
Machupo ≃	248	12.34 S	64.25 W
Machynlleth	42	52.35 N	3.51 W
Maciá, Arg.	252	32.10 S	59.23 W
Macia, Moç.	156	25.03 S	33.10 E
Maciel, Arroyo ≃, Ur.	258	33.42 S	57.59 W
Maciel, Arroyo ≃, Ur.	258	33.36 S	56.31 W
Măcin	38	45.15 N	28.08 E
Macina → Massina ◈[1]	150	14.30 N	5.00 W
Macintyre ≃	166	28.38 N	149.41 E
Maçka	130	40.48 N	39.38 E
Mačkassy	80	52.46 N	45.34 E
Mackay, Austl.	166	21.09 S	149.11 E
Mackay, Id., U.S.	202	43.54 N	113.36 W
MacKay ≃	184	57.03 N	111.55 W
Mackay, Lake ⊜	162	22.30 S	129.00 E
MacKay Lake ⊜	176	63.55 N	110.25 W
Mackenrode	54	51.33 N	10.33 E
Mackenzie	246	6.00 N	58.17 W
Mackenzie ≃, Austl.	166	23.38 S	149.46 E
Mackenzie ≃, N.T., Can.	176	69.15 N	134.08 W
MacKenzie Bay ⊂, Ant.	9	68.20 S	71.15 E
Mackenzie Bay ⊂, Can.	180	69.00 N	136.30 W
Mackenzie Delta ≚[2]	180	68.50 N	135.25 W
Mackenzie Mountains ⋏	180	64.00 N	130.00 W
Mackeyville	210	41.03 N	77.28 W
Mackinac, Straits of ⊔	190	45.49 N	84.42 W
Mackinac Bridge ◈[5]	190	45.50 N	84.45 W
Mackinac Island	190	45.50 N	84.37 W
Mackinac Island I	190	45.51 N	84.38 W
Mackinac Island State Park ♦	190	45.52 N	84.40 W
Mackinaw	190	40.32 N	89.21 W
Mackinaw ≃	194	40.33 N	89.44 W
Mackinaw City	190	45.47 N	84.43 W
Mackinnon Road	154	3.44 S	39.03 E
Macklin	184	52.20 N	109.56 W
Mačkovci	61	46.47 N	16.09 E
M'ačkovo, Ross.	82	55.13 N	38.40 E
M'ačkovo, Ross.	82	56.21 N	39.03 E
Macksville, Austl.	166	30.43 S	152.55 E
Macksville, Ks., U.S.	198	38.57 N	98.58 W
Maclean	166	29.28 S	153.13 E
Macleantown	158	32.47 S	27.45 E
Maclear	158	31.02 S	28.23 E
Macleay ≃	166	30.52 S	153.01 E
Macleod	274b	37.43 S	145.04 E
Macleod, Lake ⊜	162	24.00 S	113.35 E
Maclovia Herrera	232	29.05 N	105.08 W
Macmillan ≃	180	62.52 N	135.55 W
Macocolo	152	6.47 S	16.08 E
Macolin	58	47.09 N	7.14 E
Macolla, Punta >	241s	12.06 N	70.13 W
Macolo	152	7.05 S	16.48 E
Macomb	190	40.27 N	90.40 W
Macomb □[6]	214	42.40 N	82.54 W
Macomb Mall ◈[9]	281	42.32 N	82.55 W
Macomer	71	40.16 N	8.47 E
Macomia	154	12.15 S	40.08 E
Macon, Bel.	50	50.03 N	4.13 E
Mâcon, Fr.	58	46.18 N	4.50 E
Macon, Ga., U.S.	192	32.50 N	83.37 W
Macon, Il., U.S.	219	39.42 N	88.59 W
Macon, Ms., U.S.	194	33.06 N	88.33 W
Macon, Mo., U.S.	194	39.44 N	92.28 W
Macon □[6], Il., U.S.	219	39.51 N	89.32 W
Macon □[6], Mo., U.S.	219	39.50 N	92.20 W
Macon, Bayou ≃	194	31.55 N	91.33 W
Macon Creek ≃	216	41.58 N	83.38 W
Macondo	152	12.35 S	23.44 E
Macondo ≃	152	13.23 S	23.03 E
Mâconnais, Monts du ⋏	58	46.18 N	4.45 E
Macorís, Cabo >	238	19.47 N	70.28 W
Macosquin	48	55.06 N	6.43 W
Macossa	156	17.52 S	33.56 E
Macouba, Pointe de >	240e	14.53 N	61.09 W
Macoun Lake ⊜	184	56.32 N	103.50 W
Macoupin □[6]	219	39.17 N	89.53 W
Macoupin Creek ≃	219	39.11 N	90.36 W
Macovane	156	21.28 S	35.04 E
Macpherson, Mount ∧[2]	162	21.49 S	121.35 E
Macquarie ≃, Austl.	166	41.44 S	147.08 E
Macquarie ≃, Austl.	166	30.07 S	147.24 E
Macquarie, Lake ⊜	170	33.05 S	151.35 E
Macquarie Fields	274a	33.59 S	150.53 E
Macquarie Harbour ⊂	166	42.19 S	145.23 E
Macquarie Island I	9	54.30 S	158.56 E
Macquarie Marshes ⩸	166	30.50 S	147.32 E
Macquarie Pass National Park ♦	170	34.34 S	150.39 E
Macquarie Ridge ✦[3]	9	57.00 S	159.00 E
Macquarie University ʊ[2]	274a	33.46 S	151.06 E
MacRitchie Reservoir ⊜[1]	271c	1.21 N	103.50 E
Mac. Robertson Land ◈[1]	9	68.10 S	65.00 E
Macrohon	116	10.05 N	124.56 E
Macroom	48	51.54 N	8.57 W
Mactan Island I	116	10.18 N	123.58 E
MacTier	212	45.08 N	79.47 W
Macuco de Minas	256	21.46 S	44.47 W
Macucuau ≃	246	0.37 S	61.24 W
Macuelizo	236	15.18 N	88.31 W
Macugnaga	58	45.58 N	7.58 E
Macujer	246	0.23 N	72.55 W
Macul	286e	33.30 S	70.34 W
Maculabo Island I	116	14.24 N	122.49 E
Macumba ≃	162	27.52 S	137.12 E
Macungie	208	40.30 N	75.33 W
Macunqiao	100	33.50 N	116.13 E
Macuro	246	10.39 N	61.56 W
Macusani	248	14.05 S	70.26 W
Macuspana	234	17.46 N	92.36 W
Macusse	152	17.51 S	20.21 E
Macuto	286c	10.37 N	66.53 W
Macuze	156	17.42 S	37.11 E
Macy	216	40.57 N	86.07 W
Mad ≃, On., Can.	212	44.25 N	79.54 W
Mad ≃, Ca., U.S.	204	40.57 N	124.07 W
Mad ≃, N.Y., U.S.	212	43.20 N	75.44 W
Mad ≃, Oh., U.S.	188	39.46 N	84.11 W
Mad ≃, Vt., U.S.	188	44.18 N	72.41 W
Mada ≃	150	7.59 N	7.55 E
Ma'dabā	132	31.43 N	35.48 E
Madagascar (Madagasikara) □[1], Afr.	138	19.00 S	46.00 E
Madagascar (Madagasikara) □[1], Afr.	157b	19.00 S	46.00 E
Madagascar Basin ✦[1]	12	27.00 S	53.00 E
Madagascar Plateau ✦[3]	10	30.00 S	45.00 E
Madagasikara → Madagascar □[1]	157b	19.00 S	46.00 E
Madagaskar → Madagascar □[1]	157b	19.00 S	46.00 E
Madagiz	84	40.19 N	46.44 E
Madagoi, Bohol ∨	144	0.44 N	42.56 E
Madā'in Şāliḥ	128	26.48 N	37.53 E
Madajevo	80	54.48 N	44.31 E
Madama	146	21.58 N	13.39 E
Madame, Isle I	186	45.33 N	61.02 W
Madan	38	41.30 N	24.57 E
Madanapalle	122	13.33 N	78.30 E
Madang, Pap. N. Gui.	164	5.15 S	145.50 E
Madang, Zhg.	100	29.58 N	116.40 E
Madang □[5]	164	5.00 S	145.30 E
Madanpur	272b	22.40 N	88.32 E
Madanpur Dabās ◈[8]	272a	28.43 N	77.02 E
Madaoua	150	14.05 N	5.58 E
Mādār Gāng ≃[1]	126	22.12 N	89.04 E
Mādāri Hāt	124	26.42 N	89.17 E
Mādārīpur	124	23.10 N	90.12 E
Madarounfa	150	13.18 N	7.09 E
Mādārpur	272b	22.54 N	88.27 E
Madau Island I	164	8.58 S	152.28 E
Madawaska, On., Can.	212	45.30 N	77.59 W
Madawaska, Me., U.S.	186	47.21 N	68.19 W
Madawaska ≃	212	45.27 N	76.21 W
Madawaska Highlands ⋏[1]	212	45.15 N	77.35 W
Madawaska Lake ⊜	212	45.20 N	78.23 W
Madaxmaroodi	144	2.39 N	44.36 E
Madaya, Mya.	110	22.13 N	96.07 E
Maḍāyā, Sūrīy.	132	33.41 N	36.06 E
Madbar	140	6.19 N	30.40 E
Mad Creek ≃	210	42.55 N	77.59 W
Maddalena, Colle della (Col de Larche))(	62	44.25 N	6.53 E
Maddalena, Isola I	71	41.14 N	9.25 E
Maddaloni	68	41.02 N	14.23 E
Maddela	116	16.21 N	121.41 E
Madden, Mount ∧	162	33.12 S	119.51 E
Maddington	168a	32.03 S	115.59 E
Maddock	198	47.57 N	99.31 W
Maddy, Loch ⊂	46	57.36 N	7.08 W
Made	52	51.41 N	4.46 E
Madeir	140	7.50 N	29.12 E
Madeira	218	39.11 N	84.21 W
Madeira I	148	32.44 N	17.00 W
Madeira ≃	242	3.22 S	58.45 W
Madeira, Arquipélago da II	148	32.40 N	16.45 W
Madeira Beach	220	27.48 N	82.48 W
Madeirinha ≃	248	8.31 S	60.46 W
Madeirinha, Paraná ≃[1]	246	3.25 S	58.51 W
Mädelegabel ∧	58	47.18 N	10.18 E
Madeleine, Îles de la II	186	47.30 N	61.45 W
Madeleine, Pointe >	275a	45.27 N	73.57 W
Madeleine-Centre	186	49.15 N	65.21 W
Madeley, Eng., U.K.	42	52.59 N	2.20 W
Madeley, Eng., U.K.	42	52.39 N	2.28 W
Madelia	190	44.03 N	94.25 W
Madeline Island I	190	46.50 N	90.40 W
Maden, Tür.	130	38.23 N	39.40 E
Maden, Tür.	130	40.11 N	40.25 E
Madenijet	86	47.53 N	78.37 E
Madera, Méx.	232	29.12 N	108.07 W
Madera, Ca., U.S.	226	36.57 N	120.03 W
Madera, Pa., U.S.	214	40.49 N	78.26 W
Madera □[6]	226	37.15 N	119.45 W
Madera Canal ≡	226	37.05 N	119.59 W
Madera Lake ⊜[1]	226	37.02 N	119.59 W
Madera Peak ∧	226	37.32 N	119.23 W
Maderas, Islas → Madeira, Arquipélago da II	148	32.40 N	16.45 W
Maderas, Volcán ∧[1]	236	11.27 N	85.31 W
Maderno	64	45.38 N	10.35 E
Madgaon (Margao)	122	15.18 N	73.57 E
Madh ◈[8]	272c	19.08 N	72.47 E
Madhepura	124	25.55 N	86.47 E
Madhkūr, Bi'r ▼[4]	142	30.42 N	32.32 E
Mādhopur	123	32.22 N	75.36 E
Madhubani	124	26.22 N	86.05 E
Madhudaha	272b	22.31 N	88.25 E
Madhugiri	122	13.40 N	77.12 E
Madhumati ≃[1]	126	22.53 N	89.52 E
Madhupar	126	22.54 N	86.28 E
Madhupur	126	24.16 N	86.39 E
Madhya Bhārat Pathār ◈[1]	124	25.00 N	77.00 E
Madhyamgrām	272b	22.42 N	88.27 E
Madhya Pradesh □[3]	118	23.00 N	79.00 E
Madia	154	7.08 S	26.00 E
Madian	106	32.15 N	119.58 E
Madibi	152	4.18 S	18.24 E
Madibira	154	8.12 S	34.49 E
Madibogo	158	26.25 S	25.10 E
Madida	98	42.57 N	130.48 E
Madidi ≃	248	12.32 S	66.52 W
Madill	196	34.05 N	96.46 W
Madimba, Ang.	152	6.31 S	14.21 E
Madimba, R.D.C.	152	4.58 S	15.08 E
Madina	150	13.24 N	8.51 W
Madina do Boé	150	11.45 N	14.13 W
Madinani	150	9.37 N	6.57 W
Madinat al-Abyār	146	32.11 N	20.36 E
Madīnat ash-Sha'b (Al-Ittihad)	144	12.50 N	44.56 E
Madīnat ath Thawrah	130	35.52 N	38.34 E
Madine, Lac de ⊜	56	48.54 N	5.42 E
Madingo	152	4.07 S	11.22 E
Madingou	152	4.09 S	13.34 E
Madingzi	104	42.08 N	120.52 E
Madi Opei	154	3.37 N	33.05 E
Madirobe	157b	16.04 S	46.15 E
Madirovalo	157b	16.26 S	46.30 E
Madison, Al., U.S.	194	34.41 N	86.44 W
Madison, Ca., U.S.	226	38.41 N	121.58 W
Madison, Ct., U.S.	207	41.16 N	72.35 W
Madison, Fl., U.S.	192	30.28 N	83.24 W
Madison, Ga., U.S.	192	33.35 N	83.28 W
Madison, Il., U.S.	219	38.40 N	90.09 W
Madison, In., U.S.	218	38.44 N	85.22 W
Madison, Ks., U.S.	198	38.08 N	96.08 W
Madison, Me., U.S.	188	44.47 N	69.52 W
Madison, Md., U.S.	208	38.30 N	76.13 W
Madison, Mn., U.S.	198	45.00 N	96.11 W
Madison, Mo., U.S.	219	39.28 N	92.12 W
Madison, Ne., U.S.	198	41.49 N	97.27 W
Madison, N.J., U.S.	210	40.45 N	74.25 W
Madison, N.Y., U.S.	210	42.53 N	75.30 W
Madison, N.C., U.S.	192	36.23 N	79.57 W
Madison, Oh., U.S.	214	41.46 N	81.03 W
Madison, Pa., U.S.	279b	40.15 N	79.41 W
Madison, S.D., U.S.	198	44.00 N	97.06 W
Madison, Va., U.S.	188	38.22 N	78.15 W
Madison, W.V., U.S.	188	38.04 N	81.49 W
Madison, Wi., U.S.	216	43.04 N	89.24 W
Madison □[6], Il., U.S.	219	38.49 N	89.58 W
Madison □[6], In., U.S.	218	40.10 N	85.41 W
Madison □[6], N.Y., U.S.	210	43.05 N	75.42 W
Madison □[6], Oh., U.S.	218	39.53 N	83.27 W
Madison □[6], Tx., U.S.	222	30.58 N	95.55 W
Madison ≃	202	45.56 N	111.30 W
Madison, West Fork ≃	202	44.55 N	111.35 W
Madisonburg, Oh., U.S.	214	40.51 N	81.55 W
Madisonburg, Pa., U.S.	210	40.55 N	77.31 W
Madison Heights, Mi., U.S.	216	42.29 N	83.06 W
Madison Heights, Va., U.S.	192	37.25 N	79.07 W
Madison Mills	218	39.40 N	83.20 W
Madison-on-the-Lake	214	41.42 N	81.24 W
Madison Park	276	40.26 N	74.19 W
Madison Range ⋏	202	45.15 N	111.20 W
Madison Square Garden ♦	276	40.45 N	74.00 W
Madisonville, Ky., U.S.	194	37.19 N	87.29 W
Madisonville, La., U.S.	194	30.24 N	90.09 W
Madisonville, Tn., U.S.	192	35.31 N	84.21 W
Madisonville, Tx., U.S.	222	30.56 N	95.54 W
Madiun	115a	7.37 S	111.31 E
Madiun ≃	115a	7.23 S	111.27 E
Madiyi	102	28.14 N	110.30 E
Madjingo	152	1.23 N	14.06 E
Madjoari	150	11.26 N	1.15 E
Madley, Mount ∧	162	24.31 S	123.58 E
Madoc	212	44.30 N	77.28 W
Mado Gashi	154	0.44 N	39.10 E
Madoi	102	34.53 N	98.24 E
Madol	140	9.02 N	27.46 E
Madon ≃	58	48.36 N	6.06 E
Madona	76	56.51 N	26.13 E
Madonie ⋏	70	37.52 N	13.58 E
Madonna (Unserfrau)	64	46.43 N	10.52 E
Madonna della Guardia ʊ[1]	62	44.29 N	8.51 E
Madonna della Quercia ʊ[1]	66	42.25 N	12.06 E
Madonna dell'Olmo	62	44.25 N	7.32 E
Madonna del Sasso ʊ[1]	58	46.11 N	8.33 E
Madonna di Campiglio	64	46.14 N	10.49 E
Madonna di Tirano	64	46.13 N	10.09 E
Madora	76	53.09 N	30.11 E
Madougou	150	14.24 N	3.05 W
Madrakah	144	21.59 N	39.59 E
Madrakah, Ra's al- >	118	19.00 N	57.50 E
Madras → Chennai, India	122	13.05 N	80.17 E
Madras, Or., U.S.	202	44.38 N	121.07 W
Madras → Tamil Nādu □[3]	122	11.00 N	78.15 E
Madre, Laguna ⊂, Méx.	232	25.00 N	97.40 W
Madre, Laguna ⊂, Tx., U.S.	196	27.00 N	97.35 W
Madre, Sierra ⋏	116	16.20 N	122.00 E
Madre de Chiapas, Sierra ⋏	232	15.30 N	92.35 W
Madre de Deus de Minas	256	21.29 S	44.20 W
Madre de Dios □[5]	248	12.00 S	70.15 W
Madre de Dios ≃	248	10.23 S	65.24 W
Madre de Dios, Isla I	254	50.15 S	75.05 W
Madre del Sur, Sierra ⋏	234	17.00 N	100.00 W
Madre Occidental, Sierra ⋏	232	25.00 N	105.00 W
Madre Oriental, Sierra ⋏	232	22.00 N	99.30 W
Madre Vieja ≃	236	14.01 N	91.26 W
Madrid, Col.	246	4.44 N	74.16 W
Madrid, Esp.	34	40.24 N	3.41 W
Madrid, Esp.	266a	40.24 N	3.41 W
Madrid, Pil.	116	9.15 N	126.00 E
Madrid, Al., U.S.	194	31.02 N	85.23 W
Madrid, Ia., U.S.	190	41.52 N	93.49 W
Madrid, Ne., U.S.	198	40.51 N	101.32 W
Madrid □[3]	34	40.30 N	3.40 W
Madridejos, Esp.	34	39.28 N	3.32 W
Madridejos, Pil.	116	11.18 N	123.44 E
Madrigalejo	34	39.09 N	5.37 W
Madrillon	284c	38.55 N	77.14 W
Madriz □[5]	236	13.30 N	86.30 W
Madroñera	34	39.26 N	5.46 W
Madruga	240p	22.55 N	81.51 W
Madrūsah	146	24.48 N	14.32 E
Madsen	184	50.58 N	93.55 W
Madsūs, Bi'r ▼[4]	142	29.15 N	32.19 E
Maducang Island I	116	10.42 N	120.15 E
Maduda	152	4.55 S	13.06 E
Maduo	152	1.24 S	20.44 E
Madura, Austl.	162	31.55 S	127.00 E
Madura → Madurai, India	122	9.56 N	78.07 E
Madura I	115a	7.00 S	113.20 E
Madura, Selat ⊔	115a	7.25 S	113.25 E
Madurai	122	9.56 N	78.07 E
Madurāntakam	122	12.31 N	79.54 E
Madureira, Serra de ⋏	287a	22.49 S	43.31 W
Maduru ≃	122	7.52 N	81.31 E
Madwar al-Bighāl ∧[2]	142	29.09 N	29.54 E
Madžalis	84	42.08 N	47.50 E
Mãe, Ilha da I	287a	22.59 S	43.04 W
Maeander Reef ✦[2]	116	8.05 N	119.18 E
Maebaru	92	33.33 N	130.12 E
Maebashi	94	36.23 N	139.04 E
Maeda	270	34.55 N	135.08 E
Mãe dos Homens	256	22.52 S	46.37 W
Maegye-ri	98	34.45 N	126.18 E
Mae Hong Son	110	19.16 N	97.56 E
Mae Klong ≃	110	13.21 N	100.00 E
Maenclochog	42	51.54 N	4.48 W
Maengsan	98	39.40 N	126.30 E
Maeno ◈[8]	268	35.46 N	139.42 E
Maenza	66	41.31 N	13.11 E
Mae Ramat	110	16.58 N	98.31 E
Mae Rim	110	18.54 N	98.57 E
Maerkansu	85	39.19 N	73.53 E
Ma'erna	102	31.13 N	102.02 E
Maer Shan ∧	102	26.18 N	100.20 E
Mae Sariang	110	18.10 N	97.56 E
Maeser	200	40.28 N	109.35 W
Mae Sot	110	16.43 N	98.34 E
Maesteg	42	51.37 N	3.40 W
Maestra, Sierra ⋏	240p	20.00 N	76.45 W
Maestre de Campo Island I	116	12.56 N	121.42 E
Maestu	34	42.44 N	2.27 W
Mae Tha	110	18.28 N	99.08 E
Maevarano ≃	157b	14.35 S	47.58 E
Maevatanana	157b	16.56 S	46.49 E
Maéwo I	175f	15.10 S	168.10 E
Ma'fan	146	25.55 N	14.29 E
Mafang	105	40.02 N	117.01 E
Mafangchang	107	29.24 N	106.06 E
Mafangcun	105	40.09 N	116.24 E
Ma Faro ✦[2]	122	5.50 N	73.26 E
Mafeking	184	52.41 N	101.06 W
Mafembage	152	14.32 S	21.42 E
Mafengtun	104	40.49 N	122.54 E
Mafeteng	158	29.51 S	27.15 E
Maffliers	261	49.05 N	2.19 E
Maffra	166	37.58 S	146.59 E
Mafia Channel ⊔	154	8.10 S	39.40 E
Mafia Island I	154	7.50 S	39.50 E
Mafikeng	156	25.53 S	25.39 E
Mafou ≃	150	10.32 N	10.08 W
Mafra, Bra.	252	26.07 S	49.49 W
Mafra, Port.	34	38.56 N	9.20 W
Magadan	74	59.34 N	150.48 E
Magadi	154	1.54 S	36.17 E
Magadi, Lake ⊜	154	1.52 S	36.17 E
Magaguadavic Lake ⊜	186	45.43 N	67.12 W
Magai-butsu ʊ[1]	96	33.05 N	131.45 E
Magalhães Bastos ◈[8]	287a	22.53 S	43.23 W
Magalhães de Almeida	250	3.24 S	42.12 W
Magaliesberg ⋏	158	25.50 S	27.30 E
Magallanes → Punta Arenas, Chile	254	53.09 S	70.55 W
Magallanes, Pil.	116	12.50 N	123.50 E
Magallanes, Estrecho de (Strait of Magellan) ⊔	254	54.00 S	71.00 W
Magallanes y de la Antártica Chilena □[4]	254	53.00 S	72.00 W
Maganga	154	0.51 N	26.22 E
Magangué	246	9.14 N	74.45 W
Magansk	88	55.52 N	93.15 E
Maganuy ≃	116	6.55 N	124.30 E
Magara, India	126	22.34 N	87.34 E
Mağara, Tür.	130	36.43 N	33.52 E
Magaramkent	84	41.37 N	48.21 E
Magaria	150	13.00 N	8.54 E
Magat ≃	116	17.02 N	121.49 E
Magazine Mountain ∧	194	35.10 N	93.38 W
Magazzolo ≃	70	37.25 N	13.15 E
Magboro	273a	6.43 N	3.24 E
Magburaka	150	8.43 N	11.57 W
Magdagači	89	53.27 N	125.48 E
Magdalena, Arg.	258	35.04 S	57.32 W
Magdalena, Bol.	248	13.20 S	64.08 W
Magdalena, Méx.	234	20.55 N	103.57 W
Magdalena, Perú	248	6.21 S	77.49 W
Magdalena, Perú	286d	12.06 S	77.05 W
Magdalena, N.M., U.S.	200	34.07 N	107.14 W
Magdalena □[5]	246	10.00 N	74.00 W
Magdalena ≃, Col.	246	11.06 N	74.51 W
Magdalena ≃, Méx.	232	30.48 N	112.32 W
Magdalena, Bahía ⊂	232	24.35 N	112.00 W
Magdalena, Isla I, Chile	254	44.40 S	73.10 W
Magdalena, Isla I, Méx.	232	24.55 N	112.15 W
Magdalena, Punta >	246	3.56 N	77.21 W
Magdalena Contreras ◈[8]	286a	19.18 N	99.17 W
Magdalena de Kino	232	30.38 N	110.57 W
Magdalena Peñasco	234	17.14 N	97.34 W
Magdalena Teitipac	234	16.54 N	96.34 W
Magdalena Tequisistlán	234	16.22 N	95.15 W
Magdalen Laver	260	51.45 N	0.11 E
Magdeburg	54	52.07 N	11.38 E
Magdeburger Börde ≚	54	52.00 N	11.30 E
Magdeburgo → Magdeburg	54	52.07 N	11.38 E
Magdiwang	116	12.30 N	122.31 E
Magdonskij, porog ∟	88	57.45 N	100.55 E
Māge	110	26.33 N	98.33 E
Magé □[7]	287a	22.41 S	43.07 W
Magee	194	31.52 N	89.44 W
Magee, Island >[1]	48	54.49 N	5.42 W
Magelang	115a	7.28 S	110.13 E
Magellan, Strait of → Magallanes, Estrecho de ⊔	254	54.00 S	71.00 W
Magellan-Strasse → Magallanes, Estrecho de ⊔	254	54.00 S	71.00 W
Magén	132	31.18 N	34.26 E
Magenta	62	45.28 N	8.53 E
Magenta, Lake ⊜	162	33.26 S	119.10 E
Magerøy I	24	71.03 N	25.45 E
Magetan	115a	7.39 S	111.20 E
Magezhuang	105	40.08 N	117.59 E
Maggia	58	46.15 N	8.42 E
Maggia ≃	58	46.09 N	8.48 E
Maggia, Valle ∨	58	46.17 N	8.40 E
Maggie Creek ≃	204	40.43 N	116.05 W
Maggiorasca, Monte ∧	62	44.33 N	9.29 E
Maggiore ≃	267a	41.54 N	12.16 E
Maggiore, Lago ⊜	36	46.00 N	8.40 E
Maggiore, Monte ∧	68	41.14 N	14.12 E
Maghāghah	142	28.39 N	30.50 E
Maghama	150	15.31 N	12.51 W
Maghar	132	32.53 N	35.24 E
Maghdūshah	132	33.31 N	35.23 E
Maghera	48	54.51 N	6.40 W
Magherafelt	48	54.45 N	6.36 W
Maghniyya	148	34.50 N	1.50 W
Magholpur ◈[8]	272a	28.42 N	77.06 E
Maghull	44	53.32 N	2.57 W
Magician Lake ⊜	216	42.04 N	86.10 W
Magic Mountain ♦	228	34.26 N	118.36 W
Magic Reservoir ⊜[1]	202	43.17 N	114.23 W
Magill, Lac ⊜	206	45.35 N	71.17 W
Magill Heights	279b	40.37 N	79.52 W
Magill Lake ⊜	184	54.45 N	94.58 W
Maginu	268	35.35 N	139.36 E
Magione	66	43.08 N	12.12 E
Magisano	68	39.01 N	16.37 E
Magiscatzín	234	22.48 N	98.42 W
Magiss Lake ⊜	184	52.59 N	91.40 W
Maglaj	38	44.33 N	18.06 E
Magliana ◈[8]	267a	41.50 N	12.25 E
Magliana, Fosso ≃	267a	41.49 N	12.25 E
Magliano dei Marsi	66	42.05 N	13.22 E
Magliano in Toscana	66	42.36 N	11.17 E
Magliano Sabina	66	42.22 N	12.29 E
Maglie	68	40.07 N	18.19 E
Maglód	264c	47.27 N	19.21 E
M'aglovo	265a	59.53 N	30.41 E
Magnago	266b	45.35 N	8.48 E
Magnanville	261	48.58 N	1.41 E
Magnet	184	51.19 N	99.30 W
Magnetawan ≃	190	45.46 N	80.37 W
Magnetic Island I	166	19.08 S	146.50 E
Magnetic Springs	214	40.21 N	83.16 W
Magnetischer Nordpol → North Magnetic Pole ◈	16	77.19 N	101.49 W
Magnetischer Südpol → South Magnetic Pole ◈	9	65.18 S	139.30 E
Magnières	58	48.27 N	6.34 E
Magnitka	86	55.21 N	59.43 E
Magnitogorsk	86	53.27 N	59.04 E
Magnitostroj	80	51.43 N	53.05 E
Magnolia, Ar., U.S.	194	33.16 N	93.14 W
Magnolia, De., U.S.	208	39.04 N	75.28 W
Magnolia, Ma., U.S.	283	42.35 N	70.43 W
Magnolia, Mn., U.S.	198	43.38 N	96.04 W
Magnolia, Ms., U.S.	194	31.08 N	90.27 W
Magnolia, N.J., U.S.	285	39.51 N	75.02 W
Magnolia, Oh., U.S.	214	40.39 N	81.17 W
Magnolia, Tx., U.S.	222	30.13 N	95.45 W
Magnor	26	59.57 N	12.12 E
Magny-en-Vexin	50	49.09 N	1.47 E
Magny-le-Hongre	261	48.52 N	2.49 E
Magny-les-Hameaux	261	48.44 N	2.04 E
Mago	89	53.15 N	140.13 E
Magog	206	45.16 N	72.09 W
Magog ≃	206	45.24 N	71.54 W
Magog, Lake ⊜	206	45.18 N	72.03 W
Magoito	266c	38.52 N	9.26 W
Magome ◈[8]	268	35.35 N	139.43 E
Mago National Park ♦	144	5.30 N	36.15 E
Magonoy	116	6.54 N	124.33 E
Magoro	154	1.44 N	34.06 E
Magothy Bay ⊂	208	37.10 N	75.55 W
Magothy River ⊂	208	39.04 N	76.28 W
Magoúla	267c	38.04 N	23.32 E
Magoye	154	16.00 S	27.37 E
Magozal, Méx.	232	21.34 N	97.59 W
Magozal, Méx.	234	21.34 N	97.59 W
M'agozero	76	60.21 N	34.50 E
Magpie	186	50.19 N	64.30 W
Magpie ≃, On., Can.	190	47.56 N	84.50 W
Magpie ≃, P.Q., Can.	186	50.19 N	64.27 W
Magpie, Lac ⊜	186	51.00 N	64.41 W
Magpie Ouest ≃	186	51.02 N	64.42 W
Magra	126	22.59 N	88.22 E
Magra ≃	64	44.03 N	9.58 E
Magra Hāt	126	22.14 N	88.23 E
Magrath	182	49.25 N	112.52 W
Magrè (Margreid)	64	46.17 N	11.12 E
Magro ≃	34	39.11 N	0.25 W
Magruder Mountain ∧	204	37.25 N	117.33 W
Magsaysay (Linugos)	116	9.01 N	125.11 E
Magsingal	116	17.41 N	120.25 E
Magstadt	56	48.45 N	8.58 E
Magu ≃	250	2.56 S	41.55 W
Maguan	102	22.59 N	104.19 E
Maguanying	271a	39.52 N	116.17 E
Maguari, Cabo >	250	0.18 S	48.22 W
Magude	156	25.02 S	32.40 E
Magudu	158	27.31 S	31.40 E
Magueyes	196	25.44 N	97.47 W
Maguindanao □[4]	116	6.55 N	124.20 E
Magumeri	146	12.08 N	12.50 E
Māgura	124	23.29 N	89.25 E
Maguru	150	12.28 N	6.35 E
Maguse Lake ⊜	176	61.40 N	95.10 W
Maguzhan	120	31.15 N	88.00 E
Magway, Mya.	110	20.09 N	94.55 E
Magway, Mya.	110	20.30 N	94.30 E
Magwe	154	4.08 N	32.17 E
Magwood Park ♦	275b	43.39 N	79.30 W
Magyarország → Hungary □[1]	30	47.00 N	20.00 E
Mahābād	128	36.45 N	45.43 E
Mahābaleshwar	122	17.55 N	73.40 E
Mahabe	157b	17.05 S	45.20 E
Mahābhārat Lek ⋏	124	27.40 N	84.30 E
Mahabo, Madag.	157b	23.40 S	46.08 E
Mahabo, Madag.	157b	20.23 S	44.40 E
Mahād	122	18.05 N	73.25 E
Mahadday Weyn	144	2.58 N	45.32 E
Mahādebpur	126	23.51 N	89.53 E
Mahādeo Hills ⋏[2]	122	22.22 S	78.34 E
Mahādeo Range ⋏	122	17.50 N	74.15 E
Mahaffey	214	40.52 N	78.43 W
Mahagi	154	2.18 N	30.59 E
Mahagi Port	154	2.09 N	31.14 E
Mahai	102	38.17 N	94.13 E
Mahaica-Berbice □[4]	246	6.20 N	57.50 W
Mahaicony Village	246	6.36 N	57.48 W
Mahajamba ≃	157b	15.33 S	47.08 E
Mahajamba, Helodranon' i ⊂	157b	15.24 S	47.05 E
Mahājan	123	28.47 N	73.50 E
Mahajanga	157b	15.43 S	46.19 E
Mahajanga □[4]	157b	17.00 S	46.00 E
Mahajilo ≃	157b	19.42 S	45.22 E
Maḥajjah	132	32.57 N	36.14 E
Mahākālī □[8]	124	29.30 N	80.30 E
Mahākālī (Sārda) ≃	124	27.21 N	81.23 E
Mahakam ≃	112	0.35 S	117.17 E
Mahālandi	126	24.04 N	88.07 E
Mahalatswe	156	23.05 S	26.51 E
Mahalla el-Kubra → Al-Maḥallah al-Kubrā	142	30.58 N	31.10 E
Maḥallāt	128	33.55 N	50.27 E
Maḥallat Kayl	142	31.01 N	30.17 E
Maḥallat Marḥūm	142	30.48 N	30.57 E
Maḥallat Minūf	142	30.53 N	30.58 E
Maḥallat Zayyād	142	31.02 N	31.14 E
Maham	124	28.59 N	76.18 E
Mahamba	158	27.07 S	31.10 E
Mahānadi ≃	118	20.19 N	86.45 E
Mahānadpati	126	23.00 N	88.16 E
Mahānanda ≃	124	24.29 N	88.18 E
Mahanay Island I	116	10.12 N	124.14 E
Mahanoro	157b	19.54 S	48.48 E
Mahanoy City	208	40.48 N	76.08 W
Mahanoy Creek ≃	208	40.42 N	76.51 W
Mahantango Creek ≃	208	40.47 N	76.56 W
Mahantango Mountain ∧	208	40.40 N	76.45 W
Mahao	89	43.10 N	127.59 E
Mahape	272c	19.07 N	73.01 E
Mahārājganj, India	124	26.07 N	84.29 E
Mahārājganj, India	124	27.09 N	83.34 E
Mahārājpur, India	124	25.01 N	79.44 E
Mahārājpur, India	272a	28.39 N	77.20 E
Mahārāshtra □[3]	122	19.00 N	76.00 E
Maḥārīq, Wādī ∨	142	27.48 N	31.47 E
Mahārlū, Daryācheh-ye ⊜	128	29.25 N	52.50 E
Mahāsamund	120	21.06 N	82.06 E
Maha Sarakham	110	16.11 N	103.18 E
Maha Sawat, Khlong ≡	269a	13.47 N	100.28 E
Mahasoa	157b	22.12 S	46.06 E
Mahasolo	157b	19.07 S	46.22 E
Mahates	246	10.14 N	75.12 W
Mahatsinjo	157b	21.26 S	45.51 E
Maḥaṭṭat al-Ḥafīf	132	32.12 N	37.08 E
Mahaut	240d	15.21 N	61.25 W
Mahavavy ≃, Madag.	157b	15.57 S	45.54 E
Mahavavy ≃, Madag.	157b	13.00 S	48.55 E

Symbols in the index entries represent the broad categories identified in the key at the right. Symbols with superior numbers (⋏[1]) identify subcategories (see complete key on page *I · 1).*

Symbole im Register stellen die rechts im Schlüssel erklärten Kategorien dar. Symbole mit hochgestellten Ziffern (⋏[1]) bezeichnen Unterabteilungen einer Kategorie (vgl. vollständiger Schlüssel auf Seite *I · 1).*

Los símbolos incluídos en el texto del índice representan las grandes categorías identificadas con la clave a la derecha. Los símbolos con numeros en su parte superior (⋏[1]) identifican las subcategorías (véase la clave completa en la página *I · 1).*

Les symboles de l'index représentent les catégories indiquées dans la légende à droite. Les symboles suivis d'un indice (⋏[1]) représentent des sous-catégories (voir légende complète à la page *I · 1).*

Os símbolos incluídos no texto do índice representam as grandes categorias identificadas com a chave à direita. Os símbolos com números em sua parte superior (⋏[1]) identificam as subcategorias (veja-se a chave completa à página *I · 1).*

English	Deutsch	Español	Français	Português
∧ Mountain	Berg	Montaña	Montagne	Montanha
⋏ Mountains	Gebirge	Montañas	Montagnes	Montanhas
)(Pass	Paß	Paso	Col	Passo
∨ Valley, Canyon	Tal, Cañon	Valle, Cañón	Vallée, Canyon	Vale, Canhão
≚ Plain	Ebene	Llano	Plaine	Planície
> Cape	Kap	Cabo	Cap	Cabo
I Island	Insel	Isla	Île	Ilha
II Islands	Inseln	Islas	Îles	Ilhas
⊻ Other Topographic Features	Andere Topographische Objekte	Otros Elementos Topográficos	Autres données topographiques	Outros acidentes topográficos

Maha-Malo I · 105

ESPAÑOL

Nombre	Página	Lat. °′	Long. °′ W = Oeste
Mahaweli ≃	122	8.27 N	81.13 E
Mahaxai	110	17.25 N	105.12 E
Maḥbas, Wādī al- V	140	15.50 N	29.45 E
Mahbūbābād	122	17.37 N	80.01 E
Mahbūbnagar	122	16.44 N	77.59 E
Mahd adh-Dhahab	128	23.30 N	40.52 E
Mahdalynivka	78	48.55 N	34.54 E
Mahdāt, Bi'r al- ⊤[4]	142	30.44 N	32.32 E
Mahdia, Guy.	246	5.16 N	59.09 W
Mahdia, Tun.	148	35.30 N	11.04 E
Mahe	122	11.42 N	75.32 E
Mahébourg	157c	20.24 S	57.42 E
Mahé Island I	138	4.40 S	55.28 E
Mahendraganj	124	25.20 N	89.45 E
Mahendragarh	124	28.17 N	76.09 E
Mahendra Giri ∧	122	18.58 N	84.21 E
Mahendranagar	124	28.52 N	80.17 E
Mahenge, Tan.	154	7.38 S	36.16 E
Mahenge, Tan.	154	8.41 S	36.43 E
Maheno	172	45.10 S	170.50 E
Maheriv	78	50.08 N	23.43 E
Mahesāna	120	23.36 N	72.24 E
Mahesgādi	272b	22.39 N	88.33 E
Maheshmunda	126	24.13 N	86.24 E
Maheshtala	272b	22.30 N	88.15 E
Maheshwar	120	22.11 N	75.35 E
Mahespur	124	23.21 N	88.55 E
Mahgawān	124	26.29 N	78.37 E
Mahi ≃	120	22.16 N	72.58 E
Mahia Peninsula ➤[1]	172	39.10 S	177.53 E
Mahiāri	272b	22.35 N	88.14 E
Māhikpur	272b	22.32 N	88.14 E
Mahilāra	126	22.56 N	90.16 E
Mahilëu̯	76	53.54 N	30.21 E
Mahilëu̯ □[8]	76	53.45 N	30.30 E
Māhīm ⊸[8]	272c	19.03 N	72.49 E
Māhīm ≃	272c	19.03 N	72.51 E
Māhīm Bay C	272c	19.02 N	72.50 E
Mahina, Mali	150	13.46 N	10.51 W
Mahina, Poly. fr.	174s	17.31 S	149.30 W
Mahinerangi, Lake ⊜	172	45.51 S	169.57 E
Mahinog	116	9.09 N	124.47 E
Mahīshādal	126	22.11 N	87.59 E
Mahishdānga	272b	22.54 N	88.11 E
Mahlabatini	158	28.14 S	31.30 E
Mahlangasi	158	27.37 S	31.42 E
Mahlberg	58	48.17 N	7.48 E
Mahlow	54	52.22 N	13.24 E
Mahlsdorf	54	52.47 N	11.13 E
Mahlsdorf ⊸[8]	264a	52.31 N	13.37 E
Mahlsdorf-Süd ⊸[8]	264a	52.29 N	13.36 E
Mahmūdābād, India	124	27.18 N	81.07 E
Maḥmūdābād, Īrān	128	36.38 N	52.15 E
Maḥmūd-e Rāqī	120	35.01 N	69.20 E
Maḥmūdīyah, Tur'at al- ≋	142	31.11 N	29.53 E
Mahmudiye	130	39.30 N	31.00 E
Mahmūdpur, India	272a	28.46 N	77.22 E
Mahmudpur, India	272b	22.41 N	88.09 E
Mahmutbey ⊸[8]	267b	41.03 N	28.49 E
Mahmutşevketpaşa	130	41.05 N	29.19 E
Mahmutşevketpaşa ⊸[8]	267b	41.09 N	29.11 E
Mahnomen	198	47.18 N	95.58 W
Mahoba	124	25.17 N	79.52 E
Mahogany Mountain ∧	202	43.14 N	117.16 W
Mahomet	216	40.11 N	88.24 W
Mahone Bay	186	44.27 N	64.23 W
Mahone Bay C	186	44.30 N	64.15 W
Mahoning □[6]	214	41.06 N	80.39 W
Mahoning ≃	214	40.58 N	80.23 W
Mahoning, West Branch ≃	214	41.12 N	80.57 W
Mahoning Creek ≃	214	40.55 N	79.27 W
Mahoning Creek Lake ⊜[1]	214	40.50 N	79.10 W
Mahony Lake ⊜	180	65.30 N	125.20 W
Mahood Falls	182	51.50 N	120.39 W
Mahood Lake ⊜	182	51.55 N	120.24 W
Mahopac	210	41.22 N	73.44 W
Mahopac Falls	210	41.22 N	73.46 W
Mahora	34	39.13 N	1.44 W
Mahoras Brook ≃	276	40.25 N	74.08 W
Mahrāt, Jabal ⋏[1]	144	17.05 N	51.30 E
Mahrauli ⊸[8]	272a	28.31 N	77.11 E
Mahrauni	124	24.35 N	78.43 E
Mähren → Morava □[9]	30	49.20 N	17.00 E
Mahres	148	34.32 N	10.30 E
Mähring	60	49.55 N	12.32 E
Mahuiling	100	29.24 N	115.48 E
Māhul ⊸[8]	272c	19.01 N	72.53 E
Mahulia	126	22.39 N	86.24 E
Mahur Island I	164	2.50 S	152.40 E
Mahuta	154	10.52 S	39.27 E
Mahuva	120	21.05 N	71.48 E
Mahwa	124	27.03 N	76.56 E
Mahwah	276	41.06 N	74.09 W
Mahwah ≃	276	41.06 N	74.10 W
Mai, Île de I	275a	45.36 N	73.50 W
Maia, Am. Sam.	174y	14.13 S	169.28 W
Maia, Port.	34	41.14 N	8.37 W
Mai Aini	144	14.47 N	39.06 E
Maiala National Park ♠	171a	27.19 S	152.46 E
Maianga	152	14.12 S	21.45 E
Maiano	64	46.11 N	13.04 E
Maiauatá	250	1.51 S	49.02 W
Maicao	246	11.23 N	72.13 W
Maîche	58	47.15 N	6.48 E
Maichen	102	20.29 N	109.59 E
Maici ≃	248	6.30 S	61.43 W
Maicuru ≃	250	2.14 S	54.17 W
Maida	68	38.51 N	16.22 E
Maidan ♠	272b	22.33 N	88.21 E
Maiden	192	35.34 N	81.12 W
Maidenhead	42	51.32 N	0.44 W
Maiden Newton	42	50.46 N	2.35 W
Maidstone, Austl.	274b	37.47 S	144.52 E
Maidstone, On., Can.	214	42.13 N	82.53 W
Maidstone, Sk., Can.	184	53.06 N	109.18 W
Maidstone, Eng., U.K.	42	51.17 N	0.32 E
Maidstone □[8]	260	51.17 N	0.35 E
Maiduguri	146	11.51 N	13.10 E
Maie	154	2.46 N	30.34 E
Maiella, Montagna della ⋏	66	42.05 N	14.07 E
Maienfeld	58	47.00 N	9.32 E
Maierato	68	38.42 N	16.11 E
Maifeld ⊸[1]	56	50.20 N	7.20 E
Maigatari	150	12.46 N	9.27 E
Maignelay	50	49.33 N	2.31 E
Maigo	116	8.10 N	123.57 E
Mai Gudo ∧	144	7.29 N	37.12 E
Maigue ≃	48	52.39 N	8.48 W
Maihar	124	24.16 N	80.45 E
Maihara	94	35.19 N	136.17 E
Maijoma	196	28.55 N	104.21 W
Maikala Plateau ⋏[1]	124	22.30 N	81.00 E
Maikala Range ⋏	122	22.30 N	81.30 E
Maikammer	56	49.18 N	8.08 E
Maiko ≃	154	0.14 N	25.33 E
Maiko, Parc National de la ♠	154	0.30 S	27.45 E
Maikoor, Pulau I	164	6.15 S	134.15 E
Mailand → Milano	62	45.28 N	9.12 E
Mailāni	124	28.17 N	80.21 E
Mailasqui	256	23.33 S	47.04 W
Maili	229c	21.25 N	158.10 W
Maillane	62	43.50 N	4.47 E
Mailley-et-Chazelot	58	47.32 N	6.03 E
Maillezais	32	46.22 N	0.44 W
Mailly-le-Camp	50	48.40 N	4.13 E
Mailly-le-Château	50	47.36 N	3.38 E
Mailly-Maillet	50	50.04 N	2.36 E
Mailsi	123	29.48 N	72.11 E
Maimbung	116	5.56 N	121.02 E

FRANÇAIS

Nom	Page	Lat. °′	Long. °′ W = Ouest
Mai Mefales	144	14.59 N	38.16 E
Mā'īn	132	31.41 N	35.44 E
Main ≃, Dtsch.	30	50.00 N	8.18 E
Main ≃, N. Ire., U.K.	48	54.43 N	6.18 W
Maināguri	124	26.34 N	88.49 E
Mainau	58	47.42 N	9.11 E
Mainbernheim	56	49.43 N	10.13 E
Mainburg	60	48.38 N	11.47 E
Main Camp	174o	2.01 N	157.25 W
Main Canal ≋, Ca., U.S.	226	37.25 N	121.05 W
Main Canal ≋, Ca., U.S.	226	37.23 N	120.26 W
Main Canal ≋, Wa., U.S.	224	47.07 N	120.44 W
Main Channel ⊔	190	45.22 N	81.50 W
Maincourt-sur-Yvette	261	48.43 N	1.58 E
Main Creek ≃	276	40.34 N	74.11 W
Maincy	261	48.33 N	2.42 E
Mai-Ndombe, Lac ⊜	152	2.00 S	18.20 E
Main-Donau-Kanal ≋	60	49.02 N	11.36 E
Main Duck Island I	212	43.56 N	76.37 W
Maine	210	42.11 N	76.03 W
Maine □[9]	32	48.15 N	0.05 W
Maine □[3], U.S.	178	45.15 N	69.15 W
Maine □[3], U.S.	188	45.15 N	69.15 W
Maine ≃	48	52.09 N	9.45 W
Maine, Gulf of C	178	43.00 N	68.00 W
Maine-et-Loire □[5]	32	47.25 N	0.30 W
Mainesburg	210	41.47 N	77.07 W
Maïné-Soroa	146	13.12 N	12.02 E
Maineville	218	39.18 N	84.13 W
Mainguerin	261	48.32 N	1.51 E
Mainhardt	56	49.04 N	9.33 E
Mainit	116	9.32 N	125.32 E
Mainit, Lake ⊜	116	9.26 N	125.32 E
Mainland	285	40.15 N	75.22 W
Mainland I, Scot., U.K.	46	59.00 N	3.15 W
Mainland I, Scot., U.K.	46a	60.16 N	1.16 W
Mainleus	54	50.06 N	11.22 E
Mainoru	164	14.02 S	134.05 E
Mainpuri	124	27.14 N	79.01 E
Main Range National Park ♠	171a	28.01 S	152.22 E
Maintal	56	50.09 N	8.54 E
Maintenon	50	48.35 N	1.35 E
Maintirano	157b	18.03 S	44.01 E
Main Topsail ∧	186	49.08 N	56.33 W
Mainvilliers	50	48.27 N	1.28 E
Mainz	56	50.01 N	8.16 E
Maio I	150a	15.15 N	23.10 W
Maiolati Spontini	66	43.28 N	13.06 E
Maiori	68	40.39 N	14.38 E
Maiori, Nuraghe ⊥	71	40.56 N	9.06 E
Maipa	164	8.21 S	146.33 E
Maipo ≃	252	33.37 S	71.39 W
Maipo, Volcán ∧[1]	252	34.10 S	69.50 W
Maipú, Arg.	252	36.52 S	57.52 W
Maipú, Arg.	252	32.58 S	68.47 W
Maipú, Chile	252	33.31 S	70.46 W
Maiqihamiao	89	43.22 N	120.46 E
Maiquetía	246	10.36 N	66.57 W
Maira ≃	62	44.49 N	7.38 E
Maira, Valle V	62	44.30 N	7.08 E
Mairābāri	120	26.28 N	92.26 E
Mairi	250	11.43 S	40.08 W
Mairinque	256	23.33 S	47.10 W
Mairiporã	256	23.19 S	46.35 W
Mairiporã □[7]	287b	23.24 S	46.37 W
Mairipotaba	255	17.18 S	49.28 W
Maisach	60	48.13 N	11.16 E
Maisaka	94	34.41 N	137.37 E
Maishi	100	29.11 N	113.58 E
Maišiagala	76	54.52 N	25.04 E
Maiskhāl Island I	120	21.36 N	91.56 E
Maison de Pierre, Lac de la ⊜	206	46.53 N	74.42 W
Maisonneuve, Parc ♠	275a	45.33 N	73.34 W
Maisons-Alfort	261	48.48 N	2.26 E
Maisons-Laffitte	50	48.57 N	2.09 E
Maisons-Laffitte, Château de ⊥	261	48.57 N	2.09 E
Maisse	50	48.24 N	2.23 E
Maissin	56	49.58 N	5.11 E
Maitani	270	34.49 N	135.22 E
Maitengwe	156	20.06 S	27.13 E
Maitengwe ≃	156	19.59 S	26.26 E
Maithon Reservoir ⊜[1]	126	23.50 N	86.43 E
Maitland, Austl.	168b	34.22 S	137.40 E
Maitland, Austl.	170	32.44 S	151.33 E
Maitland, N.S., Can.	186	45.19 N	63.30 W
Maitland, On., Can.	212	44.38 N	75.37 W
Maitland, Fl., U.S.	220	28.37 N	81.21 W
Maitland ≃	190	43.45 N	81.43 W
Maitland, Lake ⊜	162	27.11 S	121.03 E
Maitri ʋ[3]	9	70.46 S	11.44 E
Maixie	100	27.38 N	115.29 E
Maíz ≃	236	11.17 N	83.52 W
Maíz, Islas del II	236	12.15 N	83.00 W
Maizefield	158	26.28 S	29.31 E
Maizhokunggar	120	29.50 N	91.45 E
Maizières-lès-Metz	56	49.13 N	6.09 E
Maizières-lès-Vic	58	48.43 N	6.46 E
Maizuru	96	35.28 N	135.24 E
Maja ≃, Ross.	74	60.24 N	134.30 E
Maja ≃, Ross.	89	54.31 N	134.41 E
Majābirah, Minqār al- ≛[4]	142	30.16 N	29.49 E
Majačnyj	86	52.41 N	55.44 E
Majadahonda	266a	40.29 N	3.52 W
Majagua	240p	21.55 N	79.00 W
Majagual	246	8.33 N	74.38 W
Majalaya	115a	7.03 S	107.45 E
Majalengka	115a	6.50 S	108.13 E
Majana, Ensenada de C	240p	22.41 N	82.45 W
Majanji	154	0.15 N	33.59 E
Majari ≃	246	3.29 N	60.58 W
Majayjay	116	14.09 N	121.28 E
Majchura	85	39.02 N	68.35 E
Majdantal	85	43.41 N	68.02 E
Majd el Kurūm	132	32.55 N	35.15 E
Majé	256	22.39 S	43.02 W
Majeigha	140	11.33 N	24.40 E
Majenang	115a	7.18 S	108.45 E
Majene	112	3.33 S	118.57 E
Majenica	216	40.46 N	85.27 W
Majevica ⋏	38	44.30 N	18.55 E
Maji	144	6.11 N	35.38 E
Majia	100	32.32 N	118.50 E
Majia ≃	98	38.09 N	117.53 E
Majiacun	106	30.08 N	119.58 E
Majiahe	102	35.20 N	104.46 E
Majian, Zhg.	100	29.19 N	119.36 E
Majian, Zhg.	100	29.43 N	120.00 E
Majiang, Zhg.	102	23.48 N	111.09 E
Majiang, Zhg.	110	26.28 N	107.28 E
Majiangzong	120	30.27 N	90.03 E
Majiaoba	102	32.14 N	104.35 E
Majiaping	102	36.31 N	103.20 E
Majiasi	105	39.03 N	117.05 E
Majiawopu	104	41.46 N	121.06 E
Majiayan	100	27.26 N	112.56 E
Majiazhai	104	42.22 N	124.04 E
Majiazhou	100	26.46 N	114.47 E
Majidun Creek ≃	273a	6.38 N	3.28 E
Majie, Zhg.	102	23.50 N	105.07 E
Majie, Zhg.	102	25.03 N	103.45 E
Majin	100	29.18 N	118.24 E
Majin ≃	100	29.00 N	118.21 E
Majinzhuangzi	104	41.55 N	123.53 E
Maji Shan I	106	31.26 N	120.06 E
Majītha	123	31.46 N	74.57 E
Majja	74	61.44 N	130.18 E
Majkain	86	51.27 N	75.52 E
Majkop	84	44.35 N	40.07 E
Majkor	85	59.01 N	55.54 E
Majli-Saj	85	41.17 N	72.29 E

PORTUGUÊS

Nome	Página	Lat. °′	Long. °′ W = Oeste
Majlispur	126	24.13 N	90.53 E
Majlybas	86	45.49 N	62.39 E
Majmak	85	42.40 N	71.15 E
Majna, Ross.	80	54.07 N	47.37 E
Majna, Ross.	86	53.00 N	91.28 E
Majnan	272b	22.59 N	88.09 E
Majnic, ozero ⊜	180	63.15 N	176.40 E
Majno-Gytkino	180	63.36 N	176.30 E
Majŏn-ni, C.M.I.K.	98	39.06 N	127.07 E
Majŏn-ni, Taehan	271b	37.36 N	126.41 E
Major, Puig ∧	34	39.48 N	2.48 E
Majorca → Mallorca I	34	39.30 N	3.00 E
Major Creek ≃	169	36.51 S	145.05 E
Major Isidoro	250	9.32 S	37.00 W
Majorque, Île → Mallorca I	34	39.30 N	3.00 E
Majrūr	140	14.01 N	30.27 E
Majrūr, Wādī V	140	15.44 N	26.26 E
Majseevičy	76	53.13 N	28.17 E
Majsk	86	57.49 N	77.16 E
Majskij, Ross.	83	47.43 N	40.03 E
Majskij, Ross.	84	43.38 N	44.04 E
Majskij, Ross.	89	52.18 N	129.38 E
Majskij, Ross.	89	49.00 N	140.10 E
Majskoje, Kaz.	86	50.55 N	78.15 E
Majskoje, Ross.	82	56.08 N	37.55 E
Majtan	86	45.46 N	74.20 E
Majtobe	85	43.01 N	70.35 E
Māju	126	22.37 N	88.05 E
Majuba Hill ⊥	158	27.28 S	29.51 E
Majuqiao	105	39.46 N	116.32 E
Majuro I[1]	14	7.09 N	171.12 E
Majuzigou	104	41.49 N	121.38 E
Maka	150	13.40 N	14.17 W
Makabana	152	2.48 S	12.29 E
Makabe	94	36.16 N	140.06 E
Makadasa ≃	116	7.22 N	124.36 E
Makaha, Hi., U.S.	229c	21.28 N	158.13 W
Makaha, Zimb.	154	17.17 S	32.37 E
Makaha Point ➤	229b	22.08 N	159.44 W
Makah Bay C	224	48.19 N	124.40 W
Makah Indian Reservation ⊸[4]	224	48.20 N	124.41 W
Makahuena Point ➤	229b	21.52 N	159.27 W
Makak	152	3.33 N	11.02 E
Makala	273b	4.25 S	15.17 E
Makalamabedi	156	20.19 S	23.51 E
Makale	112	3.06 S	119.51 E
Makallé	252	27.13 S	59.17 W
Makālu ∧	124	27.54 N	87.06 E
Makamba	154	4.08 S	29.49 E
Makanapur	272a	28.38 N	77.21 E
Makanči	86	46.48 N	82.00 E
Makanya	154	4.20 S	37.51 E
Makanza	152	1.36 N	19.07 E
Makaoo Indian Reserve ⊸[4]	184	53.40 N	110.02 W
Makapu Point ➤	174v	18.59 S	169.56 W
Makapuu Head ➤	229c	21.19 N	157.39 W
Makarakomburu, Mount ∧	175e	9.43 S	160.02 E
Makarakskij	86	55.36 N	88.03 E
Makarapan Mountain ∧	246	4.00 N	58.51 W
Makarewa	172	46.20 S	168.21 E
Makari	146	12.35 N	14.28 E
Makar-Ib	24	63.39 N	49.24 E
Makaricha	24	66.15 N	58.20 E
Makariv	78	50.28 N	29.49 E
Makarje	80	58.35 N	48.11 E
Makarjev	80	57.52 N	43.48 E
Makarjevo	80	56.06 N	45.06 E
Makarov	89	48.38 N	142.48 E
Makarovo, Ross.	80	52.18 N	43.20 E
Makarovo, Ross.	82	54.22 N	36.40 E
Makarovo, Ross.	88	57.29 N	107.52 E
Makarska	36	43.18 N	17.02 E
Makasar → Ujungpandang	112	5.07 S	119.24 E
Makasar, Selat (Makassar Strait) ⊔	112	2.00 S	117.30 E
Makaševka	80	51.30 N	42.36 E
Makassar Strait → Makasar, Selat ⊔	112	2.00 S	117.30 E
Makasuko	154	6.00 S	34.56 E
Makat	80	47.39 N	53.19 E
Makatea I	14	15.50 S	148.15 W
Makati	269f	14.34 N	121.02 E
Makaw, Mya.	110	26.27 N	96.42 E
Makaw, R.D.C.	152	3.29 S	18.19 E
Makawao	229a	20.51 N	156.18 W
Makaweli	229b	21.55 N	159.38 W
Makay, Massif du ⋏	157b	21.15 S	45.15 E
Makaya	152	3.22 S	18.02 E
Makedonija → Macedonia □[1]	38	41.50 N	22.00 E
Makefu	174v	18.59 S	169.55 W
Makemie Park	208	37.55 N	75.34 W
Makemo I[1]	14	16.35 S	143.40 W
Makena	229a	20.39 N	156.27 W
Makeni	150	8.53 N	12.03 W
Makere	154	4.17 S	30.25 E
Maketu	172	37.46 S	176.27 E
Makeyevka → Makiyivka, Ukr.	83	48.02 N	37.58 E
Makeyevka → Makiyivka, Ukr.	83	48.02 N	37.58 E
Makgadikgadi ≚	156	20.45 S	25.30 E
Makgadikgadi Pans Game Reserve ⊸[4]	156	20.30 S	24.45 E
Makhachkala → Machačkala	84	42.58 N	47.30 E
Makhad	123	33.08 N	71.44 E
Makhaleng ≃	158	30.20 S	27.23 E
Mākhālpur	272b	22.56 N	88.10 E
Makham	110	12.40 N	102.12 E
Makhdūmnagar	124	26.28 N	82.46 E
Makhfar al-Quwayrah	132	29.48 N	35.19 E
Makhfar Ramn	132	29.42 N	35.25 E
Makhrūq, Wādī al- V	132	31.30 N	37.10 E
Makhyah, Wādī V	144	17.40 N	49.01 E
Maki, Indon.	164	3.11 S	134.14 E
Maki, Nihon	92	37.45 N	138.53 E
Maki, Nihon	94	37.05 N	138.23 E
Maki, Nihon	270	34.52 N	135.04 E
Makika, Lua ≛[6]	229a	20.34 N	156.34 W
Makikihi	172	44.38 S	171.09 E
Makilala	116	6.55 N	125.05 E
Makindu	154	2.17 S	37.49 E
Makino, Nihon	94	35.28 N	136.05 E
M'akino, Ross.	265b	55.48 N	37.22 E
Makinsk	86	52.37 N	70.26 E
Makio-dam ⊸[6]	94	35.50 N	137.36 E
Makioka	94	35.45 N	138.43 E
Makira □[4]	175e	11.00 S	162.30 E
Makira Harbour C	175e	10.25 S	161.29 E
M'akiševo	76	56.34 N	28.53 E
M'akit	74	61.24 N	152.09 E
Makiyivka, Ukr.	78	50.40 N	31.50 E
Makiyivka, Ukr.	83	49.14 N	37.59 E
Makiyivka, Ukr.	83	48.02 N	37.58 E
Makkah (Mecca)	144	21.27 N	39.49 E
Makkavejevo	88	51.44 N	113.58 E
Makkum	52	53.04 N	5.24 E
Makó, Magy.	30	46.13 N	20.29 E
Mako, Sén.	150	12.52 N	12.21 W
Makoaneng ∧	158	29.47 S	28.57 E
Makobe Lake ⊜	190	47.27 N	80.25 W
Makoka	154	2.34 S	25.29 E
Makok-ni	271b	37.43 N	126.38 E
Makokou	152	0.34 N	12.52 E
Makoli	154	17.27 S	26.05 E
Makongai Island I	175g	17.27 S	178.58 E
Makongo	154	3.25 N	26.22 E
Makongolosi	154	8.24 S	33.09 E
Makopse	84	43.59 N	39.13 E
Makorako	172	39.09 S	176.02 E
Makoro	154	3.08 N	29.44 E
Makoshika State Park ♠	198	47.03 N	104.41 W
Makoshyne	78	51.27 N	32.18 E
Makotuku	172	40.07 S	176.14 E
Makoua	152	0.01 N	15.39 E
Makov	30	49.23 N	18.30 E
Makovskoje	86	58.12 N	90.52 E
Maków Mazowiecki	30	52.52 N	21.06 E
Maków Podhalański	30	49.44 N	19.41 E
Makrai	124	22.04 N	77.06 E
Makrampur	126	22.44 N	90.14 E
Makrāna	120	27.03 N	74.43 E
Makran Coast ≛[2]	128	25.15 N	61.00 E
Makrany	78	51.50 N	24.14 E
M'aksa	76	58.54 N	38.12 E
Maksaticha	76	57.48 N	35.53 E
Maksimicha	88	53.15 N	108.43 E
Maksimkin Jar	86	58.42 N	86.48 E
Maksimovka, Ross.	80	52.59 N	51.10 E
Maksimovka, Ross.	89	46.04 N	137.51 E
Maksimovo	82	56.20 N	35.58 E
Maksudangarh	124	24.03 N	77.15 E
Maksymovychi	78	51.13 N	29.37 E
Maktar	148	35.51 N	9.12 E
Maktau	154	3.24 S	38.08 E
Mākū, Īrān	128	39.17 N	44.31 E
Maku, Zhg.	105	39.33 N	114.46 E
Makuhari	268	35.39 N	140.03 E
Makuliro	154	9.35 S	37.26 E
Makumbako	154	8.51 S	34.50 E
Makumbi	152	5.51 S	20.41 E
Makung (P'enghu)	100	23.34 N	119.34 E
Makunudu I	122	6.25 N	72.41 E
Makunudu Atoll I[1]	122	6.20 N	72.36 E
Makuragi-san ∧	96	35.32 N	133.08 E
Makurazaki	92	31.16 N	130.19 E
Makurdi	150	7.45 N	8.32 E
Makushin Volcano ∧[1]	180	53.53 N	166.50 W
Makušino	86	55.13 N	67.13 E
Makuyuni	154	3.33 S	36.06 E
Makwa Lake ⊜	184	54.04 N	109.15 W
Makwassie	158	27.26 S	26.00 E
Makwende-Bayo	154	7.08 S	28.06 E
Makwiro	154	17.58 S	30.28 E
Māl, India	124	26.52 N	88.44 E
Mal, Maur.	150	16.58 N	13.23 W
Mala, Perú	248	12.39 S	76.38 W
Malå, Sve.	26	65.11 N	18.44 E
Mala ≃	248	12.40 S	76.41 W
Mala, Punta ➤	246	7.28 N	80.00 W
Malabang	116	7.38 N	124.03 E
Malabar, Austl.	274a	33.58 S	151.15 E
Malabar, Fl., U.S.	220	28.00 N	80.33 W
Malabar Coast ≛[2]	122	11.00 N	75.00 E
Malabar Farm State Park ♠	214	40.38 N	82.25 W
Malabar Hill ∧[2]	272c	18.57 N	72.48 E
Malabar Point ➤	272c	18.57 N	72.47 E
Mala Bilozirka	78	47.14 N	34.56 E
Malabo	152	3.45 N	8.47 E
Mal Abrigo	258	34.09 S	56.57 W
Malabrigo Point ➤	116	13.36 N	121.15 E
Malabuyoc	116	9.39 N	123.19 E
Malaca, Estrecho de → Malacca, Strait of ⊔	110	2.30 N	101.20 E
Malacacheta	255	17.50 S	42.05 W
Malacañang Palace ʋ	269f	14.36 N	120.59 E
Malacatepec, Volcán ∧[1]	286a	19.10 N	99.16 W
Malacca, Strait of ⊔	110	2.30 N	101.20 E
Malachovka	82	55.39 N	38.00 E
Malachovo, Ross.	82	54.45 N	37.27 E
Malachovo, Ross.	82	54.22 N	37.31 E
Malachovskij	80	49.08 N	41.43 E
Malacky	30	48.27 N	17.00 E
Mālād ⊸[8]	272c	19.11 N	72.51 E
Malad ≃	200	41.35 N	112.07 W
Malad City	202	42.11 N	112.15 W
Malad Creek ≃	272c	19.08 N	72.48 E
Mala Divytsya	78	50.41 N	32.10 E
Maladzečna	76	54.19 N	26.49 E
Malafede ≃	267a	41.47 N	12.24 E
Málaga, Col.	246	6.42 N	72.44 W
Málaga, Esp.	34	36.43 N	4.25 W
Malaga, Ca., U.S.	226	36.42 N	119.46 W
Malaga, N.J., U.S.	208	39.34 N	75.02 W
Malaga, N.M., U.S.	196	32.13 N	104.04 W
Málaga □[4]	34	36.50 N	4.40 W
Malagarasi	154	5.06 S	30.50 E
Malagarasi ≃	154	5.12 S	29.47 E
Malagash	186	45.46 N	63.23 W
Malagasy Republic → Madagascar □[1]	157b	19.00 S	46.00 E
Malago ≃	116	10.55 N	123.02 E
Malagón	34	39.10 N	3.51 W
Malagrotta ⊸[8]	66	41.53 N	12.20 E
Mal'agurt	80	57.39 N	52.32 E
Malahat	224	48.32 N	123.34 W
Malahide	48	53.27 N	6.09 W
Mălăiești	38	46.59 N	29.33 E
Malaimbandy	157b	20.20 S	45.36 E
Malaisie → Malaysia □[1]	112	2.30 N	112.30 E
Malaita □[4]	175e	9.00 S	161.00 E
Malaita I	175e	9.00 S	161.00 E
Malaja Bessergenovka	83	47.09 N	38.36 E
Malaja Borščovka	82	56.33 N	36.53 E
Malaja Bykovka	80	51.54 N	47.45 E
Malaja Čuja ≃	88	58.56 N	112.13 E
Malaja Doroginka	82	54.06 N	38.56 E
Malaja Dubna	82	55.52 N	38.58 E
Malaja Istra ≃	82	55.54 N	36.50 E
Malaja Ižmora	80	53.32 N	42.48 E
Malaja Jekaterinovka	80	51.26 N	44.17 E
Malaja Kinel' ≃	80	53.29 N	51.30 E
Malaja Kokšaga ≃	80	56.09 N	47.53 E
Malaja Konkudera ≃	88	57.26 N	112.37 E
Malaja Kuril'skaja Gr'ada (Habomai-Shotō) II	92a	43.30 N	146.10 E
Malaja Laba ≃	84	44.16 N	40.53 E
Malaja Neva ≃[1]	265a	59.57 N	30.15 E
Malaja Ochta ⊸[8]	265a	59.56 N	30.24 E
Malaja Orlovka	80	47.18 N	41.24 E
Malaja Pera	24	64.11 N	54.47 E
Malaja Serdoba	80	52.28 N	44.56 E
Malaja Sestra ≃	82	56.17 N	35.57 E
Malaja Višera	76	58.51 N	32.14 E
Malaka → Melaka	114	2.12 N	102.15 E
Malaka, Sempitan ⊔	114	5.44 N	95.30 E
Malakāl	140	9.31 N	31.39 E
Malākand	123	34.34 N	71.56 E
Mala Kapela ⋏	36	44.50 N	15.30 E
Malakka, Strasse von → Malacca, Strait of ⊔	110	2.30 N	101.20 E
Malakoff, Fr.	261	48.49 N	2.19 E
Malakoff, Tx., U.S.	222	32.10 N	96.00 W
Malakpur ⊸[8]	272a	28.42 N	77.12 E
Malakula □[8]	175f	16.20 S	167.20 E
Malakula I	175f	16.15 S	167.30 E
Malakwāl	123	32.34 N	73.13 E
Malala	164	5.15 S	147.10 E
Malalag	116	6.36 N	125.24 E
Malalbergo	64	44.43 N	11.32 E
Malamala	112	3.21 S	120.55 E
Mala Mala Game Reserve ⊸[4]	156	24.52 S	31.30 E
Malamaui Island I	116	6.44 N	121.58 E
Malambo	246	10.52 N	74.47 W
Malambo, Arroyo ≃	258	33.43 S	58.46 W
Malambunga	116	9.02 N	117.38 E
Malamocco	64	45.22 N	12.20 E
Malampaya Sound ⊔	116	10.51 N	119.20 E
Malān	110	25.37 N	96.21 E
Malān, Rās ➤	128	25.18 N	65.11 E
Malanao Island I	116	9.27 N	118.37 E
Malanas ≃	116	17.41 N	120.43 E
Mālancha	272b	22.55 N	88.26 E
Mālancha ≃[1]	126	21.40 N	89.20 E
Mālandighi	126	23.33 N	87.24 E
Malandji	152	5.56 S	22.18 E
Malang	115a	7.59 S	112.37 E
Malang, Gunung ∧	115a	7.02 S	107.01 E
Malangali	154	8.34 S	34.51 E
Malangas	116	7.37 N	123.01 E
Malanggwā	124	26.52 N	85.34 E
Malangka, Tanjung ➤	112	1.20 N	120.48 E
Malan Guan)(	105	40.16 N	117.39 E
Malanipa Island I	116	6.53 N	122.16 E
Malanje	152	9.32 S	16.20 E
Malanje □[5]	152	9.30 S	16.30 E
Malanut Bay C	116	9.16 N	117.59 E
Malanville	150	11.52 N	3.23 E
Malanyu	105	40.11 N	117.42 E
Malanzán	252	30.48 S	66.37 W
Mała Panew ≃	30	50.44 N	17.52 E
Malapantao, Mount ∧	116	9.54 N	122.37 E
Malapardis Brook ≃	276	40.49 N	74.25 W
Mälaren ⊜	40	59.30 N	17.12 E
Malargüe	252	35.28 S	69.35 W
Mälar-See → Mälaren ⊜	40	59.30 N	17.12 E
Malartic	190	48.08 N	78.08 W
Malartic, Lac ⊜	190	48.15 N	78.07 W
Malaryta	78	51.47 N	24.05 E
Malasia → Malaysia □[1]	112	2.30 N	112.30 E
Malasiqui	116	15.55 N	120.25 E
Malaspina	254	44.56 S	66.54 W
Malaspina Glacier ⊓	180	59.50 N	140.30 W
Malaspina Strait ⊔	182	49.44 N	124.20 W
Malassis	261	48.38 N	2.03 E
Malāṭīyah	142	28.42 N	30.51 E
Mala Tokmachivka	78	47.32 N	35.54 E
Malatya	130	38.21 N	38.19 E
Malatya □[4]	130	38.30 N	38.10 E
Malau	175f	15.10 S	166.48 E
Malaucène	62	44.10 N	5.08 E
Malaunay	50	49.32 N	1.02 E
Malaut	123	30.13 N	74.29 E
Malavalli	122	12.23 N	77.05 E
Mala Vyska	78	48.39 N	31.38 E
Malawali, Pulau I	116	7.03 N	117.18 E
Malawi □[1], Afr.	138	13.30 S	34.00 E
Malawi □[1], Afr.	154	13.30 S	34.00 E
Malawi, Lake → Nyasa, Lake ⊜	154	12.00 S	34.30 E
Malawiya	140	15.16 N	36.12 E
Malaya → Semenanjung Malaysia □[9]	114	4.00 N	102.00 E
Malayagiri ∧	120	21.23 N	85.16 E
Malayal	116	7.12 N	121.57 E
Malaybalay	116	8.09 N	125.05 E
Malāyer	128	34.17 N	48.50 E
Malay Peninsula ➤[1]	110	6.00 N	101.00 E
Malay Reef ✣[2]	166	17.59 S	149.18 E
Malaysia □[1], Asia	108	2.30 N	112.30 E
Malaysia □[1], Asia	112	2.30 N	112.30 E
Malazgirt	130	39.09 N	42.31 E
Malbaie ≃	186	47.39 N	70.09 W
Malbaie, La C	186	48.35 N	64.14 W
Malbon	166	21.04 S	140.18 E
Malbooma	162	30.41 S	134.11 E
Malborghetto Valbruna	64	46.30 N	13.26 E
Malbork	30	54.02 N	19.01 E
Malbrán	252	29.21 S	62.27 W
Malbuisson	58	46.48 N	6.18 E
Malbun	58	47.35 N	9.33 E
Malcesine	64	45.46 N	10.48 E
Mal'cevo	265b	55.56 N	37.57 E
Mal'čevskaja	78	49.04 N	40.21 E
Mal'čevsko-Polnenskaja	83	48.58 N	40.12 E
Malchanskij chrebet ⋏	88	50.45 N	109.30 E
Malchin	54	53.44 N	12.46 E
Malchiner See ⊜	54	53.43 N	12.38 E
Malching	60	48.19 N	13.12 E
Malchow	54	53.28 N	12.25 E
Malchow ⊸[8]	264a	52.35 N	13.29 E
Malčin	88	49.44 N	93.18 E
Malcolm	162	28.56 S	121.30 E
Malcolm, Point ➤	162	33.48 S	123.45 E
Malcolm Island I	182	50.40 N	127.00 W
Malcom	190	41.42 N	92.33 W
Malcompeth → Mahābaleshwar	122	17.55 N	73.40 E
Malcontenta	64	45.25 N	12.13 E
Malczyce	30	51.14 N	16.29 E
Māldah	124	25.02 N	88.09 E
Maldegem	50	51.13 N	3.27 E
Malden, Ma., U.S.	207	42.25 N	71.04 W
Malden, Mo., U.S.	194	36.33 N	89.57 W
Malden I	14	4.03 S	154.59 W
Malden ≃	283	42.24 N	71.05 W
Malden Bridge	210	42.28 N	73.35 W
Malden on Hudson	210	42.06 N	73.56 W
Maldivas → Maldives □[1]	12	3.15 N	73.00 E
Maldive Islands → Maldives □[1]	12	3.15 N	73.00 E
Mal di Ventre, Isola di I	71	39.59 N	8.18 E
Maldives □[1]	12	3.15 N	73.00 E
Maldon, Austl.	169	37.00 S	144.04 E
Maldon, Eng., U.K.	42	51.45 N	0.40 E
Maldon □[8]	260	51.43 N	0.40 E
Maldonado	252	34.54 S	54.57 W
Maldonado, Punta ➤	234	16.20 N	98.35 W
Male, It.	64	46.21 N	10.55 E
Male', Mald.	12	4.10 N	73.30 E
Male, Mya.	110	23.02 N	95.58 E
Maléa, Ákra ➤	38	36.26 N	23.12 E
Malea, Dolok ∧	114	0.56 N	99.38 E
Malebo, Pool ⊜	152	4.17 S	15.20 E
Malediven → Maldives □[1]	12	3.15 N	73.00 E
Mālegaon	122	20.33 N	74.32 E
Malegno, It.	64	45.56 N	10.14 E
Malegno, It.	64	46.40 N	11.08 E
Malehra	124	24.34 N	79.19 E
Maleit, Lake ⊜	140	7.55 N	28.35 E
Malek, Kaz.	85	40.47 N	68.37 E
Malek, Sūd.	140	6.04 N	31.36 E
Malé Karpaty ⋏	30	48.30 N	17.20 E
Malek Dīn	120	32.25 N	68.04 E
Malek Kandī	128	37.09 N	46.06 E
Malek Sīāh, Kūh-e ∧	128	29.51 N	60.52 E
Malela, R.D.C.	154	2.28 S	26.09 E
Malela, R.D.C.	154	4.22 S	26.08 E
Malema	154	14.57 S	37.20 E
Malen'ga	24	63.50 N	36.25 E
Malengoya	154	3.32 N	25.25 E
Malente	54	54.10 N	10.33 E
Maleo	62	45.10 N	9.46 E
Male Polissya ⊸[1]	78	50.10 N	25.00 E
Māler Kotla	124	30.31 N	75.53 E
Malesco	58	46.08 N	8.30 E
Malesherbes	50	48.18 N	2.25 E
Malestroit	32	47.49 N	2.23 W
Maleta	88	50.50 N	108.25 E
Maletto	70	37.49 N	14.52 E
Malfa	70	38.35 N	14.50 E
Malgas	158	34.18 S	20.35 E
Malgersdorf	60	48.32 N	12.45 E
Malgobek	84	43.32 N	44.34 E
Malgomaj ⊜	26	64.47 N	16.12 E
Malha Wells	140	15.08 N	26.12 E
Malheur ≃	202	44.03 N	116.59 W
Malheur, North Fork ≃	202	43.45 N	118.04 W
Malheur, South Fork ≃	202	43.33 N	118.10 W
Malheureux, Cap ➤	157c	19.59 S	57.36 E
Malheur Lake ⊜	202	43.20 N	118.45 W
Mali, Guinée	150	12.05 N	12.18 W
Mali, R.D.C.	154	2.48 S	26.08 E
Mali □[1], Afr.	134	17.00 N	4.00 W
Mali □[1], Afr.	150	17.00 N	4.00 W
Mali ≃	102	25.43 N	97.29 E
Maliangping	102	31.29 N	111.20 E
Malianjingzi	102	41.32 N	95.23 E
Malibamatšo ≃	158	29.20 S	29.28 E
Malibu	228	34.02 N	118.42 W
Malibu Lake ⊜[1]	228	34.07 N	118.45 W
Malien ≃	269d	25.11 N	121.41 E
Malienkang	269d	25.10 N	121.39 E
Maligay Bay C	116	7.30 N	123.14 E
Malighati	126	22.33 N	87.40 E
Maligne ≃	182	52.56 N	118.02 W
Maligne Lake ⊜	182	52.40 N	117.31 W
Malīhābād	124	26.55 N	80.43 E
Māliḥah, Wādī V	142	29.21 N	32.35 E
Malik	112	0.34 S	123.14 E
Malik, Wādī al- V	140	18.02 N	30.58 E
Mali Kyun I	110	13.06 N	98.16 E
Malili	112	2.38 S	121.06 E
Målilla	26	57.23 N	15.48 E
Malimba, Monts ⋏	154	7.32 S	29.30 E
Malim Nawar	114	4.21 N	101.07 E
Malimono	116	9.34 N	125.25 E
Malin, Ire.	48	55.18 N	7.15 W
Malin, Or., U.S.	202	42.00 N	121.24 W
Malinalco ⊥	234	18.57 N	99.30 W
Malinaltepec	234	17.03 N	98.40 W
Malinau	112	3.35 N	116.38 E
Malin Beg	48	54.40 N	8.48 W
Malindang, Mount ∧	116	8.13 N	123.38 E
Malindi	154	3.13 S	40.07 E
Malindi Marine National Park ♠	154	3.15 S	40.10 E
Malines → Mechelen	50	51.02 N	4.28 E
Malinga	152	2.25 S	12.14 E
Malingping	115a	6.46 S	106.01 E
Malingsbosjön ⊜	40	59.55 N	15.27 E
Malin Head ➤	48	55.23 N	7.24 W
Malinki	82	54.05 N	38.59 E
Malinniki	82	56.17 N	38.24 E
Malino, Indon.	112	5.15 S	119.51 E
Malino, Ross.	82	55.06 N	38.11 E
Malino, Ross.	265b	55.58 N	37.13 E
Malino, Bukit ∧	112	0.45 N	120.47 E
Malinoa I	174w	21.02 S	175.08 W
Malinovka, Ross.	80	51.47 N	43.26 E
Malinovka, Ross.	86	53.24 N	87.17 E
Malinta	216	41.19 N	84.02 W
Malinyi	154	8.56 S	36.08 E
Malipāra	272b	22.57 N	88.14 E
Mali Rajinac ∧	36	44.48 N	15.02 E
Malita	116	6.25 N	125.36 E
Malitbog	116	10.10 N	125.00 E
Maliuchang	107	29.05 N	104.07 E
Maliuping	107	29.55 N	106.23 E
Ma Liu Shui	271d	22.25 N	114.12 E
Malivo	82	55.07 N	39.02 E
Maliwun	110	10.14 N	98.37 E
Maliyivka	78	47.29 N	32.43 E
Malizhen	102	23.10 N	104.35 E
Maljamar	196	32.51 N	103.46 W
Malka, Ross.	74	53.20 N	157.30 E
Malka, Ross.	84	43.47 N	43.21 E
Malka ≃	84	43.44 N	44.15 E
Malkāpur	120	20.53 N	76.12 E
Malkara	130	40.53 N	26.54 E
Malkerns	158	26.32 S	31.11 E
Malko Tărnovo	38	41.59 N	27.32 E
Mallāḥ	132	32.30 N	36.51 E
Mallaig, Ab., Can.	182	54.13 N	111.22 W
Mallaig, Scot., U.K.	46	57.00 N	5.50 W
Mallala	168b	34.26 S	138.30 E
Mallaoua	150	13.02 N	9.36 E
Mallapunyah	164	16.59 S	135.49 E
Mallaranny	48	53.54 N	9.49 W
Mallard Reservoir ⊜[1]	282	38.01 N	122.03 W
Mallawī	142	27.44 N	30.50 E
Mallee Cliffs National Park ♠	166	34.15 S	142.40 E
Mallemort	62	43.44 N	5.11 E
Mallersdorf-Pfaffenberg	60	48.47 N	12.16 E
Mallery Lake ⊜	176	63.55 N	98.25 W
Malles Venosta (Mals)	64	46.41 N	10.32 E
Mallet	252	25.55 S	50.50 W
Mallig	116	17.08 N	121.41 E
Malligasta	252	29.11 S	67.26 W
Mallina	162	20.53 S	118.02 E
Malling	41	56.02 N	10.10 E
Malliss, Dtsch.	54	53.13 N	11.19 E
Malliss, Dtsch.	54	53.13 N	11.19 E
Mallnitz	64	46.59 N	13.10 E
Mallorca I	34	39.30 N	3.00 E
Mallorytown	212	44.29 N	75.53 W
Mallow	48	52.08 N	8.39 W
Mallwood	216	42.51 N	89.02 W
Malm	26	64.04 N	11.13 E
Malmbäck	26	57.35 N	14.28 E
Malmberget	24	67.10 N	20.40 E
Malmédy	56	50.25 N	6.02 E
Malmesbury, S. Afr.	158	33.28 S	18.44 E
Malmesbury, Eng., U.K.	42	51.36 N	2.06 W
Malmesbury, Vale of V	42	51.22 N	2.10 W
Malmköping	40	59.08 N	16.44 E
Malmlången ⊜	40	59.27 N	14.42 E
Malmö	41	55.36 N	13.00 E
Malmöhus Län □[6]	26	55.45 N	13.30 E
Malmsbury	169	37.12 S	144.23 E
Malmsbury Reservoir ⊜[1]	169	37.13 S	144.22 E
Malmslätt	26	58.25 N	15.30 E
Malmstrom Air Force Base ■	202	47.30 N	111.10 W
Malmyž	80	56.31 N	50.41 E
Malna	116	8.08 N	124.27 E
Malnate	62	45.48 N	8.53 E
Malnoue	261	48.50 N	2.36 E
Malo	64	45.39 N	11.24 E
Malo I	175f	15.40 S	167.11 E
Malo, Arroyo ≃	258	33.43 S	58.52 W
Maloarchangel'sk	76	52.24 N	36.30 E
Maloarchangel'skoje	88	50.24 N	108.50 E
Maloba	154	6.18 S	27.39 E
Malodel'skaja	80	50.11 N	43.53 E
Maloduša	76	52.09 N	30.14 E
Maloelap I[1]	14	8.45 N	171.03 E
Maloja	58	46.24 N	9.41 E
Malojapass)(	58	46.24 N	9.41 E
Malojaroslavec	82	55.01 N	36.28 E
Malojaz	86	55.13 N	58.09 E
Maloje Goloustnoje	88	52.18 N	105.18 E
Maloje Kozino	80	56.26 N	43.41 E
Maloje-Ščerbedino	80	51.59 N	42.50 E
Maloje Skuratovo	76	53.33 N	37.00 E
Malokaterynivka	78	47.39 N	35.16 E
Malokirsanovka	83	47.28 N	38.31 E
Malokrasnojarka	86	56.28 N	76.01 E
Malo-les-Bains	50	51.03 N	2.24 E
Malolo	154	7.18 S	36.35 E
Malolos, Guam	174p	13.18 N	144.46 E
Malolos, Pil.	116	14.51 N	120.49 E
Malom	164	3.10 S	151.50 E
Maloma	158	27.00 S	31.40 E
Malombe, Lake ⊜	154	14.38 S	35.12 E
Malomykhaylivka	78	48.06 N	36.23 E
Malomykolaivka	83	48.18 N	39.01 E
Malonabatovskij	80	48.57 N	43.40 E
Malone, Fl., U.S.	192	30.57 N	85.09 W
Malone, N.Y., U.S.	188	44.50 N	74.17 W
Malone, Tx., U.S.	222	31.55 N	96.54 W
Malone, Wa., U.S.	224	46.58 N	123.20 W
Malonno	64	46.07 N	10.18 E

Symbol	English	Deutsch	Español	Français	Português
≃	River	Fluß	Río	Rivière	Rio
≋	Canal	Kanal	Canal	Canal	Canal
⌊	Waterfall, Rapids	Wasserfall, Stromschnellen	Cascada, Rápidos	Chute d'eau, Rapides	Cascata, Rápidos
⊔	Strait	Meeresstraße	Estrecho	Détroit	Estreito
C	Bay, Gulf	Bucht, Golf	Bahía, Golfo	Baie, Golfe	Baía, Golfo
⊜	Lake, Lakes	See, Seen	Lago, Lagos	Lac, Lacs	Lago, Lagos
≚	Swamp	Sumpf	Pantano	Marais	Pântano
⊓	Ice Features, Glacier	Eis- und Gletscherformen	Accidentes Glaciales	Formes glaciaires	Acidentes glaciares
⊤	Other Hydrographic Features	Andere Hydrographische Objekte	Otros Elementos Hidrográficos	Autres données hydrographiques	Outros acidentes hidrográficos
✣	Submarine Features	Untermeerische Objekte	Accidentes Submarinos	Formes de relief sous-marin	Acidentes submarinos
□	Political Unit	Politische Einheit	Unidad Política	Entité politique	Unidade política
ʋ	Cultural Institution	Kulturelle Institution	Institución Cultural	Institution culturelle	Instituição cultural
⊥	Historical Site	Historische Stätte	Sitio Histórico	Site historique	Sítio histórico
♠	Recreational Site	Erholungs- und Ferienort	Sitio de Recreo	Centre de loisirs	Área de Lazer
⊠	Airport	Flughafen	Aeropuerto	Aéroport	Aeroporto
■	Military Installation	Militäranlage	Instalación Militar	Installation militaire	Instalação militar
⊸	Miscellaneous	Verschiedenes	Misceláneo	Divers	Diversos

Name	Page	Lat.°′	Long.°′
Malonty	61	48.41 N	14.35 E
Małopolska ◆[1]	30	50.10 N	21.30 E
Malorossijka	86	53.12 N	62.30 E
Malošujka	24	63.45 N	37.22 E
Malotkavičy	76	52.07 N	25.56 E
Malott	182	48.16 N	119.42 W
Måløv	41	55.45 N	12.20 E
Małowice	30	51.34 N	15.27 E
Måløy	26	61.56 N	5.07 E
Malozemel'skaja Tundra ◆[1]	24	67.50 N	51.00 E
Malpaisillo	236	12.35 N	86.41 W
Malpartida de Plasencia	34	39.59 N	6.02 W
Malpas, Austl.	166	34.43 S	140.37 E
Malpas, Eng., U.K.	44	53.01 N	2.46 W
Malpaso	234	22.37 N	102.46 W
Malpe	122	13.21 N	74.43 E
Malpelo, Isla de I	242	3.59 N	81.35 W
Malpensa, Aeroporto della ⊠	62	45.38 N	8.44 E
Malpeque Bay c	186	46.30 N	63.47 W
Malprabha ≃	122	16.12 N	76.03 E
Mālpura	120	26.17 N	75.23 E
Mals → Malles Venosta	64	46.41 N	10.32 E
Mälsåker slott ⊥	40	59.23 N	17.18 E
Malsch	56	48.53 N	8.19 E
Malše (Maltsch) ≃	61	48.58 N	14.28 E
Målselva ≃	24	69.14 N	18.30 E
Malsfeld	56	51.06 N	9.32 E
Malta, Bra.	250	6.54 S	37.31 W
Malta, Lat.	76	56.21 N	27.10 E
Malta, Öst.	64	46.57 N	13.30 E
Malta, Il., U.S.	216	41.56 N	88.52 W
Malta, Mt., U.S.	202	48.21 N	107.52 W
Malta, Oh., U.S.	188	39.38 N	81.51 W
Malta □[1], Europe	22	35.50 N	14.35 E
Malta □[1], Europe	36	35.50 N	14.35 E
Malta I	36	35.53 N	14.27 E
Malta ≃	76	56.44 N	26.53 E
Malta Channel ʊ	36	36.20 N	15.00 E
Maltahöhe	156	24.50 S	17.00 E
Maltatal V	64	47.03 N	13.24 E
Maltby	44	53.26 N	1.11 W
Malte → Malta □[1]	36	35.50 N	14.35 E
Malte Brun ∧	172	43.34 S	170.18 E
Maltepe ◆[8]	267b	40.55 N	29.08 E
Malton	44	54.08 N	0.48 W
Malton ◆[8]	275b	43.42 N	79.38 W
Maltrata	234	18.48 N	97.16 W
Maltsch (Malše) ≃	61	48.58 N	14.28 E
Malugou	89	43.39 N	128.27 E
Maluku □[4]	164	5.00 S	130.00 E
Maluku (Moluccas) II	108	2.00 S	128.00 E
Maluku, Laut (Molucca Sea) ⊤[2]	108	0.00	125.00 E
Maluku-Maes	152	4.06 S	15.31 E
Ma'lūlā	130	33.50 N	36.33 E
Ma'lūlā, Jabal ∧	132	33.54 N	36.36 E
Malu Mare	38	44.15 N	23.51 E
Malumfashi	150	11.47 N	7.37 E
Malunda	112	3.00 S	118.50 E
Malung	26	60.40 N	13.44 E
Maluso	116	6.33 N	121.53 E
Malūṭ	140	10.26 N	32.12 E
Maluti	126	24.09 N	87.41 E
Maluwe	150	8.40 N	2.17 W
Maluzhen	106	31.20 N	121.16 E
Malvaglia	58	46.25 N	8.59 E
Malvaglio	266b	45.31 N	8.47 E
Malvagna	70	37.55 N	15.04 E
Mālvan	122	16.04 N	73.28 E
Malveira	266c	38.45 N	9.27 W
Malvern, Austl.	274b	37.52 S	145.02 E
Malvern, Ar., U.S.	194	34.21 N	92.48 W
Malvern, Ia., U.S.	198	41.00 N	95.35 W
Malvern, Oh., U.S.	214	40.41 N	81.10 W
Malvern, Pa., U.S.	285	40.02 N	75.31 W
Malvern ◆[8]	273d	26.12 S	28.06 E
Malverne	276	40.40 N	73.40 W
Malvern Hills ⋏[2]	42	52.05 N	2.21 W
Malvérnia	156	22.06 S	31.42 E
Malvern Link	42	52.08 N	2.18 W
Malvinas	252	29.37 S	58.59 W
Malvinas, Islas → Falkland Islands □[2]	254	51.45 S	59.00 W
Malvito	68	39.36 N	16.03 E
Malwal	140	9.19 N	31.35 E
Mālwa Plateau ⋏[1]	124	23.50 N	77.30 E
Malybaj	85	43.30 N	78.25 E
Malý Dunaj ≃	30	47.45 N	18.09 E
Malyi Nesvetaj ≃	83	47.32 N	39.49 E
Malyj, ostrov I	76	60.02 N	28.02 E
Malyja Haradzjacičy	76	52.33 N	28.20 E
Malyj An'uj ≃	74	68.30 N	160.49 E
Malyj Čeremšan ≃	80	54.18 N	50.01 E
Malyj Chamar-Daban, chrebet ⋏	88	51.00 N	105.00 E
Malyj Civil' ≃	80	55.54 N	47.28 E
Malyje Alabuchi	80	51.33 N	42.10 E
Malyje Čany, ozero ⊜	86	54.33 N	78.02 E
Malyje Jagury	80	45.26 N	43.01 E
Malyje Kamkaly	86	44.44 N	71.31 E
Malyje Karmakuly	72	72.23 N	52.44 E
Malyje Porogi	265a	59.47 N	30.42 E
Malyj Irgiz ≃	80	52.12 N	47.58 E
Malyj Jenisej (Ka-Chem) ≃	88	51.43 N	94.26 E
Malyj Jugan ≃	86	60.40 N	73.54 E
Malyj Kundyš ≃	80	56.22 N	47.53 E
Malyj Šantar, ostrov I	89	54.30 N	137.36 E
Malyj Sarybulak	86	52.10 N	72.35 E
Malyj Tajmyr, ostrov I	74	78.08 N	107.12 E
Malyj T'uters, ostrov I	76	59.49 N	26.56 E
Malyj Uran ≃	80	52.30 N	53.01 E
Malyj Uzen' ≃	80	48.50 N	49.39 E
Malyj Zelenčuk ≃	84	44.24 N	41.56 E
Malyn', Ross.	82	54.36 N	38.40 E
Malyn, Ukr.	78	50.46 N	29.15 E
Malynivka	78	49.47 N	36.43 E
Malyševo	76	57.50 N	35.36 E
Malzéville	58	48.43 N	6.12 E
Mama	88	58.18 N	112.54 E
Mama ≃	88	58.18 N	112.55 E
Ma Ma Creek ≃	171a	27.35 S	152.13 E
Mamadyš	80	55.44 N	51.25 E
Mamagota	175e	6.46 S	155.24 E
Mamahuolang	104	42.24 N	124.12 E
Mamajiecun	104	41.26 N	122.51 E
Mamakan	88	57.48 N	114.01 E
Mamaku	172	38.06 S	176.05 E
Mamakwash Lake ⊜	184	51.38 N	92.56 W
Mamala Bay c	229a	21.18 N	157.57 W
Mamalu Bay c	229a	20.37 N	156.09 W
Mamanguape	250	6.50 S	35.07 W
Mama'o, Hakau ⊤[2]	174w	21.00 S	175.12 W
Mamara	248	14.14 S	72.35 W
Mamaroneck	210	40.56 N	73.43 W
Mamaroneck ≃	276	40.57 N	73.44 W
Mamaroneck Harbor c	276	40.56 N	73.43 W
Mamasa	112	2.56 S	119.22 E
Mamasa ≃	112	3.30 S	119.42 E
Mamba	94	36.07 N	138.55 E
Mambaí	255	14.28 S	46.07 W
Mambajao	116	9.15 N	124.43 E
Mambajao, Mount ∧	116	9.10 N	124.44 E
Mambali	154	4.33 S	32.41 E
Mambalot	116	8.51 N	117.55 E
Mambare ≃	164	8.20 S	147.55 E
Mambasa	154	1.21 N	29.03 E
Mamberamo ≃	164	1.26 S	137.53 E
Mambéré ≃	152	3.31 N	16.03 E
Mambili ≃	152	0.07 N	16.08 E
Mambrui	154	3.07 S	40.09 E
Mambucaba	256	23.01 S	44.31 W
Mambucaba ≃	256	23.02 S	44.32 W
Mamburao	116	13.14 N	120.35 E
Mambusao ≃	116	11.24 N	122.41 E
Mamdūḥ, Rujm ∧	132	32.14 N	36.15 E
Mamedkala	84	42.10 N	48.06 E
Mamehaktebo	112	0.08 N	115.32 E
Mamelodi	158	25.42 S	28.21 E
Ma-Me-O Beach	182	52.58 N	113.59 W
Mamera	286c	10.27 N	66.59 W
Mamera, Quebrada ≃	286c	10.27 N	66.59 W
Mamers	50	48.21 N	0.23 E
Mamfe	152	5.46 N	9.17 E
Mamiá ≃	250	1.55 S	55.07 W
Mamiá, Lago ⊜	246	4.15 S	63.03 W
Mamiao	98	35.04 N	116.10 E
Mamie	192	36.07 N	75.50 W
Mamiña	248	20.05 S	69.14 W
Maminigui	150	7.24 N	5.50 W
Mamirolle	58	47.12 N	6.10 E
Mamisonskij, pereval)(	84	42.43 N	43.48 E
Maml'utka	86	54.57 N	68.35 E
Mammendorf	60	48.12 N	11.09 E
Mammola	68	38.22 N	16.15 E
Mammoth, Az., U.S.	200	32.43 N	110.38 W
Mammoth, W.V., U.S.	188	38.15 N	81.22 W
Mammoth Cave National Park ♠	194	37.08 N	86.13 W
Mammoth Lakes	204	37.38 N	118.58 W
Mammoth Pool Reservoir ⊜[1]	226	37.20 N	119.20 W
Mammoth Spring	194	36.29 N	91.32 W
Mamoiada	71	40.13 N	9.17 E
Mamonovo, Ross.	76	54.28 N	19.57 E
Mamonovo, Ross.	265b	55.36 N	37.49 E
Mamonovo, Ross.	265b	55.41 N	37.19 E
Mamont	279b	40.29 N	79.36 W
Mamontovo, Ross.	86	52.43 N	81.37 E
Mamontovo, Ross.	86	51.45 N	81.25 E
Mamoré ≃	248	10.23 S	65.23 W
Mamori, Lago ⊜	246	3.38 S	60.07 W
Mamoriá ≃	248	7.30 S	66.21 W
Mamou, Guinée	150	10.23 N	12.05 W
Mamou, La., U.S.	194	30.38 N	92.25 W
Mamoutzou	157a	12.47 S	45.14 E
Mampikony	157b	16.06 S	47.38 E
Mampong	150	7.04 N	1.24 W
Mamraš	84	41.44 N	48.19 E
Mamre	158	33.30 S	18.29 E
Mamry, Jezioro ⊜	30	54.08 N	21.42 E
Mamuchi	98	35.41 N	118.17 E
Mamué	152	13.35 S	13.13 E
Mamuil, Paso de)(	254	39.35 S	71.28 W
Mamuju	112	2.41 S	118.54 E
Mamulique	196	26.08 N	100.20 W
Ma'mūn	140	12.15 N	22.41 E
Mamuno	156	22.16 S	20.01 E
Mamuripi (Manuripe) ≃	248	11.06 S	67.36 W
Mamuru ≃	250	2.42 S	56.44 W
Mamykovo	80	54.38 N	50.37 E
Mamyl'	24	61.57 N	56.41 E
Man, C. Iv.	150	7.24 N	7.33 W
Man, India	120	33.51 N	78.32 E
Man, W.V., U.S.	192	37.44 N	81.52 W
Man (Île de) → Isle of Man □[2]	44	54.15 N	4.30 W
Man, Isle of → Isle of Man □[2]	44	54.15 N	4.30 W
Mana, Guy. fr.	250	5.40 N	53.47 W
Mana, Hi., U.S.	229b	22.02 N	159.46 W
Mana ≃, Guy. fr.	250	5.44 N	53.54 W
Mana ≃, Ross.	86	55.57 N	92.28 E
Manabí □[4]	246	0.40 S	80.05 W
Manacacías ≃	246	4.23 N	72.04 W
Manacapuru	246	3.18 S	60.37 W
Manacapuru ≃	246	3.18 S	60.38 W
Manacle Point ›	42	50.03 N	5.03 W
Manacor	34	39.34 N	3.12 E
Manado	112	1.29 N	124.51 E
Managua	236	12.09 N	86.17 W
Managua □[5]	236	12.00 N	86.25 W
Managua, Aeropuerto ⊠	286b	23.00 N	82.17 W
Managua, Lago de ⊜	236	12.20 N	86.20 W
Manahawkin	208	39.41 N	74.15 W
Manahawkin Bay c	208	39.40 N	74.12 W
Manaia	172	39.33 S	174.08 E
Manā'if, Bi'r al- ⊤[4]	142	30.31 N	32.12 E
Manajenki	76	53.42 N	36.27 E
Manakalampona ∧	157b	15.23 S	48.50 E
Manakara	157b	22.08 S	48.01 E
Manakau	172	40.43 S	175.13 E
Manakau ∧	172	42.14 S	173.37 E
Manākhah	144	15.07 N	43.44 E
Manalapan Brook ≃	276	40.24 N	74.23 W
Manāli	123	32.15 N	77.10 E
Manama → Al-Manāmah	128	26.13 N	50.35 E
Manamansalo I	26	64.21 N	27.04 E
Manambaho ≃	157b	17.41 S	44.04 E
Manambato, Madag.	157b	13.14 S	49.54 E
Manambato, Madag.	157b	13.43 S	49.07 E
Manambolo ≃	157b	19.18 S	44.24 E
Manambolosy	157b	16.02 S	49.40 E
Manam Island I	164	4.05 S	145.05 E
Mánamo, Caño ≃[1]	246	9.55 N	62.16 W
Manamoc Island I	116	11.19 N	120.41 E
Manana Island I	229c	21.20 N	157.40 W
Mananantanana ≃	157b	21.25 S	45.33 E
Mananao	116	13.30 N	120.34 E
Mananara	157b	16.10 S	49.46 E
Mananara ≃	157b	23.21 S	47.42 E
Manandaza	157b	19.19 S	45.23 E
Mananjary	157b	21.13 S	48.20 E
Manankoro	150	10.28 N	7.27 W
Manantenina	157b	24.17 S	47.19 E
Manantiales Behr	254	45.41 S	67.31 W
Manaoag	116	16.03 N	120.29 E
Manáos → Manaus	246	3.08 S	60.01 W
Manapatrana	157b	21.40 S	47.35 E
Manapiare ≃	246	5.04 N	66.30 W
Manapire ≃	246	7.42 N	66.07 W
Manapla	116	10.58 N	123.07 E
Mana Point ›	229b	22.03 N	159.47 W
Mana Pools National Park ♠	154	16.00 S	28.35 E
Manapouri	172	45.34 S	167.36 E
Manapouri, Lake ⊜	172	45.30 S	167.30 E
Manappārai	122	10.36 N	78.25 E
Manaquiri, Lago ⊜	246	3.29 S	60.31 W
Manār ≃	122	18.39 N	77.44 E
Manaravolo	157b	23.59 S	45.39 E
Manas, Som.	144	2.57 N	43.28 E
Manas, Zhg.	86	44.18 N	86.13 E
Manās ≃, Asia	120	26.13 N	90.38 E
Manas ≃, Zhg.	86	45.38 N	85.12 E
Manas, gora ∧	85	42.18 N	71.01 E
Manasarowar Lake → Mapam Yumco ⊜	120	30.42 N	81.27 E
Manas Hu ⊜	86	45.45 N	85.55 E
Manāslu ∧	124	28.33 N	84.33 E
Manasota Key I	220	26.58 N	82.23 W
Manasquan	208	40.07 N	74.02 W
Manasquan ≃	208	40.06 N	74.02 W
Manassa	200	37.10 N	105.56 W
Manassas	208	38.45 N	77.28 W
Manassas National Battlefield Park ♠	208	38.50 N	77.32 W
Manassas Park	208	38.46 N	77.27 W
Manastash Creek ≃	224	46.59 N	120.35 W
Manastash Creek, North Fork ≃	224	46.57 N	120.44 W
Manastash Creek, South Fork ≃	224	46.57 N	120.44 W
Manastash Ridge ∧	224	46.55 N	120.30 W
Mânăstirea	38	44.13 N	26.54 E
Manatang	112	8.26 S	124.28 E
Manatawny	208	40.17 N	75.41 W
Manatawny Creek ≃	208	40.14 N	75.39 W
Manatee □[6]	220	27.26 N	82.25 W
Manatee ≃	220	27.32 N	82.38 W
Manatee, Lake ⊜[1]	220	27.29 N	82.20 W
Manatí, Col.	246	10.27 N	74.58 W
Manatí, Cuba	240p	21.19 N	76.56 W
Manatí, P.R.	240m	18.26 N	66.29 W
Manatí ≃	240p	21.40 N	79.50 W
Manatí, Bahía de c	240p	21.24 N	76.48 W
Manatuto	112	8.30 S	126.01 E
Manaul	116	12.27 N	121.25 E
Manaung	110	18.51 N	93.44 E
Manaus	246	3.08 S	60.01 W
Manavgat	130	36.47 N	31.26 E
Manawa	190	44.27 N	88.55 W
Mānāwāla	123	31.35 N	73.41 E
Manawan Lake ⊜	184	55.24 N	103.14 W
Manāwar	120	22.14 N	75.05 E
Manawatu ≃	172	40.28 S	175.13 E
Manawoka, Pulau I	164	4.05 S	131.20 E
Manay	116	7.13 N	126.32 E
Manayunk ◆[8]	285	40.01 N	75.13 W
Manazuru	94	35.09 N	139.08 E
Manazuru-misaki ›	94	35.08 N	139.10 E
Manban	102	23.04 N	103.11 E
Mānbāzār	126	23.04 N	86.39 E
Manbian	102	24.19 N	100.32 E
Manbij	130	36.31 N	37.57 E
Manby	44	53.22 N	0.06 E
Mancelona	190	44.54 N	85.03 W
Mancha Blanca	254	40.47 S	65.27 W
Mancha Real	34	37.47 N	3.37 W
Manchaug	207	42.05 N	71.44 W
Manche □[5]	32	49.00 N	1.10 W
Mancheng	105	38.56 N	115.20 E
Mancherāl	122	18.52 N	79.26 E
Manchester, Eng., U.K.	44	53.28 N	2.15 W
Manchester, Eng., U.K.	262	53.28 N	2.15 W
Manchester, Ct., U.S.	207	41.46 N	72.31 W
Manchester, Ga., U.S.	192	32.51 N	84.37 W
Manchester, Il., U.S.	219	39.33 N	90.20 W
Manchester, Ia., U.S.	190	42.29 N	91.27 W
Manchester, Ky., U.S.	192	37.09 N	83.45 W
Manchester, Md., U.S.	208	39.39 N	76.53 W
Manchester, Ma., U.S.	207	42.34 N	70.46 W
Manchester, Mi., U.S.	216	42.09 N	84.02 W
Manchester, N.H., U.S.	188	42.59 N	71.27 W
Manchester, N.Y., U.S.	210	42.58 N	77.13 W
Manchester, Oh., U.S.	218	38.41 N	83.36 W
Manchester, Pa., U.S.	208	40.03 N	76.43 W
Manchester, Tn., U.S.	194	35.28 N	86.05 W
Manchester, Vt., U.S.	210	43.09 N	73.04 W
Manchester, Wa., U.S.	224	47.33 N	122.33 W
Manchester □[8]	262	53.27 N	2.13 W
Manchester Bridge	210	41.41 N	73.52 W
Manchester City Football Ground ♠	262	53.27 N	2.14 W
Manchester Docks ◆[5]	262	53.28 N	2.17 W
Manchester International Airport ⊠	44	53.21 N	2.15 W
Manchester Race Course ♠	262	53.30 N	2.16 W
Manchester Ship Canal ≂	262	53.19 N	2.57 W
Manchester United Football Ground ♠	262	53.28 N	2.18 W
Manching	60	48.43 N	11.30 E
Manchioneal	241q	18.02 N	76.17 W
Manchón	236	14.23 N	92.02 W
Manchouli → Manzhouli	88	49.35 N	117.22 E
Manchuria □[9]	90	47.00 N	125.00 E
Manciano	66	42.35 N	11.31 E
Mancieulles	56	49.17 N	5.53 E
Máncora	246	4.06 S	81.05 W
Mancos	200	37.20 N	108.17 W
Mancos ≃	200	36.59 N	108.59 W
Mand	128	26.07 N	62.03 E
Mānd ≃, India	120	21.42 N	83.15 E
Mand ≃, Īrān	128	28.11 N	51.17 E
Manda, India	126	22.06 N	86.14 E
Manda, Tan.	154	7.58 S	32.26 E
Manda, Tan.	154	8.30 S	32.44 E
Manda, Tan.	154	10.28 S	34.35 E
Manda, Tchad	146	9.12 N	18.10 E
Manda, Jabal ∧	140	8.39 N	24.27 E
Mandabe, Madag.	157b	21.03 S	44.55 E
Mandabe, Madag.	157b	20.55 S	45.49 E
Mandach	102	44.28 N	108.11 E
Mandaguari	255	23.32 S	51.42 W
Mandai Orchard Gardens ♠	271c	1.24 N	103.47 E
Manda Island I	154	2.15 S	40.57 E
Mandal	26	58.02 N	7.27 E
Mandal, Jibāl ∧[2]	140	12.09 N	29.31 E
Mandala, Puncak ∧	164	4.44 S	140.20 E
Mandalay	110	22.00 N	96.05 E
Mandalay □[5]	110	21.00 N	96.00 E
Mandale	216	41.01 N	84.20 W
Mandale Station ◆[5]	272c	19.03 N	72.56 E
Mandalgov'	102	45.45 N	106.12 E
Mandalī	128	33.45 N	45.32 E
Mandalkia	272b	22.43 N	88.08 E
Mandal-Ovoo	102	44.35 N	104.05 E
Mandalselva ≃	26	58.02 N	7.28 E
Mandaluyong	269f	14.35 N	121.02 E
Mandan	198	46.49 N	100.53 W
Mandanici	70	38.00 N	15.19 E
Mandāoli ◆[8]	272a	28.38 N	77.18 E
Mandaon	116	12.14 N	123.17 E
Mandapur	126	23.00 N	88.29 E
Mandar, Teluk c	112	3.40 S	119.15 E
Mandara Mountains (Monts Mandara) ⋏	146	10.45 N	13.40 E
Mandas	71	39.38 N	9.07 E
Mandatoriccio	68	39.28 N	16.50 E
Mandau ≃	114	0.48 N	101.47 E
Mandaue	116	10.20 N	123.56 E
Mandāwar	124	29.30 N	78.08 E
Mandeb, Bab el ʊ	144	12.40 N	43.20 E
Mandehu	104	42.07 N	121.33 E
Mandel	128	33.17 N	61.52 E
Mandélia	146	11.43 N	15.15 E
Mandelieu	62	43.33 N	6.56 E
Mandello del Lario	58	45.54 N	9.19 E
Mandera	154	3.56 N	41.52 E
Manderfeld	56	50.20 N	6.20 E
Manderscheid	56	50.05 N	6.49 E
Manderson	202	44.16 N	107.57 W
Mandeure	58	47.27 N	6.48 E
Mandeville, P.Q., Can.	206	46.22 N	73.22 W
Mandeville, Jam.	241q	18.02 N	77.30 W
Mandeville, N.Z.	172	46.00 S	168.49 E
Mandeville, La., U.S.	194	30.21 N	90.03 W
Mandi	123	31.43 N	76.55 E
Mandiana	150	10.38 N	8.41 W
Mandiangin	112	2.01 S	102.58 E
Mandi Angin, Gunong ∧	114	4.42 N	102.52 E
Mandi Bahāuddīn	123	32.35 N	73.30 E
Mandi Būrewāla	123	30.09 N	72.41 E
Mandi Dabwāli	123	29.58 N	74.42 E
Mandié	154	16.30 S	33.30 E
Mandimba	154	14.21 S	35.39 E
Mandini	158	29.09 S	31.25 E
Mandioli, Pulau I	108	0.44 S	127.14 E
Mandioré, Lagoa ⊜	248	18.08 S	57.33 W
Mandira ⊜[1]	124	22.20 N	84.35 E
Mandiri ≃	115a	7.02 S	106.32 E
Mandi Sādiqganj	123	30.10 N	73.44 E
Mandjafa	146	11.11 N	15.25 E
Mandjé, Lac ⊜	152	2.50 S	10.22 E
Mandji	152	1.36 S	10.26 E
Mandla	124	22.36 N	80.23 E
Mandora	162	19.44 S	120.51 E
Mandoto	157b	19.34 S	46.17 E
Mandoul ≃	146	8.56 N	17.58 E
Mandouri	150	10.51 N	0.49 E
Mándra, Ellás	267c	38.04 N	23.30 E
Māndrā, India	272b	22.55 N	88.07 E
Mandra, Pāk.	123	33.22 N	73.14 E
Mandrare ≃	157b	25.10 S	46.27 E
Mandres-les-Roses	261	48.42 N	2.33 E
Mandriola ◆[8]	267a	41.45 N	12.30 E
Mandriole	64	44.33 N	12.14 E
Mandrioli, Passo dei)(	66	43.48 N	11.55 E
Mandritsara	157b	15.50 S	48.49 E
Mandronarivo	157b	21.07 S	45.38 E
Mandsaur	120	24.04 N	75.04 E
Māndu	122	22.22 N	75.23 E
Mandu, Ribeirão do ≃	256	22.14 S	45.55 W
Manduba, Ponta ›	256	24.05 S	46.18 W
Manduhu	104	41.36 N	122.38 E
Mandun	102	22.17 N	100.05 E
Mandurah	168a	32.32 S	115.43 E
Manduria	68	40.24 N	17.38 E
Māndvi, India	120	21.15 N	73.18 E
Māndvi, India	120	22.50 N	69.22 E
Mandvi ◆[8]	272c	18.57 N	72.50 E
Mandya	122	12.33 N	76.54 E
Mané	150	12.59 N	1.21 W
Måne ≃	26	59.00 N	9.40 E
Manea	42	52.30 N	0.11 E
Manebach	54	50.41 N	10.51 E
Manek Urai	114	5.23 N	102.14 E
Manendragarh	124	23.13 N	82.13 E
Manera	157b	22.55 S	44.20 E
Manerbio	64	45.21 N	10.08 E
Manětím	60	49.59 N	13.14 E
Manevychi	78	51.17 N	25.33 E
Manfalūṭ	142	27.19 N	30.58 E
Manfredonia	68	41.38 N	15.55 E
Manfredonia, Golfo di c	68	41.35 N	16.05 E
Manga, Bra.	255	14.46 S	43.56 W
Manga, Burkina	150	11.40 N	1.04 W
Manga, Ur.	258	34.49 S	56.06 W
Manga ◆[1]	146	15.00 N	14.00 E
Mangabeiras, Chapada das ⋏[2]	250	10.00 S	46.30 W
Mangagoy	116	8.11 N	126.21 E
Mangahao ≃	172	40.23 S	175.50 E
Mangai	164	2.45 S	151.05 E
Mangaia I	14	21.55 S	157.55 W
Mangakino	172	38.22 S	175.47 E
Mangala	152	1.02 N	23.50 E
Mangalagiri	122	16.26 N	80.33 E
Mangaldai	120	26.26 N	92.02 E
Mangaldan	116	16.04 N	120.24 E
Mangalia	38	43.50 N	28.35 E
Mangalkot	126	23.33 N	87.54 E
Mangalmé	146	12.21 N	19.37 E
Mangalore	122	12.52 N	74.53 E
Mangalpaita	126	23.19 N	89.11 E
Mangalvedha	122	17.31 N	75.28 E
Mangamahu	172	39.49 S	175.22 E
Manganês ≃	250	10.21 S	48.27 W
Manganji	268	35.40 N	139.26 E
Mangaoka	157b	12.19 S	49.07 E
Mangapehi	172	38.31 S	175.18 E
Mangaratiba	256	22.57 S	44.02 W
Mangart, Monte (Mangrt) ∧	64	46.25 N	13.40 E
Mangatarem	116	15.47 N	120.17 E
Mangawān	124	24.41 N	81.33 E
Mangaweka	172	39.48 S	175.47 E
Mangaweka ∧	172	39.49 S	176.05 E
Mangcao Point ›	116	11.02 N	123.54 E
Mangchang	102	25.08 N	107.31 E
Mangde ≃	124	27.35 N	90.28 E
Mange, S.L.	150	8.55 N	12.51 W
Mange, R.D.C.	152	0.54 N	20.30 E
Mange, Zhg.	120	32.25 N	83.35 E
Mangeigne	146	10.31 N	21.19 E
Mangerton Mountain ∧	48	51.57 N	9.29 W
Mangfall ≃	64	47.51 N	12.08 E
Manggar	112	2.53 S	108.16 E
Manggeng	114	3.36 N	96.55 E
Manggonggri	164	3.30 S	133.19 E
Mangguar, Tanjung ›	164	2.53 S	134.51 E
Mangham	194	32.18 N	91.46 W
Mangichu ≃	126	23.24 N	90.48 E
Mangindrano	157b	14.17 S	48.58 E
Mangin Range ⋏	110	24.20 N	95.42 E
Mangistau □[8]	86	44.00 N	54.30 E
Mangkalihat, Tanjung ›	112	1.02 N	118.59 E
Mangkutana	112	2.24 S	120.48 E
Manglares, Cabo ›	246	1.36 N	79.02 W
Mangla Reservoir ⊜[1]	123	33.10 N	73.40 E
Manglaur	124	29.48 N	77.52 E
Manglisi	84	41.43 N	44.24 E
Mangnai	120	37.40 N	91.50 E
Mangniu ≃, Zhg.	104	41.45 N	120.53 E
Mangniu ≃, Zhg.	105	39.04 N	116.26 E
Mangnuiyingzi	104	41.37 N	120.43 E
Mango	220	28.00 N	82.19 W
Mangochi	154	14.28 S	35.16 E
Mango Island I	175g	17.27 S	179.09 W
Mangoky ≃, Madag.	157b	21.29 S	43.41 E
Mangoky ≃, Madag.	157b	23.27 S	45.13 E
Mangole, Pulau I	112	1.53 S	125.50 E
Mangombe	154	1.25 S	26.54 E
Mangone	68	39.12 N	16.20 E
Mangonia Park	220	26.46 N	80.05 W
Mangonui	172	34.59 S	173.32 E
Mangoplah	171b	35.23 S	147.15 E
Mangoro ≃	157b	20.00 S	48.45 E
Mangotsfield	42	51.28 N	2.28 W
Mangoupa	140	5.53 N	24.40 E
Mangrol	120	21.07 N	70.07 E
Mangrove Cay I	238	24.10 N	77.45 W
Mangrove Creek ≃	170	33.28 S	151.10 E
Mangrove Creek Dam ◆[6]	170	33.13 S	151.07 E
Mangrove Mountain	170	33.19 S	151.14 E
Mangrove Point ›	220	26.56 N	82.08 W
Mangrt (Monte Mangart) ∧	64	46.25 N	13.40 E
Mangrullo, Cuchilla ⋏[2]	258	34.34 S	56.42 W
Mangrūl Pīr	122	20.19 N	77.21 E
Mångsälven ≃	40	59.59 N	14.36 E
Mangsang	112	2.10 S	104.00 E
Mangu ≃	273b	4.24 S	15.24 E
Mangualde	34	40.36 N	7.46 W
Mangueira, Lagoa c	252	33.06 S	52.48 W
Mangueirinha	252	25.57 S	52.09 W
Manguéni, Plateau du ⋏[1]	146	22.35 N	12.40 E
Mangui	89	52.03 N	122.13 E
Manguito	240p	22.35 N	80.55 W
Mangulile	236	15.03 N	86.49 W
Mangum	196	34.52 N	99.30 W
Mangungu	152	5.13 S	19.35 E
Mangut, Ross.	86	55.47 N	70.46 E
Mangut, Ross.	88	49.46 N	112.38 E
Mangya	90	37.40 N	90.50 E
Man'gyŏng	98	35.52 N	126.48 E
Manhan ≃	207	42.17 N	72.38 W
Manhartsberg ∧	61	48.32 N	15.44 E
Manhasset	276	40.47 N	73.42 W
Manhasset Bay c	276	40.50 N	73.43 W
Manhasset Hills	276	40.46 N	73.41 W
Manhasset Neck ›[1]	276	40.50 N	73.42 W
Manhattan, Il., U.S.	216	41.25 N	87.59 W
Manhattan, Ks., U.S.	198	39.11 N	96.34 W
Manhattan, Mt., U.S.	202	45.51 N	111.19 W
Manhattan □[8]	276	40.46 N	73.55 W
Manhattan Beach	228	33.53 N	118.24 W
Manhattan Beach State Park ♠	280	33.54 N	118.25 W
Manhattan Bridge ◆[5]	276	40.42 N	73.59 W
Manhattan College ɤ[2]	276	40.53 N	73.54 W
Manheim	208	40.09 N	76.23 W
Manhiça	156	25.24 S	32.48 E
Mān Hpāng	110	22.41 N	98.36 E
Manhuaçu	255	20.15 S	42.02 W
Manhuaçu ≃	255	19.30 S	41.06 W
Manhumirim	255	20.22 S	41.57 W
Maní, P.R.	240m	18.15 N	67.10 W
Mani, R.D.C.	154	6.27 S	25.20 E
Mānī', Jabal al- ∧	132	33.19 N	36.17 E
Mania ≃	157b	19.42 S	45.22 E
Maniago	64	46.10 N	12.43 E
Maniamba	154	12.43 S	35.00 E
Manianga	273b	4.10 S	15.19 E
Manica □[5]	156	19.00 S	33.15 E
Manicahan	116	7.01 N	122.12 E
Manicaland □[4]	154	19.30 S	32.15 E
Manicani Island I	116	10.59 N	125.38 E
Manicaragua	240p	22.09 N	79.58 W
Manic Deux, Réservoir ⊜[1]	186	49.25 N	68.25 W
Manicoré	248	5.49 S	61.17 W
Manicoré ≃	248	5.51 S	61.19 W
Manicouagan ≃	186	49.11 N	68.13 W
Manicouagan, Réservoir ⊜[1]	186	51.30 N	68.19 W
Manic Trois, Réservoir ⊜[1]	186	50.00 N	68.40 W
Maniema □[4]	154	3.00 S	26.30 E
Manifold ≃	44	53.03 N	1.47 W
Maniganggo	102	32.01 N	99.11 E
Manignan	150	10.00 N	7.50 W
Manigotagan	184	51.06 N	96.18 W
Manigotagan ≃	184	51.07 N	96.20 W
Manihāri	124	25.21 N	87.38 E
Manihiki I[1]	14	10.24 S	161.01 W
Manika, Plateau de la ⋏[1]	154	10.00 S	26.00 E
Manikanāli	126	23.19 N	87.03 E
Mānikganj	124	23.52 N	90.00 E
Mānikpur	124	25.04 N	81.07 E
Manila, Pil.	116	14.35 N	121.00 E
Manila, Pil.	269f	14.35 N	121.00 E
Manila, Ar., U.S.	194	35.52 N	90.10 W
Manila, Ut., U.S.	200	40.59 N	109.43 W
Manila Bay c	116	14.30 N	120.45 E
Manila Cathedral ɤ[1]	269f	14.35 N	120.59 E
Manila International Airport ⊠	269f	14.31 N	121.01 E
Manilla, Austl.	166	30.45 S	150.43 E
Manilla, In., U.S.	218	39.34 N	85.37 W
Manilla, Ia., U.S.	198	41.53 N	95.13 W
Manille → Manila	116	14.35 N	121.00 E
Manily	74	62.29 N	165.36 E
Mani Majra	123	30.43 N	76.50 E
Manimbaya, Tanjung ›	112	0.01 N	119.36 E
Manimpé	150	14.09 N	5.31 W
Maningory ≃	157b	17.13 S	49.28 E
Maningrida	164	12.03 S	134.13 E
Maninjau, Danau ⊜	112	0.20 S	100.11 E
Manino	76	53.58 N	34.20 E
Manipa, Pulau I	164	3.17 S	127.35 E
Manipa, Selat ʊ	164	3.20 S	127.23 E
Manipur □[3]	120	25.00 N	94.00 E
Manipur ≃	110	22.52 N	94.05 E
Manique de Baixo	266c	38.44 N	9.22 W
Maniquin Island I	116	11.36 N	121.45 E
Manirāmpur	126	23.01 N	89.14 E
Manisa	130	38.36 N	27.26 E
Manisa □[4]	130	38.50 N	28.10 E
Manissauá-Miçu ≃	250	10.58 S	53.20 W
Manistee	190	44.14 N	86.19 W
Manistee ≃	190	44.15 N	86.21 W
Manistique	190	45.57 N	86.14 W
Manistique ≃	190	45.57 N	86.15 W
Manistique, West Branch ≃	190	46.02 N	86.09 W
Manistique Lake ⊜	190	46.15 N	85.45 W
Manito	194	40.25 N	89.46 W
Manitoba □[4], Can.	176	54.00 N	97.00 W
Manitoba □[4], Can.	184	54.00 N	97.00 W
Manitoba, Lake ⊜	184	51.00 N	98.45 W
Manitou	184	49.15 N	98.31 W
Manitou ≃, On., Can.	184	48.58 N	93.20 W
Manitou ≃, P.Q., Can.	186	50.18 N	65.15 W
Manitou, Lac ⊜, P.Q., Can.	186	50.29 N	63.54 W
Manitou, Lac ⊜, P.Q., Can.	186	50.54 N	65.18 W
Manitou, Lac ⊜, P.Q., Can.	206	46.03 N	74.23 W
Manitou, Lake ⊜, On., Can.	190	45.48 N	82.00 W
Manitou, Lake ⊜, In., U.S.	216	41.03 N	86.11 W
Manitou Beach, Sk., Can.	184	51.43 N	105.26 W
Manitou Beach, Mi., U.S.	216	41.58 N	84.19 W
Manitou Lake ⊜, On., Can.	190	46.01 N	79.00 W
Manitou Lake ⊜, Sk., Can.	184	52.45 N	109.45 W
Manitoulin Island I	190	45.50 N	82.20 W
Manitou Springs	200	38.51 N	104.55 W
Manitouwabing Lake ⊜	212	45.29 N	79.54 W
Manitowaning	190	45.45 N	81.49 W
Manitowik Lake ⊜	190	48.10 N	84.24 W
Manitowish Waters	190	46.09 N	89.53 W
Manitowoc	190	44.05 N	87.39 W
Manitowoc ≃	190	44.05 N	87.39 W
Maniwaki	188	46.23 N	75.58 W
Ma'nīyā	142	30.50 N	30.39 E
Manizales	246	5.05 N	75.32 W
Manja, Madag.	157b	21.26 S	44.20 E
Manjā, Urd.	132	31.45 N	35.51 E
Manjacaze	156	24.44 S	33.53 E
Manjakandriana	157b	18.55 S	47.47 E
Manjeri	122	11.07 N	76.07 E
Manjiang	98	41.57 N	127.36 E
Manjimup	162	34.14 S	116.09 E
Manjing	107	29.55 N	104.07 E
Mānjra ≃	122	18.49 N	77.52 E
Manjuyod	116	9.41 N	123.09 E
Mank	61	48.06 N	15.20 E
Mankanaj	86	48.58 N	60.58 E
Månkarbo	40	60.14 N	17.28 E
Mān Kāt	110	22.05 N	98.01 E
Mankato, Ks., U.S.	198	39.47 N	98.12 W
Mankato, Mn., U.S.	190	44.09 N	93.59 W
Mankayane	158	26.42 S	31.00 E
Mankent	85	42.25 N	69.50 E
Mankera	123	31.23 N	71.26 E
Mankim	152	5.01 N	12.00 E
Mankinholes	262	53.42 N	2.03 W
Man'kivka, Ukr.	78	48.58 N	30.20 E
Man'kivka, Ukr.	83	49.34 N	38.27 E
Mankono	150	8.04 N	6.12 W
Mankota	184	49.25 N	107.04 W
Man'kovo	83	49.24 N	40.17 E
Man'kovo-Ber'ozovskaja	80	48.47 N	41.33 E
Mankoya	154	14.47 S	24.48 E
Mānkundu	272b	22.50 N	88.22 E
Mānkur, India	126	22.30 N	87.54 E
Mānkur, India	126	23.20 N	87.33 E
Manlaj	102	44.07 N	106.50 E
Manley	262	53.14 N	2.45 W
Manley Hot Springs	180	65.00 N	150.37 W
Manleys Corner	283	42.03 N	71.04 W
Manlius	210	43.00 N	75.58 W
Manlleu	34	42.00 N	2.17 E
Manly, Austl.	170	33.48 S	151.17 E
Manly, Austl.	171a	27.28 S	153.15 E
Manly, Ia., U.S.	190	43.17 N	93.12 W
Manly Warringah War Memorial Park ♠	274a	33.46 S	151.15 E
Manmād	122	20.15 N	74.27 E
Mann ≃	164	12.20 S	134.07 E
Mann, Mount ∧	162	25.59 S	129.42 E
Manna, Indon.	112	4.27 S	102.55 E
Mān Na, Mya.	110	23.27 N	97.14 E
Mannahill	166	32.26 S	139.59 E
Mannar	122	8.59 N	79.54 E
Mannar, Gulf of c	122	8.30 N	79.00 E
Mannārgudi	122	10.40 N	79.26 E
Mannar Island I	122	9.03 N	79.50 E
Mann Creek ≃	281	42.32 N	83.44 W
Männedorf	58	47.15 N	8.42 E
Mannersdorf am Leithagebirge	61	47.58 N	16.36 E
Mannersdorf an der Rabnitz	61	47.25 N	16.31 E
Mannford	196	36.09 N	96.23 W
Mannheim	56	49.29 N	8.29 E
Manni	120	34.48 N	87.15 E
Manning, Ia., U.S.	198	41.54 N	95.03 W
Manning, N.D., U.S.	198	47.13 N	102.46 W
Manning, S.C., U.S.	192	33.41 N	80.12 W
Manning, Cape ›	174o	2.02 N	157.26 W
Manning Provincial Park ♠	224	49.07 N	120.54 W
Manning Strait ʊ	175e	7.24 S	158.00 E
Mannington	188	39.31 N	80.20 W
Manningtree	42	51.57 N	1.04 E
Mannō	96	34.11 N	133.51 E
Mann Ranges ⋏	162	26.00 S	129.30 E
Mannsville	212	43.42 N	76.03 W
Mannswörth ◆[8]	264b	48.09 N	16.31 E
Mannu ≃, It.	71	39.16 N	9.00 E
Mannu ≃, It.	71	40.50 N	8.23 E
Mannu, Capo ›	71	40.02 N	8.22 E
Mannu, Monte ∧	71	40.23 N	8.25 E
Mannum	166	34.55 S	139.18 E
Mannus	171b	35.48 S	147.57 E
Mannus Creek ≃	171b	35.58 S	148.03 E
Mannville	182	53.20 N	111.10 W
Mano	150	8.02 N	12.06 W
Mano ≃	150	6.56 N	11.31 W
Manoa	248	9.40 S	65.27 W
Manoel Ribas	252	24.31 S	51.39 W
Manohardi	126	24.08 N	90.43 E
Manoharpur, India	124	22.23 N	85.12 E
Manoharpur, India	126	21.59 N	87.18 E
Manokin ≃	208	38.05 N	75.55 W
Manokotak	180	58.40 N	159.09 W
Manokwari	164	0.52 S	134.05 E
Manolo Fortich (Maluko)	116	8.25 N	124.58 E
Manoma ≃	89	49.18 N	136.37 E
Manombo	157b	22.57 S	43.28 E
Manomet	207	41.55 N	70.34 W
Manomet Hill ∧[2]	207	41.55 N	70.36 W
Manong	114	4.36 N	100.53 E
Manonga ≃	154	4.08 S	34.12 E
Manono	154	7.18 S	27.25 E
Manono I	175a	13.50 S	172.05 W
Manoora	168b	34.00 S	138.49 E
Manoppello	66	42.15 N	14.03 E
Manor, Sk., Can.	184	49.36 N	102.05 W
Manor, Pa., U.S.	214	40.20 N	79.40 W
Manor, Tx., U.S.	222	30.20 N	97.33 W
Manorbier	42	51.39 N	4.48 W
Manorhamilton	48	54.18 N	8.10 W
Manorhaven	276	40.50 N	73.42 W
Manor Hill	214	40.38 N	77.55 W
Manori ◆[8]	272c	19.12 N	72.47 E
Manori Creek c	272c	19.12 N	72.48 E
Manorina National Park ♠	171a	27.23 S	152.47 E
Manori Point ›	272c	19.11 N	72.47 E
Manoron	110	11.38 N	99.04 E
Manorville	214	40.47 N	79.31 W
Manosque	62	43.50 N	5.47 E
Manotick	212	45.13 N	75.41 W
Manouane ≃	186	49.30 N	71.11 W
Manouane, Lac ⊜	186	50.41 N	70.45 W
Manouanis ≃	186	50.28 N	70.08 W
Manouanis, Lac ⊜	186	50.51 N	70.20 W
Manown	279b	40.13 N	79.54 W
Manpaka	273b	4.18 S	15.12 E
Manpitou	100	22.17 N	112.52 E
Manp'o	98	41.10 N	126.17 E
Mānpur, India	122	20.22 N	80.43 E
Mānpur, India	124	23.46 N	81.08 E
Manqabād	142	27.12 N	31.07 E
Manqaṭīn	142	28.20 N	30.40 E
Manquehue, Cerro ∧	286e	33.21 S	70.36 W
Manra I[1]	14	4.27 S	171.15 W
Manresa	34	41.44 N	1.50 E
Manresa Island I	276	41.04 N	73.25 W
Mānsa, India	120	23.26 N	72.40 E
Mānsa, India	123	29.59 N	75.23 E
Mansa (Fort Rosebery), Zam.	154	11.12 S	28.53 E
Mansabá	150	12.18 N	15.15 W
Mansafīs	142	28.00 N	30.49 E
Mansalay	116	12.31 N	121.26 E
Mansara	150	13.20 N	4.39 W
Manse ≃	50	47.08 N	0.25 E
Manseau	206	46.22 N	72.00 W
Mānsehra	123	34.20 N	73.12 E
Mansein	110	25.12 N	95.58 E
Mansel Island I	176	62.00 N	79.50 W
Mansfeld	54	51.35 N	11.27 E
Mansfield, Austl.	169	37.03 S	146.05 E
Mansfield, Eng., U.K.	44	53.09 N	1.11 W
Mansfield, Ar., U.S.	194	35.04 N	94.13 W
Mansfield, Ga., U.S.	192	33.31 N	83.44 W
Mansfield, Il., U.S.	216	40.12 N	88.30 W
Mansfield, La., U.S.	194	32.02 N	93.42 W
Mansfield, Ma., U.S.	207	42.02 N	71.13 W
Mansfield, Mo., U.S.	194	37.06 N	92.34 W
Mansfield, N.J., U.S.	285	40.05 N	74.43 W
Mansfield, Oh., U.S.	214	40.45 N	82.30 W
Mansfield, Pa., U.S.	210	41.48 N	77.04 W
Mansfield, Tx., U.S.	222	32.33 N	97.08 W
Mansfield, Mount ∧	188	44.33 N	72.49 W
Mansfield Center	207	41.45 N	72.11 W
Mansfield Hollow Lake ⊜[1]	207	41.45 N	72.11 W
Mansfield Hollow State Park ♠	207	41.46 N	72.10 W
Mansfield Municipal Airport ⊠	283	42.00 N	71.12 W
Mansfield Woodhouse	44	53.11 N	1.12 W
Man Shan I	106	31.14 N	120.17 E
Mansieville Location	273d	26.05 S	27.45 E
Mānsinhapur	272b	22.39 N	88.09 E
Mansión	236	10.06 N	85.22 W
Manskoje belogorje ⋏	88	54.35 N	94.00 E
Mansle	32	45.53 N	0.11 E
Manso ≃	248	14.42 S	56.16 W
Mansôa	150	12.10 N	14.36 W
Manson, Ia., U.S.	198	42.32 N	94.32 W
Manson, Wa., U.S.	182	47.53 N	120.09 W
Manson ≃	182	55.42 N	123.47 W
Manson Creek	182	55.41 N	124.29 W
Mansonville	206	45.03 N	72.23 W
Mansourah	34	36.04 N	4.28 E
Mansucum	246	9.02 N	77.49 W
Mansura → Al-Manṣūrah, Miṣr	142	31.03 N	31.23 E
Mansura, La., U.S.	194	31.03 N	92.02 W

Symbols in the index entries represent the broad categories identified in the key at the right. Symbols with superior numbers (⋏[1]) identify subcategories (see complete key on page *I · 1).*

Symbole im Register stellen die rechts im Schlüssel erklärten Kategorien dar. Symbole mit hochgestellten Ziffern (⋏[1]) bezeichnen Unterabteilungen einer Kategorie (vgl. vollständiger Schlüssel auf Seite *I · 1).*

Los símbolos incluídos en el texto del índice representan las grandes categorías identificadas con la clave a la derecha. Los símbolos con numeros en su parte superior (⋏[1]) identifican las subcategorías (véase la clave completa en la página *I · 1).*

Les symboles de l'index représentent les catégories indiquées dans la légende à droite. Les symboles suivis d'un indice (⋏[1]) représentent des sous-catégories (voir légende complète à la page *I · 1).*

Os símbolos incluídos no texto do índice representam as grandes categorias identificadas com a chave à direita. Os símbolos com números em sua parte superior (⋏[1]) identificam as subcategorias (veja-se a chave completa à página *I · 1).*

∧ Mountain	Berg	Montaña	Montagne	Montanha
⋏ Mountains	Gebirge	Montañas	Montagnes	Montanhas
)(Pass	Paß	Paso	Col	Passo
V Valley, Canyon	Tal, Cañon	Valle, Cañón	Vallée, Canyon	Vale, Canhão
⩦ Plain	Ebene	Llano	Plaine	Planície
› Cape	Kap	Cabo	Cap	Cabo
I Island	Insel	Isla	Île	Ilha
II Islands	Inseln	Islas	Îles	Ilhas
⊥ Other Topographic Features	Andere Topographische Objekte	Otros Elementos Topográficos	Autres données topographiques	Outros acidentes topográficos

ESPAÑOL

Nombre	Página	Lat.°′	Long.°′ W = Oeste
Manṣūrīyah, Tur'at al- ≊	142	31.03 N	31.24 E
Mansurovo	82	55.52 N	36.36 E
Manta, Ec.	246	0.57 S	80.44 W
Manta, It.	62	44.37 N	7.29 E
Manta, Bahía de c	246	0.54 S	80.42 W
Mantabuan Island I	116	5.02 N	120.13 E
Mantagao ≃	184	51.50 N	97.48 W
Mantalingajan, Mount ʌ	116	8.48 N	117.40 E
Mantalingajan Range ⩓	116	8.46 N	117.40 E
Mantanani Besar, Pulau I	112	6.45 N	116.17 E
Mantangule Island I	116	8.10 N	117.10 E
Mantantale	152	2.10 S	20.06 E
Mantare	154	2.43 S	33.13 E
Mantaro ≃	248	12.15 S	73.58 W
Manteca	226	37.47 N	121.12 W
Mantecal	246	7.33 N	69.09 W
Mantel	60	49.39 N	12.03 E
Mantena	255	18.47 S	40.59 W
Manteno	216	41.15 N	87.49 W
Manteo	192	35.54 N	75.40 W
Mantes-Chérence, Aérodrome de ⊠	261	49.05 N	1.41 E
Mantes-la-Jolie	50	48.59 N	1.43 E
Mantes-la-Ville	261	48.58 N	1.42 E
Manteswar	126	23.26 N	88.06 E
Manteuil-le-Haudouin	50	49.08 N	2.48 E
Manthelan	50	47.08 N	0.47 E
Manti	200	39.16 N	111.38 W
Manticao	116	8.24 N	124.17 E
Mantilla -•-[8]	286b	23.04 N	82.20 W
Mantin	114	2.49 N	101.54 E
Mantiqueira, Serra da ⩓	256	22.00 S	44.45 W
Mantok	112	1.09 S	123.14 E
Manton	190	44.24 N	85.23 W
Mantorville	190	44.04 N	92.45 W
Mantos Blancos	252	23.25 S	70.05 W
Mantou	104	42.27 N	122.26 E
Mantova	64	45.09 N	10.48 E
Mantova □[4]	64	45.10 N	10.47 E
Māntri	126	21.39 N	86.49 E
Mänttä	26	62.02 N	24.38 E
Mantua, Cuba	240p	22.17 N	84.17 W
Mantua → Mantova, It.	64	45.09 N	10.48 E
Mantua, N.J., U.S.	208	39.47 N	75.10 W
Mantua, Oh., U.S.	214	41.17 N	81.13 W
Mantua, Va., U.S.	284c	38.51 N	77.15 W
Mantua ≃	240p	22.12 N	84.25 W
Mantua Creek ≃	285	39.51 N	75.14 W
Mantua Creek, Chestnut Branch ≃	285	39.47 N	75.10 W
Mantua Creek, Porch Branch ≃	285	39.46 N	75.07 W
Mantua Hills	284c	38.51 N	77.16 W
Mantua Terrace	285	39.48 N	75.10 W
Manturovo, Ross.	78	51.28 N	37.07 E
Manturovo, Ross.	80	58.20 N	44.46 E
Mäntyharju	26	61.25 N	26.53 E
Mäntyluoto	26	61.35 N	21.29 E
Manu	248	12.15 S	70.50 W
Manú ≃	248	12.16 S	70.51 W
Manu, Parque Nacional del ♠	248	12.15 S	71.40 W
Manuae I[1], Cook Is.	14	19.21 S	158.56 W
Manuae I[1], Poly. fr.	14	16.30 S	154.40 W
Manua Islands II	174y	14.13 S	169.35 W
Manuel	234	22.44 N	98.19 W
Manuel Alves ≃	250	11.19 S	48.28 W
Manuel Alves Grande ≃	250	7.27 S	47.35 W
Manuel Antonio, Parque Nacional ♠	236	9.25 N	84.10 W
Manuel Avila Camacho, Presa ⊜[1]	234	18.55 N	98.10 W
Manuel Benavides	232	29.05 N	103.55 W
Manuel Derqui	252	27.50 S	58.48 W
Manuel Duarte	256	22.06 S	43.34 W
Manuel Ribeiro	256	22.54 S	42.47 W
Manuel Rodríguez, Isla I	254	52.35 S	73.50 W
Manuel Urbano	248	8.53 S	69.18 W
Manués-Açu ≃	250	3.22 S	57.44 W
Manuguru	122	17.59 N	80.43 E
Manuhangi I[1]	14	19.12 S	141.16 W
Manuherikia ≃	172	45.16 S	169.24 E
Manui, Pulau I	112	3.35 S	123.08 E
Manuilovskaja	76	60.29 N	40.40 E
Manu Island I	164	1.17 S	143.35 E
Manūjān	128	27.24 N	57.32 E
Manuk ≃	115a	6.14 S	108.13 E
Manuk, Pulau I	164	5.33 S	130.18 E
Manukan	116	8.31 N	123.06 E
Manukau	172	37.02 S	174.54 E
Manukau Harbour c	172	37.01 S	174.44 E
Manulla ≃	48	53.57 N	9.12 W
Manulu Lagoon c	174o	1.56 N	157.20 W
Manumuskin ≃	208	39.18 N	75.00 W
Manundi, Tanjung ›	164	0.38 S	135.22 E
Manunui	172	38.53 S	175.20 E
Manuoha ʌ	172	38.39 S	177.07 E
Manuripe (Mamuripi) ≃	248	11.06 S	67.36 W
Manuripi ≃	248	11.42 S	67.16 W
Manursing Island I	276	40.58 N	73.40 W
Manursing Island Park ♠	276	40.58 N	73.40 W
Manus □[5]	164	2.00 S	147.00 E
Mānushmuria	126	22.22 N	86.47 E
Manus Island I	164	2.05 S	147.00 E
Manutahi	172	39.40 S	174.24 E
Manutuke	172	38.41 S	177.55 E
Manvel, N.D., U.S.	198	48.04 N	97.10 W
Manvel, Tx., U.S.	222	29.28 N	95.22 W
Manville, N.J., U.S.	210	40.32 N	74.35 W
Manville, R.I., U.S.	207	41.58 N	71.28 W
Mānwat	122	19.18 N	76.30 E
Many	194	31.34 N	93.29 W
Manyal Shīḥah	273c	29.57 N	31.14 E
Manyana	156	23.23 S	21.44 E
Manyani	154	3.05 S	38.30 E
Manyara, Lake ⊜	154	3.35 S	35.50 E
Manyberries	184	49.24 N	110.42 W
Manyč ≃	72	47.15 N	40.00 E
Manyč-Gudilo, ozero ⊜	80	46.24 N	42.38 E
Manyeleti Game Reserve -•-[4]	156	25.42 S	31.30 E
Many Island Lake ⊜	184	50.08 N	110.03 W
Manyoni	154	5.45 S	34.50 E
Many Peaks	166	24.33 S	151.23 E
Manytsch → Manyč ≃	72	47.15 N	40.00 E
Manz'a	86	58.29 N	96.15 E
Mānzai	120	30.07 N	68.52 E
Manzanares	34	39.00 N	3.22 W
Manzanares ≃	34	40.19 N	3.32 W
Manzanares, Canal del ≊	266a	40.23 N	3.41 W
Manzanillo, Cuba	240p	20.21 N	77.07 W
Manzanillo, Méx.	234	19.03 N	104.20 W
Manzanillo, Bahía c	234	19.04 N	104.22 W
Manzanillo, Bahía de c	234	19.12 N	104.43 W
Manzanillo, Punta ›, Pan.	236	9.38 N	79.32 W
Manzanillo, Punta ›, Ven.	241s	11.32 N	69.17 W
Manzanillo Bay c	238	19.45 N	71.46 W
Manzanita, Or., U.S.	224	45.43 N	123.56 W
Manzanita, Wa., U.S.	224	47.42 N	122.33 W
Manzano, It.	64	45.59 N	13.23 E
Manzano, N.M., U.S.	200	34.38 N	106.20 W
Manzanola	198	38.06 N	103.51 W
Manzano Peak ʌ	200	34.35 N	106.26 W

FRANÇAIS

Nom	Page	Lat.°′	Long.°′ W = Ouest
Manzheliya	78	49.19 N	33.38 E
Manzhouli	88	49.35 N	117.22 E
Manziana	66	42.08 N	12.08 E
Manzil	128	29.15 N	63.05 E
Manzilah, Birkat al- ⊜	142	31.08 N	31.56 E
Manzilah, Buḥayrat al- ⊜	142	31.15 N	32.00 E
Manzini	158	26.30 S	31.25 E
Manzone	258	34.29 S	58.52 W
Manzurka	88	53.30 N	106.04 E
Maó, Esp.	34	39.53 N	4.15 E
Mao, Rep. Dom.	238	19.34 N	71.05 W
Mao, Tchad	136	14.07 N	15.19 E
Maoba	102	30.02 N	108.59 E
Maocifan	100	31.40 N	112.53 E
Maocun	98	34.25 N	117.16 E
Maodianzi, Zhg.	107	30.42 N	104.25 E
Maodianzi, Zhg.	107	29.45 N	104.55 E
Mao'ertuo	107	29.19 N	106.24 E
Maojiagou	104	40.58 N	120.51 E
Maojiaji	100	31.32 N	114.16 E
Maojiakou	100	29.53 N	112.58 E
Maojiaping	105	40.34 N	114.43 E
Maojiapuzi	104	41.10 N	123.32 E
Maojiatun	104	41.05 N	121.58 E
Maojiazao	98	39.53 N	113.26 E
Maoke, Pegunungan ⩓	164	4.00 S	138.00 E
Maolin, Zhg.	89	43.58 N	123.24 E
Maolin, Zhg.	100	30.32 N	118.14 E
Maomao Shan ʌ	102	37.12 N	103.10 E
Maoming	102	21.39 N	110.54 E
Maomu	102	40.18 N	99.28 E
Ma On Shan ʌ	271d	22.25 N	114.15 E
Ma On Shan Tsuen	271d	22.24 N	114.14 E
Maoping	102	30.23 N	110.33 E
Maopora, Pulau I	112	7.35 S	127.35 E
Maoshan	105	40.17 N	117.26 E
Mao Shan ⩓	106	31.43 N	119.17 E
Maoshi	100	26.57 N	113.05 E
Maospati	115a	7.36 S	111.26 E
Maouri, Dallol V	150	12.05 N	3.32 E
Maowen	102	31.30 N	103.39 E
Maoxing	89	45.32 N	124.33 E
Mao Yü I	100	23.19 N	119.19 E
Maozhou	105	38.51 N	116.06 E
Mapaga	112	0.06 S	119.48 E
Mapam Yumco ⊜	120	30.42 N	81.27 E
Mapan	112	2.21 S	111.10 E
Mapanda	152	9.32 S	24.16 E
Mapane	112	1.24 S	120.40 E
Mapanza	154	16.15 S	26.55 E
Mapaoni ≃	250	1.55 N	54.13 W
Mapari ≃, Bra.	246	1.49 S	66.48 W
Mapari ≃, Bra.	250	0.45 N	53.07 W
Mapastepec	234	15.26 N	92.54 W
Mapaville	219	38.14 N	90.29 W
Mapi	164	7.07 S	139.23 E
Mapi ≃	164	7.00 S	139.16 E
Mapia, Kepulauan II	108	0.50 N	134.20 E
Mapida	112	0.33 S	119.46 E
Mapimí	232	25.49 N	103.51 W
Mapimí, Bolsón de -•-[2]	232	26.30 N	104.00 W
Mapimí, Bufa de ʌ	196	25.47 N	103.48 W
Maping, Zhg.	100	24.16 N	117.54 E
Maping, Zhg.	100	31.36 N	113.32 E
Mapinga	154	6.36 S	39.04 E
Mapinhane	156	22.19 S	35.03 E
Mapire	246	7.45 N	64.42 W
Mapiri	248	15.15 S	68.10 W
Mapiri ≃	248	9.52 S	66.21 W
Mapixari, Ilha I	246	2.10 S	65.08 W
Maple -•-[8]	275b	43.51 N	79.31 W
Maple ≃, U.S.	198	45.47 N	98.33 W
Maple ≃, Ia., U.S.	198	42.00 N	95.59 W
Maple ≃, Mi., U.S.	190	42.59 N	84.57 W
Maple ≃, Mn., U.S.	190	44.05 N	94.00 W
Maple ≃, N.D., U.S.	198	46.56 N	96.55 W
Maple Airfield ⊠	275b	43.51 N	79.32 W
Maple Bay	224	48.49 N	123.36 W
Maple Bluff	216	43.07 N	89.22 W
Maple Creek	184	49.55 N	109.27 W
Maple Creek ≃	198	41.33 N	96.27 W
Maplecrest	210	42.17 N	74.11 W
Maple Cross	260	51.37 N	0.30 W
Mapledale	214	41.23 N	79.51 W
Maple Falls	224	48.55 N	122.04 W
Maple Glen	285	40.11 N	75.11 W
Maple Grove, On., Can.	212	43.55 N	78.44 W
Maple Grove, P.Q., Can.	206	45.19 N	73.50 W
Maple Heights	214	41.24 N	81.33 W
Maple Lake	190	45.13 N	94.00 W
Maple Lake ⊜	212	45.06 N	78.40 W
Maple Lane	216	41.45 N	86.14 W
Maple Leaf Gardens ♠	275b	43.40 N	79.23 W
Maple Meadow Brook ≃	283	42.33 N	71.09 W
Maple Mount	194	37.42 N	87.26 W
Maple Park	216	41.55 N	88.36 W
Maple Ridge	224	49.13 N	122.36 W
Maples	216	41.01 N	84.58 W
Maple Shade	285	39.57 N	74.59 W
Maple Springs	214	42.12 N	79.25 W
Maplesville	194	32.47 N	86.52 W
Mapleton, S. Afr.	158	26.20 S	28.14 E
Mapleton, Ia., U.S.	198	42.09 N	95.47 W
Mapleton, Mn., U.S.	190	43.55 N	93.57 W
Mapleton, Or., U.S.	202	44.01 N	123.51 W
Mapleton, Ut,. U.S.	200	40.07 N	111.34 W
Mapleton Depot	214	40.24 N	77.57 W
Maple Valley	224	47.25 N	122.03 W
Mapleville	207	41.56 N	71.38 W
Maplewood, Mo., U.S.	219	38.36 N	90.19 W
Maplewood, N.J., U.S.	276	40.43 N	74.14 W
Maplewood, Oh., U.S.	216	40.23 N	84.02 W
Maplewood, Wa., U.S.	224	47.30 N	122.07 W
Maplewood Terrace	279b	40.17 N	79.32 W
Mapocho ≃	286e	33.25 S	70.47 W
Mapocho, Estación -•-[5]	286e	33.26 S	70.40 W
Mapoi	154	5.28 N	27.40 E
Mapoon Aboriginal Reserve -•-[4]	164	11.40 S	142.25 E
Mappsville	208	37.51 N	75.34 W
Maprik	164	3.40 S	143.05 E
Mapuera ≃	250	1.05 S	57.02 W
Mapujiang	105	40.24 N	114.56 E
Mapulanguene	156	24.29 S	32.06 E
Mapumulo	158	29.11 S	31.02 E
Maputa	158	26.59 S	32.46 E
Maputo	156	25.58 S	32.35 E
Maputo □[5]	156	26.00 S	32.25 E
Maputo (Great Usutu) (Lusutfu) ≃	158	26.11 S	32.42 E
Maputo, Baia de c	158	25.48 S	32.51 E
Maqên Gangri ʌ	102	34.55 N	99.18 E
Maqiangou	105	39.30 N	115.02 E
Maqiao, Zhg.	100	29.48 N	114.22 E
Maqiao, Zhg.	106	30.28 N	120.42 E
Maqna	128	28.24 N	34.45 E
Maqṭeïr ⍑[4]	148	22.10 N	10.50 W
Maquan ≃	124	29.35 N	84.10 E
Maqueda	34	40.04 N	4.22 W
Maqueda Bay c	116	11.44 N	124.58 E
Maqueda Channel ʮ	116	13.42 N	124.01 E
Maquela do Zombo	152	6.03 S	15.07 E
Maquereau, Pointe au ›	186	48.12 N	64.47 W
Maquilaú ≃	246	1.23 N	63.24 W
Maquiling, Mount ʌ	116	14.08 N	121.12 E
Maquinchao	254	41.15 S	68.44 W
Maquinchao ≃	254	41.13 S	69.25 W

PORTUGUÊS

Nome	Página	Lat.°′	Long.°′ W = Oeste
Maquoketa	190	42.04 N	90.39 W
Maquoketa ≃	190	42.11 N	90.19 W
Maquoketa, North Fork ≃	190	42.05 N	90.40 W
Mar, Laguna c	286b	23.05 N	82.30 W
Mar, Serra do ⩡[4]	252	26.00 S	48.00 W
Mara, India	120	28.11 N	94.06 E
Mara, Perú	248	14.06 S	72.07 W
Mara, Zhg.	120	28.11 N	94.08 E
Mara □[4]	154	1.45 S	34.30 E
Mara ≃, Afr.	154	1.31 S	33.56 E
Mara ≃, Ross.	88	58.06 N	104.06 E
Maraã, Bra.	246	1.50 S	65.22 W
Maraa, Poly. fr.	174s	17.46 S	149.34 W
Marabá	250	5.21 S	49.07 W
Marabahan	112	3.00 S	114.45 E
Marabut	116	11.07 N	125.13 E
Maracá, Ilha de I, Bra.	246	3.25 N	61.40 W
Maracá, Ilha de I, Bra.	250	2.05 N	50.25 W
Maracaçumé ≃	250	1.23 S	45.42 W
Maracaí	255	22.36 S	50.39 W
Maracaibo	246	10.40 N	71.37 W
Maracaibo, Lago de ⊜	246	9.50 N	71.30 W
Maracaju	255	21.38 S	55.09 W
Maracaju, Serra de ⩓[2]	255	20.45 S	55.00 W
Maracalagonis	71	39.17 N	9.13 E
Maracanã	250	0.46 S	47.27 W
Maracanã -•-[8]	287a	22.54 S	43.14 W
Maracanã ≃	248	8.22 S	59.41 W
Maracanã, Estádio do ♠	287a	22.55 S	43.14 W
Maracanaú	250	3.52 S	38.38 W
Maracás	255	13.26 S	40.27 W
Maracay	246	10.15 N	67.36 W
Maracossic Creek ≃	208	37.53 N	77.11 W
Marādah	146	29.14 N	19.13 E
Maradi	150	13.29 N	7.06 E
Maradi □[5]	150	14.00 N	7.00 E
Maradi, Goulbin ≃	150	13.38 N	6.20 E
Marāghah, Sabkhat al- ⊜	130	35.39 N	37.39 E
Marāgheh	128	37.23 N	46.13 E
Maragiu, Capo ›	71	40.20 N	8.23 E
Maragogi	250	9.01 S	35.13 W
Maragogipe	255	12.46 S	38.55 W
Marahoué, Parc National de la ♠	150	7.00 N	6.00 W
Mārahra	124	27.44 N	78.35 E
Marahuaca, Cerro ʌ	246	3.34 N	65.27 W
Maraial	250	8.47 S	35.50 W
Maraiche Lake ⊜	184	54.28 N	102.01 W
Marainviller	58	48.35 N	6.36 E
Maraisburg → Roodepoort-Maraisburg	273d	26.11 S	27.56 E
Marais des Cygnes ≃	194	38.02 N	94.14 W
Marais Temps Clair ⊜	219	38.54 N	90.24 W
Marajó, Baía de c	250	1.00 S	48.30 W
Marajó, Ilha de I	250	1.00 S	49.30 W
Marakabei	158	29.32 S	28.09 E
Ma'rakah	132	33.16 N	35.18 E
Mārākand	84	38.52 N	45.14 E
Marakwini	164	3.42 S	141.31 E
Maralal	154	1.06 N	36.42 E
Maralaleng	156	25.47 S	22.45 E
Maralal Game Sanctuary -•-[4]	154	1.09 N	36.38 E
Maraldy	86	52.26 N	77.45 E
Marali	152	6.01 N	18.24 E
Maralik	84	40.35 N	43.52 E
Maralinga	162	30.10 S	131.35 E
Maralinga Lands -•-[4]	162	29.15 S	130.50 E
Maram	120	25.25 N	94.06 E
Maramag	116	7.46 N	125.00 E
Maramasike I	175e	9.32 S	161.27 E
Marambaia ≃	256	21.44 S	46.25 W
Marambaia, Ilha da I	256	23.04 S	43.58 W
Marambaia, Pico da ʌ	256	23.04 S	43.59 W
Marambaia, Restinga de ⩡[2]	256	23.04 S	43.45 W
Marambio ᵾ[3]	9	64.14 S	56.43 W
Marampa	150	8.41 N	12.28 W
Maramsilli Reservoir ⊜[1]	122	20.32 N	81.41 E
Maramureș □[6]	38	47.40 N	24.00 E
Maran	114	3.35 N	102.46 E
Mārān, Koh-i- ʌ	120	29.26 N	66.48 E
Marana, Mali	150	14.38 N	11.55 W
Marana, Az., U.S.	200	32.26 N	111.13 W
Maranalgo	162	29.23 S	117.48 E
Maranboy	164	14.30 S	132.45 E
Maranchón	34	41.03 N	2.12 W
Marand	128	38.26 N	45.46 E
Maranello	64	44.32 N	10.52 E
Marang, Malay.	114	5.12 N	103.13 E
Marang, Mya.	110	10.27 N	98.47 E
Marangá ≃	287a	22.51 S	43.23 W
Marangani	248	14.22 S	71.10 W
Marangas	116	8.40 N	117.38 E
Marange-Zondrange	56	49.07 N	6.32 E
Maranguape	250	3.53 S	38.40 W
Maranhão □[3]	250	5.00 S	45.00 W
Maranhão ≃	255	13.51 S	48.20 W
Marano	266b	45.38 N	8.38 E
Marano, Laguna di c	64	45.44 N	13.10 E
Maranoa ≃	166	27.50 S	148.37 E
Marano di Napoli	68	40.54 N	14.11 E
Marano Lagunare	64	45.46 N	13.10 E
Marañón ≃	242	4.30 S	73.27 W
Marano sul Panaro	64	44.27 N	10.58 E
Marano Vicentino	64	45.41 N	11.25 E
Marans	32	46.19 N	1.00 W
Maraoli -•-[8]	272c	19.03 N	72.54 E
Marapanim	250	0.42 S	47.42 W
Marapendi, Lagoa de c	287a	23.01 S	43.24 W
Marapi ≃	250	0.37 N	55.58 W
Marapicu, Morro do ʌ	287a	22.50 S	43.36 W
Mararoa ≃	172	45.34 S	167.36 E
Mararui	154	1.56 S	41.18 E
Maras, Perú	248	13.20 S	72.09 W
Maraş → Kahramanmaraş, Tür.	130	37.36 N	36.55 E
Marasany	80	57.27 N	54.25 E
Marasende, Pulau I	112	5.08 S	118.09 E
Mărășești	38	45.52 N	27.14 E
Maratasã ≃	250	4.14 S	42.15 W
Maratea	68	39.59 N	15.45 E
Marathon, Austl.	166	20.49 S	143.34 E
Marathon, On., Can.	190	48.43 N	86.23 W
Marathón, Ellás	38	38.10 N	23.58 E
Marathon, Fl., U.S.	220	24.42 N	81.05 W
Marathon, N.Y., U.S.	210	42.26 N	76.01 W
Marathon, Tx., U.S.	196	30.12 N	103.15 W
Marathon, Wi., U.S.	190	44.55 N	89.50 W
Maratua, Pulau I	112	2.15 N	118.36 E
Marau, Bra.	252	28.27 S	52.12 W
Maraú, Bra.	255	14.06 S	39.00 W
Marauiá ≃	246	0.23 S	65.13 W
Marausa	70	37.56 N	12.30 E
Maravari	175e	7.51 S	156.42 E
Maravatío de Ocampo	234	19.54 N	100.27 W
Maravilha	252	26.47 S	53.09 W
Maravillas	232	27.22 N	104.29 W
Maravillas Creek ≃	196	29.34 N	102.47 W
Mara Vista	207	41.33 N	70.34 W
Marav Lake ⊜	120	29.04 N	69.18 E
Maravovo	175e	9.17 S	159.38 E
Marāwah	146	32.29 N	21.25 E
Marawi, Pil.	116	8.01 N	124.18 E

Marawī, Sūd.	140	18.29 N	31.49 E
Marawwaḥ I	128	24.18 N	53.18 E
Maraye-en-Othe	50	48.10 N	3.51 E
Marayes	252	31.29 S	67.20 W
Marayong	274a	33.45 S	150.54 E
Märäzä	84	40.33 N	48.56 E
Marazion	42	50.08 N	5.28 W
Marbach, Dtsch.	54	51.02 N	13.13 E
Marbach, Dtsch.	56	50.37 N	9.43 E
Marbach, Dtsch.	56	51.28 N	8.50 E
Marbach, Schw.	58	46.52 N	7.55 E
Marbach am Neckar	56	48.56 N	9.14 E
Marbache	56	48.48 N	6.05 E
Marbais	50	50.33 N	4.31 E
Marbeck	52	51.49 N	6.52 E
Marbella	34	36.31 N	4.53 W
Marble, Mn., U.S.	190	47.19 N	93.17 W
Marble, N.C., U.S.	192	35.10 N	83.55 W
Marble, Pa., U.S.	214	41.20 N	79.26 W
Marble Arch ⊥	146	30.29 N	18.35 E
Marble Bar	162	21.11 S	119.44 E
Marble Canyon V	200	36.30 N	111.50 W
Marble Falls	196	30.34 N	98.16 W
Marble Hall	156	24.57 S	29.13 E
Marblehead, Il., U.S.	219	39.50 N	91.22 W
Marblehead, Ma., U.S.	207	42.30 N	70.51 W
Marblehead, Oh., U.S.	214	41.32 N	82.44 W
Marblehead Neck ›[1]	283	42.29 N	70.51 W
Marble Hill	194	37.18 N	89.58 W
Marble Lake ⊜	216	41.54 N	84.54 W
Marblemount	224	48.31 N	121.26 W
Marble Rock	190	42.57 N	92.52 W
Marbleton	206	45.37 N	71.35 W
Marburg, Austl.	171a	27.34 S	152.35 E
Marburg, Dtsch.	56	50.49 N	8.46 E
Marburg, S. Afr.	158	30.44 S	30.26 E
Marburg, Lake ⊜[1]	208	39.48 N	76.53 W
Marburg an der Drau → Maribor	36	46.33 N	15.39 E
Marbury	208	38.34 N	77.09 W
Marc ≃	50	50.43 N	3.50 E
Marca, Ponta da ›	152	16.31 S	11.42 E
Marcal ≃	30	47.41 N	17.32 E
Marcala	236	14.07 N	88.00 W
Marcali	30	46.35 N	17.25 E
Marcallo con Casone	266b	45.29 N	8.52 E
Marcaria	64	45.07 N	10.32 E
Marceau, Lac ⊜	186	51.25 N	66.41 W
Marcedusa	68	39.02 N	16.50 E
Marcelin	184	52.55 N	106.47 W
Marceline	194	39.42 N	92.56 W
Marcelino Ramos	252	27.28 S	51.54 W
Marcella	276	40.59 N	74.28 W
Marcellina	66	42.01 N	12.48 E
Marcellus, Mi., U.S.	216	42.01 N	85.48 W
Marcellus, N.Y., U.S.	210	42.59 N	76.20 W
Marcellus Falls	210	43.00 N	76.20 W
Marcevo	83	47.15 N	38.53 E
March, Dtsch.	58	48.03 N	7.47 E
March, Eng., U.K.	42	52.33 N	0.06 E
March (Morava) ≃	30	48.10 N	16.59 E
Marcha	74	60.37 N	123.18 E
Marcha ≃	74	63.28 N	118.50 E
March Air Force Base ■	228	33.54 N	117.15 W
Marchais	261	48.31 N	2.03 E
Marchal	152	5.16 S	14.58 E
Marchamat	85	40.30 N	72.19 E
Marchand	214	40.51 N	79.02 W
Marchaux	58	47.19 N	6.08 E
Marche □[4]	66	43.30 N	13.15 E
Marche □[9]	32	46.05 N	2.10 E
Marche-en-Famenne	56	50.12 N	5.20 E
Marchegg	61	48.17 N	16.55 E
Marche-les-Dames	56	50.29 N	4.58 E
Marchémoret	261	49.03 N	2.46 E
Marchena	34	37.20 N	5.24 W
Marchena, Isla I	246a	0.21 N	90.29 W
Marchenoir	50	47.49 N	1.24 E
Marchesato -•-[1]	68	39.07 N	16.58 E
Marchfeld -•-[1]	264b	48.17 N	16.31 E
Marchienne-au-Pont	50	50.24 N	4.23 E
Marchinbar Island I	164	11.15 S	136.45 E
Mar Chiquita, Laguna c	252	37.37 S	57.24 W
Mar Chiquita, Laguna ⊜	252	30.42 S	62.36 W
Marchtrenk	61	48.11 N	14.07 E
Marchykhyna Buda	78	51.58 N	34.03 E
Marciana	66	42.47 N	10.10 E
Marciana Marina	66	42.48 N	10.12 E
Marcianise	68	41.02 N	14.17 E
Marciano della Chiana	66	43.18 N	11.47 E
Marcigny	32	46.17 N	4.02 E
Marcillac-Vallon	32	44.29 N	2.28 E
Marcilloles	62	45.20 N	5.11 E
Marcilly	261	49.02 N	2.53 E
Marcilly-la-Campagne	50	48.50 N	1.13 E
Marcilly-le-Hayer	50	48.21 N	3.38 E
Marcilly-sur-Eure	50	48.49 N	1.21 E
Marck	50	50.57 N	1.57 E
Marckolsheim	58	48.10 N	7.33 E
Marco, Bra.	250	3.08 S	40.09 W
Marco, It.	64	45.51 N	11.01 E
Marco, Fl., U.S.	220	25.58 N	81.43 W
Marcoing	50	50.07 N	3.11 E
Marco Island I	220	25.55 N	81.45 W
Marcola	202	44.10 N	122.51 W
Marcona	248	15.03 S	75.01 W
Marco Polo, Aeroporto ⊠	64	45.30 N	12.21 E
Marco Polo Bridge -•-[5]	271a	39.52 N	116.12 E
Marcos Juárez	252	32.42 S	62.06 W
Marcos Paz	258	34.46 S	58.50 W
Marcos Paz □[5]	288	34.49 S	58.49 W
Marcotte, Lac ⊜	206	46.47 N	73.12 W
Marcoussis	261	48.39 N	2.14 E
Marcq	261	48.52 N	1.49 E
Marcq-en-Barœul	50	50.40 N	3.05 E
Marčugi	82	55.21 N	38.33 E
Mârculești	38	47.52 N	28.14 E
Marcus	198	42.49 N	95.48 W
Marcus Baker, Mount ʌ	180	61.26 N	147.45 W
Marcus Hook	208	39.49 N	75.25 W
Marcus Hook Creek ≃	285	39.49 N	75.25 W
Marcus Island → Minami-Tori-shima I	14	24.18 N	153.58 E
Marcy, Mount ʌ	188	44.07 N	73.56 W
Marda	162	30.13 S	119.17 E
Mardalsfossen ∟	26	62.30 N	8.07 E
Mardān	123	34.12 N	72.02 E
Mardarivka	78	47.32 N	29.44 E
Mar de Cães, Vala de ≊	266c	38.51 N	8.59 W
Mar de Espanha	256	21.52 S	43.00 W
Mardela Springs	208	38.27 N	75.45 W
Mar del Plata	252	38.00 S	57.33 W
Marden	42	51.10 N	0.29 E
Mardie	162	21.11 S	115.57 E
Mardin	130	37.18 N	40.44 E
Mardin □[4]	128	37.25 N	41.00 E
Mar Dyke ≃	260	51.29 N	0.14 E
Maré I	175f	21.30 S	168.00 E
Mare a Brăilei, Insula I	38	45.00 N	28.00 E
Marea de Portillo	240p	19.55 N	77.11 W
Marecchia ≃	66	44.04 N	12.34 E
Marechal Cândido Rondon	252	24.34 S	54.04 W
Marechal Deodoro	250	9.43 S	35.54 W
Marechal Taumaturgo	248	8.57 S	72.48 W
Maree, Loch ⊜	46	57.42 N	5.30 W

Mareeba	166	17.00 S	145.26 E
Mareetsane	158	26.09 S	25.25 E
Mareil-en-France	261	49.04 N	2.26 E
Mareil-le-Guyon	261	48.47 N	1.51 E
Mareil-Marly	261	48.53 N	2.05 E
Mare Island I	226	38.06 N	122.16 W
Mare Island Naval Shipyard ■	226	38.06 N	122.17 W
Mare Island Strait ʮ	282	38.06 N	122.17 W
Mareje, Gunung ʌ	115b	8.46 S	116.08 E
Marek	112	4.48 S	120.21 E
Maremma -•-[1]	66	42.30 N	11.30 E
Marene	62	44.39 N	7.44 E
Marengo, Il., U.S.	216	42.14 N	88.36 W
Marengo, In., U.S.	218	38.22 N	86.20 W
Marengo, Ia., U.S.	190	41.47 N	92.04 W
Marengo, Mi., U.S.	216	42.17 N	84.51 W
Marengo, Oh., U.S.	214	40.24 N	82.49 W
Marengo ⊥	62	44.49 N	8.40 E
Marengo Cave ⩡[5]	218	38.23 N	86.21 W
Marenisco	190	46.22 N	89.41 W
Marennes	32	45.50 N	1.06 W
Marerano	157b	21.23 S	44.52 E
Maresias	256	23.48 S	45.33 W
Marettimo	70	37.58 N	12.04 E
Marettimo, Isola I	70	37.58 N	12.03 E
Mareuil-en-Brie	50	48.57 N	3.45 E
Mareuil-lès-Meaux	261	48.56 N	2.52 E
Mareuil-sur-Aÿ	50	49.03 N	4.02 E
Mareuil-sur-Belle	32	45.28 N	0.28 E
Marevo	76	57.19 N	32.05 E
Marey-sur-Tille	58	47.35 N	5.03 E
Marfa	196	30.18 N	104.01 W
Marfinka	83	47.36 N	38.32 E
Marfino	80	46.25 N	48.44 E
Mar Forest -•-[3]	46	57.00 N	3.35 W
Margai Caka ⊜	120	35.00 N	87.00 E
Margam, Īrān	84	39.09 N	44.57 E
Margam, Wales, U.K.	42	51.34 N	3.44 W
Margao → Madgaon	122	15.18 N	73.57 E
Margaree	186	46.24 N	61.05 W
Margaree Harbour	186	46.26 N	61.07 W
Margaret ≃	162	18.10 S	125.37 E
Margaret, Mount ʌ	224	46.18 N	122.08 W
Margaret Bay	182	51.20 N	127.29 W
Margaret Creek ≃	166	29.26 S	137.07 E
Margarethenhöhe -•-[8]	263	51.26 N	6.58 E
Margaret River, Austl.	162	33.57 S	115.04 E
Margaret River, Austl.	162	18.38 S	126.52 E
Margaret Roding	260	51.47 N	0.19 E
Margaretting	260	51.41 N	0.25 E
Margarettsville	208	36.32 N	77.21 W
Margaretville	210	42.08 N	74.38 W
Margarita, Bahía → Marguerite Bay c	9	68.30 S	68.30 W
Margarita, Isla de I	246	11.00 N	64.00 W
Margarita Belén	252	27.16 S	58.58 W
Margarita Peak ʌ	228	33.26 N	117.23 W
Margaritovka	83	46.55 N	38.52 E
Margate, S. Afr.	158	30.55 S	30.15 E
Margate, Eng., U.K.	42	51.24 N	1.24 E
Margate, Fl., U.S.	220	26.14 N	80.12 W
Margate City	208	39.19 N	74.30 W
Margecany	30	48.54 N	21.01 E
Margelan → Margilan	85	40.28 N	71.44 E
Margeride, Monts de la ⩓	32	44.50 N	3.30 E
Margès	62	45.09 N	5.03 E
Māngherita, India	120	27.17 N	95.41 E
Margherita → Jamaame, Som.	144	0.04 N	42.45 E
Margherita di Savoia	68	41.23 N	16.09 E
Margherita Peak ʌ	154	0.22 N	29.51 E
Marghī	120	34.58 N	66.31 E
Marghita	38	47.21 N	22.21 E
Margi ≃	70	37.16 N	14.58 E
Margilan	85	40.28 N	71.44 E
Margit Híd -•-[5]	264c	47.31 N	19.02 E
Margit-sziget I	264c	47.32 N	19.03 E
Margny-lès-Compiègne	50	49.26 N	2.49 E
Margone	62	45.13 N	7.11 E
Margonin	30	52.59 N	17.05 E
Margos	248	10.04 S	76.26 W
Margosatubig	116	7.34 N	123.10 E
Margot Lake ⊜	184	52.28 N	93.10 W
Māngow, Dasht-e -•-[2]	128	30.45 N	63.10 E
Margreid → Magrè	64	46.17 N	11.12 E
Marguerite, Pic → Margherita Peak ʌ	154	0.22 N	29.51 E
Marguerite Bay c	9	68.30 S	68.30 W
Marguerittes	62	43.51 N	4.27 E
Margut	56	49.35 N	5.16 E
Margyang	124	29.57 N	90.09 E
Marhanets'	78	47.38 N	34.40 E
Mari	164	9.10 S	141.40 E
Maria	116	9.12 N	123.39 E
Maria, Îles II	14	21.48 S	154.41 W
Mariabrunn -•-[8]	264b	48.12 N	16.14 E
María Cleofas, Isla I	234	21.16 N	106.14 W
Maria da Fé	256	22.18 S	45.23 W
María Elena	252	22.21 S	69.40 W
Maria Enzersdorf	61	48.06 N	16.17 E
Maria Gail	64	46.36 N	13.52 E
Mariager	26	56.39 N	10.00 E
Mariāhu	124	25.37 N	82.37 E
María Ignacia (Vela)	252	37.24 S	59.30 W
Maria Island I, Austl.	164	14.52 S	135.40 E
Maria Island I, Austl.	166	42.39 S	148.04 E
Maria Island National Park ♠	166	42.39 S	148.06 E
Mariakani	154	3.52 S	39.28 E
Maria Laach ᵾ[1]	56	50.24 N	7.14 E
María la Baja	246	9.59 N	75.17 W
Maria Lanzendorf	264b	48.06 N	16.25 E
Maria Luggau	64	46.42 N	12.45 E
María Madre, Isla I	234	21.35 N	106.33 W
María Magdalena, Isla I	234	21.25 N	106.24 W
Marian, Lake ⊜	220	27.52 N	81.06 W
Mariana	255	20.23 S	43.25 W
Mariana Basin ✣[1]	14	17.30 N	145.00 E
Mariana Islands II	108	16.00 N	145.30 E
Mariana Ridge ✣[3]	14	17.00 N	146.00 E
Mariana Trench ✣[1]	14	15.00 N	147.30 E
Mariāni	120	26.40 N	94.20 E
Marian Lake ⊜	176	63.00 N	116.10 W
Marianna, Ar., U.S.	194	34.46 N	90.45 W
Marianna, Fl., U.S.	192	30.46 N	85.13 W
Mariannelund	26	57.37 N	15.34 E
Mariannhill	158	29.52 S	30.50 E
Mariano Acosta	258	34.43 S	58.48 W
Mariano Comense	62	45.42 N	9.11 E
Mariano del Friuli	64	45.55 N	13.27 E
Mariano I. Loza	252	29.22 S	58.12 W
Mariano J. Haedo	288	34.38 S	58.36 W
Mariano Moreno, Arg.	252	38.44 S	70.01 W
Mariano Moreno → Moreno, Arg.	258	34.39 S	58.48 W
Marianopoli	70	37.36 N	13.55 E
Mariánské Lázně	60	49.59 N	12.43 E
Mariar	164	2.48 S	132.50 E
Mariarano	157b	15.29 S	46.42 E
Marias ≃	202	47.56 N	110.30 W
Marias, Dry Fork ≃	202	48.22 N	111.45 W
Marías, Islas II	234	21.25 N	106.28 W
Maria Saal	61	46.41 N	14.21 E
Marias Pass)(	202	48.19 N	113.21 W
Maria Stein	216	40.24 N	84.28 W
María Teresa	252	34.01 S	61.54 W
Maria-Theresiopel → Subotica	38	46.06 N	19.39 E

Mariato, Punta ›	246	7.13 N	80.53 W
Maria van Diemen, Cape ›	172	34.28 S	172.39 E
Mariaville	210	42.49 N	74.08 W
Mariazell	61	47.47 N	15.19 E
Ma'rib	144	15.30 N	45.20 E
Maribo	41	54.46 N	11.31 E
Maribojoc Bay c	116	9.42 N	123.50 E
Maribor	36	46.33 N	15.39 E
Maribyrnong	274b	37.46 S	144.54 E
Maricá, Bra.	256	22.55 S	42.49 W
Marica, Ross.	78	51.45 N	35.16 E
Maricá □[7]	287a	22.57 S	42.59 W
Marica (Évros) (Meriç) ≃	38	40.52 N	26.12 E
Maricá, Lagoa de c	256	22.56 S	42.50 W
Maricaban Island I	116	13.39 N	120.53 E
Maricao	240m	18.11 N	66.59 W
Maricás, Ilhas II	256	23.01 S	42.55 W
Maricha Bil ⊜	272b	22.55 N	88.31 E
Marico ≃	156	24.12 S	26.52 E
Maricopa, Az., U.S.	200	33.03 N	112.02 W
Maricopa, Ca., U.S.	204	35.03 N	119.24 W
Maricopa Indian Reservation -•-[4]	200	33.02 N	112.05 W
Maricunga, Salar de ≚	252	26.55 S	69.05 W
Maridagao ≃	116	7.13 N	124.41 E
Marīdī	154	4.55 N	29.28 E
Maridi ≃	140	6.05 N	29.24 E
Marié ≃	246	0.27 S	66.26 W
Marie Byrd Land -•-[1]	9	80.00 S	120.00 W
Marie Curtis Park ♠	275b	43.35 N	79.33 W
Mariedamm	40	58.51 N	15.09 E
Mariefred	40	59.16 N	17.13 E
Marie-Galante I	241o	15.56 N	61.16 W
Mariehamn	26	60.06 N	19.57 E
Marieholm	41	55.52 N	13.09 E
Mariel	240p	22.59 N	82.45 W
Mari El → Marij El □[3]	80	56.30 N	48.00 E
Marie Lake ⊜	184	54.37 N	110.18 W
Marie-Lefranc, Lac ⊜	206	46.08 N	75.00 W
Mariembourg	50	50.06 N	4.31 E
Marienbad → Mariánské Lázně	60	49.59 N	12.43 E
Marienbaum	52	51.41 N	6.22 E
Marienberg, Dtsch.	54	50.39 N	13.10 E
Marienberg, Pap. N. Gui.	164	3.55 S	144.15 E
Marien-Berg ʌ[2]	264a	52.22 N	13.32 E
Marienborn	54	52.12 N	11.08 E
Marienburg → Malbork	30	54.02 N	19.01 E
Mariendorf -•-[8]	264a	52.26 N	13.23 E
Marienfelde -•-[8]	54	52.25 N	13.22 E
Marienhafe	52	53.31 N	7.16 E
Marienheide	56	51.05 N	7.32 E
Marienmünster	52	51.50 N	9.13 E
Mariental, Dtsch.	54	52.16 N	10.59 E
Mariental, Namibia	156	24.36 S	17.59 E
Marienville	214	41.28 N	79.07 W
Maries □[6]	219	38.15 N	91.56 W
Maries ≃	194	38.30 N	92.01 W
Mariestad	40	58.43 N	13.51 E
Marieta ≃	246	5.02 N	66.38 W
Marietta, Ga., U.S.	192	33.57 N	84.33 W
Marietta, In., U.S.	218	39.26 N	85.53 W
Marietta, Mn., U.S.	198	45.00 N	96.25 W
Marietta, Oh., U.S.	188	39.24 N	81.27 W
Marietta, Ok., U.S.	196	33.56 N	97.06 W
Marietta, Pa., U.S.	208	40.03 N	76.33 W
Marietta, Tx., U.S.	222	33.10 N	94.33 W
Marietta, Wa., U.S.	224	48.47 N	122.34 W
Marieville	206	45.26 N	73.10 W
Mariga ≃	150	9.40 N	5.55 E
Marignane	62	43.25 N	5.13 E
Marignier	58	46.06 N	6.31 E
Marigny-le-Châtel	50	48.24 N	3.44 E
Marigny-L'Église	50	47.22 N	3.56 E
Marigot, Dom.	240d	15.32 N	61.18 W
Marigot, Guad.	238	18.04 N	63.06 W
Marihatag	116	8.48 N	126.18 E
Mariinsk	86	56.13 N	87.45 E
Mariinskoje	89	51.43 N	140.13 E
Marijampole	76	54.33 N	23.21 E
Marijec	80	56.32 N	49.50 E
Marij El □[3], Ross.	72	56.30 N	48.00 E
Marij El □[3], Ross.	80	56.30 N	48.00 E
Marikana	158	25.42 S	27.30 E
Marikina	269f	14.38 N	121.06 E
Marikina ≃	269f	14.33 N	121.04 E
Marília	255	22.13 S	49.56 W
Marilla	210	42.50 N	78.33 W
Mari-Malmyž	80	56.30 N	50.52 E
Marimari ≃	246	3.58 S	58.49 W
Marimba	152	8.28 S	17.08 E
Marín	34	42.23 N	8.42 W
Marin □[6]	226	38.03 N	122.33 W
Marina	226	36.41 N	121.48 W
Marina -•-[8]	282	37.47 N	122.27 W
Marina del Rey	280	33.50 N	118.25 W
Marina del Rey c	280	33.58 N	118.27 W
Marina di Andora	62	43.57 N	8.08 E
Marina di Campo	66	42.44 N	10.14 E
Marina di Caronia	70	38.02 N	14.28 E
Marina di Carrara	64	44.02 N	10.02 E
Marina di Cecina	66	43.18 N	10.29 E
Marina di Gioiosa Ionica	68	38.18 N	16.20 E
Marina di Grosseto	66	42.43 N	10.59 E
Marina di Massa	64	44.00 N	10.06 E
Marina di Minturno	66	41.16 N	13.45 E
Marina di Orosei	71	40.22 N	9.43 E
Marina di Palma -•-[8]	70	37.10 N	13.43 E
Marina di Pietrasanta	64	43.56 N	10.12 E
Marina di Pisa	66	43.40 N	10.16 E
Marina di Ragusa	70	36.47 N	14.33 E
Marina di Ravenna	66	44.29 N	12.17 E
Marina Fall ∟	246	5.22 N	59.29 W
Mar'ina Horka	76	53.31 N	28.09 E
Marin City	282	37.52 N	122.21 W
Marinduque □[4]	116	13.25 N	121.55 E
Marinduque Island I	116	13.24 N	121.58 E
Marine	219	38.47 N	89.46 W
Marine City	214	42.43 N	82.29 W
Marine-Ehrenmal ⊥	54	54.23 N	10.15 E
Marineland of the Pacific ᵾ[3]	228	33.44 N	118.24 W
Marinella	70	37.35 N	12.50 E
Marine Museum ᵾ	280	33.43 N	118.17 W
Marineo	70	37.57 N	13.25 E
Marine Park ♠	283	42.20 N	71.01 W
Marine Parkway Bridge -•-[5]	276	40.34 N	73.53 W
Mariners Museum ᵾ	208	37.03 N	76.30 W
Marines	50	49.09 N	1.59 E
Marinette	190	45.06 N	87.37 W
Maringá	255	23.25 S	51.55 W
Maringa ≃	152	1.14 N	19.48 E
Maringouin	194	30.29 N	91.31 W
Marínguè	154	17.55 S	34.24 E
Marinha Grande	34	39.45 N	8.56 W
Marinho ≃	287a	23.00 S	43.27 W
Marin Mall -•-[9]	282	37.56 N	122.31 W
Marino, It.	66	41.46 N	12.39 E
Marino, Vanuatu	175f	15.00 S	168.09 E
Marinovka	80	48.41 N	43.49 E
Marin Peninsula ›[1]	282	37.51 N	122.31 W
Marinskij Posad	80	56.07 N	47.43 E
Marintu	112	0.34 N	110.00 E
Marinwood	226	38.02 N	122.32 W
Mario, Monte ʌ[2]	267a	41.55 N	12.27 E
Marion, Austl.	168b	35.01 S	138.34 E
Marion, Al., U.S.	194	32.37 N	87.19 W
Marion, Ar., U.S.	194	35.12 N	90.11 W
Marion, Ct., U.S.	207	41.33 N	72.55 W
Marion, Il., U.S.	194	37.43 N	88.55 W
Marion, In., U.S.	216	40.33 N	85.39 W

≃ River	Fluß	Río	Rivière	Rio	✣ Submarine Features	Untermeerische Objekte	Accidentes Submarinos	Formes de relief sous-marin	Acidentes submarinos
≊ Canal	Kanal	Canal	Canal	Canal	□ Political Unit	Politische Einheit	Unidad Politica	Entité politique	Unidade política
∟ Waterfall, Rapids	Wasserfall, Stromschnellen	Cascada, Rápidos	Chute d'eau, Rapides	Cascata, Rápidos	ᵾ Cultural Institution	Kulturelle Institution	Institución Cultural	Institution culturelle	Institução cultural
ʮ Strait	Meeresstraße	Estrecho	Détroit	Estreito	⊥ Historical Site	Historische Stätte	Sitio Histórico	Site historique	Sitio histórico
c Bay, Gulf	Bucht, Golf	Bahía, Golfo	Baie, Golfe	Baía, Golfo	♠ Recreational Site	Erholungs- und Ferienort	Sitio de Recreo	Centre de loisirs	Area de Lazer
⊜ Lake, Lakes	See, Seen	Lago, Lagos	Lac, Lacs	Lago, Lagos	⊠ Airport	Flughafen	Aeropuerto	Aéroport	Aeroporto
≚ Swamp	Sumpf	Pantano	Marais	Pântano	■ Military Installation	Militäranlage	Instalación Militar	Installation militaire	Instalação militar
⍓ Ice Features, Glacier	Eis- und Gletscherformen	Accidentes Glaciales	Formes glaciaires	Acidentes glaciares	-•- Miscellaneous	Verschiedenes	Misceláneo	Divers	Diversos
⍑ Other Hydrographic Features	Andere Hydrographische Objekte	Otros Elementos Hidrográficos	Autres données hydrographiques	Outros acidentes hidrográficos					

I · 108 Mari-Mass

ENGLISH Name Page Lat.°′ Long.°′ — DEUTSCH Name Seite Breite°′ Länge°′ E = Ost

Name	Page	Lat.°′	Long.°′
Marion, Ia., U.S.	190	42.02 N	91.35 W
Marion, Ks., U.S.	198	38.20 N	97.01 W
Marion, Ky., U.S.	194	37.19 N	88.04 W
Marion, La., U.S.	194	32.54 N	92.14 W
Marion, Ma., U.S.	207	41.42 N	70.45 W
Marion, Mi., U.S.	190	44.06 N	85.08 W
Marion, Ms., U.S.	194	32.25 N	88.38 W
Marion, N.Y., U.S.	210	43.08 N	77.11 W
Marion, N.C., U.S.	192	35.41 N	82.00 W
Marion, N.D., U.S.	198	46.36 N	98.19 W
Marion, Oh., U.S.	214	40.35 N	83.07 W
Marion, S.C., U.S.	192	34.10 N	79.24 W
Marion, S.D., U.S.	198	43.25 N	97.15 W
Marion, Va., U.S.	192	36.50 N	81.30 W
Marion, Wi., U.S.	190	44.40 N	88.53 W
Marion □[6], Fl., U.S.	220	29.00 N	82.03 W
Marion □[6], Il., U.S.	219	38.38 N	88.57 W
Marion □[6], In., U.S.	218	39.46 N	86.09 W
Marion □[6], Mo., U.S.	219	39.50 N	91.37 W
Marion □[6], Oh., U.S.	214	40.35 N	83.08 W
Marion □[6], Or., U.S.	224	45.06 N	122.47 W
Marion □[6], Tx., U.S.	222	32.48 N	94.33 W
Marion, Lake ⊜	220	28.05 N	81.32 W
Marion, Lake ⊜[1]	192	33.30 N	80.25 W
Marion Bay ⊂	166	42.48 S	147.55 E
Marion Center	214	40.46 N	79.03 W
Marion Downs	166	23.22 S	139.39 E
Marion Heights	210	40.48 N	76.28 W
Marion Hill	214	40.44 N	80.18 W
Marion Junction	194	32.26 N	87.14 W
Marion Lake ⊜[1]	198	38.24 N	97.08 W
Marion Reef ✢[2]	166	19.10 S	152.17 E
Marion Station	208	38.02 N	75.46 W
Marionville	194	37.00 N	93.38 W
Mariópolis	252	26.20 S	52.33 W
Maripa	246	7.26 N	65.09 W
Maripá de Minas	256	21.48 S	42.58 W
Maripasoula	250	3.38 N	54.02 W
Maripipi Island I	116	11.47 N	124.19 E
Mariposa	226	37.29 N	119.57 W
Mariposa □[6]	226	37.29 N	119.58 W
Mariposa Creek ≃	226	37.14 N	120.26 W
Mariposa Slough ≃	226	37.12 N	120.46 W
Mariquita	246	5.12 N	74.54 W
Marisa	112	0.28 N	121.56 E
Marisa ≃	112	0.28 N	121.56 E
Mariscal Estigarribia	252	22.02 S	60.38 W
Marisco, Ponta do ≻	287a	23.01 S	43.17 W
Mariškino	82	55.21 N	38.37 E
Marismas del Guadalquivir ≋	34	37.00 N	6.15 W
Marissa	219	38.15 N	89.45 W
Maritime Alps (Alpes Maritimes) (Alpi Marittime) ⋏	62	44.15 N	7.10 E
Maritime Atlas → Atlas Tellien ⋏	148	36.00 N	3.00 E
Maritimes, Alpes → Maritime Alps ⋏	62	44.15 N	7.10 E
Marittime, Alpi → Maritime Alps ⋏	62	44.15 N	7.10 E
Mari-Turek	80	56.47 N	49.36 E
Maritzburg → Pietermaritzburg	158	29.37 S	30.16 E
Mariupol'	83	47.06 N	37.33 E
Mariusa, Caño ≃[1]	246	9.43 N	61.26 W
Mariusa, Isla I	241r	9.39 N	61.19 W
Marīvān	128	35.31 N	46.10 E
Mariveles	116	14.26 N	120.29 E
Märjamaa	76	58.54 N	24.26 E
Marjanovka	86	54.58 N	72.38 E
Marjanskaja	78	45.06 N	38.38 E
Marjevka	86	53.46 N	67.24 E
Marjino, Ross.	82	54.28 N	37.12 E
Marjino, Ross.	89	48.31 N	130.38 E
Marjino, Ross.	265a	59.50 N	29.56 E
Marjino, Ross.	265a	59.54 N	31.00 E
Marjino, Ross.	265b	55.52 N	37.18 E
Marjinskaja	84	43.53 N	43.29 E
Marjinsko	76	58.49 N	28.32 E
Mār Jirjis, Jūn ⊂	132	33.54 N	35.33 E
Marj 'Uyūn	132	33.22 N	35.35 E
Marka, Som.	144	1.43 N	44.53 E
Mārkā, Urd.	132	31.59 N	35.59 E
Markā I	144	18.13 N	41.19 E
Mark Acres	279b	40.21 N	79.42 W
Markakol', ozero ⊜	86	48.45 N	85.48 E
Markala	150	13.41 N	6.05 W
Markam	102	29.40 N	98.30 E
Markansu	85	39.18 N	73.20 E
Mārkāpur	122	15.44 N	79.17 E
Markaryd	26	56.26 N	13.36 E
Markazī □[4]	128	34.30 N	50.30 E
Markdale	212	44.19 N	80.39 W
Markdorf	58	47.43 N	9.23 E
Marked Tree	194	35.31 N	90.25 W
Markelo	52	52.14 N	6.30 E
Markelovo	86	56.42 N	83.33 E
Marken I	52	52.28 N	5.03 E
Markendorf	54	51.59 N	13.10 E
Markermeer ⊜	52	52.33 N	5.15 E
Markesan	190	43.42 N	88.59 W
Märket I	40	60.18 N	19.08 E
Market Bosworth	42	52.37 N	1.24 W
Market Deeping	42	52.41 N	0.19 W
Market Drayton	42	52.54 N	2.29 W
Market Harborough	42	52.29 N	0.55 W
Markethill	48	54.18 N	6.31 W
Market Lavington	42	51.18 N	1.59 W
Market Rasen	44	53.24 N	0.21 W
Market Weighton	44	53.52 N	0.40 W
Markfield	42	52.40 N	1.17 W
Markgröningen	56	48.54 N	9.05 E
Markham, On., Can.	212	43.52 N	79.16 W
Markham, Il., U.S.	278	41.35 N	87.41 W
Markham, Tx., U.S.	222	28.57 N	96.04 W
Markham ≃	164	6.35 S	146.25 E
Markham, Mount ∧	9	82.51 S	161.21 E
Markham Bay ⊂	176	63.30 N	71.48 W
Markinch	46	56.12 N	3.08 W
Märkisch Buchholz	54	52.07 N	13.46 E
Markit	85	38.55 N	77.38 E
Markivka	83	49.31 N	39.34 E
Markkleeberg	54	51.17 N	12.23 E
Markland Dam ◆[6]	218	38.47 N	84.58 W
Markle, In., U.S.	216	40.50 N	85.20 W
Markle, Pa., U.S.	279b	40.34 N	79.39 W
Markleeville	226	38.41 N	119.46 W
Markleville	218	39.58 N	85.36 W
Markley Canyon V	282	38.00 N	121.50 W
Marklohe	52	52.40 N	9.09 E
Marknesse	52	52.43 N	5.52 E
Markneukirchen	54	50.18 N	12.19 E
Markoldendorf	52	51.48 N	9.46 E
Markópoulon	267c	37.54 N	23.54 E
Markounda	152	7.37 N	16.59 E
Markovo, Ross.	74	64.40 N	170.25 E
Markovo, Ross.	80	57.01 N	40.30 E
Markovo, Ross.	82	55.52 N	39.17 E
Markovo, Ross.	88	57.20 N	107.04 E
Markoy	150	14.39 N	0.02 E
Markranstädt	54	51.18 N	12.13 E
Marks, Ross.	80	51.42 N	46.46 E
Marks, Ms., U.S.	194	34.15 N	90.16 W
Marks Tey	42	51.52 N	0.47 E
Marksuhl	56	50.55 N	10.11 E
Marksville	194	31.07 N	92.03 W
Markt Bibart	56	49.39 N	10.26 E
Marktbreit	56	49.40 N	10.08 E
Markt Erlbach	56	49.29 N	10.38 E
Marktheidenfeld	56	49.50 N	9.36 E
Markt Indersdorf	60	48.22 N	11.23 E
Marktl	60	48.15 N	12.51 E
Marktleugast	54	50.10 N	11.38 E
Marktleuthen	54	50.08 N	12.00 E
Marktoberdorf	58	47.47 N	10.37 E
Marktredwitz	60	50.00 N	12.06 E
Markt Rettenbach	58	47.57 N	10.23 E
Marktschellenberg	64	47.42 N	13.02 E
Markt Schwaben	60	48.11 N	11.51 E
Mark Twain Cave ⊥[5]	219	39.42 N	91.21 W
Mark Twain Lake ⊜[1]	219	39.30 N	91.45 W
Mark Twain State Park ♠	219	39.29 N	91.48 W
Markundi	140	11.33 N	23.49 E
Markvue Manor	279b	40.20 N	79.46 W
Mark West Creek ≃	226	38.30 N	122.42 W
Marl	52	51.38 N	7.05 E
Marlasi	164	5.30 S	134.38 E
Marlboro, Ab., Can.	182	53.33 N	116.45 W
Marlboro, N.J., U.S.	208	40.18 N	74.14 W
Marlboro, N.Y., U.S.	210	41.36 N	73.58 W
Marlboro, Oh., U.S.	214	40.53 N	81.12 W
Marlboro, Pa., U.S.	285	39.54 N	75.42 W
Marlborough, Austl.	166	22.49 S	149.53 E
Marlborough, Guy.	246	7.29 N	58.38 W
Marlborough, Eng., U.K.	42	51.26 N	1.43 W
Marlborough, Ct., U.S.	207	41.37 N	72.27 W
Marlborough, Ma., U.S.	207	42.20 N	71.33 W
Marlborough Downs ⋏[1]	42	51.30 N	1.45 W
Marldon	42	50.28 N	3.36 W
Marle	50	49.44 N	3.46 E
Marlenheim	58	48.37 N	7.30 E
Marles-en-Brie	261	48.44 N	2.53 E
Marles-les-Mines	50	50.30 N	2.31 E
Marlette	190	43.19 N	83.04 W
Marlette Lake ⊜	226	39.10 N	119.54 W
Marley, Il., U.S.	278	41.33 N	87.55 W
Marley, Md., U.S.	208	39.09 N	76.35 W
Marley Creek ≃	278	41.31 N	87.57 W
Marley Neck ≻[1]	284b	39.12 N	76.33 W
Marlieux	58	46.04 N	5.04 E
Marlin	222	31.18 N	96.53 W
Marlinton	188	38.13 N	80.05 W
Marl-Loemühle, Flughafen ⊠	263	51.39 N	7.10 E
Marlow, Dtsch.	54	54.09 N	12.34 E
Marlow, Eng., U.K.	42	51.35 N	0.48 W
Marlow, Ok., U.S.	196	34.38 N	97.57 W
Marlpit Hill	260	51.13 N	0.04 E
Marlton	208	39.53 N	74.55 W
Marlton Heights	285	39.40 N	75.21 W
Marly	50	50.20 N	3.32 E
Marly, Forêt de ♠	261	48.52 N	2.03 E
Marly-la-Ville	261	49.05 N	2.30 E
Marly-le-Roi	50	48.52 N	2.05 E
Marma, Sve.	26	61.16 N	16.52 E
Marma, Sve.	40	60.30 N	17.25 E
Marmaduke	194	36.11 N	90.22 W
Marmagne	58	46.50 N	4.21 E
Marmande	32	44.30 N	0.10 E
Marmara, Sea of → Marmara Denizi ⊤[2]	130	40.40 N	28.15 E
Marmara Adası I	130	40.38 N	27.37 E
Marmara Denizi (Sea of Marmara) ⊤[2]	130	40.40 N	28.15 E
Marmara Ereğlisi	130	40.58 N	27.57 E
Marmara Gölü ⊜	130	38.37 N	28.02 E
Marmaris	130	36.51 N	28.16 E
Marmarītā	130	34.47 N	36.15 E
Marmarth	198	46.17 N	103.55 W
Marmaton ≃	194	38.00 N	94.19 W
Marmelopolis	256	22.27 S	45.10 W
Marmelos	248	6.08 S	61.50 W
Marmelos, Rio dos ≃	248	6.06 S	61.46 W
Marmet	188	38.14 N	81.34 W
Marmion Lake ⊜[1]	190	48.54 N	91.30 W
Marmirolo	64	45.13 N	10.45 E
Marmolada ∧	64	46.26 N	11.51 E
Marmora, On., Can.	212	44.29 N	77.41 W
Marmora, N.J., U.S.	208	39.16 N	74.38 W
Marmore	66	42.33 N	12.43 E
Marmore ≃	62	45.44 N	7.37 E
Marmore, Cascàta delle ⌞	66	42.33 N	12.43 E
Marmot Bay ⊂	180	58.00 N	152.20 W
Marmot Island I	180	58.13 N	151.51 W
Marmoutier	58	48.41 N	7.23 E
Mar Muerto, Laguna ⊂	234	16.10 N	94.10 W
Marnate	266b	45.38 N	8.54 E
Marnay	58	47.17 N	5.46 E
Marnaz	58	46.04 N	6.32 E
Marne, Dtsch.	52	53.57 N	9.00 E
Marne, Mi., U.S.	216	43.02 N	85.49 W
Marne □[5]	32	48.55 N	4.10 E
Marne ≃, Austl.	168b	34.40 S	139.18 E
Marne ≃, Fr.	32	48.49 N	2.24 E
Marne à la Saône, Canal de la ≍	58	48.44 N	4.36 E
Marne au Rhin, Canal de la ≍	56	48.35 N	7.47 E
Marneuli	84	41.28 N	44.50 E
Marnhull	42	50.58 N	2.18 W
Marnitz	54	53.19 N	11.56 E
Maroa, Il., U.S.	219	40.02 N	88.57 W
Maroa, Ven.	246	2.43 N	67.33 W
Maroala	157b	15.23 S	47.59 E
Maroantsetra	157b	15.26 S	49.44 E
Marobi Raghza	120	32.36 N	69.52 E
Maroc → Morocco □[1]	148	32.00 N	5.00 W
Maroelaboom	156	19.15 S	18.53 E
Marofandilia	157b	20.07 S	44.34 E
Maroglio ≃	70	37.03 N	14.15 E
Marokko → Morocco □[1]	148	32.00 N	5.00 W
Marol ◆[8]	272c	19.07 N	72.53 E
Marolambo	157b	20.02 S	48.07 E
Maroldsweisach	56	50.12 N	10.39 E
Marolles-en-Brie	261	48.44 N	2.33 E
Marolles-en-Hurepoix	261	48.34 N	2.18 E
Marolles-les-Braults	50	48.15 N	0.19 E
Maromandia	157b	14.13 S	48.08 E
Maromme	50	49.28 N	1.02 E
Maromokotro ∧	157b	14.01 S	48.59 E
Marondera	154	18.10 S	31.36 E
Marone	64	45.44 N	10.05 E
Marong	102	31.07 N	99.20 E
Maronghi Creek ≃	171a	26.58 S	152.22 E
Maroni (Marowijne) ≃	250	5.45 N	53.58 W
Maroon	171a	28.10 S	152.44 E
Maroon, Mount ∧	171a	28.13 S	152.44 E
Maroondah Aqueduct ≍[1]	274b	37.42 S	145.01 E
Maros	112	5.00 S	119.34 E
Maros (Mureș) ≃	38	46.15 N	20.13 E
Maroseranana	157b	18.32 S	48.51 E
Marostica	64	45.45 N	11.39 E
Marosvásárhely → Târgu Mureș	38	46.33 N	24.33 E
Marotandrano	157b	16.10 S	48.50 E
Marotiri, Îles II	14	27.55 S	143.26 W
Marotta	66	43.46 N	13.08 E
Maroua	146	10.36 N	14.20 E
Maroubra	274a	33.57 S	151.16 E
Marouini ≃	250	3.18 N	54.04 W
Marovato, Madag.	157b	13.59 S	48.36 E
Marovato, Madag.	157b	15.48 S	48.05 E
Marovato, Madag.	157b	16.28 S	48.25 E
Marovoay	157b	16.06 S	46.39 E
Marovoay Nord	157b	16.57 S	44.34 E
Marowijne □[5]	250	5.40 N	54.20 W
Marowijne (Maroni) ≃	250	5.45 N	53.58 W
Marpent	50	50.18 N	4.05 E
Marpingen	56	49.27 N	7.03 E
Marple	44	53.24 N	2.03 W
Marquam	224	45.04 N	122.41 W
Marquand	194	37.25 N	90.10 W
Marquard	158	28.54 S	27.28 E
Marquardt	54	52.27 N	12.57 E
Marquartstein	64	47.45 N	12.28 E
Marquesas Islands → Marquises, Îles II	6	9.00 S	139.30 W
Marquesas Keys II	220	24.34 N	82.08 W
Marquette, Ks., U.S.	198	38.33 N	97.50 W
Marquette, Mi., U.S.	190	46.32 N	87.23 W
Marquette Park ♠	278	41.46 N	87.42 W
Márquez, Perú	286d	11.57 S	77.08 W
Marquez, Tx., U.S.	222	31.14 N	96.15 W
Marquion	50	50.13 N	3.05 E
Marquis	241k	12.06 N	61.37 W
Marquis, Cape ≻	241f	14.03 N	60.54 W
Marquise	50	50.49 N	1.42 E
Marquises, Îles (Marquesas Islands) II	6	9.00 S	139.30 W
Marrabel	168b	34.08 S	138.53 E
Marra Creek ≃	166	30.05 S	147.05 E
Marradi	66	44.04 N	11.37 E
Marradong	168a	32.52 S	116.27 E
Marrah, Jabal ∧	140	13.04 N	24.21 E
Marra Hills ⋏[2]	140	6.05 N	27.33 E
Marrakech	148	31.38 N	8.00 W
Marrakech □[4]	148	31.30 N	8.05 W
Marramarra National Park ♠	170	33.32 S	151.04 E
Marrawah	166	40.56 S	144.41 E
Marree	166	29.39 S	138.04 E
Marrero	194	29.53 N	90.06 W
Marrickville	274a	33.55 S	151.09 E
Marromeu	156	18.20 S	35.56 E
Marrowstone Island I	224	48.04 N	122.41 W
Marrubiu	71	39.45 N	8.38 E
Marruecos → Morocco □[1]	148	32.00 N	5.00 W
Marrupa	154	13.08 S	37.30 E
Mars	214	40.41 N	80.00 W
Marsā al-Burayqah	146	30.25 N	19.34 E
Marsabit	154	2.20 N	37.59 E
Marsabit National Park ♠	154	2.20 N	38.00 E
Marsac-en-Livradois	62	45.29 N	3.44 E
Marṣafā wa Kafr Aḥmad Ḥashīsh	142	30.25 N	31.15 E
Marsal	56	48.48 N	6.36 E
Marsala	70	37.48 N	12.26 E
Marsā Maṭrūḥ	140	31.21 N	27.14 E
Marsā Maṭrūḥ □[4]	142	29.00 N	30.00 E
Marsange ≃	261	48.43 N	2.45 E
Marsangue ≃	261	48.40 N	2.47 E
Marsannay-la-Côte	58	47.16 N	4.59 E
Marsanne	62	44.39 N	4.52 E
Marsassoum	150	12.50 N	16.00 W
Mars'aty	86	60.05 N	60.29 E
Marsberg, Dtsch.	52	51.28 N	8.50 E
Marsberg, Dtsch.	56	51.28 N	8.51 E
Marscheid ◆[8]	263	51.14 N	7.14 E
Marsciano	66	42.54 N	12.20 E
Marsden, Austl.	166	33.45 S	147.32 E
Marsden, Eng., U.K.	262	53.36 N	1.56 W
Marsden, Point ≻	168b	35.35 S	137.38 E
Marsden Park	274a	33.42 S	150.50 E
Marsdiep Ʉ	52	52.59 N	4.45 E
Marseille	62	43.18 N	5.24 E
Marseille-en-Beauvaisis	50	49.35 N	1.57 E
Marseille-Marignane, Aéroport de ⊠	62	43.27 N	5.13 E
Marseilles, Il., U.S.	216	41.19 N	88.42 W
Marseilles, Oh., U.S.	214	40.42 N	83.23 W
Marsella → Marseille	62	43.18 N	5.24 E
Marsfield	274a	33.47 S	151.07 E
Marsfjället ∧	24	65.05 N	15.28 E
Marshall, Liber.	150	6.10 N	10.23 W
Marshall, Ar., U.S.	194	35.54 N	92.37 W
Marshall, Il., U.S.	194	39.23 N	87.41 W
Marshall, Mi., U.S.	216	42.16 N	84.57 W
Marshall, Mn., U.S.	198	44.26 N	95.47 W
Marshall, Mo., U.S.	194	39.07 N	93.11 W
Marshall, N.C., U.S.	192	35.47 N	82.41 W
Marshall, Tx., U.S.	194	32.32 N	94.22 W
Marshall, Va., U.S.	188	38.51 N	77.51 W
Marshall, Wi., U.S.	216	43.10 N	89.04 W
Marshall □[6], Il., U.S.	216	41.02 N	89.24 W
Marshall □[6], In., U.S.	216	41.21 N	86.19 W
Marshall ≃	162	22.59 S	136.59 E
Marshall Bennett Islands II	164	8.50 S	151.50 E
Marshallberg	192	34.43 N	76.30 W
Marshall Canyon Regional Park ♠	280	34.09 N	117.43 W
Marshall Gold Discovery State Historical Park ♠	226	38.48 N	120.53 W
Marshall Hall	208	38.41 N	77.06 W
Marshall Islands □[1]	14	11.00 N	168.00 E
Marshall Islands II	14	9.00 N	168.00 E
Marshalls Creek	210	41.03 N	75.08 W
Marshallton, De., U.S.	208	39.43 N	75.39 W
Marshallton, Pa., U.S.	210	40.47 N	76.33 W
Marshallton, Pa., U.S.	285	39.57 N	75.41 W
Marshalltown	190	42.02 N	92.54 W
Marshallville, Ga., U.S.	192	32.27 N	83.56 W
Marshallville, Oh., U.S.	214	40.54 N	81.44 W
Marshbank Metropolitan Park ♠	281	42.36 N	83.23 W
Marsh Creek ≃, Ca., U.S.	282	37.53 N	121.49 W
Marsh Creek ≃, Mi., U.S.	281	42.06 N	83.13 W
Marsh Creek ≃, Pa., U.S.	214	41.03 N	77.36 W
Marsh Creek ≃, Pa., U.S.	285	40.03 N	75.43 W
Marsh Creek ≃, Wi., U.S.	216	42.13 N	89.04 W
Marsh Creek Lake ⊜[1]	208	40.04 N	75.44 W
Marshes Creek ≃	276	40.36 N	74.13 W
Marshfield, Eng., U.K.	42	51.28 N	2.19 W
Marshfield, Ma., U.S.	207	42.05 N	70.42 W
Marshfield, Mo., U.S.	194	37.20 N	92.54 W
Marshfield, Wi., U.S.	190	44.40 N	90.10 W
Marshfield Airport ⊠	283	42.06 N	70.40 W
Marshfield Center	283	42.07 N	70.43 W
Marshfield Hills	207	42.08 N	70.44 W
Marsh Harbour	238	26.33 N	77.03 W
Marsh Hill	210	41.29 N	76.58 W
Mars Hill, In., U.S.	218	39.43 N	86.09 W
Mars Hill, Me., U.S.	186	46.30 N	67.52 W
Mars Hill, N.C., U.S.	192	35.49 N	82.32 W
Marsh Island I	194	29.35 N	91.53 W
Marsh Lake ⊜	180	60.25 N	134.18 W
Marsh Peak ∧	200	40.43 N	109.50 W
Marshside	262	53.40 N	2.58 W
Marshville	192	34.59 N	80.22 W
Marshyhope Creek ≃	208	38.32 N	75.45 W
Marsica ◆[1]	66	41.50 N	13.45 E
Marsico Nuovo	68	40.25 N	15.44 E
Marsico Vetere	68	40.23 N	15.49 E
Marsillargues	62	43.40 N	4.11 E
Marsimang, Tanjung ≻	164	3.27 S	130.49 E
Marsing	202	43.32 N	116.48 W
Marske-by-the-Sea	44	54.36 N	1.01 W
Mars-la-Tour	56	49.06 N	5.54 E
Marson	56	48.55 N	4.32 E
Marssum	52	53.12 N	5.42 E
Märsta	40	59.37 N	17.51 E
Marstal	41	54.51 N	10.31 E
Marsteller	214	40.39 N	78.48 W
Märstetten	58	47.36 N	9.04 E
Marston	262	53.16 N	2.30 W
Marston Moor ≚	44	53.57 N	1.17 W
Marston Moor Battlesite ⊥	44	53.57 N	1.17 W
Marstons Mills	207	41.39 N	70.25 W
Marstrand	26	57.53 N	11.35 E
Marsyāṅgdī ≃	124	28.05 N	84.28 E
Mart	222	31.32 N	96.50 W
Marta	66	42.32 N	11.55 E
Marta ≃	66	42.14 N	11.42 E
Martaban	110	16.32 N	97.37 E
Martaban, Gulf of ⊂	110	16.30 N	97.00 E
Martano	68	40.12 N	18.18 E
Martap	152	6.54 N	13.03 E
Martapura, Indon.	112	3.25 S	114.51 E
Martapura, Indon.	112	4.19 S	104.22 E
Marte	146	12.22 N	13.51 E
Marteg ≃	42	52.20 N	3.33 W
Martel, Fr.	32	44.56 N	1.37 E
Martel, Oh., U.S.	214	40.40 N	82.55 W
Martelange	56	49.50 N	5.44 E
Martell	226	38.22 N	120.48 W
Martello	64	46.34 N	10.47 E
Martello, Val V	64	46.31 N	10.45 E
Martemjanovskij	86	55.54 N	80.22 E
Marten ◆[8]	263	51.31 N	7.23 E
Marten Lake ⊜	190	46.42 N	79.41 W
Marten Mountain ∧	182	55.28 N	114.43 W
Marte R. Gomez, Presa ⊜[1]	196	26.10 N	99.00 W
Martfeld	52	52.52 N	9.04 E
Marthaguy Creek ≃	166	30.16 S	147.35 E
Martha Lake	224	47.51 N	122.20 W
Marthall	262	53.17 N	2.18 W
Martham	42	52.42 N	1.38 E
Marthasville	219	38.37 N	91.03 W
Martha's Vineyard I	207	41.25 N	70.40 W
Martí, Cuba	240p	21.09 N	77.27 W
Martí, Cuba	240p	22.57 N	80.55 W
Martí, Pico ∧	240p	20.01 N	76.35 W
Martignacco	64	46.05 N	13.08 E
Martignat	58	46.13 N	5.36 E
Martigny	58	46.06 N	7.04 E
Martigny-les-Bains	58	48.06 N	5.49 E
Martigues	62	43.24 N	5.03 E
Martil	34	35.37 N	5.17 W
Martim Francisco	256	22.31 S	46.57 W
Martin, Slvk.	30	49.05 N	18.55 E
Martin, Ky., U.S.	192	37.34 N	82.45 W
Martin, Mi., U.S.	216	42.32 N	85.38 W
Martin, N.D., U.S.	198	47.49 N	100.06 W
Martin, Oh., U.S.	214	41.33 N	83.20 W
Martin, S.D., U.S.	198	43.10 N	101.43 W
Martin, Tn., U.S.	194	36.20 N	88.51 W
Martin □[6]	220	27.07 N	80.31 W
Martín ≃	34	41.18 N	0.19 W
Martín, Arroyo ≃	288	34.51 S	58.04 W
Martin, Isle I	46	57.55 N	5.14 W
Martina	58	46.53 N	10.30 E
Martina Franca	68	40.42 N	17.21 E
Martinborough	172	41.13 S	175.28 E
Martín Chico, Punta ≻	258	34.10 S	58.13 W
Martindale	196	29.50 N	97.51 W
Martindale Creek ≃, Austl.	170	32.32 S	150.42 E
Martindale Creek ≃, In., U.S.	218	39.48 N	85.09 W
Martindale Pond ⊜	284a	43.11 N	79.16 W
Martin-Église	50	49.54 N	1.09 E
Martinengo	62	45.34 N	9.46 E
Mărtinești	38	45.30 N	27.18 E
Martinez, Ca., U.S.	226	38.01 N	122.07 W
Martinez, Ga., U.S.	192	33.31 N	82.04 W
Martínez ◆[8]	258	34.29 S	58.30 W
Martínez de la Torre	234	20.04 N	97.03 W
Martín García, Isla I	258	34.13 S	58.15 W
Martinho Campos	255	19.20 S	45.13 W
Martinica → Martinique □[2]	240e	14.40 N	61.00 W
Martini Creek ≃	282	37.33 N	122.31 W
Martinique □[2], N.A.	230	14.40 N	61.00 W
Martinique □[2], N.A.	240e	14.40 N	61.00 W
Martinique Passage Ʉ	238	15.10 N	61.15 W
Martin Lake ⊜[1], Al., U.S.	194	32.50 N	85.55 W
Martin Lake ⊜[1], Tx., U.S.	222	32.15 N	94.35 W
Martin Marietta Corporation ʊ[3]	284b	39.20 N	76.26 W
Martinniemi	26	65.13 N	25.18 E
Martinópole	250	3.15 S	40.41 W
Martin Peninsula ≻[1]	9	74.25 S	114.10 W
Martín Pérez ≃	286b	23.07 N	82.20 W
Martin Point ≻	180	70.08 N	143.16 W
Martin Run ≃	279a	41.27 N	82.12 W
Martins	250	6.05 S	37.55 W
Martinsberg	61	48.22 N	15.09 E
Martins Brook ≃	283	42.34 N	71.06 W
Martinsburg, Mo., U.S.	219	39.06 N	91.38 W
Martinsburg, N.Y., U.S.	212	43.44 N	75.28 W
Martinsburg, Oh., U.S.	214	40.16 N	82.21 W
Martinsburg, Pa., U.S.	214	40.18 N	78.19 W
Martinsburg, W.V., U.S.	188	39.27 N	77.57 W
Martins Creek	208	40.47 N	75.11 W
Martins Creek ≃	210	41.37 N	75.46 W
Martinscroft	262	53.24 N	2.31 W
Martins Ferry	214	40.05 N	80.43 W
Martins Mills	222	32.25 N	95.47 W
Martins Pond ⊜	283	42.36 N	71.08 W
Martinstein	56	49.48 N	7.32 E
Martinsthal	56	50.03 N	8.07 E
Martinsville, Austl.	170	33.03 S	151.25 E
Martinsville, Il., U.S.	194	39.20 N	87.52 W
Martinsville, In., U.S.	218	39.25 N	86.25 W
Martinsville, N.J., U.S.	276	40.36 N	74.34 W
Martinsville, Oh., U.S.	218	39.19 N	83.48 W
Martinsville, Va., U.S.	192	36.41 N	79.52 W
Martinton	216	40.55 N	87.44 W
Martintown	206	45.09 N	74.42 W
Martin Van Buren National Historic Site ⊥	210	42.22 N	73.43 W
Martin Vaz, Ilhas II	244	20.30 S	28.51 W
Martis	71	40.47 N	8.49 E
Martisovo	76	56.34 N	31.55 E
Martock	42	50.59 N	2.46 W
Martofte	41	55.33 N	10.40 E
Marton, N.Z.	172	40.05 S	175.23 E
Marton, Eng., U.K.	262	53.12 N	2.13 W
Martorell	266d	41.28 N	1.56 E
Martorelles de Baix	266d	41.32 N	2.14 E
Martos	34	37.43 N	3.58 W
Martova	78	49.57 N	36.57 E
Martre, Lac la ⊜	176	63.15 N	117.55 W
Martti	24	67.28 N	28.28 E
Martūbah	146	32.35 N	22.46 E
Martuk	86	50.46 N	56.31 E
Martuni	84	40.08 N	45.19 E
Martvili	84	42.25 N	42.22 E
Martville	210	43.17 N	76.38 W
Martynivka	78	49.38 N	31.18 E
Martynovo	80	50.43 N	50.23 E
Martynovskij	80	50.29 N	42.18 E
Martynovychi	78	51.17 N	29.37 E
Maru	150	12.22 N	6.22 E
Marua	164	9.30 S	149.20 E
Marudi	112	4.11 N	114.19 E
Marudu, Telukan ⊂	112	6.45 N	116.55 E
Marugame	96	34.17 N	133.47 E
Maruggio	68	40.19 N	17.34 E
Maruia	172	42.11 S	172.13 E
Maruia ≃	172	41.47 S	172.12 E
Maruim	250	10.45 S	37.05 W
Maruko	94	36.19 N	138.16 E
Marula	154	20.26 S	28.06 E
Marulan	170	34.43 S	150.00 E
Marulan South	170	34.46 S	150.02 E
Marum	52	53.08 N	6.16 E
Marum, Mont ∧	175f	16.15 S	168.07 E
Marunga	152	17.27 S	20.02 E
Marungu	154	3.44 S	30.48 E
Marungu ⋏	154	7.42 S	30.00 E
Maruoka	94	36.09 N	136.16 E
Mårup	41	55.57 N	10.35 E
Marusino	265b	55.42 N	37.59 E
Maruškino	82	55.36 N	37.12 E
Ma'rūt	120	31.34 N	67.03 E
Marutea I[1]	14	17.00 S	143.10 W
Maruyama	94	35.01 N	139.58 E
Maruyama ≃	96	35.39 N	134.50 E
Marv Dasht	128	29.50 N	52.40 E
Marve ◆[8]	272c	19.12 N	72.49 E
Marvejols	32	44.33 N	3.18 E
Marvell	194	34.33 N	90.54 W
Marvel Loch	162	31.28 S	119.28 E
Marviken	40	58.34 N	16.51 E
Marvila ◆[8]	266c	38.44 N	9.06 W
Marville	56	49.27 N	5.27 E
Marvin Creek ≃	214	41.48 N	78.26 W
Marvine, Mount ∧	200	38.40 N	111.39 W
Mar Vista ◆[8]	280	34.00 N	118.27 W
Mārwār	120	25.44 N	73.36 E
Marwayne	184	53.32 N	110.20 W
Marwitz	264a	52.41 N	13.09 E
Marwitzer Heide ◆[3]	264a	52.40 N	13.06 E
Marwood	214	40.48 N	79.47 W
Marxhagen	54	53.37 N	12.36 E
Marxloh ◆[8]	263	51.31 N	6.46 E
Mary	128	37.36 N	61.50 E
Mary ≃, Austl.	164	12.53 S	131.38 E
Mary ≃, Austl.	166	25.26 S	152.55 E
Mar'yanivka	78	50.28 N	24.48 E
Mary Anne Group II	162	21.13 S	115.32 E
Maryborough, Austl.	166	25.32 S	152.42 E
Maryborough, Austl.	169	37.03 S	143.45 E
Maryborough → Port Laoise, Ire.	48	53.02 N	7.17 W
Mary D	208	40.45 N	76.04 W
Marydale	158	29.23 S	22.05 E
Marydel	208	39.06 N	75.44 W
Maryfield	184	49.48 N	101.32 W
Maryhill	224	45.41 N	120.49 W
Mar'yinka	83	47.56 N	37.31 E
Maryj □[8]	128	37.30 N	62.30 E
Mary Jane, Lake ⊜	220	28.22 N	81.11 W
Mary Kathleen	166	20.49 S	139.58 E
Maryknoll	210	41.11 N	73.50 W
Mary Lake ⊜	212	45.15 N	79.15 W
Maryland	210	42.32 N	74.53 W
Maryland □[3], U.S.	178	39.00 N	76.45 W
Maryland □[3], U.S.	188	39.00 N	76.45 W
Maryland, University of (Baltimore County Campus) ʊ[2], Md., U.S.	284b	39.15 N	76.43 W
Maryland, University of ʊ[2], Md., U.S.	284c	38.59 N	76.57 W
Maryland City	208	39.05 N	76.49 W
Maryland Gardens Park ♠	275b	43.47 N	79.32 W
Maryland Heights	219	38.42 N	90.25 W
Maryland Historical Society ʊ	284b	39.18 N	76.37 W
Maryland Line	208	39.42 N	76.39 W
Maryland Park	284c	38.53 N	76.54 W
Marylebone	262	53.34 N	2.38 W
Maryneal	196	32.14 N	100.27 W
Marynivka	78	47.46 N	30.53 E
Marypark	46	57.26 N	3.21 W
Maryport	44	54.43 N	3.30 W
Marys ≃, Il., U.S.	194	37.53 N	89.47 W
Marys ≃, Nv., U.S.	204	41.04 N	115.16 W
Marys Creek ≃	202	42.18 N	115.48 W
Mary's Igloo	180	65.09 N	165.04 W
Marys Peak ∧	202	44.30 N	123.33 W
Marystown	186	47.10 N	55.09 W
Marysvale	200	38.26 N	112.13 W
Marysville, Austl.	169	37.31 S	145.45 E
Marysville, B.C., Can.	182	49.38 N	115.57 W
Marysville, N.B., Can.	186	45.59 N	66.35 W
Marysville, Ca., U.S.	226	39.08 N	121.35 W
Marysville, Ks., U.S.	198	39.50 N	96.38 W
Marysville, Mi., U.S.	214	42.54 N	82.29 W
Marysville, Oh., U.S.	214	40.14 N	83.22 W
Marysville, Pa., U.S.	208	40.20 N	76.55 W
Marysville, Wa., U.S.	224	48.03 N	122.10 W
Maryūṭ, Buḥayrat ⊜	142	31.08 N	29.56 E
Maryvale	171a	28.05 S	152.15 E
Maryvale ◆[8]	275b	43.46 N	79.18 W
Maryville, Mo., U.S.	194	40.20 N	94.52 W
Maryville, Tn., U.S.	192	35.45 N	83.58 W
Marywell	46	57.02 N	2.42 W
Marywood	216	41.48 N	88.18 W
Marzabotto	64	44.20 N	11.12 E
Marzagão	255	17.59 S	48.39 W
Marzahn ◆[8]	264a	52.33 N	13.33 E
Marzahna	54	52.00 N	12.46 E
Marzahne	54	52.31 N	12.31 E
Marzal, Aven de ⊥[5]	62	44.22 N	4.31 E
Marzo, Punta ≻	246	6.50 N	77.42 W
Marzolara	64	44.38 N	10.10 E
Marzūq	146	25.55 N	13.55 E
Marzūq, Ḥamādat ◆[2]	146	26.10 N	12.45 E
Marzūq, Ṣaḥrā' ◆[2]	146	24.30 N	13.00 E
Masa	152	3.45 S	15.29 E
Masachapa	236	11.47 N	86.31 W
Masada → Meẓada, Ḥorvot ⊥	132	31.19 N	35.21 E
Mas'adah (Cæsarea Philippi)	132	33.14 N	35.45 E
Más Afuera, Isla → Alejandro Selkirk, Isla I	244	33.45 S	80.46 W
Masagua	236	14.12 N	90.51 W
Masaguisi	116	12.41 N	121.32 E
Masai	114	1.29 N	103.53 E
Masai Mara Game Reserve ◆[4]	154	1.15 S	35.15 E
Masai Steppe ⋏[1]	154	4.45 S	37.00 E
Masak	85	43.37 N	78.18 E
Masaka	154	0.20 S	31.44 E
Masaki, Nihon	96	33.47 N	132.42 E
Masaki, Nihon	268	35.13 N	140.02 E
Masalembu Besar, Pulau I	112	5.34 S	114.26 E
Masallı	84	39.03 N	48.40 E
Masalok, Puntan ≻	174n	15.01 N	145.41 E
Masamba	112	2.32 S	120.20 E
Masan	98	35.11 N	128.32 E
Masandra	78	44.32 N	34.12 E
Masangwe ∧	154	5.28 S	30.05 E
Masānjor	126	24.07 N	87.19 E
Masapelid Island I	116	9.42 N	125.39 E
Masapun	112	7.47 S	126.38 E
Masarah	142	27.29 N	30.50 E
Masaran	115a	7.28 S	110.55 E
Ma'ṣarat Samālūṭ	142	28.19 N	30.43 E
Masaryktown	220	28.26 N	82.27 W
Masasi	154	10.43 S	38.48 E
Masatepe	236	11.55 N	86.09 W
Más a Tierra, Isla → Róbinson Crusoe, Isla I	244	33.38 S	78.52 W
Masaya	236	11.58 N	86.06 W
Masaya □[5]	236	12.00 N	86.10 W
Masba	146	11.30 N	13.00 E
Masbate	116	12.22 N	123.36 E
Masbate □[4]	116	12.20 N	123.30 E
Masbate Island I	116	12.15 N	123.30 E
Masbate Pass Ʉ	116	12.30 N	123.35 E
Mascali	70	37.45 N	15.12 E
Mascarene Basin ✢[1]	12	15.00 S	56.00 E
Mascarene Islands II	157c	21.00 S	57.00 E
Mascarene Plateau ✢[3]	12	10.00 S	60.00 E
Mascasín	252	31.22 S	66.59 W
Maschen	52	53.24 N	10.02 E
Maschito	68	40.54 N	15.50 E
Mascot, Austl.	274a	33.56 S	151.12 E
Mascot, Tn., U.S.	192	36.03 N	83.44 W
Mascota	234	20.32 N	104.49 W
Mascota ≃	234	20.38 N	104.59 W
Mascotte	220	28.35 N	81.53 W
Mascouche	206	45.45 N	73.36 W
Mascouche ≃	206	45.41 N	73.40 W
Mascoutah	219	38.29 N	89.47 W
Mascuppic Lake ⊜	283	42.41 N	71.23 W
Mase	102	27.16 N	104.08 E
Masefield	184	49.09 N	107.48 W
Masela, Pulau I	164	8.09 S	129.50 E
Maselheim, Dtsch.	58	48.08 N	9.53 E
Maselheim, Dtsch.	64	48.08 N	9.53 E
Masenberg ∧	61	47.21 N	15.53 E
Maser	64	45.48 N	11.59 E
Maserada sul Piave	64	45.45 N	12.17 E
Maseru	158	29.28 S	27.30 E
Masevaux	58	47.47 N	7.00 E
Masha	100	27.26 N	117.50 E
Mashaba	154	20.02 S	30.29 E
Mashaba Mountains ⋏	154	18.45 S	30.32 E
Mash'abbe' Sade	132	31.00 N	34.47 E
Mashābih I	128	25.37 N	36.29 E
Mashalah	142	30.44 N	31.08 E
Masham	44	54.13 N	1.40 W
Mashan, Zhg.	89	45.13 N	130.35 E
Mashan, Zhg.	100	27.33 N	113.46 E
Mashan, Zhg.	102	23.50 N	108.16 E
Mashar	140	9.14 N	26.52 E
Mashbury	260	51.47 N	0.24 E
Mashel ≃	224	46.51 N	122.20 W
Mashenqiao	105	40.04 N	117.36 E
Masherbrum ∧	123	35.43 N	76.18 E
Masheve	78	52.06 N	32.48 E
Mashgharah	132	33.32 N	35.39 E
Mashhad, Īrān	128	36.18 N	59.36 E
Mash-had, Yis.	132	32.44 N	35.19 E
Mashi, Nig.	150	13.00 N	7.54 E
Mashi, Zhg.	100	29.05 N	114.22 E
Mashi, Zhg.	100	25.01 N	114.09 E
Mashike	92a	43.51 N	141.31 E
Mashiko	94	36.28 N	140.06 E
Mashita ≃	94	35.40 N	137.10 E
Mashivka	78	49.26 N	34.52 E
Mashīz	128	29.56 N	56.37 E
Mashkai ≃	128	26.02 N	65.19 E
Māshkel, Hāmūn-i- ⊜	128	28.15 N	63.00 E
Māshkel, Rūd-i- (Māshkīd) ≃	128	28.02 N	63.25 E
Mashki Chāh	128	29.01 N	62.27 E
Māshkīd (Rūd-i-Māshkel) ≃	128	28.02 N	63.25 E
Mashonaland North □[4]	154	16.30 S	30.00 E
Mashonaland South □[4]	154	18.15 S	30.45 E
Mashpee	207	41.38 N	70.28 W
Mashra'ur-Raqq	140	8.25 N	29.16 E
Mashtūl as-Sūq	142	30.22 N	31.22 E
Mashū-ko ⊜	92a	43.35 N	144.32 E
Masibi	152	11.08 S	22.42 E
Masihi	114	2.47 N	99.40 E
Masīlah, Wādī al- V	144	15.10 N	51.08 E
Masi-Manimba	152	4.46 S	17.55 E
Masin	164	6.15 S	139.19 E
Masina	272b	22.55 N	88.32 E
Masindi	154	1.41 N	31.43 E
Masini Port	154	1.42 N	32.05 E
Masinloc	116	15.32 N	119.57 E
Masīr	142	31.03 N	31.00 E
Maṣīrah I	118	20.25 N	58.50 E
Maṣīrah, Khalīj ⊂	118	20.10 N	58.15 E
Masis	84	40.00 N	44.29 E
Masisea	248	8.36 S	74.19 W
Masisi	154	1.24 S	28.49 E
Masjed-e Soleymān	128	31.58 N	49.18 E
Masjid Tanah	114	2.21 N	102.07 E
Mask, Lough ⊜	48	53.35 N	9.20 W
Maska	150	11.20 N	7.20 E
Maskan, Ras ≻	144	11.10 N	43.33 E
Maskanah	130	36.01 N	38.05 E
Maskin	128	23.35 N	56.39 E
Maškino	82	54.53 N	36.08 E
Maskinongé □[6]	206	46.35 N	73.30 W
Maskinongé ≃, P.Q., Can.	206	46.10 N	73.01 W
Maskinongé ≃, P.Q., Can.	206	45.49 N	74.40 W
Maskinongé, Lac ⊜	206	46.19 N	73.23 W
Maškoviči	82	54.11 N	36.17 E
Masku	26	60.34 N	22.06 E
Maskūtān	128	26.51 N	59.49 E
Maskwa ≃	184	50.33 N	96.08 W
Masl'anino	86	54.20 N	84.13 E
Masl'anskaja	86	55.56 N	70.08 E
Maslova	265a	59.47 N	30.48 E
Maslovka	78	51.33 N	39.14 E
Maslovo	86	60.07 N	60.30 E
Masnières	50	50.07 N	3.13 E
Maso	150	7.14 N	2.53 W
Masoala	157b	15.59 S	50.10 E
Masoala, Cap ≻	157b	15.59 S	50.13 E
Masoala, Presqu'île de ≻[1]	157b	15.40 S	50.12 E
Masoarivo	157b	19.03 S	44.19 E
Masomeloka	157b	20.17 S	48.37 E
Mason, Mi., U.S.	216	42.34 N	84.26 W
Mason, Oh., U.S.	218	39.21 N	84.18 W
Mason, Tn., U.S.	194	35.24 N	89.31 W
Mason, Tx., U.S.	196	30.44 N	99.13 W
Mason, W.V., U.S.	188	39.01 N	82.01 W
Mason □[6], Il., U.S.	219	40.18 N	90.04 W
Mason □[6], Ky., U.S.	218	38.35 N	83.48 W
Mason □[6], Wa., U.S.	224	47.20 N	123.09 W
Mason, Lake ⊜	162	27.39 S	119.34 E
Mason Bay ⊂	172	46.56 S	167.44 E
Mason City, Il., U.S.	219	40.12 N	89.41 W
Mason City, Ia., U.S.	190	43.09 N	93.12 W
Mason City, Ne., U.S.	198	41.13 N	99.18 W
Masone	62	44.30 N	8.42 E
Masonicus Brook ≃	276	41.06 N	74.09 W
Mason Lake ⊜	224	47.20 N	122.57 W
Masons Creek ≃	285	39.59 N	74.51 W
Mason Valley V	226	39.07 N	119.10 W
Masonville, N.J., U.S.	285	39.59 N	74.52 W
Masonville, N.Y., U.S.	210	42.15 N	75.23 W
Maspeth ◆[8]	276	40.43 N	73.55 W
Masqaṭ (Muscat)	128	23.37 N	58.35 E
Maṣra'	142	27.14 N	31.02 E
Massa	64	44.01 N	10.09 E
Massa-Carrara □[4]	64	44.15 N	10.03 E
Massachusetts □[3], U.S.	178	42.15 N	71.50 W
Massachusetts □[3], U.S.	207	42.15 N	71.50 W
Massachusetts (Boston), University of ʊ[2]	283	42.19 N	71.03 W
Massachusetts Bay ⊂	207	42.20 N	70.50 W
Massachusetts Correctional Institution ʊ	283	42.07 N	71.18 W
Massachusetts Institute of Technology ʊ[2]	283	42.21 N	71.06 W
Massaciuccoli, Lago di ⊜	66	43.50 N	10.20 E
Massacre Lake ⊜	204	41.39 N	119.35 W
Massa Fermana	66	43.09 N	13.28 E
Massa Fiscaglia	66	44.48 N	12.01 E
Massafra	68	40.35 N	17.07 E
Massaguet	146	12.28 N	15.26 E
Massakory	146	13.00 N	15.44 E
Massalassef	146	11.43 N	17.08 E
Massa Lombarda	66	44.27 N	11.49 E
Massa Lubrense	68	40.36 N	14.20 E
Massa Marittima	66	43.03 N	10.53 E
Massa Martana	66	42.46 N	12.31 E
Massangano	152	9.37 S	14.15 E
Massangena	156	21.32 S	32.57 E
Massapê	250	3.31 S	40.19 W
Massapequa	210	40.40 N	73.28 W
Massapequa Park	276	40.40 N	73.27 W

Symbols in the index entries represent the broad categories identified in the key at the right. Symbols with superior numbers (⋏[1]) identify subcategories (see complete key on page *I · 1*).

Symbole im Register stellen die rechts im Schlüssel erklärten Kategorien dar. Symbole mit hochgestellten Ziffern (⋏[1]) bezeichnen Unterabteilungen einer Kategorie (vgl. vollständiger Schlüssel auf Seite *I · 1*).

Los símbolos incluídos en el texto del índice representan las grandes categorías identificadas con la clave a la derecha. Los símbolos con numeros en su parte superior (⋏[1]) identifican las subcategorías (véase la clave completa en la página *I · 1*).

Les symboles de l'index représentent les catégories indiquées dans la légende à droite. Les symboles suivis d'un indice (⋏[1]) représentent des sous-catégories (voir légende complète à la page *I · 1*).

Os símbolos incluídos no texto do índice representam as grandes categorias identificadas com a chave à direita. Os símbolos com números em sua parte superior (⋏[1]) identificam as subcategorias (veja-se a chave completa à página *I · 1*).

	English	Deutsch	Español	Français	Português
∧	Mountain	Berg	Montaña	Montagne	Montanha
⋏	Mountains	Gebirge	Montañas	Montagnes	Montanhas
)(	Pass	Paß	Paso	Col	Passo
V	Valley, Canyon	Tal, Cañon	Valle, Cañón	Vallée, Canyon	Vale, Canhão
≚	Plain	Ebene	Llano	Plaine	Planície
≻	Cape	Kap	Cabo	Cap	Cabo
I	Island	Insel	Isla	Île	Ilha
II	Islands	Inseln	Islas	Îles	Ilhas
⊥	Other Topographic Features	Andere Topographische Objekte	Otros Elementos Topográficos	Autres données topographiques	Outros acidentes topográficos

ESPAÑOL	FRANÇAIS	PORTUGUÊS
Nombre / Página / Lat.°' / Long.°' W=Oeste	Nom / Page / Lat.°' / Long.°' W=Ouest	Nome / Página / Lat.°' / Long.°' W=Oeste

Column 1 (Español)

Nombre	Página	Lat.°'	Long.°' W=Oeste
Massapequa Reserve County Park ♦	276	40.42 N	73.27 W
Massapoag Brook ≃	283	42.09 N	71.09 W
Massapoag Lake ⊘	283	42.06 N	71.11 W
Massara	156	18.20 S	34.09 E
Massarosa	66	43.52 N	10.20 E
Massasoit State Park ♦	207	41.53 N	71.01 W
Massaua — Mitsiwa	144	15.38 N	39.28 E
Massawa — Mitsiwa	144	15.38 N	39.28 E
Massawippi ≃	206	45.22 N	71.51 W
Massawippi, Lake ⊘	206	45.14 N	72.00 W
Massay	50	47.09 N	2.00 E
Massé, Ruisseau ≃	275a	45.28 N	73.17 W
Massello	62	44.57 N	7.04 E
Massen	52	51.32 N	7.38 E
Massena, Ia., U.S.	198	41.15 N	94.46 W
Massena, N.Y., U.S.	206	44.55 N	74.53 W
Massenya	146	11.24 N	16.10 E
Masset	182	54.02 N	132.09 W
Masset Inlet c	182	53.42 N	132.20 W
Masseube	32	43.26 N	0.35 E
Massey	190	46.12 N	82.05 W
Massiac	32	45.15 N	3.12 E
Massiaru	76	58.00 N	24.35 E
Massico, Monte ∧	68	41.10 N	13.55 E
Massieville	218	39.16 N	82.58 W
Massif Central — Central, Massif ↗	32	45.00 N	3.10 E
Massillon	214	40.48 N	81.32 W
Massima Camp	152	1.27 S	11.42 E
Massina ≃	273b	4.22 S	15.22 E
Massina ✦[1]	150	14.30 N	5.00 W
Massing	60	48.24 N	12.36 E
Massinga	156	23.20 S	35.25 E
Massingir	156	23.51 S	32.04 E
Massive, Mount ∧	200	39.12 N	106.28 W
Masson, Lac ⊘	206	46.03 N	74.02 W
Masson Island I	9	66.08 S	96.34 E
Massy	261	48.44 N	2.17 E
Maştâbah	144	20.49 N	39.20 E
Maştaġa	84	40.32 N	50.00 E
Masterson	196	35.38 N	101.58 W
Masterton	172	40.57 S	175.40 E
Mas-Thibert	62	43.34 N	4.44 E
Mastic Point	192	25.03 N	77.57 W
Mastigouche ≃	206	46.20 N	73.24 W
Mastigouche Nord ≃	206	46.24 N	73.25 W
Mastok	76	53.59 N	30.28 E
Mastüj	123	36.17 N	72.31 E
Mastüj ≃	123	35.54 N	71.46 E
Mastung	128	29.48 N	66.51 E
Mastürah	128	23.06 N	38.50 E
Masty	76	53.25 N	24.32 E
Masu	146	12.10 N	13.19 E
Masua	126	24.16 N	90.46 E
Masuho	94	35.34 N	138.28 E
Masuika	152	7.37 S	22.32 E
Masuku	154	17.12 S	27.07 E
Masüleh	128	37.10 N	48.59 E
Masulipatam — Machilīpatnam	128	16.10 N	81.08 E
Masura	126	23.16 N	90.24 E
Masurai, Gunung ∧	112	2.30 S	101.51 E
Masury	214	41.12 N	80.32 W
Masvingo	156	20.05 S	30.50 E
Maşyâf	130	35.03 N	36.21 E
Maszewo, Pol.	52	53.29 N	15.02 E
Maszewo, Pol.	52	52.06 N	14.55 E
Mat, Indon.	38	41.39 N	19.34 E
Mata, Indon.	115b	8.12 S	122.56 E
Mata, R.D.C.	152	7.53 S	21.58 E
Mata Amarilla	234	49.36 S	71.13 W
Mataba, Mount ∧	269f	14.42 N	121.10 E
Matabeleland North □[4]	154	19.00 S	27.15 E
Matabeleland South □[4]	154	21.00 S	29.15 E
Matabuena	34	41.10 N	3.40 W
Matachel ≃	34	38.50 N	6.17 W
Matachewan	190	47.56 N	80.39 W
Matacuni ≃	246	3.02 N	65.16 W
Matad	88	46.58 N	115.18 E
Mata de Plátano, Quebrada ≃	286c	10.35 N	66.46 W
Matadero Creek ≃	282	37.26 N	122.08 W
Mata de São João	255	12.31 S	38.17 W
Matadi	152	5.49 S	13.27 E
Matador	196	34.00 N	100.49 W
Matagalpa	236	12.55 N	85.55 W
Matagalpa □[5]	236	13.00 N	85.30 W
Matagami	176	49.45 N	77.38 W
Matag-ob	116	11.07 N	124.29 E
Matagorda ≃	196	28.41 N	95.58 W
Matagorda □[6]	222	28.57 N	96.00 W
Matagorda Bay c	196	28.35 N	96.20 W
Matagorda Island I	196	28.15 N	96.30 W
Matagorda Peninsula ↘[1]	196	28.32 N	96.07 W
Mata Grande	250	9.07 S	37.44 W
Mathiae, Pointe ↘	174s	17.49 S	149.17 W
Mataiea[1]	14	17.45 S	149.23 W
Mataiva[1]	14	45.53 N	78.43 E
Matajing	112	29.32 N	104.00 E
Matak, Pulau I	112	3.18 N	106.16 E
Matakana, Austl.	168	33.00 S	145.54 E
Matakana, N.Z.	172	36.21 S	174.43 E
Matakana Island I	172	37.35 S	176.05 E
Matakitaki ≃	172	41.48 S	172.19 E
Matala	152	14.45 S	15.04 E
Matale	122	7.28 N	80.37 E
Matam	150	15.40 N	13.15 W
Matamar	126	33.36 N	131.28 E
Matamata, Cerro ∧	236	9.47 N	83.15 W
Matameye	150	13.26 N	8.28 E
Matamoras	210	41.22 N	74.42 W
Matamoros, Méx.	232	25.53 N	97.30 W
Matamoros, Méx.	232	25.32 N	103.15 W
Matan	112	1.52 S	110.00 E
Matana, Danau ⊘	112	2.28 S	121.20 E
Matanalem, Cape ↘	248	2.28 S	149.57 E
Matandu ≃	154	8.45 S	39.19 E
Matane	186	48.51 N	67.32 W
Matang, Malay.	114	4.49 N	100.41 E
Matang, Zhg.	100	22.20 N	110.47 E
Matang, Zhg.	100	32.20 N	120.14 E
Matani	172	37.49 S	175.25 E
Matanni	123	33.48 N	71.34 E
Matanuska ≃	180	61.30 N	149.15 W
Matanza — San Justo	258	34.40 S	58.33 W
Matanza ↘[5]	258	34.34 S	58.22 W
Matanzas, Aeródromo ☒	288	34.44 S	58.30 W
Matanzas, Cuba	238	23.03 N	81.35 W
Matanzas, Méx.	234	22.01 N	101.38 W
Matanzas ≃	232	25.32 N	103.15 W
Matanzas, Bahía de c	240p	23.04 N	81.30 W
Matapa	156	23.13 S	25.12 E
Matapalo, Cabo ↘	236	8.22 N	83.19 W
Matape ≃	232	27.56 N	110.52 W
Matapédia	186	47.58 N	66.56 W
Matapédia, Lac ⊘	186	48.32 N	67.32 W
Matapédia ≃	186	48.06 N	66.57 W
Mata Point ↘	174r	19.07 S	169.51 W
Matapu	172	39.29 S	174.14 E
Mataquito ≃	252	34.59 S	72.12 W
Matará, Perú	248	7.16 S	78.16 W
Matara, S. Lan.	122	5.56 N	80.33 E

Column 2 (Français)

Nom	Page	Lat.°'	Long.°' W=Ouest
Mataram	115b	8.35 S	116.07 E
Matarani	248	17.00 S	72.06 W
Mataranka	164	14.56 S	133.07 E
Matârimah, Ra's ↘	142	29.27 N	32.42 E
Matarinao Bay c	116	11.14 N	125.34 E
Mataró	34	41.32 N	2.27 E
Matarraña ≃	34	41.14 N	0.22 E
Matas ↙	266d	41.30 N	2.16 E
Matasiri, Pulau I	112	4.48 S	115.46 E
Matata	172	37.53 S	176.45 E
Matatepai, Pointe ↘	174x	9.43 S	139.02 W
Matatiele	158	30.24 S	28.43 E
Mātāfīla Dam ←[6]	124	25.06 N	78.22 E
Matatindoc Point ↘	116	9.43 N	122.23 E
Matatula, Cape ↘	174u	14.15 S	170.34 W
Mataura	172	46.11 S	168.52 E
Mataura ≃, Bra.	248	5.30 S	60.45 W
Mataura ≃, N.Z.	172	46.34 S	168.43 E
Matâutu	175a	13.57 S	171.56 W
Mataval, Baie de c	174s	17.30 S	149.30 W
Matavera	174k	21.13 S	159.44 W
Mataveri	174z	27.10 S	109.27 E
Mataveri Airstrip ☒	174z	27.10 S	109.25 W
Matawai	172	38.21 S	177.32 E
Matawan ≃	208	40.24 N	74.13 W
Matawin ≃	206	46.54 N	72.56 W
Matāy	142	28.25 N	30.46 E
Matbül	142	31.05 N	31.02 E
Matča	85	39.27 N	69.39 E
Matchaponix Brook ≃	276	40.23 N	74.23 W
Matchi-Manitou, Lac ⊘	190	48.00 N	77.04 W
Matching Green	260	51.47 N	0.13 E
Matching Tye	260	51.47 N	0.12 E
Mateare	236	12.14 N	86.26 W
Mateba, Île de I	152	5.54 S	12.50 E
Matehuala	234	23.39 N	100.39 W
Mateke Hills ↗[2]	156	21.48 S	31.00 E
Mateko	152	4.03 S	18.56 E
Matelica	66	43.15 N	13.00 E
Matemo, Ilha I	154	12.13 S	40.36 E
Matera	68	40.40 N	16.37 E
Matera □[4]	68	40.30 N	16.25 E
Matese, Lago del ⊘	68	41.25 N	14.25 E
Matese, Monti del ∧	66	41.27 N	14.22 E
Matészalka	30	47.57 N	22.19 E
Matete	273b	4.24 S	15.20 E
Matetsi	154	18.16 S	25.56 E
Mateur	148	37.03 N	9.40 E
Matewan	192	37.37 N	82.09 W
Matfield	207	42.02 N	70.59 W
Matfors	26	62.21 N	17.02 E
Matha	32	45.52 N	0.19 W
Mathbaria	126	22.18 N	89.57 E
Mathematicians Seamounts ↙[3]	16	15.00 N	111.00 W
Mather, Mb., Can.	184	49.06 N	99.07 W
Mather, Pa., U.S.	188	39.56 N	80.04 W
Mather Air Force Base ⊡	282	38.34 N	121.13 W
Mather Gorge V	284c	38.59 N	77.15 W
Matheson	190	48.32 N	80.23 W
Matheson Island	184	51.44 N	96.55 W
Matheu	258	34.22 S	58.51 W
Mathews	208	37.26 N	76.19 W
Mathews ≃[6]	208	37.25 N	76.23 W
Mathews, Lake ⊘	228	33.51 N	117.25 W
Mathi	62	45.15 N	7.32 E
Mathis	196	28.05 N	97.49 W
Mâthle	272b	22.35 N	88.11 E
Mathry	42	51.57 N	5.05 W
Mathura, India	122	10.57 N	78.27 E
Mathura, India	124	27.30 N	77.41 E
Mathura Bil ⊘	272b	22.56 N	88.23 E
Mathurai — Madurai	122	9.56 N	78.07 E
Mathurâpur, Bngl.	126	24.02 N	88.47 E
Mathurâpur, Bngl.	126	23.17 N	89.15 E
Mati	116	6.57 N	126.13 E
Matiacoali	150	12.12 N	1.02 E
Matiakhola	126	23.16 N	86.53 E
Matianhe ≃	124	26.56 N	88.43 E
Matiate ≃	126	25.36 N	68.27 E
Matigny	261	49.00 N	2.59 E
Matinecock	276	40.53 N	73.33 W
Matinenda Lake ⊘	190	46.22 N	82.57 W
Matinha	250	3.06 S	45.02 W
Matinicock Point ↘	276	40.54 N	73.38 W
Matinicus Island I	188	43.54 N	68.53 W
Matipó	68	40.02 N	16.08 E
Matir Târis	142	29.22 N	30.54 E
Matiyure ≃	246	7.36 N	67.33 W
Matjiesfontein	158	33.14 S	20.35 E
Matkasel'kja	26	61.58 N	30.33 E
Matla ≃	126	22.04 N	88.33 E
Matlabas ≃	156	23.39 S	27.45 E
Matlacha	208	26.37 N	82.05 W
Matlacha Pass ↗	220	26.37 N	82.04 W
Matlamanyane	156	19.33 S	25.57 E
Matlapa	234	21.23 N	98.50 W
M'atlevo	58	54.54 N	35.18 E
Matlock, Eng., U.K.	44	53.08 N	1.32 W
Matlock, Wa., U.S.	226	47.14 N	123.25 W
Matlock, Mount ∧	169	37.35 S	146.11 E
Matmata	148	33.33 N	9.58 E
Matnog	116	12.35 N	124.05 E
Mato, Cerro ∧	246	7.09 N	65.07 W
Matobe	175g	7.15 N	151.04 E
Matobe	208	37.13 N	75.29 W
Matobo ≃	156	25.53 S	32.45 E
Mato Grosso ≃	242	12.00 S	57.00 W
Mato Grosso, Planalto do ∧	242	15.30 S	56.00 W
Mato Grosso do Sul □[3]	242	20.00 S	55.00 W
Mato-Rio ≃	156	25.58 S	32.26 E
Mato Verde	250	15.23 S	42.52 W
Mato Mole, Serra do ∧[2]	256	23.05 S	46.12 W
Matochkin Šar ≃	72	73.16 N	55.21 E
Matočkin Šar, proliv ↗	72	73.20 N	55.21 E
Matões	250	5.32 S	43.11 W
Matola	156	25.58 S	32.28 E
Matosinhos	255	19.35 S	44.07 W
Matopos ≃	156	20.24 S	28.28 E
Matosinhos	34	41.11 N	8.42 W
Matoug	148	35.24 N	8.48 E
Matouji	98	35.02 N	115.07 E
Matou, T'aiwan	100	23.09 N	120.20 E
Matouzhen, Zhg.	100	30.16 N	116.27 E
Matouzhen, Zhg.	100	31.24 N	116.58 E
Matoury	250	4.51 S	52.20 W
Matouzi	100	29.18 N	119.48 E
Matova	107	33.05 N	114.09 E
Matra ∧	98	35.02 N	115.07 E
Mátra ∧	30	47.55 N	20.00 E

Column 3 (Português)

Nome	Página	Lat.°'	Long.°' W=Oeste
Matrah	128	23.38 N	58.34 E
Matraville	274a	33.54 S	151.18 E
Matrei am Brenner	64	47.08 N	11.27 E
Matrei in Osttirol	64	47.00 N	12.32 E
Matru	150	7.36 N	12.11 W
Matsap	158	28.38 S	22.47 E
Matsapha	158	26.29 S	31.23 E
Matsari	152	5.21 N	12.14 E
Matsena	150	13.05 N	10.05 E
Matsiatra ≃	157b	21.25 S	45.33 E
Matsieng	158	29.36 S	27.32 E
Matsknutsgårdarna	40	60.28 N	15.22 E
Matsqui	224	49.12 N	122.25 W
Matsu — Matsu Tao I	100	26.09 N	119.56 E
Matsubara	96	34.34 N	135.33 E
Matsubushi	268	35.55 N	139.49 E
Matsuda	94	35.21 N	139.09 E
Matsudai	94	37.08 N	138.37 E
Matsudo	94	35.47 N	139.54 E
Matsudo Race Track ◈	268	35.48 N	139.55 E
Matsue	96	35.28 N	133.04 E
Matsugasaki	268	35.53 N	139.58 E
Matsukawa, Nihon	94	36.19 N	138.48 E
Matsukawa, Nihon	94	36.25 N	137.51 E
Matsumae	92	41.26 N	140.07 E
Matsumoto	94	36.14 N	137.58 E
Matsunoyama	94	37.05 N	138.37 E
Matsuno	96	33.13 N	132.42 E
Matsuōji	268	35.08 N	140.01 E
Matsuoka	94	36.05 N	136.28 E
Matsusaka	94	34.34 N	136.32 E
Matsu-san ∧	270	34.38 N	135.44 E
Matsushima	92	38.22 N	141.04 E
Matsu Tao I	100	26.09 N	119.56 E
Matsutō	94	36.31 N	136.34 E
Matsuura	96	33.22 N	129.42 E
Matsuyama	96	33.50 N	132.45 E
Matsuzaki	94	34.45 N	138.47 E
Mattagami ≃	176	50.43 N	81.29 W
Mattagami Heights	190	48.29 N	81.22 W
Mattagami Lake ⊘	190	47.54 N	81.35 W
Mattamuskeet, Lake ⊘	208	35.30 N	76.11 W
Mattapan	283	42.16 N	71.06 W
Mattaponi ≃	208	37.32 N	76.46 W
Mattaponi ≃	208	37.31 N	76.47 W
Mattarana	62	44.15 N	9.37 E
Mattarello	64	46.00 N	11.07 E
Mattawa, On., Can.	190	46.19 N	78.42 W
Mattawa, Wa., U.S.	202	46.44 N	119.54 W
Mattawamkeag	188	45.30 N	68.21 W
Mattawamkeag ≃	188	45.30 N	68.24 W
Mattawan	216	42.12 N	85.47 W
Mattawoman Creek ≃	208	38.34 N	77.12 W
Matterhorn (Cervino) ∧, Europe	58	45.59 N	7.43 E
Matterhorn ∧, Nv., U.S.	204	41.49 N	115.23 W
Mattersburg	61	47.44 N	16.25 E
Mattertal V	58	46.10 N	7.49 E
Matteson	216	41.30 N	87.42 W
Matteson Lake ⊘	216	41.56 N	85.12 W
Matthew Flinders Memorial ⊥	169	38.19 S	145.04 E
Matthews	216	40.23 N	85.29 W
Matthews Mountain ∧	194	37.29 N	90.21 W
Matthews Ridge	246	7.30 N	60.10 W
Matthew Town	238	20.57 N	73.40 W
Matthias Church ↟	264c	47.30 N	19.02 E
Matthiessen State Park ♦	216	41.17 N	89.01 W
Mattī, Sabkhat ≃	128	23.30 N	52.00 E
Mattie, Lake ⊘	220	28.08 N	81.46 W
Mattighofen	61	48.06 N	13.04 E
Mattigxofen ←	56	48.06 N	13.09 E
Mattinata	68	41.42 N	16.03 E
Mattishall	42	52.39 N	1.02 E
Mattituck	207	40.59 N	72.32 W
Mattole ≃	204	40.18 N	124.21 W
Mat:oon, Il., U.S.	194	39.28 N	88.22 W
Mat:oon, Wi., U.S.	190	45.01 N	89.02 W
Mat:ox Creek ≃	208	38.12 N	76.58 W
Mat:ox Draw ≃	198	38.03 N	101.11 W
Mat:see	64	47.58 N	13.06 E
Mat:see	60	47.59 N	13.07 E
Mat:ydale	210	43.05 N	76.08 W
Matu	112	2.41 N	111.32 E
Matuba	156	24.27 S	32.55 E
Matucana	248	11.51 S	76.24 W
Matudo — Matsudo	94	35.47 N	139.54 E
Matue — Matsue	96	35.28 N	133.04 E
Mat:ku Island I	175g	19.10 S	179.46 E
Matumoto — Matsumoto	94	36.14 N	137.58 E
Matunuck	207	41.23 N	71.32 W
Matūrín	246	9.45 N	63.11 W
Maturín ↘[9]	246	9.50 N	63.00 W
Maturuca	246	4.22 N	60.10 W
Matusadona National Park ♦	154	16.25 S	28.35 E
Mat:tina	255	19.13 S	45.58 W
Mat:tuba	154	14.46 S	35.59 E
Mat:tum, Mount ∧	116	6.22 N	125.05 E
Mat:uzaka	94	34.34 N	136.32 E
Matveyevka	80	52.33 N	53.23 E
Matvejev Kurgan	83	47.35 N	38.52 E
Matvejevo, Ross.	76	57.47 N	57.51 E
Matxixako, Cabo ↘	34	43.27 N	2.45 W
Mátyásföld ←[8]	264c	47.31 N	19.12 E
Matyšsiv	76	50.27 N	25.18 E
Matysivo	58	49.03 N	31.34 E
Mau	124	25.17 N	81.23 E
Maú (Ireng) ≃	246	3.33 N	59.51 W
Mauá, Bra.	256	23.40 S	46.27 W
Mauá, Moç.	154	13.51 S	37.10 E
Mauá ←[13]	287a	23.40 S	46.27 W
Mau Aimma	124	25.42 N	81.55 E
Mauban	116	14.12 N	121.44 E
Maubara	112	8.37 S	125.12 E
Maubeuge	32	50.17 N	3.58 E
Maubin	110	16.44 N	95.39 E
Maubourguet	32	43.28 N	0.02 E
Maués	246	3.24 S	57.42 W
Maués ≃	246	3.22 S	57.44 W
Mauga Silisili ∧	175a	13.35 S	172.27 W

Column 4

Nome	Página	Lat.°'	Long.°' W=Oeste
Maughold	44	54.18 N	4.17 W
Maug Islands II	108	20.01 N	145.13 E
Mauguio	62	43.37 N	4.01 E
Mauguio, Étang de c	62	43.35 N	4.02 E
Maui □[6]	229a	20.53 N	156.30 W
Maui I	229a	20.45 N	156.15 W
Mauk	115a	6.04 S	106.30 E
Maulbach	56	50.43 N	9.04 E
Maulbronn	56	49.00 N	8.49 E
Maulde	50	50.30 N	3.26 E
Mauldin	192	34.46 N	82.18 W
Maule	50	48.55 N	1.51 E
Maule □[4]	252	35.30 S	71.30 W
Maule ≃	252	35.19 S	72.25 W
Maule, Laguna del ⊘	252	36.04 S	70.30 W
Maulén	32	46.56 N	0.45 W
Mauléon-Licharre	32	43.14 N	0.53 W
Maulette	261	48.48 N	1.37 E
Maulvi Bâzâr	126	24.29 N	91.47 E
Maumaupaki ∧	172	36.58 S	175.35 E
Maumee	214	41.33 N	83.39 W
Maumee ≃	214	41.42 N	83.28 W
Maumee Bay c	214	41.43 N	83.26 W
Maumelle, Lake ⊘[1]	194	34.55 N	92.40 W
Maumere	115b	8.37 S	122.14 E
Maun	156	20.00 S	23.25 E
Mauna Kea ∧	229d	19.50 N	155.28 W
Maunaloa	229a	21.08 N	157.13 W
Mauna Loa ∧[1]	229d	19.29 N	155.36 W
Maunalua Bay c	229e	21.17 N	157.44 W
Maunath Bhanjan	124	25.57 N	83.33 E
Maunatlala	156	22.32 S	27.28 E
Maunahaumi ∧	172	38.18 S	177.40 E
Maunga Roa ∧	174k	21.13 S	159.48 W
Maungatapere	172	35.45 S	174.12 E
Maungaturoto	172	36.06 S	174.22 E
Maungdaw	110	20.50 N	92.21 E
Maungmagan	110	14.09 N	98.06 E
Maungu	154	3.33 S	38.45 E
Maunoir, Lac ⊘	180	67.30 N	125.00 W
Maupihaa I[1]	14	16.50 S	153.55 W
Maupin	224	45.10 N	121.04 W
Maur	123	30.05 N	75.15 E
Maur, Pulau I	114	2.12 N	103.51 E
Mau Rānīpur	124	25.15 N	79.08 E
Maurecourt	261	49.00 N	2.04 E
Maure-de-Bretagne	32	47.54 N	1.59 W
Mauregard	261	49.02 N	2.35 E
Maurepas	261	48.45 N	1.55 E
Maurepas, Lake ⊘	194	30.15 N	90.30 W
Maures ∧	62	43.16 N	6.23 E
Mauretanien — Mauritania □[1]	134	20.00 N	12.00 W
Mauri ≃	248	17.18 S	68.41 W
Mauri, Passo della ʮ	64	46.27 N	12.31 E
Mauriac	32	45.13 N	2.20 E
Maurice — Mauritius □[1]	157c	20.17 S	57.33 E
Maurice ≃	208	39.13 N	75.02 W
Maurice, Lake ⊘	162	29.28 S	130.58 E
Maurice K. Goddard State Park ♦	214	41.23 N	81.10 W
Mauricetown	208	39.17 N	74.58 W
Mauriceville	172	40.47 S	175.42 E
Mauricio — Mauritius □[1]	157c	20.17 S	57.33 E
Maurienne V	62	45.13 N	6.30 E
Mauritania — Mauritanie □[1]	134	20.00 N	12.00 W
Mauritania — Mauritania □[1]	134	20.00 N	12.00 W
Mauritius □[1], Afr.	157c	20.17 S	57.33 E
Mauritius I, Afr.	157c	20.17 S	57.33 E
Mauron	32	48.05 N	2.18 W
Maurs	32	44.43 N	2.11 E
Maurua I — Maupiti I	14	16.26 S	152.15 W
Maury ≃	192	37.37 N	79.27 W
Maury Channel ʮ	176	75.44 N	94.40 W
Maury Island I	224	47.20 N	122.24 W
Maussane	62	43.43 N	4.48 E
Mauston	190	43.47 N	90.04 W
Mautau, Pointe ↘	174x	9.42 S	138.58 W
Mautern	61	48.24 N	15.35 E
Mautern in Steiermark	64	47.24 N	14.50 E
Mauth	56	48.53 N	13.35 E
Mauthausen	61	48.14 N	14.32 E
Mauvais Coulee ≃	198	48.21 N	99.06 W
Mauvaise Terre Creek ≃	219	39.43 N	90.38 W
Mauvaise Terre Lake ⊘	219	39.42 N	90.12 W
Mauvezin	32	43.44 N	0.53 E
Mauzé-sur-le-Mignon	32	46.12 N	0.41 W
Mava	164	6.50 S	145.25 E
Mavanza	156	21.13 S	35.11 E
Mävelikara	122	9.16 N	76.33 E
Maverick	200	33.43 N	109.32 W
Mavinga	152	15.50 S	20.21 E
Mavita	156	19.33 S	33.10 E
Mavrovouni	36	39.40 N	22.48 E
Mawa	152	2.45 N	26.42 E
Mawai	114	2.16 N	103.57 E
Ma Wan I	271d	22.21 N	114.03 E
Mawana	124	29.06 N	77.55 E
Mawanga	152	4.58 S	15.28 E
Mawasangka	116	5.17 S	122.18 E
Mawchi	110	18.49 N	97.08 E
Mawddach ≃	44	52.43 N	4.03 W
Mawdesley	259	53.38 N	2.47 W
Mawdesley Lake ⊘	184	54.01 N	100.39 W
Mawi	272a	28.14 N	77.20 E
Mawjib, Wâdī al- V	132	31.28 N	35.34 E
Mawkhi	110	19.40 N	97.17 E
Mawlaik	110	23.38 N	94.26 E
Mawlamyine	110	16.30 N	97.38 E
Mawlawine (Moulmein)	110	16.30 N	97.38 E
Mawr, Wâdī V	144	15.41 N	43.42 E
Mawshij	144	13.41 N	43.19 E
Mawson ◉	9	67.40 S	63.43 E
Mawson Escarpment ↗	9	73.05 S	68.10 E
Mawson Peninsula ↘[1]	9	68.50 S	154.11 E
Maw Taung ∧	110	11.45 N	99.35 E
Max	198	47.49 N	101.18 W
Maxaranguape	250	5.31 S	35.16 W
Maxcanú	232	20.35 N	90.00 W
Maxéville	32	48.43 N	6.10 E
Maxhütte-Haidhof	56	49.18 N	12.04 E
Maxia, Punta ∧	68	39.26 N	9.14 E
Maximiliansau	57	49.04 N	8.18 E
Maximo	214	40.53 N	81.17 W
Maximo Paz	258	34.56 S	58.37 W
Maxinkuckee, Lake ⊘	216	41.12 N	86.24 W
Maxixe	156	23.51 S	35.21 E
Maxton	192	34.44 N	79.20 W
Maxville	206	45.17 N	74.51 W
Maxwell, Ca., U.S.	226	39.16 N	122.11 W

Column 5

Nome	Página	Lat.°'	Long.°' W=Oeste
Maxwell, In., U.S.	218	39.51 N	85.46 W
Maxwell, Ia., U.S.	190	41.53 N	93.23 W
Maxwell, Ne., U.S.	198	41.04 N	100.31 W
Maxwell, N.M., U.S.	196	36.32 N	104.32 W
Maxwell, Tx., U.S.	222	29.53 N	97.48 W
Maxwell Air Force Base ⊡	194	32.23 N	86.21 W
Maxwell Bay c	176	74.35 N	89.00 W
May	196	31.59 N	98.55 W
May ≃, Austl.	162	17.07 S	123.50 E
May ≃, Ab., Can.	182	55.43 N	111.22 W
May ≃, Pap. N. Gui.	164	4.35 S	141.35 E
May, Cape ↘[1]	208	38.58 N	74.55 W
May, Isle of I	46	56.11 N	2.34 W
May, Mount ∧	182	54.02 N	119.58 W
Maya, Pulau I	112	1.10 S	109.35 E
Maya, Ross.	80	57.14 N	41.13 E
Mayachka ∧	83	48.44 N	37.33 E
Mayaguana	238	22.23 N	72.57 W
Mayaguana Passage ʮ	238	22.32 N	73.15 W
Mayagüez	240m	18.12 N	67.09 W
Mayagüez ↘[9]	240m	18.12 N	67.10 W
Mayagüez, Bahía de c	240m	18.12 N	67.10 W
Mayahi	150	13.58 N	7.40 E
Mayajigua	240p	22.14 N	79.04 W
Mayaky, Ukr.	78	46.25 N	30.16 E
Mayaky, Ukr.	83	48.57 N	37.37 E
Mayala	273b	4.21 S	15.09 E
Mayales, Punta ↘	236	11.52 N	85.26 W
Mayama	152	3.51 S	14.54 E
Mayamba	152	4.46 S	16.52 E
Mayamey	128	36.24 N	55.42 E
Mayaro ≃	70	37.39 N	12.35 E
Mayaro Bay c	241r	10.15 N	60.58 W
Mayarí	240p	20.40 N	75.41 W
Mayarí Arriba	240p	20.28 N	75.32 W
Maybee	216	42.00 N	83.30 W
Maybeury	192	37.22 N	81.22 W
Maybole	46	55.21 N	4.41 W
Maybrook	210	41.29 N	74.13 W
Maychew	144	13.02 N	39.34 E
Maydelle	222	31.48 N	95.18 W
Maydena	166	42.45 S	146.30 E
Maydh	144	11.00 N	47.07 E
Maydolong	116	11.30 N	125.30 E
Maydos	36	40.11 N	26.22 E
Mayen	56	50.19 N	7.13 E
Mayence — Mainz	56	50.01 N	8.16 E
Mayenne	32	48.18 N	0.37 W
Mayenne □[5]	32	48.05 N	0.40 W
Mayenne ≃	32	47.30 N	0.33 W
Mayer	200	34.23 N	112.14 W
Mayerling	61	48.03 N	16.06 E
Mayersville	194	32.54 N	91.03 W
Mayerthorpe	182	53.57 N	115.08 W
Mayet	50	47.46 N	0.17 E
Mayfa'h ↟, S. Afr.	273d	26.12 S	28.01 E
Mayfair ↟[8], Pa., U.S.	279f	40.02 N	75.03 W
Mayfield, N.Z.	172	43.49 S	171.25 E
Mayfield, Eng., U.K.	42	51.01 N	0.15 E
Mayfield, Eng., U.K.	44	53.01 N	1.45 W
Mayfield, Scot., U.K.	45	55.52 N	3.02 W
Mayfield, In., U.S.	218	40.11 N	85.27 W
Mayfield, Ky., U.S.	194	36.44 N	88.38 W
Mayfield, N.Y., U.S.	210	43.06 N	74.16 W
Mayfield, Oh., U.S.	215	41.31 N	81.26 W
Mayfield, Pa., U.S.	210	41.33 N	75.32 W
Mayfield Creek ≃	194	36.57 N	89.05 W
Mayfield Dam ←[2]	224	46.31 N	122.32 W
Mayfield Heights	215	41.31 N	81.27 W
Mayfield Lake ⊘[1]	224	46.31 N	122.34 W
Mayflower	194	34.57 N	92.25 W
Mayford	260	51.18 N	0.34 W
May Inlet c	176	76.15 N	100.45 W
Maying	98	36.36 N	103.57 E
Maykop — Majkop	84	44.35 N	40.07 E
Mayland	260	51.39 N	0.47 E
Maymont	182	52.33 N	107.40 W
Maymyo	110	22.02 N	96.28 E
Mayn ≃	74	64.42 N	173.40 E
Maynard, Ma., U.S.	207	42.26 N	71.27 W
Maynard, Mn., U.S.	198	44.54 N	95.28 W
Maynard, Oh., U.S.	214	40.04 N	80.53 W
Maynardville	192	36.15 N	83.47 W
Mayne ≃	166	26.15 S	141.55 E
Maynooth	46	53.23 N	6.35 W
Mayo, Yk., Can.	180	63.35 N	135.54 W
Mayo, Fl., U.S.	208	30.03 N	83.10 W
Mayo, Md., U.S.	208	38.53 N	76.30 W
Mayo ≃, Arg.	234	45.40 S	70.15 W
Mayo ≃, Col.	246	1.40 N	77.17 W
Mayo ≃, Perú	248	6.37 S	76.16 W
Mayor Buratovich	252	39.16 S	62.37 W
Mayo Reservoir ⊘[1]	192	36.33 N	78.53 W
Mayon Volcano ∧[1]	116	13.15 N	123.41 E
Mayor Pablo Lagerenza	254	19.56 S	60.47 W
Mayotte I[1], Afr.	138	12.50 S	45.10 E
Mayotte □[1], Afr.	138	12.50 S	45.10 E
Mayoumba — Mayumba	152	3.25 S	10.39 E
Mayoyao	269b	16.47 N	121.11 E
Maypearl	222	32.18 N	96.59 W
Mayport Naval Station ⊡	192	30.22 N	81.24 W
Mayrān, Desierto de ≃	232	25.45 N	102.45 W

Column 6

Nome	Página	Lat.°'	Long.°' W=Oeste
Mãyûram	122	11.06 N	79.40 E
Mayville, Mi., U.S.	216	43.20 N	83.21 W
Mayville, N.D., U.S.	198	47.29 N	97.19 W
Mayville, N.Y., U.S.	214	42.15 N	79.30 W
Mayville, Wi., U.S.	190	43.29 N	88.32 W
Maywood, Ca., U.S.	280	33.59 N	118.11 W
Maywood, Il., U.S.	216	41.52 N	87.50 W
Maywood, Mo., U.S.	219	39.57 N	91.36 W
Maywood, Ne., U.S.	198	40.39 N	100.37 W
Maywood, N.J., U.S.	276	40.54 N	74.03 W
Maywood, N.Y., U.S.	210	42.42 N	73.52 W
Maywood Race Track ♦	278	41.44 N	87.50 W
Mayyit, Al-Bahr al- — Dead Sea ⊘	132	31.30 N	35.30 E
Maza, Arg.	252	36.50 S	63.19 W
Maza, Ross.	80	57.14 N	41.13 E
Mazabuka	154	15.51 S	27.46 E
Mazagan — El-Jadida	148	33.16 N	8.30 W
Mazagão	250	0.07 S	51.17 W
Mazagão ←[3]	272c	18.57 N	72.50 E
Mazagão Velho	250	0.13 S	51.25 W
Mazamet	32	43.30 N	2.24 E
Mazamitla	234	19.55 N	103.02 W
Mazan	62	44.04 N	5.08 E
Mãzandarān □[4]	128	36.30 N	53.30 E
Mazanovo	89	51.40 N	128.52 E
Mazar, Jabal ∧	132	33.34 N	36.03 E
Mazar ∧	148	31.50 N	1.36 E
Mazara, Val di ←[1]	70	37.39 N	12.35 E
Mazar-e Sharīf	120	36.42 N	67.06 E
Mazargues	62	43.15 N	5.24 E
Mazaro ≃	70	37.39 N	12.35 E
Mazarredo	254	47.05 S	66.42 W
Mazarrón	34	37.30 N	1.19 W
Mazarrón, Golfo de c	34	37.20 N	1.18 W
Mazaruni ≃	246	6.25 N	58.38 W
Mazatenango	236	14.32 N	91.30 W
Mazatlán	234	23.13 N	106.25 W
Mazatlán Villa de Flores	234	18.02 N	96.54 W
Mazatzal Mountains ∧	200	34.00 N	111.55 W
Mazatzal Peak ∧	200	34.03 N	111.28 W
Maze	94	35.52 N	137.10 E
Maze ≃	261	49.00 N	2.04 E
Mažeikiai	76	56.19 N	22.20 E
Mazenod	184	49.53 N	106.14 W
Mazeppa, Mn., U.S.	190	44.16 N	92.32 W
Mazeppa, Pa., U.S.	169	40.59 N	76.59 W
Mazhan, Zhg.	100	23.27 N	114.00 E
Mazhan, Zhg.	98	32.35 N	109.01 E
Mazhang, Zhg.	104	42.23 N	122.26 E
Mazhangfang, Zhg.	104	40.44 N	120.53 E
Mazhuang, Zhg.	98	37.47 N	115.17 E
Mazhuang, Zhg.	100	32.54 N	114.03 E
Mazhuang, Zhg.	105	39.11 N	116.15 E
Mazïr, Khubb al- ⊘	128	27.45 N	43.55 E
Mazıdağı	130	37.30 N	40.30 E
Mazıgou	105	37.30 N	40.30 E
Mazilovo ←[8]	265b	55.44 N	37.26 E
Mazlīnān	128	36.16 N	56.46 E
Mazinan Lake ⊘	212	44.55 N	77.12 W
Mazırbe	76	57.41 N	22.17 E
Mazocco	154	11.40 S	35.48 E
Mazoe ≃	154	16.32 S	33.25 E
Mazomanie	190	43.10 N	89.47 W
Mazomba ≃	154	7.48 S	35.39 E
Mazon	216	41.14 N	88.25 W
Mazon, East Fork ≃	216	41.11 N	88.18 W
Mazon, West Fork ≃	216	41.11 N	88.27 W
Mazong Shan ∧	88	41.58 N	97.10 E
Mazong Shan ∧	102	41.50 N	97.30 E
Mazou ≃	148	40.15 N	2.59 E
Mazra'at al-Bayt Jinn	132	33.19 N	35.55 E
Mazsalaca	76	57.52 N	25.03 E
Mazunga	156	21.45 S	29.52 E
Mazurskie, Pojezierze ∧	30	53.45 N	21.00 E
Mazury ✦[1]	30	53.45 N	21.00 E
Mazyr	78	52.03 N	29.14 E
Mazzarino	70	37.18 N	14.13 E
Mazzarrà Sant'andrea	70	38.05 N	15.08 E
Mba	132	31.30 N	35.30 E
Mbabo, Tchabal ∧	150	7.16 N	12.06 E
Mbabane	158	26.18 S	31.06 E
Mbaïki	152	3.53 N	18.00 E
Mbakaou, Barrage de ←[2]	152	6.15 N	12.46 E
Mbala (Abercorn)	154	8.50 S	31.22 E
Mbalam	152	2.13 N	13.49 E
Mbale	154	1.05 N	34.10 E
Mbalmayo	152	3.31 N	11.30 E
Mbalo	175g	10.14 S	161.33 E
Mbam ≃	152	4.25 N	11.21 E
Mbamba Bay	154	11.17 S	34.46 E
Mbandaka (Coquilhatville)	152	0.04 N	18.16 E
Mbandjok	152	4.27 N	11.54 E
Mbanga	152	4.30 N	9.34 E
Mbanika Island I	175g	9.05 S	159.12 E
M'banza Congo	152	6.15 S	14.15 E
Mbanza-Ngungu	152	5.15 S	14.52 E
Mbarara	154	0.37 S	30.39 E
Mbari ≃	152	4.34 N	22.43 E
Mbé, Camer.	152	7.51 N	13.36 E
Mbé, Congo	152	3.25 S	15.23 E
Mbeni ≃	273b	4.03 S	15.35 E
Mbemkuru ≃	154	9.22 S	39.54 E
Mbemba	273b	4.50 S	14.55 E
Mbengga I	175g	18.23 S	178.08 E
Mbenguë	150	10.00 N	5.54 W
Mbéni	157b	11.28 S	43.24 E
Mbereshi Mission	154	9.45 S	28.47 E
Mbeya	154	8.54 S	33.27 E
Mbeya □[4]	154	8.20 S	33.00 E
Mbinda	152	2.05 S	12.51 E
Mbini	152	1.35 N	9.37 E
Mbini ≃	152	1.37 N	9.39 E
Mbirizi	154	0.23 S	31.22 E
Mbó ≃	152	4.11 S	14.55 E
Mbogo	154	7.06 S	33.26 E
Mboki	152	5.19 N	25.58 E
Mbol	152	4.08 S	23.09 E

Legend

≃ River	Fluß	Río	Rivière	Rio
≖ Canal	Kanal	Canal	Canal	Canal
ʮ Waterfall, Rapids	Wasserfall, Stromschnellen	Cascada, Rápidos	Chute d'eau, Rapides	Cascata, Rápidos
ʯ Strait	Meeresstraße	Estrecho	Détroit	Estreito
c Bay, Gulf	Bucht, Golf	Bahía, Golfo	Baie, Golfe	Baía, Golfo
⊘ Lake, Lakes	See, Seen	Lago, Lagos	Lac, Lacs	Lago, Lagos
≃ Swamp	Sumpf	Pantano	Marais	Pântano
⧈ Ice Features, Glacier	Eis- und Gletscherformen	Accidentes Glaciales	Formes glaciaires	Acidentes glaciares
Other Hydrographic Features	Andere Hydrographische Objekte	Otros Elementos Hidrográficos	Autres données hydrographiques	Outros acidentes hidrográficos
↙ Submarine Features	Untermeerische Objekte	Accidentes Submarinos	Formes de relief sous-marin	Acidentes submarinos
□ Political Unit	Politische Einheit	Unidad Política	Entité politique	Unidade política
↟ Cultural Institution	Kulturelle Institution	Institución Cultural	Institution culturelle	Instituição cultural
♦ Historical Site	Historische Stätte	Sitio Histórico	Site historique	Sítio Histórico
♦ Recreational Site	Erholungs- und Ferienort	Sitio de Recreo	Centre de loisirs	Área de Lazer
☒ Airport	Flughafen	Aeropuerto	Aéroport	Aeroporto
⊡ Military Installation	Militäranlage	Instalación Militar	Installation militaire	Instalação militar
⊙ Miscellaneous	Verschiedenes	Misceláneo	Divers	Diversos

		ENGLISH				DEUTSCH			Länge⁰ʳ
Name	Page	Lat.⁰ʳ	Long.⁰ʳ		Name	Seite	Breite⁰ʳ	E = Ost	

Symbols in the index entries represent the broad categories identified in the key at the right. Symbols with superscript numbers (ʌ¹) identify subcategories (see complete key on page I · 1).

Symbole im Register stellen die rechts im Schlüssel erklärten Kategorien dar. Symbole mit hochgestellten Ziffern (ʌ¹) bezeichnen Unterabteilungen einer Kategorie (vgl. vollständiger Schlüssel auf Seite I · 1).

Los símbolos incluidos en el texto del índice representan las grandes categorías identificadas con la clave a la derecha. Los símbolos con números en su parte superior (ʌ¹) identifican las subcategorías (véase la clave completa en la página I · 1).

Les symboles de l'index représentent les catégories indiquées dans la légende à droite. Les symboles suivis d'un indice (ʌ¹) représentent les sous-catégories (voir légende complète à la page I · 1).

Os símbolos incluídos no texto do índice representam as grandes categorias identificadas com a chave à direita. Os símbolos com números em sua parte superior (ʌ¹) identificam as subcategorias (veja-se a chave completa à página I · 1).

ʌ Mountain	Berg	Montaña	Montagne	Montanha
ʌ Mountains	Gebirge	Montañas	Montagnes	Montanhas
⋊ Pass	Paß	Paso	Col	Passo
V Valley, Canyon	Tal, Cañon	Valle, Cañón	Vallée, Canyon	Vale, Canhão
⌐ Plain	Ebene	Llano	Plaine	Planície
⊦ Kap	Kap	Cabo	Cap	Cabo
I Island	Insel	Isla	Île	Ilha
II Islands	Inseln	Islas	Îles	Ilhas
≃ Other Topographic Features	Andere Topographische Objekte	Otros Elementos Topográficos	Autres données topographiques	Outros acidentes topográficos

ESPAÑOL	FRANÇAIS	PORTUGUÊS
Nombre Página Lat.°′ Long.°′ W=Oeste	Nom Page Lat.°′ Long.°′ W=Ouest	Nome Página Lat.°′ Long.°′ W=Oeste

Column 1

Melozitna ≃ 180 64.46 N 155.29 W
Melrose, Austl. 162 27.56 S 121.19 E
Melrose, Austl. 166 32.42 S 146.58 E
Melrose, Scot., U.K. 46 55.36 N 2.44 W
Melrose, Ma., U.S. 207 42.27 N 71.04 W
Melrose, Mn., U.S. 198 45.40 N 94.48 W
Melrose, N.M., U.S. 196 34.25 N 103.37 W
Melrose, N.Y., U.S. 210 42.50 N 73.37 W
Melrose, Oh., U.S. 216 41.05 N 84.25 W
Melrose, Wi., U.S. 190 44.07 N 90.59 W
Melrose ◄•⁸ 276 40.49 N 73.55 W
Melrose Abbey ⌂¹ 46 55.37 N 2.45 W
Melrose Park, Fl., U.S. 220 26.06 N 80.12 W
Melrose Park, Il., U.S. 216 41.54 N 87.51 W
Melrose Park, N.Y., U.S. 212 42.54 N 76.32 W
Melrose Park, Pa., U.S. 285 40.04 N 75.08 W
Mels 58 47.03 N 9.25 E
Melstone 202 46.36 N 107.52 W
Melsungen 56 51.08 N 9.32 E
Meltaus 24 66.54 N 25.22 E
Meltham, Eng., U.K. 44 53.35 N 1.51 W
Meltham, Eng., U.K. 262 53.36 N 1.51 W
Melton, Austl. 168b 34.05 S 137.59 E
Melton, Austl. 169 37.41 S 144.35 E
Melton Constable 42 52.53 N 1.01 E
Melton Hill Lake ⊜¹ 192 36.00 N 84.15 W
Melton Mowbray 42 52.46 N 0.53 W
Melton Reservoir ⊜¹ 169 37.43 S 144.32 E
Melúa 246 3.55 N 72.50 W
Meluan 112 1.52 N 111.56 E
Meluco 154 12.36 S 39.38 E
Melülì ≃ 154 16.28 S 39.44 E
Melun, Fr. 50 48.32 N 2.40 E
Melun, Mya. 110 20.14 N 93.24 E
Melunga 152 17.16 S 16.24 E
Melür 122 10.03 N 78.20 E
Melvaig 46 57.48 N 5.49 W
Melvern 198 38.30 N 95.38 W
Melvern Lake ⊜¹ 198 38.30 N 95.50 W
Melvich 46 58.33 N 3.55 W
Melville, Austl. 168a 32.03 S 115.49 E
Melville, Sk., Can. 184 50.55 N 102.48 W
Melville, La., U.S. 194 30.41 N 91.44 W
Melville, N.Y., U.S. 276 40.47 N 73.24 W
Melville ◄•⁸ 273d 26.11 S 28.00 E
Melville, Cape ›, Austl. 164 14.11 S 144.30 E
Melville, Cape ›, Pil. 116 7.49 N 117.01 E
Melville, Détroit de — Viscount Melville Sound ⊔ 176 74.10 N 108.00 W
Melville, Lake ⊜ 176 53.45 N 59.30 W
Melville Bugt c 176 75.30 N 63.00 W
Melville Hall Airport ⊠ 240d 15.33 N 61.18 W
Melville Hills ⊼² 180 69.15 N 124.00 W
Melville Island I, Austl. 164 11.40 S 131.00 E
Melville Island I, N.T., Can. 16 75.15 N 110.00 W
Melville Peninsula ›¹ 176 68.00 N 84.00 W
Melville Sound ⊔, N.T., Can. 176 68.05 N 107.30 W
Melville Sound ⊔, On., U.S. 212 44.57 N 81.05 W
Melvin, Il., U.S. 216 40.34 N 88.15 W
Melvin, Ky., U.S. 192 37.21 N 82.41 W
Melvin, Tx., U.S. 196 31.13 N 99.35 W
Melvin, Lough ⊜ 48 54.26 N 8.10 W
Melvindale 281 42.16 N 83.10 W
Melvin Lake ⊜ 184 57.08 N 100.15 W
Melyana 148 36.15 N 2.15 E
Mélykút 30 46.13 N 19.24 E
Melzo 62 45.30 N 9.25 E
Memala 112 1.44 S 112.36 E
Mémar Co ⊜ 120 34.15 N 82.20 E
Memari 126 23.12 N 88.07 E
Memba 154 14.11 S 40.30 E
Membalong 112 3.09 S 107.38 E
Memboro 115b 9.22 S 119.32 E
Membre 56 49.52 N 4.54 E
Même ≃ 50 48.11 N 0.39 E
Memel — Klaipéda, Liet. 76 55.43 N 21.07 E
Memel, S. Afr. 158 27.43 S 29.30 E
Memel — Nemunas ≃ 76 55.18 N 21.23 E
Memele ≃ 76 56.24 N 24.10 E
Memewin, Lac ⊜ 190 46.29 N 78.42 W
Memmert I 52 53.38 N 6.53 E
Memmingen 58 47.59 N 10.11 E
Memo ≃ 246 9.16 N 66.40 W
Memori, Tanjung › 104 0.52 S 134.08 E
Memorial Bridge ◄•⁵ 269a 13.44 N 100.30 E
Memorial Stadium ◄ 280 32.20 N 76.36 W
Mémot 110 11.49 N 106.11 E
Mempawah 112 0.20 N 108.58 E
Memphis, Fl., U.S. 220 27.32 N 82.33 W
Memphis, Mi., U.S. 222 42.54 N 82.46 W
Memphis, Mo., U.S. 194 40.27 N 92.10 W
Memphis, Tn., U.S. 194 35.08 N 90.02 W
Memphis, Tx., U.S. 196 34.43 N 100.32 W
Memphis — Mit Ruhaynah ⊐ 142 29.51 N 31.15 E
Memphis Naval Air Station ⊠ 194 35.21 N 89.52 W
Memphremagog, Lake ⊜ 206 45.09 N 72.15 W
Memsie 46 57.39 N 2.02 W
Mena, Ityo. 144 6.25 N 39.51 E
Mena, Ukr. 78 51.31 N 32.13 E
Mena, Ar., U.S. 194 34.35 N 94.14 W
Manado — Manado 112 1.29 N 124.51 E
Menaggio 58 46.01 N 9.14 E
Menahga 198 46.45 N 95.06 W
Menai 274a 34.01 S 151.01 E
Menai Bridge 44 53.14 N 4.10 W
Menai Strait ⊔ 44 53.12 N 4.12 W
Ménaka 150 15.55 N 2.24 E
Menaldum 52 53.12 N 5.39 E
Menan 202 43.43 N 111.59 W
Menands 210 42.41 N 73.43 W
Menangina 162 29.50 S 121.14 E
Menanticco Creek ≃ 208 39.20 N 74.50 W
Menarandra ≃ 157b 25.17 S 44.30 E
Menard 196 30.55 N 99.47 W
Menard ⊡⁶ 219 40.01 N 89.51 W
Menard Creek ≃ 222 30.29 N 94.50 W
Menars 50 47.54 N 1.24 E
Menasha 190 44.13 N 88.26 W
Menate 112 0.14 S 110.02 E
Menawashei 140 12.40 N 24.59 E
Menchang 105 38.54 N 117.01 E
Menchykury 78 47.04 N 34.48 E
Mencué 254 40.20 S 70.00 W
Mend 89 43.40 N 123.08 E
Mendanau, Pulau I 112 2.56 S 107.45 E
Mendarik, Pulau I 112 0.59 N 104.18 E
Mendatai 102 38.51 N 94.39 E
Mendawai ≃ 112 3.17 S 113.16 E
Mendawai 112 2.59 S 113.16 E
Mendaya 115a 8.23 S 114.42 E
Mende 50 44.30 N 3.30 E
Mendebo ⊼ 144 6.30 N 39.30 E
Mendel ⊼ 32 46.14 N 11.13 E
Mendelejevsk 26 55.53 N 52.19 E
Menden 56 51.26 N 7.47 E
Menden ◄•⁸ 56 51.26 N 7.48 E
Mendenhall, Ms. 194 31.57 N 89.52 W
Mendenhall, Pa., U.S. 285 39.51 N 75.38 W

Column 2

Mendenhall, Cape › 180 59.51 N 166.15 W
Mendes 256 22.32 S 43.44 W
Méndez 232 25.07 N 98.34 W
Mendez-Nuñez 116 14.08 N 120.54 E
Mendham 112 40.46 N 74.36 W
Mendi, Ityo. 144 9.50 N 35.06 E
Mendi, Pap. N. Gui. 56 6.10 S 143.40 E
Mendig 56 50.21 N 7.15 E
Mendip Hills ⊼² 42 51.15 N 2.40 W
Mendocino 204 39.18 N 123.47 W
Mendocino, Cape › 204 40.25 N 124.25 W
Mendocino Fracture Zone ✦ 16 40.00 N 145.00 W
Mendola ⊼ 70 37.44 N 13.32 E
Mendon, Il., U.S. 219 40.05 N 91.17 W
Mendon, Ma., U.S. 207 42.06 N 71.33 W
Mendon, Mi., U.S. 216 42.00 N 85.27 W
Mendon, N.Y., U.S. 210 43.00 N 77.34 W
Mendon, Oh., U.S. 216 40.11 N 79.41 W
Mendota, Ca., U.S. 226 36.45 N 120.22 W
Mendota, Il., U.S. 216 41.32 N 89.07 W
Mendota, Lake ⊜ 216 43.05 N 89.25 W
Mendota Dam ◄•⁶ 226 36.48 N 120.22 W
Mendoza, Arg. 252 32.53 S 68.49 W
Mendoza, Perú 248 6.20 S 77.30 W
Mendoza, Ur. 258 34.17 S 56.13 W
Mendoza ⊡⁴ 252 34.30 S 68.30 W
Mendoza ≃ 252 32.21 S 68.18 W
Mendoza, Arroyo de ≃ 258 34.21 S 56.18 W
Mendrisio 58 45.52 N 8.59 E
Mend'ukino 82 54.47 N 38.51 E
Mendung 112 0.31 N 103.13 E
Ménéac 32 35.14 N 25.47 E
Mene de Mauroa 246 10.43 N 71.01 W
Mene Grande 246 9.49 N 70.56 W
Menemen 130 38.36 N 27.04 E
Menen 50 50.48 N 3.07 E
Meneng Point › 174b 0.32 S 166.57 E
Menes 115a 6.23 S 105.53 E
Menfi 70 37.36 N 12.53 E
Mengalum, Pulau I 112 6.16 N 115.12 E
Mengban 102 23.08 N 100.13 E
Mengbang 102 21.28 N 101.19 E
Mengcheng 100 33.16 N 116.33 E
Mengchi ⊡⁷ 107 29.47 N 104.53 E
Mengcun 98 38.06 N 117.05 E
Mengdapu 104 41.35 N 123.12 E
Mengede ◄•⁸ 263 51.34 N 7.23 E
Mengen, Dtsch. 58 48.03 N 9.23 E
Mengen, Tür. 130 40.56 N 32.04 E
Mengeringhausen 56 51.22 N 8.59 E
Mengerskirch-Hämmern 54 50.24 N 11.07 E
Menges Mills 208 39.52 N 76.54 W
Menggala 112 4.28 S 105.17 E
Menggu 102 26.34 N 102.57 E
Menggubao 104 42.27 N 122.23 E
Menggudai 102 38.10 N 108.15 E
Menghai 102 22.00 N 100.25 E
Menghe 106 32.03 N 119.47 E
Menghun 102 21.44 N 100.27 E
Mengjiacun 106 31.33 N 118.46 E
Mengjiagang 89 46.22 N 130.40 E
Mengjiatai 104 42.06 N 123.21 E
Mengjiawan 102 38.35 N 109.25 E
Mengjiawopeng 104 42.19 N 121.51 E
Mengjiayuanjia 105 43.52 N 118.08 E
Mengjiazhai 269b 31.18 N 121.19 E
Mengkibol 112 2.00 N 103.37 E
Mengkuang 114 3.11 N 102.24 E
Menglian 102 22.20 N 99.38 E
Menglinghausen ◄•⁸ 263 51.28 N 7.25 E
Mengluchang 107 29.19 N 103.35 E
Mengmucun 106 31.59 N 119.01 E
Mengong 152 2.56 N 11.25 E
Mengqigou 104 42.00 N 121.08 E
Mengqingxi 102 24.07 N 110.33 E
Meng Shan ⊼, Zhg. 98 35.44 N 117.45 E
Meng Shan ⊼, Zhg. 107 31.50 N 107.10 E
Mengtong 107 30.44 N 105.53 E
Mengwang 102 22.26 N 100.34 E
Mengyin 98 35.45 N 117.57 E
Mengzhe 102 22.02 N 100.16 E
Mengzi 102 24.10 N 99.46 E
Menihek Lakes ⊜ 176 54.00 N 66.35 W
Ménil-la-Tour 56 48.46 N 5.52 E
Menindee 166 32.24 S 142.26 E
Menindee Lake ⊜ 166 32.21 S 142.23 E
Meningie 166 35.42 S 139.20 E
Menjiangangzi 106 42.29 N 131.19 E
Menkoutang 106 31.01 N 119.27 E
Menlo 224 46.37 N 123.38 W
Menlo Park 226 37.27 N 122.10 W
Menlo Park Mall ◄•⁹ 276 40.32 N 74.20 W
Menlo Park Terrace 276 40.32 N 74.21 W
Mennecy 261 48.34 N 2.26 E
Mennetou-sur-Cher 50 47.16 N 1.53 E
Menno 198 43.14 N 97.34 W
Menominee ≃ 190 45.06 N 87.36 W
Menominee ⊡ 190 45.00 N 88.45 W
Menominee Indian Reservation ⊠⁴ 190 45.00 N 88.45 W
Menominee Falls 216 43.02 N 87.54 W
Menomonie 190 44.52 N 91.55 W
Menongue 152 14.36 S 17.48 E
Menor, Mar c 34 37.43 N 0.48 W
Menorca I 34 40.00 N 4.00 E
Menslage 52 52.41 N 7.49 E
Menstrup 41 55.13 N 11.36 E
Menteith, Lake ⊜ 180 62.40 N 143.07 W
Mentawai, Kepulauan II 112 2.00 S 99.30 E
Mentawai, Selat ⊔ 108 1.45 S 100.00 E
Mentekab 114 3.29 N 102.21 E
Mentelle, peski ⊼² 80 47.20 N 50.40 E
Menteng ◄•⁸ 269e 6.12 S 106.50 E
Menteroda 54 51.18 N 10.33 E
Menthon-Saint-Bernard 62 45.51 N 6.12 E
Menton 62 43.47 N 7.30 E
Mentone, Austl. 274b 37.59 S 145.05 E

Column 3

Menzelinsk 80 55.43 N 53.08 E
Menzel Temime 148 36.47 N 10.59 E
Menzenschwand 58 47.49 N 8.04 E
Menzies 162 29.41 S 121.02 E
Menzies, Mount ⊼ 9 73.33 S 61.50 E
Menziken 58 47.14 N 8.12 E
Meobaai c 156 24.25 S 14.34 E
Meoa Ägri 272a 28.42 N 77.23 E
Meoio 64 45.37 N 12.27 E
Meo'n ≃ 42 50.48 N 1.15 W
Meopham 260 51.22 N 0.22 E
Meopham Station 260 51.23 N 0.21 E
Meoqui 232 28.17 N 105.29 W
Meota 184 53.02 N 108.27 W
Méouge ≃ 62 44.16 N 5.50 E
Méounes-lès-Montrieux 62 43.17 N 5.58 E
Mepal 42 52.24 N 0.07 E
Mepisckaro, gora ⊼ 84 41.50 N 42.40 E
Meppel 52 52.42 N 6.11 E
Meppen 52 52.41 N 7.17 E
Meqerghane, Sebkha ⊜ 148 26.19 N 1.20 E
Mequinenza, Embalse de ⊜¹ 34 41.20 N 0.05 E
Mequon 216 43.13 N 87.59 W
Mer 50 47.42 N 1.30 E
Mera ≃ 58 46.11 N 9.25 E
Merah 112 0.50 N 116.48 E
Merai 164 4.50 S 152.20 E
Meräker 26 63.26 N 11.45 E
Merakurak 115a 6.53 S 111.59 E
Meramangye, Lake ⊜ 162 28.25 S 132.13 E
Merambéllou, Kólpos c 32 35.14 N 25.47 E
Meramec ≃ 194 38.23 N 90.21 W
Meramec Caverns ⊐⁵ 219 38.15 N 91.06 W
Meramec State Park ⊠⁵ 219 38.15 N 91.05 W
Meran — Merano, It. 64 46.40 N 11.09 E
Meran, Nig. 273a 6.38 N 3.16 E
Meranggau 112 2.09 S 102.47 E
Merano (Meran) 64 46.40 N 11.09 E
Merapi, Gunung ⊼ 115a 8.03 S 114.15 E
Merapoh 114 4.41 N 101.59 E
Merasheen 186 47.25 N 54.21 W
Merasheen Island I 186 47.30 N 54.15 W
Merate 62 45.42 N 9.25 E
Meratus, Pegunungan ⊼ 112 2.45 S 115.40 E
Merauke 164 8.28 S 140.20 E
Merauke ≃ 164 8.30 S 140.24 E
Merbau, Indon. 114 1.07 N 102.33 E
Merbau, Indon. 114 2.16 N 99.50 E
Merca — Marka 144 1.43 N 44.53 E
Mercaderes 246 1.47 N 77.10 W
Mercantour, Parc National du ♦ 62 44.10 N 7.00 E
Mercāra 122 12.25 N 75.44 E
Mercatale 66 43.15 N 12.08 E
Mercato San Saverino 66 40.47 N 14.46 E
Mercato Saraceno 66 43.57 N 12.12 E
Merced 226 37.18 N 120.28 W
Merced ≃ 226 37.15 N 120.40 W
Merced ⊡ 226 37.21 N 120.58 W
Merced, Lake ⊜ 282 37.43 N 122.29 W
Merced, North Fork ≃ 226 37.37 N 120.03 W
Merced, South Fork ≃ 226 37.39 N 119.53 W
Merced Airport ⊠ 226 37.17 N 120.31 W
Mercedario, Cerro ⊼ 252 31.59 S 70.07 W
Mercedes, Arg. 252 29.12 S 58.05 W
Mercedes, Arg. 252 33.40 S 65.28 W
Mercedes, Arg. 258 34.39 S 59.27 W
Mercedes, Pil. 116 14.07 N 123.01 E
Mercedes, Tx., U.S. 196 26.08 N 97.54 W
Mercedes, Ur. 258 33.16 S 58.01 W
Mercer, N.Z. 172 37.16 S 175.03 E
Mercer, Mo., U.S. 194 40.30 N 93.31 W
Mercer, Pa., U.S. 214 41.13 N 80.14 W
Mercer, Wi., U.S. 190 46.09 N 90.03 W
Mercer ⊡, N.J., U.S. 208 40.13 N 74.45 W
Mercer ⊡⁶, Oh., U.S. 216 40.33 N 84.34 W
Mercer Island 224 47.34 N 122.15 W
Mercersburg 208 39.50 N 77.54 W
Mercerville 208 40.14 N 74.41 W
Mercês, Bra. 256 21.12 S 43.21 W
Merchants Bay c 176 67.07 N 62.50 W
Merchants Millpond ⊜ 208 36.26 N 76.41 W
Merchtem 50 50.58 N 4.14 E
Mercier (Saint-Philomène) 271c 45.19 N 73.45 W
Mercier, Pont ◄•⁵ 275a 45.25 N 73.39 W
Mercoal 182 53.10 N 117.05 W
Mercogliano 66 40.56 N 14.44 E
Mercury Islands II 172 36.35 S 175.55 E
Mercy, Cape › 176 64.53 N 63.32 W
Mercy Bay c 180 74.05 N 119.00 W
Mercy-le-Bas 56 49.23 N 5.45 E
Merdeka Bridge ◄•⁵ 271c 13.03 N 103.53 E
Méré, Fr. 261 48.47 N 1.49 E
Mere, Eng., U.K. 42 51.06 N 2.16 W
Mere, Eng., U.K. 262 53.20 N 2.25 W
Mereclough 262 53.46 N 2.11 W
Meredith, Austl. 169 37.51 S 144.04 E
Meredith, Cape › 254 52.15 S 60.39 W
Meredith, Lake ⊜¹ 196 35.36 N 101.42 W
Meredosia 219 39.50 N 90.34 W
Meredosia Lake ⊜ 219 39.52 N 90.33 W
Mereeg 144 3.46 N 47.18 E
Merefa 78 49.49 N 36.03 E
Mere Lava I 175l 14.25 S 168.03 E
Mereni 38 46.58 N 29.04 E
Mer'enkurkku (Norra Kvarken) ⊔ 26 63.36 N 20.43 E
Merevari ≃ 246 4.28 N 63.57 W
Méréville 50 48.19 N 2.05 E
Merewether 260 32.57 S 151.44 E
Mereworth 260 51.15 N 0.24 E
Mergozzo 62 45.58 N 8.26 E
Mergui (Myeik) 110 12.26 N 98.36 E
Mergui Archipelago II 110 12.00 N 98.00 E
Méri 152 10.52 N 14.08 E
Meribah 166 34.42 S 140.51 E
Meribel ≃ 138 7.40 N 33.55 E
Meriç 130 41.11 N 26.25 E
Meriç (Marica) (Évros) ≃ 130 40.52 N 26.12 E

Column 4

Meridale 210 42.22 N 74.57 W
Meriden, Eng., U.K. 42 52.26 N 1.37 W
Meriden, Ct., U.S. 207 41.32 N 72.48 W
Meriden, N.J., U.S. 276 40.57 N 74.28 W
Meriden, Ga., U.S. 228 39.09 N 121.55 W
Meridian, Ga., U.S. 192 33.17 N 81.22 W
Meridian, Id., U.S. 202 43.36 N 116.23 W
Meridian, Ms., U.S. 194 32.21 N 88.42 W
Meridian, N.Y., U.S. 210 43.09 N 76.32 W
Meridian, Pa., U.S. 214 40.51 N 79.58 W
Meridian, Tx., U.S. 222 31.55 N 97.39 W
Meridian Hills 218 39.53 N 86.09 W
Meridian Naval Air Station ⊠ 194 32.33 N 88.34 W
Meridianville 194 34.51 N 86.34 W
Mériel 261 49.05 N 2.12 E
Mesabi Range ⊼² 190 47.30 N 92.50 W
Mérignac 32 44.50 N 0.42 W
Merigold 194 33.50 N 90.43 W
Merikarvia 26 61.51 N 21.30 E
Merimbula 166 36.53 S 149.54 E
Mering 60 48.16 N 10.59 E
Meringa 146 10.44 N 12.09 E
Merin Gubai 144 1.26 N 44.20 E
Meringur 166 34.24 S 141.16 E
Merinos 198 41.28 N 103.21 W
Merion Station 285 39.59 N 75.15 W
Merir I 108 4.19 N 132.19 E
Merishausen 58 47.45 N 8.37 E
Merit 222 33.13 N 96.17 W
Merivale Gardens 212 45.19 N 75.44 W
Meriwether Farms 285 39.58 N 75.34 W
Merizo 174p 13.16 N 144.40 E
Merke 85 42.52 N 73.11 E
Merkel 196 32.28 N 100.00 W
Merkem 50 50.57 N 2.51 E
Merkendorf 56 49.12 N 10.42 E
Merkine 76 54.10 N 24.10 E
Merklin 80 49.34 N 13.07 E
Merklingen 58 48.30 N 9.44 E
Merkourovoúni ⊼ 267c 37.54 N 23.48 E
Merksem 50 51.15 N 4.27 E
Merksplas 50 51.22 N 4.52 E
Merkulaivičy 76 52.58 N 30.36 E
Merkys ≃ 76 54.10 N 24.11 E
Merlebach 56 49.10 N 11.26 E
Merlejevo 82 55.05 N 37.13 E
Merlimau, Pulau I 271c 1.17 N 103.42 E
Merlin, On., Can. 214 42.14 N 82.14 W
Merlin, Or., U.S. 202 42.31 N 123.25 W
Merlin Seamount ✦³ 14 9.05 S 150.44 W
Merlo, Arg. 252 32.21 S 65.02 W
Merlo, Arg. 258 34.40 S 58.45 W
Merlo, Aeródromo ⊠ 258 34.41 S 58.45 W
Merlynston 274b 37.43 S 144.58 E
Mermaid Beach 171a 28.03 S 153.27 E
Mern 41 55.03 N 12.04 E
Mernye 30 46.29 N 17.50 E
Meron, Hare ⊼ 132 32.59 N 35.26 E
Merotai Besar 112 4.26 N 117.46 E
Merouana 148 35.38 N 5.55 E
Merouane, Chott ⊜ 148 34.00 N 6.02 E
Mer'oža ≃ 76 59.02 N 36.23 E
Merredin 162 31.29 S 118.16 E
Merrick ⊼ 44 55.08 N 4.29 W
Merrick Bay c 276 40.38 N 73.33 W
Merrickville 212 44.55 N 75.50 W
Merriewold Lake 212 41.27 N 74.12 W
Merrill, Ia., U.S. 198 42.43 N 96.14 W
Merrill, Mi., U.S. 190 43.24 N 84.19 W
Merrill, Or., U.S. 202 42.01 N 121.35 W
Merrill, Wi., U.S. 190 45.11 N 89.41 W
Merrillan 190 44.27 N 90.50 W
Merrill C. Meigs Field ⊠ 278 41.52 N 87.37 W
Merrill Lake ⊜¹ 208 41.55 N 77.24 W
Merrillville 216 41.28 N 87.19 W
Merrimac ≃ 207 42.49 N 70.49 W
Merrimack 188 42.52 N 71.30 W
Merrimack College ⊻² 283 42.40 N 71.07 W
Merriman, S. Afr. 158 32.23 S 23.08 E
Merriman, Ne., U.S. 198 42.55 N 101.42 W
Merrionette Park 278 41.41 N 87.42 W
Merriott 42 50.54 N 2.48 W
Merritt, B.C., Can. 182 50.07 N 120.47 W
Merritt, Wa., U.S. 224 47.47 N 120.51 W
Merritt, Lake ⊜¹ 282 37.48 N 122.15 W
Merritt Island 220 28.21 N 80.42 W
Merritt Island I 220 28.33 N 80.40 W
Merritt Reservoir ⊜¹ 198 42.38 N 100.55 W
Merrouge 194 32.46 N 91.47 W
Merrygoen 166 31.51 S 149.14 E
Merrylands 274a 33.50 S 150.59 E
Merrymeeting Park ⊐³ 283 42.16 N 71.01 W
Merryville 194 30.45 N 93.33 W
Mersa Fatma 144 14.55 N 40.18 E
Mersa Matruh — Marsā Matrūh 140 31.21 N 27.14 E
Mersch 52 49.45 N 6.06 E
Merscheid ◄•⁸ 263 51.10 N 7.01 E
Mersea Island I 42 51.47 N 0.55 E
Merseburg 54 51.21 N 11.59 E
Mersey ≃, N.S., Can. 186 44.02 N 64.43 W
Mersey ≃, Eng., U.K. 44 53.25 N 3.00 W
Mersey Tunnel ◄•⁵ 262 53.24 N 2.59 W
Mersin — İçel 130 36.48 N 34.38 E
Mers-les-Bains 50 50.04 N 1.14 E
Mersrags 76 57.20 N 23.08 E
Merta 120 26.39 N 74.02 E
Merta Road 120 26.43 N 73.55 E
Merthyr Tydfil 42 51.46 N 3.23 W
Merti 154 1.04 N 38.40 E
Mertingen 60 48.34 N 10.47 E
Mértola 32 37.38 N 7.40 W
Mertz Glacier Tongue 9 67.40 S 144.45 E
Mertzon 196 31.16 N 100.49 W
Mertztown 208 40.30 N 75.40 W
Méru 50 49.14 N 2.08 E
Meru, Kenya 154 0.03 N 37.39 E
Meru, Mount ⊼ 154 3.14 S 36.45 E
Meru National Park ⊠ 154 0.10 N 38.15 E
Meruoca 250 3.28 S 40.28 W
Mervans 50 46.48 N 5.11 E
Merville 50 50.38 N 2.38 E
Mervin 184 53.20 N 108.53 W
Merwede ≃ 52 51.49 N 4.42 E
Merwin, Lake ⊜¹ 226 45.57 N 122.26 W
Méry, Bela. 76 55.37 N 27.38 E

Column 5

Mery, Ross. 82 55.49 N 36.36 E
Méry-la-Bataille 50 49.33 N 2.38 E
Méry-sur-Oise 261 49.04 N 2.11 E
Méry-sur-Seine 50 48.30 N 3.53 E
Merzen 52 52.29 N 7.50 E
Merzenich 56 50.50 N 6.32 E
Merzhausen 58 47.58 N 7.49 E
Merzifon 130 40.53 N 35.29 E
Merzig 56 49.27 N 6.36 E
Mesa, Micron. 175c 7.21 N 151.51 E
Mesa, Moç. 154 13.00 S 39.33 E
Mesa, S. Afr. 158 26.29 S 26.59 E
Mesa, Az., U.S. 200 33.25 N 111.49 W
Mesa, Ca., U.S. 204 41.15 N 1.48 W
Mesa, Cerro ⊼ 254 48.45 S 71.29 W
Mesa del Nayar 194 22.16 N 104.35 W
Mesachie Lake 224 48.49 N 124.07 W
Mesa de Santa Rita 234 23.04 N 105.31 W
Mes'agutovo 86 55.35 N 58.20 E
Mesa Mountain ⊼ 200 37.55 N 106.38 W
Mesarás, Kólpos c 38 34.58 N 24.36 E
Mesa Verde National Park ⊠ 200 37.13 N 108.30 W
Mescalero 200 33.09 N 105.46 W
Mescalero Apache Indian Reservation ⊠⁴ 200 33.12 N 105.40 W
Meščerino, Ross. 76 53.37 N 37.23 E
Meščerino, Ross. 82 55.11 N 38.21 E
Meščerskij 265b 55.40 N 37.25 E
Meščerskoje 82 55.17 N 37.38 E
Meschede 56 51.20 N 8.17 E
Meschetskij chrebet ⊼ 84 41.48 N 42.30 E
Mescit Tepe ⊼ 130 40.22 N 41.11 E
Meschow 76 53.49 N 12.58 E
Meščovsk 76 54.19 N 35.40 E
Meščura 24 63.20 N 50.52 E
Mesé Atet 110 18.38 N 97.39 E
Mesen-Bucht — Mezenskaja guba c 24 66.40 N 43.45 E
Mesero 266b 45.30 N 8.51 E
Mesewa 144 15.38 N 39.28 E
Mesfinto 144 13.20 N 37.19 E
Mesgouez, Lac ⊜ 176 51.24 N 75.05 W
Meshamasic ⊼ 207 41.38 N 72.32 W
Mesilla 200 32.16 N 106.48 W
Mesillas, Méx. 234 23.14 N 106.03 W
Mesillas, Méx. 234 23.33 N 103.35 W
Mesima ≃ 68 38.30 N 15.55 E
Meslay-du-Maine 32 47.57 N 0.33 W
Mesola 64 44.55 N 12.14 E
Mesolcina, Valle V 58 46.20 N 9.10 E
Mesolóngion 38 38.21 N 21.17 E
Mesopotamia 214 41.27 N 80.57 W
Mesopotamia ⊡⁹ 128 34.00 N 44.00 E
Mesoraca 68 39.05 N 16.48 E
Mesótopos 38 39.05 N 25.54 E
Mespelbrunn ⊼ 54 49.56 N 9.19 E
Mesquita, Bra. 255 19.13 S 42.35 W
Mesquita, Bra. 255 22.48 S 43.26 W
Mesquite, Nv., U.S. 204 36.48 N 114.03 W
Mesquite, Tx., U.S. 196 32.46 N 96.35 W
Messach Mellet ⊼² 146 24.30 N 11.35 E
Messalo ≃ 154 11.40 S 40.26 E
Messancy 56 49.36 N 5.49 E
Mesquita, Bra. 255 22.48 S 43.26 W
Messina, S. Afr. 158 22.23 S 30.00 E
Messina, Stretto di ⊔ 68 38.15 N 15.35 E
Messina, Str. di — Messina, Stretto di ⊔ 68 38.15 N 15.35 E
Messini 38 37.04 N 22.00 E
Messiniakós Kólpos c 38 36.58 N 22.00 E
Messingham 44 53.32 N 0.40 W
Messix Peak ⊼ 202 41.29 N 112.31 W
Messkirch 58 47.59 N 9.07 E
Messojacha ≃ 26 68.33 N 80.40 E
Messondo 152 3.32 N 10.50 E
Messstetten 58 48.11 N 8.58 E
Messy 261 48.59 N 2.42 E
Mesta (Néstos) ≃ 38 40.44 N 24.44 E
Mestanza 32 38.35 N 4.04 W
Mestghanem 148 35.56 N 0.05 E
Mestia 84 43.03 N 42.43 E
Mestlin 54 53.35 N 11.56 E
Mesto Touškov 80 49.46 N 13.22 E
Mestre 64 45.29 N 12.15 E
Mestrino 66 45.27 N 11.46 E
Mesudji ≃ 112 4.08 S 105.52 E
Mesvin 56 50.25 N 3.57 E
Meszah Peak ⊼ 180 58.28 N 131.26 W

Column 6

Metharaw 110 16.12 N 98.08 E
Metheringham 44 53.08 N 0.24 W
Methil 46 56.10 N 3.01 W
Methler 263 51.35 N 7.37 E
Methlick 46 57.25 N 2.14 W
Methóni 38 36.50 N 21.43 E
Methow ≃ 202 48.03 N 119.53 W
Methuen 207 42.43 N 71.11 W
Methven, N.Z. 172 43.38 S 171.39 E
Methven, Scot., U.K. 46 56.25 N 3.34 W
Methwold 42 52.31 N 0.33 E
Metica ≃ 246 4.09 N 72.55 W
Metiskow 184 52.24 N 110.38 W
Metković 36 43.03 N 17.39 E
Metlakatla, B.C., Can. 182 54.20 N 130.27 W
Metlakatla, Ak., U.S. 182 55.08 N 131.35 W
Metlaoui 148 34.20 N 8.24 E
Metlatonoc 234 17.11 N 98.20 W
Metlika 36 45.39 N 15.19 E
Metliili ech Chaâmba 148 32.18 N 3.40 E
Metnitz 61 46.59 N 14.13 E
Meto, Bayou ≃ 194 34.05 N 91.26 W
Metolius ≃ 202 44.36 N 121.17 W
Metompkin Bay c 208 37.43 N 75.35 W
Metompkin Inlet c 208 37.41 N 75.35 W
Metro 115a 5.05 S 105.20 E
Metropolis 194 37.09 N 88.43 W
Metropolitan 190 46.00 N 87.53 W
Metropolitan Beach ◄ 281 42.35 N 82.48 W
Metropolitan Museum of Art ◄ 276 40.47 N 73.58 W
Metropolitan Oakland International Airport ⊠ 226 37.43 N 122.13 W
Metschow 54 53.49 N 12.58 E
Metsemotlhaba 160 24.01 S 24.40 E
Metsera 154 2.35 S 26.07 E
Métsovon 38 39.46 N 21.11 E
Mettawa 278 42.14 N 87.56 W
Metten 60 48.52 N 12.55 E
Mettendorf 56 49.57 N 6.19 E
Mettet 192 32.23 N 82.03 W
Mettet 56 50.19 N 4.40 E
Mettetal Airport ⊠ 281 42.21 N 83.27 W
Mettingen 52 52.18 N 7.46 E
Mettlach 56 49.30 N 6.36 E
Mettmann 56 51.15 N 6.58 E
Mettmenstetten 58 47.14 N 8.27 E
Mettupalaiyam 122 11.18 N 76.57 E
Mettur 122 11.48 N 77.48 E
Metu 138 8.20 N 35.36 E
Metuchen 210 40.32 N 74.21 W
Metuge 154 12.58 S 40.20 E
Metulla 132 33.17 N 35.35 E
Metung 169 37.53 S 147.53 E
Metz 50 49.08 N 6.10 E
Metzervisse 56 49.19 N 6.17 E
Metzger 224 45.26 N 122.45 W
Metzingen 54 48.32 N 9.17 E
Metzkausen 263 51.16 N 6.57 E
Metztitlán 234 20.36 N 98.45 W
Metztitlán, Laguna ⊜ 234 20.40 N 98.50 W
Meu ≃ 158 27.56 S 28.50 E
Meulaboh 114 4.09 N 96.08 E
Meulan 50 49.01 N 1.54 E
Meulebeke 50 50.57 N 3.17 E
Meung-sur-Loire 50 47.50 N 1.42 E
Meureudu 114 5.09 N 96.16 E
Meursault 50 46.59 N 4.46 E
Meuse ⊡⁵ 48 48.47 N 5.16 E
Meuse (Maas) ≃ 50 51.49 N 5.01 E
Meuselbach 54 50.37 N 11.08 E
Meuselwitz 54 51.02 N 12.17 E
Meux Creek ≃ 212 44.07 N 81.02 W
Mevagissey 42 50.16 N 4.48 W
Mevang 152 0.07 N 11.05 E
Mewatt Plain ⊼ 120 ...
Mexia 196 31.41 N 96.29 W
Mexiana, Ilha I 250 0.02 S 49.35 W
Mexicali 200 32.40 N 115.29 W
Mexican Hat 200 37.09 N 109.52 W
Mexicaltzingo 234 19.13 N 99.35 W
Mexico, Me., U.S. 188 44.33 N 70.32 W
Mexico, Mo., U.S. 194 39.10 N 91.52 W
Mexico, N.Y., U.S. 210 43.27 N 76.13 W
Mexico ⊡¹, N.A. 230 23.00 N 102.00 W
México (Mexico) ⊡¹, N.A. 230 23.00 N 102.00 W
México (Mexico) ⊡³ 234 19.24 N 99.09 W
México, Golfo de — Mexico, Gulf of c 230 25.00 N 90.00 W
México — Ciudad de México 234 19.24 N 99.09 W
Mexiko 234 19.24 N 99.09 W
México, Golf von — Mexico, Gulf of c 230 25.00 N 90.00 W
Mexico, Gulf of c 230 25.00 N 90.00 W
Mexico Basin ✦¹ 16 24.00 N 92.00 W
Mexico Beach 192 29.56 N 85.25 W
Mexico City — Ciudad de México 234 19.24 N 99.09 W
Mexiko 234 19.24 N 99.09 W
Mexique, Golfe du — Mexico, Gulf of c 230 25.00 N 90.00 W
Mexticacán 234 21.13 N 102.43 W
Mey, Castle of ◄¹ 46 58.39 N 3.14 W
Meyers 154 ...
Meymac 50 45.32 N 2.09 E
Meyrargues 62 43.38 N 5.32 E
Meyrueis 50 44.11 N 3.26 E
Meza 175b 7.20 N 134.27 E
Mezada (Masada), Horvot ⊐ 132 31.19 N 35.21 E
Mezdra 36 43.09 N 23.42 E
Mezcala 234 17.56 N 99.37 W

Symbol	English	Deutsch	Español	Français	Português
≃	River	Fluß	Río	Rivière	Rio
≤	Canal	Kanal	Canal	Canal	Canal
↯	Waterfall, Rapids	Wasserfall, Stromschnellen	Cascada, Rápidos	Chute d'eau, Rapides	Cascata, Rápidos
⊔	Strait	Meeresstraße	Estrecho	Détroit	Estreito
c	Bay, Gulf	Bucht, Golf	Bahía, Golfo	Baie, Golfe	Baía, Golfo
⊜	Lake, Lakes	See, Seen	Lago, Lagos	Lac, Lacs	Lago, Lagos
⊒	Swamp	Sumpf	Pantano	Marais	Pântano
⊠	Ice Features, Glacier	Eis und Gletscherformen	Accidentes Glaciares	Formes glaciaires	Acidentes glaciares
⊡	Other Hydrographic Features	Andere Hydrographische Objekte	Otros Elementos Hidrográficos	Autres données hydrographiques	Outros acidentes hidrográficos
✦	Submarine Features	Untermeerische Objekte	Accidentes Submarinos	Formes de relief sous-marin	Acidentes submarinos
⊡	Political Unit	Politische Einheit	Unidad Política	Entité politique	Unidade política
⊻	Cultural Institution	Kulturelle Institution	Institución Cultural	Institution culturelle	Instituição cultural
⊐	Historical Site	Historische Stätte	Sitio Histórico	Site historique	Sítio histórico
⊐	Recreational Site	Erholungs- und Ferienort	Sitio de Recreo	Centre de loisirs	Sítio de Recreio
⊠	Airport	Flughafen	Aeropuerto	Aéroport	Aeroporto
■	Military Installation	Militäranlage	Instalación Militar	Installation militaire	Instalação militar
◄	Miscellaneous	Verschiedenes	Misceláneo	Divers	Diversos

Column 1

Name	Page	Lat.	Long.
Mezcala ≃	234	18.00 N	99.47 W
Mezcalapa	234	17.37 N	93.22 W
Mezcalapa ≃	234	18.00 N	92.54 W
Mezdra	38	43.09 N	23.42 E
Meždurečensk	86	53.42 N	88.03 E
Meždurečenskij	86	59.36 N	65.53 E
Méze	32	43.25 N	3.36 E
Mézel	62	43.59 N	6.12 E
Mezen'	24	65.50 N	44.13 E
Mezen' ≃	24	66.11 N	43.59 E
Mézenc, Mont ▲	62	44.55 N	4.11 E
Mezenskaja guba c	24	66.40 N	43.45 E
Mezhova	78	48.16 N	36.44 E
Mezhyrich	78	50.43 N	34.29 E
Mezidin Lake ◎	182	56.04 N	129.18 W
Mežica	61	46.31 N	14.52 E
Mézières-en-Brenne	32	46.49 N	1.13 E
Mézières-sur-Seine	261	48.58 N	1.48 E
Mézilhac	62	44.48 N	4.21 E
Mézin	32	44.03 N	0.16 E
Mezinovs·ij	76	55.30 N	40.21 E
Mezőberény	30	46.50 N	21.02 E
Mezőcsát	30	47.49 N	20.55 E
Mezőkovácsháza	30	46.25 N	20.55 E
Mezőkövesd	30	47.50 N	20.34 E
Mezőtúr	30	47.00 N	20.38 E
Mežoz'ornyj	86	54.59 N	59.23 E
Mezquital	234	23.29 N	104.23 W
Mezquital del Oro	232	22.35 N	104.54 W
Mezquital del Oro	234	21.10 N	103.23 W
Mezquitic	234	22.23 N	103.41 W
Mezraa	130	41.12 N	35.08 E
Mézy	261	49.00 N	1.53 E
Mezzana	64	46.19 N	10.48 E
Mezzano	64	46.09 N	11.48 E
Mezzenile	64	45.17 N	7.23 E
Mezzocorona	64	46.13 N	11.07 E
Mezzoiuso	70	37.52 N	13.28 E
Mezzola, Lago di ◎	58	46.10 N	9.26 E
Mezzoldo	58	46.01 N	9.40 E
Mezzolombardo	64	46.13 N	11.05 E
Mezzomerico	266b	45.37 N	8.36 E
Mfangani Island I	154	0.28 S	34.01 E
Mfolozi ≃	158	28.25 S	32.26 E
Mfou	152	3.43 N	11.38 E
Mfuwe	154	13.04 S	31.46 E
Mgači	89	51.05 N	142.17 E
Mgeni ≃	158	29.48 S	31.02 E
Mgeta	154	8.19 S	36.08 E
Mglin	76	53.04 N	32.51 E
M'Goun, Irhil ▲	148	31.31 N	6.25 W
M'hai, B'nom ▲	110	11.21 N	107.50 E
Mhasvad	122	17.38 N	74.47 E
Mhlatuze ≃	158	28.47 S	32.06 E
Mhlume	158	26.02 S	31.50 E
Mholach, Beinn ▲²	46	58.14 N	6.31 W
Mhòr, Beinn ▲	46	57.17 N	7.19 W
Mhòr, Loch ◎	46	57.14 N	4.26 W
Mhow	122	22.33 N	75.46 E
Mi ≃, Zhg.	98	37.12 N	119.10 E
Mi ≃, Zhg.	100	27.09 N	112.51 E
Mia, Oued V	148	30.47 N	4.54 E
Miacatlán	234	18.46 N	99.22 W
Mia-dong ≃⁶	271b	37.37 N	127.01 E
Miagao	116	10.39 N	122.14 E
Miahuatlán de Porfirio Díaz	234	16.20 N	96.36 W
Miajadas	34	39.09 N	5.54 W
Miaméré	146	8.52 N	19.50 E
Miami, Mb., Can.	184	49.21 N	98.11 W
Miami, Az., U.S.	200	33.23 N	110.52 W
Miami, Fl., U.S.	220	25.46 N	80.11 W
Miami, In., U.S.	216	40.36 N	86.06 W
Miami, Ok., U.S.	196	36.52 N	94.52 W
Miami, Tx., U.S.	196	35.42 N	100.38 W
Miami □⁶, Oh., U.S.	218	40.45 N	86.04 W
Miami □⁶, Oh., U.S.	218	40.02 N	84.13 W
Miami ≃	224	45.33 N	123.53 W
Miami Beach, On., Can.	212	44.13 N	79.29 W
Miami Beach, Fl., U.S.	220	25.47 N	80.07 W
Miami Canal ≃	220	25.47 N	80.51 W
Miami Creek ≃	226	37.21 N	119.44 W
Miami International Airport ✈	220	25.48 N	80.17 W
Miami Lakes	220	25.53 N	80.18 W
Miamisburg	218	39.38 N	84.17 W
Miamisburg Mound State Memorial ⊥	218	39.38 N	84.17 W
Miami Shores	220	25.51 N	80.11 W
Miami Springs	220	25.49 N	80.17 W
Miami State Recreation Area ♦	216	40.40 N	85.55 W
Miamiville	218	39.13 N	84.18 W
Miàn Channún	123	30.27 N	72.22 E
Mianchi	102	34.48 N	111.49 E
Mīāndoāb	128	36.58 N	46.06 E
Miandrivazo	157b	19.31 S	45.28 E
Miandube	89	39.05 N	121.06 E
Miane	64	37.26 N	47.42 E
Mīāneh	128	37.26 N	47.42 E
Miang, Phu ▲	110	17.42 N	101.01 E
Miangas, Pulau I	8	5.35 N	126.35 E
Mianhu	100	23.28 N	116.09 E
Mianhuadi	104	41.15 N	120.49 E
Miàni	123	32.32 N	73.04 E
Miàni Hōr c	120	25.34 N	66.19 E
Mianning	102	28.39 N	102.09 E
Mianus ≃	207	41.03 N	73.35 W
Mianus, East Branch ≃	276	41.06 N	73.35 W
Mianus Reservoir ◎¹	276	41.08 N	73.37 W
Miānwāli	123	32.35 N	71.33 E
Mianxian	102	33.09 N	106.40 E
Mianyang, Zhg.	102	30.23 N	113.25 E
Mianyang, Zhg.	102	31.30 N	104.49 E
Mianzhu	102	31.20 N	104.09 E
Miao Dao I	98	37.56 N	120.45 E
Miaodao Qundao II	98	38.10 N	120.40 E
Miao'ergou	96	45.32 N	83.52 E
Miaofengshan	104	40.04 N	116.13 E
Miaogou	104	41.12 N	120.40 E
Miaojiagou	104	41.28 N	123.22 E
Miaojiatun	104	40.54 N	120.55 E
Miaokou	98	35.48 N	114.09 E
Miaoli	100	24.34 N	120.49 E
Miao Ling ⚞	102	26.15 N	107.26 E
Miaopu	104	31.00 N	118.44 E
Miaoqian	100	30.33 N	117.44 E
Miaotou	98	30.58 N	120.33 E
Miaowan	100	33.07 N	114.41 E
Miaoyang	98	40.49 N	124.24 E
Miaozhen	106	31.43 N	121.21 E
Miaozigou	107	30.17 N	104.35 E
Miarayon	98	8.04 N	124.50 E
Marinarivo, Madag.	157b	16.38 S	48.15 E
Marinarivo, Madag.	157b	20.13 S	47.31 E
Miarinavaratra	157b	20.13 S	47.31 E
Miass	86	36.34 N	137.53 E
Miass ≃	86	56.06 N	64.30 E
Miasteczko Krajeńskie	30	53.06 N	17.01 E
Miboro-dam ≃⁶	94	36.08 N	136.56 E
Mibu	94	36.25 N	139.48 E
Mibu ≃	94	35.18 N	136.38 E
Mica	156	24.10 S	30.48 E
Mica Mountain ▲	200	32.13 N	110.33 W
Micang Shan ⚞	102	32.30 N	107.10 E
Micanopy	192	29.30 N	82.16 W
Micanzas	156	18.10 S	36.35 E
Mičavičevnik	34	64.14 N	57.58 E
Miccosukee, Lake ◎	192	30.34 N	83.58 W
Miccosukee Indian Reservation □⁴	220	26.10 N	80.50 W
Michael, Mount ▲	164	6.25 S	145.20 E
Michael J. Kirwan Reservoir ◎¹	214	41.10 N	81.10 W
Michajlov	58	54.14 N	39.02 E

Column 2

Name	Page	Lat.	Long.
Michajlovka, Kaz.	85	43.06 N	71.36 E
Michajlovka, Kaz.	85	42.50 N	75.42 E
Michajlovka, Kaz.	86	53.51 N	76.32 E
Michajlovka, Kyrg.	85	42.37 N	78.20 E
Michajlovka, Ross.	78	49.53 N	39.38 E
Michajlovka, Ross.	86	59.36 N	65.53 E
Michajlovka, Ross.	80	50.05 N	43.15 E
Michajlovka, Ross.	86	51.49 N	79.45 E
Michajlovka, Ross.	86	56.26 N	78.53 E
Michajlovka, Ross.	80	50.26 N	104.10 E
Michajlovka, Ross.	88	55.30 N	114.09 E
Michajlovka, Ross.	88	51.07 N	119.20 E
Michajlovka, Ross.	88	43.56 N	132.00 E
Michajlovka, Ross.	265a	60.04 N	30.14 E
Michajlovka, Ross.	265a	59.43 N	30.01 E
Michajlovo-	80	56.56 N	45.04 E
Aleksandrovskij	83	49.13 N	40.15 E
Michajlovka	85	50.17 N	55.23 E
Michajlovskaja	80	50.58 N	41.52 E
Michajlovski, Ross.	76	60.05 N	43.29 E
Michajlovski, Ross.	76	51.41 N	79.47 E
Michajlovskoje, Ross.	76	58.23 N	37.40 E
Michajlovskoje, Ross.	80	56.11 N	45.47 E
Michajlovskoje, Ross.	265b	55.50 N	36.20 E
Michajlovskoje, Ross.	82	55.27 N	38.26 E
Michaíli	82	55.17 N	39.05 E
Michalkovo	82	54.11 N	37.33 E
Michalevo	30	48.45 N	21.55 E
Michalovce	30	48.45 N	21.55 E
Michalovy Hory	60	49.55 N	12.47 E
Michaud, Point ➤	186	45.34 N	60.40 W
Micheal Peak ▲	182	53.35 N	126.26 W
Michel	182	49.43 N	114.49 W
Michelago	171b	35.43 S	149.10 E
Michelau	56	50.10 N	11.06 E
Micheldever	42	51.09 N	1.15 W
Micheldorf in Oberösterreich	61	47.52 N	14.08 E
Michelsneukirchen	60	49.08 N	12.33 E
Michelson, Mount ▲	180	69.19 N	144.17 W
Michel'sonovskij	265b	55.42 N	37.54 E
Michelstadt	56	49.41 N	9.00 E
Michendorf	54	52.18 N	13.01 E
Miches	238	18.59 N	69.03 W
Micheta	84	41.52 N	44.44 E
Michiana Regional Airport ⚹	216	41.42 N	86.19 W
Michgamme ≃	190	46.04 N	88.13 W
Michigan	198	48.01 N	98.07 W
Michigan □³, U.S.	178	44.00 N	85.00 W
Michigan ≃	200	40.52 N	106.20 W
Michigan, Lake ◎	190	44.00 N	87.00 W
Michigan, University of ♦²	281	42.17 N	83.44 W
Michigan Center	216	42.13 N	84.19 W
Michigan City	216	41.42 N	86.53 W
Michigan International Speedway ♦	216	42.03 N	84.15 W
Michigan Stadium ♦	281	42.16 N	83.45 W
Michigan State Fair Grounds ♦	281	42.27 N	83.07 W
Michigantown	216	40.19 N	86.23 W
Michika	146	10.38 N	13.24 E
Michillinda	280	34.07 N	118.05 W
Michinmahuida, Volcán ▲¹	254	42.49 S	72.28 W
Michipicoten Bay c	190	47.55 N	84.56 W
Michipicoten Island I	190	47.45 N	85.45 W
Michnevo	82	55.07 N	37.58 E
Michninskaja	24	60.26 N	46.14 E
Michoacán	204	32.28 N	115.20 W
Michoacán □³	234	19.10 N	101.50 W
Michoacanejo	234	21.33 N	102.36 W
Michow	30	51.32 N	22.19 E
Mchurinsk	80	52.54 N	40.30 E
Mickle Fell ▲	44	54.37 N	2.18 W
Mickleham	260	51.16 N	0.19 W
Mickleover	42	52.54 N	1.32 W
Mickleton, Eng., U.K.	42	52.05 N	1.46 W
Mickleton, N.J., U.S.	285	39.47 N	75.14 W
Mickle Trafford	262	53.13 N	2.50 W
Micklefield	263	53.48 N	86.16 W
Mico, Montañas del ⚞	236	15.30 N	88.55 W
Miconge	152	4.58 S	12.51 E
Micoud	241f	13.50 N	60.54 W
Micronesia II	14	11.00 N	159.00 E
Micronesia, Federated States of □¹	14	5.00 N	152.00 E
Mičurinsk	82	52.54 N	40.30 E
Midai, Pulau I	112	3.00 N	107.47 E
Midale	184	49.22 N	103.27 W
Midar	148	34.58 N	3.30 W
Mid-Atlantic Ridge ⚞³	8	0.00	20.00 W
Midbar Yehuda → Wilderness of Judæa ◆²	132	31.30 N	35.18 E
Middalya	162	23.55 S	114.45 E
Middelburg, Ned.	52	51.30 N	3.37 E
Middelburg, S. Afr.	158	25.47 S	29.28 E
Middelburg, S. Afr.	158	31.30 S	25.00 E
Middelfart	41	55.30 N	9.45 E
Middelharnis	52	51.45 N	4.11 E
Middelkerke	52	51.11 N	2.49 E
Middelkerke-Vliegveld ✈	50	51.12 N	2.52 E
Middelstum	52	53.20 N	6.38 E
Middelwater	158	23.17 S	30.16 E
Middelwit	156	24.58 S	27.00 E
Middenbeemster	52	52.33 N	4.55 E
Middenin	158	27.43 S	28.02 E
Middenmeer	52	52.47 N	5.00 E
Middle ≃, B.C., Can.	182	54.50 N	125.08 W
Middle ≃, In., U.S.	226	38.03 N	121.31 W
Middle ≃, Mn., U.S.	194	44.29 N	93.24 W
Middle ≃, Mn., U.S.	198	48.22 N	97.44 W
Middle Alkali Lake ◎	204	41.28 N	120.04 W
Middle America Trench ✶	16	15.00 N	95.00 W
Middle Andaman I	110	12.30 N	92.50 E
Middle Barton	42	51.56 N	1.22 W
Middle Bass	214	41.41 N	82.50 W
Middle Bass Island I	214	41.41 N	82.49 W
Middle-Bay	186	51.28 N	57.30 W
Middle Bay c	278	40.37 N	73.36 W
Middle Bosque ≃	222	31.31 N	97.16 W
Middlebourne	188	39.29 N	80.54 W
Middlebranch	214	40.54 N	81.20 W
Middle Breakwater ✶⁵	280	33.43 N	118.13 W
Middle Brook	186	48.45 N	54.05 W
Middle Brook ≃, N.J., U.S.	276	40.34 N	74.41 W
Middle Brook ≃, N.Y., U.S.	276	40.33 N	74.33 W
Middle Brook, East Branch ≃	276	40.37 N	74.35 W
Middle Brook, West Branch ≃	276	40.37 N	74.35 W
Middleburg, Md.	285	39.35 N	77.12 W

Column 3

Name	Page	Lat.	Long.
Middlebury, Vt., U.S.	188	44.00 N	73.10 W
Middlebush	276	40.29 N	74.32 W
Middle Caicos I	238	21.47 N	71.43 W
Middle Cape ➤	220	25.09 N	81.09 W
Middle Castor ≃	212	45.16 N	75.24 W
Middle Channel ≃¹, N.T., Can.	180	69.21 N	135.33 W
Middle Channel ≃¹, Mi., U.S.	281	42.33 N	82.42 W
Middle Concho ≃	196	31.27 N	100.25 W
Middle Creek ≃, U.S.	208	39.41 N	76.18 W
Middle Creek ≃, Pa., U.S.	278	40.46 N	76.52 W
Middle Creek ≃, Pa., U.S.	210	41.28 N	75.11 W
Middle Fabius ≃	194	39.58 N	91.35 W
Middle Falls	263	43.07 N	73.32 W
Middlefield, Ct., U.S.	207	41.31 N	72.42 W
Middlefield, N.Y., U.S.	210	42.41 N	74.50 W
Middlefield, Oh., U.S.	214	41.27 N	81.04 W
Middle Fork Reservoir ◎¹	216	39.51 N	84.51 W
Middle Ground ✶¹	272c	18.55 N	72.51 E
Middle Ground ✶²	174g	28.15 N	177.25 W
Middle Grove, Mo., U.S.	219	39.24 N	92.16 W
Middle Grove, N.Y., U.S.	210	43.05 N	73.55 W
Middle Haddam	207	41.33 N	72.33 W
Middleham	44	54.17 N	1.49 W
Middle Harbour c	274a	33.48 S	151.14 E
Middle Head ➤	274a	33.50 S	151.16 E
Middle Hope	186	45.34 N	74.01 W
Middle Island	210	40.53 N	72.56 W
Middle Island I, Austl.	162	34.07 S	123.12 E
Middle Island I, On., Can.	214	41.41 N	82.41 W
Middle Level Main Drain ≃	42	52.43 N	0.22 E
Middle Loup ≃	198	41.17 N	98.23 W
Middle Maitland ≃	212	43.51 N	81.19 W
Middlemarch	172	45.31 S	170.07 E
Middlemount	166	22.49 S	148.40 E
Middle Musquodoboit	186	45.03 N	63.09 W
Middle Nodaway ≃	194	40.54 N	94.50 W
Middle Pease ≃	196	34.15 N	100.07 W
Middle Point	216	40.51 N	84.27 W
Middleport, N.Y., U.S.	210	43.12 N	78.28 W
Middleport, Oh., U.S.	188	39.00 N	82.02 W
Middleport, Pa., U.S.	208	40.44 N	76.05 W
Middle Raccoon ≃	194	41.34 N	94.12 W
Middle Reservoir ◎¹	283	42.27 N	71.07 W
Middle River	208	39.20 N	76.26 W
Middle River ≃	208	39.19 N	76.25 W
Middle River Neck ✶¹	284b	39.22 N	76.23 W
Middle River Rouge ≃	281	42.20 N	83.15 W
Middle Rouge Parkway ♦	281	42.22 N	83.21 W
Middle Run ≃	285	39.41 N	75.43 W
Middlesboro	192	36.36 N	83.43 W
Middlesbrough	44	54.35 N	1.14 W
Middlesex, Belize	232	17.02 N	88.31 W
Middlesex, N.J., U.S.	276	40.34 N	74.29 W
Middlesex, N.Y., U.S.	210	42.42 N	77.16 W
Middlesex, N.C., U.S.	192	35.47 N	78.12 W
Middlesex □⁶, On., Can.	212	43.00 N	81.08 W
Middlesex □⁶, Ct., U.S.	207	41.33 N	72.39 W
Middlesex □⁶, Ma., U.S.	207	42.30 N	71.25 W
Middlesex □⁶, N.J., U.S.	276	40.29 N	74.27 W
Middlesex □⁶, Va., U.S.	208	37.40 N	76.35 W
Middlesex Fells Reservation ♦	283	42.27 N	71.07 W
Middlesex Reservoir ◎¹	276	40.37 N	74.19 W
Middle Stewiacke	186	45.13 N	63.08 W
Middle Swan	168a	31.52 S	116.00 E
Middle Thames ≃	212	42.59 N	80.58 W
Middleton, Austl.	166	22.22 S	141.32 E
Middleton, N.S., Can.	186	44.57 N	65.04 W
Middleton, Eng., U.K.	42	53.33 N	2.13 W
Middleton, Id., U.S.	200	43.42 N	116.37 W
Middleton, Ma., U.S.	283	42.35 N	71.01 W
Middleton, Mi., U.S.	190	43.11 N	84.42 W
Middleton, Tn., U.S.	194	35.03 N	88.53 W
Middleton, Wi., U.S.	216	43.05 N	89.30 W
Middleton-in-Teesdale	44	54.38 N	2.04 W
Middleton Island I	180	59.25 N	146.25 W
Middleton-on-the-Wolds	44	53.56 N	0.33 W
Middleton Pond ◎	283	42.36 N	71.02 W
Middleton Reef ✶¹	160	29.28 S	159.06 E
Middleton Saint George	44	54.30 N	1.28 W
Middleton, N. Ire., U.K.	48	54.18 N	6.50 W
Middletown, Ca., U.S.	226	38.45 N	122.36 W
Middletown, Ct., U.S.	207	41.33 N	72.39 W
Middletown, De., U.S.	208	39.26 N	75.43 W
Middletown, In., U.S.	219	40.11 N	89.35 W
Middletown, In., U.S.	216	40.03 N	85.32 W
Middletown, Ky., U.S.	208	38.14 N	85.32 W
Middletown, Md.	208	39.26 N	77.32 W
Middletown, Mo., U.S.	194	39.07 N	91.24 W
Middletown, N.J., U.S.	276	40.23 N	74.07 W
Middletown, N.Y., U.S.	210	41.26 N	74.25 W
Middletown, Oh., U.S.	216	39.30 N	84.23 W
Middletown, Pa., U.S.	208	40.11 N	76.43 W
Middletown, R.I., U.S.	207	41.30 N	71.17 W
Middletown, Va., U.S.	208	39.03 N	78.16 W
Middletown Park ♦	276	40.09 N	85.26 W
Middle Tuolumne ≃	226	37.50 N	120.01 W
Middleville, Mi., U.S.	216	42.42 N	85.27 W
Middleville, N.Y., U.S.	210	43.08 N	74.58 W
Middleville, N.Y., U.S.	276	43.08 N	74.58 W
Middlewich	44	53.11 N	2.27 W
Middle Yegua Creek ≃			
Middle Yuba ≃	226	39.19 N	96.47 W
Middlewit	226	39.24 N	121.12 W
Midelt	148	32.41 N	4.43 W
Midfield	282	33.28 N	86.55 W
Midge Hall	262	53.43 N	2.45 W
Midgic	186	45.59 N	64.18 W
Mid Glamorgan □⁴	42	51.38 N	3.25 W
Midhurst, On., Can.	212	44.27 N	79.44 W
Midhurst, Eng., U.K.	42	50.59 N	0.45 W
Midi, Aiguille du ▲	62	45.51 N	6.53 E
Midi, Canal du ≃	32	43.26 N	1.58 E
Midi de Bigorre, Pic du ▲	32	42.56 N	0.08 E
Mid Illovo	158	29.59 S	30.25 E
Mid-Indian Basin ✶¹	12	10.00 S	80.00 E
Mid-Indian Ridge ✶³	8	12.00 S	66.00 E
Midland, Austl.	168a	31.53 S	115.59 E
Midland, On., Can.	204	32.33 N	114.48 W
Midland, Mi., U.S.	190	43.36 N	84.14 W
Midland, N.C., U.S.	192	35.13 N	80.30 W
Midland, Pa., U.S.	214	40.37 N	80.26 W
Midland, S.D., U.S.	198	44.04 N	101.09 W
Midland, Tx., U.S.	196	31.59 N	102.04 W
Midland, Wa., U.S.	210	41.40 N	85.42 W
Midland Bay c	212	44.47 N	79.52 W

Column 4

Name	Page	Lat.	Long.
Midland Beach ●⁸	276	40.34 N	74.05 W
Midland City	219	40.09 N	89.08 W
Midland Park, Mi., U.S.	216	42.23 N	85.22 W
Midland Park, N.J., U.S.	276	40.59 N	74.08 W
Midland Park Lake ◎	212	44.44 N	79.53 W
Midlands □⁴	154	19.00 S	29.45 E
Midleton	48	51.55 N	8.10 W
Midlothian, Il., U.S.	216	41.37 N	87.43 W
Midlothian, Tx., U.S.	222	32.28 N	96.59 W
Midlothian Creek ≃, Pa.	278	41.39 N	87.40 W
Midium	52	53.43 N	5.37 E
Midkese	182	50.55 N	114.05 W
Midkese ≃	154	6.46 S	37.54 E
Midland Sound ☌	182	50.51 N	114.05 W
Midongy Nord	157b	20.45 S	46.13 E
Midongy Sud	157b	23.35 S	47.01 E
Midori	96	34.43 N	132.37 E
Midori ●³	268	35.33 N	139.34 E
Midori ≃	92	32.42 N	130.37 E
Midou ≃	32	43.54 N	0.30 W
Mid-Pacific Mountains ✶³	14	20.00 N	170.00 E
Midpines	226	37.32 N	119.55 W
Midreshet Ben Gurion	132	30.51 N	34.46 E
Midsayap	116	7.12 N	124.32 E
Midshipman Point ➤	282	38.07 N	122.27 W
Midsland	52	53.22 N	5.16 E
Midsomer Norton	42	51.18 N	2.28 W
Midu	102	25.22 N	100.31 E
Midvale, De., U.S.	285	39.39 N	75.37 W
Midvale, Oh., U.S.	214	40.26 N	81.22 W
Midville	192	32.49 N	82.14 W
Midway, B.C., Can.	182	49.01 N	118.47 W
Midway, B.C., Can.	202	49.01 N	118.46 W
Midway, Al., U.S.	194	32.04 N	85.31 W
Midway, Fl., U.S.	192	30.28 N	84.28 W
Midway, Ky., U.S.	208	38.09 N	84.41 W
Midway, Pa., U.S.	279b	40.22 N	80.17 W
Midway, Pa., U.S.	222	31.02 N	95.45 W
Midway, Ut., U.S.	200	40.30 N	111.28 W
Midway City	280	33.45 N	118.00 W
Midway Islands □², Oc.	6	28.13 N	177.22 W
Midway Islands □², Oc.	174g	28.13 N	177.22 W
Midway Mall ●⁹	279a	41.24 N	82.07 W
Midway Naval Station ■	174g	28.13 N	177.26 W
Midway Park	192	34.43 N	77.21 W
Midwest	200	43.24 N	106.16 W
Midwest City	196	35.26 N	97.24 W
Midwolda	52	53.12 N	7.00 E
Midyat	130	37.25 N	41.23 E
Midyobe	152	1.21 N	10.18 E
Midžor (Midžur) ▲	38	43.23 N	22.42 E
Mie	96	32.58 N	131.35 E
Mie □⁵	92	34.30 N	136.30 E
Miechów	30	50.23 N	20.01 E
Międzybórz	30	51.24 N	17.40 E
Międzychód	30	52.36 N	15.55 E
Międzylesie	30	50.10 N	16.40 E
Międzyrzec Podlaski	30	52.00 N	22.47 E
Międzyrzecz	30	52.28 N	15.35 E
Międzyzdroje	30	53.55 N	14.28 E
Miehuanu	100	31.19 N	117.44 E
Miejska Górka	30	51.40 N	16.58 E
Mielan	32	43.26 N	0.19 E
Mielec	30	50.18 N	21.25 E
Mielno	30	54.16 N	16.01 E
Mien ≃	208	37.40 N	76.35 W
Mienga	152	17.17 S	19.48 E
Mienhua Yü I	100	25.29 N	122.06 E
Mient'ienhuo Shan ⚞	269d	25.11 N	121.30 E
Miercurea-Ciuc	38	46.21 N	25.48 E
Mieres	34	43.15 N	5.46 W
Mierlo	52	51.27 N	5.37 E
Mieroszów	30	50.41 N	16.10 E
Miersdorf	264a	52.20 N	13.37 E
Miersig	38	46.49 N	22.11 E
Mier y Noriega	234	23.25 N	100.07 W
Miesaituo	120	35.52 N	93.40 E
Miesbach	64	47.47 N	11.50 E
Miesenbach	61	47.42 N	15.48 E
Mieso	144	9.15 N	40.48 E
Miesterhorst	54	52.27 N	11.09 E
Mieszkowice	30	52.46 N	14.30 E
Mifflin, Oh., U.S.	214	40.47 N	82.22 W
Mifflin, Pa., U.S.	208	40.34 N	77.24 W
Mifflin □⁶	208	40.38 N	77.33 W
Mifflinburg	208	40.55 N	77.02 W
Mifflintown	208	40.34 N	77.24 W
Mifflinville	210	41.01 N	76.18 W
Miftah, Wâdi V	142	30.15 N	31.46 E
Migdal	132	32.50 N	35.30 E
Migdal Ha'Emeq	132	32.41 N	35.15 E
Migennes	50	47.58 N	3.31 E
Migliarino	64	44.48 N	11.56 E
Miglionico	66	40.34 N	16.30 E
Mignano Monte Lungo	68	41.23 N	13.58 E
Mignone ≃	68	42.11 N	11.44 E
Mignovillard	58	46.48 N	6.08 E
Migori ≃	154	0.59 S	34.15 E
Miguel Alemán, Presa ◎¹	234	18.13 N	96.32 W
Miguel Alves	250	4.10 S	42.54 W
Miguel Auza	232	24.18 N	103.25 W
Miguel Calmon	250	11.26 S	40.36 W
Miguel de la Borda	238	9.09 N	80.19 W
Migueles, Arroyo de ≃	266a		
Miguelete	259	34.51 S	56.13 W
Miguelete, Arroyo ≃	258	34.14 S	57.54 W
Miguelópolis	258	20.11 S	48.02 W
Miguelópolis	232	26.30 N	108.35 W
Miguel Pereira	258	22.25 S	43.22 W
Miguel Riglos	252	36.51 S	63.42 W
Migulinskaja	80	49.42 N	41.16 E
Migvie	46	57.08 N	2.56 W
Migyaunglaung	110	14.40 N	98.09 E
Mihaeşti	38	45.07 N	25.00 E
Mihailevitza	32	44.38 N	23.32 W
Mihailovgrad □⁴	38	43.24 N	23.14 E
Mihalgazi	130	40.02 N	30.34 E
Mihálovce	30	48.45 N	21.55 E
Mihama, Nihon	94	34.46 N	136.54 E
Mihama, Nihon	94	35.36 N	135.56 E
Mihama, Nihon	96	33.54 N	135.08 E
Mihara, Nihon	96	34.24 N	133.05 E
Mihara, Nihon	96	34.44 N	131.34 E
Mihara-yama ▲¹	94	34.43 N	139.24 E
Mihla	54	51.04 N	10.18 E
Miho	94	36.00 N	140.18 E
Mihonoseki	96	35.33 N	133.14 E
Mihuanc ≃⁶	98	39.07 N	116.27 E
Mijaly	84	47.44 N	53.50 E
Mijares ≃	34	39.55 N	0.01 W
Mijdahah	144	14.40 N	49.02 E
Mijdrecht	52	52.12 N	4.52 E
Mijiang	102	24.30 N	108.29 E
Mijares	38	44.06 N	28.11 E
Mikabo-yama ▲	94	36.09 N	138.55 E
Mikame	96	33.24 N	132.23 E
Mikamo, Nihon	96	35.09 N	133.37 E

Column 5 (ENGLISH / DEUTSCH cross-reference)

ENGLISH Name	Page	Lat.	Long.	DEUTSCH Name	Seite	Breite	Länge (E=Ost)
Mikamo, Nihon	96	34.05 N	133.57 E	Milford Lake ◎¹	198	39.15 N	97.00 W
Mikasa	92a	43.14 N	141.53 E	Milford on Sea	42	50.44 N	1.36 W
Mikaševičy	76	52.13 N	27.28 E	Milford Ridge	284b	39.21 N	76.45 W
Mikata	94	35.33 N	135.55 E	Milford Sound	172	44.40 S	167.54 E
Mikata-ko ◎	94	35.34 N	135.53 E	Milford Sound ☌	172	44.35 S	167.47 E
Mikawa, Nihon	276	40.59 N	74.08 W	Milford Station	186	45.03 N	63.26 W
Mikawa, Nihon	94	36.29 N	136.29 E	Milgis ≃	154	1.48 N	38.06 E
Mikawa, Nihon	96	33.37 N	132.58 E	Milgoo ▲	162	28.51 S	118.07 E
Mikawa-wan c	94	34.43 N	137.10 E	Mil'guvejem ≃	180	68.22 N	171.30 E
Mikawa-wan-kokutei-kōen ♦	94	34.42 N	137.10 E	Milh, Bahr al- ◎	128	32.40 N	43.35 E
Mikazuki	96	34.58 N	134.27 E	Mîlh, Wâdi al- ≃			
Mikese	154	6.46 S	37.54 E	Milhat Ashqar ☶, 'Irâq	128	35.18 N	41.55 E
Mikhaylov- Kotsyubyns'ke	78	51.27 N	31.04 E	Milhat Ashqar ☶, 'Irâq	130	35.18 N	41.55 E
Mikhaylov, Cape ➤	9	66.51 S	118.33 E	Milhaud	62	43.47 N	4.18 E
Mikhrot Shelomo Hamelekh (Timna') (King Solomon's Mines) ⊥	132	29.45 N	34.56 E	Mili I¹	14	6.08 N	171.55 E
Midongy Sud	157b	23.35 S	47.01 E	Milian ≃	112	5.13 N	117.25 E
Miki, Nihon	96	34.48 N	134.59 E	Milicia ≃	70	38.04 N	13.33 E
Miki, Nihon	96	34.17 N	134.05 E	Milicz	30	51.32 N	17.17 E
Mikinai	38	37.44 N	22.45 E	Milieu, Rivière du ≃	206	46.47 N	73.56 W
Mikindani	154	10.17 S	40.07 E	Milili	142	30.36 N	31.03 E
Mikinduri	154	0.07 N	37.50 E	Miling	162	30.30 S	116.21 E
Mikkabi	94	34.48 N	137.33 E	Milis	71	40.03 N	8.38 E
Mikkaichi	270	34.26 N	119.55 W	Militello in Val di Catania	70	37.16 N	14.48 E
Mikkeli	26	61.41 N	27.15 E	Militello Rosmarino	70	38.03 N	14.41 E
Mikkelin lääni □⁴	26	62.00 N	27.30 E	Milk ≃	182	48.05 N	106.15 W
Mikkwa ≃	176	58.25 N	114.45 W	Milk Creek ≃, Co., U.S.	200	40.24 N	107.45 W
Mikołajki	30	53.49 N	21.36 E	Milk Creek ≃, Or., U.S.	224	45.15 N	122.41 W
Mikołów	30	50.11 N	18.55 E	Milk Hill ▲²	42	51.23 N	1.51 W
Mikomeseng	152	2.08 N	10.37 E	Mil'kovo	74	54.43 N	158.37 E
Mikomoto-jima I	94	34.34 N	138.56 E	Milk River	182	49.09 N	112.05 W
Mikonos	38	37.26 N	25.20 E	Milk River Ridge Reservoir ◎¹	182	49.22 N	112.35 W
Mikonos I	38	37.29 N	25.25 E	Mill ≃, Ct., U.S.	276	41.08 N	73.16 W
Mikope	152	5.03 S	20.48 E	Mill ≃, Ma., U.S.	207	41.08 N	72.37 W
Mikrá Préspa, Límni ◎	38	40.46 N	21.04 E	Mill ≃, Ma., U.S.	283	42.38 N	70.41 W
Mikre	38	43.02 N	24.31 E	Mill ≃, Ma., U.S.	283	42.38 N	70.57 W
Miksimil	126	22.52 N	89.23 E	Mill ≃, Ma., U.S.	283	42.08 N	71.21 W
Mikšino	76	57.15 N	35.43 E	Mill ≃, Ma., U.S.	283	42.40 N	70.52 W
Mikulášovice	54	50.58 N	14.21 E	Mill ≃, N.Y., U.S.	276	40.38 N	73.39 W
Mikulino	76	55.02 N	31.07 E	Millard	198	41.13 N	96.07 W
Mikulkin, mys ➤	24	67.48 N	46.40 E	Millau	32	44.06 N	3.05 E
Mikulov	61	48.49 N	16.39 E	Mill Bay	224	48.39 N	123.34 W
Mikumi	154	7.24 S	36.59 E	Millbourne	192	37.59 N	79.36 W
Mikumi National Park ♦	154	7.12 S	37.05 E	Millbrae	285	39.58 N	75.15 W
Mikun'	24	62.21 N	50.06 E	Millbrook, On., Can.	226	37.35 S	122.23 W
Mikuni	94	36.13 N	136.09 E	Millbrook, Eng., U.K.	42	50.20 N	4.13 W
Mikuni-sammyaku ⚞	94	36.46 N	138.50 E	Millbrook, Ma., U.S.	283	42.03 N	70.41 W
Mikuni-tōge ⤬	94	36.46 N	138.50 E	Millbrook, N.J., U.S.	276	40.52 N	74.33 W
Mikuni-yama ▲	94	35.59 N	138.43 E	Millbrook, N.Y., U.S.	210	41.47 N	73.41 W
Mikura-jima I	92	33.52 N	139.36 E	Mill Brook ≃, Ma., U.S.	283	42.31 N	71.18 W
Mila	190	45.45 N	93.39 W	Mill Brook ≃, N.J., U.S.	276	40.53 N	74.28 W
Miladummadulu Atoll I¹	122	6.15 N	73.15 E	Mill Brook ≃, N.J., U.S.	276	40.25 N	74.06 W
Milagre	256	21.18 S	47.00 W	Mill Creek ≃, Austl.	274a	33.59 S	151.01 E
Milagres	250	7.17 S	38.57 W	Mill Creek ≃, Ca.	226	36.49 N	119.21 W
Milagro	246	2.07 S	79.36 W	Mill Creek ≃, De., U.S.	285	39.42 N	75.36 W
Milagros	116	12.13 N	123.30 E	Mill Creek ≃, Il., U.S.	219	39.50 N	91.24 W
Milam □⁶	222	30.47 N	96.57 W	Mill Creek ≃, In., U.S.	216	39.30 N	86.57 W
Milan → Milano, It.	62	45.28 N	9.12 E	Millbury, Ma., U.S.	207	42.11 N	71.45 W
Milan, Ga., U.S.	192	32.01 N	83.03 W	Millbury, Oh., U.S.	214	41.33 N	83.25 W
Milan, In., U.S.	218	39.07 N	85.07 W	Mill City	202	44.45 N	122.29 W
Milan, Mi., U.S.	216	42.05 N	83.40 W	Mill Creek ≃, Pa., U.S.	214	40.27 N	77.56 W
Milan, Mo., U.S.	194	40.12 N	93.07 W	Mill Creek ≃, Pa., U.S.	207	40.27 N	111.54 W
Milan, N.M., U.S.	200	35.11 N	117.44 E	Mill Creek ≃, W.V., U.S.			
Milan, Tn., U.S.	194	35.55 N	88.45 W	Mill Creek ≃, Austl.	188	38.43 N	79.58 W
Milando	152	8.45 S	17.36 E	Mill Creek ≃, Ca.	226	36.49 N	119.21 W
Milan Federal Correctional Institution ⊶	281	42.06 N	83.40 W	Mill Creek ≃, De., U.S.	285	39.42 N	75.39 W
Milang	168b	35.25 S	138.58 E	Mill Creek ≃, Il., U.S.	219	39.50 N	91.24 W
Milano (Milan), It.	62	45.28 N	9.12 E	Mill Creek ≃, In., U.S.			
Milano (Milan), It.	266b	45.28 N	9.12 E	Milan, Tx., U.S.	194	39.30 N	86.57 W
Milano, Tx., U.S.	222	30.43 N	96.52 W	Mill Creek ≃, Mo., U.S.			
Milanoa	157b	13.35 S	49.47 E	Mill Creek ≃, N.J., U.S.	276	40.44 N	74.18 W
Milano Marittima	64	44.16 N	12.21 E	Mill Creek ≃, Oh.	279a	41.06 N	80.39 W
Milanville	210	41.40 N	75.03 W	Mill Creek ≃, Oh.	214	41.23 N	83.42 W
Milas	130	37.19 N	27.47 E	Mill Creek ≃, Or.	224	45.04 N	123.01 W
Milašević	76	53.41 N	32.15 E	Mill Creek ≃, Or.	218	38.28 N	84.20 W
Mil'atino, Ross.	54	54.29 N	34.18 E	Mill Creek ≃, Pa.	210	40.48 N	74.03 W
Mil'atino, Ross.	76	53.41 N	32.15 E	Mill Creek ≃, Ca., U.S.	226	36.49 N	119.21 W
Milavidy	76	52.55 N	25.44 E	Mill Creek ≃, Or.	226	36.49 N	119.21 W
Milazzo	70	38.18 N	15.14 E	Mill Creek, North Fork ≃	192	37.59 N	79.36 W
Milazzo, Capo di ➤	70	38.16 N	15.14 E	Mill Creek, South Fork ≃	224	45.36 N	121.12 W
Milazzo, Golfo di c	70	38.13 N	15.16 E	Millcreek Township	214	42.05 N	80.10 W
Milbank	198	45.13 N	96.38 W	Milledgeville, Ga., U.S.	192	33.04 N	83.13 W
Milborne Port	42	50.58 N	2.27 W	Milledgeville, Oh., U.S.	214	39.36 N	83.36 W
Milburn	214	40.14 N	83.09 W	Mille Îles, Rivière des ≃	206	45.35 N	73.43 W
Milburn Creek ≃	218	38.23 N	84.32 W	Mille Lacs, Lac des ◎	190	48.50 N	90.30 W
Milden	184	51.29 N	107.31 W	Mille Lacs Kathio State Park ♦	190	46.08 N	93.43 W
Mildenau	54	50.35 N	13.17 E	Millendon	168a	31.48 S	116.02 E
Mildenhall	42	52.21 N	0.30 E	Millendreath	43	50.20 N	4.25 W
Mildmay	212	44.03 N	81.07 W	Miller, Mount ▲	219	38.15 N	87.38 W
Mildred, Il., U.S.	219	39.46 N	89.38 W	Millers ≃	283	42.34 N	72.15 W
Mildred, Pa., U.S.	210	41.28 N	76.18 W	Mill Hall	208	41.06 N	77.29 W
Mildura	166	34.12 S	142.09 E	Miller, S.D., U.S.	198	44.31 N	98.59 W
Mil düzü ≃	84	40.00 N	48.08 E	Miller, Mount ▲	180	61.00 N	142.18 W
Mile	102	24.26 N	103.26 E	Miller Mountain ▲	204	37.48 N	117.29 W
Milena	70	37.28 N	13.44 E	Millersburg, In., U.S.	216	41.31 N	85.41 W
Milendella	66	40.34 N	139.12 E	Millers Place	210	40.58 N	72.59 W
Milepa	154	14.30 S	36.12 E	Milldale	207	41.33 N	72.53 W
Miles, Austl.	166	26.49 S	150.11 E	Millers Tavern	208	37.47 N	76.58 W
Miles, Tx., U.S.	196	31.36 N	100.11 W	Miller, Mount ▲	222	32.10 N	96.42 W
Miles City	198	46.25 N	105.50 W	Millers Falls	207	42.35 N	72.29 W
Milesburg	208	40.56 N	77.47 W	Millersburg, Oh., U.S.	214	40.33 N	81.55 W
Miles Standish State Forest ♦	207	41.50 N	70.40 W	Millersburg, Ky., U.S.	208	38.18 N	84.09 W
Mileševka ≃	36	43.21 N	19.40 E	Millersburg, Pa., U.S.	208	40.32 N	76.57 W
Miletto, Monte ▲	68	41.27 N	14.22 E	Mill Creek ≃, Va., U.S.	208	37.54 N	77.10 W
Miletus (Milet) ⊥	130	37.28 N	27.15 E	Mill Brook ≃	192	33.04 N	83.13 W
Mil'atino	54	54.29 N	34.18 E	Milledgeville, Oh., U.S.	214	39.36 N	83.36 W
Milevsko	60	49.27 N	14.22 E	Miller House	180	65.32 N	145.11 W
Milford, Ut., U.S.	200	38.24 N	113.00 W	Miller Mountain ▲	204	37.48 N	117.29 W
Milford, Eng., U.K.	42	51.11 N	0.38 W	Miller Peak ▲	200	31.23 N	110.17 W
Milford Center	214	40.10 N	83.26 W	Miller Place	210	40.58 N	72.59 W
Milford Cross Roads	273b	41.13 N	73.00 W	Millers River ≃	283	42.34 N	72.15 W
Milford Haven	42	51.42 N	5.03 W	Millersburg, In., U.S.	216	41.31 N	85.41 W

Symbols in the index entries represent the broad categories identified in the key at the right. Symbols with superior numbers (≃¹) identify subcategories (see complete key on page I · 1).

Symbole im Register stellen die rechts im Schlüssel erklärten Kategorien dar. Symbole mit hochgestellten Ziffern (≃¹) bezeichnen Unterabteilungen einer Kategorie (vgl. vollständigen Schlüssel auf Seite I · 1).

Los símbolos incluidos en el texto del índice representan las grandes categorías identificadas con la clave a la derecha. Los símbolos con numeros en su parte superior (≃¹) identifican las subcategorías (véase la clave completa en la página I · 1).

Les symboles de l'index représentent les catégories indiquées dans la légende à droite. Les symboles suivis d'un indice (≃¹) représentent des sous-catégories (voir légende complète à la page I · 1).

Os símbolos incluídos no texto do índice representam as grandes categorias identificadas com a chave à direita. Os símbolos com números em sua parte superior (≃¹) identificam as subcategorias (veja-se a chave completa à página I · 1).

▲ Mountain	Berg	Montaña	Montagne	Montanha
⚞ Mountains	Gebirge	Montañas	Montagnes	Montanhas
⤬ Pass	Paß	Paso	Col	Passo
V Valley, Canyon	Tal, Cañon	Valle, Cañón	Vallée, Canyon	Vale, Canhão
≃ Plain	Ebene	Llano	Plaine	Planície
➤ Cape	Kap	Cabo	Cap	Cabo
I Island	Insel	Isla	Île	Ilha
II Islands	Inseln	Islas	Îles	Ilhas
⊥ Other Topographic Features	Andere Topographische Objekte	Otros Elementos Topográficos	Autres données topographiques	Outros acidentes topográficos

Nombre	Página	Lat.	Long. W = Oeste	Nom	Page	Lat.	Long. W = Ouest	Nome	Página	Lat.	Long. W = Oeste

ENGLISH: Name / Page / Lat.°′ / Long.°′ — DEUTSCH: Name / Seite / Breite°′ / Länge°′ E = Ost

Name	Page	Lat.°′	Long.°′
Mitchell Corners	212	43.57 N	78.48 W
Mitchell Field ⊠	278	41.55 N	88.15 W
Mitchell Lake ⊜, B.C., Can.	182	52.53 N	120.36 W
Mitchell Lake ⊜, On., Can.	212	44.34 N	78.58 W
Mitchell Point ≻	214	42.26 N	82.26 W
Mitchellville	190	41.40 N	93.21 W
Mitchelstown	48	52.16 N	8.16 W
Mīt Fāris	142	31.02 N	31.36 E
Mīt Ghamr	142	30.43 N	31.16 E
Mīt Ḥalfah	273c	30.10 N	31.14 E
Mīt Ḥamal	142	30.26 N	31.32 E
Mithapur	120	22.25 N	69.00 E
Mitha Tiwāna	123	32.15 N	72.07 E
Mithi	120	24.44 N	69.48 E
Míthimna	38	39.22 N	26.10 E
Mitiaro I	14	19.49 S	157.43 W
Mitidja, Plaine de la ≚	34	36.45 N	3.00 E
Mitilíni	38	39.06 N	26.32 E
Mitino	265b	55.51 N	37.21 E
Mitis, Lac ⊜	186	48.17 N	67.45 W
Mitishto ≃	184	54.50 N	98.58 W
Mitiškovo	76	54.40 N	33.31 E
Mitiwanga	214	41.22 N	82.27 W
Mitkof Island I	180	56.45 N	132.50 W
Mitla ⊥	234	16.55 N	96.17 W
Mitla, Laguna ⊂	234	17.03 N	100.25 W
Mitla, Mamarr (Mitla Pass))(	142	30.00 N	32.53 E
Mitla Pass → Mitla, Mamarr)(	142	30.00 N	32.53 E
Mito, Nihon	94	34.49 N	137.19 E
Mito, Nihon	94	36.22 N	140.28 E
Mito, Nihon	96	34.40 N	131.59 E
Mitō, Nihon	96	34.13 N	131.21 E
Mito, Nihon	268	35.10 N	139.37 E
Mitomi	94	35.47 N	138.44 E
Mitoya	96	35.17 N	132.52 E
Mitra, Monte ∧	152	1.23 N	9.57 E
Mitra do Bispo ∧	256	22.10 S	44.34 W
Mitre ∧	172	40.48 S	175.27 E
Mitre, Península ≻[1]	254	54.48 S	65.40 W
Mitre Peak ∧	172	44.38 S	167.50 E
Mitrofania Island I	180	55.51 N	158.49 W
Mitrofanovka	78	49.58 N	39.42 E
Mitrofanovo	24	63.13 N	56.00 E
Mīt Ruhaynah	273c	29.51 N	31.15 E
Mīt Ruhaynah (Memphis) ⊥	142	29.51 N	31.15 E
Mitry-le-Neuf	261	48.57 N	2.36 E
Mitry-Mory	261	48.59 N	2.37 E
Mitsamiouli	157a	11.23 S	43.18 E
Mitsinjo	157b	16.01 S	45.52 E
Mitsio, Nosy I	157b	12.54 S	48.36 E
Mitsiwa (Massawa)	144	15.38 N	39.28 E
Mitsiwa Channel ᛘ	144	15.30 N	40.00 E
Mitsu, Nihon	96	34.47 N	134.33 E
Mitsu, Nihon	96	34.48 N	133.56 E
Mitsubori	268	35.56 N	139.56 E
Mitsue	94	34.29 N	136.10 E
Mitsugi	96	34.30 N	133.09 E
Mitsuike Park ♠	268	35.31 N	139.39 E
Mitsukaidō	94	36.01 N	139.59 E
Mitsuke	92	37.32 N	138.56 E
Mitsumarenge-dake ∧	94	36.23 N	137.35 E
Mitsushima	92	34.16 N	129.19 E
Mitsuzaku	268	35.25 N	140.00 E
Mitsuzawa Park Race Track ♠	268	35.27 N	139.36 E
Mitta, Oued el V	148	34.20 N	6.44 E
Mittagong	170	34.27 S	150.27 E
Mittagskogel (Kepa) ∧	61	46.31 N	13.57 E
Mittainville	261	48.40 N	1.39 E
Mitta Mitta ≃	171b	36.12 S	147.11 E
Mitte ◆[8]	264a	52.31 N	13.24 E
Mittelberg	58	47.20 N	10.10 E
Mittelfischach	56	49.02 N	9.52 E
Mittelfranken □[5]	56	49.20 N	10.40 E
Mittellandkanal ≡	30	52.16 N	11.41 E
Mittelmeer → Mediterranean Sea ⩡[2]	10	35.00 N	20.00 E
Mittelsaida	54	50.46 N	13.18 E
Mittelstetten	60	48.15 N	11.06 E
Mittenwald	64	47.27 N	11.15 E
Mittenwalde, Dtsch.	54	53.11 N	13.39 E
Mittenwalde, Dtsch.	54	52.16 N	13.32 E
Mitterndorf	64	47.33 N	13.55 E
Mittersill	64	47.16 N	12.29 E
Mitterskirchen	60	48.21 N	12.44 E
Mitterteich	60	49.57 N	12.15 E
Mittewald an der Drau	64	46.46 N	12.36 E
Mittweida	54	50.59 N	12.59 E
Mitú	246	1.08 N	70.03 W
Mitumba, Monts ⋀	154	6.00 S	29.00 E
Mituo	107	28.53 N	105.37 E
Mitwaba	154	8.38 S	27.20 E
Mitwitz	56	50.15 N	11.12 E
Mityana	154	0.24 N	32.03 E
Mīt Yazīd	142	30.30 N	31.20 E
Mitzic	152	0.47 N	11.34 E
Miura	94	35.08 N	139.37 E
Miura-chosuichi ⊜[1]	94	35.49 N	137.23 E
Miura-dam ◆[6]	94	35.49 N	137.24 E
Miura-hantō ≻[1]	94	35.15 N	139.39 E
Mius	80	51.26 N	47.56 E
Mius ≃	83	47.18 N	38.49 E
Miusskij liman ⊂[1]	83	47.15 N	38.40 E
Miusyns'k	83	48.05 N	38.53 E
Miwa, Nihon	94	35.11 N	136.47 E
Miwa, Nihon	94	36.39 N	140.18 E
Miwa, Nihon	96	35.12 N	135.14 E
Miwa, Nihon	96	34.13 N	132.06 E
Miwa, Nihon	96	34.39 N	132.51 E
Miwa, Nihon	270	34.31 N	135.51 E
Mi-Wuk Village	226	38.05 N	120.13 W
Mixcoac ◆[3]	286a	19.23 N	99.12 W
Mixcoac, Presa de ⊜[1]	286a	19.22 N	99.14 W
Mixco Viejo ⊥	236	14.52 N	90.40 W
Mixian	100	34.31 N	113.22 E
Mixin	107	30.23 N	105.46 E
Mixquiahuala	234	20.14 N	99.13 W
Mixtán	234	17.55 N	95.51 W
Mixteco ≃	234	18.11 N	98.30 W
Mixtlán	234	20.26 N	104.25 W
Miya	94	36.05 N	137.15 E
Miya ≃, Nihon	94	36.28 N	137.15 E
Miya ≃, Nihon	94	34.32 N	136.44 E
Miyagawa, Nihon	94	36.19 N	137.09 E
Miyagawa, Nihon	94	34.22 N	136.21 E
Miyagi □[5]	92	38.22 N	140.52 E
Miyagi-jima I	174m	26.21 N	127.57 E
Miyāh, Wādī al- V	140	25.00 N	33.23 E
Miyahara	268	35.56 N	139.37 E
Miyajima	96	34.18 N	132.19 E
Miyake	270	34.35 N	135.47 E
Miyake-jima I	92	34.05 N	139.32 E
Miyako	92	39.38 N	141.57 E
Miyakojima ◆[8]	270	34.43 N	135.33 E
Miyako-jima I	175d	24.47 N	125.20 E
Miyakonojō	92	31.44 N	131.04 E
Miyako-rettō II	175d	24.24 N	125.00 E
Miyama, Nihon	92	34.06 N	136.14 E
Miyama, Nihon	94	36.00 N	136.22 E
Miyama, Nihon	94	35.33 N	136.45 E
Miyama, Nihon	96	35.16 N	135.33 E
Miyama, Nihon	96	33.59 N	135.22 E
Miyāni	120	21.51 N	69.23 E
Miyanojō	92	31.54 N	130.27 E
Miyanoura-dake ∧	93b	30.20 N	130.31 E
Miyara	175d	24.20 N	124.14 E
Miyata	96	33.44 N	130.40 E
Miyazaki, Nihon	92	31.54 N	131.26 E
Miyazaki, Nihon	94	35.56 N	136.05 E
Miyazakino-hana ≻	96	34.04 N	135.05 E
Miyazu	96	35.32 N	135.11 E
Miyi	102	27.00 N	102.08 E
Miyoshi, Nihon	96	33.57 N	133.03 E
Miyoshi, Nihon	96	34.48 N	132.51 E
Miyoshi, Nihon	96	34.02 N	133.52 E
Miyoshi, Nihon	268	35.50 N	139.31 E
Miyota	94	36.18 N	138.30 E
Miyun	105	40.22 N	116.50 E
Miyun Shuiku ⊜[1]	105	40.30 N	116.58 E
Mizan Teferi	144	6.53 N	35.28 E
Mizdah	146	31.26 N	12.59 E
Mize	194	31.52 N	89.33 W
Mizen Head ≻, Ire.	48	52.51 N	6.01 W
Mizen Head ≻, Ire.	48	51.27 N	9.49 W
Mižèvičy	76	52.59 N	25.05 E
Mizhhir'ya	78	48.32 N	23.30 E
Mizhi	102	37.49 N	110.02 E
Mizil	38	45.00 N	26.26 E
Mizoch	78	50.24 N	26.09 E
Mizoguchi	96	35.21 N	133.26 E
Mizonokuchi	268	35.36 N	139.37 E
Mizonuma	268	35.48 N	139.36 E
Mizoram □[3]	120	23.30 N	93.00 E
Mizpah	208	39.29 N	74.50 W
Mizpah Creek ≃	198	46.16 N	105.17 W
Mizpé Ramon	132	30.36 N	34.48 E
Mizque	248	17.56 S	65.19 W
Mizque ≃	248	18.39 S	64.20 W
Mizue ◆[8]	268	35.41 N	139.54 E
Mizuho, Nihon	94	35.46 N	139.21 E
Mizuho, Nihon	96	35.10 N	135.22 E
Mizuho, Nihon	96	34.51 N	132.31 E
Mizukaidō → Mitsukaidō	94	36.01 N	139.59 E
Mizuko	268	35.50 N	139.34 E
Mizumaki	96	33.51 N	130.42 E
Mizunami	94	35.22 N	137.15 E
Mizunoko-jima I	96	33.02 N	132.11 E
Mizusawa	92	39.08 N	141.08 E
Mizushima-nada ⊂	96	34.25 N	133.40 E
Mizutori	270	34.47 N	135.45 E
Mizuwake-tōge)(	96	33.15 N	131.17 E
Mjadzel	76	54.53 N	26.57 E
Mjaleškavičy	78	51.56 N	28.59 E
Mjälgen	40	60.33 N	15.07 E
Mjällom	26	62.59 N	18.26 E
Mjangad	86	48.15 N	91.57 E
Mjanyana	158	31.50 S	28.10 E
Mjölby	26	58.19 N	15.08 E
Mjøndalen	26	59.45 N	10.01 E
Mjörn ⊜	26	57.54 N	12.25 E
Mjøsa ⊜	26	60.40 N	11.00 E
Mkalama	154	4.07 S	34.38 E
Mkata	154	5.47 S	38.17 E
Mkhondvo ≃	158	26.39 S	31.25 E
Mkokotoni	154	5.52 S	39.15 E
Mkomazi ≃	158	30.12 S	30.50 E
Mkomazi Game Reserve ◆[4]	154	4.10 S	38.10 E
Mkulwe	154	8.35 S	32.19 E
Mkumvura ≃	154	15.55 S	31.07 E
Mkunumbi	154	2.18 S	40.42 E
Mkushi	154	13.40 S	29.20 E
Mkushi ≃	154	14.40 S	29.07 E
Mkushi River	154	13.32 S	29.45 E
Mkuze	158	27.37 S	32.02 E
Mkuze ≃	158	27.53 S	32.29 E
Mkuzi Game Reserve ◆[4]	158	27.40 S	32.15 E
Mkwaja	154	5.47 S	38.51 E
Mkwaya	154	10.06 S	39.40 E
Mladá Boleslav	54	50.23 N	14.59 E
Mladenovac	38	44.26 N	20.42 E
Mladotice	60	49.58 N	13.18 E
Mlala Hills ⋀[2]	154	6.47 S	31.45 E
M'Lang	116	6.55 N	124.53 E
M'Lang ≃	116	6.52 N	124.45 E
Mlanje Peak → Sapitwa ∧	154	15.57 S	35.36 E
Mlava ≃	38	44.45 N	21.13 E
Mława	30	53.06 N	20.23 E
Mlawula	158	26.11 S	32.01 E
Mliba	158	26.14 S	31.36 E
Mljet, Otok I	36	42.45 N	17.30 E
Mljet Nacionalni Park ♠	36	42.47 N	17.25 E
Mljetski Kanal ᛘ	36	42.48 N	17.35 E
Mlyniv	78	50.31 N	25.37 E
Mmabatho	156	25.51 S	25.38 E
Mmadinare	156	21.57 S	27.52 E
Mnazi	154	8.54 S	39.06 E
Mnevniki ◆[8]	265b	55.45 N	37.28 E
Mnichov	60	50.03 N	12.49 E
Mníšek pod Brdy	30	49.52 N	14.16 E
Mo	24	66.15 N	14.08 E
Mo ≃	150	8.45 N	0.11 E
Moa	240p	20.40 N	74.56 W
Moa ≃, Afr.	150	6.59 N	11.36 W
Moa ≃, Bra.	248	7.39 S	72.41 W
Moa, Pulau I	164	8.10 S	127.56 E
Moab	200	38.34 N	109.32 W
Moabi	152	2.15 S	11.00 E
Moaco ≃	248	7.41 S	68.18 W
Moa Island I	164	10.12 S	142.16 E
Moala Island I	175g	18.36 S	179.53 E
Moalboal	116	9.56 N	123.23 E
Moama	166	36.07 S	144.47 E
Moamba	156	25.35 S	32.13 E
Moana	168b	35.13 S	138.29 E
Moanda	152	1.34 S	13.11 E
Moanza	152	5.25 S	17.30 E
Moar Lake ⊜	184	52.00 N	95.09 W
Moate	48	53.23 N	7.43 W
Moatize	154	16.08 S	33.45 E
Moawhango	172	39.35 S	175.52 E
Moba, Nig.	273a	6.27 N	3.28 E
Moba, R.D.C.	154	7.03 S	29.47 E
Mobara	94	35.25 N	140.18 E
Mobārakpur	126	22.58 N	89.10 E
Mobaye	152	4.19 N	21.11 E
Mobayi-Mbongo	152	4.18 N	21.11 E
Mobberley	262	53.19 N	2.20 W
Mobeetie	196	35.31 N	100.26 W
Mobeka	152	1.53 N	19.46 E
Mobenzélé	152	0.54 N	17.51 E
Moberly	194	39.25 N	92.26 W
Moberly ≃	182	56.12 N	120.55 W
Moberly Lake	182	55.48 N	121.45 W
Moberly Lake ⊜	182	55.49 N	121.45 W
Mobile, Al., U.S.	194	30.41 N	88.02 W
Mobile, Az., U.S.	200	33.03 N	112.16 W
Mobile ≃	194	30.29 N	88.01 W
Mobile Bay ⊂	194	30.25 N	88.00 W
Mobjack	208	37.23 N	76.21 W
Mobjack Bay ⊂	208	37.19 N	76.21 W
Mobridge	198	45.32 N	100.25 W
Moca, P.R.	240m	18.24 N	67.07 W
Moca, Rep. Dom.	238	19.24 N	70.31 W
Moča ≃	82	55.25 N	37.28 E
Mocajuba	250	2.35 S	49.30 W
Mocal ≃	236	14.00 N	88.33 W
Močalejevka	80	53.38 N	51.46 E
Močališče	80	56.21 N	48.23 E
Moçambique	154	15.03 S	40.45 E
Moçambique → Mozambique □[1]	138	18.15 S	35.00 E
Mocanaqua	210	41.08 N	76.08 W
Mocassins, Lac des ⊜	206	46.35 N	74.25 W
Mo Cay	110	10.08 N	106.20 E
Moccasin, Ca., U.S.	226	37.49 N	120.18 W
Moccasin, Il., U.S.	219	39.09 N	88.45 W
Moc Chau	110	20.51 N	104.37 E
Moccoidumis	144	1.36 N	44.26 E
Mocha → Al-Makhā'	144	13.19 N	43.15 E
Mocha, Isla I	252	38.22 S	73.56 W
Moche ≃	248	8.10 S	79.03 W
Moche ⊥	248	8.06 S	79.05 W
Mocheng	106	31.35 N	120.43 E
Mochh	123	32.45 N	71.31 E
Mochigase	96	35.20 N	134.12 E
Mochitlan	234	17.30 N	99.18 W
Mochizuki	94	36.16 N	138.22 E
Mocho, Arroyo ≃	226	37.41 N	121.55 W
Mochonap ᛘ	175c	7.41 N	151.48 E
Mochov	54	50.08 N	14.50 E
Mochtín	60	49.22 N	13.21 E
Mochudi	156	24.28 S	26.05 E
Močily	82	54.20 N	38.41 E
Mocímboa da Praia	154	11.20 S	40.21 E
Mocímboa do Rovuma	154	11.20 S	39.18 E
Möckeln ⊜, Sve.	26	56.40 N	14.10 E
Möckeln ⊜, Sve.	40	59.18 N	14.30 E
Möckern	54	52.08 N	11.57 E
Mockfjärd	40	60.30 N	14.58 E
Mockhorn Island I	208	37.13 N	75.53 W
Möckmühl	56	49.19 N	9.22 E
Mockrehna	54	51.30 N	12.49 E
Mocksville	192	35.53 N	80.33 W
Moclips	224	47.14 N	124.12 W
Môco, Serra do ∧	152	12.28 S	15.10 E
Mocoa	246	1.09 N	76.37 W
Mococa	256	21.28 S	47.01 W
Mocoduene	156	23.40 S	35.10 E
Mocoretá	252	30.38 S	57.58 W
Mocorito	232	25.29 N	107.55 W
Moctezuma, Méx.	232	29.48 N	109.42 W
Moctezuma, Méx.	234	22.45 N	101.05 W
Moctezuma ≃, Méx.	232	29.09 N	109.40 W
Moctezuma ≃, Méx.	234	21.59 N	98.34 W
Mocuba	154	16.50 S	36.59 E
Močurica ≃	38	42.31 N	26.32 E
Modane	62	45.12 N	6.40 E
Modāsa	120	23.28 N	73.18 E
Modau ≃	56	49.49 N	8.28 E
Modbury	42	50.21 N	3.53 W
Modder ≃	158	29.02 S	24.37 E
Modderbee	273d	26.10 S	28.24 E
Modder East	273d	26.11 S	28.26 E
Modderfontein	273d	26.06 S	28.09 E
Modderfontein ≃	273d	26.13 S	28.10 E
Modderrivier	158	29.02 S	24.38 E
Model City	284a	43.11 N	78.59 W
Modena, It.	64	44.40 N	10.55 E
Modena, N.Y., U.S.	210	41.40 N	74.07 W
Modena □[4]	64	44.30 N	10.54 E
Moder ≃	56	48.49 N	8.06 E
Möderbrugg	61	47.17 N	14.29 E
Modern Art, Museum of ⊽	276	40.46 N	73.58 W
Modeste, Mount ∧	224	48.37 N	124.06 W
Modesto, Ca., U.S.	226	37.38 N	120.59 W
Modesto, Il., U.S.	219	39.29 N	89.59 W
Modesto City-County Airport ⊠	226	37.39 N	120.57 W
Modesto Main Canal ≡	226	37.39 N	120.27 W
Modesto Reservoir ⊜[1]	226	37.26 N	121.58 W
Modica	70	36.52 N	14.46 E
Modigliana	66	44.09 N	11.47 E
Modinagar	124	28.51 N	77.37 E
Modione ≃	70	37.34 N	12.49 E
Modjamboli	152	2.28 N	22.06 E
Modjeska	280	33.43 N	117.37 W
Mödling	61	48.05 N	16.17 E
Mödling ≃	264b	48.04 N	16.22 E
Modoc	218	40.02 N	85.07 W
Modon ≃	50	47.16 N	1.27 E
Modowi	164	4.05 S	134.39 E
Modra, Slvk.	30	48.21 N	17.17 E
Modra, Tchad	146	20.43 N	17.42 E
Modra špilja ⊥[5]	36	43.00 N	16.02 E
Mödrath	56	50.53 N	6.43 E
Modriča	38	44.57 N	18.18 E
Modřice	61	49.07 N	16.37 E
Mo Duc	110	14.57 N	108.53 E
Modugno	68	41.05 N	16.47 E
Moe	169	38.10 S	146.15 E
Moe ≃, Austl.	169	38.08 S	146.17 E
Moe ≃, P.Q., Can.	206	45.19 N	71.49 W
Moecherville	216	41.44 N	88.17 W
Moeda	255	20.20 S	44.03 W
Moehau ∧	172	36.35 S	175.24 E
Moel Fferna ∧	42	52.57 N	3.18 W
Moelv	26	60.56 N	10.42 E
Moema	255	19.50 S	45.24 W
Moen	50	50.46 N	3.24 E
Moena	64	46.22 N	11.39 E
Moengo	250	5.37 N	54.24 W
Moen-jo-Daro ⊥	120	27.18 N	68.15 E
Moenkopi	200	36.06 N	111.13 W
Moenkopi Wash V	200	35.54 N	111.26 W
Moeraki Point ≻	172	45.22 S	170.52 E
Moerbeke, Bel.	50	50.45 N	3.55 E
Moerbeke, Bel.	50	51.10 N	3.56 E
Moerdijk	52	51.43 N	4.38 E
Moerewa	172	35.23 S	174.02 E
Moergestel	52	51.33 N	5.11 E
Moero, Lago → Mweru, Lake ⊜	154	9.00 S	28.45 E
Moers	56	51.27 N	6.37 E
Moersbach ≃	263	51.33 N	6.36 E
Moesa ≃	58	46.13 N	9.03 E
Moffat	44	55.20 N	3.27 W
Moffat Peak ∧	172	45.02 S	168.07 E
Moffatt	222	31.12 N	97.28 W
Moffatt, Lac ⊜	206	45.34 N	71.19 W
Moffat Water ≃	44	55.18 N	3.25 W
Moffet Point ≻	180	55.26 N	162.32 W
Moffett Field Naval Air Station ■	226	37.24 N	122.03 W
Moffit	198	46.40 N	100.17 W
Mofoluku	273a	6.33 N	3.20 E
Moga	123	30.48 N	75.10 E
Mogadiscio → Muqdisho	144	2.04 N	45.22 E
Mogadishu → Muqdisho	144	2.04 N	45.22 E
Mogador → Essaouira	148	31.30 N	9.47 W
Mogadore	214	41.02 N	81.23 W
Mogadore Reservoir ⊜[1]	214	41.04 N	81.21 W
Mogadouro	34	41.20 N	6.39 W
Mogalakwena ≃	156	23.00 S	28.40 E
Mogalo	152	3.10 N	19.04 E
Mogami ≃	92	38.55 N	139.48 E
Mogan Shan ∧	106	30.36 N	119.52 E
Mogapinyana	156	22.19 S	27.27 E
Mogaung	110	25.18 N	96.56 E
Mogdy	89	50.35 N	133.51 E
Mogees	285	40.06 N	75.19 W
Møgeltønder	41	54.56 N	8.49 E
Mogenstrup	41	55.11 N	11.53 E
Mogent ≃	266d	41.33 N	2.15 E
Moggio Udinese	64	46.25 N	13.12 E
Mogi, Serra do ⋀	287b	23.47 S	46.20 W
Mogielnica	30	51.42 N	20.43 E
Mogilev → Mahilëu	76	53.54 N	30.21 E
Mogilno	30	52.40 N	17.58 E
Mogincual	154	15.35 S	40.25 E
Moglal, Wādī V	140	19.18 N	34.29 E
Moglia	64	44.56 N	10.55 E
Mogliano Veneto	64	45.33 N	12.14 E
Mogoča	88	53.44 N	119.44 E
Mogoča ≃	76	58.00 N	36.26 E
Mogočin	86	57.43 N	83.34 E
Mogod	88	48.24 N	103.00 E
Mogogh	140	8.26 N	31.19 E
Mogojto	88	54.25 N	110.27 E
Mogojtuj	88	51.17 N	114.55 E
Mogok	110	22.55 N	96.30 E
Mogollon Mountains ⋀	200	33.25 N	108.40 W
Mogollon Rim ⊥[4]	200	34.25 N	110.50 W
Mogor	120	32.52 N	67.47 E
Mogorella	71	39.52 N	8.51 E
Mogoro	71	39.41 N	8.47 E
Mogotes	246	6.30 N	72.58 W
Mogotón ∧	236	13.45 N	86.23 W
Mograt Island I	140	19.30 N	33.15 E
Mogroum	146	11.06 N	15.25 E
Moguer	34	37.16 N	6.50 W
Mogyoród	264c	47.36 N	19.15 E
Mogyoródi-patak ≃	264c	47.36 N	19.05 E
Mogzon	88	51.45 N	111.58 E
Mohács	30	45.59 N	18.42 E
Mohaka	172	39.07 S	177.11 E
Mohaka ≃	172	39.07 S	177.12 E
Mohall	198	48.45 N	101.30 W
Moḥammadābād	128	30.53 N	61.28 E
Mohammedia (Fedala)	148	33.44 N	7.24 W
Mohana	124	25.54 N	77.45 E
Mohangi	154	0.03 N	29.05 E
Mohania	124	25.11 N	83.37 E
Mohanpur, Bngl.	126	23.24 N	90.36 E
Mohanpur, India	126	21.51 N	87.26 E
Mohanpur, India	272a	28.44 N	77.10 E
Mohave, Lake ⊜[1]	204	35.25 N	114.38 W
Mohawk, Mi., U.S.	190	47.18 N	88.21 W
Mohawk, N.Y., U.S.	210	43.00 N	75.00 W
Mohawk ≃	210	42.47 N	73.42 W
Mohawk, East Branch ≃	212	43.22 N	75.28 W
Mohawk, Lake ⊜	276	41.02 N	74.41 W
Mohawk Dam ◆[6]	214	40.20 N	82.05 W
Mohawk Mountain ∧	207	41.49 N	73.17 W
Mohawk Point ≻	212	42.51 N	79.29 W
Mohe	89	53.29 N	122.19 E
Moheda	26	57.00 N	14.34 E
Mohegan	207	41.28 N	72.06 W
Mohegan Lake	210	41.19 N	73.51 W
Mohelnice	30	49.46 N	16.55 E
Moher, Cliffs of ⊥[4]	48	52.57 N	9.26 W
Mohican ≃	214	40.22 N	82.09 W
Mohican, Black Fork ≃	214	40.35 N	82.17 W
Mohican, Cape ≻	180	60.12 N	167.28 W
Mohican, Clear Fork ≃	214	40.35 N	82.12 W
Mohican, Jerome Fork ≃	214	40.45 N	82.23 W
Mohican, Lake Fork ≃	214	40.27 N	82.12 W
Mohican, Muddy Fork ≃	214	40.45 N	82.08 W
Mohican State Park ♠	214	40.37 N	82.16 W
Mohicanville Dam ◆[6]	214	40.44 N	82.09 W
Mohili ◆[8]	272c	19.06 N	72.53 E
Mohill	48	53.54 N	7.52 W
Mohlakeng	273d	26.13 S	27.42 E
Möhlau	54	51.44 N	12.21 E
Möhlin	58	47.34 N	7.51 E
Möhne ≃	52	51.27 N	7.57 E
Möhnestausee ⊜[1]	52	51.29 N	8.08 E
Mohns Ridge ✦[3]	16	72.30 N	5.00 E
Mohnton	208	40.17 N	75.59 W
Mohnyin	110	24.47 N	96.22 E
Moho ≃	236	16.04 N	88.52 W
Mohokare (Caledon) ≃	158	30.31 S	26.05 E
Moholm	40	58.37 N	14.02 E
Mohon	56	49.45 N	4.44 E
Mohorn	54	51.00 N	13.28 E
Mohoro	154	8.08 S	39.10 E
Möhringen	58	47.57 N	8.46 E
Mohrsville	208	40.28 N	75.59 W
Mohyla-Bel'mak, hora ∧[2]	78	47.20 N	36.35 E
Mohyla-Mechetna, hora ∧[2]	83	48.16 N	38.53 E
Mohyliv	78	48.52 N	34.29 E
Mohyliv-Podil's'kyy	78	48.27 N	27.48 E
Moi	26	58.28 N	6.32 E
Moiano, It.	68	40.39 N	14.28 E
Moiano, It.	68	41.05 N	14.32 E
Moindou	175f	21.42 S	165.41 E
Moinești	38	46.28 N	26.29 E
Moingbi	140	5.46 N	28.49 E
Moio Alcantara	70	37.54 N	15.03 E
Moiporá	255	16.34 S	50.42 W
Moira	48	54.30 N	6.17 W
Moira ≃	212	44.09 N	77.23 W
Moiraba	250	2.27 S	49.25 W
Moira Lake ⊜	212	44.29 N	77.27 W
Moirans	62	45.20 N	5.34 E
Moirans-en-Montagne	58	46.26 N	5.44 E
Mõisaküla	76	58.06 N	25.11 E
Moisdon	32	47.37 N	1.22 W
Moisejevka	86	58.05 N	76.16 E
Moisejevo Alabuška	76	51.54 N	42.06 E
Moisenay	261	48.34 N	2.44 E
Moisés Ville	252	30.43 S	61.29 W
Moisie	186	50.11 N	66.05 W
Moisie ≃	176	50.11 N	66.05 W
Moisie, Baie de ⊂	186	50.16 N	65.56 W
Moisling ◆[8]	54	53.50 N	10.38 E
Moison Creek ≃	281	42.18 N	82.40 W
Moissac	32	44.06 N	1.05 E
Moïssala	146	8.21 N	17.46 E
Moisselles	261	49.03 N	2.20 E
Moisson	261	49.05 N	1.40 E
Moisson, Forêt de ♠	261	49.03 N	1.39 E
Moissy-Cramayel	261	48.38 N	2.36 E
Moita	34	38.39 N	8.59 W
Moitaco	246	8.01 N	64.21 W
Moivre ≃	56	48.52 N	4.28 E
Mojácar	34	37.08 N	1.51 W
Mojana, Brazo ≃[1]	246	9.02 N	74.46 W
Mojave	228	35.03 N	118.10 W
Mojave ≃	204	35.06 N	116.04 W
Mojave Desert ◆[2]	204	35.00 N	117.00 W
Mojave River Forks Reservoir ⊜[1]	228	34.20 N	117.15 W
Moji	85	38.59 N	74.24 E
Mojiang	102	23.28 N	101.39 E
Mojicuaçu ≃	255	20.53 S	48.10 W
Moji das Cruzes	256	23.31 S	46.11 W
Mojiguaçu	256	22.22 S	46.57 W
Mojimirim	256	22.26 S	46.57 W
Mojjero ≃	74	68.44 N	103.42 E
Mojnalyk	88	51.18 N	95.33 E
Mojo	144	8.36 N	39.07 E
Mojoagung	115a	7.34 S	112.21 E
Mojokerto	115a	7.28 S	112.26 E
Mojosari	115a	7.31 S	112.33 E
Mojstrana	64	46.27 N	13.56 E
Moju	250	1.53 S	48.46 W
Moju ≃	250	1.40 S	48.25 W
Mojynkum	85	43.48 N	73.41 E
Mojynkum, peski ◆[2]	86	44.20 N	71.00 E
Mojynty	86	47.13 N	73.21 E
Mōka	94	36.26 N	140.01 E
Mokai	172	38.32 S	175.54 E
Mokāma	124	25.24 N	85.55 E
Mokambo	154	12.25 S	28.21 E
Mokane	219	38.40 N	91.52 W
Mokapu Peninsula ≻[1]	229c	21.27 N	157.45 W
Mokaria	152	2.00 N	23.20 E
Mokarta, Castello di ⊥	70	37.48 N	12.45 E
Mokau	172	38.41 S	174.37 E
Mokau ≃	172	38.42 S	174.37 E
Moke	102	30.14 N	100.01 E
Mokelumne ≃	226	38.13 N	121.28 W
Mokelumne, Middle Fork ≃	226	38.22 N	120.37 W
Mokelumne, North Fork ≃	226	38.22 N	120.37 W
Mokelumne, South Fork ≃	226	38.23 N	120.35 W
Mokelumne Aqueduct ≡[1]	226	37.54 N	122.07 W
Mokelumne Hill	226	38.18 N	120.42 W
Mokena	216	41.31 N	87.53 W
Mokhotlong	158	29.22 S	29.02 E
Mokil I[1]	14	6.40 N	159.47 E
Mokimbo	154	6.20 S	28.42 E
Mokino	80	57.27 N	49.11 E
Moklakan	88	54.56 N	118.56 E
Möklinta	40	60.05 N	16.32 E
Moknine	148	35.38 N	10.54 E
Mokochu, Khao ∧	110	15.56 N	99.06 E
Mokohinau Islands II	172	35.55 S	175.07 E
Mokokchūng	120	26.20 N	94.32 E
Mokolo, Cam.	146	10.45 N	13.48 E
Mokolo, R.D.C.	152	1.57 N	18.05 E
Mokolo ≃	156	23.14 S	27.43 E
Mokombe	152	0.14 S	23.48 E
Mokoreta ≃	172	46.21 S	168.51 E
Mokou	273b	4.13 S	15.13 E
Mokpalin	110	17.26 N	96.53 E
Mokp'o	98	34.48 N	126.22 E
Mokraja Jel'muta	80	46.51 N	41.41 E
Mokraja Ol'chovka	80	50.28 N	44.59 E
Mokra Sura ≃	78	48.19 N	35.09 E
Mokra Volnovakha ≃	83	47.30 N	37.15 E
Mokrisset	34	34.59 N	5.20 W
Mokri Yaly ≃	78	48.05 N	36.44 E
Mokrous	80	51.14 N	47.37 E
Mokrousovo	86	55.48 N	66.45 E
Mokroyelanchyk	83	47.42 N	38.31 E
Mokrušinskoje	86	57.31 N	93.11 E
Mokryj Gašun	80	46.53 N	42.45 E
Mokryj Jelančik ≃	83	47.08 N	38.20 E
Mokryj Kor	82	54.34 N	37.58 E
Mokša ≃	80	54.44 N	41.53 E
Mokšan	80	53.26 N	44.37 E
Moku	154	2.57 N	29.22 E
Mokuleia	229c	21.35 N	158.09 W
Mokumbusu	152	1.44 N	21.04 E
Mokvyn	78	50.57 N	26.48 E
Mokwa	150	9.20 N	5.02 E
Mol	56	51.11 N	5.06 E
Mola di Bari	68	41.04 N	17.05 E
Molale	144	10.08 N	39.42 E
Molalla	224	45.08 N	122.34 W
Molalla ≃	224	45.18 N	122.43 W
Molalla, North Fork ≃	224	45.05 N	122.29 W
Molanda	152	2.28 N	20.48 E
Molango	234	20.53 N	98.46 W
Molanosa	184	54.30 N	105.33 W
Moláoi	38	36.48 N	22.52 E
Molara, Isola I	71	40.52 N	9.43 E
Molaretto	62	45.10 N	7.00 E
Molat, Otok I	36	44.15 N	14.49 E
Molbergen	52	52.51 N	7.55 E
Molčanovka	83	46.52 N	38.37 E
Molčanovo	86	57.35 N	83.48 E
Mold	44	53.10 N	3.08 W
Moldary	86	50.47 N	78.29 E
Moldau → Vltava ≃	30	50.21 N	14.30 E
Moldavia □[9]	38	47.00 N	27.15 E
Moldavia → Moldova □[1]	38	47.00 N	29.00 E
Moldavija → Moldova □[1]	38	47.00 N	29.00 E
Molde	26	62.44 N	7.11 E
Moldotau, chrebet ⋀	85	41.35 N	74.40 E
Moldova □[1], Europe	22	47.00 N	29.00 E
Moldova □[1], Europe	38	47.00 N	29.00 E
Moldova ≃	38	46.54 N	26.58 E
Moldova Nouă	38	44.44 N	21.40 E
Moldoveanu, Vârful ∧	38	45.36 N	24.44 E
Môle ≃, Fr.	62	43.15 N	6.32 E
Mole ≃, Eng., U.K.	42	50.57 N	3.54 W
Mole ≃, Eng., U.K.	42	51.24 N	0.21 W
Môle, Cap du ≻	238	19.50 N	73.25 W
Mole Creek	166	41.33 S	146.24 E
Moledet	132	32.35 N	35.26 E
Molega Lake ⊜	186	44.22 N	64.53 W
Mole Game Reserve ◆[4]	150	9.30 N	2.00 W
Molegbe	152	4.14 N	20.53 E
Molenbeek-St.-Jean	50	50.51 N	4.19 E
Molepolole	156	24.25 S	25.30 E
Moléson ∧	58	46.33 N	7.01 E
Molėtai	76	55.14 N	25.25 E
Mole Valley □[8]	260	51.16 N	0.18 W
Molfetta	68	41.12 N	16.36 E
Molibagu	112	0.23 N	123.59 E
Molières-sur-Cèze	62	44.15 N	4.09 E
Molimiao	89	43.34 N	121.54 E
Molina	252	35.07 S	71.17 W
Molina de Aragón	34	40.51 N	1.53 W
Molina de Segura	34	38.03 N	1.12 W
Molina di Ledro	64	45.56 N	10.46 E
Molinara	68	41.18 N	14.54 E
Moline, Il., U.S.	190	41.30 N	90.30 W
Moline, Ks., U.S.	198	37.21 N	96.18 W
Moline, Mi., U.S.	216	42.44 N	85.39 W
Molinella	64	44.37 N	11.40 E
Molinges	58	46.21 N	5.46 E
Molingguan	106	31.50 N	118.50 E
Molini di Tures (Mühlen)	64	46.54 N	11.56 E
Molinière Point ≻	241k	12.05 N	61.45 W
Molino	194	30.43 N	87.18 W
Molino de Rosas ◆[8]	286a	19.22 N	99.13 W
Molinos	252	25.25 S	66.19 W
Molins de Rei	34	41.25 N	2.01 E
Moliro	154	8.13 S	30.34 E
Molise □[4]	66	41.35 N	14.30 E
Moliterno	68	40.14 N	15.52 E
Mölkau	54	51.20 N	12.26 E
Molkom	40	59.36 N	13.43 E
Möll ≃	64	46.50 N	13.26 E
Mollahasan	130	39.22 N	42.37 E
Mollāhāt	126	22.56 N	89.48 E
Mollakendi	130	38.36 N	39.20 E
Mollaro	64	46.16 N	11.05 E
Möllbrücke	64	46.50 N	13.22 E
Mölle	41	56.17 N	12.29 E
Möllen	263	51.35 N	6.42 E
Möllenbeck, Dtsch.	54	53.17 N	11.44 E
Möllenbeck, Dtsch.	54	53.23 N	13.20 E
Mollendo	248	17.02 S	72.01 W
Möllenhagen	54	53.32 N	12.56 E
Möllensee ⊜	264a	52.26 N	13.51 E
Mollepata	248	13.31 S	72.32 W
Moller, Port ⊂	180	55.51 N	160.25 W
Möllersdorf	264b	48.02 N	16.18 E
Mollet del Vallès	266d	41.33 N	2.13 E
Mollia	62	45.49 N	8.02 E
Molliens-Vidame	50	49.53 N	2.01 E
Mollington	262	53.13 N	2.55 W
Mollis	58	47.05 N	9.04 E
Mölln, Dtsch.	54	53.37 N	10.41 E
Molln, Öst.	61	47.53 N	14.15 E
Mollösund	26	58.04 N	11.28 E
Mollusk	208	37.43 N	76.32 W
Molly Ann Brook ≃	276	40.55 N	74.11 W
Mölnbo	40	59.03 N	17.25 E
Mölndal	26	57.39 N	12.01 E
Mölnlycke	26	57.39 N	12.09 E
Mölntorp	40	59.33 N	16.15 E
Molocaboc Island I	116	10.58 N	123.34 E
Molochans'k	78	47.12 N	35.36 E
Molochio	68	38.18 N	16.02 E
Molochna ≃	78	46.42 N	35.20 E
Molochnyy lyman ⊜	78	46.30 N	35.20 E
Moločnoje	76	59.17 N	39.41 E
Molócuè ≃	154	17.03 S	38.52 E
Molodežnaja ⊽[3]	9	67.35 S	46.35 E
Molodi	82	55.17 N	37.31 E
Molodo	150	14.14 N	6.02 W
Molodogvardejskoje	86	54.03 N	70.44 E
Molodohvariys'k	83	48.20 N	39.40 E
Molodoj Tud	76	56.26 N	33.36 E
Molod'ožnyj	89	50.23 N	136.48 E
Mologa ≃	76	58.50 N	37.11 E
Molokai I	229a	21.07 N	157.00 W
Molokai Fracture Zone ✦	16	23.00 N	130.00 W
Molokča ≃	82	56.15 N	38.45 E
Molokini I	229a	20.38 N	156.30 W
Molokovo, Ross.	76	58.10 N	36.45 E
Molokovo, Ross.	82	55.34 N	37.52 E
Moloma ≃	24	58.20 N	48.28 E
Molong	166	33.06 S	148.52 E
Molonglo ≃	171b	35.15 S	148.58 E
Molopo ≃	156	28.30 S	20.13 E
Molotov → Perm'	86	58.00 N	56.15 E
Molotovsk → Severodvinsk	24	64.34 N	39.50 E
Molou	146	13.42 N	21.44 E
Moloundou	152	2.03 N	15.10 E
Molowaie	152	5.47 S	23.20 E
Moloy	58	47.32 N	4.55 E
Molsheim	58	48.32 N	7.29 E
Molson Lake ⊜	184	54.12 N	96.45 W
Molteno	158	31.22 S	26.22 E
Moltrasio	58	45.52 N	9.05 E
Molu, Pulau I	164	6.45 S	131.33 E
Molucas, Islas → Maluku II	108	2.00 S	128.00 E
Molucas, Mar de la → Maluku, Laut ⩡[2]	108	0.00	125.00 E
Moluccas → Maluku II	108	2.00 S	128.00 E
Molucca Sea → Maluku, Laut ⩡[2]	108	0.00	125.00 E
Molukken → Maluku II	108	2.00 S	128.00 E
Molumbo	154	15.27 S	30.15 E
Molundo	116	7.56 N	124.23 E
Moluques → Maluku II	108	2.00 S	128.00 E
Molveno, Lago di ⊜	64	46.08 N	10.57 E
Molvoticy	76	57.25 N	32.20 E
Molžaninovo	82	55.56 N	37.22 E
Moma, Moç.	154	16.44 S	39.14 E
Moma, R.D.C.	152	1.36 S	23.57 E
Moma ≃	74	66.26 N	143.06 E
Momanga	156	18.12 S	21.42 E
Momats ≃	164	5.20 S	137.47 E
Momax	234	21.56 N	103.19 W
Momba ≃	154	8.28 S	32.40 E
Mombaça	250	5.45 S	39.38 W
Mombaça, Corrego ≃	287b	23.46 S	46.47 W
Mombachito, Cerro ∧	236	12.24 N	85.34 W
Mombacho, Volcán ∧[1]	236	11.50 N	85.58 W
Mombango	152	1.45 N	24.26 E
Mombaruzzo	62	44.46 N	8.27 E
Mombasa	154	4.03 S	39.40 E
Mombetsu	92a	44.21 N	143.22 E
Mombo	154	4.53 S	38.17 E
Mombongo	152	1.39 N	23.09 E
Momboyo ≃	152	0.16 S	19.00 E
Mombuey	34	42.02 N	6.20 W
Mombum	164	8.23 S	138.51 E
Momčilgrad	38	41.32 N	25.25 E
Momence	216	41.10 N	87.39 W
Momfafa, Tanjung ≻	164	0.18 S	131.20 E
Momi	175g	17.55 S	177.17 E
Momignies	50	50.02 N	4.10 E
Mömlingen	56	49.52 N	9.05 E
Mommark	41	54.55 N	10.03 E
Mommenheim	56	48.45 N	7.39 E
Momo	152	1.52 N	11.48 E
Momotombo, Volcán ∧[1]	236	12.26 N	86.33 W
Momozaka	270	34.51 N	135.02 E
Mompog Island I	116	13.31 N	122.11 E
Mompog Pass ᛘ	116	13.34 N	122.13 E
Mompono	152	0.04 N	21.48 E
Mompós	246	9.14 N	74.26 W
Momskij chrebet ⋀	74	66.00 N	146.00 E
Mon	110	18.31 N	96.38 E
Mon □[8]	110	17.30 N	97.00 E
Møn I	41	55.00 N	12.20 E
Mon ≃	110	20.20 N	94.54 E
Mona	200	39.48 N	111.51 W
Mona, Canal de la ᛘ	238	18.30 N	67.45 W
Mona, Isla de I	238	18.05 N	67.54 W
Mona, Punta ≻	236	9.38 N	82.37 W
Monaca	214	40.41 N	80.16 W
Monach, Sound of ᛘ	46	57.34 N	7.35 W
Monach Islands II	46	57.31 N	7.40 W
Monaci, Fiume dei ≃	70	37.24 N	14.48 E
Monaco	62	43.42 N	7.23 E
Monaco □[1], Europe	22	43.45 N	7.25 E
Monaco □[1], Europe	62	43.45 N	7.25 E
Monadhliath Mountains ⋀	46	57.10 N	4.00 W
Monadnock Mountain ∧	207	42.52 N	72.07 W
Monagas □[3]	246	9.20 N	63.00 W
Monaghan	48	54.15 N	6.58 W
Monaghan □[6]	48	54.10 N	7.00 W
Monagrillo	236	7.59 N	80.26 W
Monahans	196	31.35 N	102.53 W
Monahans Draw V	196	31.55 N	101.46 W
Monahans Sandhills State Park ♠	196	31.38 N	102.50 W
Monakino	89	43.24 N	133.29 E
Mona Lake ⊜	216	43.11 N	86.17 W
Monamolin	48	52.33 N	6.20 W
Monango	198	46.10 N	98.35 W
Monapo	154	14.57 S	40.17 E
Monapo ≃	154	15.07 S	40.33 E
Mona Quimbundo	152	9.55 S	19.58 E
Monar, Loch ⊜	46	57.25 N	5.06 W
Monarch	192	34.43 N	81.35 W
Monarch Mountain ∧	182	51.54 N	125.53 W
Monarch Pass)(	200	38.30 N	106.19 W
Monaro Range ⋀	171b	36.22 S	149.03 E
Monarto South	168b	35.08 S	139.08 E
Monaš	80	46.58 N	50.36 E
Monashee Mountains ⋀	182	50.30 N	118.30 W
Monashee Provincial Park ♠	182	50.28 N	118.11 W
Monash University ⊽[2]	274b	37.55 S	145.08 E
Monasterace	68	38.27 N	16.33 E
Monasterevin	48	53.07 N	7.02 W
Monasterolo di Savigliano	62	44.40 N	7.37 E
Monastir, It.	71	39.23 N	9.02 E
Monastir → Bitola, Mak.	38	41.01 N	21.20 E
Monastir, Tun.	148	35.47 N	10.50 E
Monastyrščina	76	54.21 N	31.50 E
Monastyryshche	78	49.00 N	29.49 E
Monastyrys'ka	78	49.06 N	25.11 E
Monatélé	152	4.16 N	11.12 E
Mona Vale	170	33.41 S	151.18 E
Monbulk	274b	37.52 S	145.25 E
Monbulk Creek ≃	274b	37.54 S	145.15 E
Moncada	116	15.44 N	120.34 E
Moncalieri	62	45.00 N	7.41 E
Moncalvo	62	45.03 N	8.16 E
Monção, Bra.	250	3.30 S	45.15 W
Moncão, Port.	34	42.05 N	8.29 W
Monceau-sur-Sambre	50	50.25 N	4.22 E
Mončegorsk	24	67.54 N	32.58 E
Mönch ∧	58	46.34 N	7.59 E
Mönchdorf	61	48.21 N	14.48 E
Mönchengladbach	56	51.12 N	6.28 E
Mönchengladbach, Flughafen ⊠	263	51.14 N	6.29 E
Mönchhof	61	47.52 N	16.56 E
Monchique	34	37.19 N	8.33 W
Mönchweiler	58	48.06 N	8.25 E
Moncks Corner	192	33.11 N	80.00 W
Monclova	232	26.54 N	101.25 W
Moncontour	32	48.21 N	2.39 W
Moncoutant	32	46.43 N	0.35 W
Moncton	186	46.06 N	64.47 W
Mondaí	252	27.05 S	53.25 W
Mondaino	66	43.51 N	12.41 E
Mondavio	66	43.40 N	12.58 E
Monday ≃	252	25.33 S	54.41 W
Mondego ≃	34	40.09 N	8.52 W
Mondego, Cabo ≻	34	40.11 N	8.55 W

Symbols in the index entries represent the broad categories identified in the key at the right. Symbols with superior numbers (⋀[1]) identify subcategories (see complete key on page I · 1).

Symbole im Register stellen die rechts im Schlüssel erklärten Kategorien dar. Symbole mit hochgestellten Ziffern (⋀[1]) bezeichnen Unterabteilungen einer Kategorie (vgl. vollständiger Schlüssel auf Seite I · 1).

Los símbolos incluídos en el texto del índice representan las grandes categorías identificadas con la clave a la derecha. Los símbolos con numeros en su parte superior (⋀[1]) identifican las subcategorías (véase la clave completa en la página I · 1).

Les symboles de l'index représentent les catégories indiquées dans la légende à droite. Les symboles suivis d'un indice (⋀[1]) représentent des sous-catégories (voir légende complète à la page I · 1).

Os símbolos incluídos no texto do índice representam as grandes categorias identificadas com a chave à direita. Os símbolos com números em sua parte superior (⋀[1]) identificam as subcategorias (veja-se a chave completa à página I · 1).

English	Deutsch	Español	Français	Português
∧ Mountain	Berg	Montaña	Montagne	Montanha
⋀ Mountains	Gebirge	Montañas	Montagnes	Montanhas
)(Pass	Paß	Paso	Col	Passo
V Valley, Canyon	Tal, Cañon	Valle, Cañón	Vallée, Canyon	Vale, Canhão
≚ Plain	Ebene	Llano	Plaine	Planície
≻ Cape	Kap	Cabo	Cap	Cabo
I Island	Insel	Isla	Île	Ilha
II Islands	Inseln	Islas	Îles	Ilhas
⊥ Other Topographic Features	Andere Topographische Objekte	Otros Elementos Topográficos	Autres données topographiques	Outros acidentes topográficos

Mond-Monu I · 115

ESPAÑOL — Nombre / Página / Lat.°′ / Long.°′ W = Oeste
FRANÇAIS — Nom / Page / Lat.°′ / Long.°′ W = Ouest
PORTUGUÊS — Nome / Página / Lat.°′ / Long.°′ W = Oeste

Mondello 70 38.13 N 13.20 E
Mondeodo 112 3.33 S 122.12 E
Mondeor 273d 26.17 S 28.00 E
Mondimbi 152 1.43 N 22.58 E
Mondo, Tan. 154 4.59 S 35.54 E
Mondo, Tchad 146 13.47 N 15.32 E
Mondolè, Monte ʌ 62 44.13 N 7.46 E
Mondolfo 66 43.45 N 13.06 E
Mondombe 152 0.53 S 22.45 E
Mondoñedo 34 43.26 N 7.22 W
Mondorf-les-Bains 56 49.31 N 6.16 E
Mondoro 150 14.40 N 1.57 W
Mondoubleau 50 47.59 N 0.54 E
Mondovi 190 44.34 N 91.40 W
Mondragon, Fr. 62 44.14 N 4.43 E
Mondragon, Pil. 116 12.31 N 124.45 E
Mondragone 68 41.07 N 13.53 E
Mondrain Island I 162 34.08 S 122.15 E
Mondsee 64 47.52 N 13.21 E
Mondsee ⊜ 64 47.49 N 13.23 E
Monds Island I 285 39.50 N 75.19 W
Mondy 88 51.40 N 100.59 E
Monee 216 41.25 N 87.45 W
Moneglia 62 44.14 N 9.30 E
Monemvasía 38 36.41 N 23.03 E
Monero 200 36.54 N 106.52 W
Moneron, ostrov I 89 46.17 N 141.15 E
Monesiglio 62 44.28 N 8.07 E
Monessen 214 40.08 N 79.53 W
Monesterio 34 38.05 N 6.16 W
Monestier-de-Clermont 62 44.54 N 5.38 E
Monetnyj 86 57.03 N 60.53 E
Monett 194 36.55 N 93.55 W
Monette 194 35.53 N 90.20 W
Money Creek ≏ 216 40.40 N 88.58 W
Moneygall 48 52.53 N 7.57 W
Moneymore 48 54.42 N 6.40 W
Monfalcone 64 45.49 N 13.32 E
Monferrato □[9] 62 44.55 N 8.05 E
Monflanquin 32 44.32 N 0.46 E
Monforte 34 39.03 N 7.26 W
Monforte de Lemos 34 42.31 N 7.30 W
Monforte San Giorgio 70 38.09 N 15.23 E
Monfort Heights 218 39.12 N 84.37 W
Monga 152 4.12 N 22.49 E
Mongaguá 256 24.06 S 46.37 W
Mongai-Musenge 152 4.04 S 19.34 E
Mongala ≏ 152 1.53 N 19.46 E
Mongalla 154 5.12 N 31.46 E
Mongalla Game Reserve ◆[4] 154 5.12 N 31.33 E
Mongandjo 152 1.21 N 24.20 E
Mongarlowe ≏ 170 35.15 S 149.52 E
Mongat 266d 41.28 N 2.17 E
Mongaup ≏ 210 41.25 N 74.45 W
Mongaup Valley 210 41.40 N 74.47 W
Mongbwalu 154 1.57 N 30.02 E
Mongbyŏn-ni 271b 37.40 N 126.44 E
Mong Cai 110 21.32 N 107.58 E
Monge ʌ 266c 38.46 N 9.26 W
Monger, Îles II 186 51.05 N 58.45 W
Mongeri 150 8.19 N 11.44 W
Mongers Lake ⊜ 162 29.15 S 117.05 E
Monggon Qulu 89 48.35 N 119.49 E
Monggŭmp'o 98 38.09 N 124.47 E
Mōng Hai 110 20.46 N 99.49 E
Mōng Hawm 110 23.51 N 98.20 E
Monghidoro 66 44.13 N 11.19 E
Mōng Hpāyak 110 20.53 N 99.54 E
Mōng Hsat 110 20.32 N 99.15 E
Monghyr
→ Munger 124 25.23 N 86.28 E
Mongi ≏ 164 6.35 S 147.35 E
Mongiana 68 38.31 N 16.19 E
Mongibello
→ Etna, Monte ʌ[1] 70 37.46 N 15.00 E
Mongiuffi 70 37.55 N 15.17 E
Mōng Küng 110 21.36 N 97.32 E
Mōng Ma 110 21.37 N 99.54 E
Mōng Mit 110 23.07 N 96.41 E
Mōng Nai 110 20.31 N 97.52 E
Mōng Nawng 110 21.39 N 98.08 E
Mongo, Tchad 146 12.11 N 18.42 E
Mongo, In., U.S. 216 41.41 N 85.17 W
Mongo ≏ 150 9.34 N 12.11 W
Mongoj 88 53.57 N 113.50 E
Mongol Altajn nuruu ⋏ 90 46.30 N 93.00 E
Mongol Ard Uls
→ Mongolia □[1] 90 46.00 N 105.00 E
Mongolei
→ Mongolia □[1] 90 46.00 N 105.00 E
Mongol els ◆[2] 88 47.45 N 94.30 E
Mongolia (Mongol Ard Uls) □[1] 90 46.00 N 105.00 E
Mongolie
→ Mongolia □[1] 90 46.00 N 105.00 E
Mongomo 152 1.38 N 11.19 E
Möngön Mor't 88 48.11 N 108.29 E
Mongororo 146 12.01 N 22.28 E
Mongoumba 152 3.38 N 18.36 E
Mōng Pai 110 19.44 N 97.05 E
Mōng Pan 110 20.19 N 98.22 E
Mōng Pawn 110 20.49 N 97.28 E
Mōng Ping 110 22.22 N 99.02 E
Mongpong ≏ 116 12.44 N 120.48 E
Mongrando 62 45.31 N 8.00 E
Mōng Si 110 23.40 N 98.23 E
Mong Tung Hang 271d 22.20 N 114.02 E
Mongu 152 15.15 S 23.09 E
Mônguа 152 16.43 S 15.23 E
Monguelfo (Welsberg) 64 46.45 N 12.06 E
Monguno 146 12.40 N 13.38 E
Mōng Yai 110 22.25 N 98.02 E
Mōng Yawng 110 21.11 N 100.22 E
Monheim, Dtsch. 56 48.50 N 10.51 E
Monheim, Dtsch. 56 51.05 N 6.52 E
Moniaive 44 55.12 N 3.55 W
Mönichkirchen 61 47.31 N 16.02 E
Monico 190 45.34 N 89.09 W
Monida Pass)(202 44.33 N 112.18 W
Mon Idée 50 49.53 N 4.23 E
Monie 152 4.00 S 17.22 E
Monie Bay c 208 38.13 N 75.51 W
Monie Creek ≏ 208 38.14 N 75.50 W
Monifieth 46 56.29 N 2.49 W
Monimail 46 56.18 N 3.08 W
Moninger 214 40.14 N 80.13 W
Monino 82 55.50 N 38.11 E
Moniquirá 246 5.52 N 73.36 W
Mõniste 76 57.35 N 26.33 E
Monistrol-d'Allier 62 44.57 N 3.38 E
Monistrol-sur-Loire 62 45.17 N 4.10 E
Monitor Range ⋏ 204 38.45 N 116.30 W
Monitor Valley V 204 39.00 N 116.40 W
Monívea 48 53.23 N 8.43 W
Monjolo 256 22.49 S 42.57 W
Monk, Pointe > 275a 45.29 N 73.57 W
Monkayo 116 7.50 N 126.03 E
Mönkebude 54 53.46 N 13.57 E
Monken Hadley ◆[8] 260 51.40 N 0.11 W
Monkey Bay 154 14.05 S 34.55 E
Monkey River 236 16.22 N 88.29 W
Mońki 30 53.24 N 22.49 E
Monkira 166 24.49 S 140.34 E
Monkoto 152 1.38 S 20.39 E
Monks Heath 262 53.16 N 2.14 W
Monkton 212 43.35 N 81.05 W
Monmouth, Wales, U.K. 42 51.50 N 2.43 W
Monmouth, Il., U.S. 190 40.54 N 90.38 W
Monmouth, In., U.S. 216 40.52 N 84.57 W
Monmouth, Or., U.S. 202 44.50 N 123.13 W
Monmouth □[6] 208 40.16 N 74.17 W
Monmouth Beach 276 40.19 N 73.58 W
Monmouth Hills 276 40.24 N 74.00 W
Monmouth Junction 208 40.22 N 74.32 W
Monmouth Mountain ʌ 182 51.00 N 123.47 W
Monnickendam 52 52.27 N 5.02 E
Monnow ≏ 42 51.48 N 2.42 W
Mono □[5] 150 6.45 N 1.50 E
Mono □[6] 226 38.18 N 119.22 W
Mono ≏ 150 6.17 N 1.51 E
Mono, Caño ≏ 246 4.25 N 67.47 W
Mono, Punta > 236 11.36 N 83.39 W
Monobe 96 33.42 N 133.53 E
Monobe ≏ 96 33.32 N 133.41 E
Monocacy ≏ 208 39.13 N 77.27 W
Monocacy Station 208 40.16 N 75.46 W
Monogarovo 82 54.42 N 38.45 E
Mono Island I 175e 7.21 S 155.34 E
Mono Lake ⊜ 204 38.00 N 119.00 W
Monomoy Island I 207 41.35 N 69.59 W
Monomoy Point > 207 41.33 N 70.02 W
Monon 216 40.52 N 86.52 W
Monona, Ia., U.S. 190 43.03 N 91.23 W
Monona, Wi., U.S. 216 43.03 N 89.20 W
Monona, Lake ⊜ 216 43.03 N 89.22 W
Monongahela 214 40.12 N 79.55 W
Monongahela ≏ 188 40.27 N 80.00 W
Monongahela Brook ≏ 285 39.47 N 75.09 W
Monopoli 68 40.57 N 17.19 E
Monor 30 47.21 N 19.27 E
Mono Road Station 275b 43.51 N 79.51 W
Monòver 34 38.26 N 0.50 W
Monowai, Lake ⊜ 172 45.52 S 167.27 E
Monponsett 207 42.01 N 70.50 W
Monponsett Pond ⊜ 283 42.01 N 70.51 W
Monreal 34 42.42 N 1.30 W
Monreal del Campo 34 40.47 N 1.21 W
Monreale 70 38.05 N 13.17 E
Monreale, Castello di ⊥ 71 39.38 N 8.49 E
Monroe, Ct., U.S. 207 41.19 N 73.12 W
Monroe, Fl., U.S. 220 25.52 N 81.06 W
Monroe, Ga., U.S. 192 33.47 N 83.42 W
Monroe, In., U.S. 216 40.44 N 84.56 W
Monroe, Ia., U.S. 190 41.31 N 93.06 W
Monroe, La., U.S. 194 32.30 N 92.07 W
Monroe, Mi., U.S. 214 41.54 N 83.23 W
Monroe, Ne., U.S. 198 41.28 N 97.35 W
Monroe, N.J., U.S. 276 41.06 N 74.38 W
Monroe, N.Y., U.S. 210 41.19 N 74.11 W
Monroe, N.C., U.S. 192 34.59 N 80.32 W
Monroe, Oh., U.S. 218 39.26 N 84.21 W
Monroe, Or., U.S. 202 44.18 N 123.17 W
Monroe, Ut,. U.S. 200 38.37 N 112.07 W
Monroe, Va., U.S. 192 37.30 N 79.07 W
Monroe, Wa., U.S. 224 47.51 N 121.58 W
Monroe, Wi., U.S. 190 42.36 N 89.38 W
Monroe □[6], Fl., U.S. 220 25.10 N 81.10 W
Monroe □[6], Il., U.S. 219 38.20 N 90.09 W
Monroe □[6], In., U.S. 218 39.10 N 86.26 W
Monroe □[6], Mi., U.S. 216 41.55 N 83.26 W
Monroe □[6], Mo., U.S. 219 39.30 N 92.00 W
Monroe □[6], N.Y., U.S. 210 43.10 N 77.36 W
Monroe □[6], Pa., U.S. 210 40.59 N 75.12 W
Monroe, Lake ⊜ 220 28.52 N 81.16 W
Monroe Bridge 207 42.43 N 72.56 W
Monroe Center, Ct., U.S. 207 41.20 N 73.12 W
Monroe Center, Il., U.S. 216 42.06 N 89.00 W
Monroe City, In., U.S. 194 38.36 N 87.21 W
Monroe City, Mo., U.S. 219 39.39 N 91.44 W
Monroe City, Tx., U.S. 222 29.47 N 94.35 W
Monroe Lake ⊜[1] 218 39.05 N 86.25 W
Monroe Manor 216 41.36 N 86.40 W
Monroeton 210 41.43 N 76.30 W
Monroeville, Al., U.S. 194 31.31 N 87.19 W
Monroeville, In., U.S. 216 40.58 N 84.52 W
Monroeville, N.J., U.S. 208 39.37 N 75.09 W
Monroeville, Oh., U.S. 214 41.14 N 82.41 W
Monroeville, Pa., U.S. 214 40.26 N 79.47 W
Monroeville Mall ◆[9] 279b 40.26 N 79.48 W
Monrovia, Liber. 150 6.18 N 10.47 W
Monrovia, Ca., U.S. 228 34.08 N 117.59 W
Monrovia, In., U.S. 218 39.34 N 86.28 W
Monrovia Mountain Park ♠ 280 34.10 N 118.10 W
Monrovia Peak ʌ 280 34.13 N 117.58 W
Mons (Bergen), Bel. 50 50.27 N 3.56 E
Mons, Fr. 62 43.41 N 6.43 E
Monschau 56 50.33 N 6.14 E
Monse 112 4.07 S 123.15 E
Monsefú 248 6.52 S 79.52 W
Monselice 64 45.14 N 11.45 E
Monsenhor Hipólito 250 6.59 S 41.07 W
Monsenhor Paulo 256 21.46 S 45.33 W
Monsenhor Tabosa 250 4.47 S 40.04 W
Monsey 210 41.06 N 74.04 W
Monsheim 56 49.38 N 8.12 E
Møns Klint ⊥[4] 41 54.58 N 12.33 E
Monsols 58 46.13 N 4.31 E
Monson, Me., U.S. 188 45.17 N 69.30 W
Monson, Ma., U.S. 207 42.06 N 72.19 W
Monster 52 52.02 N 4.10 E
Mönsterås 26 57.02 N 16.26 E
Monsummano Terme 66 43.52 N 10.49 E
Montà 62 44.48 N 7.57 E
Montabaur 56 50.26 N 7.50 E
Montafon V 58 47.02 N 9.57 E
Montagano 66 41.39 N 14.40 E
Montagnana 64 45.14 N 11.28 E
Montagnareale 70 38.07 N 14.57 E
Montagne d'Ambre, Parque National de la ♠ 157b 12.40 S 49.05 E
Montagnola ⋏ 66 43.17 N 11.11 E
Montagrier 32 45.16 N 0.29 E
Montagu 158 33.45 S 20.08 E
Montague, P.E., Can. 186 46.10 N 62.39 W
Montague, Ca., U.S. 204 41.43 N 122.31 W
Montague, Ma., U.S. 207 42.32 N 72.32 W
Montague, Mi., U.S. 190 43.25 N 86.21 W
Montague, Tx., U.S. 196 33.40 N 97.43 W
Montague, Isla I 232 31.45 N 114.48 W
Montague City 207 42.35 N 72.35 W
Montague Island I 180 60.00 N 147.30 W
Montague Peak ʌ 180 60.15 N 147.01 W
Montagu Island I 18 58.25 S 26.20 W
Montaigle, Château de ⊥ 56 50.18 N 4.49 E
Montaigu 32 46.59 N 1.19 W
Montaigut-en-Combraille 32 46.11 N 2.48 E
Montainville 261 48.53 N 1.52 E
Montaione 66 43.33 N 10.55 E
Montajtas 85 42.06 N 68.58 E
Montalba 222 31.53 N 95.38 W
Montalbán 34 40.50 N 0.48 W
Montalbancito 286c 10.28 N 66.59 W
Montalbano Elicona 70 38.02 N 15.01 E
Montalbano Ionico 68 40.17 N 16.34 E
Montalcino 66 43.03 N 11.29 E
Montaldo di Cosola 62 44.40 N 9.11 E
Montale 66 43.56 N 11.01 E
Montalegre 34 41.49 N 7.48 W
Montalet-le-Bois 261 49.03 N 1.50 E
Montalieu-Vercieu 62 45.49 N 5.24 E
Montallegro 70 37.23 N 13.21 E
Mont Alto 208 39.50 N 77.33 W
Montalto ʌ 68 38.10 N 15.55 E
Montalto delle Marche 66 42.59 N 13.36 E
Montalto di Castro 66 42.21 N 11.37 E
Montalto Ligure 62 43.56 N 7.51 E
Montalto Uffugo 68 39.25 N 16.10 E
Montalvin Manor 226 37.59 N 122.21 W
Montana, Blg. 38 43.25 N 23.13 E
Montana, Schw. 58 46.18 N 7.29 E
Montana, Ak., U.S. 180 62.05 N 150.04 W
Montana □[3], U.S. 178 47.00 N 110.00 W
Montana □[3], U.S. 202 47.00 N 110.00 W
Montana de Oro State Park ♠ 226 35.15 N 120.50 W
Montana Indian Reserve ◆[4] 182 52.43 N 113.25 W
Montanaro 62 45.14 N 7.51 E
Montánchez 34 39.13 N 6.09 W
Montandon 210 40.58 N 76.51 W
Montanha 255 18.08 S 40.21 W
Montano Antilia 68 40.10 N 15.22 E
Montara 226 37.33 N 122.31 W
Montara Beach ♠ 282 37.33 N 122.31 W
Montara Mountain ⋏ 282 37.32 N 122.27 W
Montargil 34 39.05 N 8.10 W
Montargis 50 48.00 N 2.45 E
Montataire 50 49.16 N 2.26 E
Montauban 32 44.01 N 1.21 E
Montauban, Lac ⊜ 206 46.52 N 72.10 W
Montauban-les-Mines 206 46.50 N 72.20 W
Montauk 207 41.02 N 71.57 W
Montauk, Lake ⊜ 207 41.04 N 71.55 W
Montauk Point > 207 41.04 N 71.52 W
Montauroux 62 43.37 N 6.46 E
Monta Vista 282 37.19 N 122.03 W
Montazzoli 66 41.57 N 14.26 E
Montbard 50 47.37 N 4.20 E
Montbarrey 58 47.01 N 5.39 E
Montbazon 50 47.17 N 0.43 E
Montbéliard 58 47.31 N 6.48 E
Mont Belvieu 222 29.50 N 94.53 W
Montbenoît 58 46.59 N 6.28 E
Montblanc 34 41.22 N 1.10 E
Mont Blanc, Tunnel du ◆[5] 58 45.50 N 6.53 E
Mont-Bonvillers 56 49.20 N 5.51 E
Montbovon 58 46.29 N 7.03 E
Montbozon 58 47.28 N 6.16 E
Montbrison 62 45.36 N 4.03 E
Montbron 32 45.40 N 0.30 E
Montbronn 56 48.59 N 7.19 E
Montcada i Reixas 266d 41.29 N 2.11 E
Montcalm □[6] 206 46.20 N 74.20 W
Montceau-les-Mines 58 46.40 N 4.22 E
Montcenis 58 46.47 N 4.23 E
Mont Cenis, Col du)(62 45.15 N 6.54 E
Mont Cenis, Lac du ⊜ 62 45.14 N 6.55 E
Montcevelles, Lac ⊜ 186 51.07 N 60.38 W
Montchanin, Fr. 58 46.45 N 4.27 E
Montchanin, De., U.S. 285 39.47 N 75.35 W
Montchauvet 261 48.54 N 1.38 E
Montclair, Ca., U.S. 228 34.06 N 117.41 W
Montclair, N.J., U.S. 210 40.49 N 74.12 W
Montclair State College ◆[2] 276 40.51 N 74.12 W
Mont Clare 285 40.08 N 75.30 W
Montcornet 50 49.41 N 4.01 E
Montdale 210 41.32 N 75.37 W
Mont-de-Marsan 32 43.53 N 0.30 W
Montdidier 50 49.39 N 2.34 E
Mont-Dore 175f 22.16 S 166.34 E
Monte, Castel del ⊥ 68 41.05 N 16.16 E
Monte, Cima del ʌ 66 42.47 N 10.23 E
Monte, Laguna del ⊜, Arg. 252 37.00 S 62.28 W
Monte, Laguna del ⊜, Arg. 258 35.28 S 58.49 W
Montea ʌ 68 39.40 N 15.57 E
Monte Adone, Galleria di ◆[5] 64 44.21 N 11.25 E
Monteagle 194 35.15 N 85.50 W
Monteagudo 248 19.49 S 63.59 W
Monte Albán ⊥ 234 17.02 N 96.45 W
Monte Alegre, Bra. 250 2.01 S 54.04 W
Monte Alegre, Bra. 250 6.04 S 35.20 W
Monte Alegre de Goiás 255 13.14 S 47.10 W
Monte Alegre de Minas 255 18.52 S 48.52 W
Monte Alegre de Sergipe 250 10.02 S 37.33 W
Monte Alegre do Piauí 250 9.46 S 45.18 W
Monte Alegre do Sul 256 22.40 S 46.41 W
Monte Azul 255 15.09 S 42.53 W
Monte Azul Paulista 255 20.55 S 48.38 W
Montebello, P.Q., Can. 206 45.39 N 74.56 W
Montebello, It. 62 45.00 N 9.06 E
Montebello, P.R. 240m 18.22 N 66.31 W
Montebello, Ca., U.S. 228 34.00 N 118.06 W
Montebello Iónico 68 37.59 N 15.45 E
Monte Bello Islands II 162 20.25 S 115.32 E
Montebello Vicentino 64 45.27 N 11.23 E
Montebelluna 64 45.47 N 12.03 E
Monte Belo 256 21.20 S 46.23 W
Montebruno 62 44.31 N 9.15 E
Monte Buey 252 32.55 S 62.27 W
Montecalvo Irpino 68 41.11 N 15.02 E
Monte Campatri 267a 41.48 N 12.44 E
Montecarlo 252 26.34 S 54.47 W
Monte Carlo ◆[8] 62 43.44 N 7.25 E
Monte Carmelo 255 18.43 S 47.29 W
Montecarotto 66 43.31 N 13.04 E
Monte Caseros 252 30.15 S 57.39 W
Montecassiano 66 43.21 N 13.26 E
Montecassino, Abbazia di ⊍[1] 66 41.29 N 13.48 E
Montecastrilli 66 42.39 N 12.29 E
Montecatini-Terme 66 43.53 N 10.46 E
Monte Cavallo 66 42.59 N 13.00 E
Montecchio 66 43.51 N 12.46 E
Montecchio Emilia 64 44.42 N 10.27 E
Montecchio Maggiore 64 45.30 N 11.24 E
Montecelio 66 42.01 N 12.44 E
Monte Ceneri, Passo)(58 46.08 N 8.55 E
Montechiaro d'Asti 62 45.01 N 8.07 E
Montechiarugolo 64 44.42 N 10.25 E
Monte Chingolo ◆[8] 288 34.45 S 58.20 W
Monteciccardo 66 43.49 N 12.48 E
Montecilfone 66 41.54 N 14.50 E
Montecillos, Cordillera de ⋏ 236 14.25 N 87.51 W
Montecito 204 34.26 N 119.37 W
Monte Comán 252 34.36 S 67.54 W
Montecorice 68 40.14 N 14.59 E
Montecorvino Pugliano 68 40.41 N 14.57 E
Montecorvino Rovella 68 40.42 N 14.59 E
Montecosaro 66 43.19 N 13.37 E
Monte Creek 182 50.39 N 119.57 W
Montecreto 64 44.14 N 10.41 E
Montecristi, Ec. 246 1.03 S 80.40 W
Monte Cristi, Rep. Dom. 238 19.52 N 71.39 W
Monte Cristo 248 14.43 S 61.14 W
Montecristo, Isola di I 36 42.20 N 10.19 E
Montecuccolo ⊍[1] 64 44.19 N 10.50 E
Montedinove 66 42.58 N 13.35 E
Monte di Procida 68 40.48 N 14.03 E
Monte do Carmo 250 10.45 S 48.07 W
Montedoro 70 37.27 N 13.49 E
Monte Escobedo 234 22.18 N 103.35 W
Monte Estoril 266c 38.42 N 9.24 W
Montefalcione 68 40.58 N 14.53 E
Montefalco 66 42.54 N 12.39 E
Montefalcone di Val Fortore 68 41.20 N 15.00 E
Montefano 66 43.25 N 13.26 E
Montefeltro ◆[1] 66 43.50 N 12.15 E
Montefiascone 66 42.32 N 12.02 E
Montefiorino 64 44.22 N 10.37 E
Monteforte d'Alpone 64 45.25 N 11.17 E
Monteforte Irpino 68 40.54 N 14.42 E
Montefrío 34 37.19 N 4.01 W
Montegallo 66 42.50 N 13.19 E
Montegiordano 68 40.02 N 16.32 E
Montegiorgio 66 43.08 N 13.32 E
Monte Giovi, Passo di (Jaufen Pass))(64 46.50 N 11.19 E
Montego Bay 241q 18.28 N 77.55 W
Montegranaro 66 43.14 N 13.38 E
Monte Grande 252 30.06 S 70.31 W
Monte Grimano 66 43.52 N 12.29 E
Montegrotto Terme 64 45.19 N 11.46 E
Montegut 194 29.28 N 90.33 W
Monteiasi 68 40.30 N 17.23 E
Monteiro 250 7.53 S 37.07 W
Monteiro Lobato 256 22.58 S 45.50 W
Monteith, Mount ʌ 182 55.45 N 122.30 W
Montejicar 34 37.34 N 3.30 W
Montejinni 164 16.40 S 131.45 E
Montelavar 266c 38.51 N 9.20 W
Monteleone di Puglia 68 41.10 N 15.15 E
Monteleone di Spoleto 66 42.39 N 12.58 E
Monteleone Rocco Doria 71 40.29 N 8.34 E
Monteleone Sabino 66 42.14 N 12.51 E
Montelepre 70 38.05 N 13.10 E
Montelíbano 246 8.05 N 75.29 W
Montélimar 62 44.34 N 4.45 E
Montelindo ≏ 252 23.56 S 57.12 W
Montella 68 40.51 N 15.01 E
Montellano 34 37.00 N 5.34 W
Montello, Nv., U.S. 204 41.15 N 114.11 W
Montello, Wi., U.S. 190 43.47 N 89.19 W
Monteluco ⊍[1] 66 42.43 N 12.45 E
Montelungo 64 44.24 N 9.54 E
Montelupo Fiorentino 66 43.44 N 11.01 E
Montemaggiore Belsito 70 37.51 N 13.46 E
Montemagno 62 44.59 N 8.20 E
Monte Maíz 252 33.12 S 62.36 W
Montemarano 68 40.55 N 15.00 E
Montemarciano 66 43.38 N 13.19 E
Montemayor, Meseta de ⋏[1] 254 44.20 S 66.10 W
Montemesola 68 40.34 N 17.20 E
Montemiletto 68 41.01 N 14.54 E
Montemilone 68 41.02 N 15.58 E
Montemor 266c 38.49 N 9.12 W
Montemor ʌ 266c 38.49 N 9.12 W
Montemorelos 232 25.12 N 99.49 W
Montemor-o-Novo 34 38.39 N 8.13 W
Montemor-o-Velho 34 40.10 N 8.41 W
Montemurro 68 40.18 N 15.59 E
Montendre 32 45.17 N 0.24 W
Montenegro 252 29.42 S 51.28 W
Montenegro
→ Crna Gora □[3] 38 42.30 N 19.18 E
Montenero 66 43.30 N 10.21 E
Montenero ʌ 68 39.13 N 16.35 E
Montenero di Bisaccia 66 41.57 N 14.47 E
Monteodorisio 66 42.05 N 14.39 E
Monte Oliveto Maggiore, Abbazia del ⊍[1] 66 43.12 N 11.32 E
Monte Pascoal, Parque Nacional de ♠ 255 16.54 S 39.24 W
Monte Patria 252 30.42 S 70.58 W
Montepescali 66 42.53 N 11.05 E
Monte Porzio Catone 267a 41.49 N 12.43 E
Monteprandone 66 42.55 N 13.50 E
Montepuez 154 13.07 S 39.00 E
Montepuez ≏ 154 12.32 S 40.27 E
Montepulciano 66 43.05 N 11.47 E
Monte Quemado 252 25.48 S 62.52 W
Monterado 112 0.45 N 109.08 E
Monterchi 66 43.29 N 12.07 E
Montereale 66 42.31 N 13.15 E
Montereale Valcellina 64 46.10 N 12.39 E
Montereau 50 47.51 N 2.34 E
Montereau-Faut-Yonne 50 48.23 N 2.57 E
Montereau-sur-le-Jard 261 48.35 N 2.40 E
Monterey, Ca., U.S. 226 36.36 N 121.53 W
Monterey, In., U.S. 216 41.09 N 86.28 W
Monterey, Ky., U.S. 218 38.25 N 84.52 W
Monterey, Ma., U.S. 207 42.10 N 73.12 W
Monterey, N.Y., U.S. 210 42.18 N 77.03 W
Monterey, Tn., U.S. 194 36.08 N 85.16 W
Monterey, Va., U.S. 188 38.24 N 79.34 W
Monterey □[6] 226 36.40 N 121.38 W
Monterey Bay c 226 36.45 N 121.55 W
Monterey Park 228 34.03 N 118.07 W
Monterey Peninsula Airport ⊠ 226 36.35 N 121.51 W
Montería 246 8.46 N 75.53 W
Monteriggioni 66 43.23 N 11.13 E
Montero 248 17.20 S 63.15 W
Monte Romano 66 42.16 N 11.54 E
Monteroni d'Arbia 66 43.14 N 11.25 E
Monteroni di Lecce 68 40.19 N 18.06 E
Monteros 252 27.10 S 65.30 W
Monterosso al Mare 62 44.09 N 9.39 E
Monterosso Almo 70 37.05 N 14.46 E
Monterosso Calabro 68 38.43 N 16.17 E
Monterotondo 66 42.03 N 12.37 E
Monterotondo Marittimo 66 43.09 N 10.51 E
Monterrey, Méx. 232 25.40 N 100.19 W
Monterrey, Méx. 234 16.05 N 93.23 W
Monterrico, Hipódromo de ♠ 286d 12.06 S 76.59 W
Monterubbiano 66 43.05 N 13.43 E
Montes Altos 250 5.50 S 47.04 W
Monte San Biagio 66 41.21 N 13.21 E
Monte San Giovanni Campano 66 41.38 N 13.31 E
Montesano 224 46.58 N 123.36 W
Montesano sulla Marcellana 68 40.16 N 15.42 E
Monte San Savino 66 43.20 N 11.43 E
Monte Santa Maria Tiberina 66 43.26 N 12.09 E
Monte Sant'Angelo 68 41.42 N 15.57 E
Monte Santo 250 10.26 S 39.20 W
Monte Santo de Minas 256 21.12 S 46.59 W
Monte Santu, Capo di > 71 40.05 N 9.44 E
Montesarchio 68 41.04 N 14.38 E
Montescaglioso 68 40.33 N 16.40 E
Montes Claros 255 16.43 S 43.52 W
Montescudaio 66 43.18 N 10.40 E
Montese 64 44.16 N 10.56 E
Monte Sereno 226 37.15 N 122.01 W
Monte Sião 256 22.26 S 46.34 W
Montesilvano Marina 66 42.31 N 14.09 E
Montespaccato ◆[8] 267a 41.54 N 12.23 E
Montespertoli 66 43.38 N 11.04 E
Montespluga 58 46.30 N 9.21 E
Montets, Col des)(58 46.00 N 6.55 E
Monteux 62 44.02 N 5.00 E
Montevago 70 37.42 N 12.58 E
Montevallo 194 33.06 N 86.51 W
Montevarchi 66 43.31 N 11.34 E
Monteverde 68 41.00 N 15.32 E
Monte Verde ≏ 256 21.55 S 43.33 W
Monteverde Nuovo ◆[8] 267a 41.51 N 12.27 E
Montevergine, Santuario di ⊍[1] 68 40.55 N 14.45 E
Montevideo, Mn., U.S. 198 44.56 N 95.43 W
Montevideo, Ur. 258 34.53 S 56.11 W
Montevideo □[5] 258 34.50 S 56.12 W
Montevideo, Cerro de ʌ[2] 258 33.54 S 56.15 W
Monte Vista 200 37.34 N 106.08 W
Montévrain 261 48.53 N 2.45 E
Montezemolo 62 44.22 N 8.08 E
Montezuma, Ga., U.S. 192 32.18 N 84.01 W
Montezuma, In., U.S. 194 39.47 N 87.22 W
Montezuma, Ia., U.S. 190 41.35 N 92.31 W
Montezuma, Ks., U.S. 198 37.35 N 100.26 W
Montezuma, N.Y., U.S. 210 43.00 N 76.42 W
Montezuma, Oh., U.S. 216 40.29 N 84.33 W
Montezuma Castle National Monument ♠ 200 34.38 N 110.49 W
Montezuma Creek ≏ 200 37.17 N 109.20 W
Montezuma Hills ⋏[2] 282 38.07 N 121.51 W
Montezuma Slough ≏ 226 38.04 N 121.52 W
Montfaucon, Fr. 56 49.17 N 5.08 E
Montfaucon, Fr. 62 45.10 N 4.18 E
Montfaucon, Schw. 58 47.17 N 7.03 E
Montfermeil 261 48.54 N 2.34 E
Montfleur 58 46.19 N 5.26 E
Montfort, Fr. 32 48.08 N 1.58 W
Montfort, Wi., U.S. 190 42.58 N 90.25 W
Montfort-l'Amaury 50 48.47 N 1.49 E
Montfort-le-Rotrou 50 48.03 N 0.25 E
Montfort-sur-Risle 50 49.18 N 0.40 E
Montfrin 62 43.53 N 4.36 E
Montgé 261 49.02 N 2.45 E
Montgenèvre 62 44.56 N 6.43 E
Montgenèvre, Col de)(62 44.56 N 6.44 E
Montgeron 261 48.42 N 2.27 E
Montgeroult 261 49.05 N 2.00 E
Montgesoye 58 47.05 N 6.12 E
Montgomery
→ Sāhīwāl, Pāk. 123 30.40 N 73.06 E
Montgomery, Wales, U.K. 42 52.33 N 3.03 W
Montgomery, Al., U.S. 194 32.23 N 86.18 W
Montgomery, Il., U.S. 216 41.43 N 88.20 W
Montgomery, La., U.S. 194 31.40 N 92.53 W
Montgomery, Mi., U.S. 216 41.46 N 84.48 W
Montgomery, Mn., U.S. 190 44.26 N 93.34 W
Montgomery, N.Y., U.S. 210 41.31 N 74.14 W
Montgomery, Oh., U.S. 218 39.13 N 84.21 W
Montgomery, Pa., U.S. 210 41.10 N 76.52 W
Montgomery, Tx., U.S. 222 30.23 N 95.42 W
Montgomery, W.V., U.S. 188 38.11 N 81.19 W
Montgomery □[6], Il., U.S. 219 39.09 N 89.29 W
Montgomery □[6], Md., U.S. 208 39.05 N 77.09 W
Montgomery □[6], Mo., U.S. 219 38.57 N 91.27 W
Montgomery □[6], N.Y., U.S. 210 42.57 N 74.22 W
Montgomery □[6], Oh., U.S. 218 39.45 N 84.15 W
Montgomery □[6], Pa., U.S. 208 40.07 N 75.21 W
Montgomery □[6], Tx., U.S. 222 30.18 N 95.30 W
Montgomery City 219 38.58 N 91.30 W
Montgomery Dam ◆[6] 214 40.39 N 80.24 W
Montgomery Knolls 284b 39.14 N 76.48 W
Montgomery Mall ◆[9] 284c 39.01 N 77.09 W
Montgomery Square 284c 39.04 N 77.09 W
Montgomeryville 285 40.15 N 75.15 W
Montgomeryville Airport ⊠ 285 40.15 N 75.14 W
Montguyon 32 45.13 N 0.11 W
Monthermé 56 49.53 N 4.44 E
Monthey 58 46.15 N 6.57 E
Monthois 56 49.19 N 4.43 E
Monthureux-sur-Saône 58 48.02 N 5.58 E
Monthyon 261 49.00 N 2.50 E
Monti 71 40.49 N 9.19 E
Monticelli d'Ongina 64 45.05 N 9.56 E
Monticello, Ar., U.S. 194 33.37 N 91.47 W
Monticello, Fl., U.S. 192 30.32 N 83.52 W
Monticello, Ga., U.S. 192 33.18 N 83.41 W
Monticello, Il., U.S. 194 40.01 N 88.34 W
Monticello, In., U.S. 216 40.44 N 86.45 W
Monticello, Ia., U.S. 190 42.14 N 91.11 W
Monticello, Ky., U.S. 194 36.49 N 84.50 W
Monticello, Mn., U.S. 190 45.18 N 93.47 W
Monticello, Ms., U.S. 194 31.33 N 90.06 W
Monticello, Mo., U.S. 219 40.07 N 91.42 W
Monticello, N.Y., U.S. 210 41.39 N 74.41 W
Monticello, Ut,. U.S. 200 37.52 N 109.20 W
Monticello, Wi., U.S. 190 42.44 N 89.35 W
Monticello ⊥ 188 38.00 N 78.30 W
Monticello Conte Otto 64 45.35 N 11.35 E
Monticello Dam ◆[6] 226 38.30 N 122.07 W
Monticello Woods 284c 38.47 N 77.10 W
Montichiari 64 45.25 N 10.23 E
Monticiano 66 43.08 N 11.11 E
Montiel, Campo de ≚ 34 38.46 N 2.44 W
Montier-en-Der 58 48.29 N 4.46 E
Montieri 66 43.08 N 11.01 E
Montieri, Poggio di ʌ 66 43.08 N 11.00 E
Montiers-sur-Saulx 58 48.32 N 5.16 E
Montignac 32 45.04 N 1.10 E
Montigny 58 48.31 N 6.48 E
Montigny-Devant-Sassey 56 49.26 N 5.09 E
Montigny-le-Bretonneux 261 48.46 N 2.02 E
Montigny-le-Roi 58 48.00 N 5.30 E
Montigny-lès-Cormeilles 261 48.59 N 2.12 E
Montigny-lès-Metz 56 49.06 N 6.09 E
Montigny-sur-Aube 58 47.57 N 4.46 E
Montijo, Esp. 34 38.55 N 6.37 W
Montijo, Pan. 236 7.59 N 81.03 W
Montijo, Port. 34 38.42 N 8.58 W
Montijo, Aeroporto ⊠ 266c 38.42 N 9.02 W
Montijo, Golfo de c 246 7.40 N 81.07 W
Montilla 34 37.35 N 4.38 W
Montividiu 255 17.24 S 51.14 W
Montivilliers 50 49.33 N 0.12 E
Montjay-la-Tour 261 48.55 N 2.40 E
Montjoie, Lac ⊜, P.Q., Can. 206 46.17 N 75.08 W
Montjoie, Lac ⊜, P.Q., Can. 206 45.25 N 72.06 W
Mont-Joli 186 48.35 N 68.11 W
Montjovet 62 45.43 N 7.40 E
Montjuich, Estadio de ♠ 266d 41.22 N 2.09 E
Montjuich, Faro de ◆[5] 266d 41.21 N 2.11 E
Montjuich, Parque de ♠ 266d 41.21 N 2.09 E
Mont-Laurier 176 46.33 N 75.30 W
Montlebon 58 47.02 N 6.37 E
Montlhéry 50 48.38 N 2.16 E
Montlhéry, Tour de ♠ 261 48.38 N 2.16 E
Montlignon 261 49.01 N 2.17 E
Montlouet 261 48.31 N 1.43 E
Mont-Louis 32 42.31 N 2.07 E
Montlouis-sur-Loire 50 47.23 N 0.50 E
Montluçon 32 46.21 N 2.36 E
Montluel 62 45.51 N 5.03 E
Montmagny, P.Q., Can. 186 46.59 N 70.33 W
Montmagny, Fr. 261 48.58 N 2.21 E
Montmajour, Abbaye de ⊍[1] 62 43.43 N 4.40 E
Montmartre ◆[8] 261 48.53 N 2.21 E
Montmédy 56 49.31 N 5.22 E
Montmélian 62 45.30 N 6.04 E
Montmeló 266d 41.33 N 2.15 E
Montmerle-sur-Saône 58 46.05 N 4.46 E
Montmin 62 45.48 N 6.16 E
Montmirail, Fr. 50 48.52 N 3.32 E
Montmirail, Fr. 50 48.06 N 0.48 E
Montmirey-le-Château 58 47.13 N 5.32 E
Montmoreau-Saint-Cybard 32 45.24 N 0.08 E
Montmorenci 216 40.28 N 87.02 W
Montmorency, Austl. 274b 37.43 S 145.07 E
Montmorency
→ Beauport, P.Q., Can. 186 46.52 N 71.11 W
Montmorency, Fr. 261 49.00 N 2.20 E
Montmorency ≏ 186 46.53 N 71.07 W
Montmorency, Forêt de ♠ 261 49.02 N 2.16 E
Montmorillon 32 46.26 N 0.52 E
Montmort 50 48.55 N 3.49 E
Monto 166 24.52 S 151.07 E
Montodine 62 45.17 N 9.42 E
Montoggio 62 44.31 N 9.03 E
Montoire-sur-le-Loir 50 47.45 N 0.52 E
Montone 66 43.22 N 12.20 E
Montone ≏ 66 44.24 N 12.14 E
Montopoli in Val d'Arno 66 43.40 N 10.45 E
Mont Orford, Parc du ♠ 206 45.22 N 72.05 W
Montorio al Vomano 66 42.35 N 13.38 E
Montorio nei Frentani 66 41.46 N 14.55 E
Montoro 34 38.01 N 4.23 W
Mont'Orso, Galleria di ◆[5] 66 41.20 N 13.15 E
Montour □[6] 210 40.58 N 76.37 W
Montour Falls 210 42.20 N 76.50 W
Montour Run ≏, Pa., U.S. 279b 40.36 N 79.57 W
Montour Run ≏, Pa., U.S. 279b 40.31 N 80.08 W
Montoursville 210 41.15 N 76.55 W
Mont Park 274b 37.43 S 145.04 E
Montparnasse, Gare ◆[5] 261 48.51 N 2.19 E
Mont Peko, Parc National du ♠ 150 7.00 N 7.15 W
Montpelier, Jam. 241q 18.22 N 77.56 W
Montpelier, Id., U.S. 202 42.19 N 111.17 W
Montpelier, In., U.S. 216 40.33 N 85.16 W
Montpelier, Md., U.S. 284c 39.04 N 76.51 W
Montpelier, Ms., U.S. 194 33.43 N 88.56 W
Montpelier, Oh., U.S. 216 41.35 N 84.36 W
Montpelier, Vt., U.S. 188 44.15 N 72.34 W
Montpellier 62 43.36 N 3.53 E
Montpellier-Fréjorgues, Aéroport de ⊠ 62 43.33 N 4.00 E
Montpezat-sous-Bauzon 62 44.43 N 4.12 E
Mont-Pichet 261 48.53 N 2.54 E
Montpon-Ménesterol 32 45.00 N 0.10 E
Montpont-en-Bresse 58 46.33 N 5.09 E
Montréal, P.Q., Can. 206 45.31 N 73.34 W
Montréal, P.Q., Can. 275a 45.31 N 73.34 W
Montréal, Fr. 50 47.32 N 4.02 E
Montreal, Wi., U.S. 190 46.25 N 90.14 W
Montreal ≏, On., Can. 190 47.14 N 84.39 W
Montreal ≏, On., Can. 190 47.08 N 79.27 W
Montreal ≏, Sk., Can. 184 55.06 N 105.19 W
Montreal ≏, U.S. 190 46.44 N 90.25 W
Montréal, Base des Forces Canadiennes ■ 275a 45.31 N 73.25 W
Montréal, Île de I 206 45.30 N 73.40 W
Montréal, Université de ⊍[2] 275a 45.30 N 73.37 W
Montréal-Est 206 45.38 N 73.31 W
Montreal International Airport ⊠ 206 45.28 N 73.45 W
Montreal Lake 184 54.03 N 105.46 W
Montreal Lake ⊜ 184 54.20 N 105.40 W
Montreal Lake Indian Reserve ◆[4] 184 54.00 N 105.45 W
Montréal-Nord 206 45.36 N 73.38 W
Montréal-Ouest 275a 45.27 N 73.39 W
Montreal Water Works Aqueduct ≖[1] 275a 45.26 N 73.36 W
Montrésor 50 47.09 N 1.12 E
Montresta 71 40.22 N 8.30 E
Montret 58 46.41 N 5.07 E
Montreuil 261 48.52 N 2.26 E
Montreuil-Bellay 32 47.08 N 0.09 W
Montreuil-sous-Bois 50 48.52 N 2.26 E
Montreuil-sur-Mer 50 50.28 N 1.46 E
Montreux 58 46.26 N 6.55 E
Montrevel-en-Bresse 58 46.20 N 5.08 E
Montrichard 50 47.21 N 1.11 E
Montriond 58 46.12 N 6.41 E
Mont-Rolland 206 45.57 N 74.07 W
Montrond-les-Bains 62 45.38 N 4.14 E
Montrose, Austl. 274b 37.49 S 145.21 E
Montrose, Scot., U.K. 46 56.43 N 2.29 W
Montrose, Ca., U.S. 228 34.12 N 118.13 W
Montrose, Co., U.S. 200 38.28 N 107.52 W
Montrose, Ia., U.S. 190 40.31 N 91.24 W
Montrose, Mi., U.S. 190 43.10 N 83.53 W
Montrose, N.Y., U.S. 210 41.15 N 73.56 W
Montrose, Oh., U.S. 214 41.08 N 81.37 W
Montrose, Pa., U.S. 210 41.50 N 75.52 W
Montrose, S.D., U.S. 198 43.41 N 97.11 W
Montrose Harbor c 278 41.58 N 87.38 W
Montrose Hill 279b 40.30 N 79.51 W
Montross 208 38.05 N 76.49 W
Montrouge 261 48.49 N 2.19 E
Mont-Royal 206 45.31 N 73.39 W
Mont Royal, Parc ♠ 275a 45.31 N 73.35 W
Mont Royal Tunnel ◆[5] 275a 45.31 N 73.38 W
Montry 261 48.53 N 2.50 E
Monts 50 47.17 N 0.37 E
Monts, Pointe des > 186 49.20 N 67.23 W
Mont-Saint-Aignan 50 49.28 N 1.05 E
Mont-Sainte-Anne, Parc du ♠ 186 47.08 N 70.55 W
Mont-Saint-Hilaire 206 45.34 N 73.11 W
Mont-Saint-Martin 56 49.32 N 5.47 E
Mont-Saint-Michel
→ Le Mont-Saint-Michel ⊍[1] 32 48.38 N 1.32 W
Mont-Saint-Vincent 58 46.38 N 4.29 E
Montsauche 50 47.13 N 4.01 E
Montsec 56 48.53 N 5.43 E
Montserrat □[2], N.A. 230 16.45 N 62.12 W
Montserrat □[2], N.A. 238 16.45 N 62.12 W
Montserrat, Monasterio de ⊍[1] 34 41.36 N 1.49 E
Montsoult 261 49.04 N 2.19 E
Montsûrs 28 48.08 N 0.33 W
Mont-sur-Vaudrey 58 46.58 N 5.36 E
Mont-Tremblant, Parc provincial du ♠ 206 46.42 N 74.20 W
Montuenga 34 41.03 N 4.37 W
Montvale, N.J., U.S. 276 41.02 N 74.01 W
Montvale, Va., U.S. 192 37.23 N 79.43 W
Montverde 220 28.36 N 81.41 W
Montville, Ct., U.S. 207 41.27 N 72.08 W
Montville, N.J., U.S. 276 40.54 N 74.23 W
Montville, Oh., U.S. 214 41.36 N 81.03 W
Montville Airpark ⊠ 276 40.56 N 74.20 W
Monument, S. Afr. 273d 26.06 S 27.43 E

Symbol	English	Deutsch	Español	Français	Português
≏	River	Fluß	Río	Rivière	Rio
≖	Canal	Kanal	Canal	Canal	Canal
∟	Waterfall, Rapids	Wasserfall, Stromschnellen	Cascada, Rápidos	Chute d'eau, Rapides	Cascata, Rápidos
⊔	Strait	Meeresstraße	Estrecho	Détroit	Estreito
c	Bay, Gulf	Bucht, Golf	Bahía, Golfo	Baie, Golfe	Baía, Golfo
⊜	Lake, Lakes	See, Seen	Lago, Lagos	Lac, Lacs	Lago, Lagos
≡	Swamp	Sumpf	Pantano	Marais	Pântano
⊓	Ice Features, Glacier	Eis- und Gletscherformen	Accidentes Glaciales	Formes glaciaires	Acidentes glaciares
⊽	Other Hydrographic Features	Andere Hydrographische Objekte	Otros Elementos Hidrográficos	Autres données hydrographiques	Outros acidentes hidrográficos
◆	Submarine Features	Untermeerische Objekte	Accidentes Submarinos	Formes de relief sous-marin	Acidentes submarinos
□	Political Unit	Politische Einheit	Unidad Politica	Entité politique	Unidade política
⊍	Cultural Institution	Kulturelle Institution	Institución Cultural	Institution culturelle	Institução cultural
⊥	Historical Site	Historische Stätte	Sitio Histórico	Site historique	Sitio histórico
♠	Recreational Site	Erholungs- und Ferienort	Sitio de Recreo	Centre de loisirs	Area de Lazer
⊠	Airport	Flughafen	Aeropuerto	Aéroport	Aeroporto
■	Military Installation	Militäranlage	Instalación Militar	Installation militaire	Instalação militar
◆	Miscellaneous	Verschiedenes	Misceláneo	Divers	Diversos

Name	Page	Lat.°′	Long.°′
Monument, Or., U.S.	202	44.49 N	119.25 W
Monument, Pa., U.S.	214	41.07 N	77.42 W
Monument Beach	207	41.43 N	70.36 W
Monument Draw V, U.S.	196	32.27 N	102.20 W
Monument Draw V, Tx., U.S.	196	30.51 N	102.33 W
Monument Hill State Historic Site ⊥	222	29.53 N	96.54 W
Monumento	256	22.44 S	43.51 W
Monument Peak ∧, Co., U.S.	200	39.43 N	107.55 W
Monument Peak ∧, Id., U.S.	202	42.07 N	114.14 W
Monument Valley V	200	37.05 N	110.20 W
Monundilla, Mount ∧	170	32.45 S	150.29 E
Monveda	152	2.57 N	21.27 E
Monymusk	46	57.13 N	2.31 W
Monyo	110	17.59 N	95.30 E
Monywa	110	22.05 N	95.08 E
Monza	62	45.35 N	9.16 E
Monze	154	16.16 S	27.28 E
Monzen	92	37.17 N	136.46 E
Monzie	46	56.24 N	3.48 W
Monzón, Esp.	34	41.55 N	0.12 E
Monzón, Perú	248	9.10 S	76.23 W
Moóca ◆[8]	287b	23.33 S	46.35 W
Moóca, Ribeirão da ≃	287b	23.36 S	46.35 W
Moodie Island I	176	64.37 N	65.30 W
Moodus	207	41.30 N	72.27 W
Moodus Reservoir ⊜[1]	207	41.30 N	72.24 W
Moody	222	31.18 N	97.21 W
Moody Air Force Base ■	192	30.59 N	83.11 W
Moody Wood Dale Airport ⊠	278	41.59 N	87.58 W
Mooers	206	44.58 N	73.35 W
Mooi ≃, S. Afr.	158	26.53 S	26.56 E
Mooi ≃, S. Afr.	158	28.45 S	30.34 E
Mooirivier	158	29.13 S	29.50 E
Mook	52	51.45 N	5.54 E
Mookane	156	24.59 S	24.33 E
Mooketsi	156	23.35 S	30.05 E
Moolawatana	166	29.55 S	139.43 E
Moolman	158	27.10 S	30.53 E
Mooloogool	162	26.06 S	119.05 E
Moon	214	40.31 N	80.14 W
Moon ≃	212	45.08 N	79.59 W
Moon, Mountains of the → Ruwenzori Range ⩘	154	0.23 N	29.54 E
Moonachie	276	40.50 N	74.02 W
Moonah Creek ≃	166	22.03 S	138.33 E
Moon Crest	279b	40.32 N	80.11 W
Moondarra Reservoir ⊜[1]	169	38.04 S	146.22 E
Moonee Valley Racecourse ♦	274b	37.46 S	144.56 E
Moonie	166	27.43 S	150.22 E
Moonie ≃	166	29.19 S	148.43 E
Moon Island I, On., Can.	212	45.09 N	80.01 W
Moon Island I, Ma., U.S.	283	42.18 N	71.00 W
Moon Run	214	40.27 N	80.06 W
Moonta	168b	34.04 S	137.35 E
Moor, Kepulauan II	164	2.57 S	135.45 E
Moora	162	30.39 S	116.00 E
Moorabbin	169	37.56 S	145.02 E
Moorabbin Airport ⊠	274b	37.59 S	145.09 E
Mooraberree	166	25.14 S	140.59 E
Moorabool ≃	169	38.09 S	144.19 E
Moorarie	162	25.56 S	117.35 E
Moorbad Lobenstein	54	50.26 N	11.38 E
Moorburg	52	53.17 N	7.53 E
Moorcroft	198	44.15 N	104.56 W
Moordorf	52	53.28 N	7.23 E
Moordrecht	52	51.59 N	4.40 E
Moore, Austl.	171a	26.53 S	152.18 E
Moore, Eng., U.K.	262	53.21 N	2.38 W
Moore, Id., U.S.	202	43.44 N	113.21 W
Moore, Mt., U.S.	202	46.58 N	109.41 W
Moore, Ok., U.S.	196	35.20 N	97.29 W
Moore, Tx., U.S.	196	29.03 N	99.01 W
Moore ≃	162	31.22 S	115.29 E
Moore, Lake ⊜	162	29.50 S	117.35 E
Moorea I	174s	17.32 S	149.50 W
Moorebank	274a	33.56 S	150.56 E
Moore Creek ≃	212	45.29 N	77.58 W
Moorefield, Ky., U.S.	218	38.16 N	83.55 W
Moorefield, Oh., U.S.	214	40.12 N	81.10 W
Moorefield, W.V., U.S.	188	39.03 N	78.58 W
Moore Haven	220	26.49 N	81.05 W
Moore Haven Lock ◆[5]	220	26.51 N	81.05 W
Moore Lake ⊜, On., Can.	212	45.26 N	78.01 W
Moore Lake ⊜, On., Can.	212	44.48 N	78.48 W
Moore Lake ⊜, Mi., U.S.	281	42.37 N	83.36 W
Mooreland, In., U.S.	218	39.59 N	85.15 W
Mooreland, Ok., U.S.	196	36.26 N	99.12 W
Moore Point ➤	275b	43.48 N	79.03 W
Moore Reservoir ⊜[1]	188	44.25 N	71.50 W
Mooresburg	210	40.59 N	76.43 W
Moores Creek National Battlefield ♦	192	34.24 N	78.08 W
Moores Hill	218	39.06 N	85.05 W
Moore Station	222	32.11 N	95.35 W
Moorestown	208	39.58 N	74.56 W
Moorestown Mall ◆[9]	285	39.56 N	74.58 W
Mooresville, In., U.S.	218	39.36 N	86.22 W
Mooresville, N.C., U.S.	192	35.35 N	80.48 W
Mooreville	281	42.06 N	83.44 W
Moorfoot Hills ⩘[2]	46	55.45 N	3.02 W
Moorhead, Mn., U.S.	198	46.52 N	96.46 W
Moorhead, Ms., U.S.	194	33.27 N	90.30 W
Mooring	222	30.41 N	96.33 W
Mooringsport	194	32.41 N	93.57 W
Moormerland	52	53.20 N	7.27 E
Moornanyah Lake ⊜	166	33.02 S	143.58 E
Moorooka	171a	27.32 S	153.02 E
Mooroolbark	274b	37.47 S	145.19 E
Moorpark	228	34.17 N	118.53 W
Moorreesburg	158	33.08 S	18.40 E
Moorrege	52	53.40 N	9.39 E
Moorriem	52	53.15 N	8.19 E
Moorsel	50	50.57 N	4.06 E
Moorside	262	53.34 N	2.04 W
Moorslede	50	50.53 N	3.04 E
Moos → Moso, It.	64	46.41 N	12.23 E
Moos → Moso in Passiria, It.	64	46.50 N	11.10 E
Moosach ◆[8]	60	48.11 N	11.31 E
Moosbrunn	264b	48.01 N	16.28 E
Moosburg	61	46.39 N	14.10 E
Moosburg an der Isar	60	48.29 N	11.57 E
Moose ≃, Me., U.S.	188	45.40 N	69.42 W
Moose ≃, N.Y., U.S.	212	43.37 N	75.22 W
Moose Creek	206	45.15 N	74.58 W
Moose Creek ≃	206	45.23 N	75.04 W
Moosehead Lake ⊜	188	45.40 N	69.40 W
Mooseheart	216	41.49 N	88.20 W
Moose Heights	182	53.05 N	122.30 W
Moose Hill ∧[2]	283	42.07 N	71.13 W
Moose Island I	184	51.42 N	97.10 W
Moose Jaw	184	50.23 N	105.32 W
Moose Jaw ≃	184	50.34 N	105.17 W
Moose Lake, Mb., Can.	184	53.43 N	100.20 W
Moose Lake, Mn., U.S.	190	46.27 N	92.45 W
Moose Lake ⊜, Ab., Can.	182	54.15 N	110.55 W
Moose Lake ⊜, Mb., Can.	184	53.55 N	99.45 W
Moose Lake ⊜, On., Can.	212	45.09 N	78.28 W
Mooselookmeguntic Lake ⊜	188	44.53 N	70.48 W
Moose Mountain ∧	184	49.45 N	102.37 W
Moose Mountain Creek ≃	184	49.12 N	102.10 W
Moose Mountain Provincial Park ♦	184	49.48 N	102.25 W
Moose Pass	180	60.29 N	149.22 W
Moosinning	60	48.17 N	11.51 E
Moosomin	184	50.07 N	101.40 W
Moosomin Indian Reserve ◆[4]	184	53.06 N	108.14 W
Moosonee	176	51.17 N	80.39 W
Moosup	207	41.42 N	71.52 W
Mooti	144	0.35 N	41.56 E
Moots Creek ≃	216	40.32 N	86.47 W
Mootwingee National Park ♦	166	31.07 S	142.23 E
Mopane	156	22.37 S	29.52 E
Mopeia Velha	156	17.59 S	35.44 E
Mopipi	156	21.07 S	24.55 E
Mopo	100	33.07 N	113.02 E
Moppo → Mokp'o	98	34.48 N	126.22 E
Mopti	150	14.30 N	4.12 W
Mopti □[4]	150	14.40 N	4.15 W
Moqokorei	144	4.04 N	46.08 E
Moquegua	248	17.12 S	70.56 W
Moquegua □[5]	248	16.50 S	70.55 W
Mór	30	47.23 N	18.12 E
Mor ≃	126	24.01 N	88.03 E
Mòr, Glen V	46	57.10 N	4.40 W
Mor, Sgurr ∧	46	57.42 N	5.03 W
Mora, Cam.	146	11.03 N	14.09 E
Mora, Esp.	34	39.41 N	3.46 W
Mora, India	272c	18.54 N	72.56 E
Mora, Port.	34	38.56 N	8.10 W
Mora, Sve.	26	61.00 N	14.33 E
Mora, Mn., U.S.	190	45.52 N	93.17 W
Mora, N.M., U.S.	200	35.58 N	105.19 W
Mora ≃	196	35.44 N	104.23 W
Mora, Arroyo de la ≃	196	34.05 N	104.18 W
Moraby	40	60.23 N	15.35 E
Morač ≃	76	52.35 N	27.35 E
Morača, Manastir ᵾ[1]	38	42.44 N	19.20 E
Morada	226	38.01 N	121.15 W
Morādābād	124	28.50 N	78.47 E
Morada Nova	250	5.07 S	38.23 W
Morada Nova de Minas	255	18.37 S	45.22 W
Moradel, Montaña de ∧	236	15.06 N	86.16 W
Mora de Rubielos	34	40.15 N	0.45 W
Moraduccio	66	44.10 N	11.29 E
Morafenobe	157b	17.49 S	44.55 E
Morąg	30	53.56 N	19.56 E
Moraga	226	37.50 N	122.08 W
Mórahalom	30	46.13 N	19.54 E
Moraine	218	39.42 N	84.13 W
Moraine Hills State Park ♦	216	42.18 N	88.15 W
Moraine State Park ♦	214	40.56 N	80.07 W
Morainvilliers	261	48.56 N	1.56 E
Morākhi ≃	126	24.01 N	88.10 E
Morākhi Reservoir ⊜[1]	126	24.10 N	87.15 E
Mor'akovskij Zaton	86	56.45 N	84.41 E
Moral de Calatrava	34	38.50 N	3.35 W
Moraleda, Canal ʯ	254	44.30 S	73.30 W
Morales, Guat.	236	15.29 N	88.49 W
Morales, Perú	248	6.28 S	76.28 W
Morales, Arroyo ≃	258	34.48 S	58.36 W
Morales, Laguna ⊂	234	23.35 N	97.47 W
Moramanga	157b	18.56 S	48.12 E
Moran, Ks., U.S.	198	37.54 N	95.10 W
Moran, Mi., U.S.	190	45.59 N	84.49 W
Moran, Tx., U.S.	196	32.33 N	99.10 W
Moran ≃	164	15.16 S	125.33 E
Moranbah	166	22.00 S	148.02 E
Morangis	261	48.42 N	2.20 E
Morangup Hill ∧[2]	168a	31.41 S	116.19 E
Morann	214	40.48 N	78.21 W
Morano Calabro	68	39.50 N	16.08 E
Morano sul Po	62	45.10 N	8.22 E
Moran State Park ♦	224	48.41 N	122.52 W
Morant Bay	241q	17.53 N	76.25 W
Morant Cays II	238	17.24 N	75.59 W
Morant Point ➤	241q	17.55 N	76.10 W
Morar, Loch ⊜	46	56.57 N	5.43 W
Mörarp	41	56.04 N	12.52 E
Morasverdes	34	40.36 N	6.16 W
Morat, Lac de (Murtensee) ⊜	58	46.55 N	7.05 E
Moratalla	34	38.12 N	1.53 W
Morattico	208	37.47 N	76.37 W
Moratuwa	122	6.46 N	79.53 E
Morava □[9]	30	49.30 N	17.00 E
Morava (March) ≃	30	48.10 N	16.59 E
Morāveh Tappeh	128	37.55 N	55.57 E
Moravia, C.R.	236	9.51 N	83.26 W
Moravia, Ia., U.S.	190	40.53 N	92.48 W
Moravia, N.Y., U.S.	210	42.42 N	76.25 W
Moravia → Morava □[9]	30	49.20 N	17.00 E
Moravian Indian Reserve ◆[4]	214	42.34 N	81.53 W
Moravská Dyje ≃	61	48.51 N	15.30 E
Moravská Ostrava → Ostrava	30	49.50 N	18.17 E
Moravská Třebová	30	49.45 N	16.40 E
Moravské Budějovice	61	49.03 N	15.49 E
Moravský Krumlov	61	49.03 N	16.19 E
Morawa	162	29.13 S	116.00 E
Morawhanna	246	8.16 N	59.45 W
Moraya	248	21.45 S	65.32 W
Morayfield	171a	27.07 S	152.57 E
Moray Firth ⊂[1]	46	57.50 N	3.30 W
Morazán, Guat.	236	14.56 N	90.09 W
Morazán, Hond.	236	15.17 N	87.34 W
Morbach	56	49.48 N	7.07 E
Morbegno	58	46.08 N	9.34 E
Morbi	120	22.49 N	70.50 E
Morbihan □[5]	32	47.55 N	2.50 W
Mörbisch am See	61	47.45 N	16.40 E
Morbras ≃	261	48.47 N	2.29 E
Mörbylånga	26	56.31 N	16.23 E
Morcenx	32	44.02 N	0.55 W
Morciano di Romagna	66	43.55 N	12.38 E
Morcone	68	41.20 N	14.40 E
Morcote	58	45.56 N	8.55 E
Morcy	80	51.18 N	47.51 E
Morden	184	49.11 N	98.05 W
Morden ◆[8]	260	51.24 N	0.12 W
Mordialloc	169	38.00 S	145.05 E
Mordino	24	61.21 N	51.52 E
Mordoğan	130	38.30 N	26.37 E
Mordovija □[3], Ross.	72	54.30 N	44.00 E
Mordovija □[3], Ross.	80	54.30 N	44.00 E
Mordovo, Ross.	80	51.07 N	45.48 E
Mordovo, Ross.	80	52.05 N	40.46 E
Mordovo-Adel'akovo	80	53.47 N	51.36 E
Mordovskij Buguruslan	80	53.48 N	52.31 E
Mordovskij zapovednik ◆[4]	80	54.48 N	43.20 E
Mordves	82	54.34 N	38.13 E
Mordvinia → Mordovija □[3]	80	54.30 N	44.00 E
Mordy	30	52.13 N	22.31 E
More, Ben ∧, Scot., U.K.	46	56.21 N	4.35 W
More, Ben ∧, Scot., U.K.	46	56.25 N	6.01 W
More, Loch ⊜	46	58.17 N	4.52 W
More Assynt, Ben ∧	46	58.08 N	4.53 W
Moreau ≃, Mo., U.S.	219	38.33 N	92.06 W
Moreau ≃, S.D., U.S.	198	45.18 N	100.43 W
Moreau, North Fork ≃	198	45.09 N	102.50 W
Moreau, South Fork ≃	198	45.09 N	102.50 W
Moreau Peak ∧	198	45.21 N	103.43 W
Moreauville	194	31.02 N	91.58 W
Morec	80	51.03 N	44.03 E
Morecambe	44	54.04 N	2.53 W
Morecambe Bay ⊂	44	54.07 N	3.00 W
Moree, Austl.	166	29.28 S	149.51 E
Morée, Fr.	50	47.54 N	1.14 E
Morehead, Pap. N. Gui.	164	8.40 S	141.35 E
Morehead, Ky., U.S.	218	38.11 N	83.25 W
Morehead ≃	164	9.00 S	141.25 E
Morehead City	192	34.43 N	76.43 W
Morehouse	194	36.50 N	89.41 W
Moreira César	256	22.55 S	45.22 W
Moreland, Austl.	274b	37.45 S	144.58 E
Moreland, Ga., U.S.	192	33.17 N	84.46 W
Moreland, Ky., U.S.	194	37.30 N	84.48 W
Moreland Hills	279a	41.27 N	81.29 W
Morelia	234	19.42 N	101.07 W
Morell	186	46.25 N	62.42 W
Morella, Austl.	166	22.59 S	143.52 E
Morella, Esp.	34	40.37 N	0.06 W
Morello ≃	70	37.29 N	14.08 E
Morelos, Méx.	196	28.25 N	100.53 W
Morelos, Méx.	232	26.42 N	107.40 W
Morelos, Méx.	234	22.53 N	102.37 W
Morelos □[3]	234	18.45 N	99.00 W
Moremi Wildlife Reserve ◆[4]	156	19.10 S	23.15 E
Morena	124	26.30 N	78.09 E
Morena, Sierra ∧	282	37.25 N	122.18 W
Morena, Sierra ⩘	34	38.00 N	5.00 W
Morenci, Az., U.S.	200	33.04 N	109.21 W
Morenci, Mi., U.S.	216	41.43 N	84.13 W
Moreni	38	45.00 N	25.39 E
Moreno	258	34.39 S	58.48 W
Moreno □[5]	288	34.36 S	58.48 W
Moreno, Bahía ⊂	252	23.35 S	70.30 W
Moreno Valley	228	33.56 N	117.09 W
Møre og Romsdal □[6]	26	62.40 N	7.50 E
Mores	71	40.33 N	8.50 E
Moresby Island I, B.C., Can.	182	52.50 N	131.55 W
Moresby Island I, B.C., Can.	224	48.40 N	123.20 W
Mores Island I	238	26.18 N	77.33 W
Moresnet	56	50.43 N	5.59 E
Morestel	62	45.40 N	5.28 E
Moreton, Austl.	164	12.28 S	142.38 E
Moreton, Eng., U.K.	44	53.24 N	3.07 W
Moreton, Eng., U.K.	260	51.44 N	0.14 E
Moreton, Cape ➤	171a	27.02 S	153.28 E
Moreton Bay ⊂	171a	27.20 S	153.15 E
Moretonhampstead	42	50.40 N	3.45 W
Moreton-in-Marsh	42	51.59 N	1.42 W
Moreton Island I	171a	27.10 S	153.25 E
Moreton Island National Park ♦	171a	27.09 S	153.25 E
Moret-sur-Loing	50	48.22 N	2.49 E
Moretta	62	44.46 N	7.32 E
Moreuil	50	49.46 N	2.29 E
Morey Park	210	42.33 N	73.43 W
Morey Peak ∧	204	38.37 N	116.17 W
Morez	58	46.31 N	6.02 E
Morfa Nefyn	42	52.56 N	4.33 W
Mörfelden-Walldorf	56	49.58 N	8.34 E
Morga	80	54.26 N	46.29 E
Morgan, Austl.	166	34.02 S	139.40 E
Morgan, Ga., U.S.	192	31.32 N	84.35 W
Morgan, Ky., U.S.	218	38.36 N	84.23 W
Morgan, Mn., U.S.	198	44.25 N	94.55 W
Morgan, Pa., U.S.	279b	40.22 N	80.08 W
Morgan, Tx., U.S.	222	32.01 N	97.37 W
Morgan, Ut,. U.S.	200	41.02 N	111.40 W
Morgan □[6], Il., U.S.	219	39.44 N	90.14 W
Morgan □[6], In., U.S.	218	39.30 N	86.25 W
Morgan, Mount ∧	171b	35.44 S	148.47 E
Morgan City, Al., U.S.	194	34.28 N	86.34 W
Morgan City, La., U.S.	194	29.41 N	91.12 W
Morgan Creek ≃	196	32.19 N	100.55 W
Morganfield	194	37.41 N	87.55 W
Morgan Hill	226	37.07 N	121.39 W
Morganito	246	5.04 N	67.44 W
Morgan Park ◆[8]	278	41.42 N	87.40 W
Morgan's Bay	158	32.43 S	28.20 E
Morgan's Point	222	29.41 N	94.59 W
Morgans Point ➤	212	42.52 N	79.21 W
Morgan State College ᵾ[2]	284b	39.21 N	76.35 W
Morgantina ⊥	70	37.25 N	14.29 E
Morganton	192	35.44 N	81.41 W
Morgantown, In., U.S.	218	39.22 N	86.15 W
Morgantown, Ky., U.S.	194	37.13 N	86.41 W
Morgantown, Md., U.S.	208	38.21 N	76.58 W
Morgantown, Ms., U.S.	194	31.18 N	89.54 W
Morgantown, Ms., U.S.	194	31.34 N	91.20 W
Morgantown, Oh., U.S.	218	39.08 N	83.13 W
Morgantown, Pa., U.S.	208	40.09 N	75.54 W
Morgantown, W.V., U.S.	188	39.37 N	79.57 W
Morganville	208	40.23 N	74.15 W
Morgan Whyalla Pipeline ≍[1]	168b	33.48 S	138.56 E
Morganza	194	30.44 N	91.35 W
Morgårdshammar	40	60.09 N	15.23 E
Morgauši	80	55.58 N	46.47 E
Morgenzon	158	26.45 S	29.36 E
Morges	58	46.31 N	6.30 E
Morgex	62	45.45 N	7.02 E
Morghāb (Murgab) ≃	128	38.18 N	61.12 E
Morghar	126	23.40 N	89.37 E
Morghūm, Kūh-e ∧	128	33.06 N	57.30 E
Morgongåva	40	59.56 N	16.57 E
Morgongiori	71	39.45 N	8.46 E
Morguilla, Punta ➤	252	37.46 S	73.40 W
Morhange	56	48.55 N	6.38 E
Mori, It.	64	45.51 N	10.59 E
Mori, Nihon	92a	42.06 N	140.35 E
Mori, Nihon	94	34.50 N	137.56 E
Mori, Nihon	270	34.32 N	135.00 E
Mori ≃	164	10.00 S	148.30 E
Moriah	241r	11.15 N	60.43 W
Moriah, Mount ∧	204	39.17 N	114.12 W
Morialta Conservation Park ♦	168b	34.55 S	138.40 E
Moriarty	200	34.59 N	106.02 W
Moriarty, Mount ∧	224	49.08 N	124.26 W
Morib	114	2.45 N	101.26 E
Moribaya	150	9.53 N	9.33 W
Morice ≃	182	54.24 N	126.45 W
Morice Lake ⊜	182	54.00 N	127.37 W
Morichal Largo ≃	246	9.27 N	62.25 W
Moricsala rezervāts ♦	76	57.17 N	22.11 E
Morie, Loch ⊜	46	57.44 N	4.28 W
Morienval	50	49.18 N	2.56 E
Morigerati	68	40.08 N	15.33 E
Moriguchi	96	34.44 N	135.34 E
Morija	158	29.34 S	27.31 E
Moriki	150	12.52 N	6.30 E
Morin Dawa	89	48.28 N	124.27 E
Moringen	52	51.42 N	9.52 E
Morino, It.	66	41.53 N	13.25 E
Morino, Ross.	76	57.54 N	30.22 E
Morinville	182	53.48 N	113.39 W
Morioka	92	39.42 N	141.09 E
Morīri, Tso ⊜	120	32.54 N	78.20 E
Morisset	170	33.06 S	151.29 E
Moriston ≃	46	57.12 N	4.36 W
Moritzburg ⊥	54	51.09 N	13.40 E
Morivione ◆[8]	266b	45.26 N	9.12 E
Morivs'k	78	51.06 N	30.50 E
Moriya	94	35.56 N	140.00 E
Moriyama	94	35.04 N	135.59 E
Moriyama-chūtonchi, Rikujō-jieitai- ■	94	35.12 N	136.57 E
Moriyoshi-zan ∧	92	39.58 N	140.33 E
Morki	80	56.25 N	49.01 E
Morkill ≃	182	53.42 N	120.30 W
Morkiny Gory	76	57.33 N	36.18 E
Mörkö I	40	58.59 N	17.40 E
Morkoka ≃	74	65.10 N	115.52 E
Mørkøv	41	55.40 N	11.32 E
Morlaix	32	48.35 N	3.50 W
Morlanwelz	50	50.27 N	4.14 E
Morles	56	50.38 N	9.51 E
Morley, Eng., U.K.	44	53.46 N	1.36 W
Morley, Mi., U.S.	190	43.29 N	85.26 W
Morley, N.Y., U.S.	212	44.40 N	75.12 W
Morley Green	262	53.20 N	2.16 W
Mörlunda	26	57.19 N	15.51 E
Mormal'	76	52.45 N	29.53 E
Mormanno	68	39.53 N	16.00 E
Mormant	50	48.36 N	2.53 E
Mormoiron	62	44.04 N	5.11 E
Mormon Lake ⊜	200	34.57 N	111.27 W
Mormon Peak ∧	204	36.57 N	114.30 W
Mormon Reservoir ⊜[1]	202	43.16 N	114.49 W
Mormon Slough ≃	226	37.57 N	121.18 W
Mormon Station Historical State Monument ♦	226	39.00 N	119.50 W
Mormugao	122	15.24 N	73.48 E
Morna	272a	28.35 N	77.22 E
Mornant	62	45.37 N	4.40 E
Mornas	62	44.12 N	4.44 E
Morne-à-l'Eau	241o	16.21 N	61.31 W
Morne Trois Pitons National Park ♦	240d	15.19 N	61.19 W
Morney	166	25.22 S	141.28 E
Morningdale	207	42.18 N	71.45 W
Morningside	284c	38.50 N	76.53 W
Morningside Park ♦	275b	43.47 N	79.12 W
Morningstar ≃	48	52.27 N	8.41 W
Morning Sun	190	41.05 N	91.15 W
Mornington	169	38.13 S	145.03 E
Mornington, Isla I	254	49.45 S	75.23 W
Mornington Island I	164	16.33 S	139.24 E
Mornington Island Aboriginal Land Trust ◆[4]	164	16.20 S	139.20 E
Mornington Peninsula ➤[1]	169	38.20 S	145.05 E
Morno	150	8.41 N	1.31 W
Mornou, Hadjer ∧	146	17.12 N	23.08 E
Moro, Indon.	114	0.46 N	103.43 E
Moro, Or., U.S.	224	45.29 N	120.43 W
Moro ≃	150	7.25 N	11.03 W
Morobe	164	7.45 S	147.35 E
Morobe □[5]	164	7.00 S	146.30 E
Morocco	216	40.56 N	87.27 W
Morocco (Al-Magreb) □[1], Afr.	134	32.00 N	5.00 W
Morocco (Al-Magreb) □[1], Afr.	148	32.00 N	5.00 W
Morococala	248	18.10 S	66.44 W
Morococha	248	11.37 S	76.09 W
Moro Creek ≃	194	33.18 N	92.22 W
Morogoro	154	6.49 S	37.40 E
Morogoro □[4]	154	8.00 S	37.15 E
Moro Gulf ⊂	116	6.51 N	123.00 E
Moroka	273d	26.16 S	27.52 E
Morokweng	158	26.12 S	23.45 E
Moroleón	234	20.08 N	101.12 W
Morombe	157b	21.45 S	43.22 E
Morón, Arg.	258	34.39 S	58.37 W
Morón, Cuba	240p	22.06 N	78.38 W
Mörön, Mong.	88	48.15 N	100.23 E
Mörön, Mong.	88	47.24 N	110.16 E
Mörön, Mong.	88	49.38 N	100.10 E
Morón, Ven.	246	10.29 N	68.11 W
Morón □[5]	288	34.37 S	58.37 W
Mörön ≃	88	47.14 N	110.37 E
Morón, Aeródromo ⊠	288	34.41 S	58.38 W
Morón, Arroyo ≃	288	34.33 S	58.37 W
Morona ≃	246	4.45 S	77.04 W
Morona-Santiago □[4]	246	2.30 S	78.00 W
Morondava	157b	20.17 S	44.17 E
Morón de Almazán	34	41.25 N	2.25 W
Morón de la Frontera	34	37.08 N	5.27 W
Morones, Sierra ⩘	234	21.45 N	103.10 W
Morong	116	14.41 N	120.16 E
Morongo Indian Reservation ◆[4]	204	33.59 N	116.50 W
Moroni, Comores	157a	11.41 S	43.16 E
Moroni, Ut,. U.S.	200	39.31 N	111.35 W
Moron Us ≃, Zhg.	90	34.42 N	94.50 E
Moron Us ≃, Zhg.	120	34.42 N	94.50 E
Moros ≃	34	41.03 N	4.15 W
Morošečnoje	74	56.24 N	156.12 E
Morotai I	108	2.20 N	128.25 E
Moroto	154	2.32 N	34.39 E
Moroto ∧	154	2.32 N	34.46 E
Morouba	152	6.11 N	20.13 E
Morovis	240m	18.20 N	66.24 W
Morowali	112	1.52 S	121.30 E
Moroyama	94	35.56 N	139.19 E
Morozivka	83	49.28 N	39.54 E
Morozkovo	86	59.29 N	61.01 E
Morozovka	78	50.09 N	39.38 E
Morozovsk	80	48.22 N	41.50 E
Morozovskaja	24	61.10 N	50.18 E
Morpeth, On., Can.	214	42.23 N	81.51 W
Morpeth, Eng., U.K.	44	55.10 N	1.41 W
Morphett Vale	168b	35.07 S	138.31 E
Morra, Monte ∧	267a	42.02 N	12.50 E
Morral	214	40.41 N	83.12 W
Morral, Arroyo del ≃	266d	41.29 N	2.03 E
Morrelganj	126	22.28 N	89.51 E
Morrice	216	42.50 N	84.11 W
Morrill	198	41.57 N	103.55 W
Morrilton	194	35.09 N	92.44 W
Morrin	182	51.40 N	112.47 W
Morrinhos, Bra.	250	3.14 S	40.07 W
Morrinhos, Bra.	255	17.44 S	49.07 W
Morrinsville	172	37.39 S	175.32 E
Morris, Mb., Can.	184	49.21 N	97.22 W
Morris, Ct., U.S.	207	41.41 N	73.11 W
Morris, Il., U.S.	216	41.21 N	88.25 W
Morris, In., U.S.	218	39.16 N	85.10 W
Morris, Mn., U.S.	198	45.35 N	95.54 W
Morris, N.Y., U.S.	210	42.32 N	75.14 W
Morris, Ok., U.S.	196	35.36 N	95.51 W
Morris, Pa., U.S.	210	41.36 N	77.18 W
Morris □[6], N.J., U.S.	210	40.48 N	74.29 W
Morris □[6], Tx., U.S.	222	33.05 N	94.45 W
Morris ≃	184	49.21 N	97.22 W
Morris, Mount ∧	162	26.09 S	131.04 E
Morrisburg	212	44.54 N	75.11 W
Morrisdale	214	40.56 N	78.13 W
Morris Dam ◆[6]	280	34.11 N	117.53 W
Morris Jesup, Kap ➤	16	83.38 N	33.52 W
Morris Lake ⊜	276	41.03 N	74.37 W
Morrison, Arg.	252	32.36 S	62.50 W
Morrison, Il., U.S.	190	41.48 N	89.57 W
Morrison, Mo., U.S.	219	38.40 N	91.38 W
Morrison, Point ➤	168b	35.44 S	137.47 E
Morrison Creek ≃	275b	43.28 N	79.39 W
Morrison Lake ⊜, On., Can.	212	44.52 N	79.28 W
Morrison Lake ⊜, Mi., U.S.	216	42.53 N	85.13 W
Morrisonville	219	39.25 N	89.27 W
Morris Park ♦	285	39.59 N	75.15 W
Morris Plains	210	40.49 N	74.28 W
Morris Reservoir ⊜[1]	228	34.12 N	117.52 W
Morris Run	210	41.40 N	77.01 W
Morristown, Az., U.S.	200	33.51 N	112.37 W
Morristown, Il., U.S.	216	42.10 N	89.03 W
Morristown, In., U.S.	218	39.40 N	85.41 W
Morristown, Mn., U.S.	190	44.14 N	93.26 W
Morristown, N.J., U.S.	210	40.47 N	74.28 W
Morristown, N.Y., U.S.	212	44.35 N	75.38 W
Morristown, Oh., U.S.	214	40.04 N	81.05 W
Morristown, S.D., U.S.	198	45.56 N	101.43 W
Morristown, Tn., U.S.	192	36.12 N	83.17 W
Morristown Airport ⊠	276	40.48 N	74.25 W
Morristown National Historical Park ♦	210	40.46 N	74.32 W
Morrisville, N.Y., U.S.	210	42.53 N	75.38 W
Morrisville, Pa., U.S.	208	40.12 N	74.47 W
Morrisville, Vt., U.S.	188	44.33 N	72.35 W
Morrito	236	11.37 N	85.05 W
Morro	246	2.39 S	80.19 W
Morro, Castillo del (Morro Castle) ⊥	286b	23.09 N	82.21 W
Morro, Punta ➤	232	19.39 N	90.42 W
Morro Agudo	287a	22.45 S	43.29 W
Morro Bay	226	35.21 N	120.50 W
Morro Bay ⊂	226	35.20 N	120.51 W
Morro Bay State Park ♦	226	35.20 N	120.52 W
Morro Creek ≃	226	35.23 N	120.52 W
Morro do Chapéu	250	11.33 S	41.09 W
Morro d'Oro	66	42.39 N	13.54 E
Morro Mazatán	234	16.07 N	95.27 W
Morrone del Sannio	66	41.43 N	14.47 E
Morropón	248	5.15 S	80.00 W
Morro Rock ∧	226	35.22 N	120.52 W
Morros	250	2.52 S	44.03 W
Morrosquillo, Golfo de ⊂	246	9.35 N	75.40 W
Morrow, La., U.S.	194	30.49 N	92.04 W
Morrow, Oh., U.S.	218	39.21 N	84.07 W
Morrow □[6]	214	40.33 N	82.50 W
Morrow Island I	282	38.07 N	122.05 W
Morrow Mountain State Park ♦	192	35.23 N	80.05 W
Morrow Point Reservoir ⊜[1]	200	38.25 N	107.30 W
Mörrum	26	56.11 N	14.45 E
Morrumbala	154	17.22 S	35.36 E
Morrumbene	156	23.39 S	35.20 E
Mörrumsån ≃	26	56.09 N	14.44 E
Mors I	26	56.50 N	8.45 E
Morsains	50	48.48 N	3.32 E
Morsang-sur-Orge	261	48.40 N	2.21 E
Moršansk	80	53.26 N	41.49 E
Morsbach	56	50.52 N	7.43 E
Morschwiller-le-Bas	58	47.45 N	7.16 E
Morščichino	265b	55.56 N	37.20 E
Morse, Sk., Can.	184	50.25 N	107.03 W
Morse, La., U.S.	194	30.07 N	92.29 W
Morse, Tx., U.S.	196	36.04 N	101.29 W
Morse Mill	219	38.17 N	90.40 W
Mörsenbroich ◆[8]	263	51.15 N	6.48 E
Morse Reservoir ⊜[1]	218	40.06 N	86.02 W
Morses Pond ⊜	283	42.18 N	71.19 W
Morsi	120	21.21 N	78.00 E
Morskaja Masel'ga	24	63.06 N	34.54 E
Morskoj Bir'učok, ostrov I	84	44.42 N	47.02 E
Morson	184	49.03 N	94.18 W
Morsott	36	35.40 N	8.01 E
Morstein	285	40.01 N	75.35 W
Mort	272a	28.43 N	77.25 E
Morta	272a	28.44 N	77.27 E
Mortagne	32	48.31 N	0.33 E
Mortagne ≃	58	48.33 N	6.27 E
Mortagne-au-Perche	50	48.31 N	0.33 E
Mortagne-sur-Sèvre	32	47.00 N	0.57 W
Mortain	32	48.39 N	0.56 W
Mortana	162	33.02 S	134.07 E
Mortara	62	45.15 N	8.44 E
Morteau	58	47.04 N	6.37 E
Mortefontaine	50	49.07 N	2.36 E
Mortegliano	64	45.57 N	13.10 E
Morte Point ➤	42	51.11 N	4.13 W
Morteratsch, Piz ∧	58	46.22 N	9.51 E
Morteros	252	30.42 S	62.00 W
Mortes, Rio das ≃, Bra.	255	11.45 S	50.44 W
Mortes, Rio das ≃, Bra.	256	21.18 S	43.58 W
Mortesoro	140	10.12 N	34.09 E
Mort-Homme, Forêt du ◆[3]	56	49.15 N	5.15 E
Mortimer	42	51.22 N	1.04 W
Mortlach	184	50.28 N	106.03 W
Mortlake, Austl.	166	38.05 S	142.48 E
Mortlake, Austl.	274a	33.51 S	151.07 E
Mortlake ◆[8]	260	51.28 N	0.16 W
Mortlock ≃	168a	31.42 S	116.55 E
Mortlock Islands II	14	5.27 N	153.40 E
Mortlock North ≃	168a	31.38 S	116.42 E
Mortola Inferiore	62	43.47 N	7.33 E
Morton, Il., U.S.	190	40.36 N	89.27 W
Morton, Mn., U.S.	198	44.33 N	94.59 W
Morton, Ms., U.S.	194	32.21 N	89.39 W
Morton, N.Y., U.S.	210	43.20 N	78.00 W
Morton, Pa., U.S.	285	39.55 N	75.20 W
Morton, Tx., U.S.	196	33.43 N	102.45 W
Morton, Wa., U.S.	224	46.33 N	122.16 W
Morton, Mount ∧[2]	274b	37.56 S	145.20 E
Morton Arboretum ♦	278	41.49 N	88.04 W
Morton Craig Range ⩘	162	28.12 S	124.41 E
Morton Grove	216	42.02 N	87.46 W
Morton National Park ♦	170	35.00 S	150.10 E
Mortons Gap	194	37.14 N	87.28 W
Mortorio, Isola I	71	41.05 N	9.36 E
Mortornès del Vallès	266d	41.33 N	2.16 E
Mortrée	50	48.38 N	0.05 E
Mörtschach	64	46.55 N	12.55 E
Mortsel	50	51.10 N	4.28 E
M'ortvyj Donec ≃	83	47.15 N	39.14 E
Morty	80	55.49 N	51.44 E
Morua	175f	16.54 S	168.32 E
Morumbi ◆[8]	287b	23.36 S	46.42 E
Morumbi, Estádio do ♦	287b	23.37 S	46.43 W
Morungaba	256	22.52 S	46.48 W
Morungole ∧	154	3.49 N	34.02 E
Moruya	166	35.55 S	150.05 E
Morvan ⩘	32	47.05 N	4.00 E
Morvant	241r	10.39 N	61.28 W
Morven, Austl.	166	26.25 S	147.07 E
Morven, N.Z.	172	44.50 S	171.07 E
Morven, Ga., U.S.	192	30.56 N	83.29 W
Morven, N.C., U.S.	192	34.51 N	80.00 W
Morven ∧, Scot., U.K.	46	58.14 N	3.42 W
Morven ∧, Scot., U.K.	46	57.07 N	3.02 W
Morwell	169	38.14 S	146.24 E
Morwell ≃	169	38.10 S	146.23 E
Morwenstow	42	50.54 N	4.33 W
Moryń	30	52.49 N	14.13 E
Moržēnga	76	59.37 N	40.12 E
Morzhovoi	180	54.55 N	163.18 W
Morzine	58	46.11 N	6.43 E
Moržovec, ostrov I	24	66.44 N	42.35 E
Moša ≃, Ross.	24	62.25 N	39.46 E
M'oša ≃, Ross.	80	55.25 N	49.22 E
Mosal'sk	76	54.29 N	34.59 E
Mosambik → Mozambique □[1]	138	18.15 S	35.00 E
Mošanicy	82	54.56 N	38.23 E
Mosås	40	59.12 N	15.08 E
Mosbach	56	49.21 N	9.08 E
Mosborough	44	53.19 N	1.22 W
Mosby	26	58.14 N	7.54 E
Mosby Woods	284c	38.52 N	77.18 W
Moscavide	266c	38.47 N	9.06 W
Mosciano Sant'Angelo	66	42.45 N	13.53 E
Moščnyj, ostrov I	76	60.01 N	27.50 E
Moscos Islands II	110	14.00 N	97.45 E
Moscou → Moskva	82	55.45 N	37.35 E
Moscow → Moskva, Ross.	82	55.45 N	37.35 E
Moscow, Id., U.S.	202	46.43 N	116.59 W
Moscow, In., U.S.	218	39.29 N	85.34 W
Moscow, Oh., U.S.	218	38.51 N	84.13 W
Moscow, Pa., U.S.	210	41.20 N	75.31 W
Moscow, Tx., U.S.	222	30.55 N	94.50 W
Moscow Air Terminal ⊠	265b	55.48 N	37.32 E
Moscow Circus ♦	265b	55.43 N	37.33 E
Moscow Mills	219	38.56 N	90.55 W
Moscow Station ◆[5]	265a	59.56 N	30.22 E
Moscow Victory Park ♦	265a	59.52 N	30.20 E
Moscow Zoo ♦	265b	55.46 N	37.34 E
Moscú → Moskva	82	55.45 N	37.35 E
Moscufo	66	42.25 N	14.03 E
Mosel	54	50.47 N	12.28 E
Mosel (Moselle) ≃	32	50.22 N	7.36 E
Moselebe ≃	156	25.03 S	23.13 E
Moselle, Ms., U.S.	194	31.30 N	89.16 W
Moselle, Mo., U.S.	219	38.23 N	90.54 W
Moselle □[5]	56	49.00 N	6.30 E
Moselle (Mosel) ≃	32	50.22 N	7.36 E
Moselotte ≃	58	48.01 N	6.38 E
Mošenskoje	76	58.31 N	34.35 E
Möser	54	52.13 N	11.48 E
Mosermandl ∧	64	47.12 N	13.24 E
Mosers River	186	44.59 N	62.15 W
Moses Lake	202	47.07 N	119.16 W
Moses Lake ⊜[1]	202	47.10 N	119.20 W
Moses Point	180	64.42 N	162.03 W
Moses Power Plant ◆[6]	284a	43.09 N	79.02 W
Mosetse	156	20.37 S	26.32 E
Mosgiel	172	45.53 S	170.21 E
Moshannon	214	41.02 N	78.00 W
Moshannon Creek ≃	214	41.04 N	78.06 W
Moshanpu	100	29.34 N	112.41 E
Moshaweng ≃	158	26.35 S	22.50 E
Mosheim, Tn., U.S.	192	36.11 N	82.57 W
Mosheim, Tx., U.S.	222	31.38 N	97.36 W
Moshi	154	3.21 S	37.20 E
Moshi ≃	150	9.18 N	4.38 E
Moshiyu	104	41.15 N	124.05 E
Moshny	78	49.32 N	31.44 E
Mosier	224	45.41 N	121.23 W
Mosier Hill ∧[2]	214	40.06 N	80.24 W
Mosina	30	52.16 N	16.51 E
Mosinee	190	44.47 N	89.42 W
Mosjøen	24	65.50 N	13.10 E
Moskal'onki	86	54.59 N	71.54 E
Moskal'vo	89	53.35 N	142.30 E
Moskau → Moskva	82	55.45 N	37.35 E
Moskenesøya I	24	67.59 N	13.00 E
Moskháton	267c	37.57 N	23.41 E
Moškino	80	57.45 N	45.20 E
Moskito-Golf → Mosquitos, Golfo de los ⊂	236	9.00 N	81.15 W
Moškovo	86	55.18 N	83.37 E
Moskovskaja Slav'anka	265a	59.45 N	30.30 E
Moskovskaja vozvyšennost' ⩘[1]	76	56.15 N	37.30 E
Moskva (Moscow), Ross.	82	55.45 N	37.35 E
Moskva (Moscow), Ross.	265b	55.45 N	37.35 E
Moskva ≃	76	55.05 N	38.50 E
Moskva, Gorod □[7]	265b	55.45 N	37.35 E
Moskva, pik ∧	85	38.57 N	71.49 E
Moskva Oblast' □[4]	76	55.30 N	37.30 E
Moskvy, kanal imeni ≍	82	56.43 N	37.08 E
Mosman	170	33.49 S	151.14 E
Mosman Park	168a	32.01 S	115.46 E
Moso (Moos)	64	46.41 N	12.23 E
Moso in Passiria (Moos)	64	46.50 N	11.10 E
Mošok	80	55.48 N	41.17 E
Mosolovo	80	54.17 N	40.32 E
Mosomane	156	24.04 S	26.15 E
Mosoni-Duna ≃	61	47.54 N	17.17 E
Mosonmagyaróvár	30	47.51 N	17.17 E
Mosonszolnok	61	47.51 N	17.11 E
Mosopa	156	24.50 S	25.31 E
Mospyne	83	47.53 N	38.03 E
Mosqueiro	250	1.10 S	48.28 W
Mosquera	246	2.30 N	78.29 W
Mosquero	196	35.46 N	103.57 W
Mosquic, Lac ⊜	206	46.39 N	74.28 W
Mosquito, Punta ➤	246	9.07 N	77.53 W
Mosquito, Riacho ≃	252	22.02 S	57.57 W
Mosquito Brook ≃	283	42.40 N	71.02 W
Mosquito Creek ≃, Ia., U.S.	198	41.11 N	95.50 W
Mosquito Creek ≃, Oh., U.S.	214	41.10 N	80.45 W
Mosquito Creek ≃, Pa., U.S.	214	41.07 N	78.07 W
Mosquito Creek Lake ⊜[1]	214	41.22 N	80.45 W
Mosquito Creek State Park ♦	214	41.22 N	80.45 W
Mosquito Indian Reserve ◆[4]	184	52.30 N	108.15 W
Mosquito Lagoon ⊂	220	28.45 N	80.45 W
Mosquitos, Costa de □[9]	236	13.00 N	83.45 W
Mosquitos, Golfo de los ⊂	236	9.00 N	81.15 W
Moss	26	59.26 N	10.42 E
Mossaka	152	1.13 S	16.48 E
Mossâmedes	255	16.07 S	50.11 W
Mossbank, Sk., Can.	184	49.55 N	105.59 W
Moss Bank, Eng., U.K.	262	53.29 N	2.44 W
Mossbank, Scot., U.K.	46a	60.27 N	1.12 W
Moss Bank Park ♦	262	53.36 N	2.28 W
Moss Beach	282	37.32 N	122.31 W
Mossburn	172	45.40 S	168.15 E
Mosselbaai (Mossel Bay)	158	34.11 S	22.08 E
Mosselbaai ⊂	158	34.06 S	22.20 E
Mossendjo	152	2.57 S	12.44 E
Mosses, Col des)(	58	46.24 N	7.06 E
Mossgiel	166	33.15 S	144.34 E
Moss Hill	222	30.15 N	94.45 W
Mossig ≃	58	48.33 N	7.30 E
Mössingen	58	48.24 N	9.03 E
Moss Landing	226	36.48 N	121.47 W
Mossleigh	182	50.43 N	113.20 W
Mossley	262	53.32 N	2.02 W
Mossley Hill ◆[8]	262	53.23 N	2.55 W
Mossman	164	16.28 S	145.22 E
Mossmans Brook ≃	276	41.03 N	74.27 W
Moss Moor ◆[3]	262	53.37 N	2.00 W
Moss Mountain ∧	194	34.50 N	92.40 W
Mossø ⊜	41	56.02 N	9.48 E
Mosson ≃	62	43.33 N	3.54 E
Mossoró	250	5.11 S	37.20 W
Mosso Santa Maria	62	45.38 N	8.08 E
Moss Point	194	30.24 N	88.32 W
Moss Point ➤	279a	41.37 N	81.32 W
Moss Side	262	53.46 N	2.57 W
Mossuril	154	14.58 S	40.42 E
Moss Vale	170	34.33 S	150.22 E
Mossy ≃, Mb., Can.	184	51.39 N	99.55 W
Mossy ≃, Sk., Can.	184	54.05 N	103.00 W
Mossyrock	224	46.31 N	122.29 W

Symbols in the index entries represent the broad categories identified in the key at the right. Symbols with superior numbers (⩘[1]) identify subcategories (see complete key on page I · 1).

Symbole im Register stellen die rechts im Schlüssel erklärten Kategorien dar. Symbole mit hochgestellten Ziffern (⩘[1]) bezeichnen Unterabteilungen einer Kategorie (vgl. vollständiger Schlüssel auf Seite I · 1).

Los símbolos incluídos en el texto del índice representan las grandes categorías identificadas con la clave a la derecha. Los símbolos con numeros en su parte superior (⩘[1]) identifican las subcategorías (véase la clave completa en la página I · 1).

Les symboles de l'index représentent les catégories indiquées dans la légende à droite. Les symboles suivis d'un indice (⩘[1]) représentent des sous-catégories (voir légende complète à la page I · 1).

Os símbolos incluídos no texto do índice representam as grandes categorias identificadas com a chave à direita. Os símbolos com números em sua parte superior (⩘[1]) identificam as subcategorias (veja-se a chave completa à página I · 1).

∧ Mountain	Berg	Montaña	Montagne	Montanha
⩘ Mountains	Gebirge	Montañas	Montagnes	Montanhas
)(Pass	Paß	Paso	Col	Passo
V Valley, Canyon	Tal, Cañon	Valle, Cañón	Vallée, Canyon	Vale, Canhão
≃ Plain	Ebene	Llano	Plaine	Planície
➤ Cape	Kap	Cabo	Cap	Cabo
I Island	Insel	Isla	Île	Ilha
II Islands	Inseln	Islas	Îles	Ilhas
⊥ Other Topographic Features	Andere Topographische Objekte	Otros Elementos Topográficos	Autres données topographiques	Outros acidentes topográficos

ESPAÑOL Nombre	Página	Lat.°'	Long.°' W=Oeste
FRANÇAIS Nom	Page	Lat.°'	Long.°' W=Ouest
PORTUGUÊS Nome	Página	Lat.°'	Long.°' W=Oeste

Symbol key / legend

Symbol	English	German	Spanish	French	Portuguese
≃ River	River	Fluß	Río	Rivière	Rio
≈ Canal	Canal	Kanal	Canal	Canal	Canal
ᴸ Waterfall, Rapids	Waterfall, Rapids	Wasserfall, Stromschnellen	Cascada, Rápidos	Chute d'eau, Rapides	Cascata, Rápidos
⋃ Strait	Strait	Meeresstraße	Estrecho	Détroit	Estreito
◡ Bay, Gulf	Bay, Gulf	Bucht, Golf	Bahía, Golfo	Baie, Golfe	Baía, Golfo
⊚ Lake, Lakes	Lake, Lakes	See, Seen	Lago, Lagos	Lac, Lacs	Lago, Lagos
≅ Swamp	Swamp	Sumpf	Pantano	Marais	Pântano
⧖ Ice Features, Glacier	Ice Features, Glacier	Eis- und Gletscherformen	Accidentes Glaciales	Formes glaciaires	Acidentes glaciares
▴ Other Hydrographic Features	Other Hydrographic Features	Andere Hydrographische Objekte	Otros Elementos Hidrográficos	Autres données hydrographiques	Outros acidentes hidrográficos
✦ Submarine Features	Submarine Features	Untermeerische Objekte	Accidentes Submarinos	Formes de relief sous-marin	Acidentes submarinos
⯈ Political Unit	Political Unit	Politische Einheit	Unidad Política	Entité politique	Unidade política
🏛 Cultural Institution	Cultural Institution	Kulturelle Institution	Institución Cultural	Institution culturelle	Instituição cultural
♦ Historical Site	Historical Site	Historische Stätte	Sitio Histórico	Site historique	Sítio histórico
♦ Recreational Site	Recreational Site	Erholungs- und Ferienort	Sitio de Recreo	Centre de loisirs	Área de Lazer
▪ Military Installation	Military Installation	Militäranlage	Instalación Militar	Installation militaire	Instalação militar
✈ Airport	Airport	Flughafen	Aeropuerto	Aéroport	Aeroporto
◂ Miscellaneous	Miscellaneous	Verschiedenes	Misceláneo	Divers	Diversos

Name	Page	Lat.°′	Long.°′
Muda ≐	114	5.33 N	100.22 E
Mudan ≐	89	46.22 N	129.33 E
Mudanjiang	89	44.35 N	129.36 E
Mudanya	130	40.22 N	28.52 E
Mudau	56	49.32 N	9.11 E
Mudaysīsāt, Jabal ∧	132	31.39 N	36.14 E
Mud Creek ≐, N.A.	206	45.01 N	72.24 W
Mud Creek ≐, U.S.	198	43.17 N	96.15 W
Mud Creek ≐, Il., U.S.	219	38.21 N	89.48 W
Mud Creek ≐, In., U.S.	216	41.06 N	86.21 W
Mud Creek ≐, In., U.S.	216	40.26 N	85.55 W
Mud Creek ≐, Ne., U.S.	198	41.01 N	98.54 W
Mud Creek ≐, N.Y., U.S.	210	42.17 N	77.13 W
Mud Creek ≐, N.Y., U.S.	210	42.59 N	77.23 W
Mud Creek ≐, N.Y., U.S.	210	43.05 N	78.43 W
Mud Creek ≐, Ok., U.S.	196	33.55 N	97.28 W
Mud Creek ≐, S.D., U.S.	198	45.11 N	98.24 W
Mud Creek ≐, Tx., U.S.	222	31.48 N	94.58 W
Muddus Nationalpark ♦	24	67.00 N	20.16 E
Muddy ≐, Nv., U.S.	204	36.27 N	114.22 W
Muddy ≐, Wa., U.S.	224	46.04 N	122.01 W
Muddy Boggy Creek ≐	196	34.03 N	95.47 W
Muddy Branch ≐	284c	39.03 N	77.18 W
Muddy Brook ≐	276	41.07 N	73.20 W
Muddy Creek ≐, U.S.	276	41.03 N	74.02 W
Muddy Creek ≐, Mo., U.S.	194	38.51 N	93.03 W
Muddy Creek ≐, Mt., U.S.	202	47.56 N	111.46 W
Muddy Creek ≐, Oh., U.S.	214	41.27 N	83.03 W
Muddy Creek ≐, Pa., U.S.	208	39.47 N	76.18 W
Muddy Creek ≐, Ut,. U.S.	200	38.24 N	110.42 W
Muddy Creek ≐, Wy., U.S.	198	42.35 N	104.57 W
Muddy Creek ≐, Wy., U.S.	200	41.59 N	106.08 W
Muddy Creek ≐, Wy., U.S.	200	41.32 N	110.13 W
Muddy Creek ≐, Wy., U.S.	200	41.01 N	107.42 W
Muddy Creek ≐, Wy., U.S.	202	43.17 N	108.14 W
Muddy Fork ≐	224	46.22 N	121.34 W
Muddy Gut ⊂	284b	39.17 N	76.26 W
Muddy Peak ∧	204	36.18 N	114.42 W
Müden, Dtsch.	52	52.52 N	10.07 E
Müden, Dtsch.	54	52.31 N	10.22 E
Mudersbach	56	50.50 N	7.57 E
Mudgee	166	32.36 S	149.35 E
Mudgeeraba	171a	28.04 S	153.22 E
Mudhol	122	16.21 N	75.17 E
Mud Island I	171a	27.20 S	153.15 E
Mud Islands II	169	38.17 S	144.45 E
Mudjatik ≐	184	56.02 N	107.36 W
Mudjuga	24	63.46 N	39.15 E
Mud Lake ⊜, Id., U.S.	202	43.53 N	112.24 W
Mud Lake ⊜, Nv., U.S.	204	37.52 N	117.04 W
Mud Lake ⊜, N.Y., U.S.	212	44.30 N	75.28 W
Mud Lake Reservoir ⊜[1]	198	45.50 N	98.10 W
Mudon	110	16.15 N	97.44 E
Mudongzhen	102	29.35 N	106.51 E
Mudu	106	31.15 N	120.30 E
Mudug □[4]	144	6.15 N	48.00 E
Mudurnu	130	40.28 N	31.13 E
Mudurnu ≐	130	40.49 N	30.33 E
M'ud'ur'um ≐	85	40.53 N	76.36 E
Mueda	154	11.39 S	39.33 E
Muelle de los Bueyes	236	12.04 N	84.32 W
Mueller, Mount ∧[2]	162	19.54 S	127.51 E
Muenster	196	33.39 N	97.23 W
Mu'er	107	29.48 N	106.37 E
Muerte, Valle de la → Death Valley V	204	36.30 N	117.00 W
Muerto ≐	252	23.02 S	62.29 W
Muerto, Mar → Dead Sea ⊜	132	31.30 N	35.30 E
Mufulira	154	12.33 S	28.14 E
Mufuma	152	9.04 S	17.06 E
Mufu Shan ∧	100	29.02 N	113.54 E
Mufu Shan ⋀	100	29.00 N	114.00 E
Muğan düzü ≚	84	39.40 N	48.15 E
Mugang	100	29.44 N	115.14 E
Mugazine	158	26.07 S	32.30 E
Mugegawa	94	35.31 N	136.51 E
Mugello V	66	43.55 N	11.30 E
Mügeln	54	51.14 N	13.02 E
Muger ≐	144	9.54 N	37.57 E
Müggelberge ∧[2]	264a	52.25 N	13.39 E
Müggelheim ◆[8]	264a	52.25 N	13.40 E
Muggia	64	45.36 N	13.46 E
Muggio	266b	45.36 N	9.14 E
Mughal Sarāi	124	25.18 N	83.07 E
Mugi, Nihon	94	35.34 N	137.01 E
Mugi, Nihon	96	33.40 N	134.25 E
Mu Gia, Deo)(	110	17.40 N	105.47 E
Muginga	152	8.20 S	17.37 E
Muğla	130	37.12 N	28.22 E
Muğla □[4]	130	37.10 N	28.30 E
Mugodžarskaja	86	48.36 N	58.27 E
Mugodžary, gory ⋀[2]	86	49.00 N	58.40 E
Mugombazi	154	5.50 S	30.14 E
Mugo-ri	98	38.58 N	126.31 E
Mugrejevskij	80	56.36 N	42.21 E
Mugron	32	43.45 N	0.45 W
Mugu Karṇālī ≐	124	29.38 N	81.52 E
Mugur-Aksy	86	50.21 N	90.30 E
Mūḩ, Sabkhat al- ⊜	130	34.30 N	38.20 E
Muhala	154	5.40 S	28.43 E
Muhamdi	124	27.57 N	80.13 E
Muḩammad, Ra's ›	140	27.44 N	34.15 E
Muhammadābād	124	26.02 N	83.23 E
Muhammadpur	126	23.24 N	89.36 E
Muḩammad Qawl	140	20.54 N	37.05 E
Muḩavec ≐	76	52.05 N	23.39 E
Muḩayshir, Birkat ⊜	142	30.43 N	31.56 E
Muheza	154	5.10 S	38.47 E
Muḩīṭ, Maṣrif al- ≡	273c	30.07 N	31.06 E
Mühlacker	56	48.57 N	8.50 E
Mühlau	54	50.54 N	12.45 E
Mühlbach am Hochkönig	64	47.22 N	13.08 E
Muhlbach-sur-Munster	58	48.02 N	7.05 E
Mühlberg	54	51.26 N	13.13 E
Mühldorf	61	48.22 N	15.21 E
Mühldorf am Inn	60	48.15 N	12.32 E
Mühlen → Molini di Tures	64	46.54 N	11.56 E
Mühlenbeck	54	52.40 N	13.22 E
Mühlenbecker See ⊜	264a	52.41 N	13.24 E
Muhlenberg	210	41.14 N	76.09 W
Mühlen-Berg ∧[2]	264a	52.23 N	13.15 E
Mühlen Eichsen	54	53.45 N	11.15 E
Mühlenfliess ≐	264a	52.26 N	13.41 E
Mühlenrahmede	263	51.16 N	7.40 E
Mühlhausen, Dtsch.	54	51.12 N	10.27 E
Mühlhausen, Dtsch.	60	49.10 N	11.27 E
Mühlhausen, Dtsch.	263	51.33 N	7.44 E
Mühlhausen im Täle	56	48.34 N	9.39 E
Mühlheim	56	50.07 N	8.50 E
Mühlheim an der Donau	58	48.01 N	8.53 E
Mühlig-Hofmann Mountains ⋀	9	72.00 S	5.20 E
Mühlleiten	264b	48.10 N	16.34 E
Mühltroff	54	50.32 N	11.55 E
Mühlviertel ◆[1]	30	48.25 N	14.10 E
Muhola	26	63.20 N	25.05 E
Muhoro	154	1.01 S	34.07 E
Muhos	26	64.48 N	25.59 E
Muḩradah	130	35.15 N	36.35 E
Mühringen	58	48.25 N	8.46 E
Muhu I	76	58.38 N	23.15 E
Muhula	154	13.53 S	39.30 E
Muhulu	154	1.03 S	27.17 E
Muhutwe	154	1.33 S	31.42 E
Muhu väin Ц	76	58.45 N	23.20 E
Muhuwesi ≐	154	11.16 S	37.58 E
Muick, Loch ⊜	46	56.55 N	3.10 W
Muiden	52	52.19 N	5.04 E
Muiderslot ⊥	52	52.20 N	5.10 E
Muides-sur-Loire	50	47.40 N	1.31 E
Muié	152	14.25 S	20.36 E
Mui Hopohoponga Point ›	174w	21.09 S	175.02 W
Muikaichi	96	34.21 N	131.56 E
Muikamachi	94	37.04 N	138.53 E
Muine Bheag (Bagenalstown)	48	52.41 N	6.58 W
Muir, Mi., U.S.	216	42.59 N	84.56 W
Muir, Pa., U.S.	208	40.36 N	76.31 W
Muir, Mount ∧	180	61.06 N	148.24 W
Muir Beach	282	37.52 N	122.35 W
Muirdrum	46	56.31 N	2.42 W
Muirkirk, Scot., U.K.	46	55.31 N	4.04 W
Muirkirk, Md., U.S.	284c	39.03 N	76.53 W
Muir of Ord	46	57.31 N	4.27 W
Muiron Islands II	162	21.35 S	114.20 E
Muir Seamount ✧[3]	16	33.41 N	62.30 W
Muirtown	46	56.16 N	3.45 W
Muir Woods	282	37.53 N	122.34 W
Muir Woods National Monument ♦	226	37.54 N	122.33 W
Muiskraal	158	33.56 S	21.13 E
Muisne	246	0.36 N	80.02 W
Muite	154	14.02 S	39.00 E
Mui Wo	271d	22.16 N	113.59 E
Muizen, Bel.	50	51.01 N	4.31 E
Muizen, Bel.	56	50.46 N	5.10 E
Muja, Ityo.	144	12.02 N	39.29 E
Muja, Ross.	88	56.24 N	115.39 E
Muja ≐	88	56.24 N	115.39 E
Mujāhidpur ◆[8]	272a	28.34 N	77.13 E
Mujang-ni	98	35.26 N	126.32 E
Mujezerskij	24	63.57 N	31.55 E
Mujiapucun	104	41.06 N	122.48 E
Mujiayu	105	40.24 N	116.55 E
Mujimbeji Mission	154	12.11 S	24.57 E
Mujnak	86	43.48 N	59.02 E
Muju	98	36.02 N	127.40 E
Mukacheve	78	48.27 N	22.45 E
Mukah	112	2.54 N	112.06 E
Mukaishima	96	34.20 N	133.10 E
Mukalla → Al-Mukallā	144	14.32 N	49.08 E
Mukandpur ◆[8]	272a	28.44 N	77.11 E
Mukandwara	120	24.49 N	75.59 E
Mukawa	94	35.47 N	138.23 E
Mukāwir	132	31.34 N	35.38 E
Mukāwir ⊥	132	31.34 N	35.38 E
Mukawwar I	140	20.48 N	37.13 E
Mukdahan	110	16.32 N	104.43 E
Mukden → Shenyang	104	41.48 N	123.27 E
Muke Arba	144	8.57 N	42.09 E
Mukebo	154	6.49 S	28.03 E
Mukeriān	123	31.57 N	75.37 E
Mukharram al-Fawqānī	130	34.49 N	37.04 E
Mukhmās	132	31.52 N	35.17 E
Mukho	98	37.33 N	129.06 E
Mukilteo	224	47.56 N	122.18 W
Mukinbudin	162	30.54 S	118.13 E
Mukinge Hill	154	13.29 S	25.52 E
Mukō	96	34.56 N	135.42 E
Muko ≐	96	34.41 N	135.23 E
Mukomuko	112	2.35 S	101.07 E
Mukomwenze	154	6.52 S	27.16 E
Mukoshima-rettō II	14	27.37 N	142.10 E
Mukry	128	37.36 N	65.44 E
Muksi-ri	98	39.52 N	125.54 E
Muksu ≐	85	39.15 N	71.23 E
Muksūdpur	126	23.18 N	89.51 E
Muktāgācha	124	24.46 N	90.14 E
Muktsar	123	30.29 N	74.31 E
Mukuku	154	12.09 S	29.49 E
Mukuleshi ≐	154	10.21 S	24.30 E
Mukur	86	48.03 N	54.30 E
Mukusaki	115b	8.33 S	121.37 E
Mukutan	154	0.38 N	36.16 E
Mukutawa ≐	184	53.10 N	97.28 W
Mukwela	154	17.02 S	26.39 E
Mukwonago	216	42.51 N	88.19 W
Mūl	122	20.04 N	79.40 E
Mula, Esp.	34	38.03 N	1.30 W
Mula, Zhg.	102	29.40 N	100.39 E
Mula ≐, India	122	19.32 N	74.50 E
Mula ≐, India	122	18.34 N	74.20 E
Mūla ≐, Pāk.	120	27.57 N	67.36 E
Mulādi	126	22.54 N	90.25 E
Muladu I	122	7.01 N	72.59 E
Mulaly	86	45.27 N	78.19 E
Mulan	89	45.57 N	128.03 E
Muland ◆[8]	272c	19.10 N	72.57 E
Mulanda	152	14.41 S	21.48 E
Mulanje, Malaŵi	154	16.03 S	35.31 E
Mulanje, Moç.	154	16.03 S	35.45 E
Mulargia, Lago ⊜[1]	71	39.37 N	9.14 E
Mulas, Punta ›	240m	18.09 N	65.27 W
Mulas, Punta de ›	240p	21.01 N	75.35 W
Mulatos	232	28.39 N	108.51 W
Mulayit Taung ∧	110	16.11 N	98.32 E
Mulazzo	64	44.19 N	9.53 E
Mulbāgal	122	13.10 N	78.24 E
Mulben	46	57.31 N	3.06 W
Mulberry, Ar., U.S.	194	35.30 N	94.03 W
Mulberry, Fl., U.S.	220	27.53 N	81.58 W
Mulberry, In., U.S.	216	40.20 N	86.39 W
Mulberry, Oh., U.S.	218	39.11 N	84.14 W
Mulberry ≐	194	35.28 N	94.03 W
Mulberry Creek ≐, Al., U.S.	194	32.27 N	86.52 W
Mulberry Creek ≐, Tx., U.S.	196	34.37 N	100.55 W
Mulberry Fork ≐	194	33.33 N	87.11 W
Mulberry Grove	219	38.55 N	89.16 W
Mulberry Mountain ∧	194	35.42 N	92.56 W
Mulchatna ≐	180	59.39 N	157.08 W
Mulchén	252	37.43 S	72.14 W
Mulda, Dtsch.	54	50.48 N	13.25 E
Mul'da, Ross.	24	67.28 N	63.34 E
Mulde ≐	54	51.52 N	12.15 E
Muldenstein	54	51.40 N	12.19 E
Muldersdrif se Loop ≐	273d	26.06 S	27.51 E
Muldersvlei	158	30.41 S	22.13 E
Muldoon	222	29.49 N	97.04 W
Muldraugh	194	37.56 N	85.59 W
Muldrow	194	35.24 N	94.35 W
Mule, Lac la ⊜	186	51.33 N	65.35 W
Muleba	154	1.49 S	31.40 E
Mule Creek ≐	198	37.05 N	99.00 W
Mulegé	232	26.53 N	112.01 W
Mulegns	58	46.33 N	9.37 E
Mulei	86	43.49 N	90.11 E
Mules (Mauls)	64	46.51 N	11.31 E
Mules, Pulau I	115b	8.54 S	120.17 E
Muleshoe	196	34.13 N	102.43 W
Mulevala	154	16.30 S	37.30 E
Mulga Downs	162	22.08 S	118.26 E
Mulgathing	162	30.15 S	134.00 E
Mulgathing Rocks ∧	162	30.14 S	133.58 E
Mulghar	126	22.46 N	89.45 E
Mulgoa	170	33.50 S	150.40 E
Mulgoa Creek ≐	274a	33.46 S	150.39 E
Mulgowie	171a	27.43 S	152.22 E
Mulgrave, Austl.	274b	37.56 S	145.12 E
Mulgrave, N.S., Can.	186	45.37 N	61.23 W
Mulgrave Hills ⋀[2]	180	67.42 N	163.24 W
Mulgul	162	24.49 S	118.26 E
Mulhacén ∧	34	37.03 N	3.19 W
Mulhall	196	36.03 N	97.24 W
Mülhausen → Mulhouse	58	47.45 N	7.20 E
Mülheim	56	49.54 N	7.01 E
Mülheim an der Ruhr	56	51.24 N	6.54 E
Mülheimer Ruhrtalbrüke ◆[5]	263	51.23 N	6.54 E
Mülheim-Karlich	56	50.21 N	7.28 E
Mulhouse (Mülhausen)	58	47.45 N	7.20 E
Muli	102	27.50 N	101.15 E
Muling, Zhg.	89	44.56 N	130.31 E
Muling, Zhg.	89	44.31 N	130.13 E
Muling ≐	89	45.53 N	133.30 E
Mulini, Capo ›	70	37.34 N	15.10 E
Mulino	224	45.13 N	122.34 W
Mulinu'u, Cape ›	175a	13.26 S	172.43 W
Mulita ≐	116	7.18 N	124.52 E
Mulkear ≐	48	52.40 N	8.33 W
Mūlki	122	13.06 N	74.48 E
Mull, Island of I	46	56.27 N	6.00 W
Mull, Sound of Ц	46	56.32 N	5.50 W
Mullagh	48	53.49 N	6.57 W
Mullaghareirk Mountains ⋀	48	52.20 N	9.10 W
Mullaghcleevaun ∧	48	53.06 N	6.24 W
Mullaghmore ∧	48	54.52 N	6.51 W
Mullaloo Point ›	168a	31.48 S	115.44 E
Mullan	202	47.28 N	115.48 W
Mullen	198	42.02 N	101.02 W
Müllenbach	56	50.19 N	6.55 E
Mullengudgery	166	31.41 S	147.26 E
Mullens	192	37.34 N	81.22 W
Muller, Pegunungan ⋀	112	0.40 N	113.50 E
Muller Creek ≐	162	22.29 S	134.30 E
Muller Range ⋀	164	5.35 S	142.15 E
Mullerup	41	55.30 N	11.13 E
Mullet Key I	220	27.37 N	82.44 W
Mullet Peninsula ›[1]	48	54.12 N	10.00 W
Mullett Lake ⊜	190	45.30 N	84.30 W
Mullewa	162	28.33 S	115.31 E
Mull Head ›, Scot., U.K.	46	59.23 N	2.54 W
Mull Head ›, Scot., U.K.	46	58.58 N	2.43 W
Müllheim	58	47.48 N	7.38 E
Mullhyttan	40	59.09 N	14.41 E
Mullica ≐	208	39.33 N	74.25 W
Mullica, Alquatka Branch ≐	285	39.47 N	74.48 W
Mullica, Sleeper Branch ≐	285	39.39 N	74.40 W
Mullica Hill	208	39.44 N	75.13 W
Mulligan ≐	166	25.00 S	138.30 E
Mulliken	216	42.45 N	84.53 W
Mullin	196	31.33 N	98.40 W
Mullinahone	48	52.30 N	7.30 W
Mullinavat	48	52.21 N	7.10 W
Mullingar	48	53.32 N	7.20 W
Mullins	192	34.12 N	79.15 W
Mullinville	198	37.35 N	99.28 W
Mullion	42	50.01 N	5.15 W
Mulloon Creek ≐	171b	35.12 S	149.38 E
Mullovka	80	54.13 N	49.25 E
Müllrose	54	52.14 N	14.25 E
Mullsjö	26	57.55 N	13.53 E
Mullumbimby	166	28.33 S	153.30 E
Mullum Mullum Creek ≐	274b	37.44 S	145.10 E
Mulobezi	154	16.48 S	25.09 E
Mulonda Funda	154	11.06 S	25.28 E
Mulondo	152	15.39 S	15.14 E
Mulongo	154	7.50 S	27.00 E
Mulshi Lake ⊜[1]	122	18.30 N	73.30 E
Multai	120	21.46 N	78.15 E
Multān	123	30.11 N	71.29 E
Multen ⊜	40	59.10 N	14.37 E
Multia	26	62.25 N	24.47 E
Multnomah □[6]	224	45.30 N	122.22 W
Multnomah Channel ≐[1]	224	45.51 N	122.52 W
Multnomah Falls ⌞	224	45.35 N	122.07 W
Mulu, Gunong ∧	112	4.04 N	114.56 E
Mulumbe, Monts ⋀	154	8.16 S	28.16 E
Mulungushi	154	14.40 S	28.50 E
Mulungushi Dam ◆[6]	154	14.40 S	28.50 E
Mulvane	198	37.28 N	97.14 W
Mulwad	140	18.39 N	30.35 E
Mulyah Mountain ∧	166	30.37 S	144.31 E
Muma	152	3.24 N	23.15 E
Mumbai (Bombay), India	122	18.58 N	72.50 E
Mumbai (Bombay), India	272c	18.58 N	72.50 E
Mumbles Head ›	42	51.35 N	3.59 W
Mumbondo	152	10.09 S	14.15 E
Mumbra	272c	19.11 N	73.01 E
Mumbwa	154	14.59 S	27.04 E
Mumcular	130	37.05 N	27.40 E
Mume	154	9.40 S	27.26 E
Mumen	102	32.09 N	106.28 E
Mumeng	164	7.00 S	146.35 E
Mumford, N.Y., U.S.	210	42.59 N	77.52 W
Mumford, Tx., U.S.	222	30.44 N	96.34 W
Mumias	154	0.20 N	34.29 E
Mümling ≐	56	49.50 N	9.09 E
Mumoni ∧	154	0.31 S	38.01 E
Mumra	80	45.47 N	47.41 E
Mumu	140	12.06 N	23.42 E
Mumungwe	156	21.59 S	26.24 E
Mun ≐	110	15.19 N	105.30 E
Mun, Jabal ∧	140	14.08 N	22.42 E
Munā, Ar. Su.	144	21.25 N	39.52 E
Muna, Méx.	232	20.29 N	89.43 W
Muna ≐	74	67.52 N	123.06 E
Muna, Pulau I	112	5.00 S	122.30 E
Muna, Selat Ц	112	5.15 S	122.10 E
Munā al-Amīr	142	29.54 N	31.15 E
Munābāo	120	25.45 N	70.17 E
Munajly	86	46.47 N	54.31 E
Munakata	96	33.50 N	130.35 E
Munam-ni	98	38.41 N	126.54 E
Munam-san ∧	98	40.26 N	127.22 E
Munbong-ni	271b	37.43 N	126.49 E
Muncar	115a	8.26 S	114.20 E
Münchberg	54	50.11 N	11.47 E
Müncheberg	54	52.30 N	14.08 E
Münchehofe	264a	52.30 N	13.40 E
München (Munich)	60	48.08 N	11.34 E
Münchenbernsdorf	54	50.49 N	11.56 E
Münchenbuchsee	58	47.01 N	7.27 E
Münchendorf	264b	48.02 N	16.23 E
München-Erding, Flughafen ⊠	60	48.22 N	11.48 E
München-Gladbach → Mönchengladbach	56	51.12 N	6.28 E
München-Riem, Flughafen ⊠	60	48.08 N	11.41 E
Münchenstein	58	47.31 N	7.37 E
Münchhausen	56	50.57 N	8.43 E
Munchique, Cerro ∧	246	2.32 N	76.57 W
Munchique, Parque Nacional ♦	246	2.30 N	77.10 W
Munch'ŏn	98	39.16 N	127.15 E
Muncie	216	40.11 N	85.23 W
Muncusun	130	38.54 N	35.38 E
Muncy	210	41.12 N	76.47 W
Muncy Creek ≐	210	41.13 N	76.48 W
Muncy Valley	210	41.21 N	76.35 W
Mundare	182	53.36 N	112.20 W
Mundaring	168a	31.54 S	116.10 E
Munday	196	33.26 N	99.37 W
Mundelein	216	42.15 N	88.00 W
Mündelheim ◆[8]	263	51.21 N	6.41 E
Münden	56	51.25 N	9.39 E
Munderfing	60	48.05 N	13.11 E
Munderkingen	58	48.14 N	9.38 E
Munderoo ∧	171b	35.48 S	147.47 E
Mundesley	42	52.53 N	1.26 E
Mundijong	168a	32.18 S	115.59 E
Mundiwindi	162	23.52 S	120.09 E
Mūndka ◆[8]	272a	28.41 N	77.02 E
Mundo ≐	34	38.19 N	1.40 W
Mundolsheim	58	48.39 N	7.42 E
Mundon Hill	260	51.41 N	0.42 E
Mundo Novo	255	11.52 S	40.28 W
Mundra	120	22.51 N	69.44 E
Mundrabilla	162	31.52 S	127.51 E
Mundubbera	166	25.36 S	151.18 E
Mundybaš	86	53.14 N	87.19 E
Mundytau, gora ∧	85	38.00 N	68.27 E
Munene	154	20.38 S	30.03 E
Munenga	152	10.02 S	14.41 E
Munera	34	39.02 N	2.28 W
Munford	194	35.26 N	89.48 W
Munfordville	194	37.16 N	85.53 W
Mungallala	166	26.27 S	147.33 E
Mungallala Creek ≐	166	28.05 S	147.15 E
Mungana	166	17.07 S	144.24 E
Mungaoli	124	24.25 N	78.06 E
Mungári	154	17.12 S	33.31 E
Mungar Junction	166	25.36 S	152.36 E
Mungau	152	13.56 S	21.55 E
Mungbere	154	2.38 N	28.30 E
Mungeli	124	22.04 N	81.41 E
Munger	124	25.23 N	86.28 E
Mungeranie	162	28.00 S	138.36 E
Mungindi	166	28.58 S	148.59 E
Munglinup	162	33.43 S	120.51 E
Mungo	152	11.49 S	16.16 E
Mungo National Park ♦	166	33.44 S	143.02 E
Mungra Badshāhpur	124	25.40 N	82.11 E
Mungun-Tajga, gora ∧	86	50.16 N	90.05 E
Mun'gyŏng	98	36.44 N	128.07 E
Munhall	214	40.23 N	79.54 W
Munhamade	154	16.37 S	36.58 E
Munhango	152	12.12 S	18.42 E
Munhango ≐	152	11.20 S	19.50 E
Munhoz	256	22.37 S	46.22 W
Munhye-ri	98	38.10 N	127.19 E
Munich → München	60	48.08 N	11.34 E
Muniesa	34	41.02 N	0.48 W
Munim ≐	250	2.45 S	44.04 W
Munirka ◆[8]	272a	28.34 N	77.10 E
Munising	190	46.24 N	86.38 W
Munith	216	42.23 N	84.15 W
Muñiz	258	34.33 S	58.42 W
Muniz Freire	255	20.28 S	41.25 W
Munkács → Mukacheve	78	48.27 N	22.45 E
Munka-Ljungby	41	56.15 N	12.58 E
Munkebjerg ∧[2]	41	55.41 N	9.37 E
Munkebo	41	55.27 N	10.34 E
Munkedal	26	58.29 N	11.41 E
Munkerud	40	59.50 N	13.31 E
Munkfors	40	59.50 N	13.32 E
Munksund	26	65.17 N	21.29 E
Munktorp	40	59.32 N	16.08 E
Munku-Sardyk, gora ∧	88	51.45 N	100.32 E
Munlochy	46	57.32 N	4.15 W
Münnerstadt	56	50.15 N	10.11 E
Munnsville	210	42.58 N	75.35 W
Muñoz	116	15.43 N	120.54 E
Munozero	24	67.05 N	34.12 E
Muñoz Gamero, Península ›[1]	254	52.30 S	73.10 W
Munpal-li	271b	37.45 N	126.43 E
Munro ◆[8]	288	34.32 S	58.31 W
Munroe Falls	214	41.08 N	81.26 W
Munro Lake ⊜	184	54.38 N	95.16 W
Munsan	98	37.51 N	126.48 E
Munsarpur	126	24.18 N	88.26 E
Munsey Park	276	40.48 N	73.41 W
Munshiganj	124	23.33 N	90.32 E
Münsing	64	47.54 N	11.22 E
Münsingen, Dtsch.	58	48.25 N	9.29 E
Münsingen, Schw.	58	46.53 N	7.34 E
Munsö I	40	59.23 N	17.35 E
Munson, Ab., Can.	182	51.34 N	112.45 W
Munson, Pa., U.S.	214	40.57 N	78.10 W
Munson Knob ∧[2]	214	40.40 N	81.54 W
Munsons Corners	210	42.35 N	76.13 W
Münster, Dtsch.	52	51.57 N	7.37 E
Munster, Dtsch.	52	52.59 N	10.05 E
Münster, Dtsch.	56	49.55 N	8.52 E
Munster, Fr.	56	48.55 N	6.54 E
Munster, Fr.	58	48.03 N	7.08 E
Münster, Schw.	58	46.29 N	8.16 E
Munster, In., U.S.	216	41.33 N	87.30 W
Münster □[5]	52	51.50 N	7.25 E
Munster □[9]	48	52.25 N	8.20 W
Munster ≐	48	52.33 N	7.12 W
Münsterkirche †[1]	263	51.27 N	7.01 E
Münsterland ◆[1]	52	52.00 N	7.30 E
Münsterlingen	58	47.38 N	9.14 E
Münstermaifeld	56	50.15 N	7.22 E
Münstertal	58	47.51 N	7.47 E
Muntadgin	162	31.45 S	118.34 E
Muntahak ∧	114	1.52 N	103.47 E
Munte	112	0.30 N	119.55 E
Muntele Mare, Vârful ∧	38	46.29 N	23.14 E
Muntendam	52	53.07 N	6.53 E
Muntok	112	2.04 S	105.11 E
Mununzi	154	0.36 N	29.15 E
Munuscong Lake ⊜	190	46.10 N	84.08 W
Münzenberg	56	50.27 N	8.46 E
Münzkirchen	60	48.29 N	13.34 E
Munzur Dağları ⋀	130	39.30 N	39.10 E
Munzur Vadisi Milli Parkı ♦	130	39.25 N	39.30 E
Muolea Point ›	229a	20.41 N	156.01 W
Muong Het	110	20.49 N	104.01 E
Muong Hinh	110	19.49 N	105.03 E
Muong Khoua	110	21.05 N	102.31 E
Muong Saiapoun	110	18.24 N	101.31 E
Muong Te	110	22.28 N	102.37 E
Muonio	24	67.57 N	23.42 E
Muotathal	58	46.59 N	8.46 E
Mupa	152	16.10 S	15.44 E
Mupa, Parque Nacional da ♦	152	16.00 S	15.35 E
Muping	98	37.24 N	121.35 E
Mupini	156	17.50 S	19.40 E
Mup'ungjang	98	35.58 N	127.49 E
Muqaddam, Wādī V	140	18.04 N	31.30 E
Muqaṭṭa'	140	14.40 N	35.51 E
Muqaybirah, Bi'r al- ⊤[4]	142	30.53 N	32.50 E
Muqayshiṭ I	128	24.10 N	53.45 E
Muqdisho (Mogadishu)	144	2.04 N	45.22 E
Muqi	98	41.46 N	124.39 E
Muqsam, Jabal ∧	140	13.38 N	27.42 E
Müqtädir	84	41.41 N	48.46 E
Muquequete	152	14.50 S	14.16 E
Muqui	255	20.57 S	41.20 W
Mur (Mura) ≐	30	46.18 N	16.53 E
Mura (Mur) ≐, Europe	30	46.18 N	16.53 E
Mura ≐, Ross.	88	58.27 N	98.34 E
Muradiye, Tür.	84	38.59 N	43.46 E
Muradiye, Tür.	130	38.39 N	27.21 E
Murādnagar	124	28.47 N	77.30 E
Murafa ≐	78	48.13 N	28.14 E
Murāgācha	126	23.32 N	88.24 E
Muraglione, Passo del)(	66	43.56 N	11.39 E
Murai Reservoir ⊜[1]	271c	1.24 N	103.41 E
Murajá	250	0.47 S	47.57 W
Murakami	92	38.14 N	139.29 E
Murallón, Cerro ∧	254	49.48 S	73.25 W
Murambi	154	1.46 S	30.23 E
Muramvya	154	3.16 S	29.37 E
Murana	164	3.33 S	133.49 E
Murang'a	154	0.43 S	37.09 E
Murano, Isola di I	64	45.28 N	12.21 E
Muranskij porog ⌞	88	58.02 N	112.16 E
Muraoka	96	35.28 N	134.35 E
Muraši	24	59.24 N	48.55 E
Muraški	265b	55.59 N	37.45 E
Murat	32	45.07 N	2.52 E
Murat ≐	84	38.39 N	39.50 E
Murat Dağı ∧	130	38.55 N	29.43 E
Muratkovo	86	58.26 N	62.23 E
Muratlı	130	41.10 N	27.30 E
Muratove	83	48.48 N	38.45 E
Muratpur	272b	22.59 N	88.27 E
Murau	61	47.07 N	14.10 E
Muravera	71	39.25 N	9.34 E
Muravjovka	89	49.50 N	127.44 E
Muravjovo	76	56.14 N	34.14 E
Murayama	92	38.28 N	140.22 E
Murayama-chosuichi ⊜[1]	268	35.45 N	139.25 E
Muraysah, Ra's al- ›	146	31.55 N	25.02 E
Murča	34	41.24 N	7.27 W
Murcanyo	144	11.41 N	50.27 E
Mūrcheh Khvort	128	33.06 N	51.30 E
Murchin	54	53.54 N	13.44 E
Murchison, Austl.	166	36.37 S	145.14 E
Murchison, N.Z.	172	41.48 S	172.20 E
Murchison, Tx., U.S.	222	32.17 N	95.45 W
Murchison ≐	162	27.42 S	114.09 E
Murchison, Mount ∧, Austl.	162	26.46 S	116.25 E
Murchison, Mount ∧, N.Z.	172	43.01 S	171.22 E
Murchison Falls → Kabalega Falls ⌞	154	2.17 N	31.41 E
Murchison Range ⋀	162	20.11 S	134.26 E
Murcia, Esp.	34	37.59 N	1.07 W
Murcia, Pil.	116	10.36 N	123.02 E
Murcia □[3], Esp.	34	38.00 N	1.30 W
Murcia □[3], Esp.	148	37.55 N	1.30 W
Murciélago, Islas II	236	10.51 N	85.57 W
Murcielagos Bay ⊂	116	8.39 N	123.33 E
Mur-de-Barrez	32	44.51 N	2.39 E
Murdeduke, Lake ⊜	169	38.11 S	143.53 E
Murder Creek ≐, Al., U.S.	194	31.04 N	87.06 W
Murder Creek ≐, N.Y., U.S.	210	43.05 N	78.31 W
Murderkill ≐	208	39.03 N	75.24 W
Murdo	198	43.53 N	100.42 W
Murdock	220	27.00 N	82.08 W
Mure	94	36.45 N	138.14 E
Mureaux, Aérodrome des ⊠	261	49.00 N	1.57 E
Mureck	61	46.42 N	15.46 E
Mürefte	130	40.40 N	27.14 E
Mureș □[6]	38	46.35 N	24.40 E
Mureș (Maros) ≐	38	46.15 N	20.13 E
Muret	32	43.28 N	1.21 E
Murewa	154	17.39 S	31.47 E
Murfreesboro, Ar., U.S.	194	34.03 N	93.41 W
Murfreesboro, N.C., U.S.	192	36.26 N	77.05 W
Murfreesboro, Tn., U.S.	194	35.50 N	86.23 W
Murg	58	47.33 N	8.01 E
Murg ≐	56	48.55 N	8.10 E
Murgab	85	38.10 N	73.59 E
Murgab (Morghāb) ≐, Asia	128	38.18 N	61.12 E
Murgab ≐, Taj.	120	38.20 N	72.30 E
Murgenella	164	11.33 S	132.55 E
Murgeni	38	46.12 N	28.01 E
Murgenthal	58	47.16 N	7.50 E
Murgha Faqīrzai	120	31.03 N	67.48 E
Murgha Kibzai	120	30.44 N	69.25 E
Murgon	166	26.15 S	151.57 E
Muri, Cook Is.	174k	21.14 S	159.43 W
Muri, Nig.	146	9.11 N	10.53 E
Muri, Schw.	58	46.56 N	7.29 E
Muri, Schw.	58	47.16 N	8.21 E
Muria, Gunung ∧	115a	6.36 S	110.53 E
Muriaé	255	21.08 S	42.22 W
Muriaé ≐	255	21.43 S	41.22 W
Murias de Paredes	34	42.51 N	6.11 W
Muribeca	250	10.26 S	36.59 W
Muribeca dos Guararapes	250	8.10 S	35.01 W
Murici	250	9.19 S	35.56 W
Muricizal ≐	250	6.40 S	48.40 W
Murīdke	123	31.48 N	74.16 E
Muriége	152	9.58 S	21.11 E
Muriel Lake ⊜	182	54.10 N	110.40 W
Murih, Pulau I	112	1.54 N	108.38 E
Murila	152	10.44 S	20.20 E
Murilo I[1]	14	8.40 N	152.11 E
Mūrinda	123	30.47 N	76.29 E
Murinja	88	54.47 N	107.21 E
Murino, Ross.	88	51.30 N	104.23 E
Murino, Ross.	265a	60.03 N	30.27 E
Murinskij ≐	265a	60.01 N	30.28 E
Muriqui	256	22.56 S	43.57 W
Muriqui ≐	287a	22.52 S	43.02 W
Murisengo	62	45.05 N	8.08 E
Mūrītāniyā → Mauritania □[1]	134	20.00 N	12.00 W
Müritz ⊜	54	53.25 N	12.43 E
Muriwai	172	38.46 S	177.55 E
Murkong Selek	120	27.49 N	95.16 E
Murlīganj	124	25.54 N	86.59 E
Murlo	66	43.09 N	11.23 E
Murmansk	24	68.58 N	33.05 E
Murmansk Oblast' □[4]	24	68.00 N	35.00 E
Murmansk Rise ✧[3]	12	75.00 N	37.00 E
Murmerwoude	52	53.16 N	6.00 E
Murmino	80	54.36 N	40.03 E
Murnau	64	47.40 N	11.12 E
Murnei	140	12.57 N	22.52 E
Murō	94	34.34 N	136.02 E
Murō-Akame-Aoyama-kokutei-kōen ♦	94	34.30 N	136.10 E
Muro Lucano	68	40.45 N	15.29 E
Murom	80	55.34 N	42.02 E
Muromcevo	86	56.23 N	75.14 E
Muroran	92a	42.18 N	140.59 E
Muros	34	42.47 N	9.02 W
Muros e Noia, Ría de ⊂[1]	34	42.45 N	9.00 W
Muroto	96	33.18 N	134.09 E
Muroto-Anan-kaigan-kokutei-kōen ♦	96	33.41 N	134.32 E
Muroto-zaki ›	96	33.15 N	134.11 E
Murovani Kurylivtsi	78	48.43 N	27.31 E
Murowana Goślina	30	52.35 N	17.01 E
Murphy, Id., U.S.	202	43.13 N	116.33 W
Murphy, Mo., U.S.	219	38.29 N	90.29 W
Murphy, N.C., U.S.	192	35.05 N	84.02 W
Murphy Lake ⊜	182	52.03 N	121.14 W
Murphys	226	38.08 N	120.27 W
Murphysboro	194	37.45 N	89.20 W
Murphy Slough ≐	226	36.28 N	120.00 W
Murr ≐	56	48.57 N	9.16 E
Murr, Wādī V	142	28.27 N	32.18 E
Murrah, Qārat al- ∧[2]	142	30.00 N	32.41 E
Murrah al-Kubrā, Al-Buḩayrah al- (Great Bitter Lake) ⊜	142	30.20 N	32.23 E
Murrah aṣ-Ṣughrā, Al-Buḩayrah al- (Little Bitter Lake) ⊜	142	30.13 N	32.33 E
Murra Murra	166	28.16 S	146.48 E
Murrāt, Ābār ⊤[4]	140	21.03 N	32.55 E
Murray, Ia., U.S.	190	41.02 N	93.56 W
Murray, Ky., U.S.	194	36.36 N	88.18 W
Murray, Ut,. U.S.	200	40.40 N	111.53 W
Murray ≐, Austl.	166	35.22 S	139.22 E
Murray ≐, Austl.	168a	32.35 S	115.46 E
Murray ≐, B.C., Can.	182	55.40 N	121.10 W
Murray, Lake ⊜	164	7.00 S	141.30 E
Murray, Lake ⊜[1]	192	34.04 N	81.23 W
Murray, Mount ∧, Yk., Can.	180	60.54 N	128.49 W
Murray, Mount ∧, Pap. N. Gui.	164	6.46 S	144.01 E
Murray Bay → La Malbaie	186	47.39 N	70.10 W
Murray Bridge	168b	35.07 S	139.17 E
Murray Canal ≡	212	44.04 N	77.35 W
Murray City	188	39.30 N	82.09 W
Murray Downs	162	21.04 S	134.40 E
Murray Fracture Zone ✧	16	34.00 N	135.00 W
Murray Harbour	186	46.00 N	62.31 W
Murray Head ›	186	46.00 N	62.28 W
Murray Maxwell Bay ⊂	176	70.00 N	80.00 W
Murray Mouth ≐[1]	168b	35.34 S	138.54 E
Murray River	186	46.01 N	62.37 W
Murraysburg	158	31.58 S	23.47 E
Murrayville, B.C., Can.	224	49.10 N	122.36 W
Murrayville, Il., U.S.	194	39.35 N	90.15 W
Murrébuè	154	13.02 S	40.30 E
Murree	123	33.54 N	73.24 E
Mürren	58	46.34 N	7.54 E
Murrhardt	56	48.59 N	9.34 E
Murrí ≐	246	6.33 N	76.52 W
Murrieta	228	33.33 N	117.12 W
Murro di Porca, Capo ›	70	37.00 N	15.20 E
Murrumbidgee ≐	166	34.43 S	143.12 E
Murrumburrah	166	34.33 S	148.21 E
Murrupula	154	15.27 S	38.47 E
Murrurundi	166	31.46 S	150.50 E
Murry Hill	279b	40.17 N	80.09 W
Murrysville	279b	40.25 N	79.41 W
Mursal	130	39.11 N	37.59 E
Mursala, Pulau I	114	1.38 N	98.32 E
Murshidābād	126	24.11 N	88.16 E
Mürşitpınar	130	36.54 N	38.19 E
Murska Sobota	36	46.40 N	16.10 E
Murskij, porog ⌞	88	58.27 N	98.30 E
Mursko Središće	61	46.31 N	16.27 E
Murtajāpur	122	20.44 N	77.23 E
Murtal	266c	38.42 N	9.22 W
Murtee	166	31.35 S	143.30 E
Murten	58	46.56 N	7.07 E
Murtensee → Morat, Lac de ⊜	58	46.55 N	7.05 E
Murter, Otok I	36	43.48 N	15.37 E
Murtle Lake ⊜	182	52.08 N	119.38 W
Murtoa	166	36.37 S	142.28 E
Murton	44	54.49 N	1.24 W
Murtosa	34	40.44 N	8.38 W
Muru	140	6.36 N	29.15 E
Muru ≐	248	8.09 S	70.45 W
Muru, Capu di ›	36	41.44 N	8.40 E
Murud	122	18.19 N	72.58 E
Murud, Gunong ∧	112	3.52 N	115.30 E
Murukta	74	67.46 N	102.01 E
Murung ≐	112	0.12 S	114.03 E
Murupara	172	38.28 S	176.42 E
Mururoa I[1]	6	21.52 S	138.55 W
Murutinga	246	3.26 S	59.12 W
Murvaul, Lake ⊜[1]	222	32.03 N	94.28 W
Murvaul Creek ≐	194	32.05 N	94.12 W
Murwāra	124	23.51 N	80.24 E
Murwillumbah	166	28.19 S	153.24 E
Mürz ≐	61	47.24 N	15.17 E
Mürzsteg	61	47.40 N	15.29 E
Mürzzuschlag	61	47.36 N	15.41 E
Muş	130	38.44 N	41.30 E
Muş □[4]	128	39.00 N	42.00 E
Musa	152	2.40 N	19.18 E
Mūša ≐, Europe	76	56.24 N	24.10 E
Musa ≐, Pap. N. Gui.	164	9.25 S	148.50 E
Mūsā, Jabal (Mount Sinai) ∧	140	28.32 N	33.59 E
Mūsā, 'Uyūn (Springs of Moses) ⊤[4]	142	29.52 N	32.39 E
Musabeyli	130	39.51 N	34.37 E
Musadi	152	2.34 S	22.47 E
Musaid	146	31.35 N	25.03 E
Mūsa Khel	123	32.38 N	71.44 E
Mūsa Khel Bāzār	120	30.52 N	69.49 E
Musala ∧	38	42.11 N	23.34 E
Musan	98	42.14 N	129.13 E
Musandam Peninsula ›[1]	128	26.18 N	56.24 E
Musao	154	7.43 S	26.17 E
Mūsā Qal'eh	120	32.22 N	64.46 E
Mūsā Qal'eh ≐	128	32.05 N	64.51 E
Musar	272b	22.54 N	88.14 E
Musasa	154	3.21 S	31.33 E
Musashi → Iruma, Nihon	94	35.50 N	139.24 E
Musashi, Nihon	96	33.30 N	131.43 E
Musashimurayama	268	35.45 N	139.23 E
Musashino	94	35.42 N	139.34 E
Musashino-daichi ⋀[1]	268	35.45 N	139.35 E
Musau	58	47.32 N	10.40 E
Musay'īd	128	24.59 N	51.32 E
Musaymīr	144	13.27 N	44.37 E
Mūsāzai	120	30.23 N	66.32 E
Muscat → Masqaṭ	128	23.37 N	58.35 E
Muscat and Oman → Oman □[1]	118	22.00 N	58.00 E
Muscatatuck ≐	218	38.46 N	86.10 W
Muscatatuck, Grassy Fork ≐	218	38.45 N	85.07 W
Muscatatuck, Vernon Fork ≐	218	38.46 N	85.54 W
Muscatine	190	41.25 N	91.03 W
Müsch	56	50.23 N	6.49 E
Mus-Chaja, gora ∧	74	62.35 N	140.50 E
Muschu Island I	164	3.25 S	143.35 E
Muschwitz	54	51.11 N	12.07 E
Muscle Shoals	194	34.44 N	87.40 W
Musclow, Mount ∧	182	53.17 N	127.09 W
Musclow Lake ⊜	184	51.25 N	94.56 W
Muscoda	190	43.11 N	90.26 W
Musconetcong ≐	210	40.36 N	75.11 W
Musconetcong, Lake ⊜	276	40.54 N	74.42 W
Muscongus Bay ⊂	188	43.55 N	69.20 W
Muscote Bay ⊂	212	44.06 N	77.18 W
Muscowpetung Indian Reserve ◆[4]	184	50.45 N	104.15 W
Muscoy	228	34.09 N	117.20 W
Muse	214	40.17 N	80.12 W
Musengezi ≐	154	15.43 S	31.14 E
Musgrave, Austl.	164	14.47 S	143.30 E
Musgrave, B.C., Can.	224	48.45 N	123.32 W
Musgrave, Mount ∧	172	43.48 S	170.43 E
Musgrave Ranges ⋀	162	26.10 S	131.50 E
Musgravetown	186	48.24 N	53.53 W
Mūshā	142	27.08 N	31.18 E
Mushābani	126	22.31 N	86.27 E
Mushāsh, Jabal al- ∧[2]	142	28.54 N	31.11 E
Mushenge	152	4.32 S	21.21 E
Mushie	152	3.01 S	16.54 E
Mushima	154	14.13 S	25.05 E
Mushin	150	6.32 N	3.22 E
Mūsi ≐, India	122	16.41 N	79.40 E
Musi ≐, Indon.	112	2.20 S	104.56 E
Musicians Seamounts ✧[3]	6	31.00 N	162.00 W
Muskauer Heide ◆[3]	54	51.25 N	14.40 E
Muskeg ≐	182	54.01 N	119.03 W

Symbols in the index entries represent the broad categories identified in the key at the right. Symbols with superior numbers (⋀[1]) identify subcategories (see complete key on page *I · 1).*

Symbole im Register stellen die rechts im Schlüssel erklärten Kategorien dar. Symbole mit hochgestellten Ziffern (⋀[1]) bezeichnen Unterabteilungen einer Kategorie (vgl. vollständiger Schlüssel auf Seite *I · 1).*

Los símbolos incluídos en el texto del índice representan las grandes categorías identificadas con la clave a la derecha. Los símbolos con numeros en su parte superior (⋀[1]) identifican las subcategorías (véase la clave completa en la página *I · 1).*

Les symboles de l'index représentent les catégories indiquées dans la légende à droite. Les symboles suivis d'un indice (⋀[1]) représentent des sous-catégories (voir légende complète à la page *I · 1).*

Os símbolos incluídos no texto do índice representam as grandes categorias identificadas com a chave à direita. Os símbolos com números em sua parte superior (⋀[1]) identificam as subcategorias (veja-se a chave completa à página *I · 1).*

∧	Mountain	Berg	Montaña	Montagne	Montanha
⋀	Mountains	Gebirge	Montañas	Montagnes	Montanhas
)(	Pass	Paß	Paso	Col	Passo
V	Valley, Canyon	Tal, Cañon	Valle, Cañón	Vallée, Canyon	Vale, Canhão
≚	Plain	Ebene	Llano	Plaine	Planície
›	Cape	Kap	Cabo	Cap	Cabo
I	Island	Insel	Isla	Île	Ilha
II	Islands	Inseln	Islas	Îles	Ilhas
⊥	Other Topographic Features	Andere Topographische Objekte	Otros Elementos Topográficos	Autres données topographiques	Outros acidentes topográficos

ESPAÑOL / FRANÇAIS / PORTUGUÊS

Nombre / Nom / Nome	Página / Page / Página	Lat.°′	Long.°′ W = Oeste / W = Ouest / W = Oeste
Muskeget Channel ⋓	207	41.25 N	70.20 W
Muskeget Island I	207	41.20 N	70.18 W
Muskeg Lake Indian Reserve ◆[4]	184	52.58 N	106.57 W
Muskego	216	42.54 N	88.08 W
Muskego Lake ⊜	216	42.53 N	88.07 W
Muskegon	216	43.14 N	86.14 W
Muskegon □[6]	216	43.12 N	86.08 W
Muskegon ≐	190	43.14 N	86.20 W
Muskegon County Airport ⊠	216	43.10 N	86.14 W
Muskegon Heights	216	43.12 N	86.14 W
Muskegon Lake ⊜	216	43.14 N	86.17 W
Muskegon State Park ♠	216	43.14 N	86.20 W
Mušketova, gora ∧	88	53.35 N	113.32 E
Muskingum □[6]	214	40.06 N	81.51 W
Muskingum ≐	188	39.27 N	81.30 W
Muskingum Brook ≐	285	39.48 N	74.44 W
Muskira	124	25.40 N	79.48 E
Muskö I	40	59.00 N	18.06 E
Muskoday Indian Reserve ◆[4]	184	53.06 N	105.30 W
Muskogee	196	35.44 N	95.22 W
Muskoka □[6]	212	45.05 N	79.03 W
Muskoka, Lake ⊜	212	45.00 N	79.25 W
Muskoka, North Branch ≐	212	45.02 N	79.19 W
Muskoka, South Branch ≐	212	45.02 N	79.19 W
Muskosh Channel ⋓	212	44.55 N	79.53 W
Muskowekwan Indian Reserve ◆[4]	184	51.19 N	104.06 W
Muskrat Creek ≐	202	43.09 N	108.11 W
Muskrat Dam Lake ⊜	184	53.25 N	91.40 W
Muskrat Lake ⊜	190	45.40 N	76.55 W
Muskwa ≐	176	58.45 N	122.35 W
Muskwa Lake ⊜	182	56.09 N	114.38 W
Muslimbāgh	120	30.49 N	67.45 E
Musl'umovo	80	55.18 N	53.12 E
Muşmuş	132	32.32 N	35.09 E
Musocco ◆[8]	266b	45.30 N	9.08 E
Musofu Mission	154	13.31 S	29.02 E
Musoma	154	1.30 S	33.48 E
Musone ≐, It.	64	45.50 N	11.55 E
Musone ≐, It.	66	43.28 N	13.38 E
Musoshi	154	11.54 S	27.46 E
Musquanousse, Lac ⊜	186	50.22 N	61.05 W
Musquapsink Brook ≐	276	40.59 N	74.01 W
Musquaro, Lac ⊜	186	50.38 N	61.05 W
Musquash ≐	212	44.57 N	79.52 W
Musquash Brook ≐	283	42.42 N	71.26 W
Musquashcut Pond ⊜	283	42.13 N	70.46 W
Musquodoboit Harbour	186	44.47 N	63.09 W
Mussau Island I	164	1.30 S	149.40 E
Musselburgh	46	55.57 N	3.04 W
Musselkanaal	52	52.56 N	7.00 E
Musselshell ≐	202	47.21 N	107.58 W
Mussende	152	10.32 S	16.05 E
Mussidan	32	45.02 N	0.22 E
Mussolo	152	9.59 S	17.19 E
Mussomeli	70	37.35 N	13.45 E
Mussoorie	124	30.27 N	78.05 E
Mussuco	152	17.08 S	19.05 E
Mussum	52	51.48 N	6.34 E
Mussuma	152	14.14 S	21.59 E
Mussy-sur-Seine	58	47.58 N	4.30 E
Mustafakemalpaşa	130	40.02 N	28.24 E
Mustafa Kemal Paşa ≐	130	40.07 N	28.33 E
Mustafino	80	55.01 N	53.38 E
Mustahil	144	5.12 N	44.17 E
Müstair	58	46.37 N	10.27 E
Mustajevo	80	51.48 N	53.25 E
Mustajõe	76	57.59 N	26.58 E
Mustāng	124	29.11 N	83.58 E
Mustang Draw V	196	32.12 N	101.36 W
Mustang Island I	196	27.45 N	97.10 W
Mustāy	142	30.37 N	31.09 E
Musters, Lago ⊜	254	45.27 S	69.13 W
Mustinka ≐	198	45.45 N	96.38 W
Mustjala	76	58.28 N	22.14 E
Mustla	76	58.14 N	25.52 E
Musṭurud	273c	30.08 N	31.17 E
Mustvee	76	58.51 N	26.56 E
Musu-dan ›	98	40.50 N	129.43 E
Musun	84	39.42 N	43.49 E
Müsuslü	84	40.28 N	47.55 E
Muswellbrook	166	32.16 S	150.53 E
Muszyna	30	49.21 N	20.54 E
Mūt, Miṣr	140	25.29 N	28.59 E
Mut, Tür.	130	36.39 N	33.27 E
Muta	61	46.37 N	15.10 E
Mutá, Ponta do ›	255	13.52 S	38.56 W
Mu'tah	132	31.06 N	35.42 E
Mutalau	174v	18.56 S	169.50 W
Mutambara	154	19.36 S	32.33 E
Mutanchiang → Mudanjiang	89	44.35 N	129.36 E
Mutanda, Moç.	156	21.02 S	33.31 E
Mutanda, R.D.C.	152	5.17 S	16.34 E
Mutanda Mission	154	12.24 S	26.16 E
Mutankiang → Mudanjiang	89	44.35 N	129.36 E
Mutarammil, Jabal al- ∧	132	31.04 N	36.06 E
Mutare	154	18.58 S	32.40 E
Mutbīn	132	33.09 N	36.15 E
Mutějovice	54	50.09 N	13.41 E
Mutha	154	1.48 S	38.26 E
Muthill	46	56.19 N	3.50 W
Mutiko	154	1.39 S	28.12 E
Muting	164	7.23 S	140.20 E
Mutis, Gunung ∧	112	9.34 S	124.14 E
Mutlu (Rezovska) ≐	38	41.59 N	28.01 E
Mutoko	154	17.24 S	32.13 E
Mutombo-Mukulu	152	7.58 S	24.00 E
Mutoraj	74	61.20 N	100.30 E
Mutoto	152	5.42 S	22.42 E
Mutouchengzi	98	41.20 N	119.59 E
Mutouhao	107	28.49 N	105.04 E
Mutsamudu	157a	12.09 S	44.25 E
Mutshatsha	152	10.39 S	24.27 E
Mutsu	92	41.17 N	141.10 E
Mutsuai	268	35.08 N	139.38 E
Mutsumi	96	34.26 N	131.34 E
Mutsuura ◆[8]	268	35.19 N	139.37 E
Mutsu-wan ⊂	92	41.05 N	140.55 E
Muttaburra	166	22.36 S	144.33 E
Muttekopf ∧	58	47.16 N	10.39 E
Muttenz	58	47.32 N	7.39 E
Mutters	64	47.14 N	11.23 E
Mutterstadt	56	49.26 N	8.21 E
Muttonbird Islands II	172	47.15 S	167.24 E
Muttontown	276	40.49 N	73.33 W
Muttra → Mathura	124	27.30 N	77.41 E
Mutual, Oh., U.S.	218	40.05 N	83.38 W
Mutual, Pa., U.S.	279b	40.14 N	79.30 W
Mutūbis	142	31.18 N	30.31 E
Mutuca, Ribeirão da ≐	256	21.36 S	45.39 W
Mutuco, Lago ⊜	250	1.21 N	50.24 W
Mutuípe	255	13.15 S	39.31 W
Mutum	255	19.49 S	41.26 W
Mutum ≐	246	4.25 S	68.03 W
Mutum Biyu	146	8.38 N	10.46 E
Mutumbo	152	13.14 S	17.17 E
Mutunópolis	255	13.40 S	49.15 W
Muturi	164	2.06 S	133.43 E
Muturi ≐	164	2.13 S	133.40 E
Mututi, Ilha do I	250	0.45 S	51.00 W
Mutzig	58	48.32 N	7.28 E
Mutzschen	54	51.16 N	12.53 E
Mu Us Shamo ◆[2]	102	38.45 N	109.10 E
Mūvattupula	122	9.58 N	76.35 E
Muvukoni	154	0.24 S	38.14 E
Muwopu	104	41.03 N	121.12 E
Muxaluando	152	8.07 S	14.17 E
Muxihe	100	31.03 N	115.21 E
Muxima	152	9.31 S	13.56 E
Muyaga	154	3.14 S	30.33 E
Muyang	100	27.06 N	119.34 E
Muyang ≐	100	27.00 N	119.41 E
Muyinga	154	2.51 S	30.20 E
Muymano ≐	248	11.27 S	69.03 W
Muy Muy	236	12.46 N	85.38 W
Muyua Island I	164	9.05 S	152.50 E
Muyuka	152	4.17 N	9.25 E
Muyumba	154	7.15 S	26.59 E
Mužač'	82	54.22 N	36.21 E
Muzaffarābād	123	34.22 N	73.28 E
Muzaffargarh	123	30.04 N	71.12 E
Muzaffarnagar	124	29.28 N	77.41 E
Muzaffarpur	124	26.07 N	85.24 E
Muzambinho	256	21.22 S	46.32 W
Muzambinho ≐	256	21.15 S	46.26 W
Muzambo ≐	256	21.17 S	46.16 W
Muzat ≐	90	41.15 N	83.27 E
Muzayrīb	132	32.42 N	36.01 E
Muzbek, gora ∧	85	40.23 N	69.39 E
Muzbel' ◆[1]	86	50.15 N	70.50 E
Muzeze	152	15.03 S	17.43 E
Muzhen	100	30.43 N	117.56 E
Muži	74	65.22 N	64.40 E
Mužiči	84	43.03 N	44.59 E
Mužiksu	86	47.42 N	84.58 E
Muzillac	32	47.33 N	2.29 W
Muzkol, chrebet ⋏	85	38.25 N	73.30 E
Muzoka	154	16.41 S	27.19 E
Muzon, Cape ›	182	54.41 N	132.44 W
Muztag ∧, Zhg.	120	36.03 N	80.07 E
Muztag ∧, Zhg.	120	36.25 N	87.25 E
Muztagata ∧	85	38.17 N	75.11 E
Muz Tau ∧	86	43.50 N	85.40 E
Muzūrah	142	28.53 N	30.48 E
Muzzana del Turgnano	64	45.49 N	13.08 E
Mvam	152	0.13 S	9.39 E
Mvangan	152	2.38 N	11.44 E
Mvela	154	14.46 S	35.16 E
Mvengué	152	3.17 N	11.01 E
Mvolo	140	6.03 N	29.56 E
Mvomero	154	6.20 S	37.25 E
Mvoti ≐	158	29.24 S	31.22 E
Mvoung ≐	152	0.04 N	12.18 E
Mvouti	152	4.15 S	12.29 E
Mvuha	154	7.12 S	37.51 E
Mvuma	154	19.19 S	30.35 E
Mwadi-Kalumba	152	7.53 S	18.46 E
Mwadui	154	3.33 S	33.36 E
Mwali (Mohéli) I	157a	12.15 S	43.45 E
Mwami	154	16.40 S	29.46 E
Mwanangumune	152	15.31 S	23.30 E
Mwango	152	6.51 S	24.13 E
Mwanza, Malaŵi	154	15.37 S	34.31 E
Mwanza, Tan.	154	2.31 S	32.54 E
Mwanza, R.D.C.	154	7.54 S	26.45 E
Mwanza, Zam.	152	17.02 S	24.27 E
Mwanza □[4]	154	2.45 S	32.45 E
Mwanza Gulf ⊂	154	2.35 S	32.51 E
Mwaya, Tan.	154	9.33 S	33.57 E
Mwaya, Tan.	154	8.55 S	36.50 E
Mweelrea ∧	48	53.38 N	9.50 W
Mwehu	154	5.44 S	26.40 E
Mweka	152	4.51 S	21.34 E
Mwemena	154	10.19 S	27.28 E
Mwenda	154	12.01 S	28.44 E
Mwendjila	152	7.12 S	18.51 E
Mwene-Ditu	152	7.03 S	23.27 E
Mwenezi	154	21.22 S	30.45 E
Mwenga	154	3.02 S	28.26 E
Mwepo	154	11.56 S	26.11 E
Mwerasandu	154	0.59 S	30.23 E
Mwereni	154	4.20 S	39.08 E
Mweru, Lake ⊜	154	9.00 S	28.45 E
Mweru Wantipa, Lake ⊜	154	8.45 S	29.40 E
Mweru Wantipa National Park ♠	154	8.45 S	29.30 E
Mwetshi	152	4.42 S	22.39 E
Mwilambwe	154	8.07 S	25.00 E
Mwilitau Islands II	164	2.50 S	146.20 E
Mwimbi	154	8.39 S	31.40 E
Mwingi	154	0.56 S	38.04 E
Mwinilunga	152	11.44 S	24.26 E
Mwitikira	154	6.31 S	35.39 E
Mwombezhi ≐	154	12.52 S	25.00 E
Myaing	110	21.37 N	94.51 E
Myājlār	120	26.15 N	70.23 E
Myakka ≐	220	26.56 N	82.11 W
Myakka, Lake ⊜	220	27.16 N	82.17 W
Myakka City	220	27.20 N	82.09 W
Myakka River State Park ♠	220	27.15 N	82.17 W
Myall Lakes National Park ♠	166	32.28 S	152.22 E
Myall Range ⋏	170	32.58 S	151.22 E
Myanaung	110	18.17 N	95.19 E
Myanmar (Burma) □[1]	110	22.00 N	98.00 E
Myaungmya	110	16.36 N	94.56 E
Myawadi	110	16.41 N	98.31 E
Mybster	46	58.27 N	3.25 W
Myckelgensjö	26	63.34 N	17.37 E
Myebon	110	20.03 N	93.22 E
Myeik → Mergui	110	12.26 N	98.36 E
Myers, Ky., U.S.	218	38.21 N	83.57 W
Myers, N.Y., U.S.	210	42.32 N	76.32 W
Myerstown	208	40.22 N	76.19 W
Myingyan	110	21.28 N	95.23 E
Myinmoletkat Taung ∧	110	13.28 N	98.48 E
Myitkyinā	110	25.23 N	97.24 E
Myitnge ≐	110	21.52 N	95.59 E
Myitta	110	14.10 N	98.31 E
Myittha	110	21.25 N	96.08 E
Myittha ≐	110	23.12 N	94.17 E
Myjava	30	48.45 N	17.34 E
Myjeldino	24	61.46 N	54.48 E
Mykhaylivka, Ukr.	78	49.19 N	36.28 E
Mykhaylivka, Ukr.	78	47.16 N	35.14 E
Mykhaylivka, Ukr.	83	48.44 N	37.16 E
Mykil's'ke-na-Dnipri	78	48.12 N	35.12 E
Mykolayiv, Ukr.	78	49.32 N	23.58 E
Mykolayiv, Ukr.	78	46.58 N	32.00 E
Mykolayiv □[4]	78	47.15 N	31.45 E
Mykolayivka, Ukr.	78	47.38 N	33.12 E
Mykolayivka, Ukr.	78	47.06 N	34.14 E
Mykolayivka, Ukr.	78	44.58 N	33.37 E
Mykolayivka, Ukr.	78	46.23 N	29.24 E
Mykolayivka, Ukr.	78	47.33 N	30.25 E
Mykolayivka, Ukr.	78	51.04 N	34.02 E
Mykolayivka, Ukr.	83	47.39 N	37.41 E
Mykolayivka, Ukr.	83	48.51 N	37.46 E
Mykulyntsi	78	49.24 N	25.38 E
Myla	24	65.25 N	50.48 E
Mylau	54	50.37 N	12.16 E
Myl'džino	86	59.03 N	78.29 E
Myllendonk, Schloss ⊥	263	51.13 N	6.29 E
Myllykoski	26	60.47 N	26.48 E
Myllymäki	26	62.32 N	24.17 E
Mylor	168b	35.03 S	138.45 E
Mymensingh	124	24.45 N	90.24 E
Mynämäki	26	60.40 N	22.00 E
Mynaral	86	45.25 N	73.41 E
Mynbulak, gora ∧	85	41.43 N	69.49 E
Mynfontein	158	30.55 S	23.57 E
Mynydd Bach ∧[2]	42	52.15 N	4.05 W
Mynydd Eppynt ∧	42	52.05 N	3.30 W
Mynydd Hiraethog ∧	44	53.05 N	3.33 W
Mynydd Pencarreg ∧[2]	42	52.04 N	4.04 W
Mynydd Preseli ∧	42	51.58 N	4.42 W
Myōgata	94	35.51 N	137.02 E
Myōgi	94	36.17 N	138.49 E
Myōgi-Arafune-Saku-kōgen-kokutei-kōen ♠	94	36.12 N	138.10 E
Myōgi-san ∧	94	36.17 N	138.44 E
Myo-gyi	110	21.27 N	96.22 E
Myohaung	110	20.36 N	93.10 E
Myohyang-san ∧	98	40.02 N	126.17 E
Myohyang-sanmaek ⋏	98	40.30 N	127.00 E
Myojin-dake ∧	270	34.57 N	135.36 E
Myōjin-san ∧	96	33.34 N	133.04 E
Myōken-san ∧	96	35.24 N	134.39 E
Myōken-zan ∧	270	34.56 N	135.28 E
Myōken-zan ∧[2]	270	34.30 N	134.57 E
Myōkō	94	36.56 N	138.13 E
Myōkō-kōgen	94	36.52 N	138.12 E
Myōkō-san ∧	94	36.52 N	138.07 E
Myōnmong-ni ◆[8]	271b	37.35 N	127.05 E
Myponga	168b	35.24 S	138.28 E
Myponga Reservoir ⊜[1]	168b	35.24 S	138.26 E
Myra ⊥	130	36.15 N	29.54 E
Mýrdalsjökull ⍓	24a	63.40 N	19.05 W
Myrhorod	78	49.58 N	33.36 E
Myrivs'ke	78	48.05 N	33.23 E
Myrnam	182	53.40 N	111.14 W
Myrnyy	78	50.57 N	28.34 E
Myronivka	78	49.39 N	30.59 E
Myronivs'kyy	83	48.29 N	38.17 E
Myroodah	162	18.08 S	124.16 E
Myropil'	78	50.07 N	27.41 E
Myropillya	78	51.02 N	35.16 E
Myrskylä (Mörskom)	26	60.40 N	25.51 E
Myrtle Beach	192	33.41 N	78.53 W
Myrtle Beach Air Force Base ■	192	33.41 N	78.56 W
Myrtle Beach State Park ♠	192	33.37 N	78.58 W
Myrtle Creek	202	43.01 N	123.17 W
Myrtle Grove	194	30.25 N	87.18 W
Myrtle Point	202	43.03 N	124.08 W
Myrtle Springs	222	32.37 N	95.56 W
Myrtletowne	204	40.47 N	124.04 W
Myrtleville	170	34.29 S	149.49 E
Myšega	82	54.31 N	37.02 E
Mysen	26	59.33 N	11.20 E
Myshuryn Rih	78	48.50 N	33.58 E
Mysia □[9]	130	39.15 N	28.00 E
Mysingen ⋓	40	59.00 N	18.15 E
Myski	86	53.42 N	87.48 E
Myškino	76	57.47 N	38.27 E
Myśla ≐	54	52.40 N	14.29 E
Myślenice	30	49.51 N	19.56 E
Myślibórz	30	52.55 N	14.52 E
Mysłowice	30	50.15 N	19.07 E
Mysore	122	12.18 N	76.39 E
Mys Šmidta	180	68.56 N	179.26 W
Mystic, Ct., U.S.	207	41.21 N	71.58 W
Mystic, Ia., U.S.	190	40.46 N	92.56 W
Mystic ≐	283	42.23 N	71.03 W
Mystic Seaport ⊍	207	41.22 N	71.58 W
Mys Vchodnoj	74	73.53 N	86.43 E
Mysy	24	60.34 N	53.57 E
Mys Želanija	72	76.56 N	68.35 E
Myszków	30	50.36 N	19.20 E
Myszyniec	30	53.24 N	21.21 E
Myt	80	56.48 N	42.21 E
My Tho	110	10.21 N	106.21 E
Mytholm	262	53.44 N	2.01 W
Mytholmroyd	262	53.44 N	1.59 W
Mytilene → Mitilíni	38	39.06 N	26.32 E
Mytišči	82	55.55 N	37.46 E
Mytishchi → Mytišči	82	55.55 N	37.46 E
Mytišino	76	54.48 N	34.01 E
Mýto	60	49.47 N	13.44 E
Myton	200	40.11 N	110.03 W
Mývatn ⊜	24a	65.37 N	16.58 W
Myzove	78	51.22 N	24.31 E
M'zab, Oued V	148	32.19 N	5.24 E
Mže ≐	60	49.46 N	13.25 E
Mzenga	154	6.56 S	38.43 E
Mziha	154	5.54 S	37.47 E
Mzimba	154	11.52 S	33.34 E
Mzimkulu ≐	158	30.44 S	30.28 E
Mzimvubu ≐	158	31.38 S	29.32 E
Mzintlava ≐	158	31.12 S	29.18 E
Mzuzu	154	11.27 S	33.55 E
Mzymta ≐	84	43.27 N	39.56 E

N

Na I	174r	6.52 N	158.22 E
Na (Tengtiao) ≐	110	22.05 N	103.09 E
Naab ≐	60	49.01 N	12.02 E
Naach, Jbel ∧	34	34.53 N	3.22 W
Naachtpunkt Brook ≐	276	40.54 N	74.15 W
Naaldwijk	52	52.00 N	4.12 E
Naalehu	229d	19.03 N	155.35 W
Na'ām	140	9.42 N	28.27 E
Na'âma, Sebkhet en ≡	148	33.20 N	0.16 W
Naaman Creek ≐	285	39.48 N	75.27 W
Naaman Creek, South Branch ≐	285	39.49 N	75.27 W
Naamans Garden	285	39.49 N	75.31 W
Naantali	26	60.27 N	22.02 E
Naarden	52	52.17 N	5.09 E
Naarn ≐	61	48.11 N	14.49 E
Naas	48	53.13 N	6.39 W
Naas ≐	171b	35.36 S	149.04 E
Naast, Bel.	50	50.33 N	4.05 E
Naast, Scot., U.K.	46	57.47 N	5.39 W
Na'aẓuẓ, Har ∧	132	30.01 N	35.00 E
Nabā, Jabal an- (Mount Nebo) ∧	132	31.46 N	35.45 E
Nababiep	156	29.36 S	17.46 E
Nabābpur	272b	22.42 N	88.12 E
Nabaganga ≐[1]	126	22.59 N	89.34 E
Nabagram	126	24.12 N	88.06 E
Nabalat Al-Ḥajanah	140	13.13 N	29.02 E
Nabari	94	34.37 N	136.05 E
Nabari ≐	94	34.45 N	136.01 E
Nabarūh	142	31.06 N	31.18 E
Nabas	116	11.50 N	122.05 E
Nabasta	126	23.15 N	88.01 E
Nabawa	162	28.31 S	114.47 E
Nabb	218	38.36 N	85.38 W
Nabberu, Lake ⊜	162	25.36 S	120.30 E
Nabburg	60	49.28 N	12.11 E
Nabeba, Mont ∧	152	1.57 N	13.50 E
Nabeina	174t	1.26 N	173.05 E
Naberera	154	4.12 S	36.56 E
Naberežnoje	265b	55.57 N	37.58 E
Naberežnyje Čelny	80	55.42 N	52.19 E
Nabesna	180	62.22 N	143.00 W
Nabesna ≐	180	63.03 N	141.52 W
Nabeul	148	36.27 N	10.44 E
Nābha	123	30.22 N	76.09 E
Nab Hill ∧[2]	262	53.47 N	1.57 W
Nabigou	152	1.12 S	9.31 E
Nabī Hārūn, Jabal an- ∧	132	30.19 N	35.24 E
Nabileque ≐	248	20.55 S	57.49 W
Nabire	164	3.22 S	135.29 E
Nabī Shu'ayb, Jabal an- ∧	144	15.17 N	43.59 E
Nabisipi ≐	186	50.14 N	62.13 W
Nabiswera	154	1.28 N	32.16 E
Nabī Yūnus, Ra's an- ›	132	33.39 N	35.24 E
Nabnasset	207	42.36 N	71.25 W
Nabnasset Pond ⊜	283	42.37 N	71.26 W
Nabogame	232	26.14 N	106.57 W
Naboomspruit	156	24.32 S	28.36 E
Nabordo	150	10.10 N	9.20 E
Nabou	150	11.27 N	2.43 W
Nabq	140	28.04 N	34.25 E
Nabua	116	13.24 N	123.22 E
Nabula	120	31.55 N	80.10 E
Nābulus	132	32.13 N	35.16 E
Nabunturan	116	7.35 N	125.58 E
Nacajuca	234	18.08 N	93.01 W
Nacala	154	14.34 S	40.41 E
Nacala-Velha	154	14.32 S	40.37 E
Načalovo	80	46.20 N	48.11 E
Nacaome	236	13.31 N	87.30 W
Nacasio Reservoir ⊜[1]	226	38.05 N	122.44 W
Nacastillo	234	19.35 N	104.55 W
Nacchie	144	7.23 N	40.10 E
Nacereddine	34	36.08 N	3.26 E
Nachabinka ≐	265b	55.51 N	37.12 E
Nachabino	82	55.51 N	37.11 E
Naches	224	46.43 N	120.41 W
Naches ≐	202	46.38 N	120.31 W
Nachi-katsuura	92	33.30 N	135.55 E
Nāchinda	126	21.53 N	87.46 E
Nachingwea	154	10.23 S	38.46 E
Nāchna	120	27.30 N	71.43 E
Náchod	30	50.25 N	16.10 E
Nachodka	89	42.48 N	132.52 E
Nachrodt-Wiblingwerde	263	51.19 N	7.37 E
Nächstebreck ◆[8]	263	51.18 N	7.14 E
Nachterstedt	54	51.49 N	11.20 E
Nachuge	110	10.45 N	92.22 E
Nachvak Fiord ⊂[2]	176	59.03 N	63.45 W
Naci, Pil.	116	14.19 N	120.46 E
Naci, Pil.	116	6.19 N	124.46 E
Nacimiento	252	37.30 S	72.40 W
Nacimiento ≐	226	35.49 N	120.45 W
Nacimiento, Lake ⊜[1]	226	35.45 N	121.00 W
Načinskij Golec, gora ∧	89	52.24 N	118.53 E
Nacka	40	59.18 N	18.10 E
Naco, Méx.	232	31.20 N	109.56 W
Naco, Az., U.S.	200	31.20 N	109.56 W
Nacogdoches	222	31.36 N	94.39 W
Nacogdoches □[6]	222	31.40 N	94.45 W
Nacogdoches, Lake ⊜[1]	222	31.37 N	94.50 W
Nácori Chico	232	29.39 N	109.01 W
Nacozari de García	232	30.24 N	109.39 W
Ñacunday	252	26.01 S	54.46 W
Nada	222	29.24 N	96.23 W
Nada ◆[8]	270	34.44 N	135.14 E
Nadābhānga	272b	22.24 N	88.14 E
Nadachi	94	37.09 N	138.06 E
Nadaleen Mountain ∧	180	64.15 N	133.04 W
Nadasaki	96	34.32 N	133.52 E
Nádasd	61	46.58 N	16.37 E
Nadbai	124	27.14 N	77.12 E
Nadder ≐	42	51.03 N	1.48 W
Nadela	34	42.58 N	7.30 W
Nadelkap → Agulhas, Cape ›	158	34.52 S	20.00 E
Naden Harbour ⊂	182	54.00 N	132.35 W
Nadeždinskoje	89	48.18 N	133.11 E
Nadi, Fiji	175g	17.48 S	177.25 E
Nadi, Sūd.	140	18.40 N	33.42 E
Nadiād	120	22.42 N	72.52 E
Nadi Bay ⊂	175g	17.44 S	177.25 E
Nādir, Miṣr	142	30.33 N	30.51 E
Nadir, Vir. Is., U.S.	240m	18.19 N	64.53 W
Nădlac	38	46.10 N	20.45 E
Nador	148	35.12 N	2.55 W
Nador □[4]	148	35.09 N	3.04 W
Nadporožje	76	60.28 N	34.17 E
Nadrin	56	50.10 N	5.41 E
Nadterečnaja	84	43.37 N	45.22 E
Nadvirna	78	48.38 N	24.34 E
Nadvoicy	24	63.52 N	34.15 E
Nadym	72	65.35 N	72.42 E
Nadym ≐	74	66.12 N	72.00 E
Nadyrovo	80	54.53 N	52.28 E
Naeba-san ∧	94	36.51 N	138.41 E
Nae-dong	98	37.16 N	126.27 E
Naejang-san Kukrip Kongwŏn ♠	98	35.28 N	126.52 E
Naenwa	120	25.46 N	75.51 E
Nærbø	26	58.40 N	5.39 E
Næsby	41	55.25 N	10.22 E
Næstved	41	55.14 N	11.46 E
Nafada	146	11.08 N	11.20 E
Nafadji	150	12.37 N	11.37 W
Nafarros	266c	38.49 N	9.25 W
Nafāzah, 'Alam ∧[2]	142	30.30 N	29.42 E
Näfels	58	47.06 N	9.04 E
Nafī	128	24.57 N	43.42 E
Nafīshah	142	30.34 N	32.15 E
Naftalan	84	40.31 N	46.50 E
Naftan, Puntan I ›	174n	15.05 N	145.45 E
Nāfūrah	146	29.20 N	21.20 E
Nafūsah, Jabal ⋏[2]	146	31.50 N	12.00 E
Nāg	120	27.24 N	65.08 E
Naga, Nihon	96	34.16 N	135.26 E
Naga, Pil.	116	13.37 N	123.11 E
Naga, Pil.	116	10.13 N	123.45 E
Nâga, Kreb en ⩡[4]	148	24.00 N	6.00 W
Naga, Oued en V	148	27.53 N	7.10 W
Nagaga	154	10.54 S	39.07 E
Nagahama, Nihon	94	35.23 N	136.16 E
Nagahama, Nihon	96	33.36 N	132.29 E
Nagahama, Nihon	174m	26.25 N	127.44 E
Naga Hills ⋏	110	26.00 N	95.00 E
Nagai, Nihon	92	38.06 N	140.02 E
Nagai, Nihon	268	35.12 N	139.37 E
Nagai Island I	180	55.11 N	159.55 W
Nagai Park ♠	270	34.36 N	135.31 E
Nagaizumi	94	35.08 N	138.54 E
Nāgāland □[3]	120	26.00 N	95.00 E
Nagambie	169	36.47 S	145.10 E
Nagannu-shima I	174m	26.16 N	127.33 E
Nagano	94	36.39 N	138.11 E
Nagano □[5]	94	36.00 N	138.00 E
Nagano-dam ◆[6]	94	35.50 N	136.33 E
Naganohara	94	36.33 N	138.38 E
Nagao, Nihon	96	34.16 N	134.10 E
Nagao, Nihon	270	34.50 N	135.43 E
Nagao-hana ›	96	35.32 N	134.01 E
Nagaoka	92	37.27 N	138.51 E
Nagaokakyō	94	34.55 N	135.42 E
Nagaon	120	26.20 N	92.40 E
Nāgappattinam	122	10.46 N	79.50 E
Nagar, India	123	32.07 N	77.10 E
Nagar, India	124	27.26 N	77.06 E
Nagara	270	34.26 N	135.44 E
Nagara ≐	94	35.01 N	136.43 E
Nagareyama	94	35.51 N	139.54 E
Nāgārjuna Sāgar ⊜[1]	122	16.35 N	79.21 E
Nagarote	236	12.16 N	86.34 W
Nagar Pārkar	120	24.22 N	70.45 E
Nāgarpur	124	24.03 N	89.53 E
Nagar Untāri	124	24.17 N	83.30 E
Nagarzê	124	28.59 N	90.25 E
Nagas	116	13.06 N	123.18 E
Nagasaka	94	35.49 N	138.22 E
Nagasaki	92	32.48 N	129.55 E
Nagasawa	268	35.12 N	139.41 E
Nagashima	94	35.05 N	136.42 E
Naga-shima I, Nihon	96	33.49 N	132.05 E
Naga-shima I, Nihon	96	34.41 N	134.15 E
Nagashino ⊥	94	34.56 N	137.32 E
Nagasin Lake ⊜	190	47.44 N	83.37 W
Nagasu, Nihon	96	32.56 N	130.27 E
Nagasu → Usa, Nihon	96	33.31 N	131.22 E
Nagata ◆[8]	270	34.40 N	135.09 E
Nagataki	270	34.23 N	135.20 E
Nagatino ◆[8]	265b	55.41 N	37.41 E
Nagato, Nihon	94	36.15 N	138.16 E
Nagato, Nihon	96	34.21 N	131.10 E
Nagatsuda ◆[8]	268	35.32 N	139.30 E
Nāgaur	120	27.12 N	73.44 E
Nāgāvali ≐	122	18.13 N	83.56 E
Nagavskaja	80	47.47 N	42.50 E
Nagawa	94	36.05 N	137.41 E
Nagawicka Lake ⊜	216	43.05 N	88.23 W
Nagcarlan	116	14.08 N	121.25 E
Nagda	120	23.27 N	75.25 E
Nagele	52	52.37 N	5.44 E
Nāgercoil	122	8.10 N	77.26 E
Nagi	96	35.07 N	134.11 E
Nagiba	116	13.41 N	120.53 E
Nagibino	86	55.46 N	72.43 E
Nagichot	154	4.16 N	33.34 E
Nagīna	124	29.27 N	78.27 E
Nāgirāt	126	23.38 N	89.18 E
Nagi-san ∧	96	35.10 N	134.11 E
Nagiso	94	35.36 N	137.37 E
Nagla	272a	28.31 N	77.22 E
Naglarby	40	60.25 N	15.34 E
Nagles Mountains ⋏	48	52.05 N	8.30 W
Nagłowice	30	50.41 N	20.06 E
Nago	174m	26.35 N	127.59 E
Nāgod	124	24.34 N	80.36 E
Nagog Pond ⊜	283	42.31 N	71.26 W
Nagoja → Nagoya	94	35.10 N	136.55 E
Nagold	56	48.33 N	8.43 E
Nagold ≐	56	48.52 N	8.42 E
Nagorje	76	56.55 N	38.16 E
Nagorno-Karabakh □[9]	84	40.00 N	46.40 E
Nagornyj, Ross.	74	55.58 N	124.57 E
Nagornyj, Ross.	265a	59.43 N	30.16 E
Nagorsk	24	59.18 N	50.48 E
Nagorskoje	82	56.54 N	38.06 E
Nago-wan ⊂	174m	26.34 N	127.57 E
Nagoya	94	35.10 N	136.55 E
Nagoya-kūkō ⊠	94	35.15 N	136.55 E
Nāgpur	120	21.09 N	79.06 E
Nagqu	120	31.34 N	92.00 E
Nagrai	123	34.23 N	72.41 E
Nāgrākāta	124	26.54 N	88.55 E
Nagrota	123	32.03 N	76.05 E
Nagu I	26	60.10 N	21.48 E
Nagua	238	19.23 N	69.50 W
Naguabo	240m	18.13 N	65.44 W
Naguilian	116	17.01 N	121.50 E
Nagumbuaya Point ›	116	13.34 N	124.21 E
Naguri	94	35.53 N	139.11 E
Naguri I	122	6.39 N	72.55 E
Nagyatád	30	46.14 N	17.22 E
Nagybajom	30	46.23 N	17.31 E
Nagybánya → Baia Mare	38	47.40 N	23.35 E
Nagycenk	61	47.36 N	16.42 E
Nagyecsed	30	47.52 N	22.24 E
Nagykálló	30	47.53 N	21.51 E
Nagykanizsa	30	46.27 N	17.00 E
Nagykáta	30	47.25 N	19.45 E
Nagy-Kevély ∧[2]	264c	47.37 N	18.59 E
Nagykőrös	30	47.02 N	19.43 E
Nagy-Milic ∧	30	48.35 N	21.28 E
Nagytarcsa	264c	47.32 N	19.17 E
Nagytétény ◆[8]	264c	47.24 N	18.58 E
Nagyvarad → Oradea	38	47.03 N	21.57 E
Naha	174m	26.13 N	127.40 E
Naha Airfield ⊠	174m	26.13 N	127.40 E
Nahabuan	112	0.49 N	114.05 E
Nahakki	123	34.25 N	71.20 E
Nahalal	132	32.41 N	35.12 E
Naḥal 'Oz	132	31.28 N	34.30 E
Naḥam	132	31.46 N	35.00 E
Nāhan	124	30.33 N	77.18 E
Nahang (Nihing) ≐	128	26.00 N	62.44 E
Nahanni National Park ♠	180	61.40 N	126.00 W
Nahant	207	42.25 N	70.55 W
Nahant Bay ⊂	207	42.27 N	70.55 W
Nahant Beach ⩡[2]	283	42.27 N	70.56 W
Nahari	96	33.25 N	134.01 E
Nahari ≐	96	33.25 N	134.01 E
Nahariyya	132	33.00 N	35.05 E
Naharpur ◆[8]	272a	28.42 N	77.07 E
Nahāta	126	23.20 N	89.31 E
Nahāvand	128	34.12 N	48.22 E
Nahcotta	224	46.30 N	124.02 W
Nahe	89	48.28 N	124.52 E
Nahe ≐	56	49.58 N	7.57 E
Naḥf	132	32.56 N	35.19 E
Nahirne	78	45.26 N	28.27 E
Nahma	190	45.50 N	86.39 W
Nahmer ◆[8]	263	51.20 N	7.35 E
Nahmer ≐	263	51.21 N	7.35 E
Nahoe	174x	9.45 S	138.55 W
Nahoï, Cap ›	175f	14.39 S	166.37 E
Nahol'chyk	83	48.01 N	39.04 E
Nahol'na ≐	83	47.57 N	38.58 E
Nahol'no-Tarasivka	83	48.00 N	39.29 E
Nahon ≐	50	47.14 N	1.39 E
Nahrīn	120	36.01 N	69.06 E
Nahr Ouassel, Oued ≐	148	35.42 N	2.33 E
Nahualate ≐	236	14.03 N	91.32 W
Nahuatzén	234	19.42 N	101.50 W
Nahuel Huapi	254	41.03 S	71.09 W
Nahuel Huapi, Lago ⊜	254	40.58 S	71.30 W
Nahuel Huapi, Parque Nacional ♠	254	41.00 S	71.48 W
Nahuel Niyeu	254	40.30 S	66.33 W
Nahunta	192	31.12 N	81.58 W
Nāhyā	142	30.03 N	31.07 E
Naia ≐	66	42.46 N	12.22 E
Naica	232	27.53 N	105.31 W
Naicam	184	52.25 N	104.30 W
Nai Ga	102	27.48 N	97.30 E
Naiguatá, Pico ∧	286c	10.33 N	66.46 W
Naihāti, Bngl.	126	22.49 N	89.37 E
Naihāti, India	126	22.54 N	88.25 E
Naij Gol ≐, Zhg.	102	36.20 N	94.49 E
Naij Gol ≐, Zhg.	120	36.20 N	94.49 E
Naikliu	112	9.30 S	123.50 E
Naikoon Provincial Park ♠	182	53.50 N	131.50 W
Naila	54	50.19 N	11.42 E
Nailin	98	41.53 N	119.15 E
Nails Creek ≐	222	30.16 N	96.44 W
Nailsea	42	51.26 N	2.43 W
Nailsworth	42	51.42 N	2.14 W
Nā'im, Jabal an- ∧	132	31.04 N	35.55 E
Naiman Qi	89	42.55 N	120.43 E
Nain, Nf., Can.	176	56.32 N	61.41 W
Nā'īn, Īrān	128	32.52 N	53.05 E
Nain ⊜	40	60.14 N	13.50 E
Naini Tāl	124	29.23 N	79.27 E
Nainpur	124	22.26 N	80.07 E
Nairai I	175g	17.49 S	179.24 E
Nairn, Scot., U.K.	46	57.35 N	3.53 W
Nairn, La., U.S.	194	29.27 N	89.38 W
Nairn ≐	46	57.35 N	3.52 W
Nairne	168b	35.02 S	138.54 E
Nairobi	154	1.17 S	36.49 E
Nairobi Airport ⊠	276	41.08 N	74.21 W
Nairobi National Park ♠	154	1.24 S	36.50 E
Naissaar I	76	59.33 N	24.32 E
Naita ∧	144	5.30 N	35.18 E
Naitamba Island I	175g	17.31 S	179.17 W
Naivasha	154	0.43 S	36.26 E
Naivasha, Lake ⊜	154	0.46 S	36.21 E
Naivos	114	2.30 N	96.10 E
Naizifang	105	39.36 N	116.47 E
N'aizishen	89	43.41 N	127.29 E
Najac	32	44.13 N	1.59 E
Najafābād	128	32.37 N	51.21 E
Najafgarh ◆[8]	272a	28.37 N	76.59 E
Najafgarh Drain ≍	272a	28.43 N	77.14 E
Najasa ≐	240p	20.42 N	77.55 W
Najd □[9]	118	25.00 N	44.30 E
Nájera	34	42.25 N	2.44 W
Najhā	132	33.23 N	36.22 E
Naj'Ḥammādī	140	26.03 N	32.15 E
Najībābād	124	29.38 N	78.20 E
Najin	98	42.15 N	130.18 E
Najinkouzi	89	50.23 N	126.57 E
Najio	270	34.50 N	135.18 E
Najstenjarvi	24	62.16 N	32.38 E
Naju	98	35.03 N	126.43 E
Najza, gora ∧	86	49.24 N	70.42 E
Naka, Nihon	94	36.27 N	140.30 E
Naka, Nihon	96	35.02 N	134.55 E
Naka, Nihon	268	35.49 N	140.03 E
Naka, Nihon	270	34.50 N	135.48 E
Naka, Nihon	270	34.42 N	135.45 E
Naka, Nihon	270	34.50 N	135.56 E
Naka ◆[8]	268	35.27 N	139.39 E
Naka ≐, Nihon	94	36.20 N	140.36 E
Naka ≐, Nihon	96	33.56 N	134.42 E
Naka ≐, Nihon	268	35.39 N	139.51 E
Nakadōri-shima I	92	32.57 N	129.04 E
Nakagami	268	35.49 N	139.21 E
Nakagawa	94	35.38 N	137.56 E
Nakagawa ◆[8]	268	35.33 N	139.35 E
Nakagō	94	36.58 N	138.14 E
Nakagusuku	174m	26.15 N	127.49 E
Nakagusuku-wan ⊂	174m	26.14 N	127.53 E
Nakagyō ◆[8]	270	35.01 N	135.45 E
Nakaheji	96	33.47 N	135.31 E
Nakai	94	35.20 N	139.14 E
Nakaizu	94	34.57 N	139.00 E
Nakajima, Nihon	94	37.07 N	136.51 E
Nakajima, Nihon	96	33.58 N	132.07 E
Nakajima, Nihon	268	35.26 N	139.56 E
Nakajima, Nihon	268	35.18 N	139.58 E
Naka-jima I	96	33.58 N	132.37 E
Nakajō, Nihon	92	38.03 N	139.24 E
Nakajō, Nihon	94	36.36 N	138.02 E
Nakakawane	94	35.03 N	138.05 E
Nāka Khārari	120	25.15 N	66.44 E
Nakalele Point ›	229a	21.02 N	156.35 W
Nākālia	126	24.02 N	89.40 E
Nakama, Nihon	96	33.50 N	130.43 E
Nakama, Nihon	174m	26.16 N	127.44 E
Nakaminato	94	36.21 N	140.36 E
Nakamura	96	32.59 N	132.56 E
Nakanai Mountains ⋏	164	5.35 S	151.10 E
Nakano, Nihon	94	36.45 N	138.22 E
Nakano, Nihon	268	35.20 N	139.54 E
Nakano, Nihon	270	34.58 N	135.58 E
Nakano ◆[8]	268	35.42 N	139.42 E
Nakanobu ◆[8]	268	35.36 N	139.43 E
Nakanojō	94	36.35 N	138.51 E
Nakano-shima I	93b	29.49 N	129.52 E
Nakanoshima-suidō ⋓	93b	29.44 N	129.49 E
Nakanougan-jima I	175d	24.11 N	123.33 E
Nakaosu	174m	26.37 N	128.02 E
Nakaōzō ◆[8]	270	34.51 N	135.11 E
Nakape	140	5.47 N	28.37 E
Nakashibetsu	92a	43.33 N	144.59 E
Nākāsipāra	126	23.35 N	88.21 E
Nakasongola	154	1.19 N	32.28 E
Nakatō	268	35.45 N	139.24 E
Nakatomi, Nihon	94	35.28 N	138.26 E
Nakatomi, Nihon	268	35.49 N	139.30 E
Nakatosa	96	33.20 N	133.14 E
Nakatsu, Nihon	96	33.34 N	131.13 E
Nakatsu, Nihon	96	33.57 N	135.18 E
Nakatsu, Nihon	268	35.30 N	139.20 E
Nakatsu ≐	94	37.00 N	138.39 E
Nakatsue	96	33.08 N	130.56 E
Nakatsugawa	94	35.29 N	137.30 E
Nakatsumine-yama ∧	96	33.58 N	134.31 E
Nakauchigami	270	34.56 N	135.10 E
Naka-umi ⊂	96	35.28 N	133.12 E
Nakayama, Nihon	96	33.38 N	132.42 E
Nakayama, Nihon	96	35.31 N	133.35 E
Nakayama ◆[8]	268	35.31 N	139.33 E
Nakayama ≐	96	33.55 N	133.08 E
Nakazato, Nihon	94	36.05 N	138.50 E
Nakazato, Nihon	94	37.03 N	138.42 E
Nakazuma	268	35.58 N	139.35 E
Nakéty	175f	21.33 S	166.03 E
Nakfa	144	16.43 N	38.32 E
Nakhichevan → Naxçıvan Muxtar Respublikası □[3]	84	39.20 N	45.30 E
Nakhola	120	26.07 N	92.11 E
Nakhon Nayok	110	14.12 N	101.13 E
Nakhon Pathom	110	13.49 N	100.03 E
Nakhon Phanom	110	17.24 N	104.47 E
Nakhon Ratchasima	110	14.58 N	102.07 E
Nakhon Sawan	110	15.41 N	100.07 E
Nakhon Si Thammarat	110	8.26 N	99.58 E
Nakhon Thai	110	17.07 N	100.50 E
Nakhtarana	120	23.20 N	69.15 E
Nakina	176	50.10 N	86.42 W
Nakkaş ≐	267b	41.00 N	28.45 E
Nakło nad Notecią	30	53.08 N	17.35 E
Naknek	180	58.44 N	157.02 W
Naknek Lake ⊜	180	58.40 N	156.15 W
Nako	150	10.38 N	3.04 W
Nakodar	123	31.07 N	75.29 E
Nakonde	154	9.20 S	32.42 E
Nakoso-no-seki-ato ⊥	94	36.53 N	140.46 E
Nakou	100	27.09 N	117.38 E
Nakskov	41	54.50 N	11.09 E
Nakskov Fjord ⊂	41	54.50 N	11.02 E
Näkten ⊜	26	62.52 N	14.38 E
Naktong-gang ≐	98	35.07 N	128.57 E
Nakūr	124	29.55 N	77.18 E
Nakuru	154	0.17 S	36.04 E
Nakuru, Lake ⊜	154	0.22 S	36.05 E
Nakusp	182	50.15 N	117.48 W
Nāl ≐	120	26.02 N	65.19 E
Nālāgarh	123	31.03 N	76.43 E
Nalajch	88	47.45 N	107.16 E
Nālanda	124	25.07 N	85.25 E
Nalao	102	24.22 N	105.23 E
Nalázi	156	24.03 S	33.20 E
Nalbach	56	49.23 N	6.47 E
Nalbāri	120	26.25 N	91.26 E
Nalcayec, Isla I	254	46.06 S	73.49 W
Nalchik → Nal'čik	84	43.29 N	43.37 E
Nālchiti	124	22.38 N	90.17 E
Nal'čik	84	43.29 N	43.37 E
Naldānga	126	23.26 N	89.11 E
Nāldera	123	31.11 N	77.11 E
Näldsjön ⊜	26	63.23 N	14.17 E
Nałęczów	30	51.18 N	22.11 E
Nalgonda	122	17.03 N	79.16 E
Nalgora	126	22.52 N	90.39 E
Nalhāti	126	24.18 N	87.49 E
Naliagrām	126	23.36 N	89.37 E
Naliang	102	21.43 N	107.51 E
Nālikul	272b	22.49 N	88.11 E
Nalinnes	50	50.19 N	4.26 E
Nalisan	104	42.06 N	122.12 E
Nallamalla Hills ⋏	122	15.30 N	78.45 E
Nalles (Nals)	64	46.32 N	11.12 E
Nallıhan	130	40.11 N	31.21 E
Na Logu	64	46.23 N	13.45 E
Nalolo	152	15.35 S	23.07 E
Nalón ≐	34	43.32 N	6.04 W
Nalong	102	23.35 N	106.05 E
Nalusa	152	14.55 S	22.13 E
Nālūt	146	31.52 N	10.59 E
Nalžovské Hory	60	49.20 N	13.33 E
Nam ≐	110	21.33 N	98.38 E
Namaacha	156	25.58 S	32.01 E
Namachire	152	11.26 S	22.43 E
Namacunde	152	17.18 S	15.50 E
Namacurra	154	17.29 S	37.01 E
Namadgi National Park ♠	171b	35.45 S	148.57 E
Namak, Daryācheh-ye ⊜	128	34.30 N	51.50 E
Namak, Kavīr-e ◆[2]	128	34.45 N	57.45 E
Namakan Lake ⊜	190	48.27 N	92.35 W
Nāmakkal	122	11.14 N	78.10 E

≐ River	Fluß	Río	Rivière	Rio	✦ Submarine Features	Untermeerische Objekte	Accidentes Submarinos / Formes de relief sous-marin / Acidentes submarinos
≍ Canal	Kanal	Canal	Canal	Canal	□ Political Unit	Politische Einheit	Unidad Politica / Entité politique / Unidade política
⌞ Waterfall, Rapids	Wasserfall, Stromschnellen	Cascada, Rápidos	Chute d'eau, Rapides	Cascata, Rápidos	⊍ Cultural Institution	Kulturelle Institution	Institución Cultural / Institution culturelle / Instituição cultural
⋓ Strait	Meeresstraße	Estrecho	Détroit	Estreito	⊥ Historical Site	Historische Stätte	Sitio Histórico / Site historique / Sitio histórico
⊂ Bay, Gulf	Bucht, Golf	Bahía, Golfo	Baie, Golfe	Baía, Golfo	♠ Recreational Site	Erholungs- und Ferienort	Sitio de Recreo / Centre de loisirs / Area de Lazer
⊜ Lake, Lakes	See, Seen	Lago, Lagos	Lac, Lacs	Lago, Lagos	⊠ Airport	Flughafen	Aeropuerto / Aéroport / Aeroporto
≡ Swamp	Sumpf	Pantano	Marais	Pântano	■ Military Installation	Militäranlage	Instalación Militar / Installation militaire / Instalação militar
⍓ Ice Features, Glacier	Eis- und Gletscherformen	Accidentes Glaciales	Formes glaciaires	Acidentes glaciares	◆ Miscellaneous	Verschiedenes	Misceláneo / Divers / Diversos
╤ Other Hydrographic Features	Andere Hydrographische Objekte	Otros Elementos Hidrográficos	Autres données hydrographiques	Outros acidentes hidrográficos			

Symbols in the index entries represent the broad categories identified in the key at the right. Symbols with superior numbers (⋏[1]) identify subcategories (see complete key on page *I · 1)*.

Symbole im Register stellen die rechts im Schlüssel erklärten Kategorien dar. Symbole mit hochgestellten Ziffern (⋏[1]) bezeichnen Unterabteilungen einer Kategorie (vgl. vollständiger Schlüssel auf Seite *I · 1)*.

Los símbolos incluídos en el texto del índice representan las grandes categorías identificadas con la clave a la derecha. Los símbolos con numeros en su parte superior (⋏[1]) identifican las subcategorías (véase la clave completa en la página *I · 1)*.

Les symboles de l'index représentent les catégories indiquées dans la légende à droite. Les symboles suivis d'un indice (⋏[1]) représentent des sous-catégories (voir légende complète à la page *I · 1)*.

Os símbolos incluídos no texto do índice representam as grandes categorias identificadas com a chave à direita. Os símbolos com números em sua parte superior (⋏[1]) identificam as subcategorias (veja-se a chave completa à página *I · 1)*.

∧ Mountain	Berg	Montaña	Montagne	Montanha
⋏ Mountains	Gebirge	Montañas	Montagnes	Montanhas
)(Pass	Paß	Paso	Col	Passo
V Valley, Canyon	Tal, Cañon	Valle, Cañón	Vallée, Canyon	Vale, Canhão
≚ Plain	Ebene	Llano	Plaine	Planície
≻ Cape	Kap	Cabo	Cap	Cabo
I Island	Insel	Isla	Île	Ilha
II Islands	Inseln	Islas	Îles	Ilhas
⊥ Other Topographic Features	Andere Topographische Objekte	Otros Elementos Topográficos	Autres données topographiques	Outros acidentes topográficos

Natu-Neue *I* · *121*

ESPAÑOL — Nombre, Página, Lat.°′, Long.°′ W = Oeste
FRANÇAIS — Nom, Page, Lat.°′, Long.°′ W = Ouest
PORTUGUÊS — Nome, Página, Lat.°′, Long.°′ W = Oeste

Natural Bridge State Resort Park ♦	192	37.47 N	83.42 W
Naturaliste, Cape ≻	162	33.32 S	115.01 E
Naturaliste Channel ⊔	162	25.25 S	113.00 E
Naturita	200	38.13 N	108.34 W
Naturita Creek ≃	200	38.13 N	108.32 W
Naturno (Naturns)	64	46.39 N	11.00 E
Natzungen	52	51.36 N	9.14 E
Nau	85	40.09 N	69.22 E
Nau, Cap de la ≻	34	38.44 N	0.14 E
Naucalpan de Juárez	286a	19.28 N	99.14 W
Naucelle	32	44.12 N	2.20 E
Nauchnyy	78	44.44 N	34.01 E
Naude	272c	19.03 N	73.06 E
Nauders	58	46.53 N	10.30 E
Nauen	54	52.36 N	12.52 E
Nauener Luch ≡	264a	52.37 N	12.55 E
Nauener Stadtforst ♦	264a	52.38 N	12.58 E
Naugachhia	124	25.24 N	87.06 E
Naugatuck	207	41.30 N	73.05 W
Naugatuck ≃	207	41.19 N	73.05 W
Naughton	190	46.24 N	81.12 W
Naugol'noje	82	56.22 N	38.11 E
Naui	140	18.28 N	30.43 E
Naujamiestis	76	55.41 N	24.04 E
Naujan	116	13.20 N	121.18 E
Naujan, Lake ⊜	116	13.10 N	121.21 E
Naujoji Akmenė	76	56.19 N	22.55 E
Naukan	180	66.01 N	169.43 W
Naulavaara ∧ [2]	26	63.53 N	28.13 E
Naulila	152	17.12 S	14.42 E
Naumburg, Dtsch.	54	51.09 N	11.48 E
Naumburg, Dtsch.	56	51.15 N	9.10 E
Naumovščina	76	58.23 N	28.20 E
Naunak	86	59.00 N	80.13 E
Naundorf	54	50.56 N	13.25 E
Naunglon	110	16.48 N	97.45 E
Naungpale	110	19.33 N	97.08 E
Naunhof	54	51.16 N	12.35 E
Naupada ✦ [8]	272c	19.04 N	72.50 E
Nā'ūr	132	31.53 N	35.50 E
Nauraushaun Brook ≃	276	41.03 N	73.59 W
Nauroth	56	50.42 N	7.52 E
Nauroz Kalāt	128	28.47 N	65.38 E
Naurskaja	84	43.38 N	45.19 E
Nauru □ [1], Oc.	14	0.32 S	166.55 E
Nauru □ [1], Oc.	174b	0.32 S	166.55 E
Naurzumskij zapovednik ♦	86	51.30 N	64.20 E
Naushahro Fīroz	120	26.50 N	68.07 E
Naushon Island I	207	41.29 N	70.45 W
Nauški	88	50.28 N	106.07 E
Nausori	175g	18.02 S	178.32 E
Naussac, Barrage de ✦ [6]	62	44.46 N	3.49 E
Naustdal	26	61.31 N	5.43 E
Nauta	246	4.32 S	73.33 W
Nautanwa	124	27.26 N	83.25 E
Nautilus Park	207	41.22 N	72.05 W
Nautla	234	20.13 N	96.47 W
Nauvoo	190	40.33 N	91.23 W
Nava, It.	62	44.06 N	7.22 E
Nava, Méx.	232	28.25 N	100.46 W
Nava, Arroyo de la ≃	266a	40.31 N	3.46 W
Nava, Colle di)(	62	44.05 N	7.53 E
Nava del Rey	34	41.20 N	5.05 W
Navadwip	126	23.25 N	88.22 E
Navael'nja	76	53.28 N	25.35 E
Navahermosa	34	39.38 N	4.28 W
Navahrudak	76	53.36 N	25.50 E
Navajo	200	35.55 N	109.01 W
Navajo ≃	200	37.01 N	107.10 W
Navajo Creek ≃	200	36.59 N	111.24 W
Navajo Hopi Joint Use Area ✦ [4]	200	36.15 N	110.30 W
Navajo Indian Reservation ✦ [4]	200	36.25 N	110.00 W
Navajo Mountain ∧	200	37.02 N	110.52 W
Navajo National Monument ♦	200	36.40 N	110.33 W
Navajo Reservoir ⊜ [1]	200	36.55 N	107.30 W
Naval	116	11.34 N	124.23 E
Navalmoral de la Mata	34	39.54 N	5.32 W
Naval Ordnance Test Station ■	228	35.32 N	117.05 W
Navalvillar de Pela	34	39.06 N	5.28 W
Navan	48	53.39 N	6.41 W
Navapolack	76	55.31 N	28.38 E
Navāpur	122	21.09 N	73.48 E
Navarin, mys ≻	180	62.16 N	179.10 E
Navarino → Pílos	38	36.55 N	21.43 E
Navarino, Isla I	254	55.05 S	67.40 W
Navarra □ [4]	34	42.40 N	1.30 W
Navarre, Austl.	169	36.54 S	143.07 E
Navarre, Oh., U.S.	214	40.43 N	81.31 W
Navarro	258	35.01 S	59.16 W
Navarro □ [6]	222	32.05 N	96.30 W
Navarro ≃	204	39.11 N	123.45 W
Navarro, Cañada ≃	258	35.00 S	59.18 W
Navarro, Laguna ⊜	258	35.01 S	59.18 W
Navarro Mills Lake ⊜ [1]	222	31.56 N	96.45 W
Navasëlki, Bela.	76	52.02 N	24.21 E
Navasëlki, Bela.	76	52.24 N	28.33 E
Navašino	80	55.32 N	42.12 E
Navasota	222	30.23 N	96.05 W
Navasota ≃	222	30.20 N	96.09 W
Navassa	192	34.15 N	78.00 W
Navassa Island I	238	18.24 N	75.01 W
Nave	64	45.35 N	10.17 E
Nävekvarn	40	58.38 N	16.49 E
Navenne	58	47.36 N	6.10 E
Naver ≃	46	58.32 N	4.15 W
Naver, Loch ⊜	46	58.17 N	4.23 W
Navesink	276	40.23 N	74.02 W
Navesink River c	276	40.23 N	73.58 W
Navesnoje	76	52.17 N	37.57 E
Nâves-Parmelan	58	45.56 N	6.11 E
Navesti ≃	76	58.30 N	24.54 E
Navestock	260	51.39 N	0.13 E
Navestock Side	260	51.39 N	0.16 E
Navia, Arg.	252	34.47 S	66.35 W
Navia, Esp.	34	43.32 N	6.43 W
Navia ≃	34	43.33 N	6.44 W
Navidad	252	33.57 S	71.50 W
Navidad ≃	196	28.41 N	96.35 W
Navidad, Bahía de c	234	19.17 N	104.50 W
Navidad Bank ✧ [3]	238	20.00 N	68.50 W
Navio, Riacho do ≃	250	8.39 S	38.36 W
Naviraí	255	23.08 S	54.13 W
Navis	64	47.07 N	11.32 E
Naviti I	175g	17.07 S	177.15 E
Navl'a	76	52.51 N	34.30 E
Navl'a ≃	76	52.42 N	34.01 E
Năvodari	38	44.19 N	28.36 E
Navoi	72	40.15 N	65.15 E
Navojoa	232	27.06 N	109.26 W
Navolato	232	24.47 N	107.42 W
Navoloki	80	57.28 N	41.59 E
Navotas	269f	14.39 N	120.57 E
Návpaktos	38	38.23 N	21.50 E
Návplion	38	37.34 N	22.48 E
Navrongo	150	10.54 N	1.06 W
Navsāri	120	20.51 N	72.55 E
Navua	175g	18.14 S	178.10 E
Navy Island I	284a	43.04 N	79.01 W
Navy Pier ✦ [5]	278	41.53 N	87.36 W
Navy Yard City	224	47.32 N	122.41 W
Nawa, Nihon	96	35.30 N	133.30 E
Nawa → Naha, Nihon	174m	26.13 N	127.40 E
Nawá, Sūrīy.	132	32.53 N	36.03 E
Nawābganj, Bngl.	124	24.36 N	88.17 E
Nawābganj, Bngl.	126	23.40 N	90.10 E
Nawābganj, India	124	28.33 N	79.38 E
Nawābganj, India	124	26.52 N	82.08 E
Nawābganj, India	124	26.56 N	81.13 E
Nawābshāh	120	26.15 N	68.25 E
Nawāda	124	24.53 N	85.32 E
Nāwah	120	32.19 N	67.53 E
Nawa Kot	120	28.20 N	71.22 E
Nawalapitiya	122	7.03 N	80.32 E
Nawalgarh	120	27.51 N	75.16 E
Nawān Kot	123	31.06 N	71.32 E
Nawanshahr	123	31.07 N	76.08 E
Nawāpāra, Bngl.	126	23.02 N	89.23 E
Nawāpāra, India	122	20.58 N	81.51 E
Nawapārā, India	126	23.29 N	88.15 E
Nawasā al-Ghayṭ	142	30.58 N	31.19 E
Nawāshahr	123	34.10 N	73.16 E
Nawāṣīf, Harrat ⩠ [9]	144	21.20 N	42.10 E
Nawāy	142	27.47 N	30.46 E
Nawiliwili Bay c	229b	21.57 N	159.21 W
Nawinda Kuta	152	16.25 S	24.28 E
Nawŏn-ni	98	36.25 N	126.40 E
Naxçıvan	84	39.13 N	45.24 E
Naxçıvan Muxtar Respublikası □ [3]	84	39.20 N	45.30 E
Naxera	208	37.20 N	76.27 W
Naxi	107	28.47 N	105.22 E
Náxos	38	37.06 N	25.23 E
Náxos I	38	37.02 N	25.35 E
Naxos ⊥	70	37.49 N	15.17 E
Nayābās	272a	28.35 N	77.19 E
Nayāgaon	126	23.32 N	90.46 E
Nayāgarh	120	20.08 N	85.06 E
Nayāgrām	126	22.02 N	87.11 E
Nayak	120	34.44 N	66.57 E
Nayāpāra	126	21.35 N	87.01 E
Nayarit	204	32.20 N	115.19 W
Nayarit □ [3]	234	22.00 N	105.00 W
Nayau Island I	175g	17.58 S	179.03 W
Nāy Band, Īrān	128	32.20 N	57.34 E
Nāy Band, Īrān	128	27.23 N	52.38 E
Nāy Band, Kūh-e ∧	128	32.26 N	57.22 E
Nayland	42	51.59 N	0.52 E
Naylor	194	36.34 N	90.36 W
Nayong	102	26.50 N	105.13 E
Nayoro	92a	44.21 N	142.28 E
Nazālī Ṭāhā'	142	28.11 N	30.42 E
Nazaré, Bra.	250	6.23 S	47.40 W
Nazaré, Bra.	255	13.02 S	39.00 W
Nazaré, Port.	34	39.36 N	9.04 W
Nazaré da Mata	250	7.44 S	35.14 W
Nazaré do Piauí	250	6.59 S	42.40 W
Nazareno	256	21.13 S	44.37 W
Nazaré Paulista	256	23.11 S	46.24 W
Nazareth, Bel.	50	50.58 N	3.36 E
Nazareth, Pa., U.S.	208	40.44 N	75.18 W
Nazareth, Vanuatu	175f	15.29 S	168.10 E
Nazareth → Nazerat, Yis.	132	32.42 N	35.18 E
Nazareth Bank ✧ [4]	12	14.30 S	60.45 E
Nazário	255	16.36 S	49.54 W
Nazarjevo, Ross.	82	55.22 N	36.24 E
Nazarjevo, Ross.	265b	55.59 N	37.16 E
Nazarovo	86	56.01 N	90.26 E
Nazarovskij	78	49.33 N	40.56 E
Nazas	232	25.14 N	104.08 W
Nazas ≃	232	25.35 N	105.00 W
Nazca	248	14.50 S	74.57 W
Nazca Ridge ✧ [3]	18	22.00 S	82.00 W
Naze	93b	28.23 N	129.30 E
Nazeing	260	51.44 N	0.03 E
N'azepetrovsk	86	56.03 N	59.36 E
Nazerat (Nazareth)	132	32.42 N	35.18 E
Nazerat 'Illit	132	32.42 N	35.19 E
Nazija	76	59.50 N	31.35 E
Nazik Gölü ⊜	130	38.50 N	42.16 E
Nazilli	130	37.55 N	28.21 E
Nazimicha	265b	55.59 N	38.08 E
Nazımiye	130	39.11 N	39.50 E
Nazimovo	86	59.30 N	90.58 E
Nazina	86	60.07 N	78.52 E
Nāzira	120	26.55 N	94.44 E
Nāzir Hāt	120	22.38 N	91.47 E
Nāzirpur	126	22.43 N	89.58 E
Nazko ≃	182	53.07 N	123.34 W
Nazlat al-'Amūdayn	142	28.14 N	30.42 E
Nazlat al-Badramān	142	27.40 N	30.44 E
Nazlat as-Sammān	273c	29.59 N	31.08 E
Nazlat Khalīfah	273c	30.01 N	31.10 E
Nazlat Quftan Bāshā	142	28.57 N	30.49 E
Nazlat Thābit	142	28.25 N	30.47 E
Nazran'	84	43.13 N	44.46 E
Nazret	144	8.33 N	39.16 E
Nazyvajevsk	86	55.34 N	71.21 E
N. B. C. Studios ʊ [3]	280	34.09 N	118.20 W
Nchanga	154	12.30 S	27.53 E
Nchelenge	154	9.20 S	28.50 E
Ncue	152	2.01 N	10.28 E
Ndabala	154	13.28 S	29.50 E
Ndala	154	4.46 S	33.16 E
N'dalatando	152	9.18 S	14.54 E
Ndali	150	9.51 N	2.43 E
Ndanda	152	5.12 N	22.21 E
Ndande	150	15.16 N	16.30 W
Ndarassa	152	6.49 N	22.15 E
Ndélé	146	8.24 N	20.39 E
Ndélélé	152	4.02 N	14.56 E
Ndemba	152	0.11 N	14.19 E
Ndendé	152	2.23 S	11.23 E
Ndikiniméki	152	4.46 N	10.50 E
Ndindi	152	3.46 S	11.09 E
N'Djamena	146	12.07 N	15.03 E
Ndji ≃	152	6.47 N	22.14 E
Ndjili ✦ [8]	273b	4.20 S	15.22 E
Ndjili ≃	273b	4.19 S	15.24 E
Ndjili, Grande Île de la I	273b	4.19 S	15.24 E
Ndjim ≃	152	4.38 N	11.24 E
Ndjo	152	1.15 S	14.30 E
Ndjolé	152	0.11 S	10.45 E
Ndogo, Lagune c	152	2.35 S	10.00 E
Ndola	154	12.58 S	28.38 E
Ndolo ✦ [8]	273b	4.19 S	15.19 E
Ndona	115b	8.46 S	121.45 E
Ndongo	152	2.19 S	13.38 E
Ndouba	152	0.11 S	14.09 E
Ndougou	152	1.39 S	9.40 E
Ndu	152	4.41 N	22.49 E
Nduguti	154	4.18 S	34.42 E
Nduindui	175f	15.24 S	167.46 E
Ndumbwe	154	10.14 S	39.58 E
Ndumu Game Reserve ✦ [4]	158	26.53 S	32.15 E
Nduye	154	1.50 N	29.01 E
Ne	268	35.47 N	140.03 E
Nea ≃	26	63.13 N	11.02 E
Neabul Creek ≃	166	27.45 S	147.32 E
Néa Erithraía	267c	38.05 N	23.49 E
Néa Filadhélfia	267c	38.02 N	23.44 E
Neagari	94	36.27 N	136.27 E
Neagh, Lough ⊜	48	54.38 N	6.24 W
Neah Bay	224	48.22 N	124.37 W
Néa Ionía	267c	38.02 N	23.45 E
Neajlov ≃	38	44.11 N	26.12 E
Néa Khalkidhón	267c	38.02 N	23.43 E
Neale, Lake ⊜	162	24.22 S	130.00 E
Neales ≃	162	28.08 S	136.47 E
Neales Flat	168b	34.15 S	139.10 E
Néa Liósia	267c	38.02 N	23.42 E
Neamț □ [6]	38	47.00 N	26.30 E
Neandertal, Naturschutzgebiet ♦	263	51.15 N	7.00 E
Néa Páfos (Paphos)	130	34.45 N	32.25 E
Neapel → Napoli	68	40.51 N	14.17 E
Néa Pendéli	267c	38.04 N	23.52 E
Néa Péramos	267c	38.00 N	23.26 E
Neápolis, Ellás	38	36.30 N	23.04 E
Neápolis, Ellás	38	35.15 N	25.37 E
Neapolis, Oh., U.S.	216	41.29 N	83.52 W
Near Islands II	181a	52.40 N	173.30 E
Near North Side ✦ [8]	278	41.54 N	87.38 W
Néa Smírni	267c	37.57 N	23.43 E
Neasons Hill	214	41.37 N	80.08 W
Neatahwanta, Lake ⊜	210	43.18 N	76.27 W
Neath	42	51.40 N	3.48 W
Neath ≃	42	51.37 N	3.50 W
Neauphle-le-Château	50	48.49 N	1.54 E
Neauphle-le-Vieux	261	48.49 N	1.52 E
Neavitt	208	38.43 N	76.16 W
Neba	94	35.15 N	137.35 E
Nebaj	236	15.24 N	91.08 W
Nebbou	150	11.18 N	1.53 W
Nebelhorn ∧	58	47.25 N	10.20 E
Nebesnaja, gora ∧	86	43.19 N	80.44 E
Nebeur	36	36.17 N	8.47 E
Nebine Creek ≃	166	29.07 S	146.56 E
Nebit-Dag	128	39.30 N	54.22 E
Neblina, Pico da ∧	246	0.48 N	66.02 W
Nebo	194	39.27 N	90.47 W
Nebo, Mount ∧, Ut., U.S.	200	39.49 N	111.46 W
Nebo, Mount → Nabā, Jabal an- ∧, Urd.	132	31.46 N	35.45 E
Nebolči	76	59.08 N	33.18 E
Nebra	54	51.17 N	11.34 E
Nebraska	218	39.04 N	85.28 W
Nebraska □ [3], U.S.	178	41.30 N	100.00 W
Nebraska □ [3], U.S.	198	41.30 N	100.00 W
Nebraska City	198	40.40 N	95.51 W
Nebrodi ⋏	70	37.54 N	14.35 E
Nebyloje	80	56.22 N	39.59 E
Nečajevka	80	53.17 N	44.27 E
Nečajevo	82	54.42 N	37.23 E
Necaxa ≃	234	20.16 N	97.27 W
Necedah	190	44.01 N	90.04 W
Nechajevskij	80	50.25 N	41.44 E
Nechako ≃	182	53.56 N	122.42 W
Nechako Plateau ⋏ [1]	182	54.00 N	124.30 W
Nechako Range ⋏	182	53.20 N	124.30 W
Nechako Reservoir ⊜ [1]	182	53.25 N	125.10 W
Nechayane	78	46.57 N	31.33 E
Neche	198	48.59 N	97.33 W
Neches	222	31.52 N	95.30 W
Neches ≃	194	29.55 N	93.52 W
Nechí	246	8.07 N	74.46 W
Nechí ≃	246	8.08 N	74.46 W
Nechisar National Park ♦	144	6.00 N	37.50 E
Nechmeya	36	36.36 N	7.31 E
Nechranice, vodní nádrž ⊜ [1]	54	50.20 N	13.20 E
Neckar ≃	30	49.31 N	8.26 E
Neckarbischofsheim	56	49.17 N	8.57 E
Neckarelz	56	49.20 N	9.06 E
Neckargemünd	56	49.23 N	8.47 E
Neckarsteinach	56	49.25 N	8.53 E
Neckarsulm	56	49.12 N	9.13 E
Neckartailfingen	56	48.36 N	9.16 E
Neckartenzlingen	56	48.35 N	9.14 E
Neck Creek ≃	276	40.36 N	74.12 W
Necker	284b	39.23 N	76.29 W
Necker Island I, Br. Vir. Is.	240m	18.33 N	64.21 W
Necker Island I, Hi., U.S.	14	23.35 N	164.42 W
Necker Ridge ✧ [3]	14	22.00 N	167.15 W
Necochea	252	38.33 S	58.45 W
Necrópolis ✦	266a	40.25 N	3.38 W
Nedalssjön ⊜	26	62.56 N	12.11 E
Nedanchychi	78	51.30 N	30.37 E
Ned Brown Preserve ♦	278	42.02 N	88.01 W
Nedel'noje	82	54.50 N	36.39 E
Nederland	194	29.58 N	93.59 W
Nederland → Netherlands □ [1]	30	52.15 N	5.30 E
Nederlandse Antillen → Netherlands Antilles □ [2]	241s	12.15 N	69.00 W
Neder Rijn ≃ [1]	52	51.58 N	5.20 E
Nederweert	52	51.17 N	5.45 E
Nederzwalm-Hermelgem	50	50.53 N	3.41 E
Nedlands	168a	31.59 S	115.49 E
Nedlitz	54	52.04 N	12.14 E
Nedlitz ✦ [8]	264a	52.26 N	13.03 E
Nêdong	120	29.14 N	91.46 E
Nedre Soppero	24	68.01 N	21.44 E
Nedre Vättern ⊜	40	59.49 N	15.40 E
Nédroma	148	35.01 N	1.45 W
Nedrow	210	42.58 N	76.08 W
Nedryhayliv	78	50.50 N	33.53 E
Nedstrand	26	59.21 N	5.51 E
Neebish Island I	190	46.16 N	84.09 W
Neede	52	52.08 N	6.36 E
Needham, In., U.S.	218	39.32 N	85.58 W
Needham, Ma., U.S.	207	42.17 N	71.14 W
Needham Market	42	52.09 N	1.03 E
Needhams Point ≻	241g	13.05 N	59.36 W
Needle Mountain ∧	202	44.05 N	109.37 W
Needles	204	34.50 N	114.36 W
Needling Hill ∧ [2]	168a	31.53 S	116.56 E
Needville	222	29.23 N	95.50 W
Neelyton	214	40.10 N	77.50 W
Ñeembucú □ [5]	252	27.00 S	58.00 W
Neenah	190	44.11 N	88.27 W
Neepawa	184	50.13 N	99.29 W
Neerabup National Park ♦	168a	31.41 S	115.43 E
Neerim South	169	38.01 S	145.58 E
Neermoor	52	53.18 N	7.26 E
Neeroeteren	56	51.05 N	5.42 E
Neerpelt	56	51.13 N	5.25 E
Neersen	263	51.15 N	6.29 E
Nee Soon	271c	1.24 N	103.49 E
Neetze	52	53.15 N	10.39 E
Neetze ≃	54	53.20 N	10.28 E
Nefedjevo, Ross.	82	54.39 N	37.56 E
Nefedjevo, Ross.	265b	55.54 N	37.10 E
Neffs	208	40.42 N	75.37 W
Neffsville	208	40.06 N	76.18 W
Nef'odovo	86	58.48 N	72.34 E
Nefta	148	33.52 N	7.33 E
Neftçala	84	39.23 N	49.16 E
Nefteabad	85	40.12 N	70.34 E
Neftegorsk	84	44.22 N	39.42 E
Neftekumsk	84	44.45 N	44.48 E
Nefyn	42	52.57 N	4.31 W
Nefza	36	36.58 N	9.05 E
Negage	152	7.45 S	15.16 E
Négala	150	12.52 N	8.27 W
Negapatam → Nāgappattinam	122	10.46 N	79.50 E
Negara, Indon.	112	2.37 S	115.06 E
Negara, Indon.	115a	8.22 S	114.37 E
Negara ≃	112	3.00 S	114.45 E
Negast	54	54.15 N	13.01 E
Negaunee	190	46.29 N	87.36 W
Negba	132	31.40 N	34.41 E
Negele	144	5.20 N	39.36 E
Negenborn	52	51.53 N	9.34 E
Negeribatin	112	4.35 S	104.32 E
Negeri Sembilan □ [3]	114	2.45 N	102.10 E
Negev Desert → HaNegev ✦ [1]	132	30.30 N	34.55 E
Negishi	268	35.51 N	139.23 E
Negley	214	40.47 N	80.32 W
Negola	152	14.10 S	14.30 E
Negomano	154	11.27 S	38.31 E
Negombo	122	7.13 N	79.50 E
Negotin	38	44.14 N	22.32 E
Negra, Laguna ⊜	252	34.03 S	53.40 W
Negra, Ponta ≻	256	22.58 S	42.42 W
Negra, Punta ≻, Belize	232	16.17 N	88.34 W
Negra, Punta ≻, Perú	248	6.06 S	81.09 W
Negrais	266c	38.53 N	9.17 W
Negras, Lomas ∧ [2]	286d	11.55 S	77.06 W
Negreira	34	42.54 N	8.44 W
Nègres, Pointe des ≻	240e	14.36 N	61.06 W
Negrești	38	46.50 N	27.27 E
Negrești-Oaș	38	47.52 N	23.25 E
Negrine	148	34.30 N	7.30 E
Negritos	246	4.38 S	81.19 W
Negro ≃, Arg.	254	41.02 S	62.47 W
Negro ≃, Bol.	248	9.49 S	65.42 W
Negro ≃, Bol.	248	14.11 S	63.07 W
Negro ≃, Bra.	248	5.15 S	70.53 W
Negro ≃, Bra.	248	19.13 S	57.17 W
Negro ≃, Bra.	250	9.15 S	47.34 W
Negro ≃, Bra.	252	26.01 S	50.30 W
Negro ≃, Col.	246	5.44 N	74.39 W
Negro ≃, N.A.	236	13.02 N	87.17 W
Negro ≃, Para.	252	24.23 S	57.11 W
Negro ≃, S.A.	246	3.08 S	59.55 W
Negro ≃, S.A.	252	33.24 S	58.22 W
Negro, Baia del c	144	7.55 N	49.55 E
Negro, Cerro ∧, Arg.	254	46.55 S	70.12 W
Negro, Cerro ∧, Arg.	254	44.09 S	69.30 W
Negro, Cerro ∧, Méx.	234	17.19 N	97.25 W
Negro, Mar → Black Sea ∓ [2]	22	43.00 N	35.00 E
Negros I	116	10.00 N	123.00 E
Negros Occidental □ [4]	116	10.20 N	123.00 E
Negros Oriental □ [4]	116	9.40 N	123.00 E
Negru Vodă	38	43.50 N	28.12 E
Neguac	186	47.15 N	65.05 W
Nehalem	224	45.43 N	123.53 W
Nehalem ≃	224	45.40 N	123.56 W
Neharèlae	76	53.36 N	27.04 E
Nehawka	198	40.49 N	95.59 W
Nehbandān	128	31.32 N	60.02 E
Neheim-Hüsten	56	51.27 N	7.57 E
Nehonsey Brook ≃	285	39.49 N	75.18 W
Néhoué, Baie de c	175f	20.21 S	164.09 E
Nehru Planetarium ʊ	272c	18.59 N	72.49 E
Neiba	238	18.28 N	71.25 W
Neichiang → Neijiang	107	29.35 N	105.03 E
Neidpath	184	50.13 N	107.15 W
Neige, Crêt de la ∧	58	46.16 N	5.56 E
Neiges, Piton des ∧	157c	21.05 S	55.29 E
Neihart	202	46.56 N	110.44 W
Neihe ≃	100	22.54 N	115.38 E
Neihu	269d	25.05 N	121.34 E
Neihuang	98	35.59 N	114.55 E
Neijiang	107	29.35 N	105.03 E
Neikiang → Neijiang	107	29.35 N	105.03 E
Neilburg	184	52.50 N	109.38 W
Neillsville	190	44.33 N	90.35 W
Neilston	46	55.47 N	4.27 W
Neimen	263	51.29 N	7.48 E
Nei Monggol Zizhiqu (Inner Mongolia) □ [4]	90	43.00 N	115.00 E
Nein	132	32.38 N	35.21 E
Neindorf	54	52.20 N	10.50 E
Neinstedt	54	51.45 N	11.05 E
Neiqiu	98	37.17 N	114.31 E
Neira	246	5.10 N	75.32 W
Neirone	62	44.27 N	9.11 E
Neishuishan	269d	25.09 N	121.43 E
Neisse (Nysa Łużycka) ≃	30	52.04 N	14.46 E
Neiva	246	2.56 N	75.18 W
Neiwufuquan	105	40.11 N	117.39 E
Neixiang	102	33.12 N	111.57 E
Neixpa ≃	234	18.05 N	102.46 W
Neizeng Shan ∧	100	24.02 N	117.32 E
Neja, Ross.	80	58.24 N	46.31 E
Neja, Ross.	80	58.18 N	43.54 E
Neja ≃	80	57.48 N	43.42 E
Nejapa de Madero	234	16.37 N	95.59 W
Nejd → Najd □ [9]	118	25.00 N	44.30 E
Nejdek	54	50.17 N	12.42 E
Nejo	144	9.30 N	35.30 E
Nejva ≃	86	57.54 N	62.18 E
Nejvo-Šajtanskij	86	57.44 N	61.15 E
Nekalagba	154	2.50 N	28.01 E
Nekemte	144	9.02 N	36.31 E
Nekhab ⊥	140	25.10 N	32.48 E
Nekhvoroshcha	78	49.09 N	34.44 E
Nekoosa	190	44.18 N	89.54 W
Nekor, Oued ≃	34	35.14 N	3.45 W
Neko-zaki ≻	96	35.40 N	134.46 E
Nekrasino	82	56.18 N	36.33 E
Nekrasovka	265b	55.41 N	37.56 E
Nekrasovo, Ross.	80	51.10 N	45.18 E
Nekrasovo, Ross.	82	54.30 N	38.57 E
Nekrasovskoje	80	57.41 N	40.22 E
Nekselø I	41	55.47 N	11.18 E
Neksø	26	55.04 N	15.09 E
Nela Park ♦	279a	41.33 N	81.33 W
Nel'aty	88	56.29 N	115.41 E
Nelichu ∧	140	6.08 N	34.25 E
Nelidovo	76	56.13 N	32.46 E
Neligh	198	42.07 N	98.01 W
Nel'kan	74	57.40 N	136.13 E
Nellie	214	40.20 N	82.04 W
Nellikuppam	122	11.46 N	79.41 E
Nellingen	56	48.33 N	9.47 E
Nellis Air Force Base ■	204	36.14 N	115.02 W
Nelliston	210	42.56 N	74.37 W
Nellis Weapons Range ■	204	37.15 N	116.20 W
Nellore	122	14.26 N	79.58 E
Nel'ma	89	47.39 N	139.09 E
Nelson, B.C., Can.	182	49.29 N	117.17 W
Nelson, N.Z.	172	41.17 S	173.17 E
Nelson, Eng., U.K.	44	53.51 N	2.13 W
Nelson, Ne., U.S.	198	40.12 N	98.04 W
Nelson, Pa., U.S.	210	41.59 N	77.14 W
Nelson ≃	184	57.04 N	92.30 W
Nelson, Cape ≻, Austl.	166	38.26 S	141.33 E
Nelson, Cape ≻, Pap. N. Gui.	164	9.00 S	149.15 E
Nelson, Estrecho ⊔	254	51.37 S	75.00 W
Nelson Creek ≃	222	30.56 N	95.31 W
Nelson House	184	55.47 N	98.51 W
Nelson Island I	180	60.35 N	164.45 W
Nelson-Kennedy Ledges State Park ♦	214	41.18 N	81.04 W
Nelson Lake ⊜	184	55.44 N	100.00 W
Nelson Lakes National Park ♦	172	41.50 S	172.40 E
Nelson Reservoir ⊜ [1]	202	48.30 N	107.34 W
Nelson's Dockyard ⊥	240c	17.00 N	61.46 W
Nelsonville, N.Y., U.S.	210	41.25 N	73.57 W
Nelsonville, Oh., U.S.	188	39.27 N	82.14 W
Nelspoort	158	32.07 S	23.00 E
Nelspoortjie	158	29.58 S	22.25 E
Nelspruit	156	25.30 S	30.58 E
Néma, Maur.	150	16.37 N	7.15 W
Nema, Ross.	80	57.31 N	50.31 E
Néma, Dahr ⩠ [4]	150	16.40 N	7.13 W
Nemadji ≃	190	46.41 N	92.02 W
Nemah	224	46.31 N	123.51 W
Nemaha	198	40.20 N	95.40 W
Neman	76	55.02 N	22.02 E
Nëman (Nemunas) ≃	76	55.18 N	21.23 E
Nematābād ✦ [8]	267d	35.38 N	51.21 E
Nembe	150	4.35 N	6.26 E
Nembrala	112	10.53 S	122.50 E
Nembro	62	45.45 N	9.45 E
Nemčinovka	265b	55.43 N	37.23 E
Nemda ≃, Ross.	80	57.35 N	48.56 E
Nemda ≃, Ross.	80	57.21 N	43.08 E
Nemegosenda ≃	190	48.31 N	82.53 W
Nemegt uul ⋏	102	43.40 N	101.10 E
Nemeiben Lake ⊜	184	55.20 N	105.20 W
Nemenčinė	76	54.51 N	25.29 E
Nementcha, Monts de ⋏	148	34.52 N	7.05 E
Nemeriči	76	53.51 N	33.59 E
Nemi	66	41.43 N	12.43 E
Nemi, Lago di ⊜	267a	41.43 N	12.42 E
Nemira Mare, Vârful ∧	38	46.15 N	26.19 E
Nemirovo	82	55.54 N	36.12 E
Nemo	222	32.16 N	97.39 W
Nemoli	68	40.04 N	15.48 E
Nemor ≃	89	48.23 N	124.32 E
Nemours	50	48.16 N	2.42 E
Nemovychi	78	51.16 N	26.38 E
Nemrut Gölü ⊜	130	38.37 N	42.12 E
Nemuna, Bjeshkët e ⋏	38	42.27 N	19.47 E
Nemunas (Nëman) ≃	76	55.18 N	21.23 E
Nemuro	92a	43.20 N	145.35 E
Nemuro-hantō ≻ [1]	92a	43.21 N	145.42 E
Nemuro Strait ⊔	92a	44.00 N	145.20 E
Nemyriv, Ukr.	78	50.07 N	23.25 E
Nemyriv, Ukr.	78	48.58 N	28.50 E
Nemzeti Museum ʊ	264c	47.29 N	19.05 E
Nen ≃	89	45.25 N	124.40 E
Nena Creek ≃	224	45.07 N	121.07 W
Nenagh	48	52.52 N	8.12 W
Nenagh ≃	48	52.56 N	8.17 W
Nenana	180	64.34 N	149.07 W
Nenana ≃	180	64.30 N	149.00 W
Nenaševo	82	54.34 N	37.28 E
Nenasi	114	3.08 N	103.27 E
Nendaz	58	46.11 N	7.18 E
Nendeln	58	47.12 N	9.32 E
Nendo I	14	10.45 S	165.54 E
Nene ≃	42	52.48 N	0.13 E
Nenggiri ≃	114	4.53 N	101.48 E
Nengjia	104	41.38 N	120.46 E
Nengo ≃	152	14.27 S	22.09 E
Nengonengo I [1]	14	18.47 S	141.48 W
Nenneper Fleuth ≃	263	51.32 N	6.26 E
Nennhausen	54	52.36 N	12.30 E
Neno	154	15.24 S	34.39 E
Nentershausen	56	51.01 N	9.56 E
Nentón ≃	236	15.48 N	91.52 W
Nenzing	58	47.11 N	9.42 E
Neo	94	35.38 N	136.37 E
Neo ≃	94	35.24 N	136.34 E
Neoch I [1]	175c	7.03 N	151.56 E
Neodesha	198	37.25 N	95.40 W
Neoga	194	39.19 N	88.27 W
Neola, Ia., U.S.	198	41.26 N	95.36 W
Neola, Ut., U.S.	200	40.26 N	110.01 W
Neoneli	71	40.04 N	8.57 E
Néon Fáliron	267c	37.57 N	23.40 E
Néon Karlovásion	38	37.48 N	26.44 E
Néon Psikhikón	267c	38.00 N	23.47 E
Neopit	190	44.58 N	88.49 W
Neópolis	250	10.18 S	36.35 W
Neoshera	123	33.09 N	74.14 E
Neosho	194	36.52 N	94.22 W
Neosho ≃	194	35.48 N	95.18 W
Neotsu	224	45.00 N	123.58 W
Nepa ≃	88	59.16 N	108.16 E
Nepal (Nepāl) □ [1], Asia	118	28.00 N	84.00 E
Nepal (Nepāl) □ [1], Asia	124	28.00 N	84.00 E
Nepālgañj	124	28.03 N	81.37 E
Nepa Nagar	120	21.28 N	76.23 E
Nepaug Reservoir ⊜ [1]	207	41.48 N	72.57 W
Nepean	212	45.18 N	75.47 W
Nepean ≃	170	33.27 S	150.53 E
Nepean, Point ≻	169	38.18 S	144.39 E
Nepean Bay c	168b	35.42 S	137.44 E
Nepean Island I	174c	29.04 S	167.58 E
Nepean Reservoir ⊜ [1]	170	34.22 S	150.35 E
Nepecino	82	55.12 N	38.37 E
Nepeña	248	9.10 S	78.23 W
Nepewassi Lake ⊜	190	46.20 N	80.40 W
Nephi	200	39.42 N	111.50 W
Nephin ∧	48	54.01 N	9.22 W
Nephin Beg Range ⋏	48	54.00 N	9.35 W
Nepi	66	42.14 N	12.21 E
Nepisiguit ≃	186	47.37 N	65.38 W
Nepisiguit Bay c	186	47.46 N	65.32 W
Népliget ♦	264c	47.29 N	19.07 E
Nepoko ≃	154	1.40 N	27.01 E
Nepomuceno	256	21.14 S	45.15 W
Nepomuk	60	49.29 N	13.36 E
Neponset ≃	283	42.17 N	71.02 W
Neponset Reservoir ⊜ [1]	283	42.05 N	71.15 W
Neponset River Reservation ♦	283	42.13 N	71.08 W
Neppermin	54	53.56 N	14.02 E
Nepr'adva ≃	76	53.40 N	38.39 E
Nép-sziget I	264c	47.34 N	19.05 E
Neptune, N.J., U.S.	208	40.12 N	74.02 W
Neptune, Oh., U.S.	216	40.36 N	84.30 W
Neptune Beach	192	30.18 N	81.23 W
Neptune City	208	40.12 N	74.02 W
Neqarot, Nahal V	132	30.40 N	35.15 E
Nera ≃, Europe	38	44.49 N	21.22 E
Nera ≃, It.	66	42.26 N	12.24 E
Nérac	32	44.08 N	0.20 E
Nerákion	267c	38.01 N	23.27 E
Nerang	171a	28.00 S	153.20 E
Nerang ≃	171a	28.03 S	153.17 E
Neratovice	54	50.14 N	14.31 E
Nerča ≃	88	51.56 N	116.40 E
Nerchau	54	51.16 N	12.47 E
Nerčinsk	88	51.58 N	116.35 E
Nerčinskij Zavod	88	51.19 N	119.36 E
Nère ≃	50	47.34 N	2.18 E
Nerechta	80	57.28 N	40.34 E
Nerenstetten	56	48.31 N	10.06 E
Neresheim	56	48.45 N	10.15 E
Nereta	76	56.13 N	25.18 E
Nereto	66	42.49 N	13.49 E
Neretva ≃	36	43.01 N	17.27 E
Nerevoznoje	80	56.53 N	53.54 E
Nerima ✦ [8]	268	35.44 N	139.39 E
Neris (Vilija) ≃	76	54.54 N	23.53 E
Nerito	66	42.32 N	13.28 E
Nerja	34	36.44 N	3.52 W
Nerka, Lake ⊜	180	59.30 N	158.45 W
Nerl', Ross.	76	57.03 N	37.59 E
Nerl', Ross.	80	56.40 N	40.24 E
Nerl' ≃, Ross.	76	57.07 N	37.39 E
Nerl' ≃, Ross.	80	56.11 N	40.34 E
Nero, ozero ⊜	80	57.07 N	39.27 E
Neroj	88	54.28 N	97.49 E
Néronde	62	45.50 N	4.14 E
Nérondes	32	47.00 N	2.49 E
Nerópolis	255	16.25 S	49.14 W
Nerriga	170	35.07 S	150.05 E
Nerrima	162	18.24 S	124.29 E
Nerrimunga Creek ≃	170	34.57 S	150.04 E
Nersingen	58	48.25 N	10.07 E
Nerskaja ≃	82	55.23 N	38.35 E
Nerul	272c	19.02 N	73.01 E
Nerus ≃	114	5.20 N	103.05 E
Nerussa ≃	76	52.33 N	33.47 E
Nerva	34	37.42 N	6.32 W
Nervi	62	44.23 N	9.02 E
Nervia ≃	62	43.47 N	7.38 E
Nerviano	266b	45.33 N	8.58 E
Nerville-la-Forêt	261	49.05 N	2.17 E
Nes, Ned.	52	53.04 N	5.51 E
Nes, Ned.	52	53.26 N	5.45 E
Nes, Nor.	26	60.34 N	9.59 E
Nes', Ross.	24	66.37 N	44.36 E
Nes, Har ∧	132	30.22 N	34.37 E
Nesbyen	26	60.34 N	9.09 E
Neščarda, vozero ⊜	76	55.54 N	29.04 E
Neschwitz	54	51.16 N	14.20 E
Nesco	208	39.38 N	74.41 W
Nescochague Creek ≃	285	39.39 N	74.41 W
Nescochague Creek, Great Swamp Branch ≃	285	39.41 N	74.43 W
Nesconset	276	40.51 N	73.09 W
Nescopeck	210	41.03 N	76.13 W
Nescopeck Creek ≃	210	41.03 N	76.14 W
Nescopeck Mountain ∧	210	41.03 N	76.05 W
Nesebăr	38	42.39 N	27.44 E
Neshaminy Creek ≃	208	40.04 N	74.55 W
Neshaminy Hills	285	40.10 N	74.57 W
Neshaminy Mall ✦ [9]	285	40.08 N	74.57 W
Neshaminy State Park ♦	285	40.05 N	74.55 W
Neshaminy Woods	285	40.10 N	74.57 W
Neshannock Creek ≃	214	40.59 N	80.21 W
Neshcheretove	83	49.24 N	38.48 E
Nesher	132	32.46 N	35.03 E
Nesjøen ⊜ [1]	26	63.02 N	12.01 E
Neškan	180	67.03 N	173.01 W
Neskaupstaður	24a	65.10 N	13.43 W
Neskowin	224	45.06 N	123.58 W
Neskynpil'gyn, laguna c	180	66.57 N	172.45 W
Nesle	50	49.46 N	2.55 E
Nesna	24	66.12 N	13.02 E
Nespelem	182	48.10 N	118.58 W
Nesque ≃	62	43.59 N	4.59 E
Nesquehoning	210	40.51 N	75.48 W
Ness	262	53.17 N	3.03 W
Ness, Loch ⊜	46	57.15 N	4.30 W
Ness City	198	38.27 N	99.54 W
Nesse ≃	54	50.59 N	10.32 E
Nesselrode, Mount ∧	180	58.58 N	134.18 W
Nesselwang	58	47.37 N	10.30 E
Nesselwängle	58	47.29 N	10.37 E
Nesslau	58	47.13 N	9.13 E
Nessmersiel	52	53.40 N	7.21 E
Nesso	58	45.55 N	9.08 E
Neštěmice	54	50.40 N	14.07 E
Nesterkovo	76	59.10 N	30.33 E
Nesterov	76	54.38 N	22.34 E
Nesterovka	80	52.26 N	53.42 E
Nesterovo, Ross.	80	54.31 N	41.49 E
Nesterovo, Ross.	82	56.45 N	36.30 E
Nesterovo, Ross.	88	52.22 N	107.53 E
Nestiary	80	56.34 N	45.21 E
Neston	44	53.18 N	3.04 W
Nestore ≃	66	43.21 N	12.15 E
Néstos (Mesta) ≃	38	40.41 N	24.44 E
Nestoyita	78	47.47 N	29.21 E
Nesttun	26	60.19 N	5.20 E
Nestucca ≃	224	45.12 N	123.57 W
Nesvetaj	83	47.27 N	39.40 E
Nes Ziyyona	132	31.55 N	34.48 E
Netanya	132	32.20 N	34.51 E
Netarhāt	124	23.29 N	84.16 E
Netarts	224	45.26 N	123.56 W
Netarts Bay c	224	45.24 N	123.56 W
Netcong	210	40.53 N	74.42 W
Nethan ≃	46	55.42 N	3.52 W
Nether Alderley	262	53.17 N	2.14 W
Netherdale	166	21.08 S	148.32 E
Netherlands (Nederland) □ [1], Europe	22	52.15 N	5.30 E
Netherlands (Nederland) □ [1], Europe	30	52.15 N	5.30 E
Netherlands Antilles (Nederlandse Antillen) □ [2], N.A.	230	12.15 N	68.45 W
Netherlands Antilles (Nederlandse Antillen) □ [2], N.A.	241s	12.15 N	68.45 W
Netherton	262	53.30 N	2.58 W
Nethy Bridge	46	57.16 N	3.38 W
Netia	154	14.48 S	39.59 E
Netley Marsh	42	50.53 N	1.32 W
Neto ≃	68	39.13 N	17.08 E
Netolice	61	49.03 N	14.12 E
Netphen	56	50.55 N	8.06 E
Netra	56	51.06 N	10.05 E
Netrakona	124	24.53 N	90.43 E
Netstal	58	47.03 N	9.03 E
Nettancourt	56	48.52 N	4.57 E
Nette	52	52.02 N	10.05 E
Nette ✦ [8]	263	51.33 N	7.25 E
Nettelstedt	52	52.18 N	8.41 E
Nettersheim	56	50.30 N	6.38 E
Nettetal	56	51.18 N	6.16 E
Nettilling Fiord c [2]	176	66.02 N	68.12 W
Nettilling Lake ⊜	176	66.30 N	70.40 W
Nett Lake ⊜	190	48.10 N	93.10 W
Nett Lake Indian Reservation ✦ [4]	190	48.06 N	93.10 W
Nettlebed	42	51.35 N	1.00 W
Nettle Creek ≃	218	40.03 N	83.48 W
Nettleden	260	51.47 N	0.32 W
Nettleham	44	53.16 N	0.29 W
Nettlestead	260	51.15 N	0.25 E
Nettlestead Green	260	51.14 N	0.25 E
Nettleton	194	34.05 N	88.37 W
Nettuno	66	41.27 N	12.39 E
Nettuno, Grotta di ⩠ [5]	71	40.34 N	8.09 E
Netzschkau	54	50.36 N	12.14 E
Neualbenreuth	60	49.59 N	12.27 E
Neu-Anspach	56	50.17 N	8.29 E
Neuastenberg	56	51.10 N	8.29 E
Neubeckum	52	51.48 N	8.01 E
Neubeuern	64	47.47 N	12.08 E
Neubrandenburg	54	53.33 N	13.15 E
Neubraunschweig → New Brunswick □ [4]	186	46.30 N	66.15 W
Neubritannien → New Britain I	164	6.00 S	150.00 E
Neubukow	54	54.02 N	11.40 E
Neuburg am Inn	60	48.30 N	13.27 E
Neuburg an der Donau	60	48.44 N	11.11 E
Neuburg-Steinhausen	54	53.58 N	11.38 E
Neuchâtel	58	46.59 N	6.56 E
Neuchâtel □ [3]	58	47.00 N	6.55 E
Neuchâtel, Lac de ⊜	58	46.52 N	6.50 E
Neu Darchau	54	53.14 N	10.53 E
Neu-Delhi → New Delhi	124	28.36 N	77.12 E
Neudenau	56	49.17 N	9.16 E
Neudietendorf	54	50.55 N	10.55 E
Neudorf, Sk., Can.	184	50.44 N	102.59 W
Neudorf, Dtsch.	54	50.29 N	12.58 E
Neudorf ✦ [8]	263	51.25 N	6.47 E
Neudörfl	61	47.48 N	16.17 E
Neudrossenfeld	60	50.01 N	11.30 E
Neue Hebriden → Vanuatu □ [1]	175f	16.00 S	167.00 E
Neuemühle	264a	52.18 N	13.39 E
Neuenburg, Dtsch.	52	53.23 N	7.57 E
Neuenbürg, Dtsch.	56	48.50 N	8.35 E
Neuenburg, Dtsch.	58	47.49 N	7.35 E
Neuenburg → Neuchâtel, Schw.	58	46.59 N	6.56 E
Neuendettelsau	56	49.17 N	10.47 E
Neuendorf	54	54.31 N	13.05 E
Neuendorfer See ⊜	54	52.07 N	13.55 E
Neuenegg	58	46.54 N	7.18 E
Neuenhagen bei Berlin	54	52.32 N	13.41 E
Neuenhaus	52	52.30 N	6.59 E
Neuenhof ✦ [8]	263	51.10 N	7.13 E
Neuenhoven	263	51.08 N	6.31 E
Neue Niers ≃	263	51.16 N	6.26 E
Neuenkamp ✦ [8]	263	51.26 N	6.44 E
Neuenkirchen, Dtsch.	52	52.30 N	8.04 E
Neuenkirchen, Dtsch.	52	51.50 N	8.26 E
Neuenkirchen, Dtsch.	52	53.14 N	8.31 E
Neuenkirchen, Dtsch.	52	53.02 N	9.42 E
Neuenkirchen, Dtsch.	52	52.14 N	7.22 E
Neuenkirchen, Dtsch.	52	53.46 N	8.53 E
Neuenkirchen, Dtsch.	54	54.32 N	13.20 E
Neuenrade	56	51.17 N	7.47 E
Neuensalz	54	50.30 N	12.13 E

≃ River	Fluß	Río	Rivière	Rio
≅ Canal	Kanal	Canal	Canal	Canal
⌞ Waterfall, Rapids	Wasserfall, Stromschnellen	Cascada, Rápidos	Chute d'eau, Rapides	Cascata, Rápidos
⊔ Strait	Meeresstraße	Estrecho	Détroit	Estreito
c Bay, Gulf	Bucht, Golf	Bahía, Golfo	Baie, Golfe	Baía, Golfo
⊜ Lake, Lakes	See, Seen	Lago, Lagos	Lac, Lacs	Lago, Lagos
≡ Swamp	Sumpf	Pantano	Marais	Pântano
⊼ Ice Features, Glacier	Eis- und Gletscherformen	Accidentes Glaciales	Formes glaciaires	Acidentes glaciares
∓ Other Hydrographic Features	Andere Hydrographische Objekte	Otros Elementos Hidrográficos	Autres données hydrographiques	Outros acidentes hidrográficos

✧ Submarine Features	Untermeerische Objekte	Accidentes Submarinos	Formes de relief sous-marin	Acidentes submarinos
□ Political Unit	Politische Einheit	Unidad Politica	Entité politique	Unidade política
ʊ Cultural Institution	Kulturelle Institution	Institución Cultural	Institution culturelle	Instituição cultural
⊥ Historical Site	Historische Stätte	Sitio Histórico	Site historique	Sitio histórico
♦ Recreational Site	Erholungs- und Ferienort	Sitio de Recreo	Centre de loisirs	Area de Lazer
⊠ Airport	Flughafen	Aeropuerto	Aéroport	Aeroporto
■ Military Installation	Militäranlage	Instalación Militar	Installation militaire	Instalação militar
✦ Miscellaneous	Verschiedenes	Misceláneo	Divers	Diversos

Symbols in the index entries represent the broad categories identified in the key at the right. Symbols with superior numbers (≮1) identify subcategories (see complete key on page I · 1).

Symbole im Register stellen die rechts im Schlüssel erklärten Kategorien dar. Symbole mit hochgestellten Ziffern (≮1) bezeichnen Unterteilungen einer Kategorie (vgl. vollständiger Schlüssel auf Seite I · 1).

Los símbolos incluídos en el texto del índice representan las grandes categorías identificadas con la clave a la derecha. Los símbolos con números en su parte superior (≮1) identifican las subcategorías (véase la clave completa en la página I · 1).

Les symboles de l'index représentent les catégories indiquées dans la légende à droite. Les symboles suivis d'un indice (≮1) représentent des sous-catégories (voir légende complète à la page I · 1).

Os símbolos incluídos no texto do índice representam as grandes categorias identificadas com a chave à direita. Os símbolos com números em sua parte superior (≮1) identificam as subcategorias (veja-se a chave completa à página I · 1).

∧ Mountain	Berg	Montaña	Montagne	Montanha
≮ Mountains	Gebirge	Montañas	Montagnes	Montanhas
✕ Pass	Paß	Paso	Col	Passo
▽ Valley, Canyon	Tal, Cañon	Valle, Cañón	Vallée, Canyon	Vale, Canhão
≏ Plain	Ebene	Llano	Plaine	Planicie
⮝ Cape	Kap	Cabo	Cap	Cabo
I Island	Insel	Isla	Île	Ilha
II Islands	Inseln	Islas	Îles	Ilhas
⮱ Other Topographic Features	Andere Topographische Objekte	Otros Elementos Topográficos	Autres données topographiques	Outros acidentes topográficos

ESPAÑOL

Nombre	Página	Lat. °'	Long. °' W = Oeste
New Tazewell	192	36.27 N	83.33 W
New Terrell City Lake ⊜[1]	222	32.44 N	96.14 W
New Thunderchild Indian Reserve ◆[4]	184	53.30 N	108.50 W
Newtok	180	60.56 N	164.38 W
Newton, Eng., U.K.	44	53.57 N	2.27 W
Newton, Eng., U.K.	262	53.16 N	2.43 W
Newton, Ga., U.S.	192	31.18 N	84.20 W
Newton, Il., U.S.	194	38.59 N	88.09 W
Newton, Ia., U.S.	190	41.41 N	93.02 W
Newton, Ks., U.S.	198	38.02 N	97.20 W
Newton, Ma., U.S.	207	42.20 N	71.12 W
Newton, Ms., U.S.	194	32.19 N	89.09 W
Newton, N.J., U.S.	210	41.03 N	74.45 W
Newton, N.C., U.S.	192	35.40 N	81.13 W
Newton, Tx., U.S.	194	30.50 N	93.45 W
Newton □[6]	216	40.46 N	87.27 W
Newton Abbot	42	50.32 N	3.36 W
Newton Arlosh	44	54.53 N	3.15 W
Newton Aycliffe	44	54.36 N	1.32 W
Newton Brook ◆[8]	275b	43.48 N	79.24 W
Newton Center	283	42.20 N	71.12 W
Newton Falls, N.Y., U.S.	188	44.12 N	74.59 W
Newton Falls, Oh., U.S.	214	41.11 N	80.58 W
Newton Ferrers	42	50.18 N	4.02 W
Newton Flotman	42	52.32 N	1.16 E
Newton Hamilton	214	40.24 N	77.51 W
Newton Highlands	283	42.19 N	71.13 W
Newton-le-Willows	44	53.28 N	2.37 W
Newton Longville	42	51.58 N	0.46 W
Newton Lower Falls	283	42.19 N	71.23 W
Newtonmore	46	57.04 N	4.08 W
Newton Stewart	44	54.57 N	4.29 W
Newtonsville	218	39.11 N	84.05 W
Newton Upper Falls	283	42.19 N	71.13 W
Newtonville, On., Can.	212	43.56 N	78.30 W
Newtonville, Ma., U.S.	283	42.21 N	71.13 W
Newtonville, N.J., U.S.	208	39.33 N	74.51 W
New Toronto ◆[8]	275b	43.36 N	79.30 W
Newtown, Austl.	169	38.09 S	144.20 E
Newtown, Nf., Can.	186	49.12 N	53.31 W
Newtown, Eng., U.K.	262	53.21 N	2.00 W
Newtown, Wales, U.K.	42	52.32 N	3.19 W
Newtown, Ct., U.S.	207	41.24 N	73.18 W
Newtown, In., U.S.	216	40.12 N	87.08 W
Newtown, Ky., U.S.	218	38.13 N	84.57 W
New Town, N.D., U.S.	198	47.58 N	102.29 W
Newtown, Pa., U.S.	208	40.14 N	74.56 W
Newtown ◆[8]	274a	33.54 S	151.11 E
Newtownabbey	48	54.42 N	5.54 W
Newtownards	48	54.36 N	5.41 W
Newtownbutler	48	54.12 N	7.23 W
Newtown Creek ≏, N.Y., U.S.	276	40.44 N	73.58 W
Newtown Creek ≏, Pa., U.S.	285	40.13 N	74.56 W
Newtown Crommelin	48	54.59 N	6.13 W
Newtown Forbes	48	53.46 N	7.50 W
Newtownhamilton	48	54.12 N	6.35 W
Newtown Mount Kennedy	48	53.05 N	6.07 W
Newtown Saint Boswells	46	55.34 N	2.40 W
Newtown Square	208	39.59 N	75.24 W
Newtownstewart	48	54.43 N	7.24 W
New Tredegar	42	51.43 N	3.14 W
New Tripoli	208	40.41 N	75.45 W
New Troy	216	41.53 N	86.33 W
New Truxton	219	38.58 N	91.15 W
New Ulm, Mn., U.S.	190	44.18 N	94.27 W
New Ulm, Tx., U.S.	222	29.53 N	96.29 W
New Utrecht ◆[8]	276	40.36 N	73.59 W
New Vernon	276	40.45 N	74.30 W
New Vienna	218	39.19 N	83.41 W
Newville, In., U.S.	216	41.21 N	84.51 W
Newville, Pa., U.S.	208	40.10 N	77.23 W
New Vineyard	188	44.48 N	70.07 W
New Waltham	44	53.32 N	0.04 W
New Washington, Pil.	116	11.39 N	122.26 E
New Washington, In., U.S.	218	38.33 N	85.32 W
New Washington, Oh., U.S.	214	40.57 N	82.51 W
New Waterford, N.S., Can.	186	46.15 N	60.05 W
New Waterford, Oh., U.S.	214	40.50 N	80.36 W
New Waverly, In., U.S.	216	40.46 N	86.12 W
New Waverly, Tx., U.S.	222	30.32 N	95.29 W
New Westminster	224	49.12 N	122.55 W
New Whiteland	218	39.33 N	86.05 W
New Wilmington	214	41.07 N	80.19 W
New Windsor → Windsor, Eng., U.K.	42	51.29 N	0.38 W
New Windsor, Md., U.S.	208	39.32 N	77.06 W
New Windsor, N.Y., U.S.	210	41.30 N	74.01 W
New Woodbine Racetrack ♠	275b	43.43 N	79.36 W
New Woodstock	210	42.50 N	75.51 W
New World Island I	186	49.35 N	54.40 W
New Year Creek ≏	222	30.08 N	96.12 W
New York, N.Y., U.S.	210	40.43 N	74.01 W
New York, N.Y., U.S.	276	40.43 N	74.01 W
New York □[6]	276	40.47 N	73.58 W
New York □[3], U.S.	178	43.00 N	75.00 W
New York □[3], U.S.	188	43.00 N	75.00 W
New York, City College of ⚱[2]	276	40.49 N	73.57 W
New York, Polytechnic Institute of ⚱[2]	276	40.42 N	73.59 W
New York, State University of (Stony Brook) ⚱[2], N.Y., U.S.	276	40.55 N	73.08 W
New York, State University of (Buffalo) ⚱[2], N.Y., U.S.	284a	42.57 N	78.49 W
New York, State University of, College at Buffalo ⚱[2]	284a	42.56 N	78.53 W
New York at Buffalo, State University of ⚱[2]	284a	42.56 N	78.49 W
New York Mills, Mn., U.S.	198	46.31 N	95.22 W
New York Mills, N.Y., U.S.	210	43.06 N	75.18 W
New York State Barge Canal ≊	210	43.05 N	78.43 W
New York Stock Exchange ⚱	276	40.42 N	74.01 W
New Zealand □[1]	172	41.00 S	174.00 E
Nexapa ≏	234	18.07 N	98.46 W
Nexon	32	45.41 N	1.11 E
Ney	216	41.23 N	84.32 W
Neyagawa	96	34.46 N	135.38 E
Neye	263	51.07 N	7.22 E
Neyestausee ⊜[1]	263	51.08 N	7.24 E
Ney Lake ⊜	184	54.38 N	92.25 W
Neyland	42	51.43 N	4.57 W
Neylandville	222	33.12 N	96.00 W
Neyrīz	128	29.12 N	54.19 E
Neyshābūr	128	36.12 N	58.50 E
Neyyāttinkara	122	8.24 N	77.05 E

FRANÇAIS

Nom	Page	Lat. °'	Long. °' W = Ouest
Nezahualcóyotl	234	19.27 N	99.03 W
Nezahualcóyotl, Presa ⊜[1]	234	17.10 N	93.40 W
Nezamajevskaja	78	46.09 N	40.16 E
Nezameno-toko ♠	94	35.46 N	137.42 E
Nežárka ≏	61	49.11 N	14.41 E
Nezavertailovca	38	46.37 N	29.56 E
Nezlobnaja	84	44.08 N	43.23 E
Neznanka ≏	265b	55.34 N	37.21 E
Neznanovo	80	54.02 N	40.06 E
Nezperce	202	46.14 N	116.14 W
Nez Perce Indian Reservation ◆[4]	202	46.20 N	116.30 W
Nez Perce National Historical Park ♠	202	45.50 N	116.15 W
Nezpique, Bayou ≏	194	30.12 N	92.35 W
Nezvěstice	60	49.39 N	13.32 E
Ngabang	112	0.23 N	109.57 E
Ngabé	152	3.12 S	16.11 E
Ngabordamlu, Tanjung ›	164	6.56 S	134.11 E
Ngadda ≏	146	12.40 N	13.50 E
Ngadirojo	115a	8.13 S	111.19 E
Ngadza	152	5.10 N	20.12 E
Ngahere	172	42.24 S	171.27 E
Ngala	146	12.20 N	14.10 E
Ngale	152	2.56 N	21.20 E
Ngali	152	2.27 S	19.20 E
Ngaliema, Baie de ⊂	273b	4.19 S	15.16 E
Ngalipaeng	112	3.24 N	125.37 E
Ngaloa Harbour ⊂	175g	19.06 S	178.11 E
Ngamaba	273b	4.14 S	15.16 E
Ngamba ◆[8]	273b	4.15 S	15.18 E
Ngambé	152	4.14 N	10.37 E
Ngamdu	146	11.48 N	12.18 E
Ngami, Lake ⊜	156	20.37 S	22.40 E
Ngamiland □[5]	156	19.09 S	22.47 E
Ngamo	154	19.08 S	27.32 E
Ngamouéri	273b	4.14 S	15.14 E
Ngamring	124	29.14 N	87.10 E
Nganda ʌ	154	10.25 S	33.50 E
Ngangala	154	4.42 N	31.55 E
Ngangla Ringco ⊜	120	31.40 N	83.00 E
Nganglong Kangri ʌ	120	32.45 N	81.12 E
Nganglong Kangri ⋀	120	32.00 N	83.00 E
Ngangzê Co ⊜	120	31.05 N	86.55 E
Nganjuk	115a	7.36 S	111.55 E
Ngao	110	18.46 N	99.59 E
Ngaoui, Mont ʌ	152	6.40 N	14.57 E
Ngaoundéré	152	7.19 N	13.35 E
Ngapali	110	18.26 N	94.19 E
Ngapara	172	44.57 S	170.45 E
Ngape	110	20.04 N	94.38 E
Ngaputaw	110	16.32 N	94.42 E
Ngara	154	2.28 S	30.39 E
Ngaramasch	175b	6.54 N	134.08 E
Ngarimbi	154	8.28 S	38.36 E
Ngaruawahia	172	37.40 S	175.09 E
Ngaruroro ≏	172	39.34 S	176.56 E
Ngasamo	154	2.33 S	33.53 E
Ngat ≏	110	19.09 N	99.01 E
Ngatangiia	174k	21.14 S	159.43 W
Ngatangiia Harbour ⊂	174k	21.14 S	159.45 W
Ngatea	172	37.17 S	175.30 E
Ngathainggyaung	110	17.24 N	95.05 E
Ngatik I[1]	14	5.51 N	157.16 E
Ngau I	175g	18.02 S	179.18 E
Ngauruhoe, Mount ʌ	172	39.09 S	175.38 E
Ngau Tau Kok → Kwun Tong	271d	22.19 N	114.12 E
Ngawen	115a	7.00 S	111.18 E
Ngawi	115a	7.24 S	111.26 E
Ngay Nua	110	21.50 N	101.54 E
Ngebard ✤[2]	175b	7.50 N	134.32 E
Ngebel	115a	7.46 S	111.37 E
Ngele	152	0.29 S	20.25 E
Ngemlis II	175b	7.07 N	134.15 E
Ngerengere	154	6.45 S	38.07 E
Ngerkeel	175b	7.25 N	134.30 E
Ngermechau	175b	7.35 N	134.39 E
Ngeruktabel I	175b	7.15 N	134.24 E
Ngetbong	175b	7.37 N	134.35 E
Ngetera	146	12.31 N	12.38 E
Nggamea Island I	175g	16.46 S	179.46 W
Nggatokae Island I	175e	8.46 S	158.11 E
Nggela Pile I	175e	9.05 S	160.15 E
Nggela Sule I	175e	9.05 S	160.15 E
Nggelelevu I	175g	16.05 S	179.09 W
Nggwavuma ≏	158	26.58 S	32.17 E
Nghia Dan	110	19.18 N	105.26 E
Nghia Hanh	110	15.03 N	108.47 E
Nghia Lo	110	21.36 N	104.31 E
Ngiap ≏	110	18.24 N	103.36 E
Ngidinga	152	5.37 S	15.17 E
Ngimbang	115a	7.17 S	112.12 E
Ng'iro ʌ	154	2.08 N	36.51 E
Ng'iro, Ewaso ≏, Kenya	154	0.28 N	39.55 E
Ngiro, Ewaso ≏, Kenya	154	2.04 S	36.07 E
Ngkesol ✤[2]	175b	7.57 N	134.41 E
Ngkesol, Toachel ʮ	175b	7.52 N	134.36 E
Ngo	152	2.29 S	15.45 E
Ngoangoa ≏	140	5.48 N	25.09 E
Ngoboli	154	4.57 N	32.37 E
Ngoko ≏, Afr.	152	1.40 N	16.03 E
Ngoko ≏, Congo	152	0.25 S	15.29 E
Ngol-Kedju Hill ʌ[2]	152	6.20 N	9.45 E
Ngolo	146	9.56 N	22.16 E
Ngom ≏	102	31.11 N	97.15 E
Ngomahuru	154	20.26 S	30.43 E
Ngomba	154	8.23 S	32.53 E
Ngomba ʌ	154	5.43 S	35.52 E
Ngombe, R.D.C.	152	6.35 S	20.42 E
Ngombe, R.D.C.	273b	4.24 S	15.11 E
Ngome	158	27.46 S	31.28 E
Ngomedzap	152	3.15 N	11.12 E
Ngomeni, Ras ›	154	2.59 S	40.14 E
Ngong	154	1.22 S	36.39 E
Ngongotaha	172	38.05 S	176.12 E
Ngono ≏	154	1.08 S	31.35 E
Ngonye Falls ⌊	152	16.40 S	23.35 E
Ngop	140	6.16 N	30.12 E
Ngora	154	1.27 N	33.46 E
Ngorengore	154	1.02 S	35.30 E
Ngoring Hu ⊜	102	34.50 N	97.35 E
Ngoro	115a	7.41 S	112.16 E
Ngorongoro Crater ≐[6]	154	3.10 S	35.35 E
Ngote	154	2.14 N	30.48 E
Ngoto	152	4.00 N	17.21 E
Ngotwane ≏	156	23.35 S	26.58 E
Ngoulémakong	152	3.07 N	11.25 E
Ngouma	150	15.38 N	3.22 W
Ngounié □[4]	152	1.30 S	11.00 E
Ngounié ≏	152	0.37 S	10.18 E
Ngouri	146	13.38 N	15.22 E
Ngouroundou	152	6.27 N	22.37 E
Ngourti	146	15.19 N	13.12 E
Ngoywa	154	5.56 S	32.48 E
Ngozi	154	2.54 S	29.50 E
Ngqeleni	158	31.40 S	29.02 E
Ngudiabaka ≏	273b	4.25 S	15.11 E
Nguélémendouka	152	4.23 N	12.55 E
Ngugha ≏	156	19.21 S	23.15 E
Nguigmi	146	14.15 N	13.07 E
Nguila	152	4.43 N	11.41 E
Nguiu	164	11.45 S	130.38 E
Ngulu I[1]	108	8.27 N	137.29 E
Ngum ≏	110	18.09 N	103.06 E
Nguna, Île I	175f	17.26 S	168.21 E
Ngunga	154	3.41 S	33.34 E
Ngunju, Tanjung ›	115b	10.19 S	120.28 E
Ngunut	115a	8.06 S	112.01 E
Ngurore	146	9.18 N	12.14 E
Nguru	146	12.52 N	10.27 E
Ngwempisi ≏	158	26.42 S	31.26 E
Ngweni	158	27.56 S	32.15 E
Ngwenya ʌ	158	26.11 S	31.02 E
Ngwerere	154	15.18 S	28.20 E

PORTUGUÊS

Nome	Página	Lat. °'	Long. °' W = Oeste
Ngweze ≏	154	17.40 S	25.07 E
Nha Be	269c	10.42 N	106.44 E
Nhabe ≏, Bots.	156	20.22 S	22.58 E
Nha Be ≏, Viet	269c	10.39 N	106.44 E
Nhacoongo	156	24.18 S	35.14 E
Nhamacolomo	156	18.05 S	34.26 E
Nhamundá	250	2.14 S	56.43 W
Nhamundá ≏	246	2.12 S	56.41 W
Nha Nam	110	21.27 N	106.06 E
Nhandeara	255	20.40 S	50.02 W
Nhareia	152	11.25 S	17.03 E
Nha Trang	110	12.15 N	109.11 E
Nhia ≏	152	10.15 S	14.12 E
Nhill	166	36.20 S	141.39 E
Nhlangano	158	27.06 S	31.12 E
Nhlazatshe	158	28.10 S	31.14 E
Nhoma ≏	156	18.52 S	20.53 E
Nhon Trach	269c	10.43 N	106.51 E
Nhulunbuy	164	12.11 S	136.47 E
Nhundo	152	14.25 S	21.23 E
Nhunguaçu	256	22.21 S	42.53 W
Niabembe	154	2.14 S	27.44 E
Niafounké	150	15.56 N	4.00 W
Niagara	190	45.46 N	87.59 W
Niagara □[6], On., Can.	212	43.05 N	79.20 W
Niagara □[6], N.Y., U.S.	210	43.10 N	78.42 W
Niagara ≏	212	43.15 N	79.04 W
Niagara County Historical Center ⚱	284a	43.10 N	78.43 W
Niagara Falls, On., Can.	212	43.06 N	79.04 W
Niagara Falls, On., Can.	284a	43.06 N	79.04 W
Niagara Falls, N.Y., U.S.	210	43.05 N	79.03 W
Niagara Falls, N.Y., U.S.	284a	43.05 N	79.03 W
Niagara Falls ⌊	212	43.05 N	79.04 W
Niagara Falls Airport ⊠	284a	43.02 N	79.08 W
Niagara Falls International Airport ⊠	284a	43.06 N	78.56 W
Niagara-on-the-Lake	212	43.15 N	79.04 W
Niagara University ⚱[2]	284a	43.08 N	79.02 W
Niagassola	150	12.19 N	9.07 W
Niah	112	3.52 N	113.44 E
Niakaramandougou	150	8.40 N	5.17 W
Niamey	150	13.31 N	2.07 E
Niamey □[5]	150	14.00 N	2.00 E
Niamtougou	150	9.46 N	1.06 E
Nianbadu	100	28.17 N	118.28 E
Niandan ≏	150	10.30 N	10.26 W
Niandan Koro	150	11.05 N	9.15 W
Nianforando	150	9.32 N	10.31 W
Niangara	154	3.42 N	27.52 E
Niangay, Lac ⊜	150	15.50 N	3.00 W
Niangmake	102	30.14 N	99.40 E
Niangnianggong	104	41.00 N	121.13 E
Niangniangmiao	98	42.34 N	118.05 E
Niangniangwa	105	40.33 N	117.30 E
Niangoloko	150	10.17 N	4.55 W
Niangua ≏	194	37.58 N	92.48 W
Niangzizhuang	105	40.02 N	118.05 E
Nia-Nia	154	1.24 N	27.36 E
Nianpan	104	41.48 N	124.02 E
Niantic, Ct., U.S.	207	41.19 N	72.11 W
Niantic, Il., U.S.	219	39.51 N	89.10 W
Nianyugou	104	42.00 N	123.59 E
Nianyushan	100	29.11 N	117.04 E
Nianzhuang	98	34.19 N	117.47 E
Nianzigang	100	31.03 N	114.18 E
Nianzishan	89	47.32 N	122.52 E
Niapu	154	2.25 N	26.28 E
Niari □[5]	152	3.15 S	12.30 E
Niari ≏	152	3.56 S	12.12 E
Niaro	140	10.38 N	31.31 E
Nias, Pulau I	114	1.05 N	97.35 E
Niassa □[5]	154	13.30 S	36.00 E
Niatupo	246	9.33 N	78.54 W
Nibbiano	62	44.54 N	9.19 E
Nibe	26	56.59 N	9.38 E
Nibong Tebal	114	5.10 N	100.29 E
Nibra	272b	22.36 N	88.16 E
Nic	84	40.56 N	47.41 E
Nīca	76	56.19 N	21.04 E
Nica ≏	86	57.29 N	64.33 E
Nicaea → İznik	130	40.26 N	29.43 E
Nicaragua □[1], N.A.	230	13.00 N	85.00 W
Nicaragua □[1], N.A.	236	13.00 N	85.00 W
Nicaragua, Lago de ⊜	236	11.30 N	85.30 W
Nicaro	240p	20.42 N	75.33 W
Nicastro	68	38.59 N	16.20 E
Ničatka, ozero ⊜	88	57.45 N	117.30 E
Nice	62	43.42 N	7.15 E
Nice-Côte d'Azur, Aéroport de ⊠	62	43.40 N	7.14 E
Niceville	194	30.31 N	86.28 W
Nichelino	62	44.59 N	7.38 E
Nicheng	106	30.55 N	121.49 E
Nichihara	96	34.33 N	131.50 E
Nichinan, Nihon	92	31.36 N	131.23 E
Nichinan, Nihon	96	35.09 N	133.16 E
Nicholas □[6]	218	38.20 N	84.02 W
Nicholas Channel ʮ	238	23.25 N	80.05 W
Nicholasville	192	37.52 N	84.34 W
Nicholls	192	31.31 N	82.38 W
Nicholl's Town	238	25.08 N	78.00 W
Nichols, Ca., U.S.	282	38.02 N	121.59 W
Nichols, Fl., U.S.	220	27.54 N	82.02 W
Nichols, N.Y., U.S.	210	42.01 N	76.22 W
Nichols Brook ≏	283	42.37 N	70.59 W
Nicholson, Austl.	162	18.02 S	128.54 E
Nicholson, Ky., U.S.	218	38.54 N	84.33 W
Nicholson, Ms., U.S.	194	30.28 N	89.41 W
Nicholson, Pa., U.S.	210	41.37 N	75.46 W
Nicholson ≏, Austl.	162	17.34 S	128.38 E
Nicholson ≏, Austl.	166	17.31 S	139.36 E
Nicholson Island I	212	43.56 N	77.31 W
Nicholson Range ⋀	162	27.15 S	116.45 E
Nicholson River Aboriginal Reserve ◆[4]	162	18.00 S	137.30 E
Nichols Run ≏	284b	39.03 N	77.18 W
Nickerie □[5]	250	5.40 N	56.50 W
Nickerie ≏	250	5.59 N	57.00 W
Nickerson	198	38.08 N	98.05 W
Nickol Bay ⊂	162	20.39 S	116.52 E
Nicktown	214	40.37 N	78.48 W
Nicobar Islands II	110	8.00 N	93.30 E
Nicola	182	50.10 N	120.40 W
Nicola ≏	182	50.25 N	121.18 W
Nicolae Bălcescu	38	47.34 N	26.52 E
Nicolai Mountain ʌ	224	46.05 N	123.28 W
Nicola Lake ⊜	182	50.10 N	120.25 W
Nicola Mameet Indian Reserve ◆[4]	182	50.11 N	120.49 W
Nicolaus	226	38.54 N	121.35 W
Nicolet	206	46.13 N	72.37 W
Nicolet □[6]	206	46.15 N	72.20 W
Nicolet ≏	206	46.14 N	72.39 W
Nicolet, Lac ⊜	206	45.50 N	71.33 W
Nicolet, Lake ⊜	190	46.20 N	84.15 W
Nicolet Centre ≏	206	45.46 N	71.50 W
Nicolet Sud-Ouest ≏	206	46.13 N	72.36 W
Nicoll Bay ⊂	276	40.43 N	73.07 W
Nicollet	190	44.16 N	94.11 W
Nicoll Point ›	276	40.42 N	73.09 W
Nicolosi	70	37.37 N	15.01 E
Nicosia, It.	70	37.45 N	14.24 E
Nicosia (Levkosía), Kípros	130	35.10 N	33.22 E
Nicosia (Lefkoşa), Kıbrıs	130	35.10 N	33.22 E
Nicotera	68	38.34 N	15.57 E
Nicoya	236	10.09 N	85.27 W
Nicoya, Golfo de ⊂	236	9.47 N	84.48 W
Nicoya, Península de ›[1]	236	10.00 N	85.25 W
Nictheroy → Niterói	256	22.53 S	43.07 W
Nida	76	55.18 N	21.01 E
Nida ≏	30	50.18 N	20.52 E
Nidadavole	122	16.55 N	81.40 E
Nidau	58	47.07 N	7.14 E
Nidd ≏	44	54.01 N	1.12 W
Nidda	56	50.24 N	9.00 E
Nidda ≏	56	50.06 N	8.34 E
Nidder ≏	56	50.12 N	8.47 E
Nidderau	56	50.14 N	8.52 E
Nide	102	31.51 N	96.19 E
Nideggen	56	50.47 N	6.29 E
Nidelva ≏	26	58.24 N	8.48 E
Nidwalden □[3]	58	46.55 N	8.28 E
Nidzica	30	53.22 N	20.26 E
Niebüll	41	54.48 N	8.50 E
Nied ≏	56	49.23 N	6.40 E
Nied Allemande ≏	56	49.10 N	6.26 E
Nieddu, Monte ʌ	71	40.45 N	9.34 E
Niedenstein	56	51.14 N	9.19 E
Niederanven	56	49.39 N	6.16 E
Niederau	54	51.10 N	13.32 E
Niederaula	56	50.48 N	9.36 E
Niederbayern □[5]	60	48.45 N	12.45 E
Niederbipp	58	47.16 N	7.39 E
Niederbobritzsch	54	50.54 N	13.26 E
Niederbonsfeld	263	51.23 N	7.08 E
Niederbronn-Les-Bains	56	48.57 N	7.38 E
Niederdonk	263	51.14 N	6.41 E
Niederelfringhausen	263	51.21 N	7.10 E
Niedereschach	58	48.08 N	8.32 E
Niedere Tauern ⋀	30	47.18 N	14.00 E
Niederfinow	54	52.50 N	13.55 E
Niederfrohna	54	50.53 N	12.43 E
Niedergörsdorf	54	51.59 N	13.00 E
Niederhaverbeck	52	53.09 N	9.54 E
Niederheimbach	56	50.02 N	7.48 E
Niederhone	56	51.13 N	10.06 E
Niederkassel	56	50.49 N	7.02 E
Nieder-Kassel ◆[8]	263	51.14 N	6.45 E
Niederkrüchten	56	51.12 N	6.13 E
Niederlande → Netherlands □[1]	30	52.15 N	5.30 E
Niederländische Antillen → Netherlands Antilles □[2]	241s	12.15 N	69.00 W
Niederlausitz □[9]	54	51.40 N	14.15 E
Niederlehme	54	52.19 N	13.39 E
Niedermarschacht	52	53.25 N	10.21 E
Niederndodeleben	54	52.08 N	11.30 E
Nieder-Neuendorf	264a	52.37 N	13.12 E
Niedernhall	56	49.17 N	9.36 E
Niedernwöhren	52	52.21 N	9.08 E
Niederoderwitz	54	50.57 N	14.44 E
Nieder-Ohmen	56	50.38 N	9.02 E
Nieder-Olm	56	49.55 N	8.11 E
Niederorschel	54	51.22 N	10.25 E
Niederösterreich □[3]	61	48.20 N	15.50 E
Niedersachsen □[3]	30	52.40 N	9.00 E
Niedersachswerfen	54	51.33 N	10.46 E
Niederschöneweide ◆[8]	264a	52.27 N	13.31 E
Niederschönhausen ◆[8]	54	52.35 N	13.23 E
Niedersonthofen	58	47.38 N	10.13 E
Niederstetten	56	49.24 N	9.55 E
Niederstotzingen	56	48.32 N	10.14 E
Niedersulz	61	48.29 N	16.40 E
Niedertrebra	54	51.04 N	11.35 E
Niederurnen	58	47.07 N	9.03 E
Niederwald	58	46.26 N	8.12 E
Niederwalgern	56	50.44 N	8.41 E
Niederweningen	58	47.30 N	8.23 E
Niederwerrn	56	50.04 N	10.11 E
Niederwiesa	54	50.51 N	13.01 E
Niederwürschnitz	54	50.43 N	12.45 E
Niederzier	56	50.53 N	6.28 E
Nied Française ≏	56	49.10 N	6.26 E
Niedu	100	25.28 N	114.08 E
Niefang	152	1.50 N	10.14 E
Niefern-Öschelbronn	56	48.55 N	8.47 E
Nieheim	52	51.48 N	9.06 E
Niekerkshoop	158	29.19 S	22.51 E
Niel	50	51.07 N	4.20 E
Niellé	150	10.12 N	5.38 W
Niellim	146	9.42 N	17.49 E
Niem	152	6.12 N	15.14 E
Niemba	154	5.57 S	28.26 E
Niemegk	54	52.04 N	12.41 E
Niemeyer ◆[8]	287a	23.00 S	43.15 W
Niemodlin	30	50.39 N	17.37 E
Niéna	150	11.26 N	6.21 W
Nienberge	52	52.00 N	7.34 E
Nienborg-Wigbold	52	52.08 N	7.06 E
Nienburg, Dtsch.	52	52.38 N	9.13 E
Nienburg, Dtsch.	54	51.50 N	11.46 E
Niendorf	54	53.59 N	10.50 E
Nienhagen, Dtsch.	52	52.33 N	10.05 E
Nienhagen, Dtsch.	54	51.57 N	11.09 E
Niénokoué, Mont ʌ[2]	150	5.26 N	7.10 W
Niepars	54	54.19 N	12.56 E
Niepkuhlen ≏	263	51.29 N	6.31 E
Niepołomice	30	50.03 N	20.13 E
Nieppe	50	50.42 N	2.50 E
Nier ≏	48	52.17 N	7.48 W
Niéré	146	14.30 N	21.09 E
Niéré, Hadjer ʌ	146	14.21 N	21.40 E
Niéri Ko ≏	150	13.21 N	13.23 W
Niers ≏	52	51.43 N	5.57 E
Nierst	263	51.19 N	6.43 E
Nierstein	56	49.52 N	8.20 E
Niesen ʌ	58	46.39 N	7.39 E
Niesky	54	51.17 N	14.49 E
Nieszawa	30	52.50 N	18.55 E
Nieto, Cañada de ≏	258	34.00 S	58.15 W
Nieu Bethesda	158	31.51 S	24.34 E
Nieuw-Amsterdam, Ned.	52	52.44 N	6.51 E
Nieuw Amsterdam, Sur.	250	5.53 N	55.05 W
Nieuw-Buinen	52	52.57 N	6.55 E
Nieuwefontein	158	28.01 S	19.06 E
Nieuwegein	52	52.03 N	5.05 E
Nieuwe-Niedorp	52	52.45 N	4.54 E
Nieuwe-Pekela	52	53.04 N	6.58 E
Nieuweschans	52	53.11 N	7.12 E
Nieuwkoop	52	52.08 N	4.47 E
Nieuw Nickerie	250	5.57 N	56.59 W
Nieuwolda	52	53.14 N	6.59 E
Nieuwoudtville	158	31.23 S	19.07 E
Nieuwpoort, Bel.	50	51.08 N	2.45 E
Nieuwpoort, Ned. Ant.	241s	12.03 N	68.49 W
Nieuwpoort-Bad	50	51.09 N	2.42 E
Nieuw-Schoonebeek	52	52.38 N	6.59 E
Nieuw-Vennep	52	52.16 N	4.38 E
Nieuw-Weerdinge	52	52.52 N	6.59 E
Nieva ≏	246	4.35 S	77.53 W
Nievenheim	56	51.07 N	6.46 E
Nievería	286d	11.59 S	76.55 W
Nièvre □[5]	32	47.05 N	3.30 E
Nièvre ≏	50	47.10 N	3.13 E
Niga	150	13.38 N	5.27 W
Nigan	126	23.30 N	87.59 E
Niğde	130	37.59 N	34.42 E
Niğde □[4]	130	38.15 N	34.15 E
Nigei Island I	182	50.55 N	127.50 W
Nigel	158	26.30 S	28.28 E
Niger □[1]	134	16.00 N	8.00 E
Niger ≏	150	5.33 N	6.33 E
Niger Delta ≚[2]	150	4.50 N	6.00 E
Nigeria □[1]	134	10.00 N	8.00 E
Nigerian Museum ⚱	273a	6.20 N	3.24 E
Nigg	46	57.43 N	4.00 W
Nighāsan	124	28.14 N	80.52 E
Nightcaps	172	45.58 S	168.02 E
Nighthawk	182	48.58 N	119.38 W
Night Hawk Lake ⊜	190	48.28 N	81.00 W
Nightingale Island I	10	37.24 S	12.28 W
Nightmute	180	60.29 N	164.43 W
Nigríta	38	40.55 N	23.30 E
Nihe	104	41.27 N	121.13 E
Nihing (Nahang) ≏	128	26.00 N	62.44 E
Nihoa I	14	23.06 N	161.58 W
Nihommatsu	92	37.35 N	140.26 E
Nihon → Japan □[1]	92	36.00 N	138.00 E
Nihonbashi ◆[8]	268	35.41 N	139.47 E
Nihon-kai → Japan, Sea of ⍑[2]	90	40.00 N	135.00 E
Nihon University ⚱[2]	268	35.42 N	139.45 E
Nihtaur	124	29.20 N	78.23 E
Nihuil, Embalse del ⊜[1]	252	35.05 S	68.45 W
Niida ≏	96	33.11 N	132.58 E
Niigata	92	37.55 N	139.03 E
Niigata □[5]	94	37.08 N	138.30 E
Niihama	96	33.58 N	133.16 E
Niihari	94	36.07 N	140.09 E
Niiharu	94	36.41 N	138.55 E
Niihau I	229b	21.55 N	160.10 W
Nii-jima I	92	34.22 N	139.16 E
Niimi	96	34.59 N	133.28 E
Niinisalo	26	61.50 N	22.29 E
Niitsu	92	37.48 N	139.07 E
Niiza	94	35.48 N	139.34 E
Níjar	34	36.58 N	2.12 W
Nijiaqiao	269b	31.14 N	121.21 E
Nijil	132	30.31 N	35.33 E
Nijkerk	52	52.13 N	5.30 E
Nijlen	56	51.10 N	4.39 E
Nijmegen	52	51.50 N	5.50 E
Nijo Castle ⊥	270	35.01 N	135.45 E
Nijvel → Nivelles	50	50.36 N	4.20 E
Nijverdal	52	52.22 N	6.27 E
Níkaia	267c	37.58 N	23.39 E
Nikel'	24	69.24 N	30.12 E
Nikel'tau	86	50.23 N	58.13 E
Nikiforovo	265b	55.50 N	38.05 E
Nikiniki	112	9.49 S	124.28 E
Nikip Lake ⊜	184	52.53 N	91.53 W
Nikitovka	78	50.23 N	38.25 E
Nikitsch	61	47.32 N	16.40 E
Nikitskoje, Ross.	82	55.18 N	38.28 E
Nikitskoje, Ross.	82	55.13 N	35.46 E
Nikki	150	9.56 N	3.12 E
Nikkō	94	36.45 N	139.37 E
Nikkō-kokuritsu-kōen ♠	94	36.49 N	139.33 E
Niklā al-'Inab	142	30.55 N	30.46 E
Niklasdorf	61	47.24 N	15.10 E
Nikobaren → Nicobar Islands II	110	8.00 N	93.30 E
Nikolai	180	62.58 N	154.09 W
Nikolajevka, Kaz.	86	49.10 N	81.59 E
Nikolajevka, Ross.	80	46.21 N	47.44 E
Nikolajevka, Ross.	80	52.28 N	49.14 E
Nikolajevka, Ross.	80	52.11 N	48.04 E
Nikolajevka, Ross.	80	53.08 N	47.12 E
Nikolajevka, Ross.	83	47.18 N	38.50 E
Nikolajevka, Ross.	86	56.29 N	95.06 E
Nikolajevka, Ross.	86	54.57 N	75.44 E
Nikolajevka, Ross.	88	55.46 N	98.10 E
Nikolajevka, Ross.	89	48.34 N	134.47 E
Nikolajevo	76	58.16 N	29.29 E
Nikolajevo-Kozlovskij	83	47.13 N	38.21 E
Nikolajevsk	80	50.01 N	45.28 E
Nikolajevskaja	80	47.37 N	41.29 E
Nikolajevsk-Na-Amure	89	53.08 N	140.44 E
Nikolajevskoje, Ross.	78	45.08 N	39.36 E
Nikolajevskoje, Ross.	88	51.04 N	111.48 E
Nikolajevskoje, Ross.	88	52.21 N	117.00 E
Nikolassee ◆[8]	264a	52.26 N	13.12 E
Nikolayev → Mykolayiv	78	46.58 N	32.00 E
Nikolo-Berezovec	76	58.38 N	42.17 E
Nikolo-Berjozovka	80	56.06 N	54.17 E
Nikolo-Chovanskoje	265b	55.36 N	37.27 E
Nikologory	80	56.09 N	41.59 E
Nikolo-Kropotki	82	56.44 N	37.55 E
Nikolo-L'vovsk	89	43.54 N	131.23 E
Nikolo-Makarovo	80	57.38 N	43.34 E
Nikolsdorf	64	46.47 N	12.55 E
Nikol'sk, Ross.	24	59.30 N	45.27 E
Nikol'sk, Ross.	80	53.45 N	46.05 E
Nikolski	180	52.56 N	168.52 W
Nikol'skij, Ross.	24	60.55 N	34.00 E
Nikol'skij, Ross.	86	56.18 N	68.58 E
Nikol'skij Toržok	76	59.53 N	38.46 E
Nikol'skoje, Ross.	74	55.12 N	166.00 E
Nikol'skoje, Ross.	76	52.39 N	36.04 E
Nikol'skoje, Ross.	76	55.26 N	35.04 E
Nikol'skoje, Ross.	76	59.23 N	44.36 E
Nikol'skoje, Ross.	76	59.30 N	42.32 E
Nikol'skoje, Ross.	78	50.35 N	41.10 E
Nikol'skoje, Ross.	80	47.46 N	46.24 E
Nikol'skoje, Ross.	80	52.37 N	43.49 E
Nikol'skoje, Ross.	82	54.51 N	35.53 E
Nikol'skoje, Ross.	82	54.27 N	36.24 E
Nikol'skoje, Ross.	82	54.30 N	36.50 E
Nikol'skoje, Ross.	82	54.03 N	37.10 E
Nikol'skoje, Ross.	82	54.18 N	35.53 E
Nikol'skoje, Ross.	82	55.37 N	36.41 E
Nikol'skoje, Ross.	82	55.15 N	36.04 E
Nikol'skoje, Ross.	82	56.09 N	36.43 E
Nikol'skoje, Ross.	82	55.53 N	36.26 E
Nikol'skoje, Ross.	86	57.12 N	84.21 E
Nikol'skoje, Ross.	86	52.02 N	55.43 E
Nikol'skoje, Ross.	265a	59.41 N	30.47 E
Nikol'skoje, Ross.	265b	55.46 N	37.54 E
Nikol'skoje-na-Čeremšane	80	54.03 N	49.14 E
Nikol'skoje-Ur'upino	265b	55.48 N	37.13 E
Nikonga ≏	154	4.40 S	31.28 E
Nikonorovka	83	49.07 N	39.59 E
Nikonova Gora	76	60.22 N	36.07 E
Nikonovskoje	82	55.17 N	38.10 E
Nikopol, Blg.	38	43.42 N	24.54 E
Nikopol', Ukr.	78	47.35 N	34.25 E
Niksar	130	40.36 N	36.58 E
Nīkshahr	128	26.13 N	60.12 E
Nikšić	38	42.46 N	18.56 E
Nikulino, Ross.	76	55.16 N	33.46 E
Nikulino, Ross.	80	58.05 N	44.14 E
Nikulino, Ross.	82	56.48 N	35.50 E
Nikulino ◆[8]	265b	55.40 N	37.28 E
Nikulkino	82	56.07 N	38.38 E
Nikul'skoje	82	55.10 N	38.41 E
Nikumaroro I[1]	14	4.40 S	174.32 W
Nikunau I	14	1.23 S	176.26 E
Nil → Nile ≏	140	30.10 N	31.06 E
Nīl, Nahr an- → Nile ≏	140	30.10 N	31.06 E
Nila, Pulau I	164	6.44 S	129.31 E
Nilakka ⊜	26	63.07 N	26.33 E
Niland	204	33.14 N	115.31 W
Nil Blanc → White Nile ≏	140	15.38 N	32.31 E
Nile □[5]	154	3.00 N	31.30 E
Nile (Nahr an-Nīl) ≏	140	30.10 N	31.06 E
Niles, Il., U.S.	216	42.01 N	87.48 W
Niles, Mi., U.S.	216	41.49 N	86.15 W
Niles, Oh., U.S.	214	41.10 N	80.45 W
Niles Canyon V	282	37.36 N	121.56 W
Niles Pond ⊜	283	42.35 N	70.40 W
Nilgani	272b	22.46 N	88.26 E
Nilgaut, Lac ⊜	190	46.36 N	77.15 W
Nīlgiri	126	21.28 N	86.46 E
Nilka	86	43.47 N	82.20 E
Nilkitkwa ≏	182	55.27 N	126.43 W
Nillahcootie, Lake ⊜[1]	169	36.54 S	146.00 E
Nilo → Nile ≏	140	30.10 N	31.06 E
Nilo Azul → Blue Nile ≏	140	15.38 N	32.31 E
Nilo Blanco → White Nile ≏	140	15.38 N	32.31 E
Nilópolis	256	22.49 S	43.25 W
Nilópolis □[7]	287a	22.49 S	43.26 W
Nilphāmāri	124	25.56 N	88.51 E
Nilsiä	26	63.12 N	28.05 E
Niltepec	234	16.34 N	94.37 W
Nilüfer ≏	130	40.18 N	28.27 E
Nīlwāl ◆[8]	272a	28.40 N	76.59 E
Nilwood	219	39.24 N	89.49 W
Nima	96	35.09 N	132.24 E
Nīmach	120	24.28 N	74.52 E
Niman ≏	89	51.24 N	132.45 E
Nimančik	89	52.09 N	133.47 E
Nimba, Mount ʌ	150	7.37 N	8.25 W
Nimbāhera	120	24.37 N	74.41 E
Nimba Range ⋀	150	7.30 N	8.30 W
Nimboran, Pegunungan ⋀	164	2.45 S	140.20 E
Nimelen ≏	89	52.27 N	136.32 E
Nîmes	62	43.50 N	4.21 E
Nimis	64	46.12 N	13.16 E
Nimishillen Creek ≏	214	40.38 N	81.22 W
Nimisila	214	40.56 N	81.34 W
Nimisila Reservoir ⊜[1]	214	40.57 N	81.31 W
Nīm Ka Thāna	120	27.44 N	75.48 E
Nimmitabel	166	36.31 S	149.16 E
Nimmonsburg	210	42.09 N	75.55 W
Nimpkish Lake ⊜	182	50.25 N	126.59 W
Nimrod Lake ⊜[1]	194	34.55 N	93.20 W
Nīmrūz □[4]	128	30.30 N	62.00 E
Nims ≏	56	49.51 N	6.28 E
Nimta	272b	22.40 N	88.25 E
Nimule	154	3.36 N	32.03 E
Nimule National Park ♠	154	3.50 N	31.35 E
Nimy	50	50.28 N	3.57 E
Niña Bonita, Presa ⊜[1]	286b	23.02 N	82.29 W
Nīnah, Wādī V	146	30.02 N	15.22 E
Nīnawā □[4]	128	36.10 N	42.35 E
Nīnawá (Nineveh) ⊥	128	36.25 N	43.10 E
Nin Bay ⊂	116	12.13 N	123.15 E
Ninda	152	14.47 S	21.24 E
Nindigully	166	28.21 S	148.49 E
Nindiri	236	12.00 N	86.08 W
Nine Ashes	260	51.42 N	0.18 E
Nine Degree Channel ʮ	122	9.00 N	73.00 E
Ninemile Creek ≏, N.Y., U.S.	210	43.11 N	75.20 W
Ninemile Creek ≏, N.Y., U.S.	210	43.06 N	76.14 W
Ninemile Creek ≏, N.Y., U.S.	210	43.24 N	76.38 W
Nine Mile Creek ≏, Ut,. U.S.	200	39.50 N	109.53 W
Ninemile Island I	279b	40.29 N	79.52 W
Nine Mile Lake ⊜	212	44.57 N	79.34 W
Nine Mile Point ›	212	44.09 N	76.34 W
Ninepin Group II	271d	22.16 N	114.21 E
Nineteen Hundred Five Memorial Cemetery ◆	265a	59.51 N	30.27 E
Ninette	184	49.24 N	99.38 W
Ninetyeast Ridge ✤[3]	6	4.00 S	90.00 E
Ninety Mile Beach ≐[2], Austl.	166	38.13 S	147.23 E
Ninety Mile Beach ≐[2], N.Z.	172	34.48 S	173.00 E
Ninety Six	192	34.10 N	82.01 W
Nineveh, In., U.S.	218	39.22 N	86.05 W
Nineveh, N.Y., U.S.	210	42.12 N	75.36 W
Nineveh → Nīnawá ⊥	128	36.25 N	43.10 E
Ninfa ⊥	66	41.36 N	12.58 E
Ninfas, Punta ›	254	42.56 S	64.20 W
Ninfield	42	50.53 N	0.25 E
Ninga	184	49.13 N	99.51 W
Ningaloo	162	22.42 S	113.40 E
Ning'an	89	44.22 N	129.25 E
Ningari	150	14.40 N	3.16 W
Ningbo	100	29.52 N	121.31 E
Ningcheng (Tianyi)	98	41.33 N	119.20 E
Ningde	100	26.43 N	119.33 E
Ningdu	100	26.31 N	115.58 E
Ningerum	164	5.41 S	141.08 E
Ninggang	100	26.50 N	114.02 E
Ningguo	106	30.38 N	118.58 E
Ninghai	100	29.17 N	121.25 E
Ninghe (Lutai)	105	39.20 N	117.48 E
Ninghepu	105	40.43 N	116.07 E
Ninghua	100	26.15 N	116.38 E
Ningi	150	11.04 N	9.32 E
Ningjin, Zhg.	98	37.37 N	114.55 E
Ningjin, Zhg.	98	37.39 N	116.48 E
Ningjing Shan ⋀	102	29.45 N	98.45 E
Ningling	98	34.27 N	115.21 E
Ningming	102	22.07 N	107.05 E
Ningnan	102	27.11 N	102.36 E
Ningpo → Ningbo	100	29.52 N	121.31 E
Ningqiang	102	32.44 N	106.19 E
Ningshan	102	33.04 N	108.39 E
Ningsia → Yinchuan	102	38.30 N	106.18 E
Ningsia Hui Autonomous Region → Ningxia Huizu Zizhiqu □[4]	102	37.00 N	106.00 E
Ningwu	102	39.01 N	112.21 E
Ningxi	100	28.35 N	121.00 E
Ningxia Huizu Zizhiqu (Ningsia Hui) □[4]	102	37.00 N	106.00 E
Ningxian	102	35.31 N	108.01 E
Ningxiang	100	28.15 N	112.33 E
Ningyang	98	35.47 N	116.47 E
Ningyō-tōge)(	96	35.19 N	133.56 E
Ningyuan	102	25.37 N	111.46 E
Ningyuanbao	102	38.38 N	102.30 E
Ningyuanpu	105	40.44 N	114.54 E
Ninh Binh	110	20.15 N	105.59 E
Ninh Hoa	110	12.29 N	109.08 E
Ninhue	252	36.24 S	72.24 W
Ninigo Group II	164	1.15 S	144.15 E
Ninilchik	180	60.03 N	151.41 W
Ninnescah ≏	198	37.20 N	97.10 W
Ninnescah, North Fork ≏	198	37.34 N	97.42 W
Ninnescah, South Fork ≏	198	37.34 N	97.42 W
Ninnis Glacier Tongue ⍓	9	68.12 S	147.12 E
Ninocminda	84	41.18 N	43.35 E
Ninohe	92	40.16 N	141.18 E
Ninomiya, Nihon	94	35.18 N	139.16 E
Ninomiya, Nihon	94	36.22 N	139.58 E
Ninove	50	50.50 N	4.01 E
Niny	84	44.29 N	43.57 E
Nio	96	34.12 N	133.39 E
Nioaque	248	21.08 S	55.48 W
Nioaque ≏	248	20.46 S	56.04 W
Niobe	214	42.01 N	79.27 W
Niobrara	198	42.45 N	98.01 W
Niobrara ≏	198	42.45 N	98.00 W
Nioka	154	2.10 N	30.39 E
Nioki	152	2.43 S	17.41 E
Niokolo Koba	150	13.04 N	12.43 W
Niokolo Koba, Parc National du ♠	150	13.00 N	13.00 W
Niono	150	14.15 N	6.00 W
Nionsamoridougou	150	8.43 N	8.50 W
Nioro du Rip	150	13.45 N	15.48 W
Nioro du Sahel	150	15.15 N	9.35 W

	English	Deutsch	Español	Français	Português
≏	River	Fluß	Río	Rivière	Rio
≊	Canal	Kanal	Canal	Canal	Canal
⌊	Waterfall, Rapids	Wasserfall, Stromschnellen	Cascada, Rápidos	Chute d'eau, Rapides	Cascata, Rápidos
ʮ	Strait	Meeresstraße	Estrecho	Détroit	Estreito
⊂	Bay, Gulf	Bucht, Golf	Bahía, Golfo	Baie, Golfe	Baía, Golfo
⊜	Lake, Lakes	See, Seen	Lago, Lagos	Lac, Lacs	Lago, Lagos
⩩	Swamp	Sumpf	Pantano	Marais	Pântano
⍓	Ice Features, Glacier	Eis- und Gletscherformen	Accidentes Glaciales	Formes glaciaires	Acidentes glaciares
⍑	Other Hydrographic Features	Andere Hydrographische Objekte	Otros Elementos Hidrográficos	Autres données hydrographiques	Outros acidentes hidrográficos
✤	Submarine Features	Untermeerische Objekte	Accidentes Submarinos	Formes de relief sous-marin	Acidentes submarinos
□	Political Unit	Politische Einheit	Unidad Politica	Entité politique	Unidade política
⚱	Cultural Institution	Kulturelle Institution	Institución Cultural	Institution culturelle	Institução cultural
⊥	Historical Site	Historische Stätte	Sitio Histórico	Site historique	Sitio histórico
♠	Recreational Site	Erholungs- und Ferienort	Sitio de Recreo	Centre de loisirs	Area de Lazer
⊠	Airport	Flughafen	Aeropuerto	Aéroport	Aeroporto
■	Military Installation	Militäranlage	Instalación Militar	Installation militaire	Instalação militar
◆	Miscellaneous	Verschiedenes	Misceláneo	Divers	Diversos

ENGLISH / DEUTSCH

Name	Page	Lat.°′	Long.°′
Niort	32	46.19 N	0.27 W
Niota	192	35.30 N	84.32 W
Nioût ▾[4]	150	16.03 N	6.52 W
Nipan	166	24.47 S	150.01 E
Nipāni	122	16.24 N	74.23 E
Nipawin	184	53.22 N	104.00 W
Nipawin Provincial Park ♦	184	54.00 N	104.40 W
Nipe, Bahía de c	240p	20.47 N	75.42 W
Nipekamew ≃	184	54.59 N	104.52 W
Nipekamew Lake ⊜	184	54.24 N	104.58 W
Nipepe	154	14.01 S	37.55 E
Nipigon	190	49.01 N	88.16 W
Nipigon, Lake ⊜	176	49.50 N	88.30 W
Nipigon Bay c	190	48.53 N	87.50 W
Nipin ≃	184	55.45 N	109.02 W
Nipisi Lake ⊜	182	55.47 N	114.57 W
Nipissing □[6]	212	45.30 N	78.50 W
Nipissing, Lake ⊜	190	46.17 N	80.00 W
Nipissis, Lac ⊜	186	51.02 N	66.10 W
Nipisso, Lac ⊜	186	50.52 N	65.50 W
Nipomo	204	35.02 N	120.28 W
Nippenicket, Lake ⊜	283	41.58 N	71.03 W
Nippers Harbour	186	49.48 N	55.52 W
Nippersink Creek ≃	216	42.23 N	88.22 W
Niqiu	100	33.25 N	115.38 E
Niquelândia	255	14.27 S	48.27 W
Niquero	240p	20.03 N	77.35 W
Niquivil	252	30.25 S	68.42 W
Nīr	128	38.02 N	47.59 E
Nīr, Jabal an- ⋏[2]	128	24.10 N	43.20 E
Nīra ≃	122	17.59 N	75.07 E
Nir'am	132	31.31 N	34.35 E
Nirasaki	94	35.42 N	138.27 E
Nirayama	94	35.03 N	138.57 E
Nirgua	246	10.09 N	68.34 W
Nirim	132	31.20 N	34.24 E
Nirmal	122	19.06 N	78.21 E
Nirmāli	124	26.19 N	86.35 E
Nirsa	126	23.47 N	86.43 E
Niš	38	43.19 N	21.54 E
Nisa	34	39.31 N	7.39 W
Niṣāb, Ar. Su.	128	29.11 N	44.43 E
Niṣāb, Yaman	144	14.31 N	46.30 E
Nišava ≃	38	43.22 N	21.46 E
Nisbet	210	41.13 N	77.07 W
Niscemi	70	37.09 N	14.23 E
Nischintāpur	272b	22.26 N	88.22 E
Niṣf Thānī Bashbīsh	142	31.07 N	31.11 E
Nish → Niš	38	43.19 N	21.54 E
Nishan	120	33.35 N	85.30 E
Nishi ◆[8], Nihon	268	35.27 N	139.38 E
Nishi ◆[8], Nihon	270	34.41 N	135.30 E
Nishiarai ◆[8]	268	35.47 N	139.47 E
Nishiazai	94	35.31 N	136.10 E
Nishibetsuin	270	34.58 N	135.31 E
Nishi-Chūgoku-sanchi-kokutei-kōen ♦	96	34.40 N	132.10 E
Nishigō	94	37.09 N	140.10 E
Nishiiyayama	96	33.53 N	133.49 E
Nishiizu	94	34.46 N	138.47 E
Nishi-jima I	96	34.39 N	134.29 E
Nishikata	94	36.28 N	139.45 E
Nishikatsura	94	35.31 N	138.51 E
Nishiki	96	34.16 N	131.57 E
Nishiki ≃	96	34.09 N	132.15 E
Nishikiori	270	34.29 N	135.34 E
Nishikyō ◆[8]	270	34.59 N	135.40 E
Nishimori ◆[8]	270	34.45 N	135.01 E
Nishinari ◆[8]	270	34.38 N	135.28 E
Nishinasuno	94	36.53 N	139.59 E
Nishinomiya	96	34.43 N	135.20 E
Nishinoomote	93b	30.44 N	131.00 E
Nishio	94	34.52 N	137.03 E
Nishitoda ◆[8]	270	34.43 N	135.00 E
Nishitosa	96	33.09 N	132.47 E
Nishiwaki	96	34.59 N	134.58 E
Nishiyodogawa ◆[8]	270	34.42 N	135.27 E
Nisinomiya → Nishinomiya	96	34.43 N	135.20 E
Nísiros I	38	36.35 N	27.10 E
Niska Lake ⊜	184	55.35 N	108.38 W
Niskayuna	210	42.46 N	73.50 W
Nisling ≃	180	62.27 N	139.30 W
Nismes	56	50.05 N	4.33 E
Nispen	52	51.29 N	4.28 E
Nisporeni	38	47.06 N	28.11 E
Nisqually ≃	224	47.06 N	122.42 W
Nisqually Indian Reservation ◆[4]	224	47.02 N	122.42 W
Nisqually Reach c	224	47.07 N	122.45 W
Nissan ≃	26	56.40 N	12.51 E
Nissequogue	276	40.54 N	73.12 W
Nissequogue ≃	276	40.54 N	73.13 W
Nissequogue, Northeast Branch ≃	276	40.50 N	73.13 W
Nissequogue River State Park ♦	276	40.51 N	73.13 W
Nisser ⊜	26	59.10 N	8.30 E
Nisshin	94	35.08 N	137.02 E
Nissoria	70	37.39 N	14.27 E
Nissum Bredning c	26	56.38 N	8.22 E
Nissum Fjord c[2]	26	56.21 N	8.14 E
Nisswa	190	46.31 N	94.17 W
Nistelrode	52	51.43 N	5.33 E
Nister ≃	56	50.47 N	7.43 E
Nistru (Dnister) ≃	78	46.18 N	30.17 E
Nisutlin ≃	180	60.10 N	132.30 W
Nita, Indon.	115b	8.40 S	122.11 E
Nita, Nihon	96	35.12 N	133.01 E
Nitalas	272c	19.06 N	73.08 E
Nītaure	76	57.10 N	25.10 E
Niterói	256	22.53 S	43.07 W
Niterói □[7]	287a	22.56 S	43.04 W
Nith ≃, On., Can.	212	43.12 N	80.22 W
Nith ≃, Scot., U.K.	44	55.00 N	3.35 W
Nithāri	272a	28.35 N	77.21 E
Nithāri ◆[8]	272a	28.42 N	77.03 E
Nithi River	182	54.01 N	125.01 W
Nithsdale V	44	55.14 N	3.46 W
Nitibe	112	9.19 S	124.12 E
Nitinat	224	48.55 N	124.29 W
Nitinat ≃	224	48.49 N	124.37 W
Nitinat Lake ⊜	182	48.45 N	124.45 W
Niton	42	50.35 N	1.16 W
Nitra	30	48.20 N	18.05 E
Nitra ≃	30	47.46 N	18.10 E
Nitro	188	38.24 N	81.50 W
Nitry	50	47.40 N	3.53 E
Nitta	94	36.17 N	139.18 E
Nittälven ≃	40	59.51 N	14.50 E
Nittany Mountain ∧	210	41.00 N	77.25 W
Nittedal	26	60.04 N	10.53 E
Nittenau	60	49.12 N	12.16 E
Nittendorf	60	49.02 N	11.58 E
Niu Aunfo Point ›	174w	21.04 S	175.20 W
Niubaotun	105	39.46 N	116.41 E
Niubu	100	31.02 N	117.39 E
Niuchutuncun	104	41.28 N	122.58 E
Niudouguang	100	24.51 N	115.44 E
Niue □[2], Oc.	14	19.02 S	169.52 W
Niue □[2], Oc.	174v	19.02 S	169.52 W
Niu'erhe	89	51.30 N	121.49 E
Niufentai	89	47.05 N	120.02 E
Niufozhen	107	29.23 N	105.02 E
Niuhang	100	28.44 N	115.51 E
Niuhuaxi	107	29.29 N	103.48 E
Niujie	102	27.47 N	104.16 E
Niujingjie	110	25.46 N	100.33 E
Niuke	120	30.41 N	82.01 E
Niulakita I	14	10.45 S	179.30 E
Niulan ≃	102	27.28 N	103.10 E
Niulanshan	105	40.13 N	116.39 E
Niumaowu	98	40.58 N	124.59 E
Niupeng	106	31.32 N	121.50 E
Niupichang	107	30.35 N	103.40 E
Niushitun	98	35.18 N	114.24 E
Niut, Gunung ∧	112	1.00 N	109.55 E
Niutan	107	29.05 N	105.21 E
Niutao I	14	6.06 S	177.17 E
Niuti	100	32.58 N	113.35 E
Niutian	100	27.17 N	115.44 E
Niutoushan	89	45.09 N	126.45 E
Niutou Shan I	100	29.07 N	121.56 E
Niutuo	105	39.15 N	116.20 E
Niutuoshan	106	31.04 N	119.37 E
Niuxichang	107	28.47 N	104.31 E
Niuxintai	104	41.21 N	123.53 E
Niuxintun	104	41.56 N	121.21 E
Niuyuanzi	105	40.20 N	117.47 E
Niuzhuang, Zhg.	98	37.21 N	118.29 E
Niuzhuang, Zhg.	104	40.58 N	122.32 E
Nivå	41	55.56 N	12.31 E
Nivala	26	63.55 N	24.58 E
Nive ≃, Austl.	166	26.02 S	146.25 E
Nive ≃, Fr.	32	43.30 N	1.29 W
Nivelles (Nijvel)	50	50.36 N	4.20 E
Nivernais □[9]	32	47.00 N	3.30 E
Nivernais, Canal du ≡	50	47.40 N	3.40 E
Niverville, Mb., Can.	184	49.37 N	97.01 W
Niverville, N.Y., U.S.	210	42.26 N	73.40 W
Nivillers	50	49.28 N	2.10 E
Nivnoje	76	53.11 N	32.35 E
Nivskij	24	67.16 N	32.23 E
Niwāno	128	26.22 N	62.43 E
Nixa	194	37.02 N	93.17 W
Nixi	102	27.58 N	99.27 E
Nixis	107	30.08 N	106.19 E
Nixizhen	107	29.02 N	104.16 E
Nixon, Nv., U.S.	204	39.49 N	119.21 W
Nixon, Pa., U.S.	214	40.45 N	79.56 W
Nixon, Tx., U.S.	222	29.16 N	97.45 W
Niyodo	96	33.32 N	133.08 E
Niyodo ≃	96	33.27 N	133.29 E
Niyor	114	2.05 N	103.17 E
Niyu Shan I	100	27.51 N	121.03 E
Niža	24	66.20 N	43.16 E
Nizāmābād	122	18.40 N	78.07 E
Nizamghāt	120	28.16 N	95.42 E
Nizām Sāgar ⊜[1]	122	18.10 N	77.55 E
Nīzgān ≃	128	33.13 N	63.40 E
Nizhniy Tagil → Nižnij Tagil	86	57.55 N	59.57 E
Nizhyn	78	51.03 N	31.54 E
Nizino	265a	59.50 N	29.53 E
Nizip	130	37.01 N	37.46 E
Nízke Tatry ⋏	30	48.54 N	19.40 E
Nízke Tatry, národní park ♦	30	47.48 N	19.35 E
Nižn'aja	80	56.34 N	49.07 E
Nižn'aja Čvorovaja	86	59.11 N	77.31 E
Nižnaja Dobrinka	80	50.18 N	45.42 E
Nižn'aja Grajvoronka	78	51.47 N	37.45 E
Nižn'aja Irga	86	56.51 N	57.26 E
Nižn'aja Karelina	88	57.55 N	107.44 E
Nižn'aja Keul'skaja, šivera ʟ	88	58.25 N	102.46 E
Nižnaja Matrenka	80	52.16 N	40.06 E
Nižn'aja Omka	86	55.26 N	74.55 E
Nižn'aja Omra	24	62.46 N	55.46 E
Nižn'aja Ošma	80	55.44 N	51.18 E
Nižn'aja Peša	24	66.43 N	47.36 E
Nižn'aja Pojma	88	56.11 N	97.13 E
Nižn'aja Pokrovka	80	51.40 N	50.07 E
Nižn'aja Šachtama	88	51.24 N	117.40 E
Nižn'aja Salda	86	58.05 N	60.43 E
Nižn'aja Syzran'	80	53.04 N	48.34 E
Nižn'aja Tavda	86	57.40 N	66.12 E
Nižn'aja Tunguska ≃	74	65.48 N	88.04 E
Nižn'aja Tura	86	58.37 N	59.49 E
Nižn'aja Vol'dža	86	58.19 N	79.20 E
Nižn'aja Zaimka	88	56.09 N	98.14 E
Nižneangarsk	88	55.47 N	109.33 E
Nižnebakanskij	78	44.52 N	37.52 E
Nižnečujskij	85	43.12 N	74.21 E
Nižnedevick	78	51.33 N	38.20 E
Nižne-Gnilovskoj ◆[8]	83	47.11 N	39.36 E
Nižnegnutov	80	48.02 N	42.22 E
Nižneilimsk	88	57.11 N	103.16 E
Nižneje Al'kejevo	80	54.46 N	50.03 E
Nižn'eje Gir'unino	88	51.12 N	116.58 E
Nižneje Kučukovo	80	56.13 N	52.57 E
Nižneje Kujto, ozero ⊜	24	64.58 N	31.38 E
Nižneje M'ačkovo	82	55.33 N	37.59 E
Nižneje Romanovo	86	59.47 N	69.35 E
Nižneje Sančelejevo	80	53.40 N	49.27 E
Nižnekamsk	80	55.32 N	51.58 E
Nižnekamskoje vodochranilišče ⊜[1]	24	55.50 N	53.00 E
Nižnekundr'učen-Skaja	80	47.45 N	40.57 E
Nižnelemskij	24	64.01 N	56.16 E
Nižne-Mit'akin Pervyj	83	48.41 N	40.02 E
Nižne-Nagol'naja	83	49.00 N	39.59 E
Nižneoz'ornoje	80	51.37 N	53.56 E
Nižne-Podpol'nyj	83	47.12 N	40.01 E
Nižnetambovskoje	89	50.54 N	138.13 E
Nižnetroickij	80	54.20 N	53.41 E
Nižneudinsk	88	54.54 N	99.03 E
Nižnevartovsk	74	60.56 N	76.31 E
Nižnij Baskunčak	80	48.13 N	46.50 E
Nižnij Časučej	88	50.31 N	115.08 E
Nižnij Čir	80	48.22 N	43.03 E
Nižnij Čulym	86	54.37 N	78.56 E
Nižnije Černi	80	47.41 N	43.26 E
Nižnije Čeršely	80	54.40 N	52.08 E
Nižnije Ostrovcy	82	55.35 N	38.01 E
Nižnije Sergi	86	56.40 N	59.18 E
Nižnije Timers'any	80	54.34 N	47.45 E
Nižnije V'azovyje	80	55.49 N	48.32 E
Nižnij Ingaš	88	56.12 N	96.31 E
Nižnij Kisl'aj	78	50.50 N	40.11 E
Nižnij Kuranach	74	58.49 N	125.32 E
Nižnij Lomov	80	53.32 N	43.41 E
Nižnij Mamon	78	50.11 N	40.30 E
Nižnij Novgorod (Gorky)	80	56.20 N	44.00 E
Nižnij Novgorod Oblast' □[4]	80	56.30 N	45.00 E
Nižnij Odes	24	63.40 N	54.52 E
Nižnij Ol'šan	78	50.45 N	38.55 E
Nižnij P'andž	120	37.08 N	68.32 E
Nižnij Paramonov	80	47.57 N	41.55 E
Nižnij Serebr'akov	80	47.58 N	41.02 E
Nižnij Škaft	80	53.36 N	45.40 E
Nižnij Stan	88	52.18 N	115.44 E
Nižnij Tagil	86	57.55 N	59.57 E
Nižnij Takanyš	80	55.57 N	51.04 E
Nižnij Ufalej	86	55.55 N	59.59 E
Nižnij V'aloz'orskij	24	66.44 N	35.10 E
Nizwā	128	22.56 N	57.32 E
Nizy-le-Comte	50	49.34 N	4.03 E
Nizza Monferrato	62	44.46 N	8.21 E
Niẕẕana	132	30.53 N	34.27 E
Niẕẕana, Naḥal V	132	30.57 N	34.23 E
Niẕẕanim	132	31.43 N	34.38 E
Njassa-See → Nyasa, Lake ⊜	154	12.00 S	34.30 E
Njasviž	76	53.13 N	26.40 E
Njazidja (Grande Comore) I	157a	11.35 S	43.20 E
Njinjo	154	8.48 S	38.54 E
Njoko ≃	152	17.10 S	24.05 E
Njombe	154	9.20 S	34.46 E
Njombe ≃	154	6.56 S	35.06 E
Njupeskär ʟ	26	61.38 N	12.41 E
Njurunda	26	62.16 N	17.22 E
Nkambe	152	6.38 N	10.40 E
Nkandla	158	28.37 S	31.05 E
Nkawkaw	150	6.33 N	0.47 W
Nkayi	154	19.00 S	28.54 E
Nkhata Bay	154	11.33 S	34.18 E
Nkhotakota	154	12.57 S	34.17 E
Nkolabona	152	1.14 N	11.43 E
Nkomi, Lagune c	152	1.35 S	9.17 E
Nkongsamba	152	4.57 N	9.56 E
Nkonko	154	6.20 S	34.58 E
Nkoso	152	2.42 S	22.39 E
Nkoto	152	1.56 S	19.41 E
Nkunga	152	4.41 S	18.34 E
Nkurenkuru	152	17.38 S	18.35 E
Nkwalini	158	28.45 S	31.33 E
Nmai ≃	102	25.42 N	97.30 E
Nnewi	150	6.00 N	6.59 E
Nō	94	37.06 N	137.59 E
Noābād	272b	22.34 N	88.31 E
Noailles	50	49.20 N	2.12 E
Noākhāli	124	22.49 N	91.06 E
Noak Hill ◆[8]	260	51.37 N	0.14 E
Noale	64	45.32 N	12.04 E
Noāmundi	124	22.09 N	85.32 E
Noank	207	41.19 N	71.59 W
Noarlunga	168b	35.11 S	138.30 E
Noasca	62	45.27 N	7.19 E
Noatak	180	67.34 N	162.59 W
Noatak ≃	180	67.00 N	162.30 W
Nobby	171a	27.51 S	151.54 E
Nobel	212	45.25 N	80.06 W
Nobeoka	92	32.35 N	131.40 E
Nobidome	268	35.48 N	139.35 E
Nobidome-yōsui ≡[1]	268	35.44 N	139.27 E
Nōbi-heiya ≚	94	35.15 N	136.45 E
Nobili	150	11.33 N	1.12 W
Nobitz	54	50.58 N	12.29 E
Noble, Il., U.S.	194	38.41 N	88.13 W
Noble, Ok., U.S.	196	35.08 N	97.23 W
Noble □[6]	216	41.24 N	85.25 W
Noble Park	274b	37.58 S	145.10 E
Noblestown	279b	40.24 N	80.12 W
Noblesville	218	40.02 N	86.00 W
Nobleton, On., Can.	212	43.54 N	79.40 W
Nobleton, Fl., U.S.	220	28.38 N	82.15 W
Noboribetsu	92a	42.27 N	141.11 E
Noborito	268	35.37 N	139.34 E
Nobres	248	14.44 S	56.20 W
Nobsa	246	5.46 N	72.57 W
Nocatee	220	27.09 N	81.52 W
Noccundra	166	27.50 S	142.36 E
Nocé	50	48.22 N	0.42 E
Noce ≃	64	46.09 N	11.04 E
Nocera Inferiore	68	40.44 N	14.38 E
Nocera Superiore	68	40.44 N	14.40 E
Nocera Tirinese	68	39.02 N	16.09 E
Nocera Umbra	66	43.05 N	12.47 E
Noceto	64	44.48 N	10.11 E
Nochistlán	234	21.22 N	102.51 W
Nochten	54	51.26 N	14.36 E
Noci	68	40.48 N	17.08 E
Nociglia	68	40.02 N	18.20 E
Nockamixon Lake ⊜[1]	208	40.28 N	75.14 W
Nockamixon State Park ♦	208	40.27 N	75.16 W
Nockatunga	166	27.43 S	142.43 E
Nocona	196	33.47 N	97.43 W
Nocupétaro	234	18.48 N	101.04 W
Noda	94	35.56 N	139.52 E
Nodagawa	96	35.31 N	135.06 E
Nodaway ≃	194	39.54 N	94.58 W
Nodera	270	34.45 N	134.56 E
Nods	58	47.06 N	6.20 E
Noé, Ouadi V	146	15.39 N	21.19 E
Noel	194	36.32 N	94.29 W
Noenieput	158	27.29 S	20.06 E
Noepoli	68	40.05 N	16.20 E
Noer	41	54.27 N	10.00 E
Noetinger	252	32.22 S	62.19 W
Nœux-les-Mines	50	50.29 N	2.40 E
Nofels	58	47.15 N	9.34 E
Nogah	132	31.37 N	34.42 E
Nogajskaja step' ≚	84	44.17 N	46.05 E
Nogales, Chile	252	32.44 S	71.15 W
Nogales, Méx.	232	31.20 N	110.56 W
Nogales, Méx.	234	18.49 N	97.10 W
Nogales, Az., U.S.	200	31.20 N	110.56 W
Nogami	94	36.07 N	139.07 E
Nogangjin	98	39.30 N	125.23 E
Nogara, It.	64	45.11 N	11.04 E
Nogara, Ityo.	144	13.53 N	36.32 E
Nogaro	32	43.46 N	0.02 W
Nōgata	96	33.44 N	130.44 E
Nogent-en-Bassigny	58	48.02 N	5.21 E
Nogent-le-Roi	50	48.39 N	1.32 E
Nogent-le-Rotrou	50	48.19 N	0.50 E
Nogent-sur-Marne	261	48.50 N	2.29 E
Nogent-sur-Oise	50	49.16 N	2.28 E
Nogent-sur-Seine	50	48.29 N	3.30 E
Nogent-sur-Vernisson	50	47.51 N	2.45 E
Nogi	94	36.14 N	139.44 E
Nogies Creek ≃	212	44.35 N	78.31 W
Noginsk	82	55.51 N	38.27 E
Nogisaki	268	35.57 N	139.58 E
Nogliki	89	51.48 N	143.10 E
Nogmung	102	27.30 N	97.49 E
Nogoa ≃	166	23.33 S	148.32 E
Nōgohaku-san ∧	94	35.46 N	136.31 E
Nogoon Nuur	86	49.33 N	90.17 E
Nogoyá	252	32.24 S	59.48 W
Nógrád □[6]	30	48.00 N	19.35 E
Noguera Pallaresa ≃	34	42.15 N	0.54 E
Noguera Ribagorzana ≃	34	41.40 N	0.43 E
Nohain ≃	50	47.24 N	2.55 E
Nohar	123	29.11 N	74.46 E
Noheji	92	40.52 N	141.08 E
Nohfelden	56	49.35 N	7.09 E
Nohili Point ›	229b	22.04 N	159.47 W
Nohjhīl	124	27.51 N	77.39 E
Nohta	124	23.40 N	79.34 E
Nohwa-do I	98	34.12 N	126.35 E
Noia	34	42.47 N	8.53 W
Noicattaro	68	41.02 N	16.59 E
Noichi	96	33.33 N	133.42 E
Noir, Causse ⋏[1]	32	44.10 N	3.15 E
Noir, Isla I	254	54.29 S	73.02 W
Noire ≃, P.Q., Can.	190	45.54 N	76.57 W
Noire ≃, P.Q., Can.	206	45.33 N	72.58 W
Noire ≃, P.Q., Can.	206	46.39 N	72.08 W
Noire, Mer du → Black Sea ▾[2]	22	43.00 N	35.00 E
Noire, Montagne ∧	206	46.14 N	74.18 W
Noire, Montagne ⋏	32	43.28 N	2.18 E
Noirétable	62	45.49 N	3.46 E
Noirmoutier	32	47.00 N	2.14 W
Noirmoutier, Île de I	32	47.00 N	2.15 W
Noiseau	261	48.47 N	2.33 E
Noisiel	261	48.51 N	2.37 E
Noisy ≃	212	44.19 N	80.08 W
Noisy-le-Grand	261	48.51 N	2.33 E
Noisy-le-Roi	261	48.51 N	2.04 E
Noisy-le-Sec	261	48.53 N	2.28 E
Nojember'an	84	41.12 N	45.01 E
Nojima-zaki ›	94	34.56 N	139.53 E
Nojiri-ko ⊜	94	36.49 N	138.13 E
Nojon	102	43.10 N	102.07 E
Nojon uul ⋏	102	43.10 N	101.30 E
Nokami	96	34.15 N	135.20 E
Nokaneng	156	19.40 S	22.16 E
Nōke	270	34.26 N	135.29 E
Nokha Mandi	120	27.35 N	73.29 E
Nokia	26	61.28 N	23.30 E
Nokilalaki, Bulu ∧	112	1.13 S	120.08 E
Nok Kundi	128	28.46 N	62.46 E
Nokogiri-yama ∧[2]	268	35.09 N	139.51 E
Nokomis, Sk., Can.	184	51.30 N	105.00 W
Nokomis, Fl., U.S.	220	27.07 N	82.26 W
Nokomis, Il., U.S.	219	39.18 N	89.17 W
Nokomis Lake ⊜	184	56.58 N	103.02 W
Nokou	146	14.35 N	14.47 E
Nokpan-ni ◆[8]	271b	37.36 N	126.56 E
Nokrek ∧	124	25.27 N	90.20 E
Nokuku	175f	14.53 S	166.35 E
Nola, Centraf.	152	3.32 N	16.04 E
Nola, It.	68	40.55 N	14.33 E
Nolan ≃	222	32.07 N	97.26 W
Nolan Creek ≃	222	31.02 N	97.26 W
Nolands Fork ≃	218	39.41 N	85.07 W
Nolanville	222	31.05 N	97.36 W
Nolay	58	46.57 N	4.38 E
Nole	62	45.15 N	7.35 E
Noli	62	44.12 N	8.26 E
Noli, Capo di ›	62	44.12 N	8.25 E
Nolichucky ≃	192	36.07 N	83.14 W
Nolin ≃	194	37.13 N	86.15 W
Nolin Lake ⊜[1]	194	37.20 N	86.10 W
Nolinsk	80	57.33 N	49.57 E
Nomad	164	6.18 S	142.14 E
Nomahegan Brook ≃	276	40.41 N	74.18 W
Nomans Land I	207	41.15 N	70.49 W
Nombre de Dios, Méx.	234	23.51 N	104.14 W
Nombre de Dios, Pan.	236	9.35 N	79.28 W
Nombre de Dios, Cordillera ⋏	236	15.35 N	86.55 W
Nome	180	64.30 N	165.24 W
Nomény	56	48.54 N	6.14 E
Nomexy	58	48.18 N	6.23 E
Nomgon, Mong.	102	45.26 N	105.08 E
Nomgon, Mong.	102	42.50 N	105.07 E
Nomgon uul ⋏	102	42.50 N	104.20 E
Nomingue, Petit lac ⊜	206	46.21 N	75.00 W
Nomini Bay c	208	38.09 N	76.43 W
Nominingue	206	46.24 N	75.02 W
Nominingue, Lac ⊜	206	46.26 N	74.59 W
Nomoneas II	175c	7.24 N	151.53 E
Nomozaki	92	32.35 N	129.45 E
Nomtsas	156	24.22 S	16.47 E
Nomura	96	33.22 N	132.38 E
Nona, Lake ⊜	220	28.24 N	81.15 W
Nonacho Lake ⊜	176	61.42 N	109.40 W
Nonancourt	50	48.46 N	1.12 E
Nonant-le-Pin	50	48.42 N	0.13 E
Nonantola	64	44.41 N	11.02 E
Nonburg	24	65.34 N	50.32 E
Nonceveux	56	50.28 N	5.44 E
Nondalton	180	60.00 N	154.49 W
Nondwa	154	6.26 S	35.20 E
Nondweni	158	28.11 S	30.49 E
None	62	44.56 N	7.32 E
Nonette ≃	50	49.12 N	2.24 E
None-yama ∧	96	33.29 N	134.10 E
Nong'an	89	44.25 N	125.10 E
Nong Bua Lamphu	110	17.11 N	102.25 E
Nong Han	110	17.21 N	103.07 E
Nong Hèt	110	19.29 N	103.59 E
Nong Khai	110	17.52 N	102.44 E
Nongoma	158	27.58 S	31.35 E
Nongpoh	120	25.54 N	91.53 E
Nongstoin	120	25.31 N	91.16 E
Nonnenhorn	58	47.34 N	9.36 E
Nonnevitz	54	54.39 N	13.17 E
Nonning	166	32.30 S	136.30 E
Nonnweiler	56	49.36 N	6.58 E
Nono	144	8.32 N	37.26 E
Nonoai	252	27.21 S	52.47 W
Nonoava	232	27.28 N	106.44 W
Nonoc Island I	116	9.51 N	125.37 E
Nono de Julho, Túnel ◆[5]	287b	23.34 S	46.39 W
Nonogasta	252	29.18 S	67.30 W
Nonoichi	94	36.32 N	136.37 E
Nonouti I[1]	14	0.40 S	174.21 E
Nonsan	98	36.12 N	127.05 E
Nonsuch Bay c	240c	17.03 N	61.42 W
Non Sung	110	15.11 N	102.16 E
Nonthaburi	110	13.50 N	100.29 E
Nonthaburi □[4]	269a	13.52 N	100.27 E
Nontron	32	45.32 N	0.40 E
Nonvianuk Lake ⊜	180	59.00 N	155.15 W
Noojee	169	37.55 S	146.00 E
Nookawarra	162	26.19 S	116.52 E
Nooksack	224	48.55 N	122.19 W
Nooksack ≃	224	48.46 N	122.35 W
Nooksack, Middle Fork ≃	224	48.50 N	122.08 W
Nooksack, North Fork ≃	224	48.50 N	122.11 W
Nooksack, South Fork ≃	224	48.50 N	122.11 W
Noonamah	164	12.38 S	131.04 E
Noonan	198	48.53 N	103.00 W
Noon Hill ∧[2]	283	42.09 N	71.19 W
Noonkanbah	162	18.30 S	124.50 E
Noorat	169	38.12 S	142.56 E
Noord-Beveland I	52	51.35 N	3.45 E
Noord-Brabant □[4]	52	51.30 N	5.00 E
Noord-Holland □[4]	52	52.40 N	4.50 E
Noordhollands Kanaal ≡	52	52.33 N	4.50 E
Noordhorn	52	53.16 N	6.24 E
Noordoewer	156	28.45 S	17.37 E
Noordoost Polder ◆[1]	52	52.42 N	5.45 E
Noordpunt ›	241s	12.23 N	69.10 W
Noord-Scharwoude	52	52.43 N	4.47 E
Noordwijk aan Zee	52	52.14 N	4.26 E
Noordwijk-Binnen	52	52.13 N	4.27 E
Noordwijkerhout	52	52.15 N	4.30 E
Noordwolde	52	52.54 N	6.09 E
Noormarkku	26	61.35 N	21.52 E
Noorvik	180	66.50 N	161.12 W
Noosaville	166	26.24 S	153.04 E
Nootka Island I	182	49.32 N	126.42 W
Nootka Sound ʮ	182	49.33 N	126.38 W
Nopaltepec	234	18.17 N	95.59 W
No Point, Point ›	276	41.09 N	73.08 W
Nóqui	152	5.51 S	13.25 E
Nora, Sve.	40	59.31 N	15.02 E
Nora, In., U.S.	218	39.55 N	86.08 W
Nora ≃	89	52.26 N	129.58 E
Nora ⊥	71	39.00 N	9.01 E
Nor Ačin	84	40.19 N	44.35 E
Norah Head ›	170	33.17 S	151.35 E
Nora Islands II	144	16.02 N	40.03 E
Norala	116	6.28 N	124.38 E
Noralee	182	53.59 N	126.26 W
Noranda	190	48.15 N	79.02 W
Noraskög ⋏	40	59.39 N	14.50 E
Nora Springs	190	43.08 N	93.00 W
Norberg	40	60.04 N	15.56 E
Norberto de la Riestra	252	35.16 S	59.46 W
Norborne	194	39.18 N	93.40 W
Norcan Lake ⊜	212	45.10 N	76.53 W
Norcatur	198	39.50 N	100.11 W
Norchia ⊥	66	42.20 N	11.57 E
Norcia	66	42.48 N	13.05 E
Norco	228	33.56 N	117.33 W
Norcott, Mount ∧	162	32.07 S	121.59 E
Norcross	192	33.56 N	84.12 W
Nord □[4], Cam.	146	9.00 N	13.30 E
Nord □[4], N. Cal.	175f	21.00 S	165.00 E
Nord □[5]	50	50.20 N	3.40 E
Nord, Canal du ≡	50	50.16 N	3.05 E
Nord, Cap → Nordkapp ›	24	71.11 N	25.48 E
Nord, Gare ◆[5]	261	48.53 N	2.21 E
Nord, Grand lac du ⊜	186	50.54 N	67.06 W
Nord, Petit lac du ⊜	186	50.50 N	67.10 W
Nord, Rivière du ≃	206	45.31 N	74.20 W
Nordamerika → North America ⊥[1]	16	45.00 N	100.00 W
Nordanholen	40	60.30 N	14.57 E
Nordausques	50	50.49 N	2.05 E
Nordaustlandet I	12	79.48 N	22.24 E
Nordbögge	263	51.37 N	7.44 E
Nordborg	41	55.03 N	9.45 E
Nordby	41	55.58 N	10.34 E
Nord Dakota → North Dakota □[3]	198	47.30 N	100.15 W
Norddeich	52	53.37 N	7.09 E
Nordegg	182	52.28 N	116.04 W
Nordegg ≃	182	52.53 N	115.18 W
Norden, Dtsch.	52	53.36 N	7.12 E
Norden, Eng., U.K.	262	53.38 N	2.13 W
Norden, Ca., U.S.	226	39.20 N	120.22 W
Nordendorf	56	48.36 N	10.50 E
Nordenham	52	53.29 N	8.28 E
Nordenšel'da, archipelag II	74	76.45 N	96.00 E
Nordenskiold ≃	180	62.05 N	136.18 W
Norderney	52	53.42 N	7.08 E
Norderney I	52	53.42 N	7.10 E
Norderstapel	41	54.21 N	9.14 E
Norderstedt	52	53.43 N	10.00 E
Nordfjord c[2]	26	61.54 N	5.12 E
Nordfjordeid	26	61.54 N	6.00 E
Nordfold	24	67.46 N	15.12 E
Nordfriesische Inseln → North Frisian Islands II	24	54.50 N	8.12 E
Nordfriesland ◆[1]	41	54.40 N	9.10 E
Nordhalben	54	50.22 N	11.30 E
Nordhausen	54	51.30 N	10.47 E
Nordheim, Dtsch.	56	49.07 N	9.08 E
Nordheim, Tx., U.S.	222	28.55 N	97.36 W
Nordheim von der Rhön	56	50.28 N	10.11 E
Nordhelle ∧[2]	263	51.09 N	7.46 E
Nordholz	52	53.47 N	8.36 E
Nordhorn	52	52.27 N	7.05 E
Nordic Park	278	41.57 N	88.02 W
Nordingrå	26	62.56 N	18.16 E
Nordirland → Northern Ireland □[8]	48	54.40 N	6.45 W
Nordiyya	132	32.19 N	34.54 E
Nordkanal ≡	263	51.10 N	6.42 E
Nordkapp ›	24	71.11 N	25.48 E
Nordkinnhalvøya ›[1]	24	70.55 N	27.45 E
Nordkirchen	52	51.44 N	7.31 E
Nord-Kivu □[4]	154	0.30 S	28.30 E
Nordkjosbotn	24	69.13 N	19.30 E
Nord-Korea → Korea, North □[1]	98	40.00 N	127.00 E
Nordland	224	48.03 N	122.41 W
Nordland □[6]	24	67.00 N	14.40 E
Nördliche Dwina → Severnaja Dvina ≃	24	64.32 N	40.30 E
Nördliches Eismeer → Arctic Ocean ▾[1]	16	85.00 N	170.00 E
Nördlingen	56	48.51 N	10.30 E
Nordmaling	26	63.34 N	19.30 E
Nordmark	40	59.50 N	14.06 E
Nordmarka ◆[1]	26	60.00 N	10.25 E
Nordostrundingen ›	16	81.36 N	12.09 W
Nord-Ostsee-Kanal ≡	30	53.53 N	9.08 E
Nord-Ouest □[4]	152	6.30 N	10.30 E
Nordpfälzer Bergland ⋏	56	49.40 N	7.40 E
Nordradde ≃	52	52.43 N	7.17 E
Nordreisa	24	69.46 N	21.03 E
Nordre Strømfjord c[2]	176	67.50 N	52.00 W
Nordrhein-Westfalen □[3]	30	51.30 N	7.30 E
Nordsee → North Sea ▾[2]	22	55.20 N	3.00 E
Nordstemmen	52	52.09 N	9.46 E
Nordstrand I	41	54.30 N	8.53 E
Nordstrandischmoor I	41	54.33 N	8.48 E
Nord-Trøndelag □[6]	24	64.25 N	12.00 E
Nordvik	74	74.02 N	111.32 E
Nordwalde	52	52.05 N	7.28 E
Nordwest-Kap → North West Cape ›	162	21.45 S	114.10 E
Nore	26	60.10 N	9.01 E
Nore ≃	48	52.25 N	6.58 W
Noremberg → Nürnberg	60	49.27 N	11.04 E
Norf	263	51.09 N	6.43 E
Norf ≃	263	51.11 N	6.44 E
Norfolk, Ct., U.S.	207	41.59 N	73.12 W
Norfolk, Ma., U.S.	283	42.07 N	71.19 W
Norfolk, Ne., U.S.	198	42.02 N	97.25 W
Norfolk, Va., U.S.	208	36.50 N	76.17 W
Norfolk □[6], Eng., U.K.	42	52.35 N	1.00 E
Norfolk □[6], Ma., U.S.	207	42.10 N	71.15 W
Norfolk Broads ◆[1]	42	52.40 N	1.30 E
Norfolk-Insel → Norfolk Island □[2]	174c	29.02 S	167.57 E
Norfolk International Airport ⊠	208	36.54 N	76.12 W
Norfolk Island □[2], Oc.	14	29.02 S	167.57 E
Norfolk Island □[2], Oc.	174c	29.02 S	167.57 E
Norfolk Island Aerodome ⊠	174c	29.03 S	167.56 E
Norfolk Naval Shipyard ■	208	36.49 N	76.18 W
Norfolk Naval Station ■	208	36.57 N	76.18 W
Norfolk Ridge ✧[3]	14	29.00 S	168.00 E
Norfork Lake ⊜[1]	194	36.25 N	92.10 W
Norg	52	53.04 N	6.27 E
Norge	208	37.22 N	76.46 W
Norge → Norway □[1]	24	62.00 N	10.00 E
Norham	44	55.43 N	2.10 W
Norheimsund	26	60.22 N	6.08 E
Noria de Ángeles	234	22.27 N	101.56 W
Norikura-dake ∧	94	36.06 N	137.33 E
Noril'sk	74	69.20 N	88.06 E
Noring, Gunong ∧	114	5.24 N	101.44 E
Norland, On., Can.	212	44.43 N	78.49 W
Norland, Fl., U.S.	220	25.57 N	80.12 W
Norlane	169	38.06 S	144.21 E
Norley	262	53.15 N	2.39 W
Norlina	192	36.26 N	78.11 W
Norma, It.	66	41.35 N	12.58 E
Norma, N.J., U.S.	208	39.29 N	75.05 W
Normal, Al., U.S.	194	34.47 N	86.34 W
Normal, Il., U.S.	216	40.30 N	88.59 W
Norman, Ar., U.S.	194	34.27 N	93.40 W
Norman, In., U.S.	218	38.57 N	86.16 W
Norman, Ok., U.S.	196	35.13 N	97.26 W
Norman ≃	166	17.28 S	140.49 E
Norman, Lake ⊜[1]	192	35.35 N	80.55 W
Normanby, Austl.	171a	27.28 S	153.01 E
Normanby, N.Z.	172	39.32 S	174.17 E
Normanby ≃	164	14.25 S	144.08 E
Normanby Island I	164	10.05 S	151.05 E
Norman Creek c	284b	39.18 N	76.25 W
Normandie □[9]	32	49.00 N	0.05 W
Normandie, Collines de ⋏[2]	32	48.40 N	0.30 W
Normandien	158	27.57 S	29.47 E
Normandy → Normandie □[9]	32	49.00 N	0.05 W
Normandy Heights	284b	39.17 N	76.48 W
Normandy Park	224	47.27 N	122.21 W
Normangee	222	31.02 N	96.07 W
Normanhurst	274a	33.43 S	151.06 E
Normanhurst, Mount ∧	162	25.04 S	122.32 E
Norman Island I	240m	18.20 N	64.37 W
Normannische Inseln → Channel Islands II	28	49.20 N	2.20 W
Norman Park	192	31.16 N	83.41 W
Normans Kill ≃	210	42.36 N	73.44 W
Normanton, Austl.	166	17.40 S	141.05 E
Normanton, Eng., U.K.	44	53.41 N	1.27 W
Normanville	168b	35.27 S	138.19 E
Norman Wells	180	65.17 N	126.51 W
Nor Marsh ≡≡	260	51.24 N	0.38 E
Nornalup	162	35.00 S	116.49 E
Norogachi	232	27.15 N	107.07 W
Noroton ≃	276	41.03 N	73.31 W
Noroton Point ›	276	41.03 N	73.26 W
Norovlin	88	48.40 N	112.00 E
Noroy-le-Bourg	58	47.37 N	6.18 E
Norphlet	194	33.18 N	92.39 W
Norquay	184	51.53 N	102.05 W
Ñorquinco	254	41.51 S	70.54 W

DEUTSCH

Name	Seite	Breite°′	Länge°′ E = Ost
Norra Barken ⊜	40	60.07 N	15.31 E
Norra Björkfjärden c	40	59.27 N	17.28 E
Norrahammar	26	57.42 N	14.06 E
Norra Hörken ⊜	40	60.04 N	14.53 E
Norra Kvarken (Merenkurkku) ʮ	26	63.36 N	20.43 E
Norra Kvills Nationalpark ♦	26	57.44 N	15.37 E
Norrälgen ⊜	40	59.50 N	14.34 E
Norra Rörum	41	56.01 N	13.30 E
Norra Storfjället ∧	24	65.52 N	15.18 E
Norra Yngern ⊜	40	59.09 N	17.22 E
Norrboda	40	60.28 N	18.25 E
Norrbotten □[9]	26	66.45 N	23.00 E
Norrbottens Län □[6]	24	66.00 N	20.00 E
Nørre Åby	41	55.27 N	9.54 E
Nørre Alslev	41	54.54 N	11.54 E
Nørre Broby	41	55.15 N	10.14 E
Nørre Nærå	41	55.34 N	10.17 E
Norrent-Fontes	50	50.35 N	2.24 E
Nørre Snede	41	55.58 N	9.25 E
Nørresundby	26	57.04 N	9.55 E
Nørre Vejrup	41	55.31 N	8.47 E
Norrfjärden	26	65.25 N	21.27 E
Norridge	216	41.57 N	87.49 W
Norridgewock	188	44.42 N	69.47 W
Norris	192	36.11 N	84.04 W
Norris, Lake ⊜	220	28.57 N	81.32 W
Norris Arm	186	49.05 N	55.15 W
Norris Bridge ◆[5]	208	37.37 N	76.26 W
Norris City	194	37.58 N	88.19 W
Norris Dam State Park ♦	192	36.14 N	84.07 W
Norrish Creek ≃	224	49.10 N	122.08 W
Norris Lake ⊜[1]	192	36.20 N	83.55 W
Norris Point	186	49.31 N	57.53 W
Norristown	208	40.07 N	75.20 W
Norrköping	40	58.36 N	16.11 E
Norroway Brook ≃	283	42.11 N	71.03 W
Norrskedika	40	60.17 N	18.17 E
Norrsundet	26	60.56 N	17.08 E
Norrtälje	40	59.46 N	18.42 E
Norrtäljeviken c	40	59.47 N	18.53 E
Norseman	162	32.12 S	121.46 E
Norsewood	172	40.04 S	176.13 E
Norsjå ⊜	26	59.18 N	9.20 E
Norsjö	26	64.55 N	19.29 E
Norsk	89	52.20 N	129.55 E
Norsminde	41	56.01 N	10.16 E
Norsup	175f	16.05 S	167.23 E
Norte, Cabo ›, Bra.	250	1.40 N	49.55 W
Norte, Cabo ›, Chile	174z	27.03 S	109.24 W
Norte, Cabo → Nordkapp ›, Nor.	24	71.11 N	25.48 E
Norte, Canal ʮ	288	34.37 S	58.15 W
Norte, Canal do ʮ	250	0.30 N	50.30 W
Norte, Cayo I	240m	18.20 N	65.15 W
Norte, Estación del ◆[5], Esp.	266a	40.25 N	3.43 W
Norte, Estación del ◆[5], Esp.	266d	41.24 N	2.02 E
Norte, Mar del → North Sea ▾[2]	22	55.20 N	3.00 E
Norte, Punta ›	254	42.04 S	63.45 W
Norte, Serra do ⋏[1]	248	11.20 S	59.00 W
Norte de Santander □[3]	238	9.15 N	73.00 W
Norte de Santander □[5]	246	8.00 N	73.00 W
Nortelândia	248	14.25 S	56.48 W
Nörten-Hardenberg	52	51.38 N	9.56 E
North, S.C., U.S.	192	33.36 N	81.06 W
North, Va., U.S.	208	37.26 N	76.24 W
North ≃, Nf., Can.	176	57.30 N	62.05 W
North ≃, On., Can.	212	44.44 N	79.39 W
North ≃, Al., U.S.	194	33.15 N	87.30 W
North ≃, Ia., U.S.	194	41.31 N	93.27 W
North ≃, Ma., U.S.	283	42.10 N	70.43 W
North ≃, Mo., U.S.	219	39.52 N	91.27 W
North ≃, Wa., U.S.	224	46.45 N	123.53 W
North, Cape ›	186	47.02 N	60.25 W
North Abington	207	42.07 N	70.57 W
North Adams, Ma., U.S.	207	42.42 N	73.06 W
North Adams, Mi., U.S.	216	41.58 N	84.32 W
North Albany	202	44.39 N	123.06 W
Northallerton	44	54.20 N	1.26 W
Northam, Austl.	168a	31.39 S	116.40 E
Northam, S. Afr.	156	25.03 S	27.11 E
Northam, Eng., U.K.	42	51.02 N	4.12 W
North America ⊥[1]	4	45.00 N	100.00 W
North America ⊥[1]	16	45.00 N	100.00 W
North American Basin ✧[1]	8	30.00 N	60.00 W
North Amherst	207	42.24 N	72.31 W
North Amityville	276	40.41 N	73.25 W
Northampton, Austl.	162	28.21 S	114.37 E
Northampton, Eng., U.K.	42	52.14 N	0.54 W
Northampton, Md., U.S.	284c	38.52 N	76.49 W
Northampton, Ma., U.S.	207	42.19 N	72.38 W
Northampton, N.Y., U.S.	207	40.54 N	72.40 W
Northampton, Pa., U.S.	208	40.41 N	75.29 W
Northampton □[6], N.C., U.S.	208	36.28 N	77.21 W
Northampton □[6], Pa., U.S.	210	40.45 N	75.18 W
Northampton □[6], Va., U.S.	208	37.20 N	75.50 W
Northamptonshire □[6]	42	52.20 N	0.50 W
North Andaman I	110	13.15 N	92.55 E
North Andover	207	42.41 N	71.08 W
North Andrews Gardens	220	26.12 N	80.07 W
North Anna ≃	192	37.48 N	77.25 W
North Anson	188	44.51 N	69.54 W
North Apollo	214	40.35 N	79.33 W
North Arlington	276	40.47 N	74.08 W
North Arm ≃[1]	224	49.12 N	123.10 W
North Asheboro	192	35.44 N	79.49 W
North Atlanta	192	33.51 N	84.20 W
North Attleboro	207	41.59 N	71.20 W
North Attleboro National Fish Hatchery ♦	283	42.00 N	71.17 W
North Auburn	274a	33.50 S	151.02 E
North Augusta	192	33.30 N	81.57 W
North Aulatsivik Island I	176	59.50 N	64.00 W
North Aurora	216	41.48 N	88.19 W
North Australian Basin ✧[1]	14	14.30 S	116.30 E
Northaw	260	51.42 N	0.09 W
North Babylon	276	40.42 N	73.19 W
North Balabac Strait ʮ	116	8.10 N	117.04 E
North Baltimore	216	41.10 N	83.40 W
North Balwyn	274b	37.48 S	145.05 E
North Bannister	168a	32.35 S	116.26 E
North Bārākpur	126	22.46 N	88.22 E
North Bass Island I	214	41.43 N	82.49 W
North Battleford	184	52.47 N	108.17 W
North Bay, On., Can.	190	46.19 N	79.28 W
North Bay, N.Y., U.S.	210	43.14 N	75.45 W
North Bay, Wi., U.S.	216	42.46 N	87.47 W
North Bay c, On., Can.	212	44.53 N	79.48 W
North Bay c, Wa., U.S.	224	46.59 N	124.04 W
North Bay Shore	276	40.45 N	73.16 W
North Bay Village	220	25.51 N	80.08 W
North Beach	168a	31.52 S	115.45 E
North Beach ◆[8]	282	37.48 N	122.25 W
North Beach Peninsula ›[1]	224	46.30 N	124.02 W

Symbols in the index entries represent the broad categories identified in the key at the right. Symbols with superior numbers (⋏[1]) identify subcategories (see complete key on page *I · 1).*

Symbole im Register stellen die rechts im Schlüssel erklärten Kategorien dar. Symbole mit hochgestellten Ziffern (⋏[1]) bezeichnen Unterabteilungen einer Kategorie (vgl. vollständiger Schlüssel auf Seite *I · 1).*

Los símbolos incluídos en el texto del índice representan las grandes categorías identificadas con la clave a la derecha. Los símbolos con numeros en su parte superior (⋏[1]) identifican las subcategorías (véase la clave completa en la página *I · 1).*

Les symboles de l'index représentent les catégories indiquées dans la légende à droite. Les symboles suivis d'un indice (⋏[1]) représentent des sous-catégories (voir légende complète à la page *I · 1).*

Os símbolos incluídos no texto do índice representam as grandes categorias identificadas com a chave à direita. Os símbolos com números em sua parte superior (⋏[1]) identificam as subcategorias (veja-se a chave completa à página *I · 1).*

	English	Deutsch	Español	Français	Português
∧	Mountain	Berg	Montaña	Montagne	Montanha
⋏	Mountains	Gebirge	Montañas	Montagnes	Montanhas
)(	Pass	Paß	Paso	Col	Passo
V	Valley, Canyon	Tal, Cañon	Valle, Cañón	Vallée, Canyon	Vale, Canhão
≚	Plain	Ebene	Llano	Plaine	Planície
›	Cape	Kap	Cabo	Cap	Cabo
I	Island	Insel	Isla	Île	Ilha
II	Islands	Inseln	Islas	Îles	Ilhas
⊥	Other Topographic Features	Andere Topographische Objekte	Otros Elementos Topográficos	Autres données topographiques	Outros acidentes topográficos

ESPAÑOL · FRANÇAIS · PORTUGUÊS

Nombre / Nom / Nome	Página / Page	Lat.°′	Long.°′ W = Oeste / W = Ouest
North Belle Vernon	214	40.08 N	79.52 W
North Bellmore	276	40.41 N	73.32 W
North Bend, B.C., Can.	182	49.53 N	121.27 W
North Bend, Ne., U.S.	198	41.27 N	96.46 W
North Bend, Oh., U.S.	218	39.09 N	84.44 W
North Bend, Or., U.S.	202	43.24 N	124.13 W
North Bend, Pa., U.S.	214	41.21 N	77.42 W
North Bend, Wa., U.S.	224	47.29 N	121.47 W
North Benfleet	260	51.35 N	0.32 E
North Bengal Plains ≚	124	26.20 N	88.30 E
North Bennington	210	42.55 N	73.14 W
North Bergen	276	40.47 N	74.02 W
North Berwick, Scot., U.K.	46	56.04 N	2.44 W
North Berwick, Me., U.S.	188	43.18 N	70.44 W
North Bethlehem	210	42.40 N	73.50 W
North Bihar Plains ≚	124	26.20 N	86.00 E
North Billerica	207	42.35 N	71.17 W
North Bloomfield	214	41.27 N	80.52 W
North Boggy Creek ≃	196	34.23 N	96.04 W
North Bonneville	224	45.38 N	121.58 W
Northborough	207	42.19 N	71.38 W
North Bosque ≃	196	31.40 N	97.24 W
North Boston	210	42.41 N	78.47 W
North Bourke	166	30.03 S	145.57 E
North Box Hill	274b	37.48 S	145.07 E
North Braddock	279b	40.23 N	79.50 W
North Branch, Mi., U.S.	190	43.13 N	83.11 W
North Branch, Mn., U.S.	190	45.30 N	92.58 W
North Branch, N.J., U.S.	210	40.36 N	74.41 W
North Branch Canal ≍	224	47.12 N	120.40 W
North Branford	207	41.19 N	72.46 W
North Breakers ✢[2]	174g	28.14 N	177.25 W
Northbridge, Austl.	274a	33.49 S	151.13 E
Northbridge, Ma., U.S.	207	42.09 N	71.39 W
North Bristol	214	41.24 N	80.52 W
Northbrook, On., Can.	212	44.44 N	77.10 W
Northbrook, Il., U.S.	216	42.07 N	87.49 W
Northbrook, Pa., U.S.	285	39.55 N	75.41 W
North Brookfield, Ma., U.S.	207	42.16 N	72.05 W
North Brookfield, N.Y., U.S.	210	42.51 N	75.24 W
North Brunswick	208	40.28 N	74.28 W
North Buganda □[5]	154	1.00 N	32.15 E
North Caicos I	238	21.56 N	71.59 W
North Caldwell	276	40.51 N	74.16 W
North Canadian ≃	196	35.17 N	95.31 W
North Canton, Ct., U.S.	207	41.53 N	72.53 W
North Canton, Ga., U.S.	192	34.14 N	84.29 W
North Canton, Oh., U.S.	214	40.52 N	81.24 W
North Cape	216	42.47 N	88.05 W
North Cape ≻, P.E., Can.	186	47.05 N	64.00 W
North Cape ≻, N.Z.	172	34.25 S	173.02 E
North Cape → Nordkapp ≻, Nor.	24	71.11 N	25.48 E
North Cape ≻, Pap. N. Gui.	164	2.32 S	150.49 E
North Cape ≻, Mi., U.S.	216	41.44 N	83.25 W
North Cape May	208	38.58 N	74.57 W
North Captiva Island I	220	26.35 N	82.13 W
North Caribou Lake ⊜	176	52.50 N	90.40 W
North Carolina □[3], U.S.	178	35.30 N	80.00 W
North Carolina □[3], U.S.	192	35.30 N	80.00 W
North Carver	207	41.55 N	70.48 W
North Cascades National Park ♠	224	48.30 N	121.00 W
North Castor ≃	212	45.16 N	75.24 W
North Catasauqua	208	40.40 N	75.29 W
North Chagrin Reservation ♠	279a	41.34 N	81.26 W
North Channel ʮ, On., Can.	190	46.02 N	82.50 W
North Channel ʮ, On., Can.	212	44.10 N	76.45 W
North Channel ʮ, U.K.	44	55.10 N	5.40 W
North Channel ʮ, N.Y., U.S.	276	40.36 N	73.53 W
North Channel ≃[1]	281	42.38 N	82.40 W
North Charleroi	214	40.09 N	79.54 W
North Charleston	192	32.51 N	79.58 W
North Chatham	210	42.29 N	73.38 W
North Chelmsford	207	42.38 N	71.23 W
North Chicago	216	42.19 N	87.50 W
North Chili	210	43.06 N	77.45 W
Northchurch	260	51.46 N	0.36 W
North City	224	47.45 N	122.18 W
North Cleveland	222	30.21 N	95.06 W
Northcliff ◄[8]	273d	26.09 S	27.58 E
Northcliffe	162	34.36 S	116.07 E
North Clymer	214	42.04 N	79.34 W
North Cohasset	283	42.15 N	70.50 W
North Cohocton	210	42.34 N	77.28 W
North College Hill	218	39.13 N	84.33 W
North Collins	210	42.35 N	78.56 W
North Commerce Lake ⊜	281	42.35 N	83.30 W
North Concho ≃	196	31.27 N	100.25 W
North Conway	188	44.03 N	71.07 W
North Cotabato □[4]	116	7.15 N	124.50 E
Northcote	274b	37.46 S	145.00 E
North Cray ◄[8]	260	51.26 N	0.08 E
North Creek	188	43.41 N	73.59 W
North Creek ≃	278	41.33 N	87.37 W
Northcrest	222	31.38 N	97.06 W
North Crossett	194	33.09 N	91.56 W
North Crosswicks	285	40.10 N	74.39 W
North Croton Creek ≃	196	33.24 N	100.00 W
North Dakota □[3], U.S.	178	47.30 N	100.15 W
North Dakota □[3], U.S.	198	47.30 N	100.15 W
North Dandalup	168a	32.31 S	115.58 E
North Dandalup ≃	168a	32.36 S	115.53 E
North Dartmouth	207	41.38 N	70.58 W
North Dighton	207	41.51 N	71.07 W
North Dorset Downs ⋏[1]	42	50.47 N	2.30 W
North Downs ⋏[1]	42	51.20 N	0.10 E
North Dum Dum	126	22.38 N	88.23 E
North Eagle Butte	198	45.02 N	101.15 W
North East, Md., U.S.	208	39.36 N	75.56 W
North East, Pa., U.S.	214	42.12 N	79.50 W
North-East □[5]	156	21.00 S	27.30 E
Northeast Cape	180	63.18 N	168.42 W
Northeast Cape ≻	180	63.17 N	168.45 W
Northeast Cape Fear ≃	192	34.11 N	77.57 W
Northeast Creek ≃	284b	39.18 N	76.29 W
North Eastern □[4]	154	1.00 N	40.15 E
Northeastern University ʊ[2]	283	42.20 N	71.05 W
North Eastham	207	41.51 N	69.59 W
Northeast Henrietta	210	43.04 N	77.36 W
Northeast Islands II	175c	7.36 N	151.57 E
North Easton	207	42.04 N	71.06 W
Northeast Pass ʮ	175c	7.30 N	151.59 E
North East Point ≻, Ba.	238	21.20 N	73.01 W
North East Point ≻, Ba.	238	22.43 N	73.50 W
North East Point ≻, Kiribati	174o	1.57 N	157.16 W
Northeast Point ≻, St. Vin.	241h	13.03 N	61.13 W
Northeast Providence Channel ʮ	238	25.40 N	77.09 W
North Edwards	228	35.01 N	117.44 W
North Egremont	207	42.11 N	73.26 W
Northeim	52	51.42 N	10.00 E
North Elkhorn Creek ≃	218	38.13 N	84.48 W
North Elm Creek ≃	222	30.53 N	97.00 W
North English	190	41.30 N	92.04 W
Northern □[4], Ghana	150	9.30 N	1.00 W
Northern □[4], Malaŵi	154	11.00 S	34.00 E
Northern □[4], S.L.	150	9.15 N	11.45 W
Northern □[4], S. Afr.	156	23.30 S	29.30 E
Northern □[4], Zam.	154	11.00 S	31.00 E
Northern □[5]	154	2.50 N	32.45 E
Northern Arm	186	49.10 N	55.23 W
Northern Cape □[4]	156	29.00 S	21.00 E
Northern Cheyenne Indian Reservation ◄[4]	202	45.31 N	106.45 W
Northern Circārs ⋏[2]	122	18.00 N	83.15 E
Northern Cook Islands II	14	10.00 S	161.00 W
Northern Division □[5]	175g	16.30 S	179.30 E
Northern Dvina → Severnaja Dvina ≃	24	64.32 N	40.30 E
Northern Indian Lake ⊜	176	57.20 N	97.20 W
Northern Ireland □[8]	48	54.40 N	6.45 W
Northern Light Lake ⊜	190	48.15 N	90.38 W
Northern Mariana Islands □[2]	14	16.00 N	149.00 E
Northern Samar □[4]	116	12.30 N	124.30 E
Northern Territory □[8]	160	20.00 S	134.00 E
North Esk ≃, Scot., U.K.	46	56.44 N	2.28 W
North Esk ≃, Scot., U.K.	46	55.54 N	3.04 W
North Essendon	274b	37.45 S	144.54 E
North Evans	210	42.42 N	78.56 W
Northey Island I	260	51.44 N	0.43 E
North Fabius ≃	194	39.54 N	91.30 W
North Fairfield	214	41.06 N	82.36 W
North Fair Oaks	282	37.28 N	122.12 W
North Falmouth	207	41.38 N	70.37 W
North Ferriby	44	53.43 N	0.30 W
Northfield, B.C., Can.	224	49.11 N	123.59 W
Northfield, Ct., U.S.	207	41.41 N	73.06 W
Northfield, Il., U.S.	278	42.05 N	87.46 W
Northfield, Ma., U.S.	207	42.41 N	72.27 W
Northfield, Mn., U.S.	190	44.27 N	93.09 W
Northfield, N.J., U.S.	208	39.22 N	74.33 W
Northfield, Oh., U.S.	214	41.20 N	81.32 W
Northfield, Vt., U.S.	188	44.09 N	72.39 W
Northfield Airport ⊠	279a	41.17 N	81.31 W
Northfield Center	279a	41.19 N	81.32 W
Northfield Park Race Track ♠	279a	41.21 N	81.31 W
Northfield Village	279a	41.21 N	81.31 W
Northfield Woods	278	42.05 N	87.52 W
North Fiji Basin ✢[1]	14	16.00 S	174.00 E
North Fitzroy	274b	37.47 S	144.59 E
Northfleet	42	51.27 N	0.21 E
North Flinders Range ⋏	166	31.00 S	139.00 E
North Fond du Lac	190	43.48 N	88.29 W
Northford	207	41.23 N	72.47 W
North Foreland ≻	42	51.23 N	1.27 E
North Fork	226	37.13 N	119.30 W
North Fork ≃	194	36.13 N	92.17 W
North Fork Lake ⊜[1]	226	38.56 N	121.00 W
North Fork Reservoir ⊜[1]	224	45.13 N	122.15 W
North Fork Village	218	39.21 N	83.02 W
North Fort Myers	220	26.40 N	81.52 W
North Freedom	190	43.27 N	89.52 W
North Frisian Islands II	24	54.50 N	8.12 E
Northgate	216	43.01 N	85.36 W
Northgate ◄[9]	282	38.00 N	122.33 W
North Georgetown	214	40.51 N	80.59 W
North Glanford	212	43.11 N	79.54 W
North Glen Ellyn	278	41.54 N	88.04 W
Northglenn	200	39.53 N	104.59 W
North Gower	212	45.08 N	75.43 W
North Grafton	207	42.14 N	71.42 W
North Granby	207	41.59 N	72.49 W
North Grand Island Bridge ◄[5]	284a	43.04 N	78.59 W
North Great River	276	40.44 N	73.10 W
North Greece	212	43.15 N	77.44 W
North Grosvenordale	207	41.59 N	71.53 W
North Grove	216	40.37 N	85.58 W
North Gulfport	194	30.24 N	89.06 W
North Hadley	207	42.23 N	72.36 W
North Haledon	276	40.57 N	74.11 W
North Hampton	218	39.59 N	83.56 W
North Hanover	283	42.08 N	70.52 W
North Harbor ⊂	269f	14.36 N	120.57 E
North Harbour ⊂	274a	33.49 S	151.17 E
North Haven	207	41.23 N	72.51 W
North Head ≻, Austl.	274a	33.49 S	151.18 E
North Head ≻, N.Z.	172	36.25 S	174.03 E
North Henderson	192	36.21 N	78.22 W
North Henik Lake ⊜	176	61.45 N	97.40 W
North Hero	188	44.49 N	73.17 W
North Highlands	226	38.41 N	121.22 W
North Hill	42	50.34 N	4.25 W
North Hills, De., U.S.	285	39.46 N	75.30 W
North Hills, Il., U.S.	278	42.18 N	88.01 W
North Hills, N.Y., U.S.	276	40.47 N	73.41 W
North Hinksey	42	51.45 N	1.16 W
North Hogan Creek ≃	218	39.03 N	84.54 W
North Hollywood ◄[8]	280	34.10 N	118.23 W
North Holmwood	260	51.13 N	0.20 W
North Honcut Creek ≃	226	39.19 N	121.36 W
North Hoosick	210	42.56 N	73.21 W
North Hornell	210	42.21 N	77.40 W
North Horr	154	3.19 N	37.04 E
North Houston	222	29.54 N	95.31 W
Northiam	42	50.59 N	0.36 E
North Industry	214	40.44 N	81.22 W
North Irwin	279b	40.20 N	79.43 W
North Island I, India	122	10.08 N	72.20 E
North Island I, Kenya	154	4.04 N	36.03 E
North Island I, N.Z.	172	39.00 S	176.00 E
North Island Naval Air Station ■	228	32.42 N	117.12 W
North Islet I	116	8.56 N	120.02 E
North Jackson	214	41.06 N	80.52 W
North Java	210	42.41 N	78.20 W
North Judson	216	41.12 N	86.46 W
North Kenai	180	60.44 N	151.19 W
North Kingstown	207	41.38 N	71.25 W
North Kingsville	214	41.54 N	80.42 W
North Knife Lake ⊜	176	58.05 N	97.05 W
North Knob ʌ	210	41.43 N	75.33 W
North Korea → Korea, North □[1]	98	40.00 N	127.00 E
North La Junta	198	37.59 N	103.31 W
North Lake	216	43.09 N	88.22 W
North Lake ⊜, N.Y., U.S.	276	41.09 N	73.41 W
North Lake ⊜, Tx., U.S.	222	32.57 N	96.58 W
North Lakhimpur	120	27.14 N	94.07 E
Northland ◄[9]	281	42.27 N	83.13 W
North Landing ≃	208	36.31 N	76.01 W
North Laramie ≃	198	42.08 N	104.56 W
North Las Vegas	204	36.11 N	115.07 W
North La Veta Pass)(	200	37.37 N	105.11 W
North Lawrence	214	40.51 N	81.38 W
Northleach	42	51.51 N	1.50 W
North Lewisburg	216	40.13 N	83.33 W
North Liberty	216	41.32 N	86.25 W
North Lima	214	40.56 N	80.39 W
North Lindenhurst	276	40.42 N	73.22 W
North Line Island I	276	40.38 N	73.29 W
Northline Terrace	222	29.55 N	95.25 W
North Little Rock	194	34.46 N	92.16 W
North Llano ≃	196	30.30 N	99.46 W
North Logan	202	41.46 N	111.48 W
North Loon Mountain ʌ	202	45.07 N	115.52 W
North Loup	198	41.29 N	98.46 W
North Loup ≃	198	41.17 N	98.23 W
North Luangwa National Park ♠	154	11.50 S	32.15 E
North Luconia Shoals ✢[2]	108	5.40 N	112.35 E
North Macmillan ≃	180	63.03 N	133.18 W
North Madison	214	41.48 N	81.03 W
North Magnetic Pole ◄	16	77.19 N	101.49 W
North Malosmadulu Atoll I[1]	122	5.35 N	72.55 E
North Mamm Peak ʌ	200	39.23 N	107.52 W
North Manchester	216	41.00 N	85.46 W
North Manitou Island I	190	45.06 N	86.01 W
North Mankato	190	44.10 N	94.02 W
North Manly	274a	33.46 S	151.16 E
North Maroota	170	33.29 S	150.56 E
North Marshfield	283	42.08 N	70.46 W
North Marysville	224	48.07 N	122.09 W
North Massapequa	276	40.42 N	73.27 W
Northmead, Austl.	274a	33.47 S	151.00 E
Northmead, S. Afr.	273d	26.10 S	28.20 E
North Merrick	276	40.41 N	73.33 W
North Miami	220	25.53 N	80.11 W
North Miami Beach	220	25.55 N	80.09 W
North Middleboro	207	41.56 N	70.58 W
North Milk ≃	202	49.08 N	112.23 W
North Mokelumne ≃	226	38.08 N	121.35 W
North Moose Lake ⊜	184	54.08 N	100.13 W
North Moreau Creek ≃	194	38.30 N	92.18 W
North Muskegon	216	43.15 N	86.16 W
North Myrtle Beach	192	33.49 N	78.40 W
North Nahanni ≃	180	62.05 N	124.30 W
North Naples	220	26.13 N	81.47 W
North Narrabeen	274a	33.42 S	151.18 E
North Nemah ≃	224	46.30 N	123.53 W
North New Hyde Park	276	40.44 N	73.41 W
North New River Canal ≍	220	26.05 N	80.12 W
North Newton	198	38.04 N	97.21 W
North Niles	216	41.52 N	86.15 W
North Norwich	210	42.37 N	75.31 W
North Oaks	222	30.22 N	97.41 W
North Ockendon ◄[8]	260	51.32 N	0.18 E
North Ogden	200	41.18 N	111.57 W
North Olmsted	214	41.24 N	81.55 W
Northolt Aerodrome ⊠	260	51.33 N	0.23 W
Northome	190	47.52 N	94.16 W
Northop	262	53.12 N	3.08 W
North Ore Creek ≃	281	42.43 N	83.47 W
North Orwell	210	41.55 N	76.19 W
North Ossetia → Severnaja Osetija □[3]	84	43.00 N	44.15 E
Northowram	262	53.44 N	1.50 W
North Oxford	207	42.09 N	71.52 W
North Palisade ʌ	204	37.06 N	118.31 W
North Palm Beach	220	26.49 N	80.04 W
North Para ≃	168b	34.36 S	138.45 E
North Park ◄[8]	278	41.59 N	87.43 W
North Park ♠	279b	40.36 N	80.00 W
North Park Lake ⊜	279b	40.36 N	80.00 W
North Parramatta	274a	33.48 S	151.00 E
North Patchogue	276	40.47 N	73.00 W
North Peak ʌ, Ak., U.S.	180	62.34 N	162.23 W
North Peak ʌ, Ca., U.S.	282	37.33 N	122.28 W
North Pease ≃	196	34.15 N	100.07 W
North Pelham, N.H., U.S.	283	42.46 N	71.21 W
North Pelham, N.Y., U.S.	276	40.55 N	73.48 W
North Pembroke	207	42.05 N	70.47 W
North Pender Island I	224	48.49 N	123.17 W
North Perry	214	41.47 N	81.07 W
North Petherton	42	51.06 N	3.01 W
North Philadelphia ◄[8]	285	39.58 N	75.09 W
North Philadelphia Airport ⊠	285	40.05 N	75.01 W
North Pine ≃	171a	27.17 S	153.01 E
North Pine Grove	214	41.24 N	79.13 W
North Piney Creek ≃	200	42.31 N	110.05 W
North Pitcher	210	42.37 N	75.49 W
North Plainfield	210	40.37 N	74.25 W
North Plains	224	45.35 N	122.59 W
North Plains ≚	200	34.40 N	108.15 W
North Platte	198	41.07 N	100.45 W
North Platte ≃	178	41.07 N	100.42 W
North Pleasureville	218	38.22 N	85.07 W
North Plympton	283	41.59 N	70.48 W
North Point, Zhg.	271d	22.17 N	114.12 E
Northpoint, Pa., U.S.	214	40.54 N	79.08 W
North Point ≻, Barb.	241g	13.20 N	59.36 W
North Point ≻, Md., U.S.	284b	39.12 N	76.27 W
North Point ≻, Mi., U.S.	190	45.02 N	83.16 W
North Pole	180	64.45 N	147.21 W
North Pole ◄	16	90.00 N	0.00
Northport, Al., U.S.	194	33.13 N	87.34 W
North Port, Fl., U.S.	220	27.03 N	82.15 W
Northport, Mi., U.S.	190	45.07 N	85.37 W
Northport, N.Y., U.S.	210	40.53 N	73.20 W
Northport, Wa., U.S.	202	48.54 N	117.46 W
North Portal	184	49.00 N	102.33 W
Northport Bay ⊂	276	40.55 N	73.23 W
Northport Harbor ⊂	276	40.53 N	73.22 W
North Powder	202	45.01 N	117.55 W
North Pownal	207	42.47 N	73.15 W
North Prairie	216	42.56 N	88.24 W
North Providence	207	41.50 N	71.25 W
North Puyallup	224	47.12 N	122.17 W
North Queensferry	46	56.01 N	3.25 W
North Quincy	219	39.58 N	91.24 W
North Raccoon ≃	198	41.50 N	94.08 W
North Raisin ≃	206	45.09 N	74.43 W
North Ram ≃	182	52.16 N	115.38 W
North Randall	279a	41.27 N	81.32 W
North Reading	207	42.34 N	71.04 W
North Reservoir ⊜[1]	283	42.28 N	71.07 W
North Rhine-Westphalia → Nordrhein-Westfalen □[3]	30	51.30 N	7.30 E
North Richland Hills	222	32.50 N	97.13 W
North Richmond	282	37.57 N	122.22 W
Northridge, Oh., U.S.	218	39.59 N	83.46 W
Northridge, Oh., U.S.	218	39.48 N	84.11 W
Northridge ◄[8]	280	34.14 N	118.33 W
Northridge Fashion Center ◄[9]	280	34.13 N	118.33 W
North Ridge Village	218	39.57 N	86.09 W
North Ridgeville	214	41.23 N	82.01 W
North Rim	200	36.12 N	112.03 W
North River ⊂	208	37.25 N	76.25 W
North Riverside	278	41.50 N	87.49 W
North Riverside Park Mall ◄[9]	278	41.51 N	87.49 W
North Robinson	214	40.48 N	82.51 W
North Rocks	274a	33.46 S	151.02 E
North Ronaldsay I	46	59.22 N	2.26 W
North Ronaldsay Firth ʮ	46	59.20 N	2.25 W
North Rose	210	43.11 N	76.53 W
North Royalton	214	41.18 N	81.43 W
North Rustico	186	46.27 N	63.19 W
North Ryde	274a	33.48 S	151.07 E
North Salem	214	40.09 N	81.33 W
North Salt Lake	200	40.50 N	111.54 W
North San Juan	226	39.22 N	121.06 W
North Santiam ≃	202	44.41 N	123.00 W
North Saskatchewan ≃	176	53.15 N	105.05 W
North Saugeen ≃	212	44.19 N	81.17 W
North Scituate, Ma., U.S.	207	42.13 N	70.47 W
North Scituate, R.I., U.S.	207	41.49 N	71.35 W
North Sea ⊤[2]	22	56.00 N	3.00 E
North Seaton Colliery	44	55.11 N	1.32 W
North Sentinel Island I	110	11.33 N	92.15 E
North Shields	44	55.01 N	1.27 W
Norths Highland ⋏[1]	9	66.40 S	126.00 E
North Shoal Lake ⊜	184	50.29 N	97.40 W
North Shore	216	42.16 N	88.23 W
Northshore ◄[9]	283	42.32 N	70.57 W
North Shore Channel ≍	278	42.05 N	87.41 W
North Shores	216	41.50 N	83.25 W
North Shoshone Peak ʌ	204	39.09 N	117.29 W
North Siberian Lowland → Severo-Sibirskaja nizmennost' ≚	74	73.00 N	100.00 E
Northside	174h	2.47 S	171.43 W
North Singa	126	23.16 N	89.30 E
North Sioux City	198	42.31 N	96.28 W
North Skunk ≃	190	41.15 N	92.02 W
North Solomons □[5]	175e	6.00 S	155.00 E
North Somercotes	44	53.28 N	0.08 E
North Sound ʮ, Antig.	240c	17.07 N	61.45 W
North Sound ʮ, Ire.	48	53.11 N	9.43 W
North Sound ʮ, Scot., U.K.	46	59.18 N	2.46 W
North Spicer Island I	176	68.30 N	78.55 W
North Spirit Lake ⊜	184	52.30 N	92.53 W
North Spot I	236	16.15 N	88.11 W
North Springfield, Pa., U.S.	214	41.59 N	80.26 W
North Springfield, Va., U.S.	284c	38.48 N	77.12 W
North Stamford Reservoir ⊜[1]	276	41.08 N	73.32 W
North Star, De., U.S.	285	39.46 N	75.43 W
North Star, Oh., U.S.	216	40.19 N	84.34 W
North Sterling Reservoir ⊜[1]	198	40.47 N	103.17 W
North Stradbroke Island I	171a	27.35 S	153.28 E
North Sudbury	283	42.24 N	71.24 W
North Sulphur ≃	196	33.23 N	95.18 W
North Sunday Creek ≃	202	46.27 N	105.54 W
North Sunderland	44	55.34 N	1.39 W
North Swansea	207	41.46 N	71.15 W
North Sydenham ≃	214	42.35 N	82.23 W
North Sydney, Austl.	274a	33.50 S	151.13 E
North Sydney, N.S., Can.	186	46.13 N	60.15 W
North Syracuse	210	43.08 N	76.07 W
North Tamborine	171a	27.56 S	153.11 E
North Taranaki Bight ⊂[3]	172	38.42 S	174.15 E
North Tarrytown	276	41.05 N	73.51 W
North Tawton	42	50.48 N	3.53 W
North Tea Lake ⊜	190	45.56 N	79.03 W
North Terre Haute	194	39.31 N	87.21 W
North Tewksbury	283	42.38 N	71.14 W
North Thames ≃	212	42.59 N	81.16 W
North Thompson ≃	182	50.41 N	120.21 W
North Thoresby	44	53.28 N	0.03 W
North Tidworth	42	51.16 N	1.40 W
North Toe ≃	192	36.00 N	82.16 W
North Tolsta	46	58.20 N	6.13 W
North Tonawanda	210	43.02 N	78.51 W
North Towanda	210	41.47 N	76.28 W
North Troy	206	44.59 N	72.24 W
North Truro	207	42.02 N	70.05 W
North Tule Draw V	196	34.30 N	101.36 W
North Tunica	194	34.42 N	90.23 W
North Turramurra	274a	33.43 S	151.09 E
North Twin Lake ⊜	186	49.16 N	55.56 W
North Tyne ≃	44	54.59 N	2.08 W
North Ubian Island I	116	6.09 N	120.27 E
North Uist I	46	57.36 N	7.18 W
Northumberland	210	40.53 N	76.47 W
Northumberland □[6], On., Can.	212	44.10 N	78.00 W
Northumberland □[6], Eng., U.K.	44	55.15 N	2.05 W
Northumberland □[6], Pa., U.S.	210	40.49 N	76.39 W
Northumberland □[6], Va., U.S.	208	37.50 N	76.25 W
Northumberland Isles II	166	21.40 S	150.00 E
Northumberland National Park ♠	44	55.15 N	2.20 W
Northumberland Strait ʮ	186	46.00 N	63.30 W
North Umpqua ≃	202	43.16 N	123.27 W
North Uxbridge	207	42.05 N	71.38 W
Northvale	276	41.00 N	73.56 W
North Valley Hills ⋏[2]	285	40.02 N	75.40 W
North Valley Stream	276	40.41 N	73.42 W
North Vancouver	224	49.19 N	123.04 W
North Vandergrift	279b	40.36 N	79.34 W
North Vernon	218	39.00 N	85.37 W
North Versailles	279b	40.22 N	79.48 W
North Vietnam → Vietnam □[1]	108	16.00 N	108.00 E
Northville, Mi., U.S.	216	42.25 N	83.29 W
Northville, N.Y., U.S.	210	43.13 N	74.10 W
Northville Downs ♠	281	42.26 N	83.29 W
Northvue	214	40.54 N	79.56 W
North Wabasca Lake ⊜	182	56.00 N	113.55 W
North Wales	208	40.12 N	75.16 W
Northwall	46	59.16 N	2.17 W
North Walsham	42	52.50 N	1.24 E
North Wantagh	276	40.41 N	73.30 W
North Warren	214	41.52 N	79.09 W
North Washington, Pa., U.S.	214	41.03 N	79.49 W
North Washington, Pa., U.S.	279b	40.32 N	79.36 W
North Watuppa Pond ⊜	207	41.42 N	71.06 W
Northway	180	62.58 N	141.56 W
North Weald Bassett	42	51.43 N	0.10 E
North Webster	216	41.19 N	85.41 W
North Weissport	210	40.50 N	75.41 W
North-West □[4]	156	26.30 S	25.00 E
Northwest ≃	208	36.31 N	76.05 W
North West Cape ≻, Austl.	162	21.45 S	114.10 E
Northwest Cape ≻, Ak., U.S.	180	63.46 N	171.45 W
Northwest Cape ≻, Fl., U.S.	220	25.13 N	81.11 W
North Westchester	207	41.34 N	72.24 W
North Western	210	43.20 N	75.22 W
North-Western □[4]	154	13.00 S	25.00 E
Northwestern University ʊ[2], Il., U.S.	278	42.04 N	87.40 W
Northwestern University (Chicago Campus) ʊ[2], Il., U.S.	278	41.54 N	87.37 W
Northwest Frontier □[4]	120	34.30 N	72.00 E
Northwest Gander ≃	186	48.50 N	55.00 W
Northwest Harbor ⊂	284b	39.16 N	76.35 W
Northwest Head ≻	116	10.08 N	118.45 E
Northwest Miramichi ≃	186	46.58 N	65.35 W
Northwest Pacific Basin ✢[1]	6	40.00 N	155.00 E
North West Point ≻	174o	2.02 N	157.29 W
Northwest Providence Channel ʮ	238	26.10 N	78.20 W
North West River	176	53.32 N	60.08 W
Northwest Territories □[4]	176	70.00 N	100.00 W
North Weymouth	283	42.15 N	70.57 W
Northwich	44	53.16 N	2.32 W
North Wichita ≃	196	33.43 N	99.29 W
North Wilbraham	207	42.09 N	72.25 W
North Wildwood	208	39.00 N	74.47 W
North Wilkesboro	192	36.09 N	81.08 W
North Willow Creek ≃	202	46.51 N	107.54 W
North Wilmington	283	42.34 N	71.09 W
North Windham, Ct., U.S.	207	41.44 N	72.09 W
North Windham, Me., U.S.	188	43.50 N	70.26 W
Northwold	42	52.33 N	0.35 E
Northwood, Eng., U.K.	42	50.44 N	1.19 W
Northwood, Ia., U.S.	190	43.26 N	93.13 W
Northwood, Mi., U.S.	216	42.19 N	85.38 W
Northwood, N.D., U.S.	198	47.44 N	97.33 W
Northwood, Oh., U.S.	214	41.36 N	83.28 W
Northwood ◄[8]	260	51.37 N	0.25 W
North Woodslee	281	42.13 N	82.43 W
Northwood Village	284c	39.02 N	77.01 W
North Yamhill ≃	224	45.13 N	123.08 W
North Yelta	168b	34.03 S	137.37 E
North York	212	43.46 N	79.25 W
North York Moors ⋏[2]	44	54.24 N	0.53 W
North York Moors National Park ♠	44	54.23 N	0.50 W
North Yorkshire □[6]	44	54.15 N	1.30 W
North Yuba ≃	226	39.22 N	121.08 W
North Zulch	222	30.55 N	96.07 W
Norton, N.B., Can.	186	45.38 N	65.42 W
Norton, Eng., U.K.	44	54.09 N	0.47 W
Norton, Eng., U.K.	262	53.20 N	2.40 W
Norton, Ks., U.S.	198	39.50 N	99.53 W
Norton, Ma., U.S.	207	41.58 N	71.11 W
Norton, Oh., U.S.	214	41.01 N	81.39 W
Norton, Vt., U.S.	206	45.00 N	71.47 W
Norton, Va., U.S.	192	36.56 N	82.37 W
Norton, Zimb.	154	17.53 S	30.42 E
Norton Air Force Base ■	228	34.06 N	117.14 W
Norton Basin ⊂	276	40.36 N	73.47 W
Norton Bay ⊂	180	64.45 N	161.15 W
Norton Creek ≃	281	42.34 N	83.34 W
Norton Fitzwarren	42	51.02 N	3.09 W
Norton Grove	207	42.00 N	71.12 W
Norton Heath	260	51.43 N	0.19 E
Norton Hill	210	42.25 N	74.04 W
Norton Pond ⊜	206	44.56 N	71.51 W
Norton Reservoir ⊜[1]	283	41.59 N	71.12 W
Norton Shores	216	43.10 N	86.15 W
Norton Sound ʮ	180	63.50 N	164.00 W
Nortonville, On., Can.	275b	43.43 N	79.44 W
Nortonville, Ks., U.S.	198	39.25 N	95.20 W
Nortorf, Dtsch.	30	54.10 N	9.50 E
Nortorf, Dtsch.	52	53.55 N	9.16 E
Nort-sur-Erdre	32	47.26 N	1.30 W
Noruega → Norway □[1]	24	62.00 N	10.00 E
Noruega, Mar de → Norwegian Sea ⊤[2]	10	70.00 N	2.00 E
Norumbega Reservoir ⊜[1]	283	42.20 N	71.18 W
Nørup	41	55.43 N	9.19 E
Norval	212	43.39 N	79.51 W
Norvalspont	158	30.38 S	25.27 E
Norvège → Norway □[1]	24	62.00 N	10.00 E
Norvegia, Cape ≻	9	71.25 S	12.18 W
Norvell	216	42.10 N	84.11 W
Norvelt	214	40.12 N	79.32 W
Nörvenich	56	50.49 N	6.39 E
Norvin Green State Forest ♠	276	41.03 N	74.20 W
Norwalk, Ca., U.S.	228	33.54 N	118.04 W
Norwalk, Ct., U.S.	207	41.07 N	73.24 W
Norwalk, Ia., U.S.	190	41.28 N	93.40 W
Norwalk, Oh., U.S.	214	41.14 N	82.36 W
Norwalk ≃	207	41.06 N	73.25 W
Norwalk Harbor ⊂	276	41.06 N	73.24 W
Norwalk Islands II	276	41.03 N	73.23 W
Norway, In., U.S.	216	40.47 N	86.46 W
Norway, Ia., U.S.	190	41.54 N	91.55 W
Norway, Me., U.S.	188	44.12 N	70.32 W
Norway, Mi., U.S.	190	45.47 N	87.54 W
Norway (Norge) □[1], Europe	22	62.00 N	10.00 E
Norway (Norge) □[1], Europe	24	62.00 N	10.00 E
Norway Bay ⊂	176	71.08 N	104.35 W
Norway House	184	53.59 N	97.50 W
Norway Lake ⊜	212	45.20 N	76.43 W
Norwegen → Norway □[1]	24	62.00 N	10.00 E
Norwegian Basin ✢[1]	10	68.00 N	2.00 W
Norwegian Sea ⊤[2]	10	70.00 N	2.00 E
Norwegian Trench ✢[1]	10	59.00 N	4.30 E
Norwell	283	42.09 N	70.47 W
Norwich, On., Can.	212	42.59 N	80.36 W
Norwich, Eng., U.K.	42	52.38 N	1.18 E
Norwich, Ct., U.S.	207	41.32 N	72.05 W
Norwich, Ks., U.S.	198	37.27 N	97.50 W
Norwich, N.Y., U.S.	210	42.31 N	75.31 W
Norwich Airport ⊠	42	52.41 N	1.15 E
Norwin Heights	279b	40.20 N	79.44 W
Norwood, On., Can.	212	44.23 N	77.59 W
Norwood, Co., U.S.	200	38.07 N	108.17 W
Norwood, Ma., U.S.	207	42.11 N	71.12 W
Norwood, Mn., U.S.	190	44.46 N	93.55 W
Norwood, N.J., U.S.	276	40.59 N	73.57 W
Norwood, N.Y., U.S.	188	44.45 N	74.59 W
Norwood, N.C., U.S.	192	35.13 N	80.07 W
Norwood, Oh., U.S.	218	39.10 N	84.27 W
Norwood, Pa., U.S.	285	39.53 N	75.17 W
Norwood ◄[8]	273d	26.10 S	28.04 E
Norwood Memorial Airport ⊠	283	42.11 N	71.10 W
Norwood Park ◄[8]	278	41.59 N	87.48 W
Norwood Pond ⊜	283	42.35 N	70.52 W
Norwoodville	190	41.39 N	93.33 W
Noryang	98	34.56 N	127.52 E
Nosaka	94	35.39 N	140.34 E
Nosappu-misaki ≻	92a	43.23 N	145.49 E
Nosate	266b	45.33 N	8.43 E
Nosbonsing, Lake ⊜	190	46.12 N	79.13 W
Nose	96	34.58 N	135.24 E
Nose ◄[8]	270	34.49 N	135.09 E
Nose Creek ≃	182	54.52 N	119.38 W
Noshiro	92	40.12 N	140.02 E
Nosivka	78	50.55 N	31.35 E
Noska ≃	86	58.53 N	68.40 E
Nosop (Nossob) ≃	156	26.55 S	20.37 E
Nosova	86	59.30 N	63.13 E
Nosovaja, Ross.	24	68.15 N	54.35 E
Nosovaja, Ross.	80	57.15 N	45.35 E
Nosovo, Ross.	76	57.07 N	27.50 E
Nosovo, Ross.	83	47.16 N	38.40 E
Nosovščina	24	62.56 N	37.03 E
Noṣratābād	128	29.54 N	59.59 E
Noss, Isle of I	46a	60.09 N	1.01 W
Nossa Senhora da Aparecida	256	22.02 S	42.48 W
Nossa Senhora das Dores	250	10.29 S	37.13 W
Nossa Senhora do Amparo	256	22.22 S	44.05 W
Nossa Senhora do Livramento	248	15.48 S	56.22 W
Nossa Senhora do Ó ◄[8]	287b	23.30 S	46.41 W
Nossebro	26	58.11 N	12.43 E
Nossen	54	51.03 N	13.17 E
Nossentiner Heide ◄[3]	54	53.35 N	12.25 E
Noss Head ≻	46	58.28 N	3.04 W
Nossob	156	22.18 S	17.10 E
Nossob (Nosop) ≃	156	26.55 S	20.37 E
Nossombougou	150	13.06 N	7.56 W
Nošul'	24	60.09 N	49.28 E
Nosy Varika	157b	20.35 S	48.32 E
Notasulga	194	32.33 N	85.40 W
Notch Cliff	284b	39.27 N	76.31 W
Notch Hill	182	50.52 N	119.26 W
Notch Peak ʌ	200	39.08 N	113.24 W
Noteć ≃	30	52.44 N	15.26 E
Notigi Lake ⊜	184	55.57 N	99.18 W
Notikewin ≃	176	57.15 N	117.05 W
Nótion Aiyaíon □[4]	38	37.00 N	25.30 E
Noto, It.	70	36.53 N	15.04 E
Noto, Nihon	92	37.18 N	137.09 E
Noto, Golfo di ⊂	70	36.50 N	15.12 E
Noto, Val di ◄[1]	70	37.05 N	14.35 E
Noto Antica ⊥	70	36.56 N	15.02 E
Notodden	26	59.34 N	9.17 E
Notogawa	94	35.10 N	136.10 E
Noto-hantō ≻[1]	92	37.20 N	137.00 E
Noto-hantō-kokutei-kōen ♠	94	37.10 N	136.50 E
Noto-jima	94	37.08 N	137.00 E
Noto-jima I	94	37.07 N	137.00 E
Nōtori-dake ʌ	94	35.37 N	138.15 E
Notoro-ko ⊜	92a	44.05 N	144.10 E
Notozero, ozero ⊜	24	66.28 N	32.05 E
Notre-Dame	186	46.19 N	64.43 W
Notre-Dame ʊ[1]	261	48.51 N	2.21 E
Notre-Dame, Bois ♠	261	48.45 N	2.35 E
Notre-Dame, Monts ⋏	186	48.10 N	68.00 W
Notre-Dame, Ruisseau ≃	275a	45.41 N	73.26 W
Notre Dame Bay ⊂	186	49.45 N	55.15 W
Notre-Dame-de-Bellecombe	62	45.48 N	6.31 E
Notre-Dame-de-Lorette ʊ[1]	50	50.25 N	2.42 E
Notre-Dame-de-Lourdes	184	49.32 N	98.33 W
Notre-Dame-de-Pierreville	206	46.06 N	72.53 W
Notre-Dame-des-Victoires ◄[8]	275a	45.35 N	73.34 W
Notre-Dame-du-Haut ʊ[1]	58	47.43 N	6.37 E
Notre-Dame-du-Laus	188	46.05 N	75.37 W
Notre-Dame-du-Nord	190	47.36 N	79.30 W
Notrees	196	31.55 N	102.45 W
Notreure ≃	50	47.41 N	2.36 E
Notsu	96	33.02 N	131.42 E
Notsuharu	96	33.09 N	131.32 E
Nottawa	216	41.55 N	85.27 W
Nottawa Creek ≃	216	42.01 N	85.24 W
Nottawasaga ≃	212	44.32 N	80.01 W
Nottawasaga Bay ⊂	212	44.35 N	80.15 W
Nottaway ≃	176	51.22 N	79.55 W
Nottingham, Eng., U.K.	42	52.58 N	1.10 W
Nottingham, Pa., U.S.	208	39.45 N	76.01 W
Nottingham, Pa., U.S.	285	40.07 N	74.58 W
Nottingham Island I	176	63.20 N	77.55 W
Nottingham Park	278	41.46 N	87.48 W
Nottingham Road	158	29.22 S	30.00 E
Nottinghamshire □[6]	44	53.00 N	1.00 W
Notting Hill	274b	37.54 S	145.08 E
Nottleben	54	50.58 N	10.50 E
Nottoway	192	37.08 N	78.05 W
Nottoway ≃	192	36.33 N	76.55 W
Nottuln	52	51.55 N	7.22 E
Notukeu Creek ≃	184	49.55 N	106.30 W
Nouâdhibou	148	20.54 N	17.04 W
Nouâdhibou, Râs ≻	148	20.46 N	17.03 W
Nouakchott	150	18.06 N	15.57 W
Nouâmghâr	150	19.22 N	16.31 W
Nouan-le-Fuzelier	50	47.32 N	2.02 E
Nouans-les-Fontaines	50	47.08 N	1.18 E
Nouméa	175f	22.16 S	166.27 E
Noun ≃	152	4.55 N	11.06 E
Nouna	150	12.44 N	3.52 W
Nounsley	260	51.46 N	0.36 E
Noupoort	158	31.10 S	24.57 E
Nous	158	28.44 S	19.52 E
Nouveau Brunswick → New Brunswick □[4]	186	46.30 N	66.15 W
Nouveau Mexique → New Mexico □[3]	178	34.30 N	106.00 W
Nouveau-Québec, Cratère du ≗[6]	176	61.17 N	73.40 W
Nouvelle	186	48.08 N	66.19 W
Nouvelle ≃	186	48.07 N	66.18 W
Nouvelle-Calédonie → New Caledonia □[2]	175f	21.30 S	165.30 E
Nouvelle-Calédonie (New Caledonia) I	175f	21.30 S	165.30 E
Nouvelle Écosse → Nova Scotia □[4]	186	45.00 N	63.00 W
Nouvelle-France, Cap de ≻	176	62.27 N	73.42 W
Nouvelle Galles du Sud → New South Wales □[3]	166	33.00 S	146.00 E
Nouvelle-Orléans → New Orleans	194	29.58 N	90.07 W
Nouvelles-Hébrides → Vanuatu □[1]	175f	16.00 S	167.00 E
Nouvelle Zélande → New Zealand □[1]	172	41.00 S	174.00 E
Nouvelle Zemble → Novaja Zeml'a II	72	74.00 N	57.00 E
Nouvion-en-Ponthieu	50	50.12 N	1.47 E
Nouvion-sur-Meuse	56	49.42 N	4.48 E
Nouzonville	56	49.49 N	4.45 E
Nova, Magy.	61	46.41 N	16.41 E
Nova, Oh., U.S.	214	41.02 N	82.18 W
Nova América	255	15.01 S	49.56 W
Nova Andradina	255	22.10 S	53.15 W
Nova Astrakhan'	83	49.07 N	38.36 E
Novabad, Taj.	85	39.01 N	70.09 E
Novabad, Taj.	85	38.37 N	68.45 E
Nová Baňa	30	48.26 N	18.39 E
Nova Bila	78	49.46 N	39.11 E
Nova Borova	78	50.42 N	28.39 E
Nová Bystřice	61	49.01 N	15.06 E
Nova Cachoeirinha ◄[8]	287b	23.28 S	46.40 W
Nova Caipemba	152	7.26 S	14.38 E
Novacella ʊ[1]	64	46.44 N	11.39 E
Nova Era	255	19.45 S	43.03 W
Nova Esperança	255	23.08 S	52.13 W
Novafeltria	66	43.53 N	12.17 E
Nova Friburgo	256	22.16 S	42.32 W

Symbol	English	Deutsch	Español	Français	Português
≃	River	Fluß	Río	Rivière	Rio
≍	Canal	Kanal	Canal	Canal	Canal
ʟ	Waterfall, Rapids	Wasserfall, Stromschnellen	Cascada, Rápidos	Chute d'eau, Rapides	Cascata, Rápidos
ʮ	Strait	Meeresstraße	Estrecho	Détroit	Estreito
⊂	Bay, Gulf	Bucht, Golf	Bahía, Golfo	Baie, Golfe	Baía, Golfo
⊜	Lake, Lakes	See, Seen	Lago, Lagos	Lac, Lacs	Lago, Lagos
≡	Swamp	Sumpf	Pantano	Marais	Pântano
⊓	Ice Features, Glacier	Eis- und Gletscherformen	Accidentes Glaciales	Formes glaciaires	Acidentes glaciares
⊤	Other Hydrographic Features	Andere Hydrographische Objekte	Otros Elementos Hidrográficos	Autres données hydrographiques	Outros acidentes hidrográficos
✢	Submarine Features	Untermeerische Objekte	Accidentes Submarinos	Formes de relief sous-marin	Acidentes submarinos
□	Political Unit	Politische Einheit	Unidad Politica	Entité politique	Unidade política
ʊ	Cultural Institution	Kulturelle Institution	Institución Cultural	Institution culturelle	Instituição cultural
⊥	Historical Site	Historische Stätte	Sitio Histórico	Site historique	Sitio histórico
♠	Recreational Site	Erholungs- und Ferienort	Sitio de Recreo	Centre de loisirs	Area de Lazer
⊠	Airport	Flughafen	Aeropuerto	Aéroport	Aeroporto
■	Military Installation	Militäranlage	Instalación Militar	Installation militaire	Instalação militar
◄	Miscellaneous	Verschiedenes	Misceláneo	Divers	Diversos

ENGLISH / DEUTSCH

Name / Name	Page / Seite	Lat.°′ / Breite°′	Long.°′ / Länge°′ E = Ost
Nova Goa → Panaji	122	15.29 N	73.50 E
Nova Gorica	64	45.57 N	13.39 E
Nova Gradiška	36	45.16 N	17.23 E
Nova Granada	255	20.29 S	49.19 W
Nova Iguaçu	256	22.45 S	43.27 W
Nova Iguaçu □[7]	287a	22.45 S	43.29 W
Nova Ivanivka	78	45.55 N	29.05 E
Novaja, Ross.	82	55.13 N	38.54 E
Novaja, Ross.	265b	55.48 N	38.03 E
Novaja ◆[8]	265a	60.02 N	30.28 E
Novaja Binaradka	80	53.48 N	49.56 E
Novaja Čigla	78	51.13 N	40.28 E
Novaja Derevn'a, Ross.	82	54.01 N	38.53 E
Novaja Derevn'a, Ross.	88	57.15 N	103.08 E
Novaja Kalitva	78	50.06 N	40.01 E
Novaja Kazanka	80	48.57 N	49.36 E
Novaja Kazmaska	80	56.49 N	53.31 E
Novaja Kriuša	78	50.16 N	41.16 E
Novaja Ladoga	76	60.05 N	32.16 E
Novaja L'al'a	86	59.03 N	60.36 E
Novaja Maluksa	76	59.39 N	31.21 E
Novaja Malykla	80	54.13 N	49.57 E
Novaja Mojgora	82	54.27 N	38.32 E
Novaja Porubežka	80	51.45 N	49.40 E
Novaja Ropša	265a	59.45 N	29.53 E
Novaja Sibir', ostrov I	74	75.00 N	149.00 E
Novaja Slobodka	82	54.56 N	36.47 E
Novaja Šul'ba	86	50.33 N	81.20 E
Novaja Uda	88	54.07 N	103.33 E
Novaja Usman'	78	51.37 N	39.24 E
Novaja Zeml'a II	72	74.00 N	57.00 E
Nova Kakhovka	78	46.45 N	33.23 E
Nováky	30	48.43 N	18.34 E
Nova Lamego	150	12.19 N	14.11 W
Novale (Rauth)	64	46.24 N	11.30 E
Novalesa	62	45.11 N	7.01 E
Novaliches Reservoir ⊜[1]	269f	14.43 N	121.05 E
Nova Lima	255	19.59 S	43.51 W
Nova Lisboa → Huambo	152	12.44 S	15.47 E
Novalukoml'	76	54.40 N	29.08 E
Nova Lusitânia	156	19.54 S	34.35 E
Nova Mambone	156	20.59 S	35.01 E
Nova Mayachka	78	46.36 N	33.14 E
Nova Milanese	266b	45.35 N	9.12 E
Nova Nabúri	154	16.46 S	38.57 E
Nova Odesa	78	47.19 N	31.47 E
Nova Odessa	256	23.09 S	46.51 W
Nova Olinda	250	7.06 S	39.40 W
Nova Olinda do Norte	246	3.45 S	59.03 W
Nová Paka	30	50.29 N	15.31 E
Nova Ponente (Deutschnofen)	64	46.25 N	11.25 E
Nova Ponte	255	19.08 S	47.41 W
Nova Praha	78	48.33 N	32.54 E
Nova Prata	252	28.47 S	51.36 W
Novar	212	45.27 N	79.15 W
Novara	62	45.28 N	8.38 E
Novara □[4]	62	45.35 N	8.35 E
Novara di Sicilia	70	38.01 N	15.08 E
Nová Role	54	50.15 N	12.47 E
Nova Roma	255	13.51 S	46.57 W
Nova Russas	250	4.42 S	40.34 W
Nova Scotia □[4], Can.	176	45.00 N	63.00 W
Nova Scotia □[4], Can.	186	45.00 N	63.00 W
Nova Siri	68	40.09 N	16.32 E
Nova Sloboda	78	51.23 N	34.08 E
Nova Sofala	156	20.09 S	34.42 E
Nova Soure	250	11.14 S	38.29 W
Novate Mezzola	58	46.15 N	9.27 E
Novate Milanese	266b	45.32 N	9.08 E
Nova Timboteua	250	1.12 S	47.24 W
Novato	226	38.06 N	122.34 W
Novato Creek ≃	282	38.06 N	122.29 W
Nova Ushytsya	78	48.49 N	27.16 E
Nova Vandúzi	156	18.57 S	33.16 E
Nova Varoš	38	43.28 N	19.48 E
Nova Venécia	255	18.43 S	40.24 W
Nova Viçosa	255	17.53 S	39.22 W
Nova Vida	248	10.11 S	62.47 W
Nova Vida, Cachoeira ⌞	248	9.25 S	63.36 W
Nova Vodolaha	78	49.43 N	35.52 E
Novayanysol'	83	47.17 N	37.16 E
Nova Zagora	38	42.29 N	26.01 E
Nova Zburivka	78	46.28 N	32.24 E
Nove	64	45.43 N	11.40 E
Nové Hrady	61	48.47 N	14.37 E
Novelda	34	38.23 N	0.46 W
Novellara	64	44.51 N	10.44 E
Novelty	219	40.00 N	92.12 W
Nové Město	30	50.21 N	16.09 E
Nové Město nad Váhom	30	48.46 N	17.49 E
Nové Město na Moravě	30	49.34 N	16.04 E
Nové Mlýny, údolní nádrž ⊜[1]	61	48.54 N	16.34 E
Noventa di Piave	64	45.39 N	12.31 E
Noventa Padovana	64	45.24 N	11.58 E
Noventa Vicentina	64	45.17 N	11.32 E
Noves	62	43.52 N	4.54 E
Nové Sedlo	54	50.10 N	12.42 E
Nové Strašecí	54	50.07 N	13.53 E
Nové Údolí	60	48.48 N	13.48 E
Nové Zámky	30	47.59 N	18.11 E
Novgorod	76	58.31 N	31.17 E
Novgorod Oblast' □[4]	76	58.15 N	33.00 E
Novhorodka	78	48.21 N	32.39 E
Novhorod-Sivers'kyy	78	51.59 N	33.16 E
Novhorods'ke	83	48.20 N	37.50 E
Novi	216	42.28 N	83.28 W
Novi Basy	78	50.53 N	34.51 E
Novi Bečej	38	45.36 N	20.08 E
Novi Beograd	38	44.49 N	20.27 E
Novi Bilokorovychi	78	51.07 N	28.02 E
Novice	196	31.59 N	99.37 W
Novičicha	86	52.13 N	81.24 E
Novi di Modena	64	44.54 N	10.54 E
Novigrad, Hrv.	36	45.19 N	13.34 E
Novigrad, Hrv.	36	44.11 N	15.33 E
Novikovo, Ross.	86	58.15 N	80.39 E
Novikovo, Ross.	89	46.23 N	143.20 E
Novi Ligure	62	44.46 N	8.47 E
Noville	56	50.40 N	5.23 E
Novi Lyon Drain ≋	281	42.30 N	83.38 W
Novinger	194	40.13 N	92.42 W
Novinka	76	59.49 N	33.20 E
Novion-Porcien	50	49.36 N	4.25 E
Novi Pazar, Blg.	38	43.21 N	27.12 E
Novi Pazar, Jugo.	38	43.08 N	20.31 E
Novi Sad	38	45.15 N	19.50 E
Novi Sanzhary	78	49.21 N	34.19 E
Novi Vinodolski	36	45.08 N	14.48 E
Novki	80	56.22 N	41.06 E
Novl'anka	80	55.48 N	41.44 E
Novlenskoje	76	59.37 N	39.20 E
Novo ≃, Bra.	248	4.55 S	70.33 W
Novo ≃, Bra.	250	4.30 S	53.50 W
Novo ≃, Bra.	250	6.22 S	55.42 W
Novo ≃, Bra.	256	21.23 S	42.44 W
Novo, Lago ⊜	250	1.30 N	50.40 W
Nôvo Acôrdo	255	13.10 S	46.48 W
Novoaleksandrovka, Kaz.	86	51.47 N	68.49 E
Novoaleksandrovka, Ross.	80	51.56 N	52.26 E
Novoaleksandrovo	265b	55.59 N	37.33 E
Novoaleksandrovsk	80	45.29 N	41.16 E
Novoaleksejevka, Kaz.	86	52.56 N	64.41 E
Novoaleksejevka, Kaz.	86	52.47 N	74.54 E
Novoaleksejevka, Kaz.	86	50.08 N	55.39 E
Novoaltajsk	86	53.24 N	83.58 E
Novoamvrosiyivs'ke	83	47.49 N	38.29 E
Novoanninskij	80	50.32 N	42.41 E
Novoarchangel'skoje	265b	55.55 N	37.33 E
Novo Aripuanã	246	5.08 S	60.22 W
Novoarkhanhel's'k	78	48.39 N	30.48 E
Novoasbest	86	57.44 N	60.45 E
Novoaydar	83	48.57 N	39.00 E
Novoazovs'k	83	47.08 N	38.05 E
Novobatajsk	83	46.54 N	39.47 E
Novobelaja	78	49.49 N	39.18 E
Novobessergenovka	83	47.11 N	38.51 E
Novobogatinskoje	80	47.22 N	51.11 E
Novobogordskoje	80	53.11 N	53.56 E
Novobohdanivka	78	47.06 N	35.29 E
Novoborove	83	49.15 N	38.33 E
Novo Brasil	255	16.11 S	50.38 W
Novobratcevskij	82	55.51 N	37.23 E
Novoburejskij	89	49.49 N	129.54 E
Novočeboksarsk	80	56.08 N	47.30 E
Novo Čeremšansk	80	54.21 N	50.10 E
Novočerkassk	83	47.25 N	40.06 E
Novočernorečenskij	86	56.16 N	91.06 E
Novocharitonovo	82	55.35 N	38.30 E
Novocherkassk → Novočerkassk	83	47.25 N	40.06 E
Novochop'orsk	80	51.07 N	41.37 E
Novochop'orskij	80	51.06 N	41.33 E
Novochovrino ◆[8]	265b	55.52 N	37.30 E
Novociml'anskaja	80	47.59 N	42.17 E
Novo Cruzeiro	255	17.29 S	41.53 W
Novodanylivka	78	46.38 N	35.00 E
Novoderev'ankov-Skaja	78	46.19 N	38.45 E
Novodevičje	80	53.37 N	48.52 E
Novodolinka	86	51.12 N	72.33 E
Novodolinskij	86	49.44 N	72.45 E
Novodoroninskoje	88	51.08 N	112.08 E
Novodruzhes'k	83	48.58 N	38.21 E
Novodubovoje	76	52.19 N	39.13 E
Novodugino	76	55.38 N	34.18 E
Novodvinsk	24	64.26 N	40.47 E
Novodžerelijevskaja	78	45.46 N	38.41 E
Novoekonomichne	83	48.18 N	37.15 E
Novofetinino	82	56.14 N	39.17 E
Novogaritovo	80	52.47 N	40.07 E
Novogirejevo ◆[8]	265b	55.45 N	37.49 E
Novogorbovo	82	55.43 N	36.29 E
Novogornyj	86	55.37 N	60.47 E
Novogrigorjevskaja	80	49.26 N	43.37 E
Novogroznenskij	84	43.15 N	46.15 E
Novo Hamburgo	252	29.41 S	51.08 W
Novo Horizonte	255	21.28 S	49.13 W
Novohrad-Volyns'kyy	78	50.36 N	27.36 E
Novohrodivka	83	48.13 N	37.20 E
Novohryhorivka, Ukr.	78	46.24 N	34.59 E
Novohryhorivka, Ukr.	83	48.34 N	37.25 E
Novohupalivka	78	48.02 N	35.26 E
Novoiljinsk	88	51.42 N	108.41 E
Novoiljinskij	86	57.54 N	55.30 E
Novoivanivka	78	49.44 N	33.28 E
Novoivanovka	85	43.08 N	71.26 E
Novoivanovskoje	265b	55.43 N	37.22 E
Novoizborsk	76	57.50 N	27.59 E
Novojampol'	89	52.55 N	127.38 E
Novojamskoje	76	52.14 N	34.28 E
Novoje, Ross.	82	55.38 N	38.55 E
Novoje, Ross.	86	58.53 N	68.40 E
Novoje Alechnovo	82	56.02 N	36.49 E
Novojegorjevskoje	86	51.46 N	80.53 E
Novoje Koval'ovo	265a	59.59 N	30.34 E
Novoje Leušino	80	56.48 N	40.32 E
Novojenisejsk	86	58.16 N	92.24 E
Novoje Pavšino	82	54.15 N	37.07 E
Novoje Zarečje	76	57.43 N	34.22 E
Novokačalinsk	89	45.06 N	132.01 E
Novokadinsk	88	54.46 N	101.24 E
Novokamala	88	55.58 N	94.58 E
Novokarasuk	86	56.16 N	71.46 E
Novokaširovo	80	54.58 N	52.32 E
Novokaširsk	82	54.51 N	38.15 E
Novokazalinsk	86	45.50 N	62.10 E
Novokijevskij	80	50.27 N	43.08 E
Novokorsunskaja	78	45.38 N	39.09 E
Novokrasne	78	48.01 N	31.21 E
Novokrasnyanka	83	49.08 N	38.18 E
Novokručininskij	88	51.46 N	113.48 E
Novokubanka	86	51.40 N	70.44 E
Novokujbyševsk	80	53.07 N	49.58 E
Novokurovka	89	48.51 N	134.20 E
Novokuzneck	86	53.45 N	87.06 E
Novokuznetsk → Novokuzneck	86	53.45 N	87.06 E
Novolakskoje	84	43.07 N	46.29 E
Novolazarevskaja ʋ[3]	9	70.45 S	11.50 E
Novoleuškovskaja	78	45.59 N	39.58 E
Novoli	68	40.23 N	18.03 E
Novol'vovsk	76	53.55 N	38.47 E
Novomalorossijskaja	78	45.38 N	39.53 E
Novomansurkino	80	53.52 N	51.52 E
Novomargaritovka	83	46.54 N	38.50 E
Novomariinka	88	55.27 N	96.01 E
Novomarkovka	86	51.44 N	72.17 E
Novomel'nikov	84	43.56 N	45.09 E
Novomelovatka	78	50.27 N	40.46 E
Novomelovoje	78	51.23 N	38.13 E
Novo Mesto	36	45.48 N	15.10 E
Novomichajlovka	86	55.13 N	81.57 E
Novomichajlovskij	78	44.15 N	38.51 E
Novomichajlovskoje	82	55.25 N	37.10 E
Novominskaja	78	46.19 N	38.57 E
Novomoskovsk, Ross.	82	54.05 N	38.13 E
Novomoskovs'k, Ukr.	78	48.37 N	35.12 E
Novomykhaylivka, Ukr.	78	47.19 N	36.04 E
Novomykhaylivka, Ukr.	83	47.51 N	37.29 E
Novomykil's'ke	83	49.21 N	39.51 E
Novomykolayivka, Ukr.	78	46.13 N	32.45 E
Novomykolayivka, Ukr.	78	47.59 N	35.55 E
Novomyrhorod	78	48.47 N	31.39 E
Novomyšastovskaja	78	45.12 N	38.35 E
Novonagajevo	80	55.56 N	54.15 E
Novonikolajevka, Kaz.	85	42.26 N	70.28 E
Novonikolajevka, Ross.	83	46.59 N	39.36 E
Novonikolajevskij	80	50.58 N	42.22 E
Novonikolayevsk → Novosibirsk	86	55.02 N	82.55 E
Novonikol'skoje, Ross.	76	59.25 N	33.13 E
Novonikol'skoje, Ross.	80	49.09 N	45.00 E
Novonikol'skoje, Ross.	86	59.46 N	79.12 E
Novonikol'skoje, Ross.	265b	55.50 N	37.15 E
Novookhtyrka	83	48.55 N	38.49 E
Novooleksandrivka, Ukr.	83	48.17 N	39.37 E
Novooleksandrivka, Ukr.	83	49.08 N	39.17 E
Novooleksiyivka, Ukr.	78	46.06 N	32.30 E
Novooleksiyivka, Ukr.	78	46.13 N	34.39 E
Novo Oriente	250	5.32 S	40.42 W
Novoorsk	86	51.23 N	58.58 E
Novopavlovka	88	51.13 N	109.14 E
Novopavlovskaja	84	43.58 N	43.38 E
Novopavlovskoje	88	50.56 N	111.35 E
Novopetrovo	86	57.11 N	69.10 E
Novopetrovskoje	82	55.59 N	36.28 E
Novopiscovo	76	57.19 N	41.54 E
Novopodrezkovo	82	55.57 N	37.21 E
Novopokrovka, Kaz.	86	53.43 N	67.45 E
Novopokrovka, Kaz.	86	50.41 N	80.28 E
Novopokrovka, Kyrg.	85	42.52 N	74.45 E
Novopokrovka, Ross.	89	45.52 N	134.28 E
Novopokrovka, Ukr.	78	48.03 N	34.37 E
Novopokrovskoje	80	51.35 N	43.36 E
Novopolevodino	80	51.46 N	47.29 E
Novopskov	83	49.33 N	39.05 E
Novorajčichinsk	89	49.47 N	129.38 E
Novor'ažsk	80	53.44 N	40.07 E
Novorepnoje	80	51.06 N	48.24 E
Novorossijka	85	42.44 N	76.07 E
Novorossijsk	78	44.45 N	37.45 E
Novorossijskoje	86	50.13 N	58.00 E
Novorossiysk → Novorossijsk	78	44.45 N	37.45 E
Novorozsosh	83	49.32 N	39.15 E
Novorudnyj	86	51.30 N	58.10 E
Novorybinka	86	51.51 N	71.14 E
Novorybnoje	74	72.50 N	105.50 E
Novoržev	76	57.02 N	29.20 E
Novošachtinsk	83	47.47 N	39.56 E
Novosaratovka	265a	59.50 N	30.32 E
Novoščerbinovskaja	78	46.28 N	38.38 E
Novosel'e	86	54.10 N	76.53 E
Novoselenginsk	88	51.06 N	106.37 E
Novoselickoje	84	44.45 N	43.26 E
Novoselivka	83	49.04 N	37.42 E
Novoselivs'ke	78	45.26 N	33.34 E
Novoselje	265a	59.48 N	30.05 E
Novoselki, Ross.	82	55.08 N	37.33 E
Novoselki, Ross.	82	54.49 N	38.55 E
Novosel'nyj	86	50.00 N	54.38 E
Novoselovo	82	56.04 N	39.04 E
Novoselytsya, Ukr.	78	48.14 N	26.17 E
Novoselytsya, Ukr.	78	49.48 N	25.03 E
Novosemejkino	80	53.23 N	50.22 E
Novosergijevka, Ross.	80	52.06 N	53.39 E
Novosergijevka, Ross.	265a	59.54 N	30.34 E
Novoseslavino	80	53.21 N	40.26 E
Novošešminsk	80	55.04 N	51.15 E
Novoshakhtinsk → Novošachtinsk	83	47.47 N	39.56 E
Novosibirsk	86	55.02 N	82.55 E
Novosibirskije ostrova II	74	75.00 N	142.00 E
Novosibirsk Oblast' □[4]	86	55.00 N	80.00 E
Novosibirskoje vodochranilišče ⊜[1]	86	54.35 N	82.35 E
Novosil'	76	52.58 N	37.03 E
Novosil's'ke	78	45.20 N	28.33 E
Novosil'skoje	78	51.56 N	38.31 E
Novosokol'niki	76	56.21 N	30.10 E
Novos'olki, Ross.	76	56.01 N	33.37 E
Novos'olki, Ross.	80	55.48 N	42.41 E
Novos'olki, Ross.	80	54.50 N	39.46 E
Novos'olki, Ross.	265a	59.42 N	30.17 E
Novos'olovo, Ross.	86	55.04 N	91.07 E
Novos'olovo, Ross.	88	56.04 N	107.42 E
Novospasovka	83	47.42 N	39.04 E
Novospasskoje	80	53.08 N	47.45 E
Novostril'tsivka	83	49.20 N	39.55 E
Novostrojevo	76	54.27 N	21.50 E
Novosvitlivka	83	48.30 N	39.30 E
Novosysojevka	89	44.14 N	133.22 E
Novotavolžanka	78	50.22 N	36.50 E
Novotitarovskaja	78	45.14 N	39.00 E
Novotroick, Ross.	86	56.11 N	78.41 E
Novotroick, Ross.	86	51.12 N	58.20 E
Novotroickoje, Kaz.	85	43.42 N	73.46 E
Novotroickoje, Ross.	80	58.28 N	47.06 E
Novo-Troitsk → Novotroick	86	51.12 N	58.20 E
Novotroyits'ke, Ukr.	78	46.22 N	34.20 E
Novotroyits'ke, Ukr.	83	47.43 N	37.35 E
Novotulka, Ross.	80	52.38 N	48.45 E
Novotulka, Ross.	80	50.50 N	47.34 E
Novotul'skij	82	54.10 N	37.43 E
Novoukolovo	78	51.02 N	38.25 E
Novoukrayinka	78	48.19 N	31.32 E
Novouljanovsk	80	54.08 N	48.24 E
Novoural'sk	86	51.15 N	57.16 E
Novouzensk	80	50.28 N	48.08 E
Novovaršavka	86	54.11 N	74.42 E
Novovasylivka, Ukr.	78	46.51 N	36.46 E
Novovasylivka, Ukr.	78	46.48 N	35.44 E
Novov'atsk	80	58.29 N	49.44 E
Novov'azniki	80	56.12 N	42.10 E
Novovolyns'k	78	50.50 N	24.05 E
Novovoronežskij	78	51.16 N	39.11 E
Novovorontsovka	78	47.29 N	33.54 E
Novovoskresenovka	85	42.50 N	73.32 E
Novovoskresens'ke	78	47.21 N	33.37 E
Novozacharkino	80	52.11 N	48.29 E
Novozagorje	82	55.39 N	38.38 E
Novozavidovskij	82	56.33 N	36.26 E
Novožilovskaja	24	64.50 N	51.20 E
Novozizevka	80	50.48 N	49.08 E
Novozybkov	76	52.32 N	31.56 E
Novska	36	45.21 N	16.59 E
Nový Bohumín	30	49.56 N	18.20 E
Nový Bor	54	50.45 N	14.33 E
Novy Dvor	76	52.50 N	24.21 E
Novyj	86	55.39 N	86.39 E
Novyja Dzjanisavičy	76	54.12 N	29.13 E
Novyj Afon	84	43.06 N	40.48 E
Novyja Valosavičy	76	54.46 N	28.50 E
Novyj Bor	24	66.43 N	52.16 E
Novyj Bujan	80	53.41 N	50.04 E
Novyje Ajbesi	80	54.49 N	47.02 E
Novyje Burasy	80	52.08 N	46.06 E
Novyje Gorki	80	56.42 N	41.06 E
Novyje Maty	80	55.15 N	54.04 E
Novyje Salty	80	54.06 N	53.26 E
Novyje Z'atcy	80	57.27 N	52.36 E
Nový Jičín	30	49.36 N	18.00 E
Novyj Jegorlyk	80	46.24 N	41.54 E
Novyj Karačaj	84	43.49 N	41.56 E
Novyj Karamass	80	56.11 N	48.58 E
Novyj Kiner	80	56.24 N	49.44 E
Novyj Multan	80	57.09 N	52.19 E
Novyj Nekouz	76	57.54 N	38.04 E
Novyj Oskol	78	50.46 N	37.53 E
Novyj Port	74	67.40 N	72.52 E
Novyj Put'	85	43.29 N	73.52 E
Novyj Ropsk	76	52.18 N	32.19 E
Novyj Stan	82	56.18 N	37.00 E
Novyj Tap	86	57.04 N	67.49 E
Novyj Terek ≃	84	43.37 N	47.25 E
Novyj Tevriz	86	59.04 N	78.08 E
Novyj Uzen'	72	43.18 N	52.48 E
Novyj Vas'ugan	86	58.34 N	76.29 E
Novy Pahost	76	55.30 N	27.29 E
Novy Torjal	80	57.00 N	48.44 E
Novyy Buh	78	47.41 N	32.30 E
Novyy Bykiv	78	50.36 N	31.39 E
Novyy Svit	83	47.48 N	38.00 E
Novyy Yarychiv	78	49.55 N	24.18 E
Nowa Dęba	30	50.26 N	21.46 E
Nowaja Semlja → Novaja Zeml'a II	72	74.00 N	57.00 E
Nowa Ruda	30	50.35 N	16.31 E
Nowa Sól (Neusalz)	30	51.48 N	15.44 E
Nowata	196	36.42 N	95.38 W
Nowater Creek ≃	202	43.57 N	108.00 W
Nowbarān	128	35.08 N	48.42 E
Nowe	30	53.40 N	18.43 E
Nowe Miasto Lubawskie	30	53.27 N	19.35 E
Nowe Miasto nad Pilicą	30	51.38 N	20.35 E
Nowendoc	166	31.32 S	151.43 E
Nowe Warpno	30	53.44 N	14.16 E
Nowfel low Shātow	128	34.23 N	50.32 E
Nowgong	124	25.04 N	79.27 E
Nowingi	166	34.36 S	142.14 E
Nowitna ≃	180	65.55 N	154.17 W
Nowogard	30	53.40 N	15.08 E
Nowogród	30	53.15 N	21.53 E
Nowogrodziec	30	51.12 N	15.25 E
Nowokusnezk → Novokuzneck	86	53.45 N	87.06 E
Nowood ≃	202	44.17 N	107.58 W
Nowosibirsk → Novosibirsk	86	55.02 N	82.55 E
Nowra	170	34.53 S	150.36 E
Nowrangapur	122	19.14 N	82.33 E
Nowshāk ∧	123	36.26 N	71.50 E
Nowshera	123	34.01 N	71.59 E
Nowy Dwór Gdański	30	54.13 N	19.06 E
Nowy Dwór Mazowiecki	30	52.26 N	20.43 E
Nowy Sącz	30	49.38 N	20.42 E
Nowy Sącz □[4]	30	49.30 N	20.15 E
Nowy Staw	30	54.09 N	19.00 E
Nowy Targ	30	49.29 N	20.02 E
Nowy Tomyśl	30	52.20 N	16.07 E
Now Zād	120	32.24 N	64.28 E
Noxapater	194	32.59 N	89.03 W
Noxe ≃	50	48.33 N	3.35 E
Noxen	210	41.25 N	76.03 W
Noxon	202	48.00 N	115.47 W
Noxon Reservoir ⊜[1]	202	47.54 N	115.40 W
Noxubee ≃	194	32.50 N	88.10 W
Noy ≃	110	17.05 N	105.02 E
Noya ≃	152	0.58 N	9.48 E
Noyant	50	47.31 N	0.08 E
Noye ≃	50	49.51 N	2.20 E
Noyelles-sur Mer	50	50.11 N	1.43 E
Noyers	50	47.42 N	4.00 E
Noyers, Ruisseau des	275a	45.21 N	73.22 W
Noyers-sur-Jabron	62	44.10 N	5.50 E
Noyes Island I	182	55.30 N	133.40 W
Noyon	50	49.35 N	3.00 E
Nožaj-Jurt	84	43.05 N	46.24 E
Nozawa-onsen	94	36.55 N	138.27 E
Nozay, Fr.	32	47.34 N	1.38 W
Nozay, Fr.	261	48.40 N	2.14 E
Nozeroy	58	46.47 N	6.02 E
Nozori-dam ◆[6]	94	36.43 N	138.39 E
Nozori-ko ⊜	94	36.42 N	138.39 E
Nozuta	268	35.35 N	139.27 E
Nqamakwe	158	32.12 S	27.56 E
Nqutu	158	28.13 S	30.32 E
N'Riquinha	152	15.45 S	21.42 E
N'Rougas	158	29.07 S	21.09 E
Nsa, Oued en V	148	32.28 N	5.24 E
Nsaba	150	5.39 N	0.45 W
Nsah	152	2.22 S	15.19 E
Nsang	152	2.02 N	10.56 E
Nsanje	154	16.55 S	35.12 E
Nsawam	150	5.50 N	0.20 W
Nsefu Game Reserve ◆[4]	154	13.07 S	32.10 E
Nsele ≃	152	4.14 S	15.33 E
Nseleni	158	28.33 S	31.39 E
Nsok	152	1.08 N	11.16 E
Nsoko	158	27.02 S	31.57 E
Nsontin	152	3.09 S	18.00 E
Nsouélé	273b	4.12 S	15.11 E
Nsukka	150	6.52 N	7.24 E
Nsuta	150	5.17 N	1.58 W
Ntakat	150	16.49 N	11.43 W
Ntambanana	158	28.36 S	31.45 E
Ntandembele	152	2.11 S	17.08 E
Ntcheu	154	14.49 S	34.38 E
Ntem ≃	152	2.15 N	9.45 E
Ntoum	152	0.23 N	9.47 E
Ntsama	152	0.32 S	14.38 E
N'Tsaoueni	157a	11.27 S	43.18 E
Ntui	152	4.27 N	11.38 E
Ntumba	154	8.20 S	32.05 E
Ntusi	154	0.03 N	31.13 E
Ntwetwe Pan ≍	156	20.30 S	25.20 E
Nuala	154	13.27 S	28.16 E
Nuanchitang	104	41.02 N	120.41 E
Nuanetsi ≃	156	22.40 S	31.50 E
Nuangola	210	41.09 N	75.58 W
Nuanli	102	23.26 N	100.51 E
Nuannuan	269d	25.06 N	121.44 E
Nuanshui	100	28.53 N	117.51 E
Nuanzhouying	100	25.22 N	117.22 E
Nuasjärvi ⊜	26	64.10 N	28.05 E
Nuatabu	174t	1.33 N	172.59 E
Nuatja	150	6.57 N	1.10 E
Nu'aymah	132	32.38 N	36.10 E
Nūbah	142	30.29 N	31.33 E
Nūbah, Jibāl an- ⋀	140	11.00 N	30.45 E
Nūbārīyah, Tur'at an- ≋	142	30.43 N	30.46 E
Nubian Desert ◆[2]	140	20.30 N	33.00 E
Ñuble ≃	252	36.39 S	72.27 W
Nubra ≃	123	34.39 N	77.36 E
Nucet	38	46.28 N	22.35 E
Nucetto	62	44.20 N	8.04 E
Nucha → Şeki	84	41.12 N	47.12 E
Nuchatlitz Inlet ⊂	182	49.45 N	126.55 W
N'uchča	24	63.27 N	46.28 E
Nuch'ŏn-ni	98	38.14 N	126.16 E
Nucla	200	38.16 N	108.32 W
Núcleo Colonial São Bento	287a	22.44 S	43.18 W
N'učpas	24	60.51 N	51.18 E
Nucuray ≃	246	5.02 S	75.34 W
Nuda, Monte la ∧	64	44.17 N	10.15 E
Nudaybah	142	30.59 N	30.22 E
Nüdlingen	56	50.13 N	10.08 E
Nudol' ≃	82	56.07 N	36.42 E
Nudol'-Šarino	82	56.06 N	36.31 E
Nudow	264a	52.20 N	13.10 E
Nueces ≃	196	27.50 N	97.30 W
Nueces Plains ≍	196	28.30 N	99.15 W
Nueltin Lake ⊜	176	60.20 N	99.50 W
Nuenen	52	51.29 N	5.33 E
Nü'er ≃	98	40.57 N	121.19 E
Nü'erhe	104	41.04 N	121.00 E
Nuestra Señora de Talavera	252	25.26 S	63.48 W
Nueva, Isla I	254	55.13 S	66.30 W
Nueva Antioquia	246	6.05 N	69.26 W
Nueva Asunción □[5]	248	21.00 S	61.00 W
Nueva Atzacoalco ◆[8]	286a	19.29 N	99.05 W
Nueva Brunswick → New Brunswick □[4]	186	46.30 N	66.15 W
Nueva Caledonia → New Caledonia □[2]	175f	21.30 S	165.30 E
Nueva Chicago ◆[8]	288	34.40 S	58.30 W
Nueva Ciudad Guerrero	232	26.35 N	99.15 W
Nueva Concepción	236	14.08 N	89.18 W
Nueva Cuadrilla	234	18.04 N	101.33 W
Nueva Ecija □[4]	116	15.35 N	121.00 E
Nueva Escocia → Nova Scotia □[4]	186	45.00 N	63.00 W
Nueva Esparta □[3]	246	11.00 N	64.00 W
Nueva Francia	252	28.11 S	64.12 W
Nueva Galia	252	35.07 S	65.15 W
Nueva Germania	252	23.54 S	56.45 W
Nueva Gerona	240p	21.53 N	82.48 W
Nueva Guinea, Isla → New Guinea I	164	5.00 S	140.00 E
Nueva Hébridas → Vanuatu □[1]	175f	16.00 S	167.00 E
Nueva Helvecia	258	34.19 S	57.13 W
Nueva Imperial	252	38.44 S	72.57 W
Nueva Italia de Ruiz	234	19.01 N	102.06 W
Nueva Loja	246	0.06 N	76.52 W
Nueva Lubecka	254	44.32 S	70.24 W
Nueva Ocotepeque	236	14.24 N	89.13 W
Nueva Palmira	258	33.53 S	58.25 W
Nueva Paz	240p	22.46 N	81.45 W
Nueva Pompeya ◆[8]	288	34.39 S	58.25 W
Nueva Rosita	232	27.57 N	101.13 W
Nueva San Salvador	236	13.41 N	89.17 W
Nueva Segovia □[5]	236	13.40 N	86.10 W
Nueva Siberia, Islas → Novosibirskije ostrova II	74	75.00 N	142.00 E
Nueva Venecia	236	14.03 N	91.33 W
Nueva Vizcaya □[4]	116	16.25 N	121.10 E
Nueva Zelandia → New Zealand □[1]	172	41.00 S	174.00 E
Nueva Zembla, Isla de → Novaja Zeml'a II	72	74.00 N	57.00 E
Nueve, Canal Numero ≋	252	36.11 S	57.18 W
Nueve de Julio	252	35.27 S	60.52 W
Nuevitas	240p	21.33 N	77.16 W
Nuevitas, Bahía de ⊂	240p	21.30 N	77.12 W
Nuevo	228	33.48 N	117.09 W
Nuevo, Bajo ✦[4]	238	15.55 N	78.30 W
Nuevo, Cayo I	232	21.51 N	92.05 W
Nuevo, Golfo ⊂	254	42.42 S	64.36 W
Nuevo Berlín	252	32.59 S	58.03 W
Nuevo Camarón	196	27.05 N	99.55 W
Nuevo Casas Grandes	232	30.25 N	107.55 W
Nuevo Chagres	236	9.14 N	80.05 W
Nuevo Delicias	232	26.15 N	102.50 W
Nuevo Laredo	232	27.30 N	99.31 W
Nuevo Léon	204	32.20 N	115.12 W
Nuevo León □[3]	232	25.40 N	100.00 W
Nuevo Morelos	234	17.31 N	95.02 W
Nuevo Necaxa	234	20.13 N	98.00 W
Nuevo Poblado el Oro	196	26.50 N	101.19 W
Nuevo Primero de Mayo	196	26.01 N	98.02 W
Nuevo Progreso	232	18.38 N	92.18 W
Nuevo Rocafuerte	246	0.56 S	75.24 W
Nuevo Saucillo	196	27.20 N	104.54 W
Nufcor	273d	26.17 S	27.44 E
Nugaal □[4]	144	8.30 N	49.00 E
Nugaaleed, Dooxo V	144	8.35 N	48.35 E
Nugget Point ≻	172	46.27 S	169.49 E
Nûgssuaq ≻[1]	176	70.25 N	52.30 W
Nugu ⊜[1]	122	11.58 N	76.28 E
Nuguria Islands II	14	3.20 S	154.45 E
Nūh	124	28.07 N	77.01 E
Nūh, Rās ≻	128	25.05 N	62.24 E
Nuhaka	172	39.03 S	177.45 E
Nuhaydāt as-Sūd, Jabal an- ∧	142	28.01 N	32.21 E
Nuhūd, Jabal an- ∧	140	14.50 N	29.53 E
Nui I[1]	14	7.15 S	177.10 E
Nuia	76	58.04 N	25.33 E
Nuits-Saint-Georges	58	47.08 N	4.57 E
Nuits-sur-Armançon	50	47.44 N	4.12 E
N'uja	74	60.32 N	116.14 E
N'uja ≃	74	60.32 N	116.20 E
Nujiang	102	29.58 N	97.25 E
N'uk, ozero ⊜	24	64.27 N	31.45 E
Nuka Island I	180	59.21 N	150.42 W
Nukan	175c	7.23 N	151.53 E
Nukata	94	34.55 N	137.17 E
Nukatl', chrebet ⋀	84	42.15 N	46.35 E
Nukey Bluff ⊥[4]	166	32.33 S	135.40 E
Nukhayb	128	32.02 N	42.15 E
Nukhaylah ⊤[4]	140	19.03 N	26.19 E
Nukhaylah, Wādī an- V	132	31.27 N	35.49 E
N'uksenica	24	60.25 N	44.13 E
Nuku'alofa	174w	21.08 S	175.12 W
Nukufetau I[1]	14	8.00 S	178.22 E
Nukuhu	164	5.35 S	149.25 E
Nukulaelae I[1]	14	9.23 S	179.52 E
Nukumanu Islands II	14	4.30 S	159.30 E
Nukunonu I	14	9.12 S	171.54 W
Nukunuku	174w	21.08 S	175.18 W
Nukuoro I[1]	14	3.51 N	154.58 E
Nukus	72	42.50 N	59.29 E
Nul	175f	16.49 S	168.24 E
Nulato	180	64.43 N	158.06 W
Nullagine	162	21.53 S	120.06 E
Nullagine ≃	162	20.43 S	120.33 E
Nullarbor	162	31.26 S	130.55 E
Nullarbor National Park ♠	162	31.30 S	130.30 E
Nullarbor Plain ≍	162	31.00 S	129.00 E
Nulltown	218	39.35 N	85.10 W
Nul'vand	85	38.16 N	70.32 E
Nulvi	71	40.47 N	8.45 E
Num, Mios I	164	1.30 S	135.13 E
Numabin Bay ⊂	184	56.30 N	103.08 W
Numakuma	96	34.23 N	133.20 E
Numan	146	9.28 N	12.02 E
Numana	66	43.31 N	13.37 E
Numancia	116	9.52 N	125.58 E
Numancia ⊥	34	41.48 N	2.25 W
Numansdorp	52	51.44 N	4.26 E
Numara I	122	6.26 N	73.03 E
Numata, Nihon	92a	43.48 N	141.57 E
Numata, Nihon	94	36.38 N	139.03 E
Numata, Nihon	96	34.27 N	132.24 E
Numatinna ≃	140	7.14 N	27.37 E
Numazu	94	35.06 N	138.52 E
Numbargulme, Mount ∧	164	14.56 S	145.03 E
Number 5 Mine	214	41.08 N	80.11 W
Nümbrecht	56	50.54 N	7.32 E
Numedal V	26	60.06 N	9.06 E
Numeralla	171b	36.11 S	149.20 E
Numeralla ≃	171b	36.06 S	149.11 E
Numfoor, Pulau I	164	1.03 S	134.54 E
Numidia	210	40.53 N	76.24 W
Numila	229b	21.54 N	159.33 W
Nu Mine	214	40.48 N	79.18 W
Numto	74	63.40 N	71.20 E
Numurkah	166	36.06 S	145.26 E
Nun ≃[1]	150	4.20 N	6.00 E
Nun'amo	180	65.37 N	170.40 W
Nunapitchuk	180	60.54 N	162.29 W
Nunawading	169	37.49 S	145.10 E
Nünchritz	54	51.18 N	13.23 E
Nunda	210	42.34 N	77.56 W
Nundah	171a	27.24 S	153.04 E
Nundu	154	3.49 S	29.05 E
Nuneaton	42	52.32 N	1.28 W
Núñes, Isla I	254	53.31 S	73.48 W
Núñez ◆[8]	288	34.33 S	58.27 W
Nunez ≃	150	10.36 N	14.40 W
Nungarin	162	31.11 S	118.06 E
Nungesser Lake ⊜	184	51.28 N	93.35 W
Nungwe	154	2.46 S	32.01 E
Nunica	216	43.04 N	86.04 W
Nunivak Island I	180	60.00 N	166.30 W
Nunjiang	89	49.10 N	125.11 E
Nunjikompita	162	32.16 S	134.19 E
Nunkini	232	20.20 N	90.11 W
Nunkun ∧	123	33.59 N	76.01 E
Nunligran	180	64.48 N	175.24 W
Nunnelly	194	35.51 N	87.28 W
Ñuñoa	286e	33.28 S	70.36 W
Nunshan	89	48.59 N	125.14 E
Nunspeet	52	52.23 N	5.46 E
Nuomin ≃	89	48.06 N	124.26 E
Nuomin Dashan ∧	89	50.15 N	122.46 E
Nuon ≃	150	6.30 N	8.36 W
Nuoro	71	40.19 N	9.20 E
Nuoro □[4]	71	40.10 N	9.20 E
Nuqruș, Jabal ∧	140	24.49 N	34.36 E
Nuquí	246	5.42 N	77.17 W
Nura	86	48.53 N	62.20 E
Nura ≃	86	50.30 N	69.59 E
Nurallao	71	39.47 N	9.05 E
Nuraminis	71	39.26 N	9.01 E
Nuratau, chrebet ⋀	85	40.20 N	67.15 E
Nuraxi, Nuraghe su ⊥	71	39.42 N	9.00 E
N'urba	74	63.17 N	118.20 E
Nürburg	56	50.21 N	6.57 E
Nürburgring ♠	56	50.21 N	6.58 E
Nur Dağları ⋀	130	36.45 N	36.20 E
Nure ≃	62	45.03 N	9.49 E
Nurek	85	38.23 N	69.19 E
Nurekskoje vodochranilišče ⊜[1]	85	38.30 N	69.30 E
Nuremberg → Nürnberg, Dtsch.	60	49.27 N	11.04 E
Nuremberg, Pa., U.S.	210	40.56 N	76.10 W
Nürenbei	107	30.11 N	106.04 E
Nūrestān □[9]	123	35.30 N	70.45 E
Nurettin	130	39.14 N	42.25 E
Nurhak	130	37.58 N	37.25 E
Nuria, Monte ∧	66	42.21 N	13.05 E
Nuriootpa	168b	34.29 S	139.00 E
Nurlat	80	54.26 N	50.46 E
Nurlaty	80	55.37 N	48.18 E
Nūrmahal	123	31.06 N	75.36 E
Nurmes	26	63.33 N	29.07 E
Nurmijärvi	26	60.28 N	24.48 E
Nūrnagar	126	22.20 N	89.03 E
Nürnberg	60	49.27 N	11.04 E
Nürnberg, Flughafen ⊠	60	49.30 N	11.06 E
Nūrpur, India	123	31.10 N	76.29 E
Nūrpur, India	123	32.18 N	75.54 E
Nurpur, India	126	22.13 N	88.05 E
Nūrpur, Pāk.	123	31.53 N	71.54 E
Nurrari Lakes ⊜	162	29.01 S	130.05 E
Nurri	71	39.43 N	9.14 E
Nurri, Mount ∧[2]	166	31.42 S	146.02 E
Nursery	222	28.56 N	97.06 W
Nürtingen	56	48.38 N	9.20 E
Nus	62	45.45 N	7.28 E
Nūsah	144	14.00 N	46.43 E
Nusa Tenggara Barat □[4]	115b	8.50 S	117.30 E
Nusa Tenggara Timur □[4]	112	9.30 S	122.00 E
Nusaybin	130	37.03 N	41.13 E
Nuşayrīyah, Jabal an- ⋀	130	35.30 N	36.12 E
Nusco	68	40.53 N	15.05 E
Nushagak ≃	180	59.00 N	158.30 W
Nushagak Bay ⊂	180	58.40 N	158.40 W
Nushagak Peninsula ≻[1]	180	58.30 N	159.00 W
Nu Shan ⋀	102	27.00 N	99.00 E
Nüshan Hu ⊜	100	32.57 N	118.03 E
Nu-shima I	96	34.10 N	134.50 E
Nushki	120	29.33 N	66.01 E
Nusplingen	58	48.08 N	8.53 E
Nušpoly	82	56.39 N	37.44 E
Nussdorf ◆[8]	264b	48.15 N	16.22 E
Nussdorf am Attersee	64	47.53 N	13.31 E
Nuta ≃	96	34.23 N	133.04 E
Nutauge, laguna ⊂	180	67.55 N	176.45 W
Nutepel'men, Ross.	180	67.26 N	174.56 W
Nutepelmen, Ross.	180	65.31 N	178.30 W
Nutfield	260	51.14 N	0.07 W
Nuth	56	50.55 N	5.54 E
Nuthe ≃, Dtsch.	54	51.58 N	11.53 E
Nuthe ≃, Dtsch.	54	52.23 N	13.04 E
Nut Lake Indian Reserve ◆[4]	184	52.20 N	103.30 W
Nutley	210	40.49 N	74.09 W
Nutrioso	200	33.57 N	109.12 W
Nut Swamp Brook ≃	276	40.21 N	74.06 W
Nuttby Mountain ∧[2]	186	45.33 N	63.13 W
Nutter Fort	188	39.15 N	80.19 W
Nutting Lake	207	42.32 N	71.16 W
Nutting Lake ⊜	283	42.32 N	71.16 W
Nutwood	219	39.05 N	90.39 W
Nutwood Downs	164	15.49 S	134.10 E
Nutzotin Mountains ⋀	180	62.10 N	141.40 W
Nu'ūmīyah, Wādī an- V	142	29.31 N	31.17 E
Nuupere, Pointe ≻	174s	17.36 S	149.47 W
Nu'uuli	174u	14.18 S	170.42 W
N'uvčim	24	61.22 N	50.42 E
Nuwākoṭ	124	28.08 N	83.53 E
Nuwaybi' al-Muzayyinah	140	28.58 N	34.39 E
Nuwerus	158	31.08 S	18.24 E
Nuweveldberge ⋀	158	32.13 S	22.10 E
Nuxis	71	39.09 N	8.44 E
Nuyakuk Lake ⊜	180	60.00 N	158.40 W
Nuyts, Point ≻	162	35.04 S	116.37 E
Nuyts Archipelago II	162	32.35 S	133.17 E
Nūzvīd	122	16.47 N	80.51 E
N'Vinda	152	13.04 S	18.57 E
Nwa	152	6.30 N	11.00 E
Nxainxai	156	19.50 S	21.13 E
Nxai Pan National Park ♠	156	19.45 S	24.50 E
Nxaunxau	156	18.19 S	21.04 E
Nyaake	150	4.52 N	7.37 W
Nyabéssan	152	2.24 N	10.24 E
Nyabing	162	33.32 S	118.09 E
Nyac	180	61.01 N	159.57 W
Nyack	210	41.05 N	73.55 W
Nyack Beach State Park ♠	276	41.07 N	73.55 W
Nyadiri ≃	154	16.44 S	32.33 E
Nyahanga	154	2.23 S	33.33 E
Nyahua	154	5.24 S	33.19 E
Nyahururu Falls	154	0.02 N	36.22 E
Nyah West	166	35.11 S	143.22 E
Nyainqêntanglha Feng ∧	124	30.22 N	90.35 E
Nyainqêntanglha Shan ⋀	120	30.00 N	90.00 E
Nyainrong	120	32.09 N	92.11 E
Nyakabindi	154	2.38 S	33.59 E
Nyakakiri	154	2.15 S	31.28 E
Nyakanazi	154	3.00 S	31.15 E
Nyakrom	150	5.37 N	0.48 W
Nyakulenga	152	13.03 S	23.29 E
Nyala	140	12.03 N	24.53 E
Nyalam	120	28.11 N	85.58 E
Nyalas	114	2.26 N	102.28 E
Nyamandhlovu	154	19.50 S	28.16 E
Nyamina	150	13.19 N	6.59 W
Nyamlell	140	9.07 N	26.58 E
Nyamougo	154	1.29 S	34.33 E
Nyamtumbo	154	10.29 S	36.02 E
Nyamwage	154	8.08 S	39.00 E
Nyandekwa	154	3.55 S	32.30 E
Nyanding, Khawr V	140	8.40 N	32.41 E
Nyang ≃	124	29.25 N	94.22 E
Nyanga □[4]	152	3.00 S	11.00 E
Nyanga ≃	152	2.58 S	10.15 E
Nyanga, Lake ⊜	162	29.57 S	126.10 E
Nyangana	156	18.00 S	20.41 E
Nyangui ∧	154	17.53 S	32.44 E
Nyanji Mission	154	14.23 S	31.48 E
Nyanza	154	2.21 S	29.45 E
Nyanza □[4]	154	0.30 S	34.30 E
Nyanza-Lac	154	4.21 S	29.36 E
Nyasa, Lake (Lake Malawi) ⊜	154	12.00 S	34.30 E
Nyaunglebin	110	17.57 N	96.44 E
Nyavikungu	154	11.26 S	25.54 E
Nyazura	154	18.43 S	32.10 E
Nyazvidzi ≃	154	20.00 S	32.17 E
Nybergsund	26	61.15 N	12.19 E
Nyborg	41	55.19 N	10.48 E
Nybro	26	56.45 N	15.54 E
Nyda	74	66.36 N	72.54 E
Nyêmo	124	29.25 N	90.08 E
Nyengo Swamp ≡	152	14.51 S	22.07 E
Nyeri	154	0.25 S	36.57 E
Nyerol	140	8.41 N	32.02 E
Nyfer ≃	42	52.02 N	4.50 W
Nygčigen, mys ≻	180	65.05 N	172.06 W
Nyhammar	40	60.17 N	14.58 E
Nyhyttan	40	59.40 N	14.48 E
Nyiel	140	6.06 N	31.13 E
Nyika National Park ♠	154	10.48 S	33.48 E
Nyika Plateau ⋀[1]	154	10.40 S	33.50 E
Nyimba	154	14.35 S	30.52 E
Nyingchi	120	29.32 N	94.25 E
Nyíradony	30	47.41 N	21.55 E
Nyírbátor	30	47.50 N	22.08 E

Symbols in the index entries represent the broad categories identified in the key at the right. Symbols with superior numbers (⋀[1]) identify subcategories (see complete key on page *I · 1).*

Symbole im Register stellen die rechts im Schlüssel erklärten Kategorien dar. Symbole mit hochgestellten Ziffern (⋀[1]) bezeichnen Unterabteilungen einer Kategorie (vgl. vollständiger Schlüssel auf Seite *I · 1).*

Los símbolos incluídos en el texto del índice representan las grandes categorías identificadas con la clave a la derecha. Los símbolos con numeros en su parte superior (⋀[1]) identifican las subcategorías (véase la clave completa en la página *I · 1).*

Les symboles de l'index représentent les catégories indiquées dans la légende à droite. Les symboles suivis d'un indice (⋀[1]) représentent des sous-catégories (voir légende complète à la page *I · 1).*

Os símbolos incluídos no texto do índice representam as grandes categorias identificadas com a chave à direita. Os símbolos com números em sua parte superior (⋀[1]) identificam as subcategorias (veja-se a chave completa à página *I · 1).*

Symbol	English	Deutsch	Español	Français	Português
∧	Mountain	Berg	Montaña	Montagne	Montanha
⋀	Mountains	Gebirge	Montañas	Montagnes	Montanhas
)(	Pass	Paß	Paso	Col	Passo
V	Valley, Canyon	Tal, Cañon	Valle, Cañón	Vallée, Canyon	Vale, Canhão
≍	Plain	Ebene	Llano	Plaine	Planície
≻	Cape	Kap	Cabo	Cap	Cabo
I	Island	Insel	Isla	Île	Ilha
II	Islands	Inseln	Islas	Îles	Ilhas
⊥	Other Topographic Features	Andere Topographische Objekte	Otros Elementos Topográficos	Autres données topographiques	Outros acidentes topográficos

ESPAÑOL

Nombre	Página	Lat.°′	Long.°′ W = Oeste
Nyíregyháza	30	47.59 N	21.43 E
Nykøbing, Dan.	26	56.48 N	8.52 E
Nykøbing, Dan.	41	55.55 N	11.41 E
Nykøbing, Dan.	41	54.46 N	11.53 E
Nyköping	40	58.45 N	17.00 E
Nykroppa	40	59.38 N	14.18 E
Nykvarn	40	59.11 N	17.26 E
Nyland	26	63.00 N	17.46 E
Nyland Acres	228	34.14 N	119.09 W
Nylga, Ross.	80	56.46 N	52.22 E
Nylga, Ross.	89	51.38 N	127.35 E
Nylstroom	156	24.42 S	28.20 E
Nymagee	166	32.04 S	146.20 E
Nymboida ≃	166	29.39 S	152.30 E
Nymburk	30	50.11 N	15.03 E
Nynäshamn	40	58.54 N	17.57 E
Nyngan	166	31.34 S	147.11 E
Nyoma	120	33.11 N	78.38 E
Nyon	58	46.23 N	6.14 E
Nyong ≃	152	3.17 N	9.54 E
Nyons	62	44.22 N	5.08 E
Nyord I	41	55.03 N	12.13 E
Nyou	150	12.46 N	1.56 W
Nýřany	60	49.43 N	13.12 E
Nyrov	24	60.42 N	56.40 E
Nýrsko	60	49.18 N	13.09 E
Nyš	89	51.31 N	142.46 E
Nysa, Pol.	30	50.29 N	17.20 E
Nyša, Ross.	80	56.23 N	51.51 E
Nysa Kłodzka ≃	30	50.49 N	17.50 E
Nysa Łużycka (Neisse) ≃	30	52.04 N	14.46 E
Nyslott → Savonlinna	26	61.52 N	28.53 E
Nysø	41	55.08 N	12.02 E
Nyssa	202	43.52 N	116.59 W
Nysted	41	54.40 N	11.45 E
Nytva	86	57.56 N	55.20 E
Nyūdō-zaki ›	92	40.00 N	139.42 E
Nyugati Pályaudvar ⬥[5]	264c	47.31 N	19.04 E
Nyūkawa	94	36.10 N	137.19 E
Nyumba ya Mungu Dam ⬥[6]	154	3.51 S	37.28 E
Nyungwe	154	10.16 S	34.07 E
Nyunzu	154	5.57 S	28.01 E
Nyuri	120	27.42 N	92.13 E
Nyūzen	94	36.56 N	137.30 E
Nyvång	41	56.08 N	12.54 E
Nyvrovo	89	54.19 N	142.36 E
Nyzhankovychi	78	49.40 N	22.47 E
Nyzhni Sirohozy	78	46.50 N	34.23 E
Nyzhniy Rohachyk	78	47.21 N	34.02 E
Nyzhn'obaranykivka	83	49.05 N	39.51 E
Nyzhn'ohirs'kyy	78	45.27 N	34.44 E
Nyzhn'oteple	83	48.48 N	39.23 E
Nyzhnya Duvanka	83	49.35 N	38.10 E
Nyzhnya Krynka	83	48.07 N	38.11 E
Nyzhnya Vil'khova	83	48.44 N	39.35 E
Nyzhnye	83	48.46 N	38.37 E
Nyzy	78	50.47 N	34.46 E
Nzaba	273b	4.06 S	15.16 E
Nzébéla	150	8.05 N	9.06 W
Nzega	154	4.13 S	33.11 E
Nzéla	152	1.25 S	12.39 E
Nzérékoré	150	7.45 N	8.49 W
N'zeto	152	7.14 S	12.52 E
Nzheleledam ⊜[1]	156	22.44 S	30.06 E
Nzi ≃	150	5.57 N	4.50 W
Nzima	154	3.03 S	32.48 E
Nziro	152	3.17 N	24.06 E
Nzo ≃	150	6.16 N	7.03 W
Nzoia ≃	154	0.03 N	33.57 E
Nzubuka	154	4.45 S	32.50 E
Nzwani (Anjouan) I	157a	12.15 S	44.25 E

O

Nombre	Página	Lat.°′	Long.°′ W = Oeste
Oa, Mull of ›	46	55.35 N	6.20 W
Oacoma	198	43.47 N	99.23 W
Oadby	42	52.36 N	1.04 W
Oad Street	260	51.20 N	0.41 E
Oahe, Lake ⊜[1]	198	45.30 N	100.25 W
Oahe Dam ⬥[6]	198	44.21 N	100.23 W
Oahu I	229c	21.30 N	158.00 W
Oak ≃	184	49.51 N	100.28 W
O-Akan-dake ∧	92a	43.27 N	144.10 E
Oakbank, Austl.	162	33.03 S	140.35 E
Oakbank, Austl.	168b	34.59 S	138.51 E
Oak Bay	224	48.27 N	123.18 W
Oak Beach	276	40.38 N	73.17 W
Oak Bluffs	207	41.27 N	70.33 W
Oakboro	192	35.13 N	80.19 W
Oak Brook	278	41.49 N	87.55 W
Oakbrook Center ⬥[9]	278	41.52 N	87.57 W
Oakbrook Terrace	278	41.52 N	87.58 W
Oakburn	184	50.35 N	100.32 W
Oak City, N.C., U.S.	192	35.57 N	77.18 W
Oak City, Ut,. U.S.	200	39.22 N	112.20 W
Oak Creek, Co., U.S.	200	40.16 N	106.57 W
Oak Creek, Wi., U.S.	216	42.53 N	87.55 W
Oak Creek ≃, U.S.	198	45.39 N	100.31 W
Oak Creek ≃, Az., U.S.	200	34.41 N	111.56 W
Oak Creek ≃, Co., U.S.	200	40.25 N	106.50 W
Oak Creek ≃, Ks., U.S.	198	39.29 N	98.28 W
Oak Creek ≃, N.D., U.S.	198	48.38 N	100.24 W
Oak Creek ≃, Tx., U.S.	196	31.48 N	100.13 W
Oakdale, Ca., U.S.	226	37.46 N	120.50 W
Oakdale, Ct., U.S.	207	41.27 N	72.09 W
Oakdale, Il., U.S.	219	38.16 N	89.30 W
Oakdale, La., U.S.	194	30.48 N	92.39 W
Oakdale, Ma., U.S.	207	42.23 N	71.47 W
Oakdale, Ne., U.S.	198	42.04 N	97.58 W
Oakdale, N.J., U.S.	285	39.59 N	74.49 W
Oakdale, N.Y., U.S.	210	40.44 N	73.08 W
Oakdale, Pa., U.S.	214	40.23 N	80.11 W
Oakdale, Tn., U.S.	192	35.59 N	84.33 W
Oakdale Woods	278	41.56 N	87.58 W
Oakengates	42	52.42 N	2.28 W
Oakes	198	46.08 N	98.05 W
Oakesdale	202	47.07 N	117.14 W
Oakey	171a	27.26 S	151.43 E
Oakeys Brook ≃	276	40.25 N	74.30 W
Oakfield, Me., U.S.	188	46.05 N	68.09 W
Oakfield, N.Y., U.S.	210	43.03 N	78.16 W
Oakfield, Wi., U.S.	190	43.41 N	88.32 W
Oakford, Il., U.S.	219	40.06 N	89.58 W
Oakford, In., U.S.	216	40.25 N	86.06 W
Oakford, Pa., U.S.	208	40.09 N	74.58 W
Oak Forest	216	41.36 N	87.44 W
Oakgrove, Eng., U.K.	262	53.13 N	2.07 W
Oak Grove, La., U.S.	194	32.51 N	91.23 W
Oak Grove, Or., U.S.	224	45.25 N	122.38 W
Oak Hall	208	37.56 N	75.33 W
Oakham	42	52.40 N	0.43 W
Oak Harbor, Oh., U.S.	214	41.30 N	83.09 W
Oak Harbor, Wa., U.S.	224	48.17 N	122.38 W
Oak Hill, De., U.S.	285	39.44 N	75.36 W
Oak Hill, Fl., U.S.	220	28.51 N	80.51 W
Oak Hill, Mi., U.S.	190	44.13 N	86.18 W
Oak Hill, N.Y., U.S.	210	42.25 N	74.09 W
Oak Hill, Oh., U.S.	188	38.54 N	82.34 W
Oak Hill, W.V., U.S.	188	37.58 N	81.08 W
Oakhurst, Ca., U.S.	226	37.19 N	119.40 W
Oakhurst, N.J., U.S.	208	40.16 N	74.01 W
Oakhurst, Tx., U.S.	222	30.44 N	95.19 W
Oak Island I, N.S., Can.	186	44.31 N	64.18 W
Oak Island I, N.Y., U.S.	276	40.39 N	73.18 W
Oak Knolls	204	34.51 N	120.27 W

FRANÇAIS

Nom	Page	Lat.°′	Long.°′ W = Ouest
Oak Lake	184	49.47 N	100.38 W
Oak Lake ⊜, Mb., Can.	184	49.40 N	100.45 W
Oak Lake ⊜, On., Can.	184	50.26 N	93.50 W
Oak Lake ⊜, On., Can.	212	44.36 N	77.55 W
Oakland, On., Can.	214	42.09 N	82.36 W
Oakland, Ca., U.S.	226	37.48 N	122.16 W
Oakland, Ca., U.S.	282	37.48 N	122.16 W
Oakland, Fl., U.S.	220	28.33 N	81.38 W
Oakland, Il., U.S.	194	39.39 N	88.01 W
Oakland, Ia., U.S.	198	41.18 N	95.23 W
Oakland, Me., U.S.	188	44.32 N	69.43 W
Oakland, Md., U.S.	188	39.24 N	79.24 W
Oakland, Md., U.S.	284c	38.51 N	76.55 W
Oakland, Ms., U.S.	194	34.03 N	89.54 W
Oakland, Ne., U.S.	198	41.50 N	96.28 W
Oakland, N.J., U.S.	210	41.00 N	74.15 W
Oakland, Or., U.S.	202	43.25 N	123.17 W
Oakland, Pa., U.S.	210	41.57 N	75.36 W
Oakland, Pa., U.S.	214	40.59 N	80.22 W
Oakland, Tx., U.S.	222	29.36 N	96.50 W
Oakland □[6]	216	42.40 N	83.23 W
Oakland ⬥[8]	279b	40.26 N	79.58 W
Oakland-Alameda County Coliseum ♠	282	37.45 N	122.12 W
Oakland Army Base ■	282	37.49 N	122.19 W
Oakland Beach	214	41.37 N	80.18 W
Oakland City	194	38.20 N	87.20 W
Oakland Gardens ⬥[8]	276	40.45 N	73.45 W
Oakland Mall ⬥[9]	281	42.32 N	83.07 W
Oakland Park	220	26.10 N	80.07 W
Oakland-Pontiac Airport ⊠	281	42.40 N	83.24 W
Oaklands	168b	35.00 S	137.41 E
Oaklands ⬥[8]	273d	26.09 S	28.04 E
Oakland Southwest Airport ⊠	281	42.30 N	83.37 W
Oakland University ♁[2]	281	42.41 N	83.13 W
Oak Lane Manor	285	39.47 N	75.32 W
Oak Lawn, Il., U.S.	216	41.43 N	87.45 W
Oaklawn, Ks., U.S.	198	37.36 N	97.17 W
Oaklawn, Md., U.S.	284c	38.47 N	76.57 W
Oakleigh	169	37.54 S	145.06 E
Oakleigh South	274b	37.56 S	145.05 E
Oakley, Eng., U.K.	42	51.15 N	1.11 W
Oakley, Scot., U.K.	46	56.04 N	3.33 W
Oakley, Ca., U.S.	226	37.58 N	121.43 W
Oakley, Id., U.S.	202	42.14 N	113.52 W
Oakley, Il., U.S.	219	39.53 N	88.48 W
Oakley, Ks., U.S.	198	39.08 N	100.51 W
Oakley Park	216	42.34 N	83.30 W
Oaklyn	285	39.54 N	75.05 W
Oakman	194	33.42 N	87.23 W
Oakmont	214	40.31 N	79.50 W
Oak Mountain State Park ♠	194	33.22 N	86.41 W
Oakmulgee Creek ≃	194	32.28 N	87.09 W
Oak Neck ›[1]	276	40.54 N	73.34 W
Oak Neck Point ›	276	40.55 N	73.34 W
Oakohay Creek ≃	194	31.44 N	89.25 W
Oak Orchard Creek ≃	210	43.22 N	78.12 W
Oak Orchard Swamp ⠿	210	43.07 N	78.18 W
Oakover ≃	162	20.43 S	120.33 E
Oak Park, Austl.	274b	37.43 S	144.55 E
Oak Park, Ca., U.S.	228	34.11 N	118.45 W
Oak Park, Il., U.S.	216	41.53 N	87.47 W
Oak Park, Mi., U.S.	216	42.27 N	83.10 W
Oak Park, Pa., U.S.	285	40.15 N	75.18 W
Oak Point	184	50.30 N	98.00 W
Oak Ridge, N.J., U.S.	210	41.03 N	74.29 W
Oakridge, Or., U.S.	202	43.44 N	122.27 W
Oak Ridge, Pa., U.S.	214	41.00 N	79.18 W
Oak Ridge, Tn., U.S.	192	36.00 N	84.16 W
Oak Ridge Lake	276	41.00 N	74.32 W
Oak Ridge National Laboratory ♁[3]	192	36.00 N	84.15 W
Oak Ridge Reservoir ⊜[1]	276	41.03 N	74.30 W
Oaks	285	40.08 N	81.28 W
Oaks Corners	210	42.56 N	77.01 W
Oak Shades	276	40.26 N	74.13 W
Oakton	284c	38.52 N	77.18 W
Oaktown	194	38.52 N	87.26 W
Oakura	172	39.07 S	173.57 E
Oak Valley, N.J., U.S.	208	39.48 N	75.09 W
Oak Valley, Va., U.S.	284c	38.54 N	77.18 W
Oak View, Ca., U.S.	228	34.24 N	119.18 W
Oak View, Md., U.S.	284c	39.01 N	76.59 W
Oakview, N.J., U.S.	285	39.51 N	75.09 W
Oakview Beach	212	44.29 N	80.03 W
Oakville, Mb., Can.	184	49.56 N	97.58 W
Oakville, On., Can.	212	43.27 N	79.41 W
Oakville, Ct., U.S.	207	41.35 N	73.05 W
Oakville, In., U.S.	218	40.05 N	85.23 W
Oakville, Mo., U.S.	219	38.28 N	90.18 W
Oakville, Wa., U.S.	224	46.50 N	123.13 W
Oakwood, On., Can.	212	44.20 N	78.53 W
Oakwood, N.J., U.S.	285	39.52 N	74.50 W
Oakwood, Oh., U.S.	214	41.23 N	81.29 W
Oakwood, Oh., U.S.	216	41.05 N	84.22 W
Oakwood, Oh., U.S.	218	39.44 N	84.10 W
Oakwood, Tx., U.S.	222	31.35 N	95.50 W
Oakwood Beach	208	39.33 N	75.31 W
Oakwood Park ♠	279a	41.26 N	82.06 W
Oamaru	172	45.06 S	170.58 E
Ōamishirasato	94	35.31 N	140.19 E
Ōana	268	35.45 N	140.04 E
Oancea	38	45.55 N	28.06 E
Ōarai	94	36.18 N	140.34 E
Oaro	172	42.31 S	173.30 E
Ōasa	96	34.46 N	132.28 E
Oat Creek ≃	226	38.50 N	121.56 W
Oates Coast ⊥[2]	9	70.00 S	160.00 E
Oatka Creek ≃	210	43.01 N	77.44 W
Oatlands	166	42.18 S	147.21 E
Oatley	274a	33.59 S	151.05 E
Oatley Park ♠	274a	33.59 S	151.04 E
Oatman	200	35.01 N	114.22 W
Oaxaca □[3]	234	17.00 N	96.30 W
Oaxaca de Juárez	234	17.03 N	96.43 W
Ob' ≃	72	66.45 N	69.30 E
Oba ≃	190	48.55 N	84.17 W
Obaba	152	2.00 S	16.10 E
Obabika Lake ⊜	190	47.05 N	80.17 W
Obal'	76	55.22 N	29.17 E
Obal' ≃	76	55.24 N	29.02 E
Obala	152	4.10 N	11.32 E
Oba Lake ⊜	190	48.38 N	84.18 W
Obama, Nihon	92	32.43 N	130.13 E
Obama, Nihon	94	35.30 N	135.45 E
Obama-wan ⊂	94	35.30 N	135.42 E
Oban, Austl.	166	21.14 S	139.03 E
Oban, Nig.	150	5.17 N	8.35 E
Oban, Scot., U.K.	46	56.25 N	5.29 W
Obanazawa	92	38.36 N	140.24 E
Obando	269f	14.43 N	120.56 E
Oban Hills ⋏[2]	150	5.35 N	8.35 E
Obara	94	35.15 N	137.18 E
O Barco de Valdeorras	34	42.25 N	6.59 W
Obata	94	34.30 N	136.40 E
Ob' Bay ⊂	9	70.35 S	163.22 E
Obbo	144	3.36 N	38.54 E
Obbola	26	63.42 N	20.19 E
Obdach	61	47.04 N	14.41 E
Obed	182	53.33 N	117.12 W
Obed ≃	192	36.04 N	84.39 W
Obeliai	76	55.56 N	25.48 E
Obelisk ∧	172	45.20 S	169.12 E
Oberá	252	27.29 S	55.08 W
Oberägeri	58	47.08 N	8.37 E
Oberalppass)(	58	46.39 N	8.40 E
Oberalpstock ∧	58	46.44 N	8.46 E
Oberammergau	64	47.35 N	11.04 E
Oberasbach	56	49.25 N	10.58 E

PORTUGUÊS

Nome	Página	Lat.°′	Long.°′ W = Oeste
Oberau	64	47.33 N	11.08 E
Oberaudorf	64	47.39 N	12.10 E
Oberbauer	263	51.17 N	7.26 E
Oberbayern □[5]	60	48.15 N	11.45 E
Oberbieber	56	50.28 N	7.29 E
Oberbonsfeld	263	51.22 N	7.08 E
Oberbrügge	263	51.11 N	7.34 E
Obercunnersdorf	54	51.02 N	14.40 E
Oberderdingen	56	49.04 N	8.48 E
Oberdiessbach	58	46.51 N	7.38 E
Oberding	60	48.19 N	11.51 E
Oberdolling	60	48.50 N	11.35 E
Oberdorla	54	51.10 N	10.25 E
Oberdrauburg	64	46.45 N	12.58 E
Oberelfringhausen	263	51.20 N	7.11 E
Ober Engadin V	58	46.37 N	9.58 E
Oberengstringen	58	47.25 N	8.28 E
Oberer See → Superior, Lake ⊜	190	48.00 N	88.00 W
Obere Saaletalsperre ⊜[1]	54	50.30 N	11.42 E
Oberfranken □[5]	60	49.50 N	11.20 E
Obergeis	56	50.54 N	9.35 E
Ober-Grafendorf	61	48.09 N	15.33 E
Obergum	52	53.20 N	6.31 E
Obergünzburg	58	47.51 N	10.25 E
Obergurgl	64	46.52 N	11.01 E
Obergurig	54	51.07 N	14.24 E
Oberhaan	263	51.13 N	7.02 E
Oberhaching	60	48.02 N	11.37 E
Oberharmersbach	58	48.22 N	8.07 E
Oberhaslach	58	48.33 N	7.20 E
Oberhausen	56	51.28 N	6.50 E
Oberhof	54	50.41 N	10.44 E
Oberhofen	58	46.44 N	7.40 E
Oberinntal V	64	47.13 N	10.45 E
Oberjettingen	56	48.34 N	8.46 E
Oberjoch	58	47.31 N	10.23 E
Ober-Kassel ⬥[8]	263	51.14 N	6.46 E
Oberkirch	58	48.31 N	8.05 E
Oberkirchbach	264b	48.17 N	16.12 E
Oberkirchen	56	51.09 N	8.22 E
Oberkochen	56	48.47 N	10.06 E
Oberkotzau	54	50.16 N	11.56 E
Oberlaa ⬥[8]	264b	48.08 N	16.24 E
Oberlaapark ♠	264b	48.08 N	16.25 E
Oberlausitz □[9]	54	51.15 N	14.00 E
Oberlin, Ks., U.S.	198	39.49 N	100.31 W
Oberlin, La., U.S.	194	30.37 N	92.45 W
Oberlin, Oh., U.S.	214	41.17 N	82.13 W
Oberlin, Pa., U.S.	208	40.14 N	76.49 W
Oberloisdorf	61	47.27 N	16.30 E
Oberlungwitz	54	50.47 N	12.44 E
Obermarchtal	58	48.14 N	9.34 E
Obermassfeld-Grimmenthal, Dtsch.	54	50.32 N	10.26 E
Obermassfeld-Grimmenthal, Dtsch.	54	50.32 N	10.26 E
Obermeiser	56	51.26 N	9.19 E
Obermieming	64	47.18 N	10.59 E
Obermodern	58	48.51 N	7.32 E
Ober-Mörlen	56	50.22 N	8.42 E
Obermoschel	56	49.44 N	7.46 E
Obermühl	61	48.27 N	13.55 E
Obernai	58	48.28 N	7.29 E
Obernbeck	52	52.12 N	8.41 E
Obernberg am Inn	60	48.19 N	13.20 E
Obernburg am Main	56	49.50 N	9.08 E
Oberndorf	52	53.45 N	9.08 E
Oberndorf am Neckar	58	48.18 N	8.34 E
Oberndorf bei Salzburg	64	47.57 N	12.56 E
Oberndorf in Tirol	64	47.30 N	12.23 E
Oberne	171b	35.24 S	147.50 E
Oberne Hill ∧[2]	171b	35.26 S	147.53 E
Obernhausen	56	50.29 N	9.56 E
Obernkirchen	52	52.16 N	9.07 E
Obernzell	60	48.34 N	13.39 E
Oberoderwitz	54	50.58 N	14.42 E
Oberon	170	33.43 S	149.52 E
Oberösterreich □[3]	30	48.15 N	14.00 E
Oberpfalz □[5]	60	49.30 N	12.10 E
Oberpleis	56	50.43 N	7.16 E
Oberpullendorf	61	47.31 N	16.31 E
Ober-Ramstadt	56	49.49 N	8.44 E
Oberried	58	46.44 N	7.58 E
Oberriet	58	47.19 N	9.33 E
Oberrimsingen	58	47.59 N	7.40 E
Oberröblingen	54	51.26 N	11.18 E
Oberrot	56	49.01 N	9.40 E
Ober Sankt Veit ⬥[8]	264b	48.11 N	16.16 E
Oberscheidental	56	49.30 N	9.09 E
Oberscheinfeld	56	49.42 N	10.26 E
Oberscheld	56	50.44 N	8.20 E
Oberschleissheim	60	48.15 N	11.34 E
Oberschöneweide ⬥[8]	264a	52.28 N	13.31 E
Oberseebach	56	48.58 N	7.59 E
Oberspier	54	51.19 N	10.51 E
Oberstadtfeld	56	50.10 N	6.46 E
Oberstaufen	58	47.33 N	10.01 E
Oberstdorf	58	47.24 N	10.16 E
Obersteinbach	56	49.02 N	7.41 E
Oberstenfeld	56	49.01 N	9.19 E
Oberstreu	56	50.24 N	10.17 E
Obersuhl	56	50.56 N	10.02 E
Obersulm	56	49.08 N	9.27 E
Obertheres	56	50.01 N	10.26 E
Oberthulba	56	50.12 N	9.58 E
Obertilliach	64	46.42 N	12.37 E
Obertraubling	60	48.58 N	12.10 E
Obertraun	64	47.33 N	13.41 E
Obertrum	64	47.56 N	13.05 E
Obertrumer See ⊜	60	47.58 N	13.06 E
Obertyn	78	48.42 N	25.11 E
Oberueckersee ⊜	54	53.12 N	13.52 E
Oberursel	56	50.11 N	8.35 E
Oberuzwil	58	47.26 N	9.08 E
Obervellach	64	46.56 N	13.12 E
Oberviechtach	60	49.28 N	12.25 E
Obervolta → Burkina Faso □[1]	150	13.00 N	1.30 W
Oberwald	58	46.32 N	8.21 E
Oberwart	61	47.17 N	16.13 E
Oberweissbach	54	50.35 N	11.08 E
Oberwengern	263	51.23 N	7.22 E
Oberwesel	56	50.06 N	7.43 E
Oberwiesenthal	54	50.25 N	12.59 E
Oberwolfach	58	48.19 N	8.12 E
Oberwölz Stadt	61	47.13 N	14.17 E
Oberzeiring	61	47.15 N	14.29 E
Obetz	218	39.52 N	82.57 W
Obey, East Fork ≃	192	36.27 N	85.07 W
Obey, West Fork ≃	192	36.27 N	85.09 W
Obgruiten	263	51.13 N	7.01 E
Obhausen	54	51.23 N	11.39 E
Obi	150	8.22 N	8.46 E
Obi, Kepulauan II	164	1.30 S	127.45 E
Obi, Pulau I	164	1.30 S	127.45 E
Obi, Selat ⊎	164	0.52 S	127.33 E
Obiaruku	150	5.51 N	6.09 E
Obichingou ≃	85	38.53 N	70.01 E
Óbidos	250	1.55 S	55.31 W
Obi-Garm	85	38.43 N	69.42 E
Obihiro	92a	42.55 N	143.12 E
Obikanda	85	39.10 N	67.10 E
Obikhody	78	51.02 N	28.59 E
Obilatu, Pulau I	108	1.25 S	127.20 E
Obil'noje	80	47.31 N	44.25 E
Obing	60	48.00 N	12.24 E
Obion	194	36.15 N	89.11 W
Obion ≃	194	35.55 N	89.39 W
Obion, Middle Fork ≃	194	36.13 N	88.56 W
Obion, Rutherford Fork ≃	194	36.17 N	89.01 W
Obion, South Fork ≃	194	36.17 N	89.03 W
Obion Creek ≃	194	36.35 N	89.11 W

Obiou, Grande Tête de l' ∧	62	44.46 N	5.50 E
Obira	92a	44.00 N	141.35 E
Obitsu ≃	94	35.24 N	139.54 E
Objačevo	24	60.20 N	49.34 E
Oblačnaja, gora ∧	89	43.45 N	134.10 E
Öblarn	61	47.27 N	13.59 E
Oblastnaja	80	56.59 N	52.37 E
Oblivskaja	80	48.32 N	42.30 E
Oblong	194	39.00 N	87.54 W
Oblučje	89	49.03 N	131.04 E
Obninsk	82	55.05 N	36.37 E
Obnora ≃	76	58.14 N	40.58 E
Obnova	38	43.26 N	24.59 E
Obo	154	5.24 N	26.30 E
Obobogorap	158	27.18 S	20.04 E
Obock	144	11.59 N	43.16 E
Obojan'	78	51.13 N	36.16 E
Ō-boke ♠	96	33.55 N	133.46 E
Obokote	154	0.52 S	26.19 E
Oboldino	265b	55.53 N	37.56 E
Obolon'	78	49.36 N	32.52 E
Oborniki	30	52.39 N	16.51 E
Obot	144	4.30 N	37.20 E
Obouya	152	0.56 S	15.43 E
Oboz'orskij	24	63.28 N	40.18 E
Obra ≃	30	52.36 N	15.28 E
Obrazcovo-Travino	80	45.58 N	48.02 E
Obree, Mount ∧	164	9.30 S	148.05 E
Obrenovac	38	44.39 N	20.12 E
O'Brien	202	42.04 N	123.42 W
O'Brien Coulee V	202	48.38 N	110.22 W
Obrighoven-Lackhausen	52	51.40 N	6.38 E
Obrovac	36	44.12 N	15.41 E
Obručeva, gora ∧	88	53.36 N	113.52 E
Obručevka	85	42.30 N	69.05 E
Obruk	130	38.10 N	33.12 E
Obryta	54	53.13 N	14.59 E
Obryvistoje	89	48.46 N	144.40 E
Obša ≃	76	55.55 N	32.32 E
Obšarovka	80	53.07 N	48.52 E
Obščij Syrt ∧	80	52.00 N	51.30 E
Observation Peak ∧	204	40.46 N	120.10 W
Observatoire, Caye de l' I	160	21.25 S	158.50 E
Observatory Inlet ⊂	182	55.10 N	129.54 W
Obskaja guba ⊂	72	69.00 N	73.00 E
Obsteig	64	47.18 N	10.56 E
Obtove	78	51.37 N	33.13 E
Ob' Trench ✢[1]	14	33.00 S	98.00 E
Ōbu	94	35.00 N	136.58 E
Obu ⬥[8]	270	34.44 N	135.09 E
Obuasi	150	6.14 N	1.39 W
Obubra	150	6.05 N	8.21 E
Obuchova	76	56.06 N	32.22 E
Obuchovka	86	46.13 N	81.05 E
Obuchovo, Ross.	82	55.50 N	38.16 E
Obuchovo, Ross.	82	56.09 N	36.55 E
Óbuda ⬥[8]	264c	47.33 N	19.02 E
Óbudai-sziget I	264c	47.33 N	19.04 E
Obudu	150	6.40 N	9.09 E
Obukhiv	78	50.08 N	30.37 E
Obukhovychi	78	51.00 N	29.46 E
Obuse	94	36.42 N	138.19 E
Obushkong Lake ⊜	190	47.42 N	80.48 W
Obuškovo	82	55.47 N	37.02 E
Obu-tōge)(	270	34.44 N	135.10 E
Obva ≃	86	58.32 N	55.18 E
Obvinsk	86	58.29 N	54.51 E
Obwalden □[3]	58	46.50 N	8.14 E
Obytichna kosa ›[2]	78	46.33 N	36.13 E
Obytichna zatoka ⊂	78	46.35 N	36.00 E
Obžericha	80	57.11 N	42.58 E
Očakovo ⬥[8]	265b	55.41 N	37.27 E
Ocala	192	29.11 N	82.08 W
Ocallí	248	6.09 S	78.18 W
Očamčira	84	42.44 N	41.28 E
Ocamo ≃	246	2.48 N	65.14 W
Ocampo, Méx.	232	28.11 N	108.23 W
Ocampo, Méx.	232	27.20 N	102.21 W
Ocampo, Méx.	234	22.50 N	99.20 W
Ocampo, Méx.	234	21.39 N	101.30 W
Ocaña, Col.	246	8.15 N	73.20 W
Ocaña, Esp.	34	39.56 N	3.31 W
Ocate Creek ≃	196	36.17 N	104.30 W
Occaquan ≃	208	38.40 N	77.14 W
Occaquan Reservoir ⊜[1]	208	38.43 N	77.22 W
Očchamuri	84	41.52 N	41.50 E
Occhieppo Inferiore	62	45.33 N	8.01 E
Occhiobello	64	44.55 N	11.35 E
Occhito, Lago di ⊜[1]	66	41.35 N	14.54 E
Occidental, Cordillera ⋏, Col.	246	5.00 N	76.00 W
Occidental, Cordillera ⋏, Perú	248	10.00 S	77.00 W
Occidental College ♁[2]	280	34.08 N	118.13 W
Occidental de Zapata, Ciénaga ⠿	240p	22.25 N	81.20 W
Occimiano	62	45.03 N	8.30 E
Occoquan	208	38.41 N	77.15 W
Occoquan Bay ⊂	208	38.37 N	77.13 W
Ocean □[6]	208	39.58 N	74.12 W
Oceana	192	37.41 N	81.37 W
Oceana Naval Air Station ■	208	36.50 N	76.02 W
Ocean Bay Park	276	40.39 N	73.08 W
Ocean Beach	276	40.38 N	73.18 W
Ocean Bluff	207	42.05 N	70.39 W
Ocean Breeze Park	220	27.15 N	80.14 W
Ocean Cape ›	180	59.30 N	139.45 W
Ocean City, Md., U.S.	208	38.20 N	75.05 W
Ocean City, N.J., U.S.	208	39.16 N	74.34 W
Ocean City, Wa., U.S.	224	47.04 N	124.09 W
Ocean Falls	182	52.21 N	127.40 W
Ocean Gate	208	39.55 N	74.08 W
Ocean Grove, Austl.	169	38.16 S	144.32 E
Ocean Grove, Ma., U.S.	207	41.43 N	71.12 W
Ocean Heights	207	41.24 N	70.33 W
Ocean Island → Banaba I	174d	0.52 S	169.35 E
Ocean Lake ⊜[1]	202	43.11 N	108.36 W
Oceano	204	35.06 N	120.37 W
Ocean Park, B.C., Can.	224	49.02 N	122.53 W
Ocean Park, Wa., U.S.	224	46.29 N	124.02 W
Ocean Park ♠	271d	22.15 N	114.09 E
Ocean Port	276	40.19 N	74.00 W
Ocean Shores	224	47.01 N	124.09 W
Oceanside, Ca., U.S.	228	33.11 N	117.22 W
Oceanside, N.Y., U.S.	210	40.38 N	73.38 W
Ocean Springs	194	30.24 N	88.49 W
Ocean View, De., U.S.	208	38.32 N	75.05 W
Ocean View, N.J., U.S.	208	39.10 N	74.44 W
Oceanville	208	39.28 N	74.27 W
Oceola	214	40.51 N	83.06 W
Očer	80	57.53 N	54.42 E
O. C. Fisher Lake ⊜[1]	196	31.30 N	100.30 W
Ocha	89	53.34 N	142.56 E
Ocha, Mochun ⊎	175c	7.09 N	151.53 E
Ochagavía, Canal ≅	286e	33.30 S	70.49 W
Ochakiv	78	46.37 N	31.33 E
Ochanomizu Women's University ♁[2]	268	35.43 N	139.44 E
Ochansk	86	57.43 N	55.23 E
Ochapowace Indian Reserve ⬥[4]	184	50.30 N	102.24 W
Ocheretyne	83	48.14 N	37.36 E
Ocheyedan	198	43.24 N	95.32 W
Ocheyedan ≃	198	43.08 N	95.09 W
Ochi, Nihon	96	33.32 N	133.15 E

Ōchi, Nihon	96	35.04 N	132.36 E
Ōchi, Nihon	96	34.16 N	134.18 E
Ochiai	96	35.01 N	133.45 E
Ochiai ⬥[8]	268	35.43 N	139.42 E
O'Chiese Indian Reserve ⬥[4]	182	52.50 N	115.28 W
Ochil Hills ⋏[2]	46	56.14 N	3.40 W
Ochiltree	44	55.28 N	4.23 W
Ōchise ≃	94	35.03 N	137.46 E
Ochlocknee	192	30.58 N	84.03 W
Ochlockonee ≃	192	29.58 N	84.21 W
Ochoco Creek ≃	202	44.19 N	120.53 W
Ochoco Mountains ⋏	202	44.30 N	120.35 W
Ochopee	220	25.54 N	81.18 W
Ocho Rios	241q	18.25 N	77.07 W
Ochota ≃	74	59.20 N	143.04 E
Ochotsk	74	59.23 N	143.18 E
Ochotskisches Meer → Okhotsk, Sea of ⊤[2]	74	53.00 N	150.00 E
Ochotskoje more → Okhotsk, Sea of ⊤[2]	74	53.00 N	150.00 E
Ochre River	184	51.03 N	99.47 W
Ochsenfurt	56	49.40 N	10.03 E
Ochsenhausen	58	48.04 N	9.56 E
Ochsenwerder ⬥[8]	52	53.28 N	10.05 E
Ochta ≃	265a	59.57 N	30.24 E
Ochtrup	52	52.13 N	7.11 E
Ochvat	76	56.46 N	32.27 E
Oci ≃	152	15.14 S	15.16 E
Ocilla	192	31.35 N	83.15 W
Ock ≃	42	51.39 N	1.17 W
Ockelbo	26	60.53 N	16.43 E
Öckerö	26	57.43 N	11.39 E
Ockham	260	51.18 N	0.27 W
Ockholm	41	54.40 N	8.49 E
Ockies	158	31.31 S	21.41 E
Ocklawaha, Lake ⊜[1]	192	29.30 N	81.50 W
Ocmulgee ≃	192	31.58 N	82.32 W
Ocmulgee National Monument ♠	192	32.43 N	83.38 W
Ocna Mureș	38	46.23 N	23.51 E
Ocnița	38	48.24 N	27.29 E
Ocoa, Bahía de ⊂	238	18.22 N	70.39 W
Ocoee	220	28.34 N	81.32 W
Ocoee (Toccoa) ≃	192	35.12 N	84.40 W
Ocoña	248	16.26 S	73.07 W
Ocoña ≃	248	16.28 S	73.07 W
Oconee	219	39.17 N	89.07 W
Oconee ≃	192	31.58 N	82.32 W
Oconee, Lake ⊜[1]	192	33.30 N	83.15 W
Ocongate	248	13.38 S	71.24 W
O'Connell	170	33.32 S	149.44 E
Oconomowoc	216	43.06 N	88.29 W
Oconomowoc ≃	216	43.07 N	88.37 W
Oconomowoc Lake	216	42.37 N	88.28 W
Oconomowoc Lake ⊜	216	43.06 N	88.27 W
Oconto	190	44.53 N	87.51 W
Oconto ≃	190	44.53 N	87.50 W
Oconto, North Branch ≃	190	45.00 N	88.23 W
Oconto Falls	190	44.52 N	88.08 W
Ocós	236	14.31 N	92.11 W
Ocosingo	232	16.54 N	92.07 W
Ocotal	236	13.38 N	86.29 W
Ocotepec	234	17.13 N	93.09 W
Ocotepeque □[5]	236	14.30 N	89.00 W
Ocotlán	234	20.21 N	102.46 W
Ocotlán de Morelos	234	16.48 N	96.40 W
Ocoyoacac	234	19.16 N	99.26 W
Ocozocoautla [de Espinosa]	234	16.46 N	93.22 W
Ocracoke	192	35.06 N	75.58 W
Ocracoke Island I	192	35.09 N	75.53 W
Ocre, Monte ∧	66	42.15 N	13.26 E
Ocros	248	10.24 S	77.24 W
Octoraro Creek ≃	208	39.39 N	76.09 W
Octoraro Creek, East Branch ≃	208	39.49 N	76.02 W
Octoraro Creek, West Branch ≃	208	39.49 N	76.05 W
Octoraro Lake ⊜[1]	208	39.48 N	76.02 W
Ocú	236	7.57 N	80.47 W
Ocuilán de Arteaga	234	18.58 N	99.25 W
Ocumare del Tuy	246	10.07 N	66.46 W
Ocuri	248	18.50 S	65.50 W
Ocussi	112	9.12 S	124.21 E
Oda, Ghana	150	5.55 N	0.59 W
Oda, Nihon	96	33.34 N	132.48 E
Ōda, Nihon	96	35.11 N	132.30 E
Oda ≃	96	34.37 N	133.44 E
Oda, Jabal ∧	140	20.21 N	36.39 E
Ŏdaejin	98	41.34 N	129.40 E
Odae-san Kukrip Kongwŏn ♠	98	37.46 N	128.37 E
Ōdai	94	34.24 N	136.25 E
Ōdaigahara-zan ∧	92	34.11 N	136.05 E
Odaka	92	37.34 N	141.00 E
Ödåkra	41	56.06 N	12.44 E
Odanakumadona	156	20.53 S	24.45 E
Ōdate	92	40.16 N	140.34 E
Odawara	94	35.15 N	139.10 E
Odayeri ⬥[8]	267b	41.14 N	28.51 E
Odda	26	60.04 N	6.33 E
Odden	41	55.58 N	11.22 E
Odder	41	55.58 N	10.10 E
Oddville	218	38.27 N	84.15 W
Odebolt	198	42.18 N	95.15 W
Ödeby	40	59.24 N	15.25 E
Odei ≃	184	56.06 N	96.55 W
Odeleite, Ribeira de ≃	34	37.21 N	7.27 W
Odell, Il., U.S.	216	41.00 N	88.31 W
Odell, Ne., U.S.	198	40.03 N	96.48 W
Odell, Or., U.S.	224	45.37 N	121.32 W
Odell, Tx., U.S.	196	34.21 N	99.25 W
Odell Lake ⊜	202	43.34 N	122.00 W
Odelzhausen	60	48.19 N	11.12 E
Odem	196	27.57 N	97.34 W
Odemira	34	37.36 N	8.38 W
Ödemiș	130	38.13 N	27.59 E
Ödenburg → Sopron	30	47.41 N	16.36 E
Odendaalsrus	158	27.48 S	26.45 E
Odensbacken	40	59.10 N	15.32 E
Odense	41	55.24 N	10.23 E
Odense ≃	41	55.26 N	10.26 E
Odense Fjord ⊂	41	55.30 N	10.34 E
Odenthal	56	51.02 N	7.07 E
Odenton	208	39.05 N	76.42 W
Odenwald ⋏	56	49.40 N	9.00 E
Oder ≃, Dtsch.	52	51.40 N	10.06 E
Oder (Odra) ≃, Europe	30	53.32 N	14.38 E
Oderberg	54	52.52 N	14.02 E
Oderbruch ⬥[1]	54	52.40 N	14.15 E
Oderen	58	47.55 N	6.59 E
Oder-Havel-Kanal ≅	54	52.52 N	14.02 E
Oder-Spree-Kanal ≅	54	52.23 N	13.41 E
Odertalsperre ⬥[6]	54	51.38 N	10.30 E
Oderzo	64	45.47 N	12.29 E
Odesa	78	46.28 N	30.44 E
Odesa □[4]	78	47.30 N	30.00 E
Ödeshög	26	58.14 N	14.39 E
Odessa, On., Can.	212	44.17 N	76.43 W
Odessa → Odesa, Ukr.	78	46.28 N	30.44 E
Odessa, De., U.S.	208	39.27 N	75.39 W
Odessa, Fl., U.S.	220	28.11 N	82.35 W
Odessa, Mo., U.S.	194	38.59 N	93.57 W
Odessa, N.Y., U.S.	210	42.20 N	76.47 W
Odessa, Tx., U.S.	196	31.50 N	102.22 W
Odessa, Wa., U.S.	202	47.20 N	118.41 W
Odessa Lake ⊜	212	44.19 N	76.41 W
Odesskoje	86	54.13 N	72.58 E
Odiakwe	156	20.01 S	25.17 E
Odib, Wādī V	140	22.38 N	36.06 E
Odiel ≃	34	37.10 N	6.54 W
Odienné	150	9.30 N	7.34 W

Odiham	42	51.15 N	0.57 W
Odin	219	38.37 N	89.03 W
Odin, Mount ∧	182	50.33 N	118.08 W
Odincovo, Ross.	82	54.40 N	38.00 E
Odincovo, Ross.	82	55.41 N	37.17 E
Odiongan	116	12.24 N	121.59 E
Odiongan Bay ⊂	116	12.25 N	121.58 E
Odivelas	266c	38.47 N	9.11 W
Odobești	38	45.45 N	27.04 E
Odojev	76	53.56 N	36.41 E
Odolanów	30	51.35 N	17.39 E
Ōdomari-chosuichi ⊜	96	34.43 N	132.18 E
Odon	194	38.50 N	86.59 W
Ŏdŏngk	110	11.48 N	104.45 E
O'Donnell	196	32.57 N	101.49 W
O'Donnell ≃	162	18.22 S	126.36 E
Odoorn	52	52.51 N	6.51 E
Odorheiu Secuiesc	38	46.18 N	25.18 E
Odra (Oder) ≃	30	53.32 N	14.38 E
Odra Port	54	53.52 N	14.14 E
Odrinhas	266c	38.53 N	9.22 W
Odrzywół	30	51.32 N	20.33 E
Ødsted	41	55.39 N	9.25 E
Odum	192	31.39 N	82.01 W
Odžaci	38	45.30 N	19.16 E
Odzala, Parc National d' ♠	152	1.00 N	15.00 E
Odzi	154	18.58 S	32.23 E
Odzi ≃	154	19.45 S	32.24 E
Odziba	152	3.35 S	15.31 E
Ōe	96	35.23 N	135.09 E
Oebisfelde	54	52.25 N	10.59 E
Oedelem	50	51.10 N	3.20 E
Oederan	54	50.52 N	13.09 E
Oeding	52	51.56 N	6.49 E
Oedt	56	51.19 N	6.22 E
Oegstgeest	52	52.10 N	4.29 E
Oeiras, Bra.	250	7.01 S	42.08 W
Oeiras, Port.	266c	38.41 N	9.21 W
Oeiras do Pará	250	1.58 S	49.51 W
Oelde	52	51.49 N	8.08 E
Oelemari ≃	250	3.13 N	54.09 W
Oella	284b	39.16 N	76.47 W
Oels → Oleśnica	30	51.13 N	17.23 E
Oelsig	54	51.41 N	13.22 E
Oelsnitz, Dtsch.	54	50.24 N	12.10 E
Oelsnitz, Dtsch.	54	50.43 N	12.41 E
Oelwein	190	42.40 N	91.54 W
Oenpelli	164	12.20 S	133.04 E
Oensingen	58	47.17 N	7.44 E
Oepping	60	48.36 N	13.56 E
Oeraro-do I	98	34.27 N	127.30 E
Oer-Erkenschwick	52	51.39 N	7.15 E
Oerlenbach	56	50.09 N	10.08 E
Oerlinghausen	52	51.57 N	8.39 E
Oermten	263	51.29 N	6.27 E
Oesede	52	52.12 N	8.04 E
Oeslau	54	50.17 N	11.01 E
Oespel ⬥[8]	263	51.30 N	7.23 E
Oeste, Canal del ≅	266a	40.32 N	3.42 W
Oeste, Parque del ♠	266a	40.26 N	3.44 W
Oesterdam ⬥[5]	52	51.29 N	4.15 E
Oestrich	263	51.22 N	7.38 E
Oestrich ⬥[8]	263	51.34 N	7.22 E
Oestrum ⬥[8]	263	51.25 N	6.40 E
Ōetaka-yama ∧	96	35.04 N	132.26 E
Oettingen in Bayern	56	48.57 N	10.36 E
Oetz	64	47.12 N	10.54 E
Oeuf ≃	50	48.11 N	2.21 E
Oeventrop	56	51.23 N	8.08 E
Oeversee	41	54.42 N	9.26 E
Ōe-yama ∧	96	35.27 N	135.07 E
Oeyŏn-do I	98	36.14 N	126.05 E
Of	130	40.57 N	40.18 E
O'Fallon, Il., U.S.	219	38.35 N	89.54 W
O'Fallon, Mo., U.S.	219	38.48 N	90.41 W
O'Fallon Creek ≃	198	46.50 N	105.09 W
Ofanto ≃	68	41.22 N	16.13 E
Ofaqim	132	31.17 N	34.37 E
Ofenpass → Fuorn, Pass dal)(	58	46.37 N	10.15 E
Offa	150	8.09 N	4.44 E
Offaly □[6]	48	53.20 N	7.30 W
Offanengo	62	45.22 N	9.44 E
Offemont	58	47.40 N	6.53 E
Offenbach	56	50.08 N	8.47 E
Offenburg	58	48.28 N	7.57 E
Offendorf	58	48.43 N	7.55 E
Offerdal	26	63.28 N	14.00 E
Offham	260	51.17 N	0.23 E
Officer	274b	38.04 S	145.25 E
Officer Creek ≃	162	27.45 S	132.24 E
Offida	66	42.56 N	13.41 E
Offingen	58	48.29 N	10.21 E
Offranville	50	49.52 N	1.03 E
Offutt Air Force Base ■	198	41.08 N	95.56 W
Oficina Alemania	252	25.10 S	69.55 W
Oficina Alianza	248	20.46 S	69.42 W
Oficina Chile	252	25.09 S	69.54 W
Oficina Pedro de Valdivia	252	22.36 S	69.40 W
Oficina Victoria	248	20.44 S	69.42 W
Ofin	273a	6.33 N	3.30 E
Öflingen	58	47.35 N	7.55 E
Ofotfjorden ⊂[2]	24	68.23 N	16.10 E
Oftringen	58	47.19 N	7.56 E
Ofu	174y	14.10 S	169.42 W
Ofu I	174y	14.11 S	169.42 W
Ōfukuroshinden	268	35.53 N	139.27 E
Ōfuna	268	35.21 N	139.32 E
Ōfunato	92	39.04 N	141.43 E
Oga	92	39.53 N	139.51 E
Ogaden ⬥[1]	144	8.00 N	44.00 E
Oga-hantō ›[1]	92	39.55 N	139.50 E
Ōgaki, Nihon	94	35.21 N	136.37 E
Ōgaki, Nihon	96	34.06 N	132.30 E
Ogallala	198	41.07 N	101.43 W
Ogan ≃	112	3.01 S	104.44 E
Ogano	94	36.01 N	139.00 E
Ogasa	94	34.41 N	138.06 E
Ogasawara-guntō (Bonin Islands) II	14	27.00 N	142.10 E
Ōgata, Nihon	94	37.13 N	138.20 E
Ōgata, Nihon	96	33.01 N	133.01 E
Ogata, Nihon	96	32.58 N	131.29 E
Ōga-tō ∧	94	36.13 N	138.06 E
Ogatsu	92	38.31 N	141.28 E
Ogawa, Nihon	92	32.35 N	130.43 E
Ogawa, Nihon	94	36.10 N	140.21 E
Ogawa, Nihon	94	36.37 N	137.58 E
Ogawa, Nihon	94	36.03 N	139.16 E
Ogawa, Nihon	94	36.45 N	140.08 E
Ogawa, Nihon	268	35.44 N	139.28 E
Ogawara-ko ⊜	92	40.47 N	141.20 E
Ogbomosho	150	8.08 N	4.15 E
Ogden, Ia., U.S.	190	42.02 N	94.01 W
Ogden, Ks., U.S.	198	39.06 N	96.42 W
Ogden, Pa., U.S.	208	39.49 N	75.27 W
Ogden, Ut,. U.S.	200	41.13 N	111.58 W
Ogden, Mount ∧	180	58.26 N	133.23 W
Ogden Dunes	216	41.38 N	87.12 W
Ogden Island I	212	44.52 N	75.12 W
Ogden Reservoir ⊜[1]	262	53.42 N	2.22 W
Ogdensburg, N.J., U.S.	210	41.04 N	74.35 W
Ogdensburg, N.Y., U.S.	212	44.41 N	75.29 W
Ogeechee ≃	192	31.51 N	81.06 W
Ōge-jima I	96	34.12 N	134.38 E
Ogema	184	49.35 N	104.55 W
Oggersheim	56	49.29 N	8.22 E
Oghi Fort	123	34.31 N	73.01 E
Ogibalovo	76	60.34 N	39.40 E
Ogidaki Mountain ∧[2]	190	46.58 N	83.58 W
Ogies	158	26.02 S	29.04 E
Ogi-jima I	96	34.26 N	134.04 E
Ogijo	273a	6.42 N	3.31 E

≃	River	Fluß	Río	Rivière	Rio
≅	Canal	Kanal	Canal	Canal	Canal
⌊	Waterfall, Rapids	Wasserfall, Stromschnellen	Cascada, Rápidos	Chute d'eau, Rapides	Cascata, Rápidos
⊎	Strait	Meeresstraße	Estrecho	Détroit	Estreito
⊂	Bay, Gulf	Bucht, Golf	Bahía, Golfo	Baie, Golfe	Baía, Golfo
⊜	Lake, Lakes	See, Seen	Lago, Lagos	Lac, Lacs	Lago, Lagos
⠿	Swamp	Sumpf	Pantano	Marais	Pântano
⊓	Ice Features, Glacier	Eis- und Gletscherformen	Accidentes Glaciales	Formes glaciaires	Acidentes glaciares
⊤	Other Hydrographic Features	Andere Hydrographische Objekte	Otros Elementos Hidrográficos	Autres données hydrographiques	Outros acidentes hidrográficos

✢	Submarine Features	Untermeerische Objekte	Accidentes Submarinos	Formes de relief sous-marin	Acidentes submarinos
□	Political Unit	Politische Einheit	Unidad Politica	Entité politique	Unidade política
♁	Cultural Institution	Kulturelle Institution	Institución Cultural	Institution culturelle	Instituição cultural
⊥	Historical Site	Historische Stätte	Sitio Histórico	Site historique	Sitio histórico
♠	Recreational Site	Erholungs- und Ferienort	Sitio de Recreo	Centre de loisirs	Area de Lazer
⊠	Airport	Flughafen	Aeropuerto	Aéroport	Aeroporto
■	Military Installation	Militäranlage	Instalación Militar	Installation militaire	Instalação militar
⬥	Miscellaneous	Verschiedenes	Misceláneo	Divers	Diversos

Name	Page	Lat.°′	Long.°′
Ogilvie, Austl.	162	28.09 S	114.38 E
Ogilvie, Mn., U.S.	190	45.49 N	93.25 W
Ogilvie ⩶	180	65.52 N	137.16 W
Ogilvie Mountains ⩘	180	65.00 N	139.30 W
Ogilville	218	39.08 N	86.01 W
Ōgimi	174m	26.42 N	128.07 E
Ōgino-sen ⋏	96	35.26 N	134.26 E
Ogle □⁶	216	42.01 N	89.20 W
Oglesby, Il., U.S.	216	41.17 N	89.03 W
Oglesby, Tx., U.S.	222	31.25 N	97.31 W
Oglethorpe	192	32.17 N	84.03 W
Ogliastra ←¹	71	39.56 N	9.37 E
Ogliastro Cilento	68	40.21 N	15.03 E
Oglio ⩶	64	45.02 N	10.39 E
Ogmore	166	22.37 S	149.40 E
Ogmore ⩶	42	51.28 N	3.38 W
Ogmore Vale	42	51.38 N	3.31 W
Ogni	86	51.54 N	83.31 E
Ognica	54	53.07 N	14.27 E
Ognon ⩶	58	47.20 N	5.29 E
Ogn'or Jar	86	58.23 N	79.29 E
Ogn'ovka	86	49.36 N	83.25 E
Ōgo	94	36.25 N	139.10 E
Ōgo ⬥⁸	270	34.49 N	135.06 E
Ōgo ⩶	270	34.47 N	135.04 E
Ogoamas, Bulu ⋏	112	0.40 N	120.12 E
Ogōchi-dam ⬥⁶	94	35.47 N	139.04 E

| ⋏ Mountain — Berg — Montaña — Montagne — Montanha |
| ⋏ Mountains — Gebirge — Montañas — Montagnes — Montanhas |
| ⋊ Pass — Paß — Paso — Col — Passo |
| V Valley, Canyon — Tal, Cañon — Valle, Cañón — Vallée, Canyon — Vale, Canhão |
| ⩶ Plain — Ebene — Llano — Plaine — Planície |
| ⊃ Cape — Kap — Cabo — Cap — Cabo |
| I Island — Insel — Isla — Île — Ilha |
| II Islands — Inseln — Islas — Îles — Ilhas |
| ⊥ Other Topographic Features — Andere Topographische Objekte — Otros Elementos Topográficos — Autres données topographiques — Outros acidentes topográficos |

ESPAÑOL				FRANÇAIS				PORTUGUÊS			
Nombre	Página	Lat.°′	Long.°′ W = Oeste	Nom	Page	Lat.°′	Long.°′ W = Ouest	Nome	Página	Lat.°′	Long.°′ W = Oeste

Nombre	Página	Lat.	Long.
Ommaney, Cape ‣	180	56.10 N	134.39 W
Ommanney Bay c	176	73.07 N	100.11 W
Omme ≃	41	55.53 N	8.40 E
Ömmen	52	52.32 N	6.25 E
Ömnödelger	88	47.52 N	109.55 E
Ömnögov'	86	49.06 N	91.43 E
Ömnögov' □⁴	102	43.00 N	104.00 E
Omø I	41	55.09 N	11.10 E
Omo ≃	144	4.31 N	35.59 E
Omoa, Bahía de c	236	15.45 N	88.10 W
Omodeo, Lago ⊜	71	40.08 N	8.55 E
Omogo	96	33.41 N	133.02 E
Omoi ≃	94	36.09 N	139.41 E
Omoko	150	5.20 N	6.39 E
Omole	273a	6.38 N	3.22 E
Omoloj ≃	74	71.10 N	132.08 E
Omolon ≃	74	68.42 N	158.36 E
Omo National Park ♦	144	6.00 N	35.45 E
Omono ≃	92	39.46 N	140.03 E
Omont	50	49.36 N	4.44 E
Ōmori ⊶⁸	268	35.34 N	139.44 E
Omotegō	94	37.03 N	140.18 E
Omoy	152	1.21 S	13.09 E
Omrel'kaj ≃	180	68.31 N	170.30 E
Omro	190	44.02 N	88.44 W
Omsino	80	58.36 N	50.28 E
Omsk	86	55.00 N	73.24 E
Omsk Oblast' □⁴	86	56.00 N	73.00 E
Omsukčan	74	62.32 N	155.48 E
O-mu, Mya.	110	22.58 N	99.18 E
Ōmu, Nihon	92a	44.34 N	142.58 E
Omu-Aran	150	8.09 N	5.07 E
Ōmuda			
— Ōmuta	96	33.02 N	130.27 E
Omul, Vârful ⋀	38	45.26 N	25.26 E
Omulew ≃	52	53.05 N	21.32 E
Ōmura	92	32.54 N	129.57 E
Ōmura-wan c	92	32.57 N	129.52 E
Ōmuro	268	35.54 N	139.58 E
Omurtag	38	43.06 N	26.25 E
Omusati □⁴	156	18.00 S	14.45 E
Ōmuta	96	33.02 N	130.27 E
Ōmyō	94	35.38 N	136.30 E
Omutinskij	86	56.31 N	67.41 E
Omutninsk	86	58.40 N	52.12 E
Ōmyōnbo	98	41.16 N	127.36 E
On	110	21.40 N	106.35 E
Ona, Nor.	26	62.52 N	6.34 E
Ona ≃, Ross.	86	52.34 N	89.50 E
Ona ≃, Ross.			
— Bir'usa ≃, Ross.	88	57.43 N	95.24 E
Onabas	232	29.27 N	109.32 W
Onadikondo	152	3.52 S	24.10 E
Onaga	198	39.29 N	96.10 W
Onagawa	92	38.26 N	141.27 E
Onahama	94	36.57 N	140.54 E
Onalaska, Tx., U.S.	222	30.48 N	95.07 W
Onalaska, Wa., U.S.	224	46.34 N	122.43 W
Onamia	190	46.04 N	93.40 W
Onancock	208	37.42 N	75.44 W
Onangué, Lac ⊜	152	0.57 S	10.04 E
Onaping ≃	190	46.37 N	81.18 W
Onaping Lake ⊜	190	47.00 N	81.30 W
Onari	268	35.55 N	139.37 E
Onatchiway, Lac ⊜	186	49.00 N	71.03 W
Onawa	198	42.01 N	96.05 W
Onaway	190	45.21 N	84.13 W
Oncativo	252	31.55 S	63.40 W
Once, Canal Numero ≅	252	36.09 S	58.36 W
Onchâi	272b	22.57 N	89.18 E
Onchan	44	54.11 N	4.27 W
Onch'ŏn-dong	98	40.51 N	129.07 E
Oncócua	152	16.34 S	13.28 E
Onda, Esp.	34	39.58 N	0.15 W
Onda, India	126	23.08 N	87.12 E
Ondangwa	156	17.55 S	16.00 E
Ondas, Rio de ≃	255	12.08 S	45.00 W
Ondava ≃	30	48.27 N	21.48 E
Onderdijk	52	52.45 N	5.07 E
Onderstedorings	158	30.13 S	20.37 E
Ondjiva	152	17.03 S	15.47 E
Ondo, Nig.	150	7.04 N	4.47 E
Ondo, Nihon	96	34.12 N	132.32 E
Ondo-ōhashi ⊶⁵	96	34.12 N	132.33 E
Ondörchaan	88	47.19 N	110.39 E
Ondörchangaj	88	49.20 N	94.50 E
Ondör-Öne	102	45.51 N	103.11 E
Ondöršireet	88	47.27 N	104.50 E
Ondör-Ulaan	88	48.03 N	100.30 E
Ondozero, ozero ⊜	62	63.48 N	33.20 E
O'Neals	226	37.08 N	119.42 W
One Arrow Indian Reserve ⊶⁴	182	52.48 N	106.03 W
Oneco, Ct., U.S.	207	41.41 N	71.48 W
Oneco, Fl., U.S.	220	27.26 N	82.32 W
Onega	24	63.55 N	38.05 E
Onega ≃	24	63.58 N	37.55 E
Onega, Lake — Onežskoje ozero ⊜	24	61.30 N	35.45 E
Oneglia	62	43.53 N	8.02 E
One Hundred and Two ≃	194	39.44 N	94.43 W
One Hundred and Two, West Fork ≃	194	40.26 N	94.49 W
One Hundred Fifty Mile House	182	52.06 N	121.55 W
One Hundred Mile House	182	51.39 N	121.18 W
Oneida, Il., U.S.	190	41.04 N	90.13 W
Oneida, Ky., U.S.	192	37.16 N	83.38 W
Oneida, N.Y., U.S.	210	43.05 N	75.39 W
Oneida, Oh., U.S.	218	39.24 N	84.33 W
Oneida, Tn., U.S.	192	36.29 N	84.30 W
Oneida ≃	210	43.10 N	75.20 W
Oneida ≃	210	43.12 N	76.17 W
Oneida Castle	210	43.05 N	75.40 W
Oneida County □⁶	210	43.09 N	75.23 W
Oneida Creek ≃	210	43.10 N	75.44 W
Oneida Indian Reserve ⊶⁴	190	44.30 N	88.10 W
Oneida Indian Reserve ⊶⁴	214	42.49 N	81.24 W
Oneida Lake ⊜	210	43.13 N	76.00 W
O'Neil Forebay ⊜¹	226	37.05 N	121.03 W
O'Neill	198	42.27 N	98.38 W
Onekama	190	44.21 N	86.12 W
Onekotan, ostrov I	74	49.25 N	154.45 E
Onema	152	4.33 S	24.31 E
Onemen, zaliv c	180	64.45 N	176.35 E
Oneonta, Al., U.S.	194	33.56 N	86.28 W
Oneonta, N.Y., U.S.	210	42.27 N	75.03 W
Oneroa I	174k	21.15 S	159.43 W
Onești	38	46.14 N	26.44 E
One Tree Hill	184	34.43 S	138.46 E
One Tree Hill ⋀²	274b	37.52 S	145.19 E
One Tree Hill Lookout ♦	169	36.48 S	144.18 E
Onexai ‣	174w	21.05 S	175.07 W
Onex	56	46.10 N	6.06 E
Onežskaja guba c	24	64.20 N	36.30 E
Onežskij poluostrov ‣¹	24	64.35 N	38.00 E
Onežskoje ozero (Lake Onega) ⊜	24	61.30 N	35.45 E
Onga	96	33.54 N	130.39 E
Onganbira	172	39.55 S	176.25 E
Ongaonga	172	39.55 S	176.25 E
Ongarue	172	38.43 S	175.17 E
Ong Con, Cu Lao I	269c	10.45 N	106.50 E
Ongea Lévu ‣	175g	19.08 S	178.24 W
Ongeluks ≃	158	32.24 S	19.46 E
Ongers ≃	158	31.04 S	23.13 E
Ongerup	158	33.58 S	118.29 E
Ongjin	98	37.57 N	125.21 E
Ongoka	154	1.23 S	26.02 E
Ongole	122	15.31 N	80.04 E
Ongon	102	45.21 N	113.09 E
Onguday	86	50.45 N	86.09 E
Oni	84	42.34 N	43.27 E
Onich	46	56.42 N	5.13 W
Onida	198	44.42 N	100.03 W
Onifai	71	40.24 N	9.39 E
Oniferi	71	40.16 N	9.10 E
Onigajō-yama ⋀	96	33.07 N	132.41 E
Onilahy ≃	157b	23.34 S	43.45 E
Onin, Jazirah ‣¹	164	2.50 S	132.05 E
Onion Creek ≃	222	30.12 N	97.35 W
Onion Peak ⋀	224	45.49 N	123.53 W
Onishi	94	36.09 N	139.04 E
Onistagane, Lac ⊜	186	50.42 N	71.19 W
Onitsha	150	6.09 N	6.47 E
Onji	270	34.37 N	135.38 E
Onjuku	94	35.11 N	140.22 E
Onkaparinga ≃	168b	35.10 S	138.28 E
Onkivesi ⊜	26	63.18 N	27.18 E
Onko	152	4.07 S	19.59 E
Onley	208	37.41 N	75.42 W
Onna	174m	26.30 N	127.51 E
Onnaing	50	50.23 N	3.36 E
Onno	58	45.55 N	9.17 E
Onny ≃	42	52.23 N	2.45 W
Ōno-I-Lau I	14	20.39 S	178.42 W
Onojō	96	33.32 N	130.28 E
Onolimbu	114	1.03 N	97.53 E
Onomi	96	33.21 N	133.09 E
Onomichi	96	34.25 N	133.12 E
Onon	88	49.08 N	112.38 E
Onon ≃	88	51.42 N	115.50 E
Onondaga, Mi., U.S.	216	42.26 N	84.33 W
Onondaga, N.Y., U.S.	210	43.00 N	76.11 W
Onondaga □⁶	210	43.03 N	76.09 W
Onondaga Creek ≃	210	43.04 N	76.11 W
Onondaga Indian Reservation ⊶⁴	210	42.55 N	76.09 W
Onor	89	50.11 N	142.40 E
Onota Lake ⊜	207	42.28 N	73.17 W
Ōnō-Ōhara ≃	94	36.33 N	138.56 E
Onoto	244	9.36 N	65.12 W
Onotoa I¹	14	1.52 S	175.34 E
Onoway	182	53.42 N	114.12 W
Ons, Illa de I	34	42.23 N	8.56 W
Onsbjerg	41	55.51 N	10.35 E
Onseepkans	158	28.46 S	19.14 E
Onsen	96	35.33 N	134.29 E
Onset	207	41.44 N	70.39 W
Onslow	162	21.39 S	115.06 E
Onslow Bay c	192	34.20 N	77.20 W
Onslow Village	260	51.14 N	0.36 W
Onsted	216	42.00 N	84.11 W
Onstwettingen	58	48.17 N	9.00 E
Onstwedde	52	53.02 N	7.02 E
On-take ⋀	92	31.35 N	130.39 E
Ontake-san ⋀	94	35.53 N	137.29 E
Ontario, Ca., U.S.	228	34.03 N	117.39 W
Ontario, In., U.S.	216	41.43 N	85.23 W
Ontario, N.Y., U.S.	210	43.13 N	77.17 W
Ontario, Or., U.S.	214	40.45 N	82.35 W
Ontario, Or., U.S.	224	44.01 N	116.57 W
Ontario □⁶	176	51.00 N	85.00 W
Ontario, Lake ⊜	212	43.45 N	78.00 W
Ontario Agricultural Museum ♦	212	43.30 N	79.56 W
Ontario Center	210	43.14 N	77.19 W
Ontario International Airport ⊠	228	34.04 N	117.36 W
Ontario Place ⊠	275b	43.38 N	79.25 W
Ontario Science Centre ⋆	275b	43.43 N	79.21 W
Ontelaunee, Lake ⊜	208	40.27 N	75.55 W
Ontinyent (Onteniente)	34	38.49 N	0.37 W
Ontojärvi ⊜	26	64.09 N	29.09 E
Ontonagon	190	46.52 N	89.18 W
Ontonagon, East Branch ≃	190	46.42 N	89.11 W
Ontonagon, Middle Branch ≃	190	46.49 N	89.10 W
Ontonagon, West Branch ≃	190	46.42 N	89.11 W
Ontong Java I¹	175e	5.20 S	159.30 E
Ontur	82	55.51 N	36.31 E
Onufrievka	78	48.54 N	33.26 E
Ōnuma	268	35.32 N	139.25 E
Onverwacht	250	5.36 N	55.12 W
Onward	216	40.42 N	86.12 W
Ōnyang, Taehan	98	36.47 N	127.00 E
Ōnyang, Taehan	98	35.34 N	129.07 E
Onzain	50	47.30 N	1.11 E
Onzo ≃	152	8.12 S	13.16 E
Oobagooma	162	16.46 S	123.59 E
Oodnadatta	162	27.33 S	135.28 E
Ood Weyne	144	9.25 N	45.04 E
Ōoka	94	36.30 N	137.59 E
Ooldea	162	30.27 S	131.50 E
Oolitic	216	38.54 N	86.31 W
Oologah	196	36.26 N	95.42 W
Oologah Lake ⊜¹	196	36.38 N	95.33 W
Ooma	174d	0.53 S	169.36 E
Oombergen	50	50.54 N	3.50 E
Oona River	182	53.57 N	130.18 W
Ooratippra	162	21.55 S	136.00 E
Ooratippra Creek ≃	162	21.55 S	136.05 E
Oorlogskloof ≃	158	31.52 S	19.01 E
Oos	56	48.47 N	8.11 E
Oos-Londen — East London	158	33.00 S	27.55 E
Oostakker	50	51.05 N	3.45 E
Oostburg, Ned.	52	51.20 N	3.30 E
Oostburg, Wi., U.S.	190	43.37 N	87.47 W
Oost-Cappel	50	50.55 N	2.36 E
Oostduinkerke	50	51.07 N	2.41 E
Oostelijk Flevoland			
Oostende (Ostende)	52	52.30 N	5.40 E
Oosterbeek	52	51.59 N	6.17 E
Oosterbeek	52	51.50 N	3.48 E
Oosterhuizen	52	51.59 N	5.50 E
Oosterhout	52	51.38 N	4.51 E
Oosterschelde c	52	51.33 N	4.00 E
Oosterscheldedam ⁴	52	51.38 N	3.41 E
Oosterwolde	52	52.59 N	6.17 E
Oosterzele	50	50.57 N	3.48 E
Oostham	52	51.05 N	5.18 E
Oostkamp	50	51.09 N	3.14 E
Oostmalle	56	51.18 N	4.44 E
Oostrozebeke	50	50.55 N	3.20 E
Oost-Souburg	52	51.27 N	3.35 E
Oost-Vlaanderen □⁴	50	51.00 N	3.45 E
Oostmarsum	52	52.25 N	6.54 E
Ootsa Lake	182	53.47 N	126.03 W
Ootsa Lake ⊜	182	53.49 N	126.18 W
Ootsi	156	25.02 S	25.45 E
Ootua, Mont ⋀	174x	9.47 S	138.58 W

Nom	Page	Lat.	Long.
Opaka	38	43.27 N	26.10 E
Opaia	152	0.37 S	24.21 E
Opaca, Cordillera ⋀	236	14.30 N	88.20 W
Opa Cliffs	226	36.57 N	121.57 W
Opa e, Côte d' ⊥²	50	50.40 N	1.35 E
Opaenica	30	52.19 N	16.23 E
Opa icha	265b	55.49 N	37.15 E
Opa-Locka	220	25.54 N	80.15 W
Opari	154	3.56 N	32.03 E
Oparino	24	59.52 N	48.17 E
Opasatica, Lac ⊜	186	33.07 N	132.41 W
Opasatika Lake ⊜	190	49.04 N	83.08 W
Opasquia	184	53.16 N	93.35 W
Opasquia Lake ⊜	184	53.18 N	93.34 W
Opatija	36	45.21 N	14.19 E
Opatów	30	50.49 N	21.26 E
Opava ≃	30	49.56 N	17.54 E
Opava ≃	30	49.50 N	18.13 E
Opečenskij Posad	76	58.16 N	34.07 E
Opeepeesway Lake ⊜	190	47.38 N	82.14 W
Opeilu	273a	6.42 N	3.18 E
Opelika	194	32.38 N	85.22 W
Opelousas	194	30.32 N	92.04 W
Open Bay c	164	4.50 S	151.20 E
Open Door	258	34.30 S	59.05 W
Opeongo ≃	190	45.42 N	77.57 W
Opeongo Lake ⊜	190	45.42 N	78.23 W
Opequon Creek ≃	188	39.35 N	77.52 W
Opf·kon	58	47.26 N	8.35 E
Op·hain-Bois-Seigneur-Isaac	50	50.40 N	4.21 E
Op·hasselt	50	50.49 N	3.53 E
Op·heim	202	48.51 N	106.24 W
Op·herdicke	263	51.29 N	7.38 E
Op·heusden	52	51.56 N	5.38 E
Ophir, Ak., U.S.	180	63.10 N	156.31 W
Ophir, Or., U.S.	224	42.34 N	124.22 W
Ophirton ⊶⁸	273d	26.14 S	28.01 E
Ophthalmia Range ⋀	162	23.17 S	119.30 E
Opi	66	41.47 N	13.50 E
Opienge	154	0.12 N	27.30 E
Opihikao	229d	19.25 N	154.53 W
Opinaca ≃	176	52.15 N	78.02 W
Opinan	46	57.43 N	5.47 W
Opinicon Lake ⊜	212	44.33 N	76.20 W
Opiscotéo, Lac ⊜	176	53.10 N	68.10 W
Opishnya	78	49.58 N	34.37 E
Opladen	56	51.04 N	7.00 E
Opmeer	52	52.43 N	4.56 E
Opobo	150	4.34 N	7.27 E
Opobo Town	150	4.30 N	7.30 E
Opočka	76	56.43 N	28.38 E
Opoczno	30	51.23 N	20.17 E
Opol	116	8.31 N	124.34 E
Opole (Oppeln)	30	50.41 N	17.55 E
Opole ⁴	30	50.30 N	17.45 E
Opole Lubelskie	30	51.09 N	21.58 E
Opono — Lapu-Lapu	116	10.19 N	123.57 E
Opononu, Lake ⊜	156	18.08 S	15.45 E
Opopeo	234	19.24 N	101.36 W
Oporto — Porto	34	41.11 N	8.36 W
Opotiki	172	38.00 S	177.17 E
Opoul	50	42.51 N	2.50 E
Oppach	54	51.03 N	14.30 E
Oppdal	26	62.36 N	9.40 E
Oppelhain	54	51.33 N	13.35 E
Oppeln — Opole	30	50.41 N	17.55 E
Oppenau	58	48.28 N	8.10 E
Oppenberg	61	47.29 N	14.16 E
Oppenheim, Dtsch.	56	49.51 N	8.21 E
Oppenheim, N.Y., U.S.	210	43.04 N	74.42 W
Oppenheim Park ⊠	284a	49.09 N	78.54 W
Oppenhuizen	52	53.00 N	5.42 E
Oppido Lucano	68	40.47 N	16.00 E
Oppido Mamertina	68	38.16 N	16.00 E
Oppio	66	44.03 N	10.50 E
Oppland □⁶	26	61.10 N	9.40 E
Opportunity, Mt., U.S.	202	46.07 N	112.49 W
Opportunity, Wa., U.S.	202	47.39 N	117.14 W
Opsa	76	55.32 N	26.47 E
Opsterland □⁴	52	53.02 N	6.08 E
Optic Lake ⊜	184	54.46 N	101.13 W
Opua Lake ⊜¹	196	36.40 N	101.10 W
Opua	172	35.19 S	174.07 E
Op·nake	172	39.27 S	173.51 E
Op·nohu, Baie d' c	174s	17.30 S	149.51 W
Op·wo	152	18.03 S	13.45 E
Opwijk	50	50.58 N	4.11 E
Oquawka	190	40.55 N	90.56 W
Oquendo, Perú	286d	11.58 S	77.08 W
Oquendo, Pil.	116	12.08 N	124.32 E
O'Quinn	222	29.50 N	96.58 W
Or' ≃	86	51.12 N	58.30 E
Or', Côte d' ⊥	58	47.10 N	4.50 E
Or', Étang d' ⊜	64	43.33 N	4.00 E
Ora (Auer), It.	64	46.21 N	11.18 E
Ora, L'byā	148	28.33 N	19.24 E
Ōra, Nihon	174m	26.33 N	128.02 E
Ora Banda	162	30.22 S	121.04 E
Oracle	200	32.36 N	110.46 W
Oradell	284	40.57 N	74.02 W
Oradell Reservoir ⊜¹	276	40.58 N	74.01 W
Oræfajökull ⋀¹	24a	64.00 N	16.38 W
Orahovica	36	45.31 N	17.53 E
Orai	124	25.59 N	79.28 E
Oraibi Wash V	200	35.26 N	110.49 W
Oraison	62	43.55 N	5.55 E
Oran — Wahran, Alg.	148	35.43 N	0.43 W
Oran, Mo., U.S.	194	37.05 N	89.39 W
Oran, Sebkha d' ⊜	34	35.32 N	0.48 W
Orange, Austl.	166	33.17 S	149.06 E
Orange, Ca., U.S.	228	33.47 N	117.51 W
Orange, Ct., U.S.	207	41.16 N	73.01 W
Orange, Ma., U.S.	207	42.35 N	72.18 W
Orange, N.J., U.S.	284	40.46 N	74.14 W
Orange, Oh., U.S.	279a	41.26 N	91.29 W
Orange, Tx., U.S.	194	30.05 N	93.44 W
Orange, Va., U.S.	188	38.14 N	78.06 W
Orange □⁶, Fl., U.S.	220	28.32 N	81.16 W
Orange □⁶, In., U.S.	216	38.33 N	86.28 W
Orange □⁶, N.Y., U.S.	210	41.24 N	74.20 W
Orange (Oranje) ≃	156	28.41 S	16.28 E
Orange, Cabo ‣	250	4.24 N	51.33 W
Orange Bowl ♦	220	25.46 N	80.14 W
Orangeburg, Ky., U.S.	218	38.35 N	83.39 W
Orangeburg, N.Y., U.S.	276	41.03 N	73.57 W
Orangeburg, S.C., U.S.	192	33.29 N	80.51 W
Orange City, Fl., U.S.	220	28.57 N	81.17 W
Orange City, Ia., U.S.	198	43.00 N	96.03 W
Orange County Airport ⊠	228	33.40 N	117.52 W
Orange Cove	226	36.37 N	119.19 W
Orange Free State □⁴, S. Afr.	158	28.30 S	27.00 E
Orange Free State — Free State □⁴, S. Afr.	158	28.30 S	27.00 E
Orange Grove	198	27.57 N	97.56 W
Orange Grove ⊶⁸	273d	26.10 S	28.05 E
Orange Lake, Fl., U.S.	192	29.25 N	82.13 W
Orange Lake, N.Y., U.S.	210	41.33 N	74.06 W
Orange Lake ⊜	192	29.29 N	82.10 W

Nome	Página	Lat.	Long.
Orangemouth — Oranjemund	156	28.38 S	16.24 E
Orange Park	192	30.09 N	81.42 W
Orange Park Acres	280	33.48 N	117.47 W
Orange Reservoir ⊜¹	276	40.46 N	74.17 W
Orangevale	226	38.40 N	121.13 W
Orangeville, On., Can.	212	43.55 N	80.06 W
Orangeville, Oh., U.S.	214	41.20 N	80.37 W
Orangeville, Ut., U.S.	200	39.13 N	111.03 W
Orange Walk	232	18.06 N	88.33 W
Orango Grande I	150	11.10 N	16.08 W
Orani, It.	71	40.15 N	9.11 E
Orani, Pil.	116	14.49 N	120.32 E
Oranienbaum	54	51.48 N	12.24 E
Oranienburg	54	52.45 N	13.14 E
Oranje ≃	52	52.55 N	6.28 E
Oranje — Orange ≃	156	28.41 S	16.28 E
Oranjefontein	156	23.25 S	27.41 E
Oranje Gebergte ⋀	250	3.00 N	55.05 W
Oranjemund	156	28.38 S	16.24 E
Oranjerivier	158	29.40 S	24.12 E
Oranjestad	241s	12.33 N	70.06 W
Oranjeville	158	27.00 S	28.15 E
Oranki	80	55.53 N	43.44 E
Oranmore	48	53.16 N	8.54 W
Oranžerei	80	45.50 N	47.36 E
Or 'Aqiva	132	32.30 N	34.55 E
Orarak	140	6.15 N	32.23 E
Orari ≃	172	44.15 S	171.25 E
Oras	116	12.09 N	125.26 E
Oras ≃	116	12.08 N	125.26 E
Oras Bay c	116	12.07 N	125.28 E
Orăștie	38	45.50 N	23.12 E
Orașul Stalin — Brașov	38	45.39 N	25.37 E
Orativ	78	49.12 N	29.32 E
Oratório, Ribeirão do ≃	287b	23.37 S	46.32 W
Oravais (Oravainen)	26	63.18 N	22.23 E
Oravita	38	45.02 N	21.41 E
Orawia	172	46.03 S	167.49 E
Orba ≃	62	44.53 N	8.37 E
Orba Co ⊜	120	34.32 N	81.03 E
Orbassano	62	45.01 N	7.32 E
Orbe	56	46.43 N	6.32 E
Orbe ≃	56	46.47 N	6.39 E
Orbec-en-Auge	50	49.01 N	0.25 E
Orbetello	66	42.27 N	11.13 E
Orbetello, Laguna di ⊜	66	42.27 N	11.14 E
Orbey	58	48.08 N	7.10 E
Orbieu ≃	32	43.14 N	2.54 E
Orbigny	50	47.12 N	1.14 E
Órbigo ≃	34	41.58 N	5.40 W
Orbigus	50	49.09 N	0.14 E
Orbisonia	214	40.15 N	77.54 W
Orbost	166	37.42 S	148.27 E
Orbyhus	40	60.14 N	17.42 E
Orcadas ⋀³	9	60.45 S	44.43 W
Orcades, Islas — Orkney Islands II	46	59.00 N	3.00 W
Orcadas del Sur, Islas — South Orkney Islands II	9	60.35 S	45.30 W
Orcades du Sud, Îles — South Orkney Islands II	9	60.35 S	45.30 W
Orcas	224	48.36 N	122.57 W
Orcas Island I	224	48.39 N	122.55 W
Orcement	261	48.35 N	1.49 E
Orcera	34	38.19 N	2.39 W
Orchamps	58	47.09 N	5.40 E
Orchard, Ne., U.S.	198	42.20 N	98.14 W
Orchard, Tx., U.S.	222	29.36 N	95.58 W
Orchard City	200	38.49 N	107.58 W
Orchard Hills, Austl.	274a	33.47 S	150.43 E
Orchard Hills, Pa., U.S.	279b	40.36 N	79.32 W
Orchard Island	216	40.28 N	83.53 W
Orchard Lake	281	42.35 N	83.21 W
Orchard Lake Village	281	42.34 N	83.21 W
Orchard Mesa	200	39.02 N	108.33 W
Orchard Park	210	42.46 N	78.44 W
Orchard Park Airport ⊠			
Orchard Peak ⋀	284a	42.48 N	78.45 W
Orchards	224	45.40 N	122.33 W
Orchard Valley	188	41.05 N	104.48 W
Orchard View	285	40.04 N	74.53 W
Orchha	124	25.21 N	78.39 E
Orchies	50	50.28 N	3.14 E
Orchon	88	49.09 N	105.21 E
Orchon ≃	88	50.21 N	106.05 E
Orchon Tuul	88	48.58 N	104.59 E
Orchyk ≃	78	49.05 N	34.54 E
Orčik ≃	78	48.53 N	34.54 E
Orcières	62	44.41 N	6.20 E
Orco ≃	62	45.10 N	7.52 E
Orcopampa	248	15.30 S	72.21 W
Orcutt	226	34.52 N	120.26 W
Orcula	204	41.17 N	124.03 W
Ord	198	41.36 N	98.55 W
Ord ≃	160	15.30 S	128.21 E
Ord, Mount ⋀	162	17.20 S	125.34 E
Ordal	261	51.12 N	56.54 E
Orde ≃	46	57.16 N	112.38 W
Orderville	200	37.16 N	112.38 W
Ordes	34	43.04 N	8.24 W
Ordesa, Parque Nacional de ♦	34	42.39 N	0.02 E
Ord Mountains ⋀	228	34.40 N	116.49 W
Ord Mountains ⋀	228	34.42 N	117.10 W
Ordoqui	252	35.54 S	61.10 W
Ord River	160	17.23 S	128.51 E
Ordu	130	41.00 N	37.54 E
Ordu □⁴	130	40.45 N	37.30 E
Ordubad	84	38.56 N	46.02 E
Ordway	188	38.13 N	103.46 W
Ordynskoje	86	54.22 N	81.56 E
Ordžonikidze — Vladikavkaz, Ross.	84	43.03 N	44.40 E
Ordžonikidze — Vladikavkaz, Ross.	84	43.00 N	44.40 E
Ordžonikidze, Ukr.	78	47.40 N	34.04 E
Ordžonikidze — Yenakiyeve, Ukr.	83	48.14 N	38.13 E
Ordžonikidzeabad	86	38.34 N	69.01 E
Ordžonikidzevskaja	84	43.18 N	45.03 E
Ordžonikidzevskij, Ross.	86	61.41 N	24.21 E
Ordžonikidzevskij, Ross.	84	43.51 N	41.54 E
Oreana	226	40.13 N	119.17 W
Oreälven ≃	26	63.32 N	19.44 E
Orebro	40	59.16 N	15.13 E
Örebro Län □⁶	40	59.30 N	15.00 E
Orechovka	80	53.59 N	48.11 E
Orechovno	76	58.49 N	29.20 E
Orechovo-Zujevo	82	55.49 N	38.59 E
Ore City	222	32.48 N	94.43 W
Oredež ≃	76	59.24 N	30.02 E
Orefield	208	40.37 N	75.43 W
Oregon, Il., U.S.	190	42.00 N	89.19 W
Oregon, Mo., U.S.	194	39.59 N	95.08 W
Oregon, Oh., U.S.	214	41.39 N	83.29 W
Oregon, Wi., U.S.	190	42.55 N	89.23 W
Oregon □⁴, U.S.	178	44.00 N	121.00 W
Oregon, In., U.S.	216	41.43 N	85.10 W

Nome	Página	Lat.	Long.
Orland Lake	278	41.38 N	87.52 W
Orlando, S. Afr.	273d	26.14 S	27.55 E
Orlando, Fl., U.S.	220	28.32 N	81.22 W
Orlando, Capo d' ‣	70	38.10 N	14.45 E
Orlando Darn ⁴	273d	26.16 S	27.56 E
Orlando International Airport ⊠	220	28.26 N	81.19 W
Orlando Naval Training Center ▪	220	28.34 N	81.20 W
Orlando West Extension	273d	26.15 S	27.54 E
Orland Park	216	41.37 N	87.51 W
Orland Square ⊶⁹	278	41.36 N	87.51 W
Orléanais □⁹	50	47.50 N	2.00 E
Orléans, On., Can.	212	45.28 N	75.31 W
Orléans, Fr.	50	47.55 N	1.54 E
Orleans, Ca., U.S.	204	41.18 N	123.32 W
Orleans, In., U.S.	218	38.39 N	86.27 W
Orleans, Ma., U.S.	207	41.47 N	69.59 W
Orleans, Ne., U.S.	198	40.07 N	99.27 W
Orleans, Vt., U.S.	188	44.49 N	72.12 W
Orléans ≃, N.Y., U.S.	210	43.15 N	78.12 W
Orleans □⁶, Vt., U.S.	206	44.47 N	72.12 W
Orléans, Canal d' ≅	50	47.54 N	1.55 E
Orléans, Île d' I	186	46.55 N	70.58 W
Orencik	130	39.16 N	29.33 E
Oreng, Indon.	114	4.03 N	97.28 E
Oreng, Indon.	114	4.33 N	96.49 E
Orense	252	38.40 S	59.47 W
Orense ≃	34	42.15 N	7.30 W
Örensehir	130	39.00 N	36.39 E
Orepuki	172	46.15 S	167.44 E
Oreški	82	55.43 N	36.21 E
Orestes	216	40.16 N	85.43 W
Orestes Pereyra	232	26.31 N	105.40 W
Orestimba Creek ≃	226	37.25 N	121.00 W
Øresund ≅			
— The Sound ⊔	41	55.50 N	12.40 E
Oreti ≃	172	46.28 S	168.17 E
Oreto ≃	70	38.06 N	13.24 E
Orewa	172	36.34 S	174.42 E
Orfanoú, Kólpos c	38	40.40 N	23.50 E
Orford, Eng., U.K.	42	52.06 N	1.31 E
Orford, Eng., U.K.	262	53.25 N	2.35 W
Orford, Mont ⋀	206	45.19 N	72.15 W
Orford Ness ‣	42	52.05 N	1.34 E
Orfordville	190	42.37 N	89.15 W
Organ Needle ⋀	200	32.21 N	106.33 W
Organ Pipe Cactus National Monument ♦	200	32.00 N	112.55 W
Orgaz	34	39.39 N	3.54 W
Orge ≃	261	48.42 N	2.24 E
Orgelet	58	46.31 N	5.37 E
Orgiano	64	45.20 N	11.26 E
Orgères-en-Beauce	50	48.09 N	1.42 E
Orgeval	50	48.55 N	1.59 E
Orgiano	64	45.21 N	11.28 E
Órgiva	34	36.54 N	3.25 W
Orgnac, Aven d' ⊥⁵	62	44.19 N	4.27 E
Orgnac-l'Aven	62	44.19 N	4.27 E
Orgon	62	43.47 N	5.02 E
Orgosolo	71	40.12 N	9.21 E
Orgtrud	82	56.12 N	40.37 E
Orgün	120	32.51 N	69.07 E
Orhaneli	130	39.54 N	29.00 E
Orhangazi	130	40.30 N	29.18 E
Orhanlar	130	39.34 N	27.37 E
Orhei	38	47.23 N	28.49 E
Oria, It.	68	40.30 N	17.38 E
Oria, R.D.C.	154	3.17 N	30.41 E
Oriçanga, Rio do ≃	256	22.18 S	47.03 W
Orichuna ≃	244	7.25 N	68.58 W
Oriči	80	58.24 N	49.05 E
Orick	204	41.17 N	124.03 W
Oricola	66	42.02 N	13.02 E
Orient, Ia., U.S.	198	41.12 N	94.24 W
Orient, N.Y., U.S.	207	41.08 N	72.18 W
Orient, Oh., U.S.	218	39.48 N	83.09 W
Orient, Wa., U.S.	182	48.53 N	118.13 W
Oriental, Mex.	234	19.22 N	97.37 W
Oriental, N.C., U.S.	192	35.01 N	76.41 W
Oriental, Cordillera ⋀, Col.	246	6.00 N	73.00 W
Oriental, Cordillera ⋀, Perú	246	11.00 S	74.00 W
Oriental, Pico ⋀	286c	10.32 N	66.50 W
Oriental de Zapata, Ciénaga ⊜	240p	22.15 N	80.50 W
Oriental Park	214	42.09 N	79.22 W
Oriente	252	38.44 S	60.37 W
Orientos	166	28.05 S	141.14 E
Origgio	266b	45.36 N	9.01 E
Origny-en-Thiérache	50	49.54 N	4.01 E
Origny-Sainte-Benoite	50	49.50 N	3.30 E
Orikhiv	78	47.34 N	35.47 E
Orikivi	83	48.17 N	39.13 E
Oril' ≃	78	49.10 N	34.54 E
Orillia	212	44.37 N	79.25 W
Orimattila	26	60.48 N	25.45 E
Orin	202	42.40 N	105.10 W
Orinduik	246	4.42 N	60.01 W
Orini	172	37.34 S	175.18 E
Orino, ozero ⊜	82	57.06 N	116.30 E
Orinoco ≃	244	9.00 N	61.30 W
Orinoco, Delta del ⊶²	244	9.15 N	61.30 W
Oriola (Orihuela)	34	38.05 N	0.57 W
Oriole, Md., U.S.	208	38.10 N	75.53 W
Oriole, Pa., U.S.	281	41.08 N	77.13 W
Oriole Park ⊶⁴	284b	40.18 N	76.37 W
Oriolo	68	40.03 N	16.27 E
Oriomo ≃	164	8.50 S	143.15 E
Orion, Il., U.S.	190	41.21 N	90.23 W
Orion, Pil.	116	14.37 N	120.34 E
Oripää	26	60.51 N	22.41 E
Oriskany	210	43.09 N	75.19 W
Oriskany Battlefield State Historic Site ♦	210	43.11 N	75.23 W
Oriskany Creek ≃	210	43.10 N	75.20 W
Oriskany Falls	210	42.56 N	75.27 W
Orissa □⁴	118	20.00 N	84.00 E
Orissaare	16	58.34 N	23.05 E
Orissa Coast Canal ≅	126	21.51 N	87.41 E
Oristano	71	39.54 N	8.36 E
Oristano, Golfo di c	71	39.50 N	8.22 E
Örizenthépter	61	46.51 N	16.25 E
Orituco ≃	246	9.37 N	66.23 W
Orivesi	26	61.41 N	24.21 E
Orivesi ⊜	26	62.16 N	29.24 E
Oriximiná	250	1.45 S	55.52 W
Orizaba	234	18.51 N	97.06 W
Orizaba, Pico de (Volcán Citlatépetl) ⋀¹	234	19.01 N	97.16 W
Orizona	255	17.03 S	48.18 W
Orjahovo	38	43.45 N	23.57 E
Orjen ⋀	36	42.35 N	18.33 E
Orjiva	198	48.05 N	100.09 W
Orkanger	26	63.19 N	9.52 E
Örkelljunga	41	56.17 N	13.17 E
Orkla ≃	26	63.18 N	9.50 E
Orkney, Sk., Can.	182	49.26 N	107.55 W
Orkney ⊶⁸	158	26.59 S	26.39 E
Orkney I	46	59.00 N	3.00 W
Orkney Islands II	46	59.00 N	3.00 W
Orla	52	50.46 N	11.31 E
Orlamünde	54	50.47 N	11.31 E
Orland, Ca., U.S.	226	39.44 N	122.11 W
Orland, In., U.S.	216	41.43 N	85.10 W

Nome	Página	Lat.	Long.
Orland Park	216	41.37 N	87.51 W
Orléans □⁹	50	47.50 N	2.00 E
Orleans, Île d' I	186	46.55 N	70.58 W
— Ech Cheliff	148	36.10 N	1.20 E
Orlík, Kaz.	86	48.17 N	51.32 E
Orlík, Ross.	88	52.30 N	99.55 E
Orlinaja, gora ⋀	180	62.35 N	178.30 E
Orlinga ≃	88	56.03 N	105.53 E
Orlinga ≃	88	56.03 N	105.53 E
Orlová	30	49.50 N	18.24 E
Orlov Gaj	80	50.57 N	48.12 E
Orlová	30	49.50 N	18.24 E
Orlovista	220	28.32 N	81.28 W
Orlovka, Ross.	78	51.02 N	40.32 E
Orlovka, Ross.	59	59.03 N	85.59 E
Orlovo, Ross.	80	51.16 N	43.46 E
Orlovo, Ross.	78	51.45 N	39.33 E
Orlovskij	80	46.52 N	42.03 E
Orlu	150	5.47 N	7.02 E
Orly	261	48.45 N	2.24 E
Ormanli	38	41.10 N	31.39 E
Ormāra	124	25.09 N	64.38 E
Ormāra, Rās ‣	128	25.09 N	64.35 E
Ormea	62	44.09 N	7.54 E
Ormesby	44	54.33 N	1.11 W
Ormesby Saint Margaret	42	52.40 N	1.42 E
Ormiston	184	49.45 N	105.22 W
Ormoc	116	11.00 N	124.37 E
Ormoc Bay c	116	10.58 N	124.35 E
Ormond	274b	37.54 S	145.03 E
Ormond Beach	192	29.17 N	81.03 W
Ormož	36	46.25 N	16.09 E
Ormsby	214	41.48 N	78.33 W
Ormsby □⁶	226	39.11 N	119.46 W
Ormsjön ⊜	26	64.23 N	16.03 E
Ormstown	206	45.08 N	74.00 W
Ormtjärnkampen Nasjonalpark ♦	26	61.12 N	9.48 E
Ornain ≃	58	48.46 N	4.47 E
Ornans	58	47.06 N	6.09 E
Ornäs	40	60.31 N	15.32 E
Ornavasso	58	45.58 N	8.24 E
Orne □⁴	50	48.40 N	0.05 E
Orne ≃, Fr.	32	48.40 N	0.05 E
Orne ≃, Fr.	58	49.18 N	6.11 E
Orne ≃, Fr.	58	49.18 N	6.11 E
Orneta	30	54.08 N	20.08 E
Ornö I	40	59.04 N	18.24 E
Örnsköldsvik	26	63.18 N	18.43 E
Oro	98	39.03 N	123.15 E
Oro ≃	164	9.00 S	148.30 E
Oro □⁵	41	55.46 N	11.49 E
Oro ≃	164	46.00 N	10.00 E
Orobie, Alpi ⋀	58	46.00 N	10.00 E
Oročanskij Golec, gora ⋀	88	53.29 N	114.18 E
Orocovis	240m	18.14 N	66.23 W
Orocué	246	4.48 N	71.20 W
Orocuina	236	13.26 N	87.06 W
Orodara	150	10.59 N	4.55 W
Orofino	202	46.28 N	116.15 W
Orogen Zizhiqi	88	50.34 N	123.43 E
Orog nuur ⊜, Mong.	88	45.02 N	100.40 E
Orog nuur ⊜, Mong.	102	50.10 N	91.00 E
Oro Grande	228	34.35 N	117.20 W
Orohena, Mont ⋀	174s	17.37 S	149.28 W
Orok, Oldoinyo ⋀	154	2.29 S	36.46 E
Oro'ol	174m	26.12 N	127.39 E
Oromo	96	59.21 N	56.35 E
Oromocto	186	45.51 N	66.29 W
Oromocto Lake ⊜	186	45.36 N	67.00 W
Oron, Nig.	150	4.48 N	8.14 E
Oron, Ross.	88	57.11 N	116.28 E
Oron-la-Ville	56	46.34 N	6.50 E
Orono, On., Can.	212	43.59 N	78.37 W
Orono, Me., U.S.	188	44.53 N	68.40 W
Oronoque ≃	246	2.45 N	57.25 W
Oronsay I	46	56.01 N	6.16 W
Orontes — Asī ≃	130	36.02 N	35.58 E
Oropa, Santuario di ♦	58	45.38 N	7.58 E
Oropeso	234	18.50 N	101.48 W
Oroquieta	116	8.29 N	123.48 E
Orós	250	6.15 S	39.05 W
Orós, Açude ⊜¹	250	6.15 S	39.05 W
Orosei	71	40.23 N	9.42 E
Orosei, Golfo di c	71	40.15 N	9.44 E
Orosháza	30	46.34 N	20.40 E
Orosí, Volcán ⋀¹	236	10.59 N	85.29 W
Oroszlány	30	47.30 N	18.19 E
Orotelli	71	40.30 N	9.07 E
Orote Peninsula ‣¹	174p	13.26 N	144.38 E
Oroville, Ca., U.S.	226	39.31 N	121.33 W
Oroville, Wa., U.S.	182	48.55 N	119.26 W
Oroville, Lake ⊜¹	226	39.33 N	121.28 W
Orowoc Creek ≃	276	40.38 N	73.21 W
Orpheus Island I	166	18.37 S	146.30 E
Orphin	261	48.31 N	1.47 E
Orpington ⊶⁸	260	51.22 N	0.06 E
Orqohan	88	49.34 N	121.13 E
Orr	190	48.03 N	92.50 W
Orrawa	172	43.29 S	170.19 E
Orrefors	41	56.50 N	15.45 E
Orrefors	41	56.50 N	15.45 E
Orrin Reservoir ⊜¹	46	57.30 N	4.45 W
Orrin, Glen V	46	57.30 N	4.45 W
Orrío	266d	41.31 N	2.15 E
Orr Lake ≃, Mb., Can.	184	56.07 N	97.11 W
Orr Lake ≃, On., Can.	212	44.37 N	79.47 W
Orrstown	208	40.04 N	77.25 W
Orrtanna	208	39.53 N	77.17 W
Orrum	192	34.28 N	79.01 W
Orrville, Al., U.S.	194	32.18 N	87.15 W
Orrville, Oh., U.S.	214	40.50 N	81.45 W
Orša, Bela.	279b	60.73 N	15.33 E
Orša, Sve.	26	61.07 N	14.37 E

Name	Page	Lat.°′	Long.°′
Orša ≃	82	56.48 N	36.11 E
Orsago	64	45.56 N	12.25 E
Orsan	62	44.08 N	4.40 E
Oršanka	80	56.55 N	47.53 E
Orsara di Puglia	68	41.17 N	15.16 E
Orsasjön ⊜	26	61.07 N	14.34 E
Orsay	50	48.42 N	2.11 E
Orsett	260	51.31 N	0.22 E
Orsières	58	46.02 N	7.09 E
Orsjön ⊜	26	61.35 N	16.20 E
Orsk	86	51.12 N	58.34 E
Örskär I	40	60.31 N	18.23 E
Ørslev	41	55.02 N	11.59 E
Orsogna	66	42.13 N	14.17 E
Orsomarso	68	39.48 N	15.55 E
Orson	210	41.49 N	75.27 W
Orşova	38	44.42 N	22.24 E
Ørsta	26	62.12 N	6.09 E
Ørsted	41	55.20 N	10.04 E
Örsundaån ≃	40	59.44 N	17.21 E
Örsundsbro	40	59.44 N	17.18 E
Orta	130	40.38 N	33.06 E
Orta, Lago d' ⊜	62	45.49 N	8.24 E
Ortaca	130	36.49 N	28.47 E
Ortakent	130	37.02 N	27.21 E
Ortaklar	130	37.53 N	27.30 E
Ortaköy, Tür.	130	40.17 N	35.16 E
Ortaköy, Tür.	130	38.44 N	34.03 E
Ortaköy, Tür.	130	38.00 N	34.23 E
Ortaköy, Tür.	130	40.27 N	38.02 E
Ortaköy •8	267b	41.03 N	29.01 E
Orta Nova	68	41.19 N	15.42 E
Orta San Giulio	62	45.48 N	8.25 E
Orte	66	42.27 N	12.23 E
Ortega	246	3.56 N	75.13 W
Ortegal, Cabo >	34	43.45 N	7.53 W
Orteguaza ≃	246	0.43 N	75.16 W
Ortelsburg → Szczytno	30	53.34 N	21.00 E
Ortenberg, Dtsch.	56	50.21 N	9.02 E
Ortenberg, Dtsch.	58	48.27 N	7.58 E
Ortenburg	60	48.33 N	13.14 E
Orth	54	54.27 N	11.03 E
Orthez	32	43.29 N	0.46 W
Orthon ≃	248	10.50 S	66.04 W
Ortigalita Creek ≃	226	36.57 N	120.52 W
Ortigalita Peak ∧	226	36.48 N	120.55 W
Ortigara, Monte ∧	64	46.00 N	11.29 E
Ortigueira	34	43.41 N	7.51 W
Orting	224	47.05 N	122.12 W
Ortisei (Sankt Ulrich)	64	46.34 N	11.40 E
Ortiz, Méx.	232	28.17 N	110.43 W
Ortiz, Ven.	246	9.37 N	67.17 W
Ortles (Otler) ∧	64	46.31 N	10.33 E
Ortles ⩘	64	46.30 N	10.40 E
Örtofta	41	55.47 N	13.14 E
Ortolo ≃	71	41.30 N	8.55 E
Ortona	66	42.21 N	14.24 E
Ortona Lock •5	220	26.47 N	81.18 W
Orton Park ♦	275b	43.46 N	79.12 W
Ortonura	85	41.29 N	76.12 E
Ortonville, Mi., U.S.	216	42.51 N	83.26 W
Ortonville, Mn., U.S.	198	45.18 N	96.26 W
Ortonville State Recreation Area ♦	216	42.52 N	83.26 W
Ortoterek	85	41.56 N	71.21 E
Orto-Tokoj	85	42.21 N	76.01 E
Ortovero	62	44.03 N	8.07 E
Ortrand	54	51.22 N	13.45 E
Örträsk	26	64.08 N	18.59 E
Ortueri	71	40.02 N	8.59 E
Ortúzar, Canal ≊	286e	33.33 S	70.47 W
Örtze ≃	52	52.40 N	9.57 E
Oruanui	172	38.35 S	176.02 E
Oruba	273a	6.35 N	3.25 E
Orudjevo	82	56.26 N	37.32 E
Orūmīyeh (Reẕā'īyeh)	128	37.33 N	45.04 E
Orūmīyeh, Daryācheh-ye (Lake Urmia) ⊜	128	37.40 N	45.30 E
Orune	71	40.24 N	9.22 E
Oruro	248	17.59 S	67.09 W
Oruro □5	248	18.40 S	67.30 W
Or'us-Mijele ≃	88	58.35 N	121.30 E
Orust I	26	58.10 N	11.38 E
Orūzgān (Qala-i-Hazār Qadam)	120	32.56 N	66.38 E
Orūzgān □4	120	33.15 N	66.00 E
Orval, Abbaye d' ʊ1	56	49.38 N	5.22 E
Orvanne ≃	50	48.22 N	2.50 E
Orvieto	66	42.43 N	12.07 E
Orvilla	208	40.16 N	75.17 W
Orvilliers	261	48.52 N	1.39 E
Orvin ≃	50	48.28 N	3.23 E
Orvinio	66	42.08 N	12.56 E
Orviston	214	41.06 N	77.45 W
Orvyn, gora ∧	180	65.14 N	175.20 W
Orwell, N.Y., U.S.	212	43.35 N	76.00 W
Orwell, Oh., U.S.	214	41.32 N	80.52 W
Orwell ≃	42	51.57 N	1.17 E
Orwigsburg	208	40.39 N	76.06 W
Orwin	208	40.35 N	76.31 W
Orxon ≃	88	49.00 N	117.41 E
Or Yehuda	132	32.01 N	34.51 E
Orynyn	78	48.46 N	26.24 E
Oryu-dong •8	271b	37.29 N	126.51 E
Orževka	80	52.43 N	42.55 E
Orzhiv	78	50.45 N	26.07 E
Orzhytsya	78	49.48 N	32.42 E
Orzinuovi	62	45.24 N	9.55 E
Orzyc ≃	30	52.47 N	21.13 E
Orzysz	30	53.49 N	21.56 E
Oš, Kyrg.	85	40.33 N	72.48 E
Os, Nor.	26	62.30 N	11.12 E
Oš □4	85	40.00 N	72.30 E
Ōsa, Nihon	96	35.05 N	133.34 E
Osa, Ross.	86	57.17 N	55.26 E
Osa, Ross.	88	53.24 N	103.53 E
Oša ≃	86	57.13 N	73.41 E
Osa, Península de >1	236	8.34 N	83.31 W
Osage, Ia., U.S.	190	43.17 N	92.48 W
Osage, Mo., U.S.	219	38.25 N	92.02 W
Osage, N.J., U.S.	285	39.51 N	75.01 W
Osage, Wy., U.S.	198	43.58 N	104.25 W
Osage □6	219	38.27 N	91.50 W
Osage ≃	194	38.35 N	91.57 W
Osage Beach	194	38.09 N	92.37 W
Osage City	198	38.38 N	95.49 W
Osaka, Nihon	94	35.57 N	137.16 E
Ōsaka, Nihon	96	34.40 N	135.30 E
Ōsaka, Nihon	270	34.40 N	135.30 E
Ōsaka □5	96	34.30 N	135.30 E
Osaka Castle ⊥	270	34.41 N	135.32 E
Ōsaka-heiya ≚	270	34.43 N	135.30 E
Ōsaka International Airport ⊠	270	34.47 N	135.26 E
Ōsaka-kō ⊂	270	34.38 N	135.26 E
Ōsaka-kokusai-kūkō ⊠	96	34.47 N	135.26 E
Osakarovka	86	50.32 N	72.39 E
Ōsaka-tōge)(	270	34.56 N	135.18 E
Osaka University ʊ2	270	34.42 N	135.30 E
Ōsaka-wan ⊂	96	34.30 N	135.18 E
Ōsakiga-hana >	96	35.11 N	132.25 E
Ōsaki-Kami-jima I	96	34.14 N	132.54 E
Osakis	198	45.52 N	95.09 W
Ōsaki-Shimo-jima I	96	34.10 N	132.50 E
Osăm ≃	38	43.42 N	24.51 E
Osan	98	37.11 N	127.04 E
Osanovo	82	54.12 N	38.41 E
Osasco	256	23.32 S	46.46 W
Osasco □7	287b	23.32 S	46.46 W
Ōsawano	94	36.34 N	137.12 E
Osawatomie	198	38.29 N	94.57 W
Ōsa-yama ∧	96	34.45 N	132.12 E
Osbaldeston	262	53.47 N	2.32 W
Osborne, Ks., U.S.	198	39.26 N	98.41 W
Osborne, Pa., U.S.	279b	40.32 N	80.10 W
Osbourn Seamount ✦3	14	26.00 S	174.50 W
Osburger Hochwald ⩘	56	49.40 N	6.50 E
Osburn	202	47.30 N	115.59 W
Osby	26	56.22 N	13.59 E
Osbyholm	41	55.51 N	13.36 E
Oscar Peak ∧	182	54.51 N	129.07 W
Oscarville	180	60.43 N	161.46 W
Oscawana Lake	210	41.23 N	73.52 W
Osceola, Ar., U.S.	194	35.42 N	89.58 W
Osceola, In., U.S.	216	41.39 N	86.04 W
Osceola, Ia., U.S.	190	41.02 N	93.45 W
Osceola, Mo., U.S.	194	38.02 N	93.42 W
Osceola, Ne., U.S.	198	41.10 N	97.32 W
Osceola, Pa., U.S.	210	41.59 N	77.21 W
Osceola, Tx., U.S.	222	32.08 N	97.14 W
Osceola, Wi., U.S.	190	45.19 N	92.42 W
Osceola □6	220	28.00 N	81.15 W
Osceola Mills	214	40.51 N	78.16 W
Oščepkovo	86	56.29 N	70.42 E
Oschatz	54	51.17 N	13.07 E
Oschersleben	54	52.01 N	11.13 E
Oschiri	71	40.43 N	9.06 E
Oscoda	190	44.26 N	83.20 W
Öse ≃	263	51.26 N	7.49 E
Osečenka	76	57.33 N	34.48 E
Osečina	38	44.23 N	19.36 E
Osejevskaja	82	55.53 N	38.10 E
Ošejkino	82	56.15 N	35.54 E
Osek	54	50.37 N	13.40 E
Ösel → Saaremaa I	76	58.25 N	22.30 E
Osen	24	64.17 N	10.30 E
Osetrovo	88	56.47 N	105.47 E
Ōse-zaki >	94	35.02 N	138.47 E
Osgood, In., U.S.	218	39.07 N	85.17 W
Osgood, Oh., U.S.	216	40.20 N	84.30 W
Osgoode	212	45.08 N	75.36 W
Osh → Oš	85	40.33 N	72.48 E
Oshakati	156	17.47 S	15.41 E
Oshamambe	92a	42.30 N	140.22 E
Oshana □4	156	18.00 S	15.30 E
O'Shanassy ≃	166	18.59 S	138.46 E
O'Shaughnessy Dam •6	226	37.57 N	119.47 W
O'Shaughnessy Reservoir ⊜1	214	40.12 N	83.09 W
Oshawa	212	43.54 N	78.51 W
Oshawa Creek ≃	212	43.52 N	78.49 W
Oshibe •8	270	34.45 N	135.04 E
Oshigambo	156	17.47 S	16.05 E
Oshika, Nihon	92	38.16 N	141.32 E
Ōshika, Nihon	94	35.34 N	138.02 E
Oshika-hantō >1	92	38.20 N	141.30 E
Oshikango	156	17.25 S	15.56 E
Oshikoto □4	156	18.30 S	17.30 E
Ōshima, Nihon	92	33.03 N	129.33 E
Ōshima, Nihon	94	37.07 N	138.30 E
Ōshima, Nihon	94	34.45 N	139.22 E
Ōshima, Nihon	96	33.55 N	132.15 E
Ō-shima I, Nihon	92a	41.30 N	139.22 E
Ō-shima I, Nihon	94	34.43 N	139.23 E
Ō-shima I, Nihon	94	36.15 N	136.07 E
Ō-shima I, Nihon	96	33.54 N	130.26 E
Ō-shima I, Nihon	96	34.30 N	131.25 E
Ō-shima I, Nihon	96	34.00 N	133.22 E
Ō-shima I, Nihon	96	34.09 N	133.04 E
Ō-shima I, Nihon	96	33.38 N	134.30 E
Oshima-hantō >1	92a	42.00 N	140.30 E
Oshimizu	94	36.49 N	136.46 E
Oshino	94	35.28 N	138.51 E
Oshivre •8	272c	19.09 N	72.51 E
Oshkosh, Ne., U.S.	198	41.24 N	102.20 W
Oshkosh, Wi., U.S.	190	44.01 N	88.32 W
Oshnovīyeh	128	37.02 N	45.06 E
Oshodi	273a	6.34 N	3.21 E
Oshoek	158	26.13 S	30.59 E
Oshogbo	150	7.47 N	4.34 E
Oshtemo	216	42.15 N	85.41 W
Oshtorān Kūh ∧	128	33.20 N	49.16 E
Oshtorīnān	128	34.01 N	48.38 E
Oshwe	152	3.24 S	19.30 E
Osi	150	8.08 N	5.14 E
Osica de Jos	38	44.15 N	24.17 E
Osich'ŏn-ni	98	41.25 N	128.16 E
Osiek	30	50.31 N	21.28 E
Osiglia	62	44.17 N	8.12 E
Osijek	38	45.33 N	18.41 E
Osilinka ≃	182	56.05 N	124.29 W
Osilo	71	40.45 N	8.40 E
Osimo	66	43.29 N	13.29 E
Osini	71	39.50 N	9.29 E
Osinki	80	52.51 N	49.30 E
Osinniki, Ross.	80	58.03 N	47.02 E
Osinniki, Ross.	86	53.37 N	87.21 E
Osinovka, Ross.	88	50.34 N	109.27 E
Osinovka, Ross.	88	56.19 N	101.56 E
Osinovskij chrebet ⩘	180	67.10 N	175.00 E
Osinów Dolny	54	52.48 N	14.10 E
Osio Sotto	62	45.36 N	9.35 E
Osipaonica	38	44.33 N	21.04 E
Osipenko → Berdyans'k	78	46.45 N	36.49 E
Osipovo Selo	76	56.51 N	30.30 E
Osire	156	20.59 S	17.19 E
Osivān	120	26.43 N	72.55 E
Oskaloosa, Ia., U.S.	190	41.17 N	92.38 W
Oskaloosa, Ks., U.S.	198	39.12 N	95.18 W
Oskar-Fredriksborg	40	59.24 N	18.26 E
Oskarshamn	26	57.16 N	16.26 E
Oskarström	26	56.48 N	12.58 E
Oskil (Oskol) ≃	78	49.06 N	37.25 E
Os'kino	78	51.14 N	39.02 E
Oskol (Oskil) ≃	78	49.06 N	37.25 E
Oskolkovo	24	67.58 N	53.42 E
Oskū	128	37.55 N	46.06 E
Oskuj	76	59.17 N	32.05 E
Oskuja ≃	76	59.14 N	31.54 E
Osl'anka, gora ∧	86	59.10 N	58.33 E
Oslava ≃	61	49.05 N	16.22 E
Ösling •1	56	49.55 N	6.00 E
Oslo	26	59.55 N	10.45 E
Oslob	116	9.31 N	123.26 E
Oslofjorden ⊂2	26	59.20 N	10.35 E
Os'ma ≃, Ross.	76	54.55 N	33.24 E
Ošma ≃, Ross.	80	57.52 N	47.45 E
Osmānābād	122	18.10 N	76.02 E
Osmancık	130	40.59 N	34.49 E
Osmaneli	130	40.22 N	30.01 E
Osmaniye	130	37.05 N	36.14 E
Osmanpaşa	130	39.38 N	34.58 E
Osmeña	116	10.11 N	125.31 E
Osmington	42	50.38 N	2.22 W
Os'mino	76	59.01 N	29.06 E
Osminog, gora ∧	180	67.54 N	176.50 E
Ösmo	40	58.59 N	17.54 E
Osmond	198	42.21 N	97.35 W
Osmore ≃	248	17.33 S	71.12 W
Osmoy	261	48.52 N	1.43 E
Osmussaar I	76	59.18 N	23.22 E
Osnabrück	52	52.16 N	8.02 E
Ośno	30	52.28 N	14.50 E
Osny	261	49.04 N	2.04 E
Oso	224	48.16 N	121.56 W
Oso ≃	154	1.09 S	27.22 E
Oso, Gran Lago del → Great Bear Lake ⊜	176	66.00 N	120.00 W
Ošoba	85	40.44 N	70.26 E
Osogna	58	46.18 N	9.00 E
Osoppo	64	46.15 N	13.05 E
Osorakan-zan ∧	96	34.36 N	132.08 E
Osore-yama ∧	92	41.18 N	141.05 E
Osorio, Quebrada ≃	286c	10.36 N	66.56 W
Osório Fonseca	250	3.40 S	58.13 W
Osorno, Chile	254	40.34 S	73.09 W
Osorno, Esp.	34	42.24 N	4.22 W
Osorno, Volcán ∧1	254	41.06 S	72.30 W
Osorun	273a	6.33 N	3.29 E
Os'otr ≃	82	54.58 N	38.46 E
Osoyoos	182	49.02 N	119.28 W
Osoyoos Indian Reserve •4	182	49.08 N	119.30 W
Osoyoos Lake ⊜	182	49.00 N	119.26 W
Osøyra	26	60.11 N	5.28 E
Ospedaletti	62	43.48 N	7.43 E
Ospedaletto, It.	64	46.03 N	11.33 E
Ospedaletto, It.	64	46.17 N	13.07 E
Ospino	246	9.18 N	69.27 W
Ospitale di Cadore	64	46.20 N	12.19 E
Ospitaletto	64	45.33 N	10.04 E
Osprey	220	27.11 N	82.29 W
Osprey Reef ✦2	164	13.55 S	146.38 E
Ospwagan Lake ⊜	184	55.35 N	98.03 W
Oss	52	51.46 N	5.31 E
Ossa, Mount ∧	166	41.54 S	146.01 E
Ossabaw Island I	192	31.47 N	81.06 W
Osse ≃, Fr.	32	44.07 N	0.17 E
Osse ≃, Nig.	150	6.10 N	5.20 E
Ossenberg	263	51.34 N	6.35 E
Ossendrecht	52	51.24 N	4.19 E
Osseo, Mi., U.S.	216	41.53 N	84.33 W
Osseo, Wi., U.S.	190	44.34 N	91.13 W
Ossett	44	53.41 N	1.35 W
Ossi	71	40.40 N	8.35 E
Ossiacher See ⊜	64	46.40 N	13.55 E
Ossian, In., U.S.	216	40.52 N	85.09 W
Ossian, Ia., U.S.	190	43.08 N	91.45 W
Ossian, Loch ⊜	46	56.46 N	4.38 W
Ossining	210	41.09 N	73.51 W
Ossipee	188	43.41 N	71.07 W
Ossjøen ⊜	26	61.13 N	11.53 E
Ossling	54	51.21 N	14.09 E
Ossmannstedt, Dtsch.	54	51.01 N	11.26 E
Ossmannstedt, Dtsch.	54	51.01 N	11.26 E
Ossona	266b	45.30 N	8.54 E
Ossora	74	59.20 N	163.13 E
Ossum-Bösinghoven	263	51.18 N	6.39 E
Ošta	24	60.49 N	35.32 E
Ostaboningue, Lac ⊜	190	47.09 N	78.53 W
Östanå, Sve.	40	59.33 N	18.35 E
Östanå, Sve.	40	60.38 N	16.48 E
Östanbyn	40	60.39 N	16.48 E
Ostankino •8	265b	55.49 N	37.37 E
Östansjö	40	59.03 N	14.59 E
Ostap'ye	78	49.33 N	33.46 E
Ostaškov	76	57.09 N	33.06 E
Ostašovo	82	55.52 N	35.52 E
Ostbevern	52	52.02 N	7.50 E
Østbirk	41	55.58 N	9.46 E
Ostbüren	263	51.31 N	7.46 E
Østby	26	61.15 N	12.32 E
Ostchinesisches Meer → East China Sea ▿2	90	30.00 N	126.00 E
Oste ≃	52	53.51 N	8.59 E
Osted	41	55.34 N	11.58 E
Osteen	220	28.50 N	81.09 W
Ostellato	66	44.45 N	11.56 E
Ostende → Oostende	50	51.13 N	2.55 E
Ostenfelde	52	51.52 N	8.04 E
Oster	78	50.57 N	30.53 E
Oster ≃, Dtsch.	60	48.43 N	13.29 E
Oster ≃, Ukr.	78	50.56 N	30.52 E
Osterath	56	51.16 N	6.37 E
Osterbönen	263	51.37 N	7.48 E
Osterburg, Dtsch.	54	52.47 N	11.44 E
Osterburg, Pa., U.S.	214	40.16 N	78.31 W
Osterburken	56	49.26 N	9.26 E
Österbybruk	40	60.12 N	17.54 E
Österbymo	26	57.50 N	15.16 E
Ostercappeln	52	52.20 N	8.13 E
Österdalälven ≃	26	60.33 N	15.08 E
Østerdalen V	26	61.15 N	11.10 E
Österfärnebo	40	60.18 N	16.48 E
Osterfeld	54	51.05 N	11.56 E
Osterfeld •8	263	51.30 N	6.53 E
Östergötland □9	26	58.24 N	15.34 E
Östergötlands Län □6	26	58.25 N	15.45 E
Österhaninge	40	59.08 N	18.12 E
Osterhofen	60	48.42 N	13.01 E
Øster Højst	41	55.00 N	9.03 E
Osterholz-Scharmbeck	52	53.14 N	8.47 E
Osterley Park ♦	260	51.30 N	0.21 W
Österlövsta	40	60.26 N	17.47 E
Ostermundigen	58	46.58 N	7.29 E
Osternienburg	54	51.48 N	12.01 E
Osterode, Dtsch.	52	51.44 N	10.11 E
Osterode → Ostróda, Pol.	30	53.43 N	19.59 E
Osterøya I	26	60.33 N	5.35 E
Österreich → Austria □1	30	47.20 N	13.20 E
Österreichisches Freilichtmuseum ʊ	61	47.10 N	15.19 E
Osterrönfeld	41	54.17 N	9.41 E
Östersjön → Baltic Sea ▿2	24	57.00 N	19.00 E
Österskär	40	59.28 N	18.18 E
Östersund	26	63.11 N	14.39 E
Östervåla	40	60.11 N	17.11 E
Osterville	207	41.37 N	70.23 W
Osterwick	52	52.01 N	7.13 E
Osterwieck	54	51.58 N	10.42 E
Ostfeld •8	263	51.40 N	7.45 E
Ostfildern	56	48.43 N	9.16 E
Østfold □6	26	59.20 N	11.30 E
Ostfriesische Inseln II	52	53.44 N	7.25 E
Ostfriesland □9	52	53.20 N	7.40 E
Ost-Ghats → Eastern Ghāts ⩘	122	14.00 N	78.50 E
Östhammar	40	60.16 N	18.22 E
Ostheim vor der Rhön	56	50.27 N	10.14 E
Osthofen	56	49.42 N	8.19 E
Ostia, Bonifica di •1	267a	41.46 N	12.18 E
Ostia Antica ⊥	66	41.45 N	12.16 E
Ostiano	64	45.13 N	10.15 E
Ostiglia	64	45.04 N	11.08 E
Ostky	78	51.16 N	27.22 E
Östliche Sierra Madre → Madre Oriental, Sierra ⩘	232	22.00 N	99.30 W
Östmark	26	60.17 N	12.45 E
Ost'or	76	54.01 N	32.48 E
Ost'or ≃	76	53.47 N	31.46 E
Ostpeene ≃	54	53.43 N	12.46 E
Ostra	66	43.37 N	13.09 E
Östraby	41	55.46 N	13.41 E
Ostrach	58	47.57 N	9.23 E
Ostrach ≃	58	48.04 N	9.24 E
Östra Grevie	41	55.28 N	13.08 E
Östra Husby	40	58.35 N	16.33 E
Östra Laxsjön ⊜	40	58.54 N	14.42 E
Östra Ljungby	41	56.11 N	13.04 E
Ostrander	214	40.15 N	83.12 W
Östra Ringsjön ⊜	41	55.52 N	13.32 E
Ostrau → Ostrava, Česká Rep.	30	49.50 N	18.17 E
Ostrau, Dtsch.	54	51.12 N	13.09 E
Ostrava	30	49.50 N	18.17 E
Ostra Vetere	66	43.36 N	13.03 E
Ostrhauderfehn	52	53.08 N	7.37 E
Östrich	263	51.40 N	6.55 E
Ostricourt	50	50.27 N	3.02 E
Östringen	56	49.13 N	8.43 E
Ostritz	54	51.01 N	14.56 E
Ostróda	30	53.43 N	19.59 E
Ostrogožsk	78	50.52 N	39.05 E
Ostroh	78	50.20 N	26.31 E
Ostrokonje	76	59.52 N	42.02 E
Ostrołęka	30	53.06 N	21.34 E
Ostrołęka □4	30	53.00 N	21.30 E
Ostroróg	30	52.39 N	16.27 E
Ostrov, Česká Rep.	54	50.17 N	12.57 E
Ostrov, Rom.	38	44.06 N	27.22 E
Ostrov, Ross.	76	57.20 N	28.22 E
Ostrov, Ross.	76	60.34 N	37.55 E
Ostrov, Ross.	265b	55.35 N	37.51 E
Ostrov I	30	47.55 N	17.35 E
Ostrov'anskij	80	46.45 N	42.13 E
Ostrovki	265a	59.48 N	30.50 E
Ostrovskaja	80	50.26 N	44.27 E
Ostrovskoje	80	57.48 N	42.15 E
Ostrov-Zalit	76	58.01 N	28.04 E
Ostrowiec Świętokrzyski	30	50.57 N	21.23 E
Ostrów Lubelski	30	51.30 N	22.52 E
Ostrów Mazowiecka	30	52.49 N	21.54 E
Ostrów Wielkopolski	30	51.39 N	17.49 E
Ostrzeszów	30	51.25 N	17.57 E
Ostsee → Baltic Sea ▿2	24	57.00 N	19.00 E
Ostseebad Ahrenshoop	54	54.23 N	12.25 E
Ostseebad Boltenhagen	54	54.00 N	11.12 E
Ostseebad Dierhagen	54	54.18 N	12.22 E
Ostseebad Graal-Müritz	54	54.15 N	12.12 E
Ostseebad Nienhagen	54	54.09 N	11.58 E
Ostseebad Rerik	54	54.06 N	11.37 E
Ostseebad Wustrow	54	54.21 N	12.23 E
Ost-Sümmern	263	51.26 N	7.44 E
Osttirol □9	64	46.55 N	12.30 E
Ostúa ≃	236	14.17 N	89.33 W
Ostuacán	234	17.25 N	93.18 W
Ostula	234	18.30 N	103.28 W
Ostuni	68	40.44 N	17.35 E
Ostwald	58	48.33 N	7.43 E
Osu	98	35.31 N	127.18 E
Osuga	76	56.02 N	34.18 E
Osuga ≃	76	57.16 N	34.49 E
Ōsuka	94	34.41 N	137.59 E
O'Sullivan, Lac ⊜	190	47.37 N	76.05 W
Osum ≃	38	40.48 N	19.52 E
Ōsumi	270	34.50 N	135.45 E
Ōsumi-hantō >1	92	31.20 N	130.55 E
Ōsumi-kaikyō ȣ	92	31.00 N	131.00 E
Ōsumi-shotō II	93b	30.30 N	130.00 E
Osuna	34	37.14 N	5.07 W
Osupugo ∧	154	1.40 S	35.49 E
Osvaldo Cruz	255	21.47 S	50.50 W
Ošvor	24	66.58 N	62.53 E
Oswaldtwistle	44	53.43 N	2.26 W
Oswaldtwistle Moor •3	262	53.43 N	2.23 W
Oswald West State Park ♦	224	45.45 N	123.58 W
Oswayo	214	41.55 N	78.01 W
Oswayo Creek ≃	210	42.02 N	78.21 W
Oswegatchie ≃	188	44.42 N	75.30 W
Oswegatchie, Middle Branch ≃	212	44.07 N	75.19 W
Oswegatchie, West Branch ≃	188	44.18 N	75.20 W
Oswego, Il., U.S.	216	41.40 N	88.21 W
Oswego, In., U.S.	216	41.19 N	85.47 W
Oswego, Ks., U.S.	198	37.10 N	95.06 W
Oswego, N.Y., U.S.	212	43.27 N	76.30 W
Oswego □6	212	43.22 N	76.15 W
Oswego ≃, N.J., U.S.	208	39.40 N	74.32 W
Oswego ≃, N.Y., U.S.	212	43.28 N	76.31 W
Oswestry	42	52.52 N	3.04 W
Oświęcim	30	50.03 N	19.12 E
Osyka	194	31.00 N	90.28 W
Osynyve	83	49.34 N	39.05 E
Osypenko	78	46.54 N	36.49 E
Ota, Nihon	94	35.58 N	136.04 E
Ōta, Nihon	94	36.18 N	139.22 E
Ōta, Nihon	96	33.31 N	131.33 E
Ōta •8	268	35.34 N	139.43 E
Ōta ≃, Nihon	94	34.40 N	137.54 E
Ōta ≃, Nihon	96	34.22 N	132.25 E
Otaci	38	48.25 N	27.47 E
Otago Peninsula >1	172	45.52 S	170.40 E
Otahuhu	172	36.57 S	174.51 E
Ōtake	96	34.12 N	132.13 E
Otaki, N.Z.	172	40.45 S	175.09 E
Ōtaki, Nihon	94	35.17 N	140.15 E
Ōtaki, Nihon	94	35.48 N	137.33 E
Ōtaki, Nihon	94	35.57 N	138.56 E
Ōtaki ≃	94	35.49 N	137.40 E
Ōtaki-yama ∧	96	34.07 N	134.08 E
Ōta-Koizumi-hikojō ♦	94	36.16 N	139.24 E
Otane	172	39.53 S	176.38 E
Otanmäki	26	64.07 N	27.06 E
Otar	85	43.33 N	75.13 E
Otari	94	36.46 N	137.54 E
Otaru	92a	43.13 N	141.00 E
Otatara	172	46.26 S	168.18 E
Otatitlán	234	18.12 N	96.02 W
Otautau	172	46.09 S	168.00 E
Otava	26	61.39 N	27.04 E
Otava ≃	30	49.27 N	14.12 E
Otavalo	246	0.14 N	78.16 W
Otavi	156	19.39 S	17.20 E
Ōtawara	94	36.52 N	140.02 E
Otawa-yama ∧	270	34.28 N	135.53 E
Otay	228	32.35 N	117.03 W
Otchinjau	152	16.30 S	13.57 E
Oteapan	234	18.00 N	94.39 W
Otego	210	42.23 N	75.10 W
Otego Creek ≃	210	42.25 N	75.07 W
Otélé	152	3.35 N	11.15 E
Otematata	172	44.37 S	170.16 E
Oteotea	175e	9.05 S	161.11 E
Otepää	76	58.03 N	26.30 E
Oteros ≃	232	26.55 N	108.22 W
Otford, Austl.	170	34.12 S	151.01 E
Otford, Eng., U.K.	42	51.19 N	0.12 E
Otgon	88	47.11 N	97.33 E
Otgon Tenger uul ∧	88	47.36 N	97.36 E
Otham	260	51.15 N	0.35 E
Othello	202	46.49 N	119.10 W
Othery	42	51.05 N	2.53 W
Othfresen	52	52.00 N	10.23 E
Óthiris, Óros ⩘	38	39.02 N	22.37 E
Othis	261	49.04 N	2.41 E
Othonoí I	38	39.50 N	19.26 E
Oti ≃	150	8.40 N	0.13 E
Otibanda	164	7.15 S	146.30 E
Otinapa	232	24.11 N	105.02 W
Otira	172	42.50 S	171.33 E
Otis, Co., U.S.	198	40.08 N	102.57 W
Otis, In., U.S.	216	41.36 N	86.54 W
Otis, Ks., U.S.	198	38.32 N	99.03 W
Otis, Ma., U.S.	207	42.11 N	73.05 W
Otisco	218	38.32 N	85.40 W
Otisco Lake ⊜	210	42.52 N	76.18 W
Otish, Monts ⩘	176	52.22 N	70.30 W
Otis Reservoir ⊜1	207	42.09 N	73.02 W
Otisville	210	41.28 N	74.32 W
Otjassy	80	53.14 N	41.39 E
Otjikondo	156	19.50 S	15.23 E
Otjimbingue	156	22.19 S	16.10 E
Otjinene	156	21.13 S	18.42 E
Otjiwarongo	156	20.29 S	16.36 E
Otjozondjou ≃	156	20.18 S	20.50 E
Otjozondjupa □4	156	20.00 S	18.00 E
Otley	44	53.54 N	1.41 W
Otmanlı	130	41.52 N	34.37 E
Otm'ok, pereval)(	85	42.20 N	73.10 E
Otmuchów	30	50.28 N	17.10 E
Otnes	26	61.45 N	11.14 E
Otnice	61	49.05 N	16.49 E
Ōtō	96	33.41 N	135.35 E
Otočac	36	44.52 N	15.14 E
Otog Qi	102	39.08 N	108.00 E
Ōtomi	175d	24.19 N	123.54 E
Oton	116	10.42 N	122.29 E
Otonabee ≃	212	44.08 N	78.14 W
Otoque, Isla I	236	8.36 N	79.36 W
Ōtori-kita	270	34.33 N	135.27 E
Otorma	80	53.32 N	42.32 E
Otoro ≃	236	15.00 N	88.16 W
Otorohanga	172	38.11 S	175.12 E
Otoskwin ≃	176	52.13 N	88.06 W
Otowa	94	34.51 N	137.18 E
Otowa-yama ∧	270	34.58 N	135.51 E
Otowa-yama-tunnel •5	94	34.58 N	135.51 E
Ōtoyo	96	33.46 N	133.40 E
Otra ≃	26	58.09 N	8.00 E
Otradnaja	84	44.23 N	41.31 E
Otradnoje	265a	59.47 N	30.49 E
Otradnyj	80	53.22 N	51.21 E
Otranto	68	40.09 N	18.30 E
Otranto, Capo d' >	68	40.06 N	18.31 E
Otranto, Strait of ȣ	38	40.00 N	19.00 E
Otricoli	66	42.25 N	12.29 E
Otrokovice	30	49.13 N	17.31 E
Ötscher ∧	61	47.52 N	15.12 E
Otsego	216	42.27 N	85.41 W
Otsego □6	210	42.42 N	74.56 W
Otsego Lake ⊜	210	42.45 N	74.52 W
Otselic ≃	210	42.20 N	75.58 W
Ōtsu, Nihon	96	35.00 N	135.52 E
Ōtsu, Nihon	268	35.16 N	139.42 E
Ōtsu ≃	270	34.30 N	135.24 E
Ōtsuchi	92	39.21 N	141.54 E
Ōtsuki	94	35.36 N	138.57 E
Ōtsu-shima I	96	34.00 N	131.42 E
Otta, Nig.	150	6.42 N	3.10 E
Otta, Nor.	26	61.46 N	9.32 E
Otta ≃	26	61.46 N	9.31 E
Ottakring •8	264b	48.12 N	16.19 E
Ottana	71	40.14 N	9.02 E
Ottarnic Pond ⊜	283	42.46 N	71.25 W
Ottati	68	40.28 N	15.19 E
Ottavia •8	267a	41.58 N	12.24 E
Ottaviano	68	40.51 N	14.28 E
Ottawa, On., Can.	212	45.25 N	75.42 W
Ottawa, Il., U.S.	216	41.20 N	88.50 W
Ottawa, Ks., U.S.	198	38.36 N	95.16 W
Ottawa, Oh., U.S.	216	41.01 N	84.02 W
Ottawa □6, Mi., U.S.	216	42.57 N	86.02 W
Ottawa □6, Oh., U.S.	214	41.31 N	82.56 W
Ottawa ≃, Can.	176	45.20 N	73.58 W
Ottawa ≃, Oh., U.S.	214	41.44 N	83.28 W
Ottawa ≃, Oh., U.S.	216	41.00 N	84.15 W
Ottawa-Carleton □6	212	45.15 N	75.45 W
Ottawa Hills	214	41.39 N	83.38 W
Ottawa International Airport ⊠	212	45.19 N	75.40 W
Ottawa Islands II	176	59.30 N	80.10 W
Ottbergen	52	51.42 N	9.18 E
Ottenby	26	56.14 N	16.25 E
Ottendorf-Okrilla	54	51.11 N	13.50 E
Ottenhöfen	58	48.34 N	8.09 E
Ottenschlag	61	48.25 N	15.13 E
Ottensheim	61	48.20 N	14.11 E
Ottenstein Stausee ⊜1	61	48.37 N	15.17 E
Otter ≃	42	50.46 N	3.17 W
Otterbach ≃	56	49.07 N	8.21 E
Otterbäcken	40	58.57 N	14.02 E
Otterbein	216	40.29 N	87.06 W
Otterburn	44	55.14 N	2.10 W
Otterburne	184	49.30 N	97.03 W
Otterburn Park	206	45.33 N	73.13 W
Otter Creek	192	29.19 N	82.46 W
Otter Creek ≃, On., Can.	212	44.06 N	81.07 W
Otter Creek ≃, Il., U.S.	219	39.18 N	90.07 W
Otter Creek ≃, In., U.S.	218	38.58 N	85.37 W
Otter Creek ≃, Ia., U.S.	190	41.20 N	93.30 W
Otter Creek ≃, Mo., U.S.	219	39.31 N	91.51 W
Otter Creek ≃, Mt., U.S.	202	45.36 N	106.17 W
Otter Creek ≃, N.Y., U.S.	212	43.43 N	75.23 W
Otter Creek ≃, Ut., U.S.	200	38.10 N	112.02 W
Otter Creek ≃, Vt., U.S.	188	44.13 N	73.17 W
Otter Creek Reservoir ⊜1	200	38.12 N	111.59 W
Otterfing	64	47.55 N	11.41 E
Otterhöfen	56	48.33 N	8.12 E
Otter-Lake, P.Q., Can.	188	45.51 N	76.26 W
Otter Lake, Mi., U.S.	190	43.13 N	83.28 W
Otter Lake ⊜, On., Can.	212	44.47 N	76.07 W
Otter Lake ⊜, On., Can.	212	45.17 N	79.56 W
Otter Lake ⊜, Sk., Can.	184	55.35 N	104.39 W
Otter Lake ⊜1	219	39.26 N	89.54 W
Otterlo	52	52.06 N	5.45 E
Otterndorf	52	53.48 N	8.53 E
Otterøya I	26	62.42 N	6.48 E
Otter River	207	42.35 N	72.03 W
Ottersberg	52	53.06 N	9.08 E
Ottershaw	260	51.22 N	0.32 W
Ottersleben	54	52.05 N	11.34 E
Ottersweier	58	48.40 N	8.07 E
Otter Tail ≃	198	46.16 N	96.36 W
Otter Tail Lake ⊜	198	46.23 N	95.40 W
Otterup	41	55.31 N	10.24 E
Otterville, On., Can.	212	42.55 N	80.36 W
Otterville, Il., U.S.	219	39.03 N	90.24 W
Otterville, Mo., U.S.	194	38.41 N	93.00 W
Ottery ≃	42	50.39 N	4.20 W
Ottery Saint Mary	42	50.45 N	3.17 W
Ottignies	56	50.40 N	4.34 E
Ottine	222	29.36 N	97.35 W
Ottmarsbocholt	52	51.49 N	7.32 E
Ottnang	60	48.06 N	13.40 E
Ottnaren ⊜	40	60.29 N	16.37 E
Otto, N.Y., U.S.	210	42.21 N	78.50 W
Otto, Tx., U.S.	222	31.27 N	96.49 W
Ottobeuren	58	47.56 N	10.18 E
Ottobeuren, Klosterkirche ʊ1	58	47.56 N	10.18 E
Ottobiano	62	45.09 N	8.50 E
Ottobrunn	60	48.04 N	11.40 E
Ottone	62	44.37 N	9.20 E
Ottosdal	158	26.58 S	26.00 E
Ottoshoop	156	25.45 S	25.59 E
Ottoville	216	40.55 N	84.20 W
Ottuk, Kyrg.	85	42.18 N	76.18 E
Ottuk, Kyrg.	85	41.38 N	75.51 E
Ottumwa	190	41.00 N	92.22 W
Ottweiler	56	49.24 N	7.09 E
Otty Lake ⊜	212	44.50 N	76.13 W
Otu, Nig.	150	8.14 N	3.24 E
Otu → Ōtsu, Nihon	96	35.00 N	135.52 E
Otukpa	150	7.09 N	7.41 E
Otumpa	252	27.19 S	62.13 W
Otun	273a	6.42 N	3.22 E
Otuquis, Bañados de ≋	248	19.20 S	58.30 W
Oturkpo	150	7.14 N	8.08 E
Otway, Bahía ȣ	254	53.20 S	74.00 W
Otway, Cape >	166	38.52 S	143.31 E
Otway, Seno ⊂	254	53.05 S	71.30 W
Otway Range ⩘	169	38.30 S	143.50 E
Otwock	30	52.07 N	21.16 E
Otyniya	78	48.44 N	24.51 E
Ötztal V	64	47.05 N	10.55 E
Ötztaler Ache ≃	64	47.14 N	10.50 E
Ötztaler Alpen (Alpi Venoste) ⩘	64	46.45 N	10.55 E
Ou ≃, Lao	110	20.04 N	102.13 E
Ou ≃, Zhg.	100	28.01 N	120.44 E
Ou ≃, Zhg.	100	26.02 N	113.09 E
Oua ≃	152	0.43 N	12.55 E
Ouachita ≃	194	31.38 N	91.49 W
Ouachita, Lake ⊜1	194	34.40 N	93.25 W
Ouachita Mountains ⩘	194	34.40 N	94.25 W
Ouaco	175f	20.50 S	164.29 E
Ouadâne	148	20.56 N	11.37 W
Ouadda	152	8.04 N	22.24 E
Ouaddaï □5	146	13.00 N	21.00 E
Ouadey, Ouadi el V	146	13.34 N	18.03 E
Ouagadougou	150	12.22 N	1.31 W
Ouahigouya	150	13.35 N	2.25 W
Ouahran → Wahran	148	35.43 N	0.43 W
Ouaka □5	152	6.00 N	21.00 E
Ouaka ≃	152	4.59 N	19.56 E
Oualâta	150	17.18 N	7.02 W
Ouâlata, Ḍahr ♠4	150	17.48 N	7.24 W
Oualé ≃	150	10.52 N	0.51 E
Oualidia	148	32.44 N	9.08 W
Ouallam	150	14.19 N	2.05 E
Ouallene	148	24.37 N	1.14 E
Oualto	150	9.01 N	10.06 W
Ouanary	250	4.13 N	51.40 W
Ouanda Djallé	146	8.54 N	22.48 E
Ouandago	146	7.10 N	18.42 E
Ouandja ≃	146	9.35 N	21.43 E
Ouandja-Vakaga, Réserve de la •4	146	9.00 N	21.30 E
Ouango	152	4.19 N	22.33 E
Ouangolodougou	150	9.58 N	5.09 W
Ouaninou	150	8.11 N	7.51 W
Ouanne ≃	50	47.57 N	2.47 E
Ouan Taredert	148	27.33 N	9.32 E
Ouaquaga	210	42.08 N	75.39 W
Ouara ≃	154	5.05 N	24.26 E
Ouarâne •1	134	21.00 N	10.30 W
Ouararda, Passe de)(	148	21.01 N	13.03 W
Ouareau ≃	206	45.56 N	73.25 W
Ouareau, Lac ⊜1	206	46.17 N	74.09 W
Ouargaye	150	11.32 N	0.01 E
Ouarkoye	150	12.05 N	3.40 W
Ouarkziz, Jbel ⩘	148	28.50 N	9.00 W
Ouarsenis, Djebel ∧	34	35.53 N	1.38 E
Ouarville	50	48.21 N	1.46 E
Ouarzazate	148	30.57 N	6.50 W
Ouarzazate □4	148	30.55 N	6.45 W
Ouassoulou ≃	150	11.35 N	8.11 W
Ouatcha	150	13.22 N	9.18 E
Oubangui (Ubangi) ≃	152	0.30 S	17.42 E
Ouche ≃	58	47.06 N	5.16 E
Oucques	50	47.49 N	1.18 E
Ōuda	94	34.28 N	135.56 E
Oudaze Lake ⊜	212	45.27 N	79.11 W
Oud-Beijerland	52	51.49 N	4.25 E
Ouddorp	52	51.48 N	3.56 E
Oude IJssel (Issel) ≃	52	52.00 N	6.10 E
Oudenaarde	50	50.51 N	3.36 E
Oudenbosch	52	51.35 N	4.31 E
Oudenburg	50	51.11 N	3.00 E
Oude-Pekela	52	53.04 N	6.58 E
Oude Rijn ≃	52	52.05 N	4.20 E
Oudeschild	52	53.02 N	4.50 E
Oude-Tonge	52	51.41 N	4.12 E
Oudewater	52	52.02 N	4.52 E
Oud-Gastel	52	51.35 N	4.27 E
Oudjda → Oujda	148	34.41 N	1.45 W
Oud-Loosdrecht	52	52.13 N	5.04 E
Oudtshoorn	158	33.35 S	22.14 E
Oudyoumoudi	150	14.04 N	0.28 W
Oued Athmenia	34	36.15 N	6.17 E
Oued Cheham	36	36.23 N	7.46 E
Oued edh Dheheb, Khlij ⊂	148	23.45 N	15.47 W
Oued Fodda	34	36.11 N	1.32 E
Oued Meliz	36	36.27 N	8.34 E
Oued Rhiou	34	35.58 N	0.55 E
Oued Tlelat	34	35.34 N	0.27 W
Oued Zarga	36	36.40 N	9.25 E
Oued-Zem	148	32.55 N	6.33 W
Ouellé	150	7.18 N	4.01 W
Ouémé □5	150	7.00 N	2.35 E
Ouémé ≃	150	6.29 N	2.32 E
Ouen, Île I	175f	22.26 S	166.49 E
Ouenkoro	150	13.23 N	3.50 W
Ouenza, Djebel ∧	36	35.57 N	8.05 E
Ouenzé •8	273b	4.14 S	15.17 E
Ouessa	150	11.03 N	2.47 W
Ouessant, Île d' (Ushant) I	32	48.28 N	5.05 W
Ouesso	152	1.37 N	16.04 E
Ouest □4	152	5.23 N	10.45 E
Ouest, Pointe de l' >	186	49.52 N	64.31 W
Ouest, Rivière de l' ≃	206	45.39 N	74.21 W
Ouezzane	148	34.52 N	5.35 W
Ouffet	56	50.26 N	5.28 E
Ouganda → Uganda □1	154	1.00 N	32.00 E
Ougarou	150	12.09 N	0.56 E
Oughter, Lough ⊜	48	54.00 N	7.30 W
Oughterard	48	53.25 N	9.17 W
Oughtibridge	44	53.26 N	1.33 W
Ouham □5	152	7.00 N	18.00 E
Ouham ≃	136	9.18 N	18.14 E
Ouham-Pendé □5	152	7.00 N	16.00 E
Ouidah	150	6.22 N	2.05 E
Ouidi	146	14.07 N	12.58 E
Ouimet Canyon V	190	48.47 N	88.40 W
Ouistreham	32	49.17 N	0.15 W
Oujda	148	34.41 N	1.45 W
Oujda □4	148	34.05 N	2.10 W
Oulad Naïl, Monts des ⩘	148	34.33 N	3.28 E
Oulainen	26	64.16 N	24.48 E
Oulangan kansallispuisto ♦	24	66.12 N	29.30 E
Oulchy-le-Château	50	49.12 N	3.21 E
Oule ≃	62	44.25 N	5.21 E
Ouled Agla	34	35.58 N	4.45 E
Ouleout Creek ≃	210	42.20 N	75.18 W
Oulins	50	48.52 N	1.28 E
Oullins	62	45.43 N	4.48 E
Oulou, Bahr ≃	146	9.48 N	21.32 E
Oulton Broad	42	52.31 N	1.42 E
Oulu	26	65.01 N	25.28 E
Oulujärvi ⊜	26	64.20 N	27.15 E
Oulujoki ≃	26	65.01 N	25.25 E
Oulun lääni □4	24	65.00 N	27.00 E
Oulx	62	45.02 N	6.50 E
Oumba	152	4.55 N	19.04 E
Oum-Chalouba	146	15.48 N	20.46 E
Oumé	150	6.23 N	5.25 W
Oum El Bouagui	148	35.53 N	7.07 E
Oum er Rbia, Oued ≃	148	33.19 N	8.21 W
Oum-Hadjer	146	13.18 N	19.41 E
Oum Hadjer, Ouadi V	146	16.38 N	20.14 E
Oumiao	102	31.55 N	112.09 E
Oumm ed Droûs Guebli, Sebkhet ⊜	148	24.03 N	11.45 W
Oumm ed Droûs Telli, Sebkhet ⊜	148	24.20 N	11.30 W
Ounâne, Bîr ▿4	148	21.28 N	3.56 W
Ounara	148	31.33 N	9.28 W
Ounasjoki ≃	24	66.30 N	25.45 E
Oundle	42	52.29 N	0.29 W
Ounianga Kébir	146	19.04 N	20.29 E
Ouolossébougou	150	12.00 N	7.55 W
Our ≃	56	49.53 N	6.18 E
Ouragahio	150	6.19 N	5.56 W
Ōura-wan ⊂	174m	26.32 N	128.04 E
Ouray	200	38.01 N	107.40 W
Ouray, Mount ∧	200	38.25 N	106.14 W
Ource ≃	58	48.06 N	4.23 E
Ourcq ≃	50	49.01 N	3.01 E
Ourcq, Canal de l' ≊	50	48.51 N	2.22 E
Ourém	250	1.33 S	47.06 W
Ourense	34	42.20 N	7.51 W
Ouri	146	21.34 N	19.13 E

Symbols in the index entries represent the broad categories identified in the key at the right. Symbols with superior numbers (⩘1) identify subcategories (see complete key on page *I · 1*).

Symbole im Register stellen die rechts im Schlüssel erklärten Kategorien dar. Symbole mit hochgestellten Ziffern (⩘1) bezeichnen Unterabteilungen einer Kategorie (vgl. vollständiger Schlüssel auf Seite *I · 1*).

Los símbolos incluídos en el texto del índice representan las grandes categorías identificadas con la clave a la derecha. Los símbolos con numeros en su parte superior (⩘1) identifican las subcategorías (véase la clave completa en la página *I · 1*).

Les symboles de l'index représentent les catégories indiquées dans la légende à droite. Les symboles suivis d'un indice (⩘1) représentent des sous-catégories (voir légende complète à la page *I · 1*).

Os símbolos incluídos no texto do índice representam as grandes categorias identificadas com a chave à direita. Os símbolos com números em sua parte superior (⩘1) identificam as subcategorias (veja-se a chave completa à página *I · 1*).

∧	Mountain	Berg	Montaña	Montagne	Montanha
⩘	Mountains	Gebirge	Montañas	Montagnes	Montanhas
)(	Pass	Paß	Paso	Col	Passo
V	Valley, Canyon	Tal, Cañon	Valle, Cañón	Vallée, Canyon	Vale, Canhão
≚	Plain	Ebene	Llano	Plaine	Planície
>	Cape	Kap	Cabo	Cap	Cabo
I	Island	Insel	Isla	Île	Ilha
II	Islands	Inseln	Islas	Îles	Ilhas
♠	Other Topographic Features	Andere Topographische Objekte	Otros Elementos Topográficos	Autres données topographiques	Outros acidentes topográficos

ESPAÑOL

Nombre	Página	Lat.°′	Long.°′ W = Oeste
Ouri, Tarso ʌ	**146**	21.25 N	18.56 E
Ouricuri	**250**	7.53 S	40.05 W
Ourimbah	**170**	33.22 S	151.23 E
Ourinhos	**255**	22.59 S	49.52 W
Ourique	**34**	37.39 N	8.13 W
Ournie	**171b**	35.56 S	147.51 E
Ouro, Paraná do ≃	**248**	8.29 S	70.30 W
Ouro, Ponta do ≻	**158**	26.51 S	32.54 E
Ouro Branco	**250**	6.42 S	36.57 W
Ouro Fino	**256**	22.17 S	46.22 W
Ouro Preto	**255**	20.23 S	43.30 W
Ouro Preto ≃	**248**	11.02 S	65.13 W
Ouroufa, Vallée d' ∨	**150**	14.42 N	7.00 E
Ours, Grand Lac de l' → Great Bear Lake ⊜	**176**	66.00 N	120.00 W
Oursi	**150**	14.41 N	0.27 W
Ourthe ≃	**56**	50.38 N	5.35 E
Ourthe Occidentale ≃	**56**	50.08 N	5.41 E
Ourthe Orientale ≃	**56**	50.08 N	5.41 E
Ourville-en-Caux	**50**	49.44 N	0.36 E
Ōu-sammyaku ⋏	**92**	38.45 N	140.50 E
Ouse ≃, On., Can.	**212**	44.17 N	78.03 W
Ouse ≃, Eng., U.K.	**42**	50.47 N	0.03 E
Ouse ≃, Eng., U.K.	**44**	53.42 N	0.41 W
Oust ≃	**32**	47.39 N	2.06 W
Outaouais, Rivière des → Ottawa ≃	**176**	45.20 N	73.58 W
Outardes, Baie aux ⊂	**186**	49.02 N	68.30 W
Outardes, Rivière aux ≃	**176**	49.04 N	68.28 W
Outardes Est, Rivière aux ≃	**206**	45.06 N	74.04 W
Outardes Quatre, Réservoir ⊜[1]	**186**	49.50 N	68.58 W
Outardes Trois, Barrage ◆[6]	**186**	49.34 N	68.48 W
Outarville	**50**	48.13 N	2.01 E
Outcalt	**276**	40.23 N	74.24 W
Outeniekwaberge ⋏	**158**	33.53 S	22.35 E
Outerbridge Crossing ◆[5]	**276**	40.31 N	74.15 W
Outer Harbour	**168b**	34.47 S	138.30 E
Outer Hebrides II	**46**	57.45 N	7.00 W
Outer Island I	**190**	47.03 N	90.30 W
Outer Santa Barbara Passage ʯ	**228**	33.10 N	118.30 W
Outer Sister Island I	**166**	39.39 S	148.00 E
Outjo	**156**	20.08 S	16.08 E
Outlane	**262**	53.39 N	1.53 W
Outlet Bay ⊂	**208**	37.22 N	75.49 W
Outlook, Sk., Can.	**184**	51.30 N	107.03 W
Outlook, Mt., U.S.	**198**	48.53 N	104.46 W
Outokumpu	**26**	62.44 N	29.01 E
Outpost Mountain ʌ	**180**	69.08 N	151.12 W
Outreau	**50**	50.42 N	1.35 E
Outremont	**206**	45.31 N	73.38 W
Outside Canal ≅	**226**	37.13 N	121.02 W
Out Skerries II	**46a**	60.25 N	0.42 W
Outwell	**42**	52.37 N	0.14 E
Ouvéa I	**175f**	20.30 S	166.35 E
Ouvéa, Lagon d' ⊂	**175f**	20.33 S	166.27 E
Ouvèze ≃	**62**	43.59 N	4.51 E
Ouvidor	**255**	18.14 S	47.50 W
Ouye, Forêt de l' ♠	**261**	48.32 N	2.00 E
Ouyen	**166**	35.04 S	142.20 E
Ouzinkie	**180**	57.55 N	152.30 W
Ouzouer-le-Marché	**50**	47.55 N	1.32 E
Ouzouer-sur-Loire	**50**	47.46 N	2.29 E
Ouzzal, Oued i-n- ∨	**148**	21.35 N	2.00 E
Ovabağ	**130**	37.43 N	39.59 E
Ovacık, Tür.	**130**	39.22 N	39.13 E
Ovacık, Tür.	**130**	41.05 N	32.55 E
Ovada	**62**	44.38 N	8.38 E
Ovakent	**130**	38.06 N	28.02 E
Oval	**210**	41.09 N	77.11 W
Ovalau I	**175g**	17.40 S	178.48 E
Ovalle	**252**	30.36 S	71.12 W
Ovamboland □[9]	**156**	17.45 S	16.30 E
Ovana, Cerro ʌ	**246**	4.38 N	66.57 W
Ovar	**34**	40.52 N	8.38 W
Ovaro	**64**	46.29 N	12.52 E
Ovčinino	**82**	56.02 N	39.03 E
Ovcyno	**265a**	59.48 N	30.37 E
Övedskloster	**41**	55.41 N	13.38 E
Ovejas	**246**	9.32 N	75.14 W
Ovelgönne	**52**	53.20 N	8.25 E
Ovenden	**262**	53.44 N	1.53 W
Oveng	**152**	2.25 N	12.16 E
Overath	**56**	50.55 N	7.14 E
Overberge	**263**	51.37 N	7.41 E
Overbrook	**198**	38.46 N	95.33 W
Overbrook ◆[8], Pa., U.S.	**279b**	40.24 N	79.59 W
Overbrook ◆[8], Pa., U.S.	**285**	39.58 N	75.16 W
Overdinkel	**52**	52.14 N	7.01 E
Overflakkee I	**52**	51.45 N	4.10 E
Overflowing ≃	**184**	53.10 N	101.05 W
Overhalla	**24**	64.30 N	11.57 E
Overijse	**56**	50.46 N	4.32 E
Overijssel □[4]	**52**	52.25 N	6.30 E
Over Jerstal	**41**	55.12 N	9.18 E
Överkalix	**24**	66.21 N	22.56 E
Overland	**219**	38.42 N	90.21 W
Overland Park	**198**	38.58 N	94.40 W
Overlea	**208**	39.22 N	76.31 W
Overloon	**52**	51.35 N	5.57 E
Övermark (Ylimarkku)	**26**	62.38 N	21.30 E
Overpeck Creek ≃	**276**	40.51 N	74.02 W
Overpelt	**56**	51.13 N	5.25 E
Overseal	**42**	52.44 N	1.34 W
Overstrand	**42**	52.56 N	1.20 E
Overton, Eng., U.K.	**42**	51.15 N	1.15 W
Overton, Ne., U.S.	**198**	40.44 N	99.32 W
Overton, Nv., U.S.	**204**	36.32 N	114.26 W
Overton, Tx., U.S.	**222**	32.16 N	94.58 W
Overton Arm ⊂	**204**	36.20 N	114.25 W
Övertorneå	**24**	66.23 N	23.40 E
Överum	**26**	57.59 N	16.19 E
Over Wallop	**42**	51.09 N	1.35 W
Ovett	**194**	31.29 N	89.01 W
Ovid, Mi., U.S.	**216**	43.00 N	84.22 W
Ovid, N.Y., U.S.	**210**	42.40 N	76.49 W
Ovidiopol'	**78**	46.17 N	30.27 E
Oviedo, Esp.	**34**	43.22 N	5.50 W
Oviedo, Fl., U.S.	**220**	28.40 N	81.13 W
Oviglio	**62**	44.52 N	8.29 E
Oviken	**26**	62.59 N	14.24 E
Oviksfjällen ⋏	**26**	63.02 N	13.51 E
Ovilla	**222**	32.32 N	96.53 W
Ovindoli	**66**	42.08 N	13.31 E
Ovinišče	**76**	58.22 N	37.02 E
Ovino	**76**	59.41 N	33.11 E
Ovìši	**76**	57.34 N	21.45 E
Övörchangaj □[4]	**102**	46.00 N	102.30 E
Øvre Anarjokka Nasjonalpark ♠	**24**	69.00 N	25.00 E
Øvre Ardal	**26**	61.19 N	7.48 E
Øvre Dividal Nasjonalpark ♠	**24**	68.39 N	19.45 E
Øvre Pasvik Nasjonalpark ♠	**24**	69.06 N	28.55 E
Øvre Rendal	**26**	61.53 N	11.05 E
Övre Vättern ⊜	**40**	59.52 N	15.40 E
Ovruch	**78**	51.21 N	28.49 E
Ovs'anikovo	**76**	60.09 N	45.16 E
Ovs'anka, Ross.	**86**	55.57 N	92.33 E
Ovs'anka, Ross.	**89**	53.35 N	126.57 E
Ovs'annikovo	**82**	56.54 N	37.33 E
Ovstug	**76**	53.24 N	33.52 E
Ōwada	**268**	35.49 N	139.33 E
Owaka	**172**	46.27 S	169.40 E
Owambo ≃	**156**	18.45 S	17.03 E
Owando	**152**	0.29 S	15.55 E
Owaneco	**219**	39.29 N	89.12 W
Owariashi	**94**	35.12 N	137.02 E
Owasco	**210**	42.51 N	76.28 W

FRANÇAIS

Nom	Page	Lat.°′	Long.°′ W = Ouest
Owasco Inlet ≃	**210**	42.45 N	76.28 W
Owasco Lake ⊜	**210**	42.52 N	76.32 W
Owasco Outlet ≃	**210**	43.04 N	76.39 W
Owase	**92**	34.04 N	136.12 E
Owasso	**196**	36.16 N	95.51 W
Owatonna	**190**	44.05 N	93.13 W
Owbeh	**128**	34.22 N	63.10 E
Owe	**272c**	19.04 N	73.04 E
Owego	**210**	42.06 N	76.15 W
Owego Creek, East Branch ≃	**210**	42.10 N	76.15 W
Owego Creek, West Branch ≃	**210**	42.10 N	76.15 W
Owel, Lough ⊜	**48**	53.34 N	7.25 W
Owen, Austl.	**168b**	34.16 S	138.33 E
Owen, Dtsch.	**56**	48.35 N	9.27 E
Owen, In., U.S.	**218**	38.27 N	85.34 W
Owen, Wi., U.S.	**190**	44.57 N	90.33 W
Owen □[6]	**218**	38.33 N	84.49 W
Owen, Mount ʌ	**172**	41.33 S	172.32 E
Owenboy ≃	**48**	51.48 N	8.18 W
Owendo	**152**	0.17 N	9.30 E
Owenea ≃	**48**	54.47 N	8.26 W
Owen Falls Dam ◆[6]	**154**	0.27 N	33.11 E
Owen Fracture Zone ✣	**12**	12.00 N	58.00 E
Owenkillew ≃	**48**	54.44 N	7.18 W
Owenmore ≃	**48**	54.07 N	9.50 W
Owen River	**172**	41.39 S	172.27 E
Owens ≃	**204**	36.31 N	117.57 W
Owensboro	**194**	37.46 N	87.06 W
Owens Creek ≃, Ca., U.S.	**226**	37.13 N	120.42 W
Owens Creek ≃, Md., U.S.	**208**	39.33 N	77.20 W
Owens Lake ⊜	**204**	36.25 N	117.56 W
Owen Sound	**212**	44.34 N	80.56 W
Owen Sound ⊂	**212**	44.40 N	80.55 W
Owen Stanley Range ⋏	**164**	9.20 S	147.55 E
Owensville, In., U.S.	**194**	38.16 N	87.41 W
Owensville, Mo., U.S.	**219**	38.20 N	91.30 W
Owensville, Oh., U.S.	**218**	39.07 N	84.08 W
Owenton, Ky., U.S.	**218**	38.32 N	84.50 W
Owenton, Va., U.S.	**208**	37.53 N	77.06 W
Owentown	**222**	32.26 N	95.12 W
Owerri	**150**	5.29 N	7.02 E
Owhango	**172**	39.00 S	175.23 E
Owikeno Lake ⊜	**182**	51.41 N	127.00 W
Owings	**208**	38.43 N	76.36 W
Owings Mills	**284b**	39.25 N	76.46 W
Owingsville	**188**	38.08 N	83.45 W
Owl ≃, Ab., Can.	**182**	54.54 N	111.57 W
Owl ≃, Mb., Can.	**176**	57.51 N	92.44 W
Owl Creek ≃, U.S.	**198**	44.41 N	103.29 W
Owl Creek ≃, Mt., U.S.	**202**	45.18 N	107.21 W
Owl Creek ≃, Wy., U.S.	**202**	43.41 N	108.11 W
Owl Creek, South Fork ≃	**202**	43.43 N	108.32 W
Owl Creek Mountains ⋏	**202**	43.30 N	108.35 W
Owo	**150**	7.15 N	5.37 E
Oworonsoki	**273a**	6.33 N	3.24 E
Owosso	**216**	42.59 N	84.10 W
Owuru ≃	**273a**	6.39 N	3.27 E
Owyhee	**204**	41.56 N	116.05 W
Owyhee ≃	**202**	43.46 N	117.02 W
Owyhee, Lake ⊜[1]	**202**	43.28 N	117.20 W
Owyhee, South Fork ≃	**202**	42.26 N	116.53 W
Oxapampa	**248**	10.34 S	75.24 W
Öxarfjörður ⊂	**24a**	66.15 N	16.45 W
Oxbow, Sk., Can.	**184**	49.14 N	102.11 W
Oxbow, Mi., U.S.	**281**	42.38 N	83.28 W
Oxbow, N.Y., U.S.	**212**	44.17 N	75.37 W
Oxbow Lake ⊜	**281**	42.38 N	83.28 W
Ox Creek ≃	**198**	48.37 N	100.17 W
Oxelösund	**40**	58.40 N	17.06 E
Oxford, N.S., Can.	**186**	45.44 N	63.52 W
Oxford, N.Z.	**172**	43.18 S	172.11 E
Oxford, Eng., U.K.	**42**	51.46 N	1.15 W
Oxford, Al., U.S.	**194**	33.36 N	85.50 W
Oxford, Ct., U.S.	**207**	41.26 N	73.07 W
Oxford, Fl., U.S.	**220**	28.55 N	82.02 W
Oxford, In., U.S.	**216**	40.31 N	87.14 W
Oxford, Ia., U.S.	**190**	41.43 N	91.47 W
Oxford, Ks., U.S.	**198**	37.16 N	97.10 W
Oxford, Ky., U.S.	**218**	38.16 N	84.30 W
Oxford, Me., U.S.	**188**	44.07 N	70.29 W
Oxford, Md., U.S.	**208**	38.41 N	76.10 W
Oxford, Ma., U.S.	**207**	42.07 N	71.51 W
Oxford, Mi., U.S.	**216**	42.49 N	83.15 W
Oxford, Ms., U.S.	**194**	34.21 N	89.31 W
Oxford, Ne., U.S.	**198**	40.15 N	99.38 W
Oxford, N.J., U.S.	**210**	40.48 N	74.59 W
Oxford, N.Y., U.S.	**210**	42.26 N	75.35 W
Oxford, N.C., U.S.	**192**	36.18 N	78.35 W
Oxford, Oh., U.S.	**218**	39.30 N	84.44 W
Oxford, Pa., U.S.	**208**	39.47 N	75.58 W
Oxford, Wi., U.S.	**190**	43.46 N	89.34 W
Oxford □[6]	**212**	43.08 N	80.50 W
Oxford Falls	**274a**	33.44 S	151.15 E
Oxford House	**184**	54.56 N	95.16 W
Oxford House Indian Reserve ◆[4]	**184**	54.54 N	95.15 W
Oxford Junction	**190**	41.59 N	90.57 W
Oxford Lake ⊜	**184**	54.51 N	95.37 W
Oxford Peak ʌ	**202**	42.16 N	112.06 W
Oxfordshire □[6]	**42**	51.50 N	1.15 W
Oxford Valley Mall ◆[9]	**285**	40.11 N	74.53 W
Oxhey	**260**	51.39 N	0.23 W
Oxie	**41**	55.33 N	13.04 E
Oxkutzcab	**232**	20.18 N	89.25 W
Oxley	**166**	34.12 S	144.06 E
Oxley Creek ≃	**171a**	27.32 S	153.00 E
Oxnard	**228**	34.11 N	119.10 W
Oxon Hill	**284c**	38.48 N	76.59 W
Oxon Run ≃	**284b**	38.49 N	77.00 W
Ox Pasture Brook ≃	**283**	42.45 N	70.54 W
Oxshott	**260**	51.20 N	0.21 W
Oxted	**42**	51.16 N	0.01 W
Oxtongue ≃	**212**	45.19 N	79.01 W
Oxtongue Lake ⊜	**212**	45.22 N	78.55 W
Oxus → Amu Darya ≃	**72**	43.40 N	59.01 E
Oya, Malay.	**112**	2.52 N	111.53 E
Ōya, Nihon	**96**	35.20 N	134.40 E
Oya ≃	**112**	2.52 N	111.52 E
Oyabe	**94**	36.40 N	136.52 E
Oyabe ≃	**94**	36.48 N	137.04 E
Ōya-ji ʊ[1]	**94**	36.38 N	139.48 E
Ōyake-yama ʌ[2]	**270**	34.48 N	135.51 E
Oyalı	**130**	37.14 N	41.45 E
Oyama, B.C., Can.	**182**	50.07 N	119.22 W
Oyama, Nihon	**94**	36.18 N	139.48 E
Ōyama, Nihon	**94**	36.36 N	137.18 E
Oyama, Nihon	**94**	35.21 N	139.00 E
Oyama, Nihon	**268**	35.36 N	139.22 E
Ōyamada	**94**	34.46 N	136.13 E
Ōyamazaki	**270**	34.54 N	135.42 E
Oyameyo, Volcán ʌ[1]	**286a**	19.10 N	99.11 W
Oyan	**152**	0.02 N	10.17 E
Ōyano	**92**	32.35 N	130.26 E
Oyapock (Oiapoque) ≃	**250**	4.08 N	51.40 W
Oyashirazu ♠	**94**	36.59 N	137.40 E
Oybin	**54**	50.50 N	14.44 E
Oye-et-Pallet	**58**	46.51 N	6.20 E
Oyem	**152**	1.37 N	11.35 E
Oyen	**184**	51.22 N	110.28 W
Øyeren ⊜	**26**	59.48 N	11.14 E
Oykel ≃	**46**	57.56 N	4.25 W
Oykel Bridge	**46**	57.58 N	4.43 W
Oy-Mittelberg	**58**	47.38 N	10.28 E
Oymyakon → Ojm'akon	**74**	63.28 N	142.49 E
Oyo, Congo	**152**	0.01 N	15.54 E

PORTUGUÊS

Nome	Página	Lat.°′	Long.°′ W = Oeste
Oyo, Nig.	**150**	7.51 N	3.56 E
Oyo ≃	**115a**	7.57 S	110.22 E
Ōyodo	**96**	34.23 N	135.48 E
Oyodo ◆[8]	**270**	34.43 N	135.30 E
Ōyodo ≃	**92**	31.53 N	131.28 E
Oyón	**248**	10.39 S	76.47 W
Oyonnax	**58**	46.15 N	5.40 E
Ōyorogi-san ʌ	**96**	35.05 N	132.51 E
Oyotún	**248**	6.51 S	79.19 W
Oyster	**208**	37.17 N	75.55 W
Oyster Bay	**210**	40.51 N	73.31 W
Oyster Bay ⊂	**276**	40.55 N	73.30 W
Oyster Bay Cove	**276**	40.52 N	73.31 W
Oyster Bay Harbor ⊂	**276**	40.53 N	73.32 W
Oyster Creek	**222**	29.00 N	95.20 W
Oyster Creek ≃	**222**	28.59 N	95.18 W
Oyster Point ʌ	**282**	37.50 N	121.52 W
Oyster Point ≻	**168b**	34.55 S	137.48 E
Oyster Rock I[2]	**272c**	18.54 N	72.50 E
Oysterville	**224**	46.33 N	124.02 W
Øystese	**26**	60.23 N	6.13 E
Oyten	**52**	53.04 N	9.01 E
Ozaki	**268**	35.59 N	139.51 E
Ozamiz	**116**	8.08 N	123.50 E
Ozanne ≃	**50**	48.11 N	1.22 E
Ozark, Al., U.S.	**194**	31.27 N	85.38 W
Ozark, Ar., U.S.	**194**	35.29 N	93.49 W
Ozark, Mo., U.S.	**194**	37.01 N	93.12 W
Ozark National Scenic Riverways ♠	**194**	37.10 N	91.10 W
Ozark Plateau ⋏[1]	**194**	37.00 N	93.00 W
Ozark Reservoir ⊜[1]	**194**	35.35 N	94.00 W
Ozarks, Lake of the ⊜[1]	**194**	38.10 N	92.50 W
Ozaukee □[6]	**216**	44.14 N	88.00 W
Ózd	**30**	48.14 N	20.18 E
Oze ≃	**96**	34.12 N	132.14 E
Ozeblin ʌ	**36**	44.35 N	15.53 E
Ozek	**86**	46.35 N	60.41 E
Ozereckoje	**82**	56.04 N	37.23 E
Oželje	**82**	54.48 N	38.17 E
Oželki	**82**	55.51 N	38.52 E
Ozerišče	**76**	54.48 N	33.13 E
Ozerki, Ross.	**80**	51.13 N	53.56 E
Ozerki, Ross.	**80**	51.32 N	45.16 E
Ozerki, Ross.	**80**	52.01 N	45.29 E
Ozerki, Ross.	**86**	53.38 N	83.44 E
Ozerki, Ross.	**265a**	59.54 N	30.44 E
Ozerna ≃	**82**	55.44 N	36.08 E
Ozerne	**78**	50.11 N	28.42 E
Ozerninskoje vodochranilišče ⊜[1]	**82**	55.45 N	36.15 E
Ozernovskij	**74**	51.30 N	156.31 E
Ozernyj	**180**	66.24 N	179.06 W
Ozero	**80**	56.58 N	44.43 E
Ozery	**82**	54.51 N	38.34 E
Ozette Lake ⊜	**224**	48.06 N	124.38 W
Ozgoryš	**85**	41.15 N	74.45 E
Ozieri	**71**	40.35 N	9.00 E
Ozimek	**30**	50.41 N	18.13 E
Ozinki	**80**	51.12 N	49.45 E
Ozirs'k	**78**	51.43 N	26.24 E
Ožogino, ozero ⊜	**74**	69.16 N	146.36 E
Ozoir-la-Ferrière	**261**	48.46 N	2.40 E
Ozona, Fl., U.S.	**220**	28.04 N	82.46 W
Ozona, Tx., U.S.	**196**	30.42 N	101.12 W
Ozone Park ◆[8]	**276**	40.40 N	73.51 W
Ozorków	**30**	51.58 N	19.19 E
Oz'ornaja	**86**	51.08 N	60.50 E
Oz'ornoje, Kaz.	**86**	53.25 N	63.15 E
Oz'ornoje, Ross.	**80**	51.41 N	44.55 E
Oz'ornoje, Ross.	**80**	51.46 N	51.28 E
Oz'ornoje, Ross.	**86**	56.48 N	71.15 E
Oz'ornyj	**80**	57.10 N	40.59 E
Oz'orsk	**76**	54.25 N	22.01 E
Oz'orskij	**89**	46.36 N	143.08 E
Ozouer-le-Voulgis	**261**	48.40 N	2.47 E
Özpınar	**130**	37.57 N	42.16 E
Ōzu, Nihon	**92**	32.52 N	130.52 E
Ōzu, Nihon	**96**	33.30 N	132.33 E
Ozubulu	**150**	5.57 N	6.51 E
Ozuluama	**234**	21.40 N	97.51 W
Ozumba	**234**	19.03 N	98.48 W
Ozurgeti	**84**	41.56 N	42.00 E

P

Nome	Página	Lat.°′	Long.°′ W = Oeste
Pâ	**150**	11.33 N	3.15 W
Paagoumène	**175f**	20.29 S	164.11 E
Paal	**56**	51.02 N	5.11 E
Paama □[8]	**175f**	16.28 S	168.18 E
Paama I	**175f**	16.28 S	168.14 E
Paar ≃	**60**	48.45 N	11.33 E
Paardekraal Monument ⊥	**273d**	26.06 S	27.47 E
Paaren	**264a**	52.39 N	12.59 E
Paarl	**158**	33.45 S	18.56 E
Paasbach ≃	**263**	51.25 N	7.11 E
Paauilo	**229d**	20.02 N	155.22 W
Pabarabuk	**164**	6.05 S	144.05 E
Pabbay I, Scot., U.K.	**46**	56.51 N	7.35 W
Pabbay I, Scot., U.K.	**46**	57.46 N	7.15 W
Pabbi	**123**	34.01 N	71.47 E
Pabbiring, Kepulauan II	**112**	4.55 S	119.25 E
Pabean	**112**	6.50 S	115.19 E
Pabellón, Punta ≻	**254**	43.14 S	74.23 W
Pabellón de Arteaga	**234**	22.10 N	102.21 W
Pabellones, Ensenada ⊂	**232**	24.27 N	107.36 W
Pabianice	**30**	51.40 N	19.22 E
Pabillonis	**71**	39.35 N	8.43 E
Pablo	**202**	47.36 N	114.07 W
Pābna	**124**	24.00 N	89.15 E
Pabo	**154**	3.00 N	32.09 E
Pabradė	**76**	54.59 N	25.44 E
Paca	**115b**	8.29 S	120.11 E
Pacaás Novas, Parque Nacional ♠	**248**	11.10 S	63.30 W
Pacaás Novos ≃	**248**	10.51 S	65.20 W
Pacaás Novos, Serra dos ⋏	**248**	10.45 S	64.15 W
Pacaembu	**255**	21.34 S	51.17 W
Pacaembú, Estádio do ♠	**287b**	23.33 S	46.39 W
Pacajá ≃	**250**	1.56 S	50.50 W
Pacajus	**250**	4.10 S	38.28 W
Pacaltsdorp	**158**	34.00 S	22.28 E
Pacaraima, Sierra de → Pakaraima Mountains ⋏	**246**	5.30 N	60.40 W
Pacarán	**248**	12.52 S	76.03 W
Pacaraos	**248**	11.11 S	76.44 W
Pacasmayo	**248**	7.24 S	79.34 W
Pacatuba	**250**	3.58 S	38.37 W
Pace, Fl., U.S.	**194**	30.35 N	87.09 W
Pace, Ms., U.S.	**194**	33.47 N	90.51 W
Paceco	**70**	37.59 N	12.33 E
Pačelma, Ross.	**80**	53.15 N	43.21 E
Pačelma, Ross.	**80**	53.20 N	43.20 E
Pacet	**115a**	6.45 S	107.03 E
Pachača	**74**	60.34 N	169.03 E
Pachacamac ⊥	**248**	12.14 S	76.52 W
Pachamba	**126**	24.12 N	86.16 E
Pachaug Pond ⊜	**207**	41.34 N	71.54 W
Pacheco	**226**	37.59 N	122.04 W
Pacheco, Isla I	**254**	52.17 S	74.45 W
Pacheco Creek ≃	**226**	36.58 N	121.28 W
Pacheco Pass)(	**226**	37.03 N	121.13 W
Pāchh Elāsin	**126**	24.08 N	89.54 E
Pachino	**70**	36.43 N	15.05 E
Pachitea ≃	**248**	8.46 S	74.32 W
Pachiza	**248**	7.16 S	76.46 W
Pachkoli ◆[8]	**272c**	19.08 N	72.54 E
Pachmarhi	**124**	22.28 N	78.26 E
Pacho	**246**	5.08 N	74.10 W
Pachomovo	**82**	54.38 N	37.33 E
Pachor	**124**	23.42 N	76.44 E

Pāchora	**122**	20.40 N	75.21 E
Pachotnyj Ugol	**80**	52.58 N	41.56 E
Pachra ≃	**82**	55.32 N	37.59 E
Pachtaabad	**85**	38.28 N	68.10 E
Pachuca [de Soto]	**234**	20.07 N	98.44 W
Paciência ◆[8]	**256**	22.55 S	43.38 W
Pacific, B.C., Can.	**182**	54.46 N	128.17 W
Pacific, Mo., U.S.	**219**	38.28 N	90.44 W
Pacific, Wa., U.S.	**224**	47.15 N	122.14 W
Pacific □[6]	**224**	46.30 N	123.39 W
Pacifica	**226**	37.37 N	122.29 W
Pacific-Antarctic Ridge ✣[3]	**6**	62.00 S	157.00 W
Pacific Beach	**224**	47.12 N	124.12 W
Pacific City	**224**	45.12 N	123.57 W
Pacific Creek ≃	**200**	42.08 N	109.24 W
Pacific Gardens	**226**	37.58 N	121.20 W
Pacific Grove	**226**	36.38 N	121.56 W
Pacific Missile Test Center ■	**228**	34.07 N	119.07 W
Pacífico, Océano → Pacific Ocean ⊤[1]	**6**	10.00 S	150.00 W
Pacific Ocean ⊤[1]	**4**	10.00 S	150.00 W
Pacific Ocean ⊤[1]	**6**	10.00 S	150.00 W
Pacifico Mountain ʌ	**228**	34.23 N	118.02 W
Pacific Palisades ◆[8]	**280**	34.03 N	118.32 W
Pacific Ranges ⋏	**182**	50.45 N	125.30 W
Pacific Rim National Park ♠	**182**	48.45 N	125.40 W
Pacifique, Océan → Pacific Ocean ⊤[1]	**6**	10.00 S	150.00 W
Pacijan Island I	**116**	10.39 N	124.20 E
Pacinan, Tanjung ≻	**115a**	7.36 S	114.02 E
Paciran	**115a**	6.52 S	112.20 E
Pacitan	**115a**	8.12 S	111.07 E
Pack	**61**	46.58 N	14.59 E
Packanack Lake ⊜	**276**	40.56 N	74.15 W
Packard Mountain ʌ[2]	**207**	42.28 N	72.21 W
Páckevei-Duna ≃[1]	**264c**	47.19 N	19.02 E
Pack Monadnock Mountain ʌ	**207**	42.52 N	71.52 W
Packsattel)(	**61**	46.58 N	14.58 E
Packwood	**224**	46.36 N	121.40 W
Packwood Lake ⊜	**224**	46.35 N	121.34 W
Pacllón	**248**	10.18 S	77.07 W
Pacock Brook ≃	**276**	41.05 N	74.31 W
Paço de Arcos	**266c**	38.42 N	9.17 W
Paço do Lumiar	**250**	2.31 S	44.07 W
Pacohuaras ≃	**248**	10.04 S	65.46 W
Pacoima ◆[8]	**280**	34.16 N	118.26 W
Pacolet ≃	**192**	34.50 N	81.27 W
Pacolet Mills	**192**	34.55 N	81.44 W
Pacora	**246**	9.05 N	79.17 W
Pacov	**30**	49.28 N	15.00 E
Pacquet	**186**	49.59 N	55.53 W
Pacuare ≃	**236**	10.14 N	83.17 W
Pacuí ≃	**255**	16.46 S	45.01 W
Pacuneiro ≃	**255**	13.02 S	53.25 W
Pacy-sur-Eure	**50**	49.01 N	1.23 E
Paczkow	**30**	50.27 N	17.00 E
Padada	**116**	6.42 N	125.22 E
Padada ≃	**116**	6.42 N	125.23 E
Padaido, Kepulauan II	**164**	1.15 S	136.30 E
Padam	**123**	33.28 N	76.53 E
Padamarang, Pulau I	**112**	4.07 S	121.24 E
Padamo ≃	**246**	2.54 N	65.17 W
Padampur	**120**	20.59 N	83.04 E
Padang, Indon.	**112**	1.39 S	108.55 E
Padang, Indon.	**112**	2.59 N	105.40 E
Padang, Indon.	**112**	6.11 S	120.26 E
Padang, Indon.	**112**	0.57 S	100.21 E
Padang, Pulau I	**114**	1.10 N	102.20 E
Padang Besar	**114**	6.40 N	100.19 E
Padangbetuah	**112**	3.39 S	102.13 E
Padang Endau	**114**	2.40 N	103.37 E
Padangpanjang	**112**	0.27 S	100.25 E
Padangsidempuan	**114**	1.22 N	99.16 E
Padangtiji	**114**	5.22 N	95.50 E
Padangtikar, Pulau I	**112**	0.50 S	109.30 E
Padang Tungku	**114**	4.14 N	101.59 E
Padany	**24**	63.17 N	33.22 E
Padas	**115a**	7.25 S	111.32 E
Padas ≃	**112**	5.14 N	115.34 E
Padasjoki	**26**	61.21 N	25.17 E
Padauari ≃	**246**	0.15 S	64.05 W
Padborg	**41**	54.49 N	9.22 E
Padcaya	**248**	21.52 S	64.48 W
Paddington ◆[8]	**260**	51.31 N	0.10 W
Paddington Station ◆[5]	**260**	51.31 N	0.11 W
Paddle ≃	**182**	54.05 N	114.15 W
Paddle Prairie	**176**	57.57 N	117.29 W
Paddock Lake	**216**	42.34 N	88.06 W
Paddock Wood	**42**	51.11 N	0.23 E
Padea	**38**	44.01 N	23.52 E
Padea-besar I	**112**	3.30 S	123.05 E
Padeghar	**272c**	18.58 N	73.03 E
Paden City	**188**	39.36 N	80.56 W
Paderborn	**52**	51.43 N	8.45 E
Paderno Dugnano	**266b**	45.34 N	9.10 E
Paderno Ponchielli	**64**	45.14 N	9.55 E
Padghe	**272c**	19.03 N	73.07 E
Padibe	**154**	3.28 N	32.50 E
Padiham	**44**	53.49 N	2.19 W
Padilla	**248**	19.19 S	64.20 W
Padilla Bay ⊂	**224**	48.35 N	122.32 W
Padjelanta Nationalpark ♠	**24**	67.28 N	16.41 E
Padle	**272c**	19.09 N	73.03 E
Padloping Island I	**176**	67.07 N	62.35 W
Padma → Ganges ≃	**124**	23.22 N	90.32 E
Padola	**64**	46.36 N	12.28 E
Padoue → Padova	**64**	45.25 N	11.53 E
Padova	**64**	45.25 N	11.53 E
Padova □[4]	**64**	45.21 N	11.49 E
Padovka	**80**	52.28 N	49.31 E
Pādra	**120**	22.14 N	73.05 E
Padrão, Ponta do ≻	**152**	6.03 S	12.18 E
Padrauna	**124**	26.55 N	83.59 E
Padre Bernardo	**255**	15.21 S	48.30 W
Padre Brito	**256**	21.18 S	43.59 W
Padre Burgos	**116**	10.02 N	125.01 E
Padre Island I	**196**	27.00 N	97.15 W
Padre Island National Seashore ♠	**196**	27.00 N	97.25 W
Padre Miguel ◆[8]	**287a**	22.53 S	43.26 W
Padre Paraíso	**255**	17.06 S	41.31 W
Padria	**71**	40.24 N	8.38 E
Padrón	**34**	42.44 N	8.40 W
Padrone, Cape ≻	**158**	33.46 S	26.30 E
Padrt'	**60**	49.40 N	13.46 E
Padstow, Austl.	**274a**	33.57 S	151.02 E
Padstow, Eng., U.K.	**42**	50.33 N	4.56 W
Padsville	**76**	55.09 N	27.58 E
Padua → Padova	**64**	45.25 N	11.53 E
Paducah, Ky., U.S.	**194**	37.05 N	88.36 W
Paducah, Tx., U.S.	**196**	34.00 N	100.18 W
Padula	**68**	40.20 N	15.39 E
Paduli	**68**	41.10 N	14.53 E
Padunskaja	**86**	55.02 N	85.02 E
Paea	**174s**	17.41 S	149.35 W
Paedun	**98**	35.03 N	128.21 E
Paekakariki	**172**	40.59 S	174.57 E
Paektu-san ʌ	**98**	42.00 N	128.03 E
Paengaroa	**172**	37.49 S	176.25 E
Paengnyŏng-do I	**98**	37.57 N	124.40 E
Paerdegat Basin ⊂	**276**	40.37 N	73.54 W
Paeroa	**172**	37.23 S	175.40 E
Paesana	**62**	44.41 N	7.16 E
Paese	**64**	45.40 N	12.10 E
Paestum ⊥	**68**	40.25 N	15.00 E
Paete	**116**	14.23 N	121.29 E
Páez ≃	**246**	2.28 N	75.34 W
Pafúri	**156**	22.27 S	31.21 E
Pag	**36**	44.27 N	15.04 E

Pag, Otok I	**36**	44.30 N	15.00 E
Paga	**150**	10.58 N	1.06 W
Pagadenbaru	**115a**	6.28 S	107.48 E
Pagadian	**116**	7.49 N	123.25 E
Pagadian Bay ⊂	**116**	7.48 N	123.31 E
Pagai Selatan, Pulau I	**112**	3.00 S	100.20 E
Pagai Utara, Pulau I	**112**	2.42 S	100.07 E
Pagalungan	**116**	7.04 N	124.41 E
Pagan	**110**	21.10 N	94.51 E
Pagan I	**108**	18.07 N	145.46 E
Pagancillo	**252**	29.34 S	68.03 W
Paganella ʌ	**64**	46.08 N	11.02 E
Pagani	**68**	40.45 N	14.37 E
Paganica	**66**	42.21 N	13.28 E
Paganico	**66**	42.56 N	11.16 E
Pagaralam	**112**	4.01 S	103.16 E
Pagasitikós Kólpos ⊂	**38**	39.15 N	22.51 E
Pagatan	**112**	3.36 S	115.56 E
Pagato ≃	**184**	55.49 N	102.05 W
Pagato Lake ⊜	**184**	56.08 N	102.30 W
Pagbilao	**116**	13.58 N	121.41 E
Pagbilao Grande Island I	**116**	13.55 N	121.46 E
Pagdanan Bay ⊂	**116**	10.31 N	119.15 E
Page, Az., U.S.	**200**	36.54 N	111.28 W
Page, N.D., U.S.	**198**	47.09 N	97.34 W
Page Field ⊠	**220**	26.35 N	81.52 W
Pagégiai	**76**	55.09 N	21.54 E
Pageland	**192**	34.46 N	80.23 W
Page Manor	**218**	39.45 N	84.06 W
Pager ≃	**154**	3.09 N	32.30 E
Pagerdewa	**112**	3.46 S	105.18 E
Paget, Mount ʌ	**244**	54.26 S	36.33 W
Paghmān	**120**	34.36 N	68.57 E
Paglia ≃	**66**	42.42 N	12.11 E
Pagliara	**70**	37.59 N	15.22 E
Paglieta	**66**	42.10 N	14.30 E
Pagliete, Bonifica delle ◆[1]	**267a**	41.53 N	12.12 E
Pagny-sur-Moselle	**56**	48.59 N	6.01 E
Pago Bay ⊂	**174p**	13.25 N	144.48 E
Pagoda Peak ʌ	**200**	40.10 N	107.20 W
Pagoda Point ≻	**110**	15.57 N	94.15 E
Pagon, Bukit ʌ	**112**	4.18 N	115.19 E
Pago Pago	**174u**	14.16 S	170.42 W
Pago Pago Harbor ⊂	**174u**	14.17 S	170.40 W
Pago Pago International Airport ⊠	**174u**	14.20 S	170.43 W
Pagosa Springs	**200**	37.16 N	107.00 W
Pagote	**272c**	18.54 N	72.59 E
Pagouda	**150**	9.45 N	1.19 E
Pagri	**124**	27.44 N	89.09 E
Pagsangahan	**116**	13.13 N	122.33 E
Pagsanjan	**116**	14.15 N	121.25 E
Paguate	**200**	35.08 N	107.22 W
Pagudpud	**116**	18.34 N	120.47 E
Pagueras, Torrente de ≃	**266d**	41.28 N	1.58 E
Paguyaman ≃	**112**	0.31 N	122.38 E
Pagwi	**164**	4.03 S	143.02 E
Pah	**84**	39.08 N	39.40 E
Pahādi ◆[8]	**272c**	19.10 N	72.51 E
Pahala	**229d**	19.12 N	155.28 W
Pahalgam	**123**	34.02 N	75.20 E
Pahang □[3]	**114**	3.30 N	102.45 E
Pahang ≃	**114**	3.32 N	103.28 E
Páhara, Laguna ⊂	**236**	14.18 N	83.15 W
Pahāsu	**124**	28.11 N	78.03 E
Pahau Point ≻	**229b**	21.49 N	160.15 W
Pahi	**114**	5.28 N	102.13 E
Pahia Point ≻	**172**	46.19 S	167.41 E
Pahiatua	**172**	40.27 S	175.50 E
Pahlād Garhi	**272a**	28.40 N	77.21 E
Pahlavī → Bandar-e Anzalī	**128**	37.28 N	49.27 E
Pahoa	**229d**	19.29 N	154.57 W
Pahokee	**220**	26.49 N	80.39 W
Pahost, Bela.	**76**	53.51 N	29.09 E
Pahost, Bela.	**76**	52.51 N	27.39 E
Pahraničny	**76**	53.07 N	23.58 E
Pahrump	**204**	36.12 N	115.58 W
Pahsimeroi ≃	**202**	44.41 N	114.03 W
Pahuatlán de Valle	**234**	20.17 N	98.09 W
Pahvant Range ⋏	**200**	38.45 N	112.15 W
Pai	**110**	19.19 N	98.27 E
Pai ≃	**110**	19.09 N	97.33 E
Pai, Ilha do I	**287a**	22.59 S	43.05 W
Paia	**229a**	20.54 N	156.22 W
Paianía	**267c**	37.57 N	23.51 E
Paicines	**226**	36.44 N	121.17 W
Paico	**248**	14.02 S	73.39 W
Paide	**76**	58.54 N	25.33 E
Paidorzu, Monte ʌ	**71**	40.30 N	9.05 E
Paifangchang	**107**	30.31 N	106.38 E
Paige	**222**	30.13 N	97.07 W
Paignton	**42**	50.26 N	3.34 W
Paiguano	**252**	30.01 S	70.32 W
Paihia	**172**	35.17 S	174.05 E
Paiho	**100**	23.21 N	120.25 E
Paiján	**248**	7.44 S	79.19 W
Päijänne ⊜	**26**	61.35 N	25.30 E
Pāikgācha	**126**	22.35 N	89.20 E
Paikü Co ⊜	**124**	28.48 N	85.36 E
Pail	**123**	32.38 N	72.27 E
Paila ≃	**248**	16.02 S	64.12 W
Paila, Sierra la ⋏	**196**	25.50 N	101.30 W
Pailin	**110**	12.51 N	102.36 E
Pailitas	**246**	8.58 N	73.38 W
Paillaco	**254**	40.04 S	72.53 W
Pailolo Channel ʯ	**229a**	21.05 N	156.42 W
Pailoutou	**106**	30.56 N	121.16 E
Pailoutun	**104**	40.44 N	122.49 E
Paimboeuf	**32**	47.17 N	2.02 W
Paimio	**26**	60.27 N	22.42 E
Paimpol	**32**	48.46 N	3.03 W
Painan	**112**	1.21 S	100.34 E
Paincourt	**214**	42.23 N	82.17 W
Painesdale	**190**	47.02 N	88.40 W
Painesville	**214**	41.43 N	81.14 W
Painscastle	**42**	52.07 N	3.12 W
Painshawfield	**44**	54.56 N	1.54 W
Painswick	**42**	51.48 N	2.11 W
Paint ≃	**190**	45.58 N	88.15 W
Paint Creek ≃, Mi., U.S.	**281**	42.06 N	83.36 W
Paint Creek ≃, Oh., U.S.	**218**	39.18 N	82.56 W
Paint Creek ≃, Pa., U.S.	**214**	41.10 N	79.28 W
Paint Creek ≃, Tx., U.S.	**196**	30.18 N	99.54 W
Paint Creek, East Fork ≃	**218**	39.32 N	83.25 W
Paint Creek, North Fork ≃	**218**	39.18 N	83.02 W
Paint Creek Lake ⊜[1]	**218**	39.15 N	83.22 W
Painted Desert ◆[2]	**200**	36.00 N	111.20 W
Painted Post	**210**	42.09 N	77.05 W
Painted Rock Reservoir ⊜[1]	**200**	33.00 N	112.50 W
Painten	**60**	49.00 N	11.49 E
Painter	**208**	37.35 N	75.47 W
Painter Creek ≃	**218**	40.05 N	84.21 W
Paintertown	**279b**	40.21 N	79.42 W
Paint Lake ⊜	**184**	55.28 N	97.57 W
Paint Rock	**196**	31.30 N	99.55 W
Paint Rock ≃	**194**	34.28 N	86.28 W
Paintsville	**192**	37.48 N	82.48 W
Paiolinho	**256**	21.52 S	45.54 W
Pai Pobre, Morro do ʌ	**287b**	23.40 S	46.55 W
Paisco	**64**	46.04 N	10.17 E
Paisha	**100**	23.40 N	119.35 E
Paisley, Austl.	**274b**	37.51 S	144.51 E
Paisley, On., Can.	**212**	44.18 N	81.16 W
Paisley, Scot., U.K.	**46**	55.50 N	4.26 W
Paisley, Fl., U.S.	**220**	28.59 N	81.32 W
Paisley, Or., U.S.	**202**	42.41 N	120.32 W

Païta, N. Cal.	**175f**	22.08 S	166.22 E
Paita, Perú	**248**	5.06 S	81.07 W
Paita, Bahía de ⊂	**248**	5.04 S	81.05 W
Paitan	**100**	23.31 N	113.46 E
Paitan ≃	**116**	6.30 N	117.30 E
Paitan, Teluk ⊂	**116**	6.45 N	117.20 E
Paiton	**115a**	7.43 S	113.30 E
Paiva	**256**	21.18 S	43.25 W
Paiva ≃	**34**	41.04 N	8.16 W
Paizhou	**100**	30.13 N	113.56 E
Paj	**24**	61.13 N	34.24 E
Pajala	**24**	67.11 N	23.22 E
Pajan	**246**	1.34 S	80.25 W
Pajapan	**234**	18.15 N	94.42 W
Pajares, Puerto de)(	**34**	43.00 N	5.46 W
Pajaro	**226**	36.54 N	121.39 W
Pajaro ≃	**226**	36.51 N	121.48 W
Pajaros Point ≻	**240m**	18.31 N	64.18 W
Paj-Choj ⋏[2]	**72**	69.00 N	63.00 E
Pajdugina ≃	**86**	58.50 N	81.47 E
Pajęczno	**30**	51.09 N	19.00 E
Pajeú ≃	**250**	8.55 S	38.42 W
Pajiangkou	**100**	23.46 N	113.14 E
Pajjer, gora ʌ	**24**	66.42 N	64.25 E
Pajtug	**85**	40.53 N	72.15 E
Pak ≃	**110**	21.05 N	102.31 E
Páka, Magy.	**61**	46.36 N	16.39 E
Paka, Malay.	**114**	4.39 N	103.26 E
Paka ≃	**114**	4.40 N	103.27 E
Pākāla	**122**	13.28 N	79.07 E
Pakaljubičy	**76**	52.30 N	31.02 E
Pakaraima Mountains ⋏	**246**	5.30 N	60.40 W
Pākaur	**124**	24.38 N	87.51 E
Pak Ban	**110**	21.14 N	102.28 E
Pakch'ŏn	**98**	39.45 N	125.35 E
Pak Chong	**110**	14.42 N	101.25 E
Pakeng	**140**	6.55 N	30.40 E
Pakenham, Austl.	**169**	38.04 S	145.29 E
Pakenham, On., Can.	**212**	45.20 N	76.17 W
Pākhāl ⊜[1]	**122**	17.57 N	79.59 E
Pákhi	**267c**	37.59 N	23.22 E
Pákhi I	**267c**	37.58 N	23.22 E
Pákhna	**130**	34.46 N	32.48 E
Pakhoi → Beihai	**102**	21.29 N	109.05 E
Pakin I[1]	**14**	7.04 N	157.48 E
Pakipaki	**172**	39.41 S	176.48 E
Pakistan (Pākistān) □[1], Asia	**118**	30.00 N	70.00 E
Pakistan (Pākistān) □[1], Asia	**120**	30.00 N	70.00 E
Pakistan, East → Bangladesh □[1]	**120**	24.00 N	90.00 E
Pak Kong	**271d**	22.23 N	114.15 E
Pak Kret	**269a**	13.55 N	100.30 E
Pak Kwo Chau I	**271d**	22.16 N	114.20 E
Paklenica Nacionalni Park ♠	**36**	44.21 N	15.23 E
Pakokku	**110**	21.20 N	95.05 E
Pakość	**30**	52.49 N	18.05 E
Pakouabo	**150**	7.10 N	5.48 W
Pakowki Lake ⊜	**184**	49.22 N	110.57 W
Pākpattan	**123**	30.21 N	73.24 E
Pak Phanang	**110**	8.21 N	100.12 E
Pak Phayun	**110**	7.21 N	100.19 E
Pak Phraek	**110**	8.13 N	100.12 E
Pakrac	**36**	45.26 N	17.12 E
Pākrāganj	**126**	24.00 N	90.41 E
Pakruojis	**76**	55.58 N	23.52 E
Paks	**30**	46.39 N	18.53 E
Pak Sane → Muang Pakxan	**110**	18.22 N	103.39 E
Pāksey	**126**	24.05 N	89.03 E
Pak Thong Chai	**110**	14.43 N	102.01 E
Paktīā □[4]	**120**	33.30 N	69.30 E
Paktīkā □[4]	**120**	32.30 N	68.45 E
Pākundia	**126**	24.20 N	90.42 E
P'akupur ≃	**74**	65.00 N	77.48 E
Pakwach	**154**	2.28 N	31.30 E
Pakwash Lake ⊜	**184**	50.45 N	93.30 W
Pakxé	**110**	15.07 N	105.47 E
Pala, Mya.	**110**	12.51 N	98.40 E
Pala, Tchad	**146**	9.22 N	14.54 E
Pala, Ca., U.S.	**228**	33.22 N	117.05 W
Palaau State Park ♠	**229a**	21.11 N	157.00 W
Palabek	**154**	3.26 N	32.34 E
Palacca Point ≻	**238**	21.15 N	73.26 W
Palacios	**196**	28.42 N	96.13 W
Palacios ≃	**248**	16.36 S	64.18 W
Paladru	**62**	45.28 N	5.33 E
Palagano	**64**	44.20 N	10.39 E
Palagianello	**68**	40.37 N	16.58 E
Palagiano	**68**	40.35 N	17.02 E
Palagonia	**70**	37.19 N	14.45 E
Palagruža, Otoci II	**36**	42.24 N	16.15 E
Palai	**122**	9.44 N	76.41 E
Palai, Punta ʌ	**71**	40.20 N	8.55 E
Palaia	**66**	43.36 N	10.46 E
Palaiá Epídhavros	**38**	37.38 N	23.09 E
Palaiá Psará	**38**	38.46 N	25.36 E
Palaikhóri	**130**	34.55 N	33.05 E
Pala Indian Reservation ◆[4]	**228**	33.21 N	117.04 W
Palaiokhóra	**38**	35.14 N	23.41 E
Palaión Fáliron	**267c**	37.55 N	23.41 E
Palaiseau	**50**	48.43 N	2.15 E
Pālakodu	**122**	16.32 N	81.44 E
Pālam ◆[8]	**272a**	28.35 N	77.05 E
Palam Airport ⊠	**123**	28.35 N	77.07 E
Palamás	**38**	39.28 N	22.05 E
Palamós	**34**	41.51 N	3.08 E
Pālampur	**123**	32.07 N	76.32 E
Palamuse	**76**	58.41 N	26.35 E
Palamut	**130**	38.59 N	27.41 E
Palana	**74**	59.07 N	159.58 E
Palanan, Mount ʌ	**116**	17.03 N	122.15 E
Palanan Bay ⊂	**116**	17.09 N	122.27 E
Palanan Point ≻	**116**	17.09 N	122.30 E
Palanas	**116**	12.09 N	123.55 E
Palandöken Dağları ⋏	**130**	39.47 N	41.15 E
Pālang	**126**	23.13 N	90.21 E
Pālang ≃[1]	**126**	23.15 N	90.21 E
Palanga	**76**	55.55 N	21.03 E
Palanganene	**152**	6.26 S	18.50 E
Palangkaraya	**112**	2.16 S	113.56 E
Palani	**122**	10.28 N	77.32 E
Pālanpur	**120**	24.10 N	72.26 E
Palanquinos	**34**	42.27 N	5.31 W
Palanzano	**64**	44.26 N	10.11 E
Palaoa Point ≻	**229a**	20.44 N	156.58 W
Palapag	**116**	12.33 N	125.07 E
Palapye	**156**	22.37 S	27.06 E
Pālār ≃	**122**	12.28 N	80.10 E
Palasan Island I	**116**	14.52 N	122.03 E
Palas de Rei	**34**	42.52 N	7.52 W
Palāshdānga	**126**	23.24 N	87.22 E
Palāspol	**126**	22.43 N	89.05 E
Palasthali	**126**	23.51 N	87.03 E
Palata	**66**	41.53 N	14.47 E
Palatcy	**86**	49.09 N	83.43 E
Palatine	**216**	42.06 N	88.02 W
Palatine Bridge	**210**	42.55 N	74.35 W
Palatka, Ross.	**74**	60.06 N	150.54 E
Palatka, Fl., U.S.	**192**	29.38 N	81.38 W
Palau, It.	**71**	41.11 N	9.23 E
Palau, Méx.	**196**	27.54 N	101.26 W
Palau □[1], Oc.	**14**	5.00 N	137.00 E
Palau (Belau) □[1], Oc.	**175b**	7.30 N	134.30 E
Palauig	**116**	15.26 N	119.54 E
Palaui Island I	**116**	18.33 N	122.08 E
Palau Islands II	**175b**	7.30 N	134.30 E
Palauk	**110**	13.16 N	98.38 E
Pal'avaam ≃	**180**	68.50 N	170.45 E
Pal'avaamskij chrebet ⋏	**180**	68.20 N	177.00 E
Palavas-les-Flots	**62**	43.32 N	3.56 E
Palaw	**110**	12.58 N	98.39 E
Palawai Basin ≚[1]	**229a**	20.47 N	156.55 W
Palawan □[4]	**116**	10.00 N	118.50 E

≃ River	Fluß	Río	Rivière	Rio
≅ Canal	Kanal	Canal	Canal	Canal
∟ Waterfall, Rapids	Wasserfall, Stromschnellen	Cascada, Rápidos	Chute d'eau, Rapides	Cascata, Rápidos
ʯ Strait	Meeresstraße	Estrecho	Détroit	Estreito
⊂ Bay, Gulf	Bucht, Golf	Bahía, Golfo	Baie, Golfe	Baía, Golfo
⊜ Lake, Lakes	See, Seen	Lago, Lagos	Lac, Lacs	Lago, Lagos
≚ Swamp	Sumpf	Pantano	Marais	Pântano
⋇ Ice Features, Glacier	Eis- und Gletscherformen	Accidentes Glaciales	Formes glaciaires	Acidentes glaciares
⊤ Other Hydrographic Features	Andere Hydrographische Objekte	Otros Elementos Hidrográficos	Autres données hydrographiques	Outros acidentes hidrográficos

✣ Submarine Features	Untermeerische Objekte	Accidentes Submarinos	Formes de relief sous-marin	Acidentes submarinos
□ Political Unit	Politische Einheit	Unidad Politica	Entité politique	Unidade política
ʊ Cultural Institution	Kulturelle Institution	Institución Cultural	Institution culturelle	Instituição cultural
⊥ Historical Site	Historische Stätte	Sitio Histórico	Site historique	Sitio histórico
♠ Recreational Site	Erholungs- und Ferienort	Sitio de Recreo	Centre de loisirs	Area de Lazer
⊠ Airport	Flughafen	Aeropuerto	Aéroport	Aeroporto
■ Military Installation	Militäranlage	Instalación Militar	Installation militaire	Instalação militar
◆ Miscellaneous	Verschiedenes	Misceláneo	Divers	Diversos

ENGLISH — DEUTSCH
Name | Page | Lat.°′ | Long.°′ — Name | Seite | Breite°′ | Länge°′ E = Ost

Palawan I 116 9.30 N 118.30 E
Palawan Passage ʯ 116 10.00 N 118.00 E
Palayan 116 15.33 N 121.06 E
Pālayankottai 122 8.43 N 77.44 E
Palazzo Adriano 70 37.41 N 13.23 E
Palazzolo Acreide 70 37.04 N 14.54 E
Palazzolo dello Stella 64 45.48 N 13.05 E
Palazzolo sull'Oglio 62 45.36 N 9.53 E
Palazzolo Vercellese 62 45.11 N 8.14 E
Palazzo San Gervasio 68 40.56 N 16.00 E
Palazzuolo sul Senio 66 44.07 N 11.33 E
P'albong-san ∧ 98 40.16 N 127.57 E
Palca, Bol. 248 16.34 S 67.59 W
Palca, Perú 248 11.21 S 75.31 W
Palcamayo 248 11.18 S 75.46 W
Pal'co 76 53.17 N 34.56 E
Paldi 224 48.48 N 123.51 W
Paldiski 76 59.20 N 24.06 E
Pāldor ∧ 124 28.16 N 85.11 E
Palech 80 56.48 N 41.51 E
Palel 120 24.27 N 94.02 E
Paleleh 112 1.04 N 121.57 E
Palembang 112 2.55 S 104.45 E
Palena 66 41.59 N 14.08 E
Palena ≃ 254 43.50 S 72.59 W
Palena, Lago (Lago General Vintter) ⊜ 254 43.55 S 71.40 W
Palencia 34 42.01 N 4.32 W
Palencia □[4] 34 42.25 N 4.35 W
Palen Lake ⊜ 204 33.46 N 115.12 W
Palenque 232 17.31 N 91.58 W
Palenque ⊥ 232 17.30 N 92.00 W
Palenque, Punta › 238 18.14 N 70.09 W
Palenville 210 42.10 N 74.01 W
Paleparto, Monte ∧ 68 39.28 N 16.34 E
Palermo, Col. 246 2.54 N 75.26 W
Palermo, It. 70 38.07 N 13.21 E
Palermo, Ca., U.S. 226 39.26 N 121.33 W
Palermo, Ur. 252 33.48 S 55.59 W
Palermo □[4] 70 37.49 N 13.35 E
Palermo ◆[8] 288 34.35 S 58.25 W
Palermo, Golfo di ⊂ 70 38.08 N 13.26 E
Palese, Aeroporto di ⊠ 68 41.10 N 16.47 E
Palesse 76 53.05 N 31.17 E
Palestina, Bra. 255 20.23 S 49.25 W
Palestina, Méx. 196 29.10 N 100.55 W
Palestine, Ar., U.S. 194 34.58 N 90.54 W
Palestine, Il., U.S. 194 39.00 N 87.36 W
Palestine, Oh., U.S. 218 40.03 N 84.45 W
Palestine, Tx., U.S. 222 31.45 N 95.37 W
Palestine □[9] 132 32.00 N 35.15 E
Palestine, Lake ⊜[1] 222 32.06 N 95.27 W
Palestrina 66 41.50 N 12.53 E
Paletwa 110 21.18 N 92.51 E
Palézieux 58 46.33 N 6.50 E
Palfau 61 47.42 N 14.48 E
Pālghāt 122 10.47 N 76.39 E
Palgrave, Mount ∧ 162 23.22 S 115.58 E
Palgrave Point › 156 20.45 S 13.20 E
Palhais 266c 38.37 N 9.03 W
Palhano 250 4.44 S 37.57 W
Palhano ≃ 250 4.33 S 37.42 W
Pāli, India 120 25.46 N 73.20 E
Pali, India 124 25.51 N 76.33 E
Paliano 66 41.48 N 13.03 E
Palidoro ◆[8] 66 41.56 N 12.11 E
Palikea ∧ 229c 21.26 N 158.06 W
Palima 112 4.20 S 120.22 E
Palimanan 115a 6.42 S 108.26 E
Palimbang 116 6.12 N 124.12 E
Palimé 150 6.54 N 0.38 E
Palín 236 14.24 N 90.42 W
Palinges 32 46.33 N 4.13 E
Palinuro 68 40.02 N 15.17 E
Palinuro, Capo › 68 40.02 N 15.16 E
Palisade, Co., U.S. 200 39.06 N 108.21 W
Palisade, Ne., U.S. 198 40.20 N 101.06 W
Palisades, Id., U.S. 202 43.21 N 111.13 W
Palisades, N.Y., U.S. 276 41.01 N 73.55 W
Palisades Amusement Park ♦ 276 40.50 N 73.59 W
Palisades Interstate Park ♦ 210 40.56 N 73.55 W
Palisades Park, Mi., U.S. 216 42.18 N 86.19 W
Palisades Park, N.J., U.S. 276 40.50 N 73.59 W
Palisades Reservoir ⊜[1] 202 43.15 N 111.05 W
Paliseul 56 49.54 N 5.08 E
Pālitāna 120 21.31 N 71.50 E
Palivere 76 58.59 N 23.52 E
Palizada 232 18.15 N 92.05 W
Palizzi 68 37.58 N 15.59 E
Paljakka ∧[2] 26 64.41 N 28.08 E
Pälkäne 26 61.20 N 24.16 E
Palk Bay ⊂ 122 9.30 N 79.15 E
Palkino, Ross. 76 57.32 N 28.01 E
Palkino, Ross. 80 58.15 N 42.56 E
Pālkonda 122 18.36 N 83.45 E
Pālkonda Range ⋏ 122 14.05 N 79.05 E
Palk Strait ʯ 122 10.00 N 79.45 E
Palla Bianca (Weisskugel) ∧ 64 46.48 N 10.44 E
Pallagorio 68 39.18 N 16.54 E
Pallamana 168b 35.02 S 139.12 E
Pallasca 248 8.15 S 78.01 W
Pallas Grean 48 52.33 N 8.22 W
Pallaskenry 48 52.39 N 8.52 W
Pallas-Ounastunturin kansallispuisto ♦ 24 68.06 N 24.00 E
Pallasovka 80 50.03 N 46.53 E
Pallastunturi ∧ 24 68.06 N 24.00 E
Pallejà 266d 41.25 N 2.00 E
Pallës, Bishti i › 38 41.24 N 19.24 E
Palling 182 54.21 N 125.55 W
Pallíni 267c 38.00 N 23.53 E
Pallinup ≃ 162 34.29 S 118.54 E
Pallisa 154 1.10 N 33.42 E
Palliser, Cape › 172 41.37 S 175.17 E
Palliser Bay ⊂ 172 41.25 S 175.05 E
Pallu 123 28.56 N 74.13 E
Palluau 32 46.48 N 1.37 W
Palma, Bra. 255 21.22 S 42.19 W
Palma, Moç. 154 10.46 S 40.29 E
P'al'ma, Ross. 24 62.26 N 35.53 E
Palma ≃ 255 12.33 S 47.52 W
Palma, Badia de ⊂ 34 39.27 N 2.35 E
Palmácia 250 4.08 S 38.50 W
Palma del Río 34 37.42 N 5.17 W
Palma [de Mallorca] 34 39.34 N 2.39 E
Palma di Montechiaro 70 37.11 N 13.46 E
Palmaḥim 132 31.56 N 34.42 E
Palmanova 64 45.54 N 13.19 E
Palma Pegada 234 22.42 N 101.48 W
Palmar ≃ 246 10.10 N 71.50 W
Palmar, Lago Artificial del ⊜[1] 252 33.05 S 57.10 W
Palmar Camp 232 16.26 N 88.53 W
Palmar de Cariaco 286c 10.34 N 66.55 W
Palmar de los Sepúlveda 232 25.43 N 107.55 W
Palmar de Varela 246 10.45 N 74.45 W
Palmarejo 240m 18.03 N 67.05 W
Palmares, Bra. 250 8.41 S 35.36 W
Palmares, C.R. 236 9.21 N 83.40 W
Palmares, C.R. 236 10.03 N 84.26 W
Palmares do Sul 252 30.16 S 50.31 W
Palmaria, Isola I 62 44.02 N 9.51 E
Palmarito 246 7.37 N 70.10 W
Palmarola, Isola I 66 40.56 N 12.51 E
Palmar Sur 236 8.58 N 83.29 W
Palmas, Bra. 250 10.08 S 48.18 W
Palmas, Bra. 252 26.30 S 52.00 W
Palmas, Méx. 234 22.49 N 103.57 W
Palmas, Golfo di ⊂ 71 39.02 N 8.31 E
Palmas, Ilha das I, Bra. 287a 23.02 S 43.12 W
Palmas, Ilha das I, Bra. 287a 23.04 S 43.31 W
Palmas Bellas 236 9.14 N 80.05 W
Palmas de Monte Alto 255 14.16 S 43.10 W
Palma Sola 220 27.31 N 82.38 W
Palma Soriano 240p 20.13 N 76.00 W
Palm Bay 220 28.02 N 80.35 W
Palm Beach, Austl. 170 33.36 S 151.19 E
Palm Beach, Austl. 171a 28.08 S 153.28 E
Palm Beach, Fl., U.S. 220 26.42 N 80.02 W
Palm Beach □[6] 220 26.38 N 80.27 W
Palm Beach Gardens 220 26.49 N 80.06 W
Palm Beach International Airport ⊠ 220 26.41 N 80.05 W
Palm City 220 27.09 N 80.16 W
Palmdale, Ca., U.S. 228 34.34 N 118.06 W
Palmdale, Fl., U.S. 220 26.56 N 81.18 W
Palmdale, Pa., U.S. 208 40.18 N 76.37 W
Palmdale, Lake ⊜[1] 228 34.33 N 118.07 W
Palm Desert 204 33.43 N 116.23 W
Palmeira, Bra. 252 25.25 S 50.00 W
Palmeira, C.V. 150a 16.46 N 22.59 W
Palmeira das Missões 252 27.55 S 53.17 W
Palmeira d'Oeste 255 20.23 S 50.47 W
Palmeira dos Índios 250 9.25 S 36.37 W
Palmeirais 250 5.58 S 43.04 W
Palmeiral 256 21.38 S 46.31 W
Palmeiras 255 12.31 S 41.34 W
Palmeiras ≃, Bra. 250 12.22 S 47.08 W
Palmeiras ≃, Bra. 255 15.25 S 51.10 W
Palmeirina 250 8.56 S 36.17 W
Palmeirinhas, Ponta das › 152 9.05 S 13.00 E
Palmela ≃ 256 21.38 S 45.23 W
Palmelo 255 17.20 S 48.27 W
Palmer, Austl. 168b 34.51 S 139.10 E
Palmer, P.R. 240m 18.22 N 65.46 W
Palmer, Ak., U.S. 180 61.36 N 149.07 W
Palmer, Il., U.S. 219 39.27 N 89.24 W
Palmer, Ma., U.S. 207 42.09 N 72.19 W
Palmer, Ms., U.S. 194 31.16 N 89.15 W
Palmer, Ne., U.S. 198 41.13 N 98.15 W
Palmer, Tn., U.S. 194 35.21 N 85.34 W
Palmer, Tx., U.S. 222 32.26 N 96.40 W
Palmer ≃, Austl. 162 24.46 S 133.25 E
Palmer ≃, Austl. 164 15.34 S 142.26 E
Palmer ≃, P.Q., Can. 206 46.19 N 71.27 W
Palmer ʋ[3] 9 64.46 S 64.03 W
Palmerah ◆[8] 269e 6.12 S 106.47 E
Palmer Heights 208 40.42 N 75.16 W
Palmer Lake 200 38.52 N 104.48 W
Palmer Land ◆[1] 9 71.30 S 65.00 W
Palmer Mill Brook ≃ 283 41.58 N 70.52 W
Palmer Park 284c 38.55 N 76.52 W
Palmer Park ♦ 281 42.26 N 83.07 W
Palmerston, On., Can. 212 43.50 N 80.51 W
Palmerston, N.Z. 172 45.29 S 170.43 E
Palmerston I[1] 14 18.04 S 163.10 W
Palmerston, Cape › 166 21.32 S 149.29 E
Palmerston Lake ⊜ 212 45.01 N 76.50 W
Palmerston North 172 40.21 S 175.37 E
Palmerton 210 40.48 N 75.36 W
Palmerville 164 15.59 S 144.05 E
Palmetto, Fl., U.S. 220 27.31 N 82.34 W
Palmetto, Ga., U.S. 192 33.31 N 84.40 W
Palmetto, La., U.S. 194 30.43 N 91.54 W
Palmford 158 27.11 S 29.42 E
Palm Harbor 220 28.04 N 82.45 W
Palmi 68 38.21 N 15.51 E
Palminópolis 255 16.47 S 50.08 W
Palmira, Arg. 252 33.03 S 68.34 W
Palmira, Col. 246 3.32 N 76.16 W
Palmira, Cuba 240p 22.14 N 80.23 W
Palmira, Ec. 246 2.05 S 78.43 W
Palmira, Méx. 196 28.58 N 100.47 W
Palmitas 252 33.31 S 57.49 W
Palmitos 252 27.05 S 53.08 W
Palmnicken → Jantarnyj 76 54.52 N 19.57 E
Palmoli 66 41.56 N 14.32 E
Palm River 220 27.56 N 82.23 W
Palms ◆[8] 280 34.02 N 118.25 W
Palm Shores 220 28.11 N 80.35 W
Palm Springs, Ca., U.S. 204 33.49 N 116.32 W
Palm Springs, Fl., U.S. 220 26.39 N 80.06 W
Palmyra → Tudmur, Sūrīy. 130 34.33 N 38.17 E
Palmyra, Il., U.S. 219 39.26 N 89.59 W
Palmyra, In., U.S. 218 38.24 N 86.06 W
Palmyra, Mi., U.S. 216 41.52 N 83.56 W
Palmyra, Mo., U.S. 219 39.47 N 91.31 W
Palmyra, N.J., U.S. 208 40.00 N 75.01 W
Palmyra, N.Y., U.S. 210 43.03 N 77.14 W
Palmyra, Oh., U.S. 214 41.07 N 81.02 W
Palmyra, Pa., U.S. 208 40.18 N 76.35 W
Palmyra, Va., U.S. 192 37.51 N 78.15 W
Palmyra, Wi., U.S. 216 42.52 N 88.35 W
Palmyra ⊥ 130 34.33 N 38.17 E
Palmyra Atoll I[1] 14 5.52 N 162.06 W
Palo, It. 66 41.56 N 12.06 E
Palo, Pil. 116 11.10 N 124.59 E
Palo Alto, Méx. 196 26.32 N 99.45 W
Palo Alto, Ca., U.S. 226 37.26 N 122.08 W
Palo Alto, Pa., U.S. 208 40.41 N 76.11 W
Palo Alto Airport ⊠ 282 37.28 N 122.07 W
Palo Blanco, Méx. 196 26.45 N 101.32 W
Palo Blanco, P.R. 240m 18.26 N 66.39 W
Palo Blanco Creek ≃ 196 27.10 N 97.52 W
Paločka 86 58.25 N 84.32 E
Palo del Colle 68 41.03 N 16.42 E
Palo Duro Canyon State Park ♦ 196 34.55 N 101.42 W
Palo Duro Creek ≃, U.S. 196 36.39 N 100.58 W
Palo Duro Creek ≃, Tx., U.S. 196 35.00 N 101.54 W
Paloe, Pulau I 115b 8.20 S 121.43 E
Paloemeu ≃ 250 3.21 N 55.26 W
Palo Flechado Pass)(200 36.25 N 105.20 W
Paloh, Indon. 112 1.43 N 109.18 E
Paloh, Malay. 112 2.25 N 111.15 E
Paloh, Malay. 114 2.11 N 103.12 E
Paloich, Sūd. 140 6.45 N 30.08 E
Paloich, Sūd. 140 10.28 N 32.32 E
Palojoensuu 24 68.17 N 23.05 E
Paloma Creek ≃ 226 36.15 N 121.26 W
Palomares Creek ≃ 282 37.42 N 122.02 W
Palomar Mountain ∧ 204 33.22 N 116.50 W
Palomar Mountain State Park ♦ 228 33.19 N 116.53 W
Palomar Park 282 37.29 N 122.16 W
Palomas 196 28.43 N 103.45 W
Palomas Viejo 232 31.44 N 107.37 W
Palombara Sabina 66 42.04 N 12.46 E
Palominos, Isla I 240m 18.21 N 65.34 W
Palomonte 68 40.40 N 15.17 E
Palompon 116 11.03 N 124.23 E
Palo Negro 246 10.11 N 67.33 W
Palo Pinto 196 32.46 N 98.18 W
Palo Pinto Reservoir ⊜[1] 196 32.38 N 98.18 W
Palopo 112 3.00 S 120.12 E
Palora ≃ 246 1.51 S 77.49 W
Palos, Cuba 240p 22.48 N 81.44 W
Palos → Palos de la Frontera, Esp. 34 37.14 N 6.53 W
Palos, Cabo de › 34 37.38 N 0.41 W
Palo Santo 252 25.34 S 59.21 W
Palos de la Frontera 34 37.14 N 6.53 W
Palos Gardens 278 41.40 N 87.48 W
Palos Heights 216 41.40 N 87.47 W
Palos Hills 278 41.41 N 87.49 W
Palos Hills ♦ 278 41.42 N 87.53 W
Palos Park 278 41.40 N 87.49 W
Palos Verdes Estates 228 33.48 N 118.23 W
Palos Verdes Hills ⋏[2] 280 33.46 N 118.21 W
Palos Verdes Point › 228 33.47 N 118.26 W
Palotai-sziget I 264c 47.35 N 19.05 E
Paloúkia 267c 37.58 N 23.31 E
Palouse 202 46.54 N 117.04 W
Palouse ≃ 202 46.35 N 118.13 W
Palouse, South Fork ≃ 202 46.53 N 117.22 W
Palo Verde 204 33.25 N 114.43 W
Palo Verde, Parque Nacional ♦ 236 10.15 N 85.10 W
P'alovskoje vodochranilišče ⊜[1] 82 56.03 N 37.40 E
Palpa 248 14.32 S 75.11 W
Palpalá 252 24.15 S 65.12 W
Pålsboda 40 59.04 N 15.20 E
Pālsit 126 23.12 N 88.03 E
Paltamo 26 64.25 N 27.50 E
Palten ≃ 61 47.34 N 14.20 E
Palu, Indon. 112 0.53 S 119.53 E
Palu, Tür. 130 38.42 N 39.57 E
Palu ≃ 112 0.52 S 119.51 E
Palu, Teluk ⊂ 112 0.40 S 119.45 E
Paluan 116 13.25 N 120.28 E
Paluan Bay ⊂ 116 13.23 N 120.25 E
Palù del Fersina 64 46.08 N 11.21 E
Paludi 68 39.32 N 16.41 E
Paluga 24 65.16 N 45.11 E
Paluke 150 5.02 N 8.06 W
Paluška ∧ 61 48.45 N 14.24 E
Paluxy ≃ 196 32.15 N 97.43 W
Paluzza 64 46.32 N 13.01 E
Palvantaš 85 40.34 N 72.12 E
Palvār, Kūh-e ∧ 128 30.04 N 57.28 E
Palvart 128 38.11 N 64.34 E
Palwal 124 28.09 N 77.20 E
Pal-Waukee Airport ⊠ 278 42.07 N 87.54 W
Pam 175f 20.16 S 164.19 E
Pama 150 11.15 N 0.42 E
Pama ≃ 152 4.23 N 18.27 E
Pamaluan 112 1.04 S 116.39 E
Pamanukan 115a 6.16 S 107.49 E
Pamarayan 115a 6.16 S 106.17 E
Pam'ati 13 Borcov 86 56.13 N 92.20 E
Pam'atnaja 86 56.01 N 65.42 E
Pam'at' Parižskoj Kommuny 80 56.06 N 44.31 E
Pāmban Channel ʯ 122 9.17 N 79.10 E
Pāmban Island I 122 9.15 N 79.20 E
Pambeguwa 150 10.40 N 8.19 E
Pambuhan 116 13.59 N 123.05 E
Pambuhan ≃ 116 12.34 N 124.55 E
Pambujan 116 12.34 N 124.56 E
Pamekasan 115a 7.10 S 113.28 E
Pamenang 112 2.07 S 102.31 E
Pameungpeuk 115a 7.38 S 107.43 E
Pamiers 32 43.07 N 1.36 E
Pamir ⋏ 118 38.00 N 73.00 E
Pamlico ≃ 192 35.20 N 76.30 W
Pamlico Sound ʯ 192 35.20 N 75.55 W
Pamotan 115a 6.46 S 111.29 E
Pampa 196 35.32 N 100.57 W
Pampã ≃ 255 17.43 S 40.36 W
Pampa ◆[1] 252 35.00 S 63.00 W
Pampa Almirón 252 26.42 S 59.08 W
Pampacolca 248 15.43 S 72.33 W
Pampa del Castillo 254 45.48 S 68.05 W
Pampa del Chañar 252 30.11 S 68.43 W
Pampa del Indio 252 26.02 S 59.55 W
Pampa del Infierno 252 26.31 S 61.10 W
Pampa de los Guanacos 252 26.14 S 61.51 W
Pampa Grande 248 18.05 S 64.06 W
Pampana ≃ 150 8.24 N 12.00 W
Pampanga □[4] 116 15.05 N 120.40 E
Pampanga ≃ 116 14.47 N 120.39 E
Pampanua 112 4.14 S 120.08 E
Pamparato 62 44.17 N 7.55 E
Pampas 248 12.24 S 74.54 W
Pampas ≃ 248 13.23 S 73.15 W
Pampas del Heath, Santuario Nacional ♦ 248 12.40 S 68.15 W
Pampeluna → Pamplona 34 42.49 N 1.38 W
Pamphylia □[9] 130 37.00 N 31.00 E
Pamplico 192 33.59 N 79.34 W
Pamplona, Col. 246 7.23 N 72.39 W
Pamplona, Esp. 34 42.49 N 1.38 W
Pampoenpoort 158 31.03 S 22.40 E
Pampow 54 53.32 N 14.15 E
Pāmpur 123 34.01 N 74.56 E
Pamukkale (Hierapolis) ⊥ 130 37.58 N 29.19 E
Pamukova 130 40.31 N 30.09 E
Pamunkey ≃ 208 37.32 N 76.48 W
Pana 219 39.23 N 89.04 W
Panabá 232 21.17 N 88.16 W
Panabo 116 7.19 N 125.42 E
Panaca 204 37.47 N 114.23 W
Panacan 116 9.16 N 118.25 E
Panacea 192 30.02 N 84.23 W
Panache, Lake ⊜ 190 46.15 N 81.20 W
Panadura 122 6.43 N 79.54 E
Panaeati Island I 164 10.40 S 152.20 E
Panāgar 124 23.18 N 79.59 E
Panagjurište 38 42.30 N 24.11 E
Panagtaran Point › 116 9.41 N 118.45 E
Panahan 112 1.44 S 111.49 E
Panaitan, Pulau I 115a 6.36 S 105.12 E
Panaitan, Selat ʯ 115a 6.40 S 105.16 E
Panaji (Panjim) 122 15.29 N 73.50 E
Pānākua 272b 22.23 N 88.21 E
Panamá, Bra. 255 18.11 S 49.21 W
Panamá, Pan. 236 8.58 N 79.32 W
Panama, Il., U.S. 219 39.02 N 89.32 W
Panama, N.Y., U.S. 214 42.04 N 79.29 W
Panama, Ok., U.S. 194 35.10 N 94.40 W
Panamá □[4] 236 8.48 N 79.55 W
Panama (Panamá) □[1], N.A. 230 9.00 N 80.00 W
Panama (Panamá) □[1], N.A. 246 9.00 N 80.00 W
Panamá, Bahía de ⊂ 246 8.50 N 79.20 W
Panamá, Canal de ≅ 236 9.20 N 79.55 W
Panamá, Golfo de ⊂ 246 8.00 N 79.30 W
Panamá, Istmo de ⊥[3] 246 9.00 N 80.00 W
Panama Basin ✣[1] 18 5.00 N 83.30 W
Panama City 194 30.09 N 85.39 W
Panamá Vieja ⊥ 236 9.00 N 79.29 W
Panambi 252 28.18 S 53.30 W
Panamint Range ⋏ 204 36.30 N 117.20 W
Panamint Valley V 204 36.15 N 117.20 W
Pan'an 100 29.06 N 120.27 E
Panao, Perú 248 9.49 S 76.00 W
Pan'ao, Zhg. 107 30.09 N 103.37 E
Panaon Island I 116 10.03 N 125.13 E
Panarea, Isola I 70 38.38 N 15.04 E
Panaro ≃ 64 44.55 N 11.25 E
Panarukan 115a 7.42 S 113.56 E
Panasoffkee, Lake ⊜ 220 28.47 N 82.08 W
Panatinane Island I 164 11.15 S 153.10 E
Panay I 116 11.15 N 122.30 E
Panay ≃ 116 11.35 N 122.43 E
Panay Gulf ⊂ 116 10.15 N 122.15 E
Panayía 38 39.59 N 25.24 E
Panay Island I 116 13.58 N 124.20 E
Pancalieri 62 44.50 N 7.35 E
Pancas 266c 38.48 N 8.55 W
Pančevo 38 44.52 N 20.39 E
Panchagarh 124 26.20 N 88.34 E
Pānchāl 126 23.15 N 87.18 E
Pānchet Hill ∧[2] 126 23.37 N 86.47 E
Pānchet Reservoir ⊜[1] 126 23.40 N 86.45 E
Pancheve 78 48.44 N 31.51 E
Pānchghara 272b 22.44 N 88.16 E
Panchgram 126 24.12 N 88.01 E
Panch'iao 269d 25.01 N 121.27 E
Panchla 126 22.32 N 88.09 E
Panchor 114 2.10 N 102.43 E
Pancho Simón ≃ 286b 23.03 N 82.21 W
Pānchur 272b 22.32 N 88.16 E
Pānchuria 272b 22.33 N 88.29 E
Panciu 38 45.55 N 27.05 E
Panda 156 24.02 S 34.45 E
Pandakan 115a 7.39 S 112.41 E
Pandamatenga 156 18.35 S 25.42 E
Pandan, Malay. 112 3.09 N 113.22 E
Pandan, Pil. 116 11.43 N 122.06 E
Pandan, Pil. 116 14.03 N 124.10 E
Pandan, Selat ʯ 271c 1.15 N 103.44 E
Pandanan Island I 116 8.17 N 117.13 E
Pandan Bay ⊂ 116 11.43 N 122.04 E
Pandan Reservoir ⊜[1] 271c 1.19 N 103.44 E
Pandaria 124 22.14 N 81.25 E
Pandarochan Bay ⊂ 116 12.12 N 121.10 E
Pandasan 112 6.28 N 116.32 E
Pan de Azúcar 252 34.48 S 55.14 W
Pan de Azucar, Cerro ∧ 286e 33.19 S 70.42 W
Pan de Azucar Island I 116 11.17 N 123.10 E
Pandegelang 115a 6.18 S 106.06 E
Pandėlys 76 56.01 N 25.13 E
Pāndharkawada 122 20.01 N 78.32 E
Pandharpur 122 17.40 N 75.20 E
Pāndhurna 122 21.36 N 78.31 E
Pandian 98 36.38 N 116.27 E
Pandino 62 45.24 N 9.33 E
Pando 252 34.43 S 55.57 W
Pando □[5] 248 11.20 S 67.40 W
Pando, Cerro ∧ 236 8.55 N 82.43 W
Pandora 216 40.56 N 83.57 W
Pandu 152 5.01 N 19.16 E
Pandua, India 124 25.08 N 88.10 E
Pāndua, India 126 23.05 N 88.17 E
P'andž (Panj) ≃ 120 37.06 N 68.20 E
Panebianco ≃ 70 37.24 N 15.04 E
Panelas 250 8.40 S 36.01 W
Paneveggio 64 46.18 N 11.44 E
Panevėžys 76 55.44 N 24.21 E
Panfang 100 27.54 N 115.57 E
Panfilov 86 44.10 N 80.01 E
Panfilovo 80 50.26 N 42.55 E
Pāng ≃ 110 20.58 N 98.30 E
Panga 154 1.51 N 26.25 E
Pangala 152 3.19 S 14.34 E
Pangalanes, Canal des ≅ 157b 22.40 S 47.50 E
Pangandaran 115a 7.41 S 108.39 E
Pangani 154 5.26 S 38.58 E
Pangani ≃ 154 5.26 S 38.58 E
Panganiran 116 13.02 N 123.26 E
Pangantocan 116 7.50 N 124.49 E
Panganuran 116 7.24 N 122.03 E
Pangasinan □[4] 116 16.00 N 120.20 E
Pangbourne 42 51.29 N 1.05 W
Pangburn 194 35.25 N 91.50 W
Pange 56 49.05 N 6.22 E
Pangfou → Bengbu 100 32.58 N 117.24 E
Pangga, Tanjung › 115b 8.55 S 116.02 E
Panggezhuang, Zhg. 105 39.38 N 116.19 E
Panggezhuang, Zhg. 105 39.16 N 115.49 E
Panghkam 110 23.53 N 97.37 E
Pangi 154 3.11 S 26.38 E
Pangian 112 1.06 S 119.24 E
Pangjiabu 105 40.36 N 115.27 E
Pangkah 115a 6.58 S 109.10 E
Pangkajene 112 4.50 S 119.32 E
Pangkalanbrandan 114 4.01 N 98.17 E
Pangkalanbuun 112 2.41 S 111.37 E
Pangkalansusu 114 4.06 N 98.14 E
Pangkalaseang, Tanjung › 112 0.42 S 123.26 E
Pangkalpinang 112 2.08 S 106.08 E
Pangkatan 114 2.09 N 100.00 E
Pangke 114 1.01 N 103.10 E
Pangkor, Pulau I 114 4.13 N 100.33 E
Panglao 116 9.35 N 123.45 E
Panglao Island I 116 9.35 N 123.48 E
Pangman 184 49.39 N 104.38 W
Pangnirtung 176 66.08 N 65.44 W
Pango Aluquém 152 8.43 S 14.27 E
Pangŏjin 98 35.29 N 129.26 E
Pangong Tso ⊜ 120 33.45 N 78.43 E
Pangp'u → Bengbu 100 32.58 N 117.24 E
Pāngsa 126 23.47 N 89.25 E
Pangtara 110 20.57 N 96.40 E
Pangubatan 116 6.57 N 125.47 E
Panguil Bay ⊂ 116 8.01 N 123.43 E
Panguipulli 254 39.38 S 72.20 W
Panguipulli, Lago ⊜ 254 39.43 S 72.13 W
Panguiranan 116 12.04 N 123.19 E
Panguitch 200 37.49 N 112.26 W
Pangururan 114 2.37 N 98.42 E
Pangutaran 116 6.18 N 120.35 E
Pangutaran Group II 116 6.15 N 120.30 E
Pangutaran Island I 116 6.18 N 120.34 E
Pangutaran Passage ʯ 116 6.13 N 120.30 E
Pangzidian 107 30.38 N 105.04 E
Panhandle 196 35.20 N 101.22 W
Paniai, Danau ⊜ 164 3.50 S 136.15 E
Pania-Mutombo 152 5.11 S 23.51 E
Paniau ∧ 229b 21.57 N 160.05 W
Panié, Mont ∧ 175f 20.36 S 164.46 E
Pānihāti 126 22.42 N 88.22 E
Panika 80 50.59 N 50.11 E
Panindícuaro 234 19.59 N 101.46 W
Panino, Ross. 76 56.25 N 34.34 E
Panino, Ross. 78 51.38 N 40.08 E
Panino-Nesterovo 82 55.23 N 38.11 E
Panīpāt 124 29.23 N 76.58 E
Paniqui 116 15.40 N 120.35 E
Panissières 62 45.47 N 4.20 E
Panitan 116 11.28 N 122.46 E
Panitian 116 9.05 N 118.05 E
Panj (P'andž) ≃ 120 37.06 N 68.20 E
Panjāb 120 34.22 N 67.01 E
Panjang 115a 5.28 S 105.18 E
Panjang, Pulau I 112 2.44 N 108.55 E
Panjang, Selat ʯ 114 0.40 N 102.30 E
Panje 272c 18.54 N 72.57 E
Panjgūr 128 26.58 N 64.06 E
Panji 114 2.34 N 97.50 E
Panjiapie 100 32.54 N 120.42 E
Panjiatun 104 41.04 N 121.38 E
Panjim → Panaji 122 15.29 N 73.50 E
Pānjkora ≃ 123 34.39 N 71.44 E
Panjnad ≃ 123 28.57 N 70.30 E
Panjpāi 120 29.55 N 66.30 E
Panjshār ≃ 120 34.38 N 69.42 E
Pankakoski 26 63.19 N 30.09 E
Panke ≃ 264a 52.32 N 13.22 E
Panker 54 54.20 N 10.34 E
Pānkhāli 126 22.37 N 89.31 E
Pankof, Cape › 180 54.40 N 163.04 W
Pankow ◆[8] 54 52.34 N 13.25 E
Pankratovo 76 59.10 N 43.30 E
Pankshin 150 9.20 N 9.24 E
Panlong, Zhg. 100 25.52 N 114.52 E
Panlong, Zhg. 106 31.58 N 121.35 E
Panlong, Zhg. 106 31.11 N 121.16 E
Panlong (Lo) ≃ 110 21.18 N 105.25 E
Panlongzhen 107 29.31 N 105.17 E
P'anmunjŏm 98 37.57 N 126.40 E
Panna 124 24.43 N 80.12 E
Pannawonica 162 21.44 S 116.22 E
Panni 68 41.13 N 15.16 E
Panningen 52 51.20 N 5.59 E
Pannonhalma ʋ[1] 30 47.28 N 17.50 E
Panoche Creek ≃ 226 36.44 N 120.31 W
Panola 194 31.58 N 86.23 W
Panola □[6] 222 32.07 N 94.30 W
Páno Lévkara 130 34.52 N 33.18 E
Panopah 112 1.56 S 111.11 E
Páno Panayiá 130 34.55 N 32.38 E
Páno Plátres 130 34.53 N 32.52 E
Panora 198 41.41 N 94.21 W
Panorama 255 21.21 S 51.51 W
Pánormos 38 37.38 N 25.02 E
Panovo, Ross. 24 59.48 N 46.27 E
Panovo, Ross. 88 58.58 N 101.58 E
P'anp'yŏng-ni 98 40.28 N 125.49 E
Panruti 122 11.46 N 79.33 E
Pansfelde 54 51.39 N 11.16 E
Panshan 104 41.12 N 122.04 E
Panshanger Aerodrome ⊠ 260 51.48 N 0.08 W
Pansik, Rápido ⌞ 236 14.30 N 85.15 W
Pansionat 265b 55.59 N 37.41 E
Pānskura 126 22.25 N 87.42 E
Pantabañgan 116 15.50 N 121.09 E
Pantalica, Necropoli di ⊥ 70 37.08 N 15.01 E
Pantanal Matogrossense, Parque Nacional do ♦ 248 17.35 S 57.40 W
Pantanaw 110 16.59 N 95.28 E
Pântano 256 22.23 S 46.01 W
Pântano, Ribeirão do ≃ 256 22.15 S 45.59 W
Pantar, Pulau I 112 8.25 S 124.07 E
Pantayivka 78 48.41 N 32.53 E
Panteleymonivka 83 48.12 N 37.59 E
Pantelleria 70 36.50 N 11.57 E
Pantelleria, Isola di I 70 36.47 N 12.00 E
Panteón Nacional ⊥ 286c 10.31 N 66.55 W
Pantepec ≃ 234 20.56 N 97.44 W
Pantha 110 23.49 N 94.33 E
Pantheon ⊥ 267a 41.55 N 12.29 E
Panther Creek ≃, Id., U.S. 202 45.19 N 114.24 W
Panther Creek ≃, Ky., U.S. 194 37.45 N 87.19 W
Panther Creek, South Fork ≃ 194 37.42 N 87.05 W
Panther Lake 210 43.19 N 75.54 W
Pantin 50 48.54 N 2.24 E
Pantitlán ◆[8] 286a 19.25 N 99.05 W
Panto, Tanjung › 115a 6.51 S 105.54 E
Panton, Mount ∧[2] 162 17.21 S 129.13 E
Pantonlabu 114 5.08 N 97.28 E
Pantry Brook ≃ 283 42.24 N 71.22 W
Panu 152 3.48 S 19.07 E
Pánuco 234 22.03 N 98.10 W
Pánuco ≃ 234 22.16 N 97.47 W
Panuke Lake ⊜ 186 44.48 N 64.07 W
Panukulan 116 14.56 N 121.49 E
Pānuria 126 23.49 N 86.58 E
Panvel 122 18.59 N 73.06 E
Panvel ≃ 272c 19.01 N 73.04 W
Panvel Creek ≃ 272c 18.59 N 73.00 E
Panwāri 124 25.27 N 79.29 E
Panxi 106 30.35 N 119.20 E
Panxian 102 25.50 N 104.36 E
Panxidu 98 35.39 N 115.52 E
Panyabungan 114 0.51 N 99.33 E
Panyam 150 9.25 N 9.13 E
Panyang 140 10.04 N 29.58 E
Panyčevo 86 57.05 N 81.49 E
Panyu 100 22.57 N 113.20 E
Panyutyne 78 48.56 N 36.17 E
Panzerstausee ⊜[1] 263 51.11 N 7.16 E
Panzhuang 105 39.20 N 117.28 E
Panzi 152 7.13 S 17.58 E
Panzós 236 15.24 N 89.40 W
Pao ≃, Thai 110 16.13 N 103.43 E
Pao ≃, Ven. 246 8.33 N 68.01 W
Pao ≃, Ven. 246 8.06 N 64.17 W
Paochi → Baoji 102 34.23 N 107.09 E
Pão de Açúcar 250 9.45 S 37.26 W
Pão de Açúcar (Sugar Loaf) ∧ 287a 22.57 S 43.09 W
Paoki → Baoji 102 34.23 N 107.09 E
Paola, It. 68 39.22 N 16.03 E
Paola, Ks., U.S. 198 38.34 N 94.52 W
Paoli, In., U.S. 218 38.33 N 86.28 W
Paoli, Pa., U.S. 208 40.02 N 75.28 W
Paoli, Wi., U.S. 216 42.56 N 89.32 W
Paonia 200 38.52 N 107.35 W
Pāonta Sāhib 124 30.27 N 77.37 E
Paopao 174s 17.31 S 149.49 W
Paoshenmiao 98 41.12 N 118.17 E
Paotai Yingzi 98 41.48 N 115.12 E
Paoting → Baoding 105 38.52 N 115.29 E
Paotow → Baotou 102 40.40 N 109.59 E
Paoua 152 7.15 N 16.26 E
Paoying → Baoying 100 33.16 N 119.20 E
P'aozero, ozero ⊜ 24 66.05 N 30.58 E
Paozi 104 42.13 N 122.19 E
Pap 85 40.53 N 71.07 E
Pápa 30 47.19 N 17.28 E
Papa, Sound of ʯ 46a 60.18 N 1.41 W
Papagaio 250 6.01 S 45.21 W
Papagaio ≃, Bra. 246 1.53 S 62.35 W
Papagaio ≃, Bra. 248 12.56 S 58.18 W
Papagayo ≃ 234 16.46 N 99.43 W
Papagayo, Golfo de ⊂ 236 10.42 N 85.50 W
Papago Indian Reservation ◆[4] 200 32.20 N 112.00 W
Papaikou 229d 19.47 N 155.05 W
Papakating Creek ≃ 276 41.11 N 74.38 W
Papakura 172 37.04 S 174.57 E
Papalia 112 5.58 S 124.01 E
Papaloapan ≃ 234 18.42 N 95.38 W
Papanoa 234 17.21 N 101.02 W
Papantla de Olarte 234 20.27 N 97.19 W
Papar, Indon. 115a 7.41 S 112.04 E
Papar, Malay. 112 5.44 N 115.56 E
Papara, Poly. fr. 174s 17.44 S 149.21 W
Papara, Sol.Is. 175e 7.02 S 156.48 E
Paparoa 172 36.06 S 174.14 E
Paparoa National Park ♦ 172 42.05 S 171.25 E
Paparoa Range ⋏ 172 42.00 S 171.35 E
Papasidero 68 39.52 N 15.54 E
Papa Stour I 46a 60.20 N 1.42 W
Papatoetoe 172 36.58 S 174.52 E
Papawai Point › 229a 20.47 N 156.33 W
Papa Westray I 46 59.21 N 2.54 W
Papeari 174s 17.45 S 149.21 W
Papeete 174s 17.32 S 149.34 W
Papelón 286c 10.27 N 66.47 W
Papenburg 52 53.05 N 7.23 E
Papendrecht 52 51.50 N 4.40 E
Papenoo 174s 17.30 S 149.25 W
Papenoo ≃ 174s 17.30 S 149.25 W
Papetoai 174s 17.29 S 149.52 W
Papey I 24a 64.37 N 14.11 W
Paphlagonia □[9] 130 41.10 N 32.45 E
Paphos → Néa Páfos 130 34.45 N 32.25 E
Papilė 76 56.09 N 22.48 E
Papillion 198 41.09 N 96.02 W
Papineau 216 40.58 N 87.43 W
Papineau □[6] 206 45.50 N 75.00 W
Papineau, Lac ⊜ 206 45.48 N 74.46 W
Papineau Creek ≃ 212 45.13 N 77.43 W
Papineau-Labelle, Réserve ♦ 188 45.55 N 75.20 W
Papineau Lake ⊜ 212 45.20 N 77.50 W
Papineauville 206 45.37 N 75.01 W
Paposo 252 25.01 S 70.28 W
Papouasie Nouvelle-Guinée → Papua New Guinea □[1] 164 6.00 S 150.00 E
Papozze 64 44.59 N 12.02 E
Pappenheim 56 48.56 N 10.58 E
Paps of Jura ⋏ 46 55.55 N 6.00 W
Papua, Gulf of ⊂ 164 8.30 S 145.00 E
Papua Neuguinea → Papua New Guinea □[1] 164 6.00 S 150.00 E
Papua New Guinea □[1] 164 6.00 S 147.00 E
Papuasia Nueva Guinea → Papua New Guinea □[1] 164 6.00 S 150.00 E
Papucaia 256 22.37 S 42.44 W
Papudo 252 32.31 S 71.27 W
Papulovo 24 60.34 N 48.00 E
Papun 110 18.04 N 97.27 E
Papunáua ≃ 246 2.09 N 70.32 W
Papunya 162 23.16 S 131.54 E
Papurí ≃ 246 0.36 N 69.11 W
Paquequer ≃ 256 22.12 S 42.54 W
Paquequer, Serra do ⋏ 256 22.12 S 42.40 W
Paquera 236 9.50 N 84.56 W
Paquetá, Ilha de I 287a 22.46 S 43.06 W
Par 42 50.21 N 4.43 W
Pará → Belém 250 1.27 S 48.29 W
Pará □[3] 250 4.00 S 53.00 W
Para □[5] 250 5.30 N 55.15 W
Pará ≃, Bra. 250 1.30 S 48.55 W
Pará ≃, Bra. 255 19.13 S 45.07 W
Para ≃, Ross. 80 54.23 N 40.52 E
Pará, Ilha do I 250 0.18 S 51.15 W
Para, Pulau I 112 3.05 N 125.30 E
Parabel' 86 58.43 N 81.31 E
Parabel' ≃ 86 58.44 N 81.35 E
Parabiago 62 45.33 N 8.57 E
Parabita 68 40.03 N 18.08 E
Paraburdoo 162 23.14 S 117.48 E
Paracale 116 14.17 N 122.48 E
Paracambi 256 22.37 S 43.43 W
Paracari ≃ 250 4.36 S 57.47 W
Paracas, Bahía de ⊂ 248 13.50 S 76.17 W
Paracas, Península de ›[1] 248 13.48 S 76.24 W
Paracatu 255 17.13 S 46.52 W
Paracatu ≃, Bra. 255 16.30 S 45.04 W
Paracatu ≃, Bra. 255 16.35 S 45.06 W
Paracel Islands → Xisha Qundao II 108 16.30 N 112.15 E
Parachilna 166 31.08 S 138.23 E
Pārachinār 120 33.54 N 70.06 E
Paracho de Verduzco 234 19.39 N 102.04 W
Parachute 200 39.27 N 108.03 W
Paraćin 38 43.52 N 21.24 E
Parácuaro 234 20.09 N 100.46 W
Paracuellos de Jarama 266a 40.30 N 3.32 W
Paracuru 250 3.24 S 39.04 W
Parád 30 47.55 N 20.02 E
Parada, Punta › 248 15.22 S 75.12 W
Paradas 34 37.18 N 5.30 W
Paradise, Guy. 246 6.45 N 58.00 W
Paradise, Ca., U.S. 204 39.44 N 121.38 W
Paradise, Mt., U.S. 202 47.23 N 114.48 W
Paradise, Nv., U.S. 204 36.09 N 115.10 W
Paradise, Pa., U.S. 208 40.01 N 76.08 W
Paradise, Tx., U.S. 222 33.09 N 97.41 W
Paradise Hill, Sk., Can. 184 53.32 N 109.28 W
Paradise Hill, Ak., U.S. 180 62.25 N 160.03 W
Paradise Island I 240b 25.05 N 77.19 W
Paradise Mountain ∧ 171a 27.45 S 152.02 E
Paradise Valley, Az., U.S. 200 33.31 N 111.56 W
Paradise Valley, Nv., U.S. 204 41.29 N 117.32 W
Parado 115b 8.45 S 118.36 E
Parado ≃ 250 10.17 S 55.39 W
Pāradwīp 120 20.16 N 86.37 E
Parafield 168b 34.47 S 138.38 E
Parafiyivka 78 50.53 N 32.38 E
Parağaçay 84 39.07 N 45.56 E
Paragon 218 39.23 N 86.33 W
Paragonah 200 37.53 N 112.46 W
Paragould 194 36.03 N 90.30 W
Paraguá ≃, Bol. 248 13.34 S 61.53 W
Paragua ≃, Ven. 246 6.55 N 62.55 W
Paraguaçu 256 21.33 S 45.44 W
Paraguaçu ≃ 255 12.45 S 38.54 W
Paraguaçu Paulista 255 22.25 S 50.34 W
Paraguaipoa 246 11.21 N 71.57 W
Paraguaná, Península de ›[1] 246 11.55 N 70.00 W
Paraguarí 252 25.38 S 57.09 W
Paraguarí □[5] 252 26.00 S 57.10 W
Paraguay □[1], S.A. 244 23.00 S 58.00 W
Paraguay □[1], S.A. 252 23.00 S 58.00 W
Paraguay (Paraguai) ≃ 18 27.18 S 58.38 W
Parahyba → João Pessoa 250 7.07 S 34.52 W
Parai, Represa do ⊜[1] 256 23.20 S 45.35 W
Paraíba □[3] 250 7.15 S 36.30 W
Paraíba do Sul 256 22.09 S 43.17 W
Paraíba do Sul ≃ 255 21.37 S 41.03 W
Paraibano 250 6.30 S 44.01 W
Paraibuna 256 23.23 S 45.39 W
Paraibuna ≃, Bra. 256 22.06 S 43.08 W
Paraibuna ≃, Bra. 256 23.22 S 45.40 W
Paraibuna, Represa do ⊜[1] 256 23.25 S 45.30 W
Paraíso, Bra. 255 19.03 S 52.59 W
Paraíso, Bra. 256 22.19 S 45.42 W
Paraíso, C.R. 236 9.50 N 83.51 W
Paraíso, Méx. 234 18.24 N 93.14 W
Paraiso, Pan. 236 9.02 N 79.38 W
Paraíso do Norte 255 23.13 S 52.38 W
Paraíso Garcia 256 21.32 S 43.53 W
Paraíso Novillero 234 18.16 N 95.59 W
Paraisópolis 256 22.33 S 45.47 W
Paraitinga ≃, Bra. 256 23.34 S 46.02 W
Paraitinga ≃, Bra. 256 23.22 S 45.40 W
Parakan 115a 7.17 S 110.06 E
Parakou 150 9.21 N 2.37 E
Paralía Aspropírgos 267c 38.02 N 23.35 E
Paralímni 130 35.02 N 33.59 E
Parama Island I 164 9.00 S 143.25 E
Paramakkudi 122 9.33 N 78.36 E
Paramaribo 250 5.50 N 55.10 W
Parambu 250 6.13 S 40.43 W
Paramillo, Parque Nacional ♦ 246 7.15 N 76.15 W
Paramirim 255 13.26 S 42.15 W
Paramirim ≃ 250 11.34 S 43.18 W
Paramithiá 38 39.28 N 20.30 E
Paramonga 248 10.40 S 77.50 W
Paramoti 250 4.06 S 39.15 W
Paramount 228 33.53 N 118.09 W
Paramus 210 40.56 N 74.04 W
Paramušir, ostrov I 74 50.25 N 155.50 E
Paramus Park ◆[9] 276 40.57 N 74.04 W
Paran, Naḥal (Wādī al-Jirāfī) V 132 30.24 N 35.10 E
Paraná, Arg. 252 31.44 S 60.32 W
Paranã, Bra. 255 12.33 S 47.52 W
Paraná □[3] 252 24.00 S 51.00 W
Paranã ≃, Bra. 255 12.30 S 48.14 W
Paraná ≃, S.A. 18 33.43 S 59.15 W
Paraná, Pico ∧ 252 25.16 S 48.48 W
Paranabi 256 23.54 S 45.14 W
Paraná Bravo ≃[1] 258 33.53 S 58.27 W
Paranacito ≃ 258 33.44 S 58.33 W
Paraná de las Palmas ≃[1] 258 34.18 S 58.33 W
Paranaguá 252 25.31 S 48.30 W
Paranaguá, Baía de ⊂ 252 25.29 S 48.33 W
Paraná Guazú ≃[1] 258 34.00 S 58.25 W
Paranaíba 255 19.40 S 51.11 W
Paranaíba ≃ 255 20.07 S 51.05 W
Paranaidji 250 6.33 S 47.27 W

Symbols in the index entries represent the broad categories identified in the key at the right. Symbols with superior numbers (⋏[1]) identify subcategories (see complete key on page *I · 1*).

Symbole im Register stellen die rechts im Schlüssel erklärten Kategorien dar. Symbole mit hochgestellten Ziffern (⋏[1]) bezeichnen Unterabteilungen einer Kategorie (vgl. vollständiger Schlüssel auf Seite *I · 1*).

Los símbolos incluídos en el texto del índice representan las grandes categorías identificadas con la clave a la derecha. Los símbolos con numeros en su parte superior (⋏[1]) identifican las subcategorías (véase la clave completa en la página *I · 1*).

Les symboles de l'index représentent les catégories indiquées dans la légende à droite. Les symboles suivis d'un indice (⋏[1]) représentent des sous-catégories (voir légende complète à la page *I · 1*).

Os símbolos incluídos no texto do índice representam as grandes categorias identificadas com a chave à direita. Os símbolos com números em sua parte superior (⋏[1]) identificam as subcategorias (veja-se a chave completa à página *I · 1*).

∧ Mountain	Berg	Montaña	Montagne	Montanha
⋏ Mountains	Gebirge	Montañas	Montagnes	Montanhas
)(Pass	Paß	Paso	Col	Passo
V Valley, Canyon	Tal, Cañon	Valle, Cañón	Vallée, Canyon	Vale, Canhão
≃ Plain	Ebene	Llano	Plaine	Planície
› Cape	Kap	Cabo	Cap	Cabo
I Island	Insel	Isla	Île	Ilha
II Islands	Inseln	Islas	Îles	Ilhas
⊥ Other Topographic Features	Andere Topographische Objekte	Otros Elementos Topográficos	Autres données topographiques	Outros acidentes topográficos

Para-Pawn *I* · 133

ESPAÑOL

Nombre	Página	Lat.°′	Long.°′ W = Oeste
Paranaíta ≃	250	9.28 S	56.43 W
Paranam	250	5.37 N	55.06 W
Paraná Miní ≃ [1]	258	34.13 S	58.25 W
Paranapanema ≃	255	22.40 S	53.09 W
Paranapiacaba	256	23.47 S	46.19 W
Paranapiacaba, Serra do ϰ	252	24.20 S	49.00 W
Parañaque	269f	14.30 N	120.59 E
Paranavaí	255	23.04 S	52.28 W
Parang, Pil.	116	7.23 N	124.16 E
Parang, Pil.	116	5.55 N	120.54 E
Parang, Pulau I	115a	5.45 S	110.14 E
Paran'ga	80	56.43 N	49.24 E
Parângu Mare, Vârful ∧	38	45.22 N	23.33 E
Paranhos	255	23.55 S	55.25 W
Paranjang	98	37.08 N	126.55 E
Paranoá, Lago do ⊜	255	15.48 S	47.50 W
Párao de Masa, Puerto de)(	34	42.38 N	3.46 W
Paraopeba	255	19.18 S	44.25 W
Parapara	246	9.44 N	67.18 W
Paraparaumu	172	40.55 S	175.01 E
Paraparaumu Beach	172	40.54 S	174.59 E
Parapayè	58	45.55 N	7.32 E
Parapetí ≃	248	18.58 S	62.21 W
Parara	112	2.37 S	120.07 E
Parás, Méx.	196	26.30 N	99.31 W
Paras, Perú	248	13.30 S	74.35 W
Parasan	116	8.05 N	123.33 E
Parāsī	124	27.32 N	83.40 E
Parāsia	124	22.12 N	78.46 E
Parasida	126	23.46 N	87.20 E
Parasnāth	124	23.59 N	86.02 E
Paratei	256	23.14 S	46.00 W
Parateí ≃	256	23.12 S	46.00 W
Parati	256	23.13 S	44.43 W
Paratico	64	45.39 N	9.57 E
Parati-Mirim	256	23.14 S	44.38 W
Paratinga	255	12.42 S	43.10 W
Paratoo	166	32.42 S	139.22 E
Parauapebas ≃	250	5.35 S	49.41 W
Parauari ≃	250	4.36 S	57.47 W
Paraúna	255	17.02 S	50.26 W
Paravani, ozero ⊜	84	41.26 N	43.48 E
Para Wirra Recreation Park ♠	168b	34.43 S	138.50 E
Paray-le-Monial	32	46.27 N	4.07 E
Parbakalan	114	2.38 N	98.27 E
Pārbati ≃	124	25.51 N	76.36 E
Pārbatipur	124	25.39 N	88.55 E
Parbhani	122	19.16 N	76.47 E
Parbig	86	57.14 N	81.24 E
Parbig ≃	86	57.37 N	82.18 E
Parbold	262	53.36 N	2.46 W
Parburuan	114	1.52 N	99.55 E
Parcani	38	46.49 N	29.31 E
Parchen	54	52.21 N	12.05 E
Parchim	54	53.25 N	11.51 E
Parchment	216	42.19 N	85.34 W
Parcines (Partschins)	64	46.41 N	11.04 E
Parczew	30	51.39 N	22.54 E
Pardee Reservoir ⊜ [1]	226	38.16 N	120.51 W
Pardeeville	190	43.32 N	89.18 W
Pardes Hanna-Karkur	132	32.28 N	34.58 E
Pārdi	122	20.31 N	72.57 E
Parding	120	32.52 N	88.39 E
Pardo ≃, Bra.	250	5.21 S	52.53 W
Pardo ≃, Bra.	252	29.59 S	52.23 W
Pardo ≃, Bra.	255	15.48 S	44.48 W
Pardo ≃, Bra.	255	20.10 S	48.38 W
Pardo ≃, Bra.	255	22.55 S	49.58 W
Pardo ≃, Bra.	255	15.39 S	38.57 W
Pardo ≃, Bra.	255	21.46 S	52.09 W
Pardo ≃, Bra.	256	23.32 S	45.30 W
Pardo ≃, Bra.	256	21.25 S	42.39 W
Pardomuan	114	2.06 N	98.20 E
Pardubice	30	50.02 N	15.47 E
Pare	115a	7.46 S	112.11 E
Parèčča	76	53.55 N	24.07 E
Parece Vela → Okino-Tori-shima I	90	20.25 N	136.00 E
Parecis	248	14.09 S	56.56 W
Parecis ≃	248	12.56 S	56.43 W
Parecis, Chapada dos ϰ	248	13.00 S	60.00 W
Parede	266c	38.41 N	9.21 W
Paredes de Nava	34	42.09 N	4.41 W
Paredón	232	25.56 N	100.58 W
Parelhas	250	6.41 S	36.39 W
Parelheiros ◆ [8]	256	23.51 S	46.44 W
Pareloup, Lac de ⊜	32	44.15 N	2.45 E
Paremata	172	41.07 S	174.52 E
Parempei I	174r	7.01 N	158.15 E
Paren'	74	62.28 N	163.05 E
Paren' ≃	74	62.25 N	163.10 E
Parengarenga Harbour c	172	34.31 S	172.57 E
Parent	176	47.55 N	74.37 W
Parent, Lac ⊜	190	48.38 N	77.03 W
Parentis-en-Born	32	44.21 N	1.05 W
Pareora	172	44.30 S	171.12 E
Parepare	112	4.01 S	119.38 E
Parera	252	35.08 S	64.32 W
Parets del Vallès	266d	41.34 N	2.14 E
Parey	54	52.22 N	11.59 E
Parfenjevo, Ross.	24	61.21 N	42.43 E
Parfenjevo, Ross.	80	58.29 N	43.25 E
Parfentevo	82	55.06 N	38.49 E
Parfino	76	57.58 N	31.41 E
Parforce-Heide ◆ [3]	264a	52.22 N	13.10 E
Párga	38	39.17 N	20.23 E
Pārgaon	272c	18.59 N	73.05 E
Pargarutan	114	1.28 N	99.20 E
Pargas (Parainen)	26	60.18 N	22.18 E
Pargey Creek ≃	285	39.49 N	75.18 W
Pargny-sur-Saulx	56	48.46 N	4.50 E
Pargolovo ◆ [8]	265a	60.04 N	30.18 E
Parham	240c	17.05 N	61.46 W
Parhebangan	114	2.15 N	98.45 E
Pari ◆ [8]	287b	23.32 S	46.37 W
Paria ≃	200	36.52 N	111.36 W
Paria, Gulf of c	246	10.20 N	62.00 W
Paria, Península de › [1]	241r	10.40 N	62.10 W
Pariaguán	246	8.51 N	64.43 W
Pariaman	112	0.38 S	100.08 E
Pariamanu ≃	248	12.26 S	69.16 W
Paricutín ∧ [1]	234	19.28 N	102.15 W
Parida, Isla I	236	8.07 N	82.20 W
Pariette Draw V	200	40.02 N	109.45 W
Parigi, Indon.	112	0.48 S	120.10 E
Parigi, Indon.	115a	6.12 S	106.22 E
Parigné-L'Évêque	50	47.56 N	0.22 E
Parika	246	6.52 N	58.25 W
Parikkala	26	61.33 N	29.30 E
Parima ≃	246	3.34 N	63.47 W
Parima, Sierra ϰ	246	2.30 N	64.00 W
Pariñas, Punta ›	246	4.40 S	81.20 W
Parintins	250	2.36 S	56.44 W
Paripiranga	250	10.41 S	37.52 W
Pariquera-Açu	252	24.43 S	47.53 W
Paris, On., Can.	212	43.12 N	80.23 W
Paris, Fr.	50	48.52 N	2.20 E
Paris, Fr.	261	48.52 N	2.20 E
Paris, Ar., U.S.	194	35.17 N	93.43 W
Paris, Id., U.S.	202	42.13 N	111.24 W
Paris, Il., U.S.	194	39.36 N	87.41 W
Paris, Ky., U.S.	218	38.12 N	84.15 W
Paris, Me., U.S.	188	44.15 N	70.30 W
Paris, Mo., U.S.	219	39.28 N	92.00 W
Paris, Oh., U.S.	214	40.48 N	81.10 W
Paris, Pa., U.S.	214	40.24 N	80.31 W
Paris, Tn., U.S.	194	36.18 N	88.19 W
Paris, Tx., U.S.	196	33.39 N	95.33 W
Paris □ [5]	261	48.52 N	2.20 E
Paris, Port de c	261	48.57 N	2.17 E
Parish	210	43.24 N	76.07 W

FRANÇAIS

Nom	Page	Lat.°′	Long.°′ W = Ouest
Parisien de Pantin, Cimetière ◆	261	48.54 N	2.23 E
Parisienne, Ile I	190	46.41 N	84.44 W
Paris-le-Bourget, Aéroport de ⊠	50	48.52 N	2.25 E
Parismina	236	10.12 N	83.38 W
Parismina ≃	236	10.19 N	83.21 W
Paris-Orly, Aéroport de ⊠	50	48.43 N	2.22 E
Paris-Plage, Aéroport ⊠	50	50.31 N	1.38 E
Parit	112	3.10 S	104.38 E
Parita, Bahía de c	236	8.08 N	80.24 W
Parit Bunga	114	2.04 N	102.33 E
Parit Buntar	114	5.07 N	100.30 E
Pariti	112	10.01 S	123.43 E
Parit Jawa	114	1.57 N	102.39 E
Park ≃	198	48.28 N	97.09 W
Park, North Branch ≃	198	48.26 N	97.27 W
Park, South Branch ≃	198	48.26 N	97.27 W
Parka	154	4.31 N	27.20 E
Parkano	26	62.01 N	23.01 E
Parkchester	285	40.00 N	75.35 W
Park City, Il., U.S.	216	42.21 N	87.53 W
Park City, Ks., U.S.	198	37.48 N	97.19 W
Park City, Mt., U.S.	202	45.37 N	108.55 W
Park City, Ut,. U.S.	200	40.38 N	111.29 W
Park Creek ≃	285	40.13 N	75.08 W
Parkdale, P.E., Can.	186	46.15 N	63.07 W
Parkdale, Mo., U.S.	219	38.29 N	90.32 W
Parkdale, Or., U.S.	224	45.31 N	121.35 W
Parkdene	273d	26.14 S	28.16 E
Parkent	85	41.18 N	69.40 E
Parker, Az., U.S.	200	34.09 N	114.17 W
Parker, Co., U.S.	198	39.31 N	104.45 W
Parker, Fl., U.S.	194	30.07 N	85.36 W
Parker, Pa., U.S.	214	41.05 N	79.41 W
Parker, S.D., U.S.	198	43.23 N	97.08 W
Parker □ [6]	222	32.48 N	97.42 W
Parker ≃	207	42.45 N	70.49 W
Parker, Cape ›	176	75.04 N	79.40 W
Parker, Lake ⊜	220	28.04 N	81.56 W
Parker City	218	40.11 N	85.12 W
Parker Dam	204	34.17 N	114.08 W
Parker Dam ◆ [6]	200	34.18 N	114.10 W
Parker Ford	285	40.12 N	75.35 W
Parker Peak ∧	198	43.24 N	103.41 W
Parker Range	162	31.38 S	119.35 E
Parker River National Wildlife Refuge ◆ [4]	283	42.45 N	70.48 W
Parkersburg, Il., U.S.	194	38.36 N	88.03 W
Parkersburg, Ia., U.S.	190	42.34 N	92.47 W
Parkersburg, W.V., U.S.	188	39.16 N	81.33 W
Parkers Creek ≃	285	40.00 N	74.53 W
Parkers Prairie	198	46.09 N	95.19 W
Parkerville	168a	31.53 S	116.09 E
Parker Volcano ∧ [1]	116	6.07 N	124.54 E
Parkes	166	33.08 S	148.11 E
Parkesburg	208	39.57 N	75.55 W
Park Falls	190	45.56 N	90.26 W
Parkfield	226	35.54 N	120.25 W
Park Forest	216	41.28 N	87.38 W
Parkgate, Eng., U.K.	262	53.18 N	3.05 W
Parkgate, Eng., U.K.	262	53.16 N	2.20 W
Park Hall	208	38.13 N	76.25 W
Parkhill, On., Can.	190	43.09 N	81.41 W
Parkhill, Pa., U.S.	214	40.22 N	78.52 W
Parkhill Gardens	273d	26.14 S	28.11 E
Parkhomenko	83	48.34 N	39.43 E
Parkhomivka	78	50.08 N	35.01 E
Parkin	194	35.15 N	90.34 W
Park Lake	216	42.48 N	84.27 W
Parkland, Pa., U.S.	285	40.09 N	74.56 W
Parkland, Wa., U.S.	224	47.09 N	122.25 W
Parklawn	284c	38.50 N	77.09 W
Park Layne	218	39.53 N	84.03 W
Parklea	274a	33.44 S	150.57 E
Parkman	214	41.22 N	81.03 W
Park Meadows	279b	40.18 N	79.44 W
Park Orchards	274b	37.46 S	145.13 E
Park Plateau ϰ [1]	198	37.15 N	104.45 W
Park Range ϰ	200	40.40 N	106.40 W
Park Rapids	198	46.55 N	95.03 W
Park Ridge, Il., U.S.	216	42.00 N	87.50 W
Park Ridge, N.J., U.S.	276	41.02 N	74.02 W
Park Ridge Farms	285	40.10 N	74.42 W
Park River	198	48.23 N	97.44 W
Parkrose	224	45.33 N	122.33 W
Park Rynie	158	30.25 S	30.35 E
Parks	180	57.38 N	154.00 W
Parks Creek ≃	212	44.17 N	77.21 W
Park Shore Resort	216	41.55 N	85.59 W
Parkside, Md., U.S.	284c	39.02 N	77.06 W
Parkside, Pa., U.S.	285	39.52 N	75.23 W
Parksley	208	37.46 N	75.39 W
Park Station ◆ [5]	273d	26.12 S	28.03 E
Parkstein	60	49.44 N	12.04 E
Parkstetten	60	48.55 N	12.36 E
Parkston	198	43.23 N	97.59 W
Parksville, B.C., Can.	182	49.19 N	124.19 W
Parksville, N.Y., U.S.	210	41.51 N	74.45 W
Parktown ◆ [8]	273d	26.11 S	28.03 E
Parktown North ◆ [8]	273d	26.09 S	28.02 E
Parkview	279b	40.30 N	79.56 W
Parkville, Md., U.S.	208	39.22 N	76.32 W
Parkville, Mo., U.S.	194	39.11 N	94.40 W
Parkwater	202	47.40 N	117.19 W
Parkway, Ca., U.S.	226	38.29 N	121.27 W
Parkway, Mo., U.S.	219	38.20 N	90.57 W
Parkwood	284c	39.01 N	77.05 W
Parla	34	40.14 N	3.46 W
Parlākimidi	122	18.47 N	84.06 E
Parle, Lac qui ⊜	198	45.07 N	96.00 W
Parli	122	18.51 N	76.32 E
Parliament, Houses of ʋ	260	51.30 N	0.07 W
Parlier	226	36.36 N	119.31 W
Parma, It.	64	44.48 N	10.20 E
Parma, Id., U.S.	202	43.47 N	116.56 W
Parma, Mi., U.S.	216	42.15 N	84.35 W
Parma, Mo., U.S.	194	36.36 N	89.48 W
Parma, Oh., U.S.	214	41.24 N	81.43 W
Parma □ [4]	64	44.40 N	10.10 E
Parma ≃	64	44.56 N	10.26 E
Parma Heights	214	41.23 N	81.45 W
Parmain	261	49.07 N	2.12 E
Parmatown Mall ◆ [9]	279a	41.23 N	81.44 W
Parnaguá	250	10.13 S	44.38 W
Parnahyba → Parnaíba	250	2.54 S	41.47 W
Parnaíba	250	2.54 S	41.47 W
Parnaíba ≃	250	3.00 S	41.50 W
Parnaibinha ≃	250	9.17 S	45.55 W
Parnamirim	250	8.05 S	39.34 W
Parnarama	250	5.41 S	43.06 W
Parnassós ∧	38	38.32 N	22.35 E
Parnassus	172	42.43 S	173.18 E
Parndorf	61	47.59 N	16.51 E
Parnell	216	40.14 N	88.42 W
Párnis ∧	38	38.11 N	23.42 E
Párnis Óros ϰ	267c	38.07 N	23.44 E
Parnon ϰ	38	37.05 N	22.40 E
Pärnu	76	58.24 N	24.32 E
Pärnu ≃	76	58.23 N	24.29 E
Pärnu-Jaagupi	76	58.37 N	24.30 E
Pärnu laht c	76	58.15 N	24.25 E
Paro	124	27.26 N	89.25 E
Pārola	120	20.53 N	75.07 E
Paromaj	89	52.50 N	143.02 E
Paroo	162	26.16 S	119.46 E
Paroo ≃	166	31.28 S	143.32 E
Parorā	272b	22.48 N	88.09 E
Páros	38	37.04 N	25.08 E
Páros I	38	37.08 N	25.12 E
Parow	158	33.53 S	18.37 E
Parowan	200	37.50 N	112.49 W

PORTUGUÊS

Nome	Página	Lat.°′	Long.°′ W = Oeste
Parpaillon ϰ	62	44.30 N	6.40 E
Parpan	58	46.46 N	9.33 E
Parr	216	41.02 N	87.13 W
Parral, Chile	252	36.09 S	71.50 W
Parral → Hidalgo del Parral, Méx.	232	26.56 N	105.40 W
Parral, Oh., U.S.	214	40.33 N	81.30 W
Parral ≃	232	27.39 N	105.07 W
Parramatta	170	33.49 S	151.00 E
Parramatta ≃	274a	33.51 S	151.14 E
Parramatta Park ♠	274a	33.49 S	151.00 E
Parramore Island I	208	37.32 N	75.38 W
Parras de la Fuente	232	25.25 N	102.11 W
Parrett ≃	42	51.13 N	3.01 W
Parrish, Al., U.S.	194	33.43 N	87.17 W
Parrish, Fl., U.S.	220	27.35 N	82.25 W
Parris Island Marine Corps Recruit Depot ■	192	32.21 N	80.41 W
Parrita	236	9.30 N	84.19 W
Parrita ≃	236	9.29 N	84.19 W
Parrsboro	186	45.24 N	64.20 W
Parry, Cape ›	176	70.08 N	124.24 W
Parry, Mount ∧	182	52.53 N	128.45 W
Parry Bay c	176	68.07 N	82.00 W
Parry Channel ʊ	16	74.20 N	98.00 W
Parry Island I	212	45.18 N	80.10 W
Parry Island Indian Reserve ◆ [4]	212	45.18 N	80.10 W
Parry Peninsula › [1]	180	69.45 N	124.30 W
Parry Sound	212	45.21 N	80.02 W
Parry Sound □ [6]	212	45.25 N	79.55 W
Parry Sound ʊ	212	45.21 N	80.06 W
Parryville	208	40.49 N	75.40 W
Parsberg	60	49.09 N	11.43 E
Parsdorf	60	48.09 N	11.47 E
Parseierspitze ∧	58	47.10 N	10.28 E
Parsęta ≃	30	54.12 N	15.33 E
Parshād	120	24.11 N	73.42 E
Parshall	198	47.57 N	102.08 W
Parshallville	281	42.41 N	83.46 W
Paršino	88	59.10 N	111.48 E
Parsippany	210	40.51 N	74.25 W
Parsippany, Lake ⊜	276	40.51 N	74.26 W
Parsnāth ∧	124	23.53 N	86.08 E
Parsnip ≃	182	55.10 N	123.00 W
Parsoburan	114	2.19 N	99.20 E
Parsonage Island I	276	40.37 N	73.37 W
Parsons, Ks., U.S.	198	37.20 N	95.15 W
Parsons, Tn., U.S.	194	35.38 N	88.07 W
Parsons, W.V., U.S.	188	39.05 N	79.40 W
Parsons, Mount ∧ [2]	164	13.33 S	135.09 E
Parson's Pond	186	50.02 N	57.43 W
Parsons Pond ⊜	186	50.00 N	57.35 W
Parsons Range ϰ	164	13.30 S	135.15 E
Parsteiner See ⊜	54	52.55 N	13.59 E
Pärsti	76	58.25 N	25.32 E
Partābpur	124	23.29 N	83.13 E
Partanna	70	37.43 N	12.53 E
Partāppur	126	21.48 N	86.44 E
Partenen	58	46.58 N	10.03 E
Parthala	272a	28.36 N	77.24 E
Parthe ≃	54	51.22 N	12.21 E
Parthenay	32	46.39 N	0.15 W
Partington	262	53.25 N	2.26 W
Partinico	70	38.03 N	13.07 E
Partizansk	89	43.08 N	133.09 E
Partizánske	30	48.39 N	18.23 E
Partizanskoje	86	55.30 N	94.24 E
Parton	44	54.34 N	3.35 W
Partridge, Point ›	224	48.13 N	122.46 W
Partridge Creek ≃	212	44.44 N	77.13 W
Partridge Crop Lake ⊜	184	55.38 N	97.27 W
Partridge Point ›	186	50.09 N	56.10 W
Partry	48	53.41 N	9.19 W
Partschins → Parcines	64	46.41 N	11.04 E
Paru ≃, Bra.	250	1.33 S	52.38 W
Parú ≃, Ven.	246	4.20 N	66.27 W
Parubcan	116	13.43 N	123.45 E
Paru de Este ≃	250	1.10 N	54.40 W
Paru de Oeste ≃	250	1.30 S	56.00 W
Parung	115a	6.25 S	106.42 E
Pårup, Dan.	41	55.24 N	10.20 E
Pårup, Dan.	41	56.08 N	9.21 E
Parūr	122	10.09 N	76.14 E
Paruro	248	13.46 S	71.51 W
Parutyne	78	46.43 N	31.53 E
Parvān □ [4]	120	35.15 N	69.30 E
Pārvatīpuram	122	18.47 N	83.26 E
Parvin State Park ♠	208	39.30 N	75.09 W
Părvomaj	38	42.06 N	25.13 E
Paryang	120	30.11 N	83.09 E
Paryčy	76	52.48 N	29.25 E
Påryd	26	56.34 N	15.55 E
Parys	158	27.04 S	27.16 E
Paša ≃	76	60.29 N	32.55 E
Paşabahçe ◆ [8]	267b	41.06 N	29.05 E
Pasacao	116	13.31 N	123.03 E
Pasaco	236	13.59 N	90.12 W
Pasadena, Nf., Can.	186	49.01 N	57.36 W
Pasadena, Ca., U.S.	228	34.08 N	118.08 W
Pasadena, Md., U.S.	208	39.06 N	76.34 W
Pasadena, Tx., U.S.	222	29.41 N	95.12 W
Pasado, Cabo ›	246	0.22 S	80.30 W
Pasaje	246	3.20 S	79.49 W
Pasaje ≃	252	25.35 S	63.57 W
Pasaje Talavera ≃ [1]	258	33.53 S	58.55 W
Pa Sak ≃	110	14.21 N	100.35 E
Paşaköy	130	35.09 N	33.36 E
Pasaleng Bay c	116	18.36 N	120.56 E
Paşalimanı Adası I	130	40.28 N	27.37 E
Pasān	124	22.51 N	82.12 E
Pasanauri	84	42.21 N	44.41 E
Pasangkayu	112	1.10 S	119.20 E
Pasarbantal	112	2.45 S	101.20 E
Pasarseluma	112	4.09 S	102.32 E
Pasar Senen Station ◆ [5]	269e	6.10 S	106.50 E
Pasarsorkam	114	1.53 N	98.34 E
Pasarwajo	112	5.29 S	122.50 E
Pasatiempo	226	37.02 N	122.02 W
Pasaunda	272a	28.42 N	77.21 E
Pasawng	110	18.52 N	97.18 E
Pasay	269f	14.33 N	121.00 E
Pasayten ≃	224	49.08 N	120.35 W
Pasayten, Middle Fork ≃	224	48.53 N	120.37 W
Pasayten, West Fork ≃	224	48.53 N	120.37 W
Pascack Brook ≃	276	40.59 N	73.59 W
Pascagama, Lac ⊜	190	48.34 N	75.36 W
Pascagoula	194	30.21 N	88.33 W
Pascagoula ≃	194	30.21 N	88.34 W
Pascalis, Lac ⊜	190	48.16 N	77.24 W
Paşcani	38	47.15 N	26.44 E
Pasching	61	48.15 N	14.12 E
Pasco	202	46.13 N	119.05 W
Pasco □ [5]	248	10.30 S	75.15 W
Pasco □ [6]	220	28.20 N	82.27 W
Pascoag	207	41.57 N	71.42 W
Pascoe Vale	274b	37.44 S	144.56 E
Pascua ≃	254	48.13 S	73.22 W
Pascua, Isla de (Easter Island) (Rapa Nui) I	174z	27.07 S	109.22 W
Pas-de-Calais □ [5]	50	50.30 N	2.20 E
Pas-en-Artois	50	50.09 N	2.30 E
Pasewalk	54	53.30 N	14.00 E
Pashmāl	123	35.26 N	72.36 E
Pasian di Prato	64	46.03 N	13.11 E
Pasiano di Pordenone	64	45.51 N	12.37 E
Pasig	116	14.33 N	121.05 E
Pasig ≃	269f	14.36 N	120.58 E
Pāsighāt	120	28.04 N	95.20 E
Pašija	86	58.26 N	58.16 E
P'asina ≃	74	73.50 N	87.10 E

Pasinler (Hasankale)	130	39.59 N	41.41 E
Pašino	86	55.11 N	83.00 E
P'asino, ozero ⊜	74	69.45 N	87.45 E
P'asinskij zaliv c	74	74.00 N	86.00 E
Pasirganting	112	2.02 S	100.53 E
Pasir Gudang	271c	1.27 N	103.53 E
Pasirian	115a	8.13 S	113.06 E
Pasir Mas	114	6.02 N	102.08 E
Pasir Panjang	271c	1.17 N	103.47 E
Pasirpengarayan	114	0.51 N	100.16 E
Pasir Puteh, Malay.	114	5.50 N	102.24 E
Pasir Puteh, Malay.	271c	1.26 N	103.56 E
Påskallavik	26	57.10 N	16.27 E
Paskeville	168b	34.02 S	137.54 E
Paškovo, Ross.	80	53.39 N	42.25 E
Paškovo, Ross.	89	48.54 N	130.42 E
Paškovskij	78	45.02 N	39.06 E
Pasłęk	30	54.05 N	19.39 E
Pasłęka ≃	30	54.26 N	19.45 E
Pasley, Cape ›	162	33.57 S	123.31 E
Pasley Bay c	176	70.40 N	96.27 W
Pašman, Otok I	36	43.58 N	15.21 E
Pasmore ≃	166	31.07 S	139.48 E
Pašn'a	24	63.21 N	56.28 E
Pasni	128	25.16 N	63.28 E
Paso de Indios	254	43.52 S	69.06 W
Paso del Cerro	252	31.29 S	55.50 W
Paso del Macho	234	18.58 N	96.43 W
Paso de los Libres	252	29.43 S	57.05 W
Paso de los Toros	252	32.49 S	56.31 W
Paso del Rey	288	34.39 S	58.46 W
Paso del Toro	234	19.02 N	96.07 W
Paso de Ovejas	234	19.17 N	96.26 W
Paso de Patria	252	27.13 S	58.35 W
Paso de San Antonio	196	29.05 N	103.55 W
Paso Hondo	232	15.49 N	92.02 W
Paso Limay	254	40.33 S	70.26 W
Pasorapa	248	18.16 S	64.37 W
Paso Robles	226	35.37 N	120.41 W
Paso Seco	240m	17.59 N	66.23 W
Paso Severino, Embalse ⊜ [1]	258	34.15 S	56.18 W
Pašozero	76	60.02 N	34.37 E
Pasqua Indian Reserve ◆ [4]	184	50.45 N	104.02 W
Pasque Island I	207	41.27 N	70.50 W
Pasquel, Punta ›	232	25.30 N	111.01 W
Pasquia Hills ϰ [2]	184	53.13 N	102.37 W
Pasquotank □ [6]	208	36.26 N	76.26 W
Pasquotank ≃	192	36.10 N	76.03 W
Pasrūr	123	32.16 N	74.40 E
Passadumkeag	188	45.11 N	68.37 W
Passadumkeag Mountain ∧ [2]	188	45.10 N	68.20 W
Passage East	48	52.13 N	6.59 W
Passagem Franca	250	6.10 S	43.47 W
Passage Point ›	176	73.29 N	115.17 W
Passage West	48	51.52 N	8.20 W
Passaic	210	40.51 N	74.07 W
Passaic □ [6]	210	40.55 N	74.10 W
Passaic ≃	276	40.43 N	74.07 W
Passaic Falls ⌊	276	40.55 N	74.11 W
Passamaquoddy Bay c	186	45.06 N	66.59 W
Passa Quatro	256	22.23 S	44.58 W
Passa Três	256	22.42 S	44.00 W
Passau	60	48.35 N	13.28 E
Passa Vinte	256	22.13 S	44.15 W
Pass Creek ≃	198	43.45 N	101.28 W
Passero, Capo ›	70	36.40 N	15.09 E
Passignano sul Trasimeno	66	43.11 N	12.08 E
Passirio (Passer) ≃	64	46.41 N	11.10 E
Pass Island	186	47.29 N	56.11 W
Pašskij Perevoz	76	60.24 N	32.59 E
Passo Corese	66	42.09 N	12.39 E
Passo Fundo	252	28.15 S	52.24 W
Passopisciaro	70	37.52 N	15.02 E
Passo Real, Reprêsa do ⊜ [1]	252	28.55 S	53.10 W
Passos	255	20.43 S	46.37 W
Passow	54	53.08 N	14.06 E
Passy	58	45.55 N	6.41 E
Passy ◆ [8]	261	48.52 N	2.17 E
Pastavy	76	55.07 N	26.50 E
Pastaza □ [4]	246	1.45 S	76.50 W
Pastaza ≃	246	4.50 S	76.25 W
Pastecho ≃	182	56.07 N	114.15 W
Pasteur, Lac ⊜	186	50.13 N	66.58 W
Pastillo	240m	17.59 N	66.29 W
Pasto	246	1.13 N	77.17 W
Pastol Bay c	180	63.07 N	163.15 W
Pastora Peak ∧	200	36.47 N	109.10 W
Pastoria Creek ≃	228	35.01 N	118.51 W
Pastos Bons	250	6.36 S	44.05 W
Pastrana	34	40.25 N	2.55 W
Pastrengo	64	45.29 N	10.48 E
Pašukovo	82	55.55 N	38.16 E
Pasuquin	116	18.20 N	120.37 E
Pasuruan	115a	7.38 S	112.54 E
Pasvalys	76	56.04 N	24.24 E
Pásztó	30	47.55 N	19.42 E
Pata	116	5.51 N	121.10 E
Patacamaya	248	17.14 S	67.55 W
Pātāchārkuchi	120	26.31 N	91.16 E
Patagonia	200	31.32 N	110.45 W
Patagonia ◆ [1]	254	44.00 S	68.00 W
Pataha Creek ≃	202	46.31 N	117.59 W
Pata Island I	116	5.49 N	121.10 E
Pātan, India	120	23.50 N	72.07 E
Pātan, India	124	23.18 N	79.42 E
Patapsco	208	39.32 N	76.53 W
Patapsco ≃	208	39.09 N	76.27 W
Patapsco, Cooks Branch ≃	284b	39.27 N	76.53 W
Patapsco, Davis Branch ≃	284b	39.19 N	76.51 W
Patapsco, North Branch ≃	208	39.21 N	76.53 W
Patapsco, Rockburn Branch ≃	284b	39.14 N	76.43 W
Patapsco, Soapstone Branch ≃	284b	39.13 N	76.43 W
Patapsco, South Branch ≃	208	39.21 N	76.53 W
Patapsco River Neck › [1]	284b	39.14 N	76.27 W
Patapsco Valley State Park ♠	208	39.20 N	76.55 W
Patargān, Daqq-e ⩸	128	33.30 N	60.40 E
Pătârlagele	38	45.19 N	26.22 E
Pataudi	124	28.19 N	76.47 E
Pataula Creek ≃	192	31.46 N	85.02 W
Patay	50	48.03 N	1.42 E
Pataz	248	7.44 S	77.37 W
Patchewollock	166	35.23 S	142.11 E
Patchogue	210	40.45 N	73.00 W
Patchogue Bay c	276	40.44 N	73.01 W
Patchway	42	51.32 N	2.34 W
Pat Cleburne, Lake ⊜ [1]	222	32.25 N	97.30 W
Pate	154	2.08 S	41.00 E
Patea	172	39.45 S	174.28 E
Patea ≃	172	39.46 S	174.29 E
Patearoa	172	45.16 S	170.03 E
Pategi	150	8.44 N	5.44 E
Pate Island I	154	2.07 S	41.03 E
Pateley Bridge	44	54.05 N	1.45 W
Patel Nagar ◆ [8]	272a	28.39 N	77.10 E
Patensie	158	33.46 S	24.49 E
Patéras Óros ϰ	267c	38.07 N	23.25 E
Patergassen	64	46.49 N	13.52 E
Paterna	34	39.30 N	0.26 W
Paternal ◆ [8]	288	34.36 S	58.28 W
Paternion	64	46.43 N	13.38 E
Paternò	70	37.34 N	14.54 E
Pateros, Pil.	269f	14.33 N	121.04 E
Pateros, Wa., U.S.	202	48.03 N	119.54 W
Patersdorf	60	49.01 N	12.59 E
Paterson, Austl.	170	32.36 S	151.37 E

Paterson, S. Afr.	158	33.26 S	25.58 E
Paterson, N.J., U.S.	210	40.55 N	74.10 W
Paterson ≃	170	32.43 S	151.39 E
Paterson, Cape ›	169	38.40 S	145.36 E
Paterson Inlet c	172	46.55 S	168.03 E
Paterswolde	52	53.08 N	6.35 E
Pātghāti	126	22.53 N	89.55 E
Pathalgaon	124	22.34 N	83.28 E
Pathānkot	123	32.17 N	75.39 E
Pathānkot Airport ⊠	123	32.15 N	75.37 E
Pātharghāra	272b	22.34 N	88.35 E
Patharia	124	23.54 N	79.12 E
Pathein (Bassein)	110	16.47 N	94.44 E
Pathfinder Reservoir ⊜ [1]	200	42.30 N	106.50 W
Pathfinder Seamount ✢ [3]	16	50.55 N	143.15 W
Pathiong	140	6.46 N	30.54 E
Pathiu	110	10.42 N	99.19 E
Path of Condie	46	56.15 N	3.30 W
Pāthrāil	126	24.12 N	89.56 E
Pathro ≃	126	24.12 N	86.48 E
Pathum Thani	110	14.01 N	100.32 E
Pati, Indon.	112	0.33 S	111.19 E
Pati, Indon.	115a	6.45 S	111.01 E
Patía	246	2.04 N	77.04 W
Patía ≃	246	2.13 N	78.40 W
Patiāla	123	30.19 N	76.24 E
Patiāla ∧	123	32.32 N	72.11 E
Pati do Alferes	256	22.25 S	43.25 W
P'atigorsk	84	44.03 N	43.04 E
Pātihāl	272b	22.39 N	88.08 E
Patikul	116	6.04 N	121.06 E
Patillas	240m	18.00 N	66.01 W
P'atimarskoje	80	49.31 N	50.32 E
Patinti, Selat ʊ	164	0.30 S	127.45 E
Patipāda	272c	19.04 N	73.05 E
Pati Point ›	174p	13.36 N	144.57 E
Pātiram	124	25.19 N	88.45 E
Patire, Convento del ʋ [1]	68	39.34 N	16.35 E
Pativilca	248	10.42 S	77.47 W
Pativilca ≃	248	10.44 S	77.48 W
Pātkai Range ϰ	120	27.00 N	96.00 E
Pat Mayse Reservoir ⊜ [1]	196	33.40 N	95.35 W
Pátmos I	38	37.20 N	26.33 E
Patna, India	124	25.36 N	85.07 E
Patna, India	126	21.56 N	87.52 E
Pātna, India	272b	22.59 N	88.18 E
Patna, Scot., U.K.	44	55.21 N	4.30 W
Patnāgarh	122	20.43 N	83.09 E
Patnanongan Island I	116	14.48 N	122.11 E
P'atnica, Ross.	82	54.46 N	38.09 E
P'atnica, Ross.	82	56.05 N	36.48 E
P'atnickoje, Ross.	78	50.25 N	37.51 E
P'atnickoje, Ross.	82	54.20 N	35.53 E
Pātnoli	272c	18.57 N	73.05 E
Patnoñgon	116	10.55 N	122.00 E
Patnos	84	39.14 N	42.52 E
Pato Branco	252	26.13 S	52.40 W
Patoka	219	38.45 N	89.05 W
Patoka ≃	194	38.25 N	87.44 W
Patoka Lake ⊜ [1]	194	38.20 N	86.40 W
Patokino	82	56.27 N	39.06 E
Patomskoje nagorje ϰ [1]	88	59.00 N	115.00 E
Paton, Île I	275a	45.31 N	73.45 W
Patonga	154	2.46 N	33.18 E
Patos	250	7.01 S	37.16 W
Patos, Lagoa dos c	252	31.06 S	51.15 W
Patos, Río de los ≃	252	31.18 S	69.25 W
Patos, Rio dos ≃	248	13.33 S	56.29 W
Patos de Minas	255	18.35 S	46.32 W
Patos Island I	224	48.47 N	122.56 W
P'atovskij	82	54.41 N	36.04 E
Patquía	252	30.03 S	66.53 W
Pátrai	38	38.15 N	21.44 E
Patraïkós Kólpos c	38	38.14 N	21.15 E
Patras → Pátrai	38	38.15 N	21.44 E
Pātrasāer	124	23.13 N	87.31 E
Patricio Lynch, Isla I	254	48.37 S	75.26 W
Patrick Air Force Base ■	220	28.15 N	80.36 W
Patrick Henry International Airport ⊠	208	37.08 N	76.30 W
Patrick Point ›	214	42.35 N	81.28 W
Patrington	44	53.41 N	0.02 W
Patriot	218	38.50 N	84.49 W
Patrocínio	255	18.57 S	46.59 W
Patrocínio Paulista	255	20.38 S	47.17 W
Patsaliga Creek ≃	194	31.22 N	86.31 W
Patscherkofel ∧	64	47.13 N	11.28 E
Pattada	71	40.35 N	9.06 E
Pattani	110	6.52 N	101.16 E
Pattani ≃	110	6.53 N	101.16 E
Patten	188	45.59 N	68.26 W
Pattenburg	210	40.38 N	75.01 W
Pattensen	52	52.15 N	9.46 E
Pattenville	283	42.35 N	71.14 W
Patterdale	44	54.32 N	2.56 W
Patterson, Ca., U.S.	226	37.28 N	121.07 W
Patterson, Ga., U.S.	192	31.23 N	82.08 W
Patterson, Il., U.S.	219	39.29 N	90.29 W
Patterson, La., U.S.	194	29.41 N	91.18 W
Patterson, N.Y., U.S.	210	41.30 N	73.36 W
Patterson, Oh., U.S.	216	40.47 N	83.32 W
Patterson ≃	274b	38.05 S	145.07 E
Patterson, Mount ∧	180	64.04 N	134.39 W
Patterson Creek ≃	188	39.34 N	78.44 W
Patterson Gardens	216	41.56 N	83.25 W
Patterson Heights	214	40.45 N	80.19 W
Patterson Island I	190	48.39 N	87.00 W
Patterson Park ♠	284b	39.17 N	76.35 W
Pattersonville	210	42.53 N	74.05 W
Patti, India	123	31.17 N	74.51 E
Patti, India	124	25.55 N	82.12 E
Patti, It.	70	38.08 N	14.58 E
Patti, Golfo di c	36	38.12 N	15.05 E
Pattison, Ms., U.S.	194	31.53 N	90.53 W
Pattison, Tx., U.S.	222	29.49 N	95.60 W
Pattoki	123	31.01 N	73.51 E
Patton	214	40.37 N	78.39 W
Patton, Cape ›	169	38.42 S	143.50 E
Patton Park ♠	281	42.19 N	83.10 W
Pattonsburg	194	40.02 N	94.08 W
Patton Seamounts ✢ [3]	16	54.20 N	149.30 W
Pattscheid ◆ [8]	263	51.05 N	7.03 E
Pattukkottai	122	10.26 N	79.19 E
Pattullo, Mount ∧	180	56.14 N	129.39 W
Patu	250	6.06 S	37.38 W
Pātua	126	22.06 N	90.23 E
Patuākhāli	124	22.21 N	90.21 E
Patuca ≃	236	15.50 N	84.17 W
Patuca, Punta ›	236	15.51 N	84.18 W
Patuha, Gunung ∧	115a	7.10 S	107.23 E
Pātul	272b	22.45 N	88.10 E
Patul, Cerro ∧	246	2.40 S	79.03 W
Pātuli	126	23.33 N	88.15 E
Patulul	236	14.25 N	91.10 W
Patumahoe	172	37.11 S	174.50 E
Pātūr	122	20.27 N	76.56 E
Patusi	164	2.10 S	147.10 E
Patutu ∧	172	39.15 S	175.51 E
Patuxent ≃	208	38.18 N	76.25 W
Patuxent, Western Branch ≃	208	38.47 N	76.43 W
Patuxent River Naval Air Test Center ■	208	38.17 N	76.25 W
Patuxent Wildlife Research Center ʋ [3]	284c	39.03 N	76.48 W
Patvinsuon kansallispuisto ♠	24	63.10 N	30.55 E
Patwāri	272a	28.35 N	77.27 E
Pátzcuaro	234	19.31 N	101.36 W

Pátzcuaro, Lago de ⊜	234	19.35 N	101.35 W
Patzicía	236	14.38 N	90.56 W
Patzig	54	54.28 N	13.24 E
Patzún	236	14.41 N	91.01 W
Pau	32	43.18 N	0.22 W
Pau, Gave de ≃	32	43.33 N	1.12 W
Pau Brasil	255	15.27 S	39.39 W
Paucarbamba	248	12.25 S	74.36 W
Paucarpata	248	16.26 S	71.30 W
Paucartambo	248	13.18 S	71.40 W
Paudash Lake ⊜	212	44.58 N	78.04 W
Pau dos Ferros	250	6.07 S	38.10 W
Pauh	112	2.08 S	102.48 E
Pauhunri ∧	124	27.58 N	88.50 E
Pauini	248	7.40 S	66.58 W
Pauini ≃, Bra.	246	1.42 S	62.50 W
Pauini ≃, Bra.	248	7.47 S	67.05 W
Pauk	110	21.27 N	94.27 E
Pauksa Taung ∧	110	19.55 N	94.18 E
Paul	202	42.36 N	113.46 W
Paul, Lac à ⊜	186	49.52 N	70.46 W
Paula Lima	256	21.35 S	43.29 W
Paularo	64	46.32 N	13.07 E
Paulaya ≃	236	15.51 N	85.06 W
Paulding, Ms., U.S.	194	32.01 N	89.02 W
Paulding, Oh., U.S.	216	41.08 N	84.34 W
Paulding □ [6]	216	41.08 N	84.35 W
Paulhan	32	43.32 N	3.27 E
Paulicéia	255	21.17 S	51.51 W
Paulilatino	71	40.05 N	8.46 E
Paulina Peak ∧	202	43.41 N	121.15 W
Pauline, Mount ∧	182	53.33 N	119.54 W
Paulinenaue	54	52.40 N	12.43 E
Paulínia	256	22.45 S	47.10 W
Paulino Neves	250	2.43 S	42.33 W
Paulins Kill	210	41.03 N	74.49 W
Paulins Kill ≃	210	40.55 N	75.05 W
Paulinzella ⊥	54	50.42 N	11.06 E
Paulis → Isiro	154	2.47 N	27.37 E
Paulistana	250	8.09 S	41.09 W
Paulistas	255	18.25 S	42.52 W
Paullina	198	42.58 N	95.41 W
Paull Lake ⊜	184	56.08 N	104.50 W
Paullo	62	45.25 N	9.24 E
Paulo Afonso	250	9.21 S	38.14 W
Paulo Afonso, Cachoeira de ⌊	250	9.24 S	38.13 W
Paulo de Faria	255	20.02 S	49.24 W
Pauloff Harbor (Pavlof Harbor)	180	54.27 N	162.42 W
Paulpietersburg	158	27.30 S	30.51 E
Paul Roux	158	28.18 S	27.59 E
Paul-Sauvé, Parc ♠	275a	45.28 N	74.02 W
Paulsboro	208	39.49 N	75.14 W
Pauls Cross Roads	208	37.52 N	76.53 W
Paul Seamount ✢ [3]	14	23.26 N	172.36 W
Paulstown → Whitehall	48	52.41 N	7.01 W
Pauls Valley	196	34.44 N	97.13 W
Paulton, Eng., U.K.	42	51.18 N	2.30 W
Paulton, Pa., U.S.	279b	40.34 N	79.34 W
Pauma Indian Reservation ◆ [4]	228	33.22 N	116.58 W
Pāunān	272b	22.57 N	88.17 E
Paung	110	16.37 N	97.28 E
Paungbyin	110	24.16 N	94.49 E
Paungde	110	18.29 N	95.30 E
Paunggyi	110	17.19 N	96.11 E
Paup	164	3.15 S	142.35 E
Paupack	210	41.24 N	75.14 W
Pauri	124	30.09 N	78.47 E
Pausa, Dtsch.	54	50.35 N	12.00 E
Pausa, Perú	248	15.16 S	73.20 W
Pausin	264a	52.38 N	13.03 E
Paute	246	2.47 S	78.50 W
Paute ≃	246	2.46 S	78.16 W
Pauto ≃	246	5.09 N	70.55 W
Pautou → Baotou	102	40.40 N	109.59 E
Pauwalu Point ›	229a	20.52 N	156.08 W
Pauwela	229a	20.56 N	156.19 W
Pauwela Point ›	229a	20.57 N	156.19 W
Pavai ◆ [8]	272c	19.07 N	72.55 E
Pavai Lake ⊜	272c	19.07 N	72.55 E
Pavda	86	59.15 N	59.30 E
Pāveh	128	35.03 N	46.22 E
Pavel'cevo	82	56.15 N	36.26 E
Pavelec	76	53.50 N	39.16 E
Pavelec Station ◆ [5]	265b	55.44 N	37.38 E
Pavia	62	45.10 N	9.10 E
Pavia □ [4]	62	45.07 N	9.08 E
Pavia, Naviglio di ≊	266b	45.27 N	9.11 E
Pavia di Udine	64	45.59 N	13.17 E
Pavilion, B.C., Can.	182	50.52 N	121.50 W
Pavilion, N.Y., U.S.	210	42.52 N	78.01 W
Pavilion Key I	220	25.42 N	81.22 W
Pavillion	200	43.14 N	108.41 W
Pavilly	50	49.34 N	0.58 E
Pāvilosta	76	56.53 N	21.14 E
Pavino	24	59.07 N	46.07 E
Pavione, Monte ∧	64	46.07 N	11.50 E
Pavlice	61	48.59 N	15.53 E
Pavlikeni	38	43.14 N	25.18 E
Pavliščevo, Ross.	82	55.11 N	35.59 E
Pavliščevo, Ross.	82	55.34 N	35.59 E
Pavlivka, Ukr.	78	47.45 N	37.14 E
Pavlivka, Ukr.	83	48.08 N	39.33 E
Pavlivka, Ukr.	83	49.36 N	38.42 E
Pavlodar	86	52.18 N	76.57 E
Pavlodar □ [8]	86	52.00 N	76.00 E
Pavlof Bay c	180	55.30 N	161.32 W
Pavlof Volcano ∧ [1]	180	55.24 N	161.52 W
Pavlogradka	86	54.12 N	73.33 E
Pavlohrad	78	48.32 N	35.53 E
Pavlopil'	83	47.16 N	37.47 E
Pavlovka, Kaz.	86	52.32 N	63.06 E
Pavlovka, Ross.	80	52.41 N	47.09 E
Pavlovka, Ross.	86	55.25 N	56.33 E
Pavlovka, Ross.	86	51.55 N	54.47 E
Pavlovo, Ross.	76	60.05 N	45.17 E
Pavlovo, Ross.	80	55.58 N	43.04 E
Pavlovo, Ross.	265a	59.56 N	30.40 E
Pavlovo, Ross.	265a	59.49 N	30.54 E
Pavlovsk, Ross.	76	59.41 N	30.27 E
Pavlovsk, Ross.	78	50.27 N	40.08 E
Pavlovsk, Ross.	86	53.20 N	82.59 E
Pavlovskaja	78	46.08 N	39.48 E
Pavlovskaja Sloboda	82	55.49 N	37.05 E
Pavlovskij	80	57.50 N	54.51 E
Pavlovskij Posad	82	55.47 N	38.40 E
Pavlysh	78	48.55 N	33.21 E
Pavne	272c	19.05 N	73.01 E
Pavo	192	31.02 N	84.04 W
Pavón, Arg.	258	34.23 S	59.03 W
Pavón, Col.	246	3.37 N	72.15 W
Pavón, Arroyo ≃	258	34.30 S	57.05 W
Pavona	267a	41.43 N	12.37 E
Pavonia	214	40.49 N	82.26 W
Pavšino	265b	55.49 N	37.21 E
Pavšozero	76	60.38 N	35.34 E
Pavullo nel Frignano	64	44.20 N	10.50 E
Pavuna, Arroio ≃	287a	22.58 S	43.23 W
Pavuvu Island I	175e	9.03 S	159.06 E
Pavy	76	58.03 N	29.30 E
Pawai, Pulau I	271c	1.12 N	103.43 E
Pawan ≃	112	1.51 S	109.57 E
Pawāyān	124	28.04 N	80.06 E
Pawcatuck	207	41.22 N	71.50 W
Paw Creek	192	35.16 N	80.56 W
Päwesin	54	52.31 N	12.42 E
Pawhuska	196	36.40 N	96.20 W
Pawling	210	41.33 N	73.36 W
Pawn ≃	110	18.53 N	97.19 E
Pawnee, Il., U.S.	219	39.35 N	89.34 W
Pawnee, Ok., U.S.	196	36.20 N	96.48 W
Pawnee ≃	198	38.10 N	99.06 W
Pawnee City	198	40.06 N	96.09 W
Pawnee Creek ≃	198	40.34 N	103.14 W

≃	River	Fluß	Río	Rivière	Rio
≊	Canal	Kanal	Canal	Canal	Canal
⌊	Waterfall, Rapids	Wasserfall, Stromschnellen	Cascada, Rápidos	Chute d'eau, Rapides	Cascata, Rápidos
ʊ	Strait	Meeresstraße	Estrecho	Détroit	Estreito
c	Bay, Gulf	Bucht, Golf	Bahía, Golfo	Baie, Golfe	Baía, Golfo
⊜	Lake, Lakes	See, Seen	Lago, Lagos	Lac, Lacs	Lago, Lagos
⩸	Swamp	Sumpf	Pantano	Marais	Pântano
⍓	Ice Features, Glacier	Eis- und Gletscherformen	Accidentes Glaciales	Formes glaciaires	Acidentes glaciares
⍑	Other Hydrographic Features	Andere Hydrographische Objekte	Otros Elementos Hidrográficos	Autres données hydrographiques	Outros acidentes hidrográficos

✢	Submarine Features	Untermeerische Objekte	Accidentes Submarinos	Formes de relief sous-marin	Acidentes submarinos
□	Political Unit	Politische Einheit	Unidad Política	Entité politique	Unidade política
ʋ	Cultural Institution	Kulturelle Institution	Institución Cultural	Institution culturelle	Instituição cultural
⊥	Historical Site	Historische Stätte	Sitio Histórico	Site historique	Sitio histórico
♠	Recreational Site	Erholungs- und Ferienort	Sitio de Recreo	Centre de loisirs	Area de Lazer
⊠	Airport	Flughafen	Aeropuerto	Aéroport	Aeroporto
■	Military Installation	Militäranlage	Instalación Militar	Installation militaire	Instalação militar
◆	Miscellaneous	Verschiedenes	Misceláneo	Divers	Diversos

Name / Name	Page / Seite	Lat.°′ / Breite°′	Long.°′ / Länge°′ E = Ost
Pawnee Rock	198	38.15 N	98.58 W
Pawni	122	20.47 N	79.38 E
Pawota	110	17.46 N	97.17 E
Paw Paw, Il., U.S.	216	41.41 N	88.59 W
Paw Paw, Mi., U.S.	216	42.13 N	85.53 W
Paw Paw, W.V., U.S.	188	39.31 N	78.27 W
Paw Paw ≃	216	42.07 N	86.29 W
Paw Paw Creek ≃	216	40.52 N	85.58 W
Paw Paw Lake	216	42.12 N	86.15 W
Paw Paw Lake ⊜	216	42.12 N	86.16 W
Pawtucket	207	41.52 N	71.22 W
Pawtucket Falls ⌞	207	42.39 N	71.20 W
Paxoí I	38	39.12 N	20.12 E
Paxson	180	63.02 N	145.30 W
Paxton, Austl.	170	32.54 S	151.16 E
Paxton, Il., U.S.	216	40.27 N	88.05 W
Paxton, Ma., U.S.	207	42.18 N	71.55 W
Paxton, Ne., U.S.	198	41.07 N	101.21 W
Paxtonia	208	40.19 N	76.48 W
Paxtonville	208	40.46 N	77.05 W
Paya	236	15.37 N	85.17 W
Paya Besar	114	3.47 N	103.16 E
Payadapu	114	3.05 N	97.23 E
Payāgpur	124	27.25 N	81.48 E
Payagyi	110	17.29 N	96.32 E
Payakumbuh	112	0.14 S	100.38 E
Paya Lebar	271c	1.22 N	103.53 E
Paya Lebar Airport ⊠	271c	1.21 N	103.54 E
Payamlı	130	37.01 N	38.35 E
Payangan	115b	8.26 S	115.15 E
Payas, Cerro ʌ	236	15.50 N	85.00 W
Payerne	58	46.49 N	6.56 E
Payeti	115b	9.41 S	120.20 E
Payette	202	44.04 N	116.55 W
Payette ≃	202	44.05 N	116.57 W
Payette, Middle Fork ≃	202	44.05 N	116.07 W
Payette, North Fork ≃	202	44.05 N	116.07 W
Payette, South Fork ≃	202	44.06 N	116.00 W
Payette Lake ⊜[1]	202	44.57 N	116.05 W
Paylampur	272b	22.47 N	88.16 E
Payne	216	41.04 N	84.43 W
Payne ≃	206	45.14 N	75.08 W
Payne, Lac ⊜	176	59.25 N	74.00 W
Payne Bay c	176	60.00 N	70.00 W
Payneham	168b	34.53 S	138.38 E
Paynes Creek ≃	204	40.16 N	122.11 W
Paynes Find	162	29.15 S	117.41 E
Paynesville, S. Afr.	273d	26.14 S	28.28 E
Paynesville, Mn., U.S.	198	45.22 N	94.42 W
Paynesville, Mo., U.S.	219	39.16 N	90.54 W
Paynetown State Recreation Area ♠	218	39.05 N	86.27 W
Paynton	184	53.01 N	108.56 W
Paysandú	252	32.19 S	58.05 W
Pays-Bas → Netherlands □[1]	30	52.15 N	5.30 E
Payson, Az., U.S.	200	34.13 N	111.19 W
Payson, Il., U.S.	219	39.49 N	91.14 W
Payson, Ut., U.S.	200	40.02 N	111.43 W
Payún, Cerro ʌ	252	36.30 S	69.18 W
Paz ≃	236	13.45 N	90.08 W
Paz, Cañada de la ≃	288	34.53 S	58.38 W
Paz, Rio da ≃	250	9.14 S	52.01 W
Pazar, Tür.	130	41.11 N	40.53 E
Pazar, Tür.	130	40.17 N	36.18 E
Pazarbaşı Burnu >	130	41.10 N	30.11 E
Pazarcık	130	37.31 N	37.19 E
Pazardžik	38	42.12 N	24.20 E
Pazarköy, Tür.	130	40.55 N	32.11 E
Pazarköy, Tür.	130	39.51 N	27.24 E
Pazarören	130	38.41 N	36.11 E
Pazaryeri, Tür.	130	38.05 N	28.14 E
Pazaryeri, Tür.	130	40.00 N	29.54 E
Paz de Ariporo	246	5.53 N	71.54 W
Paz de Río	246	5.59 N	72.47 W
Pazifischer Ozean → Pacific Ocean ⊤[1]	6	10.00 S	150.00 W
P'ažijeva Sel'ga	24	61.29 N	34.29 E
Pazin	36	45.14 N	13.56 E
Pazña	248	18.36 S	66.55 W
Paznauntal V	58	47.03 N	10.20 E
Pčevža	76	59.23 N	32.20 E
Pčevža ≃	76	59.21 N	31.54 E
Pchery	54	50.10 N	14.08 E
Pcič	76	52.09 N	28.52 E
Pcič ≃	76	52.09 N	28.52 E
Pe	110	13.28 N	98.31 E
Pea	174w	21.10 S	175.14 W
Pea ≃	194	31.01 N	85.51 W
Peabody, Ks., U.S.	198	38.10 N	97.06 W
Peabody, Ma., U.S.	207	42.31 N	70.55 W
Peace ≃, Can.	176	59.00 N	111.25 W
Peace ≃, Fl., U.S.	220	26.55 N	82.05 W
Peace Arch ⊥	224	49.00 N	122.45 W
Peace Bridge ◆[5]	284a	42.54 N	78.55 W
Peace Canyon Dam ◆[6]	182	55.59 N	121.59 W
Peace Dale	207	41.27 N	71.29 W
Peacehaven	42	50.47 N	0.01 E
Peace River	182	56.14 N	117.17 W
Peach Creek	188	37.52 N	81.59 W
Peach Creek ≃, Tx., U.S.	222	30.07 N	95.10 W
Peach Creek ≃, Tx., U.S.	222	29.24 N	97.19 W
Peach Creek, Sandy Fork ≃	222	29.34 N	97.19 W
Peachdale	158	26.30 S	24.42 E
Peachland	182	49.46 N	119.44 W
Peach Orchard	192	33.28 N	82.04 W
Peach Springs	200	35.31 N	113.25 W
Peacock Hills ⋏[2]	176	66.05 N	110.45 W
Peacock Point >, On., Can.	212	42.47 N	79.59 W
Peacock Point >, Wake I.	174a	19.16 N	166.37 E
Peacock Sound ʯ	9	72.55 S	100.00 W
Pea Hill Branch ≃	284c	38.45 N	76.57 W
Peak Charles National Park ♠	162	32.55 S	121.06 E
Peak Crossing	171a	27.47 S	152.44 E
Peak Dale	262	53.17 N	1.52 W
Peak District National Park ♠	44	53.17 N	1.45 W
Peak Downs	166	22.12 S	148.10 E
Peake Creek ≃	162	28.05 S	136.07 E
Peaked Mountain ʌ	186	46.34 N	68.49 W
Peak Forest	262	53.19 N	1.50 W
Peak Forest Canal ≊	262	53.29 N	2.06 W
Peak Hill, Austl.	162	25.38 S	118.43 E
Peak Hill, Austl.	166	32.44 S	148.12 E
Peakhurst	274a	33.58 S	151.04 E
Peakview	171b	36.04 S	149.24 E
Peäldoajvi ʌ	24	69.11 N	26.36 E
Peale, Mount ʌ	200	38.26 N	109.14 W
Peale Island I	174a	19.19 N	166.35 E
Peapack Brook ≃	276	40.41 N	74.39 W
Pearblossom	228	34.30 N	117.55 W
Pearce	200	31.54 N	109.49 W
Pearce, Royal Australian Air Force Station ■	168a	31.41 S	116.01 E
Pearce Point >	164	14.25 S	129.21 E
Peard Bay c	180	70.51 N	159.10 W
Pea Ridge ʌ	218	38.25 N	83.36 W
Pea Ridge National Military Park ♠	194	36.29 N	94.06 W
Pearisburg	192	37.19 N	80.44 W
Pearl, Il., U.S.	194	39.28 N	90.38 W
Pearl, Ms., U.S.	194	32.16 N	90.07 W
Pearl ≃	194	30.11 N	89.32 W
Pearl, Lake ⊜	283	42.04 N	71.21 W
Pearland	222	29.33 N	95.17 W
Pearl and Hermes Atoll I[1]	14	27.55 N	175.45 W
Pearl Bank ✢[4]	116	5.49 N	119.42 E
Pearl Beach	214	42.37 N	82.35 W
Pearl City	229c	21.23 N	157.58 W
Pearl Creek ≃	198	44.15 N	98.08 W
Pearl Harbor c	229c	21.22 N	157.58 W
Pearl Harbor Naval Station ■	229c	21.21 N	157.57 W
Pearl Peak ʌ	204	40.14 N	115.32 W
Pearl River, La., U.S.	194	30.22 N	89.44 W
Pearl River, N.Y., U.S.	210	41.03 N	74.01 W
Pearns Point >	240c	17.05 N	61.54 W
Pearsall	196	28.53 N	99.05 W
Pearse Island I	182	54.51 N	130.21 W
Pearsoll Peak ʌ	202	42.18 N	123.50 W
Pearson	192	31.17 N	82.51 W
Pearson Lake ⊜	184	56.15 N	97.15 W
Pearston	158	32.35 S	25.08 E
Peary Land ◆[1]	16	83.00 N	35.00 W
Pease ≃	196	34.12 N	99.07 W
Pease Air Force Base ■	188	43.06 N	70.49 W
Peasedown Saint John	42	51.19 N	2.27 W
Peaster	222	32.52 N	97.52 W
Peat Inn	46	56.17 N	2.53 W
Pebane	154	17.10 S	38.08 E
Pebas	246	3.20 S	71.49 W
Pebble Beach	226	36.34 N	121.57 W
Pebble Island I	254	51.18 S	59.35 W
Peć	38	42.40 N	20.19 E
Pecan Bayou ≃	196	31.28 N	98.43 W
Pecangakan	115a	6.41 S	110.42 E
Pecan Gap	196	33.26 N	95.51 W
Peçanha	255	18.33 S	42.34 W
Peças, Ilha das I	252	25.26 S	48.19 W
Pecatonica	190	42.18 N	89.21 W
Pecatonica ≃	190	42.27 N	89.05 W
Pecatu	115b	8.50 S	115.07 E
Peccioli	66	43.33 N	10.43 E
Pécel	264c	47.29 N	19.21 E
Peçenek	130	40.25 N	32.19 E
Pečenga	24	69.33 N	31.07 E
Pečerniki	82	54.39 N	39.14 E
Pečernikovskije Vyselki	82	54.10 N	39.10 E
Pechanga Indian Reservation ◆[4]	228	33.27 N	117.04 W
Peche Island I	281	42.21 N	82.56 W
Pechenihy	78	49.52 N	36.55 E
Pechenizhyn	78	48.32 N	24.54 E
Pecheniz'ke vodoskhovyshche ⊜[1]	78	50.05 N	36.47 E
Pechera	78	48.52 N	28.42 E
Pechincha ◆[8]	287a	22.56 S	43.21 W
Pechora → Pečora ≃	24	68.13 N	54.15 E
Pechorka ≃	265b	55.35 N	38.03 E
Pechra-Jakovlevskaja	265b	55.48 N	37.58 E
Pechra-Pokrovskoje	265b	55.50 N	37.57 E
Pechu	84	43.24 N	40.49 E
Peči	80	54.48 N	44.19 E
Pecica	38	46.10 N	21.05 E
Pečicy	82	55.36 N	38.27 E
Pecixe, Ilha de I	150	11.50 N	16.05 W
Peck	190	43.15 N	82.49 W
Peck Bay c	208	39.16 N	74.37 W
Peck-Berge ⋏[2]	264a	52.36 N	13.34 E
Peckeloh	52	52.01 N	8.07 E
Peckelsheim	52	51.36 N	9.07 E
Pecket Well	262	53.46 N	2.00 W
Peck Lake ⊜	210	43.07 N	74.25 W
Peckman ≃	276	40.53 N	74.13 W
Peconic ≃	207	40.55 N	72.37 W
Pečora	24	65.10 N	57.11 E
Pečora ≃	24	68.13 N	54.15 E
Pecora, Capo >	71	39.27 N	8.23 E
Pecoraro, Monte ʌ	68	38.32 N	16.20 E
Pečoro-Ilyčskij zapovednik ◆[4]	24	62.20 N	59.00 E
Pečorskaja guba c	24	68.40 N	54.45 E
Pečorskoje more ⊤[2]	24	70.00 N	54.00 E
Pečory	76	57.49 N	27.36 E
Pecos, N.M., U.S.	200	35.34 N	105.40 W
Pecos, Tx., U.S.	196	31.25 N	103.29 W
Pecos ≃	178	29.42 N	101.22 W
Pecos National Monument ♠	200	35.26 N	105.56 W
Pecos Plains ≚	196	33.20 N	104.30 W
Pecq	50	50.41 N	3.20 E
Pecquencourt	50	50.23 N	3.13 E
Pecqueuse	261	48.39 N	2.03 E
Pécs	30	46.05 N	18.13 E
Pedana	122	16.16 N	81.10 E
Pedara	70	37.38 N	15.04 E
Pedas	114	2.37 N	102.04 E
Pedasí	246	7.32 N	80.02 W
Pedaso	66	43.06 N	13.50 E
Peddāpuram	122	17.05 N	82.08 E
Pedder, Lake ⊜[1]	166	42.54 S	146.12 E
Peddie	158	33.12 S	27.07 E
Peddocks Island I	283	42.17 N	70.56 W
Pededze ≃	76	56.56 N	26.54 E
Pedernales, Arg.	252	35.15 S	59.39 W
Pedernales, Méx.	234	19.08 N	101.28 W
Pedernales, Rep. Dom.	238	18.02 N	71.45 W
Pedernales, Ven.	246	9.58 N	62.16 W
Pedernales ≃	196	30.26 N	98.04 W
Pedernales, Salar de ≚	252	26.15 S	69.10 W
Pedernales Falls State Park ♠	196	30.20 N	98.14 W
Pederobba	64	45.53 N	11.58 E
Pedersborg	41	55.27 N	11.34 E
Pederstrup	41	54.54 N	11.16 E
Pedesina	58	46.05 N	9.33 E
Pedhoulás	130	34.58 N	32.50 E
Pedja ≃	76	58.25 N	26.11 E
Pedley	228	33.59 N	117.28 W
Pé do Morro	256	22.20 S	44.57 W
Pedra	250	8.30 S	36.57 W
Pedra Azul	255	16.01 S	41.16 W
Pedra Bela	256	22.47 S	46.27 W
Pedra Branca	250	5.27 S	39.43 W
Pedra de Guaratiba ◆[8]	256	23.00 S	43.39 W
Pedra Grande, Recifes da ✢[2]	255	17.45 S	38.58 W
Pedra Lume	150a	16.46 N	22.54 W
Pedralva	256	22.14 S	45.28 W
Pedras	250	2.48 S	57.16 W
Pedras, Rio das ≃	287a	22.51 S	43.01 W
Pedras de Fogo	250	7.23 S	35.07 W
Pedra Selada	256	22.21 S	44.26 W
Pedras Negras	248	12.51 S	62.54 W
Pedras Salgadas	34	41.32 N	7.36 W
Pedraza	246	10.11 N	74.55 W
Pedregal, Pan.	236	8.22 N	82.26 W
Pedregal, Ven.	246	11.01 N	70.08 W
Pedregulho	255	20.16 S	47.29 W
Pedreira	256	22.43 S	46.55 W
Pedreira ≃	250	0.12 N	50.47 W
Pedreiras	250	4.34 S	44.39 W
Pedriceña	232	25.06 N	103.47 W
Pedricktown	208	39.46 N	75.24 W
Pedrinhas	250	11.12 S	37.41 W
Pedro, Point >	122	9.50 N	80.14 E
Pedro Afonso	250	8.59 S	48.11 W
Pedro Antonio de los Santos	234	21.36 N	98.58 W
Pedro Avelino	250	5.31 S	36.23 W
Pedro Bay	180	59.47 N	154.07 W
Pedro Betancourt	240p	22.44 N	81.17 W
Pedro Cays II	238	17.00 N	77.50 W
Pedro de Olla, Cerro ʌ	234	17.07 N	97.40 W
Pedro do Rio	256	22.20 S	43.09 W
Pedrógão Grande	34	39.55 N	8.09 W
Pedro Gomes	255	18.04 S	54.32 W
Pedro II	250	4.25 S	41.28 W
Pedro II, Ilha I	246	1.10 N	66.40 W
Pedro Juan Caballero	252	22.34 S	55.37 W
Pedro Leopoldo	255	19.38 S	44.03 W
Pedro Luro	252	39.29 S	62.41 W
Pedro Muñoz	34	39.24 N	2.58 W
Pedro Osório	252	31.51 S	52.45 W
Pedro R. Fernández	252	28.45 S	58.39 W
Pedro Teixeira	256	21.43 S	43.44 W
Pedro Velho	250	6.26 S	35.14 W
Peebinga	166	34.56 S	140.55 E
Peebles, Scot., U.K.	46	55.39 N	3.12 W
Peebles, Oh., U.S.	218	38.56 N	83.24 W
Peedamullah	162	21.50 S	115.38 E
Pee Dee ≃	192	34.43 N	79.52 W
Peekaboo Mountain ʌ[2]	188	45.45 N	67.53 W
Peekskill	210	41.17 N	73.55 W
Peel, Austl.	170	33.19 S	149.38 E
Peel, I. of Man	44	54.13 N	4.40 W
Peel □[6]	212	43.45 N	79.47 W
Peel ≃	180	67.37 N	134.40 W
Peel Channel ≃[1]	180	68.13 N	135.00 W
Peel Fell ʌ	44	55.17 N	2.35 W
Peel Inlet c	168a	32.35 S	115.44 E
Peel Island I	171a	27.30 S	153.22 E
Pe Ell	224	46.34 N	123.17 W
Peel Point >	176	73.22 N	114.35 W
Peel Sound ʯ	176	73.15 N	96.30 W
Peene ≃	54	54.09 N	13.46 E
Peenemünde	54	54.08 N	13.46 E
Peepeekisis Indian Reserve ◆[4]	184	50.52 N	103.24 W
Peer	56	51.08 N	5.28 E
Peerless	202	48.46 N	105.49 W
Peers	182	53.40 N	116.00 W
Peesane	184	52.52 N	103.36 W
Peetz	198	40.57 N	103.06 W
Peetzsee ⊜	264a	52.26 N	13.50 E
Pefferlaw	212	44.19 N	79.12 W
Pefferlaw Brook ≃	212	44.15 N	79.13 W
Pegasus, Port c	172	47.12 S	167.41 E
Pegasus Bay c	172	43.20 S	173.00 E
Pegau	54	51.10 N	12.14 E
Pegli	62	44.26 N	8.48 E
Peglia, Monte ʌ	66	42.49 N	12.13 E
Pegnitz	60	49.45 N	11.33 E
Pegnitz ≃	60	49.29 N	11.00 E
Pego	34	38.51 N	0.07 W
Pegolotte	64	45.12 N	12.02 E
Pegswood	44	55.11 N	1.38 W
Pegtymel' ≃	180	69.25 N	174.35 E
Pegtymel'skij chrebet ⋏	180	68.30 N	177.00 E
Pegu → Bago	110	17.20 N	96.29 E
Pegu ≃	110	16.47 N	96.13 E
Pegueros	234	20.57 N	102.40 W
Peguis Indian Reserve ◆[4]	184	51.20 N	97.35 W
Pegu Yoma ⋏	110	19.00 N	95.50 E
Pegwell Bay c	42	51.18 N	1.26 E
Pegyš	24	63.26 N	50.30 E
Pehčevo	38	41.46 N	22.54 E
Pehladpur ◆[8]	272a	28.35 N	77.06 E
Pehlivanköy	130	41.21 N	26.55 E
Pehowa	124	29.59 N	76.35 E
Pehuajó	252	35.48 S	61.53 W
Pehula	26	61.17 N	22.42 E
Peian → Bei'an	89	48.16 N	126.36 E
Peiching → Beijing	105	39.55 N	116.25 E
Peigan Indian Reserve ◆[4]	182	49.35 N	113.40 W
Peihai → Beihai	102	21.29 N	109.05 E
Peij	52	51.06 N	5.53 E
Peijiatun	98	39.19 N	121.41 E
Peikang	100	23.34 N	120.18 E
Peikang ≃	100	23.31 N	120.08 E
Peikant'ang Tao I	100	26.13 N	119.59 E
Peilstein im Mühlviertel	60	48.37 N	13.53 E
Peinan	100	22.47 N	121.07 E
Peinan ≃	100	22.46 N	121.10 E
Peine	52	52.19 N	10.13 E
Peine, Pointe à >	240d	15.23 N	61.15 W
Peinnechaung I	110	19.59 N	93.04 E
Peio	64	46.22 N	10.40 E
Peip'ing → Beijing	105	39.55 N	116.25 E
Peipsi järv (Čudskoje ozero) ⊜	76	58.45 N	27.25 E
Peipus, Lake → Čudskoje ozero ⊜	76	58.45 N	27.25 E
Peïra-Cava	62	43.56 N	7.22 E
Peirce, Cape >	180	58.35 N	161.47 W
Peisey-Nancroix	62	45.33 N	6.45 E
Peissenberg	64	47.48 N	11.04 E
Peissenberg ʌ, Dtsch.	60	47.48 N	11.01 E
Peissenberg ʌ, Dtsch.	64	47.48 N	11.01 E
Peiting	58	47.47 N	10.55 E
Peit'ou ◆[8]	269d	25.08 N	121.30 E
Peitz	54	51.51 N	14.24 E
Peixe	255	12.03 S	48.32 W
Peixe, Rio do ≃, Bra.	255	21.31 S	51.58 W
Peixe, Rio do ≃, Bra.	255	14.06 S	50.51 W
Peixe, Rio do ≃, Bra.	256	23.24 S	45.28 W
Peixe, Rio do ≃, Bra.	256	21.55 S	43.21 W
Peixe, Rio do ≃, Bra.	256	22.23 S	46.51 W
Peixe, Rio do ≃, Bra.	256	23.12 S	46.06 W
Peixe, Rio do ≃, Bra.	256	21.38 S	45.11 W
Peixe-Boi	250	1.12 S	47.18 W
Peixes, Rio dos ≃	250	10.42 S	57.56 W
Peixian (Yunhe), Zhg.	98	34.21 N	117.59 E
Peixian, Zhg.	98	34.44 N	116.59 E
Peixoto, Reprêsa de ⊜[1]	255	20.10 S	47.20 W
Peixoto de Azevedo ≃	250	10.06 S	55.31 W
Peiziyan	98	35.07 N	115.01 E
Pejantan, Pulau I	112	0.07 N	107.14 E
Pejelagartero	234	18.04 N	93.45 W
Pek ≃	38	44.46 N	21.33 E
Pekalongan	115a	6.53 S	109.40 E
Pekan	114	3.30 N	103.25 E
Pekanbaru	112	0.32 N	101.27 E
Pekanheran	112	0.21 S	102.26 E
Pekin, Il., U.S.	190	40.34 N	89.38 W
Pekin, In., U.S.	218	38.29 N	86.01 W
Pekin, N.Y., U.S.	284a	43.10 N	78.53 W
Pekin, Oh., U.S.	214	40.43 N	81.07 W
Pékin → Beijing, Zhg.	105	39.55 N	116.25 E
Peking → Beijing	105	39.55 N	116.25 E
Peking National Library ʋ	271a	39.56 N	116.22 E
Peking Railway Station ◆[5]	271a	39.54 N	116.26 E
Peking University ʋ[2]	271a	39.59 N	116.18 E
Peking Zoo ♠	271a	39.56 N	116.19 E
Peklino	76	53.33 N	33.32 E
Pekša ≃	80	55.53 N	39.40 E
Pektubajevo	80	57.02 N	48.23 E
Pekul'nej, chrebet ⋏	180	66.00 N	175.00 E
Pekul'nejskoje, ozero ⊜	180	62.40 N	177.00 E
Péla	150	7.37 N	9.07 W
Pelabuhandagang	112	1.08 S	103.05 E
Pelabuhan Kelang	114	3.00 N	101.24 E
Pelabuhanratu	115a	6.59 S	106.33 E
Pelabuhanratu, Teluk c	115a	7.03 S	106.27 E
Pel'a-Chovanskaja	80	54.36 N	44.56 E
Pelado, Volcán ʌ[1]	286a	19.09 N	99.13 W
Pelagie, Isole II	70a	35.40 N	12.40 E
Pelago	66	43.46 N	11.30 E
Pelahatchie	194	32.18 N	89.47 W
Pelahiyivka	83	48.06 N	38.36 E
Pelaihari	112	3.48 S	114.45 E
Pelalawan	112	0.27 N	102.05 E
Pelat, Mont ʌ	62	44.16 N	6.42 E
Pelawan	114	2.47 N	102.55 E
Pełczyce	30	53.03 N	15.18 E
Pélé, Mont ʌ	152	3.15 S	11.14 E
Pelechuco	248	14.48 S	69.04 W
Peleduj	74	59.36 N	112.45 E
Pelée, Montagne ʌ	240e	14.48 N	61.10 W
Pelee, Point >	214	41.54 N	82.30 W
Pelee Island I	214	41.46 N	82.39 W
Pelee Passage ʯ	214	41.52 N	82.37 W
Pelega, Vârful ʌ	38	45.22 N	22.54 E
Pelekech ʌ	154	3.48 N	35.04 E
Peleliu → Beliliou I	175b	7.01 N	134.15 E
Peleng, Pulau I	112	1.20 S	123.10 E
Peleng, Selat ʯ	112	1.10 S	122.45 E
Pelf, Monte ʌ	64	46.14 N	12.12 E
Pelham, On., Can.	212	43.02 N	79.17 W
Pelham, Al., U.S.	194	33.17 N	86.48 W
Pelham, Ga., U.S.	192	31.07 N	84.09 W
Pelham, Ma., U.S.	207	42.23 N	72.24 W
Pelham, N.H., U.S.	207	42.44 N	71.19 W
Pelham, N.Y., U.S.	276	40.54 N	73.48 W
Pelham Bay c	276	40.52 N	73.47 W
Pelham Bay Park ♠	276	40.52 N	73.49 W
Pelham Manor	276	40.53 N	73.48 W
Pelhřimov	30	49.26 N	15.13 E
Pelican	180	57.57 N	136.14 W
Pelican ≃	198	46.17 N	96.08 W
Pelican, Punta >	200	31.19 N	113.43 W
Pelican Bay c	184	52.45 N	100.20 W
Pelican Island I, Mo., U.S.	219	38.52 N	90.18 W
Pelican Island I, Tx., U.S.	222	29.20 N	94.48 W
Pelican Lagoon c	168b	35.50 S	137.47 E
Pelican Lake	190	45.30 N	89.10 W
Pelican Lake ⊜, Ab., Can.	182	55.47 N	113.15 W
Pelican Lake ⊜, Mb., Can.	184	49.20 N	99.35 W
Pelican Lake ⊜, Mb., Can.	184	53.50 N	96.08 W
Pelican Lake ⊜, Mb., Can.	184	52.30 N	100.20 W
Pelican Lake ⊜, Sk., Can.	184	55.08 N	103.00 W
Pelican Lake ⊜, Sk., Can.	184	50.32 N	106.00 W
Pelican Lake ⊜, Mn., U.S.	190	48.05 N	92.54 W
Pelican Lake ⊜, S.D., U.S.	198	44.52 N	97.11 W
Pelican Mountain ʌ	182	55.35 N	113.40 W
Pelican Narrows	184	55.10 N	102.56 W
Pelican Point >	168b	34.48 S	138.29 E
Pelican Rapids, Mb., Can.	184	52.45 N	100.42 W
Pelican Rapids, Mn., U.S.	198	46.34 N	96.04 W
Pelileo	246	1.19 S	78.32 W
Pelinia	38	47.53 N	27.50 E
Pelister ʌ	38	41.00 N	21.12 E
Pelješac, Poluotok >[1]	36	42.58 N	17.20 E
Pelkosenniemi	24	67.07 N	27.30 E
Pelkum, Dtsch.	52	51.39 N	7.46 E
Pelkum, Dtsch.	263	51.40 N	7.24 E
Pella, S. Afr.	158	29.01 S	19.06 E
Pella, Ia., U.S.	190	41.24 N	92.54 W
Pélla ⊥	38	40.45 N	22.33 E
Pellaro	68	38.01 N	15.39 E
Pell City	194	33.35 N	86.17 W
Pellechia, Monte ʌ	66	42.07 N	12.52 E
Pellegrini	252	36.16 S	63.09 W
Pellegrini, Lago ⊜	252	38.40 S	68.00 W
Pellegrino, Cozzo ʌ	68	39.45 N	16.03 E
Pellegrino, Monte ʌ	70	38.10 N	13.21 E
Pellegrino Parmense	64	44.44 N	9.55 E
Pellendorf	264b	48.06 N	16.27 E
Peller, Monte ʌ	64	46.18 N	10.57 E
Pellestrina, Litorale di ⊥[2]	64	45.16 N	12.18 E
Pelletier Lake ⊜	184	56.30 N	97.00 W
Pellice ≃	62	44.50 N	7.38 E
Pellingen	56	49.40 N	6.40 E
Pell Lake	216	42.32 N	88.21 W
Pello	24	66.47 N	24.00 E
Pellston	190	45.33 N	84.47 W
Pellworm I	30	54.31 N	8.38 E
Pelly	184	51.52 N	101.55 W
Pelly ≃	180	62.47 N	137.19 W
Pelly Bay c	176	68.53 N	89.51 W
Pelly Crossing	180	62.50 N	136.35 W
Pelly Lake ⊜	176	65.59 N	101.12 W
Pelly Mountains ⋏	180	62.00 N	133.00 W
Pelón, Cerro ʌ	234	20.05 N	99.55 W
Peloncillo Mountains ⋏	200	32.15 N	109.00 W
Pelopónnisos □[4]	38	37.30 N	22.30 E
Pelopónnisos (Peloponnesus) >[1]	38	37.30 N	22.00 E
Peloritani, Monti ⋏	70	38.03 N	15.20 E
Pelotas	252	31.46 S	52.20 W
Pelotas ≃	252	27.28 S	51.55 W
Pelplin	30	53.56 N	18.42 E
Pelque ≃	254	51.03 S	70.58 W
Pelsin	54	53.48 N	13.40 E
Pelusium Bay → Ţīnah, Khalīj aț- c	140	31.08 N	32.40 E
Pel'ušn'a	76	58.56 N	32.52 E
Pélussin	62	45.25 N	4.41 E
Pelvo d'Elva ʌ	62	44.33 N	7.02 E
Pelym	86	59.38 N	63.05 E
Pemadumcook Lake ⊜	188	45.40 N	68.55 W
Pemalang	115a	6.54 S	109.22 E
Pemalang, Ujung >	115a	6.47 S	109.29 E
Pemali ≃	115a	6.47 S	109.01 E
Pemangkat	112	1.10 N	108.58 E
Pematang	112	0.12 S	102.04 E
Pematangsiantar	114	2.57 N	99.03 E
Pematangtanahjawa	114	2.53 N	99.12 E
Pemba, Moç.	154	12.58 S	40.30 E
Pemba, Zam.	154	16.31 S	27.22 E
Pemba I	154	5.10 S	39.48 E
Pemba Channel ʯ	154	5.10 S	39.20 E
Pembarisan, Pegunungan ⋏	115a	7.13 S	108.45 E
Pemberton, Austl.	162	34.28 S	116.01 E
Pemberton, B.C., Can.	182	50.20 N	122.48 W
Pemberton, Eng., U.K.	262	53.32 N	2.41 W
Pemberton, N.J., U.S.	208	39.58 N	74.41 W
Pemberton, Oh., U.S.	216	40.18 N	84.02 W
Pemberton Airport ⊠	285	39.59 N	74.41 W
Pemberton Heights	285	39.58 N	74.41 W
Pemberville	214	41.24 N	83.27 W
Pembina	198	48.57 N	97.14 W
Pembina ≃, Ab., Can.	182	54.45 N	114.15 W
Pembina ≃, N.A.	184	48.57 N	97.14 W
Pembina Hills ⋏[2]	198	49.10 N	98.25 W
Pembine	190	45.38 N	87.59 W
Pembrey	42	51.42 N	4.16 W
Pembroke, On., Can.	190	45.49 N	77.07 W
Pembroke, Wales, U.K.	42	51.41 N	4.55 W
Pembroke, Ga., U.S.	192	32.08 N	81.37 W
Pembroke, Ky., U.S.	194	36.46 N	87.21 W
Pembroke, Me., U.S.	188	44.57 N	67.09 W
Pembroke, N.Y., U.S.	210	43.00 N	78.27 W
Pembroke, N.C., U.S.	192	34.40 N	79.11 W
Pembroke, Va., U.S.	192	37.19 N	80.38 W
Pembroke, Cape >	176	62.56 N	81.55 W
Pembroke Castle ⊥	42	51.41 N	4.56 W
Pembroke Dock	42	51.42 N	4.56 W
Pembroke Pines	220	26.00 N	80.13 W
Pembrokeshire Coast National Park ♠	42	51.47 N	5.06 W
Pembuang	112	2.34 S	112.19 E
Pembuang ≃	112	3.24 S	112.33 E
Pembury	42	51.09 N	0.20 E
Pemfling	60	49.16 N	12.37 E
Pemichigamau Lake ⊜	184	56.16 N	99.33 W
Pemigewasset ≃	188	43.26 N	71.40 W
Pemmican Portage	184	53.56 N	102.17 W
Pemuco	252	36.58 S	72.06 W
Pemynoos Indian Reserve ◆[4]	182	50.29 N	121.15 W
Pemzašen	84	40.35 N	43.57 E
Pena, Parque de ♠	266c	38.47 N	9.23 W
Peña Barroza	248	22.10 S	67.25 W
Peña Blanca	236	8.27 N	81.40 W
Peñafiel, Esp.	34	41.36 N	4.07 W
Penafiel, Port.	34	41.12 N	8.17 W
Pen'agino	265b	55.50 N	37.21 E
Peña Gorda, Cerro ʌ	234	20.44 N	104.50 W
Peña Grande ◆[8]	266a	40.29 N	3.44 W
Pen'akša	80	56.22 N	44.56 E
Peñalara ʌ	34	40.51 N	3.57 W
Peñalolén	286e	33.29 S	70.32 W
Pena-Lunanga	154	4.16 S	28.10 E
Penalva	250	3.18 S	45.10 W
Penambulai, Pulau I	164	6.24 S	134.48 E
Penang → George Town	114	5.25 N	100.20 E
Penanjung, Teluk c	115a	7.45 S	108.37 E
Penápolis	255	21.24 S	50.04 W
Peñaranda de Bracamonte	34	40.54 N	5.12 W
Pen Argyl	210	40.52 N	75.15 W
Penaron	114	4.38 N	97.40 E
Peñarroya-Pueblonuevo	34	38.18 N	5.16 W
Penarth	42	51.27 N	3.11 W
Peñas, Cabo de >	34	43.39 N	5.51 W
Penas, Golfo de c	254	47.22 S	74.50 W
Penasco	200	36.10 N	105.41 W
Peñasco, Rio ≃	196	32.45 N	104.19 W
Penataquit Creek ≃	276	40.43 N	73.14 W
Penbrook	208	40.16 N	76.50 W
Pencader	42	52.01 N	4.16 W
Pencahue	252	35.24 S	71.49 W
Pence	190	46.25 N	90.16 W
Pen Centre ◆[9]	284a	43.08 N	79.14 W
Penchard	261	48.59 N	2.52 E
Penck Trough V	9	73.00 S	2.45 W
Penco	252	36.44 S	72.59 W
Pencoed	42	51.32 N	3.30 W
Pendang, Indon.	112	1.28 S	114.51 E
Pendang, Malay.	114	6.00 N	100.28 E
Pendé ≃	146	7.55 N	16.36 E
Pendéli	267c	38.03 N	23.52 E
Pendelikón Óros ⋏	267c	38.06 N	23.54 E
Pendembu, S.L.	150	8.06 N	10.42 W
Pendembu, S.L.	150	9.06 N	12.12 W
Pendências	250	5.15 S	36.43 W
Pendeng	114	4.06 N	97.36 E
Pender	198	42.06 N	96.42 W
Pender Bay c	162	16.45 S	122.42 E
Pendhar	272c	19.04 N	73.06 E
Pendjari ≃	150	10.54 N	0.51 E
Pendjari, Parc National de la ♠	150	11.20 N	1.15 E
Pendlebury	262	53.31 N	2.20 W
Pendle Hill	274a	33.48 S	150.57 E
Pendle Hill ʌ[2]	44	53.52 N	2.17 W
Pendleton, In., U.S.	218	39.59 N	85.44 W
Pendleton, N.Y., U.S.	284a	43.05 N	78.44 W
Pendleton, Or., U.S.	202	45.40 N	118.47 W
Pendleton, S.C., U.S.	192	34.39 N	82.47 W
Pendleton □[6]	218	38.42 N	84.22 W
Pendolo	112	2.05 S	120.42 E
Pendopo	112	3.17 S	103.52 E
Pend Oreille ≃	202	49.04 N	117.37 W
Pend Oreille, Lake ⊜	202	48.10 N	116.11 W
Pend Oreille, Mount ʌ	202	48.25 N	116.10 W
Pendotiba ≃	287a	22.53 S	43.02 W
Pendžikent	85	39.29 N	67.35 E
Penebel	115b	8.25 S	115.09 E
Penedo	250	10.17 S	36.36 W
Penedono	34	40.59 N	7.24 W
Penela	34	40.02 N	8.23 W
Penelope	222	31.52 N	96.56 W
Penetang Harbour c	212	44.47 N	79.57 W
Penetanguishene	212	44.47 N	79.55 W
Penfield, Il., U.S.	216	40.18 N	87.57 W
Penfield, N.Y., U.S.	210	43.07 N	77.28 W
Penfield, Oh., U.S.	214	41.10 N	82.08 W
Penfield, Pa., U.S.	214	41.13 N	78.34 W
Penganga ≃	122	19.53 N	79.09 E
Pengastulan	115b	8.11 S	114.55 E
Peng Chau I	271d	22.17 N	114.02 E
P'engchia Yü I	100	25.38 N	122.04 E
Penge, S. Afr.	156	24.22 S	30.13 E
Penge, R.D.C.	154	5.31 S	24.37 E
Penge ◆[8]	260	51.25 N	0.04 W
Penggong	106	30.27 N	119.57 E
Penggongmiao	100	26.07 N	113.34 E
Penghu	100	25.24 N	118.11 E
P'enghu Ch'üntao (Pescadores) II	100	23.30 N	119.30 E
P'enghu Shuitao ʯ	100	23.30 N	119.50 E
Pengiki, Pulau I	112	0.15 N	108.03 E
Pengjiachang	107	30.36 N	103.53 E
Pengjialouzi	104	41.56 N	123.40 E
Pengjiawan	100	32.16 N	114.04 E
Pengjiawu	105	39.41 N	117.10 E
Pengkalan Baharu	114	4.28 N	100.38 E
Pengkou	100	25.32 N	116.42 E
Penglai (Dengzhou)	98	37.48 N	120.42 E
Penglaizhen	107	30.36 N	105.14 E
Penglang	106	31.23 N	121.05 E
Pengnan	107	30.25 N	105.53 E
Pengpu → Bengbu	100	32.58 N	117.24 E
Pengshan	107	30.13 N	103.52 E
Pengshi	100	30.28 N	113.10 E
Pengshui	102	29.18 N	108.09 E
Penguin	166	41.07 S	146.04 E
Pengwaluote Shan ʌ	120	33.30 N	86.35 E
Pengxi	102	30.49 N	105.40 E
Pengxian	102	31.00 N	103.50 E
Pengze	100	29.53 N	116.33 E
Pengzhai	100	24.23 N	115.06 E
Pengzhuangzi	105	40.06 N	114.51 E
Penha	252	26.46 S	48.39 W
Penha ◆[8]	287a	22.49 S	43.17 W
Penha de França ◆[8]	287b	23.32 S	46.32 W
Penha Longa, Bra.	256	22.04 S	43.05 W
Penhalonga, Zimb.	154	18.54 S	32.40 E
Penhold	182	52.08 N	113.52 W
Penhold, Canadian Forces Base ■	182	52.12 N	113.53 W
Penhorn Creek ≃	276	40.45 N	74.05 W
Penhsi → Benxi	104	41.18 N	123.45 E
Penibética, Cordillera ⋏	34	37.00 N	4.00 W
Peniche	34	39.21 N	9.23 W
Penicuik	46	55.50 N	3.14 W
Penida, Nusa I	115b	8.44 S	115.32 E
Penig	54	50.56 N	12.41 E
Peningo Neck >[1]	276	40.57 N	73.41 W
Peninjai	112	1.26 S	101.50 E
Peninsula Lake ⊜	212	45.20 N	79.05 W
Peninsula State Park ♠	190	45.09 N	87.14 W
Peníscola	34	40.21 N	0.25 E
Penistone	44	53.32 N	1.37 W
Penitas	196	26.17 N	98.27 W
Penitencia Creek ≃	282	37.27 N	121.55 W
Penitente, Serra do ⋏[2]	250	8.45 S	46.20 W
Penjamillo [de Degollado]	234	20.06 N	101.54 W
Pénjamo	234	20.26 N	101.44 W
Penketh	262	53.23 N	2.40 W
Penki → Benxi	104	41.18 N	123.45 E
Penkino	82	54.50 N	38.53 E
Penkridge	42	52.44 N	2.07 W
Penkun	54	53.17 N	14.14 E
Pen Lake ⊜	212	45.28 N	78.23 W
Penllyn	285	40.10 N	75.15 W
Penmaenmawr	44	53.16 N	3.54 W
Penmarc'h, Pointe de >	32	47.48 N	4.22 W
Penn	279b	40.20 N	79.38 W
Penna, Punta della >	66	42.10 N	14.43 E
Pennabilli	66	43.49 N	12.16 E
Penn Acres	285	39.40 N	75.34 W
Pennant Hills	274a	33.44 S	151.04 E
Pennant Hills Park ♠	274a	33.45 S	151.06 E
Pennant Point >	186	44.26 N	63.39 W
Pennant Station	184	50.33 N	108.12 W
Pennask Lake ⊜	182	50.00 N	120.05 W
Pennask Mountain ʌ	182	49.53 N	120.07 W
Penn Brook ≃	283	42.44 N	70.59 W
Penn Cove c	224	48.14 N	122.41 W
Penn Cove Park	224	48.14 N	122.41 W
Penndel	285	40.09 N	74.55 W
Penne	66	42.27 N	13.55 E
Penne, Punta >	68	40.41 N	17.56 E
Penne-d'Agenais	32	44.23 N	0.49 E
Pennedepie	50	49.25 N	0.11 E
Pennel Creek ≃	198	46.34 N	104.52 W
Penneru ≃	122	14.35 N	80.10 E
Pennes (Pens)	64	46.47 N	11.25 E
Pennes, Val di V	64	46.47 N	11.25 E
Penneshaw	168b	35.44 S	137.56 E
Penngrove	226	38.18 N	122.40 W
Penn Hills	214	40.28 N	79.51 W
Penn Hills Center ◆[9]	279b	40.28 N	79.50 W
Pennines ⋏	44	54.10 N	2.05 W
Pennines, Alpes ⋏	58	46.05 N	7.50 E
Penningby	40	59.41 N	18.40 E
Penningby slott ⊥	40	59.41 N	18.40 E
Pennington, N.J., U.S.	208	40.19 N	74.47 W
Pennington, Tx., U.S.	222	31.11 N	95.14 W
Pennington ≃[1]	150	4.45 N	5.35 E
Pennington Gap	192	36.45 N	83.01 W
Pennino, Monte ʌ	66	43.06 N	12.53 E
Penn Run	214	40.37 N	79.01 W
Pennsauken	208	39.58 N	75.04 W
Pennsauken Creek ≃	285	39.59 N	75.03 W
Pennsauken Creek, North Branch ≃	285	39.58 N	75.01 W
Pennsauken Creek, South Branch ≃	285	39.58 N	75.01 W
Pennsboro	188	39.17 N	80.58 W
Penns Brook ≃	276	40.43 N	74.32 W
Pennsburg	208	40.23 N	75.29 W
Pennsbury Heights	285	40.12 N	74.49 W
Pennsbury Manor ⊥	285	40.08 N	74.46 W
Penn's Cave ⊥[5]	210	40.53 N	77.36 W
Penns Creek	210	40.52 N	77.04 W
Penns Creek ≃	210	40.48 N	76.51 W
Pennsdale	210	41.15 N	76.48 W
Penns Grove	208	39.43 N	75.28 W
Pennside	208	40.20 N	75.53 W
Penns Neck	276	40.20 N	74.38 W
Pennsuco	220	25.53 N	80.22 W
Pennsville	208	39.39 N	75.31 W
Penns Woods	279b	40.21 N	79.46 W
Pennsylvania □[3], U.S.	178	40.45 N	77.30 W
Pennsylvania □[3], U.S.	188	40.45 N	77.30 W
Pennsylvania, University of ʋ[2]	285	39.57 N	75.12 W
Pennsylvania Canal ≊	285	40.13 N	74.47 W
Pennsylvania Station ◆[5]	276	40.45 N	74.00 W
Penn Valley, Ca., U.S.	226	39.12 N	121.11 W
Penn Valley, Pa., U.S.	285	40.01 N	75.16 W
Penn Valley Terrace	285	40.11 N	74.47 W
Pennville	216	40.29 N	85.08 W
Penn Wynne	285	39.59 N	75.16 W
Penny	182	53.50 N	121.17 W
Penn Yan	210	42.39 N	77.03 W
Pennycutaway ≃	184	56.43 N	92.44 W
Penny Hill	285	39.46 N	75.30 W
Penny Ice Cap ⊓	176	67.10 N	66.00 W
Pennypack Creek ≃	285	40.02 N	75.00 W
Pennypack Park ♠	285	40.04 N	75.03 W
Penny Strait ʯ	176	76.30 N	97.00 W
Peno	76	56.55 N	32.45 E
Penobscot	210	41.10 N	75.52 W
Penobscot ≃	188	44.30 N	68.50 W
Penobscot, East Branch ≃	186	45.35 N	68.32 W
Penobscot, West Branch ≃	188	45.35 N	68.32 W
Penobscot Bay c	188	44.15 N	68.52 W
Peno Creek ≃	219	39.32 N	91.16 W
Pen'ok	86	55.30 N	81.34 E
Penola	166	37.23 S	140.50 E
Peñoles	196	25.39 N	104.30 W
Peñón Blanco	232	24.47 N	104.02 W
Penong	162	31.55 S	133.01 E
Penonomé	236	8.31 N	80.22 W
Penrhyn I[1]	14	9.00 S	158.00 W
Penrhyn Bay	44	53.19 N	3.45 W
Penrhyndeudraeth	42	52.56 N	4.04 W
Penrith, Austl.	170	33.45 S	150.42 E
Penrith, Eng., U.K.	44	54.40 N	2.44 W
Penryn, Eng., U.K.	42	50.09 N	5.06 W
Penryn, Ca., U.S.	226	38.51 N	121.10 W
Penryn, Pa., U.S.	208	40.12 N	76.22 W
Pens → Pennes	64	46.47 N	11.25 E
Pensacola	194	30.25 N	87.13 W
Pensacola Bay c	194	30.25 N	87.06 W
Pensacola Mountains ⋏	9	83.45 S	55.00 W
Pensacola Naval Air Station ■	194	30.21 N	87.19 W
Pensacola Seamount ✢[3]	14	18.17 N	157.20 W
Pensaukee ≃	190	44.49 N	87.55 W
Pensby	262	53.21 N	3.06 W
Pense	184	50.25 N	105.00 W
Penshaw	44	54.53 N	1.29 W
Pensiangan	112	4.33 N	116.19 E
Pensilva	42	50.30 N	4.25 W
Pensilvania	246	5.31 N	75.05 W
Pentagna	256	22.09 S	43.45 W
Pentagon ʋ	284c	38.52 N	77.03 W
Pentagon Mountain ʌ	202	47.56 N	113.07 W
Pentecost □[8]	175f	15.45 S	168.12 E
Pentecoste	250	3.48 S	39.17 W
Pentecôte I	175f	15.42 S	168.10 E
Pentecôte ≃	186	49.47 N	67.10 W
Pentecôte, Lac ⊜	186	49.53 N	67.20 W
Penticton	182	49.30 N	119.35 W
Penticton Indian Reserve ◆[4]	182	49.30 N	119.40 W
Pentire Point >	42	50.36 N	4.55 W
Pentland	166	20.32 S	145.24 E
Pentland Firth ʯ	46	58.44 N	3.07 W
Pentland Hills ⋏[2]	46	55.48 N	3.23 W
Pentling	60	48.59 N	12.04 E
Pentraeth	44	53.17 N	4.12 W
Pentre Halkyn	262	53.15 N	3.12 W
Pentucket, Lake ⊜	283	42.47 N	71.05 W
Pentucket Pond ⊜	283	42.44 N	71.00 W
Pentwater	190	43.46 N	86.25 W
Penuba	112	0.20 S	104.28 E
Peñuelas	240m	18.03 N	66.43 W
Penuguan	112	2.27 S	104.31 E
Penukonda	122	14.05 N	77.35 E
Penunjok, Tanjong >	114	4.22 N	103.29 E
Pènwègon	110	18.13 N	96.34 E

Symbols in the index entries represent the broad categories identified in the key at the right. Symbols with superior numbers (⋏[1]) identify subcategories (see complete key on page *I · 1).*

Symbole im Register stellen die rechts im Schlüssel erklärten Kategorien dar. Symbole mit hochgestellten Ziffern (⋏[1]) bezeichnen Unterabteilungen einer Kategorie (vgl. vollständiger Schlüssel auf Seite *I · 1).*

Los símbolos incluídos en el texto del índice representan las grandes categorías identificadas con la clave a la derecha. Los símbolos con numeros en su parte superior (⋏[1]) identifican las subcategorías (véase la clave completa en la página *I · 1).*

Les symboles de l'index représentent les catégories indiquées dans la légende à droite. Les symboles suivis d'un indice (⋏[1]) représentent des sous-catégories (voir légende complète à la page *I · 1).*

Os símbolos incluídos no texto do índice representam as grandes categorias identificadas com a chave à direita. Os símbolos com números em sua parte superior (⋏[1]) identificam as subcategorias (veja-se a chave completa à página *I · 1).*

ʌ Mountain	Berg	Montaña	Montagne	Montanha
⋏ Mountains	Gebirge	Montañas	Montagnes	Montanhas
)(Pass	Paß	Paso	Col	Passo
V Valley, Canyon	Tal, Cañon	Valle, Cañón	Vallée, Canyon	Vale, Canhão
≚ Plain	Ebene	Llano	Plaine	Planície
> Cape	Kap	Cabo	Cap	Cabo
I Island	Insel	Isla	Île	Ilha
II Islands	Inseln	Islas	Îles	Ilhas
⊥ Other Topographic Features	Andere Topographische Objekte	Otros Elementos Topográficos	Autres données topographiques	Outros acidentes topográficos

ESPAÑOL

Nombre	Página	Lat.°′	Long.°′ W = Oeste
Penwell	196	31.44 N	102.35 W
Peny	78	51.04 N	35.54 E
Penyagolosa ∧	34	40.13 N	0.21 W
Penyal d'Ifac ♦	34	38.38 N	0.05 E
Penyengat	114	0.54 N	102.20 E
Pen-y-Ghent ∧	44	54.09 N	2.14 W
Penygroes, Wales, U.K.	42	51.49 N	4.02 W
Penygroes, Wales, U.K.	44	53.04 N	4.17 W
Penyu, Kepulauan II	164	5.22 S	127.46 E
Penyu, Teluk c	115a	7.45 S	109.15 E
Penza	80	53.13 N	45.00 E
Penzance	42	50.07 N	5.33 W
Penza Oblast' □[4]	80	53.00 N	45.00 E
Penzberg	64	47.45 N	11.23 E
Penžina ≃	74	62.28 N	165.18 E
Penzing ◆[8]	264b	48.12 N	16.18 E
Penzino	80	52.07 N	50.27 E
Penžinskaja guba c	74	61.00 N	162.00 E
Penžinskij chrebet ⋏	74	62.30 N	167.00 E
Penzlin	54	53.30 N	13.05 E
Péone	62	44.07 N	6.54 E
Peoples Creek ≃	202	48.24 N	108.19 W
Peoples Ditch ≊	226	36.15 N	119.41 W
Peoria, Az., U.S.	200	33.34 N	112.14 W
Peoria, Il., U.S.	190	40.41 N	89.35 W
Peoria, Oh., U.S.	216	40.19 N	83.27 W
Peoria Heights	190	40.44 N	89.34 W
Peotillos	234	22.30 N	100.37 W
Peotone	216	41.19 N	87.47 W
Peover Eye ≃	262	53.15 N	2.31 W
Peover Heath	262	53.15 N	2.19 W
Pepa	154	7.42 S	29.47 E
Pepacton Reservoir ⊜[1]	210	42.06 N	74.54 W
Pepaw ≃	184	52.40 N	102.23 W
Pepel	150	8.35 N	13.03 W
Peper	140	7.04 N	33.00 E
Pepin	190	44.26 N	92.08 W
Pepin, Lake ⊜	190	44.30 N	92.15 W
Pepinster	56	50.34 N	5.49 E
Pepperell	207	42.40 N	71.35 W
Pepper Park State Recreation Area ♦	220	27.30 N	80.18 W
Pepper Pike	279a	41.28 N	81.27 W
Peqi'in Hadasha	132	32.59 N	35.20 E
Peqin	38	41.03 N	19.45 E
Pequannock	210	40.57 N	74.17 W
Pequannock ≃	276	40.58 N	74.17 W
Pequanticut Brook ≃	283	42.01 N	71.08 W
Pequea Creek ≃	208	39.53 N	76.22 W
Pequeno ≃	287a	22.55 S	43.25 W
Pequeri	256	21.50 S	43.06 W
Pequest ≃	210	40.50 N	75.05 W
Pequez	208	39.53 N	76.22 W
Pequizeiro	250	8.32 S	48.58 W
Pequop Mountains ⋏	204	40.45 N	114.40 W
Pequot Lakes	190	46.36 N	94.18 W
Perabumulih	112	3.27 S	104.15 E
Perak □[3]	114	5.00 N	101.00 E
Perak ≃	114	3.58 N	100.53 E
Perak, Kuala c	114	4.00 N	100.47 E
Peralba, Monte ∧	64	46.37 N	12.43 E
Perales de Alfambra	34	40.38 N	1.00 W
Perales del Rio	266a	40.19 N	3.38 W
Peralillo	252	34.29 S	71.29 W
Peralta	200	34.50 N	106.41 W
Pérama	267c	37.58 N	23.34 E
Perambalur	122	11.14 N	78.53 E
Perämeri (Bottenviken) c	26	65.00 N	23.00 E
Peranāmbattu	122	12.56 N	78.43 E
Peraní, Ákra ›	267c	37.54 N	23.31 E
Perarolo di Cadore	64	46.24 N	12.21 E
Peräseinäjoki	26	62.34 N	23.04 E
Percé	186	48.31 N	64.13 W
Percée, Pointe ∧	58	45.57 N	6.33 E
Perch ≃	212	44.00 N	76.05 W
Perchas	240m	18.19 N	66.59 W
Perchau	61	47.06 N	14.27 E
Perchauer Sattel)(	61	47.07 N	14.27 E
Perche, Collines du ⋏[2]	50	48.25 N	0.40 E
Perche Creek ≃	194	38.49 N	92.24 W
Perch Lake ⊜	212	44.07 N	75.54 W
Perchtoldsdorf	61	48.07 N	16.17 E
Perchuškovo	265b	55.41 N	37.10 E
Percival Lakes ⊜	162	21.25 S	125.00 E
Percy Creek ≃	212	44.15 N	77.49 W
Percy Isles II	166	21.39 S	150.16 E
Percy Lake ⊜	212	45.13 N	78.22 W
Percy Reach ⊜	212	44.15 N	77.45 W
Perdagangan-tomuon	114	3.09 N	99.20 E
Perdasdefogu	71	39.41 N	9.26 E
Perdeberg	158	28.59 S	25.05 E
Perdekop	158	27.13 S	29.38 E
Perdices, Arroyo de las ≃	288	34.41 S	58.22 W
Perdida ≃	250	9.13 S	47.59 W
Perdido	194	31.00 N	87.37 W
Perdido ≃, Bra.	248	22.10 S	57.33 W
Perdido ≃, U.S.	194	30.29 N	87.26 W
Perdido, Arroyo ≃	254	42.55 S	67.00 W
Perdido, Arroyo del ≃	258	33.37 S	57.23 W
Perdido, Cuchilla del ⋏[2]	258	33.43 S	57.17 W
Perdido, Monte ∧	34	42.40 N	0.05 E
Perdido Bay c	194	30.21 N	87.27 W
Perdifumo	68	40.16 N	15.01 E
Perdix	208	40.22 N	76.57 W
Perdizes	255	19.21 S	47.17 W
Perdreauville	261	48.58 N	1.38 E
Perdu, Lac ⊜	186	50.44 N	70.14 W
Perdue	184	52.04 N	107.32 W
Perebrody	78	51.43 N	27.00 E
Perechyn	78	48.44 N	22.26 E
Peredel	76	55.12 N	35.41 E
Peredel'cy	82	55.36 N	37.21 E
Peredelkino	265b	55.39 N	37.21 E
Peredmistne	78	45.57 N	34.37 E
Peregino	76	57.27 N	31.21 E
Perehins'ke	78	48.49 N	24.12 E
Perehonivka	78	48.32 N	30.31 E
Pereira	246	4.49 N	75.43 W
Pereira Barreto	255	20.38 S	51.07 W
Pereiro	250	6.03 S	38.28 W
Perejaslavka	89	47.58 N	135.06 E
Perejaslavskaja	78	45.51 N	39.02 E
Perejež'na	24	59.43 N	48.12 E
Perekopivka	78	50.37 N	33.25 E
Perekopnoje	80	51.13 N	48.04 E
Perekopskaja	80	49.21 N	43.20 E
Père-Lachaise, Cimetière du ◆	261	48.51 N	2.25 E
Perelazovskij	80	49.09 N	42.33 E
Perelazy	76	53.02 N	31.28 E
Perelesinskij	78	51.44 N	40.07 E
Perel'ub	80	51.52 N	50.22 E
Pere Marquette ≃	190	43.57 N	86.27 W
Pere Marquette, Big South Branch ≃	190	43.56 N	86.10 W
Pere Marquette State Park ♦	219	39.00 N	90.30 W
Perem'otnoje	80	51.11 N	50.49 E
Peremyshlyany	78	49.41 N	24.33 E
Peremyšl'	82	54.16 N	36.10 E
Perené ≃	248	11.09 S	74.18 W
Perenjori	162	29.26 S	116.17 E
Pereputje	92a	46.17 N	141.54 E
Pererov	78	52.04 N	28.00 E
Pereščepnoje	80	50.32 N	45.06 E
Pereshchepyne	78	49.01 N	35.22 E
Pereslavl'-Zalesskij	82	56.44 N	38.51 E
Peresypkino Pervoje	80	52.55 N	42.55 E
Peretrusovo	82	56.51 N	36.53 E
Perevals'k	83	48.26 N	38.47 E
Perevoz, Ross.	80	55.36 N	44.32 E
Perevoz, Ross.	88	59.00 N	116.57 E

FRANÇAIS

Nom	Page	Lat.°′	Long.°′ W = Ouest
Perevoz, Ross.	265a	59.43 N	30.47 E
Pereyaslav-Khmel'nyts'kyy	78	50.06 N	31.30 E
Pereyra, Arroyo ≃	288	34.47 S	58.08 W
Pereyra, Punta ›	258	34.14 S	58.04 W
Pérez	252	33.00 S	60.46 W
Perfugas	71	40.50 N	8.53 E
Perg	61	48.15 N	14.37 E
Pergamino	252	33.53 S	60.35 W
Pergamum ⊥	130	39.10 N	27.13 E
Pergau ≃	114	5.23 N	102.02 E
Pergine Valdarno	66	43.28 N	11.41 E
Pergine Valsugana	64	46.04 N	11.14 E
Pergola	66	43.34 N	12.50 E
Pergusa, Lago di ⊜	70	37.31 N	14.18 E
Perham	198	46.35 N	95.34 W
Perho	26	63.13 N	24.25 E
Peri	64	45.39 N	10.54 E
Peri ≃	130	38.50 N	39.35 E
Peribán de Ramos	234	19.32 N	102.28 W
Péribonca ≃	176	48.45 N	72.05 W
Péribonca, Lac ⊜	186	50.04 N	71.15 W
Perico, Arg.	252	24.23 S	65.06 W
Perico, Cuba	240p	22.46 N	81.01 W
Pericos	232	25.03 N	107.42 W
Pericumã ≃	250	2.17 S	44.42 W
Peridot	200	33.18 N	110.27 W
Périers	32	49.11 N	1.25 W
Perigiraja	112	0.16 S	103.30 E
Périgord □[9]	32	45.20 N	1.00 E
Perigoso, Canal ⊔	250	0.05 N	49.40 W
Périgueux	32	45.11 N	0.43 E
Perijá, Serranía De ⋏	246	10.00 N	73.00 W
Perim → Barīm I	144	12.39 N	43.25 E
Peri-Mirim	250	2.38 S	44.54 W
Perinaldo	62	43.52 N	7.40 E
Peringat	114	6.02 N	102.17 E
Periprava	38	45.24 N	29.32 E
Perisher Valley ♦	171b	36.23 S	145.24 E
Peristérion	267c	38.01 N	23.42 E
Perito	68	40.18 N	15.09 E
Perito Moreno	254	46.36 S	70.56 W
Peritoró	250	4.20 S	44.18 W
Perivale ◆[8]	260	51.32 N	0.19 W
Periyakulam	122	10.07 N	77.33 E
Periyār ≃	122	10.11 N	76.13 E
Perkasie	208	40.22 N	75.17 W
Perkins	196	35.58 N	97.02 W
Perkinsfield	212	44.42 N	79.57 W
Perkins Observatory ⊕[3]	214	40.14 N	83.02 W
Perkinston	194	30.46 N	89.08 W
Perkinsville, In., U.S.	218	40.09 N	85.52 W
Perkinsville, N.Y., U.S.	210	42.32 N	77.38 W
Perkiomen Creek ≃	208	40.07 N	75.28 W
Perkiomen Creek, East Branch ≃	208	40.15 N	75.27 W
Perkiomen Junction	285	40.06 N	75.28 W
Perkiomen Valley Airport ⊠	285	40.12 N	75.25 W
Perl	56	49.28 N	6.23 E
Perlas, Archipiélago de las II	246	8.25 N	79.00 W
Perlas, Laguna de c	236	12.30 N	83.40 W
Perlas, Punta de ›	236	12.23 N	83.30 W
Perleberg	54	53.04 N	11.51 E
Perlesreut	60	48.47 N	13.27 E
Perlez	38	45.12 N	20.24 E
Perlis □[3]	114	6.30 N	100.15 E
Perl'ovka	78	51.51 N	38.51 E
Perm'	86	58.00 N	56.15 E
Permanente Creek ≃	282	37.25 N	122.05 W
Permas	24	59.20 N	45.34 E
Përmet	38	40.14 N	20.21 E
Permisi	80	54.06 N	45.48 E
Perm' Oblast' □[4]	86	58.00 N	58.00 E
Pernambuco → Recife	250	8.03 S	34.54 W
Pernambuco □[3]	250	8.00 S	37.00 W
Pernate	266b	45.27 N	8.41 E
Pernatty Lagoon ⊜	166	31.31 S	137.14 E
Pernay	50	47.27 N	0.30 E
Pernegg an der Mur	61	47.22 N	15.21 E
Pernes-les-Fontaines	62	44.00 N	5.03 E
Pernik	38	42.36 N	23.02 E
Pernink	54	50.20 N	12.45 E
Perniö	26	60.12 N	23.08 E
Pernitz	61	47.54 N	15.58 E
Pernovo	82	55.58 N	39.10 E
Pero	266b	45.31 N	9.05 E
Peroba, Ribeirão do ≃	287b	23.27 S	46.22 W
Pérols, Étang de c	62	43.33 N	3.56 E
Peron, Cape ›	168a	32.17 S	115.41 E
Péronne	50	49.56 N	2.56 E
Peron Peninsula ›[1]	162	25.55 S	113.30 E
Pero Pinheiro	266c	38.51 N	9.20 W
Perosa Argentina	62	44.58 N	7.10 E
Perote	234	19.34 N	97.14 W
Peroto	248	14.50 S	64.31 W
Pérou → Peru □[1]	242	10.00 S	76.00 W
Pérouges	58	45.54 N	5.11 E
Peroulaz	62	45.42 N	7.19 E
Perovo ◆[8]	265b	55.44 N	37.46 E
Perow	182	54.31 N	126.26 W
Perpendicular, Point ›	170	35.06 S	150.48 E
Perpignan	32	42.41 N	2.53 E
Perranporth	42	50.20 N	5.09 W
Perrault Falls	184	50.19 N	93.11 W
Perray ≃	261	48.31 N	1.42 E
Perrero	62	44.56 N	7.05 E
Perriers-sur-Andelle	50	49.25 N	1.22 E
Perrignier	58	46.18 N	6.27 E
Perrigny	58	46.40 N	5.35 E
Perrin	196	33.02 N	98.04 W
Perrine	220	25.36 N	80.21 W
Perrineville	208	40.13 N	74.26 W
Perris	228	33.46 N	117.13 W
Perris, Lake ⊜[1]	228	33.50 N	117.10 W
Perro, Laguna del ⊜	200	34.40 N	105.57 W
Perro, Punta del ›	34	36.45 N	6.25 W
Perros, Bahía de c	240p	22.25 N	78.30 W
Perros-Guirec	32	48.49 N	3.27 W
Perrot, Île I	206	45.22 N	73.57 W
Perry, Fl., U.S.	192	30.07 N	83.34 W
Perry, Ga., U.S.	192	32.27 N	83.43 W
Perry, Il., U.S.	219	39.47 N	90.45 W
Perry, Ia., U.S.	190	41.50 N	94.06 W
Perry, Ks., U.S.	198	39.04 N	95.23 W
Perry, Me., U.S.	186	44.58 N	67.04 W
Perry, Mi., U.S.	216	42.49 N	84.13 W
Perry, Mo., U.S.	219	39.25 N	91.40 W
Perry, N.Y., U.S.	210	42.42 N	78.00 W
Perry, Oh., U.S.	214	41.45 N	81.08 W
Perry, Ok., U.S.	196	36.17 N	97.17 W
Perry, Tx., U.S.	222	31.25 N	96.55 W
Perry, Ut,. U.S.	200	41.27 N	112.02 W
Perry □[6]	208	40.25 N	77.11 W
Perrydale	224	45.02 N	123.15 W
Perry Hall	208	39.24 N	76.27 W
Perry Heights	214	40.47 N	81.28 W
Perry-Jōriku-kinenhi ⊥	94	35.14 N	139.43 E
Perry Lake ⊜[1]	198	39.20 N	95.30 W
Perryman	208	39.28 N	76.12 W
Perrymont	279b	40.33 N	80.02 W
Perryopolis	214	40.05 N	79.45 W
Perry Park	218	38.33 N	85.00 W
Perry Point	208	39.33 N	76.04 W
Perrysburg, N.Y., U.S.	210	42.27 N	79.00 W
Perrysburg, Oh., U.S.	214	41.33 N	83.37 W
Perry's Landing Monument ⊥	268	35.13 N	139.43 E
Perry's Victory and International Peace Memorial ⊥	214	41.33 N	82.50 W
Perrysville	214	40.39 N	82.18 W

PORTUGUÊS

Nome	Página	Lat.°′	Long.°′ W = Oeste
Perryton	196	36.24 N	100.48 W
Perryville, Ak., U.S.	180	55.54 N	159.10 W
Perryville, Ar., U.S.	194	35.00 N	92.48 W
Perryville, Ky., U.S.	192	37.39 N	84.57 W
Perryville, Md., U.S.	208	39.33 N	76.04 W
Perryville, Mo., U.S.	194	37.43 N	89.51 W
Perryville, N.Y., U.S.	210	43.01 N	75.48 W
Peršamajski	76	53.54 N	25.23 E
Persan	50	49.09 N	2.16 E
Perşani, Munţii ⋏	38	45.40 N	25.15 E
Persberg	40	59.45 N	14.15 E
Perschling ≃	61	48.20 N	15.58 E
Perşembe	130	41.04 N	37.46 E
Persepolis → Takht-e Jamshīd ⊥	128	29.57 N	52.52 E
Perseverance, Mount ∧	171a	27.25 S	152.10 E
Perseverancia	248	14.44 S	62.48 W
Pershagen	40	59.10 N	17.39 E
Pershing	218	39.49 N	84.53 W
Pershore	42	52.07 N	2.05 W
Pershotravens'k, Ukr.	78	50.12 N	27.39 E
Pershotravens'k, Ukr.	78	48.22 N	36.24 E
Pershotravneve, Ukr.	78	51.24 N	28.53 E
Pershotravneve, Ukr.	83	47.03 N	37.18 E
Pershyttan	40	59.30 N	15.00 E
Persia	198	41.34 N	95.34 W
Persia → Iran □[1]	128	32.00 N	53.00 E
Persian Gulf (Arabian Gulf) c	128	27.00 N	51.00 E
Pérsico, Golfo → Persian Gulf c	128	27.00 N	51.00 E
Persimmon Creek ≃	194	31.31 N	86.50 W
Persique, Golfe → Persian Gulf c	128	27.00 N	51.00 E
Persischer Golf → Persian Gulf c	128	27.00 N	51.00 E
Perštejn	54	50.23 N	13.08 E
Perstorp	41	56.08 N	13.23 E
Pertandangan, Tanjung ›	114	2.41 N	100.14 E
Pertek	130	38.50 N	39.22 E
Perth, Austl.	168a	31.56 S	115.50 E
Perth, On., Can.	212	44.54 N	76.15 W
Perth, Scot., U.K.	46	56.24 N	3.28 W
Perth, N.Y., U.S.	210	43.03 N	74.12 W
Perth □[6]	212	43.30 N	81.05 W
Perth Amboy	210	40.30 N	74.15 W
Perth-Andover	186	46.45 N	67.42 W
Perth Basin ✦[1]	14	28.30 S	110.00 E
Perthes	58	48.39 N	4.49 E
Perth International Airport ⊠	168a	31.57 S	115.58 E
Perthois ◆[1]	58	48.40 N	4.45 E
Pertokar	144	16.59 N	37.28 E
Pertominsk	24	64.47 N	38.25 E
Pertovo	80	54.22 N	41.31 E
Pertuis	62	43.41 N	5.30 E
Pertusato, Capo ›	71	41.21 N	9.10 E
Peru, Il., U.S.	216	41.19 N	89.07 W
Peru, In., U.S.	216	40.45 N	86.04 W
Peru, Ne., U.S.	198	40.28 N	95.44 W
Peru, N.Y., U.S.	188	44.34 N	73.31 W
Peru (Perú) □[1], S.A.	242	10.00 S	76.00 W
Peru (Perú) □[1], S.A.	248	10.00 S	76.00 W
Peruaçu ≃	255	15.11 S	44.07 W
Peru Basin ✦[1]	18	15.00 S	85.00 W
Peruc	54	50.19 N	13.59 E
Perućac, Jezero ⊜[1]	38	43.55 N	19.10 E
Peru-Chile Trench ✦[1]	18	20.00 S	73.00 W
Perugia	66	43.08 N	12.22 E
Perugia □[4]	66	43.03 N	12.33 E
Perugorría	252	29.20 S	58.37 W
Peruíbe	252	24.19 S	47.00 W
Peruípe ≃	255	17.43 S	39.16 W
Perumalpār I[1]	122	11.10 N	72.04 E
Peruque Creek ≃	219	38.53 N	90.39 W
Perus ◆[8]	256	23.25 S	46.45 W
Perušić	36	44.39 N	15.23 E
Péruwelz	50	50.31 N	3.35 E
Pervaja Maja	86	48.55 N	67.25 E
Pervari	128	37.54 N	42.36 E
Pervenchères	50	48.26 N	0.26 E
Pervesinka	80	52.13 N	43.15 E
Pervijze	50	51.05 N	2.47 E
Pervoavgustovskij	76	52.14 N	35.03 E
Pervoje Pole	180	63.05 N	179.19 E
Pervomajevka	85	42.05 N	69.53 E
Pervomajka	86	51.17 N	70.08 E
Pervomajsk, Ross.	80	54.53 N	43.49 E
Pervomajsk, Ross.	88	58.02 N	94.05 E
Pervomajskij, Kyrg.	85	42.51 N	74.04 E
Pervomajskij, Ross.	76	54.04 N	32.29 E
Pervomajskij, Ross.	80	53.22 N	51.38 E
Pervomajskij, Ross.	80	51.22 N	48.54 E
Pervomajskij, Ross.	80	53.15 N	40.18 E
Pervomajskij, Ross.	82	55.57 N	37.52 E
Pervomajskij, Ross.	82	54.03 N	37.32 E
Pervomajskij, Ross.	82	55.32 N	37.09 E
Pervomajskij, Ross.	86	53.41 N	55.57 E
Pervomajskij, Ross.	86	51.32 N	55.06 E
Pervomajskij, Ross.	86	59.29 N	61.24 E
Pervomajskij, Ross.	86	54.52 N	61.08 E
Pervomajskij, Ross.	88	51.44 N	115.39 E
Pervomajskoje, Ross.	76	52.56 N	33.36 E
Pervomajskoje, Ross.	80	55.05 N	47.22 E
Pervomajskoje, Ross.	80	46.03 N	42.13 E
Pervomajskoje, Ross.	80	46.21 N	43.37 E
Pervomajskoje, Ross.	80	48.50 N	41.14 E
Pervomajskoje, Ross.	80	51.28 N	47.37 E
Pervomajskoje, Ross.	80	50.56 N	46.46 E
Pervomajskoje, Ross.	86	53.45 N	84.08 E
Pervomajskoje, Ross.	86	57.06 N	86.12 E
Pervomays'k, Ukr.	78	48.04 N	30.52 E
Pervomays'k, Ukr.	83	48.37 N	38.35 E
Pervomays'ke	78	45.43 N	33.51 E
Pervomays'kyy, Ukr.	78	49.24 N	36.12 E
Pervomays'kyy, Ukr.	83	47.58 N	38.47 E
Pervoural'sk	86	56.54 N	59.58 E
Pervušino	80	58.02 N	41.56 E
Pervyj Kuril'skij proliv ⊔	74	50.50 N	156.36 E
Perwenitz	264a	52.40 N	13.01 E
Fes'	76	58.55 N	34.19 E
Fes' ≃	76	59.08 N	35.18 E
Fesa ≃	66	43.44 N	11.01 E
Fes'akov, ostrov I	24	68.47 N	57.35 E
Fesangrohan ≃	269e	6.11 S	106.45 E
Fesaro	66	43.54 N	12.55 E
Pesaro e Urbino □[4]	66	43.40 N	12.38 E
Pesca	246	5.33 N	73.03 W
Pescadero	226	37.15 N	122.22 W
Pescadero Creek ≃, Ca., U.S.	226	37.16 N	122.25 W
Pescadero Creek ≃, Ca., U.S.	226	36.42 N	121.17 W
Pescadores → P'enghu Ch'üntao II	100	23.30 N	119.30 E
Pescadores, Punta ›, Méx.	232	23.46 N	109.43 W
Pescadores, Punta ›, Perú	248	16.21 S	73.15 W
Pescaglia	66	43.58 N	10.25 E
Pesčanka	80	51.18 N	43.40 E
Pesčanoje, Kaz.	86	53.01 N	76.19 E
Pesčanoje, Ross.	24	62.09 N	35.48 E
Pesčanokopskoje	80	46.12 N	41.04 E
Pescantina	64	45.29 N	10.51 E
Pesčanyje, ostrova II	83	46.52 N	38.17 E
Pescara	66	42.28 N	14.13 E
Pescara □[4]	66	42.20 N	13.57 E
Pescara ≃	66	42.28 N	14.13 E
Pescasseroli	66	41.48 N	13.47 E
Pesch	263	51.11 N	6.32 E
Pesch, Schloss ⊥	263	51.18 N	6.39 E
Peschici	68	41.57 N	16.01 E
Peschiera del Garda	64	45.26 N	10.42 E
Peschio, Monte ∧	267a	41.43 N	12.46 E
Pescia	66	43.54 N	10.41 E
Pescina	66	42.02 N	13.39 E
Pescocostanzo	66	41.53 N	14.04 E
Pescolanciano	66	41.41 N	14.20 E
Pescopagano	68	40.50 N	15.24 E
Pescorocchiano	66	42.12 N	13.09 E
Pesco Sannita	68	41.14 N	14.49 E
Pesé	236	7.54 N	80.37 W
Pesek, Pulau I	271c	1.17 N	103.41 E
Peseux	58	46.59 N	6.53 E
Peshastin	224	47.34 N	120.36 W
Peshastin Creek ≃	224	47.33 N	120.35 W
Peshāwar	123	34.01 N	71.33 E
Peshīn Jān	128	33.25 N	61.28 E
Peshkopi	38	41.41 N	20.26 E
Peshtigo	190	45.03 N	87.44 W
Peshtigo ≃	190	44.58 N	87.40 W
Pesio ≃	62	44.28 N	7.53 E
Pesjane	82	56.01 N	38.48 E
Peski, Bela.	76	53.21 N	24.38 E
Peski, Ross.	80	51.16 N	42.27 E
Peski, Ross.	82	55.13 N	38.46 E
Peški, Ross.	82	56.08 N	37.04 E
Peskovatskoje	82	54.03 N	36.16 E
Peškovka, Kaz.	86	53.45 N	62.23 E
Peskovka, Ross.	86	59.04 N	52.22 E
Peškovo	83	47.02 N	39.24 E
Peškovo Grecovo	82	54.26 N	37.36 E
Pesmes	58	47.17 N	5.34 E
Pesnica	61	46.36 N	15.41 E
Pesnica ≃	61	46.24 N	16.05 E
Pešnoj, poluostrov ›[2]	80	46.52 N	51.42 E
Pesočenskij	82	54.10 N	36.06 E
Pesočn'a	80	54.07 N	40.50 E
Pesočnoje	80	58.01 N	39.10 E
Pesočnyj	76	60.07 N	30.08 E
Peso da Régua	34	41.10 N	7.47 W
Pespire	236	13.35 N	87.22 W
Pesqueira	250	8.22 S	36.42 W
Pesquería	196	25.47 N	100.03 W
Pesquería ≃	196	25.54 N	99.11 W
Pessac	32	44.48 N	0.38 W
Pessin	54	52.38 N	12.40 E
Pessinetto	62	45.17 N	7.24 E
Pest □[6]	30	47.25 N	19.20 E
Pest ◆[8]	264c	47.30 N	19.04 E
Pest'aki	80	56.43 N	42.40 E
Peštera	38	42.02 N	24.18 E
Pesterzsébet ◆[8]	264c	47.26 N	19.07 E
Pesthidegkút ◆[8]	264c	47.34 N	18.58 E
Pestimre ◆[8]	264c	47.24 N	19.12 E
Pestlőrinc ◆[8]	264c	47.26 N	19.12 E
Pestovo, Ross.	76	58.36 N	35.48 E
Pestovo, Ross.	80	57.12 N	46.44 E
Pestovskoje vodochranilišče ⊜[1]	82	56.06 N	37.40 E
Pestravka	80	52.24 N	49.58 E
Pestrecy	80	55.46 N	49.39 E
Pestrikovo	82	55.05 N	38.53 E
Pestújhely ◆[8]	264c	47.32 N	19.07 E
Petacalco, Bahía c	234	17.57 N	102.05 W
Petah Tiqwa	132	32.05 N	34.53 E
Petäjävesi	26	62.15 N	25.12 E
Petal	194	31.20 N	89.15 W
Petalcingo	232	17.17 N	92.27 W
Petaling Jaya	114	3.05 N	101.39 E
Petalión, Kólpos c	38	37.59 N	24.02 E
Petaluma	226	38.13 N	122.38 W
Petaluma ≃	226	38.06 N	122.30 W
Pétange	56	49.34 N	5.52 E
Petare	246	10.29 N	66.49 W
Petatlán	234	17.31 N	101.16 W
Petauke	154	14.15 S	31.20 E
Petawawa	190	45.54 N	77.17 W
Petawawa ≃	190	45.55 N	77.15 W
Pété	146	10.58 N	14.30 E
Petegem	50	50.58 N	3.32 E
Petén □[5]	236	16.15 N	89.50 W
Petén Itzá, Lago ⊜	232	16.59 N	89.50 W
Petenwell Lake ⊜[1]	190	44.10 N	89.57 W
Peter and Paul Fortress ⊥	265a	59.57 N	30.19 E
Peterboro	210	42.58 N	75.41 W
Peterborough, Austl.	166	32.58 S	138.50 E
Peterborough, On., Can.	212	44.18 N	78.19 W
Peterborough, Eng., U.K.	42	52.35 N	0.15 W
Peterborough, N.H., U.S.	188	42.52 N	71.57 W
Peterborough □[6]	212	44.33 N	78.15 W
Peterculter	46	57.05 N	2.16 W
Peterhead	46	57.30 N	1.49 W
Peter Hill ∧	46	56.58 N	2.42 W
Peter I Island I	9	68.47 S	90.35 W
Peter Island I	240m	18.22 N	64.35 W
Peter Lake ⊜, N.T., Can.	176	63.08 N	92.48 W
Peter Lake ⊜, Sk., Can.	184	57.15 N	103.53 W
Peterlee	44	54.46 N	1.19 W
Peter Lougheed Provincial Park ♦	182	50.45 N	115.15 W
Peterman	194	31.35 N	87.15 W
Petermann Ranges ⋏	162	25.00 S	129.46 E
Petermann Reserve ◆[4]	162	25.00 S	130.15 E
Peter Pond Lake ⊜	184	55.55 N	108.44 W
Peter Pond Lake Indian Reserve ◆[4]	184	55.55 N	109.00 W
Petersberg	56	50.33 N	9.43 E
Peters Brook ≃	276	40.33 N	74.37 W
Petersburg, Ak., U.S.	180	56.49 N	132.57 W
Petersburg, Il., U.S.	219	40.00 N	89.50 W
Petersburg, In., U.S.	194	38.29 N	87.16 W
Petersburg, Mi., U.S.	216	41.54 N	83.42 W
Petersburg, Ne., U.S.	198	41.51 N	98.04 W
Petersburg, N.J., U.S.	208	39.15 N	74.43 W
Petersburg, N.Y., U.S.	210	42.44 N	73.20 W
Petersburg, Oh., U.S.	214	40.54 N	80.31 W
Petersburg, Pa., U.S.	214	40.34 N	78.03 W
Petersburg, Tn., U.S.	194	35.19 N	86.38 W
Petersburg, Tx., U.S.	196	33.52 N	101.36 W
Petersburg, Va., U.S.	208	37.13 N	77.24 W
Petersburg, W.V., U.S.	188	38.59 N	79.07 W
Petersburg National Battlefield ♦	208	37.14 N	77.22 W
Peters Canyon Reservoir ⊜[1]	280	33.47 N	117.45 W
Peters Creek ≃, Ca., U.S.	282	37.15 N	122.13 W
Peters Creek ≃, Pa., U.S.	279b	40.18 N	79.52 W
Peters Creek, Piney Fork ≃	279b	40.16 N	79.58 W
Petersdorf	54	54.29 N	11.04 E
Petersfield, S. Afr.	273d	26.14 S	28.26 E
Petersfield, Eng., U.K.	42	51.00 N	0.56 W
Petershagen, Dtsch.	52	52.23 N	8.58 E
Petershagen, Dtsch.	54	52.24 N	14.20 E
Petershagen, Dtsch.	54	52.31 N	13.46 E
Petersham, Austl.	274a	33.54 S	151.09 E
Petersham, Ma., U.S.	207	42.29 N	72.11 W
Petershausen	60	48.25 N	11.28 E
Peters Hill ∧[2]	168b	34.11 S	138.50 E
Peterson	198	42.55 N	95.20 W
Peterson Air Force Base ■	198	38.49 N	104.42 W
Peters Pond ⊜	283	42.43 N	71.16 W
Peterswald Hill ∧[2]	162	26.43 S	123.39 E
Peter the Great Bay → Petra Velikogo, zaliv c	89	42.40 N	132.00 E
Peter the Great Monument ⊥	265a	59.56 N	30.18 E
Pétervására	30	48.01 N	20.06 E
Petilia Policastro	68	39.07 N	16.47 E
Pétionville	238	18.31 N	72.17 W
Petit	273d	26.06 S	28.22 E
Petit Bois Island I	194	30.12 N	88.26 W
Petit-Bourg	241o	16.12 N	61.36 W
Petit-Canal	241o	16.23 N	61.29 W
Petitcodiac	186	45.56 N	65.10 W
Petitcodiac ≃	186	45.50 N	64.33 W
Petit Cul-de-Sac Marin c	241o	16.12 N	61.33 W
Petite Nation, Rivière de la ≃	206	45.35 N	75.06 W
Petite Rivière du Chêne ≃	206	46.34 N	72.02 W
Petite Rivière Noire, Piton de la ∧	157c	20.24 S	57.24 E
Petite Rivière Rouge ≃	206	45.45 N	75.00 W
Petites-Anses	241o	15.51 N	61.39 W
Petite Sauldre ≃	50	47.26 N	2.05 E
Petite Terre, Îles de la II	241o	16.10 N	61.07 W
Petit Forte	186	47.24 N	54.40 W
Petit-Fort-Philippe	50	51.00 N	2.07 E
Petit-Goâve	238	18.26 N	72.52 W
Petit Jean ≃	194	35.10 N	92.56 W
Petit Jean State Park ♦	194	35.06 N	92.57 W
Petit Loango	152	2.16 S	9.35 E
Petit Loango, Parc National du ♦	152	2.15 S	9.36 E
Petit Mécatina, Île du I	186	50.33 N	59.20 W
Petit Morin ≃	50	48.56 N	3.07 E
Petitot ≃	176	60.14 N	123.29 W
Petit Piton ∧	241f	13.50 N	61.04 W
Petit Rhône ≃	62	43.27 N	4.24 E
Petit-Saint-Bernard, Col du)(	62	45.41 N	6.53 E
Petitsikapau Lake ⊜	176	54.45 N	66.25 W
Petkeljärven kansallispuisto ♦	24	62.35 N	31.12 E
Petkus	54	51.59 N	13.21 E
Petlād	120	22.28 N	72.48 E
Petlalcingo	234	18.05 N	97.54 W
Peto	232	20.08 N	88.55 W
Petoh	114	2.53 N	103.15 E
Petone	172	41.13 S	174.52 E
Petorca	252	32.15 S	70.56 W
Petoskey	190	45.22 N	84.57 W
Petownikip Lake ⊜	184	52.56 N	92.02 W
Petra → Baṭrā ⊥	132	30.20 N	35.26 E
Petralia Soprana	70	37.47 N	14.06 E
Petralia Sottana	70	37.48 N	14.05 E
Petras, Mount ∧	9	75.52 S	128.38 W
Petra Velikogo, zaliv (Peter the Great Bay) c	89	42.40 N	132.00 E
Petre, Point ›	212	43.50 N	77.09 W
Petrecovo	24	61.18 N	57.07 E
Petrella, Monte ∧	66	41.18 N	13.40 E
Petrella Salto	66	42.18 N	13.04 E
Petrella Tifernina	66	41.41 N	14.42 E
Petrič	38	41.24 N	23.13 E
Petrie	171a	27.16 S	152.59 E
Petrified Forest National Park ♦	200	34.55 N	109.49 W
Petrila	38	45.27 N	23.25 E
Petrinja	36	45.26 N	16.17 E
Petriščevo, Ross.	82	54.37 N	36.57 E
Petriščevo, Ross.	82	55.30 N	36.18 E
Petrítis, Ákra ›	267c	37.56 N	23.24 E
Petrivka, Ukr.	78	46.54 N	30.44 E
Petrivka, Ukr.	83	48.53 N	39.52 E
Petrivka, Ukr.	83	48.48 N	39.16 E
Petrivs'ke	78	49.10 N	36.54 E
Petrodvorec	76	59.53 N	29.54 E
Petroglyphs Provincial Park ♦	212	44.33 N	77.53 W
Petrograd → Sankt-Peterburg	76	59.55 N	30.15 E
Petrohué	254	41.08 S	72.25 W
Petrolândia	250	9.05 S	38.18 W
Petrólea	246	8.30 N	72.35 W
Petroleum	216	40.36 N	85.09 W
Petrolia, On., Can.	214	42.52 N	82.09 W
Petrolia, Pa., U.S.	214	41.01 N	79.43 W
Petrolia, Tx., U.S.	196	34.01 N	98.14 W
Petrolina	250	9.24 S	40.30 W
Petrolina de Goiás	255	16.06 S	49.20 W
Petronà	68	39.03 N	16.45 E
Petrona, Punta ›	240m	17.56 N	66.23 W
Petronila Creek ≃	196	27.32 N	97.32 W
Petropavlivka, Ukr.	78	48.27 N	36.26 E
Petropavlivka, Ukr.	83	49.43 N	37.42 E
Petropavlovka, Ross.	78	50.06 N	40.54 E
Petropavlovka, Ross.	88	50.38 N	105.19 E
Petropavlovsk, Kaz.	86	54.54 N	69.06 E
Petropavlovsk, Ross.	86	56.20 N	57.09 E
Petropavlovsk-Kamčatskij	74	53.01 N	158.39 E
Petropavlovskoje, Ross.	86	52.04 N	84.08 E
Petropavlovskoje, Ross.	88	58.13 N	108.59 E
Petrópolis	256	22.31 S	43.10 W
Petros	192	36.05 N	84.26 W
Petroşani	38	45.25 N	23.22 E
Petrosino	70	37.43 N	12.29 E
Petro-Slav'anka	265a	59.48 N	30.31 E
Petroso, Monte ∧	66	41.44 N	13.55 E
Petroúpolis	267c	38.03 N	23.41 E
Petrovac	38	44.22 N	21.27 E
Petrove	78	48.20 N	33.16 E
Petrovgrad → Zrenjanin	38	45.23 N	20.24 E
Petrovka	80	53.13 N	51.58 E
Petrovo, Ross.	76	58.22 N	35.09 E
Petrovo, Ross.	82	55.00 N	38.08 E
Petrovo, Ross.	88	54.30 N	105.15 E
Petrovo-Dal'neje	265b	55.45 N	37.11 E
Petrovsk	80	52.19 N	45.23 E
Petrovskaja	78	45.25 N	37.57 E
Petrovs'ke	83	48.18 N	38.52 E
Petrovskij, Ross.	80	56.39 N	40.19 E
Petrovskij, Ross.	80	50.45 N	41.59 E
Petrovskij, Ross.	82	54.29 N	36.59 E
Petrovskoje, Ross.	80	52.39 N	40.15 E
Petrovskoje, Ross.	80	57.01 N	39.16 E
Petrovskoje, Ross.	82	55.27 N	38.21 E
Petrovskoje, Ross.	82	55.32 N	36.59 E
Petrovskoje, Ross.	265b	55.36 N	37.53 E
Petrovsko-Razumovskoje ◆[8]	265b	55.50 N	37.34 E
Petrovsk-Zabajkal'skij	88	51.17 N	108.50 E
Petrov Val	80	50.09 N	45.12 E
Petrozavodsk	24	61.47 N	34.20 E
Petrozsény → Petroşani	38	45.25 N	23.22 E
Petrun'	24	66.28 N	60.43 E
Petrusburg	158	29.08 S	25.27 E
Petrušino	265a	59.48 N	30.50 E
Petrus Steyn	158	27.38 S	28.08 E
Petrusville	158	30.05 S	24.41 E
Petrykaŭ	76	52.08 N	28.30 E
Petrykivka	78	48.43 N	34.37 E
Petschora → Pečora ≃	24	68.13 N	54.15 E
Petten	52	52.45 N	4.39 E
Pettenbach	61	47.57 N	14.01 E
Petteril ≃	44	54.54 N	2.55 W
Petticoat Creek ≃	275b	43.48 N	79.06 W
Pettigoe	48	54.33 N	7.50 W
Pettinascura, Monte ∧	68	39.22 N	16.37 E
Pettineo	70	37.58 N	14.17 E
Pettisville	216	41.31 N	84.13 W
Pettnau	64	47.18 N	11.08 E
Pettneu am Arlberg	58	47.09 N	10.20 E
Pettus	196	28.37 N	97.48 W
Petty Harbour	186	47.28 N	52.43 W
Petty Island I	285	39.58 N	75.07 W
Petua	272b	22.25 N	88.27 E
Petuchovo	86	55.06 N	67.58 E
Petuški	80	55.55 N	39.28 E
Petworth	42	50.59 N	0.38 W
Petzow	264a	52.21 N	12.56 E
Peudada	114	5.12 N	96.35 E
Peuerbach	60	48.20 N	13.46 E
Peuetsagoe, Gunung ∧	114	4.55 N	96.20 E
Peureulak	114	4.48 N	97.53 E
Peureulak ≃	114	4.54 N	97.53 E
Peureulak, Ujung ›	114	4.54 N	97.54 E
Peusangan ≃	114	5.16 N	96.51 E
Peusangan, Ujung ›	114	5.16 N	96.50 E
Pevek	74	69.42 N	170.17 E
Pevely	219	38.17 N	90.23 W
Pevensey	42	50.49 N	0.20 E
Pevensey Levels ≋	42	50.50 N	0.20 E
Peveragno	62	44.20 N	7.37 E
Pewamo	216	43.00 N	84.50 W
Pewaukee	216	43.04 N	88.15 W
Pewaukee Lake ⊜	216	43.04 N	88.19 W
Pewee Valley	218	38.18 N	85.29 W
Pews Creek ≃	276	40.27 N	74.06 W
Pewsey	42	51.21 N	1.46 W
Pewsey, Vale of ∨	42	51.20 N	1.48 W
Péyia	130	34.53 N	32.23 E
Peyrolles-en-Provence	62	43.39 N	5.35 E
Peyruis	62	44.02 N	5.56 E
Peza ≃	24	65.36 N	44.35 E
Pezas	86	54.39 N	87.46 E
Pezawa Taung ∧	110	19.33 N	94.31 E
Pézenas	32	43.27 N	3.25 E
Peženga	76	59.10 N	44.16 E
Pezinok	30	48.18 N	17.17 E
Pezu	123	32.19 N	70.44 E
Pezzana	62	45.16 N	8.29 E
Pfäfers	58	46.59 N	9.30 E
Pfaffenhausen	58	48.07 N	10.27 E
Pfaffenhofen an der Ilm	60	48.31 N	11.30 E
Pfaffenhofen an der Roth	58	48.21 N	10.10 E
Pfaffenhoffen	56	48.51 N	7.37 E
Pfaffenöden ∧[2]	264b	48.04 N	16.33 E
Pfäffikersee ⊜	58	47.21 N	8.48 E
Pfäffikon	58	47.22 N	8.47 E
Pfaffing	64	48.03 N	12.07 E
Pfaffnau	58	47.14 N	7.54 E
Pfaffstätten	264b	48.01 N	16.16 E
Pfalzdorf	52	51.42 N	6.11 E
Pfänder ∧	58	47.30 N	9.47 E
Pfarrkirchen	60	48.27 N	12.56 E
Pfarrweisach	56	50.09 N	10.44 E
Pfastatt	58	47.47 N	7.18 E
Pfatter	60	48.58 N	12.23 E
Pfaueninsel, Schloss ⊥	264a	52.26 N	13.07 E
Pfeddersheim	56	49.38 N	8.16 E
Pfeffenhausen	60	48.40 N	11.58 E
Pfeiffer-Big Sur State Park ♦	226	36.15 N	121.47 W
Pferderennbahn ♦	263	51.31 N	7.32 E
Pfinztal	56	48.59 N	8.33 E
Pflugerville	222	30.26 N	97.37 W
Pförring	60	48.49 N	11.41 E
Pforzen	58	47.55 N	10.37 E
Pforzheim	56	48.54 N	8.42 E
Pfreimd	60	49.30 N	12.11 E
Pfreimd ≃	60	49.29 N	12.11 E
Pfrimm ≃	56	49.39 N	8.22 E
Pfronten	58	47.34 N	10.33 E
Pfuhl	58	48.24 N	10.02 E
Pfullendorf	58	47.55 N	9.15 E
Pfullingen	58	48.28 N	9.13 E
Pfunds	58	46.58 N	10.33 E
Pfungstadt	56	49.48 N	8.36 E
Pfyn	58	47.36 N	8.57 E
Pha-an	110	16.53 N	97.38 E
Phachi ≃	110	13.56 N	99.24 E
Phaéton, Port c	174s	17.44 S	149.21 W
Phagwāra	123	31.14 N	75.46 E
Phala	156	23.45 S	26.57 E
Phalaborwa	156	23.55 S	31.13 E
Phalanx	214	41.15 N	80.58 W
Phalempin	50	50.31 N	3.01 E
Phālia	123	32.26 N	73.35 E
Phalodi	120	27.08 N	72.22 E
Phalsbourg	56	48.46 N	7.16 E
Phalta	126	22.17 N	88.07 E
Phaltan	122	17.59 N	74.26 E
Phalti	272b	22.46 N	88.34 E
Phan	110	19.28 N	99.43 E
Phanat Nikhom	110	13.27 N	101.11 E
Phangan, Ko I	110	9.45 N	100.04 E
Phang Hoei, Khao ∧	110	15.15 N	101.23 E
Phangnga	110	8.28 N	98.32 E
Phaniang ≃	110	16.49 N	102.24 E
Phanom Dongrak, Thiu Khao ⋏	110	14.25 N	103.30 E
Phanom Thuan	110	14.07 N	99.42 E
Phan Rang	110	11.34 N	108.59 E
Phan Thiet	110	10.56 N	108.06 E
Phan Thong	110	13.28 N	101.06 E
Phantom Lake	216	42.52 N	88.21 W
Pharenda	124	27.06 N	83.17 E
Phariāro	120	27.12 N	68.59 E
Pharr	196	26.11 N	98.11 W
Phasi Charoen	269a	13.43 N	100.26 E
Phasi Charoen, Khlong ≊	269a	13.44 N	100.30 E
Phat Diem	110	20.06 N	106.06 E
Phato	110	9.48 N	98.48 E
Phatthalung	110	7.37 N	100.05 E
Phayao	110	19.10 N	99.55 E
Pheasant Creek ≃	184	50.35 N	103.28 W
Pheba	194	33.35 N	88.56 W
Phelan	228	34.25 N	117.34 W
Phelps, N.Y., U.S.	210	42.57 N	77.03 W
Phelps, Tx., U.S.	222	30.42 N	95.27 W
Phelps, Wi., U.S.	190	46.03 N	89.05 W
Phelps Lake ⊜	192	35.46 N	76.27 W
Phenix City	192	32.28 N	85.00 W
Phepane ≃	156	25.50 S	22.45 E
Phet Buri ≃	110	13.13 N	99.59 E
Phetchabun	110	16.25 N	101.08 E
Phetchabun, Thiu Khao ⋏	110	16.20 N	100.55 E
Phetchaburi	110	13.06 N	99.57 E
Phibun Mangsahan	110	15.14 N	105.14 E
Phichai	110	17.17 N	100.05 E
Phichit	110	16.26 N	100.22 E
Philadelphia, S. Afr.	158	33.40 S	18.36 E
Philadelphia, Il., U.S.	219	39.58 N	90.07 W
Philadelphia, Ms., U.S.	194	32.46 N	89.07 W
Philadelphia, Mo., U.S.	219	39.50 N	91.44 W
Philadelphia, N.Y., U.S.	212	44.09 N	75.42 W
Philadelphia, Pa., U.S.	208	39.57 N	75.09 W
Philadelphia, Pa., U.S.	285	39.57 N	75.09 W
Philadelphia, Tn., U.S.	192	35.40 N	84.24 W
Philadelphia □[6]	285	39.57 N	75.07 W
Philadelphia International Airport ⊠	208	39.53 N	75.14 W
Philadelphia Museum of Art ⊕	285	39.58 N	75.11 W

Symbol	English	Deutsch	Español	Français	Português
≃	River	Fluß	Río	Rivière	Rio
≊	Canal	Kanal	Canal	Canal	Canal
∟	Waterfall, Rapids	Wasserfall, Stromschnellen	Cascada, Rápidos	Chute d'eau, Rapides	Cascata, Rápidos
⊔	Strait	Meeresstraße	Estrecho	Détroit	Estreito
c	Bay, Gulf	Bucht, Golf	Bahía, Golfo	Baie, Golfe	Baía, Golfo
⊜	Lake, Lakes	See, Seen	Lago, Lagos	Lac, Lacs	Lago, Lagos
≋	Swamp	Sumpf	Pantano	Marais	Pântano
⊓	Ice Features, Glacier	Eis- und Gletscherformen	Accidentes Glaciales	Formes glaciaires	Acidentes glaciares
⊤	Other Hydrographic Features	Andere Hydrographische Objekte	Otros Elementos Hidrográficos	Autres données hydrographiques	Outros acidentes hidrográficos
✦	Submarine Features	Untermeerische Objekte	Accidentes Submarinos	Formes de relief sous-marin	Acidentes submarinos
□	Political Unit	Politische Einheit	Unidad Politica	Entité politique	Unidade política
⊕	Cultural Institution	Kulturelle Institution	Institución Cultural	Institution culturelle	Instituição cultural
⊥	Historical Site	Historische Stätte	Sitio Histórico	Site historique	Sitio histórico
♦	Recreational Site	Erholungs- und Ferienort	Sitio de Recreo	Centre de loisirs	Area de Lazer
⊠	Airport	Flughafen	Aeropuerto	Aéroport	Aeroporto
■	Military Installation	Militäranlage	Instalación Militar	Installation militaire	Instalação militar
◆	Miscellaneous	Verschiedenes	Misceláneo	Divers	Diversos

I · 136 Phil-Pine

ENGLISH Name Page Lat.°′ Long.°′ — DEUTSCH Name Seite Breite°′ Länge°′ E = Ost

Philadelphia Naval Shipyard ■ 285 39.53 N 75.11 W
Philadelphia Park Race Track ♦ 285 40.07 N 74.57 W
Philae ⊥ 140 24.01 N 32.53 E
Phil Campbell 194 34.21 N 87.42 W
Philip 198 44.02 N 101.39 W
Philipp 194 33.45 N 90.12 W
Philippeville → Skikda, Alg. 148 36.50 N 6.58 E
Philippeville, Bel. 50 50.12 N 4.32 E
Philippi 188 39.09 N 80.02 W
Philippi, Lake ⊜ 166 24.22 S 139.00 E
Philippine Basin ✢1 14 17.00 N 132.00 E
Philippine International Convention Center ♦ 269f 14.32 N 120.59 E
Philippinen → Philippines □1 116 13.00 N 122.00 E
Philippines (Pilipinas) □1, Asia 108 13.00 N 122.00 E
Philippines (Pilipinas) □1, Asia 116 13.00 N 122.00 E
Philippines, University of the ✢2 269f 14.39 N 121.04 E
Philippine Sea ⩶2 14 20.00 N 135.00 E
Philippine Trench ✢1 14 9.00 N 127.00 E
Philippolis 158 30.19 S 25.13 E
Philippopolis → Plovdiv 38 42.09 N 24.45 E
Philippsburg 56 49.14 N 8.27 E
Philippsreut 60 48.52 N 13.41 E
Philippsthal, Dtsch. 56 50.51 N 10.00 E
Philippsthal, Dtsch. 264a 52.20 N 13.09 E
Philipsburg, P.Q., Can. 206 45.02 N 73.05 W
Philipsburg, Ned. Ant. 238 17.59 N 63.10 W
Philipsburg, Mt., U.S. 202 46.19 N 113.17 W
Philipsburg, Pa., U.S. 214 40.53 N 78.13 W
Philipsburg Manor ⊥ 276 41.05 N 73.52 W
Philipse Manor Hall State Historic Site ⊥ 276 40.56 N 73.54 W
Philip Smith Mountains ⩘ 180 68.30 N 148.00 W
Philipstown 158 30.26 S 24.29 E
Phillaur 123 31.01 N 75.47 E
Phillip Island I 169 38.29 S 145.14 E
Phillips, Me., U.S. 188 44.49 N 70.20 W
Phillips, Tx., U.S. 196 35.41 N 101.21 W
Phillips, Wi., U.S. 190 45.41 N 90.24 W
Phillipsburg, Ga., U.S. 192 31.34 N 83.31 W
Phillipsburg, Ks., U.S. 198 39.45 N 99.19 W
Phillipsburg, N.J., U.S. 210 40.41 N 75.11 W
Philmont 210 42.14 N 73.39 W
Philo, Il., U.S. 194 40.01 N 88.09 W
Philo, Oh., U.S. 188 39.51 N 81.54 W
Philomath 202 44.32 N 123.21 W
Philpots Island I 176 74.48 N 80.00 W
Phimai 110 15.13 N 102.30 E
Phinga 272b 22.41 N 88.25 E
Phitsanulok 110 16.50 N 100.15 E
Phnom Penh → Phnum Pénh 110 11.33 N 104.55 E
Phnum Pénh 110 11.33 N 104.55 E
Phnum Tbêng Méanchey 110 13.49 N 104.58 E
Pho ≃ 124 27.41 N 89.53 E
Phoenicia 210 42.05 N 74.18 W
Phoenix, Az., U.S. 200 33.26 N 112.04 W
Phoenix, Il., U.S. 278 41.36 N 87.38 W
Phoenix, Md., U.S. 208 39.30 N 76.36 W
Phoenix, N.Y., U.S. 210 43.13 N 76.18 W
Phoenix Islands II 14 4.00 S 172.00 W
Phoenix Lake ⊜1 282 37.57 N 122.35 W
Phoenix Park ♦ 281 42.24 N 83.27 W
Phoenixville 208 40.07 N 75.30 W
Phon 110 15.49 N 102.36 E
Phong ≃ 110 16.23 N 102.56 E
Phôngsali 110 21.41 N 102.06 E
Phong Tho 110 22.32 N 103.21 E
Phon Phisai 110 18.01 N 103.05 E
Phosphate Hill 166 21.52 S 139.51 E
Phrae 110 18.09 N 100.08 E
Phra Khanong ✢8 269a 13.42 N 100.35 E
Phra Nakhon → Krung Thep 110 13.45 N 100.31 E
Phra Nakhon Si Ayutthaya 110 14.21 N 100.33 E
Phran Krata 110 16.40 N 99.36 E
Phrao 110 19.22 N 99.13 E
Phra Pradaeng 269a 13.40 N 100.32 E
Phra Rop, Khao ∧ 110 13.11 N 99.31 E
Phrom Phiram 110 17.02 N 100.12 E
Phrygia □9 130 39.00 N 30.00 E
Phsar Réam 110 10.30 N 103.37 E
Phu Cat 110 14.01 N 109.03 E
Phu Huu, Viet 110 18.58 N 105.31 E
Phu Huu, Viet 269c 10.43 N 106.47 E
Phuket 110 7.53 N 98.24 E
Phuket, Ko I 110 8.00 N 98.22 E
Phularwān 123 32.22 N 73.00 E
Phulbari 126 21.52 N 88.08 E
Phulbāria 126 23.22 N 89.50 E
Phuljhuri 126 22.12 N 90.04 E
Phulkusma 126 22.43 N 86.52 E
Phu Loc 110 16.16 N 107.53 E
Phūlpur 124 25.33 N 82.06 E
Phulra 123 34.20 N 73.03 E
Phultala 126 22.59 N 89.28 E
Phu Ly 110 20.32 N 105.56 E
Phum Duang ≃ 110 9.10 N 99.20 E
Phumĭ Bâ Khăm 110 13.51 N 107.22 E
Phumĭ Banam 110 11.19 N 105.18 E
Phumĭ Béng 110 13.05 N 104.18 E
Phumĭ Châmbák 110 11.14 N 104.49 E
Phumĭ Chângho Ândêng 110 12.39 N 104.35 E
Phumĭ Chhuk 110 10.50 N 104.28 E
Phumĭ Chruŏy Slêng 110 13.14 N 105.57 E
Phumĭ Dăk Dăm 110 12.20 N 107.21 E
Phumĭ Kâmpóng Srâlau 110 14.05 N 105.46 E
Phumĭ Kâmpóng Trâbâk 110 13.06 N 105.14 E
Phumĭ Kântuŏt Sâmraông 110 14.12 N 104.37 E
Phumĭ Kaôh Kért 110 13.47 N 104.32 E
Phumĭ Kaôh Kŏng 110 11.26 N 103.11 E
Phumĭ Khpôb 110 11.02 N 105.12 E
Phumĭ Krêk 110 11.46 N 105.56 E
Phumĭ Lvéa Kraôm 110 13.21 N 102.54 E
Phumĭ Moŭng 110 13.45 N 103.33 E
Phumĭ Narŭng 110 13.53 N 105.34 E
Phumĭ Phnum Srâlau 110 11.03 N 103.42 E
Phumĭ Prêk Kák 110 12.15 N 105.32 E
Phumĭ Prêk Sândêk 110 11.51 N 105.22 E
Phumĭ Prey Toch 110 12.54 N 103.23 E
Phumĭ Puŏk Chăs 110 13.26 N 103.44 E
Phumĭ Rôluŏs Chăs 110 13.19 N 104.00 E
Phumĭ Sâmraông 110 14.11 N 103.31 E
Phumĭ Spœ Tbong 110 12.20 N 105.19 E
Phumĭ Srê Kôkir 110 13.08 N 106.04 E
Phumĭ Srê Rônéam 110 12.16 N 106.25 E
Phumĭ Tbêng 110 13.35 N 104.55 E
Phumĭ Thalabârĭvăt 110 13.33 N 105.57 E
Phumĭ Thmâ Pôk 110 13.57 N 103.04 E
Phumĭ Tnaôt 110 12.56 N 104.34 E
Phumĭ Tœk Choŭ 110 13.36 N 103.24 E
Phu My 110 14.10 N 109.03 E
Phung Hiep 110 9.49 N 105.50 E
Phuntsholing 124 26.53 N 89.23 E
Phuoc Binh 110 11.50 N 106.58 E
Phuoc Khanh 269c 10.40 N 106.48 E
Phuoc Long 110 9.26 N 105.28 E
Phuoc Long Xa 269c 10.49 N 106.46 E
Phuoc Luong 269c 10.45 N 106.48 E
Phu Quoc 110 10.13 N 103.58 E
Phu Quoc, Dao I 110 10.12 N 104.00 E
Phurphura 272b 22.44 N 88.08 E
Phu Tho 110 21.24 N 105.13 E
Phu Tho Hoa 269c 10.46 N 106.38 E
Phu Tho Race Track ♦ 269c 10.46 N 106.40 E
Phutthaisong 110 15.32 N 103.01 E
Phu Vang 110 16.31 N 107.37 E
Phu Yen 110 21.16 N 104.39 E
Pi ≃ 100 32.26 N 116.34 E
Pia 154 4.00 N 26.17 E
Piabas 250 1.12 S 46.54 W
Piabetá 256 22.37 S 43.10 W
Piabonha ≃ 256 22.07 S 43.08 W
Piaçabuçu 250 10.24 S 36.25 W
Piacatuba 256 21.29 S 42.47 W
Piacenza 62 45.01 N 9.40 E
Piacenza □4 62 44.53 N 9.35 E
Piacouadie, Lac ⊜ 186 51.16 N 70.54 W
Piadena 64 45.08 N 10.22 E
Piaggine 68 40.21 N 15.23 E
Piako ≃ 172 37.12 S 175.30 E
Pialba 166 25.17 S 152.51 E
Piāli ≃ 272b 22.23 N 88.35 E
Piana 36 42.14 N 8.38 E
Piana, Isola I 71 40.58 N 8.13 E
Piana Crixia 62 44.29 N 8.18 E
Piana degli Albanesi 70 38.00 N 13.17 E
Piana degli Albanesi, Lago di ⊜ 70 37.58 N 13.18 E
Piana Mwanga 154 7.40 S 28.10 E
Piancastagnaio 66 42.51 N 11.41 E
Piancó 250 7.12 S 37.57 W
Pian Creek ≃ 166 30.02 S 148.12 E
Pian di Sco 66 43.38 N 11.33 E
Pianella 66 42.24 N 14.02 E
Pianello Val Tidone 62 44.57 N 9.24 E
Pianezza 62 45.06 N 7.33 E
Pianguan 102 39.24 N 111.30 E
Pianjiaojie 102 26.01 N 100.32 E
Piankatank ≃ 208 37.32 N 76.18 W
Pianling 104 41.24 N 123.58 E
Piano 64 45.46 N 11.08 E
Piano d'Arta 64 46.29 N 13.01 E
Piano del Voglio 66 44.10 N 11.13 E
Pianoro 64 44.22 N 11.20 E
Pianosa, Isola I, It. 36 42.35 N 10.04 E
Pianosa, Isola I, It. 66 42.13 N 15.45 E
Pianosinatico 66 44.07 N 10.44 E
Pianottoli-Caldarello 71 41.29 N 9.03 E
Pians 58 47.08 N 10.30 E
Pianu, Mochun ⩌ 175c 7.20 N 151.26 E
Piapot 184 49.59 N 109.07 W
Piapot Indian Reserve ✢4 184 50.45 N 104.26 W
Piasa 219 39.07 N 90.07 W
Piasa Creek ≃ 219 38.56 N 90.17 W
Piaseczno 30 52.05 N 21.01 E
Piashti, Lac ⊜ 186 50.29 N 62.52 W
Piaski 30 51.08 N 22.51 E
Piat 116 17.48 N 121.29 E
Piatã 255 13.09 S 41.48 W
Piatra-Neamț 38 46.56 N 26.22 E
Piatra-Olt 38 44.24 N 24.16 E
Piatt □6 219 40.00 N 88.35 W
Piau 256 21.31 S 43.19 W
Piauí □3 250 7.00 S 43.00 W
Piauí ≃, Bra. 250 6.38 S 42.42 W
Piauí ≃, Bra. 255 16.41 S 41.53 W
Piauí, Morro do ∧ 255 14.59 S 47.31 W
Piaus ≃ 255 12.27 S 49.32 W
Piave ≃ 64 45.32 N 12.44 E
Piawaning 162 30.51 S 116.22 E
Piaxtla ≃ 232 23.42 N 106.49 W
Piazza Armerina 70 37.23 N 14.22 E
Piazzi, Isla I 254 51.45 S 74.05 W
Piazzola sul Brenta 64 45.32 N 11.47 E
Piberegg 61 47.05 N 15.05 E
Pibor ≃ 140 8.26 N 33.13 E
Pibor Post 140 6.48 N 33.08 E
Pibroch 182 54.16 N 113.52 W
Pic ≃ 190 48.36 N 86.18 W
Pica 248 20.30 S 69.21 W
Picacho 200 32.42 N 111.29 W
Picacho, Cerro del ∧ 286a 19.35 N 99.08 W
Pičajevo 80 53.15 N 42.12 E
Picanoc ≃ 190 46.05 N 76.03 W
Picardie □9 50 49.45 N 2.50 E
Picatinny Arsenal ■ 276 40.57 N 74.33 W
Picatinny Lake ⊜ 276 40.57 N 74.33 W
Picayune 194 30.31 N 89.40 W
Piccadilly 186 48.34 N 58.55 W
Piccadilly Station ✢5 262 53.28 N 2.14 W
Piccione 66 43.11 N 12.31 E
Piccolo, Mar ⩶2 68 40.29 N 17.16 E
Piccotts End 260 51.46 N 0.28 W
Pic de Tio ∧ 150 8.52 N 8.54 W
Piceance Creek ≃ 200 40.05 N 108.14 W
Picentini, Monti ⩘ 68 40.45 N 15.00 E
Picerno 68 40.38 N 15.38 E
Pičeury 80 54.19 N 45.50 E
Pīch ≃ 123 34.52 N 71.09 E
Pichana ≃ 246 3.31 S 71.43 W
Pichanal 252 23.19 S 64.13 W
Picheng 106 32.07 N 119.42 E
Picher 196 36.59 N 94.49 W
Pichhor 124 25.58 N 78.24 E
Pichilemu 252 34.23 S 72.00 W
Pichileufú, Arroyo ≃ 254 40.35 S 70.39 W
Pichimá 246 4.24 N 77.21 W
Pichi-Mahuida 252 38.50 S 64.57 W
Pichincha □4 246 0.10 S 78.40 W
Pichis ≃ 248 9.59 S 74.59 W
Pichl bei Wels 60 48.11 N 13.54 E
Pichor 124 25.11 N 78.11 E
Pichtovka 86 56.00 N 82.42 E
Pichucalco 234 17.31 N 93.09 W
Picinguaba 256 23.22 S 44.50 W
Picinisco 66 41.39 N 13.52 E
Pic Island I 190 48.43 N 86.38 W
Pickardville 182 54.03 N 113.53 W
Pickaway □6 218 39.36 N 82.57 W
Pickens, Ms., U.S. 194 32.53 N 89.58 W
Pickens, S.C., U.S. 192 34.53 N 82.42 W
Pickens, W.V., U.S. 188 38.39 N 80.12 W
Pickensville 194 33.14 N 88.16 W
Pickerel ≃ 190 45.55 N 80.50 W
Pickerel Lake ⊜ 184 52.36 N 99.30 W
Pickering, On., Can. 212 43.52 N 79.02 W
Pickering, Eng., U.K. 44 54.14 N 0.46 W
Pickering, Vale of V 44 54.12 N 0.45 W
Pickering Beach 212 43.50 N 78.59 W
Pickering Brook 168a 32.03 S 116.08 E
Pickering Creek ≃ 285 40.08 N 75.30 W
Pickering Creek Reservoir ⊜1 285 40.07 N 75.30 W
Pickett, Lake ⊜ 220 28.36 N 81.07 W
Pickford 190 46.09 N 84.21 W
Pičkir'ajevo 80 54.12 N 42.27 E
Pickle Crow 176 51.30 N 90.04 W
Pickmere 262 53.17 N 2.28 W
Pick Mere ⊜ 262 53.17 N 2.29 W
Pickstown 198 43.04 N 98.31 W
Pickton 222 33.02 N 95.24 W
Pickwick Lake ⊜1 194 34.55 N 88.10 W
Pickwick Landing Dam ✢6 194 35.00 N 88.21 W
Picnic Point ≻ 274b 37.57 S 145.00 E
Pico 66 41.27 N 13.34 E
Pico ∧ 150a 14.56 N 24.21 W
Pico I 148a 38.28 N 28.20 W
Pico, Ponta do ∧ 148a 38.28 N 28.25 W
Pico da Neblina, Parque Nacional ♦ 246 0.30 N 66.00 W
Pico de Orizaba, Parque Nacional ♦ 234 19.05 N 97.16 W
Pico Rivera 228 33.58 N 118.05 W
Picos 250 7.05 S 41.28 W
Picota 248 6.55 S 76.20 W
Pico Truncado 254 46.48 S 67.58 W
Picquigny 50 49.57 N 2.09 E
Picton, Austl. 170 34.11 S 150.36 E
Picton, On., Can. 212 44.00 N 77.08 W
Picton, N.Z. 172 41.18 S 174.01 E
Picton, Eng., U.K. 262 53.14 N 2.51 W
Picton, Isla I 254 55.02 S 66.57 W
Picton Bay ⊂ 212 44.03 N 77.08 W
Picton Junction 168a 33.21 S 115.41 E
Pictou 186 45.41 N 62.43 W
Pictou Island I 186 45.50 N 62.34 W
Picture Butte 182 49.53 N 112.47 W
Pictured Rocks National Lakeshore ♦ 190 46.35 N 86.20 W
Picture Rocks 210 41.17 N 76.43 W
Picúa, Punta ≻ 240m 18.25 N 65.46 W
Picuí 250 6.31 S 36.21 W
Picunda 84 43.12 N 40.21 E
Picún Leufú 254 39.31 S 69.15 W
Picún Leufú, Arroyo ≃ 254 39.31 S 69.08 W
Picuris Indian Reservation ✢4 200 36.12 N 105.42 W
Pidálion, Akrotírion ≻ 130 34.56 N 34.05 E
Pidarak 128 25.51 N 63.14 E
Pidbyzh 78 49.22 N 23.15 E
Piddle ≃ 42 50.42 N 2.04 W
Piddletrenthide 42 50.48 N 2.25 W
Pide Adası I 267b 40.53 N 29.04 E
Pidhaytsi 78 49.16 N 25.08 E
Pidhorodna 78 48.07 N 30.51 E
Pidhorodne 78 48.34 N 35.08 E
Pidie, Ujung ≻ 114 5.30 N 95.53 E
Piding 64 47.46 N 12.55 E
Pidkamin' 78 49.57 N 25.19 E
Pidlisne 78 48.47 N 32.15 E
Pidurutalagala ∧ 122 7.00 N 80.46 E
Pidvolochys'k 78 49.33 N 26.09 E
Piedade 287a 22.41 S 43.05 W
Piedade ✢8 287a 22.53 S 43.19 W
Piedade do Baruel 287b 23.37 S 46.18 W
Piedade do Rio Grande 256 21.28 S 44.12 W
Piedecuesta 246 6.59 N 73.03 W
Piedicavallo 62 45.42 N 7.57 E
Piedicroce 36 42.23 N 9.23 E
Piediluco 66 42.32 N 12.45 E
Piedimonte Etneo 70 37.48 N 15.12 E
Piedimonte Matese 68 41.21 N 14.22 E
Piedimonte San Germano 66 41.30 N 13.45 E
Piedimulera 58 46.01 N 8.16 E
Piè di Ripa 66 43.15 N 13.29 E
Piedmont, Al., U.S. 194 33.55 N 85.36 W
Piedmont, Ca., U.S. 226 37.49 N 122.13 W
Piedmont, Mo., U.S. 194 37.09 N 90.41 W
Piedmont, Oh., U.S. 214 40.11 N 81.12 W
Piedmont, S.C., U.S. 192 34.54 N 82.21 W
Piedmont Lake ⊜1 214 40.08 N 81.11 W
Piedra, C.R. 236 9.29 N 83.40 W
Piedra, Ca., U.S. 226 36.48 N 119.22 W
Piedra ≃ 200 37.01 N 107.24 W
Piedra, Cerro ∧ 252 37.41 S 73.07 W
Piedra Azul, Quebrada ≃ 286c 10.36 N 66.57 W
Piedrabuena 34 39.02 N 4.10 W
Piedra del Águila 254 40.03 S 70.05 W
Piedra del Águila, Embalse ⊜1 254 40.30 S 70.20 W
Piedrafita, Puerto de)(34 42.40 N 7.01 W
Piedrahita 34 40.28 N 5.19 W
Piedra Roja 236 8.38 N 81.48 W
Piedras, Arroyo de las ≃ 288 34.43 S 58.19 W
Piedras, Punta ≻, Arg. 258 35.25 S 57.08 W
Piedras, Punta ≻, Ven. 246 10.40 N 61.40 W
Piedras Blancas 252 31.11 S 59.56 W
Piedras Blancas, Point ≻ 226 35.40 N 121.17 W
Piedras Coloradas 252 32.23 S 57.36 W
Piedras Negras, Guat. 232 17.11 N 91.15 W
Piedras Negras, Méx. 232 28.42 N 100.31 W
Piedras Negras ⊥ 232 17.12 N 91.15 W
Piedra Sola 252 32.04 S 56.21 W
Piegaro 66 42.58 N 12.05 E
Pie Island I 190 48.15 N 89.05 W
Pieksämäki 26 62.18 N 27.08 E
Piéla 150 12.42 N 0.08 W
Pielach ≃ 61 48.15 N 15.22 E
Pielavesi 26 63.14 N 26.45 E
Pielavesi ⊜ 26 63.18 N 26.35 E
Pielinen ⊜ 26 63.15 N 29.40 E
Pieljekaise Nationalpark ♦ 24 66.18 N 16.58 E
Piemonte □4 36 45.00 N 8.00 E
Pienaarsrivier 156 25.15 S 28.18 E
Piendamó 246 2.38 N 76.30 W
Pieniężno 30 54.15 N 20.08 E
Pieniński Park Narodowy ♦ 30 49.25 N 20.25 E
Pieni-Salpausselkä ∧ 26 61.08 N 27.20 E
Piennes 56 49.19 N 5.47 E
Pieńsk 30 51.15 N 15.03 E
Pienza 66 43.04 N 11.41 E
Pierce, Co., U.S. 200 40.38 N 104.45 W
Pierce, Fl., U.S. 220 27.50 N 81.58 W
Pierce, Id., U.S. 202 46.29 N 115.47 W
Pierce, Ne., U.S. 198 42.11 N 97.31 W
Pierce, Tx., U.S. 222 29.14 N 96.12 W
Pierce □6 224 47.04 N 122.07 W
Pierce, Lake ⊜ 220 27.58 N 81.31 W
Pierce City 194 36.56 N 94.00 W
Pierce Lake ⊜, Can. 184 54.10 N 92.56 W
Pierce Lake ⊜, Sk., Can. 184 54.30 N 109.42 W
Pierceton 216 41.12 N 85.42 W
Piermont 210 41.03 N 73.55 W
Pierowall 46 59.20 N 2.59 W
Pierpont, Oh., U.S. 214 41.45 N 80.34 W
Pierpont, S.D., U.S. 198 45.29 N 97.49 W
Pierre 198 44.22 N 100.21 W
Pierre, Bayou ≃, La., U.S. 194 31.51 N 93.06 W
Pierre, Bayou ≃, Ms., U.S. 194 31.55 N 91.11 W
Pierre-Buffière 32 45.42 N 1.21 E
Pierreclos 58 46.20 N 4.41 E
Pierre-de-Bresse 58 46.53 N 5.15 E
Pierrefeu-du-Var 62 43.13 N 6.08 E
Pierrefitte-sur-Aire 56 48.54 N 5.20 E
Pierrefitte-sur-Sauldre 50 47.30 N 2.09 E
Pierrefitte-sur-Seine 261 48.58 N 2.22 E
Pierrefonds, P.Q., Can. 206 45.29 N 73.52 W
Pierrefonds, Fr. 50 49.21 N 2.59 E
Pierrefontaine-les-Varans 58 47.13 N 6.33 E
Pierrelatte 62 44.23 N 4.42 E
Pierrelaye 261 49.01 N 2.09 E
Pierre Part 194 29.57 N 91.12 W
Pierre Pertuis, Col de)(58 47.12 N 7.11 E
Pierrepont Manor 212 43.44 N 76.04 W
Pierre-sur-Haute ∧ 62 45.39 N 3.49 E
Pierreville, P.Q., Can. 206 46.04 N 72.49 W
Pierreville, Trin. 241r 10.18 N 61.01 W
Pierron 219 38.47 N 89.36 W
Pierron, Lac ⊜ 206 46.53 N 74.20 W
Pierry 50 49.01 N 3.56 E
Pierson 192 29.14 N 81.27 W
Piersonville 285 40.10 N 74.42 W
Pierz 190 45.58 N 94.06 W
Piesendorf 64 47.17 N 12.43 E
Pieskow 54 52.16 N 14.04 E
Piesport 56 49.53 N 6.55 E
Piešťany 30 48.36 N 17.50 E
Piesting ≃ 61 48.02 N 16.30 E
Pietarsaari → Jakobstad 26 63.40 N 22.42 E
Pieterburen 52 53.24 N 6.27 E
Pieterlen 58 47.11 N 7.20 E
Pietermaritzburg 158 29.37 S 30.16 E
Pietersburg 156 23.54 S 29.25 E
Pietrabbondante 66 41.45 N 14.23 E
Pietracamela 66 42.31 N 13.33 E
Pietracatella 66 41.35 N 14.52 E
Pietra del Pertusillo, Lago di ⊜ 68 40.17 N 15.58 E
Pietragalla 68 40.45 N 15.53 E
Pietra Ligure 62 44.09 N 8.17 E
Pietralunga 66 43.26 N 12.26 E
Pietramala 66 44.10 N 11.20 E
Pietramelara 68 41.16 N 14.11 E
Pietramontecorvino 68 41.32 N 15.07 E
Pietrapaola 68 39.29 N 16.49 E
Pietrapertosa 68 40.31 N 16.04 E
Pietraperzia 70 37.25 N 14.08 E
Pietrasanta 64 43.57 N 10.14 E
Pietrelcina 68 41.12 N 14.51 E
Piet Retief 158 27.01 S 30.50 E
Pietrosu, Vârful ∧, Rom. 38 47.36 N 24.38 E
Pietrosu, Vârful ∧, Rom. 38 47.08 N 25.11 E
Pieve 64 45.46 N 10.45 E
Pieve d'Alpago 64 46.10 N 12.21 E
Pieve del Cairo 62 45.03 N 8.48 E
Pieve di Cadore 64 46.26 N 12.22 E
Pieve di Cento 64 44.43 N 11.18 E
Pieve di Soligo 64 45.53 N 12.10 E
Pieve di Teco 62 44.03 N 7.56 E
Pieve Fosciana 64 44.08 N 10.25 E
Pievepelago 64 44.12 N 10.37 E
Pieve Porto Morone 62 45.07 N 9.26 E
Pieve Santo Stefano 66 43.40 N 12.02 E
Piffard 210 42.50 N 77.51 W
Pigari 80 51.24 N 49.42 E
Pigeon, Mi., U.S. 190 43.49 N 83.16 W
Pigeon, Pa., U.S. 214 41.32 N 79.03 W
Pigeon ≃, Mb., Can. 184 52.15 N 97.00 W
Pigeon ≃, On., Can. 212 44.22 N 78.31 W
Pigeon ≃, N.A. 190 48.00 N 89.34 W
Pigeon ≃, U.S. 192 36.00 N 83.11 W
Pigeon ≃, U.S. 216 41.46 N 85.47 W
Pigeon ≃, Mi., U.S. 190 43.56 N 83.17 W
Pigeon ≃, Mi., U.S. 190 45.27 N 84.33 W
Pigeon ≃, Mi., U.S. 216 42.54 N 86.11 W
Pigeon Bay ⊂ 214 42.01 N 82.40 W
Pigeon Cove 207 42.40 N 70.38 W
Pigeon Creek ≃, Al., U.S. 194 31.20 N 86.42 W
Pigeon Creek ≃, In., U.S. 194 37.59 N 87.35 W
Pigeon Creek ≃, In., U.S. 216 41.41 N 85.17 W
Pigeon Creek ≃, Pa., U.S. 279b 40.12 N 79.55 W
Pigeon Creek ≃, Pa., U.S. 285 40.12 N 75.35 W
Pigeon Forge 192 35.47 N 83.33 W
Pigeon Lake ⊜, Ab., Can. 182 53.00 N 114.00 W
Pigeon Lake ⊜, On., Can. 212 44.30 N 78.30 W
Pigeon Run ≃ 285 40.06 N 75.35 W
Pigeon Swamp ≋ 276 40.23 N 74.29 W
Pigezhuang 105 39.39 N 116.15 E
Pigg ≃ 192 37.00 N 79.29 W
Piggott 194 36.22 N 90.11 W
Piggs Peak 158 25.38 S 31.15 E
Pigkawagan 116 7.12 N 124.32 E
Piglio 66 41.49 N 13.08 E
Pigna 62 43.56 N 7.40 E
Pignans 62 43.18 N 6.13 E
Pignataro Maggiore 68 41.11 N 14.10 E
Pignola 68 40.34 N 15.47 E
Pigs, Bay of → Cochinos, Bahía de ⊂ 240p 22.07 N 81.10 W
Pigüé 252 37.37 S 62.25 W
Pigŭm-do I 98 34.45 N 125.55 E
Pihama 172 39.30 S 173.56 E
Piha Passage ⩌ 174w 21.07 S 175.05 W
Pihāri 124 27.38 N 80.12 E
Pihlajavesi ⊜ 26 61.45 N 28.50 E
Pihlava 26 61.33 N 21.36 E
Pihtipudas 26 63.23 N 25.34 E
Pihuamo 234 19.15 N 103.23 W
P'ihyŏn 98 40.01 N 124.37 E
Piikkiö 26 60.26 N 22.31 E
Piippola 26 64.10 N 25.58 E
Pijijiapan 234 15.42 N 93.14 W
Pijnacker 52 52.02 N 4.27 E
Pijol, Pico ∧ 236 15.06 N 87.35 W
Pikal'ovo 76 59.31 N 34.06 E
Pikangikum 184 51.49 N 94.00 W
Pikangikum Lake ⊜ 184 51.48 N 94.00 W
Pike 210 42.33 N 78.09 W
Pike □6, Il., U.S. 219 39.36 N 90.48 W
Pike □6, Mo., U.S. 219 39.21 N 91.10 W
Pike □6, Oh., U.S. 218 39.05 N 83.06 W
Pike □6, Pa., U.S. 210 41.19 N 74.48 W
Pike ≃, N.A. 206 45.04 N 73.06 W
Pike ≃, Wi., U.S. 190 45.26 N 87.52 W
Pike, North Branch ≃ 190 45.30 N 88.01 W
Pike, South Branch ≃ 190 45.30 N 88.01 W
Pike Creek ≃, On., Can. 281 42.19 N 82.51 W
Pike Creek ≃, De., U.S. 285 39.42 N 75.42 W
Pike Lake ⊜ 212 44.46 N 76.21 W
Pikelot I 14 8.05 N 147.38 E
Pike Lowe ∧2 262 53.42 N 2.34 W
Pike Run ≃ 276 40.25 N 74.38 W
Pikes Peak 218 39.08 N 86.09 W
Pikes Peak ∧ 200 38.51 N 105.03 W
Pikes Rocks ∧2 214 41.56 N 79.24 W
Pikesville 208 39.22 N 76.43 W
Piketberg 158 32.54 S 18.46 E
Piketon 218 39.04 N 83.00 W
Piketown 208 40.23 N 76.45 W
Pikeville, Ky., U.S. 192 37.28 N 82.31 W
Pikeville, Tn., U.S. 194 35.36 N 85.11 W
Pikkola 265a 59.42 N 30.08 E
Pikou 98 39.24 N 122.20 E
Pikounda 152 0.33 N 16.42 E
Pikwitonei 184 55.35 N 97.09 W
Pila, Arg. 252 36.01 S 58.08 W
Pila, It. 62 45.41 N 7.18 E
Piła (Schneidemühl), Pol. 30 53.10 N 16.44 E
Piła □4 30 53.15 N 16.30 E
Pilanesberg ∧ 156 25.14 S 27.04 E
Pilanesberg Game Reserve ✢4 156 25.15 S 27.05 E
Pilão Arcado 250 9.56 S 42.29 W
Pilar, Arg. 252 31.41 S 63.54 W
Pilar, Arg. 252 31.27 S 61.15 W
Pilar, Arg. 258 34.27 S 58.54 W
Pilar, Bra. 250 9.36 S 35.56 W
Pilar, Bra. 287a 22.42 S 43.19 W
Pilar, Para. 252 26.52 S 58.23 W
Pilar, Pil. 116 11.29 N 123.00 E
Pilar, Pil. 116 9.52 N 126.06 E
Pilar □5 288 34.28 S 58.52 W
Pilar Bay ⊂ 116 11.34 N 123.00 E
Pilarcitos Creek ≃ 282 37.28 N 122.27 W
Pilarcitos Lake ⊜ 282 37.33 N 122.25 W
Pilar de Goiás 255 14.41 S 49.27 W
Pilar do Sul 255 23.49 S 47.42 W
Pilares 196 30.24 N 104.52 W
Pilas Group II 116 6.45 N 121.35 E
Pilas Island I 116 6.38 N 121.37 E
Pilatus ∧ 58 46.59 N 8.15 E
Pilawa 30 51.58 N 21.31 E
Pilaya ≃ 248 20.55 S 64.04 W
Pilcher Park ♦ 278 41.32 N 88.01 W
Pilchuck ≃ 224 47.55 N 122.02 W
Pilchuck Creek ≃ 224 48.12 N 122.13 W
Pilcomayo ≃ 18 25.21 S 57.42 W
Pilcomayo, Brazo Norte ≃ 252 24.56 S 58.16 W
Pilcomayo, Brazo Sur ≃ 252 24.56 S 58.16 W
Pil'dozero 24 65.43 N 33.28 E
Piles Creek ≃ 276 40.37 N 74.12 W
Pilga 162 21.29 S 119.25 E
Pilger 198 42.00 N 97.03 W
Pilgrim Gardens 285 39.57 N 75.19 W
Pilgrim Memorial Monument ⊥ 207 42.04 N 70.12 W
Pilgrims Hatch 260 51.38 N 0.17 E
Pilgrim's Rest 156 24.55 S 30.44 E
Pil'gyn 180 69.18 N 179.08 E
Pili 116 13.33 N 123.16 E
Pīlībhīt 124 28.38 N 79.48 E
Pilica ≃ 30 51.52 N 21.17 E
Pilipinas → Philippines □1 116 13.00 N 122.00 E
Pilis ⩘ 264c 47.37 N 18.59 E
Pilisborosjenő 264c 47.36 N 19.00 E
Pilkhua 124 28.43 N 77.39 E
Pillaro 246 1.10 S 78.32 W
Pillar Point ≻ 282 37.30 N 122.30 W
Pillar Point ≻1 212 43.59 N 76.09 W
Pillau → Baltijsk 76 54.39 N 19.55 E
Pilley's Island 186 49.31 N 55.44 W
Pilliga 166 30.21 S 148.54 E
Pillings Pond ⊜ 283 42.32 N 71.02 W
Pillon, Col du)(58 46.22 N 7.13 E
Pillow 208 40.38 N 76.48 W
Pillsbury Sound ⩌ 240m 18.20 N 64.49 W
Pil'na 80 55.33 N 45.55 E
Pílos 38 36.55 N 21.43 E
Pilot ∧ 166 36.45 S 148.13 E
Pilot Butte 184 50.28 N 104.25 W
Pilot Grove 194 38.52 N 92.54 W
Pilot Hill 226 38.50 N 121.02 W
Pilot Knob 194 37.37 N 90.38 W
Pilot Knob ∧, Ar., U.S. 194 35.42 N 93.57 W
Pilot Knob ∧, Id., U.S. 202 45.54 N 115.42 W
Pilot Mound 184 49.16 N 98.55 W
Pilot Mountain 192 36.23 N 80.28 W
Pilot Peak ∧, Nv., U.S. 204 41.02 N 114.06 W
Pilot Peak ∧, Nv., U.S. 204 38.21 N 117.58 W
Pilot Peak ∧, Wy., U.S. 202 44.58 N 109.53 W
Pilot Point, Ak., U.S. 180 57.34 N 157.35 W
Pilot Point, Tx., U.S. 196 33.23 N 96.57 W
Pilot Rock 202 45.29 N 118.49 W
Pilot Rock ∧ 200 35.09 N 109.53 W
Pilot Station 180 61.56 N 162.54 W
Pilottown 194 29.10 N 89.15 W
Pilpah Range ⩘ 166 20.23 S 138.34 E
Pilsen → Plzeň 60 49.45 N 13.23 E
Pilsensee ⊜ 60 48.01 N 11.11 E
Pilsting 60 48.42 N 12.39 E
Pilsum 52 53.29 N 7.04 E
Piltene 76 57.13 N 21.40 E
Pilu ≃ 110 19.33 N 97.24 E
Piluchang 107 29.13 N 105.37 E
Pil'ugino 80 53.25 N 52.26 E
Pilusi 106 32.05 N 120.05 E
Pilzno 30 49.59 N 21.17 E
Pim ≃ 74 61.18 N 71.57 E
Pima 200 32.53 N 109.49 W
Pimah 110 15.36 N 107.25 E
Pimba 166 31.15 S 136.47 E
Pimelles 50 47.50 N 4.10 E
Pimenta Bueno ≃ 248 11.39 S 61.11 W
Pimenteira, Vereda ≃ 250 9.58 S 42.46 W
Pimenteiras 250 6.14 S 41.25 W
Pimentel, Bra. 250 3.43 S 45.30 W
Pimentel, Perú 248 6.50 S 79.57 W
Pimlico Race Course ♦ 284b 39.21 N 76.40 W
Pimmit Hills 284c 38.54 N 77.12 W
Pimmit Run ≃ 284c 38.55 N 77.07 W
Pimu-Lendo 152 1.46 N 20.54 E
Pimville ✢8 273d 26.16 S 27.54 E
Pina 34 41.29 N 0.32 W
Pina ≃ 76 52.10 N 26.14 E
Pinacanauan ≃ 116 17.37 N 121.44 E
Pináculo, Cerro ∧ 254 50.45 S 72.16 W
Pinalón, Cerro ∧ 236 15.05 N 89.55 W
Pinamalayan 116 13.02 N 121.29 E
Pinang → George Town 114 5.25 N 100.20 E
Pinang □3 114 5.20 N 100.20 E
Pinang, Pulau I 114 5.23 N 100.15 E
Pinangah 112 5.12 N 116.50 E
Pınarbaşı, Tür. 130 41.36 N 33.07 E
Pınarbaşı, Tür. 130 38.44 N 36.24 E
Pinar del Río 240p 22.25 N 83.42 W
Pinar del Río □4 240p 22.30 N 83.45 W
Pinardville 188 42.59 N 71.30 W
Pınarhisar 130 41.37 N 27.30 E
Pınarlar 130 38.53 N 39.29 E
Pinas, Arg. 252 31.09 S 65.29 W
Piñas, Ec. 246 3.42 S 79.42 W
Piñas, Cerro ∧ 236 15.25 N 85.47 W
Pinatubo, Mount ∧ 116 15.08 N 120.21 E
Pinazo, Arroyo ≃ 288 34.24 S 58.48 W
Pinchbeck 42 52.48 N 0.09 W
Pincher Creek 182 49.29 N 113.57 W
Pinchi Lake ⊜ 182 54.35 N 124.20 W
Pinckney 216 42.27 N 83.56 W
Pinckney State Recreation Area ♦ 216 42.25 N 84.04 W
Pinckneyville 194 38.04 N 89.22 W
Pinconning 190 43.51 N 83.57 W
Pincourt 206 45.23 N 74.00 W
Pinčuga 86 58.23 N 96.59 E
Pińczów 30 50.32 N 20.35 E
Pindaíba, Ribeirão ≃ 255 14.18 S 51.45 W
Pindale 110 21.11 N 95.51 E
Pindamonhangaba 256 22.55 S 45.28 W
Pindar 162 28.29 S 115.48 E
Pindaré ≃ 250 3.17 S 44.47 W
Pindaré-Mirim 250 3.37 S 45.21 W
Pind Dādan Khān 123 32.35 N 73.03 E
Pinde → Píndhos Óros ⩘ 38 39.49 N 21.14 E
Pinder Point ≻ 192 26.28 N 78.39 W
Píndhos Óros (Pindus Mountains) ⩘ 38 39.49 N 21.14 E
Pindi Bhattiān 123 31.54 N 73.16 E
Pindiga 146 9.59 N 10.54 E
Pindi Gheb 123 33.14 N 72.16 E
Pindo → Píndhos Óros ⩘ 38 39.49 N 21.14 E
Pindobaçu 250 10.44 S 40.21 W
Pindorama de Goiás 250 10.55 S 47.40 W
Pinduši 24 62.56 N 34.35 E
Pindus Mountains → Píndhos Óros ⩘ 38 39.49 N 21.14 E
Pindwāra 120 24.48 N 73.04 E
Pine ≃, B.C., Can. 182 56.08 N 120.41 W
Pine ≃, Mb., Can. 184 52.00 N 100.09 W
Pine ≃, On., Can. 212 44.20 N 79.52 W
Pine ≃, Mi., U.S. 190 44.15 N 85.55 W
Pine ≃, Mi., U.S. 190 43.35 N 84.08 W
Pine ≃, Mi., U.S. 190 46.03 N 84.40 W
Pine ≃, Mi., U.S. 190 44.26 N 83.21 W
Pine ≃, Mi., U.S. 214 42.49 N 82.29 W
Pine ≃, Wi., U.S. 190 44.08 N 88.54 W
Pine ≃, Wi., U.S. 190 45.50 N 88.08 W
Pine ≃, Wi., U.S. 190 43.12 N 90.18 W
Pine Apple 194 31.52 N 86.59 W
Pine Banks Park ♦ 283 42.26 N 71.04 W
Pine Barrens ✢1 208 39.48 N 74.35 W
Pine Beach 206 45.32 N 73.57 W
Pine Bluff 194 34.13 N 92.00 W
Pine Bluffs 198 41.10 N 104.04 W
Pine Brook 276 40.52 N 74.20 W
Pine Brook ≃, U.S. 276 41.04 N 74.05 W
Pine Brook ≃, Ma., U.S. 283 42.00 N 70.47 W
Pine Brook ≃, N.J., U.S. 276 40.19 N 74.20 W
Pine Bush 210 41.36 N 74.17 W
Pine Castle 220 28.28 N 81.22 W
Pine City, Mn., U.S. 190 45.49 N 92.58 W
Pine City, N.Y., U.S. 210 42.02 N 76.52 W
Pinecliff Lake ⊜ 276 41.08 N 74.23 W
Pinecraft 220 27.19 N 82.30 W
Pine Creek 164 13.49 S 131.49 E
Pine Creek ≃, Ab., Can. 182 54.56 N 112.31 W
Pine Creek ≃, Ca., U.S. 204 40.40 N 120.46 W
Pine Creek ≃, Ca., U.S. 282 37.58 N 122.02 W
Pine Creek ≃, Nv., U.S. 204 40.36 N 116.10 W
Pine Creek ≃, Pa., U.S. 210 41.10 N 77.16 W
Pine Creek ≃, Pa., U.S. 279b 40.30 N 79.57 W
Pine Creek ≃, Pa., U.S. 285 40.05 N 75.37 W
Pine Creek, West Branch ≃ 210 41.43 N 77.38 W
Pine Creek Indian Reserve ✢4 184 52.03 N 100.14 W
Pine Creek Lake ⊜1 196 34.05 N 95.05 W
Pine Creek Point ≻ 276 41.07 N 73.16 W
Pine Crest, Fl., U.S. 220 28.01 N 82.32 W
Pinecrest, Va., U.S. 208 38.50 N 77.09 W
Pinecrest Lake ⊜ 226 38.12 N 119.58 W
Pine Crest Point ≻ 284a 42.52 N 79.11 W
Pinedale 200 42.52 N 109.51 W
Pine Falls 184 50.35 N 96.15 W
Pine Flat Lake ⊜1 226 36.52 N 119.18 W
Pinega 24 64.42 N 43.19 E
Pinega ≃ 24 64.08 N 41.54 E
Pine Glen 212 45.19 N 75.43 W
Pine Grove, On., Can. 275b 43.48 N 79.35 W
Pine Grove, Ca., U.S. 226 38.25 N 120.39 W
Pine Grove, Fl., U.S. 220 28.16 N 81.11 W
Pine Grove, N.J., U.S. 285 39.53 N 74.52 W
Pine Grove, Pa., U.S. 208 40.32 N 76.23 W
Pine Grove, W.V., U.S. 188 39.33 N 80.40 W
Pine Grove Mills 214 40.44 N 77.53 W
Pine Hill, Austl. 166 23.39 S 146.58 E
Pine Hill, Al., U.S. 194 31.58 N 87.35 W
Pine Hill, N.J., U.S. 208 39.47 N 74.59 W
Pine Hill, N.Y., U.S. 210 42.08 N 74.29 W
Pinehill, Tx., U.S. 222 32.06 N 94.36 W
Pine Hills 220 28.33 N 81.27 W
Pinehouse Lake 184 55.31 N 106.36 W
Pinehouse Lake ⊜ 184 55.32 N 106.35 W
Pinehurst, Ga., U.S. 192 32.11 N 83.45 W
Pinehurst, Id., U.S. 202 45.15 N 116.20 W
Pinehurst, Ma., U.S. 207 42.31 N 71.13 W
Pinehurst, N.Y., U.S. 284a 42.44 N 78.57 W
Pinehurst, N.C., U.S. 192 35.11 N 79.28 W
Pinehurst, Tx., U.S. 222 30.10 N 95.41 W
Pinehurst Lake ⊜ 182 54.39 N 111.25 W
Pine Island, Mn., U.S. 190 44.12 N 92.38 W
Pine Island, N.Y., U.S. 210 41.17 N 74.27 W
Pine Island I 220 26.35 N 82.06 W
Pine Island Bay ⊂ 9 74.50 S 102.05 W
Pine Island Bayou ≃ 194 30.10 N 94.07 W
Pine Island Creek ≃ 283 42.47 N 70.48 W
Pine Island Dam ✢6 214 40.08 N 80.43 W
Pine Island Sound ⩌ 220 26.33 N 82.10 W
Pine Lake, In., U.S. 216 41.38 N 86.45 W
Pine Lake, Ma., U.S. 283 42.23 N 71.27 W
Pine Lake ⊜, On., Can. 212 44.57 N 79.27 W
Pine Lake ⊜, Mi., U.S. 281 42.35 N 83.20 W
Pine Lake ⊜, N.Y., U.S. 210 43.12 N 74.31 W
Pineland 194 31.14 N 93.58 W
Pine Lawn 219 38.41 N 90.16 W
Pinellas □6 220 27.53 N 82.43 W
Pinellas, Point ≻ 220 27.42 N 82.38 W
Pinellas Park 220 27.50 N 82.41 W
Pine Marsh ≋ 276 40.37 N 73.34 W
Pine Meadow Lake ⊜ 276 41.11 N 74.07 W
Pine Mountain ∧, U.S. 192 36.55 N 83.20 W
Pine Mountain ∧, Ca., U.S. 226 35.41 N 121.05 W
Pine Mountain ∧, Ca., U.S. 280 34.13 N 117.54 W
Pine Mountain ∧, Ct., U.S. 207 41.58 N 72.56 W
Pine Mountain ∧, Ga., U.S. 192 32.51 N 84.47 W
Pine Mountain ∧, Or., U.S. 202 43.47 N 120.54 W
Pine Mountain ∧, Wy., U.S. 200 41.02 N 109.01 W
Pine Nut Mountains ⩘ 226 39.00 N 119.25 W
Pine Orchard Meadows 284b 39.17 N 76.52 W
Pine Pass)(182 55.22 N 122.40 W
Pine Plains 210 41.59 N 73.40 W
Pine Point, Austl. 168b 34.34 S 137.52 E
Pine Point, N.T., Can. 176 61.01 N 114.15 W
Pine Point Park ♦ 275b 43.43 N 79.33 W
Pine Portage Dam ✢6 176 49.18 N 88.19 W
Pine Prairie 194 30.47 N 92.25 W
Piner 218 38.50 N 84.32 W
Pine Rest 283 42.23 N 71.26 W
Pine Ridge, Pa., U.S. 285 39.55 N 75.22 W
Pine Ridge, S.D., U.S. 198 43.01 N 102.33 W
Pine Ridge, Va., U.S. 284c 38.52 N 77.14 W
Pine Ridge ∧ 198 42.40 N 103.00 W
Pine Ridge Estates 276 41.02 N 73.41 W
Pine Ridge Indian Reservation ✢4 198 43.25 N 102.21 W
Pine River, Mb., Can. 184 51.47 N 100.32 W
Pine River, Mn., U.S. 190 46.43 N 94.24 W
Piñero 258 34.32 S 58.45 W
Pinerolo 62 44.53 N 7.21 E
Piñeros, Isla I 240m 18.15 N 65.35 W
Pinerovka 80 51.34 N 43.04 E
Pine Run ≃ 279b 40.37 N 79.35 W
Pines ≃ 283 42.27 N 70.58 W
Pines, Isle of → Juventud, Isla de la I 240p 21.40 N 82.50 W
Pines, Lake O' The ⊜1 222 32.46 N 94.35 W
Pines, Point of ≻ 283 42.26 N 70.58 W
Pine Shores 220 27.17 N 82.32 W
Pines Lake ⊜ 276 41.00 N 74.16 W
Pines Run ≃ 285 39.50 N 75.05 W
Pine Swamp Knob ∧ 188 39.33 N 79.31 W
Pineto 66 42.36 N 14.04 E
Pinetop 200 34.07 N 109.56 W
Pinetops 192 35.47 N 77.38 W
Pinetown 158 29.52 S 30.46 E
Pine Tree Hill ∧ 114 3.43 N 101.42 E
Pine Valley, Md., U.S. 284b 39.26 N 76.39 W
Pine Valley, N.Y., U.S. 210 42.14 N 76.51 W
Pine Valley V 204 38.25 N 113.40 W
Pine Village 216 40.27 N 87.15 W
Pineville, Ky., U.S. 192 36.45 N 83.41 W
Pineville, La., U.S. 194 31.19 N 92.26 W
Pineville, Mo., U.S. 194 36.35 N 94.23 W
Pineville, N.C., U.S. 192 35.04 N 80.53 W

Symbols in the index entries represent the broad categories identified in the key at the right. Symbols with superior numbers (⩘1) identify subcategories (see complete key on page *I · 1).*

Symbole im Register stellen die rechts im Schlüssel erklärten Kategorien dar. Symbole mit hochgestellten Ziffern (⩘1) bezeichnen Unterabteilungen einer Kategorie (vgl. vollständiger Schlüssel auf Seite *I · 1).*

Los símbolos incluídos en el texto del índice representan las grandes categorías identificadas con la clave a la derecha. Los símbolos con numeros en su parte superior (⩘1) identifican las subcategorías (véase la clave completa en la página *I · 1).*

Les symboles de l'index représentent les catégories indiquées dans la légende à droite. Les symboles suivis d'un indice (⩘1) représentent des sous-catégories (voir légende complète à la page *I · 1).*

Os símbolos incluídos no texto do índice representam as grandes categorias identificadas com a chave à direita. Os símbolos com números em sua parte superior (⩘1) identificam as subcategorias (veja-se a chave completa à página *I · 1).*

∧ Mountain	Berg	Montaña	Montagne	Montanha
⩘ Mountains	Gebirge	Montañas	Montagnes	Montanhas
)(Pass	Paß	Paso	Col	Passo
V Valley, Canyon	Tal, Cañon	Valle, Cañón	Vallée, Canyon	Vale, Canhão
⩦ Plain	Ebene	Llano	Plaine	Planície
≻ Cape	Kap	Cabo	Cap	Cabo
I Island	Insel	Isla	Île	Ilha
II Islands	Inseln	Islas	Îles	Ilhas
⊥ Other Topographic Features	Andere Topographische Objekte	Otros Elementos Topográficos	Autres données topographiques	Outros acidentes topográficos

Pine-Pluc I · 137

ESPAÑOL — Nombre | Página | Lat.°′ | Long.°′ W = Oeste
FRANÇAIS — Nom | Page | Lat.°′ | Long.°′ W = Ouest
PORTUGUÊS — Nome | Página | Lat.°′ | Long.°′ W = Oeste

Nombre / Nom / Nome	Página / Page	Lat.°′	Long.°′
Pineville, Pa., U.S.	208	40.18 N	75.00 W
Pineville, W.V., U.S.	192	37.34 N	81.32 W
Pinewood, Fl., U.S.	220	25.53 N	80.14 W
Pinewood, S.C., U.S.	192	33.44 N	80.27 W
Piney	50	48.22 N	4.20 E
Piney ≃	194	35.49 N	87.33 W
Piney Branch ≃	284c	38.56 N	77.18 W
Piney Creek ≃, Tx., U.S.	222	31.03 N	94.34 W
Piney Creek ≃, Wy., U.S.	202	44.34 N	106.32 W
Piney Fork	214	40.15 N	80.50 W
Piney Point	222	29.46 N	95.31 W
Piney Point ≻	208	38.08 N	76.32 W
Piney Run ≃	284c	38.58 N	77.17 W
Piney Woods	194	32.03 N	89.59 W
Pinfold	262	53.36 N	2.55 W
Ping ≃, Thai	110	15.42 N	100.09 E
Ping ≃, Zhg.	100	25.59 N	115.07 E
Pinga	154	1.01 S	28.42 E
Ping'an, Zhg.	89	45.20 N	123.42 E
Ping'an, Zhg.	104	41.11 N	123.26 E
Ping'an, Zhg.	107	30.36 N	104.42 E
Ping'anbu	98	41.45 N	116.13 E
Ping'ancheng	105	40.03 N	117.48 E
Ping'andi	104	42.34 N	121.52 E
Pingaring	162	32.45 S	118.37 E
Pingba, Zhg.	100	31.19 N	113.18 E
Pingba, Zhg.	102	26.22 N	106.09 E
Pingchang	102	31.35 N	107.03 E
Pingchao	106	32.07 N	120.45 E
Pingding	98	37.48 N	113.37 E
Pingdingpu	104	42.22 N	123.55 E
Pingdingshan, Zhg.	98	41.26 N	124.45 E
Pingdingshan, Zhg.	100	33.45 N	113.17 E
Pingding Shan ∧	89	46.38 N	128.27 E
Pingdu	98	36.47 N	119.54 E
Pingelap I[1]	14	6.13 N	160.42 E
Pingelly	162	32.32 S	117.05 E
Pingfang, Zhg.	100	30.07 N	113.48 E
Pingfang, Zhg.	104	41.17 N	120.40 E
Pingfang, Zhg.	104	41.28 N	120.48 E
Pingfang, Zhg.	104	42.14 N	120.38 E
Pingfang, Zhg.	104	42.27 N	120.38 E
Pingfang, Zhg.	271a	39.56 N	116.33 E
Pingfangdu	104	41.45 N	121.12 E
Pingfangzi	104	41.31 N	121.21 E
Pinggau	61	47.27 N	16.04 E
Pinggu	105	40.09 N	117.07 E
Pingguo	102	23.19 N	107.39 E
Pinghai, Zhg.	100	25.14 N	119.15 E
Pinghai, Zhg.	100	22.39 N	114.53 E
Pinghe, Zhg.	100	24.25 N	117.22 E
Pinghe, Zhg.	102	22.51 N	102.30 E
Pinghe ≃	100	24.25 N	116.36 E
P'inghsiang → Pingxiang	102	22.09 N	106.43 E
Pinghu, Zhg.	100	26.46 N	118.48 E
Pinghu, Zhg.	100	30.56 N	115.22 E
Pinghu, Zhg.	100	22.42 N	114.08 E
Pinghu, Zhg.	106	30.42 N	121.01 E
Pingjiang	100	28.44 N	113.34 E
Pingjing	105	39.20 N	116.06 E
Pinglan	100	22.22 N	113.27 E
Pingle, Zhg.	102	24.37 N	110.40 E
Pingle, Zhg.	102	24.31 N	106.59 E
Pingli	102	32.19 N	109.21 E
Pingliang	102	35.32 N	106.41 E
Pinglidian	98	37.17 N	119.59 E
Pingling	100	23.39 N	114.23 E
Pinglucheng	102	39.50 N	112.19 E
Pingluo	102	38.57 N	106.35 E
Pingluopu	104	41.56 N	123.20 E
Pingnan, Zhg.	100	26.56 N	119.02 E
Pingnan, Zhg.	102	23.30 N	110.30 E
Pingqiao	100	33.24 N	119.13 E
Pingquan	98	40.59 N	118.34 E
Pingrup	162	33.32 S	118.31 E
Ping Shan, Zhg.	271d	22.27 N	114.00 E
Pingshan, Zhg.	100	25.36 N	117.52 E
Pingshan, Zhg.	100	23.26 N	113.15 E
Pingshan, Zhg.	100	22.43 N	114.22 E
Pingshan, Zhg.	102	38.15 N	114.10 E
Pingshang	98	35.11 N	119.07 E
Pingshi, Zhg.	100	32.32 N	113.03 E
Pingshi, Zhg.	100	25.20 N	113.02 E
Pingshui	100	29.53 N	120.38 E
Pingtaizi	105	40.44 N	116.25 E
Pingtan, Zhg.	100	25.31 N	119.47 E
Pingtan, Zhg.	100	23.04 N	114.38 E
Pingtan, Zhg.	107	29.50 N	105.56 E
Pingtan, Zhg.	107	29.38 N	105.16 E
Pingtan Dao I	100	25.33 N	119.48 E
Pingtang	102	25.50 N	107.19 E
Pingtian	100	25.19 N	113.31 E
P'ingtung	100	22.40 N	120.29 E
Pingües, Cayos II	240p	20.47 N	78.15 W
Pingwang	106	30.59 N	120.38 E
Pingwu	102	32.29 N	104.37 E
Pingxiang, Zhg.	100	27.38 N	113.50 E
Pingxiang, Zhg.	102	22.09 N	106.43 E
Pingyang, Zhg.	89	48.13 N	124.23 E
Pingyang, Zhg.	100	27.41 N	120.33 E
Pingyao, Zhg.	102	37.16 N	112.09 E
Pingyao, Zhg.	106	30.24 N	119.58 E
Pingyi	98	35.34 N	117.37 E
Pingyin	98	36.19 N	116.22 E
Pingyu	100	32.57 N	114.41 E
Pingyuan, Zhg.	98	37.11 N	116.25 E
Pingyuan, Zhg.	100	24.36 N	115.54 E
Pingzhai	102	24.07 N	104.22 E
Pingzhuang	98	42.03 N	119.22 E
Pinhal	256	22.12 S	46.45 W
Pinhal, Ribeirão do ≃	256	22.42 S	46.42 W
Pinhal Novo	34	38.38 N	8.55 W
Pinhalzinho	256	22.46 S	46.36 W
Pinhão	250	10.34 S	37.44 W
Pinheiral	256	22.31 S	43.59 W
Pinheirinhos	256	22.26 S	44.59 W
Pinheiro	250	2.31 S	45.05 W
Pinheiro de Loures	266c	38.50 N	9.12 W
Pinheiro Machado	252	31.34 S	53.23 W
Pinheiros, Bra.	255	18.21 S	40.14 W
Pinheiros, Bra.	256	22.32 S	44.54 W
Pinheiros ≃	287b	23.32 S	46.44 W
Pinhel	34	40.46 N	7.04 W
Pinhoe	42	50.44 N	3.27 W
Pinhuã ≃	248	6.21 S	65.00 W
Pini, Pulau I	110	0.08 N	98.40 E
Pinillos	246	8.55 N	74.28 W
Piniós ≃	38	39.54 N	22.45 E
Pinitos, Sierra de ⩘	200	31.08 N	110.50 W
Pinjar, Lake ⊜	168a	31.38 S	115.49 E
Pinjarra	168a	32.37 S	115.53 E
Pinjor Garden ♦	123	30.47 N	76.47 E
Pinka ≃	61	47.00 N	16.35 E
Pinkafeld	61	47.22 N	16.07 E
Pinkiang → Harbin	89	45.45 N	126.41 E
Pinlaung	110	20.08 N	96.47 E
Pinlebu	110	24.05 N	95.21 E
Pinn ≃	260	51.31 N	0.29 W
Pinnacle ∧, N.Z.	172	41.49 S	173.17 E
Pinnacle ∧, N.Y., U.S.	188	43.13 N	74.23 W
Pinnacle ∧, Va., U.S.	188	39.08 N	78.26 W
Pinnacle Buttes ∧	202	43.44 N	109.57 W
Pinnacle Island I	180	60.12 N	172.46 W
Pinnacle Peak ∧	224	46.45 N	121.43 W
Pinnacles National Monument ♦	226	36.28 N	121.19 W
Pinnaroo	166	35.16 S	140.55 E
Pinneberg	52	53.40 N	9.47 E
Pinner ➜[8]	260	51.36 N	0.23 W
Pino, Sierra del ⩘	196	28.15 N	103.03 W
Pin Oak Creek ≃	222	31.57 N	96.28 W
Pinocchio	66	43.35 N	13.30 E
Pinochle Peak ∧	224	45.43 N	123.36 W
Pinole	226	38.00 N	122.17 W
Pinole Creek ≃	282	38.01 N	122.18 W
Pinole Point ≻	282	38.01 N	122.22 W
Pinole Ridge ∧	282	37.59 N	122.15 W
Pinos	234	22.18 N	101.34 W
Pinos, Mount ∧	228	34.50 N	119.09 W
Pinos, Point ≻	226	36.38 N	121.56 W
Pinos Puente	34	37.15 N	3.45 W
Pinotepa de Don Luis	234	16.25 N	97.55 W
Pinrang	112	3.48 S	119.38 E
Pins, Île de → Juventud, Isla de la I	240p	21.40 N	82.50 W
Pins, Île des I	175f	22.37 S	167.30 E
Pins, Pointe aux ≻	214	42.15 N	81.51 W
Pins, Rivière des ≃	206	46.01 N	72.03 W
Pinsk	76	52.07 N	26.04 E
Pinson	194	33.41 N	86.41 W
Pinsot	62	45.21 N	6.06 E
Pinta, Isla I	246a	0.35 N	90.44 W
Pintada Arroyo ∨	196	34.53 N	104.39 W
Pintado	258	33.50 S	56.18 W
Pintado ≃	255	13.33 S	50.16 W
Pintado, Arroyo de ≃	258	34.08 S	56.14 W
Pintado, Cuchilla del ⩘[2]	258	34.12 S	56.25 W
Pintados	248	20.37 S	69.38 W
Pintados, Salar de ≡	248	20.30 S	69.42 W
Pintasan	112	5.26 N	117.43 E
Pinteus	266c	38.52 N	9.09 W
Pintlala Creek ≃	194	32.21 N	86.30 W
Pinto Butte ∧	184	49.22 N	107.25 W
Pinto Creek ≃, Ab., Can.	182	53.51 N	117.35 W
Pinto Creek ≃, Sk., Can.	184	49.40 N	106.42 W
Pintos, Arroyo de ≃	258	33.55 S	56.51 W
Pintos Negreiros	256	22.18 S	45.13 W
Pintoyacu ≃, Ec.	246	2.07 S	76.03 W
Pintoyacu ≃, Perú	246	3.35 S	73.55 W
Pinturas ≃	254	46.35 S	70.18 W
Pintuyan	116	9.57 N	125.15 E
Pin'ug	24	60.15 N	47.48 E
Pinukpuk	116	17.35 N	121.22 E
Pinwherry	44	55.09 N	4.50 W
Pinxton	44	53.06 N	1.19 W
Pinzano al Tagliamento	64	46.11 N	12.57 E
Pinzgau ∨	64	47.15 N	12.40 E
Pinzón, Isla I	246a	0.36 S	90.40 W
Piobbico	66	43.35 N	12.31 E
Pioche	204	37.55 N	114.27 W
Pio IX	250	6.50 S	40.37 W
Piolenc	62	44.11 N	4.46 E
Piombino	66	42.55 N	10.32 E
Piombino, Canale di ꭒ	66	42.53 N	10.30 E
Pioneer, Austl.	162	31.48 S	121.43 E
Pioneer, Ca., U.S.	226	38.25 N	120.33 W
Pioneer, Oh., U.S.	216	41.40 N	84.33 W
Pioneer Mine	182	50.46 N	122.46 W
Pioneer Mountains ⩘	202	45.40 N	113.00 W
Pioneer Park ♦	273d	26.14 S	28.04 E
Pioner, ostrov I	74	79.50 N	92.30 E
Pionerskij	76	54.57 N	20.20 E
Pionierbivak	164	2.16 S	138.02 E
Pionki	30	51.30 N	21.27 E
Pio Pico State Historical Monument ♦	280	33.59 N	118.04 W
Piopio	172	38.28 S	175.01 E
Pioppo	70	38.03 N	13.14 E
Piora, Mount ∧	164	6.45 S	146.00 E
Pioraco	66	43.11 N	12.59 E
Piorini ≃	246	3.23 S	63.30 W
Piorini, Lago ⊜	246	3.34 S	63.15 W
Piotrków Trybunalski	30	51.25 N	19.42 E
Piotrków Trybunalski □[4]	30	51.30 N	19.45 E
Piotta	58	46.31 N	8.40 E
Pio V. Corpus (Limbujan)	116	11.53 N	124.03 E
Piove di Sacco	64	45.18 N	12.02 E
Piovene-Rocchette	64	45.45 N	11.25 E
Pio XII	250	3.53 S	45.17 W
Pipa	107	29.07 N	105.05 E
Pipalkoti	124	30.26 N	79.27 E
Pipanaco, Salar de ≡	252	28.07 S	66.25 W
Pīpār	120	26.23 N	73.32 E
Piparia	124	22.45 N	78.21 E
Pīpar Road	120	26.27 N	73.27 E
Pipas	152	14.56 S	12.12 E
Pipe Creek ≃, In., U.S.	194	40.08 N	85.52 W
Pipe Creek ≃, In., U.S.	216	40.45 N	86.13 W
Pipe Creek ≃, In., U.S.	218	39.26 N	85.06 W
Piper City	216	40.45 N	88.11 W
Pipe Spring National Monument ♦	200	36.43 N	112.33 W
Pipestem Creek ≃	198	46.54 N	98.43 W
Pipestem State Park ♦	192	37.32 N	81.00 W
Pipestone	198	44.00 N	96.19 W
Pipestone ≃	176	52.53 N	89.23 W
Pipestone Creek ≃, Can.	184	49.42 N	100.45 W
Pipestone Creek ≃, Mi., U.S.	216	42.04 N	86.24 W
Pipestone National Monument ♦	198	44.00 N	96.18 W
Pipi ≃	146	7.27 N	22.48 E
Pipinas	258	35.32 S	57.20 W
Piping Brook ≃	276	41.08 N	73.37 W
Pipiriki	172	39.29 S	175.03 E
Piplān	123	32.17 N	71.21 E
Piplūn	126	23.21 N	88.07 E
Pipmuacan, Réservoir ⊜[1]	186	49.35 N	70.30 W
Pipri	124	23.58 N	82.40 E
Pipriac	28	47.49 N	1.57 W
Piqiang	85	40.20 N	77.38 E
Piqiao	106	31.34 N	119.27 E
Piqua	218	40.08 N	84.14 W
Piquet Carneiro	250	5.48 S	39.25 W
Piquete	256	22.36 S	45.11 W
Piquete, Ribeirão ≃	256	22.36 S	45.01 W
Piquiri ≃, Bra.	248	17.39 S	55.09 W
Piquiri ≃, Bra.	248	17.18 S	56.44 W
Piquiri ≃, Bra.	252	24.03 S	54.14 W
Pira	150	8.30 N	1.44 E
Piracaia	256	23.03 S	46.21 W
Piracanjuba	255	17.18 S	49.01 W
Piracanjuba ≃	255	18.14 S	48.48 W
Piracão ≃	287a	23.02 S	43.36 W
Piracicaba	255	22.43 S	47.38 W
Piracicaba ≃	255	22.36 S	48.19 W
Piraçununga	255	21.59 S	47.25 W
Piracuruca	250	3.56 S	41.42 W
Pirae	174s	17.32 S	149.33 W
Piraeus → Piraiévs	38	37.57 N	23.38 E
Pirahmet	130	38.11 N	39.51 E
Piraí	256	22.38 S	43.54 W
Piraí ≃	256	22.28 S	43.50 W
Piraí do Sul	252	24.31 S	49.56 W
Piraiévs (Piraeus)	38	37.57 N	23.38 E
Piraino	70	38.10 N	14.52 E
Piraju	255	23.12 S	49.23 W
Pirajuba	255	19.54 S	48.42 W
Pirajucara, Ribeirão ≃	287b	23.34 S	46.43 W
Pirajuí	255	21.59 S	49.29 W
Pirakata	126	22.34 N	87.11 E
Piramida, gora ∧	88	54.15 N	95.45 E
Piramidal'nyj, pik ∧	85	39.34 N	69.57 E
Pirámide de Cuicuilco ⊥	286a	19.18 N	99.11 W
Pirámide de Santa Cecilia ⊥	286a	19.33 N	99.09 W
Pirámide de Tenayuca ⊥	286a	19.32 N	99.11 W
Piram Island I	120	21.36 N	72.41 E
Piran	36	45.32 N	13.34 E
Piraña, Arroyo ≃	288	34.24 S	58.30 W
Pirané	252	25.43 S	59.06 W
Piranga	255	20.41 S	43.18 W
Pirangaí	256	22.34 S	44.37 W
Piranguçu	256	22.31 S	45.30 W
Piranguinho	256	22.24 S	45.32 W
Piranhas	255	16.31 S	51.51 W
Piranhas ≃, Bra.	250	5.15 S	36.45 W
Piranhas ≃, Bra.	250	8.40 S	49.28 W
Piranhas ≃, Bra.	250	5.56 S	48.15 W
Piranji ≃	250	4.23 S	37.48 W
Pīrān Shahr	128	36.41 N	45.08 E
Pirapemas	250	3.43 S	44.14 W
Pirapetinga ≃	256	21.37 S	42.32 W
Pirapetinga, Ribeirão ≃	256	21.49 S	43.36 W
Pirapó ≃	255	22.30 S	52.01 W
Pirapora	255	17.21 S	44.56 W
Pirapora do Bom Jesus	256	23.24 S	47.00 W
Pirapora do Bom Jesus □[7]	287b	23.24 S	46.56 W
Piraputanga	255	20.26 S	55.32 W
Piracuara	252	25.26 S	49.04 W
Piracuê ≃	287a	23.01 S	43.37 W
Pirarajá	252	33.44 S	54.45 W
Pirata, Monte ∧[2]	240m	18.06 N	65.33 W
Pirate Creek ≃	282	37.33 N	121.52 W
Piratinga ≃	255	15.41 S	46.07 W
Piratini	252	31.27 S	53.06 W
Piratini ≃	252	28.06 S	55.27 W
Piratininga	287a	22.57 S	43.04 W
Piratininga, Lagoa ⊂	256	22.57 S	43.05 W
Piratuba	252	27.27 S	51.48 W
Piratuba, Lago ⊂	250	1.37 N	50.10 W
Piratucu ≃	250	1.59 S	56.58 W
Piraúba	256	21.17 S	43.02 W
Piraube, Lac ⊜	186	50.33 N	71.42 W
Piray ≃	248	16.32 S	63.45 W
Piraziz	130	40.58 N	38.08 E
Pirbright	260	51.18 N	0.39 W
Pirdop	38	42.42 N	24.11 E
Pirenópolis	255	15.51 S	48.57 W
Pires, Ribeirão ≃	287b	23.43 S	46.25 W
Pires do Rio	255	17.18 S	48.17 W
Pírgos	38	37.41 N	21.28 E
Piriá	250	1.40 S	50.02 W
Piriápolis	252	34.54 S	55.17 W
Piribebuy	252	25.29 S	57.03 W
Pirin ⩘	38	41.40 N	23.30 E
Pirinççi ➜[8]	267b	41.10 N	28.50 E
Pirineos → Pyrenees ⩘	34	42.40 N	1.00 E
Piripiri	250	4.16 S	41.47 W
Piritiba	250	11.44 S	40.34 W
Píritu, Ven.	246	11.22 N	69.08 W
Píritu, Ven.	246	9.23 N	69.12 W
Pirituba ➜[8]	287b	23.29 S	46.43 W
Pīr Mahal	123	30.46 N	72.26 E
Pirmasens	56	49.12 N	7.36 E
Pirna	54	50.58 N	13.56 E
Piroči	82	55.04 N	38.57 E
Pirogovskij	265b	55.59 N	37.44 E
Pirogovskoje vodochranilišče ⊜[1]	82	55.58 N	37.40 E
Pirojpur	126	22.34 N	89.59 E
Pirón ≃	34	41.23 N	4.31 W
Pirongia	172	38.00 S	175.12 E
Pirot	38	43.09 N	22.35 E
Pirovano	252	36.30 S	61.34 W
Pirovskoje	86	57.37 N	92.16 E
Pīr Panjāl Range ⩘	123	33.37 N	74.32 E
Pirpirituba	250	6.46 S	35.30 W
Pirreşit Tepe ∧	84	38.56 N	43.55 E
Pirsaat	84	39.54 N	49.24 E
Pirsaatçay ≃	84	39.53 N	49.19 E
Pirtleville	200	31.22 N	109.34 W
Piru, Indon.	164	3.04 S	128.12 E
Piru, Ca., U.S.	228	34.25 N	118.48 W
Piru, Lake ⊜[1]	228	34.30 N	118.45 W
Piru, Teluk ⊂	164	3.10 S	128.08 E
Piru Creek ≃	228	34.23 N	118.47 W
Pisa	66	43.43 N	10.23 E
Pisa □[4]	66	43.25 N	10.43 E
Pisa ∧[2]	26	63.13 N	28.18 E
Pisa ≃	30	53.15 N	21.52 E
Pisa, Certosa di ʊ[1]	66	43.45 N	10.31 E
Pisa, Mount ∧	172	44.52 S	169.11 E
Pisagua	248	19.36 S	70.13 W
Pisam-bong ∧	98	40.41 N	126.34 E
Pisang, Pulau I	164	1.23 S	128.55 E
Pisarevka	78	49.53 N	40.12 E
Pisarve	272c	19.06 N	73.05 E
Pisau, Tanjong ≻	116	6.04 N	118.03 E
Piščalje	80	58.14 N	48.42 E
Piscasaw Creek ≃	216	42.16 N	88.49 W
Piscataway	210	40.29 N	74.23 W
Piscataway Creek ≃, Md., U.S.	208	38.42 N	77.02 W
Piscataway Creek ≃, Va., U.S.	208	37.54 N	76.50 W
Pişchia	38	45.55 N	21.20 E
Pisciotta	68	40.06 N	15.14 E
Pisco	248	13.42 S	76.13 W
Pisco ≃	248	13.42 S	76.15 W
Pişcolt	38	47.35 N	22.18 E
Piscovo	80	57.11 N	40.32 E
Piseco Lake ⊜	210	43.23 N	74.36 W
Písek	30	49.19 N	14.10 E
Pisgah, Md., U.S.	208	38.32 N	77.08 W
Pisgah, Oh., U.S.	218	39.19 N	84.22 W
Pisgah Forest	192	35.15 N	82.42 W
Pishan	120	37.37 N	78.18 E
Pishchana	78	48.08 N	29.44 E
Pishchane, Ukr.	78	49.44 N	31.50 E
Pishchane, Ukr.	83	49.34 N	37.51 E
Pishchanka	78	48.12 N	28.53 E
Pishīn	120	30.35 N	67.00 E
Pishīn Lora (Lowrah) ≃	120	29.09 N	64.55 E
Pisidia □[9]	130	37.30 N	31.00 E
Pisinemo	200	32.02 N	112.18 W
Pising	112	5.05 S	121.54 E
Piskivka	78	50.42 N	29.38 E
Pisky, Ukr.	78	50.23 N	33.27 E
Pisky, Ukr.	83	49.26 N	38.59 E
Pisky-Rad'kivs'ki	83	49.17 N	37.36 E
Pismo Beach	226	35.08 N	120.38 W
Pišnur	80	57.47 N	47.58 E
Piso, Lake ⊜	150	6.48 N	11.17 W
Pisogne	64	45.48 N	10.06 E
Pisqui ≃	248	7.45 S	75.01 W
Pissila	150	13.10 N	0.49 W
Pissos	32	44.19 N	0.47 W
Pistakee Highlands	216	42.25 N	88.11 W
Pistakee Lake ⊜	216	42.23 N	88.12 W
Pisticci	68	40.23 N	16.34 E
Pistoia	66	43.55 N	10.54 E
Pistoia □[4]	64	43.58 N	10.50 E
Pistolet Bay ⊂	186	51.32 N	55.50 W
Pistuk Peak ∧	180	59.43 N	159.42 W
Pisuerga ≃	34	41.33 N	4.52 W
Pisz	30	53.38 N	21.49 E
Pit ≃	204	40.45 N	122.22 W
Pit, North Fork ≃	204	41.28 N	120.33 W
Pit, South Fork ≃	204	41.28 N	120.33 W
Pita	150	11.05 N	12.24 W
Pital	246	2.16 N	75.49 W
Pitalito	246	1.51 N	76.02 W
Pitampura Kālan ➜[8]	272a	28.42 N	77.08 E
Pitanga	252	24.46 S	51.44 W
Pitangueiras	255	21.02 S	48.13 W
Pitangueiras, Ribeirão das ≃	256	21.27 S	44.27 W
Pitangui	255	19.40 S	44.54 W
Pitcairn	279b	40.24 N	79.46 W
Pitcairn □[2], Oc.	6	25.04 S	130.05 W
Pitcairn □[2], Oc.	174e	25.04 S	130.05 W
Pitcher	210	42.35 N	75.52 W
Pitch Place	260	51.16 N	0.36 W
Piteå	26	65.20 N	21.30 E
Piteälven ≃	24	65.14 N	21.32 E
Piteglio	66	44.01 N	10.46 E
Pitelino	80	54.34 N	41.49 E
Piterka	80	50.42 N	47.27 E
Piteşti	38	44.52 N	24.52 E
Pithapuram	122	17.07 N	82.16 E
Pithara	162	30.24 S	116.40 E
Pithiviers	50	48.10 N	2.15 E
Pithorāgarh	124	29.35 N	80.13 E
Piti, Lagoa ⊜	158	26.34 S	32.53 E
Pitigliano	66	42.38 N	11.40 E
Pitim	80	53.12 N	42.21 E
Pitinga ≃	246	1.32 S	59.49 W
Pitiquito	232	30.42 N	112.02 W
Pitjantjatjara Lands ➜[4]	162	27.00 S	130.30 E
Pitk'aranta	24	61.34 N	31.27 E
Pitkas Point	180	62.02 N	163.17 W
Pitlochry	46	56.43 N	3.45 W
Pitman	208	39.43 N	75.07 W
Pitman Airport ⊠	285	39.45 N	75.08 W
Pitmedden	46	57.20 N	2.11 W
Pitner Ditch ≅	216	41.14 N	86.53 W
Pitogo	116	10.08 N	124.33 E
Pitomača	36	45.57 N	17.14 E
Pitou, Zhg.	100	25.01 N	114.35 E
Pitou, Zhg.	100	23.34 N	116.05 E
Pitou, Zhg.	100	24.26 N	114.22 E
Pitrufquén	254	38.59 S	72.39 W
Pitsea	260	51.34 N	0.31 E
Pitseng	158	28.58 S	28.16 E
Pitsford Reservoir ⊜[1]	42	52.20 N	0.52 W
Pitt ≃	224	49.12 N	122.47 W
Pitt, Mount ∧	174c	29.01 S	167.56 E
Pittem	50	51.00 N	3.16 E
Pitten ≃	61	47.44 N	16.14 E
Pittenweem	46	56.12 N	2.44 W
Pitti Island I	122	10.50 N	72.38 E
Pitt Island I	182	53.35 N	129.45 W
Pitt Lake ⊜	182	49.25 N	122.32 W
Pitt Meadows	224	49.13 N	122.39 W
Pittsboro, In., U.S.	218	39.51 N	86.28 W
Pittsboro, Ms., U.S.	194	33.56 N	89.20 W
Pittsboro, N.C., U.S.	192	35.43 N	79.10 W
Pittsburg, Ca., U.S.	226	38.01 N	121.53 W
Pittsburg, In., U.S.	216	40.37 N	86.42 W
Pittsburg, Ks., U.S.	198	37.24 N	94.42 W
Pittsburg, N.H., U.S.	206	45.03 N	71.23 W
Pittsburg, Tx., U.S.	222	32.59 N	94.57 W
Pittsburgh, Pa., U.S.	214	40.26 N	79.59 W
Pittsburgh, Pa., U.S.	279b	40.26 N	79.59 W
Pittsburgh, University of ʊ[2]	279b	40.27 N	79.58 W
Pittsburgh-Monroeville Airport ⊠	279b	40.27 N	79.46 W
Pittsfield, Il., U.S.	219	39.36 N	90.48 W
Pittsfield, Me., U.S.	188	44.46 N	69.23 W
Pittsfield, Ma., U.S.	207	42.27 N	73.14 W
Pittsfield, N.H., U.S.	188	43.18 N	71.19 W
Pittsfield, Pa., U.S.	214	41.50 N	79.23 W
Pittsford, Mi., U.S.	216	41.52 N	84.28 W
Pittsford, N.Y., U.S.	210	43.05 N	77.31 W
Pitt Stadium ♦	279b	40.27 N	79.58 W
Pittston	210	41.19 N	75.47 W
Pittsview	194	32.11 N	85.09 W
Pittsville	208	38.23 N	75.24 W
Pittsworth	166	27.43 S	151.38 E
Pitt Water ⊂	170	33.37 S	151.18 E
Pituil	252	28.34 S	67.27 W
Pitumarca	248	13.59 S	71.25 W
Pituri Creek ≃	166	22.58 S	138.50 E
Pitzbach ≃	64	47.13 N	10.46 E
Pitztal ∨	64	47.07 N	10.47 E
Pium	250	10.27 S	49.11 W
Pium ≃	250	10.12 S	49.57 W
Piura	248	5.12 S	80.38 W
Piura □[5]	248	5.10 S	80.00 W
Piura ≃	248	5.32 S	80.53 W
Piute Peak ∧	204	35.27 N	118.24 W
Piute Reservoir ⊜[1]	200	38.17 N	112.12 W
Piva ≃	38	43.21 N	18.51 E
Pivan'	89	50.29 N	137.06 E
Pivdennyy Buh ≃	78	46.59 N	31.58 E
Piverone	62	45.27 N	8.00 E
Pivijay	246	10.28 N	74.37 W
Piwniczna	30	49.27 N	20.42 E
Pixian	102	30.49 N	103.49 E
Pixley	226	35.58 N	119.17 W
Pižanka	80	57.28 N	48.33 E
Pižma	80	57.52 N	47.06 E
Pižma ≃	80	57.37 N	48.58 E
Pizzighettone	62	45.11 N	9.47 E
Pizzillo, Monte ∧	70	37.48 N	15.01 E
Pizzo	68	38.44 N	16.10 E
Pizzoferrato	66	41.55 N	14.14 E
Pizzoli	66	42.26 N	13.18 E
Pizzone	66	41.40 N	14.02 E
Pjalka	24	66.43 N	40.59 E
Pjana ≃	80	55.40 N	45.57 E
Pjaršai	76	54.02 N	26.41 E
Pjöngjang → P'yŏngyang	98	39.01 N	125.45 E
P. K. le Rouxdam ⊜[1]	158	30.12 S	24.54 E
Placanica	68	38.25 N	16.27 E
Place Bonaventure ➜[9]	275a	45.30 N	73.34 W
Placentia, Nf., Can.	186	47.14 N	53.58 W
Placentia, Ca., U.S.	228	33.52 N	117.52 W
Placentia Bay ⊂	186	47.15 N	54.30 W
Placer, Pil.	116	11.52 N	123.55 E
Placer, Pil.	116	9.39 N	125.36 E
Placer □[6]	226	38.54 N	121.04 W
Placeres del Oro ≃	234	18.27 N	100.57 W
Placeres de Picacho	234	23.11 N	105.42 W
Placerville	226	38.43 N	120.47 W
Placetas	240p	22.19 N	79.40 W
Place Versailles ➜[9]	275a	45.35 N	73.32 W
Plachino	76	54.28 N	39.20 E
Placid, Lake ⊜	220	27.14 N	81.22 W
Placida	220	26.49 N	82.15 W
Plácido de Castro	248	10.20 S	67.11 W
Plácido Rosas	252	32.45 S	53.44 W
Placita de Morelos	234	18.31 N	103.42 W
Plačkovica ⩘	38	41.45 N	22.35 E
Plaffeien	58	46.44 N	7.17 E
Plages, Lac des ⊜	206	45.59 N	74.54 W
Plage-Sainte-Cécile	50	50.34 N	1.35 E
Plailly	261	49.06 N	2.35 E
Plai Mat ≃	110	15.22 N	102.45 E
Plain	224	47.46 N	120.39 W
Plain City, Oh., U.S.	214	40.06 N	83.16 W
Plain City, Ut., U.S.	200	41.17 N	112.05 W
Plain Dealing	194	32.54 N	93.41 W
Plaines, Île aux I	275a	45.21 N	73.50 W
Plainfield, Ct., U.S.	207	41.40 N	71.54 W
Plainfield, Il., U.S.	216	41.37 N	88.12 W
Plainfield, In., U.S.	218	39.42 N	86.23 W
Plainfield, Ma., U.S.	207	42.30 N	72.55 W
Plainfield, N.J., U.S.	210	40.37 N	74.26 W
Plainfield, Oh., U.S.	214	40.13 N	81.43 W
Plainfield, Pa., U.S.	208	40.12 N	77.17 W
Plainfield, Wi., U.S.	190	44.12 N	89.29 W
Plains, Ga., U.S.	192	32.02 N	84.23 W
Plains, Ks., U.S.	198	37.15 N	100.35 W
Plains, Mt., U.S.	202	47.27 N	114.52 W
Plains, Tx., U.S.	196	33.11 N	102.50 W
Plainsboro	208	40.20 N	74.36 W
Plainview, Ca., U.S.	226	36.08 N	119.08 W
Plainview, Il., U.S.	219	39.10 N	89.59 W
Plainview, Mn., U.S.	190	44.09 N	92.10 W
Plainview, Ne., U.S.	198	42.20 N	97.47 W
Plainview, N.Y., U.S.	210	40.46 N	73.28 W
Plainview, Tx., U.S.	196	34.11 N	101.42 W
Plainville, Ct., U.S.	207	41.40 N	72.51 W
Plainville, Il., U.S.	219	39.47 N	91.11 W
Plainville, In., U.S.	194	38.48 N	87.09 W
Plainville, Ks., U.S.	198	39.14 N	99.17 W
Plainville, Ma., U.S.	207	42.00 N	71.20 W
Plainville, N.Y., U.S.	210	43.10 N	76.27 W
Plainwell	216	42.26 N	85.38 W
Plaisance, Baie de ⊂	186	47.18 N	61.53 W
Plaisir	261	48.49 N	1.57 E
Plaistow	207	42.50 N	71.05 W
Plakhtiyivka	78	46.07 N	29.43 E
Plaksino	76	56.11 N	30.42 E
Plamondon	182	54.51 N	112.19 W
Plampang	115b	8.48 S	117.48 E
Planá	60	49.52 N	12.44 E
Plana, Illa I	34	38.10 N	0.28 W
Planada	226	37.18 N	120.19 W
Planalto, Bra.	252	27.20 S	53.03 W
Planalto, Bra.	255	14.39 S	40.29 W
Planches	50	48.42 N	0.22 E
Plandome	276	40.48 N	73.42 W
Plandome Heights	276	40.48 N	73.42 W
Plandome Manor	276	40.49 N	73.42 W
Plan-d'Orgon	62	43.48 N	5.00 E
Plane ≃	54	52.23 N	12.30 E
Planegg	60	48.06 N	11.25 E
Planers'ke	78	44.57 N	35.14 E
Planeta Rica	246	8.25 N	75.36 W
Plangeross	64	46.59 N	10.52 E
Plankenfels	60	49.53 N	11.20 E
Plankinton	198	43.42 N	98.29 W
Plano, Il., U.S.	216	41.39 N	88.32 W
Plano, Tx., U.S.	222	33.01 N	96.41 W
Plansee ⊜	64	47.28 N	10.48 E
Plantagenet	206	45.32 N	75.00 W
Plantation, Fl., U.S.	220	24.59 N	80.33 W
Plantation, Fl., U.S.	220	26.07 N	80.14 W
Plantation, Ky., U.S.	218	38.17 N	85.36 W
Plantation Key I	220	24.58 N	80.33 W
Plant City	220	28.01 N	82.06 W
Plantersville, Al., U.S.	194	32.39 N	86.55 W
Plantersville, Ms., U.S.	194	34.12 N	88.39 W
Plantersville, Tx., U.S.	222	30.20 N	95.52 W
Planting Fields Arboretum State Park ♦	276	40.52 N	73.33 W
Plantsite	200	33.03 N	109.19 W
Plantsville	207	41.35 N	72.53 W
Plaquemine	194	30.17 N	91.14 W
Plaridel, Pil.	116	10.32 N	124.46 E
Plaridel, Pil.	116	8.37 N	123.43 E
Plasencia	34	40.02 N	6.05 W
Plaški	36	45.05 N	15.22 E
Plassenburg ⊥	60	50.06 N	11.28 E
Plassey	126	23.47 N	88.15 E
Plast	86	54.22 N	60.50 E
Plaster Rock	186	46.54 N	67.24 W
Plastovo	82	54.17 N	37.03 E
Plastun	89	44.45 N	136.19 E
Plastunovskaja	78	45.18 N	39.16 E
Plasy	60	49.56 N	13.24 E
Plata	54	53.33 N	11.30 E
Plata, Isla de la I	246	1.16 S	81.06 W
Plata, Río de la ⊂[1]	258	35.00 S	57.00 W
Plata, Río de la ≃	240m	18.29 N	66.15 W
Platani ≃	70	37.24 N	13.16 E
Platania	68	39.00 N	16.19 E
Plátanos	288	34.47 S	58.11 W
Plátanos, Arroyo ≃	288	34.45 S	58.08 W
Plate, Île I	275a	45.22 N	73.48 W
Platea	214	41.57 N	80.20 W
Plateau Creek ≃	200	39.11 N	108.18 W
Plateaux □[5]	152	2.15 S	15.30 E
Platì	68	38.13 N	16.03 E
Platinum	180	59.01 N	161.49 W
Platnirovskaja	78	45.23 N	39.23 E
Plato	246	9.47 N	74.47 W
Platono-Petrovka	83	46.59 N	39.28 E
Platonovka	80	52.43 N	41.57 E
Platón Sánchez	234	21.17 N	98.22 W
Platovo	83	48.05 N	39.53 E
Platrand	158	27.08 S	29.29 E
Platt	260	51.17 N	0.20 E
Platta	58	46.40 N	8.51 E
Platte	198	43.23 N	98.50 W
Platte ≃, U.S.	194	39.16 N	94.50 W
Platte ≃, Mn., U.S.	190	45.47 N	94.17 W
Platte ≃, Ne., U.S.	198	41.04 N	95.53 W
Platte ≃, Wi., U.S.	190	42.37 N	90.40 W
Platte Center	198	41.32 N	97.29 W
Platte City	194	39.22 N	94.46 W
Platte Creek ≃	198	43.19 N	99.00 W
Platte Island I	138	5.52 S	55.23 E
Plattekill	210	41.37 N	74.05 W
Platteville, Co., U.S.	200	40.12 N	104.49 W
Platteville, Wi., U.S.	190	42.44 N	90.28 W
Platt Hall ⊥	262	53.27 N	2.13 W
Plattling	60	48.47 N	12.53 E
Plattsburg	194	39.33 N	94.26 W
Plattsburgh	188	44.41 N	73.27 W
Plattsburgh Air Force Base ■	188	44.40 N	73.28 W
Plattsmouth	198	41.00 N	95.52 W
Plattsville	212	43.18 N	80.37 W
Platveld	156	19.58 S	17.07 E
Plau	54	53.27 N	12.16 E
Plaue, Dtsch.	54	52.24 N	12.25 E
Plaue, Dtsch.	54	50.47 N	10.54 E
Plauen	54	50.30 N	12.08 E
Plauer See ⊜	54	53.30 N	12.20 E
Plav	38	42.36 N	19.56 E
Plave	64	46.02 N	13.36 E
Plaviņas	76	56.37 N	25.43 E
Plavsk	76	53.43 N	37.18 E
Plaxtol	260	51.15 N	0.18 E
Playa Azul	234	17.59 N	102.24 W
Playa Baracoa	286b	23.03 N	82.34 W
Playa Bonita	236	9.39 N	84.27 W
Playa de Fajardo	240m	18.20 N	65.38 W
Playa de Guayanés	240m	18.04 N	65.49 W
Playa de Guayanilla	240m	18.01 N	66.46 W
Playa del Carmen	232	20.36 N	87.06 W
Playa del Rey ➜[8]	280	33.58 N	118.26 W
Playa de Naguabo	240m	18.12 N	65.43 W
Playa de Ponce	240m	17.59 N	66.37 W
Playa Noriega, Laguna ⊜	232	29.10 N	111.50 W
Playas Lake ⊜	200	31.50 N	108.34 W
Playa Vicente	234	17.50 N	95.49 W
Play Cu	110	13.59 N	108.00 E
Playford ≃	162	19.03 S	135.35 E
Playgreen Lake ⊜	184	54.00 N	98.10 W
Playland ♦	276	40.58 N	73.41 W
Plaza	198	48.01 N	101.57 W
Plaza at Mid Island ➜[9]	276	40.46 N	73.32 W
Plaza de Caisán	236	8.46 N	82.45 W
Plaza de Mayo ♦	288	34.36 S	58.23 W
Plaza de Toros ♦	266a	40.26 N	3.39 W
Plaza de Toros Las Arenas ♦	266d	41.23 N	2.09 W
Plaza de Toros Monumental ♦	266d	41.24 N	2.11 E
Plaza Huincul	252	38.55 S	69.09 W
Plaza Park	285	40.04 N	74.53 W
Plazas de Soberanía en el Norte de África → Spanish North Africa □[2]	34	35.53 N	5.19 W
Pleasant	275b	43.41 N	79.49 W
Pleasant, Lake ⊜[1]	200	33.53 N	112.16 W
Pleasant, Mount ∧	192	37.44 N	79.10 W
Pleasant, Mount ∧[2]	186	45.26 N	66.49 W
Pleasant Bay	186	46.49 N	60.48 W
Pleasantdale, Sk., Can.	184	52.35 N	104.30 W
Pleasantdale, N.Y., U.S.	210	42.47 N	73.40 W
Pleasant Gap	214	40.52 N	77.44 W
Pleasant Garden	192	35.57 N	79.45 W
Pleasant Grove, Ca., U.S.	226	38.49 N	121.29 W
Pleasant Grove, Ut., U.S.	200	40.21 N	111.44 W
Pleasant Grove Creek ≃	226	38.48 N	121.32 W
Pleasant Hill, Ca., U.S.	226	37.56 N	122.03 W
Pleasant Hill, Il., U.S.	219	39.26 N	90.52 W
Pleasant Hill, La., U.S.	194	31.49 N	93.31 W
Pleasant Hill, Mo., U.S.	194	38.47 N	94.16 W
Pleasant Hill, N.C., U.S.	208	36.32 N	77.32 W
Pleasant Hill, Oh., U.S.	218	40.03 N	84.20 W
Pleasant Hill Lake ⊜[1]	214	40.38 N	82.21 W
Pleasant Hills	214	40.20 N	79.57 W
Pleasant Lake, In., U.S.	216	41.34 N	85.00 W
Pleasant Lake, Mi., U.S.	216	42.23 N	84.22 W
Pleasant Lake ⊜	216	42.13 N	83.56 W
Pleasant Mills	216	40.47 N	84.51 W
Pleasant Mount	210	41.44 N	75.26 W
Pleasanton, Ca., U.S.	226	37.39 N	121.52 W
Pleasanton, Ks., U.S.	198	38.10 N	94.42 W
Pleasanton, Tx., U.S.	196	28.58 N	98.28 W
Pleasanton Ridge ∧	282	37.40 N	121.55 W
Pleasant Plains, Il., U.S.	219	39.52 N	89.55 W
Pleasant Plains, N.J., U.S.	208	40.00 N	74.13 W
Pleasant Point	172	44.16 S	171.08 E
Pleasant Prairie	216	42.33 N	87.57 W
Pleasant Ridge	281	42.31 N	83.10 W
Pleasant Unity	214	40.15 N	79.28 W
Pleasant Valley, N.Y., U.S.	210	41.44 N	73.49 W
Pleasant Valley, Oh., U.S.	218	39.22 N	83.03 W
Pleasant Valley, Pa., U.S.	279b	40.31 N	75.18 W
Pleasantville, Ia., U.S.	190	41.23 N	93.16 W
Pleasantville, Md., U.S.	284b	39.11 N	76.38 W
Pleasantville, N.J., U.S.	208	39.23 N	74.31 W
Pleasantville, N.Y., U.S.	210	41.07 N	73.47 W
Pleasantville, Pa., U.S.	214	41.35 N	79.34 W
Pleasington	262	53.44 N	2.34 W
Pleasure Beach	207	41.18 N	72.08 W
Pleasure Ridge Park	218	38.09 N	85.51 W
Pleasureville	218	38.33 N	85.04 W
Pléaux	32	45.08 N	2.14 E
Plechanovo	82	54.14 N	37.33 E
Plechanovskoje	76	52.39 N	39.50 E
Plechovo	78	51.07 N	35.18 E
Plechý (Plöckenstein) ∧	60	48.46 N	13.51 E
Pledger	222	29.11 N	95.55 W
Pleebo	150	4.35 N	7.40 W
Pleiku → Play Cu	110	13.59 N	108.00 E
Pleinfeld	56	49.06 N	10.59 E
Pleissa	54	50.50 N	12.46 E
Pleisse ≃	54	51.20 N	12.22 E
Pléneuf	32	48.36 N	2.33 W
Plenty	184	51.47 N	108.36 W
Plenty ≃, Austl.	162	23.25 S	136.31 E
Plenty ≃, Austl.	274b	37.45 S	145.07 E
Plenty, Bay of ⊂	172	37.40 S	177.00 E
Plentywood	198	48.46 N	104.33 W
Plered	115a	6.38 S	107.23 E
Pleščanicy	76	54.25 N	27.50 E
Pleščejevo, ozero ⊜	82	56.46 N	38.47 E
Pleseck	24	62.43 N	40.20 E
Plešivka	82	54.23 N	37.09 E
Plesná ≃	54	50.07 N	12.28 E
Pless, Dtsch.	58	48.05 N	10.08 E
Pless → Pszczyna, Pol.	30	49.59 N	18.57 E
Plessa	54	51.28 N	13.37 E
Plessisville	206	46.14 N	71.47 W
Pleszew	30	51.54 N	17.48 E
Pletenevka	82	54.31 N	36.06 E
Pletenyy Tashlyk	78	48.29 N	31.40 E
Pleternica	38	45.17 N	17.48 E
Plétipi, Lac ⊜	176	51.44 N	70.06 W
Plettenberg	56	51.13 N	7.52 E
Plettenbergbaai	158	34.04 S	23.22 E
Pleurs	50	48.41 N	3.52 E
Pleven	38	43.25 N	24.37 E
Plevna, Mo., U.S.	219	39.58 N	92.05 W
Plevna, Mt., U.S.	198	46.25 N	104.31 W
Pleyben	32	48.14 N	3.58 W
Pleystein	60	49.39 N	12.25 E
Pliening	60	48.12 N	11.48 E
Pliezhausen	56	48.33 N	9.12 E
Plimmerton	172	41.05 S	174.52 E
Plimoth Plantation ⊥	207	41.57 N	70.38 W
Plintovka	265a	60.01 N	30.46 E
Pliszka ≃	54	52.14 N	14.42 E
Plitvička Jezera Nacionalni Park ♦	36	44.53 N	15.38 E
Plješevica ⩘	36	44.40 N	15.45 E
Pljevlja	38	43.21 N	19.21 E
Ploaghe	71	40.40 N	8.45 E
Plochingen	56	48.42 N	9.25 E
Płock	30	52.33 N	19.43 E
Płock □[4]	30	52.25 N	19.45 E
Plöckenpass)(	64	46.36 N	12.58 E
Plöckenstein (Plechý) ∧	60	48.46 N	13.51 E
Plockton	46	57.20 N	5.39 W
Ploćno ∧	36	43.36 N	17.34 E
Plodorodnoje	80	46.44 N	41.06 E
Ploegsteert	50	50.43 N	2.53 E
Ploërmel	32	47.56 N	2.24 W
Ploeşti → Ploieşti	38	44.56 N	26.02 E
Plogastel-Saint-Germain	28	47.59 N	4.16 W
Ploieşti	38	44.56 N	26.02 E
Plomárion	38	38.59 N	26.22 E
Plomb du Cantal ∧	32	45.03 N	2.46 E
Plombières-les-Bains	58	47.58 N	6.29 E
Plombières-lès-Dijon	58	47.20 N	4.58 E
Plomer	258	34.48 S	59.02 W
Plomer, Point ≻	166	31.19 S	152.58 E
Plön	54	54.09 N	10.25 E
Plonge, Lac la ⊜	184	55.08 N	107.25 W
Płońsk	30	52.38 N	20.23 E
Pl'os	80	57.27 N	41.31 E
Plose, Cima delle ∧	64	46.42 N	11.44 E
Ploskij	78	46.17 N	40.15 E
Ploskoje	76	52.45 N	38.21 E
Ploskoš'	76	56.46 N	31.16 E
Pl'oso	76	59.47 N	35.43 E
Plössberg, Dtsch.	60	49.47 N	12.19 E
Plössberg, Dtsch.	60	49.47 N	12.19 E
Plotbišče	80	56.50 N	50.35 E
Plotina	83	48.33 N	40.05 E
Plotnica	76	52.03 N	26.39 E
Plottier	252	38.58 S	68.14 W
Płoty	30	53.49 N	15.16 E
Plötz	54	51.38 N	11.56 E
Plouay	32	47.55 N	3.20 W
Ploučnice ≃	54	50.47 N	14.13 E
Ploudalmézeau	32	48.32 N	4.39 W
Plouguenast	32	48.17 N	2.43 W
Plouha	32	48.41 N	2.56 W
Plovdiv	38	42.09 N	24.45 E
Plovdiv □[4]	38	42.08 N	24.32 E
Plover ≃	190	44.29 N	89.35 W
Plover Islands II	180	71.15 N	155.30 W
Pluckemin	276	40.39 N	74.39 W

Symbol	English	Deutsch	Español	Français	Português
≃	River	Fluß	Río	Rivière	Rio
≅	Canal	Kanal	Canal	Canal	Canal
↳	Waterfall, Rapids	Wasserfall, Stromschnellen	Cascada, Rápidos	Chute d'eau, Rapides	Cascata, Rápidos
ꭒ	Strait	Meeresstraße	Estrecho	Détroit	Estreito
⊂	Bay, Gulf	Bucht, Golf	Bahía, Golfo	Baie, Golfe	Baía, Golfo
⊜	Lake, Lakes	See, Seen	Lago, Lagos	Lac, Lacs	Lago, Lagos
≡	Swamp	Sumpf	Pantano	Marais	Pântano
⍓	Ice Features, Glacier	Eis- und Gletscherformen	Accidentes Glaciales	Formes glaciaires	Acidentes glaciares
⊤	Other Hydrographic Features	Andere Hydrographische Objekte	Otros Elementos Hidrográficos	Autres données hydrographiques	Outros acidentes hidrográficos
✢	Submarine Features	Untermeerische Objekte	Accidentes Submarinos	Formes de relief sous-marin	Acidentes submarinos
□	Political Unit	Politische Einheit	Unidad Política	Entité politique	Unidade política
ʊ	Cultural Institution	Kulturelle Institution	Institución Cultural	Institution culturelle	Instituição cultural
⊥	Historical Site	Historische Stätte	Sitio Histórico	Site historique	Sitio histórico
♦	Recreational Site	Erholungs- und Ferienort	Sitio de Recreo	Centre de loisirs	Area de Lazer
⊠	Airport	Flughafen	Aeropuerto	Aéroport	Aeroporto
■	Military Installation	Militäranlage	Instalación Militar	Installation militaire	Instalação militar
➜	Miscellaneous	Verschiedenes	Misceláneo	Divers	Diversos

I · 138 **Plum-Pont**

ENGLISH: Name, Page, Lat.°′, Long.°′ — DEUTSCH: Name, Seite, Breite°′, Länge°′ E = Ost

Name	Page	Lat.°′	Long.°′
Plum, Pa., U.S.	214	40.31 N	79.45 W
Plum, Pa., U.S.	214	41.35 N	79.51 W
Plum, Tx., U.S.	222	29.56 N	96.58 W
Pluma Hidalgo	234	15.55 N	96.25 W
Plumas	184	50.25 N	99.02 W
Plumbridge	48	54.46 N	7.15 W
Plum Brook ≃	281	42.34 N	82.58 W
Plum Creek ≃, Il., U.S.	278	41.33 N	87.29 W
Plum Creek ≃, Ne., U.S.	198	41.52 N	96.44 W
Plum Creek ≃, Oh., U.S.	279a	41.18 N	82.09 W
Plum Creek ≃, Pa., U.S.	279b	40.31 N	79.51 W
Plum Creek ≃, S.D., U.S.	198	44.13 N	100.43 W
Plum Creek ≃, Tx., U.S.	196	29.38 N	97.36 W
Plum Creek, Clear Fork ≃	222	29.45 N	97.37 W
Plumerville	194	35.09 N	92.38 W
Plum Grove	222	30.15 N	95.05 W
Plum Grove Estates	278	42.04 N	88.02 W
Plum Island	283	42.49 N	70.59 W
Plum Island I, Ma., U.S.	207	42.45 N	70.48 W
Plum Island I, N.Y., U.S.	207	41.11 N	72.12 W
Plum Island Airport ⊠	283	42.48 N	70.50 W
Plum Island Sound ʊ	283	42.45 N	70.48 W
Plum Island State Park ♦	283	42.42 N	70.47 W
Plumley	262	53.17 N	2.25 W
Plummer	202	47.20 N	116.53 W
Plummers Landing	218	38.19 N	83.33 W
Plumper Sound ʊ	224	48.47 N	123.13 W
Plum Point ›	276	40.50 N	40.43 W
Plumpton	274a	33.45 S	150.50 E
Plumridge Lakes ⊜	162	29.30 S	125.25 E
Plum Run ≃	279b	40.15 N	80.13 W
Plumsteadville	208	40.23 N	75.09 W
Plumtree	154	20.30 S	27.50 E
Plumville	214	40.48 N	79.11 W
Plumwood	218	40.01 N	83.23 W
Plungė	76	55.55 N	21.51 E
Pl'uskovo	76	52.46 N	33.49 E
Pl'ussa	76	58.26 N	29.21 E
Pl'ussa ≃	76	59.19 N	28.11 E
Plutarco Elías Calles, Presa ⊜[1]	232	29.10 N	109.40 W
Pluvigner	32	47.46 N	3.01 E
Plym ≃	42	50.22 N	4.07 W
Plymouth, Monts.	238	16.42 N	62.13 W
Plymouth, Trin.	241r	11.13 N	60.47 W
Plymouth, Eng., U.K.	42	50.23 N	4.10 W
Plymouth, Ca., U.S.	226	38.29 N	120.51 W
Plymouth, Ct., U.S.	207	41.40 N	73.03 W
Plymouth, Il., U.S.	194	40.17 N	90.55 W
Plymouth, In., U.S.	216	41.20 N	86.18 W
Plymouth, Ma., U.S.	207	41.57 N	70.40 W
Plymouth, Mi., U.S.	216	42.22 N	83.28 W
Plymouth, Ne., U.S.	198	40.18 N	96.59 W
Plymouth, N.H., U.S.	188	43.45 N	71.41 W
Plymouth, N.Y., U.S.	210	42.37 N	75.36 W
Plymouth, N.C., U.S.	192	35.52 N	76.44 W
Plymouth, Oh., U.S.	214	41.00 N	82.40 W
Plymouth, Pa., U.S.	210	41.14 N	75.56 W
Plymouth, Wi., U.S.	190	43.44 N	87.58 W
Plymouth □[6]	207	41.58 N	70.41 W
Plymouth ≃	283	42.12 N	70.54 W
Plymouth Airport ⊠	42	50.25 N	4.06 W
Plymouth Bay c	207	41.57 N	70.37 W
Plymouth Harbor c	283	41.58 N	70.39 W
Plymouth Meeting	285	40.06 N	75.16 W
Plymouth Meeting Mall ⬥[9]	285	40.07 N	75.17 W
Plymouth Rock ⊥	207	41.57 N	70.39 W
Plymouth Valley	285	40.07 N	75.23 W
Plympton, Eng., U.K.	42	50.23 N	4.03 W
Plympton, Ma., U.S.	207	41.57 N	70.48 W
Plymptonville	214	41.03 N	78.28 W
Plymstock	42	50.22 N	4.04 W
Plynlimon ∧	42	52.28 N	3.47 W
Plyskiv	78	49.23 N	29.18 E
Plysky	78	51.07 N	32.24 E
Plzeň	60	49.45 N	13.23 E
Pniewy	30	52.31 N	16.15 E
Pô	150	11.10 N	1.09 W
Po ≃, It.	36	44.57 N	12.04 E
Po ≃, Zhg.	100	28.57 N	116.39 E
Po, Foci del (Mouths of the Po) ≃[1]	64	44.52 N	12.30 E
Pô, Parc National de ♦	150	11.30 N	1.15 W
Poá	256	23.32 S	46.20 W
Poá ≃	287b	23.37 S	46.45 W
Poana ≃	250	0.56 N	57.03 W
Poarta Orientală, Pasul)(	38	45.06 N	22.18 E
Poás, Volcán ∧[1]	236	10.11 N	84.13 W
Pobé, Bénin	150	6.58 N	2.41 E
Pobé, Burkina	150	13.53 N	1.45 W
Pobeda, gora ∧	74	65.12 N	146.12 E
Pobeda Ice Island I	9	64.30 S	97.00 E
Pobedino	74	49.51 N	142.49 E
Pobedy, pik ∧	72	42.02 N	80.05 E
Pobershau	54	50.38 N	13.13 E
Poběžovice	60	49.31 N	12.48 E
Poblado Cerro Gordo	240m	18.29 N	66.20 W
Poblado Jacaguas	240m	18.03 N	66.32 W
Poblado Medianía Alta	240m	18.26 N	65.50 W
Poblado Sábalos	240m	18.11 N	67.09 W
Poblado Santana	240m	18.27 N	66.40 W
Poblet	258	35.04 S	57.57 W
Pobra de Trives	34	42.20 N	7.15 W
Pocahontas, Ar., U.S.	194	36.15 N	90.58 W
Pocahontas, Il., U.S.	219	38.49 N	89.32 W
Pocahontas, Ia., U.S.	198	42.44 N	94.40 W
Pocahontas State Park ♦	208	37.23 N	77.34 W
Pocantico Hills	276	41.06 N	73.50 W
Pocantico Lake ⊜	276	41.07 N	73.50 W
Poção	250	8.11 S	36.42 W
Pocasset	207	41.41 N	70.37 W
Pocatalico ≃	188	38.29 N	81.49 W
Pocatello	202	42.52 N	112.26 W
Počep	76	52.56 N	33.27 E
Pocé-sur-Cisse	50	47.26 N	0.59 E
Pochayiv	78	50.01 N	25.31 E
Pöchlarn	61	48.12 N	15.13 E
Pochvistnevo	80	53.38 N	52.08 E
Pocinhos, Bra.	250	7.04 S	36.03 W
Pocinhos, Bra.	256	21.56 S	46.25 W
Počinki	80	54.42 N	44.51 E
Počinnaja Sopka	76	58.25 N	34.22 E
Počinok	76	54.25 N	32.27 E
Pocitos, Salar ≚	252	24.30 S	67.03 W
Pockau	54	50.42 N	13.14 E
Pocking, Dtsch.	60	48.24 N	13.19 E
Pöcking, Dtsch.	64	47.58 N	11.18 E
Pocklington	44	53.56 N	0.46 W
Pocoata	248	18.41 S	66.11 W
Poço da Cruz, Açude ⊜[1]	250	8.30 S	37.35 W
Poço do Bispo ⬥[8]	266c	38.44 N	9.06 W
Poções	255	14.31 S	40.21 W
Poço Fundo	256	21.48 S	45.58 W
Poço Fundo, Cachoeira do ⌞	256	22.10 S	44.13 W
Pocol	64	46.31 N	12.07 E
Pocola	194	35.13 N	94.28 W
Pocomoke ≃	208	37.58 N	75.39 W
Pocomoke City	208	38.04 N	75.34 W
Pocomoke Sound ʊ	208	37.52 N	75.49 W
Pocona	248	17.39 S	65.24 W
Poconé	248	16.15 S	56.37 W
Pocono International Raceway ♦	210	41.03 N	75.31 W
Pocono Lake	210	41.06 N	75.31 W

Name	Page	Lat.°′	Long.°′
Pocono Manor	210	41.06 N	75.22 W
Pocono Mountains ⋀[2]	210	41.10 N	75.20 W
Pocono Pines	210	41.05 N	75.29 W
Pocono Summit	210	41.07 N	75.25 W
Pocopson	285	39.54 N	75.37 W
Pocopson Creek ≃	285	39.54 N	75.37 W
Poço Redondo	250	9.49 S	37.41 W
Poços de Caldas	256	21.48 S	46.34 W
Poço Verde	250	10.42 S	38.11 W
Pocrane	255	19.37 S	41.37 W
Pocrí	236	8.16 N	80.33 W
Podbel'skaja	80	53.37 N	51.50 E
Podberezje, Ross.	76	56.57 N	30.38 E
Podberezje, Ross.	82	56.46 N	37.10 E
Podbořany	54	50.11 N	13.25 E
Podborki	82	54.11 N	35.56 E
Podborovje	76	59.30 N	35.02 E
Podbužje	76	53.30 N	34.56 E
Podčerje	24	63.57 N	57.34 E
Podchožeje	82	54.19 N	38.34 E
Podčinnyj	80	50.52 N	45.13 E
Poddębice	30	51.53 N	18.58 E
Poddemjur	24	64.05 N	53.26 E
Poddolgoje	76	53.12 N	38.04 E
Poddorje	76	57.28 N	31.07 E
Poděbrady	30	50.08 N	15.07 E
Po della Donzella ≃	64	44.48 N	12.25 E
Po delle Tolle ≃	64	44.50 N	12.28 E
Podensac	32	44.39 N	0.22 W
Podenzano	62	44.57 N	9.41 E
Podersdorf am See	61	47.51 N	16.50 E
Podgorenskij	78	50.24 N	39.39 E
Podgorica	38	42.26 N	19.14 E
Podgornaja	78	50.28 N	41.10 E
Podgornoje, Kaz.	85	42.55 N	72.25 E
Podgornoje, Ross.	78	51.43 N	39.07 E
Podgornoje, Ross.	78	50.27 N	39.37 E
Podgornoje, Ross.	80	46.33 N	43.07 E
Podgornoje, Ross.	86	57.47 N	82.36 E
Podhůří	60	49.28 N	13.40 E
Podi	112	1.08 S	121.16 E
Po di Goro ≃	64	44.48 N	12.27 E
Podillya □[9]	78	48.50 N	27.30 E
Podil's'ka vysochyna ⋀[1]	78	49.00 N	27.00 E
Po di Volano ≃	64	44.49 N	12.15 E
Podjom-Michajlovka	80	52.49 N	50.32 E
Podjuchy ⬥[8]	54	53.20 N	14.36 E
Podkamennaja Tunguska	74	61.36 N	90.09 E
Podkamennaja Tunguska ≃	74	61.36 N	90.18 E
Podkoren	64	46.30 N	13.45 E
Podkumok ≃	84	44.14 N	43.36 E
Podlasie ⬥[1]	30	52.30 N	23.00 E
Podlesnoje	80	51.50 N	47.03 E
Podlopatki	88	50.55 N	107.05 E
Podmošje	82	56.23 N	37.24 E
Podol'sk	82	55.26 N	37.33 E
Podor, Maur.	150	16.40 N	15.00 W
Podor, Sén.	150	16.40 N	14.57 W
Podora	24	62.22 N	54.19 E
Podosinovec	24	60.17 N	47.04 E
Podoz'orskij	80	57.14 N	40.20 E
Podporožje	24	60.53 N	34.07 E
Podravina ⬥[1]	36	45.40 N	17.40 E
Podravska Slatina	38	45.42 N	17.42 E
Podrezčicha	24	59.22 N	51.28 E
Podstepnoje	80	51.08 N	51.28 E
Podt'osovo	88	58.36 N	92.06 E
Pod'uga	24	61.06 N	40.53 E
Podujevo	38	42.55 N	21.11 E
Poduškino	265b	55.43 N	37.17 E
Podu Turcului	38	46.12 N	27.23 E
Podymachino	88	56.59 N	106.11 E
Podyvotje	78	52.03 N	34.08 E
Poe	216	40.56 N	85.05 W
Poechos, Embalse ⊜[1]	246	4.40 S	80.30 W
Poel I	54	54.00 N	11.26 E
Poeldijk	52	52.01 N	4.12 E
Poelela, Lagoa ⊜	156	24.38 S	35.00 E
Poelkapelle	50	50.55 N	2.57 E
Poestenkill	210	42.41 N	73.34 W
Poesten Kill ≃	210	42.43 N	73.42 W
Poetto	71	39.12 N	9.10 E
Pofadder	158	29.10 S	19.22 E
Pogamasing Lake ⊜	190	46.57 N	81.50 W
Pogan, Zhg.	100	28.18 N	116.46 E
Pogan, Zhg.	100	27.40 N	116.46 E
Pogăniș ≃	38	45.41 N	21.22 E
Pogar	76	52.33 N	33.16 E
Poge, Cape ›	207	41.25 N	70.27 W
Poggendorf	54	54.03 N	13.07 E
Poggiardo	68	40.03 N	18.23 E
Poggibonsi	66	43.28 N	11.09 E
Poggio	64	44.30 N	10.00 E
Poggio Berni	66	44.02 N	12.24 E
Poggio Bustone	66	42.30 N	12.53 E
Poggio Imperiale	68	41.49 N	15.22 E
Poggiomarino	68	40.48 N	14.32 E
Poggio Mirteto	66	42.16 N	12.41 E
Poggio Moiano	66	42.12 N	12.53 E
Poggioreale	70	37.47 N	13.01 E
Poggio Renatico	64	44.46 N	11.29 E
Poggiorsini	68	40.55 N	16.15 E
Poggio Rusco	64	44.59 N	11.07 E
Poggio Sannita	66	41.47 N	14.25 E
Pöggstall	61	48.19 N	15.12 E
Pogibi	89	52.12 N	141.42 E
Pogil-to I	98	34.09 N	126.33 E
Pogliano	266b	45.32 N	8.59 E
Pogny	56	48.52 N	4.29 E
Pogoanele	38	44.54 N	27.00 E
Pogodajevo	80	51.37 N	51.04 E
Pogoniani	38	40.00 N	20.25 E
Pogoreloje Gorodišče	76	56.08 N	34.56 E
Pogoso	152	6.46 S	17.12 E
Pogost, Ross.	80	57.39 N	42.33 E
Pogost, Ross.	82	56.52 N	39.04 E
Pogožeje	78	51.36 N	37.16 E
Pogradec	38	40.54 N	20.39 E
Po Grande ≃	64	44.57 N	12.26 E
Pograničnoje	80	50.32 N	48.38 E
Pograničnyj, Ross.	80	46.57 N	45.46 E
Pograničnyj, Ross.	89	44.25 N	131.24 E
Pogromni Volcano ∧[1]	180	54.33 N	164.45 W
Pogromnoje	80	52.35 N	52.32 E
Pogruznaja	80	54.14 N	50.29 E
Poh	112	0.46 S	122.49 E
P'ohang	98	36.03 N	129.20 E
Pohatcong Creek ≃	210	40.37 N	75.11 W
Pohénégamook	186	47.31 N	69.16 W
Pohick Creek ≃	284c	38.46 N	77.14 W
Pohick Creek, Rabbit Branch ≃	284c	38.48 N	77.17 W
Pohick Creek, Sideburn Branch ≃	284c	38.48 N	77.17 W
Pohjanmaa ⬥[1]	26	64.00 N	25.00 E
Pohjois-Karjalan lääni □[4]	24	63.00 N	30.00 E
Pöhl, Talsperre ⬥[6]	54	50.33 N	12.12 E
Pöhla	54	50.31 N	12.49 E
Pöhlde	52	51.37 N	10.18 E
Pohl-Göns	56	50.28 N	8.39 E
Pohlheim	56	50.34 N	8.45 E
Pohnpei I	174r	6.55 N	158.15 E
Pohořelice	61	48.59 N	16.32 E
Pohorje ⋀	61	46.30 N	15.20 E
Pohrebyshche	78	49.29 N	29.16 E
Pohri	124	25.32 N	77.21 E
Pohsien → Boxian	100	33.53 N	115.45 E
Pohue Bay c	229d	19.00 N	155.48 W
Poiana Mare	38	43.55 N	23.04 E
Poiana Ruscă, Munții ⋀	38	45.41 N	22.30 E
Pöide	76	58.31 N	23.03 E
Poigny-la-Forêt	261	48.41 N	1.45 E
Poim	80	53.01 N	43.11 E

Name	Page	Lat.°′	Long.°′
Poing	64	48.10 N	11.49 E
Poinsett, Cape ›	9	65.42 S	113.18 E
Poinsett, Lake ⊜, Fl., U.S.	220	28.20 N	80.50 W
Poinsett, Lake ⊜, S.D., U.S.	198	44.34 N	97.05 W
Point	222	32.56 N	95.52 W
Point Arena	204	38.54 N	123.41 W
Point Au Fer Island I	194	29.15 N	91.15 W
Point Baker	180	56.21 N	133.37 W
Pointblank	222	30.45 N	95.13 W
Point Chautauqua	214	42.14 N	79.28 W
Point Comfort	196	28.41 N	96.33 W
Point Cook	274b	37.56 S	144.45 E
Point Cook Royal Australian Air Force Station ■	169	37.56 S	144.45 E
Point du Jour, Ruisseau du ≃	206	45.50 N	73.25 W
Pointe-à-la-Frégate	186	49.12 N	64.55 W
Pointe-à-la-Garde	186	48.05 N	66.32 W
Pointe a la Hache	194	29.34 N	89.47 W
Pointe-à-Maurier	186	50.20 N	59.48 W
Pointe-à-Pitre	241o	16.14 N	61.32 W
Pointe-à-Pitre-le Raizet, Aéroport de ⊠	241o	16.17 N	61.32 W
Pointe-au-Chêne	206	45.38 N	74.45 W
Pointe Aux Peaux Farms	216	41.57 N	83.16 W
Pointe-aux-Trembles	206	45.39 N	73.30 W
Pointe-Calumet	275a	45.30 N	73.58 W
Pointe-Claire	206	45.26 N	73.50 W
Pointe-des-Cascades	275a	45.20 N	73.58 W
Pointe-des-Galets → Le Port	157c	20.55 S	55.18 E
Pointe-du-Moulin	275a	45.22 N	73.52 W
Point Edward	214	43.00 N	82.24 W
Pointe-Noire, Congo	152	4.48 S	11.51 E
Pointe-Noire, Guad.	241o	16.14 N	61.47 W
Point Enterprise	222	31.40 N	96.26 W
Pointers	208	39.35 N	75.26 W
Point Fortin	241r	10.11 N	61.41 W
Point Hope	180	68.21 N	166.41 W
Point Imperial ∧	200	36.16 N	111.58 W
Point Independence	207	41.44 N	70.39 W
Point Lake ⊜	176	65.15 N	113.04 W
Point Leamington	186	49.20 N	55.24 W
Point Lookout, Md., U.S.	208	38.02 N	76.19 W
Point Lookout, N.Y., U.S.	276	40.35 N	73.35 W
Point Marion	188	39.44 N	79.53 W
Point McLeay	168b	35.32 S	139.06 E
Point Nepean National Park ♦	169	38.25 S	144.45 E
Point of Rocks	208	39.16 N	77.32 W
Point O'Woods	276	40.39 N	73.08 W
Point Pass	168b	34.05 S	139.03 E
Point Pelee National Park ♦	214	41.57 N	82.30 W
Point Peninsula ›[1]	212	44.01 N	76.15 W
Point Pleasant, Md., U.S.	284b	39.11 N	76.35 W
Point Pleasant, N.J., U.S.	208	40.04 N	74.04 W
Point Pleasant, Oh., U.S.	218	38.54 N	84.14 W
Point Pleasant, Pa., U.S.	208	40.25 N	75.04 W
Point Pleasant, W.V., U.S.	188	38.50 N	82.08 W
Point Pleasant Beach	208	40.05 N	74.02 W
Point Reyes National Seashore ♦	204	38.00 N	122.58 W
Point Roberts	224	48.59 N	123.04 W
Point Salines International Airport ⊠	241k	12.01 N	61.47 W
Point Samson	162	20.36 S	117.12 E
Point Sapin	186	46.58 N	64.50 W
Point View Reservoir ⊜[1]	276	40.58 N	74.15 W
Point Whiteshed	180	60.28 N	145.57 W
Poirino	62	44.55 N	7.51 E
Poisevo	80	55.32 N	53.30 E
Poison Creek ≃	202	43.15 N	108.09 W
Poison Spider Creek ≃	200	42.46 N	106.31 W
Poisson Blanc, Réservoir du ⊜[1]	188	46.00 N	75.45 W
Poissonnier Point ›	162	19.57 S	119.11 E
Poissons	58	48.25 N	5.13 E
Poissy	50	48.56 N	2.03 E
Poitiers	32	46.35 N	0.20 E
Poitou □[9]	32	46.20 N	0.30 W
Poix	50	49.47 N	1.59 E
Poix-Terron	56	49.39 N	4.39 E
Pojarkovo	89	49.38 N	128.38 E
Pojma ≃	88	56.54 N	97.48 E
Pojo	248	17.45 S	64.49 W
Pojoaque Valley	200	35.59 N	106.00 W
Pojuca	255	12.21 S	38.20 W
Pojuca ≃	255	12.34 S	38.03 W
Pokagon State Park ♦	216	41.43 N	85.01 W
Pokaran	120	26.55 N	71.55 E
Pokataroo	166	29.35 S	148.42 E
Pokatejeva	88	56.59 N	97.25 E
Pokatilovka, Kaz.	80	51.06 N	51.53 E
Pokatilovka, Kaz.	86	45.23 N	80.10 E
Poke Run ≃	279b	40.30 N	79.33 W
Pokharā	124	28.14 N	83.59 E
Pokharia	126	23.55 N	86.37 E
Poko, Sūd.	140	5.38 N	31.50 E
Poko, R.D.C.	154	3.09 N	26.53 E
Pokoinu	174k	21.12 S	159.49 W
Pokojnoje	84	44.48 N	44.16 E
Pokok Sena	114	6.10 N	100.32 E
Pokrov	82	55.55 N	39.10 E
Pokrovka, Kaz.	86	54.17 N	68.15 E
Pokrovka, Kaz.	86	49.28 N	81.28 E
Pokrovka, Kyrg.	85	42.20 N	78.01 E
Pokrovka, Kyrg.	85	42.45 N	71.36 E
Pokrovka, Ross.	80	48.22 N	46.04 E
Pokrovka, Ross.	80	53.47 N	53.19 E
Pokrovka, Ross.	89	43.57 N	131.39 E
Pokrovsk	74	61.29 N	129.06 E
Pokrovskaja Arčada	80	52.56 N	44.13 E
Pokrovs'ke, Ukr.	78	47.59 N	36.14 E
Pokrovs'ke, Ukr.	78	46.32 N	31.38 E
Pokrovs'ke, Ukr.	78	49.44 N	38.13 E
Pokrovs'ke, Ukr.	83	48.37 N	38.09 E
Pokrovskoje, Ross.	76	52.38 N	36.51 E
Pokrovskoje, Ross.	80	54.04 N	43.37 E
Pokrovskoje, Ross.	80	53.54 N	40.26 E
Pokrovskoje, Ross.	82	56.25 N	37.03 E
Pokrovskoje, Ross.	82	55.53 N	36.19 E
Pokrovskoje, Ross.	83	47.25 N	38.54 E
Pokrovskoje, Ross.	86	57.14 N	66.48 E
Pokrovskoje, Ross.	265a	59.44 N	30.46 E
Pokrovskoje ⬥[8]	265b	55.37 N	37.37 E
Pokrovsko-Strešnevo ⬥[8]	265b	55.49 N	37.29 E
Pokrovsk-Ural'skij	86	60.10 N	59.49 E
Pokur	74	61.02 N	75.26 E
Pola → Pula, Hrv.	64	44.52 N	13.50 E
Pola, Pil.	116	13.09 N	121.26 E
Pola, Ross.	76	57.56 N	31.50 E
Pola ≃	76	58.04 N	31.37 E
Pola Bay c	116	13.10 N	121.28 E
Polacca	200	35.50 N	110.22 W
Polacca Wash V	200	35.22 N	110.50 W
Polack	76	55.31 N	28.46 E
Pola de Laviana	34	43.15 N	5.34 W
Pola de Lena	34	43.10 N	5.49 W
Pola de Siero	34	43.23 N	5.40 W
Polān	128	25.35 N	61.12 E
Polanco	252	33.54 S	55.09 W
Poland, Kiribati	174o	1.59 N	157.32 W

Name	Page	Lat.°′	Long.°′
Poland, N.Y., U.S.	210	43.13 N	75.03 W
Poland, Oh., U.S.	214	41.01 N	80.37 W
Poland (Polska) □[1], Europe	22	52.00 N	19.00 E
Poland (Polska) □[1], Europe	30	52.00 N	19.00 E
Polangui	116	13.17 N	123.29 E
Polanów	30	54.08 N	16.39 E
Polapare ≃	115b	9.43 S	119.06 E
Pol'arnik	180	67.03 N	178.53 W
Pol'arnyj, Ross.	24	69.12 N	33.22 E
Pol'arnyj, Ross.	74	69.10 N	178.48 E
Pol'arnyj Ural ⋀	24	66.55 N	64.30 E
Polatlı	130	39.36 N	32.09 E
Polba	272b	22.57 N	88.18 E
Polbain	46	58.02 N	5.23 W
Polbeth	46	55.52 N	3.33 W
Polch	56	50.18 N	7.18 E
Polcirkeln	24	66.34 N	21.05 E
Polcura	252	37.17 S	71.43 W
Połczyn Zdrój	30	53.46 N	16.06 E
Polden Hills ⋀[2]	42	51.08 N	2.50 W
Poldnevica	80	58.37 N	46.38 E
Pol'dorak	85	39.25 N	69.56 E
Poleang	112	4.42 S	121.46 E
Polebridge	182	48.45 N	114.17 W
Polecat Creek ≃	196	36.00 N	95.57 W
Poledník ∧	60	49.04 N	13.24 E
Polee, Pulau I	164	2.12 S	130.15 E
Polegate	42	50.49 N	0.15 E
Pol-e Khomrī	120	35.56 N	68.43 E
Pole Moor	262	53.39 N	1.54 W
Polen → Poland □[1]	30	52.00 N	19.00 E
Polenezköy ⬥[8]	267b	41.07 N	29.12 E
Pol-e Safīd	128	36.06 N	53.01 E
Polesden Lacey ⊥	260	51.15 N	0.22 W
Polesella	64	44.58 N	11.45 E
Polesine ⬥[1]	64	45.00 N	11.45 E
Polesine Parmense	64	45.01 N	10.04 E
Polessk [Labiau]	76	54.52 N	21.05 E
Polesworth	42	52.37 N	1.36 W
Polesye ⬥[1]	72	52.00 N	27.00 E
Polevaja	78	51.37 N	36.30 E
Polevskoj	86	56.26 N	60.11 E
Polewali	112	3.25 S	119.20 E
Pol-e Žahāb	128	34.28 N	45.52 E
Polgár	30	47.52 N	21.08 E
Polgooth	42	50.19 N	4.48 W
Pŏlgyo	98	34.52 N	127.21 E
Poli, Cam.	146	8.29 N	13.15 E
Poli, Zhg.	98	35.43 N	119.47 E
Poli, Zhg.	98	35.57 N	118.17 E
Polia	68	38.45 N	16.19 E
Políaigos I	38	36.46 N	24.38 E
Policastro, Golfo di c	68	40.00 N	15.30 E
Policastro Bussentino	68	40.09 N	15.32 E
Police	30	53.35 N	14.33 E
Polička	30	49.43 N	16.16 E
Policoro	68	40.13 N	16.41 E
Polignac	62	45.04 N	3.52 E
Polignano a Mare	68	41.00 N	17.13 E
Poligny	58	46.50 N	5.43 E
Polihale State Park ♦	229b	22.05 N	159.45 W
Políkastron	38	41.00 N	22.34 E
Polikhnítos	38	39.05 N	26.11 E
Polillo	116	14.43 N	121.56 E
Polillo Island I	116	14.50 N	121.57 E
Polillo Islands II	116	14.50 N	122.05 E
Polillo Strait ʊ	116	14.44 N	121.51 E
Polinesia Francesa → French Polynesia □[2]	14	15.00 S	140.00 W
Polinik ∧	64	46.54 N	13.09 E
Polinyà de Vallès	266d	41.33 N	2.10 E
Pólis	130	35.02 N	32.25 E
Polis'ke	78	51.14 N	29.22 E
Polist' ≃	76	58.06 N	31.31 E
Polistena	68	38.25 N	16.05 E
Politécnico Nacional, Instituto ◈[2]	286a	19.30 N	99.08 W
Politotdel'skoje	83	47.33 N	39.05 E
Pölitz → Police	30	53.35 N	14.33 E
Polivanovo	80	53.36 N	47.23 E
Políyiros	38	40.23 N	23.27 E
Polizzi Generosa	70	37.49 N	14.00 E
Polizzo, Monte ∧	70	37.52 N	12.47 E
Polk, Ne., U.S.	198	41.04 N	97.47 W
Polk, Oh., U.S.	214	40.57 N	82.13 W
Polk, Pa., U.S.	214	41.22 N	79.55 W
Polk □[6], Fl., U.S.	220	28.01 N	81.37 W
Polk □[6], Or., U.S.	224	45.00 N	123.23 W
Polk □[6], Tx., U.S.	222	30.45 N	94.48 W
Polk City	220	28.10 N	81.49 W
Pol'kino	74	71.10 N	99.13 E
Polkton	192	35.00 N	80.12 W
Polla	68	40.30 N	15.30 E
Pollāchi	122	10.40 N	77.01 E
Pöllau	61	47.18 N	15.51 E
Pöllauberg	61	47.19 N	15.52 E
Polleben	54	51.34 N	11.36 E
Pollenfeld	60	48.57 N	11.12 E
Pollenza	66	43.16 N	13.21 E
Pollica	68	40.11 N	15.03 E
Pollina	70	37.59 N	14.09 E
Polling	64	47.48 N	11.09 E
Pollino, Monte ∧	68	39.55 N	16.11 E
Polloc Harbor c	116	7.23 N	124.12 E
Pollock, La., U.S.	194	31.31 N	92.24 W
Pollock, S.D., U.S.	198	45.54 N	100.17 W
Pollock Pines	226	38.46 N	120.34 W
Pollock Run ≃	279b	40.14 N	79.47 W
Pollok	222	31.27 N	94.52 W
Pollutri	66	42.08 N	14.35 E
Pollux ∧	172	44.14 S	168.53 E
Polmak	24	70.04 N	28.00 E
Polmont	46	55.59 N	3.42 W
Polná	30	49.29 N	15.43 E
Polnaja ≃	83	48.54 N	39.50 E
Pol'noje-Jaltunovo	80	53.59 N	41.52 E
Polnovo-Seliger	76	57.32 N	32.55 E
Polo, Il., U.S.	190	41.59 N	89.34 W
Polo, Mo., U.S.	194	39.33 N	94.02 W
Polochic ≃	236	15.28 N	89.22 W
Polock	86	52.46 N	59.42 E
Pologne → Poland □[1]	30	52.00 N	19.00 E
Pologoje Zajmišče	80	48.29 N	45.57 E
Pologrudovo	86	57.07 N	74.13 E
Polohy	78	47.29 N	36.15 E
Polom, Ross.	24	59.13 N	50.50 E
Polom, Ross.	80	57.47 N	53.29 E
Polo Magnético del Sur → South Magnetic Pole ⬥	9	65.18 S	139.30 E
Pölömäki ∧[2]	26	63.21 N	27.03 E
Polomet' ≃	76	57.41 N	32.12 E
Polomolok	116	6.14 N	125.03 E
Polonia → Poland □[1]	30	52.00 N	19.00 E
Polonia, Arroyo ≃	258	34.10 S	57.15 W
Polonio, Cabo ›	252	34.24 S	53.46 W
Polonnaruwa	122	7.56 N	81.00 E
Polonnaruwa ⊥	122	7.56 N	81.00 E
Polonne	78	50.07 N	27.30 E
Pološkovo	82	54.08 N	35.53 E
Polo Sur → South Pole ⬥	9	90.00 S	0.00
Polotn'anyj	82	54.45 N	36.00 E
Polotsk → Polock	76	55.31 N	28.46 E
Polovinnoje, Ross.	86	54.43 N	63.50 E
Polovinnoje, Ross.	86	53.46 N	79.15 E
Polovo	76	57.03 N	32.27 E
Polovynkyne	83	49.14 N	38.55 E
Polperro	42	50.19 N	4.31 W
Polruan	42	50.19 N	4.36 W
Pöls	61	47.13 N	14.35 E
Pölsbach ≃	61	47.11 N	14.45 E

Name	Page	Lat.°′	Long.°′
Polska → Poland □[1]	30	52.00 N	19.00 E
Polski Trămbeš	38	43.22 N	25.38 E
Polson	202	47.41 N	114.09 W
Polster ∧	61	47.32 N	14.58 E
Polsum	52	51.37 N	7.03 E
Poltava	78	49.35 N	34.34 E
Poltava □[4]	78	49.45 N	34.00 E
Poltavka	86	54.22 N	71.45 E
Poltevy Pen'ki	80	54.35 N	42.06 E
Poltimore	188	45.47 N	75.43 W
Põltsamaa	76	58.38 N	25.58 E
Põltsamaa ≃	76	58.27 N	26.09 E
Poludino	86	54.51 N	69.55 E
Poluj ≃	74	66.31 N	66.33 E
Polunočnoje	72	60.52 N	60.25 E
Polur	122	12.30 N	79.08 E
Polur'adinki	82	54.51 N	38.41 E
Poluškino	265b	55.41 N	38.05 E
Pol'ustrovo ⬥[8]	265a	59.58 N	30.25 E
Põlva	76	58.03 N	27.03 E
Polvaredas	258	35.35 S	59.30 W
Polverigi	66	43.31 N	13.23 E
Polvijärvi	26	62.51 N	29.22 E
Polvilho	287b	23.23 S	46.50 W
Polvoranca	266a	40.19 N	3.48 W
Polynesia II	14	4.00 S	156.00 W
Polynesian Cultural Center ◈	229c	21.39 N	157.55 W
Polynésie française → French Polynesia □[2]	14	15.00 S	140.00 W
Polynnoje	80	46.51 N	46.56 E
Polysajevo	86	54.35 N	86.14 E
Pölzig	54	50.57 N	12.11 E
Poma, Lago ⊜[1]	70	37.55 N	13.06 E
Pomabamba	248	8.50 S	77.28 W
Pomacanchi	248	14.02 S	71.34 W
Pomahaka ≃	172	46.09 S	169.34 E
Pomarance	66	43.18 N	10.52 E
Pomarico	68	40.31 N	16.33 E
Pomarkku	26	61.42 N	22.00 E
Pomata	248	16.16 S	69.18 W
Pomáz	264c	47.39 N	19.02 E
Pomba ≃	256	21.24 S	42.32 W
Pombais, Ribeira de ≃	266c	38.48 N	9.07 W
Pombal, Bra.	250	6.46 S	37.47 W
Pombal, Port.	34	39.55 N	8.38 W
Pombia	266b	45.39 N	8.38 E
Pomellen	54	53.20 N	14.23 E
Pomene	156	22.53 S	35.33 E
Pomerania □[9]	30	54.00 N	16.00 E
Pomeranian Bay c	54	54.00 N	14.15 E
Pomerene	200	31.59 N	110.17 W
Pomerode	252	26.45 S	49.11 W
Pomeroon ≃	246	7.37 N	58.45 W
Pomeroon-Supenaam □[4]	246	7.20 N	58.50 W
Pomeroy, S. Afr.	158	28.33 S	30.26 E
Pomeroy, N. Ire., U.K.	48	54.36 N	6.55 W
Pomeroy, Ia., U.S.	198	42.33 N	94.41 W
Pomeroy, Oh., U.S.	188	39.01 N	82.02 W
Pomeroy, Pa., U.S.	208	39.58 N	75.53 W
Pomeroy, Wa., U.S.	202	46.28 N	117.36 W
Pomezia	66	41.40 N	12.30 E
Pomfret, S. Afr.	156	25.50 S	23.32 E
Pomfret, Ct., U.S.	207	41.53 N	71.57 W
Pomfret, Md., U.S.	208	38.34 N	77.01 W
Pomi	38	47.42 N	23.19 E
Pomichna	78	48.14 N	31.26 E
Pomigliano	68	40.54 N	14.23 E
Pominovo	82	55.26 N	39.11 E
Pomio	164	5.30 S	151.30 E
Pommard	58	47.01 N	4.47 E
Pomme de Terre ≃, Mn., U.S.	198	45.10 N	96.05 W
Pomme de Terre ≃, Mo., U.S.	194	38.11 N	93.24 W
Pomme de Terre Lake ⊜[1]	194	37.51 N	93.19 W
Pommelsbrunn	60	49.30 N	11.31 E
Pommera	50	50.10 N	2.26 E
Pommern → Pomerania □[9]	30	54.00 N	16.00 E
Pommersche Bucht → Pomeranian Bay c	54	54.00 N	14.15 E
Pommersfelden	56	49.46 N	10.49 E
Pomona, Namibia	156	27.09 S	15.18 E
Pomona, Ca., U.S.	228	34.03 N	117.45 W
Pomona, Ks., U.S.	198	38.36 N	95.27 W
Pomona, N.J., U.S.	208	39.28 N	74.34 W
Pomona, N.Y., U.S.	276	41.10 N	74.02 W
Pomona College ◈[2]	280	34.06 N	117.44 W
Pomona Estates	273d	26.06 S	28.15 E
Pomona Lake ⊜[1]	198	38.40 N	95.35 W
Pomona Park	192	29.30 N	81.35 W
Pomongo	152	5.00 S	19.08 E
Pomorie	38	42.33 N	27.39 E
Pomorskij proliv ʊ	24	68.30 N	50.00 E
Pomoryany	78	49.38 N	24.56 E
Pomorze → Pomerania □[9]	30	54.00 N	16.00 E
Pomozdino	24	62.12 N	54.06 E
Pompano Beach	220	26.14 N	80.07 W
Pompano Beach Highlands	220	26.16 N	80.06 W
Pompei	68	40.45 N	14.30 E
Pompei ⊥	68	40.45 N	14.30 E
Pompéia	255	22.08 S	50.10 W
Pompejevka	89	48.23 N	130.46 E
Pompeston Creek ≃	285	40.01 N	75.01 W
Pompéu	255	19.12 S	44.59 W
Pompey, Fr.	56	48.46 N	6.07 E
Pompey, N.Y., U.S.	210	42.54 N	76.01 W
Pomponio Creek ≃	282	37.18 N	122.25 W
Pomponio State Beach ♦	282	37.17 N	122.24 W
Pomponne	261	48.53 N	2.41 E
Pompon-yama ∧	270	34.56 N	135.37 E
Pomposa	66	44.49 N	12.11 E
Pomposa, Abbazia di ◈[1]	64	44.49 N	12.11 E
Pompton ≃	276	40.54 N	74.16 W
Pompton Lakes	210	41.00 N	74.17 W
Pompton Lakes ⊜	276	41.00 N	74.17 W
Pomquet	186	45.38 N	61.51 W
Pomssen	54	51.14 N	12.37 E
Ponape → Pohnpei I	174r	6.55 N	158.15 E
Ponask Lake ⊜	184	54.00 N	92.41 W
Ponass Lakes ⊜	184	52.18 N	103.58 W
Ponazyrevo	80	58.21 N	46.19 E
Ponca	198	42.33 N	96.42 W
Ponca City	196	36.42 N	97.05 W
Ponca Creek ≃	198	42.48 N	98.05 W
Ponce	240m	18.01 N	66.37 W
Ponce, Aeropuerto ⊠	240m	18.01 N	66.34 W
Ponce de Leon	194	30.43 N	85.56 W
Ponce de Leon Bay c	220	25.21 N	81.07 W
Ponce de Leon Inlet c	192	29.04 N	80.55 W
Poncé-sur-le-Loir	50	47.46 N	0.40 E
Poncha Pass)(	200	38.25 N	106.05 W
Ponchatoula	194	30.26 N	90.26 W
Poncin	58	46.05 N	5.24 E
Poncitlán	234	20.22 N	102.55 W
Pond ≃	194	37.32 N	87.21 W
Pond Brook ≃, N.J., U.S.	276	41.02 N	74.15 W
Pond Brook ≃, Oh., U.S.	279a	41.17 N	81.24 W
Pondcreek	196	36.40 N	97.48 W
Pond Creek ≃, U.S.	196	36.40 N	97.33 W
Pond Creek ≃, Tx., U.S.	222	31.02 N	96.46 W
Pond Eddy	210	41.27 N	74.49 W
Ponder	222	33.11 N	97.17 W

Name	Seite	Breite°′	Länge°′ E = Ost
Pondera Coulee V	202	48.16 N	111.03 W
Ponders End ⬥[8]	260	51.39 N	0.03 W
Pondicherry	122	11.56 N	79.53 E
Pondicherry □[8]	122	11.56 N	79.50 E
Pond Inlet	176	72.41 N	78.00 W
Pond Inlet c	176	72.46 N	77.00 W
Pondok Tanjong	114	5.00 N	100.44 E
Pondoland □[9]	158	31.10 S	29.30 E
Pondosa	204	41.12 N	121.41 W
Pond Run ≃	285	40.13 N	74.44 W
Poneas Island I	116	9.55 N	125.57 E
Ponente, Capo ›	70a	35.31 N	12.31 E
Ponente, Riviera di ≛[2]	62	44.10 N	8.20 E
Ponérihouen	175f	21.05 S	165.24 E
Poneto	216	40.39 N	85.13 W
Ponežukaj	78	44.53 N	39.22 E
Ponferrada	34	42.33 N	6.35 W
Pong	110	19.10 N	100.17 E
Pongani	164	9.05 S	148.35 E
Pongara, Pointe ›	152	0.21 N	9.21 E
Pongaroa	172	40.33 S	176.11 E
Pongau V	64	47.21 N	13.14 E
Pong Dam ⬥[6]	123	31.59 N	75.57 E
Ponghyŏn	98	37.49 N	125.36 E
Pongo ≃	140	8.42 N	27.40 E
Pongolo ≃	158	26.57 S	32.17 E
Pon'goma	24	65.21 N	34.25 E
Pong Tamale	150	9.41 N	0.49 W
Ponhook Lake ⊜	186	44.19 N	64.53 W
Poni ≃	208	38.07 N	77.26 W
Poniatowa	30	51.11 N	22.05 E
Poniec	30	51.47 N	16.50 E
Ponil Creek ≃	196	36.29 N	104.48 W
Poninka	78	50.12 N	27.32 E
Ponino	80	58.16 N	52.49 E
Ponitz, Dtsch.	54	50.51 N	12.25 E
Pönitz, Dtsch.	54	54.03 N	10.40 E
Ponizovje	76	55.17 N	31.04 E
Ponkapoag Pond ⊜	283	42.12 N	71.06 W
Pônley	110	12.26 N	104.27 E
Ponnaiyār ≃	122	11.46 N	79.47 E
Ponnāni	122	10.46 N	75.54 E
Ponnūru Nidubrolu	122	16.04 N	80.34 E
Pono	164	6.22 S	134.36 E
Ponoj	24	67.05 N	41.07 E
Ponoj ≃	24	66.59 N	41.17 E
Ponoka	182	52.42 N	113.35 W
Ponomar'ovka, Ross.	80	53.19 N	54.08 E
Ponomar'ovka, Ross.	86	56.08 N	82.23 E
Ponornytsya	78	51.43 N	32.49 E
Ponorogo	115a	7.52 S	111.27 E
Ponpāj	272b	22.56 N	88.15 E
Pons	32	45.35 N	0.33 W
Ponsacco	66	43.37 N	10.38 E
Ponson Island I	116	10.46 N	124.32 E
Ponsul ≃	34	39.40 N	7.31 W
Pont	62	45.34 N	7.07 E
Pont-à-Celles	50	50.30 N	4.21 E
Ponta Delgada	148a	37.44 N	25.40 W
Ponta Delgada □[5]	148a	37.40 N	25.30 W
Ponta de Pedras	250	1.23 S	48.52 W
Ponta Grossa	252	25.05 S	50.09 W
Pontalete	256	21.27 S	45.40 W
Pontalina	255	17.31 S	49.27 W
Pontallier-sur-Saône	58	47.18 N	5.25 E
Pont-à-Marcq	50	50.31 N	3.07 E
Pont-à-Mousson	56	48.54 N	6.04 E
Ponta Negra	256	22.57 S	35.10 W
Pontão	34	39.55 N	8.22 W
Ponta Porã	255	22.32 S	55.43 W
Pontardawe	42	51.44 N	3.51 W
Pontardulais	42	51.43 N	4.03 W
Pontarlier	58	46.54 N	6.22 E
Pontas de Pedra	250	7.38 S	34.48 W
Pontassieve	66	43.46 N	11.26 E
Pontaubert	50	47.29 N	3.52 E
Pont-Audemer	50	49.21 N	0.31 E
Pontault-Combault	261	48.47 N	2.36 E
Pontaumur	32	45.52 N	2.40 E
Pont-Aven	32	47.51 N	3.45 W
Pontbriand	206	46.09 N	71.15 W
Pont Canavese	62	45.25 N	7.36 E
Pontcarré	261	48.48 N	2.42 E
Pontcharra	62	45.26 N	6.01 E
Pontchartrain	261	48.48 N	1.54 E
Pontchartrain, Lake ⊜	194	30.10 N	90.10 W
Pontchâteau	32	47.26 N	2.05 W
Pont-Croix	32	48.02 N	4.29 W
Pont-d'Ain	58	46.03 N	5.20 E
Pont d'Arc ♦	62	44.23 N	4.26 E
Pont-de-Bonne	56	50.27 N	5.17 E
Pont-de-Chéruy	62	45.45 N	5.11 E
Pont-de-l'Arche	50	49.18 N	1.10 E
Pont-de-Pany	58	47.18 N	4.49 E
Pont-de-Poitte	58	46.35 N	5.41 E
Pont-de-Roide	58	47.23 N	6.46 E
Pont-de-Ruan	50	47.15 N	0.35 E
Pont-de-Salars	32	44.17 N	2.44 E
Pont-de-Vaux	58	46.26 N	4.56 E
Pont-de-Veyle	58	46.16 N	4.53 E
Ponte a Elsa	66	43.41 N	10.54 E
Ponte Alta do Bom Jesus	255	12.06 S	46.29 W
Ponte Alta do Norte	250	10.45 S	47.34 W
Ponte a Moriano	66	43.54 N	10.31 E
Ponteareas	34	42.11 N	8.30 W
Pontebba	64	46.30 N	13.18 E
Ponte Branca	255	16.27 S	52.40 W
Ponte Caffaro	64	45.50 N	10.32 E
Pontecagnano	68	40.39 N	14.52 E
Ponte-Caldelas	34	42.23 N	8.30 W
Pontecchio Marconi	64	44.25 N	11.15 E
Pontecchio Polesine	64	45.01 N	11.49 E
Pontecorvo	66	41.27 N	13.40 E
Pontecurone	62	44.57 N	8.56 E
Ponte da Barca	34	41.48 N	8.25 W
Ponte d'Arbia	66	43.10 N	11.28 E
Ponte delle Arche	64	46.02 N	10.52 E
Ponte dell'Olio	62	44.52 N	9.39 E
Pontedera	66	43.40 N	10.38 E
Ponte de Sor	34	39.15 N	8.01 W
Pontedeume	34	43.24 N	8.10 W
Ponte di Barbarano	64	45.23 N	11.34 E
Ponte di Legno	64	46.16 N	10.31 E
Ponte di Nava	62	44.08 N	7.53 E
Ponte di Piave	64	45.43 N	12.28 E
Ponte do Lima	34	41.46 N	8.35 W
Ponte do Púngoè	156	19.30 S	34.32 E
Pontefract	44	53.42 N	1.18 W
Ponte Galeria ⬥[8]	267a	41.49 N	12.21 E
Ponte Gardena (Waidbruck)	64	46.36 N	11.32 E
Ponte Ghiereto	66	43.59 N	11.15 E
Pontegrande	58	45.59 N	8.09 E
Ponte in Valtellina	64	46.12 N	9.59 E
Ponteix	184	49.45 N	107.29 W
Pontelagoscuro	64	44.53 N	11.36 E
Ponteland	44	55.03 N	1.44 W
Pontelandolfo	68	41.17 N	14.41 E
Pontelongo	64	45.15 N	12.02 E
Ponte nell'Alpi	64	46.11 N	12.16 E
Ponte Nova	255	20.24 S	42.54 W
Pont-en-Royans	62	45.04 N	5.21 E
Ponte Nuovo	66	43.01 N	12.28 E
Pontenure	62	44.59 N	9.47 E
Pontepetri	66	44.02 N	10.53 E
Pontericcioli	66	43.26 N	12.38 E
Ponte Rocchetta	64	46.14 N	11.04 E
Ponterwyd	42	52.25 N	3.50 W
Ponte San Giovanni	66	43.05 N	12.26 E
Ponte San Pietro	62	45.42 N	9.35 E
Pontesbury	42	52.39 N	2.54 W
Ponte Selva	64	45.52 N	9.54 E
Ponte Serrada	252	26.52 S	51.58 W
Pontestura	62	45.08 N	8.20 E
Ponte Tresa	58	45.58 N	8.52 E
Pontevedra, Arg.	258	34.45 S	58.42 W
Pontevedra, Esp.	34	42.26 N	8.38 W
Pontevedra, Pil.	116	10.22 N	122.52 E
Pontevedra □[4]	34	42.30 N	8.40 W

Symbols in the index entries represent the broad categories identified in the key at the right. Symbols with superior numbers (⋀[1]) identify subcategories (see complete key on page *I · 1).*

Symbole im Register stellen die rechts im Schlüssel erklärten Kategorien dar. Symbole mit hochgestellten Ziffern (⋀[1]) bezeichnen Unterabteilungen einer Kategorie (vgl. vollständiger Schlüssel auf Seite *I · 1).*

Los símbolos incluídos en el texto del índice representan las grandes categorías identificadas con la clave a la derecha. Los símbolos con numeros en su parte superior (⋀[1]) identifican las subcategorías (véase la clave completa en la página *I · 1).*

Les symboles de l'index représentent les catégories indiquées dans la légende à droite. Les symboles suivis d'un indice (⋀[1]) représentent des sous-catégories (voir légende complète à la page *I · 1).*

Os símbolos incluídos no texto do índice representam as grandes categorias identificadas com a chave à direita. Os símbolos com números em sua parte superior (⋀[1]) identificam as subcategorias (veja-se a chave completa à página *I · 1).*

∧ Mountain	Berg	Montaña	Montagne	Montanha
⋀ Mountains	Gebirge	Montañas	Montagnes	Montanhas
)(Pass	Paß	Paso	Col	Passo
V Valley, Canyon	Tal, Cañon	Valle, Cañón	Vallée, Canyon	Vale, Canhão
≚ Plain	Ebene	Llano	Plaine	Planície
› Cape	Kap	Cabo	Cap	Cabo
I Island	Insel	Isla	Île	Ilha
II Islands	Inseln	Islas	Îles	Ilhas
≛ Other Topographic Features	Andere Topographische Objekte	Otros Elementos Topográficos	Autres données topographiques	Outros acidentes topográficos

ESPAÑOL (Nombre, Página, Lat.°′, Long.°′ W = Oeste) — **FRANÇAIS** (Nom, Page, Lat.°′, Long.°′ W = Ouest) — **PORTUGUÊS** (Nome, Página, Lat.°′, Long.°′ W = Oeste)

Nombre / Nom / Nome	Página / Page	Lat.°′	Long.°′
Pontevedra, Ría de c[1]	34	42.22 N	8.45 W
Ponte Vedra Beach	192	30.14 N	81.23 W
Pont-Évêque	62	45.32 N	4.55 E
Pontevico	64	45.16 N	10.05 E
Pontfaverger-Moronvilliers	50	49.18 N	4.19 E
Pontgibaud	32	45.50 N	2.52 E
Ponthévrard	261	48.33 N	1.55 E
Ponthierry	261	48.32 N	2.33 E
Ponthierville → Ubundu	154	0.21 S	25.29 E
Pontiac, Il., U.S.	216	40.52 N	88.37 W
Pontiac, Mi., U.S.	216	42.38 N	83.17 W
Pontiac ▫[6]	212	46.30 N	77.00 W
Pontiac Lake	281	42.40 N	83.28 W
Pontiac Lake ⊜	281	42.40 N	83.28 W
Pontiac Lake State Recreation Area ♦	216	42.41 N	83.28 W
Pontiac Mall ◆[9]	281	42.39 N	83.20 W
Pontiac State Recreation Area ♦	281	42.41 N	83.28 W
Pontianak	112	0.02 S	109.20 E
Pontian Kechil	114	1.29 N	103.23 E
Pontida	62	45.43 N	9.30 E
Pontigny	50	47.55 N	3.43 E
Pontinha ◆[8]	266c	38.46 N	9.11 W
Pontinia	66	41.24 N	13.02 E
Pontivy	32	48.04 N	2.59 W
Pont-l'Abbé	32	47.52 N	4.13 W
Pont-lès-Moulins	58	47.19 N	6.22 E
Pont-l'Évêque	50	49.18 N	0.11 E
Pontlevoy	50	47.23 N	1.15 E
Pontoise	50	49.03 N	2.06 E
Pontoise-Cormeilles-en-Vexin, Aérodrome ⊠	261	49.06 N	2.02 E
Ponton Creek ≃	162	31.10 S	124.25 E
Pontonnyj	265a	59.47 N	30.38 E
Pontoon Beach	219	38.43 N	90.04 W
Pontorson	32	48.33 N	1.31 W
Pontotoc, Ms., U.S.	194	34.14 N	88.59 W
Pontotoc, Tx., U.S.	196	30.54 N	98.59 W
Pontremoli	62	44.22 N	9.53 E
Pont-Remy	50	50.03 N	1.55 E
Pontresina	58	46.28 N	9.53 E
Pontrhydfendigaid	42	52.17 N	3.51 W
Pont-Rouge	206	46.45 N	71.42 W
Pont-Royal	62	43.43 N	5.11 E
Ponts	34	41.55 N	1.12 E
Pont-Sainte-Marie	50	48.19 N	4.06 E
Pont-Sainte-Maxence	50	49.18 N	2.36 E
Pont-Saint-Esprit	62	44.15 N	4.39 E
Pont-Saint-Martin	62	45.36 N	7.48 E
Pont-Scorff	28	47.50 N	3.24 W
Ponts Quentin, Ruisseau des ≃	261	48.44 N	1.48 E
Pont-sur-Yonne	50	48.17 N	3.12 E
Pontuda, Ilha I	287a	23.02 S	43.18 W
Pontus ▫[9]	130	40.15 N	38.00 E
Pontvallain	50	47.45 N	0.12 E
Pont-Viau ◆[8]	275a	45.34 N	73.41 W
Pontyberem	42	51.17 N	4.09 W
Pontycymer	42	51.37 N	3.34 W
Pontypool	42	51.43 N	3.02 W
Pontypridd	42	51.37 N	3.22 W
Pony	202	45.39 N	111.53 W
Ponyri	76	52.19 N	36.20 E
Ponza	66	40.54 N	12.58 E
Ponza, Isola di I	66	40.55 N	12.57 E
Ponziane, Isole II	66	40.55 N	12.57 E
Ponzone	62	44.35 N	8.27 E
Poochera	162	32.43 S	134.51 E
Pool ▫[5]	152	3.30 S	15.00 E
Poole	42	50.43 N	1.59 W
Poole, Mount ∧	166	29.37 S	141.46 E
Poole Bay c	42	50.42 N	1.52 W
Pooler	192	32.06 N	81.14 W
Poole's Cavern ⊥[5]	262	53.14 N	1.56 W
Pooles Island I	208	39.17 N	76.16 W
Poolesville	208	39.08 N	77.25 W
Poolewe	46	57.45 N	5.37 W
Pooley Island I	182	52.44 N	128.16 W
Pool's Cove	186	47.41 N	55.26 W
Poolville	222	32.58 N	97.52 W
Poona → Pune	122	18.32 N	73.52 E
Pooncarie	166	33.23 S	142.34 E
Poondinna, Mount ∧	162	27.20 S	129.59 E
Poopo	248	18.23 S	66.59 W
Poopó, Lago ⊜	248	18.45 S	67.07 W
Pooraka	168b	34.50 S	138.37 E
Poor Knights Islands II	172	35.30 S	174.45 E
Poor Man Indian Reserve ◆[4]	184	51.30 N	104.23 W
Poor Meadow Brook ≃	283	42.01 N	70.55 W
Poortjie	158	30.13 S	22.44 E
Poowong	169	38.21 S	145.46 E
Popa, Isla I	236	9.11 N	82.07 W
Popasna	83	48.37 N	38.20 E
Popasne	78	48.48 N	35.31 E
Popayán	246	2.27 N	76.36 W
Pope	194	34.12 N	89.56 W
Pope Creek ≃	226	38.37 N	122.17 W
Popelnaste	78	48.39 N	33.43 E
Poperečnoje	88	52.23 N	110.42 E
Poperinge	50	50.51 N	2.43 E
Popești	38	47.14 N	22.25 E
Popești-Leordeni	38	44.23 N	26.10 E
Pope Valley	226	38.37 N	122.26 W
Popham Bay c	176	64.10 N	65.10 W
Popigaj	74	71.55 N	110.47 E
Popigaj ≃	74	72.54 N	106.36 E
Popil'nya	78	49.57 N	29.27 E
Popiltah Lake ⊜	166	33.10 S	141.43 E
Popinci	38	42.25 N	24.17 E
Popki	80	50.11 N	44.30 E
Popkum	224	49.12 N	121.44 W
Poplar, Ca., U.S.	226	36.03 N	119.08 W
Poplar, Mt., U.S.	198	48.06 N	105.11 W
Poplar, Wi., U.S.	190	46.35 N	91.47 W
Poplar ◆[8]	260	51.31 N	0.01 W
Poplar ≃, Can.	184	53.00 N	97.24 W
Poplar ≃, N.A.	198	48.05 N	105.11 W
Poplar ≃, Mn., U.S.	198	47.51 N	96.04 W
Poplar, West Fork ≃	198	48.31 N	105.22 W
Poplar Bluff	194	36.45 N	90.23 W
Poplar Grove	216	42.22 N	88.49 W
Poplar Heights	284c	38.53 N	77.12 W
Poplar Hill	184	52.05 N	94.18 W
Poplar Mountain ∧	194	36.43 N	85.03 W
Poplar Point	184	50.04 N	97.57 W
Poplar Ridge	210	42.44 N	76.37 W
Poplar Springs	208	39.21 N	77.06 W
Poplarville	194	30.50 N	89.32 W
Poplevinskij	76	53.41 N	39.33 E
Popocatépetl, Volcán ∧[1]	234	19.02 N	98.38 W
Popof Island I	180	55.17 N	160.25 W
Popoh	115a	8.15 S	111.48 E
Popokabaka	152	5.42 S	16.35 E
Popoli	66	42.10 N	13.50 E
Popondetta	164	8.46 S	148.14 E
Popova	89	42.58 N	131.42 E
Popovka, Ross.	76	60.08 N	39.21 E
Popovka, Ross.	80	49.14 N	41.12 E
Popovkino	82	56.07 N	36.01 E
Popovo	38	43.21 N	26.13 E
Poppberg ∧	60	49.25 N	11.35 E
Poppel	56	51.27 N	5.02 E
Poppenhausen	56	50.06 N	10.08 E
Poppenricht	60	49.29 N	11.48 E
Poppi	66	43.43 N	11.46 E
Popple ≃	190	45.50 N	88.21 W
Poprad	30	49.03 N	20.18 E
Poprad ≃	30	49.38 N	20.42 E
Popricani	38	47.18 N	27.31 E
Pŏpsŏng	98	35.22 N	126.27 E
Pŏptong	98	38.59 N	127.05 E
Poptún	236	16.21 N	89.26 W
Populonia	66	42.59 N	10.29 E
Poputnaja	84	44.31 N	41.27 E
Poquessing Creek ≃	285	40.03 N	74.58 W
Poquetanuck	207	41.29 N	72.02 W
Poquonock	207	41.54 N	72.40 W
Poquonock Bridge	207	41.20 N	72.01 W
Poquoson	208	37.07 N	76.21 W
Poquoson ≃	208	37.10 N	76.24 W
Poquott	276	40.57 N	73.05 W
Porādaha	126	23.51 N	89.01 E
Porādiha	126	21.33 N	86.26 E
Porāli Nai ≃	120	25.58 N	66.26 E
Poranga	250	4.44 S	40.55 W
Porangahau	172	40.18 S	176.37 E
Porangatu	255	13.26 S	49.10 W
Porazava	76	52.56 N	24.22 E
Porbandar	120	21.38 N	69.36 E
Porce ≃	246	7.28 N	74.53 W
Porchaman	128	33.08 N	63.51 E
Porcher Island I	182	53.57 N	130.30 W
Porcheville	261	48.58 N	1.47 E
Porchov	76	57.46 N	29.34 E
Porcia	64	45.57 N	12.36 E
Porciúncula	255	20.58 S	42.02 W
Porco	248	19.50 S	65.59 W
Porcos, Rio dos ≃	255	12.42 S	45.07 W
Porcuna	34	37.52 N	4.11 W
Porcupine ≃	180	66.35 N	145.15 W
Porcupine Brook ≃	283	42.46 N	71.13 W
Porcupine Creek ≃	202	48.07 N	106.20 W
Porcupine Creek, Middle Fork ≃	202	48.31 N	106.30 W
Porcupine Creek, West Fork ≃	202	48.31 N	106.30 W
Porcupine Dome ∧	180	65.31 N	145.31 W
Porcupine Hills ⋏[2]	184	52.30 N	101.45 W
Porcupine Mountains State Park ♦	190	46.47 N	89.50 W
Pordenone	64	45.57 N	12.39 E
Pordenone ▫[4]	64	46.00 N	12.45 E
Pordim	38	43.23 N	24.51 E
Poreč	36	45.13 N	13.37 E
Porecatu	255	22.43 S	51.24 W
Porečje, Ross.	76	55.43 N	35.33 E
Porečje, Ross.	76	56.06 N	30.29 E
Porečje-Rybnoje	80	57.06 N	39.23 E
Poreckoje	80	55.12 N	46.20 E
Porez	80	57.40 N	51.10 E
Porgera	164	5.28 S	143.12 E
Pori	26	61.29 N	21.47 E
Poricy Brook ≃	276	40.21 N	74.05 W
Poringland	42	52.33 N	1.21 E
Porirua	172	41.08 S	174.51 E
Porjaguba	24	66.47 N	33.45 E
Porkkala	26	59.59 N	24.26 E
Porlamar	246	10.57 N	63.51 W
Porlezza	58	46.03 N	9.07 E
Porlock	42	51.14 N	3.36 W
Porma ≃	34	42.29 N	5.28 W
Pornassio	62	44.04 N	7.52 E
Pörnbach	60	48.37 N	11.28 E
Pornic	32	47.07 N	2.06 W
Poro ∧	154	1.14 N	36.37 E
Porog, Ross.	24	63.50 N	38.29 E
Porog, Ross.	76	59.16 N	33.24 E
Porogi	265a	59.46 N	30.47 E
Poro Island I	116	10.40 N	124.27 E
Porokylä	26	63.33 N	29.06 E
Poroma	248	18.29 S	65.30 W
Poronaj ≃	89	49.14 N	143.06 E
Poronajsk	89	49.14 N	143.04 E
Porong	115a	7.32 S	112.41 E
Porong ≃	115a	7.32 S	112.51 E
Poropotank ≃	208	37.27 N	76.42 W
Poroshkove	78	48.41 N	22.45 E
Porosozero	24	62.43 N	32.42 E
Poroto Mountains ⋏	154	9.00 S	33.45 E
Porožskij	88	56.04 N	101.46 E
Porpoise Bay c	9	66.30 S	128.30 E
Porpoise Channel ⊔	276	40.55 N	73.09 W
Porquerolles	62	43.00 N	6.12 E
Porquerolles, Île de I	62	43.00 N	6.13 E
Porrentruy	58	47.25 N	7.05 E
Porretta Terme	64	44.09 N	10.59 E
Porsangen c[2]	24	70.58 N	27.00 E
Porsangerhalvøya >[1]	24	70.50 N	25.00 E
Porsea	114	2.27 N	99.09 E
Porsgrunn	26	59.09 N	9.40 E
Porsuk ≃	130	39.42 N	31.59 E
Port → Le Port	157c	20.55 S	55.18 E
Portachuelo	248	17.21 S	63.24 W
Portacloy	48	54.19 N	9.48 W
Port Adelaide	168b	34.51 S	138.30 E
Portadown	48	54.26 N	6.27 W
Portaferry	48	54.23 N	5.33 W
Portage, In., U.S.	216	41.34 N	87.10 W
Portage, Mi., U.S.	216	42.12 N	85.34 W
Portage, Oh., U.S.	216	41.20 N	83.39 W
Portage, Pa., U.S.	214	40.23 N	78.40 W
Portage, Ut,. U.S.	200	41.58 N	112.14 W
Portage, Wi., U.S.	190	43.32 N	89.27 W
Portage ▫[6]	214	41.09 N	81.15 W
Portage ≃, Mi., U.S.	216	41.57 N	85.38 W
Portage ≃, Oh., U.S.	214	41.31 N	83.05 W
Portage, East Branch ≃	216	41.17 N	83.31 W
Portage, Middle Branch ≃	216	41.22 N	83.28 W
Portage, North Branch ≃	216	41.25 N	83.27 W
Portage, South Branch ≃	216	41.22 N	83.30 W
Portage Bay c	184	51.33 N	98.50 W
Portage Des Sioux	219	38.55 N	90.20 W
Portage Lake ⊜, Mi., U.S.	190	47.04 N	88.30 W
Portage Lake ⊜, Mi., U.S.	216	42.03 N	85.31 W
Portage Lake ⊜, Mi., U.S.	216	42.25 N	83.54 W
Portage Lakes	214	40.59 N	81.32 W
Portage Lakes ⊜	214	40.59 N	81.32 W
Portage Lakes State Park ♦	214	40.57 N	81.32 W
Portage-la-Prairie	184	49.59 N	98.18 W
Portage Park ◆[8]	278	41.57 N	87.46 W
Portageville, Mo., U.S.	194	36.25 N	89.41 W
Portageville, N.Y., U.S.	210	42.34 N	78.02 W
Portal, Ga., U.S.	192	32.32 N	81.55 W
Portal, N.D., U.S.	198	48.59 N	102.32 W
Port Alberni	224	49.14 N	124.48 W
Portal del Infierno ∟	236	14.22 N	85.38 W
Portalegre, Bra.	250	6.02 S	38.00 W
Portalegre, Port.	34	39.17 N	7.26 W
Portales	196	34.11 N	103.20 W
Port Alexander	180	56.15 N	134.39 W
Port Alfred (Kowie)	158	33.36 S	26.55 E
Port Alice	182	50.23 N	127.27 W
Port Allegany	214	41.48 N	78.16 W
Port Allen	194	30.27 N	91.12 W
Port Alma, Austl.	166	23.35 S	150.51 E
Port Alma, On., Can.	214	42.11 N	82.15 W
Port Alsworth	180	60.12 N	154.20 W
Port Angeles	224	48.07 N	123.25 W
Port Angeles Harbor c	224	48.07 N	123.24 W
Port Anson	186	49.32 N	55.50 W
Port Antonio	241q	18.11 N	76.28 W
Port Aransas	196	27.50 N	97.04 W
Portarlington, Austl.	169	38.07 S	144.39 E
Portarlington, Ire.	48	53.10 N	7.11 W
Port Arthur, Austl.	166	43.09 S	147.51 E
Port Arthur → Thunder Bay, On., Can.	190	48.23 N	89.15 W
Port Arthur, Tx., U.S.	194	29.53 N	93.55 W
Port Arthur → Lüshun, Zhg.	98	38.48 N	121.16 E
Port Ashton	180	60.04 N	148.01 W
Port Askaig	46	55.51 N	6.07 W
Port Augusta	166	32.30 S	137.46 E
Port au Port	186	48.33 N	58.44 W
Port au Port Bay c	186	48.40 N	58.45 W
Port au Port Peninsula >[1]	186	48.35 N	59.00 W
Port-au-Prince	238	18.32 N	72.20 W
Port-au-Prince, Baie de c	238	18.40 N	72.30 W
Port Austin	190	44.02 N	82.59 W
Port-aux-Basques → Channel-Port-aux-Basques	186	47.34 N	59.09 W
Portavogie	48	54.27 N	5.27 W
Porta Westfalica	52	52.14 N	8.55 E
Porta Westfalica ♦	52	52.14 N	8.55 E
Port Bannatyne	46	55.52 N	5.05 W
Port Barre	194	30.33 N	91.57 W
Port Bell	154	0.17 N	32.39 E
Port-Bergé	157b	15.33 S	47.40 E
Port Blair	110	11.40 N	92.45 E
Port Blakely	224	47.37 N	122.28 W
Port Blandford	186	48.21 N	54.10 W
Port Bolivar	222	29.23 N	94.46 W
Port Borden	186	46.15 N	63.42 W
Port-Bouët	150	5.15 N	3.58 W
Port Broughton	166	33.36 S	137.56 E
Port Burwell	212	42.39 N	80.49 W
Port Byron, Il., U.S.	190	41.36 N	90.20 W
Port Byron, N.Y., U.S.	210	43.02 N	76.37 W
Port Campbell	169	38.37 S	143.00 E
Port Campbell National Park ♦	169	38.38 S	142.55 E
Port Canning	126	22.18 N	88.40 E
Port Carbon	208	40.42 N	76.10 W
Port Carling	212	45.07 N	79.35 W
Port-Cartier	186	50.01 N	66.52 W
Port-Cartier Sept-Îles, Réserve ♦	186	50.35 N	67.10 W
Port Chalmers	172	45.49 S	170.37 E
Port Charlotte	220	26.58 N	82.05 W
Port Chester	210	41.00 N	73.39 W
Port Chester Harbor c	276	40.59 N	73.40 W
Port Clements	182	53.42 N	132.11 W
Port Clinton, Austl.	168b	34.14 S	138.01 E
Port Clinton, Oh., U.S.	214	41.30 N	82.56 W
Port Clinton, Pa., U.S.	208	40.35 N	76.02 W
Port Clyde	188	43.55 N	69.15 W
Port Colborne	212	42.53 N	79.14 W
Port Colden	210	40.45 N	74.57 W
Port Columbus International Airport ⊠	218	40.00 N	82.53 W
Port Coquitlam	224	49.16 N	122.46 W
Port Costa	282	38.03 N	122.11 W
Port Crane	210	42.10 N	75.50 W
Port Credit	212	43.33 N	79.35 W
Port-Cros	62	43.00 N	6.23 E
Port-Cros, Île de I	62	43.00 N	6.24 E
Port-Cros, Parc National de ♦	62	43.01 N	6.24 E
Port-Daniel, Réserve ♦	186	48.18 N	64.55 W
Port-de-Bouc	62	43.24 N	4.59 E
Port-de-Paix	238	19.57 N	72.50 W
Port Deposit	208	39.36 N	76.06 W
Port Dickinson	210	42.08 N	75.53 W
Port Dickson	114	2.31 N	101.48 E
Porte Crayon, Mount ∧	188	38.56 N	79.27 W
Port Edward, B.C., Can.	182	54.14 N	130.18 W
Port Edward, S. Afr.	158	31.02 S	30.13 E
Port Edward → Weihai, Zhg.	98	37.28 N	122.07 E
Port Edwards	190	44.21 N	89.51 W
Portegolpe	236	10.20 N	85.46 W
Porteiras	250	7.31 S	39.07 W
Porteirinha	255	15.44 S	43.02 W
Portel, Bra.	250	1.57 S	50.49 W
Portel, Port.	34	38.18 N	7.42 W
Portela, Aeroporto da ⊠	266c	38.46 N	9.08 W
Port Elgin, N.B., Can.	186	46.03 N	64.05 W
Port Elgin, On., Can.	190	44.26 N	81.24 W
Port Elizabeth, St. Vin.	241h	13.03 N	61.13 W
Port Elizabeth, S. Afr.	158	33.58 S	25.40 E
Port Elizabeth, N.J., U.S.	208	39.18 N	74.58 W
Port Ellen	46	55.39 N	6.12 W
Port Elliot	168b	35.32 S	138.41 E
Port-en-Bessin	32	49.21 N	0.45 W
Porter, In., U.S.	216	41.36 N	87.04 W
Porter, Ok., U.S.	196	35.52 N	95.31 W
Porter, Tx., U.S.	222	30.06 N	95.14 W
Porter, Wa., U.S.	224	46.56 N	123.18 W
Porter ▫[6]	216	41.28 N	87.04 W
Port'Ercole	66	42.23 N	11.12 E
Porter Corners	210	43.09 N	73.53 W
Porter Creek ≃	279a	41.41 N	81.56 W
Port Erin	44	54.06 N	4.44 W
Porter Lake ⊜	184	56.21 N	107.20 W
Porter Point >	241h	13.23 N	61.11 W
Porter Springs	222	31.16 N	95.36 W
Porters Retreat	170	34.00 S	149.48 E
Porters Run ≃	279b	40.27 N	79.33 W
Portersville	214	40.56 N	80.09 W
Porterville, S. Afr.	158	33.00 S	19.00 E
Porterville, Ca., U.S.	204	36.03 N	119.00 W
Porterville, Ms., U.S.	194	32.41 N	88.28 W
Portes-lés-Valence	62	44.52 N	4.53 E
Port Essington	182	54.09 N	129.57 W
Portete, Bahía c	246	12.13 N	71.55 W
Port-Étienne → Nouâdhibou	148	20.54 N	17.04 W
Port Ewen	210	41.54 N	73.58 W
Port-Eynon	42	51.33 N	4.13 W
Port-Eynon Point >	42	51.32 N	4.12 W
Portezuelo	234	20.25 N	102.31 W
Port Fairy	166	38.23 S	142.14 E
Port Fitzroy	172	36.10 S	175.21 E
Port Gamble	224	47.51 N	122.34 W
Port Gamble Indian Reservation ◆[4]	224	47.53 N	122.34 W
Port Gentil	152	0.43 S	8.47 E
Port Germein	166	33.01 S	138.00 E
Port Gibson, Ms., U.S.	194	31.57 N	90.59 W
Port Gibson, N.Y., U.S.	210	43.02 N	77.09 W
Port Glasgow	46	55.57 N	4.41 W
Portglenone	48	54.52 N	6.29 W
Port Graham	180	59.21 N	151.50 W
Port Greville	186	45.24 N	64.33 W
Porth	42	51.38 N	3.25 W
Port Hacking	274a	34.04 S	151.08 E
Port Hacking Point >	170	34.05 S	151.10 E
Port Harcourt	150	4.43 N	7.05 E
Port Hardy	182	50.43 N	127.29 W
Port Hawkesbury	186	45.37 N	61.21 W
Porthcawl	42	51.29 N	3.43 W
Port Hedland	162	20.19 S	118.34 E
Port Heiden	180	56.55 N	158.41 W
Port Henry	188	44.02 N	73.27 W
Port Hill	186	46.35 N	63.53 W
Porthleven	42	50.05 N	5.19 W
Porthmadog	42	52.55 N	4.08 W
Porth Neigwl c	42	52.48 N	4.34 W
Port Hood	186	46.01 N	61.32 W
Port Hope, On., Can.	212	43.57 N	78.18 W
Port Hope, Mi., U.S.	190	43.56 N	82.42 W
Port Howe	238	24.15 N	75.21 W
Port Hueneme	228	34.08 N	119.11 W
Port Hughes	168b	34.04 S	137.32 E
Port Huron	214	42.58 N	82.25 W
Portici	68	40.49 N	14.20 E
Portico di Romagna	66	44.01 N	11.47 E
Portigliola	68	38.14 N	16.13 E
Port-Ilič	84	38.53 N	48.48 E
Portimão	34	37.08 N	8.32 W
Portinho, Rio do ≃	287a	23.03 S	43.35 W
Port Isaac	42	50.35 N	4.49 W
Port Isabel	196	26.04 N	97.12 W
Portishead	42	51.30 N	2.46 W
Port Jefferson, N.Y., U.S.	210	40.56 N	73.03 W
Port Jefferson, Oh., U.S.	216	40.19 N	84.05 W
Port Jefferson Harbor c	276	40.58 N	73.05 W
Port Jefferson Station	210	40.55 N	73.02 W
Port Jervis	210	41.22 N	74.41 W
Port Julia	168b	34.40 S	137.52 E
Port-Katon	83	46.52 N	38.46 E
Port Kembla	170	34.29 S	150.54 E
Port Kennedy	285	40.06 N	75.25 W
Port Kenny	162	33.10 S	134.42 E
Portknockie	46	57.41 N	2.51 W
Port Láirge → Waterford	48	52.15 N	7.06 W
Port Lambton	214	42.39 N	82.30 W
Portland, Austl.	166	38.21 S	141.36 E
Portland, Austl.	170	33.22 S	150.00 E
Portland, N.Z.	172	35.48 S	174.19 E
Portland, Ar., U.S.	194	33.14 N	91.30 W
Portland, Ct., U.S.	207	41.34 N	72.38 W
Portland, In., U.S.	216	40.26 N	84.58 W
Portland, Me., U.S.	188	43.39 N	70.15 W
Portland, Mi., U.S.	216	42.52 N	84.54 W
Portland, Mo., U.S.	219	38.42 N	91.43 W
Portland, N.Y., U.S.	214	42.22 N	79.28 W
Portland, N.D., U.S.	198	47.29 N	97.22 W
Portland, Or., U.S.	224	45.31 N	122.40 W
Portland, Pa., U.S.	210	40.55 N	75.06 W
Portland, Tn., U.S.	194	36.34 N	86.30 W
Portland, Tx., U.S.	196	27.52 N	97.19 W
Portland, Wi., U.S.	216	43.12 N	88.58 W
Portland, Bill of >	42	50.31 N	2.27 W
Portland, Cape >	166	40.45 S	147.57 E
Portland, Isle of I	42	50.33 N	2.27 W
Portland Bay c	166	38.19 S	141.47 E
Portland Bight c[3]	241q	17.53 N	77.08 W
Portland Canal c	182	55.10 N	130.08 W
Portland Creek Pond ⊜	186	50.12 N	57.34 W
Portland Inlet c	182	54.50 N	130.15 W
Portland International Airport ⊠	224	45.35 N	122.36 W
Portland Island I	172	39.17 S	177.52 E
Portland Mills	214	41.23 N	78.50 W
Portland Point >	241q	17.42 N	77.11 W
Portlandville	210	42.32 N	74.58 W
Port Laoise (Maryborough)	48	53.02 N	7.17 W
Port Lavaca	196	28.36 N	96.37 W
Portlaw	48	52.17 N	7.19 W
Port-Lesney	58	47.00 N	5.49 E
Portlethen	46	57.03 N	2.06 W
Port Leyden	212	43.35 N	75.21 W
Port Lincoln	166	34.44 S	135.52 E
Port Lions	180	57.52 N	152.53 W
Portlock Reefs ✣[2]	164	9.30 S	144.45 E
Port Logan	44	54.43 N	4.56 W
Port Loko	150	8.46 N	12.47 W
Port-Louis, Fr.	32	47.43 N	3.21 W
Port-Louis, Guad.	241o	16.25 N	61.32 W
Port Louis, Maus.	157c	20.10 S	57.30 E
Port Ludlow	224	47.55 N	122.40 W
Port-Lyautey → Kenitra	148	34.16 N	6.40 W
Port MacDonnell	166	38.03 S	140.42 E
Port Macquarie	166	31.26 S	152.55 E
Port Madison Indian Reservation ◆[4]	224	47.45 N	122.35 W
Portmahomack	46	57.49 N	3.50 W
Port Maitland	186	43.59 N	66.09 W
Port Maria	241q	18.22 N	76.54 W
Portmarnock	48	53.25 N	6.08 W
Port Matilda	214	40.48 N	78.03 W
Port Mayaca	220	27.08 N	80.12 W
Port McNeill	182	50.35 N	127.06 W
Port McNicoll	212	44.45 N	79.49 W
Port Melbourne	274b	37.51 S	144.56 E
Port Mellon	182	49.32 N	123.29 W
Port-Menier	186	49.48 N	64.20 W
Port Moller	180	55.59 N	160.34 W
Port Monmouth	276	40.25 N	74.05 W
Port Moody	224	49.17 N	122.51 W
Port Morant	241q	17.54 N	76.19 W
Portmore	241q	17.58 N	76.53 W
Port Moresby	164	9.30 S	147.10 E
Port Moresby ▫[5]	164	9.30 S	147.10 E
Port Morien	186	46.08 N	59.52 W
Port Morris	276	40.54 N	74.41 W
Port Mouton	186	43.56 N	64.51 W
Port Murray	210	40.47 N	74.54 W
Portnaguran	46	58.17 N	6.13 W
Portnahaven	46	55.41 N	6.31 W
Port Neches	194	29.59 N	93.57 W
Port Neill	166	34.07 S	136.20 E
Port Nelson	184	57.03 N	92.36 W
Portneuf	206	46.42 N	71.53 W
Portneuf ▫[6]	206	46.45 N	72.00 W
Portneuf ≃, P.Q., Can.	186	48.38 N	69.05 W
Portneuf ≃, P.Q., Can.	206	46.42 N	71.53 W
Portneuf ≃, Id., U.S.	202	42.58 N	112.35 W
Portneuf, Lac ⊜	186	49.08 N	70.18 W
Portneuf-Station	206	46.43 N	71.54 W
Portneuf-sur-Mer	186	48.37 N	69.06 W
Port Neville	182	50.29 N	126.05 W
Port Noarlunga	168b	35.09 S	138.28 E
Port Nolloth	156	29.17 S	16.51 E
Port Norris	208	39.14 N	75.02 W
Porto, Bra.	250	3.54 S	42.42 W
Porto, Port.	34	41.11 N	8.36 W
Porto, Bonifica di ◆[1]	267a	41.48 N	12.16 E
Porto Acre	248	9.34 S	67.31 W
Porto Alegre, Bra.	252	30.04 S	51.11 W
Porto Alegre, S. Tom./P.	152	0.02 N	6.32 E
Porto Amboim	152	10.44 S	13.44 E
Porto Azzurro	66	42.46 N	10.24 E
Portobello	46	55.58 N	3.07 W
Porto Belo, Bra.	252	27.10 S	48.33 W
Portobelo, Pan.	236	9.33 N	79.39 W
Porto Calvo	250	9.04 S	35.24 W
Porto Ceresio	58	45.54 N	8.55 E
Port O'Connor	196	28.27 N	96.24 W
Porto das Caixas	256	22.42 S	42.53 W
Porto d'Ascoli	66	42.55 N	13.53 E
Porto das Flôres	256	22.05 S	43.34 W
Porto das Gabarras	250	3.07 S	44.34 W
Pôrto de Mós	34	39.36 N	8.39 W
Porto de Moz	250	1.45 S	52.14 W
Porto de Pedras	250	9.10 S	35.17 W
Porto di Potenza Picena	66	43.21 N	13.42 E
Porto di Traiano, Necropoli del ⊥	267a	41.46 N	12.16 E
Porto dos Gaúchos	250	11.29 S	57.22 W
Porto Empedocle	70	37.17 N	13.32 E
Porto Esperança	248	19.37 S	57.27 W
Porto Esperidião	248	15.51 S	58.28 W
Porto Farina	36	37.10 N	10.12 E
Porto Feliz	255	23.13 S	47.32 W
Portoferraio	66	42.49 N	10.19 E
Porto Ferreira	255	21.51 S	47.28 W
Portofino	62	44.18 N	9.12 E
Port of Ness	46	58.29 N	6.13 W
Porto Franco	250	6.20 S	47.24 W
Port of Spain	241r	10.39 N	61.31 W
Porto Garibaldi	66	44.41 N	12.14 E
Porto Grande	250	0.42 N	51.24 W
Portogruaro	64	45.47 N	12.50 E
Porto Inglês	150a	15.08 N	23.13 W
Portola	204	39.48 N	120.28 W
Portola State Park ♦	226	37.15 N	122.13 W
Portola Valley	226	37.23 N	122.13 W
Porto Lucena	252	27.51 S	55.01 W
Pörtom (Pirttikylä)	26	62.42 N	21.37 E
Portomaggiore	64	44.42 N	11.48 E
Porto Maurizio	62	43.52 N	8.01 E
Porto Mendes	252	24.30 S	54.20 W
Porto Murtinho	248	21.42 S	57.52 W
Porto Nacional	250	10.42 S	48.25 W
Porto-Novo, Bénin	150	6.29 N	2.37 E
Porto Novo, Bra.	256	23.40 S	45.28 W
Porto Novo, India	122	11.29 N	79.46 E
Porto Novo Creek c	273a	6.26 N	3.20 E
Portopalo, It.	70	36.41 N	15.08 E
Porto Palo, It.	70	37.34 N	12.54 E
Port Orange	192	29.06 N	80.59 W
Port Orchard	224	47.32 N	122.38 W
Porto Real	256	22.25 S	44.20 W
Porto Real do Colégio	250	10.11 S	36.49 W
Porto Recanati	66	43.26 N	13.40 E
Port Orford	202	42.44 N	124.29 W
Porto Rico	152	6.08 S	12.30 E
Porto Rico → Puerto Rico ▫[2]	240m	18.15 N	66.30 W
Portorož	64	45.31 N	13.36 E
Porto Salvo	266c	38.43 N	9.18 W
Porto San Giorgio	66	43.11 N	13.48 E
Porto Santana	250	0.03 S	51.11 W
Porto Sant'Elpidio	66	43.15 N	13.45 E
Porto Santo I	148	33.04 N	16.20 W
Porto Santo Stefano	66	42.26 N	11.07 E
Porto São José	255	22.43 S	53.10 W
Portoscuso	71	39.12 N	8.23 E
Porto Seguro, Bra.	255	16.26 S	39.05 W
Porto-Séguro, Togo	150	6.12 N	1.29 E
Porto Torres	71	40.50 N	8.24 E
Porto União	252	26.15 S	51.05 W
Porto Válter	248	8.15 S	72.45 W
Porto Valtravaglia	58	45.58 N	8.41 E
Porto-Vecchio	36	41.35 N	9.16 E
Porto Velho	248	8.46 S	63.54 W
Porto Velho do Cunha	256	21.50 S	42.32 W
Portovenere	62	44.03 N	9.51 E
Portoviejo	246	1.03 S	80.27 W
Portpatrick, Scot., U.K.	44	54.51 N	5.07 W
Port Patrick, Vanuatu	175f	20.08 S	169.47 E
Port Penn	208	39.31 N	75.34 W
Port Perry	212	44.06 N	78.57 W
Port Phillip Bay c	169	38.07 S	144.48 E
Port Pirie	166	33.11 S	138.01 E
Port Providence	285	40.08 N	75.30 W
Portraine	48	53.30 N	6.07 W
Port Reading	276	40.33 N	74.15 W
Portree	46	57.24 N	6.12 W
Port Renfrew	224	48.33 N	124.25 W
Port Republic	208	39.31 N	74.29 W
Port Rexton	186	48.23 N	53.20 W
Port Richey	220	28.16 N	82.43 W
Port Richmond	208	37.33 N	76.49 W
Port Robinson	284a	43.02 N	79.13 W
Port Rowan	214	42.37 N	80.28 W
Port Royal, Jam.	241q	17.56 N	76.51 W
Port Royal, Ky., U.S.	218	38.33 N	85.04 W
Port Royal, Pa., U.S.	208	40.32 N	77.23 W
Port Royal, S.C., U.S.	192	32.22 N	80.41 W
Port Royal, Va., U.S.	208	38.10 N	77.11 W
Port-Royal-des-Champs, Abbaye de ♥[1]	261	48.45 N	2.01 E
Port Royal National Historic Park ♦	186	44.44 N	65.40 W
Portrush	48	55.12 N	6.40 W
Port Said → Būr Sa'īd	142	31.16 N	32.18 E
Port-Sainte-Marie	32	44.15 N	0.24 E
Port Saint Joe	192	29.49 N	85.18 W
Port Saint Johns	158	31.38 S	29.33 E
Port-Saint-Louis	62	43.23 N	4.48 E
Port Saint Lucie	220	27.20 N	80.20 W
Port Saint Mary	44	54.05 N	4.43 W
Port-Saint-Servan	186	51.19 N	58.02 W
Port Salerno	220	27.08 N	80.12 W
Portsalon	48	55.13 N	7.37 W
Port Sanilac	190	43.25 N	82.32 W
Port Saunders	186	50.39 N	57.18 W
Pörtschach	61	46.37 N	14.08 E
Portsea	169	38.19 S	144.43 E
Port Seton	46	55.58 N	2.57 W
Port Shepstone	158	30.46 S	30.22 E
Portslade	42	50.50 N	0.11 W
Portsmouth, Dom.	240d	15.35 N	61.28 W
Portsmouth, Eng., U.K.	42	50.48 N	1.05 W
Portsmouth, N.H., U.S.	188	43.04 N	70.45 W
Portsmouth, Oh., U.S.	218	38.43 N	82.59 W
Portsmouth, R.I., U.S.	207	41.36 N	71.15 W
Portsmouth, Va., U.S.	208	36.50 N	76.17 W
Portsmouth Naval Shipyard ■	188	43.05 N	70.45 W
Portsoy	46	57.41 N	2.41 W
Port Stanley, On., Can.	214	42.40 N	81.13 W
Port Stanley → Stanley, Falk. Is.	254	51.42 S	57.51 W
Portstewart	48	55.11 N	6.43 W
Port Sudan → Būr Sūdān	140	19.37 N	37.14 E
Port Sulphur	194	29.28 N	89.41 W
Port Sunlight	262	53.21 N	2.59 W
Port-sur-Saône	58	47.41 N	6.03 E
Port Talbot	42	51.36 N	3.47 W
Port Taufiq → Būr Tawfīq	128	29.57 N	32.34 E
Porttipahdan tekojärvi ⊜[1]	24	68.08 N	26.40 E
Port Tobacco River c	208	38.27 N	77.02 W
Port Townsend	224	48.07 N	122.45 W
Port Trevorton	208	40.42 N	76.52 W
Portugal ▫[1], Europe	22	39.30 N	8.00 W
Portugal ▫[1], Europe	34	39.30 N	8.00 W
Portugal, Cachoeira ∟	248	9.55 S	64.16 W
Portugal Cove South	186	46.42 N	53.15 W
Portugalete	34	43.19 N	3.01 W
Portuguesa ▫[3]	246	9.10 N	69.15 W
Portuguesa ≃	246	7.57 N	67.32 W
Portuguese Guinea → Guinea-Bissau ▫[1]	150	12.00 N	15.00 W
Portumna	48	53.06 N	8.13 W
Port Union, Nf., Can.	186	48.30 N	53.05 W
Port Union, On., Can.	275b	43.47 N	79.08 W
Port-Vendres	32	42.31 N	3.07 E
Port Victoria → Victoria	138	4.38 S	55.27 E
Port Vila	175f	17.44 S	168.19 E
Portville	210	42.02 N	78.20 W
Port Vincent	168b	34.47 S	137.51 E
Port-Vladimir	24	69.25 N	33.06 E
Port Vue	279b	40.20 N	79.52 W
Port Waikato	172	37.23 S	174.44 E
Port Wakefield, Austl.	168b	34.11 S	138.09 E
Port Wakefield, Ak., U.S.	180	58.03 N	153.03 W
Port Washington, B.C., Can.	224	48.49 N	123.19 W
Port Washington, N.Y., U.S.	210	40.49 N	73.41 W
Port Washington, Oh., U.S.	214	40.27 N	81.37 W
Port Washington, Wi., U.S.	190	43.23 N	87.52 W
Port Weld	114	4.50 N	100.38 E
Port Welshpool	169	38.42 S	146.28 E
Port Wentworth	192	32.08 N	81.09 W
Port William, Scot., U.K.	44	54.46 N	4.35 W
Port William, Oh., U.S.	218	39.33 N	83.47 W
Port Wing	190	46.46 N	91.23 W
Porum	196	35.21 N	95.15 W
Porus	241q	18.02 N	77.25 W
Porvenir, Chile	254	53.18 S	70.22 W
Porvenir, Méx.	232	31.15 N	105.51 W
Porvoo (Borgå)	26	60.24 N	25.40 E
Porvoonjoki ≃	26	60.23 N	25.40 E
Porz	56	50.53 N	7.03 E
Porzdni	80	57.00 N	42.33 E
Porzuna	34	39.09 N	4.09 W
Posada	71	40.38 N	9.43 E
Posada ≃	71	40.39 N	9.45 E
Posadas, Arg.	252	27.23 S	55.53 W
Posadas, Esp.	34	37.48 N	5.06 W
Posavina V	36	45.10 N	17.20 E
Poščharv	85	38.24 N	71.10 E
Poschiavino ≃	58	46.12 N	10.10 E
Poschiavo	58	46.18 N	10.04 E
Pošechon'e	76	58.30 N	39.07 E
Posen → Poznań, Pol.	30	52.25 N	16.55 E
Posen, Il., U.S.	278	41.37 N	87.40 W
Posen, Mi., U.S.	190	45.15 N	83.41 W
Poseritz	54	54.18 N	13.16 E
Posesión, Bahía c	254	52.17 S	69.14 W
Posevnaja	86	54.18 N	83.20 E
Poshan → Boshan	98	36.29 N	117.50 E
Poshiwu	106	30.22 N	119.36 E
Posieux	58	46.46 N	7.06 E
Posina	64	45.47 N	11.15 E
Pösing	60	49.14 N	12.33 E
Posio	26	66.06 N	28.09 E
Positano	68	40.38 N	14.29 E
Posjet	89	42.39 N	130.50 E
Poso	112	1.23 S	120.44 E
Poso, Danau ⊜	112	1.52 S	120.35 E
Poso, Teluk c	112	1.15 S	120.55 E
Poso Creek ≃	226	35.41 N	119.22 W
Posof	130	41.31 N	42.42 E
Pos'olki	80	53.08 N	46.29 E
Pos'olok	265a	59.43 N	30.12 E
Posŏng	98	34.47 N	127.04 E
Posooy, Mount ∧	116	17.21 N	120.48 E
Pospelicha	86	51.57 N	81.46 E
Possagno	64	45.51 N	11.51 E
Posse, Bra.	255	14.05 S	46.22 W
Posse, Bra.	256	22.16 S	43.06 W
Possel	152	5.01 N	19.15 E
Possendorf	54	50.57 N	13.42 E
Posses	256	21.43 S	46.08 W
Possession Islands II	9	71.27 S	171.08 E
Possession Sound ⊔	224	48.00 N	122.20 W
Possidhonia ⊥	38	37.40 N	24.00 E
Pössneck	54	50.42 N	11.37 E
Possruck (Kozjak) ⋏	61	46.37 N	15.28 E
Possum Kingdom Lake ⊜[1]	196	32.55 N	98.28 W
Post	196	33.11 N	101.22 W
Posta	66	42.31 N	13.06 E
Postal (Burgstall)	64	46.36 N	11.11 E
Postau	60	48.39 N	12.20 E
Postbauer	60	49.19 N	11.21 E
Post Creek ≃	210	42.09 N	77.02 W
Poste-de-la-Baleine	176	55.17 N	77.45 W
Postelle	192	35.02 N	84.22 W
Poste Ramartina	157b	19.38 S	45.58 E
Posterholt	52	51.07 N	6.03 E
Post Falls	202	47.43 N	116.57 W
Postiglione	68	40.33 N	15.13 E
Postmasburg	158	28.18 S	23.05 E
Postojna	36	45.47 N	14.13 E
Postojnska jama ⊥[7]	36	45.47 N	14.12 E
Postoloprty	54	50.20 N	13.40 E
P'ostraja Dresva	74	61.34 N	156.41 E
Postrevalle	248	18.29 S	63.51 W
Postsee ⊜	54	54.13 N	10.13 E
Poststadion ♦	264a	52.32 N	13.21 E
Postville	190	43.05 N	91.34 W
Pota	115b	8.20 S	120.46 E
Potaizi	104	41.34 N	121.08 E
Potake Pond ⊜	276	41.08 N	74.13 W
Pótam	232	27.36 N	110.23 W
Potanino	76	60.16 N	32.47 E
Potaro ≃	246	5.22 N	58.54 W
Potaro Landing	246	5.23 N	59.08 W
Potaro-Siparuni ▫[4]	246	5.00 N	59.30 W
Potato Creek ≃, Ga., U.S.	192	32.47 N	84.21 W
Potato Creek ≃, Pa., U.S.	214	41.53 N	78.23 W
Potawatomie Woods ♦	278	42.08 N	87.53 W
Potchefstroom	158	26.46 S	27.01 E
Poté	255	17.49 S	41.49 W
Poteau	194	35.03 N	94.37 W
Poteau ≃	194	35.23 N	94.26 W
Poteet	196	29.02 N	98.34 W
Potengi ≃	250	5.47 S	35.16 W
Pötenitz	54	53.57 N	10.58 E
Pötenitzer Wiek c	54	53.55 N	10.55 E
Potenji	250	7.06 S	40.00 W
Potenza	68	40.38 N	15.49 E
Potenza ▫[4]	68	40.30 N	15.50 E
Potenza ≃	66	43.25 N	13.40 E
Potenza Picena	66	43.22 N	13.37 E
Poteriteri, Lake ⊜	172	46.06 S	167.08 E
Potes	34	43.09 N	4.37 W
Potfontein	158	30.12 S	24.08 E
Potgietersrus	156	24.15 S	28.55 E
Poth	196	29.04 N	98.05 W
Potholes Reservoir ⊜[1]	202	47.01 N	119.19 W
Poti	84	42.09 N	41.40 E
Poti ≃	250	5.02 S	42.50 W
Potic Creek ≃	210	42.16 N	73.55 W
Potiraguá	255	15.36 S	39.53 W
Potirendaba	255	21.08 S	49.08 W
Potiskum	146	11.43 N	11.05 E
Potiyivka	78	50.37 N	28.58 E
Potlatch	202	46.55 N	116.53 W
Potlatch ≃	202	46.28 N	116.46 W
Po Toi Island I	271d	22.10 N	114.15 E
Po Toi Island Group II	271d	22.11 N	114.16 E
Potol Point >	116	11.56 N	121.57 E
Potomac, Il., U.S.	216	40.18 N	87.48 W
Potomac, Md., U.S.	284c	39.01 N	77.12 W
Potomac ≃	188	38.00 N	76.18 W
Potomac, South Branch ≃	188	39.31 N	78.35 W
Potomac, South Branch, North Fork ≃	188	38.59 N	79.11 W
Potomac, South Branch, South Fork ≃	188	39.04 N	78.59 W
Potomac Creek ≃	208	38.21 N	77.18 W
Potomac Creek, Long Branch ≃	208	38.23 N	77.29 W
Potomac Heights	208	38.36 N	77.08 W
Poto-Poto ◆[8]	273b	4.15 S	15.18 E
Potosí, Bol.	248	19.35 S	65.45 W

	English	Deutsch	Español	Français	Português
≃	River	Fluß	Río	Rivière	Rio
≅	Canal	Kanal	Canal	Canal	Canal
∟	Waterfall, Rapids	Wasserfall, Stromschnellen	Cascada, Rápidos	Chute d'eau, Rapides	Cascata, Rápidos
⊔	Strait	Meeresstraße	Estrecho	Détroit	Estreito
c	Bay, Gulf	Bucht, Golf	Bahía, Golfo	Baie, Golfe	Baía, Golfo
⊜	Lake, Lakes	See, Seen	Lago, Lagos	Lac, Lacs	Lago, Lagos
⁝⁝	Swamp	Sumpf	Pantano	Marais	Pântano
⊓	Ice Features, Glacier	Eis- und Gletscherformen	Accidentes Glaciales	Formes glaciaires	Acidentes glaciares
⊽	Other Hydrographic Features	Andere Hydrographische Objekte	Otros Elementos Hidrográficos	Autres données hydrographiques	Outros acidentes hidrográficos
✣	Submarine Features	Untermeerische Objekte	Accidentes Submarinos	Formes de relief sous-marin	Acidentes submarinos
▫	Political Unit	Politische Einheit	Unidad Politica	Entité politique	Unidade política
♥	Cultural Institution	Kulturelle Institution	Institución Cultural	Institution culturelle	Instituição cultural
⊥	Historical Site	Historische Stätte	Sitio Histórico	Site historique	Sitio histórico
♦	Recreational Site	Erholungs- und Ferienort	Sitio de Recreo	Centre de loisirs	Area de Lazer
⊠	Airport	Flughafen	Aeropuerto	Aéroport	Aeroporto
■	Military Installation	Militäranlage	Instalación Militar	Installation militaire	Instalação militar
◆	Miscellaneous	Verschiedenes	Misceláneo	Divers	Diversos

ENGLISH Name	Page	Lat.°'	Long.°'	DEUTSCH Name	Seite	Breite°'	Länge°' E = Ost

Name	Page	Lat.°'	Long.°'
Potosi, Mo., U.S.	194	37.56 N	90.47 W
Potosí □[5]	248	20.40 S	67.00 W
Pototan	116	10.55 N	122.40 E
Potrerillos, Chile	252	26.26 S	69.29 W
Potrerillos, Hond.	236	15.11 N	87.58 W
Potrerillos Arriba	236	8.41 N	82.30 W
Potrero	236	10.28 N	85.47 W
Potrero ⬥[8]	282	37.48 N	122.24 W
Potrero de Gallegos	234	22.38 N	103.41 W
Potrero del Llano	196	29.12 N	104.28 W
Potrero Grande	236	9.00 N	83.11 W
Potrite	248	61.32 S	16.10 W
Potro, Cerro del ʌ	252	28.24 S	69.39 W
Potsdam, Dtsch.	54	52.24 N	13.04 E
Potsdam, N.Y., U.S.	188	44.40 N	74.58 W
Potsdam, Oh., U.S.	218	39.58 N	84.25 W
Potsdam, Staatsforst ♠	264a	52.26 N	13.04 E
Potshausen	52	53.11 N	7.37 E
Pott, Île I	175f	19.35 S	163.36 E
Pottawatomie Creek ≃	198	38.29 N	94.55 W
Pottawatomi Indian Reservation ⬥[4]	198	39.20 N	95.50 W
Pottendorf	61	47.55 N	16.23 E
Potten End	260	51.46 N	0.31 W
Pottenhofen	61	48.46 N	16.33 E
Pottenstein	60	49.46 N	11.25 E
Potter	198	41.13 N	103.18 W
Potter □[6]	214	41.47 N	78.01 W
Potter Hollow	210	42.25 N	74.13 W
Potter Lake	216	42.50 N	88.21 W
Potter Point ›	274a	34.03 S	151.13 E
Potters Bar	42	51.42 N	0.11 W
Potters Mills	208	40.48 N	77.32 W
Potter Street	260	51.46 N	0.08 E
Pottersville	276	40.42 N	74.43 W
Potterville	216	42.38 N	84.45 W
Pöttmes	60	48.35 N	11.06 E
Potton	42	52.08 N	0.14 W
Potts Camp	194	34.38 N	89.18 W
Potts Creek ≃	192	37.45 N	80.00 W
Potts Grove	210	41.00 N	76.48 W
Potts Hill Reservoirs ⊜[1]	274a	33.54 S	151.02 E
Pott Shrigley	262	53.19 N	2.05 W
Pottstown	208	40.14 N	75.39 W
Pottstown Landing	285	40.14 N	75.40 W
Pottstown Limerick Airport ⊠	285	40.14 N	75.34 W
Pottstown Municipal Airport ⊠	285	40.16 N	75.40 W
Pottsville	208	40.41 N	76.11 W
Potwin	198	37.56 N	97.01 W
Pötzleinsdorf ⬥[8]	264b	48.15 N	16.19 E
Pötzleinsdorfer Park ♠	264b	48.14 N	16.18 E
P'otzu	100	23.28 N	120.14 E
Pouancé	32	47.44 N	1.11 W
Pouce-Coupe	182	55.43 N	120.08 W
Pouce Coupé ≃	182	56.08 N	119.52 W
Pouch	54	51.37 N	12.24 E
Pouch Cove	186	47.46 N	52.46 W
Pouembout	175f	21.08 S	164.53 E
Poughkeepsie	210	41.42 N	73.55 W
Poughquag	210	41.37 N	73.41 W
Pouilly-en-Auxois	58	47.16 N	4.33 E
Pouilly-sur-Loire	50	47.17 N	2.57 E
Pouilly-sur-Meuse	56	49.32 N	5.07 E
Poulain, Étang ⊜	261	48.43 N	1.44 E
Poulan	192	31.30 N	83.47 W
Poulaphouca Reservoir ⊜[1]	48	53.08 N	6.31 W
Poulin-de-Courval, Lac ⊜	186	48.52 N	70.27 W
Poulsbo	224	47.44 N	122.38 W
Poulter, Lac ⊜	190	47.07 N	76.45 W
Poultney	188	43.31 N	73.14 W
Poulton-le-Fylde	44	53.51 N	2.59 W
Poum	175f	20.14 S	164.02 E
Poŭn	98	36.29 N	127.43 E
Pound	192	37.07 N	82.36 W
Poundmaker Indian Reserve ⬥[4]	184	52.51 N	109.00 W
Poundstock	42	50.46 N	4.33 W
Pouoanuu, Mont ʌ	174x	9.49 S	139.07 W
Pourri, Mont ʌ	62	45.32 N	6.52 E
Pouru-Saint-Rémy	56	49.41 N	5.05 E
Pourville-sur-Mer	50	49.55 N	1.02 E
Pouso Alegre	256	22.13 S	45.56 W
Pouso Alto	256	22.11 S	44.58 W
Pouso Redondo	252	27.15 S	49.57 W
Pouso Sêco	256	22.41 S	44.10 W
Pouss	146	10.51 N	15.03 E
Poutasi	175a	14.01 S	171.41 W
Poŭthĭsăt	110	12.32 N	103.55 E
Poŭthĭsăt ≃	110	12.41 N	104.09 E
Pouxeux	58	48.06 N	6.34 E
Pouzauges	32	46.47 N	0.50 W
Považská Bystrica	30	49.08 N	18.27 E
Povenec	24	62.51 N	34.45 E
Poverello, Monte ʌ	70	38.05 N	15.22 E
Poverennyj	80	46.45 N	43.12 E
Poverty Bay c	172	38.42 S	177.58 E
Povetkino	82	54.20 N	38.23 E
Poviglio	64	44.51 N	10.32 E
Povljen ⋏	38	43.55 N	19.30 E
Póvoa, Mouchão da I	266c	38.51 N	9.03 W
Povoação	148a	37.45 N	25.15 W
Póvoa de Santa Iria	266c	38.52 N	9.04 W
Póvoa de Santo Adrião	266c	38.48 N	9.10 W
Póvoa de Varzim	34	41.23 N	8.46 W
Povorino	80	51.12 N	42.14 E
Povorotnyj, mys ›	89	42.42 N	133.04 E
Povorsk	78	51.16 N	25.07 E
Povrly	54	50.40 N	14.10 E
Povungnituk	176	60.02 N	77.10 W
Povungnituk, Rivière de ≃	176	60.03 N	77.15 W
Powassan	190	46.05 N	79.22 W
Poway	228	32.57 N	117.02 W
Powder ≃, U.S.	178	46.44 N	105.26 W
Powder ≃, Or., U.S.	202	44.45 N	117.03 W
Powder, Dry Fork ≃	200	43.47 N	106.15 W
Powder, Middle Fork ≃	200	43.42 N	106.33 W
Powder, North Fork ≃	202	43.42 N	106.33 W
Powder, Red Fork ≃	202	43.39 N	106.47 W
Powder, South Fork ≃	202	43.40 N	106.30 W
Powder Horn Lake ⊜	278	41.38 N	87.32 W
Powderly, Ky., U.S.	194	37.09 N	87.10 W
Powderly, Tx., U.S.	196	33.49 N	95.31 W
Powdermaker Ditch ≊	279a	41.30 N	82.02 W
Powder Mill Village	284c	39.03 N	76.57 W
Powder River Pass)(	202	44.09 N	107.04 W
Powell, Oh., U.S.	214	40.09 N	83.05 W
Powell, Pa., U.S.	210	41.42 N	76.31 W
Powell, Tx., U.S.	222	32.07 N	96.20 W
Powell, Wy., U.S.	202	44.45 N	108.45 W
Powell ≃	192	36.29 N	83.42 W
Powell, Lake ⊜[1]	200	37.25 N	110.45 W
Powell, Mount ʌ	200	39.46 N	106.20 W
Powell Creek ≃, Austl.	166	25.02 S	143.40 E
Powell Creek ≃, Oh., U.S.	216	41.17 N	84.21 W
Powellhurst	224	45.30 N	122.32 W
Powell Lake ⊜	182	50.11 N	124.24 W
Powell River	182	49.52 N	124.33 W
Powells Valley	208	40.26 N	76.56 W
Powellton	188	38.05 N	81.19 W
Powellville	208	38.19 N	75.22 W
Powers, Mi., U.S.	190	45.41 N	87.31 W
Powers, Or., U.S.	202	42.53 N	124.04 W
Powers Lake, N.D., U.S.	198	48.33 N	102.38 W
Powers Lake, Wi., U.S.	216	42.33 N	88.17 W
Powers Lookout ♠	169	36.50 S	146.22 E
Powhatan, La., U.S.	194	31.52 N	93.12 W
Powhatan, Va., U.S.	192	37.32 N	77.55 W
Powhatan Mill	284b	39.20 N	76.43 W
Powhatan Point	188	39.51 N	80.48 W
Powis, Vale of V	42	52.38 N	3.08 W
Powissett Brook ≃	283	42.16 N	71.14 W
Powlett ≃	169	38.35 S	145.32 E
Pownal	210	42.45 N	73.14 W
Powys □[6]	42	52.17 N	3.20 W
Poxoréo	255	15.50 S	54.23 W
Poya	175f	21.19 S	165.07 E
Poyang Hu ⊜	100	29.00 N	116.25 E
Poyan Reservoir ⊜[1]	271c	1.23 N	103.40 E
Poyen	194	34.19 N	92.38 W
Poygan, Lake ⊜	190	44.09 N	88.50 W
Poyle	260	51.28 N	0.31 W
Poynette	190	43.23 N	89.24 W
Poynor	222	32.04 N	95.36 W
Poynton	44	53.21 N	2.07 W
Poyntz Pass	48	54.18 N	6.23 W
Poyraz ⬥[8]	267b	41.12 N	29.07 E
Poyraz Burnu ›	267b	41.12 N	29.08 E
Poysdorf	61	48.40 N	16.38 E
Pozantı	130	37.25 N	34.52 E
Požarevac	38	44.37 N	21.11 E
Poza Rica	234	20.33 N	97.27 W
Požarskoje	89	46.16 N	134.04 E
Pozdejevka	89	50.36 N	128.56 E
Požega	38	43.50 N	20.02 E
Poznań	30	52.25 N	16.55 E
Poznań □[4]	30	52.20 N	16.55 E
Pozo Alcón	34	37.42 N	2.56 W
Pozo Almonte	248	20.16 S	69.48 W
Pozoblanco	34	38.22 N	4.51 W
Pozo-Cañada	34	38.48 N	1.45 W
Pozo Colorado	252	23.28 S	58.51 W
Pozo del Molle	252	32.02 S	62.55 W
Pozo del Tigre	252	24.54 S	60.19 W
Pozo Hondo	252	27.10 S	64.30 W
Pozos, Punta ›	254	47.57 S	65.47 W
Pozsony → Bratislava	30	48.09 N	17.07 E
Pozuelo de Alarcón, Esp.	34	40.26 N	3.49 W
Pozuelo de Alarcón, Esp.	266a	40.26 N	3.49 W
Pozuelos	246	10.11 N	64.39 W
Pozuelos, Laguna ⊜	252	22.22 S	66.01 W
Pozuzo	248	10.04 S	75.32 W
Pozuzo ≃	248	9.52 S	75.12 W
Požva	86	59.05 N	56.05 E
Pozzallo	70	36.43 N	14.51 E
Pozzillo, Lago di ⊜	70	37.40 N	14.35 E
Pozzolo Formigaro	62	44.48 N	8.47 E
Pozzomaggiore	71	40.24 N	8.39 E
Pozzuoli	68	40.49 N	14.07 E
Pozzuolo del Friuli	64	45.59 N	13.12 E
Pra ≃, Ghana	150	5.01 N	1.37 W
Pra ≃, Ross.	80	54.45 N	41.01 E
Prabuty	30	53.46 N	19.10 E
Praça Cruzeiro	256	22.43 S	42.38 W
Praça Sêca ⬥[8]	287a	22.54 S	43.21 W
Prachatice	30	49.01 N	14.00 E
Prachin Buri	110	14.03 N	101.22 E
Prachuap Khiri Khan	110	11.49 N	99.48 E
Prackenbach	60	49.06 N	12.50 E
Pracuí ≃	250	2.26 S	51.19 W
Pracupi ≃	250	2.06 S	51.30 W
Pradelles	62	44.46 N	3.53 E
Pradera	246	3.25 N	76.15 W
Prades	32	42.37 N	2.26 E
Pradleves	62	44.25 N	7.17 E
Prado	255	17.21 S	39.13 W
Prado, Museo del ⊍	266a	40.25 N	3.41 W
Prado Dam ⬥[6]	280	33.54 N	117.39 W
Prado Flood Control Basin ≚[1]	280	33.54 N	117.38 W
Prados	255	21.03 S	44.05 W
Prads	62	44.13 N	6.27 E
Præstø	41	55.07 N	12.03 E
Prag → Praha	54	50.05 N	14.26 E
Praga → Praha	54	50.05 N	14.26 E
Pragelato	62	45.01 N	6.57 E
Pragersko	61	46.23 N	15.40 E
Praglia, Monastero di ⊍[1]	64	45.23 N	11.45 E
Prägraten	64	47.01 N	12.23 E
Prague → Praha, Česká Rep.	54	50.05 N	14.26 E
Prague, Ne., U.S.	198	41.18 N	96.48 W
Prague, Ok., U.S.	196	35.29 N	96.41 W
Praha (Prague)	54	50.05 N	14.26 E
Praha ʌ	60	49.40 N	13.49 E
Prahova □[6]	38	45.00 N	26.00 E
Prahova ≃	38	44.43 N	26.27 E
Prahran	274b	37.51 S	144.59 E
Praia	150a	14.55 N	23.31 W
Praia a Mare	68	39.54 N	15.47 E
Praia da Cruz Quebrada	266c	38.42 N	9.14 W
Praia da Enseada	256	23.29 S	45.05 W
Praia das Maçãs	266c	38.50 N	9.28 W
Praia da Vitória	148a	38.44 N	27.04 W
Praia de Araçatiba	256	23.15 S	44.21 W
Praia Funda, Ponta da ›	287a	23.05 S	43.33 W
Praia Grande, Bra.	252	29.12 S	49.57 W
Praia Grande, Bra.	256	24.01 S	46.25 W
Praiano	68	40.37 N	14.32 E
Praikalogu	115b	9.45 S	119.25 E
Prainha	250	1.48 S	53.29 W
Prainha Nova	248	7.16 S	60.23 W
Prairie	166	20.52 S	144.36 E
Prairie ≃, Mi., U.S.	216	41.55 N	85.38 W
Prairie ≃, Mn., U.S.	190	47.18 N	93.29 W
Prairie ≃, Wi., U.S.	190	45.10 N	89.42 W
Prairie City, Il., U.S.	190	40.37 N	90.28 W
Prairie City, Ia., U.S.	190	41.35 N	93.14 W
Prairie City, Or., U.S.	202	44.27 N	118.42 W
Prairie Creek ≃, Fl., U.S.	220	26.59 N	81.56 W
Prairie Creek ≃, Il., U.S.	216	41.21 N	88.12 W
Prairie Creek ≃, Il., U.S.	216	40.55 N	87.49 W
Prairie Creek ≃, Il., U.S.	278	41.36 N	87.40 W
Prairie Creek ≃, Mi., U.S.	216	42.59 N	85.01 W
Prairie Creek ≃, Ne., U.S.	198	41.22 N	97.32 W
Prairie Creek Reservoir ⊜[1]	218	40.08 N	85.17 W
Prairie Dog Creek ≃	198	40.00 N	99.23 W
Prairie du Chien	190	43.03 N	91.08 W
Prairie du Sac	190	43.17 N	89.43 W
Prairie Elk Creek ≃	198	48.00 N	105.51 W
Prairie Grove	194	35.58 N	94.19 W
Prairie Hill	222	31.39 N	96.47 W
Prairie Lea	222	29.44 N	97.45 W
Prairie River	184	52.52 N	103.00 W
Prairies, Coteau des ⋏[2]	198	44.30 N	96.45 W
Prairies, Lake of the ⊜[1]	184	51.05 N	101.25 W
Prairies, Rivière des ≃	275a	45.42 N	73.29 W
Prairie View, Il., U.S.	278	42.12 N	87.57 W
Prairie View, Tx., U.S.	222	30.05 N	95.59 W
Prairie Village	198	38.59 N	94.38 W
Prajekan	115a	7.47 S	113.59 E
Prakhon Chai	110	14.37 N	103.05 E
Pralboino	64	45.16 N	10.13 E
Prali	62	44.54 N	7.03 E
Pralls Island I	276	40.37 N	74.12 W
Pralognan-la-Vanoise	62	45.23 N	6.43 E
Pram	60	48.14 N	13.37 E
Pram ≃	60	48.28 N	13.26 E
Pramaggiore, Monte ʌ	64	46.22 N	12.33 E
Prambachkirchen	60	48.19 N	13.55 E
Prambanan	115a	7.45 S	110.30 E
Pr'amicyno	78	51.39 N	35.56 E
Pramort	54	54.26 N	12.55 E
Prampram	150	5.42 N	0.07 E
Pran Buri	110	12.23 N	99.55 E
Pran Buri ≃	110	12.24 N	100.00 E
Prang	150	7.59 N	0.53 W
Prangli I	76	59.38 N	25.02 E
Prānhita ≃	122	18.49 N	79.55 E
Pranzo	64	45.55 N	10.48 E
Prapa, Khlong ≊	269a	13.46 N	100.32 E
Prapat	114	2.40 N	98.56 E
Praraye	58	45.55 N	7.32 E
Prärien → Great Plains ≚	16	42.00 N	100.00 W
Praskoveja	84	44.43 N	44.12 E
Praslin, Lac ⊜	186	50.03 N	69.48 W
Praslin Island I	138	4.19 S	55.44 E
Prasonísi, Ákra ›	38	35.52 N	27.46 E
Praszka	30	51.04 N	18.26 E
Prat, Isla I	254	48.15 S	75.00 W
Prata, Bra.	250	7.41 S	37.06 W
Prata, Bra.	255	19.18 S	48.55 W
Prata, Bra.	287a	22.45 S	43.25 W
Prata, Rio da ≃, Bra.	255	17.28 S	46.35 W
Prata, Rio da ≃, Bra.	255	18.49 S	49.54 W
Prata, Rio da ≃, Bra.	287a	22.56 S	43.34 W
Pratāpgarh, India	120	24.02 N	74.47 E
Pratāpgarh, India	124	25.54 N	81.58 E
Pratāpnagar	126	22.23 N	89.13 E
Pratápolis	255	20.45 S	46.52 W
Pratas Island → Tungsha Tao I	90	20.42 N	116.43 E
Pratau	54	51.50 N	12.38 E
Pratella	68	41.24 N	14.11 E
Prater ♠	264b	48.12 N	16.25 E
Prathet Thai → Thailand □[1]	110	15.00 N	100.00 E
Pratinha	255	19.46 S	46.24 W
Prato	66	43.53 N	11.06 E
Prato □[4]	64	44.00 N	11.05 E
Prato allo Stelvio	64	46.37 N	10.35 E
Pratola Peligna	66	42.06 N	13.52 E
Pratola Serra	68	40.59 N	14.51 E
Pratolino	66	43.52 N	11.18 E
Pratomagno ⋏	66	43.39 N	11.39 E
Pratt	198	37.38 N	98.44 W
Pratteln	58	47.31 N	7.42 E
Prättigau V	58	46.55 N	9.45 E
Pratt's Bottom ⬥[8]	260	51.20 N	0.07 E
Prattsburg	210	42.31 N	77.17 W
Prattsville	210	42.18 N	74.26 W
Prattville	194	32.27 N	86.27 W
Pratudão ≃	255	13.56 S	44.55 W
Prauthoy	58	47.40 N	5.17 E
Pravaja Mama ≃	88	57.10 N	111.54 E
Pravda	89	47.00 N	142.01 E
Pravdinsk, Ross.	76	54.27 N	21.01 E
Pravdinsk, Ross.	80	56.32 N	43.34 E
Pravdinskij	82	56.04 N	37.51 E
Pravia	34	43.29 N	6.07 W
Prawet Buri Rom, Khlong ≊	269a	13.42 N	100.35 E
Prawle Point ›	42	50.13 N	3.42 W
Praya	115b	8.42 S	116.17 E
Pr'aža	24	61.42 N	33.35 E
Praz-sur-Arly	62	45.50 N	6.34 E
Prazzo	62	44.29 N	7.03 E
Preakness Brook ≃	276	40.54 N	74.15 W
Preakness Mountain ʌ	276	40.58 N	74.13 W
Preakness Valley Park ♠	276	40.55 N	74.14 W
Preble, In., U.S.	216	40.50 N	85.01 W
Preble, N.Y., U.S.	210	42.44 N	76.09 W
Preble □[6]	218	39.45 N	84.38 W
Preci	66	42.53 N	13.02 E
Prečistoje, Ross.	76	55.41 N	34.56 E
Prečistoje, Ross.	76	55.31 N	32.22 E
Prečistoje, Ross.	80	58.27 N	40.19 E
Précy-sous-Thil	50	47.23 N	4.19 E
Précy-sur-Marne	261	48.56 N	2.47 E
Précy-sur-Oise	50	49.12 N	2.22 E
Preda	58	46.36 N	9.46 E
Predappio	66	44.06 N	11.58 E
Predazzo	64	46.19 N	11.36 E
Predeal	38	45.30 N	25.35 E
Prédecelle ≃	261	48.35 N	2.07 E
Předenice	60	49.37 N	13.24 E
Predeşti	38	44.21 N	23.36 E
Predgornoje	86	47.10 N	81.02 E
Predigtstuhl ʌ	61	48.48 N	15.22 E
Předin	61	49.12 N	15.40 E
Predivinsk	86	57.04 N	93.27 E
Predlitz [-Turrach]	64	47.04 N	13.55 E
Predoi (Prettau)	64	47.02 N	12.06 E
Predore	64	45.40 N	10.01 E
Preeceville	184	51.58 N	102.40 W
Pré-en-Pail	32	48.27 N	0.12 W
Preesall	44	53.55 N	2.58 W
Preetz	54	54.14 N	10.16 E
Pregarten	61	48.21 N	14.32 E
Pregel → Pregol'a ≃	76	54.41 N	20.22 E
Pregnana	266b	45.31 N	9.00 E
Pregol'a ≃	76	54.41 N	20.22 E
Pregonero	246	8.01 N	71.46 W
Pregos	256	21.46 S	42.54 W
Pregradnaja	84	43.58 N	41.12 E
Pregradnoje	80	45.49 N	41.45 E
Preguiças ≃	250	2.34 S	42.44 W
Preila	76	55.22 N	21.04 E
Preiļi	76	56.18 N	26.43 E
Preissac, Lac ⊜	190	48.20 N	78.20 W
Prekestolen ♠	26	59.00 N	6.01 E
Preko	36	44.05 N	15.11 E
Prekomurje ⬥[1]	61	46.40 N	16.10 E
Prĕk Poŭthĭ	110	11.51 N	105.07 E
Prelate	184	50.51 N	109.23 W
Přelouč	30	50.02 N	15.34 E
Premana	58	46.03 N	9.25 E
Prembun	115a	7.43 S	109.48 E
Prémery	50	47.10 N	3.20 E
Premià de Dalt	266d	41.31 N	2.21 E
Premià de Mar	266d	41.29 N	2.21 E
Premnitz	54	52.32 N	12.19 E
Prémont, P.Q., Can.	206	46.22 N	73.03 W
Premont, Tx., U.S.	196	27.21 N	98.07 W
Prémontré	50	49.33 N	3.24 E
Premuda, Otok I	36	44.20 N	14.37 E
Prenestini, Monti ⋏	66	41.50 N	12.55 E
Prenjas	38	41.04 N	20.32 E
Prentice	190	45.32 N	90.17 W
Prentiss	194	31.35 N	89.52 W
Prenton	262	53.22 N	3.03 W
Prenzlau	54	53.19 N	13.52 E
Prenzlauer Berg ⬥[8]	264a	52.32 N	13.26 E
Preobraženije	89	42.57 N	133.55 E
Preobraženovka	89	48.04 N	131.55 E
Preobrazhenne	83	49.32 N	38.10 E
Preparis Island I	110	14.52 N	93.41 E
Preparis North Channel ɥ	110	15.27 N	94.05 E
Preparis South Channel ɥ	110	14.40 N	94.00 E
Přerov	30	49.27 N	17.27 E
Prerow	54	54.26 N	12.35 E
Pré-Saint-Didier	62	45.46 N	6.59 E
Presanella, Cima ʌ	64	46.13 N	10.40 E
Prescot	44	53.26 N	2.48 W
Prescott, On., Can.	212	44.43 N	75.31 W
Prescott, Az., U.S.	200	34.32 N	112.28 W
Prescott, Ar., U.S.	194	33.48 N	93.22 W
Prescott, Or., U.S.	224	46.02 N	122.53 W
Prescott, Wi., U.S.	190	44.44 N	92.48 W
Prescott and Russell □[6]	206	45.25 N	75.00 W
Prescott Island I	176	73.01 N	96.50 W
Preševo	38	42.18 N	21.39 E
Presho	198	43.54 N	100.03 W
Presicce	68	39.54 N	18.16 E
Presidencia de la Plaza	252	27.01 S	59.51 W
Presidencia Roca	252	26.08 S	59.36 W
Presidencia Roque Sáenz Peña	252	26.47 S	60.27 W
Presidente Costa e Silva, Ponte ⬥[5]	287a	22.53 S	43.10 W
Presidente Derqui	258	34.29 S	58.51 W
Presidente Dutra	250	5.15 S	44.30 W
Presidente Epitácio	255	21.46 S	52.06 W
Presidente Getúlio	252	27.03 S	49.37 W
Presidente Hayes □[5]	252	24.00 S	59.00 W
Presidente Nicolás Avellaneda, Parque ♠	288	34.39 S	58.29 W
Presidente Olegário	255	18.25 S	46.25 W
Presidente Prudente	255	22.07 S	51.22 W
Presidente Ríos, Lago ⊜	254	46.28 S	74.25 W
Presidente Roosevelt, Estação ⬥[5]	287b	23.33 S	46.36 W
Presidente Venceslau	255	21.52 S	51.50 W
Presidential Heights	279b	40.34 N	80.03 W
President Roxas	116	11.26 N	122.56 E
Presidio	196	29.33 N	104.22 W
Presidio ≃	234	23.06 N	106.17 W
Presidio of San Francisco ■	226	37.48 N	122.28 W
Presles	56	50.23 N	4.35 E
Presles-en-Brie	261	48.43 N	2.45 E
Presnogor'kovka	86	54.30 N	65.45 E
Presnovka	86	54.40 N	67.09 E
Presolana, Passo della)(	64	45.55 N	10.06 E
Prešov	30	49.00 N	21.15 E
Prespa, Lake ⊜	38	40.55 N	21.00 E
Prespansko Jezero → Prespa, Lake ⊜	38	40.55 N	21.00 E
Presque Isle	186	46.40 N	68.00 W
Presque Isle ›[1]	214	42.09 N	80.06 W
Presque Isle ≃	190	46.43 N	89.59 W
Presque Isle State Park ♠	214	42.09 N	80.06 W
Presqu'ile Bay c	212	44.01 N	77.43 W
Presqu'ile Peninsula ›[1]	212	44.00 N	77.41 W
Presqu'ile Provincial Park ♠	212	44.00 N	77.42 W
Pressana	64	45.17 N	11.24 E
Pressath	60	49.46 N	11.56 E
Pressbaum	61	48.11 N	16.05 E
Pressburg → Bratislava	30	48.09 N	17.07 E
Pressel	54	51.34 N	12.41 E
Pressig	54	50.21 N	11.19 E
Prestatyn	44	53.20 N	3.24 W
Prestbury	262	53.17 N	2.09 W
Prestea	150	5.27 N	2.08 W
Presteigne	42	52.17 N	3.00 W
Přeštice	60	49.34 N	13.20 E
Presto	279b	40.23 N	80.07 W
Preston, Austl.	169	37.45 S	145.01 E
Preston, Eng., U.K.	42	50.39 N	2.25 W
Preston, Eng., U.K.	44	53.46 N	0.12 W
Preston, Eng., U.K.	44	53.46 N	2.42 W
Preston, Ga., U.S.	192	32.03 N	84.32 W
Preston, Id., U.S.	202	42.05 N	111.52 W
Preston, Ia., U.S.	190	42.03 N	90.24 W
Preston, Ks., U.S.	198	37.45 N	98.33 W
Preston, Md., U.S.	208	38.42 N	75.54 W
Preston, Mn., U.S.	190	43.40 N	92.04 W
Preston, Wa., U.S.	224	47.31 N	121.55 W
Preston □[8]	262	53.48 N	2.42 W
Preston ≃, Austl.	168a	33.20 S	115.40 E
Preston ≃, P.Q., Can.	206	46.05 N	75.04 W
Preston, Cape ›	162	20.51 S	116.12 E
Preston, Lac ⊜	206	46.05 N	75.04 W
Preston, Lake ⊜, Austl.	168a	32.59 S	115.42 E
Preston, Lake ⊜, Fl., U.S.	220	28.18 N	81.08 W
Preston Airport ⊠	276	40.22 N	74.15 W
Preston Brook	262	53.19 N	2.39 W
Preston Brook Canal Tunnel ⬥[5]	262	53.19 N	2.38 W
Preston Heights	216	41.28 N	88.08 W
Preston Hollow	210	42.27 N	74.13 W
Preston North End Football Ground ♠	262	53.47 N	2.42 W
Prestonpans	46	55.57 N	3.00 W
Preston Peak ʌ	204	41.50 N	123.37 W
Prestonsburg	192	37.39 N	82.46 W
Prestrud Inlet c	9	78.18 S	156.00 W
Preststranda	26	59.06 N	9.04 E
Prestville	182	55.44 N	118.37 W
Prestwich	44	53.32 N	2.17 W
Prestwick	46	55.29 N	4.37 W
Prestwick Airport ⊠	46	55.30 N	4.36 W
Preto ≃, Bra.	246	1.41 S	63.48 W
Preto ≃, Bra.	248	8.03 S	62.54 W
Preto ≃, Bra.	250	11.21 S	43.52 W
Preto ≃, Bra.	250	3.32 S	43.46 W
Preto ≃, Bra.	255	13.37 S	48.06 W
Preto ≃, Bra.	255	17.00 S	46.12 W
Preto ≃, Bra.	255	18.44 S	50.23 W
Preto ≃, Bra.	255	20.08 S	49.38 W
Preto ≃, Bra.	256	22.14 S	43.07 W
Preto ≃, Bra.	256	22.01 S	43.20 W
Preto do Igapó-açu ≃	246	4.26 S	59.48 W
Pretoria	158	25.45 S	28.10 E
Pretoriusvlei	158	28.30 S	22.59 E
Prettau → Predoi	64	47.02 N	12.06 E
Prettin	54	51.39 N	12.55 E
Prettyboy Reservoir ⊜[1]	208	39.38 N	76.45 W
Pretty Prairie	198	37.46 N	98.01 W
Pretzfeld	60	49.45 N	11.11 E
Pretzier	54	52.49 N	11.15 E
Pretzsch	54	51.42 N	12.48 E
Preussisch Eylau → Bagrationovsk	76	54.23 N	20.39 E
Preussisch-Oldendorf	52	52.18 N	8.30 E
Preussisch-Ströhen	52	52.29 N	8.40 E
Prevalje	61	46.32 N	14.55 E
Préveza	38	38.57 N	20.44 E
Prévost	206	45.52 N	74.05 W
Prevost Island I	224	48.50 N	123.22 W
Prey Lvéa	110	11.10 N	104.57 E
Prey Nób	110	10.38 N	103.47 E
Prey Vêng	110	11.29 N	105.19 E
Prezza, Monte ʌ	66	42.02 N	13.49 E
Priaral'skije Karakumy, peski ⬥[2]	86	47.00 N	63.30 E
Priargunsk	88	50.27 N	119.00 E
Priay	58	46.00 N	5.17 E
Pribilof Islands II	180	57.00 N	170.00 W
Priboj	38	43.35 N	19.31 E
Příbram	30	49.42 N	14.01 E
Pribylovo	76	60.26 N	28.40 E
Priccio, Cozzo ʌ	70	37.01 N	14.46 E
Price, Austl.	168b	34.17 S	138.00 E
Price, Tx., U.S.	222	32.08 N	94.57 W
Price, Ut,. U.S.	200	39.35 N	110.48 W
Price ≃	200	39.10 N	110.06 W
Price, Cape ›	110	13.34 N	93.03 E
Price Bend c	276	40.55 N	73.24 W
Price Island I	182	52.23 N	128.36 W
Prichard	194	30.44 N	88.04 W
Prichsenstadt	56	49.49 N	10.21 E
Prickly Point ›	241k	11.59 N	61.45 W
Priddy	196	31.40 N	98.31 W
Priego	34	40.27 N	2.18 W
Priego de Córdoba	34	37.26 N	4.11 W
Priekule, Lat.	76	56.26 N	21.35 E
Priekule, Liet.	76	55.33 N	21.19 E
Prienai	76	54.38 N	23.57 E
Prien am Chiemsee	64	47.51 N	12.20 E
Prieros	54	52.13 N	13.46 E
Prieska	158	29.40 S	22.42 E
Priest ≃	202	48.11 N	116.53 W
Priestewitz	54	51.15 N	13.30 E
Priest Island I	46	57.58 N	5.30 W
Priest Lake ⊜	202	48.34 N	116.52 W
Priestley, Mount ʌ	182	55.13 N	128.53 W
Priest Rapids Lake ⊜[1]	202	46.45 N	119.55 W
Priest River	202	48.10 N	116.54 W
Prieta, Loma ʌ	226	37.07 N	121.51 W
Prieta, Peña ʌ	34	43.01 N	4.44 W
Prieto ≃	240m	18.15 N	66.54 W
Prieto Diaz	116	13.02 N	124.12 E
Prievidza	30	48.47 N	18.37 E
Prignitz ⬥[1]	54	53.05 N	12.15 E
Priiskovyj, Ross.	86	54.39 N	88.42 E
Priiskovyj, Ross.	88	51.57 N	116.39 E
Prijedor	36	44.59 N	16.43 E
Prijepolje	38	43.23 N	19.39 E
Prijutnoje	80	46.06 N	43.31 E
Prijutovo	80	53.54 N	53.56 E
Prikaspijskaja nizmennost' ≚	80	48.00 N	52.00 E
Prikro	150	7.39 N	3.59 W
Prilep	38	41.20 N	21.33 E
Prilepy	82	54.03 N	37.42 E
Prilly	58	46.32 N	6.36 E
Priluki, Ross.	76	59.16 N	39.53 E
Priluki, Ross.	82	54.51 N	37.53 E
Prima Porta ⬥[8]	267a	42.00 N	12.29 E
Primavera	250	0.56 S	47.06 W
Přimda	60	49.41 N	12.41 E
Primeira Cruz	250	2.30 S	43.26 W
Primeiro de Maio	255	22.48 S	51.01 W
Primera	196	26.14 N	97.43 W
Primero ≃	252	31.00 S	63.12 W
Primero de Mayo	196	27.12 N	101.15 W
Primghar	198	43.05 N	95.37 W
Primolano	64	45.58 N	11.42 E
Primorje [Warnicken]	76	54.57 N	20.02 E
Primorka	83	47.16 N	39.03 E
Primorsk, Ross.	76	54.44 N	20.01 E
Primorsk, Ross.	76	60.22 N	28.36 E
Primorsk, Ross.	80	49.16 N	45.03 E
Primorskij	89	43.07 N	131.38 E
Primorskij chrebet ⋏	88	52.30 N	106.00 E
Primorskij Kraj □[8]	89	45.25 N	135.25 E
Primorsko	38	42.10 N	27.51 E
Primorsko-Achtarsk	78	46.03 N	38.11 E
Primos	285	39.55 N	75.18 W
Primrose, S. Afr.	273d	26.12 S	28.10 E
Primrose, Pa., U.S.	210	40.42 N	76.17 W
Primrose, Pa., U.S.	279b	40.21 N	80.16 W
Primrose Brook ≃	276	40.43 N	74.31 W
Primrose Lake ⊜	184	54.55 N	109.45 W
Prims ≃	56	49.20 N	6.44 E
Primstal	56	49.32 N	6.58 E
Prince, Lake ⊜[1]	208	36.48 N	76.38 W
Prince Albert, On., Can.	212	44.05 N	78.58 W
Prince Albert, Sk., Can.	184	53.12 N	105.46 W
Prince Albert, S. Afr.	158	33.13 S	22.02 E
Prince Albert Mountains ⋏	9	76.00 S	161.30 E
Prince Albert National Park ♠	184	54.00 N	106.25 W
Prince Albert Road	158	33.01 S	21.40 E
Prince Albert Sound ɥ	176	70.25 N	115.00 W
Prince Alexander Mountains ⋏	164	3.30 S	142.50 E
Prince Alfred Hamlet	158	33.18 S	19.20 E
Prince Charles Island I	176	67.50 N	76.00 W
Prince Charles Mountains ⋏	9	72.00 S	67.00 E
Prince-de-Galles, Île du → Prince of Wales Island I, Austl.	164	10.40 S	142.10 E
Prince-de-Galles, Île du → Prince of Wales Island I, N.T., Can.	176	72.40 N	99.00 W
Prince Edward □[6]	212	44.00 N	77.15 W
Prince Edward Bay c	212	43.57 N	76.57 W
Prince Edward Island □[4], Can.	176	46.20 N	63.20 W
Prince Edward Island □[4], Can.	186	46.20 N	63.20 W
Prince Edward Island National Park ♠	186	46.31 N	63.26 W
Prince Edward Islands II	6	46.35 S	37.56 E
Prince Edward Park ♠	274a	34.02 S	151.03 E
Prince Edward Point ›	212	43.56 N	76.52 W
Prince Frederick	208	38.32 N	76.35 W
Prince Gallitzin State Park ♠	214	40.40 N	78.32 W
Prince George, B.C., Can.	182	53.55 N	122.45 W
Prince George, Va., U.S.	208	37.13 N	77.17 W
Prince George □[6]	208	37.13 N	77.10 W
Prince Georges □[6]	208	38.49 N	76.45 W
Prince Georges Plaza ⬥[9]	284c	38.58 N	76.57 W
Prince Leopold Island I	176	74.02 N	89.55 W
Prince of Wales, Cape ›	180	65.40 N	168.05 W
Prince of Wales Island I, Austl.	164	10.40 S	142.10 E
Prince of Wales Island I, N.T., Can.	176	72.40 N	99.00 W
Prince of Wales Island I, Ak., U.S.	180	55.47 N	132.50 W
Prince of Wales Strait ɥ	176	73.00 N	117.00 W
Prince Olav Coast ⊥[2]	9	68.30 S	42.30 E
Prince Patrick Island I	16	76.45 N	119.30 W
Prince Regent ≃	164	15.28 S	125.05 E
Prince Regent Inlet c	176	73.00 N	90.30 W
Prince Regent Nature Reserve ♠	164	15.30 S	125.30 E
Prince Rupert	182	54.19 N	130.19 W
Prince Rupert Bay c	240d	15.34 N	61.29 W
Prince Rupert Bluff Point ›	240d	15.35 N	61.29 W
Princesa, Puerto c	116	9.45 N	118.43 E
Princesa Astrid, Costa → Princess Astrid Coast ⊥[2]	9	70.45 S	12.30 E
Princesa Carlota, Bahía → Princess Charlotte Bay c	164	14.25 S	144.00 E
Princesa Isabel	250	7.44 S	38.00 W
Princesa Marta, Costa → Princess Martha Coast ⊥[2]	9	72.00 S	7.30 W
Princesa Ragnhild, Costa → Princess Ragnhild Coast ⊥[2]	9	70.15 S	27.30 E
Princes Bay c	276	40.31 N	74.12 W
Princes Risborough	42	51.44 N	0.51 W
Princess Anne	208	38.12 N	75.41 W
Princess Astrid Coast ⊥[2]	9	70.45 S	12.30 E
Princess Charlotte Bay c	164	14.25 S	144.00 E
Princess Martha Coast ⊥[2]	9	72.00 S	7.30 W
Princess Ragnhild Coast ⊥[2]	9	70.15 S	27.30 E
Princess Ranges ⋏	162	26.08 S	121.55 E
Princess Royal Channel ɥ	182	53.10 N	128.37 W
Princess Royal Island I	182	52.57 N	128.49 W
Princes Town	241r	10.16 N	61.23 W
Princeton, B.C., Can.	182	49.27 N	120.31 W
Princeton, Nf., Can.	186	48.25 N	53.36 W
Princeton, On., Can.	212	43.10 N	80.32 W
Princeton, Ca., U.S.	226	39.24 N	122.00 W
Princeton, Fl., U.S.	220	25.32 N	80.24 W
Princeton, Il., U.S.	190	41.22 N	89.27 W
Princeton, In., U.S.	194	38.21 N	87.34 W
Princeton, Ky., U.S.	194	37.06 N	87.52 W
Princeton, Me., U.S.	188	45.13 N	67.34 W
Princeton, Mi., U.S.	190	46.17 N	87.28 W
Princeton, Mn., U.S.	190	45.34 N	93.34 W
Princeton, Mo., U.S.	194	40.24 N	93.34 W
Princeton, N.J., U.S.	208	40.20 N	74.39 W
Princeton, N.C., U.S.	192	35.27 N	78.09 W
Princeton, Tx., U.S.	222	33.11 N	96.30 W
Princeton, W.V., U.S.	192	37.21 N	81.06 W
Princeton, Wi., U.S.	190	43.51 N	89.07 W
Princeton Airfield ⊠	276	40.24 N	74.39 W
Princeton Battlefield Park ⊥	276	40.20 N	74.41 W
Princeton Junction	208	40.19 N	74.37 W
Princeton Township	276	40.22 N	74.40 W
Princeton University ⊍[2]	276	40.21 N	74.39 W
Princetown	42	50.33 N	4.00 W
Princeville, P.Q., Can.	206	46.10 N	71.53 W
Princeville, Il., U.S.	190	40.56 N	89.45 W
Princeville, N.C., U.S.	192	35.53 N	77.31 W
Prince William □[6]	208	38.42 N	77.27 W
Prince William Forest Park ♠	208	38.36 N	77.23 W
Prince William Sound ɥ	180	60.40 N	147.00 W
Príncipe I	152	1.37 N	7.25 E
Príncipe Alberto, Montes → Prince Albert Mountains ⋏	9	76.00 S	161.30 E
Príncipe Carlos, Montes → Prince Charles Mountains ⋏	9	72.00 S	67.00 E
Principe Channel ɥ	182	53.28 N	130.00 W
Príncipe da Beira	248	12.25 S	64.25 W
Príncipe de Gales, Isla → Prince of Wales Island I, Austl.	164	10.40 S	142.10 E
Príncipe de Gales, Isla → Prince of Wales Island I, N.T., Can.	176	72.40 N	99.00 W
Príncipe Eduardo, Isla → Prince Edward Island □[4]	186	46.20 N	63.20 W
Príncipe Olav, Costa → Prince Olav Coast ⊥[2]	9	68.30 S	42.30 E
Príncipe Patricio, Isla → Prince Patrick Island I	16	76.45 N	119.30 W
Prineville	202	44.18 N	120.51 W
Prineville Reservoir ⊜[1]	202	44.08 N	120.42 W
Prineville Southeast	202	44.17 N	120.53 W
Pringgabaja	115b	8.34 S	116.37 E
Pringsewu	112	5.24 S	104.55 E
Pringy	261	48.31 N	2.34 E
Prinsenbeek	52	51.36 N	4.42 E
Prinses Margrietkanaal ≊	52	53.10 N	5.55 E
Prinshof	158	32.06 S	20.53 E
Prinzapolka	236	13.24 N	83.34 W
Prinzapolka ≃	236	13.24 N	83.34 W
Prinzessin Astrid-Küste → Princess Astrid Coast ⊥[2]	9	70.45 S	12.30 E
Prinzessin Charlotte Bucht → Princess Charlotte Bay c	164	14.25 S	144.00 E
Prinzessin Martha-Küste → Princess Martha Coast ⊥[2]	9	72.00 S	7.30 W
Prinzessin Ragnhild-Küste → Princess Ragnhild Coast ⊥[2]	9	70.15 S	27.30 E
Priobskoje plato ⋏[1]	86	52.40 N	83.00 E
Prioksko-Terrasnyj zapovednik ⬥[4]	82	54.51 N	37.36 E
Priolo Gargallo	70	37.09 N	15.11 E
Prior, Cabo ›	34	43.34 N	8.19 W
Priort	264a	52.31 N	12.58 E
Priozernyj	80	47.23 N	45.14 E
Prioz'ornyj	86	47.50 N	84.13 E
Prioz'orsk	24	61.02 N	30.04 E
Pripet → Prypjac' ≃	78	51.21 N	30.09 E
Pripet Marshes → Polesje ⬥[1]	72	52.00 N	27.00 E
Pripol'arnyj Ural ⋏	24	65.00 N	60.00 E
Prirečje	88	55.07 N	101.03 E
Prirečnoje	80	51.03 N	52.26 E
Přísečnice	54	50.27 N	13.06 E
Priselje	76	55.09 N	32.49 E
Prislon	82	56.48 N	37.16 E
Pristan'-Prževal'sk	85	42.34 N	78.18 E
Pristen'	78	51.15 N	36.41 E
Priština	38	42.39 N	21.10 E
Pritchett	198	37.22 N	102.51 W
Přítluky	61	48.51 N	16.46 E
Pritzerbe	54	52.30 N	12.27 E
Pritzier	54	53.22 N	11.04 E
Pritzwalk	54	53.09 N	12.10 E
Priural'nyj	80	51.29 N	53.06 E
Privas	62	44.44 N	4.36 E
Priverno	66	41.28 N	13.11 E
Privodino	24	61.05 N	46.28 E
Privokzal'nyj, Ross.	82	55.59 N	35.56 E
Privokzal'nyj, Ross.	86	58.53 N	60.43 E
Privol'naja	78	46.09 N	38.42 E
Privol'noje	80	50.57 N	46.06 E
Privolžje	80	52.52 N	48.37 E
Privolžsk	80	57.23 N	41.17 E
Privolžskaja vozvyšennost' ⋏[1]	80	52.00 N	46.00 E
Privolžskij, Ross.	80	46.24 N	48.00 E
Privolžskij, Ross.	80	51.24 N	46.02 E
Privolžskoje	80	51.06 N	45.57 E
Prizren	38	42.12 N	20.44 E
Prizzi	70	37.43 N	13.26 E
Prizzi, Lago di ⊜	70	37.44 N	13.25 E
Prnjavor	36	44.52 N	17.40 E
Probolinggo	115a	7.45 S	113.13 E
Proboštov	54	50.39 N	13.50 E
Probstzella	54	50.32 N	11.22 E
Probus	42	50.17 N	4.57 W
Procchio	66	42.47 N	10.15 E
Prochladnoje	86	48.30 N	82.41 E
Prochladnyj	84	43.46 N	44.00 E
Prochorkino	86	59.34 N	79.26 E
Prochorovka	82	54.07 N	38.11 E
Prochowice	30	51.17 N	16.22 E
Procida	68	40.46 N	14.02 E

Symbols in the index entries represent the broad categories identified in the key at the right. Symbols with superior numbers (⋏[1]) identify subcategories (see complete key on page *I · 1)*.

Symbole im Register stellen die rechts im Schlüssel erklärten Kategorien dar. Symbole mit hochgestellten Ziffern (⋏[1]) bezeichnen Unterabteilungen einer Kategorie (vgl. vollständiger Schlüssel auf Seite *I · 1)*.

Los símbolos incluídos en el texto del índice representan las grandes categorías identificadas con la clave a la derecha. Los símbolos con numeros en su parte superior (⋏[1]) identifican las subcategorías (véase la clave completa en la página *I · 1)*.

Les symboles de l'index représentent les catégories indiquées dans la légende à droite. Les symboles suivis d'un indice (⋏[1]) représentent des sous-catégories (voir légende complète à la page *I · 1)*.

Os símbolos incluídos no texto do índice representam as grandes categorias identificadas com a chave à direita. Os símbolos com números em sua parte superior (⋏[1]) identificam as subcategorias (veja-se a chave completa à página *I · 1)*.

	English	Deutsch	Español	Français	Português
ʌ	Mountain	Berg	Montaña	Montagne	Montanha
⋏	Mountains	Gebirge	Montañas	Montagnes	Montanhas
)(	Pass	Paß	Paso	Col	Passo
V	Valley, Canyon	Tal, Cañon	Valle, Cañón	Vallée, Canyon	Vale, Canhão
≚	Plain	Ebene	Llano	Plaine	Planície
›	Cape	Kap	Cabo	Cap	Cabo
I	Island	Insel	Isla	Île	Ilha
II	Islands	Inseln	Islas	Îles	Ilhas
⊥	Other Topographic Features	Andere Topographische Objekte	Otros Elementos Topográficos	Autres données topographiques	Outros acidentes topográficos

ESPAÑOL

Nombre	Página	Lat.°′	Long.°′ W = Oeste
Procida, Isola di I	68	40.45 N	14.01 E
Procter	182	49.37 N	116.57 W
Proctor, Mn., U.S.	190	46.44 N	92.13 W
Proctor, Vt., U.S.	188	43.39 N	73.02 W
Proctor Brook ≃	283	42.32 N	70.54 W
Proctor Lake ⊜	228	35.07 N	118.21 W
Proctor Lake ⊜[1]	196	32.02 N	98.32 W
Proddatūr	122	14.44 N	78.33 E
Proença-a-Nova	34	39.45 N	7.55 W
Profen	54	51.07 N	12.13 E
Pro Football Hall of Fame ʊ	214	40.49 N	81.25 W
Prognoj	83	48.45 N	39.51 E
Progreso, Méx.	196	27.28 N	100.59 W
Progreso, Méx.	232	21.17 N	89.40 W
Progreso, Méx.	234	23.48 N	103.18 W
Progreso, Méx.	234	20.15 N	99.12 W
Progreso, Ur.	258	34.40 S	56.13 W
Progress, Ross.	89	49.42 N	129.39 E
Progress, Or., U.S.	224	45.28 N	122.47 W
Progress, Pa., U.S.	208	40.08 N	76.34 W
Project City	204	40.41 N	122.21 W
Prokopjeva	88	58.03 N	100.39 E
Prokopjevsk	86	53.53 N	86.45 E
Prokopyevsk → Prokopjevsk	86	53.53 N	86.45 E
Prokuplje	38	43.14 N	21.36 E
Prokuševo	76	59.55 N	34.56 E
Prokutkino	86	56.19 N	69.46 E
Proletarij	76	58.26 N	31.44 E
Proletarsk, Ross.	80	46.42 N	41.44 E
Proletarsk, Taj.	85	40.10 N	69.30 E
Proletarskij, Ross.	78	50.47 N	35.47 E
Proletarskij, Ross.	82	55.01 N	37.23 E
Prolysovo	76	52.54 N	34.09 E
Prome (Pyè)	110	18.49 N	95.13 E
Promised Land State Park ♠	210	41.18 N	75.11 W
Promissão	255	21.32 S	49.52 W
Promontogno	58	46.21 N	9.34 E
Prompton	210	41.35 N	75.19 W
Prompton Lake ⊜[1]	210	41.36 N	75.20 W
Prompton Lake State Park ♠	210	41.37 N	75.22 W
Promyšlennaja	86	54.55 N	85.40 E
Promyšlennovskij	86	55.29 N	86.12 E
Promyšlennyj	24	67.35 N	63.55 E
Promyslovka	80	45.44 N	47.10 E
Pron'a ≃	80	54.21 N	40.24 E
Pron'a Gorodišče	82	54.15 N	38.43 E
Pronin	80	49.12 N	42.11 E
Pronja ≃	76	53.25 N	31.01 E
Pronsfeld	56	50.10 N	6.20 E
Pronsk	76	54.07 N	39.37 E
Prony, Baie du c	175f	22.22 S	166.53 E
Prophet ≃	176	58.45 N	122.45 W
Prophetstown	190	41.40 N	89.56 W
Propriá	250	10.13 S	36.51 W
Propriano	36	41.40 N	8.55 E
Prorer Wiek c	54	54.27 N	13.38 E
Prorva	86	46.03 N	53.15 E
Proryvnoje	86	54.23 N	64.26 E
Prösen	54	51.25 N	13.30 E
Proserpine	166	20.24 S	148.34 E
Prosigk	54	51.42 N	12.03 E
Proskurov → Khmel'nyts'kyy	78	49.25 N	27.00 E
Prosna ≃	30	52.10 N	17.39 E
Prosnica	80	58.26 N	50.15 E
Prosotsáni	38	41.10 N	23.59 E
Prospect, Austl.	168b	34.54 S	138.35 E
Prospect, Austl.	274a	33.48 S	150.56 E
Prospect, Ct., U.S.	207	41.30 N	72.58 W
Prospect, N.Y., U.S.	210	43.18 N	75.09 W
Prospect, Oh., U.S.	214	40.27 N	83.11 W
Prospect, Pa., U.S.	214	40.54 N	80.03 W
Prospect Bay c	208	38.56 N	76.14 W
Prospect Creek ≃	274a	33.55 S	150.59 E
Prospect Heights	278	42.05 N	87.56 W
Prospect Hill	168b	35.13 S	138.44 E
Prospect Hill ∧[2], Ma., U.S.	207	41.21 N	70.45 W
Prospect Hill ∧[2], Ma., U.S.	283	42.23 N	71.15 W
Prospect Hill Park ♠	283	42.23 N	71.15 W
Prospect Park, N.J., U.S.	276	40.56 N	74.10 W
Prospect Park, Pa., U.S.	214	41.31 N	78.13 W
Prospect Park, Pa., U.S.	285	39.53 N	75.18 W
Prospect Park ♠	276	40.40 N	73.58 W
Prospect Park Lake ⊜	276	40.39 N	73.57 W
Prospect Plains	276	40.19 N	74.28 W
Prospect Point	276	40.58 N	74.38 W
Prospect Point ≻	276	40.52 N	73.43 W
Prospect Reservoir ⊜[1]	274a	33.49 S	150.54 E
Prospectville	285	40.13 N	75.11 W
Prosper	222	33.14 N	96.48 W
Prosperi Airport ⊠	278	41.33 N	87.47 W
Prosperidad	116	8.34 N	125.52 E
Prosser	202	46.12 N	119.46 W
Prosser Creek Reservoir ⊜[1]	226	39.22 N	120.08 W
Prostějov	30	49.29 N	17.07 E
Prostki	30	53.43 N	22.26 E
Proston	166	26.10 S	151.36 E
Prosyana	78	48.07 N	36.23 E
Prosyane	78	49.42 N	35.47 E
Prošyka	76	54.29 N	29.08 E
Proszowice	30	50.12 N	20.18 E
Protasovo, Ross.	82	54.48 N	38.35 E
Protasovo, Ross.	82	54.11 N	37.00 E
Protasovo, Ross.	82	56.08 N	37.36 E
Protea	273d	26.17 S	27.51 E
Protection	198	37.12 N	99.29 W
Protection Island I	224	48.07 N	122.55 W
Protem	158	34.16 S	20.05 E
Protivín	61	49.12 N	14.13 E
Protoka ≃	78	45.43 N	37.46 E
Protva	82	55.01 N	36.41 E
Protva ≃	82	54.51 N	37.16 E
Protville	36	36.54 N	10.01 E
Prötzel	54	52.38 N	13.59 E
Proud Lake State Recreation Area ♠	281	42.34 N	83.33 W
Proulxville	206	46.40 N	72.30 W
Provadija	38	43.11 N	27.26 E
Provencal	194	31.39 N	93.12 W
Provence □[9]	62	44.00 N	6.00 E
Provence, Alpes de ⩘	62	43.40 N	6.00 E
Provenchères-sur-Fave	58	48.19 N	7.05 E
Providence, Ky., U.S.	194	37.23 N	87.45 W
Providence, R.I., U.S.	207	41.49 N	71.24 W
Providence, Ut,. U.S.	200	41.42 N	111.48 W
Providence □[6]	207	41.52 N	71.36 W
Providence ≃	207	41.43 N	71.21 W
Providence Forge	208	37.26 N	77.02 W
Providence Island I	138	9.14 S	51.02 E
Providência, Bra.	256	21.40 S	42.35 W
Providencia, Chile	286e	33.26 S	70.37 W
Providencia, Méx.	196	27.06 N	103.32 W
Providencia, Isla de I	236	13.21 N	81.22 W
Providenciales I	238	21.47 N	72.17 W
Providenija	180	64.23 N	173.18 W
Providenija, buchta c	180	64.30 N	173.20 W
Provincetown	207	42.03 N	70.10 W
Provins	50	48.33 N	3.18 E
Provo	200	40.14 N	111.39 W
Provo ≃	200	40.14 N	111.44 W
Provost	184	52.21 N	110.16 W
Provost, Lac ⊜	206	46.22 N	74.00 W
Proyizhdzhe	83	49.25 N	38.58 E
Prozor	36	43.49 N	17.37 E
Pru ≃	150	7.58 N	0.53 W
Prudence Island I	207	41.37 N	71.19 W
Prudentópolis	252	25.12 S	50.57 W

FRANÇAIS

Nom	Page	Lat.°′	Long.°′ W = Ouest
Prudentov	80	49.39 N	46.19 E
Prudhoe	44	54.58 N	1.51 W
Prudhoe Bay c	180	70.20 N	148.20 W
Prudhoe Island I	166	21.19 S	149.40 E
Prudišči	82	54.24 N	38.26 E
Prudki	82	54.46 N	36.29 E
Prudnik	30	50.19 N	17.34 E
Prudyanka	78	50.14 N	36.09 E
Pruggern	64	47.25 N	13.52 E
Prüm	56	50.12 N	6.25 E
Prüm ≃	56	49.49 N	6.28 E
Pruna, Punta sa ∧	71	40.11 N	9.26 E
Prunay-le-Temple	261	48.52 N	1.40 E
Prunay-sous-Ablis	261	48.32 N	1.48 E
Prunedale	226	36.47 N	121.40 W
Prunéřov	54	50.25 N	13.16 E
Prunières	62	44.33 N	6.20 E
Prunn, Schloss ⊥	60	48.57 N	11.44 E
Pruszków	30	52.11 N	20.48 E
Prut ≃	78	45.30 N	28.12 E
Pruth → Prut ≃	78	45.30 N	28.12 E
Prutz	58	47.05 N	10.40 E
Pružany	76	52.33 N	24.28 E
Pryadivka	78	48.55 N	34.41 E
Pryazovs'ka vysochyna ⩘[1]	83	47.30 N	37.30 E
Pryazovs'ke	78	46.43 N	35.38 E
Prychornomors'ka nyzovyna ≚	78	47.00 N	33.00 E
Prydniprovs'ka nyzovyna ≚	78	50.00 N	32.00 E
Prydniprovs'ka vysochyna ⩘[1]	78	49.00 N	32.00 E
Prydz Bay c	9	69.00 S	76.00 E
Prykolotne	78	50.09 N	37.21 E
Pryluky	78	50.36 N	32.24 E
Prymors'k	78	46.44 N	36.20 E
Prymors'ke	83	47.11 N	37.42 E
Prymors'kyy	78	45.07 N	35.29 E
Pryor	196	36.19 N	95.19 W
Pryor Creek ≃	202	45.54 N	108.19 W
Pryor Mountain ∧[2]	222	31.43 N	95.12 W
Prypjac' (Pryp'yat') ≃	78	51.21 N	30.09 E
Pryputni	78	50.57 N	32.14 E
Pryp'yat'	78	51.26 N	30.10 E
Pryp'yat' (Prypjac') ≃	78	51.21 N	30.09 E
Pryshyb	78	47.16 N	35.21 E
Prysor ≃	42	52.56 N	4.00 W
Prystin	83	49.36 N	37.38 E
Pryvillya, Ukr.	83	49.01 N	38.18 E
Pryvillya, Ukr.	83	48.52 N	37.16 E
Pryvil'ne	78	47.29 N	32.17 E
Pryvitne	78	44.50 N	34.41 E
Przasnysz	30	53.01 N	20.55 E
Przedbórz	30	51.06 N	19.53 E
Przemków	30	51.32 N	15.48 E
Przemocze	54	53.27 N	14.55 E
Przemyśl	30	49.47 N	22.47 E
Przemyśl □[4]	30	50.00 N	22.40 E
Przeworsk	30	50.05 N	22.29 E
Przewóz	54	51.29 N	14.59 E
Przybiernów	54	53.46 N	14.46 E
Przysucha	30	51.22 N	20.38 E
Pšagar	85	39.58 N	68.08 E
Psakhná	38	38.35 N	23.38 E
Psará I	38	38.35 N	25.37 E
Psárion	38	37.20 N	21.51 E
Psebaj	84	44.07 N	40.47 E
Pšecha ≃	78	44.47 N	39.48 E
Psekups ≃	78	45.00 N	39.09 E
Pselec	78	51.17 N	36.32 E
Psikhikón	267c	38.01 N	23.46 E
Pšiš ≃	78	45.01 N	39.18 E
Pšiš, gora ∧	84	43.24 N	41.12 E
Psittália I	267c	37.56 N	23.35 E
Pskem	85	41.56 N	70.22 E
Pskem ≃	85	41.38 N	70.01 E
Pskent	85	40.54 N	69.20 E
Pskov	76	57.50 N	28.20 E
Pskov Oblast' □[4]	76	57.00 N	29.00 E
Pskovskoje ozero ⊜	76	58.00 N	28.00 E
Pskowsee → Pskovskcje ozero ⊜	76	58.00 N	28.00 E
Ps'ol ≃	78	49.02 N	33.33 E
Pšov	54	50.10 N	13.29 E
Pszczyna	30	49.59 N	18.57 E
Ptarmigan, Cape ≻	176	71.04 N	118.07 W
Ptolemaís	38	40.31 N	21.41 E
Ptolemais ⊥	146	32.43 N	20.57 E
Ptuj	36	46.25 N	15.52 E
Pu ≃, Zhg.	104	41.21 N	122.47 E
Pu ≃, Zhg.	107	30.25 N	103.49 E
Puah, Pulau I	112	0.30 S	122.34 E
Puakonikai	174d	0.52 S	169.36 E
Puamau, Baie c	174x	9.46 S	138.52 W
Puán, Arg.	252	37.33 S	62.43 W
Puan, Taehan	98	35.45 N	126.44 E
Pubāil	126	23.56 N	90.29 E
Pubnico	186	43.42 N	65.47 W
Pucallpa	248	8.23 S	74.32 W
Pucara	248	18.43 S	64.11 W
Pucarani	248	16.23 S	68.30 W
Puccha ≃	248	9.05 S	76.54 W
Puccia, Serra di ∧	70	37.44 N	13.56 E
Puce	214	42.18 N	82.47 W
Puces ≃	281	42.18 N	82.47 W
Pučevejem ≃	180	68.48 N	170.30 E
Pučež	80	56.59 N	43.11 E
Puchberg am Schneeberg	61	47.47 N	15.54 E
Pucheng, Zhg.	100	27.55 N	118.31 E
Pucheng, Zhg.	102	34.59 N	109.29 E
Pucheta	252	29.54 S	57.34 W
Puchheim	60	48.09 N	11.20 E
Púchov	30	49.08 N	18.20 E
Pucioasa	38	45.04 N	25.26 E
Pucio Point ≻	116	11.46 N	121.51 E
Pučišća	36	43.21 N	16.44 E
Puck	30	54.44 N	18.27 E
Puckapunyal	169	37.01 S	145.03 E
Pucketa Creek ≃	279b	40.33 N	79.45 W
Pudahuel	286e	33.26 S	70.46 W
Pudding ≃	224	45.18 N	122.43 W
Puddingstone Reservoir ⊜[1]	280	34.05 N	117.48 W
Puddington	262	53.15 N	3.00 W
Puddletown	42	50.45 N	2.21 W
Pūdeh Tal ≃	128	31.03 N	62.15 E
Pudem	80	58.18 N	52.10 E
Pudi	102	27.58 N	99.05 E
Pudimoe	158	27.26 S	24.44 E
Puding	102	26.21 N	105.40 E
Pudino	86	57.34 N	79.24 E
Pudops Dam ⊷[6]	186	48.09 N	56.50 W
Pudož	24	61.48 N	36.32 E
Pudsey	44	53.48 N	1.40 W
Pudu ≃	102	26.19 N	102.45 E
Puduari ≃	246	2.08 S	61.15 W
Puduhe	102	25.39 N	102.39 E
Pudukkottai	122	10.23 N	78.49 E
Puebla □[3]	234	18.50 N	98.00 W
Puebla de Alcocer	34	38.59 N	5.15 W
Puebla de Don Fadrique	34	37.58 N	2.26 W
Puebla de Don Rodrigo	34	39.05 N	4.37 W
Puebla de Sanabria	34	42.03 N	6.38 W
Puebla [de Zaragoza]	234	19.03 N	98.12 W
Pueblito de Ponce	240m	18.26 N	66.58 W
Pueblo	198	38.15 N	104.36 W
Pueblo Libertador	252	30.13 S	59.23 W
Pueblo Libre	286d	12.05 S	77.04 W
Pueblo Mountain ∧	202	42.06 N	118.39 W
Pueblo Nuevo, Col.	246	8.31 N	75.15 W
Pueblo Nuevo, Méx.	234	20.31 N	101.22 W
Pueblo Nuevo, Nic.	236	13.23 N	86.29 W
Pueblo Nuevo, P.R.	240m	18.28 N	66.51 W
Pueblo Nuevo, Ur.	258	34.26 S	56.29 W

PORTUGUÊS

Nome	Página	Lat.°′	Long.°′ W = Oeste
Pueblo Nuevo, Ven.	246	11.58 N	69.55 W
Pueblo Nuevo ⊷[8]	266a	40.26 N	3.39 W
Pueblo Nuevo Tiquisate	236	14.17 N	91.22 W
Pueblo of Acoma	200	35.03 N	107.35 W
Pueblo Reservoir ⊜[1]	198	38.15 N	104.45 W
Puebloviejo, Ec.	246	1.34 S	79.30 W
Pueblo Viejo, Méx.	234	17.33 N	100.05 W
Pueblo Viejo, Méx.	234	16.14 N	94.39 W
Pueblo Viejo, Laguna c	234	22.10 N	97.53 W
Pueblo Yaqui	232	27.19 N	110.01 W
Puelches	252	38.09 S	65.55 W
Puente Alto	252	33.37 S	70.35 W
Puente de Arganda	266a	40.19 N	3.31 W
Puente de Ixtla	234	18.37 N	99.20 W
Puente del Arzobispo	34	39.48 N	5.10 W
Puente Genil	34	37.23 N	4.47 W
Puente Hills ⩘[2]	280	34.00 N	117.55 W
Puente Hills Mall ⊷[9]	280	33.59 N	117.56 W
Puente la Reina	34	42.40 N	1.49 W
Puente Negro	196	27.55 N	101.01 W
Puente Nuevo, Embalse de ⊜[1]	34	38.00 N	5.00 W
Puente Piedra	286d	11.57 S	77.05 W
Pueo Point ≻	229b	21.54 N	160.04 W
Pu'er	102	23.07 N	101.00 E
Puerca, Punta ≻	240m	18.14 N	65.36 W
Puerco ≃	200	34.53 N	110.07 W
Puerco, Rio ≃	200	34.22 N	106.50 W
Pu'erdu	102	28.08 N	104.24 E
Puerto Acosta	248	15.32 S	69.15 W
Puerto Adela	252	24.33 S	54.22 W
Puerto Aisén	254	45.24 S	72.42 W
Puerto Alegre	248	13.53 S	61.36 W
Puerto Ángel	234	15.40 N	96.29 W
Puerto Arista	234	15.56 N	93.48 W
Puerto Armuelles	236	8.17 N	82.52 W
Puerto Asís	246	0.30 N	76.31 W
Puerto Ayacucho	246	5.40 N	67.35 W
Puerto Ayora, Ec.	246a	0.45 S	90.19 W
Puerto Ayora, Ec.	246a	0.45 S	90.19 W
Puerto Bahía Negra	248	20.15 S	58.12 W
Puerto Baquerizo Moreno	246a	0.54 S	89.36 W
Puerto Barrios	236	15.43 N	88.36 W
Puerto Bermejo	252	26.56 S	58.30 W
Puerto Bermúdez	248	10.20 S	74.54 W
Puerto Berrío	246	6.29 N	74.24 W
Puerto Bolívar, Col.	246	12.15 N	71.58 W
Puerto Bolívar, Ec.	246	3.16 S	79.59 W
Puerto Boyacá	246	5.45 N	74.39 W
Puerto Busch	248	20.02 S	57.55 W
Puerto Cabello	246	10.28 N	68.01 W
Puerto Cabezas	236	14.02 N	83.23 W
Puerto Carreño	246	6.12 N	67.22 W
Puerto Casado	252	22.20 S	57.55 W
Puerto Castilla	236	16.01 N	86.01 W
Puerto Chicama	248	7.42 S	79.27 W
Puerto Colombia	246	10.59 N	74.58 W
Puerto Constanza	258	33.50 S	59.03 W
Puerto Cortés	236	15.48 N	87.56 W
Puerto Cumarebo	246	11.29 N	69.21 W
Puerto de Eten	248	6.54 S	79.52 W
Puerto Delicia	252	26.12 S	54.35 W
Puerto de Lomas	248	15.34 S	74.50 W
Puerto Delón	236	14.22 N	85.53 W
Puerto del Rosario	148	28.30 N	13.52 W
Puerto Deseado	254	47.45 S	65.54 W
Puerto El Triunfo	236	13.17 N	88.33 W
Puerto Escondido	234	15.50 N	97.10 W
Puerto Españа → Port of Spain	241r	10.39 N	61.31 W
Puerto Esperanza	252	26.01 S	54.39 W
Puerto Felipe, Bahía → Port Phillip Bay c	169	38.07 S	144.48 E
Puerto Fonciere	252	22.29 S	57.48 W
Puerto Francisco de Orellana	246	0.28 S	76.58 W
Puerto Gonzalo Moreno	248	11.06 S	66.10 W
Puerto Guaraní	248	21.18 S	57.55 W
Puerto Heath	248	12.30 S	68.40 W
Puerto Iguazú	252	25.34 S	54.34 W
Puerto Inca	248	9.22 S	74.58 W
Puerto Ingeniero Ibáñez	254	46.18 S	71.56 W
Puerto Inírida	246	3.53 N	67.52 W
Puerto Jiménez	236	8.33 N	83.19 W
Puerto Juárez	232	21.11 N	86.49 W
Puerto la Cruz	246	10.13 N	64.38 W
Puerto la Plata, Zona Nacional □[5]	288	34.52 S	57.52 W
Puerto Leda	248	20.41 S	58.02 W
Puerto Leguízamo	246	0.12 S	74.46 W
Puerto Lempira	236	15.13 N	83.47 W
Puerto Libertad, Arg.	252	25.55 S	54.36 W
Puerto Libertad, Méx.	232	29.55 N	112.43 W
Puerto Limón, Col.	246	3.23 N	73.30 W
Puerto Limón, C.R.	236	10.00 N	83.02 W
Puertollano	34	38.41 N	4.07 W
Puerto Lobos	254	42.00 S	65.06 W
Puerto López	246	4.05 N	72.58 W
Puerto Madero	236	14.44 N	92.25 W
Puerto Madryn	254	42.46 S	65.03 W
Puerto Maldonado	248	12.36 S	69.11 W
Puerto Manatí	240p	21.22 N	76.50 W
Puerto Mihanovich	248	20.52 S	57.59 W
Puerto Montt	254	41.28 S	72.57 W
Puerto Morazán	236	12.51 N	87.11 W
Puerto Morelos	232	20.50 N	86.52 W
Puerto Nariño	246	4.56 N	67.48 W
Puerto Natales	254	51.44 S	72.31 W
Puerto Nuevo, Punta ≻	240m	18.30 N	66.24 W
Puerto Octay	254	40.58 S	72.54 W
Puerto Ordaz → Ciudad Guayana	246	8.22 N	62.40 W
Puerto Padre	240p	21.12 N	76.36 W
Puerto Páez	246	6.13 N	67.28 W
Puerto Palmer, Pico ∧	196	27.08 N	101.47 W
Puerto Peñasco	232	31.20 N	113.33 W
Puerto Pilón	236	9.22 N	79.48 W
Puerto Pinasco	252	22.43 S	57.50 W
Puerto Pirámide	254	42.34 S	64.17 W
Puerto Piray	252	26.28 S	54.42 W
Puerto Píritu	246	10.04 N	65.03 W
Puerto Plata	238	19.48 N	70.41 W
Puerto Portillo	248	9.46 S	72.45 W
Puerto Princesa, Pil.	116	9.44 N	118.44 E
Puerto Princesa, Pil.	116	10.06 N	125.29 E
Puerto Real, Esp.	34	36.32 N	6.11 W
Puerto Real, P.R.	240m	18.05 N	67.11 W
Puerto Rico, Arg.	252	26.48 S	55.02 W
Puerto Rico, Bol.	248	11.05 S	67.38 W
Puerto Rico, Col.	246	1.54 N	75.10 W
Puerto Rico □[2], N.A.	230	18.15 N	66.30 W
Puerto Rico □[2], N.A.	240m	18.15 N	66.30 W
Puerto Rico Trench ✣[1]	16	20.00 N	66.00 W
Puerto Rondón	246	6.17 N	71.06 W
Puerto Saavedra	252	38.47 S	73.24 W
Puerto Salgar	246	5.28 N	74.39 W
Puerto Sandino	236	12.12 N	86.46 W
Puerto San José	236	13.55 N	90.49 W
Puerto San Julián	254	49.18 S	67.43 W
Puerto Santa Cruz	254	50.01 S	68.31 W
Puerto Sastre	252	22.06 S	57.59 W
Puerto Siles	248	12.48 S	65.05 W
Puerto Suarez	248	18.57 S	57.51 W
Puerto Supe	248	10.49 S	77.45 W
Puerto Tejada	246	3.14 N	76.24 W
Puerto Tolosa	246	0.59 S	74.09 W
Puerto Umbría	246	0.52 N	76.33 W
Puerto Vallarta	234	20.37 N	105.15 W
Puerto Varas	254	41.19 S	72.59 W
Puerto Victoria, Arg.	252	26.20 S	54.39 W
Puerto Victoria, Perú	248	9.54 S	74.58 W

Puerto Viejo, C.R.	236	10.26 N	83.59 W
Puerto Viejo, C.R.	236	9.39 N	82.45 W
Puerto Villamil	246a	0.56 S	91.01 W
Puerto Villamizar	246	8.19 N	72.26 W
Puerto Villarroel	248	16.50 S	64.47 W
Puerto Visser	254	45.24 S	67.08 W
Puerto Wilches	246	7.21 N	73.54 W
Puerto Williams	254	54.56 S	67.37 W
Puerto Ybapobó	252	23.42 S	57.12 W
Pueyrredón, Lago (Lago Cochrane) ⊜	254	47.20 S	72.00 W
Puffendorf	56	50.56 N	6.13 E
Puffing Billy Railroad Station ⊷[5]	274b	37.55 S	145.21 E
Pugačov	80	52.01 N	48.50 E
Pugač'ovo	80	56.35 N	53.02 E
Puge, Tan.	154	4.45 S	33.07 E
Puge, Zhg.	102	27.28 N	102.31 E
Puget, Cape ≻	180	59.52 N	148.26 W
Puget Island I	224	46.10 N	123.23 W
Puget Sound ɥ	224	47.50 N	122.30 W
Puget Sound Naval Shipyard ■	224	47.33 N	122.38 W
Puget-sur-Argens	62	43.27 N	6.41 E
Puget-Théniers	62	43.57 N	6.54 E
Puget-Ville	62	43.17 N	6.08 E
Pugh, Mount ∧	224	48.08 N	121.22 W
Pughtown	285	40.10 N	75.40 W
Puglia □[4]	68	41.15 N	16.15 E
Pugong-ni	271b	37.43 N	126.58 E
Pugŏ-ri	98	42.01 N	129.59 E
Pugwash	186	45.51 N	63.40 W
Puḫavičy	76	53.32 N	28.15 E
Puhe	104	41.57 N	123.36 E
Puhi	229b	21.58 N	159.23 W
Puhja	76	58.20 N	26.19 E
Puhos	26	62.05 N	29.54 E
Puhosjärvi ⊜	26	65.19 N	27.55 E
Puica	248	15.04 S	72.42 W
Puiești	38	46.25 N	27.33 E
Puigcerdá	34	42.26 N	1.56 E
Puigmal ∧	34	42.23 N	2.07 E
Puimoisson	62	43.52 N	6.08 E
Puinahua, Canal de ≃[1]	248	5.20 S	74.13 W
Puinān	272b	22.56 N	88.13 E
Puir	89	53.10 N	141.25 E
Puisaye, Collines de la ⩘[2]	50	47.40 N	3.15 E
Puiseaux	50	48.12 N	2.28 E
Puiseaux ≃	50	48.00 N	2.44 E
Puiseux-en-France	261	49.04 N	2.29 E
Puiseux-Pontoise	261	49.03 N	2.01 E
Puisieux	50	50.07 N	2.42 E
Puits ≃	50	48.31 N	4.15 E
Pujada Bay c	116	6.51 N	126.14 E
Pujehun	150	7.21 N	11.42 W
Puji, Zhg.	100	27.59 N	113.25 E
Puji, Zhg.	100	29.58 N	112.32 E
Pujiang, Zhg.	100	29.28 N	119.53 E
Pujiang, Zhg.	107	30.12 N	103.30 E
Pujilí	246	0.57 S	78.41 W
Pujon	115a	7.50 S	112.28 E
Pujun	112	1.20 S	114.20 E
Pujut	114	1.25 N	100.39 E
Pujut, Tanjung ≻	115a	5.52 S	106.02 E
Pukaki, Lake ⊜	172	44.07 S	170.10 E
Pukalani	229a	20.50 N	156.20 W
Pukaskwa ≃	190	48.00 N	85.53 W
Pukaskwa National Park ♠	190	48.20 N	85.50 W
Pukch'ang	98	39.36 N	126.17 E
Pukchin	98	40.10 N	125.43 E
Pukch'ŏn	98	36.13 N	126.45 E
Pukch'ŏng	98	40.15 N	128.20 E
Pukë	38	42.03 N	19.54 E
Pukeashun Mountain ∧	182	51.12 N	119.14 W
Pukekohe	172	37.12 S	174.55 E
Puketeraki Range ⩘	172	42.58 S	172.12 E
Puketoi Range ⩘	172	40.30 S	176.05 E
Pukeuri Junction	172	45.02 S	171.02 E
Pukhan-gang ≃	98	37.31 N	127.18 E
Pŭkhan-san ∧	271b	37.41 N	127.00 E
Pukhrāyān	124	26.14 N	79.51 E
Pukoo	229d	21.04 N	156.48 W
Pukou, Zhg.	100	26.16 N	119.35 E
Pukou, Zhg.	106	32.07 N	118.43 E
Puksoozero	24	62.38 N	40.36 E
Puksubaek-san ∧	98	40.42 N	127.44 E
Puktae-ch'ŏn ≃	98	40.28 N	129.00 E
Pula, Hrv.	36	44.52 N	13.50 E
Pula, It.	71	39.01 N	9.00 E
Pulacayo	248	20.25 S	66.41 W
Pulandian Wan c	98	39.18 N	121.35 E
Pulanduta Point ≻	116	11.54 N	123.10 E
Pulangi ≃	116	7.18 N	124.50 E
Pulangpisau	112	2.46 S	114.14 E
Pulap I[1]	14	7.35 N	149.24 E
Púlar, Cerro ∧	252	24.11 S	68.04 W
Pulaski, In., U.S.	216	40.59 N	86.40 W
Pulaski, Mi., U.S.	216	42.07 N	84.40 W
Pulaski, N.Y., U.S.	212	43.34 N	76.07 W
Pulaski, Oh., U.S.	216	41.30 N	84.26 W
Pulaski, Pa., U.S.	214	41.07 N	80.26 W
Pulaski, Tn., U.S.	194	35.11 N	87.01 W
Pulaski, Va., U.S.	192	37.02 N	80.46 W
Pulaski, Wi., U.S.	190	44.40 N	88.14 W
Pulaski □[6]	216	41.03 N	86.36 W
Pulau ≃	164	5.50 S	138.15 E
Pulaukida	112	2.44 S	102.34 E
Pulaukijang	112	0.42 S	103.12 E
Pulaumerak, Indon.	115a	5.56 S	106.00 E
Pulaumerak, Indon.	115a	5.56 S	106.00 E
Pulauraja	114	2.42 N	99.37 E
Puławy	30	51.25 N	21.57 E
Pulborough	42	50.58 N	0.30 W
Pul'chakim	85	38.10 N	67.21 E
Pulehu Gulch V	229a	20.50 N	156.28 W
Pulfero	64	46.11 N	13.29 E
Pulga	123	31.59 N	77.26 E
Pulgaon	122	20.44 N	78.20 E
Pulham Market	42	52.26 N	1.14 E
Pulheim	56	51.00 N	6.47 E
Puli	100	23.58 N	120.57 E
Pulicat	122	13.25 N	80.19 E
Pulicat Lake c	122	13.40 N	80.10 E
Pulichatum	128	35.57 N	61.07 E
Puliciano	66	43.23 N	11.51 E
Puliyangudi	122	9.10 N	77.25 E
Pulj → Pula	64	44.52 N	13.50 E
Pulkau	61	48.42 N	15.51 E
Pulkau ≃	61	48.43 N	16.21 E
Pulkkila	26	64.16 N	25.52 E
Pulkovo ⊷[8]	265a	59.46 N	30.20 E
Pullman, Mi., U.S.	216	42.29 N	86.05 W
Pullman, Wa., U.S.	202	46.43 N	117.10 W
Pullman ⊷[8]	278	41.43 N	87.36 W
Púllo	248	15.14 S	73.50 W
Pully	58	46.31 N	6.39 E
Pul'mo	78	51.31 N	23.47 E
Pulo ⊥	68	41.12 N	16.34 E
Pulo Anna I	108	4.40 N	131.58 E
Pulog, Mount ∧	116	16.36 N	120.54 E
Pulogadung ⊷[8]	269e	6.11 S	106.54 E
Pulon'ga	24	66.17 N	40.02 E
Púlpito do Sul	152	15.46 S	12.00 E
Pulsano	68	40.23 N	17.22 E
Pulsen	54	51.23 N	13.26 E
Pulsnitz	54	51.11 N	14.01 E
Pulsnitz ≃	54	51.27 N	13.30 E
Pulteney	210	42.31 N	77.10 W
Pulteneyville	210	43.17 N	77.11 W
Pułtusk	30	52.43 N	21.05 E
Pulü, Zhg.	107	29.50 N	106.11 E
Pulu, Zhg.	120	36.11 N	81.30 E
Pulupandan	116	10.31 N	122.48 E
Pulur	130	40.10 N	39.53 E
Pulusuk I	14	6.42 N	149.19 E
Pulversheim	58	47.51 N	7.18 E
Puma Yumco ⊜	124	28.35 N	90.20 E
Pumbi	152	3.26 N	22.11 E
Pumei	102	23.28 N	105.15 E
Pumphrey	284b	39.13 N	76.38 W
Pumpkin Buttes ∧	200	43.44 N	105.54 W
Pumpkin Center	228	35.18 N	119.05 W
Pumpkin Creek ≃, Mt., U.S.	198	46.15 N	105.45 W
Pumpkin Creek ≃, Ne., U.S.	198	41.38 N	103.01 W
Pumsaint	42	52.03 N	3.58 W
Pumsi	80	57.12 N	51.39 E
Puná, Isla I	246	2.50 S	80.08 W
Punaauia	174s	17.38 S	149.36 W
Punaauia, Pointe de ≻	174s	17.38 S	149.36 W
Punakha	124	27.37 N	89.52 E
Punaluu	229c	21.35 N	157.53 W
Punan, Indon.	112	1.20 N	115.34 E
Punan, Indon.	112	3.24 N	116.16 E
Punan, Zhg.	100	24.39 N	117.41 E
Punata	248	17.32 S	65.50 W
Pūnch	123	33.46 N	74.06 E
Pūnch ≃	123	33.12 N	73.40 E
Puncha	126	23.10 N	86.39 E
Punchaw	182	53.28 N	123.13 W
Punchbowl	274a	33.56 S	151.03 E
Pundaguitan	116	6.22 N	126.10 E
Punda Maria	156	22.40 S	31.05 E
Pünderich	56	50.02 N	7.08 E
Pūndri	124	29.45 N	76.33 E
Punduga	76	60.08 N	40.12 E
Pune (Poona)	122	18.32 N	73.52 E
P'ungam-ni	98	37.43 N	128.11 E
Pungan	85	40.45 N	70.49 E
Punganūru	122	13.22 N	78.35 E
Pungarancho ≃	234	18.47 N	100.41 W
Pungești	38	46.42 N	27.20 E
Punggol	271c	1.25 N	103.55 E
Punggol ≃	271c	1.25 N	103.54 E
Pungki	114	4.17 N	96.13 E
Pungo ≃	192	35.23 N	76.33 W
Pungo Andongo	152	9.40 S	15.35 E
Púngoè ≃	154	19.50 S	34.48 E
P'ungsan, C.M.I.K.	98	40.47 N	128.10 E
P'ungsan, C.M.I.K.	98	38.28 N	125.01 E
P'ungsong-ni	98	39.56 N	127.11 E
Punia	154	1.28 S	26.27 E
Punilla, Sierra de la ⩘	252	28.55 S	69.00 W
Puning	100	23.18 N	116.12 E
Punitaqui	252	30.50 S	71.16 W
Punjab □[3]	123	31.00 N	75.30 E
Punjab □[4]	120	31.00 N	72.00 E
Punkaharju ♠	26	61.47 N	29.20 E
Punkalaidun	26	61.07 N	23.06 E
Punnichy	184	51.23 N	104.18 W
Puno	248	15.50 S	70.02 W
Puno □[5]	248	15.00 S	70.00 W
Punta, Castillo de la ⊥	286b	23.09 N	82.21 W
Punta, Cerro de ∧	240m	18.10 N	66.36 W
Punta Alegre	240p	22.23 N	78.49 W
Punta Alta	254	38.53 S	62.05 W
Punta Arenas	254	53.09 S	70.55 W
Punta Banda, Cabo ≻	232	31.45 N	116.45 W
Punta Brava ⊷[8]	286b	23.01 N	82.30 W
Punta Cardón	246	11.38 N	70.14 W
Punta Colnett	232	31.05 N	116.05 W
Punta de Agua Creek (Tramperos Creek) ≃	196	35.32 N	102.27 W
Punta de Bombón	248	17.11 S	71.48 W
Punta de Díaz	252	28.03 S	70.37 W
Punta del Cobre	252	27.30 S	70.16 W
Punta del Este	252	34.58 S	54.57 W
Punta Delgada	254	42.46 S	63.38 W
Punta de los Llanos	252	30.09 S	66.33 W
Punta de Mata	246	9.43 N	63.38 W
Punta de Piedras	246	10.54 N	64.06 W
Punta Flecha	116	7.23 N	123.25 E
Punta Gorda, Belize	232	16.07 N	88.48 W
Punta Gorda, Nic.	236	11.31 N	83.47 W
Punta Gorda, Fl., U.S.	220	26.55 N	82.02 W
Punta Gorda ≃	236	11.30 N	83.47 W
Punta Gorda, Bahía de c	236	11.15 N	83.45 W
Punta Negra, Salar de ≚	252	24.35 S	69.00 W
Punta Prieta	232	28.58 N	114.17 W
Punta Raisi, Aeroporto di ⊠	70	38.11 N	13.06 E
Puntarenas	236	9.58 N	84.50 W
Puntarenas □[4]	236	9.00 N	83.15 W
Punta Santiago	240m	18.10 N	65.45 W
Puntas del Sauce	258	33.51 S	57.01 W
Punto Fijo	246	11.42 N	70.13 W
Puntzi Lake ⊜	182	52.12 N	124.02 W
Punung	115a	8.08 S	111.01 E
Punxsutawney	214	40.56 N	78.58 W
Puolanka	26	64.52 N	27.40 E
Puolo Point ≻	229b	21.54 N	159.36 W
Puper	164	0.10 S	131.18 E
Pup'yŏng	271b	37.30 N	126.43 E
Puqi, Zhg.	100	28.11 N	121.01 E
Puqi, Zhg.	100	29.43 N	113.53 E
Puqian, Zhg.	100	23.34 N	114.38 E
Puqian, Zhg.	102	20.03 N	110.36 E
Puquio	248	14.42 S	74.08 W
Pur ≃	74	67.31 N	77.55 E
Purabiya Plain ≚	124	25.50 N	82.30 E
Puracé, Volcán ∧[1]	246	2.21 N	76.23 W
Purandarpur	126	23.51 N	87.36 E
Pūranpur	124	28.31 N	80.09 E
Purari ≃	164	7.25 S	145.05 E
Purba	114	2.54 N	98.42 E
Purbashthāli	126	23.28 N	88.21 E
Purbeck, Isle of I	42	50.38 N	2.00 W
Purbolinggo	115a	7.24 S	109.22 E
Purcell	196	35.00 N	97.21 W
Purcell Mountains ⩘	182	50.00 N	116.30 W
Purcellville	188	39.08 N	77.42 W
Purchase	276	41.02 N	73.43 W
Purchena	34	37.21 N	2.22 W
Purdon	222	31.57 N	96.37 W
Purdoški	80	54.40 N	43.32 E
Purdy	194	36.49 N	93.55 W
Purech	80	56.39 N	43.05 E
Pureora ∧	172	38.33 S	175.38 E
Purépero	234	19.55 N	102.01 W
Purfleet	42	51.29 N	0.15 E
Purga	171a	27.43 S	152.44 E
Purga Creek ≃	171a	27.42 S	152.45 E
Purgatoire ≃	198	38.04 N	103.10 W
Purgatory Brook ≃	283	42.11 N	71.11 W
Pürgg	61	47.32 N	14.04 E
Purgstall an der Erlauf	61	48.03 N	15.08 E
Puri	120	19.48 N	85.51 E
Purial, Sierra del ⩘	240p	20.12 N	74.42 W
Purificación, Col.	246	3.51 N	74.55 W
Purificación, Méx.	234	19.43 N	104.38 W
Purificación ≃, Méx.	232	23.58 N	98.42 W
Purificación ≃, Méx.	234	19.18 N	104.54 W
Purikari neem ≻	76	59.40 N	25.43 E
Purísima	196	29.09 N	100.46 W
Purísima, Sierra de la ⩘	196	26.30 N	101.44 W
Purisima Creek ≃	282	37.24 N	122.26 W
Purísima de Bustos	234	21.02 N	101.52 W
Purkersdorf	61	48.12 N	16.11 E
Purleigh	260	51.41 N	0.40 E
Purley	222	33.05 N	95.16 W
Purley ⊷[8]	260	51.20 N	0.07 W
Purling	210	42.17 N	74.00 W
Purmerend	52	52.31 N	4.57 E
Pūrna ≃, India	122	19.07 N	77.02 E
Pūrna ≃, India	122	21.05 N	76.00 E
Pūrnia	124	25.47 N	87.31 E
Puronga	76	60.09 N	40.54 E
Purranque	254	40.55 S	73.10 W
Purrorumba Hill ∧	171b	35.10 S	149.23 E
Purros	156	18.38 S	12.59 E
Purrumbete, Lake ⊜	169	38.17 S	143.14 E
Pursat → Poŭthĭsăt	110	12.32 N	103.55 E
Purton	42	51.36 N	1.52 W
Puruándiro	234	20.05 N	101.30 W
Puruarán	234	19.06 N	101.32 W
Puruí ≃	246	1.40 S	68.08 W
Purukcahu	112	0.35 S	114.35 E
Puruliya	126	23.20 N	86.22 E
Puruni ≃	246	6.00 N	59.12 W
Purus (Purús) ≃	242	3.42 S	61.28 W
Puruvesi ⊜	26	61.50 N	29.27 E
Purvis	194	31.08 N	89.24 W
Purwakarta	115a	6.34 S	107.26 E
Purwantoro	115a	7.51 S	111.15 E
Purwareja	115a	7.28 S	109.25 E
Purwodadi, Indon.	115a	7.49 S	110.00 E
Purwodadi, Indon.	115a	7.05 S	110.54 E
Purwokerto	115a	7.25 S	109.14 E
Purworejo	115a	7.43 S	110.01 E
Pusa	112	1.36 N	111.17 E
Pusad	122	19.54 N	77.35 E
Pusan	98	35.06 N	129.03 E
Pusan □[4]	98	35.10 N	129.05 E
Pūsa Road	124	25.59 N	85.41 E
Pusat Gayo, Pegunungan ⩘	114	4.15 N	97.05 E
Puščino	82	54.50 N	37.36 E
Pusgo Point ≻	116	13.31 N	122.38 E
Pushang	98	36.08 N	119.42 E
Pushkar	120	26.30 N	74.33 E
Pushkarivka	78	48.40 N	34.16 E
Pushkin → Puškin	76	59.43 N	30.25 E
Pushkin Airport ⊠	265a	59.41 N	30.21 E
Pushkin Drama Theatre ʊ	265a	59.56 N	30.21 E
Pushthrough	186	47.39 N	56.10 W
Puskiakiwenin Indian Reserve ⊷[4]	184	53.57 N	110.26 W
Puškin	76	59.43 N	30.25 E
Puškino, Ross.	80	51.14 N	46.59 E
Puškino, Ross.	82	56.01 N	37.51 E
Puškino, Ross.	82	56.36 N	35.46 E
Puškinskij	265a	59.43 N	30.18 E
Puškinskije Gory	76	57.01 N	28.54 E
Puskwaskau ≃	182	55.29 N	118.10 W
Puslinch Lake ⊜	212	43.25 N	80.16 W
Pusŏng-ni	98	40.19 N	127.19 E
Püspökladány	30	47.19 N	21.07 E
Pussay	50	48.21 N	2.00 E
Püssi	76	59.24 N	27.01 E
Pustertal V	64	46.45 N	12.20 E
Pustin'	76	59.54 N	35.32 E
Pustomyty	78	49.42 N	23.56 E
Pustoš'	76	60.07 N	42.45 E
Pustoška	76	56.20 N	29.22 E
Pustozersk	24	67.33 N	52.27 E
Pusur ≃[1]	126	21.45 N	89.30 E
Puszczykowo	30	52.17 N	16.52 E
Putaendo	252	32.38 S	70.44 W
Putah Creek ≃	226	38.33 N	121.42 W
Putai	100	23.23 N	120.09 E
Putana, Volcán ∧[1]	252	22.43 S	67.54 W
Putang ≃	269e	6.13 S	106.54 E
Putangqiao	106	31.34 N	118.59 E
Putao	102	27.21 N	97.24 E
Putaruru	172	38.03 S	175.47 E
Put'atin	89	42.52 N	132.25 E
Put'atino	80	54.10 N	41.07 E
Putbus	54	54.21 N	13.28 E
Puteaux	261	48.53 N	2.14 E
Puteran, Pulau I	115a	7.05 S	114.00 E
Putfontein Landbouhoewes	273d	26.08 S	28.24 E
Putgarten	54	54.40 N	13.25 E
Puth Kalān ⊷[8]	272a	28.43 N	77.05 E
Putian, Zhg.	100	25.26 N	119.01 E
Putian, Zhg.	100	29.16 N	114.58 E
Putifigari	71	40.34 N	8.27 E
Putignano	68	40.51 N	17.07 E
Putilkovo	265b	55.52 N	37.23 E
Putina	248	14.55 S	69.52 W
Put-in-Bay	214	41.39 N	82.49 W
Putincevo	86	49.50 N	84.22 E
Puting, Tanjung ≻	112	3.31 S	111.46 E
Putla de Guerrero	234	17.02 N	97.56 W
Putlitz	54	53.15 N	12.02 E
Putnam, Ct., U.S.	207	41.54 N	71.54 W
Putnam, Tx., U.S.	196	32.22 N	99.12 W
Putnam □[6], N.Y., U.S.	210	41.26 N	73.41 W
Putnam □[6], Oh., U.S.	216	41.01 N	84.03 W
Putnam Lake	210	41.28 N	73.35 W
Putnam Lake ⊜	276	41.05 N	73.38 W
Putnam Valley	210	41.20 N	73.52 W
Putnamville Reservoir ⊜[1]	283	42.36 N	70.57 W
Putney, Ga., U.S.	192	31.29 N	84.07 W
Putney, Vt., U.S.	188	42.58 N	72.31 W
Putney ⊷[8]	260	51.28 N	0.13 W
Putney Island I	126	21.42 N	89.20 E
Puto	175e	5.41 S	154.43 E
Putorana, plato ⩘[1]	74	69.00 N	95.00 E
Putorino	172	39.08 S	177.00 E
Putre	248	18.12 S	69.35 W
Putri Narrows ɥ	271c	1.27 N	103.42 E
Putsonderwater	158	29.09 S	21.51 E
Pütt	263	51.11 N	6.59 E
Puttalam	122	8.02 N	79.49 E
Puttalam Lagoon c	122	8.07 N	79.47 E
Putte, Bel.	56	51.04 N	4.38 E
Putte, Ned.	52	51.22 N	4.23 E
Puttelange-lès-Farschviller	56	49.03 N	6.56 E
Putten	52	52.15 N	5.36 E
Putten I	52	51.50 N	4.15 E
Puttgarden	54	54.30 N	11.13 E
Püttlingen	56	49.17 N	6.53 E
Puttūr	122	13.27 N	79.33 E
Putty	170	32.57 S	150.40 E
Putty Creek ≃	170	33.05 S	150.37 E
Putú	252	35.13 S	72.17 W
Putumayo □[8]	246	0.30 N	76.00 W
Putumayo (Içá) ≃	246	3.07 S	67.58 W
Putuo	100	29.58 N	122.17 E
Putu Range ⩘	150	5.30 N	8.10 W
Pütürge	130	38.12 N	38.53 E
Putussibau	112	0.50 N	112.56 E
Putyla	78	48.01 N	25.03 E
Putyvl'	78	51.21 N	33.52 E
Putzkau	54	51.06 N	14.13 E
Putzu Idu	71	40.02 N	8.25 E
Pu'uhonua o Honaunau National Historical Park ♠	229d	19.25 N	155.54 W
Puu Kaaumakua ∧	229c	21.30 N	157.54 W
Puu Keahiakahoe ∧	229c	21.23 N	157.49 W
Puukohola Heiau National Historic Site ⊥	229d	20.00 N	155.46 W
Puukolii	229a	20.56 N	156.40 W
Puu Kukui ∧	229a	20.52 N	156.35 W
Puula ⊜	26	61.50 N	26.42 E
Puumala	26	61.32 N	28.11 E
Puunene	229a	20.51 N	156.27 W
Pu'upu'a	175a	13.34 S	172.09 W
Puurmani	76	58.34 N	26.17 E
Puurs	50	51.05 N	4.17 E
Puuwai	229b	21.54 N	160.12 W
Puxi	100	25.10 N	119.08 E
Puxian	102	36.30 N	111.02 E
Puxico	194	36.56 N	90.09 W
Puxingchang	107	30.41 N	105.06 E
Puyallup	224	47.11 N	122.17 W
Puyallup ≃	224	47.15 N	122.24 W
Puyang	98	35.42 N	114.59 E

Symbol	English	Deutsch	Español	Français	Português
≃	River	Fluß	Río	Rivière	Rio
≊	Canal	Kanal	Canal	Canal	Canal
ʟ	Waterfall, Rapids	Wasserfall, Stromschnellen	Cascada, Rápidos	Chute d'eau, Rapides	Cascata, Rápidos
ɥ	Strait	Meeresstraße	Estrecho	Détroit	Estreito
c	Bay, Gulf	Bucht, Golf	Bahía, Golfo	Baie, Golfe	Baía, Golfo
⊜	Lake, Lakes	See, Seen	Lago, Lagos	Lac, Lacs	Lago, Lagos
≚	Swamp	Sumpf	Pantano	Marais	Pântano
✱	Ice Features, Glacier	Eis- und Gletscherformen	Accidentes Glaciales	Formes glaciaires	Acidentes glaciares
⊤	Other Hydrographic Features	Andere Hydrographische Objekte	Otros Elementos Hidrográficos	Autres données hydrographiques	Outros acidentes hidrográficos
✣	Submarine Features	Untermeerische Objekte	Accidentes Submarinos	Formes de relief sous-marin	Acidentes submarinos
□	Political Unit	Politische Einheit	Unidad Politica	Entité politique	Unidade política
ʊ	Cultural Institution	Kulturelle Institution	Institución Cultural	Institution culturelle	Instituição cultural
⊥	Historical Site	Historische Stätte	Sitio Histórico	Site historique	Sitio histórico
♠	Recreational Site	Erholungs- und Ferienort	Sitio de Recreo	Centre de loisirs	Area de Lazer
⊠	Airport	Flughafen	Aeropuerto	Aéroport	Aeroporto
■	Military Installation	Militäranlage	Instalación Militar	Installation militaire	Instalação militar
⊷	Miscellaneous	Verschiedenes	Misceláneo	Divers	Diversos

	ENGLISH				DEUTSCH		
	Name	Page	Lat.°′	Long.°′	Name	Seite	Breite°′	Länge°′ E = Ost

ESPAÑOL Nombre	Página	Lat.°'	Long.°' W=Oeste
Quilino	252	30.12 S	64.29 W
Quillabamba	248	12.49 S	72.43 W
Quillacollo	248	17.26 S	66.17 W
Quillagua	248	21.39 S	69.33 W
Quillan	32	42.52 N	2.11 E
Quillebeuf-sur-Seine	50	49.29 N	0.31 E
Quill Lake	184	52.05 N	104.15 W
Quillota	252	32.53 S	71.16 W
Quilmes	258	34.44 S	58.16 W
Quilmes □⁵	288	34.44 S	58.16 W
Quilmes, Aeródromo ⚓	288	34.42 S	58.15 W
Quilombo ≃	258	23.52 S	46.21 W
Quilon	122	8.53 N	76.36 E
Quilotoa Wash V	228	32.56 N	112.46 W
Quilpie	166	26.37 S	144.15 E
Quilpué	252	33.03 S	71.27 W
Quilty	48	52.47 N	9.26 W
Quimarí, Alto de ⚤	246	8.07 N	76.23 W
Quimbango	152	11.01 S	17.26 E
Quimbaya	246	4.38 N	75.47 W
Quimbele	152	6.28 S	16.13 E
Quimbonge	152	13.59 S	16.05 E
Quimbonbo	152	8.36 S	18.30 E
Quimbumbe	152	7.50 S	14.03 E
Quimby	198	42.39 N	95.38 W
Quime	248	17.02 S	67.15 W
Quimichis	234	22.21 N	105.32 W
Quimilí	252	27.38 S	62.25 W
Quimper	32	48.00 N	4.06 W
Quimperlé	32	47.52 N	3.33 W
Quinalasag Island I	116	13.56 N	123.38 E
Quinault	224	47.28 N	123.50 W
Quinault, Lake ⚌	224	47.23 N	124.18 W
Quinault, North Fork	224	47.32 N	123.40 W
Quinault Indian Reservation ⁴	224	47.24 N	124.10 W
Quinby Inlet c	208	37.28 N	75.40 W
Quincampoix	50	49.32 N	1.11 E
Quince Mil	248	13.16 S	70.38 W
Quinches	248	12.13 S	76.05 W
Quincy, Ca., U.S.	204	39.56 N	120.56 W
Quincy, Fl., U.S.	192	30.35 N	84.35 W
Quincy, Il., U.S.	219	39.56 N	91.24 W
Quincy, Ky., U.S.	218	38.37 N	83.07 W
Quincy, Ma., U.S.	207	42.15 N	71.00 W
Quincy, Mi., U.S.	216	41.56 N	84.53 W
Quincy, Oh., U.S.	216	40.17 N	83.58 W
Quincy, Or., U.S.	224	46.08 N	123.09 W
Quincy, Pa., U.S.	208	39.48 N	77.35 W
Quincy, Wa., U.S.	202	47.14 N	119.51 W
Quincy Bay c	207	42.17 N	70.58 W
Quincy-sous-Sénart	261	48.40 N	2.33 E
Quincy-Voisins	261	48.54 N	2.53 E
Quindanning	168a	33.03 S	116.34 E
Quindío □⁵	246	4.30 N	75.40 W
Quinebaug	207	41.57 N	71.57 W
Quinebaug ≃	207	41.33 N	72.03 W
Quines	252	32.13 S	65.48 W
Quingey	58	47.06 N	5.53 E
Quingyi □	100	31.12 N	118.29 E
Quinhagak	192	59.45 N	161.43 W
Qui Nhon	110	13.46 N	109.14 E
Quinilban Islands II	116	11.27 N	120.48 E
Quinjenje	152	12.49 S	14.55 E
Quinlan	222	32.55 N	96.08 W
Quinn ≃	204	40.52 N	119.03 W
Quiñones, Arroyo de los ≃	266a	40.33 N	3.34 W
Quinson	62	43.42 N	6.02 E
Quinta da Boa Vista ⸱	287a	22.54 S	43.15 W
Quintanar de la Orden	34	39.34 N	3.03 W
Quintana Roo □³	232	19.40 N	88.30 W
Quinta Normal de Agricultura ⸱	286e	33.27 S	70.42 W
Quintana, Bay of c	244	44.07 N	75.11 W
Quintero	198	39.04 N	100.13 W
Quintero	252	32.47 S	71.32 W
Quintette Mountain ∧	182	54.52 N	120.53 W
Quintin	32	48.24 N	2.55 W
Quintino Sella, Canale ≈	266b	45.29 N	8.38 E
Quinto	34	41.25 N	0.29 W
Quinto ≃	252	34.14 S	64.10 W
Quinto Creek ≃	226	37.11 N	121.02 W
Quinto de Noviembre, Presa ⊕⁴	236	13.59 N	88.44 W
Quinton, Sk., Can.	184	51.23 N	104.24 W
Quinton, N.J., U.S.	208	39.41 N	75.29 W
Quinton, Ok., U.S.	196	35.07 N	95.22 W
Quinto Romano ⸱⁸	266b	45.29 N	9.06 E
Quinzano d'Oglio	64	45.19 N	10.00 E
Quinzáu	152	6.51 S	12.46 E
Quinze, Lac des ⚌	190	47.35 N	79.05 W
Quionga	154	10.37 S	40.30 E
Quipapá	268	8.50 S	36.02 W
Quipeio	152	12.25 S	15.30 E
Quipemba	152	12.13 S	15.32 E
Quipit c	116	8.04 N	122.29 E
Quipungo	152	14.51 S	14.30 E
Quiquive ⚌	248	14.39 S	67.38 W
Quirauk Mountain ∧	208	39.42 N	77.31 W
Quiriguá I	236	15.17 N	89.04 W
Quirihue	252	36.17 S	72.32 W
Quirima	152	10.48 S	18.09 E
Quirimbo	152	12.20 S	40.36 E
Quirindi	166	31.31 S	150.41 E
Quirino □⁵	116	16.25 N	121.35 E
Quirinópolis	255	18.32 S	50.30 W
Quiriquire	246	9.59 N	63.13 W
Quiririm ⸱⁸	287a	22.48 N	45.37 W
Quirke Lake ⚌	190	46.28 N	82.33 W
Quiroga, Esp.	34	42.29 N	7.16 W
Quiroga, Méx.	234	19.40 N	101.32 W
Quirpon Island I	188	51.35 N	55.25 W
Quirra, Salto di ⊹¹	71	39.35 N	9.33 E
Quissac	62	43.55 N	4.00 E
Quissanga	154	12.25 S	40.29 E
Quissico	156	24.42 S	34.44 E
Quissonga	152	10.01 S	15.07 E
Quistello	64	45.00 N	11.00 E
Quitapa	152	10.23 S	18.14 E
Quitaque	196	34.22 N	101.04 W
Quitasueño ⊹⁴	236	14.20 N	81.15 W
Quiteraju	154	11.48 S	40.25 E
Quitilipi	252	26.52 S	60.13 W
Quitman, Ga., U.S.	192	30.47 N	83.33 W
Quitman, Ms., U.S.	192	32.02 N	88.43 W
Quitman, Tx., U.S.	196	32.47 N	95.27 W
Quitman, Lake ⚌¹	192	32.49 N	95.27 W
Quito	246	0.13 S	78.30 W
Quitzdorf, Speicherbecken ⊕¹	54	51.17 N	14.45 E
Quivilla	248	9.32 S	76.41 W
Quixadá	268	4.58 S	39.01 W
Quixeramobim	250	5.12 S	39.17 W
Quixeré	250	5.04 S	37.59 W
Quixico	152	7.59 S	14.25 E
Quixinge	152	9.12 S	16.23 E
Quizenga	152	9.14 S	15.40 E
Quladian, Zhg.	89	43.13 N	116.57 E
Qujiang, Zhg.	100	28.15 N	115.45 E
Qujiang, Zhg.	100	24.41 N	113.35 E
Qujing	102	25.32 N	103.41 E
Qujiu	102	22.28 N	107.40 E
Qukou	102	39.46 N	117.07 E
Qulay'ah, Ra's al- ⊁	128	28.53 N	48.18 E
Qulin	194	36.36 N	90.14 W

FRANÇAIS Nom	Page	Lat.°'	Long.°' W=Ouest
Qulubbā	142	27.45 N	30.50 E
Qulūd, Jabal ∧²	140	11.41 N	29.31 E
Qulūsanā	142	28.21 N	30.44 E
Qulzum, Bahr al- c	142	29.55 N	32.31 E
— Zya, Zhg.	90	34.42 N	94.50 E
Qumar, Zhg.	120	34.39 N	95.00 E
Qumarlêb	102	34.35 N	95.27 E
Qumbu	158	31.10 S	28.48 E
Qumrān, Khirbat ⸱	132	31.44 N	35.27 E
Qunayfidhah, Nafūd ⸱⁸	128	24.45 N	45.30 E
Qunbush Al-Hamrā'	142	29.00 N	30.59 E
Qungtag	120	29.59 N	87.33 E
Qunshen'guan	105	39.49 N	117.59 E
Quobba, Point ⊁	164	24.23 S	113.24 E
Quoich ⚌	176	64.00 N	93.30 W
Quoich, Loch ⚌	46	57.04 N	5.17 W
Quoile ⚌	48	54.21 N	5.42 W
Quoin Point ⊁	158	34.46 S	19.37 E
Quonochontaug	207	41.21 N	71.43 W
Quorn	166	32.21 S	138.03 E
Quorndon	42	52.45 N	1.09 W
Quoxo ⚌	156	22.16 S	24.02 E
Qurayyah, Wādī V	132	30.26 N	34.01 E
Qurayyāt	128	23.17 N	58.55 E
Qurdūd	140	10.17 N	29.56 E
Qurrāsah	142	14.38 N	32.12 E
Qurün Harhash ∧²	142	28.09 N	31.42 E
Qūs	140	25.55 N	32.45 E
Qusar	84	41.25 N	48.26 E
Quşayr ad-Daffah ⸱	128	37.59 N	45.03 E
Qūshchī	107	30.41 N	106.02 E
Qutang	100	32.30 N	120.21 E
Qutbapur ⸱⁸	272a	28.35 N	77.01 E
Qutb Minar ⸱¹	272a	28.32 N	77.11 E
Qutdilgssat	176	70.04 N	53.01 W
Quthing	158	30.30 S	27.36 E
Qutūr	142	30.30 N	30.57 E
Quwaysinā	142	30.34 N	31.09 E
Quxi, Zhg.	100	28.00 N	120.31 E
Quxi, Zhg.	100	23.36 N	116.26 E
Quxia	106	32.06 N	120.09 E
Quxian, Zhg.	100	28.58 N	118.52 E
Quxian, Zhg.	102	30.51 N	106.59 E
Quxingji	98	34.52 N	114.39 E
Quxiong	102	31.09 N	96.00 E
Qüxü	120	29.22 N	90.43 E
Quyang	98	38.34 N	114.42 E
Qūyjāq-e-Bālā	84	39.16 N	47.07 E
Quyuyó	252	26.14 S	57.01 W
Quzhou	98	36.46 N	114.57 E
Quzong	102	30.08 N	96.00 E

R			
Rââ	41	56.00 N	12.44 E
Raab			
— Györ, Magy.	30	47.42 N	17.38 E
Raab, Öst.	60	48.21 N	13.39 E
Raab (Rába) ≃	30	47.42 N	17.38 E
Raabs an der Thaya	61	48.51 N	15.30 E
Raadal ⸱⁸	263	51.24 N	6.56 E
Raahe	26	64.41 N	24.29 E
Rääkkylä	26	62.19 N	29.37 E
Raalte	52	52.24 N	6.16 E
Raamsdonksveer	52	51.41 N	4.56 E
Ra'ananna	132	32.11 N	34.53 E
Raas, Pulau I	115a	7.09 S	114.32 E
Raasay I	46	57.23 N	6.04 W
Raasay, Sound of ⋃	46	57.27 N	6.06 W
Raasdorf	264b	48.15 N	16.34 E
Raasiku	76	59.22 N	25.11 E
Rab, Otok I	36	44.46 N	14.46 E
Raba	115b	8.27 S	118.46 E
Rába (Raab) ≃			
Europe	30	47.42 N	17.38 E
Raba ≃, Pol.	30	50.09 N	20.30 E
Rababale	144	8.17 N	48.18 E
Rabaçal ≃	34	41.30 N	7.12 W
Rábade	34	43.07 N	7.37 W
Rábahidvég	61	47.04 N	16.45 E
Rabak	140	13.09 N	32.44 E
Rababa	144	3.58 S	39.37 E
Rababa ≃	36	46.21 N	14.11 E
Rabat, Magreb	148	34.02 N	6.51 W
Rabat, Malta	36	35.52 N	14.25 E
Rabat (Victoria), Malta	36	36.02 N	14.14 E
Rabaul	148	33.57 N	6.50 W
Rabaul	64	4.12 S	152.12 E
Rabbit ≃	216	42.38 N	86.06 W
Rabbit, Lac ⚌	190	47.30 N	78.22 W
Rabbit Creek ≃, S.D., U.S.	198	45.13 N	102.10 W
Rabbit Creek ≃, Tx., U.S.	222	32.26 N	94.47 W
Rabbit Ears Pass ⋌	203	40.23 N	106.37 W
Rabbit Lake ⚌, On., Can.	190	47.00 N	79.37 W
Rabbit Lake ⚌, Ca., U.S.	228	34.27 N	117.01 W
Rabbits Creek ≃	222	29.59 N	96.55 W
Rábca ≃	76	54.39 N	21.34 E
R'aboceva	76	54.39 N	36.10 E
Rabeira, Ponta da ⊁	287a	22.49 S	43.10 W
Rabenau	54	50.57 N	13.38 E
Rabette, Ruisseau la ≃	261	48.35 N	2.00 E
Rābi', Ash-Shallāl al- (Fourth Cataract) ⋃	140	18.47 N	32.03 E
Rabigh	128	22.48 N	39.01 E
Rabinal	236	15.06 N	90.27 W
Rabiusa ≃	58	46.48 N	9.20 E
Rabka	30	49.36 N	19.56 E
Rabkavi Banhatti	122	16.28 N	75.06 E
Rabnabad Channel ⋃	124	21.50 N	90.19 E
Rabnabad Islands II	126	21.58 N	90.24 E
Rábnita (Rybnica)	80	47.46 N	29.00 E
Raboočostrovsk	76	64.52 N	34.42 E
Raboči	86	59.07 N	79.00 E
Rabong, Gunong ∧	114	4.48 N	102.07 E
Rabotki	80	56.03 N	44.38 E
R'abovskij	80	50.01 N	41.53 E
Rabun Bald ∧	192	34.58 N	83.18 W
Rabwah	124	31.45 N	72.55 E
Raby	262	53.19 N	3.02 W
Rabyānah ⊺⁴	146	24.15 N	22.00 E
Rabyānah, Sahrā' ⊹	146	24.30 N	21.00 E
Racale	36	39.58 N	18.06 E
Racalmuto	70	37.24 N	13.44 E
Racari	80	46.46 N	25.45 E
Raccoon ≃	216	39.47 N	87.23 W
Raccoon Creek ≃, Oh., U.S.	214	40.02 N	82.24 W
Raccoon Creek ≃, Pa., U.S.	214	40.38 N	80.22 W
Raccoon Creek ≃, Va., U.S.	208	36.48 N	77.10 W
Raccoon Creek, South Branch ≃	285	39.44 N	75.15 W
Raccoon Creek State Park ⸱	214	40.30 N	80.24 W
Raccoon Island I	285	40.18 N	74.34 W
Race, Cape ⊁	186	46.40 N	53.10 W
Raceland	194	29.43 N	90.35 W

PORTUGUÊS Nome	Página	Lat.°'	Long.°' W=Oeste
Race Point ⊁	207	42.04 N	70.14 W
Racette, Lac ⚌	206	46.34 N	74.03 W
Racette, Ruisseau ≃	206	46.36 N	74.04 W
Raceview	273d	26.17 S	28.08 E
Rach'a ⁸	76	60.05 N	30.49 E
Rach Gia	110	10.01 N	105.05 E
Rach Gia, Vinh c	110	10.00 N	105.00 E
Rachmanovka	80	51.57 N	49.29 E
Rachmanovo	82	55.44 N	38.37 E
Raciaz	30	52.47 N	20.06 E
Racibórz (Ratibor)	30	50.06 N	18.13 E
Racine, Pa., U.S.	214	40.49 N	80.20 W
Racine, Wi., U.S.	216	42.43 N	87.46 W
Racine □⁶	216	42.45 N	88.05 W
Racines	64	46.52 N	11.18 E
Račinskij chrebet ⊀	84	42.30 N	43.30 E
Rackerby	226	39.26 N	121.20 W
Racksund ⋃	26	39.26 N	121.20 W
Răckeve	30	47.10 N	18.56 E
Rackwick	46	58.52 N	3.23 W
Rackwitz	54	51.26 N	12.23 E
R'ad ≃	76	57.56 N	35.04 E
Rāda	40	60.00 N	13.36 E
Radama, Nosy II	157b	14.00 S	47.47 E
Radama, Presqu'île ⊁¹	157b	14.16 S	47.53 E
Rādasjön ⚌	40	59.58 N	13.38 E
Radaškovičy	76	54.09 N	27.14 E
Rādāuți	38	47.51 N	25.55 E
Radcuza ≃	60	49.45 N	13.23 E
Radčenskoje	78	49.48 N	40.32 E
Radcliff	194	37.50 N	85.56 W
Radcliffe	44	53.34 N	2.20 W
Radcliffe on Trent	42	52.57 N	1.03 W
Radda in Chianti	66	43.29 N	11.22 E
Radclusa	70	37.28 N	14.32 E
Radde	26	59.21 N	10.51 E
Radebaugh	279b	40.19 N	79.35 W
Radeberg	54	51.07 N	13.55 E
Radebeul	54	51.06 N	13.40 E
Radeburg	54	51.13 N	13.43 E
Radeče	36	46.04 N	15.11 E
Radegast	54	51.39 N	12.05 E
Radekhiv	78	50.18 N	24.37 E
Radenci	61	46.38 N	16.03 E
Radenthein	64	46.48 N	13.43 E
Radevormwald	56	51.12 N	7.21 E
Radford	192	37.07 N	80.34 W
Rādhanagar, India	126	22.38 N	87.19 E
Rādhānagar, India	272b	22.27 N	88.28 E
Radici, Foce delle ⋌	66	44.12 N	10.31 E
Radičofani	66	42.54 N	11.46 E
Radicondoli	66	43.16 N	11.02 E
Rădinesti	38	44.48 N	23.46 E
Radiščevo	80	52.51 N	47.53 E
Radisson	184	52.27 N	107.23 W
Radium Hot Springs	182	50.38 N	116.03 W
Rad'kovka	78	51.06 N	36.58 E
Radlett	42	51.42 N	0.20 W
Radlett Aerodrome ⚓	260	51.43 N	0.19 W
Radley Run ≃	285	39.54 N	75.37 W
Radlje ob Dravi	61	46.37 N	15.13 E
Rådmansö¹	40	59.45 N	18.55 E
Radnevo	38	42.18 N	25.56 E
Radnice	60	49.51 N	13.37 E
Radnor, Oh., U.S.	214	40.23 N	83.09 W
Radnor, Pa., U.S.	285	40.02 N	75.21 W
Radnor Forest ∧	42	52.18 N	3.10 W
Radnor Mere ⚌	262	53.17 N	2.14 W
Rădoaia	80	47.44 N	28.09 E
Radofinnikovo	76	59.09 N	30.55 E
Radogošča	76	59.47 N	34.51 E
Radolfzell	58	47.44 N	8.58 E
Radom, Pol.	30	51.25 N	21.10 E
Radom □⁴	30	51.25 N	21.15 E
Radomicko	54	52.10 N	14.58 E
Radomir	38	42.33 N	22.58 E
Radomka ≃	78	51.56 N	32.32 E
Radomski	30	51.05 N	21.26 E
Radomsko	30	51.05 N	19.25 E
Radomyšl'	30	50.12 N	29.14 E
Radomyśl Wielki	30	50.12 N	21.16 E
Radošice	60	49.33 N	13.39 E
Radošina	30	48.38 N	17.57 E
Radovići	38	42.23 N	18.42 E
Radovis	38	41.38 N	22.28 E
Radowo	54	53.24 N	15.36 E
Radstadt	64	47.23 N	13.27 E
Radstädter Tauern ⋌	64	47.15 N	13.34 E
Radstock, Cape ⊁	162	33.12 S	134.20 E
Racuha ≃	152	12.25 N	44.15 E
Racul¹	236	14.25 N	91.06 W
Racushne	78	47.49 N	30.29 E
Racutino	78	46.39 N	33.57 E
Racvilišikis	76	55.50 N	23.31 E
Radville	184	49.27 N	104.17 W
Radway	182	54.04 N	112.57 W
Radykovskoje	80	45.56 N	41.57 E
Radymno	30	49.57 N	22.48 E
Radviliškis	76	55.48 N	23.31 E
Radyr	42	51.31 N	3.15 W
Radziejów	30	52.38 N	18.32 E
Radzyń Chelmiński	30	53.24 N	18.56 E
Radzyń Podlaski	30	51.48 N	22.38 E
Rae	176	62.50 N	116.03 W
Rãe Bareli	124	26.13 N	81.14 E
Rae Isthmus ⊁³	176	66.55 N	86.30 W
Rãenda	126	22.18 N	89.51 E
Raeren	52	50.41 N	6.07 E
Raesfeld	52	51.46 N	6.50 E
Raeside, Lake ⚌	162	29.30 S	122.00 E
Rae Strait ⋃	176	68.45 N	95.00 W
Raevski	82	54.04 N	54.57 E
Rafaela	252	31.16 S	61.29 W
Rafael Calzada	258	34.48 S	58.22 W
Rafael Castillo	288	34.43 S	58.34 W
Rafael Perazza	258	34.32 S	56.47 W
Rafah	132	31.18 N	34.15 E
Rafaï	144	4.59 N	23.56 E
Rafaïfadai	75	37.24 N	30.31 E
Raffelberg, Rennbahn ⸱	263	51.26 N	6.50 E
Raffili Mission	140	6.53 N	27.58 E
Rarhā'	128	29.42 N	43.30 E
Rafinesque, Mount ∧	181a	76.20 N	71.10 W
Rafsanjān	128	30.24 N	56.01 E
Rafz	58	47.37 N	8.32 E
Ragada	64	47.44 N	10.38 E
Ragang, Mount ∧	116	7.43 N	124.32 E
Ragay	116	13.49 N	122.47 E
Ragay Gulf c	116	13.30 N	122.45 E
Rāgeleje	41	56.06 N	12.10 E
Ragewitz	54	51.14 N	12.51 E
Ragged, Mount ∧	162	33.27 S	123.26 E
Ragged Island I	238	22.12 N	75.44 W
Ragged Island Range II	238	22.10 N	75.45 W
Ragged Lake ⚌	212	45.28 N	78.38 W
Ragged Top Mountain ∧	228	33.38 N	116.12 W
Raghabpur	272b	22.25 N	88.24 E
Raghunāthbāri	126	22.12 N	87.47 E
Raghunāthpur, India	126	23.33 N	86.40 E
Raghunāthpur, India	126	22.14 N	89.31 E
Ragland	194	33.44 N	86.09 W
Ragnitz	61	46.50 N	15.35 E
Rago Nasjonalpark ♦	24	67.26 N	16.00 E
Ragow	264a	52.17 N	13.33 E
Ragozino	86	59.15 N	77.52 E
Ragozýeden	40	60.29 N	14.05 E
Raguda, Ghubbet c	144	10.45 N	46.34 E
Raguli	80	51.42 N	12.17 E
Ragusa	70	36.55 N	14.44 E
— Dubrovnik, Hrv.	38	42.38 N	18.07 E
Ragusa, It.	70	36.55 N	14.44 E
Ragusa □⁴	70	36.55 N	14.36 E
Rahad ≃	76	55.34 N	24.36 E
Raha	112	4.51 S	122.43 E
Rahad, Nahr ar- (Rahad) ≃	140	14.28 N	33.31 E
Rahad al-Bardī	140	11.18 N	23.53 E
Rahad Game Reserve ♦⁴	140	13.06 N	35.05 E
Rahat, Harrat ∧⁹	144	22.20 N	40.05 E
Rahatgarh	124	22.15 N	77.14 E
Rāhatgarh	124	23.47 N	78.22 E
Rahbah	130	34.30 N	36.09 E
Rahden	52	52.26 N	8.36 E
Rahīm Ki Bāzār	124	24.19 N	69.09 E
Rahīmyār Khān	124	28.25 N	70.18 E
Rahm ➤⁸, Dtsch.	263	51.26 N	6.26 E
Rahm ➤⁸, Dtsch.	263	51.32 N	7.23 E
Rahmde ≃	263	51.17 N	7.41 E
Rahmen See ⚌	264a	52.45 N	13.25 E
Rahns	285	40.12 N	75.27 W
Rahnsdorf ⸱⁸	264a	52.26 N	13.42 E
Rahon	76	59.21 N	10.51 E
Rahotu	172	39.20 S	173.48 E
Rahouia ≃	34	35.32 N	1.01 E
Rähnwäli	123	32.15 N	74.10 E
Rahway	210	40.36 N	74.16 W
Rahway ≃	276	40.35 N	74.12 W
Rahway, East Branch ≃	276	40.42 N	74.18 W
Rahway, Robinsons Branch ≃	276	40.37 N	74.17 W
Rahway, South Branch ≃	276	40.36 N	74.17 W
Rahway, West Branch ≃	276	40.42 N	74.18 W
Rahway River Parkway ♦	276	40.41 N	74.19 W
Raiana ≃	66	42.06 N	13.49 E
Raiatea I	14	16.50 S	151.25 W
Raichūr	122	16.12 N	77.22 E
Raidi	76	59.21 N	51.41 E
Raidiġhi	126	22.00 N	88.26 E
Raiding	61	47.34 N	16.32 E
Raiganj	124	25.37 N	88.07 E
Raigarh	122	21.54 N	83.24 E
Raijua, Pulau I	112	10.37 S	121.36 E
Raik	123	30.39 N	75.36 E
Railroad Canyon Reservoir ⚌¹	228	33.42 N	117.16 W
Railroad Creek ≃	224	48.12 N	120.36 W
Rail Road Flat	226	38.20 N	120.30 W
Railroad Valley V	204	38.25 N	115.40 W
Railton	166	41.21 S	146.25 E
Raimangal ≃	126	21.47 N	89.08 E
Rain			
— Riva di Tures, It.	64	46.57 N	12.04 E
Rainbach im Innkreis	60	48.27 N	13.32 E
Rainbow	166	35.54 S	142.01 E
Rainbow Bridge ♦⁵	284a	43.05 N	79.04 W
Rainbow Bridge National Monument ♦	200	37.06 N	110.57 W
Rainbow Lakes ≌	182	52.23 N	119.59 W
Rainbow Lakes	276	40.52 N	74.28 W
Rainbow Park ♦	276	41.46 N	87.33 W
Rainbow Shores	212	43.37 N	76.12 W
Rainelle	188	37.58 N	80.46 W
Rainford	44	53.30 N	2.48 W
Rainham ≃⁸	260	51.31 N	0.12 E
Rainham	260	51.22 N	0.37 E
Rainhill	262	53.26 N	2.46 W
Rainhill Stoops	262	53.25 N	2.45 W
Rainier, Or., U.S.	224	46.05 N	122.56 W
Rainier, Wa., U.S.	224	46.53 N	122.41 W
Rainier, Mount ∧	224	46.52 N	121.46 W
Rainow	262	53.17 N	2.06 W
Rainsboro	214	39.13 N	83.23 W
Rainsford Island I	283	42.18 N	70.57 W
Rainworth	43	53.07 N	1.08 W
Rainy ≃, Mi., U.S.	216	45.55 N	84.13 W
Rainy ≃, Can.	212	45.32 N	79.30 W
Rainy Lake ⚌, N.A.	184	48.42 N	93.10 W
Rainy Pass ⋌	190	52.38 N	88.32 W
Rainy River	190	48.43 N	94.34 W
Raipur, India	124	23.03 N	90.46 E
Raipur, India	124	21.14 N	81.38 E
Raipur, India	126	22.06 N	88.07 E
Raipur, India	126	22.48 N	88.23 E
Raipura	126	24.00 N	90.46 E
Rais ≃	76	59.22 N	53.10 E
Rais el Aïoun	34	35.57 N	5.59 E
Raisdorf	54	54.18 N	10.15 E
Raisen	124	23.20 N	77.48 E
Raisin ≃, On., Can.	206	45.05 N	74.23 W
Raisin ≃, Mi., U.S.	216	41.53 N	83.23 W
Rāisinghnagar	124	29.32 N	73.27 E
Raismes	50	50.24 N	3.29 E
Raita ≃	80	51.50 N	49.53 E
Raitenbuch	60	48.58 N	11.06 E
Raivavae I	14	23.52 S	147.40 W
Raja, Gili I	115a	7.14 S	113.47 E
Raja, Ujung ⊁	114	3.45 N	96.33 E
Rajabāri	126	23.23 N	90.28 E
Rajabhat Khāwa	126	26.35 N	89.24 E
Rājahmundry	122	16.59 N	81.47 E
Rajāng ≃	112	2.04 N	111.12 E
Rājapur	122	16.39 N	73.31 E
Rājapur Uplands ⁴¹	126	22.15 N	88.10 E
Rājasthān □³	124	27.00 N	74.00 E
Rājāuri	123	33.23 N	74.18 E
Rājbāri	126	23.45 N	89.39 E
Rajčichinsk	89	49.46 N	129.25 E
Rājendrapur	126	24.06 N	90.27 E
Rajevskij	86	54.04 N	54.56 E
Rāj Gangpur	124	22.11 N	84.36 E
Rājganj ≃¹	126	22.21 N	90.16 E
Rājgarh, India	123	28.38 N	75.23 E
Rājgarh, India	124	23.56 N	76.58 E
Rājgarh, India	124	27.14 N	76.38 E
Rajghat ≃¹	272a	28.39 N	77.15 E
Rājgīr	124	25.02 N	85.25 E
Rajgorodok	80	48.48 N	52.53 E
Rajgród	30	53.44 N	22.42 E
Rājhāt	272b	22.56 N	88.21 E
Rajhrad	61	49.05 N	16.37 E
Rājibpur	272b	22.49 N	88.23 E
Rajik	112	2.36 S	105.56 E
Rajka	30	48.00 N	17.12 E
Rājkot	120	22.18 N	70.47 E
Rajkuzi	265a	59.47 N	29.57 E
Rājmahāl	124	25.03 N	87.50 E
Rājmahāl Hills ∧²	124	25.03 N	87.20 E
Rājnagar	126	23.57 N	87.19 E
Rāj Nāndgaon	120	21.06 N	81.02 E
Rajokri ⸱⁸	272a	28.31 N	77.07 E
Rāj-Oleksandrivka	83	48.48 N	37.51 E
Rājpipla	124	21.47 N	73.34 E
Rājpur, India	120	21.56 N	75.08 E
Rājpur, India	126	22.25 N	88.25 E
Rājpur, India	272a	28.41 N	77.12 E
Rājpur ⸱⁸	272a	28.41 N	77.11 E
Rājpura	124	30.29 N	76.36 E
Rājshāhi	124	24.22 N	88.36 E
Rājshāhi □⁵	124	25.15 N	89.15 E
Rajula	123	21.03 N	71.26 E
Raka	120	29.26 N	85.50 E
Raka ≃	124	29.24 N	87.58 E
Rakaia ≃	172	43.45 S	172.01 E
Rakaia ≃	172	43.56 S	172.13 E
Rakamaz	30	48.08 N	21.30 E
Rakata, Pulau I	115a	6.10 S	105.26 E
Rakha La ×	124	27.53 N	87.34 E
Rakhawt, Wādī V	144	17.40 N	51.40 E
Rakhine □⁵	110	19.00 N	94.15 E
Rakhiv	78	48.03 N	24.12 E
Rakhmanivka	78	47.48 N	33.13 E
Rakhneh	131	31.39 N	59.13 E
Rakhni	120	30.03 N	69.55 E
Rakhny-Lisovi	78	48.47 N	28.29 E
Rakhshān ≃	128	27.10 N	63.25 E
Raki	76	51.34 N	35.42 E
Rakitnoje, Ross.	78	50.51 N	35.50 E
Rakitnoje, Ross.	89	45.36 N	134.17 E
Rakke	76	58.59 N	26.15 E
Rakkestad	26	59.26 N	11.21 E
Rakonewice	30	52.10 N	16.16 E
Rakops	156	21.00 S	24.32 E
Rákoscsaba ⸱⁸	264c	47.29 N	19.17 E
Rákoshegy ⸱⁸	264c	47.28 N	19.14 E
Rákoskeresztúr ⸱⁸	264c	47.29 N	19.15 E
Rákoskert ⸱⁸	264c	47.29 N	19.18 E
Rákosliget ⸱⁸	264c	47.30 N	19.16 E
Rákospalota ⸱⁸	264c	47.34 N	19.08 E
Rákos-patak ≃	264c	47.33 N	19.04 E
Rákosszentmihály	264c	47.32 N	19.11 E
Rakovnická plošina �	60	50.08 N	13.47 E
Rakovník	54	50.05 N	13.43 E
Rakovski	38	42.18 N	24.58 E
Raksa	80	53.33 N	41.37 E
Raksakiny	86	60.37 N	73.52 E
Rakūša	80	47.03 N	52.47 E
Rākvåg	26	63.46 N	10.05 E
Rakvere	76	59.22 N	26.20 E
Rakwa	164	2.42 S	134.30 E
Raleigh, Nf., Can.	188	51.34 N	55.44 W
Raleigh, Ms., U.S.	194	32.02 N	89.31 W
Raleigh, N.C., U.S.	192	35.46 N	78.38 W
Raleigh ≃, N.J., U.S.	210	41.03 N	74.22 W
Raleighvallen Voltz Berg, Natuurreservaat ♦, Sur.	246	4.45 N	56.05 W
Raleighvallen Voltz Berg, Natuurreservaat ♦, Sur.			
Ralik Chain II	14	8.00 N	167.00 E
Ralls	196	33.40 N	101.23 W
Ralls □⁶	194	39.34 N	91.30 W
Ralston, Ne., U.S.	198	41.12 N	96.02 W
Ralston, Pa., U.S.	208	41.31 N	76.57 W
Rama, Nic.	236	12.09 N	84.15 W
Rama ≃	132	32.56 N	35.22 E
Ráma ≃	38	43.50 N	17.52 E
Ramacca	70	37.23 N	14.42 E
Rāmachandrapuram	116	16.51 N	82.01 E
Ramādah	144	13.36 N	108.29 W
Rāmallāh	132	31.54 N	35.12 E
Rāmanāgaram	122	12.43 N	77.18 E
Rāmanathapuram	122	9.23 N	78.50 E
Rāmanuj Ganj	124	23.48 N	83.42 E
Ramapo ≃	210	41.06 N	74.16 W
Ramapo Mountains ⊁	276	41.06 N	74.14 W
Ramat HaSharon	132	32.08 N	34.50 E
Ramat HaShofet	132	32.36 N	35.05 E
Ramatlabama	158	25.36 S	25.34 E
Ramat VI Bridge ≃⁵	286a	13.48 N	100.32 E
Rambervillers	58	48.21 N	6.38 E
Rambi I	175g	16.30 S	179.59 E
Rambla ≃	34	37.47 N	0.44 W
Rambouillet	32	48.39 N	1.49 E
Rambouillet, Château de ⸱			
Rambouillet, Forêt de ♦³			
Rambutyo Island I	164	2.20 S	147.50 E
Ram Head ⊁, S. Afr.	158	31.48 S	29.22 E
Ram Head ⊁, Eng., U.K.	42	50.19 N	4.13 W
Ramenje, Ross.	76	58.50 N	39.51 E
Ramenje, Ross.	76	55.53 N	38.10 E
Ramenki ⸱⁸	265b	55.41 N	37.31 E
Ramenskoje	82	55.34 N	38.14 E
Rameswaram	122	9.17 N	79.18 E
Ramey	214	40.48 N	78.23 W
Rāmganj	126	23.06 N	90.51 E
Rāmgarh, Bngl.	120	22.59 N	91.44 E
Rāmgarh, India	120	27.22 N	70.30 E
Rāmgarh, India	120	27.15 N	75.11 E
Rāmgarh, India	124	23.38 N	85.31 E
Rāmgarh, India	124	24.34 N	87.15 E
Rāmgarh, India	124	22.42 N	87.04 E
Rāmgarh Hills ∧²	124	27.14 N	76.38 E
Ram Head ⊁	240m	18.18 N	64.42 W
Rāmhormoz	128	31.16 N	49.36 E
Ramingstein	64	47.04 N	13.53 E
Ramírez, Méx.	196	25.57 N	97.46 W
Ramírez, Méx.	236	27.20 N	100.58 W
Ramiriqui	246	5.24 N	73.20 W
Ramis ≃	144	7.59 N	41.34 E
Rāmjībanpur	126	22.50 N	87.37 E
Ramla	132	31.55 N	34.52 E
Ramlu ∧	144	13.24 N	41.51 E
Ramm, Jabal ∧	132	29.35 N	35.24 E
Rämmen	40	60.07 N	14.08 E
Ramnäs	38	45.39 N	27.19 E
Rāmnagar, India	123	32.49 N	75.19 E
Rāmnagar, India	124	25.17 N	83.02 E
Rāmnagar, India	126	29.24 N	79.07 E
Rāmnagar, India	126	21.41 N	87.33 E
Rāmnagar, India	272b	22.23 N	88.19 E
Ramnäs	40	59.46 N	16.12 E
Râmnicu Sărat	38	45.23 N	27.03 E
Râmnicu Vâlcea	38	45.06 N	24.22 E
Ramo	144	6.42 N	41.23 E
Ramon'	78	51.54 N	39.20 E
Ramon, Har ∧	132	30.30 N	34.38 E
Ramon, Makhtésh ⸱	132	30.36 N	34.49 E
Ramon, Nahal V	132	30.36 N	34.55 E
Ramona, Ca., U.S.	228	33.02 N	116.52 W
Ramona, Ks., U.S.	196	36.31 N	95.55 W
Ramona, S.D., U.S.	198	44.07 N	97.12 W
Ramor, Lough ⚌	48	53.49 N	7.05 W
Ramos ≃	234	22.50 N	101.55 W
Ramos ≃⁵	45.15	5.43 N	43.15 W
Ramos ≃¹	150	5.06 N	5.22 E
Ramosch	58	46.50 N	10.22 E
Ramos Island I	116	8.06 N	117.02 E
Ramos Mejía	288	34.38 S	58.34 W
Ramotswa	156	24.56 S	25.50 E
Rampal	126	22.34 N	89.39 E
Rampart	86	65.30 N	150.11 W
Ramparts ≃	180	66.11 N	129.03 W
Rampillon	50	48.33 N	3.04 E
Rampside	54	54.05 N	3.10 W
Rāmpur, India	123	31.27 N	77.38 E
Rāmpur, India	126	23.49 N	77.27 E
Rāmpur, India	124	28.49 N	79.02 E
Rāmpur, India	123	30.17 N	75.14 E
Rāmpura Phūl	123	30.17 N	75.14 E
— Rājshāhi	124	24.22 N	88.36 E
Rāmpur Hāt	126	24.10 N	87.47 E
Ramrath	263	51.06 N	6.41 E
Ramree Island I	110	19.06 N	93.48 E
Ramrikhi □¹	126	25.17 N	89.00 E
Ramsay Range ⊀	162	18.31 S	127.03 E
Ramsbeck	56	51.18 N	8.24 E
Ramsberg	40	59.46 N	15.17 E
Ramsbottom	44	53.40 N	2.19 W
Ramsden Bellhouse	260	51.37 N	0.29 E
Ramsden Heath	260	51.38 N	0.28 E
Ramseur	192	35.44 N	79.39 W
Ramsey, I. of Man	44	54.20 N	4.21 W
Ramsey, Eng., U.K.	42	52.27 N	0.07 W
Ramsey, Il., U.S.	219	39.08 N	89.06 W
Ramsey, N.J., U.S.	210	41.03 N	74.08 W
Ramsey Creek ≃	276	39.03 N	89.04 W
Ramsey Island I	42	51.52 N	5.10 W
Ramsey Lake State Park ♦, Austl.	274a	33.59 S	151.08 E
Ramsgate, Eng., U.K.	42	51.20 N	1.25 E
Ramsgate, S. Afr.	158	30.53 S	30.20 E
Ramshai	126	26.44 N	88.51 E
Ramshyttan	40	60.18 N	15.13 E
Ramshorn Peak ∧	202	45.09 N	111.06 W
Ramsin-e			
Ramstein-Miesenbach	56	49.27 N	7.33 E
Ramten	41	56.25 N	10.39 E
Ramu ≃	160	4.00 S	144.41 E
Ramu, Kenya	144	3.56 N	41.11 E
Ramvik	40	62.49 N	17.51 E
Ramville, Îlet I	240e	14.42 N	60.53 W
Ramygala	76	55.31 N	24.18 E
Ramzaj	80	53.16 N	44.44 E
Rānāghāt	124	23.11 N	88.35 E
Rana Kao, Volcán ∧¹	174z	27.11 S	109.27 W
Ranat	122	47.02 N	11.13 E
Rānāvāv	120	21.33 N	69.45 E
Rânau, Danau ⚌	112	4.50 S	103.55 E
Ranau	112	5.57 N	116.41 E
Rancagua	252	34.10 S	70.45 W
Rancaqua ≃	252	34.22 S	71.12 W
Rancheria ≃	180	60.13 N	129.07 W
Ranchester	202	44.54 N	107.10 W
Ranchi	120	23.23 N	85.23 E
Rānchī	124	23.23 N	85.20 E
Ranchi Plateau ≈¹	124	23.00 N	85.00 E
Rancho Colorado	234	28.48 N	112.28 W
Rancho Cordova	226	38.35 N	121.18 W
Rancho Nuevo, Méx.	234	19.29 N	99.17 W
Rancho Nuevo, Méx.	232	21.38 N	100.15 W
Rancho Palos Verdes	228	33.45 N	118.24 W
Rancho Santa Fe	228	33.01 N	117.12 W
Rancho Veloz	240p	22.50 N	80.23 W
Rancocas Creek ≃	285	40.00 N	74.59 W
Rancocas Creek, North Branch ≃	285	40.00 N	74.59 W
Rancocas Creek, South Branch ≃	208	40.00 N	74.52 W
Rancocas Creek, Southwest Branch ≃	285	39.57 N	74.48 W
Rancocas Heights	285	39.59 N	74.51 W
Rancocas Woods	285	40.00 N	74.55 W
Rancocas State Park ♦	285	40.00 N	74.51 W
Rancul	252	35.03 S	64.42 W

ESPAÑOL Nombre	Página	Lat.°	Long.° W=Oeste
Redwood Creek ≃, Ca., U.S.	282	37.31 N	122.12 W
Redwood Creek ≃, Ca., U.S.	282	37.52 N	122.35 W
Redwood Estates	226	37.10 N	121.59 W
Redwood Falls	198	44.32 N	95.07 W
Redwood National Park ♦	204	41.30 N	124.05 W
Redwood Point ►	282	37.32 N	122.12 W
Redwood Regional Park ♦	282	37.38 N	122.10 W
Redwood Terrace	282	37.19 N	122.18 W
Redwood Valley	204	39.15 N	123.12 W
Ree, Lough ☒	48	53.35 N	8.00 W
Reed City	190	43.52 N	85.30 W
Reeder	198	46.06 N	102.56 W
Reeders	210	41.01 N	75.20 W
Reed Lake ⊘, Mb., Can.	184	54.37 N	100.30 W
Reed Lake ⊘, Sk., Can.	184	50.24 N	107.05 W
Reedley	226	36.35 N	119.26 W
Reedsburg, Oh., U.S.	214	40.49 N	82.07 W
Reedsburg, Wi., U.S.	190	43.31 N	90.00 W
Reeds Peak ▲	200	33.09 N	107.51 W
Reedsport	202	43.42 N	124.05 W
Reedsville, Pa., U.S.	208	40.39 N	77.35 W
Reedsville, Wi., U.S.	190	44.09 N	87.57 W
Reedurban	214	40.47 N	81.26 W
Reedville	208	37.50 N	76.16 W
Reedy Creek ≃	220	28.04 N	81.21 W
Reedy Creek Swamp ☒	220	28.17 N	81.31 W
Reedy Lake ⊘	220	27.44 N	81.22 W
Reefton	172	42.07 S	171.52 E
Reelfoot Lake ⊘	194	36.25 N	89.22 W
Reepham	42	52.46 N	1.07 E
Reersø ►¹	41	55.31 N	11.06 E
Rees	52	51.45 N	6.23 E
Reese	190	43.27 N	83.41 W
Reese	204	40.39 N	116.54 W
Reese Air Force Base ■	196	33.36 N	102.02 W
Reeseville	190	43.18 N	88.50 W
Reetz	54	53.11 N	11.52 E
Refaa, Djebel ▲	34	35.34 S	5.52 E
Refahiye	130	39.54 N	38.46 E
Reform	194	33.22 N	88.00 W
Reforma de Pineda	234	16.24 N	94.28 W
Refton	208	39.57 N	76.14 W
Refuge Cove	182	50.07 N	124.50 W
Refugio, Isla I	254	43.58 S	73.12 W
Refugio Creek ≃	282	38.01 N	122.17 W
Rega ≃	54	54.10 N	15.18 E
Regan	34	35.38 N	5.46 W
Regalbuto	70	37.39 N	14.38 E
Regau	62	47.59 N	13.41 E
Regen	60	48.59 N	13.07 E
Regen ≃	60	48.59 N	13.07 E
Regência	255	19.36 S	39.49 W
Regency Estates	284c	39.03 N	77.10 W
Regeneração	255	6.15 S	42.41 W
Regensburg	60	49.01 N	12.06 E
Regensdorf	58	47.26 N	8.28 E
Regenstauf	60	49.08 N	12.08 E
Regent, Austl.	274b	37.44 S	145.00 E
Regent, N.D., U.S.	198	46.25 N	102.33 W
Regent Park	284c	39.02 N	77.10 W
Regents Park ♦	273d	26.15 S	28.04 E
Regent's Park ♦	260	51.32 N	0.09 W
Regentville	274a	33.47 S	150.40 E
Reggâne	148	26.42 N	0.10 E
Regge ≃	52	52.31 N	6.22 E
Reggello	66	43.41 N	11.32 E
Reggio di Calabria	68	38.07 N	15.39 E
Reggio di Calabria ☐⁴	68	38.10 N	16.00 E
Reggiolo	66	44.55 N	10.48 E
Reggio nell'Emilia	66	44.43 N	10.36 E
Reggio nell'Emilia ☐⁴	66	44.37 N	10.37 E
Regharen	40	58.54 N	15.46 E
Reghin	38	46.47 N	24.42 E
Regina, Sk., Can.	184	50.25 N	104.39 W
Regina, Guy. fr.	252	4.19 N	52.08 W
Regina, S. Afr.	158	27.02 S	26.30 E
Regina Beach	184	50.47 N	105.00 W
Regina Elena, Canale ☒	266b	45.41 N	8.39 E
Región Metropolitana ☐⁴	252	33.30 S	70.30 W
Regis-Breitingen	54	51.05 N	12.26 E
Registro	252	24.30 S	47.50 W
Registro do Araguaia	255	15.44 S	51.50 W
Regiwar	120	25.57 N	65.44 E
Regla ►⁸	286b	23.08 N	82.20 W
Regnéville	32	49.01 N	1.33 W
Regnitz ≃	56	49.54 N	10.49 E
Rego Park ►⁸	284b	40.44 N	73.52 W
Regozero	24	65.44 N	31.10 E
Regresso, Cachoeira do ☒	250	0.58 S	54.51 W
Regstrup	41	55.40 N	11.37 E
Reguengos de Monsaraz	34	38.25 N	7.32 W
Rehau	60	50.15 N	12.02 E
Rehback ►⁵	56	49.27 N	8.27 E
Rehberge ▲²	56	52.35 N	13.11 E
Rehberge, Volkspark ♦	264a	52.33 N	13.20 E
Rehburg	52	52.29 N	9.13 E
Rehden	52	52.37 N	8.29 E
Rehe	56	50.38 N	8.07 E
Rehefeld-Zaunhaus	54	50.43 N	13.42 E
Rehfelde	54	52.30 N	13.54 E
Rehli	124	23.38 N	79.05 E
Rehme	52	52.12 N	8.49 E
Rehna	54	53.47 N	11.03 E
Rehoboth	156	23.18 S	17.03 E
Rehoboth Bay c	208	38.40 N	75.06 W
Rehoboth Beach	208	38.43 N	75.04 W
Rehoboth Seamount ⁺³	16	37.30 N	59.50 W
Rehon	132	31.54 N	34.49 E
Rehti	124	22.44 N	77.26 E
Reiche Ebrach ≃	56	49.49 N	10.58 E
Reiche Liesing ≃	264b	48.08 N	16.16 E
Reichelsheim	56	49.43 N	8.50 E
Reichenau, Dtsch.	58	47.41 N	9.03 E
Reichenau, Schw.	58	46.49 N	9.24 E
Reichenau an der Rax	61	47.42 N	15.50 E
Reichenbach, Dtsch.	54	51.08 N	14.48 E
Reichenbach, Dtsch.	54	50.37 N	12.18 E
Reichenbach — Dzierżoniów, Pol.	30	50.44 N	16.39 E
Reichenbach, Schw.	58	46.38 N	7.42 E
Reichenberg — Liberec	30	50.46 N	15.03 E
Reichenhofen	56	47.54 N	10.09 E
Reichensachsen	58	51.09 N	9.59 E
Reichen Spitze ▲	64	47.09 N	12.10 E
Reichertshausen	60	48.28 N	11.31 E
Reichertsheim	60	48.40 N	12.22 E
Reichertshofen	60	48.40 N	11.28 E
Reichling ⊘¹	61	47.53 N	14.27 E
Reichsbrücke ►⁵	264b	48.14 N	16.25 E
Reichshoffen	56	48.56 N	7.40 E
Reichstädt	54	50.52 N	13.38 E
Reid	162	30.49 S	128.26 E
Reid, Mount ▲, Austl.	162	17.58 S	101.34 W
Reid, Mount ▲, Ak., U.S.	182	55.42 N	131.15 W
Reid Lake ⊘	182	50.02 N	108.05 W
Reidsville, Ga., U.S.	192	32.05 N	82.07 W
Reidsville, N.C., U.S.	192	36.21 N	79.39 W
Reiffton	208	40.19 N	75.53 W

FRANÇAIS Nom	Page	Lat.°	Long.° W=Ouest
Reigate	42	51.14 N	0.13 W
Reigate and Banstead ☐⁸	260	51.17 N	0.12 W
Reignac-sur-Indre	50	47.13 N	0.55 E
Reignier	58	46.08 N	6.16 E
Reigoldswil	58	47.24 N	7.41 E
Reihoku	92	32.31 N	130.02 E
Reims	50	49.15 N	4.02 E
Reims, Montagne de ▲²	50	49.08 N	4.00 E
Reina Alejandra — Queen Alexandra Range ▲	9	84.00 S	168.00 E
Reina Carlota, Estrecho de la — Queen Charlotte Sound ☒	182	51.30 N	129.30 W
Reinach, Schw.	58	47.30 N	7.35 E
Reinach, Schw.	58	47.15 N	8.11 E
Reina Fiabola — Queen Fiabola Mountains ▲	9	71.30 S	35.40 E
Reina Maria, Costa de la — Queen Mary Coast ▲²	9	67.00 S	96.00 E
Reina Maud, Tierras de la — Queen Maud Land ▲¹	9	72.30 S	12.00 E
Reinbeck	190	42.19 N	92.35 W
Reinbek	52	53.31 N	10.14 E
Reinberg	54	54.12 N	13.15 E
Reindeer ≃	184	55.36 N	103.11 W
Reindeer Island I	184	52.25 N	98.00 W
Reindeer Lake ⊘	176	57.15 N	102.40 W
Reindeer Station	180	68.42 N	134.06 W
Reine Charlotte, Détroit de la — Queen Charlotte Sound ☒	182	51.30 N	129.30 W
Reinerton	208	40.36 N	76.34 W
Reinfeld	52	53.49 N	10.28 E
Reinhardswald ▲	52	51.30 N	9.30 E
Reinhardtsdorf	54	50.53 N	14.11 E
Reinheim	56	49.49 N	8.50 E
Reinickendorf ►⁸	264a	52.35 N	13.21 E
Reinosa	34	43.00 N	4.08 W
Reino Unido — United Kingdom ☐¹	28	54.00 N	2.00 W
Reinsdorf, Dtsch.	54	50.42 N	12.33 E
Reinsdorf, Dtsch.	54	51.54 N	12.37 E
Reinshagen ►⁸	263	51.10 N	7.09 E
Reinstorf	54	53.50 N	11.38 E
Reis	130	38.16 N	31.35 E
Reisaelva ≃	24	69.48 N	21.00 E
Reisbach	60	48.34 N	12.38 E
Reischach	60	48.17 N	12.44 E
Reisdorf, Camp ■	273b	4.21 S	15.15 E
Reisholz ►⁸	263	51.11 N	6.52 E
Reisjärvi	26	63.37 N	24.54 E
Reiss	46	58.28 N	3.10 W
Reisterstown	208	39.28 N	76.49 W
Reisterstown Road Plaza ►⁹	284b	39.02 N	76.42 W
Reitano	70	37.58 N	14.20 E
Reitdiep ≃	52	53.20 N	6.30 E
Reith bei Seefeld	64	47.18 N	11.12 E
Reit im Winkl	64	47.40 N	12.28 E
Reitz	158	27.53 S	28.31 E
Reivilo	158	27.36 S	24.08 E
Rejinagar	126	23.53 N	88.15 E
Rejmyra	40	58.50 N	15.55 E
Rejowiec Fabryczny	30	51.08 N	23.13 E
Rejštejn	60	49.09 N	13.31 E
Rekarne ≃	40	59.26 N	16.20 E
Rekarne ≃	40	59.17 N	16.25 E
Reken	52	51.50 N	7.02 E
Rekjoäti	272b	22.37 N	88.28 E
Reliance, N.T., Can.	176	62.42 N	109.08 W
Reliance, S.D., U.S.	200	43.53 N	99.36 W
Relief Reservoir ⊘¹	226	38.16 N	119.44 W
Religione, Punta ►	70	36.42 N	14.46 E
Reliz Creek ≃	226	36.19 N	121.18 W
Rellingen	52	53.39 N	9.49 E
Rellinghausen ►⁸	263	51.25 N	7.04 E
Reloncaví, Seno c	254	41.40 S	72.35 W
Remada	148	32.19 N	10.24 E
Remagen, Dtsch.	30	50.34 N	7.13 E
Remagen, Dtsch.	56	50.34 N	7.13 E
Rémalard	50	48.26 N	0.47 E
Remanso	255	9.37 S	42.07 W
Remarde ≃	261	48.35 N	2.15 E
Remarkable, Mount ▲	162	32.48 S	138.10 E
Rembang	115a	6.42 S	111.20 E
Rembau	114	2.35 N	102.06 E
Rembchi	34	35.04 N	1.26 W
Remda	54	50.46 N	11.13 E
Remecó	52	37.38 S	63.39 W
Remedios, Col.	246	7.02 N	74.41 W
Remedios, Cuba	240p	22.30 N	79.33 W
Remedios, Punta ►	236	13.31 N	89.49 W
Remedios, Santuario de los ♦	286a	19.28 N	99.15 W
Remedios de Escalada ►⁸	258	34.43 S	58.23 W
Remer	190	47.03 N	93.54 W
Remeshk	128	26.50 N	58.49 E
Remhoogte	158	29.33 S	23.01 E
Rémilly	56	49.01 N	6.24 E
Reminderville	214	40.16 N	81.23 W
Remington, Ind., U.S.	216	40.45 N	87.09 W
Remington, Va., U.S.	188	38.32 N	77.48 W
Remiremont	56	48.01 N	6.35 E
Remo	259	4.53 S	52.17 W
Remontnoje	80	46.33 N	43.39 E
Remoulins	62	43.56 N	4.34 E
Rempang, Pulau I	114	1.05 N	104.10 E
Remptendorf	54	50.31 N	11.39 E
Rems ≃	56	48.50 N	9.12 E
Remscheid	56	51.11 N	7.11 E
Remsen, Ia., U.S.	198	42.48 N	95.58 W
Remsen, N.Y., U.S.	210	43.20 N	75.11 W
Remsfeld	56	51.00 N	9.28 E
Remuna	126	21.33 N	86.54 E
Rémuzat	62	44.24 N	5.21 E
Renaix — Ronse	50	50.45 N	3.36 E
Renala Khurd	124	30.53 N	73.36 E
Rena Point ►	116	16.10 N	119.45 E
Renard Islands II	166	10.50 S	153.05 E
Renata	182	49.26 N	118.06 W
Renca	286e	33.23 S	70.43 W
Renchen	56	48.35 N	8.01 E
Rencontre East	186	47.38 N	55.12 W
Rencun	92	36.19 N	113.50 E

PORTUGUÊS Nome	Página	Lat.°	Long.° W=Oeste
Renda, Ityo.	144	14.30 N	39.53 E
Renda, Lat.	76	57.09 N	22.22 E
Rende	68	39.19 N	16.11 E
Rendena, Valle V	64	46.08 N	10.42 E
Rend Lake ⊘¹	194	38.05 N	88.58 W
Rendova Island I	175e	8.32 S	157.20 E
Rendsburg	41	54.18 N	9.40 E
Renens	58	46.32 N	6.35 E
Renesse	52	51.44 N	3.46 E
Renews	186	46.56 N	52.56 W
Renfrew, On., Can.	212	45.28 N	76.41 W
Renfrew, Scot., U.K.	46	55.53 N	4.24 W
Renfrew, Pa., U.S.	214	40.46 N	79.58 W
Renfrew ☐⁶	212	45.25 N	77.05 W
Rengam	114	1.53 N	103.24 E
Ren'gang	106	32.01 N	120.50 E
Rengasdengklok	115a	6.09 S	107.17 E
Rengat	112	0.24 S	102.33 E
Rengat	115a	7.04 S	112.00 E
Rengen	26	64.05 N	14.03 E
Rengezhuang	105	40.29 N	118.10 E
Rengit	112	1.41 N	103.09 E
Rengkang	112	1.07 N	112.10 E
Rengo	252	34.25 S	70.52 W
Rengsdorf	56	50.30 N	7.29 E
Reng Tläng ▲	120	21.59 N	92.36 E
Renhe, Zhg.	100	33.32 N	114.02 E
Renhe, Zhg.	100	22.47 N	114.02 E
Renhechang	107	30.30 N	105.56 E
Renheji	100	31.56 N	115.07 E
Renhua	100	25.06 N	113.44 E
Renhuai	102	27.48 N	106.18 E
Reni	188	45.27 N	28.17 E
Renick	188	37.59 N	80.21 W
Renish Point ►	46	57.44 N	6.59 W
Renjiawopeng	104	41.27 N	122.18 E
Renjiaxu	106	30.49 N	121.00 E
Renju	100	24.51 N	115.54 E
Renko	26	60.54 N	24.17 E
Renkum	52	51.58 N	5.45 E
Renliuchang	107	29.13 N	106.39 E
Renlong	107	30.32 N	105.47 E
Renmark	162	34.11 S	140.45 E
Renmei	100	25.50 N	117.56 E
Renmin	89	46.37 N	125.32 E
Renna, Monte ▲	70	36.52 N	14.41 E
Rennau	54	52.17 N	10.55 E
Rennell, Islas II	254	52.00 S	74.00 W
Rennell and Bellona ☐⁴	175e	10.45 S	160.00 E
Rennell Sound ☒	182	53.25 N	132.40 W
Renner	222	32.59 N	96.47 W
Rennerdale	279b	40.24 N	80.08 W
Rennerod	56	50.36 N	8.04 E
Renner Springs	166	18.20 S	133.48 E
Rennertshofen	60	48.45 N	11.02 E
Rennes	32	48.05 N	1.41 W
Rennick Bay c	9	70.18 S	161.45 E
Rennick Glacier ⊠	9	70.30 S	161.45 E
Rennie	184	49.51 N	95.33 W
Rennie's Mill	271d	22.18 N	114.15 E
Renningen	56	48.46 N	8.56 E
Renntier-See — Reindeer Lake ⊘	176	57.15 N	102.40 W
Rennweg	64	47.01 N	13.37 E
Reno, Nv., U.S.	226	39.31 N	119.48 W
Reno, Pa., U.S.	214	41.25 N	79.45 W
Reno, Tx., U.S.	222	32.56 N	97.05 W
Reno ≃	66	44.37 N	12.16 E
Reno Beach	214	41.40 N	83.15 W
Reno Hill ▲	200	42.35 N	106.03 W
Reno International ☒	226	39.30 N	119.46 W
Renoster ≃	158	31.37 S	20.37 E
Renous	186	46.49 N	65.48 W
Renous ≃	186	46.50 N	65.50 W
Renovo	214	41.19 N	77.45 W
Renqiao	100	33.27 N	117.16 E
Renqiu	98	38.43 N	116.05 E
Rens	41	54.54 N	9.06 E
Renshou, Zhg.	100	29.59 N	104.08 E
Renshou, Zhg.	107	30.00 N	104.08 E
Rensjön	24	68.05 N	19.49 E
Rensselaer, In., U.S.	216	40.56 N	87.09 W
Rensselaer, Mo., U.S.	191	39.40 N	91.33 W
Rensselaer, N.Y., U.S.	210	42.38 N	73.44 W
Rensselaer ☐⁶	210	42.43 N	73.40 W
Rensselaer Falls	212	44.35 N	75.18 W
Rensselaerville	210	42.30 N	74.08 W
Rentería	34	43.19 N	1.54 W
Rentfort ►⁸	263	51.35 N	6.57 E
Renton	224	47.28 N	122.12 W
Rentuo	107	29.14 N	106.23 E
Rentweinsdorf	56	50.04 N	10.47 E
Renun ≃	114	3.05 N	97.55 E
Renville	198	44.47 N	95.12 W
Renwez	52	49.50 N	4.36 E
Renwick, N.Z.	172	41.30 S	173.50 E
Renwick, Ia., U.S.	198	42.49 N	93.58 W
Renxiahaushen Park ♦	271d	22.31 N	114.10 E
Réo, Burkina	150	12.19 N	2.28 W
Reo, Indon.	115b	8.19 S	120.30 E
Reola ►⁸	272a	28.34 N	76.59 E
Repaupo	284b	39.48 N	75.18 W
Repbäcken	40	59.48 N	15.20 E
Repentigny	212	45.44 N	73.28 W
Repetek	106	38.34 N	63.11 E
Repky	76	60.10 N	29.52 E
Repojoki ≃	24	68.24 N	25.52 E
Repjovka, Ross.	80	53.09 N	48.06 E
Repolka	76	59.16 N	29.34 E
Reporoa	172	38.26 S	176.21 E
Reposaari	26	61.37 N	21.27 E
Reppen — Rzepin	54	52.20 N	14.49 E
Republic, Ks., U.S.	200	39.57 N	97.49 W
Republic, Mi., U.S.	190	46.24 N	87.58 W
Republic, Mo., U.S.	194	37.07 N	93.28 W
Republic, Wa., U.S.	202	48.39 N	118.44 W
República Centroafricana — Central African Republic ☐¹	136	7.00 N	21.00 E
Republican Airport ☒	198	40.44 N	73.25 W
Republican, North Fork ≃	198	40.01 N	101.59 W
Republican, South Fork ≃	198	40.01 N	101.59 W
Republic Observatory ♦	273d	26.11 S	28.05 E
Republic Steel Corporation ►³	279a	41.09 N	81.40 W
Repulse Bay ☒	166	20.36 S	148.43 E
Repulse Bay c	166	22.30 S	148.50 E
Repvåg	24	70.45 N	25.41 E
Requena, Esp.	34	39.29 N	1.06 W
Requena, Perú	248	4.58 S	73.50 W
Requista	62	44.02 N	2.32 E
Rère ≃	50	47.22 N	1.52 E
Reriutaba	250	4.10 S	40.35 W
Reşadiye	130	40.24 N	40.40 E

Nombre	Página	Lat.°	Long.°
Reşadiye ►⁸	267b	41.05 N	29.15 E
Reşadiye Yarımadası ►¹	130	36.40 N	27.45 E
Resang, Tanjong ►	114	2.35 N	103.51 E
Resarö	40	59.26 N	18.20 E
Rescalda	266b	45.38 N	8.56 E
Rescaldina	266b	45.37 N	8.57 E
Rescue	208	36.59 N	76.33 W
Research	274b	37.42 S	145.11 E
Reseda ►⁸	280	34.12 N	118.31 W
Resen	38	41.05 N	21.00 E
Resende	256	22.28 S	44.27 W
Reserva	252	24.38 S	50.52 W
Reserva, Parque de la ♦	286d	12.04 S	77.02 W
Reserve, La., U.S.	194	30.03 N	90.33 W
Reserve, N.M., U.S.	200	33.43 N	108.45 W
Reserve Township	279b	40.29 N	79.59 W
Reservoir	274b	37.43 S	145.00 E
Reservoir Pond ⊘	283	42.10 N	71.07 W
Rešetnikovo	82	56.27 N	36.34 E
Reshetylivka	78	49.34 N	34.04 E
Reshui	98	42.09 N	119.18 E
Reshuitang	102	24.10 N	103.09 E
Resia, Lago di ⊘¹	64	46.47 N	10.32 E
Resia, Passo di (Reschenpass))(	64	46.50 N	10.30 E
Resipol, Beinn ▲	46	56.43 N	5.39 W
Resistencia	252	27.27 S	58.59 W
Resița	38	45.17 N	21.53 E
Resiutta	64	46.23 N	13.13 E
Resko	30	53.47 N	15.25 E
Rešma	80	57.24 N	42.34 E
Resolute	176	74.41 N	94.54 W
Resolution Island I, N.T., Can.	176	61.30 N	65.00 W
Resolution Island I, N.Z.	172	45.40 S	166.40 E
Resolven	42	51.42 N	3.42 W
Resort, Loch c	46	58.03 N	7.06 W
Rešotkino	76	56.30 N	27.19 E
Resplandes	256	6.17 S	45.13 W
Resplendor	255	19.20 S	41.15 W
Ressa ≃	76	54.45 N	35.10 E
Ressaca, Ribeirão da ☒	287b	23.38 S	46.51 W
Resse	263	51.54 N	7.07 E
Ressons-sur-Matz	54	53.49 N	35.15 E
Resthaven	216	41.16 N	88.09 W
Restigouche (Ristigouche) ≃	186	48.04 N	66.20 W
Restinga Seca	252	29.49 S	53.23 W
Reston, Mb., Can.	184	49.35 N	101.02 W
Reston, Scot., U.K.	46	55.51 N	2.11 W
Reston, Va., U.S.	208	38.58 N	77.20 W
Restoule Lake ⊘	190	46.03 N	79.47 W
Restrepo, Col.	246	4.15 N	73.33 W
Restrepo, Col.	246	3.48 N	76.31 W
Resuttano	70	37.41 N	14.02 E
Retalhuleu	236	14.32 N	91.41 W
Retalhuleu ☐⁵	236	14.30 N	91.45 W
Retamosa	252	33.55 S	54.44 W
Retem, Oued er V	148	33.30 N	5.45 E
Retence	54	50.38 N	13.46 E
Retford	44	53.20 N	0.56 W
Rethem	52	52.47 N	9.23 E
Rethel	50	49.31 N	4.22 E
Rethem	52	52.45 N	9.23 E
Réthimnon	38	35.22 N	24.29 E
Retiche, Alpi — Rhaetian Alps ▲	58	46.30 N	10.00 E
Retie	58	51.16 N	5.04 E
Retiers	50	47.55 N	1.23 W
Retiro, Estación ►⁵	288	34.36 S	58.22 W
Retiro, Parque del ♦	266a	40.25 N	3.41 W
Retournac	62	45.12 N	4.02 E
Retreat	222	39.20 N	96.29 W
Retreat	170	34.07 S	149.38 E
Retsof	210	42.50 N	77.53 W
Rettenberg	58	47.35 N	10.17 E
Rettendon	260	51.39 N	0.33 E
Rettendon Place	260	51.37 N	0.32 E
Rettert	56	50.30 N	8.05 E
Rettin	54	54.08 N	11.00 E
Return Creek ≃	226	37.56 N	119.28 W
Retz	61	48.45 N	15.57 E
Retzow	52	52.37 N	12.41 E
Reuden	54	52.04 N	12.18 E
Reungeut	114	4.34 N	96.22 E
Reus	34	41.09 N	1.07 E
Reuschenberg	263	51.10 N	6.42 E
Reusel	58	51.21 N	5.22 E
Reuss ≃	58	47.28 N	8.14 E
Reuterstadt Stavenhagen	54	53.42 N	12.53 E
Reuth	56	50.17 N	7.37 E
Reutlingen	56	48.29 N	9.11 E
Reutov	82	55.46 N	37.52 E
Reutte	64	47.29 N	10.43 E
Reuver	58	51.17 N	6.05 E
Revadim	132	31.46 N	34.48 E
Revakino	82	55.22 N	37.40 E
Reval — Tallinn	76	59.25 N	24.45 E
Revda, Ross.	80	56.48 N	59.57 E
Réveillon, Ruisseau ≃	261	48.42 N	2.30 E
Revel	62	43.27 N	2.00 E
Revelganj	124	25.47 N	84.40 E
Revelstoke	182	50.59 N	118.12 W
Revelstoke, Lake ⊘¹	202	51.30 N	119.25 W
Reventazón	248	6.10 S	80.58 W
Reventazón ≃	244	10.00 N	83.00 W
Revere, Ross.	78	55.45 N	40.38 E
Revere, Pa., U.S.	208	40.31 N	75.10 W
Revere Beach ▲²	283	42.25 N	70.59 W
Revermont ▲²	62	46.27 N	5.25 E
Revesby	274a	33.57 S	151.01 E
Revest-du-Bion	62	44.05 N	5.33 E
Revigny-sur-Ornain	54	48.50 N	4.59 E
Revillagigedo, Islas II	232	19.00 N	111.30 W
Revillagigedo Channel ☒	182	55.10 N	131.13 W
Revillagigedo Island I	182	55.35 N	131.23 W
Revin	50	49.56 N	4.38 E
Revloc	214	40.29 N	78.45 W
Řevničov	60	50.08 N	13.45 E
Revol'ucii, pik ▲	85	38.31 N	72.21 E
Revolución, Museo de la ♦	286b	23.08 N	82.22 W
Revolution, Museum of the ♦	265b	55.46 N	37.36 E
Revúca	60	48.41 N	20.07 E
Revúdossjön ⊘	54	53.15 N	15.17 E
Rewa	124	24.32 N	81.18 E
Rewari	124	28.11 N	76.37 E
Rex, Mount ▲²	9	74.57 S	76.00 W
Rexburg	202	43.49 N	111.47 W
Rexdale ►⁸	275b	43.43 N	79.34 W
Rexford, Ks., U.S.	200	39.28 N	100.45 W
Rexford, Mt., U.S.	202	48.52 N	115.13 W
Reşadiye	130	40.24 N	40.40 E

Nome	Página	Lat.°	Long.°
Rexton	186	46.39 N	64.52 W
Rexville	210	42.05 N	77.40 W
Rey, Arroyo del ≃	288	34.46 S	58.27 W
Rey, Embalse del ⊘¹	266a	40.18 N	3.32 W
Rey, Estrecho del — King Sound ☒	162	17.00 S	123.30 E
Rey, Isla del I	246	8.22 N	78.55 W
Rey, Laguna del ⊘	196	27.01 N	103.26 W
Rey Bouba	146	8.40 N	14.11 E
Reyes	248	14.19 S	67.23 W
Reyes, Point ►	204	38.00 N	123.01 W
Reyes Peak ▲	228	34.38 N	119.17 W
Reyhanlı	130	36.18 N	36.32 E
Rey Jorge, Estrecho — King George Sound ☒	162	35.03 S	117.57 E
Rey Jorge, Isla — King George Island I	9	62.00 S	58.15 W
Reykjanes ►¹	24a	63.49 N	22.43 W
Reykjanes Ridge ►³	10	62.00 N	27.00 W
Reykjavik	24a	64.09 N	21.51 W
Reynella	168b	35.06 S	138.32 E
Reyno	194	36.21 N	90.45 W
Reynolds, Ga., U.S.	192	32.33 N	84.05 W
Reynolds, In., U.S.	216	40.44 N	86.52 W
Reynolds, N.D., U.S.	198	47.57 N	97.45 W
Reynolds Channel ☒	276	40.36 N	73.40 W
Reynolds Creek ≃, Austl.	171a	27.56 S	152.36 E
Reynolds Creek ≃, On., Can.	212	43.00 N	80.58 W
Reynoldsville	214	41.05 N	78.53 W
Reynosa	232	26.07 N	98.18 W
Reyssouze ≃	58	46.27 N	4.54 E
Rež	86	57.23 N	61.24 E
Reža ≃	82	54.54 N	62.18 E
Reza, gora (Küh-e Rīzeh) ▲	128	33.47 N	58.05 E
Rezé	32	47.12 N	1.34 W
Rēzekne	76	56.30 N	27.19 E
Rēzekne ≃	76	56.46 N	26.58 E
Rezina	38	47.44 N	28.58 E
Rezino	76	55.51 N	75.18 E
Rezovo	38	41.59 N	28.02 E
Rezovska (Mutlu) ≃	38	41.59 N	28.01 E
Režvānshahr	128	37.33 N	49.09 E
Rezzato	64	45.31 N	10.19 E
Rezzoaglio	62	44.32 N	9.23 E
Rezzonico	62	46.04 N	9.16 E
Rhade	52	53.19 N	9.07 E
Rhadeswood Reservoir ⊘¹	262	53.29 N	1.56 W
Rhaetian Alps (Rätische Alpen) (Alpi Retiche) ▲	58	46.30 N	10.00 E
Rhallamane, Sebkha de ≊	148	23.41 N	9.50 W
Rhame	198	46.13 N	103.39 W
Rharbi, Île I	148	34.39 N	11.03 E
Rharbi, Zahrez ⊘	148	34.50 N	3.10 E
Rhauderfehn	52	53.08 N	7.35 E
Rhaunen	56	49.51 N	7.20 E
Rhayader	42	52.18 N	3.30 W
Rhea Creek ≃	202	45.30 N	119.46 W
Rhede, Dtsch.	52	53.03 N	7.16 E
Rhede, Dtsch.	52	51.50 N	6.42 E
Rheden	52	52.01 N	6.02 E
Rheems	208	40.08 N	76.34 W
Rheidol ≃	42	52.25 N	4.05 W
Rheims — Reims	50	49.15 N	4.02 E
Rhein	184	51.19 N	102.10 W
Rhein — Rhine ≃	30	51.52 N	6.02 E
Rheinau	56	48.41 N	7.56 E
Rheinbach	56	50.37 N	6.57 E
Rheinberg	52	51.33 N	6.35 E
Rheinböllen	56	50.00 N	7.40 E
Rheinbreitbach	56	50.37 N	7.13 E
Rheinbrohl	56	50.30 N	7.19 E
Rheinbrücke ►⁵	263	51.12 N	6.44 E
Rheindürkheim	56	49.42 N	8.21 E
Rheine	56	52.17 N	7.26 E
Rheineck	58	47.28 N	9.35 E
Rheinen	263	51.27 N	7.38 E
Rheinfelden, Dtsch.	58	47.33 N	7.47 E
Rheinfelden, Schw.	58	47.33 N	7.47 E
Rheinhausen ►⁸	263	51.24 N	6.43 E
Rhein-Herne-Kanal ☒	263	51.27 N	6.47 E
Rheinkamp	56	51.30 N	6.37 E
Rheinland-Pfalz ☐³	56	50.00 N	7.00 E
Rheinsberg	54	53.06 N	12.53 E
Rheinstetten	56	48.58 N	8.18 E
Rheinwald V	58	46.32 N	9.17 E
Rheinwaldhorn ▲	58	46.30 N	9.01 E
Rhêmes-Notre-Dame	62	45.34 N	7.07 E
Rhenen	52	51.57 N	5.34 E
Rheurdt	263	51.27 N	6.28 E
Rheydt	56	51.10 N	6.29 E
Rheydt, Schloss ⊥	263	51.11 N	6.29 E
Rhin ≃, Dtsch.	54	52.50 N	12.50 E
Rhin — Rhine ≃, Europe	30	51.52 N	6.02 E
Rhinau	56	48.19 N	7.42 E
Rhine	210	43.17 N	88.09 W
Rhine (Rhein) (Rhin) ≃	30	51.52 N	6.02 E
Rhinebeck	210	41.55 N	73.57 W
Rhinecliff	210	41.55 N	73.57 W
Rhineland	222	33.30 N	99.31 W
Rhinelander	190	45.38 N	89.24 W
Rhin Kanal ☒	54	52.47 N	12.24 E
Rhinluch ☒	54	52.50 N	12.45 E
Rhinns of Kells ▲	46	55.09 N	4.20 W
Rhinns Point ►	46	55.40 N	6.30 W
Rhino Camp	154	2.58 N	31.24 E
Rhinow	54	52.45 N	12.20 E
Rhiou, Oued ≃	34	36.00 N	0.55 E
Rhir, Cap ►	148	30.38 N	9.54 W
Rhis, Oued ≃	34	35.14 N	3.31 E
Rho	66	45.32 N	9.02 E
Rhode Island ☐³, U.S.	178	41.40 N	71.30 W
Rhode Island ☐³, U.S.	207	41.40 N	71.30 W
Rhode Island I	207	41.37 N	71.15 W
Rhodes, Austl.	274a	33.50 S	151.05 E
Rhodes — Ródhos, Ellás	38	36.26 N	28.13 E
Rhodes — Ródhos I	38	36.10 N	28.00 E
Rhodes, Eng., U.K.	262	53.34 N	2.14 W
Rhodesia — Zimbabwe ☐¹	38	36.10 N	28.00 E
Rhodesia Inyanga National Park ♦	154	18.12 S	32.45 E
Rhodes Matopos National Park ♦	154	20.33 S	28.20 E
Rhodes Peak ▲	202	46.41 N	114.47 W
Rhodes's Tomb ⌂	154	20.30 S	28.30 E
Rhododendron	202	45.20 N	121.55 W
Rhododendron State Park ♦	207	42.47 N	72.12 W
Rhodon, Ruisseau de ≃	261	48.42 N	2.04 E

Nome	Página	Lat.°	Long.°
Rhodope Mountains (Rodopi) (Orosirá Rodhópis) ▲	38	41.30 N	24.30 E
Rhodt	56	49.16 N	8.07 E
Rhome	222	33.03 N	97.28 W
Rhön ▲	56	50.30 N	9.50 E
Rhondda	42	51.40 N	3.27 W
Rhône ☐⁵	32	45.55 N	4.40 E
Rhône ≃	32	43.20 N	4.50 E
Rhône au Rhin, Canal du ☒	58	47.06 N	5.19 E
Rhône à Sète, Canal du ☒	62	43.25 N	3.42 E
Rhoose	42	51.24 N	3.20 W
Rhosesmor	262	53.10 N	3.10 W
Rhosllanerchrugog	44	53.00 N	3.03 W
Rhosneigr	44	53.14 N	4.31 W
Rhos-on-Sea	44	53.19 N	3.45 W
Rhossili	42	51.34 N	4.17 W
Rhourde-el-Baguel	148	31.24 N	6.57 E
Rhuddlan	44	53.16 N	3.28 W
Rhüden	52	51.56 N	10.07 E
Rhue ≃	62	45.23 N	2.29 E
Rhyl	44	53.19 N	3.29 W
Rhymney	42	51.46 N	3.18 W
Rhymney ≃	42	51.28 N	3.10 W
Rhynie	46	57.19 N	2.50 W
Riaba	152	3.23 N	8.46 E
Riachão	250	7.22 S	46.37 W
Riachão do Dantas	250	11.04 S	37.44 W
Riachão do Jacuípe	250	11.48 S	39.21 W
Riacho de Santana	255	13.37 S	42.57 W
Riacho Grande	256	23.48 S	46.35 W
Riachos, Islas de los ℿ	254	41.10 S	62.08 W
Riachuelo, Bra.	250	10.44 S	37.11 W
Riachuelo, Chile	254	40.49 S	73.21 W
Riachuelo, Ur.	254	34.28 S	57.43 W
Riachuelo ≃	288	34.38 S	58.22 W
Riachuelo, Arroyo ≃	255	34.27 S	57.44 W
Rialma	255	15.18 S	49.34 W
Rialto, Bra.	256	22.35 S	44.16 W
Rialto, Ca., U.S.	228	34.06 N	117.22 W
Riamkanan, Waduk ⊘¹	112	3.30 S	115.05 E
Riangnapi ℿ	255	15.29 S	49.28 W
Riãng	120	27.32 N	92.56 E
Riangnom	140	9.55 N	30.01 E
Riaño	34	42.58 N	5.01 W
Riasi	124	33.05 N	74.50 E
Riau ≃⁴	112	1.00 N	102.00 E
Riau, Kepulauan ℿ	112	1.00 N	104.30 E
Riaz	58	46.30 N	7.04 E
Riaza	34	41.17 N	3.28 W
Riaza ≃	34	41.42 N	3.55 W
Ribadavia	34	42.17 N	8.08 W
Ribadeo	34	43.32 N	7.02 W
Ribadesella	34	43.28 N	5.04 W
Ribas de Jarama	266a	40.23 N	3.31 W
Ribas do Rio Pardo	255	20.27 S	53.46 W
Ribauê	154	14.57 S	38.17 E
Ribble ≃	44	53.44 N	2.50 W
Ribble Valley ☐⁸	262	53.46 N	2.40 W
Ribble Valley ☐⁸	262	53.46 N	2.31 W
Ribblesdale V	44	54.05 N	2.20 W
Ribchester	262	53.49 N	2.32 W
Ribe ☐⁵	41	55.21 N	8.46 E
Ribe ☐⁶	41	55.35 N	8.50 E
Ribe ≃	41	55.21 N	8.40 E
Ribeauvillé	58	48.12 N	7.19 E
Ribécourt	54	49.31 N	2.55 E
Ribeira	252	24.40 S	49.01 W
Ribeira do Iguape ≃	252	24.40 S	47.24 W
Ribeira do Pombal	250	10.50 S	38.32 W
Ribeira Grande, C.V.	150a	17.11 N	25.04 W
Ribeira Grande, Port.	148	38.31 N	28.43 W
Ribeirão	250	8.31 S	35.23 W
Ribeirão das Lajes, Reprêsa do ⊘¹	256	22.45 S	43.55 W
Ribeirão de São Joaquim	256	22.17 S	44.11 W
Ribeirão do Pinhal	255	23.24 S	50.18 W
Ribeirão Pires	256	23.43 S	46.25 W
Ribeirão Prêto	256	21.10 S	47.48 W
Ribeirão Vermelho	255	21.11 S	45.03 W
Ribeiro Gonçalves	255	7.32 S	45.14 W
Ribeiros	50	41.28 N	8.28 W
Ribémont	50	49.48 N	3.28 E
Ribera	70	37.30 N	13.16 E
Riberalta	248	11.00 S	66.06 W
Ribérac	62	45.14 N	0.20 E
Ribes de Freser	266c	42.18 N	2.10 E
Ribnica	66	45.44 N	14.44 E
Ribnica, Slvn.	66	46.32 N	15.16 E
Ribnitz-Damgarten	54	54.15 N	12.28 E
Ribstone Creek ≃	184	52.51 N	110.05 W
Ricadi	68	38.37 N	15.52 E
Ricardo Flores Magón	232	29.58 N	106.58 W
Ricardos, Estany de la ⊘	266d	41.18 N	2.07 E
Ricaurte	172	43.32 S	172.36 E
Riccall	44	53.50 N	1.04 W
Riccarton	172	43.32 S	172.36 E
Riccione	66	43.59 N	12.39 E
Rice	216	42.15 N	90.36 W
Rice Creek ≃	210	42.16 N	84.57 W
Rice Lake, Mi., U.S.	190	47.42 N	82.08 W
Rice Lake ⊘, On., Can.	212	44.08 N	78.13 W
Rice Lake Indian Reserve ►⁴	212	44.10 N	78.12 W
Riceville, Ia., U.S.	198	43.22 N	92.33 W
Riceville, Tn., U.S.	192	35.22 N	84.41 W
Rich, Cape ►	212	44.43 N	80.38 W
Richan	184	49.59 N	92.49 W
Richard B. Russell Lake ⊘¹	192	34.18 N	82.39 W
Richard Collinson Inlet c	176	72.45 N	113.45 W
Richards-Gebaur Air Force Base ■	194	38.51 N	94.33 W
Richard's Bay	158	28.47 S	32.06 E
Richard's Harbour	186	47.37 N	56.34 W
Richards Island I	180	69.20 N	134.34 W
Richardson	222	32.57 N	96.43 W
Richardson ≃	176	58.30 N	111.30 W
Richardson Bay c	282	37.52 N	122.29 W
Richardson Mountains ▲, Can.	180	67.15 N	136.30 W
Richardson Mountains ▲, N.Z.	172	44.40 S	168.31 E
Richardson Park	285	39.44 N	75.35 W
Richardton	198	46.53 N	102.19 W
Richardville	214	41.16 N	79.01 W
Richboro	284	40.13 N	75.00 W
Richelieu, P.Q., Can.	212	45.27 N	73.15 W
Richelieu, Fr.	32	47.01 N	0.19 E
Richelieu ≃	212	46.03 N	73.07 W
Richelieu ☐⁶	212	45.30 N	73.30 W
Richer	184	49.39 N	96.28 W
Richey	198	47.38 N	105.04 W

Símbolo	ESPAÑOL	Fluß	Río	Rivière	Rio
≃	River	Fluß	Río	Rivière	Rio
☒	Canal	Kanal	Canal	Canal	Canal
↳	Waterfall, Rapids	Wasserfall, Stromschnellen	Cascada, Rápidos	Chute d'eau, Rapides	Cascata, Rápidos
L	Strait	Meeresstraße	Estrecho	Détroit	Estreito
c	Bay, Gulf	Bucht, Golf	Bahía, Golfo	Baie, Golfe	Baía, Golfo
⊘	Lake, Lakes	See, Seen	Lago, Lagos	Lac, Lacs	Lago, Lagos
☒	Swamp	Sumpf	Pantano	Marais	Pântano
⊠	Ice Features, Glacier	Eis- und Gletscherformen	Accidentes Glaciares	Formes glaciaires	Acidentes glaciares
►	Other Hydrographic Features	Andere Hydrographische Objekte	Otros Elementos Hidrográficos	Autres données hydrographiques	Outros acidentes hidrográficos

Símbolo	Submarine				
✦	Submarine Features	Untermeerische Objekte	Formes de relief sous-marin	Accidentes Submarinos	
☐	Political Unit	Politische Einheit	Unidad Política	Entité politique	Unidade política
⌂	Cultural Institution	Kulturelle Institution	Institución Cultural	Institution culturelle	Instituição cultural
⊥	Historical Site	Historische Stätte	Sitio Histórico	Site historique	Sitio histórico
♦	Recreational Site	Erholungs- und Ferienort	Sitio de Recreo	Centre de loisirs	Area de Lazer
☒	Airport	Flughafen	Aeropuerto	Aéroport	Aeroporto
■	Military Installation	Militärinstallation	Instalación Militar	Installation militaire	Instalação militar
►	Miscellaneous	Verschiedenes	Misceláneo	Divers	Diversos

Name	Page	Lat.	Long.
Richfield, Id., U.S.	202	43.02 N	114.09 W
Richfield, Mn., U.S.	190	44.53 N	93.16 W
Richfield, Oh., U.S.	214	41.14 N	81.39 W
Richfield, Pa., U.S.	208	40.41 N	77.07 W
Richfield, Ut., U.S.	200	38.46 N	112.05 W
Richfield Springs	210	42.51 N	74.59 W
Richford, N.Y., U.S.	210	42.21 N	76.12 W
Richford, Vt., U.S.	206	44.59 N	72.40 W
Rich Fountain	219	38.24 N	91.53 W
Richgrove	226	35.48 N	119.07 W
Richhill, N. Ire., U.K.	48	54.23 N	6.33 W
Rich Hill, Mo., U.S.	194	38.05 N	94.12 W
Richibucto	186	46.41 N	64.52 W
Richland, Ga., U.S.	78	51.07 N	34.30 E
Richky	192	32.05 N	84.40 W
Richland, Mi., U.S.	216	42.22 N	85.27 W
Richland, Mo., U.S.	194	37.51 N	92.24 W
Richland, N.J., U.S.	208	39.29 N	74.52 W
Richland, N.Y., U.S.	210	43.34 N	76.03 W
Richland, Pa., U.S.	208	40.21 N	76.16 W
Richland, Tx., U.S.	222	31.56 N	96.26 W
Richland, Tx., U.S.	222	32.57 N	95.49 W
Richland, Wa., U.S.	200	46.17 N	119.17 W
Richland ◆⁶	214	40.46 N	82.31 W
Richland Center	190	43.20 N	90.23 W
Richland Creek ≃, Il., U.S.	219	38.14 N	89.54 W
Richland Creek ≃, Tn., U.S.	194	35.02 N	86.55 W
Richland Creek ≃, Tx., U.S.	222	31.58 N	96.03 W
Richland Creek Lake @¹	222	32.00 N	96.13 W
Richlands, N.C., U.S.	192	34.53 N	77.32 W
Richlands, Va., U.S.	192	37.05 N	81.47 W
Richland Springs	196	31.16 N	98.57 W
Richmond, Austl.	166	20.44 S	143.08 E
Richmond, Austl.	170	33.36 S	150.46 E
Richmond, B.C., Can.	224	49.09 N	123.06 W
Richmond, On., Can.	212	45.11 N	75.50 W
Richmond, P.Q., Can.	206	45.40 N	72.09 W
Richmond, N.Z.	172	41.20 S	173.11 E
Richmond, S. Afr.	158	31.23 S	23.56 E
Richmond, S. Afr.	158	29.54 S	30.08 E
Richmond, Eng., U.K.	44	54.24 N	1.44 W
Richmond, Ca., U.S.	226	37.56 N	122.20 W
Richmond, Il., U.S.	216	42.28 N	88.18 W
Richmond, In., U.S.	216	39.49 N	84.53 W
Richmond, Ks., U.S.	198	38.24 N	95.15 W
Richmond, Ky., U.S.	212	37.44 N	84.17 W
Richmond, Me., U.S.	188	44.05 N	69.47 W
Richmond, Ma., U.S.	207	42.22 N	73.22 W
Richmond, Mi., U.S.	214	42.48 N	82.45 W
Richmond, Mn., U.S.	190	45.27 N	94.31 W
Richmond, Oh., U.S.	214	39.16 N	93.58 W
Richmond, Tx., U.S.	222	29.34 N	95.45 W
Richmond, Ut., U.S.	200	41.55 N	111.48 W
Richmond, Vt., U.S.	188	44.24 N	72.59 W
Richmond, Va., U.S.	208	37.33 N	77.27 W
Richmond □⁶, P.Q., Can.	206	45.40 N	72.00 W
Richmond □⁶, N.Y., U.S.	210	40.38 N	74.05 W
Richmond □⁶, Va., U.S.	208	37.32 N	77.28 W
Richmond ◆⁸, Eng., U.K.	42	51.28 N	0.18 W
Richmond ◆⁸, Ca., U.S.	282	37.46 N	122.29 W
Richmond ◆⁸, Pa., U.S.	285	39.59 N	75.06 W
Richmond, Mount ▲	172	41.25 S	173.24 E
Richmond Point ▸	282	37.55 N	122.23 W
Richmond Beach	224	47.46 N	122.23 W
Richmond Creek ≃	276	40.34 N	74.11 W
Richmond Heights, Fl., U.S.	220	25.37 N	80.22 W
Richmond Heights, Mo., U.S.	219	38.37 N	90.19 W
Richmond Heights, Oh., U.S.	214	41.33 N	81.30 W
Richmond Highlands	224	47.45 N	122.20 W
Richmond Hill, On., Can.	212	43.52 N	79.27 W
Richmond Hill, Ga., U.S.	192	31.56 N	81.18 W
Richmond Hill ◆⁸	276	40.42 N	73.49 W
Richmond International Airport ◆	208	37.30 N	77.19 W
Richmond Mall ◆⁹	279a	41.32 N	81.30 W
Richmond National Battlefield Park ◆	208	37.30 N	77.23 W
Richmond Park ◆	260	51.26 N	0.16 W
Richmond Peak ▲	241h	13.17 N	61.13 W
Richmond Range ▲	172	41.27 S	173.30 E
Richmond Royal Australian Air Force Base ◆	170	33.37 S	150.48 E
Richmond-San Rafael Bridge ◆⁸	282	37.56 N	122.27 W
Richmondtown Restoration □	276	40.34 N	74.09 W
Richmond Valley ◆⁸	276	40.31 N	74.13 W
Richmondville	210	42.38 N	74.33 W
Richrath	263	51.08 N	6.56 E
Rich Square	192	36.16 N	77.17 W
Rich Stadium ◆	284	42.57 N	78.47 W
Richtenberg	54	54.12 N	12.53 E
Richterswil	54	47.13 N	8.42 E
Richton Park	194	31.20 N	88.56 W
Richvale, On., Can.	212	41.29 N	87.42 W
Richvale, Ca., U.S.	226	39.30 N	121.45 W
Richview	219	38.23 N	89.11 W
Richville, N.Y., U.S.	212	44.25 N	75.23 W
Richville, Oh., U.S.	214	40.45 N	81.27 W
Richwood, N.J., U.S.	285	39.43 N	75.10 W
Richwood, W.V., U.S.	188	38.13 N	80.32 W
Richwood Village	222	29.04 N	95.25 W
Ricinskij zapovednik □	84	43.25 N	40.30 E
Rickenbacker Air Force Base ◆	218	39.48 N	82.56 W
Rickenpass ⋊	58	47.04 N	9.21 E
Ricken Tunnel ◆⁵	58	47.12 N	9.05 E
Ricketts Glen State Park ◆	208	41.20 N	76.18 W
Ricketts Point ▸	274b	38.00 S	145.02 E
Rickleån ≃	36	64.05 N	20.44 E
Rickling	54	54.01 N	10.13 E
Rickmansworth	42	51.39 N	0.29 W
Rico	200	37.41 N	108.01 W
Ricoa ≃	241s	11.30 N	69.12 W
Ricobayo, Embalse de �@¹	34	41.30 N	5.55 W
Ricupe	152	14.37 S	21.25 E
Ridà I	144	14.38 N	44.54 E
Ridanna (Ridnaun)	60	46.48 N	11.15 E
Riddarhyttan	40	59.48 N	15.33 E
Ridderkerk	52	51.52 N	4.35 E
Riddes	58	46.10 N	7.13 E
Riddle	200	42.57 N	123.22 W
Riddle Mountain ▲	208	43.10 N	78.15 W
Riddlewood	285	39.54 N	75.26 W
Riddon, Loch c	46	55.57 N	5.12 W
Rideau ≃	212	45.27 N	75.42 W
Ridge, Eng., U.K.	260	51.41 N	0.16 W
Ridge, Tx., U.S.	222	31.09 N	96.19 W
Ridge Acres	276	40.41 N	74.32 W
Ridgecrest, Ca., U.S.	226	35.37 N	117.40 W
Ridgecrest, Wa., U.S.	224	47.45 N	122.21 W
Ridgedale	184	53.04 N	104.09 W
Ridge Farm	194	39.53 N	87.39 W
Ridgefield, Ct., U.S.	207	41.17 N	73.30 W

Name	Page	Lat.	Long.
Ridgefield, Il., U.S.	216	42.16 N	88.22 W
Ridgefield, N.J., U.S.	210	40.50 N	74.00 W
Ridgefield, Wa., U.S.	224	45.48 N	122.44 W
Ridgefield Park	276	40.51 N	74.01 W
Ridgeland, Ms., U.S.	194	32.25 N	90.07 W
Ridgeland, S.C., U.S.	192	32.28 N	80.58 W
Ridgely, Md., U.S.	208	38.56 N	75.53 W
Ridgely, Tn., U.S.	194	36.15 N	89.29 W
Ridge Manor	220	28.31 N	82.10 W
Ridgeport	210	43.13 N	77.43 W
Ridgetown	212	42.26 N	81.53 W
Ridgeville, Mb., Can.	184	49.04 N	97.01 W
Ridgeville, In., U.S.	216	40.17 N	85.01 W
Ridgeville, S.C., U.S.	192	33.05 N	80.18 W
Ridgeville Corners	214	41.26 N	84.15 W
Ridgeway, On., Can.	284a	42.53 N	79.03 W
Ridgeway, Il., U.S.	216	41.59 N	83.51 W
Ridgeway, Mo., U.S.	194	40.22 N	93.56 W
Ridgeway, N.J., U.S.	208	40.01 N	74.17 W
Ridgeway, Oh., U.S.	216	40.30 N	83.34 W
Ridgeway, Tx., U.S.	222	33.15 N	95.46 W
Ridgeway, Wi., U.S.	190	43.00 N	89.59 W
Ridgeway Ditch ≃	279a	41.25 N	82.20 W
Ridgewood	210	40.58 N	74.07 W
Ridgewood ◆⁸	276	40.42 N	73.53 W
Ridgewood Farm	285	39.57 N	75.34 W
Ridgewood Reservoir ◎¹	276	40.41 N	73.53 W
Ridgway, Co., U.S.	200	38.09 N	107.45 W
Ridgway, Il., U.S.	194	37.47 N	88.16 W
Ridgway, Pa., U.S.	208	41.25 N	78.43 W
Riding Mountain ▲	184	50.37 N	99.37 W
Riding Mountain National Park ◆	184	50.55 N	100.25 W
Ridlwajär	124	27.57 N	83.26 E
Ridley Creek ≃	285	39.51 N	75.21 W
Ridley Creek State Park ◆	285	39.57 N	75.27 W
Ridnaun → Ridanna	60	46.55 N	11.15 E
Riebeek-Kasteel	158	33.23 S	18.53 E
Riebeek-Oos	158	33.10 S	26.10 E
Riebeek-Wes	158	33.21 S	18.52 E
Riecawr, Loch ◎	44	55.13 N	4.27 W
Riedau	60	48.18 N	13.38 E
Riedelbach	56	50.18 N	8.23 E
Rieden	60	49.19 N	11.57 E
Riedenburg	60	48.58 N	11.41 E
Rieder	54	51.44 N	11.10 E
Riederalp	58	46.23 N	8.01 E
Riedern	56	49.40 N	9.23 E
Ried im Innkreis	60	48.13 N	13.30 E
Ried im Oberinntal	58	47.03 N	10.39 E
Riedisheim	58	47.45 N	7.22 E
Riedlingen	58	48.09 N	9.28 E
Riedstadt	56	49.50 N	8.30 E
Riegel	58	48.09 N	7.45 E
Riegelsville, N.J., U.S.	210	40.49 N	74.52 W
Riegelsville, Pa., U.S.	208	40.36 N	75.12 W
Riegelwood	192	34.20 N	78.15 W
Riegersburg	61	47.00 N	15.56 E
Riegersburg, Schloss ⌂	61	47.01 N	15.56 E
Riegersdorf	64	46.33 N	13.47 E
Riehen	58	47.35 N	7.39 E
Rieka	36	45.20 N	14.27 E
Rijeka → Rijeka	36	45.20 N	14.27 E
Rielasingen-Worblingen	58	47.44 N	8.50 E
Riemke ◆⁸	263	51.30 N	7.13 E
Riemst	56	50.48 N	5.36 E
Rieneck	56	50.05 N	9.38 E
Rienza (Rienz) ≃	64	46.43 N	11.39 E
Rienzi	194	34.45 N	88.31 W
Riesa	54	51.18 N	13.17 E
Riesco, Isla I	254	53.00 S	72.30 W
Rieseby	41	54.32 N	9.48 E
Riesel	222	31.28 N	96.56 W
Riese Pio X	64	45.44 N	11.55 E
Riestedt	54	51.29 N	11.21 E
Riet ≃, S. Afr.	158	31.20 S	20.17 E
Riet ≃, S. Afr.	158	29.00 S	23.54 E
Rietavas	76	55.44 N	21.56 E
Rietberg	52	51.47 N	8.25 E
Rietbron	158	32.54 S	23.10 E
Rietfontein	158	21.58 S	20.58 E
Riethuiskraal	158	34.20 S	21.22 E
Rieti	66	42.24 N	12.51 E
Rieti □⁴	66	42.18 N	12.52 E
Rietschen	54	51.23 N	14.47 E
Rietspruit ≃, S. Afr.	273d	26.19 S	28.18 E
Rietspruit ≃, S. Afr.	158	27.35 S	27.38 E
Rietvlei	158	30.29 S	29.51 E
Rietzsee See ◎	54	52.29 N	12.39 E
Rievaulx Abbey ◆¹	44	54.16 N	1.07 W
Riez	62	43.49 N	6.06 E
Riezlern	58	47.21 N	10.11 E
Rif	148	35.00 N	4.00 W
Rifle Lake ◎¹	214	44.13 N	84.15 W
Riffart	224	46.30 N	122.20 W
Rifiano (Riffian)	64	46.42 N	11.11 E
Rifle	200	39.32 N	107.46 W
Rifle ≃	190	44.04 N	83.49 W
Rifstangi ▸	34a	66.35 N	16.11 W
Rift Valley □⁴	154	0.30 N	36.00 E
Rift Valley V	10	3.00 S	29.00 E
Rift Valley Lakes National Park ◆	144	7.30 N	38.30 E
Riga, Lat.	76	56.57 N	24.06 E
Riga, Ross.	88	56.46 N	106.17 E
Riga, Mi., U.S.	216	41.49 N	83.50 W
Rīga, Gulf of (Rīgas jūras līcis) (Rīa iahl) c	76	57.30 N	23.35 E
Riga, Mount ▲	162	21.59 S	116.25 E
Rigacikun	150	10.40 N	7.28 E
Rigaih	114	4.40 N	95.34 E
Rīgān	128	28.37 N	58.58 E
Rīgas jūras līcis → Riga, Gulf of c	76	57.30 N	23.35 E
Rīga Station ◆⁵	265b	55.48 N	37.38 E
Rigaud ≃	208	45.29 N	74.18 W
Rigby	202	43.40 N	111.54 W
Riggins	202	45.25 N	116.19 W
Riggisberg	58	46.48 N	7.29 E
Rigi ▲	58	47.03 N	8.30 E
Rignac	62	44.24 N	2.17 E
Rignano Flaminio	66	42.12 N	12.29 E
Rignano Garganico	68	41.40 N	15.35 E
Rignano sull'Arno	66	43.43 N	11.27 E
Rigney	58	47.23 N	6.11 E
Rigney Bluff	210	43.19 N	77.38 W
Rigny-Ussé	62	47.15 N	0.18 E
Rigo	164	9.47 S	147.34 E
Rigolet	176	54.20 N	58.35 W
Rig-Rig	150	14.16 N	14.22 E
Rigside	46	55.36 N	3.47 W
Riguldi	76	59.08 N	23.33 E
Rīh, Jazīrat ar- I	128	15.10 N	42.12 E
Rihand ≃	124	24.33 N	82.58 E
Rihand Dam ◆⁶	124	24.05 N	82.45 E
Riihimäki	60	60.45 N	24.46 E
Rïiser-Larsen Peninsula ▸¹	9	68.55 S	34.00 E
Rijau	150	11.07 N	5.14 E
Riječki Zaljev c	36	45.15 N	14.25 E
Rijeka	36	45.20 N	14.27 E
Rijen	52	51.35 N	4.55 E
Rijkevorsel	52	51.21 N	4.46 E
Rijksdorp	52	52.09 N	4.25 E

Name	Page	Lat.	Long.
Rijssel → Lille	50	50.38 N	3.04 E
Rijssen	52	52.18 N	6.30 E
Rijswijk	52	52.04 N	4.20 E
Rikers Island I	276	40.47 N	73.53 W
Rikers Island Channel ⨆	276	40.47 N	73.52 W
Rikkavesi ◎	26	62.50 N	28.44 E
Rikugārsen	24	68.24 N	18.12 E
Rikuchū-kaigan-kokuritsu-kōen ◆	92	39.25 N	141.57 E
Rikuzen-takata	92	39.01 N	141.38 E
Rila ◆⁴	38	42.08 N	23.33 E
Riley	198	39.17 N	96.49 W
Riley, Mount ▲	200	31.55 N	107.07 W
Riley, Point ▸	168b	33.53 S	137.36 E
Riley Creek ≃	216	41.02 N	84.00 W
Riley Lake ◎	212	44.50 N	79.11 W
Rileys Range ▲	170	34.21 S	150.10 E
Rilievo	70	37.55 N	12.33 E
Rillieux	62	45.49 N	4.54 E
Rillington	44	54.09 N	0.42 W
Rillito	204	40.17 N	79.44 W
Rilton	214	40.17 N	79.44 W
Rilly-la-Montagne	50	49.10 N	4.03 E
Rilski manastir ◆¹	38	42.08 N	23.20 E
Rima ≃	150	13.04 N	5.10 E
Rímac	286d	12.03 S	77.03 W
Rímac ≃	248	12.02 S	77.09 W
Rimachi, Laguna ◎	246	4.25 S	76.43 W
Rímah, Jabal ar- ▲	132	32.19 N	36.52 E
Rima San Giuseppe	62	45.52 N	8.00 E
Rimatara I	14	22.38 S	152.51 W
Rimavská Sobota	30	48.23 N	20.02 E
Rimbey	182	52.38 N	114.14 W
Rimbo	40	59.45 N	18.22 E
Rimé, Ouadi V	146	14.02 N	18.03 E
Rimersburg	214	41.02 N	79.30 W
Rimforsa	26	58.08 N	15.40 E
Rimi	150	12.58 N	7.43 E
Rimini	66	44.04 N	12.34 E
Rimini □⁴	66	44.00 N	12.35 E
Rimo Glacier ◊	123	35.25 N	77.30 E
Rimogne	56	49.50 N	4.33 E
Rimouski	186	48.26 N	68.33 W
Rimouski, Réserve ◆	186	48.27 N	68.32 W
Rimpar	56	49.51 N	9.57 E
Rimrock Lake ◎¹	224	46.38 N	121.12 W
Rimsko-Korsakovka	80	51.34 N	48.31 E
Rin → Rhine ≃	30	51.52 N	6.02 E
Rinbung	124	29.21 N	89.57 E
Rinca, Pulau I	115b	8.37 S	119.48 E
Rinca, Pulau I	115b	8.42 S	119.42 E
Rinchnach	60	48.57 N	13.12 E
Rinçin Lchumbe	88	51.07 N	99.40 E
Rincón, C.R.	236	8.42 N	83.29 W
Rincon, P.R.	240m	18.20 N	67.15 W
Rincon, Ga., U.S.	192	32.17 N	81.14 W
Rincon, N.M., U.S.	200	32.40 N	107.03 W
Rincón, Bahía de c	240m	17.58 N	66.20 W
Rinconada	252	22.26 S	66.10 W
Rinconada, Hipódromo de la ◆	286c	10.26 N	66.56 W
Rincón de la Vieja, Parque Nacional ◆	236	10.48 N	85.18 W
Rincón del Bonete, Lago Artificial de ◎¹	252	32.45 S	56.00 W
Rincón del Ocote, Cerro ▲	236	13.36 N	87.10 W
Rincón de Romos	234	22.14 N	102.18 W
Rincon Indian Reservation ◆⁴	228	33.15 N	116.57 W
Rindown Castle ⌂¹	48	53.32 N	7.59 W
Rīngas	120	27.21 N	75.34 E
Ringdove	175f	16.38 S	168.09 E
Ringe	41	55.14 N	10.29 E
Ringebu	26	61.31 N	10.10 E
Ringenwalde	54	53.03 N	13.42 E
Ringertown	279b	40.25 N	79.36 W
Ringford	44	54.54 N	4.03 W
Ringgau ◆¹	56	51.04 N	10.04 E
Ringgold, Gunung ▲	115a	7.43 S	113.50 E
Ringgold, Ga., U.S.	192	34.54 N	85.06 W
Ringgold, La., U.S.	194	32.19 N	93.16 W
Ringgold, Tx., U.S.	196	33.49 N	97.56 W
Ringgold Isles II	175g	16.15 S	179.25 W
Ringim	150	12.08 N	9.10 E
Ringkøbing	41	56.05 N	8.15 E
Ringkøbing □⁶	26	56.00 N	8.15 E
Ringkøbing Fjord c²	26	56.00 N	8.15 E
Ringlet	114	4.25 N	101.23 E
Ringling Museums ⨆	220	27.23 N	82.34 W
Ringmer	42	50.53 N	0.04 E
Ringoes	208	40.26 N	74.52 W
Rings Island	283	42.49 N	70.52 W
Ringsted, Dan.	41	55.27 N	11.49 E
Ringsted, Ia., U.S.	198	43.17 N	94.30 W
Ringvassøy I	24	69.55 N	19.15 E
Ringwood, Austl.	169	37.49 S	145.14 E
Ringwood, Eng., U.K.	42	50.51 N	1.47 W
Ringwood, N.J., U.S.	210	41.06 N	74.14 W
Ringwood Manor ⊥	276	41.08 N	74.15 W
Ringwood North	274b	37.47 S	145.14 E
Ringwood State Park ◆	210	41.08 N	74.16 W
Riñihue	254	39.49 S	72.27 W
Riñihue, Lago ◎	254	39.50 S	72.18 W
Rinjani, Gunung ▲	115b	8.24 S	116.28 E
Rinkenæs	41	54.54 N	9.34 E
Rinkerode	52	51.50 N	7.41 E
Rinnes, Ben ▲	46	57.23 N	3.15 W
Rinnthal	56	49.13 N	7.55 E
Rinsumageest	52	53.18 N	5.57 E
Rinteln	52	52.11 N	9.04 E
Rinxent	50	50.48 N	1.44 E
Rio, Fl., U.S.	220	27.13 N	80.14 W
Rio, Wi., U.S.	190	43.27 N	89.15 W
Río Azul	252	25.43 S	50.47 W
Riobamba	246	1.40 S	78.38 W
Río Blanco, Chile	252	32.55 S	70.19 W
Río Blanco (Tenango de Río Blanco), Méx.	234	18.50 N	97.09 W
Río Bonito	228	33.25 N	105.43 W
Rio Bonito	287b	23.43 S	46.41 W
Río Branco, Bra.	248	9.58 S	67.48 W
Rio Branco, Bra.	252	32.34 S	53.25 W
Río Bravo, Méx.	196	26.02 N	98.06 W
Río Bravo, Méx.	232	25.59 S	98.06 W
Rio Brilhante	251	21.48 S	54.33 W
Río Caribe	242	10.42 N	63.07 W
Río Casca	208	20.13 S	42.39 W
Río Cauto	240p	20.35 N	76.44 W
Río Ceballos	252	31.10 S	64.20 W
Río Chico, Arg.	254	41.43 S	70.30 W
Río Chico, Ven.	246	10.18 N	65.59 W
Río Claro, Bra.	254	22.24 S	47.33 W
Rio Claro, Bra.	256	22.43 S	44.09 W
Rio Claro, Bra.	241r	10.18 N	61.11 W
Rio Claro, Represa do ◎¹	256	23.39 S	45.54 W
Rio Colorado	252	39.01 S	64.05 W
Rio Comprido ◆⁸	287a	22.55 S	43.12 W
Río Cuarto	252	33.08 S	64.21 W
Rio das Flores	256	22.10 S	43.33 W
Rio das Pedras	158	23.12 S	35.23 E
Rio de Janeiro, Bra.	256	22.54 S	43.14 W
Rio de Janeiro, Bra.	255	22.00 S	42.30 W
Río de Janeiro □³	255	22.00 S	42.30 W
Rio de Janeiro ◆⁸	287a	22.57 S	43.13 W
Rio de Jesús	236	7.59 N	81.10 W
Rio de Mouro	266c	38.46 N	9.20 W
Río de Oro	246	8.17 N	73.23 W
Río do Prado	255	16.35 S	40.34 W
Rio do Sul	252	27.13 S	49.39 W
Rio Douro	287a	22.39 S	43.32 W
Río Espera	255	20.51 S	43.29 W
Río Gallegos	254	51.38 S	69.13 W
Río Grande, Arg.	254	53.47 S	67.42 W
Río Grande, Bra.	252	32.02 S	52.05 W
Río Grande, Méx.	234	15.59 N	97.27 W
Río Grande, Méx.	234	23.50 N	103.02 W
Río Grande, Nic.	236	12.53 N	86.32 W
Río Grande, P.R.	240m	18.23 N	65.50 W
Río Grande, N.J., U.S.	208	39.00 N	74.52 W
Río Grande, Ven.	286c	10.35 N	66.57 W
Río Grande → Grande, Rio ≃	178	25.57 N	97.09 W
Río Grande, Ponte do ◆⁵	287b	23.46 S	46.31 W
Río Grande City	196	26.22 N	98.49 W
Río Grande da Serra, Bra.	256	23.44 S	46.24 W
Río Grande da Serra, Bra.	287b	23.44 S	46.24 W
Río Grande da Serra ◆⁸	287b	23.45 S	46.23 W
Río Grande do Norte □³	250	5.45 S	36.00 W
Río Grande do Sul □³	252	32.02 S	52.05 W
Río Grande do Sul □³	252	30.00 S	54.00 W
Riogrande	226	22.11 S	42.30 W
Ríohacha	246	11.33 N	72.55 W
Río Hato	236	8.23 N	80.10 W
Río Hondo, Méx.	286a	19.25 N	99.16 W
Río Hondo, Tx., U.S.	196	26.14 N	97.34 W
Rioja	248	6.05 S	77.09 W
Río Jaguari, Reservatório do ◎¹	256	22.55 S	46.25 W
Río Jueyes	240m	18.01 N	66.20 W
Riola	64	44.16 N	11.04 E
Río Lagartos	232	21.36 N	88.10 W
Riolândia	255	19.59 S	49.40 W
Río Largo	250	9.29 S	35.51 W
Riola Sardo	71	39.59 N	8.32 E
Río Linda	226	38.41 N	121.26 W
Riolo Terme	66	44.16 N	11.43 E
Río Luján ≃	258	34.17 S	58.54 W
Riom	32	45.54 N	3.07 E
Riomaggiore	64	44.06 N	9.44 E
Río Mayo	254	45.41 S	70.16 W
Río Mulatos	248	19.42 S	66.47 W
Río Muni □⁴	152	1.30 N	10.30 E
Riondel	182	49.46 N	116.52 W
Río Negro, Bra.	252	26.06 S	49.48 W
Río Negro, Chile	254	40.47 S	73.14 W
Ríonegro, Col.	246	6.09 N	75.22 W
Ríonegro, Col.	246	7.16 N	73.09 W
Río Negro, Bahía de c	240m	17.58 N	66.20 W
Río Negro □⁴	254	40.00 S	67.00 W
Río Negro, Pantanal do ≡	248	19.00 S	56.00 W
Rionero in Vulture	68	40.56 N	15.41 E
Rionero Sannitico	66	41.42 N	14.08 E
Rioni ≃	84	42.08 N	41.39 E
Río Novo	255	21.29 S	43.08 W
Río Novo do Sul	255	20.52 S	40.56 W
Ríopar	34	38.30 N	2.27 W
Río Pardo	252	29.59 S	52.22 W
Rio Pardo de Minas	255	15.37 S	42.33 W
Río Pico	254	44.13 S	71.21 W
Río Piedras, Arg.	252	25.18 S	64.54 W
Río Piedras, P.R.	240m	18.24 N	66.03 W
Río Pilcomayo, Parque Nacional ◆	252	25.10 S	58.00 W
Río Piracicaba	255	19.55 S	43.11 W
Rio Pomba	256	21.17 S	43.11 W
Río Prêto	256	22.06 S	43.50 W
Rio Prêto → São José do Rio Prêto, Bra.	256	22.10 S	42.57 W
Río Real	250	11.28 S	37.56 W
Río Saliceto	64	44.49 N	10.49 E
Río San Juan □⁵	236	11.10 N	84.30 W
Río Segundo	252	31.40 S	63.55 W
Ríosucio, Col.	246	5.25 N	75.42 W
Ríosucio, Col.	246	7.27 N	77.07 W
Río Terceiro	252	32.11 S	64.06 W
Ríoverde	234	21.56 N	99.59 W
Río Verde de Mato Grosso	255	18.55 S	54.52 W
Río Vista, Ca., U.S.	226	38.09 N	121.41 W
Río Vista, Tx., U.S.	222	32.14 N	97.23 W
Rioz	58	47.25 N	6.04 E
Riozinho ≃, Bra.	246	2.55 S	67.07 W
Riozinho ≃, Bra.	250	7.06 S	51.40 W
Riozinho ≃, Bra.	248	8.25 S	45.43 W
Rip ◆¹	54	50.24 N	14.18 E
Ripacandida	68	40.55 N	15.43 E
Ripatti, Punta dei ▸	66	42.02 N	11.25 E
Ripatransone	66	43.00 N	13.46 E
Ripky	78	51.48 N	31.05 E
Ripley, Eng., U.K.	42	51.18 N	0.30 W
Ripley, Il., U.S.	219	40.01 N	90.38 W
Ripley, Ms., U.S.	194	34.44 N	88.57 W
Ripley, N.Y., U.S.	214	42.16 N	79.42 W
Ripley, Oh., U.S.	218	38.45 N	83.51 W
Ripley, Tn., U.S.	194	35.45 N	89.31 W
Ripley □⁶	216	39.05 N	85.15 W
Ripoll	34	42.12 N	2.12 E
Ripollet	262	41.30 N	2.09 E
Ripon, P.Q., Can.	206	45.47 N	75.06 W
Ripon, Eng., U.K.	44	54.08 N	1.31 W
Ripon, Ca., U.S.	226	37.44 N	121.07 W
Ripon, Wi., U.S.	190	43.50 N	88.50 W
Riposto	70	37.44 N	15.12 E
Rippling Ridge	284b	39.11 N	76.37 W
Rippond 1	44	53.41 N	1.57 W
Rippowam ≃	207	41.03 N	73.33 W
Riquewihr	58	48.10 N	7.18 E
Ririba, Laga	154	3.34 N	37.15 E
Risālpur Cantonment	123	34.04 N	72.00 E
Risaralda □⁵	246	5.00 N	76.00 W
Risbäck	26	64.42 N	15.32 E
Risca	42	51.37 N	3.07 W
Rischenau	52	51.52 N	9.04 E
Risco, Ilha do I	266b	33.06 N	16.19 W
Rishã', Wādī ar- V	128	25.40 N	44.05 E
Rishiri-Rebun-Sarobetsu-kokuritsu-kōen ◆	92a	45.10 N	141.35 E
Rishiri-suidō ⨆	92a	45.09 N	141.15 E
Rishiri-tō I	92a	45.11 N	141.15 E
Rishon LeZiyyon	132	31.58 N	34.48 E
Rishra	272b	22.43 N	88.21 E
Rishworth, Wādī V	142	29.29 N	31.16 E
Rishton	260	53.46 N	2.25 W
Rising	262	52.41 N	1.57 W

Name	Page	Lat.	Long.
Rishworth Moor ◆³	262	53.39 N	2.01 W
Risinge	40	58.42 N	15.51 E
Rising Star	196	32.05 N	98.57 W
Rising Sun, In., U.S.	218	38.56 N	84.51 W
Rising Sun, Md., U.S.	208	39.41 N	76.03 W
Risingon, Oh., U.S.	214	41.16 N	83.25 W
Risle ≃	50	49.26 N	0.23 E
Risnov	35	45.26 N	14.37 E
Risøi	41	55.42 N	12.06 E
Rison, Ar., U.S.	194	33.57 N	92.11 W
Rison, Md., U.S.	208	38.32 N	77.10 W
Risør	26	58.43 N	9.14 E
Ris-Orangis	50	48.39 N	2.25 E
Riss ≃	58	48.17 N	9.49 E
Rissani	148	31.23 N	4.09 W
Risskov ◆⁸	41	56.11 N	10.14 E
Risstissen	58	48.16 N	9.49 E
Risti	76	58.59 N	24.03 E
Ristigouche (Restigouche) ≃	186	48.04 N	66.20 W
Ristiina	26	61.30 N	27.16 E
Ristijärvi	26	64.30 N	28.13 E
Ristina	41	54.50 N	10.38 E
Ristna ▸	76	58.56 N	22.05 E
Risum-Lindholm	41	54.45 N	8.53 E
Rita Blanca Creek ≃	196	35.40 N	102.29 W
Ritchie, S. Afr.	158	29.02 S	24.38 E
Ritchie, Md., U.S.	284c	38.52 N	76.52 W
Ritchie Branch ≃	284c	38.53 N	76.52 W
Ritchie's Archipelago II	272a	28.43 N	77.06 E
Ritidian Point ▸	174p	13.39 N	144.51 E
Ritscher Upland ▵¹	9	73.20 S	9.30 W
Ritsumeikan University ◆²	270	35.01 N	135.46 E
Ritsurin-kōen ◆	96	34.19 N	134.02 E
Ritta Island I	220	26.44 N	80.44 W
Ritter, Mount ▲	226	37.42 N	119.12 W
Rittergrün	52	53.11 N	8.45 E
Rittershude	52	50.29 N	12.47 E
Rittman	214	40.58 N	81.46 W
Rittö	94	35.01 N	136.00 E
Ritzville	202	47.07 N	118.23 W
Riu	120	28.19 N	95.03 E
Riva	64	45.53 N	10.50 E
Rivadavia, Arg.	252	35.28 S	62.57 W
Rivadavia, Arg.	252	33.11 S	68.28 W
Rivadavia, Arg.	252	24.11 S	62.53 W
Rivadavia, Chile	252	31.33 S	68.37 W
Riva del Garda	64	45.53 N	10.50 E
Riva del Sole	66	42.46 N	10.52 E
Riva di Tures (Rain)	64	46.56 N	11.58 E
Rivanazzano	62	44.56 N	9.01 E
Rivanna ≃	192	37.45 N	78.10 W
Rivare	216	40.49 N	84.50 W
Rivarolo Canavese	64	45.19 N	7.43 E
Rivarolo Mantovano	64	45.04 N	10.26 E
Rivas	236	11.26 N	85.50 W
Rivas □⁵	236	11.25 N	85.50 W
Rivasdale	287d	26.17 S	27.56 E
Rivash	128	35.26 N	58.26 E
Rivas-Vaciamadrid	266a	40.20 N	3.31 W
Riva Trigoso	62	44.16 N	9.26 E
Rive, Île de la ◆⁸	273b	4.21 S	15.26 E
Rive d'Arcano	64	46.08 N	13.02 E
Rive-de-Gier	62	45.32 N	4.37 E
Rivello	68	40.04 N	15.45 E
Rivera, Arg.	252	37.12 S	63.14 W
Rivera, Col.	246	2.47 N	75.15 W
Rivera, Ur.	252	30.54 S	55.31 W
Riverbank	226	37.44 N	120.56 W
Rivera ◆⁸	226	33.59 N	118.04 W
Riverbank	226	37.44 N	120.56 W
Riverdale, Il., U.S.	216	41.38 N	87.37 W
Riverdale, Md., U.S.	284c	38.57 N	76.56 W
Riverdale, N.J., U.S.	276	40.59 N	74.18 W
Riverdale, N.D., U.S.	198	47.29 N	101.22 W
Riverdale Heights	284c	38.58 N	76.55 W
River Drive Park	212	44.08 N	79.31 W
Riverea, Oh., U.S.	279a	41.25 N	81.51 W
River Falls, Al., U.S.	194	31.21 N	86.32 W
River Falls, Wi., U.S.	190	44.51 N	92.37 W
River Forest	278	41.53 N	87.48 W
River Grove	278	41.56 N	87.50 W
Riverhaven	218	41.05 N	80.40 W
Riverhead, Eng., U.K.	260	51.17 N	0.10 E
Riverhead, N.Y., U.S.	207	40.55 N	72.40 W
River Hébert	186	45.42 N	64.23 W
River Hills	279d	43.09 N	87.54 W
River John	186	45.45 N	63.04 W
River Jordan	224	48.25 N	124.03 W
River Lea Navigation ≃	260	51.40 N	0.02 W
River Meadow Brook ≃	283	42.38 N	71.17 W
Rivermont	283	42.13 N	71.17 W
Rivero, Isla I	254	45.20 S	73.57 W
River Oaks	226	38.33 N	121.31 W
River Pines, Ca., U.S.	226	38.33 N	120.40 W
River Pines, Ma., U.S.	283	42.35 N	71.17 W
River Plaza	207	40.21 N	74.04 W
River Ridge Estates	284c	38.48 N	77.00 W
River Road	284c	38.48 N	77.00 W
River Rouge	282	42.16 N	83.08 W
River Rouge Park	282	42.21 N	83.15 W
Rivers, Lake of the ◎	184	49.49 N	105.45 W
Riversdale, N.Z.	172	45.54 S	168.44 E
Riversdale, S. Afr.	158	34.07 S	21.15 E
Riverside, Ct., U.S.	207	41.02 N	73.35 W
Riverside, Il., U.S.	278	41.50 N	87.49 W
Riverside, Md., U.S.	284b	39.14 N	76.41 W
Riverside, Mi., U.S.	216	42.17 N	86.24 W
Riverside, Mo., U.S.	219	39.10 N	94.37 W
Riverside, N.J., U.S.	208	40.02 N	74.57 W
Riverside International Raceway ◆	228	33.57 N	117.17 W
Riverside Manors	284c	38.53 N	76.55 W
Riverside Park ◆, Mi., U.S.	281	42.21 N	83.09 W

Name	Page	Lat.	Long.
Riverview, Mi., U.S.	216	42.10 N	83.10 W
Riverview Park ◆	279b	40.29 N	80.01 W
Riverwood, Austl.	274a	33.57 S	151.03 E
Riverwood, In., U.S.	218	40.06 N	85.58 W
Riverwoods	278	42.09 N	87.54 W
Rives, Fr.	62	45.21 S	5.30 E
Rives, Tn., U.S.	194	36.21 N	89.02 W
Rivesaltes	32	42.46 N	2.52 E
Rives Junction	216	42.23 N	84.27 W
Rive Sud, Canal de la ⨆	275a	45.25 N	73.41 W
Rivesville	188	39.31 N	80.07 W
Riviera, Az., U.S.	204	35.04 N	114.35 W
Riviera, Tx., U.S.	196	27.18 N	97.49 W
Riviera ◆⁸	58	46.15 N	8.58 E
Riviera Beach, Fl., U.S.	220	26.46 N	80.03 W
Riviera Beach, Md., U.S.	208	39.10 N	76.30 W
Rivière-au-Tonnerre	186	50.16 N	64.47 W
Rivière-Bleue	186	47.26 N	69.03 W
Rivière-Bois-Clair	206	46.34 N	71.50 W
Rivière-de-la-Chaloupe	186	49.08 N	62.32 W
Rivière-des-Prairies	275a	45.39 N	73.33 W
Rivière-du-Loup	186	47.50 N	69.32 W
Rivière du Rempart	157c	20.06 S	57.41 E
Rivière-Matane	186	48.39 N	67.20 W
Rivière-Mékinac	206	46.47 N	72.48 W
Rivière-Pentecôte	186	49.47 N	67.10 W
Rivière-Pilote	240e	14.29 N	60.54 W
Rivière-Salée	240e	14.32 N	60.59 W
Rivière-Verte	186	47.19 N	68.09 W
Riviersonderend	158	34.09 S	19.55 E
Rivignano	64	45.59 S	13.03 E
Rivinton Reservoirs ◎¹	262	53.37 N	2.34 W
Rivoli	62	45.04 N	7.31 E
Rivoli Bay c	166	37.32 S	140.04 E
Rivolta d'Adda	64	45.28 N	9.31 E
Rivoltella	64	45.28 N	10.33 E
Riwaka	172	41.05 S	173.00 E
Rixford	214	41.55 N	78.30 W
Rixheim	58	47.46 N	7.24 E
Riyadh → Ar-Riyāḍ	128	24.38 N	46.43 E
Rīyāq	132	33.51 N	36.00 E
Rizal, Pil.	116	15.43 N	121.06 E
Rizal □⁴	269f	14.33 N	121.00 E
Rizal → Pasay, Pil.	269f	14.33 N	121.00 E
Rizal ◆⁸	269f	14.33 N	121.10 E
Rizal Memorial Stadium ◆	269f	14.34 N	120.59 E
Rize	130	41.02 N	40.31 E
Rize □⁴	40	40.55 N	40.55 E
Rīzeh, Kūh-e (gora Reza) ▲	128	37.47 N	58.05 E
Rizhao	98	35.27 N	119.29 E
Rizzíconi	68	38.24 N	15.58 E
Rizzíco, Capo ▸	68	38.54 N	17.06 E
Rjukan	26	59.52 N	8.34 E
Rkīz, Lac ◎	150	16.50 N	15.19 W
Rô	175f	21.22 S	167.50 E
Roa, Nor.	34	41.42 N	3.55 W
Roa, Nor.	26	60.17 N	10.37 E
Roa, R.D.C.	154	3.49 N	24.56 E
Roade	42	52.09 N	0.53 W
Roadford Reservoir ◎¹	42	50.43 N	4.13 W
Roadhead	44	55.03 N	2.46 W
Roadknight, Point ▸	169	38.26 S	144.11 E
Roadside	44	58.33 S	28.52 E
Road Town	240m	18.27 N	64.37 W
Roag, East Loch c	46	58.14 N	6.48 W
Roag, West Loch c	46	58.13 N	6.53 W
Roaming Rock, Lake ◎¹	214	41.38 N	80.49 W
Roaming Shores	214	41.38 N	80.49 W
Roana	64	45.52 N	11.28 E
Roan Cliffs ▲⁴	200	39.20 N	109.43 W
Roan Fell ▲	44	55.13 N	2.52 W
Roan Mountain	192	36.11 N	82.04 W
Roann	216	40.54 N	85.55 W
Roanne	32	46.02 N	4.04 E
Roanoke, Al., U.S.	194	33.09 N	85.22 W
Roanoke, Il., U.S.	216	40.47 N	89.11 W
Roanoke, In., U.S.	216	40.58 N	85.22 W
Roanoke, Va., U.S.	192	37.16 N	79.56 W
Roanoke, Va., U.S. (Staunton) ≃	214	36.28 N	76.44 W
Roanoke Island I	192	35.56 N	76.43 W
Roanoke Rapids	192	36.27 N	77.39 W
Roan Plateau ▵¹	200	39.22 N	109.40 W
Roans Prairie	222	30.35 N	95.58 W
Roanwater	48	51.28 N	9.00 W
Roatán, Isla de I	236	16.23 N	86.35 W
Robã Oued Yahia	36	36.05 N	0.38 E
Robalo ≃	254	54.56 S	67.43 W
Robbennelland I	158	33.49 S	18.22 E
Robbers Cave State Park ◆	196	34.42 N	95.07 W
Robbins, Il., U.S.	278	41.39 N	87.42 W
Robbins Ditch ≃	284	41.21 N	86.43 W
Robbins Island I	166	40.41 S	144.57 E
Robbins Rest	276	40.39 N	73.10 W
Robbinsville, N.J., U.S.	208	40.13 N	74.37 W
Robbinsville, N.C., U.S.	192	35.19 N	83.48 W
Robbio	62	45.17 N	8.35 E
Robe, Austl.	166	37.10 S	139.45 E
Robe, Ityo.	144	7.07 N	40.02 E
Robe ≃	48	53.38 N	9.16 W
Robe, Mount ▲	168	31.40 S	141.22 E
Robecchetto con Induno	266b	45.32 N	8.46 E
Robecco d'Oglio	64	45.15 N	10.18 E
Robecco sul Naviglio	64	45.26 N	8.53 E
Röbel	54	53.23 N	12.36 E
Rober	194	31.40 N	93.58 W
Röbergel ▲²	58	46.53 N	9.56 E
Robert, Havre du c	240e	14.40 N	60.56 W
Robert ≃	92	32.43 N	84.00 W
Roberta	192	32.43 N	84.01 W
Robert E. Lee Birthplace ⊥	208	38.10 N	76.49 W
Robert E. Lee's Memorial Stadium ◆	284c	38.53 N	76.58 W

		English	Deutsch	Español	Français	Português
▲		Mountain	Berg	Montaña	Montagne	Montanha
▲		Mountains	Gebirge	Montañas	Montagnes	Montanhas
⋊		Pass	Paß	Paso	Col	Passo
V		Valley, Canyon	Tal, Cañon	Valle, Cañón	Vallée, Canyon	Vale, Canhão
▵		Plain	Ebene	Llano	Plaine	Planície
▸		Cape	Kap	Cabo	Cap	Cabo
I		Island	Insel	Isla	Île	Ilha
II		Islands	Inseln	Islas	Îles	Ilhas
⊥		Other Topographic Features	Andere Topographische Objekte	Otros Elementos Topográficos	Autres données topographiques	Outros acidentes topográficos

ESPAÑOL — Nombre · Página · Lat.°' · Long.°' W = Oeste
FRANÇAIS — Nom · Page · Lat.°' · Long.°' W = Ouest
PORTUGUÊS — Nome · Página · Lat.°' · Long.°' W = Oeste

Robert H. Treman State Park ♦	210	42.24 N	76.35 W
Robert Lee	196	31.54 N	100.29 W
Robert Louis Stevenson Memorial State Park ♦	226	38.40 N	122.36 W
Robert Louis Stevenson's Tomb ⊥	175a	13.50 S	171.44 W
Robert Morse College ʊ[2]	279b	40.31 N	80.12 W
Robert Moses State Park ♦	210	40.37 N	73.16 W
Robert Mueller Municipal Airport ⊠	222	30.18 N	97.42 W
Roberto Payró	258	35.10 S	57.39 W
Robert Point ›	168a	32.31 S	115.42 E
Roberts, Id., U.S.	202	43.43 N	112.07 W
Roberts, Il., U.S.	216	40.37 N	88.11 W
Roberts, Mt., U.S.	202	45.21 N	109.10 W
Roberts, Mount ∧	171a	28.13 S	152.28 E
Roberts, Point ›	224	49.00 N	123.06 W
Robert's Arm	186	49.29 N	55.49 W
Robertsbridge	42	50.59 N	0.29 E
Roberts Canyon V	280	34.11 N	117.54 W
Roberts Creek Mountain ∧	204	39.52 N	116.18 W
Robertsdale, Al., U.S.	194	30.33 N	87.42 W
Robertsdale, Pa., U.S.	214	40.11 N	78.06 W
Robertsfield	150	6.15 N	10.24 W
Robertsfors	26	64.11 N	20.51 E
Robertsganj	124	24.42 N	83.04 E
Robertsham ◄[8]	273d	26.15 S	28.00 E
Robertsholm	40	60.35 N	76.16 E
Robert S. Kerr Lake ⊜[1]	194	35.25 N	95.00 W
Roberts Mountain ∧	180	60.03 N	166.16 W
Robertson, Austl.	170	34.35 S	150.35 E
Robertson, S. Afr.	158	33.46 S	19.50 E
Robertson □[6], Ky., U.S.	218	38.32 N	84.04 W
Robertson □[6], Tx., U.S.	222	31.00 N	96.30 W
Robertson, Lac ⊜	186	51.00 N	59.10 W
Robertson Bay ⊂	9	71.25 S	170.00 E
Robertson Range ⋏	162	23.10 S	121.00 E
Robertsonville	206	46.09 N	71.13 W
Roberts Park	278	41.44 N	87.49 W
Roberts Peak ∧	182	52.57 N	120.32 W
Robertsport	150	6.45 N	11.22 W
Robertstown	168b	34.00 S	139.05 E
Robertsville	214	40.46 N	81.11 W
Robertville	56	50.27 N	6.07 E
Roberval	176	48.31 N	72.13 W
Robin Hood's Bay	44	54.25 N	0.33 W
Robins Air Force Base ■	192	32.38 N	83.35 W
Robins Island I	207	40.58 N	72.28 W
Robinson, Il., U.S.	194	39.00 N	87.44 W
Robinson, Tx., U.S.	222	31.28 N	97.06 W
Robinson ≃	164	16.03 S	137.16 E
Robinson, Lake ⊜[1]	192	34.26 N	80.10 W
Robinson Brook ≃	283	43.02 N	71.13 W
Robinson Creek ≃	226	38.16 N	119.15 W
Róbinson Crusoe, Isla (Isla Más a Tierra) I	244	33.38 S	78.52 W
Robinson Gorge National Park ♦	166	25.15 S	149.10 E
Robinson Lake ⊜	222	29.35 N	94.36 W
Robinson Lake Aerodrome ⊠	273d	26.08 S	27.42 E
Robinson Pond ⊜	283	42.48 N	71.23 W
Robinson Range ⋏	162	25.45 S	119.00 E
Robinson Run ≃	279b	40.23 N	80.06 W
Robinson Run, North Branch ≃	279b	40.23 N	80.11 W
Robinsons	186	48.15 N	58.48 W
Robinvale	166	34.36 S	142.46 E
Robleda	34	40.23 N	6.36 W
Robledo	34	38.46 N	2.26 W
Roblin	184	51.14 N	101.21 W
Roboré	248	18.20 S	59.45 W
Röbrinken	40	58.36 N	15.53 E
Rob Roy Island I	175e	7.25 S	157.35 E
Robson, Mount ∧	182	53.07 N	119.09 W
Robstown	196	27.47 N	97.40 W
Roby, Eng., U.K.	262	53.25 N	2.51 W
Roby, Il., U.S.	219	39.44 N	89.24 W
Roby, Tx., U.S.	196	32.44 N	100.22 W
Roby Mill	262	53.34 N	2.44 W
Roca, Cabo da ›	34	38.47 N	9.30 W
Roçado	250	6.40 S	44.19 W
Rocafuerte	246	0.55 S	80.28 W
Roça Grande	256	21.36 S	42.58 W
Rocanville	184	50.24 N	101.43 W
Roca Partida, Isla I	232	19.01 N	112.02 W
Roca Partida, Punta ›	234	18.42 N	95.10 W
Rocas, Atol das I[1]	250	3.52 S	33.59 W
Roccabernarda	68	39.08 N	16.52 E
Roccacasale	66	42.07 N	13.53 E
Roccadaspide	68	40.26 N	15.12 E
Rocca di Cambio	66	42.14 N	13.29 E
Rocca di Mezzo	66	42.12 N	13.31 E
Rocca di Neto	68	39.11 N	17.00 E
Rocca di Papa	66	41.46 N	12.42 E
Roccafluvione	66	42.51 N	13.29 E
Roccagloriosa	68	40.06 N	15.26 E
Roccalbegna	66	42.47 N	11.30 E
Roccalumera	70	37.58 N	15.24 E
Rocca Massima	66	41.41 N	12.55 E
Roccamena	70	37.50 N	13.09 E
Roccamonfina	68	41.17 N	13.59 E
Roccanova	68	40.13 N	16.12 E
Roccapalumba	70	37.48 N	13.39 E
Rocca Pia	66	41.56 N	13.59 E
Rocca Pietore	64	46.26 N	11.59 E
Roccaprebalza	64	44.31 N	9.57 E
Rocca Priora	267a	41.48 N	12.45 E
Roccaraso	66	41.51 N	14.05 E
Rocca San Casciano	66	44.03 N	11.50 E
Rocca Santa Maria	66	42.41 N	13.30 E
Roccasecca	66	41.33 N	13.40 E
Roccasecca dei Volsci	66	41.29 N	13.13 E
Roccastrada	66	43.00 N	11.10 E
Roccavione	62	44.19 N	7.29 E
Roccavivara	66	41.50 N	14.36 E
Roccelito, Monte ∧	70	37.50 N	13.47 E
Roccella Ionica	68	38.19 N	16.24 E
Roccella Valdemone	70	37.56 N	15.00 E
Rocchetta Sant'Antonio	68	41.06 N	15.27 E
Rocciamelone ∧	62	45.12 N	7.05 E
Ročegda	24	62.42 N	43.23 E
Roch ≃	44	53.34 N	2.18 W
Rocha, Bra.	256	21.28 S	45.49 W
Rocha, Ur.	252	34.29 S	54.20 W
Rocha Miranda ◄[8]	287a	22.52 S	43.22 W
Rocha Sobrinho	287a	22.47 S	43.25 W
Rochdale, Eng., U.K.	44	53.38 N	2.09 W
Rochdale, Ma., U.S.	207	42.11 N	71.54 W
Rochdale, N.Y., U.S.	210	41.43 N	73.50 W
Rochdale □[8]	262	53.37 N	2.08 W
Rochdale Canal ≍	262	53.43 N	1.54 W
Roche	42	50.24 N	4.48 W
Rochebrune, Grand Pic de ∧	62	44.49 N	6.51 E
Rochechouart	32	45.50 N	0.50 E
Rochedinho	255	20.14 S	54.33 W
Rochedo	255	19.57 S	54.52 W
Rochedo de Minas	256	21.38 S	43.01 W
Rochefort, Bel.	56	50.10 N	5.13 E
Rochefort, Fr.	32	45.57 N	0.58 W
Rochefort-en-Yvelines	50	48.35 N	1.59 E
Rochefort-Montagne	32	45.41 N	2.48 E
Rochefort-sur-Nenon	58	47.07 N	5.34 E
Roche Harbor	224	48.36 N	123.08 W
Rochehaut	56	49.51 N	5.00 E
Roche-la-Molière	62	45.26 N	4.19 E
Roche-lez-Beaupré	58	47.17 N	6.07 E
Rochelle, Ga., U.S.	192	31.57 N	83.27 W
Rochelle, Il., U.S.	216	41.55 N	89.04 W
Rochelle, Tx., U.S.	196	31.13 N	99.13 W
Rochelle Park	276	40.54 N	74.04 W
Rochemaure	62	44.35 N	4.42 E
Roche-Percée	184	49.03 N	102.45 W
Rochepot, Château de la ⊥	58	46.57 N	4.40 E
Rocher Fendu, Rapides du ∟	275a	45.19 N	73.57 W
Rochester, Austl.	166	36.22 S	144.42 E
Rochester, Eng., U.K.	42	51.24 N	0.30 E
Rochester, Eng., U.K.	44	55.16 N	2.16 W
Rochester, Il., U.S.	219	39.45 N	89.32 W
Rochester, In., U.S.	216	41.03 N	86.12 W
Rochester, Ma., U.S.	207	41.43 N	70.49 W
Rochester, Mi., U.S.	214	42.40 N	83.08 W
Rochester, Mn., U.S.	190	44.01 N	92.28 W
Rochester, N.H., U.S.	188	43.18 N	70.58 W
Rochester, N.Y., U.S.	210	43.09 N	77.36 W
Rochester, Oh., U.S.	214	41.07 N	82.18 W
Rochester, Pa., U.S.	214	40.42 N	80.17 W
Rochester, Tx., U.S.	196	33.19 N	99.51 W
Rochester, Wa., U.S.	224	46.49 N	123.05 W
Rochester, Wi., U.S.	216	42.44 N	88.13 W
Rochester City Airport ⊠	260	51.21 N	0.30 E
Rochester Hills	214	42.40 N	83.09 W
Rochester Mills	214	40.49 N	78.59 W
Rochester-Monroe County Airport ⊠	210	43.07 N	77.40 W
Rochester-Utica State Recreation Area ♦	214	42.39 N	83.04 W
Rochetaillée	62	45.25 N	4.27 E
Rocheuses → Rocky Mountains ⋏	16	48.00 N	116.00 W
Rochford	42	51.36 N	0.43 E
Rochford □[8]	260	51.36 N	0.39 E
Rochfortbridge	48	53.23 N	7.17 W
Rochlitz	54	51.03 N	12.47 E
Rochon, Lac ⊜	206	46.43 N	75.14 W
Rock	190	46.04 N	87.09 W
Rock □[6]	216	42.41 N	89.05 W
Rock ≃, U.S.	190	41.29 N	90.37 W
Rock ≃, U.S.	198	43.05 N	96.27 W
Rockall I	22	57.35 N	13.48 W
Rockall Rise ✣[3]	10	59.00 N	14.00 W
Rockanje	52	51.53 N	4.05 E
Rockaway, N.J., U.S.	210	40.54 N	74.30 W
Rockaway, Or., U.S.	224	45.36 N	123.56 W
Rockaway ≃	210	40.51 N	74.21 W
Rockaway Inlet ⊂	276	40.34 N	73.55 W
Rockaway Neck	276	40.51 N	74.21 W
Rockaway Park ◄[8]	276	40.35 N	73.50 W
Rockaway Point ◄[8]	276	40.33 N	73.55 W
Rockaway Point ›	276	40.33 N	73.56 W
Rockaways' Playland ♦	276	40.35 N	73.49 W
Rockbank	274b	37.43 S	144.39 E
Rock Bay	182	50.20 N	125.29 W
Rockbridge	219	39.16 N	90.12 W
Rock Bridge State Park ♦	219	38.53 N	92.19 W
Rock Brook ≃	276	40.25 N	74.40 W
Rock Candy Mountain ∧	224	47.01 N	123.07 W
Rockcastle ≃	192	36.58 N	84.21 W
Rock City Falls	210	43.04 N	73.55 W
Rockcliffe Park	212	45.27 N	75.41 W
Rockcorry	48	54.07 N	7.01 W
Rock Creek, B.C., Can.	182	49.06 N	118.58 W
Rock Creek, Oh., U.S.	214	41.39 N	80.51 W
Rock Creek ≃, N.A.	202	48.25 N	107.05 W
Rock Creek ≃, U.S.	208	39.43 N	77.13 W
Rock Creek ≃, U.S.	284c	38.54 N	77.04 W
Rock Creek ≃, Ca., U.S.	226	37.55 N	120.58 W
Rock Creek ≃, Co., U.S.	198	40.20 N	102.31 W
Rock Creek ≃, Il., U.S.	216	41.12 N	87.59 W
Rock Creek ≃, In., U.S.	216	40.42 N	86.35 W
Rock Creek ≃, In., U.S.	216	40.49 N	85.23 W
Rock Creek ≃, Mt., U.S.	202	45.31 N	108.49 W
Rock Creek ≃, Mt., U.S.	202	46.43 N	113.40 W
Rock Creek ≃, Nv., U.S.	204	40.39 N	116.54 W
Rock Creek ≃, Or., U.S.	202	45.34 N	120.25 W
Rock Creek ≃, Or., U.S.	202	42.39 N	119.08 W
Rock Creek ≃, Or., U.S.	224	45.51 N	123.12 W
Rock Creek ≃, S.D., U.S.	198	43.44 N	97.58 W
Rock Creek ≃, Ut,. U.S.	200	40.17 N	110.30 W
Rock Creek ≃, Wa., U.S.	202	46.55 N	117.56 W
Rock Creek ≃, Wa., U.S.	202	45.42 N	120.29 W
Rock Creek ≃, Wy., U.S.	200	41.54 N	106.08 W
Rock Creek Butte ∧	202	44.49 N	118.07 W
Rock Creek Hills	284c	39.01 N	77.04 W
Rock Creek Park ♦	284c	38.58 N	77.03 W
Rock Cut State Park ♦	216	42.20 N	89.00 W
Rockdale, Austl.	170	33.57 S	151.08 E
Rockdale, Il., U.S.	216	41.30 N	88.06 W
Rockdale, Md., U.S.	284b	39.21 N	76.45 W
Rockdale, Pa., U.S.	285	39.53 N	75.26 W
Rockdale, Tx., U.S.	222	30.39 N	97.00 W
Rockdale, W.V., U.S.	214	40.18 N	80.35 W
Rockefeller Center ʊ	276	40.45 N	74.00 W
Rockefeller Park ♦	279a	41.32 N	81.38 W
Rockefeller Plateau ⋏[1]	9	80.00 S	135.00 W
Rockenhausen	56	49.38 N	7.49 E
Rockensüss	56	51.03 N	9.50 E
Rockfall	207	41.31 N	72.41 W
Rock Falls	190	41.46 N	89.41 W
Rock Ferry	262	53.22 N	3.00 W
Rockfield	216	40.38 N	86.34 W
Rock Flat	171b	36.21 S	149.12 E
Rock Flat Creek ≃	171b	36.07 S	149.12 E
Rockford, Al., U.S.	194	32.53 N	86.13 W
Rockford, Il., U.S.	216	42.16 N	89.05 W
Rockford, In., U.S.	218	38.59 N	85.54 W
Rockford, Ia., U.S.	190	43.03 N	92.56 W
Rockford, Mi., U.S.	190	43.07 N	85.33 W
Rockford, Oh., U.S.	216	40.41 N	84.38 W
Rockford, Tn., U.S.	192	35.49 N	83.56 W
Rock Forest	206	45.20 N	71.59 W
Rockglen, Sk., Can.	184	49.10 N	105.57 W
Rock Glen, N.Y., U.S.	210	42.41 N	78.07 W
Rock Hall	208	39.08 N	76.14 W
Rockhammar	40	59.32 N	15.26 E
Rockhampton	166	23.23 S	150.31 E
Rockhampton Downs	162	18.57 S	135.01 E
Rock Hill, N.Y., U.S.	210	41.38 N	74.36 W
Rock Hill, S.C., U.S.	192	34.55 N	81.01 W
Rockhill Furnace	214	40.15 N	77.54 W
Rockingham, Austl.	168a	32.17 S	115.44 E
Rockingham, N.C., U.S.	192	34.56 N	79.46 W
Rockingham □[6]	207	42.50 N	71.15 W
Rockingham Bay ⊂	166	18.10 S	146.05 E
Rockingham Forest ◄[3]	42	52.30 N	0.37 W
Rockingham Park ♦	283	42.47 N	71.14 W
Rockingham State Historic Site ⊥	276	40.24 N	74.37 W
Rock Island, P.Q., Can.	206	45.01 N	72.06 W
Rock Island, Il., U.S.	190	41.30 N	90.34 W
Rock Island, Tx., U.S.	222	29.32 N	96.35 W
Rocklake	198	48.47 N	99.15 W
Rock Lake ⊜, Mb., Can.	184	49.11 N	99.12 W
Rock Lake ⊜, On., Can.	212	45.30 N	78.23 W
Rock Lake ⊜, Il., U.S.	278	41.40 N	88.03 W
Rock Lake ⊜, N.D., U.S.	198	48.50 N	99.10 W
Rock Lake ⊜, Wi., U.S.	216	43.04 N	88.56 W
Rockland, On., Can.	188	45.33 N	75.17 W
Rockland, De., U.S.	285	39.47 N	75.34 W
Rockland, Id., U.S.	202	42.34 N	112.52 W
Rockland, Me., U.S.	188	44.06 N	69.06 W
Rockland, Ma., U.S.	207	42.07 N	70.55 W
Rockland, Mi., U.S.	190	46.44 N	89.10 W
Rockland, N.Y., U.S.	210	41.58 N	74.54 W
Rockland □[6]	210	41.09 N	73.59 W
Rockland Lake	276	41.09 N	73.55 W
Rockland Lake ⊜	276	41.08 N	73.55 W
Rockland Lake State Park ♦	276	41.08 N	73.55 W
Rocklands Reservoir ⊜[1]	166	37.15 S	142.00 E
Rockledge, Fl., U.S.	220	28.21 N	80.43 W
Rockledge, Pa., U.S.	285	40.03 N	75.05 W
Rockleigh	276	41.00 N	73.55 W
Rocklin	226	38.47 N	121.14 W
Rockmart	192	34.00 N	85.02 W
Rock Meadow Brook ≃	283	42.16 N	71.13 W
Rock of Cashel ⊥	48	52.31 N	7.53 W
Rock Point	208	38.16 N	76.50 W
Rock Point Provincial Park ♦	212	42.51 N	79.33 W
Rock Pond ⊜	283	42.44 N	71.00 W
Rockport, Il., U.S.	219	39.32 N	91.00 W
Rockport, Ky., U.S.	194	37.20 N	86.59 W
Rockport, Me., U.S.	188	44.11 N	69.04 W
Rockport, Ma., U.S.	207	42.39 N	70.37 W
Rock Port, Mo., U.S.	194	40.24 N	95.30 W
Rockport, Tx., U.S.	196	28.01 N	97.03 W
Rock Rapids	198	43.25 N	96.10 W
Rock River	200	41.44 N	105.58 W
Rock Run	208	39.59 N	75.50 W
Rock Run ≃	284c	38.58 N	77.11 W
Rock Sound	238	24.54 N	76.12 W
Rocksprings, Tx., U.S.	196	30.00 N	100.12 W
Rock Springs, Wy., U.S.	200	41.35 N	109.12 W
Rockstone	246	5.59 N	58.33 W
Rock Stream	210	42.28 N	76.56 W
Rockton, Il., U.S.	216	42.27 N	89.04 W
Rockton, Pa., U.S.	214	41.05 N	78.39 W
Rock Valley	198	43.12 N	96.17 W
Rockville, N.Z.	172	40.44 S	172.38 E
Rockville, Ct., U.S.	207	41.52 N	72.27 W
Rockville, In., U.S.	194	39.45 N	87.13 W
Rockville, Md., U.S.	208	39.05 N	77.09 W
Rockville, Ma., U.S.	283	42.08 N	71.21 W
Rockville, Pa., U.S.	208	40.20 N	76.54 W
Rockville, R.I., U.S.	207	41.27 N	71.30 W
Rockville Centre	210	40.39 N	73.38 W
Rockwall	222	32.55 N	96.27 W
Rockwall □[6]	222	32.55 N	96.23 W
Rockwell, Ia., U.S.	190	42.59 N	93.11 W
Rockwell, N.C., U.S.	192	35.33 N	80.24 W
Rockwell, Lake ⊜	214	41.12 N	81.19 W
Rockwell City	198	42.23 N	94.38 W
Rockwell International Corporation ʊ[3]	280	33.52 N	117.51 W
Rockwood, On., Can.	212	43.37 N	80.08 W
Rockwood, Me., U.S.	188	45.41 N	69.44 W
Rockwood, Mi., U.S.	216	42.04 N	83.14 W
Rockwood, Or., U.S.	224	45.31 N	122.28 W
Rockwood, Pa., U.S.	188	39.54 N	79.09 W
Rockwood, Tn., U.S.	192	35.51 N	84.41 W
Rockwood Lake ⊜	276	41.06 N	73.38 W
Rockwood Lake Brook ≃	276	41.03 N	73.36 W
Rocky	196	35.09 N	99.03 W
Rocky ≃, Ab., Can.	182	53.08 N	117.59 W
Rocky ≃, Mi., U.S.	216	41.57 N	85.39 W
Rocky ≃, N.C., U.S.	192	35.37 N	79.09 W
Rocky ≃, Oh., U.S.	214	41.30 N	81.49 W
Rocky, East Branch ≃	279a	41.24 N	81.53 W
Rocky, West Branch ≃	214	41.24 N	81.53 W
Rocky Arroyo V	196	32.32 N	104.21 W
Rocky Boy's Indian Reservation ◄[4]	202	48.18 N	109.45 W
Rocky Branch ≃	284c	38.53 N	77.19 W
Rocky Cape National Park ♦	166	40.56 S	145.35 E
Rocky Comfort Creek ≃	192	32.59 N	82.25 W
Rocky Coulee V	202	47.10 N	119.16 W
Rocky Creek ≃	192	35.53 N	80.47 W
Rockyford, Ab., Can.	182	51.13 N	113.08 W
Rocky Ford, Co., U.S.	198	38.06 N	103.43 W
Rocky Ford Creek ≃	216	41.19 N	83.37 W
Rocky Fork Lake ⊜	218	39.11 N	83.28 W
Rocky Fork State Park ♦	218	39.11 N	83.30 W
Rocky Gorge Reservoir ⊜[1]	208	39.07 N	76.54 W
Rocky Grove	214	41.25 N	79.49 W
Rocky Gully	162	34.30 S	116.48 E
Rocky Harbour	186	49.36 N	57.55 W
Rocky Harbour ⊂	271d	22.20 N	114.19 E
Rocky Hill, Ct., U.S.	207	41.40 N	72.39 W
Rocky Hill, N.J., U.S.	276	40.24 N	74.38 W
Rocky Island Lake ⊜[1]	190	46.56 N	83.04 W
Rocky Lake ⊜	184	54.08 N	101.30 W
Rocky Mount, N.C., U.S.	192	35.57 N	77.48 W
Rocky Mount, Va., U.S.	192	36.59 N	79.53 W
Rocky Mountain ∧	202	47.49 N	112.49 W
Rocky Mountain House	182	52.22 N	114.55 W
Rocky Mountain National Park ♦	200	40.19 N	105.42 W
Rocky Mountains ⋏	16	48.00 N	116.00 W
Rocky Point, N.Y., U.S.	207	40.57 N	72.56 W
Rocky Point, Wa., U.S.	224	47.35 N	122.41 W
Rocky Point ›, Ba.	192	26.00 N	77.25 W
Rocky Point ›, Ire.	48	54.42 N	8.48 W
Rocky Point ›, Namibia	156	19.03 S	12.30 E
Rocky Point ›, Norf. I.	174c	29.03 S	167.55 E
Rocky Point ›, Ak., U.S.	180	64.25 N	163.10 W
Rocky Point ›, Ma., U.S.	207	41.57 N	70.35 W
Rocky Point ›, N.Y., U.S.	276	40.55 N	73.32 W
Rocky Ridge	214	41.32 N	83.13 W
Rocky Ridge ∧	282	37.48 N	122.03 W
Rocky River	214	41.28 N	81.50 W
Rocky River Reservation ♦	279a	41.27 N	81.50 W
Rocky Run ≃, N.D., U.S.	198	47.38 N	99.02 W
Rocky Run ≃, Pa., U.S.	285	39.54 N	75.28 W
Rocky Run ≃, Va., U.S.	284c	38.58 N	77.15 W
Rocky Saugeen ≃	212	44.13 N	80.53 W
Rocky Top ∧	202	44.47 N	122.17 W
Roclenge-sur-Geer	56	50.45 N	5.36 E
Rocosas, Montañas → Rocky Mountains ⋏	16	48.00 N	116.00 W
Rocquencourt	261	48.50 N	2.07 E
Rocroi	50	49.55 N	4.31 E
Roda	192	36.58 N	82.49 W
Roda ≃	54	50.52 N	11.44 E
Rodach	56	50.20 N	10.46 E
Rodach ≃, Dtsch.	54	50.09 N	11.10 E
Rodach ≃, Dtsch.	56	50.08 N	10.52 E
Rodakove	83	48.33 N	39.02 E
Rodalben	56	49.14 N	7.38 E
Rodalquilar	34	37.40 N	2.08 W
Rodas	240p	22.20 N	80.33 W
Rodas → Ródhos I	38	36.10 N	28.00 E
Rodaun ◄[8]	264b	48.08 N	16.16 E
Rødberg	26	60.16 N	8.58 E
Rødby	41	54.42 N	11.24 E
Rødbyhavn	41	54.39 N	11.21 E
Roddickton	186	50.52 N	56.08 W
Rødding	41	55.23 N	9.06 E
Rodeiro	256	21.12 S	42.52 W
Rødekro	41	55.04 N	9.21 E
Rodel	46	57.41 N	7.05 W
Roden	52	53.07 N	6.26 E
Roden ≃	42	52.43 N	2.36 W
Rodenberg	52	52.18 N	9.21 E
Rodenkirchen, Dtsch.	52	53.24 N	8.26 E
Rodenkirchen, Dtsch.	56	50.54 N	6.59 E
Rödentel	54	50.17 N	11.01 E
Rodeo, Arg.	252	30.12 S	69.06 W
Rodeo, Méx.	232	25.11 N	104.34 W
Rodeo, Ca., U.S.	226	38.01 N	122.15 W
Rodeo, N.M., U.S.	200	31.50 N	109.01 W
Rodeo Lagoon ⊂	282	37.50 N	122.31 W
Röderau	54	51.19 N	13.19 E
Roderick ≃	162	26.57 S	116.13 E
Roderick Island I	182	52.40 N	128.22 W
Rödermark	56	49.59 N	8.50 E
Rodewisch	54	50.32 N	12.24 E
Rodez	32	44.21 N	2.35 E
Rodgau	56	50.02 N	8.54 E
Rodheim-Bieber	56	50.37 N	8.35 E
Rodhópis, Orosirá → Rhodope Mountains ⋏	38	41.30 N	24.30 E
Ródhos (Rhodes)	38	36.26 N	28.13 E
Ródhos (Rhodes) I	38	36.10 N	28.00 E
Rodi Garganico	68	41.55 N	15.53 E
Roding	60	49.12 N	12.32 E
Roding ≃	42	51.31 N	0.06 E
Rodinka	80	57.24 N	43.34 E
Rodino, Ross.	76	58.57 N	44.59 E
Rodino, Ross.	86	52.30 N	80.15 E
Rodionovo-Nesvetajskaja	83	47.36 N	39.42 E
Rodleben	54	51.54 N	12.12 E
Rodman	180	57.28 N	135.21 W
Rodman Naval Station ■	236	8.56 N	79.36 W
Rodn'a	76	56.22 N	34.55 E
Rodnei, Munții ⋏	38	47.35 N	24.40 E
Rodney, On., Can.	214	42.34 N	81.41 W
Rodney, Ms., U.S.	194	31.51 N	91.11 W
Rodney, Cape ›, N.Z.	172	36.17 S	174.49 E
Rodney, Cape ›, Ak., U.S.	180	64.39 N	166.24 W
Rodney Bay ⊂	241f	14.05 N	60.58 W
Rodney Village	208	39.07 N	75.31 W
Rodničok	80	51.26 N	42.54 E
Rodniki, Ross.	80	57.06 N	41.44 E
Rodniki, Ross.	265b	55.39 N	38.04 E
Rodnikovka	86	50.39 N	57.12 E
Rodolfo, Lago → Rudolf, Lake ⊜	144	3.30 N	36.05 E
Rodonit, Kep i ›	38	41.35 N	19.27 E
Rødovre	41	55.41 N	12.29 E
Rodrigo de Freitas, Lagoa ⊂	287a	22.58 S	43.13 W
Rodrigues I	12	19.42 S	63.25 E
Rodríguez, Méx.	196	27.10 N	100.01 W
Rodríguez, Ur.	258	34.23 S	56.33 W
Rodríguez, Arroyo ≃	288	34.52 S	58.02 W
Roduco	208	36.27 N	76.48 W
Rødven	26	62.38 N	7.33 E
Rødvig	41	55.15 N	12.23 E
Rodyns'ke	83	48.25 N	37.19 E
Roe ≃	48	55.07 N	6.59 W
Roebling	208	40.06 N	74.47 W
Roebourne	162	20.47 S	117.09 E
Roebuck Bay ⊂	162	18.04 S	122.17 E
Roehampton ◄[8]	260	51.27 N	0.14 W
Roe Island I	282	38.04 N	122.02 W
Roeland Park	198	39.02 N	94.37 W
Roelands	168a	33.18 S	115.50 E
Roeliff Jansen Kill ≃	210	42.11 N	73.52 W
Roelofarendsveen	52	52.12 N	4.38 E
Roelofskamp	158	26.10 S	24.24 E
Roen, Monte ∧	64	46.22 N	11.11 E
Roer (Rur) ≃	56	51.12 N	5.59 E
Roermond	52	51.12 N	6.00 E
Roesbrugge-Haringe	50	50.55 N	2.37 E
Roeselare (Roulers)	50	50.57 N	3.08 E
Roesinger, Lake ⊜	224	47.58 N	121.55 W
Roessleville	210	42.41 N	73.48 W
Roes Welcome Sound ⊍	176	64.00 N	88.00 W
Roetgen	56	50.39 N	6.12 E
Rœulx	50	50.30 N	4.06 E
Roff	196	34.37 N	96.50 W
Röfors	40	58.57 N	14.37 E
Rofrano	68	40.12 N	15.25 E
Rogačevo	82	56.26 N	37.10 E
Rogačovka	78	51.30 N	39.34 E
Rogagua, Laguna ⊜	248	13.43 S	66.54 W
Rogaguado, Laguna ⊜	248	12.52 S	65.43 W
Rogaland □[6]	26	59.00 N	6.15 E
Rogalik	83	48.56 N	40.03 E
Rogans Hill	274a	33.44 S	151.01 E
Rogan's Seat ∧	44	54.25 N	2.07 W
Rogart	46	58.00 N	4.08 W
Rogäsen	54	52.19 N	12.20 E
Rogaška Slatina	36	46.14 N	15.38 E
Rogatica	38	43.48 N	19.00 E
Rogätz	54	52.19 N	11.46 E
Rogen ⊜	26	62.19 N	12.23 E
Roger, Lac ⊜	190	47.50 N	78.51 W
Roger Island I	283	42.43 N	70.50 W
Rogers, Ar., U.S.	194	36.19 N	94.07 W
Rogers, Ct., U.S.	207	41.50 N	71.54 W
Rogers, Oh., U.S.	214	40.48 N	80.38 W
Rogers, Tx., U.S.	222	30.55 N	97.13 W
Rogers, Mount ∧	192	36.39 N	81.33 W
Rogers City	190	45.25 N	83.49 W
Rogers Lake ⊜	228	34.52 N	117.51 W
Rogers Park ◄[8]	278	42.01 N	87.40 W
Rogers Pass)(	182	51.17 N	117.31 W
Rogersville, N.B., Can.	186	46.44 N	65.26 W
Rogersville, Al., U.S.	194	34.49 N	87.17 W
Rogersville, Tn., U.S.	192	36.24 N	83.00 W
Roggenburg	58	48.17 N	10.14 E
Roggeveldberge ⋏	158	32.17 S	20.08 E
Roggewein, Cabo ›	174z	27.07 S	109.15 W
Roggiano Gravina	68	39.37 N	16.09 E
Roghudi	68	38.03 N	15.55 E
Rogliano, Fr.	36	42.57 N	9.25 E
Rogliano, It.	68	39.11 N	16.20 E
Rognac	62	43.29 N	5.14 E
Rognedino	76	53.48 N	33.33 E
Rögnitz ≃	54	53.19 N	10.57 E
Rognon ≃	58	48.23 N	5.10 E
Rogny	50	47.45 N	2.53 E
Rogojampi	115a	8.19 S	114.17 E
Rogovatoje	78	51.14 N	38.22 E
Rogovo	82	55.13 N	37.05 E
Rogovskaja	78	45.44 N	38.44 E
Rogovskoje	80	58.33 N	50.43 E
Rogožkino	83	47.10 N	39.21 E
Rogoźno	30	52.46 N	17.00 E
Rogue ≃, Mi., U.S.	190	43.04 N	85.35 W
Rogue ≃, Or., U.S.	202	42.26 N	124.25 W
Rogue River	202	42.26 N	123.10 W
Rohan'	78	49.54 N	36.29 E
Rohatyn	78	49.25 N	24.37 E
Rohdenhaus	263	51.18 N	7.01 E
Rohilkhand Plains ≚	124	28.20 N	79.30 E
Rohinjan	272c	19.06 N	73.04 E
Rohitpur	126	23.42 N	90.19 E
Rohl ≃	140	6.22 N	29.46 E
Röhlinghausen ◄[8]	263	51.30 N	7.10 E
Rohnert Park	226	38.20 N	122.42 W
Rohoziv	78	50.14 N	31.03 E
Rohrbach in Oberösterreich	60	48.34 N	13.59 E
Rohrbach-lès-Bitche	56	49.03 N	7.16 E
Rohrbeck	264a	52.32 N	13.02 E
Rohrberg	54	52.42 N	11.02 E
Röhrenfurth	56	51.09 N	9.32 E
Rohri	120	27.41 N	68.54 E
Rohr in Niederbayern	60	48.46 N	11.58 E
Röhrmoos	60	48.20 N	11.28 E
Röhrnbach	60	48.44 N	13.32 E
Röhrsdorf	54	50.51 N	12.50 E
Rohtak	123	28.54 N	76.34 E
Rohunta, Laguna ⊂	236	15.12 N	83.30 W
Roi, Île du → King Island I	166	39.50 S	144.00 E
Roia (Roya) ≃	62	43.48 N	7.35 E
Roi Et	110	16.03 N	103.40 E
Roi Georges, Îles du II	14	14.32 S	145.08 W
Roi Léopold, Monts du → King Leopold Ranges ⋏	160	17.30 S	125.45 E
Roine ⊜	26	61.24 N	24.06 E
Roinville	261	48.32 N	2.03 E
Roisel	50	49.57 N	3.06 E
Roissy	261	48.47 N	2.39 E
Roissy-en-France	261	49.00 N	2.31 E
Roitzsch	54	51.34 N	12.16 E
Roja	76	57.30 N	22.49 E
Rojas	252	34.12 S	60.44 W
Rojo → Red ≃	178	31.00 N	91.40 W
Rojo, Cabo ›, Méx.	234	21.33 N	97.20 W
Rojo, Cabo ›, P.R.	240m	17.56 N	67.11 W
Rojo, Mar → Red Sea ⍑[2]	136	20.00 N	38.00 E
Rokan	112	0.34 N	100.25 E
Rokan ≃	114	2.00 N	100.52 E
Rokan-kanan ≃	114	1.23 N	100.56 E
Rokan-kiri ≃	114	1.23 N	100.56 E
Röke	41	56.14 N	13.30 E
Rokeby National Park ♦	164	13.40 S	142.55 E
Rokel ≃	150	8.33 N	12.48 W
Rokewood	169	37.54 S	143.43 E
Rokewood Junction	169	37.51 S	143.41 E
Rokhah	120	35.16 N	69.28 E
Rokiškis	76	55.58 N	25.35 E
Rokkō-san ∧	96	34.46 N	135.16 E
Rokkō-sanchi ⋏	270	34.45 N	135.13 E
Roklum	54	52.04 N	10.44 E
Rokuan kansallispuisto ♦	26	64.32 N	26.33 E
Rokugō	94	35.29 N	138.27 E
Rokugō ◄[8]	268	35.33 N	139.43 E
Rokusei	94	36.58 N	136.52 E
Rokycany	60	49.45 N	13.36 E
Rokytná ≃	61	49.05 N	16.22 E
Rokytne, Ukr.	78	49.42 N	30.27 E
Rokytne, Ukr.	78	51.17 N	27.14 E
Rolampont	58	47.57 N	5.16 E
Roland, Mb., Can.	184	49.25 N	97.55 W
Roland, Ar., U.S.	194	34.54 N	92.29 W
Roland, Ia., U.S.	190	42.09 N	93.30 W
Roland, Lake ⊜[1]	284b	39.23 N	76.38 W
Roland C. Nickerson State Park ♦	207	41.46 N	70.03 W
Rolândia	255	23.18 S	51.22 W
Roland Park ◄[8]	284b	39.22 N	76.39 W
Roland Run ≃	284b	39.23 N	76.39 W
Rolava ≃	54	50.15 N	12.51 E
Røldal	26	59.49 N	6.48 E
Roldán	252	32.54 S	60.54 W
Roldanillo	246	4.24 N	76.09 W
Rolde	52	52.58 N	6.38 E
Roldskov ◄[3]	26	56.48 N	9.50 E
Rolette	198	48.39 N	99.50 W
Roleystone	168a	32.08 S	116.04 E
Rolfe	198	42.48 N	94.31 W
Roll, Az., U.S.	200	32.45 N	113.59 W
Roll, In., U.S.	216	40.33 N	85.23 W
Rolla, B.C., Can.	182	55.54 N	120.09 W
Rolla, Ks., U.S.	198	37.07 N	101.07 W
Rolla, Mo., U.S.	194	37.57 N	91.46 W
Rolla, N.D., U.S.	198	48.51 N	99.37 W
Rolle	58	46.28 N	6.20 E
Rolle, Passo di)(	64	46.18 N	11.47 E
Rolleboise	261	49.01 N	1.36 E
Rolleston, Austl.	166	24.28 S	148.37 E
Rolleston, N.Z.	172	43.35 S	172.23 E
Rolling Acres	284b	39.17 N	76.52 W
Rollingbay	224	47.39 N	122.30 W
Rolling Fork	194	32.54 N	90.52 W
Rolling Fork ≃	194	37.55 N	85.50 W
Rolling Hills	280	33.46 N	118.21 W
Rolling Hills Estates	280	33.47 N	118.21 W
Rolling Meadows	216	42.05 N	88.00 W
Rolling Prairie	216	41.40 N	86.37 W
Rolling River Indian Reserve ◄[4]	184	50.27 N	100.00 W
Rollingstone	166	19.03 S	146.24 E
Rollingwood	282	37.57 N	122.20 W
Rollins	182	47.54 N	114.11 W
Rollins Reservoir ⊜[1]	226	39.08 N	120.57 W
Rolvsøya I	24	71.00 N	24.00 E
Rom → Roma	66	41.54 N	12.29 E
Roma, Austl.	166	26.35 S	148.47 E
Roma (Rome), It.	66	41.54 N	12.29 E
Roma (Rome), It.	267a	41.54 N	12.29 E
Roma, Leso.	158	29.27 S	27.45 E
Roma, Tx., U.S.	196	26.25 N	99.01 W
Roma □[4]	66	41.58 N	12.40 E
Romagna □[9]	64	44.30 N	12.15 E
Romagnano Sesia	62	45.38 N	8.23 E
Romagne-sous-Montfaucon	56	49.20 N	5.05 E
Romain, Cape ›	192	33.00 N	79.22 W
Romaine ≃	176	50.18 N	63.47 W
Romainmôtier	58	46.42 N	6.29 E
Romainville	261	48.53 N	2.26 E
Romakloster	26	57.31 N	18.27 E
Roman	38	46.55 N	26.56 E
Roman ≃	42	51.51 N	0.57 E
Romanche ≃	62	45.05 N	5.43 E
Romanche Gap ✣[1]	10	0.10 S	18.15 W
Romang, Pulau I	164	7.35 S	127.26 E
Romang, Selat ⊍	164	7.30 S	127.00 E
Romania (România) □[1], Europe	22	46.00 N	25.30 E
Romania (România) □[1], Europe	38	46.00 N	25.30 E
Romankivtsi	78	48.29 N	27.13 E
Roman-Kosh, hora ∧	78	44.37 N	34.15 E
Roman Nose Mountain ∧	202	43.55 N	123.44 W
Romano, Cape ›	220	25.50 N	81.41 W
Romano, Cayo I	240p	22.04 N	77.50 W
Romano Banco	266b	45.25 N	9.06 E
Romano di Lombardia	62	45.31 N	9.45 E
Romanova	88	57.04 N	103.24 E
Romanovka, Ross.	80	51.24 N	47.23 E
Romanovka, Ross.	80	51.45 N	42.45 E
Romanovka, Ross.	80	49.47 N	45.05 E
Romanovka, Ross.	86	54.38 N	76.03 E
Romanovka, Ross.	88	53.14 N	112.46 E
Romanovka, Ross.	265a	60.03 N	30.42 E
Romanovo, Ross.	82	56.39 N	39.14 E
Romanovo, Ross.	86	52.37 N	81.14 E
Romanovo, Ross.	86	59.09 N	61.30 E
Romanovo, Ross.	86	53.58 N	80.30 E
Romans d'Isonzo	64	45.53 N	13.26 E
Romanshorn	58	47.34 N	9.22 E
Romans-sur-Isère	62	45.03 N	5.03 E
Romansville	285	39.57 N	75.45 W
Romanzof Mountains ⋏	180	69.00 N	144.00 W
Romaški	80	50.13 N	46.41 E
Romaškino	80	52.29 N	51.48 E
Romaškovo	265b	55.44 N	37.20 E
Romayor	222	30.27 N	94.50 W
Rombari	154	4.33 N	31.02 E
Romblon	116	12.35 N	122.15 E
Romblon □[4]	116	12.30 N	122.10 E
Romblon Island I	116	12.33 N	122.17 E
Romblon Passage ⊍	116	12.27 N	122.12 E
Rombo, Ilhéus do II	150a	14.58 N	24.40 W
Rome → Roma, It.	66	41.54 N	12.29 E
Rome, Ga., U.S.	192	34.15 N	85.09 W
Rome, Il., U.S.	190	40.53 N	89.30 W
Rome, Ms., U.S.	194	33.57 N	90.28 W
Rome, N.Y., U.S.	210	43.12 N	75.27 W
Rome, Oh., U.S.	214	41.36 N	80.52 W
Rome, Pa., U.S.	210	41.51 N	76.21 W
Rome, Wi., U.S.	216	42.58 N	88.38 W
Rome City	216	41.29 N	85.22 W
Romeleåsen ⋏[2]	41	55.34 N	13.33 E
Romenay	58	46.30 N	5.04 E
Romeno	64	46.24 N	11.07 E
Romentino	62	45.28 N	8.42 E
Romeo	214	42.48 N	83.00 W
Romeoville	216	41.38 N	88.05 W
Römerberg	56	49.17 N	8.24 E
Romero, Isla I	258	33.48 S	59.20 W
Römerstein	58	48.30 N	9.31 E
Rometan	128	39.56 N	64.23 E
Rometta	70	38.10 N	15.25 E
Romfartuna	40	59.44 N	16.35 E
Romford ◄[8]	260	51.35 N	0.11 E
Römhild	54	50.24 N	10.32 E
Romiley	262	53.25 N	2.05 W
Romilly, Mount ∧[2]	162	20.27 S	126.34 E
Romilly-sur-Seine	50	48.31 N	3.43 E
Romit	85	38.44 N	69.17 E
Romit, zapovednik ♦	85	38.52 N	69.20 E
Romita	234	20.52 N	101.31 W
Romitorio	267a	42.01 N	12.39 E
Rommani	148	34.34 N	6.37 W
Romme	40	60.26 N	15.30 E
Rommerskirchen	56	51.02 N	6.40 E
Romney, In., U.S.	216	40.14 N	86.54 W
Romney, W.V., U.S.	188	39.20 N	78.45 W
Romney Marsh ≡	42	51.03 N	0.55 E
Romny, Ross.	89	50.44 N	129.15 E
Romny, Ukr.	78	50.45 N	33.30 E
Rømø I	26	55.08 N	8.31 E
Romodan	78	49.59 N	33.19 E
Romodanovo	80	54.26 N	45.20 E
Romoland	228	33.45 N	117.10 W
Romont	58	46.42 N	6.55 E
Romorantin-Lanthenay	50	47.22 N	1.45 E
Rompin, Malay.	114	2.42 N	102.31 E
Rompin, Malay.	114	2.48 N	103.29 E
Rompin ≃	114	2.49 N	103.29 E
Romrod	56	50.43 N	9.13 E
Romsdalen V	26	62.15 N	8.05 E
Romsdalsfjorden ⊂[2]	26	62.39 N	7.15 E
Romsey, Austl.	169	37.21 S	144.45 E
Romsey, Eng., U.K.	42	50.59 N	1.30 W
Romsø I	41	55.31 N	10.48 E
Romulus, Mi., U.S.	216	42.13 N	83.23 W
Romulus, N.Y., U.S.	210	42.45 N	76.50 W
Røn, Nor.	26	61.03 N	9.03 E
Ron, Viet	110	17.53 N	106.27 E
Ron, Mui ›	110	18.07 N	106.27 E
Rona, Schw.	58	46.34 N	9.38 E
Rona, R.D.C.	154	2.14 N	30.52 E
Rona I, Scot., U.K.	46	57.34 N	5.59 W
Rona I, Scot., U.K.	46	59.07 N	5.49 W
Ronald	224	47.14 N	121.01 W
Ronan	202	47.31 N	114.06 W
Ronas Hill ∧[2]	46a	60.31 N	1.28 W
Ronas Voe ⊂	46a	60.32 N	1.29 W
Ronay I	46	57.29 N	7.11 W
Roncade	64	45.38 N	12.22 E
Roncador, Cayos de ✣[4]	236	13.32 N	80.03 W
Roncador, Serra do ⋏[1]	242	12.00 S	52.00 W
Roncador Reef ✣[2]	175e	6.13 S	159.22 E
Roncegno	64	46.03 N	11.25 E
Ronceverte	192	37.44 N	80.27 W
Ronchamp	58	47.42 N	6.39 E
Ronchi dei Legionari	64	45.50 N	13.30 E
Ronchin	50	50.36 N	3.06 E
Ronchis	64	45.49 N	13.00 E
Ronciglione	66	42.17 N	12.13 E
Ronco	58	46.08 N	8.44 E
Ronco Canavese	62	45.30 N	7.32 E
Roncofreddo	66	44.02 N	12.20 E
Roncone	64	45.59 N	10.40 E
Ronco Scrivia	62	44.37 N	8.59 E
Roncq	50	50.45 N	3.07 E
Rond, Sommet ∧	206	45.05 N	72.33 W
Ronda	34	36.44 N	5.10 W
Rondane ∧	26	61.55 N	9.45 E
Rondane Nasjonal Park ♦	26	61.50 N	9.50 E
Rønde	41	56.18 N	10.29 E
Ronde, Pointe ›	240d	15.33 N	61.29 W
Rondeau Harbour ⊂	214	42.18 N	81.53 W
Rondeau Provincial Park ♦	214	42.16 N	81.51 W
Rondebult	273d	26.18 S	28.14 E
Ronde Island I	241k	12.18 N	61.35 W
Rondissone	62	45.15 N	7.58 E
Rondon	255	23.23 S	52.48 W
Rondônia □[3]	248	11.00 S	63.00 W
Rondonópolis	255	16.28 S	54.38 W
Rondout	278	42.17 N	87.53 W
Rondout Creek ≃	210	41.55 N	73.53 W
Rondout Reservoir ⊜[1]	210	41.50 N	74.29 W
Rone ≃	50	50.46 N	3.27 E
Ronehamn	26	57.10 N	18.29 E
Rong ≃	102	24.32 N	109.15 E
Ronga	80	56.43 N	48.32 E
Rongai	154	0.10 S	35.51 E
Rong'an	102	25.10 N	109.20 E
Rongbaca	102	31.48 N	99.40 E
Rongchang	107	29.24 N	105.36 E
Rongcheng, Zhg.	98	37.08 N	122.23 E
Rongcheng, Zhg.	105	39.03 N	115.52 E
Rongding	107	28.57 N	103.40 E
Ronge, Lac la ⊜	184	55.10 N	105.00 W
Rongelap I[1]	14	11.20 N	166.50 E
Rongjiang	102	25.52 N	108.37 E
Rongkop	115a	8.10 S	110.45 E
Rongola	158	27.22 S	31.37 E
Rongotea	172	40.18 S	175.25 E

≃ River	Fluß	Río	Rivière	Rio
≍ Canal	Kanal	Canal	Canal	Canal
∟ Waterfall, Rapids	Wasserfall, Stromschnellen	Cascada, Rápidos	Chute d'eau, Rapides	Cascata, Rápidos
⊍ Strait	Meeresstraße	Estrecho	Détroit	Estreito
⊂ Bay, Gulf	Bucht, Golf	Bahía, Golfo	Baie, Golfe	Baía, Golfo
⊜ Lake, Lakes	See, Seen	Lago, Lagos	Lac, Lacs	Lago, Lagos
≡ Swamp	Sumpf	Pantano	Marais	Pântano
⊓ Ice Features, Glacier	Eis- und Gletscherformen	Accidentes Glaciales	Formes glaciaires	Acidentes glaciares
⍑ Other Hydrographic Features	Andere Hydrographische Objekte	Otros Elementos Hidrográficos	Autres données hydrographiques	Outros acidentes hidrográficos
✣ Submarine Features	Untermeerische Objekte	Accidentes Submarinos	Formes de relief sous-marin	Acidentes submarinos
□ Political Unit	Politische Einheit	Unidad Politica	Entité politique	Unidade política
ʊ Cultural Institution	Kulturelle Institution	Institución Cultural	Institution culturelle	Institução cultural
⊥ Historical Site	Historische Stätte	Sitio Histórico	Site historique	Sitio histórico
♦ Recreational Site	Erholungs- und Ferienort	Sitio de Recreo	Centre de loisirs	Area de Lazer
⊠ Airport	Flughafen	Aeropuerto	Aéroport	Aeroporto
■ Military Installation	Militäranlage	Instalación Militar	Installation militaire	Instalação militar
◄ Miscellaneous	Verschiedenes	Misceláneo	Divers	Diversos

ENGLISH: Name | Page | Lat.°′ | Long.°′
DEUTSCH: Name | Seite | Breite°′ | Länge°′ E = Ost

Name	Page	Lat.°′	Long.°′
Rõngu	76	58.09 N	26.15 E
Rongui, Ilha I	154	10.50 S	40.40 E
Rongwanshi	100	28.10 N	112.57 E
Rongxian, Zhg.	102	22.50 N	110.38 E
Rongxian, Zhg.	107	29.28 N	104.25 E
Ronkiti Harbor c	174r	6.48 N	158.10 E
Ronkonkoma	276	40.48 N	73.06 W
Ronkonkoma, Lake ⊜	276	40.50 N	73.07 W
Rønne	26	55.06 N	14.42 E
Rönne ≃	41	56.16 N	12.50 E
Ronneburg	54	50.51 N	12.10 E
Ronneby	26	56.12 N	15.18 E
Ronne Entrance c	9	72.30 S	74.00 W
Ronne Ice Shelf ⊓	9	78.30 S	61.00 W
Ronnenberg	52	52.20 N	9.40 E
Rönneshytta	40	58.56 N	15.02 E
Rönninge	40	59.12 N	17.44 E
Ronroni	175e	9.37 S	159.58 E
Rönsahl	263	51.07 N	7.30 E
Ronsdorf ✦[8]	263	51.14 N	7.12 E
Ronse (Renaix-Gleiche)	50	50.45 N	3.36 E
Röntgenmuseum ʊ	263	51.12 N	7.16 E
Ronuro ≃	255	11.56 S	53.33 W
Roodepoort □[5]	273d	26.10 S	27.52 E
Roodepoort-Maraisburg	158	26.11 S	27.54 E
Roodeschool	52	53.25 N	6.45 E
Roodhouse	219	39.29 N	90.22 W
Roof Butte ∧	200	36.28 N	109.05 W
Rooiberge ∧	158	28.27 S	28.26 E
Rooiboklaagte ≃	156	20.50 S	21.00 E
Rooidam	158	28.07 S	21.15 E
Rooilyf	158	28.49 S	21.57 E
Rooiwal	158	27.18 S	27.32 E
Rooks Creek ≃	216	40.57 N	88.44 W
Rookwood Cemetery ✦	274a	33.53 S	151.04 E
Roon, Pulau I	164	2.23 S	134.33 E
Rooniu, Mont ∧	174s	17.49 S	149.12 W
Roordahuizum	52	53.06 N	5.46 E
Roorkee	124	29.52 N	77.53 E
Roosboom	158	28.36 S	29.44 E
Roosendaal	52	51.32 N	4.28 E
Roosevelt, Az., U.S.	200	33.40 N	111.08 W
Roosevelt, Mn., U.S.	198	48.48 N	95.05 W
Roosevelt, N.J., U.S.	208	40.13 N	74.28 W
Roosevelt, N.Y., U.S.	276	40.40 N	73.35 W
Roosevelt, Ok., U.S.	196	34.50 N	99.01 W
Roosevelt, Ut,. U.S.	200	40.17 N	109.59 W
Roosevelt ≃	248	7.35 S	60.20 W
Roosevelt Beach	210	43.19 N	78.52 W
Roosevelt Campobello International Park ♦	186	44.52 N	66.58 W
Roosevelt Field ✦[9]	276	40.45 N	73.37 W
Roosevelt Island I	9	79.30 S	162.00 W
Roosevelt Park	216	43.11 N	86.15 W
Roosevelt Park ♦	276	40.33 N	74.21 W
Roosevelt Roads Naval Station ■	240m	18.15 N	65.38 W
Roosevelt Terrace	226	38.08 N	122.16 W
Root	58	47.07 N	8.23 E
Root ≃, N.T., Can.	180	62.50 N	123.40 W
Root ≃, Mn., U.S.	190	43.46 N	91.15 W
Root ≃, Wi., U.S.	216	42.44 N	87.47 W
Root, North Branch ≃	190	43.49 N	92.10 W
Root, South Branch ≃	190	43.44 N	91.58 W
Root Lake ⊜	184	54.04 N	101.24 W
Rootstown	214	41.05 N	81.14 W
Rooty Hill	170	33.46 S	150.50 E
Ropang	115b	8.52 S	117.29 E
Ropaži	76	57.08 N	24.30 E
Ropča	24	63.02 N	52.16 E
Ropczyce	30	50.03 N	21.37 E
Roper	192	35.52 N	76.36 W
Roper ≃	164	14.43 S	135.27 E
Roper Bar	164	14.44 S	134.44 E
Roper Valley	164	14.56 S	134.00 E
Ropes Creek ≃	274a	33.43 S	150.47 E
Ropesville	196	33.26 N	102.09 W
Roppe	58	47.40 N	6.55 E
Ropša	265a	59.44 N	29.52 E
Roque	250	3.01 S	45.23 W
Roquebillière	62	44.01 N	7.18 E
Roquebrune-Cap-Martin	62	43.46 N	7.28 E
Roquebrune-sur-Argens	62	43.26 N	6.38 E
Roquefavour, Aqueduc de ≡[1]	62	43.31 N	5.19 E
Roquefort	32	44.02 N	0.19 W
Roquemaure	62	44.03 N	4.47 E
Roque Pérez	258	35.25 S	59.20 W
Roquestéron	62	43.52 N	7.00 E
Roquevaire	62	43.21 N	5.36 E
Rora Head >	46	58.52 N	3.25 W
Roraima □[3]	246	1.00 N	61.00 W
Roraima, Mount ∧	246	5.12 N	60.44 W
Rörbäcksnäs	26	61.08 N	12.49 E
Roreto Chisone	62	44.59 N	7.06 E
Rorey Lake ⊜	180	66.55 N	128.25 W
Rorke Lake ⊜	184	54.33 N	92.30 W
Rorke's Drift ⊥	158	28.20 S	30.32 E
Rorketon	184	51.26 N	99.32 W
Røros	26	62.35 N	11.20 E
Rorschach	58	47.29 N	9.30 E
Rørvig	41	55.57 N	11.46 E
Rørvik	24	64.51 N	11.14 E
Ros'	76	53.17 N	24.24 E
Ros' ≃	78	49.39 N	31.35 E
Rosà, It.	64	45.43 N	11.45 E
Rosa, Zam.	154	9.38 S	31.21 E
Rosa, Cap >	36	36.58 N	8.14 E
Rosa, Lake ⊜	238	21.00 N	73.30 W
Rosa, Monte ∧	58	45.55 N	7.53 E
Rosairinho	266c	38.40 N	9.01 W
Rošal'	80	55.40 N	39.51 E
Rosales, Méx.	232	28.12 N	105.33 W
Rosales, Pil.	116	15.54 N	120.38 E
Rosalia	202	47.14 N	117.22 W
Rosalie, Lake ⊜	220	27.58 N	81.28 W
Rosalind Bank ✈[4]	238	16.30 N	80.30 W
Rosamond, Ca., U.S.	228	34.51 N	118.09 W
Rosamond, Il., U.S.	219	39.23 N	89.10 W
Rosamond Lake ⊜	228	34.50 N	118.04 W
Rosamorada	234	22.08 N	105.12 W
Rosana	255	22.33 S	53.00 W
Rosander, Mount ∧	224	48.46 N	124.42 W
Rosanky	222	29.56 N	97.18 W
Rosanna	274b	37.45 S	145.04 E
Rosans	62	44.23 N	5.28 E
Rosario, Arg.	252	32.57 S	60.40 W
Rosário, Bra.	250	2.57 S	44.14 W
Rosario, Méx.	232	27.37 N	109.16 W
Rosario, Méx.	234	23.00 N	105.52 W
Rosario, Para.	252	24.27 S	57.03 W
Rosario, Pil.	116	13.51 N	121.12 E
Rosario, Pil.	116	16.14 N	120.29 E
Rosario, Ur.	258	34.19 S	57.21 W
Rosario, Ven.	246	10.19 N	72.19 W
Rosario ≃, Arg.	252	24.50 S	65.43 W
Rosario ≃, Ur.	258	34.26 S	57.21 W
Rosario, Bahía c	232	29.52 N	115.45 W
Rosario, Cayo el I	240p	21.38 N	81.53 W
Rosario, Islas del II	246	10.10 N	75.46 W
Rosario Bank ✈[2]	238	18.30 N	84.05 W
Rosario de Arriba	232	30.01 N	115.40 W
Rosario de la Frontera	252	25.48 S	64.58 W
Rosario de Lerma	252	24.59 S	65.35 W
Rosario del Tala	252	32.18 S	59.09 W
Rosário de Minas	256	21.43 S	43.38 W
Rosário do Sul	252	30.15 S	54.55 W
Rosário Oeste	248	14.50 S	56.25 W
Rosario Strait ʯ	224	48.30 N	122.45 W
Rosarito, Méx.	204	32.20 N	117.02 W
Rosarito, Méx.	232	26.27 N	111.38 W
Rosarito, Embalse de ⊜[1]	34	40.05 N	5.15 W
Rosarno	68	38.29 N	15.59 E
Rosas	196	26.09 N	103.27 W
Rosazza	62	45.41 N	7.58 E
Rošča	82	54.47 N	36.51 E
Rosche	54	52.59 N	10.45 E
Roščino	76	60.15 N	29.37 E
Rosciolo	66	42.07 N	13.20 E
Roscoe, Il., U.S.	216	42.25 N	89.01 W
Roscoe, N.Y., U.S.	210	41.55 N	74.54 W
Roscoe, Pa., U.S.	214	40.04 N	79.51 W
Roscoe, S.D., U.S.	198	45.26 N	99.20 W
Roscoe, Tx., U.S.	196	32.26 N	100.32 W
Roscoe ≃	180	69.40 N	120.57 W
Roscoe Village ⊥	214	40.18 N	81.54 W
Roscoff	32	48.44 N	3.59 E
Roscommon, Ire.	48	53.38 N	8.11 W
Roscommon, Mi., U.S.	190	44.29 N	84.35 W
Roscommon □[6]	48	53.45 N	8.15 W
Roscrea	48	52.57 N	7.47 W
Rosdorf	52	51.30 N	9.53 E
Rose, It.	68	39.24 N	16.17 E
Rose, N.Y., U.S.	210	43.09 N	76.53 W
Rose, Monte ∧	70	37.39 N	13.25 E
Rose, Mount ∧	226	39.21 N	119.55 W
Rose, Pointe de la >	240e	14.40 N	60.53 W
Roseau, Dom.	240d	15.18 N	61.24 W
Roseau, Mn., U.S.	198	48.50 N	95.45 W
Roseau ≃, Dom.	240d	15.18 N	61.24 W
Roseau ≃, N.A.	198	49.08 N	97.15 W
Roseau ≃, St. Luc.	241f	13.58 N	61.02 W
Rosebank ✦[8]	273d	26.09 S	28.02 E
Rosebank Station	275b	43.47 N	79.07 W
Roseberry Lakes ⊜	184	52.40 N	92.30 W
Roseberth	166	25.47 S	139.37 E
Rosebery	166	41.46 S	145.32 E
Rosebery ✦[8]	274a	33.55 S	151.12 E
Rose-Blanche	186	47.37 N	58.41 W
Roseboom	210	42.45 N	74.47 W
Roseboro	192	34.57 N	78.30 W
Rose Bowl ♦	280	34.10 N	118.09 W
Rosebud, Austl.	169	38.21 S	144.54 E
Rosebud, Mo., U.S.	219	38.23 N	91.24 W
Rosebud, Mt., U.S.	202	46.16 N	106.26 W
Rose Bud, Pa., U.S.	214	40.45 N	78.33 W
Rosebud, S.D., U.S.	198	43.13 N	100.51 W
Rosebud, Tx., U.S.	222	31.04 N	96.58 W
Rosebud ≃	182	51.25 N	112.37 W
Rosebud Creek ≃	202	46.16 N	106.28 W
Rosebud Indian Reservation ✦[4]	198	43.25 N	100.28 W
Roseburg	202	43.13 N	123.20 W
Rosebush	190	43.41 N	84.46 W
Rose City	190	44.25 N	84.07 W
Rose Creek ≃, U.S.	198	40.04 N	97.07 W
Rose Creek ≃, Ca., U.S.	226	38.07 N	120.24 W
Rosecroft Raceway ♦	284c	38.48 N	76.58 W
Rosedale, Austl.	166	24.38 S	151.55 E
Rosedale, Ab., Can.	182	51.25 N	112.38 W
Rosedale, B.C., Can.	224	49.11 N	121.48 W
Rosedale, In., U.S.	194	39.37 N	87.17 W
Rosedale, La., U.S.	194	30.27 N	91.27 W
Rosedale, Md., U.S.	284b	39.19 N	76.30 W
Rosedale, Ms., U.S.	194	33.51 N	91.01 W
Rosedale ✦[8], On., Can.	275b	43.41 N	79.22 W
Rosedale ✦[8], N.Y., U.S.	276	40.39 N	73.45 W
Rosedale Estates	284c	38.47 N	76.58 W
Rosedale Hills	218	39.42 N	86.07 W
Rosedene	158	32.01 S	22.07 E
Rosehall	246	6.16 N	57.21 W
Rosehearty	46	57.42 N	2.07 W
Rose-Hill, Maus.	157c	20.14 S	57.27 E
Rose Hill, N.C., U.S.	192	34.49 N	78.01 W
Rose Hill, Va., U.S.	192	36.40 N	83.22 W
Rosehill Cemetery ✦	278	41.59 N	87.41 W
Rosehill Racecourse ♦	274a	33.49 S	151.02 E
Rose Hills Memorial Park ✦	280	34.01 N	118.02 W
Roseira	256	22.54 S	45.18 W
Rose Island I, Am. Sam.	14	14.32 S	168.08 W
Rose Island I, Ba.	192	25.06 N	77.14 W
Rose Lake	182	54.24 N	126.02 W
Roseland, Ca., U.S.	226	38.30 N	122.55 W
Roseland, In., U.S.	216	41.42 N	86.15 W
Roseland, La., U.S.	194	30.45 N	90.30 W
Roseland, N.J., U.S.	276	40.49 N	74.17 W
Roseland, Oh., U.S.	214	40.47 N	82.32 W
Roseland ✦[8]	278	41.42 N	87.38 W
Roselawn	216	41.09 N	87.19 W
Roselle, Il., U.S.	216	41.59 N	88.04 W
Roselle, N.J., U.S.	276	40.39 N	74.15 W
Roselle Field ⊠	278	41.59 N	88.06 W
Rosellen	263	51.08 N	6.43 E
Roselle Park	276	40.39 N	74.15 W
Rosellerheide	263	51.07 N	6.44 E
Rose Lodge	224	45.01 N	123.52 W
Rosemary	182	50.46 N	112.05 W
Rosemary Brook ≃	283	42.19 N	71.15 W
Rosemead	280	34.04 N	118.04 W
Rosemère	206	45.38 N	73.48 W
Rosemont, Ca., U.S.	226	38.34 N	121.20 W
Rosemont, Il., U.S.	278	41.59 N	87.52 W
Rosemont, Ky., U.S.	218	38.01 N	84.32 W
Rosemont, Oh., U.S.	214	41.03 N	80.53 W
Rosemont, Pa., U.S.	285	40.01 N	75.19 W
Rosemont Horizon ♦	278	42.00 N	87.53 W
Rosenberg	222	29.33 N	95.48 W
Rosendaël	50	51.02 N	2.24 E
Rosendal, Nor.	26	59.59 N	6.01 E
Rosendal, S. Afr.	158	28.30 S	27.55 E
Rosendale	210	41.51 N	74.05 W
Roseneath	273d	26.17 S	28.11 E
Rosenfeld	58	48.17 N	8.43 E
Rosengarten, Dtsch.	52	53.23 N	9.54 E
Rosengarten, Dtsch.	56	49.04 N	9.44 E
Rosenhayn	208	39.28 N	75.07 W
Rosenheim	64	47.51 N	12.07 E
Rosenhügel ✦[8]	263	51.10 N	7.12 E
Rosenow	54	53.38 N	13.02 E
Rosenthal, Dtsch.	54	50.51 N	14.04 E
Rosenthal, Dtsch.	56	50.58 N	8.52 E
Rosenthal ✦[8]	264a	52.36 N	13.23 E
Rose Peak ∧	200	33.26 N	109.22 W
Rosepine	194	30.55 N	93.17 W
Rose Point >	182	54.13 N	131.35 W
Rosersberg	40	59.35 N	17.53 E
Rosersberg ⊥	40	59.34 N	17.50 E
Roses, Golf de c	34	42.10 N	3.15 E
Roseto	210	40.52 N	75.12 W
Roseto Capo Spulico	68	39.59 N	16.36 E
Roseto degli Abruzzi	66	42.41 N	14.01 E
Roseto Valfortore	68	41.22 N	15.06 E
Rosetown	184	51.33 N	108.00 W
Rose Tree	285	39.56 N	75.23 W
Rose Tree Park ♦	285	39.56 N	75.24 W
Rosetta → Rashīd	142	31.24 N	30.25 E
Rosetta Branch → Rashīd, Far' ≃	142	31.30 N	30.21 E
Rosetta Mouth → Rashīd, Maṣabb ≃[1]	142	31.30 N	30.20 E
Rosettenville ✦[8]	273d	26.15 S	28.03 E
Rosevale	171a	27.51 S	152.29 E
Rose Valley, Sk., Can.	184	52.18 N	103.50 W
Rose Valley, Pa., U.S.	285	39.53 N	75.23 W
Rose Valley, Pa., U.S.	285	40.10 N	75.13 W
Rose Valley, Wa., U.S.	224	46.06 N	122.50 W
Roseville, Austl.	274a	33.47 S	151.11 E
Roseville, Ca., U.S.	226	38.45 N	121.17 W
Roseville, Il., U.S.	190	40.43 N	90.39 W
Roseville, Mi., U.S.	214	42.29 N	82.56 W
Roseville, Mn., U.S.	190	45.00 N	93.09 W
Roseville, Oh., U.S.	188	39.48 N	82.04 W
Roseville, Pa., U.S.	210	41.51 N	76.57 W
Roseville Park	285	39.42 N	75.43 W
Rosewood, Austl.	171a	27.39 S	152.35 E
Rosewood, Austl.	171b	35.41 S	147.52 E
Rosewood, Oh., U.S.	216	40.13 N	83.58 W
Rosewood Heights	219	38.53 N	90.05 W
Roseworthy	168b	34.32 S	138.44 E
Roshage >	26	57.07 N	8.38 E
Roshanara Gardens ♦	272a	28.40 N	77.12 E
Rosharon	222	29.21 N	95.28 W
Rosheim	58	48.30 N	7.28 E
Rosherville Dam ⊜[1]	273d	26.14 S	28.07 E
Rosh Ha'Ayin	132	32.06 N	34.57 E
Rosholt, S.D., U.S.	198	45.52 N	96.43 W
Rosholt, Wi., U.S.	190	44.37 N	89.18 W
Rosh Pinna	132	32.58 N	35.32 E
Rosica ≃	38	43.15 N	25.42 E
Rosice	30	49.11 N	16.23 E
Rosiclare	194	37.25 N	88.20 W
Rosières-aux-Salines	58	48.36 N	6.20 E
Rosières-en-Santerre	50	49.49 N	2.43 E
Rosiers, Rivière des ≃	206	45.59 N	72.07 W
Rosignano Marittimo	66	43.24 N	10.28 E
Rosignano Solvay	66	43.23 N	10.26 E
Rosignol	246	6.17 N	57.32 W
Roșiori de Vede	38	44.07 N	25.00 E
Rositz	54	51.01 N	12.22 E
Roskilde	41	55.39 N	12.05 E
Roskilde □[6]	41	55.30 N	12.05 E
Roskilde Fjord c	41	55.56 N	12.00 E
Roskow	54	52.28 N	12.42 E
Roslagen □[9]	40	59.30 N	18.40 E
Roslags-Bro	40	59.50 N	18.44 E
Rosl'akovo	24	69.03 N	33.09 E
Rosl'atino	76	59.46 N	44.15 E
Roslavl'	76	53.57 N	32.52 E
Roslev	26	56.42 N	8.59 E
Roslindale ✦[8]	283	42.18 N	71.07 W
Roslyn, N.Y., U.S.	276	40.48 N	73.39 W
Roslyn, Pa., U.S.	208	40.07 N	75.08 W
Roslyn, Pa., U.S.	285	39.57 N	75.36 W
Roslyn, Wa., U.S.	224	47.13 N	120.59 W
Roslyn Estates	276	40.47 N	73.40 W
Roslyn Harbor	276	40.49 N	73.38 W
Roslyn Heights	276	40.47 N	73.38 W
Rosmalen	52	51.43 N	5.22 E
Rosman	192	35.08 N	82.49 W
Rosmead	158	31.29 S	25.08 E
Ros Mhic Thriúin → New Ross	48	52.24 N	6.56 W
Røsnæs >[1]	41	55.44 N	10.59 E
Rosne, Ruisseau le ≃	261	48.58 N	2.25 E
Rosneath	46	56.01 N	4.49 W
Rosny-sous-Bois	261	48.53 N	2.29 E
Rosny-sur-Seine	50	49.00 N	1.38 E
Rosolina	64	45.05 N	12.15 E
Rosolini	70	36.49 N	14.57 E
Rošore	85	38.20 N	72.19 E
Rosporden	32	47.58 N	3.50 W
Rösrath	56	50.54 N	7.11 E
Ross, Austl.	166	42.02 S	147.29 E
Ross, N.Z.	172	42.54 S	170.49 E
Ross, Ca., U.S.	226	37.55 N	122.32 W
Ross, In., U.S.	278	41.32 N	87.23 W
Ross, Oh., U.S.	218	39.19 N	84.39 W
Ross □[6]	218	39.20 N	83.06 W
Ross ≃	180	61.59 N	132.26 W
Ross, Cape >	116	10.56 N	119.13 E
Ross, Mount ∧	172	41.28 S	175.21 E
Ross, Point >	174c	29.04 S	167.56 E
Ross, Pointe >	275a	45.21 N	73.48 W
Rossa	58	46.22 N	9.08 E
Rossach	56	50.09 N	10.56 E
Rossano	68	39.35 N	16.39 E
Rossasna	76	54.39 N	30.53 E
Rossau	54	52.47 N	11.38 E
Rossbach	54	51.15 N	11.53 E
Ross Behy	48	52.02 N	9.58 W
Ross-Béthio	150	16.16 N	16.08 W
Rossburg	216	40.17 N	84.38 W
Rossburn	184	50.40 N	100.52 W
Ross Carbery	48	51.35 N	9.01 W
Rosscott Manor	285	39.39 N	75.44 W
Ross Dam ✦[6]	224	48.44 N	121.04 W
Rossdorf	56	49.51 N	8.45 E
Rosseau	212	45.16 N	79.39 W
Rosseau, Lake ⊜	212	45.10 N	79.35 W
Rossel, Cap >	175f	20.23 S	166.36 E
Rossell y Rius	252	33.11 S	55.42 W
Rossen ⊜	40	60.19 N	16.26 E
Rossendale □[8]	262	53.43 N	2.14 W
Rosser	222	32.28 N	96.27 W
Rosses Bay c	48	55.02 N	8.27 W
Rosses Point	48	54.18 N	8.33 W
Rossford	214	41.37 N	83.33 W
Ross Fork Creek ≃	202	47.05 N	109.43 W
Rosshaupten	58	47.39 N	10.43 E
Rosshyttan	40	60.04 N	16.21 E
Ross Ice Shelf ⊓	9	81.30 S	175.00 W
Rossiglione	62	44.34 N	8.40 E
Rossignol, Lake ⊜	186	44.10 N	65.10 W
Rossija → Russia □[1]	72	60.00 N	80.00 E
Rössing	156	22.31 S	14.52 E
Rossio, Estação do ✦[5]	266c	38.43 N	9.09 W
Ross Island I, Ant.	9	77.30 S	168.00 E
Ross Island I, Mb., Can.	184	54.14 N	97.45 W
Rossiter	214	40.53 N	78.55 W
Rossitten → Rybačij	76	55.09 N	20.51 E
Rossla	54	51.28 N	11.04 E
Ross Lake ⊜[1]	224	48.53 N	121.04 W
Ross Lake National Recreation Area ♦	224	48.45 N	121.00 W
Rossland	182	49.05 N	117.48 W
Rosslare	48	52.17 N	6.23 W
Rosslare Harbour	48	52.15 N	6.22 W
Rosslau	54	51.53 N	12.14 E
Rosslea	48	54.14 N	7.11 W
Rossleben, Dtsch.	54	51.18 N	11.26 E
Rossleben, Dtsch.	54	51.18 N	11.26 E
Rosslyn Farms	279b	40.26 N	80.05 W
Rossmoor	280	33.47 N	118.05 W
Rossmore	274a	33.57 S	150.46 E
Rossmoyne	208	40.13 N	76.57 W
Rosso	150	16.30 N	15.49 W
Rossön	26	63.55 N	16.21 E
Ross-on-Wye	42	51.55 N	2.35 W
Rossoš', Ross.	78	50.12 N	39.34 E
Rossoš', Ross.	78	51.08 N	38.29 E
Rossouw	158	31.09 S	27.18 E
Ross R. Barnett Reservoir ⊜[1]	194	32.30 N	90.00 W
Ross River	180	61.59 N	132.27 W
Ross-Schelfeis → Ross Ice Shelf ⊓	9	81.30 S	175.00 W
Ross Sea ⊤[2]	9	76.00 S	175.00 W
Rosstal	56	49.25 N	10.52 E
Rosston	218	40.03 N	86.17 W
Ross Township	279b	40.32 N	80.01 W
Rossu, Capu >	36	42.14 N	8.33 E
Røssvatnet ⊜	24	65.45 N	14.00 E
Rossville, Ga., U.S.	192	34.58 N	85.17 W
Rossville, Il., U.S.	216	40.22 N	87.40 W
Rossville, In., U.S.	216	40.25 N	86.35 W
Rossville, Ks., U.S.	198	39.08 N	95.57 W
Rossville, Md., U.S.	284b	39.20 N	76.29 W
Rosswein	54	51.03 N	13.10 E
Røst II	24	67.28 N	11.59 E
Rostāg	120	37.07 N	69.49 E
Röstånga	41	56.00 N	13.17 E
Rostavytsya ≃	78	49.44 N	30.01 E
Rosthern	184	52.40 N	106.17 W
Rostherne	262	53.21 N	2.23 W
Rostherne Mere ⊜	262	53.21 N	2.23 W
Roštkala	120	37.16 N	71.49 E
Rostock	54	54.05 N	12.07 E
Rostov	80	57.11 N	39.25 E
Rostov-na-Donu	83	47.14 N	39.42 E
Rostov Oblast' □[4]	78	48.00 N	40.00 E
Rostrataville	158	26.49 S	25.39 E
Rostraver Airport ⊠	279b	40.13 N	79.50 W
Rostrevor	48	54.06 N	6.12 W
Rosvinskoje	24	66.32 N	52.26 E
Roswell, Ga., U.S.	192	34.01 N	84.21 W
Roswell, N.M., U.S.	196	33.23 N	104.31 W
Roswell, Oh., U.S.	214	40.28 N	81.21 W
Rosyth	46	56.03 N	3.26 W
Rot ≃	58	48.19 N	9.54 E
Rota	34	36.37 N	6.21 W
Rota I	108	14.10 N	145.12 E
Rot am See	56	49.15 N	10.01 E
Rotan	196	32.51 N	100.27 W
Rotanda	156	19.33 S	32.50 E
Rot an der Rot	58	48.01 N	10.02 E
Rotary Island I	285	40.14 N	74.49 W
Rotbach ≃	263	51.34 N	6.41 E
Rotberg	264a	52.21 N	13.31 E
Rote-Erde, Stadion ♦	263	51.30 N	7.27 E
Rotenburg	52	53.06 N	9.24 E
Rotenburg an der Fulda	56	51.00 N	9.45 E
Roter Main ≃	60	50.04 N	11.24 E
Rotes Meer → Red Sea ⊤[2]	136	20.00 N	38.00 E
Roth, Dtsch.	56	50.46 N	7.42 E
Roth, Dtsch.	60	49.15 N	11.06 E
Roth ≃	58	48.27 N	10.10 E
Rötha	54	51.12 N	12.25 E
Rothaargebirge ⋏	56	51.05 N	8.15 E
Rothbury	44	55.19 N	1.55 W
Rothbury Forest ✦[3]	44	55.18 N	1.54 W
Rothemühl	54	53.36 N	13.49 E
Röthenbach, Dtsch.	58	47.37 N	9.59 E
Röthenbach, Schw.	58	46.51 N	7.45 E
Röthenbach an der Pegnitz	60	49.29 N	11.15 E
Rothenburg	54	51.20 N	14.58 E
Rothenburg ob der Tauber	56	49.23 N	10.10 E
Rothenfels	56	49.54 N	9.35 E
Rothenkirchen	54	50.33 N	12.30 E
Rothenschirmbach	54	51.27 N	11.33 E
Rothenstein ∧[2]	263	51.07 N	7.41 E
Rother ≃, Eng., U.K.	42	50.54 N	0.42 E
Rother ≃, Eng., U.K.	42	50.57 N	0.32 W
Rothera ʊ[3]	9	67.34 S	68.08 W
Rotherham, N.Z.	172	42.42 S	172.57 E
Rotherham, Eng., U.K.	44	53.26 N	1.20 W
Rothes	46	57.31 N	3.13 W
Rothesay, N.B., Can.	186	45.23 N	66.00 W
Rothesay, Scot., U.K.	46	55.51 N	5.03 W
Röthlein	56	49.59 N	10.13 E
Rothneusiedl ✦[8]	264b	48.08 N	16.23 E
Rothrist	58	47.19 N	7.53 E
Rothsay, Austl.	162	29.17 S	116.53 E
Rothsay, Mn., U.S.	198	46.28 N	96.16 W
Rothschild	190	44.53 N	89.37 W
Rothsville	208	40.09 N	76.15 W
Rothwell, N.B., Can.	186	46.04 N	66.04 W
Rothwell, Eng., U.K.	42	52.25 N	0.48 W
Rothwell, Eng., U.K.	44	53.46 N	1.29 W
Roti, Pulau I	112	10.45 S	123.10 E
Roti, Selat ʯ	112	10.25 S	123.25 E
Roto	166	33.03 S	145.28 E
Rotoiti, Lake ⊜, N.Z.	172	38.02 S	176.25 E
Rotoiti, Lake ⊜, N.Z.	172	41.50 S	172.50 E
Rotomanu	172	42.39 S	171.32 E
Rotonda	68	39.57 N	16.02 E
Rotondella	68	40.10 N	16.32 E
Rotondo, Monte ∧	36	42.13 N	9.03 E
Rotoroa, Lake ⊜	172	41.52 S	172.38 E
Rotorua	172	38.09 S	176.15 E
Rotorua, Lake ⊜	172	38.05 S	176.16 E
Rotowaro	172	37.36 S	175.05 E
Rott	64	47.54 N	10.59 E
Rott ≃	60	48.27 N	13.26 E
Rottach-Egern	64	47.41 N	11.46 E
Rott am Inn	64	47.59 N	12.07 E
Röttenbach	60	49.09 N	11.02 E
Rottenbach-Tremersdorf	56	50.21 N	10.56 E
Rottenbuch	64	47.44 N	10.58 E
Rottenburg am Neckar	58	48.28 N	8.56 E
Rottenburg an der Laaber	60	48.42 N	12.02 E
Rottenmann	61	47.31 N	14.22 E
Rotterdam, Ned.	52	51.55 N	4.28 E
Rotterdam, N.Y., U.S.	210	42.48 N	73.59 W
Rotterdam, Luchthaven ⊠	52	51.58 N	4.30 E
Rotterdam Junction	210	42.52 N	74.03 W
Rotthalmünster	60	48.21 N	13.12 E
Rotthausen ✦[8]	263	51.30 N	7.05 E
Rottingdean	42	50.48 N	0.04 W
Röttingen	56	49.31 N	9.58 E
Rottleberode	54	51.31 N	10.57 E
Rottnest Island I	168a	32.00 S	115.30 E
Rottofreno	62	45.03 N	9.34 E
Rottum	263	51.36 N	7.42 E
Rottumeroog I	52	53.33 N	6.35 E
Rottumerplaat I	52	53.32 N	6.30 E
Rottweil	58	48.10 N	8.37 E
Rotuma I	14	12.30 S	177.05 E
Rotwand ∧	64	47.39 N	11.56 E
Rötz	60	49.21 N	12.32 E
Roubaix	50	50.42 N	3.10 E
Roubideau Creek ≃	200	38.44 N	108.10 W
Roubidoux Creek ≃	194	37.51 N	92.13 W
Roubion ≃	62	44.31 N	4.42 E
Rouceux	58	48.22 N	5.41 E
Roudnice [nad Labem]	54	50.22 N	14.16 E
Rouen	50	49.26 N	1.05 E
Rougé	32	47.47 N	1.27 W
Rouge ≃, On., Can.	212	43.48 N	79.07 W
Rouge ≃, P.Q., Can.	206	45.39 N	74.42 W
Rouge ≃, P.Q., Can.	206	45.33 N	74.20 W
Rouge → Red ≃, U.S.	178	31.00 N	91.40 W
Rouge, Bell Branch ≃	281	42.23 N	83.16 W
Rouge, Lac ⊜	206	46.56 N	74.38 W
Rouge, Mer → Red Sea ⊤[2]	136	20.00 N	38.00 E
Rouge, River ≃	281	42.17 N	83.06 W
Rougeau, Forêt de ♦	261	48.35 N	2.30 E
Rougemont, Fr.	58	47.29 N	6.21 E
Rougemont, Schw.	58	46.29 N	7.12 E
Rougemont-le-Château	58	47.44 N	6.58 E
Rough ≃	194	37.29 N	87.08 W
Rough And Ready	226	39.14 N	121.08 W
Rough River Lake ⊜[1]	194	37.40 N	86.25 W
Rouiba	34	36.44 N	3.17 E
Rouillac	32	45.47 N	0.04 W
Rouillon	261	48.33 N	2.00 E
Roulans	58	47.19 N	6.14 E
Rouleau	184	50.11 N	104.55 W
Roulers → Roeselare	50	50.57 N	3.08 E
Roulette	214	41.46 N	78.09 W
Roumanie → Romania □[1]	38	46.00 N	25.30 E
Round Harbour	186	49.51 N	55.40 W
Roundhead	216	40.34 N	83.50 W
Round Hill Head >	166	24.10 S	151.53 E
Round Hill Regional Park ♦	279b	40.15 N	79.51 W
Round Knowe ∧[2]	48	55.08 N	6.55 W
Round Lake, Il., U.S.	278	42.21 N	88.05 W
Round Lake, Mn., U.S.	198	43.32 N	95.28 W
Round Lake, N.Y., U.S.	210	42.56 N	73.47 W
Round Lake ⊜, Nf., Can.	186	51.08 N	56.33 W
Round Lake ⊜, On., Can.	190	45.38 N	77.32 W
Round Lake ⊜, On., Can.	212	44.30 N	77.52 W
Round Lake ⊜, On., Can.	212	45.28 N	79.24 W
Round Lake ⊜, Sk., Can.	184	50.33 N	102.23 W
Round Lake ⊜, Il., U.S.	278	42.22 N	88.05 W
Round Lake ⊜, Mi., U.S.	216	41.58 N	84.17 W
Round Lake Beach	216	42.22 N	88.05 W
Round Lake Park	216	42.21 N	88.04 W
Round Mound ∧[2]	198	38.55 N	99.39 W
Round Mountain	204	38.42 N	117.04 W
Round Mountain ∧, Austl.	166	30.27 S	152.14 E
Round Mountain ∧, Austl.	171b	36.15 S	148.34 E
Round Pond ⊜, Nf., Can.	186	48.10 N	56.00 W
Round Pond ⊜, Ma., U.S.	283	42.36 N	70.49 W
Round Rock	222	30.30 N	97.40 W
Roundstone	48	53.23 N	9.53 W
Round Top	210	42.16 N	74.02 W
Round Top ∧[2]	208	40.30 N	76.42 W
Round Top Regional Park ♦	282	37.51 N	122.12 W
Roundup	202	46.26 N	108.32 W
Round Valley Indian Reservation ✦[4]	204	39.50 N	123.20 W
Round Valley Reservoir ⊜[1]	210	40.36 N	74.50 W
Roundwood	48	53.04 N	6.13 W
Roura	250	4.44 N	52.20 W
Rourkela → Raurkela	124	22.13 N	84.53 E
Rousay I	46	59.10 N	3.02 W
Rouse Hill	274a	33.41 S	150.56 E
Rouses Point	206	45.00 N	73.22 W
Rouseville	214	41.28 N	79.41 W
Rousies	50	50.16 N	4.00 E
Rousseau, Lake ⊜[1]	220	29.02 N	82.32 W
Rousset, Col de)(	62	44.50 N	5.24 E
Roussigny	261	48.39 N	2.06 E
Roussillon, Fr.	62	45.22 N	4.49 E
Roussillon, Fr.	62	43.54 N	5.17 E
Roussillon □[9]	32	42.30 N	2.30 E
Roussy-le-Village	56	49.27 N	6.10 E
Routhierville	186	48.11 N	67.09 W
Routot	50	49.23 N	0.44 E
Rouveen	52	52.36 N	6.11 E
Rouvignies	50	50.20 N	3.26 E
Rouville □[6]	206	45.23 N	73.04 W
Rouvray	50	47.25 N	4.06 E
Rouvray, Lac ⊜	186	49.18 N	70.49 W
Rouxville	158	30.29 S	26.46 E
Rouyn	190	48.15 N	79.01 W
Rouzerville	208	39.44 N	77.32 W
Rovaniemi	24	66.34 N	25.48 E
Rovasenda	62	45.32 N	8.19 E
Rovato	64	45.34 N	10.00 E
Rove, Tunnel du ✦[5]	62	43.22 N	5.17 E
Rovegno	62	44.35 N	9.17 E
Rovellasca	62	45.40 N	9.03 E
Rovello Porro	62	45.39 N	9.02 E
Roven'ki	78	49.56 N	38.54 E
Roven'ky	83	48.05 N	39.21 E
Rovenskaja Slabada	76	52.13 N	30.19 E
Roverbella	64	45.16 N	10.46 E
Rovere	66	42.10 N	13.31 E
Roverè della Luna	64	46.15 N	11.10 E
Roveredo	58	46.14 N	9.08 E
Rovereto	64	45.53 N	11.02 E
Roverè Veronese	64	45.36 N	11.03 E
Rövershagen	54	54.10 N	12.15 E
Roversi	252	27.35 S	61.57 W
Roverud	26	60.15 N	12.03 E
Roviano	66	42.01 N	13.00 E
Rovigo	64	45.04 N	11.47 E
Rovigo □[4]	64	45.02 N	11.50 E
Rovinj	36	45.05 N	13.38 E
Rovira	246	4.14 N	75.14 W
Rovnoje, Kyrg.	85	42.53 N	73.32 E
Rovnoje, Ross.	80	50.47 N	46.05 E
Rovubu (Ruvubu) ≃	154	2.23 S	30.47 E
Rovuma (Ruvuma) ≃	154	10.29 S	40.28 E
Rów	54	52.58 N	14.45 E
Rowan □[6]	218	38.17 N	83.26 W
Rowan Lake ⊜	184	49.18 N	93.32 W
Rowanty Creek ≃	208	36.58 N	77.21 W
Rowena, Austl.	166	29.49 S	148.54 E
Rowena, Tx., U.S.	196	31.39 N	100.03 W
Rowe Park ♦	273a	6.30 N	3.23 E
Rowhill	273d	26.14 S	28.26 E
Rowland, N.C., U.S.	192	34.32 N	79.17 W
Rowland, Pa., U.S.	210	41.28 N	75.03 W
Rowland Flat	168b	34.35 S	138.56 E
Rowland Heights	280	33.58 N	117.54 W
Rowlands Gill	44	54.54 N	1.45 W
Rowlesburg	188	39.20 N	79.40 W
Rowlett	222	32.54 N	96.33 W
Rowlett, Isla I	254	44.48 S	74.25 W
Rowlett Creek ≃	222	32.49 N	96.31 W
Rowley	207	42.43 N	70.52 W
Rowley ≃, N.T., Can.	176	70.16 N	77.45 W
Rowley ≃, Ma., U.S.	283	42.43 N	70.49 W
Rowley Island I	176	69.08 N	78.50 W
Rowley Shoals ✈[2]	162	17.30 S	119.00 E
Rowntree Mill Park ♦	275b	43.45 N	79.35 W
Rowsburg	214	40.52 N	82.10 W
Rowville	274b	37.56 S	145.14 E
Roxa, Ilha I	150	11.15 N	15.40 W
Roxana	219	38.50 N	90.04 W
Roxas, Pil.	108	11.35 N	122.45 E
Roxas, Pil.	116	17.08 N	121.36 E
Roxas, Pil.	116	12.35 N	121.31 E
Roxas, Pil.	116	10.20 N	119.21 E
Roxas (Capiz), Pil.	116	11.35 N	122.45 E
Roxboro, P.Q., Can.	275a	45.31 N	73.48 W
Roxboro, N.C., U.S.	192	36.23 N	78.58 W
Roxborough	241r	11.15 N	60.35 W
Roxborough ✦[8]	285	40.02 N	75.13 W
Roxburgh, N.Z.	172	45.32 S	169.19 E
Roxburgh, Scot., U.K.	46	55.34 N	2.30 W
Roxbury, Ct., U.S.	207	41.33 N	73.18 W
Roxbury, N.Y., U.S.	210	42.17 N	74.33 W
Roxbury, Pa., U.S.	214	40.07 N	77.40 W
Roxbury, Va., U.S.	208	37.28 N	77.09 W
Roxbury ✦[8], Ma., U.S.	283	42.20 N	71.06 W
Roxbury ✦[8], N.Y., U.S.	276	40.34 N	73.54 W
Roxby Downs	162	30.43 S	136.46 E
Roxel	52	51.57 N	7.32 E
Roxen ⊜	26	58.30 N	15.41 E
Roxie	194	31.30 N	91.04 W
Roxo, Cap >	150	12.20 N	16.43 W
Roxton	196	33.33 N	95.44 W
Roxton Pond (Sainte-Pudentienne)	206	45.29 N	72.40 W
Roxwell	260	51.45 N	0.23 E
Roy, N.M., U.S.	196	35.56 N	104.11 W
Roy, Ut,. U.S.	200	41.09 N	112.01 W
Roy, Wa., U.S.	224	47.00 N	122.32 W
Roya (Roia) ≃	62	43.48 N	7.35 E
Royal	198	43.03 N	95.17 W
Royal Albert Hall ʊ	260	51.30 N	0.11 W
Royal Australian Naval College ʊ[2]	170	35.07 S	150.42 E
Royal Bangkok Sports Club ♦	269a	13.44 N	100.33 E
Royal Botanic Gardens ♦, Austl.	274a	33.52 S	151.13 E
Royal Botanic Gardens ♦, Austl.	274b	37.50 S	144.59 E
Royal Canal ≡	48	53.21 N	6.15 W
Royal Center	216	40.51 N	86.29 W
Royal Chitwan National Park ♦	124	27.30 N	84.30 E
Royal City	202	46.54 N	119.38 W
Royale, Isle I	190	48.00 N	89.00 W
Royal Gorge V	200	38.17 N	105.45 W
Royal Island I	192	25.31 N	76.51 W
Royalla	171b	35.31 S	149.09 E
Royal Leamington Spa	42	52.18 N	1.31 W
Royal Natal National Park ♦	158	28.45 S	28.57 E
Royal National Park ♦	170	34.10 S	151.05 E
Royal Naval College ■	260	51.29 N	0.01 W
Royal Oak, B.C., Can.	224	48.30 N	123.23 W
Royal Oak, Md., U.S.	208	38.44 N	76.10 W
Royal Oak, Mi., U.S.	216	42.29 N	83.08 W
Royal Oak Township	281	42.27 N	83.10 W
Royal Ontario Museum ʊ	275b	43.40 N	79.24 W
Royal Palms State Beach ♦	280	33.44 N	118.19 W
Royal Park ♦	274b	37.47 S	144.57 E
Royal Roads c	224	48.26 N	123.26 W
Royalton, In., U.S.	218	39.56 N	86.21 W
Royalton, Mn., U.S.	190	45.49 N	94.17 W
Royalton, Pa., U.S.	208	40.11 N	76.44 W
Royal Tunbridge Wells	42	51.08 N	0.16 E
Royal Turf Club ♦	269a	13.46 N	100.32 E
Royan	32	45.37 N	1.01 W
Royaume-Uni → United Kingdom □[1]	28	54.00 N	2.00 W
Roybon	62	45.15 N	5.15 E
Royce Brook ≃	276	40.32 N	70.35 W
Roydon, Eng., U.K.	42	51.46 N	0.03 E
Roydon, Eng., U.K.	42	52.50 N	0.32 E
Roye	50	49.42 N	2.48 E
Royersford	208	40.11 N	75.32 W
Royerton	216	40.15 N	85.21 W
Roy Hill	162	22.38 S	119.57 E
Roylyanka	78	46.17 N	29.46 E
Royse City	222	32.58 N	96.19 W
Royston, Eng., U.K.	42	52.03 N	0.01 W
Royston, Eng., U.K.	44	53.37 N	1.27 W
Royston, Ga., U.S.	192	34.17 N	83.06 W
Royton	44	53.34 N	2.08 W
Rožaj	38	42.50 N	20.10 E
Różan	30	52.53 N	21.25 E
Rozay-en-Brie	50	48.41 N	2.58 E
Roždestvenka, Kaz.	86	50.52 N	71.22 E
Roždestvenka, Ross.	86	55.21 N	77.29 E
Roždestvenka, Ross.	86	55.42 N	70.00 E
Roždestveno, Ross.	76	57.44 N	37.57 E
Roždestveno, Ross.	80	53.15 N	50.04 E
Roždestveno, Ross.	82	56.51 N	36.33 E
Roždestveno, Ross.	82	55.57 N	36.23 E
Roždestvenskaja Chava	78	51.38 N	39.40 E
Roždestvenskoje, Ross.	80	58.09 N	45.35 E
Roždestvenskoje, Ross.	80	52.47 N	42.10 E
Roždestvenskoje, Ross.	80	51.14 N	42.10 E
Roždestvo	76	57.36 N	33.48 E
Rozdil'na	78	46.51 N	30.05 E
Rozdol'ne, Ukr.	78	45.47 N	33.29 E
Rozdol'ne, Ukr.	83	47.37 N	38.01 E
Rozdory	78	48.21 N	35.42 E
Rozel	43b	49.14 N	2.03 W
Rozelle	274a	33.52 S	151.10 E
Roželov	60	49.33 N	13.48 E
Rozewie, Przylądek >	30	54.51 N	18.21 E
Rozhnof, Cape >	180	55.58 N	160.58 W
Rozhnyativ	78	48.56 N	24.09 E
Rozhyshche	78	50.54 N	25.15 E
Rozivka	78	47.23 N	37.04 E
Rožki	80	56.41 N	50.31 E
Rozkishne	83	48.30 N	39.18 E
Rožkov	80	51.39 N	52.19 E
Rožmberk ⊜	61	49.04 N	14.47 E
Rožmberk nad Vltavou	61	48.39 N	14.22 E
Rožmitál pod Třemšínem	60	49.36 N	13.52 E
Rožňava	30	48.40 N	20.32 E
Roznov	38	46.50 N	26.31 E
Rožnov pod Radhoštěm	30	49.28 N	18.10 E
Rożnów	30	49.46 N	20.42 E
Rozoy-sur-Serre	50	49.43 N	4.08 E
Rozsypne	83	48.08 N	38.34 E
Roztocze ⋏[2]	30	50.30 N	23.20 E
Roztoky	54	50.09 N	14.22 E
Rozzano	62	45.20 N	9.06 E
Rrëshen	38	41.47 N	19.54 E
Rrogozhinë	38	41.05 N	19.40 E
Rtiščevo	80	52.16 N	43.47 E
Ru ≃	100	32.43 N	115.01 E
Ru, Tanjong >	114	2.50 N	101.17 E
Ruabon	42	52.59 N	3.02 W
Ruacaná	152	17.25 S	14.12 E
Ruacana Falls L	152	17.22 S	14.12 E
Ruaha National Park ♦	154	7.30 S	34.40 E
Ruahine Range ⋏	172	40.00 S	176.06 E
Ruahmi, Ra's >	142	28.44 N	32.50 E
Ruanda	154	10.33 S	34.57 E
Ruanda → Rwanda □[1]	154	2.00 S	30.00 E
Ruango	164	5.35 S	150.10 E
Ruapehu, Mount ∧	172	39.17 S	175.34 E
Ruapuke Island I	172	46.47 S	168.30 E
Ruatahuna	172	38.33 S	176.57 E
Ruatapu	172	42.48 S	170.53 E
Ruathair, Loch an ⊜	46	58.18 N	3.56 W
Ruatoria	172	37.53 S	178.20 E
Ruawai	172	36.08 S	174.02 E
Rub' al Khali → Ar-Rub' al-Khālī ✦[2]	118	20.00 N	51.00 E
Rubanivka	78	47.00 N	34.10 E
Rubbestadneset	26	59.49 N	5.17 E
Rubcovsk	86	51.33 N	81.10 E
Rubeho Mountains ⋏	154	6.55 S	36.30 E
Rubel'	78	51.58 N	27.04 E
Rübeland	54	51.45 N	10.50 E
Rubelles	261	48.34 N	2.41 E
Rubery ✦[8]	42	52.24 N	2.00 W
Rubeshibe	92a	43.47 N	143.38 E
Rubežinskoje	80	51.26 N	51.59 E
Rubí, Esp.	266d	41.29 N	2.02 E
Rubi, R.D.C.	154	2.49 N	25.14 E
Rubí ≃, Esp.	266d	41.26 N	2.00 E
Rubi ≃, R.D.C.	152	2.48 N	23.54 E
Rubiana	62	45.08 N	7.23 E
Rubiataba	255	15.08 S	49.48 W
Rubicon ≃	226	39.00 N	120.44 W
Rubicone ≃	66	44.08 N	12.28 E
Rubidoux	228	33.59 N	117.24 W
Rubiera	64	44.39 N	10.45 E
Rubim	255	16.23 S	40.32 W
Rubino	150	6.04 N	4.18 W
Rubio	246	7.43 N	72.22 W
Rubio Woods ♦	278	41.38 N	87.46 W
Rubizhne	83	49.01 N	38.23 E
Rubl'ovo	82	55.47 N	37.21 E
Rublyivka	78	49.15 N	33.19 E
Ruboani	140	8.06 N	30.45 E
Rubona	154	0.33 N	30.10 E

Symbols in the index entries represent the broad categories identified in the key at the right. Symbols with superior numbers (⋏[1]) identify subcategories (see complete key on page *I · 1*).

Symbole im Register stellen die rechts im Schlüssel erklärten Kategorien dar. Symbole mit hochgestellten Ziffern (⋏[1]) bezeichnen Unterabteilungen einer Kategorie (vgl. vollständiger Schlüssel auf Seite *I · 1*).

Los símbolos incluídos en el texto del índice representan las grandes categorías identificadas con la clave a la derecha. Los símbolos con numeros en su parte superior (⋏[1]) identifican las subcategorías (véase la clave completa en la página *I · 1*).

Les symboles de l'index représentent les catégories indiquées dans la légende à droite. Les symboles suivis d'un indice (⋏[1]) représentent des sous-catégories (voir légende complète à la page *I · 1*).

Os símbolos incluídos no texto do índice representam as grandes categorias identificadas com a chave à direita. Os símbolos com números em sua parte superior (⋏[1]) identificam as subcategorias (veja-se a chave completa à página *I · 1*).

English	Deutsch	Español	Français	Português
∧ Mountain	Berg	Montaña	Montagne	Montanha
⋏ Mountains	Gebirge	Montañas	Montagnes	Montanhas
)(Pass	Paß	Paso	Col	Passo
V Valley, Canyon	Tal, Cañon	Valle, Cañón	Vallée, Canyon	Vale, Canhão
≚ Plain	Ebene	Llano	Plaine	Planície
> Cape	Kap	Cabo	Cap	Cabo
I Island	Insel	Isla	Île	Ilha
II Islands	Inseln	Islas	Îles	Ilhas
≗ Other Topographic Features	Andere Topographische Objekte	Otros Elementos Topográficos	Autres données topographiques	Outros acidentes topográficos

ESPAÑOL / FRANÇAIS / PORTUGUÊS — Nombre / Nom / Nome	Página / Page	Lat.°′	Long.°′ W=Oeste/Ouest
Rubondo Island I	154	2.20 S	31.52 E
Rubondo Island National Park ♦	154	2.20 S	31.52 E
Rubtsi	83	49.12 N	37.33 E
Rubtsovsk — Rubcovsk	86	51.33 N	81.10 E
Ruby, Ak., U.S.	180	64.44 N	155.30 W
Ruby, N.Y., U.S.	210	42.01 N	74.01 W
Ruby ≃	202	45.34 N	112.21 W
Ruby Creek ≃	224	48.43 N	120.59 W
Ruby Dome ʌ	204	40.37 N	115.28 W
Ruby Lake ⊜	204	40.10 N	115.30 W
Ruby Mountains ʌ	204	40.25 N	115.35 W
Ruby Valley V	204	40.30 N	115.15 W
Rucava	76	56.09 N	21.10 E
Ruchan'	76	53.33 N	32.48 E
Ruche	261	49.02 N	2.27 E
Rucheng	100	25.34 N	113.47 E
Ruciane-Nida	30	53.39 N	21.35 E
Ručji ⊷⁸	265a	60.01 N	30.24 E
Ručjuvom	24	66.42 N	61.08 E
Rucphen	51	52.34 N	4.34 E
Ruda	64	45.50 N	13.24 E
Rudall	166	33.41 S	136.16 E
Rudall ≃	162	22.16 S	122.47 E
Rudall River National Park ♦	162	22.25 S	122.40 E
Ruda Śląska	30	50.18 N	18.51 E
Rudauli	124	26.45 N	81.45 E
Rudaymat al-Liwā'	132	33.01 N	36.35 E
Rūdbār, Afg.	128	30.09 N	62.36 E
Rūdbār, Īrān	128	36.48 N	49.24 E
Rudbøl	41	54.54 N	8.45 E
Ruddervoorde	50	51.06 N	3.12 E
Ruddiman Terrace	216	43.12 N	86.17 W
Rudelsburg ⊥	54	51.07 N	11.43 E
Ruden I	54	54.12 N	13.46 E
Rudersberg	54	48.53 N	9.32 E
Rüdersdorf, Dtsch.	54	52.29 N	13.47 E
Rüdersdorf, Öst.	61	47.03 N	16.07 E
Rüdersdorf, Forst ⊷³	264a	52.26 N	13.50 E
Rüdesheim am Rhein	56	49.59 N	7.56 E
Rudewa	154	10.06 S	34.39 E
Rudge Ramos	287b	23.41 S	46.34 W
Rudiškes	76	54.31 N	24.50 E
Rudivka	83	49.24 N	38.27 E
Rudkino	78	51.27 N	39.01 E
Rudkøbing	41	54.56 N	10.43 E
Rudky	78	49.39 N	23.29 E
Rudn'a, Ross.	76	54.57 N	31.06 E
Rudn'a, Ross.	80	50.48 N	44.33 E
Rudnaja Pristan'	89	44.22 N	135.48 E
Rudnica ≃	265b	53.43 N	37.56 E
Rudnevo	82	54.44 N	38.09 E
Rudničnyj, Kaz.	86	44.40 N	78.55 E
Rudničnyj, Ross.	24	59.38 N	52.27 E
Rudničnyj, Ross.	86	56.08 N	86.12 E
Rudničnyj, Ross.	86	59.42 N	60.18 E
Rudnik	30	52.28 N	22.15 E
Rüdnitz	54	52.43 N	13.37 E
Rudnyj, Kaz.	86	52.57 N	63.07 E
Rudnyj, Ross.	89	44.21 N	134.58 E
Rudnytsya	78	48.15 N	28.53 E
Rudo	38	43.37 N	19.22 E
Rudolf, Lake (Lake Turkana) ⊜	144	3.30 N	36.00 E
Rudolfov	61	48.59 N	14.34 E
Rudolph	216	41.17 N	83.40 W
Rudolstadt	54	50.43 N	11.20 E
Rudong, Zhg.	102	21.39 N	111.23 E
Rudong, Zhg.	106	32.19 N	121.12 E
Rudova	80	53.07 N	42.23 E
Rudow ⊷⁸	54	52.25 N	13.30 E
Rūdsar	128	37.08 N	50.18 E
Ruds Vedby	41	55.33 N	11.23 E
Rudyard, Mi., U.S.	190	46.13 N	84.36 W
Rudyard, Mt., U.S.	202	48.33 N	110.33 W
Rudyerd Bay c	182	55.35 N	130.44 W
Rudzensk	76	53.36 N	27.52 E
Rue, Fr.	56	50.16 N	1.40 E
Rue, Schw.	58	46.37 N	6.50 E
Ruecas ≃	34	39.00 N	5.55 W
Ruel-Malmaison	261	48.53 N	2.11 E
Ruen ʌ	38	42.10 N	22.31 E
Ruenya (Luenha) ≃	154	16.24 S	33.48 E
Rufā'ah	140	14.46 N	33.22 E
Ruffano	39	39.59 N	18.15 E
Ruffec	32	46.01 N	0.12 E
Ruffieu	58	46.00 N	5.40 E
Ruffieux	58	45.51 N	5.50 E
Ruffin	192	33.01 N	80.48 W
Ruffle Bar I	278	40.36 N	46.51 W
Rufford	262	48.58 N	2.49 W
Rufford Old Hall ⊥	262	53.38 N	2.49 W
Ruffs Dale	279b	40.10 N	79.37 W
Rufidschi — Rufiji ≃	154	8.00 S	39.20 E
Rufina	154	8.00 S	39.20 E
Rufino	252	34.16 S	62.42 W
Rufisque	154	14.44 N	17.17 W
Rufunsa	154	15.05 S	29.40 E
Rufus	224	45.41 N	120.44 W
Rufus, Mount ʌ	168b	34.20 S	139.07 E
Rugao	106	32.25 N	120.38 E
Rugby, Eng., U.K.	42	52.23 N	1.15 W
Rugby, N.D., U.S.	198	48.22 N	99.59 W
Rugeley	42	52.46 N	1.55 W
Rügen I	54	54.25 N	13.24 E
Rüggeberg	263	51.16 N	7.22 E
Rugged Mountain ʌ	182	50.02 N	126.41 W
Ruggles Beach	216	41.22 N	82.29 W
Rugles	50	48.49 N	0.42 E
Rugufu ≃	154	5.10 S	30.14 E
Ruguj	76	59.28 N	32.50 E
Ruhama	132	31.30 N	34.42 E
Ruhea	124	26.19 N	88.25 E
Ruhengeri	154	1.30 S	29.38 E
Ruhla	54	50.53 N	10.22 E
Ruhland	54	51.27 N	13.52 E
Ruhlsdorf	264a	52.23 N	13.16 E
Ruhmannsfelden	60	48.59 N	12.59 E
Ruhner Berge ʌ²	54	53.17 N	11.55 E
Ruhnu saar I	76	57.48 N	23.15 E
Ruhpolding	60	47.45 N	12.38 E
Ruhr ≃	52	51.27 N	6.44 E
Ruhrort ⊷⁸	263	51.26 N	6.45 E
Ruhr-Universität ∨²	263	51.27 N	7.16 E
Ruhstorf an der Rott	60	48.26 N	13.20 E
Ruhudji ≃	154	8.52 S	36.01 E
Ruhuhu ≃	154	10.31 S	34.34 E
Ruhuhu National Park ♦	122	6.30 N	81.30 E
Rui'an	100	27.49 N	120.38 E
Ruichang	100	29.41 N	115.40 E
Ruicheng	102	34.45 N	110.45 E
Ruidoso	200	33.19 N	105.40 W
Ruidoso, Río ≃	200	33.19 N	105.08 W
Ruidoso Downs	200	33.19 N	105.36 W
Ruifeng Sha I	106	31.25 N	121.36 E
Ruihong	108	28.45 N	116.00 E
Ruijin	100	25.50 N	116.00 E
Ruinen	51	52.46 N	6.21 E
Ruiselede ⊷⁸	50	51.03 N	3.24 E
Ruivo, Pico ʌ	148	32.45 N	16.56 W
Ruiz	234	21.57 N	105.09 W
Ruiz, Nevado del ʌ¹	246	4.54 N	75.18 W
Ruiz de Montoya	252	26.59 S	55.03 W
Rūjiena	76	57.54 N	25.21 E
Rujm ar-Rashīd, Jabal ʌ	132	31.53 N	36.18 E
Rujm as-Sakhrī	132	31.02 N	35.43 E
Rukan-shō ⊷²	174m	26.06 N	127.32 E
Ruki ≃	154	0.05 N	18.17 E
Rukni ≃	126	23.33 N	86.33 E
Rukungiri	154	0.48 S	29.55 E
Rukwa ⊷⁴	154	7.00 S	31.30 E
Rukwa, Lake ⊜	154	8.00 S	32.25 E
Rule	196	33.11 N	99.53 W
Rule Creek ≃	198	38.02 N	103.02 W
Ruleville	194	33.43 N	90.33 W
Rully	52	52.20 N	8.04 E
Rully	58	46.52 N	4.45 E
Rulo	198	40.03 N	95.25 W
Rülzheim	56	49.09 N	8.16 E
Rum	61	47.08 N	16.51 E
Rum I	46	57.00 N	6.20 W
Rum, Jabal ʌ	132	45.11 N	93.23 W
Rum, Sound of ᶸ	46	56.56 N	6.14 W
Rumaa	38	45.00 N	19.49 E
Rumaat	164	5.49 S	132.48 E
Rumah	128	25.34 N	47.09 E
Rumahtinggih	164	6.23 S	140.17 E
Rum'ancevo, Ross.	82	55.38 N	37.26 E
Rum'ancevo, Ross.	82	55.58 N	36.32 E
Rumänien — Romania ⊡¹	38	46.00 N	25.30 E
Rumaysh	132	33.05 N	35.22 E
Rumbek	140	6.48 N	29.41 E
Rumbeke	50	50.56 N	3.10 E
Rumberpon, Pulau I	164	1.50 S	134.15 E
Rumbling Bridge	46	56.10 N	3.35 W
Rumburk	54	50.57 N	14.32 E
Rum Cay I	238	23.40 N	74.53 W
Rumelange	56	49.28 N	6.02 E
Rumelifeneri ⊷⁸	267b	41.14 N	29.06 E
Rumelihisarı ⊷⁸	267b	41.05 N	29.03 E
Rumelihisarı ⊥	267b	41.05 N	29.03 E
Rumelikavağı ⊷⁸	267b	41.11 N	29.04 E
Rumford	188	44.33 N	70.33 W
Rumford ≃	283	41.58 N	71.11 W
Rumia	30	54.35 N	18.25 E
Rumilly	58	45.48 N	4.16 E
Rumilly	62	45.52 N	5.57 E
Rumiñahui ʌ¹	82	56.31 N	38.47 E
Rum Jungle	164	13.01 S	131.00 E
R'umki	265a	59.47 N	30.22 E
Rümlang	58	47.26 N	8.32 E
Rummah, Wādī ar- V	128	26.12 N	44.04 E
Rummānah, Bi'r ar- ⊤⁴	142	31.00 N	32.40 E
Rummel	214	40.13 N	78.48 W
Rummelsburg ⊷⁸	264a	52.30 N	13.29 E
Rummenohl ⊷⁸	263	51.17 N	7.32 E
Rumney	42	51.31 N	3.07 W
Rumoi	92a	43.56 N	141.39 E
Rumont	56	48.50 N	5.17 E
Rump Mountain ʌ	154	11.01 S	33.52 E
Rumphi	154	11.01 S	33.52 E
Rumson	208	40.22 N	73.59 W
Rumst	50	51.05 N	4.25 E
Rumula	164	16.35 S	145.20 E
Runan	100	33.01 N	114.22 E
Runaway, Cape ⊁	172	37.32 S	177.59 E
Runazi	154	2.47 S	31.28 E
Runcorn ⊷⁸	44	53.20 N	2.44 W
Rundēni	76	56.16 N	27.52 E
Rundu	156	17.52 S	19.43 E
Rundvik	26	63.32 N	19.26 E
Rûng, Kaôh I	120	10.44 N	103.14 E
Rungan ≃	120	26.38 N	65.43 E
Rungis	261	48.45 N	2.21 E
Rungis-Halles, Marché de ⩗	261	48.46 N	2.21 E
Rungsted	41	55.53 N	12.33 E
Rungus Point ⊁	116	13.43 N	123.58 E
Rungwa, Tan.	154	7.21 S	31.40 E
Rungwa, Tan.	154	6.57 S	33.31 E
Rungwa ≃	154	7.36 S	31.50 E
Rungwa Game Reserve ⊷⁴	154	7.00 S	34.10 E
Rungwe	154	9.00 S	33.40 E
Runhällen	28	60.02 N	16.49 E
Runheji	100	32.30 N	116.05 E
Runn ⊜	56	50.24 N	8.10 E
Runnemede	285	39.51 N	75.04 W
Running Springs	228	34.12 N	117.07 W
Running Water Draw V	196	33.58 N	101.30 W
Runnymede ⊷⁸	260	51.24 N	0.32 W
Runnymede ⊥	42	51.26 N	0.34 W
Rünthe	263	51.39 N	7.39 E
Runwell	260	51.37 N	0.32 E
Ruo ≃, Afr.	154	16.33 S	35.09 E
Ruo'ergai	102	41.00 N	100.17 E
Ruoheng	100	28.24 N	121.31 E
Ruokolahti	26	61.17 N	28.50 E
Ruoqiang	96	38.30 N	88.05 E
Ruoti	68	40.43 N	15.41 E
Ruovesi	26	61.59 N	24.05 E
Rupanco	254	40.45 S	72.42 W
Rupanco, Lago ⊜	254	40.49 S	72.28 W
Rupat, Pulau I	114	1.50 N	101.35 E
Rupat, Selat ᶸ	114	1.50 N	101.28 E
Rupdia	126	23.08 N	89.18 E
Rupea	38	46.02 N	25.13 E
Rupert, Id., U.S.	202	42.37 N	113.40 W
Rupert, Vt., U.S.	210	43.15 N	73.13 W
Rupert, W.V., U.S.	188	37.57 N	80.41 W
Rupert, Rivière de ≃	176	51.29 N	78.45 W
Rupert Coast ⊼²	166	20.53 S	142.23 E
Rupganj	126	23.42 N	90.31 E
Rūpnagar	124	30.59 N	76.31 E
Rūpnārāyan ≃	126	22.15 N	88.02 E
Ruponda	154	10.15 S	38.42 E
Ruppertenrod	56	50.37 N	9.05 E
Ruppiner See ⊜	54	52.54 N	12.50 E
Rupprechtseck ʌ	61	47.14 N	14.00 E
Rupt de Mad ≃	56	49.00 N	6.02 E
Rupt-sur-Moselle	58	47.56 N	6.48 E
Rupununi ≃	248	4.03 N	58.34 W
Ruqād, Wādī ar- V	132	32.44 N	35.46 E
Rur (Roer) ≃	52	51.12 N	5.59 E
Rural Hall	192	36.14 N	80.17 W
Rural Retreat	192	36.53 N	81.16 W
Rural Ridge	279b	40.35 N	79.50 W
Rural Valley	214	40.48 N	79.18 W
Ruri ≃	154	0.30 N	30.52 E
Ruri-kei ⊥	96	35.03 N	135.26 E
Rurrenabaque	248	14.28 S	67.34 W
Rurstausee ⊜¹	56	50.36 N	6.22 E
Rururtu I	158	22.25 S	151.20 W
Rusambo	154	16.35 S	32.12 E
Rusape	154	18.32 S	32.07 E
Rusava ≃	61	49.19 N	17.34 E
Rush, Ire.	48	53.32 N	6.06 W
Rush, N.Y., U.S.	210	42.59 N	77.39 W
Rush, Pa., U.S.	210	41.47 N	76.03 W
Rush ≃	218	39.37 N	85.27 W
Rush ≃, N.D., U.S.	198	47.00 N	96.54 W
Rush ≃, Wi., U.S.	190	44.34 N	92.19 W
Rushan (Xiacun)	98	36.54 N	121.29 E
Rush Center	198	38.27 N	99.18 W
Rush City	190	45.41 N	92.57 W
Rush Creek ≃, Co., U.S.	198	38.22 N	102.32 W
Rush Creek ≃, Ne., U.S.	198	41.27 N	102.32 W
Rush Creek ≃, N.Y., U.S.	284a	42.00 N	78.52 W
Rush Creek ≃, Oh., U.S.	188	39.38 N	82.33 W
Rush Creek ≃, Ok., U.S.	214	40.34 N	83.20 W
Rushden	42	52.17 N	0.36 W
Rushford, Mn., U.S.	190	43.48 N	91.45 W
Rushford, Tn., U.S.	210	42.23 N	78.15 W
Rushford Lake ⊜¹	214	42.23 N	78.12 W
Rush Hill	219	39.13 N	91.43 W
Rush Lake ⊜, On., Can.	190	47.48 N	82.12 W
Rush Lake ⊜, Wi., U.S.	190	43.56 N	88.49 W
Rushland	285	40.15 N	75.02 W
Rushmore	198	43.37 N	95.48 W
Rusholme ⊷⁸	262	53.27 N	2.12 W
Rush Springs	196	34.46 N	97.57 W
Rushsylvania	216	40.27 N	83.40 W
Rushville, Il., U.S.	219	40.07 N	90.33 W
Rushville, In., U.S.	218	39.36 N	85.26 W
Rushville, Ne., U.S.	198	42.43 N	102.27 W
Rushville, N.Y., U.S.	210	42.45 N	77.13 W
Rusinga Island I	154	0.24 S	34.10 E
Rusizi (Ruzizi) ≃	154	3.16 S	29.14 E
Rusk	222	31.47 N	95.09 W
Rusk ⊡⁶	222	32.10 N	94.50 W
Ruskin, B.C., Can.	224	49.12 N	122.28 W
Ruskin, Fl., U.S.	220	27.43 N	82.26 W
Ruskington	44	53.02 N	0.23 W
Rusné	76	55.18 N	21.22 E
Rušoni ≃	76	56.11 N	27.02 E
Rusovce	61	48.04 N	17.10 E
Ruspina	272b	22.29 N	88.21 E
Russas	250	4.56 S	37.58 W
Russbach ≃	56	48.10 N	16.58 E
Russee	41	54.18 N	10.06 E
Russell, Mb., Can.	184	50.47 N	101.15 W
Russell, On., Can.	212	45.15 N	75.22 W
Russell, N.Z.	172	35.16 S	174.07 E
Russell, Ia., U.S.	190	40.58 N	93.11 W
Russell, Ks., U.S.	198	38.53 N	98.51 W
Russell, Ky., U.S.	188	38.31 N	82.41 W
Russell, Mn., U.S.	198	44.19 N	95.57 W
Russell, Pa., U.S.	214	41.56 N	79.08 W
Russell, Cape ⊁	176	75.15 N	117.35 W
Russell, Mount ʌ	180	62.48 N	151.52 W
Russell Cave National Monument ♦	194	34.54 N	85.48 W
Russell Creek ≃	194	37.14 N	85.30 W
Russell Gardens	276	40.47 N	73.43 W
Russell Island I	176	73.55 N	98.25 W
Russell Islands II	175e	9.04 S	159.12 E
Russellkonda	124	19.56 N	84.35 E
Russell Lake ⊜	184	56.15 N	101.30 W
Russell Range ʌ	162	33.24 S	123.28 E
Russells Point	216	40.28 N	83.54 W
Russell Springs	194	37.03 N	85.05 W
Russellton	214	40.37 N	79.50 W
Russellville, Al., U.S.	194	34.30 N	87.43 W
Russellville, Ar., U.S.	194	35.16 N	93.08 W
Russellville, Ky., U.S.	194	36.50 N	86.53 W
Russellville, Mo., U.S.	194	38.30 N	92.26 W
Russellville, Oh., U.S.	218	38.51 N	83.47 W
Russellville, Or., U.S.	224	45.31 N	122.33 W
Rüsselsheim	56	50.00 N	8.25 E
Russi	64	44.22 N	12.02 E
Russia ⊡¹, Europe	72	60.00 N	80.00 E
Russia ⊡¹, Europe	74	60.00 N	100.00 E
Russian ≃	204	38.27 N	123.08 W
Russian Mission	180	61.47 N	161.19 W
Russiaville	218	40.25 N	86.16 W
Russka	76	58.59 N	28.30 E
Russkaja Bujlovka	78	50.59 N	40.03 E
Russkaja Gavan'	74	76.10 N	62.35 E
Russkaja Poľana	86	53.47 N	73.53 E
Russkaja Talovka	80	49.59 N	49.05 E
Russkaja Žuravka	80	50.21 N	40.33 E
Russkij	89	43.03 N	131.50 E
Russkij, ostrov I	74	77.00 N	96.00 E
Russkij Aktaš	80	55.02 N	52.07 E
Russkij Brod	76	52.36 N	37.22 E
Russkij Kameškir	80	52.56 N	46.06 E
Russkij Turek	80	57.03 N	50.13 E
Russkij Vožoj	80	56.57 N	53.22 E
Russkij Zavorot, mys ⊁	24	68.58 N	54.34 E
Russko-Dobrino	80	57.45 N	38.56 E
Russko-Vysockoje	265a	59.42 N	29.56 E
Rust, Öst.	61	47.48 N	16.41 E
Rust, Tn., U.S.	210	41.48 N	76.19 W
Rustam	123	34.21 N	72.17 E
Rustavi	84	41.33 N	45.02 E
Rustburg	192	37.16 N	79.06 W
Rustenburg	156	25.37 S	27.08 E
Rustic Canyon V	280	34.04 N	118.31 W
Rustig	158	27.22 S	27.06 E
Ruston, La., U.S.	194	32.31 N	92.38 W
Ruston, Wa., U.S.	224	47.17 N	122.30 W
Rusville	273d	26.10 S	28.18 E
Ruszów	54	51.21 N	15.09 E
Ruta	34	37.19 N	4.22 W
Rütenbrock	52	52.50 N	7.10 E
Rutenga	156	21.08 S	30.45 E
Rutherford, Ca., U.S.	226	38.28 N	122.25 W
Rutherford, N.J., U.S.	210	40.49 N	74.06 W
Rutherford, Tn., U.S.	194	36.07 N	88.59 W
Rutherfordton	192	35.22 N	81.57 W
Rutherglen, Scot., U.K.	46	55.50 N	4.12 W
Ruther Glen, Va., U.S.	208	37.56 N	77.27 W
Ruthin	44	53.07 N	3.18 W
Ruthven, On., Can.	217	42.03 N	82.40 W
Ruthven, U.K.	46	57.04 N	4.00 W
Rūti	58	47.16 N	8.51 E
Rutigliano	68	41.01 N	17.00 E
Rutino	68	40.18 N	15.04 E
Rutland, B.C., Can.	182	49.54 N	119.24 W
Rutland, Fl., U.S.	220	28.51 N	82.13 W
Rutland, Ma., U.S.	210	42.22 N	71.56 W
Rutland, N.D., U.S.	198	46.03 N	97.30 W
Rutland, Vt., U.S.	188	43.36 N	72.58 W
Rutland ⊡⁶	210	43.37 N	73.15 W
Rutland Island I	110	11.25 N	92.40 E
Rutland State Park ♦	207	42.23 N	72.01 W
Rutland Water ⊜¹	42	52.39 N	0.38 W
Rutledge, Ga., U.S.	192	33.37 N	83.36 W
Rutledge, Pa., U.S.	285	39.54 N	75.20 W
Rutledge, Tn., U.S.	192	36.16 N	83.30 W
Rutog	120	33.27 N	79.43 E
Rutshuru	154	1.11 S	29.27 E
Rüttenscheid ⊷⁸	263	51.26 N	7.00 E
Rutter	190	46.06 N	80.40 W
Rutul	84	41.33 N	47.25 E
Ruukki	26	64.40 N	25.06 E
Ruurlo	52	52.05 N	6.26 E
Ruvo del Monte	68	40.51 N	15.32 E
Ruvo di Puglia	68	41.07 N	16.29 E
Ruvu	154	6.48 S	38.39 E
Ruvu ≃	154	6.23 S	38.52 E
Ruvubu (Rovubu) ≃	154	2.23 S	30.47 E
Ruvuma ≃¹	154	11.00 S	36.00 E
Ruvuma (Rovuma) ≃	154	10.29 S	40.28 E
Ruwayān, Wādī ar- ≃⁷	142	29.07 N	30.10 E
Ruwaybah ⊤⁴	140	15.39 N	28.45 E
Ruwayfi, Jabal ar- ʌ	132	31.12 N	36.00 E
Ruwenzori National Park ♦	154	0.15 S	30.00 E
Ruwenzori Range ʌ	154	0.23 N	29.54 E
Ruwer	56	49.47 N	6.43 E
Ruwer ≃	56	49.47 N	6.42 E
Ruya (Luia) ≃	154	16.34 S	33.12 E
Ruyang	100	34.10 N	112.26 E
Ruy Barbosa	250	12.18 S	40.27 W
Ruyigi	154	3.29 S	30.15 E
Ruyton-Eleven-Towns	42	52.48 N	2.54 W
Ruza	82	55.42 N	36.12 E
Ruza ≃	82	55.38 N	36.17 E
Ruzajevka, Kaz.	86	52.49 N	66.57 E
Ruzajevka, Ross.	80	54.04 N	44.57 E
Ružany	76	52.52 N	24.53 E
Ružomberok	30	49.05 N	19.18 E
Ruzsa	30	56.18 N	43.14 E
Ruzyně ⊷⁸	54	50.06 N	14.17 E
Ruzzah, Jabal ʌ²	142	30.01 N	36.04 E
Rwamagana	154	1.57 S	30.34 E
Rwanda ⊡¹, Afr.	138	2.00 S	30.00 E
Rwanda ⊡¹, Afr.	154	2.00 S	30.00 E
Rwashamaire	154	0.49 S	30.08 E
Ry	41	56.05 N	9.46 E
Ryal Fold	262	53.41 N	2.30 W
Ryan	196	34.01 N	97.57 W
Ryan ≃	182	50.25 N	122.43 W
Ryan Field ♦	278	42.04 N	87.41 W
Ryan, Loch c	44	54.58 N	5.02 W
Ryan Peak ʌ	202	43.54 N	114.25 W
Ryans Creek ≃	169	36.43 S	146.12 E
Ryarsh	260	51.19 N	0.24 E
Ryasnopil'	78	47.04 N	31.12 E
Ryazan' — R'azan'	80	54.38 N	39.44 E
Rybačij, poluostrov ⊁¹	24	69.42 N	32.36 E
Rybačje	86	46.27 N	81.32 E
Rybačje ≃	86	46.27 N	81.32 E
Rybakovo ⊷⁸	265a	60.00 N	30.30 E
Rybackoje ⊷⁸	265a	59.50 N	30.30 E
Rybakvka	78	46.37 N	31.20 E
Rybinsk	78	58.03 N	38.52 E
Rybinsker Stausee — Rybinskoje vodochranilišče ⊜¹	76	58.30 N	38.25 E
Rybinskije Budy	78	51.13 N	35.57 E
Rybinskoje	86	55.47 N	94.47 E
Rybinskoje vodochranilišče ⊜¹	76	58.30 N	38.25 E
Rybkino	80	54.15 N	43.46 E
Rybnaja Sloboda	80	55.28 N	50.09 E
Rybnik	30	50.06 N	18.32 E
Rybnoje, Ross.	76	54.44 N	39.30 E
Rybnoje, Ross.	86	58.08 N	94.30 E
Rybnovsk	89	53.12 N	141.50 E
Ryburn ≃	262	53.43 N	1.53 W
Rybuška	80	51.17 N	45.26 E
Rychwał	30	52.05 N	18.09 E
Ryčkovo	58	55.09 N	61.43 E
Rycroft	182	55.45 N	118.43 W
Ryd	28	56.28 N	14.41 E
Rydaholm	28	56.59 N	14.16 E
Rydal, Austl.	170	33.29 S	150.02 E
Rydal, Austl.	285	40.06 N	75.06 W
Rydalmere ≃	274a	33.49 S	151.02 E
Rydbo	28	59.28 N	18.11 E
Ryde, Austl.	170	33.49 S	151.06 E
Ryde, Eng., U.K.	42	50.44 N	1.10 W
Ryde ⊷⁸	274a	33.49 S	151.06 E
Ryder's Hill ʌ²	42	50.31 N	3.53 W
Ryderwood	224	46.22 N	123.02 W
Rydgóvård	41	55.28 N	13.35 E
Rydzyna	30	51.48 N	16.40 E
Rye, Austl.	169	38.23 S	144.49 E
Rye, Eng., U.K.	42	50.57 N	0.44 E
Rye, N.Y., U.S.	210	40.58 N	73.41 W
Rye, Tx., U.S.	222	30.27 N	94.46 W
Rye ≃	44	54.10 N	0.44 W
Ryegate	202	46.17 N	109.15 W
Rye Hills-Rye Brook	276	41.00 N	73.41 W
Rye Lake ⊜	276	41.04 N	73.43 W
Ryeosu — Yŏsu	94	34.44 N	127.44 E
Rye Patch Reservoir ⊜¹	204	40.38 N	118.18 W
Ryer Island I	282	38.05 N	122.01 W
Ryes	32	49.19 N	0.37 W
Ryfylke ⊷¹	28	59.20 N	6.30 E
Ryfylke ⊷⁹	28	59.10 N	6.05 E
Rygge	28	59.23 N	10.43 E
Rygnestad	28	59.16 N	7.29 E
Rykaartspos	158	26.32 S	26.39 E
Ryker Lake ⊜	276	41.03 N	74.33 W
Rykerts	182	49.00 N	116.35 W
Ryki	30	51.39 N	21.56 E
Rykovo	265b	58.09 N	38.13 E
Ryley	182	53.17 N	112.26 W
Rylovići	38	42.25 N	18.35 E
Ryl'sk	78	51.34 N	34.43 E
Rylstone	170	32.48 S	149.58 E
Rymařov	30	49.56 N	17.16 E
Ryn	30	53.56 N	21.33 E
Rynfield	273d	26.09 S	28.20 E
Ryńsk	30	53.09 N	18.57 E
Ryn-Peski ⊷²	80	48.30 N	47.00 E
Ryō	270	34.44 N	135.42 E
Ryōgami-sanchi ʌ²	98	36.00 N	138.05 E
Ryōhaku-sanchi ʌ²	96	36.20 N	136.45 E
Ryojun — Lüshun	98	38.48 N	121.16 E
Ryōtsu	98	38.05 N	138.26 E
Ryōyō	100	31.18 N	118.26 E
Rypin	30	53.04 N	19.25 E
Rysjö	28	62.01 N	15.30 E
Ryšňa	76	55.37 N	27.28 E
Rysy ʌ	30	49.12 N	20.04 E
Ryton, Eng., U.K.	44	54.58 N	1.46 W
Ryton-on-Dunsmore	42	52.22 N	1.25 W
Rytterne	28	59.31 N	16.22 E
Ryūga-dake ʌ	96	33.54 N	140.11 E
Ryūgasaki	98	35.54 N	140.11 E
Ryūjin	96	33.54 N	135.32 E
Ryukyu Islands — Nansei-shotō II	196	26.30 N	128.00 E
Ryukyu Trench ⊷¹	174m	24.26 N	125.00 E
Ryūō, Ross.	270	34.26 N	135.42 E
Ryūō, Nihon	94	35.39 N	136.07 E
Ryūsen	270	34.28 N	135.37 E
Ryūyō	94	34.40 N	137.48 E
Rżaksa	80	52.09 N	42.02 E
Rżanica	76	53.26 N	33.55 E
Ržava	78	51.14 N	36.43 E
Rzepin	30	52.22 N	14.50 E
Rzeszów ≃⁴	30	50.00 N	22.00 E
Rzeszów ⊡⁴	30	50.00 N	22.00 E
Ržev	76	56.16 N	34.20 E
Rzhyshchiv	78	49.58 N	31.03 E
Ržovka ⊷⁸	265a	59.58 N	30.30 E

S

Nombre / Nom / Nome	Página / Page	Lat.°′	Long.°′ W=Oeste
Sa	110	18.34 N	100.45 E
Sa ≃	105	40.22 N	117.58 E
Sa'ad	132	31.28 N	34.32 E
Sa'ādatābād	128	30.06 N	53.08 E
Sääksjärvi ⊜	26	61.24 N	22.24 E
Saal	54	54.19 N	12.29 E
Saalach ≃	64	47.51 N	13.00 E
Saal an der Donau	60	48.54 N	11.56 E
Saal an der Saale	56	50.19 N	10.21 E
Saalbach	64	47.23 N	12.38 E
Saalburg	54	50.30 N	11.43 E
Saaldorf, Dtsch.	54	50.27 N	11.41 E
Saaldorf, Dtsch.	64	47.52 N	12.56 E
Saale ≃	54	51.57 N	11.55 E
Saaler Bodden c	54	54.14 N	12.26 E
Saales	58	48.21 N	7.07 E
Saaletalsperre ⊜⁶	54	50.30 N	11.43 E
Saalfeld	54	50.39 N	11.22 E
Saalfelden	64	47.25 N	12.51 E
Saamar	88	50.08 N	106.10 E
Saâne ≃, Fr.	50	49.54 N	0.56 E
Saane (Sarine) ≃, Schw.	58	46.59 N	7.15 E
Saanen	58	46.29 N	7.16 E
Saanenmöser	58	46.31 N	7.18 E
Saanich Inlet c	224	48.38 N	123.30 W
Saar — Saarland ⊡³	56	49.20 N	7.00 E
Saar (Sarre) ≃	56	49.42 N	6.34 E
Saarbrücken	56	49.14 N	6.59 E
Saarburg	56	49.36 N	6.33 E
Sääre	76	57.56 N	22.02 E
Saarekouis — Saarlouis	56	49.21 N	6.45 E
Saaremaa I	76	58.25 N	22.30 E
Saarijärvi	26	62.43 N	25.16 E
Saaristomeren kansallispuisto ♦	26	59.50 N	21.50 E
Saarland ⊡³	56	49.20 N	7.00 E
Saarlautern — Saarlouis	56	49.21 N	6.45 E
Saarlouis	56	49.21 N	6.45 E
Saarmund	264a	52.19 N	13.07 E
Saarn ⊷⁸	263	51.24 N	6.53 E
Saarnberg ⊷⁸	263	51.25 N	6.53 E
Saas Almagell	58	46.07 N	7.58 E
Saas Grund	58	46.07 N	7.55 E
Saastal V	58	46.10 N	7.56 E
Saatli	84	39.56 N	48.23 E
Saavedra	252	37.45 S	62.22 W
Saba I	238	17.38 N	63.10 W
Saba ≃, Nihon	96	35.30 N	131.30 E
Saba ≃, Ross.	76	59.08 N	29.00 E
Sabā', Wādī al- V	128	28.35 N	36.35 E
Šabac	38	44.45 N	19.42 E
Sabadell	34	41.33 N	2.06 E
Sabae	94	35.57 N	136.11 E
Saba'ah	142	30.15 N	32.33 E
Sabah ⊡³	112	5.20 N	117.10 E
Sabajevo	80	54.15 N	45.06 E
Sabak, Cape ⊁	181a	52.20 N	173.45 E
Sabak Bernam	114	3.46 N	100.59 E
Sabal	112	0.59 S	123.14 E
Sabalán, Kūh-e ʌ	84	38.15 N	47.48 E
Sabalana, Kepulauan II	112	6.45 S	118.50 E
Sabalgarh	124	26.15 N	77.24 E
Sabana, Archipiélago de II	240m	23.00 N	80.00 W
Sabana de La Mar	240	19.04 N	69.24 W
Sabana de Mendoza	246	9.26 N	70.46 W
Sabanagrande, Hond.	236	13.50 N	87.15 W
Sabanagrande, P.R.	240f	18.05 N	66.58 W
Sabanalamar, Ensenada c	240p	21.36 N	78.44 W
Sabanalarga	246	10.38 N	74.55 W
Sabana Llana	240f	18.02 N	66.05 W
Sabaneta, Rep. Dom.	240	19.09 N	69.30 W
Sabaneta, Ven.	246	8.44 N	69.56 W
Sabaneta, Puntan ⊁	174a	15.17 N	145.49 E
Sabang (Dampalas), Indon.	114	0.11 N	119.51 E
Sabang (Dampelas), Indon.	114	5.55 N	95.19 E
Sabanözü	130	40.29 N	33.18 E
Sabará	255	19.54 S	43.48 W
Sabarei	154	4.20 N	36.55 E
Sabari ≃	122	17.34 N	81.15 E
Sabarmati ≃	132	22.18 N	72.22 E
Sabastīyah (Samaria) ⊥	132	32.17 N	35.12 E
Sab'atayn, Ramlat as- ⊷⁸	144	15.30 N	46.10 E
Sabáthu	124	30.59 N	76.59 E
Sabáudia	68	41.18 N	13.01 E
Sabaudia, Lago di c	68	41.16 N	13.02 E
Sábava Wanak	154	10.33 N	44.08 E
Sabaya	248	19.01 S	68.23 W
Sabáyah, Jabal ʌ	142	28.43 N	34.02 E
Sabbioneta	64	44.59 N	10.29 E
Sabčat Bela	140	34.05 N	0.20 E
Sabderat	140	15.27 N	36.51 E
Sabetha	198	39.54 N	95.48 W
Sabhā, Lībiyā	146	27.03 N	14.26 E
Sabhā, Al-Urd.	132	32.19 N	36.29 E
Sabi (Save) ≃, Afr.	156	21.00 S	35.02 E
Sabi ≃, India	124	28.29 N	76.44 E
Sabicu	240p	22.54 N	80.06 W
Sabidana, Jabal ʌ	140	18.04 N	36.50 E
Sabie	156	25.10 S	30.47 E
Sabillasville	208	39.42 N	77.27 W
Sabina	216	39.29 N	83.38 W
Sabina ⊷⁹	68	42.15 N	12.42 E
Sabinal	222	29.19 N	99.28 W
Sabinal, Cayo I	240p	21.38 N	77.18 W
Sabinas	234	27.51 N	101.07 W
Sabinas ≃	232	27.37 N	100.42 W
Sabinas Hidalgo	234	26.30 N	100.10 W
Sabine ⊡⁶	222	31.00 N	93.45 W
Sabine ≃	222	29.44 N	93.54 W
Sabine, Cowleech Fork ≃	222	33.03 N	95.59 W
Sabine, Mount ʌ, Ant.	9	71.55 N	169.33 E
Sabine, Mount ʌ, Austl.	169	38.38 S	143.44 E
Sabine, South Fork ≃	222	32.52 N	96.10 W
Sabine Bay c	176	75.35 N	109.30 W
Sabine Lake ⊜	222	29.50 N	93.50 W
Sabine Pass ᶸ	194	29.44 N	93.52 W
Sabine Peninsula ⊁¹	176	76.20 N	109.30 W
Sabini, Monti ʌ	68	42.13 N	12.50 E
Sabinópolis	255	18.40 S	43.06 W
Sabinov	30	49.06 N	21.06 E
Sabinsville	210	41.52 N	77.31 W
Sabir, Jabal ʌ	144	13.30 N	44.03 E
Şabirabad	84	40.01 N	48.29 E
Sabla	38	43.32 N	28.32 E
Sabl'a, gora ʌ	24	64.48 N	58.50 E
Sablayan	116	12.50 N	120.46 E
Sable, Anse au c	275a	46.21 N	73.56 W
Sable, Cape ⊁	186	43.25 N	65.35 W
Sable, Cape ⊁¹	220	25.12 N	81.05 W
Sable, Île de ⊤	158	19.15 S	159.56 E
Sable, Rivière du ≃	176	53.30 N	68.21 W
Sable Island I	186	43.55 N	59.50 W
Sables, River aux ≃	190	46.13 N	82.04 W
Sablé-sur-Sarthe	32	47.50 N	0.20 W
Sabljinskoje	84	44.31 N	43.14 E
Šablykino	76	52.51 N	35.12 E
Sabo	152	7.50 N	17.49 E
Sabocero	236	6.32 S	39.54 W
Sabogal ≃	236	10.55 N	84.43 W
Sáboli ⊷⁸	272a	28.43 N	77.18 E
Sabonkafi	150	14.38 N	8.45 E
Sabor ≃	34	41.10 N	7.07 W
Sabou	150	12.04 N	2.14 W
Sabourin, Lac ⊜	176	47.58 N	77.41 W
Sabra, Tanjung ⊁	164	2.17 S	132.19 E
Sabrātah	146	32.47 N	12.29 E
Sabres	32	44.09 N	0.44 W
Sabrevois	206	45.12 N	73.14 W
Sabrina Coast ⊼²	9	67.00 S	119.30 E
Sabuda, Pulau I	164	2.38 S	131.36 E
Sabugal	34	40.21 N	7.05 W
Sabugo	266c	38.49 N	9.18 W
Sabuk	273b	4.27 S	15.10 E
Sabula	190	42.04 N	90.10 W
Sabunçu, Azer.	84	40.26 N	49.56 E
Sabunçu, Tür.	130	39.33 N	30.12 E
Saburovo	265b	55.38 N	37.42 E
Sabyā	144	17.09 N	42.37 E
Sabzevār	128	36.13 N	57.42 E
Sac ⊡⁶	194	38.01 N	93.43 W
Sacaba	248	17.23 S	66.02 W
Sacaca	248	18.05 S	66.26 W
Sacacomie, Lac ⊜	206	46.31 N	73.14 W
Sacagawea ≃	202	47.27 N	107.58 W
Sacagawea Peak ʌ	202	45.15 N	111.17 W
Sacanche	248	7.05 S	76.44 W
Sacandaga ≃	210	43.19 N	73.50 W
Sacandaga, West Branch ≃	210	43.22 N	74.17 W
Scandica	152	5.58 S	15.56 E
Sacaola	152	12.57 S	22.25 E
Sacarana	248	12.52 S	67.22 W
Sacatón	200	33.05 N	111.44 W
Sacavém	266c	38.47 N	9.06 W
Sacheere	84	42.19 N	43.23 E
Sac City	198	42.25 N	94.59 W
Sacco ≃	68	41.24 N	13.32 E
Sacedón	34	40.29 N	2.43 W
Sacele	38	45.37 N	25.42 E
Sacelu	38	45.04 N	23.35 E
Saç Geçidi ⊼	130	39.54 N	42.22 E
Sachalin, ostrov I	89	51.00 N	143.00 E
Sachalin, ostrov (Sakhalin) I	89	51.00 N	143.00 E
Sachalinskij zaliv c	89	53.45 N	141.30 E
Sachand	85	34.50 N	71.28 E
Sachnovyj	252	26.41 S	61.50 W
Saché	32	47.15 N	0.33 E
Sachigo ≃	176	55.06 N	88.58 W
Sachigo Lake ⊜	184	53.49 N	92.08 W
Sachovskaja	76	56.02 N	35.29 E
Sachrinán	85	40.44 N	72.03 E
Sachrisabz	126	39.03 N	66.50 E
Sachs	188	39.33 N	78.49 W
Sachse	222	32.59 N	96.36 W
Sachseln	58	46.52 N	8.15 E
Sachsen ⊡³	54	51.00 N	13.30 E
Sachsen ⊡⁹	30	50.45 N	12.30 E
Sachsen-Anhalt ⊡³	54	52.00 N	11.30 E
Sachsenburg	64	46.49 N	13.21 E
Sachsenhagen	52	52.24 N	9.16 E
Sachsenhausen, Dtsch.	264c	50.06 N	8.41 E
Sachsenhausen, Dtsch.	264b	52.46 N	13.14 E
Sachs Harbour	176	72.00 N	125.00 W
Sächsische Schweiz ⊷¹	54	50.55 N	14.10 E
Šachterskij	89	64.42 N	177.40 E
Šachtinsk	86	49.43 N	72.36 E
Šachty	84	47.42 N	40.13 E
Sachu ≃	85	57.40 N	46.37 E
Sack, Bela.	76	53.00 N	27.41 E
Sack, Ross.	80	54.01 N	41.53 E
Sackets Harbor	210	43.56 N	76.07 W
Sackville	186	45.54 N	64.22 W
Saclay	261	48.44 N	2.10 E
Saco, Me., U.S.	188	43.30 N	70.26 W
Saco, Mt., U.S.	202	48.27 N	107.20 W
Saco ≃	207	43.30 N	70.22 W
Saco Bay c	207	43.30 N	70.19 W
Saco Island I	116	6.06 N	121.44 E
Sacotes	266c	38.48 N	9.20 W
Sacra Familia do Tinguá	255	22.29 S	43.36 W
Sacramento, Bra.	255	19.53 S	47.27 W
Sacramento, Ca., U.S.	226	38.34 N	121.29 W
Sacramento ⊡⁶	226	38.35 N	121.30 W
Sacramento ≃	226	38.03 N	121.56 W
Sacramento, Pampa del ≃	248	8.00 S	75.50 W
Sacramento Metropolitan Airport ⊷	282	38.42 N	121.35 W
Sacramento Mountains ʌ	200	32.45 N	105.30 W
Sacramento River Deep Water Ship Channel ≃	282	38.15 N	121.40 W
Sacramento South	282	38.14 N	121.26 W
Sacramento Valley V	204	39.15 N	122.00 W
Sacramento Wash V	228	34.43 N	114.28 W
Sacré-Coeur	206	48.14 N	69.49 W
Sacré-Cœur ⊥	261	48.53 N	2.21 E
Sacred Heart	198	44.47 N	95.21 W
Sacriston	44	54.49 N	1.37 W

Legend

Symbol	English	Deutsch	Español	Français	Português
≃	River	Fluß	Río	Rivière	Rio
≋	Canal	Kanal	Canal	Canal	Canal
ᴸ	Waterfall, Rapids	Wasserfall, Stromschnellen	Cascada, Rápidos	Chute d'eau, Rapides	Cascata, Rápidos
ᶸ	Strait	Meeresstraße	Estrecho	Détroit	Estreito
c	Bay, Gulf	Bucht, Golf	Bahía, Golfo	Baie, Golfe	Baía, Golfo
⊜	Lake, Lakes	See, Seen	Lago, Lagos	Lac, Lacs	Lago, Lagos
⊶	Swamp	Sumpf	Pantano	Marais	Pântano
⊠	Ice Features, Glacier	Eis- und Gletscherformen	Formas Glaciares	Formes glaciaires	Formas glaciares
⊷	Other Hydrographic Features	Andere Hydrographische Objekte	Otros Elementos Hidrográficos	Autres données hydrographiques	Outros acidentes hidrográficos
✦	Submarine Features	Untermeerische Objekte	Accidentes Submarinos	Formes de relief sous-marin	Acidentes submarinos
⊡	Political Unit	Politische Einheit	Unidad Política	Entité politique	Unidade política
⊥	Cultural Institution	Kulturelle Institution	Institución Cultural	Institution culturelle	Instituição cultural
⊥	Historical Site	Historische Stätte	Sitio Histórico	Site historique	Sitio histórico
♦	Recreational Site	Erholungs- und Ferienort	Sitio de Recreo	Centre de loisirs	Area de Lazer
⊷	Airport	Flughafen	Aeropuerto	Aéroport	Aeroporto
⊷	Military Installation	Militäranlage	Instalación Militar	Installation militaire	Instalação militar
⊷	Miscellaneous	Verschiedenes	Misceláneo	Divers	Diversos

ENGLISH — Name / Page / Lat.°′ / Long.°′
DEUTSCH — Name / Seite / Breite°′ / Länge°′ E = Ost

Sacro, Monte ∧ **68** 40.13 N 15.20 E
Sacro Monte ✝[1] **62** 45.49 N 8.15 E
Sacrow ◄[8] **264a** 52.26 N 13.06 E
Sacrower-Paretzer Kanal ≊ **264a** 52.28 N 12.55 E
Sacrower See ⊜ **264a** 52.27 N 13.06 E
Săcueni **38** 47.21 N 22.06 E
Sacul **222** 31.50 N 94.56 W
Sacupana **246** 8.35 N 61.39 W
Sada, Esp. **34** 43.21 N 8.15 W
Sada, Nihon **96** 35.15 N 132.43 E
Sádaba **34** 42.17 N 1.16 W
Sadābād, India **124** 27.27 N 78.03 E
Sa'dābād, Īrān **128** 29.23 N 51.07 E
Sa'dābād, Īrān **128** 34.51 N 50.36 E
Ṣadad **130** 34.18 N 36.56 E
Ṣa'dah **144** 16.52 N 43.37 E
Sadaik Taung ∧ **110** 15.09 N 98.12 E
Sadali **71** 39.49 N 9.16 E
Sada-misaki ≻ **96** 33.20 N 132.01 E
Sada-misaki-hantō ≻[1] **96** 33.26 N 132.13 E
Sadamitsu **96** 34.02 N 134.04 E
Sadane ≃ **115a** 6.01 S 106.37 E
Sadang ≃ **112** 3.43 S 119.27 E
Sadanga **116** 17.09 N 121.02 E
Sadani **154** 6.03 S 38.47 E
Sadao **110** 6.38 N 100.26 E
Sadarpur, Bngl. **126** 23.28 N 90.02 E
Sādarpur, India **272a** 28.33 N 77.21 E
Sadčikovka **86** 53.01 N 63.27 E
Sadda **120** 33.42 N 70.20 E
Saddle ≃ **276** 40.52 N 74.07 W
Saddleback, Mount ∧ **168a** 32.58 S 116.28 E
Saddle Brook **276** 40.54 N 74.06 W
Saddlebunch Keys II **220** 24.37 N 81.37 W
Saddle Lake Indian Reserve ◄[4] **182** 54.00 N 111.40 W
Saddle Mountain ∧, Co., U.S. **200** 38.50 N 105.28 W
Saddle Mountain ∧, Or., U.S. **224** 45.58 N 123.41 W
Saddle Mountains ⋏ **202** 46.50 N 119.55 W
Saddle Mountain State Park ♠ **224** 45.58 N 123.41 W
Saddle Peak ∧ **110** 13.09 N 93.01 E
Saddle River **276** 40.54 N 74.05 W
Saddle Rock **276** 40.48 N 73.45 W
Saddleworth, Austl. **168b** 34.05 S 138.47 E
Saddleworth, Eng., U.K. **262** 53.33 N 1.59 W
Saddleworth Moor ◄[3] **262** 53.33 N 1.57 W
Sa Dec **110** 10.18 N 105.46 E
Sadelkow **54** 53.36 N 13.26 E
Sādhaura **124** 30.23 N 77.13 E
Sādhuhāti **126** 23.34 N 89.01 E
Sadieville **218** 38.23 N 84.32 W
Sadiola **150** 13.53 N 11.42 W
Sādiqābād **120** 28.18 N 70.08 E
Sadiya **120** 27.50 N 95.40 E
Sa'dīyah, Wādī V **144** 20.35 N 39.38 E
Sa'dīyāt, Ra's as- ≻ **132** 33.41 N 35.25 E
Sadler Lake ⊜ **184** 55.17 N 103.45 W
Sado I **92** 38.00 N 138.25 E
Sado ≃ **34** 38.29 N 8.55 W
Sado-kaikyō ⊔ **92** 37.50 N 138.40 E
Sadon **84** 42.51 N 44.00 E
Sadovoje, Ross. **80** 46.56 N 44.23 E
Sadovoje, Ross. **80** 47.46 N 44.30 E
Sadovoje Pervoje **78** 51.33 N 40.29 E
Sadowara **92** 32.02 N 131.26 E
Ṣādri **120** 25.11 N 73.26 E
Šadrina **89** 51.33 N 130.22 E
Šadrino **86** 55.52 N 91.06 E
Šadrinsk **86** 56.05 N 63.38 E
Sadsburyville **208** 39.59 N 75.53 W
Sādulpur **123** 28.38 N 75.24 E
Sädvaluspen **24** 66.24 N 16.51 E
Sæby, Dan. **26** 57.20 N 10.32 E
Sæby, Dan. **41** 55.33 N 11.19 E
Saegertown **214** 41.43 N 80.09 W
Sae Islands II **164** 0.45 S 145.15 E
Saeki → Saiki, Nihon **96** 32.57 N 131.54 E
Saeki, Nihon **96** 34.22 N 132.11 E
Saeki, Nihon **96** 34.51 N 134.06 E
Saengil-to I **98** 34.19 N 126.59 E
Saerbeck **52** 52.10 N 7.38 E
Saerluojia Hu ⊜ **120** 33.55 N 86.55 E
Særslev, Dan. **41** 55.31 N 10.11 E
Særslev, Dan. **41** 55.43 N 11.23 E
Saeul **56** 49.44 N 5.59 E
Ṣafā, Tulūl aṣ- ∧[1] **132** 33.02 N 37.12 E
Safad → Ẕefat **132** 32.58 N 35.30 E
Safājah, Jazīrat I **140** 26.45 N 33.59 E
Safakulevo **86** 54.59 N 62.33 E
Ṣafānīyah **142** 28.49 N 30.48 E
Safdar Jang Airport ⊠ **272a** 28.37 N 77.13 E
Safdar Jang's Tomb ⊥ **272a** 28.36 N 77.13 E
Safed Koh Range ⋏ **123** 33.58 N 70.25 E
Safe Harbor Dam ◄[6] **208** 39.59 N 76.28 W
Safenbach ≃ **61** 47.06 N 16.05 E
Safety Bay **168a** 32.18 S 115.43 E
Safety Harbor **220** 27.59 N 82.41 W
Säffle **26** 59.08 N 12.56 E
Safford **200** 32.50 N 109.42 W
Saffron Walden **42** 52.01 N 0.15 E
Safi **148** 32.20 N 9.17 W
Safi □[4] **148** 32.05 N 9.00 W
Safia **164** 9.35 S 148.40 E
Ṣafīābād **128** 36.45 N 57.58 E
Safīd ≃ **120** 36.44 N 65.38 E
Safīd Kūh, Selseleh-ye ⋏ **128** 34.30 N 63.30 E
Safidon **124** 29.25 N 76.40 E
Safiental V **58** 46.40 N 9.18 E
Safioune, Sebkhet ≝ **148** 32.16 N 5.27 E
Safipur **126** 23.01 N 90.22 E
Ṣāfītā **130** 34.49 N 36.07 E
Safonovo, Ross. **24** 65.42 N 47.39 E
Safonovo, Ross. **76** 55.06 N 33.15 E
Safonovo, Ross. **82** 55.33 N 38.17 E
Safrakköyü ◄[8] **267b** 41.00 N 28.47 E
Safranbolu **130** 41.15 N 32.45 E
Ṣaft al-'Inab **142** 30.49 N 30.41 E
Ṣaft al-Khammār **142** 28.02 N 30.42 E
Ṣaft al-Laban **273c** 30.02 N 31.10 E
Ṣaft al-Mulūk **142** 30.49 N 30.41 E
Ṣaft Rāshīn **142** 28.58 N 30.55 E
Ṣaft Turāb **142** 30.54 N 31.07 E
Ṣafwān **128** 30.07 N 47.43 E
Saga, Kaz. **86** 50.23 N 64.15 E
Saga, Kaz. **86** 49.25 N 55.17 E
Saga, Nihon **92** 33.15 N 130.18 E
Saga, Nihon **96** 33.05 N 133.06 E
Saga, Zhg. **120** 29.30 N 85.22 E
Saga □[5] **96** 33.21 N 130.28 E
Sagaba **152** 11.17 S 23.07 E
Sagae **92** 38.22 N 140.17 E
Sagaing **110** 21.52 N 95.59 E
Sagaing □[8] **110** 24.00 N 95.00 E
Sagak, Cape ≻ **180** 52.48 N 169.08 W
Šagalaherang **115a** 6.40 S 107.39 E
Šagalakasa **80** 46.54 N 50.43 E
Sagamāthā □[8] **124** 27.15 N 86.45 E
Sagami ≃ **94** 35.19 N 139.22 E
Sagamihara **94** 35.34 N 139.23 E
Sagamihara-daichi ⋏[1] **268** 35.27 N 139.27 E
Sagamiko **94** 35.37 N 139.12 E
Sagami-ko ⊜ **94** 35.35 N 139.16 E
Sagami-nada ⊂ **94** 35.00 N 139.30 E
Sagami-wan ⊂ **94** 35.15 N 139.25 E
Sagamore, Ma., U.S. **207** 41.46 N 70.31 W
Sagamore, Pa., U.S. **214** 40.46 N 79.13 W
Sagamore Beach **207** 41.47 N 70.31 W
Sagamore Hill National Historic Site ⊥ **276** 40.53 N 73.30 W
Sagamore Hills **279a** 41.02 N 81.26 W
Sagan → Żagań **30** 51.37 N 15.19 E
Šagan ≃, Kaz. **86** 50.37 N 79.15 E
Sagån ≃, Sve. **40** 59.35 N 16.54 E
Saganaga Lake ⊜ **190** 48.14 N 90.52 W
Saganashkee Slough ≃ **278** 41.41 N 87.53 W
Saganash Lake ⊜ **190** 49.04 N 82.35 W
Saganoseki **96** 33.15 N 131.53 E
Saganthit Kyun I **110** 11.56 N 98.29 E
Sagaon **272c** 19.12 N 73.06 E
Sāgar, India **122** 14.10 N 75.02 E
Sāgar, India **124** 23.50 N 78.43 E
Sagara **94** 34.41 N 138.12 E
Sagaranten **115a** 7.13 S 106.52 E
Sagard **54** 54.31 N 13.33 E
Sāgardīghi **126** 24.17 N 88.06 E
Sagaredžo **84** 41.44 N 45.20 E
Sāgar Island I **126** 21.43 N 88.06 E
Sagarmatha → Everest, Mount ∧ **124** 27.59 N 86.56 E
Sagarmatha National Park ♠ **124** 27.50 N 86.45 E
Sāgar Plateau ⋏[1] **124** 23.30 N 78.30 E
Sagavanirktok ≃ **180** 70.20 N 148.00 W
Sagay **116** 10.57 N 123.25 E
Sage, Mount ∧ **240m** 18.25 N 64.39 W
Sage Creek ≃, N.A. **202** 48.58 N 110.06 W
Sage Creek ≃, U.S. **202** 44.50 N 108.26 W
Sage Creek ≃, Mt., U.S. **202** 47.16 N 109.43 W
Sage Creek ≃, Mt., U.S. **202** 48.20 N 110.03 W
Sagemace Bay ⊂ **184** 51.49 N 100.03 W
Sagerton **196** 33.05 N 99.58 W
Saggaubach ≃ **61** 46.43 N 15.24 E
Sag Harbor **207** 40.59 N 72.17 W
Ṣaghbīn **132** 33.37 N 35.42 E
Ṣaghīr, Al-Baḥr aṣ- ≊ **142** 31.09 N 31.56 E
Sagil **86** 50.20 N 91.40 E
Saginaw, Mi., U.S. **190** 43.25 N 83.56 W
Saginaw, Tx., U.S. **222** 32.52 N 97.22 W
Saginaw ≃ **190** 43.39 N 83.51 W
Saginaw Bay ⊂ **190** 43.50 N 83.40 W
Sagiz, Kaz. **80** 47.31 N 53.16 E
Sagiz, Kaz. **86** 48.12 N 54.56 E
Sağkaya **130** 37.11 N 35.41 E
Sagleipie **150** 7.00 N 8.52 W
Saglek Bay ⊂ **176** 58.35 N 63.00 W
Šaglyteniz, ozero ⊜ **86** 54.08 N 69.52 E
Šagonar **86** 51.32 N 92.48 E
Sagrado **64** 45.52 N 13.29 E
Sagres **34** 37.00 N 8.56 W
Sag Sag **164** 5.35 S 148.20 E
Sagsaj **86** 48.54 N 89.37 E
Sagsajn ≃ **102** 44.50 N 96.26 E
Sagu, Indon. **112** 8.15 S 123.13 E
Şagu, Rom. **38** 46.03 N 21.17 E
Saguache **200** 38.05 N 106.05 W
Saguache Creek ≃ **200** 37.52 N 105.51 W
Sagua de Tánamo **240p** 20.35 N 75.14 W
Sagua la Chica ≃ **240p** 22.45 N 79.39 W
Sagua la Grande **240p** 22.49 N 80.05 W
Saguaro National Park ♠ **200** 32.12 N 110.38 W
Saguenay ≃ **176** 48.08 N 69.44 W
Saguna **272b** 22.59 N 88.29 E
Sagunay Lake **216** 41.43 N 86.34 W
Sagunt **34** 39.41 N 0.16 W
Saguny **78** 50.36 N 39.43 E
Sagutjevo **76** 52.28 N 33.28 E
Sāgwāra **120** 23.41 N 74.01 E
Sagy **261** 49.03 N 1.57 E
Sa'gya **120** 28.55 N 88.05 E
Sagyndyk, mys ≻ **84** 44.02 N 50.52 E
Sagyz ≃ **86** 47.32 N 53.20 E
Sah **150** 15.38 N 4.03 W
Saḥāb **132** 31.53 N 36.00 E
Sahaba **140** 18.55 N 30.28 E
Sahagún, Col. **246** 8.57 N 75.27 W
Sahagún, Esp. **34** 42.22 N 5.02 W
Saḥam **132** 32.42 N 35.47 E
Saḥam al-Jawlān **132** 32.46 N 35.56 E
Sahana Ambodipont **157b** 14.37 S 50.11 E
Sahand, Kūh-e ∧ **128** 37.44 N 46.27 E
Sahara ◄[2] **10** 26.00 N 13.00 E
Sahāranpur **124** 29.58 N 77.33 E
Sahara Occidental → Western Sahara □[2] **148** 24.30 N 13.00 W
Sahara Occidentale → Western Sahara □[2] **148** 24.30 N 13.00 W
Saharsa **124** 25.53 N 86.36 E
Sahasinaka **157b** 21.49 S 47.49 E
Sahasrail **126** 23.19 N 89.43 E
Sahaswān **124** 28.05 N 78.45 E
Ṣahbuz **84** 39.25 N 45.34 E
Šahel ◄[1] **134** 17.00 N 2.00 E
Sahel, Canal du ≊ **150** 13.44 N 6.05 W
Sahel, Oued ≃ **34** 36.26 N 4.33 E
Sāhibabad **272a** 28.40 N 77.22 E
Sahibābad ◄[8] **272a** 28.45 N 77.05 E
Sāhibganj **124** 25.15 N 87.39 E
Sāhibi ≃ **124** 28.29 N 76.44 E
Şahin **130** 41.01 N 26.50 E
Sāhīwāl, Pāk. **123** 30.40 N 73.06 E
Sāhīwāl, Pāk. **123** 31.58 N 72.20 E
Sahlenburg **52** 53.52 N 8.38 E
Ṣaḥneh **128** 34.29 N 47.41 E
Ṣaḥrā', Bi'r ⊤[4] **140** 22.52 N 28.37 E
Ṣahrajat al-Kubrā wa Kafr Jirjis Yūsuf **142** 30.38 N 31.17 E
Sahtlam **224** 48.48 N 123.54 W
Sahuaripa **232** 29.03 N 109.14 W
Sahuarita **200** 31.57 N 110.58 W
Sahuayo de José María Morelos **234** 20.04 N 102.43 W
Sahul Shelf ✣[4] **14** 12.30 S 125.00 E
Sahunivka **78** 49.17 N 32.23 E
Sa Huynh **110** 14.40 N 109.04 E
Ṣahwat al-Qamḥ **132** 32.36 N 36.23 E
Šahy **30** 48.05 N 18.57 E
Saï **150** 13.50 N 5.00 W
Sai ≃, India **124** 25.39 N 82.47 E
Sai ≃, Nihon **94** 36.36 N 136.35 E
Sai ≃, Nihon **94** 36.37 N 138.14 E
Saibai Island I **164** 9.24 S 142.40 E
Sai Buri **110** 6.42 N 101.37 E
Sai Buri ≃ **110** 6.43 N 101.39 E
Saïda **148** 34.50 N 0.09 E
Saidābād, Bngl. **126** 24.18 N 89.43 E
Sa'īdābād, Īrān **267d** 35.40 N 51.11 E
Saidaiji **96** 34.39 N 134.02 E
Saïdia **148** 35.04 N 2.15 W
Sa'īdīyeh **128** 36.26 N 48.48 E
Saido **268** 35.52 N 139.41 E
Saidor **164** 5.35 S 146.30 E
Saidpur, Bngl. **124** 25.47 N 88.54 E
Saidpur, India **124** 25.33 N 83.11 E
Saidu **123** 34.45 N 72.21 E
Saigawa **96** 33.39 N 130.57 E
Saignelégier **58** 47.15 N 7.00 E
Saignon **62** 43.52 N 5.26 E
Saigō **92** 36.12 N 133.20 E
Saigon → Thanh Pho Ho Chi Minh **269c** 10.45 N 106.40 E
Sai Gon ≃ **269c** 10.45 N 106.45 E
Saihaku **96** 35.20 N 133.20 E
Saihan Toroi **102** 41.41 N 100.26 E
Saijō, Nihon **96** 33.55 N 133.11 E
Saijō, Nihon **96** 34.56 N 133.07 E
Saijō ≃ **96** 34.48 N 132.51 E
Saikai-kokuritsu-kōen ♠ **92** 33.12 N 129.22 E
Sai Keng **271d** 22.26 N 114.16 E
Saiki **96** 32.57 N 131.54 E
Saiki-wan ⊂ **96** 33.00 N 131.58 E
Sai Kung **271d** 22.23 N 114.15 E
Saileati **85** 38.57 N 74.45 E
Sailkupa **126** 23.41 N 89.15 E
Saillans **62** 44.42 N 5.11 E
Sailly **261** 49.02 N 1.48 E
Sailmouille, Ruisseau ≃ **261** 48.37 N 2.17 E
Sailolof **164** 1.15 S 130.46 E
Sailor Creek ≃ **202** 42.56 N 115.29 W
Ṣail-sous-Couzan **62** 45.44 N 3.57 E
Šaim **86** 60.21 N 64.14 E
Saima **98** 41.00 N 124.14 E
Saimaa ⊜ **26** 61.15 N 28.15 E
Saimaa Canal ≊ **26** 61.05 N 28.18 E
Saimbeyli **130** 38.00 N 36.06 E
Saín Alto **234** 23.35 N 103.15 W
Saindak **128** 29.17 N 61.34 E
Ṣā'īn Dezh **128** 36.40 N 46.33 E
Sainghin-en-Weppes **50** 50.33 N 2.54 E
Sainjang **98** 39.15 N 125.51 E
Sainō-ha'iji ⊥ **96** 35.29 N 133.39 E
Sains-du-Nord **50** 50.06 N 4.00 E
Sains-en-Gohelle **50** 50.27 N 2.41 E
Sains-Richaumont **50** 49.49 N 3.42 E
Saint Abb's Head ≻ **46** 55.54 N 2.09 W
Sainte-Adèle **206** 45.57 N 74.07 W
Sainte-Adresse **50** 49.30 N 0.05 E
Saint-Adrien **206** 45.49 N 71.43 W
Saint-Affrique **32** 43.57 N 2.53 E
Saint-Agapit **206** 46.34 N 71.27 W
Saint Agatha **212** 43.26 N 80.36 W
Sainte-Agathe, Mb., Can. **184** 49.34 N 97.10 W
Sainte-Agathe, Fr. **62** 45.49 N 3.37 E
Sainte-Agathe [-de-Lotbinière] **206** 46.23 N 71.24 W
Sainte-Agathe-des-Monts **206** 46.03 N 74.17 W
Sainte-Agnès, Fr. **62** 43.48 N 7.28 E
Saint Agnes, Eng., U.K. **42** 50.18 N 5.13 W
Saint Agnes I **42a** 49.54 N 6.20 W
Saint-Agrève **62** 45.01 N 4.24 E
Saint-Aignan **50** 47.16 N 1.23 E
Saint-Aimé (Massueville) **206** 45.55 N 72.56 W
Saint Albans, Austl. **169** 37.44 S 144.48 E
Saint Albans, Austl. **170** 33.17 S 150.59 E
Saint Alban's, Nf., Can. **186** 47.52 N 55.51 W
Saint Albans, Eng., U.K. **42** 51.46 N 0.21 W
Saint Albans, Mo., U.S. **219** 38.35 N 90.46 W
Saint Albans, Vt., U.S. **188** 44.48 N 73.05 W
Saint Albans, W.V., U.S. **188** 38.23 N 81.50 W
Saint Albans □[8] **260** 51.45 N 0.20 W
Saint Albans ◄[8] **276** 40.42 N 73.46 W
Saint Albans, Cape ≻ **168b** 35.49 S 138.07 E
Saint Albans Cathedral ✝[1] **260** 51.45 N 0.20 W
Saint Albert, Ab., Can. **182** 53.38 N 113.38 W
Saint-Albert, P.Q., Can. **206** 46.00 N 72.05 W
Saint Aldhelm's Head ≻ **42** 50.34 N 2.04 W
Saint-Alexandre-de-Kamouraska **186** 47.41 N 69.38 W
Saint-Alexis-des-Monts **206** 46.28 N 73.08 W
Saint-Amable **275a** 45.39 N 73.18 W
Saint-Amand **56** 48.49 N 4.36 E
Saint-Amand-en-Puisaye **50** 47.31 N 3.04 E
Saint-Amand-les-Eaux **50** 50.26 N 3.26 E
Saint-Amand-Longpré **50** 47.41 N 1.01 E
Saint-Amand-Montrond **32** 46.44 N 2.30 E
Saint-Amant-Roche-Savine **62** 45.34 N 3.38 E
Saint-Amarin **58** 47.53 N 7.01 E
Saint-Ambroix **62** 44.15 N 4.11 E
Sainte-Amélie **184** 50.59 N 99.21 W
Saint-Amour **58** 46.26 N 5.21 E
Saint-André **157c** 20.57 S 55.39 E
Saint-André, Cap ≻ **157b** 16.11 S 44.27 E
Saint-André, Ruisseau ≃ **275a** 45.22 N 73.29 W
Saint-André-Avellin **206** 45.43 N 75.03 W
Saint-André-de-l'Eure **50** 48.54 N 1.17 E
Saint-André-de-Valborgne **62** 44.09 N 3.41 E
St.-André-Est **206** 45.34 N 74.20 W
Saint-André-les-Alpes **62** 43.58 N 6.30 E
Saint-André-les-Vergers **50** 48.17 N 4.03 E
Saint Andrew **241g** 13.15 N 59.33 W
Saint Andrew, Mount ∧ **241h** 13.11 N 61.13 W
Saint Andrew Lakes ⊜ **212** 44.36 N 76.40 W
Saint Andrews, N.B., Can. **186** 45.05 N 67.03 W
Saint Andrews, Scot., U.K. **46** 56.20 N 2.48 W
Saint Andrews, S.C., U.S. **192** 32.46 N 79.59 W
Saint Andrews Bay ⊂ **46** 56.22 N 2.50 W
Saint Andrew's Cathedral ✝[1] **271c** 1.18 N 103.51 E
Saint Andrews Channel ⊔ **186** 46.03 N 60.38 W
Saint Ann **219** 38.43 N 90.22 W
Sainte-Anne, Guad. **241o** 16.14 N 61.23 W
Saint Anne, Guernsey **43b** 49.42 N 2.12 W
Sainte-Anne, Mart. **240e** 14.26 N 60.53 W
Saint Anne, Il., U.S. **216** 41.01 N 87.42 W
Sainte-Anne ≃ **206** 46.33 N 72.12 W
Saint Anne, Cathedral of ✝[1] **273b** 4.18 S 15.19 E
Sainte Anne, Lac ⊜, Ab., Can. **182** 53.43 N 114.27 W
Sainte-Anne, Lac ⊜, P.Q., Can. **186** 50.05 N 67.50 W
Sainte-Anne-de-Beaupré **186** 47.02 N 70.56 W
Sainte-Anne-de-Bellevue **275a** 45.24 N 73.57 W
Sainte-Anne-de-la-Pérade **206** 46.35 N 72.12 W
Sainte-Anne-de-Madawaska **186** 47.15 N 68.02 W
Sainte-Anne-des-Chênes **184** 49.40 N 96.40 W
Sainte-Anne-des-Monts **186** 49.08 N 66.30 W
Sainte-Anne-des-Plaines **206** 46.46 N 73.48 W
Saint Anne of the Congo ✝[1] **273b** 4.16 S 15.17 E
Saint Anne's **44** 53.45 N 3.02 W
Saint Ann's Bay **241q** 18.26 N 77.08 W
Saint Anns Bay ⊂ **186** 46.20 N 60.30 W
Saint Ann's Head ≻ **42** 51.41 N 5.10 W
Saint-Anselme **186** 46.37 N 70.58 W
Saint Ansgar **190** 43.22 N 92.55 W
Saint-Anthème **62** 45.31 N 3.55 E
Saint Anthony, N.B., Can. **186** 46.22 N 64.45 W
Saint Anthony, Nf., Can. **186** 51.22 N 55.35 W
Saint Anthony, Id., U.S. **202** 43.57 N 111.40 W
Saint-Antoine, P.Q., Can. **206** 45.46 N 73.59 W
Saint-Antoine, Fr. **62** 45.10 N 5.13 E
Saint-Antonin **32** 44.09 N 1.45 E
Saint-Apollinaire (Francoeur) **206** 46.37 N 71.31 W
Saint Arnaud, Austl. **166** 36.37 S 143.15 E
Saint Arnaud, N.Z. **172** 41.48 S 172.50 E
Saint-Arnoult, Forêt de ♠ **261** 48.35 N 1.55 E
Saint-Arnoult-en-Yvelines **50** 48.34 N 1.56 E
Saint Arvans **42** 51.40 N 2.41 W
Saint Asaph **44** 53.16 N 3.26 W
Saint-Astier **32** 45.09 N 0.32 E
Saint Athan **42** 51.24 N 3.25 W
Saint-Auban **62** 43.51 N 6.44 E
Saint-Aubert, Mont ∧[2] **50** 50.39 N 3.24 E
Saint Aubert Island I **219** 38.40 N 91.52 W
Saint-Aubin, Fr. **50** 49.53 N 0.53 E
Saint-Aubin, Fr. **58** 47.02 N 5.20 E
Saint Aubin, Jersey **43b** 49.11 N 2.10 W
Saint-Aubin, Schw. **58** 46.54 N 6.47 E
Saint-Aubin-lès-Elbeuf **50** 49.18 N 1.01 E
Saint-Aubin-sur-Aire **58** 48.42 N 5.27 E
Saint-Augustin **157b** 23.33 S 43.46 E
Saint-Augustin ≃ **176** 51.14 N 58.41 W
Saint-Augustin-Deux-Montagnes **275a** 45.38 N 73.59 W
Saint Augustine **192** 29.53 N 81.18 W
Saint-Augustin Nord-Ouest ≃ **186** 51.16 N 58.42 W
Saint-Augustin-Saguenay **186** 51.14 N 58.39 W
Saint-Aulaye **32** 45.12 N 0.08 E
Saint Austell **42** 50.20 N 4.48 W
Saint-Avertin **50** 47.22 N 0.44 E
Saint-Avold **56** 49.06 N 6.42 E
Saint-Ay **50** 47.51 N 1.45 E
Saint-Aygulf **62** 43.23 N 6.44 E
Saint Barbe **186** 51.12 N 56.46 W
Saint Barnabas Chapel ✝[1] **174c** 29.02 S 167.55 E
Saint-Barthélemy I **238** 17.54 N 62.50 W
Saint-Basile **186** 47.21 N 68.14 W
Saint-Basile-de-Portneuf **206** 46.45 N 71.49 W
Saint-Basile-le-Grand **206** 45.32 N 73.17 W
Saint Bathans, Mount ∧ **172** 44.44 S 169.46 E
Sainte-Baume, Chaîne de la ⋏ **62** 43.20 N 5.45 E
Saint-Béat **32** 42.55 N 0.42 E
Saint Bees **44** 54.30 N 3.37 W
Saint Bees Head ≻ **44** 54.32 N 3.38 W
Saint Benedict **214** 40.38 N 78.44 W
Saint-Benoît, Fr. **261** 48.40 N 1.55 E
Saint-Benoît, Réu. **157c** 21.02 S 55.43 E
Saint-Benoît-du-Sault **32** 46.27 N 1.23 E
Saint-Benoît-en-Woëvre **56** 48.59 N 5.47 E
Saint Bernard **218** 39.10 N 84.29 W
Saint-Bernard, Île I **275a** 45.23 N 73.45 W
Saint-Bernard-de-Dorchester **206** 46.30 N 71.08 W
Saint-Béron **62** 45.30 N 5.43 E
Saint-Blaise, P.Q., Can. **206** 45.13 N 73.17 W
Saint-Blaise, Schw. **58** 47.01 N 6.59 E
Saint-Blaise-la-Roche **58** 48.24 N 7.10 E
Saint Blaize, Cape ≻ **158** 34.11 S 22.10 E
Saint Blazey **42** 50.22 N 4.43 W
Saint-Blin **58** 48.16 N 5.25 E
Saint-Bonaventure, P.Q., Can. **206** 45.58 N 72.41 W
Saint Bonaventure, N.Y., U.S. **210** 42.05 N 78.28 W
Saint-Boniface-de-Shawinigan **206** 46.30 N 72.49 W
Saint-Bonnet **62** 44.41 N 6.05 E
Saint-Bonnet-de-Joux **58** 46.29 N 4.27 E
Saint-Bonnet-le-Château **62** 45.25 N 4.04 E
Saint-Bonnet-le-Froid **62** 45.09 N 4.27 E
Saint Boswells **46** 55.34 N 2.39 W
Saint Brendan's **186** 48.52 N 53.40 W
Saint-Brice-sous-Forêt **261** 49.00 N 2.21 E
Saint Bride, Mount ∧ **182** 51.30 N 115.57 W
Saint Bride's **186** 46.55 N 54.10 W
Saint Brides Bay ⊂ **42** 51.48 N 5.15 W
Saint Bride's Major **42** 51.28 N 3.38 W
Saint-Brieuc **32** 48.31 N 2.47 W
Saint-Brieux **184** 52.38 N 104.52 W
Saint-Broing-les-Moines **58** 47.41 N 4.50 E
Saint-Bruno **206** 45.32 N 73.21 W
Saint-Bruno, Mont ∧[2] **275a** 45.33 N 73.19 W
Saint-Calais **50** 47.55 N 0.45 E
Saint-Calixte-de-Kilkenny **206** 45.57 N 73.51 W
Saint-Cannat **62** 43.37 N 5.18 E
Saint-Casimir **206** 46.40 N 72.08 W
Saint-Cassien, Lac de ⊜[1] **62** 43.35 N 6.48 E
Saint Catharines **212** 43.10 N 79.15 W
Saint Catharines Airport ⊠ **284a** 43.11 N 79.10 W
Saint Catherine **220** 28.37 N 82.08 W
Saint Catherine, Monastery of → Qiddīsah Kātrīnā, Dayr al- ✝[1] **140** 28.29 N 34.01 E
Saint Catherine, Mount ∧ **241k** 12.10 N 61.40 W
Sainte-Catherine-de-Fierbois **50** 47.09 N 0.39 E
Saint Catherines Island I **192** 31.38 N 81.10 W
Saint Catherine's Point ≻ **42** 50.34 N 1.15 W
Saint-Célestin (Annaville) **206** 46.13 N 72.26 W
Saint-Céré **32** 44.52 N 1.53 E
Saint-Cergue **58** 46.27 N 6.09 E
Saint-Césaire **206** 45.25 N 73.00 W
Saint-Cézaire-sur-Siagne **62** 43.39 N 6.48 E
Saint-Chamas **62** 43.33 N 5.02 E
Saint-Chamond **62** 45.28 N 4.30 E
Saint-Chaptes **62** 43.58 N 4.17 E
Saint Charles, Ar., U.S. **194** 34.22 N 91.08 W
Saint Charles, Id., U.S. **202** 42.06 N 111.23 W
Saint Charles, Il., U.S. **216** 41.54 N 88.18 W
Saint Charles, Md., U.S. **208** 38.36 N 76.56 W
Saint Charles, Mi., U.S. **190** 43.17 N 84.08 W
Saint Charles, Mn., U.S. **190** 43.58 N 92.03 W
Saint Charles, Mo., U.S. **219** 38.47 N 90.28 W
Saint Charles □[6] **219** 38.47 N 90.43 W
Saint-Charles ≃ **275a** 45.40 N 73.27 W
Saint-Charles, Lac ⊜ **206** 46.55 N 71.23 W
Saint-Charles-de-Drummond **206** 45.54 N 72.28 W
Saint Charles Mesa **198** 38.15 N 104.32 W
Saint-Charles-sur-Richelieu **206** 45.41 N 73.11 W
Saint-Chef **62** 45.38 N 5.22 E
Saint-Chély-d'Apcher **32** 44.48 N 3.17 E
Saint-Chéron **261** 48.33 N 2.07 E
Saint-Christophe-en-Bazelle **50** 47.11 N 1.43 E
Saint-Christophe-Nevis → Saint Kitts and Nevis □[1] **238** 17.20 N 62.45 W
Saint Christopher (Saint Kitts) I **238** 17.20 N 62.45 W
Saint Christopher-Nevis → Saint Kitts y Nevis □[1] **238** 17.20 N 62.45 W
Saint-Chrysostome **206** 45.06 N 73.46 W
Saint-Ciers-sur-Gironde **32** 45.18 N 0.37 W
Saint Clair, Mi., U.S. **214** 42.48 N 82.29 W
Saint Clair, Mo., U.S. **219** 38.20 N 90.58 W
Saint Clair, Pa., U.S. **208** 40.43 N 76.11 W
Saint Clair, Pa., U.S. **279b** 40.16 N 79.33 W
Saint Clair □[6], Il., U.S. **219** 38.31 N 90.00 W
Saint Clair □[6], Mi., U.S. **214** 42.50 N 82.42 W
Saint Clair ≃ **214** 42.37 N 82.31 W
Saint Clair, Lake ⊜ **214** 42.25 N 82.41 W
Saint Clair Beach **281** 42.19 N 82.51 W
Saint Clair Flats **214** 42.32 N 82.37 W
Saint Clair Flats ≚ **281** 42.35 N 82.36 W
Saint Clair Flats Canal ≊ **214** 42.20 N 82.58 W
Saint Clair Flats State Wildlife Area ◄[4] **281** 42.36 N 82.40 W
Saint Clair Haven **214** 42.34 N 82.47 W
Saint Clair Shores **214** 42.29 N 82.53 W
Saint-Clair-sur-Epte **50** 49.12 N 1.41 E
Saint Clairsville, Oh., U.S. **214** 40.04 N 80.54 W
Saint Clairsville, Pa., U.S. **214** 40.09 N 78.31 W
Saint Clair Tunnel ◄[5] **214** 42.57 N 82.25 W
Saint-Claud **32** 45.53 N 0.23 E
Saint-Claude, Mb., Can. **184** 49.40 N 98.22 W
Saint-Claude, Fr. **58** 46.23 N 5.52 E
Saint-Claude, Guad. **241o** 16.02 N 61.42 W
Saint-Claude, Ruisseau ≃ **275a** 45.25 N 73.28 W
Saint Clears **42** 51.50 N 4.30 W
Saint-Clément **58** 48.32 N 6.36 E
Saint Clements **212** 43.31 N 80.39 W
Saint Clements Bay ⊂ **208** 38.17 N 76.42 W
Sainte-Clothilde **206** 45.59 N 72.14 W
Sainte-Clotilde-de-Châteauguay **206** 45.10 N 73.41 W
Saint-Cloud, Fr. **50** 48.50 N 2.11 E
Saint Cloud, Fl., U.S. **220** 28.14 N 81.16 W
Saint Cloud, Mn., U.S. **190** 45.33 N 94.09 W
Saint-Cloud, Parc de ♠ **261** 48.50 N 2.13 E
Saint-Colomban-des-Villards **62** 45.18 N 6.14 E
Sainte-Colombe **58** 47.52 N 4.32 E
Saint Columb Major **42** 50.26 N 4.56 W
Saint Combs **46** 57.39 N 1.54 W
Saint-Constant **206** 45.22 N 73.37 W
Saint-Cosme-en-Vairais **50** 48.16 N 0.28 E
Sainte-Croix, P.Q., Can. **206** 46.38 N 71.44 W
Sainte-Croix, Schw. **58** 46.49 N 6.31 E
Saint Croix I **241n** 17.45 N 64.45 W
Saint Croix ≃, N.A. **186** 45.10 N 67.10 W
Saint Croix ≃, U.S. **190** 44.45 N 92.49 W
Sainte-Croix, Barrage de ◄[6] **62** 43.45 N 6.08 E
Sainte-Croix-aux-Mines **58** 48.16 N 7.13 E
Saint Croix Falls **190** 45.24 N 92.38 W
Saint Croix Island I **158** 33.48 S 25.45 E
Saint Croix Island National Monument ♠ **188** 45.08 N 67.08 W
Saint Croix National Scenic Riverway ♠ **190** 46.00 N 92.25 W
Saint Croix State Park ♠ **190** 46.00 N 92.40 W
Sainte-Croix-Vallée-Francaise **62** 44.11 N 3.44 E
Saint-Cuthbert **206** 46.09 N 73.14 W
Saint-Cyprien **32** 44.52 N 1.02 E
Saint-Cyrille-de-Wendover **206** 45.56 N 72.26 W
Saint-Cyr-l'École **50** 48.48 N 2.04 E
Saint-Cyr-l'École, Aérodrome de ⊠ **261** 48.49 N 2.04 E
Saint Cyr Range ⋏ **180** 61.10 N 131.10 W
Sainte-Cyr-sous-Dourdan **261** 48.34 N 2.02 E
Saint-Cyr-sur-Loire **50** 47.24 N 0.40 E
Saint-Cyr-sur-Mer **62** 43.11 N 5.43 E
Saint-Dalmas-de-Tende **62** 44.03 N 7.35 E
Saint-Damien-de-Brandon **206** 46.20 N 73.29 W
Saint David, Az., U.S. **200** 31.54 N 110.12 W
Saint David, Il., U.S. **190** 40.29 N 90.02 W
Saint David's, Nf., Can. **186** 48.12 N 58.52 W
Saint Davids, On., Can. **284a** 43.10 N 79.06 W
Saint David's, Wales, U.K. **42** 51.54 N 5.16 W
Saint Davids, Pa., U.S. **285** 40.02 N 75.22 W
Saint David's Cathedral ✝[1] **42** 51.54 N 5.16 W
Saint David's Head ≻ **42** 51.55 N 5.19 W
Saint David's Island I **240a** 32.22 N 64.39 W
Saint Day **42** 50.14 N 5.11 W
Saint-Denis, Fr. **50** 48.56 N 2.22 E
Saint-Denis, Réu. **157c** 20.52 S 55.28 E
Saint-Denis, Basilique ✝[1] **261** 48.56 N 2.22 E
Saint-Denis-de-l'Hôtel **50** 47.52 N 2.07 E
Saint-Denis-en-Bugey **58** 45.57 N 5.20 E
Saint-Denis-Rivière-Richelieu **206** 45.47 N 73.09 W
Saint Dennis **42** 50.23 N 4.53 W
Saint-Didier-en-Velay **62** 45.18 N 4.17 E
Saint-Didier-les-Bains **62** 44.00 N 5.07 E
Saint-Dié **58** 48.17 N 6.57 E
Saint-Disdier **62** 44.44 N 5.54 E
Saint-Dizier **58** 48.38 N 4.57 E
Saint Dogmaels **42** 52.05 N 4.40 W
Saint-Donat-de-Montcalm **206** 46.19 N 74.13 W
Saint-Donat-sur-l'Herbasse **62** 45.07 N 5.00 E
Sainte-Dorothée ◄[8] **275a** 45.32 N 73.49 W
Saint-Dyé-sur-Loire **50** 47.39 N 1.29 E
Saint-Édouard-de-Maskinongé **206** 46.20 N 73.09 W
Saint Edward **198** 41.34 N 97.52 W
Saint-Égrève **62** 45.14 N 5.41 E
Saint Eleanor's **186** 46.25 N 63.49 W
Saint Elias, Cape ≻ **180** 59.52 N 144.30 W
Saint Elias, Mount ∧ **180** 60.18 N 140.55 W
Saint Elias Mountains ⋏ **180** 60.30 N 139.30 W
Saint-Élie **250** 4.50 N 53.17 W
Saint Elmo **219** 39.01 N 88.50 W
Saint-Éloi **186** 48.02 N 69.14 W
Saint-Émile-de-Montcalm **206** 46.06 N 74.00 W
Saint-Émile-de-Québec **206** 46.52 N 71.20 W
Saint-Émile-de-Suffolk **206** 45.56 N 74.55 W
Sainte-Enimie **32** 44.22 N 3.26 E
Saint-Épain **50** 47.08 N 0.32 E
Saint-Esprit ≃ **206** 45.52 N 73.27 W
Saint-Étienne **62** 45.26 N 4.24 E
Saint-Étienne-de-Lugdarès **62** 44.39 N 3.57 E
Saint-Étienne-de-Saint-Geoirs **62** 45.20 N 5.21 E
Saint-Étienne-des-Grès **206** 46.26 N 72.46 W
Saint-Étienne-de-Tinée **62** 44.15 N 6.55 E
Saint-Étienne-du-Rouvray **50** 49.23 N 1.06 E
Saint-Étienne-en-Dévoluy **62** 44.42 N 5.56 E
Saint-Étienne-le-Laus **62** 44.30 N 6.10 E
Saint-Étienne-les-Orgues **62** 44.03 N 5.47 E
Saint-Étienne-lès-Remiremont **58** 48.02 N 6.37 E
Saint-Eugène **206** 45.30 N 74.28 W
Saint-Eustache **206** 45.34 N 73.54 W
Saint-Evroult-Notre-Dame-du-Bois **50** 48.48 N 0.28 E
Saint-Fabien **186** 48.18 N 68.52 W
Saint Faith's **158** 30.30 S 30.12 E
Saint-Fargeau **50** 47.38 N 3.04 E
Saint-Fargeau-Ponthierry **261** 48.33 N 2.32 E
Saint-Félicien, P.Q., Can. **176** 48.39 N 72.26 W
Saint-Félicien, Fr. **62** 45.05 N 4.38 E
Sainte-Félicité **186** 48.54 N 67.20 W
Saint-Félix **62** 45.48 N 5.58 E
Saint-Félix-de-Kingsey **206** 45.48 N 72.12 W
Saint-Félix-de-Valois **206** 46.10 N 73.26 W
Saint-Ferdinand (Bernierville) **206** 46.06 N 71.34 W
Saintfield **48** 54.28 N 5.50 W
Saint Fillans **46** 56.23 N 4.07 W
Saint-Firmin **62** 44.47 N 6.02 E
Saint-Firmin-sur-Loire **50** 47.37 N 2.44 E
Saint-Flavien **206** 46.31 N 71.36 W
Saint-Florent **36** 42.41 N 9.18 E
Saint-Florentin **50** 48.00 N 3.44 E
Saint-Florent-sur-Cher **32** 46.59 N 2.15 E
Saint-Floris, Parc National ♠ **146** 9.40 N 21.35 E
Saint-Flour **32** 45.02 N 3.05 E
Saint-Fons **62** 45.42 N 4.52 E
Saint-Fortunat **206** 45.58 N 71.36 W
Sainte-Foy **206** 46.47 N 71.17 W
Sainte-Foy-la-Grande **32** 44.50 N 0.13 E
Sainte-Foy-l'Argentière **62** 45.42 N 4.28 E
Sainte-Foy-lès-Lyon **62** 45.44 N 4.48 E
Sainte-Foy-Tarentaise **62** 45.35 N 6.53 E
Saint Francis, Ks., U.S. **198** 39.46 N 101.47 W
Saint Francis, S.D., U.S. **198** 43.08 N 100.54 W
Saint Francis, Wi., U.S. **216** 42.58 N 87.52 W
Saint Francis ≃, N.A. **186** 47.10 N 68.57 W
Saint Francis ≃, U.S. **194** 34.38 N 90.35 W
Saint Francis, Cape ≻, Nf., Can. **186** 47.50 N 52.47 W
Saint Francis, Cape ≻, S. Afr. **158** 34.14 S 24.49 E
Saint Francis, Lake ⊜ **206** 45.08 N 74.25 W
Saint Francis Bay ⊂ **158** 34.35 S 25.10 E
Saint Francisville **194** 30.46 N 91.22 W
Saint-François **241o** 16.15 N 61.17 W
Saint-François ≃ **206** 46.07 N 72.55 W
Saint-François, Lac ⊜ **206** 45.55 N 71.10 W
Saint-François de Boundji **152** 1.03 S 15.22 E
Saint-François-de-Laval ◄[8] **275a** 45.40 N 73.34 W
Saint-François-du-Lac **206** 46.04 N 72.50 W
Saint Francois Mountains ⋏[2] **194** 37.30 N 90.35 W
Saint-François-sur-Bugeon **62** 45.24 N 6.21 E
Saint-Front **62** 44.59 N 4.08 E
Saint-Gabriel **206** 46.17 N 73.23 W
Saint-Gabriel-de-Gaspé **186** 48.31 N 64.32 W
Saint-Gabriel-de-Rimouski **186** 48.25 N 68.10 W
Saint-Gall → Sankt Gallen **58** 47.25 N 9.23 E
Saint-Galmier **62** 45.35 N 4.19 E
Sainte-Gauburge-Sainte-Colombe **50** 48.42 N 0.26 E
Saint-Gaudens **32** 43.07 N 0.44 E
Saint-Gaudens National Historic Site ⊥ **188** 43.29 N 72.19 W
Saint-Gaultier **32** 46.38 N 1.25 E
Saint-Gély-du-Fesc **62** 43.42 N 3.48 E
Saint-Genest-Lerpt **62** 45.27 N 4.20 E
Saint-Genest-Malifaux **62** 45.20 N 4.25 E
Sainte-Geneviève, P.Q., Can. **275a** 45.29 N 73.52 W
Sainte Genevieve, Mo., U.S. **194** 37.59 N 90.03 W
Sainte-Geneviève-de-Batiscan **206** 46.32 N 72.20 W
Sainte-Geneviève-des-Bois **50** 48.38 N 2.20 E
Saint-Gengoux-le-National **58** 46.37 N 4.39 E
Saint-Genis-de-Saintonge **32** 45.29 N 0.34 W
Saint-Genis-Laval **62** 45.41 N 4.48 E
Saint-Genis-Pouilly **58** 46.15 N 6.01 E
Saint-Genix-sur-Guiers **62** 45.36 N 5.38 E
Saint-Geoire-en-Valdaine **62** 45.27 N 5.38 E
Saint George, Austl. **166** 28.02 S 148.35 E
Saint George, Ber. **240a** 32.22 N 64.40 W
Saint George, N.B., Can. **186** 45.08 N 66.49 W
Saint George, On., Can. **212** 43.15 N 80.15 W
Saint George, Pa., U.S. **214** 41.15 N 79.47 W
Saint George, S.C., U.S. **192** 33.11 N 80.34 W
Saint George, Ut,. U.S. **200** 37.06 N 113.34 W
Saint George ◄[8] **276** 40.39 N 74.05 W
Saint George, Cape ≻, Nf., Can. **186** 48.27 N 59.15 W
Saint George, Cape ≻, Pap. N. Gui. **164** 4.52 S 152.52 E
Saint George, Cape ≻, Fl., U.S. **192** 29.35 N 85.04 W
Saint George, Point ≻ **204** 41.47 N 124.15 W
Saint George Island, Ak., U.S. **180** 56.36 N 169.32 W
Saint George Island, Md., U.S. **208** 38.07 N 76.29 W
Saint George Island I, Ak., U.S. **180** 56.35 N 169.35 W
Saint George Island I, Fl., U.S. **192** 29.39 N 84.55 W
Saint George's, Nf., Can. **186** 48.26 N 58.29 W
Saint-Georges, P.Q., Can. **188** 46.07 N 70.40 W
Saint-Georges, P.Q., Can. **206** 46.37 N 72.40 W
Saint-Georges, Fr. **58** 48.40 N 6.56 E
Saint George's, Gren. **241k** 12.03 N 61.45 W
Saint-Georges, Guy. fr. **250** 3.54 N 51.48 W
Saint Georges, De., U.S. **208** 39.33 N 75.39 W

Symbols in the index entries represent the broad categories identified in the key at the right. Symbols with superior numbers (⋏[1]) identify subcategories (see complete key on page *I · 1).*

Symbole im Register stellen die rechts im Schlüssel erklärten Kategorien dar. Symbole mit hochgestellten Ziffern (⋏[1]) bezeichnen Unterabteilungen einer Kategorie (vgl. vollständiger Schlüssel auf Seite *I · 1).*

Los símbolos incluídos en el texto del índice representan las grandes categorías identificadas con la clave a la derecha. Los símbolos con numeros en su parte superior (⋏[1]) identifican las subcategorías (véase la clave completa en la página *I · 1).*

Les symboles de l'index représentent les catégories indiquées dans la légende à droite. Les symboles suivis d'un indice (⋏[1]) représentent des sous-catégories (voir légende complète à la page *I · 1).*

Os símbolos incluídos no texto do índice representam as grandes categorias identificadas com a chave à direita. Os símbolos com números em sua parte superior (⋏[1]) identificam as subcategorias (veja-se a chave completa à página *I · 1).*

∧	Mountain	Berg	Montaña	Montagne	Montanha
⋏	Mountains	Gebirge	Montañas	Montagnes	Montanhas
)(	Pass	Paß	Paso	Col	Passo
V	Valley, Canyon	Tal, Cañon	Valle, Cañón	Vallée, Canyon	Vale, Canhão
≚	Plain	Ebene	Llano	Plaine	Planície
≻	Cape	Kap	Cabo	Cap	Cabo
I	Island	Insel	Isla	Île	Ilha
II	Islands	Inseln	Islas	Îles	Ilhas
⊥	Other Topographic Features	Andere Topographische Objekte	Otros Elementos Topográficos	Autres données topographiques	Outros acidentes topográficos

ESPAÑOL Nombre / FRANÇAIS Nom / PORTUGUÊS Nome	Página / Page / Página	Lat.°′	Long.°′ W = Oeste / W = Ouest / W = Oeste
Saint Georges Basin ⊂	170	35.07 S	150.36 E
Saint George's Bay ⊂, Nf., Can.	186	48.20 N	59.00 W
Saint Georges Bay ⊂, N.S., Can.	186	45.50 N	61.45 W
Saint George's Channel ʊ, Europe	28	52.00 N	6.00 W
Saint George's Channel ʊ, Pap. N. Gui.	164	4.30 S	152.30 E
Saint-Georges-de-Reneins	58	46.04 N	4.43 E
Saint-Georges-de-Windsor	206	45.42 N	71.50 W
Saint-Georges-en-Couzan	62	45.42 N	3.56 E
Saint Georges Head ›	170	35.12 S	150.42 E
Saint George's Island I	240a	32.22 N	64.40 W
Saint George Sound ʊ	192	29.47 N	84.42 W
Saint-Gérard, Bel.	56	50.21 N	4.45 E
Saint-Gérard, P.Q., Can.	206	45.46 N	71.25 W
Saint-Germain ≃	206	45.55 N	72.30 W
Saint-Germain, Forêt de ♠	261	48.55 N	2.05 E
Saint-Germain-de-Calberte	62	44.13 N	3.48 E
Saint-Germain-de-Grantham	206	45.50 N	72.34 W
Saint-Germain-de-Joux	58	46.11 N	5.44 E
Saint-Germain-des-Champs	50	47.25 N	3.55 E
Saint-Germain-du-Bois	58	46.45 N	5.15 E
Saint-Germain-du-Plain	58	46.42 N	4.58 E
Saint-Germain-en-Laye	50	48.54 N	2.05 E
Saint-Germain-en-Laye, Château de ⊥	261	48.54 N	2.06 E
Saint-Germain-Laval	62	45.50 N	4.01 E
Saint-Germain-Laxis	261	48.35 N	2.43 E
Saint-Germain-Lembron	32	45.28 N	3.14 E
Saint-Germain-lès-Arlay	58	46.46 N	5.34 E
Saint-Germain-lès-Corbeil	261	48.37 N	2.29 E
Saint-Germain-l'Herm	32	45.28 N	3.33 E
Saint-Germain-sur-Morin	261	48.53 N	2.51 E
Saint Germans	42	50.24 N	4.18 W
Saint-Germer-de-Fly	50	49.27 N	1.47 E
Saint-Gervais-d'Auvergne	32	46.02 N	2.49 E
Saint-Gervais-les-Bains	62	45.54 N	6.43 E
Saint-Gervasy	62	43.53 N	4.29 E
Saint-Géry	32	44.29 N	1.35 E
Saint-Gilles, Bel.	50	50.49 N	4.20 E
Saint-Gilles, P.Q., Can.	206	46.31 N	71.22 W
Saint-Gilles, Fr.	62	43.41 N	4.26 E
Saint-Gilles-Croix-de-Vie	32	46.42 N	1.57 W
Saint-Gingolph	58	46.24 N	6.52 E
Saint-Girons	32	42.59 N	1.09 E
Saint-Gobain	50	49.36 N	3.23 E
Saint Gotthard Pass → San Gottardo, Passo del)(	58	46.33 N	8.34 E
Saint Govan's Head ›	42	51.36 N	4.55 W
Saint-Gratien	261	48.58 N	2.17 E
Saint-Grégoire (Larochelle)	206	46.16 N	72.30 W
Saint Gregory, Mount ∧	186	49.19 N	58.13 W
Saint-Guénolé	32	47.49 N	4.20 W
Saint-Guillaume-d'Upton	206	45.53 N	72.46 W
Saint-Héand	62	45.31 N	4.22 E
Saint Helena	226	38.30 N	122.28 W
Saint Helena □[2]	10	15.57 S	5.42 W
Saint Helena, Mount ∧	226	38.40 N	122.38 W
Saint Helena Sound ʊ	192	32.27 N	80.25 W
Sainte-Hélène, Île I	275a	45.31 N	73.32 W
Sainte-Hélène-de-Bagot	206	45.44 N	72.44 W
Saint Helens, Austl.	166	41.20 S	148.15 E
Saint Helens, Eng., U.K.	42	50.42 N	1.06 W
Saint Helens, Eng., U.K.	44	53.28 N	2.44 W
Saint Helens, Or., U.S.	224	45.51 N	122.48 W
Saint Helens □[8]	262	53.28 N	2.45 W
Saint Helens, Mount ∧[1]	224	46.12 N	122.11 W
Saint Helens Canal ≊	262	53.27 N	2.42 W
Saint Helier	43b	49.11 N	2.06 W
Saint Henry	216	40.25 N	84.38 W
Sainte-Hermine	32	46.33 N	1.04 W
Saint-Hilaire-du-Harcouët	32	48.35 N	1.06 W
Saint-Hilarion	261	48.37 N	1.44 E
Saint-Hippolyte, Fr.	58	47.19 N	6.49 E
Saint-Hippolyte, Fr.	62	43.38 N	4.45 E
Saint-Hippolyte-de-Kilkenny	206	45.56 N	74.01 W
Saint-Hippolyte-du-Fort	62	43.58 N	3.51 E
Saint-Honorat, Mont ∧	62	44.05 N	6.46 E
Saint-Hubert, Bel.	56	50.01 N	5.23 E
Saint-Hubert, P.Q., Can.	206	45.30 N	73.25 W
Saint-Hubert, Étang de ⊜	261	48.43 N	1.51 E
Saint-Hubert-le-Roi	261	48.43 N	1.52 E
Saint-Hugues	206	45.48 N	72.52 W
Saint-Hyacinthe	206	45.37 N	72.57 W
Saint-Hyacinthe □[6]	206	45.40 N	73.05 W
Saint-Ignace, N.B., Can.	186	46.42 N	65.05 W
Saint Ignace, Mi., U.S.	190	45.52 N	84.43 W
Saint Ignace Island I	190	48.48 N	87.55 W
Saint Ignatius, Guy.	246	3.20 N	59.47 W
Saint Ignatius, Mt., U.S.	202	47.19 N	114.05 W
Saint-Imier	58	47.09 N	7.00 E
Saint-Imier, Vallon de ∨	58	47.10 N	7.00 E
Saint-Isidore	186	47.33 N	65.03 W
Saint-Isidore-d'Auckland	206	45.16 N	71.31 W
Saint-Isidore-de-Laprairie	275a	45.18 N	73.41 W
Saint Ives, Austl.	274a	33.44 S	151.10 E
Saint Ives, Eng., U.K.	32	50.12 N	5.29 W
Saint Ives, Eng., U.K.	42	52.20 N	0.05 W
Saint Ives Bay ⊂	42	50.14 N	5.28 W
Saint Jacob	219	38.43 N	89.46 W
Saint Jacobs	212	43.32 N	80.33 W
Saint-Jacques	206	45.57 N	73.34 W
Saint-Jacques ≃	275a	45.26 N	73.29 W
Saint James, Il., U.S.	219	38.57 N	88.51 W
Saint James, Mi., U.S.	190	45.45 N	85.30 W
Saint James, Mn., U.S.	198	43.58 N	94.37 W
Saint James, Mo., U.S.	194	37.59 N	91.36 W
Saint James, N.Y., U.S.	210	40.52 N	73.09 W
Saint James, Cape ›	182	51.56 N	131.01 W
Saint James City	220	26.29 N	82.04 W
Saint James Islands II	240m	18.19 N	64.50 W
Saint-Janvier	275a	45.43 N	73.56 W
Saint-Jean □[6]	206	45.15 N	73.20 W
Saint-Jean ≃, P.Q., Can.	186	48.46 N	64.26 W
Saint-Jean ≃, P.Q., Can.	186	50.17 N	64.20 W
Saint-Jean, Île I	275a	45.41 N	73.39 W
Saint-Jean, Lac ⊜	176	48.35 N	72.05 W
Saint-Jean, Rapides de ʟ	275a	45.19 N	73.15 W
Saint-Jean Airport ⊠	275a	45.18 N	73.17 W
Saint-Jean-aux-Bois	50	49.21 N	2.55 E
Saint-Jean-Baptiste	184	49.16 N	97.21 W
Saint-Jean-Baptiste-de-Rouville	206	45.31 N	73.07 W
Saint-Jean-Cap-Ferrat	62	43.41 N	7.20 E
Saint-Jean-d'Angély	32	45.57 N	0.31 W
Saint-Jean-d'Assé	50	48.09 N	0.07 E
Saint-Jean-de-Bournay	62	45.29 N	5.08 E
Saint-Jean-de-Braye	50	47.54 N	1.58 E
Saint-Jean-de-la-Roulle	50	47.55 N	1.52 E
Saint-Jean-de-Losne	58	47.06 N	5.15 E
Saint-Jean-de-Luz	32	43.23 N	1.40 W
Saint-Jean-de-Maurienne	62	45.17 N	6.21 E
Saint-Jean-de-Monts	32	46.48 N	2.03 W
Saint-Jean-des-Piles	206	46.41 N	72.45 W
Saint-Jean-du-Gard	62	44.06 N	3.53 E
Saint-Jean-en-Royans	62	45.01 N	5.18 E
Saint-Jean-Pied-de-Port	32	43.10 N	1.14 W
Saint-Jean-Port-Joli	186	47.13 N	70.16 W
Saint-Jean-Soleymieux	62	45.30 N	4.02 E
Saint-Jean-sur-Richelieu	206	45.19 N	73.16 W
Saint-Jeoire	58	46.09 N	6.28 E
Saint-Jérôme	206	45.47 N	74.00 W
Saint Jo	196	33.41 N	97.31 W
Saint Joachim	214	42.16 N	82.38 W
Saint Joe	216	41.18 N	84.54 W
Saint Joe ≃	202	47.21 N	116.42 W
Saint John, N.B., Can.	186	45.16 N	66.03 W
Saint John, Jersey	43b	49.15 N	2.08 W
Saint John, In., U.S.	216	41.27 N	87.28 W
Saint John, Ks., U.S.	198	38.00 N	98.45 W
Saint John, N.D., U.S.	198	48.56 N	99.42 W
Saint John, Wa., U.S.	202	47.05 N	117.34 W
Saint John I	240m	18.20 N	64.45 W
Saint John ≃, Liber.	150	6.40 N	9.10 W
Saint John ≃, N.A.	186	45.15 N	66.04 W
Saint John, Cape ›	186	50.00 N	55.32 W
Saint John, Lake ⊜, Nf., Can.	186	48.23 N	54.41 W
Saint John, Lake ⊜, On., Can.	212	44.41 N	79.20 W
Saint John Bay ⊂	186	50.54 N	57.08 W
Saint John Island I	186	50.49 N	57.14 W
Saint John's, Antig.	240c	17.06 N	61.51 W
Saint John's, Nf., Can.	186	47.34 N	52.43 W
Saint Johns → Saint-Jean-sur-Richelieu, P.Q., Can.	206	45.19 N	73.16 W
Saint John's, I. of Man	44	54.13 N	4.38 W
Saint Johns, Az., U.S.	200	34.30 N	109.21 W
Saint Johns, Mi., U.S.	216	43.00 N	84.33 W
Saint Johns, Mo., U.S.	219	38.42 N	90.20 W
Saint Johns, Oh., U.S.	216	40.33 N	84.05 W
Saint Johns ≃, Ca., U.S.	226	36.25 N	119.25 W
Saint Johns ≃, Fl., U.S.	192	30.24 N	81.24 W
Saint Johnsburg	210	43.05 N	78.53 W
Saint Johnsbury	188	44.25 N	72.00 W
Saint Johns Creek ≃	219	38.34 N	91.01 W
Saint John's Jerusalem ⊥	260	51.25 N	0.14 E
Saint Johns Marsh ≡	220	27.45 N	80.40 W
Saint John's Point ›	48	54.13 N	5.40 W
Saint John's University ᵾ[2]	276	40.43 N	73.48 W
Saint Johnsville	210	42.59 N	74.41 W
Saint Joseph, N.B., Can.	186	45.59 N	64.34 W
Saint Joseph, Dom.	240d	15.26 N	61.26 W
Saint-Joseph, Mart.	240e	14.40 N	61.03 W
Saint-Joseph, N. Cal.	175f	20.27 S	166.36 E
Saint-Joseph, Réu.	157c	21.22 S	55.36 E
Saint Joseph, Il., U.S.	194	40.06 N	88.02 W
Saint Joseph, La., U.S.	194	31.55 N	91.14 W
Saint Joseph, Mi., U.S.	216	42.05 N	86.29 W
Saint Joseph, Mn., U.S.	190	45.33 N	94.19 W
Saint Joseph, Mo., U.S.	194	39.46 N	94.50 W
Saint Joseph, Tn., U.S.	194	35.02 N	87.30 W
Saint Joseph □[6], In., U.S.	216	41.41 N	86.15 W
Saint Joseph □[6], Mi., U.S.	216	41.55 N	85.31 W
Saint Joseph ≃, U.S.	216	42.07 N	86.29 W
Saint Joseph ≃, U.S.	216	41.05 N	85.08 W
Saint Joseph, East Branch ≃	216	41.39 N	84.34 W
Saint-Joseph, Île I	275a	45.41 N	73.42 W
Saint-Joseph, Lac ⊜	206	46.54 N	71.38 W
Saint Joseph, Lake ⊜	176	51.05 N	90.35 W
Saint Joseph, West Branch ≃	216	41.39 N	84.34 W
Saint Joseph Bay ⊂	192	29.47 N	85.21 W
Saint Joseph Channel ʊ	190	46.19 N	84.04 W
Saint-Joseph-d'Alma → Alma	186	48.33 N	71.39 W
Saint-Joseph-de-Beauce	186	46.18 N	70.53 W
Saint-Joseph-de-Mékinac	206	46.55 N	72.42 W
Saint-Joseph-de-Sorel	206	46.02 N	73.07 W
Saint-Joseph-du-Lac	275a	45.32 N	74.00 W
Saint Joseph Island I	190	46.13 N	83.57 W
Saint Joseph's University ᵾ[2]	285	40.00 N	75.14 W
Saint-Jouin-Bruneval	50	49.39 N	0.10 E
Saint-Jovite	206	46.07 N	74.36 W
Sainte-Julie	206	45.35 N	73.19 W
Saint-Julien	58	46.23 N	5.27 E
Saint-Julien-Chapteuil	62	45.02 N	4.04 E
Saint-Julien-du-Sault	50	48.02 N	3.18 E
Saint-Julien-du-Verdon	62	43.55 N	6.32 E
Saint-Julien-en-Beauchêne	62	44.37 N	5.42 E
Saint-Julien-en-Born	32	44.04 N	1.14 W
Saint-Julien-en-Genevois	58	46.08 N	6.05 E
Saint-Julien-en-Jarez	62	45.28 N	4.31 E
Saint-Julien-les-Villas	50	48.16 N	4.06 E
Saint-Julien-Molin-Molette	62	45.19 N	4.37 E
Sainte-Julienne	206	45.58 N	73.43 W
Saint-Junien	32	45.53 N	0.54 E
Saint Just, P.R.	240m	18.23 N	66.00 W
Saint Just, Eng., U.K.	42	50.07 N	5.42 W
Saint-Just-en-Chaussée	50	49.30 N	2.26 E
Saint-Just-en-Chevalet	32	45.55 N	3.50 E
Saint-Justin	206	46.15 N	73.05 W
Saint-Just-Malmont	62	45.20 N	4.19 E
Saint-Just-sur-Loire	62	45.29 N	4.16 E
Saint Keverne	42	50.03 N	5.06 W
Saint Kilda, Austl.	168b	34.44 S	138.32 E
Saint Kilda, Austl.	169	37.52 S	144.59 E
Saint Kilda, N.Z.	172	45.54 S	170.30 E
Saint Kilda I	28	57.49 N	8.36 W
Saint Kitts	168b	34.21 S	139.04 E
Saint Kitts → Saint Christopher I	238	17.20 N	62.45 W
Saint Kitts and Nevis □[1], N.A.	230	17.20 N	62.45 W
Saint Kitts and Nevis □[1], N.A.	238	17.20 N	62.45 W
Saint-Lambert, P.Q., Can.	206	45.30 N	73.30 W
Saint-Lambert, Fr.	261	48.44 N	2.01 E
Saint Landry	194	30.50 N	92.15 W
Saint-Laurent, Mb., Can.	184	50.24 N	97.56 W
Saint-Laurent, P.Q., Can.	206	45.30 N	73.40 W
Saint-Laurent, Fr.	58	48.09 N	6.27 E
Saint-Laurent → Saint Lawrence ≃	176	49.30 N	67.00 W
Saint-Laurent-Blangy	50	50.18 N	2.48 E
Saint-Laurent-de-Chamousset	62	45.44 N	4.28 E
Saint-Laurent-du-Maroni	250	5.30 N	54.02 W
Saint-Laurent-du-Maroni □[8]	250	4.00 N	53.30 W
Saint-Laurent-du-Pont	62	45.23 N	5.44 E
Saint-Laurent-du-Var	62	43.40 N	7.11 E
Saint-Laurent-en-Caux	50	49.45 N	0.53 E
Saint-Laurent-en-Grandvaux	58	46.35 N	5.57 E
Saint-Laurent-et-Benon	32	45.09 N	0.49 W
Saint-Laurent-les-Bains	62	44.37 N	3.58 E
Saint-Laurent-sur-Saône	58	46.18 N	4.50 E
Saint Lawrence, Austl.	166	22.21 S	149.31 E
Saint Lawrence, Nf., Can.	186	46.55 N	55.24 W
Saint Lawrence □[6]	212	44.30 N	75.27 W
Saint Lawrence ≃	176	49.30 N	67.00 W
Saint Lawrence, Cape ›	186	47.03 N	60.37 W
Saint Lawrence, Gulf of ⊂	186	48.00 N	62.00 W
Saint Lawrence, Lake ⊜	206	44.56 N	75.04 W
Saint Lawrence Island I	180	63.30 N	170.30 W
Saint Lawrence Islands National Park ♠	212	44.18 N	76.08 W
Saint-Lawrence Seaway ≊	275a	45.43 N	73.25 W
Saint-Lazare	184	50.26 N	101.16 W
Saint-Lazare, Gare ◆[5]	261	48.53 N	2.20 E
Saint-Léandre	186	48.44 N	67.36 W
Saint-Léger-en-Yvelines	50	48.43 N	1.46 E
Saint-Léger-sur-Dheune	58	46.51 N	4.38 E
Saint Leo	220	28.20 N	82.15 W
Saint Leon	218	39.17 N	84.57 W
Saint-Léonard, N.B., Can.	186	47.10 N	67.56 W
Saint-Léonard, P.Q., Can.	206	45.35 N	73.35 W
Saint Leonard, Md., U.S.	208	38.28 N	76.30 W
Saint-Léonard-d'Aston	206	46.06 N	72.22 W
Saint Leonards, Eng., U.K.	42	50.49 N	1.51 W
Saint Leonards, Eng., U.K.	42	50.51 N	0.34 E
Saint-Leu-d'Esserent	50	49.13 N	2.25 E
Saint-Leu-la-Forêt	50	49.01 N	2.15 E
Saint-Liboire	206	45.39 N	72.46 W
Saint-Lô	32	49.07 N	1.05 W
Saint-Louis, Sk., Can.	184	52.56 N	105.49 W
Saint-Louis, Fr.	58	47.35 N	7.34 E
Saint-Louis, Guad.	241o	15.57 N	61.19 W
Saint-Louis, Réu.	157c	21.16 S	55.25 E
Saint-Louis, Sén.	150	16.02 N	16.30 W
Saint Louis, Mi., U.S.	190	43.24 N	84.36 W
Saint Louis, Mo., U.S.	219	38.37 N	90.11 W
Saint Louis, Tx., U.S.	222	32.18 N	95.20 W
Saint-Louis □[4]	150	16.00 N	14.30 W
Saint Louis □[6]	219	38.39 N	90.25 W
Saint-Louis ≃, P.Q., Can.	275a	45.19 N	73.53 W
Saint Louis ≃, U.S.	190	46.45 N	92.06 W
Saint-Louis, Lac ⊜	206	45.24 N	73.48 W
Saint-Louis, Pointe ›	275a	45.19 N	73.53 W
Saint Louis Crossing	218	39.19 N	85.51 W
Saint-Louis-de-Champlain	206	46.25 N	72.36 W
Saint-Louis-de-Kent	186	46.44 N	64.58 W
Saint Louis Park	190	44.56 N	93.20 W
Saint Louisville	214	40.10 N	82.25 W
Saint-Loup-sur-Aujon	58	47.53 N	5.05 E
Saint-Loup-sur-Semouse	58	47.53 N	6.16 E
Saint-Luc, P.Q., Can.	206	45.22 N	73.18 W
Saint-Luc, Schw.	58	46.13 N	7.36 E
Sainte-Luce	240e	14.28 N	60.56 W
Saint Lucia □[1], N.A.	230	13.53 N	60.58 W
Saint Lucia □[1], N.A.	241f	13.53 N	60.58 W
Saint Lucia, Cape ›	158	28.25 S	32.25 E
Saint Lucia, Lake ⊜	158	28.05 S	32.26 E
Saint Lucia Channel ʊ	238	14.09 N	60.57 W
Saint Lucia Estuary	158	28.22 S	32.25 E
Saint Lucia Game Reserve ◆[4]	158	28.10 S	32.28 E
Sainte-Lucie, Fr.	36	41.42 N	9.22 E
Saint Lucie, Fl., U.S.	220	27.29 N	80.20 W
Saint Lucie □[6]	220	27.23 N	80.26 W
Saint Lucie Canal ≊	220	27.10 N	80.15 W
Saint Lucie Inlet ⊂	220	27.10 N	80.10 W
Saint Lucie Lock ◆[5]	220	27.07 N	80.17 W
Saint-Lucien	261	48.39 N	1.38 E
Saint-Lupicin	58	46.24 N	5.47 E
Sainte-Magnance	50	47.27 N	4.04 E
Saint Magnus Bay ⊂	46a	60.24 N	1.34 W
Saint Magnus Cathedral ᵾ[1]	46	58.58 N	2.57 W
Saint-Malo, P.Q., Can.	206	45.12 N	71.30 W
Saint-Malo, Fr.	32	48.39 N	2.01 W
Saint-Malo, Golfe de ⊂	32	48.45 N	2.00 W
Saint-Mamert-du-Gard	62	43.53 N	4.12 E
Saint-Mammès	50	48.23 N	2.49 E
Saint-Mandé	261	48.50 N	2.25 E
Saint-Mandrier-sur-Mer	62	43.04 N	5.56 E
Saint-Marc	238	19.07 N	72.42 W
Saint-Marc, Canal de ʊ	238	18.50 N	72.45 W
Saint-Marc-des-Carrières	206	46.41 N	72.03 W
Saint-Marcel	58	46.47 N	4.54 E
Saint-Marcellin	62	45.09 N	5.19 E
Saint-Marcelline-de-Kildare	206	46.07 N	73.36 W
Saint-Marc-sur-Richelieu	275a	45.41 N	73.12 W
Saint-Mard	261	49.02 N	2.42 E
Saint Margaret Bay ⊂	186	51.01 N	56.58 W
Saint Margaret's at Cliffe	42	51.09 N	1.24 E
Saint Margarets Bay ⊂	186	44.35 N	64.00 W
Saint Margaret's Hope	46	58.49 N	2.57 W
Sainte-Marguerite ≃	176	50.09 N	66.36 W
Sainte-Marguerite, Baie ⊂	186	50.06 N	66.36 W
Sainte-Marguerite-sur-Mer	50	49.55 N	0.57 E
Sainte-Marie	240e	14.47 N	61.00 W
Sainte-Marie, Cap ›	157b	25.36 S	45.08 E
Sainte-Marie-aux-Mines (Markirch)	58	48.15 N	7.11 E
Saint Maries	202	47.18 N	116.33 W
Saint Maries ≃	202	47.19 N	116.33 W
Saint-Marin → San Marino □[1]	66	43.56 N	12.25 E
Saint Marks, S. Afr.	158	32.01 S	27.22 E
Saint Marks, Fl., U.S.	192	30.09 N	84.12 W
Saint Marks ≃	192	30.08 N	84.12 W
Sainte-Marthe-de-Gaspé	186	49.12 N	66.10 W
Sainte-Marthe-sur-le-Lac	275a	45.32 N	73.56 W
Saint-Martin (Sint Maarten) I	238	18.04 N	63.04 W
Saint-Martin, Cap ›	240e	14.52 N	61.13 W
Saint Martin, Lake ⊜	184	51.37 N	98.29 W
Saint-Martin-Boulogne	50	50.43 N	1.38 E
Saint-Martin-d'Ardèche	62	44.18 N	4.35 E
Saint-Martin-d'Auxigny	50	47.12 N	2.25 E
Saint-Martin-de-Belleville	62	45.23 N	6.30 E
Saint-Martin-de-Bossenay	50	48.26 N	3.41 E
Saint-Martin-de-Bréthencourt	261	48.31 N	1.56 E
Saint-Martin-de-Crau	62	43.38 N	4.49 E
Saint-Martin-de-Londres	62	43.47 N	3.44 E
Saint-Martin-de-Nigelles	261	48.37 N	1.37 E
Saint-Martin-d'Entraunes	62	44.08 N	6.46 E
Saint-Martin-des-Champs	261	48.53 N	1.43 E
Saint-Martin-de-Valamas	62	44.56 N	4.22 E
Saint-Martin-d'Hères	62	45.10 N	5.46 E
Saint-Martin-du-Puy	50	47.20 N	3.52 E
Saint-Martin-du-Tertre	261	49.06 N	2.21 E
Saint-Martin-du-Var	62	43.49 N	7.12 E
Sainte-Martine	206	45.15 N	73.48 W
Saint-Martin-en-Bresse	58	46.49 N	5.04 E
Saint-Martin-la-Garenne	261	49.02 N	1.41 E
Saint-Martin-la-Plaine	62	45.32 N	4.36 E
Saint Martins, N.B., Can.	186	45.21 N	65.32 W
Saint Martin's, Eng., U.K.	42	52.55 N	2.59 W
Saint Martin's I	42a	49.58 N	6.20 W
Saint Martins Keys II	220	28.47 N	82.44 W
Saint-Martin-Vésubie	62	44.04 N	7.15 E
Saint Martinville	194	30.07 N	91.49 W
Saint Mary	194	37.52 N	89.58 W
Saint Mary ≃, B.C., Can.	182	49.37 N	115.38 W
Saint Mary ≃, N.A.	182	49.37 N	112.52 W
Saint Mary, Cape ›	150	13.28 N	16.40 W
Saint Mary, Mount ∧	164	8.10 S	147.00 E
Saint Mary Bourne	42	51.16 N	1.24 W
Saint Mary Cray ◆[8]	260	51.23 N	0.07 E
Saint Mary Lake ⊜	202	48.40 N	113.30 W
Saint Marylebone ◆[8]	260	51.31 N	0.10 W
Saint Mary of the Lake Seminary ᵾ[2]	278	42.17 N	88.00 W
Saint Mary Peak ∧	166	31.30 S	138.33 E
Saint Mary Reservoir ⊜[1]	182	49.19 N	113.12 W
Saint Marys, Austl.	166	41.35 S	148.10 E
Saint Marys, Austl.	170	33.47 S	150.47 E
Saint Mary's, Nf., Can.	186	46.55 N	53.34 W
Saint Mary's, On., Can.	212	43.16 N	81.08 W
Saint Marys, Ak., U.S.	180	62.04 N	163.10 W
Saint Marys, Ga., U.S.	192	30.43 N	81.32 W
Saint Marys, Ks., U.S.	198	39.11 N	96.04 W
Saint Marys, Oh., U.S.	216	40.32 N	84.23 W
Saint Marys, Pa., U.S.	214	41.25 N	78.33 W
Saint Marys, W.V., U.S.	188	39.23 N	81.12 W
Saint Marys □[6]	208	38.17 N	76.38 W
Saint Mary's I	42a	49.55 N	6.18 W
Saint Marys ≃, N.S., Can.	186	45.02 N	61.54 W
Saint Marys ≃, N.A.	190	45.58 N	83.54 W
Saint Marys ≃, U.S.	192	30.43 N	81.27 W
Saint Marys ≃, U.S.	216	41.05 N	85.08 W
Saint Marys ≃, Md., U.S.	208	38.06 N	76.26 W
Saint Mary's, Cape ›, Nf., Can.	186	46.49 N	54.12 W
Saint Marys, Cape ›, N.S., Can.	186	44.05 N	66.13 W
Saint Marys, North Prong ≃	192	30.22 N	82.06 W
Saint Marys, South Prong ≃	192	30.22 N	82.06 W
Saint Mary's Bay	42	51.00 N	0.58 E
Saint Mary's Bay ⊂, Nf., Can.	186	46.50 N	53.47 W
Saint Marys Bay ⊂, N.S., Can.	186	44.25 N	66.10 W
Saint Marys City	208	38.11 N	76.26 W
Saint Mary's Hoo	260	51.28 N	0.36 E
Saint Marys Lake ⊜	278	42.17 N	87.59 W
Saint Mary's Marshes ≡	260	51.28 N	0.35 E
Saint-Mathieu	32	45.42 N	0.46 E
Saint-Mathieu, Pointe de ›	32	48.20 N	4.46 W
Saint-Mathieu-de-Laprairie	275a	45.19 N	73.31 W
Saint Matthew Island I	180	60.30 N	172.45 W
Saint Matthews, Ky., U.S.	218	38.15 N	85.39 W
Saint Matthews, S.C., U.S.	192	33.39 N	80.46 W
Saint Matthias Group II	164	1.30 S	149.40 E
Saint-Maur-des-Fossés	50	48.48 N	2.30 E
Sainte-Maure-de-Touraine	32	47.07 N	0.37 E
Saint-Maurice, Fr.	261	48.49 N	2.25 E
Saint-Maurice, Schw.	58	46.13 N	7.00 E
Saint-Maurice □[6]	206	46.35 N	73.00 W
Saint-Maurice ≃	176	46.21 N	72.31 W
Saint-Maurice, Parc de ♠	206	46.52 N	73.10 W
Saint-Maurice-en-Montagne	58	46.34 N	5.50 E
Saint-Maurice-Montcouronne	261	48.35 N	2.07 E
Saint Mawes	42	50.09 N	5.01 W
Saint Mawgan	42	50.28 N	4.58 W
Saint-Max	58	48.42 N	6.13 E
Sainte-Maxime	62	43.18 N	6.38 E
Saint-Maximin-la-Sainte-Baume	62	43.27 N	5.52 E
Saint-Méen-le-Grand	32	48.11 N	2.12 W
Saint Meinrad	194	38.10 N	86.48 W
Sainte-Menehould	56	49.05 N	4.54 E
Saint-Menges	56	49.44 N	4.56 E
Sainte-Mère-Église	32	49.25 N	1.19 W
Saint Merryn	42	50.31 N	4.58 W
Saint-Méry	261	48.35 N	2.50 E
Sainte-Mesme	261	48.32 N	1.58 E
Saint-Mesmes	261	48.59 N	2.42 E
Saint Michael, Ak., U.S.	180	63.29 N	162.02 W
Saint Michael, Pa., U.S.	214	40.20 N	78.46 W
Saint Michaels	208	38.47 N	76.13 W
Saint-Michel, Fr.	50	49.55 N	4.08 E
Saint-Michel, Fr.	62	45.13 N	6.28 E
Saint-Michel ◆[8]	275a	45.35 N	73.35 W
Saint-Michel-de-Napierville	206	45.14 N	73.34 W
Saint-Michel-des-Saints	206	46.41 N	73.55 W
Saint-Michel-sur-Meurthe	58	48.19 N	6.54 E
Saint-Michel-sur-Orge	261	48.38 N	2.18 E
Saint-Mihiel	56	48.54 N	5.33 E
Saint Monance	46	56.12 N	2.46 W
Sainte-Monique-des-Deux-Montagnes	275a	45.40 N	74.00 W
Sainte-Montaine	50	47.29 N	2.19 E
Saint-Moritz → Sankt Moritz	58	46.30 N	9.50 E
Saint-Narcisse	206	46.34 N	72.28 W
Saint-Nazaire	32	47.17 N	2.12 W
Saint-Nazaire-en-Royans	62	45.04 N	5.15 E
Saint-Nazaire-le-Désert	62	44.34 N	5.17 E
Saint Nazianz	190	44.00 N	87.55 W
Saint Neots	42	52.14 N	0.17 W
Saint-Nicéphore	206	45.50 N	72.25 W
Saint-Nicolas → Sint-Niklaas, Bel.	50	51.10 N	4.08 E
Saint-Nicolas, Bel.	56	50.38 N	5.32 E
Saint-Nicolas, P.Q., Can.	206	46.42 N	71.24 W
Saint-Nicolas-aux-Bois	50	49.36 N	3.25 E
Saint-Nicolas-d'Aliermont	50	49.53 N	1.13 E
Saint-Nizier-du-Moucherotte	62	45.10 N	5.38 E
Saint-Nom-la-Bretèche	261	48.51 N	2.01 E
Saint Nora Lake ⊜	212	45.08 N	78.49 W
Saint-Norbert-d'Arthabaska	206	46.07 N	71.50 W
Sainte-Odile ᵾ[1]	58	48.26 N	7.24 E
Saint-Omer	50	50.45 N	2.15 E
Saintonge □[9]	32	45.30 N	0.30 W
Saint-Ouen, Fr.	50	50.02 N	2.03 E
Saint-Ouen, Fr.	261	48.54 N	2.20 E
Saint-Ouen-l'Aumône	50	49.03 N	2.06 E
Saint-Pacôme	186	47.24 N	69.57 W
Saint-Pamphile	186	46.58 N	69.47 W
Saint Pancras ◆[8]	260	51.32 N	0.07 W
Saint Paris	218	40.07 N	83.57 W
Saint-Pascal	186	47.32 N	69.49 W
Saint-Paterne	50	48.24 N	0.07 E
Saint-Pathus	261	49.04 N	2.48 E
Saint-Patrice, Lac ⊜	190	46.22 N	77.20 W
Saint Paul, Ab., Can.	182	53.59 N	111.17 W
Saint-Paul, Fr.	62	43.42 N	7.07 E
Saint-Paul, Fr.	62	44.31 N	6.45 E
Saint-Paul, Réu.	157c	21.00 S	55.16 E
Saint Paul, In., U.S.	218	39.25 N	85.28 W
Saint Paul, Ks., U.S.	198	37.31 N	95.10 W
Saint Paul, Mn., U.S.	190	44.57 N	93.05 W
Saint Paul, Ne., U.S.	198	41.13 N	98.27 W
Saint Paul, Or., U.S.	224	45.12 N	122.58 W
Saint Paul, Va., U.S.	192	36.54 N	82.18 W
Saint-Paul ≃, Can.	176	51.26 N	57.40 W
Saint Paul ≃, Liber.	150	6.23 N	10.48 W
Saint Paul, Cape ›	150	5.49 N	0.57 E
Saint-Paul, Île I	6	38.43 S	77.29 E
Saint-Paul, Lac ⊜	206	46.18 N	72.29 W
Saint Paul Bay ⊂	116	10.14 N	118.54 E
Saint-Paul-de-Chester (Chesterville)	206	45.57 N	71.49 W
Saint-Paul-en-Jarez	62	45.29 N	4.35 E
Saint-Paul-et-Valmalle	62	43.38 N	3.40 E
Saint-Paulien	62	45.08 N	3.49 E
Saint-Paulin	206	46.25 N	73.01 W
Saint Paul Island	180	57.07 N	170.17 W
Saint Paul Island I, N.S., Can.	186	47.15 N	60.10 W
Saint Paul Island I, Ak., U.S.	180	57.10 N	170.15 W
Saint Pauls	192	34.48 N	78.58 W
Saint Paul's Cathedral ᵾ[1]	260	51.31 N	0.06 W
Saint Paul's Cray ◆[8]	260	51.24 N	0.07 E
Saint Pauls Inlet ⊂	186	49.50 N	57.45 W
Saint Paul's Point ›	174e	25.04 S	130.05 W
Saint-Paul-Trois-Châteaux	62	44.21 N	4.46 E
Saint-Péravy-la-Colombe	50	48.00 N	1.42 E
Saint-Péray	62	44.57 N	4.50 E
Saint-Père	50	47.28 N	3.46 E
Saint Peter, Il., U.S.	219	38.52 N	88.51 W
Saint Peter, Mn., U.S.	190	44.19 N	93.57 W
Saint Peter, Lake ⊜	212	45.18 N	78.02 W
Saint Peter Island I	162	32.17 S	133.35 E
Saint Peter Port	43b	49.27 N	2.32 W
Saint Peters, N.S., Can.	186	45.40 N	60.52 W
Saint Peters, Mo., U.S.	219	38.48 N	90.37 W
Saint Peters, Pa., U.S.	285	40.11 N	75.44 W
Saint Peters Bay	186	46.25 N	62.35 W
Saint Petersburg → Sankt-Peterburg, Ross.	76	59.55 N	30.15 E
Saint Petersburg, Fl., U.S.	220	27.46 N	82.40 W
Saint Petersburg, Pa., U.S.	214	41.10 N	79.37 W
Saint Petersburg Beach	220	27.43 N	82.44 W
Saint Peter's College ᵾ[2]	276	40.44 N	74.05 W
Saint-Philippe-d'Argenteuil	206	45.37 N	74.25 W
Saint-Philippe-de-Laprairie	275a	45.21 N	73.28 W
Saint-Pie	206	45.30 N	72.54 W
Saint-Pierre, P.Q., Can.	275a	45.27 N	73.39 W
Saint-Pierre, Fr.	62	45.40 N	3.45 E
Saint-Pierre, It.	62	45.42 N	7.14 E
Saint-Pierre, Mart.	240e	14.45 N	61.11 W
Saint-Pierre, Réu.	157c	21.19 S	55.29 E
Saint-Pierre, St. P./M.	186	46.47 N	56.11 W
Saint-Pierre I	186	46.47 N	56.11 W
Saint-Pierre ≃	275a	45.23 N	73.34 W
Saint-Pierre, Lac ⊜, P.Q., Can.	186	50.08 N	68.26 W
Saint-Pierre, Lac ⊜, P.Q., Can.	206	46.12 N	72.52 W
Saint Pierre and Miquelon (Saint-Pierre-et-Miquelon) □[2], N.A.	176	46.55 N	56.20 W
Saint Pierre and Miquelon (Saint-Pierre-et-Miquelon) □[2], N.A.	186	46.55 N	56.20 W
Saint-Pierre-d'Albigny	62	45.34 N	6.09 E
Saint-Pierre-de-Bœuf	62	45.22 N	4.45 E
Saint-Pierre-de-Broughton	206	46.15 N	71.12 W
Saint-Pierre-de-Chartreuse	62	45.20 N	5.49 E
Saint-Pierre-des-Corps	50	47.23 N	0.44 E
Saint-Pierre-de-Vacquière	62	43.52 N	4.13 E
Saint-Pierre-du-Vauvray	50	49.14 N	1.13 E
Saint-Pierre-Église	32	49.40 N	1.24 W
Saint-Pierre-en-Port	50	49.48 N	0.29 E
Saint-Pierre-et-Miquelon → Saint Pierre and Miquelon □[2]	186	46.55 N	56.20 W
Saint Pierre Island I	138	9.19 S	50.43 E
Saint Pierre-Jolys	184	49.26 N	96.59 W
Saint Pierre-le-Moûtier	32	46.48 N	3.07 E
Saint-Pierre-lès-Elbeuf	50	49.16 N	1.03 E
Saint-Pierre-sur-Dives	28	49.01 N	0.02 W
Saint-Pierreville	62	44.49 N	4.29 E
Saint-Point, Lac de ⊜	58	46.49 N	6.19 E
Saint-Pol-de-Léon	32	48.41 N	3.59 W
Saint-Pol-sur-Mer	50	51.02 N	2.21 E
Saint-Pol-sur-Ternoise	50	50.23 N	2.20 E
Saint-Polycarpe	206	45.18 N	74.18 W
Saint-Pons	32	43.29 N	2.46 E
Saint-Pourçain-sur-Sioule	32	46.19 N	3.17 E
Saint-Prex	58	46.29 N	6.28 E
Saint-Priest	62	45.42 N	4.57 E
Saint-Priest-en-Jarez	62	45.28 N	4.22 E
Saint-Prix	261	49.01 N	2.16 E
Saint-Prosper-de-Dorchester	188	46.13 N	70.29 W
Saint-Quentin, N.B., Can.	186	47.30 N	67.23 W
Saint-Quentin, Fr.	50	49.51 N	3.17 E
Saint-Quentin, Canal de ≊	50	49.36 N	3.11 E
Saint-Quentin, Étang de ⊜	261	48.47 N	2.01 E
Saint-Rambert-d'Albon	62	45.17 N	4.49 E
Saint-Rambert-en-Bugey	58	45.57 N	5.26 E
Saint-Rambert-sur-Loire	62	45.30 N	4.15 E
Saint-Raphaël	62	43.25 N	6.46 E
Saint-Raymond	206	46.54 N	71.50 W
Saint-Rédempter-de-Lévis	206	46.42 N	71.17 W
Saint Regis	202	47.17 N	115.06 W
Saint-Régis ≃, P.Q., Can.	275a	45.24 N	73.34 W
Saint Regis ≃, N.A.	188	45.00 N	74.39 W
Saint Regis ≃, Mt., U.S.	202	47.18 N	115.05 W
Saint Regis, West Branch ≃	188	44.47 N	74.46 W
Saint Regis Falls	188	44.40 N	74.32 W
Saint Regis Indian Reservation ◆[4]	206	44.58 N	74.39 W
Saint-Rémi	206	45.16 N	73.37 W
Saint-Rémi-d'Amherst	206	46.01 N	74.46 W
Saint-Rémy (lès-Chevreuse), Fr.	50	48.42 N	2.05 E
Saint-Rémy, Fr.	58	46.46 N	4.50 E
Saint Remy, N.Y., U.S.	210	41.54 N	74.01 W
Saint-Rémy-de-Provence	62	43.47 N	4.50 E
Saint-Rémy-en-Bouzemont	58	48.38 N	4.39 E
Saint-Rémy-l'Honoré	261	48.45 N	1.53 E
Saint-Rémy-sur-Avre	50	48.46 N	1.15 E
Saint-Renan	32	48.26 N	4.37 W
Saint-Révérien	50	47.13 N	3.30 E
Saint-Rhémy	62	45.50 N	7.11 E
Saint-Riquier	50	50.08 N	1.57 E
Saint Robert	194	37.50 N	92.09 W
Saint-Roch-de-l'Achigan	206	45.51 N	73.36 W
Saint-Romain-de-Colbosc	50	49.32 N	0.22 E
Saint-Romain-le-Puy	62	45.33 N	4.07 E
Saint-Romans	62	45.07 N	5.19 E
Saint-Romuald	206	46.45 N	71.14 W
Sainte-Rosalie	206	45.38 N	72.54 W
Sainte-Rose	241o	16.20 N	61.42 W
Sainte-Rose ◆[8]	275a	45.36 N	73.47 W
Sainte-Rose-du-Lac	184	51.03 N	99.32 W
Saintry-sur-Seine	261	48.36 N	2.30 E
Saintes, Bel.	50	50.42 N	4.10 E
Saintes, Fr.	32	45.45 N	0.38 W
Saint-Saëns	50	49.40 N	1.17 E
Saint Sampson	43b	49.29 N	2.31 W
Saint-Satur	50	47.20 N	2.51 E
Saint-Saturnin-d'Apt	62	43.56 N	5.23 E
Saint-Sauveur, Fr.	50	47.37 N	3.12 E
Saint-Sauveur, Fr.	58	47.48 N	6.23 E
Saint-Sauveur-des-Monts	206	45.52 N	74.10 W
Saint-Sauveur-sur-Tinée	62	44.05 N	7.06 E
Saint-Savin	32	46.34 N	0.52 E
Saint-Savinien	32	45.53 N	0.41 W
Saint Saviour	43b	49.11 N	2.06 W
Saint Sebastian Bay ⊂	158	34.25 S	21.00 E
Saint-Sébastien	206	45.07 N	73.09 W
Saint-Sébastien, Cap ›	157b	12.26 S	48.44 E
Saint-Seine-l'Abbaye	58	47.26 N	4.47 E
Saint Séverin	56	50.32 N	5.25 E
Saint Shotts	186	46.38 N	53.35 W
Sainte-Sigolène	62	45.14 N	4.15 E
Saint-Siméon	186	47.50 N	69.53 W
Saint-Simon	50	49.45 N	3.10 E
Saint Simons Island	192	31.09 N	81.22 W
Saint Simons Island I	192	31.14 N	81.21 W
Saint-Sixte ≃	206	45.39 N	75.08 W
Saintes-Maries, Golfe des ⊂	62	43.25 N	4.31 E
Saintes-Maries-de-la-Mer	62	43.27 N	4.26 E
Sainte-Sophie-de-Mégantic	206	46.09 N	71.42 W
Saint-Soupplets	261	49.02 N	2.48 E
Saint Stanislas Bay ⊂	174o	1.53 N	157.30 W
Saint-Stanislas-de-Kosta	206	45.11 N	74.08 W

English	Deutsch	Español	Français	Português
≃ River	Fluß	Río	Rivière	Rio
≊ Canal	Kanal	Canal	Canal	Canal
ʟ Waterfall, Rapids	Wasserfall, Stromschnellen	Cascada, Rápidos	Chute d'eau, Rapides	Cascata, Rápidos
ʊ Strait	Meeresstraße	Estrecho	Détroit	Estreito
⊂ Bay, Gulf	Bucht, Golf	Bahía, Golfo	Baie, Golfe	Baía, Golfo
⊜ Lake, Lakes	See, Seen	Lago, Lagos	Lac, Lacs	Lago, Lagos
≡ Swamp	Sumpf	Pantano	Marais	Pântano
⊓ Ice Features, Glacier	Eis- und Gletscherformen	Accidentes Glaciales	Formes glaciaires	Acidentes glaciares
⊤ Other Hydrographic Features	Andere Hydrographische Objekte	Otros Elementos Hidrográficos	Autres données hydrographiques	Outros acidentes hidrográficos
✢ Submarine Features	Untermeerische Objekte	Accidentes Submarinos	Formes de relief sous-marin	Acidentes submarinos
□ Political Unit	Politische Einheit	Unidad Politica	Entité politique	Unidade política
ᵾ Cultural Institution	Kulturelle Institution	Institución Cultural	Institution culturelle	Instituição cultural
⊥ Historical Site	Historische Stätte	Sitio Histórico	Site historique	Sitio histórico
♠ Recreational Site	Erholungs- und Ferienort	Sitio de Recreo	Centre de loisirs	Area de Lazer
⊠ Airport	Flughafen	Aeropuerto	Aéroport	Aeroporto
■ Military Installation	Militäranlage	Instalación Militar	Installation militaire	Instalação militar
◆ Miscellaneous	Verschiedenes	Misceláneo	Divers	Diversos

Name	Page	Lat.°'	Long.°'
Saint Stephen, N.B., Can.	186	45.12 N	67.17 W
Saint Stephen, S.C., U.S.	192	33.24 N	79.55 W
Saint-Sulpice-de-Favières	261	48.33 N	2.11 E
Saint-Sulpice-les-Feuilles	32	46.19 N	1.22 E
Sainte-Suzanne	58	47.30 N	6.46 E
Saint-Sylvestre	206	46.22 N	71.14 W
Saint-Symphorien, Fr.	32	44.26 N	0.30 W
Saint-Symphorien, Fr.	261	48.31 N	1.46 E
Saint-Symphorien-d'Ozon	62	45.38 N	4.52 E
Saint-Symphorien-sur-Coise	62	45.38 N	4.27 E
Sainte-Thècle	206	46.49 N	72.31 W
Saint-Théodore-d'Acton	206	45.41 N	72.35 W
Sainte-Thérèse	206	45.38 N	73.51 W
Sainte-Thérèse, Île I, P.Q., Can.	275a	45.41 N	73.28 W
Sainte-Thérèse, Île I, P.Q., Can.	275a	45.22 N	73.15 W
Saint-Thibault-des-Vignes	261	48.52 N	2.41 E
Saint Thomas, On., Can.	212	42.47 N	81.12 W
Saint Thomas, Mo., U.S.	219	38.22 N	92.13 W
Saint Thomas, N.D., U.S.	198	48.37 N	97.26 W
Saint Thomas → Charlotte Amalie, Vir. Is., U.S.	240m	18.21 N	64.56 W
Saint Thomas I	240m	18.21 N	64.55 W
Saint-Timothée	206	45.18 N	74.02 W
Saint-Tite	206	46.44 N	72.34 W
Saint-Tite-des-Caps	186	47.08 N	70.47 W
Saint-Trivier-de-Courtes	58	46.28 N	5.05 E
Saint-Trivier-sur-Moignans	58	46.04 N	4.54 E
Saint-Tropez	62	43.16 N	6.38 E
Saint Tudy	42	50.33 N	4.43 W
Sainte-Tulle	62	43.47 N	5.46 E
Saint-Ubald	206	46.45 N	72.16 W
Saint-Urbain-de-Charlevoix	186	47.33 N	70.32 W
Saint-Ursanne	58	47.22 N	7.10 E
Saint-Uze	62	45.11 N	4.52 E
Saint-Valérien	50	48.11 N	3.06 E
Saint-Valéry-en-Caux	50	49.52 N	0.44 E
Saint-Valéry-sur-Somme	50	50.11 N	1.38 E
Saint-Vallier, Fr.	58	46.38 N	4.22 E
Saint-Vallier, Fr.	62	45.10 N	4.49 E
Saint-Vallier-de-Thiey	62	43.42 N	6.51 E
Saint-Varent	32	46.53 N	0.14 W
Saint-Venant	50	50.37 N	2.33 E
Saint-Véran	62	44.42 N	6.52 E
Sainte-Victoire, Montagne ∧	62	43.32 N	5.39 E
Saint-Victoret	62	43.25 N	5.14 E
Saint-Vincent, It.	62	45.45 N	7.39 E
Saint Vincent, Mn., U.S.	198	48.58 N	97.13 W
Saint Vincent I	241h	13.15 N	61.12 W
Saint-Vincent, Baie de ⊂	175f	22.00 S	166.05 E
Saint-Vincent, Cap ≻	157b	21.57 S	43.16 E
Saint Vincent, Cape ≻, Austl.	166	43.18 S	145.50 E
Saint Vincent, Cape → São Vicente, Cabo de ≻, Port.	34	37.01 N	9.00 W
Saint Vincent, Gulf ⊂	168b	35.00 S	138.05 E
Saint Vincent and the Grenadines □[1], N.A.	230	13.15 N	61.12 W
Saint Vincent and the Grenadines □[1], N.A.	241h	13.15 N	61.12 W
Saint-Vincent-de-Paul ◆[8]	275a	45.37 N	73.39 W
Saint-Vincent-de-Tyrosse	32	43.40 N	1.18 W
Saint Vincent Passage ⊌	238	13.30 N	61.00 W
Saint Vincent's	186	46.48 N	53.38 W
Saint-Vit	58	47.11 N	5.49 E
Saint-Vith	56	50.17 N	6.08 E
Saint-Vivien-de-Médoc	32	45.26 N	1.02 W
Saint-Vrain	261	48.33 N	2.20 E
Saint Walburg	184	53.39 N	109.12 W
Saint-Wandrille-Rançon	50	49.32 N	0.46 E
Saint-Wenceslas ≃	206	46.18 N	72.23 W
Saint Williams	212	42.40 N	80.25 W
Saint-Witz	261	49.05 N	2.34 E
Saint-Yrieix-la-Perche	32	45.31 N	1.12 E
Saint-Yvon	186	49.10 N	64.48 W
Saint-Zacharie	62	43.23 N	5.43 E
Saint-Zénon	206	46.33 N	73.49 W
Sāinthiya	126	23.57 N	87.40 E
Saipan I	174n	15.12 N	145.45 E
Saipan Channel ⊌	174n	15.05 N	145.41 E
Saipan International Airport ⊠	174n	15.07 N	145.43 E
Saiqi	100	27.00 N	119.43 E
Saishu-to → Cheju-do I	90	33.20 N	126.30 E
Saita	96	34.08 N	133.49 E
Saita ≃	96	34.08 N	133.38 E
Saitama □[5]	94	36.00 N	139.30 E
Saitama University ✿[2]	268	35.52 N	139.36 E
Saito	92	32.06 N	131.24 E
Saiwai ◆[8]	268	35.33 N	139.41 E
Saiwa Swamp National Park ♠	154	1.06 N	35.12 E
Saiyidān ◆[8]	272a	28.40 N	77.05 E
Sai Yok	110	14.07 N	99.08 E
Sajak	86	47.02 N	77.22 E
Sajam	164	0.53 S	132.41 E
Sajama	248	18.07 S	69.00 W
Sajama, Nevado ∧	248	18.06 S	68.54 W
Sajan → Sayan Mountains ⋏	88	52.45 N	96.00 E
Sajanogorsk	86	53.08 N	91.29 E
Sajano-Šušenskoje vodochranilišče ⊜[1]	86	52.20 N	92.25 E
Sajantuj	88	51.44 N	107.30 E
Sajasan	84	43.03 N	46.17 E
Sajat	128	38.47 N	63.53 E
Sajchan	88	48.40 N	102.39 E
Sajchandulaan	102	44.40 N	109.01 E
Sajchan-Ovoo	102	45.27 N	103.54 E
Sajchin	80	48.50 N	46.47 E
Ṣajen	115a	7.40 S	112.31 E
Šajgino	80	57.46 N	46.51 E
Ṣajīd I	144	16.52 N	41.50 E
Šajmak'	120	37.27 N	74.44 E
Sajnšand	102	44.52 N	110.09 E
Sajó (Slaná) ≃	30	47.56 N	21.08 E
Sajószentpéter	30	48.13 N	20.44 E
Sajram	85	42.18 N	69.45 E
Sajukino	80	52.47 N	41.59 E
Sājūr (Bağırsak) ≃	130	36.40 N	38.05 E
Sak ≃	158	30.02 S	20.40 E
Saka, Kenya	154	0.09 S	39.20 E
Saka, Nihon	96	34.20 N	132.31 E
Sakado	94	35.57 N	139.24 E
Sakae, Nihon	94	35.50 N	140.15 E
Sakae, Nihon	94	36.58 N	138.35 E
Sa Kaeo	110	13.49 N	102.04 E
Sakahogi	94	35.26 N	136.59 E
Sakai, Nihon	94	36.10 N	136.14 E
Sakai, Nihon	94	36.16 N	139.15 E

Name	Page	Lat.°'	Long.°'
Sakai, Nihon	94	36.06 N	139.48 E
Sakai, Nihon	96	34.35 N	135.28 E
Sakai, Nihon	268	35.25 N	139.22 E
Sakai ≃	94	35.18 N	139.29 E
Sakaide	96	34.19 N	133.52 E
Sakaigawa	94	35.35 N	138.37 E
Sakaiminato	96	35.33 N	133.15 E
Sakākah	128	29.59 N	40.06 E
Sakakawea, Lake ⊜[1]	198	47.50 N	102.20 W
Sakaki	94	36.28 N	138.11 E
Sakakita	94	36.25 N	138.01 E
Sakala, Pulau I	112	6.54 S	116.15 E
Sakami ≃	176	53.40 N	76.40 W
Sakami, Lac ⊜	176	53.15 N	76.45 W
Sakania	154	12.45 S	28.34 E
Sakar	128	38.56 N	63.45 E
Sakar ⋏	38	41.59 N	26.16 E
Sakaraha	157b	22.55 S	44.32 E
Sakar-Čaga	128	37.38 N	61.40 E
Sakar Island I	164	5.25 S	148.05 E
Sakartvelo → Georgia □[1]	22	42.00 N	44.00 E
Sakarya	130	40.46 N	30.24 E
Sakarya □[4]	130	40.45 N	30.35 E
Sakarya ≃	130	41.07 N	30.39 E
Sakashita	94	35.34 N	137.32 E
Sakassou	150	7.27 N	5.18 W
Sakata	92	38.55 N	139.50 E
Sakauchi	94	35.36 N	136.25 E
Sakawa	96	33.30 N	133.17 E
Sakawa ≃	94	35.15 N	139.11 E
Sakchu	98	40.23 N	125.01 E
Sakesar	123	32.33 N	71.56 E
Sakété	150	6.43 N	2.40 E
Sakhā	142	31.05 N	30.57 E
Sakhalin → Sachalin, ostrov I	89	51.00 N	143.00 E
Sākhar	120	32.57 N	65.32 E
Sakhi Sarwar	120	29.59 N	70.18 E
Sakhnin	132	32.52 N	35.17 E
Sakhnovshchyna	78	49.08 N	35.53 E
Ṣakhrīyāt, Jabal aṣ- ∧	132	31.01 N	36.21 E
Sakht Sar	128	36.53 N	50.41 E
Ṣāki ◆[8]	272c	19.06 N	72.53 E
Šakiai	76	54.57 N	23.03 E
Sākib	132	32.17 N	35.49 E
Sakiet Sidi Youssef	36	36.13 N	8.22 E
Sakijang Bendera, Pulau I	271c	1.13 N	103.51 E
Sakijang Pelepah, Pulau I	271c	1.13 N	103.52 E
Sakishima-shotō II	175d	24.46 N	124.00 E
Sakito	92	33.02 N	129.32 E
Sakkara → Ṣaqqārah	142	29.51 N	31.13 E
Sakmara ≃	86	51.46 N	55.01 E
Sako	270	34.53 N	135.47 E
Sakon Nakhon	110	17.10 N	104.09 E
Sakonnet	207	41.28 N	71.12 W
Sakonnet Point ≻	207	41.27 N	71.12 W
Sakoyra	150	14.17 N	1.24 E
Sakra, Pulau I	271c	1.16 N	103.42 E
Sakrand	120	26.08 N	68.16 E
Sakrivier	158	30.54 S	20.28 E
Saks	194	33.42 N	85.52 W
Saksahan' ≃	78	47.53 N	33.18 E
Saksauldala ◆[2]	86	44.30 N	73.00 E
Sakskøbing	41	54.48 N	11.39 E
Sakti	124	22.02 N	82.58 E
Saku, Nihon	94	36.09 N	138.30 E
Saku, Nihon	94	36.13 N	138.29 E
Sakubva	154	19.00 S	32.10 E
Sakugi	96	34.52 N	132.43 E
Sakuma	94	35.05 N	137.48 E
Sakuma-dam ◆[6]	94	35.05 N	137.47 E
Sakuma-ko ⊜[1]	94	35.08 N	137.47 E
Sakura	94	35.43 N	140.14 E
Sakura ≃	94	36.05 N	140.14 E
Sakurae	96	34.57 N	132.20 E
Sakurai	96	34.30 N	135.51 E
Sakura-tōge)(	270	34.36 N	135.53 E
Saku-shima I	94	34.43 N	137.03 E
Sakutō	96	35.01 N	134.14 E
Sakwaso Lake ⊜	184	53.01 N	91.55 W
Saky	78	45.09 N	33.35 E
Säkylä	26	61.02 N	22.20 E
Sakyō ◆[8]	270	35.02 N	135.48 E
Sal I	150a	16.45 N	22.55 W
Sal ≃	80	47.31 N	40.45 E
Sal, Cay I	238	23.42 N	80.24 W
Sal, Ponta do ≻	266c	38.41 N	9.22 W
Sal, Punta ≻	236	15.53 N	87.37 W
Šal'a, Ross.	86	57.15 N	58.43 E
Šal'a, Slvk.	30	48.09 N	17.52 E
Sala, Sve.	40	59.55 N	16.36 E
Sala, Ouadi V	146	17.00 N	20.53 E
Sala Baganza	64	44.43 N	10.14 E
Salabangka, Kepulauan II	112	3.02 S	122.25 E
Salaberry, Île de I	206	45.17 N	74.07 W
Salaberry-de-Valleyfield	206	45.15 N	74.08 W
Salaca ≃	76	57.45 N	24.21 E
Salacgrīva	76	57.45 N	24.21 E
Sala Consilina	68	40.24 N	15.36 E
Salada, Laguna ⊜, Arg.	258	35.17 S	59.24 W
Salada, Laguna ⊜, Méx.	232	32.20 N	115.40 W
Saladas	252	28.15 S	58.38 W
Saladillo	252	35.38 S	59.46 W
Saladillo ≃, Arg.	252	33.25 S	63.02 W
Saladillo ≃, Arg.	252	29.05 S	63.25 W
Saladillo, Arroyo ≃	258	35.33 S	59.04 W
Saladillo de Rodríguez, Arroyo ≃	258	35.29 S	59.01 W
Saladillo Dulce, Arroyo ≃	252	31.25 S	60.33 W
Salado, Arg.	252	28.18 S	67.15 W
Salado, Tx., U.S.	222	30.57 N	97.32 W
Salado ≃, Arg.	252	38.49 S	64.57 W
Salado ≃, Arg.	252	31.42 S	60.44 W
Salado ≃, Arg.	252	35.44 S	57.21 W
Salado ≃, Arg.	252	29.13 S	66.34 W
Salado ≃, Cuba	240p	20.36 N	76.56 W
Salado ≃, Méx.	232	26.52 N	99.19 W
Salado ≃, Méx.	234	18.44 N	103.36 W
Salado ≃, Méx.	234	17.55 N	96.58 W
Salado, Arroyo ≃, Arg.	254	41.37 S	65.02 W
Salado, Arroyo ≃, Arg.	254	40.35 S	66.33 W
Salado, Rio ≃	200	34.16 N	106.52 W
Salado Creek ≃, Tx., U.S.	196	29.14 N	98.25 W
Salado Creek ≃, Tx., U.S.	222	30.59 N	97.25 W
Salaga	150	8.33 N	0.31 W
Salagle	144	1.50 N	42.17 E
Sālah	132	32.38 N	36.46 E
Ṣalāh ad-Dīn □[4]	128	34.15 N	43.55 E
Salahin	144	2.57 N	46.26 E
Sala'ilua	175a	13.41 S	172.34 W
Salair	86	54.13 N	85.47 E
Salairskij kr'až ∧	86	54.15 N	85.30 E
Sălaj □[6]	38	47.15 N	23.00 E
Salak	114	2.34 N	98.20 E
Salak, Gunung ∧	115a	6.42 S	106.44 E
Šalakas	76	55.35 N	26.08 E
Šalakuša	24	62.15 N	40.17 E
Salal	146	14.51 N	17.13 E
Salala, Chile	252	30.41 S	71.32 W
Salala, Liber.	150	6.40 N	10.05 W
Salālah, Sūd.	140	21.19 N	36.13 E
Ṣalālah, 'Umān	118	17.00 N	54.06 E
Salamá, Guat.	236	15.06 N	90.16 W
Salamá, Hond.	236	14.50 N	86.36 W

Name	Page	Lat.°'	Long.°'
Salamajärven kansallispuisto ♠	26	63.20 N	24.40 E
Salaman	115a	7.35 S	110.08 E
Salamanca, Chile	252	31.47 S	70.58 W
Salamanca, Esp.	34	40.58 N	5.39 W
Salamanca, Méx.	234	20.34 N	101.12 W
Salamanca, Perú	248	15.31 S	72.50 W
Salamanca, Perú	286d	12.05 S	77.00 W
Salamanca, N.Y., U.S.	210	42.09 N	78.42 W
Salamanca □[4]	34	40.45 N	6.00 W
Salamanga	158	26.28 S	32.39 E
Salamat □[5]	146	11.00 N	20.30 E
Salamat, Bahr ≃	146	9.27 N	18.06 E
Salāmbek	120	28.18 N	65.09 E
Salamina	246	5.25 N	75.29 W
Salamínos, Órmos ⊂	267c	37.56 N	23.27 E
Salamís	38	37.58 N	23.29 E
Salamís I	38	37.54 N	23.26 E
Salamis ⊥	130	35.10 N	33.54 E
Salamīyah	130	35.01 N	37.03 E
Salām Khān	120	31.47 N	66.45 E
Salamonia	216	40.23 N	84.52 W
Salamonie ≃	216	40.50 N	85.43 W
Salamonie Lake ⊜[1]	216	40.46 N	85.37 W
Salāmūn	142	31.04 N	31.28 E
Salandra	68	40.31 N	16.19 E
Sālang, Tūnel-e ◆[5]	120	35.19 N	69.02 E
Salani	175a	14.00 S	171.33 W
Salantai	76	56.04 N	21.32 E
Salaparuta	70	37.47 N	13.00 E
Salaquí	246	7.18 N	77.33 W
Salaquí ≃	246	7.27 N	77.07 W
Salāqūs	142	28.44 N	30.50 E
Salar	85	41.21 N	69.22 E
Salara	64	44.59 N	11.25 E
Sălard	38	47.13 N	22.03 E
Salarjovo	265b	55.37 N	37.26 E
Salas	248	6.16 S	79.37 W
Salas de los Infantes	34	42.01 N	3.17 W
Salat ≃	32	43.10 N	0.58 E
Salatiga	115a	7.19 S	110.30 E
Salauš	80	55.59 N	52.53 E
Salavat	86	53.21 N	55.55 E
Salavaux	58	46.55 N	7.02 E
Salaverry	248	8.14 S	78.58 W
Salavina	252	28.48 S	63.25 W
Salawati I	164	1.07 S	130.52 E
Salawe	154	3.19 S	32.52 E
Salay	116	8.52 N	124.47 E
Salāya	120	22.19 N	69.35 E
Sala y Gómez, Isla I	18	26.28 S	105.28 W
Sala y Gomez Ridge ⩩[3]	18	25.00 S	98.00 W
Salazgor'	80	54.07 N	43.09 E
Salba	88	53.14 N	92.36 E
Salbani	126	22.38 N	87.20 E
Salbohed	40	59.55 N	16.19 E
Salbosjön ⊜	40	59.50 N	14.54 E
Ṣalbris	50	47.26 N	2.03 E
Šalbuzdag, gora ∧	84	41.19 N	47.48 E
Salcajá	236	14.53 N	91.27 W
Salccantay, Nevado ∧	248	13.20 S	72.33 W
Salcedo, Pil.	116	11.09 N	125.40 E
Salcedo, Rep. Dom.	238	19.23 N	70.25 W
Salcha ≃	180	64.29 N	147.00 W
Salching	60	48.49 N	12.34 E
Ṣalcia	38	43.57 N	24.56 E
Šalčininkai	76	54.18 N	25.23 E
Salcombe	42	50.13 N	3.47 W
Ṣalda ≃	86	58.48 N	61.20 E
Šaldaj	86	51.56 N	78.48 E
Saldaña	34	42.31 N	4.44 W
Saldaña ≃	246	4.01 N	74.52 W
Saldanha	158	33.00 S	17.56 E
Ṣaldanhabaai ⊂	158	33.04 S	18.00 E
Šaldež	80	56.52 N	44.46 E
Saldungaray	252	38.12 S	61.47 W
Saldus	76	56.40 N	22.30 E
Sale, Austl.	166	38.06 S	147.04 E
Sale, It.	62	44.59 N	8.48 E
Salé, Magreb	148	34.04 N	6.50 W
Sale, Eng., U.K.	44	53.26 N	2.19 W
Salebabu, Pulau I	108	3.55 N	126.40 E
Salechard	74	66.33 N	66.40 E
Sale Creek	194	35.22 N	85.06 W
Salée, Rivière ⊌	241o	16.17 N	61.33 W
Saleh, Teluk ⊂	115b	8.34 S	117.57 E
Salelologa	175a	13.44 S	172.10 W
Salem, On., Can.	212	43.42 N	80.27 W
Salem, Dtsch.	58	47.46 N	9.16 E
Salem, India	122	11.39 N	78.10 E
Salem, S. Afr.	158	33.28 S	26.29 E
Salem, Sve.	40	59.13 N	17.44 E
Salem, Ar., U.S.	194	36.22 N	91.49 W
Salem, Il., U.S.	219	38.37 N	88.56 W
Salem, In., U.S.	218	38.03 N	86.15 W
Salem, Ia., U.S.	190	40.51 N	91.37 W
Salem, Ky., U.S.	194	37.15 N	88.14 W
Salem, Ma., U.S.	207	42.31 N	70.53 W
Salem, Mi., U.S.	281	42.24 N	83.34 W
Salem, Mo., U.S.	194	37.38 N	91.32 W
Salem, N.H., U.S.	207	42.47 N	71.12 W
Salem, N.J., U.S.	208	39.34 N	75.28 W
Salem, N.Y., U.S.	210	43.10 N	73.19 W
Salem, Oh., U.S.	214	40.54 N	80.51 W
Salem, Or., U.S.	224	44.56 N	123.02 W
Salem, S.D., U.S.	198	43.43 N	97.23 W
Salem, Ut,. U.S.	200	40.03 N	111.40 W
Salem, Va., U.S.	192	37.17 N	80.03 W
Salem, W.V., U.S.	188	39.16 N	80.33 W
Salem, Wi., U.S.	216	42.33 N	88.06 W
Salem □[6]	208	39.34 N	75.20 W
Salem ≃	208	39.34 N	75.31 W
Salem Airfield ⊠	281	42.25 N	83.34 W
Sale Marasino	64	45.43 N	10.06 E
Salem Canal ≋	285	39.41 N	75.31 W
Salem Depot	283	42.47 N	71.12 W
Salem Harbor ⊂	283	42.31 N	70.53 W
Salem Heights	214	40.54 N	80.53 W
Salemi	70	37.49 N	12.48 E
Salem Maritime National Historic Site ⊥	207	42.31 N	70.53 W
Salem State College ✿[2]	283	42.30 N	70.54 W
Salem Upland ⋏[1]	194	37.25 N	91.30 W
Sälen, Sve.	26	61.10 N	13.16 E
Salen, Scot., U.K.	46	56.43 N	5.47 W
Salen, Scot., U.K.	46	56.31 N	5.57 W
Salentina, Penisola ≻[1]	68	40.25 N	18.00 E
Salentine, Murge ◆[1]	68	40.02 N	18.13 E
Salento	68	40.15 N	15.11 E
Salernes	62	43.33 N	6.14 E
Salerno	68	40.41 N	14.47 E
Salerno □[4]	68	40.27 N	15.16 E
Salerno, Golfo di ⊂	68	40.32 N	14.42 E
Salers	32	45.08 N	2.30 E
Salesbury	262	53.47 N	2.30 W
Salesópolis	256	23.32 S	45.51 W
Salève, Mont ∧	58	46.07 N	6.10 E
Salford	44	53.28 N	2.18 W
Salford □[8]	262	53.28 N	2.23 W
Ṣalfords	260	51.12 N	0.10 W
Šalgačova	24	62.19 N	39.35 E
Salgado	250	11.02 S	37.28 W
Salgan	80	55.14 N	45.30 E
Ṣalgar	246	5.58 N	75.59 W
Šalgija	86	47.35 N	70.36 E
Salgótarján	30	48.07 N	19.48 E
Salgueiro	250	8.04 S	39.06 W
Salher ∧	122	20.43 N	73.56 E
Salhyr ≃	78	45.38 N	35.01 E
Sali, Alg.	148	26.58 N	0.01 W
Ṣali, Hrv.	36	43.56 N	15.10 E
Šali, Ross.	80	55.41 N	49.40 E
Šali, Ross.	84	43.08 N	45.54 E
Salí ≃	252	27.33 S	64.57 W
Salice Salentino	68	40.23 N	17.58 E

Name	Page	Lat.°'	Long.°'
Salice Terme	62	44.55 N	9.01 E
Salici, Monte ∧	70	37.44 N	14.38 E
Salida, Ca., U.S.	226	37.42 N	121.05 W
Salida, Co., U.S.	200	38.32 N	105.59 W
Salies-de-Béarn	32	43.29 N	0.55 W
Ṣalīf	144	15.18 N	42.40 E
Salignac-Eyvignes	32	44.59 N	1.19 E
Salihli	130	38.29 N	28.09 E
Salihorsk	76	52.48 N	27.32 E
Şālikha	126	23.18 N	89.22 E
Šalikovo	82	55.30 N	36.13 E
Salim	140	12.52 N	28.40 E
Salima	154	13.47 S	34.26 E
Salīmah, Wāḥat ‡[4]	140	21.22 N	29.19 E
Salimani	157a	11.47 S	43.17 E
Salimbatu	112	2.57 N	117.21 E
Salimgarh Fort ⊥	272a	28.40 N	77.14 E
Salimi	152	9.24 S	23.35 E
Salin	110	20.35 N	94.39 E
Salina, Ks., U.S.	198	38.50 N	97.36 W
Salina, Ok., U.S.	196	36.17 N	95.09 W
Salina, Pa., U.S.	214	40.31 N	79.30 W
Salina, Ut,. U.S.	200	38.57 N	111.51 W
Salina, Canale di ⊌	70	38.32 N	14.54 E
Salina, Isola I	70	38.34 N	14.50 E
Salina Cruz	234	16.10 N	95.12 W
Salina Point ≻	238	22.13 N	74.18 W
Salinas, Bra.	255	16.10 S	42.17 W
Salinas, Ec.	246	2.13 S	80.58 W
Salinas, P.R.	240m	17.59 N	66.18 W
Salinas, Ca., U.S.	226	36.40 N	121.39 W
Salinas ≃, Bra.	255	16.37 S	42.18 W
Salinas (Chixoy) ≃, N.A.	232	16.28 N	90.33 W
Salinas ≃, Ca., U.S.	226	36.45 N	121.48 W
Salinas, Pampa de las ≚	252	31.58 S	66.42 W
Salinas, Ponta das ≻	152	12.50 S	12.56 E
Salinas, Sierra de ⋏	226	36.18 N	121.20 W
Salinas de Garci Mendoza	248	19.38 S	67.43 W
Salinas de Hidalgo	234	22.38 N	101.43 W
Salinas del Rey	196	27.38 N	102.24 W
Salinas Municipal Airport ⊠	226	36.40 N	121.40 W
Salinas National Monument ♠	200	34.05 N	106.14 W
Salinas Valley V	226	36.15 N	121.15 W
Salinas Victoria	196	25.53 N	100.19 W
Salin-de-Giraud	62	43.25 N	4.44 E
Salindres	62	44.10 N	4.10 E
Saline, La., U.S.	194	32.09 N	92.58 W
Saline, Mi., U.S.	216	42.10 N	83.46 W
Saline ≃, Ar., U.S.	194	33.44 N	93.58 W
Saline ≃, Ar., U.S.	194	33.10 N	92.08 W
Saline ≃, Il., U.S.	194	37.35 N	88.08 W
Saline ≃, Ks., U.S.	198	38.51 N	97.30 W
Saline ≃, Mi., U.S.	216	41.59 N	83.37 W
Saline, North Fork ≃	194	37.44 N	88.19 W
Saline Bayou ≃	194	31.45 N	92.58 W
Saline di Volterra	66	43.22 N	10.49 E
Saline Lake ⊜[1]	194	31.55 N	92.55 W
Salines, Point ≻	241k	12.00 N	61.48 W
Salines, Pointe des ≻	240e	14.24 N	60.53 W
Salineville	214	40.37 N	80.51 W
Salingyi	110	21.58 N	95.03 E
Ṣalinópolis	250	0.37 S	47.20 W
Šalinskoje	86	55.43 N	93.46 E
Salins-les-Bains	58	46.57 N	5.53 E
Salins-les-Thermes	62	45.28 N	6.32 E
Salipolo	112	3.45 S	119.29 E
Salisbury, Austl.	168b	34.46 S	138.38 E
Salisbury, Dom.	240d	15.26 N	61.27 W
Salisbury, Eng., U.K.	42	51.05 N	1.48 W
Salisbury, Ct., U.S.	207	41.59 N	73.25 W
Salisbury, Md., U.S.	208	38.21 N	75.35 W
Salisbury, Ma., U.S.	207	42.50 N	70.51 W
Salisbury, Mo., U.S.	194	39.25 N	92.48 W
Salisbury, N.C., U.S.	192	35.40 N	80.28 W
Salisbury, Pa., U.S.	188	39.45 N	79.04 W
Salisbury → Harare, Zimb.	154	17.50 S	31.03 E
Salisbury Cathedral ✿[1]	42	51.05 N	1.48 W
Salisbury Center	210	43.09 N	74.47 W
Salisbury Hall ⊥	260	51.43 N	0.16 W
Salisbury Island I, Austl.	162	34.21 S	123.32 E
Salisbury Island I, N.T., Can.	176	63.30 N	77.00 W
Salisbury Mills	210	41.26 N	74.08 W
Salisbury Plain ≚	42	51.12 N	1.55 W
Salisbury Plain ≃	283	42.02 N	70.58 W
Salish Mountains ⋏	202	48.15 N	114.45 W
Salito ≃	70	37.29 N	13.46 E
Salitpa	194	31.37 N	88.01 W
Salitre ≃	250	9.29 S	40.39 W
Ṣalix	214	40.18 N	78.46 W
Šalkar	80	48.03 N	48.56 E
Šalkar, ozero ⊜	80	50.33 N	51.40 E
Šalkar-Jega-Kara, ozero ⊜	86	50.45 N	60.54 E
Salkehatchie ≃	192	32.37 N	80.53 W
Ṣalkhad	132	32.29 N	36.43 E
Salkhia	272b	22.35 N	88.21 E
Salkum	224	46.31 N	122.37 W
Salla	24	66.50 N	28.40 E
Salladasburg	210	41.17 N	77.14 W
Sallagriffon	62	43.53 N	6.54 E
Sallanches	58	45.56 N	6.38 E
Salland ◆[1]	52	52.20 N	6.20 E
Salles-Curan	32	44.11 N	2.47 E
Salles-sous-Bois	62	44.27 N	4.56 E
Sallgast	54	51.35 N	13.51 E
Salling ◆[1]	26	56.40 N	9.00 E
Salliqueló	252	36.45 S	62.56 W
Sallisaw	196	35.27 N	94.47 W
Sallisaw Creek ≃	194	35.23 N	94.52 W
Salluit	176	62.14 N	75.38 W
Sallūm	140	19.23 N	37.06 E
Sallūm, Khalīj as- ⊂	146	31.41 N	25.21 E
Salm ≃	56	49.51 N	6.51 E
Salmās	128	38.11 N	44.47 E
Salmchâteau	56	50.16 N	5.54 E
Salme	76	58.10 N	22.15 E
Salmi	24	61.22 N	31.53 E
Salmo	182	49.12 N	117.17 W
Salmon	202	45.10 N	113.53 W
Salmon ≃, B.C., Can.	182	54.05 N	122.34 W
Salmon ≃, N.B., Can.	186	46.06 N	65.56 W
Salmon ≃, On., Can.	212	44.11 N	77.15 W
Salmon ≃, N.A.	188	45.02 N	74.31 W
Salmon ≃, Ct., U.S.	207	41.29 N	72.29 W
Salmon ≃, Id., U.S.	202	45.51 N	116.46 W
Salmon ≃, N.Y., U.S.	212	43.35 N	76.12 W
Salmon ≃, Or., U.S.	224	45.03 N	124.00 W
Salmon ≃, Or., U.S.	224	45.22 N	122.02 W
Salmon, East Fork ≃	202	44.16 N	114.19 W
Salmon, Middle Fork ≃	202	45.18 N	114.36 W
Salmon, North Branch ≃	212	43.32 N	75.48 W
Salmon, South Fork ≃	202	45.23 N	115.31 W
Salmon Arm	182	50.42 N	119.16 W
Salmon-Bay	186	51.26 N	57.36 W
Salmon Creek ≃, N.Y., U.S.	210	43.16 N	77.02 W
Salmon Creek ≃, N.Y., U.S.	210	43.19 N	77.43 W
Salmon Creek ≃, Wa., U.S.	224	46.26 N	122.52 W
Salmon Creek ≃, Wa., U.S.	224	45.44 N	122.45 W
Salmon Falls Creek ≃	202	42.43 N	114.51 W
Salmon Falls Creek Reservoir ⊜[1]	202	42.08 N	114.45 W
Salmon Gums	162	32.59 S	121.38 E

Name	Page	Lat.°'	Long.°'
Salmon Lake ⊜	212	44.49 N	78.28 W
Salmon Mountain ∧	188	45.14 N	71.08 W
Salmon Mountains ⋏	204	41.00 N	123.00 W
Salmon Peak ∧	196	29.28 N	100.10 W
Salmon Point ≻	212	43.52 N	77.14 W
Salmon River Mountains ⋏	202	44.45 N	115.30 W
Salmon River Reservoir ⊜[1]	212	43.32 N	75.52 W
Salmon Valley	182	54.05 N	122.41 W
Salmyš ≃	86	52.01 N	55.21 E
Sal'nytsya	78	49.44 N	28.02 E
Salo, Centraf.	152	3.12 N	16.07 E
Salò, It.	64	45.36 N	10.31 E
Salo, Suomi	26	60.23 N	23.08 E
Salobel'ak	80	57.07 N	48.05 E
Salobra ≃	248	20.12 S	56.29 W
Salomatino	80	50.01 N	44.50 E
Salome	200	33.46 N	113.36 W
Salomon, Cap ≻	240e	14.30 N	61.06 W
Salomon, Îles → Solomon Islands □[1]	175e	8.00 S	159.00 E
Salomón, Islas → Solomon Islands □[1]	175e	8.00 S	159.00 E
Salomone, Monte ∧	267a	41.47 N	12.44 E
Salomon-Inseln → Solomon Islands □[1]	175e	8.00 S	159.00 E
Salon ≃	58	47.32 N	5.41 E
Salona	210	41.05 N	77.28 W
Salon-de-Provence	62	43.38 N	5.06 E
Salonga ≃	152	0.10 S	19.50 E
Salonga, Parc National de la ♠	152	1.45 S	21.20 E
Salonika → Thessaloníki	38	40.38 N	22.56 E
Salonta	38	46.48 N	21.40 E
Salor ≃	34	39.39 N	7.03 W
Salorno (Salurn)	64	46.14 N	11.13 E
Saloslovo	265b	55.42 N	37.09 E
Ṣaloum ≃	150	13.50 N	16.45 W
Šalovka ≃	265b	55.47 N	38.12 E
Salpausselkä ∧	26	61.00 N	26.30 E
Ṣalpazarı	130	40.59 N	39.10 E
Ṣalqīn	130	36.08 N	36.27 E
Sal Rei	150a	16.11 N	22.55 W
Salsacate	252	31.19 S	65.05 W
Salsette Island I	272c	19.10 N	72.53 E
Salsilgo, Qawz ⊥[8]	140	10.49 N	22.54 E
Salsipuedes, Canal ⊌	232	28.37 N	113.00 W
Salsipuedes, Punta ≻, C.R.	236	8.28 N	83.37 W
Salsipuedes, Punta ≻, Méx.	232	32.05 N	116.53 W
Ṣal'sk	80	46.28 N	41.33 E
Šal'skij	24	61.48 N	35.58 E
Sal'sko-Manyčskaja gr'ada ∧	80	46.40 N	42.30 E
Salso ≃	70	37.06 N	13.57 E
Salsomaggiore Terme	64	44.49 N	9.59 E
Salt ≃, U.S.	202	43.08 N	111.02 W
Salt ≃, Az., U.S.	200	33.23 N	112.18 W
Salt ≃, Ky., U.S.	194	38.00 N	85.57 W
Salt ≃, Mi., U.S.	281	42.39 N	82.47 W
Salt ≃, Mo., U.S.	219	39.28 N	91.04 W
Salt, Elk Fork ≃	219	39.28 N	91.53 W
Salt, Middle Fork ≃	219	39.28 N	91.49 W
Salt, North Fork ≃	219	39.30 N	91.47 W
Salt, South Fork ≃	219	39.28 N	91.49 W
Salta	252	24.47 S	65.25 W
Salta □[4]	252	25.00 S	64.30 W
Saltaim, ozero ⊜	86	56.10 N	71.45 E
Saltair	224	48.57 N	123.46 W
Saltaire	276	40.39 N	73.12 W
Saltanovka	76	52.47 N	34.17 E
Saltara	66	43.45 N	12.54 E
Salt Ash, Austl.	170	32.47 S	151.55 E
Saltash, Eng., U.K.	42	50.24 N	4.12 W
Saltbæk Vig ⊂	41	55.43 N	11.12 E
Salt Basin ⊜	196	31.50 N	105.00 W
Saltburn-by-the-Sea	44	54.35 N	0.58 W
Salt Cay I	240b	25.06 N	77.18 W
Saltcoats, Sk., Can.	184	51.03 N	102.12 W
Saltcoats, Scot., U.K.	46	55.38 N	4.47 W
Salt Creek ≃, On., Can.	275b	43.48 N	79.42 W
Salt Creek ≃, Ca., U.S.	204	36.15 N	116.49 W
Salt Creek ≃, Il., U.S.	194	40.08 N	89.50 W
Salt Creek ≃, Il., U.S.	278	41.49 N	87.50 W
Salt Creek ≃, In., U.S.	216	41.37 N	87.09 W
Salt Creek ≃, In., U.S.	218	38.50 N	86.32 W
Salt Creek ≃, In., U.S.	218	39.27 N	85.09 W
Salt Creek ≃, Ks., U.S.	198	39.06 N	97.44 W
Salt Creek ≃, N.M., U.S.	196	33.35 N	104.23 W
Salt Creek ≃, Ok., U.S.	196	36.32 N	96.43 W
Salt Creek ≃, Or., U.S.	202	43.43 N	122.26 W
Salt Creek ≃, Or., U.S.	224	45.09 N	123.13 W
Salt Creek ≃, Wy., U.S.	202	43.41 N	106.20 W
Salt Creek, Middle Fork ≃	218	39.04 N	86.15 W
Salt Creek, North Fork ≃, Il., U.S.	216	40.13 N	88.50 W
Salt Creek, North Fork ≃, In., U.S.	218	39.08 N	86.21 W
Salt Creek, West Branch ≃	278	42.02 N	88.01 W
Salt Creek South Fork ≃	218	39.02 N	86.16 W
Salt Draw V	196	31.19 N	103.28 W
Saltee Islands II	48	52.07 N	6.36 W
Salten	41	56.05 N	9.35 E
Saltfleet	44	53.25 N	0.11 E
Saltford	42	51.24 N	2.27 W
Salt Fork Lake ⊜[1]	214	41.07 N	81.30 W
Salt Fork State Park ♠	214	40.06 N	81.29 W
Saltholm I	41	55.38 N	12.46 E
Saltillo, Méx.	232	25.25 N	101.00 W
Saltillo, Ms., U.S.	194	34.22 N	88.40 W
Saltillo, Pa., U.S.	214	40.13 N	78.01 W
Saltillo, Tn., U.S.	194	35.22 N	88.12 W
Saltillo, Tx., U.S.	222	33.11 N	95.20 W
Salt Island I	240m	18.23 N	64.31 W
Salt Lake	158	29.16 S	24.00 E
Salt Lake ⊜	196	34.05 N	103.05 W
Salt Lake City	200	40.45 N	111.53 W
Salto, Arg.	252	34.17 S	60.15 W
Salto, Ur.	252	31.23 S	57.58 W
Salto ≃	66	42.23 N	12.54 E
Salto, Lago del ⊜	66	42.15 N	13.02 E
Salto da Divisa	255	16.00 S	39.57 W
Salto de las Rosas	252	34.43 S	68.14 W
Salto del Fraile ≻	286d	12.11 S	77.03 W
Salto del Guairá	252	24.03 S	54.17 W
Salto Grande	255	22.54 S	49.59 W
Salto Grande, Embalse ⊜[1]	252	31.00 S	57.55 W
Salton City	204	33.19 N	115.59 W
Salton Sea ⊜	204	33.19 N	115.50 W
Salton Sea State Recreation Area ♠	204	33.29 N	115.53 W
Saltonstall, Lake ⊜	283	42.47 N	71.04 W
Sāltora	126	23.32 N	86.56 E
Saltoro Range ⋏	123	35.17 N	77.03 E
Salto Santiago, Represa de ⊜[1]	252	25.40 S	52.30 W
Salt Pan Creek ≃	274a	33.59 S	151.02 E

Name	Seite	Breite°'	Länge°' E = Ost
Saltpeter Creek ⊂	284b	39.20 N	76.22 W
Salt Point	210	41.44 N	73.42 W
Saltpond	150	5.12 N	1.04 W
Salt Range ⋏	123	32.40 N	72.35 E
Salt River Indian Reservation ◆[4]	200	33.31 N	111.48 W
Saltsburg	214	40.29 N	79.27 W
Saltsjöbaden	40	59.17 N	18.18 E
Salt Slough ≃	226	37.18 N	120.54 W
Saltspring Island I	224	48.47 N	123.30 W
Salt Springs Reservoir ⊜[1]	226	38.30 N	120.11 W
Saltville	192	36.52 N	81.45 W
Salt Wells Creek ≃	200	41.39 N	108.59 W
Saltykovka, Ross.	80	52.07 N	44.05 E
Saltykovka, Ross.	265b	55.46 N	37.55 E
Saluda, S.C., U.S.	192	34.00 N	81.46 W
Saluda, Va., U.S.	208	37.36 N	76.35 W
Saluda ≃	192	34.00 N	81.04 W
Saludecio	66	43.52 N	12.40 E
Saluën → Salween ≃	12	16.31 N	97.37 E
Salue Timpaus, Selat ⊌	112	1.55 S	124.00 E
Salug	116	8.07 N	122.47 E
Saluggia	62	45.14 N	8.00 E
Sālūmbar	120	24.08 N	74.03 E
Salunga	208	40.06 N	76.26 W
Saluping Island I	116	6.20 N	122.02 E
Salūq 'Atīq	130	36.36 N	39.07 E
Sālūr	122	18.32 N	83.13 E
Salurn → Salorno	64	46.14 N	11.13 E
Salussola	62	45.27 N	8.07 E
Salutaris	256	22.10 S	43.17 W
Saluzzo	62	44.39 N	7.29 E
Salvación, Bahía ⊂	254	50.55 S	75.05 W
Salvado, Mount ∧	162	25.15 S	121.01 E
Salvador, Bra.	255	12.59 S	38.31 W
Salvador, Pil.	116	7.54 N	123.50 E
Salvador, El → El Salvador □[1]	236	13.50 N	88.55 W
Salvador, Lake ⊜	194	29.45 N	90.15 W
Salvador Island I	116	15.31 N	119.55 E
Salvador María	258	35.18 S	59.10 W
Salvador Mazza	252	22.04 S	63.43 W
Salvage	186	48.41 N	53.38 W
Salvail ≃	206	45.49 N	72.58 W
Salvaterra	250	0.46 S	48.31 W
Salvaterra de Magos	34	39.01 N	8.48 W
Salvatierra	234	20.13 N	100.53 W
Salve	68	39.51 N	18.17 E
Salviac	32	44.41 N	1.16 E
Salwā, Dawḥat ⊂	128	25.30 N	50.40 E
Salwā Baḥrī	140	24.44 N	32.56 E
Salween ≃	12	16.31 N	97.37 E
Salyan, Azer.	84	39.34 N	48.58 E
Salyān, Nepāl	124	28.22 N	82.10 E
Salyer	204	40.53 N	123.35 W
Salyersville	192	37.45 N	83.04 W
Salza ≃, Dtsch.	54	51.32 N	11.50 E
Salza ≃, Öst.	61	47.40 N	14.43 E
Salzach ≃	30	48.12 N	12.56 E
Salza Irpina	68	40.55 N	14.53 E
Salzbergen	52	52.19 N	7.20 E
Salzböde ≃	56	50.40 N	8.42 E
Salzbrunn	156	24.23 S	18.00 E
Salzburg	64	47.48 N	13.02 E
Salzburg □[3]	64	47.25 N	13.15 E
Salzgitter	52	52.10 N	10.25 E
Salzgitter-Bad ◆[8]	52	52.04 N	10.23 E
Salzgitter-Barum ◆[8]	52	52.07 N	10.25 E
Salzgitter-Immendorf ◆[8]	52	52.09 N	10.26 E
Salzgitter-Lebenstedt ◆[8]	52	52.09 N	10.20 E
Salzgitter-Thiede ◆[8]	52	52.11 N	10.29 E
Salzgitter-Watenstedt ◆[8]	54	52.06 N	10.22 E
Salzhaff ⊂	54	54.06 N	11.36 E
Salzhausen	52	53.13 N	10.09 E
Salzhemmendorf	52	52.04 N	9.35 E
Salzkammergut ◆[1]	64	47.45 N	13.30 E
Salzkotten	52	51.40 N	8.36 E
Salzmünde	54	51.31 N	11.49 E
Salzwedel	54	52.51 N	11.09 E
Salzweg	60	48.37 N	13.29 E
Sam, Gabon	152	0.58 N	11.16 E
Sām, India	120	26.50 N	70.31 E
Samā	132	32.28 N	36.14 E
Sama ≃	248	18.10 S	70.40 W
Sam A. Baker State Park ♠	194	37.16 N	90.34 W
Samacá	246	5.29 N	73.29 W
Samacèvičy	76	53.13 N	31.50 E
Samacimbo	152	13.33 S	16.59 E
Samādūn	142	30.20 N	30.57 E
Samagaltaj	88	50.36 N	95.03 E
Samah	146	28.12 N	19.09 E
Samāika ◆[8]	272a	28.32 N	77.05 E
Samaipata	248	18.09 S	63.52 W
Samal (Peñaplata)	116	7.05 N	125.42 E
Samalá ≃	236	14.11 N	91.47 W
Samalanga	114	5.13 N	96.22 E
Ṣamalayuca	200	31.21 N	106.28 W
Šamaldy-Saj	85	41.12 N	72.11 E
Samales Group II	116	6.00 N	121.45 E
Samalga Pass ⊌	180	52.48 N	169.25 W
Samal Island I	116	7.03 N	125.44 E
Sāmalkot	122	17.03 N	82.11 E
Samālūt	142	28.18 N	30.42 E
Samambaia ≃	255	22.45 S	53.21 W
Samāna, India	124	30.09 N	76.12 E
Samaná, Rep. Dom.	238	19.13 N	69.19 W
Samaná, Bahía de ⊂	238	19.10 N	69.25 W
Samaná, Cabo ≻	238	19.18 N	69.09 W
Samana Cay I	238	23.06 N	73.42 W
Samandağı	130	36.07 N	35.56 E
Samandıra	130	40.59 N	29.13 E
Samandıra ≃	267b	40.59 N	29.15 E
Samangān	120	36.16 N	68.01 E
Samangān □[4]	120	36.15 N	67.40 E
Samangwa	152	4.24 S	24.10 E
Samani	92a	42.07 N	142.56 E
Samaniego	246	1.20 N	77.35 W
Samanlı Dağları ⋏	130	40.36 N	29.30 E
Samannūd	142	30.58 N	31.15 E
Samar	132	29.49 N	35.01 E
Samar □[4]	116	11.50 N	125.00 E
Samar I	116	12.00 N	125.00 E
Samara	80	53.12 N	50.09 E
Samara ≃, Ross.	80	53.10 N	50.04 E
Samara ≃, Ukr.	78	48.27 N	35.07 E
Samarai	164	10.37 S	150.40 E
Samara Oblast' □[4]	80	53.30 N	50.30 E
Samarate	62	45.38 N	8.47 E
Samarga	89	47.17 N	138.48 E
Samarga ≃	89	47.15 N	138.46 E
Samaria, Id., U.S.	202	42.07 N	112.20 W
Samaria, Mi., U.S.	216	41.48 N	83.35 W
Samaria (As-Sāmirah) □[9]	132	32.15 N	35.10 E
Samaria, Mount ∧	169	36.52 S	146.03 E
Samaria Gorge → Farángi Samariás V	38	35.18 N	24.00 E
Samariapo	246	5.15 N	67.48 W
Samarinda	112	0.30 S	117.09 E
Samarka	89	44.44 N	134.13 E
Samarkand	85	39.40 N	66.48 E
Samarkand □[4]	85	39.40 N	67.15 E
Sāmarrā'	128	34.12 N	43.52 E
Samar Sea ‡[2]	116	12.15 N	124.15 E
Samarskoje, Kaz.	86	49.00 N	83.23 E
Samarskoje, Ross.	83	46.56 N	39.41 E
Ṣamarskoje, Ross.	86	52.02 N	58.10 E
Šamary	86	57.21 N	58.14 E
Samasata	123	29.21 N	71.33 E
Samassi	71	39.29 N	8.54 E
Samastīpur	124	25.51 N	85.47 E
Samatya ◆[8]	267b	41.00 N	28.56 E

Symbols in the index entries represent the broad categories identified in the key at the right. Symbols with superior numbers (⋏[1]) identify subcategories (see complete key on page *I · 1).*

Symbole im Register stellen die rechts im Schlüssel erklärten Kategorien dar. Symbole mit hochgestellten Ziffern (⋏[1]) bezeichnen Unterabteilungen einer Kategorie (vgl. vollständiger Schlüssel auf Seite *I · 1).*

Los símbolos incluídos en el texto del índice representan las grandes categorías identificadas con la clave a la derecha. Los símbolos con numeros en su parte superior (⋏[1]) identifican las subcategorías (véase la clave completa en la página *I · 1).*

Les symboles de l'index représentent les catégories indiquées dans la légende à droite. Les symboles suivis d'un indice (⋏[1]) représentent des sous-catégories (voir légende complète à la page *I · 1).*

Os símbolos incluídos no texto do índice representam as grandes categorias identificadas com a chave à direita. Os símbolos com números em sua parte superior (⋏[1]) identificam as subcategorias (veja-se a chave completa à página *I · 1).*

∧ Mountain	Berg	Montaña	Montagne	Montanha
⋏ Mountains	Gebirge	Montañas	Montagnes	Montanhas
)(Pass	Paß	Paso	Col	Passo
V Valley, Canyon	Tal, Cañon	Valle, Cañón	Vallée, Canyon	Vale, Canhão
≚ Plain	Ebene	Llano	Plaine	Planície
≻ Cape	Kap	Cabo	Cap	Cabo
I Island	Insel	Isla	Île	Ilha
II Islands	Inseln	Islas	Îles	Ilhas
⊥ Other Topographic Features	Andere Topographische Objekte	Otros Elementos Topográficos	Autres données topographiques	Outros acidentes topográficos

ESPAÑOL — Nombre | Página | Lat.°′ | Long.°′ W = Oeste

FRANÇAIS — Nom | Page | Lat.°′ | Long.°′ W = Ouest

PORTUGUÊS — Nome | Página | Lat.°′ | Long.°′ W = Oeste

Nombre	Página	Lat.°′	Long.°′ W = Oeste
Samaúna	248	7.50 S	60.02 W
Samawāri	120	28.34 N	66.46 E
Şamaxı	84	40.38 N	48.39 E
Samba, Centraf.	152	6.49 N	21.12 E
Samba, India	123	32.34 N	75.07 E
Samba, R.D.C.	152	0.14 N	21.19 E
Samba, R.D.C.	154	4.38 S	26.22 E
Samba Caju	152	8.46 S	15.24 E
Sambaetiba	256	22.41 S	42.48 W
Sambaíba	250	7.08 S	45.21 W
Sambalpur	120	21.27 N	83.58 E
Sambar, Tanjung ›	112	2.59 S	110.19 E
Sambas	112	1.20 N	109.15 E
Sambava	157b	14.16 S	50.10 E
Sambawizi	154	18.21 S	26.16 E
Şambayat	130	37.41 N	38.03 E
Sambāza	120	31.49 N	69.20 E
Sambek, Ross.	83	47.20 N	39.01 E
Sambek, Ross.	83	47.45 N	39.48 E
Sambek ≏	83	47.16 N	39.01 E
Sambesi → Zambezi ≏	138	18.55 S	36.04 E
Sambhal	124	28.35 N	78.33 E
Sāmbhar	120	26.55 N	75.12 E
Sāmbhar Lake ⊜	120	26.58 N	75.05 E
Sambia → Zambia □[1]	154	14.30 S	27.30 E
Sambiase	68	38.58 N	16.17 E
Sambir	78	49.32 N	23.11 E
Sambit, Pulau I	112	1.46 N	119.03 E
Sambito ≏	250	5.40 S	42.10 W
Sambo	152	12.57 S	16.05 E
Samboan	116	9.32 N	123.18 E
Samboja	112	1.02 S	117.02 E
Sambolabbo	152	7.05 N	11.59 E
Sâmbor	110	12.46 N	105.58 E
Samborombón ≏	252	35.43 S	57.20 W
Samborombón, Bahía c	252	36.00 S	57.12 W
Samborondón	246	1.57 S	79.44 W
Sambre ≏	32	50.28 N	4.52 E
Sambre à l'Oise, Canal de la ≊	50	49.39 N	3.20 E
Sambreville	56	50.26 N	4.37 E
Sambriāl	123	32.28 N	74.21 E
Sambú ≏	246	8.05 N	78.18 W
Sambuca di Sicilia	70	37.39 N	13.07 E
Sambuca Pistoiese	66	44.06 N	11.00 E
Sambughetti, Monte ∧	70	37.50 N	14.22 E
Sambungo	152	8.39 S	20.43 E
Sambusu	156	17.50 S	19.20 E
Samch'ŏk	98	37.27 N	129.10 E
Sam Chom, Khao ∧	110	8.07 N	99.26 E
Samch'ŏnp'o	98	34.57 N	128.03 E
Samdžir, gora ∧	88	52.32 N	93.53 E
Same	154	4.04 S	37.44 E
Same ≏	94	36.54 N	140.49 E
Samedan	58	46.33 N	9.52 E
Samegawa	94	37.02 N	140.31 E
Sāmen	128	34.12 N	48.42 E
Samene, Oued V	148	26.49 N	7.08 E
Samer	50	50.38 N	1.45 E
Sameru Dando ∧	124	27.02 N	90.20 E
Samet'	80	57.49 N	40.44 E
Samford	171a	27.23 S	152.53 E
Samfya	154	11.21 S	29.32 E
Samga	98	35.25 N	128.05 E
Samho	98	39.56 N	127.53 E
Saminka ≏	265b	55.45 N	37.17 E
Samiria ≏	246	4.42 S	74.13 W
Samish	224	48.35 N	122.33 W
Samish ≏	224	48.38 N	122.29 W
Samish, Lake ⊜	224	48.39 N	122.24 W
Samish Bay c	224	48.36 N	122.28 W
Samj	132	32.27 N	36.30 E
Samka	110	20.09 N	96.57 E
Şämkir	84	40.50 N	46.02 E
Samlesbury	262	53.46 N	2.38 W
Samlesbury Aerodrome ⊠	262	53.47 N	2.34 W
Samlesbury Bottoms	262	53.45 N	2.34 W
Samlesbury Higher Hall ⊥	262	53.46 N	2.34 W
Şamlı	130	39.48 N	27.51 E
Sammamish, Lake ⊜	224	47.36 N	122.06 W
Sammichele di Bari	68	40.53 N	16.57 E
Samnangjin	98	35.23 N	128.50 E
Samnaun	58	46.56 N	10.22 E
Samnaungruppe ⋏	58	47.00 N	10.25 E
Sam Ngao	110	17.15 N	99.01 E
Samnū	146	27.17 N	14.53 E
Samnye	98	35.55 N	127.05 E
Samo	164	3.58 S	152.51 E
Samoa → Western Samoa □[1]	175a	13.55 S	172.00 W
Samoa → American Samoa □[2]	175a	14.20 S	170.00 W
Samoa americane → American Samoa □[2]	175a	14.20 S	170.00 W
Samoa Basin ⊹[1]	14	16.00 S	166.00 W
Samoa i Sisifo → Western Samoa □[1]	175a	13.55 S	172.00 W
Samoa Islands II	175a	14.00 S	171.00 W
Samo Alto	252	30.25 S	70.58 W
Samoa Occidental → Western Samoa □[1]	175a	13.55 S	172.00 W
Samoa Occidentales → Western Samoa □[1]	175a	13.55 S	172.00 W
Samobor	36	45.48 N	15.43 E
Samoded	24	63.38 N	40.29 E
Samoëns	58	46.05 N	6.44 E
Samofalovka	80	48.57 N	44.13 E
Samoggia ≏	64	44.41 N	11.15 E
Samojlovka	80	51.12 N	43.43 E
Samokov	38	42.20 N	23.33 E
Samolaco	58	46.15 N	9.21 E
Samora ≏	266c	38.50 N	8.57 W
Sámos	38	37.45 N	27.00 E
Sámos I	38	37.48 N	26.44 E
Samosdelka	80	46.02 N	47.53 E
Samoset	220	27.28 N	82.32 W
Samosir, Pulau I	114	2.35 N	98.50 E
Samothrace → Samothráki I	38	40.30 N	25.32 E
Samothráki	38	40.28 N	25.31 E
Samothráki (Samothrace) I	38	40.30 N	25.32 E
Samouco	266c	38.43 N	9.00 W
Samovol'no-Ivanovka	80	52.33 N	50.53 E
S'amozero	24	61.54 N	33.18 E
Sampacho	252	33.23 S	64.43 W
Sampaga	112	2.19 S	119.07 E
Sampaio Correia	256	22.52 S	42.36 W
Sampalan	115b	8.41 S	115.34 E
Sampanahan	112	2.38 S	116.11 E
Sampang	115a	7.12 S	113.14 E
Sampara ≏	112	3.49 S	122.28 E
Sampawams Creek ≏	276	40.41 N	73.19 W
Sam Pervyj	86	45.28 N	56.06 E
Sampéyre	62	44.34 N	7.11 E
Sampford Peverell	42	50.56 N	3.22 W
Sampieri	70	36.43 N	14.44 E
Sampit	112	2.32 S	112.57 E
Sampit ≏	112	2.44 S	112.54 E
Sampit, Teluk c	112	3.05 S	113.03 E
Sampolawa	112	5.36 S	122.43 E
Sampson	279b	40.10 N	79.53 W
Sampson State Park ♠	210	42.44 N	76.55 W
Sampués	246	9.11 N	75.23 W
Sampur	80	52.19 N	41.37 E
Sampwe	154	9.20 S	27.26 E
Samrāla	123	30.51 N	76.11 E
Sam Rayburn Reservoir ⊜[1]	194	31.27 N	94.37 W
Samre	144	13.07 N	39.10 E
Samreboi	150	5.36 N	2.34 W
Samro, ozero ⊜	76	58.57 N	28.49 E
Samrong, Khlong ≊	269a	13.39 N	100.34 E
Sams ≏	224	47.38 N	124.01 W
Samsang	120	30.31 N	82.37 E
Samsø I	41	55.52 N	10.37 E
Samsø Bælt ʊ	41	55.48 N	10.47 E
Samson, Al., U.S.	194	31.06 N	86.02 W
Sam Son, Viet	110	19.44 N	105.54 E
Samson I	42a	49.56 N	6.22 W
Samson Indian Reserve ◆[4]	182	52.48 N	113.10 W
Samsonovka	85	42.44 N	70.32 E
Samsonvale, Lake ⊜[1]	171a	27.15 S	152.55 E
Samsonville	210	41.53 N	74.18 W
Sams Point ∧	210	41.40 N	74.22 W
Samsu	98	41.19 N	127.59 E
Samsun	130	41.17 N	36.20 E
Samsun □[4]	130	41.15 N	36.00 E
Samsun Körfezi c	130	41.18 N	36.21 E
Samtens	54	54.21 N	13.17 E
Samthar	124	25.51 N	78.55 E
Samtown	194	31.16 N	92.26 W
Samtredia	84	42.10 N	42.20 E
Samu	112	2.01 S	115.57 E
Samūdragarh	126	23.21 N	88.20 E
Samuel, Mount ∧	162	19.41 S	134.09 E
Samuel P. Taylor State Park ♠	226	38.01 N	122.44 W
Samugheo	71	39.57 N	8.56 E
Samuhú	252	27.31 S	60.24 W
Samui, Ko I	110	9.30 N	100.00 E
Samukawa	94	35.22 N	139.23 E
Samundri	123	31.04 N	72.58 E
Samur ≏	84	41.53 N	48.32 E
Samur-Abşeron kanalı ≊	84	41.38 N	48.25 E
Samus'	86	56.46 N	84.44 E
Samusele	152	10.06 S	24.05 E
Samut Prakan	110	13.36 N	100.36 E
Samut Prakan □[4]	269a	13.35 N	100.35 E
Samut Sakhon	110	13.32 N	100.17 E
Samut Songkhram	110	13.24 N	100.00 E
Samuyi Shankou)(	124	29.55 N	84.46 E
S'amža	76	60.01 N	41.02 E
San	150	13.18 N	4.54 W
San (Xan) ≏, Asia	110	13.32 N	105.58 E
San ≏, Europe	30	50.44 N	21.50 E
San ≏, Zhg.	100	33.02 N	119.21 E
Saña, Perú	248	6.55 S	79.35 W
Şan'ā', Yaman	144	15.23 N	44.12 E
Şana ≏, Bos.	36	45.03 N	16.23 E
Šan'a ≏, Ross.	82	54.41 N	35.55 E
Sanaag □[4]	144	10.30 N	47.45 E
Sanaba	150	12.25 N	3.49 W
Sanaba ≏	150	15.06 N	10.55 W
Şanabū	142	27.30 N	30.47 E
Sanada	94	36.27 N	138.20 E
Sanae ᵾ[3]	9	70.30 S	2.30 W
Sanafā	142	30.47 N	31.21 E
Şanāfīr I	128	27.55 N	34.40 E
Sanaga ≏	152	3.35 N	9.38 E
Sanage-yama ∧	94	35.12 N	137.10 E
Sanagōchi	96	33.59 N	134.28 E
San Agustín, Arg.	252	38.01 S	58.21 W
San Agustín, Arg.	252	31.59 S	64.23 W
San Agustín, Bol.	248	21.05 S	67.45 W
San Agustín, Col.	246	1.53 N	76.16 W
San Agustín, Méx.	200	31.31 N	106.15 W
San Agustin, Pil.	116	16.30 N	121.45 E
San Agustin, Pil.	116	12.25 N	120.59 E
San Agustin, Cape ›	116	6.16 N	126.11 E
San Agustin, Plains of ≚	200	33.50 N	108.00 W
San Agustín Atenango	234	17.38 N	97.59 W
San Agustín de Valle Fértil	252	30.38 S	67.27 W
San Agustín Loxicha	234	16.01 N	96.38 W
San Agustín Tlaxiaca	234	20.07 N	98.53 W
Sanak Islands II	180	54.25 N	162.35 W
San Alberto	196	27.30 N	101.20 W
San Alejo	236	13.26 N	87.58 W
Şān al-Ḥajar, Birkat ⊜	142	31.03 N	31.54 E
Şān al-Ḥajar al-Qiblīyah	142	30.58 N	31.52 E
Sanalona, Presa ⊜[1]	232	24.53 N	107.00 W
San Ambrosio, Isla I	244	26.21 S	79.52 W
Sanam Chai, Khlong ≊	269a	13.38 N	100.27 E
Sanana	112	2.04 S	125.58 E
Sanana, Pulau I	112	2.12 S	125.55 E
Sānand	120	22.59 N	72.23 E
Sanandaj	128	35.19 N	47.00 E
Sanandita	248	21.40 S	63.35 W
San Andreas	226	38.11 N	120.40 W
San Andreas Fault V	226	36.20 N	121.00 W
San Andreas Lake ⊜	282	37.36 N	122.26 W
San Andrés, Col.	236	12.35 N	81.42 W
San Andrés, Col.	246	6.49 N	72.52 W
San Andrés, Méx.	232	27.14 N	114.14 W
San Andrés, Pan.	236	8.36 N	82.44 W
San Andrés, Isla de I	236	12.32 N	81.42 W
San Andrés, Laguna c	234	22.40 N	97.52 W
San Andrés Calpan	234	19.06 N	98.27 W
San Andrés Cohamiata	234	22.12 N	104.03 W
San Andrés de Giles	258	34.27 S	59.27 W
San Andres Mountains ⋏	200	32.55 N	106.45 W
San Andres Point ›	116	13.34 N	121.52 E
San Andrés Sajcabajá	236	15.13 N	90.55 W
San Andrés Timilpan	234	19.52 N	99.45 W
San Andrés Totoltepec ◆[8]	286a	19.15 N	99.10 W
San Andrés Tuxtla	234	18.27 N	95.13 W
San Andrés y Providencia □[8]	238	12.30 N	81.45 W
Sananduva	252	27.57 S	51.48 W
San Angel → Álvaro Obregón ◆[8]	286a	19.21 N	99.12 W
San Angelo	196	31.27 N	100.26 W
San Anselmo	226	37.58 N	122.33 W
San Antero	246	9.23 N	75.46 W
San Antonio, Arg.	252	28.57 S	65.20 W
San Antonio, Arg.	252	28.56 S	65.06 W
San Antonio, Belize	236	16.15 N	89.02 W
San Antonio, Chile	252	27.53 S	70.03 W
San Antonio, Chile	252	33.35 S	71.38 W
San Antonio, Col.	246	3.55 N	75.28 W
San Antonio, C.R.	236	10.12 N	85.26 W
San Antonio, N. Mar. Is.	174n	15.08 N	145.43 E
San Antonio, Perú	248	6.22 S	76.21 W
San Antonio, Pil.	116	12.25 N	124.17 E
San Antonio, Pil.	116	14.57 N	120.05 E
San Antonio, P.R.	240m	18.30 N	67.07 W
San Antonio, Fl., U.S.	220	28.20 N	82.16 W
San Antonio, N.M., U.S.	200	35.06 N	106.22 W
San Antonio, Tx., U.S.	196	29.25 N	98.29 W
San Antonio, Ur.	252	31.22 S	57.48 W
San Antonio, Ur.	258	34.27 S	56.05 W
San Antonio □[7]	286b	22.55 N	82.29 W
San Antonio ≏, Méx.	196	29.13 N	103.47 W
San Antonio ≏, Méx.	232	31.00 N	116.15 W
San Antonio ≏, Ca., U.S.	226	35.52 N	120.48 W
San Antonio ≏, Tx., U.S.	196	28.30 N	96.50 W
San Antonio ≏[1]	288	34.24 S	58.31 W
San Antonio, Cabo ›	252	36.40 S	56.42 W
San Antonio, Cabo de ›	240p	21.52 N	84.57 W
San Antonio, Lake ⊜[1]	226	35.55 N	121.00 W
San Antonio, Mount ∧	228	34.17 N	117.39 W
San Antonio, Punta ›, Méx.	232	26.31 N	111.28 W
San Antonio, Punta ›, Méx.	232	29.46 N	115.42 W
San Antonio, Rio ≏	200	37.11 N	105.55 W
San Antonio Bay c, Pil.	116	8.38 N	117.35 E
San Antonio Bay c, Tx., U.S.	196	28.20 N	96.45 W
San Antonio Canyon V	280	34.12 N	117.40 W
San Antonio Creek ≏	226	38.09 N	122.33 W
San Antonio Dam ◆[5]	280	34.09 N	117.41 W
San Antonio de Areco	258	34.15 S	59.28 W
San Antonio de Galipán	286c	10.33 N	66.53 W
San Antonio de los Baños	240p	22.53 N	82.30 W
San Antonio de los Cobres	252	24.11 S	66.21 W
San Antonio del Táchira	246	7.50 N	72.27 W
San Antonio de Padua, Arg.	258	34.40 S	58.42 W
San Antonio de Padua, Méx.	234	22.35 N	104.30 W
San Antonio de Padua, Mission ᵾ[1]	226	36.01 N	121.15 W
San Antonio de Tamanaco	246	9.41 N	66.03 W
San Antonio El Bravo	232	30.10 N	104.42 W
San Antonio Eloxochitlán	234	18.11 N	96.52 W
San Antonio Heights	228	34.10 N	117.40 W
San Antonio Mountain ∧	200	36.52 N	106.02 W
San Antonio Nogalar	234	23.04 N	98.22 W
San Antonio Oeste	254	40.44 S	64.56 W
San Antonio Reservoir ⊜[1]	226	37.35 N	121.50 W
San Antonio Someyucan	286a	19.27 N	99.16 W
San Antonio Suchitepéquez	236	14.32 N	91.25 W
San Antonio Tecómitl ◆[8]	286a	19.13 N	98.59 W
San Antonio Ticino	266b	45.35 N	8.46 E
San Ardo	226	36.01 N	120.54 W
Sanaroa Island I	164	9.35 S	151.00 E
Sanary-sur-Mer	62	43.07 N	5.48 E
Sanatoga	285	40.15 N	75.36 W
Sanatoga Creek ≏	285	40.14 N	75.36 W
Sanatorium	194	31.53 N	89.46 W
San Augustine	194	31.31 N	94.06 W
San Augustin Pass)(	200	32.26 N	106.34 W
Sanaur	124	30.18 N	76.27 E
Sanāw	144	17.50 N	51.00 E
Sanāwad	120	22.11 N	76.04 E
Sanāwān	123	30.19 N	70.59 E
Sanbao, Zhg.	102	43.00 N	93.19 E
Sanbao, Zhg.	105	40.20 N	116.02 E
Sanbaoyingzi	104	41.34 N	120.56 E
San Bartolomeo in Galdo	68	41.24 N	15.01 E
San Basilio	71	39.32 N	9.11 E
San Benedetto, Alpe di ⋏	66	43.53 N	11.43 E
San Benedetto del Tronto	66	42.57 N	13.53 E
San Benedetto in Alpe	66	43.59 N	11.41 E
San Benedetto Po	64	45.02 N	10.55 E
San Benedicto, Isla I	232	19.18 N	110.49 W
San Benigno Canavese	62	45.13 N	7.46 E
San Benito, Bol.	248	17.31 S	65.55 W
San Benito, Guat.	232	16.55 N	89.54 W
San Benito, Perú	248	7.26 S	78.56 W
San Benito, Tx., U.S.	196	26.07 N	97.37 W
San Benito □[6]	226	36.51 N	121.24 W
San Benito ≏	226	36.53 N	121.34 W
San Benito Mountain ∧	226	36.22 N	120.38 W
San Bernard ≏	222	28.52 N	95.27 W
San Bernardino, Schw.	58	46.28 N	9.12 E
San Bernardino, Ca., U.S.	228	34.07 N	117.18 W
San Bernardino □[6]	228	34.40 N	117.17 W
San Bernardino, Passo del)(	58	46.30 N	9.11 E
San Bernardino Mountains ⋏	204	34.10 N	116.45 W
San Bernardino National Forest ♠	280	34.12 N	117.38 W
San Bernardino Strait ʊ	116	12.32 N	124.10 E
San Bernardo, Arg.	252	27.17 S	60.42 W
San Bernardo, Chile	252	33.36 S	70.43 W
San Bernardo, Méx.	232	25.59 N	105.33 W
San Bernardo, Isla I	236	11.32 N	85.06 W
San Bernardo, Islas de II	246	9.45 N	75.50 W
San Bernardo del Viento	246	9.21 N	75.57 W
Sanbe-yama ∧	96	35.08 N	132.37 E
San Biagio	66	44.35 N	11.52 E
San Biagio di Callalta	64	45.41 N	12.22 E
San Biagio Platani	70	37.31 N	13.32 E
San Biagio Saracinisco	66	41.37 N	13.55 E
San Blas, Méx.	232	26.05 N	108.46 W
San Blas, Méx.	234	21.31 N	105.16 W
San Blas, Cape ›	192	29.40 N	85.22 W
San Blas, Golfo de c	246	9.30 N	79.00 W
San Blas, Serranía De ⋏	246	9.18 N	79.00 W
San Blas de los Sauces	252	28.24 S	67.05 W
San Bonifacio	64	45.24 N	11.16 E
San Borja	248	14.49 S	66.51 W
Sanborn, Ia., U.S.	198	43.10 N	95.39 W
Sanborn, Mn., U.S.	198	44.12 N	95.07 W
Sanborn, N.Y., U.S.	210	43.08 N	78.53 W
Sanborn, N.D., U.S.	198	46.56 N	98.13 W
San Bovio	266b	45.28 N	9.19 E
San Bruno	226	37.37 N	122.24 W
San Bruno, Point ›	282	37.39 N	122.22 W
San Bruno Mountain ∧	282	37.42 N	122.25 W
Sanbu	94	35.39 N	140.23 E
San Buenaventura, Bol.	248	14.28 S	67.35 W
San Buenaventura, Méx.	232	27.05 N	101.32 W
San Buenaventura → Ventura, Ca., U.S.	228	34.17 N	119.18 W
San Buono	66	41.59 N	14.34 E
San Calogero	68	38.34 N	16.01 E
San Calogero, Monte ∧	70	37.57 N	13.44 E
San Candido (Innichen)	64	46.44 N	12.17 E
Sancang	100	32.45 N	120.43 E
San Carlo	58	46.25 N	8.32 E
San Carlos, Arg.	252	27.45 S	55.54 W
San Carlos, Arg.	252	33.46 S	69.02 W
San Carlos, Arg.	252	25.56 S	65.56 W
San Carlos, Chile	252	36.25 S	71.58 W
San Carlos, Chile	286e	33.36 S	70.35 W
San Carlos, Méx.	232	29.01 N	100.51 W
San Carlos, Méx.	232	24.35 N	98.56 W
San Carlos, Nic.	236	11.07 N	84.47 W
San Carlos, Pan.	236	8.29 N	79.57 W
San Carlos, Para.	252	22.16 S	57.18 W
San Carlos, Pil.	116	10.30 N	123.25 E
San Carlos, Pil.	116	15.55 N	120.20 E
San Carlos, Az., U.S.	200	33.20 N	110.27 W
San Carlos, Ca., U.S.	226	37.29 N	122.15 W
San Carlos, Ur.	252	34.48 S	54.55 W
San Carlos, Ven.	246	9.40 N	68.36 W
San Carlos ≏, C.R.	236	10.47 N	84.12 W
San Carlos ≏, Az., U.S.	200	33.16 N	110.27 W
San Carlos ≏, Ven.	246	9.07 N	68.25 W
San Carlos, Riacho ≏	252	22.51 S	57.51 W
San Carlos Airport ⊠	282	37.31 N	122.15 W
San Carlos Bay c	220	26.28 N	82.03 W
San Carlos Borromeo, Mission ᵾ[1]	226	36.34 N	121.55 W
San Carlos Centro	252	31.44 S	61.06 W
San Carlos de Bariloche	254	41.09 S	71.18 W
San Carlos de Bolívar	252	36.15 S	61.06 W
San Carlos de Chena	286e	33.35 S	70.44 W
San Carlos de Guaroa	246	3.44 N	73.14 W
San Carlos del Zulia	246	9.01 N	71.55 W
San Carlos de Río Negro	246	1.55 N	67.04 W
San Carlos Indian Reservation ◆[4]	200	33.23 N	110.09 W
San Carlos Reservoir ⊜[1]	200	33.13 N	110.24 W
San Carlos Viejo, Canal ≊	286e	33.25 S	70.38 W
San Carpoforo Creek ≏	226	35.47 N	121.19 W
San Casciano dei Bagni	66	42.52 N	11.53 E
San Casciano in Val di Pesa	66	43.39 N	11.11 E
San Cataldo, It.	68	40.23 N	18.17 E
San Cataldo, It.	70	37.29 N	13.59 E
San Cayetano	252	38.20 S	59.37 W
Sancergues	50	47.09 N	2.55 E
Sancerre	50	47.20 N	2.51 E
Sancerrois, Collines du ⋏[2]	50	47.25 N	2.45 E
San Cesario di Lecce	68	40.18 N	18.10 E
San Cesario sul Panaro	64	44.34 N	11.02 E
Sancey-le-Grand	58	47.18 N	6.35 E
Sancha, Zhg.	105	40.27 N	116.26 E
Sancha, Zhg.	106	31.52 N	119.06 E
Sancha ≏	102	26.55 N	106.06 E
Sanchaba	107	30.19 N	104.14 E
Sanchahe	89	44.59 N	126.04 E
Sanchakou	105	39.47 N	117.19 E
Sanchang	106	31.54 N	121.15 E
Sanchazi	104	41.07 N	124.15 E
Sanchazicun	104	42.03 N	123.59 E
Sanchenglong	89	44.02 N	120.58 E
Sánchez	238	19.14 N	69.36 W
Sanchez Creek ≏	222	32.36 N	97.50 W
Sánchez Magallanes	234	18.14 N	93.52 W
Sānchi	124	23.29 N	77.44 E
Sanchih	100	25.16 N	121.30 E
San Chirico Raparo	68	40.11 N	16.05 E
Sanch'ŏng	98	35.26 N	127.54 E
Sanchung	269d	25.04 N	121.30 E
Sanch'ungch'iao	269d	25.12 N	121.35 E
San Cipirello	70	37.58 N	13.10 E
San Ciro de Acosta	234	21.38 N	99.49 W
San Clemente, Esp.	34	39.24 N	2.26 W
San Clemente, Ca., U.S.	228	33.25 N	117.36 W
San Clemente, Arroyo de ≏	266d	41.20 N	2.00 E
San Clemente, Cerro ∧	254	46.36 S	73.20 W
San Clemente a Casauria ᵾ[1]	66	42.14 N	13.55 E
San Clemente Island I	228	32.54 N	118.29 W
Sancoins	32	46.50 N	2.55 E
San Colombano al Lambro	62	45.11 N	9.29 E
San Cono	70	37.17 N	14.22 E
Sanco Point ›	116	8.15 N	126.27 E
San Cosme	252	27.22 S	58.31 W
San Cosmo Albanese	68	39.35 N	16.25 E
San Costantino Albanese	68	40.02 N	16.18 E
San Cristóbal, Arg.	252	30.19 S	61.14 W
San Cristóbal, Cuba	240p	22.43 N	83.03 W
San Cristóbal, Rep. Dom.	238	18.25 N	70.06 W
San Cristóbal, Ven.	246	7.46 N	72.14 W
San Cristobal I	175e	10.36 S	161.45 E
San Cristóbal, Bahía c	232	27.23 N	114.38 W
San Cristóbal, Cerro ∧, Chile	286e	33.25 S	70.39 W
San Cristóbal, Cerro ∧, Perú	286d	12.02 S	77.01 W
San Cristóbal, Isla I	246a	0.50 S	89.26 W
San Cristóbal, Nevis → Saint Kitts and Nevis □[1]	238	17.20 N	62.45 W
San Cristóbal, Volcán ∧[1]	236	12.42 N	87.01 W
San Cristóbal de la Barranca	234	21.03 N	103.26 W
San Cristóbal de la Laguna	148	28.29 N	16.19 W
San Cristóbal de las Casas	234	16.45 N	92.38 W
San Cristóbal Totonicapán	236	14.55 N	91.26 W
San Cristobal Trench ⊹[1]	14	11.15 S	162.45 E
San Cristóbal Verapaz	236	15.23 N	90.24 W
San Cristobal Wash V	200	32.47 N	113.44 W
San Croce, Monte ∧	66	41.17 N	13.58 E
Sancti Spíritus	240p	21.56 N	79.27 W
Sancti Spíritus □[4]	240p	22.00 N	79.20 W
San Cugat, Riera de ≏	266d	41.29 N	2.11 E
Sančursk	80	56.57 N	47.15 E
Sancy, Puy de ∧	32	45.32 N	2.49 E
Sand, Dtsch.	56	48.32 N	7.55 E
Sand, Nor.	26	59.29 N	6.15 E
Sand ≏, Ab., Can.	184	54.22 N	111.05 W
Sand ≏, S. Afr.	156	22.25 S	30.05 E
Sand ≏, S. Afr.	158	28.05 S	26.25 E
Sanda, Nihon	96	34.53 N	135.14 E
Sanda, Nihon	268	35.28 N	139.21 E
Sandafā al-Fa'r	142	28.32 N	30.40 E
Sandai	112	1.15 S	110.31 E
Sanda Island I	44	55.18 N	5.34 W
Sandakan	112	5.50 N	118.07 E
Sandakan, Pelabuhan c	116	5.45 N	118.05 E
San Damián	248	12.02 S	76.24 W
San Damiano d'Asti	62	44.50 N	8.04 E
San Damiano Macra	62	44.29 N	7.16 E
Sândăn	110	12.42 N	106.01 E
Sandan, Chāh ⫪[4]	128	28.59 N	63.27 E
Sandane	26	61.46 N	6.13 E
San Daniele del Friuli	64	46.09 N	13.00 E
Sandan-kyō ♠	96	34.38 N	132.13 E
Sandanski	38	41.34 N	23.17 E
Sandaogang	89	46.08 N	130.05 E
Sandaogou, Zhg.	104	41.39 N	121.45 E
Sandaogou, Zhg.	105	39.33 N	115.27 E
Sandaohe	86	44.21 N	85.37 E
Sandaoliangzi	104	41.20 N	122.07 E
Sandaolingzi	104	40.58 N	124.08 E
Sandaozhen	89	47.25 N	126.25 E
Sandaré	150	14.42 N	10.18 W
Sandared	26	57.43 N	12.47 E
Sandarne	26	61.16 N	17.10 E
Sand Arroyo V	196	37.29 N	101.29 W
Sandata	80	46.16 N	41.46 E
Sandau	54	52.47 N	12.02 E
Sandaun □[5]	164	4.00 S	141.30 E
Sanday I	46	59.15 N	2.35 W
Sanday Sound c	46	59.11 N	2.31 W
Sandbach	44	53.09 N	2.22 W
Sandbank	46	55.59 N	4.58 W
Sandbanks Provincial Park ♠	212	43.55 N	77.17 W
Sandbochum ◆[8]	263	51.40 N	7.41 E
Sand City	226	36.37 N	121.51 W
Sand Coulee	202	47.23 N	111.10 W
Sand Coulee Creek ≏	202	47.27 N	111.18 W
Sand Creek ≏, U.S.	200	41.13 N	105.43 W
Sand Creek ≏, In., U.S.	218	39.03 N	85.51 W
Sand Creek ≏, Ks., U.S.	198	37.26 N	98.12 W
Sand Creek ≏, Mn., U.S.	190	45.56 N	92.39 W
Sand Creek ≏, Mt., U.S.	202	47.18 N	106.45 W
Sand Creek ≏, S.D., U.S.	198	44.02 N	98.05 W
Sand Creek ≏, Wy., U.S.	200	43.27 N	105.26 W
Sand Creek ≏, Wy., U.S.	200	41.02 N	107.52 W
Sand Creek ≏, Wy., U.S.	202	44.16 N	107.55 W
Sand Cut	220	26.56 N	80.35 W
Sande, Dtsch.	52	51.45 N	8.39 E
Sande, Dtsch.	52	53.30 N	8.01 E
Sandefjord	26	59.08 N	10.14 E
San Demetrio Corone	68	39.34 N	16.22 E
San Demetrio ne'Vestini	66	42.17 N	13.34 E
Sanders, Az., U.S.	200	35.12 N	109.19 W
Sanders, Ky., U.S.	218	38.39 N	84.56 W
Sandersdorf, Dtsch.	54	51.37 N	12.15 E
Sandersdorf, Dtsch.	60	48.54 N	11.37 E
Sandersleben	54	51.40 N	11.34 E
Sanderson	196	30.08 N	102.23 W
Sanderstead ◆[8]	260	51.20 N	0.05 W
Sanderston	168b	34.46 S	139.13 E
Sandersville, Ga., U.S.	192	32.58 N	82.48 W
Sandersville, Ms., U.S.	194	31.47 N	89.01 W
Sandeshkhali	126	22.22 N	88.53 E
Sandesneben	52	53.41 N	10.30 E
Sandfly Lake ⊜	184	55.45 N	106.05 W
Sand Fork	188	38.54 N	80.45 W
Sandgate, Austl.	171a	27.20 S	153.05 E
Sandgate, Eng., U.K.	42	51.05 N	1.08 E
Sandhammaren ›	26	55.23 N	14.12 E
Sandhamn	40	59.17 N	18.55 E
Sandhead	44	54.48 N	4.58 W
Sandheuwel	158	31.46 S	20.48 E
Sandhill, On., Can.	275b	43.50 N	79.49 W
Sand Hill, Ma., U.S.	207	42.13 N	70.44 W
Sand Hill ∧[2]	210	42.31 N	77.37 W
Sand Hill ≏	198	47.36 N	96.52 W
Sand Hills ⋏[2]	198	42.00 N	101.00 W
Sandhorst	52	53.29 N	7.29 E
Sandhurst	42	51.19 N	0.48 W
Sāndi	124	27.18 N	79.57 E
Sandia	248	14.17 S	69.26 W
Sandia Crest ∧	200	35.13 N	106.27 W
Sandia Indian Reservation ◆[4]	200	35.15 N	106.30 W
Sandian	100	30.56 N	114.48 E
San Diego, Ca., U.S.	228	32.42 N	117.09 W
San Diego, Tx., U.S.	196	27.45 N	98.14 W
San Diego □[6]	228	33.00 N	117.05 W
San Diego ≏, Cuba	240p	22.20 N	83.16 W
San Diego ≏, Ca., U.S.	204	32.46 N	117.13 W
San Diego, Cabo ›	254	54.38 S	65.07 W
San Diego Aqueduct ≊[1]	228	32.55 N	116.55 W
San Diego Bay c	228	32.37 N	117.07 W
San Diego Creek ≏	196	27.47 N	98.03 W
San Diego de Alcala, Mission ᵾ[1]	228	32.48 N	117.06 W
San Diego de la Unión	234	21.28 N	100.52 W
San Diego Naval Training Center ■	228	32.44 N	117.13 W
San Dieguito ≏	228	32.58 N	117.16 W
Sandies Creek ≏	222	29.06 N	97.20 W
Sandıklı	130	38.28 N	30.17 E
Sandīla	124	27.05 N	80.31 E
Sandilands	168b	34.31 S	137.46 E
Sandilands Village	240b	25.02 N	77.18 W
San Dimas	228	34.06 N	117.48 W
San Dimas Canyon V	280	34.10 N	117.46 W
San Dimas Reservoir ⊜[1]	280	34.09 N	117.43 W
San Dionisio, Nic.	236	12.45 N	85.51 W
San Dionisio, Pil.	116	11.16 N	123.06 E
Sand Island I, Mid. Is.	174g	28.12 N	177.23 W
Sand Island I, Hi., U.S.	229c	21.18 N	157.53 W
Sand Islet I	174g	28.16 N	177.23 W
Sandiway	262	53.14 N	2.36 W
Sand Key I	220	27.53 N	82.51 W
Sandkrug	54	52.53 N	13.52 E
Sandl	61	48.33 N	14.38 E
Sand Lake	210	42.38 N	73.32 W
Sand Lake ⊜, On., Can.	184	50.05 N	94.39 W
Sand Lake ⊜, On., Can.	212	44.56 N	77.02 W
Sand Lake ⊜, On., Can.	212	44.34 N	76.15 W
Sandling ∧	64	47.39 N	13.43 E
Sandnes	26	58.51 N	5.44 E
Sandness	46a	60.17 N	1.38 W
Sandoa	152	9.41 S	22.52 E
Sandogora	80	58.12 N	40.59 E
Sandomierz	30	50.41 N	21.45 E
San Domingo Creek ≏	226	38.07 N	120.40 W
San Domino, Isola I	66	42.07 N	15.29 E
Sandon	260	51.43 N	0.32 E
Sandoná	246	1.17 N	77.28 W
San Donaci	68	40.27 N	17.55 E
San Donà di Piave	64	45.38 N	12.34 E
San Donato di Lecce	68	40.15 N	18.10 E
San Donato di Ninea	68	39.42 N	16.03 E
San Donato Milanese	62	45.24 N	9.16 E
San Donato Val di Comino	66	41.42 N	13.49 E
Sandongo	152	15.30 S	21.28 E
San Dorligo della Valle	64	45.36 N	13.51 E
Sandouping	102	30.48 N	110.49 E
Sandoval	219	38.36 N	89.06 W
Sandovalina	255	22.27 S	51.44 W
Sandover ≏	162	21.43 S	136.32 E
Sandovo	76	58.28 N	36.25 E
Sandoway	110	18.28 N	94.22 E
Sandown	42	50.39 N	1.09 W
Sandown Park Racecourse ♠, Austl.	274b	37.57 S	145.10 E
Sandown Park Race Course ♠, Eng., U.K.	260	51.22 N	0.22 W
Sand Point, Ak., U.S.	180	55.20 N	160.30 W
Sandpoint, Id., U.S.	202	48.16 N	116.33 W
Sandrancourt	261	49.02 N	1.39 E
Sandray I	46	56.53 N	7.30 W
Sandridge, Eng., U.K.	260	51.47 N	0.18 W
Sand Ridge, N.Y., U.S.	210	43.15 N	76.14 W
Sandrigo	64	45.39 N	11.36 E
Sandringham, Austl.	166	24.05 S	139.04 E
Sandringham, Austl.	169	37.57 S	145.00 E
Sandringham, Eng., U.K.	42	52.50 N	0.30 E
Sandringham ◆[8]	273d	26.09 S	28.07 E
Sandringham House ⊥	42	52.50 N	0.30 E
Sand River Valley	158	28.28 S	29.33 E
Sands Key I	220	25.30 N	80.11 W
Sandslån	26	63.01 N	17.47 E
Sandspit	182	53.14 N	131.50 W
Sands Point	276	40.51 N	73.43 W
Sands Point ›	276	40.52 N	73.44 W
Sand Springs, Ok., U.S.	196	36.08 N	96.06 W
Sand Springs, Tx., U.S.	196	32.15 N	101.22 W
Sandspruit	158	27.18 S	29.48 E
Sandspruit ≏	273d	26.07 S	28.04 E
Sandstedt	52	53.21 N	8.31 E
Sandston	208	37.31 N	77.18 W
Sandstone, Austl.	162	27.59 S	119.17 E
Sandstone, Mn., U.S.	190	46.07 N	92.52 W
Sandstone Creek ≏	216	42.23 N	84.33 W
Sandu, Zhg.	100	29.46 N	120.12 E
Sandu, Zhg.	100	26.02 N	113.16 E
Sandu, Zhg.	100	29.12 N	114.40 E
Sandu, Zhg.	102	25.59 N	107.52 E
Sanduan	104	41.10 N	121.27 E
Sandu Ao c	100	26.35 N	119.50 E
Sandugan Point ›	116	9.18 N	123.36 E
Sandumba	152	13.45 S	17.29 E
Sandun, Zhg.	106	31.52 N	121.50 E
Sandun, Zhg.	106	30.19 N	120.05 E
Sanduo	100	32.49 N	119.42 E
Sandusky, In., U.S.	218	39.25 N	85.29 W
Sandusky, Mi., U.S.	190	43.25 N	82.49 W
Sandusky, N.Y., U.S.	210	42.30 N	78.23 W
Sandusky, Oh., U.S.	214	41.26 N	82.42 W
Sandusky □[6]	214	41.21 N	83.07 W
Sandusky ≏	214	41.27 N	83.00 W
Sandusky Bay c	214	41.27 N	82.52 W
Sand uul ∧	102	43.27 N	104.04 E
Sandvig	26	55.17 N	14.47 E
Sandvika	26	59.54 N	10.31 E
Sandviken	40	60.37 N	16.46 E
Sandweiler	56	49.37 N	6.13 E
Sandwich, Eng., U.K.	42	51.17 N	1.20 E
Sandwich, Il., U.S.	216	41.38 N	88.37 W
Sandwich, Ma., U.S.	207	41.45 N	70.29 W
Sandwich Bay c, Nf., Can.	176	53.35 N	57.15 W
Sandwich Bay c, Namibia	156	23.22 S	14.30 E
Sandwich del Sur, Islas → South Sandwich Islands II	18	57.45 S	26.30 W
Sandwick, B.C., Can.	182	49.42 N	124.59 W
Sandwick, Scot., U.K.	46a	60.00 N	1.15 W
Sand Wick c	46a	60.42 N	0.52 W
Sandwīp	124	22.29 N	91.26 E
Sandwīp Channel ʊ	124	22.30 N	91.35 E
Sandwīp Island I	124	22.30 N	91.25 E
Sandy, Eng., U.K.	42	52.08 N	0.18 W
Sandy, Or., U.S.	224	45.23 N	122.15 W
Sandy, Pa., U.S.	214	41.07 N	78.47 W
Sandy, Ut,. U.S.	200	40.35 N	111.53 W
Sandy ≏, Me., U.S.	188	44.45 N	69.52 W
Sandy ≏, Or., U.S.	224	45.34 N	122.24 W
Sandy ≏, Va., U.S.	192	36.35 N	79.25 W
Sandy Bay c, Nic.	236	14.28 N	83.16 W
Sandy Bay c, Ma., U.S.	283	42.40 N	70.37 W
Sandy Bay Indian Reserve ◆[4]	184	50.33 N	98.40 W
Sandy Bay Mountain ∧	188	45.47 N	70.25 W
Sandy Beach	210	43.04 N	78.55 W
Sandy Branch ≏	284c	39.03 N	77.16 W
Sandy Cape ›, Austl.	166	41.25 S	144.45 E
Sandy Cape ›, Austl.	166	24.42 S	153.17 E
Sandy Creek	212	43.38 N	76.05 W
Sandy Creek ≏, Austl.	166	32.10 S	144.39 E
Sandy Creek ≏, U.S.	196	34.25 N	99.35 W
Sandy Creek ≏, U.S.	196	36.50 N	98.10 W
Sandy Creek ≏, Il., U.S.	219	39.34 N	90.35 W
Sandy Creek ≏, N.Y., U.S.	212	43.44 N	76.15 W
Sandy Creek ≏, N.Y., U.S.	212	43.20 N	77.55 W
Sandy Creek ≏, N.C., U.S.	192	36.08 N	78.02 W
Sandy Creek ≏, Oh., U.S.	214	40.38 N	81.26 W
Sandy Creek ≏, Pa., U.S.	214	41.18 N	79.51 W
Sandy Creek ≏, Tx., U.S.	196	30.34 N	98.26 W
Sandy Creek ≏, Tx., U.S.	222	29.02 N	96.33 W
Sandy Creek, East Branch ≏	210	43.17 N	78.03 W
Sandy Creek, North Branch ≏	212	43.51 N	75.58 W
Sandy Creek, West Branch ≏	210	43.17 N	78.03 W
Sandy Desert ◆[2]	128	28.40 N	62.30 E
Sandy Hook, Ct., U.S.	207	41.25 N	73.16 W
Sandy Hook, Ky., U.S.	192	38.05 N	83.07 W
Sandy Hook, Ms., U.S.	194	31.02 N	89.48 W
Sandy Hook ›[2]	208	40.27 N	74.00 W
Sandy Hook Bay c	276	40.26 N	74.03 W
Sandykači	128	36.33 N	62.34 E
Sandy Key I	220	25.02 N	81.01 W
Sandy Lake	214	41.20 N	80.04 W
Sandy Lake ⊜, Nf., Can.	186	49.16 N	57.00 W
Sandy Lake ⊜, On., Can.	184	53.02 N	93.00 W
Sandy Lake ⊜, On., Can.	212	44.33 N	78.24 W
Sandy Lick Creek ≏	214	41.09 N	79.05 W
Sandy Point ›, Austl.	168b	34.16 S	138.09 E
Sandy Point ›, Trin.	241r	11.09 N	60.50 W
Sandy Point ›, R.I., U.S.	207	41.14 N	71.35 W
Sandy Point Town	238	17.22 N	62.50 W
Sandy Ridge	214	40.49 N	78.14 W
Sandy Springs	192	33.55 N	84.22 W
Sandyville, Md., U.S.	208	39.31 N	76.55 W
Sandyville, Oh., U.S.	214	40.38 N	81.23 W
Sandžak ◆[1]	38	43.10 N	19.30 E
San Eladio	258	34.46 S	59.11 W
San Elizario	200	31.35 N	106.16 W
San Emigdio Creek ≏	228	35.02 N	119.11 W
San Emilio	116	17.14 N	120.37 E
Sanen ≏	115a	8.23 S	113.37 E
San Enrique	252	35.47 S	60.22 W
San Estanislao	252	24.39 S	56.26 W
San Esteban	236	15.17 N	85.52 W
San Esteban, Isla I	232	28.42 N	112.36 W
San Esteban de Gormaz	34	41.35 N	3.12 W
San Fele	68	40.49 N	15.32 E

	English	Deutsch	Español	Français	Português
≏	River	Fluß	Río	Rivière	Rio
≊	Canal	Kanal	Canal	Canal	Canal
⌞	Waterfall, Rapids	Wasserfall, Stromschnellen	Cascada, Rápidos	Chute d'eau, Rapides	Cascata, Rápidos
ʊ	Strait	Meeresstraße	Estrecho	Détroit	Estreito
c	Bay, Gulf	Bucht, Golf	Bahía, Golfo	Baie, Golfe	Baía, Golfo
⊜	Lake, Lakes	See, Seen	Lago, Lagos	Lac, Lacs	Lago, Lagos
≡	Swamp	Sumpf	Pantano	Marais	Pântano
⊓	Ice Features, Glacier	Eis- und Gletscherformen	Accidentes Glaciales	Formes glaciaires	Acidentes glaciares
⫪	Other Hydrographic Features	Andere Hydrographische Objekte	Otros Elementos Hidrográficos	Autres données hydrographiques	Outros acidentes hidrográficos
⊹	Submarine Features	Untermeerische Objekte	Accidentes Submarinos	Formes de relief sous-marin	Acidentes submarinos
□	Political Unit	Politische Einheit	Unidad Política	Entité politique	Unidade política
ᵾ	Cultural Institution	Kulturelle Institution	Institución Cultural	Institution culturelle	Instituição cultural
⊥	Historical Site	Historische Stätte	Sitio Histórico	Site historique	Sitio histórico
♠	Recreational Site	Erholungs- und Ferienort	Sitio de Recreo	Centre de loisirs	Area de Lazer
⊠	Airport	Flughafen	Aeropuerto	Aéroport	Aeroporto
■	Military Installation	Militäranlage	Instalación Militar	Installation militaire	Instalação militar
◆	Miscellaneous	Verschiedenes	Misceláneo	Divers	Diversos

San Felice (Sankt Felix) 64 46.30 N 11.08 E
San Felice Circeo 66 41.14 N 13.05 E
San Felice sul Panaro 64 44.50 N 11.08 E
San Felipe, Chile 252 32.45 S 70.44 W
San Felipe, Col. 246 1.55 N 67.06 W
San Felipe, Méx. 232 31.00 N 114.52 W
San Felipe, Méx. 234 21.29 N 101.13 W
San Felipe, Pil. 116 15.04 N 120.04 E
San Felipe, Tx., U.S. 222 29.48 N 96.06 W
San Felipe, Ven. 246 10.20 N 68.44 W
San Felipe, Castillo de ⊥ 236 15.39 N 89.01 W
San Felipe, Cayos de II 240p 21.58 N 83.30 W
San Felipe Aztatán 234 22.23 N 105.24 W
San Felipe Creek ≐ 204 33.09 N 115.46 W
San Felipe de Vichayal 248 4.52 S 81.05 W
San Felipe Indian Reservation ♦4 200 35.26 N 106.26 W
San Felipe Jalapa de Díaz 234 18.04 N 96.32 W
San Felipe Nuevo Mercurio 232 24.22 N 102.06 W
San Felipe Pueblo 200 35.27 N 106.28 W
San Félix ≐ 236 8.10 N 81.51 W
San Félix, Isla I 244 26.17 S 80.05 W
San Ferdinando di Puglia 68 41.18 N 16.04 E
San Fermín 196 26.20 N 104.49 W
San Fernando, Arg. 258 34.26 S 58.34 W
San Fernando, Chile 252 34.35 S 71.00 W
San Fernando, Esp. 34 36.28 N 6.12 W
San Fernando, Méx. 196 28.32 N 100.54 W
San Fernando, Méx. 200 31.16 N 110.36 W
San Fernando, Méx. 232 24.50 N 98.10 W
San Fernando, Méx. 234 16.52 N 93.13 W
San Fernando, Pil. 116 16.37 N 120.19 E
San Fernando, Pil. 116 12.30 N 123.46 E
San Fernando, Pil. 116 15.01 N 120.41 E
San Fernando, Trin. 241r 10.17 N 61.28 W
San Fernando, Ca., U.S. 228 34.16 N 118.26 W
San Fernando, Ven. 246 7.54 N 67.28 W
San Fernando □5 288 34.28 S 58.34 W
San Fernando, Aeródromo ⊠ 288 34.27 S 58.35 W
San Fernando Airport ⊠ 280 34.17 N 118.25 W
San Fernando Creek ≐ 196 27.28 N 97.46 W
San Fernando de Atabapo 246 4.03 N 67.42 W
San Fernando de Henares 266a 40.26 N 3.32 W
San Fernando del Valle de Catamarca 252 28.28 S 65.47 W
San Fernando Mission v1 280 34.16 N 118.28 W
San Fernando Point › 116 16.38 N 120.17 E
San Fernando Valley V 280 34.13 N 118.27 W
San Fili 68 39.20 N 16.09 E
San Filippo del Mela, It. 70 38.10 N 15.17 E
San Filippo del Mela, It. 70 38.10 N 15.17 E
Sånfjället ▲ 26 62.17 N 13.32 E
Sånfjällets Nationalpark ♦ 26 62.20 N 13.40 E
San Floriano 64 46.02 N 12.18 E
Sanford, Co., U.S. 200 37.15 N 105.54 W
Sanford, Fl., U.S. 220 28.48 N 81.16 W
Sanford, Me., U.S. 188 43.26 N 70.46 W
Sanford, Mi., U.S. 190 43.40 N 84.22 W
Sanford, N.C., U.S. 192 35.28 N 79.10 W
Sanford, Tx., U.S. 196 35.42 N 101.32 W
Sanford ≐ 162 27.22 S 115.53 E
Sanford, Mount ▲ 180 62.13 N 144.09 W
San Francesco, Convento v1, It. 66 42.28 N 12.45 E
San Francesco, Convento v1, It. 267a 42.03 N 12.46 E
San Francisco, Arg. 252 31.26 S 62.05 W
San Francisco, Col. 246 1.11 N 76.53 W
San Francisco, C.R. 236 9.49 N 85.15 W
San Francisco, El Sal. 236 13.42 N 88.06 W
San Francisco, Pan. 236 8.15 N 80.58 W
San Francisco, Pil. 116 8.30 N 125.56 E
San Francisco, Pil. 116 10.04 N 125.09 E
San Francisco, Ca., U.S. 226 37.46 N 122.25 W
San Francisco, Ca., U.S. 282 37.46 N 122.25 W
San Francisco □6 226 37.45 N 122.22 W
San Francisco ≐, Arg. 252 23.16 S 64.03 W
San Francisco → São Francisco ≐, Bra. 242 10.30 S 36.24 W
San Francisco ≐, U.S. 200 32.59 N 109.22 W
San Francisco, Arroyo ≐ 288 34.43 S 58.19 W
San Francisco, Paso de ⟩⟨ 252 26.53 S 68.19 W
San Francisco, University of v2 282 37.46 N 122.26 W
San Francisco Bay c 226 37.43 N 122.17 W
San Francisco Creek ≐ 196 29.53 N 102.19 W
San Francisco Culhuacán ♦8 286a 19.20 N 99.08 W
San Francisco de Borja 232 27.53 N 106.41 W
San Francisco de Horizonte 196 25.56 N 103.26 W
San Francisco de Lajas 234 23.07 N 105.07 W
San Francisco de la Paz 236 14.55 N 86.14 W
San Francisco del Chañar 252 29.47 S 63.56 W
San Francisco del Monte de Oro 252 32.36 S 66.08 W
San Francisco del Oro 232 26.52 N 105.51 W
San Francisco del Rincón 234 21.01 N 101.51 W
San Francisco de Macoris 238 19.18 N 70.15 W
San Francisco de Mostazal 252 33.59 S 70.43 W
San Francisco el Grande, Iglesia de v1 266a 40.25 N 3.43 W
San Francisco International Airport ⊠ 226 37.37 N 122.23 W
San Francisco Ixhuatán 234 16.22 N 94.29 W
San Francisco Libre 236 12.30 N 86.18 W
San Francisco Maritime National Historical Park ♦ 282 37.48 N 122.27 W
San Francisco-Oakland Bay Bridge ♦5 282 37.48 N 122.22 W
San Francisco State Fish and Game Refuge ♦4 282 37.35 N 122.25 W
San Francisco State University v2 282 37.43 N 122.28 W
San Francisco Tlalcilalcalpa 234 19.18 N 99.46 W
San Francisco Tlaltenco ♦8 286a 19.17 N 99.01 W
San Francisco Zoological Gardens ♦ 282 37.44 N 122.30 W
San Francisquito Creek ≐ 282 37.28 N 122.07 W
San Franco, Cerro ▲ 236 15.25 N 87.18 W
San Fratello 70 38.01 N 14.36 E
San Fratello ≐ 70 38.02 N 14.34 E
Sanga, Ang. 152 11.07 S 15.22 E
Sanga, Burkina 150 11.10 N 0.10 E
Sanga, Mali 150 14.28 N 3.19 W
Sanga, R.D.C. 154 7.02 S 28.21 E
San Gabriel, Ec. 246 0.36 N 77.49 W
San Gabriel, Ca., U.S. 228 34.05 N 118.06 W
San Gabriel ≐, Ca., U.S. 280 33.45 N 118.07 W
San Gabriel ≐, Tx., U.S. 222 30.46 N 97.01 W
San Gabriel, Isla I 258 34.28 S 57.54 W
San Gabriel, North Fork ≐, Ca., U.S. 280 34.15 N 117.52 W
San Gabriel, North Fork ≐, Tx., U.S. 196 30.38 N 97.41 W
San Gabriel, South Fork ≐ 196 30.38 N 97.41 W
San Gabriel Arcangel, Mission v1 280 34.06 N 118.06 W
San Gabriel Chilac 234 18.19 N 97.21 W
San Gabriel Dam ♦6 280 34.13 N 117.52 W
San Gabriel Mountains ⩘ 228 34.20 N 118.00 W
San Gabriel Peak ▲ 280 34.15 N 118.06 W
San Gabriel Reservoir ⊜1 228 34.13 N 117.51 W
Sängäçal burnu › 84 40.07 N 49.30 E
San Galgano, Abbazia di v1 66 43.10 N 11.10 E
Şangaly 24 61.08 N 43.19 E
Sangamankanda Point › 122 7.01 N 81.52 E
Sangamner 122 19.34 N 74.13 E
Sangamon □6 219 39.47 N 89.40 W
Sangamon ≐ 194 40.07 N 90.20 W
Sangamon, South Fork ≐ 219 39.48 N 89.32 W
Sanga Puitã 255 22.40 S 55.36 W
Sangar 74 63.55 N 127.31 E
Sangar Saray 120 34.24 N 70.38 E
Sangasanga-dalam 112 0.40 S 117.14 E
Sanga Sanga Island I 116 5.04 N 119.47 E
Sangat 123 30.05 N 74.50 E
Sangatte 50 50.56 N 1.45 E
San Gavino Monreale 71 39.33 N 8.47 E
Sangay ▲1 246 2.00 S 78.20 W
Sangay, Parque Nacional ♦ 246 1.50 S 78.20 W
Sangayán, Isla I 248 13.51 S 76.28 W
Sang Bast 128 35.59 N 59.46 E
Sangbé 152 6.03 N 12.28 E
Sangchris Lake ⊜1 219 39.35 N 89.30 W
Sangchris Lake State Park ♦ 219 39.38 N 89.28 W
Sangchungshih 100 25.04 N 121.29 E
Sangeang, Pulau I 115b 8.12 S 119.04 E
Sang-e Māsheh 120 33.08 N 67.27 E
San Gemini 66 42.37 N 12.33 E
San Genesio Atesino 64 46.32 N 11.20 E
Sangenjaya ♦8 268 35.38 N 139.40 E
Sanger, Ca., U.S. 226 36.42 N 119.33 W
Sanger, Tx., U.S. 196 33.21 N 97.10 W
Sangera 38 47.38 N 28.09 E
Sangerhausen 54 51.28 N 11.17 E
San Germán 240m 18.05 N 67.03 W
San Germano Vercellese 62 45.21 N 8.15 E
San Geronimo 226 38.01 N 122.39 W
San Gerónimo, Arroyo ≐ 258 33.57 S 56.05 W
Sangerville 188 45.09 N 69.21 W
Sanggan ≐ 90 40.21 N 115.21 E
Sanggar, Teluk c 115b 8.20 S 118.18 E
Sanggau 112 0.08 N 110.36 E
Sangge-ri ♦8 271b 37.41 N 127.05 E
Sanggin Dalai 102 38.11 N 105.17 E
Sanggona 112 3.52 S 121.46 E
Sangha □5, Centraf. 152 3.35 N 16.20 E
Sangha □5, Congo 152 1.00 N 15.30 E
Sangha ≐ 152 1.13 S 16.49 E
Sanghar 120 26.02 N 68.57 E
San Giacomo (Sankt Jakob in Pfitsch) 64 46.57 N 11.36 E
San Giacomo Filippo 58 46.20 N 9.21 E
Sangihe, Kepulauan II 112 3.00 N 125.30 E
Sangihe, Pulau I 112 3.35 N 125.32 E
Sangiin dalaj nuur ⊜ 88 49.17 N 99.00 E
San Gil 246 6.33 N 73.08 W
Sangilen, chrebet ⩘ 88 50.18 N 96.30 E
San Gimignano 66 43.28 N 11.02 E
San Ginesio 66 43.06 N 13.19 E
San Gion 58 46.38 N 8.50 E
San Giorgio 68 40.51 N 14.23 E
San Giorgio Canavese 62 45.20 N 7.48 E
San Giorgio della Richinvelda 64 46.03 N 12.52 E
San Giorgio del Sannio 68 41.04 N 14.51 E
San Giorgio di Lomellina 62 45.10 N 8.47 E
San Giorgio di Nogaro 64 45.50 N 13.13 E
San Giorgio di Piano 64 44.39 N 11.22 E
San Giorgio Ionico 68 40.27 N 17.23 E
San Giorgio la Molara 68 41.16 N 14.55 E
San Giorgio Lucano 68 40.07 N 16.23 E
San Giorgio Monferrato 62 45.07 N 8.23 E
San Giorgio Morgeto 68 38.23 N 16.06 E
San Giorgio Piacentino 62 44.57 N 9.44 E
San Giorgio su Legnano 266b 45.34 N 8.55 E
San Giovanni (Sankt Johann) 64 46.38 N 11.44 E
San Giovanni al Timavo (Sankt Johann in Ahrn) 64 46.58 N 11.57 E
San Giovanni a Piro 68 40.03 N 15.27 E
San Giovanni-Bianco 58 45.52 N 9.39 E
San Giovanni d'Asso 66 43.09 N 11.35 E
San Giovanni Gemini 70 37.38 N 13.39 E
San Giovanni Ilarione 64 45.30 N 11.15 E
San Giovanni in Croce 64 45.05 N 10.22 E
San Giovanni in Fiore 68 39.15 N 16.42 E
San Giovanni in Laterano v1 267a 41.53 N 12.30 E
San Giovanni in Persiceto 64 44.38 N 11.11 E
San Giovanni la Punta 70 37.35 N 15.07 E
San Giovanni Lupatoto 64 45.23 N 11.03 E
San Giovanni Rotondo 68 41.42 N 15.44 E
San Giovanni Suergiu 71 39.07 N 8.31 E
San Giovanni Valdarno 66 43.34 N 11.32 E
San Giuliano, Lago di ⊜ 68 40.37 N 16.30 E
San Giuliano Milanese 266b 45.24 N 9.17 E
San Giuliano Terme 66 43.46 N 10.26 E
San Giuseppe, It. 62 44.22 N 8.18 E
San Giuseppe, It. 70 37.58 N 13.11 E
San Giuseppe Vesuviano 68 40.50 N 14.30 E
San Giustino 66 43.33 N 12.10 E
San Giusto, Aeroporto di ⊠ 66 43.41 N 10.21 E
San Giusto Canavese 62 45.19 N 7.49 E
Sangju 98 36.26 N 128.09 E
Sāngkapura 115a 5.52 S 112.40 E
Sângkê ≐ 110 13.13 N 103.41 E
Sangkhai 110 14.39 N 103.52 E
Sangkulirang 112 0.59 N 117.58 E
Sāngla 123 31.43 N 73.23 E
Sangley Point › 259f 14.30 N 120.55 E
Sāngli 122 16.52 N 74.34 E
Sanglin 100 27.54 N 114.46 E
Sangluoshu 98 37.31 N 117.43 E
Sangmélima 152 2.56 N 11.59 E
Sangngagqoiling 120 28.33 N 93.00 E
Sangnyŏng-ni 98 38.14 N 126.54 E
Sango 270 34.36 N 135.42 E
San Godenzo 66 43.55 N 11.37 E
Sāngole 122 17.26 N 75.12 E
Sangolquí 246 0.19 S 78.27 W
San Gorgonio Mountain ▲ 204 34.06 N 116.50 W
San Gottardo, Passo del ⟩⟨ 58 46.33 N 8.34 E
Sangou 98 41.02 N 118.11 E
Sangre de Cristo Mountains ⩘ 200 37.30 N 105.15 W
San Gregorio, Arg. 252 34.19 S 62.02 W
San Gregorio, It. 66 42.19 N 13.29 E
San Gregorio, Ca., U.S. 226 37.19 N 122.23 W
San Gregorio, Ur. 252 32.37 S 55.40 W
San Gregorio, Ur. 258 33.57 S 56.45 W
San Gregorio ♦8 286a 19.15 N 99.03 W
San Gregorio, Arroyo ≐ 258 33.59 S 56.50 W
San Gregorio Creek ≐ 282 37.19 N 122.25 W
San Gregorio Magno 68 40.39 N 15.24 E
San Gregorio State Beach ♦ 282 37.19 N 122.24 W
Sangre Grande 241r 10.35 N 61.07 W
Sangro ≐ 66 42.14 N 14.32 E
Sangrūr 123 30.14 N 75.50 E
Sangsang 120 29.25 N 86.40 E
Sangshuyuan 86 42.23 N 88.30 E
Sangsues, Lac aux ⊜ 190 46.29 N 77.57 W
Sangtuda 85 38.04 N 69.04 E
Sanguandian 100 31.19 N 118.05 E
Sanguang 106 31.47 N 121.16 E
Sanguanmiao 100 32.25 N 114.04 E
Sanguanyingzi 104 41.39 N 120.44 E
Sangudo 182 53.53 N 114.54 W
Sangue, Rio do ≐ 248 11.01 S 58.39 W
Sangüesa 34 42.35 N 1.17 W
Sanguinetto 64 45.11 N 11.09 E
Sanguliu 104 40.45 N 124.14 E
Sangurli 272c 18.56 N 73.07 E
Sangutane ≐ 156 24.07 S 33.47 E
Sangvor, Taj. 85 38.47 N 71.12 E
Sangvor, Taj. 85 38.53 N 71.06 E
Sangwa 154 5.30 S 26.00 E
Sangya 120 30.52 N 91.40 E
Sangyuanbao 105 40.15 N 115.32 E
Sangyuanpu 106 31.37 N 118.53 E
Sangyuanzhen 107 30.30 N 103.26 E
Sangzhi 102 29.18 N 110.02 E
Sangzidian 98 36.46 N 116.55 E
Sanhe, Zhg. 100 24.24 N 116.34 E
Sanhe, Zhg. 105 39.59 N 117.04 E
Sanhechang, Zhg. 102 31.22 N 106.48 E
Sanhechang, Zhg. 107 30.04 N 105.01 E
Sanhecun 98 42.28 N 129.39 E
Sanheji 100 32.42 N 117.55 E
Sanhekou 106 31.50 N 120.08 E
Sanhetun 104 42.38 N 123.38 E
Sanhezhan 89 52.34 N 126.02 E
Sanhezhen 100 31.30 N 117.14 E
Sanhezhuang 105 40.04 N 116.18 E
San Hipólito, Punta › 232 26.59 N 113.59 W
Sanhsient'ai I 100 23.08 N 121.25 E
Sanhsing 100 24.40 N 121.39 E
Sanhu 100 27.55 N 115.24 E
Sanhui, Zhg. 107 30.06 N 106.26 E
Sanhui, Zhg. 107 29.57 N 105.53 E
Sanhūr 142 29.25 N 30.46 E
Sanhūr al-Madīnah 142 31.07 N 30.44 E
Sani 100 24.25 N 120.46 E
Sanibel 220 26.26 N 82.01 W
Sanibel Island I 220 26.27 N 82.06 W
Sānī Bherī ≐ 124 28.42 N 82.16 E
San Ignacio, Arg. 252 27.16 S 55.32 W
San Ignacio, C.R. 236 9.48 N 84.09 W
San Ignacio, Hond. 236 14.38 N 87.02 W
San Ignacio, Méx. 232 27.27 N 112.51 W
San Ignacio, Méx. 234 23.12 N 100.12 W
San Ignacio, Méx. 234 23.55 N 106.25 W
San Ignacio, Para. 252 26.52 S 57.03 W
San Ignacio, Perú 248 5.08 S 78.59 W
San Ignacio, Isla I 232 25.25 N 108.54 W
San Ignacio, Laguna ⊜ 232 26.54 N 113.13 W
San Ignacio de Moxo 248 14.53 S 65.36 W
San Ignacio de Velasco 248 16.23 S 60.59 W
San Ildefonso, Cape › 116 16.02 N 121.59 E
San Ildefonso, Cerro ▲ 236 15.31 N 88.17 W
San Ildefonso Indian Reservation ♦4 200 35.53 N 106.08 W
San Ildefonso la Granja 34 40.54 N 4.00 W
San Ildefonso Peninsula ›1 116 16.10 N 122.05 E
San Ildefonso Villa Alta 234 17.21 N 96.09 W
San'in-kaigan-kokuritsu-kōen ♦ 96 35.38 N 134.38 E
Sanino 265a 59.50 N 29.54 E
Sani Pass ⟩⟨ 158 29.34 S 29.19 E
San Isidro, Arg. 252 28.27 S 65.44 W
San Isidro, Arg. 258 34.27 S 58.30 W
San Isidro, C.R. 236 9.22 N 83.42 W
San Isidro, Méx. 200 31.31 N 106.18 W
San Isidro, Nic. 236 12.56 N 86.12 W
San Isidro, Perú 286d 12.07 S 77.03 W
San Isidro, Pil. 116 11.24 N 124.21 E
San Isidro, Tx., U.S. 196 26.42 N 98.27 W
San Isidro □5 288 34.29 S 58.33 W
San Isidro el Real, Catedral de v1 266a 40.25 N 3.42 W
Sanitaria Springs 210 42.09 N 75.46 W
Sanitatas 156 18.11 S 12.47 E
Sanitz 54 54.04 N 12.22 E
San Jacinto, Col. 246 9.50 N 75.08 W
San Jacinto, Méx. 196 25.29 N 103.44 W
San Jacinto, Pil. 116 12.34 N 123.44 E
San Jacinto, Ca., U.S. 228 33.47 N 116.57 W
San Jacinto □6 222 30.35 N 95.10 W
San Jacinto ≐, Ca., U.S. 228 33.43 N 117.16 W
San Jacinto ≐, Tx., U.S. 222 29.46 N 95.05 W
San Jacinto, East Fork ≐ 222 30.05 N 95.09 W
San Jacinto, West Fork ≐ 222 30.02 N 95.15 W
San Jacinto Monument ⊥ 222 29.45 N 95.01 W
San Jacinto Peak ▲ 204 33.49 N 116.41 W
San Jacinto Valley V 228 33.50 N 117.05 W
Sanjahā 142 30.50 N 31.38 E
San Javier, Arg. 252 27.53 S 55.08 W
San Javier, Arg. 252 30.35 S 59.57 W
San Javier, Bol. 248 14.34 S 64.42 W
San Javier, Bol. 248 16.20 S 62.38 W
San Javier, Méx. 196 26.16 N 99.27 W
San Javier, Ur. 252 32.41 S 58.08 W
San Javier ≐ 252 31.30 S 60.20 W
San Javier de Loncomilla 252 35.35 S 71.45 W
Sanjāwi 120 30.17 N 68.21 E
Sanje 154 0.46 S 31.30 E
San Jeronimito 234 17.33 N 101.20 W
San Jerónimo, Guat. 236 15.03 N 90.12 W
San Jerónimo, Méx. 234 17.08 N 100.28 W
San Jerónimo Norte 252 31.33 S 61.05 W
Sanjiadian, Zhg. 105 40.09 N 116.36 E
Sanjiadian, Zhg. 105 39.58 N 116.06 E
Sanjiadian, Zhg. 105 39.22 N 115.58 E
Sanjiang, Zhg. 102 25.42 N 109.23 E
Sanjiang, Zhg. 107 29.33 N 104.03 E
Sanjiangzhen 107 30.31 N 103.48 E
Sanjiaocheng 102 36.47 N 104.40 E
Sanjiaopao 104 41.22 N 122.17 E
Sanjiaoshancun 104 40.42 N 122.49 E
Sanjiazhen 107 30.17 N 105.32 E
Sanjiazi, Zhg. 104 41.53 N 121.42 E
Sanjiazi, Zhg. 104 40.42 N 123.16 E
Sanjiazi, Zhg. 104 40.54 N 121.59 E
Sanjiazi, Zhg. 104 42.33 N 121.38 E
Sanjiazi, Zhg. 104 42.02 N 122.20 E
Sanjiaziyingzi 104 41.52 N 120.49 E
Sanjie, Zhg. 100 32.35 N 118.08 E
Sanjie, Zhg. 102 25.01 N 101.02 E
Sanjō 92 37.37 N 138.57 E
San Joaquín, Bol. 248 13.04 S 64.49 W
San Joaquín, Chile 286e 33.30 S 70.37 W
San Joaquín, Para. 252 24.57 S 56.07 W
San Joaquín, Pil. 116 10.35 N 122.08 E
San Joaquin, Ca., U.S. 226 36.36 N 120.11 W
San Joaquin □6 226 37.57 N 121.17 W
San Joaquín ≐, Bol. 248 13.08 S 63.41 W
San Joaquin ≐, Ca., U.S. 226 38.03 N 121.50 W
San Joaquin, Middle Fork ≐ 226 37.32 N 119.11 W
San Joaquin, North Fork ≐ 226 37.32 N 119.11 W
San Joaquin, South Fork ≐ 226 37.26 N 119.14 W
San Joaquin Valley V 204 36.50 N 120.10 W
San Jon 196 35.06 N 103.19 W
San Jorge, Arg. 252 31.54 S 61.52 W
San Jorge, El Sal. 236 13.25 N 88.21 W
San Jorge, Nic. 236 11.27 N 85.48 W
San Jorge ≐ 246 9.07 N 74.44 W
San Jorge, Bahía de c 200 31.12 N 113.15 W
San Jorge, Cabo › 254 45.47 S 67.21 W
San Jorge, Canal de → Saint George's Channel ⊔ 28 52.00 N 6.00 W
San Jorge, Golfo c 254 46.00 S 67.00 W
San Jorge Island I 175e 8.27 S 159.35 E
San José, Arg. 252 27.46 S 55.47 W
San José, C.R. 236 9.56 N 84.05 W
San José, Méx. 196 28.16 N 100.15 W
San Jose, N. Mar. Is. 174n 15.09 N 145.43 E
San José, Para. 252 25.33 S 56.45 W
San Jose, Pil. 116 10.45 N 121.56 E
San Jose, Pil. 116 15.48 N 121.00 E
San Jose, Pil. 116 12.27 N 121.03 E
San Jose, Ca., U.S. 226 37.20 N 121.53 W
San Jose, Ca., U.S. 282 37.20 N 121.53 W
San Jose, Il., U.S. 194 40.18 N 89.36 W
San Jose, N.M., U.S. 200 35.23 N 105.28 W
San José, Ven. 286c 10.34 N 66.57 W
San José □4 236 9.40 N 84.00 W
San José □5 258 34.15 S 56.45 W
San José □7 286b 22.57 N 82.14 W
San Jose ≐, B.C., Can. 182 52.14 N 122.15 W
San José ≐, Ur. 258 34.38 S 56.29 W
San José, Arroyo ≐ 282 38.03 N 122.30 W
San José, Golfo c 254 42.20 S 64.18 W
San José, Isla I, Méx. 232 25.00 N 110.38 W
San José, Isla I, Pan. 246 8.15 N 79.07 W
San José, Laguna c 240m 18.25 N 66.01 W
San Jose, Mission v1 282 37.32 N 121.55 W
San Jose, Río ≐ 200 34.52 N 107.01 W
San Jose Arena ♦ 282 37.20 N 121.54 W
San José Ayuquila 234 17.58 N 97.57 W
San José Batuc 232 29.15 N 109.44 W
San José Buena Vista 236 13.49 N 90.19 W
San Jose Creek ≐ 280 34.01 N 118.03 W
San José de Aura 196 27.34 N 101.23 W
San José de Bácum 232 27.32 N 110.09 W
San José de Buan 116 12.02 N 125.01 E
San José de Chiquitos 248 17.51 S 60.47 W
San José de Copán 236 14.54 N 88.44 W
San José de Feliciano 252 30.23 S 58.45 W
San José de Galipán 286c 10.35 N 66.54 W
San José de Galipán, Quebrada ≐ 286c 10.37 N 66.54 W
San José de Gracia 234 20.40 N 102.35 W
San José de Guanipa 246 8.54 N 64.09 W
San José de Guaribe 246 9.52 N 65.48 W
San José de Iturbide 234 21.00 N 100.23 W
San José de Jáchal 252 30.14 S 68.45 W
San José de la Esquina 252 33.06 S 61.42 W
San José de la Parilla 234 23.44 N 104.07 W
San José de la Popa 196 26.10 N 100.47 W
San José de las Flores 234 17.20 N 95.24 W
San José de las Lajas 240p 22.58 N 82.09 W
San José de las Raíces 232 24.35 N 100.14 W
San José del Cabo 232 23.03 N 109.41 W
San José del Guaviare 246 2.35 N 72.38 W
San José de Llanetes 234 22.55 N 103.16 W
San José de los Molinos 248 13.57 S 75.41 W
San José de Lourdes 234 23.18 N 103.01 W
San José del Valle 234 23.20 N 98.24 W
San José de Mayo 258 34.20 S 56.42 W
San José de Ocuné 246 4.15 N 70.20 W
San José de Sisa 248 6.37 S 76.39 W
San José de Tiznados 246 9.23 N 67.33 W
San Jose Hills ⩘2 280 34.04 N 117.49 W
San Jose Island I 196 28.10 N 96.45 W
San Jose Municipal Airport ⊠ 226 37.22 N 121.56 W
San Jose State University v2 226 37.20 N 121.53 W
San Juan, Arg. 252 31.32 S 68.31 W
San Juan, Guat. 236 15.52 N 88.53 W
San Juan, Méx. 196 29.34 N 104.36 W
San Juan, Perú 248 15.21 S 75.10 W
San Juan, Pil. 116 13.50 N 121.24 E
San Juan, Pil. 116 16.40 N 120.20 E
San Juan, Pil. 116 8.25 N 126.20 E
San Juan, P.R. 240m 18.28 N 66.07 W
San Juan □4 252 31.00 S 69.00 W
San Juan □6 224 48.34 N 122.59 W
San Juan ≐, Arg. 252 32.17 S 67.22 W
San Juan ≐, B.C., Can. 224 48.34 N 124.24 W
San Juan ≐, Col. 246 4.03 N 77.27 W
San Juan ≐, Méx. 232 26.22 N 98.51 W
San Juan ≐, Méx. 234 18.36 N 95.40 W
San Juan ≐, Méx. 234 17.59 N 95.09 W
San Juan ≐, N.A. 236 10.56 N 83.42 W
San Juan ≐, Perú 248 13.27 S 76.11 W
San Juan ≐, Pil. 259f 14.14 N 121.01 E
San Juan ≐, S.A. 246 1.11 N 78.33 W
San Juan ≐, U.S. 200 37.18 N 110.28 W
San Juan ≐, Ur. 258 34.17 S 57.58 W
San Juan ≐, Ven. 246 10.14 N 62.38 W
San Juan, Bahía de c 240m 18.27 N 66.07 W
San Juan, Cabezas de › 240m 18.23 N 65.37 W
San Juan, Cabo ›, Arg. 254 54.44 S 63.44 W
San Juan, Cabo ›, Gui. Ecu. 152 1.08 N 9.23 E
San Juan, Embalse de ⊜1 34 40.30 N 4.15 W
San Juan, Pasaje de ⊔ 240m 18.24 N 65.37 W
San Juan, Pico ▲ 240p 21.59 N 80.09 W
San Juan, Port c 224 48.34 N 124.27 W
San Juan, Punta › 174z 27.03 S 109.22 W
San Juan Basin ⊻1 200 36.15 N 108.20 W
San Juan Bautista, Méx. 196 26.58 N 101.24 W
San Juan Bautista, Para. 252 26.38 S 57.10 W
San Juan Bautista, Ca., U.S. 226 36.51 N 121.32 W
San Juan Bautista State Historical Park ♦ 226 36.51 N 121.31 W
San Juan Capistrano 228 33.30 N 117.39 W
San Juan Capistrano Mission v1 228 33.31 N 117.40 W
San Juan Cotzal 236 15.26 N 91.01 W
San Juan Creek ≐, Ca., U.S. 226 35.40 N 120.22 W
San Juan Creek ≐, Ca., U.S. 228 33.28 N 117.41 W
San Juan de Abajo 234 20.48 N 105.13 W
San Juan de Aragón, Bosque ♦ 286a 19.28 N 99.04 W
San Juan de Aragón, Zoológico de ♦ 286a 19.28 N 99.05 W
San Juan de Colón 246 8.02 N 72.16 W
San Juan de Dios 286c 10.35 N 66.55 W
San Juan de Guadalupe 232 24.38 N 102.44 W
San Juan de la Maguana 238 18.48 N 71.14 W
San Juan de la Vega 234 20.38 N 100.46 W
San Juan del César 246 10.46 N 73.01 W
San Juan del Monte 269f 14.36 N 121.02 E
San Juan del Norte 236 10.55 N 83.42 W
San Juan del Oro ≐ 248 21.02 S 65.19 W
San Juan de los Cayos 246 11.10 N 68.25 W
San Juan de los Lagos 234 21.15 N 102.18 W
San Juan de los Lagos ≐ 234 21.18 N 102.33 W
San Juan de los Morros 246 9.55 N 67.21 W
San Juan del Río, Méx. 232 24.47 N 104.27 W
San Juan del Río, Méx. 234 20.23 N 100.00 W
San Juan del Salado 234 23.18 N 101.56 W
San Juan del Sur 236 11.15 N 85.52 W
San Juan de Lurigancho 286d 11.59 S 77.01 W
San Juan de Micay ≐ 246 3.05 N 77.32 W
San Juan de Miraflores 286d 12.11 S 76.57 W
San Juan de Payara 246 7.39 N 67.36 W
San Juan de Sabinas 196 27.55 N 101.18 W
San Juan Evangelista 234 17.54 N 95.08 W
San Juan Guichicovi 234 16.58 N 95.06 W
San Juanico 232 26.15 N 112.24 W
San Juanillo 236 10.02 N 85.44 W
San Juan Indian Reservation ♦4 200 36.03 N 106.04 W
San Juan Island I 224 48.32 N 123.05 W
San Juan Island National Historical Park ♦ 224 48.28 N 123.00 W
San Juan Islands II 224 48.36 N 122.50 W
San Juanito, Isla I 234 21.43 N 106.38 W
San Juan Ixcaquixtla 234 18.27 N 97.49 W
San Juan Ixtayopan ♦8 286a 19.14 N 99.00 W
San Juan Lachao 234 16.14 N 97.09 W
San Juan Mazatlán 234 17.02 N 95.25 W
San Juan Mountains ⩘ 200 37.35 N 107.10 W
San Juan Nepomuceno, Col. 246 9.57 N 75.05 W
San Juan Nepomuceno, Para. 252 26.06 S 55.58 W
San Juan Peyotán 234 22.24 N 104.21 W
San Juan Quiahije 234 16.17 N 97.20 W
San Juan Sacatepéquez 236 14.43 N 90.39 W
San Juan Teita 234 17.05 N 97.25 W
San Juan y Martínez 240p 22.16 N 83.50 W
San Julián, Méx. 234 21.01 N 102.10 W
San Julian, Pil. 116 11.45 N 125.27 E
San Julian, Quebrada ≐ 286c 10.37 N 66.51 W
San Justo, Arg. 252 30.47 S 60.35 W
San Justo, Arg. 258 34.40 S 58.33 W
San Justo, Aeródromo ⊠ 288 34.44 S 58.36 W
Sankanbiaiwa ▲ 150 8.56 N 10.48 W
Sankarani ≐ 150 12.01 N 8.19 W
Sankarankovil 122 9.10 N 77.33 E
Sankarpur 272b 22.51 N 88.27 E
Sānkdaha 126 22.46 N 89.10 E
Sankeng 100 23.36 N 112.48 E
Sankertown 214 40.28 N 78.35 W
Sankeshu 104 42.38 N 122.25 E
Sankeshwar 122 16.16 N 74.29 E
Sankey Brook ≐ 262 53.22 N 2.38 W
Sankh ≐ 124 22.15 N 84.48 E
Sankheda 120 22.10 N 73.35 E
Sankosh ≐ 124 26.48 N 89.56 E
Sānkra 120 21.18 N 82.39 E
Sānkrāil 272b 22.34 N 88.14 E
Sankt Aegyd am Neuwalde 61 47.52 N 15.35 E
Sankt Andrä 61 46.46 N 14.49 E
Sankt Andrä [-vor dem Hagenthale] 61 48.19 N 16.13 E
Sankt Andreasberg 54 51.43 N 10.31 E
Sankt Anton am Arlberg 58 47.08 N 10.16 E
Sankt Antönien 58 46.58 N 9.49 E
Sankt Augustin 56 50.40 N 7.16 E
Sankt Bartholomä v1 64 47.32 N 12.58 E
Sankt Blasien 58 47.46 N 8.07 E
Sankt Christopher-Nevis → Saint Kitts and Nevis □1 238 17.20 N 62.45 W
Sankt Florian v1 61 48.12 N 14.23 E
Sankt Gallen, Öst. 61 47.41 N 14.37 E
Sankt Gallen, Schw. 58 47.25 N 9.23 E
Sankt Gallen □3 58 47.10 N 9.08 E
Sankt Gallenkirch 58 47.01 N 9.59 E
Sankt Georgen, Dtsch. 58 47.59 N 7.47 E
Sankt Georgen, Öst. 61 46.43 N 14.55 E
Sankt Georgen im Attergau 64 47.56 N 13.29 E
Sankt Gertraud → Santa Gertrude 64 46.29 N 10.53 E
Sankt Gertrud ♦8 54 53.52 N 10.47 E
Sankt Gilgen 64 47.46 N 13.22 E
Sankt Goar 56 50.09 N 7.43 E
Sankt Goarshausen 56 50.09 N 7.44 E
Sankt Helena → Saint Helena □2 8 15.57 S 5.42 W
Sankt Hubert 56 51.23 N 6.26 E
Sankt Ingbert 56 49.17 N 7.06 E
Sankt Jakob → San Giacomo 64 46.57 N 11.36 E
Sankt Jakob im Lesachtal 64 46.41 N 12.56 E
Sankt Jakob im Rosental 61 46.33 N 14.03 E
Sankt Jakob in Defereggen 64 46.55 N 12.20 E
Sankt Johann → San Giovanni 64 46.38 N 11.44 E
Sankt Johann am Tauern 61 47.22 N 14.29 E
Sankt Johann im Pongau 64 47.21 N 13.12 E
Sankt Johann im Walde 64 46.54 N 12.37 E
Sankt Johann in Tirol 64 47.31 N 12.26 E
Sankt Kanzian 61 46.37 N 14.34 E
Sankt Leonhard → San Leonardo 64 46.49 N 11.15 E
Sankt Leonhard am Forst 61 48.09 N 15.17 E
Sankt Leonhard im Pitztal 64 47.04 N 10.51 E
Sankt Lorenz ♦8 54 53.51 N 10.40 E
Sankt Lorenz → Saint Lawrence ≐ 176 49.30 N 67.00 W
Sankt Lorenzen → San Lorenzo di Sebato 64 46.47 N 11.54 E
Sankt Lorenzen im Lesachtal 64 46.42 N 12.47 E
Sankt Lorenz-Golf → Saint Lawrence, Gulf of c 186 48.00 N 62.00 W
Sankt Lorenz-Insel → Saint Lawrence Island I 180 63.30 N 170.30 W
Sankt Margarethen an der Raab 61 47.03 N 15.45 E
Sankt Märgen 58 48.00 N 8.05 E
Sankt Margrethen 58 47.27 N 9.36 E
Sankt Martin 64 47.28 N 13.23 E
Sankt Martin an der Raab 61 46.55 N 16.08 E
Sankt Martin in Gsies → San Martino in Casies 64 46.49 N 12.14 E
Sankt Mauritz 52 51.57 N 7.39 E
Sankt Michael im Lungau 64 47.06 N 13.38 E
Sankt Michael in Obersteiermark 61 47.20 N 15.01 E
Sankt Michel → Mikkeli 26 61.41 N 27.15 E
Sankt Moritz 58 46.30 N 9.50 E
Sankt Niklaus 58 46.11 N 7.48 E
Sankt Nikolaus → San Nicolò d'Ultima 64 46.30 N 10.55 E
Sankt Oswald 60 48.54 N 13.25 E
Sankt Paul im Lavanttal 61 46.42 N 14.52 E
Sankt Peter 58 48.01 N 8.01 E
Sankt Peter v1 263 51.37 N 7.12 E
Sankt Peter am Kammersberg 61 47.11 N 14.11 E
Sankt Peter am Ottersbach 61 46.48 N 15.45 E
Sankt-Peterburg (Saint Petersburg), Ross. 76 59.55 N 30.15 E
Sankt-Peterburg (Saint Petersburg), Ross. 265a 59.55 N 30.15 E
Sankt-Peterburg, Gorod □6 265a 59.55 N 30.15 E
Sankt Peter in der Au 61 48.03 N 14.37 E
Sankt Peter-Ording 30 54.18 N 8.38 E
Sankt Pölten 61 48.12 N 15.37 E
Sankt-Quirinus-Dom v1 263 51.12 N 6.42 E
Sankt Stefan an der Gail 64 46.37 N 13.31 E
Sankt Stefan im Rosental 61 46.54 N 15.42 E
Sankt Ulrich → Ortisei 64 46.34 N 11.40 E
Sankt Valentin 61 48.10 N 14.32 E
Sankt Veit an der Glan 61 46.46 N 14.21 E
Sankt Veit an der Gölsen 61 48.03 N 15.40 E
Sankt Veit im Pongau 64 47.20 N 13.09 E
Sankt-Viktors-Dom v1 263 51.40 N 6.27 E
Sankt Vincent → Saint Vincent and the Grenadines □1 241h 13.15 N 61.12 W
Sankt Wallburg → Santa Valburga 64 46.33 N 11.00 E
Sankt Wendel 56 49.28 N 7.10 E
Sankt-Willibrodi-Dom v1 263 51.40 N 6.37 E
Sankt Wolfgang, Dtsch. 60 48.13 N 12.08 E
Sankt Wolfgang, Dtsch. 60 48.13 N 12.08 E
Sankt Wolfgang im Salzkammergut 64 47.44 N 13.27 E
Sankuru ≐ 152 4.17 S 20.25 E
San Lázaro 252 22.10 S 57.55 W
San Lázaro, Cabo › 232 24.48 N 112.19 W
San Lazaro Race Track ♦ 269f 14.37 N 120.59 E
San Lazzaro di Savena 64 44.28 N 11.25 E
San Leandro 226 37.43 N 122.09 W
San Leandro Creek ≐ 282 37.45 N 122.12 W
San Leo 66 43.54 N 12.21 E
San Leon 222 29.29 N 94.55 W
San Leonardo (Sankt Leonhard), It. 64 46.49 N 11.15 E
San Leonardo, Méx. 196 27.28 N 104.55 W
San Leonardo ≐ 70 37.59 N 13.41 E
San Leone 70 37.16 N 13.35 E
Sanlicheng 100 31.48 N 114.12 E
Sanlidian 100 30.48 N 118.15 E
Sanlifan 100 30.51 N 115.15 E
Sanlintang 106 31.08 N 121.29 E
Sanlipu 106 31.46 N 119.03 E
Sanliuji 100 32.08 N 116.19 E
Şanlıurfa 130 37.08 N 38.46 E
Şanlıurfa □4 130 37.20 N 39.15 E
San Lope 246 6.12 N 71.56 W
San Lorenzo, Arg. 252 28.08 S 58.46 W
San Lorenzo, Arg. 252 32.45 S 60.44 W
San Lorenzo, Bol. 248 21.26 S 64.47 W
San Lorenzo, Ec. 246 1.17 N 78.50 W
San Lorenzo, Hond. 236 13.25 N 87.27 W
San Lorenzo, It. 68 38.01 N 15.50 E
San Lorenzo, Méx. 196 25.37 N 97.55 W
San Lorenzo, Méx. 232 25.32 N 102.11 W
San Lorenzo, Nic. 236 12.23 N 85.40 W
San Lorenzo, P.R. 240m 18.11 N 65.58 W
San Lorenzo, Ca., U.S. 226 37.40 N 122.07 W
San Lorenzo, Ven. 246 9.47 N 71.04 W
San Lorenzo ≐, Méx. 232 24.15 N 107.24 W
San Lorenzo → Saint Lawrence ≐, N.A. 176 49.30 N 67.00 W
San Lorenzo ≐, Ca., U.S. 226 36.58 N 122.01 W
San Lorenzo, Bahía de c 236 13.19 N 87.30 W
San Lorenzo, Cabo › 246 1.04 S 80.56 W
San Lorenzo, Golfo del → Saint Lawrence, Gulf of c 186 48.00 N 62.00 W

Symbols in the index entries represent the broad categories identified in the key at the right. Symbols with superior numbers (⩘1) identify subcategories (see complete key on page I · 1).

Symbole im Register stellen die rechts im Schlüssel erklärten Kategorien dar. Symbole mit hochgestellten Ziffern (⩘1) bezeichnen Unterabteilungen einer Kategorie (vgl. vollständiger Schlüssel auf Seite I · 1).

Los símbolos incluídos en el texto del índice representan las grandes categorías identificadas con la clave a la derecha. Los símbolos con numeros en su parte superior (⩘1) identifican las subcategorías (véase la clave completa en la página I · 1).

Les symboles de l'index représentent les catégories indiquées dans la légende à droite. Les symboles suivis d'un indice (⩘1) représentent des sous-catégories (voir légende complète à la page I · 1).

Os símbolos incluídos no texto do índice representam as grandes categorias identificadas com a chave à direita. Os símbolos com números em sua parte superior (⩘1) identificam as subcategorias (veja-se a chave completa à página I · 1).

Symbol	English	Deutsch	Español	Français	Português
▲	Mountain	Berg	Montaña	Montagne	Montanha
⩘	Mountains	Gebirge	Montañas	Montagnes	Montanhas
⟩⟨	Pass	Paß	Paso	Col	Passo
V	Valley, Canyon	Tal, Cañon	Valle, Cañón	Vallée, Canyon	Vale, Canhão
≡	Plain	Ebene	Llano	Plaine	Planície
›	Cape	Kap	Cabo	Cap	Cabo
I	Island	Insel	Isla	Île	Ilha
II	Islands	Inseln	Islas	Îles	Ilhas
⊥	Other Topographic Features	Andere Topographische Objekte	Otros Elementos Topográficos	Autres données topographiques	Outros acidentes topográficos

ESPAÑOL: Nombre | Página | Lat.°′ | Long.°′ W = Oeste
FRANÇAIS: Nom | Page | Lat.°′ | Long.°′ W = Ouest
PORTUGUÊS: Nome | Página | Lat.°′ | Long.°′ W = Oeste

Nombre / Nom / Nome	Página / Page	Lat.°′	Long.°′
San Lorenzo, Isla I, Méx.	232	28.38 N	112.51 W
San Lorenzo, Isla I, Perú	248	12.05 S	77.15 W
San Lorenzo, Monte (Cerro Cochrane) ∧	254	47.37 S	72.19 W
San Lorenzo Bellizzi	68	39.53 N	16.20 E
San Lorenzo Creek ≃, Ca., U.S.	226	36.12 N	120.38 W
San Lorenzo Creek ≃, Ca., U.S.	282	37.39 N	122.09 W
San Lorenzo de El Escorial	34	40.35 N	4.09 W
San Lorenzo de la Parrilla	34	39.51 N	2.22 W
San Lorenzo del Vallo	68	39.40 N	16.18 E
San Lorenzo di Sebato (Sankt Lorenzen)	64	46.47 N	11.54 E
San Lorenzo in Campo	66	43.36 N	12.56 E
San Lorenzo Nuovo	66	42.41 N	11.54 E
San Lorenzo Tezonco ◆[8]	286a	19.18 N	99.04 W
San Luca	68	38.09 N	16.04 E
Sanlúcar de Barrameda	34	36.47 N	6.21 W
Sanlúcar la Mayor	34	37.23 N	6.12 W
San Lucas, Bol.	248	20.06 S	65.07 W
San Lucas, Ec.	246	3.45 S	79.15 W
San Lucas, Méx.	232	22.53 N	109.54 W
San Lucas, Ca., U.S.	226	36.08 N	121.01 W
San Lucas, Cabo ›	232	22.52 N	109.53 W
San Luis, Arg.	252	33.18 S	66.21 W
San Luis, Cuba	240p	20.12 N	75.51 W
San Luis, Cuba	240p	22.17 N	83.46 W
San Luis, Guat.	236	16.14 N	89.27 W
San Luis, Perú	286d	12.04 S	77.00 W
San Luis, Az., U.S.	200	32.04 N	111.57 W
San Luis, Co., U.S.	200	37.12 N	105.25 W
San Luis, Ven.	246	11.07 N	69.42 W
San Luis □[4]	252	34.00 S	66.00 W
San Luis ◆[8]	286b	23.05 N	82.20 W
San Luis ≃	234	17.13 N	100.55 W
San Luis, Arroyo ≃	258	34.10 S	57.44 W
San Luís, Laguna ⊜	248	13.45 S	64.00 W
San Luis, Sierra de ⋏	252	32.40 S	65.50 W
San Luis Acatlán	234	16.48 N	98.45 W
San Luis Creek ≃	200	37.42 N	105.44 W
San Luis de la Loma	234	17.18 N	100.55 W
San Luis de la Paz	234	21.18 N	100.31 W
San Luis del Cordero	232	25.26 N	104.18 W
San Luis del Palmar	252	27.31 S	58.34 W
San Luis Gonzaga	232	24.55 N	111.16 W
San Luis Gonzaga, Bahía c	232	29.48 N	114.22 W
San Luis Jilotepeque	236	14.39 N	89.44 W
San Luis Obispo	226	35.16 N	120.39 W
San Luis Obispo □[6]	226	35.30 N	120.30 W
San Luis Pass c	222	29.05 N	95.08 W
San Luis Peak ∧	200	37.59 N	106.56 W
San Luis Potosí	234	22.09 N	100.59 W
San Luis Potosí □[3]	234	22.30 N	100.30 W
San Luis Reservoir ⊜[1]	226	37.07 N	121.05 W
San Luis Rey	228	33.14 N	117.20 W
San Luis Rey ≃	204	33.12 N	117.24 W
San Luis Rey, Mission ⊍[1]	228	33.14 N	117.20 W
San Luis Río Colorado	232	32.29 N	114.48 W
San Luis Soyatlán	234	20.12 N	103.18 W
San Luis State Recreation Area ♠	226	37.04 N	121.05 W
San Luis Valley V	200	37.25 N	106.00 W
Sanluri	71	39.34 N	8.54 E
San Macario	266b	45.36 N	8.47 E
Sanmaiden	270	34.34 N	135.51 E
San Mamete	58	46.02 N	9.04 E
San Mango d'Aquino	68	39.03 N	16.11 E
San Manuel, Arg.	252	37.47 S	58.50 W
San Manuel, Méx.	234	17.37 N	93.24 W
San Manuel, Az., U.S.	200	32.35 N	110.37 W
San Marcelino	116	14.58 N	120.09 E
San Marcello Pistoiese	66	44.03 N	10.47 E
San Marcial ≃	232	28.04 N	110.44 W
San Marco, Capo ›, It.	70	37.30 N	13.01 E
San Marco, Capo ›, It.	71	39.51 N	8.26 E
San Marco Argentano	68	39.33 N	16.07 E
San Marco dei Cavoti	68	41.18 N	14.53 E
San Marco in Lamis	68	41.43 N	15.38 E
San Marco la Catola	68	41.31 N	15.00 E
San Marcos, Chile	252	30.56 S	71.03 W
San Marcos, Col.	246	8.39 N	75.08 W
San Marcos, C.R.	236	9.40 N	84.01 W
San Marcos, El Sal.	236	13.39 N	89.11 W
San Marcos, Guat.	236	14.58 N	91.48 W
San Marcos, Hond.	236	14.24 N	88.56 W
San Marcos, Hond.	236	15.17 N	88.23 W
San Marcos, Méx.	234	16.48 N	99.21 W
San Marcos, Méx.	234	20.02 N	99.20 W
San Marcos, Méx.	234	20.47 N	104.11 W
San Marcos, Ca., U.S.	228	33.08 N	117.09 W
San Marcos, Tx., U.S.	196	29.52 N	97.56 W
San Marcos □[5]	236	15.00 N	91.55 W
San Marcos ≃	196	29.29 N	97.28 W
San Marcos, Isla I	232	27.13 N	112.06 W
San Marcos, Laguna ⊜	234	20.17 N	103.33 W
San Marcos, Universidad Nacional de ⊍[2]	286d	12.04 S	77.05 W
San Marcos Arteaga	234	17.45 N	97.58 W
San Marcos de Colón	236	13.26 N	86.48 W
San Marino, S. Mar.	66	43.55 N	12.28 E
San Marino, Ca., U.S.	280	34.07 N	118.06 W
San Marino □[1], Europe	22	43.56 N	12.25 E
San Marino □[1], Europe	66	43.56 N	12.25 E
San Martín, Arg.	252	29.14 S	65.46 W
San Martín, Arg.	252	33.04 S	68.28 W
San Martín → General San Martín, Arg.	258	34.34 S	58.32 W
San Martín, Col.	246	3.42 N	73.42 W
San Martin, Ca., U.S.	226	37.05 N	121.37 W
San Martín, Ur.	258	33.45 S	57.37 W
San Martín □[5]	248	7.00 S	76.50 W
San Martín ≃, Bol.	248	11.50 S	67.16 W
San Martín ≃, Bol.	248	13.08 S	63.43 W
San Martín ⊍[3]	9	68.07 S	67.08 W
San Martín, Arroyo ≃	258	33.49 S	57.44 W
San Martín, Cuchilla ⋏[2]	258	33.45 S	57.54 W
San Martín, Lago (Lago O'Higgins) ⊜	254	49.00 S	72.40 W
San Martín, Volcán ∧[1]	234	18.33 N	95.12 W
San Martín de Bolaños	234	21.29 N	103.58 W
San Martín de las Vacas	196	25.30 N	101.20 W
San Martín de los Andes	254	40.10 S	71.21 W
San Martin de Porras	286d	12.04 S	77.04 W
San Martín de Valdeiglesias	34	40.21 N	4.24 W
San Martín Hidalgo	234	20.27 N	103.57 W
San Martino, It.	62	45.27 N	8.47 E
San Martino (Sankt Martin), It.	64	46.47 N	11.13 E
San Martino, It.	64	45.25 N	10.35 E
San Martino Buon Albergo	64	45.25 N	11.05 E
San Martino d'Agri	68	40.14 N	16.04 E
San Martino di Castrozza	64	46.16 N	11.48 E
San Martino di Lupari	64	45.39 N	11.51 E
San Martino in Badia (Sankt Martin)	64	46.41 N	11.52 E
San Martino in Casies (Sankt Martin in Gsies)	64	46.49 N	12.14 E
San Martino in Rio	64	44.44 N	10.48 E
San Martino Valle Caudina	68	41.01 N	14.39 E
San Martín Peras	234	17.19 N	98.15 W
San Marzano di San Giuseppe	68	40.27 N	17.30 E
San Mateo, Méx.	234	22.59 N	103.30 W
San Mateo, Pil.	269f	14.42 N	121.07 E
San Mateo, Ca., U.S.	226	37.33 N	122.19 W
San Mateo, Fl., U.S.	192	29.36 N	81.35 W
San Mateo, N.M., U.S.	200	35.19 N	107.38 W
San Mateo, Ven.	246	9.45 N	64.33 W
San Mateo □[6]	226	37.25 N	122.20 W
San Mateo Atenco	234	19.16 N	99.32 W
San Mateo Bridge ◆[5]	282	37.36 N	122.13 W
San Mateo Canyon V	228	33.23 N	117.36 W
San Mateo Creek ≃	282	37.34 N	122.18 W
San Mateo del Mar	234	16.12 N	95.00 W
San Mateo Ixtatán	236	15.50 N	91.29 W
San Mateo Memorial Park ♠	282	37.17 N	122.18 W
San Mateo Point ›	228	33.23 N	117.36 W
San Mateo Tecoloapan	286a	19.34 N	99.14 W
San Matías	248	16.22 S	58.24 W
San Matías, Golfo c	254	41.30 S	64.15 W
San Mauro Castelverde	70	37.55 N	14.11 E
San Mauro Forte	68	40.29 N	16.15 E
San Mauro la Bruca	68	40.07 N	15.17 E
San Mauro Marchesato	68	39.06 N	16.56 E
San Mauro Torinese	62	45.06 N	7.46 E
San Medi, Arroyo de ≃	266d	41.28 N	2.06 E
Sanmen	100	29.06 N	121.24 E
San Menaio	68	41.56 N	15.58 E
Sanmen Wan c	100	29.08 N	121.44 E
Sanmenxia (Shanxian)	102	34.45 N	111.05 E
San Michele, Sacra di ⊍[1]	62	45.11 N	7.21 E
San Michele all'Adige	64	46.12 N	11.08 E
San Michele al Tagliamento	64	45.46 N	12.59 E
San Michele di Ganzaria	70	37.17 N	14.26 E
San Michele Mondovì	62	44.23 N	7.54 E
San Michele Salentino	68	40.38 N	17.37 E
San Miguel, Arg.	252	28.00 S	57.36 W
San Miguel → General Sarmiento, Arg.	258	34.33 S	58.43 W
San Miguel, Bol.	248	16.42 S	61.01 W
San Miguel, Chile	286e	33.30 S	70.40 W
San Miguel, Ec.	246	1.44 S	79.01 W
San Miguel, El Sal.	236	13.29 N	88.11 W
San Miguel, Esp.	148	28.05 N	16.37 W
San Miguel, Méx.	232	29.10 N	101.28 W
San Miguel, Méx.	234	23.23 N	98.10 W
San Miguel, Pan.	246	8.27 N	78.56 W
San Miguel, Perú	248	13.01 S	73.58 W
San Miguel, Perú	286d	12.06 S	77.07 W
San Miguel, Pil.	116	15.09 N	120.59 E
San Miguel, Ca., U.S.	226	35.45 N	120.41 W
San Miguel ≃, Bol.	248	13.52 S	63.56 W
San Miguel (Cuilco) ≃, N.A.	236	15.56 N	92.10 W
San Miguel ≃, S.A.	246	0.08 N	75.51 W
San Miguel ≃, S.A.	248	19.15 S	59.20 W
San Miguel ≃, Co., U.S.	200	38.23 N	108.48 W
San Miguel, Cerro ∧[2]	248	19.19 S	60.36 W
San Miguel, Golfo de c	246	8.22 N	78.17 W
San Miguel, Volcán de ∧[1]	236	13.26 N	88.16 W
San Miguel Arcángel, Mission ⊍[1]	226	35.44 N	120.42 W
San Miguel Bay c	116	13.50 N	123.10 E
San Miguel Chimalapa	234	16.43 N	94.41 W
San Miguel Creek ≃	196	28.30 N	98.25 W
San Miguel de Allende	234	20.55 N	100.45 W
San Miguel de Cruces	232	24.25 N	105.51 W
San Miguel del Monte	258	35.27 S	58.48 W
San Miguel de Pallaques	248	7.00 S	78.51 W
San Miguel de Salcedo	246	1.02 S	78.34 W
San Miguel de Tucumán	252	26.49 S	65.13 W
San Miguel El Alto	234	21.01 N	102.21 W
San Miguel El Grande	234	17.02 N	97.37 W
San Miguel Island I, Pil.	116	13.23 N	123.48 E
San Miguel Island I, Ca., U.S.	204	34.02 N	120.22 W
San Miguel Islands II	116	7.45 N	118.28 E
San Miguelito	236	11.24 N	84.54 W
San Miguel Ixtahuacán	236	15.15 N	91.45 W
San Miguel Mountain ∧	228	32.42 N	116.56 W
San Miguel Sola de Vega	234	16.31 N	96.59 W
San Miguel Talea de Castro	234	17.22 N	96.15 W
San Miguel Tecuixiapan	234	17.58 N	99.27 W
San Miguel Tenango	234	16.16 N	95.36 W
San Miguel Totolapan	234	18.08 N	100.23 W
Sanming	100	26.14 N	117.36 E
San Miniato	66	43.41 N	10.51 E
San Murezzan → Sankt Moritz	58	46.30 N	9.50 E
Sannahed	40	59.06 N	15.09 E
Sannan	96	35.04 N	135.02 E
Sannār	140	13.33 N	33.38 E
San Narciso, Pil.	116	13.34 N	122.34 E
San Narciso, Pil.	116	15.01 N	120.05 E
Sannazzaro de'Burgondi	62	45.06 N	8.54 E
Sannicandro di Bari	68	41.00 N	16.48 E
Sannicandro Garganico	68	41.50 N	15.34 E
Sannicola	68	40.05 N	18.04 E
San Nicola, Isola I	66	42.07 N	15.30 E
San Nicola, Monte ∧	68	38.35 N	16.24 E
San Nicola Arcella	68	39.51 N	15.48 E
San Nicola da Crissa	68	38.40 N	16.17 E
San Nicolás, Cuba	240p	22.47 N	81.55 W
San Nicolás, Esp.	148	27.59 N	15.46 W
San Nicolás, Hond.	236	15.00 N	88.45 W
San Nicolás, Méx.	234	16.26 N	98.32 W
San Nicolás, Perú	248	15.13 S	75.12 W
San Nicolas, Pil.	116	18.09 N	120.38 E
San Nicolás ≃	234	19.40 N	105.14 W
San Nicolás de los Arroyos	252	33.20 S	60.13 W
San Nicolás de los Garza	196	25.45 N	100.18 W
San Nicolas Island I	204	33.15 N	119.31 W
Sânnicolau Mare	38	46.05 N	20.38 E
San Nicolò di Comelico	64	46.35 N	12.31 E
San Nicolò d'Ultimo (Sankt Nikolaus)	64	46.30 N	10.55 E
San Nicolò Ferrarese	64	44.42 N	11.42 E
San Nicolò Gerrei	71	39.30 N	9.18 E
Sannieshof	158	26.30 S	25.47 E
Sannikova, proliv ⊔	74	74.30 N	140.00 E
Şannīn, Jabal ∧	132	33.57 N	35.52 E
Sannio, Monti del ⋏	66	41.30 N	14.45 E
Sanniquellie	150	7.22 N	8.43 W
Sannohe	92	40.22 N	141.15 E
Sannois	261	48.58 N	2.15 E
Sannūr, Wādī V	142	28.58 N	31.03 E
Sano	94	36.19 N	139.35 E
Sañogasta	252	29.18 S	67.36 W
Sanok	30	49.34 N	22.13 E
Sânon ≃	58	48.38 N	6.20 E
San Onofre	246	9.44 N	75.32 W
San Onofre Mountain ∧	228	33.22 N	117.30 W
San Pablo, Chile	254	40.24 S	73.01 W
San Pablo, Col.	246	1.40 N	77.00 W
San Pablo, Pil.	116	14.04 N	121.19 E
San Pablo, Pil.	116	7.40 N	123.27 E
San Pablo, Ca., U.S.	226	37.57 N	122.20 W
San Pablo ◆[8]	286a	19.11 N	99.04 W
San Pablo ≃, Bol.	248	14.52 S	63.42 W
San Pablo ≃, Méx.	234	18.32 N	96.01 W
San Pablo ≃, Pan.	236	7.51 N	81.10 W
San Pablo, Point ›	282	37.58 N	122.26 W
San Pablo Autopan	234	19.21 N	99.40 W
San Pablo Bay c	226	38.06 N	122.22 W
San Pablo Creek ≃	282	37.58 N	122.30 W
San Pablo Huixtepec	234	16.50 N	96.46 W
San Pablo Reservoir ⊜[1]	282	37.56 N	122.15 W
San Pablo Ridge ∧	282	37.55 N	122.15 W
San Pablo Strait ⊔	282	37.58 N	122.26 W
San Pablo Villa de Mitla	234	16.55 N	96.24 W
Sanpāda	272c	19.04 N	73.01 E
San Pancrazio Salentino	68	40.25 N	17.50 E
San Paolo	64	46.29 N	11.15 E
San Paolo di Civitate	68	41.44 N	15.15 E
San Pascual	116	13.08 N	122.59 E
San Pasqual Indian Reservation ◆[4]	228	33.12 N	116.58 W
San Pedro, Arg.	252	33.40 S	59.40 W
San Pedro, Arg.	252	24.14 S	64.52 W
San Pedro, Arg.	252	27.57 S	65.10 W
San Pedro, Chile	252	21.57 S	68.34 W
San Pedro, Chile	252	33.54 S	71.28 W
San Pedro, Col.	246	9.24 N	75.04 W
San Pedro, C.R.	236	9.56 N	84.03 W
San Pédro, C. Iv.	150	4.44 N	6.37 W
San Pedro, Para.	252	24.07 S	56.59 W
San Pedro, Tx., U.S.	196	27.47 N	97.40 W
San Pedro, Ur.	258	34.21 S	57.51 W
San Pedro, Ven.	246	8.50 N	71.58 W
San Pedro □[5]	252	24.15 S	56.30 W
San Pedro ◆[8]	228	33.44 N	118.18 W
San Pedro ≃, Cuba	240p	21.09 N	78.30 W
San Pedro ≃, Méx.	232	30.56 N	108.08 W
San Pedro ≃, Méx.	234	21.45 N	105.30 W
San Pedro ≃, N.A.	200	32.59 N	110.47 W
San Pedro ≃, N.A.	232	17.45 N	91.25 W
San Pedro ≃, Ven.	286c	10.35 N	66.48 W
San Pedro, Arroyo ≃	258	34.21 S	57.56 W
San Pedro, Point ›, Ca., U.S.	282	37.35 N	122.31 W
San Pedro, Point ›, Ca., U.S.	282	37.59 N	122.27 W
San Pedro, Punta ›	252	25.30 S	70.38 W
San Pedro, Volcán ∧[1]	252	21.53 S	68.25 W
San Pedro Amuzgos	234	16.39 N	98.06 W
San Pedro Apóstol	234	16.44 N	96.44 W
San Pedro Ayampuc	236	14.47 N	90.27 W
San Pedro Bay c, Pil.	116	11.11 N	125.05 E
San Pedro Bay c, Ca., U.S.	228	33.45 N	118.11 W
San Pedro Breakwater ◆[5]	280	33.42 N	118.16 W
San Pedro Carchá	236	15.29 N	90.16 W
San Pedro Channel ⊔	228	33.35 N	118.25 W
San Pedro Creek ≃, Ca., U.S.	282	37.36 N	122.30 W
San Pedro Creek ≃, Tx., U.S.	222	31.34 N	95.14 W
San Pedro de Arriba	258	34.18 S	57.47 W
San Pedro de Atacama	252	22.55 S	68.13 W
San Pedro de Buena Vista	248	18.13 S	65.59 W
San Pedro de Curahuara	248	17.40 S	68.02 W
San Pedro de la Cueva	232	29.18 N	109.44 W
San Pedro de las Colonias	232	25.45 N	102.59 W
San Pedro del Gallo	232	25.33 N	104.18 W
San Pedro de Lloc	248	7.26 S	79.31 W
San Pedro del Norte	236	13.04 N	84.33 W
San Pedro del Paraná	252	26.46 S	56.15 W
San Pedro de Macorís	238	18.27 N	69.18 W
San Pedro El Alto	234	16.01 N	96.28 W
San Pedro Huamelula	234	16.02 N	95.40 W
San Pedro Jicayán	234	16.25 N	97.59 W
San Pedro Juchatengo	234	16.21 N	97.06 W
San Pedro Mártir ◆[8]	286a	19.16 N	99.10 W
San Pedro Mixtepec	234	16.00 N	97.07 W
San Pedro Peaks ⋏	200	36.07 N	106.49 W
San Pedro Pinula	236	14.40 N	89.51 W
San Pedro Pochutla	234	15.44 N	96.28 W
San Pedro Sacatepéquez	236	14.58 N	91.46 W
San Pedro Sula	236	15.27 N	88.02 W
San Pedro Tabasco	232	17.47 N	91.10 W
San Pedro Tapanatepec	234	16.21 N	94.12 W
San Pedro Tututepec	234	16.09 N	97.38 W
San Pedro Xalostoc	286a	19.32 N	99.05 W
San Pedro y Miquelón → Saint Pierre and Miquelon □[2]	186	46.55 N	56.20 W
San Pelayo	246	8.58 N	75.51 W
San Pellegrino	62	45.50 N	9.40 E
San Piero a Grado	66	43.41 N	10.21 E
San Piero in Bagno	66	43.51 N	11.58 E
San Pierre	216	41.12 N	86.53 W
San Pietro (Sankt Peter)	64	47.01 N	12.03 E
San Pietro, Isola di I	71	39.08 N	8.17 E
San Pietro a Maida	68	38.50 N	16.20 E
San Pietro di Cadore	64	46.34 N	12.35 E
San Pietro in Casale	64	44.42 N	11.24 E
San Pietro in Gu	64	45.37 N	11.40 E
San Pietro in Guarano	68	39.20 N	16.19 E
San Pietro in Palazzi	66	43.20 N	10.30 E
San Pietro in Vaticano ⊍[1]	267a	41.54 N	12.28 E
San Pietro Vara	62	44.20 N	9.35 E
San Pietro Vernotico	68	40.29 N	18.00 E
San Pitch ≃	200	39.03 N	111.51 W
Sanpoil ≃	202	47.53 N	118.41 W
San Policarpio	116	12.11 N	125.30 E
San Polo d'Enza	64	44.38 N	10.26 E
Sanpu	98	34.09 N	117.10 E
Sanqiao	106	30.35 N	119.58 E
San Quentin	282	37.56 N	122.29 W
San Quentin State Prison ⊍	282	37.56 N	122.28 W
Sanquhar	44	55.22 N	3.56 W
Sanquianga, Parque Nacional ♠	246	2.30 N	78.15 W
San Quintin	116	16.00 N	120.50 E
San Quintín, Cabo ›	232	30.21 N	116.00 W
San Quirico d'Orcia	66	43.03 N	11.36 E
Sanqutan	100	27.17 N	115.04 E
Sanquzhen	107	29.39 N	105.37 E
San Rafael, Arg.	252	34.36 S	68.20 W
San Rafael, Chile	252	35.19 S	71.32 W
San Rafael, Méx.	232	25.01 N	100.33 W
San Rafael, Méx.	234	20.12 N	96.51 W
San Rafael, Ca., U.S.	226	37.58 N	122.31 W
San Rafael, N.M., U.S.	200	35.06 N	107.52 W
San Rafael, Ven.	246	10.58 N	71.44 W
San Rafael ≃, Bol.	248	18.38 S	58.55 W
San Rafael ≃, Ut,. U.S.	200	38.47 N	110.07 W
San Rafael Bay c	282	37.58 N	122.28 W
San Rafael de las Tortillas	196	26.49 N	99.32 W
San Rafael del Norte	236	13.12 N	86.06 W
San Rafael del Sur	236	11.51 N	86.27 W
San Rafael Desert ◆[2]	200	38.40 N	110.30 W
San Rafael Hills ⋏[2]	280	34.10 N	118.12 W
San Rafael Mountains ⋏	204	34.45 N	119.50 W
San Rafael Oriente	236	13.23 N	88.21 W
San Rafael Swell ⋏[1]	200	38.40 N	110.45 W
San Rafael Tasajera	236	13.16 N	88.52 W
San Ramón, Arg.	252	27.42 S	64.17 W
San Ramón, Bol.	248	13.17 S	64.43 W
San Ramón, C.R.	236	10.06 N	84.28 W
San Ramón, Hond.	236	14.41 N	84.43 W
San Ramón, Perú	248	11.08 S	75.20 W
San Ramon, Pil.	116	13.16 N	124.05 E
San Ramon, Ca., U.S.	282	37.47 N	121.59 W
San Ramón, Ur.	252	34.18 S	55.58 W
San Ramon Creek ≃	282	37.54 N	122.03 W
San Ramón de la Nueva Orán	252	23.08 S	64.20 W
San Ramon Valley V	282	37.46 N	121.58 W
Sanrao	100	23.59 N	116.50 E
San-rei ∧	96	33.50 N	133.59 E
San Remigio	116	11.05 N	123.56 E
San Remo, Austl.	169	38.31 S	145.22 E
San Remo, It.	62	43.49 N	7.46 E
San Remo, N.Y., U.S.	210	40.52 N	73.13 W
San Roberto	68	38.18 N	15.44 E
San Rodrigo ≃	196	28.54 N	100.37 W
San Román ≃	236	16.21 N	90.22 W
San Román, Cabo ›	246	12.12 N	70.00 W
San Roque, Arg.	252	28.34 S	58.43 W
San Roque, Arg.	252	30.17 S	68.41 W
San Roque, Esp.	34	36.13 N	5.24 W
San Roque, N. Mar. Is.	174n	15.15 N	145.47 E
San Roque, Pil.	269f	14.29 N	120.54 E
San Roque, Cabo → São Roque, Cabo de ›	250	5.29 S	35.16 W
San Roque, Punta ›	232	27.11 N	114.26 W
San Rosendo	252	37.16 S	72.43 W
San Rufo	68	40.26 N	15.28 E
San Saba	196	31.11 N	98.43 W
San Saba ≃	196	31.15 N	98.35 W
San Saep, Khlong ≊	269a	13.45 N	100.36 E
San Salvador, Arg.	252	29.16 S	57.31 W
San Salvador, Arg.	252	31.37 S	58.30 W
San Salvador, El Sal.	236	13.42 N	89.12 W
San Salvador (Watling Island) I	238	24.02 N	74.28 W
San Salvador ≃	258	33.37 S	58.06 W
San Salvador, Cuchilla ⋏[2]	258	33.56 S	57.45 W
San Salvador, Volcán de ∧[1]	236	13.44 N	89.17 W
San Salvador de Jujuy	252	24.11 S	65.18 W
San Salvador el Seco	234	19.08 N	97.39 W
San Salvatore, Monte ∧	70	37.50 N	14.03 E
San Salvatore Monferrato	62	44.59 N	8.34 E
San Salvatore Telesino	68	41.14 N	14.30 E
San Salvo	66	42.03 N	14.44 E
Sansanné-Mango	150	10.21 N	0.28 E
Sans Bois Creek ≃	196	35.20 N	94.50 W
San Sebastián, El Sal.	236	13.44 N	88.50 W
San Sebastián → Donostia, Esp.	34	43.19 N	1.59 W
San Sebastián, Guat.	236	14.34 N	91.39 W
San Sebastián, Hond.	236	14.24 N	88.42 W
San Sebastián, Méx.	234	20.47 N	104.51 W
San Sebastián, P.R.	240m	18.20 N	66.59 W
San Sebastián, Bahía c	254	53.12 S	68.20 W
San Sebastián de la Gomera	148	28.06 N	17.06 W
San Sebastián del Álamo	234	21.26 N	102.21 W
San Sebastián de los Reyes	266a	40.33 N	3.38 W
San Sebastián de Yalí	236	13.18 N	86.11 W
San Sebastiano	64	45.38 N	10.16 E
San Sebastiano Curone	62	44.47 N	9.04 E
San Sebastián Tecomaxtlahuaca	234	17.21 N	98.02 W
San Sebastián Zinacatepec	234	18.20 N	97.15 W
San Secondo Parmense	64	44.55 N	10.14 E
Sansepolcro	66	43.34 N	12.08 E
San Severino Lucano	68	40.01 N	16.08 E
San Severino Marche	66	43.13 N	13.10 E
San Severo	68	41.41 N	15.23 E
Sansha	100	26.58 N	120.12 E
Sanshengchang	89	44.51 N	120.21 E
Sanshierzhan	89	53.16 N	121.49 E
Sanshijia, Zhg.	98	41.44 N	119.15 E
Sanshijia, Zhg.	98	41.05 N	119.03 E
Sanshilibao	98	39.15 N	121.48 E
Sanshiling	106	30.51 N	119.29 E
Sanshisanzhan	89	53.10 N	121.27 E
Sanshui	100	23.11 N	112.53 E
San Sigismondo (Sankt Sigmund)	64	46.49 N	11.46 E
San Simeon	226	35.39 N	121.11 W
San Simon, Méx.	204	30.30 N	115.58 W
San Simon, Az., U.S.	200	32.16 N	109.13 W
San Simón ≃, Bol.	248	13.13 S	63.31 W
San Simon ≃, Az., U.S.	200	32.50 N	109.39 W
San Simon Wash V	200	31.45 N	112.25 W
San Siro ◆[8]	266b	45.29 N	9.07 E
Sanski Most	36	44.46 N	16.40 E
Sanso	150	11.43 N	6.51 W
San Solano	252	31.29 S	65.55 W
Sansom Park Village	222	32.48 N	97.24 W
Sanson	172	40.13 S	175.25 E
San Sosti	68	39.40 N	16.02 E
San Sperate	71	39.21 N	9.00 E
Sans Souci	274a	33.59 S	151.08 E
Sans-Souci ⊥	238	19.37 N	72.12 W
Sanssouci, Schloss ⊍	54	52.24 N	13.02 E
San Stefano Ticino	266b	45.29 N	8.55 E
Santa, Perú	248	8.59 S	78.36 W
Santa, Pil.	116	17.29 N	120.26 E
Santa ≃	248	8.58 S	78.39 W
Santa, Isla del I	248	9.02 S	78.40 W
Santa Adélia	255	21.16 S	48.48 W
Santa Albertina	255	20.02 S	50.44 W
Santa Amalia	34	39.01 N	6.01 W
Santa Ana, Arg.	252	27.22 S	55.34 W
Santa Ana, Bol.	248	13.45 S	65.35 W
Santa Ana, Bol.	248	18.43 S	58.44 W
Santa Ana, Col.	246	9.19 N	74.35 W
Santa Ana, Ec.	246	1.13 S	80.23 W
Santa Ana, El Sal.	236	13.59 N	89.34 W
Santa Ana, Méx.	232	24.04 N	100.30 W
Santa Ana, Méx.	232	30.33 N	111.07 W
Santa Ana, Ca., U.S.	228	33.44 N	117.52 W
Santa Ana, Ven.	246	9.19 N	64.39 W
Santa Ana ≃, Cuba	286b	23.04 N	82.32 W
Santa Ana ≃, Ca., U.S.	228	33.38 N	117.57 W
Santa Ana, Volcán de ∧[1]	236	13.50 N	89.38 W
Santa Ana Canyon V	280	33.53 N	117.43 W
Santa Ana de Chena	286e	33.34 S	70.47 W
Santa Ana del Alto Beni	248	15.31 S	67.30 W
Santa Ana Heights	228	33.39 N	117.54 W
Santa Ana Indian Reservation ◆[4]	200	35.28 N	106.37 W
Santa Ana Island I	175e	10.50 S	162.28 E
Santa Ana Maya	234	20.00 N	101.01 W
Santa Ana Mountains ⋏	228	33.45 N	117.35 W
Santa Ana Race Track ♠	269f	14.35 N	121.01 E
Santa Ana Tlacotenco ◆[8]	286a	19.10 N	98.59 W
Santa Anita	234	20.33 N	103.27 W
Santa Anita Canyon V	280	34.12 N	118.01 W
Santa Anita Park ♠	280	34.08 N	118.03 W
Santa Anna	196	31.44 N	99.19 W
Santa Apolonia	196	25.38 N	97.59 W
Santa Bárbara, Chile	252	37.40 S	72.01 W
Santa Barbara, Col.	246	5.53 N	75.35 W
Santa Bárbara, Hond.	236	14.53 N	88.14 W
Santa Bárbara, Méx.	232	26.48 N	105.49 W
Santa Bárbara, Méx.	234	18.52 N	101.07 W
Santa Barbara, Ca., U.S.	204	34.25 N	119.42 W
Santa Bárbara, Ven.	246	3.57 N	67.06 W
Santa Bárbara, Ven.	246	7.47 N	71.10 W
Santa Bárbara □[5]	236	15.10 N	88.20 W
Santa Barbara □[6]	228	33.28 N	119.02 W
Santa Bárbara ≃	248	16.58 S	61.39 W
Santa Bárbara, Morro de ∧	287a	22.57 S	43.28 W
Santa Bárbara, Túnel ◆[5]	287a	22.56 S	43.12 W
Santa Barbara Channel ⊔	204	34.15 N	119.55 W
Santa Bárbara do Monte Verde	256	21.58 S	43.42 W
Santa Bárbara do Sul	252	28.22 S	53.15 W
Santa Barbara do Tugúrio	256	21.15 S	43.35 W
Santa Barbara Island I	228	33.28 N	119.02 W
Santa Branca	256	23.24 S	45.53 W
Santa Branca, Represa ⊜[1]	256	23.20 S	45.50 W
Santaca	158	26.36 S	32.32 E
Santa Catalina, Arg.	252	21.57 S	66.04 W
Santa Catalina, Pil.	116	9.20 N	122.51 E
Santa Catalina, Ur.	258	33.49 S	57.29 W
Santa Catalina, Arroyo ≃	288	34.46 S	58.27 W
Santa Catalina, Gulf of c	228	33.20 N	117.45 W
Santa Catalina, Isla I	232	25.40 N	110.47 W
Santa Catalina, Laguna ⊜	288	34.46 S	58.27 W
Santa Catalina Island I	228	33.23 N	118.24 W
Santa Catalina o Calovébora	236	8.47 N	81.20 W
Santa Catarina, Méx.	204	31.37 N	115.48 W
Santa Catarina, Méx.	232	25.41 N	100.28 W
Santa Catarina □[3]	252	27.00 S	50.00 W
Santa Catarina, Ilha de I	252	27.36 S	48.30 W
Santa Catarina Juquila	234	16.14 N	97.18 W
Santa Caterina di Pittinuri	71	40.06 N	8.30 E
Santa Caterina Valfurva	64	46.25 N	10.29 E
Santa Caterina Villarmosa	70	37.35 N	14.02 E
Santa Cecília	252	26.56 S	50.27 W
Santa Cesarea Terme	68	40.02 N	18.29 E
Santa Clara, Col.	246	2.43 S	69.43 W
Santa Clara, Cuba	240p	22.24 N	79.58 W
Santa Clara, Méx.	232	29.17 N	107.01 W
Santa Clara, Méx.	234	19.41 N	102.30 W
Santa Clara, Méx.	286a	19.34 N	99.04 W
Santa Clara, Ca., U.S.	226	37.20 N	121.56 W
Santa Clara, Ut,. U.S.	200	37.07 N	113.39 W
Santa Clara □[6]	226	37.20 N	121.53 W
Santa Clara ≃, Ca., U.S.	228	34.14 N	119.16 W
Santa Clara ≃, Ut,. U.S.	200	37.05 N	113.36 W
Santa Clara, Bahía de c	240p	23.05 N	80.30 W
Santa Clara, University of ⊍[2]	282	37.21 N	121.56 W
Santa Clara de Olimar	252	32.55 S	54.58 W
Santa Clara Indian Reservation ◆[4]	200	35.59 N	106.10 W
Santa Clara Valley V	226	37.10 N	121.40 W
Santa Clarita, Perú	286d	12.00 S	77.01 W
Santa Clarita, Ca., U.S.	228	34.23 N	118.32 E
Santa Clotilde	246	2.34 S	73.44 W
Santa Coloma de Cervelló	266d	41.22 N	2.01 E
Santa Coloma de Farners	34	41.52 N	2.40 E
Santa Coloma de Gramanet	266d	41.27 N	2.13 E
Santa Comba	34	43.02 N	8.49 W
Santa Comba Dão	34	40.24 N	8.08 W
Santa Cristina	64	46.34 N	11.43 E
Santa Cristina d'Aspromonte	68	38.15 N	15.58 E
Santa Croce	64	46.05 N	12.18 E
Santa Croce, Capo ›	70	37.14 N	15.15 E
Santa Croce, Lago di ⊜	64	46.10 N	12.20 E
Santa Croce Camerina	70	36.50 N	14.31 E
Santa Croce del Sannio	68	41.23 N	14.43 E
Santa Croce di Magliano	66	41.42 N	14.59 E
Santa Croce Sull'Arno	66	43.42 N	10.47 E
Santa Cruz, Bra.	250	6.13 S	36.01 W
Santa Cruz, Bra.	255	19.56 S	40.09 W
Santa Cruz, Chile	252	34.38 S	71.22 W
Santa Cruz, C.R.	236	10.16 N	85.36 W
Santa Cruz, Méx.	200	31.14 N	110.35 W
Santa Cruz, Perú	248	6.37 S	78.57 W
Santa Cruz, Pil.	116	6.50 N	125.25 E
Santa Cruz, Pil.	116	14.17 N	121.25 E
Santa Cruz, Pil.	116	13.29 N	122.02 E
Santa Cruz, Pil.	116	13.04 N	120.43 E
Santa Cruz, Pil.	116	15.46 N	119.55 E
Santa Cruz (Tubajon), Pil.	116	10.19 N	125.33 E
Santa Cruz, Ca., U.S.	226	36.58 N	122.01 W
Santa Cruz, Ven.	246	8.25 N	71.39 W
Santa Cruz, Ven.	286c	10.26 N	67.01 W
Santa Cruz □[4]	254	49.00 S	70.00 W
Santa Cruz □[5]	248	17.30 S	61.30 W
Santa Cruz □[6]	226	36.58 N	122.01 W
Santa Cruz ◆[8], Bra.	256	22.56 S	43.41 W
Santa Cruz ◆[8], India	272c	19.05 N	72.50 E
Santa Cruz ≃, Arg.	254	50.08 S	68.20 W
Santa Cruz ≃, Cuba	286b	23.04 N	82.29 W
Santa Cruz ≃, N.A.	200	32.42 N	111.33 W
Santa Cruz, Ilha I	287a	22.52 S	43.07 W
Santa Cruz, Isla I	246a	0.38 S	90.23 W
Santa Cruz, Sierra de ⋏	236	15.40 N	89.15 W
Santa Cruz Basin ✦[1]	14	12.00 S	163.00 E
Santa Cruz Cabrália	255	16.17 S	39.02 W
Santa Cruz da Graciosa	148a	39.05 N	28.01 W
Santa Cruz das Flores	148a	39.27 N	31.07 W
Santa Cruz de Goiás	255	17.19 S	48.30 W
Santa Cruz de Juventino Rosas	234	20.39 N	101.00 W
Santa Cruz de la Palma	148	28.41 N	17.45 W
Santa Cruz de la Sierra	248	17.48 S	63.10 W
Santa Cruz de la Zarza	34	39.58 N	3.10 W
Santa Cruz del Quiché	236	15.02 N	91.08 W
Santa Cruz del Sur	240p	20.43 N	78.00 W
Santa Cruz de Mudela	34	38.38 N	3.28 W
Santa Cruz de Tenerife	148	28.27 N	16.14 W
Santa Cruz de Tenerife □[4], Esp.	34	28.20 N	16.50 W
Santa Cruz de Tenerife □[4], Esp.	148	28.15 N	17.00 W
Santa Cruz do Capibaribe	250	7.57 S	36.12 W
Santa Cruz do Piauí	250	7.09 S	41.48 W
Santa Cruz do Prata	256	21.12 S	46.45 W
Santa Cruz do Rio Pardo	255	22.55 S	49.37 W
Santa Cruz do Sul	252	29.43 S	52.26 W
Santa Cruz International Airport ⊠	272c	19.05 N	72.52 E
Santa Cruz Island I	204	34.01 N	119.45 W
Santa Cruz Islands II	14	11.00 S	166.15 E
Santa Cruz Meyehualco ◆[8]	286a	19.20 N	99.03 W
Santa Cruz Mountains ⋏	226	37.15 N	122.00 W
Santa Cruz Point ›	116	15.44 N	119.52 E
Santa Cruz Tacache de Mina	234	17.51 N	98.07 W
Santadi	71	39.05 N	8.43 E
Santa Domenica Talao	68	39.49 N	15.51 E
Santa Domenica Vittoria	70	37.55 N	14.58 E
Sant Adrià de Besòs	266d	41.25 N	2.14 E
Santa Elena, Arg.	252	30.57 S	59.48 W
Santa Elena, Ec.	246	2.14 S	80.51 W
Santa Elena, El Sal.	236	13.22 N	88.25 W
Santa Elena, Méx.	196	27.59 N	103.56 W
Santa Elena, Méx.	232	27.28 N	102.33 W
Santa Elena, Méx.	234	18.39 N	101.34 W
Santa Elena ≃	248	15.42 S	67.13 W
Santa Elena, Bahía de c	246	2.06 S	80.53 W
Santa Elena, Cabo ›	236	10.54 N	85.57 W
Santa Elena, Golfo de c	236	10.59 N	85.50 W
Santa Elena, Punta ›	246	2.11 S	81.00 W
Santa Elena del Gomero	286e	33.29 S	70.46 W
Santa Elena de Uairén	246	4.37 N	61.08 W
Santa Elisabetta	70	37.26 N	13.33 E
Santa Eufemia	34	38.36 N	4.54 W
Santa Eulalia, Esp.	34	40.34 N	1.19 W
Santa Eulalia, Guat.	236	15.45 N	91.29 W
Santa Eulària del Riu	34	38.59 N	1.31 E
Santa Fe, Arg.	252	31.38 S	60.42 W
Santa Fé, Bra.	255	15.40 S	51.16 W
Santa Fé, Bra.	255	23.01 S	51.48 W
Santa Fe, Esp.	34	37.11 N	3.43 W
Santa Fe, Hond.	236	15.55 N	86.05 W
Santa Fé, Pan.	236	8.31 N	81.05 W
Santa Fe, Pil.	116	11.09 N	123.47 E
Santa Fe, Pil.	116	16.10 N	120.57 E
Santa Fe, Pil.	116	12.10 N	122.00 E
Santa Fe, Mo., U.S.	219	39.22 N	91.49 W
Santa Fe, N.M., U.S.	200	35.41 N	105.56 W
Santa Fe □[4]	252	31.00 S	61.00 W
Santa Fé ◆[8]	286b	23.05 N	82.31 W
Santa Fe ≃, Fl., U.S.	192	29.53 N	82.53 W
Santa Fe ≃, N.M., U.S.	200	35.36 N	106.20 W
Santa Fé, Aeropuerto ⊠	286b	23.04 N	82.28 W
Santa Fe, Isla I	246a	0.49 S	90.04 W
Santa Fé, Ribeirão ≃	287b	23.24 S	46.48 W
Santa Fe Baldy ∧	200	35.50 N	105.46 W
Santa Fe Dam ◆[6]	280	34.07 N	117.58 W
Santa Fe de Bogotá	246	4.36 N	74.05 W
Santa Fe de Minas	255	16.42 S	45.26 W
Santa Fé do Sul	255	20.13 S	50.56 W
Santa Fe Flood Control Basin ⌀[1]	280	34.07 N	117.58 W
Santa Fe Springs	280	33.56 N	118.04 W
Santa Filomena	250	9.07 S	45.56 W
Santa Fiora	66	42.50 N	11.35 E
Santa Flavia	70	38.05 N	13.31 E
Sant'Agata Bolognese	64	44.40 N	11.08 E
Sant'Agata de'Goti	68	41.05 N	14.30 E
Sant'Agata del Bianco	68	38.05 N	16.05 E
Sant'Agata di Militello	70	38.04 N	14.38 E
Sant'Agata di Puglia	68	41.09 N	15.23 E
Sant'Agata Feltria	66	43.52 N	12.12 E
Sant'Agata sul Santerno	66	44.26 N	11.51 E
Santa Gertrude (Sankt Gertraud)	64	46.29 N	10.53 E
Santa Gertrudis	196	26.09 N	98.44 W
Santa Giusta, Stagno di ⊜	71	39.52 N	8.35 E
Sant'Agostino	64	44.48 N	11.23 E
Sāntāhār	124	24.48 N	88.59 E
Santa Helena	250	2.14 S	45.18 W
Santa Helena de Goiás	255	17.43 S	50.35 W
Santai, Zhg.	85	39.14 N	77.42 E
Santai, Zhg.	86	44.35 N	81.18 E
Santai, Zhg.	102	31.10 N	105.02 E
Santai, Zhg.	104	41.48 N	121.53 E
Santai, Zhg.	104	41.56 N	123.11 E
Santai, Zhg.	105	38.58 N	115.49 E
Santa Inês	255	13.17 S	39.48 W
Santa Inés, Bahía c	232	26.59 N	111.59 W
Santa Inés, Isla I	254	53.45 S	72.45 W
Santa Inés Ahuatempan	234	18.25 N	98.01 W
Santa Iria de Azóia	266c	38.51 N	9.05 W
Santa Isabel, Arg.	252	36.15 S	66.56 W
Santa Isabel, Arg.	252	33.54 S	61.42 W
Santa Isabel, Bra.	256	23.19 S	46.14 W
Santa Isabel, Ec.	246	3.21 S	79.19 W

	English	Deutsch	Español	Français	Português
≃	River	Fluß	Río	Rivière	Rio
≊	Canal	Kanal	Canal	Canal	Canal
∟	Waterfall, Rapids	Wasserfall, Stromschnellen	Cascada, Rápidos	Chute d'eau, Rapides	Cascata, Rápidos
⊔	Strait	Meeresstraße	Estrecho	Détroit	Estreito
c	Bay, Gulf	Bucht, Golf	Bahía, Golfo	Baie, Golfe	Baía, Golfo
⊜	Lake, Lakes	See, Seen	Lago, Lagos	Lac, Lacs	Lago, Lagos
≡	Swamp	Sumpf	Pantano	Marais	Pântano
⊓	Ice Features, Glacier	Eis- und Gletscherformen	Accidentes Glaciales	Formes glaciaires	Acidentes glaciares
⌀	Other Hydrographic Features	Andere Hydrographische Objekte	Otros Elementos Hidrográficos	Autres données hydrographiques	Outros acidentes hidrográficos
✦	Submarine Features	Untermeerische Objekte	Accidentes Submarinos	Formes de relief sous-marin	Acidentes submarinos
□	Political Unit	Politische Einheit	Unidad Politica	Entité politique	Unidade política
⊍	Cultural Institution	Kulturelle Institution	Institución Cultural	Institution culturelle	Instituição cultural
⊥	Historical Site	Historische Stätte	Sitio Histórico	Site historique	Sitio histórico
♠	Recreational Site	Erholungs- und Ferienort	Sitio de Recreo	Centre de loisirs	Area de Lazer
⊠	Airport	Flughafen	Aeropuerto	Aéroport	Aeroporto
■	Military Installation	Militäranlage	Instalación Militar	Installation militaire	Instalação militar
◆	Miscellaneous	Verschiedenes	Misceláneo	Divers	Diversos

I · 156 **Sant-Saoj**

ENGLISH — Name, Page, Lat.°′, Long.°′
DEUTSCH — Name, Seite, Breite°′, Länge°′ E = Ost

Santa Isabel → Malabo, Gui. Ecu. **152** 3.45 N 8.47 E
Santa Isabel, Méx. **234** 23.15 N 100.52 W
Santa Isabel, P.R. **240m** 17.58 N 66.24 W
Santa Isabel I **175e** 8.00 S 159.00 E
Santa Isabel ≃ **236** 15.59 N 90.00 W
Santa Isabel, Pico de ∧ **152** 3.35 N 8.46 E
Santa Isabel Creek ≃ **196** 27.39 N 99.38 W
Santa Isabel de Sihuas **248** 16.20 S 72.06 W
Santa Isabel do Araguaia **250** 6.07 S 48.19 W
Santa Isabel do Rio Prêto **256** 22.14 S 44.05 W
Santaizi **104** 41.21 N 121.36 E
Santa Josefa **116** 8.02 N 125.57 E
Santa Julia **286e** 33.30 S 70.38 W
Santa Juliana **255** 19.19 S 47.32 W
Santal, Baie du ⊂ **175f** 20.50 S 167.05 E
Sant'Alberto **66** 44.32 N 12.09 E
Sant'Alfio **70** 37.44 N 15.08 E
Sāntalpur **120** 23.45 N 71.10 E
Santa Luce **66** 43.28 N 10.34 E
Santa Lucía, Arg. **252** 28.59 S 59.06 W
Santa Lucía, Arg. **252** 31.32 S 68.29 W
Santa Lucía, Cuba **240p** 21.02 N 76.00 W
Santa Lucía, Cuba **240p** 22.40 N 83.58 W
Santa Lucia, It. **64** 46.28 N 10.21 E
Santa Lucia, It. **64** 45.26 N 10.57 E
Santa Lucía, Ur. **258** 34.27 S 56.24 W
Santa Lucía, Ven. **246** 8.07 N 69.46 W
Santa Lucía → Saint Lucia □[1] **241f** 13.53 N 60.58 W
Santa Lucía ≃ **258** 34.48 S 56.22 W
Santa Lucia, Cabo → Saint Lucia, Cape › **158** 28.25 S 32.25 E
Santa Lucía, Cuchilla ⋏[2] **258** 34.09 S 56.11 W
Santa Lucía Chico ≃ **258** 34.21 S 56.20 W
Santa Lucía Cotzumalguapa **236** 14.20 N 91.01 W
Santa Lucia Creek ≃ **226** 36.13 N 121.30 W
Santa Lucia del Mela **70** 38.09 N 15.17 E
Santa Lucia di Piave **64** 45.51 N 12.17 E
Santa Lucia Range ⋏ **226** 36.00 N 121.20 W
Santaluz **250** 11.15 S 39.22 W
Santa Luzia, Bra. **250** 6.53 S 36.56 W
Santa Luzia, Port. **34** 37.44 N 8.24 W
Santa Luzia I **150a** 16.46 N 24.45 W
Santa Magdalena **252** 34.30 S 63.56 W
Santa-Manza, Golfu di ⊂ **71** 41.37 N 9.22 E
Santa Margarita **226** 35.23 N 120.36 W
Santa Margarita ≃ **228** 33.14 N 117.25 W
Santa Margarita, Isla I **232** 24.27 N 111.50 W
Santa Margarita Lake ⊜[1] **226** 35.20 N 120.28 W
Santa Margarita Mountains ⋏ **228** 33.30 N 117.25 W
Santa Margherita di Belice **70** 37.41 N 13.01 E
Santa Margherita Ligure **62** 44.20 N 9.12 E
Santa María, Arg. **252** 26.41 S 66.02 W
Santa Maria, Bra. **252** 29.41 S 53.48 W
Santa Maria, C.V. **150a** 16.36 N 22.54 W
Santa María, C.R. **236** 9.39 N 83.57 W
Santa María, Méx. **196** 28.02 N 101.38 W
Santa María, Pan. **236** 8.07 N 80.40 W
Santa Maria, Pil. **116** 17.22 N 120.29 E
Santa María, P.R. **240m** 18.09 N 65.26 W
Santa Maria, Schw. **58** 46.16 N 9.09 E
Santa Maria, Schw. **58** 46.36 N 10.24 E
Santa Maria, Ca., U.S. **204** 34.57 N 120.26 W
Santa Maria I, Port. **148a** 36.58 N 25.06 W
Santa Maria I, Vanuatu **175f** 14.15 S 167.30 E
Santa Maria ≃, Bra. **252** 29.48 S 54.56 W
Santa Maria ≃, Bra. **252** 21.50 S 54.53 W
Santa María ≃, Méx. **232** 31.00 N 107.14 W
Santa María ≃, Méx. **234** 21.48 N 99.10 W
Santa María ≃, Pan. **236** 8.06 N 80.29 W
Santa Maria ≃, Az., U.S. **200** 34.19 N 113.31 W
Santa María, Bahía ⊂ **232** 25.04 N 108.06 W
Santa María, Cabo → Sainte-Marie, Cap ›, Madag. **157b** 25.36 S 45.08 E
Santa María, Cabo ›, Ur. **252** 34.40 S 54.10 W
Santa Maria, Cabo de ›, Ang. **152** 13.25 S 12.32 E
Santa Maria, Cabo de ›, Moç. **158** 26.05 S 32.58 E
Santa Maria, Cabo de ›, Port. **34** 36.58 N 7.54 W
Santa Maria, Cape › **238** 23.41 N 75.19 W
Santa María, Cayo I **240p** 22.40 N 79.00 W
Santa María, Cerro ∧ **286d** 11.56 S 76.57 W
Santa Maria, Giogo di (Pass Umbrail))(**64** 46.34 N 10.25 E
Santa María, Isla I, Chile **252** 37.02 S 73.33 W
Santa María, Isla I, Ec. **246a** 1.17 S 90.26 W
Santa Maria, Isola I **71** 41.17 N 9.22 E
Santa María, Laguna de ⊜ **200** 31.07 N 107.16 W
Santa Maria, Ribeirão ≃ **250** 7.10 S 49.13 W
Santa María, Volcán ∧[1] **236** 14.45 N 91.33 W
Santa María Ajoloapan **234** 19.58 N 99.03 W
Santa Maria a Monte **66** 43.42 N 10.42 E
Santa Maria Asunción Tlaxiaco **234** 17.16 N 97.41 W
Santa Maria a Vico **68** 41.02 N 14.29 E
Santa María Ayoquezco **234** 16.41 N 96.50 W
Santa Maria Capua Vetere **68** 41.05 N 14.15 E
Santa María Chimalapa **234** 16.55 N 94.41 W
Santa María Colotepec **234** 15.53 N 96.55 W
Santa Maria da Boa Vista **250** 8.49 S 39.49 W
Santa Maria da Vitória **255** 13.24 S 44.12 W
Santa Maria degli Angeli **66** 43.03 N 12.34 E
Santa María de Huazamoto **234** 22.30 N 104.30 W
Santa María de Ipire **246** 8.49 N 65.19 W
Santa Maria de Itabira **255** 19.27 S 43.08 W
Santa Maria del Cedro **68** 39.45 N 15.50 E
Santa Maria della Versa **62** 44.59 N 9.18 E
Santa Maria delle Grazie ʊ[1] **266b** 45.27 N 9.10 E
Santa María del Oro **232** 25.56 N 105.22 W
Santa María de los Ángeles **234** 22.11 N 103.14 W
Santa María del Refugio **234** 23.44 N 101.14 W
Santa María del Río **234** 21.48 N 100.45 W
Santa María del Valle **234** 20.54 N 102.22 W
Santa Mariá de Mohovano **232** 26.42 N 103.39 W
Santa Maria di Galeria ◆[8] **267a** 42.01 N 12.19 E
Santa Maria di Leuca, Capo › **68** 39.47 N 18.22 E
Santa Maria di Licodia **70** 37.37 N 14.53 E
Santa Maria di Siponto ʊ[1] **68** 41.40 N 15.51 E
Santa Maria do Suaçuí **255** 18.12 S 42.25 W
Santa María Huazolotitlán **234** 16.17 N 97.56 W
Santa María Jalapa del Marqués **234** 16.30 N 95.28 W
Santa María la Real de Nieva **34** 41.04 N 4.24 W
Santa Maria Madalena **255** 21.57 S 42.01 W
Santa Maria Maggiore **58** 46.08 N 8.28 E
Santa Maria Maggiore ʊ[1] **267a** 41.53 N 12.30 E
Santa Maria Nuova **66** 43.29 N 13.18 E
Santa-Maria-Siché **36** 41.52 N 8.59 E
Santa María Tulpetlac **286a** 19.34 N 99.03 W
Santa María Xadani **234** 15.56 N 96.04 W
Santa María Zoquitlán **234** 16.33 N 96.23 W
Santa Marinella **66** 42.02 N 11.51 E
Santa Marta, Col. **246** 11.15 N 74.13 W
Santa Marta, Guat. **236** 13.58 N 91.18 W
Santa Marta, Cabo de › **152** 13.52 S 12.25 E
Santa Marta, Cerro ∧ **234** 18.19 N 94.48 W
Santa Marta, Ciénaga Grande ⊂ **246** 10.50 N 74.25 W
Santa Marta Grande, Cabo de › **252** 28.38 S 48.45 W
Sant'Ambrogio **64** 45.31 N 10.50 E
Santa Mónica, Méx. **196** 28.12 N 100.37 W
Santa Monica, Ca., U.S. **228** 34.01 N 118.29 W
Santa Mónica ◆[8] **286c** 10.29 N 66.53 W
Santa Monica Bay ⊂ **228** 33.54 N 118.25 W
Santa Monica Beach State Park ♦ **280** 34.01 N 118.30 W
Santa Monica Mountains ⋏ **228** 34.05 N 118.40 W
Santa Monica Mountains National Recreation Area ♦ **228** 34.05 N 118.45 W
Santa Monica Municipal Airport ⊠ **280** 34.01 N 118.27 W
Santan **112** 0.03 S 117.28 E
Santana, Bra. **255** 12.59 S 44.03 W
Sântana, Rom. **38** 46.21 N 21.30 E
Santana ◆[8] **287b** 23.29 S 46.38 W
Santana ≃ **255** 19.43 S 51.02 W
Santana, Coxilha de ⋏[2] **252** 31.15 S 55.15 W
Santana, Ilha de I **250** 2.18 S 43.41 W
Santana, Ribeirão ≃ **250** 9.47 S 50.13 W
Santana da Boa Vista **252** 30.52 S 53.07 W
Santana da Vargem **256** 21.15 S 45.30 W
Santana de Caldas **256** 21.50 S 46.24 W
Santana de Cataguases **256** 21.17 S 42.33 W
Santana de Parnaíba **256** 23.27 S 46.55 W
Santana de Parnaíba □[7] **287b** 23.27 S 46.54 W
Santana do Campestre **256** 21.16 S 42.56 W
Santana do Capivari **256** 22.14 S 44.56 W
Santana do Cariri **250** 7.11 S 39.44 W
Santana do Deserto **256** 21.57 S 43.11 W
Santana do Garambéu **256** 21.36 S 44.06 W
Santana do Ipanema **250** 9.22 S 37.14 W
Santana do Livramento **252** 30.53 S 55.31 W
Santana do Matos **250** 5.57 S 36.39 W
Santander, Col. **246** 3.01 N 76.28 W
Santander, Esp. **34** 43.28 N 3.48 W
Santander, Pil. **116** 9.25 N 123.20 E
Santander □[5] **246** 7.00 N 73.15 W
Santander Jiménez **232** 24.13 N 98.28 W
Sant'Andrea, Isola I **68** 40.03 N 17.57 E
Sant'Andrea Frius **71** 39.29 N 9.10 E
Sant Andreu de la Barca **266d** 41.27 N 1.59 E
Santa Nella **226** 37.03 N 121.02 W
Santanésia **256** 22.30 S 43.49 W
Santang **100** 28.44 N 116.32 E
Sant'Angelo, Castel ⊥ **267a** 41.55 N 12.28 E
Sant'Angelo, Monte ∧ **267a** 41.56 N 12.49 E
Sant'Angelo dei Lombardi **68** 40.56 N 15.11 E
Sant'Angelo in Vado **66** 43.40 N 12.25 E
Sant'Angelo Lodigiano **62** 45.14 N 9.24 E
Sant'Angelo Muxard **70** 37.28 N 13.32 E
Sant'Angelo Romano **267a** 42.02 N 12.42 E
Santanghu **102** 44.13 N 93.22 E
Santanilla, Islas II **238** 17.25 N 83.55 W
Santa Ninfa **70** 37.46 N 12.53 E
Sant'Antimo **68** 40.56 N 14.14 E
Sant'Antine, Nuraghe ⊥ **71** 40.29 N 8.46 E
Sant'Antioco **71** 39.04 N 8.27 E
Sant'Antioco, Isola di I **71** 39.02 N 8.25 E
Sant Antoni de Portmany **34** 38.58 N 1.18 E
Sant'Antonio Abate **68** 40.43 N 14.32 E
Sant'Antonio di Santadi **71** 39.43 N 8.29 E
Sant'Antonio Morignone **64** 46.24 N 10.21 E
Santanyi **34** 39.22 N 3.07 E
Santa Panagia, Capo › **70** 37.07 N 15.18 E
Santa Paula **228** 34.21 N 119.03 W
Santa Paula Creek ≃ **228** 34.21 N 119.03 W
Santa Perpètua de Mogoda **266d** 41.32 N 2.11 E
Santapogue Creek ≃ **276** 40.40 N 73.21 W
Santa Pola, Cap de › **34** 38.12 N 0.31 W
Sant'Apollinare in Classe ʊ[1] **66** 44.22 N 12.15 E
Santaquin **200** 39.58 N 111.47 W
Santa Quitéria **250** 4.20 S 40.10 W
Santa Quitéria do Maranhão **250** 3.31 S 42.32 W
Sant'Arcangelo **68** 40.15 N 16.17 E
Santarcangelo di Romagna **66** 44.04 N 12.27 E
Sant'Arcangelo Trimonte **68** 41.10 N 14.56 E
Santarém, Bra. **250** 2.26 S 54.42 W
Santarém, Port. **34** 39.14 N 8.41 W
Santarém □[5] **266c** 38.50 N 8.56 W
Santaren Channel U **238** 24.00 N 79.30 W
Santa Rita, Bra. **250** 7.08 S 34.58 W
Santa Rita, Bra. **287a** 22.41 S 43.28 W
Santa Rita, Col. **246** 0.33 N 73.58 W
Santa Rita, Hond. **236** 15.09 N 87.53 W
Santa Rita, Méx. **196** 27.29 N 100.33 W
Santa Rita, Méx. **232** 28.34 N 111.42 W
Santa Rita, Pil. **116** 11.27 N 124.56 E
Santa Rita, Mt., U.S. **182** 48.42 N 112.19 W
Santa Rita, Ven. **246** 10.32 N 71.32 W
Santa Rita, Punta › **258** 34.28 S 57.52 W
Santa Rita de Caldas **256** 22.02 S 46.20 W
Santa Rita de Catuna **252** 30.57 S 66.13 W
Santa Rita de Jacutinga **256** 22.09 S 44.06 W
Santa Rita del Rucio **234** 23.04 N 100.19 W
Santa Rita do Araguaia **255** 17.20 S 53.12 W
Santa Rita do Ibitipoca **256** 21.33 S 43.55 W
Santa Rita do Sapucaí **256** 22.15 S 45.42 W
Santa Rita do Weil **246** 3.29 S 69.19 W
Santa Rita Park **226** 37.02 N 120.35 W
Santa Rosa, Arg. **252** 36.37 S 64.17 W
Santa Rosa, Arg. **252** 23.22 S 64.30 W
Santa Rosa, Bol. **248** 14.10 S 66.53 W
Santa Rosa, Bol. **248** 10.36 S 67.25 W
Santa Rosa, Bol. **248** 17.07 S 63.35 W
Santa Rosa, Bra. **252** 27.52 S 54.29 W
Santa Rosa, Bra. **255** 15.01 S 47.13 W
Santa Rosa, Col. **246** 2.31 N 68.13 W
Santa Rosa, C.R. **236** 10.51 N 85.38 W
Santa Rosa, Ec. **246** 3.27 S 79.58 W
Santa Rosa, Méx. **204** 31.59 N 116.45 W
Santa Rosa, Méx. **234** 22.18 N 104.24 W
Santa Rosa, Para. **248** 21.46 S 61.43 W
Santa Rosa, Para. **252** 26.52 S 56.49 W
Santa Rosa, Ca., U.S. **226** 38.26 N 122.42 W
Santa Rosa, N.M., U.S. **196** 34.56 N 104.40 W
Santa Rosa, Tx., U.S. **196** 26.15 N 97.50 W
Santa Rosa, Ur. **258** 34.30 S 56.03 W
Santa Rosa, Ven. **246** 8.26 N 69.24 W
Santa Rosa, Ven. **246** 7.03 N 68.28 W
Santa Rosa, Ven. **286c** 10.30 N 66.46 W
Santa Rosa □[5] **236** 14.10 N 90.18 W
Santa Rosa, Mount ∧[2] **174p** 13.32 N 144.55 E
Santa Rosa, Parque Nacional ♦ **236** 10.50 N 85.45 W
Santa Rosa, Presa ⊜[1] **234** 20.58 N 103.35 W
Santa Rosa Beach **194** 30.23 N 86.13 W
Santa Rosa Creek ≃ **226** 35.34 N 121.06 W
Santa Rosa de Aguán **236** 15.57 N 85.43 W
Santa Rosa de Amanadona **246** 1.29 N 66.55 W
Santa Rosa [de Copán] **236** 14.47 N 88.46 W
Santa Rosa de Huechuraba **286e** 33.21 S 70.41 W
Santa Rosa del Conlara **252** 32.20 S 65.12 W
Santa Rosa de Leales **252** 27.09 S 65.15 W
Santa Rosa de Lima **236** 13.37 N 87.53 W
Santa Rosa de Locobe **286e** 33.26 S 70.33 W
Santa Rosa del Palmar **248** 16.54 S 62.24 W
Santa Rosa de Osos **246** 6.39 N 75.28 W
Santa Rosa de Río Primero **252** 31.09 S 63.23 W
Santa Rosa de Sucumbíos **246** 0.22 N 77.10 W
Santa Rosa de Viterbo **246** 5.53 N 72.59 W
Santa Rosa Indian Reservation ◆[4] **204** 33.35 N 116.35 W
Santa Rosa Island I, Ca., U.S. **204** 33.58 N 120.06 W
Santa Rosa Island I, Fl., U.S. **194** 30.22 N 86.55 W
Santa Rosa Jáuregui **234** 20.44 N 100.27 W
Santa Rosalía, Méx. **196** 26.08 N 98.59 W
Santa Rosalía, Méx. **232** 27.19 N 112.17 W
Santa Rosalía, Ven. **246** 9.02 N 69.01 W
Santa Rosa Range ⋏ **204** 41.35 N 117.40 W
Santa Rosa Wash V **200** 33.00 N 112.00 W
Santa Rosita **286d** 12.03 S 76.59 W
Sant'Arsenio **68** 40.28 N 15.29 E
Šantarskije ostrova II **74** 55.00 N 137.36 E
Santa Severa **66** 42.02 N 11.57 E
Santa Severina **68** 39.09 N 16.55 E
Santa Sofia **66** 43.57 N 11.54 E
Santa Susana Mountains ⋏ **228** 34.20 N 118.42 W
Santa Sylvina **252** 27.49 S 61.09 W
Santa Tecla → Nueva San Salvador **236** 13.41 N 89.17 W
Santa Teresa, Bra. **255** 19.55 S 40.36 W
Santa Teresa, Méx. **196** 29.34 N 104.39 W
Santa Teresa, Méx. **200** 30.52 N 111.33 W
Santa Teresa, Méx. **232** 25.17 N 97.51 W
Santa Teresa, Méx. **234** 22.28 N 104.44 W
Santa Teresa ≃ **255** 11.47 S 48.37 W
Santa Teresa, Embalse de ⊜[1] **34** 40.40 N 5.30 W
Santa Teresa de lo Ovalle **286e** 33.23 S 70.47 W
Santa Teresa di Riva **70** 37.57 N 15.22 E
Santa Teresa Gallura **71** 41.14 N 9.11 E
Santa Tereza de Goiás **255** 13.38 S 49.01 W
Santa Terezinha **250** 10.28 S 50.31 W
Santa Uxia **34** 42.33 N 9.00 W
Santa Valburga (Sankt Wallburg) **64** 46.33 N 11.00 E
Santa Venerina **70** 37.41 N 15.08 E
Santa Venetia **226** 38.01 N 122.31 W
Santa Vitória **255** 18.50 S 50.08 W
Santa Vitória do Palmar **252** 33.31 S 53.21 W
Santa Vittoria, Monte ∧ **71** 39.45 N 9.18 E
Santa Vittoria in Matenano **66** 43.01 N 13.29 E
Santa Ynez ≃ **204** 34.41 N 120.36 W
Santa Ynez Canyon V **280** 34.04 N 118.34 W
Santa Ysabel Indian Reservation ◆[4] **204** 33.11 N 116.41 W
Sant Bartomeu de la Quadra **266d** 41.26 N 2.02 E
Sant Boi de Llobregat **266d** 41.21 N 2.03 E
Sant Carles de la Ràpita **34** 40.37 N 0.36 E
Sant Climent de Llobregat **266d** 41.20 N 2.00 E
Sant Cugat del Vallès **266d** 41.28 N 2.05 E
Santee **228** 32.50 N 116.58 W
Santee ≃ **192** 33.14 N 79.28 W
Santee Dam ◆[6] **192** 33.24 N 80.12 W
Santee Indian Reservation ◆[4] **198** 42.45 N 97.50 W
Sant'Egidio alla Vibrata **66** 42.49 N 13.42 E
Sant'Elena **64** 45.12 N 11.43 E
Sant'Elia a Pianisi **66** 41.38 N 14.52 E
Sant'Elia Fiumerapido **66** 41.32 N 13.52 E
Sant'Elpidio a Mare **66** 43.14 N 13.41 E
Santena **62** 44.57 N 7.45 E
Santenay **58** 46.55 N 4.41 E
Santeny **261** 48.43 N 2.34 E
San Teodoro, It. **70** 37.51 N 14.42 E
San Teodoro, It. **71** 40.46 N 9.39 E
Santermo in Colle **68** 40.48 N 16.45 E
Santerno ≃ **64** 44.34 N 11.58 E
Santerre □[9] **50** 49.40 N 2.40 E
Sant'Eufemia, Golfo di ⊂ **68** 38.50 N 16.00 E
Sant'Eufemia a Maiella **66** 42.07 N 14.02 E
Sant'Eufemia d'Aspromonte **68** 38.16 N 15.52 E
Sant'Eufemia Lamezia **68** 38.55 N 16.15 E
Sant Feliu de Guíxols **34** 41.47 N 3.02 E
Sant Feliu de Llobregat **266d** 41.23 N 2.03 E
Sant Fost de Campsentelles **266d** 41.31 N 2.14 E
Sānthia, Bngl. **126** 24.03 N 89.33 E
Santhià, It. **62** 45.22 N 8.10 E
Santiago, Bol. **248** 18.19 S 59.34 W
Santiago, Bra. **252** 29.11 S 54.53 W
Santiago, Chile **252** 33.27 S 70.40 W
Santiago, Chile **286e** 33.27 S 70.40 W
Santiago → Santiago de Compostela, Esp. **34** 42.53 N 8.33 W
Santiago, Méx. **232** 23.28 N 109.43 W
Santiago, Pan. **236** 8.06 N 80.59 W
Santiago, Para. **252** 27.09 S 56.47 W
Santiago, Perú **248** 14.11 S 75.44 W
Santiago, Pil. **116** 16.41 N 121.33 E
Santiago I **150a** 15.05 N 23.40 W
Santiago ≃, Arg. **288** 34.50 S 57.57 W
Santiago ≃, Méx. **232** 25.11 N 105.26 W
Santiago ≃, S.A. **246** 4.27 S 77.38 W
Santiago, Cape › **116** 13.46 N 120.39 E
Santiago, Cerro ∧ **236** 8.33 N 81.44 W
Santiago, Isla I, Arg. **288** 34.50 S 57.53 W
Santiago, Isla I, Ec. **246a** 0.14 S 90.45 W
Santiago, Serranía de ⋏ **248** 18.25 S 59.25 W
Santiago Atitlán **236** 14.38 N 91.14 W
Santiago Chazumba **234** 18.12 N 97.40 W
Santiago Choapan **234** 17.20 N 95.57 W
Santiago Creek ≃, Ca., U.S. **228** 35.06 N 119.17 W
Santiago Creek ≃, Ca., U.S. **228** 33.46 N 117.54 W
Santiago Dam ◆[6] **280** 33.47 N 117.43 W
Santiago de Cao **248** 7.58 S 79.15 W
Santiago de Chocorvos **248** 13.50 S 75.16 W
Santiago de Chuco **248** 8.09 S 78.11 W
Santiago de Compostela **34** 42.53 N 8.33 W
Santiago de Cuba **240p** 20.01 N 75.49 W
Santiago de Cuba □[4] **240p** 20.10 N 75.55 W
Santiago de Huari **248** 19.00 S 66.48 W
Santiago de Huata **248** 16.06 S 68.53 W
Santiago de la Peña **234** 20.57 N 97.24 W
Santiago de las Vegas ◆[8] **286b** 22.58 N 82.23 W
Santiago del Estero **252** 27.47 S 64.16 W
Santiago del Estero □[4] **252** 28.00 S 63.30 W
Santiago de los Caballeros **238** 19.27 N 70.42 W
Santiago de Machaca **248** 17.05 S 69.16 W
Santiago de Méndez **246** 2.43 S 78.19 W
Santiago de Surco **286d** 12.09 S 77.01 W
Santiago do Cacém **34** 38.01 N 8.42 W
Santiago Island I **116** 16.24 N 119.56 E
Santiago Ixcuintla **234** 21.49 N 105.13 W
Santiago Ixtayutla **234** 16.33 N 97.39 W
Santiago Jamiltepec **234** 16.17 N 97.49 W
Santiago Juxtlahuaca **234** 17.20 N 98.01 W
Santiago Lachiguirí **234** 16.41 N 95.32 W
Santiago Larre **258** 35.34 S 59.10 W
Santiago Maravatío **234** 20.10 N 101.00 W
Santiago Papasquiaro **232** 25.03 N 105.25 W
Santiago Peak ∧, Ca., U.S. **228** 33.42 N 117.32 W
Santiago Peak ∧, Tx., U.S. **196** 29.47 N 103.25 W
Santiago Pinotepa Nacional **234** 16.19 N 98.01 W
Santiago Reservoir ⊜[1] **228** 33.47 N 117.43 W
Santiago Tepalcatlapan ◆[8] **286a** 19.15 N 99.08 W
Santiago Tulantepec **234** 20.02 N 98.22 W
Santiago Tutla **234** 17.10 N 95.26 W
Santiago Tuxtla **234** 18.28 N 95.18 W
Santiago Vázquez **258** 34.48 S 56.21 W
Santiago Yaveo **234** 17.19 N 95.42 W
Santiago Zacatepec **234** 17.11 N 95.51 W
Santiaguillo, Laguna ⊜ **232** 24.48 N 104.48 W
Santiam Pass)(**202** 44.25 N 121.51 W
San Tian Zhu (Three Indian Temples) ʊ[1] **106** 30.15 N 120.08 E
Santiao Chiao › **100** 25.02 N 121.59 E
Santiaoqiao **106** 31.36 N 121.22 E
Santi Filippo e Giacomo **70** 37.51 N 12.31 E
Santiguila **150** 12.42 N 7.26 W
Sant'Ilario d'Enza **64** 44.46 N 10.27 E
San Timoteo **246** 9.48 N 71.04 W
San Timoteo Canyon V **228** 34.04 N 117.17 W
Säntis ∧ **58** 47.15 N 9.21 E
Santissima Trinita di Saccargia ʊ[1] **71** 40.41 N 8.42 E
Santissimo ◆[8] **287a** 22.53 S 43.31 W
Santisteban del Puerto **34** 38.15 N 3.12 W
Sant Joan de Labritja **34** 39.05 N 1.30 E
Sant Joan Despí **266d** 41.22 N 2.04 E
Sant Jordi, Golf de ⊂ **34** 40.53 N 1.00 E
Sant Just Desvern **266d** 41.23 N 2.05 E
Sant Mateu **34** 40.28 N 0.11 E
Santō, Nihon **94** 35.21 N 136.22 E
Santō, Nihon **96** 35.19 N 134.53 E
Santo, Tx., U.S. **196** 32.36 N 98.13 W
Santo, Vanuatu **175f** 15.32 S 167.08 E
Santo Aleixo **256** 22.34 S 43.04 W
Santo Amaro, Bra. **250** 2.33 S 43.14 W
Santo Amaro, Bra. **255** 12.32 S 38.43 W
Santo Amaro ◆[8] **287b** 23.39 S 46.42 W
Santo Amaro, Ilha de I **256** 23.57 S 46.14 W
Santo Amaro das Brotas **250** 10.47 S 37.04 W
Santo Anastácio **255** 21.58 S 51.39 W
Santo André **256** 23.40 S 46.31 W
Santo Ângelo **252** 28.18 S 54.16 W
Santo Antão I **150a** 17.05 N 25.10 W
Santo Antônio, Bra. **250** 6.18 S 35.27 W
Santo António, S. Tom./P. **152** 1.39 N 7.26 E
Santo Antônio ≃, Bra. **250** 11.31 S 48.37 W
Santo Antônio ≃, Bra. **255** 17.30 S 45.37 W
Santo Antônio ≃, Bra. **287a** 22.42 S 43.37 W
Santo Antônio, Ilha de I **156** 21.58 S 35.28 E
Santo Antônio da Charneca **266c** 38.37 N 9.02 W
Santo Antônio da Patrulha **252** 29.50 S 50.32 W
Santo Antônio de Jesus **255** 12.58 S 39.16 W
Santo Antônio de Pádua **255** 21.32 S 42.11 W
Santo Antonio de Posse **256** 22.36 S 46.55 W
Santo Antônio do Amparo **255** 20.57 S 44.55 W
Santo Antônio do Aventureiro **256** 21.45 S 42.49 W
Santo Antônio do Içá **246** 3.05 S 67.57 W
Santo Antônio do Jardim **256** 22.07 S 46.41 W
Santo Antônio do Leverger **248** 15.52 S 56.05 W
Santo Antônio do Pinhal **256** 22.47 S 45.41 W
Santo Antônio do Rio Verde **255** 17.57 S 47.27 W
Santo Antônio do Sudoeste **252** 26.02 S 53.44 W
Santo Augusto **252** 27.51 S 53.47 W
Santo Corazón **248** 17.59 S 58.51 W
Santo Domingo, Cuba **240p** 22.35 N 80.15 W
Santo Domingo, Méx. **196** 25.38 N 101.05 W
Santo Domingo, Méx. **196** 25.48 N 104.28 W
Santo Domingo, Méx. **232** 25.32 N 112.02 W
Santo Domingo, Nic. **236** 12.16 N 85.05 W
Santo Domingo, Rep. Dom. **238** 18.28 N 69.54 W
Santo Domingo ≃, Méx. **234** 16.41 N 93.00 W
Santo Domingo ≃, Méx. **234** 17.40 N 98.07 W
Santo Domingo ≃, Méx. **234** 18.10 N 96.08 W
Santo Domingo ≃, Méx. **236** 16.15 N 91.17 W
Santo Domingo, Arroyo ≃ **204** 30.43 N 116.03 W
Santo Domingo, Isla → Hispaniola I **238** 19.00 N 71.00 W
Santo Domingo de la Calzada **34** 42.26 N 2.57 W
Santo Domingo de los Colorados **246** 0.15 S 79.09 W
Santo Domingo Indian Reservation ◆[4] **200** 35.30 N 106.25 W
Santo Domingo Nuxaá **234** 17.08 N 97.02 W
Santo Domingo Pueblo **200** 35.30 N 106.21 W
Santo Domingo Tehuantepec **234** 16.20 N 95.14 W
Santo Domingo Teojomulco **234** 16.36 N 97.14 W
Santo Domingo Zanatepec **234** 16.29 N 94.21 W
Santo Estêvão **255** 12.26 S 39.13 W
Sant'Olcese **62** 44.30 N 8.58 E
Santolea, Embalse de ⊜[1] **34** 40.47 N 0.19 W
Santo / Malo □[8] **175f** 15.20 S 166.55 E
San Tomé **246** 8.58 N 64.08 W
San Tommaso **66** 42.11 N 13.58 E
Sant'Omobono Imagna **62** 45.48 N 9.32 E
Santoña **34** 43.27 N 3.27 W
Santong ≃ **98** 42.39 N 126.03 E
Santo Nino Island I **116** 11.55 N 124.27 E
Sant' Onofrio ◆[8] **267a** 41.56 N 12.25 E
Santo Onofre ≃ **255** 12.34 S 43.12 W
Santop, Pic ∧ **175f** 18.39 S 169.03 E
Sant'Oreste **66** 42.14 N 12.32 E
Santorini → Thíra I **38** 36.24 N 25.29 E
Santorso **64** 45.44 N 11.23 E
Santos **256** 23.57 S 46.20 W
Santos, Arroyo de los ≃ **258** 35.28 S 57.29 W
Santos, Baía de ⊂ **256** 24.00 S 46.21 W
Santos Dumont **256** 21.28 S 43.34 W
Santos Dumont, Aeroporto ⊠ **256** 22.55 S 43.10 W
Santoshpur **272b** 22.40 N 88.10 E
Santo Stefano, Isola I **66** 40.47 N 13.27 E
Santo Stefano Belbo **62** 44.43 N 8.14 E
Santo Stefano d'Aveto **62** 44.35 N 9.27 E
Santo Stefano di Cadore **64** 46.33 N 12.32 E
Santo Stefano di Camastra **70** 38.01 N 14.21 E
Santo Stefano di Magra **64** 44.10 N 9.55 E
Santo Stefano Quisquina **70** 37.37 N 13.29 E
Santo Stino di Livenza **64** 45.44 N 12.41 E
Santos Tomás del Norte **236** 13.11 N 86.56 W
Santo Tirso **34** 41.21 N 8.28 W
Santo Tomás, Col. **246** 10.46 N 74.45 W
Santo Tomás, Méx. **232** 31.33 N 116.24 W
Santo Tomás, Nic. **236** 12.04 N 85.05 W
Santo Tomás, Perú **248** 6.36 S 77.48 W
Santo Tomás, Perú **248** 14.29 S 72.06 W
Santo Tomas, Pil. **116** 7.29 N 125.38 E
Santo Tomás ≃, Méx. **204** 31.32 N 116.40 W
Santo Tomás ≃, Perú **248** 13.47 S 72.09 W
Santo Tomás, Punta › **232** 31.34 N 116.42 W
Santo Tomas, University of ʊ[2] **269f** 14.37 N 120.59 E
Santo Tomás, Volcán ∧[1] **246a** 0.48 S 91.07 W
Santo Tomás y Principe → Sao Tome and Principe □[1] **152** 1.00 N 7.00 E
Santo Tomé, Arg. **252** 28.33 S 56.03 W
Santo Tomé, Arg. **252** 31.40 S 60.46 W
Santo Tomé de Guayana → Ciudad Guayana **246** 8.22 N 62.40 W
Sant'pietro, Lago di ⊜ **68** 41.01 N 15.30 E
Santpoort **52** 52.25 N 4.38 E
Sant Quirze de la Serra **266d** 41.32 N 2.05 E
Santuanjiang **106** 30.54 N 121.43 E
Santuario de Quillacas **248** 19.14 S 66.58 W
Santu Lussurgiu **71** 40.08 N 8.39 E
Santunying **105** 40.14 N 118.12 E
Sant Vicenç dels Horts **266d** 41.24 N 2.01 E
San Ubaldo **236** 11.51 N 85.20 W
Sanuki **268** 35.16 N 139.53 E
Sanuki-sammyaku ⋏ **96** 34.09 N 134.11 E
Şānūr **132** 32.21 N 35.15 E
San Valentino in Abruzzo Citeriore **66** 42.14 N 13.59 E
San Valentino Torio **68** 40.48 N 14.36 E
San Venanzo **66** 42.52 N 12.16 E
San Vendemiano **64** 45.54 N 12.20 E
San Vicente, Arg. **252** 28.30 S 64.09 W
San Vicente, Arg. **258** 34.58 S 58.22 W
San Vicente, El Sal. **236** 13.38 N 88.48 W
San Vicente □[5] **288** 34.56 S 58.24 W
San Vicente → Saint Vincent and the Grenadines □[1] **241h** 13.15 N 61.12 W
San Vicente, Cabo → São Vicente, Cabo de › **34** 37.01 N 9.00 W
San Vicente, Volcán de ∧[1] **236** 13.36 N 88.51 W
San Vicente Creek ≃ **282** 37.32 N 122.31 W
San Vicente de Alcántara **34** 39.21 N 7.08 W
San Vicente de Cañete **248** 13.05 S 76.24 W
San Vicente de Chucurí **246** 6.54 N 73.25 W
San Vicente de la Barquera **34** 43.26 N 4.24 W
San Vicente del Caguán **246** 2.07 N 74.46 W
San Vicente de Tagua-Tagua **252** 34.26 S 71.05 W
San Vicente Mountain ∧ **280** 34.08 N 118.31 W
San Vicente Reservoir ⊜[1] **228** 32.55 N 116.55 W
San Vicente Tancuayalab **234** 21.44 N 98.34 W
San Vigilio **64** 45.34 N 10.41 E
San Vigilio ʊ[1] **64** 46.37 N 11.07 E
San Vincenzo **66** 43.06 N 10.32 E
San Vito, C.R. **236** 8.50 N 82.58 W
San Vito, It. **71** 39.26 N 9.32 E
San Vito, Capo › **70** 38.11 N 12.44 E
San Vito, Serralta di ∧ **68** 38.46 N 16.22 E
San Vito al Tagliamento **64** 45.54 N 12.52 E
San Vito Chietino **66** 42.18 N 14.27 E
San Vito dei Normanni **68** 40.39 N 17.42 E
San Vito lo Capo **70** 38.10 N 12.45 E
San Vito Romano **66** 41.53 N 12.59 E
San Vito sullo Ionio **68** 38.43 N 16.25 E
Sanwa, Nihon **94** 37.07 N 138.21 E
Sanwa, Nihon **94** 36.12 N 139.49 E
Sanwa, Nihon **96** 34.42 N 133.15 E
San Xavier Indian Reservation ◆[4] **200** 32.05 N 111.08 W
Sanxi, Zhg. **100** 30.22 N 118.25 E
Sanxi, Zhg. **100** 27.42 N 120.04 E
Sanxing, Zhg. **106** 31.47 N 121.35 E
Sanxing, Zhg. **106** 31.58 N 121.07 E
Sanxingchang, Zhg. **107** 30.19 N 104.09 E
Sanxingchang, Zhg. **107** 30.32 N 104.38 E
Sanxingjie **106** 32.06 N 121.01 E
Sanyang, Zhg. **100** 28.37 N 116.15 E
Sanyang, Zhg. **100** 31.20 N 113.10 E
Sanyang, Zhg. **100** 27.57 N 114.22 E
Sanyangzhen **106** 31.55 N 121.29 E
Sanyanjing **104** 41.28 N 122.27 E
Sanyanqiao **100** 28.39 N 113.43 E
Sanyati ≃ **154** 16.49 S 28.45 E
San Ygnacio **196** 27.03 N 99.27 W
Sanyō, Nihon **96** 34.45 N 134.01 E
Sanyō, Nihon **96** 34.02 N 131.10 E
Sanyuan **102** 34.35 N 108.54 E
Sanyuanpu **98** 42.02 N 125.44 E
Sanyuhao **98** 42.30 N 117.34 E
Sanyuzhen **106** 32.08 N 121.19 E
Sanza **68** 40.15 N 15.33 E
Sanzao Dao I **100** 22.03 N 113.21 E
Sanza Pombo **152** 7.19 S 15.59 E
Sanzar ≃ **85** 40.00 N 67.40 E
San Zeno di Montagna **64** 45.37 N 10.43 E
Sanzha **98** 41.44 N 114.39 E
Sanzhan, Zhg. **89** 49.42 N 125.20 E
Sanzhan, Zhg. **89** 49.36 N 126.38 E
Sanzuodian **98** 41.36 N 118.49 E
São Benedito **250** 4.03 S 40.53 W
São Benedito ≃ **250** 9.11 S 57.02 W
São Benedito das Areias **256** 21.19 S 47.02 W
São Benedito do Rio Preto **250** 3.20 S 43.35 W
São Bento **250** 2.42 S 44.50 W
São Bento ≃ **256** 21.42 S 45.18 W
São Bento, Mosteiro de ʊ[1] **287a** 22.54 S 43.11 W
São Bento Abade **256** 21.35 S 45.04 W
São Bento de Caldas **256** 22.08 S 46.18 W
São Bento do Norte **250** 5.04 S 36.02 W
São Bento do Sapucaí **256** 22.42 S 45.43 W
São Bento do Sul **252** 26.15 S 49.23 W
São Bento do Una **250** 8.32 S 36.22 W
São Bernardino **287a** 22.40 S 43.26 W
São Bernardo **250** 3.22 S 42.24 W
São Bernardo do Campo **256** 23.42 S 46.33 W
São Bernardo do Campo □[7] **287b** 23.44 S 46.33 W
São Borja **252** 28.39 S 56.00 W
São Brás **250** 10.05 S 36.55 W
São Brás de Alportel **34** 37.09 N 7.53 W
Sâo Braz, Cabo de › **152** 9.59 S 13.19 E
São Caetano de Odivelas **250** 0.45 S 48.02 W
São Caetano do Sul **256** 23.36 S 46.34 W
São Caetano do Sul □[7] **287b** 23.37 S 46.33 W
São Carlos **255** 22.01 S 47.54 W
São Cristóvão **250** 11.01 S 37.12 W
São Cristóvão ◆[8] **287a** 22.54 S 43.14 W
Saodatun **104** 42.02 N 123.31 E
São Domingos, Bra. **252** 26.34 S 52.32 W
São Domingos, Bra. **255** 13.24 S 46.19 W
São Domingos, Bra. **256** 21.41 S 42.47 W
São Domingos, Gui.-B. **150** 12.22 N 16.08 W
São Domingos ≃, Bra. **248** 12.28 S 64.13 W
São Domingos ≃, Bra. **255** 13.24 S 47.12 W
São Domingos ≃, Bra. **255** 19.13 S 50.44 W
São Domingos ≃, Bra. **255** 20.03 S 53.13 W
São Domingos da Bocaina **256** 21.50 S 44.01 W
São Domingos do Capim **250** 1.41 S 47.47 W
São Domingos do Maranhão **250** 5.42 S 44.22 W
São Felipe **255** 14.49 S 41.23 W
São Félix de Balsas **250** 7.08 S 44.52 W
São Félix do Araguaia **250** 11.36 S 50.39 W
São Félix do Piauí **250** 5.56 S 42.07 W
São Filipe **150a** 14.54 N 24.31 W
São Francisco **255** 15.57 S 44.52 W
São Francisco ≃, Bra. **242** 10.30 S 36.24 W
São Francisco ≃, Bra. **255** 16.09 S 40.39 W
São Francisco ≃, Bra. **256** 21.50 S 42.42 W
São Francisco ≃, Bra. **287a** 22.57 S 43.20 W
São Francisco, Baía de ⊂ **252** 26.10 S 48.34 W
São Francisco, Ilha de I **252** 26.18 S 48.37 W
São Francisco de Assis **252** 29.33 S 55.08 W
São Francisco de Goiás **255** 15.55 S 49.16 W
São Francisco de Paula **252** 29.27 S 50.35 W
São Francisco do Croará **287a** 22.42 S 43.08 W
São Francisco do Maranhão **250** 6.15 S 42.52 W
São Francisco do Piauí **250** 7.15 S 42.32 W
São Francisco do Sul **252** 26.14 S 48.39 W
São Francisco Xavier **256** 22.54 S 45.58 W
São Gabriel **252** 30.20 S 54.19 W
São Gabriel da Palha **255** 19.01 S 40.32 W
São Gabriel de Goiás **255** 15.12 S 47.34 W
São Gonçalo, Bra. **256** 21.36 S 46.19 W
São Gonçalo, Bra. **256** 22.51 S 43.04 W
São Gonçalo □[7] **287a** 22.48 S 43.01 W
São Gonçalo do Abaeté **255** 18.20 S 45.49 W
São Gonçalo do Sapucaí **256** 21.54 S 45.36 W
São Gonçalo dos Campos **255** 12.25 S 38.58 W
Sao Hill **154** 8.20 S 35.12 E
São Jerônimo **252** 29.58 S 51.43 W
São Jerônimo, Serra de ⋏[1] **255** 16.30 S 54.50 W
São Jerônimo da Serra **255** 23.43 S 50.44 W
São João **150** 11.32 N 15.26 W
São João ≃, Bra. **255** 12.27 S 51.07 W
São João ≃, Bra. **256** 22.33 S 42.29 W
São João da Barra **255** 21.38 S 41.03 W
São João da Boa Vista **256** 21.58 S 46.47 W
São João D'Aliança **255** 14.42 S 47.32 W
São João da Madeira **34** 40.54 N 8.30 W
São João da Mata **256** 21.56 S 45.56 W
São João da Ponte **255** 15.56 S 44.01 W
São João da Serra **256** 21.28 S 43.27 W
São João das Lampas **266c** 38.52 N 9.24 W

Symbols in the index entries represent the broad categories identified in the key at the right. Symbols with superior numbers (⋏[1]) identify subcategories (see complete key on page *I · 1).*

Symbole im Register stellen die rechts im Schlüssel erklärten Kategorien dar. Symbole mit hochgestellten Ziffern (⋏[1]) bezeichnen Unterabteilungen einer Kategorie (vgl. vollständiger Schlüssel auf Seite *I · 1).*

Los símbolos incluídos en el texto del índice representan las grandes categorías identificadas con la clave a la derecha. Los símbolos con numeros en su parte superior (⋏[1]) identifican las subcategorías (véase la clave completa en la página *I · 1).*

Les symboles de l'index représentent les catégories indiquées dans la légende à droite. Les symboles suivis d'un indice (⋏[1]) représentent des sous-catégories (voir légende complète à la page *I · 1).*

Os símbolos incluídos no texto do índice representam as grandes categorias identificadas com a chave à direita. Os símbolos com números em sua parte superior (⋏[1]) identificam as subcategorias (veja-se a chave completa à página *I · 1).*

	English	Deutsch	Español	Français	Português
∧	Mountain	Berg	Montaña	Montagne	Montanha
⋏	Mountains	Gebirge	Montañas	Montagnes	Montanhas
)(	Pass	Paß	Paso	Col	Passo
V	Valley, Canyon	Tal, Cañon	Valle, Cañón	Vallée, Canyon	Vale, Canhão
≚	Plain	Ebene	Llano	Plaine	Planície
›	Cape	Kap	Cabo	Cap	Cabo
I	Island	Insel	Isla	Île	Ilha
II	Islands	Inseln	Islas	Îles	Ilhas
⊥	Other Topographic Features	Andere Topographische Objekte	Otros Elementos Topográficos	Autres données topographiques	Outros acidentes topográficos

Saoj-Saun I · 157

ESPAÑOL · FRANÇAIS · PORTUGUÊS

Nombre / Nom / Nome	Página / Page	Lat.°′	Long.°′ W = Oeste / W = Ouest
São João de Côrtes	250	2.12 S	44.32 W
São João del-Rei	255	21.09 S	44.16 W
São João de Meriti	256	22.48 S	43.22 W
São João de Meriti □[7]	287a	22.48 S	43.21 W
São João de Meriti ≃	287a	22.48 S	43.18 W
São João do Araguaia	250	5.23 S	48.46 W
São João do Jaguaribe	250	5.16 S	38.16 W
São João do Paraíso	255	15.19 S	42.01 W
São João do Piauí	250	8.21 S	42.15 W
São João do Sabugi	250	6.43 S	37.12 W
São João dos Patos	250	6.30 S	43.42 W
São João Evangelista	255	18.32 S	42.45 W
São João Nepomuceno	256	21.33 S	43.01 W
São João Novo	256	23.33 S	47.01 W
São Joaquim	252	28.18 S	49.56 W
São Joaquim, Parque Nacional de ♠	252	28.15 S	49.57 W
São Joaquim da Barra	255	20.35 S	47.53 W
São Jorge I	148a	38.38 N	28.03 W
São Jorge, Castelo de ⊥	266c	38.43 N	9.08 W
São José, Bra.	252	27.38 S	48.39 W
São José, Bra.	256	22.43 S	42.36 W
São José ≃, Bra.	255	19.10 S	40.12 W
São José ≃, Bra.	287a	22.39 S	43.27 W
São José, Ponta de ›	152	12.36 S	13.12 E
São José da Laje	250	9.01 S	36.03 W
São José de Anauá	246	1.00 N	61.23 W
São José de Encoge	152	7.38 S	14.41 E
São José de Mipibu	250	6.05 S	35.15 W
São José de Piranhas	250	7.07 S	38.30 W
São José do Alegre	256	22.19 S	45.32 W
São José do Barreiro	256	22.38 S	44.35 W
São José do Belmonte	250	7.52 S	38.46 W
São José do Campestre	250	6.18 S	35.42 W
São José do Cedro	252	26.30 S	53.30 W
São José do Egito	250	7.28 S	37.16 W
São José do Gurupi	250	1.36 S	46.13 W
São José do Norte	252	32.01 S	52.03 W
São José do Peixe	250	7.24 S	42.34 W
São José do Piriá	250	1.17 S	46.18 W
São José do Rio Pardo	256	21.36 S	46.54 W
São José do Rio Preto, Bra.	255	20.48 S	49.23 W
São José do Rio Prêto, Bra.	256	22.10 S	42.57 W
São José dos Campos	256	23.11 S	45.53 W
São José dos Lopes	256	21.48 S	43.53 W
São José dos Pinhais	252	25.31 S	49.13 W
São José do Turvo	256	22.21 S	43.59 W
São Julião da Barra	266c	38.40 N	9.21 W
São Julião do Tojal	266c	38.51 N	9.08 W
São Leopoldo	252	29.46 S	51.09 W
São Lourenço	256	22.07 S	45.03 W
São Lourenço, Pantanal de ≣	248	17.30 S	56.30 W
São Lourenço da Serra	256	23.52 S	46.57 W
São Lourenço do Oeste	252	26.24 S	52.46 W
São Lourenço do Sul	252	31.22 S	51.58 W
São Luís	250	2.31 S	44.16 W
São Luís de Montes Belos	255	16.32 S	50.20 W
São Luís do Curu	250	3.40 S	39.14 W
São Luís Do Paraitinga	256	23.14 S	45.20 W
São Luís do Quitunde	250	9.20 S	35.33 W
São Luís Gonzaga	252	28.24 S	54.58 W
São Mamede	250	6.56 S	37.06 W
São Manuel	255	22.44 S	48.34 W
São Manuel ≃	242	7.21 S	58.03 W
São Manuel do Guaiaçu	256	21.20 S	42.51 W
São Marcos ≃	255	18.15 S	47.37 W
São Mateus, Bra.	255	18.44 S	39.51 W
São Mateus, Bra.	256	22.49 S	43.23 W
São Mateus, Port.	148a	38.26 N	28.27 W
São Mateus, Braço Norte ≃	255	18.37 S	40.05 W
São Mateus de Minas	256	22.42 S	46.03 W
São Mateus do Sul	252	25.52 S	50.23 W
São Miguel	250	6.13 S	38.30 W
São Miguel I	148a	37.47 N	25.30 W
São Miguel ≃	255	16.26 S	41.00 W
São Miguel do Araguaia	255	13.19 S	50.13 W
São Miguel d'Oeste	252	26.45 S	53.34 W
São Miguel do Guamá	250	1.37 S	47.27 W
São Miguel dos Campos	250	9.47 S	36.05 W
São Miguel dos Macacos	250	1.11 S	50.28 W
São Miguel do Tapuio	250	5.30 S	41.20 W
São Miguel Paulista (Baquiriru) ◆[8]	256	23.30 S	46.26 W
Saona, Isla I	238	18.09 N	68.40 W
Saonara	64	45.22 N	11.59 E
Saône ≃	58	45.44 N	4.50 E
Saône-et-Loire □[5]	32	46.42 N	4.45 E
Saonek	164	0.28 S	130.47 E
Saoner	120	21.23 N	78.54 E
São Nicolau I	150a	16.35 N	24.15 W
São Nicolau ≃	250	5.45 S	42.02 W
São Paulo, Bra.	256	23.32 S	46.37 W
São Paulo, Bra.	287b	23.32 S	46.37 W
São Paulo □[3]	255	22.00 S	49.00 W
São Paulo □[7]	287b	23.33 S	46.38 W
São Paulo, Ribeirão de ≃	256	22.16 S	46.37 W
São Paulo de Olivença	246	3.27 S	68.48 W
São Paulo do Potengi	250	5.55 S	35.45 W
São Pedro	255	19.53 S	51.55 W
São Pedro ≃	255	16.30 S	41.17 W
São Pedro de Caldas	256	21.49 S	46.16 W
São Pedro de Viseu	250	2.33 S	49.33 W
São Pedro do Estoril	266c	38.42 N	9.22 W
São Pedro do Piauí	250	5.56 S	42.43 W
São Pedro do Sul, Bra.	252	29.37 S	54.10 W
São Pedro do Sul, Port.	34	40.45 N	8.04 W
São Rafael	250	5.47 S	36.55 W
São Raimundo das Mangabeiras	250	7.01 S	45.29 W
São Raimundo Nonato	250	9.01 S	42.42 W
Saorge	62	43.59 N	7.33 E
Saori	94	35.11 N	136.44 E
São Romão	255	16.22 S	45.04 W
São Roque, Bra.	256	23.06 S	44.42 W
São Roque, Bra.	256	23.32 S	47.08 W
São Roque, Cabo de ›	250	5.29 S	35.16 W
São Roque da Fartura	256	21.51 S	46.45 W
São Salvador → Salvador	255	12.59 S	38.31 W
São Sebastião	256	23.48 S	45.25 W
São Sebastião, Canal de ʮ	256	23.48 S	45.23 W
São Sebastião, Ilha de I	256	23.50 S	45.18 W
São Sebastião, Pico de ∧	256	23.52 S	45.23 W
São Sebastião, Ponta ›	156	22.07 S	35.30 E
São Sebastião da Bela Vista	256	22.10 S	45.45 W
São Sebastião da Boa Vista	250	1.42 S	49.31 W
São Sebastião da Grama	256	21.43 S	46.49 W
São Sebastião da Vitória	256	21.14 S	44.25 W
São Sebastião do Barreado	256	22.04 S	43.38 W
São Sebastião do Maranhão	255	18.05 S	42.35 W
São Sebastião do Paraíso	255	20.55 S	47.00 W
São Sebastião do Rio Claro	255	15.45 S	51.30 W
São Sebastião do Rio Verde	256	22.13 S	44.58 W
São Sebastião dos Robertos	256	22.13 S	46.32 W
São Sebastião do Umbuzeiro	250	8.09 S	37.01 W
São Sepé	252	30.10 S	53.34 W
São Silvestre do Jacareí	256	23.23 S	46.01 W
São Simão, Bra.	255	18.56 S	50.30 W
São Simão, Bra.	255	21.30 S	47.33 W
São Simão, Represa de ⊜[1]	255	18.40 S	50.00 W
São Tiago	255	20.55 S	44.30 W
São Timóteo	255	13.51 S	42.11 W
São Tomé, Bra.	250	5.58 S	36.04 W
São Tomé, S. Tom./P.	152	0.20 N	6.44 E
São Tomé I	152	0.12 N	6.39 E
São Tomé ≃, Bra.	250	8.10 S	58.13 W
São Tomé ≃, Bra.	256	21.26 S	46.02 W
São Tomé, Cabo de ›	255	21.59 S	40.59 W
São Tomé, Pico de ∧	152	0.16 N	6.33 E
Sao Tome and Principe (São Tomé e Principe) □[1], Afr.	138	1.00 N	7.00 E
Sao Tome and Principe (São Tomé e Principe) □[1], Afr.	152	1.00 N	7.00 E
São Tomé das Letras	256	21.43 S	44.59 W
Sao Tomé-et-Principe → Sao Tome and Principe □[1]	152	1.00 N	7.00 E
Saou	62	44.39 N	5.04 E
Saoura, Oued ∨	148	29.00 N	0.55 W
São Valério ≃	250	11.20 S	48.28 W
São Vicente	256	23.58 S	46.23 W
São Vicente I	150a	16.50 N	25.00 W
São Vicente, Cabo de (Cape Saint Vincent) ›	34	37.01 N	9.00 W
São Vicente, Ribeirão ≃	256	21.59 S	45.40 W
São Vicente de Minas	256	21.42 S	44.27 W
São Vicente Ferrer	250	7.35 S	35.30 W
Sa Pa	110	22.21 N	103.50 E
Sápai	38	41.02 N	25.41 E
Sapanca	130	40.41 N	30.16 E
Sapang Baho ≃	269f	14.33 N	121.06 E
Sapao	116	10.01 N	126.02 E
Sapão ≃	250	11.01 S	45.32 W
Saparua, Pulau I	164	3.34 S	128.40 E
Sapatgrām	124	26.20 N	90.08 E
Sapé, Bra.	250	7.06 S	35.13 W
Sape, Indon.	115b	8.34 S	118.59 E
Sapé ≃	287a	22.52 S	43.02 W
Sape, Selat ʮ	115b	8.39 S	119.18 E
Sapele	150	5.54 N	5.41 E
Sapello ≃	200	35.47 N	104.59 W
Sapelo Island I	192	31.28 N	81.15 W
Saperkino	80	54.05 N	51.38 E
Şaphane	130	39.01 N	29.14 E
Sapian Bay ⊂	116	11.33 N	122.37 E
Sapindji	152	9.39 S	23.12 E
Sapitwa ∧	154	15.57 S	35.36 E
Šapki	76	59.36 N	31.14 E
Šapkina ≃	24	66.44 N	52.25 E
Šapkino	80	51.42 N	42.24 E
Šapkovo, Ross.	76	55.47 N	33.20 E
Sapkovo, Ross.	82	54.34 N	39.10 E
Sa Pobla	34	39.46 N	3.01 E
Sapockin	76	53.50 N	23.39 E
Sapodilla Cays I	236	16.08 N	88.15 W
Saponara	70	38.11 N	15.26 E
Saponé	150	12.03 N	1.36 W
Sap'o-ri	98	40.49 N	129.31 E
Sap'ornaja	265a	59.46 N	30.41 E
Saporoschje → Zaporizhzhya	78	47.50 N	35.10 E
Saposoa	248	6.56 S	76.48 W
Sapou	175c	7.18 N	151.53 E
Sapožok	80	53.56 N	40.41 E
Sappa Creek ≃	198	40.07 N	99.38 W
Sappa Creek, Middle Fork ≃	198	39.40 N	100.53 W
Sappa Creek, North Fork ≃	198	39.47 N	100.35 W
Sappa Creek, South Fork ≃	198	39.47 N	100.35 W
Sappada	64	46.34 N	12.41 E
Sapphire Mountains ⋏	202	46.20 N	113.45 W
Sappho	224	48.04 N	124.16 W
Sappington	219	38.32 N	90.22 W
Sapporo	92a	43.03 N	141.21 E
Şapri	68	40.04 N	15.38 E
Šapša	76	60.34 N	34.01 E
Sap Songkhla, Thale ⊂	110	7.13 N	100.30 E
Šapsugskaja	78	44.45 N	38.05 E
Saptakośī ≃	124	26.31 N	86.58 E
Sapta-ri	271b	37.43 N	126.44 E
Sapu	152	12.29 S	19.26 E
Sapucaí	256	22.19 S	46.42 W
Sapucaí ≃	256	21.33 S	45.40 W
Sapucaia	256	22.00 S	42.54 W
Sapucaí-Mirim	256	22.44 S	45.45 W
Sapucaí-Mirim ≃	256	22.12 S	45.53 W
Sapudi, Pulau I	115a	7.06 S	114.20 E
Sapulpa	196	35.59 N	96.06 W
Sapulu	115a	6.54 S	112.57 E
Sapuran	115a	7.28 S	109.58 E
Sapwe	154	10.57 S	28.10 E
Sāq, Jabal ∧[2]	128	26.17 N	43.16 E
Sāqiat al-ʿAbd	140	20.48 N	30.19 E
Sāqiyat Makkī	142	30.00 N	31.13 E
Şaqqārah	142	29.51 N	31.13 E
Şaqqārah (Step Pyramid) ⊥	142	29.52 N	31.13 E
Saqqez	128	36.14 N	46.16 E
Saquarema	256	22.56 S	42.30 W
Saquarema, Lagoa de ⊂	256	22.55 S	42.33 W
Saquena	248	4.40 S	73.31 W
Saquish Neck ›[1]	283	42.00 N	70.37 W
Saquisilí	246	0.51 S	78.40 W
Sāra, Bngl.	126	24.07 N	89.02 E
Sara, Burkina	150	11.43 N	3.50 W
Sara, Pil.	116	11.16 N	123.01 E
Sara, Ross.	80	54.38 N	46.46 E
Sarāb	128	37.56 N	47.32 E
Sarabia, Méx.	234	20.31 N	101.05 W
Sarabia, Méx.	234	17.03 N	95.01 W
Sarabia ≃	234	17.11 N	94.56 W
Sarābiyūm	142	30.23 N	32.17 E
Saraburi	110	14.32 N	100.55 E
Saracena	68	39.46 N	16.09 E
Saraceno, Monte ∧	66	41.27 N	14.44 E
Saracura ≃	255	12.18 S	40.07 W
Saracuruna ≃	287a	22.41 S	43.13 W
Saraféré	150	15.50 N	3.42 W
Saragosa	196	31.01 N	103.39 W
Saragossa → Zaragoza	34	41.38 N	0.53 W
Saraguay ◆[8]	275a	45.31 N	73.45 W
Saraguro	246	3.36 S	79.13 W
Sarai	80	53.44 N	41.00 E
Sarāi Alamgir	123	32.54 N	73.45 E
Saraikela	124	22.43 N	85.57 E
Sarāi Naurang	123	32.50 N	70.47 E
Saraipāli	120	21.20 N	83.00 E
Säräisniemi	26	64.27 N	26.47 E
Sarajas de Madrid ◆[8]	266a	40.28 N	3.35 W
Sarajčik	80	47.30 N	51.43 E
Sarajevo	38	43.52 N	18.25 E
Saraj-Gir	80	53.36 N	53.24 E
Saraji	166	22.21 S	148.18 E
Sarajskij	80	47.19 N	40.45 E
Sarakhs	128	36.32 N	61.11 E
Saraktaš	86	51.50 N	56.22 E
Sarala	86	54.52 N	89.14 E
Saraland	194	30.49 N	88.04 W
Šaralday	88	51.01 N	107.38 E
Saralžin	80	49.12 N	48.55 E
Saramacca □[5]	250	5.40 N	55.40 W
Saramacca ≃	250	5.51 N	55.53 W
Saramaguacán ≃	240p	21.30 N	77.17 W
Saran, Fr.	50	47.57 N	1.53 E
Saran', Kaz.	86	49.46 N	72.52 E
Šaran, Ross.	80	54.49 N	54.00 E
Saran, Gunung ∧	112	0.25 S	111.18 E
Saranac	216	42.55 N	85.12 W
Saranac ≃	188	44.42 N	73.27 W
Saranac Lake	188	44.19 N	74.07 W
Saranakan, gora ∧	88	52.35 N	113.50 E
Saranap	282	37.53 N	122.06 W
Šaranbaš-Kn'azevo	80	54.58 N	54.09 E
Saranda	154	5.43 S	34.59 E
Sarandapótamos ≃	267c	38.03 N	23.34 E
Sarandë	38	39.52 N	20.00 E
Sarandi	252	27.56 S	52.55 W
Sarandí ◆[8]	258	34.40 S	58.21 W
Sarandí del Yi	252	33.21 S	55.38 W
Sarandí Grande	258	33.44 S	56.20 W
Sarandira	256	21.50 S	43.11 W
Šaranga	80	57.11 N	46.34 E
Sarangani Bay ⊂	116	5.57 N	125.11 E
Sarangani Island I	116	5.27 N	125.28 E
Sarangani Islands II	116	5.25 N	125.26 E
Sarangani Strait ʮ	116	5.31 N	125.23 E
Sārangarh	120	21.36 N	83.05 E
Sārangpur	124	23.34 N	76.28 E
Sārankhola	126	22.18 N	89.47 E
Saranley	144	2.22 N	42.17 E
Saranpaul'	24	64.14 N	60.53 E
Saransk	80	54.11 N	45.11 E
Sara Peak ∧	150	9.41 N	9.17 E
Saraphi	110	18.43 N	99.03 E
Sarapiquí ≃	236	10.43 N	83.56 W
Şarapó ≃	287a	22.46 S	43.37 W
Šarapovo, Ross.	80	55.17 N	44.42 E
Šarapovo, Ross.	82	55.11 N	37.16 E
Sarapuí ≃	287a	22.46 S	43.24 W
Sarapuí, Canal de ≊	287a	22.44 S	43.16 W
Sarapul	80	56.28 N	53.48 E
Sarapul'skaja vozvyšennost' ⋏[1]	80	56.15 N	53.30 E
Sarapul'skoje	89	48.52 N	135.59 E
Sarāqib	130	35.52 N	36.48 E
Sarare	246	9.47 N	69.10 W
Sarare ≃	246	7.18 N	70.41 W
Sarar Plain ≚	144	9.25 N	46.17 E
Sara Sara, Nevado ∧	248	15.19 S	73.27 W
Sarasota	220	27.20 N	82.31 W
Sarasota □[6]	220	27.10 N	82.21 W
Sarasota Bay ⊂	220	27.23 N	82.39 W
Sarasota-Bradenton Airport ⊠	220	27.24 N	82.33 W
Sarasota Springs	220	27.17 N	82.28 W
Šarašova	76	52.33 N	24.13 E
Saraswati ≃	272b	22.59 N	88.22 E
Sarata	78	46.02 N	29.38 E
Sarath	126	24.14 N	86.50 E
Saratoga, Austl.	170	33.28 S	151.21 E
Saratoga, Ca., U.S.	226	37.15 N	122.01 W
Saratoga, In., U.S.	216	40.14 N	84.55 W
Saratoga, Tx., U.S.	222	30.17 N	94.31 W
Saratoga, Wy., U.S.	200	41.27 N	106.48 W
Saratoga □[6]	210	43.00 N	73.51 W
Saratoga Battlefield Monument ⊥	210	43.05 N	73.35 W
Saratoga Creek ≃	282	37.25 N	121.58 W
Saratoga Lake ⊜	210	43.01 N	73.39 W
Saratoga National Historical Park ♠	210	43.00 N	73.38 W
Saratoga Passage ʮ	224	48.10 N	122.30 W
Saratoga Spa State Park ♠	210	43.03 N	73.50 W
Saratoga Springs	210	43.04 N	73.47 W
Šara-Togot	88	53.01 N	106.43 E
Saratok	112	1.44 N	111.20 E
Saratov	80	51.34 N	46.02 E
Saratovka	86	51.12 N	54.54 E
Saratov Oblast' □[4]	80	51.30 N	47.00 E
Saratovskoje vodochranilišče ⊜[1]	80	52.45 N	48.30 E
Saraurcu ∧	246	0.06 S	77.55 W
Sarāvān, Īrān	128	27.15 N	62.40 E
Saravan, Lao	110	15.43 N	106.25 E
Sarawak □[3]	112	2.30 N	113.30 E
Saray	130	41.26 N	27.55 E
Saraya, Guinée	150	10.46 N	10.24 W
Saraya, Sén.	150	12.50 N	11.45 W
Sarāyān	128	33.51 N	58.31 E
Saraycık	130	40.57 N	35.08 E
Saraydüzü	130	41.20 N	34.52 E
Sarā-ye Aḥmadī	128	27.56 N	56.42 E
Sarayevo → Sarajevo	38	43.52 N	18.25 E
Sarayköy	130	37.55 N	28.58 E
Sarayönü	130	38.17 N	32.25 E
Sarbaj	80	53.39 N	51.34 E
Sarbāz	128	26.39 N	61.15 E
Sarbinowo	54	52.40 N	14.40 E
Sárbogárd	30	46.53 N	18.38 E
Sarca ≃	64	45.52 N	10.52 E
Sarce ≃	50	48.09 N	4.18 E
Sarcee Indian Reserve ◆[4]	182	50.58 N	114.06 W
Sarcelle, Passe de la ʮ	175f	22.29 S	167.12 E
Sarcelles	50	49.00 N	2.23 E
Sarche di Calavino	64	46.03 N	10.57 E
Sarcidano ◆[1]	71	39.49 N	9.10 E
Šarčino	86	53.09 N	81.45 E
Sarclet	46	58.22 N	3.07 W
Sarcoxie	194	37.04 N	94.06 W
Sārda (Mahākālī) ≃	124	27.22 N	81.23 E
Sard āb)(	123	36.40 N	71.32 E
Sārda Canal ≊	124	28.08 N	80.24 E
Sardagna	64	46.03 N	11.06 E
Sardah	124	24.18 N	88.44 E
Sardaq	128	34.48 N	58.07 E
Sardara	71	39.37 N	8.49 E
Sardār Chāh	128	27.58 N	64.50 E
Sardārpur	120	22.39 N	74.59 E
Sardārshahr	120	28.26 N	74.29 E
Sar Dasht, Īrān	128	36.09 N	45.28 E
Sar Dasht, Īrān	128	32.32 N	48.52 E
Sardegna □[4]	71	40.00 N	9.00 E
Sardegna (Sardinia) I	71	40.00 N	9.00 E
Sardeh Band	120	33.17 N	68.39 E
Sardhana	124	29.09 N	77.37 E
Sardiha	126	22.22 N	87.09 E
Sardinal	236	10.31 N	85.39 W
Sardinata	246	8.05 N	72.48 W
Sardinia, N.Y., U.S.	210	42.32 N	78.31 W
Sardinia, Oh., U.S.	218	39.00 N	83.48 W
Sardinia → Sardegna I	71	40.00 N	9.00 E
Sardinien → Sardegna I	71	40.00 N	9.00 E
Sardis, B.C., Can.	224	49.08 N	121.57 W
Sardis, Al., U.S.	194	32.17 N	86.59 W
Sardis, Ga., U.S.	192	32.58 N	81.45 W
Sardis, Ky., U.S.	218	38.31 N	83.57 W
Sardis, Ms., U.S.	194	34.26 N	89.55 W
Sardis, Pa., U.S.	279b	40.29 N	79.42 W
Sardis, Tn., U.S.	194	35.27 N	88.18 W
Sardis Lake ⊜[1]	194	34.27 N	89.43 W
Şardona, Piz ∧	58	46.55 N	9.15 E
Šardonem'	24	63.56 N	44.37 E
Sarek ∧	24	67.25 N	17.46 E
Sareks Nationalpark ♠	24	67.15 N	17.30 E
Sārenga, India	126	22.46 N	87.02 E
Sārenga, India	272b	22.31 N	88.13 E
Sarentina, Valle ∨	64	46.35 N	11.25 E
Sarentino (Sarnthein)	64	46.38 N	11.21 E
Sar-e Pol	120	36.14 N	65.55 E
Sarepta	194	32.53 N	93.26 W
Sarezskoje, ozero ⊜	85	38.13 N	72.45 E
Sarezzo	64	45.39 N	10.12 E
Sargans	58	47.03 N	9.26 E
Sargasso Sea ⊤[2]	8	30.00 N	50.00 W
Sargasso Sea ⊤[2]	8	30.00 N	50.00 W
Sargatskoje	86	55.37 N	73.30 E
Sargau ≃	85	43.25 N	73.50 E
Sargé-lès-le-Mans	50	48.02 N	0.14 E
Sargent, Ga., U.S.	192	33.25 N	84.52 W
Sargent, Ne., U.S.	198	41.38 N	99.22 W
Sargent Creek ≃	226	35.57 N	120.52 W
Şargodha	123	32.05 N	72.40 E
Šargol'džin	88	52.21 N	114.42 E
Šargul', ozero ⊜	86	54.35 N	78.51 E
Šargun	85	38.37 N	67.53 E
Sarh	146	9.09 N	18.23 E
Sarhli, Djebel ∧	34	36.06 N	0.40 E
Sārī	128	36.34 N	53.04 E
Saría I	38	35.50 N	27.15 E
Saribi, Tanjung ›	164	1.36 S	135.25 E
Sarıbuğday	130	40.35 N	35.35 E
Saric	232	31.08 N	111.23 W
Saricumbe	152	12.12 S	19.46 E
Sarigan I	108	16.42 N	145.47 E
Sarıgazi ◆[8]	267b	41.01 N	29.12 E
Sarıgöl	130	38.14 N	28.43 E
Sarıkamış	130	40.20 N	42.35 E
Sarıkaya, Tür.	130	38.47 N	32.15 E
Sarıkaya, Tür.	130	39.30 N	35.24 E
Sarikei	112	2.07 N	111.31 E
Sarıköy	130	40.12 N	27.36 E
Sarilhos Grandes	266c	38.41 N	8.58 W
Sarilhos Pequenos	266c	38.41 N	8.59 W
Sarim	154	0.23 S	40.58 E
Sarimbun, Pulau I	271c	1.26 N	103.41 E
Sarina	166	21.26 S	149.13 E
Sarine (Saane) ≃	58	46.59 N	7.15 E
Sariñena	34	41.48 N	0.10 W
Sarıoğlan	130	39.05 N	35.59 E
Saripul'	85	38.26 N	70.08 E
Sarīr	146	27.36 N	22.32 E
Sarısu	84	39.01 N	42.55 E
Sarita	196	27.13 N	97.47 W
Sariwŏn	98	38.31 N	125.44 E
Sarıyar Barajı ⊜[1]	130	40.02 N	31.40 E
Şarız	130	38.30 N	36.30 E
Šarja	80	58.24 N	45.30 E
Sarju (Babaī) ≃	124	27.42 N	81.16 E
Sark I	43b	49.26 N	2.21 W
Sark ≃	44	54.58 N	3.04 W
Şarkad	30	46.44 N	21.23 E
Šarkan	80	57.18 N	53.53 E
Şarkand	86	45.26 N	79.54 E
Šarkaŭščyna	76	55.22 N	27.28 E
Şarkikaraağaç	130	38.04 N	31.23 E
Şarkışla	130	39.21 N	36.26 E
Şarköy	130	40.37 N	27.06 E
Şarlat-la-Canéda	32	44.53 N	1.13 E
Šarlauk	128	38.13 N	55.38 E
Şarles	198	48.56 N	98.59 W
Šarlyk	86	52.55 N	54.35 E
Sarmakovo	84	43.43 N	43.12 E
Sarmanovo	80	55.15 N	52.36 E
Sărmaşu	38	46.46 N	24.11 E
Sarmathura	124	26.31 N	77.22 E
Sarmatskaja ≃	83	47.20 N	38.48 E
Sármellék	30	46.44 N	17.10 E
Sarmi	164	1.51 S	138.44 E
Sarmiento	254	45.36 S	69.05 W
Sarmiento ≃	288	34.25 S	58.35 W
Sarmiento de Gambia, Cerro ∧	254	54.27 S	70.50 W
Sarmiento de Gamboa, Lago ⊜	254	51.04 S	72.45 W
Särna	26	61.41 N	13.08 E
Sarna, ozero ⊜	80	48.24 N	44.38 E
Sarnano	66	43.02 N	13.18 E
Sārnāth ⊥	124	25.24 N	83.01 E
Sarnen	58	46.54 N	8.15 E
Sărnena Gora ⋏	38	42.35 N	25.10 E
Sarner See ⊜	58	46.52 N	8.13 E
Sarnia	214	42.58 N	82.23 W
Sarnico	64	45.40 N	9.57 E
Sarno	68	40.49 N	14.37 E
Sarnow	54	53.45 N	13.37 E
Sarnowa	30	51.38 N	16.54 E
Sarnthein → Sarentino	64	46.38 N	11.21 E
Šarnutovskij	80	47.40 N	43.46 E
Sarny	78	51.21 N	26.36 E
Şaroako	112	2.31 S	121.22 E
Šaroargun ≃	84	43.02 N	45.44 E
Sarolangun	112	2.18 S	102.42 E
Saroma-ko ⊜	92a	44.08 N	143.50 E
Saron	158	33.11 S	19.01 E
Saronikós Kólpos ⊂	38	37.45 N	23.30 E
Saronno	62	45.38 N	9.02 E
Saros Körfezi ⊂	130	40.30 N	26.20 E
Sárospatak	30	48.19 N	21.34 E
Sarowbī	120	34.36 N	69.43 E
Sarpa	80	47.07 N	45.29 E
Şarpa, ozero ⊜	80	47.18 N	45.20 E
Şarpajevka	78	48.34 N	40.59 E
Sar Passage ʮ	175b	7.12 N	134.23 E
Şarpinskije ozera ⊜	80	47.30 N	45.00 E
Šar Planina ⋏	38	42.05 N	20.50 E
Sarpsborg	26	59.17 N	11.07 E
Sarpy Creek ≃	202	46.15 N	107.09 W
Sárrabus ◆[1]	71	39.23 N	9.21 E
Sarralbe	56	49.00 N	7.01 E
Sarras	62	45.11 N	4.48 E
Sarrath, Oued ∨	36	35.59 N	8.23 E
Sarratt	260	51.41 N	0.29 W
Sarre	62	45.43 N	7.15 E
Sarre (Saar) ≃	56	49.42 N	6.34 E
Sarre Blanche ≃	56	48.41 N	7.01 E
Sarrebourg	58	48.44 N	7.03 E
Sarrebruck → Saarbrücken	56	49.14 N	6.59 E
Sarreguemines	56	49.06 N	7.03 E
Sarre Rouge ≃	56	48.41 N	7.01 E
Sarre-Union	56	48.56 N	7.05 E
Sarria	34	42.47 N	7.24 W
Sarriá ◆[8]	266d	41.24 N	2.08 E
Sarro	150	13.43 N	5.15 W
Sarroch	71	39.04 N	9.00 E
Şars	86	56.33 N	57.07 E
Šarscin	76	52.39 N	31.03 E
Sarsfield	212	45.27 N	75.21 W
Sarsina	66	43.55 N	12.08 E
Sarsol	272c	19.02 N	73.01 E
Sarstedt	52	52.14 N	9.51 E
Sarstein ∧	64	47.36 N	13.41 E
Sarstoon (Sarstún) ≃	236	15.53 N	88.55 W
Sarstún (Sarstoon) ≃	236	15.53 N	88.55 W
Sarsuna	272b	22.28 N	88.18 E
Sart	56	50.31 N	5.56 E
Sartang ≃	74	67.44 N	133.12 E
Sarteano	66	42.59 N	11.52 E
Sartell	190	45.37 N	94.12 W
Sartène	36	41.36 N	8.59 E
Sarthe □[5]	32	48.00 N	0.05 E
Sarthe ≃	32	47.30 N	0.32 W
Sartičala	84	41.43 N	45.10 E
Sartilly	32	48.45 N	1.27 W
Sartirana Lomellina	62	45.07 N	8.39 E
Sartlan, ozero ⊜	86	55.00 N	78.35 E
Sartol'gen	80	48.57 N	47.03 E
Sartrouville	261	48.57 N	2.10 E
Saru	85	42.20 N	77.55 E
Sarufutsu	92a	45.16 N	142.12 E
Saruhanlı	130	38.44 N	27.34 E
Şärur, Azer.	84	39.33 N	44.58 E
Şarūr, ʿUmān	128	23.22 N	58.07 E
Šar Us ≃	88	47.08 N	97.38 E
Saru-shima I	268	35.17 N	139.42 E
Sarvadyk	80	46.07 N	44.07 E
Sárvár	30	47.15 N	16.57 E
Sarver	214	40.44 N	79.45 W
Sarvestān	128	29.16 N	53.13 E
Sárvíz ≃	30	46.24 N	18.41 E
Saryagač	85	41.27 N	69.10 E
Saryassija	85	38.25 N	67.57 E
Sarybasat	86	46.38 N	60.27 E
Sarybulak, Kaz.	85	43.24 N	71.30 E
Sarybulak, Kaz.	86	49.27 N	76.27 E
Sarybulak, Kyrg.	85	40.54 N	73.49 E
Sarych, mys ›	78	44.23 N	33.45 E
Sarychosor	85	38.32 N	69.49 E
Sarydala	85	41.11 N	70.27 E
Saryesik-Atyrau, peski ◆[2]	86	45.30 N	76.00 E
Saryg-Sep	88	51.30 N	95.36 E
Sarykamskoje ozero ⊜	72	41.56 N	57.25 E
Sarykoby	85	43.44 N	72.35 E
Sarykol'skij chrebet ⋏	120	38.00 N	74.30 E
Sarykomej	86	45.12 N	74.11 E
Sarykopa, ozero ⊜	86	50.22 N	64.08 E
Sarymogol	85	39.55 N	72.47 E
Şaryozek	86	44.22 N	77.59 E
Šarypovo	86	55.33 N	89.12 E
Saryšagan	86	46.07 N	73.38 E
Sarysu	86	48.23 N	69.59 E
Sarysu ≃	86	45.12 N	66.36 E
Sary-Taš	85	39.44 N	73.15 E
Sarytau	86	49.54 N	76.41 E
Saryžaz	72	42.55 N	79.38 E
Sarzana	64	44.07 N	9.58 E
Sarzanello, Fortezza di ⊥	64	44.08 N	9.58 E
Sarzeau	32	47.32 N	2.46 W
S'as' ≃	76	60.09 N	32.30 E
Saʿsaʿ, Sūrīy.	132	33.17 N	36.02 E
Sasa, Yis.	132	33.02 N	35.24 E
Sasabe	200	31.27 N	111.31 W
Sasabe ≃	200	30.41 N	111.56 W
Sasabeneh	144	7.55 N	43.39 E
Sasaga-mine ∧	96	33.49 N	133.17 E
Sasaginnigak Lake ⊜	184	51.36 N	95.40 W
Sasago-tunnel ◆[5]	94	35.38 N	138.47 E
Sasaguri	96	33.37 N	130.32 E
Sasak	110	0.01 S	99.42 E
Sasakwa	196	34.56 N	96.31 W
Sasamungga	175e	7.02 S	156.47 E
Sasao	270	34.57 N	135.20 E
Sasar, Tanjung ›	115b	9.17 S	119.56 E
Sāsarām	124	24.57 N	84.02 E
Sasayama	96	35.04 N	135.13 E
Sasa-yama ∧	96	33.03 N	132.40 E
Sasbach, Dtsch.	56	48.38 N	8.06 E
Sasbach, Dtsch.	58	48.08 N	7.37 E
Sasco Brook ≃	276	41.07 N	73.18 W
Sásd	30	46.15 N	18.06 E
Sasebo	92	33.10 N	129.43 E
Sasebo Naval Base ■	92	33.09 N	129.45 E
Saseenos	224	48.24 N	123.40 W
Saseginaga, Lac ⊜	190	47.06 N	78.35 W
Sashalom ◆[8]	264c	47.31 N	19.11 E
Sas-hegy ∧[2]	264c	47.23 N	19.18 E
Sashiki	174m	26.10 N	127.47 E
Sashima	94	36.08 N	139.51 E
Saskatchewan □[4], Can.	176	54.00 N	105.00 W
Saskatchewan □[4], Can.	184	54.00 N	105.00 W
Saskatchewan ≃	184	53.12 N	99.16 W
Saskatoon	184	52.07 N	106.38 W
Saskylach	74	71.55 N	114.01 E
Saslaya, Cerro ∧	238	13.45 N	85.03 W
Sasmik, Cape ›	180	51.36 N	177.55 W
Sāsni	124	27.43 N	78.05 E
Sasnovy Bor	76	52.32 N	29.36 E
Sasolburg	158	26.48 S	27.45 E
Sason	130	38.20 N	41.25 E
Sasovo	80	54.21 N	41.54 E
Saspamco	196	29.14 N	98.18 W
Saspul Gompa	123	34.15 N	77.09 E
Sassafras, Austl.	274b	37.52 S	145.21 E
Sassafras, Ky., U.S.	192	37.14 N	83.06 W
Sassafras ≃	208	39.23 N	76.02 W
Sassafras Mountain ∧	192	35.03 N	82.48 W
Sassafras Neck ›[1]	208	39.25 N	75.55 W
Sassandra	150	4.58 N	6.05 W
Sassandra ≃	150	4.58 N	6.05 W
Sassano	68	40.20 N	15.33 E
Sassari	71	40.44 N	8.33 E
Sassari □[4]	71	40.40 N	9.00 E
Sassbach ≃	61	46.43 N	15.48 E
Sasse ≃	62	44.15 N	5.55 E
Sassello	62	44.29 N	8.30 E
Sassenage	62	45.12 N	5.40 E
Sassenberg	52	51.59 N	8.02 E
Sassenheim	52	52.13 N	4.31 E
Sassnitz	54	54.31 N	13.38 E
Sassocorvaro	66	43.47 N	12.30 E
Sasso di Castalda	68	40.30 N	15.40 E
Sassoferrato	66	43.26 N	12.51 E
Sasso Marconi	64	44.24 N	11.15 E
S'as'stroj	76	60.08 N	32.34 E
Sassuolo	64	44.33 N	10.47 E
Sastobe	85	42.34 N	70.00 E
Sastown	150	4.40 N	8.26 W
Sastre	252	31.45 S	61.50 W
Sas van Gent	52	51.14 N	3.47 E
Sasyk, ozero ⊜	78	45.12 N	33.31 E
Sasykkol', ozero ⊜	86	46.35 N	81.00 E
Şasykoli	80	47.33 N	47.00 E
Šat ≃	82	54.08 N	37.47 E
Satadougou	150	12.21 N	10.07 W
Satah Mountain ∧	182	52.29 N	124.41 W
Şatakunta ◆[1]	26	61.30 N	23.00 E
Šatalovka	78	51.09 N	38.16 E
Šatalovo	76	54.20 N	32.27 E
Sata-misaki ›	92	30.59 N	130.40 E
Satāna	122	20.35 N	74.12 E
Sataniv	78	49.15 N	26.16 E
Satanta	198	37.26 N	100.59 W
Sátão	34	40.44 N	7.44 W
Sātāra, India	122	17.41 N	73.59 E
Satara, S. Afr.	156	24.29 S	31.47 E
Sataua	175a	13.28 S	172.40 W
Sātbāria, Bngl.	126	23.52 N	89.26 E
Sātbāria, India	272b	22.25 N	88.33 E
Satélite	232	31.43 N	106.23 W
Satellite Beach	220	28.10 N	80.35 W
Satellite Channel ʮ	224	48.43 N	123.30 W
Satema	152	4.18 N	21.42 E
Satengar, Pulau I	112	7.31 S	117.17 E
Säter	40	60.21 N	15.45 E
Sātgāchia	126	23.16 N	88.08 E
Sātghara	272b	22.44 N	88.21 E
Satilla ≃	192	30.59 N	81.28 W
Satilpa Creek ≃	194	31.39 N	88.05 W
Satin	222	31.21 N	97.02 W
Satipo	248	11.16 S	74.37 W
Sátiro Dias	250	11.36 S	38.36 W
Satis	80	55.02 N	43.48 E
Satīt (Tekeze) ≃	140	14.20 N	35.50 E
Satka	86	55.03 N	59.01 E
Satkānia	120	22.04 N	92.03 E
Şātkhira	124	22.43 N	89.06 E
Šatki	80	55.11 N	44.08 E
Satla Bīl ≣	126	22.54 N	90.04 E
Satluj → Sutlej ≃	120	29.23 N	71.02 E
Satna	124	24.35 N	80.50 E
Sato, Cañada de ≃	288	34.35 S	58.38 W
Satomi	94	36.43 N	140.30 E
Şátoraljaújhely	30	48.24 N	21.39 E
Šatov	61	48.48 N	16.01 E
Šatovo	82	54.56 N	37.14 E
Şatow	54	53.59 N	11.51 E
Šatpajev	86	47.55 N	67.28 E
Sātpura Range ⋏	122	22.00 N	78.00 E
Sätrabrunn	40	59.51 N	16.27 E
Şatriano di Lucania	68	40.33 N	15.33 E
Šatrovo	86	56.31 N	64.38 E
Satrup	41	54.41 N	9.35 E
Satsop ≃	224	47.03 N	123.30 W
Satsop, East Fork ≃	224	47.02 N	123.32 W
Satsop, Middle Fork ≃	224	47.05 N	123.30 W
Satsop, West Fork ≃	224	47.02 N	123.32 W
Satsuma	194	30.51 N	88.03 W
Satsuma-hantō ›[1]	92	31.25 N	130.25 E
Satsunan-shotō II	93b	29.00 N	130.00 E
Sattahip	110	12.40 N	100.54 E
Sāttānkulam	122	8.27 N	77.56 E
Satte	94	36.04 N	139.43 E
Sattel	58	47.05 N	8.42 E
Sattenapalle	122	16.24 N	80.11 E
Satthwa	110	17.46 N	94.30 E
Sattledt	61	48.04 N	14.03 E
Satui	112	3.47 S	115.27 E
Sātuli	272b	22.33 N	88.34 E
Satu Mare	38	47.48 N	22.53 E
Satu Mare □[6]	38	47.40 N	23.00 E
Şatun	110	6.37 N	100.04 E
Šatura	80	55.34 N	39.32 E
Saturna	224	48.43 N	123.11 W
Saturna Island I	224	48.47 N	123.08 W
Şaturnino M. Laspiur	252	31.42 S	62.29 W
Šaturtorf	76	55.34 N	39.26 E
Satus Creek ≃	202	46.16 N	120.07 W
Satus Peak ∧	224	46.15 N	120.45 W
Satyamangalam	122	11.31 N	77.15 E
Satzkorn	264a	52.29 N	12.59 E
Sau ≃	269c	10.46 N	106.48 E
Saualpe ⋏	61	46.55 N	14.40 E
Sauble ≃	212	44.40 N	81.17 W
Sauce, Arg.	252	30.05 S	58.46 W
Sauce, Perú	248	6.44 S	76.10 W
Sauce, Ur.	258	34.39 S	56.04 W
Sauce, Arroyo ≃	258	34.26 S	57.28 W
Sauce, Arroyo del ≃	288	34.41 S	58.50 W
Sauce Corto, Arroyo ≃	252	36.55 S	61.48 W
Saucier	194	30.38 N	89.08 W
Saucillo	232	28.01 N	105.17 W
Sauda	26	59.39 N	6.20 E
Saudade	256	21.56 S	43.03 W
Sauđárkrókur	24a	65.46 N	19.41 W
Saúde	250	10.56 S	40.24 W
Saúde ◆[8]	287b	23.37 S	46.37 W
Saudi Arabia (Al-ʿArabīyah as-Suʿūdīyah) □[1]	118	25.00 N	45.00 E
Saudi-Arabien → Saudi Arabia □[1]	118	25.00 N	45.00 E
Saudron	58	48.30 N	5.20 E
Sauer ≃, Europe	56	48.55 N	8.10 E
Sauer (Sûre) ≃, Europe	56	49.44 N	6.31 E
Sauerkohl-Berge ∧[2]	264a	52.20 N	13.45 E
Sauerlach	64	47.58 N	11.38 E
Sauerland ◆[1]	52	51.10 N	8.00 E
Saueruiná ≃	248	12.00 S	58.43 W
Sauê-Uiná ≃	248	12.24 S	58.40 W
Saug ≃	116	7.27 N	125.44 E
Saugatuck, Ct., U.S.	276	41.08 N	73.23 W
Saugatuck, Mi., U.S.	216	42.39 N	86.12 W
Saugatuck ≃	276	41.07 N	73.22 W
Saugatuck Reservoir ⊜[1]	207	41.16 N	73.22 W
Saugeen ≃	190	44.30 N	81.22 W
Saugeen Indian Reserve ◆[4]	212	44.33 N	81.18 W
Saugerties	210	42.04 N	73.57 W
Saughall	262	53.13 N	2.58 W
Saugor → Sāgar	124	23.50 N	78.43 E
Saugstad, Mount ∧	182	52.15 N	126.31 W
Saugus	207	42.27 N	71.00 W
Saugus ≃	283	42.28 N	70.58 W
Saugus Iron Works National Historic Site ⊥	283	42.28 N	71.01 W
Sauh, Tanjong ›	114	3.46 N	100.49 E
Saujil	252	28.11 S	66.14 W
Saujon	32	45.40 N	0.56 W
Sauk ≃, Mn., U.S.	198	45.36 N	94.10 W
Sauk ≃, Wa., U.S.	224	48.30 N	121.37 W
Sauk Centre	198	45.44 N	94.57 W
Sauk City	190	43.16 N	89.43 W
Sauk Rapids	190	45.35 N	94.09 W
Sauksaj ≃	85	39.11 N	72.15 E
Sauk Village	216	41.29 N	87.34 W
Saukville	190	43.22 N	87.56 W
Şaül	250	3.37 N	53.12 W
Šaul'der	85	42.47 N	68.24 E
Sauldre ≃	50	47.16 N	1.30 E
Sauldre, Canal de la ≊	50	47.36 N	2.06 E
Saulgau	58	48.01 N	9.30 E
Saulgrub	64	47.40 N	11.01 E
Saulheim	56	49.51 N	8.09 E
Saulieu	50	47.16 N	4.14 E
Saulkrasti	76	57.17 N	24.25 E
Saulnot	58	47.34 N	6.38 E
Sault-au-Mouton	186	48.33 N	69.15 W
Sault au Récollet ◆[8]	275a	45.34 N	73.39 W
Sault aux Cochons, Rivière du ≃	186	48.44 N	69.04 W
Sault-de-Vaucluse	62	44.05 N	5.25 E
Saulteaux ≃	182	55.16 N	114.25 W
Saulteaux Indian Reserve ◆[4]	184	53.08 N	108.18 W
Sault-lès-Rethel	50	49.30 N	4.22 E
Sault Sainte Marie, On., Can.	190	46.31 N	84.20 W
Sault Sainte Marie, Mi., U.S.	190	46.29 N	84.20 W
Saulx ≃, Fr.	56	48.45 N	4.35 E
Saulx ≃, Fr.	261	48.41 N	2.19 E
Saulx-de-Vesoul	58	47.42 N	6.17 E
Saulx-les-Chartreux	261	48.42 N	2.16 E
Saulxures-sur-Moselotte	58	47.57 N	6.46 E
Šaum'ani	84	41.21 N	44.46 E
Saumarez Reef ✣[2]	166	21.50 S	153.40 E
Saumlaki	164	7.57 S	131.19 E
Saumon, Rivière au ≃	206	45.41 N	71.27 W
Saumons, Rivíere aux ≃	186	49.25 N	62.15 W
Saumur	32	47.16 N	0.05 W
Saundatti	122	15.47 N	75.07 E
Saundersfoot	42	51.43 N	4.43 W
Saunders Island I, Falk. Is.	254	51.20 S	60.10 W
Saunders Island I, S. Geor.	9	57.47 S	26.27 W
Saunders Point ∧[2]	162	27.52 S	125.38 E
Saunderstown	207	41.30 N	71.25 W
Saunemin	216	40.54 N	88.24 W

Symbol	English	Deutsch	Español	Français	Português
≃	River	Fluß	Río	Rivière	Rio
≊	Canal	Kanal	Canal	Canal	Canal
ᒪ	Waterfall, Rapids	Wasserfall, Stromschnellen	Cascada, Rápidos	Chute d'eau, Rapides	Cascata, Rápidos
ʮ	Strait	Meeresstraße	Estrecho	Détroit	Estreito
⊂	Bay, Gulf	Bucht, Golf	Bahía, Golfo	Baie, Golfe	Baía, Golfo
⊜	Lake, Lakes	See, Seen	Lago, Lagos	Lac, Lacs	Lago, Lagos
≣	Swamp	Sumpf	Pantano	Marais	Pântano
⌂	Ice Features, Glacier	Eis- und Gletscherformen	Accidentes Glaciales	Formes glaciaires	Acidentes glaciares
⊤	Other Hydrographic Features	Andere Hydrographische Objekte	Otros Elementos Hidrográficos	Autres données hydrographiques	Outros acidentes hidrográficos
✣	Submarine Features	Untermeerische Objekte	Accidentes Submarinos	Formes de relief sous-marin	Acidentes submarinos
□	Political Unit	Politische Einheit	Unidad Politica	Entité politique	Unidade política
♡	Cultural Institution	Kulturelle Institution	Institución Cultural	Institution culturelle	Instituição cultural
⊥	Historical Site	Historische Stätte	Sitio Histórico	Site historique	Sítio histórico
♠	Recreational Site	Erholungs- und Ferienort	Sitio de Recreo	Centre de loisirs	Area de Lazer
⊠	Airport	Flughafen	Aeropuerto	Aéroport	Aeroporto
■	Military Installation	Militäranlage	Instalación Militar	Installation militaire	Instalação militar
◆	Miscellaneous	Verschiedenes	Misceláneo	Divers	Diversos

ESPAÑOL				FRANÇAIS				PORTUGUÊS			
Nombre	Página	Lat.°′	Long.°′ W = Oeste	Nom	Page	Lat.°′	Long.°′ W = Ouest	Nome	Página	Lat.°′	Long.°′ W = Oeste

Scott Base ⚓³ 9 77.50 S 166.25 E
Scottburgh 158 30.19 S 30.40 E
Scott City, Ks., U.S. 198 38.28 N 100.54 W
Scott City, Mo., U.S. 194 37.13 N 89.31 W
Scott Cove ⫶ 276 41.03 N 73.28 W
Scott Creek ⫶ 226 37.02 N 122.13 W
Scottdale, Mi., U.S. 216 42.03 N 86.27 W
Scottdale, Pa., U.S. 214 40.06 N 79.35 W
Scotter 44 53.29 N 0.40 W
Scott Haven 279b 40.15 N 79.47 W
Scott Island I, Ant. 9 67.24 S 179.55 W
Scott Island I, On.,
 Can. 212 44.36 N 76.20 W
Scott Islands II 182 50.48 N 128.40 W
Scott Lake 220 25.56 N 80.13 W
Scott Mountain ▲ 202 44.11 N 115.47 W
Scott Peak ▲ 202 44.21 N 112.50 W
Scott Reef ⫶² 160 14.00 S 121.50 E
Scott Run ⫶ 284c 38.58 N 77.12 W
Scotts 216 41.19 N 85.24 W
Scottsbluff 198 41.52 N 103.40 W
Scotts Bluff National
 Monument ✦ 198 41.49 N 103.41 W
Scottsboro 194 34.40 N 86.02 W
Scottsburg, In., U.S. 218 38.41 N 85.46 W
Scottsburg, N.Y.,
 U.S. 210 42.40 N 77.43 W
Scottsdale, Austl. 166 41.10 S 147.31 E
Scottsdale, Az., U.S. 200 33.30 N 111.53 W
Scotts Flat Reservoir
 ⫶¹ 226 39.17 N 120.55 W
Scotts Head ⸼ 240d 15.13 N 61.23 W
Scotts Hill 194 35.31 N 88.15 W
Scotts Level Branch
 ⫶ 284b 39.22 N 76.45 W
Scottsmoor 220 28.46 N 80.53 W
Scotts Valley 226 37.03 N 122.00 W
Scottsville, Ky., U.S. 194 36.45 N 86.11 W
Scottsville, N.Y., U.S. 210 43.01 N 77.44 W
Scott Township 279b 40.32 N 80.11 W
Scottville, Il., U.S. 219 39.29 N 90.06 W
Scottville, Mi., U.S. 190 43.57 N 86.16 W
Scourie 46 58.20 N 5.08 W
Scout Lake 184 49.22 N 106.00 W
Scrabster 46 58.37 N 3.32 W
Scranton, Ia., U.S. 198 41.54 N 94.32 W
Scranton, N.Y., U.S. 212 42.44 N 78.50 W
Scranton, N.D., U.S. 198 46.08 N 103.08 W
Scranton, Pa., U.S. 210 41.24 N 75.39 W
Scremerston 44 55.44 N 1.59 W
Screven 192 31.29 N 82.01 W
Screw 164 3.55 S 142.50 E
Scribner 198 41.40 N 96.39 W
Scridain, Loch ⫶ 46 56.21 N 6.07 W
Scripps Institution of
 Oceanography ⚓³ 226 32.52 N 117.15 W
Scrivia ⫶ 62 45.03 N 8.54 E
Scroggins 44 53.25 N 95.11 W
Scrooby 44 53.25 N 1.01 W
Scrub Island I 240m 18.28 N 64.31 W
Ščučje, Ross. 86 52.56 N 70.12 E
Ščučje, Ross. 78 51.45 N 40.29 E
Ščučje, Ross. 80 51.45 N 40.29 E
Ščučje, Ross. 86 55.17 N 63.59 E
Ščučje Ozero ⫶ 86 56.28 N 56.38 E
Ščučyn 76 53.36 N 24.45 E
Scugog ⫶ 212 44.24 N 78.45 W
Scugog, Lake ⫶ 212 44.10 N 78.51 W
Scugog Indian
 Reserve ⫶⁴ 212 44.11 N 78.54 W
Scugog Island I 212 44.10 N 78.53 W
Ščukino 82 54.28 N 37.01 E
Scunthorpe 44 53.36 N 0.38 W
Scuol (Schuls) 58 46.48 N 10.18 E
Scuppernong ⫶ 216 42.54 N 88.42 W
Scurcola Marsicana 66 42.03 N 13.20 E
Ščurovo 83 55.03 N 38.49 E
Scurrival Point ⸼ 46 57.04 N 7.31 W
Scurry 222 32.31 N 96.23 W
Scutari
 → Shkodër 38 42.05 N 19.30 E
Scutari, Lake ⫶ 122 42.12 N 19.18 E
Scvih a ⫶ 78 52.04 N 27.54 E
Ščytkavičy 76 53.13 N 28.33 E
Sé ⫶⁸ 287b 23.33 S 46.37 W
Seabeck 226 47.38 N 122.51 W
Sea Bird Island I 224 49.15 N 121.45 W
Seabird Island Indian
 Reserve ⫶⁴ 224 49.17 N 121.42 W
Seaboard 192 36.29 N 77.26 W
Sea Bright 214 40.21 N 73.58 W
Seabrook, Md., U.S. 284c 38.58 N 76.50 W
Seabrook, N.J., U.S. 208 39.30 N 75.13 W
Seabrook, Tx., U.S. 229 29.33 N 95.01 W
Seabrook, Lake ⫶ 162 30.56 S 119.40 E
Sea Cliff 210 40.50 N 73.38 W
Seacock Swamp ⫶ 284b 36.48 N 76.51 W
Seacombe 44 53.23 N 3.02 W
Sea Dog Island I 276 40.36 N 73.35 W
Seadrift 208 28.30 N 96.47 W
Seaford, Eng., U.K. 42 50.46 N 0.06 E
Seaford, De., U.S. 208 38.38 N 75.36 W
Seaford, N.Y., U.S. 276 40.39 N 73.30 W
Seaforth, Austl. 274a 33.48 S 151.15 E
Seaforth, On., Can. 190 43.33 N 81.24 W
Seaforth, Eng., U.K. 262 53.28 N 3.01 W
Seaforth, Loch ⫶ 46 57.54 N 6.40 W
Seafox Seamount ⫶
 ⫶ 14 30.30 S 172.45 W
Seager Wheeler Lake
 ⫶ 184 54.27 N 103.30 W
Seagoville 222 32.38 N 96.32 W
Seagraves 196 32.56 N 102.33 W
Seaham 44 54.52 N 1.21 W
Seaholme 274b 37.52 S 144.50 E
Seahorse Breakers
 ⫶ 115a 5.30 N 112.37 E
Seahorse Point ⸼ 176 63.47 N 80.09 W
Seahouses 44 55.35 N 1.38 W
Sea Island I 224 49.12 N 123.10 W
Sea Islands II 192 31.20 N 81.20 W
Sea Isle City 208 39.09 N 74.41 W
Seal ⫶ 260 51.17 N 0.14 E
Seal, Cape ⸼ 158 34.07 S 23.25 E
Sea Lake 166 35.30 S 142.51 E
Sealand 262 53.12 N 2.58 W
Sealark Channel ⫶ 175e 9.18 S 160.20 E
Sea Bay ⫶ 9 71.40 S 12.25 W
Sea Beach 276 40.34 N 118.06 W
Seal Beach National
 Wildlife Refuge ✦ 280 33.45 N 118.03 W
Seal Cays II 238 21.10 N 71.38 W
Seal Cove, N.B.,
 Can. 186 44.39 N 66.51 W
Seal Cove, Nf., Can. 186 49.56 N 56.23 W
Sealdah Railroad
 Station ⫶⁵ 272b 22.34 N 88.22 E
Seale 194 32.17 N 85.10 W
Sealevel 192 34.51 N 76.23 W
Seal Island I 186 43.23 N 66.01 W
Seal Islands II 282 55.10 N 162.30 W
Seal Lake ⫶ 176 54.18 N 61.40 W
Sea Lake ⫶ 276 40.48 N 119.05 W
Seal Rocks II ⫶ 162 32.28 S 152.32 E
Sealston 284b 38.22 N 77.19 W
Sealy 222 29.46 N 96.09 W
Seaman 218 38.56 N 83.34 W
Seamer 44 54.14 N 0.26 W
Seanor 222 36.23 N 52.17 W
Seara 287 27.07 S 52.17 W
Searchlight 204 35.27 N 114.55 W
Searcy 194 35.15 N 91.44 W
Searles Lake ⫶ 204 35.43 N 117.20 W
Sears Tower ⫶ 226 41.53 N 87.38 W
Searsmont 186 44.27 N 68.55 W
Sears Tower ⫶ 226 41.53 N 87.38 W
Searsport 188 44.27 N 68.55 W
Seasville Lake ⫶ 282 37.24 N 122.14 W
Seaside 44 54.24 N 3.29 W

Seashore State Park
 ✦ 208 36.54 N 76.02 W
Seaside, Ca., U.S. 226 36.36 N 121.51 W
Seaside, Or., U.S. 224 45.59 N 123.55 W
Seaside Park 208 39.55 N 74.04 W
Seaside Park ✦ 276 41.10 N 73.12 W
SeaTac 224 47.25 N 122.19 W
Seaton, Eng., U.K. 42 50.43 N 3.05 W
Seaton, Eng., U.K. 44 54.41 N 3.33 W
Seaton, Eng., U.K. 44 53.54 N 1.14 W
Seaton ⫶ 42 50.22 N 4.22 W
Seaton Delaval 44 55.04 N 1.31 W
Seaton Sluice 44 55.05 N 1.28 W
Seat Pleasant 284c 38.53 N 76.54 W
Seattle 224 47.36 N 122.19 W
Seattle, Mount ▲ 180 60.06 N 139.11 W
Seattle Heights 224 47.48 N 122.20 W
Seattle-Tacoma
 International
 Airport ⫶ 224 47.27 N 122.18 W
Seatuck National
 Wildlife Refuge ✦ 276 40.43 N 73.13 W
Seaview, Eng., U.K. 42 50.43 N 1.06 W
Sea View, Ma., U.S. 283 42.08 N 70.42 W
Seaview, N.Y., U.S. 276 40.39 N 73.09 W
Seaview, Wa., U.S. 224 46.20 N 124.03 W
Seaward Kaikoura
 Range ⫶ 172 42.14 S 173.39 E
Seaward Roads ⫶ 174g 28.13 N 177.25 W
Sea World ✦, Fl.,
 U.S. 220 28.25 N 81.28 W
Sea World ✦, Oh.,
 U.S. 214 41.21 N 81.23 W
Seba 112 10.29 S 121.50 E
Sébaco 236 12.51 N 86.06 W
Sebago Lake ⫶ 188 43.50 N 70.35 W
Se Bai ⫶ 110 15.13 N 104.47 E
Sebakor, Teluk ⫶ 164 3.35 S 132.50 E
Sebakung 112 1.37 S 116.26 E
Šebalin 80 47.22 N 43.36 E
Šebalino, Ross. 80 48.16 N 43.21 E
Šebalino, Ross. 86 51.17 N 85.40 E
Sebanga 114 1.24 N 101.10 E
Sebangan, Teluk ⫶ 112 3.15 S 113.30 E
Sébangka, Pulau I 112 1.00 N 104.50 E
Sébaou, Oued ⫶ 34 36.55 N 3.55 E
Sebarok, Pulau I 271c 1.13 N 103.48 E
Sebastian, Fl., U.S. 220 27.46 N 80.29 W
Sebastian, Tx., U.S. 196 26.20 N 97.47 W
Sebastian, Cape ⸼ 202 42.19 N 124.26 W
Sebastián Inlet ⫶ 220 27.51 N 80.26 W
Sebastián Vizcaíno,
 Bahía ⫶ 232 28.00 N 114.30 W
Sebastião de Lacerda 256 22.17 S 43.35 W
Sebastopol, Austl. 169 37.36 S 143.51 E
Sebastopol, Ms.,
 U.S. 194 32.34 N 89.20 W
Sebatik, Pulau I 112 4.10 N 117.45 E
Sebba 150 13.26 N 0.32 E
Sebderat 144 15.26 N 36.40 E
Sébé ⫶ 152 1.02 S 13.06 E
Sebec Lake ⫶ 188 45.18 N 69.18 W
Sebeka 78 46.38 N 95.05 W
Sebekino 78 50.25 N 36.56 E
Sébékoro 150 12.57 N 8.59 W
Sebenico
 → Šibenik 36 43.44 N 15.54 E
Sebera, Punta ⸼ 71 39.03 N 8.50 E
Seberi 252 27.29 S 53.24 W
Seberta 112 0.43 S 102.31 E
Sebeta 88 54.40 N 99.54 E
Sebesi, Pulau I 115a 5.57 S 105.30 E
Sebes Körös (Crişul
 Repede) ⫶ 38 46.55 N 20.59 E
Sebewaing 190 43.43 N 83.27 W
Sebež 76 56.17 N 28.29 E
Sebille Manor 281 42.39 N 82.49 W
Şebinkarahisar 130 40.18 N 38.26 E
Sebiş 38 46.23 N 22.08 E
Sebou, Oued ⫶ 148 34.15 N 6.40 W
Sebree 194 37.36 N 87.31 W
Sebrell 208 36.47 N 77.07 W
Sebring, Fl., U.S. 220 27.29 N 81.26 W
Sebring, Oh., U.S. 214 40.55 N 81.01 W
Sebringville 212 43.24 N 81.04 W
Sebuku, Pulau I, 112 4.03 N 116.56 E
 Indon.
Sebuku, Pulau I,
 Indon. 115a 5.53 S 105.31 E
Sebuku, Teluk ⫶ 112 4.00 N 118.26 E
Sebuno 89 46.27 N 141.51 E
Seč 58 49.50 N 15.40 E
Seca, Ilha I 287a 22.51 S 43.06 W
Secane 285 39.55 N 75.18 W
Secang 115a 7.23 S 110.15 E
Secas, Islas II 236 7.58 N 82.02 W
Secaucus 276 40.47 N 74.03 W
Secchia ⫶ 64 45.04 N 11.00 E
Secchevo 80 45.02 N 15.43 E
Secclantas 252 25.18 S 66.15 W
Seclin 54 50.33 N 3.02 E
Seco ⫶, Arg. 252 23.08 S 63.57 W
Seco ⫶, Arg. 254 38.34 S 67.02 W
Seco ⫶, Esp. 266d 41.30 N 2.09 E
Seco, Arroyo ⫶, Ca.,
 U.S. 226 36.25 N 121.20 W
Seco, Arroyo ⫶, N.M.,
 U.S. 220 34.05 N 118.13 W
Seco Creek ⫶, N.M. 220
Seco Creek ⫶, Tx.,
 U.S. 196 29.02 N 99.08 W
Seco Island I 112 11.19 N 121.41 E
Second ⫶ 276 40.47 N 74.09 W
Second Cliff ⫶ 283 42.12 N 70.43 W
Second Han-gang
 Bridge ⫶ 271b 37.34 N 126.54 E
Second Herring
 Brook ⫶ 283 42.09 N 70.47 W
Second Mesa 204 35.49 N 110.30 W
Second Mountain ▲ 208 40.33 N 76.30 W
Second San Diego
 Aqueduct ⫶ 228 32.41 N 117.01 W
Second Swamp ⫶ 284 37.08 N 77.12 W
Second Valley 168b 35.33 S 138.14 E
Second Watchung
 Mountain ▲ 276 40.55 N 74.13 W
Sečovce 30 48.42 N 21.40 E
Sečovská Polianka 30 48.47 N 21.42 E
Secos ⫶ 256 22.32 S 43.08 W
Secretan 184 51.38 N 105.16 W
Secretary 208 38.36 N 75.56 W
Secretary Island I 172 45.15 S 166.55 E
Section 194 34.34 N 85.59 W
Secunda Island I 196 32.32 N 120.53 W
Security 198 38.45 N 104.44 W
Security Square ⫶⁹ 284b 39.19 N 76.45 W
Šěd ⫶ 82 47.00 N 18.31 E
Seda, Lat. 76 57.40 N 25.46 E
Seda, Liet. 76 56.10 N 22.10 E
Seda, Zhg. 102 32.20 N 100.41 E

Seda ⫶ 76 57.47 N 25.15 E
Sedah 112 10.46 S 123.12 E
Sedalia, Ab., Can. 184 51.41 N 110.40 W
Sedalia, In., U.S. 216 40.25 N 86.31 W
Sedalia, Mo., U.S. 194 38.42 N 93.13 W
Sedalia, Oh., U.S. 218 39.44 N 83.29 W
Sedan, Austl. 168b 34.35 S 139.18 E
Sedan, Fr. 56 49.42 N 4.57 E
Sedan, Ks., U.S. 198 37.07 N 96.11 W
Sedan⫶a, Cape ⸼ 180 53.49 N 166.06 W
Sedan⫶a Island I 180 53.50 N 166.10 W
Sedano 34 42.43 N 3.45 W
Sedan, Tanjung ⸼ 115a 7.49 S 114.27 E
Sedano 150 14.07 N 6.44 W
Séguéla, C. Iv. 150 7.57 N 6.40 W
Séguéla, Mali 150 14.07 N 6.44 W
Séguédine 148 20.12 N 12.59 E
Séguéla, C. Iv. 150 7.57 N 6.40 W
Sedanovo 88 56.58 N 101.22 E
Sedari, Tanjung ⸼ 115a 5.57 S 107.18 E
Sedayu 115a 6.59 S 112.33 E
Sedbergh 44 54.20 N 2.31 W
Sedco Hills 228 33.39 N 117.24 W
Seddin-Berg ⫶ 264a 52.24 N 13.40 E
Seddinsee ⫶ 264a 52.23 N 13.41 E
Seddon 172 41.40 S 174.05 E
Seddonville 172 41.33 S 171.59 E
Sedé Boqér 132 30.52 N 34.47 E
Sedel'nikovo 86 56.57 N 75.18 E
Séderon 62 44.12 N 5.32 E
Sederot 132 31.31 N 34.35 E
Sedgefield, Eng.,
 U.K. 44 54.39 N 1.26 W
Sedgefield, N.J., U.S. 276 40.51 N 74.28 W
Sedgefield, N.C.,
 U.S. 192 35.10 N 80.51 W
Sedgewick 184 52.46 N 111.41 W
Sedgwick, Co., U.S. 198 40.56 N 102.31 W
Sedgwick, Ks., U.S. 198 37.55 N 97.25 W
Sedgwick, Mount ▲ 200 35.11 N 108.06 W
Sédhiou 150 12.44 N 15.33 W
Sedico 64 46.06 N 12.06 E
Sedili 71 40.10 N 8.55 E
Sedin 71 40.51 N 8.49 E
Sedlčany 30 49.40 N 14.26 E
Sedlec 208 36.46 N 76.59 W
Sedlice 60 51.33 N 14.03 E
Sedliz ⫶ 54 51.33 N 14.03 E
Sedlo ⫶ 84 44.13 N 40.52 E
Sedniv 78 51.39 N 31.34 E
Sedok ⫶ 84 44.13 N 40.52 E
Sedom (Sodom) ⫶ 132 31.04 N 35.23 E
Sedona 200 34.52 N 111.45 W
Sedot Yam 132 32.29 N 34.53 E
Sedova, pik ▲ 112 72.20 N 55.30 E
Sedrata 36 36.08 N 7.32 E
Sedriano 62 45.29 N 8.58 E
Sedrina 62 45.47 N 9.38 E
Sedro Woolley 224 48.30 N 122.14 W
Sedrun 58 46.41 N 8.46 E
Šeduva 76 55.46 N 23.46 E
Şędziszów 30 50.04 N 21.41 E
See 58 47.05 N 10.28 E
Seeberg, Dtsch. 264a 52.33 N 13.41 E
Seeberg, Schw. 58 47.09 N 7.40 E
Seebergsattel ⫶ 61 47.38 N 15.18 E
Seeber Lake ⫶ 61 43.52 N 93.03 W
Seebrook 54 47.38 N 13.30 E
Seebruck 64 47.56 N 12.28 E
Seeburg 264d 51.30 N 13.07 E
Seefeld, Dtsch. 52 53.27 N 8.21 E
Seefeld, Dtsch. 52 52.37 N 13.40 E
Seefeld in Tirol 64 47.20 N 11.11 E
Seefin ⸼² 48 52.18 N 8.32 W
Seege ⫶ 54 53.04 N 11.23 E
Seegefeld 264a 52.33 N 13.05 E
Seehausen, Dtsch. 54 51.57 N 12.55 E
Seehausen, Dtsch. 54 52.06 N 11.17 E
Seeheim 156 26.50 S 17.45 E
Seeheim-Jugenheim 54 49.45 N 8.38 E
Seehof 264a 52.24 N 13.17 E
Seeis 156 22.29 S 17.39 E
Seekaskootch Indian
 Reserve ⫶⁴ 184 53.43 N 109.55 W
Seekoegat 158 33.03 S 22.31 E
Seekoei ⫶ 158 30.18 S 25.01 E
Seekonk 207 41.48 N 71.20 W
Seelbach 54 48.18 N 7.56 E
Seeley Lake 202 47.09 N 113.29 W
Seeleys Bay 212 44.29 N 76.14 W
Seelingstädt 54 50.46 N 12.14 E
Seelow 54 52.32 N 14.23 E
Seelville, In., U.S. 194 39.29 N 87.16 W
Seelyville, Pa., U.S. 210 41.35 N 75.17 W
Seelze 52 52.24 N 9.35 E
Seemade ⫶ 144 7.10 N 48.36 E
Seemandl Butte ▲ 180 60.09 N 167.08 W
Seemanbach ⫶ 56 50.57 N 7.28 E
Seemore Downs 162 30.42 S 125.15 E
Seen 64 47.29 N 8.46 E
Seengen 64 47.19 N 8.13 E
Seeon 54 47.58 N 12.26 E
Seer Green 260 51.37 N 0.36 W
Seer⸼gu 102 32.00 N 103.33 E
Seer⸼hausen 54 51.20 N 13.22 E
Sées 56 48.36 N 0.10 E
Seese 62 47.00 N 9.18 E
Seesen 52 51.53 N 10.10 E
Seeshaupt 54 47.49 N 11.18 E
Seetal Alpen ⫶ 61 47.09 N 13.57 E
Seetaler 61 14.35 N 13.57 E
Seeula 158 53.23 N 22.29 E
Seewalchen am
 Attersee 64 47.57 N 13.35 E
Seewiesen 61 47.37 N 15.16 E
Seewinkel ⫶ 61 47.48 N 16.49 E
Seewis 62 46.57 N 9.38 E
Seez ⫶ 62 45.37 N 6.48 E
Şefaatli 130 39.31 N 34.46 E
Sefadu 150 8.39 N 10.59 W
Séfar ⫶ 156 23.02 S 27.28 E
Sefarim ⫶ 130 38.11 N 26.51 E
Seferihisar 130 38.12 N 26.50 E
Seffner 220 27.59 N 82.17 W
Sefid, Küh-e ▲ 128 30.56 N 60.35 E
Sefid Ābeh 128 30.56 N 60.35 E
Sefrou 148 33.56 N 4.50 W
Sefton, N.Z. 172 43.15 S 172.40 E
Sefton, Eng., U.K. 262 53.30 N 3.00 W
Sefton, Mount ▲ 172 43.41 S 170.03 E
Sefton Park ⫶ 262 53.23 N 3.00 W
Segal ⫶ 54 54.39 N 1.26 W
Segaluid ⫶ 116 5.43 N 117.55 E
Segama ⫶ 112 5.30 N 118.48 E
Segamat 112 2.30 N 102.49 E
Segano 100 35.33 N 136.40 E
Segarcea 38 44.06 N 23.45 E
Segawa, Oued es 148 31.39 N 2.26 E
Şegmas 148 31.39 N 2.26 E
Segni 66 41.41 N 13.01 E
Segorbe 34 39.51 N 0.30 W
Segou 150 13.27 N 6.16 W
Ségou ⫶ 150 14.00 N 5.40 E

Şegovary 24 62.23 N 42.57 E
Segovia, Col. 246 7.07 N 74.42 W
Segovia, Esp. 34 40.57 N 4.07 W
Segovia ⫶⁴ 34 41.15 N 4.00 W
Segozero, ozero ⫶ 24 63.18 N 33.45 E
Segré 266b 45.29 N 9.19 E
Segré 32 47.41 N 0.53 W
Segre ⫶ 34 41.22 N 0.20 E
Seguam Island I 180 52.17 N 172.30 W
Seguam Pass ⫶ 180 52.08 N 172.45 W
Séguédine 148 20.12 N 12.59 E
Sel⸼co, Ross. 24 63.18 N 41.22 E
Séguéla, C. Iv. 150 7.57 N 6.40 W
Sel⸼co, Ross. 53 53.22 N 34.06 E
Séguéla, Mali 150 14.07 N 6.44 W
Selcourt 273d 26.18 S 28.27 E
Ségula ⫶ 150 13.27 N 1.58 W
Selçuk ⫶ 130 37.56 N 27.22 E
Séguénéga 150 13.27 N 1.58 W
Selçuğa ⫶ 89 49.42 N 133.20 E
Seguí 252 31.57 S 60.08 W
Selçuk 130 37.56 N 27.22 E
Seguin 196 29.34 N 97.57 W
Sel'cy, Ross. 76 57.57 N 35.59 E
Séguin ⫶ 212 45.21 N 80.01 W
Sel'cy, Ross. 265a 59.57 N 30.43 E
Segula Island I 181a 52.01 N 178.07 E
Semanu 115a 8.00 S 110.39 E
Seguntur 112 1.54 N 117.47 E
Sel'co, Ross. 76 57.57 N 35.59 E
Segura 34 39.50 N 6.59 W
Selden, Ks., U.S. 198 39.32 N 100.34 W
Segura ⫶ 34 38.06 N 0.38 W
Selden, N.Y., U.S. 210 40.51 N 73.02 W
Segura, Sierra de ⫶ 34 38.00 N 2.43 W
Semau, Pulau I 112 10.13 S 123.22 E
Sehäni Kalän 272a 28.41 N 77.25 E
Selden ⫶ 212 45.21 N 80.01 W
Sehāni Khurd 272a 28.42 N 77.25 E
Selchow 264a 52.21 N 13.28 E
Sehärä Bāzär 126 23.06 N 87.49 E
Semakau, Pulau I 271c 1.12 N 103.46 E
Sehithwa 156 20.23 S 22.45 E
Selegas 71 39.34 N 9.06 E
Sehlabathebe 158 29.53 S 29.05 E
Selemadeg 115b 8.29 S 115.02 E
Sehlabathebe
 National Park ✦ 158 29.53 S 29.06 E
Selembao 273b 4.22 S 15.17 E
Sehma 54 50.32 N 13.00 E
Semenanjung
Sehnde 52 52.18 N 9.57 E
 Malaysia ⸼⁹ 114 4.00 N 102.00 E
Sehnkewin 150 5.13 N 9.12 W
Semendua 152 3.11 S 18.05 E
Sehnkwehn ⫶ 150 5.12 N 9.21 W
Semene ⫶ 62 45.05 N 11.30 E
Sehore 124 23.12 N 77.05 E
Selenga (Selenge) ⫶ 88 52.16 N 106.16 E
Semenicului, Munţii ⫶ 38 45.05 N 22.05 E
Sehwān 120 26.26 N 67.52 E
Selenge, Mong. 88 49.25 N 103.59 E
Semenivka ⫶ 78 49.36 N 33.10 E
Sehyŏn-ni 98 38.20 N 127.41 E
Selenge, R.D.C. 152 1.58 S 18.11 E
Semenivka, Ukr. 78 52.10 N 32.35 E
Seia 34 40.25 N 7.42 W
Selenge (Selenga) ⫶ 88 49.30 N 106.30 E
Semenyih 114 2.57 N 101.51 E
Seibert 198 39.18 N 102.52 W
Selenginsk 88 52.06 N 107.01 E
Semeni, Gunung ▲ 89 52.57 N 132.34 E
Seibo 268 35.50 N 139.22 E
Selenica 38 40.32 N 19.38 E
Semertak 89 52.57 N 132.34 E
Seiches-sur-le-Loir 32 47.35 N 0.22 W
Selenicä ⫶ 38 40.32 N 19.38 E
Semetovo 82 54.28 N 38.50 E
Seidan 96 34.19 N 134.45 E
Selen⸼ach ⫶ 74 67.48 N 144.54 E
Sereža⸼va 76 55.28 N 27.52 E
Seidersville 210 40.35 N 75.23 W
Selent 54 54.17 N 10.26 E
Semiahmoo Bay ⫶ 224 48.58 N 122.48 W
Seiersberg 61 47.01 N 15.24 E
Selenter See ⫶ 54 54.17 N 10.28 E
Semibalki 83 47.00 N 39.03 E
Seiffen 54 50.39 N 13.26 E
Selenter See ⫶ 54 54.17 N 10.28 E
Semibalki 83 47.00 N 39.03 E
Seiffhennersdorf 54 50.56 N 14.36 E
Sélestat 58 48.16 N 7.27 E
Semibratovo 87 57.18 N 39.32 E
Seignelay 58 47.54 N 3.36 E
 (Schlettstadt)
Semiburg 80 46.11 N 48.16 E
Seignigul, Lac ⫶ 275a 45.33 N 73.20 W
Seletar, Pulau I 271c 1.26 N 103.52 E
Semichi Islands II 181a 52.42 N 174.00 E
Seikan 54 47.54 N 3.36 E
Seletar, Pulau I 271c 1.26 N 103.52 E
Semidi Islands II 180 56.07 N 156.44 W
Seikpyu 110 20.55 N 94.47 E
Seletar Hills 271c 1.23 N 103.53 E
Semigorsk 88 56.42 N 104.41 E
Seil I 46 56.18 N 5.39 W
Seletar Reservoir ⫶¹ 271c 1.24 N 103.48 E
Semijarka 80 50.54 N 78.20 E
Seiland I 26 70.25 N 23.15 E
Selezen'ovo, Ross. 26 60.45 N 28.39 E
Semikarakorsk 83 47.31 N 40.48 E
Seilhac 32 45.22 N 1.42 E
Selezen'ovo, Ross. 76 59.12 N 42.18 E
Semilej 80 53.57 N 45.21 E
Seiling 196 36.08 N 98.55 W
Selezni, Ross. 76 55.39 N 31.29 E
Semilovo 80 55.54 N 42.10 E
Seillans 62 43.38 N 6.38 E
Selezni, Ross. 82 52.45 N 41.15 E
Semily 30 50.36 N 15.20 E
Seille ⫶, Fr. 56 49.07 N 6.11 E
Selezn'ovo 76 60.45 N 28.39 E
Seminara 66 38.20 N 15.52 E
Seille ⫶, Fr. 56 46.31 N 4.56 E
Self Defense Fleet
 Headquarters ⫶ 268 35.18 N 139.38 E
Seminary 194 31.33 N 89.29 W
Seim 140 12.20 N 23.50 E
Selfoss 34a 63.56 N 20.57 W
Seminoe Reservoir
 → Sejm ⫶ 78 51.27 N 32.34 E
Selfridge 198 46.02 N 100.55 W
 ⫶¹ 200 42.00 N 106.50 W
Sein, Île de I 32 48.02 N 4.51 W
Selfridge Air National
 Guard Base ⫶ 281 42.36 N 82.49 W
Seminoe State Park
Seinäjoki 26 62.47 N 22.50 E
Selfridge ⫶ 198 49.36 N 135.26 E
 ✦ 202 42.05 N 106.55 W
Seine ⫶, Mb., Can. 184 49.54 N 97.07 W
Selibaby 150 15.10 N 12.11 W
Seminole, Fl., U.S. 220 27.50 N 82.47 W
Seine ⫶, On., Can. 190 48.40 N 92.49 W
Selichino 90 50.22 N 137.38 E
Seminole, Ok., U.S. 196 35.13 N 96.40 W
Seine ⫶, Fr. 56 49.26 N 0.26 E
Selichovo, zaliv ⫶ 74 60.00 N 158.00 E
Seminole, Tx., U.S. 196 32.43 N 102.38 W
Seine-et-Marne ⫶⁵ 54 48.30 N 3.00 E
Selichovo 83 55.42 N 37.41 E
Seminole Draw ⫶ 196 32.27 N 102.20 W
Seine-Maritime ⫶⁵ 56 49.45 N 1.00 E
Seligental 54 49.00 N 9.56 E
Seminole Park 220 27.52 N 82.45 W
Seine-Port 54 48.33 N 2.33 E
Seliger, ozero ⫶ 76 57.13 N 33.05 E
Seminskij chrebet ⫶ 86 51.05 N 85.50 E
Seine-Saint-Denis ⫶⁵ 261 48.55 N 2.30 E
Seligman, Az., U.S. 200 35.19 N 112.52 W
Semiozerje 48 49.52 N 110.23 E
Seip Mound State
 Memorial ⫶ 218 39.20 N 83.13 W
Seligman, Mo., U.S. 194 36.31 N 93.56 W
Semioz'ornyj 80 52.22 N 64.08 E
Seipstown 208 40.35 N 75.40 W
Selim 114 3.51 N 101.29 E
Semipalatinsk ⫶⁸ 80 50.28 N 80.13 E
Seira ⫶ 62 52.53 N 11.45 E
Selimbäu 112 0.37 N 112.08 E
Semipalatinsk 80 50.28 N 80.13 E
Seimiye 130 37.24 N 27.40 E
Semirara Island I 116 12.04 N 121.23 E
Sein⸼ar 258 34.39 S 58.37 W
Selim River ⫶ 114 3.50 N 101.24 E
Semipolka 80 52.15 N 77.54 E
Seishin
 → Ch'ŏngjin 98 41.47 N 129.50 E
Sêlitovka 192 35.00 N 84.33 W
Semirara Island I 116 12.04 N 121.23 E
Seitenstetten 61 48.02 N 14.39 E
Selinsgrove 208 40.47 N 76.51 W
Semisopochnoi Island
Seitovka 60 46.43 N 48.03 E
Selinunte ⫶ 70 37.35 N 12.49 E
 I 181a 52.00 N 179.35 E
Seitsemisen
 kansallispuisto ✦ 26 61.58 N 23.20 E
Sêlişče, Ross. 76 56.50 N 33.16 E
Semitau 80 0.33 N 111.58 E
Sejaka 94 34.29 N 136.30 E
Sêlişče, Ross. 84 64.58 N 46.18 E
Semizbugy, gora ▲ 80 50.12 N 74.48 E
Seixal 34 38.38 N 9.06 W
Selişte 84 44.58 N 41.42 E
Semizovka 80 56.02 N 45.59 E
Seixas, Ponta do ⸼ 257 7.09 S 34.47 W
Selizarovo 76 56.51 N 33.27 E
Semli Kalän 124 24.16 N 76.39 E
Seize Îles, Lac des ⫶ 206 45.54 N 74.28 W
Selje 26 62.03 N 5.22 E
Semluki 83 53.03 N 39.08 E
Sejaka 94 34.29 N 136.30 E
Seljord 26 59.29 N 8.37 E
Semmenstedt 52 52.11 N 10.43 E
Sejerø I 26 55.53 N 11.09 E
Selkämeri
 (Bottenhavet) ⫶ 26 62.00 N 20.00 E
Semmering 61 47.38 N 15.49 E
Sejerø Bugt ⫶ 41 55.50 N 11.15 E
Selkirk, Mb., Can. 184 50.09 N 96.52 W
Semmes 194 30.46 N 88.16 W
Sejm ⫶ (Seym) 78 51.27 N 32.34 E
Selkirk, On., Can. 212 42.49 N 79.56 W
Semnan ⸼⁸ 128 35.34 N 53.23 E
Sejmčan 74 62.53 N 152.26 E
Selkirk, Scot., U.K. 46 55.33 N 2.50 W
Semnan 128 35.34 N 53.23 E
Sejny 30 54.06 N 23.21 E
Selkirk Mountains ⫶ 202 51.00 N 117.40 W
Semonaicha 78 50.39 N 81.54 E
Sek 148 29.59 N 2.00 W
Selkirk Provincial
 Park ✦ 212 43.33 N 76.12 W
Semonkong 158 29.51 S 28.05 E
Sekadau 112 0.01 S 110.54 E
Selkirk Shores State
 Park ✦ 212 43.33 N 76.12 W
Semord 88 56.48 N 93.09 E
Sekakes 158 29.58 S 28.27 E
Selkovka 83 55.03 N 37.46 E
Semoravia 118 5.02 S 55.30 E
Sekampung ⫶ 115a 5.36 S 105.50 E
Selkovskaja 84 43.37 N 46.20 E
Semper 265b 54.33 N 13.22 E
Sekayam ⫶ 112 0.30 N 110.25 E
Selky⸼ 80 51.47 N 82.10 E
Sempach 64 47.08 N 8.11 E
Sekayu 112 2.59 S 103.51 E
Sellafield ⫶ 44 54.25 N 3.30 W
Sempacher See ⫶ 64 47.09 N 8.09 E
Seke, Ityo. 144 9.56 N 38.19 E
Sellersburg 218 38.24 N 85.46 W
Sempang Mangayau,
 Tanjong ⸼ 112 7.02 N 116.45 E
Seke, Tan. 152 3.20 S 33.31 E
Sellersville 208 40.21 N 75.18 W
Semple Lake ⫶ 184 55.02 N 95.38 W
Seke-Banza 152 5.18 S 13.16 E
Selles-sur-Cher 56 47.16 N 1.33 E
Sempoma 112 4.28 N 118.37 E
Sekeladi ⫶ 152 2.38 S 102.14 E
Sellia Marina 66 38.53 N 16.45 E
Sena di Corno ⫶ 256 22.18 S 42.08 W
Sekenke 152 4.10 S 34.10 E
Sellin 265b 54.23 N 13.42 E
Semu ⫶ 154 10.35 S 40.12 E
Sekiardi ⫶ 130 37.33 N 30.22 E
Sellindge 260 51.06 N 1.00 E
Semuda 115a 2.51 S 112.58 E
Seki, Azer. 84 41.12 N 47.12 E
Sellore 124 20.02 N 75.48 E
Semur-en-Auxois 54 47.29 N 4.20 E
Seki, Nihon 94 34.30 N 136.55 E
Sellersburg 218 38.24 N 85.46 W
Semur⸼a 148 4.00 N 112.30 E
Seki, Tür. 130 36.58 N 36.59 E
Sellrain ⫶ 62 47.13 N 11.16 E
Semursk 74 55.34 N 128.04 E
Sekidō-san ▲ 94 36.58 N 136.59 E
Sells 200 31.55 N 111.53 W
Semuta 115a 1.18 N 110.34 E
Sekigahara 94 35.22 N 136.28 E
Selm 56 51.42 N 7.28 E
Semža 84 66.06 N 44.11 E
Sekima ⫶ 112 1.41 S 111.41 E
Selma, Al., U.S. 194 32.24 N 87.01 W
Sen ⫶ 110 12.48 N 104.34 E
Sekinomiya 94 35.29 N 134.50 E
Selma, Ca., U.S. 226 36.34 N 119.36 W
Sena, Bol. 248 11.32 S 67.11 W
Sekiya 268 35.44 N 139.47 E
Selma, In., U.S. 218 40.11 N 85.24 W
Sena, Moç. 154 17.27 S 35.00 E
Sekima ⫶ 112 1.41 S 111.41 E
Selma, N.C., U.S. 192 35.32 N 78.17 W
Sena ⫶ 32 45.33 N 4.08 E
Sekiu 202 48.16 N 124.18 W
Selma, Oh., U.S. 218 39.48 N 83.47 W
Senachwine Lake ⫶ 216 41.07 N 89.30 W
Sekiyado 268 36.06 N 139.47 E
Selmer 194 35.10 N 88.36 W
Senaki 84 42.17 N 42.04 E
Sekondi-Takoradi 150 4.59 N 1.43 W
Selmo ⫶ 130 37.47 N 41.25 E
Senaki 84 42.17 N 42.04 E
Sekota 144 12.38 N 39.03 E
Selmon ⫶ 110 12.57 N 99.12 E
Senan 54 47.55 N 3.27 E
Sekpiegu 150 9.45 N 0.05 W
Selon ⫶ 268 35.42 N 139.34 E
Senas 62 43.44 N 5.04 E
Sekretarka 80 52.30 N 54.12 E
Seloncourt 58 47.28 N 6.52 E
Senatobia 194 34.37 N 89.58 W
Sekretarka 269e 61.04 N 106.47 E
Selong 112 8.39 S 116.29 E
Senburi 110 8.06 N 99.07 E
Sekt'an ⫶ 102 37.40 N 80.53 E
Selongey 54 47.35 N 5.11 E
Senador Amaral 256 22.35 S 46.11 W
Sekumi ⫶ 152 5.00 S 17.53 E
Selopuro ⫶ 115a 8.08 S 112.22 E
Senador Canedo 255 16.42 S 49.06 W
Sel ⫶ 102 42.50 N 86.28 E
Selou⸼z, Mount ▲ 202 45.10 N 113.43 W
Senador Cörtes 256 21.52 S 43.12 W
Selai ⫶ 114 2.13 N 103.26 E
Selous Game
 Reserve ⫶⁴ 154 9.10 S 37.10 E
Senador Firmino 256 20.55 S 43.06 W
Selajar, Selat ⫶ 112 5.42 S 120.28 E
Selsdon ⫶ 260 51.21 N 0.04 W
Senador Guiomard 248 10.09 S 67.36 W
Sêlajevo 83 55.14 N 38.13 E
Selsey 42 50.44 N 0.48 W
Senador José Bento 256 22.10 S 46.15 W
Selam ⫶ 144 6.13 N 34.04 E
Selsey Bill ⸼ 42 50.43 N 0.47 W
Senador José Porfírio 250 2.35 S 51.57 W
Selangor ⸼³ 114 3.20 N 101.15 E
Selši 26 58.56 N 97.32 E
Senador Pompeu 250 5.35 S 39.22 W
Selangor ⫶ 114 3.15 N 101.25 E
Selters 56 50.33 N 8.00 E
Senanayake
 Samudra ⫶ 122 7.11 N 81.29 E
Selah 202 46.39 N 120.31 W
Selty 269e 57.19 N 52.10 E
Sendai, Nihon 95 38.15 N 140.53 E
Selaphum 110 16.02 N 103.57 E
Seltz 54 48.54 N 8.07 E
Sendai, Nihon 94 31.49 N 130.18 E
Selargius 66 39.16 N 9.15 E
Selu ⫶ 114 3.50 N 130.52 E
Sendai ⫶ 94 31.43 N 130.13 E
Selaru, Pulau I 164 8.09 S 131.00 E
Selva, Arg. 252 29.45 S 62.02 W
Sênsai ⸼ 90 31.43 N 130.13 E
Selat, Tanjung ⸼ 112 4.10 S 114.38 E
Selva ⫶ 64 46.33 N 11.46 E
Sena Madureira 248 9.04 S 68.40 W
Selatan, Tanjung ⸼ 112 4.10 S 114.38 E
Selva, Val di ⫶ 248 9.04 S 68.40 W
Sena Madureira 248 9.04 S 68.40 W
Selawik 180 66.36 N 160.00 W
Selva di Cadore 64 46.26 N 12.07 E
Senanga 154 16.07 S 23.16 E
Selawik Lake ⫶ 180 66.36 N 160.40 W
Selvagens, Ilhas ⫶ 146 30.08 N 15.55 W
Senanayake 242 63.36 N 108.55 E
Selayar, Selat ⫶ 112 5.42 S 120.28 E
Selvas ⫶ 242 5.00 S 68.00 W
Sendafa 144 9.09 N 39.02 E
Selayar ⫶ 112 5.42 S 120.28 E
Selvino 62 45.47 N 9.45 E
Sendenhorst 56 51.51 N 7.50 E
Selbeck ⫶⁸ 263 51.22 N 6.52 W
Selwyn, Austl. 166 21.32 S 140.30 E
Sendhwa 124 21.41 N 75.06 E
Selbecke ⫶⁸ 263 51.20 N 7.28 E
Selwyn, Eng., U.K. 44 53.47 N 1.04 W
Sêndrô, Forêt de ✦ 152 5.05 S 34.10 E

Selbitz 54 50.19 N 11.44 E
Selwyn, Passage ⫶ 175f 16.03 S 168.12 E
Selborne 42 51.06 N 0.56 W
Selwyn Lake ⫶ 176 59.55 N 104.35 W
Selbu 26 63.13 N 11.02 E
Selwyn Mountains ⫶ 180 63.10 N 130.20 W
Selbusjøen ⫶ 26 63.14 N 10.54 E
Selwyn Range ⫶ 166 21.35 S 140.35 E
Selby, Austl. 274b 37.55 S 145.22 E
Selyatyn 78 47.53 N 25.12 E
Selby, Eng., U.K. 44 53.48 N 1.04 W
Selydove 83 48.08 N 37.18 E
Selby, S.D., U.S. 198 45.30 N 100.01 W
Selz ⫶ 56 49.59 N 8.02 E
Selby ⫶⁸ 273d 26.13 S 28.02 E
Šemacha 86 56.15 N 59.16 E
Selbyville 208 38.27 N 75.13 W
Semal, Pulau I 164 3.08 S 132.30 E
Selchow 264a 52.21 N 13.28 E
Semakau, Pulau I 271c 1.12 N 103.46 E
Sel'co, Ross. 24 63.18 N 41.22 E
Seman ⫶ 38 40.56 N 19.24 E
Sel'co, Ross. 53 53.22 N 34.06 E
Semanggol 114 4.57 N 100.38 E
Selcourt 273d 26.18 S 28.27 E
Semangka, Teluk ⫶ 112 5.36 S 104.42 E
Selçuk ⫶ 130 37.56 N 27.22 E
Semanicha 80 57.18 N 45.24 E
Selçuk 130 37.56 N 27.22 E
Semans 184 51.25 N 104.44 W
Selçuğa ⫶ 89 49.42 N 133.20 E
Semanu 115a 8.00 S 110.39 E
Sel'cy, Ross. 76 57.57 N 35.59 E
Semarang 115a 6.58 S 110.25 E
Sel'cy, Ross. 265a 59.57 N 30.43 E
Semarang 115a 6.58 S 110.25 E
Sel'co, Ross. 76 57.57 N 35.59 E
Semaria 124 24.16 N 79.54 E
Selden, Ks., U.S. 198 39.32 N 100.34 W
Sematan 112 1.48 N 109.46 E
Selden, N.Y., U.S. 210 40.51 N 73.02 W
Semau, Pulau I 112 10.13 S 123.22 E
Seldovia 180 59.27 N 151.43 W
⫶ 154 0.14 S 116.28 E
Sele ⫶ 66 40.33 N 14.57 E
Sembabule 154 0.05 S 31.27 E
Sele, Piana del ⫶ 66 40.33 N 14.57 E
Sembadel ⫶ 62 45.16 N 3.41 E
Sele, Selat ⫶ 164 1.10 S 131.05 E
Sembakung ⫶ 112 3.47 N 117.30 E
Sele, Tanjung ⸼ 164 1.26 S 130.55 E
Sembawang 271c 1.27 N 103.50 E
Selebi Phikwe 156 22.00 S 27.50 E
Sembé 152 1.39 N 14.36 E
Selec 76 52.33 N 33.35 E
Semberong ⫶ 114 2.27 N 103.37 E
Selechov 88 52.13 N 104.08 E
Semblançay 32 47.30 N 0.35 E
Selection Park 273d 26.18 S 28.27 E
Sembo ⫶ 152 7.42 S 13.01 E
Selegas 71 39.34 N 9.06 E
Semcy 76 52.51 N 33.28 E
Selemadeg 115b 8.29 S 115.02 E
Şemdinli 128 37.18 N 44.35 E
Selembao 273b 4.22 S 15.17 E
Šemelišeks 76 54.40 N 24.40 E

⫶ River — Fluß — Río — Rivière — Rio
⚌ Canal — Kanal — Canal — Canal — Canal
↳ Waterfall, Rapids — Wasserfall, Stromschnellen — Cascada, Rápidos — Chute d'eau, Rapides — Cascata, Rápidos
⫶ Strait — Meeresstraße — Estrecho — Détroit — Estreito
⫶ Bay, Gulf — Bucht, Golf — Bahía, Golfo — Baie, Golfe — Baía, Golfo
⫶ Lake, Lakes — See, Seen — Lago, Lagos — Lac, Lacs — Lago, Lagos
☲ Swamp — Sumpf — Pantano — Marais — Pântano
⫶ Ice Features, Glacier — Eis- und Gletscherformen — Accidentes Glaciales — Formes glaciaires — Acidentes glaciares
⸼ Other Hydrographic Features — Andere Hydrographische Objekte — Otros Elementos Hidrográficos — Autres données hydrographiques — Outros Acidentes hidrográficos

✦ Submarine Features — Untermeerische Objekte — Accidentes Submarinos — Formes de relief sous-marin — Acidentes submarinos
⫶ Political Unit — Politische Einheit — Unidad Política — Entité politique — Unidade política
⫶ Cultural Institution — Kulturelle Institution — Institución Cultural — Institution culturelle — Institução cultural
⫶ Historical Site — Historische Stätte — Sitio Histórico — Site historique — Sítio histórico
✦ Recreational Site — Erholungs- und Ferienort — Sitio de Recreo — Centre de loisirs — Area de Lazer
⫶ Airport — Flughafen — Aeropuerto — Aéroport — Aeroporto
⫶ Military Installation — Militäranlage — Instalación Militar — Installation militaire — Instalação militar
⫶ Miscellaneous — Verschiedenes — Misceláneo — Divers — Diversos

ESPAÑOL: Nombre | Página | Lat.°′ | Long.°′ W = Oeste
FRANÇAIS: Nom | Page | Lat.°′ | Long.°′ W = Ouest
PORTUGUÊS: Nome | Página | Lat.°′ | Long.°′ W = Oeste

Nombre	Página	Lat.°′	Long.°′ W = Oeste
Shahryār	128	35.28 N	51.05 E
Shahu	100	30.11 N	113.39 E
Shāhzādpur	126	24.10 N	89.36 E
Shā'ib al-Banāt, Jabal ∧	140	26.59 N	33.29 E
Shaighālu	120	31.11 N	68.49 E
Shaikou	100	27.19 N	117.35 E
Sha'īrah, Jabal ∧ [2]	132	30.06 N	34.17 E
Sha'īrah, Jabal ash- ⋏	132	29.31 N	34.29 E
Shājāpur	124	23.26 N	76.16 E
Shajian	100	24.46 N	117.38 E
Shajianzi	98	41.01 N	125.26 E
Shajiazhuang	106	32.13 N	120.53 E
Shajing	100	23.36 N	114.06 E
Shajingzi	102	37.42 N	105.09 E
Shakaga-dake ∧	96	33.11 N	130.53 E
Shakaga-hana ≻	96	34.25 N	134.14 E
Shakaga-take-tunnel ◆ [5]	96	33.27 N	130.52 E
Shakardarra	123	33.14 N	71.30 E
Shakargarh	123	32.16 N	75.10 E
Shakarpura	272a	28.46 N	77.21 E
Shakarpur Khās ◆ [8]	272a	28.38 N	77.17 E
Shakaskraal	158	29.26 S	31.14 E
Shakawe	156	18.23 S	21.50 E
Shakeng	98	42.13 N	116.35 E
Shaker Heights	214	41.28 N	81.32 W
Shaker Heights Park ♠	279a	41.29 N	81.33 W
Shakespeare	212	43.22 N	80.49 W
Shākhen	128	33.22 N	59.32 E
Shakhtars'k	83	48.03 N	38.28 E
Shakhtne	83	47.57 N	38.17 E
Shakhty → Šachty	83	47.42 N	40.13 E
Shaki	150	8.39 N	3.25 E
Shākir, Jazīrat I	140	27.30 N	33.59 E
Shakopee	190	44.47 N	93.31 W
Shakotan-hantō ≻ [1]	92a	43.20 N	140.30 E
Shakou	100	24.25 N	113.32 E
Shakshūk	142	29.28 N	30.42 E
Shaktoolik	180	64.20 N	161.09 W
Shakujii ◆ [8]	268	35.45 N	139.37 E
Shakūrpur ◆ [8]	272a	28.41 N	77.09 E
Shala, Lake ⊜	144	7.25 N	38.30 E
Shalalth	182	50.44 N	122.13 W
Shalatayn, Bi'r ⊤ [4]	140	23.08 N	35.36 E
Shaleitian Dao I	98	39.03 N	118.44 E
Shaler Mountains ⋏	176	72.35 N	110.45 W
Shaleshanto	156	19.09 S	23.58 E
Shalford	260	51.13 N	0.34 W
Shālimah	142	31.14 N	30.52 E
Shalimar Railroad Station ◆ [5]	272b	22.33 N	88.19 E
Shaling, Zhg.	104	41.09 N	122.22 E
Shaling, Zhg.	104	41.20 N	123.01 E
Shalingpu	104	41.47 N	123.11 E
Shalingzi	105	40.42 N	114.55 E
Shaliuhe, Zhg.	102	36.28 N	98.57 E
Shaliuhe, Zhg.	105	39.53 N	117.56 E
Shallotte	192	33.58 N	78.23 W
Shallowater	196	33.41 N	101.59 W
Shallow Brook ≃	276	40.21 N	74.35 W
Shallow Lake	212	44.36 N	81.05 W
Shaluhe	89	51.08 N	126.00 E
Shaluli Shan ⋏	102	30.45 N	99.45 E
Shalyhyne	78	51.34 N	34.07 E
Shām, Bādiyat ash- (Syrian Desert) ◆ [2]	128	32.00 N	40.00 E
Shām, Jabal ash- ∧	128	23.13 N	57.16 E
Shama ≃	154	6.16 S	32.27 E
Shaman	85	38.50 N	75.36 E
Shamattawa	184	55.52 N	92.05 W
Shambe	140	7.07 N	30.46 E
Shambi	152	1.49 S	22.39 E
Shambu	144	9.40 N	37.03 E
Shambuanda	152	6.38 S	20.13 E
Shām Churasi	123	31.30 N	75.45 E
Shamei	100	24.32 N	118.25 E
Shamepūr ◆ [8]	272a	28.45 N	77.09 E
Shamīl	128	27.30 N	56.53 E
Shāmli	124	29.27 N	77.19 E
Shammākh	132	30.30 N	35.30 E
Shamokin	208	40.47 N	76.33 W
Shamona Creek ≃	285	40.02 N	75.43 W
Shamrayivka	78	49.46 N	29.49 E
Shamrock, Fl., U.S.	192	29.38 N	83.08 W
Shamrock, Tx., U.S.	196	35.12 N	100.14 W
Shamsābād	124	27.01 N	78.08 E
Shamsher	272a	28.44 N	77.24 E
Shamva	154	17.18 S	31.34 E
Shan □ [3]	110	22.00 N	98.00 E
Shanbiao	98	35.28 N	113.57 E
Shancheng	102	37.01 N	107.00 E
Shanchengzhen	98	42.23 N	125.26 E
Shandaken	210	42.07 N	74.23 W
Shandan	102	38.45 N	101.15 E
Shandatgyi	110	19.37 N	94.43 E
Shandī	140	16.42 N	33.26 E
Shandian ≃	98	42.23 N	116.21 E
Shandianhe	98	42.22 N	116.15 E
Shandīd	142	30.55 N	30.40 E
Shandon	226	35.39 N	120.22 W
Shandong	107	29.31 N	106.25 E
Shandong (Shantung) □ [4]	98	36.00 N	118.00 E
Shandong Bandao (Shantung Peninsula) ≻ [1]	98	37.00 N	121.00 E
Shandrivka	78	48.57 N	35.46 E
Shaner	279b	40.17 N	79.47 W
Shanesville	214	40.31 N	81.39 W
Shangalume	154	10.49 S	26.34 E
Shangani	154	19.47 S	29.22 E
Shangani ≃	154	18.41 S	27.10 E
Shang'ao	106	30.41 N	119.25 E
Shangba	106	32.11 N	118.46 E
Shangbahe	100	30.40 N	115.05 E
Shangbai	106	30.29 N	119.58 E
Shangbancheng	105	40.50 N	118.03 E
Shangbatang	102	32.46 N	96.20 E
Shangcai	100	33.16 N	114.15 E
Shangcang	105	39.54 N	117.23 E
Shangchen	106	30.07 N	119.53 E
Shangcheng	100	31.48 N	115.24 E
Shangchewan	100	29.48 N	113.01 E
Shangch'iu → Shangqiu	98	34.27 N	115.42 E
Shangchuan Dao I	102	21.42 N	112.47 E
Shangdang	106	32.06 N	119.24 E
Shangdayangqi	89	51.09 N	124.02 E
Shangdian	100	34.07 N	112.23 E
Shangdianmiao	106	30.56 N	120.51 E
Shangdouying	105	40.36 N	115.33 E
Shangdu	98	41.29 N	113.34 E
Shangduichunshi	104	41.00 N	123.02 E
Shangdundu	100	27.56 N	116.15 E
Shangfu	100	28.40 N	114.59 E
Shanggaixin	102	23.25 N	100.02 E
Shanggan	100	25.56 N	119.22 E
Shanggang	100	33.30 N	120.04 E
Shanggangzi	104	42.26 N	123.03 E
Shanggao	100	28.18 N	114.54 E
Shanggecun	106	31.49 N	119.07 E
Shanggu	98	40.47 N	118.28 E
Shangguanying	98	41.18 N	117.07 E
Shanghai, Va., U.S.	208	37.37 N	76.47 W
Shanghai, Zhg.	106	31.07 N	121.22 E
Shanghai, Zhg.	106	31.14 N	121.28 E
Shanghai, Zhg.	269b	31.14 N	121.28 E
Shanghailingao	104	41.57 N	120.55 E
Shanghai Museum ɤ	269b	31.13 N	121.28 E
Shanghai Shi (Shanghai Shih) □ [7]	106	31.10 N	121.30 E
Shanghai Station ◆ [5]	269b	31.15 N	121.28 E
Shanghang	100	25.06 N	116.25 E
Shanghe	98	37.19 N	117.07 E
Shanghekou	98	40.26 N	124.47 E
Shanghetou	105	39.12 N	116.59 E
Shanghewantun	104	41.42 N	123.23 E
Shang Hu ⊜	106	31.39 N	120.41 E
Shanghuang	106	31.33 N	119.34 E
Shanghuangqi	98	41.29 N	116.31 E
Shanghucun	105	40.45 N	115.45 E
Shangjao → Shangrao	100	28.26 N	117.58 E
Shangjiafen	104	41.18 N	121.10 E
Shangjiahe	98	41.51 N	124.28 E
Shangjiaodao	100	29.00 N	119.54 E
Shangjiatai	104	40.53 N	123.35 E
Shangjie	100	27.06 N	116.06 E
Shangjin	102	33.09 N	110.03 E
Shangjiuwu	100	33.59 N	113.01 E
Shangkasa	120	33.45 N	80.12 E
Shangkou	98	36.59 N	118.53 E
Shanglanjiagou	104	40.52 N	120.37 E
Shanglin, Zhg.	98	38.19 N	116.05 E
Shanglin, Zhg.	102	23.28 N	108.33 E
Shanglin, Zhg.	104	41.31 N	122.14 E
Shanglishi	100	27.52 N	113.46 E
Shangliuhezicun	104	41.28 N	123.32 E
Shangliulinzi	104	41.02 N	123.13 E
Shangmagushan	104	41.41 N	124.10 E
Shangmatai	105	39.22 N	117.15 E
Shangmatun	104	40.57 N	123.22 E
Shangmingdian	106	31.12 N	120.57 E
Shangmingju	105	39.41 N	115.12 E
Shangnan	102	33.31 N	110.45 E
Shangpandaoling	104	41.42 N	121.14 E
Shangpeibu	106	31.28 N	119.13 E
Shangping, Zhg.	100	25.57 N	117.33 E
Shangping, Zhg.	100	24.43 N	115.27 E
Shangping, Zhg.	100	24.29 N	114.38 E
Shangpuzi	104	41.37 N	121.35 E
Shangqianbu	106	30.27 N	120.04 E
Shangqiao	100	31.02 N	117.42 E
Shangqing, Zhg.	100	25.53 N	118.36 E
Shangqing, Zhg.	100	28.02 N	117.00 E
Shangqingshuicun	105	39.56 N	115.38 E
Shangqiu (Zhuji), Zhg.	98	34.27 N	115.42 E
Shangqiu, Zhg.	98	34.23 N	115.37 E
Shangrao	100	28.26 N	117.58 E
Shangshe	102	38.15 N	113.20 E
Shangshibatai	104	42.02 N	120.51 E
Shangshui	100	33.33 N	114.34 E
Shangsi	102	22.09 N	107.57 E
Shangtan	106	30.27 N	118.42 E
Shangtang	100	33.23 N	118.02 E
Shan Guan)(	100	27.30 N	117.06 E
Shangweiniuchang	104	40.54 N	120.44 E
Shangxian	102	33.51 N	109.54 E
Shangxingzhen	106	31.32 N	119.15 E
Shangxinhe	106	32.02 N	118.43 E
Shangxinqiu	104	42.27 N	121.37 E
Shangyangbao	98	42.30 N	124.14 E
Shangyangcun	106	30.48 N	118.40 E
Shangye	98	35.26 N	117.59 E
Shangyi (Nanhaoqian)	98	41.04 N	114.03 E
Shangying	89	44.10 N	127.17 E
Shangyinkou	102	32.52 N	103.04 E
Shangyou	100	25.51 N	114.30 E
Shangyou ≃	100	25.49 N	114.50 E
Shangyou Shuiku ⊜ [1]	100	25.52 N	114.21 E
Shangyu	100	30.02 N	120.54 E
Shangyuan	104	41.39 N	120.55 E
Shangyun	102	23.01 N	99.50 E
Shangzhai	98	39.13 N	114.17 E
Shangzhaoshugou	104	42.12 N	121.58 E
Shangzhazi	105	40.52 N	117.42 E
Shangzhenzhuang	105	40.20 N	117.06 E
Shangzhi	89	45.13 N	127.59 E
Shangzhuangtai	105	39.41 N	115.25 E
Shanhaiguan	98	40.01 N	119.44 E
Shanhaikwan → Shanhaiguan	98	40.01 N	119.44 E
Shanhecun	89	45.38 N	128.27 E
Shanhetun	89	44.44 N	127.12 E
Shanjiazhuang	105	38.52 N	115.45 E
Shanklin	42	50.38 N	1.10 W
Shankou, Zhg.	100	26.40 N	117.46 E
Shankou, Zhg.	100	28.58 N	115.12 E
Shankou, Zhg.	100	28.48 N	114.29 E
Shankou, Zhg.	102	21.38 N	109.43 E
Shanlenggang	102	28.33 N	103.23 E
Shanli	100	29.52 N	117.21 E
Shanlian	106	30.42 N	120.19 E
Shanmenjie	106	30.40 N	118.52 E
Shanmulong	102	24.39 N	98.05 E
Shannanguan	100	31.36 N	116.52 E
Shannock	207	41.26 N	71.38 W
Shannon, Ire.	48	52.43 N	8.53 W
Shannon, N.Z.	172	40.33 S	175.25 E
Shannon, S. Afr.	158	29.08 S	26.18 E
Shannon, Ga., U.S.	192	34.20 N	85.04 W
Shannon, Il., U.S.	190	42.09 N	89.44 W
Shannon, Ms., U.S.	194	34.06 N	88.42 W
Shannon ≃	48	52.36 N	9.41 W
Shannon, Lake ⊜	224	48.37 N	121.42 W
Shannon, Mouth of the ≃ [1]	48	52.30 N	9.50 W
Shannon Airport ⊠	48	52.41 N	8.55 W
Shannons Flat	171b	35.54 S	148.58 E
Shannontown	192	33.53 N	80.21 W
Shannonville	212	44.12 N	77.13 W
Shanpo	100	30.06 N	114.20 E
Shanrendong	89	46.50 N	123.08 E
Shanrenqiao	106	31.16 N	120.27 E
Shanshan	86	42.52 N	90.10 E
Shanshenmiao	105	40.45 N	117.11 E
Shanshūr	142	30.21 N	31.00 E
Shansi → Shanxi □ [4]	102	37.00 N	112.00 E
Shanting	98	35.09 N	117.29 E
Shāntipur	126	23.15 N	88.26 E
Shantou (Swatow)	100	23.23 N	116.41 E
Shantung → Shandong □ [4]	98	36.00 N	118.00 E
Shantung Peninsula → Shandong Bandao ≻ [1]	98	37.00 N	121.00 E
Shanty Bay	212	44.25 N	79.36 W
Shanwa	154	3.10 S	33.46 E
Shanwei	100	22.47 N	115.21 E
Shanxi (Shansi) □ [4]	102	37.00 N	112.00 E
Shanxian, Zhg.	98	34.48 N	116.03 E
Shanxian → Sanmenxia, Zhg.	102	34.45 N	111.05 E
Shanxiawu	100	28.52 N	113.52 E
Shanxu	102	22.21 N	107.58 E
Shanyang, Zhg.	100	26.43 N	119.13 E
Shanyang, Zhg.	102	33.35 N	109.49 E
Shanyang, Zhg.	106	31.19 N	120.16 E
Shanyao	100	25.13 N	118.55 E
Shanyaqiao	106	31.15 N	119.25 E
Shanyin	102	39.33 N	112.50 E
Shanzhangjiafen	105	40.37 N	116.44 E
Shanzui	105	40.48 N	118.13 E
Shanzuizi	104	41.55 N	120.30 E
Shaobo	100	32.30 N	119.32 E
Shaodenggao	104	42.13 N	121.47 E
Shaodian, Zhg.	98	34.08 N	118.25 E
Shaodian, Zhg.	100	33.10 N	114.18 E
Shaoguan	100	24.50 N	113.37 E
Shaogudian	98	36.57 N	115.32 E
Shaoguyingzi	104	41.33 N	120.27 E
Shaohing → Shaoxing	100	30.00 N	120.35 E
Shaohsing → Shaoxing	100	30.00 N	120.35 E
Shaojiaolou	106	31.05 N	121.32 E
Shaokuan → Shaoguan	100	24.50 N	113.37 E
Shaowu	100	27.20 N	117.28 E
Shaoxing	100	30.00 N	120.35 E
Shaoyang, Zhg.	102	27.15 N	111.28 E
Shaoyang, Zhg.	102	27.00 N	111.18 E
Shaoyun	107	29.30 N	105.57 E
Shaozihe	98	40.13 N	123.33 E
Shap	44	54.32 N	2.41 W
Shapinsay I	46	59.03 N	2.53 W
Shāpūr ≃	128	29.39 N	51.03 E
Shaq'ah, Ra's ash- ≻	130	34.19 N	35.41 E
Shaqqā	132	32.53 N	36.42 E
Shaqq al-Ju'ayfir, Wādī V	140	15.16 N	26.00 E
Shaqrā', Ar. Su.	128	25.15 N	45.15 E
Shaqrā, Lubnān	132	33.12 N	35.28 E
Shaqrā', Sūrīy.	132	32.54 N	36.14 E
Shaqrā', Yaman	144	13.21 N	45.42 E
Shaquan	86	44.33 N	83.25 E
Shaquzhen	107	30.33 N	103.45 E
Sharafābād	272a	28.36 N	77.23 E
Sharafkhāneh	128	38.11 N	45.29 E
Sharan Jogīzai	120	31.02 N	68.33 E
Sharatin Mountain ∧	180	57.49 N	152.41 W
Sharbatāt, Ra's ash- ≻	118	17.56 N	56.21 E
Sharbīn, Jabal ∧	132	33.43 N	36.21 E
Sharbot Lake	212	44.46 N	76.41 W
Sharbot Lake ⊜	212	44.46 N	76.41 W
Share	150	8.50 N	4.56 E
Sharhorod	78	48.44 N	28.05 E
Shari	92a	43.55 N	144.50 E
Shari-dake ∧	92a	43.46 N	144.43 E
Sharīṭah, Ra's ≻	128	26.23 N	56.23 E
Sharivka	78	50.01 N	35.27 E
Shark ≃	220	25.21 N	81.05 W
Shark Bay ⊂	162	25.30 S	113.30 E
Shark Point ≻, Austl.	274a	33.55 S	151.17 E
Shark Point ≻, Fl., U.S.	220	25.23 N	81.09 W
Shark River Hills	208	40.12 N	74.03 W
Sharktooth Mountain ∧	180	58.35 N	127.57 W
Sharm ash-Shaykh	140	27.51 N	34.17 E
Sharnbrook	42	52.13 N	0.32 W
Sharnūb	142	31.01 N	30.35 E
Sharon, On., Can.	214	42.53 N	81.22 W
Sharon, Ct., U.S.	207	41.52 N	73.28 W
Sharon, Ma., U.S.	207	42.07 N	71.10 W
Sharon, N.D., U.S.	198	47.35 N	97.53 W
Sharon, Pa., U.S.	214	41.13 N	80.29 W
Sharon, Tn., U.S.	194	36.14 N	88.49 W
Sharon, Wi., U.S.	216	42.30 N	88.43 W
Sharon Center	214	41.06 N	81.44 W
Sharon Hill	285	39.54 N	75.16 W
Sharon Park	218	39.23 N	84.35 W
Sharon Springs, Ks., U.S.	198	38.53 N	101.45 W
Sharon Springs, N.Y., U.S.	210	42.48 N	74.37 W
Sharon Valley	207	41.53 N	73.29 W
Sharonville	218	39.16 N	84.24 W
Sharpe, Lake ⊜ [1]	198	44.05 N	99.55 W
Sharpe Lake ⊜	184	54.24 N	93.30 W
Sharpes	220	28.25 N	80.45 W
Sharp Island I	271d	22.22 N	114.17 E
Sharpley	285	39.48 N	75.33 W
Sharp Park ♠	282	37.37 N	122.29 W
Sharp Peak ∧	116	5.58 N	125.31 E
Sharpsburg, Il., U.S.	219	39.37 N	89.21 W
Sharpsburg, Ky., U.S.	218	38.12 N	83.55 W
Sharpsburg, Pa., U.S.	279b	40.29 N	79.55 W
Sharps Hill	279b	40.30 N	79.56 W
Sharps Run ≃	285	39.54 N	74.49 W
Sharpsville, In., U.S.	216	40.22 N	86.05 W
Sharpsville, Pa., U.S.	214	41.15 N	80.28 W
Sharptown, Md., U.S.	208	38.32 N	75.43 W
Sharptown, N.J., U.S.	285	39.39 N	75.21 W
Sharqī, Al-Jabal ash- (Anti-Lebanon) ⋏	132	33.35 N	36.00 E
Sharqīyah, Aṣ-Ṣaḥrā' ash- (Arabian Desert) ◆ [2]	140	28.00 N	32.00 E
Sharqpur	123	31.28 N	74.06 E
Sharshar, Jabal ∧ [2]	140	23.52 N	30.20 E
Shartlesville	208	40.31 N	76.06 W
Shārūnah	142	28.36 N	30.51 E
Shārūnah, Wādī V	142	28.36 N	30.52 E
Shasha	144	6.20 N	35.57 E
Shashe ≃	156	22.14 S	29.20 E
Shashemene	144	7.12 N	38.43 E
Shashi	102	30.19 N	112.14 E
Shashibu	100	25.48 N	114.54 E
Shasi → Shashi	102	30.19 N	112.14 E
Shasta	204	40.36 N	122.29 W
Shasta ≃	204	41.50 N	122.35 W
Shasta, Mount ∧ [1]	204	41.20 N	122.20 W
Shasta Lake ⊜ [1]	204	40.50 N	122.25 W
Shatangjiang	106	31.25 N	120.01 E
Shaṭānūf	142	30.14 N	31.04 E
Shatawī	140	14.39 N	32.06 E
Shāṭi', Wādī ash- V	146	27.30 N	13.15 E
Shatian, Zhg.	100	25.53 N	113.44 E
Shatian, Zhg.	100	23.59 N	113.56 E
Shatila	132	33.51 N	35.30 E
Sha Tin	271d	22.23 N	114.11 E
Shats'k	78	51.31 N	23.57 E
Shats'kyy Pryrodnyy Natsional'nyy Park ♠	78	51.30 N	23.55 E
Shatt al-Arab → Arab, Shatt al- ≃	128	29.57 N	48.34 E
Shattuck	196	36.16 N	99.52 W
Shatuji	98	35.18 N	115.45 E
Shatuosi	102	31.20 N	108.51 E
Shauck	214	40.37 N	82.40 W
Shaunavon	184	49.40 N	108.25 W
Shaver Lake	226	37.09 N	119.18 W
Shaver Lake ⊜ [1]	226	37.08 N	119.17 W
Shavertown	210	41.19 N	75.55 W
Shavé Ẓiyyon	132	32.59 N	35.05 E
Shavington	44	53.04 N	2.27 W
Shaw, Eng., U.K.	44	53.34 N	2.05 W
Shaw, Ms., U.S.	194	33.36 N	90.46 W
Shaw ≃	162	20.20 S	119.17 E
Shaw Air Force Base ■	192	33.58 N	80.29 W
Shawan, Zhg.	86	44.34 N	85.48 E
Shawan, Zhg.	100	27.52 N	119.28 E
Shawan, Zhg.	107	29.25 N	103.33 E
Shawanaga Inlet ⊂	190	45.32 N	80.24 W
Shawangunk Kill ≃	210	41.41 N	74.10 W
Shawangunk Mountains ⋏	210	41.35 N	74.30 W
Shawano	190	44.46 N	88.36 W
Shawbury	42	52.47 N	2.39 W
Shaw Creek ≃	192	33.34 N	81.30 W
Shawforth	262	53.41 N	2.10 W
Shawhan	218	38.18 N	84.16 W
Shawinigan	206	46.33 N	72.45 W
Shawinigan ≃	206	46.32 N	72.46 W
Shawinigan, Lac ⊜	206	46.41 N	73.10 W
Shawinigan Falls → Shawinigan	206	46.33 N	72.45 W
Shawinigan-Sud	206	46.31 N	72.45 W
Shaw Island I	224	48.34 N	122.57 W
Shawmarī, Wādī ash- V	132	30.21 N	36.25 E
Shawmere ≃	190	48.20 N	82.28 W
Shawnee, Ks., U.S.	198	39.02 N	94.43 W
Shawnee, Oh., U.S.	188	39.36 N	82.12 W
Shawnee, Ok., U.S.	196	35.19 N	96.55 W
Shawnee, Lake ⊜	276	40.58 N	74.35 W
Shawnee Hills	214	40.07 N	83.09 W
Shawnee On Delaware	210	41.01 N	75.07 W
Shawnee State Park ♠	218	38.43 N	83.10 W
Shawneetown	194	37.42 N	88.11 W
Shawnī	142	30.45 N	30.55 E
Shawnigan Lake	224	48.38 N	123.35 W
Shawnigan Lake ⊜	224	48.37 N	123.37 W
Shawo, Som.	144	3.26 N	45.21 E
Shawo, Zhg.	98	34.28 N	114.37 E
Shawo, Zhg.	100	31.44 N	115.08 E
Shawo, Zhg.	100	28.52 N	114.47 E
Shawsheen ≃	283	42.42 N	71.08 W
Shawsheen Village	283	42.40 N	71.09 W
Shawtown	279b	40.20 N	79.42 W
Shawville	188	45.36 N	76.30 W
Shaxi, Zhg.	100	28.34 N	118.06 E
Shaxi, Zhg.	100	26.53 N	115.34 E
Shaxi, Zhg.	100	24.38 N	113.42 E
Shaxi, Zhg.	106	31.34 N	121.04 E
Shaxian	100	26.24 N	117.47 E
Shaxikou	100	26.33 N	118.02 E
Shaximiao	107	29.57 N	106.19 E
Shayang	100	30.42 N	112.33 E
Shaybārā I	128	25.27 N	36.48 E
Shay Gap	162	20.25 S	120.03 E
Shaykh, Jabal ash- (Mount Hermon) ∧	132	33.26 N	35.51 E
Shaykh, Wādī ash- V	142	28.48 N	30.55 E
Shaykh Al-Ḥadīd	130	36.30 N	36.35 E
Shaykh Miskīn	132	32.49 N	36.09 E
Shaykh Sa'd	128	32.34 N	46.17 E
Shaykh 'Uthmān	144	12.52 N	44.59 E
Shayuan	100	27.45 N	120.38 E
Shazhen	98	36.23 N	115.47 E
Shazhou	106	31.52 N	120.32 E
Shazihe	102	32.12 N	106.42 E
Shchastya	83	48.44 N	39.14 E
Shchekino → Ščokino	76	54.01 N	37.31 E
Shchelkovo → Ščolkovo	76	55.55 N	38.00 E
Shcherbakov → Rybinsk	76	58.03 N	38.52 E
Shchors	78	51.49 N	31.59 E
Shchors'k	78	48.22 N	34.06 E
Shchotove	83	48.09 N	39.04 E
She ≃	100	30.41 N	114.32 E
Sheaf ≃	44	53.23 N	1.26 W
Shea Island I	276	41.03 N	73.24 W
Sheakleyville	214	41.27 N	80.13 W
Shea Stadium ♠	276	40.45 N	73.51 W
Shebele	144	9.43 N	42.43 E
Shebele (Shabeelle) ≃	144	0.12 S	42.45 E
Shebelynka	78	49.27 N	36.30 E
Sheberghān	120	36.41 N	65.45 E
Shebeshekong ≃	212	45.26 N	80.19 W
Sheboygan	190	43.45 N	87.42 W
Sheboygan ≃	190	43.45 N	87.42 W
Sheboygan Falls	190	43.43 N	87.48 W
Shebu	100	27.40 N	112.48 E
Shechem → Nābulus	132	32.13 N	35.16 E
Shechem ⊥	132	32.13 N	35.15 E
Shecheng	102	37.14 N	113.05 E
Shedd Canyon V	226	35.39 N	120.26 W
Shedden	214	42.44 N	81.21 W
Shediac	186	46.13 N	64.32 W
Shedin Peak ∧	182	55.55 N	127.32 W
Sheekh	144	9.56 N	45.11 E
Sheelin, Lough ⊜	48	53.48 N	7.22 W
Sheenjek ≃	180	66.45 N	144.33 W
Sheep ≃	182	50.44 N	113.51 W
Sheep Creek ≃, Ab., Can.	182	54.04 N	119.00 W
Sheep Creek ≃, U.S.	202	42.27 N	115.36 W
Sheep Creek ≃, Ut,. U.S.	200	40.55 N	109.39 W
Sheep Creek ≃, Wy., U.S.	200	42.03 N	106.04 W
Sheep Haven ⊂	48	55.10 N	7.52 W
Sheepmoor	158	26.42 S	30.13 E
Sheep Mountain ∧, Az., U.S.	200	32.32 N	114.14 W
Sheep Mountain ∧, Wy., U.S.	200	43.33 N	110.32 W
Sheep Peak ∧	196	31.14 N	104.59 W
Sheepranch	226	38.13 N	120.28 W
Sheep Range ⋏	204	36.45 N	115.05 W
Sheepshead Bay ◆ [8]	276	40.35 N	73.56 W
's-Heerenberg	52	51.53 N	6.15 E
's-Heerenhoek	52	51.27 N	3.46 E
Sheerness	42	51.27 N	0.45 E
Sheet Harbour	186	44.55 N	62.32 W
Shefar'am	132	32.48 N	35.10 E
Sheffield, N.Z.	172	43.23 S	172.01 E
Sheffield, Eng., U.K.	44	53.23 N	1.28 W
Sheffield, Al., U.S.	194	34.45 N	87.41 W
Sheffield, Il., U.S.	190	41.21 N	89.44 W
Sheffield, Ia., U.S.	190	42.53 N	93.12 W
Sheffield, Ma., U.S.	207	42.06 N	73.21 W
Sheffield, Oh., U.S.	214	41.25 N	82.05 W
Sheffield, Pa., U.S.	214	41.42 N	79.02 W
Sheffield, Tx., U.S.	196	30.41 N	101.49 W
Sheffield Island I	276	41.03 N	73.25 W
Sheffield Island Harbor ⊂	276	41.03 N	73.25 W
Sheffield Lake	214	41.29 N	82.06 W
Sheffield Lake ⊜	186	49.20 N	56.35 W
Shefford	42	52.02 N	0.20 W
Shefford □ [6]	206	45.25 N	72.30 W
Shefu	100	26.11 N	115.22 E
Shegangshi	100	28.32 N	113.36 E
Shegaon	122	20.47 N	76.41 E
Sheho	184	51.38 N	103.12 W
Shehong	102	30.56 N	105.22 E
Shehongmiao	107	30.44 N	106.03 E
Shehy Mountains ⋏	48	51.48 N	9.15 W
Sheikh Hasan	144	12.04 N	35.53 E
Sheikhpura	124	25.09 N	85.51 E
Shekatika	186	51.17 N	58.20 W
Shekhūpura	123	31.42 N	73.59 E
Sheki → Şeki	84	41.12 N	47.12 E
Shekki → Zhongshan	100	22.31 N	113.22 E
Shek Kong	271d	22.26 N	114.06 E
Shek Kong Airfield ⊠	271d	22.27 N	114.05 E
Shek Kwu Chau I	271d	22.12 N	113.59 E
Shekou	100	30.44 N	114.20 E
Shek Uk Shan ∧	271d	22.27 N	114.18 E
Shelagyote Peak ∧	182	55.58 N	127.12 W
Shelbina	219	39.41 N	92.02 W
Shelbourne	169	36.52 S	144.01 E
Shelburn	194	39.11 N	87.24 W
Shelburne, N.S., Can.	186	43.46 N	65.19 W
Shelburne, On., Can.	212	44.04 N	80.12 W
Shelburne Bay ⊂	164	11.49 S	143.00 E
Shelburne Falls	207	42.36 N	72.44 W
Shelby, In., U.S.	216	41.11 N	87.20 W
Shelby, Ia., U.S.	198	41.30 N	95.27 W
Shelby, Mi., U.S.	190	43.36 N	86.21 W
Shelby, Ms., U.S.	194	33.57 N	90.46 W
Shelby, Mt., U.S.	202	48.30 N	111.51 W
Shelby, Ne., U.S.	198	41.11 N	97.25 W
Shelby, N.C., U.S.	192	35.17 N	81.32 W
Shelby, Oh., U.S.	214	40.52 N	82.39 W
Shelby □ [6], Il., U.S.	219	39.24 N	88.48 W
Shelby □ [6], In., U.S.	218	39.31 N	85.47 W
Shelby □ [6], Ky., U.S.	218	38.15 N	85.13 W
Shelby □ [6], Mo., U.S.	219	39.49 N	92.03 W
Shelby □ [6], Oh., U.S.	216	40.17 N	84.09 W
Shelby Village	281	42.38 N	83.04 W
Shelbyville, Il., U.S.	219	39.24 N	88.47 W
Shelbyville, In., U.S.	218	39.31 N	85.46 W
Shelbyville, Ky., U.S.	218	38.12 N	85.13 W
Shelbyville, Mo., U.S.	219	39.48 N	92.02 W
Shelbyville, Tn., U.S.	194	35.29 N	86.27 W
Shelbyville, Lake ⊜ [1]	219	39.30 N	88.40 W
Sheldon, Il., U.S.	216	40.46 N	87.33 W
Sheldon, Ia., U.S.	198	43.10 N	95.51 W
Sheldon, Mi., U.S.	216	42.17 N	83.28 W
Sheldon, Mo., U.S.	194	37.39 N	94.17 W
Sheldon, Tx., U.S.	222	29.52 N	95.08 W
Sheldon Brook ≃	276	41.03 N	73.52 W
Sheldon Creek ≃	212	44.07 N	79.53 W
Sheldon Point	180	62.32 N	164.52 W
Sheldon Reservoir ⊜ [1]	222	29.52 N	95.10 W
Sheldonville	283	42.02 N	71.23 W
Sheldrake ≃	276	40.57 N	73.44 W
Sheldrake Lake ⊜, On., Can.	212	44.49 N	77.16 W
Sheldrake Lake ⊜, N.Y., U.S.	276	40.57 N	73.46 W
Shelikof Strait ⋓	180	57.30 N	155.00 W
Shell ≃	184	50.58 N	101.24 W
Shell, Loch ⊂	46	58.00 N	6.30 W
Shellbrook	184	53.13 N	106.24 W
Shell Brook ≃	184	53.21 N	106.00 W
Shell Creek ≃, U.S.	200	40.56 N	108.37 W
Shell Creek ≃, Ne., U.S.	198	41.27 N	96.58 W
Shell Creek ≃, N.D., U.S.	198	47.59 N	102.17 W
Shell Creek ≃, Wy., U.S.	202	44.31 N	108.03 W
Shellen	146	9.54 N	12.00 E
Shelley, B.C., Can.	182	54.00 N	122.37 W
Shelley, Id., U.S.	202	43.22 N	112.07 W
Shellharbour	170	34.35 S	150.52 E
Shell Lake, Sk., Can.	184	53.18 N	107.04 W
Shell Lake, Wi., U.S.	190	45.44 N	91.55 W
Shell Lakes ⊜	162	29.21 S	127.25 E
Shellman	192	31.45 N	84.36 W
Shellmouth Dam ◆ [6]	184	50.58 N	101.25 W
Shellow Bowells	260	51.45 N	0.20 E
Shell Rock	190	42.42 N	92.34 W
Shell Rock ≃	190	42.38 N	92.30 W
Shellrock Peak ∧	224	46.43 N	121.14 W
Shellsburg	190	42.05 N	91.52 W
Shelocta	214	40.39 N	79.18 W
Shelter, Port ⊂	271d	22.21 N	114.17 E
Shelter Island	207	41.04 N	72.20 W
Shelter Island I, Zhg..	271d	22.20 N	114.17 E
Shelter Island I, N.Y., U.S.	207	41.04 N	72.20 W
Shelter Island Heights	207	41.05 N	72.21 W
Shelter Island Sound ⋓	207	41.03 N	72.22 W
Shelton, Ct., U.S.	207	41.18 N	73.05 W
Shelton, Ne., U.S.	198	40.47 N	98.44 W
Shelton, Wa., U.S.	224	47.13 N	123.06 W
Shemanker ≃	150	8.12 N	9.45 E
Shemogue	186	46.09 N	64.11 W
Shemya Station	181a	52.43 N	174.05 E
Shenandoah, Ia., U.S.	198	40.45 N	95.22 W
Shenandoah, Pa., U.S.	208	40.49 N	76.12 W
Shenandoah, Va., U.S.	188	38.29 N	78.37 W
Shenandoah ≃	188	39.19 N	77.44 W
Shenandoah, North Fork ≃	188	38.57 N	78.12 W
Shenandoah, South Fork ≃	188	38.57 N	78.12 W
Shenandoah Heights	210	40.49 N	76.12 W
Shenandoah National Park ♠	188	38.48 N	78.12 W
Shenango	214	41.23 N	80.24 W
Shenango ≃	214	40.57 N	80.23 W
Shenango River Lake ⊜ [1]	214	41.22 N	80.28 W
Shenchi	102	39.09 N	112.19 E
Shencottah	122	8.58 N	77.16 E
Shencun	106	31.04 N	118.51 E
Shendam	150	8.53 N	9.32 E
Shendang	106	30.34 N	120.49 E
Shending Shan ∧	89	46.38 N	133.28 E
Shenduncun	106	30.48 N	120.25 E
Shenfield	260	51.38 N	0.19 E
Shengang, Zhg.	100	27.20 N	116.18 E
Shengang, Zhg.	106	31.54 N	120.08 E
Shenge	150	7.55 N	12.57 W
Shengfang	105	39.04 N	116.42 E
Shenggongjing	106	31.07 N	119.48 E
Shenghongqing	100	30.12 N	114.56 E
Shengjiachi	107	30.28 N	105.03 E
Shengjiaqiao	106	31.27 N	121.24 E
Shengjiatun	104	41.14 N	121.22 E
Shengjin'gao	104	42.04 N	120.43 E
Shengou	100	34.08 N	113.13 E
Shengqing	104	41.34 N	121.36 E
Shengshan	106	30.50 N	120.15 E
Shengshui	98	35.45 N	119.39 E
Shengshuihezi	98	42.27 N	125.59 E
Shengsi Liedao II	100	30.42 N	122.20 E
Shengtian	100	27.14 N	113.06 E
Shengxian	100	29.36 N	120.48 E
Shengze	106	30.55 N	120.39 E
Shengzigou	104	41.35 N	124.04 E
Shenhu	100	24.38 N	118.39 E
Shenipsit Lake ⊜	207	41.53 N	72.26 W
Shenji	98	34.47 N	115.09 E
Shenjia	89	46.06 N	126.46 E
Shenjiadian	89	46.35 N	130.38 E
Shenjiatai	104	41.22 N	120.50 E
Shenjiawan	106	31.43 N	121.19 E
Shenjiazhuang	106	32.18 N	120.26 E
Shenjing, Zhg.	102	21.59 N	112.28 E
Shenjing, Zhg.	105	40.24 N	114.49 E
Shenjingzi	104	41.47 N	123.41 E
Shenk'eng	269d	25.00 N	121.36 E
Shenkou	100	28.42 N	116.02 E
Shenley	260	51.41 N	0.17 W
Shenmu	102	38.56 N	110.19 E
Shennan	105	38.59 N	114.56 E
Shenorock	210	41.20 N	73.44 W
Shenqiu	100	33.24 N	115.02 E
Shenquan	100	22.59 N	116.20 E
Shenquan Gang ⊂	100	22.54 N	116.18 E
Shensi → Shaanxi □ [4]	102	35.00 N	109.00 E
Shenton, Mount ∧	162	28.00 S	123.22 E
Shentuan	98	35.30 N	119.17 E
Shenxian, Zhg.	98	38.01 N	115.33 E
Shenxian, Zhg.	98	36.15 N	115.41 E
Shenxing	105	39.02 N	115.19 E
Shenyang (Mukden)	104	41.48 N	123.27 E
Shenze	98	38.11 N	115.11 E
Shenzhen	100	22.32 N	114.08 E
Sheoganj	120	25.09 N	73.04 E
Sheokhāla	126	22.46 N	88.10 E
Sheopur	124	25.40 N	76.42 E
Shepard	182	50.57 N	113.55 W
Shepard Island I	9	74.25 S	132.30 W
Shepards Brook ≃	283	42.08 N	71.25 W
Shepaug ≃	207	41.28 N	73.19 W
Shepetivka	78	50.11 N	27.04 E
Shepherd, Mi., U.S.	190	43.31 N	84.41 W
Shepherd, Tx., U.S.	222	30.30 N	95.01 W
Shepherd □ [8]	175f	17.05 S	168.25 E
Shepherd, Îles II	175f	16.55 S	168.36 E
Shepherdstown	188	39.25 N	77.48 W
Shepherdsville	194	37.59 N	85.42 W
Sheppard Air Force Base ■	196	33.58 N	98.30 W
Sheppard Peak ∧	180	57.41 N	132.37 W
Sheppard Pond ⊜	276	41.08 N	74.13 W
Shepparton	166	36.23 S	145.25 E
Shepperd, Lake ⊜	162	29.55 S	123.09 E
Shepperton	260	51.24 N	0.27 W
Sheppey, Isle of I	42	51.24 N	0.50 E
Sheppler Hill ∧ [2]	279b	40.09 N	79.49 W
Sheppton	210	40.53 N	76.07 W
Shepshed	42	52.47 N	1.18 W
Shepton Mallet	42	51.12 N	2.33 W
Shepway	260	51.15 N	0.33 E
Sheqi	100	33.03 N	112.57 E
Sherab	140	10.43 N	24.47 E
Sherada	144	7.21 N	36.32 E
Sheraden ◆ [8]	279b	40.28 N	80.05 W
Sherard, Cape ≻	176	74.36 N	80.25 W
Sherborn	283	42.14 N	71.22 W
Sherborne	42	50.57 N	2.31 W
Sherborne Lake ⊜	212	45.11 N	78.47 W
Sherborne Saint John	42	51.18 N	1.07 W
Sherbro ≃	150	7.45 N	12.55 W
Sherbro Island I	150	7.45 N	12.55 W
Sherbrooke, N.S., Can.	186	45.08 N	61.59 W
Sherbrooke, P.Q., Can.	206	45.25 N	71.54 W
Sherbrooke □ [6]	206	45.25 N	71.55 W
Sherbrooke Lake ⊜	186	44.40 N	64.35 W
Sherburn	198	43.39 N	94.43 W
Sherburne	210	42.40 N	75.29 W
Sherburne Reef ✢ [2]	164	3.20 S	148.00 E
Sherburn in Elmet	44	53.48 N	1.15 W
Shercock	48	54.00 N	6.54 W
Shere	260	51.13 N	0.28 W
Sheridan, Ar., U.S.	194	34.18 N	92.24 W
Sheridan, Ca., U.S.	226	38.59 N	121.22 W
Sheridan, Il., U.S.	216	41.32 N	88.41 W
Sheridan, In., U.S.	218	40.08 N	86.13 W
Sheridan, Mt., U.S.	202	45.27 N	112.11 W
Sheridan, Or., U.S.	202	45.05 N	123.23 W
Sheridan, Pa., U.S.	208	40.21 N	76.14 W
Sheridan, Tx., U.S.	222	29.29 N	96.40 W
Sheridan, Wy., U.S.	202	44.47 N	106.57 W
Sheridan, Mount ∧	202	44.16 N	110.32 W
Sheridan Park ♠	284a	42.59 N	78.54 W
Sheringa	162	33.51 S	135.15 E
Sheringham	42	52.57 N	1.12 E
Sherkston	284a	42.53 N	79.08 W
Sherlock ≃	162	20.44 S	117.35 E
Sherman, Ct., U.S.	207	41.34 N	73.29 W
Sherman, Il., U.S.	219	39.54 N	89.36 W
Sherman, Ky., U.S.	218	38.44 N	84.36 W
Sherman, Ms., U.S.	194	34.21 N	88.50 W
Sherman, N.Y., U.S.	214	42.09 N	79.35 W
Sherman, Tx., U.S.	196	33.38 N	96.36 W
Sherman □ [6]	224	45.25 N	120.49 W
Sherman Creek ≃	208	40.23 N	77.02 W
Sherman Mills	188	45.52 N	68.23 W
Sherman Mountain ∧	194	36.01 N	93.17 W
Sherman Oaks ◆ [8]	280	34.09 N	118.26 W
Sherman Reservoir ⊜ [1]	198	41.20 N	98.55 W
Sherman Station	188	45.53 N	68.25 W
Sherpur, Bngl.	124	24.41 N	89.25 E
Sherpur, Bngl.	124	25.01 N	90.01 E
Sher Qila	123	36.06 N	74.03 E
Sherrard	190	41.19 N	90.31 W
Sherridon	184	55.07 N	101.05 W
Sherrill	210	43.04 N	75.35 W
Sherrodsville	214	40.29 N	81.14 W
Sher Shāh	123	30.06 N	71.21 E
Shertallai	122	9.42 N	76.20 E
's-Hertogenbosch	52	51.41 N	5.19 E
Sherway Centre ◆ [9]	275b	43.37 N	79.33 W
Sherwood, On., Can.	275b	43.50 N	79.31 W
Sherwood, P.E., Can.	186	46.17 N	63.08 W
Sherwood, Ar., U.S.	194	34.48 N	92.13 W
Sherwood, Md., U.S.	208	38.36 N	76.19 W
Sherwood, Mi., U.S.	216	42.00 N	85.14 W
Sherwood, N.D., U.S.	198	48.57 N	101.37 W
Sherwood, Oh., U.S.	216	41.17 N	84.33 W
Sherwood, Or., U.S.	224	45.21 N	122.50 W
Sherwood, Tn., U.S.	194	35.04 N	85.55 W
Sherwood, Lake ⊜	281	42.36 N	83.33 W
Sherwood Forest, Ca., U.S.	226	37.57 N	122.17 W
Sherwood Forest, Md., U.S.	284c	39.05 N	77.01 W
Sherwood Forest ◆ [3]	44	53.08 N	1.08 W
Sherwood Island State Park ♠	276	41.07 N	73.20 W
Sherwood Manor	207	42.01 N	72.38 W
Sherwood Park, Ab., Can.	182	53.31 N	113.19 W
Sherwood Park, De., U.S.	285	39.44 N	75.39 W
Sherwood Park, N.Y., U.S.	210	42.36 N	73.43 W
Sherwood Park ♠	275b	43.43 N	79.24 W
Sherwood Point ≻	276	41.07 N	73.20 W
Sherwood Shores	196	30.36 N	98.22 W
She Shan ∧ [2]	106	31.06 N	121.11 E
Sheshea ≃	248	9.36 S	74.10 W
Shesh Gāv	120	33.45 N	68.33 E
Shestakivka	78	48.32 N	31.58 E
Shesternya	78	47.33 N	33.16 E
Shet Bandar	272c	18.58 N	72.56 E
Shetek, Lake ⊜	198	44.08 N	95.42 W
Shetland □ [4]	46a	60.30 N	1.15 W
Shetland del Sur, Islas → South Shetland Islands II	9	62.00 S	58.00 W
Shetland Islands II	46a	60.30 N	1.15 W
Shetou	106	31.39 N	119.27 E
Shetrunji ≃	120	21.19 N	72.07 E
Shetucket ≃	207	41.31 N	72.05 W
Sheva	272c	18.56 N	72.57 E
Sheva Nhava	272c	18.58 N	72.58 E
Shevaroy Hills ⋏ [2]	122	11.50 N	78.16 E
Shevchenkove, Ukr.	78	45.33 N	29.20 E
Shevchenkove, Ukr.	78	51.40 N	33.39 E
Shevchenkove, Ukr.	78	49.41 N	37.10 E
Shevchenkove Druhe	78	47.29 N	36.08 E
Shevington	262	53.34 N	2.42 W
Shevington Moor	262	53.35 N	2.41 W
Shewa □ [4]	144	9.00 N	39.00 E
Shewa Gimira	144	7.00 N	35.50 E
Shexian, Zhg.	98	36.33 N	113.40 E
Shexian, Zhg.	100	29.53 N	118.26 E
Sheyang, Zhg.	100	33.20 N	119.38 E
Sheyang, Zhg.	100	33.46 N	120.18 E
Sheyenne	198	47.49 N	99.07 W
Sheyenne ≃	198	47.05 N	96.50 W
Sheykhābād	120	34.05 N	68.45 E
Shey-Phoksundo National Park ♠	124	29.30 N	82.45 E
Shezhu	106	31.19 N	119.16 E
Shḥīm	132	33.37 N	35.29 E
Shi ≃, Zhg.	100	32.18 N	114.31 E
Shi ≃, Zhg.	100	32.32 N	115.52 E
Shiant, Sound of ⋓	46	57.55 N	6.25 W
Shiant Islands II	46	57.53 N	6.21 W
Shiawassee □ [6]	216	42.56 N	84.09 W
Shiawassee ≃	216	43.06 N	84.10 W
Shiawassee, South Branch ≃	216	42.49 N	83.56 W
Shiba	100	32.45 N	118.07 E
Shiba ≃	268	35.47 N	139.44 E
Shibadu	102	28.01 N	110.51 E
Shibakawa	94	35.13 N	138.33 E
Shibām	144	15.56 N	48.38 E
Shiban	107	30.18 N	104.28 E
Shibanxi	107	29.17 N	103.51 E
Shibaocheng	102	39.48 N	96.10 E
Shibarni	140	14.50 N	24.25 E
Shibasaki	268	35.39 N	139.34 E
Shibata	92	37.57 N	139.20 E
Shibayama	94	35.41 N	140.25 E
Shibayama-gata ⊜	94	36.21 N	136.23 E
Shibden Hall ⊥	262	53.44 N	1.51 W
Shibecha	92a	43.17 N	144.36 E
Shibetsu, Nihon	92a	43.40 N	145.08 E
Shibetsu, Nihon	92a	44.10 N	142.23 E
Shibi	100	26.43 N	120.02 E
Shibīn al-Kawm	142	30.33 N	31.01 E
Shibīn al-Qanāṭir	142	30.19 N	31.19 E
Shibing	102	26.50 N	108.04 E
Shibishan	100	29.21 N	116.45 E
Shiblanjah	142	30.28 N	31.16 E
Shibu	98	36.45 N	119.27 E
Shibukawa	94	36.29 N	139.00 E
Shibure-yama ∧	270	34.45 N	135.05 E
Shibushi	92	31.28 N	131.07 E
Shibutsu-san ∧	94	36.54 N	139.11 E
Shibuya ◆ [8]	268	35.40 N	139.42 E
Shibuzi	98	36.09 N	119.06 E
Shicha	100	28.24 N	115.50 E
Shichangyu	104	41.12 N	123.14 E
Shicheng, Zhg.	98	40.39 N	124.17 E
Shicheng, Zhg.	100	25.18 N	119.21 E

Symbol	English	Deutsch	Español	Français	Português
≃	River	Fluß	Río	Rivière	Rio
⋿	Canal	Kanal	Canal	Canal	Canal
∟	Waterfall, Rapids	Wasserfall, Stromschnellen	Cascada, Rápidos	Chute d'eau, Rapides	Cascata, Rápidos
⋓	Strait	Meeresstraße	Estrecho	Détroit	Estreito
⊂	Bay, Gulf	Bucht, Golf	Bahía, Golfo	Baie, Golfe	Baía, Golfo
⊜	Lake, Lakes	See, Seen	Lago, Lagos	Lac, Lacs	Lago, Lagos
⩸	Swamp	Sumpf	Pantano	Marais	Pântano
⊓	Ice Features, Glacier	Eis- und Gletscherformen	Accidentes Glaciales	Formes glaciaires	Acidentes glaciares
⊤	Other Hydrographic Features	Andere Hydrographische Objekte	Otros Elementos Hidrográficos	Autres données hydrographiques	Outros acidentes hidrográficos
✢	Submarine Features	Untermeerische Objekte	Accidentes Submarinos	Formes de relief sous-marin	Acidentes submarinos
□	Political Unit	Politische Einheit	Unidad Politica	Entité politique	Unidade política
ɤ	Cultural Institution	Kulturelle Institution	Institución Cultural	Institution culturelle	Instituição cultural
⊥	Historical Site	Historische Stätte	Sitio Histórico	Site historique	Sitio histórico
♠	Recreational Site	Erholungs- und Ferienort	Sitio de Recreo	Centre de loisirs	Area de Lazer
⊠	Airport	Flughafen	Aeropuerto	Aéroport	Aeroporto
■	Military Installation	Militäranlage	Instalación Militar	Installation militaire	Instalação militar
◆	Miscellaneous	Verschiedenes	Misceláneo	Divers	Diversos

Name	Page	Lat.°′	Long.°′
Shicheng, Zhg.	100	26.22 N	116.22 E
Shicheng Dao I	98	39.31 N	123.02 E
Shichisō	94	35.33 N	137.07 E
Shickley	198	40.25 N	97.43 W
Shickshinny	210	41.09 N	76.09 W
Shidai	100	30.20 N	117.56 E
Shidao	98	36.53 N	122.23 E
Shideng	102	26.44 N	99.11 E
Shidler	196	36.46 N	96.39 W
Shido	96	34.19 N	134.10 E
Shidong, Zhg.	107	28.59 N	105.27 E
Shidong, Zhg.	107	30.25 N	105.20 E
Shidongzigou	105	40.41 N	118.23 E
Shiel, Loch ⊜	46	56.47 N	5.35 W
Shiel Bridge	46	57.12 N	5.25 W
Shieldaig	46	57.31 N	5.39 W
Shieldhill	46	55.58 N	3.46 W
Shields ≃	202	45.43 N	110.28 W
Shiercun	106	30.31 N	119.34 E
Shi'er Shan ʌ	100	29.18 N	118.08 E
Shi'erwei	106	32.15 N	119.14 E
Shifang	100	25.01 N	116.14 E
Shifnal	42	52.40 N	2.21 W
Shifo	107	29.58 N	103.50 E
Shifobao	104	41.28 N	121.27 E
Shifochang	107	30.19 N	105.07 E
Shifodian	100	32.06 N	115.46 E
Shifosi	104	42.08 N	123.20 E
Shifoya	98	40.12 N	123.10 E
Shiga, Nihon	94	36.20 N	137.59 E
Shiga, Nihon	94	35.09 N	135.55 E
Shiga □[5]	96	35.15 N	136.00 E
Shigaib	140	15.01 N	23.36 E
Shigang, Zhg.	100	32.13 N	120.58 E
Shigang, Zhg.	106	32.14 N	121.00 E
Shigangmen	269b	31.21 N	121.17 E
Shigaopu	107	30.16 N	104.01 E
Shigar ≃, Asia	123	34.39 N	75.51 E
Shigar ≃, Pāk.	123	34.39 N	75.51 E
Shigaraki	94	34.52 N	136.03 E
Shigaraki-gū ʋ[1]	94	34.54 N	136.04 E
Shigenobu	96	33.48 N	132.50 E
Shigenobu ≃	96	33.48 N	132.41 E
Shigezhuang, Zhg.	105	38.57 N	116.19 E
Shigezhuang, Zhg.	105	38.59 N	115.36 E
Shigezhuang, Zhg.	105	39.18 N	116.53 E
Shigouyi	102	37.44 N	106.26 E
Shigu, Zhg.	100	29.27 N	117.14 E
Shigu, Zhg.	102	26.50 N	99.55 E
Shiguaigou	102	40.42 N	110.20 E
Shiguantun	104	41.38 N	123.39 E
Shigulingyu	105	40.38 N	116.54 E
Shiḥān ʌ	132	31.23 N	35.44 E
Shihch'i			
→ Zhongshan	100	22.31 N	113.22 E
Shihchiachuang			
→ Shijiazhuang	98	38.03 N	114.28 E
Shihe	98	39.19 N	121.52 E
Shihengyuanyu	106	31.50 N	121.45 E
Shihezi	86	44.18 N	86.02 E
Shihkiachwang			
→ Shijiazhuang	98	38.03 N	114.28 E
Shihlin ◆[8]	269d	25.06 N	121.31 E
Shihti	269d	25.02 N	121.44 E
Shihting	269d	24.59 N	121.39 E
Shihu, Zhg.	98	41.29 N	126.18 E
Shihu, Zhg.	105	40.04 N	117.17 E
Shihuajie	102	32.20 N	111.25 E
Shihudang	106	30.58 N	121.07 E
Shihuixi	107	29.02 N	105.04 E
Shihuiyaozi	104	42.08 N	123.47 E
Shihuxia	105	40.48 N	117.22 E
Shiida	96	33.39 N	131.04 E
Shijiaba	107	30.18 N	104.46 E
Shijiagangzi	104	42.19 N	123.34 E
Shijiagou	104	42.27 N	123.28 E
Shijiao	100	23.36 N	112.59 E
Shijiaqiao, Zhg.	106	30.46 N	120.06 E
Shijiaqiao, Zhg.	106	32.18 N	119.26 E
Shijiawu	105	39.21 N	116.15 E
Shijiaxiang	107	29.38 N	104.59 E
Shijiayaozhuang	106	32.13 N	120.29 E
Shijiazhai, Zhg.	98	38.56 N	114.18 E
Shijiazhai, Zhg.	269b	31.23 N	121.30 E
Shijiazhen	106	31.51 N	121.10 E
Shijiazhuang	98	38.03 N	114.28 E
Shijiazi, Zhg.	104	42.07 N	122.18 E
Shijiazi, Zhg.	104	42.39 N	122.06 E
Shijiedu	106	30.57 N	119.13 E
Shijing, Zhg.	98	35.30 N	118.57 E
Shijing, Zhg.	100	24.40 N	118.24 E
Shijing, Zhg.	105	39.54 N	114.58 E
Shijingshan	105	39.56 N	116.07 E
Shijiu Hu ⊜	106	31.28 N	118.53 E
Shijiusuo	98	35.24 N	119.29 E
Shijiu Tuo I	98	39.11 N	118.56 E
Shijōnawate	270	34.45 N	135.39 E
Shijūmagari-tōge)(	96	35.11 N	133.32 E
Shika	94	37.01 N	136.47 E
Shikami-yama ʌ	270	34.47 N	135.10 E
Shikano	96	35.28 N	134.04 E
Shikārpur, India	122	14.16 N	75.21 E
Shikārpur, India	124	28.17 N	78.01 E
Shikārpur, Pāk.	120	27.57 N	68.38 E
Shikatsu	94	35.14 N	136.53 E
Shikengkong ʌ	100	24.56 N	113.00 E
Shikewusumiao	102	40.13 N	108.52 E
Shiki	94	35.50 N	139.35 E
Shikishima	94	35.41 N	138.32 E
Shikohābād	124	27.06 N	78.36 E
Shikoku I	92	33.45 N	133.30 E
Shikoku-sanchi ʌʌ	96	33.47 N	133.30 E
Shikoma	268	35.11 N	139.56 E
Shikotsu-ko ⊜	92a	42.45 N	141.20 E
Shikotsu-Tōya-kokuritsu-kōen ♦	92a	42.47 N	141.00 E
Shikuang	106	31.54 N	121.24 E
Shil	272c	19.09 N	73.03 E
Shilabo	144	6.05 N	44.48 E
Shilbottle	44	55.23 N	1.42 W
Shildon	44	54.38 N	1.39 W
Shiliangji	100	33.54 N	115.14 E
Shilibao	105	39.55 N	116.29 E
Shiliguri	124	26.42 N	88.26 E
Shilihe	104	41.31 N	123.22 E
Shiling	106	30.26 N	119.35 E
Shilipeng	106	31.14 N	119.35 E
Shilipu, Zhg.	105	39.29 N	116.18 E
Shilipu, Zhg.	105	39.11 N	115.59 E
Shilipu, Zhg.	105	40.15 N	117.58 E
Shiliuban	100	24.08 N	117.33 E
Shillelagh	48	52.45 N	6.32 W
Shillingstone	42	50.54 N	2.14 W
Shillington	208	40.18 N	75.57 W
Shillong	120	25.34 N	91.53 E
Shilo, Canadian Forces Base ■	184	49.49 N	99.38 W
Shiloh, Il., U.S.	219	38.34 N	89.54 W
Shiloh, N.J., U.S.	208	39.27 N	75.17 W
Shiloh, Oh., U.S.	214	40.58 N	82.36 W
Shiloh, Oh., U.S.	218	39.49 N	84.13 W
Shiloh, Oh., U.S.	218	39.49 N	84.13 W
Shiloh, Pa., U.S.	208	39.59 N	76.49 W
Shiloh			
→ Saylūn, Khirbat ⊥	132	32.03 N	35.17 E
Shiloh National Military Park ♦	194	35.06 N	88.21 W
Shilong, Zhg.	100	23.07 N	113.48 E
Shilong, Zhg.	102	23.54 N	109.40 E
Shilong, Zhg.	107	30.15 N	106.34 E
Shilou	100	22.58 N	113.29 E
Shima, Nihon	92	34.13 N	136.51 E
Shima, Nihon	270	34.59 N	135.20 E
Shima, Zhg.	100	24.27 N	117.49 E
Shima, Zhg.	107	29.38 N	105.50 E
Shimabara	92	32.47 N	130.22 E
Shimachang, Zhg.	107	28.59 N	105.55 E
Shimachang, Zhg.	107	29.03 N	105.36 E
Shimada, Nihon	94	34.49 N	138.11 E
Shimada, Nihon	268	35.59 N	139.25 E
Shimagahara	94	34.46 N	136.03 E
Shima-hantō ≻[1]	94	34.26 N	136.33 E
Shimamiao	106	32.08 N	119.20 E
Shimamoto	96	34.53 N	135.40 E
Shimane □[5]	96	35.00 N	132.30 E
Shimane-hantō ≻[1]	96	35.30 N	133.00 E
Shimantan	100	33.17 N	113.28 E
Shimanto ≃	96	32.56 N	133.00 E
Shimata ≃	96	33.57 N	131.55 E
Shimbiris ʌ	144	10.44 N	47.15 E
Shimei	106	32.14 N	120.10 E
Shimen, Zhg.	98	39.44 N	118.52 E
Shimen, Zhg.	102	29.28 N	111.17 E
Shimen, Zhg.	105	40.06 N	117.42 E
Shimen, Zhg.	106	30.37 N	120.26 E
Shimen, Zhg.	107	29.36 N	106.27 E
Shimen, Zhg.	107	29.09 N	106.02 E
Shimencun, Zhg.	106	31.21 N	119.34 E
Shimencun, Zhg.	106	30.23 N	119.41 E
Shimendong	100	28.16 N	120.07 E
Shimengou	104	40.40 N	123.43 E
Shimenjie	100	29.34 N	116.44 E
Shimenlou	100	28.58 N	114.51 E
Shimenying	105	39.54 N	116.05 E
Shimenzi	89	48.30 N	121.31 E
Shimian	102	29.18 N	102.22 E
Shimiaozi	104	40.39 N	123.31 E
Shimizu, Nihon	92	35.01 N	138.29 E
Shimizu			
→ Tosa-shimizu, Nihon	92	32.46 N	132.57 E
Shimizu, Nihon	92a	43.01 N	142.53 E
Shimizu, Nihon	94	36.02 N	136.09 E
Shimizu, Nihon	94	35.01 N	138.29 E
Shimizu, Nihon	96	34.05 N	135.26 E
Shimizu-tunnel ◆[5]	94	36.52 N	138.55 E
Shimla	123	31.06 N	77.10 E
Shimminato	94	36.47 N	137.04 E
Shimobe	94	35.27 N	138.29 E
Shimoda	94	34.40 N	138.57 E
Shimodate	94	36.18 N	139.59 E
Shimofusa	94	35.52 N	140.21 E
Shimofusa-daichi ʌʌ[1]	268	35.45 N	139.58 E
Shimofusa-kōkūkichi, Kaijō-jieitai- ■	94	35.50 N	140.05 E
Shimofusa Naval Air Base ■	268	35.48 N	140.01 E
Shimoga	122	13.55 N	75.34 E
Shimogawara	268	35.56 N	139.21 E
Shimogōri	268	35.21 N	140.03 E
Shimogyō ◆[8]	270	34.59 N	135.45 E
Shimohōya	268	35.45 N	139.34 E
Shimoichi	96	34.22 N	135.47 E
Shimoigusa ◆[8]	268	35.43 N	139.37 E
Shimoji	175d	24.45 N	125.16 E
Shimoji-jima I	175d	24.49 N	125.09 E
Shimojō	94	35.24 N	137.47 E
Shimokawa	92a	44.18 N	142.39 E
Shimokita-hantō ≻[1]	92	41.15 N	141.00 E
Shimomatsu	270	34.27 N	135.23 E
Shimomizo	268	35.31 N	139.23 E
Shimoni	154	4.39 S	39.23 E
Shimoniikura	268	35.47 N	139.38 E
Shimonita	94	36.13 N	138.47 E
Shimonoseki	96	33.57 N	130.57 E
Shimookudomi	268	35.53 N	139.26 E
Shimoryūzu-zaki ≻	96	33.30 N	133.34 E
Shimosakamoto	270	35.03 N	135.53 E
Shimosuwa	94	36.04 N	138.05 E
Shimotajiri	270	34.57 N	135.28 E
Shimotomi	268	35.50 N	139.29 E
Shimotsu	96	34.10 N	135.08 E
Shimotsuchidana	268	35.24 N	139.27 E
Shimotsui	96	34.26 N	133.47 E
Shimotsuma	94	36.11 N	139.58 E
Shimotsuruma	268	35.29 N	139.28 E
Shimoya	268	35.23 N	139.21 E
Shimoyama	94	35.02 N	137.19 E
Shimoyugi	268	35.38 N	139.23 E
Shimura ◆[8]	268	35.46 N	139.41 E
Shin, Loch ⊜	46	58.06 N	4.34 W
Shinagawa ◆[8]	268	35.37 N	139.45 E
Shinan	102	22.43 N	109.54 E
Shinano	94	36.48 N	138.13 E
Shinano ≃	92	37.56 N	139.03 E
Shinarā	142	28.47 N	30.46 E
Shināṣ	128	24.46 N	56.28 E
Shinawari	123	33.32 N	70.48 E
Shinbārī	273c	30.07 N	31.09 E
Shīndand	128	33.18 N	62.08 E
Shindenbaru-kichi, Kōkū-jieitai- ■	92	32.04 N	131.30 E
Shindo	268	35.21 N	139.21 E
Shiner	222	29.25 N	97.10 W
Shingbwiyang	110	26.41 N	96.13 E
Shingishū			
→ Sinŭiju	98	40.05 N	124.24 E
Shinglehouse	214	41.57 N	78.11 W
Shingle Springs	226	38.40 N	120.56 W
Shing Mun Reservoir ⊜[1]	271d	22.23 N	114.08 E
Shingo	96	34.59 N	133.23 E
Shingū, Nihon	92	33.44 N	135.59 E
Shingū, Nihon	96	34.55 N	134.33 E
Shingū, Nihon	96	33.56 N	133.38 E
Shingwidzi	156	23.05 S	31.25 E
Shingwidzi (Singuédeze) ≃	156	23.53 S	32.17 E
Shinichi	96	34.33 N	133.16 E
Shining Tor ʌ	262	53.16 N	2.01 W
Shinīrah	132	32.22 N	36.45 E
Shinji	96	35.24 N	132.54 E
Shinji-ko ⊜	96	35.27 N	132.58 E
Shinjō, Nihon	92	38.46 N	140.18 E
Shinjō, Nihon	270	34.30 N	135.44 E
Shinjuku ◆[8]	268	35.41 N	139.42 E
Shinkawa	94	35.09 N	136.50 E
Shīnkay	120	31.57 N	67.26 E
Shinkolobwe	154	11.02 S	26.35 E
Shinmachi	94	36.16 N	139.07 E
Shinminato ≃	270	34.38 N	135.09 E
Shinnārah, Minqār ⊥[4]	142	28.52 N	30.38 E
Shinnayō	96	34.04 N	131.47 E
Shinnecock Bay c	207	40.52 N	72.28 W
Shinnel Water ≃	44	55.13 N	3.49 W
Shinness	46	58.05 N	4.28 W
Shinnston	188	39.23 N	80.18 W
Shino-jima I	94	34.39 N	137.00 E
Shinsai-bashi ◆[8]	270	34.40 N	135.31 E
Shinshār	130	34.36 N	36.44 E
Shinshiro	94	34.54 N	137.30 E
Shinshū-shinmachi	94	36.34 N	138.01 E
Shintone	94	35.50 N	140.20 E
Shinyanga	154	3.40 S	33.26 E
Shinyanga □[4]	154	3.45 S	33.00 E
Shin-yōdo ≃[1]	270	34.41 N	135.26 E
Shio	94	36.52 N	136.48 E
Shiobara	94	36.58 N	139.49 E
Shiocton	190	44.26 N	88.34 W
Shiogama	92	38.19 N	141.01 E
Shiojiri	94	36.06 N	137.58 E
Shiojiri-tōge)(	94	36.05 N	138.02 E
Shiomi-dake ʌ	94	35.34 N	138.12 E
Shionoe	96	34.10 N	134.05 E
Shiono-misaki ≻	92	33.26 N	135.45 E
Shioya	94	36.46 N	139.51 E
Shioya ◆[8]	270	34.38 N	135.06 E
Shioya-zaki ≻, Nihon	92	33.26 N	135.45 E
Shioya-zaki ≻, Nihon	94	36.59 N	140.59 E
Shiozawa	94	37.02 N	138.51 E
Shipai, Zhg.	100	23.08 N	113.21 E
Shipai, Zhg.	106	31.30 N	120.55 E
Shipanpu	107	30.28 N	104.23 E
Shipantuo	107	30.25 N	106.13 E
Ship Bottom	208	39.38 N	74.10 W
Shipbourne	260	51.15 N	0.17 E
Ship Cove	186	47.06 N	54.05 W
Shipdham	42	52.37 N	0.53 E
Shiping, Zhg.	102	28.20 N	107.42 E
Shiping, Zhg.	102	23.47 N	102.30 E
Shipley	44	53.50 N	1.47 W
Shipman, Il., U.S.	219	39.07 N	90.03 W
Shipman, Va., U.S.	192	37.43 N	78.50 W
Shippan Point ≻	276	41.01 N	73.32 W
Shippegan	186	47.45 N	64.42 W
Shippensburg	208	40.03 N	77.31 W
Shippenville	214	41.15 N	79.28 W
Shippingport	214	40.38 N	80.25 W
Shippō	94	35.10 N	136.48 E
Shiprock	200	36.47 N	108.41 W
Ship Rock ʌ	200	36.42 N	108.50 W
Shipshaw ≃	186	48.27 N	71.12 W
Shipshewana	216	41.40 N	85.34 W
Shipston-on-Stour	42	52.04 N	1.37 W
Shipton-under-Wychwood	42	51.51 N	1.35 W
Shipu, Zhg.	100	29.13 N	121.55 E
Shipu, Zhg.	106	31.15 N	121.03 E
Shiqi			
→ Zhongshan	100	22.31 N	113.22 E
Shiqian	102	27.31 N	108.20 E
Shiqiao, Zhg.	100	33.12 N	112.36 E
Shiqiao, Zhg.	100	26.58 N	114.23 E
Shiqiao, Zhg.	106	30.30 N	119.11 E
Shiqiao, Zhg.	107	30.25 N	104.31 E
Shiqiaopu	107	30.05 N	105.23 E
Shiqiaozi	104	41.27 N	123.43 E
Shiqma ≃	132	31.36 N	34.30 E
Shiquan, Zhg.	102	33.03 N	108.17 E
Shiquan, Zhg.	106	30.30 N	120.48 E
Shirahama, Nihon	94	34.54 N	139.54 E
Shirahama, Nihon	96	33.40 N	135.20 E
Shirahata-yama ʌ	96	34.54 N	134.23 E
Shiraitono-taki ʟ	94	35.18 N	138.38 E
Shirakami-misaki ≻	92a	41.24 N	140.12 E
Shirakawa, Nihon	94	37.07 N	140.13 E
Shirakawa, Nihon	94	35.35 N	137.12 E
Shirakawa, Nihon	94	36.16 N	136.54 E
Shirakawa-no-seki-ato ⊥	94	37.03 N	140.15 E
Shirakawa-tōge ʌ[2]	270	34.42 N	135.07 E
Shirako	94	35.26 N	140.23 E
Shirākol	126	22.18 N	88.16 E
Shirakura-yama ʌ	94	35.00 N	137.46 E
Shirama-yama ʌ	96	34.01 N	135.23 E
Shiramine	94	36.10 N	136.37 E
Shirane	94	35.38 N	138.28 E
Shirane-san ʌ, Nihon	94	36.38 N	138.32 E
Shirane-san ʌ, Nihon	94	36.48 N	139.22 E
Shirane-san (Kita-dake) ʌ, Nihon	94	35.40 N	138.15 E
Shiranuka	92a	42.57 N	144.05 E
Shiraoi	92a	42.33 N	141.21 E
Shiraoka	94	36.01 N	139.40 E
Shiraone	272c	19.03 N	73.01 E
Shirasawa	94	36.40 N	139.08 E
Shirati	154	1.08 S	33.59 E
Shīrāz	128	29.36 N	52.32 E
Shirbīn	142	31.11 N	31.32 E
Shirdley Hill	262	53.36 N	2.58 W
Shire (Chire) ≃	154	17.42 S	35.19 E
Shirebrook	44	53.12 N	1.13 W
Shiremanstown	208	40.13 N	76.57 W
Shiretoko-hantō ≻[1]	92a	44.00 N	145.00 E
Shiretoko-kokuritsu-kōen ♦	92a	44.08 N	145.10 E
Shiretoko-misaki ≻	92a	44.14 N	145.17 E
Shīrīn ≃	120	36.49 N	65.01 E
Shīr Kūh ʌ	128	31.34 N	54.04 E
Shirland	216	42.27 N	89.12 W
Shirley, B.C., Can.	224	48.23 N	123.54 W
Shirley, Il., U.S.	216	40.24 N	89.04 W
Shirley, In., U.S.	218	39.53 N	85.34 W
Shirley, Ma., U.S.	207	42.32 N	71.39 W
Shirley Plantation ⊥	208	37.21 N	77.15 W
Shirleysburg	214	40.18 N	77.53 W
Shiro	222	30.37 N	95.53 W
Shiroi	94	35.48 N	140.04 E
Shiroishi	92	38.00 N	140.37 E
Shirokawa	96	33.23 N	132.46 E
Shirone	92	37.46 N	139.01 E
Shirotori, Nihon	94	35.53 N	136.52 E
Shirotori, Nihon	96	34.15 N	134.20 E
Shirouma-dake ʌ	94	36.45 N	137.46 E
Shiroyama	94	35.35 N	139.19 E
Shiro-yama ʌ	270	34.38 N	135.53 E
Shirpur	120	21.21 N	74.53 E
Shirrell Heath	42	50.55 N	1.12 W
Shirshābah	142	30.47 N	31.10 E
Shīrvān	128	37.24 N	57.55 E
Shisaka-jima I	96	34.07 N	133.11 E
Shisanling	105	40.19 N	116.16 E
Shi San Ling (Ming Tombs) ⊥	105	40.19 N	116.13 E
Shisanzhan	89	51.21 N	125.43 E
Shisha Hai ⊜	271a	39.57 N	116.22 E
Shishaldin Volcano ʌ[1]	180	54.45 N	163.57 W
Shishan	104	41.16 N	121.30 E
Shishi	100	24.48 N	118.38 E
Shishikui	96	33.34 N	134.18 E
Shishi Shan ʌ	100	24.44 N	117.54 E
Shishmaref	180	66.14 N	166.09 W
Shishmaref Inlet c	180	66.07 N	165.50 W
Shishou	102	29.43 N	112.19 E
Shisht al-An'ām	142	30.52 N	30.44 E
Shisiazhan	89	51.36 N	125.42 E
Shisixian	104	40.53 N	122.59 E
Shisler Point ≻	284a	42.52 N	79.08 W
Shisui	94	35.43 N	140.16 E
Shitai	100	30.13 N	117.27 E
Shitan, Zhg.	100	27.44 N	112.42 E
Shitan, Zhg.	100	23.10 N	113.47 E
Shitang, Zhg.	100	28.16 N	121.36 E
Shitang, Zhg.	102	25.38 N	110.50 E
Shitangwan	106	31.40 N	120.13 E
Shitara	94	35.05 N	137.35 E
Shithāthah	128	32.33 N	43.29 E
Shiting, Zhg.	100	27.36 N	113.16 E
Shiting, Zhg.	105	39.31 N	115.41 E
Shitoufangzi	89	48.38 N	126.08 E
Shitougouzi	89	49.19 N	125.55 E
Shitoumiao	102	41.41 N	106.50 E
Shitoumiaozi	104	41.38 N	121.26 E
Shitoushan	105	40.27 N	116.13 E
Shitoushuangmiao	98	41.28 N	118.55 E
Shituan	107	30.09 N	105.01 E
Shitunwei	104	41.07 N	121.31 E
Shiv	120	26.11 N	71.15 E
Shivalya	126	23.50 N	89.47 E
Shively	218	38.12 N	85.49 W
Shivering, Mount ʌ	170	34.08 S	150.02 E
Shivpuri	124	25.26 N	77.39 E
Shivta, Horvot (Subeita) ⊥	132	30.53 N	34.38 E
Shivwits Plateau ʌʌ[1]	200	36.15 N	113.40 W
Shiwaku-shotō II	96	34.20 N	133.45 E
Shiwan, Zhg.	100	27.17 N	112.57 E
Shiwan, Zhg.	100	28.12 N	113.49 E
Shiwan, Zhg.	100	23.01 N	113.04 E
Shiwan, Zhg.	102	37.35 N	109.01 E
Shiwenchang	104	41.43 N	123.54 E
Shiwu	89	43.48 N	124.13 E
Shixi, Zhg.	100	28.16 N	117.45 E
Shixi, Zhg.	100	28.16 N	115.36 E
Shixia	105	40.20 N	114.59 E
Shixian	89	43.05 N	129.47 E
Shixiancun	106	31.12 N	120.29 E
Shixiechang	107	29.51 N	106.41 E
Shixing	100	24.58 N	114.03 E
Shixun	100	24.44 N	118.11 E
Shiyachang	107	30.27 N	106.31 E
Shiyan, Zhg.	102	32.38 N	110.44 E
Shiyan, Zhg.	107	30.22 N	104.27 E
Shiyangchang, Zhg.	107	29.56 N	105.37 E
Shiyangchang, Zhg.	107	30.42 N	105.57 E
Shiyanqiao	107	29.19 N	105.22 E
Shiyiwei	106	31.59 N	120.43 E
Shiyizhan	89	51.13 N	125.52 E
Shiyu	107	29.46 N	106.06 E
Shizhangzi	98	40.24 N	119.48 E
Shizheng	100	24.32 N	115.50 E
Shizhenjie	100	28.51 N	116.56 E
Shizhong, Zhg.	100	24.57 N	117.06 E
Shizhong, Zhg.	106	30.44 N	120.16 E
Shizhongtan	107	30.26 N	104.35 E
Shizhu, Zhg.	100	28.48 N	120.06 E
Shizhu, Zhg.	102	29.56 N	108.09 E
Shizhuang	106	32.08 N	120.31 E
Shizhuangzi, Zhg.	104	42.24 N	122.53 E
Shizhuangzi, Zhg.	105	40.38 N	116.59 E
Shizhuzi	104	41.18 N	121.35 E
Shizichang	107	29.32 N	106.14 E
Shizigu	105	39.23 N	118.08 E
Shizikou	100	24.12 N	113.38 E
Shizilin	106	31.26 N	121.25 E
Shizipo	105	40.21 N	115.07 E
Shizipu	106	30.59 N	119.07 E
Shizuchi-kokutei-kōen ♦	96	33.45 N	133.08 E
Shizugawa	92	38.40 N	141.27 E
Shizui, Zhg.	89	43.08 N	126.06 E
Shizui, Zhg.	98	38.52 N	113.42 E
Shizuma ≃	96	35.12 N	132.28 E
Shizunai	92a	42.20 N	142.22 E
Shizuoka	94	34.58 N	138.23 E
Shizuoka □[5]	94	35.00 N	138.00 E
Shkodër	38	42.05 N	19.30 E
Shkumbin ≃	38	41.01 N	19.26 E
Shō ≃	94	36.47 N	137.04 E
Shoal ≃	194	30.41 N	86.39 W
Shoal Cape ≻	162	33.53 S	121.07 E
Shoal Creek ≃, U.S.	194	40.28 N	92.42 W
Shoal Creek ≃, U.S.	194	34.50 N	87.33 W
Shoal Creek ≃, U.S.	194	37.05 N	94.42 W
Shoal Creek ≃, Il., U.S.	219	38.28 N	89.35 W
Shoal Creek ≃, Mo., U.S.	194	39.44 N	93.32 W
Shoal Creek, East Fork ≃	219	38.51 N	89.30 W
Shoal Creek, Middle Fork ≃	219	39.05 N	89.33 W
Shoal Creek, West Fork ≃	219	39.05 N	89.33 W
Shoal Harbour	186	48.11 N	53.59 W
Shoalhaven ≃	170	34.52 S	150.44 E
Shoalhaven Bight c[3]	170	34.52 S	150.47 E
Shoal Lake	184	50.26 N	100.34 W
Shoal Lake ⊜	184	49.32 N	95.00 W
Shoal Point ≻	276	41.08 N	73.15 W
Shoals	194	38.39 N	86.47 W
Shoals, Bay of c	168b	35.37 S	137.37 E
Shoalwater, Cape ≻	224	46.44 N	124.06 W
Shoalwater Bay c	166	22.02 S	150.25 E
Shōbara	96	34.51 N	133.01 E
Shōboku	96	35.06 N	134.07 E
Shobonier	219	38.52 N	89.05 W
Shōbu	94	36.04 N	139.36 E
Shōdai	270	34.51 N	135.42 E
Shōdo-shima I	96	34.30 N	134.17 E
Shoeburyness	42	51.32 N	0.48 E
Shoe Cove	186	49.55 N	55.33 W
Shoemakersville	208	40.30 N	75.58 W
Shōgawa	94	36.34 N	136.59 E
Shogunle	273a	6.35 N	3.21 E
Shohola	210	41.28 N	74.55 W
Shohola Creek ≃	210	41.28 N	74.55 W
Shokambetsu-dake ʌ	92a	43.43 N	141.31 E
Shokan	210	41.58 N	74.13 W
Shōkawa	94	36.02 N	136.57 E
Sholingnur	122	13.07 N	79.25 E
Shomera	132	33.05 N	35.17 E
Shomolu	273a	6.32 N	3.23 E
Shōmyō-no-taki ʟ	94	36.35 N	137.24 E
Shona, Eilean I	46	56.47 N	5.52 W
Shōnai	96	33.11 N	131.26 E
Shōnai ≃	94	35.04 N	136.50 E
Shōnan	268	35.50 N	140.02 E
Shongum	276	40.50 N	74.33 W
Shongum Lake ⊜	276	40.51 N	74.32 W
Shongwe	158	27.24 S	32.25 E
Shōō	96	35.02 N	134.08 E
Shooters Hill	170	33.54 S	149.52 E
Shooters Island I	276	40.39 N	74.10 W
Shopiere	216	42.34 N	88.57 W
Shoranūr	122	10.46 N	76.17 E
Shorāpur	122	16.31 N	76.45 E
Shoreacres, B.C., Can.	182	49.26 N	117.32 W
Shore Acres, Ca., U.S.	226	38.02 N	121.58 W
Shore Acres, Ma., U.S.	207	42.12 N	70.44 W
Shore Acres, N.J., U.S.	208	40.01 N	74.06 W
Shoreacres, Tx., U.S.	222	29.37 N	95.01 W
Shoreditch ◆[8]	260	51.32 N	0.05 W
Shoreham, Austl.	169	38.25 S	145.03 E
Shoreham, Eng., U.K.	260	51.20 N	0.11 E
Shoreham, Mi., U.S.	216	42.03 N	86.30 W
Shoreham-by-Sea	42	50.49 N	0.16 W
Shorewood, Il., U.S.	216	41.32 N	88.12 W
Shorewood, Wi., U.S.	216	43.05 N	87.53 W
Shorewood Hills	216	43.04 N	89.26 W
Shorkot	123	30.50 N	72.04 E
Shorkot Road	123	30.47 N	72.15 E
Shorne	260	51.25 N	0.26 E
Short Beach	207	41.15 N	72.50 W
Short Creek	214	40.11 N	80.55 W
Shortland Islands II	175e	6.55 S	155.53 E
Short Mountain ʌ	192	36.23 N	83.10 W
Shortsville	210	42.57 N	77.13 W
Shoshone	202	42.56 N	114.24 W
Shoshone ≃	202	44.52 N	108.11 W
Shoshone, North Fork ≃	202	44.29 N	109.18 W
Shoshone, South Fork ≃	202	44.27 N	109.14 W
Shoshone Basin ≚[1]	202	43.05 N	108.05 W
Shoshone Lake ⊜	202	44.22 N	110.43 W
Shoshone Mountains ʌʌ	204	39.00 N	117.30 W
Shoshone Peak ʌ	204	36.56 N	116.16 W
Shoshone Range ʌʌ	204	40.20 N	116.50 W
Shoshong	156	22.59 S	26.30 E
Shoshoni	200	43.14 N	108.06 W
Shostka	78	51.52 N	33.30 E
Shotley Gate	42	51.58 N	1.15 E
Shotton	262	53.12 N	3.02 W
Shotton Colliery	44	54.44 N	1.20 W
Shotts	46	55.49 N	3.48 W
Shotwick	262	53.14 N	2.59 W
Shou'anzhen	107	30.16 N	103.37 E
Shouchang	100	29.22 N	119.13 E
Shoufeng	100	23.52 N	121.30 E
Shouguang	98	36.53 N	118.42 E
Shouning	100	27.27 N	119.30 E
Shournagh ≃	48	51.53 N	8.35 W
Shoushan	104	41.12 N	123.03 E
Shouwangfen	105	40.35 N	117.48 E
Shouxian	100	32.35 N	116.47 E
Shouyang	102	37.59 N	113.09 E
Shōwa, Nihon	94	36.37 N	139.04 E
Shōwa, Nihon	96	34.43 N	133.39 E
Showell	208	38.23 N	75.12 W
Show Low	200	34.15 N	110.01 W
Shpola	78	49.01 N	31.24 E
Shpykiv	78	48.46 N	28.35 E
Shqipëri			
→ Albania □[1]	38	41.00 N	20.00 E
Shramkivka	78	50.10 N	32.05 E
Shreve	214	40.40 N	82.01 W
Shreveport	194	32.30 N	93.44 W
Shrevewood	284c	38.53 N	77.13 W
Shrewsbury, Eng., U.K.	42	52.43 N	2.45 W
Shrewsbury, Ma., U.S.	207	42.17 N	71.42 W
Shrewsbury, N.J., U.S.	208	40.19 N	74.03 W
Shrewsbury, Pa., U.S.	208	39.46 N	76.40 W
Shrewsbury River c	276	40.21 N	74.00 W
Shrewton	42	51.12 N	1.55 W
Shri Dūngargarh	120	28.05 N	74.00 E
Shri Mohangarh	120	27.17 N	71.14 E
Shriner Mountain ʌ	210	40.56 N	77.20 W
Shrīrangapattana	122	12.25 N	76.42 E
Shrivenham	42	51.36 N	1.39 W
Shropshire □[6]	42	52.40 N	2.40 W
Shropshire Union Canal ≋	262	53.17 N	2.53 W
Shrub Oak	210	41.20 N	73.49 W
Shrule	48	53.30 N	9.08 W
Shtormove	83	49.06 N	38.55 E
Shu ≃	98	34.07 N	118.30 E
Shuajingsi	102	32.00 N	103.05 E
Shuanfeng Shan ʌ	107	29.26 N	105.47 E
Shuang ≃	269d	25.00 N	121.31 E
Shuangbai	102	24.54 N	101.32 E
Shuangcheng	89	45.21 N	126.17 E
Shuangchengzi	105	40.11 N	118.03 E
Shuangdian	100	32.23 N	120.51 E
Shuangdun	106	32.13 N	121.08 E
Shuangfeng, Zhg.	102	27.24 N	112.05 E
Shuangfeng, Zhg.	106	31.31 N	121.01 E
Shuangfeng, Zhg.	106	31.31 N	121.02 E
Shuangfeng Shan ʌ	100	24.28 N	114.43 E
Shuangfengyi	107	29.27 N	105.09 E
Shuangfu	105	39.48 N	117.44 E
Shuangfuchang, Zhg.	107	29.41 N	103.31 E
Shuangfuchang, Zhg.	107	30.08 N	103.32 E
Shuanggang, Zhg.	89	45.07 N	122.59 E
Shuanggang, Zhg.	100	28.11 N	117.30 E
Shuanggetun	89	48.58 N	129.57 E
Shuanggou, Zhg.	98	34.03 N	117.37 E
Shuanggou, Zhg.	100	32.12 N	112.21 E
Shuanggou, Zhg.	100	33.16 N	118.10 E
Shuanggufen	107	29.38 N	104.11 E
Shuanghe, Zhg.	100	31.33 N	116.46 E
Shuanghe, Zhg.	100	31.41 N	112.46 E
Shuanghe, Zhg.	107	29.40 N	104.48 E
Shuanghe, Zhg.	107	30.07 N	105.10 E
Shuanghe, Zhg.	107	30.15 N	104.44 E
Shuanghechang, Zhg.	107	28.51 N	104.51 E
Shuanghechang, Zhg.	107	29.25 N	106.17 E
Shuanghechang, Zhg.	107	29.12 N	105.43 E
Shuanghechang, Zhg.	107	29.18 N	105.36 E
Shuang-hsi	269d	25.01 N	121.39 E
Shuangji ≃	100	34.05 N	114.24 E
Shuangjiang, Zhg.	100	26.48 N	116.28 E
Shuangjiang, Zhg.	102	23.37 N	99.41 E
Shuangjiang, Zhg.	107	30.13 N	105.45 E
Shuangjiangqiao	102	25.19 N	98.51 E
Shuangjianji	100	33.12 N	116.40 E
Shuangjingzi	104	42.28 N	123.42 E
Shuangkou	105	39.15 N	117.02 E
Shuangliao	89	43.31 N	123.30 E
Shuanglin	106	30.47 N	120.19 E
Shuanglingzi, Zhg.	104	40.54 N	124.10 E
Shuanglingzi, Zhg.	104	40.50 N	123.06 E
Shuangliu	107	30.34 N	103.55 E
Shuangliushu	100	31.56 N	115.12 E
Shuanglongtai	104	40.56 N	122.39 E
Shuangmiao, Zhg.	100	28.24 N	120.45 E
Shuangmiao, Zhg.	100	32.09 N	116.52 E
Shuangmiaozi, Zhg.	104	42.25 N	122.17 E
Shuangmiaozi, Zhg.	104	42.02 N	121.52 E
Shuangpai	110	25.57 N	111.32 E
Shuangpaishi	106	31.24 N	118.59 E
Shuangqiao, Zhg.	100	32.29 N	116.41 E
Shuangqiao, Zhg.	105	39.54 N	116.37 E
Shuangqiao, Zhg.	106	30.59 N	118.47 E
Shuangshanzi	98	40.21 N	119.08 E
Shuangshipu	107	29.14 N	104.42 E
Shuangshiqiao, Zhg.	107	29.22 N	105.51 E
Shuangshiqiao, Zhg.	107	29.23 N	104.29 E
Shuangshu	105	39.34 N	117.01 E
Shuangshutai	89	43.50 N	121.15 E
Shuangtaizi, Zhg.	104	41.34 N	121.12 E
Shuangtaizi, Zhg.	104	42.21 N	124.10 E
Shuangtaizi, Zhg.	104	42.25 N	123.11 E
Shuangtaizi, Zhg.	104	41.00 N	122.34 E
Shuangtaizi, Zhg.	104	41.11 N	121.14 E
Shuangtaizi ≃	104	40.59 N	121.51 E
Shuangtaizihe Kou ≃[1]	104	40.55 N	121.50 E
Shuangtang, Zhg.	100	28.01 N	116.44 E
Shuangtang, Zhg.	105	39.03 N	116.17 E
Shuangtang, Zhg.	105	38.53 N	116.54 E
Shuangtangdian	106	30.59 N	118.51 E
Shuangtuo	105	39.14 N	117.20 E
Shuangtuozhen	105	39.29 N	118.23 E
Shuangxi, Zhg.	100	27.01 N	119.03 E
Shuangxi, Zhg.	106	30.24 N	119.50 E
Shuangyang	89	43.32 N	125.42 E
Shuangyangdian	104	41.07 N	121.16 E
Shuangyaocun	105	38.55 N	117.03 E
Shuangyashan	89	46.37 N	131.22 E
Shu'ayb, Wādī V	132	31.54 N	35.38 E
Shu'ayt, Wādī V	144	18.15 N	52.00 E
Shubenacadie ≃	186	45.20 N	63.30 W
Shublik Mountains ʌʌ	180	69.31 N	145.40 W
Shubrā al-Khaymah	142	30.06 N	31.15 E
Shubrā Bābil	142	30.54 N	31.11 E
Shubrā Khalfūn	142	30.29 N	31.05 E
Shubrā Khīt	142	31.02 N	30.43 E
Shubuta	194	31.51 N	88.41 W
Shucheng	100	31.27 N	116.57 E
Shufu	85	39.27 N	75.52 E
Shufuka Shan ʌ	89	50.28 N	123.10 E
Shugudali	89	52.47 N	124.02 E
Shuheyingzi	104	42.18 N	122.16 E
Shuhezhen	106	31.35 N	121.35 E
Shūhō	96	34.13 N	131.18 E
Shuhong	100	28.39 N	120.09 E
Shuibatang	102	28.39 N	107.03 E
Shuibei, Zhg.	100	28.04 N	115.01 E
Shuibei, Zhg.	106	31.40 N	119.39 E
Shuichaoyang	100	26.22 N	117.57 E
Shuicheng	102	26.41 N	104.50 E
Shuidao	98	37.10 N	121.33 E
Shuidiangou	89	47.43 N	122.40 E
Shuidong, Zhg.	106	31.23 N	119.37 E
Shuidong, Zhg.	106	30.47 N	118.57 E
Shuidongjie	106	31.07 N	119.33 E
Shuiduixia	106	30.17 N	118.50 E
Shuihai	100	33.02 N	120.26 E
Shuihouling	100	30.43 N	116.26 E
Shuiji	100	27.26 N	118.20 E
Shuijiahuangdi	104	42.14 N	123.28 E
Shuijian	105	40.09 N	115.58 E
Shuijing	102	26.10 N	99.09 E
Shuijingtang	102	28.50 N	108.11 E
Shuikou, Zhg.	100	26.59 N	117.41 E
Shuikou, Zhg.	100	26.22 N	118.44 E
Shuikou, Zhg.	100	24.00 N	115.55 E
Shuikou, Zhg.	100	26.18 N	113.46 E
Shuikou, Zhg.	102	25.54 N	109.06 E
Shuikou, Zhg.	107	29.29 N	103.42 E
Shuikouchang	107	29.33 N	103.40 E
Shuikouguan	102	22.30 N	106.34 E
Shuikoushan	102	26.30 N	112.30 E
Shuikouxu	100	25.09 N	114.28 E
Shuiliandong	98	42.12 N	125.09 E
Shuimenzi	98	39.36 N	122.19 E
Shuimingqiao	106	31.03 N	119.09 E
Shuimoqipan	85	39.51 N	76.42 E
Shuiquan'gou	104	41.58 N	121.50 E
Shuiquanzi, Zhg.	104	42.15 N	121.32 E
Shuiquanzi, Zhg.	104	40.53 N	121.05 E
Shuitangzi	102	29.18 N	101.10 E
Shuiting	100	29.10 N	119.14 E
Shuitou, Zhg.	100	24.43 N	118.25 E
Shuitou, Zhg.	100	23.53 N	113.37 E
Shuitou, Zhg.	100	27.38 N	120.16 E
Shuitouwei	100	26.06 N	115.28 E
Shuituzhen	107	29.47 N	106.31 E
Shuiyang	106	31.14 N	118.47 E
Shuiyang ≃	106	31.14 N	118.48 E
Shuiye	98	36.08 N	114.07 E
Shuizhai	98	36.54 N	117.24 E
Shuizhuyang	100	26.59 N	119.13 E
Shujāābād	123	29.53 N	71.18 E
Shujālpur	124	23.24 N	76.43 E
Shujiawazi	104	42.20 N	121.57 E
Shuksan, Mount ʌ	224	48.50 N	121.36 W
Shulan	89	44.27 N	126.57 E
Shulaps Peak ʌ	182	50.57 N	122.31 W
Shule	85	39.23 N	76.06 E
Shule ≃	102	40.50 N	94.10 E
Shūlgareh	120	36.19 N	66.53 E
Shul'hynka	83	49.08 N	38.56 E
Shullsburg	190	42.34 N	90.13 W
Shulu (Xinji)	98	37.54 N	115.13 E
Shumagin Islands II	180	55.07 N	159.45 W
Shumatuscacant ≃	283	42.03 N	70.51 W
Shumen			
→ Šumen	38	43.16 N	26.55 E
Shums'k	78	50.07 N	26.07 E
Shūnah, Wādī ash- V	142	29.38 N	32.13 E
Shun'an	100	30.57 N	117.57 E
Shūnat Nimrīn	132	31.54 N	35.37 E
Shunayn, Sabkhat ⊜	146	30.30 N	21.00 E
Shunchang	100	26.50 N	117.48 E
Shunde	100	22.50 N	113.14 E
Shundian	100	34.15 N	113.20 E
Shundianqiao	106	31.24 N	120.41 E
Shunge	102	37.25 N	95.27 E
Shungnak	180	66.53 N	157.02 W
Shunhechang	107	29.57 N	104.42 E
Shunlongchang	107	30.04 N	103.27 E
Shunshanpu	104	42.08 N	122.21 E
Shuntianhu	100	24.08 N	114.48 E
Shunyi	105	40.08 N	116.38 E
Shuoduzong	102	30.48 N	95.47 E
Shuojiaji	100	33.42 N	119.44 E
Shuping	107	29.19 N	104.43 E
Shupiyan	123	33.43 N	74.50 E
Shuqayyiqah, Nafūd ⊥[8]	128	25.45 N	43.55 E
Shuqualak	194	32.58 N	88.34 W
Shūr ≃, Īrān	128	31.45 N	55.15 E
Shūr ≃, Īrān	128	34.38 N	51.46 E
Shūr ≃, Īrān	128	30.57 N	57.42 E
Shūr ≃, Īrān	128	35.57 N	56.24 E
Shuri	174m	26.13 N	127.43 E
Shurkhua	110	22.15 N	93.38 E
Shurugwi	154	19.40 S	30.00 E
Shūsf	128	31.48 N	60.01 E
Shūsh	128	32.11 N	48.15 E
Shushan	210	43.05 N	73.21 W
Shushan Hu ⊜	98	35.36 N	116.27 E
Shūshtar	128	32.03 N	48.51 E
Shuswap ≃	182	50.50 N	119.00 W
Shuswap Lake ⊜	182	50.57 N	119.15 W
Shuṭab	142	27.08 N	31.14 E
Shutendōji-yama ʌ	96	33.06 N	130.54 E
Shuteye Peak ʌ	226	37.21 N	119.25 W
Shutlingsloe ʌ	262	53.13 N	2.02 W
Shūtō	96	34.05 N	132.05 E
Shuwak	140	14.23 N	35.52 E
Shuwaykah	132	32.20 N	35.02 E
Shuya, Nihon	174m	26.40 N	128.06 E
Shuya			
→ Šuja, Ross.	24	61.55 N	34.12 E
Shuyak Island I	180	58.35 N	152.30 W
Shuyang	98	34.08 N	118.47 E
Shuyūkh Fawqānī	130	36.46 N	38.03 E
Shuzenji	94	34.58 N	138.56 E
Shwangliao			
→ Liaoyuan	89	42.54 N	125.07 E
Shwebo	110	22.34 N	95.42 E
Shwegun	110	17.09 N	97.39 E
Shwegyin	110	17.55 N	96.53 E
Shweli (Longchuan) ≃	102	23.56 N	96.17 E
Shwenyaung	110	20.46 N	96.57 E
Shyamdih	126	23.47 N	86.56 E
Shyok	120	34.11 N	78.08 E
Shyok ≃	120	35.13 N	75.53 E
Shypuvate	78	49.56 N	37.24 E
Shyrmivka	78	49.34 N	29.06 E
Shyroke, Ukr.	78	47.41 N	33.14 E
Shyroke, Ukr.	78	48.08 N	34.49 E
Shyrokolanivka	78	47.10 N	31.24 E
Shyrokyne	83	47.06 N	37.49 E
Shyryaeve	78	47.23 N	30.13 E
Shyshaky	78	49.53 N	34.00 E
Si ≃	98	35.11 N	116.42 E
Sia	164	6.49 S	134.19 E
Siabu	114	1.01 N	99.29 E
Siachen Glacier ⊓	123	35.30 N	77.00 E
Siagne ≃	62	43.32 N	6.57 E
Siāhān Range ʌʌ	128	27.25 N	64.30 E
Sīāh Kūh, Kavīr-e ≚	128	32.40 N	53.52 E
Sīāh Kūh, Selseleh-ye ʌʌ	128	34.00 N	64.00 E
Siak ≃	114	1.13 N	102.09 E
Siak Kecil ≃	114	1.16 N	102.08 E
Siak Sri Indrapura	114	0.46 N	102.04 E
Sialang	114	1.31 N	99.27 E
Sialejevskaja P'atina	80	53.49 N	44.32 E
Siālkot	123	32.30 N	74.31 E
Sialsūk	120	23.24 N	92.45 E
Siam			
→ Thailand □[1]	110	15.00 N	100.00 E
Siam, Gulf of			
→ Thailand, Gulf of c	110	10.00 N	101.00 E
Siamanna	71	39.55 N	8.46 E
Sian			
→ Xi'an, Zhg.	102	34.15 N	108.52 E
Si'an, Zhg.	106	30.54 N	119.39 E
Siangtan			
→ Xiangtan	100	27.51 N	112.54 E
Sianhala	150	10.03 N	6.51 W
Sianów	30	54.15 N	16.16 E
Siantan, Pulau I	112	3.10 N	106.15 E
Sianzhuang	100	33.05 N	119.13 E
Siapa ≃	246	2.07 N	66.28 W
Siargao Island I	116	9.53 N	126.02 E
Siari	123	34.56 N	76.44 E
Siasconset	207	41.15 N	69.58 W
Siasi	116	5.33 N	120.49 E
Siasi Island I	116	5.33 N	120.51 E
Šiaškotan, ostrov I	74	48.49 N	154.06 E
Siátista	38	40.16 N	21.33 E
Siaton	116	9.04 N	123.02 E
Siaton ≃	116	9.02 N	123.02 E
Siaton Point ≻	116	9.03 N	123.01 E
Siau, Pulau I	112	2.42 N	125.24 E
Siaugues-Saint-Romain	62	45.06 N	3.38 E
Šiauliai	76	55.56 N	23.19 E
Sibago Island I	116	6.45 N	122.24 E
Sibā'ī, Jabal as- ʌ	140	25.43 N	34.09 E
Sibaj	86	52.42 N	58.39 E
Sibalom	116	10.47 N	122.01 E
Sibanicú	240p	21.14 N	77.31 W
Sibao	100	25.55 N	116.42 E
Sibari	68	39.45 N	16.27 E
Sibari, Piana di ≚	68	39.45 N	16.25 E
Sibasa	156	22.53 S	30.33 E
Sibati	86	47.12 N	88.15 E
Sibayi ⊜	158	27.20 S	32.40 E
Sibay Island I	116	11.51 N	121.29 E
Sibbald	184	51.23 N	110.09 W
Sibbald Point Provincial Park ♦	212	44.19 N	79.19 W
Šibbe	85	39.53 N	72.05 E
Sibbo	26	60.22 N	25.16 E
Şibchar	126	23.21 N	90.09 E
Šibenik	36	43.44 N	15.54 E
Siberia			
→ Sibir' ◆[1]	74	65.00 N	110.00 E

Symbols in the index entries represent the broad categories identified in the key at the right. Symbols with superior numbers (ʌʌ[1]) identify subcategories (see complete key on page *I · 1).*

Symbole im Register stellen die rechts im Schlüssel erklärten Kategorien dar. Symbole mit hochgestellten Ziffern (ʌʌ[1]) bezeichnen Unterabteilungen einer Kategorie (vgl. vollständiger Schlüssel auf Seite *I · 1).*

Los símbolos incluídos en el texto del índice representan las grandes categorías identificadas con la clave a la derecha. Los símbolos con numeros en su parte superior (ʌʌ[1]) identifican las subcategorías (véase la clave completa en la página *I · 1).*

Les symboles de l'index représentent les catégories indiquées dans la légende à droite. Les symboles suivis d'un indice (ʌʌ[1]) représentent des sous-catégories (voir légende complète à la page *I · 1).*

Os símbolos incluídos no texto do índice representam as grandes categorias identificadas com a chave à direita. Os símbolos com números em sua parte superior (ʌʌ[1]) identificam as subcategorias (veja-se a chave completa à página *I · 1).*

ʌ Mountain	Berg	Montaña	Montagne	Montanha
ʌʌ Mountains	Gebirge	Montañas	Montagnes	Montanhas
)(Pass	Paß	Paso	Col	Passo
V Valley, Canyon	Tal, Cañon	Valle, Cañón	Vallée, Canyon	Vale, Canhão
≚ Plain	Ebene	Llano	Plaine	Planície
≻ Cape	Kap	Cabo	Cap	Cabo
I Island	Insel	Isla	Île	Ilha
II Islands	Inseln	Islas	Îles	Ilhas
⊥ Other Topographic Features	Andere Topographische Objekte	Otros Elementos Topográficos	Autres données topographiques	Outros acidentes topográficos

Sibe-Sing *I* · *163*

ESPAÑOL

Nombre	Página	Lat.°′	Long.°′ W = Oeste
Siberia Occidental, Llanura de → Zapadno-Sibirskaja ravnina ≚	72	60.00 N	75.00 E
Sibérie Occidental, Dépression de la → Zapadno-Sibirskaja ravnina ≚	72	60.00 N	75.00 E
Siberut, Pulau I	108	1.20 S	98.55 E
Sibi	120	29.33 N	67.53 E
Sibiči	89	46.04 N	135.22 E
Sibidiri	164	9.00 S	142.15 E
Sibigo	114	2.51 N	95.55 E
Sibillini, Monti ⋏	66	42.54 N	13.13 E
Sibir' (Siberia) ◆[1]	74	65.00 N	110.00 E
Sibir'akova, ostrov I	74	72.50 N	79.00 E
Sibircevo	89	44.12 N	132.26 E
Sibiti	152	3.41 S	13.21 E
Sibiti ≃	154	3.49 S	34.46 E
Sibiu	38	45.48 N	24.09 E
Sibiu □[6]	38	46.00 N	24.15 E
Sible Hedingham	42	51.58 N	0.35 E
Sibley, Il., U.S.	216	40.35 N	88.23 W
Sibley, Ia., U.S.	198	43.23 N	95.45 W
Sibley, La., U.S.	194	32.33 N	93.18 W
Sibley, Ms., U.S.	194	31.22 N	91.23 W
Sibley Peninsula ›[1]	190	48.25 N	88.45 W
Sibley Provincial Park ♦	190	48.25 N	88.49 W
Siboa	112	0.30 N	120.02 E
Sibochi	107	28.50 N	104.32 E
Sibolga	114	1.45 N	98.48 E
Siborang	114	1.08 N	99.26 E
Siborongborong	114	2.13 N	98.59 E
Sibpur, Bngl.	124	24.02 N	90.44 E
Sibpur, India	272b	22.24 N	88.33 E
Sibpur, India	272b	22.34 N	88.19 E
Sibsa ≃[1]	126	22.01 N	89.30 E
Sibsāgar	120	26.59 N	94.39 E
Sibu	112	2.18 N	111.49 E
Sibu, Pulau I	114	2.13 N	104.04 E
Sibuatan, Gunung ∧	114	2.56 N	98.24 E
Sibuguey ≃	116	7.38 N	122.48 E
Sibuguey Bay ⊂	116	7.30 N	122.40 E
Sibut	152	5.44 N	19.05 E
Sibuti	112	4.03 N	113.48 E
Sibutu Island I	112	4.46 N	119.29 E
Sibutu Passage ʮ	112	4.50 N	119.35 E
Sibuyan Island I	116	12.25 N	122.34 E
Sibuyan Sea ⊤[2]	116	12.50 N	122.40 E
Siby	150	12.23 N	8.20 W
Sibyŏn	98	38.19 N	126.41 E
Sicamous	182	50.50 N	119.00 W
Sicapoo, Mount ∧	116	18.01 N	120.56 E
Siccus ≃	166	31.26 S	139.30 E
Sichakou	98	41.39 N	116.26 E
Šichany	80	52.07 N	47.13 E
Sichifulo ≃	154	17.26 S	25.02 E
Si Chon	110	9.00 N	99.54 E
Sichote-Alin' ⋏	89	48.00 N	138.00 E
Sichote-Alinskij zapovednik ♦	89	45.15 N	136.15 E
Šichtovo	76	55.43 N	32.18 E
Sichuan (Szechwan) □[4]	102	31.00 N	105.00 E
Sichuan Pendi ≚[1]	102	30.00 N	105.00 E
Sichuanzhai	102	23.02 N	101.44 E
Sicié, Cap ›	62	43.03 N	5.51 E
Sicignano degli Alburni	68	40.34 N	15.18 E
Sicilia □[4]	70	37.30 N	14.00 E
Sicilia (Sicily) I	70	37.30 N	14.00 E
Sicilia, Isla de → Sicilia I	70	37.30 N	14.00 E
Sicily → Sicilia I	70	37.30 N	14.00 E
Sicily, Strait of ʮ	36	37.20 N	11.20 E
Sicily Island	194	31.50 N	91.39 W
Sicklerville	208	39.43 N	74.58 W
Sickte	54	52.13 N	10.38 E
Sicogon Island I	116	11.27 N	123.16 E
Sico Tinto ≃	236	15.58 N	84.58 W
Sicuani	248	14.16 S	71.13 W
Siculiana	70	37.20 N	13.25 E
Sicun	106	31.55 N	119.18 E
Šid	38	45.08 N	19.13 E
Sīdah, Qārat ∧[2]	142	30.16 N	29.58 E
Sidamo □[4]	144	5.00 N	39.00 E
Sidao	271a	39.51 N	116.26 E
Sidaohe	105	40.24 N	117.17 E
Sidareja	115a	7.29 S	108.47 E
Sidas	112	0.24 N	109.46 E
Sidcup ◆[8]	260	51.25 N	0.06 E
Siddeburen	52	53.15 N	6.52 E
Siddhapur	120	23.55 N	72.23 E
Siddinghausen	263	51.32 N	7.48 E
Siddington	262	53.14 N	2.14 W
Siddipet	122	18.06 N	78.51 E
Sideia Island I	164	10.35 S	150.50 E
Sidel'kino	80	54.32 N	51.08 E
Sidéradougou	150	10.40 N	4.15 W
Siderno	68	38.16 N	16.18 E
Siderópolis	252	28.35 S	49.26 W
Šiderti ≃, Kaz.	80	50.10 N	52.20 E
Šiderti ≃, Kaz.	86	52.32 N	74.50 E
Sidhauli	124	27.17 N	80.50 E
Sídheros, Ákra ›	38	35.19 N	26.19 E
Sidhi	124	24.25 N	81.53 E
Sidhirókastron	38	41.14 N	23.22 E
Sīdī 'Abd ar-Raḥmān	140	30.58 N	29.44 E
Sidi Aïch	34	36.37 N	4.42 E
Sidi Aïssa	148	35.53 N	3.48 E
Sidi Akacha	34	36.28 N	1.18 E
Sidi Ali	34	36.06 N	0.25 E
Sidi Ali, Oued V	148	34.07 N	2.05 W
Sidi Ali Ben Nasrallah	36	35.15 N	9.50 E
Sīdī Barrānī	140	31.36 N	25.55 E
Sidi bel Abbès	148	35.13 N	0.10 W
Sidi Bennour	148	32.30 N	8.30 W
Sidi Bou Zid	148	35.02 N	9.30 E
Sidi Daoud	36	37.00 N	10.55 E
Sidi el Hani, Sebkhet ⊜	36	35.33 N	10.25 E
Sīdī Ghāzī	142	31.12 N	31.03 E
Sīdī Ḥunaysh	140	31.10 N	27.37 E
Sidi Ifni	148	29.24 N	10.12 W
Sidi Kacem	148	34.15 N	5.39 W
Sidikalang	114	2.45 N	98.19 E
Sidimo	144	2.27 N	41.58 E
Sidi Mohammed Ben Ali	34	36.09 N	0.51 E
Sidi Moussa, Oued V	148	26.58 N	3.54 E
Sidi Okba	148	34.48 N	5.54 E
Sīdī Sālim	142	31.17 N	30.48 E
Sidi Slimane	148	34.15 N	5.49 W
Sidi Smaïl	148	32.49 N	8.30 W
Sidlaghatta	122	13.23 N	77.52 E
Sidlaw Hills ⋏[2]	46	56.30 N	3.10 W
Sidley, Mount ∧	9	77.02 S	126.00 W
Sidli	124	26.33 N	90.28 E
Sidman	214	40.20 N	78.45 W
Sidmouth	42	50.41 N	3.15 W
Sidnaw	190	46.30 N	88.42 W
Sidney, B.C., Can.	224	48.39 N	123.24 W
Sidney, Il., U.S.	194	40.01 N	88.04 W
Sidney, In., U.S.	216	41.06 N	85.45 W
Sidney, Ia., U.S.	198	40.44 N	95.38 W
Sidney, Mt., U.S.	198	47.43 N	104.09 W
Sidney, Ne., U.S.	198	41.08 N	102.58 W
Sidney, N.Y., U.S.	210	42.18 N	75.23 W
Sidney, Oh., U.S.	216	40.17 N	84.09 W
Sidney Center	210	42.17 N	75.15 W
Sidney Island I	224	48.37 N	123.18 W
Sidney Lanier, Lake ⊜[1]	192	34.15 N	83.57 W
Sido	150	11.40 N	7.36 W
Sidoan	112	0.16 N	120.12 E

FRANÇAIS

Nom	Page	Lat.°′	Long.°′ W = Ouest
Sidoarjo	115a	7.27 S	112.43 E
Sidon → Şaydā, Lubnān	132	33.33 N	35.22 E
Sidon, Ms., U.S.	194	33.24 N	90.12 W
Sidorovo	76	58.48 N	40.58 E
Sidory	80	50.08 N	43.19 E
Sidr, Ra's as- ›	142	29.36 N	32.40 E
Sidr, Wādī V	142	29.40 N	32.41 E
Sidra, Gulf of → Surt, Khalīj ⊂	146	31.30 N	18.00 E
Sidrolândia	255	20.55 S	54.58 W
Sidu, Zhg.	100	23.48 N	117.18 E
Sidu, Zhg.	100	24.12 N	115.15 E
Siduan	106	30.59 N	121.48 E
Siebengebirge ⋏[2]	56	50.40 N	7.14 E
Siebenlehn	54	51.01 N	13.18 E
Sieber	52	51.42 N	10.25 E
Siebnen	58	47.11 N	8.54 E
Siedenbollentin	54	53.44 N	13.23 E
Siedenburg	52	52.41 N	8.56 E
Siedlce	30	52.11 N	22.16 E
Siedlce □[4]	30	52.15 N	22.00 E
Sieg ≃	56	50.45 N	7.05 E
Siegburg	56	50.47 N	7.12 E
Siegen	56	50.52 N	8.02 E
Siegenburg	60	48.45 N	11.51 E
Siegendorf im Burgenland	61	47.47 N	16.33 E
Siegenfeld	264b	48.02 N	16.10 E
Sieghartskirchen	61	48.15 N	16.01 E
Siegsdorf	64	47.46 N	12.39 E
Sielbeck	54	54.11 N	10.37 E
Sielenbach	60	48.24 N	11.10 E
Sielow	54	51.50 N	14.22 E
Siemens, Cape ›	164	1.21 S	149.34 E
Siemensstadt ◆[8]	264a	52.32 N	13.17 E
Siemianowice Śląskie	30	50.19 N	19.01 E
Siemiatycze	30	52.26 N	22.53 E
Siĕmpang	110	14.07 N	106.23 E
Siĕmréab	110	13.22 N	103.51 E
Siems-Dänischburg ◆[8]	54	53.55 N	10.44 E
Siena	66	43.19 N	11.21 E
Siena □[4]	66	43.13 N	11.24 E
Sieniawa	30	50.11 N	22.36 E
Sienna → Siena	66	43.19 N	11.21 E
Sienyang → Xianyang	102	34.22 N	108.42 E
Sieradz	30	51.36 N	18.45 E
Sieradz □[4]	30	51.40 N	18.45 E
Sieraków	30	52.39 N	16.04 E
Sierck-les-Bains	56	49.26 N	6.21 E
Sierksdorf	54	54.04 N	10.46 E
Sierning	61	48.03 N	14.19 E
Sierpc	30	52.52 N	19.41 E
Si'erpu	104	40.47 N	120.41 E
Sierra □[6]	226	39.30 N	120.30 W
Sierra Blanca	200	31.11 N	105.21 W
Sierra Blanca Peak ∧	200	33.23 N	105.48 W
Sierra-Bullones	116	9.51 N	124.20 E
Sierra Chica	252	36.50 S	60.13 W
Sierra City	226	39.33 N	120.37 W
Sierra Colorada	254	40.35 S	67.48 W
Sierra de Agua	232	17.32 N	88.54 W
Sierra Gorda	252	22.54 S	69.19 W
Sierra Leona → Sierra Leone □[1]	150	8.30 N	11.30 W
Sierra Leone □[1], Afr.	134	8.30 N	11.30 W
Sierra Leone □[1], Afr.	150	8.30 N	11.30 W
Sierra Leone Basin ✢[1]	10	5.00 N	17.00 W
Sierra Leone Rise ✢[3]	10	5.30 N	21.00 W
Sierra Madre	228	34.09 N	118.03 W
Sierra Mojada	196	27.17 N	103.42 W
Sierra Nevada, Parque Nacional ♦	246	8.36 N	70.50 W
Sierra Peak ∧	280	33.51 N	117.39 W
Sierra San Pedro Mártir, Parque Nacional ♦	204	31.00 N	115.30 W
Sierras Bayas	252	36.57 S	60.09 W
Sierraville	226	39.35 N	120.21 W
Sierra Vista	200	31.33 N	110.18 W
Sierre	58	46.18 N	7.32 E
Siersleben	54	51.36 N	11.32 E
Siesta Key	220	27.19 N	82.34 W
Siesta Key I	220	27.16 N	82.33 W
Siete Puntas ≃	252	23.34 S	57.20 W
Siethen	264a	52.17 N	13.13 E
Siethener See ⊜	264a	52.17 N	13.12 E
Sietow	54	53.26 N	12.35 E
Sieve ≃	66	43.46 N	11.26 E
Sievering ◆[8]	264b	48.15 N	16.20 E
Siezenheim	64	47.48 N	12.59 E
Sifahandra	114	1.30 N	97.21 E
Sifangtai, Zhg.	89	46.55 N	127.00 E
Sifangtai, Zhg.	104	41.33 N	121.19 E
Sifangtai, Zhg.	104	41.02 N	122.46 E
Sifangtai, Zhg.	104	41.35 N	122.57 E
Sifen	100	27.32 N	113.30 E
Sifeni	144	12.16 N	40.21 E
Sifentoudun	106	32.18 N	121.21 E
Siffu ≃	116	17.12 N	121.48 E
Sifié	150	7.59 N	6.55 W
Sífnos I	38	36.59 N	24.40 E
Sifón Villanueva	196	27.17 N	100.17 W
Sifton	184	51.21 N	100.07 W
Sig, Alg.	34	35.32 N	0.11 W
Sig, Ross.	24	65.35 N	34.13 E
Si Galangang	114	1.15 N	99.20 E
Šigali	80	55.33 N	48.02 E
Sigean	32	43.02 N	2.59 E
Sigel	214	41.17 N	79.07 W
Sigep	110	1.02 S	98.49 E
Siggebohyttan	40	59.37 N	15.01 E
Siggelkow	54	53.23 N	11.56 E
Sighetu Marmației	38	47.56 N	23.54 E
Sighișoara	38	46.13 N	24.48 E
Sighty Crag ∧	44	55.07 N	2.37 W
Sigillo	66	43.20 N	12.44 E
Sigiriya	122	7.57 N	80.45 E
Siglan	74	59.02 N	152.25 E
Siglerville	208	40.44 N	77.31 W
Sigli	114	5.23 N	95.57 E
Sigli, Cap ›	34	36.54 N	4.46 E
Sigloy	50	47.50 N	2.14 E
Siglufjörður	24a	66.10 N	18.56 W
Sigmaringen	58	48.05 N	9.13 E
Sigmaringendorf	58	48.04 N	9.15 E
Signa	66	43.47 N	11.05 E
Signachi	84	41.37 N	45.54 E
Signalberg ∧	60	49.28 N	12.32 E
Signal Hill, Ca., U.S.	280	33.47 N	118.09 W
Signal Hill, Il., U.S.	219	38.34 N	90.05 W
Signal Hill National Historic Park ♦	186	47.35 N	52.40 W
Signal Mountain	194	35.07 N	85.20 W
Signal Mountain ∧	188	44.12 N	72.20 W
Signal Peak ∧	200	37.19 N	113.29 W
Signau	58	46.55 N	7.43 E
Signes	62	43.18 N	5.52 E
Signy ʊ[3]	9	60.43 S	45.36 W
Signy-l'Abbaye	50	49.42 N	4.25 E
Signy-Le-Petit	50	49.54 N	4.17 E
Šigony	80	53.23 N	48.42 E
Sigourney	190	41.20 N	92.12 W
Sigre ≃	236	15.49 N	84.38 W
Sigriswil	58	46.43 N	7.42 E
Sígsig	246	3.01 S	78.45 W
Sigtuna	40	59.37 N	17.43 E
Siguanea, Ensenada de la ⊂	240p	21.38 N	83.05 W
Siguatepeque	236	14.32 N	87.49 W
Siguel ≃	116	5.58 N	125.06 E
Sigüenza	34	41.04 N	2.38 W
Sigües	34	42.38 N	1.00 W
Siguiri	150	11.25 N	9.10 W
Sigulda	76	57.09 N	24.51 E

PORTUGUÊS

Nome	Página	Lat.°′	Long.°′ W = Oeste
Sigurd	200	38.50 N	111.58 W
Siguri Falls ∟	154	8.31 S	37.23 E
Sihabuhabu, Dolok ∧	114	2.10 N	99.21 E
Sihai	105	40.33 N	116.24 E
Sihala → Sri Lanka □[1]	122	7.00 N	81.00 E
Sihanoukville → Kâmpóng Saôm	110	10.38 N	103.30 E
Sihecun	105	39.56 N	117.07 E
Sihepeng	114	1.06 N	99.27 E
Sihl ≃	58	47.23 N	8.32 E
Sihlepu	158	27.42 S	32.06 E
Sihlsee ⊜	58	47.07 N	8.47 E
Sihong	100	33.28 N	118.11 E
Sihor	120	21.42 N	71.58 E
Sihorā	124	23.29 N	80.07 E
Sihu	98	34.38 N	117.59 E
Sihuas	248	8.34 S	77.37 W
Sihuas ≃	248	16.37 S	72.19 W
Sihui	102	23.19 N	112.40 E
Sihŭng ◆[8]	271b	37.28 N	126.54 E
Siikajoki ≃	26	64.50 N	24.44 E
Siilinjärvi	26	63.05 N	27.40 E
Si'īr	132	31.35 N	35.09 E
Siirt	130	37.56 N	41.57 E
Siirt □[4]	128	38.00 N	42.00 E
Sija	24	63.38 N	41.38 E
Sijā ≃	124	29.08 N	81.35 E
Sijbekarspel	52	52.43 N	4.59 E
Sijiaba	106	32.02 N	121.18 E
Sijianfang	104	42.29 N	122.17 E
Sijiao Shan I	100	30.41 N	122.28 E
Sijiazi	98	41.47 N	120.06 E
Sijing	106	31.07 N	121.16 E
Sijunjung	112	0.42 S	100.58 E
Sijupu	107	30.02 N	106.18 E
Sik	114	5.49 N	100.44 E
Sika	115b	8.45 S	122.12 E
Sikalongo	154	16.46 S	27.07 E
Sikandarābād	124	28.27 N	77.42 E
Sikandarpur, India	272a	28.42 N	77.21 E
Sikandarpur, India	272b	22.57 N	88.12 E
Sikandra	124	24.57 N	86.02 E
Sikandra Rao	124	27.42 N	78.24 E
Sikanni Chief ≃	176	58.20 N	121.50 W
Sikao	110	7.34 N	99.21 E
Sīkar	120	27.37 N	75.09 E
Sikarpur	272b	22.36 N	88.32 E
Sikasso	150	11.19 N	5.40 W
Sikasso □[4]	150	10.55 N	7.00 W
Sikelenge	152	14.50 S	24.14 E
Sikeli	112	5.16 S	121.48 E
Sikensi	150	5.40 N	4.34 W
Sikeshu	86	44.25 N	84.14 E
Sikeston	194	36.52 N	89.35 W
Sikfors	40	59.48 N	14.35 E
Si Khiu	110	14.53 N	101.44 E
Sikiá	38	40.02 N	23.56 E
Sikiang → Xi ≃	102	22.25 N	113.23 E
Sikijang	114	4.22 N	98.02 E
Siking → Xi'an	102	34.15 N	108.52 E
Síkinos	38	36.39 N	25.06 E
Síkinos I	38	36.39 N	25.06 E
Sikión ⊥	38	37.59 N	22.44 E
Sikkim □[3]	124	27.35 N	88.35 E
Siklós ⊥	30	45.55 N	18.25 E
Sikonge	154	5.38 S	32.46 E
Sikosi	156	17.59 S	23.19 E
Šikotan, ostrov (Shikotan-tō) I	92a	43.47 N	146.45 E
Sikrod	272a	28.43 N	77.11 E
Sikt'ach	74	69.55 N	125.02 E
Sikuati	112	6.53 N	116.40 E
Sikutu	112	0.53 N	120.37 E
Sil'	83	48.43 N	38.02 E
Sil ≃	34	42.27 N	7.43 W
Šila	86	56.33 N	93.02 E
Silacayoapan	234	17.30 N	98.09 W
Sila Grande ⋏	68	39.22 N	16.30 E
Sila Greca ⋏	68	39.30 N	16.30 E
Silai ≃	126	22.41 N	87.46 E
Silalahi	114	2.48 N	98.32 E
Šilalė	76	55.28 N	22.12 E
Silam, Gunong ∧	116	4.58 N	118.10 E
Silāmpur ◆[8]	272a	28.40 N	77.16 E
Silandro (Schlanders)	64	46.38 N	10.46 E
Silang	116	14.14 N	120.58 E
Silangcheng	98	42.19 N	115.43 E
Silanus	71	40.17 N	8.53 E
Silao	234	20.56 N	101.26 W
Sila Piccola ⋏	68	39.05 N	16.35 E
Silas	194	31.45 N	88.19 W
Silat	112	0.21 N	111.47 E
Sīlat az-Zahr	132	32.19 N	35.11 E
Silau ≃	114	2.58 N	99.48 E
Silaut	112	2.22 S	101.08 E
Silaw Aihagam, Gunung ∧	114	5.25 N	95.40 E
Silay	116	10.48 N	122.58 E
Silay, Mount ∧	116	10.47 N	123.14 E
Silba	36	44.23 N	14.42 E
Silbertal	58	47.05 N	9.59 E
Silchar	120	24.49 N	92.48 E
Silda, India	126	22.37 N	86.49 E
Sil'da, Ross.	86	51.46 N	59.45 E
Şile	130	41.11 N	29.36 E
Sile ≃	64	45.33 N	12.27 E
Sileby	42	52.43 N	1.06 W
Šilega	24	64.03 N	44.01 E
Silenrieux	50	50.14 N	4.24 E
Silent Lake ⊜	212	44.55 N	78.04 W
Silent Lake Provincial Park ♦	212	44.54 N	78.05 W
Siler City	192	35.43 N	79.27 W
Sileru ≃	122	17.47 N	81.24 E
Silesia □[9]	30	51.00 N	16.45 E
Silet	148	22.44 N	4.37 E
Sileti ≃	86	53.06 N	73.22 E
Siletiteniz, ozero ⊜	86	53.15 N	73.15 E
Siletz	202	44.43 N	123.55 W
Siletz ≃	202	44.54 N	124.00 W
Silex	219	39.07 N	91.03 W
Silgaḍhī	124	29.16 N	80.59 E
Silghāt	120	26.37 N	92.56 E
Silhouette I	138	4.29 S	55.14 E
Siliana	148	36.05 N	9.22 E
Siliana, Oued ≃	36	36.33 N	9.25 E
Silifke	130	36.22 N	33.56 E
Silijiang	105	39.43 N	117.28 E
Šilikti	86	47.10 N	84.32 E
Silingan, Mount ∧	116	7.46 N	122.30 E
Siling Co ⊜	120	31.50 N	89.00 E
Siliqua	71	39.18 N	8.48 E
Silistra	38	44.07 N	27.16 E
Silivri	130	41.04 N	28.15 E
Siljak ∧	38	43.45 N	21.50 E
Siljan ⊜	26	60.50 N	14.45 E
Siljansnäs	26	60.45 N	14.42 E
Šilka	88	51.51 N	116.02 E
Šilka ≃	74	53.22 N	121.32 E
Silkāripāra	126	24.14 N	87.28 E
Silkeborg	41	56.10 N	9.34 E
Silkworth	210	41.16 N	76.05 W
Sill ≃	64	47.16 N	11.25 E
Sillamäe	76	59.24 N	27.45 E
Sillānwāli	123	31.50 N	72.33 E
Sillaro ≃	64	44.34 N	11.51 E
Sille	130	37.56 N	32.26 E
Sillem Island I	176	70.55 N	71.30 W
Sillen ⊜	40	58.59 N	17.22 E
Sillenstede	52	53.34 N	7.59 E
Sillery, P.Q., Can.	206	46.46 N	71.15 W
Sillery, Fr.	50	49.12 N	4.08 E
Silli	150	11.36 N	2.30 W
Sillian	64	46.45 N	12.25 E
Sillil	144	10.59 N	43.26 E
Sillon de Talbert ›[1]	32	48.53 N	3.05 W
Silloth	44	54.52 N	3.23 W
Sillustani ⊥	248	15.45 S	70.05 W
Silly-le-Long	261	49.06 N	2.48 E
Šil'naja Balka	80	50.34 N	49.01 E
Silnice	60	48.54 N	13.44 E
Siloam Springs	194	36.11 N	94.32 W
Siloam Springs State Park ♦	219	39.53 N	90.54 W
Silogui	110	1.14 S	99.00 E
Šiloviči	76	55.24 N	32.33 E
Šilovka	80	54.03 N	48.40 E
Šilovo, Ross.	76	55.00 N	33.46 E
Šilovo, Ross.	80	54.19 N	40.53 E
Silowana Plains ≚	152	17.00 S	23.15 E
Silphuh	126	23.44 N	86.22 E
Silsbee	194	30.20 N	94.10 W
Silsby Lake ⊜	184	55.29 N	95.46 W
Silschede	263	51.21 N	7.19 E
Silsden	44	53.55 N	1.55 W
Sils im Engadin	58	46.22 N	9.46 E
Silton	184	50.48 N	104.55 W
Siluas	112	1.17 N	109.51 E
Siluko	150	6.31 N	5.09 E
Šilutė	76	55.21 N	21.29 E
Silvacane, Abbaye de ʊ[1]	62	43.44 N	5.20 E
Silvan (Miyafarkin)	130	38.08 N	41.01 E
Silvana	224	48.12 N	122.15 W
Sīlvāneh	128	37.25 N	44.51 E
Silvânia	255	16.42 S	48.38 W
Silvano d'Orba	62	44.41 N	8.40 E
Silvan Reservoir ⊜[1]	169	37.50 S	145.25 E
Silvaplana	58	46.26 N	9.47 E
Silvassa	122	20.17 N	73.00 E
Silveiras	256	22.40 S	44.52 W
Silver	196	32.04 N	100.40 W
Silverado	228	33.45 N	117.35 W
Silver Bank ✢[2]	238	20.30 N	69.45 W
Silver Bank Passage ʮ	238	20.45 N	70.15 W
Silver Bay	190	47.17 N	91.15 W
Silver Bell	200	32.23 N	111.29 W
Silver City, N.M., U.S.	200	32.46 N	108.16 W
Silver City, N.C., U.S.	192	35.00 N	79.12 W
Silver Creek, Ms., U.S.	194	31.36 N	89.59 W
Silver Creek, Ne., U.S.	198	41.18 N	97.39 W
Silver Creek, N.Y., U.S.	214	42.32 N	79.10 W
Silver Creek ≃, Az., U.S.	200	34.44 N	110.02 W
Silver Creek ≃, Ca., U.S.	226	38.47 N	120.35 W
Silver Creek ≃, Ca., U.S.	226	36.36 N	120.41 W
Silver Creek ≃, Il., U.S.	219	38.20 N	89.52 W
Silver Creek ≃, Il., U.S.	278	41.54 N	87.50 W
Silver Creek ≃, In., U.S.	218	39.36 N	84.59 W
Silver Creek ≃, In., U.S.	218	38.17 N	85.47 W
Silver Creek ≃, Ky., U.S.	192	37.48 N	84.30 W
Silver Creek ≃, Mi., U.S.	281	42.06 N	83.17 E
Silver Creek ≃, Or., U.S.	202	43.16 N	119.13 W
Silver Creek ≃, Wa., U.S.	224	46.32 N	121.55 W
Silver Creek, Muddy Fork ≃	218	38.25 N	86.44 W
Silver Creek, South Fork ≃	226	38.49 N	120.27 W
Silverdale, B.C., Can.	224	49.09 N	122.24 W
Silverdale, N.Z.	172	36.37 S	174.40 E
Silverdale, Eng., U.K.	44	54.10 N	2.49 W
Silverdale, Pa., U.S.	208	40.21 N	75.16 W
Silverdale, Wa., U.S.	224	47.38 N	122.41 W
Silverdalen	26	57.32 N	15.44 E
Silverdome ♦	281	42.39 N	83.15 W
Silver End	42	51.51 N	0.37 E
Silver Falls State Park ♦	202	44.48 N	122.50 W
Silverfields	273d	26.07 S	27.49 E
Silver Fork ≃	219	39.06 N	92.21 W
Silver Grove	218	39.02 N	84.23 W
Silver Hill	284c	38.50 N	76.56 W
Silverhope Creek ≃	224	49.18 N	121.27 W
Silver Lake, Ca., U.S.	226	38.38 N	120.07 W
Silver Lake, In., U.S.	216	41.04 N	85.53 W
Silver Lake, Ks., U.S.	198	39.06 N	95.51 W
Silver Lake, Ma., U.S.	207	42.34 N	71.11 W
Silver Lake, Mn., U.S.	190	44.54 N	94.11 W
Silver Lake, Oh., U.S.	214	41.09 N	81.27 W
Silver Lake, Or., U.S.	202	43.07 N	121.02 W
Silverlake, Wa., U.S.	224	46.17 N	122.48 W
Silver Lake, Wi., U.S.	216	42.32 N	88.09 W
Silver Lake ⊜, Ca., U.S.	226	38.39 N	120.07 W
Silver Lake ⊜, De., U.S.	208	39.11 N	75.32 W
Silver Lake ⊜, Ma., U.S.	283	42.01 N	70.48 W
Silver Lake ⊜, N.Y., U.S.	210	42.42 N	78.02 W
Silver Lake ⊜, N.Y., U.S.	276	41.03 N	73.45 W
Silver Lake ⊜, Or., U.S.	202	43.06 N	120.53 W
Silver Lake ⊜, Or., U.S.	202	43.22 N	119.24 W
Silver Lake ⊜, Wa., U.S.	224	46.17 N	122.47 W
Silver Lake ⊜, Wa., U.S.	224	48.58 N	122.04 W
Silver Lake Park ♦	276	41.03 N	73.45 W
Silver Lake Reservoir ⊜[1], Ca., U.S.	280	34.06 N	118.16 W
Silver Lake Reservoir ⊜[1], N.Y., U.S.	276	40.37 N	74.06 W
Silvermine ≃	276	41.08 N	73.26 W
Silver Mine Bay ⊂	271d	22.16 N	114.00 E
Silvermine Brook ≃	276	41.08 N	73.27 W
Silvermine Mountains ⋏	48	52.45 N	8.15 W
Silvermines	48	52.47 N	8.13 W
Silver Mountain ∧	280	34.12 N	117.52 W
Silver Peak ∧	228	33.28 N	118.35 W
Silver Peak Range ⋏	204	37.35 N	117.45 W
Silver Spring, Md., U.S.	208	38.59 N	77.01 W
Silver Spring, Pa., U.S.	208	40.04 N	76.26 W
Silver Springs, Nv., U.S.	226	39.24 N	119.13 W
Silver Springs, N.Y., U.S.	210	42.39 N	78.05 W
Silver Springs State Park ♦	216	41.38 N	88.32 W
Silver Star Mountain ∧	224	48.33 N	120.35 W
Silver Star Provincial Park ♦	182	50.22 N	119.05 W
Silverstone	42	52.05 N	1.02 W
Silver Streams	158	28.20 S	23.33 E
Silverthrone Mountain ∧	182	51.31 N	126.06 W
Silvertip Mountain ∧	202	47.47 N	113.15 W
Silverton, Austl.	166	31.53 S	141.13 E
Silverton, B.C., Can.	182	49.57 N	117.21 W
Silverton, Eng., U.K.	42	50.48 N	3.28 W
Silverton, Co., U.S.	200	37.48 N	107.39 W
Silverton, N.J., U.S.	208	40.00 N	74.08 W
Silverton, Oh., U.S.	218	39.12 N	84.24 W
Silverton, Or., U.S.	224	45.00 N	122.46 W
Silverton, Tx., U.S.	196	34.28 N	101.19 W
Silverwood Lake ⊜[1]	228	34.18 N	117.19 W
Silves	34	37.11 N	8.26 W
Silvi	66	42.34 N	14.05 E
Silvia	246	2.37 N	76.21 W
Silvianópolis	256	22.02 S	45.50 W
Silvícola	164	8.39 S	126.59 E
Silvies ≃	202	43.22 N	118.48 W
Silview	285	39.42 N	75.37 W
Silvolde	52	51.55 N	6.23 E
Silvretta Gruppe ⋏	58	46.50 N	10.10 E
Sim	86	54.59 N	57.41 E
Sim, Cap ›	148	31.23 N	9.51 W
Sima, Comores	157a	12.11 S	44.17 E
Sima, Ross.	80	56.41 N	39.33 E
Simaltala	124	24.43 N	86.33 E
Simanavičy	76	53.05 N	28.38 E
Simanggang	112	1.15 N	111.26 E
Simangumban	114	1.42 N	99.10 E
Simaničy	78	51.53 N	28.04 E
Šimanovsk	89	52.00 N	127.42 E
Simao	102	22.50 N	101.00 E
Simão Dias	250	10.44 S	37.49 W
Simão Pereira	256	21.58 S	43.19 W
Simara Island I	116	12.48 N	122.03 E
Simard, Lac ⊜	190	47.37 N	78.41 W
Simaria Kalān	124	24.04 N	84.56 E
Simatang, Pulau I	112	1.04 N	120.23 E
Simav	130	39.05 N	28.59 E
Simav ≃	130	40.23 N	28.31 E
Simav Gölü ⊜	130	39.09 N	28.55 E
Simaxis	71	39.56 N	8.41 E
Simba, Kenya	154	2.10 S	37.36 E
Simba, Tan.	154	1.44 S	34.13 E
Simba, R.D.C.	152	0.36 N	22.55 E
Simbach	60	48.34 N	12.45 E
Simbach am Inn	60	48.16 N	13.01 E
Simbario	68	38.37 N	16.20 E
Simberi Island I	164	2.40 S	152.00 E
Simbirsk → Uljanovsk	80	54.20 N	48.24 E
Simbo, Tan.	154	4.53 S	29.44 E
Simbo, Tan.	154	4.40 S	33.27 E
Simbo Island I	175e	8.17 S	156.33 E
Simbruini, Monti ⋏	66	41.55 N	13.15 E
Simbu □[5]	164	6.05 S	145.00 E
Simcoe	212	42.50 N	80.18 W
Simcoe □[6]	212	44.25 N	79.50 W
Simcoe, Lake ⊜	212	44.20 N	79.20 W
Simcoe Creek ≃	224	46.22 N	120.36 W
Simcoe Island I	212	44.10 N	76.31 W
Simcoe Point ›	275b	43.49 N	79.01 W
Simdega	124	22.37 N	84.31 E
Simen	104	40.44 N	123.49 E
Simeng	107	29.56 N	103.44 E
Simen Mountains National Park ♦	144	13.08 N	38.15 E
Simenti	150	13.00 N	13.25 W
Simeonovgrad	38	42.02 N	25.50 E
Simeri ≃	68	38.52 N	16.43 E
Simeria	38	45.51 N	23.01 E
Simeto ≃	70	37.24 N	15.06 E
Simeulue, Pulau I	114	2.33 N	96.05 E
Simeyiz	78	44.26 N	34.01 E
Simeykyne	83	48.19 N	39.32 E
Simferopol'	78	44.57 N	34.06 E
Sími	38	36.36 N	27.50 E
Sími I	38	36.35 N	27.52 E
Simi, Arroyo ≃	228	34.16 N	118.39 W
Simiane	62	43.25 N	5.26 E
Simianshan	107	28.49 N	105.09 E
Simikoṭ	124	29.58 N	81.50 E
Similaun ∧	64	46.46 N	10.53 E
Similkameen ≃	182	48.56 N	119.26 W
Simingchang	107	29.02 N	105.45 E
Simiri	150	14.08 N	2.08 E
Simisa Island I	116	5.57 N	121.35 E
Simití	246	7.58 N	73.57 W
Simi Valley	228	34.16 N	118.47 W
Simiyu ≃	154	2.33 S	33.25 E
Simizu → Shimizu	94	35.01 N	138.29 E
Simla, India	272b	22.54 N	88.22 E
Simla, India	272b	22.47 N	88.16 E
Simla, Co., U.S.	198	39.08 N	104.05 W
Simla ◆[8]	272b	22.35 N	88.22 E
Simlāpāl	126	22.55 N	87.05 E
Şimleu Silvaniei	38	47.14 N	22.48 E
Simlipālgarh	126	21.51 N	86.23 E
Simme ≃	58	46.41 N	7.38 E
Simmelsdorf	60	49.36 N	11.21 E
Simmental V	58	46.37 N	7.25 E
Simmerath	56	50.36 N	6.18 E
Simmerberg	58	47.35 N	9.56 E
Simmering ◆[8]	264b	48.11 N	16.25 E
Simmern	56	49.59 N	7.31 E
Simmesport	194	30.59 N	91.48 W
Simmie	184	49.57 N	108.06 W
Simmons Island I	282	38.06 N	121.58 W
Simmons Point ›	282	38.03 N	121.56 W
Simmonswood Moss ◆[3]	262	53.30 N	2.50 W
Simms	202	47.29 N	111.55 W
Simnas	76	54.24 N	23.39 E
Simoca	252	27.16 S	65.21 W
Simões	250	7.36 S	40.49 W
Simojärvi ⊜	26	66.06 N	27.03 E
Simojoki ≃	26	65.37 N	25.03 E
Simojovel	234	17.12 N	92.38 W
Simon, Lac ⊜, P.Q., Can.	206	46.10 N	74.45 W
Simon, Lac ⊜, P.Q., Can.	206	45.58 N	75.05 W
Simón Bolívar, Aeropuerto Internacional ⊠	286c	10.37 N	66.59 W
Simoneti	84	42.14 N	42.52 E
Simonette ≃	182	55.07 N	118.00 W
Simonhouse Lake ⊜	184	54.30 N	101.10 W
Simonicha	80	56.31 N	53.50 E
Simonoseki → Shimonoseki	96	33.57 N	130.57 E
Simonsbath	42	51.09 N	3.45 W
Simonson Brook ≃	276	40.26 N	74.37 W
Simonstone	262	53.48 N	2.20 W
Simonstorp	40	58.47 N	16.09 E
Simon's Town	158	34.14 S	18.26 E
Simonton Lake	216	41.44 N	85.59 W
Simoom Sound	182	50.45 N	126.29 W
Šimorskoje	80	55.19 N	42.02 E
Simpang, Indon.	112	1.16 S	104.05 E
Simpang, Indon.	112	1.03 S	110.06 E
Simpang, Indon.	112	0.09 N	103.15 E
Simpangampat	114	2.55 N	99.43 E
Simpang Empat	114	6.20 N	100.11 E
Simpang-kanan ≃	114	2.21 N	97.51 E
Simpang-kiri ≃	114	2.21 N	97.51 E
Simpang Rengam	114	1.50 N	103.19 E
Simpangtiga	114	2.23 N	99.47 E
Simpangulim	114	5.06 N	97.32 E
Simpele	26	61.26 N	29.22 E
Simplício Mendes	250	7.51 S	41.54 W
Simplon Pass)(	58	46.15 N	8.02 E
Simplon Tunnel ◆[5]	58	46.15 N	8.05 E
Simpnäs	40	59.52 N	19.04 E
Simp'o-ri	98	38.36 N	127.41 E
Simpson, La., U.S.	194	31.14 N	93.00 W
Simpson, Pa., U.S.	210	41.35 N	75.29 W
Simpson ≃	254	45.25 S	72.32 W
Simpson, Isla I	254	45.53 S	73.48 W
Simpson Desert ◆[2]	162	25.00 S	137.00 E
Simpson Desert National Park ♦	162	25.40 S	138.15 E
Simpson Island I	190	48.48 N	87.40 W
Simpson Lake ⊜	180	68.10 N	126.35 W
Simpson Peak ∧	180	59.44 N	131.27 W
Simpson Peninsula ›[1]	176	68.34 N	88.45 W
Simpsons Gap National Park ♦	162	23.40 S	133.45 E
Simpson Strait ʮ	176	68.27 N	97.45 W
Simpsonville, Ky., U.S.	218	38.13 N	85.21 W
Simpsonville, Md., U.S.	208	39.11 N	76.52 W
Simpsonville, S.C., U.S.	192	34.44 N	82.15 W
Simrishamn	26	55.33 N	14.20 E
Sims	216	40.30 N	85.51 W
Simsbury	207	41.52 N	72.48 W
Šimsk	76	58.13 N	30.43 E
Simssee ⊜	64	47.52 N	12.14 E
Simunjan	112	1.23 N	110.45 E
Simurāli	126	23.03 N	88.30 E
Simušir, ostrov I	74	46.58 N	152.02 E
Sīnā' □[4]	142	30.15 N	32.40 E
Sīna ≃	122	17.22 N	75.54 E
Sīnā', Shibh Jazīrat (Sinai Peninsula) ›[1]	140	29.30 N	34.00 E
Sinabang	114	2.29 N	96.23 E
Sinabelkirchen	61	47.06 N	15.50 E
Sinabung, Gunung ∧	114	3.10 N	98.24 E
Sinadhago	144	5.22 N	46.20 E
Sinagra	70	38.05 N	14.51 E
Sinai, Mount ∧, Gren.	241k	12.04 N	61.42 W
Sinai, Mount → Mūsā, Jabal ∧, Miṣr	140	28.32 N	33.59 E
Sinaia	38	45.21 N	25.33 E
Sinai Peninsula → Sīnā', Shibh Jazīrat ›[1]	140	29.30 N	34.00 E
Sin'aja ≃, Europe	76	57.10 N	28.31 E
Sin'aja ≃, Ross.	74	61.06 N	126.50 E
Sinajana	174p	13.28 N	144.45 E
Sinako, Mount ∧	116	7.30 N	125.17 E
Sinaloa □[3]	232	25.00 N	107.30 W
Sinaloa ≃	232	25.18 N	108.30 W
Sinalunga	66	43.12 N	11.44 E
Sinamaica	246	11.05 N	71.51 W
Sinamary ≃	250	5.27 N	53.00 W
Sinan, Tür.	130	37.52 N	41.00 E
Sinan, Zhg.	102	27.54 N	108.18 E
Sinanju	98	39.36 N	125.36 E
Sinanpaşa	130	38.45 N	30.15 E
Sīnarū	142	29.22 N	30.45 E
Sinatle	84	42.28 N	43.04 E
Sin'avka	83	47.17 N	39.17 E
Sīnāwin	146	31.02 N	10.36 E
Sinbad Creek ≃	282	37.35 N	121.53 W
Sinbaungwe	110	19.43 N	95.10 E
Sinbo	110	24.46 N	97.03 E
Sinbokchang	98	41.01 N	128.54 E
Sincan, Tür.	130	39.28 N	37.54 E
Sincan, Tür.	130	39.59 N	32.26 E
Sincé	246	9.15 N	75.09 W
Sincelejo	246	9.18 N	75.24 W
Sinch'ang, C.M.I.K.	98	40.07 N	128.28 E
Sinch'ang, C.M.I.K.	98	40.19 N	125.27 E
Sinch'ŏn	98	38.22 N	125.28 E
Sinch'ŏn-ni	271b	37.27 N	126.48 E
Sinclair	200	41.46 N	107.06 W
Sinclair, Lake ⊜[1]	192	33.11 N	83.16 W
Sinclair, Point ›	162	32.06 S	133.00 E
Sinclair Island I	224	48.37 N	122.40 W
Sinclair Mills	182	54.02 N	121.41 W
Sinclair's Bay ⊂	46	58.30 N	3.07 W
Sinclairville	214	42.15 N	79.15 W
Sind □[4]	120	25.30 N	69.00 E
Sind ≃	124	26.26 N	79.13 E
Sinda	89	48.57 N	136.18 E
Sindal	26	57.28 N	10.13 E
Sindangan	116	8.14 N	123.00 E
Sindangan ≃	116	8.13 N	123.00 E
Sindangan Bay ⊂	116	8.11 N	122.50 E
Sindangan Point ›	116	8.10 N	122.40 E
Sindangbarang	115a	7.27 S	107.08 E
Sindara	152	1.02 S	10.40 E
Sindari	120	25.35 N	71.55 E
Sindelfingen	56	48.42 N	9.00 E
Sindèr	150	14.29 N	1.22 E
Sindhnūr	122	15.47 N	76.46 E
Sindhulī Māńdi	124	27.16 N	85.58 E
Sindi	76	58.24 N	24.40 E
Sindia	71	40.18 N	8.39 E
Sindingale	110	18.17 N	94.25 E
Sındıran	130	39.17 N	32.41 E
Sındırgı	130	39.14 N	28.10 E
Sindiyūn	142	30.15 N	31.12 E
Sin-do I	98	39.48 N	124.14 E
Sindŏk	98	36.47 N	126.10 E
Sindor	24	62.50 N	51.57 E
Sindou	150	10.40 N	5.10 W
Sindri	126	23.45 N	86.42 E
Sind Sāgar Doāb ⋏[1]	123	31.30 N	71.30 E
Sine V	150	14.10 N	16.28 W
Sinegorje	24	59.42 N	50.40 E
Sinegorsk	89	47.10 N	142.30 E
Sinegorskij	78	48.00 N	40.53 E
Šine-Ider	88	48.56 N	99.33 E
Sinekçi	130	40.16 N	27.24 E
Sinekli	130	41.14 N	28.12 E
Sinendé	150	10.21 N	2.23 E
Sinen'kije	80	51.15 N	45.46 E
Sinepuxent Bay ⊂	208	38.16 N	75.09 W
Sines	34	37.57 N	8.52 W
Sines, Cabo de ›	34	37.57 N	8.53 W
Sinewit, Mount ∧	164	4.40 S	152.00 E
Sinez'orki	76	53.02 N	34.26 E
Sinfra	150	6.37 N	5.55 W
Singair	126	23.49 N	90.08 E
Singako	146	9.50 N	19.29 E
Singal	123	36.06 N	73.53 E
Singalamwe	156	17.41 S	23.23 E
Singālila ∧	124	27.13 N	88.01 E
Singālila Range ⋏	124	27.25 N	88.05 E
Singaparna	115a	7.21 S	108.06 E
Singapore, Sing.	114	1.17 N	103.51 E
Singapore, Sing.	271c	1.17 N	103.51 E
Singapore □[1], Asia	108	1.22 N	103.48 E
Singapore □[1], Asia	114	1.22 N	103.48 E
Singapore I	271c	1.23 N	103.48 E
Singapore ≃	271c	1.17 N	103.51 E
Singapore, National University of ʊ[2]	271c	1.18 N	103.46 E
Singapore Station ◆[5]	271c	1.17 N	103.50 E
Singapore Strait ʮ	112	1.15 N	104.00 E
Singapour → Singapore □[1]	114	1.22 N	103.48 E
Singapur → Singapore	114	1.17 N	103.51 E
Singapur → Singapore □[1]	114	1.22 N	103.48 E
Singaraja	115b	8.07 S	115.06 E
Singarka ≃	265a	59.53 N	29.54 E
Singāti	126	22.44 N	89.43 E
Singatoka	175g	18.08 S	177.30 E
Sing Buri	110	14.53 N	100.25 E
Singe	272b	22.57 N	88.26 E
Singen (Hohentwiel)	58	47.46 N	8.50 E
Singer	194	30.39 N	93.24 W
Singhi	126	23.37 N	87.48 E
Singida	154	4.49 S	34.45 E
Singida □[4]	154	5.30 S	34.30 E
Singing, India	102	28.59 N	94.50 E
Singing, India	120	28.53 N	94.47 E
Singing Tower ♦	220	27.57 N	81.34 W
Singkaling Hkāmti	110	26.00 N	95.42 E
Singkang	112	4.08 S	120.01 E
Singkawang	112	0.54 N	109.00 E
Singkep, Pulau I	112	0.30 S	104.25 E
Singkil	114	2.17 N	97.49 E
Singkuang	114	1.03 N	98.56 E
Singleton, Austl.	170	32.34 S	151.10 E
Singleton, Eng., U.K.	42	50.55 N	0.46 W
Singleton, Mount ∧, Austl.	162	29.28 S	117.18 E
Singleton, Mount ∧, Austl.	162	22.00 S	130.49 E

≃	River	Fluß	Río	Rivière	Rio
≍	Canal	Kanal	Canal	Canal	Canal
∟	Waterfall, Rapids	Wasserfall, Stromschnellen	Cascada, Rápidos	Chute d'eau, Rapides	Cascata, Rápidos
ʮ	Strait	Meeresstraße	Estrecho	Détroit	Estreito
⊂	Bay, Gulf	Bucht, Golf	Bahía, Golfo	Baie, Golfe	Baía, Golfo
⊜	Lake, Lakes	See, Seen	Lago, Lagos	Lac, Lacs	Lago, Lagos
≡	Swamp	Sumpf	Pantano	Marais	Pântano
⊓	Ice Features, Glacier	Eis- und Gletscherformen	Accidentes Glaciales	Formes glaciaires	Acidentes glaciares
⊤	Other Hydrographic Features	Andere Hydrographische Objekte	Otros Elementos Hidrográficos	Autres données hydrographiques	Outros acidentes hidrográficos

✢	Submarine Features	Untermeerische Objekte	Accidentes Submarinos	Formes de relief sous-marin	Acidentes submarinos
□	Political Unit	Politische Einheit	Unidad Politica	Entité politique	Unidade política
ʊ	Cultural Institution	Kulturelle Institution	Institución Cultural	Institution culturelle	Instituição cultural
⊥	Historical Site	Historische Stätte	Sitio Histórico	Site historique	Sitio histórico
♦	Recreational Site	Erholungs- und Ferienort	Sitio de Recreo	Centre de loisirs	Area de Lazer
⊠	Airport	Flughafen	Aeropuerto	Aéroport	Aeroporto
■	Military Installation	Militäranlage	Instalación Militar	Installation militaire	Instalação militar
◆	Miscellaneous	Verschiedenes	Misceláneo	Divers	Diversos

Symbols in the index entries represent the broad categories identified in the legend. Symbols with superior numbers (▲[1]) identify subcategories (see complete key on page I · 1).

Symbole im Register stellen die rechts im Schlüssel erklärten Kategorien dar. Symbole mit hochgestellten Ziffern (▲[1]) bezeichnen Unterteilungen einer Kategorie (vgl. vollständiger Schlüssel auf Seite I · 1).

Los símbolos incluídos en el texto del índice representan las grandes categorías identificadas con la clave a la derecha. Símbolos con numeros en su parte superior (▲[1]) identifican las subcategorías (véase la clave completa en la página I · 1).

Os símbolos incluídos no texto do índice representam as grandes categorias identificadas com a chave à direita. Os símbolos com números em sua parte superior (▲[1]) identificam as subcategorias (veja-se a chave completa à página I · 1).

Les symboles de l'index représentent les catégories identifiées dans la légende à droite. Les symboles suivis d'un indice (▲[1]) représentent des sous-catégories (voir légende complète à la page I · 1).

▲ Mountain	Berg	Montaña	Montagne	Montanha
▲ Gebirge	Gebirge	Montañas	Montagnes	Montanhas
⋈ Pass	Paß	Paso	Col	Passo
∨ Valley, Canyon	Tal, Cañon	Valle, Cañón	Vallée, Canyon	Vale, Canhão
≗ Plain	Ebene	Llano	Plaine	Planície
➤ Cape	Kap	Cabo	Cap	Cabo
I Island	Insel	Isla	Île	Ilha
II Islands	Inseln	Islas	Îles	Ilhas
⋆ Other Topographic Features	Andere Topographische Objekte	Otros Elementos Topográficos	Autres données topographiques	Outros acidentes topográficos

ESPAÑOL · FRANÇAIS · PORTUGUÊS

Nombre / Nom / Nome	Página / Page	Lat.°′	Long.°′ W = Oeste / Ouest
Slotermeer ⊜	52	52.55 N	5.40 E
Slough	42	51.31 N	0.36 W
Slough □8	260	51.32 N	0.35 W
Slough Brook ≐	276	40.45 N	74.21 W
Sloughhouse	226	38.30 N	121.12 W
Slovakia □1	22	48.30 N	20.00 E
Slovan	214	40.21 N	80.23 W
Slovechne	78	51.23 N	28.21 E
Slovenia □1, Europe	22	46.15 N	15.10 E
Slovenia (Slovenija) □1, Europe	36	46.15 N	15.10 E
Slovenj Gradec	61	46.31 N	15.05 E
Slovenska Bistrica, Slvn.	36	46.23 N	15.34 E
Slovenska Bistrica, Slvn.	61	46.23 N	15.34 E
Slovenske Gorice ⋏2	61	46.35 N	15.55 E
Slovenské rudohorie ⋏	30	48.45 N	20.00 E
Slovinka	80	58.02 N	43.07 E
Slov'yanhirs'k	83	49.02 N	37.31 E
Slov'yanka	78	48.24 N	36.43 E
Slov'yanoserbs'k	83	48.42 N	38.59 E
Slov'yans'k	83	48.52 N	37.37 E
Słowiński Park Narodowy ♦	30	54.40 N	17.25 E
Słubice	54	52.20 N	14.32 E
Sluč ≐	76	52.08 N	27.31 E
Sluch ≐	78	51.37 N	26.38 E
Sluck	76	53.01 N	27.33 E
Sl'ud'anka	88	51.38 N	103.42 E
Sluderno (Schluderns)	64	46.40 N	10.35 E
Sludy	76	58.52 N	36.52 E
Sluis	52	51.18 N	3.24 E
Sluiskil	52	51.16 N	3.50 E
Šluknov	54	51.00 N	14.27 E
Slunj	36	45.07 N	15.35 E
Słupca	30	52.19 N	17.52 E
Słupia ≐	30	54.35 N	16.50 E
Słupsk (Stolp)	30	54.28 N	17.01 E
Słupsk □4	30	54.10 N	17.15 E
Slurry	156	25.49 S	25.52 E
Šl'uz-Mokr'aki	86	59.17 N	88.50 E
Sly, Oued ≐	34	36.04 N	1.08 E
Smachtino	82	54.51 N	36.25 E
Smackover	194	33.21 N	92.43 W
Smackover Creek ≐	194	33.22 N	92.24 W
Småland □9	26	57.20 N	15.00 E
Smålandsfarvandet ⊔	41	55.05 N	11.20 E
Smålandsstenar	26	57.10 N	13.24 E
Smalininkai	76	55.05 N	22.35 E
Smaljany	76	54.36 N	30.04 E
Smaljavičy	76	54.02 N	28.05 E
Smallbridge	262	53.38 N	2.08 W
Smalleytown	276	40.39 N	74.28 W
Smallwood	210	41.40 N	74.49 W
Smallwood Reservoir ⊜1	176	54.05 N	64.30 W
Smallwood State Park ♦	208	38.33 N	77.12 W
Smara	148	26.44 N	11.41 W
Smarhon'	76	54.29 N	26.24 E
Smartt Syndicate Dam ⊜1	158	30.40 S	23.18 E
Smartville	226	39.12 N	121.18 W
Smeaton	184	53.30 N	104.49 W
Smeaton Bay ⊂	182	55.20 N	130.50 W
Smečno	54	50.10 N	14.03 E
Smedby	40	58.33 N	16.16 E
Smědeč	61	48.56 N	14.09 E
Smederevo	38	44.40 N	20.56 E
Smederevska Palanka	38	44.22 N	20.58 E
Smedjebacken	40	60.08 N	15.25 E
Šmel'ovka	80	54.47 N	49.11 E
Smelt Brook ≐, Ma., U.S.	283	42.13 N	70.58 W
Smelt Brook ≐, Ma., U.S.	283	42.00 N	70.43 W
Smelt Pond ⊜	283	41.58 N	70.43 W
Smeralda, Costa ⩠2	71	41.04 N	9.30 E
Smerwick Harbour ⊂	48	52.12 N	10.24 W
Smethport	214	41.48 N	78.26 W
Smethwick	42	52.30 N	1.58 W
Smicksburg	214	40.52 N	79.10 W
Smidovič	89	48.36 N	133.49 E
Šmidta → Mys Šmidta	180	68.56 N	179.26 W
Šmidta, mys ≻	180	68.56 N	179.30 W
Šmidta, ostrov I	74	81.08 N	90.48 E
Šmidta, poluostrov ≻1	89	54.10 N	142.40 E
Śmigiel	30	52.01 N	16.32 E
Smila	78	49.14 N	31.53 E
Smilavičy	76	53.45 N	28.01 E
Smilde	52	52.57 N	6.27 E
Smile, Ukr.	78	50.55 N	33.36 E
Smile, Ky., U.S.	218	38.15 N	83.29 W
Smiley, Sk., Can.	184	51.37 N	109.29 W
Smiley, Tx., U.S.	222	29.16 N	97.38 W
Smiltene	76	57.26 N	25.56 E
Smirnovo	86	54.31 N	69.25 E
Smirnych	89	49.43 N	142.38 E
Smir-Restinga	34	35.42 N	5.23 W
Smite ≐	44	53.04 N	0.48 W
Smith	182	55.10 N	114.02 W
Smith □6	222	32.20 N	95.15 W
Smith ≐, U.S.	192	36.29 N	79.45 W
Smith ≐, Ca., U.S.	204	41.56 N	124.12 W
Smith ≐, Mt., U.S.	202	47.25 N	111.29 W
Smith ≐, Or., U.S.	202	43.43 N	124.05 W
Smith, Cape ≻	190	45.48 N	81.35 W
Smith Arm ⊂	180	66.15 N	124.00 W
Smith Bay ⊂	180	70.51 N	154.25 W
Smithboro, Il., U.S.	219	38.54 N	89.20 W
Smithboro, N.Y., U.S.	210	42.02 N	76.24 W
Smith Canyon V	198	37.46 N	103.26 W
Smith Center	198	39.46 N	98.47 W
Smith Creek ≐, S.D., U.S.	198	43.58 N	99.20 W
Smith Creek ≐, Wa., U.S.	224	46.45 N	123.53 W
Smithdale	279b	40.14 N	79.48 W
Smithers, B.C., Can.	182	54.47 N	127.10 W
Smithers, W.V., U.S.	188	38.10 N	81.18 W
Smithers Lake ⊜1	222	29.29 N	95.38 W
Smithfield, Austl.	168b	34.41 S	138.41 E
Smithfield, Austl.	274a	33.51 S	150.57 E
Smithfield, On., Can.	212	44.04 N	77.41 W
Smithfield, S. Afr.	158	30.09 S	26.30 E
Smithfield, Eng., U.K.	44	54.59 N	2.52 W
Smithfield, N.C., U.S.	192	35.30 N	78.20 W
Smithfield, Oh., U.S.	214	40.16 N	80.46 W
Smithfield, Pa., U.S.	214	39.48 N	79.48 W
Smithfield, Ut,. U.S.	200	41.50 N	111.49 W
Smithfield, Va., U.S.	208	36.58 N	76.37 W
Smithflat	226	38.44 N	120.45 W
Smith Haven Mall ◆9	276	40.52 N	73.08 W
Smithills Hall ⊥	262	53.36 N	2.27 W
Smith Island I, Ant.	9	62.59 S	62.32 W
Smith Island I, N.C., U.S.	192	33.52 N	77.59 W
Smith Island I, Va., U.S.	208	37.10 N	75.51 W
Smith Island I, Wa., U.S.	224	48.19 N	122.50 W
Smith Island II	208	38.01 N	76.02 W
Smithland	194	37.08 N	88.24 W
Smithmill	214	40.46 N	78.25 W
Smith Mountain ∧	280	34.17 N	117.52 W
Smith Mountain Lake ⊜1	192	37.10 N	79.40 W
Smith Peak ∧	202	48.50 N	116.39 W
Smith Peninsula ≻1	9	74.25 S	61.15 W
Smith Point	222	29.27 N	94.45 W
Smith Point ≻, N.S., Can.	186	45.51 N	63.25 W
Smith Point ≻, Tx., U.S.	222	29.32 N	94.46 W
Smith Point ≻, Va. U.S.	208	37.53 N	76.14 W
Smithport	214	40.50 N	78.52 W
Smith River	204	41.55 N	124.08 W
Smiths	194	32.32 N	85.05 W
Smithsburg	208	39.39 N	77.34 W
Smiths Creek	214	42.55 N	82.36 W
Smiths Falls	212	44.54 N	76.01 W
Smiths Fork ≐	202	41.23 N	110.12 W
Smiths Grove	194	37.03 N	86.12 W
Smiths Mills	276	41.01 N	74.22 W
Smith Sound ⊔	182	51.18 N	127.48 W
Smithton, Austl.	166	40.51 S	145.07 E
Smithton, Il., U.S.	219	38.24 N	89.59 W
Smithton, Mo., U.S.	194	38.40 N	93.05 W
Smithton, Pa., U.S.	279b	40.09 N	79.44 W
Smithtown	210	40.52 N	73.13 W
Smithtown Bay ⊂	276	40.57 N	73.12 W
Smith Valley	218	39.36 N	86.12 W
Smithville, On., Can.	212	43.06 N	79.33 W
Smithville, Ga., U.S.	192	31.54 N	84.15 W
Smithville, In., U.S.	218	39.04 N	86.30 W
Smithville, Ms., U.S.	194	34.04 N	88.23 W
Smithville, Mo., U.S.	194	39.23 N	94.34 W
Smithville, N.J., U.S.	208	39.59 N	74.44 W
Smithville, N.J., U.S.	285	39.29 N	74.27 W
Smithville, Oh., U.S.	214	40.51 N	81.51 W
Smithville, Tn., U.S.	194	35.57 N	85.48 W
Smithville, Tx., U.S.	222	30.00 N	97.09 W
Smithville Flats	210	42.24 N	75.49 W
Smithville Lake ⊜1	194	39.25 N	94.30 W
Smögen	26	58.21 N	11.13 E
Smoke Creek ≐, Mt., U.S.	198	48.18 N	104.41 W
Smoke Creek ≐, N.Y., U.S.	284a	42.49 N	78.52 W
Smoke Creek, South Branch ≐	284a	42.49 N	78.49 W
Smoke Creek Desert ◆2	204	40.30 N	119.40 W
Smoke Lake ⊜	212	45.32 N	78.41 W
Smokeless	214	40.24 N	76.02 W
Smokerun	214	40.48 N	78.26 W
Smoketown	208	40.02 N	76.12 W
Smokey, Cape ≻	186	46.38 N	60.21 W
Smokey Dome ∧	202	43.29 N	114.56 W
Smoky ≐	182	56.10 N	117.21 W
Smoky Bay	162	32.22 S	133.56 E
Smoky Cape ≻	166	30.56 S	153.05 E
Smoky Hill ≐	198	39.03 N	96.48 W
Smoky Hill, North Fork ≐	198	38.55 N	101.17 W
Smoky Lake	182	54.07 N	112.28 W
Smøla I	24	63.24 N	8.00 E
Smol'aninovo	89	43.19 N	132.28 E
Smolensk	76	54.47 N	32.03 E
Smolenskaja vozvyšennost' ⋏1	76	54.30 N	33.00 E
Smolensk Oblast' □4	76	55.00 N	33.00 E
Smolenskoje	86	52.20 N	85.05 E
Smólikas ∧	38	40.06 N	20.52 E
Smoljan	38	41.35 N	24.41 E
Smolny υ	265a	59.57 N	30.24 E
Smoot	200	42.37 N	110.54 W
Smoothstone ≐	184	55.20 N	106.39 W
Smoothstone Lake ⊜	184	54.40 N	106.50 W
Smorodovka	76	57.08 N	29.52 E
Smotrych	78	48.56 N	26.34 E
Smotrych ≐	78	48.34 N	26.38 E
Smuškovoje	80	47.20 N	45.55 E
Smyčka	82	56.04 N	35.56 E
Smygehamn	41	55.21 N	13.22 E
Smygehuk ≻	41	55.21 N	13.23 E
Smyley Island I	9	72.55 S	78.00 W
Smyrna → İzmir, Tür.	130	38.25 N	27.09 E
Smyrna, De., U.S.	208	39.17 N	75.36 W
Smyrna, Ga., U.S.	192	33.53 N	84.30 W
Smyrna, N.Y., U.S.	210	42.41 N	75.34 W
Smyrna, Tn., U.S.	194	35.58 N	86.31 W
Smyrna ≐	208	39.22 N	75.31 W
Smyšl'ajevka	80	53.15 N	50.22 E
Smyth, Canal ⊔	254	52.15 S	73.40 W
Smythe, Mount ∧	176	57.54 N	124.53 W
Smythe Park ♦	275b	43.41 N	79.30 W
Smythesdale	169	37.38 S	143.41 E
Sn'adin	78	52.04 N	28.19 E
Snæfell ∧, Ísland	24a	64.48 N	15.32 W
Snaefell ∧, I. of Man	44	54.16 N	4.27 W
Snæfellsnes ≻1	24a	64.50 N	23.00 W
Snag	180	62.24 N	140.22 W
Snaght, Slieve ∧	48	55.12 N	7.20 W
Snagost'	78	51.21 N	34.54 E
Snahapish ≐	224	47.38 N	124.11 W
Snaith	44	53.41 N	1.02 W
Šn'ajevo	80	52.34 N	46.11 E
Snake ≐, Yk., Can.	180	65.58 N	134.10 W
Snake ≐, U.S.	202	46.12 N	119.02 W
Snake ≐, Ca., U.S.	226	39.07 N	121.43 W
Snake ≐, Mn., U.S.	190	45.49 N	92.46 W
Snake ≐, Mn., U.S.	198	48.26 N	97.07 W
Snake ≐, Ne., U.S.	198	42.47 N	100.48 W
Snake Bight ⊂3	220	25.10 N	80.50 W
Snake Brook ≐	283	42.18 N	71.22 W
Snake Creek ≐, Mt., U.S.	202	48.32 N	108.53 W
Snake Creek ≐, Ne., U.S.	198	42.01 N	102.45 W
Snake Creek ≐, S.D., U.S.	198	44.58 N	98.29 W
Snake Creek, South Fork ≐	198	45.02 N	98.36 W
Snake Creek Canal ≡	220	25.57 N	80.11 W
Snake Indian ≐	182	53.11 N	118.00 W
Snake Range ⋏	204	39.00 N	114.15 W
Snake Rapids ⌊	212	45.14 N	77.20 W
Snake River Plain ≚	202	43.00 N	113.00 W
Snake Valley	169	37.37 S	143.35 E
Snake Valley V	204	39.20 N	113.55 W
Snape	42	52.11 N	1.30 E
Snaptun	41	55.49 N	10.04 E
Snares Islands II	9	48.00 S	166.30 E
Snasahögarna ∧	26	63.13 N	12.21 E
Snay Pôl	110	11.40 N	105.13 E
Sneads	192	30.42 N	84.55 W
Snedsted	26	56.54 N	8.32 E
Sneedville	192	36.31 N	83.13 W
Sneek	52	53.02 N	5.40 E
Sneekermeer ⊜	52	53.02 N	5.45 E
Snee-osh-Beach	224	48.24 N	122.33 W
Sneeuberg ∧	158	32.25 S	19.12 E
Sneeuberg ⋏	158	31.46 S	24.20 E
Snekkersten	41	56.00 N	12.36 E
Snelgrove	275b	43.44 N	79.49 W
Snelling	204	37.31 N	120.26 W
Snettisham	42	52.53 N	0.30 E
Sněžka ∧	30	50.44 N	15.44 E
Snežnaja ≐	88	51.28 N	104.38 E
Snežnik ∧	36	45.35 N	14.27 E
Śniardwy, Jezioro ⊜	30	53.46 N	21.44 E
Snicarte	219	40.07 N	90.14 W
Snicarte Island I	219	40.08 N	90.12 W
Snihurivka	78	47.06 N	32.47 E
Snina	30	48.59 N	22.07 E
Snipe Keys II	220	24.40 N	81.38 W
Snipe Lake ⊜	182	55.07 N	116.46 W
Snizhne	83	48.01 N	38.46 E
Snizort, Loch ⊂	46	57.34 N	6.28 W
Snøde	41	55.05 N	10.55 E
Snodland	42	51.20 N	0.27 E
Snoghøj	41	55.31 N	9.43 E
Snøhetta ∧	26	62.20 N	9.17 E
Snohomish	224	47.54 N	122.05 W
Snohomish □6	224	48.02 N	121.41 W
Snohomish ≐	224	48.01 N	122.13 W
Snønipa ∧	26	61.42 N	6.41 E
Snook	222	30.29 N	96.28 W
Snoqualmie	224	47.31 N	121.49 W
Snoqualmie ≐	224	47.50 N	122.03 W
Snoqualmie, Middle Fork ≐	224	47.31 N	121.46 W
Snoqualmie, North Fork ≐	224	47.31 N	121.46 W
Snoqualmie, South Fork ≐	224	47.31 N	121.46 W
Snoqualmie Falls	224	47.32 N	121.49 W
Snoqualmie Mountain ∧	224	47.27 N	121.25 W
Snoqualmie Pass)(	224	47.25 N	121.25 W
Snøtinden ∧	24	66.38 N	14.00 E
Snou	76	53.13 N	26.24 E
Snov ≐	78	51.45 N	31.45 E
Snover	190	43.27 N	82.58 W
Snowbird Lake ⊜	176	60.41 N	103.00 W
Snow Canyon State Park ♦	200	37.11 N	113.42 W
Snow Creek ≐	224	47.59 N	122.53 W
Snowden, Sk., Can.	184	53.30 N	104.41 W
Snowden, Pa., U.S.	279b	40.16 N	79.58 W
Snowden Oaks	284c	39.04 N	76.52 W
Snowdenville	285	40.11 N	75.36 W
Snowdon ∧	44	53.04 N	4.05 W
Snowdonia National Park ♦	28	53.00 N	3.57 W
Snowdoun	194	32.14 N	86.17 W
Snowdrift	176	62.23 N	110.47 W
Snowflake	200	34.30 N	110.04 W
Snow Hill, Md., U.S.	208	38.10 N	75.23 W
Snow Hill, N.C., U.S.	192	35.27 N	77.40 W
Snowking Mountain ∧	224	48.24 N	121.17 W
Snow Lake	184	54.53 N	100.02 W
Snow Lakes ⊜	224	47.29 N	120.45 W
Snowmass Mountain ∧	200	39.07 N	107.04 W
Snow Mountain ∧	226	39.23 N	122.45 W
Snow Peak ∧	202	48.35 N	118.29 W
Snows Brook ≐	283	42.47 N	71.06 W
Snow Shoe	214	41.02 N	77.57 W
Snowshoe Butte ∧	224	47.13 N	121.22 W
Snowshoe Peak ∧	202	48.13 N	115.41 W
Snowtown	166	33.47 S	138.13 E
Snow Water Lake ⊜	204	41.07 N	115.00 W
Snowy ≐	166	37.48 S	148.32 E
Snowy Mountain ∧	188	43.42 N	74.23 W
Snowy Mountains ⋏	166	36.30 S	148.20 E
Snowyside Peak ∧	202	43.57 N	114.58 W
Snubba Range ⋏	171b	35.40 S	148.10 E
Snuŏl	110	12.04 N	106.26 E
Snyatyn	78	48.28 N	25.34 E
Snyder, Ok., U.S.	196	34.39 N	98.57 W
Snyder, Tx., U.S.	196	32.43 N	100.55 W
Snyder □6	210	40.47 N	77.03 W
Snydertown	210	40.53 N	76.40 W
Soacha	246	4.35 N	74.13 W
Soahany	157b	18.42 S	44.13 E
Soaker, Mount ∧	172	45.23 S	167.15 E
Soalala	157b	16.06 S	45.20 E
Soalara	157b	23.36 S	43.44 E
Soalcka	157b	18.32 S	45.15 E
Sŏam	98	38.01 N	126.43 E
Soamanonga	157b	23.52 S	44.47 E
Soān ≐	123	33.01 N	71.44 E
Soan-do I	98	34.09 N	126.39 E
Soanierana Ivongo	157b	16.55 S	49.35 E
Soanindrariny	157b	19.54 S	47.14 E
Soap Creek ≐	190	40.55 N	92.14 W
Soap Lake	202	47.23 N	119.29 W
Soasiu → Tidore	108	0.40 N	127.26 E
Soatá	246	6.20 N	72.41 W
Soavina	157b	20.23 S	46.56 E
Soavinandriana	157b	19.09 S	46.45 E
Soay I	46	57.08 N	6.14 W
Soazza	58	46.22 N	9.13 E
Sob ≐	78	48.42 N	29.17 E
Sobaek-sanmaek ⋏	98	36.00 N	128.00 E
Sobat ≐	140	9.22 N	31.33 E
Sobernheim	56	49.47 N	7.38 E
Soběšice	60	49.12 N	13.41 E
Soběslav	30	49.15 N	14.44 E
Sobger ≐	164	3.44 S	140.20 E
Sobinka	80	55.59 N	40.01 E
Sobcba Indian Reservation ◆4	228	33.47 N	116.54 W
Sobcko	140	6.49 N	24.50 E
Sobolekovo	80	55.39 N	51.53 E
Sobolev	80	51.56 N	51.43 E
Sobolevo	82	55.31 N	38.43 E
Sobolino	88	53.23 N	119.42 E
Sobolivka	78	48.36 N	29.30 E
Sobótka	30	50.55 N	16.45 E
Sobradinho	252	29.24 S	53.03 W
Sobradinho, Represa de ⊜1	250	9.40 S	42.00 W
Sobrado	34	41.02 N	8.16 W
Sobral	250	3.42 S	40.21 W
Sobrance	30	48.45 N	22.11 E
Sobrante Ridge ∧	282	37.58 N	122.15 W
Sobrarbe ◆1	34	42.22 N	0.10 E
Sobue	94	35.15 N	136.43 E
Søby	41	54.56 N	10.16 E
Sobych	78	51.52 N	33.14 E
Soča	64	46.20 N	13.39 E
Soča (Isonzo) ≐	64	45.47 N	13.32 E
Socaire	252	23.36 S	67.51 W
Socchieve	64	46.25 N	12.52 E
Soc Giang	110	22.54 N	106.01 E
Socgorodok	78	50.11 N	38.09 E
Soch	85	39.57 N	71.08 E
Soch ≐	85	40.20 N	71.02 E
Sochaczew	30	52.14 N	20.14 E
Sochaux	58	47.31 N	6.50 E
Soch'e → Shache	120	38.25 N	77.16 E
Sochi → Soči	84	43.35 N	39.45 E
Sŏch'ŏn	98	36.05 N	126.41 E
Sochondo	88	51.49 N	112.32 E
Sochondo, gora ∧	88	49.44 N	111.05 E
Soch'ŏng-do I	98	37.46 N	124.45 E
Sochor, gora ∧	88	51.18 N	105.15 E
Soči	84	43.35 N	39.45 E
Social Circle	192	33.39 N	83.43 W
Social Security Administration υ	284b	39.19 N	76.44 W
Sociedade Hípica Paulista ♦	287b	23.36 S	46.41 W
Société, Archipel de la (Society Islands) II	14	17.00 S	150.00 W
Society Hill	192	34.30 N	79.51 W
Society Islands → Société, Archipel de la II	14	17.00 S	150.00 W
Society Ridge ✦3	14	17.00 S	151.00 W
Soco ≐	238	18.27 N	69.12 W
Socoltenango	232	16.13 N	92.15 W
Socompa, Paso)(	252	24.27 S	68.18 W
Soconusco, Sierra de — Madre, Sierra ⋏	236	15.20 N	92.20 W
Socorro, Bra.	256	22.36 S	46.32 W
Socorro, Col.	246	6.29 N	73.16 W
Socorro, Pil.	116	9.37 N	125.58 E
Socorro, N.M., U.S.	200	34.03 N	106.53 W
Socorro, Tx., U.S.	200	31.39 N	106.18 W
Socorro ◆8	287b	23.39 S	46.42 W
Socorro, Isla I	232	18.45 N	110.58 W
Socota	248	6.18 S	78.44 W
Socotora, Isla → Suquṭrā I	118	12.30 N	54.00 E
Socotra → Suquṭrā I	118	12.30 N	54.00 E
Soc Trang	110	9.36 N	105.58 E
Socuéllamos	34	39.17 N	2.48 W
Soda Creek	182	52.21 N	122.18 W
Soda Creek ≐	226	38.48 N	122.29 W
Soda Lake ⊜, Ca., U.S.	204	35.08 N	116.04 W
Soda Lake ⊜, Ca., U.S.	226	35.15 N	119.53 W
Sodankylä	24	67.29 N	26.32 E
Soda Springs	202	42.39 N	111.36 W
Soddy-Daisy	194	35.16 N	85.10 W
Sodegaura	94	35.26 N	139.57 E
Söderälgen ⊜	40	59.43 N	14.35 E
Söderåsen ⋏2	41	56.04 N	13.05 E
Söderbärke	40	60.05 N	15.33 E
Söderby-Karl	40	59.53 N	18.41 E
Söderfors	40	60.23 N	17.14 E
Söderhamn	26	61.18 N	17.03 E
Söderköping	26	58.29 N	16.18 E
Södermanland □9	41	59.12 N	16.49 E
Södermanlands Län □6	40	59.15 N	16.40 E
Södernmanland □9	40	59.12 N	16.49 E
Söderslätt □9	41	55.29 N	13.15 E
Södertälje	40	59.12 N	17.37 E
Södertörn ≻1	40	59.05 N	18.00 E
Sodhra	123	32.28 N	74.11 E
Sodingen ◆8	263	51.32 N	7.15 E
Sodium	158	30.11 S	23.09 E
Sodo	144	6.52 N	37.47 E
Sodom → Sedom ⊥	132	31.04 N	35.23 E
Sodpur	272b	22.39 N	88.23 E
Södra Björkfjärden ⊂	40	59.18 N	17.32 E
Södra Hörken ⊜	40	60.02 N	15.02 E
Södra Kvarken ⊔	26	60.15 N	19.05 E
Södra Råda	40	59.01 N	14.10 E
Södra Sandby	41	55.43 N	13.20 E
Södra Vi	26	57.45 N	15.48 E
Sodražica	36	45.46 N	14.38 E
Sodus	210	43.14 N	77.03 W
Sodus Bay ⊂	210	43.15 N	76.58 W
Sodus Creek ≐	210	43.13 N	76.56 W
Sodus Point	210	43.16 N	76.59 W
Sŏdu-su ≐	98	42.05 N	129.00 E
Sodwalls	170	33.31 S	149.59 E
Sodwana Bay National Park ♦	158	27.30 S	32.39 E
Soe	112	9.52 S	124.17 E
Soeda	96	33.34 N	130.52 E
Soekmekaar	156	23.28 S	29.58 E
Soela väin ⊔	76	58.40 N	22.35 E
Soerabaja → Surabaya	115a	7.15 S	112.45 E
Soest, Dtsch.	52	51.34 N	8.07 E
Soest, Ned.	52	52.09 N	5.18 E
Soestdijk	52	52.11 N	5.18 E
Soestdijk, Paleis υ	52	52.12 N	5.15 E
Soeste ≐	52	53.10 N	7.44 E
Soesterberg	52	52.07 N	5.17 E
Soeurs, Île des I	275a	45.28 N	73.33 W
Sofádhes	38	39.20 N	22.06 E
Sofala	170	33.05 S	149.42 E
Sofala □5	156	19.00 S	35.00 E
Sofia → Sofija	38	42.41 N	23.19 E
Sofia ≐	157b	15.27 S	47.23 E
Sofiero	41	56.05 N	12.39 E
Sofija (Sofia)	38	42.41 N	23.19 E
Sofija □4	38	42.17 N	23.16 E
Sofijsk, Ross.	89	51.34 N	139.52 E
Sofijsk, Ross.	89	52.15 N	133.58 E
Sofiyivka, Ukr.	78	46.33 N	34.03 E
Sofiyivka, Ukr.	78	48.04 N	33.52 E
Sofiyivs'kyy	83	48.12 N	38.52 E
Sofjanga	24	65.52 N	31.15 E
Sofjino	82	55.30 N	38.11 E
Sofrino	82	56.09 N	37.56 E
Sofronovo	76	59.48 N	36.54 E
Sogakofe	150	6.00 N	0.36 E
Sogamoso	246	5.43 N	72.56 W
Sogamoso ≐	246	7.13 N	73.56 W
Soğanlı ≐	130	41.11 N	32.38 E
Soğanlı Geçidi)(	130	40.33 N	40.16 E
Soğanlıköy ◆8	267b	40.55 N	29.12 E
Sogcho → Sokch'o	98	38.12 N	128.36 E
Sogda	89	50.24 N	132.12 E
Sögel	52	52.50 N	7.31 E
Sogen	164	9.25 S	147.25 E
Sogindy	85	43.27 N	74.38 E
Sogliano al Rubicone	66	44.00 N	12.18 E
Sognafjorden ⊂2	26	61.06 N	5.10 E
Søgne	26	58.05 N	7.49 E
Sogne Fjord → Sognafjorden ⊂2	26	61.06 N	5.10 E
Sogn og Fjordane □6	26	61.30 N	6.50 E
Sogod, Pil.	116	10.45 N	124.00 E
Sogod, Pil.	116	10.23 N	124.59 E
Sogod Bay ⊂	116	10.15 N	125.02 E
Sogo Nur ⊜	102	42.18 N	101.08 E
Sogoža ≐	76	58.28 N	39.06 E
Sogri-san Kukrip Kongwŏn ♦	98	36.33 N	127.52 E
Soğuksu Milli Parkı ♦	130	40.25 N	32.35 E
Söğüt	130	40.00 N	30.11 E
Söğütalan	130	40.03 N	28.34 E
Söğüt Gölü ⊜	130	37.03 N	29.53 E
Söğütlü	130	40.54 N	30.29 E
Sog Xian	120	31.50 N	93.45 E
Sohāg → Sawhāj	140	26.33 N	31.42 E
Sohāgpur, India	124	23.19 N	81.21 E
Sohāgpur, India	124	22.42 N	78.12 E
Soham	42	52.20 N	0.20 E
Sohano	175e	5.27 S	154.40 E
Soharkha	272a	28.35 N	77.24 E
Soheit-Tinlot	56	50.29 N	5.22 E
Sohland	54	51.02 N	14.25 E
Söhlde	52	52.11 N	10.14 E
Sohna	124	28.15 N	77.04 E
Sŏhŭng	98	38.27 N	126.10 E
Sŏhwa-ri	98	38.15 N	128.13 E
Soignies (Zinnik)	50	50.35 N	4.04 E
Soignolles-en-Brie	261	48.39 N	2.42 E
Soin	150	12.47 N	3.49 W
Soindres	261	48.57 N	1.40 E
Soini	26	62.52 N	24.13 E
Sointula	182	50.38 N	127.01 W
Soira ∧	144	14.45 N	39.32 E
Soisalo ∧	26	62.40 N	28.10 E
Soissons	50	49.22 N	3.20 E
Soisy-sous-Montmorency	261	48.59 N	2.18 E
Soisy-sur-Seine	261	48.39 N	2.27 E
Sōja	96	34.40 N	133.45 E
Sojana	24	65.48 N	43.20 E
Sojat	120	25.55 N	73.40 E
Šojda	24	61.11 N	37.40 E
Sojiji Temple υ1	268	35.31 N	139.41 E
Sojītra	120	22.33 N	72.43 E
Šojna	24	67.52 N	44.08 E
Sŏjosŏn-man ⊂	98	39.20 N	124.50 E
Sojoton Point ≻	116	9.58 N	122.27 E
Sok ≐	80	53.24 N	50.08 E
Sōka, Nihon	94	35.49 N	139.48 E
Soka, Taehan	271b	37.30 N	126.48 E
Sokal'	78	50.29 N	24.17 E
Šokal'skogo, proliv ⊔	74	79.00 N	100.25 E
Sokch'o	98	38.12 N	128.36 E
Söke	130	37.45 N	27.24 E
Sokehs Passage ⊔	174r	7.01 N	158.11 E
Sokele	154	9.55 S	24.36 E
Sokhós	38	40.49 N	23.21 E
Sokna	26	60.14 N	9.54 E
Sokodé	150	8.59 N	1.08 E
Sokol, Ross.	74	72.24 N	126.48 E
Sokol, Ross.	76	59.28 N	40.10 E
Sokol, Ross.	89	47.14 N	142.45 E
Sokol ∧	60	49.03 N	13.31 E
Sokółka, Pol.	30	53.25 N	23.31 E
Sokolka, Ross.	80	55.34 N	51.30 E
Sokol'niki ◆8	265b	55.48 N	37.41 E
Sokolniki Park ♦	265b	55.48 N	37.41 E
Sokol'nikovo	82	55.21 N	35.49 E
Sokolo	150	14.44 N	6.08 W
Sokolohirne	78	46.29 N	34.58 E
Sokolov	54	50.09 N	12.40 E
Sokolova Hora	78	50.19 N	28.36 E
Sokolova Pustyn'	82	54.51 N	38.03 E
Sokolovka	86	55.06 N	69.12 E
Sokolovo, Ross.	24	65.21 N	56.57 E
Sokolovo, Ross.	76	52.55 N	34.39 E
Sokolovo, Ross.	80	52.49 N	42.26 E
Sokolovo, Ross.	82	56.02 N	36.55 E
Sokolovo, Ross.	86	52.33 N	84.46 E
Sokolovo-Kundr'učenskij	83	47.50 N	39.57 E
Sokołów	30	50.14 N	22.07 E
Sokołów Podlaski	30	52.25 N	22.15 E
Sokol'skoje	80	57.08 N	43.13 E
Sokone	150	13.53 N	16.22 W
Sokoto	150	13.04 N	5.16 E
Sokoto ≐	150	11.20 N	4.10 E
Sŏkp'o-ri	98	37.46 N	125.27 E
Sokrutovka	80	47.54 N	46.33 E
Šokša	76	58.24 N	42.27 E
Soksa-ri	98	40.40 N	127.17 E
Sokskije jary ⋏2	80	54.10 N	51.30 E
Sŏk-to I	98	38.40 N	125.00 E
Sokuluk	85	42.52 N	74.18 E
Sokur, Ross.	80	52.01 N	45.48 E
Sokur, Ross.	86	55.13 N	83.13 E
Sokyryany	78	48.27 N	27.25 E
Sokyryntsi	78	50.42 N	32.46 E
Sol'	30	48.56 N	21.36 E
Sol, Costa del ⩠2	34	36.40 N	4.00 W
Sola, Nor.	26	58.53 N	5.36 E
Sola, Vanuatu	175f	13.53 S	167.33 E
Sola, R.D.C.	154	5.09 S	27.06 E
Soła ≐	30	50.04 N	19.13 E
Solacolu	38	44.23 N	26.34 E
Solai	154	0.02 N	36.09 E
Šolaksaj	86	51.45 N	64.48 E
Solan	123	30.55 N	77.07 E
Solana	220	26.56 N	82.01 W
Solana Beach	228	32.59 N	117.16 W
Solander, Cape ≻	274a	34.01 S	151.14 E
Solander Island I	172	46.34 S	166.53 E
Solânea	250	6.45 S	35.39 W
Solangāri	272b	22.36 N	88.27 E
Sol'anka ≐	80	50.10 N	51.20 E
Solano	116	16.31 N	121.11 E
Solano □6	226	38.15 N	121.52 W
Solāpur	122	17.41 N	75.55 E
Solar, Morro ∧2	286d	12.11 S	77.02 W
Solarino	70	37.06 N	15.07 E
Solaro	266b	45.37 N	9.05 E
Solaro, Monte ∧	68	40.33 N	14.13 E
Solberg	26	63.47 N	17.38 E
Solbiate Arno	62	45.42 N	8.48 E
Solbiate Olona	266b	45.39 N	8.53 E
Solca, Arg.	252	30.46 S	66.28 W
Solca, Rom.	38	47.42 N	25.50 E
Solčava	61	46.25 N	14.41 E
Sol'cy	76	58.08 N	30.20 E
Solda Gölü ⊜	130	37.33 N	29.42 E
Soldatskaja	84	43.48 N	43.49 E
Soldatskoje	85	40.52 N	68.56 E
Soldatsko-Stepnoje	80	49.32 N	45.30 E
Sölde ◆8	263	51.31 N	7.35 E
Sol de Julio	252	29.33 S	63.27 W
Sölden	64	46.58 N	11.00 E
Sölderholz ◆8	263	51.29 N	7.35 E
Soldier Creek ≐	198	39.04 N	95.39 W
Soldier Field ♦	278	41.52 N	87.37 W
Soldier Key I	220	25.35 N	80.10 W
Soldier Point ≻	240c	17.02 N	61.41 W
Soldier Pond	186	47.09 N	68.34 W
Soldiers Grove	190	43.23 N	90.46 W
Soldotna	180	60.29 N	151.04 W
Sole, Val di V	64	46.20 N	10.45 E
Solebury	208	40.23 N	75.02 W
Solec Kujawski	30	53.06 N	18.14 E
Soledad, Col.	246	10.55 N	74.46 W
Soledad, Ca., U.S.	226	36.25 N	121.19 W
Soledad, Ven.	246	8.10 N	63.34 W
Soledad, Cerro ∧	196	26.29 N	103.23 W
Soledad de Doblado	234	19.03 N	96.25 W
Soledad Díez Gutiérrez	234	22.12 N	100.57 W
Soledade	252	28.50 S	52.30 W
Soledade de Minas	256	22.04 S	45.03 W
Soledad Pass)(	228	34.30 N	118.07 W
Soleduck ≐	224	47.55 N	124.35 W
Solemar	256	24.05 S	46.36 W
Solen	198	46.23 N	100.47 W
Sølen ∧	26	61.55 N	11.30 E
Solenoje	80	46.14 N	42.32 E
Solentiname, Archipiélago de II	236	11.10 N	85.00 W
Solenzara	36	41.51 N	9.23 E
Solenzo	150	12.11 N	4.05 W
Solero	62	44.55 N	8.30 E
Solers	261	48.40 N	2.43 E
Solesmes	50	50.11 N	3.30 E
Soleure → Solothurn	58	47.13 N	7.32 E
Solferino	64	45.23 N	10.34 E
Solginskij	24	61.05 N	41.19 E
Solgne	56	48.58 N	6.18 E
Solgonskij kr'až ∧	86	55.30 N	91.00 E
Solhan	130	38.58 N	41.03 E
Solheim, Nor.	26	60.53 N	5.27 E
Solheim, S. Afr.	273d	26.11 S	28.10 E
Soliera	64	44.45 N	10.55 E
Soligalič	76	59.05 N	42.17 E
Solignac-sur-Loire	62	44.58 N	3.53 E
Soligny-la-Trappe	50	48.37 N	0.32 E
Solihull	42	52.25 N	1.45 W
Solikamsk	86	59.39 N	56.47 E
Solila	157b	21.25 S	46.37 E
Sol'-Ileck	86	51.10 N	54.59 E
Soliman	148	36.42 N	10.30 E
Solimões → Amazon ≐	242	0.10 S	49.00 W
Solin ≐	50	48.02 N	2.43 E
Solingen	56	51.10 N	7.05 E
Solís, Arg.	258	34.18 S	59.20 W
Solís, Ur.	252	34.36 S	55.29 W
Solís, Presa ⊜1	234	20.05 N	100.36 W
Soliseño	196	26.01 N	97.48 W
Söll	64	47.30 N	12.11 E
Sollar	84	41.40 N	48.38 E
Sollas	46	57.39 N	7.21 W
Sollefteå	26	63.10 N	17.16 E
Sollenau	61	47.53 N	16.15 E
Sollentuna	40	59.28 N	17.54 E
Sóller	34	39.46 N	2.42 E
Søllerød	41	55.49 N	12.31 E
Sollerön I	26	60.55 N	14.37 E
Søllested	41	54.49 N	11.17 E
Solliès-Pont	62	43.11 N	6.03 E
Solling ⋏	52	51.45 N	9.35 E
Söllingen	54	52.05 N	10.55 E
Sollom	262	53.40 N	2.50 W
Sollstedt	54	51.25 N	10.31 E
Solms	56	50.32 N	8.24 E
Solna	40	59.22 N	18.01 E
Solncedar	78	44.34 N	38.01 E
Solncevo	265b	55.39 N	37.24 E
Solnečnogorsk	82	56.11 N	36.59 E
Solnhofen	56	48.53 N	10.59 E
Solo → Surakarta	115a	7.35 S	110.50 E
Solo ≐	115a	6.47 S	112.33 E
Šolochovskij	80	48.18 N	41.03 E
Solodča	80	49.39 N	44.17 E
Solodniki	80	48.25 N	45.16 E
Solofra	68	40.50 N	14.51 E
Sologne ◆1	50	47.20 N	2.00 E
Sologoncy	74	66.13 N	114.14 E
Solok	112	0.48 S	100.39 E
Sololá, Guat.	236	14.46 N	91.11 W
Solola, Som.	144	0.07 N	41.31 E
Sololá □5	236	14.40 N	91.15 W
Solomennikova	86	58.20 N	89.02 E
Solomennoje	24	61.51 N	34.19 E
Solomon, Az., U.S.	200	32.48 N	109.37 W
Solomon, Ks., U.S.	198	38.55 N	97.22 W
Solomon ≐	198	38.54 N	97.22 W
Solomon, North Fork ≐	198	39.29 N	98.26 W
Solomon, South Fork ≐	198	39.29 N	98.26 W
Solomon Basin ✦1	14	7.00 S	152.00 E
Solomon Islands □1	175e	8.00 S	159.00 E
Solomon Islands II	175e	8.00 S	159.00 E
Solomons	208	38.20 N	76.28 W
Solomon Sea ⫪2	14	8.00 S	155.00 E
Solomon's Pools → Sulaymān, Birak ⊥	132	31.41 N	35.10 E
Solon, Ia., U.S.	190	41.48 N	91.29 W
Solon, Me., U.S.	188	44.56 N	69.51 W
Solon, Oh., U.S.	214	41.23 N	81.26 W
Solon, Zhg.	89	46.36 N	121.13 E
Solone, Ukr.	78	48.13 N	34.52 E
Solone, Ukr.	83	49.18 N	37.39 E
Solone Ozero	78	45.53 N	34.27 E
Solonešnoje	86	51.40 N	84.21 E
Solonka	80	50.13 N	41.28 E
Sol'onoje	84	44.03 N	40.53 E
Sol'onoje, ozero ⊜	86	55.20 N	70.05 E
Sol'onoje Zajmišče	80	47.56 N	46.07 E
Solonópole	250	5.44 S	39.01 W
Solon Springs	190	46.21 N	91.49 W
Solopaca	68	41.11 N	14.33 E
Solor, Kepulauan II	112	8.25 S	123.30 E
Solor, Pulau I	112	8.27 S	123.05 E
Solotča	80	54.48 N	39.51 E
Solothurn	58	47.13 N	7.32 E
Solothurn □3	58	47.25 N	7.35 E
Solotvyn	78	48.42 N	24.25 E
Solotvyna	78	47.57 N	23.52 E
Soloveckije ostrova II	24	65.07 N	35.53 E
Solovjovka	76	60.46 N	30.09 E
Solovjovsk, Ross.	88	49.55 N	115.42 E
Solovjovsk, Ross.	89	54.14 N	124.26 E
Solre-le-Château	50	50.10 N	4.05 E
Solre-sur-Sambre	50	50.18 N	4.08 E
Solrød Strand	41	55.32 N	12.14 E
Solsona	34	41.59 N	1.31 E
Solt	30	46.48 N	19.00 E
Šolta, Otok I	36	43.23 N	16.15 E
Solṭānābād	128	36.23 N	58.02 E
Soltau	52	52.59 N	9.49 E
Solton	86	52.50 N	86.28 E
Solunto ⊥	70	38.06 N	13.32 E
Solus, Mount ∧	168a	32.28 S	116.13 E
Solutré-Pouilly	58	46.18 N	4.43 E
Solva	42	51.52 N	5.11 W
Solva ≐	42	51.52 N	5.17 W
Solvang	204	34.36 N	120.08 W
Solvarbo	40	60.24 N	15.40 E
Solvay	210	43.03 N	76.12 W
Sölvesborg	26	56.03 N	14.33 E
Sol'vyčegodsk	24	61.21 N	46.52 E
Solway Firth ⊂1	44	54.50 N	3.35 W
Solwezi	154	12.11 S	26.25 E
Soly	76	54.31 N	26.11 E
Solymár	264c	47.36 N	18.56 E
Solza	24	64.33 N	39.29 E
Sōma, Nihon	92	37.48 N	140.57 E
Soma, Tür.	130	39.10 N	27.36 E
Somabula	154	19.41 S	29.41 E
Sōmahara-chūtonchi, Rikujō-jieitai- ■	94	36.23 N	138.58 E
Somain	50	50.22 N	3.17 E
Somalia (Somaliya) □1, Afr.	136	6.00 N	48.00 E
Somalia (Somaliya) □1, Afr.	144	6.00 N	48.00 E
Somali Basin ✦1	12	0.00	52.00 E
Somalie → Somalia □1	144	6.00 N	48.00 E
Somaliland → Somalia □1	144	6.00 N	48.00 E
Somali Republic → Somalia □1	144	6.00 N	48.00 E
Somaliya → Somalia □1	144	6.00 N	48.00 E
Somalomo	152	3.23 N	12.44 E
Sōman	98	41.20 N	128.54 E
Somanga	154	8.24 S	39.17 E
Sombernon	58	47.18 N	4.42 E
Sombo	152	8.42 S	20.57 E
Sombor	38	45.46 N	19.07 E
Sombra	214	42.43 N	82.29 W
Sombrerete	234	23.38 N	103.39 W
Sombreretillo	196	26.19 N	99.58 W
Sombrero I	238	18.36 N	63.26 W
Sombrero Channel ⊔	110	7.41 N	93.35 E
Sombrio	252	29.07 S	49.40 W
Sombrio, Lagoa do ⊂	252	29.12 S	49.42 W
Şomcuta Mare	38	47.31 N	23.29 E
Somdari	120	25.49 N	72.35 E
Somenos	224	48.49 N	123.44 W
Somercotes	44	53.04 N	1.22 W
Somerdale, N.J., U.S.	208	39.50 N	75.01 W
Somerdale, Oh., U.S.	214	40.34 N	81.22 W
Someren	52	51.24 N	5.44 E
Somero	26	60.37 N	23.32 E
Sõmerpalu	76	57.51 N	26.48 E
Somers, Austl.	169	38.24 S	145.10 E
Somers, Ct., U.S.	207	41.59 N	72.26 W
Somers, Mt., U.S.	202	48.04 N	114.13 W
Somers, Wi., U.S.	216	42.38 N	87.54 W
Somersby	170	33.25 S	151.17 E
Somerset, Austl.	166	41.03 S	145.49 E
Somerset, Mb., Can.	184	49.24 N	98.39 W
Somerset, Co., U.S.	200	38.55 N	107.28 W
Somerset, Ky., U.S.	192	37.05 N	84.36 W
Somerset, Md., U.S.	284c	38.58 N	77.05 W
Somerset, Ma., U.S.	207	41.46 N	71.07 W
Somerset, N.J., U.S.	208	40.44 N	74.34 W
Somerset, Oh., U.S.	188	39.48 N	82.17 W
Somerset, Pa., U.S.	188	40.00 N	79.04 W
Somerset, Tx., U.S.	196	29.13 N	98.40 W
Somerset, Wi., U.S.	190	45.07 N	92.40 W
Somerset □6, Eng., U.K.	42	51.08 N	3.00 W
Somerset □6, Md., U.S.	208	38.05 N	75.41 W
Somerset □6, N.J., U.S.	208	40.34 N	74.37 W
Somerset □6, Pa., U.S.	214	40.09 N	79.00 W
Somerset Airport ⊠	276	40.37 N	74.40 W
Somerset Center	216	42.03 N	84.25 W
Somerset East	158	32.42 S	25.35 E
Somerset Hills Airport ⊠	276	40.41 N	74.32 W
Somerset Island I, Ber.	240a	32.17 N	64.52 W
Somerset Island I, N.T., Can.	176	73.15 N	93.30 W
Somerset Reservoir ⊜1	171a	27.03 S	152.35 E
Somerset West	158	34.08 S	18.50 E
Somersham	42	52.23 N	0.01 E
Somers Point	208	39.19 N	74.35 W
Somersworth	188	43.15 N	70.51 W
Somerton, Eng., U.K.	42	51.03 N	2.44 W
Somerton, Az., U.S.	200	32.35 N	114.42 W
Somerton ◆8	285	40.06 N	75.01 W
Somerton Creek ≐	208	36.32 N	76.55 W
Somervell □6	222	32.15 N	97.45 W
Somerville, Austl.	169	38.13 S	145.10 E
Somerville, Ma., U.S.	207	42.23 N	71.06 W
Somerville, N.J., U.S.	210	40.34 N	74.36 W
Somerville, Oh., U.S.	218	39.33 N	84.38 W
Somerville, Tn., U.S.	194	35.14 N	89.21 W
Somerville, Tx., U.S.	222	30.20 N	96.31 W
Somerville Lake ⊜1	222	30.18 N	96.40 W

Symbol	English	Deutsch	Español	Français	Português
≐	River	Fluß	Río	Rivière	Rio
≡	Canal	Kanal	Canal	Canal	Canal
⌊	Waterfall, Rapids	Wasserfall, Stromschnellen	Cascada, Rápidos	Chute d'eau, Rapides	Cascata, Rápidos
⊔	Strait	Meeresstraße	Estrecho	Détroit	Estreito
⊂	Bay, Gulf	Bucht, Golf	Bahía, Golfo	Baie, Golfe	Baía, Golfo
⊜	Lake, Lakes	See, Seen	Lago, Lagos	Lac, Lacs	Lago, Lagos
⩸	Swamp	Sumpf	Pantano	Marais	Pântano
⌘	Ice Features, Glacier	Eis- und Gletscherformen	Accidentes Glaciales	Formes glaciaires	Acidentes glaciares
⫪	Other Hydrographic Features	Andere Hydrographische Objekte	Otros Elementos Hidrográficos	Autres données hydrographiques	Outros acidentes hidrográficos
✦	Submarine Features	Untermeerische Objekte	Accidentes Submarinos	Formes de relief sous-marin	Acidentes submarinos
□	Political Unit	Politische Einheit	Unidad Política	Entité politique	Unidade política
υ	Cultural Institution	Kulturelle Institution	Institución Cultural	Institution culturelle	Instituição cultural
⊥	Historical Site	Historische Stätte	Sitio Histórico	Site historique	Sitio histórico
♦	Recreational Site	Erholungs- und Ferienort	Sitio de Recreo	Centre de loisirs	Area de Lazer
⊠	Airport	Flughafen	Aeropuerto	Aéroport	Aeroporto
■	Military Installation	Militäranlage	Instalación Militar	Installation militaire	Instalação militar
◆	Miscellaneous	Verschiedenes	Misceláneo	Divers	Diversos

ENGLISH

DEUTSCH

Symbols in the index entries represent the broad categories identified in the key at the right. Symbols with superior numbers (⋏[1]) identify subcategories (see complete key on page *I · 1).*

Symbole im Register stellen die rechts im Schlüssel erklärten Kategorien dar. Symbole mit hochgestellten Ziffern (⋏[1]) bezeichnen Unterabteilungen einer Kategorie (vgl. vollständiger Schlüssel auf Seite *I · 1).*

Los símbolos incluídos en el texto del índice representan las grandes categorías identificadas con la clave a la derecha. Los símbolos con numeros en su parte superior (⋏[1]) identifican las subcategorías (véase la clave completa en la página *I · 1).*

Les symboles de l'index représentent les catégories indiquées dans la légende à droite. Les symboles suivis d'un indice (⋏[1]) représentent des sous-catégories (voir légende complète à la page *I · 1).*

Os símbolos incluídos no texto do índice representam as grandes categorias identificadas com a chave à direita. Os símbolos com números em sua parte superior (⋏[1]) identificam as subcategorias (veja-se a chave completa à página *I · 1).*

∧	Mountain	Berg	Montaña	Montagne	Montanha
⋏	Mountains	Gebirge	Montañas	Montagnes	Montanhas
)(	Pass	Paß	Paso	Col	Passo
V	Valley, Canyon	Tal, Cañon	Valle, Cañón	Vallée, Canyon	Vale, Canhão
≚	Plain	Ebene	Llano	Plaine	Planície
›	Cape	Kap	Cabo	Cap	Cabo
I	Island	Insel	Isla	Île	Ilha
II	Islands	Inseln	Islas	Îles	Ilhas
±	Other Topographic Features	Andere Topographische Objekte	Otros Elementos Topográficos	Autres données topographiques	Outros acidentes topográficos

Sout-Squi I · 167

ESPAÑOL — Nombre · Página · Lat.°' · Long.°' W = Oeste
FRANÇAIS — Nom · Page · Lat.°' · Long.°' W = Ouest
PORTUGUÊS — Nome · Página · Lat.°' · Long.°' W = Oeste

Nombre / Nom / Nome	Página / Page	Lat.°'	Long.°'
South Mokelumne ≃	226	38.08 N	121.35 W
South Molton	42	51.01 N	3.50 W
South Monroe	216	41.54 N	83.25 W
Southmont	214	40.18 N	78.56 W
South Montrose	210	41.48 N	75.53 W
South Moose Lake ⊜	184	53.46 N	100.08 W
South Mountain	208	39.51 N	77.29 W
South Mountain ∧, U.S.	208	39.40 N	77.30 W
South Mountain ∧, Id., U.S.	202	42.44 N	116.54 W
South Mountain Reservation ♠	276	40.45 N	74.18 W
South Mount Vernon	214	40.23 N	82.23 W
South Nahanni ≃	176	61.03 N	123.20 W
South Naknek	180	58.43 N	157.00 W
South Nation ≃	188	45.34 N	75.06 W
South Negril Point >	241q	18.15 N	78.22 W
South New Berlin	210	42.31 N	75.23 W
South New Castle	214	40.58 N	80.21 W
South New River Canal ≊	220	26.04 N	80.12 W
South Norfolk → Chesapeake	208	36.43 N	76.15 W
South Normanton	44	53.06 N	1.20 W
South Norwalk Reservoir ⊜[1]	276	41.11 N	73.27 W
South Norwood ◆[8]	260	51.24 N	0.04 W
South Nutfield	260	51.14 N	0.08 W
South Nyack	276	41.04 N	73.55 W
South Ockendon	42	51.32 N	0.18 E
South Ogden	200	41.11 N	111.58 W
Southold	207	41.03 N	72.25 W
South Onondaga	210	42.56 N	76.13 W
South Orange	276	40.47 N	74.15 W
South Orkney Islands II	9	60.35 S	45.30 W
South Oroville	226	39.30 N	121.33 W
South Ossetia → Jugo Osetija □[9]	84	42.20 N	44.00 E
South Otselic	210	42.38 N	75.46 W
Southowram	262	53.43 N	1.50 W
South Oxhey	260	51.38 N	0.23 W
South Oyster Bay ⊂	276	40.38 N	73.28 W
South Palo Duro Creek ≃	196	36.06 N	101.29 W
South Para ≃	168b	34.36 S	138.45 E
South Para Reservoir ⊜[1]	168b	34.42 S	138.52 E
South Paris	188	44.13 N	70.30 W
South Park	216	41.44 N	88.18 W
South Park ♠, N.Y., U.S.	284a	42.50 N	78.50 W
South Park ♠, Pa., U.S.	279b	40.19 N	80.01 W
South Pasadena, Ca., U.S.	280	34.06 N	118.08 W
South Pasadena, Fl., U.S.	220	27.46 N	82.43 W
South Pass)(	200	42.22 N	108.55 W
South Pass Ʉ	175c	7.14 N	151.48 E
South Passage Ʉ, Austl.	171a	27.22 S	153.26 E
South Passage Ʉ, Oh., U.S.	214	41.35 N	82.45 W
South Patrick Shores	220	28.12 N	80.35 W
South Pekin	190	40.29 N	89.39 W
South Pender	224	48.45 N	123.14 W
South Pender Island I	224	48.45 N	123.10 W
South Perth	168a	31.59 S	115.52 E
South Petherton	42	50.58 N	2.49 W
South Philadelphia ◆[8]	285	39.56 N	75.10 W
South Philipsburg	214	40.53 N	78.13 W
South Pittsburg	194	35.00 N	85.42 W
South Plainfield	210	40.34 N	74.24 W
South Platte ≃	178	41.07 N	100.42 W
South Platte, North Fork ≃	200	39.25 N	105.10 W
South Point >, Barb.	241g	13.02 N	59.31 W
South Point >, Pil.	116	10.24 N	122.30 E
South Pole ◆	9	90.00 S	0.00
South Porcupine	190	48.28 N	81.13 W
Southport, Austl.	166	43.25 S	146.59 E
Southport, Austl.	171a	27.58 S	153.25 E
Southport, Eng., U.K.	44	53.39 N	3.01 W
Southport, Ct., U.S.	207	41.08 N	73.17 W
Southport, Fl., U.S.	194	30.17 N	85.38 W
Southport, In., U.S.	218	39.39 N	86.07 W
Southport, N.Y., U.S.	210	42.03 N	76.49 W
Southport, N.C., U.S.	192	33.55 N	78.01 W
South Portland	188	43.38 N	70.14 W
South Portsmouth	218	38.43 N	83.00 W
South Pottstown	208	40.14 N	75.39 W
South Prairie Creek ≃	224	47.08 N	122.10 W
South Raisin ≃	206	45.08 N	74.35 W
South Range	190	47.04 N	88.38 W
South Renovo	214	41.19 N	77.44 W
South Reservoir ⊜[1]	283	42.27 N	71.07 W
South Ribble □[8]	262	53.45 N	2.42 W
South River, On., Can.	190	45.50 N	79.23 W
South River, N.J., U.S.	208	40.26 N	74.23 W
South River ⊂	208	38.57 N	76.29 W
South Rockwood	216	42.04 N	83.16 W
South Ronaldsay I	46	58.46 N	2.58 W
South Roxana	219	38.50 N	90.04 W
South Royalston	207	42.37 N	72.08 W
South Rukuru ≃	154	10.46 S	34.14 E
South Russell	214	41.25 N	81.21 W
South Salmara	124	25.55 N	90.01 E
South Sand Bluff >	158	31.19 S	30.01 E
South Sandwich Islands II	18	57.45 S	26.30 W
South Sandwich Trench ✢[1]	18	56.30 S	25.00 W
South Sandy Creek ≃	212	43.43 N	76.12 W
South San Francisco	226	37.39 N	122.24 W
South San Gabriel	280	34.03 N	118.05 W
South San Jose Hills	280	34.01 N	117.55 W
South San Ramon Creek ≃	282	37.42 N	121.55 W
South Santiam ≃	202	44.41 N	123.00 W
South Saskatchewan ≃	184	53.15 N	105.05 W
South Saugeen ≃	212	44.08 N	81.02 W
South Seaville	208	39.10 N	74.45 W
South Setauket	210	40.54 N	73.06 W
South Shafter	226	35.28 N	119.17 W
South Shetland Islands II	9	62.00 S	58.00 W
South Shields	44	55.00 N	1.25 W
South Shore	218	38.43 N	82.59 W
South Shore ◆[8]	278	41.46 N	87.35 W
South Shore Mall ◆[9]	276	40.44 N	73.15 W
South Shore Plaza ◆[9]	283	42.13 N	71.01 W
Southside	174h	2.49 S	171.43 W
South Side ◆[8]	279b	40.26 N	79.58 W
Southside Place	222	29.42 N	95.26 W
South Sioux City	198	42.28 N	96.24 W
South Skunk ≃	190	41.15 N	92.02 W
South Slocan	182	49.28 N	117.32 W
South Solon	218	39.44 N	83.36 W
South Sound Ʉ	48	53.02 N	9.28 W
South Spicer Island I	176	68.06 N	79.13 W
South Standard	219	39.21 N	89.47 W
South Station ◆[5]	283	42.21 N	71.04 W
South Sterling	210	41.17 N	75.21 W
South Stony Brook	276	40.53 N	73.07 W
South Stradbroke Island I	171a	27.51 S	153.25 E
South Streator	216	40.39 N	88.23 W
South Suburban → Behāla	126	22.31 N	88.19 E
South Sulphur ≃	196	33.23 N	95.18 W
South Sunday Creek ≃	202	46.27 N	105.54 W
South Superior	200	41.45 N	108.57 W
South Swansea	207	41.43 N	71.12 W
South Taranaki Bight ⊂[3]	172	39.40 S	174.10 E
South Tasman Rise ✢[3]	6	49.00 S	148.00 E
South Temple	208	40.24 N	75.55 W
South Thompson ≃	182	50.41 N	120.21 W
South Toms River	208	39.56 N	74.12 W
South Torrington	198	42.02 N	104.10 W
South Towanda	210	41.45 N	76.27 W
South Tucson	200	32.11 N	110.58 W
South Turkeyfoot Creek ≃	216	41.25 N	83.58 W
South Twillingate Island I	186	49.37 N	54.47 W
South Tyne ≃	44	54.59 N	2.08 W
South Ubian	116	5.11 N	120.30 E
South Uist I	46	57.15 N	7.21 W
South Umpqua ≃	202	43.20 N	123.25 W
South Valley	210	42.42 N	74.43 W
South Valley Hills ⩕[2]	285	40.00 N	75.40 W
South Valley Stream	276	40.38 N	73.44 W
South Venice	220	27.03 N	82.25 W
South Ventana Cone ∧	204	36.17 N	121.38 W
South Vestal	210	42.01 N	76.00 W
South Vietnam → Vietnam □[1]	108	16.00 N	108.00 E
Southview	214	40.20 N	80.16 W
Southview Apartments	284c	38.50 N	77.00 W
South Wabasca Lake ⊜	182	55.54 N	113.45 W
South Wales	210	42.43 N	78.35 W
South Walpole	283	42.06 N	71.15 W
Southwark ◆[8]	260	51.30 N	0.06 W
South Warren Reservoir ⊜[1]	168b	34.43 S	138.55 E
Southwater	42	51.01 N	0.21 W
South Waverly	210	41.59 N	76.32 W
South Weald	260	51.37 N	0.16 E
Southwell	44	53.05 N	0.58 W
South Wellfleet	207	41.55 N	69.59 W
South Wellington	224	49.06 N	123.53 W
Southwest	214	40.12 N	79.32 W
South West Bay ⊂	240b	25.00 N	77.32 W
Southwest Branch ≃	284c	38.53 N	76.48 W
South Westbury	276	40.45 N	73.35 W
South West Cape >, Austl.	166	43.34 S	146.02 E
South West Cape >, N.Z.	172	47.17 S	167.28 E
Southwest Cape >, Ak., U.S.	180	63.18 N	171.27 W
Southwest Cape >, Vir. Is., U.S.	241n	17.41 N	64.54 W
Southwest Channel Ʉ	220	27.34 N	82.45 W
South West City	194	36.30 N	94.36 W
South Westerlo	210	42.27 N	74.02 W
Southwest Greensburg	214	40.17 N	79.33 W
Southwest Harbor	188	44.16 N	68.19 W
Southwest Indian Ridge ✢[3]	6	30.00 S	60.00 E
Southwest Miramichi ≃	186	46.58 N	65.35 W
Southwest Museum ʊ	280	34.06 N	118.13 W
Southwest National Park ♠	166	43.15 S	146.15 E
Southwest Pacific Basin ✢[1]	6	40.00 S	150.00 W
Southwest Point >, Ba.	238	25.51 N	77.13 W
South West Point >, Kiribati	174o	1.52 N	157.33 W
Southwest Point >, Pap. N. Gui.	164	2.14 S	146.34 E
South Weymouth	283	42.10 N	70.57 W
South Weymouth Naval Air Station ■	207	42.09 N	70.57 W
South Whitley	216	41.05 N	85.37 W
South Whittier	280	33.57 N	118.02 W
South Wichita ≃	196	33.43 N	99.29 W
Southwick, Eng., U.K.	42	50.50 N	0.13 W
Southwick, Ma., U.S.	207	42.03 N	72.46 W
South Williamson	192	37.40 N	82.17 W
South Williamsport	210	41.13 N	76.59 W
South Wilmington	216	41.10 N	88.16 W
South Windham	188	43.44 N	70.25 W
South Windsor	207	41.49 N	72.37 W
Southwold	42	52.20 N	1.40 E
Southwood	210	42.59 N	76.08 W
Southwood Acres	207	41.59 N	72.32 W
South Woodham Ferrers	42	51.39 N	0.37 E
South Woodslee	214	42.14 N	82.43 W
South Woodstock	207	41.56 N	71.57 W
Southworth	224	47.31 N	122.30 W
South Yadkin ≃	192	35.45 N	80.27 W
South Yamhill ≃	224	45.13 N	123.08 W
South Yarmouth	207	41.40 N	70.11 W
South Yarra	274b	37.51 S	145.00 E
South Yorkshire □[6]	44	53.30 N	1.15 W
South Yuba ≃	226	39.17 N	121.12 W
South Zeal	42	50.44 N	3.54 W
Soutpan	158	28.43 S	26.04 E
Soutpansberg ⩕	156	22.55 S	29.30 E
Souttouf, Adrar ⩕	148	22.15 N	15.40 W
Souvigny	32	46.32 N	3.11 E
Souzy-la-Briche	261	48.32 N	2.09 E
Sovata	38	46.35 N	25.04 E
Soverato	68	38.41 N	16.33 E
Sovere	64	45.49 N	10.01 E
Sovereign Hill Historical Park ⊥	169	37.37 S	143.51 E
Sovereign Mountain ∧	180	62.08 N	148.36 W
Soveria Mannelli	68	39.05 N	16.22 E
Sövestad	41	55.30 N	13.47 E
Sovetašen	84	40.06 N	44.33 E
Sovetka	83	47.30 N	39.15 E
Sovetsk, Ross.	76	53.56 N	37.39 E
Sovetsk, Ross.	76	55.05 N	21.53 E
Sovetsk, Ross.	80	57.37 N	48.58 E
Sovetskaja, Ross.	80	49.00 N	42.07 E
Sovetskaja, Ross.	84	44.46 N	41.11 E
Sovetskaja, Ross.	84	44.02 N	44.03 E
Sovetskaja Gavan'	89	48.58 N	140.18 E
Sovetskich Oficerov, pik ∧	85	38.26 N	73.18 E
Sovetskij, Ross.	76	60.32 N	28.41 E
Sovetskij, Ross.	80	56.46 N	48.32 E
Sovetskij, Ross.	86	51.04 N	56.29 E
Sovetskij, Taj.	85	38.02 N	69.35 E
Sovetskij, Taj.	85	40.11 N	71.19 E
Sovetskoje, Kaz.	85	42.17 N	70.15 E
Sovetskoje, Ross.	78	50.21 N	39.01 E
Sovetskoje, Ross.	80	51.27 N	46.44 E
Sovetskoje, Ross.	84	43.19 N	43.36 E
Sovetskoje, Ross.	84	42.52 N	45.41 E
Šovgenovskij	78	45.02 N	40.14 E
Sovicille	66	43.17 N	11.13 E
Sovico	266b	45.39 N	9.16 E
Søvik	26	62.33 N	6.18 E
Søvind	41	55.54 N	10.01 E
Sovpolje	24	65.18 N	43.55 E
Sovyets'kyy	78	45.20 N	34.56 E
Sow ≃	42	52.48 N	2.00 W
Sowa Pan ⩯	156	20.45 S	26.00 E
Sowek	164	0.49 S	135.30 E
Sowerby, Eng., U.K.	44	54.13 N	1.21 W
Sowerby, Eng., U.K.	262	53.42 N	1.56 W
Sowerby Bridge	44	53.43 N	1.54 W
Soweto	158	26.14 S	27.54 E
Sowjetisches Ehrenmal ⊥	264a	52.29 N	13.28 E
Soy	56	50.17 N	5.31 E
Sōya-kaikyō → La Perouse Strait Ʉ	89	45.45 N	142.00 E
Sōya-misaki >	92a	45.31 N	141.56 E
Soyang-chōsuji ⊜[1]	98	37.56 N	127.53 E
Soyapango	236	13.42 N	89.09 W
Soyen	64	48.07 N	12.13 E
Soyers Lake ⊜	212	45.02 N	78.37 W
Soyet	124	24.12 N	76.10 E
Soyland Moor ◆[3]	262	53.40 N	2.02 W
Soyo	152	6.07 S	12.18 E
Soyons	62	44.53 N	4.51 E
Sož (Sozh) ≃, Europe	78	51.57 N	30.48 E
Soz' ≃, Ross.	82	56.48 N	36.44 E
Sozh (Sož) ≃	78	51.57 N	30.48 E
Sozimskij	24	59.44 N	52.16 E
Šožma	24	61.56 N	40.15 E
Sozopol	38	42.25 N	27.42 E
Sozzago	266b	45.24 N	8.43 E
Spa	56	50.30 N	5.52 E
Spaatz Island I	9	73.12 S	75.00 W
Space Needle ʊ	224	47.38 N	122.23 W
Space Obelisk ⊥	265b	55.49 N	37.38 E
Spadafora	70	38.13 N	15.22 E
Spada Lake ⊜[1]	224	47.57 N	121.40 W
Spaden	52	53.34 N	8.38 E
Spahl	56	50.39 N	9.55 E
Spaichingen	58	48.04 N	8.44 E
Spain (España) □[1], Europe	22	40.00 N	4.00 W
Spain (España) □[1], Europe	34	40.00 N	4.00 W
Spakenburg	52	52.15 N	5.23 E
Spalato → Split	36	43.31 N	16.27 E
Spalding, Austl.	166	33.30 S	138.37 E
Spalding, Sk., Can.	184	52.20 N	104.30 W
Spalding, Eng., U.K.	42	52.47 N	0.10 W
Spalding, Mo., U.S.	219	39.38 N	91.32 W
Spalding, Ne., U.S.	198	41.41 N	98.21 W
Spalt	56	49.10 N	10.55 E
Spam Island I	174h	2.48 S	171.43 W
Spandau ◆[8]	54	52.33 N	13.12 E
Spandau, Berliner Forst ◆[3]	264a	52.35 N	13.11 E
Spang	41	54.56 N	9.50 E
Spangenberg	56	51.07 N	9.40 E
Spangler	214	40.38 N	78.46 W
Spaniard's Bay	186	47.37 N	53.17 W
Spanien → Spain □[1]	34	40.00 N	4.00 W
Spanish	190	46.12 N	82.21 W
Spanish ≃	190	46.11 N	82.19 W
Spanish Camp	222	29.23 N	96.10 W
Spanish Fork	200	40.06 N	111.39 W
Spanish Lake	219	38.47 N	90.12 W
Spanish North Africa □[2], Afr.	34	35.53 N	5.19 W
Spanish North Africa □[2], Afr.	134	35.53 N	5.19 W
Spanish Peak ∧	202	44.24 N	119.46 W
Spanish Point >	240a	32.18 N	64.48 W
Spanish Sahara → Western Sahara □[2]	134	24.30 N	13.00 W
Spanish Town, Br. Vir. Is.	240m	18.27 N	64.26 W
Spanish Town, Jam.	241q	17.59 N	76.57 W
Spannberg	61	48.27 N	16.44 E
Spantekow	54	53.47 N	13.32 E
Sparagio, Monte ∧	70	38.03 N	12.46 E
Sparbach	264b	48.04 N	16.11 E
Spargi, Isola I	71	41.14 N	9.21 E
Sparkford	42	51.02 N	2.34 W
Sparkill	276	41.02 N	73.56 W
Sparkle Lake	210	41.18 N	73.47 W
Sparkman	194	33.55 N	92.50 W
Sparks, Ga., U.S.	192	31.10 N	83.26 W
Sparks, Nv., U.S.	226	39.32 N	119.45 W
Sparland	190	41.02 N	89.26 W
Sparlingville	214	42.58 N	82.30 W
Sparneck	54	50.09 N	11.50 E
Sparreholm	40	59.04 N	16.49 E
Sparrow Bush	210	41.23 N	74.43 W
Sparrow Lake ⊜	212	44.49 N	79.24 W
Sparrowpit	262	53.19 N	1.52 W
Sparrows Point	208	39.13 N	76.28 W
Sparrows Point >	284b	39.12 N	76.30 W
Sparta, On., Can.	212	42.42 N	81.05 W
Sparta → Spárti, Ellás	38	37.05 N	22.27 E
Sparta, Ga., U.S.	192	33.16 N	82.58 W
Sparta, Il., U.S.	194	38.07 N	89.42 W
Sparta, Ky., U.S.	218	38.40 N	84.54 W
Sparta, Mi., U.S.	190	43.09 N	85.42 W
Sparta, N.J., U.S.	210	41.02 N	74.38 W
Sparta, N.C., U.S.	192	36.30 N	81.07 W
Sparta, Oh., U.S.	214	40.24 N	82.42 W
Sparta, Tn., U.S.	194	35.55 N	85.27 W
Sparta, Wi., U.S.	190	43.56 N	90.48 W
Sparta Brook ≃	276	41.08 N	73.52 W
Spartak Garden ♠	265a	59.51 N	30.30 E
Sparta Lake	210	41.03 N	74.34 W
Spartanburg, In., U.S.	218	40.03 N	84.51 W
Spartanburg, S.C., U.S.	192	34.56 N	81.55 W
Spartansburg	214	41.49 N	79.41 W
Spartel, Cap >	34	35.48 N	5.56 W
Spárti (Sparta)	38	37.05 N	22.27 E
Spartivento, Capo >, It.	68	37.55 N	16.04 E
Spartivento, Capo >, It.	71	38.53 N	8.50 E
Spas-Demensk	76	54.25 N	34.01 E
Spas-Klepiki	80	55.08 N	40.13 E
Spass	82	55.55 N	35.55 E
Spassk	86	49.32 N	73.17 E
Spassk-Dal'nij	89	44.37 N	132.48 E
Spasskij	86	53.42 N	59.12 E
Spasskoje, Ross.	76	53.06 N	36.24 E
Spasskoje, Ross.	80	55.52 N	45.42 E
Spasskoje, Ross.	82	54.05 N	38.28 E
Spassk-R'azanskij	80	54.24 N	40.23 E
Spas-Zaulok	82	56.29 N	36.34 E
Spáta	267c	37.48 N	23.55 E
Spátha, Ákra >	38	35.42 N	23.44 E
Spaulding	219	39.52 N	89.32 W
Spaulding, Lake ⊜[1]	226	39.20 N	120.37 W
Speaks	222	29.15 N	96.42 W
Spean, Glen V	46	56.53 N	4.45 W
Spean Bridge	46	56.53 N	4.54 W
Spear, Cape >	186	47.32 N	52.32 W
Spearfish	198	44.29 N	103.51 W
Spearman	196	36.11 N	101.11 W
Spearsville	218	39.21 N	86.11 W
Spearville	198	37.51 N	99.45 W
Spearwood	168a	32.07 S	115.47 E
Speas Artemidos (Rock Tombs) ⊥	142	27.54 N	30.52 E
Specchia	68	39.57 N	18.18 E
Spechtsbrunn	54	50.30 N	11.14 E
Spectacle Island I	283	42.19 N	70.59 W
Spectrum ♠	285	39.54 N	75.10 W
Spectrum Range ⩕	180	57.30 N	130.40 W
Spednic Lake ⊜	186	45.36 N	67.35 W
Speed	218	38.24 N	85.45 W
Speed ≃	212	43.23 N	80.22 W
Speedway	218	39.48 N	86.16 W
Speicher, Dtsch.	56	49.56 N	6.38 E
Speicher, Schw.	58	47.24 N	9.27 E
Speichersdorf	60	49.52 N	11.46 E
Speichersee ⊜	60	48.13 N	11.45 E
Speightstown	241g	13.15 N	59.39 W
Speigletown	210	42.48 N	73.38 W
Speikkogel ∧	61	47.14 N	15.03 E
Speising ◆[8]	264b	48.10 N	16.17 E
Speke ◆[8]	262	53.21 N	2.51 W
Speke Gulf ⊂	154	2.20 S	33.15 E
Speke Hall ⊥	262	53.20 N	2.52 W
Speldorf ◆[8]	263	51.25 N	6.52 E
Spelle	52	52.22 N	7.28 E
Spellen	263	51.37 N	6.37 E
Spello	66	42.59 N	12.40 E
Spelthorne □[8]	260	51.25 N	0.28 W
Spelve, Loch ⊂	46	56.22 N	5.46 W
Spenard	180	61.11 N	149.55 W
Spence Bay	176	69.32 N	93.31 W
Spencer, In., U.S.	194	39.17 N	86.45 W
Spencer, Ia., U.S.	198	43.08 N	95.08 W
Spencer, Ma., U.S.	207	42.14 N	71.59 W
Spencer, Ne., U.S.	198	42.52 N	98.42 W
Spencer, N.Y., U.S.	210	42.12 N	76.29 W
Spencer, N.C., U.S.	192	35.41 N	80.26 W
Spencer, Oh., U.S.	214	41.06 N	82.07 W
Spencer, S.D., U.S.	198	43.43 N	97.35 W
Spencer, Tn., U.S.	194	35.44 N	85.28 W
Spencer, W.V., U.S.	188	38.48 N	81.21 W
Spencer, Wi., U.S.	190	44.45 N	90.17 W
Spencer, Cape >, Austl.	166	35.18 S	136.53 E
Spencer, Cape >, N.B., Can.	186	45.12 N	65.55 W
Spencer, Cape >, Ak., U.S.	180	58.14 N	136.40 W
Spencer, Mount ∧	224	49.03 N	124.38 W
Spencer, Point >	180	65.18 N	166.50 W
Spencer Brook ≃	283	42.28 N	71.22 W
Spencer Creek ≃, On., Can.	212	43.17 N	79.54 W
Spencer Creek ≃, Mo., U.S.	219	39.33 N	91.20 W
Spencer Field ⊠	281	42.31 N	83.33 W
Spencer Gulf ⊂	166	34.00 S	137.00 E
Spencer Lake ⊜	224	47.16 N	122.57 W
Spencerport	210	43.11 N	77.48 W
Spencertown	210	42.20 N	73.33 W
Spencerville, On., Can.	212	44.51 N	75.33 W
Spencerville, In., U.S.	216	41.16 N	84.55 W
Spencerville, Md., U.S.	208	39.06 N	76.58 W
Spencerville, Oh., U.S.	216	40.42 N	84.21 W
Spences Bridge	182	50.25 N	121.21 W
Spenge	52	52.08 N	8.28 E
Spennymoor	44	54.42 N	1.35 W
Spenser Mountains ⩕	172	42.15 S	172.30 E
Sperenberg	54	52.08 N	13.22 E
Sperillen ⊜	26	60.28 N	10.03 E
Sperling	224	49.08 N	122.33 W
Sperlinga	70	37.46 N	14.21 E
Sperlonga	66	41.15 N	13.26 E
Spermaceti Cove ⊂	276	40.26 N	73.59 W
Sperone, Capo >	71	38.57 N	8.25 E
Sperrin Mountains ⩕	48	54.50 N	7.05 W
Sperry Creek ≃	279a	41.29 N	81.53 W
Sperry Rand Corporation ʊ[3]	276	40.45 N	73.42 W
Sperryville	188	38.39 N	78.13 W
Spessart ◆[1]	56	50.10 N	9.20 E
Spesutie Island I	208	39.27 N	76.05 W
Spétsai I	38	37.16 N	23.08 E
Spexard	52	51.52 N	8.24 E
Spey ≃	46	57.40 N	3.06 W
Spey Bay ⊂	46	57.41 N	3.00 W
Speyer	56	49.19 N	8.26 E
Speyerbach ≃	56	49.19 N	8.27 E
Speyside	241r	11.18 N	60.32 W
Spezia → La Spezia	62	44.07 N	9.50 E
Spezzano Albanese	68	39.40 N	16.19 E
Spezzano della Sila	68	39.18 N	16.20 E
Sphinx → Abū al-Hawl ⊥	142	29.59 N	31.08 E
Spiazzo	64	46.07 N	10.40 E
Spiceland	218	39.50 N	85.26 W
Spicer	198	45.13 N	94.56 W
Spicer Creek ≃	284a	43.02 N	78.53 W
Spicer Meadow Reservoir ⊜[1]	226	38.23 N	119.59 W
Spicheren	56	49.12 N	6.58 E
Spickard	194	40.14 N	93.35 W
Spicket ≃	283	42.42 N	71.09 W
Spieka	52	53.45 N	8.35 E
Spiekeroog I	52	53.46 N	7.42 E
Spiess Seamount ✢[3]	8	54.40 S	0.15 E
Spiez	58	46.41 N	7.39 E
Spijkenisse	52	51.51 N	4.20 E
Spilamberto	64	44.32 N	11.01 E
Spilimbergo	64	46.07 N	12.54 E
Spilinga	68	38.37 N	15.54 E
Spillersboda	40	59.42 N	18.51 E
Spillimacheen ≃	182	50.55 N	116.20 W
Spillville	190	43.12 N	91.57 W
Spilsby	44	53.11 N	0.06 E
Spinazzola	68	40.58 N	16.06 E
Spīn Būldak	120	31.01 N	66.24 E
Spincourt	56	49.20 N	5.40 E
Spindale	192	35.21 N	81.55 W
Spindoli	66	43.12 N	12.54 E
Spinea-Orgnano	64	45.29 N	12.10 E
Spinetta Marengo	62	44.53 N	8.41 E
Spinnerstown	208	40.26 N	75.26 W
Spinoso	68	40.16 N	15.58 E
Spires → Speyer	56	49.19 N	8.26 E
Spirit Lake, Id., U.S.	202	47.57 N	116.52 W
Spirit Lake, Ia., U.S.	198	43.25 N	95.06 W
Spirit Lake ⊜	224	46.16 N	122.08 W
Spirit River	182	55.47 N	118.50 W
Spiritwood	184	53.22 N	107.31 W
Spiro	194	35.14 N	94.37 W
Spirovo	76	57.26 N	34.59 E
Spišská Nová Ves	30	48.57 N	20.34 E
Spitak	84	40.51 N	44.16 E
Spital am Pyhrn	61	47.39 N	14.20 E
Spithead Ʉ	42	50.45 N	1.05 W
Spit Point >	162	20.02 S	119.00 E
Spitsbergen I	12	78.45 N	16.00 E
Spitsbergen Bank ✢[4]	12	76.00 N	23.00 E
Spittal an der Drau	64	46.48 N	13.30 E
Spittal of Glenshee	46	56.48 N	3.28 W
Spitz	61	48.22 N	15.25 E
Spitzer Berg ∧[2]	264a	52.38 N	13.35 E
Spivakivka	83	49.03 N	38.54 E
Spixworth	42	52.40 N	1.20 E
Spjelkavik	26	62.28 N	6.23 E
Splavnucha	80	51.05 N	45.22 E
Splendora	222	30.14 N	95.10 W
Split	36	43.31 N	16.27 E
Split, Cape >	186	45.20 N	64.30 W
Split Lake ⊜	184	56.08 N	96.15 W
Splitrock Reservoir ⊜[1]	276	40.58 N	74.27 W
Spluga, Passo della (Splügenpass))(	58	46.30 N	9.20 E
Splügen	58	46.33 N	9.20 E
Splügenpass (Passo della Spluga))(	58	46.30 N	9.20 E
Spodsbjerg	41	54.56 N	10.50 E
Spofford	196	29.11 N	100.25 W
Špogi	76	56.05 N	26.44 E
Spokane	202	47.39 N	117.25 W
Spokane ≃	202	47.54 N	118.20 W
Spokane, Mount ∧	202	47.55 N	117.07 W
Spokane Indian Reservation ◆[4]	202	47.55 N	118.00 W
Spokojnaja	84	44.15 N	41.25 E
Spoleto	66	42.44 N	12.44 E
Spoltore	66	42.27 N	14.08 E
Spondigna	64	46.38 N	10.37 E
Spondon	42	52.54 N	1.25 W
Sponds Hill ∧[2]	262	53.19 N	2.03 W
Spóng	110	13.27 N	105.34 E
Spoon ≃	194	40.18 N	90.04 W
Spooner	190	45.49 N	91.53 W
Sporava	76	52.25 N	25.20 E
Spořice	54	50.26 N	13.25 E
Spornitz	54	53.24 N	11.43 E
Spornoje	74	62.20 N	151.03 E
Spørring	41	56.18 N	10.09 E
Sportforum ♠	264a	52.33 N	13.29 E
Sport Hill	207	41.14 N	73.16 W
Sporting Hill	208	40.09 N	76.26 W
Sportsman's Park Race Track ♠	278	41.50 N	87.46 W
Spotorno	62	44.14 N	8.25 E
Spot Pond ⊜	283	42.27 N	71.06 W
Spotswood, Austl.	274b	37.50 S	144.53 E
Spotswood, N.J., U.S.	208	40.23 N	74.23 W
Spotsylvania	208	38.12 N	77.35 W
Spotsylvania □[6]	208	38.15 N	77.30 W
Spotsylvania Court House Battlefield ⊥	208	38.15 N	77.35 W
Sprague, Mb., Can.	184	49.02 N	95.38 W
Sprague, Wa., U.S.	202	47.18 N	117.58 W
Sprague ≃	202	42.34 N	121.51 W
Sprague, North Fork ≃	202	42.26 N	121.07 W
Sprague, South Fork ≃	202	42.26 N	121.07 W
Spragueville	207	41.53 N	71.32 W
Sprain Ridge Park ♠	276	40.59 N	73.51 W
Sprankle Mills	214	41.00 N	79.07 W
Spratly Islands II	108	10.00 N	114.00 E
Spratt Point >	212	44.36 N	80.01 W
Spray	202	44.50 N	119.47 W
Spray Lakes Reservoir ⊜[1]	182	50.55 N	115.20 W
Spreča ≃	38	44.45 N	18.06 E
Spreckels	226	36.36 N	121.34 W
Spreckelsville	229a	20.53 N	156.24 W
Spree ≃	54	52.32 N	13.13 E
Spreenhagen	54	52.20 N	13.52 E
Spreeufontein	158	33.22 S	20.45 E
Spreewald ◆[1]	54	51.50 N	14.05 E
Spremberg	54	51.34 N	14.22 E
Sprendlingen	56	49.51 N	7.59 E
Spresiano	64	45.46 N	12.16 E
Spring	222	30.04 N	95.25 W
Spring ≃, U.S.	194	36.52 N	94.44 W
Spring ≃, Ar., U.S.	194	36.08 N	91.05 W
Spring, North Fork ≃	194	37.18 N	94.21 W
Spring, South Fork ≃	194	36.19 N	91.30 W
Spring Arbor	216	42.12 N	84.33 W
Spring Bay ⊂	200	41.40 N	112.50 W
Springbok	156	29.43 S	17.55 E
Springboro, Oh., U.S.	218	39.33 N	84.14 W
Springboro, Pa., U.S.	214	41.48 N	80.22 W
Spring Branch ≃	284b	39.26 N	76.35 W
Springbrook, On., Can.	275b	43.39 N	79.47 W
Springbrook, Md., U.S.	284c	39.03 N	77.00 W
Spring Brook, N.Y., U.S.	210	42.49 N	78.40 W
Spring Brook ≃	278	41.58 N	87.59 W
Springbrook Forest	284c	39.03 N	77.01 W
Springburn	172	43.40 S	171.28 E
Spring City, Pa., U.S.	208	40.10 N	75.32 W
Spring City, Tn., U.S.	192	35.41 N	84.51 W
Spring City, Ut,. U.S.	200	39.28 N	111.29 W
Spring Coulee V	198	48.31 N	100.54 W
Spring Creek, N.Z.	172	41.28 S	173.58 E
Spring Creek, Pa., U.S.	214	41.53 N	79.32 W
Spring Creek ≃, Austl.	166	24.12 S	140.58 E
Spring Creek ≃, U.S.	198	40.30 N	101.21 W
Spring Creek ≃, Ga., U.S.	192	30.54 N	84.45 W
Spring Creek ≃, Il., U.S.	216	40.49 N	87.50 W
Spring Creek ≃, Il., U.S.	219	39.52 N	89.37 W
Spring Creek ≃, Il., U.S.	278	41.32 N	88.04 W
Spring Creek ≃, Mo., U.S.	219	38.21 N	91.10 W
Spring Creek ≃, Nv., U.S.	204	39.55 N	117.50 W
Spring Creek ≃, N.D., U.S.	198	47.15 N	101.48 W
Spring Creek ≃, Pa., U.S.	214	40.56 N	77.47 W
Spring Creek ≃, Pa., U.S.	214	41.24 N	78.57 W
Spring Creek ≃, S.D., U.S.	198	45.54 N	100.18 W
Spring Creek ≃, S.D., U.S.	198	43.52 N	102.42 W
Spring Creek ≃, Tx., U.S.	222	30.02 N	95.16 W
Springdale, Nf., Can.	186	49.30 N	56.04 W
Springdale, Ar., U.S.	194	36.11 N	94.07 W
Springdale, Oh., U.S.	218	39.17 N	84.28 W
Springdale, Pa., U.S.	214	40.32 N	79.47 W
Springdale, S.C., U.S.	192	33.57 N	81.06 W
Springdale, Ut,. U.S.	200	37.11 N	112.59 W
Springdale, Wa., U.S.	202	48.03 N	117.44 W
Spring Dale, W.V., U.S.	192	37.52 N	80.48 W
Springe	52	52.12 N	9.32 E
Springer	196	36.21 N	104.35 W
Springers Brook ≃	285	39.44 N	74.41 W
Springerville	200	34.08 N	109.17 W
Springfield, N.S., Can.	186	44.38 N	64.52 W
Springfield, On., Can.	212	42.50 N	80.56 W
Springfield, N.Z.	172	43.20 S	171.55 E
Springfield, S. Afr.	158	29.02 S	22.53 E
Springfield, Co., U.S.	198	37.24 N	102.36 W
Springfield, Fl., U.S.	194	30.09 N	85.36 W
Springfield, Ga., U.S.	192	32.22 N	81.18 W
Springfield, Il., U.S.	219	39.48 N	89.38 W
Springfield, Ky., U.S.	194	37.41 N	85.13 W
Springfield, Ma., U.S.	207	42.06 N	72.35 W
Springfield, Mi., U.S.	216	42.19 N	85.14 W
Springfield, Mn., U.S.	198	44.14 N	94.58 W
Springfield, Mo., U.S.	194	37.12 N	93.17 W
Springfield, N.J., U.S.	276	40.43 N	74.18 W
Springfield, Oh., U.S.	218	39.55 N	83.48 W
Springfield, Or., U.S.	202	44.02 N	123.01 W
Springfield, Pa., U.S.	285	39.55 N	75.19 W
Springfield, S.C., U.S.	192	33.29 N	81.16 W
Springfield, S.D., U.S.	198	42.51 N	97.53 W
Springfield, Tn., U.S.	194	36.30 N	86.53 W
Springfield, Vt., U.S.	188	43.17 N	72.28 W
Springfield, Va., U.S.	284c	38.45 N	77.13 W
Springfield, Lake ⊜[1]	219	39.44 N	89.36 W
Springfield Center	210	42.50 N	74.53 W
Springfield Estates	284c	38.47 N	77.11 W
Springfield Lake ⊜	285	40.11 N	75.00 W
Springfield Lake ⊜[1]	222	31.36 N	96.33 W
Springfield Mall ◆[9]	284c	38.46 N	77.11 W
Springfield Plateau ⩕[1]	194	37.10 N	93.30 W
Springfontein	158	30.19 S	25.36 E
Spring Garden	246	6.59 N	58.31 W
Spring Garden Brook ≃	276	40.46 N	74.23 W
Spring Garden Township	208	39.57 N	76.44 W
Spring Glen, N.Y., U.S.	210	41.40 N	74.26 W
Spring Glen, Pa., U.S.	208	40.38 N	76.37 W
Spring Glen, Ut,. U.S.	200	39.39 N	110.51 W
Spring Green	190	43.10 N	90.04 W
Spring Grove, Il., U.S.	216	42.26 N	88.13 W
Spring Grove, Mn., U.S.	190	43.33 N	91.38 W
Spring Grove, Pa., U.S.	208	39.52 N	76.51 W
Springhill, N.S., Can.	186	45.39 N	64.03 W
Spring Hill, Ca., U.S.	226	39.15 N	121.03 W
Spring Hill, Fl., U.S.	220	28.33 N	82.27 W
Springhill, La., U.S.	194	33.00 N	93.28 W
Spring Hill, Pa., U.S.	214	40.23 N	78.40 W
Spring Hill, Tn., U.S.	194	35.45 N	86.55 W
Spring Hill, Tx., U.S.	222	32.34 N	94.48 W
Springhills	216	40.16 N	83.22 W
Spring Hope	192	35.56 N	78.06 W
Springhouse, B.C., Can.	182	51.55 N	122.07 W
Spring House, Pa., U.S.	285	40.11 N	75.14 W
Spring Lake, Mi., U.S.	216	43.04 N	86.11 W
Spring Lake, N.J., U.S.	208	40.09 N	74.01 W
Spring Lake, N.C., U.S.	192	35.10 N	78.58 W
Spring Lake ⊜, Mi., U.S.	216	43.06 N	86.11 W
Spring Lake ⊜, N.J., U.S.	276	40.35 N	74.25 W
Spring Lake Heights	208	40.09 N	74.01 W
Spring Mill, Oh., U.S.	214	40.54 N	82.36 W
Spring Mill, Pa., U.S.	285	40.04 N	75.17 W
Spring Mill Reservoir ⊜[1]	262	53.39 N	2.13 W
Spring Mills	210	40.51 N	77.34 W
Spring Mill State Park ♠	218	38.43 N	86.25 W
Spring Mount	208	40.17 N	75.28 W
Spring Mountains ⩕	204	36.10 N	115.40 W
Spring Pond ⊜	283	42.30 N	70.57 W
Springport, In., U.S.	218	40.03 N	85.24 W
Springport, Mi., U.S.	216	42.22 N	84.41 W
Spring Run	214	40.09 N	83.47 W
Springs	158	26.13 S	28.25 E
Springs □[5]	273d	26.14 S	28.30 E
Springs Aerodrome ⊠	273d	26.15 S	28.24 E
Springside	285	40.04 N	74.51 W
Springs Junction	172	42.19 S	172.11 E
Springsure	166	24.07 S	148.05 E
Springton	168b	34.43 S	139.05 E
Springtown	222	32.58 N	97.41 W
Springvale, Austl.	162	17.48 S	127.41 E
Springvale, Austl.	166	23.33 S	140.42 E
Springvale, Austl.	169	37.57 S	145.09 E
Springvale, Me., U.S.	188	43.28 N	70.47 W
Springvale South	274b	37.58 S	145.09 E
Spring Valley, Ca., U.S.	228	32.44 N	116.59 W
Spring Valley, Il., U.S.	190	41.19 N	89.11 W
Spring Valley, Mn., U.S.	190	43.41 N	92.23 W
Spring Valley, N.Y., U.S.	210	41.06 N	74.02 W
Spring Valley, Oh., U.S.	218	39.36 N	84.00 W
Spring Valley, Tx., U.S.	222	29.47 N	95.31 W
Spring Valley, Wi., U.S.	190	44.50 N	92.14 W
Spring Valley V	204	39.15 N	114.25 W
Spring Valley Creek ≃	204	39.20 N	114.25 W
Springview	198	42.49 N	99.44 W
Springville, Al., U.S.	194	33.46 N	86.28 W
Springville, Ca., U.S.	204	36.08 N	118.49 W
Springville, Ia., U.S.	190	42.03 N	91.26 W
Springville, N.J., U.S.	285	39.56 N	74.52 W
Springville, N.Y., U.S.	210	42.30 N	78.40 W
Springville, Pa., U.S.	210	41.42 N	75.55 W
Springville, Ut,. U.S.	200	40.09 N	111.36 W
Springwater	210	42.38 N	77.35 W
Springwood	170	33.42 S	150.33 E
Sprint ≃	44	54.22 N	2.45 W
Sprite Creek ≃	210	43.08 N	74.44 W
Sproat Lake ⊜	182	49.16 N	125.03 W
Sprockhövel	56	51.22 N	7.15 E
Sprogels Run ≃	285	40.14 N	75.37 W
Sprogø I	41	55.20 N	10.58 E
Sprötze	52	53.18 N	9.49 E
Sproul	214	40.16 N	78.28 W
Sprout Brook ≃	276	40.54 N	74.05 W
Spruce ≃	184	53.15 N	105.43 W
Spruce Brook	186	48.45 N	58.11 W
Spruce Creek	214	40.37 N	78.08 W
Spruce Creek ≃	210	43.07 N	74.46 W
Spruce Grove	182	53.32 N	113.55 W
Spruce Knob ∧	188	38.42 N	79.32 W
Spruce Knob-Seneca Rocks National Recreation Area ♠	188	38.50 N	79.20 W
Spruce Lake	184	53.32 N	109.05 W
Spruce Mountain ∧, Az., U.S.	200	34.28 N	112.24 W
Spruce Mountain ∧, Nv., U.S.	204	40.33 N	114.49 W
Spruce Pine, Al., U.S.	194	34.23 N	87.43 W
Spruce Pine, N.C., U.S.	192	35.54 N	82.03 W
Spruce Run Reservoir ⊜[1]	210	40.40 N	74.57 W
Spruce Run State Park ♠	210	40.40 N	74.56 W
Spruce Woods Provincial Park ♠	184	49.42 N	99.05 W
Spry	208	39.55 N	76.41 W
Spry Lake ⊜	212	44.44 N	81.15 W
Spulico, Capo >	68	39.58 N	16.39 E
Spur	196	33.28 N	100.51 W
Spurfield	182	55.13 N	114.16 W
Spurger	194	30.42 N	94.11 W
Spurn Head >	44	53.34 N	0.07 E
Spurr, Mount ∧	180	61.18 N	152.15 W
Sputendorf	264a	52.20 N	13.13 E
Spuzzum	182	49.41 N	121.25 W
Spy Hill	184	50.36 N	101.41 W
Spy Pond ⊜	283	42.24 N	71.09 W
Squally Channel Ʉ	182	53.10 N	129.15 W
Squamish	182	49.42 N	123.09 W
Squamish ≃	182	49.45 N	123.09 W
Squam Lake ⊜	188	43.45 N	71.32 W
Square Butte Creek ≃	198	46.55 N	100.55 W
Square Lake ⊜	186	47.03 N	68.20 W
Squatec	186	47.53 N	68.43 W
Squaw Cap Mountain ∧	186	47.53 N	66.53 W
Squaw Creek ≃, Id., U.S.	202	43.51 N	116.22 W
Squaw Creek ≃, Il., U.S.	278	42.21 N	88.07 W
Squaw Creek ≃, Or., U.S.	202	44.27 N	121.20 W
Squaw Creek Lake ⊜[1]	222	32.19 N	97.47 W
Squaw Harbor	180	55.11 N	160.30 W
Squaw Hill ∧	200	41.48 N	105.02 W
Squaw Island I	284a	42.56 N	78.54 W
Squaw Peak ∧, Ca., U.S.	226	39.11 N	120.16 W
Squaw Peak ∧, Mt., U.S.	202	47.10 N	114.21 W
Squaw Rapids	184	53.41 N	103.20 W
Squaw Rapids Dam ◆[6]	184	53.40 N	103.25 W
Squaw Run ≃	279b	40.29 N	79.52 W
Squaw Valley State Recreation Area ♠	226	39.12 N	120.15 W
Squibnocket Point >	207	41.18 N	70.47 W
Squilax	182	50.52 N	119.35 W
Squillace	68	38.47 N	16.31 E
Squillace, Golfo di ⊂	68	38.50 N	16.50 E
Squinzano	68	40.26 N	18.03 E

≃ River	Fluß	Río	Rivière	Rio	
≊ Canal	Kanal	Canal	Canal	Canal	
⌞ Waterfall, Rapids	Wasserfall, Stromschnellen	Cascada, Rápidos	Chute d'eau, Rapides	Cascata, Rápidos	
Ʉ Strait	Meeresstraße	Estrecho	Détroit	Estreito	
⊂ Bay, Gulf	Bucht, Golf	Bahía, Golfo	Baie, Golfe	Baía, Golfo	
⊜ Lake, Lakes	See, Seen	Lago, Lagos	Lac, Lacs	Lago, Lagos	
⩯ Swamp	Sumpf	Pantano	Marais	Pântano	
⫨ Ice Features, Glacier	Eis- und Gletscherformen	Accidentes Glaciales	Formes glaciaires	Acidentes glaciares	
⫪ Other Hydrographic Features	Andere Hydrographische Objekte	Otros Elementos Hidrográficos	Autres données hydrographiques	Outros acidentes hidrográficos	
✢ Submarine Features	Untermeerische Objekte	Accidentes Submarinos	Formes de relief sous-marin	Acidentes submarinos	
□ Political Unit	Politische Einheit	Unidad Política	Entité politique	Unidade política	
ʊ Cultural Institution	Kulturelle Institution	Institución Cultural	Institution culturelle	Instituição cultural	
⊥ Historical Site	Historische Stätte	Sitio Histórico	Site historique	Sitio histórico	
♠ Recreational Site	Erholungs- und Ferienort	Sitio de Recreo	Centre de loisirs	Area de Lazer	
⊠ Airport	Flughafen	Aeropuerto	Aéroport	Aeroporto	
■ Military Installation	Militäranlage	Instalación Militar	Installation militaire	Instalação militar	
◆ Miscellaneous	Verschiedenes	Misceláneo	Divers	Diversos	

Name	Page	Lat.°′	Long.°′
Squire	192	37.14 N	81.36 W
Squires, Mount ∧	162	26.12 S	127.28 E
Squirrel ≃	180	66.57 N	160.27 W
Squirrel Hill •[8]	279b	40.26 N	79.55 W
Squirrel Hill Tunnel •[5]	279b	40.26 N	79.55 W
Squirrel's Heath •[8]	260	51.35 N	0.13 E
Sragen	115a	7.26 S	111.02 E
Srbija (Serbia) □[3]	38	44.00 N	21.00 E
Srbobran	38	45.33 N	19.48 E
Srê Âmbĕl	110	11.07 N	103.46 E
Sredec	38	42.21 N	27.10 E
Sredinnyj chrebet ⋀	74	56.00 N	158.00 E
Sredna Gora ⋀	38	42.30 N	25.00 E
Sredn'aja Achtuba	80	48.43 N	44.52 E
Sredn'aja Mokla ≃	88	55.01 N	119.37 E
Sredn'aja Nanaki, gora ∧	89	52.26 N	132.50 E
Sredn'aja Ol'okma	88	55.26 N	120.33 E
Srednegorje	76	60.34 N	29.25 E
Sredneje Kujto, ozero ⊜	24	65.08 N	31.15 E
Srednekolymsk	74	67.27 N	153.41 E
Srednerusskaja vozvyšennost' ⋀[1]	72	52.00 N	38.00 E
Srednesibirskoje ploskogorje ⋀[1]	74	65.00 N	105.00 E
Srednij Ikorec	78	51.05 N	39.45 E
Srednij Kalar	88	55.51 N	117.24 E
Srednij Ural ⋀	86	58.00 N	59.00 E
Srednij Urgal	89	51.09 N	132.59 E
Srednij Vas'ugan	86	59.16 N	78.15 E
Srê Khtŭm	110	12.10 N	106.52 E
Śrem	30	52.08 N	17.01 E
Srê Moăt	110	13.18 N	107.10 E
Sremska Mitrovica	38	44.58 N	19.37 E
Sremski Karlovci	38	45.12 N	19.57 E
Srêng ≃	110	13.21 N	103.27 E
Srêpôk ≃	110	13.33 N	106.16 E
Sretensk	88	52.15 N	117.43 E
Sretenskoje	88	56.28 N	96.25 E
Srīdharpur	126	23.04 N	89.25 E
Sri Hargobindpur	123	31.41 N	75.39 E
Sri Jayawardenepura (Kotte)	122	6.54 N	79.54 E
Srīkākulam	122	18.18 N	83.54 E
Sri Kālahasti	122	13.45 N	79.43 E
Sri Lanka □[1], Asia	118	7.00 N	81.00 E
Sri Lanka □[1], Asia	122	7.00 N	81.00 E
Srīnagar, Bngl.	126	23.32 N	90.18 E
Srīnagar, India	123	34.05 N	74.49 E
Srīnagar, India	124	30.13 N	78.47 E
Srīnagar Airport ⊠	123	34.00 N	74.52 E
Srīpur, Bngl.	126	24.12 N	90.29 E
Srīpur, Bngl.	126	23.36 N	89.24 E
Srīrampur, India	122	19.34 N	74.34 E
Srirāmpur, India	272b	22.49 N	88.29 E
Srīrangam	122	10.52 N	78.41 E
Srīvardhan	122	18.02 N	73.01 E
Srīvilliputtūr	122	9.31 N	77.38 E
Środa Śląska	30	51.10 N	16.36 E
Środa Wielkopolski	30	52.14 N	17.17 E
Srpska Crnja	38	45.43 N	20.42 E
Ssangmun-ni •[8]	271b	37.39 N	127.02 E
Ssuchunghsi	100	22.06 N	120.44 E
Ssup'ing → Siping	89	43.12 N	124.20 E
Staaken •[8]	54	52.32 N	13.08 E
Staaten ≃	164	16.24 S	141.17 E
Staaten River National Park ♦	164	16.40 S	143.00 E
Staatsburg	210	41.50 N	73.55 W
Staatz	61	48.40 N	16.29 E
Stabbursdalen Nasjonalpark ♦	24	70.06 N	24.30 E
Staberhuk ›	54	54.24 N	11.19 E
Stabroek	50	51.20 N	4.22 E
Stachy	60	49.06 N	13.40 E
Stack, Loch ⊜	46	58.20 N	4.55 W
Stack Skerry I[2]	46	59.01 N	4.31 W
Stacksteads	262	53.41 N	2.13 W
Stacyville	190	43.26 N	92.46 W
Stad-Delden	52	52.16 N	6.42 E
Stade	52	53.36 N	9.28 E
Staden, Bel.	50	50.59 N	3.01 E
Staden, Dtsch.	56	50.20 N	8.54 E
Stadion am Zoo ♦	263	51.14 N	7.07 E
Städjan ∧	26	61.55 N	12.52 E
Stadl an der Mur	61	47.05 N	13.58 E
Stadlandet ›[1]	26	62.07 N	5.18 E
Stadlau •[8]	264b	48.14 N	16.28 E
Stadl-Paura	64	48.05 N	13.53 E
Stadoličy	78	51.44 N	28.30 E
Stadskanaal	52	53.00 N	6.55 E
Stadtallendorf	56	50.50 N	9.01 E
Stadthagen	52	52.19 N	9.13 E
Stadtilm	54	50.47 N	11.05 E
Städtische Rahmede	263	51.17 N	7.40 E
Stadtkyll	56	50.21 N	6.32 E
Stadtlauringen	56	50.11 N	10.22 E
Stadtlengsfeld	56	50.47 N	10.07 E
Stadtlohn	52	51.59 N	6.55 E
Stadtoldendorf	52	51.53 N	9.37 E
Stadtprozelten	56	49.47 N	9.25 E
Stadtroda	54	50.51 N	11.44 E
Stadtsteinach	54	50.09 N	11.30 E
Stadt Wehlen	54	50.58 N	14.02 E
Stadum	41	54.44 N	9.03 E
Stäfa	58	47.15 N	8.44 E
Staffa I	46	56.25 N	6.20 W
Staffanstorp	41	55.38 N	13.13 E
Staffelberg ∧	56	50.06 N	11.02 E
Staffelde	264a	52.44 N	13.00 E
Staffelsee ⊜	64	47.42 N	11.10 E
Staffelstein	56	50.06 N	11.00 E
Staffin	46	57.37 N	6.12 W
Staffora ≃	62	45.04 N	9.01 E
Stafford, Eng., U.K.	42	52.48 N	2.07 W
Stafford, Ct., U.S.	207	41.59 N	72.17 W
Stafford, Ks., U.S.	198	37.57 N	98.36 W
Stafford, N.Y., U.S.	210	42.59 N	78.04 W
Stafford, Tx., U.S.	222	29.37 N	95.34 W
Stafford, Va., U.S.	208	38.25 N	77.24 W
Stafford □[6]	208	38.25 N	77.30 W
Staffordshire □[6]	28	52.50 N	2.00 W
Stafford Springs	207	41.57 N	72.18 W
Staffordsville	188	37.49 N	82.50 W
Staffordville	207	41.59 N	72.15 W
Stagen	112	3.18 S	116.10 E
Stag Pond ⊜	276	40.59 N	74.42 W
Stahl-Berg ∧[2]	264a	52.21 N	13.46 E
Stahlbrode	54	54.14 N	13.17 E
Stahle	52	51.50 N	9.25 E
Stahnsdorf	54	52.23 N	13.13 E
Stahringen	58	47.47 N	8.58 E
Staicele	76	57.50 N	24.45 E
Staines	42	51.26 N	0.31 W
Staines Reservoirs ⊜[1]	260	51.27 N	0.30 W
Stainforth	44	53.36 N	1.01 W
Staining	44	53.49 N	2.59 W
Stainland	262	53.40 N	1.53 W
Stainmore Forest •[3]	44	54.30 N	2.10 W
Stains	261	48.57 N	2.23 E
Stainz	61	46.54 N	15.16 E
Stairtown	222	29.43 N	97.44 W
Staked Plain → Estacado, Llano ≚	196	33.30 N	102.40 W
Stäket	40	59.28 N	17.48 E
Stakhanov	83	48.34 N	38.40 E
Stakroge	41	55.53 N	8.51 E
Stalać	38	43.40 N	21.25 E
Stalbridge	42	50.58 N	2.23 W
Stalden	58	46.14 N	7.52 E
Stalettì	68	38.46 N	16.32 E
Stalham	42	52.47 N	1.31 E
Stalheim	26	60.50 N	6.40 E
Stalhofen	61	47.05 N	15.16 E
Stalin → Varna, Blg.	38	43.13 N	27.55 E
Stalin → Brașov, Rom.	38	45.39 N	25.37 E
Stalin → Kuçovë, Shq.	38	40.48 N	19.54 E
Stalinabad → Dušanbe	85	38.35 N	68.48 E
Stalingrad → Volgograd	80	48.44 N	44.25 E
Stalino → Donets'k	83	48.00 N	37.48 E
Stalinogorsk → Novomoskovsk	82	54.05 N	38.13 E
Stalinsk → Novokuzneck	86	53.45 N	87.06 E
Stallarholmen	40	59.22 N	17.12 E
Ställberg	40	59.59 N	14.55 E
Ställdalen	40	59.56 N	14.56 E
Stallwang	60	49.03 N	12.40 E
Stalowa Wola	30	50.35 N	22.02 E
Stalybridge	44	53.29 N	2.03 W
Stambaugh	190	46.04 N	88.37 W
Stamford, Austl.	166	21.16 S	143.49 E
Stamford, Eng., U.K.	42	52.39 N	0.29 W
Stamford, Ct., U.S.	207	41.03 N	73.32 W
Stamford, N.Y., U.S.	210	42.24 N	74.36 W
Stamford, Tx., U.S.	196	32.56 N	99.48 W
Stamford, Vt., U.S.	207	42.45 N	73.04 W
Stamford, Lake ⊜[1]	196	33.05 N	99.35 W
Stamford Bridge	44	53.59 N	0.55 W
Stamford Brige Stadium ♦	260	51.29 N	0.11 W
Stamford Harbor ⊂	276	41.02 N	73.32 W
Stamford Museum ʊ	276	41.07 N	73.33 W
Stammbach	54	50.09 N	11.41 E
Stammersdorf •[8]	264b	48.18 N	16.25 E
Stammham, Dtsch.	60	48.15 N	12.53 E
Stammham, Dtsch.	60	48.52 N	11.28 E
Stammheim, Dtsch.	56	48.41 N	8.46 E
Stammheim, Schw.	58	47.38 N	8.47 E
Stampede Reservoir ⊜[1]	226	39.29 N	120.07 W
Stamping Ground	218	38.16 N	84.41 W
Stampriet	156	24.20 S	18.28 E
Stamps	194	33.21 N	93.29 W
Stams	64	47.16 N	10.59 E
Stamsried	60	49.16 N	12.32 E
Stanaford	188	37.48 N	81.09 W
Stanardsville	188	38.17 N	78.26 W
Stanberry	194	40.13 N	94.32 W
Stanborough	260	51.47 N	0.13 W
Stancija-Gorčakovo	85	40.25 N	71.45 E
Stancionno-Ojašinskij	86	55.28 N	83.53 E
Standard, Ab., Can.	182	51.07 N	112.59 W
Standard, Ak., U.S.	180	64.47 N	148.32 W
Standard, Ca., U.S.	226	37.59 N	120.20 W
Standard, Pa., U.S.	214	40.10 N	79.32 W
Standard Oil Company Refinery ʊ[3]	282	37.57 N	122.24 W
Standard Shaft	279b	40.10 N	79.32 W
Standedge Canal Tunnel •[5]	262	53.34 N	2.00 W
Standedge Railway Tunnel •[5]	262	53.34 N	2.00 W
Standerton	158	26.58 S	29.07 E
Standiford Field ⊠	218	38.11 N	85.44 W
Standing Rock Indian Reservation •[4]	198	45.50 N	101.10 W
Standing Stone Creek ≃	214	40.30 N	78.00 W
Standing Stones ⊥	46	58.12 N	6.48 W
Standish, Eng., U.K.	44	53.36 N	2.41 W
Standish, Mi., U.S.	190	43.58 N	83.57 W
Standish Monument ⊥	283	42.01 N	70.41 W
Standon	42	51.53 N	0.02 E
Stanfield, Az., U.S.	200	32.52 N	111.57 W
Stanfield, Or., U.S.	202	45.46 N	119.12 W
Stanford, S. Afr.	158	34.26 S	19.29 E
Stanford, Ca., U.S.	226	37.25 N	122.08 W
Stanford, Ky., U.S.	192	37.31 N	84.39 W
Stanford, Mt., U.S.	202	47.09 N	110.13 W
Stanford Center •[9]	282	37.27 N	122.10 W
Stanford Heights	210	42.46 N	73.53 W
Stanford le Hope	42	51.31 N	0.26 E
Stanford Linear Accelerator ʊ[3]	282	37.25 N	122.12 W
Stanford Rivers	260	51.41 N	0.13 E
Stanford University ʊ[2]	282	37.26 N	122.10 W
Stanfordville	210	41.52 N	73.43 W
Stånga	26	57.17 N	18.28 E
Stångån ≃	26	58.27 N	15.37 E
Stångby	41	55.46 N	13.10 E
Stange	26	60.43 N	11.11 E
Stanger	158	29.27 S	31.14 E
Stanghella	64	45.08 N	11.45 E
Stanhope, Eng., U.K.	44	54.45 N	2.01 W
Stanhope, Ia., U.S.	190	42.17 N	93.47 W
Stanhope, N.J., U.S.	210	40.54 N	74.42 W
Stanislaus □[6]	226	37.39 N	121.00 W
Stanislaus ≃	226	37.40 N	121.14 W
Stanislaus, Clark Fork ≃	226	38.22 N	119.52 W
Stanislaus, Middle Fork ≃	226	38.09 N	120.21 W
Stanislaus, North Fork ≃	226	38.09 N	120.21 W
Stanislaus, South Fork ≃	226	38.04 N	120.25 W
Stanislav → Ivano-Frankivs'k, Ukr.	78	48.55 N	24.43 E
Stanislav, Ukr.	78	46.34 N	32.09 E
Stanislavchyk	78	48.58 N	28.07 E
Stanisławów → Ivano-Frankivs'k	78	48.55 N	24.43 E
Stânișoara, Munții ⋀	38	47.10 N	26.00 E
Staňkov	60	49.34 N	13.04 E
Stanley, Austl.	166	40.46 S	145.18 E
Stanley, N.B., Can.	186	46.17 N	66.44 W
Stanley, Falk. Is.	254	51.42 S	57.51 W
Stanley, Zhg.	271d	22.13 N	114.12 E
Stanley, Eng., U.K.	44	54.52 N	1.42 W
Stanley, Scot., U.K.	46	56.28 N	3.27 W
Stanley, N.Y., U.S.	210	42.49 N	77.06 W
Stanley, N.C., U.S.	192	35.21 N	81.05 W
Stanley, N.D., U.S.	198	48.19 N	102.23 W
Stanley, Va., U.S.	188	38.34 N	78.30 W
Stanley, Wi., U.S.	190	44.57 N	90.56 W
Stanley ≃	171a	27.09 S	152.32 E
Stanley, Mont ∧[2]	273b	4.19 S	15.15 E
Stanley Bay ⊂	271d	22.12 N	114.12 E
Stanley Falls ∟	154	0.30 N	25.12 E
Stanley Mills	275b	43.46 N	79.44 W
Stanley Mound ∧	271d	22.14 N	114.12 E
Stanley Park ♦, B.C., Can.	224	49.19 N	123.09 W
Stanley Park ♦, Eng., U.K.	262	53.26 N	2.57 W
Stanley Park ♦, Eng., U.K.	262	53.49 N	3.02 W
Stanley Reservoir ⊜[1]	122	11.54 N	77.50 E
Stanleyville → Kisangani	154	0.30 N	25.12 E
Stanlow	44	53.17 N	2.52 W
Stanmore •[8]	260	51.37 N	0.19 W
Stannards	210	42.05 N	77.55 W
Stannington	44	55.06 N	1.40 W
Stanovoj chrebet ⋀	74	56.20 N	126.00 E
Stanovoje nagorje (Stanovoy Mountains) ⋀	88	56.00 N	114.00 E
Stanovoj Kolodez'	76	52.51 N	36.16 E
Stanovoy Mountains → Stanovoje nagorje ⋀	88	56.00 N	114.00 E
Stans	58	46.57 N	8.22 E
Stansbury	168b	34.55 S	137.47 E
Stansmore Range ⋀	162	21.23 S	128.33 E
Stansstad	58	46.59 N	8.20 E
Stanstead	206	45.01 N	72.05 W
Stanstead □[6]	206	45.10 N	72.00 W
Stanstead Abbots	42	51.47 N	0.01 E
Stansted	260	51.20 N	0.18 E
Stansted Mountfitchet	42	51.54 N	0.12 E
Stanthorpe	166	28.39 S	151.57 E
Stanton, Eng., U.K.	42	52.19 N	0.53 E
Stanton, Ca., U.S.	228	33.48 N	117.59 W
Stanton, De., U.S.	208	39.43 N	75.37 W
Stanton, Ia., U.S.	198	41.05 N	95.11 W
Stanton, Ky., U.S.	192	37.50 N	83.51 W
Stanton, Mi., U.S.	190	43.17 N	85.04 W
Stanton, Mo., U.S.	219	38.16 N	91.06 W
Stanton, Ne., U.S.	198	41.57 N	97.13 W
Stanton, N.D., U.S.	198	47.19 N	101.22 W
Stanton, Tn., U.S.	194	35.27 N	89.24 W
Stanton, Tx., U.S.	196	32.07 N	101.47 W
Stantonsburg	192	35.36 N	77.49 W
Stanwell	260	51.27 N	0.29 W
Stanwell Moor	260	51.28 N	0.30 W
Stanwood	224	48.14 N	122.22 W
Stanwyck Estates	285	39.42 N	75.33 W
Stanychno-Luhans'ke	83	48.39 N	39.30 E
Stanzach	58	47.23 N	10.34 E
Stanz im Mürztal	61	47.28 N	15.30 E
Stapelburg	54	51.53 N	10.40 E
Stapelfeld	52	53.36 N	10.13 E
Staphorst	52	52.37 N	6.12 E
Stapleford	42	52.56 N	1.16 W
Stapleford Abbotts	260	51.38 N	0.10 E
Stapleford Aerodrome ⊠	260	51.39 N	0.08 E
Stapleford Tawney	260	51.40 N	0.11 E
Staplehurst	42	51.10 N	0.33 E
Staples	198	46.21 N	94.47 W
Stapleton, Al., U.S.	194	30.44 N	87.47 W
Stapleton, Ne., U.S.	198	41.28 N	100.30 W
Stąporków	30	51.09 N	20.34 E
Star', Ross.	76	53.37 N	34.09 E
Star, Ms., U.S.	194	32.05 N	90.02 W
Star, N.C., U.S.	192	35.24 N	79.47 W
Stará Boleslav	54	50.12 N	14.42 E
Starachowice	30	51.03 N	21.04 E
Stara Fužina	64	46.17 N	13.54 E
Staraja	265a	59.55 N	30.38 E
Staraja Belica, Bela.	76	54.42 N	29.38 E
Staraja Belica, Ross.	78	51.59 N	35.13 E
Staraja Belogorka	80	52.05 N	53.17 E
Staraja Derevn'a •[8]	265a	59.59 N	30.15 E
Staraja Duginka	82	54.20 N	38.45 E
Staraja Kriuša	78	50.12 N	41.09 E
Staraja Kulatka	80	52.43 N	47.37 E
Staraja Kupavna	82	55.48 N	38.10 E
Staraja Majna	80	54.36 N	48.57 E
Staraja Poltavka	80	50.28 N	46.28 E
Staraja Porubežka	80	52.03 N	49.11 E
Staraja Račejka	80	53.22 N	48.03 E
Staraja Rudnja	76	52.50 N	30.17 E
Staraja Russa	76	58.00 N	31.23 E
Staraja Ruza	82	55.39 N	36.20 E
Staraja Sachča	80	54.25 N	49.58 E
Staraja Sitn'a	82	54.56 N	38.09 E
Staraja Terizmorga	80	54.16 N	44.32 E
Staraja Toropa	76	56.17 N	31.40 E
Staraja Veduga	78	51.48 N	38.31 E
Staraja Vičuga	80	57.16 N	41.53 E
Stara Mayachka	78	46.30 N	33.11 E
Staranzano	64	45.49 N	13.30 E
Stara Pazova	38	44.59 N	20.10 E
Stara Planina (Balkan Mountains) ⋀	38	42.45 N	25.00 E
Stará Role	54	50.14 N	12.47 E
Stara Synyava	78	49.36 N	27.37 E
Stara Ushytsya	78	48.35 N	27.07 E
Starav, Ben ∧	46	56.32 N	5.03 W
Stará Voda	60	50.00 N	12.36 E
Stara Vyzhivka	78	51.27 N	24.24 E
Stara Zagora	38	42.25 N	25.38 E
Starbejevo	265b	55.55 N	37.28 E
Starbrick	214	41.50 N	79.12 W
Starbuck, Mb., Can.	184	49.46 N	97.36 W
Starbuck, Mn., U.S.	198	45.36 N	95.31 W
Starbuck, Wa., U.S.	202	46.31 N	118.07 W
Starbuck I	14	5.37 S	155.53 W
Starchenkove	78	47.17 N	36.59 E
Star City, Sk., Can.	184	52.53 N	104.21 W
Star City, Ar., U.S.	194	33.56 N	91.50 W
Star City, In., U.S.	216	40.58 N	86.33 W
Starcross	42	50.38 N	3.27 W
Stare Czarnowo	54	53.16 N	14.45 E
Staré Sedliště	60	49.45 N	12.42 E
Starford	214	40.42 N	78.58 W
Stargard Szczeciński (Stargard in Pommern)	30	53.20 N	15.02 E
Stargo	200	33.04 N	109.21 W
Star Harbour ⊂	175e	10.47 S	162.18 E
Stari Bar	38	42.06 N	19.08 E
Starica, Ross.	76	56.30 N	34.56 E
Starica, Ross.	76	59.04 N	29.30 E
Starica, Ross.	80	48.13 N	45.56 E
Stari Grad	36	43.11 N	16.36 E
Starij R'ad	76	58.05 N	34.54 E
Starina	76	59.37 N	44.42 E
Stari Popylyukhy	78	48.18 N	28.55 E
Stari Sanzhary	78	49.25 N	34.27 E
Stari Vlah •[1]	38	43.35 N	20.15 E
Star Junction	214	40.04 N	79.46 W
Stark □[6]	214	40.48 N	81.22 W
Starke	192	29.56 N	82.06 W
Starke □[6]	216	41.18 N	86.37 W
Starkey	210	42.32 N	76.56 W
Starkville	194	33.27 N	88.49 W
Star Lake	224	47.22 N	122.18 W
Star Mountains ⋀	164	5.05 S	141.05 E
Starnberg	60	48.00 N	11.20 E
Starnberger See ⊜	64	47.55 N	11.18 E
Starnikovo	82	55.22 N	38.24 E
Staroalejskoje	86	51.00 N	82.01 E
Starobačaty	86	54.14 N	86.07 E
Starobaltačevo	86	56.01 N	55.56 E
Starobesheve	83	47.44 N	38.03 E
Starobil's'k	83	49.16 N	38.56 E
Starobin	76	52.44 N	27.28 E
Staročerkasskaja	83	47.15 N	40.03 E
Starocuruchajtuj	88	50.12 N	119.15 E
Staroderev'ankovskaja	78	46.08 N	38.58 E
Starodub	76	52.35 N	32.46 E
Starod'umejevo	80	55.16 N	54.22 E
Starogan'kino	80	53.55 N	52.15 E
Starogard Gdański	30	53.59 N	18.33 E
Staroihnativka	83	47.32 N	37.47 E
Staroje	76	59.16 N	40.40 E
Staroje Bajsarovo	80	55.31 N	53.54 E
Staroje Drožžanoje	80	54.44 N	47.34 E
Staroje Ibrajkino	80	54.52 N	51.02 E
Staroje Jaškino	80	52.49 N	52.57 E
Staroje Jermakovo	80	54.04 N	51.59 E
Staroje Oleničevo	80	45.34 N	47.11 E
Staroje Rachino	76	58.08 N	32.39 E
Staroje Šajgovo	80	54.18 N	44.26 E
Staroje Šajmurzino	80	54.45 N	47.58 E
Staroje Sindrovo	80	54.25 N	44.06 E
Staroje Sjalo	76	55.14 N	29.54 E
Staroje Slavkino	80	52.34 N	45.08 E
Staroje Ustje	80	53.28 N	41.51 E
Starojurjevo	80	53.21 N	40.42 E
Starokostyantyniv	78	49.46 N	27.13 E
Starokozache	78	46.21 N	29.59 E
Starokuručevo	80	55.09 N	54.04 E
Starolaspa	83	47.34 N	37.59 E
Staroleuškovskaja	78	45.59 N	39.44 E
Starominskaja	78	46.31 N	39.04 E
Staromlynivka	78	47.42 N	36.49 E
Staromušta	80	55.49 N	54.14 E
Staromykhaylivka	83	47.58 N	37.36 E
Staronikolajevo	82	55.37 N	36.16 E
Staro-Podgorodneje	82	54.46 N	38.57 E
Staropokrovka	85	42.50 N	75.18 E
Staroščerbinovskaja	78	46.37 N	38.40 E
Staroseslavino	80	53.12 N	40.25 E
Starošešminsk	80	55.22 N	51.15 E
Starosiedle	54	51.50 N	14.50 E
Starosoldatskoje	86	56.12 N	72.37 E
Starosubchangulovo	86	53.06 N	57.26 E
Starotimoškino	24	53.43 N	47.32 E
Starotitarovskaja	78	45.14 N	37.09 E
Staroutkinsk	86	57.14 N	59.20 E
Starovirivka	78	49.33 N	35.42 E
Starožilovo	80	54.14 N	39.55 E
Starožil'sk	80	56.34 N	47.17 E
Star Peak ∧	204	40.32 N	118.10 W
Starr	214	41.32 N	79.22 W
Starrucca	210	41.54 N	75.28 W
Start Bay ⊂	42	50.17 N	3.36 W
Start Point ›	42	50.13 N	3.38 W
Startup	224	47.52 N	121.44 W
Starvation Reservoir ⊜[1]	200	40.15 N	110.30 W
Starved Rock State Park ♦	216	41.19 N	88.58 W
Staryja Darohi	76	53.02 N	28.16 E
Staryj Ajbesi	80	54.57 N	47.03 E
Staryj Bagr'až	80	54.54 N	51.39 E
Staryj Bir'uz'ak	84	44.47 N	46.54 E
Staryj Bol'ševik	265b	55.57 N	37.47 E
Staryj Chop'or	80	51.30 N	42.58 E
Staryj Čindant	88	50.33 N	115.33 E
Staryje Burasy	80	52.16 N	46.09 E
Staryje Maty	80	55.14 N	53.55 E
Staryje Turdaki	80	53.55 N	45.29 E
Staryje Z'atcy	80	57.21 N	52.39 E
Staryj Kazangal	80	50.15 N	47.39 E
Staryj Kistruss	80	54.28 N	40.34 E
Staryj Lesken	84	43.20 N	43.55 E
Staryj Medved'	76	58.18 N	30.30 E
Staryj Oskol	78	51.19 N	37.51 E
Staryj Terek ≃	84	44.00 N	47.24 E
Staryj Tukšum	80	53.42 N	48.33 E
Starý Plzenec	60	49.42 N	13.28 E
Stary Sącz	30	49.34 N	20.38 E
Staryy Chortoryys'k	78	51.15 N	25.54 E
Staryy Krym, Ukr.	78	45.03 N	35.05 E
Staryy Krym, Ukr.	83	47.10 N	37.30 E
Staryy Merchyk	78	49.58 N	35.46 E
Staryy Sambir	78	49.27 N	22.59 E
Stassfurt	54	51.51 N	11.34 E
Staszów	30	50.34 N	21.20 E
State Center	190	42.01 N	93.09 W
State College	214	40.47 N	77.51 W
State Fair Grounds ♦	284b	39.27 N	76.38 W
Stateline, Ca., U.S.	226	38.57 N	119.57 W
State Line, Ms., U.S.	194	31.26 N	88.28 W
Stateline, Nv., U.S.	204	38.58 N	119.56 W
Staten Island I	276	40.35 N	74.09 W
Staten Island Mall •[9]	276	40.35 N	74.10 W
Statenville	192	30.42 N	83.01 W
State Park Place	219	38.40 N	90.03 W
State Road	192	36.19 N	80.52 W
Statesboro	192	32.26 N	81.47 W
Statesville	192	35.46 N	80.53 W
Stateville Correctional Center ʊ	278	41.35 N	88.06 W
Station Peak	162	21.10 S	118.11 E
Statte	68	40.34 N	17.12 E
Statue of Liberty National Monument ♦	210	40.41 N	74.03 W
Staubbachfall ∟	58	46.35 N	7.55 E
Staubun	76	52.48 N	31.25 E
Staufen	58	47.53 N	7.44 E
Staufenberg	56	50.40 N	8.43 E
Staughton Vale	169	37.51 S	144.17 E
Staunton, Il., U.S.	219	39.00 N	89.47 W
Staunton, Va., U.S.	188	38.08 N	79.04 W
Staunton → Roanoke ≃	192	35.56 N	76.43 W
Stavanger	26	58.58 N	5.45 E
Stave ≃	224	49.10 N	122.26 W
Stave Lake ⊜	182	49.15 N	122.21 W
Staveley	44	53.16 N	1.20 W
Stavelot	56	50.23 N	5.56 E
Stavely, Ab., Can.	182	50.10 N	113.38 W
Stavely, Eng., U.K.	44	54.22 N	2.49 W
Staveren	52	52.53 N	5.22 E
Stavern	26	59.00 N	10.02 E
Stavne	78	48.59 N	22.40 E
Stavropol', Ross.	72	45.02 N	41.59 E
Stavropol → Toljatti, Ross.	80	53.31 N	49.26 E
Stavropol' Kraj □[8]	84	44.38 N	43.30 E
Stavrovo	80	56.08 N	40.00 E
Stavsnäs	40	59.17 N	18.41 E
Stavyshche	78	49.23 N	30.12 E
Stawell	166	37.04 S	142.46 E
Stawell ≃	166	20.38 S	142.55 E
Stawiski	30	53.23 N	22.09 E
Stawiszyn	30	51.55 N	18.07 E
Staxigoe	46	58.28 N	3.04 W
Stayky	78	50.05 N	30.54 E
Stayner	212	44.25 N	80.05 W
Stayton	202	44.48 N	122.47 W
Stazzema	64	43.59 N	10.19 E
Steamboat	226	39.22 N	119.44 W
Steamboat Creek ≃	226	39.31 N	119.42 W
Steamboat Mountain ∧	200	41.58 N	108.58 W
Steamboat Slough ≃	226	38.11 N	121.40 W
Steamboat Springs	200	40.29 N	106.49 W
Steamburg	210	42.07 N	78.54 W
Stearns	192	36.41 N	84.28 W
Stearns Pond ⊜	283	42.37 N	71.04 W
Stębark	30	53.30 N	20.08 E
Stebbins	180	63.32 N	162.18 W
Stebliv	78	49.24 N	31.06 E
Stechow	54	52.38 N	12.28 E
Steckborn	58	47.40 N	8.55 E
Stederdorf	52	52.21 N	10.15 E
Stedum	52	53.18 N	6.41 E
Steeg	58	47.14 N	10.17 E
Steel ≃	190	48.46 N	86.54 W
Steel City	210	40.38 N	75.20 W
Steele, Mo., U.S.	194	36.05 N	89.49 W
Steele, N.D., U.S.	198	46.51 N	99.54 W
Steele •[8]	263	51.27 N	7.05 E
Steele, Mount ∧	200	41.50 N	107.00 W
Steele Creek ≃, Tx., U.S.	222	32.01 N	97.28 W
Steele Creek ≃, Tx., U.S.	222	31.13 N	96.19 W
Steeles Corners	275b	43.48 N	79.25 W
Steeleville	194	38.00 N	89.39 W
Steelhead	224	49.13 N	122.19 W
Steel's Drift	158	27.21 S	29.30 E
Steels Point ›	174c	29.02 S	168.00 E
Steels Run ≃	279b	40.25 N	79.38 W
Steelton, N.Y., U.S.	284a	42.47 N	78.49 W
Steelton, Pa., U.S.	208	40.14 N	76.50 W
Steelville	194	37.58 N	91.21 W
Steenbergen	52	51.35 N	4.19 E
Steenburg Lake ⊜	212	44.50 N	77.41 W
Steenderen	52	52.04 N	6.11 E
Steens Mountain ⋀	202	42.35 N	118.40 W
Steenvoorde	50	50.48 N	2.35 E
Steenwijk	52	52.47 N	6.08 E
Steepbank ≃	184	57.01 N	111.28 W
Steephill Lake ⊜	184	55.58 N	103.08 W
Steep Holm I	42	51.21 N	3.07 W
Steeping ≃	44	53.06 N	0.18 E
Steeple Claydon	42	51.56 N	0.59 W
Steep Point ›	162	26.08 S	113.08 E
Steep Rock	184	51.26 N	98.48 W
Stefanie, Lake → Chew Bahir ⊜, Afr.	144	4.40 N	36.50 E
Stefanie, Lake (Chew Bahir) ⊜, Afr.	144	4.40 N	36.50 E
Stefansson Island I	176	73.20 N	105.45 W
Ștefan Vodă	38	44.19 N	27.19 E
Steffisburg	58	46.47 N	7.39 E
Steg	58	47.21 N	8.56 E
Stegalovka	76	52.24 N	38.19 E
Stege	41	54.59 N	12.18 E
Stegeborg	26	58.26 N	16.35 E
Stege Bugt ⊂	41	55.01 N	12.05 E
Stegelitz	54	53.08 N	13.51 E
Steger	216	41.28 N	87.38 W
Stegersbach	61	47.10 N	16.10 E
Steglitz •[8]	264a	52.28 N	13.19 E
Stehag	41	55.54 N	13.23 E
Stehekin	224	48.18 N	120.39 W
Stehekin ≃	224	48.21 N	120.40 W
Ștei	38	46.32 N	22.28 E
Steiermark □[3]	30	47.10 N	15.10 E
Steigerwald ⋀	56	49.40 N	10.20 E
Steigra	54	51.18 N	11.39 E
Steilacoom	224	47.10 N	122.36 W
Steimbke	52	52.40 N	9.22 E
Stein, Dtsch.	56	49.25 N	11.01 E
Stein, Dtsch.	60	49.25 N	11.01 E
Stein, Ned.	56	50.57 N	5.46 E
Stein, Schw.	58	47.33 N	7.58 E
Steina	54	51.12 N	14.01 E
Steinach, Dtsch.	54	50.25 N	11.10 E
Steinach, Dtsch.	58	48.18 N	8.04 E
Steinach, Öst.	64	47.05 N	11.28 E
Steinach ≃	54	50.11 N	11.12 E
Steinamanger → Szombathely	30	47.14 N	16.38 E
Stein am Rhein	58	47.40 N	8.51 E
Steinau	56	50.23 N	9.27 E
Steinbach, Mb., Can.	184	49.32 N	96.41 W
Steinbach, Dtsch.	56	48.43 N	8.10 E
Steinberg ∧[2]	263	51.05 N	7.27 E
Steinberger Slough ≃	282	37.33 N	122.13 W
Steinbourg	56	48.46 N	7.25 E
Steindorf	61	46.42 N	14.01 E
Steinen	58	47.38 N	7.44 E
Steinernes Meer ⋀	64	47.30 N	12.58 E
Steinfeld, Dtsch.	52	52.35 N	8.12 E
Steinfeld, Dtsch.	54	50.22 N	10.44 E
Steinfeld, Öst.	64	46.45 N	13.15 E
Steinfort	56	49.40 N	5.55 E
Steinforth	263	51.09 N	6.32 E
Steinfurt	52	52.09 N	7.21 E
Steingaden	58	47.42 N	10.51 E
Steinhagen, Dtsch.	52	52.00 N	8.24 E
Steinhagen, Dtsch.	54	54.13 N	12.59 E
Steinhatchee ≃	192	29.40 N	83.24 W
Steinhausen	156	21.49 S	18.20 E
Steinhausen ʊ[1]	58	48.01 N	9.41 E
Steinheid	54	50.28 N	11.04 E
Steinheim, Dtsch.	52	51.52 N	9.05 E
Steinheim, Dtsch.	56	48.58 N	9.16 E
Steinhöfel	54	52.24 N	14.10 E
Steinhöring	60	48.05 N	12.02 E
Steinhude	52	52.27 N	9.21 E
Steinhuder Meer ⊜	52	52.28 N	9.19 E
Steinkjer	26	64.01 N	11.30 E
Steinkopf	156	29.18 S	17.43 E
Steinloge	52	52.54 N	8.19 E
Stein-Neukirch	56	50.41 N	8.03 E
Steinpass)(	64	47.39 N	12.45 E
Steinsdorf	54	52.02 N	14.40 E
Steinshamn	26	62.47 N	6.29 E
Steinstücken •[8]	264a	52.23 N	13.08 E
Steinwiesen	54	50.17 N	11.28 E
Stekene	50	51.12 N	4.02 E
Stekl'anka	76	59.08 N	41.37 E
Steklino	76	56.51 N	32.10 E
Steksovo	80	55.17 N	43.25 E
Stella, It.	62	44.24 N	8.30 E
Stella, S. Afr.	158	26.38 S	24.48 E
Stella, Ne., U.S.	198	40.13 N	95.46 W
Stella Niagara	210	43.12 N	79.02 W
Stella-Plage	50	50.29 N	1.35 E
Stellaquo Indian Reserve •[4]	182	54.03 N	124.55 W
Stellarton	186	45.34 N	62.40 W
Stelle	52	53.23 N	10.06 E
Stellenbosch	158	33.58 S	18.50 E
Steller, Mount ∧	180	60.30 N	143.02 W
Stelvio, Parco Nazionale dello ♦	64	46.30 N	10.40 E
Stelvio, Passo dello)(	64	46.32 N	10.27 E
Stemwede	52	52.25 N	8.27 E
Stenay	56	49.29 N	5.11 E
Stendal	54	52.36 N	11.51 E
Stende	76	57.09 N	22.33 E
Stenden	263	51.25 N	6.27 E
Stenhammar slott ⊥	40	59.03 N	16.31 E
Stenhouse Bay	166	35.17 S	136.56 E
Stenhousemuir	46	56.02 N	3.48 W
Stenico	64	46.03 N	10.51 E
Stenlille	41	55.32 N	11.36 E
Stenløse	41	55.46 N	12.12 E
Stenness, Loch of ⊜	46	59.00 N	3.15 W
Stenón	267c	37.58 N	23.25 E
Stenón Návstathmou ɥ	267c	37.58 N	23.33 E
Stensätra	40	60.36 N	16.44 E
Stensele	24	65.05 N	17.09 E
Stenstorp	26	58.16 N	13.43 E
Stenstrup	41	55.07 N	10.31 E
Stentrop	263	51.30 N	7.49 E
Stenungsund	26	58.05 N	11.49 E
Stepan'	78	51.10 N	26.18 E
Stepanakert → Xankändi	84	39.49 N	46.44 E
Stepanavan	84	41.00 N	44.23 E
Stepancevo, Ross.	80	56.08 N	41.42 E
Stepancevo, Ross.	82	56.22 N	36.10 E
Stepancy	78	49.42 N	31.18 E
Stepanivka	78	50.58 N	34.37 E
Stepano-Krynka	83	47.55 N	38.21 E
Stepanovka, Ross.	80	52.04 N	53.02 E
Stepanovka, Ross.	86	57.13 N	67.26 E
Stepanovo	82	55.43 N	38.28 E
Stepanovskoje	265b	55.47 N	37.10 E
Stepanščino	82	55.15 N	38.30 E
Stepenitz ≃	54	53.48 N	11.10 E
Stephans-Dom ʊ[1]	264b	48.12 N	16.23 E
Stephanskirchen	64	47.51 N	12.11 E
Stephen	198	48.27 N	96.52 W
Stephen A. Forbes State Park ♦	219	38.44 N	88.46 W
Stephen F. Austin State Historic Park ♦	222	29.48 N	96.05 W
Stephens	194	33.24 N	93.04 W
Stephens, Cape ›	172	40.42 S	173.57 E
Stephens, Port ⊂	166	32.45 S	152.05 E
Stephens City	188	39.05 N	78.13 W
Stephens Creek	166	31.50 S	141.30 E
Stephens Island I	182	54.10 N	130.45 W
Stephens Knob ∧[2]	192	36.37 N	84.20 W
Stephens Lake ⊜[1]	184	56.26 N	95.07 W
Stephens Mills	210	42.23 N	77.38 W
Stephenson	190	45.24 N	87.36 W
Stephenson, Lake ⊜	222	29.35 N	94.40 W
Stephenson, Mount ∧	9	69.49 S	69.43 W
Stephens Passage ɥ	180	57.50 N	133.50 W
Stephentown	210	42.33 N	73.23 W
Stephentown Center	210	42.34 N	73.25 W
Stephenville, Nf., Can.	186	48.33 N	58.35 W
Stephenville, Tx., U.S.	196	32.13 N	98.12 W
Stephenville Crossing	186	48.30 N	58.26 W
Stepn'ak	86	52.50 N	70.50 E
Stepney •[8]	260	51.31 N	0.02 W
Stepnica	54	53.40 N	14.36 E
Stepnoj	80	48.56 N	45.36 E
Stepnoje, Ross.	80	51.24 N	46.52 E
Stepnoje, Ross.	84	44.17 N	44.36 E
Step Pyramid → Șaqqārah ⊥	142	29.52 N	31.14 E
Steps Point ›	174u	14.22 S	170.45 W
Steptoe Valley V	204	39.25 N	114.45 W
Stepurino	76	56.24 N	35.16 E
Sterdyń	30	52.35 N	22.18 E
Stereá Ellás □[4]	38	38.30 N	23.00 E
Sterkaar	158	31.05 S	23.42 E
Sterkrade •[8]	263	51.31 N	6.51 E
Sterkspruit	158	30.32 S	27.22 E
Sterkstroom	158	31.32 S	26.32 E
Sterlibaševo	86	53.28 N	55.15 E
Sterling, S. Afr.	158	31.16 S	21.28 E
Sterling, Ak., U.S.	180	60.32 N	150.48 W
Sterling, Co., U.S.	198	40.37 N	103.12 W
Sterling, Ct., U.S.	207	41.42 N	71.49 W
Sterling, Il., U.S.	190	41.47 N	89.41 W
Sterling, Ks., U.S.	198	38.12 N	98.12 W
Sterling, Ma., U.S.	207	42.26 N	71.45 W
Sterling, Mi., U.S.	190	44.02 N	84.01 W
Sterling, Ne., U.S.	198	40.27 N	96.22 W
Sterling, N.Y., U.S.	210	43.20 N	76.39 W
Sterling, Oh., U.S.	214	40.58 N	81.51 W
Sterling, Ok., U.S.	196	34.45 N	98.10 W
Sterling, Va., U.S.	208	39.00 N	77.25 W
Sterling City	196	31.50 N	100.59 W
Sterling Creek ≃	210	43.20 N	76.42 W
Sterling Forest Lake ⊜	276	41.10 N	74.16 W
Sterling Heights	214	42.34 N	83.01 W
Sterling Junction	207	42.24 N	71.46 W
Sterling Park	282	37.41 N	122.26 W
Sterling Run	214	41.25 N	78.12 W
Sterlington	194	32.41 N	92.05 W
Sterlitamak	86	53.37 N	55.58 E
Sternberg	54	53.43 N	11.49 E
Šternberk	30	49.44 N	17.18 E
Sternstein ∧	61	48.34 N	14.16 E
Sterup	41	54.44 N	9.44 E
Sterzing → Vipiteno	64	46.54 N	11.26 E
Stęszew	30	52.18 N	16.42 E
Štětí	54	50.25 N	14.23 E
Stetson Pond ⊜	283	42.02 N	70.50 W
Stetten am kalten Markt	58	48.07 N	9.04 E
Stettin → Szczecin	30	53.24 N	14.32 E
Stettiner Haff (Zalew Szczeciński) ⊂	54	53.46 N	14.14 E
Stettler	182	52.19 N	112.43 W
Steuben □[6], In., U.S.	216	41.38 N	85.00 W
Steuben □[6], N.Y., U.S.	210	42.20 N	77.19 W
Steubenville	214	40.22 N	80.38 W
Steutz	54	51.53 N	12.05 E
Stevenage	42	51.55 N	0.14 W
Stevens, N.J., U.S.	285	40.05 N	74.49 W
Stevens, Pa., U.S.	208	40.13 N	76.09 W
Stevens, Lake ⊜	224	48.01 N	122.05 W
Stevens, Mount ∧	172	40.48 S	172.27 E
Stevens Creek ≃, Ca., U.S.	282	37.26 N	122.05 W
Stevens Creek ≃, S.C., U.S.	192	33.34 N	82.03 W
Stevens Creek Park ♦	282	37.17 N	122.04 W
Stevens Creek Reservoir ⊜[1]	282	37.17 N	122.05 W
Stevens Institute of Technology ʊ[2]	276	40.44 N	74.02 W
Stevenson, Al., U.S.	194	34.52 N	85.50 W
Stevenson, Md., U.S.	284b	39.25 N	76.43 W
Stevenson, Wa., U.S.	224	45.42 N	121.53 W
Stevenson Creek ≃	162	27.06 S	135.33 E
Stevenson Entrance ɥ	180	58.45 N	152.20 W
Stevenson Lake ⊜	184	53.56 N	96.09 W
Stevens Pass)(	224	47.45 N	121.04 W
Stevens Peak ∧	202	47.27 N	115.46 W
Stevens Point	190	44.31 N	89.34 W
Stevenston	46	55.39 N	4.45 W
Stevens Village	180	66.00 N	149.05 W
Stevensville, On., Can.	284a	42.57 N	79.04 W
Stevensville, Md., U.S.	208	38.58 N	76.18 W
Stevensville, Mi., U.S.	216	42.00 N	86.31 W
Stevensville, Mt., U.S.	202	46.30 N	114.05 W
Stevensville, Pa., U.S.	210	41.46 N	76.11 W
Stevinson	226	37.20 N	120.51 W
Stevns Klint ⊥[4]	41	55.18 N	12.27 E
Steward	216	41.51 N	89.01 W
Stewardson	219	39.15 N	88.37 W
Stewart, B.C., Can.	182	55.56 N	129.59 W
Stewart, Mn., U.S.	190	44.43 N	94.29 W
Stewart ≃	180	63.18 N	139.25 W
Stewart, Cape ›	164	11.57 S	134.45 E
Stewart, Isla I	254	54.52 S	71.12 W
Stewart, Mount ∧	166	20.12 S	145.29 E
Stewart Island I	172	47.00 S	167.50 E
Stewart Islands II	175e	8.25 S	162.52 E
Stewart Lake ⊜	219	40.09 N	90.16 W
Stewart Manor	276	40.43 N	73.41 W
Stewarton	46	55.41 N	4.31 W
Stewartstown, N. Ire., U.K.	48	54.35 N	6.41 W
Stewartstown, Pa., U.S.	208	39.45 N	76.35 W
Stewartsville, Mo., U.S.	194	39.45 N	94.29 W
Stewartsville, N.J., U.S.	208	40.41 N	75.06 W
Stewartsville, Pa., U.S.	279b	40.21 N	79.46 W
Stewart Valley	184	50.36 N	107.50 W
Stewartville	190	43.51 N	92.29 W
Stewiacke	186	45.08 N	63.21 W
Steyerberg	52	52.34 N	9.01 E
Steyning	42	50.53 N	0.20 W
Steynsburg	158	31.15 S	25.49 E
Steynsrus	158	27.58 S	27.33 E
Steyr	61	48.03 N	14.25 E
Steyr ≃	61	48.02 N	14.25 E
Steyregg	61	48.17 N	14.22 E
Steytlerville	158	33.21 S	24.21 E
Stežki	80	53.06 N	41.13 E
Stezzano	62	45.38 N	9.39 E
Sthal	126	24.12 N	89.44 E
Știa	66	43.48 N	11.42 E
Štiavnické vrchy ⋀	30	48.40 N	18.45 E
Stickle Pond ⊜	276	40.59 N	74.25 W
Stickney, Eng., U.K.	44	53.05 N	0.01 E
Stickney, Il., U.S.	216	41.49 N	87.46 W
Stickney, S.D., U.S.	198	43.35 N	98.26 W
Stidsvig	41	56.12 N	13.08 E
Stiefing ≃	61	46.47 N	15.35 E
Stiege	54	51.40 N	10.53 E
Stiene	76	57.26 N	24.34 E
Stienitzfliess ≃	264a	52.33 N	13.43 E
Stienitz-See ⊜	264a	52.30 N	13.49 E
Stiens	52	53.15 N	5.45 E
Stiepel •[8]	263	51.25 N	7.15 E
Stif	148	36.09 N	5.26 E
Stiftskirche ʊ[1]	263	51.23 N	7.00 E
Stige	41	55.26 N	10.25 E
Stigler	196	35.15 N	95.07 W
Stigliano	68	40.24 N	16.14 E
Stigtomta	40	58.48 N	16.47 E
Stih, hora ∧	78	48.37 N	23.11 E
Stikine ≃	180	56.40 N	132.30 W
Stikine Ranges ⋀	180	58.45 N	130.00 W
Stiklestad	26	63.48 N	11.33 E
Stilbaai	158	34.24 S	21.26 E
Stiles	210	40.40 N	75.30 W
Stiles Pond ⊜	283	42.41 N	71.02 W
Stilesville	210	42.05 N	75.24 W
Stilfontein	158	26.50 S	26.50 E
Stilís	38	38.55 N	22.36 E
Still	148	34.20 N	5.51 E
Stillaguamish ≃	224	48.11 N	122.22 W
Stillaguamish, North Fork ≃	224	48.11 N	122.07 W

ENGLISH	DEUTSCH	ESPAÑOL	FRANÇAIS	PORTUGUÊS
∧ Mountain	Berg	Montaña	Montagne	Montanha
⋀ Mountains	Gebirge	Montañas	Montagnes	Montanhas
)(Pass	Paß	Paso	Col	Passo
V Valley, Canyon	Tal, Cañon	Valle, Cañón	Vallée, Canyon	Vale, Canhão
≚ Plain	Ebene	Llano	Plaine	Planície
› Cape	Kap	Cabo	Cap	Cabo
I Island	Insel	Isla	Île	Ilha
II Islands	Inseln	Islas	Îles	Ilhas
⊥ Other Topographic Features	Andere Topographische Objekte	Otros Elementos Topográficos	Autres données topographiques	Outros acidentes topográficos

Symbols in the index entries represent the broad categories identified in the key at the right. Symbols with superior numbers (⋀[1]) identify subcategories (see complete key on page I · 1).

Symbole im Register stellen die rechts im Schlüssel erklärten Kategorien dar. Symbole mit hochgestellten Ziffern (⋀[1]) bezeichnen Unterabteilungen einer Kategorie (vgl. vollständiger Schlüssel auf Seite I · 1).

Los símbolos incluídos en el texto del índice representan las grandes categorías identificadas con la clave a la derecha. Los símbolos con numeros en su parte superior (⋀[1]) identifican las subcategorías (véase la clave completa en la página I · 1).

Les symboles de l'index représentent les catégories indiquées dans la légende à droite. Les symboles suivis d'un indice (⋀[1]) représentent des sous-catégories (voir légende complète à la page I · 1).

Os símbolos incluídos no texto do índice representam as grandes categorias identificadas com a chave à direita. Os símbolos com números em sua parte superior (⋀[1]) identificam as subcategorias (veja-se a chave completa à página I · 1).

ESPAÑOL — Nombre / Página / Lat.°′ / Long.°′ W = Oeste
FRANÇAIS — Nom / Page / Lat.°′ / Long.°′ W = Ouest
PORTUGUÊS — Nome / Página / Lat.°′ / Long.°′ W = Oeste

Nombre	Página	Lat.°′	Long.°′ W = Oeste
Stillaguamish, South Fork ≃	224	48.11 N	122.07 W
Stillhouse Hollow Lake ⊜[1]	222	31.00 N	97.35 W
Stilling	41	56.04 N	10.00 E
Stillman Valley	216	42.07 N	89.11 W
Stillmore	192	32.26 N	82.12 W
Still Pond	208	39.19 N	76.02 W
Still Run ≃	285	39.49 N	75.18 W
Stillwater, B.C., Can.	182	49.46 N	124.18 W
Stillwater, Mn., U.S.	190	45.03 N	92.48 W
Stillwater, N.J., U.S.	210	41.02 N	74.52 W
Stillwater, N.Y., U.S.	210	42.56 N	73.39 W
Stillwater, Oh., U.S.	214	40.20 N	81.18 W
Stillwater, Ok., U.S.	196	36.06 N	97.03 W
Stillwater, Pa., U.S.	210	41.09 N	76.22 W
Stillwater ≃, Mt., U.S.	202	45.38 N	109.17 W
Stillwater ≃, Oh., U.S.	218	39.47 N	84.12 W
Stillwater Creek ≃	214	40.25 N	81.22 W
Stillwater Range ⋏	204	39.50 N	118.15 W
Stillwell, Il., U.S.	219	40.13 N	91.11 W
Stillwell, Ok., U.S.	194	35.49 N	94.38 W
Stilo	68	38.29 N	16.28 E
Stilo, Punta ›	68	38.28 N	16.36 E
Stimberg ∧[2]	263	51.40 N	7.15 E
Stimigliano	66	42.18 N	12.34 E
Stimson, Mount ∧	202	48.31 N	113.36 W
Stînca-Costești, Lacul ⊜[1]	38	47.55 N	27.10 E
Stinchar ≃	44	55.06 N	5.00 W
Stinear Nunataks ⋏	9	69.42 S	64.40 E
Stine Canal ≅	226	35.15 N	119.08 W
Stine Mountain ∧	202	45.44 N	113.07 W
Stingray Point ›	208	37.33 N	76.18 W
Stinking Water Creek ≃	198	40.22 N	101.07 W
Stinnett	196	35.49 N	101.26 W
Stintino	71	40.56 N	8.13 E
Ştintonville	273d	26.14 S	28.13 E
Štip	38	41.44 N	22.12 E
Stiperstones ∧	42	52.35 N	2.56 W
Stiring-Wendel	56	49.12 N	6.56 E
Stírka ∧	60	49.24 N	13.34 E
Stirling, Austl.	162	21.44 S	133.45 E
Stirling, Austl.	168a	31.54 S	115.47 E
Stirling, Austl.	168b	35.00 S	138.43 E
Stirling, Ab., Can.	182	49.30 N	112.31 W
Stirling, On., Can.	212	44.18 N	77.33 W
Stirling, Scot., U.K.	46	56.07 N	3.57 W
Stirling, N.J., U.S.	210	40.40 N	74.29 W
Stirling, Mount ∧	162	31.50 S	117.38 E
Stirling Castle ⊥	46	56.07 N	3.57 W
Stirling City	204	39.54 N	121.31 W
Stirling Range ⋏	162	34.23 S	117.50 E
Stirling Range National Park ♦	162	34.22 S	118.00 E
Stirling Reservoir ⊜[1]	168a	33.08 S	116.03 E
Stirrat	192	37.43 N	82.00 W
Ştissing Mountain ∧	210	41.57 N	73.42 W
Štitary	61	48.56 N	15.51 E
Stittsville	212	45.15 N	75.55 W
Stittville	210	43.13 N	75.17 W
Stjärnhov	40	59.05 N	17.00 E
Stjärnsund, Sve.	40	60.26 N	16.12 E
Stjärnsund, Sve.	40	58.51 N	14.55 E
Stjernøya I	24	70.18 N	22.45 E
Stjørdalshalsen	26	63.28 N	10.56 E
Stöberhai ∧	54	51.39 N	10.34 E
Stobi ⊥	38	41.33 N	21.59 E
Stock	260	51.40 N	0.27 E
Stock, Étang du ⊜	56	48.45 N	6.55 E
Stockach	58	47.51 N	9.00 E
Stöckalp	58	46.48 N	8.17 E
Stockamöllan	41	55.57 N	13.22 E
Stockbridge, Eng., U.K.	42	51.07 N	1.29 W
Stockbridge, Ga., U.S.	192	33.32 N	84.14 W
Stockbridge, Ma., U.S.	207	42.17 N	73.19 W
Stockbridge, Mi., U.S.	216	42.27 N	84.10 W
Stockbridge Bowl ⊜	207	42.20 N	73.19 W
Stockbridge Indian Reservation ◄[4]	190	44.52 N	88.53 W
Stockbury	260	51.20 N	0.39 E
Stockby	40	59.20 N	17.41 E
Stockdale, Oh., U.S.	218	38.57 N	82.51 W
Stockdale, Tx., U.S.	196	29.14 N	97.57 W
Stockelsdorf	54	53.54 N	10.38 E
Stöcken	54	53.00 N	10.40 E
Stockerau	61	48.23 N	16.13 E
Stockertown	208	40.45 N	75.15 W
Stockett	202	47.21 N	111.09 W
Stockheim	56	50.19 N	9.01 E
Stockholm, Sve.	40	59.20 N	18.03 E
Stockholm, Me., U.S.	186	47.02 N	68.08 W
Stockholm, N.J., U.S.	210	41.05 N	74.31 W
Stockholm, Lake ⊜	276	41.04 N	74.32 W
Stockholms Län □[6]	40	59.30 N	18.20 E
Stock Island	220	24.34 N	81.45 W
Stockland	216	40.37 N	87.36 W
Stockport, Eng., U.K.	44	53.25 N	2.10 W
Stockport, N.Y., U.S.	210	42.19 N	73.45 W
Stockport □[8]	262	53.23 N	2.08 W
Stocksbridge	44	53.27 N	1.34 W
Stockstadt	56	49.59 N	9.04 E
Stocksund	40	59.23 N	18.04 E
Stockton, Austl.	170	32.55 S	151.47 E
Stockton, Al., U.S.	194	30.59 N	87.51 W
Stockton, Ca., U.S.	226	37.57 N	121.17 W
Stockton, Il., U.S.	190	42.20 N	90.00 W
Stockton, Ks., U.S.	198	39.26 N	99.15 W
Stockton, Md., U.S.	208	38.03 N	75.24 W
Stockton, Mo., U.S.	194	37.41 N	93.47 W
Stockton, N.J., U.S.	208	40.24 N	74.58 W
Stockton, N.Y., U.S.	214	42.19 N	79.22 W
Stockton, Ut,. U.S.	200	40.27 N	112.21 W
Stockton Heath, Eng., U.K.	44	53.22 N	2.34 W
Stockton Heath, Eng., U.K.	262	53.22 N	2.34 W
Stockton Metropolitan Airport ⊠	226	37.54 N	121.15 W
Stockton-on-Tees	44	54.34 N	1.19 W
Stockton Plateau ⋏[1]	196	30.30 N	102.30 W
Stockton Reservoir ⊜[1]	194	37.40 N	93.45 W
Stockton Springs	188	44.29 N	68.51 W
Stockum, Dtsch.	52	51.40 N	7.42 E
Stockum, Dtsch.	263	51.32 N	7.47 E
Stockum, Dtsch.	263	51.36 N	6.39 E
Stockum, Dtsch.	263	51.28 N	7.22 E
Stockum ◄[8]	263	51.16 N	6.44 E
Stockville	198	40.31 N	100.22 W
Stockwell	216	40.17 N	86.46 W
Stockwell, Lake ⊜	285	39.51 N	74.47 W
Stoco Lake ⊜	212	44.28 N	77.18 W
Stoczek Łukowski	30	51.58 N	21.58 E
Stod	60	49.39 N	13.10 E
Stoddard Mountain ∧	228	34.42 N	117.07 W
Stöde	26	62.25 N	16.35 E
Stodolišče	76	54.11 N	32.39 E
Stœng Trêng	110	13.31 N	105.58 E
Stoer	46	58.12 N	5.20 W
Stoer, Point of ›	46	58.15 N	5.21 W
Stoffberg	156	25.29 S	29.49 E
Stojba	89	52.49 N	131.43 E
Stoke	260	51.27 N	0.37 E
Stoke ≃	206	45.35 N	71.58 W
Stoke, Monts ⋏	206	45.33 N	71.42 W
Stoke D'Abernon	260	51.19 N	0.23 W
Stokenchurch	42	51.40 N	0.55 W
Stoke Newington ◄[8]	260	51.34 N	0.05 W
Stoke-on-Trent	42	53.00 N	2.10 W
Stoke Poges	260	51.33 N	0.35 W
Stokes, Mount ∧	172	41.06 S	174.06 E
Stokes Inlet c	162	33.50 S	121.08 E
Stokesley	44	54.28 N	1.11 W
Stokes Point ›	166	40.10 S	143.56 E
Stokes Range ⋏[2]	164	15.46 S	130.57 E
Stokhid ≃	78	51.52 N	25.38 E
Stokkemarke	41	54.50 N	11.23 E
Stokksnes ›	24a	64.17 N	14.54 W
Stol ∧	38	44.13 N	22.14 E
Stolac	36	43.05 N	17.58 E
Stolberg	56	50.46 N	6.13 E
Stolbišči	80	55.39 N	49.14 E
Stolboucha	86	49.59 N	84.30 E
Stolbovo	76	52.38 N	34.47 E
Stolbovoj, ostrov I	74	74.05 N	136.00 E
Stolby, zapovednik ♦	88	55.45 N	92.45 E
Stolin	78	51.53 N	26.51 E
Stollberg	54	50.42 N	12.47 E
Stöllet	26	60.24 N	13.16 E
Stol'ne	78	51.31 N	31.55 E
Stolp → Słupsk	30	54.28 N	17.01 E
Stolpe	264a	52.40 N	13.16 E
Stolpen	54	51.05 N	14.04 E
Stolper Heide ◄[3]	264a	52.39 N	13.14 E
Stolpino	80	57.24 N	42.55 E
Stolzenau	52	52.31 N	9.04 E
Ston	36	42.50 N	17.42 E
Stondon Massey	260	51.41 N	0.18 E
Stone, Eng., U.K.	42	52.54 N	2.10 W
Stone, Eng., U.K.	260	51.27 N	0.16 E
Stoneboro	214	41.20 N	80.06 W
Stone Canyon Reservoir ⊜[1]	280	34.07 N	118.28 W
Stone Corral Creek ≃	226	39.16 N	122.06 W
Stone Creek	214	40.24 N	81.34 W
Stonecutters Island I	271d	22.19 N	114.08 E
Stonefort	194	37.37 N	88.42 W
Stoneham, Ma., U.S.	283	42.28 N	71.06 W
Stoneham, Pa., U.S.	214	41.49 N	79.07 W
Stone Harbor	208	39.03 N	74.45 W
Stonehaven	46	56.57 N	2.12 W
Stonehenge	166	24.22 S	143.17 E
Stonehenge ⊥	42	51.11 N	1.49 W
Stonehill College ⊍[2]	283	42.03 N	71.05 W
Stonehouse, Eng., U.K.	42	51.45 N	2.17 W
Stonehouse, Scot., U.K.	46	55.43 N	4.00 W
Stone Indian Reserve ◄[4]	182	51.54 N	123.12 W
Stoneleigh	42	52.21 N	1.31 W
Stonelick Creek ≃	218	39.07 N	84.13 W
Stonelick State Park ♦	218	39.13 N	84.04 W
Stone Mountain	192	33.48 N	84.10 W
Stone Mountain ∧, Pa., U.S.	210	40.37 N	77.48 W
Stone Mountain ∧, Vt., U.S.	188	44.34 N	71.40 W
Stone Mountain Memorial State Park ♦	192	33.49 N	84.06 W
Stone Park	278	41.54 N	87.53 W
Stoner	182	53.36 N	122.40 W
Stoner Creek ≃	218	38.18 N	84.14 W
Stone Ridge	210	41.51 N	74.09 W
Stonerstown	214	40.13 N	78.16 W
Stones, East Fork ≃	194	35.59 N	86.27 W
Stones, West Fork ≃	194	35.59 N	86.27 W
Stones River National Battlefield ⊥	194	35.52 N	86.26 W
Stonestown ◄[9]	282	37.44 N	122.28 W
Stonevilla	279b	40.18 N	79.31 W
Stoneville	192	36.27 N	79.54 W
Stonewall, Mb., Can.	184	50.09 N	97.21 W
Stonewall, La., U.S.	194	32.16 N	93.49 W
Stonewall, Ms., U.S.	194	32.07 N	88.47 W
Stonewall, Ok., U.S.	196	34.39 N	96.31 W
Stonewall Manor	284c	38.53 N	77.14 W
Stoney Creek	212	43.13 N	79.46 W
Stoney Point ›	214	42.18 N	82.34 W
Stonington, Ct., U.S.	207	41.20 N	71.54 W
Stonington, Il., U.S.	219	39.38 N	89.11 W
Stonington, Me., U.S.	188	44.09 N	68.40 W
Stony ≃, Ak., U.S.	180	61.45 N	156.35 W
Stony ≃, Mn., U.S.	190	47.44 N	91.47 W
Stony Brook	210	40.55 N	73.08 W
Stony Brook ≃, Ct., U.S.	276	41.04 N	73.28 W
Stony Brook ≃, Ct., U.S.	276	41.08 N	73.22 W
Stony Brook ≃, Ma., U.S.	283	42.38 N	71.22 W
Stony Brook ≃, Ma., U.S.	283	42.22 N	71.16 W
Stony Brook ≃, N.J., U.S.	276	40.19 N	74.41 W
Stony Brook ≃, N.J., U.S.	276	40.56 N	74.26 W
Stony Brook Harbor c	276	40.54 N	73.10 W
Stony Brook Reservation ♦	283	42.16 N	71.09 W
Stony Creek, Ct., U.S.	207	41.15 N	72.44 W
Stony Creek, Va., U.S.	208	36.56 N	77.24 W
Stony Creek ≃, Ca., U.S.	204	39.41 N	121.58 W
Stony Creek ≃, Il., U.S.	278	41.41 N	87.51 W
Stony Creek ≃, Mi., U.S.	216	41.57 N	83.18 W
Stony Creek ≃, Mi., U.S.	216	43.00 N	84.55 W
Stony Creek ≃, N.Y., U.S.	212	43.49 N	76.14 W
Stony Creek ≃, Pa., U.S.	285	40.07 N	75.21 W
Stony Creek ≃, Va., U.S.	208	36.56 N	77.23 W
Stony Creek, Middle Fork ≃	226	39.25 N	122.31 W
Stony Creek, North Fork ≃	226	39.22 N	122.37 W
Stony Creek, South Fork ≃	226	39.22 N	122.39 W
Stony Creek Indian Reserve ◄[4]	182	53.57 N	124.07 W
Stony Creek Mills	208	40.21 N	75.52 W
Stonyford	226	39.22 N	122.32 W
Stony Gorge Reservoir ⊜[1]	226	39.34 N	122.31 W
Stony Indian Reserve ◄[4]	182	51.10 N	114.55 W
Stony Island I, Mi., U.S.	281	42.07 N	83.08 W
Stony Island I, N.Y., U.S.	212	43.53 N	76.25 W
Stony Kill ≃	210	42.24 N	73.38 W
Stony Lake ⊜, Mb., Can.	176	58.51 N	98.35 W
Stony Lake ⊜, On., Can.	212	44.33 N	78.05 W
Stony Plain	182	53.32 N	114.00 W
Stony Plain Indian Reserve ◄[4]	182	53.30 N	113.45 W
Stony Point, Austl.	169	38.22 S	145.13 E
Stony Point, Mi., U.S.	216	41.57 N	83.16 W
Stony Point, N.Y., U.S.	210	41.13 N	73.59 W
Stony Point, N.C., U.S.	192	35.51 N	81.02 W
Stony Point ›	284a	42.50 N	78.52 W
Stony Point ›[1]	212	43.52 N	76.15 W
Stony Prairie	214	41.21 N	83.10 W
Stony Rapids	176	59.16 N	105.50 W
Stony Ridge	214	41.30 N	83.30 W
Stony River	180	61.47 N	156.41 W
Stony Run	284b	39.11 N	76.42 W
Stony Run ≃	285	40.09 N	75.32 W
Stony Stratford	42	52.04 N	0.52 W
Stoober Bach ≃	61	47.27 N	16.35 E
Stop ≃	283	42.10 N	71.19 W
Stopnica	30	50.27 N	20.57 E
Stoppenberg ◄[8]	263	51.29 N	7.02 E
Stör ≃	54	53.50 N	11.29 E
Storå	40	59.43 N	15.08 E
Storå ≃	26	56.19 N	8.19 E
Stora Alvaret ≋	26	56.30 N	16.30 E
Stora Gla ⊜	26	59.30 N	12.30 E
Stora Kloten ⊜	40	59.52 N	15.16 E
Stora Le ⊜	26	59.05 N	11.53 E
Stora Lulevatten ⊜	24	67.10 N	19.16 E
Stora Mellösa	40	59.13 N	15.30 E
Stora Möja I, Sve.	26	59.26 N	18.55 E
Stora Möja I, Sve.	40	59.26 N	18.55 E
Stora Norn ⊜	40	60.14 N	15.42 E
Stora Sjöfallets Nationalpark ♦	24	67.44 N	18.16 E
Stora Skedvi	40	60.24 N	15.48 E
Stora Sundby	40	59.16 N	16.07 E
Storavan ⊜	24	65.40 N	18.15 E
Stora Vika	40	58.56 N	17.48 E
Storby	26	60.13 N	19.34 E
Stord I	26	59.53 N	5.25 E
Store Andst	41	55.29 N	9.14 E
Storebælt ʯ	41	55.30 N	11.00 E
Store Heddinge	41	55.19 N	12.25 E
Store Magleby	41	55.36 N	12.38 E
Store Merløse	41	55.33 N	11.40 E
Støren	26	63.02 N	10.18 E
Store Sotra I	26	60.18 N	5.05 E
Storeton	262	53.21 N	3.03 W
Storey □[6]	226	39.28 N	119.30 W
Storfjärden ⊜	40	60.30 N	17.23 E
Storfjorden c[2]	26	62.25 N	6.30 E
Storfors	40	59.32 N	14.16 E
Störitzsee ⊜	264a	52.23 N	13.51 E
Störkanal ≅	54	53.36 N	11.30 E
Storkerson Bay c	176	73.00 N	124.50 W
Storkerson Peninsula ›[1]	176	72.30 N	106.30 W
Storkow, Dtsch.	54	53.19 N	14.17 E
Storkow, Dtsch.	54	52.15 N	13.56 E
Storlien	26	63.19 N	12.06 E
Stormarn ◄[1]	52	53.45 N	10.20 E
Storm Bay c	166	43.10 S	147.32 E
Stormberg ∧	158	30.57 S	26.41 E
Stormberge ⋏	158	31.27 S	26.55 E
Storm King Mountain ∧	224	46.39 N	122.10 W
Storm Lake	198	42.38 N	95.12 W
Storm Mountain ∧	180	59.37 N	150.35 W
Stormont-Dundas and Glengarry □[6]	206	45.10 N	75.00 W
Stormsrivier	158	33.59 S	23.52 E
Stormsvlei	158	34.05 S	20.06 E
Stormville	210	41.34 N	73.45 W
Stornara	68	41.17 N	15.46 E
Stornarella	68	41.15 N	15.44 E
Stornorrforsen	26	63.52 N	20.03 E
Stornoway	46	58.12 N	6.23 W
Storo	64	45.51 N	10.35 E
Storoževaja	84	43.53 N	41.27 E
Storoževsk	24	61.57 N	52.16 E
Storozhynets'	78	48.10 N	25.43 E
Storrensjön ⊜	26	63.38 N	12.34 E
Storrington	42	50.55 N	0.28 W
Storrs	207	41.48 N	72.15 W
Storsjøen ⊜, Nor.	26	60.23 N	11.40 E
Storsjøen ⊜, Nor.	26	61.35 N	11.12 E
Storsjön ⊜, Sve.	26	62.48 N	13.07 E
Storsjön ⊜, Sve.	26	63.12 N	14.18 E
Storsjön ⊜, Sve.	40	60.34 N	16.44 E
Storsjön ⊜, Sve.	40	59.04 N	17.12 E
Storsteinsfjellet ∧	24	68.14 N	17.52 E
Storstrøm □[6]	41	55.00 N	11.55 E
Storstrømmen ʯ	41	54.58 N	11.55 E
Storstrømsbroen ◄[5]	41	54.58 N	11.50 E
Stort ≃	260	51.46 N	0.01 E
Storthoaks	184	49.22 N	101.38 W
Storuman	24	65.06 N	17.06 E
Storuman ⊜[1]	24	65.14 N	16.54 E
Storuman-See → Storavan ⊜	24	65.40 N	18.15 E
Storvarts gruve	26	62.38 N	11.31 E
Storvätteshågna ∧	26	62.07 N	12.27 E
Storvik	40	60.35 N	16.32 E
Storvindeln ⊜	24	65.43 N	17.05 E
Storvreta	40	59.58 N	17.42 E
Story	202	44.34 N	106.53 W
Story City	190	42.11 N	93.35 W
Stosch, Isla I	254	49.09 S	75.26 W
Stössen	54	51.06 N	11.55 E
Stotfold	42	52.01 N	0.14 W
Stötten, Dtsch.	58	47.44 N	10.42 E
Stötten, Dtsch.	64	47.44 N	10.42 E
Stotternheim	54	51.03 N	11.02 E
Stottville	210	42.17 N	73.44 W
Stoubcy	76	53.29 N	26.44 E
Stouchsburg	208	40.23 N	76.14 W
Stough Park ♦	280	34.12 N	118.18 W
Stoughton, Sk., Can.	184	49.41 N	103.03 W
Stoughton, Eng., U.K.	260	51.15 N	0.35 W
Stoughton, Ma., U.S.	207	42.07 N	71.06 W
Stoughton, Wi., U.S.	216	42.55 N	89.13 W
Stoumont	56	50.25 N	5.48 E
Stoŭng ≃	110	12.50 N	104.19 E
Stour ≃, Eng., U.K.	42	51.52 N	1.16 E
Stour ≃, Eng., U.K.	42	50.43 N	1.46 W
Stour ≃, Eng., U.K.	42	51.18 N	1.22 E
Stour ≃, Eng., U.K.	42	52.20 N	2.15 W
Stourbridge	42	52.27 N	2.09 W
Stourport-on-Severn	42	52.21 N	2.16 W
Stout Lake ⊜	184	52.08 N	94.33 W
Stoutsville	219	39.33 N	91.51 W
Stover	194	38.26 N	92.59 W
Stow, Ma., U.S.	207	42.26 N	71.30 W
Stow, N.Y., U.S.	214	42.09 N	79.25 W
Stow, Oh., U.S.	214	41.10 N	81.27 W
Stowe, Pa., U.S.	208	40.15 N	75.40 W
Stowe, Vt., U.S.	188	44.27 N	72.41 W
Stowell	194	29.47 N	94.23 W
Stowe Township	279b	40.29 N	80.04 W
Stow Maries	260	51.40 N	0.39 E
Stowmarket	42	52.11 N	1.00 E
Stow-on-the-Wold	42	51.56 N	1.44 W
Stowupland	42	52.12 N	1.01 E
Stoyoma Mountain ∧	182	49.59 N	121.13 W
Stoystown	214	40.06 N	78.57 W
Stožec	60	48.51 N	13.50 E
Stra	64	45.25 N	12.00 E
Straach	54	51.57 N	12.35 E
Strabane, N. Ire., U.K.	48	54.49 N	7.27 W
Strabane, Pa., U.S.	214	40.15 N	80.11 W
Straberg	263	51.05 N	6.45 E
Strachan	46	57.01 N	2.32 W
Strachan Island I	164	9.00 S	142.10 E
Strachur	46	56.10 N	5.04 W
Stradbally	48	53.00 N	7.08 W
Stradbroke	42	52.19 N	1.16 E
Stradella	62	45.05 N	9.18 E
Stradone	48	53.58 N	7.14 W
Stradovn'a, ozero ⊜	82	56.53 N	36.18 E
Stradzečy	76	51.56 N	23.40 E
Straelen	56	51.27 N	6.16 E
Strafford	285	40.03 N	75.25 W
Straffordville	212	42.45 N	80.47 W
Strahan	166	42.09 S	145.19 E
Straight Creek ≃	218	38.46 N	83.55 W
Strakonice	60	49.16 N	13.55 E
Stralsund	54	54.19 N	13.05 E
Strambino	62	45.23 N	7.53 E
Strand	158	34.06 S	18.50 E
Stranda	26	62.19 N	6.54 E
Strande	54	54.26 N	10.12 E
Strandhill	48	54.17 N	8.36 W
Stranger Creek ≃	198	39.00 N	95.01 W
Strangford	48	54.22 N	5.34 W
Strangford Lough ⊜	48	54.28 N	5.35 W
Strängnäs	40	59.23 N	17.02 E
Strångsjö	40	58.54 N	16.12 E
Strangways ≃	164	14.52 S	133.50 E
Strangways, Mount ∧	162	23.02 S	133.51 E
Stranorlar	48	54.48 N	7.46 W
Stranraer	44	54.55 N	5.02 W
Strasbourg, Sk., Can.	184	51.04 N	104.57 W
Strasbourg, Fr.	58	48.35 N	7.45 E
Strasbourg, Aéroport ⊠	58	48.32 N	7.38 E
Strasburg, Dtsch.	54	53.30 N	13.44 E
Strasburg, Co., U.S.	198	39.44 N	104.20 W
Strasburg, N.D., U.S.	198	46.08 N	100.09 W
Strasburg, Oh., U.S.	214	40.35 N	81.31 W
Strasburg, Pa., U.S.	208	39.58 N	76.11 W
Strasburg, Va., U.S.	188	38.59 N	78.21 W
Strășeni	38	47.08 N	28.36 E
Straševiči	76	56.49 N	34.36 E
Strašín	60	49.08 N	13.38 E
Stråssa	40	59.45 N	15.13 E
Strassburg → Strasbourg	58	48.35 N	7.45 E
Strasshof an der Nordbahn	61	48.19 N	16.39 E
Strasskirchen	60	48.50 N	12.43 E
Strata Florida Abbey ⊍[1]	42	52.16 N	3.51 W
Stratford, On., Can.	212	43.22 N	80.57 W
Stratford, N.Z.	172	39.20 S	174.17 E
Stratford, Ct., U.S.	207	41.11 N	73.08 W
Stratford, De., U.S.	285	39.40 N	75.38 W
Stratford, Ia., U.S.	190	42.16 N	93.55 W
Stratford, N.J., U.S.	208	39.49 N	75.00 W
Stratford, N.Y., U.S.	210	43.11 N	74.42 W
Stratford, Ok., U.S.	196	34.47 N	96.57 W
Stratford, Tx., U.S.	196	36.20 N	102.04 W
Stratford, Wi., U.S.	190	44.48 N	90.04 W
Stratford Centre	206	45.47 N	71.16 W
Stratford Point ›	276	41.09 N	73.06 W
Stratford Square ◄[9]	278	41.57 N	88.07 W
Stratford-upon-Avon	42	52.12 N	1.41 W
Strathalbyn	168b	35.16 S	138.54 E
Strathaven	46	55.40 N	4.04 W
Strathbogie Ranges ⋏	169	36.55 S	145.45 E
Strathclair	184	50.24 N	100.24 W
Strathclyde □[4]	46	56.00 N	5.15 W
Strathcona Provincial Park ♦	182	49.40 N	125.50 W
Strathdearn V	46	57.15 N	4.05 W
Strathdon	46	57.11 N	3.02 W
Strathearn V	46	56.18 N	3.45 W
Strathfield	170	33.52 S	151.06 E
Strathgordon	166	42.46 S	146.03 E
Strath Kanaird	46	57.59 N	5.11 W
Strathlorne	186	46.11 N	61.17 W
Strathminglo	46	56.16 N	3.16 W
Strathmoor ◄[8]	281	42.23 N	83.11 W
Strathmore, Ab., Can.	182	51.03 N	113.23 W
Strathmore, Ca., U.S.	204	36.08 N	119.03 W
Strathmore, N.J., U.S.	276	40.24 N	74.13 W
Strathmore V	46	56.39 N	3.00 W
Strathpeffer	46	57.35 N	4.33 W
Strathpine	171a	27.19 S	152.59 E
Strathroy	214	42.57 N	81.38 W
Strathy ≃	46	58.34 N	4.00 W
Strathy Point ›	46	58.35 N	4.02 W
Strattanville	214	41.12 N	79.19 W
Stratton, Eng., U.K.	42	50.50 N	4.31 W
Stratton, Eng., U.K.	42	51.44 N	1.59 W
Stratton, Co., U.S.	198	39.18 N	102.36 W
Stratton, Me., U.S.	188	45.08 N	70.26 W
Stratton, Ne., U.S.	198	40.08 N	101.13 W
Stratton, Oh., U.S.	214	40.32 N	80.38 W
Stratton Mountain ∧	188	43.05 N	72.56 W
Stratton Saint Margaret	42	51.35 N	1.45 W
Straubenhardt	56	48.51 N	8.32 E
Straubing	60	48.53 N	12.34 E
Strauch	263	51.09 N	6.56 E
Straumen	26	63.52 N	11.18 E
Straupitz	54	51.54 N	14.07 E
Strausberg	54	52.35 N	13.53 E
Straus-Berger Stadtforst ♦	264a	52.34 N	13.52 E
Strausberg-Vorstadt	264a	52.32 N	13.51 E
Straussberg	54	51.23 N	10.44 E
Straussee ⊜	264a	52.35 N	13.53 E
Straussfurt	54	51.09 N	10.59 E
Strausstown	208	40.30 N	76.11 W
Stravignano	66	43.05 N	12.49 E
Strawberry	226	38.13 N	118.35 W
Strawberry ≃, Ar., U.S.	194	35.53 N	91.13 W
Strawberry ≃, Ut,. U.S.	200	40.10 N	110.24 W
Strawberry Island I	284a	42.57 N	78.55 W
Strawberry Mountain ∧	202	44.19 N	118.43 W
Strawberry Point, Ca., U.S.	282	37.54 N	122.31 W
Strawberry Point, Ia., U.S.	190	42.41 N	91.32 W
Strawberry Point ›	283	42.15 N	70.46 W
Strawberry Reservoir ⊜[1]	200	40.11 N	111.08 W
Strawberry Valley	226	39.34 N	121.06 W
Strawbridge Lake ⊜	285	39.57 N	74.57 W
Strawn	196	32.33 N	98.29 W
Straw Pump	279b	40.19 N	79.40 W
Stráž	61	49.04 N	14.54 E
Strážnice	30	48.54 N	17.18 E
Strážov	60	49.18 N	13.15 E
Strážske	30	48.53 N	21.50 E
Streaky Bay	162	32.48 S	134.13 E
Streaky Bay c	162	32.36 S	134.08 E
Streamwood	216	42.01 N	88.10 W
Streatham, Austl.	169	37.41 S	143.04 E
Streatham, B.C., Can.	182	53.52 N	126.12 W
Streatham ◄[8]	260	51.26 N	0.08 W
Streator	216	41.07 N	88.50 W
Strebersdorf ◄[8]	264b	48.18 N	16.23 E
Středočeský Kraj □[4]	30	49.55 N	14.30 E
Stredoslovenský Kraj □[4]	30	48.50 N	19.10 E
Street	42	51.07 N	2.42 W
Streeter	198	46.39 N	99.21 W
Streetman	222	31.53 N	96.19 W
Streetsboro	214	41.14 N	81.20 W
Streets Run ≃	279b	40.23 N	79.56 W
Streetsville	212	43.35 N	79.42 W
Strehaia	38	44.37 N	23.12 E
Strehla	54	51.21 N	13.13 E
Střela ≃	60	49.55 N	13.33 E
Strelasund ʯ	54	54.20 N	13.05 E
Streleckije Vyselki	82	54.12 N	38.57 E
Strelica	78	51.37 N	38.55 E
Střelice	61	49.09 N	16.30 E
Strelitzalt	54	53.20 N	13.05 E
Strelka	86	58.05 N	93.01 E
Strelka ≃	265a	59.52 N	30.03 E
Strelka-Čun'a	74	61.45 N	102.48 E
Strelkovo	82	55.28 N	37.37 E
Strel'na, Ross.	24	66.06 N	38.40 E
Strel'na, Ross.	76	59.51 N	30.02 E
Strel'na ≃	24	66.04 N	38.39 E
Strel'skaja	24	59.28 N	47.47 E
Střelské Hoštice	60	49.18 N	13.46 E
Strem ≃	61	47.00 N	16.31 E
Strembo	64	46.09 N	10.44 E
Stremilovo	82	55.09 N	37.09 E
Strenči	76	57.37 N	25.41 E
Strengen	58	47.08 N	10.27 E
Strensall	44	54.03 N	1.02 W
Stresa	62	45.53 N	8.32 E
Strèšyn	76	52.43 N	30.05 E
Stretford	44	53.27 N	2.19 W
Stretton, Austl.	162	32.32 S	117.41 E
Stretton, Eng., U.K.	42	52.44 N	0.35 W
Stretton, Eng., U.K.	44	53.21 N	2.35 W
Streu ≃	56	50.21 N	10.16 E
Streufdorf	54	50.21 N	10.41 E
Strib	41	55.32 N	9.47 E
Striberg	40	59.33 N	14.56 E
Stříbro	60	49.46 N	13.00 E
Strichen	46	57.34 N	2.05 W
Strickherdicke	263	51.29 N	7.43 E
Strickland ≃	164	6.00 S	142.05 E
Strigno	64	46.04 N	11.31 E
Strijen	52	51.45 N	4.33 E
Striker, Lake ⊜[1]	222	31.57 N	94.59 W
Strilkove	78	45.54 N	34.53 E
Stril'tsivka	83	49.18 N	39.52 E
Strimón (Struma) ≃	38	40.47 N	23.51 E
Stringtown	218	40.05 N	86.29 W
Striven, Loch c	46	55.58 N	5.09 W
Strižament, gora ∧	84	44.46 N	42.01 E
Striži	80	58.30 N	49.13 E
Strjama ≃	38	42.10 N	24.56 E
Strobel	252	32.03 S	60.37 W
Strobel, Lago ⊜	254	48.22 S	71.12 W
Strobl	64	47.43 N	13.29 E
Strobleton	214	41.22 N	79.25 W
Strøby	41	55.23 N	12.18 E
Stroeder	254	40.11 S	62.37 W
Strofádhes, Nísoi II	38	37.15 N	21.00 E
Strogino ◄[8]	265b	55.49 N	37.25 E
Strogonof Point ›	180	56.53 N	158.49 W
Stroh	216	41.34 N	85.11 W
Ströhen	52	52.32 N	8.41 E
Stroitel'	78	50.47 N	36.26 E
Strokestown	48	53.47 N	8.08 W
Strom ≃	54	53.15 N	13.50 E
Stroma I	46	58.41 N	3.08 W
Stromberg, Dtsch.	52	51.48 N	8.12 E
Stromberg, Dtsch.	56	49.57 N	7.46 E
Stromboli, Isola I	70	38.47 N	15.13 E
Strome	182	52.48 N	112.04 W
Stromeferry	46	57.21 N	5.34 W
Strömkendorf	54	53.58 N	11.29 E
Stromness	46	58.57 N	3.18 W
Strömsberg	40	60.24 N	17.35 E
Strömsbro	40	60.42 N	17.10 E
Strömsbruk	26	61.53 N	17.19 E
Stromsburg	198	41.06 N	97.35 W
Strömsholm	40	59.32 N	16.15 E
Strömsnäsbruk	26	56.33 N	13.43 E
Strömstad	26	58.56 N	11.10 E
Strömsund	26	63.51 N	15.35 E
Strömsvattudal ⊜	26	63.56 N	15.28 E
Stromyn'	82	56.03 N	38.29 E
Strong	194	33.06 N	92.20 W
Strong ≃	194	31.51 N	90.08 W
Strong City	198	38.23 N	96.32 W
Stronghurst	190	40.44 N	90.54 W
Strongoli	68	39.15 N	17.03 E
Strongs Creek ≃	276	40.40 N	73.22 W
Strongs Neck ›[1]	276	40.58 N	73.07 W
Strongstown	214	40.33 N	78.55 W
Strongsville	214	41.18 N	81.50 W
Strongsville Airport ⊠	279a	41.19 N	81.52 W
Stronsay I	46	59.07 N	2.37 W
Stronsay Firth ʯ	46	59.02 N	2.41 W
Stronsdorf	61	48.39 N	16.18 E
Strontian	46	56.41 N	5.34 W
Strood	42	51.24 N	0.28 E
Stropkov	30	49.12 N	21.40 E
Stropnice ≃	61	48.52 N	14.30 E
Stroppiana	62	45.14 N	8.27 E
Stroud, Austl.	166	32.20 S	151.56 E
Stroud, Eng., U.K.	42	51.45 N	2.12 W
Stroud, Ok., U.S.	196	35.44 N	96.39 W
Stroudsburg	210	40.59 N	75.11 W
Strövelstorp	41	56.09 N	12.49 E
Strubenvale	273d	26.16 S	28.28 E
Strücklingen	52	53.07 N	7.40 E
Struer	26	56.29 N	8.37 E
Struga	38	41.11 N	20.40 E
Strugi-Krasnyje	76	58.17 N	29.06 E
Struisbaai	158	34.49 S	20.04 E
Struisbult	273d	26.19 S	28.29 E
Strule ≃	48	54.43 N	7.25 W
Strullendorf	56	49.51 N	10.58 E
Strum	190	44.32 N	91.23 W
Struma (Strimón) ≃	38	40.47 N	23.51 E
Strumble Head ›	42	52.02 N	5.04 W
Strumica	38	41.26 N	22.38 E
Strümp	263	51.17 N	6.40 E
Strunino	82	56.23 N	38.34 E
Strupna	82	54.43 N	38.48 E
Struthers	214	41.03 N	80.36 W
Struy	46	57.24 N	4.39 W
Strydenburg	158	29.58 S	23.40 E
Strydomsvlei	158	33.10 S	23.03 E
Strydpoort	158	27.00 S	25.58 E
Stryker, Mt., U.S.	182	48.40 N	114.46 W
Stryker, Oh., U.S.	216	41.30 N	84.24 W
Strykersville	210	42.42 N	78.27 W
Stryków	30	51.55 N	19.37 E
Stryn	26	61.55 N	6.47 E
Strynø I	41	54.54 N	10.37 E
Strypa ≃	78	48.52 N	25.26 E
Stryy	78	49.15 N	23.51 E
Stryy ≃	78	49.24 N	24.13 E
Stryzhavka	78	49.19 N	28.28 E
Strzegom	30	50.57 N	16.21 E
Strzegowo-Osada	30	52.55 N	20.18 E
Strzelce Krajeńskie	30	52.53 N	15.32 E
Strzelce Opolskie	30	50.31 N	18.19 E
Strzelecki Creek ≃	166	29.37 S	139.59 E
Strzelecki Desert ◄[2]	166	28.00 S	140.10 E
Strzeleckie, Mount ∧	162	21.10 S	133.53 E
Strzelecki National Park ♦	166	40.14 S	148.06 E
Strzelin	30	50.47 N	17.03 E
Strzelno	30	52.38 N	18.11 E
Strzyżów	30	49.52 N	21.47 E
Stuart, Fl., U.S.	220	27.11 N	80.15 W
Stuart, Ia., U.S.	198	41.30 N	94.19 W
Stuart, Ne., U.S.	198	42.35 N	99.08 W
Stuart, Va., U.S.	192	36.38 N	80.15 W
Stuart ≃	182	54.00 N	123.32 W
Stuart, Central Mount ∧	162	21.54 S	133.27 E
Stuart, Mount ∧	224	47.29 N	120.54 W
Stuart Channel ʯ	224	48.55 N	123.45 W
Stuart Island I, Ak., U.S.	180	63.35 N	162.30 W
Stuart Island I, Wa., U.S.	224	48.42 N	123.12 W
Stuart Lake ⊜	182	54.32 N	124.35 W
Stuart Mountains ⋏	172	45.00 S	167.37 E
Stuart Range ⋏	162	29.10 S	134.56 E
Stuarts Draft	192	38.01 N	79.02 W
Stubai V	64	47.06 N	11.19 E
Stubaier Alpen ⋏	64	47.10 N	11.05 E
Stubalpe ⋏	61	47.06 N	14.54 E
Stübbecken	263	51.23 N	7.36 E
Stubbekøbing	41	54.53 N	12.03 E
Stubbenfelde	54	54.02 N	14.01 E
Stubbington	42	50.50 N	1.13 W
Stubbins	262	53.39 N	2.19 W
Stubenberg	61	47.14 N	15.48 E
Stubla ≃	78	50.50 N	26.04 E
Stubner Kogel ∧	64	47.07 N	13.06 E
Studená	61	49.11 N	15.17 E
Studenec	80	54.52 N	48.16 E
Studenica, Manastir ⊍[1]	38	43.21 N	20.35 E
Studen Kladenec, Jazovir ⊜[1]	38	41.37 N	25.30 E
Studenok	78	51.42 N	34.07 E
Studholme Junction	172	44.44 S	171.08 E
Studi, Università degli ⊍[2]	266b	45.28 N	9.14 E
Studland	42	50.39 N	1.58 W
Studley	42	52.16 N	1.52 W
Stud'onoje, Ross.	80	51.36 N	53.10 E
Stud'onoje, Ross.	86	53.37 N	77.31 E
Studsvik	40	58.46 N	17.23 E
Stugudal	26	62.54 N	11.52 E
Stugun	26	63.10 N	15.36 E
Stuhleck ∧	61	47.34 N	15.47 E
Stühlingen	58	47.44 N	8.26 E
Stuhlweissenburg → Székesfehérvár	30	47.12 N	18.25 E
Stuhr	52	53.01 N	8.45 E
Stuie	182	52.22 N	126.02 W
Stukely, Lac ⊜	206	45.22 N	72.15 W
Stull ≃	184	55.10 N	92.39 W
Stull Lake ⊜	184	54.23 N	92.34 W
Stülpe	54	52.02 N	13.19 E
Stumm	64	47.17 N	11.53 E
Stump Creek	214	41.01 N	78.50 W
Stump Creek ≃	276	40.28 N	74.16 W
Stumpf	263	51.06 N	7.13 E
Stump Lake ⊜	198	47.54 N	98.24 W
Stumsdorf	54	51.37 N	12.03 E
Stuorre Tjõure ∧	26	63.56 N	13.30 E
Stupart ≃	184	56.00 N	93.22 W
Stupava	61	48.17 N	17.02 E
Stupino	82	54.53 N	38.05 E
Stuppach	56	49.27 N	9.44 E
Stura ≃	62	45.09 N	8.21 E
Stura di Ala ≃	62	45.18 N	7.24 E
Stura di Demonte ≃	62	44.40 N	7.53 E
Stura di Lanzo ≃	62	45.06 N	7.44 E
Stura di Val Grande ≃	62	45.18 N	7.24 E
Stura di Viù ≃	62	45.16 N	7.26 E
Sturbridge	207	42.06 N	72.04 W
Sturdee	162	31.52 S	132.23 E
Sturge Island I	9	67.27 S	164.18 E
Sturgeon, Mo., U.S.	219	39.14 N	92.16 W
Sturgeon, Pa., U.S.	279b	40.23 N	80.13 W
Sturgeon ≃, On., Can.	190	46.19 N	79.58 W
Sturgeon ≃, Sk., Can.	184	53.12 N	105.53 W
Sturgeon ≃, Mi., U.S.	190	45.24 N	84.38 W
Sturgeon ≃, Mi., U.S.	190	45.50 N	86.41 W
Sturgeon ≃, Mi., U.S.	190	47.02 N	88.30 W
Sturgeon Bay	190	44.50 N	87.22 W
Sturgeon Bay c	184	52.00 N	97.50 W
Sturgeon Falls	190	46.22 N	79.55 W
Sturgeon Lake ⊜, Ab., Can.	182	55.06 N	117.30 W
Sturgeon Lake ⊜, On., Can.	184	55.25 N	90.55 W
Sturgeon Lake ⊜, On., Can.	212	44.28 N	78.42 W
Sturgeon Lake ⊜, Wa., U.S.	224	45.44 N	122.48 W
Sturgeon Lake Indian Reserve ◄[4], Ab., Can.	182	55.04 N	117.29 W
Sturgeon Lake Indian Reserve ◄[4], Sk., Can.	184	53.25 N	106.05 W
Sturgeon Landing	184	54.16 N	101.49 W
Sturgeon Point ›	212	42.42 N	79.03 W
Sturgis, Sk., Can.	184	51.58 N	102.32 W
Sturgis, Ky., U.S.	194	37.32 N	87.59 W
Sturgis, Mi., U.S.	216	41.47 N	85.25 W
Sturgis, Ms., U.S.	194	33.20 N	89.02 W
Sturgis, S.D., U.S.	198	44.24 N	103.30 W
Sturla	62	44.24 N	8.59 E
Şturminster Newton	42	50.50 N	2.19 W
Štúrovo	30	47.48 N	18.49 E
Sturry	42	51.18 N	1.07 E
Sturt, Mount ∧	166	29.33 S	141.42 E
Sturt Creek	162	19.10 S	128.10 E
Sturt Creek ≃	162	20.08 S	127.24 E
Sturtevant	216	42.41 N	87.53 W
Sturt National Park ♦	166	29.00 S	141.40 E
Sturt Stony Desert ◄[2]	166	28.30 S	141.00 E
Sturup flygplats ⊠	41	55.34 N	13.21 E
Stürzelberg	263	51.08 N	6.49 E
Stutensee	56	49.05 N	8.29 E
Stutterheim	158	32.33 S	27.28 E
Stuttgart, Dtsch.	56	48.46 N	9.11 E
Stuttgart, Ar., U.S.	194	34.30 N	91.33 W
Stuttgart □[5]	56	49.00 N	9.45 E
Stuttgart, Flughafen ⊠	56	48.41 N	9.12 E
Stützengrün	54	50.32 N	12.31 E
Stützerbach	54	50.38 N	10.51 E
Stuyvesant	210	42.24 N	73.47 W
Stuyvesant Falls	210	42.21 N	73.44 W
Styal	262	53.21 N	2.15 W
Stykkishólmur	24a	65.06 N	22.48 W
Styr ≃	78	52.07 N	26.35 E
Styrum ◄[8]	263	51.27 N	6.51 E
Styx ≃, On., Can.	212	44.11 N	80.57 W
Styx ≃, Al., U.S.	194	30.31 N	87.27 W
Šu	85	43.36 N	73.45 E
Suaçuí Grande ≃	255	18.50 S	41.46 W
Suai	112	3.48 N	113.38 E
Suain	164	3.20 S	142.55 E
Suaita	246	6.07 N	73.27 W
Suakin Archipelago II	140	18.42 N	38.30 E
Sual	116	16.04 N	120.05 E
Suan	98	38.42 N	126.22 E
Suao, T'aiwan	100	24.36 N	121.51 E
Su'ao, Zhg.	100	25.38 N	119.42 E
Suapure ≃	246	6.25 N	66.23 W
Suaqui Grande	232	28.24 N	109.54 W
Suār	124	29.02 N	79.03 E
Suātala	124	23.09 N	79.02 E
Şuatima	114	4.13 N	96.04 E
Šubač	76	60.22 N	38.14 E
Subačius	76	55.46 N	24.47 E
Subah	115a	6.58 S	109.52 E
Subaio	256	22.30 S	42.50 W
Subang	115a	6.34 S	107.45 E
Şubansiri ≃	120	26.48 N	93.50 E
Šubarkuduk	86	49.13 N	56.34 E
Subar Laut, Pulau I	271c	1.13 N	103.50 E
Subarnapur	272b	22.58 N	88.34 E
Şubarnarekha ≃	120	21.34 N	87.24 E
Šubarši	86	48.35 N	57.12 E
Subashi	85	38.22 N	74.57 E
Subasio, Monte ∧	66	43.03 N	12.40 E
Subate	76	56.01 N	25.56 E
Subay', 'Urūq as- ◄[2]	144	22.15 N	43.05 E
Subbiano	66	43.34 N	11.52 E
Subbotino	86	53.04 N	91.55 E
Subchankulovo	80	54.34 N	53.49 E
Subei	102	39.27 N	95.03 E
Subeita → Shivta, Horvot ⊥	132	30.53 N	34.38 E
Suben	60	48.25 N	13.26 E
Subhepur	272a	28.45 N	77.16 E
Subi, Pulau I	112	2.55 N	108.50 E
Subiaco	66	41.55 N	13.06 E
Subic	116	14.53 N	120.14 E
Subic Bay c	116	14.45 N	120.13 E
Subic Bay Naval Base (U.S.) ■	116	14.47 N	120.16 E
Subipur	272b	22.54 N	88.08 E
Subk al-Ahad	142	30.18 N	31.02 E
Sublette	198	37.28 N	100.50 W
Sublett Range ⋏	202	42.20 N	112.50 W
Sublime	222	29.29 N	96.48 W
Subotica	38	46.06 N	19.39 E
Suburban Airport ⊠	284c	39.05 N	76.50 W
Suburban Village	285	39.58 N	75.34 W
Suca	144	6.31 N	39.14 E
Sucarnoochee ≃	194	32.25 N	88.02 W
Succasunna	210	40.52 N	74.38 W
Succor Creek ≃	202	43.38 N	116.56 W
Suceava	38	47.39 N	26.19 E

Symbol	English	Deutsch	Español	Français	Português
≃	River	Fluß	Río	Rivière	Rio
≅	Canal	Kanal	Canal	Canal	Canal
∟	Waterfall, Rapids	Wasserfall, Stromschnellen	Cascada, Rápidos	Chute d'eau, Rapides	Cascata, Rápidos
ʯ	Strait	Meeresstraße	Estrecho	Détroit	Estreito
c	Bay, Gulf	Bucht, Golf	Bahía, Golfo	Baie, Golfe	Baía, Golfo
⊜	Lake, Lakes	See, Seen	Lago, Lagos	Lac, Lacs	Lago, Lagos
≋	Swamp	Sumpf	Pantano	Marais	Pântano
⊼	Ice Features, Glacier	Eis- und Gletscherformen	Accidentes Glaciales	Formes glaciaires	Acidentes glaciares
⊤	Other Hydrographic Features	Andere Hydrographische Objekte	Otros Elementos Hidrográficos	Autres données hydrographiques	Outros acidentes hidrográficos

Symbol	English	Deutsch	Español	Français	Português
◄	Submarine Features	Untermeerische Objekte	Accidentes Submarinos	Formes de relief sous-marin	Acidentes submarinos
□	Political Unit	Politische Einheit	Unidad Politica	Entité politique	Unidade política
⊍	Cultural Institution	Kulturelle Institution	Institución Cultural	Institution culturelle	Instituição cultural
⊥	Historical Site	Historische Stätte	Sitio Histórico	Site historique	Sitio histórico
♦	Recreational Site	Erholungs- und Ferienort	Sitio de Recreo	Centre de loisirs	Area de Lazer
⊠	Airport	Flughafen	Aeropuerto	Aéroport	Aeroporto
■	Military Installation	Militäranlage	Instalación Militar	Installation militaire	Instalação militar
◄	Miscellaneous	Verschiedenes	Misceláneo	Divers	Diversos

Suceava □6 38 47.30 N 25.45 E
Suceava ≃ 38 47.32 N 26.32 E
Sucha [Beskidzka] 30 49.44 N 19.36 E
Suchaja 88 52.32 N 107.06 E
Suchań, Pol. 30 53.17 N 15.19 E
Suchan
→ Partizansk, Ross. 89 43.08 N 133.09 E
Suchana 74 68.45 N 118.00 E
Suchang 107 30.34 N 103.34 E
Süchbaatar 88 50.15 N 106.12 E
Süchbaatar □4 102 45.30 N 114.00 E
Suchdol ◆8 54 50.08 N 14.21 E
Suchdol nad Lužnicí 61 48.54 N 14.53 E
Suchedniów 30 51.03 N 20.51 E
Suchetgarh 123 32.34 N 74.40 E
Suchiapa 234 16.37 N 93.05 W
Suchiapa ≃ 234 16.36 N 93.01 W
Súchil 234 23.38 N 103.55 W
Suchiniči 76 54.06 N 35.20 E
Suchitepéquez □5 236 14.25 N 91.20 W
Suchitlán 234 19.22 N 103.43 W
Suchitoto 236 13.56 N 89.02 W
Suchobezvodnoje 80 57.03 N 44.50 E
Suchoborka 24 59.06 N 49.58 E
Suchodol, Ross. 80 53.55 N 51.14 E
Suchodol, Ross. 82 54.27 N 37.22 E
Suchodol'skij 76 53.43 N 38.17 E
Suchodrev ≃ 82 54.44 N 35.59 E
Suchoj 80 47.06 N 41.27 E
Suchoj Jelančik ≃ 83 47.16 N 38.25 E
Suchoj Log 86 56.55 N 62.01 E
Suchoj Pit 86 58.48 N 92.49 E
Suchoj Sambek ≃ 83 47.23 N 39.07 E
Suchona ≃ 24 60.46 N 46.24 E
Suchorečka 80 52.49 N 52.27 E
Suchotinka 80 52.31 N 41.35 E
Suchou
→ Suzhou 106 31.18 N 120.37 E
Suchoverkovo 76 56.37 N 35.35 E
Suchov Pervyj 80 49.59 N 43.28 E
Süchow
→ Xuzhou 98 34.16 N 117.11 E
Süchteln 56 51.17 N 6.22 E
Suchumi 84 43.01 N 41.02 E
Sucio ≃ 246 7.27 N 77.07 W
Suck ≃ 48 53.16 N 8.03 W
Sucker Creek ≃ 212 44.09 N 77.08 W
Sucker Creek Indian Reserve ◆4 182 55.28 N 116.10 W
Sucker Lake ⊜ 212 44.46 N 78.16 W
Suckling, Mount ∧ 164 9.45 S 148.55 E
Sucre, Arg. 258 34.30 S 59.07 W
Sucre, Bol. 248 19.02 S 65.17 W
Sucre, Col. 246 8.49 N 74.44 W
Sucre, Ec. 246 1.16 S 80.26 W
Sucre □3 246 10.25 N 63.30 W
Sucre □5, Col. 246 9.00 N 75.00 W
Sucre □5, Ven. 286c 10.25 N 66.50 W
Sucúa 246 2.28 S 78.10 W
Sucuaro 246 4.34 N 68.50 W
Sucumbíos □4 246 0.06 N 76.52 W
Sucunduri ≃ 248 5.50 S 59.32 W
Sucuriju 250 1.39 N 49.57 W
Sucuriú ≃ 255 20.47 S 51.38 W
Sucy-en-Brie 50 48.46 N 2.32 E
Sud □4 175f 22.00 S 166.30 E
Sud, Canal du ʮ 238 18.40 N 73.05 W
Sud, Grand Récif ⊤2 175f 23.00 S 167.02 E
Sud, Pointe > 157a 11.53 S 43.49 E
Sud, Rivière du ≃ 206 45.08 N 73.15 W
Suda 76 59.09 N 37.33 E
Suda ≃ 76 59.11 N 37.30 E
Südafrika
→ South Africa □1 156 30.00 S 26.00 E
Sudaj 76 58.58 N 43.08 E
Sudak 78 44.52 N 34.59 E
Südamerika
→ South America ◆1 18 15.00 S 60.00 W
Sudan 196 34.04 N 102.31 W
Sudan (As-Sūdān) □1, Afr. 136 15.00 N 30.00 E
Sudan (As-Sūdān) □1, Afr. 140 15.00 N 30.00 E
Sudan ◆1 10 10.00 N 20.00 E
Sudañez 248 19.06 S 64.44 W
Sudarsan 272b 22.59 N 88.17 E
Südbahnhof ◆5 264b 48.11 N 16.23 E
Südberg ◆8 263 51.11 N 7.08 E
Sudbišči 76 52.57 N 37.39 E
Sud'bodarovka 80 52.19 N 54.07 E
Südbrookmerland 52 53.29 N 7.24 E
Sudbury, On., Can. 190 46.30 N 81.00 W
Sudbury, Eng., U.K. 42 52.02 N 0.44 E
Sudbury, Ma., U.S. 207 42.23 N 71.25 W
Sudbury ≃ 283 42.28 N 71.22 W
Sudbury Center 283 42.23 N 71.25 W
Sudbury Reservoir ⊜1 207 42.19 N 71.31 W
Südchinesisches Meer
→ South China Sea ⊤2 108 10.00 N 113.00 E
Sudd
→ As-Sudd ◆1 140 8.00 N 31.00 E
Sud Dakota
→ South Dakota □3 198 44.15 N 100.00 W
Sudd an-Na'ām, Jabal ∧ 142 29.49 N 31.43 E
Suddie 246 7.07 N 58.29 W
Sude ≃ 54 53.22 N 10.45 E
Süderbrarup 41 54.38 N 9.46 E
Suderburg 52 52.54 N 10.27 E
Süderlügum 41 54.52 N 8.55 E
Suderwich 263 51.37 N 7.15 E
Sudeten
→ Sudety ⋏ 30 50.30 N 16.00 E
Sudety ⋏ 30 50.30 N 16.00 E
Süd-Georgien
→ South Georgia I 244 54.15 S 36.45 W
Sudi 154 10.06 S 39.57 E
Sudislavl' 80 57.53 N 41.43 E
Sudkamen 263 51.35 N 7.39 E
Sud-Kivu □4 154 3.00 S 28.30 E
Süd-Korea
→ Korea, South □1 98 36.30 N 128.00 E
Sudlersville 208 39.11 N 75.51 W
Südlicher Bug
→ Pivdennyy Buh ≃ 78 46.59 N 31.58 E
Südlicher Indianer-See
→ Southern Indian Lake ⊜ 176 57.10 N 98.40 W
Südlohn 52 51.57 N 6.52 E
Sudnikovo 82 55.53 N 36.02 E
Sudogda 80 55.57 N 40.50 E
Sudomskaja vozvyšennost' ⋏ 76 57.25 N 29.25 E
Sudong, Pulau I 271c 1.13 N 103.44 E
Süd-Orkney-Inseln
→ South Orkney Islands II 9 60.35 S 45.30 W
Sudost' ≃ 76 52.19 N 33.24 E
Sud-Ouest □4 152 5.10 N 9.00 E
Sud-Ouest, Pointe du > 186 49.23 N 63.36 W
Sudova Vyshnya 78 49.49 N 23.22 E
Südradde ≃ 52 52.41 N 7.34 E
Süd-Sandwich-Inseln
→ South Sandwich Islands II 18 57.45 S 26.30 W
Süd-Shetland-Inseln
→ South Shetland Islands II 9 62.00 S 58.00 W
Sudūd 142 30.25 N 30.54 E
Südwest-Kap
→ South West Cape > 166 43.34 S 146.02 E
Sudweyhe 52 52.59 N 8.53 E
Sudža 78 51.12 N 35.16 E
Sue 96 33.35 N 130.30 E
Sue ≃ 140 7.41 N 28.03 E
Sueca 34 39.12 N 0.19 W
Suecia
→ Sweden □1 24 62.00 N 15.00 E
Sue Creek c 284b 39.17 N 76.24 W
Suedberg 208 40.32 N 76.28 W
Suède
→ Sweden □1 24 62.00 N 15.00 E
Suemez Island I 182 55.17 N 133.21 W
Suèvres 50 47.40 N 1.28 E
Suez
→ As-Suways 142 29.58 N 32.33 E
Suez, Gulf of
→ Suways, Khalīj as- c 140 29.00 N 32.50 E
Suez Canal
→ Suways, Qanāt as- ≍ 142 29.55 N 32.33 E
Sūf 132 32.19 N 35.50 E
Sufaynah 128 23.09 N 40.32 E
Suffern 210 41.06 N 74.09 W
Suffern Park 276 41.07 N 74.07 W
Suffield, Ab., Can. 184 50.12 N 111.10 W
Suffield, Ct., U.S. 207 41.58 N 72.39 W
Suffield, Oh., U.S. 214 41.01 N 81.21 W
Suffield, Canadian Forces Base ■ 184 50.15 N 111.10 W
Suffolk 208 36.43 N 76.35 W
Suffolk □6, Eng., U.K. 42 52.10 N 1.00 E
Suffolk □6, Ma., U.S. 207 42.21 N 71.04 W
Suffolk □6, N.Y., U.S. 210 40.55 N 72.40 W
Suffolk, Ruisseau ≃ 206 45.48 N 74.59 W
Sūfīān 128 38.17 N 45.59 E
Sufi-Kurgan 85 40.02 N 73.30 E
Sufu
→ Kashi 85 39.29 N 75.59 E
Suga-jima I 94 34.29 N 136.53 E
Sugana, Val ✓ 64 46.00 N 11.40 E
Sugandha 272b 22.54 N 88.20 E
Sugano 268 35.44 N 139.56 E
Sugar ≃, U.S. 190 42.26 N 89.12 W
Sugar ≃, N.H., U.S. 188 43.24 N 72.24 W
Sugar ≃, N.Y., U.S. 212 43.31 N 75.19 W
Sugar City 202 43.52 N 111.44 W
Sugarcreek, Oh., U.S. 214 40.30 N 81.39 W
Sugarcreek, Pa., U.S. 214 41.25 N 79.52 W
Sugar Creek ≃, U.S. 216 40.47 N 87.45 W
Sugar Creek ≃, Il., U.S. 194 40.09 N 89.38 W
Sugar Creek ≃, Il., U.S. 219 38.28 N 89.37 W
Sugar Creek ≃, Il., U.S. 219 39.48 N 89.32 W
Sugar Creek ≃, In., U.S. 194 39.51 N 87.21 W
Sugar Creek ≃, In., U.S. 218 39.21 N 86.00 W
Sugar Creek ≃, Mi., U.S. 281 42.06 N 83.36 W
Sugar Creek ≃, N.Y., U.S. 210 42.38 N 77.09 W
Sugar Creek ≃, Oh., U.S. 214 40.31 N 81.28 W
Sugar Creek ≃, Oh., U.S. 216 40.57 N 84.11 W
Sugar Creek ≃, Oh., U.S. 218 39.27 N 83.25 W
Sugar Creek ≃, Ok., U.S. 196 35.05 N 98.10 W
Sugar Creek ≃, Pa., U.S. 210 41.47 N 76.27 W
Sugar Creek ≃, Wi., U.S. 216 42.43 N 88.19 W
Sugar Grove, Il., U.S. 216 41.45 N 88.27 W
Sugargrove, Pa., U.S. 214 41.59 N 79.21 W
Sugar Grove, Va., U.S. 192 36.46 N 81.24 W
Sugar Hill 192 34.06 N 84.02 W
Sugar Island I, On., Can. 212 44.26 N 77.17 W
Sugar Island I, Mi., U.S. 190 46.25 N 84.12 W
Sugar Land 222 29.37 N 95.38 W
Sugar Loaf 210 41.19 N 74.17 W
Sugar Loaf
→ Pão de Açúcar ∧ 287a 22.57 S 43.09 W
Sugarloaf ∧2 214 41.24 N 81.06 W
Sugarloaf Hill ∧2 274b 37.58 S 145.19 E
Sugarloaf Key I 220 24.40 N 81.32 W
Sugarloaf Mountain ∧, Ky., U.S. 218 38.13 N 83.32 W
Sugarloaf Mountain ∧, Me., U.S. 188 45.01 N 70.22 W
Sugar Loaf Mountain ∧, Md., U.S. 208 39.16 N 77.23 W
Sugar Loaf Mountain ∧, Ok., U.S. 194 35.02 N 94.28 W
Sugarloaf Mountain ∧2 220 28.39 N 81.44 W
Sugarloaf Peak ∧ 280 34.14 N 117.38 W
Sugarloaf Point >, Austl. 166 32.26 S 152.33 E
Sugar Loaf Point >, On., Can. 284a 42.52 N 79.17 W
Sugarloaf Reservoir ⊜1 169 37.41 S 145.18 E
Sugarloaf Ridge State Park ◆ 226 38.26 N 122.29 W
Sugar Notch 210 41.11 N 75.55 W
Sugar Pine Point State Park ◆ 226 39.03 N 120.07 W
Sugartown 285 40.00 N 75.31 W
Sugauli 124 26.46 N 84.44 E
Sugbai Passage ʮ 116 5.22 N 120.33 E
Sugbay 116 7.31 N 123.19 E
Sugbuhan Point > 116 10.04 N 126.04 E
Sugenheim 56 49.36 N 10.26 E
Suggi Lake ⊜ 184 54.22 N 102.47 W
Suginami ◆8 268 35.42 N 139.38 E
Sugita ◆8 268 35.23 N 139.38 E
Sugito 268 36.02 N 139.44 E
Suğla Gölü ⊜ 130 37.20 N 32.02 E
Šugnou 83 38.35 N 70.20 E
Sugod 116 12.03 N 124.09 E
Sugoj ≃ 74 64.15 N 154.29 E
Sugonovo 82 54.44 N 36.01 E
Šugozero 76 59.55 N 34.12 E
Šugurovo, Ross. 80 53.25 N 46.29 E
Šugurovo, Ross. 80 54.31 N 52.06 E
Sugut ≃ 112 6.26 N 117.43 E
Suguta ≃ 154 2.03 N 36.33 E
Suguti 154 1.44 S 33.39 E
Suhai Hu ⊜ 102 38.50 N 94.00 E
Suhaitu 102 44.50 N 93.39 E
Şuḥār 128 24.22 N 56.45 E
Suheli Island I1 122 10.03 N 72.17 E
Suhl 54 50.37 N 10.41 E
Suhlendorf 54 52.55 N 10.46 E
Suhopolje 36 45.48 N 17.30 E
Suhr 58 47.22 N 8.05 E
Suhr ≃ 58 47.25 N 8.04 E
Suhum 150 6.05 N 0.27 W
Şuhut 130 38.32 N 30.33 E
Sūi 120 28.37 N 69.19 E
Suiá-Miçu ≃ 250 11.13 S 53.15 W
Suianzhan 89 53.07 N 125.20 E
Suiattle ≃ 224 48.20 N 121.33 W
Suichang 100 28.34 N 119.14 E
Suichuan 100 26.26 N 114.32 E
Suichuan ≃ 100 26.30 N 114.45 E
Suid Afrika
→ South Africa □1 156 30.00 S 26.00 E
Suide 102 37.32 N 110.12 E
Suiding 86 44.03 N 80.49 E
Suido-suigenchi ⊜1 270 34.54 N 135.17 E
Suidvaal 158 26.52 S 29.47 E
Suifenhe 89 44.24 N 131.10 E
Suifu, Nihon 94 36.37 N 140.29 E
Suifu
→ Yibin, Zhg. 107 28.47 N 104.38 E
Suigō-kokutei-kōen ◆ 94 36.05 N 140.20 E
Suigō-Tsukuba-kokutei-kōen ◆ 94 36.00 N 140.20 E
Suihua 89 46.37 N 127.00 E
Suijiang 102 28.31 N 104.07 E
Suileng 89 47.18 N 127.10 E
Suining, Zhg. 100 33.54 N 117.56 E
Suining, Zhg. 102 26.21 N 110.00 E
Suining, Zhg. 107 30.31 N 105.34 E
Suipacha 252 34.45 S 59.41 W
Suiping 100 33.10 N 113.57 E
Suippe ≃ 50 49.25 N 3.57 E
Suippes 56 49.08 N 4.32 E
Suir ≃ 48 52.15 N 7.00 W
Suisse
→ Switzerland □1 58 47.00 N 8.00 E
Suisun Bay c 226 38.06 N 122.00 W
Suisun City 226 38.14 N 122.02 W
Suisun Creek ≃ 226 38.12 N 122.06 W
Suita 96 34.45 N 135.32 E
Suiti burnu > 84 40.12 N 50.22 E
Suitland 284c 38.50 N 76.55 W
Suixi, Zhg. 100 33.56 N 116.46 E
Suixi, Zhg. 102 21.25 N 110.15 E
Suixian, Zhg. 98 34.26 N 115.05 E
Suixian, Zhg. 100 31.42 N 113.20 E
Suiyang, Zhg. 89 44.26 N 130.53 E
Suiyang, Zhg. 102 27.56 N 107.18 E
Suiyangdian 100 32.04 N 112.55 E
Suiza
→ Switzerland □1 58 47.00 N 8.00 E
Suize ≃ 58 48.08 N 5.08 E
Suizhong 98 40.20 N 120.19 E
Šuja, Ross. 24 61.55 N 34.12 E
Šuja, Ross. 80 56.50 N 41.23 E
Šuja ≃, Ross. 24 61.54 N 34.15 E
Šuja ≃, Ross. 80 57.56 N 43.15 E
Sujānagar 126 23.57 N 89.25 E
Sujāngarh 120 27.42 N 74.28 E
Sujāwal 120 24.36 N 68.05 E
Suji 107 29.35 N 103.37 E
Sujiabu 100 31.38 N 116.22 E
Sujiaqiao 105 39.24 N 116.10 E
Sujiatun 104 41.40 N 123.22 E
Sujiawan 107 29.48 N 104.57 E
Sujiawu 105 39.17 N 115.55 E
Sujiazui 100 33.40 N 119.29 E
Šujskoje 76 59.22 N 40.59 E
Šujutkina Kosa, mys > 84 44.13 N 47.15 E
Sukabihanawa 112 9.30 S 124.57 E
Sukabumi 115a 6.55 S 106.56 E
Sukadana, Indon. 112 1.15 S 109.57 E
Sukadana, Indon. 115a 5.05 S 105.33 E
Sukadana, Teluk c 112 1.24 S 109.50 E
Sukagawa 92 37.17 N 140.23 E
Sukamandi 115a 6.20 S 107.39 E
Sukamara 112 2.43 S 111.11 E
Sukanegara 115a 7.06 S 107.07 E
Sukapura 115a 7.52 S 113.03 E
Sukaraja, Indon. 112 2.21 S 110.37 E
Sukaraja, Indon. 115a 7.27 S 108.12 E
Sukaraja, Indon. 115a 7.27 S 109.17 E
Sukarno, Pegunungan
→ Jaya, Puncak ∧ 164 4.05 S 137.11 E
Sukau 112 5.32 N 118.17 E
Sukchar 272b 22.42 N 88.22 E
Sukch'ŏn 98 39.24 N 125.38 E
Sukematsu 270 34.31 N 135.26 E
Sukeva 26 63.52 N 27.26 E
Sukha Volnovakha ≃ 83 47.37 N 38.01 E
Sukhnah, 'Ayn ⊤4 142 29.35 N 32.15 E
Sukhothai 110 17.01 N 99.49 E
Sukhumi
→ Suchumi 84 43.01 N 41.02 E
Sukhyy Torets' ≃ 83 48.49 N 37.36 E
Sukkertoppen (Maniitsoq) 176 65.25 N 52.53 W
Sukkozero 24 63.11 N 32.18 E
Sukkur 120 27.42 N 68.52 E
Sukkwan Island I 182 55.05 N 132.45 W
Suklāra 126 23.11 N 86.21 E
Sukmanovka 78 51.47 N 41.34 E
Sukodadi 115a 7.06 S 112.19 E
Sukoharjo 115a 7.41 S 110.50 E
Sukovo 82 54.54 N 38.19 E
Sukroml'a 76 56.53 N 34.44 E
Sukses 156 21.01 S 16.52 E
Suksun 86 57.07 N 57.24 E
Sukumo 92 32.56 N 132.44 E
Sukun, Pulau I 115b 8.07 S 122.08 E
Sukunka ≃ 182 55.37 N 121.37 W
Sul, Baía c 252 27.40 S 48.35 W
Sul, Canal do ʮ 250 0.10 S 49.30 W
Sula I 26 61.08 N 4.55 E
Sula ≃, Ross. 24 67.16 N 52.07 E
Sula ≃, Ukr. 78 49.40 N 32.41 E
Sula, Kepulauan II 112 1.52 S 125.22 E
Sulaco ≃ 236 15.01 N 87.44 W
Sulaimān Khel 123 33.41 N 71.01 E
Sulaimān Range ⋏ 120 30.30 N 70.10 E
Sulak, Ross. 80 51.52 N 48.21 E
Sulak, Ross. 84 43.16 N 47.32 E
Sulak ≃ 84 43.20 N 47.34 E
Sulakyurt 130 40.10 N 33.44 E
Sulang 115a 6.48 S 111.23 E
Sulat 116 11.49 N 125.27 E
Sulauan Point > 116 8.37 N 124.29 E
Sulawesi (Celebes) I 112 2.00 S 121.00 E
Sulawesi Selatan □4 112 3.30 S 120.00 E
Sulawesi Tengah □4 112 1.00 S 123.00 E
Sulawesi Tenggara □4 112 4.00 S 122.00 E
Sulawesi Utara □4 112 0.30 N 124.00 E
Sulaymān, Birak (Solomon's Pools) 132 31.41 N 35.10 E
Sulby 44 54.18 N 4.29 W
Sulcis ◆1 71 39.04 N 8.41 E
Suldalsvatnet ⊜ 26 59.35 N 6.45 E
Süldeh 128 36.34 N 52.01 E
Sulechów 30 52.06 N 15.38 E
Sulęcin 30 52.26 N 15.08 E
Suleja 86 55.09 N 58.50 E
Sulejów 30 51.22 N 19.53 E
Sulejówek 30 52.14 N 21.17 E
Sulen, Mount ∧ 164 3.25 S 142.15 E
Sule Skerry I2 46 59.05 N 4.26 W
Suleymaniye Mosque ◈1 267b 41.00 N 28.57 E
Süleymanlı 130 37.54 N 36.50 E
Sülfeld 54 53.48 N 10.14 E
Sul'gino, Ross. 82 54.33 N 37.35 E
Sul'gino, Ross. 82 55.50 N 35.55 E
Sulia 154 1.32 S 26.33 E
Suliki 112 0.06 S 100.27 E
Sulima 150 6.58 N 11.35 W
Sulin 83 48.54 N 40.07 E
Sulina 38 45.09 N 29.40 E
Sulina, Braţul ≃1 38 45.09 N 29.41 E
Sulincheer 102 42.41 N 109.20 E
Sulingen 52 52.41 N 8.47 E
Sulinskij 83 47.52 N 40.06 E
Sulitelma ∧ 24 67.08 N 16.24 E
Sulkava 26 61.47 N 28.23 E
Sullana 248 4.53 S 80.41 W
Sullane ≃ 48 51.53 N 8.56 W
Sulligent 194 33.54 N 88.08 W
Sullivan, Il., U.S. 194 39.35 N 88.36 W
Sullivan, In., U.S. 194 39.06 N 87.24 W
Sullivan, Mo., U.S. 219 38.12 N 91.09 W
Sullivan, Oh., U.S. 214 41.02 N 82.13 W
Sullivan, Wi., U.S. 216 43.00 N 88.35 W
Sullivan □6, N.Y., U.S. 210 41.39 N 74.42 W
Sullivan □6, Pa., U.S. 210 41.25 N 76.29 W
Sullivan Canyon ✓ 280 34.03 N 118.30 W
Sullivan Creek ≃ 226 37.53 N 120.25 W
Sullivan Lake ⊜ 182 52.00 N 112.00 W
Sullivanville 210 42.14 N 76.46 W
Sully-sur-Loire 50 47.46 N 2.22 E
Sulm ≃ 61 46.45 N 15.34 E
Sulmona 66 42.03 N 13.55 E
Sulot' ≃ 82 56.41 N 38.01 E
Sulphur, Yk., Can. 180 63.47 N 138.53 W
Sulphur, In., U.S. 218 38.14 N 86.28 W
Sulphur, Ky., U.S. 218 38.29 N 85.16 W
Sulphur, La., U.S. 194 30.14 N 93.22 W
Sulphur, Ok., U.S. 196 34.30 N 96.58 W
Sulphur ≃, Ab., Can. 182 53.50 N 119.10 W
Sulphur ≃, U.S. 194 33.07 N 93.52 W
Sulphur Creek ≃ 198 44.46 N 102.25 W
Sulphur Draw ✓ 196 33.12 N 102.17 W
Sulphur Springs, In., U.S. 218 40.00 N 85.26 W
Sulphur Springs, Oh., U.S. 214 40.52 N 82.52 W
Sulphur Springs, Tx., U.S. 222 33.08 N 95.36 W
Sulphur Springs Draw ✓ 196 32.12 N 101.36 W
Sulphur Springs Valley ✓ 200 31.50 N 109.50 W
Sulsul 144 5.06 N 44.55 E
Sultan 224 47.51 N 121.48 W
Sultan ≃ 224 47.52 N 121.49 W
Sultana 226 36.33 N 119.20 W
Sultanahmet Mosque ◈1 267b 41.00 N 28.58 E
Sultan Alonto, Lake ⊜ 116 7.53 N 124.15 E
Sultana Point > 168b 35.08 S 137.45 E
Sultanatābād ◆8 267d 35.46 N 51.28 E
Sultançiftliği ◆8 267b 41.02 N 29.13 E
Sultandağı 130 38.32 N 31.14 E
Sultan Dağı ∧ 130 38.58 N 27.26 E
Sultanhanı 130 38.15 N 33.33 E
Sultanhisar 130 37.53 N 28.10 E
Sultan Kudarat 116 7.17 N 124.16 E
Sultan Kudarat □4 116 6.20 N 124.20 E
Sultan Mosque ◈1 271c 1.18 N 103.52 E
Sultānpur, India 123 31.13 N 75.11 E
Sultānpur, India 124 26.16 N 82.04 E
Sultānpur Dabās ◆8 272a 28.46 N 77.03 E
Sultan sa Barongis 116 6.46 N 124.38 E
Sultan-Saly 83 47.21 N 39.35 E
Sulu 164 5.25 S 151.00 E
Sulu □4 116 6.00 N 121.00 E
Suluan Island I 116 10.46 N 125.57 E
Sulu Archipelago II 116 6.00 N 121.00 E
Sulu Basin ⊤1 12 8.00 N 121.30 E
Sulu Chi ⊜ 124 30.12 N 86.20 E
Sülüklü 130 39.05 N 30.58 E
Sul'ukta 85 39.56 N 69.34 E
Sululta 144 9.10 N 38.48 E
Suluntah 146 32.36 N 21.43 E
Suluova (Suluca) 130 40.47 N 35.42 E
Sulūq 146 31.39 N 20.15 E
Sulusaj 85 38.50 N 67.05 E
Sulusaray 130 40.00 N 36.06 E
Sulu Sea ⊤2 116 8.00 N 120.00 E
Sulutobe 86 44.38 N 66.05 E
Sulz 58 48.18 N 7.51 E
Sulz am Neckar 58 48.21 N 8.37 E
Sulzano 64 45.41 N 10.05 E
Sulzbach, Dtsch. 56 49.18 N 7.07 E
Sulzbach, Dtsch. 56 49.00 N 9.30 E
Sulzbach ≃ 60 48.36 N 13.02 E
Sulzbach am Kocher 56 48.58 N 9.50 E
Sulzbach-Rosenberg 60 49.30 N 11.45 E
Sulzberg, Dtsch. 58 47.40 N 10.21 E
Sulzberg, Dtsch. 64 47.40 N 10.21 E
Sulzberger Bay c 9 77.00 S 152.00 W
Sulzburg 58 47.50 N 7.42 E
Sülze 52 52.46 N 10.02 E
Šum, Ross. 76 59.52 N 31.46 E
Šum, Ross. 88 54.51 N 95.18 E
Suma ◆8 270 34.39 N 135.08 E
Šum'ači 76 53.52 N 32.25 E
Šumadija ◆1 38 44.10 N 20.50 E
Sumalata 112 0.59 N 122.30 E
Sumallo ≃ 224 49.14 N 121.05 W
Sumampa 252 29.22 S 63.28 W
Sumanaj 86 42.37 N 59.08 E
Sumangat, Tanjong > 116 6.35 N 117.33 E
Sumano-ura ◆ 96 34.38 N 135.08 E
Sumār 128 33.52 N 45.39 E
Sumarokovo 82 55.46 N 35.55 E
Sumas 202 49.00 N 122.15 W
Sumas ≃ 224 49.09 N 122.12 W
Sumatera (Sumatra) I 112 0.05 S 102.00 E
Sumatera Barat □4 112 0.30 S 100.30 E
Sumatera Selatan □4 112 3.00 S 104.00 E
Sumatera Utara □4 114 2.20 N 99.00 E
Sum'atino 82 55.00 N 36.21 E
Sumatou 107 30.28 N 104.03 E
Sumatra
→ Sumatera I 108 0.05 S 102.00 E
Sumava Resorts 216 41.10 N 87.26 W
Sumayh 140 12.43 N 30.53 E
Sumba I 115b 10.00 S 120.00 E
Sumba, Île I 152 1.44 N 19.32 E
Sumba, Selat ʮ 115b 9.05 S 120.00 E
Sumbar ≃ 128 38.00 N 55.17 E
Sumbawa I 115b 8.40 S 118.00 E
Sumbawa Besar 115b 8.30 S 117.26 E
Sumbawanga 154 7.58 S 31.37 E
Sumbay 248 15.58 S 71.23 W
Sumbe 152 11.13 S 13.50 E
Sümber 90 46.21 N 108.20 E
Sumbilla 34 43.10 N 1.40 W
Sumbing, Gunung ∧ 115a 7.23 S 110.04 E
Sumbu National Park ◆ 154 8.50 S 30.25 E
Sumburgh Head > 46a 59.53 N 1.20 W
Sumburgh Roost ʮ 46a 59.49 N 1.19 W
Sumbut 80 55.33 N 50.41 E
Sumbuya 150 7.39 N 11.58 W
Sumdo 120 35.01 N 78.41 E
Sumé 250 7.39 S 36.55 W
Sumedang 115a 6.52 S 107.55 E
Sümeg 30 46.59 N 17.17 E
Šumek 86 48.42 N 85.32 E
Šumen 38 43.16 N 26.55 E
Sumène 62 43.59 N 3.43 E
Sumenep 115a 7.01 S 113.52 E
Šumerl'a 80 55.30 N 46.26 E
Sumgait
→ Sumqayıt 84 40.36 N 49.38 E
Šumicha 86 55.14 N 63.19 E
Sumida ◆8 268 35.42 N 139.48 E
Sumida ≃ 268 35.40 N 139.47 E
Sumidouro 256 22.03 S 42.41 W
Sumilao 116 8.18 N 124.57 E
Šumilina 76 55.18 N 29.37 E
Šumilinskaja 80 49.58 N 41.26 E
Suminoe ◆8 270 34.36 N 135.28 E
Sumisu-jima I 90 31.27 N 140.03 E
Sumiswald 58 47.02 N 7.45 E
Sumiyoshi ◆8 270 34.36 N 135.31 E
Šumkino 86 55.03 N 65.44 E
Sumkino 86 58.09 N 68.22 E
Sumlog ≃ 116 6.53 N 126.02 E
Summer Bridge 44 54.03 N 1.41 W
Summerdale 208 40.18 N 76.56 W
Summerfield, Fl., U.S. 220 29.00 N 82.02 W
Summerfield, Mo., U.S. 219 38.17 N 91.49 W
Summerfield, N.C., U.S. 192 36.12 N 79.54 W
Summerford, Nf., Can. 186 49.29 N 54.47 W
Summerford, Oh., U.S. 218 39.55 N 83.29 W
Summerhill, Ire. 48 53.29 N 6.44 W
Summerhill, Pa., U.S. 214 40.22 N 78.46 W
Summer Island I 190 45.34 N 86.39 W
Summer Isles II 46 58.02 N 5.28 W
Summer Lake ⊜ 202 42.50 N 120.45 W
Summerland 182 49.36 N 119.41 W
Summerland Reserve ◆4 169 38.31 S 145.10 E
Sümmern 56 51.25 N 7.43 E
Summer Palace ◈ 265a 59.53 N 29.55 E
Summerseat 262 53.38 N 2.19 W
Summerside 186 46.24 N 63.47 W
Summersville, Mo., U.S. 194 37.10 N 91.39 W
Summersville, W.V., U.S. 188 38.16 N 80.51 W
Summerton 192 33.36 N 80.21 W
Summertown 194 35.26 N 87.18 W
Summerville, On., Can. 275b 43.37 N 79.34 W
Summerville, Ga., U.S. 192 34.28 N 85.20 W
Summerville, Pa., U.S. 214 41.06 N 79.11 W
Summerville, S.C., U.S. 192 33.00 N 80.11 W
Summit, Eng., U.K. 262 53.40 N 2.05 W
Summit, Ak., U.S. 180 63.20 N 149.08 W
Summit, Il., U.S. 216 41.47 N 87.48 W
Summit, Ms., U.S. 194 31.17 N 90.28 W
Summit, N.J., U.S. 210 40.44 N 74.21 W
Summit, N.Y., U.S. 210 42.35 N 74.35 W
Summit, S.D., U.S. 198 45.18 N 97.02 W
Summit, Wa., U.S. 224 47.10 N 122.21 W
Summit □6 214 41.05 N 81.31 W
Summit Creek ≃ 224 46.00 N 121.10 W
Summit Farms 284b 39.19 N 76.32 W
Summit Hill 210 40.49 N 75.52 W
Summit Lake 182 54.17 N 122.38 W
Summit Lake ⊜ 224 47.04 N 123.07 W
Summit Mountain ∧ 204 39.23 N 116.28 W
Summit Park 276 41.09 N 74.03 W
Summit Park Mall ◆9 284a 43.05 N 78.56 W
Summit Peak ∧ 200 37.21 N 106.42 W
Summit Rock ∧ 172 45.25 S 170.04 E
Summit Station 208 40.34 N 76.12 W
Summitville, In., U.S. 216 40.20 N 85.38 W
Summitville, N.Y., U.S. 210 41.37 N 74.27 W
Summitville, Oh., U.S. 214 40.41 N 80.53 W
Summt 264a 52.41 N 13.22 E
Summter See ⊜ 264a 52.42 N 13.23 E
Šumná 61 48.56 N 15.52 E
Sumnal 120 35.45 N 78.40 E
Sumner, Ia., U.S. 190 42.50 N 92.05 W
Sumner, Ms., U.S. 194 33.58 N 90.22 W
Sumner, Wa., U.S. 224 47.12 N 122.14 W
Sumner, Lake ⊜ 172 42.42 S 172.13 E
Sumner Lake ⊜1 196 34.38 N 104.25 W
Sumner Lake State Park ◆ 196 34.38 N 104.24 W
Sumner Strait ʮ 180 56.15 N 133.45 W
Sumoto 96 34.21 N 134.54 E
Sumpangbinangae 112 4.24 S 119.36 E
Šumperk 30 49.58 N 16.58 E
Sumpiuh 115a 7.37 S 109.21 E
Sumprabum 110 26.33 N 97.34 E
Sumpter 281 42.10 N 83.29 W
Sumqayıt 84 40.36 N 49.38 E
Sumqayıt ≃ 84 40.37 N 49.37 E
Sumrall 194 31.25 N 89.32 W
Sumsar 85 41.18 N 71.19 E
Š'umsi 80 57.07 N 51.37 E
Šumskij 88 54.48 N 99.09 E
Šumskij Posad 24 64.15 N 35.25 E
Šumšu, ostrov I 74 50.45 N 156.20 E
Sumter 192 33.55 N 80.20 W
Sumter □6 220 28.38 N 82.08 W
Sumustā al-Waqf 142 28.55 N 30.51 E
Sumy 78 50.55 N 34.45 E
Sumy □4 78 51.00 N 34.00 E
Sumzom 102 29.45 N 96.10 E
S'un' ≃, Ross. 80 55.44 N 54.16 E
Sun ≃, Mt., U.S. 202 47.30 N 111.19 W
Sun ≃, Zhg. 107 29.13 N 106.21 E
Suna, Kenya 154 1.05 S 34.26 E
Suna, Ross. 80 57.51 N 50.05 E
Suna ≃ 24 62.05 N 34.08 E
Sunagawa 92a 43.29 N 141.55 E
Sun' al-Heteimi ⊤4 132 31.05 N 34.00 E
Sun' al-Menī'i ⊤4 132 31.07 N 34.12 E
Sunām 123 30.08 N 75.48 E
Sunāmganj 120 25.04 N 91.24 E
Sunami 94 35.25 N 136.40 E
Sunan 98 39.13 N 125.41 E
Sunapee Lake ⊜ 188 43.23 N 72.03 W
Sunart, Loch c 46 56.41 N 5.43 W
Sunashinden 268 35.53 N 139.30 E
Sunbāţ 142 30.48 N 31.12 E
Sunbright 192 36.14 N 84.40 W
Sunburst 202 48.52 N 111.54 W
Sunbury, Austl. 169 37.35 S 144.44 E
Sunbury, Eng., U.K. 260 51.25 N 0.26 W
Sunbury, N.C., U.S. 192 36.26 N 76.36 W
Sunbury, Oh., U.S. 214 40.14 N 82.51 W
Sunbury, Pa., U.S. 210 40.51 N 76.47 W
Sunchales 252 30.56 S 61.34 W
Sunch'ang 98 35.23 N 127.07 E
Sunchild Indian Reserve ◆4 182 52.43 N 115.24 W
Sünching 60 48.53 N 12.21 E
Suncho Corral 252 27.56 S 63.27 W
Sunch'ŏn, C.M.I.K. 98 39.26 N 125.54 E
Sunch'ŏn, Taehan 98 34.57 N 127.28 E
Sun City, Az., U.S. 200 33.35 N 112.16 W
Sun City, Ca., U.S. 228 33.42 N 117.11 W
Sun City, Fl., U.S. 220 27.40 N 82.28 W
Sun City Center 220 27.43 N 82.21 W
Suncook 188 43.07 N 71.27 W
Suncook ≃ 188 43.08 N 71.28 W
Sunda, Selat (Sunda Strait) ʮ 112 6.00 S 105.45 E
Sundance 198 44.24 N 104.22 W
Sundar 112 4.54 N 115.12 E
Sundar ≃ 124 28.26 N 84.20 E
Sundarbans ◆1 126 22.00 N 89.00 E
Sundargarh 124 22.07 N 84.02 E
Sundarnagar 123 31.32 N 76.53 E
Sunda Shelf ⊤4 14 5.00 N 107.00 E
Sunda Strait
→ Sunda, Selat ʮ 112 6.00 S 105.45 E
Sunday Creek ≃ 169 37.02 S 145.05 E
Sundby, Dan. 41 54.52 N 11.48 E
Sundby, Sve. 40 59.23 N 17.03 E
Sundbyberg 40 59.22 N 17.58 E
Sundbyholm 40 59.27 N 16.37 E
Sundbyholm slott ⊥ 40 59.27 N 16.37 E
Sunde 26 59.50 N 5.43 E
Sunderland, On., Can. 212 44.16 N 79.04 W
Sunderland, Eng., U.K. 44 54.55 N 1.23 W
Sunderland, Ma., U.S. 207 42.28 N 72.34 W
Sunderland, Vt., U.S. 210 43.06 N 73.06 W
Sundern 56 51.20 N 8.00 E
Sünderup 41 54.46 N 9.27 E
Sundgau ◆1 58 47.40 N 7.15 E
Sundhouse 58 48.15 N 7.36 E
Sundi-Lutete 152 4.34 S 14.14 E
Sundown, Austl. 162 26.14 S 133.12 E
Sundown, N.Y., U.S. 210 41.53 N 74.28 W
Sundown, Tx., U.S. 196 33.27 N 102.29 W
Sundra 273d 26.51 N 80.46 E
Sundre 182 51.48 N 114.38 W
Sundridge, On., Can. 190 45.46 N 79.24 W
Sundridge, Eng., U.K. 260 51.17 N 0.08 E
Sunds 41 56.12 N 9.01 E
Sundsbruk 26 62.27 N 17.22 E
Sundsvall 26 62.23 N 17.18 E
Sundwig 263 51.23 N 7.47 E
Suneori 268 35.56 N 139.24 E
Sunfield 216 42.45 N 84.59 W
Sunfish Creek ≃ 218 39.01 N 83.03 W
Sunflower 194 33.32 N 90.32 W
Sunflower, Mount ∧ 198 39.04 N 102.01 W
Sungaianyar 112 2.55 S 116.18 E
Sungaiapit 114 1.09 N 102.10 E
Sungaibamban 114 3.26 N 99.09 E
Sungaibatu 112 0.48 N 110.45 E
Sungai Bayor 114 5.15 N 100.47 E
Sungaibuntu 115a 6.03 S 107.24 E
Sungaidareh 112 0.58 S 101.30 E
Sungaigerong 112 2.59 S 104.52 E
Sungaiguntung 112 0.18 N 103.37 E
Sungaikakap 112 0.04 S 109.10 E
Sungai Kolok 114 6.02 N 101.58 E
Sungailangsat 112 0.52 S 101.18 E
Sungai Lembing 114 3.55 N 103.02 E
Sungailiat 112 1.51 S 106.08 E
Sungailimau 112 0.31 S 100.03 E
Sungaimanasip 114 1.49 N 100.54 E
Sungainipah 114 0.57 N 98.57 E
Sungaipakning 114 1.20 N 102.09 E
Sungaipenuh 112 2.05 S 101.23 E
Sungaipenyu 112 0.16 N 109.04 E
Sungai Petani 114 5.39 N 100.30 E
Sungaipinang 112 0.48 S 114.04 E
Sungairampah 114 3.29 N 99.09 E
Sungairotan, Indon. 112 1.39 S 102.51 E
Sungairotan, Indon. 112 3.06 S 104.18 E
Sungaisalak 112 0.27 S 102.59 E
Sungaiselan 112 2.24 S 105.59 E
Sungai Siput 114 4.49 N 101.04 E
Sungaitampang 114 2.20 N 100.07 E
Sungaitiram 112 0.47 S 117.12 E
Šungaj 80 48.32 N 46.46 E
Sungari
→ Songhua ≃ 89 47.44 N 132.32 E
Sungchiang
→ Songjiang 106 31.01 N 121.14 E
Sungezhuang 105 40.15 N 116.39 E
Sungguminasa 112 5.12 S 119.27 E
Sungi ≃ 115b 8.38 S 115.06 E
Sungi Point > 116 10.55 N 125.50 E
Sungkai 114 4.00 N 101.19 E
Sung Kong I 271d 22.11 N 114.17 E
Sung Noen 110 14.54 N 101.50 E
Sungsang 112 2.22 S 104.56 E
Sungshan Domestic Airport ◆ 269d 25.04 N 121.33 E
Sungurlu 130 40.10 N 34.23 E
Sunhezhen 105 40.03 N 116.31 E
Suni 71 40.17 N 8.33 E
Suning 98 38.25 N 115.50 E
Sunjiabu 106 30.55 N 118.54 E
Sunjiadizi 104 42.09 N 124.09 E
Sunjiagou 104 40.45 N 120.39 E
Sunjiajiang 105 40.10 N 115.32 E
Sunjiakanzi 104 40.42 N 123.02 E
Sunjiawan 104 41.59 N 121.42 E
Sunjiazhai 106 30.55 N 121.52 E
Sunjikāy 140 12.20 N 29.46 E
Sunkar, gora ∧ 86 44.15 N 73.50 E
Sunken Meadow State Park ◆ 207 40.54 N 73.16 W
Sunkoši ≃ 124 26.55 N 87.09 E
Sunland ◆8 280 34.16 N 118.19 W
Sunland Park 200 31.50 N 106.45 W
Sunlight Creek ≃ 202 44.47 N 109.23 W
Sunlongwan 104 41.19 N 122.57 E
Sunman 218 39.14 N 85.05 W
Sunnansjö 40 60.13 N 14.57 E
Sunndalsøra 26 62.40 N 8.33 E
Sunne 26 59.50 N 13.09 E
Sunnemo 40 59.53 N 13.43 E
Sunnersta 40 59.48 N 17.39 E
Sunnī, Khawr ✓ 140 7.09 N 28.41 E
Sunningdale 260 51.24 N 0.38 W
Sunninghill 42 51.25 N 0.40 W
Sunnybrae 186 45.24 N 62.30 W
Sunny Corner 170 33.23 S 149.53 E
Sunny Crest 278 41.33 N 87.42 W
Sunnydale 224 47.28 N 122.20 W
Sunnyland 220 27.17 N 82.29 W
Sunnylvsfjorden c2 26 62.17 N 7.01 E
Sunnymede 182 51.17 N 111.40 W
Sunnyridge 273d 26.10 S 28.11 E
Sunnyside, Nf., Can. 186 47.51 N 53.55 W
Sunnyside, Ca., U.S. 226 32.40 N 117.01 W
Sunny Side, Tx., U.S. 222 29.54 N 96.04 W
Sunnyside, Ut., U.S. 200 39.33 N 110.23 W
Sunnyside, Wa., U.S. 202 46.19 N 120.00 W
Sunnyside ⊥ 276 41.03 N 73.52 W
Sunnyslope, Ab., Can. 182 51.40 N 113.32 W
Sunnyslope, Wa., U.S. 224 47.30 N 122.44 W
Sunnyvale, Ca., U.S. 226 37.22 N 122.02 W
Sunnyvale, Tx., U.S. 222 32.48 N 96.33 W
Sunol 282 37.36 N 121.53 W
Sunol Ridge ∧ 282 37.38 N 121.56 W
Sun Prairie 216 43.11 N 89.12 W
Sunray 196 36.01 N 101.49 W
Sunrise, Ky., U.S. 218 38.33 N 84.14 W
Sunrise, Tx., U.S. 222 31.17 N 96.53 W
Sunrise, Wy., U.S. 200 42.19 N 104.42 W
Sunrise Heights 216 42.18 N 85.09 W
Sunrise Manor 204 36.08 N 115.04 W
Sunrise Peak ∧ 224 46.20 N 121.46 W
Sun River Terrace 216 41.06 N 87.45 W
Sunset, La., U.S. 194 30.24 N 92.04 W
Sunset, Tx., U.S. 196 33.27 N 97.46 W
Sunset ◆8 282 37.45 N 122.30 W
Sunset Bay 214 42.11 N 79.24 W
Sunset Beach, Ca., U.S. 280 33.43 N 118.04 W
Sunset Beach, Hi., U.S. 229c 21.40 N 158.02 W
Sunset Country ◆1 166 35.00 S 141.30 E
Sunset Crater National Monument ◆ 200 35.18 N 111.21 W
Sunset Heights 196 31.53 N 102.22 W
Sunset Hill 276 40.26 N 74.35 W
Sunset Hills 279b 40.35 N 80.15 W
Sunset Peak ∧ 280 34.13 N 117.42 W
Sunset Prairie 182 55.50 N 120.48 W
Sunset Valley 214 40.18 N 79.44 W
Sunshine, Austl. 166 37.47 S 144.50 E
Sunshine, Austl. 169 37.47 S 144.50 E
Sunshine, Ak., U.S. 180 62.10 N 150.04 W
Sunshine Island I 271d 22.16 N 114.03 E
Sunshine Point > 281 42.36 N 82.47 W
Sunshine Skyway Bridge ◆5 220 27.37 N 82.39 W
Suntai ≃ 146 8.05 N 10.04 E
Suntar 74 62.10 N 117.40 E
Suntar-Chajata, chrebet ⋏ 74 62.00 N 143.00 E
Suntaug Lake ⊜ 283 42.32 N 71.00 W
Süntel ⋏ 52 52.12 N 9.25 E
Sun Temple ◈1 273c 29.55 N 31.11 E
Sunter ◆8 269e 6.09 S 106.50 E
Sunter, Kali ≍ 269e 6.07 S 106.50 E
Sunti ≃ 272b 22.37 N 88.34 E
Suntrana 180 63.51 N 148.51 W
Suntsar 128 25.31 N 62.00 E
Suntu 144 8.06 N 36.57 E
Sun Valley, Id., U.S. 202 43.41 N 114.21 W
Sun Valley, Nv., U.S. 226 39.34 N 119.47 W
Sun Valley ◆8 280 34.14 N 118.21 W
SunValley Center ◆9 282 37.58 N 122.03 W
Sunwapta ≃ 182 52.32 N 117.41 W
Sunwi-do I 98 37.44 N 125.15 E
Sunwu 89 49.27 N 127.20 E
Sunwui
→ Jiangmen 100 22.35 N 113.05 E
Sunyani 150 7.20 N 2.20 W
Sunying 98 34.30 N 114.21 E
Sunža ≃ 84 43.26 N 46.08 E
Sunženskij chrebet ⋏ 84 43.21 N 45.00 E

Symbols in the index entries represent the broad categories identified in the key at the right. Symbols with superior numbers (⋏1) identify subcategories (see complete key on page I · 1).

Symbole im Register stellen die rechts im Schlüssel erklärten Kategorien dar. Symbole mit hochgestellten Ziffern (⋏1) bezeichnen Unterabteilungen einer Kategorie (vgl. vollständiger Schlüssel auf Seite I · 1).

Los símbolos incluídos en el texto del índice representan las grandes categorías identificadas con la clave a la derecha. Los símbolos con numeros en su parte superior (⋏1) identifican las subcategorías (véase la clave completa en la página I · 1).

Les symboles de l'index représentent les catégories indiquées dans la légende à droite. Les symboles suivis d'un indice (⋏1) représentent des sous-catégories (voir légende complète à la page I · 1).

Os símbolos incluídos no texto do índice representam as grandes categorias identificadas com a chave à direita. Os símbolos com números em sua parte superior (⋏1) identificam as subcategorias (veja-se a chave completa à página I · 1).

∧ Mountain	Berg	Montaña	Montagne	Montanha
⋏ Mountains	Gebirge	Montañas	Montagnes	Montanhas
)(Pass	Paß	Paso	Col	Passo
✓ Valley, Canyon	Tal, Cañon	Valle, Cañón	Vallée, Canyon	Vale, Canhão
≐ Plain	Ebene	Llano	Plaine	Planície
> Cape	Kap	Cabo	Cap	Cabo
I Island	Insel	Isla	Île	Ilha
II Islands	Inseln	Islas	Îles	Ilhas
◆ Other Topographic Features	Andere Topographische Objekte	Otros Elementos Topográficos	Autres données topographiques	Outros acidentes topográficos

ESPAÑOL Nombre	Página	Lat.°′	Long.°′ W = Oeste
Sun Zhong Shan Ling (Tomb of Sun Yat Sen) ⊥	106	32.10 N	118.56 E
Suojarvi	24	62.05 N	32.21 E
Suolahti	26	62.34 N	25.52 E
Suomenlahti → Finland, Gulf of c	26	60.00 N	27.00 E
Suomenselkä ∧	26	63.59 N	27.00 E
Suomi → Finland □[1]	24	64.00 N	26.00 E
Suomussalmi	26	64.53 N	29.05 E
Suō-nada ⊤[2]	96	33.50 N	131.30 E
Suonenjoki	26	62.37 N	27.08 E
Suontee ⊜	26	61.40 N	26.30 E
Suordach	74	66.43 N	132.04 E
Suoshu	106	31.57 N	119.00 E
Supachuy	248	19.29 S	64.31 W
Supamo ≃	246	6.48 N	61.50 W
Supaul	124	26.07 N	86.36 E
Supe	144	8.37 N	35.38 E
Superbe ≃	50	48.35 N	3.53 E
Superga, Basilica di ʋ[1]	62	45.05 N	7.46 E
Superior, Az., U.S.	200	33.17 N	111.05 W
Superior, Mt., U.S.	202	47.11 N	114.53 W
Superior, Ne., U.S.	198	40.01 N	98.04 W
Superior, Wi., U.S.	190	46.43 N	92.06 W
Superior, Laguna c	234	16.20 N	94.55 W
Superior, Lake ⊜	190	48.00 N	88.00 W
Superior Lake ⊜	228	35.15 N	117.02 W
Superior Valley V	228	35.16 N	117.00 W
Supersano	68	40.01 N	18.14 E
Supetar	36	43.23 N	16.33 E
Suphan Buri	110	14.28 N	100.07 E
Suphan Buri ≃	110	13.29 N	100.17 E
Süphan Dağı ∧	84	38.56 N	42.50 E
Supino	66	41.37 N	13.14 E
Supiori I	164	0.45 S	135.30 E
Supiy ≃	78	49.38 N	31.48 E
Sūpkhār	124	22.12 N	80.56 E
Suponevo	76	53.12 N	34.18 E
Supoqiao	107	30.40 N	103.59 E
Süpplingen	54	52.14 N	10.54 E
Supraśl	30	53.13 N	23.20 E
Supraśl ≃	30	53.04 N	22.56 E
Sup'ung	98	40.27 N	124.57 E
Sup'ung-chŏsuji ⊜[1]	98	40.30 N	125.05 E
Supur	126	23.01 N	86.52 E
Suputinskij zapovednik ♠	89	43.40 N	132.20 E
Sūq-'Abs	144	15.59 N	43.04 E
Sūq ash-Shuyūkh	128	30.53 N	46.28 E
Suq'at al-Jamal	140	12.48 N	27.42 E
Suqian	100	33.59 N	118.18 E
Suqiao, Zhg.	100	34.08 N	113.47 E
Suqiao, Zhg.	105	39.03 N	116.29 E
Sūq Suwayq	128	24.23 N	38.27 E
Suquamish	224	47.43 N	122.33 W
Suquṭrā (Socotra) I	118	12.30 N	54.00 E
Ṣūr (Tyre), Lubnān	132	33.16 N	35.11 E
Ṣūr, 'Umān	118	22.35 N	59.31 E
Sur, Cabo >	174z	27.12 S	109.26 W
Sur, Campos de Hielo ⊓	254	49.10 S	73.30 W
Sur, Canal ⊍	288	34.37 S	58.15 W
Sur, Point >	226	36.18 N	121.54 W
Sura	80	53.53 N	45.45 E
Sura ◆[8]	272b	22.33 N	88.25 E
Sura ≃	80	56.06 N	46.00 E
Sura, Cape >	144	11.10 N	47.30 E
Ṣūrāb, Pāk.	120	28.29 N	66.16 E
Šurab, Taj.	85	40.03 N	70.33 E
Surabaya	115a	7.15 S	112.45 E
S'urachi, Nuraghe ⊥	71	40.01 N	8.33 E
Ṣurad	142	30.59 N	30.54 E
Surag-san ∧	271b	37.42 N	127.04 E
Surahammar	40	59.43 N	16.13 E
Sūrak	128	25.43 N	58.48 E
Surakarta	115a	7.35 S	110.50 E
Suramana	112	0.50 S	119.33 E
Surami	84	42.01 N	43.34 E
Ṣūrān, Īrān	128	27.18 N	62.04 E
Šuran, Ross.	80	55.22 N	49.50 E
Ṣūrān, Sūrīy.	130	36.34 N	37.13 E
Ṣūrān, Sūrīy.	130	35.17 N	36.45 E
Ṣuran ≃	58	46.02 N	5.19 E
Šurany	30	48.06 N	18.14 E
Surar	144	7.27 N	40.57 E
Surat, Austl.	166	27.09 S	149.04 E
Sūrat, India	120	21.10 N	72.50 E
Sūratgarh	123	29.19 N	73.54 E
Surat Thani (Ban Don)	110	9.08 N	99.19 E
Surava	80	52.57 N	41.18 E
Suraž, Bela.	76	55.25 N	30.44 E
Suraż, Pol.	30	52.58 N	22.58 E
Suraž, Ross.	76	53.01 N	32.24 E
Surbiton ◆[8]	260	51.24 N	0.18 W
Surbo	68	40.24 N	18.08 E
Surbourg	56	48.55 N	7.51 E
Surchan	80	46.39 N	49.38 E
Surchandarja □[4]	85	38.00 N	67.30 E
Surchandarja ≃	85	37.58 N	67.50 E
Surchdara	85	38.37 N	69.55 E
Ṣurchob ≃	85	38.53 N	70.03 E
Šurči	85	37.59 N	67.47 E
Surco ≃	286d	12.13 S	77.03 W
Surdulica	38	42.41 N	22.10 E
Sûre (Sauer) ≃	56	49.44 N	6.31 E
Şureanu, Munţii ⋏	38	45.38 N	23.27 E
Šureksor, ozero ⊜	86	52.16 N	75.50 E
Surendorf	41	54.28 N	10.04 E
Surendranagar	120	22.42 N	71.41 E
Suresnes	261	48.52 N	2.14 E
Suretka	236	9.34 N	82.56 W
Surf City	208	39.39 N	74.09 W
Surfers Paradise	171a	28.00 S	153.26 E
Surfside, Fl., U.S.	220	25.52 N	80.07 W
Surfside, Tx., U.S.	222	28.57 N	95.17 W
Surgères	32	46.07 N	0.45 W
Surgidero	240p	22.41 N	82.18 W
Surgijn ≃	88	47.20 N	95.50 E
Surgoinsville	192	36.28 N	82.51 W
Sürgü	130	38.01 N	37.59 E
Sürgücü	130	37.35 N	40.44 E
Surgut	74	61.14 N	73.20 E
Surhuisterveen	52	53.10 N	6.10 E
Suri	164	7.10 S	143.55 E
Suria	272b	22.51 N	88.33 E
Suriāpet	122	17.09 N	79.37 E
Suribachi-yama ∧[2]	174f	24.45 N	141.17 E
Suribao ≃	116	11.33 N	125.28 E
Surigao	116	9.45 N	125.30 E
Surigao del Norte □[4]	116	9.35 N	125.36 E
Surigao del Sur □[4]	116	9.00 N	126.00 E
Surigao Strait ⊍	116	10.15 N	125.23 E
Surikova	86	56.59 N	91.31 E
Surin	110	14.53 N	103.29 E
Surinam → Suriname □[1]	250	4.00 N	56.00 W
Suriname □[1], S.A.	242	4.00 N	56.00 W
Suriname □[1], S.A.	250	4.00 N	56.00 W
Šurinda	88	55.13 N	113.23 E
Suring	190	44.59 N	88.22 W
Sūrīyah → Syria □[1]	128	35.00 N	38.00 E
S'urkum	89	50.08 N	140.31 E
S'urkum, mys >	89	50.05 N	140.41 E
Šurma	80	56.58 N	50.21 E
Sūrmaq	128	31.03 N	52.48 E
Surmelin ≃	50	49.04 N	3.31 E
Surnadalsøra	26	62.59 N	8.39 E
Surodadi	115a	6.53 S	109.15 E
Surovaticha	80	55.45 N	43.56 E
Surovikino	80	48.36 N	42.51 E
Surovo	88	55.37 N	105.36 E
Surprise	200	33.37 N	112.19 W
Surprise, Lake ⊜	222	29.33 N	94.41 W
Surprise Valley V	204	41.35 N	120.05 W

FRANÇAIS Nom	Page	Lat.°′	Long.°′ W = Ouest
Surquillo	286d	12.07 S	77.02 W
Surrency	192	31.43 N	82.11 W
Surrey, B.C., Can.	224	49.12 N	122.53 W
Surrey, N.D., U.S.	198	48.14 N	101.07 W
Surrey □[6]	42	51.10 N	0.20 W
Surrey, University of ʋ[2]	260	51.14 N	0.36 W
Surrey Heath □[8]	260	51.23 N	0.35 W
Surry	208	37.08 N	76.50 W
Surry □[6]	208	37.10 N	76.50 W
Sursee	58	47.10 N	8.06 E
Sursés V	58	46.34 N	9.38 E
Sursk	80	53.04 N	45.42 E
Surskij Majdan	80	55.01 N	46.32 E
Surskoje	80	54.30 N	46.44 E
Surt	146	31.12 N	16.35 E
Surt, Khalīj (Gulf of Sidra) c	146	31.30 N	18.00 E
Surtainville	28	49.25 N	1.50 W
Surtanāhu	120	26.22 N	70.00 E
Surte	26	57.49 N	12.01 E
Surtsey I	24a	63.16 N	20.32 W
Suru	164	6.50 S	144.45 E
Suru ≃	123	34.45 N	76.12 E
Surubiú ≃	250	3.58 S	48.52 W
Sürüç	130	36.58 N	38.24 E
Suruga-wan c	94	34.51 N	138.33 E
Suruí	256	22.40 S	43.07 W
Suruí ≃	287a	22.42 S	43.07 W
Surulangun	112	2.37 S	102.45 E
Suru-Lere ◆[8]	273a	6.31 N	3.22 E
Surumu ≃	246	3.22 N	60.19 W
Surveyor Creek ≃	198	40.20 N	102.38 W
Surveyor Point >	168b	34.47 S	137.51 E
Survilliers	261	49.06 N	2.33 E
Surwold	52	53.00 N	7.30 E
Şury-le-Comtal	62	45.32 N	4.10 E
Šuryškary	74	65.54 N	65.22 E
Şuşa, Azer.	84	39.45 N	46.44 E
Susa, It.	62	45.08 N	7.03 E
Susa, Nihon	96	34.37 N	131.36 E
Suså ≃	41	55.11 N	11.46 E
Susa, Valle di V	62	45.09 N	7.10 E
Sūsah	146	32.54 N	21.58 E
Susak, Otok I	36	44.31 N	14.18 E
Susaki	96	33.22 N	133.17 E
Susami	96	33.33 N	135.30 E
Susamyr	85	42.09 N	73.58 E
Susamyr ≃	85	42.08 N	74.03 E
Susamyrtau, chrebet ⋏	85	42.08 N	73.15 E
Susan	208	37.22 N	76.19 W
Susan ≃	204	40.19 N	120.17 W
Susan, Port c	224	48.10 N	122.25 W
Sūsangerd	128	31.34 N	48.11 E
Susanino, Ross.	76	59.30 N	30.22 E
Susanino, Ross.	80	58.09 N	41.36 E
Susanino, Ross.	89	52.47 N	140.06 E
Susano	256	23.32 S	46.20 W
Susano □[7]	287b	23.35 S	46.18 W
Susanville	204	40.24 N	120.39 W
Šušary, Ross.	265a	59.46 N	30.21 E
Šušary, Ross.	265a	59.48 N	30.23 E
Susch	58	46.46 N	10.04 E
Susegana	64	45.51 N	12.15 E
Suşehri	130	40.11 N	38.06 E
Süsel	54	54.04 N	10.43 E
Šušenskoje	86	53.19 N	91.58 E
Sušice	60	49.14 N	13.32 E
Susitna	180	61.33 N	150.31 W
Susitna ≃	180	61.16 N	150.30 W
Susleni	38	47.25 N	28.59 E
Suslonger	80	56.18 N	48.13 E
Sušn'aki Pervoje	86	57.53 N	88.47 E
Susobana ≃	94	36.37 N	138.11 E
Susoh	114	3.43 N	96.50 E
Susong	100	30.09 N	116.06 E
Susono	94	35.09 N	138.54 E
Suspiro del Moro, Puerto)(	34	37.04 N	3.39 W
Susquehanna	210	41.56 N	75.36 W
Susquehanna □[6]	210	41.50 N	75.50 W
Susquehanna ≃	188	39.33 N	76.05 W
Susquehanna, West Branch ≃	210	40.53 N	76.47 W
Susquehanna State Park ♠	208	39.36 N	76.09 W
Susques	252	23.25 S	66.29 W
Sussa ≃	152	7.22 S	17.05 E
Süssen	56	48.41 N	9.45 E
Süssenbrunn ◆[8]	264b	48.17 N	16.30 E
Süsser See ⊜	54	51.30 N	11.40 E
Sussex, N.B., Can.	186	45.43 N	65.31 W
Sussex, N.J., U.S.	210	41.12 N	74.36 W
Sussex, Va., U.S.	208	36.54 N	77.16 W
Sussex, Wi., U.S.	216	43.08 N	88.13 W
Sussex □[6], De., U.S.	208	38.42 N	75.23 W
Sussex □[6], N.J., U.S.	210	41.08 N	74.41 W
Sussex □[6], Va., U.S.	208	36.50 N	77.15 W
Sussex, Vale of V	42	50.57 N	0.17 W
Sussex Inlet	170	35.11 S	150.36 E
Sussey	50	47.13 N	4.22 E
Sustenhorn ∧	58	46.42 N	8.28 E
Susten Pass)(	58	46.44 N	8.27 E
Susteren	52	51.04 N	5.51 E
Šustikovo	82	55.17 N	35.59 E
Susu	174m	26.47 N	128.19 E
Susubona	175e	8.18 S	159.27 E
Susui	112	4.56 N	116.41 E
Susuman	74	62.47 N	148.10 E
Susurluk	130	39.54 N	28.10 E
Şusuzmüsellim	130	41.06 N	27.03 E
Šušvė ≃	76	55.10 N	23.49 E
Susz	30	53.44 N	19.20 E
Sutāhāta	126	22.08 N	88.07 E
Sutak	123	33.12 N	77.28 E
Sutama	94	35.47 N	138.25 E
Sut-Chol'	86	51.24 N	91.17 E
Sütçüler	130	37.30 N	30.59 E
Sutera	70	37.31 N	13.44 E
Sutersville	214	40.14 N	79.48 W
Suthat, Wat ʋ[1]	269a	13.45 N	100.30 E
Sutherland, Austl.	170	34.02 S	151.04 E
Sutherland, S. Afr.	158	32.24 S	20.40 E
Sutherland, Ia., U.S.	198	42.58 N	95.29 W
Sutherland, Ne., U.S.	198	41.09 N	101.07 W
Sutherland ≃	182	54.29 N	125.05 W
Sutherland, Lake ⊜	224	48.05 N	123.42 W
Sutherland Falls ∟	172	44.48 S	167.44 E
Sutherlands	168b	34.10 S	139.13 E
Sutherlin	202	43.23 N	123.18 W
Suthiāna	272a	28.31 N	77.26 E
Sutjeska Nacionalni Park ♠	38	43.22 N	18.45 E
Sutlej (Satluj) (Langqên) ≃	120	29.23 N	71.02 E
Sutri	66	42.14 N	12.13 E
Sutrio	64	46.31 N	12.59 E
Sütschou → Xuzhou, Zhg.	98	34.16 N	117.11 E
Sutschou → Suzhou, Zhg.	106	31.18 N	120.37 E
Sutter	226	39.10 N	121.45 W
Sutter □[6]	226	39.08 N	121.37 W
Sutter Buttes ∧	226	39.12 N	121.50 W
Sutter Bypass ≃	226	38.47 N	121.38 W
Sutter Creek	226	38.23 N	120.48 W
Sutter Creek ≃	226	38.22 N	120.59 W
Sutton, Austl.	171b	35.10 S	149.15 E
Sutton, P.Q., Can.	206	45.06 N	72.37 W
Sutton, Eng., U.K.	42	52.23 N	0.07 E
Sutton, Eng., U.K.	260	51.12 N	0.26 W
Sutton, Ak., U.S.	180	61.43 N	148.53 W
Sutton, Ma., U.S.	207	42.09 N	71.45 W
Sutton, Ne., U.S.	198	40.36 N	97.51 W
Sutton, W.V., U.S.	188	38.39 N	80.42 W
Sutton ◆[8]	42	51.22 N	0.12 W
Sutton, Monts ⋏	206	45.05 N	72.30 W
Sutton-at-Home	260	51.25 N	0.14 E
Sutton Bridge	42	52.46 N	0.12 E

PORTUGUÊS Nome	Página	Lat.°′	Long.°′ W = Oeste
Sutton Coldfield	42	52.34 N	1.48 W
Sutton Courtenay	42	51.39 N	1.17 W
Sutton Forest	170	34.35 S	150.19 E
Sutton in Ashfield	44	53.08 N	1.15 W
Sutton Lake ⊜[1]	188	38.40 N	80.40 W
Sutton Lane Ends	262	53.14 N	2.06 W
Sutton Leach	262	53.26 N	2.42 W
Sutton on Sea	44	53.19 N	0.17 E
Sutton on Trent	44	53.10 N	0.49 W
Sutton Park	276	40.49 N	74.42 W
Sutton Place ⊥	260	51.16 N	0.33 W
Suttons Bay	190	44.58 N	85.39 W
Sutton Scotney	42	51.10 N	1.21 W
Sutton Valence	42	51.12 N	0.36 E
Sutton Veny	42	51.11 N	2.08 W
Sutton Weaver	262	53.18 N	2.41 W
Sutton West	212	44.18 N	79.22 W
Suttor ≃	166	21.25 S	147.45 E
Suttrop	56	51.27 N	8.22 E
Suttsu	92a	42.48 N	140.14 E
Sutwik Island I	180	56.34 N	157.05 W
Suunduk ≃	86	51.46 N	58.46 E
Suurberge ⋏	158	33.18 S	25.32 E
Suurbraak	158	34.00 S	20.39 E
Suure-Jaani	76	58.33 N	25.28 E
Suur Munamägi ∧[2]	76	57.43 N	27.04 E
Suur Pakri I	76	59.20 N	23.55 E
Suur väin ⊍	76	58.35 N	23.25 E
Suva	175g	18.08 S	178.25 E
Suvainiškis	76	56.10 N	25.17 E
Şuvälan	84	40.30 N	50.09 E
Šuvalovo Oz'orki ◆[8]	265a	60.02 N	30.18 E
Suva Planina ⋏	38	43.10 N	22.10 E
Suvarlı	130	37.32 N	37.38 E
Suvasvesi ⊜	26	62.39 N	28.12 E
Suvereto	66	43.05 N	10.40 E
Suvo	88	53.39 N	110.00 E
Suvorka	88	56.33 N	103.24 E
Suvorov	82	54.07 N	36.30 E
Suvorove	78	45.34 N	28.59 E
Suvorovo	82	56.07 N	35.54 E
Suwa, Erit.	144	14.17 N	41.06 E
Suwa, Nihon	94	36.02 N	138.08 E
Suwa-ko ⊜	94	36.05 N	138.05 E
Suwałki	30	54.07 N	22.56 E
Suwałki □[4]	30	54.10 N	22.15 E
Suwannaphum	110	15.33 N	103.47 E
Suwannee ≃	192	29.18 N	83.09 W
Suwannee Lake ⊜	184	56.08 N	100.10 W
Suwanose-jima I	93b	29.38 N	129.43 E
Suwanose-suidō ⊍	93b	29.32 N	129.40 E
Suwarrow I[1]	14	13.15 S	163.05 W
Suwaydah	130	35.46 N	39.38 E
Şuwaylih	132	32.02 N	35.50 E
Suways, Khalīj as- (Gulf of Suez) c	140	29.00 N	32.50 E
Suways, Qanāt as- (Suez Canal) ≅	142	29.55 N	32.33 E
Suwŏn	98	37.17 N	127.01 E
Suwon-dong	98	41.54 N	129.43 E
Suxi	100	29.25 N	120.07 E
Suxian	100	33.38 N	116.58 E
Suya	150	9.28 N	3.11 E
Suykbulak	86	49.48 N	80.50 E
Suyo	246	4.30 S	80.00 W
Suzak	86	44.07 N	68.28 E
Suzaka	94	36.39 N	138.19 E
Suzdal'	80	56.25 N	40.26 E
Suze ≃	58	47.08 N	7.14 E
Suze-la-Rousse	62	44.17 N	4.51 E
Suzhi	98	42.17 N	113.42 E
Suzhou (Soochow)	106	31.18 N	120.37 E
Suzhuang	105	40.04 N	116.44 E
Suzi ≃	98	41.55 N	124.17 E
Suzigou	98	40.25 N	123.25 E
S'uzikozero	24	61.48 N	37.20 E
Suz'omka	76	52.19 N	34.05 E
Suzu	92	37.25 N	137.17 E
Suzuka	94	34.51 N	136.35 E
Suzuka ≃	94	34.54 N	136.39 E
Suzuka-kokutei-kōen ♠	94	35.00 N	136.25 E
Suzuka-sammyaku ⋏	94	35.00 N	136.25 E
Suzuki	268	35.43 N	139.31 E
S'uz'um	80	58.02 N	47.32 E
Suzu-misaki >	92	37.31 N	137.21 E
Suzun	86	53.47 N	82.19 E
Suzzara	64	45.00 N	10.45 E
Sværdborg	41	55.05 N	11.54 E
Svalbard II	12	78.00 N	20.00 E
Svalöv	41	55.55 N	13.06 E
Svalyava	78	48.33 N	22.59 E
Svaneholm	41	55.30 N	13.28 E
Svaneke	26	55.08 N	15.09 E
Svanetskij chrebet ⋏	84	42.55 N	42.42 E
Svängsta	26	56.16 N	14.46 E
Svanninge	41	55.07 N	10.15 E
Svanskog	26	59.11 N	12.33 E
Svapa ≃	78	51.44 N	34.56 E
Svappavaara	24	67.39 N	21.04 E
Švarcevskij	82	54.06 N	37.59 E
Svärdsjö	26	60.45 N	15.55 E
Švaricha	80	57.33 N	49.37 E
Svartå	40	59.08 N	14.31 E
Svartälven ≃	40	59.19 N	14.35 E
Svartån ≃	40	59.37 N	16.33 E
Svarte	41	55.25 N	13.43 E
Svartenhuk >[1]	176	71.55 N	55.00 W
Svärtinge	40	58.39 N	16.00 E
Svartisen ⊓	24	66.38 N	14.00 E
Svartlöga I	40	59.34 N	19.03 E
Svartsjölandet I	40	59.22 N	17.41 E
Svataj	74	67.57 N	151.54 E
Svatava	54	50.11 N	12.35 E
Svatava ≃	54	50.11 N	12.38 E
Sv'atica ≃	80	58.22 N	51.43 E
Sv'atoj Nos, mys >, Ross.	24	68.10 N	39.45 E
Sv'atoj Nos, mys >, Ross.	74	72.52 N	140.42 E
Sv'atoj Nos, poluostrov >[1]	88	53.40 N	108.50 E
Sv'atoslavka	80	51.20 N	43.26 E
Svatove	83	49.23 N	38.13 E
Svay Chék	110	13.48 N	102.58 E
Svay Riĕng	110	11.05 N	105.48 E
Sveafallen ∟	40	59.10 N	14.22 E
Svebølle	41	55.38 N	11.20 E
Sveča	80	58.16 N	47.32 E
Svedala	41	55.30 N	13.14 E
Svėdasai	76	55.41 N	25.22 E
Sveg	26	62.02 N	14.21 E
Şvegssjön ⊜[1]	26	62.03 N	14.10 E
Švėkšna	76	55.31 N	21.37 E
Svelgen	26	61.47 N	5.15 E
Svelvik	26	59.37 N	10.24 E
Sven'	76	53.09 N	34.21 E
Švenčionėliai	76	55.10 N	26.00 E
Švenčionys	76	55.07 N	26.10 E
Svendborg	41	55.03 N	10.37 E
Svenljunga	26	57.30 N	13.07 E
Svennevad	40	59.01 N	15.22 E
Svensen	224	46.10 N	123.39 W
Svenstorp	41	55.46 N	13.15 E
Şvenstrup	26	56.59 N	9.52 E
Šventoji	76	56.02 N	21.05 E
Šventoji ≃	76	55.06 N	24.22 E
Sverbejevo	89	53.36 N	123.15 E
Sverdlovo, Ross.	80	51.16 N	44.34 E
Sverdlovo, Ross.	82	56.38 N	36.37 E
Sverdlovsk → Jekaterinburg, Ross.	86	56.51 N	60.36 E
Sverdlovs'k, Ukr.	83	48.05 N	39.40 E
Sverdrup, ostrov I	74	74.35 N	79.30 E
Sverige → Sweden □[1]	24	62.00 N	15.00 E
Şverkestaån ≃	40	59.28 N	15.28 E
Švermov	54	50.09 N	14.05 E
Svesa	78	51.57 N	33.54 E
Sveti Arhandjel Mihajlo ʋ[1]	38	42.07 N	21.28 E
Sveti Jovan Bigorski ʋ[1]	38	41.38 N	20.37 E
Sveti Nikole	38	41.52 N	21.58 E
Sveti Petar u Šumi	64	45.11 N	13.52 E
Svetlahorsk	76	52.38 N	29.42 E
Svetlaja	89	46.33 N	138.18 E
Světlá nad Sázavou	30	49.40 N	15.25 E
Svetlogorsk	76	54.57 N	20.10 E
Svetlograd	72	45.20 N	42.40 E
Svetloje	80	57.03 N	53.38 E
Svetlyj, Ross.	76	54.41 N	20.08 E
Svetlyj, Ross.	86	50.47 N	60.53 E
Svetlyj, Ross.	88	58.26 N	115.55 E
Svetlyj Jar	80	48.29 N	44.46 E
Svetogorsk	24	61.07 N	28.51 E
Svetozarevo	38	43.58 N	21.16 E
Svežen'kaja	80	54.01 N	42.26 E
Svidník	30	49.18 N	21.35 E
Švihov	60	49.29 N	13.17 E
Svijaga ≃	80	55.47 N	48.40 E
Svilajnac	38	44.14 N	21.13 E
Svilengrad	38	41.46 N	26.12 E
Svindal	26	58.30 N	7.28 E
Svinecea Mare, Vârful ∧	38	44.48 N	22.09 E
Svinesund	26	59.06 N	11.16 E
Svinninge	41	55.43 N	11.28 E
Svir	76	54.51 N	26.24 E
Svir' ≃	76	60.30 N	32.48 E
Svirica	76	60.29 N	32.51 E
Svirsk	88	53.04 N	103.21 E
Svir'stroj	76	60.48 N	33.43 E
Sviščovka	80	52.51 N	43.44 E
Svislač, Bela.	76	53.02 N	24.06 E
Svislač, Bela.	76	53.26 N	28.59 E
Svislač ≃	76	53.26 N	28.59 E
Svištov	38	43.37 N	25.20 E
Svit	30	49.03 N	20.12 E
Svitava ≃	30	49.09 N	16.38 E
Svitávka	30	49.30 N	16.37 E
Svitavy	30	49.45 N	16.27 E
Svitino	82	54.54 N	35.49 E
Svitlovods'k	78	49.04 N	33.15 E
Svjacilavičy	76	52.48 N	31.19 E
Svobidnyy port	78	46.20 N	31.51 E
Svoboda, Ross.	78	47.12 N	40.39 E
Svoboda, Ross.	78	51.58 N	36.17 E
Svobodnaja	89	46.48 N	143.23 E
Svobodne	83	47.32 N	37.34 E
Svobodnyj, Ross.	80	52.20 N	46.22 E
Svobodnyj, Ross.	89	51.24 N	128.08 E
Svoge	38	42.58 N	23.21 E
Svojna	82	54.09 N	36.39 E
Svol'na ≃	76	55.43 N	28.02 E
Svolvær	24	68.14 N	14.34 E
Svor	54	50.47 N	14.36 E
Svorkmo	26	63.10 N	9.45 E
Svratka ≃	61	49.11 N	16.38 E
Svržno	60	49.35 N	12.46 E
Svullrya	26	60.25 N	12.24 E
Svystunivka	83	49.29 N	38.20 E
Swābi	123	34.07 N	72.28 E
Swadlincote	42	52.47 N	1.33 W
Swaffham	42	52.39 N	0.41 E
Swain	210	42.29 N	77.51 W
Swain Reefs ⟡[2]	166	21.40 S	152.15 E
Swainsboro	192	32.35 N	82.20 W
Swains Island I[1]	14	11.03 S	171.05 W
Swakop ≃	156	22.38 S	14.36 E
Swakopmund	156	22.41 S	14.34 E
Swale □[8]	260	51.21 N	0.41 E
Swale ≃	44	54.06 N	1.20 W
Swale Canyon V	224	45.49 N	121.05 W
Swale Creek ≃	224	45.49 N	121.05 W
Swaledale V	44	54.25 N	1.47 W
Swallowfield	218	38.21 N	84.51 W
Swalmen	52	51.15 N	6.02 E
Swamp City	222	32.29 N	94.56 W
Swampscott	207	42.28 N	70.55 W
Swan	222	32.26 N	95.22 W
Swan ≃, Austl.	168a	32.03 S	115.45 E
Swan ≃, Can.	184	52.30 N	100.47 W
Swan ≃, Ab., Can.	182	55.31 N	115.17 W
Swan ≃, Mn., U.S.	190	47.01 N	93.16 W
Swan ≃, Mt., U.S.	202	48.04 N	114.05 W
Swan Acres	279b	40.33 N	80.02 W
Swanage	42	50.37 N	1.58 W
Swan Bay c	169	38.14 S	144.40 E
Swan Creek ≃, Austl.	171a	28.08 S	152.13 E
Swan Creek ≃, Mi., U.S.	216	41.58 N	85.19 W
Swan Creek ≃, Mi., U.S.	216	41.58 N	83.17 W
Swan Creek ≃, Oh., U.S.	216	41.39 N	83.32 W
Swan Creek ≃, S.D., U.S.	198	45.19 N	100.15 W
Swan Creek, North Branch ≃	281	42.06 N	83.23 W
Swan Creek Point >	281	42.40 N	82.39 W
Swanee → Suwannee ≃	192	29.18 N	83.09 W
Swan Hill	166	35.21 S	143.34 E
Swan Hills	182	54.43 N	115.24 W
Swan Hills ⋏[2]	182	54.48 N	115.52 W
Swanington	216	40.35 N	87.17 W
Swan Island I	169	38.15 S	144.41 E
Swan Islands → Santanilla, Islas II	238	17.25 N	83.55 W
Swank Creek ≃	224	47.07 N	120.45 W
Swan Lake, Mb., Can.	184	49.24 N	98.46 W
Swan Lake, Mt., U.S.	202	47.55 N	113.50 W
Swan Lake, N.Y., U.S.	210	41.45 N	74.47 W
Swan Lake ⊜, Mb., Can.	184	52.30 N	100.45 W
Swan Lake ⊜, On., Can.	184	54.17 N	91.12 W
Swan Lake ⊜, Il., U.S.	219	38.57 N	90.33 W
Swan Lake ⊜, Mn., U.S.	190	44.19 N	94.15 W
Swanland	44	53.44 N	0.29 W
Swanley	42	51.24 N	0.12 E
Swanlinbar	48	54.10 N	7.42 W
Swannanoa	192	35.36 N	82.23 W
Swannanoa, Lake ⊜	276	41.01 N	74.31 W
Swan Peak ∧	202	47.43 N	113.38 W
Swanquarter	192	35.24 N	76.20 W
Swan Range ⋏	202	47.50 N	113.40 W
Swan Reach	166	34.34 S	139.36 E
Swan River	184	52.06 N	101.16 W
Swansboro	192	34.41 N	77.07 W
Swanscombe	260	51.26 N	0.18 E
Swansea, Austl.	166	42.08 S	148.04 E
Swansea, Austl.	170	33.05 S	151.38 E
Swansea, Wales, U.K.	42	51.38 N	3.57 W
Swansea, Il., U.S.	219	38.32 N	89.59 W
Swansea, Ma., U.S.	207	41.44 N	71.11 W
Swansea, S.C., U.S.	192	33.44 N	81.05 W
Swansea ◆[8]	275b	43.38 N	79.28 W
Swansea Bay c	42	51.35 N	3.52 W
Swans Island I	188	44.10 N	68.25 W
Swanson Lake ⊜[1]	198	40.09 N	101.06 W
Swanton, Oh., U.S.	216	41.35 N	83.53 W
Swanton, Vt., U.S.	206	44.55 N	73.07 W
Swanville	190	45.54 N	94.38 W
Swanzey Center	207	42.49 N	72.10 W
Swarbacks Minn ⊍	46a	60.20 N	1.36 W
Swartberg	158	30.15 S	29.23 E
Swarthmore	208	39.54 N	75.21 W
Swarthmore College ʋ[2]	285	39.54 N	75.21 W
Swart-Kei ≃	158	32.09 S	27.24 E
Swart-Mfolozi ≃	158	28.22 S	31.58 E
Swartplaas	158	26.08 S	26.57 E
Swartruggens	156	25.40 S	26.42 E
Swartruggens ⋏	158	33.02 S	19.35 E
Swartswood Lake	210	41.04 N	74.51 W
Swartswood State Park ♠	210	41.05 N	74.50 W
Swartz Creek	216	42.57 N	83.49 W
Swarupkāti	126	22.45 N	90.06 E
Swarupnagar	126	22.49 N	88.52 E
Swarzędz	30	52.26 N	17.05 E
Swasey Peak ∧	200	39.23 N	113.19 W
Swasey Wash V	200	39.15 N	112.53 W
Swasiland → Swaziland □[1]	158	26.30 S	31.30 E
Swāt ≃	123	34.20 N	71.34 E
Swatara Creek ≃	208	40.11 N	76.44 W
Swa-Tenda	152	7.09 S	17.07 E
Swatow → Shantou	100	23.23 N	116.41 E
Swauger Creek ≃	226	38.16 N	119.16 W
Swauk Pass)(	224	47.21 N	120.40 W
Sway	42	50.47 N	1.37 W
Swayzee	216	40.30 N	85.49 W
Swaziland □[1], Afr.	138	26.30 S	31.30 E
Swaziland □[1], Afr.	158	26.30 S	31.30 E
Swea City	190	43.23 N	94.19 W
Swede Hill	279b	40.17 N	79.34 W
Swedeland	285	40.05 N	75.20 W
Sweden (Sverige) □[1], Europe	22	62.00 N	15.00 E
Sweden (Sverige) □[1], Europe	24	62.00 N	15.00 E
Sweden Valley	214	41.45 N	77.56 W
Swede Run ≃	285	40.02 N	74.58 W
Swedesboro	208	39.44 N	75.18 W
Swedesburg	285	40.06 N	75.20 W
Swedish Knoll ∧	200	39.16 N	111.26 W
Swedru	150	5.32 N	0.43 W
Sween, Loch c	46	55.59 N	5.39 W
Sweeney Plan	279b	40.11 N	79.48 W
Sweeny	222	29.02 N	95.41 W
Sweeny Park ♠	284a	43.02 N	78.52 W
Sweet Briar	192	37.33 N	79.04 W
Sweetgrass	182	49.00 N	111.57 W
Sweet Grass Creek ≃	202	45.47 N	109.47 W
Sweetgrass Hills ⋏[2]	202	48.55 N	111.30 W
Sweet Grass Indian Reserve ◆[4]	184	52.44 N	108.45 W
Sweetheart Abbey ʋ[1]	44	54.59 N	3.38 W
Sweet Home, Or., U.S.	202	44.23 N	122.44 W
Sweet Home, Tx., U.S.	222	29.21 N	97.04 W
Sweetsers	216	40.34 N	85.46 W
Sweet Springs	194	38.57 N	93.24 W
Sweet Valley	210	41.17 N	76.09 W
Sweetwater, Fl., U.S.	220	25.46 N	80.21 W
Sweet Water, Il., U.S.	219	40.03 N	89.42 W
Sweetwater, Tn., U.S.	192	35.36 N	84.27 W
Sweetwater, Tx., U.S.	196	32.28 N	100.24 W
Sweetwater ≃	200	42.31 N	107.02 W
Sweetwater Creek	220	27.59 N	82.33 W
Sweetwater Creek ≃, U.S.	196	35.18 N	99.57 W
Sweetwater Creek ≃, Tx., U.S.	196	32.40 N	100.06 W
Sweetwater Mountains ⋏	226	38.30 N	119.17 W
Swellendam	158	34.02 S	20.26 E
Swepsonville	192	36.01 N	79.21 W
Swerdlovsk → Jekaterinburg	86	56.51 N	60.36 E
Świdnica (Schweidnitz)	30	50.51 N	16.29 E
Świdnik	30	51.14 N	22.41 E
Świdwin	30	53.47 N	15.47 E
Świebodzice	30	50.52 N	16.19 E
Świebodzin	30	52.15 N	15.32 E
Świecie	30	53.25 N	18.28 E
Świerzawa	30	51.01 N	15.54 E
Świerzno	54	53.57 N	14.59 E
Święta	54	53.35 N	14.36 E
Świętokrzyskie, Góry ⋏	30	50.55 N	21.00 E
Świętokrzyski Park Narodowy ♠	30	50.55 N	21.00 E
Swift ≃, Eng., U.K.	42	52.23 N	1.16 W
Swift ≃, Ak., U.S.	180	61.53 N	156.18 W
Swift ≃, Ma., U.S.	207	42.12 N	72.22 W
Swift Creek ≃, Al., U.S.	194	32.25 N	86.38 W
Swift Creek ≃, N.C., U.S.	192	35.12 N	77.05 W
Swift Creek ≃, N.C., U.S.	192	35.57 N	77.35 W
Swift Creek ≃, Va., U.S.	208	37.17 N	77.15 W
Swift Current	184	50.17 N	107.50 W
Swift Current Creek ≃	184	50.40 N	107.44 W
Swifton	194	35.49 N	91.07 W
Swift Reservoir ⊜[1]	224	46.04 N	122.05 W
Swiftwater	210	41.06 N	75.20 W
Swilly ≃	48	54.57 N	7.42 W
Swilly, Lough c	48	55.10 N	7.38 W
Swimming ≃	276	40.21 N	74.05 W
Swimming River Reservoir ⊜[1]	276	40.19 N	74.07 W
Świna ≃[1]	54	53.55 N	14.17 E
Swinburne, Cape >	176	71.14 N	98.34 W
Swinden Reservoirs ⊜[1]	262	53.48 N	2.10 W
Swindle Island I	182	52.32 N	128.35 W
Swindon	42	51.34 N	1.47 W
Swinemünde → Świnoujście	30	53.53 N	14.14 E
Swineshead	42	52.56 N	0.09 W
Swinford	48	53.57 N	8.57 W
Swinging Bridge Reservoir ⊜[1]	210	41.37 N	74.48 W
Swinomish Indian Reservation ◆[4]	224	48.25 N	122.33 W
Świnoujście (Swinemünde)	30	53.53 N	14.14 E
Swinton, Eng., U.K.	44	53.28 N	1.20 W
Swinton, Eng., U.K.	262	53.31 N	2.20 W
Swinton, Scot., U.K.	46	55.43 N	2.15 W
Swissvale	279b	40.25 N	79.52 W
Swisttal	56	50.40 N	6.54 E
Switzerland □[6]	218	38.45 N	85.04 W
Switzerland □[1], Europe	22	47.00 N	8.00 E
Switzerland □[1], Europe	58	47.00 N	8.00 E
Swona I	46	58.45 N	3.03 W
Swordfish Seamount ⟡[3]	14	18.25 N	158.25 W
Swords	48	53.28 N	6.13 W
Swords Range ⋏	166	21.57 S	141.32 E
Swormville	284a	43.02 N	78.42 W
Sworton Heath	262	53.21 N	2.28 W
Swoyerville	210	41.18 N	75.52 W
Syalach	74	66.12 N	124.00 E
Syam	58	46.42 N	5.57 E
Syāmnagar	126	22.21 N	89.07 E
Syāmpur, India	126	22.18 N	88.02 E
Syampur, India	272b	22.29 N	88.13 E
Sybille Creek ≃	198	42.07 N	105.02 W
Syburg ◆[8]	263	51.25 N	7.29 E
Sycamore, Ga., U.S.	192	31.40 N	83.38 W
Sycamore, Il., U.S.	216	41.59 N	88.41 W
Sycamore, Oh., U.S.	214	40.56 N	83.10 W
Sycamore Creek ≃, Az., U.S.	200	33.38 N	111.40 W
Sycamore Creek ≃, Mi., U.S.	216	42.43 N	84.32 W
Sycamore Creek ≃, Oh., U.S.	214	40.59 N	83.12 W
Sycamore Creek ≃, Tx., U.S.	196	29.14 N	100.48 W
Sycamore Gardens	285	39.42 N	75.42 W
Sycamore Island I	279b	40.29 N	79.52 W
Sycamore Slough ≃	226	38.48 N	121.44 W
Sycan ≃	202	42.27 N	121.15 W
Sycaway	210	42.44 N	73.39 W
Syčova	86	57.35 N	69.20 E
Syčovka	76	55.50 N	34.17 E
Syców	30	51.19 N	17.43 E
Sydenham, Austl.	274b	37.42 S	144.46 E
Sydenham, On., Can.	212	44.25 N	76.36 W
Sydenham ◆[8], S. Afr.	273d	26.09 S	28.06 E
Sydenham ◆[8], Eng., U.K.	260	51.26 N	0.03 W
Sydenham ≃, On., Can.	190	42.33 N	82.25 W
Sydenham ≃, On., Can.	212	44.35 N	80.57 W
Sydenham Lake ⊜	212	44.25 N	76.35 W
Sydenham West	274b	37.41 S	144.39 E
Sydney, Austl.	170	33.52 S	151.13 E
Sydney, Austl.	274a	33.52 S	151.13 E
Sydney, N.S., Can.	186	46.09 N	60.11 W
Sydney, Fl., U.S.	220	27.58 N	82.12 W
Sydney, University of ʋ[2]	274a	33.53 S	151.11 E
Sydney Bay c, On., Can.	212	44.54 N	81.05 W
Sydney Bay c, Norf. I.	174c	29.04 S	167.57 E
Sydney Bay Bluff ±[4]	212	44.54 N	81.07 W
Sydney Harbour Bridge ◆[5]	170	33.52 S	151.12 E
Sydney Lake ⊜	184	50.40 N	94.24 W
Sydney Mines	186	46.14 N	60.14 W
Sydney Point >	174d	0.53 S	169.36 E
Syedove	83	47.03 N	38.10 E
Syevernyy	83	48.22 N	39.56 E
Syeverodonets'k	83	48.58 N	38.27 E
Syevero-Hundorivs'kyy	83	48.23 N	39.54 E
Syferbult	158	26.00 S	27.20 E
Şygan	279b	40.21 N	80.08 W
Šyičy	76	52.15 N	29.14 E
Syke	52	52.54 N	8.49 E
Sykesville, Md., U.S.	208	39.22 N	76.58 W
Sykesville, Pa., U.S.	214	41.03 N	78.49 W
Sykkylven	26	62.24 N	6.35 E
Syktyvkar	24	61.40 N	50.46 E
Sylacauga	194	33.10 N	86.15 W
Sylarna ∧	26	63.02 N	12.13 E
Sylhet	120	24.54 N	91.52 E
Syloga	24	63.50 N	43.39 E
Sylt I	30	54.54 N	8.20 E
Sylva	192	35.22 N	83.13 W
Sylva ≃	86	57.39 N	56.54 E
Sylvan Beach	210	43.11 N	75.43 W
Sylvan Glen	285	40.11 N	75.42 W
Sylvan Grove	198	39.00 N	98.23 W
Sylvan Hills	194	34.50 N	92.13 W
Sylvania, Austl.	274a	34.01 S	151.07 E
Sylvania, Ga., U.S.	192	32.45 N	81.38 W
Sylvania, Oh., U.S.	214	41.43 N	83.42 W
Sylvania, Pa., U.S.	210	41.48 N	76.51 W
Sylvania Heights	274a	34.02 S	151.06 E
Sylvan Lake, Ab., Can.	182	52.19 N	114.05 W
Sylvan Lake, Il., U.S.	278	42.15 N	88.03 W
Sylvan Lake, Mi., U.S.	281	42.37 N	83.20 W
Sylvan Lake ⊜, Ab., Can.	182	52.21 N	114.10 W
Sylvan Lake ⊜, In., U.S.	216	41.29 N	85.20 W
Sylvan Lake ⊜, Mi., U.S.	281	42.37 N	83.20 W
Sylvan Pass)(	202	44.28 N	110.08 W
Sylvan Shores	220	28.49 N	81.41 W
Sylvensteinsee ⊜[1]	64	47.34 N	11.32 E
Sylvester, Ga., U.S.	192	31.31 N	83.50 W
Sylvester, Tx., U.S.	196	32.43 N	100.15 W
Sylvester, Mount ∧[2]	186	48.11 N	55.04 W
Sylvia	198	37.57 N	98.24 W
Şym	74	60.20 N	88.23 E
Šymkent	85	42.18 N	69.36 E
Symmes Creek ≃	188	38.26 N	82.27 W
Syn'a	24	65.22 N	57.42 E
Syndal	274b	37.53 S	145.09 E
Synel'nykove	78	48.20 N	35.31 E
Şynevir	78	48.30 N	23.38 E
Šyngystaj	86	49.13 N	85.55 E
Synivka	78	50.33 N	34.06 E
Synkovo	82	55.21 N	37.38 E
Synnyr, chrebet ⋏	88	56.50 N	111.10 E
Syntul	80	55.00 N	41.18 E
Synyukha ≃	78	48.03 N	30.51 E
Syon House ⊥	260	51.29 N	0.19 W
Syosset	210	40.49 N	73.30 W
Syowa ʋ[3]	9	69.00 S	39.35 E
Syracuse → Siracusa, It.	70	37.04 N	15.18 E
Syracuse, In., U.S.	216	41.25 N	85.45 W
Syracuse, Ks., U.S.	198	37.58 N	101.45 W
Syracuse, Ne., U.S.	198	40.39 N	96.11 W
Syracuse, N.Y., U.S.	210	43.02 N	76.08 W
Syracuse Hancock International Airport ⊠, N.Y., U.S.	210	43.07 N	76.07 W
Syracuse Hancock International Airport ⊠, N.Y., U.S.	212	43.07 N	76.07 W
Syrau	54	50.32 N	12.05 E
Syrčan	80	57.22 N	50.15 E
Syrdarja	85	40.52 N	68.38 E
Syrdarja □[4]	85	40.30 N	68.40 E
Syr Darya (Syrdar'ja) ≃	72	46.03 N	61.00 E
Syre	46	58.22 N	4.14 W
Syre ≃	56	49.42 N	6.29 E
Syria (Sūrīyah) □[1], Asia	118	35.00 N	38.00 E
Syria (Sūrīyah) □[1], Asia	128	35.00 N	38.00 E
Syriam	110	16.46 N	96.15 E
Syrian Desert → Shām, Bādiyat ash- ◆[2]	128	32.00 N	40.00 E
Syrie → Syria □[1]	128	35.00 N	38.00 E
Syrien → Syria □[1]	128	35.00 N	38.00 E
Syrotyne	83	48.55 N	38.31 E
Şyrskij	76	52.34 N	39.29 E
Šyščycy	76	53.13 N	27.32 E
Sysert'	86	56.29 N	60.49 E
Sysmä	26	61.30 N	25.41 E
Sysola ≃	24	61.42 N	50.53 E
Sysslebäck	26	60.44 N	12.52 E
Syston	42	52.42 N	1.04 W
Systyg-Chem	88	52.40 N	95.30 E
Sytkivtsi	78	48.54 N	29.12 E
Syt'kovo	76	56.31 N	34.01 E
Sytykanskij, porog ∟	88	57.49 N	118.33 E
Syukunoshō	270	34.50 N	135.32 E
Syväri ⊜	26	63.16 N	28.06 E
Syvash, zatoka ⊍	78	46.00 N	34.30 E
Syvas'ke	78	46.23 N	34.34 E
Syzran'	80	53.09 N	48.27 E
Syzran' ≃	80	53.04 N	48.26 E
Szabadka → Subotica	38	46.06 N	19.39 E
Szabolcs-Szatmár-Bereg □[6]	30	48.00 N	22.10 E
Szada	264c	47.38 N	19.19 E

Symbol	English	Deutsch	Español	Français	Português
≃	River	Fluß	Río	Rivière	Rio
≅	Canal	Kanal	Canal	Canal	Canal
∟	Waterfall, Rapids	Wasserfall, Stromschnellen	Cascada, Rápidos	Chute d'eau, Rapides	Cascata, Rápidos
⊍	Strait	Meeresstraße	Estrecho	Détroit	Estreito
c	Bay, Gulf	Bucht, Golf	Bahía, Golfo	Baie, Golfe	Baía, Golfo
⊜	Lake, Lakes	See, Seen	Lago, Lagos	Lac, Lacs	Lago, Lagos
≡	Swamp	Sumpf	Pantano	Marais	Pântano
⊓	Ice Features, Glacier	Eis- und Gletscherformen	Accidentes Glaciales	Formes glaciaires	Acidentes glaciares
⊤	Other Hydrographic Features	Andere Hydrographische Objekte	Otros Elementos Hidrográficos	Autres données hydrographiques	Outros acidentes hidrográficos
⟡	Submarine Features	Untermeerische Objekte	Accidentes Submarinos	Formes de relief sous-marin	Acidentes submarinos
□	Political Unit	Politische Einheit	Unidad Politica	Entité politique	Unidade política
ʋ	Cultural Institution	Kulturelle Institution	Institución Cultural	Institution culturelle	Instituição cultural
⊥	Historical Site	Historische Stätte	Sitio Histórico	Site historique	Sitio histórico
♠	Recreational Site	Erholungs- und Ferienort	Sitio de Recreo	Centre de loisirs	Area de Lazer
⊠	Airport	Flughafen	Aeropuerto	Aéroport	Aeroporto
■	Military Installation	Militäranlage	Instalación Militar	Installation militaire	Instalação militar
◆	Miscellaneous	Verschiedenes	Misceláneo	Divers	Diversos

ENGLISH: Name · Page · Lat.°′ · Long.°′ — DEUTSCH: Name · Seite · Breite°′ · Länge°′ E = Ost

Name	Page	Lat.°′	Long.°′
Szamocin	**30**	53.02 N	17.08 E
Szamos (Someș) ≃	**38**	48.07 N	22.20 E
Szamotuły	**30**	52.37 N	16.35 E
Szarvas	**30**	46.52 N	20.34 E
Szatmárnémeti → Satu Mare	**38**	47.48 N	22.53 E
Százhalombatta	**264c**	47.20 N	18.56 E
Szczawnica	**30**	49.26 N	20.30 E
Szczecin (Stettin)	**30**	53.24 N	14.32 E
Szczecin □ 4	**30**	53.45 N	15.00 E
Szczecinek (Neustettin)	**30**	53.43 N	16.42 E
Szczeciński, Zalew (Stettiner Haff) ᑕ	**54**	53.46 N	14.14 E
Szczekociny	**30**	50.38 N	19.50 E
Szczuczyn	**30**	53.34 N	22.18 E
Szczytno	**30**	53.34 N	21.00 E
Szechwan → Sichuan □ 4	**102**	31.00 N	105.00 E
Szechwan Basin → Sichuan Pendi ≚ 1	**102**	30.00 N	105.00 E
Szécsény	**30**	48.06 N	19.31 E
Szeged	**30**	46.15 N	20.09 E
Szeghalom	**30**	47.01 N	21.11 E
Székesfehérvár	**30**	47.12 N	18.25 E
Szekszárd	**30**	46.21 N	18.42 E
Szemenyecsörnye	**61**	46.30 N	16.37 E
Szentendre	**30**	47.40 N	19.05 E
Szentendrei-Duna ≃ 1	**264c**	47.36 N	19.05 E
Szentendrei-sziget I	**264c**	47.39 N	19.07 E
Szentes	**30**	46.39 N	20.16 E
Szentgotthárd	**30**	46.57 N	16.17 E
Szentpéterfa	**61**	47.06 N	16.29 E
Szeping → Siping	**89**	43.12 N	124.20 E
Szépművészeti Museum ⊍	**264c**	47.31 N	19.05 E
Szerencs	**30**	48.09 N	21.13 E
Szigethalom	**264c**	47.20 N	19.00 E
Szigetszentmiklós	**264c**	47.21 N	19.03 E
Szilas-patak ≃	**264c**	47.36 N	19.06 E
Szlichtyngowa	**30**	51.43 N	16.15 E
Szob	**30**	47.50 N	18.52 E
Szolnok	**30**	47.10 N	20.12 E
Szombathely	**30**	47.14 N	16.38 E
Szprotawa	**30**	51.34 N	15.33 E
Sztum	**30**	53.56 N	19.01 E
Szubin	**30**	53.00 N	17.44 E
Szydłowiec	**30**	51.14 N	20.51 E
Szypliszki	**30**	54.15 N	23.05 E
T			
Ta ≃	**94**	36.17 N	139.54 E
Taacyn ≃	**102**	45.09 N	101.27 E
Taal	**116**	13.53 N	120.55 E
Taal, Lake ⊜	**116**	13.55 N	121.00 E
Taalintehdas → Dalsbruk	**26**	60.02 N	22.31 E
Taan ≃	**100**	24.24 N	120.36 E
Taancan Point ›	**116**	10.00 N	125.01 E
Taavetti	**26**	60.55 N	27.34 E
Tabacal	**252**	23.16 S	64.15 W
Tabacal, Quebrada ≃	**286c**	10.31 N	67.02 W
Tabaco	**116**	13.23 N	123.44 E
Tabacundo	**246**	0.03 N	78.12 W
Tabai ≃	**164**	3.01 S	135.52 E
Tabalosos	**248**	6.21 S	76.41 W
Tabanan	**115b**	8.32 S	115.08 E
Tabango	**116**	11.19 N	124.22 E
Tabankulu	**158**	30.58 S	29.19 E
Tábara	**34**	41.49 N	5.57 W
Tabar Island I	**164**	2.55 S	152.05 E
Tabar Islands II	**164**	2.50 S	152.00 E
Tabarka	**148**	36.57 N	8.45 E
Tabarz	**54**	50.52 N	10.31 E
Ṭabas	**128**	33.36 N	56.54 E
Tabasará ≃	**236**	8.00 N	81.39 W
Tabasco □ 3	**232**	18.15 N	93.00 W
Ṭabas Masīnā	**128**	32.48 N	60.14 E
Tabat	**86**	52.57 N	90.43 E
Tabatinga ≃	**255**	17.24 S	43.18 W
Tabayama	**94**	35.47 N	138.55 E
Tabayin	**110**	22.42 N	95.19 E
Tabb	**208**	37.08 N	76.29 W
Tabei	**98**	39.44 N	122.29 E
Tabelbala	**148**	29.23 N	3.15 W
Tabelbala, Kahal ⫠ 8	**148**	28.30 N	2.00 W
Taber	**182**	49.47 N	112.08 W
Taberg, Sve.	**26**	57.41 N	14.05 E
Taberg, Sve.	**40**	59.50 N	14.08 E
Taberg, N.Y., U.S.	**210**	43.18 N	75.37 W
Tabernacle	**285**	39.50 N	74.42 W
Tabi	**152**	8.10 S	13.18 E
Tabiang	**174d**	0.52 S	169.35 E
Tabiano Terme	**64**	44.48 N	10.02 E
Tabira	**250**	7.35 S	37.33 W
Tabiteuea	**174t**	1.25 N	173.07 E
Tabiteuea I 1	**14**	1.20 S	174.50 E
Tabla	**150**	13.46 N	3.01 E
Tabla, Cerro de la ʌ	**240m**	18.03 N	66.08 W
Tablada	**288**	34.42 S	58.32 W
Tablas, Cabo ›	**252**	31.51 S	71.34 W
Tablas Island I	**116**	12.24 N	122.02 E
Tablas Plateau ⩘ 1	**116**	9.43 N	122.43 E
Tablas Strait)(	**116**	12.40 N	121.48 E
Tablat	**34**	36.24 N	3.19 E
Table Bay ᑕ	**158**	33.53 S	18.27 E
Table Cape ›	**172**	39.06 S	178.00 E
Tableland	**162**	17.17 S	127.00 E
Table Mountain ʌ, Nf., Can.	**186**	47.43 N	59.13 W
Table Mountain ʌ, S. Afr.	**158**	33.57 S	18.25 E
Table Mountain ʌ, Az., U.S.	**200**	32.49 N	110.31 W
Table Rock	**198**	40.10 N	96.05 W
Table Rock Lake ⊜ 1	**194**	36.35 N	93.30 W
Tabletop ʌ, Austl.	**162**	22.32 S	123.55 E
Table Top ʌ, Az., U.S.	**200**	32.46 N	112.07 W
Tabletop Mountain ʌ	**171b**	35.58 S	148.30 E
Tabley Mere ⊜	**262**	53.17 N	2.25 W
Tabligbo	**150**	6.35 N	1.30 E
Tablones	**240m**	18.15 N	65.45 W
Taboan ≃	**116**	17.57 N	122.11 E
Taboão, Ribeirão do ≃	**287b**	23.40 S	46.28 W
Taboão da Serra	**256**	23.38 S	46.46 W
Taboco ≃	**248**	19.53 S	55.58 W
Taboga	**236**	8.48 N	79.33 W
Tabogon	**116**	10.57 N	124.02 E
Tábor, Česká Rep.	**30**	49.25 N	14.41 E
Tabor, Ross.	**74**	71.16 N	150.12 E
Tabor, Ia., U.S.	**198**	40.53 N	95.40 W
Tabor, N.J., U.S.	**276**	40.52 N	74.29 W
Tabor, S.D., U.S.	**198**	42.56 N	97.39 W
Tabor, Mount → Tavor, Har ʌ	**132**	32.41 N	35.23 E
Tabora	**154**	5.01 S	32.48 E
Tabora □ 4	**154**	5.15 S	32.45 E
Tabor City	**192**	34.08 N	78.52 W
Tabory	**86**	58.31 N	64.33 E
Tabou	**150**	4.25 N	7.21 W
Tabrīz	**128**	38.05 N	46.18 E
Tábua, Riacho da ≃	**250**	9.12 S	44.25 W
Tabuaço	**34**	41.07 N	7.34 W
Tabuaeran I 1	**14**	3.52 N	159.20 W
Tabuão	**256**	21.59 S	44.02 W
Tábuas	**256**	22.12 S	43.37 W
Tabu-dong	**98**	36.03 N	128.31 E
Tabuelan	**116**	10.49 N	123.52 E
Tabūk, Ar. Su.	**128**	28.23 N	36.35 E
Tabuk, Pil.	**116**	17.24 N	121.25 E
Tabuleiro	**256**	21.22 S	43.15 W
Tabuleiro do Norte	**250**	5.15 S	38.07 W
Tabuny	**86**	52.46 N	78.45 E
Tabuse	**96**	33.57 N	132.03 E
Tabuyung	**114**	0.51 N	99.00 E
Tabwémasana, Mont ʌ	**175f**	15.20 S	166.44 E
Täby	**40**	59.30 N	18.03 E
Tacagua, Quebrada ≃	**286c**	10.37 N	67.02 W
Tacámbaro de Codallos	**234**	19.14 N	101.28 W
Tacaná	**236**	15.14 N	92.05 W
Tacaná, Volcán ʌ 1	**236**	15.08 N	92.06 W
Tacañitas	**252**	28.38 S	62.36 W
Tacaratu	**250**	9.06 S	38.10 W
Taceno	**58**	46.02 N	9.21 E
Taché, Lac ⊜	**176**	64.00 N	120.00 W
Tacheng (Qoqek)	**86**	46.45 N	82.57 E
Tacherting	**60**	48.05 N	12.34 E
Tachia	**100**	24.21 N	120.37 E
Tachia ≃	**100**	24.20 N	120.33 E
Tachiaochang Airport ⊠	**107**	32.01 N	118.47 E
Tachiataš	**72**	42.22 N	59.35 E
Tachibana, Nihon	**96**	33.11 N	130.36 E
Tachibana, Nihon	**96**	33.54 N	132.17 E
Tachie ≃	**182**	54.40 N	124.50 W
Tachikawa	**94**	35.42 N	139.25 E
Tachikawa Air Base ■	**268**	35.43 N	139.25 E
Tachinger See ⊜	**60**	47.58 N	12.45 E
Táchira □ 3	**246**	7.50 N	72.05 W
Tachoshui	**100**	24.20 N	121.44 E
Tachov	**60**	49.48 N	12.38 E
Tachta, Ross.	**80**	45.54 N	42.07 E
Tachta, Ross.	**89**	53.08 N	139.53 E
Tachta-Bazar	**128**	35.57 N	62.50 E
Tachtabrod	**86**	52.38 N	67.34 E
Tachtakupyr	**86**	43.02 N	60.17 E
Tachtamygda	**89**	54.06 N	123.34 E
Tacima	**250**	6.30 S	35.39 W
Tacina ≃	**68**	38.56 N	16.53 E
Tacinskij	**80**	48.13 N	41.17 E
Taciuã, Lago ≃	**246**	4.29 S	60.35 W
Tacloban	**116**	11.15 N	125.00 E
Taclobo	**116**	12.20 N	122.34 E
Tacna, Perú	**248**	18.01 S	70.15 W
Tacna, Az., U.S.	**200**	32.41 N	113.57 W
Tacna □ 5	**248**	17.40 S	70.20 W
Tacoignières	**261**	48.50 N	1.40 E
Tacoma	**224**	47.15 N	122.26 W
Tacoma Narrows Bridge ◆ 5	**224**	47.16 N	122.33 W
Taconic	**207**	42.02 N	73.24 W
Taconic Range ⩘	**210**	42.30 N	73.20 W
Taconic State Park ♠	**210**	42.05 N	73.34 W
Tacony ◆ 8	**285**	40.02 N	75.03 W
Tacony Creek ≃	**285**	40.01 N	75.06 W
Tacony Creek Park ♠	**285**	40.02 N	75.07 W
Tacony Palmyra Bridge ◆ 5	**285**	40.01 N	75.02 W
Taco Pozo	**252**	25.37 S	63.17 W
Tacotalpa	**234**	17.36 N	92.49 W
Tacotalpa ≃	**234**	17.50 N	92.52 W
Tacuarembó	**252**	31.44 S	55.59 W
Tacuarembó ≃	**252**	32.25 S	55.29 W
Tacuarí ≃	**252**	32.46 S	53.18 W
Tacuatí	**252**	23.27 S	56.35 W
Tacuba ◆ 8	**286a**	19.28 N	99.12 W
Tacubaya ◆ 8	**286a**	19.25 N	99.12 W
Tacuparé, Cachoeira ∟	**250**	5.20 S	55.50 W
Tacurong	**116**	6.42 N	124.42 E
Tacuru, Bra.	**252**	23.38 N	55.01 W
Tacuru, Bra.	**255**	23.38 S	55.01 W
Tacurú, Laguna ⊜	**258**	34.58 S	58.25 W
Tacutu (Takutu) ≃	**246**	3.01 N	60.29 W
Tadain	**270**	34.52 N	135.24 E
Tadami	**92**	37.21 N	139.19 E
Tadaoka	**270**	34.29 N	135.24 E
Tadasuni	**71**	40.06 N	8.53 E
Tadcaster	**44**	53.53 N	1.16 W
Tademaït, Plateau du ⩘ 1	**148**	28.30 N	2.00 E
Tadenac Lake ⊜	**212**	45.03 N	79.56 W
Tādepallegūdem	**122**	16.50 N	81.30 E
Tadía, Ciénaga de ⊜	**246**	6.48 N	76.49 W
Tadine	**175f**	21.33 S	167.52 E
Tadio, Lagune ᑕ	**150**	5.11 N	5.15 W
Tadjemout	**148**	25.37 N	3.48 E
Tadjenanet	**34**	36.08 N	5.59 E
Tadjeraout, Oued V	**148**	21.17 N	1.19 E
Tadjoura	**144**	11.47 N	42.54 E
Tadjoura, Golfe de ᑕ	**144**	11.42 N	43.00 E
Tadley	**42**	51.21 N	1.08 W
Tado	**94**	35.08 N	136.38 E
Tadok	**114**	3.58 N	96.19 E
Tadotsu	**96**	34.16 N	133.45 E
Tadoule Lake ⊜	**176**	58.36 N	98.20 W
Tadoussac	**186**	48.09 N	69.43 W
Tādpatri	**122**	14.55 N	78.01 E
Taduno	**112**	1.55 S	123.05 E
Tadworth	**42**	51.17 N	0.14 W
Tadzhikistan → Tajikistan □ 1	**72**	39.00 N	71.00 E
Tadžikabad	**85**	39.07 N	70.50 E
T'aean	**98**	36.46 N	126.16 E
T'aebaek-san ʌ	**98**	37.06 N	128.55 E
T'aebaek-sanmaek ⩘	**98**	37.40 N	128.50 E
Taebu-do I	**98**	37.15 N	126.35 E
Taech'ŏn	**98**	36.22 N	126.34 E
Taech'ŏng-do I	**98**	37.49 N	124.43 E
Taedong	**98**	39.05 N	125.31 E
Taedong-gang ≃	**98**	38.42 N	125.15 E
Taegu	**98**	35.52 N	128.35 E
Taegu □ 4	**98**	35.50 N	128.35 E
Taegwan	**98**	40.13 N	125.12 E
Taehan-Min'guk → Korea, South □ 1	**98**	36.30 N	128.00 E
Taehŭksan-do I	**98**	34.40 N	125.25 E
Taehŭng	**98**	40.06 N	126.56 E
Taehwajŏn	**271b**	37.36 N	126.52 E
T'aein	**98**	35.40 N	126.55 E
Taejin	**98**	36.34 N	129.24 E
Taejŏn	**98**	36.20 N	127.26 E
Taejujŏm	**98**	38.24 N	127.58 E
T'aemo-san ʌ	**271b**	37.27 N	127.04 E
Taeng ≃	**110**	19.06 N	98.57 E
Taer	**102**	34.09 N	98.50 E
Ta'erwan	**100**	31.49 N	113.25 E
Taeryanghwa	**98**	41.14 N	129.42 E
Taf ≃	**42**	51.47 N	4.26 W
Tafahi I	**14**	15.51 S	173.43 W
Tafahnā al-ʻAzab	**142**	30.36 N	31.15 E
Tafalla	**34**	42.31 N	1.40 W
Tafanlieh	**100**	21.58 N	120.46 E
Ṭafas	**132**	32.44 N	36.04 E
Tafāsīkh, Ghurd at- ⫠ 8	**142**	29.43 N	29.45 E
Tafassasset, Oued (Oued Tafassâsset) V	**148**	20.56 N	10.12 E
Tafassâsset, Ténéré du ◆ 2	**146**	21.00 N	11.00 E
Tafea □ 8	**175f**	19.30 S	169.00 E
Tafelbaai → Table Bay ᑕ	**158**	33.53 S	18.27 E
Tafelberg ʌ	**250**	3.55 N	56.10 W
Tafermaar	**164**	6.51 S	134.06 E
Taff ≃	**42**	51.27 N	3.09 W
Tafiré	**150**	9.04 N	5.10 W
Tafí Viejo	**252**	26.44 S	65.16 W
Taflan	**130**	41.25 N	36.09 E
Tafna, Oued ≃	**34**	35.17 N	1.30 W
Tafo	**150**	6.13 N	0.22 W
Tafraoute	**148**	29.40 N	8.58 W
Taft, Īrān	**128**	31.45 N	54.14 E
Taft, Pil.	**116**	11.54 N	125.25 E
Taft, Ca., U.S.	**204**	35.08 N	119.27 W
Taft, Fl., U.S.	**220**	28.23 N	81.24 W
Taft, Ok., U.S.	**196**	35.45 N	95.32 W
Taft, Tx., U.S.	**196**	27.58 N	97.23 W
Taftān, Kūh-e ʌ	**128**	28.36 N	61.08 E
Tafton	**210**	41.25 N	75.11 W
Taga, Nihon	**94**	35.13 N	136.17 E
Taga, Nihon	**270**	34.49 N	135.49 E
Taga, W. Sam.	**175a**	13.46 S	172.28 W
Tagabukid	**116**	7.00 N	126.21 E
Taga Dzong	**124**	27.04 N	89.53 E
Tagagawik ≃	**180**	66.30 N	159.00 W
Tagaj	**80**	54.18 N	47.39 E
Tagajō	**92**	38.20 N	141.00 E
Tagan	**86**	54.57 N	77.18 E
Tagana-an	**116**	9.42 N	125.35 E
Taganrog	**83**	47.12 N	38.56 E
Taganrogskij zaliv ᑕ	**78**	47.00 N	38.23 E
Tagant □ 4	**150**	18.20 N	11.30 W
Tagânt ◆ 1	**150**	18.00 N	12.00 W
Tagapula Island I	**116**	12.04 N	124.12 E
Tågarp	**41**	55.56 N	12.57 E
Tagauayan Island I	**116**	10.58 N	121.13 E
Tagawa	**96**	33.38 N	130.49 E
Tagaytay	**116**	14.06 N	120.56 E
Tagbara	**152**	5.56 N	21.09 E
Tagbilaran	**116**	9.39 N	123.51 E
Tagdempt → Tihert	**148**	35.28 N	1.21 E
Tage	**164**	6.20 S	143.20 E
Tageren Canal ≍	**174q**	9.33 N	138.09 E
Taggia	**62**	43.52 N	7.51 E
Taghit	**148**	30.55 N	2.02 W
Taghkanic Creek ≃	**210**	42.13 N	73.45 W
Taghmon	**48**	52.18 N	6.39 W
Tagig	**269f**	14.32 N	121.04 E
Tagig ≃	**269f**	14.31 N	121.05 E
Tagish Lake ⊜	**180**	59.45 N	134.15 W
Tagliacozzo	**66**	42.04 N	13.14 E
Tagliamento ≃	**64**	45.38 N	13.06 E
Tagliata, Monte della ʌ	**64**	44.34 N	9.48 E
Taglio di Po	**64**	45.00 N	12.12 E
Tagna	**88**	53.36 N	101.54 E
Tagna ≃	**88**	53.38 N	101.53 E
Tago	**116**	9.02 N	126.13 E
Tago ≃	**116**	9.01 N	126.14 E
Tagoloan	**116**	8.32 N	124.45 E
Tagolo Point ›	**116**	8.44 N	123.23 E
Tagon Harbour ᑕ	**162**	33.53 S	123.00 E
Tagounit	**148**	29.58 N	5.36 W
Tagourâret ⍑ 4	**150**	17.45 N	7.43 W
Tagow Bāy	**120**	35.42 N	66.03 E
Tagrina, Oued V	**148**	21.00 N	6.16 E
Taguatinga	**255**	12.25 S	46.26 W
Tagubanhan Island I	**116**	11.08 N	123.07 E
Tagudin	**116**	16.56 N	120.27 E
Taguedoufat V	**150**	14.50 N	7.42 E
Taguke	**120**	32.07 N	84.35 E
Tagul ≃	**88**	55.35 N	97.45 E
Tagula Island I	**160**	11.30 S	153.30 E
Tagum	**116**	7.28 N	125.48 E
T'agun	**86**	53.56 N	85.38 E
Tagun Bay ᑕ	**116**	13.55 N	123.46 E
Tagus (Tejo) (Tajo) ≃	**34**	38.40 N	9.24 W
T'agyŏng-ni	**98**	38.04 N	126.03 E
Tah, Sebkha ⊜	**148**	27.45 N	12.42 W
Taha	**89**	47.33 N	124.14 E
Tahaa I	**14**	16.38 S	151.30 W
Tahakopa	**172**	46.31 S	169.23 E
Tahala	**148**	34.04 N	4.20 W
Tahan, Gunong ʌ	**114**	4.38 N	102.14 E
Tahanaoute	**148**	31.24 N	7.54 W
Tahāneh-ye Ney Basteh	**128**	32.59 N	60.53 E
Tahara	**94**	34.40 N	137.16 E
Tahart	**148**	22.51 N	5.12 E
Tahat ʌ	**148**	23.18 N	5.47 E
Taheke	**172**	35.27 S	173.39 E
Ṭāherī	**128**	27.42 N	52.21 E
Tahgong, Puntan ›	**174n**	15.06 N	145.39 E
Tahifet	**148**	22.58 N	5.55 E
Tahiryuak Lake ⊜	**176**	70.56 N	112.20 W
Tahiti I	**174s**	17.37 S	149.27 W
Tahkuna nina ›	**76**	59.07 N	22.36 E
Tāhlāb (Ṭālāb) ≃	**128**	28.09 N	62.45 E
Tahlequah	**196**	35.54 N	94.58 W
Ṭahmā wa Minshāt ʻAbd as-Sayyid	**142**	29.38 N	31.14 E
Tahmoor	**170**	34.13 S	150.36 E
Tahneta Pass)(	**180**	61.53 N	147.20 W
Tahoe, Lake ⊜	**226**	39.07 N	120.03 W
Tahoe City	**226**	39.10 N	120.08 W
Tahoe Lake ⊜	**176**	70.15 N	108.45 W
Tahoe Valley	**204**	38.55 N	120.00 W
Tahoka	**196**	33.10 N	101.47 W
Taholah	**224**	47.20 N	124.17 W
Tahoua	**150**	14.54 N	5.16 E
Tahoua □ 5	**150**	16.00 N	5.00 E
Tahquamenon ≃	**190**	46.34 N	85.02 W
Tahquamenon Falls State Park ♠	**190**	46.29 N	85.05 W
Tahsi	**100**	24.57 N	121.53 E
Tahsis	**182**	49.55 N	126.39 W
Ṭahṭā	**140**	26.46 N	31.30 E
Tahtaköprü	**130**	39.57 N	29.39 E
Tahtsa Lake ⊜	**182**	53.42 N	127.26 W
Tahtsa Peak ʌ	**182**	53.33 N	127.47 W
Tahu	**100**	24.26 N	120.52 E
Tahuamanu ≃	**248**	11.06 S	67.36 W
Tahuata I	**174x**	9.57 S	139.05 W
Tahulandang, Pulau I	**112**	2.20 N	125.25 E
Tahuna	**112**	3.37 N	125.29 E
Tahuofang ⊜ 1	**104**	41.55 N	124.07 E
Tahuya ≃	**224**	47.23 N	123.03 W
Ṭahwāy	**142**	30.22 N	30.52 E
Taï, C. Iv.	**150**	5.52 N	7.27 W
Tai, It.	**64**	46.25 N	12.20 E
Tai, Nihon	**270**	34.31 N	135.26 E
Tai ◆ 8	**270**	34.45 N	135.00 E
Taiaçupeba	**256**	23.40 S	46.11 W
Tai'an, Zhg.	**98**	36.12 N	117.07 E
Tai'an, Zhg.	**104**	41.23 N	122.27 E
Tai'an, Zhg.	**107**	30.05 N	105.47 E
Tai'angang	**106**	31.43 N	121.40 E
Taiarapu, Presqu'île de › 1	**174s**	17.47 S	149.14 W
Taibai	**102**	34.00 N	107.18 E
Taibai Shan ʌ, Zhg.	**98**	39.19 N	114.11 E
Taibai Shan ʌ, Zhg.	**102**	33.54 N	107.46 E
Taibon Agordino	**64**	46.18 N	12.00 E
Taibus Qi (Baochang)	**98**	41.56 N	115.22 E
Taicang	**106**	31.26 N	121.07 E
T'aichou → Taizhou	**100**	32.30 N	119.58 E
Taichu → T'aichung	**100**	24.09 N	120.41 E
T'aichung	**100**	24.09 N	120.41 E
Taicunzhen	**106**	31.27 N	119.03 E
Taiden → Taejŏn	**98**	36.20 N	127.26 E
Taiei	**94**	35.49 N	140.25 E
Taieri ≃	**172**	46.03 S	170.11 E
Taif → Aṭ-Ṭā'if	**144**	21.16 N	40.24 E
Taigu	**102**	37.28 N	112.30 E
Tai Hang	**271d**	22.17 N	114.11 E
Taihang Shan ⩘	**102**	38.00 N	114.00 E
Taihape	**172**	39.40 S	175.48 E
Taihe, Zhg.	**100**	33.11 N	115.36 E
Taihe, Zhg.	**100**	26.49 N	114.55 E
Taihe, Zhg.	**107**	30.10 N	105.56 E
Taihezhen, Zhg.	**89**	44.47 N	123.29 E
Taihezhen, Zhg.	**107**	30.07 N	103.50 E
Taihezhen, Zhg.	**107**	30.06 N	106.03 E
Taiho	**174m**	26.39 N	128.07 E
Taihoku → T'aipei	**100**	25.03 N	121.30 E
T'aihsi	**100**	23.42 N	120.11 E
T'aihsien → Taizhou	**100**	32.30 N	119.58 E
Taihu	**100**	30.26 N	116.16 E
Tai Hu ⊜	**106**	31.15 N	120.10 E
Taijiang	**102**	26.32 N	108.22 E
Taijimiao	**98**	40.55 N	113.46 E
Taijüan → Taiyuan	**102**	37.55 N	112.30 E
Taikang	**98**	34.04 N	114.50 E
Taikkyi	**110**	17.19 N	95.58 E
Taikou	**102**	31.53 N	111.07 E
Taiko-yama ʌ	**96**	35.46 N	135.12 E
Taikyu → Taegu	**98**	35.52 N	128.35 E
Tailai	**89**	46.23 N	123.27 E
Tai Lam Chung	**271d**	22.22 N	114.01 E
Tai Lam Chung Reservoir ⊜ 1	**271d**	22.23 N	114.01 E
Tailem Bend	**166**	35.16 S	139.27 E
Tailfingen	**58**	48.15 N	9.01 E
Tai Long, Zhg.	**271d**	22.25 N	114.22 E
Tai Long, Zhg.	**271d**	22.13 N	113.59 E
Tai Long Bay ᑕ	**271d**	22.24 N	114.24 E
Taima, Nihon	**96**	34.30 N	135.42 E
T'aima, T'aiwan	**100**	22.37 N	120.59 E
Taimba	**74**	60.18 N	98.58 E
Taimei	**100**	23.19 N	114.29 E
Tai Mong Tsai	**271d**	22.24 N	114.18 E
Tai Mo Shan ʌ	**271d**	22.25 N	114.07 E
Taimyr-Halbinsel → Tajmyr, poluostrov › 1	**74**	76.00 N	104.00 E
Tain	**46**	57.48 N	4.04 W
Tainaka	**270**	34.36 N	135.37 E
T'ainan	**100**	23.00 N	120.12 E
Taínaron, Ákra ›	**38**	36.22 N	22.30 E
Taining	**100**	26.54 N	117.09 E
Tain-l'Hermitage	**62**	45.04 N	4.51 E
Tai O, Zhg.	**100**	22.15 N	113.51 E
Taio, It.	**64**	46.20 N	11.04 E
Taiobeiras	**255**	15.49 S	42.14 W
Tai Pang Wan → Da Peng Wan ᑕ	**100**	22.30 N	114.24 E
T'aipei, T'aiwan	**100**	25.03 N	121.30 E
T'aipei, T'aiwan	**269d**	25.03 N	121.30 E
T'aipei □ 6	**269d**	25.00 N	121.40 E
Taipei Bridge ◆ 5	**269d**	25.04 N	121.30 E
T'aipeihsien	**100**	25.00 N	121.27 E
Taipei Institute of Technology ⊍ 2	**269d**	25.02 N	121.32 E
Taipei New Park ♠	**269d**	25.03 N	121.31 E
T'aipei Shih □ 7	**269d**	25.05 N	121.33 E
Taiping, Malay.	**114**	4.51 N	100.44 E
Taiping, Zhg.	**100**	22.49 N	113.41 E
Taiping, Zhg.	**100**	30.18 N	118.12 E
Taiping, Zhg.	**102**	22.40 N	107.05 E
Taiping, Zhg.	**107**	30.24 N	103.37 E
Taipingchang, Zhg.	**102**	27.25 N	103.04 E
Taipingchang, Zhg.	**107**	29.53 N	106.04 E
Taipingchang, Zhg.	**107**	29.55 N	103.49 E
Taipingchang, Zhg.	**107**	30.10 N	106.21 E
Taipingchang, Zhg.	**107**	30.39 N	105.54 E
Taipingchang, Zhg.	**107**	30.25 N	103.46 E
Taipingchang, Zhg.	**107**	29.33 N	103.33 E
Taipingchuan, Zhg.	**89**	44.23 N	123.11 E
Taipingchuan, Zhg.	**98**	42.36 N	127.20 E
Taipingdian	**102**	32.08 N	111.45 E
Taipingkou	**100**	29.50 N	113.35 E
Taipingling	**89**	43.26 N	128.09 E
Taipingshan, Zhg.	**98**	40.34 N	122.25 E
Taipingshan, Zhg.	**104**	41.36 N	123.41 E
Taipingshao	**98**	40.54 N	125.08 E
Taipingsi	**107**	29.24 N	103.34 E
Taipingxigou	**104**	42.36 N	121.13 E
Taipingzhai	**104**	42.14 N	124.07 E
Taipingzhen, Zhg.	**89**	46.44 N	130.44 E
Taipingzhen, Zhg.	**102**	35.42 N	107.37 E
Taipingzhen, Zhg.	**107**	29.24 N	105.47 E
Taipingzhen, Zhg.	**107**	30.26 N	104.12 E
Taipingzhuang, Zhg.	**104**	42.38 N	123.45 E
Taipingzhuang, Zhg.	**105**	40.03 N	116.24 E
Taipingzhuang, Zhg.	**105**	40.08 N	117.36 E
Tai Po Hoi ᑕ	**271d**	22.26 N	114.12 E
Tai Po Tsai	**271d**	22.21 N	114.15 E
Taipu	**250**	5.37 S	35.36 W
Taira, Nihon	**94**	36.26 N	136.57 E
Taira → Iwaki, Nihon	**94**	37.03 N	140.55 E
Tairetá	**256**	22.36 S	43.42 W
Tairiqiao	**106**	30.59 N	121.33 E
Tais	**112**	4.06 S	102.34 E
Taisen-zan ʌ	**96**	33.06 N	131.17 E
Taisha → Izumo, Nihon	**96**	35.22 N	132.46 E
Taisha, Nihon	**96**	35.24 N	132.40 E
Taishaku-kyō ♠	**96**	34.53 N	133.13 E
Taishaku-zan ʌ, Nihon	**94**	36.58 N	139.28 E
Taishaku-zan ʌ, Nihon	**270**	34.47 N	135.07 E
Taishan, Zhg.	**98**	39.01 N	113.36 E
Taishan, Zhg.	**102**	22.16 N	112.44 E
Taishanchang	**107**	30.32 N	106.42 E
Taishi, Nihon	**96**	34.50 N	134.33 E
Taishi, Nihon	**270**	34.31 N	135.39 E
Taishō	**96**	33.12 N	132.58 E
Taishō ◆ 8	**270**	34.38 N	135.27 E
Tai Shui Hang	**271d**	22.25 N	14.13 E
Taishun	**100**	27.33 N	119.43 E
Tai Tam Bay ᑕ	**271d**	22.13 N	114.13 E
Taitao, Península de › 1	**254**	46.30 S	74.25 W
Taitapu	**172**	43.40 S	172.33 E
Taitō ◆ 8	**268**	35.43 N	139.47 E
Tai Tong	**271d**	22.25 N	114.01 E
Taitouying	**98**	40.02 N	119.12 E
Taitō-zaki ›	**94**	35.18 N	140.25 E
T'aitung	**100**	22.45 N	121.09 E
Taivalkoski	**26**	65.34 N	28.15 E
Tai Wan	**271d**	22.10 N	114.15 E
Taiwan (T'aiwan) □ 1, Asia	**90**	23.30 N	121.00 E
Taiwan (T'aiwan) □ 1, Asia	**100**	23.30 N	121.00 E
T'aiwan I	**100**	23.30 N	121.00 E
Taiwan Strait)(	**100**	24.00 N	119.00 E
Tai Wan Tau	**271d**	22.18 N	114.17 E
Taixi	**100**	24.42 N	116.56 E
Taixian	**100**	32.31 N	120.09 E
Taixing	**106**	32.11 N	120.01 E
Taixizhen	**106**	31.03 N	119.49 E
Taiyang	**100**	30.12 N	119.19 E
Taiyanggong	**271a**	39.58 N	116.25 E
Taïyetos Óros ⩘	**38**	37.00 N	22.20 E
Ṭaiyiba	**132**	32.16 N	35.01 E
Taiyuan	**102**	37.55 N	112.30 E
Taizhao	**120**	30.01 N	93.08 E
Taizhou	**100**	32.30 N	119.58 E
Taizhou Liedao II	**100**	28.30 N	121.53 E
Taizi ≃	**98**	41.00 N	122.26 E
Taʻizz	**144**	13.38 N	44.04 E
Tāj al-ʻIzz	**142**	30.57 N	31.35 E
Tajarḥī	**146**	24.21 N	14.28 E
Tajbola	**24**	68.26 N	33.19 E
Tajdakovo	**82**	54.29 N	37.32 E
Tajerouine	**36**	35.54 N	8.34 E
Tajetteret, Oued V	**148**	21.20 N	7.22 E
Tajga	**86**	56.04 N	85.37 E
Tajgonos, mys ›	**74**	60.35 N	160.08 E
Tajgonos, poluostrov › 1	**74**	61.20 N	161.00 E
Tajikistan □ 1, Asia	**72**	39.00 N	71.00 E
Tajikistan □ 1, Asia	**85**	39.00 N	71.00 E
Tajikstan → Tajikistan □ 1	**72**	39.00 N	71.00 E
Tajima	**94**	37.12 N	139.46 E
Tajimi	**94**	35.19 N	137.08 E
Tajique	**200**	34.45 N	106.17 W
Tajiri	**270**	34.24 N	135.18 E
Tajitos	**232**	30.58 N	112.18 W
Tajlakdžegen	**86**	43.54 N	60.29 E
Tajlakovy	**86**	59.20 N	74.04 E
Tāj Mahal ⊥	**124**	27.10 N	78.03 E
Tajmura ≃	**72**	63.46 N	98.01 E
Tajmyr, ozero ⊜	**74**	74.30 N	102.30 E
Tajmyr, poluostrov › 1	**74**	76.00 N	104.00 E
Tajna	**88**	56.27 N	95.30 E
Tajninka	**265b**	55.54 N	37.45 E
Tajo → Tagus ≃	**34**	38.40 N	9.24 W
Tajožnyj, Ross.	**86**	56.09 N	94.29 E
Tajožnyj, Ross.	**88**	56.13 N	94.55 E
Tajpur, India	**124**	25.51 N	85.41 E
Tajpur, India	**124**	29.10 N	78.29 E
Tājpur, India	**272b**	22.44 N	88.16 E
Tajpur Khurd ◆ 8	**272a**	28.35 N	77.03 E
Tajšet	**88**	55.57 N	98.00 E
Tajsojgan	**80**	48.19 N	53.29 E
Tajturka	**88**	52.51 N	103.28 E
Tajumulco, Volcán ʌ 1	**236**	15.02 N	91.55 W
Tajuña ≃	**34**	40.07 N	3.35 W
Tājūrā', Lībiyā	**146**	32.53 N	13.21 E
Tajura, Ross.	**88**	57.00 N	106.35 E
Tajura ≃	**88**	57.00 N	106.35 E
Tajžina	**86**	53.38 N	87.28 E
Tak	**110**	16.52 N	99.08 E
Takāb	**128**	36.24 N	47.07 E
Takabanare-jima I	**174m**	26.22 N	127.59 E
Takabara	**150**	11.50 N	11.30 W
Takachiho	**92**	32.42 N	131.18 E
Takachu	**156**	22.37 S	21.58 E
Takada → Bungo-takada, Nihon	**96**	33.33 N	131.27 E
Takada → Yamato-takada, Nihon	**96**	34.31 N	135.45 E
Takagi	**268**	35.56 N	139.35 E
Takahagi	**94**	36.43 N	140.43 E
Takahama, Nihon	**94**	34.55 N	136.59 E
Takahama, Nihon	**94**	37.00 N	136.46 E
Takahama, Nihon	**96**	35.29 N	135.33 E
Takahara ≃	**94**	36.28 N	137.15 E
Takahashi	**96**	34.47 N	133.37 E
Takahashi ≃	**96**	34.31 N	133.42 E
Takahe, Mount ʌ	**9**	76.16 S	112.14 W
Takaido ◆ 8	**268**	35.40 N	139.37 E
Takaishi	**96**	34.32 N	135.26 E
Takaka	**172**	40.51 S	172.48 E
Takakkaw Falls ∟	**182**	51.30 N	116.28 W
Takalaou	**146**	10.07 N	19.48 E
Takalar	**112**	5.28 S	119.24 E
Takamatsu, Nihon	**94**	36.46 N	136.43 E
Takamatsu, Nihon	**96**	34.20 N	134.03 E
Takami-shima I	**96**	34.19 N	133.41 E
Takamiya	**96**	34.47 N	132.44 E
Takami-yama ʌ	**94**	34.25 N	136.05 E
Takamori	**94**	35.33 N	137.53 E
Takanabe	**92**	32.08 N	131.30 E
Takanawa-hantō › 1	**96**	33.58 N	132.56 E
Takanawa-san ʌ	**96**	33.56 N	132.51 E
Takane, Nihon	**94**	36.02 N	137.29 E
Takane, Nihon	**94**	35.50 N	138.25 E
Takanezawa	**94**	36.37 N	139.59 E
Takano	**96**	35.02 N	132.55 E
Takanosu	**92**	40.13 N	140.22 E
Takao → Kaohsiung	**100**	22.38 N	120.17 E
Takaoka	**94**	36.45 N	137.01 E
Takao-kokutei-kōen ♠	**94**	35.38 N	139.15 E
Takao-san ʌ, Nihon	**94**	35.38 N	139.15 E
Takao-san ʌ, Nihon	**270**	34.49 N	135.51 E
Takapau	**172**	40.02 S	176.21 E
Takapuna	**172**	36.47 S	174.47 E
Takara-jima I	**93b**	29.09 N	129.13 E
Takarazuka	**270**	34.49 N	135.21 E
Takasago	**96**	34.45 N	134.48 E
Takasaki	**94**	36.20 N	139.01 E
Takase	**96**	34.10 N	133.45 E
Takase ≃	**94**	36.28 N	137.52 E
Takashima, Nihon	**92**	32.39 N	129.45 E
Takashima, Nihon	**94**	35.18 N	136.01 E
Taka-shima I	**96**	34.50 N	131.50 E
Takashippu	**174m**	26.24 N	127.44 E
Takasu	**94**	35.57 N	136.53 E
Takata → Rikuzen-takata, Nihon	**92**	39.01 N	141.38 E
Takata → Joetsu, Nihon	**94**	37.06 N	138.15 E
Takata, Nihon	**96**	33.06 N	130.28 E
Takatō	**94**	35.50 N	138.04 E
Takatomi	**94**	35.29 N	136.47 E
Takatori	**96**	34.27 N	135.48 E
Takatori-yama ʌ	**96**	33.18 N	130.43 E
Takatori-yama ʌ 2	**268**	35.18 N	139.37 E
Takatsu ≃	**96**	34.42 N	131.49 E
Takatsuki, Nihon	**94**	35.28 N	136.14 E
Takatsuki, Nihon	**96**	34.51 N	135.37 E
Takaungu	**154**	3.41 S	39.51 E
Ta-kaw	**110**	21.36 N	98.56 E
Takayama, Nihon	**94**	36.08 N	137.15 E
Takayama, Nihon	**94**	36.37 N	138.57 E
Takayama, Nihon	**94**	36.40 N	138.21 E
Takayama, Nihon	**270**	34.45 N	135.44 E
Takayanagi, Nihon	**94**	37.13 N	138.38 E
Takayanagi, Nihon	**268**	35.25 N	139.57 E
Tak Bai	**114**	6.16 N	102.03 E
Takčijan	**85**	38.32 N	68.03 E
Takebe	**96**	34.52 N	133.54 E
Takefu	**94**	35.54 N	136.10 E
Takehara	**96**	34.21 N	132.55 E
Takeli	**85**	40.30 N	69.25 E
Takenake	**120**	34.11 N	81.20 E
Takengon	**114**	4.38 N	96.50 E
Takeno ≃	**96**	35.45 N	135.06 E
Takenotsuka ◆ 8	**268**	35.48 N	139.48 E
Takeo	**92**	33.12 N	130.01 E
Takeoka	**268**	35.12 N	139.51 E
Tåkern ⊜	**26**	58.21 N	14.48 E
Takeshi	**94**	36.17 N	138.14 E
Take-shima I	**93b**	30.49 N	130.26 E
Take-shima (Tok-to) II	**92**	37.17 N	131.53 E
Tākestān	**128**	36.04 N	49.43 E
Taketa	**96**	32.58 N	131.24 E
Taketoyo	**94**	34.51 N	136.55 E
Takêv	**110**	10.59 N	104.47 E
Take-yama ʌ 2	**268**	35.13 N	139.39 E
Takhādīd ⍑ 4	**128**	29.59 N	44.30 E
Takhār □ 4	**120**	36.30 N	69.30 E
Takhatpur	**124**	22.09 N	81.52 E
Takhli	**110**	15.15 N	100.21 E
Ta Khoa	**110**	21.13 N	104.18 E
Takht-e Jamshīd ⊥	**128**	29.57 N	52.52 E
Takht-i-Bhāi	**123**	34.17 N	71.56 E
Tāki, India	**126**	22.36 N	88.55 E
Taki, Nihon	**94**	34.30 N	136.33 E
Taki, Nihon	**96**	35.16 N	132.38 E
Taki, Pap. N. Gui.	**175e**	6.29 S	155.50 E
Takijuk Lake ⊜	**176**	66.15 N	113.05 W
Takikawa	**92a**	43.33 N	141.54 E
Takino	**96**	34.56 N	134.58 E
Takipur	**126**	24.19 N	87.58 E
Takitimu Mountains ⩘	**172**	45.41 S	167.53 E
Takla Lake ⊜	**182**	55.25 N	125.53 W
Takla Landing	**182**	55.29 N	125.58 W
Takla Makan → Taklimakan Shamo ◆ 2	**90**	39.00 N	83.00 E
Taklimakan Shamo ◆ 2	**90**	39.00 N	83.00 E
Tako	**94**	35.44 N	140.28 E
Takob	**85**	38.50 N	68.57 E
Tako-bana ›	**96**	35.36 N	133.06 E
Takolekaju, Pegunungan ⩘	**112**	2.00 S	121.00 E
Takoma Park	**284c**	38.58 N	77.00 W
Takoradi → Sekondi-Takoradi	**150**	4.59 N	1.43 W
Takotna	**180**	62.56 N	156.04 W
Takow → Kaohsiung	**100**	22.38 N	120.17 E
Takpochao, Okso ʌ	**174n**	15.11 N	145.45 E
Takrouna	**36**	36.09 N	10.20 E
Taksimo	**88**	51.03 N	107.50 E
Taksino	**82**	56.19 N	36.10 E
Takslesluk Lake ⊜	**180**	61.04 N	162.55 W
Taksony	**264c**	47.20 N	19.04 E
Taku	**92**	33.17 N	130.08 E
Taku ≃	**180**	58.26 N	133.59 W
Takuan, Mount ʌ	**175e**	6.27 S	155.36 E
Takua Pa	**110**	8.53 N	98.21 E
Taku Glacier ⊓	**180**	58.35 N	134.10 W
Takum	**150**	7.17 N	9.59 E
Takuma	**96**	34.13 N	133.40 E
Takundi	**152**	4.45 S	16.34 E
Takutea I	**14**	19.49 S	158.18 W
Takut Tangub Bay ᑕ	**116**	6.33 N	122.15 E
Takutu (Tacutu) ≃	**246**	3.01 N	60.29 W
Takuu Islands II	**14**	4.45 S	157.00 E
Takysie Lake	**182**	53.54 N	125.53 W
Tāl	**123**	34.55 N	72.13 E
Tala, Bngl.	**126**	22.46 N	89.16 E
Tāla, India	**124**	23.43 N	81.02 E
Tala, Méx.	**234**	20.40 N	103.42 W
Talā, Miṣr	**142**	30.41 N	30.56 E
Tala, Ur.	**252**	34.21 S	55.46 W
Tala, Arroyo del ≃	**258**	33.37 S	56.34 W
Ṭālāb (Tāhlāb) ≃	**128**	28.09 N	62.45 E
Talacogon	**116**	8.28 N	125.46 E
Talačyn	**76**	54.25 N	29.42 E
Talaga	**112**	2.11 S	125.53 E
Talagang	**123**	32.55 N	72.25 E
Talagante	**252**	33.40 S	70.56 W
Talagou	**104**	41.37 N	120.32 E
Ta Lai	**110**	11.24 N	107.23 E
Talaimannar	**122**	9.05 N	79.44 E
Talāja	**120**	21.21 N	72.03 E
Talak ◆ 1	**150**	18.20 N	6.00 E
Talakag	**116**	8.16 N	124.37 E
Talakan	**89**	49.38 N	133.18 E
Talakivka	**83**	47.10 N	37.43 E
Tālāla	**120**	21.02 N	70.32 E
Talalayivka	**78**	50.51 N	33.08 E
Talamanca, Cordillera de ⩘	**236**	9.30 N	83.40 W
Talamba	**123**	30.32 N	72.14 E
Talamone	**66**	42.33 N	11.08 E
Talana, It.	**71**	40.02 N	9.30 E
Talana, S. Afr.	**158**	28.10 S	30.15 E
Talandža	**89**	49.27 N	131.35 E
Talang, Gunung ʌ	**112**	0.58 S	100.39 E
Talangbatu	**112**	4.06 S	105.29 E
Talangbetutu	**112**	2.53 S	104.41 E
Talangpadang	**112**	5.21 S	104.11 E
Talangrimbo	**112**	3.29 S	105.25 E
Talant	**58**	47.19 N	5.00 E
Talap	**80**	48.26 N	48.03 E
Talara	**246**	4.34 S	81.17 W
Talarrubias	**34**	39.02 N	5.14 W
Talas	**85**	42.32 N	72.14 E
Talas □ 4	**85**	42.30 N	72.00 E
Talas ≃	**85**	44.02 N	69.37 E
Talasea	**164**	5.20 S	150.05 E
Talasskij-Alatau, chrebet ⩘	**85**	42.10 N	72.00 E
Talatakoh, Pulau I	**112**	0.22 S	122.05 E
Talʻat al-Jamāʻah, Rujm ʌ	**132**	30.23 N	35.30 E
Talata Mafara	**150**	12.35 N	6.04 E
Talaud, Kepulauan II	**108**	4.20 N	126.50 E
Talavera	**116**	15.35 N	120.55 E
Talavera de la Reina	**34**	39.57 N	4.50 W
Talawdī	**140**	10.38 N	30.23 E
Talayan	**116**	6.55 N	124.24 E
Tālbāndh	**126**	22.03 N	86.20 E
Talbingo	**171b**	35.34 S	148.18 E
Talbingo Reservoir ⊜ 1	**171b**	35.43 S	148.20 E
Talbot	**169**	37.11 S	143.43 E
Talbot ≃	**212**	44.28 N	79.10 W
Talbot, Cape ›	**164**	13.48 S	126.43 E
Talbot Brook	**168a**	32.01 S	116.40 E
Talbot Brook ≃	**168a**	32.10 S	116.49 E
Talbot Islands II	**164**	9.15 S	142.08 E
Talbot Lake ⊜, Mb., Can.	**184**	54.00 N	99.55 W
Talbot Lake ⊜, On., Can.	**212**	44.42 N	78.51 W
Talbotton	**192**	32.40 N	84.32 W
Talbotville Royal	**214**	42.48 N	81.15 W
Talbragar ≃	**166**	32.12 S	148.37 E
Talca	**252**	35.26 S	71.40 W
Talcahuano	**252**	36.43 S	73.07 W
Tālcher	**120**	20.57 N	85.13 E
Talchichitle, Isla I	**232**	24.59 N	108.04 W
Talco	**196**	33.21 N	95.06 W
Talcottville	**207**	41.49 N	72.30 W
Talcy, Château de ⊥	**50**	47.46 N	1.27 E
Taldan	**89**	53.40 N	124.48 E
Tāldāngra	**126**	23.02 N	87.06 E
Taldom	**82**	56.44 N	37.32 E
Taldyapan, Kaz.	**80**	48.07 N	47.08 E
Taldyapan, Kaz.	**80**	49.46 N	50.14 E
Taldyk, pereval)(	**85**	39.47 N	73.11 E
Taldykorgan	**86**	45.00 N	78.23 E
Taldykorgan □ 8	**86**	45.30 N	78.30 E
Taldykuduk	**80**	50.09 N	49.33 E
Tale	**150**	9.26 N	1.07 W
Taleex	**144**	9.09 N	48.26 E
Talence	**32**	44.49 N	0.35 W
Talent	**202**	42.14 N	122.47 W
Tālesh	**128**	37.48 N	48.55 E
Taley	**152**	6.40 N	16.23 E
Talgar	**85**	43.18 N	77.18 E
Talgar, pik ʌ	**85**	43.05 N	77.20 E
Talgarreg	**42**	52.08 N	4.18 W
Talgarth	**42**	52.00 N	3.15 W
Ṭalḥ, ʻIlw aṭ- ʌ 2	**142**	28.30 N	29.38 E
Talhār	**120**	24.53 N	68.49 E
Tali, Pointe de ›	**241o**	15.56 N	61.12 W
Talia, Austl.	**162**	33.19 S	134.54 E
Talia, Méx.	**196**	25.44 N	102.26 W
Taliabu, Pulau I	**112**	1.48 S	124.48 E
Talian Dao I	**98**	39.03 N	122.52 E
Talibon	**116**	10.09 N	124.19 E
Talibong, Ko I	**110**	7.15 N	99.23 E
Talica, Ross.	**76**	58.44 N	41.34 E
Talica, Ross.	**80**	58.01 N	51.30 E
Talica, Ross.	**86**	57.00 N	63.43 E
Talickij Čamlyk	**80**	52.02 N	40.32 E
Talien → Dalian	**98**	38.53 N	121.35 E
Talihina	**196**	34.45 N	95.02 W
Tālīkota	**122**	16.29 N	76.19 E
Talikud Island I	**116**	6.56 N	125.42 E
Talim Island I	**116**	14.21 N	121.14 E
Talimuashili	**85**	39.08 N	77.03 E
Taling Chan	**269a**	13.46 N	100.27 E
Taliouine	**148**	30.36 N	7.49 W
Taliparamba	**122**	12.03 N	75.21 E
Tali Post	**140**	5.54 N	30.47 E
Talisay, Pil.	**116**	10.15 N	123.51 E
Talisay, Pil.	**116**	14.08 N	122.55 E
Talisay, Pil.	**116**	10.44 N	122.58 E
Talisayan	**116**	9.00 N	124.55 E
Talisei, Pulau I	**112**	1.51 N	125.05 E
Talish-Mikeyli	**84**	39.23 N	48.22 E
Talish Mountains (Kūhhā-ye Ṭavālesh) ⩘	**128**	38.42 N	48.18 E
Talisker	**46**	57.17 N	6.27 W
Taliwang	**115b**	8.44 S	116.52 E
Tal'ka	**76**	53.22 N	28.21 E
Talkeetna	**180**	62.20 N	150.07 W
Talkeetna Mountains ⩘	**180**	62.10 N	148.15 W
Ṭalkhā	**142**	31.03 N	31.22 E
Ṭalkheh ≃	**128**	37.52 N	45.53 E
Talladale	**46**	57.42 N	5.29 W
Talladega	**194**	33.26 N	86.06 W
Tall ʻAfar	**128**	36.22 N	42.27 E
Tallaght	**48**	53.17 N	6.21 W
Tal Lah, India	**126**	22.19 N	87.18 E
Tallah, Miṣr	**142**	28.05 N	30.44 E
Tallahaga Creek ≃	**194**	32.55 N	88.58 W
Tallahala Creek ≃	**194**	31.12 N	89.05 W
Tallahassee	**192**	30.26 N	84.16 W
Tallahatchie ≃	**194**	33.33 N	90.10 W

Symbols in the index entries represent the broad categories identified in the key at the right. Symbols with superior numbers (⩘ 1) identify subcategories (see complete key on page *I · 1*).

Symbole im Register stellen die rechts im Schlüssel erklärten Kategorien dar. Symbole mit hochgestellten Ziffern (⩘ 1) bezeichnen Unterabteilungen einer Kategorie (vgl. vollständiger Schlüssel auf Seite *I · 1*).

Los símbolos incluídos en el texto del índice representan las grandes categorías identificadas con la clave a la derecha. Los símbolos con numeros en su parte superior (⩘ 1) identifican las subcategorías (véase la clave completa en la página *I · 1*).

Les symboles de l'index représentent les catégories indiquées dans la légende à droite. Les symboles suivis d'un indice (⩘ 1) représentent des sous-catégories (voir légende complète à la page *I · 1*).

Os símbolos incluídos no texto do índice representam as grandes categorias identificadas com a chave à direita. Os símbolos com números em sua parte superior (⩘ 1) identificam as subcategorias (veja-se a chave completa à página *I · 1*).

Symbol	English	Deutsch	Español	Français	Português
ʌ	Mountain	Berg	Montaña	Montagne	Montanha
⩘	Mountains	Gebirge	Montañas	Montagnes	Montanhas
)(	Pass	Paß	Paso	Col	Passo
V	Valley, Canyon	Tal, Cañon	Valle, Cañón	Vallée, Canyon	Vale, Canhão
≚	Plain	Ebene	Llano	Plaine	Planície
›	Cape	Kap	Cabo	Cap	Cabo
I	Island	Insel	Isla	Île	Ilha
II	Islands	Inseln	Islas	Îles	Ilhas
⫠	Other Topographic Features	Andere Topographische Objekte	Otros Elementos Topográficos	Autres données topographiques	Outros acidentes topográficos

Tall-Tara *I* · *173*

ESPAÑOL — Nombre, Página, Lat.°′, Long.°′ W = Oeste
FRANÇAIS — Nom, Page, Lat.°′, Long.°′ W = Ouest
PORTUGUÊS — Nome, Página, Lat.°′, Long.°′ W = Oeste

Tall al-Abyaḍ 130 36.41 N 38.57 E
Tall al-ʿAmārnah (Akhetatem) ⊥ 142 27.38 N 30.54 E
Tall al-Maskhūtah (Succotah) ⊥ 142 30.33 N 32.07 E
Tall al-Muqayyar (Ur) ⊥ 128 30.57 N 46.09 E
Tallanalla 168a 33.06 S 116.07 E
Tallangatta 166 36.13 S 147.15 E
Tallangatta Creek ≃ 171b 36.15 S 147.13 E
Tallapoosa 194 33.44 N 85.17 W
Tallapoosa ≃ 194 32.30 N 86.16 W
Tallard 62 44.28 N 6.03 E
Talla Reservoir ⊜[1] 46 55.29 N 3.24 W
Tall ar-Ratābah (Pithom) ⊥ 142 30.32 N 32.06 E
Tall ar-Rubʿ (Mendes) ⊥ 142 30.58 N 31.31 E
Tallassee 194 32.32 N 85.53 W
Tall as-Sulṭān ⊥ 132 31.52 N 35.27 E
Tall Banī ʿUmrān 142 27.40 N 30.54 E
Tall Basṭah (Bubastis) ⊥ 142 30.34 N 31.31 E
Tällberg 26 60.49 N 15.00 E
Tall Bīsah 130 34.50 N 36.44 E
Tall-e Khosrow-ye Soflá 128 30.37 N 51.35 E
Talleyville 208 39.48 N 75.32 W
Tallinn 76 59.25 N 24.45 E
Tall Kalakh 130 34.40 N 36.15 E
Tall Kayf 128 36.29 N 43.08 E
Tall Kūjik 130 36.48 N 42.04 E
Tallmadge 214 41.06 N 81.27 W
Tallman 276 41.07 N 74.06 W
Tallman Mountain State Park ♦ 276 41.01 N 73.54 W
Talloires 62 45.51 N 6.13 E
Tallong 170 34.44 S 150.05 E
Tallow 48 52.05 N 8.00 W
Tallowa Dam ◆[6] 170 34.47 S 150.18 E
Tall Rāk 142 30.54 N 31.43 E
Tall Rifʿat 130 36.28 N 37.06 E
Tall Salḥab 130 35.15 N 36.22 E
Tall Tamir 130 36.39 N 40.22 E
Tallula 219 39.56 N 89.56 W
Tallulah 194 32.24 N 91.11 W
Tally 80 53.08 N 53.04 E
Tally Ho 274b 37.52 S 145.09 E
Tālma 126 23.29 N 89.54 E
Talmage, Ca., U.S. 204 39.08 N 123.10 W
Talmage, Ne., U.S. 198 40.31 N 96.01 W
Talmage, Pa., U.S. 208 40.07 N 76.13 W
Talmalmo 171b 35.56 S 147.30 E
Talmas 50 50.02 N 2.20 E
Talmaz 38 46.38 N 29.40 E
Talʼmenka 86 53.51 N 83.35 E
Talmine 46 58.31 N 4.26 W
Talmont 32 46.28 N 1.37 W
Talʼne 78 48.53 N 30.42 E
Talʼniki 88 52.47 N 102.24 E
Talo ʌ 144 10.44 N 37.55 E
Taloda 120 21.34 N 74.13 E
Talofofo 174p 13.21 N 144.45 E
Talofofo Bay c 174p 13.20 N 144.46 E
Taloga 196 36.02 N 98.57 W
Taloje 88 55.24 N 95.40 E
Taloje Budrukh 272c 19.05 N 73.05 E
Talok 112 1.03 N 118.48 E
Talon, Lake ⊜ 190 46.18 N 79.05 W
Talonan, Tano > 115b 9.07 S 117.02 E
Tāloqān 120 36.44 N 69.33 E
Taloro ≃ 71 40.08 N 8.58 E
Talovaja 78 51.06 N 40.44 E
Talovka, Kaz. 80 50.25 N 47.35 E
Talovka, Ross. 80 49.58 N 45.01 E
Talovka, Ross. 84 44.14 N 46.36 E
Talovka, Ross. 86 51.27 N 81.54 E
Talovka, Ross. 86 57.10 N 93.09 E
Talpa 196 31.47 N 99.43 W
Talpa de Allende 234 20.23 N 104.51 W
Talquin, Lake ⊜[1] 192 30.26 N 84.33 W
Tālsa 272b 22.49 N 88.33 E
Talsarnau 42 52.54 N 4.03 W
Talsi 76 57.15 N 22.36 E
Talšik 86 53.42 N 71.53 E
Taltal 252 25.24 S 70.29 W
Taltapin Lake ⊜ 182 54.19 N 125.20 W
Taltson ≃ 176 61.23 N 112.45 W
Talu 112 0.14 N 99.59 E
Taludaa 112 0.20 N 123.28 E
Taluk 112 0.32 S 101.35 E
Talumphuk, Laem > 110 8.30 N 100.10 E
Taluti, Teluk c 164 3.21 S 129.45 E
Talvikʼulʼa 24 68.45 N 29.19 E
Talwandi Bhāi 123 30.51 N 74.56 E
Talwood 166 28.30 S 149.30 E
Taly 78 49.51 N 40.04 E
Ṭalyā 142 30.16 N 31.00 E
Tal-y-bont 42 52.29 N 3.59 W
Tama, Arg. 252 30.31 S 66.32 W
Tama, Nihon 94 35.37 N 139.27 E
Tama, Ia., U.S. 190 41.58 N 92.34 W
Tama ≃ 94 35.32 N 139.47 E
Tama Cemetery ◆ 268 35.41 N 139.31 E
Tamacuarí, Pico ʌ 246 1.15 N 64.45 W
Tamadjert 148 25.36 N 7.20 E
Tamagawa, Nihon 94 37.12 N 140.24 E
Tamagawa, Nihon 96 34.01 N 132.56 E
Tamagawa ◆[8] 268 35.37 N 139.39 E
Tamagawa-josui ≃ 268 35.42 N 139.35 E
Tamakautonga 174v 19.05 S 169.55 W
Tamaki 94 34.29 N 136.38 E
Tāmākośī ≃ 124 27.22 N 85.59 E
Tama-kyūryō ⋏[2] 268 35.35 N 139.30 E
Tamala, Austl. 162 26.42 S 113.45 E
Tamala, Ross. 80 52.33 N 43.16 E
Tamalameque 246 8.52 N 73.49 W
Tamalave, Sierra ⋏ 234 22.45 N 99.15 W
Ṭamalāy 142 30.30 N 30.51 E
Tamale 150 9.25 N 0.50 W
Tamalea 112 2.29 S 119.19 E
Tamalpais, Mount ʌ 226 37.56 N 122.35 W
Tamalpais Valley 226 37.53 N 122.32 W
Tamamura 94 36.18 N 139.07 E
Taman, Indon. 115a 7.25 S 112.41 E
Tamanʼ, Ross. 78 45.13 N 36.43 E
Tamana 92 32.55 N 130.33 E
Tamana I 14 2.29 S 175.59 E
Tamaná, Cerro ʌ 246 5.02 N 76.17 W
Tamana, Mount ʌ[2] 241r 10.28 N 61.12 W
Tamanaco ≃ 246 9.25 N 65.23 W
Tamanan 115a 8.01 S 113.49 E
Tamanar 148 31.00 N 9.35 W
Tamandourirt, Oued V 150 19.39 N 2.04 W
Tamanduateí ≃ 287b 23.36 S 46.35 W
Tamanhint 146 27.13 N 14.36 E
Tamani 150 13.20 N 6.50 W
Tamaniquá 246 2.38 S 65.44 W
Taman Negara ♦ 114 4.43 N 102.23 E
Tamano 96 34.30 N 133.56 E
Tamanquaré, Ilha I 246 0.28 S 64.55 W
Tamanskij zaliv c 78 45.18 N 36.45 E
Tamanthi 110 25.19 N 95.18 E
Tamanusi 112 1.48 S 121.18 E
Tamapatz 234 21.35 N 99.09 W
Tamaqua 208 40.47 N 75.58 W
Tamar ≃, Austl. 166 41.04 S 146.47 E
Tamar ≃, Nepāl 124 26.55 N 87.10 E
Tamar ≃, Eng., U.K. 42 50.22 N 4.10 W
Támara 246 5.50 N 72.10 W
Tamarac ≃ 198 48.29 N 97.07 W
Tamarack Lake ⊜[1] 214 41.35 N 80.05 W
Tamarite de Litera 34 41.52 N 0.26 E
Tamaroa 194 38.08 N 89.14 W
Tamarome 164 2.54 S 133.38 E
Tamarugal, Pampa del ≡ 248 21.00 S 69.25 W
Tamashima 96 34.32 N 133.40 E
Tamási 30 46.38 N 18.18 E
Tamaské 150 14.49 N 5.39 E
Tamatsukuri 94 36.06 N 140.25 E
Tamaulipas □[3] 232 24.00 N 98.45 W
Tamaya ≃ 248 8.31 S 74.13 W
Tamayu 96 35.25 N 133.01 E
Tama Zoological Park ♦ 268 35.39 N 139.24 E
Tamazula 232 24.57 N 106.57 W
Tamazula de Gordiano 234 19.38 N 103.15 W
Tamazulapan del Progreso 234 17.41 N 97.34 W
Tamazunchale 234 21.16 N 98.47 W
Tamba 96 35.09 N 135.25 E
Tambach-Dietharz 54 50.48 N 10.36 E
Tambacounda 150 13.47 N 13.40 W
Tambacounda □[4] 150 14.00 N 13.00 W
Tamba Dabatou 150 11.48 N 10.40 W
Tambak 115a 5.45 S 112.37 E
Tambakboyo 115a 6.48 S 111.50 E
Tamba-kōchi ⋏[1] 92 35.20 N 135.30 E
Tambakrejo 115a 7.16 S 111.36 E
Tambalan 112 3.08 N 115.34 E
Tambangsawah 112 3.02 S 102.11 E
Tambara, Moç. 154 16.45 S 34.15 E
Tambara, Nihon 96 33.54 N 133.04 E
Tāmbaram 122 12.55 N 80.07 E
Tambaú ≃ 256 21.34 S 47.05 W
Tambault, Île à I 275a 45.20 N 73.51 W
Tambea 112 4.12 S 121.36 E
Tambej 74 71.30 N 71.50 E
Tambelan, Kepulauan II 112 1.00 N 107.30 E
Tambelan Besar, Pulau I 112 0.58 N 107.34 E
Tambellup 162 34.02 S 117.39 E
Tamberías 252 31.28 S 69.25 W
Tambisan, Pulau I 116 5.27 N 119.10 E
Tambler 116 6.03 N 125.09 E
Tambo, Austl. 166 24.53 S 146.15 E
Tambo, Perú 248 12.56 S 74.01 W
Tambo ≃, Austl. 166 37.51 S 147.48 E
Tambo ≃, Perú 248 17.10 S 71.51 W
Tambo ≃, Perú 248 10.43 S 73.45 W
Tamboara 255 23.09 S 52.33 W
Tambo Grande 248 4.56 S 80.21 W
Tambohorano 157b 17.30 S 43.58 E
Tamboli 112 3.57 S 121.20 E
Tambolongang, Pulau I 112 6.36 S 120.24 E
Tambopata ≃ 248 12.36 S 69.11 W
Tambor 236 9.43 N 85.01 W
Tambora, Gunung ʌ 115b 8.14 S 117.55 E
Tamboril 250 4.50 S 40.20 W
Tamborine 171a 27.53 S 153.08 E
Tamborine Mountain ʌ[2] 171a 27.55 S 153.10 E
Tamboritha, Mount ʌ 166 37.28 S 146.41 E
Tamboryacu ≃ 246 2.31 S 73.40 W
Tambov 80 52.43 N 41.25 E
Tambovka, Ross. 80 47.18 N 47.23 E
Tambovka, Ross. 89 50.06 N 128.04 E
Tambov Oblastʼ □[4] 80 52.45 N 41.30 E
Tambre ≃ 34 42.49 N 8.53 W
Tambu 112 0.02 S 119.52 E
Tambu, Teluk c 112 0.02 N 119.45 E
Tambulian Point > 116 7.22 N 123.27 E
Tambunan 112 5.40 N 116.22 E
Tambura 140 5.36 N 27.28 E
Tamchaket 150 17.15 N 10.40 W
Tam Chuak, Laem > 110 8.33 N 98.12 E
Tamdhas 124 28.04 N 83.14 E
Tame 246 6.28 N 71.44 W
Tame ≃ 262 53.25 N 2.09 W
Tameapa 232 25.39 N 107.22 W
Tamedda, Djebel ʌ 148 32.48 N 0.05 E
Tâmega ≃ 34 41.05 N 8.21 W
Tameghza 148 34.23 N 7.57 E
Tamel Aike 254 48.19 S 70.58 W
Tamelelt 148 31.50 N 7.29 W
Tamenghest 148 22.56 N 5.30 E
Tamenghest, Oued V 148 22.10 N 0.10 E
Tamenuen 164 6.27 S 139.48 E
Tamerton Foliot 42 50.26 N 4.08 W
Tamesí ≃ 234 22.13 N 97.52 W
Tameside □[8] 262 53.29 N 2.03 W
Tamga, Kyrg. 85 42.09 N 77.32 E
Tamga, Ross. 89 45.34 N 133.36 E
Tamgak, Monts ⋏ 150 19.11 N 8.42 E
Tamgué, Massif du ⋏ 150 12.00 N 12.18 W
Tamiahua 234 21.16 N 97.27 W
Tamiahua, Laguna de c 234 21.35 N 97.35 W
Tamiami Canal ≊ 220 25.47 N 80.15 W
Tamiang ≃ 114 4.25 N 98.16 E
Tamica 24 64.10 N 38.05 E
Tamil Harbor c 174q 9.30 N 138.09 E
Tamil Nādu □[3] 122 11.00 N 78.15 E
Tamiment 210 41.09 N 75.02 W
Tamina 222 30.11 N 96.26 W
Tamir 88 50.24 N 107.25 E
Tamiryn ≃ 88 47.48 N 102.36 E
Tamiš (Timiș) ≃ 38 44.51 N 20.39 E
Tamitatoala ≃ 255 11.56 S 53.36 W
Ṭāmīyah 142 29.29 N 30.58 E
Tamkūhi 124 26.41 N 84.11 E
Tam Ky 110 15.34 N 108.29 E
Tamlūk 126 22.18 N 87.55 E
Tāmma 120 25.11 N 93.42 E
Tammaro ≃ 68 41.09 N 14.50 E
Tammerfors → Tampere 26 61.30 N 23.45 E
Tammisaari → Ekenäs 26 59.58 N 23.26 E
Tamms 194 37.14 N 89.16 W
Ṭammūh 273c 29.56 N 31.16 E
Tāmna 126 23.15 N 86.21 E
Tämnarån ≃ 40 60.31 N 17.39 E
Tämnaren ⊜ 40 60.10 N 17.20 E
Tamnum 144 15.07 N 50.49 E
Tamon ◆[8] 270 34.39 N 135.04 E
Tampa, Ang. 152 15.30 S 13.27 E
Tampa, Fl., U.S. 220 27.56 N 82.27 W
Tampa Bay c 220 27.45 N 82.35 W
Tampa International Airport ⊠ 220 27.59 N 82.32 W
Tampamachoco, Laguna c 234 21.00 N 97.21 W
Tampang 112 5.54 S 104.43 E
Tampaón ≃ 234 21.59 N 98.36 W
Tamparan 116 8.27 N 117.13 E
Tampere 26 61.30 N 23.45 E
Tampico, Méx. 234 22.13 N 97.51 W
Tampico, Il., U.S. 190 41.37 N 89.47 W
Tampico, In., U.S. 218 38.48 N 85.58 W
Tampin 114 2.28 N 102.14 E
Tampiquito 234 23.52 N 98.14 W
Tampulonanjing, Gunung ʌ 114 1.46 N 99.24 E
Tam Quan 110 14.35 N 109.03 E
Tamra 132 32.51 N 35.12 E
Tamrau, Pegunungan ⋏ 164 0.30 S 132.27 E
Tamri 148 30.43 N 9.43 W
Tamsagbulag 88 47.14 N 117.21 E
Tamsalu 76 59.10 N 26.06 E
Tamshiyacu 246 4.05 S 72.58 W
Tamsweg 64 47.08 N 13.48 E
Tamu 110 24.13 N 94.18 E
Tamuín 234 21.59 N 98.45 W
Tamuk Island I 116 6.27 N 121.49 E
Tamuning 174p 13.29 N 144.46 E
Tamura 268 35.22 N 139.22 E
Tamusuke 85 38.03 N 76.53 E
Tamworth, Austl. 166 31.05 S 150.55 E
Tamworth, On., Can. 212 44.29 N 77.00 W
Tamworth, Eng., U.K. 42 52.39 N 1.40 W
Tamyang 98 35.21 N 126.58 E
Tan ≃ 100 23.57 N 115.47 E
Tana, Chile 248 19.27 S 69.57 W
Tana, Nor. 24 70.28 N 28.18 E
Tana ≃, Cuba 240p 20.42 N 77.25 W
Tana ≃, Kenya 154 2.32 S 40.31 E
Tʼan a ≃, Ross. 88 58.40 N 120.30 E
Tana, Lake ⊜ 144 12.00 N 37.20 E
Tanabe, Nihon 96 34.49 N 135.46 E
Tanabe, Nihon 96 33.44 N 135.22 E
Tanabi 255 20.37 S 49.37 W
Tanacross 180 63.23 N 143.21 W
Tanafjorden c[2] 24 70.54 N 28.40 E
Tanaga Island I 180 51.50 N 178.00 W
Tanaga Volcano ʌ[1] 180 51.53 N 178.09 W
Tanagro ≃ 68 40.38 N 15.14 E
Tanaguarena 286c 10.37 N 66.49 W
Tanagura 94 37.02 N 140.23 E
Tanah, Tanjung > 115a 6.29 S 108.32 E
Tanahbala, Pulau I 110 0.25 S 98.25 E
Tanahgrogot 112 1.55 S 116.12 E
Tanahjampea, Pulau I 112 7.05 S 120.42 E
Tanahmasa, Pulau I 110 0.12 S 98.27 E
Tanahmerah, Indon. 112 3.41 N 117.31 E
Tanahmerah, Indon. 164 6.05 S 140.17 E
Tanah Merah, Malay. 114 5.48 N 102.09 E
Tanah Merah, Malay. 114 2.36 N 101.48 E
Tanahputih 114 1.41 N 101.03 E
Tanaka ◆[8] 270 34.42 N 134.59 E
Tanakeke, Pulau I 112 5.30 S 119.16 E
Tanakpur 124 29.05 N 80.07 E
Tanʿam 128 23.09 N 56.29 E
Tanami 162 19.59 S 129.43 E
Tanami Desert ◆[2] 162 20.00 S 129.30 E
Ṭanān, Miṣr 142 30.15 N 31.14 E
Tan An, Viet 110 8.46 N 105.11 E
Tan An, Viet 110 10.32 N 106.25 E
Tanana 180 65.10 N 152.05 W
Tanana ≃ 180 65.09 N 151.55 W
Tananarive → Antananarivo 157b 18.55 S 47.31 E
Tanapag 174n 15.14 N 145.45 E
Tanapag, Lagunan c 174n 15.14 N 145.44 E
Tanaro ≃ 62 45.01 N 8.47 E
Tanārūt, Wādī V 146 30.08 N 9.59 E
Tanashi 94 35.44 N 139.33 E
Tanat ≃ 42 52.46 N 3.07 W
Tanauan 116 11.07 N 125.01 E
Tanbar 166 25.50 S 141.55 E
Ṭanbidī 142 28.38 N 30.47 E
Tan Binh 269c 10.48 N 106.40 E
Tanbu, Zhg. 98 35.51 N 118.17 E
Tanbu, Zhg. 100 28.08 N 114.12 E
Tancarville 50 49.29 N 0.28 E
Tancarville, Canal de ≊ 50 49.28 N 0.28 E
Tancha 174m 26.28 N 127.50 E
Tan Chau 110 10.48 N 105.15 E
Tancheng 98 34.37 N 118.23 E
Tanchoj 88 51.33 N 105.07 E
Tanchʼŏn 98 40.27 N 128.54 E
Tancítaro 234 19.20 N 102.22 W
Tancítaro, Pico de ʌ 234 19.23 N 102.13 W
Tancochapa ≃ 234 17.59 N 94.04 W
Tanda, C. Iv. 150 7.48 N 3.10 W
Tānda, India 123 31.42 N 75.38 E
Tānda, India 124 28.59 N 78.56 E
Tānda, India 124 26.33 N 82.39 E
Tānda, Pāk. 123 32.42 N 74.22 E
Tandag 116 9.04 N 126.12 E
Tandah 142 27.41 N 30.46 E
Tandai 154 19.36 S 32.48 E
Tandaj 80 47.33 N 51.30 E
Tandala 154 9.23 S 34.14 E
Tandaltī 140 13.01 N 31.52 E
Țăndărei 38 44.38 N 27.40 E
Tandaué 152 17.00 S 18.06 E
Tandian 98 40.39 N 124.46 E
Tandil 252 37.19 S 59.09 W
Tandjilé □[5] 146 9.45 N 16.30 E
Tandjilé ≃ 146 9.45 N 15.50 E
Tāndliānwāla 123 31.02 N 73.08 E
Tando Ādam 120 25.46 N 68.40 E
Tando Allāhyār 120 25.28 N 68.43 E
Tando Bāgo 120 24.47 N 68.58 E
Tando Muhammad Khān 120 25.08 N 68.32 E
Tandou Bougou 152 3.32 S 10.53 E
Tandou Lake ⊜ 166 32.38 S 142.05 E
Tandovo, ozero ⊜ 86 55.07 N 78.02 E
Tando Zinze 152 5.22 S 12.26 E
Tandragee 48 54.20 N 6.25 W
Tandridge 260 51.14 N 0.02 W
Tandridge □[8] 260 51.17 N 0.05 W
Tandslet 41 54.55 N 9.59 E
Tandubas 116 5.10 N 120.20 E
Tandubatu Island I 116 5.13 N 120.17 E
Tandula Tank ⊜[1] 122 20.40 N 81.12 E
Tandun 112 0.36 N 100.38 E
Tāndūr 122 17.14 N 77.35 E
Tanduy ≃ 115a 7.41 S 108.47 E
Taneatua 172 38.04 S 177.01 E
Tanega-shima I 93b 30.40 N 131.00 E
Taneichi 92 40.26 N 141.43 E
Tan Emellel 148 27.30 N 9.45 E
Tanete 112 4.32 S 119.36 E
Taneum Creek ≃ 224 47.10 N 120.40 W
Tanew ≃ 30 50.31 N 22.16 E
Taneytown 208 39.39 N 77.10 W
Tanezrouft ◆[2] 148 24.00 N 0.45 W
Tanezzuft, Wādī V 146 25.51 N 10.19 E
Tanforan Park ◆[9] 282 37.38 N 122.25 W
Tang ≃, Zhg. 98 38.45 N 115.35 E
Tang ≃, Zhg. 100 32.09 N 112.25 E
Tang ≃, Zhg. 100 33.18 N 117.46 E
Tang ≃, Zhg. 104 41.15 N 123.21 E
Tang ≃, Zhg. 105 40.43 N 116.38 E
Tanga, Ross. 88 51.02 N 111.33 E
Tånga, Sve. 41 56.12 N 12.46 E
Tanga, Tan. 154 5.04 S 39.06 E
Tanga □[4] 154 5.00 S 38.15 E
Tangail 124 24.15 N 89.55 E
Tangainony 157b 22.42 S 47.45 E
Tanga Islands II 14 3.30 S 153.15 E
Tanga Langua > 241k 12.14 N 61.39 W
Tangalla 122 6.01 N 80.48 E
Tangamong Lake ⊜ 212 44.43 N 77.51 W
Tangancícuaro [de Arista] 234 19.54 N 102.08 W
Tanganika, Lago → Tanganyika, Lake ⊜ 154 6.00 S 29.30 E
Tanganjika-See → Tanganyika, Lake ⊜ 154 6.00 S 29.30 E
Tanganyika, Lake ⊜ 154 6.00 S 29.30 E
Tangarana ≃ 246 3.02 S 75.08 W
Tangarare 175e 9.35 S 159.39 E
Tanga-shima I 96 34.40 N 134.35 E
Tangba 107 30.00 N 105.46 E
Tangchi 89 47.00 N 123.46 E
Tangchigou 104 41.04 N 124.11 E
Tangcun, Zhg. 100 29.50 N 118.54 E
Tangcun, Zhg. 100 25.26 N 113.10 E
Tangdaohe 98 40.38 N 118.58 E
Tanger (Tangier) 148 35.48 N 5.45 W
Tanger □[4] 148 35.35 N 5.50 W
Tanger ≃ 54 52.33 N 11.59 E
Tangerang 115a 6.11 S 106.37 E
Tangerhütte 54 52.26 N 11.48 E
Tangerine 220 28.47 N 81.38 W
Tangʼerli 105 39.09 N 116.43 E
Tangermünde 54 52.32 N 11.58 E
Tangfang, Zhg. 102 27.00 N 101.08 E
Tangfang, Zhg. 104 41.20 N 120.34 E
Tangfang, Zhg. 105 39.29 N 118.01 E
Tangfangqiao 106 31.45 N 120.50 E
Tangfeng 98 38.07 N 115.30 E
Tanggangzi 104 41.01 N 122.54 E
Tanggeasinua, Pegunungan ⋏ 112 3.24 S 121.42 E
Tanggengtou 106 30.55 N 119.03 E
Tanggou 100 33.59 N 118.57 E
Tanggu 105 39.01 N 117.40 E
Tangguantun 98 38.43 N 116.55 E
Tanggul 115a 8.10 S 113.26 E
Tanggulashan (Tuotuoheyan) 120 34.05 N 92.45 E
Tanggula Shan ⋏ 120 33.00 N 92.00 E
Tanggula Shankou)(120 32.59 N 91.45 E
Tanggushiluke 120 38.45 N 80.55 E
Tanghe 100 32.43 N 112.48 E
Tanghekou 105 40.44 N 116.38 E
Tanghu 105 39.11 N 115.24 E
Tanghuang 106 31.41 N 119.25 E
Tangi 123 34.18 N 71.40 E
Tangier, N.S., Can. 186 44.48 N 62.42 W
Tangier → Tanger, Magreb 148 35.48 N 5.45 W
Tangier, Va., U.S. 208 37.49 N 75.59 W
Tangier Island I 208 37.50 N 76.00 W
Tangier Sound ʯ 208 38.02 N 75.58 W
Tangijatuo 107 29.36 N 106.39 E
Tangipahoa ≃ 194 30.20 N 90.18 W
Tangjia 100 22.23 N 113.36 E
Tangjiagou 100 30.48 N 117.28 E
Tangjiang 100 25.51 N 114.44 E
Tangjiapao 104 41.59 N 122.14 E
Tangjiaqiao 106 31.24 N 119.12 E
Tangjin 98 36.54 N 126.37 E
Tangjiqiaozhen 106 31.13 N 121.31 E
Tangkahan 112 1.36 S 113.52 E
Tangkak 114 2.16 N 102.33 E
Tangkou 100 30.06 N 118.11 E
Tanglad 115b 8.47 S 115.35 E
Tanglewood, Fl., U.S. 220 26.37 N 81.53 W
Tanglewood, Tx., U.S. 222 30.30 N 96.59 W
Tanglewood ♦ 207 42.21 N 73.20 W
Tangling 100 26.14 N 119.24 E
Tanglitun 104 41.45 N 123.57 E
Tangmai 102 30.08 N 95.08 E
Tangmarg 123 34.02 N 74.26 E
Tangmazhai 104 41.10 N 122.44 E
Tang Nhon Phu 269c 10.50 N 106.47 E
Tang-ni 98 34.12 N 126.52 E
Tango 96 35.44 N 135.06 E
Tango-hantō >[1] 96 35.40 N 135.10 E
Tangowahine 172 35.52 S 173.56 E
Tangpu, Zhg. 100 29.51 N 120.47 E
Tangpu, Zhg. 100 28.28 N 114.58 E
Tangqi 106 30.29 N 120.11 E
Tangqiao 106 31.13 N 119.15 E
Tangra Yumco ⊜ 120 31.00 N 86.20 E
Tangsanying 98 41.38 N 117.40 E
Tangschan → Tangshan 105 39.38 N 118.11 E
Tangse 114 5.01 N 95.55 E
Tangshan, Zhg. 105 40.10 N 116.22 E
Tangshan, Zhg. 105 39.38 N 118.11 E
Tangshan, Zhg. 106 32.05 N 119.03 E
Tang Shan ʌ 106 32.03 N 119.02 E
Tangshi 106 31.33 N 120.51 E
Tangtou, Zhg. 98 35.16 N 118.35 E
Tangtou, Zhg. 102 27.42 N 108.17 E
Tangtou, Zhg. 106 31.38 N 120.19 E
Tangtouxia 100 22.50 N 114.06 E
Tangtse 120 34.02 N 78.11 E
Tanguá 256 22.44 S 42.43 W
Tangub 116 8.03 N 123.44 E
Tanguiéta 150 10.37 N 1.16 E
Tanguip Point > 116 7.43 N 126.32 E
Tanguj 88 55.23 N 100.58 E
Tangulbei 154 0.48 N 36.17 E
Tangusu, Telukan c 116 5.27 N 119.03 E
Tangwang ≃ 89 46.40 N 129.54 E
Tangxi 100 29.04 N 119.23 E
Tangxian 98 38.45 N 114.58 E
Tangxianzhen 100 31.59 N 113.07 E
Tangyan 110 22.29 N 98.24 E
Tangyi 98 36.32 N 115.47 E
Tangyin, Zhg. 98 35.55 N 114.21 E
Tangyin, Zhg. 100 27.32 N 116.16 E
Tangyuan 89 46.42 N 129.55 E
Tangzha 106 32.05 N 120.49 E
Tanhuato 234 20.17 N 102.20 W
Taniantaweng Shan ⋏ 102 30.00 N 98.00 E
Tanigami ◆[8] 270 34.46 N 135.10 E
Tanigawa-dake ʌ 94 36.50 N 138.56 E
Tanigumi 94 35.31 N 136.36 E
Tanimbar, Kepulauan II 164 7.30 S 131.30 E
Taninges 58 46.07 N 6.36 E
Tanintharyi □[8] 110 12.00 N 99.00 E
Tanır 130 38.26 N 36.55 E
Tanis (Zoan) ⊥ 142 30.57 N 31.53 E
Tanishpa ʌ 120 31.10 N 68.24 E
Tanjay 116 9.31 N 123.09 E
Tanjiafang 98 36.41 N 118.36 E
Tanjiahe 100 31.58 N 113.56 E
Tanjiang 100 24.07 N 116.32 E
Tanjiaqiao 100 30.11 N 118.15 E
Tanjil ≃ 169 38.08 S 146.17 E
Tanjong Dawai 114 5.41 N 100.22 E
Tanjong Malim 114 3.41 N 101.31 E
Tanjore → Thanjāvūr 122 10.48 N 79.09 E
Tanjung, Indon. 112 2.11 S 115.23 E
Tanjung, Indon. 115a 6.52 S 108.52 E
Tanjung, Indon. 115b 8.21 S 116.09 E
Tanjungbalai 114 2.58 N 99.48 E
Tanjungbatu, Indon. 112 0.45 N 117.26 E
Tanjungbatu, Indon. 112 2.17 N 118.05 E
Tanjungbatu, Indon. 112 0.38 N 103.26 E
Tanjungenim 112 3.45 S 103.48 E
Tanjungkarang-Telukbetung 115a 5.27 S 105.16 E
Tanjunglabu 112 2.57 S 106.54 E
Tanjungmedan, Indon. 114 1.26 N 100.34 E
Tanjungmedan, Indon. 114 2.06 N 100.14 E
Tanjungmengedar 114 2.39 N 100.01 E
Tanjungpandan 112 2.45 S 107.39 E
Tanjungpinang 112 0.55 N 104.27 E
Tanjungpriok ◆[8] 269e 6.06 S 106.53 E
Tanjungpura 114 3.54 N 98.26 E
Tanjungpusu 112 0.01 S 113.30 E
Tanjungraja 112 3.21 S 104.40 E
Tanjungredep 112 2.09 N 117.29 E
Tanjungsamak 114 0.52 N 103.03 E
Tanjungselor 112 2.51 N 117.22 E
Tanjungslamat 114 3.49 N 98.20 E
Tanjunguban 112 1.03 N 104.14 E
Tānk 120 32.13 N 70.23 E
Tan Kena 148 26.33 N 9.35 E
Tan Kien 269c 10.42 N 106.35 E
Tankou 100 25.48 N 114.50 E
Tankwa ≃ 158 32.20 S 19.33 E
Tanlay 50 47.50 N 4.05 E
Tann, Dtsch. 56 50.38 N 10.01 E
Tann, Dtsch. 60 48.19 N 12.54 E
Tanna 54 50.30 N 11.51 E
Tanna I 175f 19.30 S 169.20 E
Tannan 96 35.05 N 135.10 E
Tännäs 26 62.27 N 12.40 E
Tanna-tunnel ◆[5] 94 35.06 N 139.00 E
Tannay 50 47.21 N 3.36 E
Tanne 54 51.41 N 10.42 E
Tannenberg → Stębark 30 53.30 N 20.08 E
Tannenbergsthal 54 50.26 N 12.27 E
Tanner 194 34.43 N 86.58 W
Tanner, Mount ʌ 182 49.40 N 118.34 W
Tannersville, N.Y., U.S. 210 42.12 N 74.08 W
Tannersville, Pa., U.S. 210 41.03 N 75.18 W
Tännesberg 60 49.32 N 12.20 E
Tännforsen ʟ 26 63.27 N 12.44 E
Tannhausen 56 48.59 N 10.21 E
Tannheim 58 47.30 N 10.31 E
Tannila 26 65.29 N 25.59 E
Tannis Bugt c 26 57.40 N 10.15 E
Tannroda 54 50.52 N 11.15 E
Tannu-Ola, chrebet ⋏ 74 51.00 N 94.00 E
Tannūrah, Raʼs > 128 26.40 N 50.30 E
Tano, Nihon 96 33.26 N 134.00 E
Tano, Nihon 270 34.57 N 135.36 E
Tano ≃ 150 5.07 N 2.56 W
Tanon Strait ʯ 116 10.20 N 123.30 E
Tânout 150 14.58 N 8.53 E
Tanpok ≃ 250 3.27 N 54.00 W
Tanque de Dolores 234 23.40 N 101.10 W
Tanque Grande, Ribeirão ≃ 287b 23.25 S 46.28 W
Tan Qui Dong 269c 10.44 N 106.42 E
Tanquinho 255 11.58 S 39.06 W
Tʼanʼ Šanʼ → Tien Shan ⋏ 90 42.00 N 80.00 E
Tansania → Tanzania □[1] 154 6.00 S 35.00 E
Tansboro 285 39.46 N 74.55 W
Tānsen 124 27.52 N 83.33 E
Tanshui 100 25.10 N 121.26 E
Tanshui ≃ 100 25.11 N 121.25 E
Tansilla 150 12.26 N 4.23 W
Tánsin, Isla de I 236 15.17 N 83.54 W
Tánsin, Laguna de c 236 15.19 N 83.58 W
Tan Son Nhut Airport ⊠ 269c 10.49 N 106.40 E
Tansyk 86 47.20 N 79.52 E
Ṭanṭā 142 30.47 N 31.00 E
Tantabogue Creek ≃ 222 31.00 N 95.21 W
Tan-Tan 148 28.26 N 11.06 W
Tan-Tan □[4] 148 28.05 N 11.00 W
Tantangara Reservoir ⊜[1] 171b 35.45 S 148.39 E
Tan Thoi Nhut 269c 10.50 N 106.36 E
Tan Thuan Dong 269c 10.45 N 106.44 E
Tāntipāra 126 23.54 N 87.22 E
Tantō 96 35.29 N 135.00 E
Tantonville 58 48.28 N 6.08 E
Tantou, Zhg. 100 29.07 N 121.09 E
Tantou, Zhg. 100 26.03 N 119.35 E
Tantou, Zhg. 100 26.53 N 115.26 E
Tantou Shan I 100 29.11 N 122.01 E
Tantoyuca 234 21.21 N 98.14 W
Tanuku 122 16.45 N 81.42 E
Tanuma 94 36.22 N 139.35 E
Tanumshede 26 58.44 N 11.19 E
Tanunda 168b 34.32 S 138.57 E
Tanʼurer ≃ 180 64.44 N 174.15 E
Tanushimaru 96 33.21 N 130.41 E
Tanvald 30 50.45 N 15.19 E
Tanwax Creek ≃ 224 46.52 N 122.27 W
Tanworth-in-Arden 42 52.20 N 1.50 W
Tanxi 100 28.58 N 115.38 E
Tanxia 100 23.58 N 115.34 E
Tanxu Shan I 106 30.37 N 121.37 E
Tanyang 98 36.57 N 128.21 E
Tanyeri 130 39.37 N 39.50 E
Tanyi 98 35.14 N 118.09 E
Tanymas ≃ 85 38.25 N 72.39 E
Tanzania □[1], Afr. 138 6.00 S 35.00 E
Tanzania □[1], Afr. 154 6.00 S 35.00 E
Tanzanie → Tanzania □[1] 154 6.00 S 35.00 E
Tanzawa-Ōyama-kokutei-kōen ♦ 94 35.30 N 139.10 E
Tanzawa-san ʌ 94 35.28 N 139.10 E
Tao ≃, Zhg. 100 25.56 N 115.06 E
Tao ≃, Zhg. 102 35.52 N 103.16 E
Tao, Ko I 110 10.05 N 99.52 E
Taoʼan 89 45.22 N 122.47 E
Taochong 100 31.04 N 118.06 E
Taochuan 102 25.07 N 111.06 E
Taocun 98 37.10 N 121.05 E
Taodigou 105 40.52 N 116.14 E
Taoʼer ≃ 89 45.42 N 124.05 E
Taoerdeng 98 40.44 N 119.02 E
Taohe 105 39.12 N 116.50 E
Taohua 106 31.23 N 120.04 E
Taohuachiyingzi 104 42.18 N 121.06 E
Taohua Dao I 100 29.48 N 122.17 E
Taohuanbuligai 104 42.13 N 122.14 E
Taohuatu 104 41.40 N 120.40 E
Taohuayuan 106 30.34 N 118.42 E
Taohuazhen 105 40.04 N 114.59 E
Taojiagou 107 29.48 N 104.48 E
Taojiahe 100 30.55 N 115.56 E
Taojialiang 104 42.36 N 121.25 E
Taolahusu 98 42.34 N 116.48 E
Taolaizhao 89 44.51 N 125.57 E
Taolakepa 120 32.05 N 85.22 E
Taole 102 38.46 N 106.40 E
Taolin 98 34.30 N 118.30 E
Taoling 100 30.21 N 118.16 E
Taoluo 98 35.17 N 119.24 E
Tʼaonan → Taoʼan 89 45.22 N 122.47 E
Taongi I[1] 14 14.37 N 168.58 E
Taormina 70 37.51 N 15.17 E
Taos, Mo., U.S. 219 38.30 N 92.04 W
Taos, N.M., U.S. 200 36.24 N 105.34 W
Taos Pueblo 200 36.26 N 105.32 W
Taoudenni 148 22.40 N 4.00 W
Taougrite 34 36.15 N 0.55 E
Taounate 148 34.25 N 4.39 W
Taounate □[4] 148 34.30 N 4.40 W
Taoura 36 36.09 N 8.03 E
Taourirt 148 34.25 N 2.53 W
Taourirt ʌ 148 24.03 N 5.02 E
Taoussa 150 16.55 N 0.35 W
Taowu 106 31.47 N 118.46 E
Taoxi, Zhg. 100 31.33 N 117.00 E
Taoxi, Zhg. 100 25.18 N 116.05 E
Taoxi, Zhg. 100 28.44 N 119.36 E
Taoxiantun 104 41.39 N 123.27 E
Taoyuan, Zhg. 100 25.48 N 117.32 E
Taoyuan, Zhg. 102 28.46 N 111.20 E
Taozhu 100 28.50 N 121.31 E
Taozhuang 106 30.58 N 120.48 E
Tapa, Eesti 76 59.16 N 25.58 E
Tapa, India 123 30.19 N 75.21 E
Tapaan Island I 116 5.28 N 120.44 E
Tapacari 248 17.31 S 66.36 W
Tapachula 232 14.54 N 92.17 W
Tapaga, Cape > 175a 14.01 S 171.23 W
Tapah 114 4.11 N 101.16 E
Tapah Road 114 4.10 N 101.12 E
Tapaje ≃ 246 2.44 N 78.07 W
Tapajós ≃ 250 2.24 S 54.41 W
Tapaktuan 114 3.16 N 97.11 E
Tapalpa 234 19.57 N 103.46 W
Tapalqué 252 36.21 S 60.01 W
Tapan 112 2.10 S 101.04 E
Tapanahony ≃ 250 4.22 N 54.27 W
Tapanui 172 45.57 S 169.16 E
Tapanuli, Teluk c 114 1.38 N 98.45 E
Tapasi 126 23.40 N 87.08 E
Tapauá 248 5.45 S 63.04 W
Tapauá ≃ 248 5.40 S 64.21 W
Tapawera 172 41.24 S 172.49 E
Tapaz 116 11.16 N 122.32 E
Tapejara 252 28.04 S 52.00 W
Tapera 252 28.38 S 52.52 W
Taperas 248 17.54 S 60.23 W
Taperoá, Bra. 250 7.12 S 36.49 W
Taperoá, Bra. 255 13.31 S 39.06 W
Tapes 252 30.40 S 51.23 W
Tapeta 150 6.29 N 8.51 W
Taphan Hin 110 16.13 N 100.26 E
Taphoen ≃ 110 14.07 N 99.25 E
Tāpi ≃, India 120 21.06 N 72.41 E
Ta Pi ≃, Thai 110 9.05 N 99.12 E
Tapiales 288 34.42 S 58.31 W
Tapiantana Channel ʯ 116 6.23 N 122.00 E
Tapiantana Group II 116 6.20 N 122.00 E
Tapiantana Island I 116 6.18 N 121.59 E
Tapiche ≃ 248 4.59 S 73.51 W
Tapili 154 3.25 N 27.40 E
Tapilula 234 17.14 N 93.02 W
Taping (Daying) ≃ 102 24.17 N 97.14 E
Tapini 164 8.20 S 147.00 E
Tapiraí 255 19.52 S 46.01 W
Tapirapé ≃ 250 10.41 S 50.38 W
Tapiratiba 256 21.28 S 46.45 W
Tapis, Gunong ʌ 114 4.03 N 102.54 E
Tapiutan Island I 116 11.12 N 119.16 E
Tapiwa 174d 0.52 S 169.35 E
Taplan National Park ♦ 110 14.20 N 102.20 E
Tāplejungg 124 27.21 N 87.40 E
Tapoa ≃ 150 12.36 N 2.29 E
Tapol 146 8.31 N 15.35 E
Tapolca 30 46.53 N 17.27 E
Tappahannock 208 37.55 N 76.51 W
Tappal 124 28.03 N 77.35 E
Tappan 210 41.01 N 73.56 W
Tappan, Lake ⊜[1] 276 41.01 N 73.59 W
Tappan Lake ⊜[1] 214 40.21 N 81.11 W
Tappan Zee c 276 41.06 N 73.53 W
Tappan Zee Bridge ◆[5] 276 41.04 N 73.54 W
Tappen 198 46.52 N 99.38 W
Tappernøje 41 55.10 N 11.59 E
Tappi-zaki > 92 41.15 N 140.21 E
Tappo 150 10.12 N 2.38 W
Tapps, Lake ⊜ 224 47.13 N 122.09 W
Tapsiā ◆[8] 272b 22.32 N 88.22 E
Tapuaenuku ʌ 172 42.00 S 173.40 E
Tapuio ≃ 250 3.41 S 44.16 W
Tapul Group II 116 5.30 N 121.00 E
Tapul Island I 116 5.43 N 120.55 E
Tapun 110 18.22 N 95.27 E
Tapurucuara 246 0.24 S 65.02 W
Taputapu, Cape > 174u 14.19 S 170.50 W
Taqāṭuʿ Hayyā 140 18.20 N 36.22 E
Taqian 100 29.03 N 117.03 E
Taqiao, Zhg. 100 31.28 N 118.25 E
Taqiao, Zhg. 100 28.24 N 117.02 E
Ṭaqṭaq 128 35.53 N 44.35 E
Taquara 252 29.39 S 50.47 W
Taquara ◆[8] 287a 22.55 S 43.21 W
Taquara, Serra da ʌ 256 22.12 S 43.53 W
Taquaras, Ponta das > 252 27.01 S 48.34 W
Taquari, Bra. 252 29.48 S 51.51 W
Taquari, Bra. 255 17.50 S 53.17 W
Taquari ≃, Bra. 248 19.15 S 57.17 W
Taquari ≃, Bra. 252 29.56 S 51.44 W
Taquari, Pantanal do ≡ 248 18.20 S 56.30 W
Taquaritinga 255 21.24 S 48.30 W
Taquaruçu ≃, Bra. 248 20.30 S 55.49 W
Taquaruçu ≃, Bra. 255 21.35 S 52.07 W
Tar ≃, Kyrg. 85 40.38 N 73.26 E
Tar ≃, N.C., U.S. 192 35.33 N 77.05 W
Tara, Austl. 166 27.17 S 150.28 E
Tara, On., Can. 212 44.28 N 81.09 W
Tara, Ross. 86 56.54 N 74.22 E
Tara, Zam. 154 16.56 S 26.47 E
Tara ⋏ 38 43.55 N 19.25 E
Tara ≃, Europe 38 43.21 N 18.51 E
Tara ≃, Ross. 86 56.42 N 74.36 E
Taraba ≃ 146 8.30 N 10.15 E
Tarabine, Oued ti-n- V 148 20.50 N 7.25 E
Tarabuco 248 19.10 S 64.57 W
Ṭarābulus (Tripoli), Lībiyā 146 32.54 N 13.11 E
Ṭarābulus (Tripoli), Lubnān 130 34.26 N 35.51 E
Ṭarābulus (Tripolitania) □[9] 146 31.00 N 15.00 E
Tarabusi Creek ≃ 281 42.24 N 83.19 W
Tarabya ◆[8] 267b 41.08 N 29.03 E
Tarach ≃ 154 4.09 N 34.56 E
Taraclia, Mol. 38 46.34 N 29.06 E
Taraclia, Mol. 38 45.54 N 28.38 E
Taradale 172 39.32 S 176.51 E
Taragaj ≃ 85 41.35 N 77.42 E
Tarāghin 146 25.59 N 14.26 E
Tarago 170 35.04 S 149.39 E
Tara Hills 282 38.00 N 122.19 W
Tarai ≡ 124 26.35 N 86.40 E
Taraia 124 26.05 N 84.53 E
Taraira (Traíra) ≃ 246 1.04 S 69.26 W
Tara Island I 116 12.17 N 120.22 E
Taraju 115a 7.27 S 107.59 E
Tarakan 112 3.18 N 117.38 E
Tarakan, Pulau I 112 3.21 N 117.36 E
Tarakanovka 82 55.07 N 35.44 E
Tārakeshwar 126 22.54 N 88.02 E
Taraklı 130 40.24 N 30.29 E
Taralga 170 34.24 S 149.49 E
Tarama 175d 24.40 N 124.41 E
Taramakau ≃ 172 42.34 S 171.08 E
Taramana 112 8.10 S 124.51 E
Tarama-shima I 175d 24.39 N 124.42 E
Tarana 170 33.32 S 149.54 E
Tārānagar 123 28.41 N 75.02 E
Taranaki, Mount ʌ 172 39.18 S 174.04 E
Tarancón 34 40.01 N 3.00 W
Tarandacuao 234 19.59 N 100.32 W
Taranga Island I 172 35.58 S 174.43 E
Tarangire National Park ♦ 154 4.00 S 36.00 E
Tarangnan 116 11.54 N 124.45 E
Tarango, Presa ⊜[1] 286a 19.22 N 99.13 W
Taranivka 78 49.37 N 36.08 E
Taransay I 46 57.54 N 7.01 W
Taranta Peligna 66 42.01 N 14.10 E
Tarantine, Murge ◆[1] 68 40.22 N 17.40 E
Taranto 68 40.28 N 17.15 E
Taranto □[4] 68 40.37 N 17.15 E
Taranto, Golfo di c 68 40.10 N 17.20 E
Tarapacá 246 2.52 S 69.44 W
Tarapoto 248 6.30 S 76.25 W
Ṭaraq al-Hbâri ◆[1] 130 34.17 N 39.16 E
Ṭaraq an-Naʿjah ◆[1] 130 34.16 N 39.53 E
Ṭaraq Sidâoui ◆[1] 130 34.33 N 39.54 E
Taraquá 246 0.06 N 68.28 W
Tarare 58 45.54 N 4.26 E
Tarariras 258 34.17 S 57.37 W
Tararua Range ⋏ 172 40.46 S 175.23 E
Tarāsa Dwīp I 110 8.15 N 93.10 E
Tarascon, Fr. 32 42.51 N 1.36 E
Tarascon, Fr. 62 43.48 N 4.40 E
Tarashcha 78 49.34 N 30.29 E
Tarasht ◆[8] 267d 35.42 N 51.21 E
Tarasivka 83 49.40 N 38.23 E
Tarasovka, Ross. 83 49.28 N 40.05 E
Tarasovka, Ross. 265b 55.58 N 37.50 E
Tarasovo, Ross. 24 66.13 N 46.39 E
Tarasovo, Ross. 24 62.49 N 41.10 E
Tarasovo, Ross. 80 58.18 N 48.45 E
Tarasovo, Ross. 88 55.52 N 107.48 E
Tarasovskij 78 48.43 N 40.22 E
Tarasp 58 46.38 N 10.25 E
Tarat 148 26.13 N 9.18 E
Tarat, Oued V 148 26.09 N 9.20 E
Tarata, Bol. 248 17.37 S 66.01 W
Tarata, Perú 248 17.28 S 70.02 W
Taratai 174t 1.32 N 173.00 E
Taratakbuluh 112 0.23 N 101.27 E
Tāratanr 126 23.58 N 86.29 E
Tarauacá 248 8.10 S 70.46 W
Tarauacá ≃ 248 7.19 S 70.15 W
Taravao, Baie de c 174s 17.43 S 149.17 W
Taravao, Isthme de ⊻[3] 174s 17.43 S 149.19 W
Taravo ≃ 36 41.42 N 8.49 E
Tarawa I[1] 174t 1.25 N 173.00 E
Tarawera 172 39.02 S 176.35 E
Tarawera, Lake ⊜ 172 38.12 S 176.27 E
Tarawera, Mount ʌ[1] 172 38.14 S 176.30 E
Tarazona 34 41.54 N 1.44 W
Tarazona de la Mancha 34 39.15 N 1.55 W

Symbol	English	Deutsch	Español	Français	Português
≃	River	Fluß	Río	Rivière	Rio
≊	Canal	Kanal	Canal	Canal	Canal
ʟ	Waterfall, Rapids	Wasserfall, Stromschnellen	Cascada, Rápidos	Chute d'eau, Rapides	Cascata, Rápidos
ʯ	Strait	Meeresstraße	Estrecho	Détroit	Estreito
c	Bay, Gulf	Bucht, Golf	Bahía, Golfo	Baie, Golfe	Baía, Golfo
⊜	Lake, Lakes	See, Seen	Lago, Lagos	Lac, Lacs	Lago, Lagos
≡	Swamp	Sumpf	Pantano	Marais	Pântano
⩀	Ice Features, Glacier	Eis- und Gletscherformen	Accidentes Glaciales	Formes glaciaires	Acidentes glaciares
⊤	Other Hydrographic Features	Andere Hydrographische Objekte	Otros Elementos Hidrográficos	Autres données hydrographiques	Outros acidentes hidrográficos
✢	Submarine Features	Untermeerische Objekte	Accidentes Submarinos	Formes de relief sous-marin	Acidentes submarinos
□	Political Unit	Politische Einheit	Unidad Política	Entité politique	Unidade política
ʊ	Cultural Institution	Kulturelle Institution	Institución Cultural	Institution culturelle	Institução cultural
⊥	Historical Site	Historische Stätte	Sitio Histórico	Site historique	Sitio histórico
♦	Recreational Site	Erholungs- und Ferienort	Sitio de Recreo	Centre de loisirs	Area de Lazer
⊠	Airport	Flughafen	Aeropuerto	Aéroport	Aeroporto
■	Military Installation	Militäranlage	Instalación Militar	Installation militaire	Instalação militar
◆	Miscellaneous	Verschiedenes	Misceláneo	Divers	Diversos

Tarba 144 0.48 N 42.39 E
Tårbæk 41 55.47 N 12.36 E
Tarbagataj, Ross. 88 51.30 N 107.22 E
Tarbagataj, Ross. 88 52.07 N 109.12 E
Tarbagataj, Ross. 88 51.12 N 109.05 E
Tarbagataj, chrebet ⋏ 86 47.12 N 83.00 E
Tarbat Ness › 46 57.51 N 3.47 W
Tarbela 123 34.08 N 72.49 E
Tarbela Reservoir ⊜[1] 123 34.10 N 72.50 E
Tarbert, Ire. 48 52.32 N 9.23 W
Tarbert, Scot., U.K. 46 55.52 N 5.26 W
Tarbert, Scot., U.K. 46 57.54 N 6.49 W
Tarbert, East Loch c 46 57.52 N 6.45 W
Tarbert, Loch c 46 55.57 N 6.00 W
Tarbert, West Loch c, Scot., U.K. 46 55.48 N 5.32 W
Tarbert, West Loch c, Scot., U.K. 46 57.55 N 6.54 W
Tarbes 32 43.14 N 0.05 E
Tarbet 46 56.12 N 4.43 W
Tarbock Green 262 53.23 N 2.49 W
Tarbolton 46 55.31 N 4.29 W
Tarboro 192 35.53 N 77.32 W
Tarbū 146 26.02 N 15.10 E
Tarcăului, Munții ⋏ 38 46.45 N 26.20 E
Tarcento 64 46.13 N 13.13 E
Tarchov Cholm, gora ∧[2] 76 57.11 N 38.25 E
Tarchovka 265a 60.04 N 29.58 E
Tarcoola 162 30.41 S 134.33 E
Tarcoon 166 30.16 S 146.43 E
Tarcutta 171b 35.17 S 147.44 E
Tarcutta Creek ≃ 171b 35.08 S 147.36 E
Tārdah 272b 22.27 N 88.31 E
Tardajos 34 42.21 N 3.49 W
Tardoki-Jani, gora ∧ 89 48.55 N 138.04 E
Tardun 162 28.48 S 115.45 E
Taredo ⬥[8] 272c 19.58 N 72.49 E
Taree 166 31.54 S 152.28 E
Tareja 74 73.20 N 90.37 E
Taremert-n-Akli, Oued V 148 25.49 N 5.17 E
Tärendö 24 67.10 N 22.38 E
Tarent, Golf von → Taranto, Golfo di c 68 40.10 N 17.20 E
Tarentaise V 62 45.30 N 6.30 E
Tarento, Golfo de → Taranto, Golfo di c 68 40.10 N 17.20 E
Tarentum 214 40.36 N 79.45 W
Tarf, Garaet et ⊜ 148 35.40 N 7.10 E
Ṭarfā', Baṭn aṭ- ≡ 128 23.50 N 51.27 E
Ṭarfā', Ra's aṭ- › 144 17.05 N 42.24 E
Ṭarfā', Wādī aṭ- V 142 28.25 N 30.50 E
Ṭarfāwī, Bi'r ⊤[4], Miṣr 140 22.55 N 28.53 E
Tarfawi, Bi'r ⊤[4], Sūd. 140 21.04 N 34.08 E
Tarfaya 148 27.58 N 12.55 W
Tarfside 46 56.54 N 2.50 W
Tarf Water ≃ 44 54.55 N 4.35 W
Targa 124 22.27 N 84.40 E
Targan ≃ 85 43.38 N 75.58 E
Target Rock National Wildlife Refuge ⬥[4] 276 40.56 N 73.26 W
Targhee Pass)(202 44.41 N 111.17 W
Targon 32 44.44 N 0.16 W
Tărgovište, Blg. 38 43.15 N 26.34 E
Târgoviște, Rom. 38 44.56 N 25.27 E
Târgu Bujor 38 45.52 N 27.54 E
Târgu Cărbunești 38 44.58 N 23.31 E
Târgu Frumos 38 47.13 N 27.00 E
Targuist 148 34.57 N 4.18 W
Târgu Jiu 38 45.02 N 23.17 E
Târgu Lăpuș 38 47.27 N 23.52 E
Târgu Mureș 38 46.33 N 24.33 E
Târgu-Neamț 38 47.12 N 26.22 E
Târgu Ocna 38 46.15 N 26.37 E
Târgu Secuiesc 38 46.00 N 26.08 E
Târgușor 38 44.28 N 28.25 E
Tarhjijt 148 29.05 N 9.24 W
Tarhu 102 41.09 N 107.58 E
Tarhūnah 146 32.26 N 13.38 E
Tari 164 5.50 S 143.00 E
Tarialan 86 49.47 N 91.55 E
Tariat 88 48.06 N 99.32 E
Táriba 246 7.49 N 72.13 W
Tarifa 34 36.01 N 5.36 W
Tarifa, Punta de › 34 36.00 N 5.37 W
Tariffville 207 41.54 N 72.45 W
Tarija 248 21.31 S 64.45 W
Tarija □[5] 248 21.30 S 64.00 W
Tarikere 122 13.43 N 75.49 E
Tariki 172 39.14 S 174.15 E
Tariku ≃ 164 3.04 S 138.09 E
Tarīm 144 16.03 N 48.59 E
Tarim ≃ 90 41.05 N 86.40 E
Tarimoro 234 20.17 N 100.45 W
Tarim Pendi ≃[1] 90 39.00 N 83.00 E
Taring 114 3.50 N 97.33 E
Tarīn Kowt 120 32.52 N 65.38 E
Taritatu ≃ 164 2.54 S 138.27 E
Tarituba 256 23.02 S 44.36 W
Tarjannevesi ⊜ 26 62.07 N 24.03 E
Tarka 150 14.37 N 7.55 E
Tarka ≃ 158 32.18 S 25.44 E
Tarka, Vallée de V 150 14.00 N 6.00 E
Tarkastad 158 32.00 S 26.16 E
Tarkazy 80 53.52 N 53.39 E
Tarkhankut, mys › 78 45.21 N 32.30 E
Tarkhūrān 128 34.41 N 50.00 E
Tarki 84 42.56 N 47.30 E
Tarkiln 207 41.57 N 71.36 W
Tarkington Bayou ≃ 222 30.10 N 94.59 W
Tarkio 194 40.26 N 95.22 W
Tarkio ≃ 198 40.10 N 95.26 W
Tarko-Sale 74 64.55 N 77.49 E
Tarkwa 150 5.19 N 1.59 W
Tarlac 116 15.29 N 120.35 E
Tarlac □[4] 116 15.30 N 120.25 E
Tarlac ≃ 116 15.45 N 120.27 E
Tarland 46 57.08 N 2.52 W
Tarlee 168b 34.16 S 138.46 E
Tarleton 44 53.41 N 2.50 W
T'arlevo 265a 59.42 N 30.27 E
Tarlo ≃ 170 34.28 S 150.04 E
Tarlo River National Park ♠ 170 34.31 S 149.55 E
Tarlscough 262 53.37 N 2.52 W
Tarm 26 55.55 N 8.32 E
Tarma 248 11.25 S 75.42 W
Tarmstedt 52 53.13 N 9.04 E
Tarn □[5] 32 43.50 N 2.00 E
Tarn ≃ 32 44.05 N 1.06 E
Tarna ≃ 30 47.31 N 19.59 E
Tärnaby 24 65.43 N 15.16 E
Tarnak ≃ 120 31.26 N 65.31 E
Țarna Mare 38 48.04 N 23.12 E
Târnava Mare ≃ 38 46.09 N 23.42 E
Târnava Mică ≃ 38 46.11 N 23.55 E
Târnăveni 38 46.20 N 24.17 E
Tårnby 41 55.38 N 12.36 E
Tarneit 274b 37.52 S 144.41 E
Tarn-et-Garonne □[5] 32 44.05 N 1.20 E
Tarnewitz 54 53.58 N 11.14 E
Tarnobrzeg 30 50.35 N 21.41 E
Tarnobrzeg □[4] 30 50.45 N 21.50 E
Tarnogród 30 50.23 N 22.45 E
Tarnogskij Gorodok 24 60.29 N 43.33 E
Tarnopol → Ternopil' 78 49.34 N 25.36 E
Târnova 38 48.10 N 27.40 E
Tarnów, Pol. 30 50.01 N 21.00 E
Tarnów, Pol. 54 52.47 N 14.58 E
Tarnów □[4] 30 50.00 N 21.00 E
Tarnowskie Góry 30 50.27 N 18.52 E
Tärnsjö 40 60.09 N 16.56 E
Tarn Tāran 123 31.27 N 74.55 E
Taro 175e 6.46 S 156.28 E
Taro ≃ 36 45.00 N 10.15 E
Taron 164 4.25 S 153.05 E
Tarong 166 26.46 S 151.51 E
Taronga Zoo ♠ 274a 33.51 S 151.15 E
Taroom 166 25.39 S 149.49 E
Tarouca 34 41.00 N 7.40 W
Taroudant 148 30.31 N 8.55 W
Ta Roun, Co ∧ 110 17.17 N 106.18 E
Tarp 41 54.40 N 9.23 E
Tarpey 226 36.47 N 119.41 W
Tarpon, Lake ⊜ 220 28.07 N 82.44 W
Tarpon Springs 220 28.08 N 82.45 W
Tarporley 44 53.09 N 2.40 W
Tarqui 246 1.35 S 75.15 W
Tarquinia 66 42.15 N 11.45 E
Tarqūmiyah 132 31.35 N 35.01 E
Tarra ≃ 246 9.05 N 72.30 W
Tarrabool Lake ⊜ 162 18.15 S 135.04 E
Tarrafal, C.V. 150a 16.58 N 25.19 W
Tarrafal, C.V. 150a 15.17 N 23.46 W
Tarragona 34 41.07 N 1.15 E
Tarragona □[4] 34 41.00 N 0.45 E
Tarraleah 166 42.18 S 146.27 E
Tarrant □[6] 222 32.47 N 97.18 W
Tarrant City 194 33.34 N 86.46 W
Tarrant Hinton 42 50.53 N 2.05 W
Tarrara Creek ≃ 208 36.33 N 77.10 W
Tarras 172 44.50 S 169.25 E
Tàrrega 34 41.39 N 1.09 E
Tarri 144 0.42 N 41.38 E
Tarrs 214 40.10 N 79.35 W
Tarrtown 214 40.51 N 79.31 W
Tarryall Creek ≃ 200 39.05 N 105.19 W
Tarrytown 210 41.04 N 73.51 W
Tarrytown Reservoir ⊜[1] 276 41.05 N 73.51 W
Tarsus 130 36.55 N 34.53 E
Tarta 128 40.02 N 52.46 E
Tartagal, Arg. 252 22.32 S 63.49 W
Tartagal, Arg. 252 28.40 S 59.52 W
Tärtär 84 40.20 N 46.55 E
Tärtär ≃ 84 40.35 N 47.22 E
Tartaro ≃ 64 45.02 N 11.30 E
Tartas ≃ 86 55.37 N 76.44 E
Tartu 76 58.23 N 26.43 E
Ṭarṭūs 130 34.53 N 35.53 E
Ṭarṭūs □[8] 130 35.00 N 36.00 E
Taruaçu 256 21.37 S 42.56 W
Tarui 94 35.22 N 136.32 E
Tarum ≃ 115a 5.59 S 107.03 E
Tarumi ⬥[8] 270 34.38 N 135.03 E
Tarumirim 255 19.16 S 41.59 W
Tarumizu 92 31.29 N 130.42 E
Tarumovka 84 44.03 N 46.33 E
Tarusa 82 54.43 N 37.11 E
Tarusa ≃ 82 54.44 N 37.11 E
Ṭārūṭ 142 30.32 N 31.28 E
Tarutao, Ko I 114 6.35 N 99.40 E
Tarutino 82 55.07 N 36.56 E
Tarutung 114 2.01 N 98.58 E
Tarutyne 78 46.12 N 29.09 E
Tarvagatajn nuruu ⋏ 88 48.20 N 99.00 E
Tarves 46 57.22 N 2.13 W
Tarvisio 64 46.30 N 13.35 E
Tarvo ≃ 248 14.47 S 61.03 W
Tarwin ≃ 169 38.42 S 145.50 E
Tarwin, East Branch ≃ 169 38.34 S 146.00 E
Tarwin, West Branch ≃ 169 38.34 S 146.00 E
Tarza 24 62.30 N 40.25 E
Tarzan 196 32.18 N 101.58 W
Tarzana ⬥[8] 280 34.10 N 118.32 W
Tarzo 64 45.58 N 12.14 E
Tas 80 48.27 N 51.02 E
Tas ≃ 42 52.36 N 1.18 E
Taşağıl 130 36.55 N 31.14 E
Tašanta 86 49.43 N 89.11 E
Tasaral 86 46.20 N 73.58 E
Tašauz 72 41.50 N 59.58 E
Tasāwah 146 25.58 N 13.30 E
Tasbuget 86 44.48 N 65.33 E
Taschkent → Taškent 85 41.20 N 69.18 E
Taşçı 130 38.13 N 35.48 E
Taşdelen 130 38.51 N 38.31 E
Tasejeva ≃ 86 58.06 N 94.01 E
Tasejevo 86 57.12 N 94.54 E
Taseko ≃ 182 52.00 N 123.40 W
Taseko Lakes ⊜ 182 51.15 N 123.35 W
Taseko Mountain ∧ 182 51.14 N 123.28 W
Tašelan 88 51.45 N 108.55 E
Tasendjanet, Oued V 148 24.36 N 1.07 E
Tāsgaon 122 17.02 N 74.36 E
Tashan, Zhg. 104 40.48 N 122.39 E
Tashan, Zhg. 104 40.51 N 120.56 E
Tashi Gang Dzong 120 27.19 N 91.34 E
Tashimalike 85 39.06 N 75.41 E
Tashiyi 100 29.43 N 112.48 E
Ṭashk, Daryācheh-ye ⊜ 128 29.45 N 53.30 E
Tashkent → Taškent 85 41.20 N 69.18 E
Tāshkurghān → Kholm 120 36.42 N 67.41 E
Tashuik'u 269d 25.13 N 121.30 E
Tasikmalaya 115a 7.20 S 108.12 E
Tasīl 132 32.50 N 35.58 E
Tåsinge I 41 55.00 N 10.36 E
Tašir 84 41.07 N 44.17 E
Taširovo 82 55.25 N 36.39 E
Tasitan 85 39.17 N 76.07 E
Tåsjö 26 64.13 N 15.54 E
Tåsjön ⊜ 26 64.15 N 15.47 E
Taskajevo 86 55.06 N 78.36 E
Taşkent, Tür. 130 36.55 N 32.31 E
Taškent (Tashkent), Uzb. 85 41.20 N 69.18 E
Taškent □[4] 85 41.00 N 69.30 E
Taškepri 128 36.18 N 62.38 E
Taşkesen 130 39.43 N 41.29 E
Taskesken 86 47.15 N 80.44 E
Taşköprü 130 41.30 N 34.14 E
Taskul 164 2.35 S 150.25 E
Taš-Kumyr 85 41.21 N 72.14 E
Taškyja 85 40.16 N 74.19 E
Tašla 80 51.47 N 52.46 E
Taşlı ≃ 267b 41.03 N 28.56 E
Tasman, Mount ∧ 172 43.34 S 170.09 E
Tasman Basin ✦[1] 6 43.00 S 158.00 E
Tasman Bay c 172 41.00 S 173.20 E
Tasmania □[3] 166 43.00 S 147.00 E
Tasmania I 166 42.00 S 147.00 E
Tasmanien → Tasmania I 166 42.00 S 147.00 E
Tasman Mountains ⋏ 172 41.07 S 172.33 E
Tasman Peninsula ›[1] 166 43.05 S 147.50 E
Tasman Sea ⊤[2] 14 40.00 S 163.00 E
Tăşnad 38 47.29 N 22.35 E
Tasoba 80 49.47 N 49.52 E
Tasotkel'skoje vodochranilišče ⊜[1] 85 43.22 N 74.00 E
Taşova 130 40.46 N 36.20 E
Tasrār Sharīf 123 33.52 N 74.46 E
Taşrumi 84 38.48 N 44.04 E
Tassajara Creek ≃ 282 37.41 N 121.53 W
Tassara 150 16.48 N 5.39 E
Tassdorf 264a 52.30 N 13.47 E
Tassialouc, Lac ⊜ 176 59.03 N 74.00 W
Tassin-la-Demi-Lune 62 45.46 N 4.47 E
Tasso Lake ⊜ 212 45.27 N 78.56 W
Tassu, Serra di lu ∧ 71 41.01 N 9.08 E
Taštagol 86 52.47 N 87.53 E
Tastiota 232 28.22 N 111.23 W
Tåstrup 41 55.39 N 12.19 E
Taštyp 86 52.48 N 89.54 E
Taşucu 130 36.19 N 33.53 E
Tata, Magreb 148 29.44 N 7.56 W
Tata, Magy. 30 47.39 N 18.18 E
Tata □[4] 148 29.40 N 7.45 W
T'at'a, vulkan ∧[1] 92a 44.21 N 146.15 E
Tataa, Pointe › 174s 17.34 S 149.37 W
Tatabánya 30 47.34 N 18.26 E
Tatahuicapan 234 18.14 N 94.45 W
Tatal 80 47.17 N 46.16 E
Tatalin ≃ 102 37.30 N 95.28 E
Tata Mailau ∧ 112 8.55 S 125.30 E
Tatamy 208 40.44 N 75.15 W
Tataouine 148 32.56 N 10.27 E
Tata Raphael, Camp ■ 273b 4.18 S 15.17 E
Tatarbunary 78 45.49 N 29.36 E
Tatarija □[3], Ross. 72 55.00 N 51.00 E
Tatarija □[3], Ross. 80 55.00 N 51.00 E
Tatarinka 76 55.58 N 33.54 E
Tatarino 78 50.36 N 39.07 E
Tatarinovo, Ross. 82 55.13 N 37.56 E
Tatarinovo, Ross. 82 56.34 N 38.25 E
Tatarischer Sund → Tatarskij proliv ⊔ 89 50.00 N 141.15 E
Tatarka, Bela. 76 53.16 N 28.48 E
Tatarka, Ross. 86 53.58 N 75.05 E
Tatarlar 130 41.46 N 26.55 E
Tatarovo ⬥[8] 265b 55.46 N 37.26 E
Tātārpur ⬥[8] 272a 28.39 N 77.07 E
Tatarsk 86 55.13 N 75.58 E
Tatarskij Kandyz 80 54.07 N 53.07 E
Tatarskij proliv (Tatar Strait) ⊔ 89 50.00 N 141.15 E
Tatarskij Sajman 80 53.18 N 47.07 E
Tatarskoje-Maklakovo 80 55.48 N 45.34 E
Tatarstan → Tatarija □[3] 80 55.00 N 51.00 E
Tatar Strait → Tatarskij proliv ⊔ 89 50.00 N 141.15 E
Tatau ≃ 112 3.07 N 112.49 E
Tatau Island I 164 2.50 S 152.00 E
Tataurovo, Ross. 76 58.44 N 43.20 E
Tataurovo, Ross. 80 57.48 N 49.34 E
Tataurovo, Ross. 88 51.37 N 112.56 E
Tate 192 34.25 N 84.22 W
Tate ≃ 166 17.22 S 143.44 E
Tatebayashi 94 36.15 N 139.32 E
Tate Gallery ♁ 260 51.29 N 0.08 W
Tateishi-misaki › 94 35.46 N 136.01 E
Tateiwa 94 37.05 N 139.32 E
Tateiwa-chosuichi ⊜[1] 96 34.33 N 132.10 E
Tateshina 94 36.16 N 138.19 E
Tateyama, Nihon 94 34.59 N 139.52 E
Tateyama, Nihon 94 36.40 N 137.19 E
Tate-yama ∧ 94 36.35 N 137.37 E
Tathlina Lake ⊜ 176 60.32 N 117.32 W
Tathlīth, Wādī V 144 20.44 N 44.17 E
Tathong Point › 271d 22.14 N 114.17 E
Tathra 166 36.44 S 149.59 E
Tatikawa → Tachikawa 94 35.42 N 139.25 E
Tatiščevo, Ross. 80 51.40 N 45.35 E
Tatiščevo, Ross. 82 56.24 N 37.31 E
Tatitlek 180 60.52 N 146.41 W
Tatla Lake 182 51.55 N 124.36 W
Tatla Lake ⊜ 182 52.00 N 124.25 W
Tatlayoko Lake 182 51.39 N 124.24 W
Tatlayoko Lake ⊜ 182 51.30 N 124.25 W
Tatlow, Mount ∧ 182 51.23 N 123.52 W
Tatnam, Cape › 176 57.16 N 91.00 W
Tatomi 94 35.36 N 138.31 E
Tatoosh Island I 224 48.24 N 124.44 W
Tatrang 120 38.28 N 85.35 E
Tatranský národní park ♠ 30 49.10 N 20.05 E
Tatrzański Park Narodowy ♠ 30 49.15 N 20.00 E
Tatsfield 260 51.18 N 0.02 E
Tatsuno, Nihon 94 35.59 N 137.59 E
Tatsuno, Nihon 96 34.52 N 134.33 E
Tatsunokuchi 94 36.27 N 136.35 E
Tatsuruhama 94 37.04 N 136.53 E
Tatsuyama 94 34.58 N 137.49 E
Tatta 120 24.45 N 67.55 E
Tattenhall 44 53.06 N 2.46 W
Tatti 85 43.12 N 73.19 E
Tatton Hall ⊥ 262 53.20 N 2.23 W
Tatton Mere ⊜ 262 53.19 N 2.22 W
Tatton Park ♠ 262 53.20 N 2.22 W
Tatu ≃ 100 24.12 N 120.29 E
Tatuapé ⬥[8] 287b 23.32 S 46.34 W
Tatuk Lake ⊜ 182 53.32 N 124.15 W
Tatum, N.M., U.S. 196 33.15 N 103.19 W
Tatum, Tx., U.S. 222 32.19 N 94.31 W
Tat'ung → Datong 102 40.05 N 113.18 E
Tat'un Shan ∧ 269d 25.11 N 121.31 E
Tatvan 130 38.30 N 42.16 E
Tatzuli ≃ 100 24.08 N 121.39 E
Tau, Am. Sam. 174y 14.14 S 169.32 W
Tau, Kaz. 80 49.40 N 47.17 E
Tau, Nor. 26 59.04 N 5.54 E
Tau I 174y 14.15 S 169.30 W
Tauá 250 6.01 S 40.26 W
Tauanap, Mochun ⊔ 175c 7.28 N 151.36 E
Taubaté 256 23.02 S 45.33 W
Tauber ≃ 56 49.46 N 9.31 E
Tauberbischofsheim 56 49.37 N 9.40 E
Taucha 54 51.23 N 12.30 E
Taučik 72 44.21 N 51.19 E
Tauer 54 51.50 N 14.28 E
Tauern-Tunnel ⬥[5] 64 47.05 N 13.05 E
Täuffelen 58 47.04 N 7.12 E
Taufkirchen, Dtsch. 60 48.21 N 12.08 E
Taufkirchen, Dtsch. 64 48.03 N 11.37 E
Taufstein ∧ 56 50.31 N 9.14 E
Taughannock Creek ≃ 210 42.33 N 76.36 W
Taughannock Falls State Park ♠ 210 42.32 N 76.35 W
Tauini ≃ 246 0.30 N 58.22 W
Taujskaja guba c 74 59.20 N 150.20 E
Taukum, peski ⬥[2] 86 44.50 N 75.30 E
Taulabé 236 14.38 N 87.59 W
Taulihawā 124 27.32 N 83.03 E
Taulov 41 55.33 N 9.37 E
Taumarunui 172 38.52 S 175.17 E
Taum Sauk Mountain ∧ 194 37.34 N 90.44 W
Taunay 248 20.18 S 56.05 W
Taunay, Cascatinha ∟ 287a 22.57 S 43.17 W
Taung 158 27.33 S 24.47 E
Taungbon 110 15.25 N 97.50 E
Taungdwingyi 110 20.01 N 95.33 E
Taunggon 110 23.38 N 96.32 E
Taunggyi 110 20.47 N 97.02 E
Taungnyo Range ⋏ 110 15.38 N 97.56 E
Taungup 110 18.51 N 94.14 E
Taungup Pass)(110 18.40 N 94.45 E
Taunsa 123 30.42 N 70.39 E
Taunsa Barrage ⬥[6] 123 30.31 N 70.51 E
Taunton, Eng., U.K. 42 51.01 N 3.06 W
Taunton, Ma., U.S. 207 41.54 N 71.05 W
Taunton, N.Y., U.S. 210 43.01 N 76.13 W
Taunton ≃ 207 41.42 N 71.10 W
Taunton, Vale of V 42 51.02 N 3.08 W
Taunton Lake ⊜ 285 39.51 N 74.51 W
Taunton Lakes 285 39.51 N 74.51 W
Taunus ⋏ 56 50.10 N 8.15 E
Taunusstein 56 50.08 N 8.08 E
Taupiri 172 37.37 S 175.11 E
Tauplitz 61 47.33 N 14.00 E
Taupo 172 38.41 S 176.05 E
Taupo, Lake ⊜ 172 38.49 S 175.55 E
Tauragė 76 55.15 N 22.17 E
Taurak 86 51.35 N 85.01 E
Tauranga 172 37.42 S 176.10 E
Taurasi 68 41.00 N 14.57 E
Taureau, Réservoir ⊜[1] 206 46.46 N 73.50 W
Tauri ≃ 164 8.08 S 146.06 E
Taurianova 68 38.21 N 16.01 E
Tauripampa 248 12.35 S 76.07 W
Taurisano 68 39.57 N 18.13 E
Taurisma 248 15.10 S 72.51 W
Tauroa Point › 172 35.10 S 173.04 E
Taurovo 86 59.36 N 73.18 E
Taurus Mountains → Toros Dağları ⋏ 130 37.00 N 33.00 E
Tauste 34 41.55 N 1.15 W
Tautira 174s 17.44 S 149.09 W
Tauxigny 50 47.13 N 0.50 E
Tavaí 252 26.07 S 55.32 W
Tavajvaam ≃ 180 64.56 N 177.30 E
Tavajza 89 45.12 N 136.44 E
Ṭavālesh, Kūhhā-ye → Talish Mountains ⋏ 128 38.42 N 48.18 E
Tavanasa 58 46.45 N 9.04 E
Tavannes 58 47.13 N 7.12 E
Tavant 50 47.07 N 0.23 E
Tavares, Bra. 250 7.38 S 37.54 W
Tavares, Fl., U.S. 220 28.48 N 81.43 W
Tavares, Ilha dos I 287a 22.49 S 43.06 W
Tavarnelle Val di Pesa 66 43.33 N 11.10 E
Tavas 130 37.34 N 29.04 E
Tavastehus → Hämeenlinna 26 61.00 N 24.27 E
Tavaux 58 47.02 N 5.24 E
Tavda 86 58.03 N 65.15 E
Tavda ≃ 72 57.47 N 67.16 E
Tave ≃ 62 44.07 N 4.42 E
Tavera ≃ 64 46.29 N 11.21 E
Taverham 42 52.41 N 1.12 E
Taverna 68 39.01 N 16.35 E
Tavern Creek ≃ 194 38.19 N 92.18 W
Tavernelle, It. 64 44.18 N 10.04 E
Tavernelle, It. 66 43.00 N 12.09 E
Tavernes 62 43.36 N 6.01 E
Tavernes de la Valldigna 34 39.04 N 0.16 W
Tavernier 220 25.00 N 80.30 W
Tavernole sul Mella 64 45.45 N 10.14 E
Taverny 50 49.02 N 2.13 E
Taveta, Kenya 154 3.24 S 37.41 E
Taveta, Tan. 154 9.01 S 35.37 E
Taveuni I 175g 16.51 S 179.58 W
Taviano 68 39.59 N 18.05 E
Tavil'dara 85 38.43 N 70.28 E
Tavira 34 37.07 N 7.39 W
Tavistock, On., Can. 212 43.19 N 80.50 W
Tavistock, Eng., U.K. 42 50.33 N 4.08 W
Tavn-Gašun 80 46.01 N 45.55 E
Tavolara, Isola I 71 40.54 N 9.42 E
Tavoliere ⬥[1] 68 41.35 N 15.25 E
Tavolžan 86 52.44 N 77.27 E
Tavor, Har (Mount Tabor) ∧ 132 32.41 N 35.23 E
Távora ≃ 34 41.09 N 7.35 W
Tavoy → Dawei 110 14.05 N 98.12 E
Tavoy Point › 110 13.32 N 98.10 E
Tavričanka 89 43.22 N 131.52 E
Tavričeskoje 86 54.35 N 73.38 E
Tavry 265a 59.55 N 30.42 E
Tavsalayihüseynan 130 38.38 N 40.32 E
Tavşanlı 130 39.33 N 29.30 E
Tavua 175g 17.27 S 177.51 E
Tavy ≃ 42 50.16 N 4.10 W
Taw ≃ 42 51.04 N 4.11 W
Tawa 172 41.10 S 174.51 E
Tawa ≃ 124 22.48 N 77.48 E
Tawaeli 112 0.43 S 119.51 E
Tawakoni, Lake ⊜[1] 222 32.55 N 96.00 W
Tawara 270 34.27 N 135.57 E
Tawarada 268 35.19 N 140.04 E
Tawaramoto 96 34.33 N 135.48 E
Tawas City 190 44.16 N 83.30 W
Tawau 112 4.15 N 117.54 E
Tawd ≃ 262 53.36 N 2.48 W
Tāwi ≃ 123 32.40 N 74.41 E
Ṭawīlah, Juzur II 140 27.35 N 33.46 E
Tawi-Tawi □[4] 116 5.20 N 120.00 E
Tawi-Tawi Group II 116 5.10 N 120.15 E
Tawi-Tawi Island I 116 5.10 N 120.00 E
Ṭawkar 140 18.26 N 37.44 E
Tawu 100 22.22 N 120.54 E
Ṭāwūq 128 35.08 N 44.27 E
Tāwurghā' 146 32.02 N 15.09 E
Ṭawwah Banī Ibrāhīm 142 28.05 N 30.41 E
Taxco de Alarcón 234 18.33 N 99.36 W
Taxenbach 64 47.17 N 12.58 E
Taxi 89 49.26 N 126.08 E
Taxila 123 33.44 N 72.49 E
Taxisco 236 14.04 N 90.28 W
Taxkorgan Tajik Zizhixian 120 37.49 N 75.14 E
Taxusi 102 32.58 N 98.10 E
Tay ≃, On., Can. 212 44.53 N 76.07 W
Tay ≃, Yk., Can. 180 62.34 N 134.22 W
Tay ≃, Scot., U.K. 46 56.22 N 3.21 W
Tay, Firth of c[1] 46 56.26 N 3.00 W
Tay, Lake ⊜ 162 32.55 S 120.48 E
Tay, Loch ⊜ 46 56.31 N 4.10 W
Tayabamba 248 8.17 S 77.18 W
Tayabas 116 14.01 N 121.35 E
Tayabas Bay c 116 13.45 N 121.45 E
Tayan 112 0.02 S 110.07 E
Tayandu, Kepulauan II 164 5.30 S 132.15 E
Tayayi 105 39.25 N 115.03 E
Tayeegle 144 4.02 N 44.31 E
Taylor, B.C., Can. 182 56.10 N 120.41 W
Taylor, Az., U.S. 200 34.27 N 110.05 W
Taylor, Ar., U.S. 194 33.06 N 93.27 W
Taylor, Mi., U.S. 216 42.14 N 83.16 W
Taylor, Mo., U.S. 219 39.56 N 91.32 W
Taylor, Ne., U.S. 198 41.46 N 99.22 W
Taylor, Pa., U.S. 210 41.23 N 75.42 W
Taylor, Tx., U.S. 222 30.34 N 97.24 W
Taylor ≃ 200 38.40 N 106.51 W
Taylor, Mount ∧, N.Z. 172 43.30 S 171.19 E
Taylor, Mount ∧, N.M., U.S. 200 35.14 N 107.37 W
Taylor Creek ≃, On., Can. 275b 43.42 N 79.20 W
Taylor Creek ≃, Il., U.S. 219 39.13 N 90.18 W
Taylor Lake Village 222 29.36 N 95.03 W
Taylor Mountain ∧ 202 44.53 N 114.13 W
Taylor Mountains ⋏ 180 60.50 N 157.20 W
Taylor Run ≃ 285 39.57 N 75.39 W
Taylors 192 34.55 N 82.17 W
Taylors Bush Park ♠ 275b 43.42 N 79.19 W
Taylors Island 208 38.28 N 76.17 W
Taylor Springs 219 39.08 N 89.30 W
Taylors Run ≃ 279b 40.11 N 79.57 W
Taylorstown 214 40.10 N 80.23 W
Taylorsville, In., U.S. 218 39.17 N 85.57 W
Taylorsville, Ky., U.S. 194 38.01 N 85.20 W
Taylorsville, Ms., U.S. 194 31.49 N 89.25 W
Taylorsville, N.C., U.S. 192 35.55 N 81.10 W
Taylorsville Dam ⬥[6] 218 39.53 N 84.10 W
Taylortown, N.J., U.S. 276 40.56 N 74.24 W
Taylortown, Oh., U.S. 214 40.28 N 80.40 W
Taylortown Reservoir ⊜[1] 276 40.58 N 74.22 W
Taylorville 219 39.32 N 89.17 W
Taylorville, Lake ⊜[1] 219 39.30 N 89.15 W
Taymā' 128 27.38 N 38.29 E
Taymouth 186 46.11 N 66.37 W
Taymyr Peninsula → Tajmyr, poluostrov ›[1] 74 76.00 N 104.00 E
Tay Ninh 110 11.18 N 106.06 E
Taynuilt 46 56.25 N 5.14 W
Tayoltita 232 24.05 N 105.56 W
Tayport 46 56.27 N 2.53 W
Táyros 267c 37.58 N 23.42 E
Tayside □[4] 46 56.30 N 3.30 W
Taytay, Pil. 116 10.49 N 119.31 E
Taytay, Pil. 116 14.34 N 121.08 E
Taytay Bay c 116 10.55 N 119.35 E
Tayu 115a 6.32 S 111.02 E
Tayüan, T'aiwan 100 25.04 N 121.11 E
Tayuan, Zhg. 89 51.27 N 124.16 E
Tayyārah 140 13.12 N 30.47 E
Ṭayyebāt 128 34.44 N 60.45 E
Taz ≃ 72 67.32 N 78.40 E
Taza 148 34.16 N 4.01 W
Taza □[4] 148 34.05 N 3.45 W
Tazawa-ko ⊜ 92 39.43 N 140.40 E
Tazenakht 148 30.35 N 7.12 W
Tazewell, Tn., U.S. 192 36.27 N 83.34 W
Tazewell, Va., U.S. 192 37.06 N 81.31 W
Tazhuang 105 39.55 N 117.13 E
Tazicheng 89 46.35 N 123.06 E
Tazigou ≃ 104 41.44 N 121.30 E
Tazin ≃ 176 60.26 N 110.45 W
Tazin Lake ⊜ 176 59.47 N 109.03 W
T'ažinskij 86 56.07 N 88.31 E
Tāzirbū ⊤[4] 146 25.45 N 21.00 E
Tazishan 107 29.28 N 104.14 E
Tazlina 180 62.04 N 145.25 W
Tazlina Lake ⊜ 180 61.50 N 146.30 W
Tazoult-Lambese 34 35.29 N 6.15 E
Tazovskaja guba c 74 69.05 N 76.00 E
Tazovskij 74 67.28 N 78.42 E
Tazovskij poluostrov ›[1] 72 68.35 N 76.00 E
Tazrouk 148 23.25 N 6.16 E
Tazumal ⊥ 236 13.59 N 89.41 W
Tāzumuddin 126 22.29 N 90.53 E
Tazungdām 102 28.02 N 97.35 E
Tbessa 148 35.28 N 8.09 E
Tbilisi 84 41.43 N 44.49 E
Tbilisskaja 78 45.23 N 40.12 E
Tchad → Chad □[1] 146 15.00 N 19.00 E
Tchad, Lac (Lake Chad) ⊜ 146 13.20 N 14.00 E
Tchaguine Golo 146 10.03 N 16.19 E
Tchamba 150 9.02 N 1.25 E
Tch'ang-Cha → Changsha 100 28.12 N 112.58 E
Tchaourou 150 8.53 N 2.36 E
Tchefuncta ≃ 194 30.22 N 90.10 W
Tchékapika 152 1.17 S 16.11 E
Tcheliabinsk → Čel'abinsk 86 55.10 N 61.24 E
Tcheng-Tcheou → Zhengzhou 102 34.48 N 113.39 E
Tchentlo Lake ⊜ 182 55.11 N 125.00 W
Tchériba 150 12.16 N 3.05 W
Tchesinkut Lake ⊜ 182 54.05 N 125.40 W
Tchetti 150 7.50 N 1.40 E
Tchibanga 152 2.51 S 11.02 E
Tchigaï, Plateau du ⋏[1] 146 21.30 N 14.50 E
Tchikala-Tcholohanga 152 12.38 S 16.03 E
Tchin-Tabáradene 150 15.58 N 5.50 E
Tchitondi 152 4.33 S 12.08 E
Tcholliré 146 8.24 N 14.10 E
Tchong-K'ing → Chongqing 107 29.34 N 106.35 E
Tchořovice 60 49.27 N 13.48 E
Tchula 194 33.10 N 90.13 W
T.C. Steele State Memorial ⊥ 218 39.08 N 86.20 W
Tczew 30 54.06 N 18.47 E
Té ≃ 110 12.27 N 106.02 E
Te, Kinh ≍ 269c 10.45 N 106.42 E
Teá ≃ 246 0.30 S 65.09 W
Teaca 38 46.55 N 24.31 E
Teacapan 234 22.33 N 105.45 W
Tea Creek ≃ 284a 43.02 N 79.06 W
Teaehoa, Pointe › 174x 9.51 S 139.01 W
Teague 222 31.37 N 96.17 W
Teahupoo 174s 17.51 S 149.13 W
Te Anau 172 45.25 S 167.43 E
Te Anau, Lake ⊜ 172 45.12 S 167.48 E
Teanaway ≃ 224 47.10 N 120.50 W
Teanaway, Middle Fork ≃ 224 47.15 N 120.53 W
Teanaway, North Fork ≃ 224 47.22 N 120.53 W
Teaneck 210 40.53 N 74.00 W
Teangue 46 57.07 N 5.50 W
Teano 68 41.15 N 14.04 E
Teapa 234 17.33 N 92.57 W
Teapa ≃ 234 17.58 N 92.54 W
Te Araroa 172 37.38 S 178.22 E
Tearinibai 174t 1.35 N 172.58 E
Te Aroha 172 37.33 S 175.43 E
Teaticket 207 41.33 N 70.35 W
Tea Tree 162 22.11 S 133.17 E
Tea Tree Gully 168b 34.49 S 138.44 E
Te Atukura ∧ 174k 21.14 S 159.45 W
Te Awamutu 172 38.01 S 175.19 E
Teba, Esp. 34 36.58 N 4.56 W
Teba, Indon. 164 1.29 S 137.54 E
Tebakang 112 1.06 N 110.30 E
Tebas 256 21.35 S 42.44 W
Tebay 44 54.26 N 2.35 W
Tebbetts 219 38.37 N 91.57 W
Teberda 84 43.28 N 41.45 E
Teberdinskij zapovednik ♠ 84 43.20 N 41.45 E
Tebicuary ≃ 252 26.36 S 58.16 W
Tebicuary-Mí ≃ 252 26.26 S 56.51 W
Tebingbulan 112 3.03 S 103.44 E
Tebingtinggi, Indon. 112 0.36 N 101.36 E
Tebingtinggi, Indon. 112 3.36 S 103.05 E
Tebingtinggi, Indon. 114 3.20 N 99.09 E
Tebingtinggi, Pulau I 114 0.54 N 102.45 E
Tébourba 36 36.49 N 9.51 E
Téboursouk 148 36.28 N 9.15 E
Téboursouk, Monts de ⋏ 36 36.30 N 9.10 E
Tebra ≃ 76 56.51 N 21.12 E
Tebstrup 41 55.59 N 9.53 E
Tebulosmta, gora ∧ 84 42.33 N 45.19 E
Tebza ≃ 80 58.23 N 41.19 E
Teča ≃ 86 56.13 N 62.58 E
Tecalitlán 234 19.26 N 103.15 W
Tecamachalco 234 18.53 N 97.44 W
Tecate 232 32.34 N 116.38 W
Tech ≃ 32 42.36 N 3.03 E
Teche, Bayou ≃ 194 29.43 N 91.13 W
Techendorf 64 46.43 N 13.17 E
Techiman 150 7.35 N 1.56 W
Techimentia 150 7.11 N 2.02 W
Techirghiol 38 44.03 N 28.36 E
Techlé 148 21.35 N 14.58 W
Techou → Dezhou 98 37.27 N 116.18 E
Tecka 254 43.29 S 70.48 W
Tecka ≃ 254 42.37 S 70.25 W
Tecklenburg 52 52.13 N 7.48 E
Teckomatorp 41 55.52 N 13.05 E
Tecolote Creek ≃ 200 35.22 N 105.15 W
Tecolotlán 234 20.13 N 104.03 W
Tecolutla ≃ 234 20.29 N 97.00 W
Tecomán 234 18.55 N 103.53 W
Tecomate, Laguna c 234 16.35 N 99.25 W
Tecominoacán 234 17.53 N 93.37 W
Tecopa 204 35.50 N 116.13 W
Tecozautla 234 20.32 N 99.38 W
Tecpan ≃ 234 17.25 N 100.40 W
Tecpan de Galeana 234 17.15 N 100.41 W
Tecpán Guatemala 236 14.46 N 91.00 W
Tecpatan 234 17.08 N 93.18 W
Tecuala 234 22.23 N 105.27 W
Tecuamburro, Volcán ∧[1] 236 14.09 N 90.24 W
Tecuautzi, Cerro ∧ 286a 19.19 N 99.00 W
Tecuci 38 45.50 N 27.26 E
Tecumseh, On., Can. 214 42.19 N 82.54 W
Tecumseh, Mi., U.S. 216 42.00 N 83.56 W
Tecumseh, Ne., U.S. 198 40.22 N 96.11 W
Tecumseh, Ok., U.S. 196 35.15 N 96.56 W
Ted Ceidaar Dabole 144 4.24 N 43.55 E
Teddington ⬥[8] 260 51.25 N 0.20 W
Tédji 146 11.46 N 21.19 E
Tedori ≃ 94 36.29 N 136.28 E
Tedrow 216 41.37 N 84.13 W
Tedžen 128 37.23 N 60.31 E
Tedžen (Harīrūd) ≃ 128 37.24 N 60.38 E
Tedženstroj 128 36.55 N 60.53 E
Teec Nos Pos 200 36.56 N 109.42 W
Teeli 86 51.07 N 90.14 E
Teels Marsh ≡ 204 38.12 N 118.21 W
Teen ⊜ 40 59.07 N 14.40 E
Teerijärvi → Terjärv 26 63.32 N 23.30 E
Tees ≃ 44 54.34 N 1.16 W
Tees Bay c 44 54.39 N 1.07 W
Teesdale V 44 54.38 N 2.07 W
Teesside → Middlesbrough 44 54.35 N 1.14 W
Tees-Side Airport ⊠ 44 54.31 N 1.25 W
Teeswater 212 44.00 N 81.17 W
Teeswater ≃ 212 44.18 N 81.17 W
Tefé 246 3.22 S 64.42 W
Tefé ≃ 242 3.35 S 64.47 W
Tefé, Lago ⊜ 246 3.27 S 64.47 W
Tefenni 130 37.18 N 29.47 E
Tefft 216 41.12 N 86.58 W
Tefle 150 5.59 N 0.35 E
Tegal 115a 6.52 S 109.08 E
Tegalombo 115a 8.04 S 111.17 E
Tégama ⬥[1] 150 15.50 N 8.12 E
Tega-numa ⊜ 268 35.51 N 140.04 E
Tegel ⬥[8] 54 52.35 N 13.17 E
Tegel, Berliner Forst ⬥[3] 264a 52.37 N 13.16 E
Tegelen 52 51.21 N 6.09 E
Tegeler See ⊜ 264a 52.35 N 13.15 E
Tegernsee 64 47.43 N 11.45 E
Tegernsee ⊜ 64 47.42 N 11.45 E
Teggiano 68 40.23 N 15.32 E
Teghra 124 25.29 N 85.57 E
Tegid, Llyn ⊜ 42 52.53 N 3.36 W
Tegina 150 10.05 N 6.14 E
Tegineneng 112 5.12 S 105.10 E
Tegistyk 85 44.02 N 68.22 E
Teglio 64 46.10 N 10.04 E
Tégua I 175l 13.15 S 166.37 E
Tegualda 254 41.02 S 73.26 W
Tegucigalpa 236 14.06 N 87.13 W
Tegul'det 86 57.19 N 88.10 E
Tehachapi 228 35.07 N 118.26 W
Tehachapi Creek ≃ 228 35.17 N 118.38 W
Tehachapi Mountains ⋏ 228 35.00 N 118.40 W
Tehachapi Pass)(228 35.06 N 118.18 W
Tehamiyam 140 18.20 N 36.32 E
Te Hapua 172 34.31 S 172.54 E
Tehar ⬥[8] 272a 28.38 N 77.07 E
Te Haroto 172 39.08 S 176.36 E
Tehata 126 23.43 N 88.32 E
Tehek Lake ⊜ 176 64.55 N 95.38 W
Teheran → Tehrān 128 35.40 N 51.26 E
Téhini 150 9.36 N 3.40 W
Tehoohaivei, Cap › 174x 9.49 S 138.54 W
Te Hope O Te Keho, Cap › 174x 10.02 S 139.06 W
Tehoru 164 3.23 S 129.30 E
Tehrān, Īrān 128 35.40 N 51.26 E
Tehrān, Īrān 267d 35.40 N 51.26 E
Tehrān □[4] 128 35.30 N 51.30 E
Tehrān, University of ♁[2] 267d 35.42 N 51.24 E
Tehran International Airport ⊠ 267d 35.41 N 51.19 E
Tehrān Pārs ⬥[8] 267d 35.44 N 51.32 E
Tehrathum 124 27.07 N 87.32 E
Tehri 124 30.23 N 78.29 E
Tehuacán 234 18.27 N 97.23 W
Tehuacana 222 31.44 N 96.33 W
Tehuacana Creek ≃, Tx., U.S. 222 31.31 N 97.02 W
Tehuacana Creek ≃, Tx., U.S. 222 31.50 N 95.59 W
Tehuantepec 234 18.41 N 103.17 W
Tehuantepec ≃ 234 16.10 N 95.07 W
Tehuantepec, Golfo de c 234 16.00 N 94.50 W
Tehuantepec, Istmo de ⊥[3] 234 17.00 N 95.00 W
Tehuantepec Ridge ✦[3] 16 13.30 N 98.00 W
Tehuelches 254 46.56 S 67.27 W
Tehuipango 234 18.31 N 97.04 W
Tehuitzingo 234 18.21 N 98.17 W
Teià 266d 41.30 N 2.19 E
Teichl ≃ 61 47.46 N 14.10 E
Teichröda 54 50.45 N 11.18 E
Teichwolframsdorf 54 50.43 N 12.14 E
Teide, Parque Nacional del ♠ 148 28.15 N 16.30 W
Teide, Pico de ∧ 148 28.16 N 16.38 W
Teifi ≃ 42 52.07 N 4.42 W
Teifiside ⬥[1] 42 52.02 N 4.22 W
Teiga Plateau ⋏[1] 140 15.38 N 25.40 E
Teign ≃ 42 50.33 N 3.29 W
Teignmouth 42 50.33 N 3.30 W
Teise ≃ 260 51.13 N 0.25 E
Teisendorf 64 47.51 N 12.49 E
Teisnach 60 49.02 N 13.00 E
Teith ≃ 46 56.08 N 3.59 W
Teixeira 250 7.13 S 37.15 W
Teixeira Pinto 150 12.10 N 13.55 W
Teixeira Soares 252 25.22 S 50.27 W
Teixeiro 34 43.07 N 8.03 W
Tejakula 115b 8.08 S 115.20 E
Tejamén 232 24.48 N 105.07 W
Tejkovo 80 56.52 N 40.34 E
Tejo → Tagus ≃ 34 38.40 N 9.24 W
Tejon Creek ≃ 228 35.08 N 118.53 W
Tejon Pass)(228 34.48 N 118.52 W
Tejupan, Punta › 234 18.20 N 103.32 W
Tejupilco de Hidalgo 234 18.54 N 100.09 W
Te Kaha 172 37.44 S 177.41 E
Tekai ≃ 114 4.14 N 102.23 E
Tékakwitha, Île I 275a 45.25 N 73.42 W
Tekam ≃ 114 3.52 N 102.27 E
Tekamah 198 41.46 N 96.13 W
Te Kao 172 34.39 S 172.57 E
Tekapo, Lake ⊜ 172 43.53 S 170.31 E
Te Karaka 172 38.28 S 177.52 E
Tekāri 124 24.56 N 84.50 E
Te Kauwhata 172 37.24 S 175.09 E
Tekax 232 20.12 N 89.17 W
Teke 130 41.04 N 29.39 E
Teke, ozero ⊜ 86 53.48 N 73.00 E
Teke Burnu › 130 38.05 N 26.36 E
Tekeli 86 44.48 N 78.57 E
Tekeli Dağı ∧ 130 40.09 N 37.28 E
Tekes 86 43.10 N 81.43 E
Tekes ≃ 86 43.36 N 82.32 E
Tekeze (Satīt) ≃ 140 14.20 N 35.50 E
Tekirdağ 130 40.59 N 27.31 E
Tekirdağ □[4] 130 41.00 N 27.30 E
Tekkali 122 18.37 N 84.14 E
Tekke 130 40.43 N 36.12 E
Tekke Burnu › 130 40.02 N 26.10 E
Tekkiraz 130 40.59 N 37.08 E
Tekman 130 39.38 N 41.31 E
Tekoa 202 47.13 N 117.04 W
Tekong, Pulau I 271c 1.24 N 104.03 E
Tekong Kechil, Pulau I 271c 1.25 N 104.01 E
Tekonsha 216 42.05 N 84.59 W
Te Kopuru 172 36.02 S 173.56 E
Tekouiat, Oued V 148 22.25 N 2.35 E
Tékro ⊤[4] 146 19.30 N 20.58 E
Tekstil'ščiki 82 55.57 N 37.49 E
Tekstil'ščiki ⬥[8] 265b 55.42 N 37.44 E
Teku 112 0.46 S 123.26 E
Te Kuiti 172 38.20 S 175.10 E
Tekukor, Pulau I 271c 1.14 N 103.50 E

Symbols in the index entries represent the broad categories identified in the key at the right. Symbols with superior numbers (⋏[1]) identify subcategories (see complete key on page I · 1).

Symbole im Register stellen die rechts im Schlüssel erklärten Kategorien dar. Symbole mit hochgestellten Ziffern (⋏[1]) bezeichnen Unterabteilungen einer Kategorie (vgl. vollständiger Schlüssel auf Seite I · 1).

Los símbolos incluídos en el texto del índice representan las grandes categorías identificadas con la clave a la derecha. Los símbolos con numeros en su parte superior (⋏[1]) identifican las subcategorías (véase la clave completa en la página I · 1).

Les symboles de l'index représentent les catégories indiquées dans la légende à droite. Les symboles suivis d'un indice (⋏[1]) représentent des souscatégories (voir légende complète à la page I · 1).

Os símbolos incluídos no texto do índice representam as grandes categorias identificadas com a chave à direita. Os símbolos com números em sua parte superior (⋏[1]) identificam as subcategorias (veja-se a chave completa à página I · 1).

	English	Deutsch	Español	Français	Português
∧	Mountain	Berg	Montaña	Montagne	Montanha
⋏	Mountains	Gebirge	Montañas	Montagnes	Montanhas
)(	Pass	Paß	Paso	Col	Passo
V	Valley, Canyon	Tal, Cañon	Valle, Cañón	Vallée, Canyon	Vale, Canhão
≃	Plain	Ebene	Llano	Plaine	Planície
›	Cape	Kap	Cabo	Cap	Cabo
I	Island	Insel	Isla	Île	Ilha
II	Islands	Inseln	Islas	Îles	Ilhas
⊥	Other Topographic Features	Andere Topographische Objekte	Otros Elementos Topográficos	Autres données topographiques	Outros acidentes topográficos

ESPAÑOL | FRANÇAIS | PORTUGUÊS

≃ River	Fluß	Río	Rivière	Rio
≏ Canal	Kanal	Canal	Canal	Canal
Ⴑ Waterfall, Rapids	Wasserfall, Stromschnellen	Cascada, Rápidos	Chute d'eau, Rapides	Cascata, Rápidos
Ⴑ Strait	Meeresstraße	Estrecho	Détroit	Estreito
c Bay, Gulf	Bucht, Golf	Bahía, Golfo	Baie, Golfe	Baía, Golfo
∅ Lake, Lakes	See, Seen	Lago, Lagos	Lac, Lacs	Lago, Lagos
≋ Swamp	Sumpf	Pantano	Marais	Pântano
Ɪ Ice Features, Glacier	Eis- und Gletscherformen	Otros Elementos Glaciales	Formes glaciaires	Acidentes glaciares
т Other Hydrographic Features	Andere Hydrographische Objekte	Otros Elementos Hidrográficos	Autres données hydrographiques	Outros acidentes hidrográficos
♣ Submarine Features	Untermeerische Objekte	Accidentes Submarinos	Formes de relief sous-marin	Acidentes submarinos
□ Political Unit	Politische Einheit	Unidad Política	Entité politique	Unidade política
⚲ Cultural Institution	Kulturelle Institution	Institución Cultural	Institution culturelle	Instituição cultural
ꞮꞮ Historical Site	Historische Stätte	Sitio Histórico	Site historique	Sitio histórico
✦ Recreational Site	Erholungs- und Ferienort	Sitio de Recreo	Centre de loisirs	Area de Lazer
✈ Airport	Flughafen	Aeropuerto	Aéroport	Aeroporto
♦ Military Installation	Militäranlage	Instalación Militar	Installation militaire	Instalação militar
✦ Miscellaneous	Verschiedenes	Misceláneo	Divers	Diversos

I · 176 Than-Tigi

ENGLISH Name Page Lat.°′ Long.°′ — DEUTSCH Name Seite Breite°′ Länge°′ E = Ost

Name	Page	Lat.°′	Long.°′
Thanjāvūr	122	10.48 N	79.09 E
Thann	58	47.49 N	7.05 E
Thannhausen	58	48.17 N	10.28 E
Thāno Bula Khān	120	25.22 N	67.50 E
Than Uyen	110	22.00 N	103.54 E
Thaoge ≃	156	20.27 S	22.36 E
Thaon-les-Vosges	58	48.15 N	6.25 E
Tha Pla	110	17.48 N	100.32 E
Thap Than ≃	110	15.21 N	104.06 E
Tharabwin West	110	12.17 N	99.03 E
Tharād	120	24.24 N	71.38 E
Tharandt	54	50.59 N	13.35 E
't Harde	52	52.25 N	5.53 E
Thar Desert (Great Indian Desert) ◈[2]	120	27.00 N	71.00 E
Thargomindah	166	28.00 S	143.49 E
Thāri Pātan ∧	124	28.58 N	82.04 E
Thar Nhom	140	7.26 N	30.29 E
Tharptown	210	40.48 N	76.34 W
Tharr, Wüste → Thar Desert ◈[2]	120	27.00 N	71.00 E
Tharrawaddy	110	17.39 N	95.48 E
Tharrawaw	110	17.41 N	95.28 E
Tharros ⊥	71	39.52 N	8.26 E
Tharsuinn, Beinn ∧	46	57.47 N	4.21 W
Tharthār, Buḥayrat ath- ⊜	128	34.00 N	43.05 E
Tharthār, Wādī ath- V	128	33.59 N	43.12 E
Tharwa	171b	35.31 S	149.04 E
Tha Sala	110	8.40 N	99.56 E
Thásos	38	40.47 N	24.42 E
Thásos I	38	40.41 N	24.47 E
Thásos ⊥	38	40.46 N	24.33 E
Tha Tako	110	15.38 N	100.29 E
Thatcham	42	51.25 N	1.15 W
Thatch Cay I	240m	18.22 N	64.52 W
Thatcher	200	32.50 N	109.45 W
Thatch Island I	276	40.38 N	73.23 W
That Khe	110	22.16 N	106.28 E
Thaton	110	16.55 N	97.22 E
That Phanom	110	16.57 N	104.44 E
Thatto Heath	262	53.26 N	2.45 W
Tha Tum	110	15.19 N	103.41 E
Thau, Bassin de c	32	43.23 N	3.36 E
Thaungdut	110	24.26 N	94.42 E
Thaungyin ≃	110	17.50 N	97.42 E
Tha Uthen	110	17.34 N	104.36 E
Thawville	216	40.41 N	88.07 W
Thaxted	42	51.57 N	0.20 E
Thaya (Dyje) ≃	61	48.37 N	16.56 E
Thayawthadangyi Kyun I	110	12.20 N	98.00 E
Thayer, Il., U.S.	219	39.32 N	89.46 W
Thayer, In., U.S.	216	41.10 N	87.20 W
Thayer, Ks., U.S.	198	37.29 N	95.28 W
Thayer, Mo., U.S.	194	36.31 N	91.32 W
Thayetchaung	110	13.52 N	98.16 E
Thayetmyo	110	19.19 N	95.11 E
Thayngen	58	47.45 N	8.42 E
Thazi	110	20.51 N	96.05 E
The Aldermen Islands II	172	36.58 S	176.05 E
Theale	42	51.27 N	1.04 W
Thealka	192	37.49 N	82.47 W
The Basin	274b	37.51 S	145.19 E
Thebes → Thívai, Ellás	38	38.21 N	23.19 E
Thebes, Il., U.S.	194	37.13 N	89.28 W
Thebes ⊥	140	25.42 N	32.37 E
The Birket ≃	262	53.24 N	3.01 W
The Bluffs ⊥[4]	210	43.22 N	76.40 W
The Bourne ≃	260	51.22 N	0.29 W
The Calvados Chain II	164	11.10 S	152.40 E
The Camels Hump ∧	169	37.23 S	144.35 E
The Capital ʊ	284c	38.53 N	77.00 W
The Cheviot ∧	44	55.28 N	2.09 W
The Citadel ⊥, Magy.	264c	47.29 N	19.03 E
The Citadel ⊥, Miṣr	273c	30.02 N	31.15 E
The Cloisters ʊ	276	40.52 N	73.56 W
The Colony	222	33.05 N	96.52 W
The Coorong c	168b	35.40 S	139.15 E
The Coteau ⩘[2]	184	51.10 N	107.30 W
The Curragh ♦	48	53.10 N	6.52 W
The Dalles	224	45.35 N	121.10 W
The Dalles Dam ◈[6]	224	45.37 N	121.08 W
The Deeps c	46a	60.09 N	1.23 W
Thedford	198	41.58 N	100.34 W
Thedinghausen	52	52.58 N	9.01 E
The Downs ⊤[3]	42	51.13 N	1.27 E
Theebine	166	25.57 S	152.33 E
The English Companys Islands II	164	11.50 S	136.32 E
The Entrance	170	33.21 S	151.30 E
Theessen	54	52.14 N	12.02 E
The Fens ◈[1]	42	52.38 N	0.02 E
The Fishing Lakes ⊜	184	50.45 N	103.51 W
The Flash ⊜	262	53.29 N	2.33 W
The Flat Tops ⩘	200	40.00 N	107.10 W
The Forest of Nisene Marks State Park ♦	226	37.03 N	121.53 W
The Glenkens ◈[1]	44	55.10 N	4.15 W
Thègon	110	18.39 N	95.25 E
The Granites	162	20.35 S	130.21 E
The Granites ∧	162	20.35 S	130.20 E
The Graves II	283	42.22 N	70.52 W
The Grove	222	31.16 N	97.32 W
The Hague → 's-Gravenhage	52	52.06 N	4.18 E
The Heads >	202	42.44 N	124.31 W
The Hermitage ʊ	265a	59.56 N	30.20 E
The Home Park ♦	260	51.28 N	0.36 W
The Hunters Hills ⩘[2]	172	44.30 S	170.50 E
Theinkun	110	11.53 N	99.09 E
The Isles Lagoon c	174o	1.50 N	157.23 W
Theiss → Tisa ≃	38	45.15 N	20.17 E
Theissen	54	51.05 N	12.06 E
The Key Indian Reserve ◈[4]	184	51.45 N	102.08 W
The Lake Fleet Islands II	212	44.18 N	76.07 W
The Lakes National Park ♦	166	38.05 S	147.40 E
The Little Minch ⊍	46	57.35 N	6.55 W
Thelon ≃	176	64.16 N	96.05 W
The Long Mynd ∧	42	52.35 N	2.48 W
The Lower Hope ≃[1]	260	51.28 N	0.28 E
Thelwall	262	53.23 N	2.32 W
The Lynd	166	18.56 S	144.30 E
Them	41	56.06 N	9.33 E
The Machars ◈[1]	44	54.50 N	4.33 W
The Mall in Columbia ◈[9]	284b	39.13 N	76.52 W
Themar	54	50.30 N	10.37 E
The Meadows Race Track ♦	279b	40.13 N	80.12 W
The Mere ⊜	262	53.20 N	2.24 W
Théméricourt	261	49.05 N	1.54 E
The Minch ⊍	46	58.10 N	5.50 W
The Mumbles	42	51.34 N	4.00 W
Then	123	32.26 N	75.44 E
The Narrows ⊍	276	40.37 N	74.03 W
The Navy Islands II	212	44.21 N	76.03 W
The Naze >	42	51.53 N	1.16 E
The Needles >	42	50.39 N	1.34 W
Thénezay	32	46.43 N	0.02 W
Thenia	148	36.43 N	3.34 E
Theniet el Hadd	148	35.47 N	2.01 E
The Oa >[1]	46	55.37 N	6.16 W
The Oaks, Austl.	170	34.04 S	150.34 E
The Oaks, Ca., U.S.	226	39.13 N	121.05 W
Theodore, Austl.	166	24.57 S	150.05 E
Theodore, Sk., Can.	184	51.25 N	102.54 W
Theodore, Al., U.S.	194	30.32 N	88.10 W
Theodore Francis Green Airport ⊠	207	41.44 N	71.26 W
Theodore Roosevelt Inaugural National Historic Site ⊥	284a	42.54 N	78.52 W
Theodore Roosevelt Island I	284c	38.54 N	77.03 W
Theodore Roosevelt Lake ⊜[1]	200	33.42 N	111.07 W
Theodore Roosevelt National Park (South Unit) ♦, N.D., U.S.	198	46.55 N	103.26 W
Theodore Roosevelt National Park (North Unit) ♦, N.D., U.S.	198	47.34 N	103.24 W
Theodor-Heuss-Brücke ◈[5]	263	51.15 N	6.45 E
Theog	123	31.07 N	77.21 E
Theólogos	38	40.39 N	24.41 E
The Orchards	284b	39.18 N	76.50 W
Théoule-sur-Mer	62	43.31 N	6.57 E
The Oval ⊥	260	51.29 N	0.07 W
The Pages II	168b	35.47 S	138.17 E
The Paps ∧	48	52.00 N	9.17 W
The Pas	184	53.50 N	101.15 W
The Peak ∧	192	36.24 N	81.39 W
Thepha	110	6.52 N	100.58 E
The Pinnacle ∧[2]	219	39.22 N	90.55 W
Thérain ≃	50	49.15 N	2.27 E
The Rajah ∧	182	53.15 N	118.31 W
The Rand → Witwatersrant ◈[1]	158	26.00 S	27.00 E
The Range	154	19.00 S	31.04 E
Theresa	212	44.12 N	75.47 W
Theresa Creek ≃	166	23.26 S	148.09 E
Theresa Park	274a	34.01 S	150.39 E
Theresienstadt → Terezín	54	50.31 N	14.08 E
The Rhins >[1]	44	54.50 N	5.00 W
The Rip c	169	38.17 S	144.37 E
Thermaïkós Kólpos c	38	40.23 N	22.47 E
Thermalito	226	39.31 N	121.36 W
Thermopílai (Thermopylae) ⊥	38	38.48 N	22.33 E
Thermopolis	200	43.38 N	108.12 W
Thermopylae → Thermopílai ⊥	38	38.48 N	22.33 E
The Road c	42a	49.56 N	6.20 W
The Rock	166	35.16 S	147.07 E
The Rockies ∧	224	46.39 N	122.22 W
Theron Mountains ⩘	9	79.05 S	28.15 W
The Rope ⊥[4]	174e	25.04 S	130.05 W
Thérouanne	50	50.38 N	2.15 E
The Savannahs ⊜	220	27.19 N	80.17 W
Theseion ⊥	267c	37.58 N	23.43 E
Thesiger Bay c	176	71.30 N	124.05 W
The Sisters ∧[2]	162	26.17 S	126.40 E
The Slot → New Georgia Sound ⊍	175e	8.00 S	158.10 E
The Sluice ≍	262	53.41 N	2.57 W
The Sny ≃	219	39.16 N	90.44 W
The Solent ⊍	42	50.46 N	1.20 W
The Sound (Øresund) ⊍	41	55.50 N	12.40 E
The Springs	207	40.52 N	72.32 W
Thesprotikón	38	39.15 N	20.47 E
Thessalía □[4]	38	39.30 N	22.30 E
Thessalía □[9]	38	39.30 N	22.15 E
Thessalon	190	46.15 N	83.34 W
Thessaloníki (Salonika)	38	40.38 N	22.56 E
Thessalonique → Thessaloníki	38	40.38 N	22.56 E
The Storr ∧	46	57.31 N	6.12 W
The Swale ⊍	42	51.22 N	0.56 E
Thet ≃	42	52.24 N	0.45 E
The Tauride Palace ʊ	265a	59.57 N	30.23 E
The Terraces ⊥[4]	162	28.40 S	121.30 E
Thetford	42	52.25 N	0.45 E
Thetford-Mines	206	46.05 N	71.18 W
The Thorofare ⊍	208	37.15 N	75.54 W
The Thumbs ∧	172	43.36 S	170.44 E
Thetis Island	224	49.59 N	123.40 W
Thetis Island I	224	49.00 N	123.41 W
The Twelve Pins ∧	48	53.31 N	9.50 W
The Twins ∧	172	41.14 S	172.39 E
Theunissen	158	28.30 S	26.41 E
Theux	56	50.32 N	5.49 E
The Valley	238	18.13 N	63.04 W
Thevenard	162	32.09 S	133.38 E
Thevenard Island I	162	21.27 S	115.00 E
The Wash c	42	52.55 N	0.15 E
The Weald ◈[1]	42	51.05 N	0.05 E
The Whirlpool ≃	284a	43.07 N	79.04 W
The Winehead ∧	210	40.58 N	77.28 W
The Wolds ⩘[2]	44	53.20 N	0.10 W
The Woodlands	222	30.09 N	95.27 W
The Wrekin ∧[2]	42	52.41 N	2.34 W
Theydon Bois	260	51.40 N	0.06 E
Theys	62	45.18 N	6.00 E
Thiais	261	48.46 N	2.23 E
Thiant	50	50.18 N	3.27 E
Thiaucourt-Regniéville	56	48.57 N	5.52 E
Thibaudeau	184	57.05 N	94.08 W
Thiberville	50	49.08 N	0.27 E
Thibodaux	194	29.47 N	90.49 W
Thicket	222	30.24 N	94.38 W
Thicket Portage	184	55.19 N	97.42 W
Thiéblemont-Farémont	58	48.41 N	4.44 E
Thief ≃	198	48.08 N	96.10 W
Thief Lake ⊜	198	48.30 N	95.55 W
Thief River Falls	198	48.07 N	96.10 W
Thiéle (Zihl) ≃	58	47.03 N	7.05 E
Thiel Mountains ⩘	9	85.15 S	91.00 W
Thielsen, Mount ∧	202	43.09 N	122.04 W
Thiendorf	54	51.17 N	13.44 E
Thiene	64	45.42 N	11.29 E
Thiensville	216	43.14 N	87.58 W
Thiérache, Collines de la ⩘[2]	50	49.50 N	3.50 E
Thierhaupten	56	48.34 N	10.54 E
Thiers	62	45.51 N	3.34 E
Thiersheim	54	50.04 N	12.07 E
Thierville-sur-Meuse	56	49.10 N	5.21 E
Thiès	150	14.48 N	16.56 W
Thiès □[4]	150	14.45 N	16.50 W
Thiesi	71	40.31 N	8.43 E
Thiessow	54	54.16 N	13.43 E
Thieux	261	49.01 N	2.40 E
Thieveley Pike ∧[2]	262	53.45 N	2.12 W
Thika	154	1.03 S	37.05 E
Thikombia Island I	175g	15.44 S	179.55 W
Thilay	56	49.52 N	4.49 E
Thilenius, Cape >	164	1.35 S	149.57 E
Thimphu	124	27.28 N	89.39 E
Thines	62	44.29 N	4.03 E
Thingvallavatn ⊜	24a	64.12 N	21.10 W
Thingvellir	24a	64.17 N	21.07 W
Thingvellir National Park ♦	24a	64.17 N	21.06 W
Thio	175f	21.37 S	166.14 E
Thionville	56	49.22 N	6.10 E
Thiou	150	13.48 N	2.40 W
Thíra	38	36.25 N	25.26 E
Thíra (Santorini) I	38	36.24 N	25.29 E
Third ≃	276	40.49 N	74.08 W
Third Cataract → Thālith, Ash-Shallāl ath- ∟	140	19.49 N	30.19 E
Third Cliff ⊥[4]	283	42.11 N	70.43 W
Third Creek ≃, Mo., U.S.	219	38.26 N	91.40 W
Third Creek ≃, N.C., U.S.	192	35.47 N	80.31 W
Third Han-gang Bridge ◈[5]	271b	37.32 N	127.00 E
Third Herring Brook ≃	283	42.07 N	70.48 W
Third Lake ⊜	206	45.14 N	71.12 W
Third Street Station ◈[5]	282	37.46 N	122.23 W
Thirlmere	170	34.12 S	150.34 E
Thirlmere ⊜	44	54.33 N	3.04 W
Thirlmere Lakes National Park ♦	170	34.14 S	150.32 E
Thiron	50	48.19 N	0.59 E
Thironne ≃	50	48.17 N	1.15 E
Thirroul	170	34.19 S	150.56 E
Thirsk	44	54.14 N	1.20 W
Thirtieth Street Station ◈[5]	285	39.57 N	75.11 W
Thirtymile Creek ≃	198	46.22 N	102.03 W
Thirtymile Point >	210	43.22 N	78.29 W
Thiruvārūr	122	10.46 N	79.39 E
Thisted	26	56.57 N	8.42 E
Thistilfjörður c	24a	66.20 N	15.25 W
Thistledown Race Track ♦	279a	41.26 N	81.32 W
Thistle Island I	166	35.00 S	136.09 E
Thistletown ◈[8]	275b	43.44 N	79.33 W
Thithia Island I	175g	17.45 S	179.18 W
Thívai (Thebes)	38	38.21 N	23.19 E
Thiverval-Grignon	261	48.51 N	1.55 E
Thiviers	32	45.25 N	0.56 E
Thizy	32	46.02 N	4.19 E
Thjórsá ≃	24a	63.47 N	20.48 W
Thlewiaza ≃	176	60.28 N	94.45 W
Thoa ≃	176	60.30 N	109.47 W
Tho Chu, Dao II	110	9.20 N	103.28 E
Thoen	110	17.36 N	99.12 E
Thohoyandou	156	23.00 S	30.29 E
Thoi Binh	110	9.21 N	105.05 E
Thoirette	58	46.16 N	5.32 E
Thoiry	261	48.52 N	1.48 E
Thoissey	58	46.10 N	4.48 E
Tholen	52	51.32 N	4.12 E
Tholen I	52	51.35 N	4.05 E
Tholey	56	49.29 N	7.02 E
Thollon	58	46.23 N	6.43 E
Thomas, Ok., U.S.	196	35.44 N	98.44 W
Thomas, Pa., U.S.	279b	40.15 N	80.06 W
Thomas, Wa., U.S.	224	47.21 N	122.13 W
Thomas, W.V., U.S.	188	39.08 N	79.29 W
Thomasboro	216	40.15 N	88.11 W
Thomas Creek ≃	202	44.40 N	122.56 W
Thomas Hill Reservoir ⊜[1]	194	39.40 N	92.40 W
Thomas J. O'Brien Lock and Dam ◈[5]	278	41.39 N	87.35 W
Thomas Lake ⊜	184	57.00 N	96.43 W
Thomas Mountains ⩘	9	75.32 S	70.57 W
Thomas Point >	208	38.54 N	76.28 W
Thomaston, Al., U.S.	194	32.15 N	87.37 W
Thomaston, Ct., U.S.	207	41.40 N	73.04 W
Thomaston, Ga., U.S.	192	32.53 N	84.19 W
Thomaston, Me., U.S.	188	44.04 N	69.10 W
Thomaston, N.Y., U.S.	276	40.47 N	73.43 W
Thomaston, Tx., U.S.	222	29.00 N	97.09 W
Thomastown, Austl.	274b	37.41 S	145.01 E
Thomastown, Ire.	48	52.31 N	7.08 W
Thomasville, Al., U.S.	194	31.54 N	87.44 W
Thomasville, Ga., U.S.	192	30.50 N	83.58 W
Thomasville, N.C., U.S.	192	35.52 N	80.04 W
Thomasville, Pa., U.S.	208	39.56 N	76.51 W
Thomes Creek ≃	204	39.59 N	122.06 W
Thom Lake ⊜	184	55.24 N	96.08 W
Thomlinson, Mount ∧	182	55.33 N	127.29 W
Thompson, Mb., Can.	184	55.45 N	97.45 W
Thompson, Ct., U.S.	207	41.57 N	71.51 W
Thompson, Ia., U.S.	190	43.22 N	93.46 W
Thompson, Mo., U.S.	219	39.11 N	91.59 W
Thompson, N.D., U.S.	198	47.46 N	97.06 W
Thompson, Oh., U.S.	214	41.41 N	81.03 W
Thompson, Pa., U.S.	210	41.52 N	75.31 W
Thompson ≃, B.C., Can.	182	50.15 N	121.33 W
Thompson ≃, U.S.	194	39.45 N	93.36 W
Thompson Creek ≃, U.S.	198	45.04 N	104.25 W
Thompson Creek ≃, Ms., U.S.	194	31.10 N	88.54 W
Thompson Falls	202	47.35 N	115.20 W
Thompson Island I	283	42.23 N	71.01 W
Thompson Pass)(	180	61.08 N	145.45 W
Thompson Peak ∧	204	41.00 N	123.03 W
Thompson Place	224	47.03 N	122.45 W
Thompson Ridge	210	41.34 N	74.20 W
Thompson Run ≃	279b	40.24 N	79.50 W
Thompsons	222	29.30 N	95.36 W
Thompsons Creek ≃	284a	43.03 N	79.08 W
Thompson Sound ⊍	172	45.09 S	166.57 E
Thompsontown	208	40.33 N	77.14 W
Thompsonville	190	44.31 N	85.56 W
Thomsen ≃	176	74.08 N	119.35 W
Thomson, Ga., U.S.	192	33.28 N	82.30 W
Thomson, Il., U.S.	190	41.58 N	90.06 W
Thomson, N.Y., U.S.	210	43.07 N	73.35 W
Thomson ≃, Austl.	166	25.11 S	142.53 E
Thomson ≃, Austl.	169	37.58 S	146.32 E
Thomson, Lake ⊜[1]	169	37.45 S	146.22 E
Thomson Lake ⊜[1]	184	49.45 N	106.35 W
Thon ≃	50	49.53 N	3.55 E
Thon Buri	110	13.43 N	100.29 E
Thônes	62	45.53 N	6.20 E
Thong	260	51.24 N	0.24 E
Thong Hoe	271c	1.25 N	103.42 E
Thong Tay Hoi	269c	10.50 N	106.39 E
Thongwa	110	16.46 N	96.32 E
Thon Lac Nghiep	110	11.20 N	108.54 E
Thonnance-lès-Joinville	58	48.27 N	5.10 E
Thonon-les-Bains	58	46.22 N	6.29 E
Thonotosassa	220	28.03 N	82.18 W
Thonze	110	17.38 N	95.47 E
Thorah Island I	212	44.27 N	79.14 W
Thorame-Haute	62	44.06 N	6.33 E
Thorburn	186	45.34 N	62.33 W
Thoreau	200	35.24 N	108.13 W
Thorembais-les-Béguines	56	50.40 N	4.49 E
Thorenc	62	43.48 N	6.49 E
Thorens-Glières	58	45.59 N	6.15 E
Thorhild	182	54.10 N	113.07 W
Thorial	140	8.40 N	29.56 E
Thorigny-sur-Marne	261	48.53 N	2.42 E
Thorigny-sur-Oreuse	50	48.17 N	3.24 E
Thórisvatn ⊜	24a	64.16 N	18.54 W
Thörl	61	47.31 N	15.13 E
Thorlákshöfn	24a	63.53 N	21.18 W
Thormanby	44	54.10 N	1.14 W
Thorn, Ned.	52	51.10 N	5.50 E
Thorn → Toruń, Pol.	30	53.02 N	18.35 E
Thornaby-on-Tees	44	54.34 N	1.18 W
Thornapple ≃, Mi., U.S.	216	42.56 N	85.28 W
Thornapple ≃, Wi., U.S.	190	45.28 N	91.16 W
Thornapple Lake ⊜	216	42.37 N	85.11 W
Thornburg	279b	40.26 N	80.05 W
Thornbury, Austl.	274b	37.45 S	145.00 E
Thornbury, On., Can.	212	44.34 N	80.26 W
Thornbury, N.Z.	172	46.17 S	168.06 E
Thornbury, Eng., U.K.	42	51.37 N	2.32 W
Thorn Creek ≃	278	41.36 N	87.35 W
Thorndale, On., Can.	212	43.06 N	81.08 W
Thorndale, Tx., U.S.	222	30.36 N	97.12 W
Thorndike	207	42.11 N	72.20 W
Thorndon	42	52.17 N	1.08 E
Thorne	44	53.37 N	0.58 W
Thorne ≃	184	54.56 N	90.35 W
Thorne Bay	182	55.44 N	132.32 W
Thorney	42	52.37 N	0.07 W
Thorngumbald	44	53.43 N	0.10 W
Thornhill, On., Can.	275b	43.48 N	79.25 W
Thornhill, S. Afr.	273d	26.07 S	28.09 E
Thornhill, Scot., U.K.	44	55.15 N	3.46 W
Thornhurst	210	41.11 N	75.35 W
Thornleigh	274a	33.44 S	151.05 E
Thornton, Austl.	171a	27.49 S	152.23 E
Thornton, Eng., U.K.	44	53.53 N	3.02 W
Thornton, Eng., U.K.	262	53.30 N	3.00 W
Thornton, Eng., U.K.	262	53.47 N	1.51 W
Thornton, Scot., U.K.	46	56.10 N	3.09 W
Thornton, Ar., U.S.	194	33.46 N	92.29 W
Thornton, Ca., U.S.	226	38.14 N	121.25 W
Thornton, Co., U.S.	200	39.52 N	104.58 W
Thornton, Il., U.S.	278	41.35 N	87.37 W
Thornton, Pa., U.S.	285	39.54 N	75.32 W
Thornton, Tx., U.S.	222	31.24 N	96.34 W
Thornton Beach ♦	282	37.42 N	122.30 W
Thornton Dale	44	54.14 N	0.43 W
Thornton Hough	262	53.19 N	3.03 W
Thornton-le-Moors	262	53.16 N	2.50 W
Thornton Moor Reservoir ⊜[1]	262	53.47 N	1.55 W
Thorntonville	196	31.34 N	102.55 W
Thornwood	210	41.07 N	73.46 W
Thornwood Common	260	51.43 N	0.08 E
Thorny Mountain ∧[2]	194	37.06 N	91.10 W
Thorofare	285	39.50 N	75.11 W
Thorold	212	43.07 N	79.12 W
Thorold South	284a	43.06 N	79.12 W
Thoronet, Abbaye du ʊ[1]	62	43.28 N	6.16 E
Thorp, Wa., U.S.	224	47.04 N	120.40 W
Thorp, Wi., U.S.	190	44.57 N	90.47 W
Thorpe	260	51.24 N	0.32 W
Thorpe-le-Soken	42	51.52 N	1.10 E
Thorp Spring	222	32.28 N	97.49 W
Thorsby, Ab., Can.	182	53.14 N	114.03 W
Thorsby, Al., U.S.	194	32.54 N	86.42 W
Thorshavn → Tórshavn	22	62.01 N	6.46 W
Thórshöfn	24a	66.13 N	15.17 W
Thorsø	41	56.18 N	9.48 E
Thorsteinson Lake ⊜	184	57.15 N	97.30 W
Thot Not	110	10.16 N	105.32 E
Thouars	32	46.59 N	0.13 W
Thouin, Cape >	162	20.20 S	118.12 E
Thoune → Thun	58	46.45 N	7.37 E
Thourotte	50	49.29 N	2.53 E
Thousand Islands II	212	44.15 N	76.12 W
Thousand Islands International Bridge ◈[5]	212	44.20 N	75.58 W
Thousand Lake Mountain ∧	200	38.25 N	111.29 W
Thousand Oaks	228	34.10 N	118.50 W
Thousand Ships Bay c	175e	8.25 S	159.40 E
Thousand Springs Creek ≃	200	41.17 N	113.51 W
Thowa ≃	154	1.33 S	40.03 E
Thowgla Creek ≃	171b	36.10 S	147.57 E
Thrace □[9]	38	41.20 N	26.45 E
Thrakikón Pélagos ⊤[2]	38	40.15 N	24.28 E
Thrall	222	30.35 N	97.18 W
Thrapston	42	52.24 N	0.32 W
Thrasher Lake ⊜	212	44.55 N	78.58 W
Thread Creek ≃	216	43.01 N	83.42 W
Thredbo Village	171b	36.29 S	148.19 E
Three Bridges	208	40.31 N	74.47 W
Three Brothers ∧	224	47.23 N	120.45 W
Three Brothers Mountain ∧	224	49.10 N	120.46 W
Three Creek ≃	208	36.47 N	77.10 W
Three Fathoms Cove c	271d	22.26 N	114.17 E
Three Fingered Jack ∧	202	44.29 N	121.50 W
Three Fingers ∧	224	48.10 N	121.41 W
Three Fools Creek ≃	224	48.53 N	120.57 W
Three Forks	202	45.53 N	111.33 W
Three Hills	182	51.42 N	113.16 W
Three Hummock Island I	166	40.26 S	144.55 E
Three Kings Islands II	172	34.10 S	172.05 E
Three Lakes	190	45.47 N	89.09 W
Three M Airport ⊠	285	40.08 N	74.51 W
Three Mile Bay	212	44.04 N	76.11 W
Three Mile Plains	186	44.58 N	64.07 W
Three Oaks	216	41.47 N	86.36 W
Three Pagodas Pass)(	110	15.18 N	98.23 E
Threepoint Lake ⊜	184	55.41 N	98.56 W
Three Points, Cape >	150	4.45 N	2.06 W
Three Rivers, Austl.	162	25.07 S	119.09 E
Three Rivers → Trois-Rivières, P.Q., Can.	206	46.21 N	72.33 W
Three Rivers, Ma., U.S.	207	42.10 N	72.21 W
Three Rivers, Mi., U.S.	216	41.56 N	85.37 W
Three Rivers, Tx., U.S.	196	28.27 N	98.10 W
Three Rivers □[8]	260	51.40 N	0.27 W
Three Sisters	158	31.54 S	23.06 E
Three Sisters ∧	202	44.10 N	121.46 W
Three Sisters Islands II	175e	10.10 S	161.57 E
Three Springs, Austl.	162	29.32 S	115.45 E
Three Springs, Pa., U.S.	214	40.12 N	77.59 W
Threlkeld	44	54.38 N	3.03 W
Throat ≃	184	51.48 N	93.30 W
Throckmorton	196	33.10 N	99.10 W
Throgs Neck ◈[8]	276	40.49 N	73.49 W
Throgs Neck Bridge ◈[5]	276	40.48 N	73.48 W
Throgs Point >	276	40.48 N	73.48 W
Throop	210	41.27 N	75.36 W
Throssel, Lake ⊜	162	27.27 S	124.16 E
Throssell Range ⩘	162	22.03 S	121.43 E
Thrushel ≃	42	50.39 N	4.15 W
Thruway Mall ◈[9]	284a	42.55 N	78.46 W
Thu, Cu Lao I	110	10.33 N	108.57 E
Thuan Chau	110	21.26 N	103.41 E
Thu Dau Mot	110	10.58 N	106.39 E
Thu Duc	269c	10.51 N	106.45 E
Thueyts	62	44.41 N	4.13 E
Thuilley-aux-Groseilles	58	48.34 N	5.58 E
Thuin	50	50.20 N	4.17 E
Thul	120	28.14 N	68.46 E
Thulaythiwāt, Tilāl ath- ∧	132	30.58 N	36.40 E
Thulba ≃	56	50.11 N	9.52 E
Thule	16	76.34 N	68.47 W
Thulī Bherī ≃	124	28.42 N	82.16 E
Thum	54	50.40 N	12.57 E
Thumb Peak ∧	116	9.48 N	118.36 E
Thumby	41	54.35 N	9.54 E
Thun	58	46.45 N	7.37 E
Thun Chang	110	19.25 N	100.53 E
Thunder Bay	190	48.23 N	89.15 W
Thunder Bay c, On., Can.	190	48.24 N	89.00 W
Thunder Bay c, On., Can.	212	44.48 N	80.03 W
Thunder Bay c, Mi., U.S.	190	45.00 N	83.22 W
Thunder Bay ≃	190	45.04 N	83.25 W
Thunder Bay, North Branch ≃	190	45.08 N	83.35 W
Thunderbird, Lake ⊜[1]	196	35.15 N	97.20 W
Thunderbolt	192	32.02 N	81.03 W
Thunder Butte ∧	198	45.19 N	101.53 W
Thunder Butte Creek ≃	198	45.13 N	101.42 W
Thunder Creek ≃, Sk., Can.	184	50.23 N	105.32 W
Thunder Creek ≃, Wa., U.S.	224	48.40 N	121.05 W
Thunder Hills ⩘[2]	184	54.30 N	106.00 W
Thunder Mountain ∧[2]	216	42.16 N	86.20 W
Thundersley	260	51.34 N	0.35 E
Thunersee ⊜	58	46.40 N	7.45 E
Thüngen	56	49.56 N	9.51 E
Thung Song	110	8.09 N	99.41 E
Thung Wa	110	7.06 N	99.46 E
Thur ≃, Fr.	58	48.05 N	7.23 E
Thur ≃, Schw.	58	47.36 N	8.35 E
Thurcroft	44	53.24 N	1.16 W
Thurgau □[3]	58	47.35 N	9.00 E
Thurgovie → Thurgau □[3]	58	47.35 N	9.00 E
Thüringen	58	47.12 N	9.45 E
Thüringen □[3]	30	51.00 N	11.00 E
Thüringer Wald ⩘	30	50.40 N	10.50 E
Thürkow	54	53.50 N	12.33 E
Thurles	48	52.41 N	7.49 W
Thurmont	208	39.37 N	77.24 W
Thurn	54	50.46 N	12.33 E
Thurn, Pass)(	64	47.19 N	12.24 E
Thurnau	60	50.01 N	11.23 E
Thurnham	260	51.17 N	0.36 E
Thurnscoe	44	53.31 N	1.19 W
Thurnwald Range ⩘	164	4.45 S	141.15 E
Thurø	41	55.03 N	10.40 E
Thurrock □[8]	260	51.30 N	0.21 E
Thursby	44	54.51 N	3.03 W
Thursday Island	164	10.35 S	142.13 E
Thurso, P.Q., Can.	206	45.36 N	75.15 W
Thurso, Scot., U.K.	46	58.35 N	3.32 W
Thurso ≃	46	58.36 N	3.30 W
Thurstaston	262	53.21 N	3.08 W
Thurston	42	52.15 N	0.49 E
Thurston □[6]	224	46.59 N	122.42 W
Thurston Island I	9	72.20 S	99.00 W
Thusis	58	46.42 N	9.26 E
Thwaites Iceberg Tongue ⊓	9	74.45 S	106.30 W
Thy ◈[1]	26	57.00 N	8.30 E
Thyborøn	26	56.42 N	8.13 E
Thylungra	166	26.04 S	143.28 E
Thyolo	154	16.10 S	35.10 E
Thyregod	41	55.54 N	9.16 E
Thysville → Mbanza-Ngungu	152	5.15 S	14.52 E
Tiadiaye	150	14.25 N	16.42 W
Tía Juana	246	10.16 N	71.22 W
Tian ≃	105	40.42 N	116.33 E
Tiana, Esp.	266d	44.29 N	2.16 E
Tiana, It.	71	40.04 N	9.08 E
Tian'anmen Square ⊥	271a	39.55 N	116.23 E
Tianbao	100	24.36 N	117.35 E
Tianchang	100	32.41 N	119.01 E
Tiancunpu	105	39.06 N	115.41 E
Tiandeng	102	23.09 N	107.10 E
Tiandong	102	23.36 N	107.08 E
Tian'e	102	25.01 N	107.20 E
Tianeti	84	42.07 N	44.59 E
Tianfanjie	100	29.20 N	116.50 E
Tiangang, Zhg.	89	43.24 N	125.54 E
Tiangang, Zhg.	89	43.55 N	127.00 E
Tiangongsi	105	39.14 N	115.53 E
Tianguá	250	3.44 S	40.59 W
Tianhe	100	27.01 N	114.30 E
Tianhekou	100	32.08 N	113.25 E
Tianhelong	89	43.56 N	120.39 E
Tianhuang	98	35.29 N	117.18 E
Tianjara, Mount ∧	170	35.11 S	150.18 E
Tianjia, Zhg.	104	41.07 N	122.03 E
Tianjia, Zhg.	107	29.40 N	105.08 E
Tianjiaba	102	32.08 N	110.03 E
Tianjiatun	104	41.39 N	123.44 E
Tianjiawopu	104	42.28 N	122.38 E
Tianjiazhen	100	29.56 N	115.26 E
Tianjin (Tientsin)	105	39.08 N	117.12 E
Tianjing	106	31.27 N	120.46 E
Tianjin Shi (Tientsin Shih) □[7]	98	39.30 N	117.15 E
Tianjun	102	37.25 N	98.58 E
Tiankai	105	39.38 N	115.51 E
Tiankoura	150	10.46 N	3.16 W
Tiankoye	150	12.35 N	12.40 W
Tianlin, Zhg.	102	24.14 N	106.03 E
Tianlin, Zhg.	107	29.49 N	105.19 E
Tian Ling ∧	89	44.22 N	129.52 E
Tianmashan	106	31.04 N	121.08 E
Tianmen	100	30.39 N	113.06 E
Tianmu Shan ⩘	100	30.25 N	119.30 E
Tianpu	106	31.56 N	121.07 E
Tianqiaochang	104	40.52 N	121.02 E
Tianqiaoling	89	43.26 N	129.38 E
Tianquan	102	30.10 N	102.48 E
Tian Shan → Tien Shan ⩘	90	42.00 N	80.00 E
Tianshenggang	106	32.03 N	120.45 E
Tianshifu	98	41.17 N	124.21 E
Tianshui	102	34.30 N	105.58 E
Tianshuijing, Zhg.	102	40.17 N	95.21 E
Tianshuijing, Zhg.	104	41.19 N	121.48 E
Tianshuituo	105	39.20 N	118.12 E
Tianshuizhan	104	41.00 N	123.34 E
Tiantai	100	29.09 N	121.02 E
Tiantang	102	22.32 N	111.55 E
Tiantou, Zhg.	100	28.48 N	120.39 E
Tiantou, Zhg.	100	26.19 N	115.57 E
Tianwangsi	106	31.45 N	119.12 E
Tianxin, Zhg.	100	27.53 N	113.06 E
Tianxin, Zhg.	100	28.11 N	114.35 E
Tianxin, Zhg.	102	27.21 N	111.00 E
Tianxingqiao	106	32.05 N	119.57 E
Tianxiyang	100	26.31 N	118.33 E
Tianyang	102	23.51 N	106.34 E
Tianyangping	107	29.11 N	105.16 E
Tianyar	115b	8.12 S	115.30 E
Tianzhen	98	40.28 N	114.06 E
Tianzhongying	100	33.13 N	115.22 E
Tianzhu, Zhg.	102	37.14 N	102.59 E
Tianzhu, Zhg.	102	26.50 N	109.00 E
Tianzhuang, Zhg.	100	25.43 N	113.40 E
Tianzhuang, Zhg.	105	39.25 N	117.54 E
Tianzhuangtai	104	40.50 N	122.08 E
Tiao ≃	106	30.56 N	120.11 E
Tiaodengchang	107	30.47 N	106.22 E
Tiarel	174s	17.32 S	149.20 W
Tiarno	64	45.53 N	10.40 E
Tiaro	166	25.44 S	152.35 E
Tiassalé	150	5.54 N	4.50 W
Tiati ∧	154	1.19 N	35.56 E
Ti'avea	175a	13.57 S	171.24 W
Tiawichi Creek ≃	222	32.19 N	94.44 W
Tiba → Chiba	94	35.36 N	140.07 E
Tibaji	252	24.30 S	50.24 W
Tibaji ≃	252	22.47 S	51.01 W
Tibari	154	5.01 N	31.43 E
Tibasti, Sarīr ◈[2]	146	24.00 N	17.00 E
Tibati	152	6.27 N	12.38 E
Tibbermore	46	56.22 N	3.32 W
Tibbie	194	31.21 N	88.14 W
Tibe	144	9.03 N	37.08 E
Tibel'ti	88	51.46 N	103.11 E
Tiber → Tevere ≃	66	41.44 N	12.14 E
Tiberias → Teverya	132	32.47 N	35.32 E
Tiberias, Lake → Kinneret, Yam ⊜	132	32.48 N	35.35 E
Tiberina, Val V	66	43.31 N	12.10 E
Tibesti ⩘	146	21.30 N	17.30 E
Tibet → Xizang Zizhiqu □[4]	90	32.00 N	88.00 E
Tibet, Lake ⊜	220	28.27 N	81.31 W
Tibet, Plateau of → Qing Zang Gaoyuan ⩘[1]	12	33.00 N	92.00 E
Tibiao	116	11.17 N	122.02 E
Tibiao Point >	116	11.18 N	122.02 E
Tibidabo ∧	266d	41.25 N	2.07 E
Tibiri, Niger	150	13.06 N	4.00 E
Tibiri, Niger	150	13.34 N	7.04 E
Tibirke	41	56.03 N	12.07 E
Tiblawan	116	6.29 N	126.06 E
Tiblemont, Lac ⊜	190	48.14 N	77.18 W
Tibnah	132	32.59 N	36.13 E
Tibnīn	132	33.12 N	35.25 E
Tibooburra	166	29.26 S	142.01 E
Tibro	26	58.26 N	14.10 E
Tiburon	226	37.52 N	122.27 W
Tiburón, Cabo >	246	8.42 N	77.24 W
Tiburón, Isla I	232	29.00 N	112.23 W
Tiburon Peninsula >[1]	282	37.53 N	122.28 W
Tiča, Jazovir ⊜[1]	38	43.05 N	26.45 E
Ticao Island I	116	12.31 N	123.42 E
Ticao Pass ⊍	116	12.38 N	123.47 E
Tice	220	26.40 N	81.48 W
Tice Creek ≃	282	37.53 N	122.03 W
Ticehurst	42	51.03 N	0.25 E
Tichigan	216	42.50 N	88.12 W
Tichigan Lake ⊜	216	42.49 N	88.13 W
Tîchît	150	18.28 N	9.30 W
Tîchît, Ḍahr ⊥[4]	150	18.30 N	9.25 W
Tichmenevo, Ross.	76	58.00 N	38.36 E
Tichmenevo, Ross.	89	49.12 N	142.54 E
Ticho	144	7.50 N	39.32 E
Tichon	24	59.23 N	46.38 E
Tichonova Pustyn'	82	54.38 N	36.09 E
Tichonovka	88	53.13 N	104.13 E
Tichookeanskij	89	43.00 N	132.24 E
Tichoreck	78	45.51 N	40.09 E
Tichtozero	24	65.35 N	30.27 E
Tichvin	76	59.39 N	33.31 E
Tichvinskaja gr'ada ∧	76	59.30 N	34.30 E
Ticino □[3]	58	46.20 N	8.45 E
Ticino ≃	36	45.09 N	9.14 E
Tickfaw	194	30.34 N	90.28 W
Tickfaw ≃	194	30.20 N	90.28 W
Tickhill	44	53.26 N	1.06 W
Ticomán ◈[8]	286a	19.31 N	99.08 W
Ticonderoga	188	43.50 N	73.25 W
Ticul	232	20.24 N	89.32 W
Tīdah	142	31.15 N	30.50 E
Tidaholm	26	58.11 N	13.57 E
Tidan ≃	40	58.42 N	13.58 E
Tiddim	110	23.23 N	93.39 E
Tide Lake ⊜	184	50.33 N	111.20 W
Tideswell	44	53.16 N	1.46 W
Tidewater	208	37.51 N	76.42 W
Tidewater ◈[1]	208	37.45 N	77.00 W
Tidikelt ≚	148	26.54 N	1.20 E
Tidioute	214	41.41 N	79.24 W
Tidirhine, Jebel ∧	148	34.50 N	4.30 W
Tidjikja	150	18.33 N	11.25 W
Tidö	40	59.30 N	16.28 E
Tidone ≃	62	45.04 N	9.32 E
Tidore	108	0.40 N	127.26 E
Tiébissou	150	7.10 N	5.13 W
Tiechang, Zhg.	98	41.44 N	126.11 E
Tiechang, Zhg.	100	24.10 N	115.30 E
Tiechang, Zhg.	102	26.34 N	103.58 E
Tiechang, Zhg.	105	40.04 N	118.12 E
Tiechangpu	107	29.29 N	104.20 E
Tiefenbach, Dtsch.	60	48.37 N	13.24 E
Tiefenbach, Dtsch.	60	49.26 N	12.35 E
Tiefenbroich	263	51.18 N	6.49 E
Tiefencastel	58	46.40 N	9.35 E
Tiefensee	54	52.41 N	13.50 E
Tiefo	107	29.45 N	104.33 E
T'iehling → Tieling	104	42.18 N	123.49 E
Tiekou	98	37.16 N	121.13 E
Tiel	52	51.54 N	5.25 E
Tieli	89	46.59 N	128.02 E
Tieling	104	42.18 N	123.49 E
Tielt	50	51.00 N	3.19 E
Tielutou	100	27.49 N	115.48 E
Tiémé	150	9.33 N	7.19 W
T'ienching → Tianjin	105	39.08 N	117.12 E
T'ienchung	100	23.52 N	120.35 E
Tienen	56	50.48 N	4.57 E
Tiénigboué	150	8.11 N	5.43 W
Tienko	150	10.14 N	7.29 W
Tien Shan ⩘	90	42.00 N	80.00 E
T'ienshui → Tianshui	102	34.30 N	105.58 E
Tientsin → Tianjin	105	39.08 N	117.12 E
Tien Yen	110	21.20 N	107.24 E
Tiepido ≃	64	44.37 N	10.59 E
Tie Plant	194	33.44 N	89.47 W
Tierga	34	41.37 N	1.36 W
Tiergarten ◈[8]	264a	52.31 N	13.21 E
Tiergarten ♦	264a	52.31 N	13.21 E
Tieroko, Tarso ∧	146	20.45 N	17.52 E
Tierp	40	60.20 N	17.30 E
Tierpark ♦	264a	52.30 N	13.32 E
Tierra Amarilla, Chile	252	27.29 S	70.17 W
Tierra Amarilla, N.M., U.S.	200	36.42 N	106.32 W
Tierra Blanca, Méx.	196	27.12 N	104.53 W
Tierra Blanca, Méx.	234	18.25 N	96.20 W
Tierra Blanca Creek ≃	196	35.00 N	101.54 W
Tierra Buena	226	39.09 N	121.40 W
Tierra Colorada, Méx.	234	17.10 N	99.35 W
Tierra Colorada, Méx.	234	17.56 N	92.39 W
Tierra Colorada, Bajo de la ≚[1]	254	42.52 S	66.48 W
Tierra de Campos ◈[1]	34	42.10 N	4.50 W
Tierra del Fuego □[8]	254	54.00 S	67.00 W
Tierra del Fuego, Isla Grande de I	254	54.00 S	69.00 W
Tierra del Fuego, Parque Nacional ♦	254	54.39 S	68.30 W
Tierra del Norte → Severnaja Zeml'a II	74	79.30 N	98.00 E
Tierralta	246	8.11 N	76.04 W
Tierra Redonda Mountain ∧	226	35.47 N	120.59 W
Tieshan	100	30.14 N	114.52 E
Tieshanguan	100	23.30 N	113.54 E
Tiétar ≃	34	39.50 N	6.01 W
Tietê	255	23.07 S	47.43 W
Tietê ≃	255	20.40 S	51.35 W
Tiéti	175f	20.57 S	165.19 E
Tieton	224	46.42 N	120.45 W
Tieton ≃	224	46.45 N	120.45 W
Tieton, South Fork ≃	224	46.38 N	121.08 W
Tietzow	264a	52.43 N	12.56 E
Tif	148	27.00 N	1.37 E
Tiffany Mountain ∧	202	48.40 N	119.56 W
Tiffin	214	41.07 N	83.11 W
Tiffin ≃	216	41.17 N	84.23 W
Tiflis → Tbilisi	84	41.43 N	44.49 E
Tifton	192	31.27 N	83.30 W
Tiftona	192	35.05 N	85.10 W
Tiga, Île I	175f	21.07 S	167.49 E
Tiga, Pulau I	112	5.43 N	115.39 E
Tigalda Island I	180	54.05 N	165.05 W
Tigapuluh, Pegunungan ⩘	112	1.05 S	102.30 E
Tigard	224	45.25 N	122.46 W
Tigasaki → Chigasaki	94	35.19 N	139.24 E
Tigbauan	116	10.41 N	122.22 E
Tigeaux	261	48.50 N	2.54 E
Tiger Lake ⊜	220	27.53 N	81.22 W
Tiger Stadium ♦	281	42.20 N	83.04 W
Tigery	261	48.38 N	2.31 E
Tighennif	148	35.20 N	0.21 E
Tighina (Bender)	38	46.48 N	29.29 E
Tighvein ∧[2]	46	55.30 N	5.10 W
Tigil'	74	57.48 N	158.40 E

Symbols in the index entries represent the broad categories identified in the key at the right. Symbols with superior numbers (⩘[1]) identify subcategories (see complete key on page *I · 1).*

Symbole im Register stellen die rechts im Schlüssel erklärten Kategorien dar. Symbole mit hochgestellten Ziffern (⩘[1]) bezeichnen Unterabteilungen einer Kategorie (vgl. vollständiger Schlüssel auf Seite *I · 1).*

Los símbolos incluídos en el texto del índice representan las grandes categorías identificadas con la clave a la derecha. Los símbolos con numeros en su parte superior (⩘[1]) identifican las subcategorías (véase la clave completa en la página *I · 1).*

Les symboles de l'index représentent les catégories indiquées dans la légende à droite. Les symboles suivis d'un indice (⩘[1]) représentent des sous-catégories (voir légende complète à la page *I · 1).*

Os símbolos incluídos no texto do índice representam as grandes categorias identificadas com a chave à direita. Os símbolos com números em sua parte superior (⩘[1]) identificam as subcategorias (veja-se a chave completa à página *I · 1).*

∧	Mountain	Berg	Montaña	Montagne	Montanha
⩘	Mountains	Gebirge	Montañas	Montagnes	Montanhas
)(	Pass	Paß	Paso	Col	Passo
V	Valley, Canyon	Tal, Cañon	Valle, Cañón	Vallée, Canyon	Vale, Canhão
≚	Plain	Ebene	Llano	Plaine	Planície
>	Cape	Kap	Cabo	Cap	Cabo
I	Island	Insel	Isla	Île	Ilha
II	Islands	Inseln	Islas	Îles	Ilhas
⊥	Other Topographic Features	Andere Topographische Objekte	Otros Elementos Topográficos	Autres données topographiques	Outros acidentes topográficos

ESPAÑOL Nombre	Página	Lat.°′	Long.°′ W = Oeste
Tiglid	148	28.31 N	10.15 W
Tiglione ≃	62	44.48 N	8.27 E
Tignale	64	45.44 N	10.44 E
Tignall	192	33.52 N	82.44 W
Tignère	152	7.22 N	12.39 E
Tignes	62	45.30 N	6.55 E
Tignish	186	46.57 N	64.02 W
Tignousti, Jebel ∧	148	31.31 N	6.44 W
Tigoda ≃	76	59.22 N	31.54 E
Tigray □[4]	144	13.40 N	40.00 E
Tigre, Arg.	258	34.25 S	58.34 W
Tigre, Col.	246	2.28 N	68.15 W
Tigre □[5]	288	34.24 S	58.37 W
Tigre ≃, Arg.	288	34.25 S	58.35 W
Tigre → Tigris ≃, Asia	128	31.00 N	47.25 E
Tigre ≃, Méx.	234	22.43 N	97.51 W
Tigre ≃, Perú	246	4.26 S	74.05 W
Tigre ≃, Ven.	246	9.20 N	62.30 W
Tigre, Cerro ∧	236	8.31 N	83.28 W
Tigre, Isla del I	258	34.47 S	56.23 W
Tigre, Punta del ›	258	34.46 S	56.33 W
Tigres, Baía dos ⊂	152	16.38 S	11.46 E
Tigris (Dicle) (Dijlah) ≃	128	31.00 N	47.25 E
Tiguabos	240p	20.14 N	75.21 W
Tiguentourine	148	27.50 N	9.18 E
Tiguesmat ⩘[2]	148	24.54 N	8.14 W
Tigy	50	47.48 N	2.12 E
Tigyaing	110	23.46 N	96.08 E
Tigzert, Oued V	148	28.20 N	9.35 W
Tigzirt	34	36.54 N	4.08 E
Tīh, Jabal at- ⩘[1]	140	29.30 N	34.00 E
Tihāmah ≚	128	26.00 N	36.30 E
Tihany ⊥	30	46.54 N	17.53 E
Tihert	148	35.28 N	1.21 E
Ṭihnāwī, Wādī aṭ- V	142	28.11 N	30.46 E
Tihua → Ürümqi	86	43.48 N	87.35 E
Tihuatlán	234	20.43 N	97.32 W
Tiilikkajärven kansallispuisto ♠	26	63.38 N	28.20 E
Tijamuchi ≃	248	14.10 S	64.58 W
Tijesno	36	43.48 N	15.39 E
Tījī	146	32.01 N	11.22 E
Tijuana	232	32.32 N	117.01 W
Tijuana ≃	204	32.33 N	117.07 W
Tijuca ◆[8]	287a	22.56 S	43.14 W
Tijuca, Barra da ⋓	287a	23.01 S	43.18 W
Tijuca, Lagoa da ⊂	287a	22.59 S	43.20 W
Tijuca, Parque Nacional da ♠	287a	22.58 S	43.15 W
Tijuca, Pico da ∧	287a	22.56 S	43.17 W
Tijucas	252	27.14 S	48.38 W
Tijucas do Sul	252	25.55 S	49.12 W
Tijuco ≃	255	18.40 S	50.05 W
Tikal ⊥	232	17.20 N	89.39 W
Tīkamgarh	124	24.44 N	78.50 E
Tikaré	150	13.17 N	1.43 W
Tikchik Lakes ⊜	180	60.07 N	158.35 W
Tikei, Île I	14	14.58 S	144.32 W
Tikhand ◆[8]	272a	28.31 N	77.17 E
Tikhoretsk → Tichoreck	78	45.51 N	40.09 E
Tikitiki	172	37.48 S	178.24 E
Tiko	152	4.05 N	9.22 E
Tikokino	172	39.49 S	176.27 E
Tikrīt	128	34.36 N	43.42 E
Tikša	24	64.07 N	32.27 E
Tikšeozero, ozero ⊜	24	66.16 N	31.53 E
Tiksi	74	71.36 N	128.48 E
Tiku	112	0.24 S	99.56 E
Til	130	38.44 N	41.49 E
Tiladummati Atoll I[1]	122	6.50 N	73.05 E
Tilamuta	112	0.30 N	122.20 E
Tilarán	236	10.28 N	84.59 W
Tilbalakan, Laguna ⊂	236	15.30 N	84.17 W
Tilbānah	142	30.59 N	31.27 E
Tilburg	52	51.34 N	5.05 E
Tilbury, On., Can.	214	42.16 N	82.26 W
Tilbury, Eng., U.K.	42	51.28 N	0.23 E
Tilcara	252	23.34 S	65.22 W
Tilcha	166	29.36 S	140.54 E
Til-Châtel	58	47.31 N	5.10 E
Tilden, Il., U.S.	219	38.12 N	89.40 W
Tilden, Ne., U.S.	198	42.02 N	97.50 W
Tilden, Tx., U.S.	196	28.28 N	98.33 W
Tilden Lake ⊜	226	38.07 N	119.36 W
Tilden Woods	284c	39.03 N	77.09 W
Tilemsès	150	15.37 N	4.44 E
Tilemsi, Vallée du V	150	16.15 N	0.02 E
Tilff	56	50.34 N	5.35 E
Tilghman Island I	208	38.42 N	76.20 W
Tilhar	124	27.59 N	79.44 E
Tilia, Oued V	148	27.27 N	0.01 W
Tiliktino	82	56.06 N	36.36 E
Tilimsen	148	34.52 N	1.15 W
Tilin	110	21.42 N	94.04 E
Tilisarao	252	32.44 S	65.18 W
Till ≃, Eng., U.K.	44	53.16 N	0.37 W
Till ≃, Eng., U.K.	44	55.41 N	2.12 W
Tillaberi	150	14.13 N	1.27 E
Tillamook	202	45.27 N	123.50 W
Tillamook □[6]	224	45.25 N	123.39 W
Tillamook ≃	224	45.28 N	123.53 W
Tillamook Bay ⊂	224	45.30 N	123.53 W
Tillamook Head ›	224	45.57 N	124.00 W
Tillanchāng Dwīp I	110	8.30 N	93.37 E
Tillberga	40	59.41 N	16.37 E
Tille ≃	58	47.07 N	5.21 E
Tillery, Lake ⊜[1]	192	35.17 N	80.05 W
Tilley	182	50.27 N	111.39 W
Tilli	126	23.57 N	89.57 E
Tillia	150	16.08 N	4.47 E
Tillicoultry	46	56.09 N	3.45 W
Tillières-sur-Avre	50	48.46 N	1.04 E
Tilling Bourne ≃	260	51.13 N	0.34 W
Tillmans Corner	194	30.43 N	88.05 W
Tillson	210	41.49 N	74.04 W
Tillsonburg	212	42.51 N	80.44 W
Tillyfourie	46	57.11 N	2.35 W
Tilogne	150	15.58 N	13.36 W
Tilomar	112	9.21 S	125.08 E
Tilos I	38	36.25 N	27.25 E
Tilpa	166	30.57 S	144.24 E
Tilrhemt	148	33.10 N	3.21 E
Tilsit → Sovetsk	76	55.05 N	21.53 E
Tilt ≃	46	56.46 N	3.50 W
Tilton, Il., U.S.	194	40.05 N	87.38 W
Tilton, Ky., U.S.	218	38.22 N	83.45 W
Tilton, N.H., U.S.	188	43.26 N	71.35 W
Tilton ≃	224	46.33 N	122.33 W
Tiltonsville	214	40.10 N	80.41 W
Tilzapotla	234	18.29 N	99.16 W
Tim	78	51.37 N	37.07 E
Tim ≃	76	52.15 N	37.22 E
Ṭimā	140	26.54 N	31.26 E
Timah, Bukit ∧[2]	271c	1.21 N	103.47 E
Timahoe	48	53.20 N	6.49 W
Timaná	246	1.58 N	75.56 W
Timane ≃	248	20.34 S	59.15 W
Timanskij kr'až ∧	24	65.00 N	51.00 E
Timar	84	38.49 N	43.27 E
Timaricha	80	57.33 N	44.47 E
Timaru	172	44.24 S	171.15 E
Timaševo, Ross.	80	53.21 N	51.12 E
Timaševo, Ross.	82	55.08 N	36.29 E
Timaševsk	78	45.37 N	38.57 E
Timau, It.	64	46.35 N	13.00 E
Timau, Kenya	154	0.05 N	37.14 E
Timavo San Giovanni	64	45.48 N	13.37 E
Timay al-Amdīd	142	30.57 N	31.32 E
Timbákion	38	35.04 N	24.46 E
Timbalier Bay ⊂	194	29.10 N	90.20 W
Timbaúba	250	7.31 S	35.19 W
Timbavati Game Reserve ◆[4]	156	24.27 S	31.27 E
Timbedgha	150	16.15 N	8.10 W
Timber	224	45.43 N	123.17 W
FRANÇAIS Nom	Page	Lat.°′	Long.°′ W = Ouest
Timber Creek	164	15.39 S	130.29 E
Timber Creek ≃	198	44.49 N	98.17 W
Timber Lake, Il., U.S.	278	42.14 N	88.07 W
Timberlake, Oh., U.S.	214	41.41 N	81.25 W
Timber Lake, S.D., U.S.	198	45.26 N	101.04 W
Timber Run ≃	284b	39.27 N	76.52 W
Timber Trails	278	41.52 N	87.57 W
Timberview	284b	39.13 N	76.45 W
Timbío	246	2.20 N	76.40 W
Timbiras	250	4.15 S	43.57 W
Timblin	214	40.58 N	79.12 W
Timbó, Bra.	252	26.50 S	49.18 W
Timbo, Guinée	150	10.38 N	11.50 W
Timbo, Liber.	150	5.37 N	9.43 W
Timbó ≃	287a	22.52 S	43.16 W
Timboon	169	38.29 S	142.59 E
Timbuctoo	285	40.00 N	74.49 W
Timbuktu → Tombouctou	150	16.46 N	3.01 W
Timbun Mata, Pulau I	112	4.39 N	118.28 E
Timel'ga	86	58.53 N	76.42 E
Timelkam	60	48.00 N	13.36 E
Times Square ⊥	276	40.45 N	74.00 W
Timétrine	150	19.27 N	0.26 W
Timétrine ⩘	150	19.20 N	0.42 W
Timeu Creek ≃	182	54.28 N	114.27 W
Timewell	219	40.00 N	90.52 W
Timgad ⊥	148	35.29 N	6.28 E
Timimoun	148	29.14 N	0.16 E
Timimoun, Sebkha de ⊜	148	29.00 N	0.05 E
Timinar	140	19.02 N	30.29 E
Timi Ouli, Ehi ∧	146	21.08 N	16.31 E
Timir'azevka	86	53.39 N	65.31 E
Timir'azevo	76	55.05 N	21.37 E
Timir'azevskij	86	56.29 N	84.54 E
Timirevo	82	55.08 N	39.10 E
Timirist, Râs ›	150	19.23 N	16.32 W
Timirjazevo	86	53.45 N	66.30 E
Timiș □[6]	38	45.40 N	21.20 E
Timiș (Tamiš) ≃	38	44.51 N	20.39 E
Timiskaming, Lake ⊜	190	47.10 N	79.25 W
Timișoara	38	45.45 N	21.13 E
Timkovo	82	55.56 N	38.37 E
Timmendorfer Strand	54	54.00 N	10.46 E
Timmernabben	26	56.58 N	16.26 E
Timmins	190	48.28 N	81.20 W
Timmonsville	192	34.08 N	79.56 W
Timms Hill ∧[2]	190	45.27 N	90.11 W
Timok ≃	38	44.13 N	22.40 E
Timon	250	5.06 S	42.49 W
Timonovo	82	56.13 N	37.02 E
Timor I	112	9.00 S	125.00 E
Timor Sea ⫪[2]	14	11.00 S	128.00 E
Timor Timur □[4]	112	8.35 S	126.00 E
Timor Trough ✢[1]	14	9.50 S	126.00 E
Timošino, Ross.	76	60.05 N	36.10 E
Timošino, Ross.	80	57.50 N	44.25 E
Timotes	246	8.59 N	70.44 W
Timothy Lake ⊜[1]	224	45.07 N	121.47 W
Timoudi	148	29.19 N	1.09 W
Timousserarène ≃	150	16.21 N	8.07 E
Timpanogos Cave National Monument ♠	200	40.18 N	111.52 W
Timpas Creek ≃	198	38.02 N	103.38 W
Timpaus, Pulau I	112	1.51 S	124.01 E
Timperley	262	53.24 N	2.19 W
Timpson	194	31.54 N	94.23 W
Timpton ≃	74	58.43 N	127.12 E
Timra	26	62.31 N	17.22 E
Timsāh, Buḥayrat at- (Lake Timsah) ⊜	142	30.34 N	32.17 E
Timsah, Lake → Timsāh, Buḥayrat at- ⊜	142	30.34 N	32.17 E
Timšer	24	62.06 N	54.40 E
Tims Ford Lake ⊜[1]	194	35.15 N	86.10 W
Timun	114	0.50 N	103.22 E
Timur	85	42.50 N	68.26 E
Timur, Banjaran ⩘	114	5.00 N	102.30 E
Timurni	124	22.22 N	77.22 E
Tīn, Ra's at- ›	146	32.37 N	23.08 E
Tina ≃	158	31.18 S	29.14 E
Tinaca Point ›	116	5.33 N	125.20 E
Tinaco	246	9.42 N	68.26 W
Tinaga Island I	116	14.28 N	122.56 E
Tīnah, Khalīj aṭ- ⊂	140	31.08 N	32.40 E
Tinahely	48	52.48 N	6.28 W
Tinaja, Punta ›	248	16.14 S	73.39 W
Tinalmud	116	13.36 N	122.53 E
Tinambac	116	13.49 N	123.19 E
Tinambung	112	3.31 S	119.01 E
Ti-n-Amzi V	150	18.20 N	4.32 E
Tinapagee	166	29.28 S	144.23 E
Tinaquillo	246	9.55 N	68.18 W
Tindari, Capo ›	70	38.10 N	15.03 E
Tinderry Peak ∧	171b	35.42 S	149.16 E
Tindila	150	10.16 N	8.15 W
Tindis	126	21.35 N	86.44 E
Tindivanam	122	12.15 N	79.39 E
Tindouf	148	27.50 N	8.04 W
Tindouf, Hamada de ◆[1]	148	27.30 N	9.00 W
Tindouf, Sebkha de ≚	148	27.45 N	7.15 W
Tineba, Pegunungan ⩘	112	1.40 S	120.25 E
Tinée ≃	62	43.55 N	7.11 E
Tineg ≃	116	17.38 N	120.37 E
Tineo	34	43.20 N	6.25 W
Ting ≃	100	24.24 N	116.35 E
Tinga ∧	146	9.21 N	23.38 E
Tingambato	234	19.30 N	101.52 W
Tinggi, Pulau I	114	2.18 N	104.07 E
Tingha	166	29.57 S	151.13 E
Tinghert, Ḥamādat (Plateau du Tinghert) ⩘[1]	148	29.00 N	9.00 E
Tinghert, Plateau du (Ḥamādat Tinghert) ⩘[1]	148	29.00 N	9.00 E
Tinghsien → Dingxian	98	38.32 N	114.59 E
Tingkar ∧	116	5.20 N	117.06 E
Ting Kau	271d	22.22 N	114.05 E
Tingkawk Sakan	110	26.04 N	96.44 E
Tingkou	98	36.34 N	119.46 E
Tinglev	41	54.56 N	9.15 E
Tinglin	106	30.53 N	121.17 E
Tingliuhe	98	39.34 N	118.49 E
Tingloy	116	13.40 N	120.52 E
Tingmerkpuk Mountain ∧	180	68.34 N	162.28 W
Tingo de Saposoa	248	7.07 S	76.38 W
Tingo María	248	9.09 S	75.56 W
Tingo María, Parque Nacional ♠	248	9.15 S	76.05 W
Tingqian	100	30.10 N	115.54 E
Tingri, Zhg.	120	28.35 N	86.38 E
Tingri, Zhg.	120	28.38 N	87.04 E
Tingsiqiao	100	29.50 N	114.12 E
Tingsryd	26	56.32 N	14.59 E
Tingstäde	26	57.44 N	18.36 E
Tingsted	41	54.49 N	11.56 E
Tinguá	256	22.36 S	43.26 W
Tingüindín	234	19.45 N	102.29 W
Tinguiririca, Volcán ∧[1]	252	34.49 S	70.21 W
Tingvoll	26	62.54 N	8.12 E
Tingvollfjorden ⊂[2]	26	62.50 N	8.11 E
Tingwick	206	45.50 N	71.58 W
Tingwon Group II	164	2.35 S	149.45 E
Tingzitou	106	30.12 N	119.46 E
Tinharé, Ilha de I	255	13.30 S	38.58 W
Tinh Bien	110	10.36 N	104.57 E
Tinian	174n	14.58 N	145.38 E
Tinian I	174n	15.00 N	145.38 E
Tinian Harbor ⊂	174n	14.57 N	145.36 E
PORTUGUÊS Nome	Página	Lat.°′	Long.°′ W = Oeste
Tinié	150	14.20 N	1.28 W
Tiniguiban	116	11.22 N	119.30 E
Tinitian	116	10.04 N	119.12 E
Tinjar ≃	112	4.04 N	114.18 E
Tinjil, Pulau I	115a	6.58 S	105.47 E
Tinker Air Force Base ■	196	35.25 N	97.24 W
Tinkers Creek ≃, Md., U.S.	284c	38.46 N	76.57 W
Tinkers Creek ≃, Oh., U.S.	214	41.22 N	81.37 W
Tinkertown	283	42.01 N	70.44 W
Tinkisso ≃	150	11.21 N	9.10 W
Tinley Creek ≃	278	41.39 N	87.45 W
Tinley Creek Woods ♠	278	41.39 N	87.47 W
Tinley Park	216	41.34 N	87.47 W
Tinniswood, Mount ∧	182	50.19 N	123.50 W
Tinnoset	26	59.43 N	9.02 E
Tinnsjø ⊜	26	59.54 N	8.55 E
Tinogasta	252	28.04 S	67.34 W
Tinompo	112	2.09 S	121.17 E
Tínos	38	37.32 N	25.10 E
Tínos I	38	37.38 N	25.10 E
Tinquipaya	248	19.11 S	65.51 W
Tin Ferhoh, Tassili ⩘	150	19.40 N	4.00 E
Tinrhir	148	31.28 N	5.30 W
Tin Sam	271d	22.22 N	114.11 E
Tinskoj	88	56.10 N	96.55 E
Tinsley	194	32.43 N	90.27 W
Tinsukia	120	27.30 N	95.22 E
Tintagel, B.C., Can.	182	54.12 N	125.35 W
Tintagel, Eng., U.K.	42	50.40 N	4.45 W
Tintagel Head ›	42	50.41 N	4.46 W
Tintaldra	171b	36.03 S	147.56 E
Tintas, Rio das ≃	287a	22.52 S	43.28 W
Tinte, Cerro ∧	248	22.40 S	67.02 W
Tintern Abbey ⊍[1]	42	51.41 N	2.40 W
Tintern Parva	42	51.42 N	2.40 W
Tintigny	56	49.41 N	5.31 E
Tintina	252	27.02 S	62.43 W
Tintinara	166	35.54 S	140.03 E
Tintioulé	150	10.13 N	9.12 W
Tinto ∧	46	55.36 N	3.39 W
Tinto ≃	34	37.12 N	6.55 W
Tinton Falls	276	40.19 N	74.04 W
Ti-n-Toumma ◆[1]	146	16.04 N	12.40 E
Tintwistle	262	53.28 N	1.58 W
Tinui	172	40.53 S	176.04 E
Tinwald	172	43.55 S	171.43 E
Ti-n-Zaouatene	150	19.55 N	2.52 E
Tinzap ≃	120	38.23 N	77.24 E
Tio	144	14.42 N	40.58 E
Tioga, Il., U.S.	219	40.13 N	91.21 W
Tioga, N.D., U.S.	198	48.23 N	102.56 W
Tioga, Pa., U.S.	210	41.55 N	77.08 W
Tioga □[6], N.Y., U.S.	210	42.06 N	76.16 W
Tioga □[6], Pa., U.S.	210	41.45 N	77.17 W
Tioga ◆[8]	285	40.00 N	75.10 W
Tioga ≃	210	42.09 N	77.05 W
Tioga Center	210	42.04 N	76.21 W
Tioga Pass)(	226	37.54 N	119.16 W
Tioga Terrace	210	42.03 N	76.07 W
Tiojala	24	61.10 N	23.52 E
Tioman, Pulau I	114	2.48 N	104.10 E
Tiona	214	41.45 N	79.03 W
Tione di Trento	64	46.02 N	10.43 E
Tionesta	214	41.30 N	79.27 W
Tionesta Creek ≃	214	41.28 N	79.22 W
Tionesta Lake ⊜[1]	214	41.28 N	79.28 W
Tioor, Pulau I	164	4.45 S	131.45 E
Tior	140	6.23 N	31.11 E
Tioro	112	4.41 S	122.36 E
Tioro, Selat ⋓	112	4.40 S	122.20 E
Tioroniaradougou	150	9.21 N	5.38 W
Tioughnioga ≃	210	42.14 N	75.51 W
Tioughnioga, East Branch ≃	210	42.36 N	76.10 W
Tipasa	34	36.35 N	2.27 E
Tipitapa	236	12.12 N	86.06 W
Tipoca, Monte ∧[2]	250	3.34 N	51.20 W
Tipp City	218	39.57 N	84.10 W
Tippecanoe, In., U.S.	216	41.12 N	86.06 W
Tippecanoe, Oh., U.S.	214	40.16 N	81.17 W
Tippecanoe □[6]	216	40.25 N	86.53 W
Tippecanoe ≃	216	40.31 N	86.47 W
Tippecanoe, Lake ⊜	216	41.20 N	85.46 W
Tippecanoe Battlefield State Memorial ⊥	216	40.31 N	86.52 W
Tippecanoe River State Park ♠	216	41.07 N	86.36 W
Tipperary, Austl.	164	13.44 S	131.02 E
Tipperary, Ire.	48	52.29 N	8.10 W
Tipperary □[6]	48	52.40 N	8.20 W
Tipton, Eng., U.K.	42	52.32 N	2.05 W
Tipton, Ca., U.S.	226	36.03 N	119.18 W
Tipton, In., U.S.	216	40.16 N	86.02 W
Tipton, Ia., U.S.	190	41.46 N	91.07 W
Tipton, Mi., U.S.	216	42.01 N	84.04 W
Tipton, Mo., U.S.	194	38.39 N	92.46 W
Tipton, Ok., U.S.	196	34.30 N	99.08 W
Tipton, Pa., U.S.	214	40.38 N	78.18 W
Tipton □[6]	216	40.17 N	86.02 W
Tipton, Mount ∧	200	35.32 N	114.12 W
Tiptonville	194	36.22 N	89.28 W
Tip Top Mountain ∧	190	48.16 N	85.59 W
Tiptree	42	51.49 N	0.45 E
Tiptūr	122	13.16 N	76.29 E
Tiputini ≃	246	0.47 S	75.32 W
Tiquicheo	234	18.53 N	100.44 W
Tira	132	32.14 N	34.57 E
Tira Chapéu, Morro ∧	256	22.45 S	44.39 W
Tiradentes	255	21.07 S	44.11 W
Tīrah, Baḥr ≅	142	31.03 N	31.15 E
Tīrān I	128	27.56 N	34.34 E
Tīrān, Maḍīq ⋓	140	27.58 N	34.28 E
Tiran, Strait of → Tīrān, Maḍīq ⋓	140	27.58 N	34.28 E
Tirana → Tiranë	38	41.20 N	19.50 E
Tiranë	38	41.20 N	19.50 E
Tirano	64	46.13 N	10.10 E
Tiraque	248	17.37 S	65.04 W
Tirari Desert ◆[2]	162	28.00 S	138.20 E
Tiraspol	38	46.51 N	29.38 E
Tirat Karmel	132	32.46 N	34.58 E
Tirat Ẕevi	132	32.25 N	35.32 E
Tirau	172	37.59 S	175.45 E
Tire	130	38.04 N	27.45 E
Tirebolu	130	41.00 N	38.48 E
Tiree I	46	56.31 N	6.49 W
Tire Hill	214	40.16 N	78.55 W
Tires (Tiers), It.	64	46.28 N	11.31 E
Tires, Port.	266c	38.43 N	9.21 W
Tires ◆[1]	148	23.30 N	13.10 W
Tirhahart, Oued V	148	23.45 N	3.10 E
Tiria, Monte ∧	71	40.23 N	9.16 E
Tirich Mīr ∧	123	36.15 N	71.50 E
Tiriro	150	10.27 N	8.39 W
Tiris Zemmour □[4]	148	24.10 N	9.30 W
Tirl'anskij	86	54.14 N	58.35 E
Tirna ≃	122	18.04 N	76.57 E
Tirnavos	38	39.45 N	22.17 E
Tirnovo → Veliko Târnovo	38	43.04 N	25.39 E
Tiro	214	40.54 N	82.46 W
Tirodi	120	21.41 N	79.42 E
Tirol □[3]	64	47.15 N	11.20 E
Tiroler Ache (Grossache) ≃	60	47.51 N	12.30 E
Tirolo (Tirol)	64	46.42 N	11.10 E
Tiros	255	19.00 S	45.58 W
Tiroungoulou	146	9.34 N	22.09 E
Tīr Pol	128	34.36 N	61.15 E
Tirrenia	66	43.38 N	10.17 E
Tirreno, Mare → Tyrrhenian Sea ⫪[2]	36	40.00 N	12.00 E
Tirry ≃	46	58.02 N	4.26 W
Tirsā, Miṣr	142	29.25 N	30.49 E
Tirsā, Miṣr	273c	29.58 N	31.12 E
Tirschenreuth	60	49.53 N	12.21 E
Tirso ≃	71	39.53 N	8.32 E
Tirsted	41	54.44 N	11.21 E
Tirstrup	41	56.18 N	10.42 E
Tīrthahalli	122	13.42 N	75.14 E
Tirua Point ›	172	38.23 S	174.38 E
Tiruchchirāppalli	122	10.49 N	78.41 E
Tiruchengodu	122	11.23 N	77.56 E
Tirukkalukkunram	122	12.37 N	80.04 E
Tirukkovilūr	122	11.57 N	79.12 E
Tiruliai	76	55.47 N	23.22 E
Tirumangalam	122	9.50 N	77.59 E
Tirunelveli	122	8.44 N	77.42 E
Tirupati	122	13.39 N	79.25 E
Tiruppattūr, India	122	12.30 N	78.34 E
Tiruppattūr, India	122	10.08 N	78.37 E
Tiruppur	122	11.06 N	77.21 E
Tirūr	122	10.54 N	75.55 E
Tiruttani	122	13.11 N	79.38 E
Tirutturaippūndi	122	10.32 N	79.39 E
Tiruvalla	122	9.23 N	76.34 E
Tiruvallūr	122	13.09 N	79.55 E
Tiruvannāmalai	122	12.13 N	79.04 E
Tiruvettipuram	122	12.40 N	79.33 E
Tirūvottiyūr	122	13.09 N	80.18 E
Tiruvur	122	17.06 N	80.38 E
Tisa (Tisza) (Tysa) ≃	38	45.15 N	20.17 E
Tis'ah	142	30.02 N	32.35 E
Tisaiyanvila	122	8.20 N	77.53 E
Tisaren ⊜	40	59.00 N	15.08 E
Tisbury	42	51.04 N	2.03 W
Tisdale	184	52.51 N	104.04 W
Tishomingo, Ms., U.S.	194	34.38 N	88.13 W
Tishomingo, Ok., U.S.	196	34.14 N	96.40 W
Tisisat Falls ↳	144	11.29 N	37.35 E
Ṭisīyah	132	32.24 N	36.27 E
Tisjön ⊜	26	60.55 N	12.58 E
Tiskilwa	190	41.17 N	89.30 W
Tiskino	86	58.05 N	83.10 E
Tiškovo, Ross.	80	46.02 N	48.36 E
Tiškovo, Ross.	82	56.05 N	37.44 E
Tisma	236	12.05 N	86.01 W
Tisnaren ⊜	40	58.57 N	15.57 E
Tišnevo	82	55.10 N	36.17 E
Tišnov	30	49.21 N	16.25 E
Tisovec	30	48.43 N	19.57 E
Tissa	146	7.26 N	10.16 E
Tissemsilt	148	35.35 N	1.50 E
Tissø ⊜	41	55.35 N	11.18 E
Tīsta ≃	124	25.23 N	89.43 E
Tisul'	86	55.45 N	88.19 E
Tisvildeleje	41	56.03 N	12.05 E
Tisza (Tisa) (Tysa) ≃	38	45.15 N	20.17 E
Tiszaföldvár	30	46.59 N	20.15 E
Tiszafüred	30	47.37 N	20.46 E
Tiszavasvári	30	47.58 N	21.22 E
Tit	148	23.00 N	5.10 E
Titaf	148	27.26 N	0.13 W
Titāgarh	126	22.45 N	88.22 E
Titano, Monte ∧	66	43.55 N	12.28 E
Titao	150	13.46 N	2.04 W
Tit-Ary	74	71.58 N	127.01 E
Titel	38	45.12 N	20.18 E
Tithwāl	123	34.24 N	73.47 E
Titicaca, Lago ⊜	248	15.50 S	69.20 W
Titicus	207	41.18 N	73.30 W
Titi Karangan	114	5.31 N	100.37 E
Titikaveka	174k	21.15 S	159.45 W
Titilāgarh	122	20.18 N	83.09 E
Titisee-Neustadt	58	47.54 N	8.13 E
Titiwangsa, Banjaran ⩘	114	4.30 N	101.25 E
Titlis ∧	58	46.47 N	8.25 E
Tito	68	40.35 N	15.40 E
Titonka	190	43.14 N	94.02 W
Titou	100	29.52 N	112.42 E
Titova Korenica	36	44.45 N	15.43 E
Titovka	83	48.59 N	39.44 E
Titovo, Ross.	80	53.17 N	43.41 E
Titovo, Ross.	82	54.19 N	36.56 E
Titovo, Ross.	82	55.35 N	39.07 E
Titovo Velenje	61	46.22 N	15.07 E
Titov Veles	38	41.41 N	21.48 E
Titov vrh ∧	38	42.00 N	20.51 E
Titran	26	63.40 N	8.18 E
Tittabawassee ≃	190	43.23 N	83.59 W
Titteri ⩘	34	36.00 N	3.30 E
Titterstone Clee Hill ∧[2]	42	52.23 N	2.35 W
Titting	60	49.00 N	11.13 E
Tittling	60	48.44 N	13.23 E
Tittmoning	60	48.04 N	12.46 E
Titu	38	44.41 N	25.32 E
Titule	154	3.17 N	25.32 E
Titus □[6]	222	33.05 N	94.58 W
Titusville, Fl., U.S.	220	28.36 N	80.48 W
Titusville, N.J., U.S.	208	40.18 N	74.52 W
Titusville, Pa., U.S.	214	41.37 N	79.40 W
Titz	56	51.01 N	6.25 E
Tiu Chung Chau I	271d	22.20 N	114.19 E
Tiumpan Head ›	46	58.16 N	6.09 W
Tiuni	120	30.57 N	77.51 E
Tiva ≃	154	2.20 S	38.48 E
Tivaouane	150	14.57 N	16.49 W
Tiveden ⩘[2]	40	58.45 N	14.40 E
Tiverton, Eng., U.K.	42	50.55 N	3.29 W
Tiverton, R.I., U.S.	207	41.37 N	71.12 W
Tivoli, Gren.	241k	12.10 N	61.37 W
Tivoli, It.	66	41.58 N	12.48 E
Tivoli, N.Y., U.S.	210	42.03 N	73.54 W
Tivoli, Tx., U.S.	196	28.27 N	96.53 W
Tivoli ♠	41	55.40 N	12.34 E
Ṭiwāl, Wādī V	146	10.22 N	22.43 E
Ṭiwāl al-'Abā ∧	130	36.20 N	39.22 E
Tiwi, Pil.	116	13.27 N	123.41 E
Ṭīwī, 'Umān	128	22.49 N	59.16 E
Tiwuronto	115b	8.48 S	120.09 E
Tixtla de Guerrero	234	17.35 N	99.26 W
Tiyās	130	34.33 N	37.40 E
Tiyo, Pegunungan ⩘	164	4.00 S	135.30 E
Tizapán ◆[8]	286a	19.20 N	99.13 W
Tizapán El Alto	234	20.10 N	103.04 W
Tizimín	232	21.10 N	88.10 W
Tizi-Ouzou	148	36.48 N	4.02 E
Tizmant ash-Sharqīyah	142	29.03 N	31.03 E
Tiznados ≃	246	8.16 N	67.47 W
Tiznit	148	29.43 N	9.44 W
Tiznit □[4]	148	29.40 N	9.45 W
Tizoc	196	25.41 N	101.59 W
Tjällmo	40	58.43 N	15.21 E
Tjeukemeer ⊜	52	52.54 N	5.50 E
Tjilatjap → Cilacap	115a	7.44 S	109.00 E
Tjirebon → Cirebon	115a	6.44 S	108.34 E
Tjolotjo	154	19.47 S	27.46 E
Tjøme I	26	59.07 N	10.24 E
Tjörn I	26	58.00 N	11.38 E
Tjörnarp	41	56.00 N	13.37 E
Tkibuli	84	42.21 N	42.59 E
Tkvarčeli	84	42.51 N	41.41 E
Tlachichuca	234	19.06 N	97.25 W
Tlacoapa	234	17.09 N	98.52 W
Tlacotalpan	234	18.37 N	95.40 W
Tlacotepec	234	17.46 N	99.59 W
Tlacuitapan	234	21.14 N	102.12 W
Tláhuac ◆[8]	286a	19.16 N	99.00 W
Tlahualilo de Zaragoza	232	26.07 N	103.27 W
Tlahuelilpan	234	20.08 N	99.14 W
Tlahuitoltepec	234	17.04 N	95.59 W
Tlajomulco de Zúñiga	234	20.28 N	103.27 W
Tlalchapa	234	18.24 N	100.28 W
Tlalcozotitlán	234	17.54 N	99.15 W
Tlalixtac de Cabrera	234	17.04 N	96.39 W
Tlalixtaquilla	234	17.21 N	98.28 W
Tlalnepantla	234	19.33 N	99.12 W
Tlalnepantla ≃	286a	19.31 N	99.16 W
Tlalpan ◆[8]	286a	19.17 N	99.10 W
Tlalpujahua	234	19.48 N	100.10 W
Tlaltenango de Sánchez Román	234	21.47 N	103.19 W
Tl'ančetamak	80	55.28 N	52.37 E
Tlapacoyan	234	19.58 N	97.13 W
Tlapa de Comonfort	234	17.33 N	98.33 W
Tlapaneco ≃	234	18.05 N	98.48 W
Tlapehuala	234	18.13 N	100.31 W
Tlapeng	156	23.15 S	21.49 E
Tlaquepaque	234	20.39 N	103.19 W
Tl'arata	84	42.07 N	46.22 E
Tlatlauquitepec	234	19.51 N	97.29 W
Tlaxcala □[3]	234	19.25 N	98.10 W
Tlaxcala de Xicotencatl	234	19.19 N	98.14 W
Tlaxcoapan	234	20.05 N	99.13 W
Tlaxco [de Morelos]	234	19.37 N	98.07 W
Tlaxmalac	234	18.21 N	99.25 W
Tlazazalca	234	19.58 N	102.04 W
Tletat ed Douair	34	35.59 N	2.55 E
Tlētē Ouāte Gharbī, Jabal ∧	130	35.20 N	39.13 E
Tlevak Strait ⋓	182	55.03 N	132.58 W
Tlhakgameng	158	26.27 S	24.21 E
Tloch	84	42.38 N	46.28 E
Tlučiná	60	49.44 N	13.14 E
Tlumach	78	48.52 N	25.01 E
Tłuszcz	30	52.26 N	21.26 E
Tmassah	146	26.22 N	15.47 E
Tmīsān	146	27.32 N	13.19 E
Tnâot ≃	110	11.29 N	104.57 E
Tnekvejem ≃	180	65.50 N	177.31 E
Toa ≃	240p	20.23 N	74.32 W
Toa Alta	240m	18.23 N	66.15 W
Toab	46a	59.53 N	1.19 W
Toa Baja	240m	18.27 N	66.15 W
Toabré ≃	236	8.56 N	80.33 W
Toachi ≃	246	0.08 N	79.18 W
Toahayaná	232	26.08 N	107.44 W
Toamasina	157b	18.10 S	49.23 E
Toamasina □[4]	157b	18.00 S	48.40 E
Toandonggu	98	40.33 N	127.35 E
Toandos Peninsula ›[1]	224	47.43 N	122.47 W
Toano, It.	64	44.23 N	10.34 E
Toano, Va., U.S.	208	37.22 N	76.48 W
Toano Draw V	204	41.27 N	114.35 W
Toano Range ⩘	204	40.50 N	114.20 W
Toast	192	36.30 N	80.37 W
Toa Vaca, Embalse ⊜[1]	240m	18.06 N	66.28 W
Toay	252	36.40 S	64.21 W
Toba, Mali	150	11.52 N	7.28 W
Toba, Nihon	94	34.29 N	136.51 E
Toba, Zhg.	102	31.18 N	97.40 E
Toba ≃	182	50.30 N	124.15 W
Toba, Danau ⊜	114	2.35 N	98.50 E
Tobacco ≃	190	43.49 N	84.24 W
Tobacco Plains Indian Reserve ◆[4]	182	49.04 N	115.06 W
Tobacco Root Mountains ⩘	202	45.35 N	112.00 W
Tobago I	241r	11.15 N	60.40 W
Toba Inlet ⊂	182	50.20 N	124.50 W
Toba Kākar Range ⩘	120	31.15 N	68.00 E
Tobalaba Eulogio Sánchez, Aeródromo ⊠	286e	33.27 S	70.33 W
Tobalai, Pulau I	164	1.37 S	128.20 E
Tobarra	34	38.35 N	1.41 W
Tobas	252	28.08 S	62.42 W
Tobašino	80	56.56 N	47.40 E
Toba Tek Singh	123	30.58 N	72.29 E
Tobe	96	33.44 N	132.47 E
Tobejuba, Isla I	246	9.20 N	60.52 W
Tobekuduk	86	49.50 N	54.15 E
Tobelo	108	1.44 N	128.01 E
Tobelombang	112	0.57 S	122.00 E
Tobercurry	48	54.03 N	8.43 W
Tobermorey	166	22.15 S	138.00 E
Tobermory, Austl.	166	27.17 S	143.41 E
Tobermory, On., Can.	190	45.15 N	81.40 W
Tobermory, Scot., U.K.	46	56.37 N	6.05 W
Toberonochy	46	56.13 N	5.38 W
Tōbetsu	92a	43.13 N	141.31 E
Tobi I	108	3.00 N	131.10 E
Tobias	198	40.25 N	97.20 W
Tobias Barreto	250	11.11 S	38.01 W
Tobiishi-bana ›	174f	24.45 N	141.17 E
Tobin, Mount ∧	204	40.22 N	117.32 W
Tobin Lake ⊜, Austl.	162	21.45 S	125.49 E
Tobin Lake ⊜, Sk., Can.	184	53.40 N	103.35 W
Tobique ≃	186	46.46 N	67.42 W
Tobi-shima I	92	39.12 N	139.34 E
Toblach → Dobbiaco	64	46.44 N	12.14 E
Tobo, Indon.	164	3.34 S	130.11 E
Tobo, Sve.	40	60.16 N	17.39 E
Toboali	112	3.00 S	106.30 E
Tobol	86	52.40 N	62.39 E
Tobol ≃	86	58.10 N	68.12 E
Toboli	112	0.43 S	120.05 E
Tobol'sk	86	58.12 N	68.16 E
Tobong-san ∧	271b	37.42 N	127.01 E
Tobor	150	12.39 N	16.16 W
Toboso	116	10.43 N	123.31 E
Tobré	150	10.12 N	2.08 E
Tobruk → Ṭubruq	146	32.05 N	23.59 E
Tobseda	24	68.36 N	52.14 E
Tōbu	94	36.21 N	138.20 E
Toburdanovo	80	55.22 N	47.38 E
Toby, Mount ∧	207	42.29 N	72.32 W
Tobyhanna	210	41.10 N	75.25 W
Tobyhanna Creek ≃	210	41.07 N	75.39 W
Tobyhanna State Park ♠	210	41.13 N	75.25 W
Tobyš ≃	24	65.30 N	51.00 E
Toca Grande, Morro da ∧	287a	22.58 S	43.31 W
Tocantínia	250	9.33 S	48.22 W
Tocantinópolis	250	6.20 S	47.25 W
Tocantins □[3]	250	10.00 S	48.00 W
Tocantins ≃, Bra.	242	1.45 S	49.10 W
Tocantins ≃, Bra.	250	5.21 S	55.58 W
Tocantinzinho ≃	255	13.57 S	48.20 W
Toccoa	192	34.34 N	83.19 W
Toccoa (Ocoee) ≃	192	35.12 N	84.40 W
Toce ≃	58	45.56 N	8.29 E
Tochapan	234	18.54 N	97.37 W
Tochcha Lake ⊜	182	54.56 N	125.54 W
Tochigi	94	36.23 N	139.44 E
Tochigi □[5]	94	36.45 N	139.45 E
Tochimilco	234	18.54 N	98.34 W
Tochio	92	37.28 N	139.00 E
Tochoj	88	50.30 N	105.00 E
Tochta	24	62.14 N	48.48 E
Tochtamyš	120	37.50 N	74.39 E
Tockholes	262	53.42 N	2.31 W
Tockoje	80	52.32 N	52.45 E
Töcksfors	26	59.30 N	11.50 E
Točnik	60	49.27 N	13.19 E
Toco, Chile	252	22.05 S	69.35 W
Toco, Trin.	241r	10.50 N	60.57 W
Tocoa	236	15.41 N	86.03 W
Tócome ≃	286c	10.29 N	66.49 W
Toconao	252	23.11 S	68.01 W
Tocopilla	252	22.05 S	70.12 W
Tocos do Moji	256	22.22 S	46.06 W
Tocuco ≃	246	9.36 N	72.15 W
Tocumwal	166	35.49 S	145.34 E
Tocuyo ≃	246	11.03 N	68.23 W
Tocuyo de la Costa	246	11.02 N	68.23 W
Toda	94	35.48 N	139.41 E
Toda Bhīm	124	26.55 N	76.49 E
Todaiji Temple ⊍[1]	270	34.42 N	135.51 E
Todang-ni	271b	37.37 N	126.50 E
Toda Rāisingh	120	26.01 N	75.29 E
Todd	214	40.16 N	78.04 W
Todd ≃	162	24.52 S	135.48 E
Todd Estates	285	39.40 N	75.43 W
Todd Fork ≃	218	39.21 N	84.08 W
Todd Fork, East Fork ≃	218	39.24 N	84.00 W
Toddington	42	51.57 N	0.32 W
Todd Point ›	284b	39.15 N	76.27 W
Toddville, Md., U.S.	208	38.17 N	76.04 W
Toddville, N.Y., U.S.	210	41.17 N	73.53 W
Todeli	112	1.40 S	124.29 E
Todenyang	154	4.32 N	35.56 E
Todi	66	42.47 N	12.24 E
Tödi ∧	58	46.49 N	8.56 E
Todmorden, Austl.	162	27.08 S	134.48 E
Todmorden, Eng., U.K.	44	53.43 N	2.05 W
Todoga-saki ›	92	39.33 N	142.05 E
Todoromi	270	34.53 N	135.28 E
Todos Santos, Bol.	248	16.48 S	65.08 W
Todos Santos, Méx.	232	23.27 N	110.13 W
Todos Santos, Bahía ⊂	232	31.48 N	116.42 W
Todro	154	3.21 N	30.14 E
Todtenhausen	52	52.20 N	8.56 E
Todtmoos	58	47.44 N	8.00 E
Todtmoos Au	58	47.42 N	7.58 E
Todtnau	58	47.50 N	7.56 E
Toe Head ›	46	57.50 N	7.08 W
Tōei	94	35.04 N	137.41 E
T'oejo	98	39.54 N	127.46 E
Toéssé	150	11.50 N	1.16 W
Toetoes Bay ⊂	172	46.38 S	168.43 E
Tofield	182	53.22 N	112.40 W
Tofino	182	49.09 N	125.54 W
Töfsingdalens Nationalpark ♠	26	62.09 N	12.30 E
Tofte	26	59.33 N	10.34 E
Toften ⊜	40	59.03 N	14.36 E
Tofterup	41	55.39 N	8.50 E
Toftlund	41	55.11 N	9.04 E
Toga	94	36.27 N	137.02 E
Toga I	175f	13.26 S	166.42 E
Togakushi	94	36.44 N	138.05 E
Togakushi-yama ∧	94	36.46 N	138.04 E
Toganas	80	50.49 N	52.02 E
Tōgane	94	35.33 N	140.22 E
Togano, Monte ∧	58	46.06 N	8.25 E
Togauchi	96	34.34 N	132.13 E
Togdheer □[4]	144	9.00 N	46.00 E
Toggenburg V	58	47.15 N	9.10 E
Togho	152	6.01 N	17.26 E
Togi	94	37.08 N	136.44 E
Togiak	180	59.04 N	160.24 W
Togiak Bay ⊂	180	59.00 N	160.30 W
Togian, Kepulauan II	112	0.20 S	122.00 E
Togian, Pulau I	112	0.22 S	121.56 E
Töging am Inn	60	48.15 N	12.35 E
Togliatti → Toljatti	80	53.31 N	49.26 E
Togni	140	18.04 N	35.13 E
Tōgō, Nihon	94	35.05 N	137.03 E
Tōgō, Nihon	96	35.28 N	133.53 E
Togo □[1], Afr.	134	8.00 N	1.10 E
Togo □[1], Afr.	150	8.00 N	1.10 E
Togochale	144	9.33 N	43.18 E
Tōgō-ike ⊜	96	35.28 N	133.54 E
Togoron	116	12.35 N	123.37 E
Tögrög, Mong.	102	45.46 N	94.48 E
Tögrög, Mong.	102	45.32 N	102.59 E
Togtoh	102	40.22 N	111.11 E
Togučin	86	55.16 N	84.23 E
Togur	86	58.24 N	82.49 E
Togura	94	36.29 N	138.09 E
Toguzak ≃	86	54.06 N	62.50 E
Toguzbulak	85	42.06 N	76.44 E
Togwotee Pass)(	202	43.45 N	110.04 W
Tōgyu-san ∧	98	35.46 N	127.40 E
Tōgyu-san Kukrip Kongwŏn ♠	98	35.52 N	127.45 E
Togyz	86	47.34 N	60.33 E
Tōhaku	96	35.30 N	133.40 E
Tohakum Peak ∧	204	40.11 N	119.27 W
Tohāna	124	29.42 N	75.54 E
Tohiea, Mont ∧	174s	17.33 S	149.49 W
Tohma ≃	130	38.31 N	38.25 E
Toholampi	26	63.46 N	24.15 E
Tohopekaliga, Lake ⊜	220	28.12 N	81.23 W
Tohor, Tanjong ›	114	1.51 N	102.42 E
T'ohyŏn-ni	98	39.53 N	124.52 E
Toi, Nihon	94	34.54 N	138.47 E
Toi, Niue	174v	18.57 S	169.51 W
Toijala	26	61.10 N	23.52 E
Toili	112	1.27 S	122.24 E
Toi-misaki ›	92	31.20 N	131.22 E
Tōin	94	35.05 N	136.35 E
Toinya	140	6.17 N	29.44 E
Toi Sar	120	31.06 N	69.54 E
Toiyabe Range ⩘	204	39.10 N	117.10 W
Tojg	128	32.04 N	61.48 E
To-jima I	96	33.12 N	132.22 E
Tojo, Indon.	112	1.17 S	121.11 E
Tōjō, Nihon	96	34.53 N	133.16 E
Tōjō, Nihon	270	34.55 N	135.04 E
Tojtepa	85	41.03 N	69.22 E
Tōju-in ⊍[1]	94	35.19 N	136.04 E
Tok	180	63.19 N	142.59 W
Tok ≃	80	52.46 N	52.22 E
Tokaanu	172	38.58 S	175.46 E
Tokachi ≃	92a	42.44 N	143.42 E
Tokachi-dake ∧	92a	43.25 N	142.41 E
Tokachi-heiya ≚	92a	43.00 N	143.30 E
Tōkagi	268	35.42 N	139.56 E
Tokai, Malay.	114	6.01 N	100.24 E
Tōkai, Nihon	94	35.00 N	136.53 E
Tōkai, Nihon	94	36.27 N	140.34 E
Tokaj ≃	78	51.18 N	41.04 E
Tokala	112	1.47 S	121.43 E
Tōkamachi	94	37.08 N	138.46 E
Tokanui	172	46.34 S	168.56 E
Tokara-kaikyō ⋓	93b	30.10 N	130.10 E
Tokara-rettō II	93b	29.36 N	129.43 E
Tokarevka	86	50.08 N	73.12 E
Tokar Game Reserve ◆[4]	140	18.15 N	37.45 E
Tokar'ovka	80	51.59 N	41.09 E
Tokar'ovo, Ross.	76	55.17 N	35.04 E
Tokar'ovo, Ross.	265b	55.38 N	37.55 E
Tokashiki-jima I	93b	26.11 N	127.21 E
Tokat	130	40.19 N	36.34 E
Tokat □[4]	130	40.25 N	36.30 E
Tŏkchŏk-kundo II	98	37.14 N	126.07 E
Tŏkch'ŏn	98	39.46 N	126.19 E
Tokeland	224	46.42 N	123.58 W
Tokelau □[2]	14	9.00 S	171.45 W
Tokelau-Inseln → Tokelau □[2]	14	9.00 S	171.45 W
Tokeneke Brook ≃	276	41.03 N	73.28 W
Tŏkhŭng-ni	98	40.02 N	127.08 E
Toki	94	35.21 N	137.11 E
Toki ≃	94	35.12 N	136.52 E
Tokio → Tōkyō	94	35.42 N	139.46 E
Toki Point ›	174a	19.19 N	166.35 E
Tokiwadaira	268	35.48 N	139.57 E
Tokke ⊜	26	59.01 N	9.15 E
Tokko	74	59.59 N	119.52 E
Tokko ≃	88	58.42 N	119.50 E
Toklar	130	38.26 N	36.01 E
Toklat ≃	180	64.27 N	150.17 W
Tokma	88	58.13 N	105.42 E
Tokmak, Kyrg.	85	42.55 N	75.18 E
Tokmak, Ukr.	78	47.15 N	35.43 E
Toko	172	39.20 S	174.24 E
Tököl	264c	47.19 N	18.58 E

≃ River	Fluß	Río	Rivière	Rio
≅ Canal	Kanal	Canal	Canal	Canal
↳ Waterfall, Rapids	Wasserfall, Stromschnellen	Cascada, Rápidos	Chute d'eau, Rapides	Cascata, Rápidos
⋓ Strait	Meeresstraße	Estrecho	Détroit	Estreito
⊂ Bay, Gulf	Bucht, Golf	Bahía, Golfo	Baie, Golfe	Baía, Golfo
⊜ Lake, Lakes	See, Seen	Lago, Lagos	Lac, Lacs	Lago, Lagos
⩧ Swamp	Sumpf	Pantano	Marais	Pântano
⊼ Ice Features, Glacier	Eis- und Gletscherformen	Accidentes Glaciales	Formes glaciaires	Acidentes glaciares
⫪ Other Hydrographic Features	Andere Hydrographische Objekte	Otros Elementos Hidrográficos	Autres données hydrographiques	Outros acidentes hidrográficos

✢ Submarine Features	Untermeerische Objekte	Accidentes Submarinos	Formes de relief sous-marin	Acidentes submarinos
□ Political Unit	Politische Einheit	Unidad Politica	Entité politique	Unidade política
⊍ Cultural Institution	Kulturelle Institution	Institución Cultural	Institution culturelle	Instituição cultural
⊥ Historical Site	Historische Stätte	Sitio Histórico	Site historique	Sitio histórico
♠ Recreational Site	Erholungs- und Ferienort	Sitio de Recreo	Centre de loisirs	Area de Lazer
⊠ Airport	Flughafen	Aeropuerto	Aéroport	Aeroporto
■ Military Installation	Militäranlage	Instalación Militar	Installation militaire	Instalação militar
◆ Miscellaneous	Verschiedenes	Misceláneo	Divers	Diversos

ENGLISH — Name | Page | Lat.°′ | Long.°′
DEUTSCH — Name | Seite | Breite°′ | Länge°′ E = Ost

Tokolimbu 112 2.48 S 121.34 E
Tokomaru 172 40.28 S 175.30 E
Tokomaru Bay 172 38.08 S 178.18 E
Tokoname 94 34.53 N 136.51 E
Toko Range ⋌ 166 23.05 S 138.20 E
Tokoro ≃ 92a 44.07 N 144.05 E
Tokoroa 172 38.14 S 175.52 E
Tokorozawa 94 35.47 N 139.28 E
Tokovs'ke 78 47.38 N 33.59 E
Toksook Bay 180 60.32 N 165.06 W
Toksovo 76 60.09 N 30.31 E
Tok-to (Take-shima) II 92 37.17 N 131.53 E
Toktogul 85 41.50 N 72.50 E
Toktogul'skoje vodochranilišče ⊜[1] 85 41.50 N 72.55 E
Toku Island I 14 18.10 S 174.11 W
Tokuji 96 34.11 N 131.40 E
Tokul Creek ≃ 224 47.35 N 121.50 W
Tokung 112 0.18 S 114.28 E
Tokuno-shima I 93b 27.45 N 128.58 E
Tokur 89 53.10 N 132.53 E
Tokura 270 34.58 N 135.18 E
Tokura-tōge)(96 35.17 N 134.31 E
Tokusaga-mine ∧ 96 34.26 N 131.41 E
Tokushima 96 34.04 N 134.34 E
Tokushima □[5] 96 33.45 N 134.00 E
Tokuyama, Nihon 94 35.42 N 136.29 E
Tokuyama, Nihon 96 34.03 N 131.49 E
Tokwe ≃ 154 21.09 S 31.30 E
Tōkyō, Nihon 94 35.42 N 139.46 E
Tōkyō, Nihon 268 35.42 N 139.46 E
Tōkyō □[5] 94 35.45 N 139.30 E
Tokyo Bay → Tōkyō-wan C 94 35.25 N 139.47 E
Tōkyō-daigaku-uchūkūkan-kenkyūsho ʋ[3] 92 31.17 N 131.05 E
Tokyo Disneyland ♦ 268 35.37 N 139.53 E
Tōkyō-kō C 268 35.37 N 139.47 E
Tōkyō-kokusai-kūkō ⊠ 94 35.45 N 140.21 E
Tokyo Station ◆[5] 268 35.41 N 139.46 E
Tokyo Tower ʋ 268 35.39 N 139.45 E
Tokyo University ʋ[2] 268 35.42 N 139.46 E
Tokyo University of Education ʋ[2] 268 35.43 N 139.44 E
Tōkyō-wan (Tokyo Bay) C 94 35.25 N 139.47 E
Tokyrau ≃ 86 46.48 N 75.24 E
Tokzār 120 35.52 N 66.26 E
Tol I 175c 7.22 N 151.37 E
Tolaga Bay 172 38.22 S 178.18 E
Tolala 112 2.56 S 121.06 E
Tolang 114 1.56 N 99.26 E
Tolbert 52 53.10 N 6.21 E
Tolbo Nuur 86 48.25 N 90.17 E
Tolbuchino 80 57.51 N 40.03 E
Tolderol Point › 168b 35.22 S 139.10 E
Toldo, Pico del ∧ 240p 20.30 N 74.54 W
Tole, Kaz. 85 42.40 N 70.08 E
Tolé, Pan. 236 8.14 N 81.41 W
Toledo, Bol. 248 18.10 S 67.25 W
Toledo, Bra. 252 24.44 S 53.45 W
Toledo, Bra. 256 22.44 S 46.23 W
Toledo, Col. 246 7.19 N 72.28 W
Toledo, Esp. 34 39.52 N 4.01 W
Toledo, Pil. 116 10.23 N 123.38 E
Toledo, Il., U.S. 194 39.16 N 88.14 W
Toledo, Ia., U.S. 190 41.59 N 92.34 W
Toledo, Oh., U.S. 214 41.39 N 83.33 W
Toledo, Or., U.S. 202 44.37 N 123.56 W
Toledo, Wa., U.S. 224 46.26 N 122.50 W
Toledo, Ur. 258 34.45 S 56.05 W
Toledo □[4] 34 39.45 N 4.00 W
Toledo □[5] 236 16.20 N 88.55 W
Toledo, Montes de ⋌ 34 39.33 N 4.20 W
Toledo Bend Reservoir ⊜[1] 194 31.30 N 93.45 W
Toledo Express Airport ⊠ 216 41.35 N 83.49 W
Tolentino 66 43.12 N 13.17 E
Tolfa 66 42.09 N 11.56 E
Tolfa, Monti della ⋌ 66 42.08 N 11.54 E
Tolga, Alg. 148 34.46 N 5.22 E
Tolga, Nor. 26 62.25 N 11.00 E
Toli 86 45.57 N 83.37 E
Toliara 157b 23.21 S 43.40 E
Toliara □[4] 157b 24.00 S 45.00 E
Tolima □[5] 246 3.45 N 75.15 W
Tolima, Nevado del ∧ 246 4.40 N 75.19 W
Tolimán, Méx. 234 20.55 N 99.56 W
Tolimán, Méx. 234 19.36 N 103.55 W
Tolitoli 112 1.02 N 120.49 E
Toljatti (Togliatti) 80 53.31 N 49.26 E
Tol'ka 74 64.02 N 81.55 E
Tolkmicko 30 54.20 N 19.31 E
Tolland 207 41.52 N 72.22 W
Tolland □[6] 207 41.52 N 72.22 W
Tollarp 26 55.56 N 13.59 E
Tollense ≃ 54 53.54 N 13.02 E
Tollensesee ⊜ 54 53.30 N 13.11 E
Tollesboro 218 38.33 N 83.34 W
Tollesbury 42 51.46 N 0.50 E
Tolleson 200 33.27 N 112.15 W
Tollhouse 226 37.01 N 119.23 W
Tolloche 252 25.30 S 63.32 W
Tølløse 41 55.37 N 11.45 E
Tollygunge ◆[8] 272b 22.30 N 88.21 E
Tolmači 76 57.26 N 35.41 E
Tolmačovo 76 58.52 N 29.55 E
Tolmezzo 64 46.24 N 13.01 E
Tolmin 36 46.11 N 13.44 E
Tolna 30 46.26 N 18.46 E
Tolna □[6] 30 46.30 N 18.35 E
Tolo 152 2.56 S 18.34 E
Tolo, Teluk C 112 2.00 S 122.30 E
Toloa, Houma › 174w 21.17 S 175.08 W
Tolokiwa Island I 164 5.20 S 147.40 E
Tolomo 89 50.03 N 137.45 E
Tolong Bay C 116 9.20 N 122.49 E
Tolongoina 157b 21.33 S 47.31 E
Tolono 194 39.59 N 88.15 W
Tolosa 34 43.08 N 2.04 W
Tolosa, Aeródromo ⊠ 288 34.53 S 57.58 W
Tolovana ≃ 180 64.51 N 149.45 W
Tolpuddle 42 50.45 N 2.18 W
Tolsan-do I 98 34.38 N 127.45 E
Tol'skij Majdan 80 54.57 N 44.39 E
Tolsta Head › 46 58.20 N 6.10 W
Tolstoj, mys › 74 59.10 N 155.12 E
Tolstopal'cevo 265b 55.38 N 37.13 E
Tolt, North Fork ≃ 224 47.42 N 121.49 W
Toltén 254 39.13 S 73.14 W
Tolten ≃ 254 39.15 S 73.14 W
Tolti 123 35.02 N 76.06 E
Tolt-Seattle Water Supply Reservoir ⊜[1] 224 47.42 N 121.39 W
Tolú 246 9.31 N 75.35 W
Toluca 216 41.00 N 89.08 W
Toluca, Nevado de ∧[1] 234 19.08 N 99.44 W
Toluca de Lerdo 234 19.17 N 99.40 W
Tolvajarvi 24 62.17 N 31.27 E
Tolvdalselva ≃ 26 58.10 N 8.00 E
Tolve 68 40.42 N 16.01 E
Tolwa 140 6.38 N 32.37 E
Tolworth ◆[8] 260 51.23 N 0.17 W
Tolyatti → Toljatti 80 53.31 N 49.26 E
Tolybaj 86 50.31 N 62.19 E
Tom' ≃, Ross. 86 56.50 N 84.27 E
Tom' ≃, Ross. 89 51.00 N 127.54 E
Toma 150 12.46 N 2.53 W
Tomago 170 32.50 S 151.44 E
Tomah 190 43.58 N 90.30 W
Tomahawk 190 45.28 N 89.43 W
Tomakivka 78 47.48 N 34.44 E
Tomakomai 92a 42.38 N 141.36 E
Tomani 112 4.50 N 115.55 E
Tomanivi ∧ 175g 17.37 S 178.01 E
Tomar, Kaz. 86 46.24 N 75.03 E
Tomar, Port. 34 39.36 N 8.25 W
Tomari 89 47.47 N 142.03 E
Tomarovka 78 50.41 N 36.14 E
Tomarza 130 38.27 N 35.49 E
Tomás Barrón (Eucaliptus) 248 17.35 S 67.31 W
Tomasboda ∧[2] 40 59.24 N 14.58 E
Tomás Gomensoro 252 30.26 S 57.26 W
Tomashhorod 78 51.19 N 27.02 E
Tomashpil' 78 48.33 N 28.31 E
Tomasine ≃ 190 46.40 N 76.16 W
Tomás Jofré 258 34.43 S 59.19 W
Tomášov 61 48.09 N 17.16 E
Tomaszów Lubelski 30 50.28 N 23.25 E
Tomaszów Mazowiecki 30 51.32 N 20.01 E
Tomatin 46 57.20 N 3.59 W
Tomatlán 234 19.56 N 105.15 W
Tomatlán ≃ 234 19.50 N 105.23 W
Tomave 248 20.06 S 66.35 W
Tomazina 255 23.46 S 49.58 W
Tomba di Nerone ◆[8] 267a 41.57 N 12.27 E
Tombadonkéa 150 11.00 N 14.23 W
Tombador, Serra do ⋌[1] 248 12.00 S 57.40 W
Tomball 222 30.06 N 95.37 W
Tombe 140 5.49 N 31.41 E
Tombigbee ≃ 194 31.04 N 87.58 W
Tombo, Punta › 254 44.03 S 65.11 W
Tombôco 152 6.48 S 13.18 E
Tombolo 64 45.38 N 11.50 E
Tombos 255 20.55 S 42.02 W
Tombouctou (Timbuktu) 150 16.46 N 3.01 W
Tombouctou □[4] 150 18.20 N 3.50 W
Tombs of the Caliphs ⊥ 273c 30.03 N 31.17 E
Tombstone 200 31.42 N 110.04 W
Tombstone Mountain ∧ 180 64.25 N 138.30 W
Tombua 152 15.49 S 11.53 E
Tom Burke 156 23.05 S 28.00 E
Tomdoun 46 57.04 N 5.03 W
Tomé 252 36.37 S 72.57 W
Tomea, Pulau I 112 5.45 S 123.56 E
Tomé-Açu 250 2.25 S 48.09 W
Tömek 130 38.02 N 32.41 E
Tomelilla 26 55.33 N 13.57 E
Tomelloso 34 39.10 N 3.01 W
Tomenaryk 86 44.02 N 67.01 E
Tomerong 170 35.04 S 150.35 E
Tomhannock Reservoir ⊜[1] 210 42.51 N 73.33 W
Tomi ≃ 152 5.07 N 19.19 E
Tomich 46 57.18 N 4.48 W
Tomichi Creek ≃ 200 38.31 N 106.58 W
Tomifobia ≃ 206 45.11 N 72.02 W
Tomiko Lake ⊜ 190 46.32 N 79.49 W
Tomilino 265b 55.39 N 37.57 E
Tomini 112 0.30 N 120.32 E
Tomini, Teluk C 112 0.20 S 121.00 E
Tominian 150 13.17 N 4.35 W
Tomintoul 46 57.14 N 3.22 W
Tomio ≃ 270 34.35 N 135.44 E
Tomioka 94 36.15 N 138.54 E
Tomisato 94 35.44 N 140.19 E
Tomiura 94 35.03 N 139.50 E
Tomiyama, Nihon 94 35.11 N 137.48 E
Tomiyama, Nihon 94 35.05 N 139.51 E
Tomizawa 94 35.14 N 138.29 E
T'omkino 76 55.05 N 35.01 E
Tomkins Cove 210 41.15 N 73.59 W
Tomkinson Ranges ⋌ 162 26.11 S 129.05 E
Tomkinsville 208 38.19 N 76.53 W
Tomlinson Run State Park ♦ 214 40.33 N 80.34 W
Tommerup Stationsby 41 55.19 N 10.13 E
Tommot 74 58.58 N 126.19 E
Tomnavoulin 46 57.18 N 3.19 W
T'omnyj 88 53.24 N 118.31 E
Tomo ≃ 246 5.20 N 67.48 W
Tomobe 94 36.20 N 140.20 E
Tomogashima-suidō ⊔ 96 34.17 N 135.00 E
Tomohon 112 1.19 N 124.49 E
Tömör Bulag 88 49.16 N 100.15 E
Tomori 174m 26.08 N 127.44 E
Tomori, Teluk C 112 1.58 S 121.28 E
Tompa 88 55.08 N 109.47 E
Tompkins, Nf., Can. 186 47.48 N 59.13 W
Tompkins, Sk., Can. 184 50.04 N 108.47 W
Tompkins □[6] 210 42.27 N 76.30 W
Tompkins County Airport ⊠ 210 42.29 N 76.57 W
Tompkinsville 194 36.42 N 85.41 W
Tompo 112 0.56 N 120.20 E
Tom Price 162 22.41 S 117.43 E
Tom Price, Mount ∧ 162 22.39 S 117.40 E
Tomptokan 74 57.06 N 133.59 E
Tomra 26 62.35 N 6.56 E
Toms ≃ 208 39.57 N 74.07 W
Toms, Ridgeway Branch ≃ 208 40.00 N 74.14 W
Toms Cove C 208 37.53 N 75.22 W
Toms Creek ≃ 208 39.38 N 77.17 W
Tomsk 86 56.30 N 84.58 E
Tomsk Oblast' □[4] 86 58.00 N 82.00 E
Toms River 208 39.58 N 74.12 W
Tom Steed Reservoir ⊜[1] 196 34.45 N 99.00 W
Tomtabacken ∧[2] 26 57.30 N 14.28 E
Tömük 130 36.41 N 34.22 E
Tomuzlovka ≃ 84 44.46 N 44.10 E
Ton 64 46.15 N 11.04 E
Tonadico 64 46.11 N 11.50 E
Tonaki-shima I 93b 26.21 N 127.09 E
Tonalá, Méx. 234 16.04 N 93.45 W
Tonalá, Méx. 234 20.37 N 103.14 W
Tonalá ≃ 234 18.13 N 94.11 W
Tonale, Passo del)(64 46.16 N 10.35 E
Tonami 94 36.38 N 136.54 E
Tonantins 246 2.47 S 67.47 W
Tonantins ≃ 246 2.47 S 67.47 W
Tonara 71 40.02 N 9.10 E
Tonasket 202 48.42 N 119.26 W
Tonate 250 4.55 N 52.22 W
Tonatico 234 18.47 N 99.41 W
Tonawanda, N.Y., U.S. 210 42.59 N 78.52 W
Tonawanda, N.Y., U.S. 210 43.01 N 78.52 W
Tonawanda Channel ≃[1] 284a 43.04 N 79.00 W
Tonawanda Creek ≃ 210 43.02 N 78.53 W
Tonawanda Indian Reservation ◆[4] 210 43.05 N 78.27 W
Tonawanda Island I 284a 43.02 N 78.53 W
Tonbara 96 35.05 N 132.47 E
Tonbo 110 18.31 N 95.05 E
Tonbridge 42 51.12 N 0.16 E
Tonbridge and Malling □[8] 260 51.16 N 0.20 E
Tonda 270 34.50 N 135.36 E
Tonda ≃ 96 33.38 N 135.24 E
Tondabayashi 96 34.30 N 135.36 E
Tondano 112 1.19 N 124.54 E
Tønder 41 54.56 N 8.54 E
Tondhre 272c 19.05 N 73.08 E
Tondi 122 9.44 N 79.01 E
Tondibi 150 16.39 N 0.14 W
Tondidji 150 13.06 N 10.20 W
Tondi Kiwindi 150 14.28 N 2.02 E
Tondoro 156 17.45 S 18.50 E
Tone, Nihon 94 36.42 N 139.13 E
Tone, Nihon 94 35.51 N 140.09 E
Tone ≃ 94 35.44 N 140.51 E
Tonekābon 128 36.49 N 50.53 E
Tone-unga ≊ 268 35.54 N 139.53 E
Tonež 78 51.49 N 27.48 E
Tonga, Cam. 152 4.58 N 10.42 E
Tonga, Sūd. 140 9.28 N 31.03 E
Tonga □[1] 14 20.00 S 175.00 W
Tongaat 158 29.37 S 31.03 E
Tonga Islands II 14 20.00 S 175.00 W
Tong'an 100 24.46 N 118.08 E
Tonganoxie 198 39.06 N 95.05 W
Tong'anqiao 106 31.22 N 120.27 E
Tonga Ridge ✤[3] 14 21.00 S 175.00 W
Tongariro, Mount ∧ 172 39.08 S 175.38 E
Tongariro National Park ♦ 172 39.15 S 175.30 E
Tongas 115a 7.44 S 113.06 E
Tongatapu □[8] 174w 21.10 S 175.10 W
Tongatapu I 174w 21.10 S 175.10 W
Tongatapu Group II 14 21.10 S 175.10 W
Tonga Trench ✤[1] 14 20.00 S 173.00 W
Tongbai, Zhg. 100 32.22 N 113.24 E
Tongbai, Zhg. 105 39.35 N 116.44 E
Tongbai Shan ∧ 100 32.20 N 113.14 E
Tongbai Shan ⋌ 100 32.20 N 113.15 E
Tongbei 89 47.45 N 126.46 E
Tongcheng, Zhg. 100 31.03 N 116.58 E
Tongcheng, Zhg. 100 32.53 N 118.58 E
Tongcheng, Zhg. 100 29.11 N 113.49 E
Tongchengzha 100 31.30 N 118.07 E
Tongchengzhuang 105 39.22 N 117.36 E
T'ongch'ŏn 98 38.54 N 127.54 E
Tongchuan 102 35.01 N 109.01 E
Tongdao 102 26.23 N 109.23 E
Tongde 102 35.17 N 100.42 E
Tongerbao 104 41.26 N 123.02 E
Tongeren 56 50.47 N 5.28 E
Tongerlo 56 51.07 N 4.54 E
Tonggou 98 41.53 N 125.46 E
Tonggu, Zhg. 100 28.33 N 114.21 E
Tonggu, Zhg. 100 21.53 N 112.55 E
Tongguan, Zhg. 100 28.29 N 112.48 E
Tongguan, Zhg. 102 34.38 N 110.20 E
Tongguan, Zhg. 102 23.18 N 101.23 E
Tongguanyi 107 29.20 N 106.23 E
Tonghai 102 24.07 N 102.49 E
Tonghaikou 100 30.14 N 113.08 E
Tonghe, Zhg. 89 45.59 N 128.45 E
Tonghe, Zhg. 100 32.56 N 112.45 E
Tongho-ri 98 35.49 N 127.54 E
Tonghua (Kuaidamao), Zhg. 98 41.40 N 125.44 E
Tonghua, Zhg. 98 41.41 N 125.55 E
Tonghui ≃ 271a 39.53 N 116.41 E
Tongi 126 23.53 N 90.24 E
Tong Island I 164 2.05 S 147.50 E
Tongjiang, Zhg. 89 47.40 N 132.30 E
Tongjiang, Zhg. 102 31.58 N 107.14 E
Tongjiangchang 107 29.37 N 103.43 E
Tongjiangkou 104 42.37 N 123.41 E
Tongjing 100 31.47 N 118.33 E
Tongjosŏn-man C 98 39.30 N 128.00 E
Tongjuzhen 98 38.36 N 117.11 E
Tongken ≃ 89 46.31 N 126.22 E
Tongli 106 31.10 N 120.43 E
Tongliang 107 29.51 N 106.03 E
Tongliao 89 43.39 N 122.14 E
Tongling, Zhg. 100 30.53 N 117.46 E
Tongling, Zhg. 102 23.28 N 109.40 E
Tonglu 100 29.48 N 119.40 E
Tonglü Yunhe ≊ 106 32.04 N 121.40 E
Tongmang-ni 98 37.37 N 126.26 E
Tongmu, Zhg. 100 27.57 N 113.55 E
Tongmu, Zhg. 102 24.09 N 110.04 E
Tongnae 98 35.12 N 129.05 E
Tongnan 107 30.11 N 105.48 E
Tongno-gang ≃ 98 40.58 N 126.04 E
Tongo 166 30.30 S 143.45 E
Tongoa I 175f 16.54 S 168.34 E
Tongobory 157b 23.32 S 44.20 E
Tongololo Creek ≃ 162 22.06 S 121.08 E
Tongoy 252 30.15 S 71.30 W
Tongqin 100 28.52 N 119.56 E
Tongquansi 107 30.23 N 104.50 E
Tongquil Island I 116 6.02 N 121.51 E
Tongren, Zhg. 102 27.38 N 109.03 E
Tongren, Zhg. 102 35.32 N 101.54 E
Tongrengchang 107 30.02 N 106.42 E
Tongsa ≃ 124 26.52 N 90.57 E
Tongsa Dzong 124 27.31 N 90.30 E
Tongsan-ni 271b 37.38 N 126.53 E
Tongshan 100 29.38 N 114.29 E
Tongshi 98 35.26 N 117.43 E
Tongshuping 100 27.17 N 114.54 E
Tongta 110 21.20 N 99.16 E
Tongtai 100 32.38 N 120.47 E
Tongtan 107 28.56 N 105.17 E
Tongtian ≃ 102 33.25 N 96.32 E
Tongue 46 58.28 N 4.25 W
Tongue ≃, U.S. 202 46.24 N 105.52 W
Tongue ≃, N.D., U.S. 198 48.56 N 97.18 W
Tongue ≃, Tx., U.S. 196 34.07 N 100.25 W
Tongue, Kyle of C 46 58.30 N 4.26 W
Tongue of the Ocean ✤[1] 238 24.30 N 77.30 W
Tongue River Reservoir ⊜[1] 202 45.06 N 106.47 W
Tongwei 102 35.07 N 105.27 E
Tongxi 107 29.59 N 106.08 E
Tongxian 105 39.55 N 116.39 E
Tongxianchang 107 30.14 N 105.24 E
Tongxiang 106 30.38 N 120.32 E
Tongxin 102 37.02 N 106.09 E
Tongxinchang 107 29.42 N 106.26 E
Tongxing 107 30.35 N 106.12 E
Tongxu 98 34.29 N 114.28 E
Tongyang-ni 98 39.08 N 126.52 E
Tongyang Yunhe ≊ 106 32.02 N 120.48 E
Tongyu 89 44.48 N 123.05 E
Tongyuan, Zhg. 100 28.04 N 116.08 E
Tongyuan, Zhg. 106 30.28 N 120.52 E
Tongyuanpu 104 40.49 N 123.54 E
Tongzhaipu 100 32.48 N 112.44 E
Tongzi 102 28.08 N 106.49 E
Tongzidixia 104 41.08 N 120.34 E
Tonica 216 41.12 N 89.04 W
Tonila 234 19.26 N 103.31 W
Tönisberg 263 51.25 N 6.30 E
Tönisheide 263 51.19 N 7.03 E
Tönisvorst 56 51.19 N 6.29 E
Tonj 140 7.17 N 28.45 E
Tonk 120 26.10 N 75.47 E
Tonkawa 196 36.40 N 97.18 W
Tonkin → Bac Phan □[9] 110 22.00 N 105.00 E
Tonkin, Gulf of C 110 20.00 N 108.00 E
Tonkino 80 57.23 N 46.28 E
Tonkou, Mont ∧ 150 7.27 N 7.39 W
Tonkwa 110 23.36 N 96.58 E
Tônlé Sab, Bœng ⊜ 110 13.00 N 104.00 E
Tonle Sap → Tônlé Sab, Bœng ⊜ 110 13.00 N 104.00 E
Tonnay-Boutonne 32 45.58 N 0.42 W
Tonneins 32 44.23 N 0.19 E
Tonner Canyon V 280 33.58 N 117.48 W
Tonnerre 50 47.51 N 3.58 E
Tönnet 40 60.14 N 13.30 E
Tönning 41 54.19 N 8.56 E
Tōno 92 39.19 N 141.32 E
Tonogaya 268 35.46 N 139.22 E
Tonopah 204 38.04 N 117.13 W
Tōnoshō, Nihon 94 35.49 N 140.42 E
Tonoshō, Nihon 96 34.29 N 134.11 E
Tonosí 246 7.24 N 80.27 W
Tonota 156 21.29 S 27.29 E
Tonquish Creek ≃ 281 42.21 N 83.22 W
Tons ≃ 124 25.17 N 82.04 E
Tonšajevo 80 57.44 N 47.00 E
Tønsberg 26 59.17 N 10.25 E
Tönsholt 263 51.38 N 6.58 E
Tonstad 26 58.40 N 6.43 E
Tonto Creek ≃ 200 33.46 N 111.15 W
Tontogany 216 41.25 N 83.44 W
Tonto National Monument ♦ 200 33.34 N 111.02 W
Tonya 130 40.53 N 39.16 E
Tonypandy 42 51.38 N 3.27 W
Tonyrefail 42 51.36 N 3.25 W
Toobeah 166 28.25 S 149.52 E
Toodyay 168a 31.33 S 116.28 E
Tooele 200 40.31 N 112.17 W
Toogoolawah 171a 27.06 S 152.23 E
Tool 222 32.16 N 96.10 W
Toolik ≃ 180 69.55 N 149.30 W
Tooma 171b 35.58 S 148.03 E
Tooma ≃ 171b 36.04 S 148.00 E
Tooma Reservoir ⊜[1] 171b 36.04 S 148.16 E
Toomebridge 48 54.45 N 6.27 W
Toompine 166 27.13 S 144.22 E
Toomsboro 192 32.49 N 83.04 W
Toomyvara 48 52.50 N 8.02 W
Toongabbie 274a 33.47 S 150.57 E
Toora 169 38.40 S 146.20 E
Toora-Chem 88 52.28 N 96.17 E
Toorak 274b 37.51 S 145.01 E
Toormakeady 48 53.39 N 9.24 W
Toosey Indian Reserve ◆[4] 182 51.56 N 122.29 W
Toot Hill 260 51.42 N 0.12 E
Tootias 144 3.57 N 43.57 E
Tootie, Mount ∧ 170 33.28 S 150.30 E
Tootsi 76 58.34 N 24.47 E
Toowoomba 171a 27.33 S 151.57 E
Topanga 228 34.06 N 118.36 W
Topanga Canyon V 280 34.05 N 118.36 W
Topanga State Park ♦ 280 34.06 N 118.33 W
Topar 86 49.32 N 72.50 E
Topawa 200 31.48 N 111.49 W
Topaz Lake ⊜ 226 38.41 N 119.32 W
Topçam 130 40.38 N 37.48 E
Topchānchi 126 23.54 N 86.12 E
Töpchin 54 52.10 N 13.34 E
Topčicha 86 52.49 N 83.10 E
Topeka, In., U.S. 216 41.32 N 85.32 W
Topeka, Ks., U.S. 198 39.02 N 95.40 W
Töpen 54 50.23 N 11.52 E
Topia 232 25.13 N 106.34 W
Topilejo ◆[8] 286a 19.12 N 99.09 W
Topino ≃ 66 43.02 N 12.30 E
Topkanovo 82 54.43 N 38.29 E
Topkapı ◆[8] 267b 41.02 N 28.54 E
Topkapi Palace ⊥ 267b 41.00 N 28.59 E
Topki 86 55.16 N 85.36 E
Topko, gora ∧ 74 57.08 N 137.24 E
Topl'a ≃ 30 48.45 N 21.45 E
Topley 182 54.30 N 126.18 W
Toplica ≃ 38 43.13 N 21.49 E
Toplița 38 46.55 N 25.21 E
T'oploje, Ross. 76 53.13 N 38.53 E
T'oploje, Ross. 76 53.37 N 37.36 E
T'oplyj Stan 80 53.58 N 50.10 E
T'oplyj Stan ◆[8] 265b 55.37 N 37.30 E
Topo ≃ 286c 10.33 N 67.00 W
Topocalma, Punta › 252 34.08 S 72.01 W
Top of Hebers 262 53.34 N 2.12 W
Topo Infiernito ∧ 286c 10.33 N 66.55 W
Topol'čany 30 48.34 N 18.10 E
Topoli 80 47.59 N 51.36 E
Topolobampo 232 25.36 N 109.03 W
Topolog 38 44.53 N 28.22 E
Topolovățu Mare 38 45.46 N 21.37 E
Topolovgrad 38 42.05 N 26.20 E
Toporok 76 58.33 N 33.28 E
Topozero, ozero ⊜ 24 65.40 N 32.00 E
Toppenish 202 46.22 N 120.18 W
Toppenish Creek ≃ 202 46.20 N 120.11 W
Toppenish Ridge ∧ 224 46.18 N 120.40 W
Toppings 262 53.37 N 2.25 W
Toprakkale 130 37.06 N 36.07 E
Tops, Mount ∧ 162 21.50 S 134.00 E
Topsa 24 62.39 N 43.34 E
Topsfield 207 42.38 N 70.57 W
Topsham, Eng., U.K. 42 50.41 N 3.27 W
Topsham, Me., U.S. 188 43.55 N 69.58 W
Top Springs 164 16.38 S 131.50 E
Topton 208 40.30 N 75.42 W
Toquima Range ⋌ 204 38.45 N 116.55 W
Toquop Wash V 204 36.45 N 114.11 W
Tor 144 7.51 N 33.35 E
Torahime 94 35.25 N 136.16 E
Torano Castello 68 39.30 N 16.08 E
Torawitan, Tanjung › 112 1.46 N 124.58 E
Toraya 248 14.03 S 73.18 W
Torbalı 130 38.10 N 27.21 E
Torbat-e Ḥeydarīyeh 128 35.16 N 59.13 E
Torbat-e Jām 128 35.14 N 60.36 E
Torbay 186 47.40 N 52.44 W
Torbay □[9] 42 50.26 N 3.34 W
Tor Bay C 42 50.25 N 3.30 W
Torbejevo, Ross. 80 54.05 N 43.15 E
Torbejevo, Ross. 82 54.44 N 36.11 E
Torbert, Mount ∧ 180 61.25 N 152.24 W
Torbino 76 58.35 N 32.53 E
Torbole 64 45.52 N 10.52 E
Torbreck, Mount ∧ 169 37.21 S 145.57 E
Torbrook 186 44.55 N 64.59 W
Torch ≃ 184 53.50 N 103.05 W
Torchany 80 55.34 N 46.36 E
Torchiarolo 68 40.29 N 18.03 E
Torch Lake ⊜ 190 45.00 N 85.19 W
Torchyn 78 50.46 N 24.59 E
Torcy 261 48.51 N 2.39 E
Torda → Turda 38 46.34 N 23.47 E
Tordera ≃ 34 41.39 N 2.47 E
Tordesillas 34 41.30 N 5.00 W
Tordino ≃ 66 42.44 N 13.59 E
Tor di Quinto ◆[8] 267a 41.56 N 12.28 E
Töre 26 65.54 N 22.39 E
Töreboda 40 58.43 N 14.08 E
Torej 88 50.33 N 104.50 E
Torekov 26 56.26 N 12.37 E
Toreno 34 42.42 N 6.30 W
Torez 83 48.01 N 38.37 E
Torfou 261 48.32 N 2.14 E
Torgau 54 51.34 N 13.00 E
Torgelow 54 53.37 N 14.00 E
Torgelower See ⊜ 54 53.34 N 12.47 E
Torgo 88 58.28 N 119.50 E
Torgun ≃ 80 50.15 N 46.18 E
Torhamn 26 56.05 N 15.50 E
Torhout 50 51.04 N 3.06 E
Toribulu 112 0.19 S 120.01 E
Toride 94 35.53 N 140.04 E
Torigakubi-misaki › 94 37.10 N 138.06 E
Torigoe 94 36.21 N 136.36 E
Toriido 270 34.25 N 135.43 E
Torii-tōge)(94 36.29 N 138.24 E
Toriki 265a 59.47 N 30.07 E
Torino (Turin) 62 45.03 N 7.40 E
Torino □[4] 62 45.08 N 7.22 E
Torino di Sangro Marina 66 42.11 N 14.32 E
Torío ≃ 34 42.35 N 5.34 W
Toriparu 255 16.20 S 53.55 W
Torit 154 4.24 N 32.34 E
Toritto 68 41.00 N 16.41 E
Toriya 94 36.59 N 136.54 E
Torjun 115a 7.10 S 113.13 E
Torkestān, Selseleh-ye Band-e ⋌ 128 35.25 N 64.15 E
Torkoviči 76 58.52 N 30.20 E
Torlino 86 58.53 N 63.46 E
Torment, Point › 162 17.02 S 123.36 E
Tormentine, Cape › 186 46.07 N 63.47 W
Tormes ≃ 34 41.18 N 6.29 W
Tormestorp 41 56.07 N 13.44 E
Tormey 282 38.03 N 122.15 W
Tormini 64 45.36 N 10.29 E
Tormosin 80 48.12 N 42.42 E
Torna 24 68.04 N 44.10 E
Torna ∧ 122 18.16 N 73.37 E
Tornado Mountain ∧ 182 49.58 N 114.39 W
Tornal'a 30 48.27 N 20.20 E
Tornareccio 66 42.02 N 14.24 E
Tornberget ∧[2] 40 59.08 N 18.01 E
Torne ≃ 44 53.36 N 0.44 W
Torneälven (Tornionjoki) ≃ 24 65.48 N 24.08 E
Torne Brook ≃ 276 41.08 N 74.10 W
Tornesch 52 53.41 N 9.43 E
Torneträsk ⊜ 24 68.20 N 19.10 E
Torngat Mountains ⋌ 176 59.00 N 64.00 W
Tornillo 200 31.27 N 106.05 W
Tornillo Creek ≃ 196 29.11 N 103.00 W
Tornimparte 66 42.17 N 13.18 E
Torning 41 56.17 N 9.20 E
Tornio 26 65.51 N 24.08 E
Tornionjoki (Torneälven) ≃ 24 65.48 N 24.08 E
Tornquist 252 38.06 S 62.14 W
Tornyiszentmiklós 61 46.31 N 16.34 E
Toro 34 41.31 N 5.24 W
Torö I 40 58.50 N 17.50 E
Toro, Arroyo ≃ 288 34.27 S 58.52 W
Toro, Cañada del ≃ 258 35.16 S 59.05 W
Toro, Cerro ∧ 234 19.10 N 104.27 W
Toro, Lago del ⊜ 254 51.14 S 72.45 W
Toro, Punta › 252 33.47 S 71.49 W
Torobuku 112 4.25 S 122.26 E
Torodi 150 13.18 N 1.40 E
Toro-iseki ⊥ 94 34.57 N 138.24 E
Torok 146 10.03 N 14.33 E
Torokina 175e 6.14 S 155.03 E
Törökszentmiklós 30 47.11 N 20.25 E
Torola ≃ 236 13.52 N 88.30 W
Torom 89 54.32 N 135.50 E
Torom ≃ 89 54.36 N 135.46 E
Toroni, Nevado ∧ 248 19.43 S 68.41 W
Toronto, Austl. 170 33.01 S 151.36 E
Toronto, On., Can. 212 43.39 N 79.23 W
Toronto, On., Can. 275b 43.39 N 79.23 W
Toronto, Ks., U.S. 198 37.47 N 95.56 W
Toronto, Oh., U.S. 214 40.27 N 80.36 W
Toronto, S.D., U.S. 198 44.34 N 96.38 W
Toronto □[6] 275b 43.44 N 79.24 W
Toronto, Canadian Forces Base ■ 212 43.45 N 79.28 W
Toronto, University of ʋ[2] 275b 43.40 N 79.24 W
Toronto Harbour C 275b 43.38 N 79.22 W
Toronto Island Airport ⊠ 275b 43.38 N 79.24 W
Toronto Lake ⊜[1] 198 37.46 N 95.57 W
Toronto Reservoir ⊜[1] 210 41.38 N 74.51 W
Toronto Zoo, Metro ♦ 275b 43.49 N 79.11 W
Toro Peak ∧ 204 33.32 N 116.25 W
Toropec 76 56.30 N 31.39 E
Toropovo 82 54.21 N 36.07 E
Tororo 154 0.42 N 34.11 E
Toros (Acho), Plaza de ♦ 286d 12.02 S 77.02 W
Toros Dağları (Taurus Mountains) ⋌ 130 37.00 N 33.00 E
Torošino 76 57.56 N 28.36 E
Torosozero 24 62.30 N 38.10 E
Torotoro 248 18.07 S 65.46 W
Toroume ∧[2] 174k 21.15 S 159.45 W
Torpa ⊥ 26 57.39 N 13.16 E
Torpè 71 40.38 N 9.40 E
Torphins 46 57.06 N 2.37 W
Tor Pignatara ◆[8] 267a 41.52 N 12.32 E
Torpo 26 60.40 N 8.43 E
Torpoint 42 50.22 N 4.11 W
Torpy ≃ 182 53.44 N 120.55 W
Torquay, Austl. 169 38.21 S 144.19 E
Torquay, Sk., Can. 184 49.08 N 103.31 W
Torquay, Eng., U.K. 42 50.28 N 3.30 W
Torquemada 34 42.02 N 4.19 W
Torraca 68 40.07 N 15.38 E
Torrance, Ca., U.S. 228 33.50 N 118.20 W
Torrance, Pa., U.S. 214 40.25 N 79.14 W
Torrance Lake ⊜ 184 57.04 N 98.12 W
Torrance Municipal Airport ⊠ 280 33.48 N 118.20 W
Torrão 34 38.18 N 8.13 W
Torre Annunziata 68 40.45 N 14.27 E
Torrebaja 34 40.07 N 1.15 W
Torrebelvicino 64 45.43 N 11.18 E
Torre Beretti 62 45.04 N 8.40 E
Torreblanca 34 40.13 N 0.12 E
Torrebruna 66 41.52 N 14.33 E
Torrecilla ∧ 34 36.41 N 5.00 W
Torrecilla en Cameros 34 42.16 N 2.37 W
Torre del Campo 34 37.46 N 3.53 W
Torre del Greco 68 40.47 N 14.22 E
Torre del Lago Puccini 66 43.50 N 10.17 E
Torre de Moncorvo 34 41.10 N 7.03 W
Torre de'Passeri 66 42.14 N 13.56 E
Torre di Mosto 64 45.41 N 12.43 E
Torre di Santa Maria 64 46.14 N 9.51 E
Torredonjimeno 34 37.46 N 3.57 W
Torre Faro ◆[8] 70 38.16 N 15.39 E
Torre Gaia ◆[8] 267a 41.51 N 12.39 E
Torregrotta 70 38.11 N 15.21 E
Torrejon Air Base ■ 266a 40.28 N 3.28 W
Torrejoncillo 34 39.54 N 6.28 W
Torrejón de Ardoz 34 40.27 N 3.29 W
Torrejón-Tiétar, Embalse de ⊜[1] 34 39.50 N 5.50 W
Torrelaguna 34 40.50 N 3.32 W
Torrelavega 34 43.21 N 4.03 W
Torrellas, Riera de ≃ 266d 41.23 N 2.01 E
Torrelles de Llobregat 266d 41.21 N 1.59 E
Torrelletes 266d 41.21 N 1.57 E
Torremaggiore 68 41.41 N 15.17 E
Torremolinos 34 36.37 N 4.30 W
Torrenieri 66 43.05 N 11.33 E
Torrens ≃ 168b 34.56 S 138.30 E
Torrens, Lake ⊜ 166 31.00 S 137.50 E
Torrens, Mount ∧ 168b 34.52 S 138.56 E
Torrens Creek 166 20.46 S 145.02 E
Torrens Creek ≃ 166 22.22 S 145.09 E
Torrens Island I 168b 34.48 S 138.32 E
Torrent, Arg. 252 28.50 S 56.28 W
Torrent, Esp. 34 39.26 N 0.28 W
Torreões 256 21.52 S 43.33 W
Torreón 232 25.33 N 103.26 W
Torre Orsaia 68 40.08 N 15.28 E
Torre Pedrera 66 44.06 N 12.31 E
Torre Pellice 62 44.49 N 7.13 E
Torreperojil 34 38.02 N 3.17 W
Torres, Arg. 258 34.26 S 59.08 W
Torres, Bra. 252 29.21 S 49.44 W
Torres, Arroyo ≃ 288 34.39 S 58.45 W
Torres, Îles II 175f 13.15 S 166.37 E
Torre Santa Susanna 68 40.28 N 17.44 E
Torresdale ◆[8] 285 40.03 N 75.00 W
Torres de Alcalá 34 35.10 N 4.16 W
Torres Martinez Indian Reservation ◆[4] 204 33.35 N 116.02 W
Torres Novas 34 39.29 N 8.32 W
Torres Strait ⊔ 164 10.25 S 142.10 E
Torres Vedras 34 39.06 N 9.16 W
Torretta 70 38.08 N 13.14 E
Torrette di Fano 66 43.47 N 13.07 E
Torrevella 34 37.59 N 0.41 W
Torricella 68 40.21 N 17.29 E
Torricella in Sabina 66 42.16 N 12.52 E
Torricella Peligna 66 42.01 N 14.15 E
Torricella Sicura 66 42.39 N 13.39 E
Torricelli Mountains ⋌ 164 3.25 S 142.20 E
Torridge ≃ 42 51.03 N 4.11 W
Torridon 46 57.33 N 5.31 W
Torridon, Loch C 46 57.35 N 5.46 W
Torriglia 62 44.31 N 9.10 E
Torrijos, Esp. 34 39.59 N 4.17 W
Torrijos, Pil. 116 13.19 N 122.05 E
Torrild 41 55.59 N 10.04 E
Torrimpietra ◆[8] 267a 41.56 N 12.13 E
Torrin 46 57.12 N 6.02 W
Tørring 41 55.51 N 9.29 E
Torrington, Ct., U.S. 207 41.48 N 73.07 W
Torrington, Wy., U.S. 198 42.03 N 104.10 W
Torrinha 255 22.26 S 48.09 W
Torrita di Siena 66 43.10 N 11.46 E
Torröjen ⊜ 26 63.55 N 12.56 E
Torrox 34 36.46 N 3.58 W
Torrvarpen ⊜ 40 59.42 N 14.30 E
Torsåker 40 60.31 N 16.29 E
Tor Sapienza ◆[8] 267a 41.54 N 12.35 E
Torsås 26 56.24 N 16.00 E
Torsburgen ⊥ 26 57.25 N 18.43 E
Torsby 26 60.08 N 13.00 E
Tors Cove 186 47.13 N 52.51 W
Torshälla 40 59.25 N 16.28 E
Tórshavn 22 62.01 N 6.46 W
Torside Reservoir ⊜[1] 262 53.29 N 1.54 W
Torsö 40 58.47 N 13.48 E
Torsö I 40 58.48 N 13.50 E
Torteval 43b 49.27 N 2.38 W
Torto ≃ 70 37.58 N 13.46 E
Tortola I 240m 18.27 N 64.36 W
Tórtolas, Cerro de las ∧ 252 29.56 S 69.54 W
Tortolì 71 39.55 N 9.39 E
Tortona 62 44.54 N 8.52 E
Tortora 68 39.56 N 15.48 E
Tortoreto 66 42.48 N 13.55 E
Tortorici 70 38.02 N 14.49 E
Tortosa 34 40.48 N 0.31 E
Tortosa, Cap de › 34 40.43 N 0.55 E
Tortue ≃ 186 50.18 N 65.23 W
Tortue, Île de la I 238 20.04 N 72.49 W
Tortue, Rivière de la ≃ 206 45.24 N 73.32 W
Tortuguero ≃ 236 10.34 N 83.31 W
Tortuguero, Laguna C 240m 18.28 N 66.26 W
Tortuguero, Parque Nacional ♦ 236 10.25 N 83.55 W
Tortuguitas 288 34.28 S 58.46 W
Tortum 130 40.19 N 41.35 E
Toru ≃ 114 1.26 N 98.46 E
Toruajgyr 85 42.32 N 76.26 E
Torue 112 0.58 S 120.18 E
Torugart, pereval (Turugart Shankou))(85 40.33 N 75.20 E
Torul 130 40.35 N 39.18 E
Toruń 30 53.02 N 18.35 E
Toruń □[4] 30 53.20 N 19.00 E
Torunos 246 8.30 N 70.04 W
Torup, Sve. 26 56.58 N 13.05 E
Torup, Sve. 41 55.34 N 13.12 E
Tõrva 76 58.00 N 25.56 E
Tory 88 51.47 N 103.00 E
Tory Island I 48 55.16 N 8.14 W
Torysa ≃ 30 48.39 N 21.21 E
Tory Sound ⊔ 48 55.14 N 8.14 W
Toržok 76 57.03 N 34.58 E
Torzym 30 52.20 N 15.04 E
Tosa, Nihon 96 33.44 N 133.32 E
Tosa, Nihon 96 33.29 N 133.25 E
T'oša ≃ 80 55.38 N 42.09 E
T'osan 98 38.18 N 126.43 E
Tosari 115a 7.53 S 112.54 E
Tosa-shimizu 92 32.46 N 132.57 E
Tosa-wan C 96 33.20 N 133.40 E
Tosayama 96 33.38 N 133.32 E
Tosa-yamada 96 33.36 N 133.41 E
Tosca 156 25.53 S 23.58 E
Toscaig 46 57.24 N 5.50 W
Toscana (Tuscany) □[4] 36 43.25 N 11.00 E
Toscano ≃ 234 18.01 N 102.32 W
Toscolano 64 45.38 N 10.37 E
Tösens 58 47.01 N 10.36 E
Toses, Collada de)(34 42.19 N 2.01 E
Tōshi-jima I 94 34.31 N 136.53 E
Toshima ◆[8] 268 35.44 N 139.43 E
To-shima I 94 34.31 N 139.17 E
Toshkivka 83 48.46 N 38.34 E
Tōshō-gū ʋ[1] 94 36.46 N 139.36 E
Tosi, Indon. 115b 9.35 S 118.57 E
Tosi, It. 66 43.45 N 11.31 E
Tosilei 144 1.25 N 41.24 E
Toškalykaja, gora ∧ 86 50.38 N 89.30 E
Tosna ≃ 265a 59.46 N 30.46 E
Tosno 76 59.33 N 30.53 E
Toson Cengel 88 48.47 N 98.15 E
Toson Hu ⊜ 102 35.18 N 98.54 E
T'osovo 76 55.37 N 34.30 E
T'osovo-Netyl'skij 76 58.57 N 31.04 E
T'osovskij 76 58.48 N 30.52 E
Töss ≃ 58 47.33 N 8.33 E
Tossens 52 53.34 N 8.16 E
Tossicia 66 42.33 N 13.39 E
Tostado 252 29.14 S 61.46 W
Tõstamaa 76 58.20 N 24.00 E
Tostedt 52 53.17 N 9.42 E
Tosterön I 40 59.25 N 17.00 E
Tostu 85 41.34 N 71.34 E
Tost uul ⋌ 102 43.15 N 100.30 E
Tosu 96 33.22 N 130.31 E
Tosya 130 41.01 N 34.02 E
Totagatic ≃ 190 46.05 N 92.11 W
Totak ⊜ 26 59.42 N 7.57 E
Totana 34 37.46 N 1.30 W
Totānāla 126 22.05 N 87.40 E
Totatiche 234 21.56 N 103.27 W
Totban 80 46.47 N 49.06 E
Toteng 156 20.22 S 22.58 E
Tôtes 50 49.41 N 1.03 E
Totes Gebirge ⋌ 30 47.42 N 13.55 E
T'otkino 78 51.17 N 34.16 E
Tot'ma 76 59.57 N 42.45 E
Totnes 42 50.25 N 3.41 W
Totness 250 5.53 N 56.19 W
Toto 152 7.08 S 14.16 E
Totonicapán 236 14.55 N 91.22 W
Totonicapán □[5] 236 15.00 N 91.20 W
Totopotomoy Creek ≃ 208 37.41 N 77.13 W
Totora, Bol. 248 17.42 S 65.09 W
Totora, Bol. 248 17.49 S 68.07 W
Totoras 252 32.35 S 61.11 W
Totos 248 13.31 S 74.30 W
Tototlán 234 20.33 N 102.48 W
Totowa 210 40.54 N 74.12 W
Totoya Island I 175g 18.57 S 179.50 W
Totson Mountain ∧ 180 64.26 N 157.15 W
Totsuka ◆[8] 268 35.24 N 139.32 E
Tottenham, Austl. 166 32.14 S 147.21 E
Tottenham, On., Can. 212 44.01 N 79.49 W
Tottenham ◆[8] 260 51.35 N 0.04 W
Tottenham Hotspur Football Ground ♦ 260 51.36 N 0.04 W
Totten Inlet C 224 47.07 N 123.02 W
Tottenville ◆[8] 276 40.31 N 74.15 W
Totteridge ◆[8] 260 51.38 N 0.12 W
Tottington 44 53.37 N 2.20 W
Totton 42 50.56 N 1.29 W
Tottori 96 35.30 N 134.14 E
Tottori □[5] 96 35.30 N 134.00 E
Tottori-sakyū ∧[2] 96 35.31 N 134.15 E
Totuskey Creek ≃ 208 37.52 N 76.45 W
Tou, Motu I 174k 21.11 S 159.48 W
Touba, C. Iv. 150 8.17 N 7.41 W
Touba, Sén. 150 14.51 N 15.53 W
Toubei 100 26.44 N 116.05 E
Toubéré Bafal 150 14.23 N 13.32 W
Toubkal, Jebel ∧ 148 31.05 N 7.55 W
Toubkal, Parc National du ♦ 148 31.05 N 7.55 W
Toubori 146 13.59 N 12.18 E
Touboro 152 7.43 N 15.12 E
T'ouch'eng 100 24.52 N 121.49 E
Touchet ≃ 202 46.02 N 118.41 W
Touchwood Hills ⋌[2] 184 51.35 N 104.17 W

Symbols in the index entries represent the broad categories identified in the key at the right. Symbols with superior numbers (⋌[1]) identify subcategories (see complete key on page *I · 1)*.

Symbole im Register stellen die rechts im Schlüssel erklärten Kategorien dar. Symbole mit hochgestellten Ziffern (⋌[1]) bezeichnen Unterabteilungen einer Kategorie (vgl. vollständiger Schlüssel auf Seite *I · 1)*.

Los símbolos incluídos en el texto del índice representan las grandes categorías identificadas con la clave a la derecha. Los símbolos con numeros en su parte superior (⋌[1]) identifican las subcategorías (véase la clave completa en la página *I · 1)*.

Les symboles de l'index représentent les catégories indiquées dans la légende à droite. Les symboles suivis d'un indice (⋌[1]) représentent des sous-catégories (voir légende complète à la page *I · 1)*.

Os símbolos incluídos no texto do índice representam as grandes categorias identificadas com a chave à direita. Os símbolos com números em sua parte superior (⋌[1]) identificam as subcategorias (veja-se a chave completa à página *I · 1)*.

	English	Deutsch	Español	Français	Português
∧	Mountain	Berg	Montaña	Montagne	Montanha
⋌	Mountains	Gebirge	Montañas	Montagnes	Montanhas
)(	Pass	Paß	Paso	Col	Passo
V	Valley, Canyon	Tal, Cañon	Valle, Cañón	Vallée, Canyon	Vale, Canhão
≚	Plain	Ebene	Llano	Plaine	Planície
›	Cape	Kap	Cabo	Cap	Cabo
I	Island	Insel	Isla	Île	Ilha
II	Islands	Inseln	Islas	Îles	Ilhas
⊥	Other Topographic Features	Andere Topographische Objekte	Otros Elementos Topográficos	Autres données topographiques	Outros acidentes topográficos

ESPAÑOL · FRANÇAIS · PORTUGUÊS

Nombre / Nom / Nome	Página / Page	Lat.°′	Long.°′ W = Oeste / Ouest
Touchwood Lake ⊜, Ab., Can.	182	54.50 N	111.23 W
Touchwood Lake ⊜, Mb., Can.	184	54.29 N	95.00 W
Toucy	50	47.44 N	3.18 E
Toudao ≏	98	42.36 N	127.11 E
Toudaogou, Zhg.	98	42.46 N	129.12 E
Toudaogou, Zhg.	104	41.37 N	121.40 E
Toudaogou, Zhg.	105	40.58 N	117.59 E
Touët-sur-Var	62	43.57 N	7.00 E
Tougan	150	13.04 N	3.04 W
Touggourt	148	33.10 N	6.00 E
Toughkenamon	285	39.50 N	75.46 W
Tougouri	150	13.19 N	0.31 W
Tougué	150	11.27 N	11.41 W
Touho	175f	20.47 S	165.14 E
Touiel, Oued V	148	31.30 N	4.46 E
Touil, Oued V	148	35.30 N	2.33 E
Touisset	207	41.43 N	71.13 W
Toukansi	100	29.22 N	119.06 E
Toukley	170	33.16 S	151.33 E
Toukoto	150	13.27 N	9.53 W
Toul	58	48.41 N	5.54 E
Toulépleu	150	6.35 N	8.25 W
Touliu	100	23.43 N	120.32 E
Toulnustouc ≏	186	49.35 N	68.24 W
Toulnustouc Nord-Est ≏	186	50.56 N	67.44 W
Toulon, Fr.	62	43.07 N	5.56 E
Toulon, Il., U.S.	190	41.05 N	89.51 W
Toulon Lake ⊜	204	40.01 N	118.40 W
Toulon-sur-Arroux	32	46.42 N	4.08 E
Touloubre ≏	62	43.33 N	5.02 E
Toulourenc ≏	62	44.14 N	5.09 E
Toulouse	32	43.36 N	1.26 E
Toumen Shan I	100	28.41 N	121.46 E
Toumfafi	150	15.02 N	5.38 E
Toumodi	150	6.33 N	5.01 W
Tounan	100	23.41 N	120.28 E
Tounassine, Hamada ◆[2]	148	28.30 N	5.00 W
Toungo	146	8.07 N	12.03 E
Toungoo	110	18.56 N	96.26 E
Toupeng	106	30.19 N	120.31 E
Touques	50	49.22 N	0.06 E
Touques ≏	50	49.22 N	0.06 E
Tour, Étang de la ⊜	261	48.40 N	1.53 E
Toura, Monts du ⩘	150	7.40 N	7.25 W
Touraine	188	45.34 N	75.47 W
Touraine □[9]	32	47.12 N	0.40 E
Tourakom	110	18.26 N	102.32 E
Tourane → Da Nang	108	16.04 N	108.13 E
Tourassine ⊤[4]	148	24.37 N	11.23 W
Tourbe ≏	56	49.10 N	4.52 E
Tourcoing	50	50.43 N	3.09 E
Touriñan, Cabo ›	34	43.03 N	9.18 W
Tournai	50	50.36 N	3.23 E
Tournan-en-Brie	50	48.44 N	2.46 E
Tourndo, Oued V	148	22.15 N	10.28 E
Tournesac ≏	50	47.27 N	4.01 E
Tournon	62	45.04 N	4.50 E
Tournus	58	46.34 N	4.54 E
Touros	250	5.12 S	35.28 W
Tou Rout	110	16.24 N	107.00 E
Tourouvre	50	48.35 N	0.40 E
Tourrette-Levens	62	43.47 N	7.16 E
Tours	50	47.23 N	0.41 E
Tours-sur-Marne	50	49.03 N	4.07 E
Tours-sur-Meymont	62	45.40 N	3.35 E
Tourteron	56	49.32 N	4.39 E
Tourves	62	43.24 N	5.56 E
Toury	50	48.12 N	1.56 E
Toussaint Creek ≏	214	41.35 N	83.04 W
Tousside, Pic ∧	146	21.02 N	16.25 E
Toussoro, Mont ∧	146	9.18 N	23.28 E
Toussus-le-Noble	261	48.45 N	2.07 E
Toussus-le-Noble, Aéroport de ⊠	261	48.45 N	2.06 E
Toustain	36	36.40 N	8.15 E
Toutai, Zhg.	89	45.40 N	124.50 E
Toutai, Zhg.	104	41.41 N	121.11 E
Toutaizi	104	42.19 N	122.49 E
Toutle	224	46.20 N	122.41 W
Toutle ≏	224	46.17 N	122.55 W
Toutle, North Fork ≏	224	46.23 N	122.34 W
Toutle, South Fork ≏	224	46.20 N	122.44 W
Toutle Mountain Range ⩘	224	46.20 N	122.30 W
Toutuohe	100	31.06 N	116.25 E
Touws ≏	158	33.45 S	21.11 E
Touwsrivier	158	33.20 S	20.00 E
Touzhan	89	49.27 N	119.41 E
Toužim	60	50.04 N	13.00 E
Töv □[4]	88	47.30 N	106.30 E
Tova	24	65.58 N	40.45 E
Tovar	246	8.20 N	71.46 W
Tovarkovo	82	54.42 N	35.57 E
Tovarkovskij	76	53.40 N	38.14 E
Tove ≏	42	52.05 N	0.38 W
Tovey	219	39.35 N	89.27 W
Tovste	78	48.50 N	25.44 E
Tovtry ⩘[1]	78	49.00 N	26.10 E
Tovuz	84	41.00 N	45.38 E
Tow	196	30.53 N	98.28 W
Tōwa	96	33.13 N	132.53 E
Towaco	210	40.55 N	74.20 W
Towada	92	40.37 N	141.13 E
Towada-Hachimantai-kokuritsu-kōen ♠	92	40.35 N	140.53 E
Towada-ko ⊜	92	40.28 N	140.55 E
Towai	172	35.29 S	174.08 E
Towamencin Creek ≏	285	40.13 N	75.23 W
Towanda, Il., U.S.	216	40.34 N	88.54 W
Towanda, Ks., U.S.	198	37.47 N	96.59 W
Towanda, Pa., U.S.	210	41.46 N	76.26 W
Towanda Creek ≏	210	41.45 N	76.26 W
Towan Head ›	42	50.25 N	5.07 W
Towar Gardens	216	42.45 N	84.28 W
Towari	112	4.36 S	121.29 E
Towcester	42	52.08 N	1.00 W
Tower	190	47.48 N	92.16 W
Tower City, N.D., U.S.	198	46.55 N	97.40 W
Tower City, Pa., U.S.	208	40.35 N	76.33 W
Tower Hamlets ◆[8]	260	51.32 N	0.03 W
Tower Hill, Austl.	166	22.03 S	144.36 E
Tower Hill, Il., U.S.	219	39.23 N	88.57 W
Towerhill Creek ≏	166	22.29 S	144.39 E
Tower of London ⊥	260	51.30 N	0.05 W
Tower Peak ∧	226	38.09 N	119.33 W
Towers of Silence ⊍[1]	272c	18.58 N	72.48 E
Tower Soudan State Park ♠	190	47.50 N	92.15 W
Towla, Mount ∧	154	21.22 S	29.52 E
Tow Law	44	54.44 N	1.49 W
Towlī	84	39.11 N	47.32 E
Town ≏	283	42.00 N	70.57 W
Town and Country	202	47.42 N	117.23 W
Town Bank	208	39.00 N	74.56 W
Town Creek ≏, Al., U.S.	194	34.46 N	87.25 W
Town Creek ≏, Al., U.S.	194	34.24 N	86.11 W
Town Creek ≏, Oh., U.S.	216	41.05 N	84.25 W
Town Creek Manor	208	38.19 N	76.27 W
Towneley Hall ⊥	262	53.46 N	2.13 W
Towner	198	48.20 N	100.24 W
Town Estates	285	40.04 N	74.52 W
Town Hill ∧[2]	240a	32.19 N	64.44 W
Townline Tunnel ◆[5]	284a	42.57 N	79.15 W
Town of Niagara	284a	43.06 N	78.59 W
Town of Pines	216	41.41 N	86.58 W
Townsend, On., Can.	212	42.54 N	80.07 W
Townsend, De., U.S.	208	39.23 N	75.41 W
Townsend, Ma., U.S.	207	42.40 N	71.42 W
Townsend, Mt., U.S.	202	46.19 N	111.31 W
Townsend, Va., U.S.	208	37.11 N	75.57 W
Townsend, Mount ∧	171b	36.25 S	148.15 E
Townsend Island I	276	40.38 N	73.26 W
Townsends Inlet ⊂	208	39.07 N	74.43 W
Townshend Island I	166	22.15 S	150.30 E
Township Line Run ≏	279b	40.13 N	79.33 W
Townsville	166	19.16 S	146.48 E
Townville	214	41.41 N	79.53 W
Towrang	170	34.42 S	149.51 E
Towrang, Mount ∧	170	34.46 S	149.51 E
Towra Point ›	274a	34.00 S	151.10 E
Towr Kham	123	34.08 N	71.05 E
Towrzī, Afg.	120	30.11 N	65.59 E
Towrzī, Afg.	128	32.38 N	65.53 E
Towson	208	39.24 N	76.36 W
Towson State College ⊍[2]	284b	39.24 N	76.37 W
Towuti, Danau ⊜	112	2.45 S	121.32 E
Toxkan (Aksaj) ≏, Asia	85	40.55 N	78.16 E
Toxkan ≏, Zhg.	90	41.08 N	80.11 E
Toyah	196	31.19 N	103.47 W
Toyah Creek ≏	196	31.18 N	103.27 W
Tōya-ko ⊜	92a	42.35 N	140.51 E
Toyama	94	36.41 N	137.13 E
Toyama □[5]	94	36.30 N	137.30 E
Toyama-heiya ≚	94	36.40 N	137.15 E
Toyama-wan ⊂	94	36.50 N	137.10 E
Toyapakeh	115b	8.41 S	115.29 E
Tōyo, Nihon	96	33.55 N	133.05 E
Tōyō, Nihon	96	33.30 N	134.16 E
Toyo ≏	94	34.47 N	137.20 E
Toyoake	94	35.03 N	137.01 E
Toyoda, Nihon	94	34.45 N	137.49 E
Toyoda, Nihon	268	35.39 N	139.23 E
Toyofuta	268	35.53 N	139.57 E
Toyohama	96	34.04 N	133.38 E
Toyohara	175d	24.15 N	123.48 E
Toyohashi	94	34.46 N	137.23 E
Toyohira	96	34.40 N	132.24 E
Toyokawa	94	34.49 N	137.24 E
Toyo-kawa-yōsui ≊	94	34.35 N	137.03 E
Toyonaka, Nihon	96	34.09 N	133.42 E
Toyonaka, Nihon	96	34.47 N	135.28 E
Toyone	94	35.09 N	137.43 E
Toyono	94	36.43 N	138.16 E
Toyooka, Nihon	94	35.33 N	137.54 E
Toyooka, Nihon	94	34.50 N	137.52 E
Toyooka, Nihon	96	35.32 N	134.50 E
Toyooka, Nihon	268	35.11 N	139.58 E
Toyosaka, Nihon	92	37.56 N	139.13 E
Toyosaka, Nihon	96	34.34 N	132.50 E
Toyosato	94	36.06 N	140.02 E
Toyoshina	94	36.18 N	137.54 E
Toyota, Nihon	94	35.05 N	137.09 E
Toyota, Nihon	94	36.46 N	138.19 E
Toyota, Nihon	96	34.12 N	131.04 E
Toyota-ko ⊜	96	34.14 N	131.08 E
Toyotomi	94	35.34 N	138.33 E
Toyotsu	96	33.40 N	130.58 E
Toyoura	96	34.08 N	130.58 E
Toy's Hill	260	51.14 N	0.06 E
Tozer, Mount ∧	164	12.45 S	143.13 E
Tozeur	148	33.55 N	8.08 E
Tozi, Mount ∧	180	65.41 N	150.58 W
Tozitna ≏	180	65.08 N	152.23 W
Tpig	84	41.47 N	47.36 E
Traar ◆[8]	263	51.23 N	6.36 E
Trabaria, Bocca)(	66	43.36 N	12.14 E
Traben-Trarbach	56	49.57 N	7.06 E
Trabia	70	37.59 N	13.39 E
Trabiju	255	22.03 S	48.18 W
Trabuco, Arroyo ≏	228	33.31 N	117.40 W
Trabzon	130	41.00 N	39.43 E
Trabzon □[4]	130	40.50 N	39.50 E
Tracadie	186	47.31 N	64.54 W
Trachselwald	58	47.01 N	7.45 E
Tra Cu	110	9.42 N	106.16 E
Tracy, P.Q., Can.	206	46.01 N	73.09 W
Tracy, Ca., U.S.	226	37.44 N	121.25 W
Tracy, Mn., U.S.	198	44.14 N	95.37 W
Tracy City	194	35.15 N	85.44 W
Tracyton	224	47.36 N	122.39 W
Tradate	62	45.43 N	8.54 E
Trade Lake ⊜	184	55.22 N	103.44 W
Tradewater ≏	194	37.31 N	88.03 W
Trading Bay ⊂	212	45.15 N	78.55 W
Tradinghouse Creek Reservoir ⊜[1]	222	31.35 N	96.55 W
Traditional Cultures, Museum of ⊍	269f	14.31 N	121.00 E
Trælleborg ⊥	41	55.23 N	11.17 E
Traer	190	42.11 N	92.27 W
Traessu, Monte ∧	71	40.28 N	8.40 E
Trafalgar, Austl.	169	38.12 S	146.09 E
Trafalgar, On., Can.	275b	43.29 N	79.43 W
Trafalgar, In., U.S.	218	39.24 N	86.09 W
Trafalgar, Cabo ›	34	36.11 N	6.02 W
Trafaria	266c	38.40 N	9.14 W
Trafford	214	40.23 N	79.45 W
Trafford □[8]	262	53.24 N	2.21 W
Trafford, Lake ⊜	220	26.25 N	81.30 W
Trafford Park	262	53.28 N	2.20 W
Trafoi	64	46.33 N	10.31 E
Tragacete	34	40.21 N	1.51 W
Tragliata ◆[8]	267a	41.58 N	12.15 E
Tragwein	61	48.20 N	14.37 E
Traição, Córrego ≏	287b	23.36 S	46.41 W
Traíd	34	40.40 N	1.49 W
Traiguén	252	38.15 S	72.41 W
Traiguén, Isla I	254	45.35 S	73.42 W
Trail	182	49.06 N	117.42 W
Trail Creek	216	41.41 N	86.51 W
Trailer Estates	220	27.24 N	82.34 W
Trail Ridge ∧	192	30.35 N	82.05 W
Traînel	50	48.25 N	3.27 E
Trainer	285	39.50 N	75.25 W
Traipu	250	9.58 S	37.01 W
Traíra (Taraira) ≏	246	1.04 S	69.26 W
Trairão ≏	250	7.20 S	51.14 W
Traíras ≏	255	14.07 S	48.31 W
Trairi	250	3.17 S	39.15 W
Traisen	61	48.02 N	15.37 E
Traisen ≏	61	48.22 N	15.46 E
Traiskirchen	61	48.01 N	16.18 E
Traismauer	61	48.21 N	15.44 E
Traîtres, Baie des ⊂	174x	9.50 S	139.02 W
Traitsching	60	49.10 N	12.39 E
Trajouce	266c	38.44 N	9.20 W
Trakai	76	54.38 N	24.56 E
Trakt	24	62.44 N	51.11 E
Träkvista	40	59.16 N	17.47 E
Tralee	48	52.16 N	9.42 W
Tralee Bay ⊂	48	52.15 N	9.59 W
Trá Lí → Tralee	48	52.16 N	9.42 W
Tramatza	71	40.00 N	8.39 E
Tramayes	58	46.18 N	4.36 E
Tramelan	58	47.13 N	7.06 E
Tra Mi	110	15.20 N	108.13 E
Tramin → Termeno	64	46.20 N	11.14 E
Trammel	192	37.00 N	82.17 W
Trammel Creek ≏	194	36.52 N	86.23 W
Tramonti di sopra	64	46.18 N	12.47 E
Tramore	48	52.10 N	7.10 W
Tramperos Creek (Punta de Agua Creek) ≏	196	35.32 N	102.27 W
Tramping Lake ⊜	184	52.08 N	108.49 W
Tramutola	68	40.19 N	15.47 E
Trăn	38	42.50 N	22.39 E
Tranås	26	58.03 N	14.59 E
Trancão ≏	266c	38.48 N	9.06 W
Trancas	252	26.13 S	65.17 W
Tranco de Beas, Embalse de ⊜[1]	34	38.10 N	2.45 W
Trancoso	34	40.47 N	7.21 W
Trand	123	34.38 N	72.59 E
Tranderup	41	54.52 N	10.22 E
Tranebjerg	41	55.50 N	10.36 E
Tranekær	41	55.00 N	10.51 E
Tranemo	26	57.29 N	13.21 E
Tranent	46	55.57 N	2.58 W
Tränental	158	27.09 S	19.33 E
Trang	110	7.33 N	99.36 E
Trangahy	157b	19.07 S	44.43 E
Trangan, Pulau I	164	6.35 S	134.20 E
Trangie	166	32.02 S	147.59 E
Tran Grande ≏	116	6.43 N	124.01 E
Trängslet	26	61.25 N	13.40 E
Trani	68	41.17 N	16.26 E
Tranmere	262	53.23 N	3.01 W
Trannon ≏	42	52.31 N	3.25 W
Tranoroa	157b	24.42 S	45.04 E
Tranquebar	122	11.02 N	79.51 E
Tranqueras	252	31.12 S	55.45 W
Tranquility	218	38.58 N	83.32 W
Tranquillity	226	36.38 N	120.15 W
Transantarctic Mountains ⩘	9	85.00 S	175.00 W
Trans-en-Provence	62	43.30 N	6.29 E
Transfer	214	41.20 N	80.26 W
Transit Airpark ⊠	284a	43.06 N	78.44 W
Transkei □[9]	158	31.20 S	29.00 E
Transquaking ≏	208	38.22 N	76.00 W
Transsylvanische Alpen → Carpații Meridionali ⩘	38	45.30 N	24.15 E
Transtrand	26	61.05 N	13.19 E
Transtrandsfjällen ∧	26	61.17 N	13.00 E
Transylvania □[9]	38	46.30 N	24.00 E
Transylvanian Alps → Carpații Meridionali ⩘	38	45.30 N	24.15 E
Tranters Creek ≏	192	35.33 N	77.05 W
Traona	58	46.09 N	9.31 E
Trapalcó, Salinas de ≚	254	39.45 S	66.45 W
Trapani	70	38.01 N	12.31 E
Trapani □[4]	70	37.50 N	12.40 E
Traphole Brook ≏	283	42.10 N	71.11 W
Trappe, Md., U.S.	208	38.39 N	76.03 W
Trappe, Pa., U.S.	208	40.12 N	75.29 W
Trappenkamp	54	54.03 N	10.16 E
Trapper Peak ∧	202	45.54 N	114.18 W
Trappes	50	48.47 N	2.00 E
Trappeto	70	38.04 N	13.03 E
Trapuá ≏	287b	23.36 S	46.17 W
Traralgon	169	38.12 S	146.32 E
Traralgon Creek ≏	169	38.10 S	146.31 E
Traras, Monts des ⩘	34	35.10 N	1.40 W
Trarza □[4]	150	17.45 N	15.45 W
Trârza ◆[1]	150	18.00 N	15.00 W
Trasacco	66	41.57 N	13.32 E
Trasadingen	58	47.40 N	8.26 E
Trascău, Munții ⩘	38	46.23 N	23.33 E
Trasimeno, Lago ⊜	66	43.08 N	12.06 E
Trask ≏	224	45.28 N	123.53 W
Träslövsläge	26	57.04 N	12.16 E
Trasna	82	54.45 N	38.42 E
Trás-os-Montes □[9]	34	41.30 N	7.15 W
Trassem	56	49.34 N	6.31 E
Trăstenik	38	43.31 N	24.28 E
Trat	110	12.14 N	102.30 E
Tratalias	71	39.06 N	8.34 E
Tratzberg, Schloss ⊥	64	47.23 N	11.44 E
Traun	61	48.13 N	14.14 E
Traun ≏, Dtsch.	60	48.00 N	12.32 E
Traun ≏, Öst.	30	48.16 N	14.22 E
Traunkirchen	64	47.50 N	13.47 E
Traunreut	64	47.56 N	12.35 E
Traunsee ⊜	64	47.51 N	13.48 E
Traunstein, Dtsch.	64	47.52 N	12.38 E
Traunstein, Öst.	61	48.26 N	15.07 E
Traunstein ∧	64	47.52 N	13.50 E
Trautenstein	54	51.41 N	10.43 E
Travagliato	64	45.31 N	10.05 E
Trave ≏	54	53.54 N	10.50 E
Travedona	62	45.48 N	8.40 E
Travellers Lake ⊜	166	33.18 S	142.00 E
Travemünde ◆[8]	54	53.57 N	10.52 E
Traver	226	36.27 N	119.29 W
Travers, Mount ∧	172	42.01 S	172.44 E
Travers, Val de V	58	46.57 N	6.38 E
Traverse, Lake ⊜	198	45.43 N	96.40 W
Traverse Bay ⊂	184	50.40 N	96.25 W
Traverse City	190	44.45 N	85.37 W
Traversella	62	45.30 N	7.45 E
Traverse Peak ∧	180	65.10 N	159.12 W
Traversetolo	64	44.38 N	10.23 E
Travers Reservoir ⊜[1]	182	50.14 N	112.51 W
Tra Vinh	110	9.56 N	106.20 E
Travis	222	31.08 N	97.00 W
Travis □[6]	222	30.18 N	97.40 W
Travis, Lake ⊜[1]	196	30.27 N	98.00 W
Travis Air Force Base ■	226	38.16 N	121.55 W
Travnik	36	44.14 N	17.40 E
Trawalla	169	37.26 S	143.29 E
Trawbreaga Bay ⊂	48	55.17 N	7.18 W
Trawick	222	31.46 N	94.45 W
Trawsfynydd	42	52.54 N	3.55 W
Trayning	162	31.07 S	117.48 E
Trazegnies	50	50.28 N	4.19 E
Trbovlje	36	46.10 N	15.03 E
Treadwell	210	42.21 N	75.03 W
Treales	262	53.47 N	2.51 W
Treasure Island	220	27.46 N	82.46 W
Treasure Island I	226	37.48 N	122.22 W
Treasure Island Naval Station ■	282	37.49 N	122.22 W
Trebatsch	54	52.05 N	14.09 E
Trebbia ≏	62	45.04 N	9.41 E
Trebbin	54	52.13 N	13.13 E
Třebechovice pod Orebem	30	50.12 N	16.00 E
Trebel	54	52.59 N	11.20 E
Trebel ≏	54	53.55 N	13.01 E
Trebelsee ⊜	54	52.28 N	12.47 E
Třebenice	54	50.29 N	14.00 E
Trebgast	60	50.04 N	11.33 E
Třebíč	30	49.13 N	15.53 E
Trebinje	38	42.43 N	18.20 E
Trebisacce	68	39.52 N	16.32 E
Trebišov	30	48.40 N	21.47 E
Trebitz	54	51.45 N	12.44 E
Trebizond → Trabzon	130	41.00 N	39.43 E
Trebjerg ∧[2]	41	55.10 N	10.14 E
Třebkov	60	49.22 N	14.04 E
Treble Mountain ∧	182	55.50 N	129.51 W
Treblinka	30	52.39 N	22.03 E
Třeboň	61	49.00 N	14.47 E
Třebouň ∧	60	50.01 N	12.59 E
Trebsen	54	51.17 N	12.45 E
Trebur	56	49.56 N	8.25 E
Trecastagni	70	37.37 N	15.05 E
Trecate	62	45.26 N	8.44 E
Trecchina	68	40.02 N	15.46 E
Trece Martires	116	14.16 N	120.50 E
Trecenta	64	45.02 N	11.28 E
Tred Avon River ⊂	208	38.42 N	76.08 W
Tredegar	42	51.47 N	3.16 W
Tredici Archi, Ponte ◆[5]	66	41.32 N	14.57 E
Treene ≏	41	54.22 N	9.05 E
Trees Mills	279b	40.23 N	80.13 W
Treffen	64	46.40 N	13.52 E
Treffort	58	46.16 N	5.22 E
Treffurt	56	51.08 N	10.14 E
Trèfle, Lac du ⊜	206	46.36 N	73.55 W
Tregaron	42	52.13 N	3.55 W
Tregnago	64	45.31 N	11.10 E
Tregosse Islets II	166	17.41 S	150.43 E
Tregubovo	76	58.59 N	31.33 E
Tréguier	32	48.47 N	3.14 W
Treharris	42	51.41 N	3.16 W
Treherne	184	49.38 N	98.41 W
Trehörningsjö	26	63.42 N	18.48 E
Treia, Dtsch.	41	54.30 N	9.17 E
Treia, It.	66	43.19 N	13.19 E
Treig, Loch ⊜	46	56.50 N	4.44 W
Treinta y Tres	252	33.14 S	54.23 W
Treis	56	50.10 N	7.17 E
Treis-Karden	56	50.11 N	7.17 E
Trekkopje	156	22.18 S	14.53 E
Trélazé	32	47.27 N	0.28 W
Trelde Næs ›	41	55.37 N	9.52 E
Trelew	254	43.15 S	65.18 W
Trelleborg	41	55.22 N	13.10 E
Treloar	219	38.39 N	91.10 W
Tremadog	42	52.56 N	4.09 W
Tremblant, Lac ⊜	206	46.15 N	74.38 W
Tremblant, Mont ∧	206	46.16 N	74.35 W
Tremblay, Hippodrome du ♠	261	48.50 N	2.29 E
Tremblay-lès-Gonesse	261	48.59 N	2.34 E
Trembleur Lake ⊜	182	54.51 N	125.07 W
Tremedal	255	14.58 S	41.24 W
Tremembé	256	22.58 S	45.33 W
Tremezzo	58	45.59 N	9.15 E
Tremino	88	56.42 N	98.04 E
Tremiti, Isole II	66	42.07 N	15.30 E
Tremo La)(	124	27.44 N	89.12 E
Tremont, Il., U.S.	190	40.31 N	89.29 W
Tremont, In., U.S.	216	41.39 N	87.02 W
Tremont, Pa., U.S.	208	40.37 N	76.23 W
Tremont ◆[8]	276	40.51 N	73.55 W
Tremont City	218	40.00 N	83.50 W
Tremonton	200	41.42 N	112.09 W
Třemošna	60	49.49 N	13.20 E
Třemošná ≏	60	49.52 N	13.32 E
Tremp	34	42.10 N	0.54 E
Trempealeau	190	44.00 N	91.26 W
Trempealeau ≏	190	44.02 N	91.32 W
Tremsbüttel	52	53.44 N	10.18 E
Trena	144	10.45 N	40.38 E
Trenčín	30	48.54 N	18.04 E
Trendelburg	52	51.34 N	9.25 E
Trenel	252	35.42 S	64.08 W
Trêng	110	12.49 N	102.54 E
Trenggalek	115a	8.03 S	111.43 E
Trenque Lauquen	252	35.58 S	62.42 W
Trent, Dtsch.	54	54.31 N	13.15 E
Trent → Trento, It.	64	46.04 N	11.08 E
Trent ≏, On., Can.	212	44.06 N	77.34 W
Trent ≏, Eng., U.K.	28	53.42 N	0.41 W
Trent ≏, N.C., U.S.	192	35.05 N	77.02 W
Trent, Vale of V	42	52.44 N	1.50 W
Trent and Mersey Canal ≊	262	53.19 N	2.39 W
Trente et un Milles, Lac des ⊜	188	46.12 N	75.49 W
Trentham	169	37.23 S	144.19 E
Trentino-Alto Adige □[4]	64	46.30 N	11.20 E
Trento	64	46.04 N	11.08 E
Trento □[4]	64	46.08 N	11.07 E
Trentola-Ducenta	68	40.59 N	14.10 E
Trenton, N.S., Can.	186	45.37 N	62.38 W
Trenton, On., Can.	212	44.06 N	77.35 W
Trenton, Fl., U.S.	192	29.36 N	82.49 W
Trenton, Ga., U.S.	192	34.52 N	85.30 W
Trenton, Il., U.S.	219	38.36 N	89.40 W
Trenton, Ky., U.S.	194	36.43 N	87.15 W
Trenton, Mi., U.S.	216	42.08 N	83.10 W
Trenton, Mo., U.S.	194	40.04 N	93.36 W
Trenton, Ne., U.S.	198	40.10 N	101.00 W
Trenton, N.J., U.S.	208	40.13 N	74.44 W
Trenton, N.C., U.S.	192	35.04 N	77.21 W
Trenton, Oh., U.S.	218	39.29 N	84.28 W
Trenton, Tn., U.S.	194	35.58 N	88.56 W
Trenton, Tx., U.S.	196	33.26 N	96.20 W
Trenton, Canadian Forces Base ■	190	44.07 N	77.33 W
Trenton Channel ≏[1]	281	42.06 N	83.11 W
Trentwood	202	47.42 N	117.13 W
Trepalade	64	45.34 N	12.24 E
Trepassey	186	46.44 N	53.22 W
Trepassey Bay ⊂	186	46.37 N	53.20 W
Treptow ◆[8]	54	52.29 N	13.29 E
Trepuzzi	68	40.24 N	18.05 E
Trequanda	66	43.11 N	11.40 E
Tresa ≏	58	46.00 N	8.43 E
Tres Algarrobos	252	35.12 S	62.46 W
Tres Árboles	252	32.24 S	56.43 W
Tres Arroyos	252	38.23 S	60.17 W
Tres Cerros	254	48.13 S	67.33 W
Treščevo	82	54.11 N	37.55 E
Tresckow	210	40.54 N	75.58 W
Tresco I	42a	49.57 N	6.19 W
Três Corações	256	21.42 S	45.16 W
Trescore Balneario	62	45.41 N	9.50 E
Três Coroas	252	29.32 S	50.48 W
Tres de Febrero → Caseros	258	34.36 S	58.33 W
Tres de Febrero □[5]	288	34.36 S	58.35 W
Três de Maio	252	27.47 S	54.14 W
Tresenda	64	46.10 N	10.05 E
Tres Esquinas	246	0.43 N	75.16 W
Três Fronteiras	255	20.13 S	50.55 W
Treshnish Isles II	46	56.30 N	6.24 W
Treshnish Point ›	46	56.33 N	6.21 W
Três Ilhas	256	22.04 S	43.29 W
Tresinaro ≏	64	44.39 N	10.47 E
Tres Isletas	252	26.21 S	60.26 W
Treskino	80	52.40 N	44.40 E
Três Lagoas	255	20.48 S	51.43 W
Tres Lagos	254	49.37 S	71.30 W
Tres Lomas	252	36.27 S	62.51 W
Três Marias	255	18.12 S	45.14 W
Três Marias, Reprêsa de ⊜[1]	255	18.12 S	45.15 W
Tres Montes, Golfo ⊂	254	46.54 S	75.00 W
Tres Montes, Península ›[1]	254	46.50 S	75.30 W
Tres Montosas ∧	200	34.06 N	107.28 W
Tres Morros, Alto de ∧	246	7.08 N	76.11 W
Tresnuraghes	71	40.15 N	8.31 E
Tres Padres, Pico ∧	286a	19.35 N	99.08 W
Tres Palacios ≏	196	28.45 N	96.09 W
Tres Palos, Laguna ⊂	234	16.46 N	99.44 W
Três Passos	252	27.27 S	53.56 W
Tres Picos	234	15.52 N	93.32 W
Tres Picos, Cerro ∧, Arg.	252	38.09 S	61.57 W
Tres Picos, Cerro ∧, Méx.	234	16.12 N	93.37 W
Tres Pinos	226	36.48 N	121.19 W
Tres Pinos Creek ≏	226	36.47 N	121.21 W
Três Pontas	256	21.22 S	45.31 W
Três Pontas, Cabo das ›	152	10.23 S	13.32 E
Tres Puntas, Cabo ›, Arg.	254	47.06 S	65.53 W
Tres Puntas, Cabo ›, Guat.	236	15.56 N	88.37 W
Três Ranchos	255	18.22 S	47.47 W
Tres Reyes Islands II	116	13.14 N	121.51 E
Três Rios, Bra.	256	22.07 S	43.12 W
Tres Ríos, C.R.	236	9.54 N	83.58 W
Tressancourt	261	48.55 N	2.00 E
Třešť	30	49.18 N	15.30 E
Tresta	46a	60.14 N	1.21 W
Tres Valles	234	18.15 N	96.08 W
Tres Vírgenes, Volcán de las ∧[1]	232	27.27 N	112.34 W
Tres Zapotes ⊥	234	18.28 N	95.24 W
Tret'akovskaja Galereja ⊍	265b	55.45 N	37.37 E
Tretet	114	4.40 N	96.51 E
Trets	62	43.27 N	5.41 E
Tretten	26	61.19 N	10.19 E
Treuchtlingen	56	48.57 N	10.54 E
Treuen	54	50.32 N	12.18 E
Treuenbrietzen	54	52.06 N	12.52 E
Trevelín	254	43.04 S	71.28 W
Trèves → Trier	56	49.45 N	6.38 E
Trevi	66	42.52 N	12.45 E
Treviglio	62	45.31 N	9.35 E
Trevignano Romano	66	42.09 N	12.15 E
Treviño	34	42.44 N	2.45 W
Treviso	64	45.40 N	12.15 E
Treviso □[4]	64	45.50 N	12.13 E
Trevor	216	42.30 N	88.07 W
Trevorton	208	40.46 N	76.40 W
Trevose	208	40.08 N	74.58 W
Trevose Head ›	42	50.33 N	5.01 W
Trevose Heights	285	40.09 N	74.59 W
Trévoux	58	45.56 N	4.46 E
Trexlertown	208	40.33 N	75.36 W
Trezevant	194	36.00 N	88.37 W
Trezzano sul Naviglio	266b	45.25 N	9.04 E
Trezzo sull'Adda	62	45.36 N	9.31 E
Trgovište	38	42.21 N	22.05 E
Trhomné	60	49.55 N	13.05 E
Trhové Sviny	61	48.51 N	14.39 E
Triabunna	166	42.30 S	147.55 E
Triadelphia Reservoir ⊜[1]	208	39.13 N	77.01 W
Trialeti	84	41.33 N	44.07 E
Trialetskij chrebet ⩘	84	41.45 N	43.50 E
Triana	66	42.47 N	11.33 E
Triánda	38	36.24 N	28.10 E
Triangle, Eng., U.K.	262	53.42 N	1.56 W
Triangle, Va., U.S.	208	38.32 N	77.20 W
Triangle Lake	210	42.32 N	74.13 W
Triangul'atorov, pik ∧	88	53.45 N	97.00 E
Triángulos, Arrecífes ✣[2]	232	20.57 N	92.16 W
Triaucourt-en-Argonne	56	48.59 N	5.04 E
Tribeni	126	22.59 N	88.24 E
Triberg	58	48.08 N	8.13 E
Tribes Hill	210	42.57 N	74.17 W
Tribobó	287a	22.52 S	43.01 W
Triborough Bridge ◆[5]	276	40.47 N	73.55 W
Tri Brata, porog ⌊	86	57.25 N	95.39 E
Tribsees	54	54.05 N	12.45 E
Tribugá, Ensenada de ⊂	246	5.45 N	77.20 W
Tribune, Sk., Can.	184	49.15 N	103.50 W
Tribune, Ks., U.S.	198	38.28 N	101.45 W
Tribune Channel ⊔	182	50.50 N	126.16 W
Tribuswinkel	264b	48.00 N	16.16 E
Tricarico	68	40.37 N	16.09 E
Tricase	68	39.56 N	18.22 E
Tricesimo	64	46.10 N	13.13 E
Trichardt	158	26.28 S	29.13 E
Trichiana	64	46.05 N	12.07 E
Trichinopoly → Tiruchchirāppalli	122	10.49 N	78.41 E
Trichūr	122	10.31 N	76.13 E
Tri Cities	222	32.09 N	95.56 W
Tricot	50	49.34 N	2.35 E
Tri County Supply Canal ≊	198	40.49 N	100.06 W
Trida	166	33.01 S	145.01 E
Trident Peak ∧	204	41.54 N	118.25 W
Triebel	54	50.21 N	12.08 E
Trieben	61	47.29 N	14.30 E
Triebes	54	50.41 N	12.01 E
Triel-sur-Seine	261	48.59 N	2.00 E
Trient → Trento	64	46.04 N	11.08 E
Triepkendorf	54	53.17 N	13.20 E
Trier	56	49.45 N	6.38 E
Trier □[5]	56	50.00 N	6.40 E
Triesen	58	47.06 N	9.31 E
Trieste (Triest) (Trst)	64	45.40 N	13.46 E
Trieste □[4]	64	45.40 N	13.50 E
Trieste, Gulf of ⊂	64	45.40 N	13.35 E
Triesting ≏	61	48.05 N	16.24 E
Trieux	56	49.20 N	5.56 E
Triftern	60	48.24 N	13.01 E
Trigal	248	18.17 S	64.08 W
Triggiano	68	41.04 N	16.55 E
Triglav ∧	64	46.23 N	13.50 E
Triglitz	54	53.12 N	12.05 E
Trigna, Pizzo ∧	70	37.58 N	13.34 E
Trigno ≏	66	42.04 N	14.48 E
Trigueros	34	37.23 N	6.50 W
Tríkala	38	39.34 N	21.46 E
Trikhonís, Límni ⊜	38	38.34 N	21.28 E
Trikora, Puncak (Wilhelmina Peak) ∧	164	4.15 S	138.45 E
Tri-Lakes	216	41.14 N	85.26 W
Trilbardou	261	48.57 N	2.48 E
Trilby	220	28.27 N	82.11 W
Trillick	48	54.27 N	7.30 W
Trilport	50	48.57 N	2.57 E
Trim	48	53.34 N	6.47 W
Triman	120	29.38 N	69.05 E
Trimbach	58	47.22 N	7.54 E
Trimble □[6]	218	38.37 N	85.20 W
Trim Creek ≏	216	41.10 N	87.38 W
Trimdon	44	54.42 N	1.25 W
Trimont	198	43.45 N	94.42 W
Trimonte	256	21.43 S	42.35 W
Trin	58	46.50 N	9.22 E
Trinchera Creek ≏	200	37.19 N	105.45 W
Trincheras, Méx.	196	25.37 N	101.55 W
Trincheras, Méx.	232	30.24 N	111.32 W
Trincomalee	122	8.34 N	81.14 E
Trincomali Channel ⊔	224	48.02 N	123.30 W
Trindade	255	16.40 S	49.30 W
Trindade I	244	20.31 S	29.19 W
Třinec	30	49.41 N	18.40 E
Tring	42	51.48 N	0.40 W
Trinidad, Bol.	248	14.47 S	64.47 W
Trinidad, Col.	246	5.25 N	71.40 W
Trinidad, Cuba	240p	21.48 N	79.59 W
Trinidad, Hond.	236	14.57 N	88.45 W
Trinidad, Co., U.S.	198	37.10 N	104.30 W
Trinidad, Tx., U.S.	222	32.08 N	96.05 W
Trinidad, Ur.	252	33.32 S	56.54 W
Trinidad I	241r	10.30 N	61.15 W
Trinidad ≏	234	17.49 N	95.09 W
Trinidad, Golfo ⊂	254	49.55 S	75.25 W
Trinidad, Isla I	252	39.08 S	61.58 W
Trinidad and Tobago □[1], N.A.	230	11.00 N	61.00 W
Trinidad and Tobago □[1], N.A.	241r	11.00 N	61.00 W
Trinità	62	44.30 N	7.45 E
Trinità, Lago della ⊜	70	37.43 N	12.46 E
Trinità d'Agultu	71	40.59 N	8.54 E
Trinitapoli	68	41.21 N	16.05 E
Trinité, Havre de la ⊂	240e	14.44 N	60.58 W
Trinity, Nf., Can.	186	48.59 N	53.55 W
Trinity, Tx., U.S.	222	30.56 N	95.22 W
Trinity □[6]	222	31.07 N	95.10 W
Trinity ≏, Ca., U.S.	204	41.11 N	123.42 W
Trinity ≏, Tx., U.S.	222	29.47 N	94.42 W
Trinity, Clear Fork ≏	196	32.46 N	97.21 W
Trinity, East Fork ≏	222	32.30 N	96.30 W
Trinity, Elm Fork ≏	222	32.47 N	96.54 W
Trinity, South Fork ≏	204	40.54 N	123.35 W
Trinity, West Fork ≏	196	32.48 N	96.51 W
Trinity Bay ⊂, Nf., Can.	186	48.00 N	53.40 W
Trinity Bay ⊂, Tx., U.S.	222	29.40 N	94.45 W
Trinity Islands II	180	56.33 N	154.25 W
Trinity Mountain ∧	202	43.36 N	115.26 W
Trinity Mountains ⩘	204	41.00 N	122.30 W
Trinity Park ♠	275b	43.39 N	79.25 W
Trinity Peak ∧	204	40.14 N	118.45 W
Trinity Site ⊥	200	33.41 N	106.28 W
Trinkat Island I	110	8.05 N	93.30 E
Trinkitat	140	18.41 N	37.43 E
Trino	62	45.12 N	8.18 E
Trins	64	47.05 N	11.25 E
Trinway	214	40.08 N	82.00 W
Triolet	157c	20.03 S	57.32 E
Triolo ≏	66	41.40 N	15.34 E
Trion	192	34.32 N	85.18 W
Trionto ≏	68	39.37 N	16.45 E
Trionto, Capo ›	68	39.37 N	16.45 E
Triora	62	43.59 N	7.46 E
Tripa ≏	114	3.53 N	96.23 E
Tripi	70	38.03 N	15.06 E
Triplett Creek ≏	218	38.10 N	83.27 W
Triplett Creek, North Fork ≏	218	38.10 N	83.31 W
Tripoli → Ṭarābulus, Lībiyā	146	32.54 N	13.11 E
Tripoli → Ṭarābulus, Lubnān	130	34.26 N	35.51 E
Tripoli, Ia., U.S.	190	42.48 N	92.15 W
Trípolis, Ellás	38	37.31 N	22.21 E
Tripolis → Ṭarābulus, Lībiyā	146	32.54 N	13.11 E
Tripolis ⊥	130	37.58 N	28.59 E
Tripolitania → Ṭarābulus □[9]	146	31.00 N	15.00 E
Triponzo	66	42.50 N	12.56 E
Tripp	198	43.13 N	97.57 W
Trippstadt	56	49.22 N	7.46 E
Trips Subdivision	281	42.34 N	83.25 W
Triptis	54	50.44 N	11.52 E
Tripura □[3]	120	24.00 N	92.00 E
Triquet, Lac ⊜	186	50.42 N	59.47 W
Trisanna ≏	58	47.07 N	10.30 E
Tristan da Cunha Group II	10	37.15 S	12.30 W
Tristan Island I	10	37.05 S	12.17 W
Tristán Suárez	258	34.53 S	58.34 W
Tristao, Îles II	150	10.53 N	14.58 W
Tristate Village	278	41.44 N	87.57 W
Triste, Golfo ⊂	246	10.40 N	68.10 W
Triśuli Gaṅggā ≏	124	27.49 N	84.47 E
Tri Ton	110	10.25 N	105.00 E
Tritriva	157b	22.46 S	46.07 E
Trittau	52	53.37 N	10.25 E
Trittenheim	56	49.49 N	6.54 E
Triuggio	266b	45.40 N	9.16 E
Triumph	194	29.20 N	89.28 W
Triunfo, Igarapé ≏	250	6.22 S	52.25 W
Trivandrum	122	8.29 N	76.55 E
Trivento	66	41.47 N	14.33 E
Trivero	62	45.40 N	8.10 E
Trivigno	68	40.35 N	15.59 E
Trnava	30	48.23 N	17.35 E
Trnovo → Veliko Târnovo	38	43.04 N	25.39 E
Tr'ochgolovyj Golec, gora ∧	88	53.22 N	107.03 E
Tr'ochsv'atskoje	82	56.29 N	37.03 E
Trochtelfingen	58	48.18 N	9.14 E
Trochu	182	51.50 N	113.13 W
Troense	41	55.02 N	10.39 E
Trofa, Arroyo de ≏	266a	40.30 N	3.45 W
Trofaiach	61	47.25 N	15.00 E
Trofarello	62	44.59 N	7.44 E
Trögd ›[1]	40	59.31 N	17.15 E
Trogen	58	47.24 N	9.28 E
Trogir	36	43.31 N	16.15 E
Troglav ∧	36	43.57 N	16.36 E
Tröglitz	54	51.04 N	12.11 E
Troia	68	41.22 N	15.18 E
Troica	76	54.24 N	40.14 E
Troice-Lykovo ◆[8]	265b	55.47 N	37.24 E
Troick, Ross.	86	54.06 N	61.35 E
Troick, Ross.	88	57.25 N	94.50 E
Troickaja	78	45.08 N	38.07 E
Troickij, Ross.	80	50.14 N	43.03 E
Troickij, Ross.	80	50.14 N	43.05 E
Troickij, Ross.	86	50.41 N	54.38 E
Troickij, Ross.	86	57.03 N	63.43 E
Troickij, Ross.	88	54.36 N	113.09 E
Troickije Rosl'ai	80	53.21 N	41.24 E
Troickij Sungur	80	53.17 N	47.37 E
Troickij Zavod	88	53.27 N	102.09 E
Troickoje, Ross.	78	51.17 N	41.28 E
Troickoje, Ross.	80	46.26 N	44.15 E
Troickoje, Ross.	80	53.22 N	48.23 E
Troickoje, Ross.	80	53.06 N	52.32 E
Troickoje, Ross.	80	53.23 N	52.48 E
Troickoje, Ross.	82	55.23 N	37.25 E
Troickoje, Ross.	82	54.52 N	37.07 E
Troickoje, Ross.	83	47.22 N	38.53 E
Troickoje, Ross.	86	52.19 N	56.23 E
Troickoje, Ross.	86	59.07 N	58.25 E
Troickoje, Ross.	86	52.58 N	84.40 E
Troickoje, Ross.	89	49.27 N	136.36 E
Troicko-Pečorsk	24	62.44 N	56.06 E
Troina	70	37.47 N	14.36 E
Troina ≏	70	37.49 N	14.46 E
Troisdorf	56	50.49 N	7.08 E
Trois Fourches, Cap des ›	148	35.26 N	2.58 W
Trois-Pistoles	186	48.07 N	69.10 W
Trois Pitons, Morne ∧	240d	15.22 N	61.20 W
Trois Ponts	56	50.22 N	5.52 E
Trois-Rivières, P.Q., Can.	206	46.21 N	72.33 W
Trois-Rivières, Guad.	241o	15.59 N	61.39 W
Trois-Rivières-Ouest	206	46.19 N	72.35 W
Troisvierges	56	50.08 N	6.00 E
Trojan	38	42.51 N	24.43 E
Trojanova Tabla ⊥	38	44.37 N	22.20 E
Trojebratskij	86	54.28 N	66.01 E
Trojekurovo, Ross.	76	53.00 N	38.58 E
Trojekurovo, Ross.	76	53.25 N	39.43 E
Tr'okhizdenka	83	48.45 N	38.58 E
Troldhede	41	55.59 N	8.45 E
Trolleholm	41	55.54 N	13.15 E
Trollhättan	26	58.16 N	12.18 E
Trollheimen ∧	26	62.51 N	9.05 E
Trombay ◆[8]	272c	19.02 N	72.57 E
Trombetas ≏	250	1.55 S	55.35 W
Tromelin, Île I	138	15.52 S	54.25 E
Tromello	62	45.12 N	8.52 E
Tromper Wiek ⊂	54	54.37 N	13.24 E
Trompia, Val V	64	45.44 N	10.12 E
Trompsburg	158	30.01 S	25.46 E
Troms □[6]	24	69.15 N	19.40 E
Tromsø	24	69.40 N	18.58 E
Trona	204	35.45 N	117.22 W
Tronador, Monte ∧	254	41.10 S	71.54 W
Troncoso	234	22.44 N	102.22 W
Trondheim	26	63.25 N	10.25 E
Trondheimsfjorden ⊂[2]	26	63.39 N	10.49 E
Trondheimsleia ⊔	26	63.30 N	9.00 E
Tronto ≏	66	42.54 N	13.55 E
Tronville-en-Barrois	56	48.43 N	5.17 E
Tronzano Vercellese	62	45.21 N	8.10 E
Troo	50	47.47 N	0.47 E
Troödos	130	34.55 N	32.53 E
Trooilapspan	158	28.40 S	21.25 E
Troon, Eng., U.K.	42	50.12 N	5.16 W
Troon, Scot., U.K.	46	55.32 N	4.40 W
Trooper	285	40.09 N	75.24 W
Troparevo	82	55.23 N	35.54 E
Tropar'ovo ◆[8]	265b	55.39 N	37.29 E
Tropas, Rio das ≏	250	6.07 S	57.28 W
Tropea	68	38.41 N	15.54 E
Trophy Mountain ∧	182	51.47 N	119.48 W
Tropic	200	37.37 N	112.04 W
Tropojë	38	42.24 N	20.10 E
Troppau → Opava	30	49.56 N	17.54 E
Trosa	40	58.54 N	17.33 E
Troškovo	80	57.19 N	46.05 E
Troškūnai	76	55.36 N	24.51 E
Trosna	76	52.26 N	35.46 E

Symbol	English	Deutsch	Español	Français	Português
≏	River	Fluß	Río	Rivière	Rio
≊	Canal	Kanal	Canal	Canal	Canal
⌊	Waterfall, Rapids	Wasserfall, Stromschnellen	Cascada, Rápidos	Chute d'eau, Rapides	Cascata, Rápidos
⊔	Strait	Meeresstraße	Estrecho	Détroit	Estreito
⊂	Bay, Gulf	Bucht, Golf	Bahía, Golfo	Baie, Golfe	Baía, Golfo
⊜	Lake, Lakes	See, Seen	Lago, Lagos	Lac, Lacs	Lago, Lagos
≡	Swamp	Sumpf	Pantano	Marais	Pântano
⩍	Ice Features, Glacier	Eis- und Gletscherformen	Accidentes Glaciales	Formes glaciaires	Acidentes glaciares
⊤	Other Hydrographic Features	Andere Hydrographische Objekte	Otros Elementos Hidrográficos	Autres données hydrographiques	Outros acidentes hidrográficos
✣	Submarine Features	Untermeerische Objekte	Accidentes Submarinos	Formes de relief sous-marin	Acidentes submarinos
□	Political Unit	Politische Einheit	Unidad Politica	Entité politique	Unidade política
⊍	Cultural Institution	Kulturelle Institution	Institución Cultural	Institution culturelle	Institução cultural
⊥	Historical Site	Historische Stätte	Sitio Histórico	Site historique	Sitio histórico
♠	Recreational Site	Erholungs- und Ferienort	Sitio de Recreo	Centre de loisirs	Area de Lazer
⊠	Airport	Flughafen	Aeropuerto	Aéroport	Aeroporto
■	Military Installation	Militäranlage	Instalación Militar	Installation militaire	Instalação militar
◆	Miscellaneous	Verschiedenes	Misceláneo	Divers	Diversos

Name	Page	Lat.°′	Long.°′
Trossingen	58	48.04 N	8.38 E
Trostan ∧	48	55.03 N	6.09 W
Tröstau	60	50.01 N	11.57 E
Trostberg	60	48.01 N	12.32 E
Trostenskoje, ozero ⊜	82	55.52 N	36.29 E
Trostyanets', Ukr.	78	50.28 N	34.59 E
Trostyanets', Ukr.	78	48.31 N	29.12 E
Trottiscliffe	260	51.19 N	0.21 E
Trotuș ≃	38	46.03 N	27.14 E
Trotwood	218	39.47 N	84.18 W
Troublesome Creek ≃	219	39.54 N	91.37 W
Troubridge Point ›	168b	35.11 S	137.41 E
Trou-du-Nord	238	19.38 N	72.01 W
Troup	222	32.08 N	95.07 W
Troup Head ›	46	57.41 N	2.18 W
Troupsburg	210	42.03 N	77.33 W
Trout	194	31.41 N	92.10 W
Trout ≃, N.T., Can.	176	61.19 N	119.51 W
Trout ≃, N.A.	206	45.05 N	74.10 W
Trout Brook ≃, Ma., U.S.	283	42.16 N	71.18 W
Trout Brook ≃, Ma., U.S.	283	42.39 N	71.16 W
Trout Creek, Mi., U.S.	190	46.28 N	89.00 W
Trout Creek, Mt., U.S.	182	47.50 N	115.35 W
Trout Creek, N.Y., U.S.	210	42.12 N	75.17 W
Trout Creek ≃, Az., U.S.	200	34.56 N	113.36 W
Trout Creek ≃, Or., U.S.	202	44.48 N	121.03 W
Trout Creek ≃, Or., U.S.	202	42.23 N	118.36 W
Trout Creek ≃, Pa., U.S.	285	40.07 N	75.24 W
Trout Creek ≃, Wa., U.S.	224	46.02 N	121.12 W
Trout Creek Pass)(	200	38.54 N	105.58 W
Troutdale	224	45.32 N	122.23 W
Trout Lake	224	45.59 N	121.31 W
Trout Lake ⊜, B.C., Can.	182	50.35 N	117.26 W
Trout Lake ⊜, N.T., Can.	176	60.35 N	121.10 W
Trout Lake ⊜, On., Can.	184	51.13 N	93.20 W
Trout Lake ⊜, On., Can.	190	46.18 N	79.20 W
Trout Lake ⊜, On., Can.	190	46.13 N	80.35 W
Trout Lake Creek ≃	224	46.00 N	121.30 W
Trout Peak ∧	202	44.36 N	109.32 W
Trout River	186	49.29 N	58.08 W
Trout Run	210	41.23 N	77.03 W
Troutville, Pa., U.S.	214	41.02 N	78.47 W
Troutville, Va., U.S.	192	37.25 N	79.52 W
Trouville-sur-Mer	50	49.22 N	0.05 E
Trowbridge	42	51.20 N	2.13 W
Troxelville	210	40.48 N	77.12 W
Troy, Al., U.S.	194	31.48 N	85.58 W
Troy, Id., U.S.	202	46.44 N	116.46 W
Troy, Il., U.S.	219	38.43 N	89.52 W
Troy, In., U.S.	194	37.59 N	86.47 W
Troy, Ks., U.S.	198	39.46 N	95.05 W
Troy, Mi., U.S.	214	42.34 N	83.09 W
Troy, Mo., U.S.	219	38.58 N	90.58 W
Troy, Mt., U.S.	202	48.27 N	115.53 W
Troy, N.H., U.S.	207	42.49 N	72.10 W
Troy, N.Y., U.S.	210	42.43 N	73.41 W
Troy, N.C., U.S.	192	35.21 N	79.53 W
Troy, Oh., U.S.	218	40.02 N	84.12 W
Troy, Pa., U.S.	210	41.47 N	76.47 W
Troy, Tn., U.S.	194	36.20 N	89.09 W
Troy, Tx., U.S.	222	31.12 N	97.18 W
Troy → Truva ⊥	130	39.57 N	26.15 E
Troyaniv	78	50.07 N	28.31 E
Troyanivka	78	51.20 N	25.17 E
Troy Brook ≃	276	40.50 N	74.22 W
Troyes	50	48.18 N	4.05 E
Troy Grove	216	41.28 N	89.05 W
Troy Hills	210	40.51 N	74.23 W
Troyits'ke, Ukr.	78	49.55 N	38.19 E
Troyits'ke, Ukr.	78	47.38 N	30.19 E
Troyits'ke, Ukr.	83	48.32 N	38.23 E
Troyits'ko-Khartsyz'k	83	47.58 N	38.16 E
Troy Lake ⊜	204	34.49 N	116.33 W
Troy Meadows ≡	276	40.50 N	74.22 W
Troy Peak ∧	204	38.19 N	115.30 W
Trpanj	36	43.00 N	17.17 E
Trst → Trieste	64	45.40 N	13.46 E
Trstená	30	49.22 N	19.37 E
Trstenik	38	43.37 N	21.00 E
Truax	184	49.55 N	104.58 W
Trubč'ovsk	76	52.37 N	33.44 E
Trubetčino	76	52.53 N	39.33 E
Trubino, Ross.	82	54.58 N	36.42 E
Trubino, Ross.	82	55.59 N	38.08 E
Trub'ož ≃	82	56.44 N	38.51 E
Truchas	200	36.02 N	105.48 W
Truchas Peak ∧	200	35.58 N	105.39 W
Truchtersheim	58	48.40 N	7.36 E
Trucial States → United Arab Emirates □[1]	128	24.00 N	54.00 E
Truckee	226	39.19 N	120.10 W
Truckee ≃	204	39.51 N	119.24 W
Trucksville	210	41.18 N	75.56 W
Trud	76	57.37 N	33.58 E
Trudfront	80	45.56 N	47.41 E
Trudnovo	86	56.39 N	91.30 E
Trudovoj	80	51.42 N	52.43 E
Trues Creek ≃	276	40.41 N	73.17 W
Truganina	274b	37.49 S	144.43 E
Truim ≃	46	57.02 N	4.10 W
Truite, Lac à la ⊜	190	47.16 N	78.17 W
Trujillo, Col.	246	4.10 N	76.19 W
Trujillo, Esp.	34	39.28 N	5.53 W
Trujillo, Hond.	236	15.55 N	86.00 W
Trujillo, Méx.	234	23.10 N	103.13 W
Trujillo, Perú	248	8.07 S	79.02 W
Trujillo, Ven.	246	9.22 N	70.26 W
Trujillo □[3]	246	9.25 N	70.30 W
Trujillo Alto	240m	18.22 N	66.01 W
Trujillo Creek ≃	196	35.28 N	102.52 W
Truk Islands → Chuuk II	175c	7.25 N	151.47 E
Truk Lagoon ⊂	175c	7.25 N	151.45 E
Trull Brook ≃	283	42.39 N	71.15 W
Truman	198	43.49 N	94.26 W
Trumann	194	35.40 N	90.30 W
Trumansburg	210	42.32 N	76.39 W
Trumbauersville	208	40.25 N	75.23 W
Trumbull	207	41.14 N	73.12 W
Trumbull □[6]	214	41.14 N	80.52 W
Trumbull, Mount ∧	200	36.25 N	113.10 W
Trumon	114	2.49 N	97.38 E
Trun, Fr.	50	48.51 N	0.02 E
Trun, Schw.	58	46.45 N	8.58 E
Trundle	166	32.55 S	147.43 E
Trung Luong	110	13.57 N	109.15 E
Trung Phan □[9]	110	15.00 N	108.00 E
Trunovskoje	80	45.29 N	42.08 E
Truro, Austl.	168b	34.25 S	139.07 E
Truro, N.S., Can.	186	45.22 N	63.16 W
Truro, Eng., U.K.	42	50.16 N	5.03 W
Truro, Ma., U.S.	207	41.59 N	70.03 W
Trusan ≃	112	4.58 N	115.11 E
Truscott	196	33.45 N	99.49 W
Trușeni	38	47.04 N	28.41 E
Trușești	38	47.46 N	27.01 E
Trusetal	54	50.47 N	10.25 E
Truskavets'	78	49.16 N	23.33 E
Truslejka	80	53.54 N	46.24 E
Trus Madi, Gunong ∧	112	5.33 N	116.31 E
Truth or Consequences (Hot Springs)	200	33.07 N	107.15 W
Trutnov	30	50.34 N	15.55 E
Truva (Troy) ⊥	130	39.57 N	26.15 E
Truxall	279b	40.33 N	79.33 W
Truxton, Mo., U.S.	219	39.00 N	91.14 W
Truxton, N.Y., U.S.	210	42.43 N	76.02 W
Truxton Wash V	200	35.38 N	114.04 W
Truyère ≃	32	44.39 N	2.34 E
Trwyn Cilan ›	42	52.46 N	4.30 W
Tryduby	78	48.06 N	30.24 E
Trylisy	78	49.59 N	29.50 E
Tryon, Ne., U.S.	198	41.33 N	100.57 W
Tryon, N.C., U.S.	192	35.12 N	82.14 W
Tryonville	214	41.42 N	79.47 W
Trypillya	78	50.07 N	30.46 E
Trysil	26	61.19 N	12.16 E
Trysilelva (Klarälven) ≃	26	59.23 N	13.32 E
Tryškiai	76	56.04 N	22.35 E
Tryweryn ≃	42	52.55 N	3.35 W
Trzcianka	30	53.03 N	16.28 E
Trzciel	30	52.23 N	15.52 E
Trzcińsko-Zdrój	30	52.58 N	14.35 E
Trzebiatów	30	54.04 N	15.14 E
Trzebiel	54	51.37 N	14.50 E
Trzebież	30	53.42 N	14.31 E
Trzebinia	30	50.10 N	19.18 E
Trzebnica	30	51.19 N	17.03 E
Trzemeszno	30	52.35 N	17.50 E
Trzęsacz	54	54.05 N	14.58 E
Tržič	36	46.22 N	14.19 E
Tsacha Lake ⊜	182	53.05 N	124.40 W
Tsala Apopka Lake ⊜	220	28.52 N	82.20 W
Tsamkong → Zhanjiang	102	21.16 N	110.28 E
Tsandi	156	17.42 S	14.50 E
Tsangano	154	15.08 S	34.32 E
Ts'anghsien → Cangzhou	98	38.19 N	116.51 E
T'sangwu → Wuzhou	102	23.30 N	111.27 E
Ts'aot'un	100	23.59 N	120.41 E
Tsarabaria	157b	13.46 S	49.58 E
Tsaramandroso	157b	16.22 S	47.02 E
Tsaratanana	157b	16.47 S	47.39 E
Tsaratanana, Massif du ⋏	157b	14.00 S	49.00 E
Tsaraxaibis	158	27.25 S	19.22 E
Tsaritsyn → Volgograd	80	48.44 N	44.25 E
Tsarychanka	78	48.57 N	34.29 E
Tsau	156	20.12 S	22.22 E
Tsaukaib	156	26.37 S	15.31 E
Tsavo	154	2.59 S	38.28 E
Tsavo East National Park ♠	154	2.11 S	38.25 E
Tsavo West National Park ♠	154	2.55 S	37.55 E
Tsawwassen	224	49.01 N	123.06 W
Tsaydaychuz Peak ∧	182	53.02 N	126.35 W
Tsayta Lake ⊜	182	55.25 N	125.30 W
Tschad → Chad □[1]	146	15.00 N	19.00 E
Tschad-See → Chad, Lake ⊜	146	13.20 N	14.00 E
Tschagguns	58	47.05 N	9.54 E
Tschamut	58	46.40 N	8.42 E
Tschangscha → Changsha	100	28.12 N	112.58 E
Tschangtschun → Changchun	89	43.53 N	125.19 E
Tscheljuskin, Kap → Čel'uskin, mys ›	74	77.45 N	104.20 E
Tschengtu → Chengdu	107	30.39 N	104.04 E
Tschenstochau → Częstochowa	30	50.49 N	19.06 E
Tschernitz	54	51.35 N	14.37 E
Tscheschkaja-Bucht → Češskaja guba ⊂	24	67.30 N	46.30 E
Tschida, Lake ⊜[1]	198	46.36 N	101.54 W
Tschingtau → Qingdao	98	36.06 N	120.19 E
Tschittagong → Chittagong	120	22.20 N	91.50 E
Tschuktschen-Meer → Chukchi Sea ⊤[2]	16	69.00 N	171.00 W
Tschungking → Chongqing	107	29.34 N	106.35 E
Tsebrykove	78	47.09 N	30.06 E
Tsekanyani	156	19.52 S	26.39 E
Tsembeyi	158	31.36 S	27.03 E
Ts'engwen ≃	100	23.03 N	120.03 E
Tsenke ≃	273b	4.24 S	15.26 E
Tses	156	25.58 S	18.08 E
Tsévié	150	6.25 N	1.13 E
Tshabong	156	26.03 S	22.29 E
Tshabuta	152	7.47 S	23.16 E
Tshane	156	24.05 S	21.54 E
Tshaneni	158	26.00 S	31.47 E
Tshangalele, Lac ⊜[1]	154	10.55 S	27.03 E
Tshangu ≃	273b	4.25 S	15.23 E
Tshela	152	4.59 S	12.56 E
Tshesebe	156	21.51 S	27.35 E
Tshibeke	154	2.44 S	28.36 E
Tshibinda	154	2.19 S	28.45 E
Tshibomba	152	9.02 S	22.34 E
Tshidilamolomo	156	25.50 S	24.41 E
Tshikapa	152	6.25 S	20.48 E
Tshilenge	152	6.15 S	23.46 E
Tshimbulu	152	6.29 S	22.51 E
Tshindjamba	152	10.54 S	22.41 E
Tshinota	152	7.01 S	20.57 E
Tshinsenda	154	12.18 S	27.58 E
Tshisuku	152	6.26 S	19.55 E
Tshitadi	152	6.45 S	21.45 E
Tshoa	152	5.34 S	12.41 E
Tshofa	154	5.14 S	25.15 E
Tshopo ≃	154	0.33 N	25.07 E
Tshuapa ≃	152	0.14 S	20.42 E
Tshukudu	156	22.30 S	23.22 E
Tshumbiri	152	2.39 S	16.14 E
Tshwaane	156	22.29 S	22.03 E
Tsiafajavona ∧	157b	19.21 S	47.15 E
Tsianaloka	157b	18.08 S	44.50 E
Tsiémé ≃	273b	4.15 S	15.18 E
Tsiga	152	1.32 S	10.11 E
Tsihombe	157b	25.18 S	45.29 E
Tsilmamo	144	6.01 N	35.17 E
Tsimanampetsotsa, Lac ⊜	157b	24.08 S	43.46 E
Tsimilofo	157b	24.59 S	45.10 E
Tsimpsean Indian Reserve •[4]	182	54.30 N	130.22 W
Tsinan → Jinan	98	36.40 N	116.57 E
Tsineng	158	27.06 S	23.04 E
Tsinghai → Qinghai □[4]	90	36.00 N	96.00 E
Tsingkiang → Qingjiang	100	33.35 N	119.02 E
Tsing Ma Bridge •[5]	271d	22.21 N	114.03 E
Tsingtao → Qingdao	98	36.06 N	120.19 E
Tsing Yi I	271d	22.21 N	114.05 E
Tsingyuan → Baoding	105	38.52 N	115.29 E
Tsining → Jining	98	35.25 N	116.36 E
Tsinjoarivo	157b	19.37 S	47.40 E
Tsinjomitondraka	157b	15.36 S	47.08 E
Tsinling Shan → Qin Ling ⋏	102	34.00 N	108.00 E
Tsintsabis	156	18.45 S	17.51 E
Tsiribihina ≃	157b	19.42 S	44.31 E
Tsiroanomandidy	157b	18.46 S	46.02 E
Tsitondroina	157b	21.19 S	46.00 E
Tsitsihar → Qiqihar	89	47.19 N	123.55 E
Tsitsikama Forest and Coastal National Park ♠	158	33.57 S	23.53 E
Tsitsutl Peak ∧	182	52.44 N	125.47 W
Tsivory	157b	24.04 S	46.05 E
Tskhinvali → Cchinvali	84	42.13 N	43.56 E
Tsna → Cna ≃	80	54.32 N	42.05 E
Tsobis	156	19.27 S	17.30 E
Tsolo	158	31.18 S	28.37 E
Tsomo	158	32.00 S	27.42 E
Tsomo ≃	158	32.25 S	27.50 E
Tsoying	100	22.41 N	120.17 E
Tsu	94	34.43 N	136.31 E
Tsubakuro-dake ∧	94	36.24 N	137.42 E
Tsubame	92	37.39 N	138.56 E
Tsubata	94	36.40 N	136.44 E
Tsuboro-suigenchi ⊜[1]	270	34.24 N	135.54 E
Tsuchiura	94	36.05 N	140.12 E
Tsuchiyama	94	34.56 N	136.17 E
Tsuda, Nihon	96	34.17 N	134.15 E
Tsuda, Nihon	270	34.49 N	135.43 E
Tsuen Wan → Quanwan	271d	22.22 N	114.07 E
Tsugaru-hantō ›[1]	92	41.00 N	140.30 E
Tsugaru-heiya ≍	92	40.49 N	140.27 E
Tsugaru-kaikyō ⊔	92a	41.35 N	141.00 E
Tsuge	94	34.37 N	135.57 E
Tsugu	94	35.10 N	137.37 E
Tsuha	174m	26.14 N	127.47 E
Tsuiki	96	33.40 N	131.03 E
Tsujidō	268	35.20 N	139.27 E
Tsukahara	268	35.18 N	139.58 E
Tsukechi	94	35.38 N	137.26 E
Tsuken-jima I	174m	26.15 N	127.57 E
Tsukigase	94	34.42 N	136.02 E
Tsukinowa-kofun ⊥	96	34.55 N	134.11 E
Tsukiyono	94	36.41 N	138.59 E
Tsukuba	94	36.13 N	140.06 E
Tsukuba-san ∧	94	36.13 N	140.06 E
Tsukude	94	34.59 N	137.25 E
Tsukui	94	35.35 N	139.16 E
Tsukumi	96	33.04 N	131.52 E
Tsukumono •[8]	270	34.50 N	135.11 E
Tsukuryne	83	48.05 N	37.18 E
Tsukushi-heiya ≍	96	33.20 N	130.30 E
Tsukushi-sanchi ⋏	92	33.30 N	130.30 E
Tsumagoi	94	36.31 N	138.32 E
Tsuman'	78	50.49 N	25.53 E
Tsumeb	156	19.13 S	17.42 E
Tsumeki-zaki ›	94	34.39 N	138.59 E
Tsumis Park	156	23.43 S	17.28 E
Tsumkwe	156	19.41 S	20.30 E
Tsuna	96	34.26 N	134.54 E
Tsunan	94	37.01 N	138.39 E
Tsunashima •[8]	268	35.32 N	139.38 E
Tsunekami-misaki ›	94	35.38 N	135.49 E
Tsuni → Zunyi	102	27.39 N	106.57 E
Tsuno-shima I	96	34.21 N	130.51 E
Tsuru	94	35.33 N	138.55 E
Tsuruga	94	35.39 N	136.04 E
Tsurugaoka-hachimangu Shrine ʊ[1]	268	35.19 N	139.33 E
Tsurugashima	268	35.56 N	139.24 E
Tsuruga-wan ⊂	94	35.45 N	136.04 E
Tsurugi	94	36.27 N	136.38 E
Tsurugi-dake ∧	94	36.37 N	137.37 E
Tsurugi-san ∧	96	33.51 N	134.06 E
Tsurugi-san-kokutei-kōen ♠	96	33.50 N	134.06 E
Tsuruhara	270	34.26 N	135.20 E
Tsuruma	268	35.51 N	139.33 E
Tsurumi •[8]	268	35.30 N	139.41 E
Tsurumi ≃	94	35.29 N	139.41 E
Tsurumi-dake ∧	96	33.17 N	131.26 E
Tsuruoka	92	38.44 N	139.50 E
Tsushima, Nihon	94	35.10 N	136.43 E
Tsushima, Nihon	96	33.05 N	132.30 E
Tsushima II	92	34.30 N	129.22 E
Tsushima-kaikyō (Eastern Channel) ⊔	92	34.00 N	129.00 E
Tsuwano	96	34.28 N	131.46 E
Tsuyama	96	35.03 N	134.00 E
Tsuyazaki	96	33.47 N	130.28 E
Tsvitkove	78	49.11 N	31.33 E
Tsvitne	78	48.57 N	32.29 E
Tsybuliv	78	49.06 N	29.50 E
Tsyurupyns'k	78	46.37 N	32.43 E
Ttruchchendūr	122	8.29 N	78.07 E
Tu → Tsu	94	34.43 N	136.31 E
Tua	152	3.38 S	16.36 E
Tua ≃	34	41.13 N	7.26 W
Tua, Tanjung ›	115a	5.54 S	105.44 E
Tua Chau	110	21.55 N	103.21 E
Tuakau	172	37.16 S	174.57 E
Tual	164	5.40 S	132.45 E
Tualatin	224	45.23 N	122.45 W
Tualatin ≃	224	45.20 N	122.39 W
Tualatin Mountains ⋏	224	45.40 N	122.50 W
Tuam	48	53.31 N	8.50 W
Tuamarina	172	41.26 S	173.57 E
Tuamotu, Îles (Tuamotu Archipelago) II	14	19.00 S	142.00 W
Tuamotu Ridge ⊹[3]	14	17.00 S	145.00 W
Tuan, Tanjong ›	114	2.23 N	101.52 E
Tuanan	112	2.07 S	114.24 E
Tuanfeng	100	30.38 N	114.51 E
Tuan Giao	110	21.35 N	103.25 E
Tuangku, Pulau I	114	2.10 N	97.16 E
Tuanlin	98	39.35 N	119.15 E
Tuannian	107	29.55 N	106.03 E
Tuanpi	100	30.44 N	115.13 E
Tuanshan	98	40.02 N	123.34 E
Tuanwang	98	36.45 N	120.38 E
Tuanxi	102	27.28 N	107.08 E
Tuapa	174v	18.57 S	169.54 W
Tuapeka Mouth	172	46.01 S	169.31 E
Tuapse	84	44.07 N	39.05 E
Tuaran	112	6.11 N	116.14 E
Tuas	114	1.19 N	103.38 E
Tuasivi	175a	13.40 S	172.07 W
Tuasivi, Cape ›	175a	13.40 S	172.07 W
Tuatapere	172	46.08 S	167.41 E
Tuath, Loch ⊔	46	56.30 N	6.12 W
Tuba	88	57.24 N	102.48 E
Tuba ≃	86	53.57 N	91.31 E
Tubac	200	31.36 N	111.02 W
Tuba City	200	36.08 N	111.14 W
T'ub'ak-Čekurča	80	56.05 N	49.56 E
Tubalan Head ›	116	6.30 N	125.35 E
Tuban	115a	6.54 S	112.03 E
Tubarão	252	28.30 S	49.01 W
Ṭūbās	132	32.19 N	35.22 E
Tubau	112	3.08 N	113.42 E
Tubbataha Reefs ⊹[2]	116	8.51 N	119.56 E
Tubbergen	52	52.25 N	6.46 E
Tubbs Island I	282	38.08 N	122.26 W
Ṭubhār	142	29.19 N	30.42 E
Tubig ≃	116	11.54 N	125.25 E
Tubigan Island I	116	6.26 N	120.47 E
Tubingantan Point ›	116	5.54 N	120.55 E
Tübingen	58	48.31 N	9.02 E
Tübingen □[5]	58	48.10 N	9.30 E
Tubinskij	86	52.53 N	58.13 E
Tubize	50	50.41 N	4.12 E
T'ub-Karagan, mys ›	84	44.39 N	50.18 E
T'ub-Karagan, poluostrov ›[1]	84	44.30 N	50.30 E
Tubli	116	13.56 N	124.09 E
Tubod	116	8.03 N	123.48 E
Tubre	64	46.39 N	10.27 E
Ṭubruq (Tobruk)	146	32.05 N	23.59 E
Tubuai I	14	23.18 S	149.30 W
Tuburan, Pil.	116	10.44 N	123.49 W
Tuburan, Pil.	116	6.39 N	122.16 E
Tubusereia	164	9.33 S	147.18 E
Tubutama	200	30.53 N	111.29 W
Tucacas	246	10.48 N	68.19 W
Tucacas, Punta ›	246	10.50 N	68.14 W
Tucalota Creek ≃	228	33.32 N	117.10 W
Tucannon ≃	202	46.33 N	118.11 W
Tucano	250	10.58 S	38.48 W
Tucava ≃	248	18.37 S	58.59 W
T'uch'ang	100	24.35 N	121.29 E
Tucheim	54	52.17 N	12.11 E
Tüchen	54	53.04 N	12.05 E
T'uch'eng, T'aiwan	269d	24.59 N	121.26 E
Tucheng, Zhg.	98	38.53 N	121.15 E
Tucheng, Zhg.	102	28.12 N	105.58 E
Tuchengzi, Zhg.	98	41.20 N	116.29 E
Tuchengzi, Zhg.	98	40.29 N	124.24 E
Tuchengzi, Zhg.	104	42.27 N	122.44 E
Tuchengzicun	104	41.52 N	120.41 E
Tuchengziwuhao	98	40.56 N	113.58 E
Tuchlovice	54	50.06 N	14.00 E
Tuchola	30	53.35 N	17.50 E
Tuchów	30	49.54 N	21.03 E
T'uchtet	86	56.32 N	89.19 E
Tuckahoe, N.J., U.S.	208	39.17 N	74.45 W
Tuckahoe, N.Y., U.S.	276	40.57 N	73.49 W
Tuckahoe ≃	208	39.17 N	74.39 W
Tuckahoe Creek ≃	208	38.49 N	75.53 W
Tuckanarra	162	27.07 S	118.05 E
Tucker Heights	210	42.55 N	73.55 W
Tuckerman	194	35.43 N	91.11 W
Tuckernuck Island I	207	41.18 N	70.15 W
Tuckerton, N.J., U.S.	208	39.36 N	74.20 W
Tuckerton, Pa., U.S.	208	40.25 N	75.57 W
Tuckfield, Mount ∧	162	18.44 S	124.54 E
Tučkovo	82	55.36 N	36.28 E
Tucson	200	32.13 N	110.55 W
Tucumã ≃[1]	246	3.58 S	66.26 W
Tucumán → San Miguel de Tucumán	252	26.49 S	65.13 W
Tucumán □[4]	252	27.00 S	65.30 W
Tucumcari	196	35.10 N	103.43 W
Tucumcari Mountain ∧	196	35.08 N	103.42 W
Tucunuco	252	30.36 S	68.38 W
Tucupido	246	9.17 N	65.47 W
Tucupita	246	9.04 N	62.03 W
Tucuruí	250	3.42 S	49.27 W
Tucuruí, Represa de ⊜[1]	250	4.40 S	49.20 W
Tucuruvi •[8]	287b	23.28 S	46.35 W
Tuczna	30	51.54 N	23.26 E
Tud ≃	42	52.38 N	1.15 E
Tudameda	112	10.52 S	122.55 E
Tudcum	252	30.14 S	69.15 W
Tudeå ≃	41	55.23 N	11.13 E
Tudela, Esp.	34	42.05 N	1.36 W
Tudela, Pil.	116	8.15 N	123.50 E
Tudela de Duero	34	41.35 N	4.35 W
Tudian	106	30.35 N	120.37 E
Tudichang	107	30.06 N	103.56 E
Tuditang	100	30.12 N	114.18 E
Tudmur (Palmyra)	130	34.33 N	38.17 E
Tudu	76	59.11 N	26.51 E
Tudweiliog	42	52.54 N	4.35 W
Tuela ≃	34	41.30 N	7.12 W
Tuen Mun	271d	22.24 N	113.58 E
Tuenno	64	46.20 N	11.01 E
Tueré ≃	250	2.48 S	50.59 W
Tuergate	85	40.28 N	75.21 E
Tufanbeyli	130	38.16 N	36.13 E
Tufānganj	124	26.19 N	89.40 E
Tuffé	50	48.07 N	0.31 E
Tufi	164	9.05 S	149.20 E
Tufo	68	41.00 N	14.47 E
Tufts University ʊ[2]	283	42.24 N	71.07 W
Tufu Point ›	174y	14.13 S	169.32 W
Tugaske	184	50.53 N	106.16 W
Tugela	158	29.09 S	31.29 E
Tugela ≃	158	29.14 S	31.30 E
Tugela Falls ⌊	158	28.45 S	28.58 E
Tugela Ferry	158	28.44 S	30.27 E
Tug Fork ≃	192	38.06 N	82.36 W
Tuggerah Lake ⊂	170	33.18 S	151.30 E
Tughlakābād •[8]	272a	28.31 N	77.16 E
Tugidak Island I	180	56.30 N	154.36 W
Tuğköyü	130	38.27 N	42.16 E
Tuglie	68	40.04 N	18.05 E
Tugnug Point ›	116	11.21 N	125.38 E
Tugolesskij Bor	80	55.33 N	39.49 E
Tugolukovo	80	51.56 N	41.40 E
Tugubun Point ›	116	7.00 N	126.27 E
Tuguegarao	116	17.37 N	121.44 E
Tugulym	86	57.04 N	64.39 E
Tugun	171a	28.09 S	153.30 E
Tugur	89	53.48 N	136.48 E
Tugur ≃	89	53.48 N	136.44 E
Tugurskij poluostrov ›[1]	89	54.00 N	137.24 E
Tuguša	88	55.57 N	96.26 E
Tugutuj	88	52.40 N	104.50 E
Tuhai ≃	98	37.55 N	118.05 E
Tuhepu	104	40.54 N	122.49 E
Tuhuangba	102	31.40 N	108.21 E
Tui	34	42.03 N	8.38 W
Tuibo	89	44.01 N	127.47 E
Tuichi ≃	248	14.36 S	67.35 W
Tuim	86	54.20 N	89.55 E
Tuineje	148	28.19 N	14.03 W
Tuira ≃	246	8.21 N	78.03 W
Tuirc, Beinn an ∧[2]	46	55.34 N	5.34 W
Tuitán	234	21.08 N	103.48 W
Tuitui	256	22.47 S	46.42 W
Tuj ≃	86	57.33 N	72.31 E
T'ujabuguz	85	40.58 N	69.15 E
Tujemojnak	86	49.20 N	62.55 E
Tuji-ri	98	41.31 N	127.12 E
Tujmazy	80	54.36 N	53.42 E
Tüjn Gol ≃	102	45.04 N	100.46 E
Tujunga •[8]	280	34.15 N	118.17 W
Tujunga Valley V	280	34.17 N	118.20 W
Tujunga Wash V	280	34.09 N	118.24 W
Tukaj	86	55.24 N	90.49 E
T'ukalinsk	86	55.52 N	72.12 E
Tukan	86	53.50 N	57.26 E
Tukan ≃	86	60.02 N	71.36 E
Tukangbesi, Kepulauan II	112	5.40 S	123.50 E
Tukayel	144	8.08 N	45.22 E
Ṭūkh, Miṣr	142	30.21 N	31.12 E
Ṭūkh, Miṣr	142	27.41 N	30.49 E
Ṭūkh al-Aqlām	142	30.52 N	31.26 E
Ṭūkh al-Khayl	142	28.06 N	30.40 E
Tukituki ≃	172	39.36 S	176.57 E
Tuk Méas	110	10.40 N	104.34 E
Tukolon'	88	55.24 N	107.42 E
Tukosméra, Mont ∧	175f	19.35 S	169.22 E
Tukpo	154	4.25 N	25.52 E
Tūkrah	146	32.32 N	20.34 E
Tuktoyaktuk	180	69.27 N	133.02 W
Tuktoyaktuk Peninsula ›[1]	180	69.45 N	131.20 W
Tukuj-Mekteb	84	44.20 N	45.11 E
Tukums	76	57.00 N	23.10 E
Tukuran	116	7.51 N	123.35 E
Tukuringra, chrebet ⋏	89	54.20 N	126.20 E
Tukuyu	154	9.15 S	33.39 E
T'uk'u Yüeh ∧	269d	25.02 N	121.38 E
Tukwila	224	47.28 N	122.15 W
Tula, Am. Sam.	174u	14.15 S	170.34 W
Tula, It.	71	40.44 N	8.59 E
Tula, Méx.	234	23.00 N	99.43 W
Tula, Nig.	146	9.50 N	11.28 E
Tula, Ross.	82	54.12 N	37.37 E
Tula ≃, Kenya	154	0.50 S	39.51 E
Tula ≃, Méx.	234	20.40 N	99.30 W
Tula ⊥	234	20.06 N	99.19 W
Tula de Allende	234	20.03 N	99.21 W
Tulaghi	175e	9.06 S	160.09 E
Tulagt Ar ≃	120	36.35 N	92.20 E
Tulai Nanshan ⋏	102	38.44 N	98.20 E
Tūlak	128	33.58 N	63.44 E
Tulalip Indian Reservation •[4]	224	48.06 N	122.15 W
Tulancingo	234	20.05 N	98.22 W
Tulangbawang ≃	112	4.24 S	105.52 E
Tula Oblast' □[4]	76	54.00 N	37.30 E
Tulaodian	104	41.13 N	121.27 E
T'ul'apsy	86	57.28 N	89.38 E
Tulare, Ca., U.S.	226	36.12 N	119.20 W
Tulare, S.D., U.S.	198	44.44 N	98.30 W
Tulare □[6]	226	36.20 N	119.18 W
Tulare Canal ≊	226	36.08 N	119.25 W
Tulare Lake Bed ⊜	226	36.03 N	119.49 W
Tulare Lake Canal ≊	226	36.04 N	119.39 W
Tularosa	200	33.04 N	106.01 W
Tularosa ≃	200	33.41 N	108.46 W
Tularosa Valley ≍[1]	200	32.45 N	106.10 W
Tulbagh	158	33.17 S	19.09 E
Tulbing	264b	48.16 N	16.09 E
Tulbinger Kogel ∧[2]	264b	48.17 N	16.09 E
Tulcán	246	0.48 N	77.43 W
Tulcea	38	45.11 N	28.48 E
Tulcea □[6]	38	45.00 N	29.00 E
Tul'chyn	78	48.39 N	28.52 E
Tulcingo de Valle	234	18.03 N	98.26 W
Tule ≃, Nic.	236	11.20 N	84.52 W
Tule ≃, Ca., U.S.	226	36.03 N	119.50 W
Tule, North Branch ≃	226	36.06 N	119.22 W
Tule, South Branch ≃	226	36.05 N	119.29 W
Tule Canal ≊	226	38.37 N	121.35 W
Tule Creek ≃	196	34.40 N	101.14 W
T'ulek	85	41.56 N	75.41 E
Tulelake	204	41.57 N	121.29 W
Tule Lake Sump ⊜[1]	204	41.54 N	121.32 W
Tulemalu Lake ⊜	176	62.58 N	99.25 W
T'ulenij, ostrov I	84	44.28 N	47.30 E
Tule River Indian Reservation •[4]	204	36.02 N	118.42 W
Tulette	62	44.17 N	4.56 E
Tule Valley V	200	39.20 N	113.25 W
T'ul'gan	86	52.22 N	56.12 E
Tul'havičy	78	51.47 N	29.38 E
Tuli	154	21.59 S	29.15 E
Tuli ≃	154	21.48 S	29.04 E
Tulia	196	34.32 N	101.45 W
Tuliahan ≃	269f	14.41 N	120.58 E
Tulica ≃	82	54.12 N	37.37 E
Tulik Volcano ∧[1]	180	53.22 N	168.03 W
Tuling	100	25.11 N	118.50 E
Tuliszków	30	52.05 N	18.17 E
Ṭūlkarm	132	32.19 N	35.02 E
T'ul'kino	86	59.49 N	56.30 E
T'ul'kubas	85	42.28 N	70.02 E
Tulla	48	52.52 N	8.45 W
Tullahoma	194	35.21 N	86.12 W
Tullamarine	274b	37.41 S	144.52 E
Tullamarine International Airport ⊠, Austl.	169	37.40 S	144.50 E
Tullamarine International Airport ⊠, Austl.	274b	37.40 S	144.50 E
Tullamore, Austl.	166	32.38 S	147.34 E
Tullamore, On., Can.	275b	43.47 N	79.46 W
Tullamore, Ire.	48	53.16 N	7.30 W
Tullaroop Creek ≃	169	36.53 S	143.53 E
Tullaroop Reservoir ⊜[1]	169	37.07 S	143.52 E
Tull Bay ⊂	208	36.30 N	76.04 W
Tulle	32	45.16 N	1.46 E
Tullgarn	40	58.57 N	17.35 E
Tullibigeal	166	33.25 S	146.44 E
Tullinge	40	59.12 N	17.53 E
Tullins	62	45.18 N	5.29 E
Tulln	61	48.20 N	16.03 E
Tullner Feld •[1]	264b	48.19 N	16.10 E
Tulloch Reservoir ⊜[1]	226	37.53 N	120.35 W
Tullock Creek ≃	202	46.08 N	107.27 W
Tullos	194	31.49 N	92.19 W
Tullow	48	52.48 N	6.44 W
Tullus	140	11.03 N	24.33 E
Tully, Austl.	166	17.56 S	145.56 E
Tully, N.Y., U.S.	210	42.47 N	76.06 W
Tully Dam •[6]	207	42.39 N	72.11 W
Tullytown	208	40.09 N	74.49 W
Ṭulmaythah	146	32.43 N	20.57 E
Tuloma ≃	24	68.52 N	32.49 E
Tulpfontein	158	32.44 S	19.43 E
Tulsa	196	36.09 N	95.59 W
Tulsequah	176	58.35 N	133.35 W
Tulsī Lake ⊜	272c	19.11 N	72.55 E
Tulsīpur	124	28.07 N	82.18 E
Tulsk	48	53.47 N	8.16 W
Tul'skij	84	44.31 N	40.10 E
Tulstrup	41	56.07 N	9.46 E
Tultepec	234	19.41 N	99.08 W
Tultitlán	286a	19.39 N	99.09 W
Tuluá	246	4.06 N	76.11 W
Tuluksak	180	61.06 N	160.58 W
Tulum	232	20.13 N	87.28 W
Tulum ⊥	232	20.12 N	87.26 W
Tulumayo ≃	248	11.10 S	75.16 W
Tulun	88	54.35 N	100.33 E
Tulungagung	115a	8.04 S	111.54 E
Tulungselapan	112	3.15 S	105.19 E
Tuluran Island I	116	10.59 N	119.17 E
Tulu Welel ∧	144	8.53 N	34.47 E
Tulyehualco •[8]	286a	19.15 N	99.01 W
Tum	164	3.38 S	130.23 E
Tuma	80	55.09 N	40.34 E
Tuma ≃	236	13.03 N	84.44 W
Tumacacori National Monument ♠	200	31.25 N	111.01 W
Tumaco	246	1.49 N	78.46 W
Tumaco, Rada de ⊂	246	1.55 N	78.45 W
Tumak	80	46.14 N	48.31 E
Tumalykol'	86	48.21 N	60.03 E
Tuman'an	84	41.00 N	44.40 E
Tuman-gang (Tumen) ≃	98	42.18 N	130.41 E
Tumannaja, gora ∧	180	66.33 N	179.43 E
Tumanovo	76	55.25 N	34.39 E
Tumanšet ≃	88	55.53 N	97.30 E
Tumanskij	180	63.58 N	178.12 E
Tumany	74	60.56 N	155.56 E
Tumarbong	116	10.23 N	119.27 E
T'um'ati → Sklad	74	71.55 N	123.33 E
Tumatumari	246	5.22 N	59.00 W
Tumauini	116	17.17 N	121.49 E
Tumba	40	59.12 N	17.49 E
Tumba, Lac ⊜	152	0.48 S	18.03 E
Tumbarumba	171b	35.47 S	148.01 E
Tumbarumba Creek ≃	171b	35.58 S	148.03 E
Tumbes	246	3.34 S	80.28 W
Tumbes □[5]	246	3.50 S	80.30 W
Tumbes (Puyango) ≃	246	3.30 S	80.27 W
Tumbes, Punta ›	252	36.37 S	73.07 W
Tumbiscatio de Ruiz	234	18.31 N	102.21 W
Tumble Mountain ∧	202	45.19 N	110.02 W
Tumbler Ridge	182	55.07 N	120.55 W
Tumblong	171b	35.09 S	148.00 E
Tumbotino	80	55.59 N	43.02 E
Tumbur	154	4.20 N	31.34 E
Tumby Bay	166	34.22 S	136.06 E
Tumča ≃	24	66.36 N	30.48 E
Tŭmch'on-ni •[8]	271b	37.34 N	126.51 E
T'umen', Ross.	86	57.09 N	65.32 E
Tumen, Zhg.	98	42.58 N	129.49 E
Tumen (Tuman-gang) ≃	98	42.18 N	130.41 E
T'umencevo	86	53.20 N	81.31 E
T'umenec, porog ⌊	88	56.38 N	99.00 E
T'umen' Oblast' □[4]	86	58.00 N	69.00 E
Tumenpu	107	29.49 N	103.39 E
Tumenskoje	82	55.00 N	38.32 E
Tumenzi	102	37.43 N	103.09 E

Name	Seite	Breite°′	Länge°′ E = Ost
Tumeremo	246	7.18 N	61.30 W
Tumiritinga	255	18.58 S	41.38 W
Tumkūr	122	13.21 N	77.05 E
Tummel ≃	46	56.38 N	3.40 W
Tumnin ≃	89	49.18 N	140.22 E
Tumon Bay ⊂	174p	13.31 N	144.48 E
Tumos ≃	156	22.55 S	14.37 E
Tumoteqi	102	40.52 N	111.28 E
Tumpang	115a	8.00 S	112.46 E
Tumpat	114	6.12 N	102.10 E
Tumsar	120	21.23 N	79.44 E
Tumtum	182	47.53 N	117.40 W
Tumu, Ghana	150	10.52 N	1.59 W
Tumu, Zhg.	105	40.23 N	115.36 E
Tumuc-Humac Mountains ⋏	250	2.20 N	55.00 W
Tumut	171b	35.18 S	148.13 E
Tumut ≃	171b	35.07 S	148.13 E
Tumut Pond Reservoir ⊜[1]	171b	35.59 S	148.25 E
Tumutuk	80	55.02 N	53.19 E
Tumwater	224	47.00 N	122.54 W
Tun ≃	110	17.25 N	98.42 E
Tuna Canyon V	280	34.03 N	118.36 W
Tunago Lake ⊜	180	66.18 N	125.50 W
Tuna-Hästberg	40	60.20 N	15.11 E
Tunapuna	241r	10.38 N	61.23 W
Tunari, Cerro ∧	248	17.18 S	66.22 W
Tunas Creek ≃	196	31.01 N	102.11 W
Tunas de Zaza	240p	21.38 N	79.33 W
Tūnat al-Jabal, Miṣr	142	27.46 N	30.44 E
Tūnat al-Jabal, Miṣr	142	28.13 N	30.43 E
Tunaydah	140	25.31 N	29.21 E
Tunbridge Wells → Royal Tunbridge Wells	42	51.08 N	0.16 E
Tunçbilek	130	39.37 N	29.29 E
Tunceli	130	39.07 N	39.32 E
Tunceli □[4]	130	39.10 N	39.30 E
Tunchang	110	19.28 N	110.08 E
T'unch'i → Tunxi	100	29.44 N	118.18 E
Tunda, Pulau I	115a	5.49 S	106.16 E
Tundazi ∧	154	17.33 S	28.05 E
Tündern	52	52.04 N	9.22 E
Tundik ≃	86	51.04 N	77.24 E
Tūndla	124	27.12 N	78.17 E
Tundubai ⊤[4]	140	18.31 N	28.33 E
Tunduru	154	11.07 S	37.21 E
Tundža ≃	38	41.40 N	26.34 E
Tune	41	55.36 N	12.11 E
Tunesien → Tunisia □[1]	148	34.00 N	9.00 E
T'unež, Ross.	82	54.37 N	38.29 E
Túnez → Tunis, Tun.	148	36.48 N	10.11 E
Túnez → Tunisia □[1]	148	34.00 N	9.00 E
T'ung ≃	74	63.46 N	121.35 E
Tunga	150	8.00 N	9.19 E
Tunga ≃	122	14.00 N	75.41 E
Tungabhadra ≃	122	15.57 N	78.15 E
Tungabhadra Reservoir ⊜[1]	122	15.16 N	76.21 E
Tungaru	140	10.14 N	30.42 E
Tungauan Bay ⊂	116	7.28 N	122.21 E
Tungchi University ʊ[2]	269b	31.18 N	121.29 E
Tungchi Yü I	100	23.15 N	119.40 E
T'ungchou → Tongxian	105	39.55 N	116.39 E
T'ungch'uan → Tongchuan	102	35.01 N	109.01 E
Tungch'üan Tao I	100	25.58 N	119.58 E
Tungelsta	40	59.06 N	18.02 E
Tung Hai → East China Sea ⊤[2]	90	30.00 N	126.00 E
Tungho	100	22.58 N	121.18 E
T'unghsien → Tongxian	105	39.55 N	116.39 E
T'unghua → Tonghua	98	41.41 N	125.55 E
Tunghwa → Tonghua	98	41.41 N	125.55 E
Tungir ≃	88	55.24 N	120.32 E
Tungirskij chrebet ⋏	88	54.40 N	119.40 E
Tungkal ≃	112	0.49 S	103.29 E
Tungkang	100	22.28 N	120.26 E
Tungkillo	168b	34.49 S	139.04 E
Tungku	112	5.01 N	118.53 E
Tungla	236	13.18 N	84.26 W
T'ungliao → Tongliao	89	43.39 N	122.14 E
Tung Lung Island I	271d	22.15 N	114.17 E
Tung O	271d	22.12 N	114.08 E
Tungokočen	88	53.33 N	115.36 E
Tungsha Tao (Pratas Island) I	90	20.42 N	116.43 E
Tungshih	100	24.15 N	120.49 E
Tungsten	180	61.57 N	128.16 W
Tungsunga, Jabal ∧	140	11.29 N	23.21 E
Tungting Tao I	100	24.10 N	118.14 E
Tungurahua □[4]	246	1.15 S	78.35 W
Tungurahua ∧[1]	246	1.27 S	78.26 W
Tungyin Tao I	100	26.22 N	120.30 E
Tuni	122	17.21 N	82.33 E
Tunia ≃	246	1.13 N	72.44 W
Tunica	194	34.41 N	90.22 W
Tunis	148	36.48 N	10.11 E
Tūnis → Tunisia □[1]	148	34.00 N	9.00 E
Tunis, Golfe de ⊂	36	37.00 N	10.30 E
Tunisia (Tunisie) □[1], Afr.	134	34.00 N	9.00 E
Tunisia (Tunisie) □[1], Afr.	148	34.00 N	9.00 E
Tunisie → Tunisia □[1]	148	34.00 N	9.00 E
Tunitas Creek ≃	282	37.21 N	122.24 W
Tunja	246	5.31 N	73.22 W
Tunjang	114	6.16 N	100.21 E
Tunka	88	51.45 N	102.32 E
Tunkás	232	20.54 N	88.45 W
Tunkhannock	210	41.32 N	75.56 W
Tunkhannock Creek ≃	210	41.32 N	75.57 W
Tunkhannock Creek, East Branch ≃	210	41.38 N	75.43 W
Tunliu	102	36.19 N	112.54 E
Tunnel	210	42.13 N	75.44 W
Tunnel Hill, Ga., U.S.	192	34.50 N	85.02 W
Tunnelhill, Pa., U.S.	214	40.29 N	78.33 W
Tunnelton, In., U.S.	218	38.46 N	86.21 W
Tunnelton, W.V., U.S.	188	39.23 N	79.44 W
Tunnsjøen ⊜	24	64.43 N	13.24 E
Tunø I	41	55.57 N	10.26 E
Tuntenhausen	64	47.56 N	12.01 E
Tuntum	250	5.14 S	44.39 W
Tuntutuliak	180	60.22 N	162.38 W
Tununak	180	60.35 N	165.16 W
Tunungayualok Island I	176	56.05 N	61.05 W
Tunuyán	252	33.34 S	69.01 W
Tunuyán ≃	252	34.03 S	66.45 W
Tunxi	100	29.44 N	118.18 E
Tuo ≃, Zhg.	100	33.16 N	117.45 E
Tuo ≃, Zhg.	102	28.57 N	105.27 E
Tuobalage	120	31.37 N	88.10 E
Tuobuja	74	62.00 N	122.02 E
Tuocheng	100	24.05 N	115.13 E
Tuoe Shan ∧	102	24.20 N	103.32 E
Tuoheji	100	33.26 N	117.26 E
Tuoj-Chaja	74	62.32 N	111.18 E
Tuoji Dao I	98	38.09 N	120.14 E
Tuokedingling	120	32.45 N	84.55 E
Tuokusidawan Ling ∧	120	37.14 N	85.47 E
Tuoli	105	39.46 N	116.01 E
Tuolumne	226	37.57 N	120.14 W
Tuolumne □[6]	226	37.59 N	120.23 W
Tuolumne ≃	226	37.36 N	121.10 W

Symbols in the index entries represent the broad categories identified in the key at the right. Symbols with superior numbers (⋏[1]) identify subcategories (see complete key on page *I · 1)*.

Symbole im Register stellen die rechts im Schlüssel erklärten Kategorien dar. Symbole mit hochgestellten Ziffern (⋏[1]) bezeichnen Unterabteilungen einer Kategorie (vgl. vollständiger Schlüssel auf Seite *I · 1)*.

Los símbolos incluídos en el texto del índice representan las grandes categorías identificadas con la clave a la derecha. Los símbolos con numeros en su parte superior (⋏[1]) identifican las subcategorías (véase la clave completa en la página *I · 1)*.

Les symboles de l'index représentent les catégories indiquées dans la légende à droite. Les symboles suivis d'un indice (⋏[1]) représentent des sous-catégories (voir légende complète à la page *I · 1)*.

Os símbolos incluídos no texto do índice representam as grandes categorias identificadas com a chave à direita. Os símbolos com números em sua parte superior (⋏[1]) identificam as subcategorias (veja-se a chave completa à página *I · 1)*.

∧	Mountain	Berg	Montaña	Montagne	Montanha
⋏	Mountains	Gebirge	Montañas	Montagnes	Montanhas
)(	Pass	Paß	Paso	Col	Passo
V	Valley, Canyon	Tal, Cañon	Valle, Cañón	Vallée, Canyon	Vale, Canhão
≍	Plain	Ebene	Llano	Plaine	Planície
›	Cape	Kap	Cabo	Cap	Cabo
I	Island	Insel	Isla	Île	Ilha
II	Islands	Inseln	Islas	Îles	Ilhas
±	Other Topographic Features	Andere Topographische Objekte	Otros Elementos Topográficos	Autres données topographiques	Outros acidentes topográficos

ESPAÑOL				FRANÇAIS				PORTUGUÊS			
Nombre	Página	Lat.°	Long.° W=Oeste	Nom	Page	Lat.°	Long.° W=Ouest	Nome	Página	Lat.°	Long.° W=Oeste

≃	River	Fluß	Río	Rivière	Rio
⧈	Canal	Kanal	Canal	Canal	Canal
ʯ	Waterfall, Rapids	Wasserfall, Stromschnellen	Cascada, Rápidos	Chute d'eau, Rapides	Cascata, Rápidos
ʮ	Strait	Meeresstraße	Estrecho	Détroit	Estreito
c	Bay, Gulf	Bucht, Golf	Bahía, Golfo	Baie, Golfe	Baía, Golfo
@	Lake, Lakes	See, Seen	Lago, Lagos	Lac, Lacs	Lago, Lagos
≋	Swamp	Sumpf	Pantano	Marais	Pântano
⧆	Ice Features, Glacier	Eis- und Gletscherformen	Accidentes Glaciares	Formes glaciaires	Acidentes glaciares
⨅	Other Hydrographic Features	Andere Hydrographische Objekte	Otros Elementos Hidrográficos	Autres données hydrographiques	Outros acidentes hidrográficos

➤	Submarine Features	Untermeerische Objekte	Accidentes Submarinos	Formes de relief sous-marin	Acidentes submarinos
⨅	Political Unit	Politische Einheit	Unidad Política	Entité politique	Unidade política
♥	Cultural Institution	Kulturelle Institution	Institución Cultural	Institution culturelle	Instituição cultural
⊥	Historical Site	Historische Stätte	Sitio Histórico	Site historique	Sítio histórico
♦	Recreational Site	Erholungs- und Ferienort	Sitio de Recreo	Centre de loisirs	Área de Lazer
■	Airport	Flughafen	Aeropuerto	Aéroport	Aeroporto
■	Military Installation	Militäranlage	Instalación Militar	Installation militaire	Instalação militar
◆	Miscellaneous	Verschiedenes	Misceláneo	Divers	Diversos

ENGLISH

Name	Page	Lat.°′	Long.°′
Uelzen, Dtsch.	263	51.33 N	7.44 E
Ueno, Nihon	94	36.05 N	138.47 E
Ueno, Nihon	94	34.45 N	136.08 E
Ueno, Nihon	270	34.53 N	135.14 E
Uenohara	94	35.37 N	139.07 E
Ueno Park ♦	268	35.43 N	139.46 E
Uenoshiba	270	34.33 N	135.28 E
Uerdingen -•- [8]	263	51.21 N	6.39 E
Uere ≃	154	3.42 N	25.24 E
Uetersen	52	53.41 N	9.39 E
Uettingen	56	49.48 N	9.43 E
Uetz	264a	52.28 N	12.56 E
Uetze	52	52.28 N	10.11 E
Ufa	86	54.44 N	55.56 E
Ufa ≃	86	54.40 N	56.00 E
Ufala, Punta ›	70	38.22 N	14.59 E
Uffculme	42	50.54 N	3.20 W
Uffenheim	56	49.32 N	10.14 E
Uffing	64	47.43 N	11.09 E
Ufita ≃	68	41.09 N	14.56 E
Ufra	128	40.00 N	53.02 E
Uft'uga ≃	76	59.46 N	39.21 E
Ugab ≃	156	21.08 S	13.40 E
Ugak Bay c	180	57.25 N	152.45 W
Ugāle	76	57.16 N	22.02 E
Ugalla ≃	154	5.08 S	30.42 E
Ugamskij chrebet ⋏	85	42.00 N	70.20 E
Uganda □ [1]	154	1.00 N	32.00 E
Uganik Island I	180	57.53 N	153.28 W
Ugărčin	38	43.06 N	24.25 E
Ugarit ⊥	130	35.35 N	35.45 E
Ugashik	180	57.32 N	157.25 W
Ugashik Bay c	180	57.34 N	157.38 W
Ugatkyn ≃	180	68.24 N	171.30 E
Ugento	68	39.56 N	18.10 E
Ugep	150	5.48 N	8.05 E
Ugerløse	41	55.35 N	11.40 E
Uggiano la Chiesa	68	40.06 N	18.27 E
Ughaybish	140	10.52 N	31.05 E
Ughelli	150	5.29 N	5.59 E
Ugie	158	31.10 S	28.13 E
Ugie ≃	46	57.30 N	1.47 W
Ugíjar	34	36.57 N	3.03 W
Ugine	62	45.45 N	6.25 E
Uglegorsk	89	49.02 N	142.03 E
Uglekamensk	89	43.13 N	133.11 E
Uglezavodsk	89	47.21 N	142.38 E
Uglič	76	57.32 N	38.19 E
Ugljan, Otok I	36	44.05 N	15.10 E
Uglovaja	80	57.01 N	52.57 E
Uglovka	76	58.14 N	33.31 E
Uglovoje	89	43.20 N	132.06 E
Uglovskoje	86	51.23 N	80.12 E
Ugodiči	80	57.10 N	39.30 E
Ugodskij Zavod	82	55.02 N	36.45 E
Ugol'naja, buchta c	180	63.00 N	179.20 E
Ugolnyy	180	62.58 N	179.17 E
Ugoma ∧	154	4.00 S	28.45 E
Ugovizza	64	46.31 N	13.29 E
Ugra	76	54.47 N	34.17 E
Ugra ≃	82	54.30 N	36.07 E
Ugr'umovo	82	55.09 N	37.40 E
Ugtaal Cajdam	88	48.17 N	105.25 E
Uguj	86	56.02 N	76.03 E
Uğurludağ	130	40.27 N	34.28 E
Ug'ut	85	41.24 N	74.50 E
Ugyak, Cape ›	180	58.17 N	154.04 W
Uh (Uzh) ≃	30	48.34 N	22.00 E
Uha-dong	98	40.41 N	125.38 E
Uhayjibah, Jabal al- ∧	132	30.11 N	34.33 E
Uherčice	61	48.55 N	15.38 E
Uherské Hradiště	30	49.05 N	17.28 E
Uherský Brod	30	49.02 N	17.39 E
Uhingen	56	48.42 N	9.35 E
Úhlava ≃	60	49.43 N	13.23 E
Uhldingen-Mühlhofen	58	47.44 N	9.15 E
Uhlenhorst	156	23.45 S	17.55 E
Ühlingen	58	47.43 N	8.19 E
Uhlman Lake ⊜	184	56.40 N	98.23 W
Uhlstädt	54	50.44 N	11.28 E
Uhniv	78	50.23 N	23.44 E
Uhrichsville	214	40.23 N	81.20 W
Uhroyidi	78	50.52 N	35.17 E
Uhyst, Dtsch.	54	51.11 N	14.13 E
Uhyst, Dtsch.	54	51.24 N	14.30 E
Uiche	152	12.03 S	21.02 E
Ui-do I	98	34.37 N	125.51 E
Uig	46	57.35 N	6.22 W
Uíge	152	7.37 S	15.03 E
Uíge □ [5]	152	7.00 S	15.30 E
Ŭijŏngbu	98	37.44 N	127.03 E
Ŭiju	98	40.12 N	124.32 E
Uil	86	49.05 N	54.40 E
Uil ≃	80	48.36 N	52.30 E
Uilpata, gora ∧	84	42.48 N	43.48 E
Uimaharju	26	62.55 N	30.15 E
Uinebona ≃	246	5.04 N	63.01 W
Uinskoje	86	56.53 N	56.35 E
Uinta ≃	200	40.14 N	109.51 W
Uintah and Ouray Indian Reservation -•- [4]	200	40.20 N	110.20 W
Uinta Mountains ⋏	200	40.45 N	110.05 W
Uiraúna	250	6.31 S	38.25 W
Uis	156	21.08 S	14.49 E
Ŭisŏng	98	36.22 N	128.41 E
Uitenhage	158	33.40 S	25.28 E
Uitgeest	52	52.32 N	4.43 E
Uithoorn	52	52.14 N	4.50 E
Uithuizen	52	53.24 N	6.40 E
Uithuizermeeden	52	53.24 N	6.42 E
Uitspanning	158	26.46 S	29.56 E
Uj ≃, Asia	86	54.17 N	64.58 E
Uj ≃, Ross.	86	57.06 N	74.12 E
Ujae I [1]	14	9.05 N	165.40 E
Ujaly	86	44.37 N	60.57 E
Ujandina ≃	74	68.23 N	145.50 E
Ujar	86	55.48 N	94.20 E
Ujarrás ⊥	236	9.51 N	83.50 W
Ujedinenija, ostrov I	72	77.28 N	82.28 E
Ujelang I [1]	14	9.49 N	160.55 E
Ujemskij	24	64.29 N	40.50 E
Újezd, Česká Rep.	54	50.03 N	14.44 E
Újezd, Česká Rep.	60	49.26 N	13.27 E
Újezd u Brna	61	49.06 N	16.45 E
Újfehértó	30	47.48 N	21.40 E
Ujgursaj	85	40.53 N	71.03 E
Ujhāni	124	28.01 N	79.01 E
Uji	96	34.53 N	135.48 E
Uji ≃	96	34.53 N	135.42 E
Uji-guntō II	92	31.11 N	129.27 E
Ujiie	94	36.41 N	139.58 E
Ujiji	154	4.55 S	29.41 E
Uji-tawara	96	34.51 N	135.52 E
Uji-yamada → Ise	94	34.29 N	136.42 E
Ujjain	120	23.11 N	75.46 E
Újkér	61	47.28 N	16.49 E
'Ujmān	128	25.25 N	55.27 E
Újpest -•- [8]	264c	47.34 N	19.06 E
Ujście	30	53.04 N	16.43 E
Ujskoje	86	54.22 N	60.00 E
Ujuk	85	43.46 N	70.58 E
Ujum	85	38.22 N	70.51 E
Ujung	112	7.04 S	120.46 E
Ujungbatu	114	0.43 N	100.31 E
Ujungbatu, Pulau I	114	2.20 N	97.24 E
Ujungberung	115a	6.55 S	107.42 E
Ujunggading	110	0.16 N	99.33 E
Ujunggenteng	115a	7.22 S	106.24 E
Ujungkulon, Semenanjung › [1]	115a	6.45 S	105.20 E
Ujungkulon National Park ♦	115a	6.40 S	105.20 E
Ujunglamuru	112	4.40 S	119.58 E
Ujungpandang (Makasar)	112	5.07 S	119.24 E
Újvidék → Novi Sad	38	45.15 N	19.50 E
Uk	88	55.04 N	98.52 E
Uka, Nihon	174m	26.48 N	128.14 E
Uka, Ross.	74	57.50 N	162.06 E
Ukamas	158	28.02 S	19.45 E
Ukara Island I	154	1.50 S	33.03 E
Ukerewe Island I	154	2.03 S	33.00 E
Ukhayḍir, Wādī V	132	30.55 N	37.01 E
Ukhra	126	23.39 N	87.14 E
Ukhrul	120	25.07 N	94.22 E
Ukhta → Uchta	24	63.33 N	53.38 E
Ukiah, Ca., U.S.	204	39.09 N	123.12 W
Ukiah, Or., U.S.	202	45.08 N	118.55 W
Ukibaru-jima I	174m	26.18 N	128.00 E
Ukiha	96	33.19 N	130.47 E
Uki Ni Masi Island I	175e	10.15 S	161.45 E
Ukmergė	76	55.15 N	24.45 E
Ukolnoi Island I	180	55.14 N	161.34 W
Ukraina → Ukraine □ [1]	22	49.00 N	32.00 E
Ukraine □ [1], Europe	22	49.00 N	32.00 E
Ukraine (Ukrayina) □ [1], Europe	78	49.00 N	32.00 E
Ukrainka	86	54.39 N	71.20 E
Ukrayins'k	83	48.06 N	37.18 E
Ukrina ≃	36	45.05 N	17.56 E
Uks'anskoje	86	55.57 N	63.01 E
Uktuz	86	55.38 N	68.30 E
Uktym	24	62.38 N	48.52 E
Uku	152	11.24 S	14.15 E
Ukui	112	0.09 S	102.11 E
Ukurejskij	88	52.24 N	116.49 E
Ukuti	154	3.39 N	33.32 E
Ukyō -•- [8]	270	35.03 N	135.42 E
Ukyr	88	49.28 N	108.52 E
Ula, Bela.	76	55.14 N	29.15 E
Ula, India	272b	22.43 N	88.33 E
Ula, Tür.	130	37.05 N	28.26 E
Ula ≃, Bela.	76	55.14 N	29.14 E
Ūla ≃, Europe	76	54.10 N	24.20 E
Ulaanbaatar	88	47.55 N	106.53 E
Ulaanbaatar □ [8]	88	47.55 N	106.53 E
Ulaanbadrach	102	44.07 N	110.11 E
Ulaan Chus	86	49.02 N	89.23 E
Ulaangom	86	49.58 N	92.02 E
Ulaan nuur ⊜	102	44.30 N	103.35 E
Ulaan Tajga ⋏	88	50.45 N	98.30 E
Ula-Chuduk	80	47.39 N	45.34 E
Ulak Island I	181a	51.22 N	179.00 W
Ulakmedan	114	2.43 N	99.38 E
Ulamba	152	9.07 S	23.40 E
Ulamona	164	5.00 S	151.15 E
Ulan, Austl.	166	32.17 S	149.44 E
Ulan, Zhg.	102	36.59 N	98.26 E
Ulan Bator → Ulaanbaatar	88	47.55 N	106.53 E
Ulanbel'	86	44.48 N	71.10 E
Ulan Buh Shamo -•- [2]	102	40.00 N	106.30 E
Ulan-Burgasy, chrebet ⋏	88	52.45 N	109.00 E
Ulan-Erge	80	46.19 N	44.53 E
Ulang ≃	236	14.27 N	83.14 W
Ulanhot → Horqin Youyi Qianqi	89	46.05 N	122.05 E
Ulānia	126	22.12 N	90.29 E
Ulaniv	78	49.42 N	28.08 E
Ulanove	78	51.46 N	34.18 E
Ulanovskij	82	54.04 N	37.51 E
Ulanów	30	50.30 N	22.16 E
Ulansuhai Nur ⊜	102	40.56 N	108.49 E
Ulan-Ude	88	51.50 N	107.37 E
Ulan Ul Hu ⊜	120	34.45 N	90.25 E
Ulan-Ušotej	88	50.45 N	105.29 E
Ular, Pulau I	271c	1.14 N	103.45 E
Ulaş	130	39.27 N	37.03 E
Ul'ašovo	24	65.27 N	56.57 E
Ulatis Creek ≃	226	38.18 N	121.00 W
Ul'atuj	88	51.09 N	116.14 E
Ulawa Island I	175e	9.46 S	161.57 E
Ulawun, Mount ∧	164	5.03 S	151.20 E
Ulaya	154	7.04 S	36.54 E
Ułazów	30	50.17 N	23.00 E
Ul'ba	86	50.16 N	83.22 E
Ul'banskij zaliv c	89	53.45 N	137.50 E
Ulchin	98	36.59 N	129.23 E
Ul'chun-Partija	88	49.56 N	112.46 E
Ulcinj	38	41.55 N	19.11 E
Ulco	158	28.21 S	24.15 E
Ulcombe	260	51.12 N	0.39 E
Ulcumayo	248	11.01 S	75.55 W
Uldum	41	55.51 N	9.36 E
Uldz ≃	88	49.56 N	115.31 E
Uleåborg → Oulu	26	65.01 N	25.28 E
Ulefoss	26	59.17 N	9.16 E
Ulen	198	47.04 N	96.15 W
Ulety	88	51.22 N	112.29 E
Ulfborg	26	56.16 N	8.20 E
Ulft	52	51.54 N	6.23 E
Ulgueira	266c	38.47 N	9.28 W
Ulhās ≃	272c	19.13 N	73.01 E
Ulhāsnagar	122	19.13 N	73.07 E
Uliast	86	48.57 N	91.17 E
Uliastaj (Džavchlant)	88	47.45 N	96.49 E
Úlice	60	49.45 N	13.09 E
Ulindi ≃	154	1.40 S	25.52 E
Ulingan	164	4.30 S	145.25 E
Ulithi I [1]	108	9.58 N	139.40 E
Ulja	74	58.51 N	141.50 E
Uljanino	82	55.21 N	38.26 E
Uljanovka	76	59.38 N	30.46 E
Uljanovo, Ross.	76	53.43 N	35.32 E
Uljanovo, Uzb.	85	40.07 N	68.30 E
Uljanovsk	80	54.20 N	48.24 E
Ul'janovskij	86	50.02 N	73.42 E
Uljanovsk Oblast' □ [4]	80	53.30 N	47.30 E
Uljanovskoje	89	46.17 N	142.13 E
Uljuan tekojärvi ⊜	26	64.19 N	25.57 E
Ul'kajak ≃	86	48.54 N	62.00 E
Ul'kan	88	57.14 N	107.19 E
Ul'kan ≃	88	55.53 N	107.45 E
Ul'ken-Karoj, ozero ⊜	86	54.00 N	71.58 E
Ulla ≃	34	42.39 N	8.44 W
Ulladulla	170	35.21 S	150.29 E
Ulladulla Head ›	170	35.22 S	150.30 E
Ullāpāra	126	24.19 N	89.34 E
Ullapool	46	57.54 N	5.10 W
Ullastrell	266d	41.31 N	1.58 E
Üllendahl -•- [8]	263	51.17 N	7.11 E
Ullerslev	41	55.22 N	10.40 E
Ullervad	40	58.40 N	13.52 E
Ullin	194	37.17 N	89.11 W
Üllő	264c	47.23 N	19.21 E
Ullswater ⊜	44	54.34 N	2.54 W
Ullučaj ≃	84	42.18 N	48.08 E
Ullŭng-do I	92	37.29 N	130.52 E
Ullvettern ⊜	40	59.27 N	14.16 E
Ullvi	40	59.42 N	16.37 E
Ulm, Dtsch.	58	48.24 N	10.00 E
Ulm, Mt., U.S.	202	47.25 N	111.30 W
Ul'ma ≃	89	51.54 N	129.18 E
Ulmarra	166	29.37 S	153.02 E
Ulmen	56	50.13 N	6.59 E
Ulmeni	38	45.04 N	26.39 E
Ulmer, Mount ∧	9	77.35 S	86.09 W
Ulongué	154	14.37 S	34.19 E
Ulpur	126	23.04 N	89.50 E
Ulricehamn	26	57.47 N	13.25 E
Ulrichskirchen	61	48.24 N	16.29 E
Ulrichstein	56	50.34 N	9.11 E
Ulrum	52	53.22 N	6.20 E
Ulsan	98	35.34 N	129.19 E
Ulsta	46a	60.30 N	1.09 W
Ulsteinvik	26	62.20 N	5.53 E
Ulster	210	41.51 N	76.30 W
Ulster □ [6]	210	41.56 N	74.00 W
Ulster □ [9]	48	54.35 N	7.00 W
Ulster ≃	56	50.51 N	9.59 E
Ulster Canal ≊	48	54.08 N	7.22 W
Ultimo, Val d' V	64	46.35 N	11.00 E
Ultraoriental, Cordillera (Serra do Divisor) ⋏	248	8.20 S	73.30 W
Ulu, Indon.	112	2.45 N	125.24 E
Ulu, Ross.	74	60.19 N	127.24 E
Ulu, Sūd.	140	10.43 N	33.29 E
Ulúa ≃	236	15.53 N	87.44 W
Ulubāria	126	22.28 N	88.06 E
Ulubat Gölü ⊜	130	40.10 N	28.35 E
Ulubey, Tür.	130	38.25 N	29.18 E
Ulubey, Tür.	130	40.53 N	37.43 E
Uluborlu	130	38.05 N	30.28 E
Uluçınar	130	36.27 N	35.51 E
Uludağ ∧	130	40.04 N	29.13 E
Uludāngar	272b	22.51 N	88.31 E
Uludere	128	37.27 N	42.51 E
Ulugan Bay c	116	10.07 N	118.47 E
Ulugqat	85	39.48 N	74.21 E
Uluinggalau ∧	175g	16.54 S	179.59 E
Ulujul ≃	86	57.46 N	85.30 E
Ulukışla, Kıbrıs	130	35.13 N	33.37 E
Ulukışla, Tür.	130	37.33 N	34.30 E
Ulul I	14	8.35 N	149.40 E
Ulu Laho, Bukit ∧	114	5.43 N	101.27 E
Ulunchan	88	54.51 N	111.02 E
Ulundi	158	28.17 S	31.26 E
Ulunga	89	46.31 N	136.56 E
Ulungur ≃	86	46.59 N	87.27 E
Ulungur Hu ⊜	86	47.15 N	87.20 E
Ulurijskij Golec, gora ∧	88	50.12 N	111.45 E
Uluru National Park ♦	162	25.20 S	131.00 E
Ulus	130	41.35 N	32.39 E
Ulusara	126	24.16 N	90.36 E
Ulut ≃	116	12.00 N	125.27 E
Ulutau, gora ∧	86	48.39 N	66.56 E
Ulutau, gory ⋏	86	49.00 N	67.00 E
Ulu Tiram	114	1.36 N	103.49 E
Ulu Yam	114	3.27 N	101.38 E
Ulva	272c	18.59 N	73.02 E
Ulva I	46	56.29 N	6.14 W
Ulvenhout	52	51.34 N	4.48 E
Ulverston	44	54.12 N	3.06 W
Ulverstone	166	41.09 S	146.10 E
Ulvöarna II	26	63.01 N	18.40 E
Ulvshale › [1]	41	55.02 N	12.16 E
Ulvshyttan	40	60.18 N	15.22 E
Ulvsund)(	41	54.59 N	12.11 E
Ulyanivka	78	50.58 N	34.18 E
Ul'yanovka	78	48.20 N	30.13 E
Ulyanovsk → Uljanovsk	80	54.20 N	48.24 E
Ulysses, Ks., U.S.	198	37.34 N	101.21 W
Ulysses, Ne., U.S.	198	41.04 N	97.12 W
Ulysses, Pa., U.S.	214	41.54 N	77.46 W
Ulytau	86	48.39 N	67.01 E
Uly-Žylanšyk ≃	86	48.51 N	63.47 E
Ulzë	38	41.41 N	19.54 E
Uma	89	52.36 N	120.37 E
Umag	36	45.25 N	13.32 E
Umaji	96	33.33 N	134.03 E
Umal'tinskij	89	51.56 N	133.36 E
Umán, Méx.	232	20.53 N	89.45 W
Uman', Ukr.	78	48.44 N	30.14 E
'Umān → Oman □ [1]	118	22.00 N	58.00 E
Uman I	175c	7.18 N	151.53 E
Umanak	176	70.40 N	52.07 W
Umanak Fjord c [2]	176	70.55 N	53.00 W
Umancevo	80	47.44 N	44.16 E
Umargāon	122	20.12 N	72.45 E
Umari	250	6.38 S	38.42 W
Umari ≃	248	7.05 S	64.34 W
'Umarī, Qā' al- ⊜	132	31.42 N	36.57 E
Umaria	124	23.32 N	80.50 E
Umarizal	250	5.59 S	37.49 W
Umarkot	120	25.22 N	69.44 E
Umatac	174p	13.18 N	144.39 E
Umatilla, Fl., U.S.	220	28.55 N	81.39 W
Umatilla, Or., U.S.	202	45.55 N	119.20 W
Umatilla ≃	202	45.55 N	119.20 W
Umatilla, Lake ⊜ [1]	202	45.44 N	120.35 W
Umatilla Indian Reservation -•- [4]	202	45.41 N	118.31 W
Umayan ≃	116	8.13 N	125.50 E
Umaze	270	34.57 N	135.03 E
Umba	24	66.41 N	34.15 E
Umbagog Lake ⊜	188	44.45 N	71.05 W
Umbai	114	2.10 N	102.20 E
Umbaúba	250	11.22 S	37.39 W
Umbelasha ≃	140	9.51 N	24.50 E
Umbertide	66	43.18 N	12.20 E
Umbogintwini	158	30.00 S	30.58 E
Umboi Island I	164	5.36 S	148.00 E
Umbrail, Pass (Giogo di Santa Maria))(	64	46.34 N	10.25 E
Umbria □ [4]	66	43.00 N	12.30 E
Umbriatico	68	39.21 N	16.55 E
Umbroli	272c	19.11 N	73.06 E
Umbukul	164	2.30 S	150.00 E
Umbuzero, ozero ⊜	24	67.43 N	34.25 E
Ume ≃	154	16.40 S	28.26 E
Umeå	26	63.50 N	20.15 E
Umeälven ≃	24	63.47 N	20.16 E
Umedani	270	34.44 N	135.51 E
Umedpur	126	22.31 N	89.59 E
Umfolozi Game Reserve -•- [4]	158	28.19 S	31.50 E
Umfors	24	65.56 N	15.00 E
Umfreville Lake ⊜	184	50.18 N	94.45 W
Umfuli ≃	154	17.30 S	29.23 E
Umgungundhlovu ⊥	158	28.27 S	31.28 E
Umguza	154	19.25 S	27.51 E
Umhausen	64	47.08 N	10.56 E
Umhlanga Rocks	158	29.43 S	31.06 E
Umi	96	33.34 N	130.30 E
Umingan	116	15.56 N	120.50 E
Umkomaas	158	30.15 S	30.42 E
Umm ad-Daraj, Jabal ∧	132	32.19 N	35.48 E
Umm 'Ajārim ⊥ [8]	142	30.50 N	32.49 E
Umm al-Abīd	146	27.31 N	15.02 E
Umm al-'Arā'is, Wādī V	146	26.26 N	13.55 E
Umm al-Arānib	146	26.08 N	14.45 E
Umm al-Birak	128	23.25 N	39.13 E
Umm al-Ḥawāyā, Jabal ∧	142	28.41 N	31.06 E
Umm al-Jimāl, Khirbat ⊥	132	32.20 N	36.22 E
Umm al-Khashab	144	17.21 N	42.32 E
Umm al-Qaywayn	128	25.35 N	55.34 E
Umm al-Qiṭṭayn	132	32.19 N	36.38 E
Umm al-Quṣūr	142	27.23 N	30.54 E
Ummanz	54	54.28 N	13.10 E
Umm Artah, Wādī V	142	28.41 N	32.37 E
Umm as-Sa'd ⊥	132	33.16 N	36.47 E
Umm Badr	140	14.14 N	27.57 E
Umm Balad, Wādī V	142	27.40 N	32.39 E
Umm Bayyū'd	140	12.05 N	31.40 E
Umm Bel	140	13.32 N	28.04 E
Umm Boim	140	11.43 N	25.57 E
Umm Dabbī	140	14.37 N	30.23 E
Umm Dam	140	13.45 N	30.59 E
Umm Dhibbān, Sūd.	140	14.14 N	29.37 E
Umm Dhibbān, Sūd.	140	15.26 N	32.51 E
Umm Digulgulaya	140	10.29 N	24.57 E
Umm Dīnār	142	30.12 N	31.04 E
Umm Durmān (Omdurman)	140	15.38 N	32.30 E
Umm el Faḥm	132	32.31 N	35.09 E
Ummeln	52	51.58 N	8.27 E
Ummendorf	54	52.09 N	11.11 E
Ummerstadt	54	50.15 N	10.48 E
Umm Habwah, Jabal ∧ [2]	142	27.23 N	31.29 E
Umm Ḥamāṭ	132	31.02 N	35.46 E
Umm Jamālah	140	11.27 N	28.12 E
Umm Kaddādah	140	13.36 N	26.42 E
Umm Khunān	273c	29.55 N	31.15 E
Umm Khushayb, Wādī V	142	30.24 N	32.43 E
Umm Kuwaykah	140	13.00 N	32.17 E
Umm Lajj	128	25.04 N	37.13 E
Umm Marahik, Jabal ∧ [2]	140	13.40 N	26.53 E
Umm Mirdi	140	18.59 N	33.32 E
Umm Mitmān ⊥ [8]	142	30.41 N	32.30 E
Umm Qantur	140	14.17 N	31.22 E
Umm Qaṣr	128	30.02 N	47.56 E
Umm Qurayn	140	9.58 N	28.55 E
Umm Quṣayr	132	31.40 N	35.53 E
Umm Raqm, Jabal ∧	142	30.14 N	31.52 E
Umm Rīshah, Birkat ⊜	142	30.21 N	30.22 E
Umm Rumaylah ⫧ [4]	140	16.55 N	31.40 E
Umm Ruwābah	140	12.54 N	31.13 E
Umm Saggāt, Wādī V	140	15.15 N	23.12 E
Umm Saysabān, Jabal ∧	132	29.45 N	35.10 E
Umm Sayyālah	140	14.25 N	31.10 E
Umm Shalīl	140	10.51 N	23.42 E
Umm Shanqah	140	13.14 N	27.14 E
Umm Shuṭūr	140	7.17 N	33.14 E
Umm Sidr, Wādī V	142	27.54 N	32.33 E
Umm Sughra ⫧ [4]	140	15.03 N	27.12 E
Umm 'Umayd, Ra's ∧	142	27.50 N	32.19 E
Umm 'Umayyid, Bi'r ⫧ [4]	142	27.53 N	32.30 E
Umm 'Umayyid, Wādī V	142	27.37 N	32.41 E
Umm Urūmah I	128	25.46 N	36.32 E
Umm Walad	132	32.39 N	36.26 E
Umm Zaytah, Jabal ∧ [2]	142	29.49 N	32.16 E
Umnak	180	53.17 N	168.20 W
Umnak Island I	180	53.25 N	168.10 W
Umnak Pass)(	180	53.20 N	167.45 W
Umnäs	24	65.24 N	16.10 E
Umniati	154	18.39 S	29.49 E
Umniati ≃	154	17.30 S	29.23 E
Um'ot, Ross.	80	54.08 N	42.42 E
Um'ot, Ross.	80	52.31 N	42.58 E
Umpferstedt	54	50.59 N	11.25 E
Umpqua ≃	202	43.42 N	124.03 W
Umpulo	152	12.38 S	17.42 E
'Umrān	144	15.50 N	43.56 E
'Umrānī, Wādī al- V	142	27.37 N	30.53 E
Umraniye	130	39.10 N	31.15 E
Umraniye -•- [8]	267b	41.01 N	29.05 E
Umred	122	20.51 N	79.20 E
Umreth	120	22.42 N	73.07 E
Umsini, Gunung ∧	164	1.22 S	133.45 E
Ŭmsŏng	98	36.56 N	127.41 E
Umstead State Park ♦	192	35.52 N	78.47 W
Umtanum Creek ≃	224	46.52 N	120.35 W
Umtata	158	31.35 S	28.47 E
Umtentweni	158	30.42 S	30.28 E
Umuahia	150	5.33 N	7.29 E
Umuarama	255	23.45 S	53.20 W
Umurbey	130	40.14 N	26.36 E
Umurlu	130	37.50 N	27.58 E
Umzimkulu	158	30.16 S	29.56 E
Umzingwani ≃	154	22.12 S	29.56 E
Umzinto	158	30.22 S	30.33 E
Una, Bra.	255	15.18 S	39.04 W
Una, India	120	20.49 N	71.02 E
Una, India	123	31.29 N	76.17 E
Una ≃	36	45.16 N	16.55 E
Una, Mount ∧	172	42.13 S	172.35 E
Una, Ribeirão ≃	287b	23.31 S	46.18 W
Unac ≃	36	44.30 N	16.09 E
Uña de Gato	196	25.58 N	99.41 W
Unadilla, Ga., U.S.	192	32.15 N	83.44 W
Unadilla, N.Y., U.S.	210	42.19 N	75.18 W
Unadilla ≃	210	42.20 N	75.25 W
Unaí	255	16.23 S	46.53 W
Unakami	94	35.46 N	140.45 E
Unalakleet	180	63.53 N	160.47 W
Unalaska	180	53.52 N	166.32 W
Unalaska Island I	180	53.45 N	166.45 W
Unanderra	170	34.27 S	150.52 E
Unango	154	12.50 S	35.20 E
Únanov	61	48.54 N	16.04 E
Unao	124	25.35 N	78.36 E
Unare ≃	246	10.03 N	65.14 W
Unauna, Pulau I	112	0.10 S	121.35 E
Unayyir, Ḥarrat al- ⊥ [9]	128	25.20 N	37.45 E
'Unayzah, Ar. Su.	128	26.06 N	43.56 E
'Unayzah, Urd.	132	30.29 N	35.48 E
'Unayzah, Jabal ∧, Asia	128	32.12 N	39.18 E
'Unayzah, Jabal ∧, Urd.	132	30.30 N	35.47 E
Unazuki	94	36.49 N	137.35 E
Uncasville	207	41.26 N	72.06 W
Unchahra	124	24.23 N	80.47 E
Ŭnch'ŏn	98	38.34 N	125.26 E
Uncia	248	18.27 S	66.37 W
Uncompahgre ≃	200	38.45 N	108.06 W
Uncompahgre Peak ∧	200	38.04 N	107.28 W
Uncompahgre Plateau ⋏ [1]	200	38.30 N	108.25 W
Uncukul'	84	42.42 N	46.48 E
Uncular	130	40.28 N	41.28 E
Unda	88	51.42 N	116.56 E
Unda ≃	88	51.25 N	116.05 E
Unden ⊜	40	58.47 N	14.26 E
Undenäs	40	58.39 N	14.25 E
Underberg	158	29.50 S	29.22 E
Under River	260	51.15 N	0.14 E
Undersåker	26	63.20 N	13.23 E
Underwood, In., U.S.	218	38.36 N	85.46 W
Underwood, N.D., U.S.	198	47.27 N	101.08 W
Underwood, Wa., U.S.	224	45.43 N	121.31 W
Undløse	41	55.36 N	11.35 E
Undory	80	54.37 N	48.25 E
Undu, Tanjung ›	115b	10.05 S	120.51 E
Undu Point ›	175g	16.08 S	179.57 W
Undva nina ›	76	58.32 N	21.55 E
Unea Island I	164	4.55 S	149.10 E
Uneča	76	52.50 N	32.40 E
Uneča ≃	76	52.50 N	31.56 E
Uneiuxi ≃	246	0.34 S	64.58 W
Úněšov	60	49.53 N	13.09 E
Unga Island I	180	55.15 N	160.45 W
Ungama Bay c	154	2.45 S	40.20 E
Ungaran	115a	7.07 S	110.24 E
Ungarie	166	33.38 S	146.58 E
Ungarn → Hungary □ [1]	30	47.00 N	20.00 E
Ungava, Péninsule d' › [1]	176	60.00 N	74.00 W
Ungava Bay c	176	59.30 N	67.30 W
Ungch'ŏn	98	35.07 N	128.44 E
Unggi	98	42.20 N	130.24 E
Ungheni	38	47.12 N	27.48 E
Ungurkuj	88	50.27 N	106.58 E
Ungvár → Uzhhorod	78	48.37 N	22.18 E
Unhos	266c	38.50 N	9.07 W
Unhošt'	54	50.04 N	14.08 E
Uni	80	57.46 N	51.30 E
União	250	4.35 S	42.52 W
União da Vitória	252	26.13 S	51.05 W
União dos Palmares	250	9.10 S	36.02 W
Unica	24	62.38 N	34.38 E
Unicoi	192	36.11 N	82.20 W
Unicorn Branch ≃	208	39.15 N	75.52 W
Unidad Santa Fe -•- [8]	286a	19.23 N	99.15 W
Uniejów	30	51.58 N	18.49 E
Unieux	62	45.24 N	4.16 E
Unije, Otok I	36	44.38 N	14.15 E
Unimak Island I	180	54.50 N	164.00 W
Unimak Pass)(	180	54.35 N	164.43 W
Unini ≃	246	1.41 S	61.31 W
Unión, Arg.	252	35.09 S	65.57 W
Union, On., Can.	212	42.42 N	81.12 W
Unión, C.R.	236	8.36 N	83.03 W
Unión, Para.	252	24.48 S	56.33 W
Union, Il., U.S.	216	42.14 N	88.33 W
Union, Ia., U.S.	190	42.14 N	93.03 W
Union, Ky., U.S.	218	38.56 N	84.40 W
Union, La., U.S.	194	30.06 N	90.54 W
Union, Ms., U.S.	194	32.34 N	89.07 W
Union, Mo., U.S.	219	38.26 N	91.00 W
Union, N.J., U.S.	210	40.41 N	74.15 W
Union, Oh., U.S.	218	39.53 N	84.18 W
Union, Or., U.S.	202	45.12 N	117.51 W
Union, S.C., U.S.	192	34.42 N	81.37 W
Union, Wa., U.S.	224	47.21 N	123.06 W
Union, W.V., U.S.	192	37.35 N	80.32 W
Union □ [6], In., U.S.	218	39.38 N	84.56 W
Union □ [6], N.J., U.S.	208	40.40 N	74.11 W
Union □ [6], Oh., U.S.	214	40.18 N	83.19 W
Union □ [6], Pa., U.S.	210	40.58 N	76.54 W
Unión -•- [8]	258	34.53 S	56.08 W
Union Bay	182	49.35 N	124.53 W
Union Beach	208	40.26 N	74.10 W
Union Bridge	208	39.34 N	77.10 W
Union Center	210	42.09 N	76.04 W
Union City, Ca., U.S.	226	37.35 N	122.04 W
Union City, Ga., U.S.	192	33.35 N	84.32 W
Union City, In., U.S.	194	40.07 N	85.05 W
Union City, Mi., U.S.	216	42.04 N	85.09 W
Union City, N.J., U.S.	276	40.46 N	74.01 W
Union City, Oh., U.S.	216	40.11 N	84.48 W
Union City, Pa., U.S.	214	41.53 N	79.50 W
Union City, Tn., U.S.	194	36.25 N	89.03 W
Union City Dam -•- [6]	214	41.55 N	79.54 W
Uniondale, S. Afr.	158	33.40 S	23.08 E
Uniondale, In., U.S.	216	40.50 N	85.15 W
Uniondale, N.Y., U.S.	276	40.42 N	73.35 W
Union Dale, Pa., U.S.	210	41.43 N	75.30 W
Unión de Reyes	240p	22.48 N	81.32 W
Unión de San Antonio	234	21.06 N	101.58 W
Union des Émirats Arabes → United Arab Emirates □ [1]	128	24.00 N	54.00 E
Unión de Tula	234	19.58 N	104.16 W
Union Flat Creek ≃	202	46.50 N	117.59 W
Union Gap	202	46.33 N	120.28 W
Union Grove, Tx., U.S.	222	32.34 N	94.55 W
Union Grove, Wi., U.S.	216	42.41 N	88.03 W
Unión Hidalgo	234	16.28 N	94.50 W
Union Hill	210	43.13 N	77.23 W
Union Lake	216	42.36 N	83.26 W
Union Lake ⊜, Mi., U.S.	216	42.03 N	85.11 W
Union Lake ⊜, Mi., U.S.	281	42.37 N	83.26 W
Union Lake ⊜, N.J., U.S.	208	39.25 N	75.03 W
Union Mills	216	41.29 N	86.46 W
Union Park	220	28.30 N	81.15 W
Union Pier	216	41.49 N	86.41 W
Union Point	192	33.36 N	83.04 W
Unionport, In., U.S.	218	40.07 N	85.06 W
Unionport, Oh., U.S.	214	40.21 N	80.51 W
Union Seamount -◊- [3]	16	49.35 N	132.45 W
Union Springs, Al., U.S.	194	32.08 N	85.42 W
Union Springs, N.Y., U.S.	210	42.50 N	76.41 W
Union Station -•- [5], On., Can.	275b	43.39 N	79.23 W
Union Station -•- [5], Ca., U.S.	280	34.04 N	118.14 W
Union Station -•- [5], D.C., U.S.	284c	38.54 N	77.00 W
Union Station -•- [5], Il., U.S.	278	41.53 N	87.38 W
Uniontown, Al., U.S.	194	32.26 N	87.30 W
Uniontown, Ky., U.S.	194	37.46 N	87.55 W
Uniontown, Md., U.S.	208	39.35 N	77.06 W
Uniontown, Oh., U.S.	214	40.58 N	81.24 W
Uniontown, Pa., U.S.	188	39.54 N	79.44 W
Union Valley Reservoir ⊜ [1]	226	38.50 N	120.26 W
Union Village	207	41.59 N	71.32 W
Unionville, On., Can.	275b	43.52 N	79.18 W
Unionville, Ct., U.S.	207	41.45 N	72.53 W
Unionville, In., U.S.	218	39.14 N	86.25 W
Unionville, Mi., U.S.	190	43.39 N	83.27 W
Unionville, Mo., U.S.	194	40.28 N	93.00 W
Unionville, N.J., U.S.	285	40.01 N	74.46 W
Unionville, N.Y., U.S.	210	41.18 N	74.34 W
Unionville, Oh., U.S.	214	41.47 N	81.00 W
Unionville, Pa., U.S.	285	39.54 N	75.44 W
Unionville Center	214	40.08 N	83.21 W
Uniopolis	216	40.36 N	84.05 W
Unipouheos Indian Reserve -•- [4]	184	53.52 N	110.21 W
Unisan	116	13.51 N	121.59 E
United	214	40.13 N	79.29 W
United Arab Emirates (Al-Imārāt al-'Arabīyah al-Muttaḥidah) □ [1], Asia	118	24.00 N	54.00 E
United Arab Emirates (Al-Imārāt al-'Arabīyah al-Muttaḥidah) □ [1], Asia	128	24.00 N	54.00 E
United Arab Republic → Egypt □ [1]	140	27.00 N	30.00 E
United Center ♦	278	41.53 N	87.40 W
United Kingdom □ [1], Europe	22	54.00 N	2.00 W
United Kingdom □ [1], Europe	28	54.00 N	2.00 W
United Kingdom Sovereign Base Area ■	130	35.00 N	33.45 E
United Nations Headquarters ʋ	276	40.45 N	73.58 W
United States □ [1]	178	38.00 N	97.00 W
United States Air Force Academy ■	200	39.00 N	104.55 W
United States Coast Guard Academy ■	207	41.22 N	72.06 W
United States Merchant Marine Academy ʋ [2]	276	40.48 N	73.46 W
United States Military Academy ■	210	41.23 N	73.58 W
United States Naval Academy ■	208	38.59 N	76.30 W
United States Steel Corporation (Lorain Plant) ʋ [3], Oh., U.S.	279a	41.27 N	82.07 W
United States Steel Corporation ʋ [3], Pa., U.S.	279b	40.20 N	79.54 W
United States Steel Corporation Fairless Works ʋ [3]	285	40.09 N	74.45 W
Unity	184	52.27 N	109.10 W
Unity Reservoir ⊜ [1]	279b	40.17 N	79.30 W
Universal City	196	29.32 N	98.17 W
Universal City ʋ [3]	280	34.09 N	118.21 W
Universal Mall -•- [9]	281	42.30 N	83.05 W
Universitaria, Ciudad ʋ [2]	266d	41.23 N	2.08 E
University	194	34.21 N	89.32 W
University City	219	38.39 N	90.19 W
University Gardens	276	40.46 N	73.43 W
University Heights, Ca., U.S.	282	37.26 N	122.12 W
University Heights, Oh., U.S.	279a	41.29 N	81.32 W

DEUTSCH

Name	Seite	Breite°′	Länge°′ E = Ost
University Park, Il., U.S.	216	41.36 N	87.39 W
University Park, Md., U.S.	284c	38.58 N	76.57 W
University Park, N.M., U.S.	200	32.06 N	106.39 W
University Park, Tx., U.S.	222	32.52 N	96.47 W
University Place	224	47.14 N	122.32 W
University View	218	40.00 N	83.03 W
Unjha	120	23.48 N	72.24 E
Unkel	56	50.35 N	7.13 E
Unken	64	47.39 N	12.43 E
Unkurda	86	55.48 N	59.24 E
Unley	168b	34.57 S	138.35 E
Unna	52	51.32 N	7.41 E
'Unnāb, Jabal al- ∧	132	29.57 N	36.55 E
'Unnāb, Wādī al- V	132	30.11 N	36.39 E
Unnão	124	26.32 N	80.30 E
Uno, Canal Numero ≊	252	36.17 S	57.08 W
Uno, Ilha I	150	11.12 N	16.15 W
Unoke	94	36.43 N	136.42 E
Ŭnp'a	98	38.26 N	125.45 E
Unpenji-san ∧	96	34.02 N	133.44 E
Unqua Point ›	276	40.39 N	73.26 W
Unquillo	252	31.14 S	64.19 W
Ŭnsan	98	39.25 N	126.01 E
Unseburg	54	51.56 N	11.30 E
Unserfrau → Madonna	64	46.43 N	10.52 E
Unsleben	56	50.22 N	10.15 E
Unst I	46a	60.45 N	0.53 W
Unstrut ≃	54	51.10 N	11.48 E
Un't	88	49.07 N	102.50 E
Unten	174m	26.41 N	128.00 E
Unterägeri	58	47.08 N	8.35 E
Unterbach, Dtsch.	263	51.12 N	6.54 E
Unterbäch, Schw.	58	46.17 N	7.48 E
Unter dem Wind, Inseln → Windward Islands II	238	13.00 N	61.00 W
Unterföhring	60	48.12 N	11.38 E
Unterfranken □ [5]	56	50.10 N	10.00 E
Unterglottertal	58	48.03 N	7.56 E
Untergriesbach	60	48.35 N	13.40 E
Untergrüne	263	51.22 N	7.39 E
Unterhaching	60	48.04 N	11.38 E
Unterhausen	58	48.26 N	9.16 E
Unterinntal V	64	47.24 N	11.47 E
Unterlaa -•- [8]	264b	48.08 N	16.25 E
Unterlüss	52	52.50 N	10.17 E
Untermauerbach	264b	48.14 N	16.12 E
Untermünkheim	56	49.09 N	9.44 E
Unteröwisheim	56	49.08 N	8.40 E
Unterrath -•- [8]	263	51.16 N	6.47 E
Unterschächen	58	46.52 N	8.47 E
Unterschleissheim, Dtsch.	60	48.17 N	11.34 E
Unterschleissheim, Dtsch.	60	48.17 N	11.34 E
Unterschneidheim	56	48.56 N	10.22 E
Unterschwaningen	56	49.04 N	10.37 E
Unterseen	58	46.41 N	7.51 E
Untertauern	64	47.18 N	13.30 E
Unterterzen	58	47.07 N	9.15 E
Unterthingau	58	47.46 N	10.31 E
Unterueckersee ⊜	54	53.17 N	13.51 E
Unterwasser	58	47.12 N	9.19 E
Unterweissbach	54	50.37 N	11.10 E
Unterwellenborn	54	50.39 N	11.26 E
Unterwössen	64	47.44 N	12.27 E
Unterzeiring	61	47.15 N	14.31 E
Untraverket	40	60.25 N	17.18 E
Unuli Horog	120	35.06 N	91.51 E
Ünye	130	41.08 N	37.17 E
Unža	80	58.01 N	44.01 E
Unža ≃	80	57.20 N	43.08 E
Unzen-Amakusa-kokuritsu-kōen ♦	92	32.45 N	130.17 E
Unzen-dake ∧	92	32.45 N	130.17 E
Unže-Pavinskaja	86	58.53 N	64.02 E
Uojan	88	56.07 N	111.38 E
Uono ≃	94	37.15 N	138.53 E
Uo-shima I	96	34.11 N	133.19 E
Uozu	94	36.48 N	137.24 E
Upa ≃	76	54.02 N	36.15 E
Upala	236	10.47 N	85.02 W
Upanema	250	5.38 S	37.15 W
Upano ≃	246	2.45 S	78.12 W
Upata	246	8.01 N	62.24 W
Upatoi Creek ≃	192	32.22 N	84.58 W
Upavon	42	51.18 N	1.49 W
Ŭpchŏ-ri	98	37.53 N	125.09 E
Upchurch	260	51.23 N	0.39 E
Upemba, Lac ⊜	154	8.36 S	26.26 E
Upemba, Parc National de l' ♦	154	9.10 S	26.35 E
Upernavik	176	72.47 N	56.10 W
Upgant-Schott	52	53.30 N	7.16 E
Uphal	140	6.58 N	34.16 E
Upham	198	48.34 N	100.43 W
Up Holland	262	53.33 N	2.44 W
Uphusen	52	53.01 N	8.58 E
Upi	116	6.57 N	124.09 E
Upía ≃	246	4.18 N	72.45 W
Upington	158	28.25 S	21.15 E
Upire ≃	246	11.27 N	68.58 W
Upland, Ca., U.S.	228	34.05 N	117.38 W
Upland, In., U.S.	216	40.28 N	85.29 W
Upland, Ne., U.S.	198	40.19 N	98.54 W
Upland, Pa., U.S.	285	39.51 N	75.23 W
Upleta	120	21.44 N	70.17 E
Upnuk Lake ⊜	180	60.21 N	158.58 W
Upolu I	175a	13.55 S	171.45 W
Upolu Point ›	229d	20.16 N	155.51 W
Uporovo	86	56.18 N	66.17 E
Upper □ [4]	150	10.30 N	1.30 W
Upper Arlington	218	40.00 N	83.03 W
Upper Arrow Lake ⊜	182	50.30 N	117.55 W
Upper Artichoke Reservoir ⊜ [1]	283	42.48 N	70.57 W
Upper Bay c	276	40.41 N	74.03 W
Upper Beaconsfield	274b	38.01 S	145.25 E
Upper Berkshire Valley	276	40.56 N	74.35 W
Upper Beverley Lake ⊜	212	44.37 N	76.05 W
Upper Black Eddy	210	40.35 N	75.07 W
Upper Blackville	186	46.39 N	65.52 W
Upper Brookville	276	40.51 N	73.34 W
Upper Canada Village ⊥	206	44.57 N	75.03 W
Upper Castlereagh	274a	33.43 S	150.40 E
Upperco	208	39.33 N	76.50 W
Upper Coliban Reservoir ⊜ [1]	169	37.18 S	144.23 E
Upper Crystal Springs Reservoir ⊜ [1]	282	37.30 N	122.20 W
Upper Darby	208	39.55 N	75.16 W
Upper Demerara-Berbice □ [4]	246	5.30 N	58.20 W
Upper des Lacs Lake ⊜ [1]	198	48.50 N	102.07 W
Upper Egypt → Aṣ-Ṣa'īd □ [9]	140	26.00 N	32.00 E
Upper End	262	53.17 N	1.52 W
Upper Erskine Lake ⊜	276	41.06 N	74.15 W
Upper Fairmount	208	38.06 N	75.47 W
Upper Falls	284b	39.26 N	76.24 W
Upper Ferntree Gully	274b	37.54 S	145.19 E
Upper Fraser	182	54.07 N	121.56 W
Upper Ganga Canal ≊	124	29.57 N	78.12 E
Upper Gap)(	212	44.06 N	76.50 W
Upper Goose Lake ⊜	184	51.44 N	92.44 W
Upper Greenwood Lake	276	41.10 N	74.22 W

Symbols in the index entries represent the broad categories identified in the key at the right. Symbols with superior numbers (⋏ [1]) identify subcategories (see complete key on page *I · 1*).

Symbole im Register stellen die rechts im Schlüssel erklärten Kategorien dar. Symbole mit hochgestellten Ziffern (⋏ [1]) bezeichnen Unterabteilungen einer Kategorie (vgl. vollständiger Schlüssel auf Seite *I · 1*).

Los símbolos incluídos en el texto del índice representan las grandes categorías identificadas con la clave a la derecha. Los símbolos con numeros en su parte superior (⋏ [1]) identifican las subcategorías (véase la clave completa en la página *I · 1*).

Les symboles de l'index représentent les catégories indiquées dans la légende à droite. Les symboles suivis d'un indice (⋏ [1]) représentent des sous-catégories (voir légende complète à la page *I · 1*).

Os símbolos incluídos no texto do índice representam as grandes categorias identificadas com a chave à direita. Os símbolos com números em sua parte superior (⋏ [1]) identificam as subcategorias (veja-se a chave completa à página *I · 1*).

∧	Mountain	Berg	Montaña	Montagne	Montanha
⋏	Mountains	Gebirge	Montañas	Montagnes	Montanhas
)(	Pass	Paß	Paso	Col	Passo
V	Valley, Canyon	Tal, Cañon	Valle, Cañón	Vallée, Canyon	Vale, Canhão
≚	Plain	Ebene	Llano	Plaine	Planície
›	Cape	Kap	Cabo	Cap	Cabo
I	Island	Insel	Isla	Île	Ilha
II	Islands	Inseln	Islas	Îles	Ilhas
⊥	Other Topographic Features	Andere Topographische Objekte	Otros Elementos Topográficos	Autres données topographiques	Outros acidentes topográficos

ESPAÑOL				FRANÇAIS				PORTUGUÊS			
Nombre	Página	Lat.°′	Long.°′ W=Oeste	Nom	Page	Lat.°′	Long.°′ W=Ouest	Nome	Página	Lat.°′	Long.°′ W=Oeste

Column 1 (ESPAÑOL)

Upper Greenwood Lake 276 41.11 N 74.23 W
Upper Hat Creek 182 50.38 N 121.35 W
Upper Humber ≃ 186 49.10 N 57.28 W
Upper Hutt 172 41.08 S 175.04 E
Upper Iowa ≃ 190 43.29 N 91.14 W
Upper Island Cove 186 47.39 N 53.12 W
Upper Keechi Creek ≃ 222 31.23 N 95.42 W
Upper Klamath Lake ☒ 202 42.23 N 122.55 W
Upper Lake 204 39.10 N 122.54 W
Upper Lake ≃ 204 41.44 N 120.08 W
Upper Lehigh 210 41.02 N 75.55 W
Upper Liard 180 60.02 N 128.55 W
Upper Machodoc Creek ≃ 208 38.18 N 77.02 W
Upper Manitou Lake ☒ 184 49.24 N 92.48 W
Upper Marlboro 208 38.46 N 76.45 W
Upper Matecumbe Key I 220 24.55 N 80.39 W
Upper Moutere 172 41.16 S 173.00 E
Upper Musquodoboit 186 45.08 N 62.57 W
Upper Mystic Lake ☒ 283 42.27 N 71.09 W
Upper Nyack 210 41.07 N 73.55 W
Upper Peirce Reservoir ☒¹ 271c 1.22 N 103.48 E
Upper Red Lake ☒ 198 48.10 N 94.40 W
Upper Rideau Lake ☒ 212 44.41 N 76.20 W
Upper River Rouge ≃ 281 42.23 N 83.16 W
Upper Saddle River 276 41.03 N 74.05 W
Upper Saint Clair 279b 40.21 N 80.05 W
Upper Sandusky 214 40.49 N 83.16 W
Upper San Leandro Reservoir ☒ 226 37.47 N 122.07 W
Upper Sheila 186 47.28 N 64.56 W
Upper Straits Lake ☒ 283 42.31 N 83.24 W
Upper Sumas 224 49.01 N 122.12 W
Upper Swan 168 31.46 S 116.01 E
Upper Takaka 172 41.02 S 172.50 E
Upper Takutu-Upper Essequibo ☐⁴ 246 3.00 N 59.00 W
Upper Tean 42 52.57 N 1.58 W
Upper Tooting ↟ 260 51.26 N 0.10 W
Upper Trajan's Wall ↟ 38 46.26 N ...
Upper Ugashik Lake ☒ 180 57.40 N 156.43 W
Upper Volta → Burkina Faso ☐¹ 150 13.00 N 1.30 W
Upper Windigo Lake ☒ 184 52.30 N 91.35 W
Upper Yarra Reservoir ☒¹ 169 37.41 S 145.56 E
Upper Yosemite Fall ✦ 226 37.45 N 119.36 W
Uppingham 42 52.35 N 0.43 W
Uppland ☐⁹ 40 59.59 N 17.48 E
Upplands 40 60.14 N 17.44 E
Upplands Väsby 40 59.52 N 17.54 E
Uppsala 40 59.52 N 17.38 E
Uppsala Län ☐⁶ 40 60.00 N 17.45 E
Upright, Cape › 180 60.17 N 172.15 W
Upsala 40 59.52 N 17.38 E
— Uppsala
Upshi 120 33.50 N 77.49 E
Upshur ☐⁶ 222 32.45 N 94.55 W
Upstart, Cape › 166 19.42 S 147.45 E
Upton, P.Q., Can. 206 45.39 N 72.41 W
Upton, Eng., U.K. 44 53.37 N 1.17 W
Upton, Eng., U.K. 44 53.14 N 0.35 W
Upton, Eng., U.K. 260 51.30 N 0.01 W
Upton, Eng., U.K. 262 53.23 N 3.06 W
Upton, Ky., U.S. 194 37.27 N 85.53 W
Upton, Ma., U.S. 207 42.10 N 71.36 W
Upton, Wy., U.S. 198 44.05 N 104.37 W
Upton Hill ☐² 169 36.52 S 145.27 E
Upton upon Severn 42 52.04 N 2.13 W
Uptown →⁸ 278 41.58 N 87.40 W
Upwell 42 52.36 N 0.12 E
Upwey 274b 37.54 S 145.20 E
Uquía, Cerro ⌃ 246 4.22 N 63.46 W
Ur
— Tall al-Muqayyar ⌂ 128 30.57 N 46.09 E
Urabá, Golfo de ⌣ 246 8.25 N 76.53 W
Urachi 84 42.21 N 47.36 E
Uracoa 246 9.00 N 62.21 W
Urad 54 52.15 N 14.67 E
Uradome-kaigan ✦ 96 35.35 N 134.21 E
Urad Zhonghou Lianheqi 102 41.42 N 108.49 E
Uraga 268 35.15 N 139.43 E
Uraga-kō ⌣ 268 35.14 N 139.44 E
Uragawara 94 37.09 N 138.26 E
Urahoro 92a 42.48 N 143.39 E
Uraj 86 60.08 N 64.48 E
Urakan 88 58.38 N 106.01 E
Urakawa 92a 42.09 N 142.47 E
Ural ≃ 72 47.00 N 51.48 E
Uralla 80 30.39 S 151.30 E
Ural Mountains
— Ural'skije gory ↗ 72 60.00 N 60.00 E
Uralo-Kl'uči 88 56.03 N 97.28 E
Uralove 72 52.11 N 33.34 E
Ural'sk 80 51.14 N 51.22 E
Ural'sk 80 51.36 N 51.40 E
Ural'skije gory (Ural Mountains) ↗ 72 60.00 N 60.00 E
Urambo 154 5.04 S 32.03 E
Uran 272c 18.52 N 72.56 E
Urana 166 35.20 S 146.16 E
Urandangi 166 21.36 S 138.18 E
Urandi 255 14.46 S 42.38 W
Urangan 166 25.18 S 152.54 E
Urania, Austl. 168b 34.31 S 137.36 E
Urania, U.S. 194 31.51 N 92.17 W
Uranium City 176 59.34 N 108.36 W
Uranquinty 171b 35.12 S 147.15 E
Urarey 78 27.26 S 122.18 E
Urariá, Paraná ≃¹ 246 3.03 S 57.43 W
Uraricaá ≃ 246 3.20 N 60.30 W
Uraricoera 246 3.27 N 60.59 W
Uraricoera ≃ 246 3.02 N 60.30 W
Uras 71 39.42 N 8.42 E
Urasaki 174m 26.40 N 127.53 E
Urasoe 174m 26.15 N 127.43 E
Ura-Tube 85 39.55 N 68.59 E
Urawakonda 122 14.17 N 77.16 E
Urawa 94 35.51 N 139.39 E
Urawa 94 35.39 N 139.54 E
'Urayfan Nāqah, Jabal ⌃ 132 30.22 N 34.27 E
'Urayyidah, Bi'r ⌃⁴ 142 29.00 N 31.58 E
'Urazmetovo 86 53.49 N 55.25 E
Urazovka 80 55.33 N 44.40 E
Urazovo 78 50.07 N 38.04 E
Urbach 56 50.53 N 7.49 E
Urban 224 48.38 N 122.40 W
Urbana, Ar., U.S. 194 33.09 N 92.26 W
Urbana, Il., U.S. 196 40.06 N 88.12 W
Urbana, Mo., U.S. 216 40.03 N 85.47 W
Urbana, Oh., U.S. 218 40.06 N 83.45 W
Urbancrest 281 40.02 N 83.05 W
Urbandale, Ia., U.S. 190 41.37 N 93.42 W
Urbandale, Mi., U.S. 284 44.09 N 86.11 W
Urbania 66 43.40 N 12.31 E
Urbanna 208 37.38 N 76.34 W
Urbano Noris 240b 20.36 N 76.13 W
Urbano Santos 250 3.13 S 43.23 W
Urbe 66 44.29 N 8.36 E
Urbe, Aeroporto dell' 267a 41.57 N 12.30 E
Urbino 66 43.43 N 12.38 E
Urbisaglia 66 43.12 N 13.18 E
Urcos 248 13.42 S 71.38 W

Column 2 (FRANÇAIS)

Urda 80 48.47 N 47.26 E
Urdaneta 116 15.59 N 120.34 E
Urdenbach →⁸ 263 51.09 N 6.53 E
Urdinarrain 252 32.41 S 58.53 W
Urdoma 24 61.47 N 48.32 E
Uržar 86 47.05 N 81.38 E
Ure ≃, Fr. 50 48.45 N 0.11 E
Ure ≃, Eng., U.K. 44 54.05 N 1.20 W
Urečča 76 52.57 N 27.54 E
Üren 142 30.58 N 30.42 E
Ureki 84 41.59 N 41.46 E
Ureliki 180 64.23 N 173.15 W
Uren' 80 57.28 N 45.49 E
Üren ☐ 40 58.59 N 16.44 E
Urèn ☐ 236 9.33 N 82.55 W
Ureña 246 7.55 N 72.28 W
Urenui 172 39.00 S 174.23 E
Uréparapara I 175f 13.32 S 167.20 E
Ures 232 29.26 N 110.24 W
Ureshino, Nihon 92 33.06 N 129.59 E
Ureshino, Nihon 94 34.34 N 136.09 E
Ureterp 52 53.05 N 6.10 E
Urga
→ Ulaanbaatar, Mong. 88 47.55 N 106.53 E
Urga, Uzb. 86 43.35 N 58.30 E
Urgamal 88 48.29 N 94.20 E
Urgenč 72 41.33 N 60.38 E
Urgnano 62 45.35 N 9.41 E
Urguenskij Golec, gora ⌃ 88 53.30 N 118.08 E
Ürgüp 130 38.38 N 34.56 E
Urgut 85 39.23 N 67.15 E
Urho Kekkosen kansallispuisto ✦ 24 68.10 N 28.30 E
Uri, India 123 34.05 N 74.02 E
Uri, It. 71 40.38 N 8.29 E
Uri ☐³ 58 46.50 N 8.40 E
Uriah 194 31.18 N 87.30 W
Uriangato 234 20.09 N 101.11 W
Uribante ≃ 246 7.18 N 70.44 W
Uribe 246 3.13 N 74.24 W
Uribelarrea 258 35.05 S 58.50 W
Uribia 246 11.43 N 72.16 W
Urich 194 38.27 N 94.00 W
Urickoje 78 52.02 N 38.11 E
Urie ≃ 46 57.19 N 2.30 W
Urimba 152 10.56 S 16.32 E
Urión ≃¹ 288 34.24 S 58.31 W
Urique 232 27.13 N 107.55 W
Urique ≃ 232 26.29 N 107.58 W
Uri-Rotstock ⌃ 58 46.52 N 8.33 E
Urituyacu ≃ 246 4.35 S 75.28 W
Uriuaná ☐ 250 2.47 S 50.29 W
Urizura 94 36.30 N 140.27 E
Urjala 26 61.05 N 23.32 E
Urk 52 52.39 N 5.36 E
Urkan ≃ 89 53.27 N 126.56 E
Urkarach 84 42.11 N 47.38 E
Urla 30 38.18 N 26.46 E
Urlati 38 44.59 N 26.14 E
Urlingford 48 52.42 N 7.35 W
Urlings 240c 17.02 N 61.52 W
Urluk 88 50.03 N 107.55 E
Urma 126 30.10 N 86.15 E
Urman, Ross. 86 54.52 N 56.53 E
'Urmān, Sūrīy. 132 32.30 N 36.41 E
Urmary 86 55.42 N 47.57 E
Urmeran 85 39.27 N 68.17 E
Urmi ≃ 89 48.44 N 134.16 E
Urmia → Orūmīyeh 128 37.33 N 45.04 E
Urmia, Lake → Orūmīyeh, Daryācheh-ye ☒ 128 37.40 N 45.30 E
Urmston 262 53.27 N 2.21 W
Urnäsch 58 47.19 N 9.17 E
Urnersee ⌣ 58 46.55 N 8.37 E
Uroyán, Montañas de ↗ 240m 18.14 N 67.02 W
Urožajnoje, Ross. 84 43.42 N 44.13 E
Urožajnoje, Ross. 84 44.47 N 44.55 E
Urquhart, Glen V 46 57.20 N 4.35 W
Urrao 246 6.20 N 76.11 W
Ur Water ≃ 44 54.53 N 3.49 W
Ursa 219 40.04 N 91.22 W
Ursberg 58 48.16 N 10.27 E
Uršel'skij 80 55.41 N 40.13 E
Ursensollen 60 49.24 N 11.46 E
Ursk 86 54.27 N 85.24 E
Ursprung 58 48.37 N 9.53 E
Urstrazym 86 52.12 N 58.50 E
Urtigueira 252 24.12 S 50.55 W
Urt Moron 120 37.00 N 93.18 E
Uruaçu 255 14.30 S 49.10 W
Uruana 255 15.30 S 49.41 W
Uruapan 204 31.38 N 116.15 W
Uruapan del Progreso 234 19.25 N 102.04 W
Urubamba 248 13.18 S 72.07 W
Urubamba ≃ 248 10.44 S 73.45 W
Urubaxi ≃ 246 0.31 S 64.50 W
Urubu ≃ 255 2.55 S 55.25 W
Urubu ≃, Bra. 250 10.51 S 49.47 W
Uruburetama 250 3.38 S 39.30 W
Urucara 246 2.32 S 57.45 W
Uruch ≃ 84 43.28 N 44.06 E
Urucu ≃ 246 4.11 S 63.36 W
Uruçuca 255 14.35 S 39.16 W
Uruçuí 250 7.14 S 44.33 W
Uruçuí, Serra da ↗² 250 9.00 S 44.45 W
Urucuia ≃ 255 16.08 S 45.05 W
Urucu-preto ≃ 248 7.20 S 64.38 W
Urucurituba 246 2.41 S 57.40 W
Uruçú 84 35.16 N 137.42 E
Uruguaiana 252 29.45 S 57.05 W
Uruguay ☐¹, S.A. 244 33.00 S 56.00 W
Uruguay (Uruguai) ☐¹ 34 34.12 S 58.18 W
Uruguay (Uruguai), gora ⌃ 88 51.25 N 102.09 E
Uru'gan ≃ 88 51.45 N 114.47 E
Urul'unguj ≃ 88 50.24 N 119.08 E
Urum, ozero ☒ 86 54.33 N 78.30 E
Urumchi — Ürümqi 120 43.48 N 87.35 E
Urundi ≃ 88 52.35 N 120.08 E
Urünqi ≃ 84 50.36 N 52.06 E
Ürümqi 120 43.48 N 87.35 E
Urung-Chaja 74 70.13 N 113.23 E
Uruoca 250 3.20 S 40.32 W
Urup 84 44.06 N 41.10 E
Urup ≃ 84 44.59 N 41.10 E
Urup, ostrov I 74 46.00 N 150.00 E
Urupá ≃ 248 10.54 S 61.57 W
Urupês 252 21.13 S 49.17 W
Uru'ping 88 52.46 N 120.00 E
Uruša 89 54.03 N 122.54 E
Uruša-Martan 84 43.08 N 45.32 E
Urusovo 82 54.15 N 38.26 E
Urussu 86 54.36 N 53.49 E
Urutaí 255 17.28 S 48.12 W
Urutai, Ilha I 250 1.07 S 51.17 W

Column 3 (PORTUGUÊS)

Urutaú 252 25.42 S 63.04 W
Uruti 172 38.57 S 174.32 E
Uru Uru, Lago ☒ 248 18.10 S 67.10 W
Uruwira 154 6.27 S 31.21 E
Uryl' 86 49.15 N 86.20 E
Uryū-yama ⌃ 270 35.03 N 135.48 E
Uryv 82 51.07 N 39.10 E
Urzajbaš 80 54.43 N 54.23 E
Urziceni 38 44.43 N 26.38 E
Ürzig 56 49.59 N 7.01 E
Urzulei 71 40.06 N 9.30 E
Uržum 80 57.08 N 50.00 E
Us ≃ 86 52.07 N 92.15 E
Usa, Nihon 96 33.31 N 131.22 E
Usa, Ross. 86 54.03 N 88.45 E
Usa ≃, Bela. 76 54.03 N 28.55 E
Usa ≃, Ross. 24 65.57 N 56.55 E
Ušačë ≃ 76 55.32 N 28.30 E
Ušača ≃ 76 55.32 N 28.30 E
Ušakovka 83 48.48 N 39.48 E
Ušakovo, Ross. 86 56.22 N 75.41 E
Ušakovo, Ross. 89 51.55 N 126.34 E
Usambara Mountains ↗ 154 4.45 S 38.30 E
Usangu Flats ≃ 154 8.30 S 34.15 E
Usanovy 86 59.28 N 73.24 E
Ušaral 85 43.54 N 70.42 E
Usarp Mountains ↗ 9 71.10 S 160.00 E
Ušava 72 62.11 N 12.40 E
Usaymīr, Wādī al- V 273c 30.04 N 31.23 E
Ušba, gora ⌃ 84 43.08 N 42.40 E
Ušbas ≃ 85 43.55 N 69.39 E
Usborne, Mount ⌃ 254 51.41 S 58.50 W
Ušče 38 43.28 N 20.37 E
Uščerpje ≃ 76 52.43 N 31.53 E
Uscio 62 44.25 N 9.10 E
Usedom 54 53.52 N 13.55 E
Usedom (Uznam) I 54 54.00 N 14.00 E
Useldange 259 49.47 N 5.59 E
Uselius 71 39.48 N 8.51 E
Usen' ≃ 86 54.44 N 53.38 E
'Usfān 144 21.55 N 39.21 E
Ushaa 152 14.55 S 23.18 E
Ushant → Ouessant, Île d' 50 48.28 N 5.05 W
Ushashi 154 2.00 S 33.57 E
'Ushayrah 144 21.46 N 40.38 E
Ushetu 154 4.10 S 32.16 E
Ushibuka 92 32.11 N 130.01 E
Ushiku 94 35.58 N 140.08 E
Ushimado 96 34.37 N 134.10 E
Ushuaia 254 54.48 S 68.18 W
Ushytsya ≃ 38 48.35 N 27.08 E
Usibelli 180 63.51 N 148.47 W
Usingen 56 50.20 N 8.32 E
Usini 71 40.40 N 8.32 E
Usinsk 24 65.58 N 56.39 E
Usk, B.C., Can. 182 54.38 N 128.25 W
Usk, Wales, U.K. 42 51.43 N 2.54 W
Usk, Wa., U.S. 202 48.18 N 117.16 W
Usk ≃ 42 51.36 N 2.58 W
Uškanij kr'až ↗ 180 65.15 N 178.35 E
Uskedal 28 59.56 N 5.52 E
Usken ☐ 40 59.56 N 16.23 E
Uskovo 265b 55.56 N 37.19 E
Uslar 56 51.39 N 9.38 E
Úslava ≃ 60 49.45 N 13.24 E
Usmajac 234 19.52 N 103.34 W
Usman', Ross. 76 52.02 N 39.44 E
Usman' ≃, Ross. 76 52.02 N 39.44 E
Usmate Velate 62 45.39 N 9.21 E
Usmyn' 76 55.52 N 31.09 E
Usoke 154 5.08 S 32.24 E
Usolje, Ross. 86 59.25 N 56.41 E
Usolje, Ross. 86 56.49 N 38.40 E
Usolje-Sibirskoje 88 52.47 N 103.38 E
Uson 116 12.13 N 123.47 E
Usovo 265b 55.44 N 37.13 E
Uspallata 252 32.35 S 69.20 W
Uspanapa ≃ 234 17.58 N 94.29 W
Uspenka, Kaz. 86 52.12 N 58.50 E
Uspenka, Ross. 86 50.38 N 41.28 E
Uspenka, Ukr. 83 48.23 N 39.10 E
Uspenskoje 86 51.16 N 53.36 E
Uspenskoje 82 54.43 N 37.04 E
Usquil 248 7.49 S 78.25 W
Ussassai 71 39.49 N 9.23 E
Usseglio 62 45.14 N 7.13 E
Ussel 50 45.33 N 2.18 E
Usson-en-Forez 50 45.23 N 3.56 E
Ussuri (Wusuli) ≃ 89 48.28 N 135.04 E
Ussurijsk 89 43.48 N 131.59 E
Ust 123 36.56 N 72.53 E
Usta ≃ 80 56.53 N 45.40 E
Ustaoset 28 60.30 N 8.04 E
Ustaritz 50 43.24 N 1.27 W
Ust'-Bagar'ak 86 56.08 N 61.52 E
Ust'-Barguzin 88 53.27 N 108.59 E
Ust'-Belaja 74 65.30 N 173.24 E
Ust'-Bol'šereck 74 52.48 N 156.14 E
Ust'-Buzulukskaja 82 50.12 N 42.17 E
Ust'-Bystr'anskaja 82 47.49 N 41.03 E
Ust'-Čaja 88 58.17 N 82.38 E
Ust'-Čarýškaja Pristan' 86 52.27 N 83.39 E
Ust'-Čaun 74 68.47 N 170.30 E
Ust'-Choperskaja 82 49.36 N 42.38 E
Ust'-Čil'ma 24 65.27 N 52.06 E
Ust'-Čižapka 88 59.02 N 79.37 E
Ust'-Čornaja 38 48.18 N 23.54 E
Ust'-Dolyssy 76 56.15 N 30.10 E
Ust'-Doneckij 82 47.39 N 40.54 E
Ust'-Džegutinskaja 84 44.05 N 41.59 E
Ust'-Elegest 88 51.32 N 94.05 E
Uster 58 47.21 N 8.43 E
Ust'-Gr'aznucha 82 50.26 N 45.14 E
Ustica 70 38.42 N 13.11 E
Ustica, Isola di I 70 38.42 N 13.11 E
Ust'-Ilga 88 55.00 N 105.02 E
— Utique ⌂ 36 37.03 N 10.03 E
Ust'-Ill'ič 86 62.32 N 56.21 E
Ust'-Ilimsk 86 57.44 N 71.10 E

Column 4

Ust'-Izes 86 55.56 N 76.56 E
Ust'-Ižora 265a 59.48 N 30.36 E
Ustja 24 61.30 N 42.36 E
Ust'-Javron'ga 24 63.25 N 44.21 E
Ustje, Ross. 76 60.49 N 32.49 E
Ustje, Ross. 76 59.38 N 39.43 E
Ustje, Ross. 80 57.47 N 39.47 E
Ustje, Ross. 82 55.16 N 36.20 E
Ustje, Ross. 86 57.46 N 94.42 E
Ustje-Kirovskoje 76 58.45 N 35.55 E
Ustka 54 54.35 N 16.50 E
Ust'-K'achta 88 50.32 N 106.16 E
Ust'-Kajtym 86 57.23 N 95.28 E
Ust'-Kalmanka 86 52.07 N 83.19 E
Ust'-Kamčatsk 74 56.15 N 162.30 E
Ust'-Kamenogorsk 86 49.58 N 82.38 E
Ust'-Kan, Ross. 86 50.57 N 84.45 E
Ust'-Kan, Ross. 86 56.31 N 93.48 E
Ust'-Karenga 86 54.26 N 116.30 E
Ust'-Karsk 88 52.43 N 118.48 E
Ust'-Katav 86 54.56 N 58.10 E
Ust'-Kulom 24 61.42 N 53.40 E
Ust'-Kurd'um 80 51.39 N 46.12 E
Ust'-Kurenga 88 57.27 N 75.34 E
Ust'-Kut 88 56.46 N 105.40 E
Ust'-Labinsk 78 45.13 N 39.42 E
Ust'-Lubija 88 52.36 N 120.16 E
Ust'-Luga 76 59.40 N 28.15 E
Ust'-Lyža 24 65.44 N 56.36 E
Ust'-Maja 74 60.25 N 134.32 E
Ust'-Naryk 86 54.20 N 87.25 E
Ust'-Nemda 80 57.03 N 50.22 E
Ust'-Nera 74 64.34 N 143.12 E
Ust'-Niman 89 51.23 N 132.42 E
Ust'-N'ukža 88 56.34 N 121.37 E
Ust'-Omčug 74 61.09 N 149.38 E
Ust'-Ordynskij 88 52.48 N 104.45 E
Ust'-Ordynskij Burjatskij Avtonomnyj Okrug ☐⁸ 88 53.30 N 104.00 E
Ust'-Oz'ornaja 86 58.54 N 117.06 E
Ust'-Oz'ornoje 86 58.54 N 87.48 E
Ust'-Paden'ga 24 61.53 N 42.36 E
Ust'-Pečengskoje 76 59.47 N 42.37 E
Ust'-Pinega 24 64.11 N 41.56 E
Ust'-Pit 86 58.59 N 91.44 E
Ust'-Pogožje 80 49.28 N 44.38 E
Ust'-Šonoša 24 61.10 N 41.18 E
Ust'-Sumy 86 54.48 N 80.26 E
Ust'-Tara 86 56.41 N 74.39 E
Ust'-Tarka 86 55.34 N 75.42 E
Ust'-Tašino 89 51.07 N 129.35 E
Ust'-Tygda 89 52.35 N 127.53 E
Ust'-Tym 86 59.26 N 80.08 E
Ust'-Tyrma 89 50.29 N 131.18 E
Ust'-Uda 88 54.10 N 103.03 E
Ust'-Ukjat 130 39.16 N 41.17 E
Ust'-Ulagan 86 50.38 N 87.58 E
Ust'-Umal'ta 89 51.07 N 133.16 E
Ust'-Undurga 89 52.07 N 118.04 E
Ust'-Unja 86 61.48 N 57.48 E
Ust'-Urt, plato ↗¹ 72 43.00 N 56.00 E
Ust'-Us 86 52.07 N 92.17 E
Ust'-Usa 24 65.59 N 56.54 E
Ust'-Uza 80 53.08 N 45.17 E
Ust'-Užna 86 58.51 N 96.26 E
Ust'-Vichoreva 86 56.47 N 101.24 E
Ust'-Voja 24 64.27 N 57.40 E
Ust'-Vyjskaja 24 62.57 N 46.41 E
Ust'-Vym 24 62.14 N 50.24 E
Ustylyh 78 50.51 N 24.09 E
Ustynivka 78 47.57 N 32.32 E
Ust'-Zaza 88 53.10 N 111.40 E
Ust'-Žuja 88 58.48 N 118.12 E

Column 5

Utinga ≃ 255 12.34 S 41.20 W
Utique 36 37.03 N 10.03 E
Utique ↟ 36 37.03 N 10.03 E
Utirik I 14 11.15 N 169.48 E
Utängan I 86 56.01 N 15.47 E
Utena 128 ...
Utenzai 123 34.11 N 71.46 E
Utica, Il., U.S. 216 41.21 N 89.00 W
Utica, Ks., U.S. 192 38.38 N 100.10 W
Utica, Mi., U.S. 281 42.37 N 83.02 W
Utica, N.Y., U.S. 210 43.06 N 75.13 W
Utica, Oh., U.S. 218 40.14 N 82.27 W
Utica, Pa., U.S. 214 41.26 N 79.58 W
Utiel 68 39.34 N 1.12 W
Utikuma Lake ☒ 176 55.50 N 115.25 W
Utila 236 16.06 N 86.55 W
Utila, Isla de I 236 16.06 N 86.56 W
Utinga ≃ 287b 23.38 S 46.32 W
Utö I 40 58.56 N 18.16 E
Utokota 156 17.50 S 20.22 E
Utonde 152 1.56 N 9.49 E
Utopia, Austl. 162 22.14 S 134.33 E
Utopia, Tx., U.S. 196 29.37 N 99.32 W
Utorgoš 76 58.17 N 30.15 E
Utraula 124 27.19 N 82.25 E
Utrecht, Ned. 52 52.05 N 5.08 E
Utrecht, S. Afr. 158 27.38 S 30.20 E
Utrecht ☐³ 52 52.05 N 5.08 E
Utrera 34 37.11 N 5.47 W
Utroja ≃ 76 57.23 N 28.09 E
Utsaladdy 224 48.15 N 122.30 W
Utsira 26 59.18 N 4.54 E
Utsjoki 24 69.53 N 27.00 E
Utsumi 94 34.21 N 133.17 E
Utsunomiya 94 36.33 N 139.52 E
Uttamapālāiyam 122 9.48 N 77.20 E
Uttaradit 110 17.38 N 100.06 E
Uttarkāshi 120 30.44 N 78.27 E
Uttarpara-Kotrung 272b 22.40 N 88.21 E
Uttar Pradesh ☐³ 120 27.00 N 80.00 E
Uttendorf, Öst. 60 48.09 N 13.07 E
Uttendorf, Öst. 64 47.17 N 12.34 E
Uttenreuth 60 49.36 N 11.05 E
Uttenweiler 58 48.09 N 9.36 E
Ütterlingsen 263 51.11 N 7.45 E
Utting 60 48.02 N 11.05 E
Uttlesford ☐⁸ 260 51.47 N 0.19 E
Uttoxeter 42 52.54 N 1.51 W
Utuado 240m 18.16 N 66.42 W
Utukok ≃ 180 70.04 N 162.18 W
Utulei 174u 14.17 S 170.40 W
Utunomiya → Utsunomiya 94 36.33 N 139.52 E
Uuidenmaan lääni ☐⁴ 26 60.30 N 25.00 E
Uulu 26 58.17 N 24.35 E
Uurainen 26 62.30 N 25.27 E
Uusikaarlepyy (Nykarleby) 26 63.32 N 22.32 E
Uusikaupunki (Nystad) 26 60.48 N 21.25 E
Uva, Ross. 80 56.59 N 52.13 E
Uvá ≃ 246 3.57 N 68.24 W
Uvalda 222 32.02 N 82.31 W
Uvalde 196 29.12 N 99.47 W
Uvaly 54 50.03 N 14.47 E
Uvarovičy 76 52.36 N 30.44 E
Uvarovka 76 55.32 N 35.37 E
Uvarovo 80 51.59 N 42.15 E
Uvas Creek ≃ 226 36.58 N 121.33 W
Uvas Reservoir ☒¹ 226 37.05 N 121.42 W
Uvat 86 59.09 N 68.54 E
'Uvda, Biq'at V 132 29.57 N 34.57 E
Uvdal 28 60.16 N 8.48 E
Uvel'skij 86 54.26 N 61.22 E
Uvernet 62 44.22 N 6.38 E
Uvero, Punta › 241s 11.21 N 68.41 W
Uvinza 154 5.06 S 30.22 E
Uvira 154 3.24 S 29.08 E
Uvod' ≃ 80 56.26 N 41.26 E
Uvongo Beach 158 30.50 S 30.20 E
Uvs nuur ☒ 74 50.20 N 92.45 E
Uwwré › 175f 18.47 S 169.16 E
Uwa 96 33.20 N 132.34 E
Uwajima 96 33.13 N 132.34 E
Uwa-kai ☌² 96 33.15 N 132.15 E
Uwayl 140 8.46 N 27.24 E
'Uwaynāt 130 35.43 N 36.05 E
'Uwayqil, Jabal ⌃ 140 21.54 N 24.58 E
Uwchland 285 40.05 N 75.42 W
Uwi, Pulau I 112 1.05 N 108.23 E
Uxbridge, On., Can. 212 44.06 N 79.07 W
Uxbridge, Ma., U.S. 207 42.04 N 71.37 W
Uxbridge →⁸ 260 51.33 N 0.29 W
Uxmal ☐ 232 20.22 N 89.46 W
Uyak Bay ☰ 180 57.36 N 153.57 W
Uyama 96 32.41 N 130.06 E
U-yin 40 57.35 N 11.58 E
Uyo 150 5.03 N 7.56 E
Uyuni 248 20.28 S 66.50 W
Uyuni, Salar de ☒ 248 20.20 S 67.42 W
Uza ≃, Ross. 80 53.28 N 45.31 E
Uza ≃, Ross. 80 55.45 N 30.45 E
Užanka 76 48.42 N 22.40 E
Užava ≃ 76 57.14 N 21.27 E
'Uzaym, Nahr al- ≃ 128 34.12 N 44.51 E
Uzbekistan ☐¹ 72 41.00 N 64.00 E
Uzboj ≃ 85 39.30 N 55.00 E
Uzda 76 53.28 N 27.13 E
Uzen ≃ 72 45.13 N 49.45 E
Uzerche 50 45.25 N 1.34 E
Uzès 50 44.01 N 4.25 E
Užgorod 38 48.37 N 22.18 E
Uzhhorod → Užhorod 78 48.37 N 22.18 E
Uznam (Usedom) I 54 54.00 N 14.00 E
Uzun 85 38.10 N 67.18 E
Uzun Ada I 130 38.42 N 26.42 E
Uzunköprü 130 41.16 N 26.42 E
Uzynkair 85 44.15 N 64.44 E
Uzyn 78 49.50 N 30.24 E

Column 6 (V)

V

Vä 26 55.59 N 14.05 E
Vääksy 26 61.11 N 25.33 E
Vaal ≃ 158 29.04 S 23.38 E
Vaala 26 64.33 N 26.50 E
Vaalbank ☒ 158 25.50 S 29.20 E
Vaaldam ☒¹ 158 26.55 S 28.15 E
Vaalkop ☒ 158 25.17 S 27.25 E
Vaalserberg ⌃² 52 50.45 N 6.01 E
Vaasa (Vasa) 26 63.06 N 21.36 E
Vaasan lääni ☐⁴ 26 63.00 N 23.00 E
Vabalninkas 76 55.58 N 24.45 E
Vabkent 128 40.02 N 64.30 E
Vác 30 47.47 N 19.08 E
Vaca, Bol. 248 19.54 S 63.48 W
Vača, Ross. 80 55.48 N 42.46 E
Vaca, Mount ⌃ 226 38.24 N 122.06 W
Vacacaí ≃ 252 29.55 S 53.06 W
Vaca Key I 220 24.43 N 81.04 W
Vacaria 252 28.30 S 50.56 W
Vacaria ≃, Bra. 255 16.39 S 42.45 W
Vacaria ≃, Bra. 255 16.39 S 42.45 W
Vacas, Arroyo de las ≃ 258 34.00 S 58.18 W
Vacaville 226 38.21 N 121.59 W
Vacca, Kaap ⊢ 158 34.21 S 21.53 E
Vaccarès, Étang de ☒ 62 43.32 N 4.34 E
Vach ≃ 74 60.45 N 76.45 E
Vacha 56 50.50 N 10.01 E
Vache, Île à I 238 18.05 N 73.38 W
Vaches, Rivière aux ≃ 206 46.02 N 72.46 W
Vachnšev 89 48.59 N 142.58 E
Vachš ≃ 72 37.06 N 68.18 E
Vachšskij chrebet ↗ 85 38.35 N 69.45 E
Vachtan 80 57.58 N 46.42 E
Vači 84 42.05 N 47.13 E
Vacía Talega, Punta ⊢ 240m 18.27 N 65.54 W
Vacoas 157c 20.18 S 57.29 E
Vad, Ross. 80 55.32 N 44.12 E
Vad, Sve. 40 60.02 N 15.39 E
Vad ≃ 80 54.33 N 42.37 E
Vada 66 43.21 N 10.28 E
Vadsbro 40 58.58 N 16.36 E
Vadsø 24 70.05 N 29.46 E
Vadstena 40 58.27 N 14.54 E
Vaduz 58 47.09 N 9.31 E
Vadvetjåkko Nationalpark ✦ 24 68.35 N 18.20 E
Væggerløse 41 54.42 N 11.56 E
Værøy I 24 67.40 N 12.39 E
Vaga ≃ 24 62.48 N 42.56 E
Vågåmo 28 61.53 N 9.06 E
Vagaj 86 57.56 N 69.01 E
Vagaj ≃ 86 57.53 N 69.01 E
Vaghena Island I 175e 7.26 S 157.46 E
Vaglia 62 43.54 N 11.17 E
Vaglio Basilicata 71 40.41 N 15.55 E
Vagney 58 48.01 N 6.43 E
Vagnhärad 40 58.55 N 17.30 E
Vágos 34 34.19 S 59.26 W
Váh ≃ 30 47.45 N 18.00 E
Vahrn — Varna 64 46.44 N 11.38 E
Vaich, Loch ☒ 46 57.43 N 4.46 W
Vaiden 194 33.19 N 89.44 W
Vaigai ≃ 122 9.17 N 79.00 E
Vaigat ☐² 178 70.11 N 53.00 W
Vaihingen an der Enz 56 48.56 N 8.58 E
Vaijāpur 122 19.55 N 74.44 E
Vail, Az., U.S. 200 32.03 N 110.42 W
Vail, Ia., U.S. 198 42.03 N 95.11 W
Vaila I 46a 60.12 N 1.37 W
Vailala ≃ 164 7.25 S 145.25 E
Vailly-sur-Aisne 50 49.25 N 3.31 E
Vailly-sur-Sauldre 50 47.27 N 2.39 E
Vail Mills 210 43.04 N 74.15 W
Vails Gate 210 41.30 N 74.02 W
Vaini 175f 21.12 S 175.11 W
Vaiont ☒¹ 64 46.16 N 12.22 E
Vaippar ≃ 122 9.01 N 78.17 E
Vair ≃ 58 48.27 N 5.52 E
Vairano Scalo 71 41.20 N 14.08 E
Vairao 175c 17.47 S 149.17 W
Vaison-la-Romaine 62 44.14 N 5.04 E
Vaitahu 174x 9.56 S 139.06 W
Vaïtogi 174u 14.21 S 170.44 W
Vajgač, ostrov I 72 70.00 N 59.00 E
Vajk' 84 39.40 N 45.30 E
Vakaga ☐⁵ 146 10.00 N 23.00 E
Vaklino 38 43.40 N 28.30 E
Vaksdal 28 60.29 N 5.44 E
Valaam, ostrov I 24 61.23 N 30.57 E
Valašská Bystřice 60 49.25 N 18.06 E
Valašské Klobouky 60 49.08 N 18.00 E
Valašské Meziříčí 60 49.28 N 17.58 E
Valatie 210 42.25 N 73.40 W
Valberg 28 59.04 N 10.13 E
Vålberg 40 59.24 N 13.12 E
Valbom 54 41.08 N 8.16 W
Valbondione 62 46.01 N 10.00 E
Valbonne 62 43.38 N 7.00 E
Valcheta 254 40.42 S 66.09 W
Valdagno 64 45.39 N 11.18 E
Valdahon 58 47.09 N 6.21 E
Valdaj, Ross. 76 57.59 N 33.14 E
Valdaj, Ross. 24 63.26 N 33.30 E

Column 7

Vaalwater 156 24.20 S 28.03 E
Vaasa (Vasa) 26 63.06 N 21.36 E
Vaasan lääni ☐⁴ 26 63.00 N 23.00 E
Vabalninkas 76 55.58 N 24.45 E
Vabkent 128 40.02 N 64.30 E
Vác 30 47.47 N 19.08 E
Vaca, Bol. 248 19.54 S 63.48 W
Vača, Ross. 80 55.48 N 42.46 E
Vaca, Mount ⌃ 226 38.24 N 122.06 W
Vacacaí ≃ 252 29.55 S 53.06 W
Vaca Key I 220 24.43 N 81.04 W
Vacaria 252 28.30 S 50.56 W
Vacaria ≃, Bra. 255 16.39 S 42.45 W
Vacas, Arroyo de las ≃ 258 34.00 S 58.18 W
Vacaville 226 38.21 N 121.59 W
Vacca, Kaap ⊢ 158 34.21 S 21.53 E
Vaccarès, Étang de ☒ 62 43.32 N 4.34 E
Vach ≃ 74 60.45 N 76.45 E
Vacha 56 50.50 N 10.01 E
Vache, Île aux I 238 18.05 N 73.38 W
Vaches, Rivière aux ≃ 206 46.02 N 72.46 W
Vachnšev 89 48.59 N 142.58 E
Vachš ≃ 72 37.06 N 68.18 E
Vachšskij chrebet ↗ 85 38.35 N 69.45 E
Vachtan 80 57.58 N 46.42 E
Vači 84 42.05 N 47.13 E
Vacoas 157c 20.18 S 57.29 E
Vad, Ross. 80 55.32 N 44.12 E
Vad, Sve. 40 60.02 N 15.39 E
Vad ≃ 80 54.33 N 42.37 E
Vadsbro 40 58.58 N 16.36 E
Vadsø 24 70.05 N 29.46 E
Vadstena 40 58.27 N 14.54 E
Vaduz 58 47.09 N 9.31 E
Vaggeryd 40 57.30 N 14.07 E
Vaghena Island I 175e 7.26 S 157.46 E
Vaglio Basilicata 71 40.41 N 15.55 E
Vagney 58 48.01 N 6.43 E
Vagnhärad 40 58.55 N 17.30 E
Vagues 258 34.19 S 59.26 W
Váh ≃ 30 47.45 N 18.00 E
Vahrn
— Varna 64 46.44 N 11.38 E
Vaich, Loch ☒ 46 57.43 N 4.46 W
Vaiden 194 33.19 N 89.44 W
Vaigai ≃ 122 9.17 N 79.00 E
Vaihingen an der Enz 56 48.56 N 8.58 E
Vaijāpur 122 19.55 N 74.44 E
Vail, Az., U.S. 200 32.03 N 110.42 W
Vail, Ia., U.S. 198 42.03 N 95.11 W
Vaila I 46a 60.12 N 1.37 W
Vailala ≃ 164 7.25 S 145.25 E
Vail Mills 210 43.04 N 74.15 W
Vails Gate 210 41.30 N 74.02 W
Vainode 56 56.26 N 21.50 E
Vaiont ☒¹ 64 46.16 N 12.22 E
Vaippar ≃ 122 9.01 N 78.17 E
Vairano Scalo 71 41.20 N 14.08 E
Vairao 175c 17.47 S 149.17 W
Vaison-la-Romaine 62 44.14 N 5.04 E
Vajta 30 46.58 N 18.40 E
Vaksdal 28 60.29 N 5.44 E
Val-Alain 206 46.24 N 71.45 W
Valamaz 80 57.40 N 52.00 E
Valandovo 38 41.19 N 22.34 E
Valašská 60 49.25 N 18.06 E
Valašské Klobouky 60 49.08 N 18.00 E
Valašské Meziříčí 60 49.28 N 17.58 E
Valatie 210 42.25 N 73.40 W
Val-Barrette 206 46.30 N 75.10 W
Valbella 58 46.45 N 9.33 E
Valbom 54 41.08 N 8.16 W
Valcanale 62 46.01 N 10.00 E
Valcheta 254 40.42 S 66.09 W
Val-d'Isère 62 45.27 N 6.59 E
Val Fabbrica 66 43.10 N 12.36 E
Valdahon 58 47.09 N 6.21 E
Valdaj, Ross. 76 57.59 N 33.14 E

Name	Page	Lat.	Long.
Valdaj, Ross.	76	57.59 N	33.14 E
Valdajskaja vozvyšennost' ⋏[2]	24	57.00 N	33.30 E
Valdarno V	66	43.35 N	11.30 E
Valdavia ≃	34	42.24 N	4.16 W
Val-David	206	46.01 N	74.12 W
Valdebeba, Arroyo de ≃	266a	41.23 N	2.10 E
Valdeblore	62	44.04 N	7.12 E
Val-de-Cães	250	1.23 S	48.29 W
Valdecañas, Embalse de ⊜[1]	34	39.45 N	5.30 W
Valdelândia	255	15.11 S	50.02 W
Val-de-Marne □[5]	261	48.47 N	2.29 E
Valdemārpils	76	57.22 N	22.35 E
Valdemarsvik	26	58.12 N	16.36 E
Valdepeñas	34	38.46 N	3.23 W
Valderaduey ≃	34	41.31 N	5.42 W
Valderas	34	42.05 N	5.27 W
Valderice	70	38.03 N	12.38 E
Valderrama	116	11.00 N	122.08 E
Valderrobres	34	40.53 N	0.09 E
Valders	190	44.03 N	87.53 W
Valdés, Península ≻[1]	254	42.30 S	64.00 W
Val-des-Bois	188	45.54 N	75.35 W
Valdese	192	35.44 N	81.33 W
Valdes Island I	224	49.04 N	123.38 W
Valdéz, Ec.	246	1.15 N	79.00 W
Valdez, Ak., U.S.	180	61.07 N	146.16 W
Valdieri	62	44.17 N	7.24 E
Val-d'Isère	62	45.27 N	6.59 E
Valdivia, Chile	254	39.48 S	73.14 W
Valdivia, Col.	246	7.11 N	75.27 W
Valdobbiadene	64	45.54 N	12.00 E
Valdoie	58	47.40 N	6.51 E
Val-d'Oise □[5]	50	49.10 N	2.10 E
Val-d'Or	190	48.07 N	77.47 W
Valdorf	52	52.09 N	8.51 E
Valdosta	192	30.49 N	83.16 W
Valdres V	26	60.55 N	9.10 E
Valdurna (Durnholz)	64	46.44 N	11.26 E
Vale, Guernsey	43b	49.29 N	2.31 W
Vale, Or., U.S.	202	43.58 N	117.14 W
Valea lui Mihai	38	47.31 N	22.09 E
Vale de Lobos	266c	38.49 N	9.17 W
Valeene	218	38.26 N	86.24 W
Valeggio sul Mincio	64	45.21 N	10.44 E
Valehouse Reservoir ⊜[1]	262	53.29 N	1.57 W
Valemount	182	52.50 N	119.15 W
Valença, Bra.	255	13.22 S	39.05 W
Valença, Bra.	256	22.15 S	43.43 W
Valença, Port.	34	42.02 N	8.38 W
Valença do Piauí	250	6.24 S	41.45 W
Valençay	50	47.09 N	1.34 E
Valence → València, Esp.	34	39.28 N	0.22 W
Valence, Fr.	62	44.56 N	4.54 E
València, Esp.	34	39.28 N	0.22 W
Valencia, Hond.	236	14.47 N	85.18 W
Valencia, Pil.	116	7.57 N	125.03 E
Valencia, Pa., U.S.	214	40.40 N	79.59 W
Valencia, Ven.	246	10.11 N	68.00 W
València □[4]	34	39.30 N	0.45 W
València, Golf de ⊂	34	39.50 N	0.30 E
Valencia, Lago de ⊜	246	10.15 N	67.45 W
Valencia, Quebrada ≃	286c	10.30 N	66.46 W
Valencia de Alcántata	34	39.25 N	7.14 W
Valencia de Don Juan	34	42.18 N	5.31 W
Valencia Island I	48	51.52 N	10.20 W
Valenciennes	50	50.21 N	3.32 E
Vălenii de Munte	38	45.12 N	26.03 E
Valensole	62	43.50 N	5.59 E
Valentano	66	42.34 N	11.49 E
Valente	250	11.34 S	39.27 W
Valentigney	58	47.28 N	6.50 E
Valentin	89	43.08 N	134.17 E
Valentín Alsina ⊸[8]	288	34.40 S	58.25 W
Valentine, Ne., U.S.	198	42.52 N	100.33 W
Valentine, Tx., U.S.	196	30.34 N	104.29 W
Valentine Mountain ∧	224	48.32 N	123.56 W
Valentinovka	265b	55.55 N	37.56 E
Valenton	261	48.45 N	2.28 E
Valenza	62	45.01 N	8.38 E
Valenzano	68	41.02 N	16.53 E
Valenzuela	269f	14.42 N	120.58 E
Våler	26	60.40 N	11.50 E
Valera	246	9.19 N	70.37 W
Valérien, Mont ∧[2]	261	48.53 N	2.13 E
Vale Royal □[8]	262	53.17 N	2.37 W
Valets, Lac ⊜	190	48.32 N	76.30 W
Valette, La → Valletta	36	35.54 N	14.31 E
Valfabbrica	66	43.09 N	12.36 E
Valflaunès	62	43.48 N	3.52 E
Valfurva	64	46.27 N	10.25 E
Valfurva V	64	46.26 N	10.26 E
Valga	76	57.47 N	26.02 E
Valge ≃	76	59.35 N	25.42 E
Valgorge	62	44.35 N	4.07 E
Valgrisanche	62	45.38 N	7.04 E
Valguarnera Caropepe	70	37.30 N	14.23 E
Valhalla, S. Afr.	158	25.49 S	28.08 E
Valhalla, N.Y., U.S.	210	41.04 N	73.46 W
Valhalla, Lake ⊜	276	40.56 N	74.22 W
Valiente, Península ≻[1]	236	9.05 N	81.51 W
Valiente, Punta ≻	236	9.11 N	81.55 W
Valier, Il., U.S.	194	38.01 N	89.03 W
Valier, Mt., U.S.	202	48.18 N	112.14 W
Valier, Pa., U.S.	214	40.55 N	79.03 W
Valili ∧	175g	16.39 S	179.10 E
Valinda	280	34.02 N	117.56 W
Valinhos	256	22.57 S	47.01 W
Valjevo	38	44.16 N	19.53 E
Valka	76	57.46 N	26.00 E
Valkeakoski	26	61.16 N	24.02 E
Valkenburg	56	50.52 N	5.50 E
Valkenswaard	52	51.21 N	5.28 E
V'alki	82	55.39 N	38.05 E
Valkininkas	76	54.21 N	24.50 E
Valky	78	49.50 N	35.37 E
Valla	40	59.02 N	16.23 E
Valladares	196	26.53 N	100.37 W
Valladolid, Ec.	246	4.33 S	79.08 W
Valladolid, Esp.	34	41.39 N	4.43 W
Valladolid, Méx.	232	20.41 N	88.12 W
Valladolid □[4]	34	41.40 N	4.50 W
Vallage ⊸[1]	58	48.24 N	5.00 E
Vallåkra	41	55.58 N	12.52 E
Vallarsa	64	45.47 N	11.07 E
Vallata	68	41.02 N	15.15 E
Vallauris	62	43.35 N	7.03 E
Vallco Fashion Park ⊸[9]	282	37.19 N	122.01 W
Valldal	26	62.20 N	7.21 E
Valldoreix	266d	41.28 N	2.04 E
Valle, Esp.	34	43.14 N	4.18 W
Valle, Lat.	76	56.30 N	24.44 E
Valle □[5]	236	13.30 N	87.35 W
Valle, Arroyo ≃	226	37.39 N	121.54 W
Vallecas ⊸[8]	266a	40.23 N	3.37 W
Valle Castellana	66	42.44 N	13.29 E
Vallecillo	196	26.40 N	99.58 W
Vallecito	226	38.07 N	120.27 W
Vallecitos	200	36.05 N	106.20 W
Vallecitos Creek ≃	282	37.36 N	121.53 W
Vallecorsa	66	41.27 N	13.24 E
Valle Crucis Abbey ♁[1]	42	52.59 N	3.12 W
Valle d'Aosta □[4]	36	45.45 N	7.25 E
Valle de Bravo	234	19.11 N	100.08 W
Valle de Guadalupe	234	21.00 N	102.37 W
Valle de Guanape	246	9.54 N	65.41 W
Valle de Juárez	234	19.53 N	102.51 W
Valle de la Pascua	246	9.13 N	66.00 W
Valle del Cauca □[5]	246	3.45 N	76.30 W
Valle de Olivos	232	27.12 N	106.17 W
Valle de Santiago	234	20.23 N	101.12 W
Valle de Zaragoza	232	27.28 N	105.49 W
Valle di Cadore	64	46.24 N	12.20 E
Valle di Sotto	64	46.25 N	10.21 E
Valledolmo	70	37.45 N	13.49 E
Valledupar	246	10.29 N	73.15 W
Valle Edén	252	31.50 S	56.09 W
Vallefiorita	68	38.46 N	16.27 E
Vallegrande	248	18.29 S	64.06 W
Valle Hermoso, Arg.	252	31.07 S	64.29 W
Valle Hermoso, Méx.	196	25.39 N	97.52 W
Vallehermoso, Pil.	116	10.20 N	123.19 E
Vallejo	226	38.06 N	122.15 W
Valle Lomellina	62	45.09 N	8.40 E
Vallelunga Pratameno	70	37.41 N	13.50 E
Valle Mosso	62	45.38 N	8.09 E
Vällen ⊜	40	60.03 N	18.20 E
Vallenar	252	28.35 S	70.46 W
Vallendar	56	50.24 N	7.37 E
Vallensbæk	41	55.38 N	12.22 E
Vallentuna	40	59.32 N	18.05 E
Vallepietra	66	41.55 N	13.14 E
Valleraugue	62	44.05 N	3.38 E
Valle Redondo	204	32.31 N	116.46 W
Vallermosa	71	39.22 N	8.48 E
Vallerotonda	66	41.33 N	13.55 E
Valleroy	56	49.12 N	5.55 E
Valles → Ciudad de Valles	234	21.59 N	99.01 W
Valles Caldera ±[6]	200	35.52 N	106.33 W
Vallet	32	47.10 N	1.16 W
Valletta	36	35.54 N	14.31 E
Valley, Al., U.S.	194	32.49 N	85.10 W
Valley, Ne., U.S.	198	41.18 N	96.20 W
Valley, Wa., U.S.	182	48.10 N	117.43 W
Valley ≃	184	51.21 N	99.55 W
Valley Bend	188	38.46 N	79.56 W
Valley Center, Ca., U.S.	228	33.13 N	117.02 W
Valley Center, Ks., U.S.	198	37.50 N	97.22 W
Valley City, N.D., U.S.	198	46.55 N	97.59 W
Valley City, Oh., U.S.	214	41.14 N	81.56 W
Valley Cottage	210	41.07 N	73.57 W
Valley Creek ≃, Pa., U.S.	285	40.06 N	75.28 W
Valley Creek ≃, Pa., U.S.	285	39.58 N	75.40 W
Valley Creek ≃, Tx., U.S.	196	31.43 N	100.02 W
Valleydale	280	34.06 N	117.56 W
Valley Falls, Ks., U.S.	198	39.20 N	95.27 W
Valley Falls, N.Y., U.S.	210	42.54 N	73.34 W
Valley Falls, R.I., U.S.	207	41.54 N	71.23 W
Valley Farms	200	32.59 N	111.26 W
Valleyfield	186	49.08 N	53.37 W
Valley Forge	208	40.05 N	75.28 W
Valley Forge Estates	285	40.05 N	75.26 W
Valley Forge National Historical Park ♦	208	40.06 N	75.27 W
Valley Grove	214	40.05 N	80.34 W
Valley Head, Al., U.S.	194	34.34 N	85.36 W
Valley Head, W.V., U.S.	188	38.32 N	80.02 W
Valley Home	226	37.50 N	120.55 W
Valley Mede	284b	39.17 N	76.50 W
Valley Mills	222	31.39 N	97.28 W
Valley of Desolation National Monument ♦	158	32.17 S	24.30 E
Valley of Fire State Park ♦	204	36.26 N	114.30 W
Valley of the Kings ⊥	140	25.45 N	32.37 E
Valley Park	219	38.32 N	90.29 W
Valley Plaza ⊸[9]	280	34.11 N	118.24 W
Valley Springs, Ca., U.S.	226	38.12 N	120.50 W
Valley Springs, S.D., U.S.	198	43.34 N	96.28 W
Valley Station	194	38.06 N	85.52 W
Valley Stream	210	40.39 N	73.42 W
Valley Stream ≃	276	40.39 N	73.45 W
Valley Stream State Park ♦	276	40.41 N	73.42 W
Valleyview, Ab., Can.	182	55.04 N	117.17 W
Valley View, Il., U.S.	216	41.50 N	88.03 W
Valley View, Oh., U.S.	279a	41.23 N	81.37 W
Valley View, Pa., U.S.	210	40.38 N	76.32 W
Valley View, Tx., U.S.	196	33.29 N	97.10 W
Vallgrund I	26	63.12 N	21.14 E
Valliant	196	34.00 N	95.05 W
Valli del Pasubio	64	45.41 N	11.15 E
Vallières	58	45.54 N	5.56 E
Vallimanca, Arroyo ≃	252	35.40 S	60.02 W
Vallio	64	45.38 N	10.23 E
Vallirana	266d	41.23 N	1.56 E
Vallø	41	55.24 N	12.15 E
Vallo della Lucania	68	40.14 N	15.17 E
Valloire	62	45.10 N	6.26 E
Vallombrosa	66	43.44 N	11.32 E
Vallonia	218	38.50 N	86.05 W
Vallon-Pont-d'Arc	62	44.24 N	4.24 E
Vallorbe	58	46.43 N	6.22 E
Vallorcine	58	46.02 N	6.56 E
Vallouise	62	44.51 N	6.29 E
Vallromanes	266d	41.32 N	2.18 E
Valls	34	41.17 N	1.15 E
Valluga ∧	58	47.09 N	10.12 E
Vallvidrera ⊸[8]	266d	41.25 N	2.07 E
Vallvidrera, Riera de ≃	266d	41.25 N	2.01 E
Val-Marie	184	49.14 N	107.44 W
Valmaseda	34	43.12 N	3.12 W
Valmeyer	219	38.17 N	90.18 W
Valmiera	76	57.33 N	25.24 E
Valmondois	261	49.06 N	2.12 E
Valmont	50	49.44 N	0.31 E
Valmontone	66	41.46 N	12.57 E
Valmy	56	49.05 N	4.46 E
Valognes	32	49.31 N	1.28 W
Valois	210	42.32 N	76.53 W
Valois, Baie de ⊂	275a	45.26 N	73.47 W
Valok	78	45.47 N	34.57 E
Valona → Vlorë	38	40.27 N	19.30 E
Valongo	34	41.11 N	8.30 W
Valoria la Buena	34	41.48 N	4.32 W
Valožyn	76	54.05 N	26.32 E
Vālpārai	122	10.22 N	76.58 E
Valparaíso, Bra.	255	21.13 S	50.51 W
Valparaíso, Chile	252	33.02 S	71.38 W
Valparaíso, Méx.	234	22.46 N	103.34 W
Valparaiso, Fl., U.S.	194	30.29 N	86.29 W
Valparaiso, In., U.S.	216	41.28 N	87.03 W
Valparaiso, Ne., U.S.	198	41.04 N	96.49 W
Valparaíso □[4]	252	32.45 S	71.20 W
Valparaíso ≃	234	22.33 N	103.39 W
Valpelline V	62	45.50 N	7.25 E
Valpovo	38	45.39 N	18.26 E
Valprato Soana	62	45.31 N	7.33 E
Valréas	62	44.23 N	4.59 E
Valrico	220	27.57 N	82.16 W
Val Roveto V	66	41.52 N	13.30 E
Vals ≃	158	27.23 S	26.30 E
Vals, Tanjung ≻	164	8.26 S	137.38 E
Val-Saint-Michel	206	46.52 N	71.27 W
Valsbaai ⊂	158	34.12 S	18.40 E
Valserine ≃	58	46.06 N	5.50 E
Valserrhein ≃	58	46.42 N	9.10 E
Valsertal V	58	46.37 N	9.10 E
Valsetz	202	44.50 N	123.39 W
Valsinni	68	40.10 N	16.26 E
Valsjöbyn	26	64.04 N	14.08 E
Valskog	40	59.27 N	15.57 E
Vals-les-Bains	62	44.40 N	4.22 E
Vals Platz	58	46.37 N	9.11 E
Vals-Près-le-Puy	62	45.01 N	3.52 E
Valstagna	64	45.51 N	11.39 E
Val-Suzon	58	47.25 N	4.54 E
Valtellina V	58	46.10 N	10.10 E
Valthermond	52	52.53 N	6.59 E
Valtice	61	48.44 N	16.45 E
Valtierrilla	234	20.32 N	101.08 W
Valtimo	26	63.40 N	28.48 E
Valtorta	58	45.59 N	9.32 E
Valtournanche	62	45.53 N	7.37 E
Valujec	76	52.46 N	33.23 E
Valujevka	80	46.44 N	43.43 E
Valujevo	265b	55.35 N	37.21 E
Valujki	78	50.13 N	38.08 E
Valvasone	64	45.59 N	12.52 E
Valverde	148	27.48 N	17.55 W
Valverde del Camino	34	37.34 N	6.45 W
Val Verde Park	228	34.27 N	118.40 W
Valyermo	228	34.26 N	117.50 W
Valyncy	76	55.42 N	28.11 E
Vamba ≃	152	7.27 S	14.17 E
Vamdrup	41	55.25 N	9.17 E
Våmhus	26	61.08 N	14.28 E
Vamizi, Ilha I	154	11.02 S	40.40 E
Vammala	26	61.20 N	22.54 E
Vamori Wash V	200	31.57 N	112.21 W
Van, Tür.	128	38.28 N	43.20 E
Van, Pa., U.S.	214	41.19 N	79.40 W
Van, Tx., U.S.	222	32.31 N	95.38 W
Van □[4]	128	39.00 N	43.45 E
Vanajavesi ⊜	26	61.09 N	24.15 E
Vanak ⊸[8]	267d	35.45 N	51.23 E
Van Alstyne	196	33.25 N	96.34 W
Vanån ≃	40	60.31 N	14.14 E
Vananda	182	49.45 N	124.33 W
Vanapa ≃	164	9.05 S	147.10 E
Vanault-les-Dames	56	48.51 N	4.46 E
Vanavana I[1]	14	20.47 S	139.09 W
Vanavara	74	60.22 N	102.16 E
Van Buren, Ar., U.S.	194	35.26 N	94.20 W
Van Buren, In., U.S.	216	40.37 N	85.30 W
Van Buren, Me., U.S.	186	47.09 N	67.56 W
Van Buren, Mo., U.S.	194	36.59 N	91.00 W
Van Buren, Oh., U.S.	216	41.08 N	83.38 W
Van Buren □[6]	216	42.14 N	86.04 W
Van Buren Point	214	42.27 N	79.25 W
Vanč	85	38.23 N	71.26 E
Vanč ≃	85	38.18 N	71.19 E
Vance Air Force Base ■	196	36.21 N	97.55 W
Vanceboro	188	45.33 N	67.25 W
Vanceburg	218	38.35 N	83.19 W
Vancleave	194	30.32 N	88.41 W
Van Cortlandt Park ♦	276	40.54 N	73.53 W
Van Cortlandtville	210	41.19 N	73.54 W
Vancouver, B.C., Can.	224	49.16 N	123.07 W
Vancouver, Wa., U.S.	224	45.38 N	122.39 W
Vancouver, Cape ≻, Austl.	162	35.01 S	118.12 E
Vancouver, Cape ≻, Ak., U.S.	180	60.33 N	165.27 W
Vancouver, Mount ∧	180	60.20 N	139.40 W
Vancouver International Airport ⊠	224	48.39 N	123.26 W
Vancouver Island I	182	49.45 N	126.00 W
Vancouver Island Ranges ⋏	182	49.25 N	125.25 W
Vancouver Lake ⊜	224	45.41 N	122.44 W
Van Daalen ≃	164	3.05 S	138.09 E
Vandalia, Il., U.S.	219	38.57 N	89.05 W
Vandalia, Mi., U.S.	216	41.55 N	85.55 W
Vandalia, Mo., U.S.	219	39.18 N	91.29 W
Vandalia, Oh., U.S.	218	39.53 N	84.11 W
Vandalia Lake ⊜[1]	219	39.01 N	89.09 W
Vändam	84	40.57 N	47.57 E
Vandavāsi	122	12.30 N	79.37 E
Vandekerckhove Lake ⊜	184	57.02 N	101.25 W
Vandel	41	55.42 N	9.13 E
Vandenberg Air Force Base ■	204	34.43 N	120.33 W
Van den Bosch, Tanjung ≻	164	4.06 S	132.55 E
Vandenesse	58	47.13 N	4.37 E
Vanderbijlpark	158	26.42 S	27.54 E
Vanderbilt, Mi., U.S.	190	45.08 N	84.39 W
Vanderbilt, Tx., U.S.	196	28.49 N	96.37 W
Vanderbilt Mansion National Historic Site ⊥	210	41.47 N	73.56 W
Vanderbilt Museum ♁	276	40.54 N	73.22 W
Vandercook Lake	216	42.11 N	84.23 W
Vandergrift	214	40.36 N	79.33 W
Vanderhoof	182	54.01 N	124.01 W
Vanderlin Island I	164	15.44 S	137.02 E
Vandervoort	194	34.22 N	94.21 W
Van Diemen, Cape ≻, Austl.	164	11.10 S	130.23 E
Van Diemen, Cape ≻, Austl.	164	16.31 S	139.41 E
Van Diemen Gulf ⊂	164	11.50 S	132.00 E
Vandling	210	41.38 N	75.29 W
Vandoeuvre-lès-Nancy	58	48.39 N	6.11 E
Vandoies (Vintl)	64	46.49 N	11.43 E
Vändra	76	58.39 N	25.02 E
Van Duzen ≃	204	40.33 N	124.08 W
Vandúzi ≃	154	18.56 S	34.01 E
Vandykpark	273d	26.16 S	28.19 E
Vandžiogala	76	55.07 N	23.58 E
Vanegas	234	23.51 N	100.52 W
Vänern ⊜	26	58.55 N	13.30 E
Vänersborg	26	58.22 N	12.19 E
Van Etten	210	42.11 N	76.33 W
Vang, Mount ∧	9	73.56 S	68.39 W
Vanga	154	4.39 S	39.13 E
Vangaindrano	157b	23.21 S	47.36 E
Vängelälven ≃	26	63.41 N	16.25 E
Van Gölü ⊜	128	38.33 N	42.46 E
Vangsnes	26	61.11 N	6.38 E
Vanguard	184	49.55 N	107.20 W
Vangunu, Mount ∧	175e	8.42 S	158.00 E
Vangunu Island I	175e	8.38 S	158.00 E
Van Hook Arm ⊂	198	47.50 N	102.25 W
Van Horn	196	31.02 N	104.49 W
Van Horne	190	42.00 N	92.05 W
Van Hornesville	210	42.54 N	74.50 W
Vani	84	42.06 N	42.30 E
Vanier	212	45.26 N	75.40 W
Vanikolo I	14	11.39 S	166.54 E
Vaniköy ⊸[8]	267b	41.04 N	29.04 E
Vanimo	164	2.40 S	141.20 E
Vanino	89	49.05 N	140.15 E
Vānīvilāsa Sāgara ⊜[1]	122	13.52 N	76.26 E
Vāniyambādi	122	12.41 N	78.37 E
Vânju Mare	38	44.26 N	22.52 E
Vankarem	180	67.51 N	175.50 W
Vankarem ≃	180	67.42 N	176.17 W
Vankarem, laguna ⊂	180	67.40 N	176.00 W
Vankaremskaja nizmennost' ≌	180	67.30 N	176.00 W
Van Kleef Aquarium ♦	271c	1.18 N	103.51 E
Vankleek Hill	206	45.31 N	74.39 W
Vanlay	50	48.02 N	4.01 E
Van Lear	192	37.46 N	82.45 W
Vanlue	216	40.58 N	83.28 W
Vanna I	24	70.09 N	19.51 E
Vännäs	26	63.55 N	19.45 E
Vanndale	194	35.18 N	90.46 W
Vanne ≃	50	48.12 N	3.16 E
Vanne et du Loing, Aqueduc de ≊[1]	261	48.36 N	2.26 E
Vannes	32	47.39 N	2.46 W
Vannes-sur-Cosson	50	47.43 N	2.13 E
Van Ninh	110	12.42 N	109.14 E
Van Norman Lakes ⊜[1]	228	34.18 N	118.28 W
Vannovka	85	42.32 N	70.21 E
Van Nuys ⊸[8]	228	34.11 N	118.26 W
Van Nuys Airport ⊠	280	34.12 N	118.29 W
Van Nuys-Sherman Oaks War Memorial Park ♦	280	34.10 N	118.27 W
Vanoi ≃	64	46.06 N	11.45 E
Vanoise, Massif de la ⋏	62	45.20 N	6.40 E
Vanoise, Parc National de la ♦	62	45.20 N	6.45 E
Van Ormer	214	40.41 N	78.30 W
Van Phong, Vung ⊂	110	12.33 N	109.18 E
Van Reenen	158	28.22 S	29.24 E
Van Reenen's Plaats	158	30.55 S	21.14 E
Van Rees, Pegunungan ⋏	164	2.35 S	138.15 E
Vanrhynsdorp	158	31.36 S	18.44 E
Vanrook	166	16.57 S	141.57 E
Vanryndam ⊜[1]	273d	26.09 S	28.21 E
Vansant	192	37.13 N	82.05 W
Van Saun Mill Brook ≃	276	40.55 N	74.03 W
Vansbro	40	60.31 N	14.13 E
Van Sciver Lake ⊜	285	40.09 N	74.48 W
Van Sickle Island I	282	38.04 N	121.53 W
Vansittart Island I	176	65.50 N	84.00 W
Vansjön ⊜	40	59.59 N	16.57 E
Vanskoje	76	58.56 N	36.52 E
Vanstadensrus	158	29.59 S	27.02 E
Vantaa (Vanda)	26	60.16 N	25.03 E
Vantaa ≃	26	60.13 N	24.59 E
Vanthali	120	21.29 N	70.20 E
Vanua Lava I	175f	13.48 S	167.28 E
Vanua Levu I	175g	16.33 S	179.15 E
Vanua Mbalavu Island I	175g	17.40 S	178.57 W
Vanuatu □[1], Oc.	14	16.00 S	167.00 E
Vanuatu □[1], Oc.	175f	16.00 S	167.00 E
Vanves	261	48.50 N	2.18 E
Van Vleck	222	29.01 N	95.53 W
Van Voorhis	279b	40.10 N	79.58 W
Van Wert	216	40.52 N	84.35 W
Van Wert □[6]	216	40.52 N	84.35 W
Vanwyksdorp	158	33.46 S	21.28 E
Vanwyksvlei	158	30.18 S	21.49 E
Vanzaghello	266b	45.35 N	8.47 E
Vanzago	266b	45.32 N	9.00 E
Van Zandt □[6]	222	32.35 N	95.50 W
Vanzylsrus	158	26.52 S	22.04 E
Vao	175f	22.39 S	167.32 E
Vapnyarka	78	48.32 N	28.44 E
Vaqueros Creek ≃	226	36.16 N	121.20 W
Var □[5]	62	43.30 N	6.20 E
Var ≃	62	43.39 N	7.12 E
Vara	26	58.16 N	12.57 E
Vara ≃	64	44.09 N	9.53 E
Varada ≃	122	14.55 N	75.40 E
Varadero	240p	23.09 N	81.16 W
Varades	32	47.23 N	1.02 W
Varages	62	43.36 N	5.58 E
Varaita ≃	62	44.49 N	7.36 E
Varaita, Valle V	62	44.35 N	7.10 E
Varakļāni	76	56.37 N	26.44 E
Varallo, It.	62	45.49 N	8.15 E
Varallo, It.	266b	45.40 N	8.38 E
Varāmīn	128	35.20 N	51.39 E
Vārānasi (Benares)	124	25.20 N	83.00 E
Varandej	24	68.48 N	58.00 E
Varangerfjorden ⊂[2]	24	70.00 N	30.00 E
Varangerhalvøya ≻[1]	24	70.25 N	29.30 E
Varangéville	56	48.38 N	6.19 E
Varano, Lago Di ⊂	68	41.53 N	15.45 E
Varano de'Melegari	64	44.41 N	10.01 E
Varapaeva	76	55.09 N	27.13 E
Varapodio	68	38.19 N	15.59 E
Varaždin	36	46.19 N	16.20 E
Varazze	62	44.22 N	8.34 E
Varberg	26	57.06 N	12.15 E
Varces	62	45.05 N	5.41 E
Varciche	84	42.08 N	42.43 E
Vardak □[4]	120	34.15 N	68.00 E
Vardaman	194	33.52 N	89.10 W
Vardar (Axiós) ≃	38	40.35 N	22.50 E
Varde	26	55.38 N	8.29 E
Vardenik	84	40.08 N	45.27 E
Vardenis	84	40.11 N	45.43 E
Vardenskij chrebet ⋏	84	39.58 N	45.25 E
Vardhoúsia Óri ⋏	38	38.44 N	22.07 E
Vardø	24	70.21 N	31.02 E
Vardūj ≃	123	37.01 N	70.47 E
Varedo	266b	45.36 N	9.09 E
Varegovo	80	57.47 N	39.17 E
Varel	52	53.22 N	8.10 E
Varela	252	34.07 S	66.27 W
Varėna	76	54.13 N	24.34 E
Varengeville-sur-Mer	50	49.55 N	0.59 E
Varenikovskaja	78	45.07 N	37.37 E
Varenna	58	46.01 N	9.17 E
Varenne ≃	50	49.53 N	1.08 E
Varennes	206	45.41 N	73.26 W
Varennes, Îles de II	275a	45.40 N	73.27 W
Varennes-en-Argonne	56	49.14 N	5.02 E
Varennes-Jarcy	261	48.41 N	2.34 E
Varennes-Saint-Sauveur	58	46.29 N	5.15 E
Varennes-sur-Allier	32	46.19 N	3.24 E
Varennes-sur-Amance	58	47.54 N	5.37 E
Varenovka	83	47.18 N	39.02 E
Vareš	38	44.09 N	18.19 E
Varese	62	45.48 N	8.48 E
Varese □[4]	62	45.48 N	8.40 E
Varese, Lago di ⊜	62	45.49 N	8.45 E
Varese Ligure	62	44.22 N	9.37 E
Varèze ≃	62	45.25 N	4.45 E
Varfolomejevka	80	50.01 N	48.12 E
Vârfurile	38	46.19 N	22.31 E
Vårgårda	26	58.02 N	12.48 E
Vargas □[5]	286c	10.34 N	66.52 W
Vargaši	86	55.23 N	65.48 E
Vargem	256	22.53 S	46.25 W
Vargem, Riacho da ≃	250	8.42 S	39.09 W
Vargem Alegre	256	22.30 S	43.55 W
Vargem do Laje	256	22.08 S	44.49 W
Vargem Grande	250	3.33 S	43.56 W
Vargem Grande ⊸[8]	287a	22.59 S	43.29 W
Vargem Grande, Ribeirão da ≃	256	22.17 S	45.40 W
Vargem Grande do Sul	256	21.50 S	46.53 W
Vargem Grande Paulista	256	23.36 S	47.01 W
Varginha	256	21.33 S	45.26 W
Vargön	26	58.22 N	12.22 E
Varigotti	62	44.11 N	8.24 E
Väringen ⊜	40	59.26 N	15.23 E
Varirata National Park ♦	164	9.20 S	147.20 E
Varjão	255	17.03 S	49.37 W
Varkallai	122	8.40 N	76.50 E
Varkaus	26	62.19 N	27.55 E
Varkhān ≃	128	32.55 N	65.30 E
Varlamovo	86	54.38 N	60.40 E
Värmdölandet I	40	59.20 N	18.33 E
Värmeln ⊜	26	59.32 N	12.54 E
Värmland □[9]	26	59.48 N	13.03 E
Värmlands Län □[6]	26	59.45 N	13.15 E
Värmlandsnäs ≻[1]	26	59.00 N	13.10 E
Varna, Blg.	38	43.13 N	27.55 E
Varna (Vahrn), It.	64	46.44 N	11.38 E
Varna, Ross.	86	53.24 N	60.58 E
Varna, N.Y., U.S.	210	42.27 N	76.26 W
Varna □[4]	38	43.24 N	27.33 E
Värnamo	26	57.11 N	14.02 E
Varnavino	80	57.24 N	45.04 E
Varnenski Zaliv ⊂	38	43.11 N	27.56 E
Varner-Hogg Plantation State Historic Park ♦	222	29.09 N	95.37 W
Varnhem	26	58.23 N	13.39 E
Varniai	76	55.45 N	22.22 E
Varnjany	76	54.44 N	26.01 E

ENGLISH

Name	Page	Lat.°′	Long.°′
Varnsdorf	54	50.52 N	14.40 E
Varnville	192	32.51 N	81.04 W
Värö	26	57.16 N	12.11 E
Városliget ♦	264c	47.31 N	19.06 E
Varpaisjärvi	26	63.22 N	27.45 E
Várpalota	30	47.12 N	18.09 E
Varpan ⊜	40	60.38 N	15.36 E
Varresbeck ⊸[8]	263	51.15 N	7.06 E
Vars, On., Can.	212	45.21 N	75.21 W
Vars, Fr.	62	44.37 N	6.41 E
Vars, Col de)(	62	44.32 N	6.42 E
Văršec	38	43.12 N	23.17 E
Varsi	62	44.40 N	9.51 E
Varsinais-Suomi ⊸[1]	26	60.40 N	22.30 E
Värska	76	57.58 N	27.38 E
Varsovie → Warszawa	30	52.15 N	21.00 E
Varsseveld	52	51.57 N	6.28 E
Vårsta	40	59.10 N	17.48 E
Varto	130	39.10 N	41.28 E
Vârtopu	38	44.12 N	23.21 E
V'artsil'a	24	62.11 N	30.41 E
Varty Lake ⊜	212	44.23 N	76.48 W
Varuna ≃	124	25.21 N	83.03 E
Varva	78	50.31 N	32.41 E
Varvarin	38	43.43 N	21.19 E
Varvarivka, Ukr.	78	48.42 N	36.02 E
Varvarivka, Ukr.	78	49.33 N	35.12 E
Varvarivka, Ukr.	83	49.05 N	38.24 E
Varysburg	210	42.46 N	78.19 W
Várzea	256	22.30 S	44.46 W
Várzea, Rio da ≃	252	27.13 S	53.19 W
Várzea Alegre	250	6.47 S	39.17 W
Várzea da Palma	255	17.36 S	44.44 W
Varzea de Sintra	266c	38.49 N	9.24 W
Várzea Grande	248	15.39 S	56.08 W
Varzeão	252	24.34 S	49.26 W
Várzea Paulista	256	23.12 S	46.50 W
Varzi, It.	62	44.49 N	9.12 E
Varzi, Ross.	80	56.03 N	52.50 E
Varzino	24	68.19 N	38.19 E
Varzo	58	46.12 N	8.15 E
Varzob	85	38.46 N	68.49 E
Varzob ≃	85	38.30 N	68.45 E
Varzuga	24	67.24 N	36.32 E
Varzy	50	47.22 N	3.23 E
Varzyk	85	41.07 N	71.14 E
Vas	64	45.56 N	11.56 E
Vas □[6]	30	47.05 N	16.45 E
Vasa → Vaasa	26	63.06 N	21.36 E
Vasai (Bassein)	122	19.21 N	72.48 E
Vasalemma	76	59.14 N	24.18 E
Vašana ≃	82	54.36 N	37.10 E
Vasar	272c	19.11 N	73.09 E
Vascão, Ribeirão do ≃	34	37.31 N	7.31 W
Vașcău	38	46.28 N	22.28 E
Väse	40	59.23 N	13.57 E
Vāshi	272c	19.04 N	72.59 E
Vashkivtsi, Ukr.	78	48.24 N	27.08 E
Vashkivtsi, Ukr.	78	48.23 N	25.30 E
Vashon	224	47.26 N	122.27 W
Vashon Heights	224	47.30 N	122.28 W
Vashon Island I	224	47.24 N	122.27 W
Vasil'euka	76	52.15 N	31.31 E
Vasilevičy	76	52.14 N	29.49 E
Vasilija, mys ≻	180	64.34 N	178.33 E
Vasiliká	38	40.28 N	23.08 E
Vasiliški	76	53.47 N	24.51 E
Vasiljevka	89	46.52 N	134.03 E
Vasiljevo, Ross.	24	60.46 N	38.59 E
Vasiljevo, Ross.	80	55.52 N	48.42 E
Vasiljevskij, ostrov I	265a	59.56 N	30.15 E
Vasiljevskij Moch	76	57.01 N	35.55 E
Vasiljevskoje, Ross.	80	56.56 N	41.40 E
Vasiljevskoje, Ross.	80	56.31 N	45.49 E
Vasiljevskoje, Ross.	82	55.00 N	37.25 E
Vasiljevskoje, Ross.	82	56.20 N	37.54 E
Vasil'sursk	80	56.08 N	46.01 E
Vasis	86	57.22 N	74.44 E
Vaška ≃	24	64.53 N	45.47 E
Vaskelovo	76	60.22 N	30.22 E
Vaskess Bay ⊂	174o	1.51 N	157.31 W
Vaslui	38	46.38 N	27.44 E
Vaslui □[6]	38	46.30 N	27.45 E
Väsman ⊜	40	60.11 N	15.04 E
Vass	192	35.15 N	79.16 W
Vassako-Bolo, Réserve Naturelle Intégrale de la ⊸[4]	146	8.10 N	19.45 E
Vassar	190	43.22 N	83.35 W
Vassdalseggi ∧	26	59.46 N	7.10 E
Vassieux-en-Vercors	62	44.53 N	5.22 E
Vassouras	256	22.25 S	43.40 W
Vassy	50	47.34 N	4.10 E
Västanfors	40	59.59 N	15.49 E
Västerås	40	59.37 N	16.33 E
Västeråsfjärden ⊂	40	59.34 N	16.34 E
Västerbotten □[9]	26	64.36 N	20.04 E
Västerbottens Län □[6]	24	64.00 N	17.30 E
Västerby	40	60.19 N	15.55 E
Västerdalälven ≃	40	60.33 N	15.08 E
Västerfärnebo	40	59.57 N	16.17 E
Västergötland □[9]	26	58.01 N	13.03 E
Västerhaninge	40	59.07 N	18.06 E
Västernorrlands Län □[6]	26	63.00 N	17.30 E
Västervik	26	57.45 N	16.38 E
Västmanland □[9]	40	59.38 N	15.15 E
Västmanlands Län □[6]	40	59.45 N	16.20 E
Vasto	66	42.07 N	14.42 E
Västra Laxsjön ⊜	40	58.54 N	14.38 E
Västra Ringsjön ⊜	41	55.53 N	13.28 E
Västra Torup	41	56.09 N	13.29 E
Vastseliina	76	57.44 N	27.17 E
Vas'ugan ≃	86	59.07 N	80.46 E
Vas'uganje ≡	86	58.00 N	77.00 E
Vas'unino	82	55.15 N	37.01 E
Vašutino	265b	55.56 N	37.26 E
Vašutkiny ozera ⊜	24	68.06 N	61.18 E
Vasvár	30	47.03 N	16.49 E
Vasylivka	78	47.26 N	35.16 E
Vasyl'kiv	78	50.12 N	30.19 E
Vasyl'kivka	78	48.13 N	36.02 E
Vát	61	47.17 N	16.47 E
Vața de Jos	38	46.10 N	22.35 E
Vatan	32	47.05 N	1.48 E
Vaternish Point ≻	46	57.36 N	6.38 W
Vatersay I	46	56.55 N	7.32 W
Vaterstetten	60	48.07 N	11.47 E
Vatican (Cité du) → Vatican City □[1]	267a	41.54 N	12.27 E
Vatican City (Città del Vaticano) □[1], Europe	66	41.54 N	12.27 E
Vatican City (Città del Vaticano) □[1], Europe	267a	41.54 N	12.27 E
Vaticano, Capo ≻	68	38.38 N	15.50 E
Vatikanstadt → Vatican City □[1]	66	41.54 N	12.27 E
V'atka → Kirov	80	58.38 N	49.42 E
V'atka ≃	80	55.36 N	51.30 E
Vatlirchvin, gora ∧	180	68.08 N	179.52 W
Vatnajökull ⊓	24a	64.25 N	16.50 W
Vatneyri	24a	65.38 N	23.57 W
Vätö I	40	59.49 N	18.57 E
Vatoa Island I	175g	19.50 S	178.13 W
Vatoloha ∧	157b	17.52 S	47.48 E
Vatomandry	157b	19.20 S	48.59 E
Vatra Dornei	38	47.21 N	25.21 E
V'atskije Pol'any	80	56.14 N	51.04 E
V'atskij uval ⋏[2]	80	57.20 N	49.10 E
V'atskoje, Ross.	80	57.52 N	40.16 E
V'atskoje, Ross.	89	48.44 N	135.43 E
Vattalkundu	122	10.10 N	77.46 E
Vättern ⊜	26	58.24 N	14.36 E
Vättersee → Vättern ⊜	26	58.24 N	14.36 E

DEUTSCH

Name	Seite	Breite°′	Länge°′ E = Ost
Vattholma	40	60.01 N	17.44 E
Vättis	58	46.55 N	9.27 E
Vatu Ira Channel ⋓	175g	17.17 S	178.31 E
Vatukoula	175g	17.31 S	177.51 E
Vatulele I	175g	18.33 S	177.37 E
Vatulino	82	55.39 N	36.09 E
Vatutine	78	49.02 N	31.04 E
Vaubecourt	56	48.56 N	5.07 E
Vauclaix	50	47.14 N	3.49 E
Vauclin, Montagne du ∧	240e	14.33 N	60.53 W
Vaucluse	274a	33.51 S	151.17 E
Vaucluse □[5]	62	44.00 N	5.10 E
Vaucluse, Fontaine de ⊥	62	43.55 N	5.08 E
Vaucluse, Plateau de ⋏[1]	62	44.00 N	5.22 E
Vaucouleurs	58	48.36 N	5.40 E
Vaucouleurs ≃	261	48.59 N	1.44 E
Vaud □[3]	58	46.40 N	6.30 E
Vaudherland	261	49.00 N	2.29 E
Vaudoy-en-Brie	50	48.41 N	3.05 E
Vaudreuil (Saint-Michel-de-Vaudreuil)	206	45.24 N	74.01 W
Vaudreuil □[6]	206	45.26 N	74.15 W
Vaudreuil, Baie de ⊂	275a	45.24 N	74.00 W
Vaufrey	58	47.21 N	6.55 E
Vaughan	212	43.47 N	79.36 W
Vaughn, N.M., U.S.	200	34.36 N	105.12 W
Vaughn, Wa., U.S.	224	47.21 N	122.46 W
Vaughnsville	216	40.53 N	84.09 W
Vaugneray	62	45.44 N	4.39 E
Vaugrigneuse	261	48.36 N	2.07 E
Vauhallan	261	48.44 N	2.12 E
Vaujours	261	48.56 N	2.35 E
Vaukavysk	76	53.10 N	24.28 E
Vaulovo	82	56.09 N	39.17 E
Vaulruz	58	46.37 N	6.59 E
Vaulx-en-Velin	62	45.47 N	4.56 E
Vaupés □[8]	246	0.45 N	70.30 W
Vaupés (Uaupés) ≃	246	0.02 N	67.16 W
Vauréal	261	49.02 N	2.02 E
Vauréal, Chute └	186	49.34 N	62.42 W
Vauvenargues	62	43.33 N	5.36 E
Vauvert	62	43.42 N	4.17 E
Vauvillers	58	47.55 N	6.06 E
Vauvise ≃	50	47.18 N	2.57 E
Vaux ≃	50	49.33 N	4.17 E
Vaux, Ru des ≃	261	48.42 N	2.00 E
Vauxhall	182	50.04 N	112.07 W
Vaux-le-Compte, Château de ⊥	50	48.36 N	2.43 E
Vaux-le-Pénil	261	48.32 N	2.41 E
Vaux-lès-Saint-Claude	58	46.22 N	5.44 E
Vaux-le-Vicomte, Château de ⊥	50	48.36 N	2.43 E
Vaux-Sous-Aubigny	58	47.39 N	5.17 E
Vaux-sur-Seine	261	49.00 N	1.58 E
Vavatenina	157b	17.28 S	49.12 E
Vava'u I	14	18.36 S	174.00 W
Vava'u Group II	14	18.40 S	174.00 W
Vavincourt	56	48.49 N	5.13 E
Vavoua	150	7.23 N	6.29 W
Vavož	80	56.47 N	51.55 E
Vavuniya	122	8.45 N	80.30 E
Vaxholm	40	59.24 N	18.20 E
Växjö	26	56.52 N	14.49 E
V'aža	78	49.16 N	41.01 E
Vaza-barris ≃	250	11.10 S	37.10 W
Vazante	255	18.00 S	46.54 W
Vazante Grande ≃	248	19.21 S	56.53 W
V'azemskij	89	47.32 N	134.48 E
Važgort	24	64.01 N	47.02 E
V'az'ma	76	55.13 N	34.18 E
V'az'ma ≃, Ross.	76	55.28 N	33.34 E
V'az'ma ≃, Ross.	82	56.29 N	35.49 E
V'azniki	80	56.15 N	42.10 E
Vazobe ∧	157b	18.25 S	47.18 E
V'azovaja	80	57.39 N	45.44 E
V'azovka, Ross.	80	48.19 N	45.36 E
V'azovka, Ross.	80	51.48 N	45.47 E
V'azovka, Ross.	80	52.52 N	48.24 E
V'azovka, Ross.	80	50.52 N	43.57 E
V'azovoje, Ross.	78	51.54 N	36.59 E
V'azovoje, Ross.	78	51.09 N	37.01 E
Vazuza ≃	76	56.10 N	34.35 E
Vazuzskoje vodochranilišče ⊜[1]	76	56.00 N	34.28 E
Vazzola	64	45.50 N	12.23 E
Veachland	218	38.12 N	85.11 W
Veado, Ilha do I	287a	22.57 S	43.06 W
Veazie	188	44.50 N	68.42 W
Veberöd	41	55.38 N	13.29 E
Veblen	198	45.51 N	97.17 W
Vecchiano	66	43.47 N	10.23 E
Vechelde	52	52.16 N	10.22 E
Vecht (Vechte) ≃	52	52.35 N	6.05 E
Vechta	52	52.43 N	8.16 E
Vechte (Vecht) ≃	52	52.35 N	6.05 E
Veckerhagen	52	51.30 N	9.35 E
Vecpiebalga	76	57.08 N	25.50 E
Vecsés	30	47.25 N	19.16 E
Vecumnieki	76	56.36 N	24.31 E
Vedado ⊸[8]	286b	23.08 N	82.24 W
Vedano al Lambro	266b	45.37 N	9.16 E
Vedano Olona	62	45.46 N	8.53 E
Vedāranniyam	122	10.22 N	79.51 E
Vedbæk	41	55.51 N	12.34 E
Vedder Crossing	224	49.06 N	121.57 W
Veddige	26	57.16 N	12.19 E
Vedea	38	44.47 N	24.37 E
Vedea ≃	38	43.43 N	25.32 E
Vedelago	64	45.41 N	12.01 E
Vedène	62	43.59 N	4.54 E
Vedeno	84	42.58 N	46.05 E
Vedeseta	58	45.53 N	9.32 E
Vedevåg	40	59.32 N	15.17 E
Vedi	84	39.56 N	44.42 E
Vedia	252	34.30 S	61.32 W
Vednoje	76	57.08 N	36.10 E
Vedomša	82	56.44 N	38.21 E
Vedrovo	80	57.33 N	42.52 E
Veedersburg	194	40.06 N	87.15 W
Veen	263	51.37 N	6.27 E
Veendam	52	53.06 N	6.58 E
Veenendaal	52	52.02 N	5.34 E
Veenhuizen	52	53.03 N	6.24 E
Veenoord	52	52.43 N	6.50 E
Veere	52	51.34 N	3.40 E
Veert	52	51.33 N	6.17 E
Vefsna ≃	24	65.50 N	13.12 E
Vega	196	35.15 N	102.26 W
Vega I	24	65.39 N	11.50 E
Vega, Arroyo de la ≃	266a	40.31 N	3.33 W
Vega Alta	240m	18.25 N	66.20 W
Vega Baja	240m	18.27 N	66.23 W
Vega Point ≻	181a	51.49 N	177.16 E
Vegår ⊜	26	58.48 N	8.47 E
Vegesack ⊸[8]	52	53.10 N	8.37 E
Veghel	52	51.37 N	5.33 E
Veglie	68	40.20 N	17.58 E
Vegreville	182	53.30 N	112.03 W
Veguita	200	34.30 N	106.46 W
Vehār Lake ⊜	272c	19.09 N	72.55 E
Vehlefanz	264a	52.43 N	13.06 E
Vehnemoor ⊸[3]	52	53.05 N	8.00 E
Veigné	50	47.17 N	0.44 E
Veil, Loch ⊜	46	56.20 N	4.25 W
Veilsdorf	54	50.24 N	10.48 E
Veinte de Noviembre	196	25.47 N	97.33 W
Veinticinco de Agosto	258	34.24 S	56.25 W
Veinticinco de Mayo, Arg.	252	35.26 S	60.10 W
Veinticinco de Mayo, Arg.	252	34.35 S	68.33 W
Veinticinco de Mayo, Ur.	258	34.12 S	56.22 W
Veintiocho de Mayo	246	3.50 S	78.52 W

Symbols in the index entries represent the broad categories identified in the key at the right. Symbols with superior numbers (⋏[1]) identify subcategories (see complete key on page *I · 1).*

Symbole im Register stellen die rechts im Schlüssel erklärten Kategorien dar. Symbole mit hochgestellten Ziffern (⋏[1]) bezeichnen Unterabteilungen einer Kategorie (vgl. vollständiger Schlüssel auf Seite *I · 1).*

Los símbolos incluídos en el texto del índice representan las grandes categorías identificadas con la clave a la derecha. Los símbolos con numeros en su parte superior (⋏[1]) identifican las subcategorías (véase la clave completa en la página *I · 1).*

Les symboles de l'index représentent les catégories indiquées dans la légende à droite. Les symboles suivis d'un indice (⋏[1]) représentent des sous-catégories (voir légende complète à la page *I · 1).*

Os símbolos incluídos no texto do índice representam as grandes categorias identificadas com a chave à direita. Os símbolos com números em sua parte superior (⋏[1]) identificam as subcategorias (veja-se a chave completa à página *I · 1).*

	English	Deutsch	Español	Français	Português
∧	Mountain	Berg	Montaña	Montagne	Montanha
⋏	Mountains	Gebirge	Montañas	Montagnes	Montanhas
)(	Pass	Paß	Paso	Col	Passo
V	Valley, Canyon	Tal, Cañon	Valle, Cañón	Vallée, Canyon	Vale, Canhão
≌	Plain	Ebene	Llano	Plaine	Planície
≻	Cape	Kap	Cabo	Cap	Cabo
I	Island	Insel	Isla	Île	Ilha
II	Islands	Inseln	Islas	Îles	Ilhas
±	Other Topographic Features	Andere Topographische Objekte	Otros Elementos Topográficos	Autres données topographiques	Outros acidentes topográficos

ESPAÑOL · FRANÇAIS · PORTUGUÊS

Nombre / Nom / Nome	Página / Page	Lat.°′	Long.°′ W = Oeste / W = Ouest
Veintiocho de Noviembre	254	51.39 S	72.18 W
Veintisiete de Abril	236	10.15 N	85.45 W
Veio ⊥	66	42.02 N	12.24 E
Veiros	250	2.05 S	52.10 W
Veisiejai	76	54.06 N	23.42 E
Veitsbronn	56	49.31 N	10.53 E
Veitsch	61	47.35 N	15.30 E
Veitschalpe ⋏	61	47.39 N	15.30 E
Veitshöchheim	56	49.50 N	9.52 E
Vejbystrand	41	56.19 N	12.45 E
Vejdelevka	78	50.09 N	38.27 E
Vejen	41	55.29 N	9.09 E
Vejer de la Frontera	34	36.15 N	5.58 W
Vejlby	41	56.12 N	10.13 E
Vejle	41	55.42 N	9.32 E
Vejle □[6]	41	55.45 N	9.30 E
Vejle Fjord ⊂	41	55.40 N	9.50 E
Vejprty	54	50.30 N	13.02 E
Vejrhøj ∧[2]	41	55.47 N	11.24 E
Vejrø ❙	41	55.02 N	11.22 E
Vekšor	24	60.33 N	49.26 E
Vel'a ≐	82	56.31 N	37.41 E
Vela Luka	36	42.58 N	16.43 E
Velapāda	272c	18.59 N	73.04 E
Velardeña	232	25.04 N	103.44 W
Velas	148a	38.41 N	28.13 W
Velas, Cabo ➤	236	10.22 N	85.53 W
Velázquez	252	34.02 S	54.17 W
Velbert	56	51.20 N	7.02 E
Velburg	60	49.14 N	11.41 E
Velddrif	158	32.47 S	18.11 E
Velden, Dtsch.	60	48.19 N	12.16 E
Velden, Dtsch.	60	49.37 N	11.31 E
Velden, Öst.	61	46.37 N	14.03 E
Veldhoven	52	51.24 N	5.24 E
Velebit ⋏	36	44.38 N	15.03 E
Velebitski Kanal ʊ	36	45.00 N	14.50 E
Velegož	82	54.42 N	37.16 E
Veleka ≐	38	42.04 N	27.58 E
Velemín	54	50.33 N	13.59 E
Velen	52	51.53 N	6.59 E
Velencei-tó ⊜	30	47.12 N	18.35 E
Velesa ≐	76	56.03 N	31.58 E
Velešín	61	48.50 N	14.28 E
Velestínon	38	39.23 N	22.45 E
Velet'ma	80	55.20 N	42.25 E
Veleųščyna	76	54.44 N	28.35 E
Vélez	246	6.01 N	73.41 W
Velez de la Gomera, Peñón de ❙	34	35.11 N	4.21 W
Vélez-Málaga	34	36.47 N	4.06 W
Vélez-Rubio	34	37.39 N	2.04 W
Velgast	54	54.16 N	12.48 E
Vel'gija	76	58.23 N	33.59 E
Velhas, Canal do ≡	287a	22.42 S	43.22 W
Velhas, Rio das ≐	255	17.13 S	44.49 W
Veličkovo	82	54.59 N	36.46 E
Velika Gorica	36	45.43 N	16.05 E
Velikaja, Ross.	24	59.13 N	49.04 E
Velikaja, Ross.	180	64.04 N	176.12 E
Velikaja ≐, Ross.	74	64.40 N	176.20 E
Velikaja ≐, Ross.	76	57.48 N	28.20 E
Velikaja Kema	89	45.30 N	137.12 E
Velika Kapela ⋏	36	45.15 N	15.00 E
Velika Morava ≐	38	44.43 N	21.03 E
Velika Plana	38	44.20 N	21.04 E
Velike Lašče	36	45.50 N	14.38 E
Veliki Bečkerek → Zrenjanin	38	45.23 N	20.24 E
Velikij Dvor	82	56.46 N	37.25 E
Velikije Luki	76	56.20 N	30.32 E
Velikij Ust'ug	24	60.48 N	46.18 E
Veliki kanal ≡	38	45.45 N	18.50 E
Veliki Stol (Hochstuhl) ∧	61	46.26 N	14.10 E
Veliki Vitorog ∧	36	44.07 N	17.03 E
Velikoarchangel'skoje	78	50.51 N	40.46 E
Velikodvorskaja	76	60.18 N	41.58 E
Velikodvorskij	80	55.15 N	40.41 E
Veliko Gradište	38	44.45 N	21.32 E
Velikoje, Ross.	76	59.32 N	36.59 E
Velikoje, Ross.	80	57.21 N	39.47 E
Velikoje, ozero ⊜, Ross.	76	57.02 N	36.34 E
Velikoje, ozero ⊜, Ross.	80	55.13 N	40.10 E
Velikonda Hills ⋏[2]	122	14.45 N	79.10 E
Velikookt'abr'skij	76	57.26 N	33.49 E
Velikorusskoje	86	54.39 N	74.38 E
Veliko Tărnovo	38	43.04 N	25.39 E
Velikovisočnoje	24	67.16 N	52.01 E
Velikovo	76	59.18 N	42.08 E
Velilla de San Antonio	266a	40.22 N	3.29 W
Veli Lošinj	36	44.31 N	14.30 E
Vélingara, Sén.	150	15.00 N	14.40 W
Vélingara, Sén.	150	13.09 N	14.07 W
Velingrad	38	42.04 N	24.00 E
Velino ≐	66	42.33 N	12.43 E
Velino, Monte ∧	66	42.09 N	13.23 E
Velіž	76	55.38 N	31.12 E
Veližany	86	57.34 N	65.49 E
Vélizy-Villacoublay	261	48.47 N	2.10 E
Veljaminovo, Ross.	82	55.12 N	37.52 E
Veljaminovo, Ross.	82	55.53 N	36.52 E
Velká Bíteš	30	49.17 N	16.13 E
Vel'ké Kapušany	30	48.33 N	22.04 E
Velké Meziříčí	30	49.21 N	16.00 E
Velké Němčie	61	48.59 N	16.40 E
Velké Pavlovice	61	48.54 N	16.49 E
Velký Bor	60	49.22 N	13.42 E
Velký Šenov	54	51.00 N	14.25 E
Velký Zvon ∧	60	49.33 N	12.39 E
Vellach ≐	61	46.35 N	14.29 E
Vella Gulf ʊ	175e	8.00 S	156.50 E
Vella Lavella ❙	175e	7.45 S	156.40 E
Vellano	66	43.57 N	10.43 E
Vellār ≐	122	11.29 N	79.46 E
Vellberg	56	49.05 N	9.53 E
Vellechevreux-et-Courbenans	58	47.33 N	6.32 E
Velletri	66	41.41 N	12.47 E
Vellinge	41	55.28 N	13.01 E
Vellmar	56	51.21 N	9.28 E
Vellore, On., Can.	275b	43.50 N	79.34 W
Vellore, India	122	12.56 N	79.08 E
Velm	264b	48.03 N	16.27 E
Velma	196	34.27 N	97.40 W
Vel'maj ≐	180	67.26 N	175.28 W
Velmede	56	51.21 N	8.22 E
Velo d'Astico	64	45.43 N	11.23 E
Velp	52	52.00 N	5.59 E
Velp ≐	56	50.58 N	5.05 E
Velpke	54	52.24 N	10.56 E
Velsen	52	52.27 N	4.39 E
Vel'sk	24	61.05 N	42.05 E
Vel't	24	68.03 N	49.55 E
Velten	54	52.41 N	13.10 E
Veltheim	52	52.11 N	8.58 E
Veltrusy	54	50.14 N	14.18 E
Veluwe ◆[1]	52	52.12 N	5.45 E
Veluwemeer ⊜	52	52.22 N	5.38 E
Velva, It.	62	44.16 N	9.33 E
Velva, N.D., U.S.	198	48.03 N	100.55 W
Velvary	54	50.15 N	14.15 E
Velyka Bahachka	78	49.47 N	33.43 E
Velyka Bilozerka	78	47.16 N	34.42 E
Velyka Blahovishchenka	78	46.51 N	34.03 E
Velyka Chernihivka	83	48.57 N	39.25 E
Velyka Danylivka	78	50.04 N	36.19 E
Velyka Dymerka	78	50.36 N	30.55 E
Velyka Hlusha	78	51.49 N	25.02 E
Velyka Korenykha	78	46.57 N	31.54 E
Velyka Koshnytsya	78	48.09 N	28.27 E
Velyka Lepetykha	78	47.11 N	33.56 E
Velyka Mykhaylivka	78	47.04 N	29.52 E
Velyka Novosilka	78	47.50 N	36.50 E
Velyka Oleksandrivka	78	47.20 N	33.18 E
Velyka Rublivka	78	49.53 N	34.49 E
Velyka Vradyyivka	78	47.52 N	30.35 E
Velyki Birky	78	49.32 N	25.45 E
Velyki Dederkaly	78	50.02 N	26.07 E
Velyki Kopani	78	46.29 N	32.59 E
Velyki Korovyntsi	78	49.59 N	28.17 E
Velyki Krynky	78	49.27 N	33.29 E
Velyki Luchky	78	48.26 N	22.35 E
Velyki Mosty	78	50.14 N	24.06 E
Velyki Sorochyntsi	78	50.03 N	33.56 E
Velykoanadol's'kyy lis ♠	83	47.42 N	37.23 E
Velykodolyns'ke	78	46.21 N	30.35 E
Velykoplos'ke	78	47.01 N	29.40 E
Velykots'k	83	49.21 N	40.02 E
Velykyy Bereznyy	78	48.53 N	22.27 E
Velykyy Burluk	78	50.05 N	37.24 E
Velykyy Bychkiv	78	47.58 N	24.03 E
Velykyy Hlubochyk	78	49.37 N	25.32 E
Velykyy Khutir	78	49.52 N	32.06 E
Velykyy Kuyal'nyk ≐	78	46.46 N	30.36 E
Velykyy Loh	83	48.15 N	39.33 E
Velykyy Sukhodil	83	48.25 N	39.53 E
Velykyy Vys' ≐	78	48.45 N	30.54 E
Velykyy Zhvanchyk	78	48.46 N	26.59 E
Velymche	78	51.36 N	24.44 E
Vémars	261	49.04 N	2.34 E
Vemdalen	26	62.27 N	13.52 E
Vemmenæs	41	54.59 N	10.40 E
Ven ❙	41	55.54 N	12.41 E
Venachar, Loch ⊜	46	56.13 N	4.19 W
Venaco	36	42.14 N	9.10 E
Venadillo	246	4.43 N	74.55 W
Venado	234	22.56 N	101.05 W
Venado, Isla ❙	241r	10.00 N	62.25 W
Venado, Isla del ❙	236	11.57 N	83.44 W
Venado Tuerto	252	33.45 S	61.58 W
Venafiorita, Aeroporto di ⊠	71	40.53 N	9.30 E
Venafro	66	41.29 N	14.02 E
Venâncio Aires	252	29.36 S	52.11 W
Venango	214	41.46 N	80.07 W
Venango □[6]	214	41.24 N	79.50 W
Venanson	62	44.03 N	7.15 E
Venant	261	48.30 N	2.06 E
Venarey-les-Laumes	58	47.32 N	4.26 E
Venaria	62	45.08 N	7.38 E
Venasca	62	44.33 N	7.24 E
Venasque	62	43.59 N	5.09 E
Vence	62	43.43 N	7.07 E
Venceslau Brás	256	22.31 S	45.21 W
Venceslau Braz	255	23.51 S	49.48 W
Vencimont	56	50.02 N	4.55 E
Venda □[9]	156	23.00 S	30.30 E
Venda Nova	34	41.40 N	7.58 W
Vendargues	62	43.39 N	3.58 E
Vendas Novas	34	38.41 N	8.28 W
Vendée □[5]	32	46.40 N	1.20 W
Vendéen, Bocage ◆[1]	32	46.40 N	1.30 W
Vendel	40	60.10 N	17.36 E
Vendelsö	40	59.12 N	18.12 E
Vendeuvre-sur-Barse	58	48.14 N	4.28 E
Vendin-lès-Béthune	50	50.32 N	2.37 E
Vendin-le-Vieil	50	50.28 N	2.52 E
Vendôme	50	47.48 N	1.04 E
Vendsyssel ◆[1]	26	57.20 N	10.00 E
Vendychany	78	48.37 N	27.48 E
Venecia, C.R.	236	10.22 N	84.17 W
Venecia → Venezia, It.	64	45.27 N	12.21 E
Venedig → Venezia	64	45.27 N	12.21 E
Venedocia	216	40.44 N	84.25 W
Venedy	219	38.24 N	89.39 W
Veneta, Laguna ⊂	64	45.25 N	12.19 E
Venetia	214	40.15 N	80.03 W
Venetian Village	216	42.24 N	88.02 W
Venetie	180	67.01 N	146.25 W
Veneto □[4]	64	45.30 N	11.45 E
Venev	82	54.21 N	38.16 E
Venezia (Venice)	64	45.27 N	12.21 E
Venezia □[4]	64	45.35 N	12.34 E
Venezuela □[1], S.A.	242	8.00 N	66.00 W
Venezuela □[1], S.A.	246	8.00 N	66.00 W
Venezuela, Golfo de ⊂	246	11.30 N	71.00 W
Venezuelan Basin ✣[1]	16	15.00 N	68.00 W
Veng	41	56.07 N	9.53 E
Vengerovo	86	55.41 N	76.45 E
Vengurla	122	15.52 N	73.38 E
Veniaminof, Mount ∧	180	56.13 N	159.18 W
Venice → Venezia, It.	64	45.27 N	12.21 E
Venice, Fl., U.S.	220	27.05 N	82.27 W
Venice, Il., U.S.	219	38.40 N	90.10 W
Venice, La., U.S.	194	29.16 N	89.21 W
Venice, Oh., U.S.	214	41.27 N	82.46 W
Venice, Pa., U.S.	279b	40.19 N	80.14 W
Venice ◆[8]	228	34.00 N	118.29 W
Venice, Gulf of ⊂	64	45.15 N	13.00 E
Venice Gardens	220	27.04 N	82.26 W
Venise → Venezia	64	45.27 N	12.21 E
Vénissieux	62	45.41 N	4.53 E
Venjan	26	60.57 N	13.55 E
Venjansjön ⊜	26	60.54 N	14.00 E
Venkatagiri	122	13.58 N	79.35 E
Venlo	52	51.24 N	6.10 E
Vennesla	26	58.17 N	7.59 E
Vennhausen ◆[8]	263	51.13 N	6.51 E
Venosa	68	40.57 N	15.49 E
Vénosc	62	44.59 N	6.07 E
Venosta, Val ∨	64	46.40 N	10.35 E
Venoste, Alpi (Ötztaler Alpen) ⋏	64	46.45 N	10.55 E
Venray	52	51.32 N	5.59 E
Vent	64	46.52 N	10.56 E
Vent, Îles du → Windward Islands ❙❙	238	13.00 N	61.00 W
Venta ≐	76	57.24 N	21.33 E
Ventanas	246	1.23 S	79.25 W
Ventasso, Monte ∧	64	44.23 N	10.17 E
Ventersburg	158	28.09 S	27.08 E
Ventersdorp	158	26.17 S	26.48 E
Venterspos	273d	26.18 S	27.39 E
Venterstad	158	30.47 S	25.48 E
Venticano	68	41.05 N	14.50 E
Ventimiglia	62	43.47 N	7.36 E
Ventimiglia di Sicilia	70	37.55 N	13.34 E
Ventnor	42	50.36 N	1.11 W
Ventnor City	208	39.20 N	74.28 W
Ventotene	66	40.48 N	13.26 E
Ventotene, Isola ❙	66	40.47 N	13.25 E
Ventoux, Mont ∧	62	44.10 N	5.17 E
Ventry	48	52.08 N	10.22 W
Ventspils	76	57.24 N	21.36 E
Ventuari ≐	246	3.58 N	67.02 W
Ventura (San Buenaventura)	228	34.16 N	119.17 W
Ventura □[6]	228	34.30 N	119.00 W
Ventura ≐	228	34.16 N	119.18 W
Venturina	66	43.02 N	10.36 E
Venus, Fl., U.S.	220	27.04 N	81.21 W
Venus, Pa., U.S.	214	41.22 N	79.29 W
Venus, Tx., U.S.	222	32.26 N	97.06 W
Vénus, Pointe ➤	174s	17.29 S	149.29 W
Venus Bay ⊂	169	38.40 S	145.43 E
Venustiano Carranza, Méx.	232	16.21 N	92.33 W
Venustiano Carranza, Méx.	234	20.31 N	97.38 W
Venustiano Carranza, Méx.	234	19.44 N	103.47 W
Venustiano Carranza, Bahía ⊂	232	19.20 N	87.35 W
Venustiano Carranza, Presa ⊜[1]	232	27.30 N	100.40 W
Venzone	64	46.20 N	13.09 E
Véore ≐	62	44.49 N	4.49 E
Vép	61	47.14 N	16.44 E
Vepryk	78	50.23 N	34.11 E
Vepsovskaja vozvyšennost' ⋏[1]	76	60.20 N	35.15 E
Ver ≐	42	51.42 N	0.20 W
Vera, Arg.	252	29.28 S	60.13 W
Vera, Esp.	34	37.15 N	1.52 W
Vera, Il., U.S.	219	39.02 N	89.07 W
Veracruz, Méx.	200	32.25 N	115.05 W
Veracruz, Méx.	234	19.12 N	96.08 W
Vera Cruz, Pa., U.S.	208	40.30 N	75.30 W
Veracruz □[3]	234	19.20 N	96.40 W
Veraguas □[4]	236	8.30 N	81.00 W
Veramejki	76	53.46 N	31.15 E
Verano Brianza	266b	45.41 N	9.14 E
Veranópolis	252	28.57 S	51.33 W
Verāval	120	20.54 N	70.22 E
Verba	78	50.17 N	25.37 E
Verbania	58	45.56 N	8.33 E
Verbank	210	41.44 N	73.43 W
Verbano-Cusio-Ossola □[4]	58	46.05 N	8.20 E
Verbeek, Pegunungan ⋏	112	2.35 S	121.25 E
Verberg ◆[8]	263	51.22 N	6.36 E
Verberie	50	49.19 N	2.44 E
Verbicaro	68	39.45 N	15.55 E
Verbier	58	46.06 N	7.13 E
Verbilki	82	56.32 N	37.36 E
Verbinskij	83	47.53 N	40.02 E
Verblyuzhka	78	48.23 N	32.54 E
Verbovskij	80	55.32 N	42.00 E
Vercelli	62	45.19 N	8.25 E
Vercelli □[4]	62	45.37 N	8.20 E
Vercel-Villedieu-le-Camp	58	47.11 N	6.24 E
Verch'aja Irmen'	86	54.35 N	82.14 E
Verchazovka	80	50.56 N	48.46 E
Vercheje Talyzino	80	55.06 N	45.49 E
Verchères	206	45.47 N	73.21 W
Verchères □[6]	206	45.45 N	73.20 W
Verchn'aja Amga	74	59.30 N	126.08 E
Verchn'aja Angara ≐	88	55.42 N	109.54 E
Verchn'aja Balkarija	84	43.06 N	43.24 E
Verchn'aja Buzinovka	80	49.04 N	43.12 E
Verchn'aja Čebula	86	56.02 N	87.36 E
Verchn'aja Chava	78	51.50 N	39.56 E
Verchn'aja Chila	88	52.06 N	115.54 E
Verchn'aja Dobrinka	80	50.46 N	45.03 E
Verchn'aja Gniluša	78	50.16 N	40.23 E
Verchn'aja Grajvoronka	78	51.41 N	37.46 E
Verchn'aja Inta	24	66.00 N	60.20 E
Verchn'aja Maza	80	52.58 N	47.56 E
Verchn'aja Orl'anka	80	53.44 N	51.04 E
Verchn'aja Pyšma	86	56.55 N	60.37 E
Verchn'aja Salda	86	58.02 N	60.33 E
Verchn'aja Serebr'akovka	80	47.21 N	42.14 E
Verchn'aja Sin'ačicha	86	57.59 N	61.40 E
Verchn'aja Sysert'	86	56.26 N	60.46 E
Verchn'aja Tajmyra ≐	74	74.15 N	99.48 E
Verchn'aja Tarka	86	56.37 N	77.30 E
Verchnaja Tereška	80	52.54 N	47.24 E
Verchn'aja Tišanka	78	51.19 N	40.32 E
Verchn'aja Tojma	24	62.13 N	45.00 E
Verchn'aja Troica	76	57.15 N	37.08 E
Verchn'aja Tura	86	58.22 N	59.49 E
Verchn'aja Zaimka	88	55.51 N	110.09 E
Verchn'aja Zima	88	53.48 N	101.47 E
Verchneaks'onovskij	80	48.21 N	42.38 E
Verchneangarskij chrebet ⋏	88	56.20 N	111.30 E
Verchne-Anikin	83	48.09 N	39.59 E
Verchnebakanskij	78	44.52 N	37.39 E
Verchneber'ozovskij	86	50.17 N	82.13 E
Verchnebuzanskij	80	46.38 N	48.02 E
Verchnecaricynskij	80	48.23 N	43.57 E
Verchnedneprovskij	76	54.59 N	33.21 E
Verchneimbatskoje	74	63.11 N	87.58 E
Verchnejarkejevo	80	55.27 N	54.19 E
Verchneje Šachlovo	82	55.02 N	37.15 E
Verchnemakejevka	78	49.10 N	41.03 E
Verchnemulomskoje vodochranilišče ⊜[1]	24	68.30 N	31.05 E
Verchnesjezžeje	80	52.44 N	51.15 E
Verchnespasskoje	80	52.39 N	41.47 E
Verchnetulomskij	24	68.38 N	31.45 E
Verchneural'sk	86	53.53 N	59.13 E
Verchneusinskoje	86	52.14 N	93.01 E
Verchnevil'ujsk	74	63.27 N	120.18 E
Verchnevolynskoje	85	40.43 N	68.51 E
Verchnij Amyl	88	53.08 N	94.30 E
Verchnij Avz'an	86	53.32 N	57.33 E
Verchnij Balyklej	80	49.34 N	45.10 E
Verchnij Baskunčak	80	48.14 N	46.44 E
Verchnij Byk	78	50.43 N	41.14 E
Verchnije Dvoriki	82	56.28 N	38.22 E
Verchnije Kigi	86	55.25 N	58.37 E
Verchnije Korobki	80	50.19 N	44.38 E
Verchnije Lipki	80	49.38 N	43.51 E
Verchnije Tatyšly	86	56.17 N	55.52 E
Verchnij Ikorec	78	51.11 N	39.46 E
Verchnij Karačan	80	51.24 N	41.46 E
Verchnij Krasnyj Pereval	89	46.33 N	134.37 E
Verchnij Kužebar	86	53.22 N	93.15 E
Verchnij Landech	80	56.51 N	42.36 E
Verchnij Leb'ažinskij	80	46.45 N	47.50 E
Verchnij Lomov	80	53.28 N	43.34 E
Verchnij Lomovec	76	52.13 N	38.37 E
Verchnij Mamon	78	50.10 N	40.23 E
Verchnij Most	76	57.31 N	28.50 E
Verchnij Nejvinskij	86	57.17 N	60.09 E
Verchnij Petr'ak	86	57.29 N	77.30 E
Verchnij Šergol'džin	88	50.12 N	108.20 E
Verchnij Tagil	86	57.22 N	59.56 E
Verchnij Takermen'	80	55.39 N	52.43 E
Verchnij Ufalej	86	56.04 N	60.14 E
Verchnij Ul'chun	88	49.34 N	112.32 E
Verchnij Uslon	80	55.47 N	48.57 E
Verchnij Zub, gora ∧	86	53.45 N	89.15 E
Verchnyje Nikul'asy	76	60.25 N	30.45 E
Verchnyj Jenisej (Ulug-Chem) ≐	88	51.47 N	92.00 E
Verchojansk	74	67.35 N	133.27 E
Verchojanskij chrebet ⋏	74	67.00 N	129.00 E
Vercholensk	88	54.06 N	105.35 E
Verchopuja	24	61.34 N	41.31 E
Verchošižemje	80	58.01 N	49.07 E
Verchososna	78	50.44 N	38.14 E
Verchoturje	86	58.52 N	60.48 E
Verchoturovo	86	58.22 N	95.21 E
Verchovažje	24	60.45 N	42.00 E
Verchovino	76	59.33 N	43.19 E
Verchovje	76	52.49 N	37.14 E
Verchovl'an'	82	55.03 N	38.21 E
Verchozim	80	52.56 N	46.23 E
Verchuba	86	50.29 N	82.26 E
Verclause	62	44.23 N	5.26 E
Vercors ◆[1]	62	44.57 N	5.25 E
Verdalsøra	26	63.48 N	11.29 E
Verde ≐, Bra.	248	11.54 S	55.48 W
Verde ≐, Bra.	248	13.33 S	58.01 W
Verde ≐, Bra.	250	10.27 S	42.16 W
Verde ≐, Bra.	255	15.07 S	48.40 W
Verde ≐, Bra.	255	17.05 S	46.05 W
Verde ≐, Bra.	255	18.01 S	50.14 W
Verde ≐, Bra.	255	19.11 S	50.44 W
Verde ≐, Bra.	255	19.55 S	49.45 W
Verde ≐, Bra.	255	21.12 S	51.53 W
Verde ≐, Bra.	256	21.34 S	45.31 W
Verde ≐, Bra.	256	21.38 S	47.03 W
Verde ≐, Méx.	234	16.45 N	98.07 W
Verde ≐, Méx.	234	20.42 N	103.14 W
Verde ≐, Méx.	234	21.37 N	99.15 W
Verde ≐, Méx.	234	15.59 N	97.47 W
Verde ≐, Para.	252	23.09 S	57.37 W
Verde ≐, S.A.	248	13.59 S	60.24 W
Verde ≐, Az., U.S.	200	33.33 N	111.40 W
Verde, Arroyo ≐, Arg.	254	41.56 S	65.03 W
Verde, Arroyo ≐, Bol.	248	11.25 S	66.20 W
Verde, Cape ➤	238	22.50 N	74.52 W
Verde, Cerro ∧	234	20.30 N	104.36 W
Verde, Costa ±[2]	71	39.34 N	8.28 E
Verde Grande ≐	255	14.35 S	43.53 W
Verde Island ❙	116	13.33 N	121.05 E
Verde Island Passage ʊ	116	13.34 N	120.51 E
Verdello	62	45.36 N	9.37 E
Verden, Dtsch.	52	52.55 N	9.13 E
Verden, Ok., U.S.	196	35.05 N	98.05 W
Verde Pequeno ≐	255	14.48 S	43.31 W
Verdesela, Pinhal da ♠	266c	38.37 N	9.08 W
Verdi	226	39.31 N	119.59 W
Verdigre	198	42.35 N	98.02 W
Verdigre Creek ≐	198	42.42 N	98.03 W
Verdigris ≐	196	35.48 N	95.19 W
Verdinho ≐	255	17.29 S	50.27 W
Verdon	198	40.08 N	95.42 W
Verdon ≐	62	43.43 N	5.46 E
Verdon, Canal du ≡	62	43.43 N	5.57 E
Verdoy	210	42.46 N	73.48 W
Verduga	76	58.46 N	29.12 E
Verdugo Mountains ⋏	280	34.13 N	118.18 W
Verdun, P.Q., Can.	206	45.27 N	73.34 W
Verdun, Fr.	32	43.52 N	1.14 E
Verdun-sur-le-Doubs	58	46.54 N	5.01 E
Verdun-sur-Meuse	56	49.10 N	5.23 E
Verdura ≐	70	37.28 N	13.12 E
Vereb'jo	76	58.41 N	32.42 E
Vereeniging	158	26.38 S	27.57 E
Veregin	184	51.35 N	102.05 W
Vereinigte Arabische Emirate → United Arab Emirates □[1]	128	24.00 N	54.00 E
Vereinigte Königreich → United Kingdom □[1]	28	54.00 N	2.00 W
Vereinigte Staaten → United States □[1]	178	38.00 N	97.00 W
Vereja, Ross.	82	55.46 N	39.06 E
Vereja, Ross.	82	55.21 N	36.11 E
Vereja, Ross.	265b	55.37 N	38.02 E
Vereščagino, Ross.	74	64.14 N	87.37 E
Vereščagino, Ross.	80	58.05 N	54.40 E
Veresegyház	264c	47.39 N	19.17 E
Veresoch	78	51.19 N	31.46 E
Veretje	82	54.08 N	36.17 E
Véretz	50	47.22 N	0.48 E
Verga	285	39.52 N	75.10 W
Verga, Cap ➤	150	10.12 N	14.27 W
Vergara	252	32.56 S	53.57 W
Vergato	64	44.17 N	11.07 E
Vergel	196	25.39 N	103.32 W
Vergeletto	58	46.14 N	8.36 E
Vergemont Creek ≐	166	24.12 S	143.17 E
Vergennes	188	44.10 N	73.15 W
Verghereto	66	43.47 N	12.00 E
Vergiate	62	45.43 N	8.42 E
Vergons	62	43.55 N	6.35 E
Vergt	32	45.02 N	0.43 E
Verhnjadzvinsk	76	55.47 N	27.56 E
Verigino	82	56.42 N	38.08 E
Verín	34	41.56 N	7.26 W
Veringenstadt	58	48.11 N	9.12 E
Verin Talin	84	40.23 N	43.53 E
Veriora	76	58.00 N	27.21 E
Veríssimo	255	19.42 S	48.18 W
Verkeerdevlei	158	28.48 S	26.48 E
Verkhivtseve	78	48.29 N	34.14 E
Verkhna Khortytsya	78	47.51 N	35.01 E
Verkhne Syn'ovydne	78	49.06 N	23.34 E
Verkhneudinsk → Ulan-Ude	88	51.50 N	107.37 E
Verkhniy Rohachyk	78	47.14 N	34.21 E
Verkhniy Ufaley → Verchnij Ufalej	86	56.04 N	60.14 E
Verkhn'odniprovs'k	78	48.39 N	34.21 E
Verkhn'osadove	78	44.42 N	33.42 E
Verkhnyachka	78	48.49 N	30.02 E
Verkhnyaya Salda → Verchn'aja Salda	86	58.02 N	60.33 E
Verkhnye	78	48.53 N	38.28 E
Verkhnye ◆[8]	83	48.53 N	38.28 E
Verkhnyeduvannyy	78	48.20 N	39.48 E
Verkhovyna	78	48.09 N	24.47 E
Verkhoyansk → Verchojansk	74	67.35 N	133.27 E
Verkykerskop	158	27.54 S	29.17 E
Verl (Senne I)	52	51.53 N	8.31 E
Vermaaklikheid	158	34.19 S	21.01 E
Vermaas	158	26.30 S	25.59 E
Vermand	50	49.52 N	3.09 E
Vermejo ≐	196	36.30 N	104.33 W
Vermelho ≐, Bra.	250	9.16 S	47.23 W
Vermelho ≐, Bra.	250	7.44 S	47.17 W
Vermelho ≐, Bra.	250	5.33 S	49.14 W
Vermelho ≐, Bra.	255	14.54 S	51.06 W
Vermenton	50	47.40 N	3.44 E
Vermette Lake ⊜	184	55.40 N	109.05 W
Vermezzo	266b	45.24 N	8.59 E
Vermiglio	64	46.18 N	10.42 E
Vermilion, Ab., Can.	182	53.22 N	110.51 W
Vermilion, Oh., U.S.	214	41.25 N	82.21 W
Vermilion □[6]	216	40.08 N	87.37 W
Vermilion ≐, Ab., Can.	184	53.44 N	110.18 W
Vermilion ≐, On., Can.	190	46.16 N	81.41 W
Vermilion ≐, Il., U.S.	216	41.19 N	89.04 W
Vermilion ≐, La., U.S.	194	29.46 N	92.09 W
Vermilion ≐, Mn., U.S.	190	48.16 N	92.30 W
Vermilion ≐, Oh., U.S.	214	41.26 N	82.22 W
Vermilion, Middle Fork ≐	216	40.12 N	87.45 W
Vermilion, North Fork ≐, Il., U.S.	216	40.49 N	88.30 W
Vermilion, North Fork ≐, Il., U.S.	216	40.13 N	87.39 W
Vermilion, South Fork ≐	216	40.49 N	88.30 W
Vermilion Bay	184	49.51 N	93.24 W
Vermilion Bay ⊂	194	29.40 N	92.00 W
Vermilion Lake ⊜, On., Can.	184	50.03 N	92.13 W
Vermilion Lake ⊜, Mn., U.S.	190	47.53 N	92.25 W
Vermilion Pass)(	182	51.14 N	116.03 W
Vermillion	198	42.46 N	96.55 W
Vermillion ≐	198	42.44 N	96.53 W
Vermillion, East Fork ≐	198	43.44 N	97.03 W
Vermillion, West Fork ≐	198	43.44 N	97.03 W
Vermillion Bluffs ±[4]	200	40.50 N	108.30 W
Vermillion Creek ≐, U.S.	200	40.46 N	108.53 W
Vermillion Creek ≐, Ks., U.S.	198	39.12 N	96.13 W
Vermont, Austl.	274b	37.50 S	145.12 E
Vermont, Il., U.S.	194	40.17 N	90.25 W
Vermont □[3], U.S.	178	43.50 N	72.45 W
Vermont □[3], U.S.	188	43.50 N	72.45 W
Vermontville	216	42.37 N	85.01 W
Vernà, Pizzo di ∧	70	38.01 N	15.15 E
Vernaison	62	45.39 N	4.49 E
Vernal	200	40.27 N	109.31 W
Vernalis	226	37.37 N	121.17 W
Vernante	62	44.15 N	7.32 E
Vernayaz	58	46.08 N	7.02 E
Vernazza	62	44.08 N	9.41 E
Verndale	198	46.24 N	95.01 W
Verne	52	51.41 N	8.34 E
Verner	190	46.25 N	80.07 W
Verneuil	32	48.44 N	0.56 E
Verneuil-L'Étang	261	48.39 N	2.50 E
Verneuil-sur-Avre	50	48.44 N	0.56 E
Verneuil-sur-Seine	261	48.59 N	1.59 E
Verneukpan	158	30.00 S	21.00 E
Verneukpan ⁝	158	30.00 S	21.10 E
Vernier	58	46.13 N	6.06 E
Verninge	41	55.18 N	10.13 E
Vernio	66	44.03 N	11.09 E
Vernole	68	40.17 N	18.18 E
Vernon, B.C., Can.	182	50.16 N	119.16 W
Vernon, On., Can.	212	45.10 N	75.28 W
Vernon, Fr.	50	49.05 N	1.29 E
Vernon, Al., U.S.	194	33.45 N	88.06 W
Vernon, Ca., U.S.	280	34.01 N	118.13 W
Vernon, Ct., U.S.	207	41.49 N	72.28 W
Vernon, Fl., U.S.	194	30.37 N	85.42 W
Vernon, Il., U.S.	219	38.48 N	89.05 W
Vernon, In., U.S.	218	38.59 N	85.36 W
Vernon, Mi., U.S.	216	42.56 N	84.02 W
Vernon, N.J., U.S.	210	41.11 N	74.29 W
Vernon, N.Y., U.S.	210	43.05 N	75.32 W
Vernon, Oh., U.S.	214	41.23 N	80.34 W
Vernon, Tx., U.S.	196	34.09 N	99.15 W
Vernon, Ut,. U.S.	200	40.05 N	112.25 W
Vernon, Lake ⊜	212	45.20 N	79.17 W
Vernon Dam ◆[6]	207	42.46 N	72.31 W
Vernon Hills	216	42.13 N	87.58 W
Vernonia	224	45.51 N	123.11 W
Vernon Lake ⊜[1]	194	31.15 N	93.25 W
Vernon River	186	46.12 N	62.50 W
Vernouillet	261	48.58 N	1.59 E
Vernoux-en-Vivarais	62	44.54 N	4.39 E
Verny	56	49.01 N	6.12 E
Vero ≐	34	42.00 N	0.10 E
Vero Beach	220	27.38 N	80.23 W
Véroia	38	40.31 N	22.12 E
Verolanuova	64	45.19 N	10.04 E
Verolavecchia	64	45.19 N	10.03 E
Veroli	66	41.41 N	13.25 E
Verona, On., Can.	212	44.29 N	76.42 W
Verona, It.	64	45.27 N	11.00 E
Verona, Ky., U.S.	218	38.49 N	84.39 W
Verona, Ms., U.S.	194	34.11 N	88.43 W
Verona, N.J., U.S.	276	40.49 N	74.14 W
Verona, N.Y., U.S.	210	43.08 N	75.34 W
Verona, Oh., U.S.	218	39.54 N	84.29 W
Verona, Pa., U.S.	279b	40.30 N	79.50 W
Verona, Wi., U.S.	216	42.59 N	89.31 W
Verona □[4]	64	45.25 N	11.02 E
Verona Beach	210	43.12 N	75.44 W
Verona Beach State Park ♠	210	43.14 N	75.44 W
Verona Park	216	42.21 N	85.09 W
Verónica	258	35.22 S	57.20 W
Verperluda, ostrov ❙	265a	59.59 N	30.01 E
Verplanck	210	41.15 N	73.58 W
Verran	166	33.51 S	136.18 E
Verrazano-Narrows Bridge ◆[5]	210	40.36 N	74.03 W
Verrès	62	45.40 N	7.42 E
Verrettes	238	19.03 N	72.28 W
Verrey-sous-Salmaise	58	47.26 N	4.40 E
Verrières, Bois de ♠	261	48.45 N	2.15 E
Verrières-le-Buisson	261	48.45 N	2.16 E
Versa ≐	62	44.54 N	8.16 E
Versailles, Fr.	50	48.48 N	2.08 E
Versailles, Il., U.S.	194	39.53 N	90.39 W
Versailles, In., U.S.	218	39.04 N	85.15 W
Versailles, Ky., U.S.	218	38.03 N	84.43 W
Versailles, Mo., U.S.	194	38.25 N	92.50 W
Versailles, N.Y., U.S.	210	42.31 N	78.59 W
Versailles, Oh., U.S.	216	40.13 N	84.29 W
Versailles, Pa., U.S.	279b	40.21 N	79.51 W
Versailles, Château de ⊥	261	48.48 N	2.07 E
Versailles, Parc de ♠	261	48.49 N	2.06 E
Versailles State Park ♠	218	39.04 N	85.13 W
Verse ≐	263	51.15 N	7.46 E
Versec → Vršac	38	45.07 N	21.18 E
Versestausee ⊜[1]	263	51.11 N	7.41 E
Versien	158	27.05 S	27.52 E
Veršina Tei	86	53.20 N	89.36 E
Veršino-Darasunskij	88	52.20 N	115.32 E
Veršino-Šachtaminskij	88	51.21 N	117.50 E
Versmold	52	52.02 N	8.09 E
Versoix	58	46.16 N	6.10 E
Ver-sur-Launette	261	49.06 N	2.41 E
Vert	261	48.57 N	1.41 E
Vert, Cap ➤	150	14.43 N	17.30 W
Vert'ačij	80	48.57 N	43.53 E
Verte, Île ❙, P.Q., Can.	186	48.02 N	69.26 W
Verte, Île ❙, P.Q., Can.	275a	45.34 N	73.30 W
Vertedero	240m	18.05 N	66.15 W
Verteillac	32	45.21 N	0.22 E
Vertientes	240p	21.16 N	78.09 W
Vertiyivka	78	51.10 N	31.51 E
Vertkovo	82	56.07 N	36.25 E
Vert-le-Grand	261	48.34 N	2.22 E
Vert-le-Petit	261	48.33 N	2.22 E
Vertlinskoje	82	56.14 N	36.58 E
Vertou	32	47.10 N	1.29 W
Vertova	62	45.48 N	9.50 E
Vert-Saint-Denis	261	48.34 N	2.37 E
Vertus	50	48.54 N	4.00 E
Verucchio	66	43.59 N	12.25 E
Verulam	158	29.45 S	31.02 E
Verulamium ⊥	42	51.45 N	0.22 W
Verviers	56	50.35 N	5.52 E
Vervins	50	49.50 N	3.54 E
Verwall Gruppe ⋏	58	47.02 N	10.10 E
Verwood	42	50.53 N	1.52 W
Veryan	42	50.13 N	4.54 W
Verzasca ≐	58	46.09 N	8.52 E
Verzegnis	64	46.25 N	12.59 E
Verzenay	50	49.10 N	4.09 E
Verzino	68	39.19 N	16.51 E
Verzuolo	62	44.36 N	7.29 E
Verzy	50	49.09 N	4.10 E
Vesanto	26	62.56 N	26.25 E
Vesava ◆[8]	272c	19.08 N	72.48 E
Vescovato, Fr.	36	42.30 N	9.26 E
Vescovato, It.	64	45.10 N	10.10 E
Vescovo di Squillace, Roccelletta del ⊥	68	38.48 N	16.35 E
Vesdre ≐	56	50.37 N	5.37 E
Vesela Hora	83	48.43 N	39.16 E
Vesele	78	47.01 N	34.55 E
Veselí nad Lužnicí	30	49.11 N	14.43 E
Veselí nad Moravou	30	48.58 N	17.22 E
Veseli Terny	78	48.07 N	33.32 E
Veselovskoje	86	54.00 N	78.43 E
Veselovskoje vodochranilišče ⊜[1]	80	47.00 N	41.18 E
Veselynove	78	47.21 N	31.14 E
Veselyy Podil	78	49.36 N	33.16 E
Vésenaz	58	46.14 N	6.12 E
Vešenskaja	80	49.38 N	41.43 E
Vesgre ≐	50	48.48 N	1.36 E
Vesijärvi ⊜	26	61.06 N	25.32 E
Vesjegonsk	76	58.40 N	37.16 E
Veškajma, Ross.	80	54.04 N	47.02 E
Veškajma, Ross.	80	54.03 N	47.08 E
Veški	265b	55.56 N	37.37 E
Vesle ≐	50	49.23 N	3.38 E
Vešn'aki ◆[8]	265b	55.44 N	37.49 E
Ves'olaja Rošča	86	53.47 N	76.22 E
Vesole, Monte ∧	68	40.24 N	15.10 E
Ves'oloje, Kaz.	85	43.19 N	77.06 E
Ves'oloje, Ross.	80	50.17 N	45.15 E
Ves'oloje, Ross.	83	47.10 N	38.45 E
Ves'olo-Voznesenka	83	47.09 N	38.20 E
Ves'olyj, Ross.	80	47.06 N	40.45 E
Ves'olyj, Ross.	83	47.20 N	39.18 E
Ves'olyj Jar, Ross.	86	51.18 N	81.07 E
Ves'olyj Jar, Ross.	89	43.57 N	135.28 E
Ves'olyj Podol	86	53.31 N	65.54 E
Ves'olyj Pos'olok ◆[8]	265a	59.54 N	30.28 E
Vesoul	58	47.38 N	6.10 E
Vespasiano	255	19.40 S	43.55 W
Vespolate	62	45.21 N	8.40 E
Vesta	236	9.43 N	83.03 W
Vest-Agder □[6]	26	58.30 N	7.10 E
Vestal	210	42.05 N	76.03 W
Vestal Center	210	42.02 N	76.01 W
Vestavia Hills	194	33.26 N	86.46 W
Vestbygd	26	58.06 N	6.35 E
Vesterålen ❙❙	24	68.45 N	15.00 E
Vester Egede	41	55.16 N	11.59 E
Vesterø Havn	26	57.18 N	10.56 E
Vester Skerninge	41	55.03 N	10.28 E
Vester Sottrup	41	54.57 N	9.43 E
Vestfjorden ⊂[2]	24	68.08 N	15.00 E
Vestfold □[6]	26	59.15 N	10.10 E
Vestmannaeyjar	24a	63.26 N	20.12 W
Vestone	64	45.42 N	10.24 E
Vestreno	58	46.06 N	9.18 E
Vestsjælland □[6]	41	55.35 N	11.30 E
Vestvågøya ❙	24	68.15 N	13.50 E
Vésubie ≐	62	43.52 N	7.12 E
Vesubio → Vesuvio ∧[1]	68	40.49 N	14.26 E
Vesuv → Vesuvio ∧[1]	68	40.49 N	14.26 E
Vesuvio (Vesuvius) ∧[1]	68	40.49 N	14.26 E
Vesuvius → Vesuvio ∧[1]	68	40.49 N	14.26 E
Vesuvius Bay	224	48.53 N	123.35 W
Veszprém	30	47.06 N	17.55 E
Veszprém □[6]	30	47.10 N	17.40 E
Vésztő	30	46.55 N	21.16 E
Vet ≐	158	27.40 S	25.40 E
Vetapālem	122	15.47 N	80.19 E
Veterans Stadium ♠	285	39.54 N	75.10 W
Vétheuil	50	49.04 N	1.42 E
Vetju	24	62.57 N	50.44 E
Vetka	76	52.33 N	31.10 E
Vetlanda	26	57.26 N	15.04 E
Vetl'anka	80	52.52 N	51.09 E
Vetluga	80	57.51 N	45.47 E
Vetluga ≐	80	56.18 N	46.24 E
Vetlužskij, Ross.	80	57.11 N	45.07 E
Vetlužskij, Ross.	80	58.23 N	45.26 E
Vetoškino	80	57.18 N	49.44 E
Vetovo	38	43.42 N	26.16 E
Vetralla	66	42.19 N	12.03 E
Vetren	38	42.16 N	24.03 E
Vetriolo	64	46.02 N	11.18 E
Vetrișoaia	38	46.26 N	28.13 E
Větřni	61	48.46 N	14.17 E
Vetryna	76	55.25 N	28.28 E
Vetschau	54	51.47 N	14.04 E
Vettisfossen ʟ	26	61.22 N	7.55 E
Vetto	64	44.29 N	10.20 E
Vettore, Monte ∧	66	42.49 N	13.16 E
Vetulonia	66	42.51 N	10.58 E
Veules-les-Roses	50	49.52 N	0.48 E
Veulettes-sur-Mer	50	49.51 N	0.36 E
Veurne (Furnes)	50	51.04 N	2.40 E
Vevay	218	38.44 N	85.04 W
Vevelstad	24	65.43 N	12.30 E
Veveno, Khawr ∨	140	6.40 N	32.58 E
Vevey	58	46.28 N	6.51 E
Vex	58	46.13 N	7.24 E
Veyle ≐	58	46.18 N	4.50 E
Veynes	62	44.32 N	5.49 E
Veyrier	62	45.53 N	6.10 E
Vézelay	50	47.28 N	3.44 E
Vézelise	58	48.29 N	6.05 E
Vézénobres	62	44.03 N	4.09 E
Vézère ≐	32	44.53 N	0.53 E
Vezirköprü	130	41.09 N	35.28 E
Vezouze ≐	58	48.35 N	6.29 E
Vezza d'Oglio	64	46.14 N	10.24 E
Vezzana, Cima della ∧	64	46.17 N	11.50 E
Vezzano	64	46.05 N	11.00 E
Vezzano Ligure	64	44.09 N	9.52 E
Viacha	248	16.39 S	68.18 W
Viadana	64	44.56 N	10.31 E
Viadutos	252	27.34 S	52.01 W
Viale	252	31.53 S	60.01 W
Vialonga	266c	38.52 N	9.05 W
Via Mala ∨	58	46.40 N	9.26 E
Viamão	252	30.05 S	51.02 W
Viamonte	252	33.44 S	63.06 W
Vian	196	35.29 N	94.58 W
Viana	250	3.13 S	45.00 W
Viana, Ilha do ❙	287a	22.52 S	43.08 W
Viana do Alentejo	34	38.20 N	8.00 W
Viana do Bolo	34	42.11 N	7.06 W
Viana do Castelo	34	41.42 N	8.50 W
Vianden	56	49.57 N	6.11 E
Vianen	52	52.00 N	5.05 E
Viangchan (Vientiane)	110	17.58 N	102.36 E
Viangphoukha	110	20.41 N	101.04 E
Viar ≐	34	37.36 N	5.50 W
Viareggio	64	43.52 N	10.14 E
Viarmes	50	49.08 N	2.22 E
Viatka → Kirov	80	58.38 N	49.42 E
Viaur ≐	32	44.08 N	2.23 E
Vibank	184	50.20 N	103.55 W
Víboras, Arroyo de las ≐	258	33.57 S	58.21 W
Viborg, Dan.	26	56.26 N	9.24 E
Viborg → Vyborg, Ross.	76	60.42 N	28.45 E
Viborg, S.D., U.S.	198	43.10 N	97.04 W
Viborg □[6]	41	56.18 N	9.27 E
Vibo Valentia	68	38.40 N	16.06 E
Vibo Valentia □[4]	68	38.40 N	16.10 E
Vibraye	50	48.03 N	0.44 E
Viburnum	194	37.42 N	91.08 W
Viby	41	55.33 N	12.02 E
Viby ◆[8]	41	56.07 N	10.10 E
Vic (Vich)	34	41.56 N	2.15 E
Vic, Étang de ⊂	62	43.29 N	3.50 E
Vicálvaro ◆[8]	266a	40.24 N	3.36 W
Vícam	232	27.35 N	110.20 W
Vicarello	66	42.10 N	12.12 E
Vicari	70	37.49 N	13.34 E
Vicchio	66	43.56 N	11.28 E
Vicco	192	37.12 N	83.03 W
Vicebsk	76	55.12 N	30.11 E
Vicebsk □[8]	76	55.20 N	29.00 E
Vic-en-Bigorre	32	43.23 N	0.03 E
Vicente, Point ➤	280	33.44 N	118.25 W
Vicente Casares	258	34.57 S	58.38 W
Vicente de Carvalho	256	23.56 S	46.19 W
Vicente Guerrero, Méx.	234	18.24 N	92.53 W
Vicente Guerrero, Méx.	234	19.08 N	98.10 W
Vicente Guerrero, Méx.	234	23.45 N	103.59 W
Vicente Guerrero, Presa ⊜[1]	234	24.00 N	98.45 W
Vicente López	258	34.32 S	58.28 W
Vicente López □[5]	288	34.32 S	58.30 W
Vicente Noble	238	18.23 N	71.11 W
Vicenza	64	45.33 N	11.33 E
Vicenza □[4]	64	45.40 N	11.27 E
Viceroy	184	49.27 N	105.22 W
Vichada □[5]	246	5.00 N	69.30 W

Symbol	English	Deutsch	Español	Français	Português
≐	River	Fluß	Río	Rivière	Rio
≡	Canal	Kanal	Canal	Canal	Canal
ʟ	Waterfall, Rapids	Wasserfall, Stromschnellen	Cascada, Rápidos	Chute d'eau, Rapides	Cascata, Rápidos
ʊ	Strait	Meeresstraße	Estrecho	Détroit	Estreito
⊂	Bay, Gulf	Bucht, Golf	Bahía, Golfo	Baie, Golfe	Baía, Golfo
⊜	Lake, Lakes	See, Seen	Lago, Lagos	Lac, Lacs	Lago, Lagos
⁝	Swamp	Sumpf	Pantano	Marais	Pântano
⊓	Ice Features, Glacier	Eis- und Gletscherformen	Accidentes Glaciales	Formes glaciaires	Acidentes glaciares
⫪	Other Hydrographic Features	Andere Hydrographische Objekte	Otros Elementos Hidrográficos	Autres données hydrographiques	Outros acidentes hidrográficos
✣	Submarine Features	Untermeerische Objekte	Accidentes Submarinos	Formes de relief sous-marin	Acidentes submarinos
□	Political Unit	Politische Einheit	Unidad Politica	Entité politique	Unidade política
⊌	Cultural Institution	Kulturelle Institution	Institución Cultural	Institution culturelle	Institução cultural
⊥	Historical Site	Historische Stätte	Sitio Histórico	Site historique	Sitio histórico
♠	Recreational Site	Erholungs- und Ferienort	Sitio de Recreo	Centre de loisirs	Area de Lazer
⊠	Airport	Flughafen	Aeropuerto	Aéroport	Aeroporto
■	Military Installation	Militäranlage	Instalación Militar	Installation militaire	Instalação militar
◆	Miscellaneous	Verschiedenes	Misceláneo	Divers	Diversos

Vichada ≐ 246 4.55 N 67.50 W
Vichadero 252 31.48 S 54.43 W
Vichigasta 252 29.29 S 67.31 W
Vichoreva ≐ 88 56.47 N 101.22 E
Vichorevka 88 56.12 N 101.09 E
Vichra ≐ 76 54.01 N 31.52 E
Vichuga → Vičuga 80 57.13 N 41.56 E
Vichuquén 252 34.53 S 72.00 W
Vichy 32 46.08 N 3.26 E
Vici 196 36.08 N 99.17 W
Vickery 214 41.23 N 82.56 W
Vicksburg, Mi., U.S. 216 42.07 N 85.31 W
Vicksburg, Ms., U.S. 194 32.21 N 90.52 W
Vicksburg, Pa., U.S. 210 40.56 N 76.59 W
Vicksburg National Military Park ♠ 194 32.24 N 90.52 W
Vico 36 42.10 N 8.48 E
Vico, Lago di ⊜ 66 42.19 N 12.10 E
Vico Canavese 62 45.30 N 7.47 E
Vico del Gargano 68 41.54 N 15.57 E
Vico Equense 68 40.40 N 14.25 E
Vicoforte 62 44.21 N 7.54 E
Vicopisano 66 43.42 N 10.35 E
Viçosa, Bra. 250 9.24 S 36.14 W
Viçosa, Bra. 255 20.45 S 42.53 W
Viçosa do Ceará 250 3.34 S 41.05 W
Vicosoprano 58 46.22 N 9.37 E
Vicovaro 66 42.01 N 12.54 E
Vicq 261 48.49 N 1.50 E
Vic-sur-Aisne 50 49.24 N 3.07 E
Vic-sur-Cère 32 44.59 N 2.37 E
Vic-sur-Seille 56 48.47 N 6.32 E
Victor, Ca., U.S. 226 38.08 N 121.12 W
Victor, Id., U.S. 202 43.36 N 111.06 W
Victor, Ia., U.S. 190 41.43 N 92.17 W
Victor, Mt., U.S. 202 46.25 N 114.08 W
Victor, N.Y., U.S. 210 42.58 N 77.24 W
Victor, Lac ⊜ 186 50.35 N 61.50 W
Victorbur 52 53.29 N 7.20 E
Victor Harbor 168b 35.34 S 138.37 E
Victoria, Arg. 252 32.37 S 60.10 W
Victoria → Vitória, Bra. 255 20.19 S 40.21 W
Victoria, B.C., Can. 224 48.25 N 123.22 W
Victoria, P.E., Can. 186 46.13 N 63.29 W
Victoria, Chile 252 38.13 S 72.20 W
Victoria, Gren. 241k 12.12 N 61.42 W
Victoria, Guinée 150 10.50 N 14.33 W
Victoria, Malay. 112 5.17 N 115.15 E
Victoria → Ciudad Victoria, Méx. 234 23.44 N 99.08 W
Victoria, Pil. 116 13.12 N 121.15 E
Victoria, Pil. 116 15.35 N 120.41 E
Victoria, Rom. 38 45.45 N 24.41 E
Victoria, Sey. 138 4.38 S 55.27 E
Victoria, Ks., U.S. 198 38.51 N 99.08 W
Victoria, Tx., U.S. 196 28.48 N 97.00 W
Victoria, Va., U.S. 192 36.59 N 78.13 W
Victoria → Xianggang, Zhg. 271d 22.17 N 114.09 E
Victoria □[3] 166 38.00 S 145.00 E
Victoria □[4] 154 20.54 S 31.21 E
Victoria □[6], On., Can. 212 44.35 N 78.50 W
Victoria □[6], Tx., U.S. 222 28.55 N 97.00 W
Victoria ◆[8] 288 34.28 S 58.31 W
Victoria ≐, Austl. 160 15.12 S 129.43 E
Victoria ≐, Nf., Can. 186 48.45 N 56.40 W
Victoria ≐, Méx. 234 21.02 N 99.50 W
Victoria, Isla I 254 45.18 S 73.58 W
Victoria, Lake ⊜, Afr. 154 1.00 S 33.00 E
Victoria, Lake ⊜, Austl. 166 34.00 S 141.16 E
Victoria, Mount ∧, Mya. 110 21.14 N 93.55 E
Victoria, Mount ∧, Pap. N. Gui. 164 8.55 S 147.35 E
Victoria, Pont ◆[5] 275a 45.29 N 73.32 W
Victoria and Albert Museum ʊ 272c 18.59 N 72.50 E
Victoria Beach 184 50.43 N 96.33 W
Victoria Beach ≛[2] 273a 6.25 N 3.25 E
Victoria de Durango → Durango 234 24.02 N 104.40 W
Victoria Falls 154 17.56 S 25.50 E
Victoria Falls ∟ 154 17.55 S 25.51 E
Victoria Falls National Park ♠ 154 17.55 S 25.40 E
Victoria Gardens ♠ 272c 18.59 N 72.50 E
Victoria Harbour 212 44.45 N 79.46 W
Victoria International Airport ⊠ 224 48.39 N 123.26 W
Victoria Island I, N.T., Can. 176 71.00 N 110.00 W
Victoria Island I, Nig. 273a 6.26 N 3.26 E
Victoria Lake ⊜ 273d 26.14 S 28.09 E
Victoria Lake ⊜[1] 186 48.18 N 57.30 W
Victoria Land ◆[1] 9 75.00 S 163.00 E
Victoria Lawn Tennis Association Courts ♠ 274b 37.51 S 145.02 E
Victoria Memorial Hall ʊ 271c 1.17 N 103.51 E
Victoria Memorial Museum ʊ 272b 22.33 N 88.21 E
Victoria Nile ≐ 154 2.14 N 31.26 E
Victoria Park 168a 31.58 S 115.55 E
Victoria Park ♠, Zhg. 271d 22.17 N 114.11 E
Victoria Park ♠, Eng., U.K. 262 53.23 N 2.34 W
Victoria Peak ∧, Belize 232 16.48 N 88.37 W
Victoria Peak ∧, B.C., Can. 182 50.03 N 126.06 W
Victoria Peak ∧, Zhg. 271d 22.17 N 114.08 E
Victoria Peaks ⋀ 116 9.22 N 118.20 E
Victoria Point 171a 27.35 S 153.18 E
Victoria Range ⋀, N.Z. 172 42.09 S 172.08 E
Victoria Range ⋀, Pil. 116 9.32 N 118.23 E
Victoria River 164 15.37 S 131.08 E
Victoria River Downs 164 16.24 S 131.00 E
Victorias 116 10.54 N 123.05 E
Victoria State Car Club Race Circuit ♠ 274b 37.45 S 145.11 E
Victoria Station ◆[5] 262 53.29 N 2.15 W
Victoria Strait ⊔ 176 69.15 N 100.30 W
Victoria Terminus ◆[5] 272c 18.57 N 72.50 E
Victoria University of Manchester ʊ[2] 262 53.28 N 2.14 W
Victoriaville 206 46.03 N 71.57 W
Victoria West 158 31.25 S 23.04 E
Victorica 252 36.13 S 65.27 W
Victorino 246 2.48 N 67.50 W
Victorino de la Plaza 252 36.36 S 62.40 W
Víctor Rosales 234 22.57 N 102.42 W
Victorville 228 34.32 N 117.17 W
Victory, Mount ∧ 164 9.10 S 149.05 E
Victory Gardens 276 40.52 N 74.32 W
Victory Heights 214 41.22 N 79.46 W
Victory Hills 279b 40.11 N 79.53 W
Victory Mills 210 43.05 N 73.36 W
Victory Monument ⊥ 269a 13.46 N 100.33 E
Vičuga 80 57.13 N 41.56 E
Vicuña 252 30.02 S 70.44 W
Vicuña Mackenna 252 33.54 S 64.23 W
Vidal, Kaap ≻ 158 28.09 S 32.33 E
Vidal Gormaz, Isla I 254 52.00 S 74.45 W
Vidalia, Ga., U.S. 192 32.13 N 82.24 W
Vidalia, La., U.S. 194 31.33 N 91.25 W
Vidal Ramos 252 27.23 S 49.22 W
Vidauban 62 43.26 N 6.26 E
Videbæk 26 56.05 N 8.38 E
Videira 252 27.00 S 51.08 W
Videle 38 44.16 N 25.31 E
Vidigueira 34 38.13 N 7.48 W
Vidim, Česká Rep. 54 50.28 N 14.31 E
Vidim, Ross. 88 56.29 N 103.09 E
Vidin 38 43.59 N 22.52 E
Vidisha 124 23.32 N 77.49 E
Vidlica 24 61.10 N 32.21 E
Vidnoje 82 55.34 N 37.41 E
Vidogošči 82 56.42 N 36.23 E
Vidor 194 30.07 N 94.00 W
Vidos ≐ 267b 40.58 N 28.53 E
Vidöstern ⊜ 26 57.04 N 14.01 E
Vidourle ≐ 62 43.32 N 4.08 E
Vidra, Rom. 38 44.16 N 26.11 E
Vidra, Rom. 38 45.55 N 26.54 E
Vidsel 24 65.51 N 20.24 E
Vidzeme □[9] 76 57.10 N 25.30 E
Vidzy 76 55.24 N 26.38 E
Vie ≐ 50 49.05 N 0.04 E
Viecht 60 48.30 N 12.04 E
Viechtach 60 49.05 N 12.53 E
Viechtwang, Öst. 61 47.55 N 13.57 E
Viechtwang, Öst. 64 47.55 N 13.57 E
Viedma 254 40.48 S 63.00 W
Viedma, Lago ⊜ 254 49.35 S 72.35 W
Viehberg ∧ 61 48.33 N 14.37 E
Vieil Armand ⊥ 58 47.52 N 7.10 E
Vieillard, Lac du ⊜ 190 47.23 N 78.02 W
Vieille Case 240d 15.36 N 61.24 W
Vieira do Minho 34 41.39 N 8.09 W
Viejo, Cerro ∧ 248 4.49 S 79.27 W
Viekšniai 76 56.16 N 22.31 E
Vielank 54 53.15 N 11.08 E
Vielha 34 42.42 N 0.48 E
Vielle-Eglise-en-Yvelines 261 48.40 N 1.53 E
Vielsalm 56 50.17 N 5.55 E
Viels-Maisons 50 48.54 N 3.24 E
Viena → Vienne ≐ 32 47.13 N 0.05 E
Vienenburg 54 51.57 N 10.34 E
Vienna, On., Can. 212 42.41 N 80.48 W
Vienna → Wien, Öst. 61 48.13 N 16.20 E
Vienna, Ga., U.S. 192 32.05 N 83.47 W
Vienna, Il., U.S. 194 37.25 N 88.54 W
Vienna, In., U.S. 218 38.39 N 85.46 W
Vienna, Md., U.S. 208 38.29 N 75.49 W
Vienna, Mo., U.S. 194 38.11 N 91.56 W
Vienna, N.J., U.S. 210 40.52 N 74.53 W
Vienna, Oh., U.S. 214 41.14 N 80.40 W
Vienna, S.D., U.S. 198 44.42 N 97.30 W
Vienna, Va., U.S. 208 38.29 N 75.49 W
Vienna, Va., U.S. 208 38.54 N 77.15 W
Vienna, W.V., U.S. 188 39.19 N 81.32 W
Vienne, Fr. 62 45.31 N 4.52 E
Vienne → Wien, Öst. 61 48.13 N 16.20 E
Vienne □[5] 32 46.35 N 0.30 E
Vienne ≐ 32 47.13 N 0.05 E
Vienne-en-Arthies 261 49.04 N 1.44 E
Vienne-le-Château 56 49.11 N 4.53 E
Vientiane → Viangchan 110 17.58 N 102.36 E
Vientos, Paso de los → Windward Passage ⊔ 238 20.00 N 73.50 W
Vieques 240m 18.09 N 65.27 W
Vieques, Aeropuerto ⊠ 240m 18.07 N 65.30 W
Vieques, Isla de I 240m 18.08 N 65.25 W
Vieques, Pasaje de ⊔ 240m 18.11 N 65.37 W
Vieques, Sonda de ⊔ 240m 18.15 N 65.23 W
Vière ≐ 56 48.46 N 4.41 E
Viereck 54 53.32 N 14.02 E
Vieremä 26 63.45 N 27.01 E
Vierfontein 158 27.03 S 26.46 E
Vierhouten 52 52.20 N 5.50 E
Vieringhausen ◆[8] 263 51.11 N 7.10 E
Vierlande ◆[1] 52 53.26 N 10.14 E
Viernau 54 50.40 N 10.32 E
Viernheim 56 49.32 N 8.34 E
Vierraden 54 53.06 N 14.17 E
Viersen 56 51.15 N 6.23 E
Vierumäki 26 61.06 N 25.57 E
Vierwaldstättersee ⊜ 58 47.00 N 8.28 E
Vierzehnheiligen ʊ[1] 56 50.08 N 11.02 E
Vierzon 50 47.13 N 2.05 E
Viesca 232 25.21 N 102.48 W
Viesecke 54 53.01 N 12.01 E
Vieselbach 54 51.00 N 11.08 E
Viesīte 76 56.21 N 25.33 E
Vieste 68 41.53 N 16.10 E
Vietgest 54 53.45 N 12.20 E
Vietnam □[1], Asia 108 16.00 N 108.00 E
Vietnam □[1], Asia 110 16.00 N 108.00 E
Vietnam Veterans Memorial ⊥ 284c 38.53 N 77.03 W
Vietri di Potenza 68 40.36 N 15.30 E
Vietri sul Mare 68 40.40 N 14.44 E
Viet Tri 110 21.18 N 105.26 E
Vieux-Condé 50 50.27 N 3.34 E
Vieux-Ferette 58 47.30 N 7.18 E
Vieux-Fort, P.Q., Can. 186 51.26 N 57.49 W
Vieux-Fort, Guad. 241o 15.57 N 61.43 W
Vieux Fort, St. Luc. 241f 13.44 N 60.57 W
Vieux-Fort, Pointe du ≻ 241o 15.57 N 61.43 W
Vieux Fort Bay ⊂ 241f 13.44 N 60.58 W
Vieux-Habitants 241o 16.04 N 61.46 W
Vieux-Thann 58 47.48 N 7.08 E
Vievis 76 54.46 N 24.48 E
View Park 280 34.00 N 118.20 W
Vieytes 258 35.16 S 57.35 W
Vif 62 45.03 N 5.40 E
Vig 41 55.51 N 11.36 E
Viga ≐ 76 59.14 N 43.41 E
Vigala 76 58.43 N 24.22 E
Vigan 116 17.34 N 120.23 E
Vigarano Mainarda 64 44.50 N 11.30 E
Vigatto 64 44.43 N 10.20 E
Vigeland 26 58.05 N 7.18 E
Vigentino ◆[8] 266b 45.25 N 9.11 E
Vigersted 41 55.29 N 11.54 E
Vigese, Monte ∧ 64 44.12 N 11.06 E
Vigésima Quinta de Abril, Ponte ◆[5] 266c 38.41 N 9.11 W
Vigevano 62 45.19 N 8.51 E
Viggianello 68 39.58 N 16.05 E
Viggiano 68 40.20 N 15.54 E
Viggiù 62 45.52 N 8.54 E
Vigia 250 0.48 S 48.08 W
Vigie Airport ⊠ 241f 14.01 N 60.59 W
Vignacourt 50 50.01 N 2.12 E
Vignale 266b 45.29 N 8.36 E
Vignanello 66 42.23 N 12.17 E
Vigneulles-lès-Hattonchâtel 56 48.59 N 5.43 E
Vigneux-sur-Seine 261 48.42 N 2.25 E
Vignola 64 44.29 N 11.00 E
Vignory 58 48.17 N 5.06 E
Vignot 56 48.46 N 5.36 E
Vigny 261 49.05 N 1.56 E
Vigo 34 42.14 N 8.43 W
Vigo, Ría de ⊂[1] 34 42.15 N 8.45 W
Vigodarzere 64 45.27 N 11.53 E
Vigo di Fassa 64 46.25 N 11.40 E
Vigolzone 62 44.55 N 9.40 E
Vigone 62 44.51 N 7.30 E
Vigonovo 64 45.23 N 12.00 E
Vigo-Rendena 64 46.05 N 10.43 E
Vigrestad 26 58.34 N 5.42 E
Viguzzolo 62 44.54 N 8.55 E
Vigy 56 49.12 N 6.18 E
Vihanti 26 64.29 N 25.00 E
Vihāri 123 30.02 N 72.21 E
Vihiers 32 47.09 N 0.32 W
Vihowa 123 31.08 N 70.30 E
Vihren ∧ 38 41.46 N 23.24 E
Vihti 26 60.25 N 24.20 E
Viiala 26 61.13 N 23.47 E
Viinijärvi 26 62.39 N 29.14 E
Viinijärvi ⊜ 26 62.44 N 29.17 E
Viipuri → Vyborg 76 60.42 N 28.45 E
Viișoara 38 46.20 N 28.26 E
Viitasaari 26 63.04 N 25.52 E
Viivikonna 76 59.19 N 27.42 E
Vijāpur 120 23.34 N 72.45 E
Vijayawāda 122 16.31 N 80.37 E
Vijosë (Aóös) ≐ 38 40.37 N 19.20 E
Vik 40 59.44 N 17.28 E
Vik ⊥ 40 59.44 N 17.27 E
Vika 40 60.31 N 15.42 E
Vikajärvi 24 66.37 N 26.12 E
Vikārābād 122 17.20 N 77.54 E
Vikbolandet ≻[1] 40 58.32 N 16.40 E
Vikeke 112 8.52 S 126.22 E
Viken 41 56.09 N 12.34 E
Viken ⊜ 26 58.39 N 14.20 E
Vikern ⊜ 40 59.30 N 14.55 E
Vikersund 26 59.59 N 10.02 E
Vikhroli ◆[8] 272c 19.07 N 72.56 E
Viking 182 53.06 N 111.46 W
Viking Village 218 39.05 N 84.18 W
Vikmanshyttan 40 60.17 N 15.49 E
Vikna 24 64.57 N 10.58 E
Vikna I 24 64.57 N 10.58 E
Vikno 78 48.34 N 25.58 E
Vikramasingapuram 122 8.43 N 77.24 E
Viksøyri 26 61.05 N 6.35 E
Viktor 24 66.09 N 58.07 E
Viktorovka 86 52.51 N 62.32 E
Viktring 61 46.35 N 14.16 E
Vikulovo 86 56.49 N 70.37 E
Vil'a 80 55.15 N 42.13 E
Vila Alferes Chamusca 156 24.29 S 33.00 E
Vila Augusta 287b 23.28 S 46.32 W
Vila Babi 287a 22.42 S 43.23 W
Vila Boacaya ◆[8] 287b 23.29 S 46.44 W
Vila Caldas Xavier 154 15.59 S 34.12 E
Vila da Maganja 154 17.18 S 37.30 E
Vila da Ribeira Brava 150a 16.37 N 24.18 W
Viladecans 266d 41.19 N 2.00 E
Viladecavalls del Vallès 266d 41.33 N 1.58 E
Vila de Manica 156 18.56 S 32.53 E
Vila de Rei 34 39.40 N 8.09 W
Vila Dirce 287b 23.35 S 46.48 W
Vila do Bispo 34 37.05 N 8.55 W
Vila do Conde 34 41.21 N 8.45 W
Vila do Porto 148a 36.56 N 25.09 W
Vila Embaú 256 22.37 S 45.02 W
Vila Flor 34 41.18 N 7.09 W
Vila Fontes 156 17.50 S 35.21 E
Vila Formosa ◆[8] 287b 23.34 S 46.33 W
Vilafranca del Penedès 34 41.21 N 1.42 E
Vila Franca de Xira 34 38.57 N 8.59 W
Vila Galvão 287b 23.27 S 46.33 W
Vila Gamito 154 14.12 S 33.00 E
Vila Gomes da Costa 156 24.19 S 33.38 E
Vila Gouveia 156 18.03 S 33.11 E
Vila Guilherme ◆[8] 287b 23.30 S 46.36 W
Vilaine ≐ 32 47.30 N 2.27 W
Vila Isabel ◆[8] 287a 22.55 S 43.15 W
Vila Jaguára ◆[8] 287b 23.31 S 46.45 W
Viļaka 76 57.11 N 27.41 E
Vilalba 34 43.18 N 7.41 W
Vila Luísa 156 25.44 S 32.40 E
Vilama, Laguna de ⊜ 252 22.36 S 66.55 W
Vila Machado 156 19.18 S 34.11 E
Vila Madalena ◆[8] 287b 23.33 S 46.42 W
Vila Maria ◆[8] 287b 23.31 S 46.34 W
Vila Mariana ◆[8] 287b 23.35 S 46.38 W
Vila Matilde ◆[8] 287b 23.32 S 46.31 W
Vilanculos 156 22.01 S 35.19 E
Viļāni 76 56.33 N 26.57 E
Vila Nova ≐ 250 0.04 S 51.13 W
Vila Nova de Famalicão 34 41.25 N 8.32 W
Vila Nova de Foz Côa 34 41.05 N 7.12 W
Vila Nova de Gaia 34 41.08 N 8.37 W
Vilanova de la Roca 266d 41.33 N 2.17 E
Vilanova i la Geltrú 34 41.14 N 1.44 E
Vila Novo de Ourém 34 39.39 N 8.35 W
Vila Paiva de Andrada 156 18.44 S 34.03 E
Vila Progresso 287a 22.55 S 43.03 W
Vila Prudente ◆[8] 287b 23.35 S 46.33 W
Vila-real, Esp. 34 39.56 N 0.06 W
Vila Real, Port. 34 41.18 N 7.45 W
Vila Real de Santo António 34 37.12 N 7.25 W
Vilar Formoso 34 40.37 N 6.50 W
Vilarinho do Monte 250 1.37 S 52.01 W
Vilassar de Dalt 266d 41.31 N 2.22 E
Vilassar de Mar 266d 41.30 N 2.24 E
Vila Vasco da Gama 154 14.54 S 32.14 E
Vila Velha, Bra. 250 3.13 N 51.13 W
Vila Velha, Bra. 255 20.20 S 40.17 W
Vila Velha de Ródão 34 39.38 N 7.40 W
Vila Verde, Port. 34 41.39 N 8.26 W
Vila Verde, Port. 266c 38.50 N 9.22 W
Vila Viçosa 34 38.47 N 8.13 W
Vilcabamba, Cordillera de ⋀ 248 12.45 S 73.20 W
Vil'cha 78 51.22 N 29.24 E
Vil'che 78 49.14 N 22.53 E
Vildbjerg 41 56.12 N 8.46 E
Vilejka 76 54.30 N 26.53 E
Vilelas 252 27.57 S 62.38 W
Vilenki 82 54.16 N 38.55 E
Vil'gort, Ross. 24 61.35 N 50.40 E
Vil'gort, Ross. 24 60.34 N 56.24 E
Vilhelmina 26 64.37 N 16.39 E
Vilhena 248 12.43 S 60.07 W
Vilija (Neris) ≐ 76 54.54 N 23.53 E
Viljandi 76 58.22 N 25.36 E
Viljoensdrif 158 26.44 S 27.55 E
Viljoenshof 158 34.40 S 19.42 E
Viljoenskroon 158 27.12 S 27.00 E
Viljoenspos 158 27.35 S 30.30 E
Vilkaviškis 76 54.39 N 23.02 E
Vil'khova ≐ 83 48.35 N 39.17 E
Vil'kickogo, ostrov I, Ross. 72 73.29 N 75.50 E
Vil'kickogo, ostrov I, Ross. 74 75.44 N 152.20 E
Vil'kickogo, proliv ⊔ 74 77.55 N 103.00 E
Vilkija 76 55.03 N 23.35 E
Villa Abecia 248 21.00 S 65.23 W
Villa Aberastain 252 31.39 S 68.35 W
Villa Acuña → Ciudad Acuña 232 29.18 N 100.55 W
Villa Adelina ◆[8] 288 34.31 S 58.32 W
Villa Adriana ⊥ 66 41.56 N 12.45 E
Villa Alejandrina 258 33.46 S 58.21 W
Villa Alemana 252 33.03 S 71.23 W
Villa Álvarez 234 19.14 N 103.43 W
Villa Ana 252 28.29 S 59.37 W
Villa Ángela 252 27.35 S 60.43 W
Villa Atamisqui 252 28.29 S 63.48 W
Villa Atuel 252 34.50 S 67.54 W
Villaba 116 11.13 N 124.23 E
Villa Ballester ◆[8] 258 34.32 S 58.33 W
Villabassa (Niederdorf) 64 46.44 N 12.10 E
Villabate 70 38.04 N 13.26 E
Villabé 261 48.35 N 2.27 E
Villa Bella 248 10.23 S 65.24 W
Villa Berthet 252 27.17 S 60.25 W
Villablino 34 42.56 N 6.19 W
Villa Borghese ʊ 267a 41.55 N 12.29 E
Villa Bosch ◆[8] 288 34.35 S 58.34 W
Villa Bruzual 246 9.20 N 69.06 W
Villa Cañás, Arg. 252 34.00 S 61.36 W
Villacañas, Esp. 34 39.38 N 3.20 W
Villa Carlos Paz 252 31.24 S 64.31 W
Villacarriedo 34 43.14 N 3.48 W
Villacarrillo 34 38.07 N 3.05 W
Villa Castelli, Arg. 252 29.00 S 68.11 W
Villa Castelli, It. 68 40.35 N 17.28 E
Villacastín 34 40.47 N 4.25 W
Villach 64 46.36 N 13.50 E
Villacidro 71 39.27 N 8.44 E
Villa Ciudadela ◆[8] 258 34.38 S 58.34 W
Villa Clara □[4] 240p 22.30 N 80.00 W
Villa Comaltitlan 236 15.13 N 92.35 W
Villa Concepción del Tío 252 31.19 S 62.50 W
Villa Constitución 252 33.14 S 60.20 W
Villa Cortese 266b 45.34 N 8.53 E
Villa Corzo 234 16.10 N 93.15 W
Villacoublay, Aérodrome de ⊠ 261 48.45 N 2.10 E
Villa Creek ≐ 226 35.27 N 120.58 W
Villa Cuauhtémoc, Méx. 234 19.24 N 99.34 W
Villa Cuauhtémoc, Méx. 234 22.11 N 97.50 W
Villada 34 42.15 N 4.58 W
Villa de Apaseo El Alto 234 20.27 N 100.37 W
Villa de Arista 234 22.39 N 100.50 W
Villa de Arriaga 234 21.54 N 101.23 W
Villadeati 62 45.04 N 8.10 E
Villa de Cos 234 23.17 N 102.21 W
Villa de Cura 246 10.02 N 67.29 W
Villa de Guadalupe 234 23.22 N 100.46 W
Villa del Carmen 252 32.57 S 65.03 W
Villa del Pueblito 234 20.32 N 100.27 W
Villa del Río 34 37.59 N 4.17 W
Villa del Rosario, Arg. 252 31.35 S 63.32 W
Villa del Rosario, Arg. 252 30.47 S 57.55 W
Villa de María 252 29.54 S 63.43 W
Villa de Mayo 258 34.30 S 58.41 W
Villa de Nova Sintra 150a 14.52 N 24.43 W
Villa de Reyes 234 21.48 N 100.56 W
Villa de San Antonio 236 14.16 N 87.36 W
Villa de San Francisco 236 14.10 N 86.58 W
Villa de Soto 252 30.51 S 64.59 W
Villa d'Este ⊥ 267a 41.57 N 12.48 E
Villa Devoto ◆[8] 288 34.36 S 58.31 W
Villa Diamante ◆[8] 288 34.41 S 58.26 W
Villa di Chiavenna 58 46.20 N 9.29 E
Villadiego 34 42.31 N 4.00 W
Villa Dolores 252 31.56 S 65.12 W
Villa Domínico ◆[8] 258 34.41 S 58.19 W
Villadose 64 45.04 N 11.53 E
Villadossola 58 46.04 N 8.16 E
Villa Elisa 252 32.10 S 58.24 W
Villa Elisa ◆[8] 258 34.50 S 58.05 W
Villa Escalante 234 19.24 N 101.39 W
Villa Flores 234 16.14 N 93.14 W
Villa Florida 252 26.23 S 57.09 W
Villafranca d'Asti 62 44.55 N 8.02 E
Villafranca del Bierzo 34 42.36 N 6.48 W
Villafranca de los Barros 34 38.34 N 6.20 W
Villafranca di Verona 64 45.21 N 10.50 E
Villafranca in Lunigiana 64 44.17 N 9.57 E
Villafranca Piemonte 62 44.47 N 7.33 E
Villafranca Sicula 70 37.35 N 13.17 E
Villafranca Tirrena 70 38.14 N 15.26 E
Villafrati 70 37.54 N 13.29 E
Villagarcía, Esp. 34 42.36 N 8.45 W
Villa García, Méx. 234 22.10 N 101.57 W
Village 196 35.33 N 97.33 W
Village Creek ≐, Ar., U.S. 194 35.28 N 91.19 W
Village Creek ≐, Tx., U.S. 222 32.46 N 97.09 W
Village Green 285 39.52 N 75.26 W
Villa General Roca 252 32.39 S 66.28 W
Village of Drummond Hill 285 39.43 N 75.42 W
Village of the Branch 276 40.51 N 73.11 W
Villa Gesell 252 37.15 S 56.55 W
Villa Giambruno 288 34.48 S 58.13 W
Villa González Ortega 234 22.30 N 101.55 W
Villagrán, Méx. 232 24.29 N 99.29 W
Villagrán, Méx. 234 20.31 N 100.59 W
Villagrande Strisaili 71 39.58 N 9.30 E
Villa Grazia 70 38.09 N 13.10 E
Villa Grove 194 39.51 N 88.09 W
Villaguay 252 31.51 S 59.01 W
Villa Guerrero, Méx. 234 21.59 N 103.36 W
Villa Guerrero, Méx. 234 18.52 N 99.39 W
Villa Guillermina 252 28.14 S 59.28 W
Villa Hayes 252 25.06 S 57.34 W
Villahermosa 234 17.59 N 92.55 W
Villa Hernandarias 252 31.13 S 59.59 W
Villa Hidalgo, Méx. 204 30.59 N 116.10 W
Villa Hidalgo, Méx. 234 21.40 N 102.36 W
Villa Hidalgo, Méx. 234 21.44 N 105.15 W
Villa Hidalgo Yalalag 234 17.11 N 96.11 W
Villa Huidobro 252 34.50 S 64.35 W
Villaines-la-Juhel 32 48.21 N 0.17 W
Villa Insurgentes 232 25.12 N 111.44 W
Villa Iris 252 38.10 S 63.15 W
Villa Jiménez 234 19.55 N 101.35 W
Villa José L. Suárez ◆[8] 288 34.32 S 58.35 W
Villa Juanita 234 17.47 N 95.09 W
Villa Juárez, Méx. 232 27.10 N 109.50 W
Villa Juárez, Méx. 234 22.20 N 100.17 W
Villa Krause 252 31.34 S 68.32 W
Villa La Angostura 254 40.47 S 71.40 W
Villalago 66 41.56 N 13.50 E
Villa Larca 252 32.37 S 64.59 W
Villa La Venta 234 18.10 N 94.07 W
Villalba, It. 70 37.39 N 13.50 E
Villalba, P.R. 240m 18.08 N 66.30 W
Villaldama 232 26.30 N 100.26 W
Villa Lia 258 34.07 S 59.26 W
Villalon 116 11.31 N 124.22 E
Villalón de Campos 34 42.06 N 5.02 W
Villalonga 254 39.53 S 62.35 W
Villalpando 34 41.52 N 5.24 W
Villa Lugano ◆[8] 288 34.41 S 58.28 W
Villalvernia 62 44.49 N 8.51 E
Villa Lynch → Lynch, Arg. ◆[8] 288 34.36 S 58.31 W
Villa Madero, Arg. 288 34.42 S 58.30 W
Villa Madero, Méx. 234 19.24 N 101.16 W
Villa Mainero 232 24.32 N 99.38 W
Villamar 71 39.37 N 8.59 E
Villa María, Arg. 252 32.25 S 63.15 W
Villa Maria, Pa., U.S. 214 41.05 N 80.30 W
Villa Maria del Triunfo 286d 12.10 S 76.56 W
Villa María Grande 252 31.39 S 59.54 W
Villa Martín, Bol. 248 20.46 S 67.47 W
Villamartín, Esp. 34 36.52 N 5.38 W
Villamarzana 64 45.01 N 11.41 E
Villamassargia 71 39.16 N 8.38 E
Villa Matoque 252 25.49 S 63.49 W
Villa Mazán 252 28.40 S 66.34 W
Villa Media Agua 252 31.59 S 68.25 W
Villa Mercedes 252 30.07 S 68.42 W
Villa Minozzo 64 44.22 N 10.28 E
Villamontes 248 21.15 S 63.30 W
Villa Morelos 234 20.00 N 101.25 W
Villandraut 32 44.28 N 0.23 W
Villa Nova, Md., U.S. 284b 39.21 N 76.44 W
Villa Nova, Oh., U.S. 216 40.33 N 84.26 W
Villanova, Pa., U.S. 208 40.02 N 75.20 W
Villanova d'Asti 62 44.57 N 7.56 E
Villanova Mondovì 62 44.21 N 7.45 E
Villanova Monferrato 62 45.11 N 8.28 E
Villanova Monteleone 71 40.30 N 8.28 E
Villanova sull'Arda 64 45.01 N 10.00 E
Villanova Tulo 71 39.47 N 9.13 E
Villanova University ʊ[2] 285 40.02 N 75.21 W
Villa Nueva, Arg. 252 32.26 S 63.15 W
Villa Nueva, Arg. 252 32.54 S 68.47 W
Villanueva, Col. 246 10.37 N 72.59 W
Villa Nueva, Guat. 236 14.31 N 90.35 W
Villanueva, Hond. 236 15.17 N 88.00 W
Villanueva, Méx. 234 22.21 N 102.53 W
Villa Nueva, Nic. 236 12.58 N 86.49 W
Villanueva, N.M., U.S. 200 35.16 N 105.21 W
Villanueva de Córdoba 34 38.20 N 4.37 W
Villanueva de la Serana 34 38.58 N 5.48 W
Villanueva de la Sierra 34 40.12 N 6.24 W
Villanueva de los Infantes 34 38.44 N 3.01 W
Villanueva del Río y Minas 34 37.39 N 5.42 W
Villa Numancia 288 34.55 S 58.24 W
Villa Obregón 234 21.07 N 102.42 W
Villa Ocampo 252 28.28 S 59.22 W
Villa Ojo de Agua 252 29.31 S 63.42 W
Villa Oliva 252 26.01 S 57.53 W
Villa Opicina 64 45.40 N 13.49 E
Villa Oropeza 248 19.10 S 65.17 W
Villa Ottone (Uttenheim) 64 46.52 N 11.57 E
Villa Papale ʊ 267a 41.45 N 12.39 E
Villa Park, Ca., U.S. 228 33.48 N 117.48 W
Villa Park, Il., U.S. 278 41.53 N 87.59 W
Villa Park Dam ◆[6] 280 33.48 N 117.46 W
Villa Pérez 240m 18.12 N 66.47 W
Villapiana 68 39.51 N 16.28 E
Villapiana Lido 68 39.48 N 16.29 E
Villapinzón 246 5.13 N 73.36 W
Villa Potenza 66 43.19 N 13.25 E
Villaputzu 71 39.26 N 9.34 E
Villa Quinteros 252 27.14 S 65.33 W
Villa Quintilio Varo ⊥ 267a 41.58 N 12.47 E
Villa Ramírez 252 32.11 S 60.12 W
Villarcayo 34 42.56 N 3.34 W
Villar-d'Arène 62 45.02 N 6.20 E
Villard-Bonnot 62 45.14 N 5.53 E
Villard-de-Lans 62 45.04 N 5.33 E
Villardefrades 34 41.43 N 5.15 W
Villar del Arzobispo 34 39.44 N 0.49 W
Villareal 116 11.34 N 124.56 E
Villa Real ◆[8] 288 34.37 S 58.31 W
Villa Regina 252 39.06 S 67.04 W
Villa Reynolds 252 33.43 S 65.23 W
Villa Rica 192 33.43 N 84.55 W
Villa Rivero 248 17.37 S 65.48 W
Villaroche 261 48.37 N 2.39 E
Villaroche ■ 261 48.37 N 2.40 E
Villa Romana del Casale ⊥ 70 37.22 N 14.20 E
Villa Rosa, Arg. 258 34.25 S 58.52 W
Villarosa, It. 70 37.35 N 14.10 E
Villar Pellice 62 44.48 N 7.09 E
Villar Perosa 62 44.56 N 7.15 E
Villarreales 196 26.07 N 100.20 W
Villarrica, Chile 254 39.16 S 72.13 W
Villarrica, Col. 246 3.58 N 74.37 W
Villarrica, Para. 252 25.45 S 56.26 W
Villarrica, Lago ⊜ 254 39.15 S 72.06 W
Villarrobledo 34 39.16 N 2.36 W
Villarrubia de los Ojos 34 39.13 N 3.36 W
Villars, Arg. 258 34.50 S 58.56 W
Villars, Schw. 58 46.18 N 7.04 E
Villars-Colmars 62 44.10 N 6.36 E
Villars-en-Azois 58 48.04 N 4.45 E
Villars-les-Dombes 58 46.00 N 5.01 E
Villars-sur-Var 62 43.56 N 7.06 E
Villa Ruiz 258 34.25 S 59.15 W
Villas 208 39.01 N 74.56 W
Villa Sáenz Peña ◆[8] 288 34.36 S 58.31 W
Villa San Andrés ◆[8] 288 34.33 S 58.32 W
Villa Sandino 236 12.03 N 84.59 W
Villa San Giovanni 68 38.13 N 15.38 E
Villa San José 252 32.12 S 58.13 W
Villa San Martín 252 28.18 S 64.12 W
Villasanta 62 45.37 N 9.18 E
Villa Santa, Montaña ∧ 236 14.12 N 86.27 W
Villa Santa Maria 66 41.57 N 14.21 E
Villa Santina 64 46.24 N 12.55 E
Villa Santo Domingo 234 23.20 N 101.44 W
Villa Santos Lugares ◆[8] 288 34.36 S 58.32 W
Villasayas 34 41.21 N 2.37 W
Villa Serrano 248 19.06 S 64.22 W
Villasimius 71 39.08 N 9.31 E
Villasis 116 15.54 N 120.35 E
Villasor 71 39.23 N 8.56 E
Villa Talavera 248 19.49 S 65.25 W
Villa Tunari 248 16.55 S 65.25 W
Villa Turdera ◆[8] 288 34.48 S 58.25 W
Villa Unión, Arg. 252 29.18 S 68.12 W
Villa Unión, Arg. 252 29.24 S 62.47 W
Villa Unión, Méx. 232 28.15 N 100.43 W
Villa Unión, Méx. 234 23.58 N 104.02 W
Villa Unión, Méx. 234 23.12 N 106.14 W
Villa Valeria 252 34.20 S 64.55 W
Villa Vallelonga 66 41.52 N 13.37 E
Villaverde ◆[8] 266a 40.21 N 3.42 W
Villaverla 64 45.39 N 11.29 E
Villa Verona 226 39.28 N 121.33 W
Villavicencio 246 4.09 N 73.37 W
Villaviciosa 34 43.29 N 5.26 W
Villaviciosa de Córdoba 34 38.05 N 5.01 W
Villa Victoria 234 18.47 N 103.24 W
Villa Viscarra 248 17.59 S 65.36 W
Villa Vomano 66 42.37 N 13.46 E
Villazón 248 22.06 S 65.36 W
Villa Zorraquín 252 31.19 S 58.02 W
Villé 58 48.20 N 7.18 E
Villebon, Lac ⊜ 190 47.58 N 77.17 W
Villebon-sur-Yvette 261 48.42 N 2.15 E
Villeconin 261 48.31 N 2.08 E
Villecresnes 261 48.43 N 2.32 E
Villecroze 62 43.35 N 6.16 E
Ville-d'Avray 261 48.50 N 2.11 E
Ville-de-Laval → Laval 206 45.35 N 73.45 W
Villedieu 32 48.50 N 1.13 W
Ville-en-Tardenois 50 49.11 N 3.48 E
Villefort 62 44.26 N 3.56 E
Villefranche 58 45.59 N 4.43 E
Villefranche-de-Rouergue 32 44.21 N 2.02 E
Villefranche-sur-Cher 50 47.18 N 1.46 E
Villefranche-sur-Mer 62 43.42 N 7.19 E
Villejuif 50 48.48 N 2.22 E
Villejust 261 48.41 N 2.14 E
Ville-Marie 190 47.19 N 79.26 W
Villemaur-sur-Vanne 50 48.15 N 3.44 E
Villemeux-sur-Eure 50 48.40 N 1.28 E
Villemoisson-sur-Orge 261 48.40 N 2.19 E
Villemomble 261 48.53 N 2.31 E
Villena 34 38.38 N 0.51 W
Ville Nacíonal 234 17.50 N 96.14 W
Villenauxe-la-Grande 50 48.35 N 3.33 E
Villeneuve, It. 62 45.42 N 7.14 E
Villeneuve, Schw. 58 46.24 N 6.55 E
Villeneuve-d'Ascq 50 50.37 N 3.10 E
Villeneuve-d'Aveyron 32 44.26 N 2.02 E
Villeneuve-de-Berg 62 44.33 N 4.30 E
Villeneuve-la-Garenne 261 48.56 N 2.20 E
Villeneuve-la-Guyard 50 48.20 N 3.04 E
Villeneuve-l'Archevêque 50 48.14 N 3.33 E
Villeneuve-le-Comte 261 48.49 N 2.50 E
Villeneuve-le-Roi 50 48.44 N 2.25 E
Villeneuve-lès-Avignon 62 43.58 N 4.48 E
Villeneuve-lès-Maguelonne 62 43.32 N 3.52 E
Villeneuve-Saint-Denis 261 48.49 N 2.48 E
Villeneuve-Saint-Georges 50 48.44 N 2.27 E
Villeneuve-sous-Dammartin 261 49.02 N 2.39 E
Villeneuve-sur-Lot 32 44.25 N 0.42 E
Villeneuve-sur-Yonne 50 48.05 N 3.18 E
Villennes-sur-Seine 261 48.56 N 2.00 E
Villenoy 50 48.57 N 2.52 E
Villeny 50 47.37 N 1.45 E
Villeparisis 50 48.56 N 2.37 E
Villepinte 261 48.58 N 2.32 E
Ville Platte 194 30.41 N 92.16 W
Villepreux 261 48.50 N 2.01 E
Villequier 50 49.31 N 0.40 E
Villeron 261 49.03 N 2.33 E
Villeroy 50 48.59 N 2.47 E
Villers-Bocage, Fr. 32 49.05 N 0.39 W
Villers-Bocage, Fr. 50 49.59 N 2.20 E
Villers-Bretonneux 50 49.52 N 2.31 E
Villers-Carbonnel 50 49.52 N 2.54 E
Villers-Cotterêts 50 49.15 N 3.05 E
Villers-devant-Orval 56 49.37 N 5.19 E
Villers-en-Arthies 261 49.05 N 1.44 E
Villersexel 58 47.33 N 6.26 E
Villers-Farlay 58 47.00 N 5.45 E
Villers-la-Ville 50 50.35 N 4.32 E
Villers-le-Lac 58 47.04 N 6.40 E
Villers-lès-Nancy 58 48.40 N 6.09 E
Villers-lès-Pots 58 47.13 N 5.21 E
Villers-Outréaux 50 50.02 N 3.18 E
Villers-Saint-Paul 50 49.17 N 2.29 E
Villers-Semeuse 56 49.44 N 4.45 E
Villerupt 56 49.28 N 5.56 E
Villerville 50 49.24 N 0.08 E
Ville-Saint-Georges → Saint-Georges 188 46.07 N 70.40 W
Villes-sur-Auzon 62 44.03 N 5.14 E
Ville-sur-Tourbe 56 49.11 N 4.47 E
Villeta 246 5.01 N 74.28 W
Villetta Barrea 66 41.47 N 13.56 E
Villeurbanne 62 45.46 N 4.53 E
Villevaudé 261 48.55 N 2.39 E
Villeziers 261 48.40 N 2.10 E
Villiers 158 27.03 S 28.35 E
Villiers-Adam 261 49.04 N 2.14 E
Villiersdorp 158 34.00 S 19.19 E
Villiers-le-Bâcle 261 48.44 N 2.08 E
Villiers-le-Bel 261 49.00 N 2.23 E
Villiers-le-Sec 261 49.04 N 2.23 E
Villiers-Saint-Frédéric 261 48.49 N 1.54 E
Villiers-Saint-Georges 50 48.39 N 3.25 E
Villiers-sur-Marne 261 48.50 N 2.33 E
Villiers-sur-Morin 261 48.52 N 2.53 E
Villigst 263 51.26 N 7.35 E
Villingen-Schwenningen 58 48.04 N 8.28 E
Villisca 198 40.55 N 94.58 W
Villmanstrand → Lappeenranta 26 61.04 N 28.11 E
Villmergen 58 47.21 N 8.15 E
Villorba 64 45.44 N 12.14 E
Villoresi, Canale ≊ 266b 45.33 N 9.19 E
Villotta 64 45.52 N 12.45 E
Vilm I 54 54.19 N 13.32 E
Vilmnitz 54 54.21 N 13.31 E
Vilna, Ab., Can. 182 54.07 N 111.55 W
Vilna → Vilnius, Liet. 76 54.41 N 25.19 E
Vilnius 76 54.41 N 25.19 E
Vil'nohirs'k 78 48.29 N 34.01 E
Vilosnes-sur-Meuse 56 49.20 N 5.14 E
Vilppula 26 62.01 N 24.31 E
Vils 58 47.33 N 10.38 E
Vils ≐, Dtsch. 60 49.09 N 11.58 E
Vils ≐, Dtsch. 60 48.37 N 13.11 E
Vils ≐, Europe 58 47.33 N 10.40 E
Vilsandi saar I 76 58.23 N 21.52 E
Vilsbiburg 60 48.27 N 12.12 E
Vilseck 60 49.37 N 11.48 E
Vil'shana 78 49.13 N 31.13 E
Vil'shanka 78 48.14 N 30.52 E
Vil'shany, Ukr. 78 50.03 N 35.53 E
Vil'shany, Ukr. 78 49.47 N 37.46 E
Vilsheim 60 48.27 N 12.07 E
Vilshofen 60 48.39 N 13.12 E
Vil'uj ≐ 74 64.24 N 126.26 E
Vil'ujsk 74 63.45 N 121.35 E
Vil'ujskoje vodochranilišče ⊜[1] 74 62.30 N 111.00 E
Viluppuram 122 11.56 N 79.29 E
Vil'va 86 58.37 N 56.52 E
Vilvoorde 50 50.56 N 4.26 E
Vimercate 62 45.37 N 9.22 E
Vimianzo 34 43.07 N 9.02 W
Vimmerby 26 57.40 N 15.51 E
Vimodrone 266b 45.31 N 9.17 E
Vimoutiers 50 48.55 N 0.12 E
Vimpeli 26 63.09 N 23.48 E
Vimperk 60 49.03 N 13.47 E
Vimy 50 50.22 N 2.49 E
Vina 204 39.55 N 122.03 W
Vina ≐ 146 7.45 N 15.36 E
Viñac 248 12.56 S 75.47 W
Viña del Mar 252 33.02 S 71.34 W
Vinadi 58 46.55 N 10.29 E
Vinadio 62 44.18 N 7.10 E
Viñales 240p 22.37 N 83.43 W
Vinalhaven 188 44.02 N 68.49 W
Vinalhaven Island I 188 44.05 N 68.52 W
Vinantes 261 49.01 N 2.44 E
Vina Roni, Mount ∧ 175e 8.10 S 157.28 E
Vinaròs 34 40.28 N 0.29 E
Vinay 62 45.13 N 5.24 E
Vinazco ≐ 234 20.56 N 97.44 W
Vincennes, Fr. 50 48.51 N 2.26 E
Vincennes, In., U.S. 194 38.40 N 87.31 W
Vincennes, Bois de ♠ 261 48.50 N 2.25 E
Vincennes, Château de ⊥ 261 48.51 N 2.26 E
Vincennes, Étang de ⊜ 261 48.47 N 2.45 E
Vincennes Bay ⊂ 9 66.30 S 109.30 E
Vincent 194 33.22 N 86.22 W
Vincent, Point ≻ 174c 29.00 S 167.55 E
Vincentown 208 39.56 N 74.44 W
Vinces 246 1.32 S 79.45 W
Vincey 58 48.20 N 6.20 E
Vinchiaturo 66 41.29 N 14.35 E
Vinchina 252 28.46 S 68.10 W
Vinchos 248 13.16 S 74.21 W
Vinci 66 43.47 N 10.55 E
Vinco 214 40.25 N 78.52 W
Vindeby 41 55.03 N 10.38 E
Vindelälven ≐ 24 63.54 N 19.52 E
Vindeln 26 64.12 N 19.44 E
Vinden, Mount ∧ 162 27.01 S 115.38 E
Vinderslev 41 56.15 N 9.26 E
Vinderup 26 56.29 N 8.47 E
Vindhya Range ⋀ 120 23.00 N 77.00 E
Vinding 41 55.41 N 9.35 E
Vindinge 41 55.19 N 10.45 E
Vine Brook ≐ 283 42.27 N 71.13 W
Vinegar Hill ∧ 202 44.43 N 118.34 W
Vine Grove 194 37.48 N 85.58 W
Vine Hill 282 38.00 N 122.06 W
Vineland, Mi., U.S. 216 42.03 N 86.30 W
Vineland, N.J., U.S. 208 39.29 N 75.01 W
Vinemont 194 34.14 N 86.51 W
Vine Valley 210 42.43 N 77.20 W
Vineyard Canyon V 226 35.46 N 120.41 W
Vineyard Haven 207 41.27 N 70.36 W
Vineyard Lake ⊜ 216 42.05 N 84.13 W
Vineyard Sound ⊔ 207 41.25 N 70.46 W
Vingåker 40 59.02 N 15.52 E
Vingeanne ≐ 58 47.21 N 5.29 E
Ving Ngün 110 22.37 N 99.16 E
Vinh 110 18.40 N 105.40 E
Vinhais 34 41.50 N 7.00 W
Vinhas, Ribeira das ≐ 266c 38.42 N 9.25 W
Vinh Chau 110 9.19 N 105.59 E
Vinhedo 256 23.01 S 46.59 W
Vinh Loc 269c 10.49 N 106.34 E
Vinh Long 110 10.15 N 105.58 E
Vinh Tuy, Viet 110 9.37 N 105.22 E
Vinh Tuy, Viet 110 17.24 N 106.36 E
Vinica 36 45.28 N 15.15 E
Vinita 196 36.38 N 95.09 W
Vinkekuil 158 32.42 S 20.27 E

Symbols in the index entries represent the broad categories identified in the key at the right. Symbols with superior numbers (⋀[1]) identify subcategories (see complete key on page *I · 1).*

Symbole im Register stellen die rechts im Schlüssel erklärten Kategorien dar. Symbole mit hochgestellten Ziffern (⋀[1]) bezeichnen Unterabteilungen einer Kategorie (vgl. vollständiger Schlüssel auf Seite *I · 1).*

Los símbolos incluídos en el texto del índice representan las grandes categorías identificadas con la clave a la derecha. Los símbolos con numeros en su parte superior (⋀[1]) identifican las subcategorías (véase la clave completa en la página *I · 1).*

Les symboles de l'index représentent les catégories indiquées dans la légende à droite. Les symboles suivis d'un indice (⋀[1]) représentent des sous-catégories (voir légende complète à la page *I · 1).*

Os símbolos incluídos no texto do índice representam as grandes categorias identificadas com a chave à direita. Os símbolos com números em sua parte superior (⋀[1]) identificam as subcategorias (veja-se a chave completa à página *I · 1).*

English	Deutsch	Español	Français	Português
∧ Mountain	Berg	Montaña	Montagne	Montanha
⋀ Mountains	Gebirge	Montañas	Montagnes	Montanhas
)(Pass	Paß	Paso	Col	Passo
V Valley, Canyon	Tal, Cañon	Valle, Cañón	Vallée, Canyon	Vale, Canhão
≚ Plain	Ebene	Llano	Plaine	Planície
≻ Cape	Kap	Cabo	Cap	Cabo
I Island	Insel	Isla	Île	Ilha
II Islands	Inseln	Islas	Îles	Ilhas
≛ Other Topographic Features	Andere Topographische Objekte	Otros Elementos Topográficos	Autres données topographiques	Outros acidentes topográficos

ESPAÑOL · FRANÇAIS · PORTUGUÊS

Nombre / Nom / Nome	Página / Page / Página	Lat.°′	Long.°′ W = Oeste / Ouest / Oeste
Vinkeveen	52	52.13 N	4.54 E
Vin'kivtsi	78	49.02 N	27.14 E
Vinkovci	38	45.17 N	18.49 E
Vinnhorst	52	52.25 N	9.43 E
Vinnitsa → Vinnytsya	78	49.14 N	28.29 E
Vinnum	263	51.41 N	7.24 E
Vinnytsya	78	49.14 N	28.29 E
Vinnytsya □[4]	78	49.00 N	28.45 E
Vinogradovo, Ross.	82	55.25 N	38.32 E
Vinogradovo, Ross.	82	55.57 N	37.32 E
Vinogrobol'	78	51.51 N	36.26 E
Vinön I	40	59.12 N	15.43 E
Vinon-sur-Verdon	62	43.43 N	5.48 E
Vinovo	62	44.57 N	7.38 E
Vinslöv	26	56.06 N	13.55 E
Vinson Massif ∧	9	78.35 S	85.25 W
Vinstra	26	61.36 N	9.45 E
Vintilă Vodă	38	45.28 N	26.44 E
Vinto	248	17.58 S	67.04 W
Vinton, Ia., U.S.	190	42.10 N	92.01 W
Vinton, La., U.S.	194	30.11 N	93.34 W
Vinton, Va., U.S.	192	37.16 N	79.53 W
Vintondale	214	40.28 N	78.55 W
Vintrosa	40	59.15 N	14.57 E
Viñuelas, Arroyo de ≃	266a	40.33 N	3.33 W
Viny	76	58.22 N	32.13 E
Vinzelberg	54	52.33 N	11.40 E
Vinzili	86	56.58 N	65.46 E
Viola, Il., U.S.	190	41.12 N	90.35 W
Viola, N.Y., U.S.	276	41.08 N	74.05 W
Viola, Wi., U.S.	190	43.30 N	90.40 W
Viola, Val V	64	46.27 N	10.15 E
Violín, Isla I	236	8.51 N	83.39 W
Viols-le-Fort	62	43.45 N	3.42 E
Viosne ≃	50	49.03 N	2.06 E
Vipava	36	45.51 N	13.58 E
Vipava ≃	64	45.54 N	13.33 E
Vipiteno (Sterzing)	64	46.54 N	11.26 E
Vipos	252	26.29 S	65.22 W
Vipperow	54	53.19 N	12.41 E
Vir, Otok I	36	44.18 N	15.04 E
Vira	58	46.08 N	8.51 E
Virac	116	13.35 N	124.15 E
Viracopos, Aeroporto de ⊠	256	23.00 S	47.08 W
Virac Point >	116	13.31 N	124.13 E
Viradouro	255	20.53 S	48.18 W
Virago Sound ⊔	182	54.00 N	132.36 W
Viramgām	120	23.07 N	72.02 E
Virandozero	24	64.05 N	35.58 E
Viranşehir	130	37.13 N	39.45 E
Vīrarājendrapet	122	12.12 N	75.48 E
Virbalis	76	54.38 N	22.49 E
Virden, Mb., Can.	184	49.51 N	100.55 W
Virden, Il., U.S.	219	39.30 N	89.46 W
Virden, N.M., U.S.	200	32.41 N	109.00 W
Vire	32	48.50 N	0.53 W
Vire ≃	32	49.20 N	1.07 W
Virelles	50	50.04 N	4.20 E
Virelles, Étang de ⊜	50	50.04 N	4.21 E
Vireux-Molhain	56	50.05 N	4.43 E
Virgem da Lapa	255	16.49 S	42.21 W
Virgen	64	47.00 N	12.27 E
Vírgen del San Cristóbal ☉[1]	286e	33.26 S	70.39 W
Vírgenes, Cabo >	254	52.22 S	68.20 W
Vírgenes, Islas → British Virgin Islands □[2], N.A.	240m	18.30 N	64.30 W
Vírgenes, Islas → Virgin Islands □[2], N.A.	240m	18.20 N	64.50 W
Virgen Tal V	64	47.00 N	12.25 E
Virgil, On., Can.	284a	43.13 N	79.08 W
Virgil, Ks., U.S.	198	37.58 N	96.00 W
Virgil, N.Y., U.S.	210	42.31 N	76.12 W
Virgilina	192	36.33 N	78.52 W
Virgilio	64	45.07 N	10.47 E
Virgin ≃	200	36.31 N	114.20 W
Virgin, North Fork ≃	200	37.10 N	113.01 W
Virginal-Samme	50	50.38 N	4.12 E
Virgin Gorda I	240m	18.30 N	64.24 W
Virgin Gorda Peak ∧	240m	18.30 N	64.24 W
Virginia, Austl.	168b	34.40 S	138.34 E
Virgínia, Bra.	256	22.20 S	45.06 W
Virginia, Ire.	48	53.49 N	7.04 W
Virginia, S. Afr.	158	28.12 S	26.49 E
Virginia, Il., U.S.	219	39.57 N	90.12 W
Virginia, Mn., U.S.	190	47.31 N	92.32 W
Virginia □[3]	178	37.30 N	78.45 W
Virginia Beach	208	36.51 N	75.58 W
Virginia City, Mt., U.S.	202	45.17 N	111.56 W
Virginia City, Nv., U.S.	226	39.18 N	119.38 W
Virginia Creek ≃	226	38.13 N	119.14 W
Virginia Falls ⌊	180	61.38 N	125.42 W
Virginia Gardens	220	25.49 N	80.17 W
Virginia Hills	208	38.47 N	77.06 W
Virginia Key I	220	25.44 N	80.09 W
Virginia Peak ∧	204	39.45 N	119.28 W
Virginia Ranch Reservoir ⊜[1]	226	39.20 N	121.19 W
Virginia Range ⋏	226	39.18 N	119.30 W
Virginiatown	190	48.08 N	79.35 W
Virginia Water	260	51.24 N	0.34 W
Virginia Water ⊜[1]	260	51.24 N	0.37 W
Virginie occidentale → West Virginia □[3]	188	38.45 N	80.30 W
Virgin Islands □[2], N.A.	230	18.20 N	64.50 W
Virgin Islands □[2], N.A.	240m	18.20 N	64.50 W
Virgin Islands II	240m	18.00 N	64.40 W
Virgin Islands National Park ♠	240m	18.20 N	64.45 W
Virginópolis	255	18.45 S	42.45 W
Virgin Passage ⊔	240m	18.20 N	65.10 W
Virginville	208	40.31 N	75.52 W
Virgolândia	255	18.27 S	42.18 W
Virieu	62	45.29 N	5.28 E
Virieu-le-Grand	62	45.51 N	5.39 E
Virihaure ⊜	24	67.20 N	16.35 E
Virje	36	46.04 N	16.59 E
Virkkala	26	60.12 N	24.01 E
Virklund	41	56.07 N	9.34 E
Virneburg	56	50.20 N	7.04 E
Virôchey	110	13.59 N	106.49 E
Viroflay	50	48.48 N	2.10 E
Viroin ≃	56	50.05 N	4.43 E
Virojoki	26	60.35 N	27.42 E
Víron	267c	37.57 N	23.45 E
Vironvay	50	49.12 N	1.13 E
Viroqua	190	43.33 N	90.53 W
Virovitica	36	45.50 N	17.23 E
Virpazar	38	42.15 N	19.05 E
Virrat	26	62.14 N	23.47 E
Virsbo	40	59.52 N	16.02 E
Virserum	26	57.19 N	15.35 E
Virtaniemi	24	68.53 N	28.27 E
Virton	56	49.34 N	5.32 E
Virtsu	76	58.34 N	23.31 E
Virú	248	8.25 S	78.45 W
Virudunagar	122	9.36 N	77.58 E
Viru-Jaagupi	76	59.15 N	26.28 E
Virulento	196	28.52 N	104.21 W
Virunga, Parc National de ♠	154	1.00 S	29.15 E
Virungu	154	7.04 S	29.46 E
Viru-Nigula	76	59.27 N	26.41 E
Virvytė ≃	76	56.13 N	22.34 E
Viry-Châtillon	50	48.40 N	2.23 E
Vis	36	43.03 N	16.12 E
Vis ≃, Fr.	62	43.56 N	3.42 E
Vis (Fish) ≃, Namibia	156	28.07 S	17.45 E
Vis ≃, S. Afr.	158	30.53 S	20.23 E
Vis, Otok I	36	43.02 N	16.11 E
Visale	175e	9.15 S	159.42 E
Visalia	226	36.19 N	119.17 W
Visalia Airport ⊠	226	36.19 N	119.23 W
Visayan Islands II	12	11.00 N	123.30 E
Visayan Sea ⊤[2]	116	11.35 N	123.51 E
Visbek	52	52.48 N	8.19 E
Visby	26	57.38 N	18.18 E
Viscaya, Bahía de → Biscay, Bay of c	32	44.00 N	4.00 W
Viscount	184	51.57 N	105.39 W
Viscount Melville Sound ⊔	176	74.10 N	108.00 W
Visé	56	50.44 N	5.42 E
Višegrad	38	43.47 N	19.17 E
Vis-en-Artois	50	50.15 N	2.56 E
Višera ≃	76	58.34 N	31.24 E
Viserba	66	44.05 N	12.32 E
Viseu, Bra.	250	1.12 S	46.07 W
Viseu, Port.	34	40.39 N	7.55 W
Vișeu ≃	38	47.55 N	24.09 E
Vișeu de Sus	38	47.44 N	24.22 E
Vishākhapatnam	122	17.42 N	83.18 E
Vishoek	158	34.08 S	18.26 E
Visim	86	57.39 N	59.30 E
Visingsö I	26	58.03 N	14.20 E
Visitation, Île de la I	275a	45.35 N	73.40 W
Viskafors	26	57.38 N	12.50 E
Viskan ≃	26	57.14 N	12.12 E
Viškil'	80	58.05 N	48.19 E
Viskinge	41	55.40 N	11.16 E
Visl'ajevo	82	54.25 N	36.43 E
Vislanda	26	56.47 N	14.27 E
Vislinskij zaliv c	30	54.27 N	19.40 E
Vismen ⊜	40	59.17 N	14.17 E
Visnagar	120	23.42 N	72.33 E
Višn'aki	265b	55.47 N	37.54 E
Višn'akovo	82	55.45 N	38.10 E
Višneva	76	54.08 N	26.14 E
Višnevoje	80	52.38 N	43.26 E
Višňové	61	48.59 N	16.09 E
Višn'ovka	86	50.49 N	72.12 E
Viso, Monte ∧	62	44.40 N	7.07 E
Visoki Dečani, Manastir ☉[1]	38	42.30 N	20.31 E
Visoko	38	43.59 N	18.11 E
Visokoi Island I	18	56.42 S	27.12 W
Visp	58	46.18 N	7.53 E
Vispa ≃	58	46.18 N	7.52 E
Visrivier	158	31.55 S	25.25 E
Vissefjärda	26	56.32 N	15.35 E
Visselhövede	52	52.59 N	9.35 E
Vissenbjerg	41	55.23 N	10.08 E
Visso	66	42.56 N	13.05 E
Vissoie	58	46.13 N	7.36 E
Vista, Ca., U.S.	228	33.12 N	117.14 W
Vista, N.Y., U.S.	210	41.12 N	73.31 W
Vista Alegre, Arg.	252	38.45 S	68.11 W
Vista Alegre, Bra.	256	21.27 S	42.35 W
Vista Alegre, Chile	286e	33.30 S	70.43 W
Vista Alegre, Perú	286d	12.09 S	77.00 W
Vista Flores	252	33.38 S	69.09 W
Vistahermosa de Negrete	234	20.16 N	102.29 W
Vista Park	228	35.21 N	118.55 W
Vistina	76	59.47 N	28.29 E
Vistre ≃	62	43.40 N	4.15 E
Vistula → Wisła ≃	30	54.22 N	18.55 E
Vit ≃	38	43.41 N	24.45 E
Vita, Mb., Can.	184	49.08 N	96.34 W
Vita, It.	70	37.52 N	12.49 E
Vita ≃	246	6.11 N	67.31 W
Vitacura	286e	33.24 S	70.36 W
Vitali	116	7.22 N	122.18 E
Vitanje	36	46.23 N	15.18 E
Vitarte	248	12.02 S	76.56 W
Vite	122	17.17 N	74.33 E
Vitebsk → Vicebsk	76	55.12 N	30.11 E
Vitebsk Station ◆[5]	265a	59.55 N	30.21 E
Vitel, Laguna ⊜	258	35.32 S	58.07 W
Viterbo	66	42.25 N	12.06 E
Viterbo □[4]	66	42.25 N	12.05 E
Vitiaz Strait ⊔	164	5.50 S	147.20 E
Vitichi	248	20.13 S	65.29 W
Vitigudino	34	41.01 N	6.26 W
Viti Levu I	175g	18.00 S	178.00 E
Vitim	74	59.28 N	112.34 E
Vitim ≃	74	59.26 N	112.34 E
Vitimskij	88	58.14 N	113.18 E
Vitimskoje ploskogorje ⋏[1]	88	54.00 N	113.30 E
Vitinia ◆[8]	267a	41.47 N	12.24 E
Vitinja)(	38	42.47 N	23.49 E
Vitis	61	48.45 N	15.10 E
Vítkov	30	49.46 N	17.45 E
Vito	175e	6.02 S	155.24 E
Vítor	248	16.26 S	71.49 W
Vitor ≃	248	16.37 S	72.19 W
Vitória, Bra.	250	2.54 S	52.01 W
Vitória, Bra.	255	20.19 S	40.21 W
Vitoria (Gasteiz), Esp.	34	42.51 N	2.40 W
Vitória, Ilha da I	256	23.45 S	45.01 W
Vitória da Conquista	255	14.51 S	40.51 W
Vitória de Santo Antão	250	8.07 S	35.18 W
Vitória do Mearim	250	3.28 S	44.53 W
Vitorino Freire	250	4.04 S	45.10 W
Vitravo ≃	68	39.11 N	17.05 E
Vitré	32	48.08 N	1.12 W
Vitrey-sur-Mance	58	47.49 N	5.45 E
Vitry-aux-Loges	50	47.56 N	2.16 E
Vitry-en-Artois	50	50.20 N	2.59 E
Vitry-la-Ville	50	48.50 N	4.28 E
Vitry-le-François	56	48.44 N	4.35 E
Vitry [-sur-Seine]	50	48.48 N	2.24 E
Vitshumbi	154	0.41 S	29.23 E
Vittangi	24	67.41 N	21.36 E
Vitteaux	58	47.24 N	4.32 E
Vittel	58	48.12 N	5.57 E
Vittinge	40	59.54 N	17.04 E
Vittoria, On., Can.	212	42.46 N	80.19 W
Vittoria, It.	70	36.57 N	14.32 E
Vittorio Veneto	64	45.59 N	12.18 E
Vittsjö	26	56.20 N	13.40 E
Vitulano	68	41.10 N	14.38 E
Vitznau	58	47.01 N	8.29 E
Viù	62	45.14 N	7.22 E
Vivarais □[9]	62	44.40 N	4.30 E
Vivarais, Monts du ⋏	62	44.55 N	4.15 E
Viveiro	34	43.40 N	7.35 W
Viver	34	39.55 N	0.36 W
Viverols	62	45.26 N	3.53 E
Viverone, Lago di ⊜	62	45.25 N	8.02 E
Vivi ≃	74	63.52 N	97.50 E
Vivian	194	32.52 N	93.59 W
Viviers	62	44.29 N	4.41 E
Viviers-du-Lac	62	45.39 N	5.54 E
Vivione, Passo del)(	64	46.02 N	10.12 E
Vivonne	32	46.26 N	0.16 E
Vivoratá	252	37.40 S	57.39 W
Vivorillo, Cayos II	236	15.50 N	83.18 W
Viwa I	175g	17.08 S	176.54 E
Vizagapatam → Vishākhapatnam	122	17.42 N	83.18 E
Vizcaíno, Desierto de ◆[2]	232	27.40 N	113.40 W
Vizcaíno, Isla I	258	33.47 S	59.15 W
Vize	130	41.34 N	27.45 E
Vize, ostrov I	72	79.30 N	77.00 E
Vizianagaram	122	18.07 N	83.25 E
Vizille	62	45.05 N	5.46 E
Vižinada	36	45.20 N	13.46 E
Vizinga	24	61.05 N	50.04 E
Vizzini	70	37.10 N	14.53 E
Vizzola	266b	45.38 N	8.42 E
Vjalikaja Berastavica	76	53.11 N	24.01 E
Vjalikaja Maščanica	76	53.58 N	29.37 E
Vjaliki Bor	78	52.02 N	29.56 E
Vjalikija Aucjuki	78	52.04 N	29.32 E
Vjalikija Radvaničy	76	52.02 N	24.02 E
Vjaseja	76	53.04 N	27.41 E
Vjatčyn	76	52.27 N	28.10 E
Vjazyn'	76	54.25 N	27.10 E
Vjulka ≃	82	56.53 N	37.57 E
Vjunka ≃	265b	55.42 N	38.01 E
Vjuny	86	55.31 N	82.55 E
Vlaanderen → Flanders □[9]	50	51.00 N	3.00 E
Vlaardingen	52	51.54 N	4.21 E
Vlachovo Březí	60	49.05 N	13.57 E
Vladař ∧	54	50.05 N	13.14 E
Vlădeasa, Vârful ∧	38	46.45 N	22.48 E
Vlădeni	38	47.25 N	27.20 E
Vladičin Han	38	42.42 N	22.04 E
Vladikavkaz	84	43.03 N	44.40 E
Vladimir	80	56.10 N	40.25 E
Vladimir Oblast' □[4]	76	56.00 N	40.30 E
Vladimirovka, Kaz.	80	50.51 N	51.08 E
Vladimirovka, Kaz.	86	53.28 N	64.02 E
Vladimirskij Tupik	76	55.42 N	33.18 E
Vladimirskoje	80	56.49 N	45.07 E
Vladivostok	89	43.10 N	131.56 E
Vladyčnoje	76	58.49 N	39.29 E
Vladykino ◆[8]	265b	55.52 N	37.36 E
Vlasenica	38	44.11 N	18.56 E
Vlašim	30	49.42 N	14.54 E
Vlaskovo	82	56.11 N	36.31 E
Vlasotince	38	42.58 N	22.08 E
Vlasovo, Ross.	74	70.48 N	135.00 E
Vlasovo, Ross.	82	56.38 N	38.14 E
Vlazoviči	76	53.01 N	32.18 E
Vledder	52	52.52 N	6.12 E
Vleesbaai c	158	34.16 S	21.57 E
Vleikolk	158	29.43 S	20.50 E
Vleuten	52	52.05 N	5.02 E
Vlieland I	52	53.15 N	5.00 E
Vlijmen	52	51.42 N	5.15 E
Vlissingen (Flushing)	52	51.26 N	3.35 E
Vlodrop	52	51.08 N	6.05 E
Vloesberg → Flobecq	50	50.44 N	3.44 E
Vlonë → Vlorë	38	40.27 N	19.30 E
Vlorë	38	40.27 N	19.30 E
Vlorës, Gji i c	38	40.25 N	19.25 E
Vlotho	52	52.10 N	8.51 E
Vltava ≃	30	50.21 N	14.30 E
Vnukovo	82	55.38 N	37.16 E
Vnukovo Airport ⊠	265b	55.37 N	37.17 E
Voca	196	31.01 N	99.11 W
Vochrinka	82	55.24 N	38.18 E
Vochtoga	76	58.47 N	41.07 E
Vočin	36	45.37 N	17.32 E
Vockerode	54	51.51 N	12.21 E
Vöckla ≃	64	48.00 N	13.36 E
Vöcklabruck	60	48.01 N	13.39 E
Vöcklamarkt	60	48.00 N	13.29 E
Vodla ≃	24	61.49 N	36.00 E
Vodlozero, ozero ⊜	24	62.20 N	36.55 E
Vodňany	30	49.09 N	14.11 E
Vodnjan	36	44.57 N	13.51 E
Vodnyj	24	63.32 N	53.18 E
Vodo	64	46.25 N	12.14 E
Vodosalma	24	64.29 N	30.44 E
Vodovatovo	80	55.24 N	43.34 E
Vodzimonje	80	56.49 N	51.38 E
Voël ≃	158	33.07 S	25.07 E
Voerde, Dtsch.	52	51.35 N	6.41 E
Voerde, Dtsch.	263	51.18 N	7.24 E
Vogelenzang	52	52.19 N	4.35 E
Vogelheim ◆[8]	263	51.29 N	6.59 E
Vogelkop → Doberai, Jazirah >[1]	164	1.30 S	132.30 E
Vogel Peak → Dimlang ∧	146	8.24 N	11.47 E
Vogelsang, Dtsch.	54	53.43 N	14.09 E
Vogelsang, Dtsch.	56	50.35 N	6.27 E
Vogelsberg ⋏	56	50.30 N	9.15 E
Vogesen → Vosges ⋏	58	48.30 N	7.10 E
Voghera	62	44.59 N	9.01 E
Vognema	76	59.59 N	38.10 E
Vogogna	58	46.01 N	8.17 E
Vogt	58	47.47 N	9.46 E
Vogtland ◆[1]	54	50.30 N	12.05 E
Vogtsburg	58	48.05 N	7.38 E
Voh	175f	20.58 S	164.42 E
Vohburg an der Donau	60	48.46 N	11.37 E
Vohenstrauss	60	49.37 N	12.21 E
Vohibinany	157b	18.49 S	49.04 E
Vohilava	157b	21.04 S	48.00 E
Vohimarina	157b	13.21 S	50.02 E
Vohipeno	157b	22.22 S	47.51 E
Vohitsora	157b	23.54 S	44.17 E
Vöhl	56	51.12 N	8.57 E
Võhma	76	58.38 N	25.33 E
Vöhrenbach	58	48.02 N	8.18 E
Vöhringen, Dtsch.	58	48.16 N	10.04 E
Vöhringen, Dtsch.	58	48.20 N	8.40 E
Vöhrum	52	52.20 N	10.10 E
Vohwinkel ◆[8]	263	51.14 N	7.09 E
Voi	154	3.23 S	38.34 E
Void	58	48.41 N	5.37 E
Voight Creek ≃	224	47.06 N	122.10 W
Voikkaa	26	60.56 N	26.37 E
Voinești	38	47.05 N	27.26 E
Voinjama	150	8.25 N	9.45 W
Voire ≃	58	48.27 N	4.25 E
Voiron	62	45.22 N	5.35 E
Voise	50	48.24 N	1.43 E
Voise ≃	50	48.35 N	1.35 E
Voisenon	261	48.34 N	2.40 E
Voisins-le-Bretonneux	50	48.45 N	2.03 E
Voiteur	58	46.45 N	5.37 E
Voitsberg	61	47.03 N	15.10 E
Voja ≃	80	57.23 N	49.55 E
Vojens	41	55.15 N	9.19 E
Vojevodskoje	86	52.47 N	85.35 E
Vojkovice	54	50.15 N	13.02 E
Vojmsjön ⊜	26	64.55 N	16.40 E
Vojnić	36	45.19 N	15.42 E
Vojnica	24	65.12 N	30.15 E
Vojtanov	54	50.06 N	12.19 E
Vojvodina □[4]	38	45.00 N	20.00 E
Voj-Vož, Ross.	24	64.20 N	55.03 E
Voj-Vož, Ross.	24	62.56 N	54.56 E
Vokeo Island I	164	3.10 S	144.05 E
Volano	66	44.48 N	12.15 E
Volant	214	41.07 N	80.16 W
Volary	60	48.55 N	13.54 E
Volcán, Arg.	252	23.54 S	65.27 W
Volcán, Pan.	236	8.46 N	82.38 W
Volcán Isluga, Parque Nacional ♠	248	19.30 S	68.30 W
Volčanka	80	52.33 N	49.59 E
Volcano, Ca., U.S.	226	38.26 N	120.37 W
Volcano, Hi., U.S.	229d	19.25 N	155.14 W
Volcano Island I	116	14.00 N	121.00 E
Volcano Islands → Kazan-rettō II	14	25.00 N	141.00 E
Volcán Poás, Parque Nacional ♠	236	10.10 N	84.15 W
Volčansk	86	59.56 N	60.04 E
Volčenskij	83	48.14 N	40.07 E
Volchonka-Zil ◆[8]	265b	55.40 N	37.37 E
Volchov	76	59.55 N	32.20 E
Volchov ≃	76	60.08 N	32.20 E
Volčicha	86	52.02 N	80.23 E
Volčij Nos, mys >	76	60.31 N	32.35 E
Volčki	80	52.29 N	40.42 E
Volda	26	62.09 N	6.06 E
Volders	64	47.17 N	11.34 E
Volendam	52	52.30 N	5.04 E
Volga, Ross.	76	57.57 N	38.24 E
Volga, Ia., U.S.	190	42.48 N	91.32 W
Volga, S.D., U.S.	198	44.19 N	96.55 W
Volga ≃, Ross.	72	45.55 N	47.52 E
Volga ≃, Ia., U.S.	190	42.45 N	91.17 W
Volga-Baltic Canal → Volgo-Baltijskij kanal ≍	24	59.00 N	38.00 E
Volgino	76	58.27 N	33.52 E
Volgo, ozero ⊜	76	56.55 N	33.10 E
Volgo-Baltijskij kanal ≍	24	59.00 N	38.00 E
Volgodonsk	80	47.33 N	42.08 E
Volgo-Donskoj sudochodnyj kanal imeni V.I. Lenina ≍	80	48.40 N	43.37 E
Volgograd (Stalingrad)	80	48.44 N	44.25 E
Volgograd Oblast' □[4]	80	49.30 N	44.00 E
Volgogradskoje vodochranilišče ⊜[1]	80	49.20 N	45.00 E
Volgorečensk	76	57.30 N	41.02 E
Volintiri	38	46.26 N	29.37 E
Volissós	38	38.29 N	25.58 E
Volkach	56	49.52 N	10.13 E
Volkel	52	51.38 N	5.40 E
Völkermarkt	61	46.39 N	14.38 E
Völkermarkter Stausee ⊜[1]	61	46.39 N	14.38 E
Völkerschlacht-Denkmal ⊥	54	51.18 N	12.24 E
Völklingen	56	49.15 N	6.50 E
Volkmarsen	56	51.24 N	9.07 E
Volkovo, Ross.	76	59.15 N	41.27 E
Volkovo, Ross.	82	55.46 N	36.15 E
Volkovo Cemetery ◆	265a	59.54 N	30.22 E
Volkovskoje	82	54.49 N	37.13 E
Volksdorf ◆[8]	52	53.39 N	10.10 E
Völksen	52	52.13 N	9.37 E
Volksrust	158	27.24 S	29.53 E
Vollenhove	52	52.41 N	5.58 E
Vollersode	52	53.18 N	8.56 E
Vollme	263	51.10 N	7.36 E
Vollore-Montagne	62	45.47 N	3.41 E
Vollore-Ville	62	45.47 N	3.36 E
Vollsjö	41	55.42 N	13.46 E
Volma ≃	76	53.35 N	28.19 E
Volmarstein	56	51.22 N	7.23 E
Volme ≃	263	51.24 N	7.27 E
Volmerange-les-Mines	56	49.27 N	6.05 E
Volmerswerth ◆[8]	263	51.11 N	6.46 E
Volmunster	56	49.07 N	7.21 E
Vol'naja Gorka	76	58.43 N	30.51 E
Volnay	58	47.00 N	4.47 E
Vol'noje, Ross.	80	47.09 N	47.38 E
Vol'noje, Ross.	86	54.17 N	71.21 E
Volnovakha	83	47.36 N	37.31 E
Vol'nyj	80	45.55 N	45.14 E
Vol'nyj, ostrov I	265a	59.58 N	30.14 E
Voločajevka Vtoraja	89	48.34 N	134.34 E
Voločanka	74	71.00 N	94.28 E
Volochys'k	78	49.32 N	26.11 E
Volockaja	76	60.17 N	42.59 E
Volodarka, Ross.	86	52.43 N	83.38 E
Volodarka, Ukr.	78	49.31 N	29.55 E
Volodarsk, Ross.	76	56.13 N	43.10 E
Volodars'k, Ukr.	83	48.06 N	39.35 E
Volodars'ke	83	47.12 N	37.20 E
Volodarskij, Ross.	80	46.24 N	48.32 E
Volodarskij, Ross.	82	55.30 N	37.57 E
Volodarskij ◆[8]	265a	59.49 N	30.05 E
Volodarskoje	86	53.18 N	68.08 E
Volodars'k-Volyns'kyy	78	50.37 N	28.25 E
Volodino	86	57.06 N	83.54 E
Volodymyrets'	78	51.25 N	26.08 E
Volodymyrivka, Ukr.	78	47.32 N	32.55 E
Volodymyrivka, Ukr.	83	47.44 N	37.23 E
Volodymyr-Volyns'kyy	78	50.51 N	24.20 E
Vologda	76	59.12 N	39.55 E
Vologda ≃	76	59.17 N	40.13 E
Vologda Oblast' □[4]	24	60.00 N	40.00 E
Voloje	76	54.09 N	34.35 E
Volokolamsk	82	56.02 N	35.57 E
Volokonovka	78	50.29 N	37.51 E
Volokovaja	24	66.28 N	48.10 E
Volonga	24	67.07 N	47.41 E
Volonne	62	44.07 N	6.01 E
Vólos	38	39.21 N	22.56 E
Vološino, Ross.	83	48.55 N	39.56 E
Vološino, Ross.	83	47.31 N	39.40 E
Vološka	24	61.20 N	40.06 E
Volos'ka Balakliya	83	49.37 N	37.20 E
Vološn'a ≃	82	55.51 N	35.54 E
Vološno	76	58.29 N	28.29 E
Volosovo	76	59.26 N	29.29 E
Volot	76	57.56 N	30.42 E
Volovets'	78	48.43 N	23.11 E
Volovo, Ross.	76	53.35 N	38.02 E
Volovo, Ross.	78	52.03 N	37.53 E
Volpago del Montello	64	45.47 N	12.07 E
Volpedo	62	44.53 N	8.59 E
Volpiano	62	45.12 N	7.46 E
Völpke	54	52.08 N	11.09 E
Völs → Fiè	64	46.31 N	11.30 E
Volsini, Monti ⋏	66	42.40 N	11.55 E
Vol'sk	80	52.02 N	47.23 E
Volstruisleegte	158	33.05 S	23.28 E
Volta □[4]	150	7.00 N	0.30 E
Volta ≃	150	5.46 N	0.41 E
Volta, Lake ⊜[1]	150	7.30 N	0.15 E
Volta Blanche (White Volta) ≃	150	9.10 N	1.15 W
Voltaggio	62	44.37 N	8.50 E
Voltago	64	46.16 N	12.00 E
Volta Grande	256	21.46 S	42.32 W
Voltaire, Cape >	164	14.16 S	125.35 E
Volta Mantovana	64	45.19 N	10.39 E
Volta Noire (Black Volta) ≃	150	8.41 N	1.33 W
Volta Redonda	256	22.32 S	44.07 W
Volta Rouge ≃	150	10.34 N	0.30 W
Volterra	66	43.24 N	10.51 E
Vol'teva	24	64.30 N	44.12 E
Voltri	62	44.26 N	8.45 E
Volturara Appula	68	41.30 N	15.03 E
Volturara Irpina	68	40.53 N	14.55 E
Volturino	68	41.28 N	15.07 E
Volturino, Monte ∧	68	40.25 N	15.49 E
Volturno ≃	66	41.01 N	13.55 E
Volubilis ⊥	148	34.00 N	5.30 W
Voluntown	207	41.34 N	71.52 W
Volusia □[6]	220	28.51 N	81.05 W
Vólvi, Límni ⊜	38	40.41 N	23.23 E
Volx	62	43.53 N	5.51 E
Volyn' □[4]	78	51.00 N	25.00 E
Volyn' □[9]	78	50.50 N	27.00 E
Volyncy	80	57.48 N	45.28 E
Volyně	60	49.10 N	13.53 E
Volynka	78	51.37 N	32.26 E
Volyňka ≃	60	49.16 N	13.54 E
Volyns'ka vysochyna ⋏[1]	78	50.30 N	25.30 E
Volzhskiy → Volžskij	80	48.50 N	44.44 E
Volžsk	80	55.53 N	48.21 E
Volžskij, Ross.	80	53.27 N	50.07 E
Volžskij, Ross.	80	48.50 N	44.44 E
Vom	150	9.41 N	8.42 E
Vomano ≃	66	42.39 N	14.02 E
Vombsjön ⊜	41	55.41 N	13.36 E
Vomp	64	47.20 N	11.41 E
Vonavona Island I	175e	8.15 S	157.05 E
Vonda	184	52.19 N	106.06 W
Vondanka	24	59.07 N	47.49 E
Vondrozo	157b	22.49 S	47.20 E
Von Frank Mountain ∧	180	63.33 N	154.20 W
Võnnu	76	58.17 N	27.05 E
Vonozero	76	60.22 N	34.26 E
Vonsild	41	55.27 N	9.29 E
Von Treuer Tableland ⋏[1]	162	26.38 S	122.53 E
Voorburg	52	52.05 N	4.23 E
Voordeelspan	158	29.05 S	21.32 E
Voorheesville	210	42.39 N	73.56 W
Voorne I	52	51.54 N	4.08 E
Voorschoten	52	52.07 N	4.27 E
Voorst	52	52.10 N	6.09 E
Voorthuizen	52	52.12 N	5.35 E
Vop' ≃	76	54.56 N	32.44 E
Vopnafjörður	24a	65.47 N	14.44 W
Vopnafjörður c	24a	65.52 N	14.40 W
Vörå (Vöyri)	26	63.09 N	22.15 E
Vor'a ≃, Ross.	76	54.54 N	35.01 E
Vor'a ≃, Ross.	82	55.52 N	38.13 E
Voranava	76	54.09 N	25.19 E
Vorarlberg □[3]	58	47.15 N	9.55 E
Vorau	61	47.25 N	15.54 E
Vorbasse	41	55.38 N	9.05 E
Vorbjovo	88	57.23 N	102.18 E
Vorchdorf	60	48.00 N	13.55 E
Vörden, Dtsch.	52	52.28 N	8.05 E
Vorden, Ned.	52	52.07 N	6.18 E
Vorder-Grauspitz ∧	58	47.03 N	9.36 E
Vorderkrimmi	64	47.14 N	12.12 E
Vordernberg	61	47.28 N	15.00 E
Vorderrhein ≃	58	46.49 N	9.25 E
Vorderriss	64	47.33 N	11.26 E
Vordingborg	41	55.01 N	11.55 E
Voreifel ⋏	56	50.15 N	7.10 E
Vóreion Aiyaíon □[4]	38	38.30 N	26.00 E
Voreppe	62	45.18 N	5.38 E
Vorey	62	45.11 N	3.54 E
Vorga	76	53.45 N	32.45 E
Vorhalle ◆[8]	263	51.23 N	7.28 E
Vorhelm	52	51.48 N	7.56 E
Vøringsfossen ⌊	26	60.26 N	7.15 E
Vórioi Sporádhes II	38	39.15 N	23.55 E
Vórios Evvoïkós Kólpos c	38	38.40 N	23.15 E
Vorkuta	24	67.27 N	63.58 E
Vorlich, Ben ∧, Scot., U.K.	46	56.20 N	4.14 W
Vorlich, Ben ∧, Scot., U.K.	46	56.17 N	4.46 W
Vorma ≃	26	60.09 N	11.27 E
Vormholz	263	51.24 N	7.18 E
Vormsi I	76	59.00 N	23.20 E
Vorobjevo, Ross.	82	56.11 N	35.45 E
Vorobjevo, Ross.	86	56.08 N	76.32 E
Vorobji	82	55.09 N	36.48 E
Vorobjovka	80	50.38 N	40.56 E
Vorob'jovo	76	59.38 N	40.55 E
Vorobyove	78	45.20 N	33.15 E
Vorokhta	78	48.18 N	24.36 E
Voron, porog ⌊	88	57.05 N	98.40 E
Vorona ≃	80	51.22 N	42.03 E
Voroncov	38	47.43 N	29.08 E
Voroncovka, Kaz.	86	48.49 N	81.32 E
Voroncovka, Ross.	78	50.37 N	40.21 E
Voroncovka, Ross.	86	59.39 N	60.14 E
Voroncovka, Ross.	88	58.51 N	112.56 E
Voroncovo, Ross.	76	57.18 N	28.42 E
Voroncovo, Ross.	80	55.16 N	40.27 E
Voronej → Voronež	78	51.40 N	39.10 E
Voronež	78	51.40 N	39.10 E
Voronež ≃	76	51.56 N	39.25 E
Voronezh → Voronež	78	51.40 N	39.10 E
Voronež Oblast' □[4]	78	51.00 N	40.00 E
Voronežskij zapovednik ◆[4]	76	51.56 N	39.37 E
Voronino	82	56.24 N	36.52 E
Voronizh	78	51.46 N	33.28 E
Voronja ≃	24	69.10 N	35.50 E
Voronjo, Ross.	24	68.27 N	35.21 E
Voronjo, Ross.	80	58.00 N	42.01 E
Voronki	82	55.48 N	37.16 E
Voron'ky	78	50.14 N	33.02 E
Voronok	76	52.23 N	32.40 E
Voronov, mys >	76	60.15 N	32.05 E
Voronovkova Niva	76	57.04 N	29.16 E
Voronovo, Ross.	82	55.19 N	37.10 E
Voronovo, Ross.	86	56.01 N	83.52 E
Voronovytsya	78	49.06 N	28.41 E
Vorontsivka	78	45.51 N	33.47 E
Voroshilov → Ussurijsk	89	43.48 N	131.59 E
Voroshilovsk → Stavropol'	72	45.02 N	41.59 E
Vorošilovgrad → Luhans'k	83	48.34 N	39.20 E
Vorotajevka	80	51.56 N	47.16 E
Vorotynec	80	56.04 N	45.52 E
Vorotynsk	82	54.25 N	36.05 E
Vorovskolesskaja	84	44.23 N	42.25 E
Vorožejka	86	58.12 N	90.02 E
Vorozhba	78	51.12 N	34.14 E
Vorpommern □[9]	54	53.40 N	13.45 E
Vorra	60	49.33 N	11.30 E
Vorsfelde	54	52.26 N	10.49 E
Vorskla ≃	78	48.53 N	34.06 E
Vorsma	80	55.59 N	43.16 E
Vorst, Bel.	56	51.04 N	5.01 E
Vorst, Dtsch.	56	51.18 N	6.25 E
Vørterkaka Nunatak ∧	9	72.20 S	27.29 E
Võrtsjärv ⊜	76	58.16 N	26.03 E
Võru	76	57.50 N	27.01 E
Voruch	85	39.52 N	70.35 E
Vorzel'	78	50.33 N	30.09 E
Vosburg	158	30.33 S	22.52 E
Voschod	80	47.24 N	41.50 E
Vösendorf	61	48.07 N	16.20 E
Vosges □[5]	58	48.10 N	6.20 E
Vosges ⋏	58	48.30 N	7.10 E
Vosja	76	59.01 N	41.11 E
Voskresenka, Ross.	80	51.01 N	46.28 E
Voskresenka, Ross.	88	53.15 N	119.31 E
Voskresenki	82	54.57 N	38.04 E
Voskresenovskoje	265a	59.43 N	30.47 E
Voskresensk	82	55.19 N	38.42 E
Voskresens'ke	78	47.02 N	32.09 E
Voskresenskoje, Ross.	76	53.12 N	38.43 E
Voskresenskoje, Ross.	76	58.54 N	38.36 E
Voskresenskoje, Ross.	76	59.26 N	37.56 E
Voskresenskoje, Ross.	76	57.49 N	37.40 E
Voskresenskoje, Ross.	80	56.51 N	45.26 E
Voskresenskoje, Ross.	80	51.51 N	46.56 E
Voskresenskoje, Ross.	82	54.07 N	37.07 E
Voskresenskoje, Ross.	82	56.20 N	38.29 E
Voskresenskoje, Ross.	86	53.08 N	56.10 E
Voslapp	52	53.36 N	8.05 E
Voss	26	60.39 N	6.26 E
Vosselaar	56	51.19 N	4.53 E
Vossman's Beacon	158	26.11 S	30.40 E
Vostočnaja Kambal'nica	24	68.18 N	46.00 E
Vostočno-Kazachstan □[8]	86	49.00 N	84.00 E
Vostočno-Kounradskij	86	47.02 N	75.07 E
Vostočno-Sibirskoje more (East Siberian Sea) ⊤[2]	12	74.00 N	166.00 E
Vostočnyj, Ross.	82	55.47 N	37.52 E
Vostočnyj, Ross.	86	58.48 N	61.52 E
Vostočnyj, Ross.	89	53.29 N	143.03 E
Vostočnyj, Ross.	89	48.17 N	142.34 E
Vostočnyj Sajan ⋏	88	53.00 N	97.00 E
Vostok I	14	10.06 S	152.23 W
Vostr'akovo	82	55.23 N	37.49 E
Vostrecovo	89	45.53 N	134.58 E
Vostrovo	86	52.09 N	80.38 E
Vosves	261	48.31 N	2.36 E
Votaw	222	30.26 N	94.41 W
Votice	30	49.38 N	14.39 E
Votkinsk	80	57.03 N	53.59 E
Votkinskoje vodochranilišče ⊜[1]	86	57.00 N	54.30 E
Vot'pa	86	60.13 N	62.57 E
Votuporanga	255	20.24 S	49.59 W
Voué	50	48.28 N	4.07 E
Vouga ≃	34	40.41 N	8.40 W
Vougba	152	5.10 N	23.06 E
Vougeot	58	47.10 N	4.58 E
Vouillé	32	46.39 N	0.10 E
Voujeaucourt	58	47.28 N	6.46 E
Voulangis	261	48.51 N	2.54 E
Voulou	146	8.33 N	22.36 E
Voulx	50	48.17 N	2.58 E
Voulzie ≃	50	48.25 N	3.12 E
Voutenay-sur-Cure	50	47.33 N	3.47 E
Vouvray	50	47.25 N	0.48 E
Vouvry	58	46.20 N	6.53 E
Vouziers	56	49.24 N	4.42 E
Vovcha ≃	78	48.00 N	36.08 E
Vovchans'k	78	50.18 N	36.57 E
Vovchoyarivka	83	48.50 N	38.22 E
Voves	50	48.16 N	1.38 E
Vovkovyntsi	78	49.13 N	27.39 E
Vovodo ≃	140	5.40 N	24.21 E
Vowinckel	214	41.25 N	79.14 W
Voxnan ≃	26	61.17 N	16.26 E
Voyageurs National Park ♠	190	48.30 N	93.00 W
Voyinka	78	45.52 N	33.59 E
Voykove	78	45.31 N	33.52 E
Voykovs'kyy	83	47.46 N	38.20 E
Voynyliv	78	49.08 N	24.30 E
Vöyri → Vörå	26	63.09 N	22.15 E
Voža ≃	82	54.38 N	39.10 E
Vožajol'	24	62.50 N	51.17 E
Vožd' Proletariata	76	55.26 N	39.19 E
Vozdviženka	80	53.10 N	54.14 E
Vozdviženskoje, Ross.	80	56.58 N	45.37 E
Vozdviženskoje, Ross.	80	45.50 N	43.40 E
Vozdviženskoje, Ross.	82	56.12 N	38.04 E
Vozdvyzhivka	78	47.46 N	36.05 E
Vože, ozero ⊜	24	60.30 N	39.00 E
Vožega	76	60.29 N	40.12 E
Vožega ≃	76	60.33 N	39.11 E
Vožgaly	80	58.09 N	50.11 E
Vožgora	24	64.32 N	48.25 E
Voznesenje	24	61.01 N	35.27 E
Voznesenka, Kaz.	86	52.24 N	70.12 E
Voznesenka, Ukr.	78	46.51 N	35.26 E
Voznesenovka	80	46.16 N	44.21 E
Voznesens'k	78	47.34 N	31.20 E
Voznesenskoje, Ross.	80	54.54 N	42.46 E
Voznesenskoje, Ross.	80	45.49 N	43.25 E
Vozroždenija, ostrov I	86	45.03 N	59.12 E
Vozroždenije	80	52.42 N	48.12 E
Vozsiyats'ke	78	47.41 N	32.07 E
Vozžajevka	89	50.44 N	128.41 E
Vrå	26	57.21 N	9.57 E
Vráble	30	48.15 N	18.19 E
Vraca	38	43.12 N	23.33 E
Vračevo	82	54.53 N	39.10 E
Vrådal	26	59.20 N	8.25 E
Vrancea □[6]	38	45.45 N	27.00 E
Vrancei, Munții ⋏	38	46.00 N	26.30 E
Vrangel'a, mys >	89	54.17 N	138.39 E
Vrangel'a, ostrov I	74	71.00 N	179.30 W
Vranje	38	42.33 N	21.54 E
Vranov	61	48.54 N	15.49 E
Vranov [nad Topl'ou]	30	48.54 N	21.41 E
Vrbas	38	45.35 N	19.39 E
Vrbas ≃	36	45.06 N	17.31 E
Vrbovec	36	45.53 N	16.25 E
Vrbovsko	36	45.23 N	15.05 E
Vrchlabí	30	50.38 N	15.37 E
Vrede	158	27.30 S	29.06 E
Vredefort	158	27.05 S	27.16 E
Vreden	52	52.02 N	6.52 E
Vredenburg	158	32.54 S	17.59 E
Vredenburgh	194	31.49 N	87.19 W
Vredendal	158	31.41 S	18.35 E
Vreed en Hoop	246	6.48 N	58.11 W
Vreeswijk	52	52.01 N	5.05 E
Vrena	40	58.52 N	16.41 E
Vresse	56	49.52 N	4.56 E
Vreta kloster ☉[1]	26	58.28 N	15.29 E
Vretstorp	40	59.02 N	14.52 E
Vrginmost	36	45.21 N	15.52 E
Vrhnika	36	45.58 N	14.18 E
Vriddhāchalam	122	11.30 N	79.20 E
Vriendschaps ≃	164	5.28 S	138.53 E
Vries	52	53.04 N	6.35 E
Vriezenveen	52	52.25 N	6.38 E
Vrigne-Meuse	56	49.42 N	4.51 E
Vrigstad	26	57.21 N	14.28 E
Vrilissia	267c	38.02 N	23.50 E
Vrille ≃	50	47.31 N	2.52 E
Vrin	58	46.39 N	9.06 E
Vrin ≃	50	48.00 N	3.20 E
Vrindāvan	124	27.35 N	77.42 E
Vrlika	36	43.55 N	16.24 E
Vrnograč	36	45.10 N	15.57 E
Vroeggedeel	158	28.02 S	22.32 E
Vron	50	50.19 N	1.45 E
Vrondádhes	38	38.24 N	26.08 E
Vroomshoop	52	52.27 N	6.34 E
Vrouenspan	158	27.50 S	20.24 E
Vroutek	54	50.08 N	13.24 E
Vršac	38	45.07 N	21.18 E
Vrsar	64	45.08 N	13.37 E
Vršič)(	64	46.26 N	13.44 E
Vrubivs'kyy	83	48.26 N	39.07 E
Vrútky	30	49.07 N	18.55 E
Vryburg	158	26.55 S	24.45 E
Vryheid	158	27.46 S	30.48 E
Vschody	76	54.42 N	34.06 E
Vselug, ozero ⊜	76	57.03 N	32.42 E
Všepadly	60	49.28 N	13.06 E
Všeruby	60	49.50 N	13.15 E
Vsetín	30	49.21 N	17.59 E
Vsevidof, Mount ∧	180	53.07 N	168.43 W
Vsevoložsk	265a	60.01 N	30.40 E
Vtoroje Potapovo	265b	55.56 N	37.58 E
Vtoryje Levyje Lamki	80	53.17 N	41.04 E
Vuadil'	85	40.11 N	71.43 E
Vuanggava Island I	175g	18.52 S	178.54 W
Vučitrn	38	42.49 N	20.58 E
Vudor, gora ∧	85	38.13 N	71.49 E
Vue-des-Alpes)(	58	47.04 N	6.53 E
Vught	52	51.40 N	5.17 E
Vuhlehirs'k	83	48.19 N	38.17 E
Vuhle-Zavod	78	52.11 N	32.53 E
Vuillafans	58	47.04 N	6.13 E
Vuitebœuf	58	46.37 N	6.34 E
Vukovar	38	45.21 N	19.00 E
Vulcan, Ab., Can.	182	50.24 N	113.15 W
Vulcan, Rom.	38	45.23 N	23.17 E
Vulcan, Mi., U.S.	190	45.46 N	87.51 W
Vulcănești	38	45.41 N	28.24 E
Vulcano, Bocche di ⊔	70	38.26 N	14.57 E
Vulcano, Isola I	70	38.24 N	14.58 E
Vulcano, Monte ∧[2]	70a	35.51 N	12.52 E
Vulci ⊥	66	42.25 N	11.35 E
Vulkanichnyy khrebet ⋏	78	48.30 N	23.00 E
Vulture, Monte ∧	68	40.57 N	15.38 E
Vul'vyvejem ≃	180	66.58 N	179.10 W
Vung Tau	110	10.21 N	107.04 E

≃ River	Fluß	Río	Rivière	Rio
≍ Canal	Kanal	Canal	Canal	Canal
⌊ Waterfall, Rapids	Wasserfall, Stromschnellen	Cascada, Rápidos	Chute d'eau, Rapides	Cascata, Rápidos
⊔ Strait	Meeresstraße	Estrecho	Détroit	Estreito
c Bay, Gulf	Bucht, Golf	Bahía, Golfo	Baie, Golfe	Baía, Golfo
⊜ Lake, Lakes	See, Seen	Lago, Lagos	Lac, Lacs	Lago, Lagos
Swamp	Sumpf	Pantano	Marais	Pântano
Ice Features, Glacier	Eis- und Gletscherformen	Accidentes Glaciales	Formes glaciaires	Acidentes glaciares
Other Hydrographic Features	Andere Hydrographische Objekte	Otros Elementos Hidrográficos	Autres données hydrographiques	Outros acidentes hidrográficos

⊤ Submarine Features	Untermeerische Objekte	Accidentes Submarinos	Formes de relief sous-marin	Acidentes submarinos
□ Political Unit	Politische Einheit	Unidad Política	Entité politique	Unidade política
☉ Cultural Institution	Kulturelle Institution	Institución Cultural	Institution culturelle	Instituição cultural
⊥ Historical Site	Historische Stätte	Sitio Histórico	Site historique	Sitio histórico
♠ Recreational Site	Erholungs- und Ferienort	Sitio de Recreo	Centre de loisirs	Area de Lazer
⊠ Airport	Flughafen	Aeropuerto	Aéroport	Aeroporto
Military Installation	Militäranlage	Instalación Militar	Installation militaire	Instalação militar
◆ Miscellaneous	Verschiedenes	Misceláneo	Divers	Diversos

I · *188* **Vuni-Wana**

ENGLISH: Name | Page | Lat.°' | Long.°'
DEUTSCH: Name | Seite | Breite°' | Länge°' E = Ost

Name	Page	Lat.°'	Long.°'
Vunindawa	175g	17.49 S	178.19 E
Vunisea Station	175g	19.03 S	178.09 E
Vuoggatjålme	24	66.36 N	16.22 E
Vuohijärvi	26	61.05 N	26.48 E
Vuohijärvi ⊜	26	61.12 N	26.42 E
Vuokatti ʌ [2]	26	64.07 N	28.14 E
Vuoksa ≃	26	61.03 N	30.11 E
Vuoksa, ozero ⊜	76	60.40 N	29.50 E
Vuoksenniska	26	61.13 N	28.49 E
Vurnary	80	55.29 N	46.58 E
Vuturu, Pizzo ʌ	70	37.56 N	14.13 E
Vuya	154	5.21 N	29.40 E
Vuyyūru	122	16.22 N	80.51 E
Vuzenica	61	46.36 N	15.10 E
Vvedenka	86	54.03 N	63.45 E
Vvedenovka	89	51.19 N	128.12 E
Vvedenskoje	82	55.42 N	36.54 E
Vyāra	120	21.07 N	73.24 E
Vyatka → Kirov	80	58.38 N	49.42 E
V'yazivok	78	49.11 N	31.25 E
Vyaz'ma → V'az'ma	76	55.13 N	34.18 E
Vyazniki → V'azniki	80	56.15 N	42.10 E
Vyborg	76	60.42 N	28.45 E
Vyborgskij zaliv c	76	60.35 N	28.24 E
Výčapy	61	49.09 N	15.53 E
Vyčegda ≃	24	61.18 N	46.36 E
Vyčegodskij	24	61.16 N	46.48 E
Vychino • [8]	265b	55.43 N	37.48 E
Východočeský Kraj □ [4]	30	50.10 N	16.00 E
Východoslovenský Kraj □ [4]	30	49.00 N	21.15 E
Vydrino, Ross.	88	51.27 N	104.39 E
Vydrino, Ross.	88	56.50 N	99.02 E
Vygoniči	76	53.08 N	34.05 E
Vygozero, ozero ⊜	24	63.35 N	34.42 E
Vyhanaščy	76	52.37 N	25.55 E
Vyhoda	78	48.56 N	23.55 E
Vyjezdnoje	80	55.23 N	43.47 E
Vyjezžij Log	86	54.58 N	93.57 E
Vyksa	80	55.18 N	42.11 E
Vylkove	78	45.25 N	29.35 E
Vylkovo	86	53.05 N	81.26 E
Vym' ≃	24	62.13 N	50.25 E
Vynnyky	78	49.48 N	24.08 E
Vynohradiv	78	48.09 N	23.02 E
Vyntja	86	60.31 N	67.18 E
Vypolzovo	76	57.53 N	33.42 E
Vyrica	76	59.25 N	30.21 E
Vyrnwy ≃	42	52.46 N	3.00 W
Vyrnwy, Lake ⊜	42	52.47 N	3.30 W
Vyša	80	53.52 N	42.24 E
Vyša ≃	80	54.02 N	42.06 E
Vyšehrad • [8]	54	50.01 N	14.27 E
Vyšelej	80	53.26 N	45.29 E
Vyselki	78	45.35 N	39.38 E
Vyšesteblijevskaja	78	45.12 N	37.00 E
Vyšgorodok	76	57.02 N	28.01 E
Vyshcha Dubechna	78	50.44 N	30.40 E
Vyshkivs'kyi, pereval)(	78	48.42 N	23.38 E
Vyshneve	78	48.27 N	33.56 E
Vyshnivchyk	78	49.02 N	26.28 E
Vyshnivets'	78	49.54 N	25.45 E
Vyška, Ross.	76	57.31 N	35.57 E
Vyška, Turk.	128	39.20 N	54.08 E
Vyskod'	76	57.46 N	30.04 E
Vyškov, Česká Rep.	30	49.16 N	17.00 E
Vyškov, Ross.	76	52.29 N	31.41 E
Vyšná Radvaň	30	49.07 N	21.56 E
Vyšneol'šanoje	76	52.08 N	37.39 E
Vyšnevolockoje vodochranilišče ⊜ [1]	76	57.35 N	34.28 E
Vyšnij Voločok	76	57.35 N	34.34 E
Vysočany • [8]	54	50.05 N	14.31 E
Vysock	76	60.36 N	28.34 E
Vysokae	76	52.22 N	23.22 E
Vysokaja, gora ʌ	89	45.59 N	136.35 E
Vysokaja Gora	80	55.56 N	49.19 E
Vysoké Mýto	30	49.57 N	16.10 E
Vysoké Tatry ⋀	30	49.12 N	20.05 E
Vysokiniči	82	54.54 N	36.55 E
Vysokogornyj	89	50.09 N	139.09 E
Vysokogorsk	89	44.23 N	135.23 E
Vysokoje, Kaz.	85	42.30 N	70.32 E
Vysokoje, Ross.	76	56.43 N	34.55 E
Vysokoje, Ross.	76	54.02 N	33.44 E
Vysokoje, Ross.	82	54.30 N	37.03 E
Vysokoje, Ross.	265b	55.59 N	37.09 E
Vysokopillya	78	47.29 N	33.32 E
Vysokovsk	82	56.19 N	36.33 E
Vysoký kámen ʌ	61	49.06 N	15.13 E
Vysots'k	78	51.43 N	26.39 E
Vyšší Brod	61	48.37 N	14.19 E
Vystupovychi	78	51.34 N	29.04 E
Vysun' ≃	78	47.07 N	32.53 E
Vytebet' ≃	76	53.53 N	35.38 E
Vytegra	24	61.00 N	36.24 E
Vytyazivka	78	48.01 N	31.53 E
Vyzhivka ≃	78	51.41 N	24.35 E
Vyzhnytsya	78	48.15 N	25.12 E
Vzmorje	89	47.51 N	142.31 E
Vzvad	76	58.10 N	31.29 E
W			
W, Parc National du ♦	150	12.50 N	2.30 E
Wa	150	10.04 N	2.29 W
Waabs	41	54.32 N	9.58 E
Waackaack Creek ≃	276	40.27 N	74.08 W
Waadt → Vaud □ [3]	58	46.40 N	6.30 E
Waajid	144	3.48 N	43.15 E
Waakirchen	64	47.46 N	11.40 E
Waal	58	48.00 N	10.46 E
Waal ≃	52	51.49 N	4.58 E
Waalre	52	51.24 N	5.26 E
Waalwijk	52	51.42 N	5.04 E
Waao	102	24.20 N	104.40 E
Waar, Meos I	164	2.05 S	134.23 E
Waarschoot	50	51.09 N	3.36 E
Waasmunster	50	51.06 N	4.05 E
Wabag	164	5.30 S	143.40 E
Wabamun	182	53.33 N	114.28 W
Wabamun Indian Reserve • [4]	182	53.30 N	114.30 W
Wabamun Lake ⊜	182	53.33 N	114.35 W
Waban	283	42.20 N	71.14 W
Waban, Lake ⊜	283	42.17 N	71.17 W
Wabana	186	47.38 N	52.57 W
Wabasca	182	56.00 N	113.53 W
Wabasca ≃	176	58.22 N	115.20 W
Wabasca Indian Reserve • [4]	182	55.53 N	113.32 W
Wabash, In., U.S.	216	40.47 N	85.49 W
Wabash, Oh., U.S.	216	40.33 N	84.45 W
Wabash □ [6]	216	40.48 N	85.49 W
Wabash ≃	194	37.46 N	88.02 W
Wabasha	190	44.23 N	92.01 W
Wabasso, Fl., U.S.	220	27.44 N	80.26 W
Wabasso, Mn., U.S.	198	44.24 N	95.15 W
Wabatongushi Lake ⊜	190	48.26 N	84.15 W
Wabe Gestro ≃	144	4.17 N	42.02 E
Wabe Mena ≃	144	5.32 N	41.11 E
Wabeno	190	45.26 N	88.39 W
Wabera	144	6.26 N	40.42 E
Wabern	56	51.06 N	9.20 E
Wabigoon Lake ⊜	184	49.44 N	92.44 W
Wabowden	184	54.55 N	98.38 W
Wabrah ╤ [4]	128	27.26 N	47.22 E
Wąbrzeźno	30	53.17 N	18.57 E
Wabu	100	32.17 N	116.55 E
Wabu Hu ⊜	100	32.23 N	116.54 E
Wabuska	226	39.08 N	119.10 W
W.A.C. Bennett Dam • [6]	182	56.01 N	122.10 W
Waccamaw ≃	192	33.21 N	79.16 W
Waccamaw, Lake ⊜	192	34.17 N	78.30 W
Waccasassa Bay c	192	29.06 N	82.52 W
Wachapreague	208	37.36 N	75.41 W
Wachapreague Inlet c	208	37.35 N	75.36 W
Wachau • [1]	61	48.18 N	15.24 E
Wachenheim	56	49.26 N	8.10 E
Wachi	96	35.15 N	135.24 E
Wąchock, Klasztory ᵾ [1]	30	51.05 N	21.01 E
Wachtberg	56	50.37 N	7.11 E
Wachtendonk	56	51.24 N	6.20 E
Wächtersbach	56	50.15 N	9.17 E
Wachusett Mountain ʌ	207	42.29 N	71.53 W
Wachusett Reservoir ⊜ [1]	207	42.23 N	71.43 W
Wacissa	192	30.21 N	83.59 W
Wackersdorf	60	49.19 N	12.11 E
Waco	222	31.32 N	97.08 W
Waco Lake ⊜ [1]	222	31.34 N	97.13 W
Waconda Lake ⊜ [1]	198	39.30 N	98.24 W
Waconia	190	44.51 N	93.47 W
Wacouno ≃	186	50.54 N	65.57 W
Wacousta	216	42.49 N	84.42 W
Wad	120	27.21 N	66.22 E
Wada, Nihon	94	35.02 N	140.01 E
Wada, Nihon	94	36.12 N	138.13 E
Wada, Nihon	268	35.12 N	139.38 E
Wada, Nihon	270	34.33 N	135.55 E
Wadagou	104	42.27 N	120.58 E
Wad Al-Ḥaddād	140	13.49 N	33.32 E
Wadamago	144	8.55 N	46.17 E
Wada-misaki ›	96	34.39 N	135.11 E
Wādat Ga	120	26.57 N	97.37 E
Wadayama	96	35.19 N	134.52 E
Wad Bandah	140	13.06 N	27.57 E
Wad Ban Naqa	140	16.30 N	33.08 E
Wadbilliga National Park ♦	166	36.20 S	149.35 E
Waddān	146	29.10 N	16.08 E
Waddān, Jabal ⋀ [2]	146	29.20 N	16.20 E
Waddeneilanden II	52	53.26 N	5.30 E
Waddenzee ╤ [2]	52	53.15 N	5.15 E
Wadderin	162	32.00 S	118.27 E
Waddesdon	42	51.51 N	0.56 W
Waddi, Chappal ʌ	152	7.02 N	11.43 E
Waddingham	44	53.27 N	0.31 W
Waddington, Eng., U.K.	44	53.10 N	0.32 W
Waddington, N.Y., U.S.	212	44.51 N	75.12 W
Waddington, Mount ʌ	182	51.23 N	125.15 W
Waddinxveen	52	52.03 N	4.40 E
Waddy	218	38.08 N	85.04 W
Wade, Mount ʌ	9	84.51 S	174.15 W
Wadebridge	42	50.32 N	4.50 W
Wadena, Sk., Can.	184	51.57 N	103.47 W
Wadena, In., U.S.	216	40.43 N	87.16 W
Wadena, Mn., U.S.	198	46.26 N	95.08 W
Wädenswil	58	47.14 N	8.40 E
Wadern	56	49.32 N	6.53 E
Wadersloh	52	51.44 N	8.15 E
Wadesboro	192	34.58 N	80.04 W
Wadeville	273d	26.16 S	28.11 E
Wadeye	164	14.13 S	129.32 E
Wadgassen	56	49.16 N	6.47 E
Wad Ḥāmid	140	16.30 N	32.48 E
Wadham Islands II	186	49.34 N	53.50 W
Wadhams	182	51.30 N	127.31 W
Wadhurst	42	51.04 N	0.21 E
Wadian	100	32.48 N	112.30 E
Wādī as-Sīr	132	31.57 N	35.49 E
Wādī Ḥalfā'	140	21.56 N	31.20 E
Wādī Jimāl, Jazīrat I	140	24.40 N	35.10 E
Wādī Mūsā	132	30.19 N	35.29 E
Wading ≃, Ma., U.S.	283	41.56 N	71.13 W
Wading ≃, N.J., U.S.	208	39.33 N	74.28 W
Wading, West Branch ≃	208	39.40 N	74.32 W
Wading River	207	40.57 N	72.50 W
Wādī Rashrāsh, Bi'r ╤ [4]	142	29.26 N	31.31 E
Wadley, Al., U.S.	194	33.07 N	85.33 W
Wadley, Ga., U.S.	192	32.52 N	82.24 W
Wad Madanī	140	14.25 N	33.28 E
Wadowice	30	49.53 N	19.30 E
Wadsworth, Il., U.S.	216	42.26 N	87.56 W
Wadsworth, Nv., U.S.	204	39.38 N	119.17 W
Wadsworth, N.Y., U.S.	210	42.49 N	77.54 W
Wadsworth, Oh., U.S.	214	41.01 N	81.43 W
Wadsworth Moor • [3]	262	53.48 N	2.02 W
Wadu I	122	5.51 N	72.58 E
Waegwan	98	35.58 N	128.24 E
Waelder	222	29.42 N	97.18 W
Waenhuiskrans	158	34.41 S	20.14 E
Wafang	98	41.44 N	118.54 E
Wafania	152	1.21 S	20.20 E
Wafrah	128	28.33 N	48.02 E
Wagadugu → Ouagadougou	150	12.22 N	1.31 W
Wāgah	123	31.36 N	74.33 E
Wagait Aboriginal Reserve • [4]	164	13.00 S	130.20 E
Wagang	102	28.04 N	103.10 E
Wagenborgen	52	53.15 N	6.56 E
Wagenfeld-Hasslingen	52	52.33 N	8.34 E
Wageningen, Ned.	52	51.58 N	5.40 E
Wageningen, Sur.	250	5.46 N	56.41 W
Wager Bay c	176	65.26 N	88.40 W
Wagerup	168a	32.55 S	115.54 E
Waggaman Heights	284c	38.49 N	76.57 W
Wagga Wagga	171b	35.07 S	147.22 E
Waggoner	219	39.23 N	89.39 W
Waghäusel	56	49.14 N	8.31 E
Wagin	162	33.18 S	117.21 E
Waging am See	64	47.56 N	12.43 E
Waginger See ⊜	64	47.56 N	12.47 E
Wägitaler See ⊜	58	47.06 N	8.55 E
Waglan Island I	271d	22.11 N	114.18 E
Wagna	61	46.46 N	15.34 E
Wagner	198	43.04 N	98.17 W
Wagner College ᵾ [2]	276	40.37 N	74.07 W
Wagoner	196	35.57 N	95.22 W
Wagon Mound	196	36.00 N	104.42 W
Wagontire Mountain ʌ	202	43.21 N	119.53 W
Wagontown	208	40.01 N	75.51 W
Wagrain	64	47.20 N	13.18 E
Wagram → Deutsch Wagram	61	48.18 N	16.34 E
Wagrien • [1]	54	54.15 N	10.45 E
Wągrowiec	30	52.49 N	17.11 E
Waha	146	28.16 N	19.54 E
Wahādurgañj	124	27.32 N	82.50 E
Wahai	164	2.48 S	129.30 E
Waharoa	172	37.46 S	175.46 E
Wāh Cantonment	123	33.48 N	72.42 E
Wahiawa	229c	21.30 N	158.01 W
Wāḥid	142	30.49 N	32.20 E
Wahkiakum □ [6]	224	46.16 N	123.28 W
Wahlen	56	49.37 N	8.51 E
Wahlstedt	54	53.57 N	10.12 E
Wahnbachstausee ⊜ [1]	56	50.48 N	7.19 E
Wahneta	220	27.57 N	81.44 W
Wahoo	198	41.12 N	96.37 W
Wahpeton	198	46.15 N	96.36 W
Wahran (Oran)	148	35.43 N	0.43 W
Wahrenbrück	54	51.33 N	13.22 E
Wahrenholz	54	52.36 N	10.36 E
Währing • [8]	264b	48.14 N	16.21 E
Wahroonga	274a	33.43 S	151.07 E
Wahweap Creek ≃	200	37.02 N	111.35 W
Wai, India	122	17.56 N	73.54 E
Wai, Indon.	164	1.42 S	127.59 E
Waialeale ʌ	229b	22.04 N	159.30 W
Waialua	229c	21.34 N	158.07 W
Waialua Bay c	229c	21.36 N	158.07 W
Waianae	229c	21.26 N	158.11 W
Waianae Range ⋀	229c	21.30 N	158.10 W
Waianapanapa State Park ♦	229a	20.47 N	156.01 W
Waiapu ≃	172	37.47 S	178.29 E
Waiatoto ≃	172	43.59 S	168.47 E
Waiau	172	42.39 S	173.03 E
Waiau ≃, N.Z.	172	42.47 S	173.22 E
Waiau ≃, N.Z.	172	46.12 S	167.38 E
Waiau ≃, N.Z.	172	38.58 S	177.24 E
Waibakul	115b	9.36 S	119.35 E
Waibeem	164	0.28 S	132.58 E
Waiblingen	56	48.50 N	9.19 E
Waibstadt	56	49.18 N	8.54 E
Waichagoumen	98	40.54 N	125.45 E
Waidbruck → Ponte Gardena	64	46.36 N	11.32 E
Waidhān	124	24.04 N	82.20 E
Waidhofen an der Thaya	61	48.49 N	15.18 E
Waidhofen an der Ybbs	61	47.58 N	14.47 E
Waidmannslust • [8]	264a	52.36 N	13.20 E
Waidring	64	47.35 N	12.34 E
Waiehu	229a	20.55 N	156.30 W
Waigang	106	31.22 N	121.11 E
Waigatsch → Vajgač, ostrov I	72	70.00 N	59.30 E
Waigeo, Pulau I	164	0.14 S	130.45 E
Waigoumen	98	41.24 N	116.13 E
Waihao Downs	172	44.48 S	170.55 E
Waihau Bay	172	37.37 S	177.55 E
Waihee	229a	20.56 N	156.30 W
Waihee Point ›	229a	20.57 N	156.31 W
Waiheke Island I	172	36.48 S	175.06 E
Waihi	172	37.24 S	175.51 E
Waihola	172	46.02 S	170.06 E
Waihopai ≃	172	41.31 S	173.44 E
Waihou ≃	172	37.10 S	175.32 E
Waihuantan	106	30.25 N	118.40 E
Waika	154	2.21 S	25.43 E
Waikabubak	115b	9.38 S	119.25 E
Waikaia	172	45.44 S	168.51 E
Waikaia ≃	172	45.53 S	168.48 E
Waikanae	172	40.53 S	175.04 E
Waikane	229c	21.30 N	157.51 W
Waikapu	229a	20.51 N	156.30 W
Waikare, Lake ⊜	172	37.26 S	175.13 E
Waikaremoana, Lake ⊜	172	38.46 S	177.07 E
Waikari	172	42.58 S	172.41 E
Waikato ≃	172	37.23 S	174.43 E
Waikelo	115b	9.24 S	119.14 E
Waikerie	166	34.11 S	139.59 E
Waikiki Beach ♦	229c	21.17 N	157.50 W
Waikino	172	37.25 S	175.46 E
Waikouaiti	172	45.36 S	170.41 E
Waikuatang	106	31.20 N	120.41 E
Wailo	144	9.25 N	48.55 E
Wailua	229b	22.03 N	159.20 W
Wailua River State Park ♦	229b	22.02 N	159.21 W
Wailuku	229a	20.53 N	156.30 W
Waimahaka	172	46.31 S	168.49 E
Waimakariri ≃	172	43.24 S	172.42 E
Waimamaku	172	35.33 S	173.29 E
Waimana	172	38.09 S	177.05 E
Waimana ≃	172	38.04 S	177.00 E
Waimanalo	229c	21.21 N	157.43 W
Waimangaroa	172	41.43 S	171.46 E
Waimangura	115b	9.30 S	119.14 E
Waimarama	172	39.48 S	176.59 E
Waimate	172	44.44 S	171.02 E
Waimea, Hi., U.S.	229c	21.38 N	158.03 W
Waimea, Hi., U.S.	229d	21.57 N	159.40 W
Waimea Canyon V	229b	22.04 N	159.39 W
Waimea Canyon State Park ♦	229b	22.04 N	159.40 W
Waimes	56	50.25 N	6.07 E
Wainfleet All Saints	44	53.07 N	0.14 E
Wainganga ≃	122	18.50 N	79.55 E
Waingapu	115b	9.39 S	120.16 E
Waini ≃	246	8.24 N	59.51 W
Wainscott	260	51.25 N	0.31 E
Wainstalls	262	53.45 N	1.56 W
Wainuiomata	172	41.16 S	174.57 E
Wainunu Bay c	175g	16.55 S	178.53 E
Wainwright, Ab., Can.	182	52.49 N	110.52 W
Wainwright, Ak., U.S.	180	70.38 N	160.01 W
Wainwright, Oh., U.S.	214	40.25 N	81.25 W
Waiohau	172	38.14 S	176.51 E
Waiotira	172	35.56 S	174.12 E
Waiouru	172	39.29 S	175.40 E
Waipa ≃	172	37.41 S	175.09 E
Waipahi	172	46.07 S	169.15 E
Waipahu	229c	21.23 N	158.00 W
Waipaoa	172	38.32 S	177.54 E
Waipara	172	43.04 S	172.45 E
Waipara ≃	172	43.09 S	172.48 E
Waipawa	172	39.56 S	176.36 E
Waipiata	172	45.11 S	170.10 E
Waipio Acres	229c	21.28 N	158.00 W
Waipio Bay c	229a	20.55 N	156.13 W
Waipiro	172	38.01 S	178.20 E
Waipu	172	35.59 S	174.27 E
Waipukurau	172	40.00 S	176.34 E
Wairakei	172	38.38 S	176.06 E
Wairarapa, Lake ⊜	172	41.13 S	175.15 E
Wairau ≃	172	41.30 S	174.04 E
Wairau Valley	172	41.34 S	173.32 E
Wairio	172	46.00 S	168.02 E
Wairoa	172	39.02 S	177.25 E
Wairoa ≃	172	39.04 S	177.26 E
Waisanzao	106	30.57 N	121.52 E
Waischenfeld	60	49.51 N	11.21 E
Waïsisi	175f	19.30 S	169.22 E
Waitahanui	172	38.47 S	176.05 E
Waitahuna	172	45.59 S	169.46 E
Waitakaruru	172	37.15 S	175.23 E
Waitaki ≃	172	44.57 S	171.09 E
Waitara, Austl.	274a	33.43 S	151.07 E
Waitara, N.Z.	172	39.00 S	174.13 E
Waitara ≃	172	38.59 S	174.14 E
Waitarere	172	40.33 S	175.12 E
Waita Reservoir ⊜ [1]	229b	21.55 N	159.27 W
Waitati	172	45.45 S	170.34 E
Waita-zan ʌ	96	33.08 N	131.10 E
Waite Hill	214	41.37 N	81.22 W
Waitemata	172	36.56 S	174.42 E
Waite Park	190	45.33 N	94.13 W
Waitoa	172	37.37 S	175.38 E
Waitotara	172	39.48 S	174.44 E
Waitotara ≃	172	39.51 S	174.41 E
Waitpinga	168b	35.37 S	138.29 E
Waitsburg	202	46.16 N	118.09 W
Waitzen → Vác	30	47.47 N	19.08 E
Waiuku	172	37.15 S	174.45 E
Waiuta	172	42.18 S	171.49 E
Waiwera South	172	46.13 S	169.30 E
Waiwo	164	0.56 S	131.03 E
Waiya	164	3.13 S	128.55 E
Waizenkirchen	60	48.20 N	13.52 E
Wajiki	96	33.51 N	134.30 E
Wajima	92	37.24 N	136.54 E
Wajir	154	1.45 N	40.04 E
Waka, Ityo.	144	7.07 N	37.26 E
Waka, Tx., U.S.	196	36.17 N	101.03 W
Waka, R.D.C.	152	1.01 N	20.13 E
Wakajabi	164	5.38 S	134.24 E
Wakakusa	94	35.36 N	138.29 E
Wakakusa-yama ʌ [2]	270	34.42 N	135.52 E
Wakamatsu → Aizu-wakamatsu	92	37.30 N	139.56 E
Wakami ≃	190	47.43 N	82.22 W
Wakami Lake ⊜	190	47.29 N	82.51 W
Wakamiya	96	33.44 N	130.37 E
Wakano-ura ♦	96	34.11 N	135.11 E
Wakarusa	216	41.32 N	86.03 W
Wakarusa ≃	198	38.57 N	95.05 W
Wakasa	96	35.20 N	134.24 E
Wakasa-wan c	92	35.45 N	135.40 E
Wakasa-wan-kokutei-kōen ♦	96	35.35 N	135.30 E
Wakatipu, Lake ⊜	172	45.05 S	168.34 E
Wakatomika Creek ≃	214	40.07 N	82.00 W
Wakato-ōhashi • [5]	96	33.54 N	130.49 E
Wakaw	184	52.39 N	105.44 W
Wakaw Lake ⊜	184	52.40 N	105.35 W
Wakayama	96	34.13 N	135.11 E
Wakayama □ [5]	96	34.00 N	135.20 E
Wakayanagi	92	38.46 N	141.08 E
Wake, Nihon	96	34.48 N	134.08 E
Wake, R.D.C.	152	0.48 S	20.10 E
WaKeeney	198	39.01 N	99.53 W
Wakefield, N.Z.	172	41.24 S	173.03 E
Wakefield, Eng., U.K.	44	53.42 N	1.29 W
Wakefield, Ks., U.S.	198	39.12 N	97.00 W
Wakefield, Ma., U.S.	207	42.30 N	71.04 W
Wakefield, Ne., U.S.	198	42.16 N	96.51 W
Wakefield, Oh., U.S.	218	38.59 N	83.01 W
Wakefield, R.I., U.S.	207	41.26 N	71.30 W
Wakefield, Va., U.S.	192	36.58 N	76.59 W
Wakefield ≃	168b	34.10 S	138.10 E
Wakefield Forest	284c	38.50 N	77.14 W
Wake Forest	192	35.58 N	78.30 W
Wake Island □ [2], Oc.	14	19.17 N	166.36 E
Wake Island □ [2], Oc.	174a	19.17 N	166.36 E
Wake Island I [1]	174a	19.18 N	166.38 E
Wake Island Air Force Base ■	174a	19.17 N	166.37 E
Wake Lagoon c	174a	19.18 N	166.36 E
Wakema	110	16.36 N	95.11 E
Wakeman	214	41.15 N	82.23 W
Wakeman ≃	182	51.00 N	126.30 W
Wakenda Creek ≃	194	39.19 N	93.16 W
Wake Village	194	33.26 N	94.07 W
Wakhān → Vākhān • [1]	120	37.00 N	73.00 E
Waki	96	34.04 N	134.09 E
Wakis	164	6.13 S	150.17 E
Wakita	196	36.53 N	97.55 W
Wakkanai	92a	45.25 N	141.40 E
Wakkerstroom	158	27.24 S	30.10 E
Wakō, Nihon	268	35.47 N	139.37 E
Wako, Pap. N. Gui.	164	6.05 S	149.05 E
Wakomata Lake ⊜	190	46.34 N	83.22 W
Wakonassin ≃	190	46.28 N	81.51 W
Wakonda	198	43.00 N	97.06 W
Wakre	164	0.19 S	131.09 E
Waku Kundo	152	11.25 S	15.07 E
Wakunai	175e	5.52 S	155.13 E
Wakusimi ≃	190	49.08 N	82.17 W
Wala ≃	154	5.46 S	32.04 E
Walachia □ [9]	38	44.00 N	25.00 E
Walamba	154	13.29 S	28.45 E
Walanae ≃	112	4.08 S	119.58 E
Walang	102	28.33 N	100.54 E
Wal Athiang	140	7.42 N	29.40 E
Walawe ≃	122	6.06 N	81.01 E
Walbeck	52	51.30 N	6.15 E
Walberswick	42	52.19 N	1.39 E
Walborn Reservoir ⊜ [1]	214	40.59 N	81.11 E
Walbran Creek ≃	224	48.34 N	124.40 W
Walbridge	214	41.35 N	83.29 W
Wałbrzych (Waldenburg)	30	50.46 N	16.17 E
Walburg	222	30.44 N	97.35 W
Walbury Hill ʌ [2]	42	51.21 N	1.30 W
Walcha	166	30.59 S	151.36 E
Walchensee ⊜	64	47.36 N	11.20 E
Walcheren I	52	51.33 N	3.35 E
Walchsee	64	47.39 N	12.19 E
Walcott, B.C., Can.	182	54.31 N	126.51 W
Walcott, Ia., U.S.	190	41.35 N	90.46 W
Walcott, N.D., U.S.	198	46.32 N	96.56 W
Walcott, Lake ⊜ [1]	202	42.40 N	113.23 W
Walcourt	50	50.15 N	4.25 E
Wałcz	30	53.17 N	16.28 E
Wald, Dtsch.	58	47.56 N	9.11 E
Wald, Dtsch.	60	49.09 N	12.20 E
Wald, Schw.	58	47.17 N	8.55 E
Wald • [8]	263	51.11 N	7.03 E
Waldai → Valdajskaja vozvyšennost' ⋀ [2]	24	57.00 N	33.30 E
Waldaist ≃	61	48.19 N	14.34 E
Wald am Schoberpass	61	47.27 N	14.40 E
Waldbauer • [8]	263	51.18 N	7.28 E
Waldbillig	56	49.47 N	6.18 E
Waldböckelheim	56	49.49 N	7.43 E
Waldbreitbach	56	50.33 N	7.25 E
Waldbröl	56	50.53 N	7.37 E
Waldbronn	56	48.56 N	8.29 E
Waldburg	58	47.45 N	9.43 E
Walddrehna	54	51.45 N	13.35 E
Waldeck, Dtsch.	56	51.12 N	9.04 E
Waldeck, Dtsch.	60	49.52 N	11.57 E
Walden, Co., U.S.	200	40.43 N	106.16 W
Walden, N.Y., U.S.	210	41.33 N	74.11 W
Walden, Lake ⊜	281	42.39 N	83.46 W
Waldenbuch	56	48.38 N	9.07 E
Waldenburg, Dtsch.	54	50.52 N	12.36 E
Waldenburg, Dtsch.	56	49.11 N	9.38 E
Waldenburg → Wałbrzych, Pol.	30	50.46 N	16.17 E
Waldenburg, Schw.	58	47.23 N	7.45 E
Walden Pond ⊜, Ma., U.S.	283	42.26 N	71.20 W
Walden Pond ⊜, Ma., U.S.	283	42.28 N	71.00 W
Walden Ridge ʌ	194	35.30 N	85.15 W
Waldershof	60	49.59 N	12.04 E
Walderslade	260	51.21 N	0.32 E
Waldheim, Sk., Can.	184	52.37 N	106.38 W
Waldheim, Dtsch.	54	51.04 N	13.01 E
Waldighoffen	58	47.33 N	7.19 E
Wald im Pinzgau	64	47.15 N	12.14 E
Waldkappel	56	51.08 N	9.52 E
Waldkirch	58	48.05 N	7.57 E
Waldkirchen	60	48.44 N	13.37 E
Waldkirchen am Wesen	60	48.26 N	13.49 E
Waldkraiburg	60	48.12 N	12.28 E
Waldmohr	56	49.23 N	7.20 E
Waldmünchen	60	49.23 N	12.43 E
Waldnaab ≃	60	49.36 N	12.08 E
Waldo, B.C., Can.	182	49.13 N	115.13 W
Waldo, Ar., U.S.	194	33.21 N	93.17 W
Waldo, Oh., U.S.	214	40.27 N	83.04 W
Waldoboro	188	44.05 N	69.22 W
Waldo Lake ⊜	283	42.07 N	71.03 W
Waldo Lake ⊜ [1]	202	43.44 N	122.03 W
Waldon ≃	42	50.51 N	4.15 W
Waldorf	208	38.37 N	76.56 W
Waldport	202	44.25 N	124.04 W
Waldron, Sk., Can.	184	50.51 N	102.30 W
Waldron, Ar., U.S.	194	34.53 N	94.05 W
Waldron, In., U.S.	218	39.27 N	85.40 W
Waldron, Mi., U.S.	216	41.43 N	84.25 W
Waldron Island I	224	48.43 N	123.02 W
Waldsassen	60	50.00 N	12.18 E
Waldshut-Tiengen	58	47.37 N	8.13 E
Waldstatt	58	47.21 N	9.17 E
Waldthurn	60	49.40 N	12.20 E
Waldviertel • [1]	61	48.40 N	15.15 E
Waldwick	276	41.00 N	74.07 W
Walea, Selat ⩌	112	0.40 S	122.00 E
Walembele	150	10.30 N	1.58 W
Walensee ⊜	58	47.07 N	9.12 E
Walenstadt	58	47.07 N	9.19 E
Wales, Ak., U.S.	180	65.36 N	168.05 W
Wales, Ma., U.S.	207	42.04 N	72.13 W
Wales, Wi., U.S.	216	43.00 N	88.23 W
Wales □ [8]	28	52.30 N	3.30 W
Wales Center	210	42.46 N	78.32 W
Wales Island I, B.C., Can.	182	54.45 N	130.30 W
Wales Island I, N.T., Can.	176	68.00 N	86.43 W
Walewale	150	10.21 N	0.48 W
Walgett	166	30.01 S	148.07 E
Walgreen Coast ± [2]	9	75.15 S	105.00 W
Walhachin	182	50.45 N	120.59 W
Walhalla, N.D., U.S.	198	48.55 N	97.55 W
Walhalla, S.C., U.S.	192	34.45 N	83.03 W
Walhalla ⊥	60	49.03 N	12.14 E
Walheim	56	50.42 N	6.10 E
Walhonding	214	40.22 N	82.09 W
Walhonding ≃	214	40.18 N	81.53 W
Wali	105	39.42 N	118.20 E
Walia	164	3.47 S	138.32 E
Walikale	154	1.25 S	28.03 E
Walincourt	50	50.04 N	3.20 E
Walis Island I	164	3.15 S	143.20 E
Walkaway	162	28.57 S	114.48 E
Walkden	44	53.32 N	2.24 W
Walkenried	54	51.35 N	10.37 E
Walker, Ia., U.S.	190	42.17 N	91.46 W
Walker, Mi., U.S.	216	43.00 N	85.46 W
Walker, Mn., U.S.	190	47.06 N	94.35 W
Walker, N.Y., U.S.	210	43.18 N	77.52 W
Walker □ [6]	222	30.42 N	95.35 W
Walker ≃	204	38.54 N	118.47 W
Walker, Lac ⊜	186	50.16 N	67.09 W
Walker, Mount ʌ [2]	171a	27.48 S	152.34 E
Walker Basin Creek ≃	228	35.20 N	118.47 W
Walker Bay c	158	34.30 S	19.20 E
Walker Creek ≃, Az., U.S.	200	36.58 N	109.42 W
Walker Creek ≃, Ma., U.S.	283	42.38 N	70.44 W
Walker Creek ≃, Wy., U.S.	198	43.09 N	104.52 W
Walker Lake ⊜, Mb., Can.	184	54.42 N	96.57 W
Walker Lake ⊜, Ak., U.S.	180	67.10 N	154.26 W
Walker Lake ⊜, Nv., U.S.	204	38.44 N	118.43 W
Walker Lake ⊜ [1]	210	40.48 N	77.11 W
Walker Point ›	158	34.05 S	22.57 E
Walker River Indian Reservation • [4]	204	39.00 N	118.40 W
Walkers Mill	279b	40.24 N	80.08 W
Walkersville	208	39.29 N	77.21 W
Walkerton, On., Can.	212	44.07 N	81.09 W
Walkerton, In., U.S.	216	41.28 N	86.28 W
Walkerton, Va., U.S.	208	37.43 N	77.01 W
Walkertown	192	36.10 N	80.09 W
Walker Valley	210	41.38 N	74.23 W
Walkerville	202	46.02 N	112.32 W
Walk Mill	262	53.46 N	2.12 W
Wall, Pa., U.S.	279b	40.24 N	79.47 W
Wall, S.D., U.S.	198	43.59 N	102.14 W
Wallace, Ca., U.S.	226	38.12 N	120.59 W
Wallace, Id., U.S.	202	47.28 N	115.55 W
Wallace, Ne., U.S.	198	40.50 N	101.09 W
Wallace, N.Y., U.S.	210	42.26 N	77.28 W
Wallace, N.C., U.S.	192	34.44 N	77.59 W
Wallaceburg	214	42.36 N	82.23 W
Wallace Lake ⊜	279a	41.22 N	81.52 W
Wallaceton	214	40.57 N	78.17 W
Wallacetown	214	42.38 N	81.28 W
Wallach	263	51.35 N	6.34 E
Wallacia	170	33.52 S	150.39 E
Wallal Downs	162	19.47 S	120.40 E
Wallam Creek ≃	166	28.40 S	147.20 E
Wallan	169	37.25 S	144.59 E
Wallangarra	166	28.56 S	151.56 E
Wallaroo	168b	33.56 S	137.38 E
Wallaroo Mines	168b	33.57 S	137.41 E
Wallasey	44	53.26 N	3.03 W
Wallau	56	50.56 N	8.28 E
Walla Walla	202	46.03 N	118.20 W
Walldorf, Dtsch.	54	50.36 N	10.23 E
Walldorf, Dtsch.	56	49.18 N	8.38 E
Walldürn	56	49.35 N	9.22 E
Walled Lake	216	42.32 N	83.28 W
Walled Lake ⊜	281	42.31 N	83.29 W
Wallen	216	41.09 N	85.09 W
Wallend	260	51.27 N	0.42 E
Wallenfels	54	50.16 N	11.28 E
Wallenhorst	52	52.21 N	8.01 E
Wallenpaupack, Lake ⊜	210	41.25 N	75.12 W
Waller	222	30.04 N	95.56 W
Waller □ [6]	222	30.00 N	96.00 W
Wallerawang	170	33.25 S	150.04 E
Wallern im Burgenland	61	47.43 N	16.56 E
Wallers	50	50.22 N	3.24 E
Wallersdorf	60	48.44 N	12.45 E
Wallersee ⊜	64	47.55 N	13.11 E
Wallerstein	56	48.53 N	10.28 E
Wallgau	64	47.31 N	11.16 E
Wallgrove	274a	33.47 S	150.51 E
Wallhausen	54	51.28 N	11.12 E
Wallhead Airport ⊠	279a	41.21 N	82.09 W
Wallingford, Eng., U.K.	42	51.37 N	1.08 W
Wallingford, Ct., U.S.	207	41.27 N	72.49 W
Wallingford, Pa., U.S.	285	39.54 N	75.22 W
Wallingford, Vt., U.S.	188	43.28 N	72.58 W
Wallington	276	40.51 N	74.06 W
Wallington • [8]	260	51.21 N	0.09 W
Wallis	222	29.37 N	96.03 W
Wallis → Valais □ [3]	58	46.10 N	7.30 E
Wallis, Îles II	14	13.18 S	176.10 W
Wallis and Futuna □ [2]	14	14.00 S	177.00 W
Wallisellen	58	47.25 N	8.36 E
Wallisville	222	29.50 N	94.44 W
Wallisville Lake ⊜ [1]	222	29.50 N	94.45 W
Wallkill	210	41.36 N	74.11 W
Wallkill ≃, U.S.	210	41.51 N	74.03 W
Wallkill ≃, U.S.	276	41.11 N	74.35 W
Wallkill, Wildcat Branch ≃	276	41.07 N	74.36 W
Wall Lake, Ia., U.S.	198	42.16 N	95.05 W
Wall Lake, Mi., U.S.	216	42.31 N	85.24 W
Wall Lake ⊜	216	42.31 N	85.23 W
Wallmer Bridge	262	53.43 N	2.48 W
Wallmerod	56	50.29 N	7.56 E
Wallops Island I	208	37.52 N	75.27 W
Wallowa	202	45.34 N	117.31 W
Wallowa ≃	202	45.43 N	117.47 W
Wallowa Mountains ⋀	202	45.10 N	117.30 W
Walls, Scot., U.K.	46a	60.14 N	1.35 W
Walls, Ms., U.S.	194	34.57 N	90.09 W
Wallsbüll	41	54.47 N	9.14 E
Wallsend, Austl.	170	32.55 S	151.40 E
Wallsend, Eng., U.K.	44	55.00 N	1.31 W
Wallstawe	54	52.47 N	11.01 E
Wall Town Drainage Ditch ≍	216	40.26 N	88.10 W
Wallula, Lake ⊜ [1]	202	46.00 N	119.00 W
Walmer, S. Afr.	158	33.59 S	25.36 E
Walmer, Eng., U.K.	42	51.13 N	1.24 E
Walmersley	262	53.37 N	2.18 W
Walney, Isle of I	44	54.07 N	3.15 W
Walnut, Ca., U.S.	228	34.01 N	117.51 W
Walnut, Il., U.S.	190	41.33 N	89.35 W
Walnut, Ia., U.S.	198	41.28 N	95.13 W
Walnut, Ks., U.S.	198	37.36 N	95.04 W
Walnut, Ms., U.S.	194	34.56 N	88.53 W
Walnut, N.C., U.S.	192	35.50 N	82.44 W
Walnut ≃	198	37.03 N	97.00 W
Walnut Canyon National Monument ♦	200	35.10 N	111.31 W
Walnut Canyon Reservoir ⊜ [1]	280	33.50 N	117.45 W
Walnut Cove	192	36.17 N	80.08 W
Walnut Creek, Ca., U.S.	226	37.54 N	122.03 W
Walnut Creek, Oh., U.S.	214	40.33 N	81.43 W
Walnut Creek ≃, Ca., U.S.	280	34.03 N	118.01 W
Walnut Creek ≃, Ca., U.S.	282	37.54 N	122.03 W
Walnut Creek ≃, Ks., U.S.	198	38.21 N	98.41 W
Walnut Creek ≃, Oh., U.S.	188	39.41 N	82.59 W
Walnut Creek ≃, Tx., U.S.	222	32.38 N	97.00 W
Walnut Creek, Middle Fork ≃	198	38.32 N	100.08 W
Walnut Creek, South Fork ≃	198	38.25 N	99.53 W
Walnut Grove, Ca., U.S.	226	38.15 N	121.31 W
Walnut Grove, Mn., U.S.	198	44.13 N	95.28 W
Walnut Grove, Ms., U.S.	194	32.35 N	89.27 W
Walnut Heights	282	37.53 N	122.08 W
Walnut Hill	219	38.29 N	89.03 W
Walnut Lake	281	42.33 N	83.19 W
Walnut Lake ⊜	281	42.33 N	83.20 W
Walnut Park	280	33.58 N	118.13 W
Walnutport	208	40.45 N	75.35 W
Walnut Ridge	194	36.04 N	90.57 W
Walnut Springs	222	32.03 N	97.45 W
Walpert Ridge ʌ	282	37.38 N	122.00 W
Walpeup	166	35.08 S	142.02 E
Walpole, Austl.	162	34.57 S	116.44 E
Walpole, Ma., U.S.	207	42.08 N	71.15 W
Walpole, N.H., U.S.	188	43.04 N	72.25 W
Walpole Island I	214	42.34 N	82.30 W
Walpole Island Indian Reserve • [4]	214	42.32 N	82.37 W
Walpole Saint Peter	42	52.42 N	0.15 E
Walsall	42	52.35 N	1.58 W
Walschleben	54	51.04 N	10.56 E
Walsden	262	53.42 N	2.06 W
Walsenburg	200	37.37 N	104.46 W
Walsh, Austl.	164	16.39 S	143.54 E
Walsh, Ab., Can.	184	49.57 N	110.03 W
Walsh, Co., U.S.	198	37.23 N	102.16 W
Walsh, Ky., U.S.	218	38.41 N	82.58 W
Walsh ≃	164	16.31 S	143.42 E
Walshaw Dean Reservoirs ⊜ [1]	262	53.48 N	2.03 W
Walshville	219	39.04 N	89.37 W
Walsingham	212	42.41 N	80.32 W
Walsleben	54	52.56 N	12.40 E
Walsoorden	52	51.23 N	4.02 E
Walsrode	52	52.52 N	9.35 E
Walston	214	40.58 N	79.01 W
Walsum	52	51.32 N	6.41 E
Walt Disney World ♦	220	28.26 N	81.35 W
Waltenhofen	64	47.40 N	10.17 E
Walterboro	192	32.54 N	80.40 W
Walter E. Long Lake ⊜ [1]	222	30.18 N	97.36 W
Walter F. George Lake ⊜ [1]	192	31.49 N	85.08 W
Walter Reed Army Medical Center ᵾ	284c	38.58 N	77.02 W
Walters	196	34.21 N	98.18 W
Waltersdorf, Dtsch.	54	50.52 N	14.38 E
Waltersdorf, Dtsch.	264a	52.22 N	13.35 E
Waltershausen	54	50.53 N	10.33 E
Waltershofen	58	47.46 N	9.55 E
Waltersville	194	32.22 N	90.52 W
Walthall	194	33.36 N	89.16 W
Waltham, Eng., U.K.	44	53.31 N	0.06 W
Waltham, Ma., U.S.	207	42.22 N	71.14 W
Waltham Abbey	42	51.42 N	0.01 E
Waltham Forest • [8]	42	51.35 N	0.01 W
Waltham on the Wolds	42	52.49 N	0.49 W
Walthamstow • [8]	260	51.35 N	0.01 W
Walthill	198	42.08 N	96.29 W
Walton, N.S., Can.	186	45.14 N	64.00 W
Walton, Eng., U.K.	42	51.24 N	0.25 W
Walton, Eng., U.K.	42	51.58 N	1.21 E
Walton, Fl., U.S.	220	27.17 N	80.15 W
Walton, In., U.S.	216	40.39 N	86.14 W
Walton, Ky., U.S.	218	38.52 N	84.36 W
Walton, N.Y., U.S.	210	42.10 N	75.07 W
Walton Hills	214	41.22 N	81.32 W
Walton-le-Dale	44	53.45 N	2.39 W
Walton on the Hill	260	51.17 N	0.15 W
Walton-on-the-Naze	42	51.51 N	1.16 E
Walton Run ≃	285	40.05 N	74.59 W
Waltonville	219	38.13 N	89.02 W
Waltrop	52	51.37 N	7.23 E
Walt Whitman Bridge • [5]	285	39.54 N	75.08 W
Walt Whitman Homes	285	39.52 N	75.11 W
Walt Whitman House State Historic Site ⊥	276	40.49 N	73.25 W
Walt Whitman Mall • [9]	276	40.50 N	73.25 W
Waltz	216	42.06 N	83.23 W
Walupt Lake ⊜	224	46.25 N	121.28 W
Walvis Bay	156	22.59 S	14.31 E
Walvis Bay □ [5]	156	22.59 S	14.31 E
Walvis Bay c	156	22.57 S	14.30 E
Walvis Ridge ✧ [3]	10	28.00 S	3.00 E
Walwa	171b	35.58 S	147.45 E
Walwen	262	53.14 N	3.15 W
Walworth, N.Y., U.S.	210	43.08 N	77.17 W
Walworth, Wi., U.S.	216	42.31 N	88.35 W
Walworth □ [6]	216	42.41 N	88.32 W
Walyunga National Park ♦	168a	31.44 S	116.04 E
Walyungup, Lake ⊜	168a	32.21 S	115.47 E
Walze	263	51.16 N	7.31 E
Walzin, Château de ⊥	56	50.13 N	4.55 E
Wama	152	12.14 S	15.33 E
Wamac	219	38.31 N	89.08 W
Wamba, Kenya	154	0.59 N	37.19 E
Wamba, Nig.	150	8.58 N	8.36 E
Wamba, R.D.C.	154	2.09 N	28.00 E
Wamba (Uamba) ≃	152	3.56 S	17.12 E
Wambel • [8]	263	51.32 N	7.32 E
Wamego	198	39.12 N	96.18 W
Wamel	52	51.53 N	5.28 E
Wamesit	283	42.37 N	71.15 W
Wami ≃	154	6.08 S	38.49 E
Wamiao	100	30.49 N	113.02 E
Wamic	224	45.13 N	121.16 W
Wamma ≃	164	3.23 S	135.13 E
Wamme ≃	56	50.10 N	5.16 E
Wamplers Lake ⊜	216	42.05 N	84.09 W
Wampool ≃	44	54.54 N	3.14 W
Wampsville	210	43.04 N	75.42 W
Wampú	236	15.01 N	85.02 W
Wampú ≃	236	14.59 N	85.03 W
Wampum	214	40.53 N	80.20 W
Wampus ≃	276	41.07 N	73.43 W
Wampus Lake Reservoir ⊜ [1]	276	41.09 N	73.43 W
Wamsasi	112	3.33 S	126.10 E
Wamsutter	200	41.40 N	107.58 W
Wamuran	171a	27.02 S	152.52 E
Wanaaring	166	29.42 S	144.09 E
Wanaka	172	44.42 S	169.09 E
Wanaka, Lake ⊜	172	44.30 S	169.08 E
Wanakah	210	42.45 N	78.54 W
Wanamassa	208	40.14 N	74.02 W
Wanamie	210	41.10 N	76.02 W
Wanamingo	190	44.18 N	92.47 W
Wan'an, Zhg.	100	26.56 N	117.22 E
Wan'an, Zhg.	100	26.30 N	114.49 E
Wan'an ≃	100	25.20 N	117.21 E

Symbols in the index entries represent the broad categories identified in the key at the right. Symbols with superior numbers (⋀ [1]) identify subcategories (see complete key on page *I · 1).*

Symbole im Register stellen die rechts im Schlüssel erklärten Kategorien dar. Symbole mit hochgestellten Ziffern (⋀ [1]) bezeichnen Unterabteilungen einer Kategorie (vgl. vollständiger Schlüssel auf Seite *I · 1).*

Los símbolos incluídos en el texto del índice representan las grandes categorías identificadas con la clave a la derecha. Los símbolos con numeros en su parte superior (⋀ [1]) identifican las subcategorías (véase la clave completa en la página *I · 1).*

Les symboles de l'index représentent les catégories indiquées dans la légende à droite. Les symboles suivis d'un indice (⋀ [1]) représentent des sous-catégories (voir légende complète à la page *I · 1).*

Os símbolos incluídos no texto do índice representam as grandes categorias identificadas com a chave à direita. Os símbolos com números em sua parte superior (⋀ [1]) identificam as subcategorias (veja-se a chave completa à página *I · 1).*

ʌ Mountain	Berg	Montaña	Montagne	Montanha
⋀ Mountains	Gebirge	Montañas	Montagnes	Montanhas
)(Pass	Paß	Paso	Col	Passo
V Valley, Canyon	Tal, Cañon	Valle, Cañón	Vallée, Canyon	Vale, Canhão
≚ Plain	Ebene	Llano	Plaine	Planície
› Cape	Kap	Cabo	Cap	Cabo
I Island	Insel	Isla	Île	Ilha
II Islands	Inseln	Islas	Îles	Ilhas
± Other Topographic Features	Andere Topographische Objekte	Otros Elementos Topográficos	Autres données topographiques	Outros acidentes topográficos

ESPAÑOL
Nombre | Página | Lat.°' | Long.°' W = Oeste

Wan'anchang 107 30.39 N 104.25 E
Wanapiri 164 4.33 S 135.59 E
Wanapitei ≃ 190 46.02 N 80.51 W
Wanapitei Lake ⊜ 190 46.45 N 80.45 W
Wanapum Lake ⊜[1] 202 47.00 N 120.00 W
Wanaque 210 41.02 N 74.17 W
Wanaque ≃ 276 40.58 N 74.17 W
Wanaque Reservoir ⊜[1] 210 41.05 N 74.17 W
Wanatah 216 41.25 N 86.53 W
Wanau 164 1.22 S 132.42 E
Wanbaoshan 89 44.12 N 125.11 E
Wanbi 166 34.46 S 140.19 E
Wanblee 198 43.34 N 101.40 W
Wanborough 42 51.33 N 1.42 W
Wanchangchang 107 29.43 N 104.19 E
Wanchese 192 35.50 N 75.38 W
Wanda 158 29.36 S 24.28 E
Wandai 164 3.41 S 136.41 E
Wandana 162 32.04 S 133.49 E
Wandawega 216 42.45 N 88.40 W
Wande 98 36.21 N 116.56 E
Wanderer 154 19.37 S 29.59 E
Wandering 168a 32.40 S 116.40 E
Wandering ≃ 182 55.05 N 112.30 W
Wanderup 41 54.41 N 9.20 E
Wandhofen 263 51.26 N 7.33 E
Wandingzhen 102 24.05 N 98.04 E
Wandlitz 54 52.45 N 13.26 E
Wandlitzer See ⊜ 264a 52.46 N 13.27 E
Wando 98 34.18 N 126.47 E
Wan-do I 98 34.21 N 126.42 E
Wandoan 166 26.08 S 149.57 E
Wandsworth ◆[8] 42 51.27 N 0.11 W
Waneta Lake ⊜ 210 42.27 N 77.06 W
Wanette 196 34.57 N 97.01 W
Wanfang 104 41.57 N 122.52 E
Wanfoxia 102 40.04 N 95.55 E
Wanfried 56 51.10 N 10.10 E
Wanfu ≃ 98 35.10 N 116.35 E
Wang ≃ 110 17.08 N 99.02 E
Wanga 154 2.58 N 29.13 E
Wangal 164 6.10 S 134.12 E
Wanganderry, Mount ∧ 170 34.20 S 150.15 E
Wanganui 172 39.56 S 175.03 E
Wanganui ≃ 172 39.56 S 175.00 E
Wang'anzhen 105 39.19 N 114.54 E
Wangaratta 166 36.22 S 146.20 E
Wangary 166 34.33 S 135.29 E
Wangbaotaicun 104 41.10 N 123.18 E
Wangbenying 105 40.28 N 116.06 E
Wangbintun 104 41.58 N 123.43 E
Wangchang, Zhg. 107 28.52 N 105.55 E
Wangchang, Zhg. 107 29.05 N 104.40 E
Wangchangtuizigou 104 41.14 N 120.32 E
Wangcheng 100 28.23 N 112.48 E
Wang Chin 110 17.53 N 99.37 E
Wangcun 98 36.41 N 117.41 E
Wangcunkou 100 28.22 N 118.59 E
Wangdain 124 29.02 N 89.15 E
Wangdalong 102 29.25 N 99.03 E
Wangdian 106 30.37 N 120.44 E
Wangdu 98 38.43 N 115.09 E
Wangdu Phodrang 124 27.29 N 89.54 E
Wange 154 2.00 S 40.55 E
Wangels 54 54.16 N 10.45 E
Wangen an der Aare 58 47.14 N 7.39 E
Wangenbourg 58 48.37 N 7.19 E
Wangen im Allgäu 58 47.41 N 9.50 E
Wangerooge 52 53.48 N 7.54 E
Wangerooge I 52 53.46 N 7.55 E
Wangersen 52 53.22 N 9.25 E
Wangfu 104 42.05 N 121.29 E
Wanggameti, Gunung ∧ 115b 10.07 S 120.14 E
Wanggangpu 104 41.38 N 123.09 E
Wanggao 102 24.38 N 111.30 E
Wanggezhuang 105 40.00 N 117.52 E
Wanggil-li 271b 37.36 N 126.39 E
Wanggoutun 104 41.40 N 121.53 E
Wanghai 98 40.26 N 120.30 E
Wanghai Shan ∧ 104 41.37 N 121.41 E
Wanghechenggou 104 41.52 N 121.13 E
Wang Hin, Khlong ≍ 269a 13.48 N 100.35 E
Wanghu 98 39.47 N 113.54 E
Wanghuzhuang 105 38.50 N 117.05 E
Wängi 58 47.30 N 8.57 E
Wangingsha 100 22.44 N 113.33 E
Wangi Wangi 170 33.04 S 151.35 E
Wangiwangi, Pulau I 112 5.20 S 123.35 E
Wangji, Zhg. 100 33.52 N 118.44 E
Wangji, Zhg. 100 34.00 N 117.46 E
Wangjia, Zhg. 106 31.59 N 121.13 E
Wangjia, Zhg. 106 32.07 N 120.59 E
Wangjiadian, Zhg. 100 31.26 N 113.58 E
Wangjiadian, Zhg. 105 40.03 N 117.29 E
Wangjiagou 104 42.33 N 123.16 E
Wangjiajing, Zhg. 98 37.49 N 115.23 E
Wangjiajing, Zhg. 98 39.56 N 122.11 E
Wangjiang 100 30.09 N 116.41 E
Wangjiangjing 106 30.53 N 120.43 E
Wang Jian Mu (Tomb of Wang Jian) ⊥ 107 30.38 N 104.04 E
Wangjiaputun 104 40.39 N 122.50 E
Wangjiapuzi, Zhg. 104 40.41 N 122.24 E
Wangjiapuzi, Zhg. 104 41.05 N 123.34 E
Wangjiaqiao 106 30.50 N 119.18 E
Wangjiashan 105 40.19 N 114.45 E
Wangjiashao 102 23.57 N 102.18 E
Wangjiatai 105 39.17 N 117.29 E
Wangjiaying, Zhg. 105 40.36 N 116.34 E
Wangjiaying, Zhg. 105 39.06 N 115.59 E
Wangjiazhai 106 31.21 N 121.37 E
Wangjiazui 106 31.16 N 120.18 E
Wangkantou 100 29.12 N 120.09 E
Wangkou 105 38.56 N 116.44 E
Wangkui 89 46.50 N 126.30 E
Wanglanzhuang 105 39.26 N 118.01 E
Wangling 100 27.13 N 113.26 E
Wangliu 100 32.25 N 115.40 E
Wangmiao 100 26.50 N 112.52 E
Wangmulazi 104 41.42 N 124.02 E
Wang Noi 110 14.13 N 100.44 E
Wangong 89 49.10 N 118.53 E
Wangpan Shan II 106 30.30 N 121.15 E
Wangpan Yang ⊂ 100 30.30 N 121.46 E
Wangpingchang 107 29.17 N 105.45 E
Wangqing 89 43.20 N 129.48 E
Wangqingmen 98 41.42 N 125.23 E
Wangqingtuo 105 39.11 N 116.53 E
Wangqinzhuang 105 39.15 N 117.05 E
Wangqucun 106 31.22 N 120.19 E
Wangs 58 47.02 N 9.26 E
Wang Saphung 110 17.18 N 101.46 E
Wangshanhutun 104 42.03 N 122.37 E
Wangshi 100 33.11 N 116.04 E
Wangsi 98 38.00 N 116.55 E
Wangsim-ni ◆[8] 271b 37.36 N 127.03 E
Wangsiying 107 30.34 N 103.29 E
Wangtai, Zhg. 98 36.05 N 119.59 E
Wangtai, Zhg. 100 26.39 N 117.57 E
Wangtan 100 29.45 N 120.40 E
Wang Thong 110 16.50 N 100.26 E
Wangtian 100 25.59 N 116.04 E
Wangting 106 31.26 N 120.26 E
Wangtongshitai 104 42.05 N 123.11 E
Wangtuan, Zhg. 98 37.32 N 116.08 E
Wangtuan, Zhg. 98 37.17 N 122.04 E
Wangtuanji 100 33.12 N 116.21 E
Wangu 107 30.19 N 106.05 E
Wanguzhen 107 29.41 N 105.57 E
Wangwenzhuang 105 38.53 N 117.15 E
Wangxiangshang 106 31.29 N 120.15 E
Wangxiangtai 105 40.02 N 115.09 E
Wangxiuqiao 106 31.38 N 121.03 E
Wangyangzhen 107 29.44 N 104.14 E
Wangyedian 98 41.36 N 118.17 E
Wangyefu 98 41.50 N 118.23 E

FRANÇAIS
Nom | Page | Lat.°' | Long.°' W = Ouest

Wangyehmiao → Horqin Youyi Qianqi 89 46.05 N 122.05 E
Wangyiguantun 104 42.36 N 123.19 E
Wangzhai 98 34.09 N 116.47 E
Wangzhimawo 105 39.39 N 117.40 E
Wangzhong 98 35.08 N 116.58 E
Wangzhuang 100 33.07 N 117.29 E
Wangzhuangbu 98 39.27 N 113.56 E
Wangzhuangji 98 34.09 N 118.23 E
Wangzhuangzi 105 39.17 N 118.14 E
Wanham 182 55.44 N 118.24 W
Wanhedian 100 32.16 N 113.16 E
Wanheimerort ◆[8] 263 51.24 N 6.46 E
Wanhsien → Wanxian 102 30.52 N 108.22 E
Wanhuyu 102 38.24 N 110.40 E
Wani 122 20.04 N 78.57 E
Wani, Gunung ∧ 112 4.29 S 123.01 E
Wanica □[5] 250 5.50 N 55.10 W
Wanie-Rukula 154 0.15 N 25.32 E
Wanigela 164 9.22 S 149.10 E
Wanipigow ≃ 184 51.11 N 96.18 W
Wanjiabu 100 28.51 N 115.39 E
Wanjiaqiao 106 30.25 N 119.07 E
Wanjiatun 98 40.03 N 119.51 E
Wanjindian 100 32.50 N 114.46 E
Wānkāner 120 22.37 N 70.56 E
Wankendorf 54 54.07 N 10.13 E
Wanle Weyne 144 2.37 N 44.54 E
Wanli, T'aiwan 269d 25.11 N 121.41 E
Wanli, Zhg. 106 31.06 N 120.16 E
Wanna 52 53.44 N 8.46 E
Wanna Lakes ⊜ 162 28.30 S 128.27 E
Wān Namton 110 22.03 N 99.33 E
Wanne-Eickel 52 51.32 N 7.09 E
Wanneroo 168a 31.45 S 115.48 E
Wannery Creek ≃ 162 22.47 S 115.43 E
Wannian 100 28.42 N 117.03 E
Wanning 110 18.53 N 110.26 E
Wannsee ◆[8] 54 52.25 N 13.09 E
Wanon Niwat 110 17.38 N 103.46 E
Wanouchi 94 35.17 N 136.38 E
Wānow 120 32.38 N 65.54 E
Wanparti 122 16.22 N 78.04 E
Wanquan 98 40.52 N 114.45 E
Wansbeck ≃ 44 55.10 N 1.34 W
Wansdorf 264a 52.38 N 13.05 E
Wan-See → Van Gölü ⊜ 128 38.33 N 42.46 E
Wanshan 107 30.23 N 106.06 E
Wanshouchang 107 29.26 N 105.55 E
Wanstead 172 40.08 S 176.32 E
Wanstead ◆[8] 260 51.34 N 0.02 E
Wantage 42 51.36 N 1.25 W
Wantagh 210 40.41 N 73.30 W
Wantan 102 30.03 N 110.18 E
Wantirna 274b 37.51 S 145.14 E
Wantirna South 274b 37.52 S 145.14 E
Wanxian, Zhg. 102 30.52 N 108.22 E
Wanxian, Zhg. 105 38.50 N 115.09 E
Wanyuan 102 32.04 N 108.02 E
Wanzai 100 28.06 N 114.27 E
Wanzarīk 146 27.31 N 13.29 E
Wanzhuang 105 39.34 N 116.36 E
Wanzleben 54 52.03 N 11.26 E
Wapack Range ⋏ 207 42.48 N 71.52 W
Wapakoneta 216 40.34 N 84.11 W
Wapanucka 196 34.22 N 96.25 W
Wapato 202 46.26 N 120.25 W
Wapawekka Hills ⋏[2] 184 54.45 N 104.20 W
Wapawekka Lake ⊜ 184 54.55 N 104.40 W
Wapella, Sk., Can. 184 50.15 N 102.00 W
Wapella, Il., U.S. 219 40.13 N 88.58 W
Wapello 190 41.10 N 91.11 W
Wapenamanda 164 5.35 S 143.55 E
Wapesi Lake ⊜ 184 50.34 N 92.21 W
Wāpi 122 20.22 N 72.54 E
Wapinda 152 3.41 S 22.48 E
Wapinitia Pass)(224 45.14 N 121.42 W
Wapisu Lake ⊜ 184 55.47 N 99.11 W
Wapiti ≃ 182 55.08 N 118.18 W
Wapizagonke, Lac ⊜ 206 46.43 N 73.02 W
Waples 222 32.29 N 97.43 W
Wapoga ≃ 164 2.42 S 136.06 E
Wappapello, Lake ⊜[1] 194 36.58 N 90.20 W
Wapping 207 41.50 N 72.33 W
Wappinger Creek ≃ 210 41.35 N 73.57 W
Wappingers Falls 210 41.35 N 73.54 W
Wapsipinicon ≃ 190 41.44 N 90.20 W
Waptus Lake ⊜ 224 47.30 N 121.10 W
Wapus ≃ 190 47.11 N 76.06 W
Wapus Lake ⊜ 184 56.27 N 102.12 W
Waqf aṣ-Ṣawwān, Jibāl ⋏ 132 30.53 N 36.48 E
Wāqid 142 30.42 N 30.44 E
Waqqāṣ 132 32.33 N 35.36 E
War 192 37.18 N 81.41 W
Wara 94 35.45 N 137.05 E
Warabi 94 35.49 N 139.41 E
Wārāh 120 27.27 N 67.48 E
Warakaraket I 164 2.15 S 130.36 E
Waramaug, Lake ⊜ 207 41.42 N 73.22 W
Warangal 122 18.00 N 79.35 E
Wararisbari, Tanjung › 164 1.05 S 136.23 E
Wārāseoni 120 21.45 N 80.02 E
Waratah, Austl. 166 41.27 S 145.32 E
Waratah, Austl. 170 32.54 S 151.44 E
Waratah Bay ⊂ 166 38.51 S 146.04 E
Warboys 42 52.24 N 0.04 W
Warbreccan 166 24.18 S 142.51 E
Warburg 52 51.29 N 9.08 E
Warburton, Austl. 162 26.07 S 126.35 E
Warburton, Austl. 169 37.46 S 145.41 E
Warburton, Pāk. 123 31.33 N 73.50 E
Warburton, Eng., U.K. 262 53.24 N 2.27 W
Warburton Aboriginal Reserve ◆[4] 162 24.00 S 128.15 E
Warburton Bay ⊂ 176 63.50 N 111.30 W
Warburton Creek ≃ 166 27.55 S 137.28 E
Warchha 123 32.25 N 71.59 E
Ward, N.Z. 172 41.50 S 174.08 E
Ward, Pa., U.S. 285 39.53 N 75.31 W
Ward ≃ 166 26.32 S 146.06 E
Ward, Mount ∧ 172 43.52 S 169.50 E
Warda 222 30.03 N 96.55 W
Ward Cove 182 55.24 N 131.44 W
Warden, S. Afr. 158 27.56 S 29.00 E
Warden, Wa., U.S. 202 46.58 N 119.02 W
Wardenburg 52 53.04 N 8.11 E
Warder 54 53.59 N 10.22 E
Wardersee ⊜ 54 53.58 N 10.26 E
Wardha 122 20.45 N 78.37 E
Wardha ≃ 122 19.38 N 79.48 E
Ward Hill ∧[2], Scot., U.K. 46 58.54 N 3.20 W
Ward Hill ∧[2], Scot., U.K. 46 58.57 N 3.09 W
Ward Hunt, Cape › 164 8.05 S 149.55 E
Ward Hunt Strait ⊔ 164 9.25 S 149.55 E
Wardle 44 53.39 N 2.08 W
Wardlow 182 50.54 N 111.33 W
Ward Mountain ∧ 202 46.10 N 114.17 W
Wardner 182 49.25 N 115.26 W
Wardour, Vale of V 42 51.05 N 2.00 W
Wards Chapel 284b 39.24 N 76.52 W
Wards Island I 276 40.47 N 73.56 W
Ward's Stone ∧ 44 54.02 N 2.38 W
Wardsville, On., Can. 214 42.39 N 81.45 W
Wardsville, Mo., U.S. 219 38.29 N 92.10 W
Wardswell Draw V 196 32.39 N 102.35 W
Wardt 52 51.41 N 6.25 E
Ware, Eng., U.K. 42 51.49 N 0.02 W
Ware, Ma., U.S. 207 42.15 N 72.14 W
Ware ≃ 207 42.11 N 72.22 W
War Eagle Creek ≃ 194 36.14 N 94.00 W
Waregem 50 50.53 N 3.25 E
Wareham, Eng., U.K. 42 50.41 N 2.07 W

PORTUGUÊS
Nome | Página | Lat.°' | Long.°' W = Oeste

Wareham, Ma., U.S. 207 41.45 N 70.43 W
Warehouse Point 207 41.55 N 72.37 W
Waremme 56 50.41 N 5.15 E
Waren, Dtsch. 54 53.31 N 12.40 E
Waren, Indon. 164 2.16 S 136.20 E
Warenai ≃ 164 2.52 S 135.55 E
Warenda 166 22.37 S 140.32 E
Warendorf 52 51.57 N 7.59 E
Ware River ⊂ 208 37.23 N 76.27 W
Ware Shoals 192 34.23 N 82.14 W
Waretown 208 39.47 N 74.11 W
Warffum 52 53.23 N 6.34 E
Warfusée-Abancourt 50 49.52 N 2.35 E
Warga 52 53.08 N 5.51 E
Wargalo 144 6.17 N 47.31 E
Wargla 148 31.59 N 5.25 E
Warialda 166 29.32 S 150.34 E
Wariap 164 1.34 S 134.11 E
Warilau 164 5.24 S 134.30 E
Warilau, Pulau I 164 5.23 S 134.33 E
Warin 54 53.48 N 11.42 E
Warinanco Park ♠ 276 40.39 N 74.14 W
Warin Chamrap 110 15.12 N 104.53 E
Waring Mountains ⋏ 180 66.50 N 159.00 W
Wāris Alīganj 124 25.01 N 85.38 E
Warka 30 51.47 N 21.10 E
Warkopi 164 1.08 S 134.07 E
Warks Burn ≃ 44 55.03 N 2.08 W
Warkworth, On., Can. 212 44.12 N 77.53 W
Warkworth, N.Z. 172 36.24 S 174.40 E
Warkworth, Eng., U.K. 44 55.21 N 1.36 W
Warland, Eng., U.K. 262 53.41 N 2.05 W
Warland, Mt., U.S. 182 48.30 N 115.17 W
Warland Reservoir ⊜[1] 262 53.41 N 2.04 W
Warley → Smethwick 42 52.30 N 1.58 W
Warley Moor Reservoir ⊜[1] 262 53.47 N 1.57 W
Warlingham 42 51.19 N 0.04 W
Warlington 42 51.39 N 1.01 W
Warman 184 52.20 N 106.34 W
Warmandi 164 0.22 S 132.39 E
Warmbad, Namibia 156 28.29 S 18.41 E
Warmbad, S. Afr. 156 24.55 S 28.15 E
Warm Baths → Warmbad 156 24.55 S 28.15 E
Warm Beach 224 48.10 N 122.21 W
War Memorial Cross ⊥ 169 37.20 S 144.36 E
Warmenhuizen 52 52.43 N 4.44 E
Warmensteinach 60 49.59 N 11.47 E
Warmeriville 50 49.21 N 4.13 E
Warmington 42 52.08 N 1.24 W
Warminster, Eng., U.K. 42 51.13 N 2.12 W
Warminster, Pa., U.S. 208 40.12 N 75.06 W
Warminster Naval Air Development Center ■ 285 40.12 N 75.09 W
Warm Springs, Ga., U.S. 192 32.53 N 84.40 W
Warm Springs, Mt., U.S. 202 46.11 N 112.48 W
Warm Springs, Or., U.S. 202 44.45 N 121.15 W
Warm Springs, Va., U.S. 192 38.02 N 79.47 W
Warm Springs ≃ 202 44.52 N 121.04 W
Warm Springs Indian Reservation ◆[4] 224 45.00 N 121.25 W
Warm Springs Reservoir ⊜[1] 202 43.37 N 118.14 W
Warnbro Sound ⊔ 168a 32.20 S 115.40 E
Warnemünde ◆[8] 54 54.10 N 12.04 E
Warner, Ab., Can. 182 49.17 N 112.12 W
Warner, N.H., U.S. 188 43.16 N 71.49 W
Warner, Ok., U.S. 196 35.29 N 95.18 W
Warner Lakes ⊜ 202 42.25 N 119.50 W
Warner Mountains ⋏ 204 41.40 N 120.20 W
Warner Peak ∧ 202 42.27 N 119.44 W
Warner Robins 192 32.37 N 83.36 W
Warners 210 43.05 N 76.20 W
Warners Pond ⊜ 283 42.28 N 71.24 W
Warnerville 210 42.34 N 74.30 W
Warnes, Arg. 252 34.55 S 60.31 W
Warnes, Bol. 248 17.30 S 63.10 W
Warnes Brook ≃ 276 40.25 N 74.18 W
Warneton 50 50.45 N 2.57 E
Warngau 64 47.50 N 11.41 E
Warnicken → Primorje 76 54.57 N 20.02 E
Warnkenhagen 54 54.00 N 11.04 E
Warnow ≃ 54 54.06 N 12.09 E
Warns 52 52.52 N 5.25 E
Warnsveld 52 52.08 N 6.13 E
Waroona 168a 32.50 S 115.55 E
Warpath ≃ 184 52.21 N 98.26 W
Warra 166 26.56 S 150.55 E
Warrabri Aboriginal Reserve ◆[4] 162 21.00 S 134.20 E
Warracknabeal 166 36.15 S 142.24 E
Warr Acres 196 35.31 N 97.37 W
Warragamba Dam ◆[6] 170 33.54 S 150.36 E
Warragul 169 38.10 S 145.56 E
Warrandyte 274b 37.45 S 145.13 E
Warrandyte South 274b 37.46 S 145.14 E
Warrāq al-ʿArab 273c 30.06 N 31.12 E
Warrāq al-Ḥaḍar, Jazīrat I 273c 30.07 N 31.13 E
Warrāq al-Hadar wa Ambūtbah wa Mīt an-Naṣārā 273c 30.06 N 31.13 E
Warrawagine 162 20.51 S 120.42 E
Warrawee 274a 33.44 S 151.07 E
Warrawolong, Mount ∧ 170 33.03 S 151.15 E
Warrawong 170 34.29 S 150.53 E
Warrego ≃ 166 30.24 S 145.21 E
Warrego Range ⋏ 166 25.00 S 146.30 E
Warren, Austl. 166 31.42 S 147.50 E
Warren, Eng., U.K. 262 53.14 N 2.10 W
Warren, Ar., U.S. 194 33.36 N 92.03 W
Warren, Il., U.S. 190 42.29 N 89.59 W
Warren, In., U.S. 216 40.40 N 85.25 W
Warren, Ma., U.S. 207 42.12 N 72.11 W
Warren, Mi., U.S. 216 42.28 N 83.01 W
Warren, Mn., U.S. 198 48.11 N 96.46 W
Warren, Mo., U.S. 219 39.47 N 91.45 W
Warren, N.J., U.S. 276 40.37 N 74.30 W
Warren, Oh., U.S. 214 41.14 N 80.49 W
Warren, Or., U.S. 224 45.49 N 122.50 W
Warren, Pa., U.S. 214 41.50 N 79.08 W
Warren, R.I., U.S. 207 41.43 N 71.16 W
Warren □[6], In., U.S. 216 40.21 N 87.17 W
Warren □[6], Mo., U.S. 219 38.45 N 91.09 W
Warren □[6], N.J., U.S. 210 40.49 N 75.05 W
Warren □[6], N.Y., U.S. 210 43.26 N 73.43 W
Warren □[6], Oh., U.S. 218 39.26 N 84.13 W
Warren □[6], Pa., U.S. 214 41.51 N 79.08 W
Warren ≃ 162 34.35 S 115.50 E
Warren City 222 32.33 N 94.54 W
Warrendale 214 40.39 N 80.04 W
Warren Dunes State Park ♠ 216 41.56 N 86.36 W
Warren H. Manning State Park ♠ 283 42.34 N 71.18 W
Warren Park 218 39.46 N 86.03 W
Warren Peaks ⋏ 198 44.29 N 104.28 W
Warrenpoint 48 54.06 N 6.15 W
Warren Point › 180 69.44 N 132.30 W
Warrens 190 44.07 N 90.29 W
Warrensburg, Il., U.S. 219 39.56 N 89.04 W
Warrensburg, Mo., U.S. 194 38.45 N 93.44 W
Warrensburg, N.Y., U.S. 188 43.29 N 73.46 W

Warrensville 210 41.19 N 76.57 W
Warrensville Heights 214 41.26 N 81.32 W
Warrenton, S. Afr. 158 28.09 S 24.47 E
Warrenton, Ga., U.S. 192 33.24 N 82.39 W
Warrenton, Mo., U.S. 219 38.48 N 91.08 W
Warrenton, N.C., U.S. 192 36.23 N 78.09 W
Warrenton, Or., U.S. 224 46.09 N 123.55 W
Warrenton, Tx., U.S. 222 30.01 N 96.44 W
Warrenton, Va., U.S. 188 38.42 N 77.47 W
Warrenville 216 41.49 N 88.10 W
Warrenzin 54 53.54 N 12.57 E
Warri 150 5.31 N 5.45 E
Warriedar Hill ∧[2] 162 29.06 S 117.06 E
Warriewood 274a 33.42 S 151.18 E
Warrill Creek ≃ 171a 27.39 S 152.44 E
Warrington, N.Z. 172 45.43 S 170.35 E
Warrington, Eng., U.K. 44 53.24 N 2.37 W
Warrington, Fl., U.S. 194 30.23 N 87.16 W
Warrington, Pa., U.S. 285 40.15 N 75.08 W
Warrington □[8] 262 53.24 N 2.33 W
Warrington Airport ⊠ 285 40.16 N 75.09 W
Warrior 194 33.48 N 86.48 W
Warrior Creek ≃ 192 31.15 N 83.34 W
Warrior Reefs ✣[2] 164 9.35 S 143.10 E
Warriors Mark 214 40.42 N 78.08 W
Warrnambool 166 38.23 S 142.29 E
Warroad 198 48.54 N 95.18 W
Warrumbungle National Park ♠ 166 31.20 S 149.00 E
Warsak 123 34.10 N 71.25 E
Warsaw → Warszawa, Pol. 30 52.15 N 21.00 E
Warsaw, Il., U.S. 190 40.21 N 91.26 W
Warsaw, In., U.S. 216 41.14 N 85.51 W
Warsaw, Ky., U.S. 218 38.47 N 84.54 W
Warsaw, Mo., U.S. 194 38.14 N 93.22 W
Warsaw, N.Y., U.S. 210 42.44 N 78.07 W
Warsaw, N.C., U.S. 192 34.59 N 78.05 W
Warsaw, Oh., U.S. 214 40.20 N 82.00 W
Warsaw, Va., U.S. 208 37.57 N 76.45 W
Warsaw Station ◆[5] 265a 59.54 N 30.19 E
Warschau → Warszawa 30 52.15 N 21.00 E
Warscheneck ∧ 61 47.39 N 14.14 E
Warshiikh 144 2.18 N 45.48 E
Warsop 44 53.13 N 1.09 W
Warspite 182 54.06 N 112.37 W
Warstein 56 51.26 N 8.21 E
Warszawa (Warsaw) 30 52.15 N 21.00 E
Warszawa □[4] 30 52.15 N 21.00 E
Warta 30 51.42 N 18.38 E
Warta ≃ 30 52.35 N 14.39 E
Wartburg, S. Afr. 158 29.25 S 30.35 E
Wartburg, Tn., U.S. 192 36.06 N 84.35 W
Wartburg ⊥ 54 50.58 N 10.18 E
Wartenberg 60 48.24 N 11.59 E
Wartenberg ◆[8] 264a 52.34 N 13.31 E
Warth 58 47.15 N 10.11 E
Warthan Creek ≃ 226 36.08 N 120.20 W
Warthausen 58 48.08 N 9.48 E
Warthe → Warta ≃ 30 52.35 N 14.39 E
Wartin 54 53.15 N 14.09 E
Warton, Eng., U.K. 44 54.09 N 2.47 W
Warton, Eng., U.K. 44 53.45 N 2.54 W
Warton Aerodrome ⊠ 262 53.45 N 2.54 W
Wartrace 194 35.31 N 86.20 W
Wartsberg ∧[2] 263 51.25 N 6.29 E
Waru 164 3.24 S 130.40 E
Warud 120 21.28 N 78.16 E
Warunta, Laguna de ⊜ 236 15.23 N 84.05 W
Waruta ≃ 164 3.18 S 140.08 E
Warwick, Austl. 171a 28.13 S 152.02 E
Warwick, P.Q., Can. 206 45.56 N 71.59 W
Warwick, Eng., U.K. 42 52.17 N 1.34 W
Warwick, Md., U.S. 208 39.25 N 75.46 W
Warwick, N.Y., U.S. 210 41.15 N 74.21 W
Warwick, R.I., U.S. 207 41.41 N 71.22 W
Warwick ≃ 208 37.05 N 76.33 W
Warwick Castle ⊥ 42 52.17 N 1.34 W
Warwick Channel ⊔ 164 13.51 S 136.16 E
Warwick Farm Racecourse and Motor Race Track ♠ 274a 33.55 S 150.57 E
Warwickshire □[6] 42 52.13 N 1.37 W
Warza 54 51.00 N 10.41 E
Wasaga Beach 212 44.31 N 80.01 W
Wasagu 150 11.25 N 5.49 E
Wasatch Mountain State Park ♠ 200 40.33 N 111.31 W
Wasatch Plateau ⋏[1] 200 39.20 N 111.30 W
Wasatch Range ⋏ 200 40.40 N 111.35 W
Wasāwewāla 123 30.28 N 73.40 E
Wasbank 158 28.24 S 30.05 E
Wasbister 46 59.10 N 3.07 W
Wascana Creek ≃ 184 50.39 N 104.55 W
Wäschenbeuren 56 48.46 N 9.41 E
Wasco, Ca., U.S. 226 35.35 N 119.20 W
Wasco, Or., U.S. 224 45.35 N 120.41 W
Wasco □[6] 224 45.10 N 121.12 W
Wase 150 9.06 N 9.59 E
Wase ≃ 146 8.27 N 10.06 E
Waseca 190 44.04 N 93.30 W
Waseda University ☉[2] 268 35.42 N 139.43 E
Wasekamio Lake ⊜ 184 56.45 N 108.45 W
Wasen 58 47.03 N 7.48 E
Wasgomuwa National Park ♠ 122 7.40 N 80.45 E
Washademoak Lake ⊜ 186 45.48 N 65.58 W
Washago 212 44.45 N 79.20 W
Washburn, Il., U.S. 190 40.55 N 89.17 W
Washburn, Me., U.S. 186 46.47 N 68.09 W
Washburn, N.D., U.S. 198 47.17 N 101.01 W
Washburn, Wi., U.S. 190 46.40 N 90.53 W
Washburn ≃ 44 53.54 N 1.39 W
Washburn, Mount ∧ 202 44.48 N 110.25 W
Washburn Lake ⊜ 176 70.03 N 106.50 W
Washdyke 172 44.21 S 171.14 E
Washicoutai 186 50.17 N 60.42 W
Washiga-take ∧ 94 35.56 N 136.58 E
Wāshīm 122 20.06 N 77.09 E
Washimiya 94 36.06 N 139.40 E
Washington, Eng., U.K. 44 54.55 N 1.30 W
Washington, Ca., U.S. 226 39.22 N 120.48 W
Washington, Ct., U.S. 207 41.37 N 73.18 W
Washington, D.C., U.S. 208 38.53 N 77.02 W
Washington, D.C., U.S. 284c 38.53 N 77.02 W
Washington, Ga., U.S. 192 33.44 N 82.44 W
Washington, Il., U.S. 190 40.42 N 89.24 W
Washington, In., U.S. 194 38.39 N 87.10 W
Washington, Ia., U.S. 190 41.17 N 91.41 W
Washington, Ks., U.S. 198 39.49 N 97.03 W
Washington, Ky., U.S. 218 38.36 N 83.48 W
Washington, La., U.S. 194 30.36 N 92.03 W
Washington, Mi., U.S. 214 42.44 N 83.02 W
Washington, Mo., U.S. 219 38.33 N 91.01 W
Washington, N.J., U.S. 210 40.45 N 74.58 W
Washington, N.C., U.S. 192 35.31 N 77.01 W
Washington, Pa., U.S. 214 40.10 N 80.14 W
Washington, Tx., U.S. 222 30.20 N 96.10 W
Washington, Ut,. U.S. 200 37.07 N 113.30 W

Washington, Va., U.S. 188 38.42 N 78.09 W
Washington □[6], Il., U.S. 219 38.21 N 89.23 W
Washington □[6], In., U.S. 218 38.36 N 86.06 W
Washington □[6], N.Y., U.S. 210 43.15 N 73.27 W
Washington □[6], Or., U.S. 224 45.33 N 123.07 W
Washington □[6], Pa., U.S. 214 40.10 N 80.15 W
Washington □[6], R.I., U.S. 207 41.28 N 71.35 W
Washington □[6], Tx., U.S. 222 30.15 N 96.20 W
Washington □[6], Wi., U.S. 216 43.14 N 88.15 W
Washington □[3], U.S. 178 47.30 N 120.30 W
Washington □[3], U.S. 202 47.30 N 120.30 W
Washington, Lake ⊜, Fl., U.S. 220 28.07 N 80.45 W
Washington, Lake ⊜, Wa., U.S. 224 47.37 N 122.15 W
Washington, Mount ∧ 188 44.15 N 71.15 W
Washington Court House 218 39.32 N 83.26 W
Washington Crossing 208 40.17 N 74.52 W
Washington Crossing State Historic Site ⊥ 208 40.17 N 74.53 W
Washington Depot 207 41.38 N 73.18 W
Washington Heights ◆[8] 276 40.52 N 73.56 W
Washington Island 190 45.23 N 86.55 W
Washington Island I 190 45.23 N 86.55 W
Washington Memorial Chapel ☉[1] 285 40.06 N 75.26 W
Washington Mills 210 43.03 N 75.16 W
Washington Monument ♠ 284c 38.53 N 77.03 W
Washington Monument State Park ♠ 208 39.30 N 77.38 W
Washington National Airport ⊠ 208 38.51 N 77.02 W
Washington-on-the-Brazos State Historic Park ♠ 222 30.20 N 96.09 W
Washington Park 219 38.38 N 90.05 W
Washington Park ♠, Il., U.S. 278 41.48 N 87.37 W
Washington Park ♠, Oh., U.S. 279a 41.27 N 81.40 W
Washington Pass)(224 48.32 N 120.39 W
Washington Place 218 39.47 N 86.01 W
Washington Rock State Park ♠ 276 40.37 N 74.28 W
Washington's Headquarters ⊥ 285 40.06 N 75.28 W
Washington Terrace 200 41.10 N 111.58 W
Washington Township 276 40.54 N 74.00 W
Washington Valley 276 40.48 N 74.32 W
Washington Valley Reservoir ⊜[1] 276 40.36 N 74.34 W
Washingtonville, N.Y., U.S. 210 41.26 N 74.10 W
Washingtonville, Oh., U.S. 214 40.54 N 80.46 W
Washingtonville, Pa., U.S. 210 41.03 N 76.40 W
Washita ≃ 196 34.12 N 96.50 W
Washoe □[6] 226 39.22 N 119.43 W
Washoe Lake ⊜ 226 39.16 N 119.48 W
Washougal 224 45.34 N 122.21 W
Washougal ≃ 224 45.35 N 122.23 W
Washow Bay ⊂ 184 51.22 N 96.47 W
Washtenaw □[6] 216 42.15 N 83.50 W
Washtucna 202 46.45 N 118.18 W
Wāshuk 128 27.44 N 64.48 E
Wasian 164 1.54 S 133.17 E
Wasilków 30 53.12 N 23.12 E
Wasilla 180 61.35 N 149.26 W
Wasior 164 2.43 S 134.30 E
Wasiri 112 7.35 S 126.38 E
Wāsiṭ □[4] 128 32.45 N 45.25 E
Waskada 184 49.06 N 100.46 W
Waskaganish 176 51.30 N 78.45 W
Waskahigan ≃ 182 54.45 N 117.12 W
Waskaiowaka Lake ⊜ 184 56.30 N 96.20 W
Waskatenau 182 54.07 N 112.47 W
Waskesiu Lake ⊜ 184 53.56 N 106.10 W
Waskom 194 32.29 N 94.04 W
Wąsosz 30 51.34 N 16.42 E
Waspam 236 14.44 N 83.58 W
Waspuk ≃ 236 14.38 N 84.26 W
Wasquehal 50 50.40 N 3.09 E
Wassaic 210 41.48 N 73.35 W
Wasselonne 58 48.38 N 7.27 E
Wassen 58 46.42 N 8.36 E
Wassenaar 52 52.07 N 4.24 E
Wassenberg 56 51.06 N 6.08 E
Wasseralfingen 56 48.52 N 10.06 E
Wasserbillig 56 49.44 N 6.30 E
Wasserburg am Inn 60 48.04 N 12.13 E
Wasserkuppe ∧ 56 50.30 N 9.56 E
Wasserkurl 263 51.33 N 7.38 E
Wasserleben 54 51.55 N 10.44 E
Wassertrüdingen 56 49.02 N 10.35 E
Wassigny 50 50.01 N 3.36 E
Wass Lake ⊜ 184 53.40 N 95.25 W
Wassmannsdorf 264a 52.22 N 13.28 E
Wassou 150 10.02 N 13.39 W
Wassy 58 48.30 N 4.57 E
Wast Water ⊜ 44 54.26 N 3.18 W
Wasu 164 6.00 S 147.15 E
Wasum 164 6.05 S 149.20 E
Wasungen 54 50.40 N 10.22 E
Watabeag Lake ⊜ 190 48.14 N 80.32 W
Watampone (Bone) 112 4.32 S 120.20 E
Watamu Marine National Park ♠ 154 3.23 S 40.00 E
Waṭan, Wādī al- V 142 30.26 N 31.49 E
Watansopeng 112 4.21 S 119.53 E
Watapi Lake ⊜ 184 55.18 N 109.35 W
Watarai 94 34.26 N 136.37 E
Watarase ≃ 94 36.13 N 139.42 E
Wataru I 122 5.43 N 73.23 E
Watatic, Mount ∧ 207 42.42 N 71.53 W
Watauga 222 32.51 N 97.15 W
Watchet 42 51.12 N 3.20 W
Watch Hill 207 41.18 N 71.51 W
Watchung 276 40.38 N 74.27 W
Watchung Reservation ♠ 276 40.41 N 74.23 W
Water 262 53.44 N 2.14 W
Waterbeach 42 52.16 N 0.11 E
Waterberg 156 20.28 S 17.13 E
Waterberge ⋏ 156 24.30 S 28.00 E
Waterberg Plateau Park ♠ 156 20.30 S 17.00 E
Waterbury, Ct., U.S. 207 41.33 N 73.02 W
Waterbury, Vt., U.S. 188 44.20 N 72.45 W
Waterdale 158 30.40 S 24.02 E
Wateree ≃ 192 33.45 N 80.37 W
Wateree Lake ⊜[1] 192 34.25 N 80.50 W
Waterend, Eng., U.K. 260 51.47 N 0.30 W
Water End, Eng., U.K. 262 53.41 N 2.15 W
Waterfall, Austl. 170 34.08 S 151.00 E
Waterfall, Pa., U.S. 214 40.08 N 78.04 W
Waterford, On., Can. 212 42.56 N 80.17 W
Waterford (Port Láirge), Ire. 48 52.15 N 7.06 W
Waterford, S. Afr. 158 33.05 S 25.00 E
Waterford, Ca., U.S. 226 37.38 N 120.46 W
Waterford, Ct., U.S. 207 41.20 N 72.09 W
Waterford, In., U.S. 216 41.40 N 86.50 W
Waterford, Mi., U.S. 216 42.42 N 83.24 W

Waterford, N.Y., U.S. 210 42.47 N 73.40 W
Waterford, Pa., U.S. 214 41.56 N 79.59 W
Waterford, Wi., U.S. 216 42.45 N 88.12 W
Waterford □[6] 48 52.10 N 7.40 W
Waterford Harbour ⊂ 48 52.10 N 6.55 W
Waterford Mills 216 41.33 N 85.50 W
Waterford Works 208 39.43 N 74.50 W
Watergate Bay ⊂ 42 50.27 N 5.05 W
Watergrasshill 48 52.01 N 8.21 W
Watergrove Reservoir ⊜[1] 262 53.39 N 2.08 W
Waterhen ≃ 184 54.38 N 107.47 W
Waterhen Lake ⊜, Mb., Can. 184 52.06 N 99.34 W
Waterhen Lake ⊜, Sk., Can. 184 54.28 N 108.25 W
Waterhouse Range ⋏ 162 24.01 S 133.25 E
Wateringbury 260 51.15 N 0.25 E
Wateringen 52 52.02 N 4.16 E
Water Island 276 40.41 N 73.02 W
Waterkloof 158 30.19 S 25.18 E
Waterloo, Austl. 164 16.38 S 129.18 E
Waterloo, Austl. 168a 33.20 S 115.47 E
Waterloo, Austl. 168b 33.59 S 138.53 E
Waterloo, Bel. 50 50.43 N 4.23 E
Waterloo, On., Can. 212 43.28 N 80.31 W
Waterloo, P.Q., Can. 206 45.21 N 72.31 W
Waterloo, S.L. 150 8.20 N 13.04 W
Waterloo, Eng., U.K. 44 53.28 N 3.02 W
Waterloo, Al., U.S. 194 34.55 N 88.03 W
Waterloo, Il., U.S. 219 38.20 N 90.08 W
Waterloo, In., U.S. 216 41.25 N 85.01 W
Waterloo, Ia., U.S. 190 42.29 N 92.20 W
Waterloo, N.Y., U.S. 210 42.54 N 76.51 W
Waterloo, Wi., U.S. 216 43.11 N 88.59 W
Waterloo □[6] 212 43.30 N 80.30 W
Waterloo Bay ⊂ 168b 35.08 S 137.26 E
Waterloo State Recreation Area ♠ 216 42.22 N 84.20 W
Waterlooville 42 50.53 N 1.02 W
Waterman, Il., U.S. 216 41.46 N 88.46 W
Waterman, Wa., U.S. 224 47.34 N 122.35 W
Waterman Mountain ∧ 228 34.20 N 117.56 W
Waterman Wash V 200 33.21 N 112.31 W
Water Mill 207 40.55 N 72.21 W
Waterport 210 43.20 N 78.16 W
Waterport Pond ⊜[1] 212 43.19 N 78.16 W
Waterproof 194 31.48 N 91.23 W
Waterside 214 40.11 N 78.23 W
Waterside Park 276 40.56 N 73.20 W
Watersmeet 190 46.16 N 89.10 W
Waterton ≃ 182 49.32 N 113.16 W
Waterton-Glacier International Peace Park ♠ 202 48.47 N 113.45 W
Waterton Lakes National Park ♠ 182 49.05 N 113.50 W
Watertown, Ct., U.S. 207 41.36 N 73.07 W
Watertown, Ma., U.S. 207 42.22 N 71.11 W
Watertown, N.Y., U.S. 212 43.58 N 75.54 W
Watertown, S.D., U.S. 198 44.53 N 97.06 W
Watertown, Wi., U.S. 216 43.11 N 88.43 W
Waterval-Boven 156 25.40 S 30.20 E
Watervale 168b 33.57 S 138.38 E
Water Valley, Ms., U.S. 194 34.09 N 89.37 W
Water Valley, N.Y., U.S. 284a 42.42 N 78.51 W
Water View 208 37.43 N 76.36 W
Waterville, N.S., Can. 186 45.03 N 64.41 W
Waterville, P.Q., Can. 206 45.16 N 71.54 W
Waterville, Ire. 48 51.49 N 10.13 W
Waterville, Ks., U.S. 198 39.41 N 96.44 W
Waterville, Me., U.S. 188 44.33 N 69.37 W
Waterville, Ma., U.S. 207 42.40 N 72.04 W
Waterville, Mn., U.S. 190 44.13 N 93.34 W
Waterville, N.Y., U.S. 210 42.55 N 75.22 W
Waterville, Oh., U.S. 216 41.30 N 83.43 W
Waterville, Pa., U.S. 210 41.19 N 77.22 W
Waterville, Wa., U.S. 202 47.38 N 120.04 W
Watervliet, Mi., U.S. 216 42.11 N 86.15 W
Watervliet, N.Y., U.S. 210 42.43 N 73.42 W
Watervliet Reservoir ⊜[1] 210 42.43 N 73.58 W
Wates, Indon. 114 1.00 N 100.16 E
Wates, Indon. 115a 7.55 S 112.07 E
Wates, Indon. 115a 7.51 S 110.10 E
Watford, On., Can. 214 42.57 N 81.53 W
Watford, Eng., U.K. 42 51.40 N 0.25 W
Watford □[8] 260 51.40 N 0.25 W
Watford City 198 47.48 N 103.16 W
Waʿth 140 8.10 N 32.07 E
Wathaman ≃ 184 57.16 N 102.52 W
Wathaman Lake ⊜ 184 56.55 N 103.43 W
Wathena 198 39.45 N 94.56 W
Watheroo 162 30.17 S 116.04 E
Watheroo National Park ♠ 162 30.14 S 115.52 E
Wathlingen 52 52.32 N 10.09 E
Wath upon Dearne 44 53.29 N 1.20 W
Wati 120 28.02 N 96.59 E
Watino 182 55.43 N 117.37 W
Watkins Glen 210 42.22 N 76.52 W
Watkins Glen International Raceway ♠ 210 42.20 N 76.55 W
Watkins Glen State Park ♠ 210 42.22 N 76.55 W
Watkins Island I 284c 39.02 N 77.17 W
Watkins Lake ⊜ 281 42.40 N 83.22 W
Watkinsville 192 33.51 N 83.24 W
Watlaar 164 5.28 S 133.07 E
Watling Island → San Salvador I 238 24.02 N 74.28 W
Watlington 42 51.37 N 1.00 W
Watoga State Park ♠ 188 38.07 N 80.05 W
Watonga 196 35.50 N 98.24 W
Watonwan ≃ 198 44.04 N 94.07 W
Watopeka ≃ 206 45.34 N 72.00 W
Watou 50 50.51 N 2.37 E
Wat Phai Tan, Khlong ≍ 269a 13.48 N 100.33 E
Watrous, Sk., Can. 184 51.40 N 105.28 W
Watrous, N.M., U.S. 200 35.47 N 104.58 W
Watsa 154 3.03 N 29.32 E
Watseka 216 40.46 N 87.44 W
Watsi Kengo 152 0.48 S 20.33 E
Watson, Austl. 162 30.29 S 131.31 E
Watson, Sk., Can. 184 52.07 N 104.31 W
Watson, In., U.S. 218 38.22 N 85.41 W
Watsonia 274b 37.43 S 145.05 E
Watson Lake 180 60.07 N 128.48 W
Watsons Bay 274a 33.51 S 151.17 E
Watsons Creek 274b 37.40 S 145.13 E
Watsons Creek ≃ 274b 37.43 S 145.16 E
Watsontown 210 41.05 N 76.51 W
Watsonville 226 36.54 N 121.45 W
Watt 222 31.39 N 96.51 W
Watten 50 50.50 N 2.13 E
Watten, Loch ⊜ 46 58.29 N 3.19 W
Wattens 64 47.17 N 11.36 E
Wattenscheid 56 51.29 N 7.08 E
Wattenwil 58 46.46 N 7.30 E
Wattignies 50 50.35 N 3.03 E
Wattiwarriganna ≃ 162 28.57 S 136.10 E
Wattle Flat 170 33.08 S 149.41 E
Wattle Glen 274b 37.40 S 145.11 E
Wattle Park ♠ 274b 37.50 S 145.07 E
Watt Mountain ∧ 240d 15.19 N 61.19 W
Watton 42 52.35 N 0.48 E
Wattrelos 50 50.42 N 3.13 E
Watts ◆[8] 280 33.56 N 118.15 W
Watts Bar Lake ⊜[1] 192 35.48 N 84.39 W
Watts Branch ≃ 284c 39.03 N 77.15 W
Wattsburg 214 42.00 N 79.49 W
Watts Island I 208 37.48 N 75.53 W
Watts Mills 192 34.31 N 82.02 W

Symbol	English	Deutsch	Español	Français	Português
≃	River	Fluß	Río	Rivière	Rio
≍	Canal	Kanal	Canal	Canal	Canal
∟	Waterfall, Rapids	Wasserfall, Stromschnellen	Cascada, Rápidos	Chute d'eau, Rapides	Cascata, Rápidos
⊔	Strait	Meeresstraße	Estrecho	Détroit	Estreito
⊂	Bay, Gulf	Bucht, Golf	Bahía, Golfo	Baie, Golfe	Baía, Golfo
⊜	Lake, Lakes	See, Seen	Lago, Lagos	Lac, Lacs	Lago, Lagos
⩸	Swamp	Sumpf	Pantano	Marais	Pântano
⌂	Ice Features, Glacier	Eis- und Gletscherformen	Accidentes Glaciales	Formes glaciaires	Acidentes glaciares
╤	Other Hydrographic Features	Andere Hydrographische Objekte	Otros Elementos Hidrográficos	Autres données hydrographiques	Outros acidentes hidrográficos

Symbol	English	Deutsch	Español	Français	Português
✣	Submarine Features	Untermeerische Objekte	Accidentes Submarinos	Formes de relief sous-marin	Acidentes submarinos
□	Political Unit	Politische Einheit	Unidad Politica	Entité politique	Unidade política
☉	Cultural Institution	Kulturelle Institution	Institución Cultural	Institution culturelle	Institução cultural
⊥	Historical Site	Historische Stätte	Sitio Histórico	Site historique	Sitio histórico
♠	Recreational Site	Erholungs- und Ferienort	Sitio de Recreo	Centre de loisirs	Area de Lazer
⊠	Airport	Flughafen	Aeropuerto	Aéroport	Aeroporto
■	Military Installation	Militäranlage	Instalación Militar	Installation militaire	Instalação militar
◆	Miscellaneous	Verschiedenes	Misceláneo	Divers	Diversos

ENGLISH

Name	Page	Lat.°′	Long.°′
Wattville	273d	26.13 S	28.18 E
Wattwil	58	47.18 N	9.06 E
Watu	152	3.18 S	20.03 E
Watubela, Kepulauan II	164	4.35 S	131.40 E
Wat Wat	164	4.29 S	152.21 E
Watzespitze ∧	58	46.59 N	10.48 E
Watzmann ∧	64	47.33 N	12.55 E
Wau	164	7.20 S	146.45 E
Waubach	56	50.55 N	6.03 E
Waubaushene	212	44.45 N	79.42 W
Waubaushene Channel ⊍	212	44.46 N	79.45 W
Waubay	198	45.19 N	97.18 W
Waubay Lake ⊜	198	45.25 N	97.25 W
Waubesa, Lake ⊜	216	43.01 N	89.20 W
Waubra	169	37.21 S	143.39 E
Waubuno Creek ≃	212	42.58 N	81.08 W
Wauchope, Austl.	162	20.36 S	134.15 E
Wauchope, Austl.	166	31.27 S	152.44 E
Wauchula	220	27.32 N	81.48 W
Wauconda, Il., U.S.	216	42.15 N	88.08 W
Wauconda, Wa., U.S.	182	48.43 N	119.00 W
Wauconda, Wa., U.S.	202	48.43 N	119.00 W
Waugh	184	49.40 N	95.13 W
Waugh Mountain ∧	202	45.29 N	114.47 W
Waukara, Bukit ∧	112	1.15 S	119.42 E
Waukaringa	166	32.18 S	139.26 E
Waukarlycarly, Lake ⊜	162	21.25 S	121.50 E
Waukegan	216	42.21 N	87.50 W
Waukena	226	36.08 N	119.31 W
Waukesha	216	43.00 N	88.13 W
Waukesha □ [6]	216	43.02 N	88.20 W
Waukomis	196	36.16 N	97.53 W
Waukon	190	43.16 N	91.28 W
Waulsort	56	50.13 N	4.52 E
Wauna	224	47.22 N	122.38 W
Waunakee	216	43.11 N	89.27 W
Wauneta	198	40.25 N	101.22 W
Waupaca	190	44.21 N	89.05 W
Waupecan Creek ≃	216	41.20 N	88.28 W
Waupoos Island I	212	43.59 N	76.58 W
Waupun	190	43.38 N	88.43 W
Wauregan	207	41.44 N	71.54 W
Waurika	196	34.10 N	97.59 W
Waurika Lake ⊜ [1]	196	34.15 N	98.05 W
Wausa	198	42.29 N	97.32 W
Wausau	190	44.57 N	89.37 W
Wausaukee	190	45.22 N	87.57 W
Wauseon	216	41.32 N	84.08 W
Waushakum Pond ⊜	283	42.16 N	71.26 W
Wautoma	190	44.04 N	89.17 W
Wauwa	154	3.27 N	27.21 E
Wauwatosa	216	43.02 N	88.00 W
Wauzeka	190	43.05 N	90.52 W
Wave Hill	162	17.29 S	130.57 E
Waveland, Ma., U.S.	283	42.17 N	70.53 W
Waveland, Ms., U.S.	194	30.17 N	89.22 W
Waveney ≃	42	52.28 N	1.45 E
Waver ≃	44	54.52 N	3.17 W
Waverley, Austl.	169	37.53 S	145.10 E
Waverley, Austl.	274a	33.54 S	151.16 E
Waverley, N.Z.	172	39.46 S	174.38 E
Waverley, S. Afr.	158	31.58 S	26.28 E
Waverley, Ma., U.S.	283	42.23 N	71.11 W
Waverley ◆ [8]	273d	26.08 S	28.04 E
Waverly, Al., U.S.	194	32.44 N	85.35 W
Waverly, Fl., U.S.	220	27.59 N	81.37 W
Waverly, Il., U.S.	219	39.35 N	89.57 W
Waverly, Ia., U.S.	190	42.43 N	92.28 W
Waverly, Ks., U.S.	198	38.23 N	95.36 W
Waverly, Mi., U.S.	216	42.44 N	84.33 W
Waverly, Mn., U.S.	190	45.04 N	93.57 W
Waverly, Mo., U.S.	194	39.12 N	93.31 W
Waverly, Ne., U.S.	198	40.55 N	96.31 W
Waverly, N.Y., U.S.	210	42.00 N	76.31 W
Waverly, Oh., U.S.	218	39.07 N	82.59 W
Waverly, Pa., U.S.	210	41.32 N	75.42 W
Waverly, Tn., U.S.	194	36.05 N	87.47 W
Waverly, Va., U.S.	208	37.02 N	77.05 W
Waverly Hall	192	32.41 N	84.44 W
Wavre	56	50.43 N	4.37 E
Wavrin	50	50.34 N	2.55 E
Wāw	140	7.42 N	28.00 E
Wāw ≃	140	7.03 N	27.13 E
Wawa, On., Can.	190	47.59 N	84.47 W
Wawa, Nig.	150	9.55 N	4.25 E
Wawa, Sūd.	140	20.26 N	30.21 E
Wawa ≃	236	13.53 N	83.28 W
Wawaka	216	41.27 N	85.28 W
Wāw al-Kabīr	146	25.20 N	16.43 E
Wawanesa	184	49.36 N	99.41 W
Wawarsing	210	41.46 N	74.21 W
Wawasee, Lake ⊜	216	41.24 N	85.41 W
Wawayanda State Park ♠	276	41.11 N	74.26 W
Wawiag ≃	190	48.25 N	91.07 W
Wawoi ≃	164	8.01 S	143.33 E
Waworada, Teluk ⊂	115b	8.44 S	118.51 E
Wawota	184	49.55 N	102.00 W
Waxahachie	222	32.23 N	96.50 W
Waxahachie, Lake ⊜ [1]	222	32.20 N	96.49 W
Waxhaw	192	34.55 N	80.44 W
Waxuecun	106	31.07 N	121.38 E
Waxweiler	56	50.05 N	6.22 E
Way, Lake ⊜	162	26.48 S	120.18 E
Waya I	175g	17.18 S	177.08 E
Wayabula	108	2.17 N	128.12 E
Wayaopu	106	30.33 N	118.53 E
Waycross	192	31.12 N	82.21 W
Wayi	154	5.11 N	30.10 E
Wayland, Ia., U.S.	190	41.08 N	91.39 W
Wayland, Ky., U.S.	192	37.26 N	82.48 W
Wayland, Ma., U.S.	283	42.21 N	71.21 W
Wayland, Mi., U.S.	216	42.40 N	85.38 W
Wayland, N.Y., U.S.	210	42.34 N	77.35 W
Wayland, Oh., U.S.	214	41.10 N	81.04 W
Waylyn	192	32.51 N	79.59 W
Waymansville	218	39.04 N	86.03 W
Waymart	210	41.34 N	75.24 W
Wayne, Ab., Can.	182	51.23 N	112.39 W
Wayne, Mi., U.S.	216	42.16 N	83.23 W
Wayne, Ne., U.S.	198	42.13 N	97.01 W
Wayne, N.J., U.S.	210	40.55 N	74.16 W
Wayne, N.Y., U.S.	210	42.28 N	77.06 W
Wayne, Oh., U.S.	214	41.18 N	83.28 W
Wayne, Ok., U.S.	196	34.55 N	97.18 W
Wayne, Pa., U.S.	208	40.02 N	75.23 W
Wayne, W.V., U.S.	188	38.13 N	82.26 W
Wayne □ [6], Il., U.S.	219	38.25 N	88.40 W
Wayne □ [6], In., U.S.	218	39.50 N	84.54 W
Wayne □ [6], Mi., U.S.	216	42.14 N	83.12 W
Wayne □ [6], N.Y., U.S.	210	43.04 N	77.00 W
Wayne □ [6], Oh., U.S.	214	40.48 N	81.56 W
Wayne □ [6], Pa., U.S.	210	41.34 N	75.16 W
Wayne City	194	38.20 N	88.35 W
Wayne Lakes	218	40.01 N	84.39 W
Waynesboro, Ga., U.S.	192	33.05 N	82.00 W
Waynesboro, Ms., U.S.	194	31.40 N	88.38 W
Waynesboro, Pa., U.S.	208	39.45 N	77.34 W
Waynesboro, Tn., U.S.	194	35.19 N	87.45 W
Waynesboro, Va., U.S.	192	38.04 N	78.53 W
Waynesburg, Oh., U.S.	214	40.40 N	81.15 W
Waynesburg, Pa., U.S.	188	39.53 N	80.10 W
Waynesfield	216	40.36 N	83.59 W
Wayne State University ⊕ [2]	281	42.21 N	83.04 W
Waynesville, Il., U.S.	194	40.15 N	89.08 W
Waynesville, Mo., U.S.	194	37.49 N	92.12 W
Waynesville, N.C., U.S.	192	35.29 N	82.59 W
Waynesville, Oh., U.S.	218	39.32 N	84.05 W
Waynoka	196	36.34 N	98.52 W
Waynoka, Lake ⊜ [1]	218	38.55 N	83.47 W
Wayoh Reservoir ⊜ [1]	262	53.39 N	2.24 W
Waza	146	11.25 N	14.34 E
Waza, Parc National de ♠	146	11.20 N	13.40 E
Wazah	120	33.22 N	69.26 E
Wāzah Khwāh	120	32.12 N	68.21 E
Waziers	50	50.23 N	3.07 E
Wāzin	146	31.57 N	10.40 E
Wazīrābād	123	32.27 N	74.07 E
Wazīrābād ◆ [8]	272a	28.43 N	77.14 E
Wāzirpur ◆ [8]	272a	28.41 N	77.10 E
Wazuka	96	34.47 N	135.55 E
Wazuka ≃	270	34.45 N	135.53 E
Wda ≃	30	53.25 N	18.29 E
Wé	175f	20.54 S	167.16 E
We, Pulau I	114	5.51 N	95.18 E
Wea Creek ≃	216	40.24 N	86.57 W
Weagamow Lake ⊜	184	52.53 N	91.22 W
Weald Park ♠	260	51.38 N	0.14 E
Wealdstone ◆ [8]	260	51.36 N	0.20 W
Weam	164	8.40 S	141.08 E
Wear ≃	44	54.55 N	1.22 W
Wearhead	44	54.45 N	2.13 W
Wearyan ≃	164	15.57 S	136.51 E
Weatherford, Ok., U.S.	196	35.31 N	98.42 W
Weatherford, Tx., U.S.	222	32.45 N	97.47 W
Weatherford, Lake ⊜ [1]	222	32.47 N	97.41 W
Weatherly	210	40.56 N	75.50 W
Weatogue	207	41.51 N	72.49 W
Weaubleau	194	37.53 N	93.32 W
Weaver, Austl.	168b	34.56 S	137.40 E
Weaver, Al., U.S.	194	33.45 N	85.48 W
Weaver, Tx., U.S.	222	33.10 N	95.25 W
Weaver ≃	44	53.18 N	2.43 W
Weaverham	44	53.16 N	2.35 W
Weaver Lake ⊜	184	52.45 N	96.35 W
Weavertown	279b	40.16 N	80.11 W
Weaverville, Ca., U.S.	204	40.43 N	122.56 W
Weaverville, N.C., U.S.	192	35.41 N	82.33 W
Webau	54	51.10 N	12.04 E
Webb, Sk., Can.	184	50.11 N	108.12 W
Webb, Ms., U.S.	194	33.56 N	90.20 W
Webb Brook ≃	283	42.32 N	71.14 W
Webb City	194	37.08 N	94.27 W
Webber Lake ⊜	184	54.28 N	94.00 W
Webberville	216	42.40 N	84.10 W
Webbwood	190	46.16 N	81.53 W
Weber ≃	200	41.13 N	112.16 W
Weber, Mount ∧	182	55.32 N	128.31 W
Weber City	192	36.37 N	82.33 W
Weber Creek ≃	226	38.46 N	121.00 W
Weber Hill	219	38.27 N	90.34 W
Weberi Bekera	144	9.39 N	39.03 E
Webster, Ab., Can.	182	55.26 N	118.42 W
Webster, Fl., U.S.	220	28.36 N	82.03 W
Webster, In., U.S.	218	39.54 N	84.57 W
Webster, Ma., U.S.	207	42.03 N	71.52 W
Webster, N.Y., U.S.	210	43.12 N	77.25 W
Webster, Pa., U.S.	214	40.11 N	79.50 W
Webster, S.D., U.S.	198	45.19 N	97.31 W
Webster, Wi., U.S.	190	45.52 N	92.22 W
Webster City	190	42.28 N	93.48 W
Webster Crossing	210	42.40 N	77.38 W
Webster Groves	219	38.35 N	90.21 W
Webster Lake ⊜	216	41.19 N	85.41 W
Websters Corners	284a	41.47 N	78.45 W
Webster Springs	188	38.28 N	80.24 W
Weches	222	31.33 N	95.14 W
Wechmar	54	50.53 N	10.47 E
Wechselburg	54	51.00 N	12.47 E
Weda	108	0.21 N	127.52 E
Wedau ◆ [8]	263	51.24 N	6.48 E
Wedau, Sportpark ♠	263	51.25 N	6.47 E
Weddell Island I	254	51.55 S	61.00 W
Weddell Sea ▼ [2]	9	72.00 S	45.00 W
Wedderburn	166	36.25 S	143.37 E
Wedding ◆ [8]	54	52.33 N	13.22 E
Weddinghofen	263	51.36 N	7.37 E
Wedel	52	53.35 N	9.41 E
Wedemark	52	52.33 N	9.44 E
Wedge, Central Mount ∧	162	22.51 S	131.50 E
Wedge Mountain ∧	182	50.10 N	122.50 W
Wedgeport	186	43.44 N	65.59 W
Wedgewood	219	38.47 N	90.17 W
Wedmore	42	51.14 N	2.49 W
Wedowee	194	33.18 N	85.29 W
Wedron	216	41.26 N	88.46 W
Weduar, Tanjung ›	164	6.00 S	132.50 E
Wedweil	140	9.00 N	27.12 E
Wedza	154	18.35 S	31.35 E
Weebo	162	28.01 S	121.03 E
Weed	204	41.25 N	122.23 W
Weed Heights	226	38.59 N	119.12 W
Weedon	206	45.42 N	71.28 W
Weedon Beck	42	52.14 N	1.05 W
Weedon Island I	220	27.51 N	82.36 W
Weed Patch	228	35.19 N	118.55 W
Weed Patch Hill ∧ [2]	218	39.10 N	86.13 W
Weedsport	210	43.02 N	76.33 W
Weedville	214	41.17 N	78.30 W
Weehawken	276	40.46 N	74.01 W
Weeim, Pulau I	164	1.29 S	130.14 E
Wee Jasper	171b	35.09 S	148.41 E
Weekapauq	207	41.20 N	71.45 W
Weeki Wachee Spring ♠	220	28.32 N	82.35 W
Weeki Wachee Swamp ≋	220	28.31 N	82.37 W
Weeks Point ›	276	40.53 N	73.39 W
Weekstown	208	39.35 N	74.36 W
Weelde	56	51.25 N	5.00 E
Weeley	42	51.51 N	1.07 E
Weel Shimbirro	144	2.23 N	44.16 E
Weems	208	37.39 N	76.26 W
Weende	52	51.33 N	9.55 E
Weenen	158	28.57 S	30.03 E
Weener	52	53.10 N	7.21 E
Weeney Bay ⊂	274a	34.01 S	151.10 E
Weeping Water	198	40.52 N	96.08 W
Weequahic Lake ⊜	276	40.42 N	74.12 W
Weert	52	51.15 N	5.43 E
Weesatche	222	28.51 N	97.27 W
Weesby	41	54.50 N	9.08 E
Weesow	264a	52.39 N	13.43 E
Weesp	52	52.17 N	5.02 E
Weetfeld ◆ [8]	263	51.38 N	7.49 E
Weethalle	166	33.53 S	146.38 E
Weeting	42	52.27 N	0.37 E
Weeton	262	53.48 N	2.56 W
Weetulta	168b	34.15 S	137.38 E
Wee Waa	166	30.14 S	149.26 E
Weeze	52	51.37 N	6.12 E
Wefensleben	54	52.11 N	11.09 E
Weferlingen	54	52.19 N	11.02 E
Wegberg	56	51.08 N	6.16 E
Wegdraai	158	28.50 S	21.52 E
Wegeleben	54	51.53 N	11.10 E
Wegendorf	264a	52.36 N	13.45 E
Wegenstedt	54	52.23 N	11.11 E
Wegeringhausen	56	51.02 N	7.45 E
Weggis	58	47.02 N	8.26 E
Węgliniec	30	51.17 N	15.13 E
Węgorzewo	30	54.14 N	21.44 E
Węgorzyno	30	53.32 N	15.33 E
Węgrów	30	52.25 N	22.01 E
Wegscheid	60	48.36 N	13.48 E
Wehdel	52	53.30 N	8.48 E
Wehebach Stausee ⊜ [1]	56	50.45 N	6.20 E
Wehingen	58	48.08 N	8.47 E
Wehofen ◆ [8]	263	51.32 N	6.46 E
Wehr	58	47.37 N	7.54 E
Wehringhausen ◆ [8]	263	51.21 N	7.27 E
Wehrsdorf	54	51.03 N	14.22 E
Wei ≃, Zhg.	98	36.51 N	115.43 E
Wei ≃, Zhg.	98	37.05 N	119.28 E
Wei ≃, Zhg.	102	34.30 N	110.20 E
Weichang (Zhuizishan)	98	42.00 N	117.32 E
Weichsel → Wisła ≃	30	54.22 N	18.55 E
Weichselboden	61	47.40 N	15.10 E
Weichuan	98	34.17 N	113.58 E
Weicun	106	31.59 N	119.55 E
Weida	54	50.45 N	12.04 E
Weida ≃	54	50.47 N	12.06 E
Weiden am See	61	47.55 N	16.52 E
Weidenberg	60	49.57 N	11.43 E
Weiden in der Oberpfalz	60	49.41 N	12.10 E
Weidenstetten	56	48.33 N	9.59 E
Weidhausen	54	50.12 N	11.08 E
Weiding	60	49.16 N	12.46 E
Weidling	264b	48.17 N	16.19 E
Weidlingau ◆ [8]	264b	48.13 N	16.13 E
Weidlingbach	264b	48.16 N	16.15 E
Weidlingerbach ≃	264b	48.18 N	16.20 E
Weifang	98	36.42 N	119.04 E
Weigelstown	208	39.59 N	76.49 W
Weigersdorf	54	51.16 N	14.39 E
Weihai	98	37.28 N	122.07 E
Weihaiwei → Weihai	98	37.28 N	122.07 E
Weiherhammer	60	49.38 N	12.04 E
Weihmichl	60	48.36 N	12.03 E
Weihnachtsinsel → Christmas Island □ [2]	112	10.30 S	105.40 E
Wei Island I	164	3.20 S	144.25 E
Weijiagou	105	40.28 N	115.08 E
Weijiatang	106	31.25 N	118.55 E
Weijiazhuang	105	39.37 N	116.22 E
Weijiazui	100	30.29 N	117.20 E
Weijingtang	106	31.27 N	120.39 E
Weikersheim	56	49.29 N	9.54 E
Weil ≃	56	50.28 N	8.16 E
Weil am Rhein	58	47.37 N	7.38 E
Weilburg	56	50.29 N	8.15 E
Weil der Stadt	56	48.45 N	8.52 E
Weiler	58	47.36 N	9.55 E
Weilerbach	56	49.29 N	7.37 E
Weilerswist	56	50.45 N	6.50 E
Weilheim	64	47.50 N	11.08 E
Weilheim an der Teck	56	48.37 N	9.32 E
Weilmoringle	166	29.15 S	146.51 E
Weilmünster	56	50.26 N	8.22 E
Weimar, Dtsch.	54	50.59 N	11.19 E
Weimar, Ca., U.S.	226	39.02 N	120.58 W
Weimar, Tx., U.S.	222	29.42 N	96.46 W
Weinan	102	34.29 N	109.29 E
Weinbach	56	50.26 N	8.18 E
Weinböhla	54	51.10 N	13.34 E
Weinel Cross Roads	279b	40.37 N	79.37 W
Weiner	194	35.37 N	90.53 W
Weinfelden	58	47.34 N	9.06 E
Weingarten, Dtsch.	56	49.05 N	8.31 E
Weingarten, Dtsch.	58	47.48 N	9.38 E
Weinheim	56	49.33 N	8.39 E
Weining, Zhg.	102	26.43 N	104.18 E
Weining, Zhg.	104	41.21 N	123.49 E
Weinsberg	56	49.10 N	9.17 E
Weinsberger Wald ◆ [3]	61	48.30 N	14.50 E
Weinstadt	56	48.49 N	9.23 E
Weinviertel ◆ [1]	61	48.38 N	16.25 E
Weipa	164	12.41 S	141.52 E
Weippe	202	46.22 N	115.56 W
Weir, India	124	27.01 N	77.11 E
Weir, Ks., U.S.	198	37.18 N	94.46 W
Weir, Ms., U.S.	194	33.16 N	89.17 W
Weir ≃, Austl.	166	28.50 S	149.06 E
Weir ≃, Mb., Can.	184	56.54 N	93.21 W
Weir ≃, Ma., U.S.	283	42.16 N	70.53 W
Weir, Lake ⊜	220	29.00 N	81.57 W
Weir River	184	56.49 N	94.04 W
Weirsdale	220	28.58 N	81.55 W
Weirton	214	40.25 N	80.35 W
Weisburd	252	27.18 S	62.36 W
Weisburg	218	39.13 N	85.03 W
Weischlitz	54	50.26 N	12.02 E
Weisendorf	56	49.37 N	10.49 E
Weiser	202	44.15 N	116.58 W
Weiser ≃	202	44.15 N	116.59 W
Weishan (Xiazhen), Zhg.	98	34.52 N	117.09 E
Weishan, Zhg.	100	29.20 N	120.25 E
Weishan, Zhg.	100	29.41 N	120.48 E
Weishan, Zhg.	102	25.15 N	100.20 E
Weishancheng	100	32.34 N	113.24 E
Weishanhe	104	40.47 N	123.31 E
Weishan Hu ⊜	98	34.40 N	117.15 E
Weishanzhuang	105	39.40 N	116.25 E
Weishi	98	34.25 N	114.11 E
Weiskirchen	56	49.33 N	6.49 E
Weismain	54	50.05 N	11.14 E
Weisner Mountain ∧	194	34.02 N	85.40 W
Weissbriach	64	46.41 N	13.15 E
Weisse Elster ≃	54	51.26 N	11.57 E
Weissenbach	264b	48.05 N	16.13 E
Weissenbach am Lech	58	47.26 N	10.39 E
Weissenberg	54	51.11 N	14.40 E
Weissenborn	54	50.52 N	13.25 E
Weissenbrunn	54	50.12 N	11.20 E
Weissenburg	58	46.39 N	7.28 E
Weissenburg in Bayern	56	49.01 N	10.58 E
Weissenfels	54	51.12 N	11.58 E
Weissenhorn	58	48.18 N	10.09 E
Weissensee	54	51.11 N	11.04 E
Weissensee ◆ [8]	264a	52.33 N	13.27 E
Weissensee ⊜	64	46.42 N	13.22 E
Weissenstadt	54	50.06 N	11.53 E
Weissenstein	64	46.41 N	13.44 E
Weissenstein ∧	58	47.15 N	7.31 E
Weissenstein Tunnel ◆ [5]	58	47.12 N	7.23 E
Weissenthurm	56	50.24 N	7.27 E
Weisser Main ≃	60	50.04 N	11.24 E
Weisser Nil → White Nile ≃	140	15.38 N	32.31 E
Weisser See → Beloje, ozero ⊜	76	60.11 N	37.37 E
Weisser Stein ∧	56	50.23 N	6.20 E
Weisses Meer → Beloje more ▼ [2]	24	65.30 N	38.00 E
Weisse Spitze ∧	64	46.52 N	12.21 E
Weissfluh ∧	58	46.50 N	9.48 E
Weisshorn ∧	58	46.06 N	7.42 E
Weissig	54	51.05 N	13.52 E
Weisskugel (Palla Bianca) ∧	64	46.48 N	10.44 E
Weiss Lake ⊜ [1]	192	34.15 N	85.35 W
Weissmeer-Ostsee Kanal → Belomorsko-Baltijskij kanal ≍	24	62.48 N	34.48 E
Weissport	210	40.50 N	75.42 W
Weisstannen	58	46.59 N	9.21 E
Weisswasser	54	51.30 N	14.38 E
Weisweiler	56	50.50 N	6.19 E
Weitang	105	40.24 N	117.24 E
Weitang ≃	104	42.19 N	122.18 E
Weitendorf	54	53.54 N	12.16 E
Weitensfeld	61	46.51 N	14.11 E
Weiterstadt	56	49.54 N	8.35 E
Weitian	100	27.43 N	118.46 E
Weitin	54	53.34 N	13.12 E
Weiting	106	31.22 N	120.47 E
Weitmar ◆ [8]	263	51.27 N	7.12 E
Weitnau	58	47.38 N	10.07 E
Weitou	100	24.34 N	118.34 E
Weitra	61	48.42 N	14.54 E
Weituo	107	30.03 N	106.08 E
Weitzgrund	54	52.11 N	12.32 E
Weiwan	98	36.43 N	115.54 E
Weixdorf	54	51.09 N	13.48 E
Weixi, Zhg.	102	27.14 N	99.12 E
Weixi, Zhg.	107	30.12 N	106.39 E
Weixian, Zhg.	98	36.57 N	115.15 E
Weixian, Zhg.	98	36.22 N	114.56 E
Weixian (Hanting), Zhg.	98	36.52 N	119.07 E
Weixin	102	27.48 N	105.06 E
Weiyuan	107	29.33 N	104.39 E
Weiyuan ≃	102	22.50 N	100.20 E
Weiyuankou	100	30.09 N	115.15 E
Weiyuanpu	98	42.39 N	124.16 E
Weiz	61	47.13 N	15.37 E
Weizhen	98	37.17 N	114.44 E
Weizhou Dao I	102	21.03 N	109.04 E
Weizhou Wan ⊂	100	24.34 N	118.30 E
Weizhuang	105	39.02 N	115.20 E
Weizi	98	40.04 N	123.10 E
Weizigou, Zhg.	104	42.25 N	122.47 E
Weizigou, Zhg.	104	41.05 N	120.38 E
Weizigou, Zhg.	104	42.05 N	120.34 E
Weizigoumen	98	41.58 N	116.49 E
Weiziyu	98	41.29 N	124.31 E
Wejherowo	30	54.37 N	18.15 E
Wekiva ≃	220	28.52 N	81.23 W
Wekiwa Springs State Park ♠	220	28.43 N	81.27 W
Wekoewa Punt ›	241s	12.14 N	68.24 W
Wekusko Lake ⊜	184	54.45 N	99.50 W
Welaka	192	29.28 N	81.40 W
Welbourn Hill	162	27.21 S	134.06 E
Welch, Ok., U.S.	196	36.52 N	95.05 W
Welch, Tx., U.S.	196	32.56 N	102.08 W
Welch, W.V., U.S.	192	37.25 N	81.35 W
Welch Creek ≃	282	37.32 N	121.51 W
Welches	224	45.19 N	121.57 W
Welch Peak ∧	224	49.10 N	121.36 W
Welcome, On., Can.	212	43.58 N	78.21 W
Welcome, Mn., U.S.	198	43.40 N	94.37 W
Welcome, S.C., U.S.	192	34.49 N	82.26 W
Welcome Lake ⊜	212	45.25 N	78.25 W
Welcome Monument ⊥	269e	6.11 S	106.49 E
Welden	58	48.27 N	10.40 E
Weldiya	144	11.50 N	39.41 E
Weldon, Sk., Can.	184	53.00 N	105.08 W
Weldon, Il., U.S.	219	40.07 N	88.45 W
Weldon, N.C., U.S.	192	36.25 N	77.35 W
Weldon, Tx., U.S.	222	31.01 N	95.34 W
Weldon ≃	194	40.06 N	93.38 W
Weldona	198	40.20 N	103.58 W
Weldon Brook ≃	276	40.58 N	74.35 W
Weleetka	196	35.20 N	96.08 W
Welega □ [4]	144	9.40 N	35.50 E
Weleri	115a	6.58 S	110.04 E
Welfare Island I	276	40.45 N	73.57 W
Welgedag	273d	26.12 S	28.30 E
Welhamgreen	260	51.44 N	0.13 W
Welheim ◆ [8]	263	51.32 N	6.59 E
Weligama	122	5.58 N	80.25 E
Welikaja → Velikaja ≃	76	57.48 N	28.20 E
Welkenraedt	56	50.40 N	5.59 E
Welker Seamount ◆ [3]	16	55.07 N	140.20 W
Welkite	144	8.15 N	37.50 E
Welkom	158	27.59 S	26.45 E
Well	52	51.34 N	6.06 E
Welland	212	42.59 N	79.15 W
Welland ≃, On., Can.	212	43.04 N	79.03 W
Welland ≃, Eng., U.K.	42	52.52 N	0.03 W
Welland Canal ≍	212	43.03 N	79.13 W
Welland Junction	284a	42.57 N	79.14 W
Wellard	168a	32.19 S	115.50 E
Wellaune	54	51.34 N	12.33 E
Wellborn, Fl., U.S.	192	30.13 N	82.49 W
Wellborn, Tx., U.S.	222	30.32 N	96.18 W
Wellerode	56	51.14 N	9.34 E
Wellers Bay ⊂	212	44.00 N	77.34 W
Wellers Creek ≃	278	42.03 N	87.53 W
Wellesbourne	42	52.12 N	1.35 W
Welles Harbor ⊂	174g	28.12 N	177.26 W
Wellesley, On., Can.	212	43.28 N	80.45 W
Wellesley, Ma., U.S.	207	42.17 N	71.17 W
Wellesley ≃	168a	33.17 S	115.44 E
Wellesley College ⊕ [2]	283	42.18 N	71.19 W
Wellesley Hills	283	42.19 N	71.17 W
Wellesley Island I	212	44.19 N	75.58 W
Wellesley Islands II	164	16.42 S	139.30 E
Wellesley Island State Park ♠	212	44.19 N	76.01 W
Wellesley Lake ⊜	180	62.30 N	139.50 W
Wellfleet	207	41.56 N	70.02 W
Well Hill	260	51.21 N	0.09 E
Wellin	56	50.05 N	5.07 E
Welling ◆ [8]	260	51.28 N	0.07 E
Wellingborough	42	52.19 N	0.42 W
Wellinghofen ◆ [8]	263	51.28 N	7.29 E
Wellington, Austl.	166	32.33 S	148.57 E
Wellington, B.C., Can.	224	49.13 N	124.01 W
Wellington, On., Can.	212	43.57 N	77.21 W
Wellington, N.Z.	172	41.18 S	174.47 E
Wellington, S. Afr.	158	33.38 S	18.57 E
Wellington, Eng., U.K.	42	52.43 N	2.31 W
Wellington, Eng., U.K.	42	50.59 N	3.14 W
Wellington, Co., U.S.	200	40.42 N	105.00 W
Wellington, Il., U.S.	216	40.32 N	87.41 W
Wellington, Ks., U.S.	198	37.15 N	97.22 W
Wellington, Mo., U.S.	194	39.08 N	93.58 W
Wellington, Nv., U.S.	226	38.45 N	119.22 W
Wellington, Oh., U.S.	214	41.10 N	82.13 W
Wellington, Tx., U.S.	196	34.51 N	100.12 W
Wellington, Ut,. U.S.	200	39.32 N	110.44 W
Wellington □ [6]	212	43.50 N	80.30 W
Wellington, Isla I	254	49.20 S	74.40 W
Wellington Bay ⊂, N.T., Can.	176	69.30 N	106.30 W
Wellington Bay ⊂, On., Can.	212	43.56 N	77.21 W
Wellington Channel ⊍	176	75.00 N	93.00 W
Wellington Point	171a	27.29 S	153.15 E
Wellington Reservoir ⊜ [1]	168a	33.24 S	116.01 E
Wellington Station	186	46.27 N	64.00 W
Wellman, Ia., U.S.	190	41.27 N	91.50 W
Wellman, Tx., U.S.	196	33.03 N	102.26 W
Wells, B.C., Can.	182	53.06 N	121.34 W
Wells, Eng., U.K.	42	51.13 N	2.39 W
Wells, Mi., U.S.	190	45.47 N	87.04 W
Wells, Mn., U.S.	190	43.44 N	93.43 W
Wells, Nv., U.S.	204	41.06 N	114.57 W
Wells, N.Y., U.S.	210	43.24 N	74.17 W
Wells, Tx., U.S.	222	31.29 N	94.56 W
Wells □ [6]	216	40.44 N	85.11 W
Wells, Lake ⊜	162	26.43 S	123.10 E
Wells, Mount ∧	168a	32.42 S	116.20 E
Wells, Mount ∧ [2]	162	17.26 S	127.14 E
Wellsboro	210	41.44 N	77.18 W
Wells Bridge	210	42.22 N	75.15 W
Wellsburg, Ia., U.S.	190	42.27 N	92.56 W
Wellsburg, N.Y., U.S.	210	42.00 N	76.43 W
Wellsburg, W.V., U.S.	214	40.16 N	80.36 W
Wells Cathedral ⊕ [1]	42	51.13 N	2.39 W
Wellsford	172	36.17 S	174.31 E
Wells Gray Provincial Park ♠	182	52.20 N	120.00 W
Wells Lake ⊜	184	57.15 N	101.00 W
Wells-next-the-Sea	42	52.58 N	0.51 E
Wells Point ›	284b	39.17 N	76.23 W
Wells State Park ♠	207	42.09 N	72.05 W
Wells Tannery	214	40.05 N	78.10 W
Wellston, Oh., U.S.	188	39.07 N	82.31 W
Wellston, Ok., U.S.	196	35.41 N	97.03 W
Wellsville, Ks., U.S.	198	38.43 N	95.04 W
Wellsville, Mo., U.S.	219	39.04 N	91.34 W
Wellsville, N.Y., U.S.	210	42.07 N	77.56 W
Wellsville, Oh., U.S.	214	40.36 N	80.38 W
Wellsville, Pa., U.S.	208	40.03 N	76.56 W
Wellsville, Ut,. U.S.	200	41.38 N	111.55 W
Wellton	200	32.40 N	114.08 W
Welmel ≃	144	5.38 N	40.47 E
Welmen	263	51.39 N	6.41 E
Welney	42	52.31 N	0.15 E
Welo □ [4]	144	11.50 N	40.20 E
Welper	263	51.25 N	7.12 E
Wels	61	48.10 N	14.02 E
Welsberg → Monguelfo	64	46.45 N	12.06 E
Welschbillig	56	49.51 N	6.34 E
Welse ≃	54	53.10 N	14.18 E
Welsford	186	45.27 N	66.20 W
Welsh	194	30.14 N	92.49 W
Welshpool, Austl.	169	38.39 S	146.26 E
Welshpool, Wales, U.K.	42	52.40 N	3.09 W
Welsickendorf	54	51.54 N	13.08 E
Welsleben	54	52.00 N	11.38 E
Weltenburg	60	48.54 N	11.50 E
Welver	52	51.38 N	7.57 E
Welverdiend	158	26.23 S	27.16 E
Welwitschia	156	20.21 S	14.57 E
Welwyn Garden City	42	51.50 N	0.13 W
Welwyn Hatfield □ [8]	260	51.47 N	0.12 W
Welzheim	56	48.53 N	9.38 E
Welzow	54	51.34 N	14.10 E
Wem	42	52.51 N	2.44 W
Wema	152	0.26 S	21.38 E
Wembere ≃	154	4.10 S	34.11 E
Wembley	182	55.09 N	119.08 W
Wembley ◆ [8]	260	51.33 N	0.18 W
Wembley Stadium ♠, S. Afr.	273d	26.14 S	28.03 E
Wembley Stadium ♠, Eng., U.K.	260	51.33 N	0.17 W
Wembury	42	50.19 N	4.05 W
Wemding	56	48.52 N	10.43 E
Wemeldinge	52	51.31 N	4.00 E
Wemme	224	45.20 N	121.57 W
Wemperhardt	56	50.09 N	6.05 E
Wemyss Bay	46	55.53 N	4.54 W
Wen ≃, Zhg.	98	36.38 N	119.22 E
Wen ≃, Zhg.	98	35.28 N	118.32 E
Wen'an	105	38.52 N	116.28 E
Wen'an Wa ≋	105	38.54 N	116.37 E
Wenas Creek ≃	224	46.42 N	120.35 W
Wenatchee	202	47.25 N	120.18 W
Wenatchee ≃	202	47.27 N	120.19 W
Wenatchee, Lake ⊜	224	47.49 N	120.47 W
Wenatchee Mountains ⋀	202	47.20 N	120.45 W
Wenchang	110	19.41 N	110.48 E
Wencheng	100	27.50 N	120.05 E
Wenchi	150	7.42 N	2.07 W
Wenchow → Wenzhou	100	28.01 N	120.39 E
Wendaohezi	104	41.46 N	124.09 E
Wendel	279b	40.18 N	79.41 W
Wendell, Id., U.S.	202	42.46 N	114.42 W
Wendell, N.C., U.S.	192	35.46 N	78.22 W
Wendelsheim	56	49.46 N	7.59 E
Wendelstein	60	49.21 N	11.08 E
Wendelstein ∧	64	47.42 N	12.00 E
Wendelville	284a	43.04 N	78.47 W
Wenden, Dtsch.	52	52.19 N	10.30 E
Wenden, Dtsch.	56	50.57 N	7.51 E
Wenden, Az., U.S.	200	33.49 N	113.32 W
Wendeng	98	37.12 N	122.04 E
Wendesi	164	2.25 S	134.13 E
Wendilou	104	41.13 N	121.08 E
Wendisch Rietz	54	52.13 N	14.01 E
Wendish Baggendorf	54	54.04 N	12.56 E
Wendji	152	0.04 S	18.10 E
Wendland ◆ [1]	54	53.00 N	11.10 E
Wendlingen	58	48.40 N	9.23 E
Wendo	144	6.38 N	38.27 E
Wendover, Eng., U.K.	42	51.46 N	0.46 W
Wendover, Ut,. U.S.	200	40.44 N	114.02 W
Wenduine	50	51.18 N	3.05 E
Wenebegon ≃	190	46.53 N	83.12 W
Wenebegon Lake ⊜	190	47.24 N	83.08 W
Wenfang	100	28.02 N	117.19 E
Weng	60	48.40 N	12.23 E
Weng ≃	100	24.10 N	113.24 E
Weng'an	102	26.53 N	107.22 E
Wengbo	120	31.23 N	86.40 E
Wengcheng	100	24.23 N	113.51 E
Wengdang	124	28.50 N	90.03 E
Wenge	152	0.03 N	24.01 E
Wengen, Dtsch.	58	47.41 N	10.09 E
Wengen, Schw.	58	46.36 N	7.56 E
Wengern	263	51.24 N	7.21 E
Wengjiabu	106	30.23 N	120.21 E
Wengong	107	30.11 N	104.09 E
Wenguantun	104	41.53 N	123.30 E
Wengyang	100	28.03 N	120.58 E
Wengyuan	100	24.21 N	114.08 E
Wenham	207	42.36 N	70.53 W
Wenham Lake ⊜	283	42.35 N	70.53 W
Wenham Swamp ≋	283	42.37 N	70.55 W
Wenheng	100	25.42 N	116.45 E
Wenī	124	28.21 N	83.34 E
Wenigzell	61	47.26 N	15.47 E
Wenjiachang	107	30.41 N	103.55 E
Wenjiang	107	30.42 N	103.49 E
Wenjiangban	100	26.01 N	117.51 E
Wenjiazhen	100	28.20 N	116.05 E
Wenling	100	28.22 N	121.20 E
Wenlock	164	13.06 S	142.58 E
Wenlock ≃	164	12.02 S	141.55 E
Wenlock Edge ⊥ [4]	42	52.30 N	2.40 W
Wenlong	100	24.48 N	114.54 E
Wenmingsi	100	25.33 N	113.20 E
Wennigsen	52	52.16 N	9.34 E
Wenning ≃	44	54.07 N	2.39 W
Wennington ◆ [8]	260	51.30 N	0.13 E
Wenniu	102	24.18 N	104.31 E
Wenns	58	47.10 N	10.44 E
Weno I	175c	7.26 N	151.52 E
Wenona, Il., U.S.	216	41.03 N	89.03 W
Wenona, Md., U.S.	208	38.08 N	75.57 W
Wenonah	208	39.47 N	75.08 W
Wenquan, Zhg.	86	44.59 N	81.04 E
Wenquan, Zhg.	100	23.37 N	113.43 E
Wenquansi	104	41.20 N	124.04 E
Wenshan	102	23.30 N	104.20 E
Wenshang	98	35.44 N	116.29 E
Wenshui, Zhg.	102	28.28 N	106.30 E
Wenshui, Zhg.	102	37.28 N	112.01 E
Wensickendorf	264a	52.45 N	13.23 E
Wensleydale V	44	54.19 N	2.00 W
Wensum ≃	42	52.37 N	1.19 E
Went ≃	44	53.39 N	0.59 W
Wentorf	52	53.30 N	10.15 E
Wentworth, Austl.	166	34.07 S	141.55 E
Wentworth, N.C., U.S.	192	36.24 N	79.46 W
Wentworth, S.D., U.S.	198	43.59 N	96.57 W
Wentworth Falls	170	33.43 S	150.22 E
Wentworth Park	273d	26.07 S	27.48 E
Wentworthville	274a	33.48 S	150.58 E
Wentzville	219	38.48 N	90.51 W
Wenxi	102	35.26 N	111.11 E
Wenxian	102	32.58 N	104.46 E
Wenxingchang	107	29.52 N	106.29 E
Wenyu ≃	105	39.56 N	116.40 E
Wenzenbach	60	49.05 N	12.12 E
Wenzhou	100	28.01 N	120.39 E
Wenzhu	100	27.01 N	113.58 E
Wenzhuangzicun	104	42.16 N	123.51 E
Weobley	42	52.09 N	2.51 W
Weohyakapka, Lake ⊜	220	27.49 N	81.25 W
Wepener	158	29.46 S	27.00 E
Wépion	56	50.25 N	4.52 E

DEUTSCH

Name	Seite	Breite°′	Länge°′ E = Ost
Weppersdorf	61	47.35 N	16.26 E
Wequetequock	207	41.21 N	71.52 W
Wera ≃	115b	8.20 S	120.43 E
Werbellin	54	52.53 N	13.41 E
Werbellinsee ⊜	54	52.54 N	13.40 E
Werben, Dtsch.	54	52.52 N	11.58 E
Werben, Dtsch.	54	51.45 N	14.10 E
Werbomont	56	50.23 N	5.41 E
Werchojansker Gebirge → Verchojanskij chrebet ⋀	74	67.00 N	129.00 E
Werda	156	25.15 S	23.16 E
Werdau	54	50.44 N	12.22 E
Werden ◆ [8]	263	51.23 N	7.00 E
Werder, Dtsch.	54	52.23 N	12.56 E
Werder, Ityo.	144	6.58 N	45.20 E
Werder ◆ [1]	54	53.40 N	13.25 E
Werdohl	56	51.15 N	7.45 E
Were Ilu	144	10.37 N	39.28 E
Werfen	64	47.28 N	13.11 E
Weri	164	3.12 S	132.38 E
Werkel	56	51.09 N	9.18 E
Werkendam	52	51.49 N	4.53 E
Werl	52	51.33 N	7.54 E
Werlaburgdorf	54	52.04 N	10.31 E
Werl-Aspe	52	52.04 N	8.43 E
Werleshausen	56	51.19 N	9.54 E
Werlte	52	52.51 N	7.41 E
Wermelskirchen	56	51.08 N	7.13 E
Wermsdorf	54	51.17 N	12.56 E
Wern ≃	56	50.02 N	9.44 E
Wernadinga	166	18.07 S	139.58 E
Wernau	58	48.42 N	9.25 E
Wernberg	64	46.37 N	13.56 E
Wernberg-Köblitz	60	49.32 N	12.10 E
Werne	52	51.40 N	7.38 E
Werne ◆ [8]	263	51.29 N	7.18 E
Werneck, Bra.	256	22.13 S	43.19 W
Werneck, Dtsch.	56	49.59 N	10.05 E
Werneuchen	54	52.38 N	13.44 E
Wernigerode	54	51.50 N	10.47 E
Wernitz	264a	52.34 N	12.55 E
Wernsdorf	264a	52.22 N	13.43 E
Wernsdorfer See ⊜	264a	52.23 N	13.42 E
Wernstein	60	48.30 N	13.28 E
Werra ≃	30	51.26 N	9.39 E
Werribee	169	37.54 S	144.40 E
Werribee ≃	169	37.59 S	144.41 E
Werribee Gorge State Park ♠	169	37.40 S	144.21 E
Werribee South	169	37.56 S	144.42 E
Werries	52	51.41 N	7.53 E
Werrington	274a	33.45 S	150.46 E
Werris Creek	166	31.21 S	150.39 E
Werschweiler	56	49.27 N	7.13 E
Wersten ◆ [8]	263	51.11 N	6.49 E
Wertach	58	47.36 N	10.25 E
Wertach ≃	58	48.24 N	10.53 E
Wertheim	56	49.46 N	9.31 E
Werther, Dtsch.	52	52.04 N	8.24 E
Werther, Dtsch.	54	51.29 N	10.46 E
Wertingen	56	48.34 N	10.41 E
Wervershoof	52	52.44 N	5.09 E
Wervik	50	50.47 N	3.02 E
Wervin	262	53.15 N	2.52 W
Werwaru	164	8.13 S	128.11 E
Weschnitz ≃	56	49.43 N	8.24 E
Weseke	52	51.54 N	6.51 E
Wesel	52	51.40 N	6.38 E
Wesel-Datteln-Kanal ≍	263	51.38 N	6.36 E
Wesenberg	54	53.17 N	12.58 E
Wesendahl	264a	52.36 N	13.49 E
Wesendorf	52	52.35 N	10.31 E
Weser ≃	52	53.32 N	8.34 E
Weser-Ems □ [5]	52	52.45 N	8.00 E
Wesergebirge ⋀	52	52.15 N	9.10 E
Wesham	262	53.48 N	2.53 W
Wesickaman Creek ≃	285	39.44 N	74.43 W
Wesī Śahar	124	28.15 N	84.23 E
Weskan	198	38.52 N	101.57 W
Weslaco	196	26.09 N	97.59 W
Weslemkoon Lake ⊜	212	45.02 N	77.25 W
Wesley, Dom.	240d	15.34 N	61.19 W
Wesley, Ia., U.S.	190	43.05 N	93.59 W
Wesleyville, Nf., Can.	186	49.09 N	53.34 W
Wesleyville, Pa., U.S.	214	42.08 N	80.00 W
Wessel, Cape ›	164	10.59 S	136.46 E
Wesseling	56	50.49 N	6.58 E
Wessel Islands II	164	11.30 S	136.25 E
Wesselsbron	158	27.50 S	25.23 E
Wesselsvlei	158	27.23 S	23.47 E
Wessington	198	44.27 N	98.41 W
Wessington Springs	198	44.04 N	98.34 W
Wessobrunn	64	47.52 N	11.01 E
Wesson	194	31.42 N	90.23 W
Wessum	52	52.05 N	6.58 E
West, Ms., U.S.	194	33.11 N	89.46 W
West, Tx., U.S.	222	31.48 N	97.05 W
West ≃, N.Y., U.S.	210	42.41 N	77.22 W
West ≃, Vt., U.S.	188	42.52 N	72.33 W
West Abington	207	42.05 N	70.58 W
Westacres	216	42.35 N	83.26 W
West Acton	207	42.28 N	71.28 W
West Alexander	214	40.06 N	80.31 W
West Alexandria	218	39.44 N	84.31 W
Westall, Point ›	162	32.55 S	134.04 E
West Allen ≃	44	54.55 N	2.19 W
West Allis	216	43.01 N	88.00 W
Westalton	219	38.51 N	90.13 W
West Amityville	276	40.41 N	73.26 W
West Andover	207	42.39 N	71.09 W
West Athens	280	33.55 N	118.18 W
West Atlantic City	208	39.23 N	74.28 W
West Babylon	210	40.43 N	73.21 W
Westbahnhof ◆ [5]	264b	48.11 N	16.20 E
West Baines ≃	164	15.36 S	129.58 E
West Bangor	210	40.52 N	75.14 W
Westbank	182	49.50 N	119.38 W
West Bank □ [9]	132	31.40 N	35.15 E
West Barnstable	207	41.42 N	70.22 W
West Barrington	207	41.44 N	71.20 W
West Bay, N.S., Can.	186	45.43 N	61.10 W
Westbay, Fl., U.S.	194	30.17 N	85.52 W
West Bay ⊂, Fl., U.S.	194	30.16 N	85.47 W
West Bay ⊂, Tx., U.S.	222	29.15 N	94.57 W
West Bay Shore	276	40.42 N	73.16 W
West Belmar	208	40.10 N	74.02 W
West Bend, Ia., U.S.	198	42.57 N	94.26 W
West Bend, Wi., U.S.	190	43.25 N	88.11 W
West Bengal □ [3]	124	24.00 N	88.00 E
West Bergholt	42	51.55 N	0.51 E
West Berlin	208	39.48 N	74.56 W
West Bernard Creek ≃	222	29.23 N	95.58 W
Westbevern	52	52.01 N	7.47 E
West Bhāgīrath Plain ⩦	126	23.30 N	88.00 E
West Bijou Creek ≃	198	39.51 N	104.08 W
West Billerica	283	42.33 N	71.19 W
West Blocton	194	33.07 N	87.07 W
West Bloomfield	210	42.54 N	77.32 W
West Bolivar	214	40.23 N	79.10 W
Westborough	207	42.16 N	71.37 W
Westbourne	184	50.09 N	98.35 W
West Bow Creek ≃	198	42.46 N	97.08 W
West Boxford	283	42.42 N	71.04 W
West Boylston	207	42.22 N	71.47 W
West Bradenton	220	27.30 N	82.37 W
West Branch, Ia., U.S.	190	41.40 N	91.20 W
West Branch, Mi., U.S.	190	44.16 N	84.14 W
West Branch Reservoir ⊜ [1]	210	41.25 N	73.42 W
West Branch State Park ♠	214	41.07 N	81.05 W
Westbridge	182	49.10 N	118.59 W

Symbols in the index entries represent the broad categories identified in the key at the right. Symbols with superior numbers (⋀ [1]) identify subcategories (see complete key on page *I · 1)*.

Symbole im Register stellen die rechts im Schlüssel erklärten Kategorien dar. Symbole mit hochgestellten Ziffern (⋀ [1]) bezeichnen Unterabteilungen einer Kategorie (vgl. vollständiger Schlüssel auf Seite *I · 1)*.

Los símbolos incluídos en el texto del índice representan las grandes categorías identificadas con la clave a la derecha. Los símbolos con numeros en su parte superior (⋀ [1]) identifican las subcategorías (véase la clave completa en la página *I · 1)*.

Les symboles de l'index représentent les catégories indiquées dans la légende à droite. Les symboles suivis d'un indice (⋀ [1]) représentent des sous-catégories (voir légende complète à la page *I · 1)*.

Os símbolos incluídos no texto do índice representam as grandes categorias identificadas com a chave à direita. Os símbolos com números em sua parte superior (⋀ [1]) identificam as subcategorias (veja-se a chave completa à página *I · 1)*.

∧ Mountain	Berg	Montaña	Montagne	Montanha
⋀ Mountains	Gebirge	Montañas	Montagnes	Montanhas
)(Pass	Paß	Paso	Col	Passo
V Valley, Canyon	Tal, Cañon	Valle, Cañón	Vallée, Canyon	Vale, Canhão
⩦ Plain	Ebene	Llano	Plaine	Planície
› Cape	Kap	Cabo	Cap	Cabo
I Island	Insel	Isla	Île	Ilha
II Islands	Inseln	Islas	Îles	Ilhas
⊥ Other Topographic Features	Andere Topographische Objekte	Otros Elementos Topográficos	Autres données topographiques	Outros acidentes topográficos

West-Whit *I* · *191*

ESPAÑOL: Nombre | Página | Lat.°′ | Long.°′ W = Oeste
FRANÇAIS: Nom | Page | Lat.°′ | Long.°′ W = Ouest
PORTUGUÊS: Nome | Página | Lat.°′ | Long.°′ W = Oeste

West Bridgewater	207	42.01 N	71.00 W
West Bridgford	42	52.56 N	1.08 W
West Bristol	285	40.06 N	74.53 W
West Bromwich	42	52.31 N	1.56 W
Westbrook, Austl.	171a	27.36 S	151.52 E
Westbrook, On., Can.	212	44.16 N	76.38 W
Westbrook, Ct., U.S.	207	41.17 N	72.26 W
Westbrook, Me., U.S.	188	43.40 N	70.22 W
Westbrook, Mn., U.S.	198	44.02 N	95.26 W
Westbrook, Tx., U.S.	196	32.21 N	101.01 W
West Brook ≃	276	41.04 N	74.18 W
West Brookfield	207	42.14 N	72.08 W
Westbrookville	210	41.30 N	74.34 W
West Burlington, Ia., U.S.	190	40.49 N	91.09 W
West Burlington, N.Y., U.S.	210	42.42 N	75.11 W
West Burra I	46a	60.05 N	1.21 W
Westbury, Eng., U.K.	42	52.41 N	2.57 W
Westbury, Eng., U.K.	42	51.16 N	2.11 W
Westbury, N.Y., U.S.	276	40.45 N	73.35 W
Westbury-on-Severn	42	51.50 N	2.24 W
West Butte ∧	202	48.57 N	111.32 W
Westby, Austl.	171b	35.30 S	147.25 E
Westby, Mt., U.S.	198	48.52 N	104.03 W
Westby, Wi., U.S.	190	43.39 N	90.51 W
West Cache Creek ≃	196	34.13 N	98.23 W
West Caicos I	238	21.39 N	72.28 W
West Calder	46	55.52 N	3.35 W
West Caldwell	276	40.50 N	74.18 W
West Cameron	208	40.45 N	76.41 W
West Camp	210	42.07 N	73.56 W
West Canada Creek ≃	188	43.01 N	74.58 W
West Cape ›	172	45.54 S	166.26 E
West Cape Howe ›	162	35.08 S	117.36 E
West Cape May	208	38.56 N	74.56 W
West Carlisle	196	33.35 N	101.56 W
West Caroline Basin ✤[1]	14	4.00 N	138.00 E
West Carrollton	218	39.40 N	84.15 W
West Carson	280	33.57 N	118.23 W
West Carthage	212	43.58 N	75.36 W
West Catfish Creek ≃	212	42.46 N	81.04 W
West Channel ≃[1]	180	68.51 N	136.10 W
West Chelmsford	283	42.37 N	71.23 W
Westchester, Il., U.S.	216	41.51 N	87.52 W
West Chester, Pa., U.S.	208	39.57 N	75.36 W
Westchester, Va., U.S.	284c	38.51 N	77.16 W
Westchester □[6]	210	41.02 N	73.46 W
Westchester ◆[8], Ca., U.S.	280	33.55 N	118.25 W
Westchester ◆[8], N.Y., U.S.	276	40.51 N	73.52 W
West Chester Airport ⊠	285	39.59 N	75.35 W
Westchester County Airport ⊠	207	41.04 N	73.43 W
Westchester Creek ≃	276	40.48 N	73.51 W
Westchester Estates	284c	38.47 N	76.55 W
Westchester Station	186	45.37 N	63.40 W
West Chester University of Pennsylvania ʋ[2]	285	39.57 N	75.36 W
West Chicago	216	41.53 N	88.12 W
West Clandon	260	51.15 N	0.30 W
West Clarksville	210	42.08 N	78.15 W
West Clear Creek ≃	200	34.34 N	111.51 W
West Cleddau ≃	42	51.46 N	4.54 W
Westcliffe	200	38.08 N	105.27 W
Westcliffe ◆[8]	273d	26.11 S	28.02 E
Westcliff-on-Sea	260	51.32 N	0.41 E
West College Corner	218	39.34 N	84.48 W
West Collingswood Heights	285	39.59 N	75.07 W
West Columbia, S.C., U.S.	192	33.59 N	81.04 W
West Columbia, Tx., U.S.	222	29.08 N	95.38 W
West Concord, Ma., U.S.	207	42.27 N	71.23 W
West Concord, Mn., U.S.	190	44.09 N	92.53 W
West Conshohocken	285	40.04 N	75.19 W
West Cote Blanche Bay ⊂	194	29.40 N	91.45 W
Westcott	260	51.13 N	0.22 W
Westcott Cove ⊂	276	41.02 N	73.30 W
West Covina	228	34.04 N	117.56 W
West Creek	208	39.38 N	74.18 W
West Creek ≃, In., U.S.	216	41.12 N	87.30 W
West Creek ≃, Pa., U.S.	214	41.30 N	78.15 W
Westdale, Ma., U.S.	283	42.01 N	70.59 W
Westdale, N.Y., U.S.	210	43.23 N	75.49 W
West Danby	210	42.19 N	76.32 W
West Davenport	210	42.27 N	74.58 W
West Deane Park ♠	275b	43.40 N	79.34 W
West Decatur	214	40.56 N	78.17 W
West Delaware Aqueduct ≊[1]	210	41.52 N	74.31 W
Westdene ◆[8]	273d	26.11 S	27.59 E
West Dennis	207	41.39 N	70.10 W
West Derby ◆[8]	262	53.26 N	2.54 W
West Derry	214	40.20 N	79.20 W
West Des Moines	190	41.34 N	93.42 W
West Ditch ≊	276	40.56 N	74.19 W
West Dolores ≃	200	37.35 N	108.21 W
West Drayton ◆[8]	260	51.30 N	0.29 W
West Duffins Creek ≃	212	43.51 N	79.04 W
West Duxbury	283	42.03 N	70.47 W
West Easton	210	40.41 N	75.14 W
West Eaton	210	42.51 N	75.39 W
Westecunk Creek ≃	208	39.37 N	74.16 W
West Edmeston	210	42.46 N	75.17 W
West Edmondale	284b	39.18 N	76.43 W
West Elizabeth	279b	40.17 N	79.54 W
West Elk Mountains ⋏	200	38.40 N	107.15 W
West Elk Peak ∧	200	38.43 N	107.13 W
West Elkton	218	39.35 N	84.33 W
West Ellicott	214	42.05 N	79.16 W
West Elmira	210	42.04 N	76.50 W
West End, Ba.	238	26.41 N	78.58 W
West End, Eng., U.K.	260	51.44 N	0.04 W
West End, Eng., U.K.	260	51.20 N	0.38 W
West End, Ar., U.S.	194	34.13 N	92.03 W
West End, Il., U.S.	216	42.17 N	89.09 W
West End, N.Y., U.S.	210	42.28 N	75.05 W
West End, N.C., U.S.	192	35.14 N	79.34 W
West End ◆[8], Eng., U.K.	260	51.32 N	0.24 W
West End ◆[8], Pa., U.S.	279b	40.27 N	80.02 W
Westende, Bel.	50	51.10 N	2.46 E
Westende, Dtsch.	263	51.25 N	7.24 E
Westendorf	64	47.26 N	12.13 E
Westenfeld ◆[8]	263	51.28 N	7.09 E
Westenholz	52	51.45 N	8.28 E
Westenschouwen	52	51.41 N	3.42 E
Westerbauer ◆[8]	263	51.20 N	7.23 E
Westerblokker	52	52.39 N	5.08 E
Westerbönen	263	51.36 N	7.46 E
Westerbork	52	52.51 N	6.37 E
Westerburg	56	50.33 N	7.58 E
Westercelle	52	52.36 N	10.05 E
Westerdale	46	58.27 N	3.30 W
Westeregeln	54	51.57 N	11.23 E
Westerham	42	51.16 N	0.05 E
Westerhausen	54	51.48 N	11.03 E
Westerholt	52	51.36 N	7.05 E
Westerholz ◆[3]	263	51.32 N	7.28 E
Westerkappeln	52	52.18 N	7.52 E
Westerland	30	54.54 N	8.18 E
Westerlo, Bel.	56	51.05 N	4.55 E
Westerlo, N.Y., U.S.	210	42.31 N	74.03 W
Westerly	207	41.22 N	71.49 W
Western	198	40.23 N	97.11 W
Western □[4], Ghana	150	5.30 N	2.30 W
Western □[4], Kenya	154	0.30 N	34.35 E
Western □[4], Sol.Is.	175e	8.00 S	157.00 E
Western □[4], Zam.	152	16.00 S	24.00 E
Western □[5], Pap. N. Gui.	164	7.00 S	142.00 E
Western □[5], Ug.	154	1.00 N	31.00 E
Western ≃	166	22.22 S	142.25 E
Western Area □[4]	150	8.20 N	13.00 W
Western Australia □[3]	160	25.00 S	122.00 E
Western Branch ≃	284c	38.55 N	76.48 W
Western Canal ≊	226	39.28 N	121.35 W
Western Cape □[4]	158	33.30 S	20.00 E
Western Channel Ʊ	98	34.40 N	129.00 E
Western Cove ⊂	168b	35.43 S	137.38 E
Western Desert → Gharbīyah, Aṣ-Ṣaḥrā' al- ◆[2]	140	27.00 N	27.00 E
Western Division □[5]	175g	18.00 S	177.30 E
Western Ghāts ⋏	122	14.00 N	75.00 E
Western Highlands □[5]	164	5.45 S	144.30 E
Western Isles □[4]	46	57.40 N	7.00 W
Westernport	188	39.29 N	79.02 W
Western Port ⊂	169	38.22 N	145.20 E
Western Port Bay ⊂	169	38.15 S	145.20 E
Western Sahara □[2], Afr.	134	24.30 N	13.00 W
Western Sahara □[2], Afr.	148	24.30 N	13.00 W
Western Samoa □[1], Oc.	14	13.55 S	172.00 W
Western Samoa □[1], Oc.	175a	13.55 S	172.00 W
Western Sayans → Zapadnyj Sajan ⋏	74	53.00 N	94.00 E
Western Shore	186	44.32 N	64.19 W
Western Springs	278	41.48 N	87.54 W
Westernville	210	43.18 N	75.23 W
Westerschelde ⊂[1]	52	51.25 N	3.45 E
Westerstede	52	53.15 N	7.55 E
Westervelt	219	39.29 N	88.52 W
Westerville	214	40.07 N	82.55 W
Westerwald ⋏	56	50.40 N	7.55 E
West European Basin ✤[1]	10	47.00 N	15.00 W
West Exeter	210	42.48 N	75.09 W
West Fairview	208	40.16 N	76.54 W
Westfalen □[9]	52	51.50 N	7.30 E
Westfalenhalle ʋ	263	51.30 N	7.27 E
West Falkland I	254	51.50 S	60.00 W
West Falls	210	42.42 N	78.41 W
West Falmouth	207	41.36 N	70.38 W
West Fargo	198	46.52 N	96.54 W
West Farleigh	260	51.15 N	0.27 E
West Farmington	214	41.23 N	80.58 W
Westfield, Eng., U.K.	42	50.55 N	0.35 E
Westfield, Il., U.S.	194	39.27 N	88.01 W
Westfield, In., U.S.	218	40.02 N	86.07 W
Westfield, Ma., U.S.	207	42.07 N	72.45 W
Westfield, N.J., U.S.	210	40.39 N	74.20 W
Westfield, N.Y., U.S.	214	42.19 N	79.34 W
Westfield, Pa., U.S.	210	41.55 N	77.32 W
Westfield, Tx., U.S.	222	30.01 N	95.24 W
Westfield, Wi., U.S.	190	43.53 N	89.29 W
Westfield ≃	207	42.05 N	72.35 W
Westfield, Middle Branch ≃	207	42.16 N	72.52 W
Westfield, West Branch ≃	207	42.13 N	72.52 W
Westfield Center	214	41.01 N	81.55 W
West Fiord ⊂[2]	176	76.02 N	90.00 W
Westford, Ma., U.S.	283	42.34 N	71.26 W
Westford, N.Y., U.S.	210	42.39 N	74.48 W
West Fork	194	35.55 N	94.11 W
West Foxboro	283	42.05 N	71.17 W
West Frankfort	194	37.53 N	88.55 W
West Friesland □[9]	52	52.45 N	4.50 E
West Frisian Islands → Waddeneilanden II	52	53.26 N	5.30 E
West Fulton	210	42.34 N	74.28 W
Westgate	166	26.35 S	146.12 E
Westgate on Sea	42	51.23 N	1.21 E
West Genesee Terrace	210	43.03 N	76.16 W
West-Ghats → Western Ghāts ⋏	122	14.00 N	75.00 E
West Gilgo Beach	276	40.37 N	73.25 W
West Glacier	202	48.29 N	113.58 W
West Glamorgan □[6]	42	51.35 N	3.35 W
West Glens Falls	210	43.18 N	73.43 W
West Glenville	210	42.56 N	74.04 W
West Goshen	207	41.49 N	73.15 W
West Granby	207	41.57 N	72.50 W
West Grand Lake ⊜	188	45.15 N	67.50 W
West Groton	207	42.36 N	71.37 W
West Grove	208	39.49 N	75.49 W
Westham	208	37.35 N	77.32 W
West Ham ◆[8]	260	51.31 N	0.01 E
West Hamburg	208	40.33 N	76.00 W
West Ham Football Club ♠	260	51.32 N	0.02 E
Westham Island I	224	49.05 N	123.10 W
West Hamlin	188	38.17 N	82.11 W
Westhampton, N.Y., U.S.	207	40.49 N	72.39 W
Westhampton, Va., U.S.	284c	38.54 N	77.11 W
West Hanningfield	260	51.40 N	0.30 E
West Hanover	283	42.07 N	70.53 W
West Harbor ⊂	276	40.54 N	73.32 W
West Harrison	218	39.15 N	84.49 W
West Hartford	207	41.45 N	72.44 W
West Hartland	207	42.00 N	72.58 W
Westhausen	56	48.53 N	10.11 E
Westhaven, Ca., U.S.	204	41.03 N	124.06 W
West Haven, Ct., U.S.	207	41.16 N	72.57 W
Westhaven, Il., U.S.	278	41.35 N	87.51 W
West Haverstraw	210	41.12 N	73.59 W
West Hazleton	210	40.57 N	75.59 W
Westhead	262	53.34 N	2.51 W
West Hebron	210	43.14 N	73.22 W
West Heidelberg	274b	37.45 S	145.02 E
Westheim	56	49.03 N	9.44 E
West Helena	194	34.33 N	90.38 W
Westhemmerde	263	51.33 N	7.47 E
West Hempstead	276	40.42 N	73.39 W
West Henrietta	210	43.02 N	77.40 W
West Hickory	214	41.34 N	79.25 W
Westhill	46	57.09 N	2.17 W
West Hill ◆[8]	275b	43.46 N	79.11 W
Westhofen	263	51.25 N	7.31 E
Westhoff	222	29.12 N	97.28 W
Westhoffen	58	48.36 N	7.26 E
West Hollywood, Ca., U.S.	228	34.05 N	118.21 W
West Hollywood, Fl., U.S.	220	26.01 N	80.10 W
Westholme	224	49.52 N	123.42 W
West Homestead	279b	40.24 N	79.55 W
Westhope, N.D., U.S.	198	48.54 N	101.01 W
Westhope, Oh., U.S.	216	41.18 N	83.57 W
West Horndon	260	51.34 N	0.21 E
West Horsley	260	51.16 N	0.27 W
Westhoughton	262	53.33 N	2.32 W
West Hoxton	274a	33.55 S	150.49 E
West Humber ≃	212	43.44 N	79.33 W
West Humble	260	51.15 N	0.20 W
West Huntington	276	40.42 N	73.18 W
West Hurley	210	42.00 N	74.06 W
Westhuyzen	158	27.30 S	25.27 E
West Hyde	260	51.37 N	0.30 W
West Ice Shelf ⍓	9	67.00 S	85.00 E
Westick	263	51.35 N	7.38 E
Westig	263	51.22 N	7.45 E
West Indies II	230	19.00 N	70.00 W
Westindische Inseln → West Indies II	230	19.00 N	70.00 W
West Irian → Irian Jaya □[4]	164	5.00 S	138.00 E
West Island I, Austl.	164	15.36 S	136.34 E
West Island I, Ma., U.S.	207	41.36 N	70.50 W
West Islip	210	40.42 N	73.18 W
West Jan Mayen Ridge ✤[3]	10	71.00 N	13.00 W
West Jefferson, N.C., U.S.	192	36.24 N	81.29 W
West Jefferson, Oh., U.S.	218	39.56 N	83.16 W
West Jordan	200	40.36 N	111.56 W
Westkapelle, Bel.	50	51.19 N	3.18 E
Westkapelle, Ned.	52	51.32 N	3.27 E
West Keansburg	276	40.27 N	74.09 W
West Kettle ≃	182	49.07 N	119.00 W
West Kilbride	46	55.42 N	4.51 W
West Kill	210	42.13 N	74.31 W
West Kingsdown	42	51.21 N	0.17 E
West Kingston	207	41.28 N	71.33 W
West Kirby	44	53.22 N	3.10 W
Westkirchen	52	51.53 N	8.02 E
West Kittanning	214	40.49 N	79.32 W
West Lafayette, In., U.S.	216	40.25 N	86.54 W
West Lafayette, Oh., U.S.	214	40.16 N	81.45 W
Westlake, La., U.S.	194	30.15 N	93.15 W
Westlake, Oh., U.S.	214	41.27 N	81.55 W
Westlake, Tx., U.S.	222	32.59 N	97.12 W
West Lake ⊜, On., Can.	212	43.56 N	77.17 W
West Lake ⊜, Fl., U.S.	220	25.12 N	80.49 W
West Lake ⊜, N.J., U.S.	276	40.58 N	74.22 W
West Lamma Channel Ʊ	271d	22.13 N	114.04 E
West Lancashire □[8]	262	53.35 N	2.50 W
Westland, Mi., U.S.	216	42.19 N	83.24 W
Westland, Pa., U.S.	214	40.17 N	80.16 W
Westland Center ◆[9]	281	42.20 N	83.23 W
Westland National Park ♠	172	43.30 S	170.10 E
Westlands	207	42.37 N	71.20 W
West Lanham Hills	284c	38.57 N	76.53 W
West Laramie	200	41.18 N	105.37 W
West Lawn	284c	38.52 N	77.11 W
West Lebanon, In., U.S.	216	40.16 N	87.23 W
West Lebanon, Pa., U.S.	214	40.35 N	79.22 W
West Leechburg	214	40.37 N	79.37 W
Westleigh, S. Afr.	158	27.31 S	27.21 E
Westleigh, Eng., U.K.	262	53.30 N	2.31 W
West Leipsic	216	41.07 N	84.00 W
Westley	226	37.33 N	121.12 W
West Leyden	212	43.28 N	75.28 W
West Liberty, Ia., U.S.	190	41.34 N	91.15 W
West Liberty, Ky., U.S.	192	37.55 N	83.15 W
West Liberty, Oh., U.S.	216	40.15 N	83.45 W
West Liberty, Pa., U.S.	214	41.00 N	80.03 W
West Liberty, W.V., U.S.	214	40.10 N	80.35 W
West Liberty ◆[8]	279b	40.24 N	80.01 W
Westliche Sahara → Western Sahara □[2]	148	24.30 N	13.00 W
Westliche Sierra Madre → Madre Occidental, Sierra ⋏	232	25.00 N	105.00 W
Westline	214	41.47 N	78.46 W
West Linn	224	45.21 N	122.36 W
West Linton	46	55.46 N	3.22 W
West Little Owyhee ≃	202	42.28 N	117.15 W
Westlock	182	54.09 N	113.52 W
West Lorne	214	42.36 N	81.36 W
West Los Angeles ◆[8]	280	34.03 N	118.28 W
West Lulworth	42	50.38 N	2.15 W
West Lunga ≃	154	13.06 S	24.39 E
West Lunga National Park ♠	154	12.55 S	25.10 E
Westmalle	52	51.18 N	4.41 E
West Malling	42	51.18 N	0.25 E
West Malling Aerodrome ⊠	260	51.16 N	0.24 E
West Manayunk	285	40.01 N	75.14 W
West Manchester	218	39.54 N	84.37 W
West Mansfield, Ma., U.S.	207	41.59 N	71.14 W
West Mansfield, Oh., U.S.	216	40.24 N	83.32 W
West Mariana Basin ✤[1]	14	15.00 N	137.00 E
West Mayfield	214	40.47 N	80.20 W
West Meadowview	216	41.08 N	87.52 W
Westmeath □[6]	48	53.30 N	7.30 W
West Medway	207	42.08 N	71.25 W
West Melbourne	220	28.04 N	80.39 W
West Memphis	194	35.08 N	90.11 W
West Meon	42	51.01 N	1.05 W
Westmere	210	42.41 N	73.52 W
West Mersea	42	51.47 N	0.55 E
West Miami	220	25.45 N	80.17 W
West Middlesex	214	41.10 N	80.27 W
West Middletown	214	40.15 N	80.25 W
West Midlands □[6]	42	52.30 N	2.00 W
West Mifflin	214	40.22 N	79.52 W
West Milford	210	41.07 N	74.22 W
West Millbury	207	42.11 N	71.48 W
West Mill Creek ≃	222	29.55 N	96.17 W
West Milton, Oh., U.S.	218	39.57 N	84.19 W
West Milton, Pa., U.S.	210	41.01 N	76.52 W
West Milwaukee	216	43.00 N	87.58 W
West Mineola	222	32.41 N	95.31 W
Westminster, Ca., U.S.	228	33.45 N	118.02 W
Westminster, Co., U.S.	200	39.50 N	105.02 W
Westminster, Md., U.S.	208	39.34 N	76.59 W
Westminster, Ma., U.S.	207	42.32 N	71.54 W
Westminster, Oh., U.S.	216	40.42 N	83.58 W
Westminster, S.C., U.S.	192	34.39 N	83.05 W
Westminster ◆[8]	260	51.30 N	0.09 W
Westminster Abbey ʋ[1]	260	51.30 N	0.07 W
Westminster Mall ◆[9]	280	33.45 N	118.01 W
West Modesto	226	37.37 N	121.02 W
West Monroe	194	32.31 N	92.08 W
Westmont, Ca., U.S.	280	33.56 N	118.18 W
Westmont, Il., U.S.	278	41.47 N	87.58 W
Westmont, N.J., U.S.	285	39.54 N	75.02 W
Westmont, Pa., U.S.	214	40.18 N	78.57 W
West Monterey	214	41.03 N	79.39 W
West Montreal ≃	190	47.56 N	80.39 W
West Moors	42	50.49 N	1.55 W
Westmoreland, Ks., U.S.	198	39.23 N	96.24 W
Westmoreland, N.Y., U.S.	210	43.07 N	75.24 W
Westmoreland, Tn., U.S.	194	36.33 N	86.14 W
Westmoreland, Va., U.S.	208	38.04 N	76.34 W
Westmoreland □[6], Pa., U.S.	214	40.18 N	79.33 W
Westmoreland □[6], Va., U.S.	208	38.10 N	76.50 W
Westmoreland City	214	40.20 N	79.41 W
Westmoreland State Park ♠	208	38.09 N	76.50 W
Westmorland	204	33.02 N	115.37 W
Westmount	206	45.29 N	73.36 W
West Mountain ∧	188	43.51 N	74.43 W
West Mud Creek ≃	222	32.07 N	95.10 W
West Mustang Creek ≃	222	29.04 N	96.26 W
West Nab ∧	262	53.35 N	1.53 W
West Nanticoke	210	40.13 N	76.01 W
West New Britain □[5]	164	5.45 S	149.30 E
West Newbury	207	42.48 N	70.59 W
West Newton, Ma., U.S.	283	42.21 N	71.14 W
West Newton, Pa., U.S.	214	40.12 N	79.46 W
West New York	276	40.47 N	74.00 W
West Nicholson	154	21.06 S	29.25 E
West Nishnabotna ≃	198	40.39 N	95.37 W
West Nodaway ≃	194	40.38 N	95.01 W
West Norriton	208	40.08 N	75.22 W
West Norwood ◆[8]	260	51.26 N	0.06 W
West Novaya Zemlya Trough ✤[1]	10	73.30 N	50.00 E
West Nueces ≃	196	29.16 N	99.56 W
West Nyack	210	41.06 N	73.58 W
West Okaw ≃	219	39.32 N	88.42 W
Weston, Austl.	170	32.49 S	151.28 E
Weston, Malay.	112	5.13 N	115.36 E
Weston, Eng., U.K.	262	53.19 N	2.44 W
Weston, Co., U.S.	200	37.07 N	104.50 W
Weston, Ct., U.S.	207	41.12 N	73.22 W
Weston, Id., U.S.	202	42.02 N	111.58 W
Weston, Ma., U.S.	207	42.22 N	71.18 W
Weston, Mi., U.S.	216	41.46 N	84.06 W
Weston, Mo., U.S.	194	39.24 N	94.54 W
Weston, Ne., U.S.	198	41.11 N	96.44 W
Weston, Oh., U.S.	216	41.20 N	83.47 W
Weston, Or., U.S.	202	45.48 N	118.25 W
Weston, Pa., U.S.	210	40.57 N	76.09 W
Weston, W.V., U.S.	188	39.02 N	80.28 W
Weston □[8]	275b	43.43 N	79.31 W
Westonaria	273d	26.19 S	27.39 E
West Oneonta	210	42.28 N	75.07 W
Westönnen	52	51.33 N	7.58 E
Weston Reservoir ⊜[1]	283	42.21 N	71.18 W
Westons Mill Pond ⊜	276	40.28 N	74.25 W
Westons Mills	210	42.04 N	78.23 W
Weston-super-Mare	42	51.21 N	2.59 W
Weston upon Trent	42	52.45 N	2.02 W
West Orange, N.J., U.S.	276	40.47 N	74.14 W
West Orange, Tx., U.S.	194	30.05 N	93.46 W
Westover, Md., U.S.	208	38.07 N	75.42 W
Westover, Pa., U.S.	214	40.45 N	78.40 W
Westover, Tn., U.S.	194	35.36 N	88.52 W
Westover, W.V., U.S.	188	39.38 N	79.58 W
Westover Air Force Base ■	207	42.12 N	72.33 W
Westoverledingen	52	53.10 N	7.28 E
Westowne	284b	39.17 N	76.43 W
West Palm Beach	220	26.42 N	80.03 W
West Palm Beach Canal ≊	220	26.38 N	80.03 W
West Paris	188	44.19 N	70.34 W
West Park	210	41.48 N	73.58 W
West Paterson	276	40.53 N	74.11 W
West Pawlet	210	43.21 N	73.15 W
West Peckham	260	51.15 N	0.22 E
West Pensacola	194	30.25 N	87.16 W
Westphalia, Ks., U.S.	198	38.10 N	95.29 W
Westphalia, Mi., U.S.	216	42.55 N	84.47 W
Westphalia, Mo., U.S.	219	38.26 N	91.59 W
West Pittsburg, Ca., U.S.	226	38.01 N	121.56 W
West Pittsburg, Pa., U.S.	214	40.55 N	80.21 W
West Pittston	210	41.19 N	75.47 W
West Plains	194	36.43 N	91.51 W
West Point, Ca., U.S.	226	38.23 N	120.31 W
West Point, Ga., U.S.	192	32.52 N	85.11 W
Westpoint, In., U.S.	216	40.21 N	87.03 W
West Point, Ia., U.S.	190	40.43 N	91.27 W
West Point, Ky., U.S.	194	37.59 N	85.56 W
West Point, Ms., U.S.	194	33.36 N	88.39 W
West Point, Ne., U.S.	198	41.50 N	96.42 W
West Point, N.Y., U.S.	210	41.23 N	73.57 W
West Point, Oh., U.S.	214	40.43 N	80.42 W
West Point, Pa., U.S.	285	40.12 N	75.18 W
West Point, Va., U.S.	208	37.31 N	76.47 W
West Point ∧	180	64.57 N	144.40 W
West Point ›, Austl.	166	35.01 S	135.57 E
West Point ›, P.E., Can.	186	46.37 N	64.25 W
West Point Lake ⊜[1]	192	33.00 N	85.10 W
West Pond ⊜	276	40.53 N	73.38 W
Westport, Nf., Can.	186	49.47 N	56.38 W
Westport, N.S., Can.	186	44.16 N	66.21 W
Westport, On., Can.	212	44.41 N	76.26 W
Westport, Ire.	48	53.48 N	9.32 W
Westport, N.Z.	172	41.45 S	171.36 E
Westport, Ct., U.S.	207	41.08 N	73.21 W
Westport, In., U.S.	218	39.10 N	85.34 W
Westport, Ky., U.S.	218	38.28 N	85.28 W
Westport, Ma., U.S.	207	41.37 N	71.04 W
Westport, Or., U.S.	224	46.07 N	123.22 W
Westport, Pa., U.S.	214	41.18 N	77.51 W
Westport, Wa., U.S.	224	46.53 N	124.06 W
Westport Point	207	41.31 N	71.04 W
West Portsmouth	218	38.45 N	83.01 W
West Prairie ≃	182	55.30 N	116.31 W
West Puente Valley	280	34.04 N	117.59 W
West Pullman ◆[8]	278	41.41 N	87.39 W
Westpunt ›	241s	12.37 N	70.03 W
West Pymble	274a	33.46 S	151.08 E
West Quoddy Head ›	188	44.49 N	66.57 W
West Rand	273d	26.07 S	27.45 E
Westray I	46	59.18 N	3.00 W
Westray Firth Ʊ	46	59.12 N	2.55 W
West Redding	207	41.19 N	73.26 W
Westrem	50	50.58 N	3.52 E
Westrich ◆[1]	56	49.15 N	7.20 E
West Richfield	214	41.14 N	81.39 W
West Richland	202	46.18 N	119.20 W
West River ⊥	208	38.52 N	76.31 W
West Road ≃	182	53.19 N	122.52 W
West Rosebud Creek ≃	202	45.29 N	109.27 W
West Roxbury ◆[8]	283	42.17 N	71.09 W
West Rupert	210	43.14 N	73.14 W
West Rutland	188	43.35 N	73.02 W
West Ryde	274a	33.48 S	151.05 E
West Sacramento	226	38.34 N	121.31 W
West Saint Marys ≃	186	45.15 N	62.04 W
West Saint Modeste	186	51.36 N	56.42 W
West Salem, Il., U.S.	194	38.31 N	88.00 W
West Salem, Oh., U.S.	214	40.58 N	82.06 W
West Salem, Wi., U.S.	190	43.53 N	91.04 W
West Salt Creek ≃	200	39.13 N	108.54 W
Westsamoa → Western Samoa □[1]	175a	13.55 S	172.00 W
West Sand Lake	210	42.39 N	73.37 W
West Saugerties	210	42.07 N	74.03 W
West Sayville	276	40.43 N	73.05 W
West Sayville County Park ♠	276	40.43 N	73.06 W
West Scenic Park	220	27.55 N	81.39 W
West Scotia Basin ✤[1]	18	57.00 S	53.00 W
West Seneca	210	42.50 N	78.45 W
West Shoal Lake ⊜	184	50.20 N	97.41 W
West Siberian Plain → Zapadno-Sibirskaja ravnina ⊻	72	60.00 N	75.00 E
Westsibirisches Flachland → Zapadno-Sibirskaja ravnina ⊻	72	60.00 N	75.00 E
West Side Canal ≊	226	35.19 N	119.23 W
West Side Tennis Club ♠	276	40.43 N	73.51 W
West Simsbury	207	41.52 N	72.51 W
West Sister Island I	214	41.44 N	83.07 W
West Slope	224	45.29 N	122.45 W
West Spanish Peak ∧	200	37.23 N	104.59 W
West Springfield, Ma., U.S.	207	42.06 N	72.37 W
West Springfield, Pa., U.S.	214	41.57 N	80.29 W
West Springfield, Va., U.S.	208	38.46 N	77.13 W
West Stewartstown	206	44.59 N	71.31 W
West Stockbridge	207	42.20 N	73.22 W
West Stony Creek ≃	210	43.15 N	74.13 W
West Suffield	207	41.59 N	72.41 W
West Sunbury	214	41.00 N	79.54 W
West Sussex □[6]	42	50.55 N	0.35 W
West Swanzey	207	42.52 N	72.20 W
West Terre Haute	194	39.27 N	87.27 W
West-Terschelling	52	53.21 N	5.13 E
West Thompson Lake ⊜[1]	207	41.57 N	71.54 W
West Thurrock	260	51.29 N	0.16 E
West Tiana	207	40.52 N	72.33 W
West Tilbury	260	51.29 N	0.24 E
West Tisbury	207	41.22 N	70.40 W
West Toodyay	168a	31.33 S	116.27 E
West Torrens	168b	34.56 S	138.32 E
Westtown, N.Y., U.S.	210	41.20 N	74.32 W
Westtown, Pa., U.S.	285	39.56 N	75.33 W
West Townsend	207	42.40 N	71.44 W
West Turffontein ◆[8]	273d	26.16 S	28.02 E
West Union, Ia., U.S.	190	42.57 N	91.48 W
West Union, Oh., U.S.	218	38.47 N	83.32 W
West Union, W.V., U.S.	188	39.17 N	80.46 W
West Union Creek ≃	282	37.25 N	122.16 W
West Unity	216	41.35 N	84.26 W
West University Place	222	29.43 N	95.26 W
West Upton	207	42.10 N	71.37 W
Westvale	210	43.02 N	76.13 W
West Valley, Mt., U.S.	202	46.08 N	113.01 W
West Valley, N.Y., U.S.	210	42.24 N	78.37 W
West Valley City	200	40.42 N	111.57 W
West Vancouver	182	49.22 N	123.12 W
West View	214	40.31 N	80.02 W
West View Amusement Park ♠	279b	40.31 N	80.02 W
Westview Heights	207	41.33 N	73.05 W
Westville, N.S., Can.	186	45.34 N	62.43 W
Westville, In., U.S.	216	41.32 N	86.54 W
Westville, N.H., U.S.	207	42.49 N	71.07 W
Westville, N.J., U.S.	285	39.52 N	75.07 W
Westville, Oh., U.S.	218	40.07 N	83.51 W
Westville, Ok., U.S.	194	35.59 N	94.34 W
Westville, Pa., U.S.	214	41.13 N	78.50 W
Westville Center	206	44.57 N	74.24 W
Westville Grove	285	39.51 N	75.07 W
Westville Lake ⊜[1]	207	42.05 N	72.05 W
Westville Oaks	285	39.51 N	75.08 W
West Virginia □[3], U.S.	178	38.45 N	80.30 W
West Virginia □[3], U.S.	188	38.45 N	80.30 W
West-Vlaanderen □[4]	50	51.00 N	3.00 E
West Walker ≃	226	38.53 N	119.10 W
West Wallsend	170	32.54 S	151.35 E
Westward Ho!	42	51.02 N	4.15 W
West Wareham	207	41.47 N	70.45 W
West Warren	207	42.12 N	72.14 W
West Warwick	207	41.42 N	71.31 W
West Water ≃	46	56.47 N	2.38 W
West Webster	210	43.12 N	77.29 W
Westwego	194	29.54 N	90.08 W
West Wellow	42	50.58 N	1.35 W
West Whittier	280	33.59 N	118.03 W
West Wickham ◆[8]	260	51.22 N	0.01 W
West Willington	207	41.52 N	72.18 W
West Willow	216	42.14 N	83.34 W
West Windsor	210	42.06 N	74.46 W
West Winfield, N.Y., U.S.	210	42.53 N	75.11 W
West Winfield, Pa., U.S.	214	40.48 N	79.42 W
Westwold	182	50.28 N	119.45 W
Westwood, Ca., U.S.	204	40.18 N	121.00 W
Westwood, In., U.S.	218	39.55 N	85.25 W
Westwood, Ma., U.S.	207	42.12 N	71.14 W
Westwood, Mi., U.S.	216	42.18 N	85.38 W
Westwood, N.J., U.S.	210	40.59 N	74.01 W
Westwood, Pa., U.S.	214	40.18 N	78.56 W
Westwood ◆[8]	280	34.04 N	118.27 W
Westwood Lakes	220	25.44 N	80.22 W
Westworth Village	222	32.45 N	97.25 W
West Wyalong	166	33.55 S	147.13 E
West Wycombe	42	51.39 N	0.49 W
West Yarmouth	207	41.39 N	70.14 W
West Yegua Creek ≃	222	30.20 N	96.52 W
West Yellow Creek ≃	194	39.38 N	93.04 W
West Yellowstone	202	44.39 N	111.06 W
West York	208	39.57 N	76.45 W
West Yorkshire □[6]	44	53.45 N	1.40 W
Wetan, Pulau I	164	7.54 S	129.32 E
Wetar, Pulau I	112	7.48 S	126.18 E
Wetar, Selat Ʊ	112	8.20 S	126.30 E
Wetaskiwin	182	52.58 N	113.22 W
Wete	154	5.04 S	39.43 E
Wethau	54	51.08 N	11.52 E
Wetherby	44	53.56 N	1.23 W
Wetherill Park	274a	33.51 S	150.54 E
Wethersfield	207	41.43 N	72.40 W
Wethmar	263	51.37 N	7.33 E
Wetiko Hills ⋏[2]	184	54.30 N	92.20 W
Wetluga → Vetluga ≃	80	56.18 N	46.24 E
Wetmore	198	39.38 N	95.48 W
Wet Mountains ⋏	200	38.00 N	105.10 W
Weto	152	7.57 N	7.50 E
Wetten	52	51.34 N	6.17 E
Wettenberg	56	50.38 N	8.39 E
Wetter, Dtsch.	56	50.54 N	8.43 E
Wetter, Dtsch.	56	51.23 N	7.23 E
Wetter ≃	56	50.18 N	8.49 E
Wetterau ◆[1]	56	50.15 N	8.50 E
Wetteren	50	51.00 N	3.53 E
Wetterhorn ∧	58	46.39 N	8.08 E
Wetterstein Gebirge ⋏	64	47.25 N	11.05 E
Wettigan	110	18.57 N	95.21 E
Wettin	54	51.35 N	11.48 E
Wettingen	58	47.28 N	8.19 E
Wettringen	52	52.12 N	7.19 E
Wettstetten	60	48.50 N	11.25 E
Wetumka	196	35.14 N	96.14 W
Wetumpka	194	32.32 N	86.12 W
Wetwang	44	54.01 N	0.34 W
Wetzikon	58	47.19 N	8.47 E
Wetzlar	56	50.33 N	8.29 E
Wetzstein ∧[2]	54	50.27 N	11.27 E
Wevelgem	50	50.48 N	3.10 E
Wevelinghoven	56	51.06 N	6.37 E
Wewahitchka	192	30.06 N	85.12 W
Wewak	164	3.35 S	143.40 E
Wewelsfleth	52	53.50 N	9.24 E
Wewer	52	51.41 N	8.42 E
Wewoka	196	35.09 N	96.29 W
Wexford, Ire.	48	52.20 N	6.27 W
Wexford, Pa., U.S.	214	40.38 N	80.03 W
Wexford □[6]	48	52.20 N	6.40 W
Wexford ◆[8]	275b	43.45 N	79.18 W
Wexford Harbour ⊂	48	52.20 N	6.24 W
Wey ≃	42	51.23 N	0.28 W
Weyakwin Lake ⊜	184	54.30 N	106.00 W
Weyanoke	284c	38.48 N	77.09 W
Weyarn	64	47.51 N	11.48 E
Weyauwega	190	44.19 N	88.56 W
Weybridge	42	51.23 N	0.28 W
Weyburn	184	49.41 N	103.52 W
Weyer ◆[8]	263	51.10 N	7.01 E
Weyer Markt	61	47.52 N	14.41 E
Weyersheim	56	48.43 N	7.48 E
Weyhausen	52	52.47 N	10.23 E
Weyhe	52	52.59 N	8.52 E
Weymouth, N.S., Can.	186	44.25 N	66.00 W
Weymouth, Eng., U.K.	42	50.36 N	2.28 W
Weymouth, Ma., U.S.	207	42.13 N	70.56 W
Weymouth, N.J., U.S.	208	39.30 N	74.46 W
Weymouth, Cape ›	164	12.37 S	143.27 E
Weymouth Back ≃	283	42.15 N	70.55 W
Weymouth Fore ≃	283	42.16 N	70.56 W
Weymouth Great Pond ⊜	283	42.12 N	71.02 W
Wezemaal	56	50.57 N	4.46 E
Wezep	52	52.27 N	6.00 E
Whakatane	172	37.58 S	177.00 E
Whakatane ≃	172	37.57 S	177.00 E
Whalan	274a	33.45 S	150.49 E
Whale Creek ≃	276	40.27 N	74.13 W
Whaley Bridge	44	53.20 N	1.59 W
Whaley Lake	210	41.33 N	73.40 W
Whaleysville	208	38.23 N	75.18 W
Whaleyville	208	36.37 N	76.41 W
Whalley	44	53.50 N	2.24 W
Whalom	207	42.34 N	71.44 W
Whalsay I	46a	60.20 N	0.59 W
Whangaehu ≃	172	40.03 S	175.06 E
Whangamata	172	37.12 S	175.52 E
Whangamomona	172	39.09 S	174.44 E
Whanganui National Park ♠	172	39.20 S	175.00 E
Whangara	172	38.34 S	178.13 E
Whangarei	172	35.43 S	174.19 E
Whangaruru Harbour ⊂	172	35.22 S	174.21 E
Whaplode	42	52.48 N	0.02 W
Wharfe ≃	44	53.51 N	1.07 W
Wharfedale V	44	54.01 N	1.56 W
Wharles	262	53.49 N	2.50 W
Wharton, N.J., U.S.	210	40.53 N	74.34 W
Wharton, Oh., U.S.	214	40.52 N	83.21 W
Wharton, Tx., U.S.	222	29.18 N	96.06 W
Wharton, W.V., U.S.	188	37.54 N	81.40 W
Wharton □[6]	222	29.17 N	96.13 W
Wharton Basin ✤[1]	12	21.00 S	100.00 E
Wharton Lake ⊜	176	64.00 N	99.55 W
Wharton State Forest ♠	285	39.45 N	74.40 W
Whataroa	172	43.17 S	170.25 E
Whatatutu	172	38.23 S	177.50 E
What Cheer	190	41.24 N	92.21 W
Whatcom □[6]	224	48.48 N	121.59 W
Whatcom, Lake ⊜	224	48.43 N	122.20 W
Whately	207	42.26 N	72.38 W
Whatley	194	31.39 N	87.42 W
Whatshan Lake ⊜	182	50.00 N	118.03 W
Whauphill	44	54.49 N	4.29 W
Wheao ≃	172	38.34 S	176.39 E
Wheatfield	216	40.33 N	87.06 W
Wheatland, Ca., U.S.	226	39.00 N	121.25 W
Wheatland, Ia., U.S.	190	41.49 N	90.50 W
Wheatland, Pa., U.S.	214	41.12 N	80.28 W
Wheatland, Wy., U.S.	200	42.03 N	104.57 W
Wheatland Hills	208	40.02 N	76.21 W
Wheatland Reservoir ⊜[1]	200	41.52 N	105.36 W
Wheatley, On., Can.	214	42.06 N	82.27 W
Wheatley, Eng., U.K.	42	51.44 N	1.08 W
Wheatley, Ar., U.S.	194	34.54 N	91.06 W
Wheatley Hill	44	54.45 N	1.23 W
Wheaton, Il., U.S.	216	41.51 N	88.06 W
Wheaton, Md., U.S.	208	39.02 N	77.03 W
Wheaton, Mn., U.S.	198	45.48 N	96.29 W
Wheaton Plaza ◆[9]	284c	39.02 N	77.03 W
Wheaton Regional Park ♠	284c	39.03 N	77.02 W
Wheat Ridge	200	39.45 N	105.04 W
Wheelbarrow Peak ∧	204	37.27 N	116.05 W
Wheeler, In., U.S.	216	41.30 N	87.10 W
Wheeler, Ms., U.S.	194	34.34 N	88.36 W
Wheeler, Tx., U.S.	196	35.26 N	100.16 W
Wheeler ≃, P.Q., Can.	176	57.02 N	67.13 W
Wheeler ≃, Sk., Can.	184	57.20 N	105.30 W
Wheeler Air Force Base ■	229c	21.29 N	158.03 W
Wheeler Dam ◆[6]	283	42.48 N	71.12 W
Wheeler Island I	282	38.05 N	121.56 W
Wheeler Lake ⊜[1]	194	34.40 N	87.05 W
Wheeler Peak ∧, Ca., U.S.	226	38.25 N	119.17 W
Wheeler Peak ∧, Nv., U.S.	204	38.59 N	114.19 W
Wheeler Peak ∧, N.M., U.S.	200	36.34 N	105.25 W
Wheelersburg	218	38.43 N	82.51 W
Wheelers Hill	274b	37.55 S	145.11 E
Wheeling, Il., U.S.	216	42.08 N	87.55 W
Wheeling, W.V., U.S.	214	40.03 N	80.43 W
Wheeling Creek ≃	214	40.03 N	80.41 W
Wheelock	222	30.54 N	96.24 W
Wheelock ≃	44	53.12 N	2.26 W
Wheelton	262	53.41 N	2.36 W
Wheelwright, Arg.	252	33.47 S	61.13 W
Wheelwright, Ky., U.S.	192	37.19 N	82.43 W
Wheelwright Park ♠	283	42.15 N	70.49 W
Wheeny Creek ≃	170	33.26 S	150.50 E
Whela Creek ≃	162	26.17 S	116.50 E
Whelan, Mount ∧[2]	166	23.25 S	138.54 E
Whelpleyhill	260	51.44 N	0.33 W
Whernside ∧	44	54.14 N	2.23 W
Whetstone Creek ≃	214	40.23 N	83.03 W
Whetstone Gulf State Park ♠	212	43.44 N	75.27 W
Whickham	44	54.56 N	1.41 W
Whidbey Island I	224	48.15 N	122.40 W
Whidbey Island Naval Air Station ■	224	48.17 N	122.37 W
Whiddon Down	42	50.43 N	3.51 W
Whigham	192	30.52 N	84.19 W
Whigville	207	41.43 N	72.56 W
Whim Creek	162	20.50 S	117.50 E
Whinham, Mount ∧	162	26.04 S	130.15 E
Whippany	210	40.49 N	74.25 W
Whippany ≃	276	40.51 N	74.21 W
Whirl Creek ≃	212	43.28 N	81.12 W
Whirlwind Reefs ✤[2]	164	4.42 S	148.16 E
Whiskey Peak ∧	200	42.18 N	107.35 W
Whiskeytown-Shasta-Trinity National Recreation Area ♠	204	40.45 N	122.15 W
Whisky Chitto Creek ≃	194	30.31 N	92.55 W
Whiston	262	53.25 N	2.50 W
Whitacres	207	41.48 N	72.39 W
Whitaker	279b	40.24 N	79.53 W
Whitakers	192	36.06 N	77.42 W

≃ River	Fluß	Río	Rivière	Rio
≊ Canal	Kanal	Canal	Canal	Canal
L Waterfall, Rapids	Wasserfall, Stromschnellen	Cascada, Rápidos	Chute d'eau, Rapides	Cascata, Rápidos
Ʊ Strait	Meeresstraße	Estrecho	Détroit	Estreito
⊂ Bay, Gulf	Bucht, Golf	Bahía, Golfo	Baie, Golfe	Baía, Golfo
⊜ Lake, Lakes	See, Seen	Lago, Lagos	Lac, Lacs	Lago, Lagos
⩨ Swamp	Sumpf	Pantano	Marais	Pântano
⍓ Ice Features, Glacier	Eis- und Gletscherformen	Accidentes Glaciales	Formes glaciaires	Acidentes glaciares
⫪ Other Hydrographic Features	Andere Hydrographische Objekte	Otros Elementos Hidrográficos	Autres données hydrographiques	Outros acidentes hidrográficos

✤ Submarine Features	Untermeerische Objekte	Accidentes Submarinos	Formes de relief sous-marin	Acidentes submarinos
□ Political Unit	Politische Einheit	Unidad Politica	Entité politique	Unidade política
ʋ Cultural Institution	Kulturelle Institution	Institución Cultural	Institution culturelle	Instituição cultural
⊥ Historical Site	Historische Stätte	Sitio Histórico	Site historique	Sitio histórico
♠ Recreational Site	Erholungs- und Ferienort	Sitio de Recreo	Centre de loisirs	Area de Lazer
⊠ Airport	Flughafen	Aeropuerto	Aéroport	Aeroporto
■ Military Installation	Militäranlage	Instalación Militar	Installation militaire	Instalação militar
◆ Miscellaneous	Verschiedenes	Misceláneo	Divers	Diversos

ENGLISH			
Name	**Page**	**Lat.°**	**Long.°**

Name	**Seite**	**Breite°**	**Länge° E = Ost**

Symbols in the index entries represent the broad categories identified in the key at the right. Symbols with superior numbers (⋌¹) identify subcategories (see complete key on page I · 1).

Symbole im Register stellen die rechts im Schlüssel erklärten Kategorien dar. Symbole mit hochgestellten Ziffern (⋌¹) bezeichnen Unterteilungen einer Kategorie (vgl. vollständiger Schlüssel auf Seite I · 1).

Los símbolos incluidos en el texto del índice representan las grandes categorías identificadas con la clave a la derecha. Los símbolos con números en su parte superior (⋌¹) identifican las subcategorías (véase la clave completa en la página I · 1).

Les symboles dans le texte de l'index représentent les catégories identifiées dans la légende à droite. Les symboles suivis d'un indice (⋌¹) représentent des sous-catégories (voir légende complète à la page I · 1).

Os símbolos incluídos no texto do índice representam as grandes categorias identificadas com a chave à direita. Os símbolos com números em sua parte superior (⋌¹) identificam as subcategorias (veja-se a chave completa na página I · 1).

Symbol	English	Español	Deutsch	Français	Português
▲	Mountain	Montaña	Berg	Montagne	Montanha
⋌	Mountains	Montañas	Gebirge	Montagnes	Montanhas
✕	Pass	Paso	Paß	Col	Passo
∨	Valley, Canyon	Valle, Cañón	Tal, Cañón	Vallée, Canyon	Vale, Canhão
≃	Plain	Llano	Ebene	Plaine	Planície
▸	Cape	Cabo	Kap	Cap	Cabo
I	Island	Isla	Insel	Île	Ilha
II	Islands	Islas	Inseln	Îles	Ilhas
⊥	Other Topographic Features	Otros Elementos Topográficos	Andere Topographische Objekte	Autres données topographiques	Outros acidentes topográficos

ESPAÑOL / FRANÇAIS / PORTUGUÊS

Nombre — Página — Lat.°′ — Long.°′ W = Oeste
Nom — Page — Lat.°′ — Long.°′ W = Ouest
Nome — Página — Lat.°′ — Long.°′ W = Oeste

Willow Brook ≃, N.J., U.S. 276 40.20 N 74.10 W
Willowbrook Mall ◆[9] 276 40.53 N 74.15 W
Willowbrook Park ♠ 276 40.36 N 74.09 W
Willow Bunch 184 49.24 N 105.37 W
Willow Bunch Lake ⊜ 184 49.27 N 105.28 W
Willow City 198 48.36 N 100.17 W
Willow Creek, Ca., U.S. 204 40.56 N 123.38 W
Willow Creek, Mt., U.S. 202 45.49 N 111.38 W
Willow Creek ≃, Ab., Can. 182 49.46 N 113.21 W
Willow Creek ≃, On., Can. 212 44.25 N 79.53 W
Willow Creek ≃, Ca., U.S. 226 39.22 N 122.05 W
Willow Creek ≃, Ca., U.S. 226 37.09 N 119.27 W
Willow Creek ≃, Il., U.S. 216 41.42 N 89.10 W
Willow Creek ≃, In., U.S. 216 41.15 N 85.08 W
Willow Creek ≃, Mi., U.S. 281 42.20 N 83.25 W
Willow Creek ≃, Mt., U.S. 202 48.10 N 111.11 W
Willow Creek ≃, Mt., U.S. 202 48.09 N 106.38 W
Willow Creek ≃, Mt., U.S. 202 46.28 N 108.28 W
Willow Creek ≃, Nv., U.S. 204 38.10 N 116.35 W
Willow Creek ≃, N.D., U.S. 198 48.34 N 100.27 W
Willow Creek ≃, Oh., U.S. 279a 41.20 N 82.03 W
Willow Creek ≃, Or., U.S. 202 44.00 N 117.13 W
Willow Creek ≃, Or., U.S. 202 45.48 N 120.01 W
Willow Creek ≃, Ut,. U.S. 200 40.02 N 109.45 W
Willow Creek, North Fork ≃ 226 37.13 N 119.30 W
Willow Creek, South Fork ≃ 226 39.32 N 122.10 W
Willowdale ◆[8] 275b 43.47 N 79.26 W
Willowdale State Forest ♠ 283 42.40 N 70.54 W
Willowdene 273d 26.18 S 27.56 E
Willowemac 210 41.55 N 74.41 W
Willowemoc Creek ≃ 210 41.53 N 74.48 W
Willow Glen ◆[8] 282 37.18 N 121.53 W
Willow Grove 208 40.08 N 75.06 W
Willow Grove Naval Air Station ■ 208 40.12 N 75.08 W
Willow Grove Park ♠ 285 40.08 N 75.08 W
Willow Hill 214 40.06 N 77.48 W
Willowick 214 41.37 N 81.28 W
Willow Lake 198 44.37 N 97.38 W
Willow Lake ⊜, N.T., Can. 176 62.11 N 119.10 W
Willow Lake ⊜, N.Y., U.S. 276 40.43 N 73.50 W
Willowlake ≃ 176 62.52 N 123.08 W
Willow Metropolitan Park ♠ 281 42.08 N 83.22 W
Willowmore 158 33.17 S 23.29 E
Willow Park 222 32.45 N 97.39 W
Willowra 162 21.15 S 132.35 E
Willowra Aboriginal Reserve ◆[4] 162 21.15 S 132.35 E
Willow Reservoir ⊜[1] 190 45.45 N 89.50 W
Willow Ridge Estates 284a 43.01 N 78.49 W
Willow River 182 54.04 N 122.28 W
Willow Run, De., U.S. 285 39.44 N 75.37 W
Willow Run, Mi., U.S. 216 42.14 N 83.35 W
Willow Run, Va., U.S. 284c 38.49 N 77.10 W
Willow Run Airport ⊠ 281 42.14 N 83.32 W
Willows 226 39.31 N 122.11 W
Willow Springs, Ca., U.S. 228 34.53 N 118.18 W
Willow Springs, Il., U.S. 278 41.44 N 87.51 W
Willow Springs, Mo., U.S. 194 36.59 N 91.58 W
Willow Springs, Pa., U.S. 279b 40.19 N 79.44 W
Willow Street 208 39.59 N 76.17 W
Willowvale 158 32.16 S 28.30 E
Willow Woods 284c 38.50 N 77.16 W
Will Rogers Beach State Park ♠ 280 34.01 N 118.30 W
Will Rogers State Park ♠ 280 34.03 N 118.31 W
Willroth 56 50.34 N 7.31 E
Wills, Lake ⊜ 162 21.25 S 128.51 E
Wills Creek ≃, Austl. 166 22.43 S 140.02 E
Wills Creek ≃, Oh., U.S. 188 40.09 N 81.55 W
Wills Creek Lake ⊜[1] 214 40.08 N 81.45 W
Willseyville 210 42.17 N 76.23 W
Willshire 216 40.45 N 84.48 W
Wills Point 222 32.43 N 96.01 W
Willston 284c 38.52 N 77.09 W
Willunga 168b 35.17 S 138.33 E
Wilmar 194 33.37 N 91.55 W
Wilmer, Al., U.S. 194 30.49 N 88.21 W
Wilmer, Pa., U.S. 285 40.07 N 75.32 W
Wilmer, Tx., U.S. 222 32.35 N 96.41 W
Wilmerding 279b 40.23 N 79.48 W
Wilmersdorf ◆[8] 264a 52.30 N 13.19 E
Wilmette 216 42.04 N 87.43 W
Wilmington, Austl. 166 32.39 S 138.07 E
Wilmington, Eng., U.K. 260 51.26 N 0.12 E
Wilmington, De., U.S. 208 39.44 N 75.32 W
Wilmington, Il., U.S. 216 41.18 N 88.08 W
Wilmington, Ma., U.S. 207 42.32 N 71.10 W
Wilmington, N.C., U.S. 192 34.13 N 77.56 W
Wilmington, Oh., U.S. 218 39.26 N 83.49 W
Wilmington, Vt., U.S. 188 42.52 N 72.52 W
Wilmington ◆[8] 280 33.47 N 118.16 W
Wilmington Manor 285 39.41 N 75.35 W
Wilmington Manor Gardens 285 39.40 N 75.34 W
Wilmore, Ky., U.S. 192 37.51 N 84.39 W
Wilmore, Pa., U.S. 214 40.23 N 78.43 W
Wilmot, Ar., U.S. 194 33.03 N 91.34 W
Wilmot, Oh., U.S. 214 40.39 N 81.38 W
Wilmot, S.D., U.S. 198 45.24 N 96.51 W
Wilmot, Wi., U.S. 216 42.31 N 88.11 W
Wilmot Woods ♠ 278 42.18 N 87.56 W
Wilmslow 44 53.20 N 2.15 W
Wilna → Vilnius 76 54.41 N 25.19 E
Wilnecote 42 52.36 N 1.40 W
Wilnsdorf 56 50.49 N 8.09 E
Wilpattu National Park ♠ 122 8.20 N 80.00 E
Wilpen 214 40.17 N 79.12 W
Wilpshire 262 53.47 N 2.28 W
Wilsall 202 45.59 N 110.39 W
Wilsdruff 54 51.05 N 13.32 E
Wilseder Berg ∧[2] 52 53.10 N 9.56 E
Wilseyville 226 38.23 N 120.31 W
Wilshamstead 42 52.05 N 0.27 W
Wilson, Austl. 166 32.00 S 138.22 E
Wilson, Ar., U.S. 194 35.34 N 90.02 W
Wilson, Ct., U.S. 207 41.48 N 72.38 W
Wilson, Il., U.S. 278 42.21 N 87.54 W
Wilson, Ks., U.S. 198 38.49 N 98.28 W
Wilson, La., U.S. 194 30.55 N 91.06 W
Wilson, N.Y., U.S. 210 43.18 N 78.49 W
Wilson, N.C., U.S. 192 35.43 N 77.54 W
Wilson, Ok., U.S. 196 34.09 N 97.25 W
Wilson, Pa., U.S. 208 40.41 N 75.14 W
Wilson, Tx., U.S. 196 33.19 N 101.44 W
Wilson ≃, Austl. 164 16.47 S 128.17 E
Wilson ≃, Austl. 166 27.38 S 141.24 E
Wilson ≃, Or., U.S. 224 45.28 N 123.53 W
Wilson, Cape › 176 66.59 N 81.28 W
Wilson, Mount ∧, Az., U.S. 200 35.59 N 114.37 W
Wilson, Mount ∧, Ca., U.S. 280 34.13 N 118.04 W
Wilson, Mount ∧, Co., U.S. 200 37.51 N 107.59 W
Wilson, Mount ∧, Nv., U.S. 204 38.15 N 114.23 W
Wilson, Mount ∧, Or., U.S. 224 45.04 N 121.39 W
Wilson, Mount ∧[2], Austl. 162 20.14 S 127.39 E
Wilson, Mount ∧[2], Austl. 168b 35.13 S 138.38 E
Wilson, Point ›, Austl. 169 38.05 S 144.30 E
Wilson, Point ›, Wa., U.S. 224 48.08 N 122.45 W
Wilson Cliffs ⊥[4] 162 22.03 S 127.09 E
Wilson Creek ≃, Tx., U.S. 222 33.07 N 96.35 W
Wilson Creek ≃, Wa., U.S. 202 47.25 N 119.07 W
Wilson Lake ⊜[1], Al., U.S. 194 34.49 N 87.30 W
Wilson Lake ⊜[1], Ks., U.S. 198 38.57 N 98.40 W
Wilson Range ⋀ 162 28.50 S 124.25 E
Wilson Run ≃, De., U.S. 285 39.48 N 75.35 W
Wilson Run ≃, Pa., U.S. 279b 40.13 N 79.37 W
Wilsons Beach 186 44.56 N 66.56 W
Wilson's Creek National Battlefield ♠ 194 37.06 N 93.27 W
Wilsons Promontory › 166 38.55 S 146.20 E
Wilsons Promontory National Park ♠ 166 39.00 S 146.25 E
Wilsonville, Il., U.S. 219 39.04 N 89.51 W
Wilsonville, Ne., U.S. 198 40.06 N 100.06 W
Wilsonville, Or., U.S. 224 45.18 N 122.46 W
Wilster 52 53.55 N 9.22 E
Wilthen 54 51.06 N 14.24 E
Wilton, Eng., U.K. 42 51.05 N 1.52 W
Wilton, Ct., U.S. 207 41.11 N 73.26 W
Wilton, Me., U.S. 188 44.35 N 70.13 W
Wilton, N.H., U.S. 207 42.50 N 71.44 W
Wilton, N.Y., U.S. 210 43.11 N 73.45 W
Wilton, N.D., U.S. 198 47.09 N 100.46 W
Wilton, Wi., U.S. 190 43.48 N 90.31 W
Wilton ≃ 164 14.45 S 134.33 E
Wilton Creek ≃ 212 44.12 N 76.56 W
Wilton Farm Acres 284b 39.18 N 76.50 W
Wilton Manors 220 26.09 N 80.08 W
Wiltshire □[6] 42 51.15 N 1.50 W
Wiltz 56 49.57 N 5.55 E
Wiluna 162 26.36 S 120.13 E
Wimapedi ≃ 184 55.27 N 99.07 W
Wimauma 220 27.42 N 82.17 W
Wimberley 196 30.00 N 98.06 W
Wimbleball Reservoir ⊜[1] 42 51.04 N 3.28 W
Wimbledon 198 47.10 N 98.27 W
Wimbledon ◆[8] 260 51.25 N 0.12 W
Wimbledon Common ♠ 260 51.26 N 0.14 W
Wimborne Minster 42 50.48 N 1.59 W
Wimereux 50 50.46 N 1.37 E
Wimmelburg 54 51.31 N 11.30 E
Wimmenau 56 48.55 N 7.25 E
Wimmera ≃ 169 36.55 S 142.56 E
Wimmis 58 46.41 N 7.38 E
Winagami Lake ⊜ 182 55.38 N 116.45 W
Winam C 154 0.15 S 34.35 E
Winamac 216 41.03 N 86.36 W
Winburg 158 28.37 S 27.00 E
Winburne 214 40.57 N 78.08 W
Wincanton 42 51.04 N 2.25 W
Wincham 262 53.16 N 2.29 W
Winchcombe 42 51.57 N 1.58 W
Winchelsea, Austl. 169 38.15 S 143.59 E
Winchelsea, Eng., U.K. 42 50.55 N 0.42 E
Winchendon 207 42.41 N 72.02 W
Winchester, On., Can. 212 45.06 N 75.21 W
Winchester, N.Z. 172 44.12 S 171.17 E
Winchester, Eng., U.K. 42 51.04 N 1.19 W
Winchester, Ca., U.S. 228 33.42 N 117.05 W
Winchester, Id., U.S. 202 46.14 N 116.37 W
Winchester, Il., U.S. 219 39.37 N 90.27 W
Winchester, In., U.S. 218 40.10 N 84.58 W
Winchester, Ky., U.S. 192 37.59 N 84.10 W
Winchester, Ma., U.S. 283 42.27 N 71.08 W
Winchester, N.H., U.S. 207 42.46 N 72.23 W
Winchester, Oh., U.S. 218 38.56 N 83.39 W
Winchester, Tn., U.S. 194 35.11 N 86.06 W
Winchester, Tx., U.S. 222 30.01 N 97.01 W
Winchester, Va., U.S. 188 39.11 N 78.10 W
Winchester Cathedral ⊛[1] 42 51.04 N 1.19 W
Winchmore Hill 260 51.39 N 0.39 W
Winchmore Hill ◆[8] 260 51.38 N 0.06 W
Wind ≃, Yk., Can. 180 65.49 N 135.18 W
Wind ≃, Wa., U.S. 224 45.43 N 121.47 W
Wind ≃, Wy., U.S. 202 43.35 N 108.13 W
Windang 170 34.32 S 150.53 E
Windau → Ventspils 76 57.24 N 21.36 E
Windber 214 40.14 N 78.50 W
Wind Cave National Park ♠ 198 43.32 N 103.25 W
Windeck 56 50.48 N 7.37 E
Winder 192 33.59 N 83.43 W
Winder, Lake ⊜ 220 28.15 N 80.51 W
Windera 166 26.03 S 151.50 E
Windermere, B.C., Can. 182 50.30 N 115.58 W
Windermere, Eng., U.K. 44 54.23 N 2.54 W
Windermere, Fl., U.S. 220 28.30 N 81.32 W
Windermere ⊜ 44 54.22 N 2.56 W
Windermere Lake ⊜ 190 47.56 N 83.47 W
Winder Village 285 40.06 N 74.52 W
Windfall, Ab., Can. 182 54.11 N 116.15 W
Windfall, In., U.S. 216 40.21 N 85.57 W
Windgap 210 40.51 N 75.18 W
Windham, Ct., U.S. 207 41.41 N 72.09 W
Windham, N.H., U.S. 283 42.48 N 71.18 W
Windham, N.Y., U.S. 210 42.19 N 74.15 W
Windham, Oh., U.S. 214 41.14 N 81.02 W
Windham □[6], Ct., U.S. 207 41.55 N 71.55 W
Windham □[6], Vt., U.S. 207 42.50 N 72.43 W
Windham Manor 284c 39.04 N 77.00 W
Windhoek 156 22.34 S 17.06 E
Windigo ≃ 184 53.22 N 91.48 W
Windigo Lake ⊜ 184 52.35 N 91.32 W
Windisch 58 47.29 N 8.13 E
Windischeschenbach 60 49.48 N 12.09 E
Windischgarsten 61 47.44 N 14.20 E
Wind Lake 216 42.49 N 88.09 W
Wind Lake ⊜ 216 42.50 N 88.09 W
Windlass Run ≃ 284b 39.24 N 76.24 W
Windleite ∧ 54 51.22 N 10.56 E
Windlesham 260 51.22 N 0.40 W
Windley Key I 220 24.57 N 80.35 W
Windmill Point ›, On., Can. 284a 42.52 N 79.01 W
Windmill Point ›, Mi., U.S. 281 42.22 N 82.55 W
Windmill Point ›, Va., U.S. 208 37.37 N 76.17 W
Windom, Mn., U.S. 198 43.51 N 95.07 W
Windom, N.Y., U.S. 210 42.47 N 78.48 W
Windom Peak ∧ 200 37.37 N 107.35 W
Windorah 166 25.26 S 142.39 E
Windorf, Dtsch. 60 48.37 N 13.13 E
Windorf, Öst. 61 48.27 N 14.02 E
Window Rock 200 35.40 N 109.03 W
Wind Point 216 42.47 N 87.45 W
Wind River Indian Reservation ◆[4] 202 43.26 N 109.00 W
Wind River Peak ∧ 200 42.42 N 109.07 W
Wind River Range ⋀ 200 43.05 N 109.25 W
Windrush ≃ 42 51.42 N 1.25 W
Windsbach 56 49.14 N 10.50 E
Windsor, Austl. 168b 34.25 S 138.20 E
Windsor, Austl. 170 33.37 S 150.49 E
Windsor, Nf., Can. 186 48.57 N 55.40 W
Windsor, N.S., Can. 186 44.59 N 64.08 W
Windsor, On., Can. 214 42.18 N 83.01 W
Windsor, On., Can. 281 42.18 N 83.01 W
Windsor, P.Q., Can. 206 45.34 N 72.00 W
Windsor, Eng., U.K. 42 51.29 N 0.38 W
Windsor, Ca., U.S. 204 38.33 N 122.49 W
Windsor, Co., U.S. 200 40.28 N 104.54 W
Windsor, Ct., U.S. 207 41.51 N 72.38 W
Windsor, Il., U.S. 194 39.26 N 88.35 W
Windsor, In., U.S. 218 40.09 N 85.12 W
Windsor, Mo., U.S. 194 38.31 N 93.31 W
Windsor, N.J., U.S. 208 40.15 N 74.35 W
Windsor, N.Y., U.S. 210 42.05 N 75.39 W
Windsor, N.C., U.S. 192 35.59 N 76.56 W
Windsor, Oh., U.S. 214 41.32 N 80.56 W
Windsor, Pa., U.S. 208 39.54 N 76.35 W
Windsor, Vt., U.S. 188 43.29 N 72.23 W
Windsor, Va., U.S. 208 36.48 N 76.44 W
Windsor, Wi., U.S. 216 43.13 N 89.20 W
Windsor, Gare ◆[5] 275a 45.30 N 73.34 W
Windsor, University of ⊛[2] 281 42.18 N 83.04 W
Windsor Airport ⊠ 214 42.17 N 82.58 W
Windsor and Maidenhead □[8] 260 51.28 N 0.37 W
Windsor Castle ⊥ 42 51.29 N 0.36 W
Windsor Forest 192 31.58 N 81.07 W
Windsor Forest ◆[3] 42 51.27 N 0.43 W
Windsor Great Park ♠ 260 51.27 N 0.37 W
Windsor Heights 214 40.12 N 80.40 W
Windsor Hills 280 33.59 N 118.21 W
Windsor Locks 207 41.55 N 72.37 W
Windsor Race Course ♠ 260 51.29 N 0.39 W
Windsor Raceway ♠ 281 42.15 N 83.05 W
Windsor Terrace 284b 39.19 N 76.43 W
Windsorton 158 28.16 S 24.44 E
Windsorville 207 41.53 N 72.32 W
Windthorst 196 33.34 N 98.26 W
Windward Islands II 238 13.00 N 61.00 W
Windward Passage ⊍ 238 20.00 N 73.50 W
Windy Hills 285 39.48 N 75.35 W
Windy Lake ⊜ 184 54.22 N 102.35 W
Windy Peak ∧, Co., U.S. 200 38.21 N 106.16 W
Windy Peak ∧, Wa., U.S. 202 48.56 N 119.58 W
Windy Run ≃ 284c 38.54 N 77.05 W
Winefred ≃ 184 56.02 N 110.36 W
Winefred Lake ⊜ 182 55.30 N 110.35 W
Winejok 140 9.01 N 27.34 E
Winesburg 214 40.37 N 81.42 W
Winfield, Ab., Can. 182 52.58 N 114.26 W
Winfield, Al., U.S. 194 33.55 N 87.49 W
Winfield, Il., U.S. 216 41.52 N 88.10 W
Winfield, Ia., U.S. 190 41.07 N 91.26 W
Winfield, Ks., U.S. 198 37.14 N 96.59 W
Winfield, Mo., U.S. 219 38.59 N 90.44 W
Winfield, N.J., U.S. 276 40.38 N 74.17 W
Winfield, Tx., U.S. 222 33.10 N 95.07 W
Winfield, W.V., U.S. 188 38.31 N 81.53 W
Wing 198 47.08 N 100.16 W
Wing ≃ 198 46.29 N 94.58 W
Wingate, Eng., U.K. 44 54.44 N 1.23 W
Wingate, Md., U.S. 208 38.16 N 76.04 W
Wingate, N.C., U.S. 192 34.59 N 80.26 W
Wingate Mountains ⋀ 164 14.29 S 130.42 E
Wingates 262 53.34 N 2.32 W
Wingdale 210 41.39 N 73.34 W
Wingecarribee ≃ 170 34.23 S 150.07 E
Wingecarribee Reservoir ⊜[1] 170 34.34 S 150.30 E
Wingello 170 34.42 S 150.09 E
Wingene 50 51.04 N 3.16 E
Wingen-sur-Moder 56 48.55 N 7.22 E
Wingerworth 44 53.12 N 1.26 W
Wingham, Austl. 166 31.52 S 152.22 E
Wingham, On., Can. 212 43.53 N 81.19 W
Wingham, Eng., U.K. 42 51.17 N 1.13 E
Wing Lake Shores 281 42.33 N 83.17 W
Wingles 50 50.29 N 2.51 E
Wingo 194 36.38 N 88.44 W
Wings Field ⊠ 285 40.08 N 75.16 W
Wingst 52 53.43 N 9.03 E
Winhole Channel ⊍ 276 43.37 N 73.48 W
Winhöring 60 48.16 N 12.39 E
Winifred 202 47.33 N 109.22 W
Winifreda 252 36.15 S 64.14 W
Winisk 176 55.15 N 85.12 W
Winisk ≃ 176 55.17 N 85.05 W
Winisk Lake ⊜ 176 52.55 N 87.22 W
Wink 196 31.45 N 103.06 W
Winkana 110 15.44 N 98.01 E
Winkelman 200 32.59 N 110.46 W
Winkelpos 158 27.35 S 26.49 E
Winklarn 60 49.26 N 12.29 E
Winkler, Mb., Can. 184 49.11 N 97.56 W
Winkler, Tx., U.S. 222 31.56 N 96.13 W
Winklern 64 46.52 N 12.52 E
Winlaw 182 49.37 N 117.34 W
Winlock 224 46.29 N 122.56 W
Winneba 150 5.25 N 0.36 W
Winnebago, Il., U.S. 190 42.15 N 89.14 W
Winnebago, Mn., U.S. 190 43.46 N 94.09 W
Winnebago, Ne., U.S. 198 42.14 N 96.28 W
Winnebago □[6] 216 42.17 N 89.06 W
Winnebago ≃ 190 43.03 N 92.57 W
Winnebago, Lake ⊜ 190 44.00 N 88.25 W
Winnebago Indian Reservation ◆[4], Ne., U.S. 198 42.15 N 96.31 W
Winnebago Indian Reservation ◆[4], Wi., U.S. 190 44.15 N 90.38 W
Winnecke, Mount ∧[2] 162 18.47 S 130.20 E
Winnecke Creek ≃ 162 18.35 S 131.34 E
Winneconne 190 44.06 N 88.42 W
Winneconnet 283 41.59 N 71.08 W
Winneconnet Pond ⊜ 283 41.58 N 71.08 W
Winnekendonk 52 51.36 N 6.17 E
Winnekenni Park ♠ 283 42.47 N 71.04 W
Winnemucca 204 40.58 N 117.44 W
Winnemucca Lake ⊜ 204 40.09 N 119.20 W
Winnenden 56 48.53 N 9.24 E
Winner 198 43.22 N 99.51 W
Winnetka 216 42.06 N 87.44 W
Winnetka ◆[8] 280 34.13 N 118.35 W
Winnett 202 47.00 N 108.21 W
Winnfield 194 31.55 N 92.38 W
Winnibigoshish, Lake ⊜ 190 47.27 N 94.12 W
Winnie 194 29.49 N 94.23 W
Winning 162 23.09 S 114.32 E
Winningen, Dtsch. 54 51.49 N 11.26 E
Winningen, Dtsch. 56 50.18 N 7.31 E
Winnipeg 184 49.53 N 97.09 W
Winnipeg ≃ 184 50.38 N 96.19 W
Winnipeg, Lake ⊜ 184 52.00 N 97.00 W
Winnipeg Beach 184 50.31 N 96.58 W
Winnipegosis 184 51.39 N 99.56 W
Winnipegosis, Lake ⊜ 184 52.30 N 100.00 W
Winnipesaukee, Lake ⊜ 188 43.35 N 71.20 W
Winnsboro, La., U.S. 194 32.09 N 91.43 W
Winnsboro, S.C., U.S. 192 34.22 N 81.05 W
Winnsboro, Tx., U.S. 222 32.57 N 95.17 W
Winnsboro, Lake ⊜[1] 222 32.55 N 95.21 W
Winnsboro Mills 192 34.21 N 81.05 W
Winnweiler 56 49.34 N 7.51 E
Winona, Ks., U.S. 198 39.03 N 101.14 W
Winona, Mi., U.S. 190 46.52 N 88.55 W
Winona, Mn., U.S. 190 44.03 N 91.38 W
Winona, Ms., U.S. 194 33.28 N 89.43 W
Winona, Mo., U.S. 194 37.00 N 91.19 W
Winona, Oh., U.S. 214 40.50 N 80.54 W
Winona, Tx., U.S. 222 32.29 N 95.10 W
Winona Lake, In., U.S. 216 41.13 N 85.49 W
Winona Lake, N.Y., U.S. 210 41.31 N 74.03 W
Winona Lake ⊜ 216 41.13 N 85.50 W
Winooski 188 44.29 N 73.11 W
Winooski ≃ 188 44.30 N 73.15 W
Winooski, North Branch ≃ 188 44.15 N 72.35 W
Winschoten 52 53.08 N 7.02 E
Winscombe 42 51.18 N 2.50 W
Winsen, Dtsch. 52 52.41 N 9.54 E
Winsen, Dtsch. 52 53.22 N 10.12 E
Winsford, Eng., U.K. 42 51.06 N 3.33 W
Winsford, Eng., U.K. 44 53.12 N 2.32 W
Winshill 42 52.48 N 1.36 W
Winside 198 42.10 N 97.10 W
Winslow, Eng., U.K. 42 51.57 N 0.54 W
Winslow, Az., U.S. 200 35.01 N 110.41 W
Winslow, Me., U.S. 188 44.32 N 69.37 W
Winslow, N.J., U.S. 285 39.39 N 74.52 W
Winslow Reef ✦[2] 14 1.36 S 174.57 W
Winsted, Ct., U.S. 207 41.55 N 73.03 W
Winsted, Mn., U.S. 190 44.57 N 94.02 W
Winston, Fl., U.S. 220 28.01 N 82.00 W
Winston, Or., U.S. 202 43.07 N 123.24 W
Winston Churchill Memorial ⊛ 219 38.52 N 91.58 W
Winston Creek ≃ 224 46.30 N 122.40 W
Winston-Salem 192 36.05 N 80.14 W
Winsum 52 53.19 N 6.31 E
Wintego Lake ⊜ 184 55.33 N 102.52 W
Winter 190 45.49 N 91.00 W
Winter Beach 220 27.43 N 80.25 W
Winterberg, Dtsch. 56 51.11 N 8.32 E
Winterberg, Dtsch. 263 51.17 N 7.18 E
Winterberg ∧[2] 263 51.20 N 7.13 E
Winterberge ⋀ 158 32.28 S 26.15 E
Winterbourne Abbas 42 50.43 N 2.34 W
Winter Creek ≃ 280 34.12 N 118.02 W
Winterfeld 54 52.44 N 11.14 E
Winter Garden 220 28.33 N 81.35 W
Winter Harbor 188 44.23 N 68.05 W
Winter Harbour 182 50.31 N 128.02 W
Winterhaven, Ca., U.S. 204 32.44 N 114.38 W
Winter Haven, Fl., U.S. 220 28.01 N 81.43 W
Winter Hill ∧[2] 262 53.38 N 2.31 W
Wintering ≃ 198 48.12 N 100.34 W
Wintering Lake ⊜ 184 55.24 N 97.42 W
Winter Island I, N.T., Can. 176 66.14 N 83.04 W
Winter Island I, Ca., U.S. 282 38.03 N 121.51 W
Winter Island I, Ma., U.S. 283 42.32 N 70.52 W
Winterlingen 58 48.11 N 9.07 E
Winter Park, Fl., U.S. 220 28.35 N 81.20 W
Winter Park, N.C., U.S. 192 34.12 N 77.53 W
Winterport 188 44.38 N 68.51 W
Winters, Ca., U.S. 226 38.31 N 121.58 W
Winters, Tx., U.S. 196 31.57 N 99.57 W
Winters Bayou ≃ 222 30.22 N 95.06 W
Winters Canal ≅ 226 38.32 N 121.58 W
Wintersdorf 54 51.03 N 12.21 E
Winterset, Ia., U.S. 190 41.19 N 94.00 W
Winterset, Oh., U.S. 214 40.06 N 81.25 W
Winter Springs 220 28.41 N 81.18 W
Winters Run ≃ 208 39.26 N 76.18 W
Winterstown 208 39.50 N 76.37 W
Wintersville 214 40.22 N 80.42 W
Winterswijk 52 51.58 N 6.44 E
Winterthur, Schw. 58 47.30 N 8.43 E
Winterthur, De., U.S. 285 39.48 N 75.35 W
Winterthur Museum ⊛ 285 39.48 N 75.36 W
Winterton, Nf., Can. 186 47.58 N 53.20 W
Winterton, S. Afr. 158 28.46 S 29.35 E
Winterton, Eng., U.K. 44 53.39 N 0.36 W
Winterton-on-Sea 42 52.43 N 1.42 E
Winterville, Ga., U.S. 192 33.58 N 83.16 W
Winterville, Ms., U.S. 194 33.30 N 91.03 W
Winterville, N.C., U.S. 192 35.31 N 77.24 W
Winthrop, Ct., U.S. 207 41.21 N 72.29 W
Winthrop, Ia., U.S. 190 42.28 N 91.44 W
Winthrop, Me., U.S. 188 44.18 N 69.58 W
Winthrop, Ma., U.S. 283 42.22 N 70.59 W
Winthrop, Mn., U.S. 190 44.32 N 94.21 W
Winthrop, Wa., U.S. 182 48.28 N 120.11 W
Winthrop, Lake ⊜ 283 42.11 N 71.25 W
Winthrop Harbor 216 42.28 N 87.49 W
Wintinna 162 27.44 S 134.07 E
Wintinna Creek ≃ 162 27.47 S 134.14 E
Winton, Austl. 166 22.23 S 143.02 E
Winton, N.Z. 172 46.09 S 168.20 E
Winton, S. Afr. 158 27.29 S 22.34 E
Winton, Ca., U.S. 226 37.23 N 120.37 W
Winton, N.C., U.S. 192 36.23 N 76.55 W
Winton, Wa., U.S. 224 47.44 N 120.44 W
Wintzenheim 58 48.04 N 7.17 E
Winwick 262 53.26 N 2.36 W
Winz 263 51.23 N 7.09 E
Winzenberg 263 51.06 N 7.38 E
Winzer 60 48.44 N 13.04 E
Winzermark 263 51.23 N 7.08 E
Wipper ≃, Dtsch. 54 51.47 N 11.42 E
Wipper ≃, Dtsch. 54 51.17 N 11.10 E
Wipper ≃, Dtsch. 263 51.07 N 7.24 E
Wipperdorf 54 51.28 N 10.42 E
Wipperfeld 263 51.05 N 7.19 E
Wipperfürth 56 51.07 N 7.23 E
Wirātnagar 124 26.29 N 87.17 E
Wīrendranagar 124 28.35 N 81.38 E
Wireton, Il., U.S. 278 41.40 N 87.42 W
Wireton, Pa., U.S. 279b 40.34 N 80.14 W
Wīrgañj 124 27.00 N 84.52 E
Wirges 56 50.28 N 7.48 E
Wiriagar ≃ 164 2.17 S 132.52 E
Wirksworth 44 53.05 N 1.34 W
Wirosari 115a 7.05 S 111.05 E
Wirral □[8] 262 53.22 N 3.05 W
Wirral ›[1] 44 53.20 N 3.03 W
Wirraminna 166 31.12 S 136.15 E
Wirrulla 162 32.24 S 134.31 E
Wisbech 42 52.40 N 0.10 E
Wisby → Visby 26 57.38 N 18.18 E
Wiscasset 188 44.00 N 69.39 W
Wischhafen 52 53.46 N 9.19 E
Wisconsin □[3], U.S. 178 44.45 N 89.30 W
Wisconsin □[3], U.S. 190 44.45 N 89.30 W
Wisconsin ≃ 190 43.00 N 91.10 W
Wisconsin, Lake ⊜[1] 190 43.24 N 89.43 W
Wisconsin Dells 190 43.37 N 89.46 W
Wisconsin Dells V 190 43.41 N 89.49 W
Wisconsin Rapids 190 44.23 N 89.49 W
Wiscoy 210 42.30 N 78.05 W
Wisdom 202 45.37 N 113.27 W
Wisdom, Lake ⊜ 164 5.20 S 147.05 E
Wise 192 36.58 N 82.34 W
Wise □[6] 222 33.07 N 97.40 W
Wise ≃ 202 45.48 N 112.57 W
Wiseman 180 67.25 N 150.06 W
Wisemans Ferry 170 33.24 S 150.59 E
Wises Landing 218 38.35 N 85.25 W
Wishart 184 51.34 N 104.00 W
Wishaw 46 55.47 N 3.56 W
Wishek 198 46.16 N 99.33 W
Wishkah ≃ 224 46.58 N 123.45 W
Wishram 224 45.39 N 120.57 W
Wiske ≃ 44 54.15 N 1.26 W
Wisła 30 49.40 N 18.52 E
Wisła ≃ 30 54.22 N 18.55 E
Wisley Aerodrome ⊠ 260 51.18 N 0.28 W
Wisley Gardens ♠ 260 51.19 N 0.29 W
Wisłok ≃ 30 50.13 N 22.32 E
Wisłoka ≃ 30 50.27 N 21.23 E
Wismar, Dtsch. 54 53.53 N 11.28 E
Wismar, Guy. 246 6.00 N 58.18 W
Wismarbucht C 54 53.57 N 11.25 E
Wisner, La., U.S. 194 31.58 N 91.39 W
Wisner, Ne., U.S. 198 41.59 N 96.54 W
Wissahickon Creek ≃ 285 40.01 N 75.12 W
Wissant 50 50.53 N 1.40 E
Wissembourg 56 49.02 N 7.57 E
Wissen 56 50.47 N 7.43 E
Wissenkerke 52 51.35 N 3.45 E
Wissey ≃ 42 52.33 N 0.21 E
Wissinoming ◆[8] 285 40.01 N 75.04 W
Wissous 261 48.44 N 2.20 E
Wister 194 34.58 N 94.43 W
Wisznice 30 51.48 N 23.12 E
Witbank 158 25.56 S 29.07 E
Witberge ⋀ 158 30.45 S 27.32 E
Witbooisvlei 156 25.04 S 18.27 E
Witchekan Lake ⊜ 184 53.25 N 107.35 W
Witches Falls National Park ♠ 171a 27.56 S 153.10 E
Witch Hazel 224 45.30 N 122.46 W
Witdraai 158 26.58 S 20.45 E
Witfield 273d 26.11 S 28.12 E
Witham 42 51.48 N 0.38 E
Witham ≃ 44 53.06 N 0.13 W
Withamsville 218 39.03 N 84.16 W
Withens Clough Reservoir ⊜[1] 262 53.42 N 2.02 W
Witheridge 42 50.55 N 3.42 W
Withernsea 44 53.44 N 0.02 E
Witherspoon, Mount ∧ 180 61.23 N 147.12 W
Withington ◆[8] 262 53.26 N 2.14 W
Withington Green 262 53.14 N 2.18 W
Withlacoochee ≃, U.S. 192 30.24 N 83.10 W
Withlacoochee ≃, Fl., U.S. 192 29.00 N 82.45 W
Withnell 262 53.42 N 2.34 W
Withokspruit ≃ 273d 26.19 S 28.21 E
Witjira National Park ♠ 162 26.25 S 135.40 E
Wit-Kei ≃ 158 32.09 S 27.24 E
Witkoppies ∧ 158 27.44 S 29.20 E
Witkowo 30 52.27 N 17.47 E
Witless Bay 186 47.16 N 52.50 W
Witley 42 51.09 N 0.38 W
Wit-Mfolozi ≃ 158 28.22 S 31.58 E
Witney 42 51.48 N 1.29 W
Witnica 30 52.40 N 14.55 E
Wit Nossob ≃ 156 23.05 S 18.45 E
Witpoort 158 27.10 S 26.08 E
Witrivier 156 24.40 S 31.00 E
Witry-lès-Reims 50 49.18 N 4.07 E
Witsand 158 34.24 S 20.50 E
Witt 219 39.15 N 89.20 W
Wittabrenna Creek ≃ 166 29.20 S 142.43 E
Witteberg ⋀ 158 28.40 S 28.02 E
Witteberge ⋀ 158 33.18 S 20.36 E
Wittelsheim 58 47.49 N 7.15 E
Witten 56 51.26 N 7.20 E
Wittenau ◆[8] 264a 52.35 N 13.20 E
Wittenberg → Lutherstadt Wittenberg, Dtsch. 54 51.52 N 12.39 E
Wittenberg, Wi., U.S. 190 44.49 N 89.10 W
Wittenberge 54 53.00 N 11.44 E
Wittenburg 54 53.31 N 11.04 E
Wittenhagen 54 54.11 N 13.05 E
Wittenheim 58 47.49 N 7.20 E
Wittenoom 162 22.17 S 118.19 E
Wittensee ⊜ 41 54.23 N 9.45 E
Wittering 42 52.37 N 0.27 W
Wittgensdorf 54 50.53 N 12.52 E
Wittichenau 54 51.23 N 14.14 E
Wittingen 54 52.43 N 10.44 E
Wittislingen 56 48.37 N 10.25 E
Wittlaer 56 51.19 N 6.44 E
Wittlich 56 49.59 N 6.53 E
Wittman 208 38.47 N 76.17 W
Wittmar 54 52.07 N 10.38 E
Wittmund 52 53.34 N 7.47 E
Witton Park ♠ 262 53.45 N 2.31 W
Wittow ›[1] 54 54.38 N 13.19 E
Wittstock 54 53.10 N 12.29 E
Witu 154 2.23 S 40.26 E
Witu Islands II 164 4.40 S 149.25 E
Witvlai 156 22.23 S 18.32 E
Witwatersrand, University of the ⊛[2] 273d 26.12 S 28.02 E
Witwatersrand Gold Mine ◆[7] 273d 26.12 S 28.11 E
Witwatersrant ◆[1] 158 26.00 S 27.00 E
Witzenhausen 56 51.20 N 9.51 E
Witzhelden 263 51.07 N 7.06 E
Witzputz 156 27.25 S 17.43 E
Wiveliscombe 42 51.03 N 3.19 W
Wivenhoe 42 51.52 N 0.58 E
Wivenhoe Reservoir ⊜[1] 171a 27.20 S 152.35 E
Wiwa Creek ≃ 184 50.02 N 106.31 W
Wixom 216 42.31 N 83.32 W
Wiżajny 30 54.23 N 22.51 E
Wizernes 50 50.43 N 2.14 E
Wjatka → V'atka ≃ 80 55.36 N 51.30 E
W. Kerr Scott Reservoir ⊜[1] 192 36.07 N 81.15 W
Wkra ≃ 30 52.27 N 20.44 E
Wladiwostok → Vladivostok 89 43.10 N 131.56 E
Władysławowo 30 54.49 N 18.25 E
Wleń 30 51.01 N 15.40 E
Wlingi 115a 8.05 S 112.19 E
Włocławek 30 52.39 N 19.02 E
Włocławek □[4] 30 52.30 N 19.05 E
Włodawa 30 51.34 N 23.32 E
Włoszczowa 30 50.52 N 19.59 E
Wnion ≃ 42 52.45 N 3.54 W
Woady Yaloak ≃ 169 38.06 S 143.33 E
Wobaer 85 39.19 N 75.32 E
Wöbbelin 54 53.24 N 11.30 E
Woburn 207 42.28 N 71.09 W
Woburn ◆[8] 275b 43.46 N 79.13 W
Woburn Sands 42 52.01 N 0.39 W
Woden, Austl. 171b 35.22 S 149.08 E
Woden, Tx., U.S. 222 31.30 N 94.32 W
Wodgina 162 21.11 S 118.40 E
Wodonga 166 36.07 S 146.54 E
Wodzisław Śląski 30 50.00 N 18.28 E
Woensdrecht 52 51.26 N 4.18 E
Woerdeke 85 39.41 N 77.53 E
Woerden 52 52.05 N 4.54 E
Woerth 56 48.56 N 7.45 E
Woëvre ◆[1] 56 49.05 N 5.40 E
Wofosi 105 40.09 N 115.18 E
Wo Fo Si (Temple of the Sleeping Buddha) ⊛[1] 105 40.01 N 116.12 E
Wognum 52 52.41 N 5.01 E
Wohlde 41 54.24 N 9.17 E
Wohlen 58 47.21 N 8.17 E
Wohlensee ⊜ 58 46.58 N 7.20 E
Wohlford, Lake ⊜[1] 228 33.10 N 116.59 W
Wohlthat Mountains ⋀ 9 71.35 S 12.20 E
Wohra ≃ 56 50.49 N 8.55 E
Woi 140 7.53 N 31.10 E
Woincourt 50 50.04 N 1.32 E
Woippy, Dtsch. 56 49.09 N 6.09 E
Woippy, Fr. 56 49.09 N 6.09 E
Wojcieszów 30 50.58 N 15.56 E
Wokalup 168a 33.06 S 115.53 E
Wokam, Pulau I 164 5.37 S 134.30 E
Wokha 120 26.06 N 94.16 E
Woking, Ab., Can. 182 55.35 N 118.46 W
Woking, Eng., U.K. 42 51.20 N 0.34 W
Woking □[8] 260 51.19 N 0.32 W
Wokingham 42 51.25 N 0.51 W
Wokingham Creek ≃ 166 22.19 S 142.30 E
Wolbach 198 41.24 N 98.24 W
Wolbeck 52 51.55 N 7.43 E
Wolbrom 30 50.24 N 19.46 E
Wolcott, Ct., U.S. 207 41.36 N 72.59 W
Wolcott, In., U.S. 216 40.45 N 87.02 W
Wolcott, N.Y., U.S. 210 43.13 N 76.48 W
Wolcott Creek ≃ 210 43.17 N 76.50 W
Wolcottsburg 210 43.04 N 78.38 W
Wolcottsville 210 43.07 N 78.31 W
Wolcottville 216 41.32 N 85.22 W
Wołcza ≃ 54 53.58 N 14.53 E
Wołczenica ≃ 54 53.52 N 14.44 E
Wołczyn 30 51.01 N 18.03 E
Woldberg ⋀[1] 52 52.25 N 5.55 E
Woldegk 54 53.27 N 13.35 E
Woldingham 260 51.17 N 0.02 W
Woleai I[1] 108 7.21 N 143.52 E
Woleu-Ntem □[4] 152 1.30 N 12.00 E
Wolf ≃, On., Can. 190 48.49 N 88.30 W
Wolf ≃, U.S. 194 35.09 N 90.04 W
Wolf ≃, Ks., U.S. 198 39.54 N 95.11 W
Wolf ≃, Ms., U.S. 194 30.21 N 89.18 W
Wolf ≃, Wi., U.S. 190 44.11 N 88.48 W
Wolf, Isla I 246a 1.23 N 91.49 W
Wolf, Volcán ∧[1] 246a 0.02 N 91.20 W
Wolfach 58 48.17 N 8.13 E
Wolf-Bay 186 50.16 N 60.08 W
Wolf Creek, Mt., U.S. 202 47.00 N 112.04 W
Wolf Creek, Or., U.S. 202 42.41 N 123.23 W
Wolf Creek ≃, U.S. 196 36.35 N 99.30 W
Wolf Creek ≃, Ca., U.S. 226 39.02 N 121.08 W
Wolf Creek ≃, Co., U.S. 200 40.12 N 108.29 W
Wolf Creek ≃, In., U.S. 216 41.15 N 87.07 W
Wolf Creek ≃, Ia., U.S. 190 42.20 N 92.09 W
Wolf Creek ≃, Mt., U.S. 198 48.05 N 105.40 W
Wolf Creek ≃, Mt., U.S. 202 47.37 N 109.38 W
Wolf Creek ≃, Oh., U.S. 214 41.16 N 83.11 W
Wolf Creek ≃, Pa., U.S. 214 41.03 N 80.07 W
Wolf Creek ≃, S.D., U.S. 198 43.21 N 97.37 W
Wolf Creek ≃, S.D., U.S. 198 44.42 N 98.40 W
Wolf Creek Lake ⊜[1] 198 38.14 N 95.41 W
Wolf Creek Pass)(200 37.29 N 106.48 W
Wolf Creek State Park ♠ 219 39.30 N 88.41 W
Wolfdale 214 40.12 N 80.17 W
Wolfe □[6] 206 45.45 N 71.30 W
Wolfeboro 188 43.35 N 71.12 W
Wolfe City 196 33.22 N 96.04 W
Wolfegg 58 47.49 N 9.47 E
Wolfe Island 212 44.12 N 76.26 W
Wolfe Island I 212 44.12 N 76.20 W
Wolfe Lake ⊜ 212 44.40 N 76.30 W
Wolfen 54 51.40 N 12.16 E
Wolfenbüttel 52 52.10 N 10.32 E
Wolfenden, Mount ∧ 182 50.26 N 127.33 W
Wolfenschiessen 58 46.55 N 8.24 E
Wolfertschwenden 58 47.53 N 10.16 E
Wolfforth 196 33.30 N 102.01 W
Wolfgangsee ⊜ 64 47.44 N 13.26 E
Wolfhagen 56 51.19 N 9.10 E
Wölfis 54 50.48 N 10.46 E
Wolf Island I 212 44.33 N 78.15 W
Wolflake, In., U.S. 216 41.20 N 85.30 W
Wolf Lake, Mi., U.S. 216 43.15 N 86.06 W
Wolf Lake ⊜, Ab., Can. 182 54.42 N 110.59 W
Wolf Lake ⊜, On., Can. 212 44.44 N 78.11 W
Wolf Lake ⊜, Yk., Can. 180 60.40 N 131.40 W
Wolf Lake ⊜, U.S. 278 41.40 N 87.31 W
Wolf Lake ⊜, N.J., U.S. 276 40.57 N 74.42 W
Wolf Mountain ∧ 180 65.17 N 154.02 W
Wolfpassing 264b 48.19 N 16.11 E
Wolf Point 202 48.05 N 105.38 W
Wolframs-Eschenbach 56 49.14 N 10.43 E
Wolfratshausen 64 47.54 N 11.25 E
Wolf Rock I[2] 28 49.57 N 5.49 W
Wolf Run 214 40.30 N 80.54 W
Wolfsberg 61 46.51 N 14.51 E
Wolfsberg ∧[2] 263 51.38 N 6.27 E
Wolfsburg 54 52.25 N 10.47 E
Wolf's Castle 42 51.54 N 4.58 W
Wolfsegg am Hausruck 60 48.06 N 13.40 E
Wolfstein 56 49.35 N 7.36 E
Wolftrap Creek ≃ 284c 38.58 N 77.17 W
Wolf Trap Farms for the Performing Arts ♠ 284c 38.56 N 77.16 W
Wolfurt 58 47.28 N 9.45 E
Wolfville 186 45.05 N 64.22 W
Wolga → Volga ≃ 72 45.55 N 47.52 E
Wolgan ≃ 170 33.12 S 150.28 E
Wolgast 54 54.03 N 13.46 E
Wolgograd → Volgograd 80 48.44 N 44.25 E
Wolgograder Stausee → Volgogradskoje vodochranilišče ⊜[1] 80 49.20 N 45.00 E
Wolhusen 58 47.04 N 8.04 E
Wolin 30 53.50 N 14.35 E
Wolin I 54 53.55 N 14.31 E
Woliński Park Narodowy ♠ 30 53.55 N 14.30 E
Wolkenstein 54 50.39 N 13.04 E
Wolkersdorf 61 48.23 N 16.31 E
Wölkisch 54 51.13 N 13.21 E
Wolkramshausen 54 51.25 N 10.44 E
Wollangambe ≃ 170 33.21 S 150.35 E
Wollaston 42 52.15 N 0.40 W
Wollaston, Islas II 254 55.40 S 67.30 W
Wollaston Beach ⊥[2] 283 42.17 N 71.01 W
Wollaston Lake ⊜, On., Can. 212 44.50 N 77.50 W
Wollaston Lake ⊜, Sk., Can. 176 58.15 N 103.20 W
Wollaston Peninsula ›[1] 176 70.00 N 115.00 W
Wollemi Creek ≃ 170 33.13 S 150.31 E
Wollemi National Park ♠ 166 32.50 S 150.30 E
Wollogorang 166 17.13 S 137.57 E
Wollombi 170 32.56 S 151.09 E
Wollombi Brook ≃ 170 32.33 S 151.04 E
Wollondilly ≃ 170 33.57 S 150.26 E
Wollongong 170 34.25 S 150.54 E
Wöllstein 56 49.49 N 7.58 E
Wolmaransstad 158 27.12 S 26.13 E

≃ River	Fiuß	Río	Rivière	Rio			
≅ Canal	Kanal	Canal	Canal	Canal			
⌊ Waterfall, Rapids	Wasserfall, Stromschnellen	Cascada, Rápidos	Chute d'eau, Rapides	Cascata, Rápidos			
⊍ Strait	Meeresstraße	Estrecho	Détroit	Estreito			
C Bay, Gulf	Bucht, Golf	Bahía, Golfo	Baie, Golfe	Baía, Golfo			
⊜ Lake, Lakes	See, Seen	Lago, Lagos	Lac, Lacs	Lago, Lagos			
⋮ Swamp	Sumpf	Pantano	Marais	Pântano			
⊓ Ice Features, Glacier	Eis- und Gletscherformen	Accidentes Glaciales	Formes glaciaires	Acidentes glaciares			
⊤ Other Hydrographic Features	Andere Hydrographische Objekte	Otros Elementos Hidrográficos	Autres données hydrographiques	Outros acidentes hidrográficos			
✦ Submarine Features	Untermeerische Objekte	Accidentes Submarinos	Formes de relief sous-marin	Acidentes submarinos			
□ Political Unit	Politische Einheit	Unidad Politica	Entité politique	Unidade política			
⊛ Cultural Institution	Kulturelle Institution	Institución Cultural	Institution culturelle	Institução cultural			
⊥ Historical Site	Historische Stätte	Sitio Histórico	Site historique	Sitio histórico			
♠ Recreational Site	Erholungs- und Ferienort	Sitio de Recreo	Centre de loisirs	Area de Lazer			
⊠ Airport	Flughafen	Aeropuerto	Aéroport	Aeroporto			
■ Military Installation	Militäranlage	Instalación Militar	Installation militaire	Instalação militar			
◆ Miscellaneous	Verschiedenes	Misceláneo	Divers	Diversos			

Symbols in the index entries represent the broad categories identified in the key at the right. Symbols with superior numbers (∧¹) identify subcategories (see complete key on page I · 1).

Symbole im Register stellen die rechts im Schlüssel erklärten Kategorien dar. Symbole mit hochgestellten Ziffern (∧¹) bezeichnen Unterteilungen einer Kategorie (vgl. vollständigen Schlüssel auf Seite I · 1).

Los símbolos incluídos en el texto del índice representan las grandes categorías identificadas con la clave a la derecha. Los símbolos con números en su parte superior (∧¹) identifican las subcategorías (véase la clave completa en la página I · 1).

Os símbolos incluídos no texto do índice representam as grandes categorias identificadas com a chave à direita. Os símbolos com números em sua parte superior (∧¹) identificam as subcategorias (veja-se a chave completa à página I · 1).

Les symboles de l'index représentent les catégories indiquées dans la légende à droite. Les symboles suivis d'un indice (∧¹) représentent des sous-catégories (voir légende complète à la page I · 1).

Symbol	English	Deutsch	Español	Français	Português
∧	Mountain	Berg	Montaña	Montagne	Montanha
∧	Mountains	Gebirge	Montañas	Montagnes	Montanhas
⋊	Pass	Paß	Paso	Col	Passo
V	Valley, Canyon	Tal, Cañon	Valle, Cañón	Vallée, Canyon	Vale, Canhão
⌐	Plain	Ebene	Llano	Plaine	Planicie
➣	Cape	Kap	Cabo	Cap	Cabo
I	Island	Insel	Isla	Île	Ilha
I	Islands	Inseln	Islas	Îles	Ilhas
≃	Other Topographic Features	Andere Topographische Objekte	Otros Elementos Topográficos	Autres données topographiques	Outros acidentes topográficos

Wyth-Yaca I · 195

ESPAÑOL — Nombre | Página | Lat.°′ | Long.°′ W = Oeste
FRANÇAIS — Nom | Page | Lat.°′ | Long.°′ W = Ouest
PORTUGUÊS — Nome | Página | Lat.°′ | Long.°′ W = Oeste

Wytheville 192 36.56 N 81.05 W
Wytschegda
— Vyčegda ≃ 24 61.18 N 46.36 E
Wyvis, Ben ʌ 46 57.42 N 4.35 W

X

Xaafuun 144 10.25 N 51.16 E
Xaafuun, Raas › 144 10.27 N 51.24 E
Xàbia 34 38.47 N 0.10 E
Xabregas ◆ [8] 266c 38.44 N 9.07 W
Xá-Cassau 152 9.02 S 20.14 E
Xaçınçay ≃ 84 40.13 N 47.18 E
Xaclbal ≃ 236 16.06 N 90.58 W
Xaçmaz 84 41.28 N 48.48 E
Xaidulla 120 36.21 N 78.02 E
Xainza 120 30.57 N 88.38 E
Xaitongmoin 124 29.22 N 88.15 E
Xai-Xai 156 25.02 S 33.34 E
Xalapa 234 19.32 N 96.55 W
Xaldan 84 40.43 N 47.15 E
Xalin 144 9.06 N 48.37 E
Xalisco 234 21.27 N 104.54 W
Xallas ≃ 34 42.54 N 9.08 W
Xalostoc 234 19.24 N 98.03 W
Xalpatlahuac 234 17.01 N 99.18 W
Xaltianguis 234 17.04 N 99.50 W
Xam (Chu) ≃ 110 19.53 N 105.45 E
Xambioá 250 6.25 S 48.40 W
Xambrê ≃ 255 24.02 S 53.59 W
Xam Nua 110 20.25 N 104.02 E
Xá-Muteba 152 9.34 S 17.50 E
Xan (San) ≃ 110 13.32 N 105.58 E
Xang ≃ 124 29.22 N 89.09 E
Xangongo 152 16.43 S 15.01 E
Xankändi
(Stepanakert) 84 39.49 N 46.44 E
Xanlar 84 40.34 N 46.20 E
Xanten 52 51.39 N 6.26 E
Xánthi 38 41.08 N 24.53 E
Xanxerê 252 26.53 S 52.23 W
Xapecó ≃ 252 27.06 S 53.01 W
Xapuri 248 10.39 S 68.31 W
Xapuri ≃ 248 10.39 S 68.30 W
Xarardheere 144 4.39 N 47.51 E
Xar Moron ≃, Zhg. 90 43.25 N 121.41 E
Xar Moron ≃, Zhg. 102 43.02 N 111.20 E
Xarrama ≃ 34 38.14 N 8.20 W
Xàtiva (Játiva) 34 38.59 N 0.31 W
Xau, Lake ⊜ 156 21.15 S 24.38 E
Xauen
— Chaouen 148 35.10 N 5.16 W
Xavante ≃ 250 11.23 S 49.41 W
Xavantes ≃ 250 10.40 S 50.41 W
Xavantina 255 21.15 S 52.48 W
Xa Vo Dat 110 11.09 N 107.31 E
Xaxim 252 26.56 S 52.31 W
Xcalak 232 18.16 N 87.50 W
X-Can 232 20.50 N 87.43 W
Xelva 34 39.45 N 0.59 W
Xenia, Il., U.S. 219 38.38 N 88.38 W
Xenia, Oh., U.S. 218 39.41 N 83.55 W
Xénô 110 16.35 N 104.50 E
Xercavins, Arroyo de
≃ 266d 41.30 N 2.02 E
Xerém 256 22.33 S 43.18 W
Xeres
— Jerez de la
Frontera 34 36.41 N 6.08 W
Xertigny 58 48.03 N 6.24 E
Xeruã ≃ 248 6.03 S 67.50 W
Xhumo 156 21.07 S 24.42 E
Xi ≃, Zhg. 100 24.34 N 117.30 E
Xi ≃, Zhg. 100 25.14 N 118.03 E
Xi ≃, Zhg. 100 30.21 N 115.06 E
Xi ≃, Zhg. 102 42.20 N 100.20 E
Xi ≃, Zhg. 102 22.25 N 113.23 E
Xi ≃, Zhg. 104 41.15 N 123.32 E
Xi ≃, Zhg. 104 41.30 N 121.26 E
Xi ≃, Zhg. 107 30.26 N 103.48 E
Xiaang 106 30.45 N 120.07 E
Xiaba 100 24.54 N 116.06 E
Xiabai, Zhg. 106 31.12 N 119.50 E
Xiabai, Zhg. 106 30.29 N 120.00 E
Xiabanghu 100 30.31 N 112.38 E
Xiabian 104 40.51 N 120.30 E
Xiabuji 100 28.19 N 116.20 E
Xiacang 105 39.47 N 117.24 E
Xiache 100 24.40 N 115.08 E
Xiachengzi 89 44.41 N 130.27 E
Xiachuan Dao I 102 21.40 N 112.37 E
Xiacun 105 40.21 N 116.14 E
Xiadao 100 26.34 N 118.16 E
Xiadian, Zhg. 98 37.06 N 120.19 E
Xiadian, Zhg. 100 31.26 N 114.17 E
Xiadian, Zhg. 105 39.57 N 116.55 E
Xiadianjie 100 25.13 N 118.27 E
Xiafeidi 98 42.18 N 124.21 E
Xiafu, Zhg. 100 25.01 N 113.41 E
Xiafu, Zhg. 100 23.52 N 115.45 E
Xiagaixin 102 22.36 N 99.59 E
Xiagang 106 31.55 N 120.13 E
Xiagezhuang 98 36.41 N 120.25 E
Xiaguan, Zhg. 98 39.07 N 114.09 E
Xiaguan, Zhg. 102 25.34 N 100.14 E
Xiaguan, Zhg. 106 32.06 N 118.44 E
Xiaguanjunchang 104 41.28 N 121.40 E
Xiaguanpi 100 24.04 N 117.06 E
Xiagucheng 102 36.47 N 102.53 E
Xiagucun 106 30.56 N 119.09 E
Xiahada 104 41.58 N 124.08 E
Xiahailangzhai 104 41.35 N 123.46 E
Xiahe 102 35.18 N 102.30 E
Xiahuangjintun 104 41.57 N 123.48 E
Xiahuayuan 105 40.29 N 115.17 E
Xiajiabaozi 98 42.16 N 124.37 E
Xiajialou 104 42.25 N 123.39 E
Xiajiang 100 27.32 N 115.08 E
Xiajiangdun 106 31.14 N 120.24 E
Xiajiangwu 106 30.29 N 119.00 E
Xiajiayuan 106 32.13 N 120.38 E
Xiajiezi 102 27.28 N 101.35 E
Xiajin 98 36.55 N 115.57 E
Xiakou 100 28.28 N 118.31 E
Xialianggang 105 39.14 N 115.07 E
Xialufang 102 31.11 N 103.38 E
Xiamaguan 102 37.14 N 106.28 E
Xiamen (Amoy) 100 24.28 N 118.07 E
Xiamen Gang c 100 24.19 N 118.10 E
Xiamianzhen 107 30.08 N 106.32 E
Xiamin'ansutai 104 41.54 N 120.53 E
Xiamocun 106 31.09 N 119.22 E
Xi'an (Sian) 102 34.15 N 108.52 E
Xian ≃ 107 29.22 N 104.44 E
Xianchenggu 98 36.53 N 115.17 E
Xiandu 100 25.04 N 117.44 E
Xianfeng, Zhg. 100 25.42 N 117.53 E
Xianfeng, Zhg. 102 29.41 N 109.02 E
Xiang ≃, Zhg. 100 25.35 N 115.49 E
Xiang ≃, Zhg. 102 29.00 N 112.56 E
Xiang'an 100 31.12 N 117.46 E
Xiangcheng, Zhg. 100 33.28 N 114.53 E
Xiangcheng, Zhg. 100 33.53 N 113.29 E
Xiangcheng, Zhg. 102 28.59 N 99.45 E
Xiangcheng, Zhg. 106 31.29 N 120.44 E
Xiangfan 102 32.03 N 112.01 E
Xiangfuguan 100 28.30 N 115.26 E
Xiangfusi 107 30.06 N 104.24 E
Xianggang (Hong
Kong) 271d 22.17 N 114.09 E
Xianggang □ [4] 100 22.15 N 114.10 E
Xianggongshi 100 28.25 N 113.32 E
Xianggongzhuang 105 39.48 N 118.19 E
Xianghe 105 39.46 N 116.59 E
Xiangheguan 100 33.08 N 113.26 E
Xianghuazhen 106 31.31 N 121.43 E
Xiangjia, Zhg. 106 31.20 N 120.31 E
Xiangjia, Zhg. 106 31.19 N 120.23 E
Xiangjiachang 107 30.08 N 104.18 E
Xiangkhoang 110 19.20 N 103.22 E
Xiangkhoang, Plateau
de ⋏ [1] 110 19.30 N 103.10 E
Xiangning 102 36.01 N 110.45 E
Xiangride 102 36.02 N 98.08 E
Xiangshan, Zhg. 100 29.28 N 121.51 E
Xiangshan, Zhg. 105 39.59 N 116.12 E
Xiangshan Gang c 100 29.38 N 121.48 E
Xiangshizhen 107 29.17 N 105.09 E
Xiangshui, Zhg. 100 23.15 N 114.10 E
Xiangshui, Zhg. 100 34.12 N 119.34 E
Xiangtan 100 27.51 N 112.54 E
Xiangtang 100 28.26 N 115.58 E
Xiangxiang 102 27.43 N 112.27 E
Xiangyang 105 39.13 N 115.25 E
Xiangyangkou 105 40.06 N 115.47 E
Xiangyin 100 28.40 N 112.53 E
Xiangyuan 102 36.32 N 113.00 E
Xiangyun 102 25.30 N 100.30 E
Xiangzhenpu 100 30.52 N 117.21 E
Xiangzhou, Zhg. 98 36.12 N 119.24 E
Xiangzhou, Zhg. 102 23.55 N 109.49 E
Xiangzhu 100 29.02 N 120.04 E
Xianinggang 100 28.20 N 112.56 E
Xianjiang 100 27.48 N 120.30 E
Xianju 100 28.51 N 120.44 E
Xianning 100 29.53 N 114.13 E
Xiannongtan Stadium
♠ 271a 39.52 N 116.23 E
Xiannübu 100 25.36 N 114.40 E
Xianru 89 43.11 N 128.02 E
Xianshichang 107 28.43 N 105.44 E
Xianshui ≃ 102 30.10 N 100.59 E
Xianshuigu 105 38.59 N 117.23 E
Xiantan, Zhg. 107 29.21 N 104.53 E
Xiantan, Zhg. 107 28.50 N 106.12 E
Xiantang 100 23.48 N 114.46 E
Xianxia Ling ⋏ 100 28.30 N 118.46 E
Xianxian 98 38.13 N 116.06 E
Xianyang, Zhg. 100 28.02 N 118.30 E
Xianyang, Zhg. 102 34.22 N 108.42 E
Xianyou 100 25.23 N 118.40 E
Xianzhong 100 28.36 N 113.48 E
Xiao ≃ 100 28.11 N 120.14 E
Xiao'an ≃ 107 29.59 N 106.13 E
Xiao'ao 100 26.14 N 119.39 E
Xiaoazhang 102 23.42 N 104.58 E
Xiaobangniulu 104 41.34 N 122.46 E
Xiaobeigou 104 41.55 N 120.46 E
Xiaobeihe, Zhg. 104 42.39 N 123.58 E
Xiaobeihe, Zhg. 104 41.22 N 122.50 E
Xiaocaohu 86 43.06 N 88.30 E
Xiaochangshan Dao I 98 39.12 N 122.41 E
Xiaocheng 100 26.20 N 119.47 E
Xiaochengdu 106 30.59 N 120.04 E
Xiaochengzi, Zhg. 89 46.33 N 122.54 E
Xiaochengzi, Zhg. 89 42.56 N 123.12 E
Xiaochi 100 30.33 N 116.23 E
Xiaochikou 100 29.46 N 115.59 E
Xiaodanyang 106 31.38 N 118.43 E
Xiaodong 102 22.14 N 108.39 E
Xiao'ergou 89 49.12 N 123.42 E
Xiaofangshen 104 42.13 N 123.54 E
Xiaofanshan 105 40.16 N 115.19 E
Xiaofen 106 31.45 N 119.39 E
Xiaofeng 106 30.36 N 119.32 E
Xiaogan 100 30.55 N 113.54 E
Xiaogangkou 100 28.14 N 115.50 E
Xiaogaojiatun 104 41.02 N 121.59 E
Xiaogencaigangzi 104 41.48 N 122.42 E
Xiaogu 107 29.08 N 104.01 E
Xiaoguai 86 45.13 N 85.02 E
Xiaogushan 98 39.49 N 123.12 E
Xiaohaizhen 106 31.58 N 120.59 E
Xiaohaladaokou 98 42.37 N 119.32 E
Xiaohan 98 35.48 N 114.52 E
Xiaohe 106 32.01 N 119.52 E
Xiaohei Shan ʌ 102 24.42 N 98.55 E
Xiaohekou 102 33.19 N 107.25 E
Xiaoheyan 98 42.26 N 119.38 E
Xiaoheying 102 32.37 N 104.23 E
Xiao Hinggan Ling
(Lesser Khingan
Range) ⋏ 89 48.45 N 127.00 E
Xiaohongmen 271a 39.49 N 116.26 E
Xiaohu 100 27.20 N 118.14 E
Xiaohuying 98 41.09 N 117.13 E
Xiaoji, Zhg. 98 36.45 N 121.01 E
Xiaoji, Zhg. 100 27.08 N 113.15 E
Xiaoji, Zhg. 100 32.38 N 119.48 E
Xiaojiachang 107 30.18 N 106.28 E
Xiaojiagang 100 31.06 N 113.55 E
Xiaojialing 100 29.35 N 116.32 E
Xiaojiang 100 25.08 N 114.59 E
Xiaojianji 100 33.23 N 116.29 E
Xiaojiawu 105 39.36 N 116.36 E
Xiaojiayingzi 98 40.17 N 118.47 E
Xiaojieling 100 31.36 N 115.09 E
Xiaojin 102 31.00 N 102.21 E
Xiaojingfang 105 39.22 N 116.34 E
Xiaojiu 89 45.15 N 127.47 E
Xiaokaoshantun 104 42.10 N 123.53 E
Xiaokuli 89 50.18 N 120.20 E
Xiaokunshan 106 31.02 N 121.07 E
Xiaolan 100 22.41 N 113.14 E
Xiaoliangshan 104 42.05 N 122.32 E
Xiaoling, Zhg. 89 45.20 N 127.18 E
Xiaoling, Zhg. 104 42.18 N 123.23 E
Xiaoling ≃ 104 41.06 N 121.07 E
Xiaolingzi 104 41.07 N 123.19 E
Xiaolinzhuang 104 41.36 N 124.01 E
Xiaolipu 98 36.24 N 116.35 E
Xiaolongtan 102 23.51 N 103.10 E
Xiaoluan ≃ 98 41.36 N 117.05 E
Xiaolüzhuang 106 31.57 N 119.25 E
Xiaomei 100 27.50 N 118.58 E
Xiaomei Guan)(100 25.17 N 114.17 E
Xiaomiaozi 98 41.24 N 114.25 E
Xiaonanhai 107 29.23 N 106.27 E
Xiaopikou 98 35.47 N 115.53 E
Xiaopingyang 102 23.22 N 109.13 E
Xiao Qaidam He ⊜ 102 37.30 N 95.12 E
Xiaoqiao 100 26.57 N 118.30 E
Xiaoqiaotou 106 30.43 N 119.27 E
Xiaoqing ≃ 98 37.17 N 118.52 E
Xiaoqingchuizi 104 42.30 N 123.39 E
Xiaoquandong 102 41.14 N 95.26 E
Xiaosanjiazi 104 42.34 N 123.23 E
Xiaosha ≃ 104 41.13 N 122.45 E
Xiaoshakou 100 29.58 N 113.16 E
Xiaoshan 106 30.10 N 120.15 E
Xiaoshangqiao 100 33.43 N 113.58 E
Xiaoshi 100 27.27 N 116.49 E
Xiaoshixiang 100 30.36 N 116.38 E
Xiaoshu 106 30.48 N 119.46 E
Xiaoshun 100 29.11 N 119.51 E
Xiaosigou 98 40.53 N 118.33 E
Xiaosijia 104 42.24 N 120.46 E
Xiaotang 98 41.38 N 119.33 E
Xiaotanghe 98 42.04 N 127.10 E
Xiaotao 100 25.46 N 117.08 E
Xiaotazi 104 42.17 N 123.08 E
Xiaotian 100 31.12 N 116.33 E
Xiaotianji 100 32.45 N 115.36 E
Xiaotun 104 42.24 N 123.44 E
Xiaotunzicun 104 41.14 N 123.20 E
Xiaowa 104 41.03 N 122.04 E
Xiaowan 100 26.53 N 116.36 E
Xiaowangmiao 100 29.41 N 121.21 E
Xiaowutai Shan ʌ 105 39.51 N 115.09 E
Xiaowutai Shan ⋏ 105 39.50 N 115.00 E
Xiaoxi 100 25.48 N 115.21 E
Xiaoxi ≃ 106 32.15 N 120.24 E
Xiaoxian 98 34.11 N 116.56 E
Xiaoxincheng 105 39.24 N 115.11 E
Xiaoxintian 271a 39.58 N 116.22 E
Xiaoxizhen 106 30.51 N 119.50 E
Xiaoyangjiadian 104 42.23 N 122.24 E
Xiaoyangqi 89 50.48 N 124.12 E
Xiaoyantai 104 41.26 N 123.10 E
Xiaoyaozhen 100 33.46 N 114.16 E
Xiaoyi 102 37.10 N 111.46 E
Xiaoying, Zhg. 98 37.18 N 118.04 E
Xiaoying, Zhg. 105 40.12 N 116.33 E
Xiaoyingcun 105 39.28 N 116.41 E
Xiaoyuan 107 30.00 N 104.56 E
Xiaozhan 105 38.55 N 117.25 E
Xiaozhang ≃ 105 39.47 N 117.22 E
Xiaozhongdian 102 27.40 N 99.46 E
Xiaozhuang 104 41.30 N 121.27 E
Xiaozhujiawan 106 31.24 N 121.01 E
Xiapu, Zhg. 100 26.52 N 120.01 E
Xiapu, Zhg. 100 27.49 N 114.26 E
Xiaqialafangzi 104 41.48 N 121.44 E
Xiaqi Dao I 100 29.42 N 122.15 E
Xiaqiubao 98 37.01 N 119.54 E
Xiasantumen 105 38.50 N 114.48 E
Xiashe 106 30.33 N 120.11 E
Xiashesi 100 27.46 N 112.57 E
Xiashi
— Haining 106 30.32 N 120.41 E
Xiashu 106 32.11 N 119.10 E
Xiashuerfowei 89 50.23 N 120.47 E
Xiashuiquan 104 41.52 N 123.38 E
Xiataizi 105 40.37 N 117.45 E
Xiatang, Zhg. 100 33.45 N 112.39 E
Xiatang, Zhg. 106 31.29 N 118.41 E
Xiatangtian 106 30.55 N 120.12 E
Xiataohuatu 104 41.42 N 120.36 E
Xiawa 98 42.39 N 120.35 E
Xiawajiang 106 30.59 N 121.51 E
Xiawaziyu 104 41.15 N 123.38 E
Xiaxi 106 31.43 N 119.45 E
Xiaxian 102 35.11 N 111.15 E
Xiaxiangcheng 102 28.42 N 99.59 E
Xiaxikou 100 26.15 N 118.59 E
Xiaxinhe 106 31.40 N 119.31 E
Xiayang, Zhg. 100 28.48 N 119.41 E
Xiayang, Zhg. 100 26.46 N 117.59 E
Xiayang, Zhg. 100 24.39 N 116.52 E
Xiayi 98 34.14 N 116.06 E
Xiaying, Zhg. 98 37.03 N 119.25 E
Xiaying, Zhg. 105 40.10 N 117.25 E
Xiayunling 105 39.43 N 115.44 E
Xiazhang 98 36.08 N 116.57 E
Xiazhen 100 28.39 N 118.21 E
Xiazhuang, Zhg. 98 35.28 N 118.43 E
Xiazhuang, Zhg. 100 27.22 N 119.01 E
Xiazhuang, Zhg. 105 39.54 N 117.01 E
Xiazhuang, Zhg. 105 39.38 N 115.26 E
Xiazikou 105 39.01 N 115.25 E
Xiban 107 30.32 N 106.12 E
Xibaqianmou 104 40.59 N 121.35 E
Xibeiyingzi 104 41.55 N 121.38 E
Xibo ≃ 98 42.17 N 118.57 E
Xibu 100 31.46 N 118.17 E
Xicang 106 31.34 N 120.29 E
Xichang, Zhg. 102 27.58 N 102.13 E
Xichang, Zhg. 104 42.15 N 124.12 E
Xicheng 89 48.10 N 125.29 E
Xichong 102 31.00 N 105.52 E
Xicicun 105 39.29 N 116.08 E
Xico 234 19.25 N 97.00 W
Xicoténcatl 234 23.00 N 98.56 W
Xicotepec de Juárez 234 20.17 N 97.57 W
Xictle, Volcán ʌ [1] 286a 19.14 N 99.14 W
Xicun 100 27.46 N 114.14 E
Xidachuan 98 41.46 N 127.34 E
Xidapo 89 43.12 N 130.02 E
Xidaying 105 39.41 N 116.14 E
Xidian 100 29.32 N 121.26 E
Xiditou 105 39.16 N 117.23 E
Xidongting Shan ʌ 106 31.07 N 120.16 E
Xié ≃ 246 0.54 N 67.11 W
Xiecun 105 39.00 N 115.31 E
Xiedian 100 33.27 N 113.28 E
Xiefang 100 26.12 N 116.41 E
Xieji 98 34.32 N 115.29 E
Xiejia 98 42.24 N 125.42 E
Xiejiagangzi 104 41.55 N 122.20 E
Xiejiapu 106 31.15 N 119.09 E
Xiejunmiao 107 30.15 N 103.40 E
Xielipuke 120 31.30 N 82.45 E
Xiemachang 107 29.46 N 106.22 E
Xiemata Shan ʌ 89 50.28 N 120.47 E
Xiepu 100 30.02 N 121.37 E
Xieqiao, Zhg. 106 32.03 N 120.22 E
Xieqiao, Zhg. 106 30.29 N 120.34 E
Xietang 106 31.18 N 120.44 E
Xiexi 106 31.54 N 118.54 E
Xiexinggou 104 41.51 N 121.05 E
Xifei ≃ 100 32.38 N 116.39 E
Xifeng, Zhg. 98 42.43 N 124.40 E
Xifeng, Zhg. 102 27.02 N 106.30 E
Xifengkou 105 40.24 N 118.19 E
Xifocun 104 41.26 N 122.33 E
Xigangzi 89 49.58 N 127.20 E
Xigaolizhuangzi 104 41.40 N 122.55 E
Xigaotan 98 38.18 N 116.13 E
Xigaotun 98 40.27 N 122.36 E
Xigazê 120 29.17 N 88.53 E
Xiguanjiatun 104 42.35 N 123.10 E
Xiguanyingzi 104 41.50 N 120.37 E
Xihaikou 104 40.50 N 121.05 E
Xihan ≃ 102 33.30 N 106.02 E
Xihe, Zhg. 100 31.01 N 118.28 E
Xihe, Zhg. 100 31.41 N 113.27 E
Xihe, Zhg. 102 34.01 N 105.17 E
Xiheying 105 39.53 N 114.42 E
Xihezhuang 105 39.20 N 118.02 E
Xi Hu ⊜ 106 30.15 N 120.08 E
Xihua 100 33.47 N 114.31 E
Xihuangcang 106 31.43 N 121.40 E
Xihuanzidong 104 41.31 N 122.28 E
Xihuashan, Zhg. 100 25.28 N 114.20 E
Xihuashan, Zhg. 105 40.07 N 116.54 E
Xihuishan 104 41.41 N 122.38 E
Xiis 144 10.53 N 46.54 E
Xiji, Zhg. 102 35.58 N 105.44 E
Xiji, Zhg. 105 39.49 N 116.52 E
Xijialong 102 23.31 N 103.51 E
Xijiang 100 25.50 N 115.49 E
Xijianshanzi 104 40.47 N 120.48 E
Xi Jiao Airfield ⊠ 271a 39.58 N 116.15 E
Xijiapuzitun 104 41.26 N 123.50 E
Xijir Ulan Hu ⊜ 120 35.12 N 90.18 E
Xikou, Zhg. 89 46.40 N 120.40 E
Xikou, Zhg. 100 28.52 N 119.11 E
Xikou, Zhg. 100 25.26 N 118.45 E
Xikou, Zhg. 100 29.14 N 114.24 E
Xikou, Zhg. 100 29.11 N 114.23 E
Xikou, Zhg. 100 29.44 N 118.02 E
Xikou, Zhg. 106 30.40 N 118.41 E
Xikouxu 100 25.24 N 117.03 E
Xikouzi 89 53.06 N 120.40 E
Xilai 107 30.20 N 103.29 E
Xilaiqiao 106 32.03 N 119.54 E
Xilaizhen 106 32.07 N 120.25 E
Xilin 120 28.33 N 87.48 E
Xi Ling (Western
Tombs) ⊥ 105 39.24 N 115.18 E
Xilintuo 120 30.08 N 88.04 E
Xilitla 234 21.20 N 98.58 W
Xiliuhe 105 38.58 N 116.32 E
Xiliushuyingzi 104 42.25 N 121.54 E
Xıllı 84 39.25 N 49.05 E
Xilókastron 38 38.05 N 22.38 E
Xiluga ≃ 98 42.21 N 118.38 E
Xiluncun 89 47.08 N 126.26 E
Ximagou 105 40.16 N 117.50 E
Ximakou 100 30.33 N 113.47 E
Ximalatu 89 47.00 N 122.01 E
Ximalin 98 40.48 N 114.29 E
Ximiao 102 41.09 N 100.17 E
Ximucheng 104 40.42 N 122.54 E
Xin ≃ 100 28.37 N 116.40 E
Xin'an, Zhg. 89 43.46 N 125.40 E
Xinan, Zhg. 100 25.26 N 117.35 E
Xin'an, Zhg. 100 26.44 N 116.13 E
Xin'an, Zhg. 100 23.02 N 114.56 E
Xin'an, Zhg. 105 39.09 N 116.38 E
Xin'an, Zhg. 106 31.47 N 120.09 E
Xin'an, Zhg. 106 31.30 N 120.22 E
Xin'an ≃ 100 29.33 N 118.58 E
Xin'andian 100 32.37 N 114.03 E
Xin'andu 100 30.52 N 116.53 E
Xin'anji 100 33.22 N 115.13 E
Xin'anjiang Shuiku
⊜ [1] 100 29.27 N 119.06 E
Xin'anpu 104 42.39 N 123.27 E
Xin'anqiao 106 32.16 N 121.07 E
Xin'ansuo 102 23.16 N 103.27 E
Xin'anzhen, Zhg. 89 44.06 N 123.46 E
Xin'anzhen, Zhg. 105 39.45 N 117.32 E
Xi'nanzhuang 105 40.48 N 118.23 E
Xinavane 156 25.02 S 32.47 E
Xinba, Zhg. 98 34.27 N 119.09 E
Xinba, Zhg. 100 30.24 N 116.52 E
Xinba, Zhg. 106 32.08 N 120.39 E
Xinba, Zhg. 106 32.16 N 119.45 E
Xinbao'an 105 40.27 N 115.24 E
Xin Barag Youqi
(Altan Emel) 88 48.41 N 116.53 E
Xin Barag Zuoqi
(Amgalang) 88 48.14 N 118.18 E
Xinbin, Zhg. 98 41.42 N 125.02 E
Xinbin, Zhg. 106 30.56 N 121.04 E
Xinbo 98 42.19 N 117.44 E
Xincai 100 32.44 N 114.59 E
Xincang, Zhg. 106 30.25 N 120.42 E
Xincang, Zhg. 106 30.44 N 121.11 E
Xinchang, Zhg. 100 29.30 N 120.53 E
Xinchang, Zhg. 102 28.03 N 103.46 E
Xinchang, Zhg. 102 25.10 N 104.18 E
Xinchang, Zhg. 106 31.42 N 121.46 E
Xinchang, Zhg. 106 31.02 N 121.38 E
Xinchang, Zhg. 107 29.20 N 104.15 E
Xinchang, Zhg. 107 29.38 N 104.33 E
Xinchang, Zhg. 107 30.29 N 106.21 E
Xinchang, Zhg. 107 30.16 N 104.29 E
Xinchangzi 107 29.40 N 103.46 E
Xincheng, Zhg. 100 25.34 N 114.36 E
Xincheng, Zhg. 102 24.09 N 108.46 E
Xincheng
(Gaobeidian), Zhg. 105 39.20 N 115.51 E
Xincheng, Zhg. 105 38.59 N 117.33 E
Xincheng, Zhg. 106 32.17 N 119.14 E
Xincheng, Zhg. 106 30.48 N 120.36 E
Xinchengzi 104 42.03 N 123.30 E
Xinchepaizi 86 44.55 N 84.30 E
Xincunji 100 32.53 N 115.31 E
Xindai 106 30.49 N 121.05 E
Xindi 104 42.21 N 120.31 E
Xindian, Zhg. 89 45.55 N 127.50 E
Xindian, Zhg. 98 37.07 N 114.49 E
Xindian, Zhg. 98 37.29 N 118.28 E
Xindian, Zhg. 100 33.07 N 112.38 E
Xindian, Zhg. 100 31.33 N 115.16 E
Xindian, Zhg. 100 33.38 N 113.51 E
Xindian, Zhg. 100 29.40 N 113.40 E
Xindian, Zhg. 105 40.11 N 116.11 E
Xindian, Zhg. 105 40.47 N 116.49 E
Xindian, Zhg. 105 39.10 N 116.27 E
Xindian, Zhg. 107 29.19 N 105.40 E
Xindianbu 100 32.24 N 116.22 E
Xindianzi, Zhg. 105 40.04 N 118.01 E
Xindianzi, Zhg. 107 28.49 N 103.35 E
Xindianzi, Zhg. 107 29.03 N 103.46 E
Xindianzi, Zhg. 107 29.52 N 106.06 E
Xindianzi, Zhg. 107 29.46 N 105.11 E
Xindianzi, Zhg. 107 29.43 N 104.01 E
Xindu 102 23.59 N 111.46 E
Xinfatuncun 104 41.13 N 122.28 E
Xinfeng, Zhg. 100 25.24 N 114.56 E
Xinfeng, Zhg. 100 27.26 N 116.40 E
Xinfeng, Zhg. 100 33.19 N 120.30 E
Xinfeng, Zhg. 100 24.04 N 114.12 E
Xinfeng, Zhg. 100 24.05 N 116.53 E
Xinfeng, Zhg. 106 31.09 N 118.40 E
Xinfeng, Zhg. 106 32.05 N 119.34 E
Xinfeng, Zhg. 106 30.43 N 120.55 E
Xinfeng ≃ 100 23.42 N 114.42 E
Xinfeng Shuiku ⊜ [1] 100 23.52 N 114.30 E
Xing'an, Zhg. 89 48.49 N 121.45 E
Xing'an, Zhg. 102 25.37 N 110.31 E
Xin'gang, Zhg. 106 31.56 N 120.57 E
Xingang, Zhg. 106 32.03 N 120.25 E
Xing'antun 89 51.31 N 120.08 E
Xingcheng 104 40.37 N 120.43 E
Xingguo 100 26.21 N 115.19 E
Xinghai 102 35.31 N 99.36 E
Xinghe 98 40.48 N 113.58 E
Xinghua 100 32.57 N 119.50 E
Xinghua Wan c 100 25.20 N 119.20 E
Xingjing 102 29.43 N 102.59 E
Xingkai Hu (ozero
Chanka) ⊜ 89 45.00 N 132.24 E
Xingliu 100 33.04 N 115.41 E
Xinglong, Zhg. 100 32.05 N 112.51 E
Xinglong, Zhg. 102 35.38 N 106.08 E
Xinglong, Zhg. 105 40.26 N 117.34 E
Xinglong, Zhg. 107 30.36 N 106.20 E
Xinglong, Zhg. 107 30.20 N 106.07 E
Xinglongchang, Zhg. 107 30.25 N 104.06 E
Xinglongchang, Zhg. 107 29.34 N 106.09 E
Xinglongchang, Zhg. 107 29.54 N 105.26 E
Xinglongcun 89 49.50 N 125.12 E
Xinglongdian, Zhg. 104 42.16 N 124.00 E
Xinglongdian, Zhg. 104 41.59 N 123.03 E
Xinglonggou, Zhg. 104 41.46 N 120.38 E
Xinglonggou, Zhg. 104 40.45 N 123.08 E
Xinglongpao 89 46.27 N 125.47 E
Xinglongtai 104 42.30 N 123.48 E
Xingning 100 24.09 N 115.45 E
Xingou, Zhg. 100 30.41 N 113.57 E
Xingou, Zhg. 100 30.08 N 112.56 E
Xingren 102 25.27 N 105.13 E
Xingrenbu 102 37.06 N 105.12 E
Xingshanbao 89 45.30 N 125.45 E
Xingtai 98 37.04 N 114.29 E
Xingtan 100 22.46 N 113.07 E
Xingtang 98 38.26 N 114.33 E
Xingtian 100 27.30 N 118.02 E
Xingu ≃ 242 1.30 S 51.53 W
Xinguan 100 33.38 N 118.05 E
Xingwenping 102 29.24 N 103.23 E
Xingxian 102 38.36 N 111.15 E
Xingxing 106 30.39 N 121.09 E
Xingyi, Zhg. 98 38.18 N 115.01 E
Xingyi, Zhg. 102 25.06 N 104.58 E
Xingzhuangzi 105 40.34 N 115.00 E
Xingzi 100 29.28 N 116.01 E
Xinhe, Zhg. 98 37.32 N 115.14 E
Xinhe, Zhg. 100 28.30 N 121.27 E
Xinhe, Zhg. 105 39.03 N 117.37 E
Xinhe, Zhg. 106 31.59 N 121.21 E
Xinhekou 89 48.22 N 130.45 E
Xinheng 100 23.38 N 116.18 E
Xinhezhen 106 31.35 N 121.31 E
Xinhezhuang 106 31.10 N 118.46 E
Xinhua 102 27.37 N 111.02 E
Xinhuai ≃ 100 34.23 N 120.05 E
Xinhuang 106 30.37 N 120.55 E
Xinhui 100 22.32 N 113.02 E
Xining (Sining) 102 36.38 N 101.55 E
Xiniu, Zhg. 100 24.10 N 113.07 E
Xiniu, Zhg. 106 31.25 N 120.07 E
Xiniuguchengzi 104 41.01 N 122.24 E
Xinji, Zhg. 98 35.19 N 115.36 E
Xinji, Zhg. 100 33.24 N 114.44 E
Xinji, Zhg. 105 39.52 N 117.10 E
Xinji, Zhg. 105 40.04 N 118.21 E
Xinjiaji 98 36.56 N 116.59 E
Xinjian, Zhg. 100 28.46 N 120.02 E
Xinjian, Zhg. 100 28.34 N 115.47 E
Xinjian, Zhg. 106 31.33 N 119.39 E
Xinjiang, Zhg. 100 24.29 N 113.52 E
Xinjiang, Zhg. 102 35.40 N 111.11 E
Xinjiang, Zhg. 106 32.05 N 120.40 E
Xinjianglang 106 30.58 N 120.54 E
Xinjiang Uygur
Zizhiqu (Sinkiang)
□ [4] 90 40.00 N 85.00 E
Xinjiapu 105 40.32 N 115.57 E
Xinjiazhuang 105 40.31 N 114.58 E
Xinjie 102 26.48 N 101.15 E
Xinjieji 89 52.08 N 126.24 E
Xinjin (Pulandian),
Zhg. 98 39.24 N 121.58 E
Xinjin, Zhg. 107 30.25 N 103.49 E
Xinjingzi 86 42.13 N 87.36 E
Xinjiulong (New
Kowloon) 271d 22.20 N 114.10 E
Xinjuntun 105 39.39 N 117.57 E
Xinkai ≃ 89 43.37 N 123.36 E
Xinkaigang 106 31.55 N 120.56 E
Xinkengdong 100 26.09 N 113.46 E
Xinle
(Dongchangshou) 98 38.24 N 114.47 E
Xinli 89 44.41 N 126.45 E
Xinlitun, Zhg. 89 43.34 N 125.18 E
Xinlitun, Zhg. 104 42.00 N 122.09 E
Xinlitun, Zhg. 104 42.15 N 122.51 E
Xinlizhuang 105 39.17 N 116.10 E
Xinmin 104 42.00 N 122.48 E
Xinmintun 104 41.39 N 123.02 E
Xinning 102 26.19 N 110.45 E
Xinping 102 24.06 N 101.58 E
Xinpu 100 24.31 N 116.08 E
Xinqianhu 98 37.59 N 118.15 E
Xinqiao, Zhg. 106 31.32 N 119.04 E
Xinqiao, Zhg. 106 31.04 N 121.18 E
Xinqiao, Zhg. 107 29.32 N 106.28 E
Xinqiao, Zhg. 107 30.10 N 103.50 E
Xinqiao, Zhg. 107 30.33 N 105.33 E
Xinqiaotou 106 31.00 N 119.24 E
Xinqiaozhen 107 29.36 N 103.39 E
Xinqiu 98 41.53 N 119.41 E
Xinqizhou 100 28.56 N 115.50 E
Xinqu 86 44.57 N 85.15 E
Xinquan 100 25.23 N 116.38 E
Xinsanyu 106 31.58 N 120.07 E
Xinshao 102 27.11 N 111.20 E
Xinshengzhen 107 29.29 N 104.39 E
Xinshi, Zhg. 106 30.37 N 120.19 E
Xinshi, Zhg. 106 32.04 N 120.02 E
Xinshizhen, Zhg. 102 28.39 N 104.02 E
Xinshizhen, Zhg. 107 30.20 N 104.35 E
Xinshu ≃ 98 34.41 N 119.12 E
Xintai 98 35.54 N 117.44 E
Xintaimen 98 40.50 N 120.23 E
Xintaizi, Zhg. 104 41.06 N 122.42 E
Xintaizi, Zhg. 104 42.07 N 123.36 E
Xintang, Zhg. 100 23.08 N 113.36 E
Xintang, Zhg. 102 30.13 N 109.30 E
Xintang, Zhg. 106 31.02 N 119.59 E
Xintangcun 106 31.53 N 119.31 E
Xintanpu 100 29.43 N 114.54 E
Xintian 102 25.53 N 112.05 E
Xintun 104 42.11 N 123.45 E
Xinvi 105 40.04 N 118.21 E
Xinwei 100 25.21 N 115.48 E
Xinwen (Suncun) 98 35.53 N 117.40 E
Xinxian, Zhg. 100 31.38 N 114.51 E
Xinxian, Zhg. 102 38.25 N 112.48 E
Xinxiang 98 35.20 N 113.51 E
Xinxim ≃ 250 7.57 S 53.20 W
Xinxing, Zhg. 89 43.16 N 129.48 E
Xinxing, Zhg. 100 22.40 N 112.52 E
Xinxing, Zhg. 102 19.57 N 109.32 E
Xinxu, Zhg. 100 22.52 N 114.20 E
Xinxu, Zhg. 100 24.57 N 117.34 E
Xinyang 100 32.08 N 114.04 E
Xinyao 100 27.39 N 118.52 E
Xinye 100 32.33 N 112.21 E
Xinyi (Xin'anzhen),
Zhg. 98 34.22 N 118.21 E
Xinyi (Dongzhen),
Zhg. 102 22.13 N 110.50 E
Xinyi ≃ 100 34.29 N 119.49 E
Xinying 102 36.03 N 105.35 E
Xinyu 100 27.49 N 114.57 E
Xinyuan 86 43.08 N 82.31 E
Xinzao 100 23.02 N 113.26 E
Xinzha 102 23.41 N 101.09 E
Xinzhai, Zhg. 98 39.24 N 118.46 E
Xinzhai, Zhg. 98 36.24 N 118.37 E
Xinzhai, Zhg. 102 24.33 N 99.08 E
Xinzhan 100 33.33 N 114.50 E
Xinzhang 105 39.05 N 116.46 E
Xinzhangzi 105 40.45 N 117.50 E
Xinzhao 102 39.32 N 107.52 E
Xinzhazhen 106 31.50 N 119.52 E
Xinzhen, Zhg. 98 35.37 N 114.03 E
Xinzhen, Zhg. 105 39.01 N 116.22 E
Xinzhen, Zhg. 106 31.24 N 121.24 E
Xinzheng 100 34.25 N 113.43 E
Xinzhou, Zhg. 100 30.50 N 114.47 E
Xinzhou, Zhg. 102 19.48 N 109.18 E
Xinzhuang, Zhg. 98 35.05 N 117.56 E
Xinzhuang, Zhg. 271a 39.56 N 116.31 E
Xinzhuangtou 105 39.25 N 115.45 E
Xinzhuangzi, Zhg. 104 41.05 N 121.23 E
Xinzhuangzi, Zhg. 105 40.14 N 116.59 E
Xinzhuangzi, Zhg. 105 40.32 N 115.10 E
Xinzhuangzi, Zhg. 105 38.52 N 117.21 E
Xinzhuangzi, Zhg. 105 39.20 N 118.25 E
Xinzo de Limia 34 42.03 N 7.43 W
Xiongdi Yu II 100 23.33 N 117.40 E
Xiongjiachang 102 26.31 N 105.39 E
Xiongxian 105 38.59 N 116.05 E
Xiongyuecheng 98 40.10 N 122.08 E
Xipamanu
(Chipamanu) ≃ 248 10.43 S 67.50 W
Xiping, Zhg. 100 28.27 N 119.29 E
Xiping, Zhg. 100 33.23 N 114.02 E
Xiping'anhe 104 40.47 N 122.01 E
Xiqia 106 31.03 N 119.37 E
Xiqilichiquan 89 49.59 N 119.27 E
Xiqin 100 26.33 N 118.06 E
Xiqing Shan ⋏ 102 35.30 N 101.30 E
Xique-Xique 250 10.50 S 42.44 W
Xırdalan 84 40.26 N 49.51 E
Xisanshilipu 100 32.40 N 117.31 E
Xisantai 98 39.38 N 121.37 E
Xishan, Zhg. 100 28.34 N 115.37 E
Xishan, Zhg. 105 39.38 N 118.10 E
Xishanqiao 106 31.57 N 118.43 E
Xishanxicun 105 40.01 N 116.50 E
Xisha Qundao
(Paracel Islands) II 108 16.30 N 112.15 E
Xishijiazi 104 41.46 N 120.55 E
Xishiqiao 106 31.53 N 120.06 E
Xishu 98 36.41 N 113.49 E
Xishui 100 30.27 N 115.13 E
Xishuiyu 105 40.25 N 116.16 E
Xisuhupu 104 41.41 N 123.14 E
Xitai 98 40.37 N 120.12 E
Xitan 100 23.47 N 117.08 E
Xitang 106 30.57 N 120.53 E
Xitangqiao, Zhg. 106 31.49 N 120.38 E
Xitangqiao, Zhg. 106 30.37 N 121.01 E
Xitaoyuan 104 40.57 N 122.11 E
Xiti 120 33.27 N 82.48 E
Xitianmu Shan ʌ 106 30.21 N 119.25 E
Xitiao ≃ 106 30.57 N 120.10 E
Xiting 106 32.07 N 121.00 E
Xitole 150 11.43 N 14.50 W
Xituan 105 39.29 N 115.47 E
Xiu ≃ 100 29.13 N 115.56 E
Xiujiangpu 104 41.17 N 123.02 E
Xiuning 100 29.47 N 118.10 E
Xiushan 102 28.29 N 108.52 E
Xiushui 100 29.04 N 114.33 E
Xiushui ≃ 104 42.03 N 122.58 E
Xiushuihe 104 42.22 N 123.01 E
Xiuyan 98 40.17 N 123.18 E
Xiva 34 39.28 N 0.43 W
Xiwei 100 25.22 N 117.46 E
Xiweizigou 104 42.01 N 121.59 E
Xiwenquan 107 29.42 N 106.07 E
Xiwu 100 29.40 N 121.30 E
Xiwukou 106 30.24 N 118.54 E
Xixabangma Feng ʌ 124 28.22 N 85.50 E
Xixi 100 26.45 N 118.42 E
Xixia 102 33.22 N 111.28 E
Xixian, Zhg. 100 32.21 N 114.44 E
Xixian, Zhg. 102 36.43 N 110.52 E
Xixiang 102 32.48 N 107.55 E
Xixiangyang 105 39.33 N 116.02 E
Xixiaojie 104 40.42 N 122.12 E
Xixiashu 106 31.57 N 119.49 E
Xixing 106 30.11 N 120.13 E
Xixona 34 38.32 N 0.30 W
Xiyang, Zhg. 98 37.37 N 113.42 E
Xiyang, Zhg. 100 25.50 N 117.25 E
Xiyang, Zhg. 106 31.49 N 120.43 E
Xiyang, Zhg. 106 31.52 N 119.23 E
Xiyang Dao I 100 26.32 N 120.04 E
Xiyangji 100 33.25 N 116.22 E
Xiyangjiao 106 31.43 N 120.23 E
Xiyangshugou 104 40.41 N 122.44 E
Xiyangzhuang 106 31.50 N 119.22 E
Xiyingzi 104 41.55 N 122.34 E
Xiyou 98 37.24 N 119.56 E
Xiyushi 106 30.36 N 119.26 E
Xizang Zizhiqu (Tibet)
□ [4] 90 32.00 N 88.00 E
Xizhi ≃ 100 23.04 N 114.31 E
Xizhimen Station ◆ [5] 271a 39.56 N 116.21 E
Xizhong Dao I 98 39.26 N 121.17 E
Xizhou 100 29.29 N 121.39 E
Xizi 98 41.48 N 119.16 E
Xocavänd 84 39.48 N 47.06 E
Xochiapa 234 17.39 N 95.46 W
Xochicalco ⊥ 234 18.48 N 99.19 W
Xochimilco ◆ [8] 286a 19.16 N 99.06 W
Xochimilco, Lago de
⊜ 286a 19.16 N 99.06 W
Xochipala 234 17.48 N 99.39 W
Xochistlahuaca 234 16.47 N 98.15 W
Xochitlán 234 19.59 N 97.36 W
Xoka 120 29.58 N 93.48 E
Xom Binh Phuoc 269c 10.40 N 106.47 E
Xom Xoai Minh 269c 10.42 N 106.50 E
Xu ≃ 100 28.17 N 116.05 E
Xuancheng 106 30.58 N 118.45 E
Xuan'en 102 30.00 N 109.20 E
Xuanfeng 100 27.42 N 114.08 E
Xuang ≃ 110 19.58 N 102.15 E
Xuanhan 102 31.24 N 107.43 E
Xuanhua 105 40.37 N 115.03 E
Xuanhuadian 100 31.42 N 114.29 E
Xuanhui ≃ 98 38.07 N 117.45 E
Xuanjiabao 106 32.17 N 120.01 E
Xuanjiangying 98 41.25 N 116.45 E
Xuan Loc 110 10.56 N 107.14 E
Xuantan 107 29.12 N 105.34 E
Xuan Thoi Thuong 269c 10.52 N 106.34 E
Xuanwei 102 26.07 N 104.05 E
Xuanzhuang 105 39.29 N 118.07 E
Xubu 98 40.02 N 113.43 E
Xuchang, Zhg. 100 34.03 N 113.49 E
Xuchang, Zhg. 107 29.06 N 104.31 E
Xucheng 98 35.56 N 116.27 E
Xuchilquitongo 234 17.15 N 96.53 W
Xucun 106 30.27 N 120.22 E
Xudat 84 41.38 N 48.42 E
Xudazhuang 100 33.44 N 117.53 E
Xuddun 144 9.09 N 47.28 E
Xuddur 144 4.07 N 43.54 E
Xueao 100 29.27 N 121.30 E
Xuebu 106 31.43 N 119.22 E
Xuecheng 98 34.50 N 117.16 E
Xuedian, Zhg. 100 34.04 N 113.04 E
Xuedian, Zhg. 100 34.30 N 113.44 E
Xuefanggou 104 41.57 N 121.01 E
Xuefeng 100 33.21 N 118.22 E
Xuehu 98 34.08 N 116.27 E
Xueshan Zhang ʌ 100 24.24 N 113.37 E
Xueshuiwen 89 49.10 N 129.45 E
Xuetangpuzi 104 40.38 N 123.53 E
Xueyanqiao 106 31.30 N 120.06 E
Xuezhen 106 31.35 N 118.38 E
Xuguanzhen 106 31.23 N 120.30 E
Xuguichenxiaodian 106 32.07 N 121.20 E
Xuguit Qi (Yakeshi) 89 49.17 N 120.41 E
Xuji 100 31.50 N 116.22 E
Xujiabu 100 29.27 N 116.18 E
Xujiadong 100 25.54 N 113.02 E
Xujiadu 100 28.18 N 114.44 E
Xujiagou 104 42.17 N 124.04 E
Xujiapuzi 104 40.44 N 123.18 E
Xujiatou 106 31.19 N 119.25 E
Xujiazhai, Zhg. 106 31.11 N 121.46 E
Xujiazhai, Zhg. 269b 31.23 N 121.17 E
Xuliying 105 39.28 N 116.02 E
Xun ≃, Zhg. 89 49.27 N 128.55 E
Xun ≃, Zhg. 102 23.28 N 111.18 E
Xungru 120 29.15 N 84.49 E
Xunhe 89 49.18 N 128.04 E
Xunhua 102 35.49 N 102.26 E
Xunjiansi 105 40.50 N 116.04 E
Xunke 89 49.35 N 128.25 E
Xunle 102 25.17 N 108.12 E
Xunmukou 98 34.03 N 114.42 E
Xunshansuo 98 37.10 N 122.29 E
Xunwu 100 24.58 N 115.38 E
Xunwu ≃ 100 24.28 N 115.26 E
Xunxian 98 35.43 N 114.31 E
Xupu, Zhg. 102 27.44 N 110.24 E
Xupu, Zhg. 106 31.45 N 120.54 E
Xushe 106 31.24 N 119.39 E
Xushi 106 31.40 N 120.57 E
Xushui 105 39.02 N 115.39 E
Xutian 98 34.10 N 114.03 E
Xuwan 100 27.55 N 116.31 E
Xuwen 102 20.21 N 110.11 E
Xuxiandai 106 30.40 N 120.47 E
Xuxiang 106 31.33 N 120.13 E
Xuyen Moc 110 10.34 N 107.25 E
Xuyi 100 33.01 N 118.29 E
Xuyong 102 28.10 N 105.24 E
Xuzhou (Süchow) 98 34.16 N 117.11 E
Xuzhuang 106 31.09 N 120.32 E

Y

Yaak 182 48.50 N 115.42 W
Yaan 102 30.03 N 103.02 E
Yaapeet 166 35.46 S 142.03 E
Yaaq-Baraawe 144 1.57 N 43.11 E
Yaba ◆ [8] 273a 6.30 N 3.23 E
Yaba College of
Technology ʊ [2] 273a 6.32 N 3.23 E
Ya'bad 132 32.27 N 35.10 E
Yabakei 96 33.27 N 131.07 E
Yabassi 152 4.28 N 9.58 E
Yabe 96 33.09 N 130.49 E
Yabe ≃ 96 33.06 N 130.26 E
Yabelo 144 4.54 N 38.05 E
Yablis 236 14.10 N 83.49 W
Yablonovy Range
— Jablonovyj
chrebet ⋏ 88 53.30 N 115.00 E
Yabluniv 78 48.24 N 24.57 E
Yablychne 78 50.18 N 35.14 E
Yabrīn ⫪ [4] 128 23.17 N 48.58 E
Yabrūd 130 33.58 N 36.40 E
Yabu, Nihon 96 35.22 N 134.47 E
Yabu, Nihon 174m 26.36 N 127.57 E
Yabucoa 240m 18.03 N 65.53 W
Yabuki 94 37.12 N 140.19 E
Yabuli 89 44.55 N 128.35 E
Yacambu, Parque
Nacional ♠ 246 9.40 N 69.42 W

Symbol	English	Deutsch	Español	Français	Português
≃	River	Fluß	Río	Rivière	Rio
⩶	Canal	Kanal	Canal	Canal	Canal
ʟ	Waterfall, Rapids	Wasserfall, Stromschnellen	Cascada, Rápidos	Chute d'eau, Rapides	Cascata, Rápidos
)(	Strait	Meeresstraße	Estrecho	Détroit	Estreito
c	Bay, Gulf	Bucht, Golf	Bahía, Golfo	Baie, Golfe	Baía, Golfo
⊜	Lake, Lakes	See, Seen	Lago, Lagos	Lac, Lacs	Lago, Lagos
⩩	Swamp	Sumpf	Pantano	Marais	Pântano
⍓	Ice Features, Glacier	Eis- und Gletscherformen	Accidentes Glaciales	Formes glaciaires	Acidentes glaciares
⫪	Other Hydrographic Features	Andere Hydrographische Objekte	Otros Elementos Hidrográficos	Autres données hydrographiques	Outros acidentes hidrográficos
✢	Submarine Features	Untermeerische Objekte	Accidentes Submarinos	Formes de relief sous-marin	Acidentes submarinos
□	Political Unit	Politische Einheit	Unidad Politica	Entité politique	Unidade política
ʊ	Cultural Institution	Kulturelle Institution	Institución Cultural	Institution culturelle	Instituição cultural
⊥	Historical Site	Historische Stätte	Sitio Histórico	Site historique	Sitio histórico
♠	Recreational Site	Erholungs- und Ferienort	Sitio de Recreo	Centre de loisirs	Area de Lazer
⊠	Airport	Flughafen	Aeropuerto	Aéroport	Aeroporto
■	Military Installation	Militäranlage	Instalación Militar	Installation militaire	Instalação militar
◆	Miscellaneous	Verschiedenes	Misceláneo	Divers	Diversos

Name	Page	Lat.°′	Long.°′
Yacaré Norte, Riacho ≃	252	22.43 S	58.14 W
Yacheng	110	18.25 N	109.11 E
Yachi ≃	102	27.18 N	107.15 E
Yachimata	94	35.39 N	140.19 E
Yachiyo, Nihon	94	35.43 N	140.07 E
Yachiyo, Nihon	94	36.10 N	139.53 E
Yacimiento Río Turbio	254	51.32 S	72.18 W
Yaco	248	17.09 S	67.24 W
Yaco (Iaco) ≃	248	9.03 S	68.34 W
Yacolt	224	45.51 N	122.24 W
Yacuiba	248	22.02 S	63.45 W
Yacuma ≃	248	13.38 S	65.23 W
Yacyretá, Isla I	252	27.25 S	56.30 W
Yada ≃	96	35.38 N	134.37 E
Yādgīr	122	16.46 N	77.08 E
Yadkin ≃	192	35.23 N	80.03 W
Yadkinville	192	36.08 N	80.39 W
Yad Mordekhay	132	31.35 N	34.34 E
Yadong	124	27.29 N	88.55 E
Yādūdah	132	32.40 N	36.04 E
Yaduty	78	51.22 N	32.19 E
Yaenengu	152	2.28 N	23.15 E
Yaeyama-rettō II	175d	24.20 N	124.00 E
Yāfā	132	32.41 N	35.17 E
Yafran	146	32.04 N	12.31 E
Yaftābād	267d	35.39 N	51.19 E
Yafuquan	85	39.12 N	76.09 E
Yagachi-shima I	174m	26.40 N	128.01 E
Yağcılar	130	39.25 N	28.23 E
Yageg	144	3.16 N	44.00 E
Yagi	96	35.04 N	135.32 E
Yagishiri-tō I	92a	44.26 N	141.25 E
Yağlıca Dağı ʌ	84	40.18 N	43.18 E
Yago	234	21.50 N	105.04 W
Yagonde	152	0.02 N	22.41 E
Yagoona	274a	33.55 S	151.02 E
Yagoua	146	10.20 N	15.14 E
Yagradagzê Shan ʌ	120	35.12 N	95.20 E
Yaguachi Nuevo	246	2.07 S	79.41 W
Yaguajay	240p	22.19 N	79.14 W
Yaguala ≃	236	15.25 N	86.40 W
Yaguará	246	2.40 N	75.31 W
Yaguaraparo	246	10.34 N	62.49 W
Yaguarí	252	31.31 S	54.58 W
Yaguarón (Jaguarão) ≃	252	32.39 S	53.12 W
Yaguas ≃	246	2.45 S	70.04 W
Yagur	132	32.44 N	35.04 E
Yahagi ≃	94	34.50 N	136.59 E
Yahagong	102	28.24 N	99.11 E
Yahara ≃	190	42.48 N	89.07 W
Yahata → Kitakyūshū	96	33.53 N	130.50 E
Yahe, Zhg.	89	45.24 N	130.24 E
Yahe, Zhg.	106	31.44 N	119.52 E
Yahila	152	0.13 N	24.28 E
Yahk	182	49.05 N	116.05 W
Yahmūm al-Asmar, Jabal ʌ	142	29.56 N	31.38 E
Yaho	268	35.41 N	139.27 E
Yahōga-take ʌ	96	33.04 N	130.50 E
Yahongqiao	105	39.45 N	117.51 E
Yahorlyts'kyy lyman C	78	46.24 N	31.50 E
Yahotyn	78	50.17 N	31.46 E
Yahualica	234	21.08 N	102.51 W
Yahuma	152	1.05 N	23.13 E
Yahyalı	130	38.07 N	35.22 E
Yai ≃	114	5.02 N	101.47 E
Yai, Khao ʌ, Asia	110	12.27 N	99.26 E
Yai, Khao ʌ, Thai	110	15.25 N	99.20 E
Yainax Butte ʌ	202	42.20 N	121.16 W
Yaita, Nihon	94	36.48 N	139.56 E
Yaita, Nihon	268	35.57 N	140.03 E
Yaitopya → Ethiopia □[1]	144	9.00 N	39.00 E
Yaizu	94	34.52 N	138.20 E
Yajiang	102	30.02 N	101.05 E
Yaka	130	41.15 N	34.01 E
Yakacık	130	36.47 N	36.10 E
Yakacık ●[8]	267b	40.55 N	29.13 E
Yakage	96	34.37 N	133.35 E
Yakak, Cape ›	180	51.38 N	177.00 W
Yakapınar	130	37.00 N	35.36 E
Yakarta → Jakarta	115a	6.10 S	106.48 E
Yake-dake ʌ	94	36.14 N	137.35 E
Yake-yama ʌ	94	36.55 N	138.03 E
Yakhchāl, Afg.	120	31.47 N	64.41 E
Yakhchāl, Afg.	128	31.47 N	64.41 E
Yakhnyky	78	50.26 N	33.10 E
Yakima	202	46.36 N	120.30 W
Yakima □[6]	224	46.34 N	121.03 W
Yakima ≃	202	46.15 N	119.02 W
Yakima Firing Center ■	202	46.44 N	120.10 W
Yakima Indian Reservation ●[4]	224	46.16 N	121.03 W
Yakkan ≃	96	33.34 N	131.22 E
Yakmach	128	28.45 N	63.51 E
Yako	150	12.58 N	2.16 W
Yakō ●[8]	268	35.32 N	139.41 E
Yakobi Island I	180	58.00 N	136.30 W
Yakoma	152	4.05 N	22.27 E
Yakou	100	24.46 N	118.46 E
Yakuendai	268	35.43 N	140.03 E
Yakuluku	154	4.20 N	28.48 E
Yakumo	92a	42.15 N	140.16 E
Yakuno	96	35.19 N	135.00 E
Yakushi-dake ʌ	94	36.28 N	137.33 E
Yakushi-ji ♦[1]	94	36.25 N	139.53 E
Yaku-shima I	93b	30.20 N	130.30 E
Yakutat	180	59.33 N	139.44 W
Yakutat Bay C	180	59.40 N	140.00 W
Yakutat Seamount ⊹[3]	16	35.15 N	48.00 W
Yakutia → Jakutija □[3]	74	67.00 N	125.00 E
Yakutsk → Jakutsk	74	62.00 N	129.40 E
Yakymivka	78	46.42 N	35.09 E
Yala, Ghana	150	10.07 N	1.52 W
Yala, Thai	110	6.33 N	101.18 E
Yalaha	220	28.44 N	81.48 W
Yalahau, Laguna C	232	21.30 N	87.15 W
Yalakdere	130	40.36 N	29.33 E
Yalama	84	41.44 N	48.34 E
Yalata	162	31.29 S	131.52 E
Yalata Aboriginal Reserve ●[4]	162	31.30 S	131.45 E
Yalca, Laguna ⊜	258	35.34 S	57.55 W
Yalding	260	51.13 N	0.26 E
Yale, B.C., Can.	182	49.34 N	121.26 W
Yale, Mi., U.S.	190	43.07 N	82.47 W
Yale, Ok., U.S.	196	36.06 N	96.41 W
Yale, Va., U.S.	208	36.50 N	77.17 W
Yale, Lake ⊜	220	28.54 N	81.45 W
Yale, Mount ʌ	200	38.51 N	106.18 W
Yale Lake ⊜[1]	224	46.00 N	122.12 W
Yalgar ≃	162	26.09 S	117.57 E
Yalgoo	162	28.20 S	116.41 E
Yalgorup National Park ♠	168a	32.55 S	115.41 E
Yali	152	0.04 N	21.03 E
Yaliji	98	36.06 N	114.56 E
Yalikamba	152	1.17 S	22.30 E
Yalinga	152	6.31 N	23.15 E
Yalisere	152	0.11 N	22.33 E
Yalleroi	166	24.04 S	145.45 E
Yallourn	169	38.11 S	146.21 E
Yallourn North	169	38.09 S	146.22 E
Yalnızçam Dağları ⋏	84	41.10 N	42.25 E
Yalobusha ≃	194	33.33 N	90.10 W
Yaloká	152	5.19 N	17.05 E
Yalong ≃	102	26.37 N	101.48 E
Yaloupi ≃	250	2.47 N	52.28 W
Yalova	130	40.39 N	29.15 E
Yalpuh, ozero ⊜	78	45.25 N	28.37 E
Yalta, Ukr.	78	44.30 N	34.10 E
Yalta, Ukr.	83	46.58 N	37.16 E
Yaltushkiv	78	48.58 N	27.30 E
Yalu	89	48.34 N	122.09 E
Yalu (Amnok-kang) ≃, Asia	98	39.55 N	124.22 E
Yalu ≃, Zhg.	89	46.56 N	123.30 E
Yalufi	152	0.45 N	24.26 E
Yalvaç	130	38.17 N	31.11 E
Yalwal Creek ≃	170	34.50 S	150.23 E
Yamachiche	206	46.16 N	72.50 W
Yamachiche ≃	206	46.16 N	72.48 W
Yamada, Nihon	92	39.28 N	141.57 E
Yamada, Nihon	94	35.49 N	140.36 E
Yamada, Nihon	94	36.34 N	137.05 E
Yamada, Nihon	96	33.33 N	130.47 E
Yamada → Tosa-yamada, Nihon	96	33.36 N	133.41 E
Yamada, Nihon	174m	26.26 N	127.47 E
Yamada, Nihon	270	34.31 N	135.39 E
Yamada, Nihon	270	34.48 N	135.32 E
Yamada ≃	270	34.47 N	135.04 E
Yamaga, Nihon	96	33.01 N	130.41 E
Yamaga, Nihon	96	33.27 N	131.30 E
Yamagata, Nihon	92	38.15 N	140.20 E
Yamagata, Nihon	94	36.38 N	140.24 E
Yamagata, Nihon	94	36.10 N	137.52 E
Yamagawa	92	31.12 N	130.39 E
Yamaguchi, Nihon	94	35.33 N	137.33 E
Yamaguchi, Nihon	96	34.10 N	131.29 E
Yamaguchi, Nihon	270	34.50 N	135.15 E
Yamaguchi □[5]	96	34.20 N	131.30 E
Yamaguchi-chosuichi ⊜[1]	268	35.46 N	139.25 E
Yama-Hita-Hiko-san-kokutei-kōen ♠	96	33.25 N	131.02 E
Yamakawa	96	34.04 N	134.15 E
Yamakita	94	35.21 N	139.05 E
Yamakuni	96	33.24 N	131.02 E
Yamakuni ≃	96	33.37 N	131.12 E
Yamām, Jabal al- ʌ	132	30.02 N	35.28 E
Yamamoto, Nihon	96	34.07 N	133.44 E
Yamamoto, Nihon	270	34.38 N	135.38 E
Yamanaka	94	36.15 N	136.22 E
Yamanakako	94	35.24 N	138.52 E
Yamanaka-ko ⊜	94	35.25 N	138.52 E
Yamanashi	94	35.40 N	138.40 E
Yamanashi □[5]	94	35.30 N	138.30 E
Yamanouchi	94	36.44 N	138.25 E
Yamasaki	96	35.00 N	134.33 E
Yamashina ●[8]	270	34.58 N	135.49 E
Yamashiro, Nihon	94	34.45 N	135.49 E
Yamashiro, Nihon	96	33.57 N	133.45 E
Yamaska (Saint-Michel)	206	46.00 N	72.55 W
Yamaska □[6]	206	46.00 N	72.45 W
Yamaska ≃	206	46.06 N	72.56 W
Yamaska, Mont ʌ[2]	206	45.27 N	72.52 W
Yamaska Nord ≃	206	45.17 N	72.51 W
Yamaska Sud-Est ≃	206	45.17 N	72.55 W
Yamate	270	34.30 N	135.27 E
Yamatengwumulu	102	38.38 N	97.05 E
Yamato, Nihon	94	35.48 N	136.54 E
Yamato, Nihon	94	35.29 N	139.29 E
Yamato, Nihon	94	37.10 N	138.56 E
Yamato, Nihon	96	33.08 N	130.26 E
Yamato ≃	96	34.36 N	135.26 E
Yamato-Aogaki-kokutei-kōen ♠	94	34.40 N	135.50 E
Yamato-kōriyama	96	34.38 N	135.47 E
Yamato-takada	96	34.31 N	135.45 E
Yamatsuri	94	36.52 N	140.25 E
Yamazaki	268	35.56 N	139.54 E
Yamba	166	29.26 S	153.22 E
Yambata	152	2.26 N	21.58 E
Yambéring	150	11.49 N	12.21 W
Yambio	154	4.34 N	28.23 E
Yambol → Jambol	38	42.29 N	26.30 E
Yamboyo	152	0.40 N	22.18 E
Yambrasbamba	248	5.45 S	77.54 W
Yambuya	154	1.16 N	24.33 E
Yamdena, Pulau I	164	7.36 S	131.25 E
Yame	96	33.28 N	130.34 E
Ya Men C	100	22.09 N	113.05 E
Yamenkou	105	39.53 N	116.12 E
Yamenying	89	43.25 N	122.19 E
Yamethin	110	20.26 N	96.09 E
Yamhill	224	45.21 N	123.11 W
Yamhill □[6]	224	45.15 N	123.20 W
Yamhill ≃	224	45.14 N	123.00 W
Yamia	150	13.24 N	10.18 E
Yamizo-san ʌ	94	36.56 N	140.17 E
Yamma Yamma, Lake ⊜	166	26.20 S	141.25 E
Yamoussoukro	150	6.49 N	5.17 W
Yampa	200	40.09 N	106.54 W
Yampa ≃	200	40.32 N	108.59 W
Yampa Plateau ⋏[1]	200	40.25 N	109.00 W
Yamparaez	248	19.10 S	65.10 W
Yampil', Ukr.	78	48.16 N	28.17 E
Yampil', Ukr.	78	49.58 N	26.14 E
Yampil', Ukr.	78	51.57 N	33.46 E
Yampil', Ukr.	83	48.56 N	37.58 E
Yamsay Mountain ʌ	202	42.56 N	121.22 W
Yamu	102	43.48 N	94.48 E
Yamuna ≃	120	25.25 N	81.50 E
Yamuna Bridge ●[5]	272a	28.40 N	77.14 E
Yamunānagar	124	30.07 N	77.18 E
Yamzho Yumco ⊜	120	28.58 N	90.44 E
Yan	114	5.48 N	100.22 E
Yan ≃, S. Lan.	122	8.55 N	81.01 E
Yan ≃, Zhg.	102	36.24 N	110.28 E
Yanac	166	36.08 S	141.26 E
Yanacachi	248	16.23 S	67.43 W
Yanachaga-Chemillen, Parque Nacional ♠	248	10.10 S	75.20 W
Yanadani	96	33.32 N	133.01 E
Yanagawa	96	33.10 N	130.24 E
Yanagi	270	34.25 N	135.56 E
Yanagimoto	270	34.34 N	135.51 E
Yanahara	96	34.55 N	134.05 E
Yanaha-shima I	174m	26.54 N	127.56 E
Yanahuara	248	16.24 S	71.33 W
Yanai	96	33.58 N	132.07 E
Yanaka	268	35.24 N	140.01 E
Yanam	122	16.44 N	82.13 E
Yan'an	102	36.36 N	109.28 E
Yanaoca	248	14.13 S	71.26 W
Yanarsu	130	38.02 N	41.33 E
Yanbian	102	26.55 N	101.30 E
Yanbu	100	23.05 N	113.10 E
Yanbuʿ al-Baḥr	128	24.05 N	38.03 E
Yanbutou	100	29.52 N	115.04 E
Yanceyville	192	36.24 N	79.20 W
Yanchang	102	36.31 N	110.08 E
Yancheng, Zhg.	100	33.36 N	113.57 E
Yancheng, Zhg.	100	33.24 N	120.09 E
Yanchep	168a	31.33 S	115.41 E
Yanchep National Park ♠	168a	31.32 S	115.40 E
Yanchi, Zhg.	102	37.52 N	107.22 E
Yanchi, Zhg.	105	40.02 N	115.53 E
Yanchuan	102	36.56 N	110.05 E
Yanco	166	34.36 S	146.25 E
Yanco Creek ≃	166	35.16 S	145.07 E
Yanda Creek ≃	166	30.28 S	145.45 E
Yandal	162	27.33 S	121.07 E
Yandama Creek ≃	166	30.00 S	140.10 E
Yandé, Île I	175f	20.03 S	163.49 E
Yande Aboriginal Reserve ●[4]	162	21.35 S	118.45 E
Yandev	150	7.20 N	9.01 E
Yandina	175e	9.07 S	159.13 E
Yandja	152	1.41 S	17.43 E
Yandongi	152	2.51 N	22.16 E
Yandoon	110	17.02 N	95.39 E
Yandua Island I	175g	16.49 S	178.18 E
Yandun	102	42.20 N	94.09 E
Yanfeng	102	25.53 N	101.01 E
Yanfolila	150	11.11 N	8.09 W
Yang ≃, Thai	110	15.44 N	104.00 E
Yang ≃, Zhg.	105	40.24 N	115.20 E
Yangambi	154	0.47 N	24.28 E
Yangan, Austl.	171a	28.12 S	152.13 E
Yang'an, Zhg.	98	37.38 N	117.09 E
Yan'gang	100	26.02 N	116.22 E
Yangarakata	154	3.01 N	30.28 E
Yangasa Levu I	175g	18.57 S	178.26 W
Yangbajain	120	30.06 N	90.33 E
Yangce	100	32.58 N	113.14 E
Yangcha	98	41.11 N	126.15 E
Yangchang	107	30.22 N	103.42 E
Yangcheng, Zhg.	102	35.29 N	112.25 E
Yangcheng, Zhg.	106	31.24 N	120.47 E
Yangcheng Hu ⊜	106	31.26 N	120.47 E
Yangchiang → Yangjiang	102	21.51 N	111.56 E
Yangch'ŏn ●[8]	271b	37.34 N	126.51 E
Yangchow → Yangzhou	100	32.24 N	119.26 E
Yangchu	98	37.11 N	120.47 E
Yangch'üan → Yangquan	98	37.52 N	113.36 E
Yangchun	102	22.10 N	111.46 E
Yangcun, Zhg.	100	28.07 N	117.40 E
Yangcun, Zhg.	100	23.26 N	114.30 E
Yangcun, Zhg.	105	39.09 N	115.50 E
Yangcunqiao	100	29.36 N	119.28 E
Yangdachengzi	89	43.59 N	124.25 E
Yangdalinzi	98	42.38 N	125.07 E
Yangdang	100	32.23 N	112.39 E
Yangdian	106	31.08 N	119.45 E
Yang'erzhuang	98	38.18 N	117.30 E
Yangfang	105	40.07 N	116.07 E
Yangfangpu	105	40.48 N	115.01 E
Yangfengang	105	39.07 N	116.52 E
Yangfenzhen	106	30.28 N	120.03 E
Yanggang Do □[4]	98	41.15 N	128.00 E
Yangganzhen	106	31.00 N	119.15 E
Yanggao	98	40.25 N	113.44 E
Yanggezhuang	105	40.09 N	116.48 E
Yanggong-ni	271b	37.39 N	126.37 E
Yanggu, Taehan	98	38.06 N	127.59 E
Yanggu, Zhg.	98	34.44 N	114.48 E
Yanggu, Zhg.	98	36.08 N	115.48 E
Yangguanpu	100	32.13 N	115.31 E
Yanghang	106	31.22 N	121.26 E
Yanghe	100	33.47 N	118.23 E
Yanghexi	102	29.39 N	108.40 E
Yanghu	100	32.34 N	116.30 E
Yanghua	107	30.11 N	104.45 E
Yanghua ≃	107	30.09 N	104.42 E
Yangi-Yul' → Jangijul'	85	41.07 N	69.03 E
Yangji, Zhg.	98	36.44 N	113.56 E
Yangji, Zhg.	98	34.25 N	116.06 E
Yangji, Zhg.	100	34.19 N	119.28 E
Yangjia, Zhg.	98	34.19 N	119.28 E
Yangjia, Zhg.	106	30.41 N	120.15 E
Yangjiachang, Zhg.	107	29.23 N	104.21 E
Yangjiachang, Zhg.	107	29.45 N	105.21 E
Yangjiafeng	100	30.49 N	112.47 E
Yangjiagou	105	39.18 N	117.54 E
Yangjiajie	107	30.18 N	104.39 E
Yangjian	106	31.39 N	120.33 E
Yangjiang	102	21.51 N	111.56 E
Yangjiaogou	98	37.16 N	118.50 E
Yangjiaqiao, Zhg.	100	27.44 N	112.46 E
Yangjiaqiao, Zhg.	106	31.53 N	121.42 E
Yangjiaqiao, Zhg.	106	32.02 N	121.26 E
Yangjiatao	105	39.49 N	117.51 E
Yangjiawopu	104	42.21 N	122.57 E
Yangjiazeng	105	40.12 N	117.04 E
Yangjiazhangzi	104	40.48 N	120.33 E
Yangjie	102	24.49 N	100.22 E
Yangjishi	100	26.39 N	113.14 E
Yangkou	100	26.47 N	117.51 E
Yangkoushi	100	28.39 N	118.53 E
Yanglinjie	100	29.07 N	113.27 E
Yangliupu, Zhg.	100	30.52 N	118.37 E
Yangliupu, Zhg.	107	30.09 N	104.03 E
Yangliuqing	105	39.08 N	117.01 E
Yangloudong	100	29.31 N	113.44 E
Yanglousi	100	29.30 N	113.38 E
Yangluo	100	30.41 N	114.34 E
Yangluomayu	104	40.47 N	122.54 E
Yangmachang	107	30.39 N	103.45 E
Yangma Dao I	98	37.28 N	121.37 E
Yangmahe	107	30.29 N	104.31 E
Yangmeisi	100	25.42 N	114.30 E
Yangmiao, Zhg.	98	34.11 N	114.53 E
Yangmiao, Zhg.	106	30.51 N	120.49 E
Yangmingshan ●[8]	269d	25.09 N	121.33 E
Yangming Shan ʌ	102	26.03 N	111.56 E
Yangmugou, Zhg.	98	40.36 N	124.28 E
Yangmugou, Zhg.	104	41.11 N	123.50 E
Yangmulin	105	40.06 N	115.12 E
Yangon (Rangoon)	110	16.47 N	96.10 E
Yangon □[8]	110	16.50 N	96.10 E
Yangor	174b	0.31 S	166.54 E
Yangpingguan	102	32.51 N	106.09 E
Yangpu	100	27.14 N	119.08 E
Yangp'yŏng	98	37.30 N	127.29 E
Yangp'yŏng-ni	98	40.53 N	127.58 E
Yangqi	106	31.23 N	119.57 E
Yangquan	98	37.52 N	113.36 E
Yangriwan	102	31.37 N	110.49 E
Yangsan	98	35.21 N	129.03 E
Yangshan, Zhg.	98	41.13 N	120.24 E
Yangshan, Zhg.	98	35.13 N	116.13 E
Yangshan, Zhg.	102	24.28 N	112.38 E
Yangshigangzi	104	41.42 N	122.59 E
Yangshitun	104	42.06 N	123.44 E
Yangshu	106	31.39 N	120.08 E
Yangshugemen	105	40.55 N	118.18 E
Yangshugoudonggou	104	41.43 N	120.41 E
Yangshuling	98	41.02 N	118.47 E
Yangshuo	102	24.45 N	110.24 E
Yangtan	106	30.42 N	119.11 E
Yangtian Zhang ʌ	100	24.37 N	115.38 E
Yangting	98	37.24 N	122.07 E
Yangtou	100	23.26 N	115.24 E
Yangtze → Chang ≃	90	31.48 N	121.10 E
Yanguan	106	30.26 N	120.32 E
Yangwan, Zhg.	100	28.22 N	116.46 E
Yangwan, Zhg.	106	31.03 N	120.22 E
Yangxi, Zhg.	100	30.11 N	118.39 E
Yangxi, Zhg.	100	27.18 N	114.10 E
Yangxian	102	33.03 N	107.47 E
Yangxiang, Zhg.	106	31.29 N	119.35 E
Yangxiang, Zhg.	106	31.12 N	121.01 E
Yangxiangtun	104	40.58 N	122.48 E
Yangxiaodian	100	31.46 N	116.45 E
Yangximu ≃	104	42.04 N	123.00 E
Yangxin, Zhg.	98	37.39 N	117.34 E
Yangxin, Zhg.	100	29.51 N	115.12 E
Yangxiudian	271a	39.44 N	116.32 E
Yangyang	98	38.04 N	128.36 E
Yangyuan (Xicheng)	98	40.01 N	114.10 E
Yangze	100	26.57 N	118.23 E
Yangzhong	106	32.16 N	119.49 E
Yangzhou	100	32.24 N	119.26 E
Yangzhuang	100	33.36 N	118.58 E
Yangzhujuanzi	104	41.38 N	122.46 E
Yangzi	100	31.19 N	112.36 E
Yangzishao	98	42.28 N	126.09 E
Yanhaiyingzi	104	41.52 N	123.05 E
Yanhe, Zhg.	100	31.16 N	115.07 E
Yanhe, Zhg.	102	28.37 N	108.35 E
Yanhecheng	105	40.04 N	115.43 E
Yanheying	98	40.02 N	119.03 E
Yanhui	98	37.54 N	113.51 E
Yanina → Ioánnina	38	39.40 N	20.50 E
Yanji, Zhg.	98	34.41 N	115.27 E
Yanji, Zhg.	98	42.57 N	129.32 E
Yanji (Longjing), Zhg.	98	42.47 N	129.26 E
Yanji, Zhg.	98	34.17 N	115.39 E
Yanjia	104	40.57 N	121.41 E
Yanjiabao	106	32.19 N	120.07 E
Yanjiadian	98	39.48 N	121.49 E
Yanjiahe	100	31.48 N	114.50 E
Yanjiajie	104	41.02 N	121.32 E
Yanjiao	105	39.56 N	116.48 E
Yanjiapu	105	39.52 N	118.00 E
Yanjiatuozi	104	42.27 N	123.47 E
Yanjiawopeng	104	40.59 N	121.17 E
Yanjin	98	35.11 N	114.11 E
Yanjing, Zhg.	102	29.00 N	98.34 E
Yanjing, Zhg.	107	29.56 N	106.21 E
Yankalilla	168b	35.28 S	138.21 E
Yankalilla Bay C	168b	35.28 S	138.15 E
Yankari Game Reserve ●[4]	146	9.45 N	10.30 E
Yankdŏk	98	39.14 N	126.41 E
Yankee Lake	210	41.35 N	74.33 W
Yankee Springs State Recreation Area ♠	216	42.38 N	85.30 W
Yankee Stadium ♠	276	40.50 N	73.56 W
Yankeetown	220	29.01 N	82.42 W
Yankton	198	42.52 N	97.23 W
Yankton Indian Reservation ●[4]	198	43.10 N	98.22 W
Yanling, Zhg.	98	34.07 N	114.11 E
Yanling, Zhg.	106	31.54 N	119.30 E
Yanliumiao	100	32.01 N	116.52 E
Yanmeimeizi	105	39.42 N	115.03 E
Yanna	166	26.56 S	146.03 E
Yannarie ≃	162	22.28 S	114.48 E
Yanqi	90	42.00 N	86.15 E
Yanqian, Zhg.	100	24.54 N	116.14 E
Yanqian, Zhg.	100	26.15 N	117.28 E
Yanqianhu	104	42.16 N	123.12 E
Yanqiao	106	31.41 N	120.17 E
Yanqidoumen	106	31.17 N	118.42 E
Yanqing	105	40.28 N	115.58 E
Yanque	248	15.39 S	71.39 W
Yanrey	162	22.31 S	114.48 E
Yanshan, Zhg.	98	38.05 N	117.13 E
Yanshan, Zhg.	100	28.18 N	117.41 E
Yanshan, Zhg.	102	23.41 N	104.21 E
Yan Shan ⋏	105	40.20 N	117.40 E
Yanshankou	105	39.59 N	117.42 E
Yanshi	100	25.17 N	117.10 E
Yanshi ≃	100	25.20 N	117.17 E
Yanshou	89	45.28 N	128.20 E
Yansi	100	29.48 N	118.20 E
Yanṭā	132	33.36 N	35.57 E
Yantabulla	166	29.21 S	145.00 E
Yantai (Chefoo), Zhg.	98	37.33 N	121.20 E
Yantai, Zhg.	105	39.47 N	116.38 E
Yantan, Zhg.	100	28.28 N	120.44 E
Yantan, Zhg.	100	28.55 N	120.11 E
Yantan, Zhg.	107	29.17 N	104.52 E
Yantian, Zhg.	100	26.53 N	119.53 E
Yantian, Zhg.	100	27.21 N	114.22 E
Yantic ≃	207	41.31 N	72.05 W
Yantietang ≊	106	31.49 N	120.46 E
Yanting	102	31.19 N	105.23 E
Yantis	222	32.56 N	95.35 W
Yantongshan, Zhg.	89	43.17 N	126.00 E
Yantongshan, Zhg.	105	40.42 N	115.06 E
Yanu	164	9.57 S	148.25 E
Yanwangshan	104	41.36 N	123.57 E
Yanweigang	98	34.30 N	119.48 E
Yanxi	100	24.46 N	117.47 E
Yanxia	100	29.34 N	114.50 E
Yanxidu	100	26.51 N	114.58 E
Yanxing	102	25.23 N	101.42 E
Yan Yean Reservoir ⊜[1]	169	37.33 S	145.08 E
Yanyegongsi	106	32.02 N	121.41 E
Yanyuan	102	27.29 N	101.32 E
Yanzhou	98	35.33 N	116.50 E
Yanziji	106	32.09 N	118.49 E
Yanzijiao	102	23.38 N	100.12 E
Yanzikou	102	27.31 N	105.21 E
Yao, Centraf.	152	5.19 N	19.36 E
Yao, Nihon	96	34.37 N	135.36 E
Yao, Tchad	146	12.51 N	17.34 E
Yao Airport ⊠	270	34.36 N	135.36 E
Yao'an	102	25.32 N	101.12 E
Yaoba	107	28.45 N	105.39 E
Yaocun, Zhg.	98	36.12 N	113.50 E
Yaocun, Zhg.	98	35.41 N	116.57 E
Yaocun, Zhg.	105	39.09 N	115.32 E
Yaodafangshen	104	42.27 N	122.59 E
Yaoerwan	105	40.49 N	115.27 E
Yaogongbu	100	29.51 N	120.18 E
Yaohongcaopao	104	40.55 N	122.26 E
Yaohuamen	106	32.08 N	118.52 E
Yaohuangdi	104	41.32 N	122.48 E
Yaojiaji	100	31.14 N	114.22 E
Yaojiaqiao	106	32.10 N	119.46 E
Yaojiatun	104	41.18 N	121.57 E
Yaojiawopeng	104	41.47 N	122.25 E
Yaojie	102	36.26 N	102.59 E
Yaoling	100	24.49 N	113.58 E
Yaolugou	98	40.34 N	119.24 E
Yaoluzi	104	41.26 N	121.34 E
Yaopi	100	26.52 N	113.38 E
Yaopu	100	32.14 N	118.20 E
Yaoqianhutun	104	41.32 N	123.36 E
Yaoshizhen	107	30.11 N	105.30 E
Yaotou	100	26.38 N	114.48 E
Yaotsu	94	35.28 N	137.09 E
Yaotun, Zhg.	89	49.28 N	127.30 E
Yaotun, Zhg.	104	40.59 N	122.18 E
Yaotutun	104	42.06 N	123.29 E
Yaoundé	152	3.52 N	11.31 E
Yaowan	98	34.12 N	118.03 E
Yaowangmiao	98	40.47 N	120.10 E
Yaoxian	102	34.56 N	108.53 E
Yaoya ≃	236	13.28 N	84.14 W
Yao Yai, Ko I	110	8.00 N	98.35 E
Yaozhan	89	52.53 N	125.13 E
Yap I	174q	9.31 N	138.06 E
Yapacaní	248	16.45 S	64.18 W
Yapacani ≃	248	16.00 S	64.25 W
Yapakopra	164	4.24 S	135.05 E
Yapehe	152	0.13 S	24.27 E
Yapei (Tamale Port)	150	9.10 N	1.10 W
Yapen, Pulau I	164	1.45 S	136.15 E
Yapen, Selat ꓤ	164	1.30 S	136.10 E
Yapero	164	4.59 S	137.11 E
Yapeyú	252	29.28 S	56.49 W
Yaphank	207	40.50 N	72.56 W
Yappar ≃	166	18.22 S	141.16 E
Yapraklı	130	40.46 N	33.47 E
Yap Trench ⊹[1]	14	8.30 N	138.00 E
Yaqian	100	26.38 N	114.30 E
Yaʿqūb	140	12.29 N	25.11 E
Yaque del Norte ≃	238	19.51 N	71.41 W
Yaqui ≃	232	27.37 N	110.39 W
Yaquina ≃	202	44.37 N	124.04 W
Yara	240p	20.16 N	76.57 W
Yaracuy □[3]	246	10.20 N	69.10 W
Yaraka	166	24.53 S	144.04 E
Yaratuar	164	2.58 S	134.40 E
Yarbasan	130	38.59 N	28.49 E
Yarcombe	42	50.52 N	3.05 W
Yardea	166	32.23 S	135.32 E
Yardımcı	130	37.00 N	38.59 E
Yardımcı Burnu ›	130	36.13 N	30.25 E
Yardımlı	84	38.55 N	48.15 E
Yardley	208	40.14 N	74.50 W
Yardville	208	40.10 N	74.39 W
Yare ≃	42	52.35 N	1.44 E
Yaremcha	78	48.27 N	24.33 E
Yarí ≃	246	0.23 S	72.16 W
Yariga-take ʌ	94	36.20 N	137.39 E
Yārik	123	32.06 N	70.47 E
Yarīm	144	14.29 N	44.21 E
Yaring	110	6.52 N	101.22 E
Yaritagua	246	10.05 N	69.08 W
Yarkand → Shache	120	38.25 N	77.16 E
Yarkand → Yarkant ≃	90	40.28 N	80.52 E
Yarkant (Yarkand) ≃	90	40.28 N	80.52 E
Yarker	212	44.23 N	76.46 W
Yarkhūn ≃	123	36.17 N	72.30 E
Yarlarweelor	162	25.35 S	117.59 E
Yarle Lakes ⊜	162	30.15 S	131.27 E
Yarloop	168a	32.57 S	115.54 E
Yarlung → Brahmaputra ≃	120	24.02 N	90.59 E
Yarma	130	37.49 N	32.54 E
Yarmolyntsi	78	49.12 N	26.50 E
Yarmouth, N.S., Can.	186	43.50 N	66.07 W
Yarmouth, Eng., U.K.	42	50.42 N	1.29 W
Yarmouth → Great Yarmouth, Eng., U.K.	42	52.37 N	1.44 E
Yarmouth, Me., U.S.	188	43.48 N	70.11 W
Yarmouth, Ma., U.S.	207	41.42 N	70.13 W
Yarmu	164	4.18 S	142.17 E
Yarmūk, Nahr al- ≃	132	32.38 N	35.34 E
Yaroslavets'	78	51.33 N	33.40 E
Yarova	83	49.03 N	37.37 E
Yarra ≃	169	37.51 S	144.54 E
Yarra Bend Park ♠	274b	37.48 S	145.01 E
Yarra Glen	169	37.40 S	145.23 E
Yarragon	169	38.12 S	146.04 E
Yarra Junction	169	37.47 S	145.37 E
Yarraloola	162	21.34 S	115.52 E
Yarram	166	38.33 S	146.41 E
Yarraman	171a	26.50 S	151.59 E
Yarrangobilly	171b	35.39 S	148.28 E
Yarrangobilly ≃	171b	35.48 N	148.23 E
Yarrangobilly Caves ⊥[5]	171b	35.44 S	148.29 E
Yarraville	274b	37.49 S	144.53 E
Yarrawonga	166	36.01 S	146.00 E
Yarra Yarra Lakes ⊜	162	29.40 S	115.47 E
Yarrow, B.C., Can.	224	49.05 N	122.02 W
Yarrow, Scot., U.K.	46	55.32 N	3.01 W
Yarrow ≃	262	53.40 N	2.49 W
Yarrowee ≃	169	37.48 S	143.56 E
Yarrow Point	224	47.39 N	122.13 W
Yarrow Reservoir ⊜[1]	262	53.38 N	2.34 W
Yarrow Water ≃	46	55.34 N	2.51 W
Yarrunga, Lake ⊜[1]	170	34.45 S	150.20 E
Yarty ≃	42	50.47 N	3.01 W
Yarumal	246	6.58 N	75.24 W
Yasa	152	3.42 S	21.24 E
Yasaka, Nihon	96	35.39 N	135.07 E
Yasaka, Nihon	96	34.46 N	132.04 E
Yasa-Lokwa	152	5.15 S	19.24 E
Yasato	94	36.14 N	140.12 E
Yasawa I	175g	16.47 S	177.31 E
Yasawa Group II	175g	17.00 S	177.23 E
Yasendu	152	0.27 N	24.20 E
Yasenivs'kyy	83	48.10 N	39.10 E
Yashanjie	106	30.51 N	119.03 E
Yashbum	144	14.19 N	46.56 E
Yashi	150	12.23 N	7.54 E
Yashikera	150	9.46 N	3.28 E
Ya-shima I	96	33.44 N	132.09 E
Yashima ♠	96	34.23 N	134.08 E
Yashio	268	35.49 N	139.51 E
Yashiro	96	34.55 N	134.58 E
Yashiro-jima I	96	33.55 N	132.15 E
Yāsīn	123	36.21 N	73.19 E
Yasinya	78	48.16 N	24.20 E
Yasku	146	12.20 N	12.30 E
Yasnohirka	83	48.47 N	37.33 E
Yasothon	110	15.45 N	104.08 E
Yass	166	34.50 S	148.55 E
Yassıada I	267b	40.51 N	29.00 E
Yassy → Iași	38	47.10 N	27.35 E
Yasu, Nihon	94	35.03 N	136.01 E
Yasu, Nihon	96	33.32 N	133.45 E
Yasuda	96	33.26 N	133.59 E
Yasugi	96	35.26 N	133.15 E
Yāsūj	128	30.40 N	51.36 E
Yasun Burnu ›	130	41.08 N	37.41 E
Yasuní ≃	246	0.56 S	75.23 W
Yasuni, Parque Nacional ♠	246	0.50 S	76.15 W
Yasuoka	94	35.22 N	137.50 E
Yasuura	96	34.17 N	132.45 E
Yasuzuka	94	37.08 N	138.28 E
Yasynivka	83	48.08 N	37.57 E
Yasynuvata	83	48.08 N	37.51 E
Yata	248	13.20 S	66.35 W
Yata ≃, Bol.	248	10.29 S	65.26 W
Yata ≃, Centraf.	146	10.23 N	22.45 E
Yatabe	94	36.02 N	140.04 E
Yatağan	130	37.20 N	28.09 E
Yatakala	150	14.48 N	0.22 E
Yata-Ngaya, Réserve de Faune de la ●[4]	146	9.15 N	23.30 W
Yāṭar	132	33.09 N	35.20 E
Yatate-yama ʌ	92	34.10 N	129.10 E
Yaté	175f	22.09 S	166.57 E
Yates □[6]	210	42.40 N	77.03 W
Yatesboro	214	40.48 N	79.20 W
Yates Center	198	37.52 N	95.43 W
Yates City	190	40.46 N	90.00 W
Yathata Island I	175g	17.15 S	179.32 W
Yathkyed Lake ⊜	176	62.41 N	98.00 W
Yating	102	25.03 N	106.05 E
Yatomi	94	35.06 N	136.43 E
Yatsuga-take ʌ	94	35.59 N	138.23 E
Yatsuga-take-chūshin-kōgen-kokutei-kōen ♠	94	36.03 N	138.20 E
Yatsuka	96	35.17 N	133.42 E
Yatsuo	94	36.34 N	137.08 E
Yatsushiro	92	32.30 N	130.36 E
Yatsushiro-kai C	92	32.20 N	130.25 E
Yaṭṭah	132	31.27 N	35.05 E
Yatta Plateau ⋏[1]	154	2.00 S	38.00 E
Yatton	42	51.24 N	2.49 W
Yatuá ≃	246	1.43 N	66.30 W
Yatusiro → Yatsushiro	92	32.30 N	130.36 E
Yauca	248	15.40 S	74.32 W
Yauca ≃	248	15.41 S	74.31 W
Yauco	240m	18.02 N	66.51 W
Yauco ≃	240m	17.59 N	66.48 W
Yauco, Embalse de ⊜[1]	240m	18.07 N	66.50 W
Yauli	248	11.41 S	76.06 W
Yaundé → Yaoundé	152	3.52 N	11.31 E
Yaupi	246	2.59 S	77.50 W
Yauri	248	14.47 S	71.29 W
Yautepec	234	18.53 N	99.04 W
Yau Tong	271d	22.18 N	114.13 E
Yauyos	248	12.24 S	75.57 W
Yāval	120	21.10 N	75.42 E
Yavarí (Javari) ≃	242	4.21 S	70.02 W
Yavarí Mirim ≃	246	4.31 S	71.44 W
Yavaros	232	26.42 N	109.31 W
Yavatmāl	122	20.24 N	78.08 E
Yaven Yaven Creek ≃	171b	35.06 S	147.46 E
Yavero ≃	248	12.06 S	72.57 W
Yavi	130	39.48 N	36.13 E
Yaví, Cerro ʌ	246	5.32 N	65.59 W
Yavita	246	2.55 N	67.26 W
Yaviza	246	8.11 N	77.41 W
Yavkine	78	47.16 N	32.37 E
Yavne	132	31.53 N	34.45 E
Yavoriv	78	49.56 N	23.23 E
Yavuzeli	130	37.20 N	37.33 E
Yavuzkemal	130	40.43 N	38.21 E
Yaw ≃	110	20.55 N	94.49 E
Yawahara	268	35.59 N	140.01 E
Yawata, Nihon	96	34.52 N	135.42 E
Yawata → Kitakyūshū, Nihon	96	33.53 N	130.50 E
Yawata, Nihon	268	35.32 N	140.08 E
Yawatahama	96	33.27 N	132.24 E
Yaxchilán ⊥	232	16.54 N	90.58 W
Yaxi	102	27.32 N	106.45 E
Yaxian	110	18.20 N	109.30 E
Yaxigang	106	31.23 N	119.10 E
Yaxley	42	52.31 N	0.16 W
Yayama	152	1.16 S	23.07 E
Yayladağı	130	35.56 N	36.01 E
Yayladere	130	39.14 N	40.03 E
Yaylak	130	37.23 N	38.20 E
Yayouta	150	8.11 N	8.30 W
Yayuan	98	41.47 N	126.11 E
Yazd	128	31.53 N	54.25 E
Yazd □[4]	128	32.00 N	54.30 E
Yazi	98	37.04 N	121.17 E
Yazichangcun	104	41.16 N	122.26 E
Yazıhan	130	38.36 N	38.11 E
Yazmān	123	29.08 N	71.45 E
Yazoo ≃	194	32.22 N	91.00 W
Yazoo City	194	32.51 N	90.24 W
Ybbs ≃	61	48.10 N	15.06 E
Ybbs an der Donau	61	48.11 N	15.05 E
Ybbsitz	61	47.56 N	14.53 E
Ybor City	220	27.57 N	82.27 W
Ybycuí	252	26.01 S	57.03 W
Yding Skovhøj ʌ[2]	41	56.00 N	9.48 E
Ydstebøhavn	26	59.08 N	5.15 E
Ydžid Parma ⋏	24	63.06 N	58.15 E
Ye	110	15.15 N	97.51 E
Yea	169	37.13 S	145.26 E
Yea ≃	169	37.11 S	145.23 E
Yeading ●[8]	260	51.32 N	0.24 W
Yeadon, Eng., U.K.	44	53.52 N	1.41 W
Yeadon, Pa., U.S.	285	39.56 N	75.15 W
Yeagertown	208	40.38 N	77.34 W
Yealm ≃	42	50.18 N	4.03 W
Yealmpton	42	50.21 N	3.59 W
Yebawgyi	110	18.40 N	94.35 E
Yebbi-Bou	146	20.58 N	18.04 E
Yébigué, Enneri V	146	22.04 N	17.49 E
Yèbles	261	48.38 N	2.46 E
Yebyu	110	14.15 N	98.12 E
Yecapixtla	234	18.53 N	98.52 W
Yecheng	120	37.54 N	77.25 E
Yech'ŏn	98	36.40 N	128.26 E
Yecla	34	38.37 N	1.07 W
Yécora	232	28.20 N	108.58 W
Yedashe	110	19.09 N	96.21 E
Yedi Göller Milli Parkı ♠	130	40.50 N	31.30 E
Yedikule ●[8]	267b	40.59 N	28.55 E
Yedikule ⊥	267b	40.59 N	28.55 E
Yédinga, Ouadi V	146	15.46 N	20.05 E
Yedseram ≃	146	12.30 N	14.05 E
Yeed	144	4.33 N	43.02 E
Yeeda	162	17.36 S	123.39 E
Yeelanna	166	34.09 S	135.45 E
Yeelirrie	162	27.17 S	120.06 E
Yeernuozha Hu ⊜	120	32.30 N	89.30 E
Yegor'yevsk → Jegorjevsk	82	55.23 N	39.02 E
Yegros	252	26.24 S	56.25 W
Yegua Creek ≃	222	30.23 N	96.18 W
Yeguas, Punta ›	258	34.55 S	56.19 W
Yeguas, Río de las ≃	34	37.22 N	4.45 W
Yehliu	269d	25.12 N	121.41 E
Yehliu Chia ›	269d	25.13 N	121.42 E
Yehud	132	32.02 N	34.53 E
Yei	154	4.05 N	30.40 E
Yei ≃	140	6.15 N	30.13 E
Yeji, Ghana	150	8.13 N	0.39 W
Yeji, Zhg.	100	31.52 N	115.55 E
Yekaterinburg → Jekaterinburg	86	56.51 N	60.36 E
Yekaterinodar → Krasnodar	78	45.02 N	39.00 E
Yekaterinoslav → Dnipropetrovs'k	78	48.27 N	34.59 E
Yekokora ≃	152	1.20 N	20.21 E
Yekumbo	152	1.02 S	23.27 E
Ye Kyun I	110	18.37 N	93.47 E
Yela Island I	160	11.21 S	154.09 E
Yelanets'	78	47.42 N	31.51 E
Yelarbon	166	28.34 S	150.45 E
Yelcho, Lago ⊜	254	43.18 S	72.18 W
Yele	150	8.25 N	11.50 W
Yelets → Jelec	76	52.37 N	38.30 E
Yélimané	150	15.08 N	10.34 W
Yelizarove	78	48.12 N	34.33 E
Yelizavethradka	78	48.48 N	32.24 E
Yell I	46a	60.36 N	1.06 W
Yellandu	122	17.36 N	80.20 E
Yellow ≃, U.S.	194	30.33 N	87.00 W
Yellow ≃, In., U.S.	216	41.16 N	86.50 W
Yellow ≃, Ia., U.S.	190	43.05 N	91.11 W
Yellow ≃, Wi., U.S.	190	44.58 N	91.18 W
Yellow ≃, Wi., U.S.	190	43.59 N	90.03 W
Yellow ≃, Wi., U.S.	190	46.01 N	92.22 W
Yellow → Huang ≃, Zhg.	90	37.32 N	118.19 E
Yellow Breeches Creek ≃	208	40.13 N	76.51 W
Yellow Creek ≃, U.S.	194	33.34 N	88.20 W
Yellow Creek ≃, Co., U.S.	200	40.10 N	108.24 W
Yellow Creek ≃, Oh., U.S.	214	40.34 N	80.40 W
Yellow Creek ≃, Tn., U.S.	194	36.26 N	87.34 W
Yellow Creek, North Fork ≃	214	40.33 N	80.42 W
Yellow Creek State Park ♠	214	40.35 N	79.02 W
Yellowdine	162	31.18 S	119.39 E
Yellow Grass	184	49.49 N	104.08 W
Yellowhead Pass)(	182	52.53 N	118.28 W
Yellow House Draw V	196	33.35 N	101.50 W
Yellowknife	176	62.27 N	114.21 W
Yellowknife ≃	176	62.31 N	114.19 W
Yellow Lake ⊜	212	44.20 N	75.36 W
Yellow Medicine ≃	198	44.44 N	95.25 W
Yellow Mountain ʌ	166	32.30 S	146.51 E
Yellow Sea ⊤[2]	90	36.00 N	123.00 E
Yellow Springs	218	39.48 N	83.53 W
Yellowstone ≃	178	47.58 N	103.59 W
Yellowstone, Clarks Fork ≃	202	45.39 N	108.43 W
Yellowstone Falls ∟	202	44.43 N	110.30 W
Yellowstone Lake ⊜	202	44.25 N	110.22 W
Yellowstone National Park	202	44.59 N	110.42 W
Yellowstone National Park ♠	202	44.30 N	110.35 W
Yellowtail Dam ●[6]	202	45.12 N	107.57 W
Yell Sound ꓤ	46a	60.32 N	1.15 W
Yellville	194	36.13 N	92.41 W
Yelm	224	46.56 N	122.36 W
Yelma	162	26.30 S	121.40 E
Yelvertoft	166	20.13 S	138.53 E
Yelverton	42	50.30 N	4.05 W
Yelwa	150	10.51 N	4.46 E
Yelyseyivka	78	47.02 N	36.24 E
Yema ≃	102	41.25 N	95.10 E
Yemadu	86	43.36 N	81.50 E
Yemagong	124	29.28 N	89.06 E
Yemaotai	104	42.20 N	122.53 E
Yemassee	192	32.41 N	80.51 W
Yematan	102	34.40 N	98.16 E
Yemen (Al-Yaman) □[1], Asia	118	15.00 N	47.00 E
Yemen (Al-Yaman) □[1], Asia	144	15.00 N	47.00 E
Yemen, People's Democratic Republic of → Yemen □[1]	144	15.00 N	47.00 E
Yemen, República Popular Democrática del → Yemen □[1]	144	15.00 N	47.00 E

Symbols in the index entries represent the broad categories identified in the key at the right. Symbols with superior numbers (⋏[1]) identify subcategories (see complete key on page I · 1).

Symbole im Register stellen die rechts im Schlüssel erklärten Kategorien dar. Symbole mit hochgestellten Ziffern (⋏[1]) bezeichnen Unterabteilungen einer Kategorie (vgl. vollständiger Schlüssel auf Seite I · 1).

Los símbolos incluídos en el texto del índice representan las grandes categorías identificadas con la clave a la derecha. Los símbolos con numeros en su parte superior (⋏[1]) identifican las subcategorías (véase la clave completa en la página I · 1).

Les symboles de l'index représentent les catégories indiquées dans la légende à droite. Les symboles suivis d'un indice (⋏[1]) représentent des sous-catégories (voir légende complète à la page I · 1).

Os símbolos incluídos no texto do índice representam as grandes categorias identificadas com a chave à direita. Os símbolos com números em sua parte superior (⋏[1]) identificam as subcategorias (veja-se a chave completa à página I · 1).

Symbol	English	Deutsch	Español	Français	Português
ʌ	Mountain	Berg	Montaña	Montagne	Montanha
⋏	Mountains	Gebirge	Montañas	Montagnes	Montanhas
)(	Pass	Paß	Paso	Col	Passo
V	Valley, Canyon	Tal, Cañon	Valle, Cañón	Vallée, Canyon	Vale, Canhão
≚	Plain	Ebene	Llano	Plaine	Planície
›	Cape	Kap	Cabo	Cap	Cabo
I	Island	Insel	Isla	Île	Ilha
II	Islands	Inseln	Islas	Îles	Ilhas
⊥	Other Topographic Features	Andere Topographische Objekte	Otros Elementos Topográficos	Autres données topographiques	Outros acidentes topográficos

ESPAÑOL

Nombre	Página	Lat. °′	Long. °′ W = Oeste
Yémen, République démocratique populaire du → Yemen □[1]	144	15.00 N	47.00 E
Yemil'chyne	78	50.52 N	27.48 E
Yen	152	2.27 N	12.41 E
Yenagoa	150	4.55 N	6.19 E
Yenakiyeve	83	48.14 N	38.13 E
Yenangyaung	110	20.28 N	94.52 E
Yenanma	110	19.46 N	94.48 E
Yen Bai	110	21.42 N	104.52 E
Yen Chau	110	21.03 N	104.18 E
Yench'eng → Yancheng	100	33.24 N	120.09 E
Yenchi → Yanji	98	42.57 N	129.32 E
Yenda	166	34.15 S	146.11 E
Yende Millimou	150	8.53 N	10.11 W
Yendéré	150	10.12 N	4.58 W
Yendi	150	9.26 N	0.01 W
Ye-ngan	110	21.09 N	96.27 E
Yenge ≃	152	0.55 S	20.40 E
Yengema	150	8.43 N	11.10 W
Yengisar	85	38.57 N	76.03 E
Yengo	152	0.22 N	15.29 E
Yengo, Mount ∧	170	32.59 S	150.51 E
Yéni	150	13.26 N	2.59 E
Yeniçağa	130	40.46 N	32.02 E
Yenice, Tür.	130	39.45 N	28.55 E
Yenice, Tür.	130	39.55 N	27.18 E
Yenice, Tür.	130	36.59 N	35.03 E
Yenice, Tür.	130	41.11 N	32.19 E
Yenice ≃	130	41.35 N	32.03 E
Yenicekale	130	37.37 N	36.37 E
Yeniceoba	130	38.53 N	32.48 E
Yenierenköy	130	35.32 N	34.11 E
Yenifoça	130	38.44 N	26.51 E
Yenikapı ◆[8]	267b	41.00 N	28.57 E
Yeniköy	130	39.46 N	28.00 E
Yeniköy ◆[8]	267b	40.59 N	28.53 E
Yenimehmetli	130	39.26 N	32.10 E
Yenipazar, Tür.	130	37.48 N	28.12 E
Yenipazar, Tür.	130	40.11 N	30.31 E
Yenişehir	130	40.16 N	29.39 E
Yenisey → Jenisej ≃	72	71.50 N	82.40 E
Yennadon	224	49.14 N	122.34 W
Yenne	62	45.42 N	5.46 E
Yennora	274a	33.52 S	150.58 E
Yenshuichen	100	23.20 N	120.16 E
Yentna ≃	180	61.34 N	150.28 W
Yeo ≃, Eng., U.K.	42	51.02 N	2.49 W
Yeo ≃, Eng., U.K.	42	51.01 N	3.50 W
Yeo ≃, Eng., U.K.	42	50.45 N	3.36 W
Yeola	122	20.02 N	74.29 E
Yeo Lake ⊜	162	28.04 S	124.23 E
Yeoman	216	40.40 N	86.43 W
Yeoval	166	32.45 S	148.40 E
Yeovil	42	50.57 N	2.39 W
Yeoville ◆[8]	273d	26.12 S	28.04 E
Yepachic	232	28.26 N	108.23 W
Yeppoon	166	23.08 S	150.45 E
Yerba Buena, Montaña ∧	236	14.05 N	87.26 W
Yerba Buena Island I	282	37.48 N	122.22 W
Yères ≃	50	50.02 N	1.19 E
Yerevan → Jerevan	84	40.11 N	44.30 E
Yerilla	162	29.28 S	121.49 E
Yering	274b	37.41 S	145.23 E
Yerington	226	38.59 N	119.09 W
Yerington Indian Reservation ◆[4]	226	39.05 N	119.12 W
Yerkes	285	40.10 N	75.27 W
Yerkes Astronomical Observatory ✥[3]	216	42.34 N	88.34 W
Yerkesik	130	37.07 N	28.17 E
Yerköy	130	39.38 N	34.29 E
Yerky	78	48.59 N	31.00 E
Yerlisu	130	40.46 N	26.39 E
Yermasóyia	130	34.43 N	33.05 E
Yermenonville	261	48.33 N	1.37 E
Yermo	204	34.54 N	116.49 W
Yeroḥam	132	31.00 N	34.55 E
Yerolimín	38	36.28 N	22.24 E
Yèrre ≃	50	48.01 N	1.16 E
Yerres	50	48.43 N	2.30 E
Yerres ≃	50	48.43 N	2.27 E
Yerseke	52	51.29 N	4.02 E
Yerupaja, Nevado ∧	248	10.16 S	76.54 W
Yerushalayim (Al-Quds) (Jerusalem)	132	31.46 N	35.14 E
Yerushalayim □[5]	132	31.45 N	35.00 E
Yerville	50	49.40 N	0.54 E
Yeryk ≃	83	48.59 N	38.30 E
Yesa, Embalse de ⊜[1]	34	42.36 N	1.09 W
Yesan	98	36.41 N	126.50 E
Yeshenpu	104	40.51 N	122.32 E
Yeshiva University ✥[2]	276	40.51 N	73.55 W
Yeshvi	272c	18.55 N	73.03 E
Yeşil ≃	130	41.24 N	36.35 E
Yeşilçonlu	130	40.13 N	28.06 E
Yeşildere	130	37.09 N	33.31 E
Yeşilhisar	130	38.21 N	35.06 E
Yeşilkent	130	36.59 N	36.10 E
Yeşilköy	130	40.57 N	28.49 E
Yeşilköy Burnu ≻	267b	40.57 N	28.50 E
Yeşilova	130	37.30 N	29.46 E
Yeşiltepe	130	37.12 N	33.02 E
Yeşilyazı	130	39.20 N	39.05 E
Yeşilyurt	130	38.18 N	38.15 E
Yeso	196	34.26 N	104.36 W
Yeso Creek ≃	196	34.13 N	104.15 W
Yesŏng-gang ≃	98	37.53 N	126.24 E
Yessentuki → Jessentuki	84	44.03 N	42.51 E
Yeste	34	38.22 N	2.18 W
Yes Tor ∧	42	50.42 N	4.00 W
Yesud HaMa'ala	132	33.03 N	35.36 E
Yetholme	170	33.27 S	149.49 E
Yetman	166	28.54 S	150.46 E
Yetminster	42	50.53 N	2.33 W
Yetsou I	152	2.08 S	10.42 E
Yettem	226	36.29 N	119.16 W
Yetti	164	3.00 S	140.53 E
Yetti ◆[1]	148	26.10 N	7.50 W
Ye-u	110	22.46 N	95.26 E
Yeu, Île d' I	32	46.42 N	2.20 W
Yevlax	84	40.36 N	47.09 E
Yevpatoriya → Yevpatoriya, Ukr.	78	45.12 N	33.22 E
Yevpatoriya, Ukr.	78	45.12 N	33.22 E
Yevsuh	83	49.13 N	39.18 E
Yevsuh ≃	83	48.47 N	39.19 E
Yexian, Zhg.	98	37.13 N	119.54 E
Yexian, Zhg.	100	33.37 N	113.20 E
Yexie	106	30.56 N	121.19 E
Yextla ≃	234	18.00 N	100.06 W
Yeysk → Jejsk	78	46.42 N	38.16 E
Yeyuan	98	36.22 N	118.27 E
Yeywa	110	21.41 N	96.24 E
Yezd → Yazd	128	31.53 N	54.25 E
Yeze Hu ⊜	106	31.08 N	120.40 E
Yezhuang	105	39.10 N	116.18 E
Yezhuhe	105	40.53 N	118.13 E
Ygatimí	252	24.05 S	55.30 W
Ygnacio Canal ≊	282	37.55 N	122.03 W
Yguazú ≃	252	25.20 S	55.00 W
Yhú	252	24.59 S	55.59 W
Yi	98	42.08 N	118.48 E
Yi ≃, Ur.	252	33.07 S	57.08 W
Yi ≃, Zhg.	98	34.07 N	118.15 E
Yi ≃, Zhg.	100	34.10 N	112.10 E
Yi ≃, Zhg.	105	39.14 N	115.46 E
Yi'an	89	47.55 N	125.20 E
Yiannitsá	38	40.48 N	22.25 E
Yíaros I	38	37.37 N	24.43 E

FRANÇAIS

Nom	Page	Lat. °′	Long. °′ W = Ouest
Yibao	106	30.25 N	119.53 E
Yibin (Ipin)	107	28.47 N	104.38 E
Yibug Caka ⊜	120	33.00 N	86.25 E
Yibutan	107	28.54 N	104.40 E
Yicanghe	100	32.47 N	120.43 E
Yichang (Ichang)	102	30.42 N	111.17 E
Yicheng, Zhg.	98	36.48 N	114.17 E
Yicheng, Zhg.	98	34.46 N	117.37 E
Yicheng, Zhg.	102	31.43 N	112.07 E
Yichexun	102	26.50 N	103.28 E
Yichuan, Zhg.	100	34.26 N	112.24 E
Yichuan, Zhg.	102	36.04 N	110.06 E
Yichun, Zhg.	90	47.42 N	128.55 E
Yichun, Zhg.	100	27.50 N	114.23 E
Yicun	105	38.57 N	115.37 E
Yidan	89	43.24 N	125.25 E
Yidie	102	37.08 N	110.30 E
Yidu, Zhg.	98	36.41 N	118.28 E
Yidu, Zhg.	102	30.22 N	111.22 E
Yidun	102	29.56 N	99.22 E
Yiewsley ◆[8]	260	51.31 N	0.28 W
Yifag	144	12.02 N	37.44 E
Yifeng, Zhg.	100	33.19 N	113.47 E
Yifeng, Zhg.	100	28.26 N	114.46 E
Yigaolou	106	30.56 N	120.20 E
Yığılca	130	40.58 N	31.27 E
Yiğitler	130	39.52 N	26.37 E
Yigou	98	35.51 N	114.20 E
Yihe	100	23.50 N	114.53 E
Yihechang	107	30.23 N	106.24 E
Yi He Yuan (Summer Palace) ✥	105	40.00 N	116.16 E
Yihezhuang, Zhg.	98	37.53 N	118.23 E
Yihezhuang, Zhg.	104	41.15 N	122.57 E
Yihuang	100	27.34 N	116.10 E
Yihuang ≃	100	28.05 N	116.18 E
Yijiangzhen	100	30.55 N	118.28 E
Yijiawan	100	27.58 N	113.01 E
Yijiazi	104	42.29 N	122.41 E
Yijingpu	105	40.08 N	117.47 E
Yijinqiao	100	30.54 N	117.12 E
Yijun	102	35.24 N	109.00 E
Yikengaolu	102	42.17 N	98.19 E
Yikou	100	26.45 N	117.00 E
Yilaha	89	48.50 N	125.10 E
Yilan	89	46.19 N	129.34 E
Yilaxi	89	43.47 N	126.08 E
Yıldız Dağı ∧	130	40.08 N	36.56 E
Yıldız Dağları ⋏	38	41.50 N	27.30 E
Yıldızeli	130	39.52 N	36.38 E
Yilehuli Shan ⋏	89	51.20 N	124.30 E
Yili	107	30.45 N	105.58 E
Yiliang, Zhg.	102	24.58 N	103.07 E
Yiliang, Zhg.	102	27.35 N	104.01 E
Yiliekede	89	48.51 N	121.37 E
Yilin	100	33.36 N	119.37 E
Yiling	100	32.30 N	119.46 E
Yiliping	120	37.55 N	93.30 E
Yilliminning	162	32.54 S	117.22 E
Yilong, Zhg.	89	47.28 N	125.23 E
Yilong, Zhg.	102	31.34 N	106.19 E
Yilong, Zhg.	102	25.20 N	103.14 E
Yimachi	104	42.11 N	122.15 E
Yimatu	104	41.55 N	121.25 E
Yimen, Zhg.	100	33.39 N	116.02 E
Yimen, Zhg.	102	24.43 N	102.10 E
Yimuhe	89	52.45 N	120.07 E
Yin ≃, Mya.	110	20.04 N	95.01 E
Yin ≃, Zhg.	98	42.19 N	118.37 E
Yinan (Jiehu)	98	35.37 N	118.30 E
Yinbaing	110	17.25 N	97.46 E
Yinchuan	102	38.30 N	106.18 E
Yindarlgooda, Lake ⊜	162	30.45 S	121.55 E
Yindi	154	1.35 N	27.40 E
Yinfang	105	39.07 N	114.52 E
Ying ≃	100	32.30 N	116.32 E
Yingcheng	100	30.57 N	113.32 E
Yingchengzi, Zhg.	89	44.08 N	125.56 E
Yingchengzi, Zhg.	98	38.58 N	121.23 E
Yingchengzi, Zhg.	104	41.50 N	124.04 E
Yingchengzi, Zhg.	104	42.22 N	124.14 E
Yingde	100	24.12 N	113.24 E
Yingen	102	41.09 N	104.45 E
Yingfang	105	40.14 N	116.17 E
Yinggehai	110	18.31 N	108.44 E
Yinghe	100	32.16 N	116.31 E
Yingjin ≃	98	42.20 N	119.19 E
Yingkoshih ≃	269d	25.06 N	121.43 E
Yingkou, Zhg.	104	40.40 N	122.14 E
Yingkou (Dashiqiao), Zhg.	104	40.38 N	122.30 E
Yingpan, Zhg.	102	25.48 N	106.18 E
Yingpan, Zhg.	102	24.44 N	99.38 E
Yingpanjie	102	25.27 N	98.24 E
Yingqiao	100	33.58 N	113.39 E
Yingshan, Zhg.	100	30.45 N	115.39 E
Yingshan, Zhg.	100	31.38 N	113.50 E
Yingshan, Zhg.	102	31.08 N	106.31 E
Yingshang	100	32.38 N	116.15 E
Yingshouyingzi, Zhg.	105	40.33 N	117.38 E
Yingshouyingzi, Zhg.	105	40.49 N	117.55 E
Yingtan	100	28.14 N	117.00 E
Yingtaogou	104	42.08 N	121.57 E
Yingtaoyuan	104	41.10 N	123.05 E
Yingtian	100	28.50 N	112.56 E
Yingxiangjie	107	29.24 N	105.11 E
Yingxianpu	104	41.20 N	121.31 E
Yining (Kuldja)	86	43.54 N	81.21 E
Yinjiadai	106	32.03 N	120.07 E
Yinjiang	102	28.02 N	108.28 E
Yinjiawopeng	104	42.34 N	121.01 E
Yinkeng	100	26.14 N	115.34 E
Yinliu	105	39.59 N	117.23 E
Yinmabin	110	22.05 N	94.54 E
Yinmahe	89	44.07 N	125.44 E
Yinmatu ≃	98	40.57 N	117.43 E
Yinnietharra	162	24.39 S	116.11 E
Yinnyein	110	16.48 N	97.23 E
Yinong	102	30.19 N	101.01 E
Yinping	98	34.15 N	118.39 E
Yinqiaotou	106	31.52 N	119.13 E
Yin Shan ⋏	102	41.48 N	109.00 E
Yinshanzhen	107	29.41 N	104.58 E
Yinwogou	98	41.55 N	117.55 E
Yinxian	100	29.50 N	121.38 E
Yinxiang	106	31.55 N	118.49 E
Yinxianji	100	32.07 N	116.32 E
Yinyangjie	104	42.16 N	121.23 E
Yinyuan	102	23.26 N	101.54 E
Yinzhan'ao	100	23.33 N	113.07 E
Yio Chu Kang	271c	1.23 N	103.51 E
Yi'ong	102	30.17 N	94.51 E
Yi'ong ≃	120	29.56 N	95.10 E
Yi Pak	271d	22.19 N	114.00 E
Yipinchang	107	29.17 N	106.34 E
Yipinglang	102	25.11 N	101.51 E
Yiqian	100	26.34 N	116.11 E
Yirba Muda	144	6.12 N	38.42 E
Yirga Alem	144	6.52 N	38.22 E
Yirkā	132	32.57 N	35.13 E
Yirol	140	6.33 N	30.30 E
Yirrkala	164	12.14 S	136.56 E
Yirshi	89	47.20 N	119.45 E
Yirwa	140	7.47 N	27.15 E
Yisaduo	102	28.50 N	96.44 E
Yishan, Zhg.	100	27.32 N	120.32 E
Yishan, Zhg.	102	24.40 N	108.35 E
Yishui	98	35.50 N	118.41 E
Yishun	271c	1.26 N	103.50 E
Yisikan	89	49.09 N	124.47 E
Yisra'el → Israel □[1]	132	31.30 N	35.00 E
Yisuhe	100	27.46 N	112.54 E
Yitajing	102	42.32 N	94.12 E
Yitang, Zhg.	98	35.10 N	118.16 E
Yitang, Zhg.	100	31.06 N	113.42 E
Yíthion	38	36.45 N	22.34 E
Yiting	100	29.15 N	119.57 E
Yitm, Wādī al- V	132	29.34 N	35.01 E
Yitong	89	43.20 N	125.17 E

PORTUGUÊS

Nome	Página	Lat. °′	Long. °′ W = Oeste
Yitong ≃	98	42.40 N	125.58 E
Yitulihe	89	50.38 N	121.34 E
Yiwu, Zhg.	100	29.18 N	120.04 E
Yiwu, Zhg.	102	43.15 N	94.45 E
Yiwu, Zhg.	102	22.00 N	101.28 E
Yiwulü Shan ⋏	104	41.42 N	121.42 E
Yixi	100	23.45 N	116.38 E
Yixian, Zhg.	100	29.55 N	117.56 E
Yixian, Zhg.	104	41.32 N	121.15 E
Yixian, Zhg.	105	39.21 N	115.29 E
Yixiken	89	52.57 N	125.40 E
Yixing	106	31.22 N	119.50 E
Yixingbu	105	39.12 N	117.12 E
Yixingchang	107	30.37 N	106.38 E
Yixu	100	26.02 N	119.16 E
Yixun ≃	98	41.16 N	117.35 E
Yiyang, Zhg.	100	28.23 N	117.25 E
Yiyang, Zhg.	102	28.36 N	112.20 E
Yiyang, Zhg.	102	34.30 N	112.10 E
Yiyuan (Nanma)	98	36.11 N	118.08 E
Yiyuankou	98	40.10 N	119.35 E
Yizhang	100	25.26 N	112.56 E
Yizheng	106	32.16 N	119.12 E
Yizikong	102	25.38 N	104.28 E
Yizre'él	132	32.33 N	35.20 E
Yizre'el, 'Émeq ≚	132	32.36 N	35.14 E
Ylakiai	76	56.17 N	21.51 E
Yläne	26	60.53 N	22.55 E
Ylihärmä	26	63.09 N	22.47 E
Yli-Kitka ⊜	26	66.08 N	28.30 E
Ylimarkku → Övermark	26	62.38 N	21.30 E
Ylistaro	26	62.57 N	22.31 E
Ylivieska	26	64.05 N	24.33 E
Ylöjärvi	26	61.33 N	23.36 E
Ymeray	261	48.31 N	1.42 E
Ymir	182	49.17 N	117.13 W
Yndin	24	61.24 N	55.10 E
Yngaren ⊜	40	58.52 N	16.35 E
Yngen ⊜	40	59.44 N	14.18 E
Yntaly	86	48.58 N	70.55 E
Ynykčanskij	74	60.15 N	137.43 E
Yoakum	222	29.17 N	97.09 W
Yobi, Indon.	164	1.43 S	138.04 E
Yobi, Indon.	164	1.42 S	136.27 E
Yockanookany ≃	194	32.40 N	89.40 W
Yoco	246	10.36 N	62.24 W
Yocona ≃	194	34.11 N	90.11 W
Yōda	268	35.24 N	139.25 E
Yoder	216	40.55 N	85.10 W
Yodo ≃	96	34.41 N	135.25 E
Yodoe	96	35.28 N	133.26 E
Yodogawa ◆[8]	270	34.42 N	135.28 E
Yoe	208	39.55 N	76.39 W
Yōga ◆[8]	268	35.38 N	139.38 E
Yogo	94	35.33 N	136.12 E
Yog Point ≻	116	14.06 N	124.12 E
Yoğuntaş	130	41.50 N	27.04 E
Yogyakarta	115a	7.48 S	110.22 E
Yogyakarta □[4]	115a	7.45 S	110.30 E
Yoho National Park ♠	182	51.26 N	116.30 W
Yoichi	92a	43.12 N	140.41 E
Yojoa, Lago de ⊜	236	14.50 N	88.00 W
Yŏju	98	37.18 N	127.37 E
Yōka	96	35.24 N	134.46 E
Yokadouma	152	3.31 N	15.03 E
Yōkaichi	94	35.06 N	136.12 E
Yōkaichiba	94	35.42 N	140.33 E
Yokamba	152	0.01 N	22.17 E
Yokana	152	0.45 N	22.53 E
Yokawa	96	34.52 N	135.06 E
Yokchi-do I	98	34.38 N	128.15 E
Yokkaichi, Nihon	94	34.58 N	136.37 E
Yokkaichi, Nihon	96	33.32 N	131.20 E
Yoko	152	2.36 S	20.06 E
Yokoate-jima I	93b	28.48 N	129.00 E
Yokohama, Nihon	94	35.27 N	139.39 E
Yokohama, Nihon	268	35.27 N	139.39 E
Yokohama-kō c	268	35.27 N	139.39 E
Yokohama National University ✥[2]	268	35.25 N	139.36 E
Yokohama Park Baseball Ground ♠	268	35.26 N	139.39 E
Yokolo	152	0.36 S	23.04 E
Yokonuma	268	35.58 N	139.27 E
Yokoshiba	94	35.40 N	140.28 E
Yokosuka	94	35.18 N	139.40 E
Yokosuka District Naval Headquarters ■	268	35.17 N	139.39 E
Yokosuka-kō c	268	35.18 N	139.39 E
Yokosuka Naval Base ■	94	35.18 N	139.41 E
Yokota, Nihon	96	35.10 N	133.06 E
Yokota, Nihon	268	35.23 N	140.01 E
Yokota, Nihon	270	34.40 N	135.55 E
Yokota Air Base ■	268	35.45 N	139.21 E
Yokote	92	39.18 N	140.34 E
Yola	146	9.12 N	12.29 E
Yolaina, Serranías de ⋏	236	11.40 N	84.20 W
Yolboyu	130	37.55 N	40.00 E
Yolo	226	38.44 N	121.48 W
Yolo □[6]	226	38.41 N	121.46 W
Yolo ≃	273b	4.19 S	15.20 E
Yolo Bypass ≃	226	38.25 N	121.40 W
Yolombó, Col.	246	6.36 N	75.01 W
Yolombo, R.D.C.	152	1.32 S	23.15 E
Yolonga	152	1.36 S	23.12 E
Yom ≃	110	15.52 N	100.16 E
Yombi	152	1.26 S	10.37 E
Yomou	150	7.34 N	9.16 W
Yona	174p	13.25 N	144.47 E
Yonabaru	174m	26.12 N	127.45 E
Yonago	96	35.26 N	133.20 E
Yonaguni	175d	24.27 N	122.57 E
Yonaguni-shima I	175d	24.27 N	123.00 E
Yonaha-dake ∧[2]	174m	26.43 N	128.13 E
Yŏnan	98	37.55 N	126.10 E
Yoncalı	130	39.01 N	38.15 E
Yoncalla	202	43.35 N	123.16 W
Yŏnch'on ◆[8]	271b	37.38 N	127.04 E
Yoneshiro ≃	92	40.13 N	140.01 E
Yonezawa	92	37.55 N	140.07 E
Yŏngam	98	34.48 N	126.40 E
Yongamp'o	98	39.55 N	124.24 E
Yŏngan, C.M.I.K.	98	41.15 N	129.30 E
Yong'an, Zhg.	100	25.58 N	117.22 E
Yongan, Zhg.	107	30.44 N	106.16 E
Yong'an, Zhg.	107	29.13 N	104.46 E
Yong'an ≃	100	28.52 N	121.04 E
Yonganbao	98	40.15 N	119.52 E
Yong'anchang	107	30.24 N	103.58 E
Yong'anshi	100	28.13 N	113.19 E
Yŏngbyŏn	98	39.49 N	125.48 E
Yongchang, Zhg.	100	29.13 N	119.20 E
Yongchang, Zhg.	102	38.17 N	101.59 E
Yongchangzhen	106	31.42 N	121.44 E
Yongcheng	100	33.58 N	116.21 E
Yongch'ŏn, C.M.I.K.	98	39.59 N	124.28 E
Yŏngch'ŏn, Taehan	98	38.07 N	127.05 E
Yŏngch'ŏn, Taehan	98	35.58 N	128.56 E
Yongch'ŏn-dong	98	41.18 N	129.40 E
Yongchuan	107	29.21 N	105.54 E
Yongchun	100	25.21 N	118.21 E
Yongdeng	102	36.48 N	103.14 E
Yongdian	98	40.34 N	124.48 E
Yongding	100	24.46 N	116.43 E
Yongding ≃, Zhg.	100	24.42 N	116.34 E
Yongding ≃, Zhg.	105	39.20 N	117.04 E
Yongdingmen Station ◆[5]	271a	39.52 N	116.23 E
Yŏngdŏk	98	36.26 N	129.23 E
Yŏngdong	98	36.10 N	127.48 E
Yŏngdŭngp'o ◆[8]	271b	37.32 N	126.54 E
Yongfeng, Zhg.	100	29.44 N	116.49 E
Yongfeng, Zhg.	100	27.19 N	115.24 E
Yongfengchang	107	30.33 N	105.05 E
Yongfu	100	25.05 N	117.20 E
Yonggang	98	38.52 N	125.21 E
Yonggangonch'ŏn	98	38.53 N	125.14 E
Yonggi	98	36.24 N	128.24 E
Yongguzhai	98	34.05 N	116.50 E
Yonghe	100	28.18 N	113.51 E
Yongheshi	100	28.18 N	113.51 E
Yonghŭng	98	39.32 N	127.13 E
Yŏnghŭng-do I	98	37.16 N	126.28 E
Yŏnghŭng-man c	98	39.15 N	127.30 E
Yongi	89	43.40 N	126.30 E
Yŏngil-man c	98	36.02 N	129.26 E
Yongji	102	34.51 N	110.29 E
Yongjia, Zhg.	100	28.11 N	120.42 E
Yongjia, Zhg.	107	29.34 N	106.01 E
Yŏngjong-do I	98	37.30 N	126.31 E
Yŏngju	98	36.50 N	128.37 E
Yongkang, Zhg.	100	32.32 N	117.24 E
Yongkang, Zhg.	100	28.53 N	120.02 E
Yongkou	100	26.16 N	118.19 E
Yongle, Zhg.	89	45.45 N	125.12 E
Yongle, Zhg.	105	39.32 N	115.59 E
Yongle ≃	100	26.54 N	113.12 E
Yongledian	105	39.43 N	116.46 E
Yonglong	106	31.34 N	121.48 E
Yonglonghe	100	30.46 N	112.48 E
Yŏngmi-dong	98	39.40 N	125.31 E
Yongnian (Linmingguan)	98	36.47 N	114.30 E
Yongnianchang	107	29.08 N	104.51 E
Yongning, Zhg.	100	24.43 N	118.42 E
Yongning, Zhg.	102	38.20 N	106.17 E
Yongning, Zhg.	102	22.42 N	108.50 E
Yongning, Zhg.	102	27.47 N	100.38 E
Yongningcheng	105	40.34 N	116.11 E
Yongningjian	98	39.56 N	121.48 E
Yong Peng	114	2.01 N	103.04 E
Yongping, Zhg.	100	28.12 N	117.45 E
Yongping, Zhg.	102	25.28 N	99.33 E
Yongqing, Zhg.	105	39.19 N	116.29 E
Yongqing, Zhg.	107	30.00 N	105.27 E
Yongquan	100	28.46 N	121.19 E
Yongren	102	26.08 N	101.40 E
Yŏngsan-gang ≃	98	34.54 N	126.32 E
Yŏngsan-ni	98	38.52 N	125.56 E
Yŏngsanp'o	98	34.58 N	126.44 E
Yongshan	102	28.15 N	103.24 E
Yongshanqiao	100	29.06 N	117.17 E
Yongsheng	102	26.42 N	100.43 E
Yongshou	102	34.43 N	108.05 E
Yongshun	102	28.57 N	109.41 E
Yongshunchang	107	30.06 N	105.26 E
Yongtai	100	25.54 N	118.58 E
Yŏngwŏl	98	37.12 N	128.28 E
Yŏngwŏn	98	39.49 N	126.32 E
Yongwŏn-ni	98	40.41 N	128.42 E
Yongxin, Zhg.	100	26.56 N	114.18 E
Yongxin, Zhg.	107	28.59 N	106.32 E
Yongxing, Zhg.	98	40.11 N	123.52 E
Yongxing, Zhg.	100	26.08 N	113.06 E
Yongxing, Zhg.	102	39.08 N	110.31 E
Yongxing, Zhg.	106	31.56 N	120.55 E
Yongxing, Zhg.	107	30.34 N	105.35 E
Yongxing, Zhg.	107	30.13 N	105.06 E
Yongxingchang, Zhg.	107	29.02 N	104.34 E
Yongxingchang, Zhg.	107	29.37 N	106.23 E
Yongxingchang, Zhg.	107	30.20 N	103.44 E
Yongxiu	100	29.04 N	115.49 E
Yŏngyang, Taehan	98	36.40 N	129.07 E
Yongyang, Zhg.	100	26.57 N	114.46 E
Yŏngyn	98	39.18 N	125.34 E
Yongyŏn-ni	98	40.44 N	126.09 E
Yongzhai	100	27.59 N	115.26 E
Yŏnhŭi-ri	271b	37.33 N	126.41 E
Yŏnhwa-san ∧	98	40.46 N	127.23 E
Yonibana	150	8.26 N	12.14 W
Yonkers	210	40.55 N	73.53 W
Yonkers Raceway ♠	276	40.55 N	73.52 W
Yonne □[5]	50	47.55 N	3.45 E
Yonne ≃	32	48.23 N	2.58 E
Yono	94	35.53 N	139.38 E
Yŏnp'yŏng-yŏlto II	98	37.38 N	125.40 E
Yonsei University ✥[2]	271b	37.34 N	126.56 E
Yoo, Enneri V	146	19.24 N	16.38 E
Yoontow	144	0.08 S	42.34 E
Yopal	246	5.21 N	72.23 W
Yop'o-ri	98	38.50 N	125.33 E
Yopurga	85	39.15 N	76.45 E
Yoqne'am	132	32.39 N	35.07 E
Yorba Linda	228	33.53 N	117.48 W
Yorii	94	36.07 N	139.12 E
Yorishima	96	34.29 N	133.35 E
York, Austl.	168a	31.53 S	116.46 E
York, On., Can.	212	43.41 N	79.29 W
York, S.L.	150	8.17 N	13.11 W
York, Eng., U.K.	44	53.58 N	1.05 W
York, Al., U.S.	194	32.29 N	88.17 W
York, In., U.S.	216	41.41 N	84.49 W
York, Ne., U.S.	198	40.52 N	97.35 W
York, N.Y., U.S.	210	42.52 N	77.53 W
York, N.D., U.S.	198	48.18 N	99.34 W
York, Pa., U.S.	208	39.57 N	76.43 W
York, S.C., U.S.	192	34.59 N	81.14 W
York □[6], On., Can.	212	43.55 N	79.25 W
York □[6], Pa., U.S.	208	39.58 N	76.44 W
York □[6], Va., U.S.	208	37.15 N	76.40 W
York ≃, On., Can.	212	45.20 N	77.35 W
York ≃, P.Q., Can.	186	48.49 N	64.34 W
York ≃, Va., U.S.	208	37.15 N	76.23 W
York, Cape ≻	164	10.42 S	142.31 E
York, Kap ≻	16	75.53 N	66.12 W
York, Vale of V	44	54.10 N	1.20 W
Yorkana	208	39.59 N	76.35 W
York Center, Il., U.S.	278	41.52 N	87.59 W
York Center, Oh., U.S.	216	40.24 N	83.27 W
Yorkdale Centre ◆[9]	275b	43.44 N	79.27 W
Yorke Peninsula ≻[1]	166	35.00 S	137.30 E
Yorketown	168b	35.02 S	137.36 E
York Factory	184	57.00 N	92.18 W
Yorkfield	278	41.52 N	87.56 W
York Haven	208	40.06 N	76.42 W
Yorklyn	285	39.48 N	75.40 W
York Minster ✥[1]	44	53.57 N	1.04 W
York New Salem	208	39.54 N	76.47 W
Yorkshire, N.Y., U.S.	210	42.31 N	78.28 W
Yorkshire, Pa., U.S.	208	39.59 N	76.41 W
Yorkshire, Va., U.S.	208	38.47 N	77.27 W
Yorkshire Dales National Park ♠	44	54.13 N	2.10 W
Yorkshire Wolds ⋏[2]	44	54.00 N	0.40 W
York Sound ⋓	160	14.50 S	125.05 E
York Springs	208	40.00 N	77.07 W
Yorkton	184	51.13 N	102.28 W
Yorktown, In., U.S.	218	40.10 N	85.29 W
Yorktown, Tx., U.S.	222	28.58 N	97.30 W
Yorktown, Va., U.S.	208	37.14 N	76.30 W
Yorktown ◆[9]	278	41.51 N	88.01 W
Yorktown Battlefield ⊥	208	37.13 N	76.31 W
Yorktown Heights	210	41.16 N	73.46 W
Yorktown Manor	207	41.38 N	71.26 W
York Township Airport ⊠	278	41.51 N	88.02 W
York University ✥[2]	275b	43.47 N	79.30 W
Yorkville, Il., U.S.	216	41.38 N	88.26 W
Yorkville, Mi., U.S.	216	42.23 N	85.24 W
Yorkville, N.Y., U.S.	210	43.06 N	75.16 W
Yorkville, Oh., U.S.	214	40.09 N	80.43 W
Yorkville ◆[8]	275b	43.40 N	79.24 W
Yoro, Hond.	236	15.09 N	87.07 W
Yoro, Mali	150	14.17 N	2.08 W
Yōrō, Nihon	94	35.18 N	136.33 E
Yoro □[5]	236	15.15 N	87.15 W
Yōrō ≃	94	35.32 N	140.04 E
Yoroi-zaki ≻	94	34.24 N	136.55 E
Yoron-jima I	93b	27.02 N	128.26 E
Yōrō-no-taki ᒪ	94	35.17 N	136.32 E
Yorosso	150	12.22 N	4.47 W
Yosemite Creek ≃	226	37.44 N	119.36 W
Yosemite National Park	226	37.45 N	119.35 W
Yosemite National Park ♠	226	37.51 N	119.33 W
Yoshida, Nihon	94	36.02 N	139.02 E
Yoshida, Nihon	94	34.46 N	138.15 E
Yoshida, Nihon	96	33.16 N	132.33 E
Yoshida, Nihon	96	34.40 N	132.42 E
Yoshida, Nihon	96	35.10 N	132.51 E
Yoshida ≃	96	34.03 N	131.02 E
Yoshii, Nihon	94	36.15 N	138.59 E
Yoshii, Nihon	96	33.20 N	130.45 E
Yoshii, Nihon	96	34.38 N	133.26 E
Yoshii, Nihon	96	34.55 N	134.06 E
Yoshii, Nihon	270	34.53 N	135.03 E
Yoshii ≃	96	34.36 N	134.03 E
Yoshikawa, Nihon	94	37.13 N	138.25 E
Yoshikawa, Nihon	94	35.53 N	139.51 E
Yoshikawa, Nihon	270	34.55 N	135.28 E
Yoshimi	94	36.02 N	139.27 E
Yoshino, Nihon	96	34.21 N	135.51 E
Yoshino, Nihon	96	34.06 N	134.23 E
Yoshino ≃, Nihon	94	34.22 N	135.40 E
Yoshino ≃, Nihon	96	34.05 N	134.36 E
Yoshinodani	94	36.17 N	136.39 E
Yoshino-Kumano-kokuritsu-kōen ♠	92	34.07 N	135.55 E
Yoshioka	94	36.27 N	139.01 E
Yoshiumi	96	34.09 N	133.03 E
Yoshiwa	96	34.29 N	132.09 E
Yoshkar-Ola → Joškar-Ola	80	56.38 N	47.52 E
Yosowilangun	115a	8.15 S	113.18 E
Yos Sudarso, Pulau (Frederik Hendrikeiland) I	164	7.50 S	138.30 E
Yŏsu	98	34.46 N	127.44 E
Yotausito	248	16.03 S	63.03 W
Yōtei-zan ∧	92a	42.49 N	140.49 E
Yotsukaidō	94	35.39 N	140.10 E
Yotvata	132	29.53 N	35.03 E
You ≃, Zhg.	100	26.23 N	118.27 E
You ≃, Zhg.	102	22.50 N	108.06 E
You ≃, Zhg.	102	28.27 N	110.24 E
Youanmi	162	28.37 S	118.49 E
Youbou	224	48.53 N	124.13 W
Youcheng	100	29.14 N	116.48 E
Youfang	106	32.09 N	119.50 E
Youghal	48	51.57 N	7.51 W
Youghal Bay c	48	51.52 N	7.50 W
Youghiogheny ≃	214	40.22 N	79.52 W
Yougoslavie → Yugoslavia □[1]	22	44.00 N	21.00 E
Youhe	100	32.19 N	113.50 E
Youjidong	104	42.12 N	121.07 E
Youkounkoun	150	12.32 N	13.08 W
Youlan	100	28.34 N	116.10 E
Young, Austl.	166	34.19 S	148.18 E
Young, Sk., Can.	184	51.47 N	105.46 W
Young, Az., U.S.	200	34.06 N	110.57 W
Young, Ur.	252	32.41 S	57.38 W
Young America	216	40.34 N	86.20 W
Younghusband Peninsula ≻[1]	166	36.00 S	139.30 E
Youngs ≃	224	46.10 N	123.49 W
Youngs, Lake ⊜	224	47.25 N	122.07 W
Youngs Creek	218	38.29 N	86.30 W
Youngs Creek ≃	219	39.21 N	91.51 W
Youngs Rock I[2]	174e	25.03 S	130.07 W
Youngstown, Ab., Can.	182	51.32 N	111.13 W
Youngstown, Fl., U.S.	192	30.21 N	85.26 W
Youngstown, N.Y., U.S.	210	43.14 N	79.03 W
Youngstown, Oh., U.S.	214	41.05 N	80.38 W
Youngstown Municipal Airport ⊠	214	41.15 N	80.41 W
Youngsville, La., U.S.	194	30.05 N	91.59 W
Youngsville, N.Y., U.S.	210	41.48 N	74.54 W
Youngsville, N.C., U.S.	192	36.01 N	78.28 W
Youngsville, Pa., U.S.	214	41.51 N	79.19 W
Youngwood	214	40.14 N	79.34 W
Youngwood Park ♠	279b	40.14 N	79.36 W
Yountville	226	38.24 N	122.22 W
Youshashan	120	38.08 N	91.10 E
Youssoufia	148	32.16 N	8.33 W
Youtingpu	107	29.26 N	105.45 E
Youville ◆[8]	275a	45.33 N	73.39 W
Youxi, Zhg.	100	28.45 N	121.06 E
Youxi, Zhg.	100	26.11 N	118.09 E
Youxi, Zhg.	107	29.12 N	106.09 E
Youxian	100	27.00 N	113.21 E
Youxizhen	107	30.35 N	106.18 E
Youyang	102	28.58 N	108.41 E
Youyi	89	46.44 N	131.44 E
Youyu	102	40.09 N	112.32 E
Youzhagou	106	31.04 N	118.46 E
Youzhou	105	40.09 N	115.42 E
Yoweragabbie	162	28.13 S	117.39 E
Yŏyang-ni	98	37.30 N	128.43 E
Yozgat	130	39.50 N	34.48 E
Yozgat □[4]	130	39.40 N	35.10 E
Ypacaraí	252	25.23 S	57.16 W
Ypané ≃	252	23.29 S	57.19 W
Ypé Jhú	252	23.54 S	55.20 W
Yport	50	49.44 N	0.19 E
Ypres → Ieper	50	50.51 N	2.53 E
Ypsilanti	216	42.14 N	83.36 W
Ypsilanti East	216	42.15 N	83.35 W
Yreka	204	41.44 N	122.38 W
Yrgajty ≃	85	43.03 N	74.43 E
Yron ≃	56	49.10 N	5.52 E
Ysabel Channel ⋓	164	2.00 S	150.00 E
Ysbyty Ystwyth	42	52.20 N	3.48 W
Yser (IJzer) ≃	50	51.09 N	2.43 E
Ysieux, Ruisseau l' ≃	261	49.09 N	2.22 E
Yssel → IJssel ≃	52	52.35 N	5.50 E
Ysselmeer → IJsselmeer ⊤[2]	52	52.45 N	5.25 E
Yssingeaux	62	45.08 N	4.07 E
Ystad	41	55.25 N	13.49 E
Ystalyfera	42	51.47 N	3.47 W
Ysterfonteinpunt ≻	158	33.22 S	18.09 E
Ystrad ≃	44	53.13 N	3.20 W
Ystrad Aeron	42	52.11 N	4.11 W
Ystradfellte	42	51.48 N	3.34 W
Ystradgynlais	42	51.47 N	3.45 W
Ystwyth ≃	42	52.24 N	4.05 W
Ytambey ≃	252	24.46 S	54.24 W
Ythan ≃	46	57.18 N	2.00 W
Ytre Arna	26	60.26 N	5.30 E
Ytterharnäs	40	60.39 N	17.21 E
Ytterhogdal	26	62.12 N	14.51 E
Yttermalung	40	60.35 N	13.50 E
Ytterselö	40	59.23 N	17.15 E
Yttre Hållsfjärden c[2]	40	59.08 N	17.40 E
Yttygran, ostrov I	180	64.36 N	172.40 W
Yū	96	34.02 N	132.13 E
Yu ≃	102	23.24 N	110.05 E
Yu, Pulau I	164	0.03 S	129.36 E
Yu'alliq, Jabal ∧	140	30.22 N	33.31 E
Yuam ≃	110	17.47 N	97.45 E
Yuan → Red ≃, Asia	110	20.17 N	106.34 E
Yuan ≃, Zhg.	100	28.09 N	115.34 E
Yuan ≃, Zhg.	102	28.58 N	111.49 E
Yuan'an	102	31.04 N	111.26 E
Yuanao	100	26.29 N	119.48 E
Yuanbachang	107	29.44 N	105.27 E
Yuanhua	106	30.25 N	120.46 E
Yuanjiang	102	23.34 N	102.03 E
Yuankeng	100	26.48 N	117.44 E
Yüanli	100	24.27 N	120.39 E
Yüanlin	100	23.58 N	120.34 E
Yuanling	102	28.20 N	110.16 E
Yuanmou	102	25.38 N	101.54 E
Yuanshancun	106	31.08 N	120.20 E
Yuanshi	98	37.45 N	114.32 E
Yuantan, Zhg.	100	32.47 N	112.53 E
Yuantan, Zhg.	100	23.39 N	113.12 E
Yuantongsi	107	30.13 N	104.15 E
Yuantouzhu	106	31.32 N	120.14 E
Yuanxiang	98	34.14 N	115.19 E
Yuanxiangzhen	106	31.39 N	119.15 E
Yuanxing	107	30.36 N	104.59 E
Yuanyang (Yangwu), Zhg.	98	35.04 N	113.57 E
Yuanyang, Zhg.	102	23.12 N	102.52 E
Yuanyangpu	107	30.10 N	105.15 E
Yuanyangqiao	107	29.41 N	106.33 E
Yuasa	96	34.02 N	135.11 E
Yuat ≃	164	4.25 S	143.55 E
Yuba	102	29.27 N	97.42 E
Yuba □[6]	226	39.16 N	121.17 W
Yuba ≃	226	39.07 N	121.36 W
Yuba City	226	39.08 N	121.36 W
Yubara	96	35.12 N	133.45 E
Yubara-chosuichi ⊜	96	35.13 N	133.43 E
Yūbari	92a	43.04 N	141.59 E
Yūbari-sanchi ⋏	92a	43.15 N	142.20 E
Yubdo	144	9.00 N	35.22 E
Yūbetsu	92a	44.14 N	143.37 E
Yūbetsu ≃	92a	44.14 N	143.37 E
Yucaipa	228	34.02 N	117.02 W
Yucatán □[3]	232	20.50 N	89.00 W
Yucatán, Canal de ⋓	238	21.45 N	85.45 W
Yucatan Peninsula (Península de Yucatán) ≻[1]	232	19.30 N	89.00 W
Yucca	200	34.52 N	114.08 W
Yucca Lake ⊜	204	36.59 N	116.01 W
Yucca Mountain ∧	204	36.56 N	116.29 W
Yucca Valley	204	34.07 N	116.35 W
Yuchaozhuang	105	39.35 N	117.50 E
Yucheng, Zhg.	98	36.56 N	116.39 E
Yucheng, Zhg.	106	30.32 N	120.51 E
Yuci	102	37.45 N	112.41 E
Yuda	92	39.20 N	140.50 E
Yudaokou	98	42.14 N	116.48 E
Yudi Shan ∧	89	52.17 N	121.52 E
Yudong	106	32.02 N	121.22 E
Yudu	100	25.59 N	115.24 E
Yue ≃	107	28.50 N	104.21 E
Yuebo	107	29.03 N	104.12 E
Yuecheng	100	32.39 N	114.49 E
Yuechi	107	30.33 N	106.26 E
Yuejiatun	104	41.10 N	120.43 E
Yuejiawopeng	104	41.35 N	122.20 E
Yuekou	100	30.32 N	113.03 E
Yuelai	106	31.56 N	121.27 E
Yuelaichang, Zhg.	107	29.44 N	106.32 E
Yuelaichang, Zhg.	107	28.53 N	106.22 E
Yuemenpu	107	30.28 N	106.34 E
Yuendumu	162	22.16 S	131.49 E
Yuendumu Aboriginal Reserve ◆[4]	162	22.20 S	131.47 E
Yuen Long	271d	22.26 N	114.02 E
Yuepu	106	31.25 N	121.26 E
Yueqing	100	28.08 N	120.58 E
Yuewang	106	31.33 N	121.09 E
Yuexi, Zhg.	100	30.50 N	116.24 E
Yuexi, Zhg.	102	28.42 N	102.28 E
Yueyang	100	29.23 N	113.06 E
Yuezi	100	24.54 N	115.02 E
Yufa	105	39.31 N	116.19 E
Yufeng	107	30.37 N	105.11 E
Yufu-dake ∧	96	33.17 N	131.24 E
Yufuin	96	33.15 N	131.20 E
Yugan	100	28.41 N	116.41 E
Yugawara	94	35.09 N	139.04 E
Yuge	96	34.15 N	133.12 E
Yugoslavia (Jugoslavija) □[1], Europe	22	44.00 N	21.00 E
Yugoslavia (Jugoslavija) □[1], Europe	38	44.00 N	21.00 E
Yugou	100	33.42 N	118.55 E
Yuguan	98	39.56 N	119.22 E
Yuguo	104	41.52 N	123.15 E
Yuhang (Linping)	106	30.25 N	120.18 E
Yuhebu	102	38.01 N	109.37 E
Yuhu	100	27.53 N	120.08 E
Yuhuaizhuang	105	39.24 N	117.40 E
Yuhuan	100	28.10 N	121.12 E
Yuhuan Dao I	100	28.08 N	121.12 E
Yuhuang Ding ∧	98	36.50 N	121.21 E
Yui	94	35.06 N	138.34 E
Yuin	162	27.58 S	116.02 E
Yujiachang	107	29.57 N	104.04 E
Yujiacun	106	31.45 N	121.48 E
Yujiang	100	28.11 N	116.47 E
Yujiaqiao	106	31.30 N	119.25 E
Yujiawan	86	44.32 N	86.45 E
Yukarıbey	130	39.15 N	27.06 E
Yukarıdudullu ◆[8]	267b	41.02 N	29.09 E
Yuke	98	37.58 N	115.39 E
Yūki, Nihon	94	36.18 N	139.53 E
Yuki, Nihon	96	34.29 N	132.16 E
Yuki, Nihon	96	34.46 N	133.17 E
Yuki, Nihon	96	33.46 N	134.36 E
Yukon, Ok., U.S.	196	35.30 N	97.45 W
Yukon, Pa., U.S.	214	40.13 N	79.41 W
Yukon □[4], Can.	176	64.00 N	135.00 W
Yukon □[4], Can.	180	64.00 N	135.00 W
Yukon ≃	180	62.33 N	163.59 W
Yukon Flats ≕	180	66.30 N	146.00 W
Yukou	105	40.12 N	117.00 E
Yukuhashi	96	33.44 N	130.59 E
Yulan	210	41.31 N	74.56 W
Yulao	102	23.31 N	111.46 E
Yulara	162	25.14 S	131.04 E
Yule ≃	162	20.41 S	118.17 E
Yule Bay c	9	70.44 S	166.40 E
Yule Island I	164	8.50 S	146.30 E
Yuli, Nig.	146	9.42 N	10.17 E
Yüli, T'aiwan	100	23.20 N	121.18 E
Yuli, Zhg.	98	37.00 N	121.25 E
Yuliang	100	29.52 N	118.30 E
Yuliangpu	89	43.26 N	121.55 E
Yulin, Zhg.	102	22.36 N	110.07 E
Yulin, Zhg.	102	38.20 N	109.29 E
Yulin, Zhg.	110	18.16 N	109.32 E
Yulincun	105	40.12 N	116.42 E
Yul-li	98	38.52 N	126.13 E
Yulong	107	29.58 N	104.22 E
Yuma, Az., U.S.	200	32.43 N	114.37 W
Yuma, Co., U.S.	198	40.08 N	102.43 W
Yuma, Bahía de c	238	18.21 N	68.35 W
Yuma Marine Corps Air Station ■	200	32.40 N	114.38 W
Yuma Proving Ground ■	204	33.05 N	114.25 W
Yumare	246	10.37 N	68.41 W
Yumbel	252	37.08 S	72.32 W
Yumbi, R.D.C.	152	1.53 S	16.32 E
Yumbi, R.D.C.	154	1.14 S	26.14 E
Yumbo	246	3.35 N	76.28 W
Yumen (Laojunmiao)	102	39.56 N	97.51 E
Yumenzhen	102	40.17 N	97.07 E
Yumesaki	96	34.58 N	134.42 E
Yumezaki ≃	96	34.47 N	134.39 E
Yumin	86	46.02 N	82.37 E
Yumurtalık	130	36.49 N	35.45 E
Yun ≃	100	30.43 N	114.04 E
Yuna, Austl.	162	28.20 S	115.00 E
Yuna, Nihon	174m	26.46 N	128.12 E
Yuna ≃	238	19.12 N	69.37 W
Yunak	130	38.49 N	31.45 E
Yunan (Ducheng)	102	23.11 N	111.29 E
Yunaska Island I	180	52.40 N	170.50 W
Yuncao	100	31.26 N	118.04 E
Yuncheng, Zhg.	98	35.35 N	115.54 E
Yuncheng, Zhg.	102	35.00 N	110.59 E
Yundamindra	162	29.07 S	122.02 E
Yundanyingzi	104	42.00 N	121.34 E

	English	Deutsch	Español	Français	Português
≃	River	Fluß	Río	Rivière	Rio
≊	Canal	Kanal	Canal	Canal	Canal
ᒪ	Waterfall, Rapids	Wasserfall, Stromschnellen	Cascada, Rápidos	Chute d'eau, Rapides	Cascata, Rápidos
⋓	Strait	Meeresstraße	Estrecho	Détroit	Estreito
c	Bay, Gulf	Bucht, Golf	Bahía, Golfo	Baie, Golfe	Baía, Golfo
⊜	Lake, Lakes	See, Seen	Lago, Lagos	Lac, Lacs	Lago, Lagos
≕	Swamp	Sumpf	Pantano	Marais	Pântano
⍓	Ice Features, Glacier	Eis- und Gletscherformen	Accidentes Glaciales	Formes glaciaires	Acidentes glaciares
⊤	Other Hydrographic Features	Andere Hydrographische Objekte	Otros Elementos Hidrográficos	Autres données hydrographiques	Outros acidentes hidrográficos

	English	Deutsch	Español	Français	Português
✢	Submarine Features	Untermeerische Objekte	Accidentes Submarinos	Formes de relief sous-marin	Acidentes submarinos
□	Political Unit	Politische Einheit	Unidad Politica	Entité politique	Unidade política
✥	Cultural Institution	Kulturelle Institution	Institución Cultural	Institution culturelle	Instituição cultural
⊥	Historical Site	Historische Stätte	Sitio Histórico	Site historique	Sitio histórico
♠	Recreational Site	Erholungs- und Ferienort	Sitio de Recreo	Centre de loisirs	Area de Lazer
⊠	Airport	Flughafen	Aeropuerto	Aéroport	Aeroporto
■	Military Installation	Militäranlage	Instalación Militar	Installation militaire	Instalação militar
◆	Miscellaneous	Verschiedenes	Misceláneo	Divers	Diversos

	ENGLISH	DEUTSCH	ESPAÑOL	FRANÇAIS	PORTUGUÊS
▲	Mountain	Berg	Montaña	Montagne	Montanha
◢	Mountains	Gebirge	Montañas	Montagnes	Montanhas
⋊	Pass	Paß	Paso	Col	Passo
≃	Valley, Canyon	Tal, Cañon	Valle, Cañón	Vallée, Canyon	Vale, Canhão
≂	Plain	Ebene	Llano	Plaine	Planície
➤	Cape	Kap	Cabo	Cap	Cabo
I	Island	Insel	Isla	Île	Ilha
II	Islands	Inseln	Islas	Îles	Ilhas
◻	Other Topographic Features	Andere Topographische Objekte	Otros Elementos Topográficos	Autres données topographiques	Outros acidentes topográficos

ESPAÑOL Nombre	FRANÇAIS Nom	PORTUGUÊS Nome	Página / Page	Lat.°'	Long.°' W=Oeste/Ouest

Legend

Symbol	English	Deutsch	Español	Français	Português
≃	River	Fluß	Río	Rivière	Rio
լ	Canal	Kanal	Canal	Canal	Canal
ᴸ	Waterfall, Rapids	Wasserfall, Stromschnellen	Cascada, Rápidos	Chute d'eau, Rápides	Cascata, Rápidos
⊂	Strait	Meeresstraße	Estrecho	Détroit	Estreito
☰	Bay, Gulf	Bucht, Golf	Bahía, Golfo	Baie, Golfe	Baía, Golfo
☰	Lake, Lakes	See, Seen	Lago, Lagos	Lac, Lacs	Lago, Lagos
☰	Swamp	Sumpf	Pantano	Marais	Pântano
▨	Ice Features, Glacier	Eis- und Gletscherformen	Formes glaciaires / Accidentes Glaciares	Formes glaciaires	Accidentes glaciares
▼	Other Hydrographic Features	Andere Hydrographische Objekte	Otros Elementos Hidrográficos	Autres données hydrographiques	Outros acidentes hidrográficos
✦	Submarine Features	Untermeerische Objekte	Accidentes Submarinos	Formes de relief sous-marin	Acidentes submarinos
□	Political Unit	Politische Einheit	Unidad Política	Entité politique	Unidade política
✠	Cultural Institution	Kulturelle Institution	Institución Cultural	Institution culturelle	Instituição cultural
⊥	Historical Site	Historische Stätte	Sitio Histórico	Site historique	Sítio histórico
⊥	Recreational Site	Erholungs- und Ferienort	Sitio de Recreo / Área de Lazer	Centre de loisirs	Centro de Recreo
✈	Airport	Flughafen	Aeropuerto	Aéroport	Aeroporto
■	Military Installation	Militäranlage	Instalación Militar	Installation militaire	Instalação militar
▪	Miscellaneous	Verschiedenes	Misceláneo	Divers	Diversos

Name	Page	Lat.°'	Long.°'	Name	Seite	Breite°'	Länge°' E = Ost

Symbols in the index entries represent the broad categories identified in the key at the right. Symbols with superior numbers (◆¹) identify subcategories (see complete key on page I · 1).

Symbole im Register stellen die rechts im Schlüssel erklärten Kategorien dar. Symbole mit hochgestellten Ziffern (◆¹) bezeichnen Unterabteilungen einer Kategorie (vgl. vollständiger Schlüssel auf Seite I · 1).

Los símbolos incluídos en el texto del índice representan las grandes categorías identificadas con la clave a la derecha. Los símbolos con numeros en su parte superior (◆¹) identifican las subcategorías (véase la clave completa en la página I · 1).

Os símbolos incluídos no texto do índice representam as grandes categorias identificadas com a chave à direita. Os símbolos com números em sua parte superior (◆¹) identificam as subcategorias (veja-se a chave completa à página I · 1).

Les symboles de l'index représentent les catégories indiquées dans la légende à droite. Les symboles suivis d'un indice (◆¹) représentent des sous-catégories (voir légende complète à la page I · 1).

▲ Mountain	Berg	Montaña	Montaña	Montagne	Montanha
⋏ Mountains	Gebirge	Montañas	Montañas	Montagnes	Montanhas
✕ Pass	Paß	Paso	Col	Passo	
∨ Valley, Canyon	Tal, Cañon	Valle, Cañón	Vallée, Canyon	Vale, Canhão	
≃ Plain	Ebene	Llano	Plaine	Planície	
⋗ Cape	Kap	Cabo	Cap	Cabo	
I Island	Insel	Isla	Île	Ilha	
II Islands	Inseln	Islas	Îles	Ilhas	
⊥ Other Topographic Features	Andere Topographische Objekte	Otros Elementos Topográficos	Autres données topographiques	Outros acidentes topográficos	

MAP COVERAGE / KARTENAUSSCHNITTE
CONTENIDO DEL ATLAS / TABLEAU D'ASSEMBLAGE / ABRANGÊNCIA DO MAPA

148   Page Reference / Seitenangabe
       Página de Referencia / Page de Référence / Página de Referência

Map Scale

• 1:300,000

1:1,000,000   1:6,000,000

1:3,000,000   1:12,000,000

Enlarged maps of Anglo-America and Europe on page XIII.
Vergrösserte Karten von Anglo-Amerika und Europa auf Seite XIII.
Mapas aumentados de América Anglosajona y Europa, página XIII.
Cartes à grande échelle de l'Âmerique anglo-saxonne et de l'Europe à la page XIII.
Mapas ampliados da América Anglo-saxônica e da Europa, página XIII.

World, Ocean, and Continent maps on page 2-19.
Weitkarten, Karten der Ozeane und Erdteile auf Seiten 2-19.
Mapas del Mundo, Océanos y Continentes, páginas 2-19.
Cartes du Monde, des Océans et des Continents aux pages 2-19.
Mapas do Mundo, dos Oceanos e dos Continentes, páginas 2-19.

Additional Pacific Ocean Island maps on pages 174-175.
Zusätzliche Karten der Inseln des Pazifischen Ozeans auf Seite 174 175.
Mapas adicionales de las Islas del Océano Pacifico, páginas 174-175.
Cartes supplémentaires des Îles de l'Océan Pacifique aux pages 174-175.
Mapas suplementais das ilhas do Oceano Pacifico, páginas 174-175.